BURTON'S LEGAL THESAURUS

Thirty-fifth Anniversary/Fifth Edition

William C. Burton, Esq.

New York Chicago San Francisco Athens London
Madrid Mexico City Milan New Delhi
Singapore Sydney Toronto

1 2 3 4 5 6 7 8 9 10 11 12 13 14 15 QVS/QVS 1 9 8 7 6 5 4 3 2 1

ISBN 978-0-07-181881-0
MHID 0-07-181881-2

Library of Congress Control Number 2013029205

Library of Congress Cataloging-in-Publication Data

Burton, William C. compiler.
Burtons legal thesaurus 5th edition: over 10,000 synonyms, terms, and expressions specifically related to the legal profession / William Burton. — 5th edition.
pages cm
ISBN 978-0-07-181881-0 (pbk.) — ISBN 0-07-181881-2
1. Law—United States—Terminology.
2. English language—Synonyms and antonyms. I. Title. II. Title: Legal thesaurus.

KF156.B856 2013
349.7301'4—dc23

2013029205

McGraw-Hill Education books are available at special quantity discounts to use as premiums and sales promotions, or for use in corporate training programs. For more information, please write to the Director of Special Sales, Professional Publishing, McGraw-Hill Education, Two Penn Plaza, New York, NY 10121-2298. Or contact your local bookstore.

This book is printed on acid-free paper.

EDITORIAL STAFF

Thirty-fifth Anniversary/Fifth Edition

by
William C. Burton, Esq.
Author

WILLIAM C. BURTON, Esq., is an attorney and a partner in the law firm of Sagat | Burton LLP. He is a former New York State Assistant Attorney General and a former New York State Assistant Special Prosecutor. As a writer, he compiled this book, which became the first legal thesaurus ever written for the legal profession. When the book was released, it was recognized as "One of the Most Innovative and Creative Projects of the Year" by the Association of American Publishers. Two decades later, he established The Burton Awards program, which rewards the finest achievements in law, including legal writing. The program is run in association with the Library of Congress. In 2011, Mr. Burton was presented the highest honor given by the second-largest association of law professors in America, The Legal Writing Institute. At that time, he was recognized for "significantly advancing the cause of legal writing in the profession of law." More recently, he was awarded the Blackstone Award by the Friends of the Law Library of Congress for "embodying and promoting the best ideals of the institution."

CONTENTS

The First and Most Comprehensive Legal Thesaurus of Its Kind

FOREWORD

In the legal community absolute understanding is the measure of perfection. Perfection in the realm of the courts is the just resolution of issues of fact and questions of law. The primary tool for resolving conflicts among civilized people is through communication by written and oral language. The root of all language is the individual word.

In the English language, each word may have several meanings. Often, it is the use of a specific word or term upon which a case or controversy may hinge. Only by using precise language can the waters remain clear and unmuddied allowing justice to take its course unfettered by those who would mislead or misrepresent.

It is through the use of such a tool as the Legal Thesaurus that one may find the precise term to fit the nuances of a particular situation. It may be too much to expect such a tool to eradicate the confusion between "scienter" and "malice." The difference between "no law" and "no unreasonable law" may also be beyond its scope. But it should clearly demonstrate that "all deliberate speed" is not synonymous with "as slowly as feasible."

William O. Douglas
Justice, U.S. Supreme Court
1939–1975

October 22, 1979

Editor's Note: Justice Douglas served for over 36 years on the Supreme Court, which is the longest term in the history of the U.S. Supreme Court. This foreword is now recorded as one of his last writings.

INTRODUCTION

Before the publication of this book, lawyers and legal writers did not have their own thesaurus to assist them as they wrote their memoranda, motions, pleadings, articles, and communications. This book was compiled specifically to address that need and to provide lawyers and legal journalists with a reference tool to find all the words to fit a thought. Through its use, the goal is to reduce ambiguities and redundancies, replacing them with clear, concise, and plain language.

The fifth edition adds many new and contemporary words that augment the previous versions of the book. It also includes many words and expressions that lawyers use frequently as they practice their profession. It even includes concepts that are examined by the highest appellate courts in the nation.

For members of the judiciary, clear and precise language is indispensable. Every written word is subject to the closest scrutiny and interpretation. Oftentimes, a decision can turn on the meaning of a single word. The words contained in cases often become precedence to shape the future.

To members of the bar, persuasive language is also extremely important. Clearly drafted arguments can be convincing and sway the outcome of pending litigation.

To students of the law, precise and accurate writing is similarly critical to convey their understanding of the law.

The concept of a legal thesaurus was born out of necessity. It had its beginning in 1974, when I was writing a memorandum of law and needed to find the precise words in a particular context. I repeatedly searched for a legal thesaurus in the stores. Finally, my mother said, "If you can't find a legal thesaurus write one yourself!" Five years later, under my direction, a staff of twelve lawyers, librarians, and trained professionals finished the book and fulfilled the need that had been foreseen.

Since the original compilation of the book thirty-five years ago, thousands of entries have been added. In each case, the broadest array of words is provided to fit the thought to be conveyed. In addition to synonyms, the entries include related words. All expressions and colloquialisms that are archaic and stilted have been omitted as synonyms. The words provided are broader than just synonyms. The words provided are often related in meaning and present a complete gamut of words the writer could be searching to find in the drafting process. A legal dictionary should be consulted to determine precise meanings, nuances, and variations in contemporary usage. Only when the true meaning of each word is understood can the appropriate synonym be selected.

At the outset, three criteria were used to select the main entries included in this book: (1) words that are strictly legal, (2) words that are not strictly legal but are commonly used in the legal profession, and (3) words that are not legal or widely used by lawyers but are sufficiently sophisticated to warrant their use. A fourth category has been added to include words that are regularly used by lawyers.

In selecting main headings, words with multiple parts of speech were evaluated. In each case, the noun, adjective, verb, or adverb form included is most commonly used by attorneys.

Whenever a main heading has more than one usage, it is divided into separate subheadings. For convenience, these subheadings are arranged alphabetically.

Under each main entry, the book also provides an alphabetical listing of associated legal concepts. In this way, writers can find complete legal concepts when only a particular word comes to mind.

Foreign phrases used in the practice of law are also included under each main heading. Most reference books list foreign phrases alphabetically under the first letter of the foreign word. This book, however, lists foreign phrases under their pivotal English concepts.

To assist the user in locating synonyms, in addition to the alphabetical arrangement of main entries of the principal words and phrases used in law, a full index includes all words, whether commonly or less frequently used in law.

Through this book I hope that legal writing is enhanced. It is a means to precision. It is a tool that can lead to perfection.

William C. Burton, Esq.
Author

ACKNOWLEDGMENTS

I dedicate this thirty-fifth anniversary edition of my book in honor of my lovely and elegant wife, Michele, and my two delightful children, Brian, who is a member of the bar, and Marni, who I am also very proud of in every way. I am so very lucky they are my family.

I gratefully acknowledge, with profound gratitude and affection, the assistance and motivation given by my loving parents, Martin and Ellen Burton. I am forever indebted to them in providing me with the educational background and resources to undertake the initial compilation of this book. I was inspired by my father's writings and encouraged by my loving and motivating mother.

A special thank-you:

To Donya Dickerson, Executive Editor, McGraw-Hill Education, for her expertise, support, and invaluable input.

To Casie Vogel, Editorial Assistant, McGraw-Hill Education, for her technical and upbeat assistance.

ABOUT THE BOOK

Here are samples of the comprehensive, easy-to-use listings. All "synonyms" include the broadest range of words the writer may be seeking. Compared with the main heading, these words are sometimes more general or narrower in scope.

MAIN ENTRY

Definition (when there is more than one meaning)

Parts of Speech

Synonyms

Associated Legal Concepts

Foreign Phrases and Translations (keyed to concepts)

refutable, suspect, unsustainable

DUE *(Owed)*, ***adjective*** chargeable, claimable, collectable, condign, *debitus*, delinquent, deserved, earned, in arrears, merited, outstanding, owing, to be paid, uncompensated, unpaid, unrewarded, unsettled

ASSOCIATED CONCEPTS: amount due, balance due, debt due, due bills, due date, due on demand, indebtedness due, justly due and owing, legally due, money due, payment due, rent due, taxes due

FOREIGN PHRASES: ***Nihil peti potest ante id tempus, quo per rerum naturam persolvi possit.*** Nothing can be demanded before the time when, in the nature of things, it can be paid.

DUE *(Regular)*, ***adjective*** according to law, allowable, appropriate, authorized, befitting, correct, expedient, fit, lawful, legal, legislated, legitimate, licit, nomothetic, permitted, proper, rightful, sanctioned, statutory

ASSOCIATED CONCEPTS: due acknowledgment, due administration of justice, due and proper care, due and reasonable care, due care, due compensation, due consideration, due course, due course of business, due course of law, due diligence, due execution, due exercise of discretion, due process of law, due proof, due proof of death, due proof of loss, due regard, holder in due course

DUE, ***noun*** accounts collectable, accounts outstanding, arrears, balance to pay, charge, claim, compensation owed, *deberi*, debit, debt, deficit, droit, entitlement, favor owed, fee, indebtedness, lawful claim, liability, obligation accrued, outstanding debt, overdue payment, pledge, right, something owed, that which is owing, vested right

lead, mulct
play upon,
trap for, sp
fraud, take

DUPLICATE
double, ec
tion, imita
repetition,
ASSOCIATED

DUPLICITY
fulness, de
duplexity,
edness, fal,
fidy, sham,

DURABLE,
ranthine, c
tinual, cont
everlasting,
well, imm
pervious to
eradicable,
terminable,
irremovabl
enduring,
gevous, m
long durati
perpetual,
resistant, r
sound, *sta*,
substantial,

INDEX ENTRY

Synonym

(Main Entry under which the synonym is listed.)

Note Readable Type

(Sample Excerpts, Exact Size)

abandon nationality expatriate
abandoned dissolute, helpless *(defenseless)*, licentious, obsolete, solitary, tainted *(corrupted)*, uncurbed, vicious, void *(empty)*. SEE MAIN ENTRY
abandoned child orphan
abandoned infant orphan
abandoned to vice profligate *(corrupt)*
abandoning cancellation
abandonment abdication, abjuration, absence *(nonattendance)*, cancellation, capitulation, cessation *(termination)*, cloture, dereliction, desertion, desuetude, disclaimer, disuse, estrangement, expense *(sacrifice)*, halt, neglect, negligence, rejection, release, renunciation, rescision, resignation *(relinquishment)*, waiver. SEE MAIN ENTRY
abandonment of a known right waiver
abandonment of a trademark SEE MAIN ENTRY
abandonment of allegiance desertion, infidelity
abase adulterate, betray *(lead astray)*,

abbreviatory compact *(pithy)*
abbreviature abridgment *(condens*
abstract, curtailment
abdere hide
abdicate abandon *(withdraw)*, cede
fect, demit, forfeit, leave *(depart)*, q
(discontinue), relinquish, renounce, r
ate, resign, retire *(conclude a career*
render *(give back)*, vacate *(void)*, wi
draw, yield *(submit)*. SEE MAIN ENTRY
abdicatio abdication, renunciation,
nation *(relinquishment)*
abdication abandonment *(disconti
ance)*, renunciation, resignation *(relin
quishment)*, waiver. SEE MAIN ENTRY
abditus latent
abduce carry away
abduct carry away, hijack, kidnap.
MAIN ENTRY
abduction taking. SEE MAIN ENTRY
abecedarian elementary, neophyte
mentary
aberemurder SEE MAIN ENTRY
aberrance deviation, error, indirect

MAIN ENTRIES

A FORTIORI, *adverb* above all, accordingly, all the more, by a stronger reason, by inference, certainly, chiefly, consequently, *ergo*, especially, even more, for a certainty, for a still stronger reason, in chief, in the main, mainly, over and above, paramountly, particularly, primarily, thus, with the greater force

A PRIORI, *adverb* accordingly, as a consequence, as a result of, as is, because of this, by reason of, consequently, deducibly, deductively, derivatively, doubtlessly, *ergo, ex concesso*, for that reason, for this reason, for which reason, from a general law to a particular instance, from cause to effect, from that cause, from this cause, in consequence, inferentially, necessarily, on account of this, on that account, on that ground, proceeding from antecedent to consequent, thusly, to that end

A SAVOIR, *adverb* below, details now to be provided, the following, hence, hereunder, hereupon, namely, next, now to be accounted for, now to be announced, now to be described, now to be enunciated, now to be itemized, now to be listed, now to be mentioned, now to be narrated, now to be presented, now to be read, now to be recited, now to be recounted, now to be reported, now to be set forth, now to be stated, now to follow, subsequently set down, the succeeding, that is, that is to say, to wit, *videlicet*

AB INITIO, *adverb* *ab origine, ab ovo*, as a start, at first, at the beginning, at the start, chiefly, first, first and foremost, first of all, firstly, for a beginning, from its birth, from the beginning, in its infancy, in the beginning, in the first place, initially, mainly, originally, primarily, principally
ASSOCIATED CONCEPTS: *ab initio*, void

ABALIENATE, *verb* assign, bequeath, convey, demise, grant, hand down, hand over, pass on, transfer, transfer by deed, transfer by will

ABALIENATION, *noun* alienation, assignation, assignment, conferment, consignment, conveyance, deeding, deliverance, delivery, grant of conveyance, transfer, the transfer of title, transmission

ABANDON *(Physically leave)*, ***verb*** abscond, absent oneself, back out, be gone, be off, cast off, decamp, defect, depart from, desert, *destituere*, disappear, emigrate, evacuate, forsake, *hominem deserere*, leave behind, leave in the lurch, make one's exit, move off, quit, remove from, retreat, run away, secede from, set off, slip away from, take leave, take one's departure, take one's leave, turn one's back on
ASSOCIATED CONCEPTS: abandoned husband, abandoned land, abandoned property, abandoned wife, desertion

ABANDON *(Relinquish)*, ***verb*** abjure, abstain, apostasize, cast aside, cast away, cast off, cease, cede, concede, demit, desert, desist, discard, discontinue, dispense with, dispose of, dispossess oneself of, disuse, divest oneself of, drop, forbear, forgo, forsake, forswear, give away, give over, give up, give up claim to, go back on, jettison, lay aside, part with, put aside, quit, render up, renounce, repudiate, resign, sacrifice, set aside, surrender, tergiversate, throw away, throw off, turn away, yield
ASSOCIATED CONCEPTS: abandon a claim, abandon a crime, renunciate a claim, surrender property

ABANDON *(Withdraw)*, ***verb*** *ab re desistere*, abdicate, back down, back off, back out, forsake, *omittere*, pull out, quit, *rem relinquere*, renege, retire, retract, retreat, stand aside, tender one's resignation, vacate office

ABANDONED, *adjective* castaway, castoff, derelict, deserted, discontinued, disregarded, disused, forsaken, ignored, neglected, obsolete, occupantless, out of use, slighted, tenantless, unattended to, uncared for, uninhabited, unoccupied, unpopulated, untenanted
ASSOCIATED CONCEPTS: abandoned claims, abandoned evidence, abandoned husband or wife, abandoned leasehold, abandoned property, abandonment of pleadings

ABANDONMENT *(Desertion)*, ***noun*** abrogation, apostasy, cession, decampment, defection, demission, departure, dereliction, disaffection, disavowal, evacuation, flight, hasty departure, relinquishment, repudiation, retirement, vacating, withdrawal
ASSOCIATED CONCEPTS: abandonment of a child, abandonment of a husband, abandonment of a property, abandonment of a wife, abandonment of land, dissolution of marriage, Enoch Arden laws
FOREIGN PHRASES: ***Occupantis fiunt derelicta.*** Things abandoned become the property of the first who is the occupant.

ABANDONMENT *(Discontinuance)*, ***noun*** abdication, abrogation, cessation, *derelictio*, desistance, discontinuation, disjunction, disruption, relinquishment, surrender, suspension, withdrawal

ASSOCIATED CONCEPTS: abandonment of a crime, abandonment of a pleading, abandonment of an easement, abandonment of assets in bankruptcy, abandonment of proscriptive rights

ABANDONMENT *(Repudiation),* ***noun*** abnegation, cancellation, declination, denial, disapprobation, disapproval, disavowal, dismissal, disownment, rejection, renouncement, renunciation, reprobation, rescission

ABANDONMENT OF A TRADEMARK, ***noun*** abjuration, disownment, disuse, divestiture, divestment, forfeiture, relinquishment, resignation, surrender

ABASE, ***verb*** abuse, adulterate, belittle, bring down, brutalize, calumniate, debase, de-civilize, defame, deform, degrade, demean, demote, derogate, diminish, discredit, disgrace, dishonor, downgrade, humble, humiliate, lower, pervert, reduce, set down, shame, take down, vitiate, vituperate, warp

ABATE *(Extinguish),* ***verb*** abolish, abrogate, annul, *cadere,* cancel, defeat, destroy, discontinue, dissolve, eliminate, exterminate, invalidate, nullify, obliterate, put an end to, quash, quell, repeal, rescind, revoke, terminate, void
ASSOCIATED CONCEPTS: abate a bequest, abate a cause of action, abate a debt, abate a devise, abate a legacy, abate an action

ABATE *(Lessen),* ***verb*** alleviate, curtail, decline, decrease, *decrescere,* diminish, *imminui,* lighten, limit, mitigate, modify, palliate, reduce, relieve, *remittere,* suppress, temper
ASSOCIATED CONCEPTS: abate a nuisance, abate a tax

ABATEMENT *(Extinguishment),* ***noun*** abolition, abrogation, annulment, cancellation, deadening, defeat, destruction, discontinuance, dissolution, elimination, extermination, invalidation, nonuse, nullification, obliteration, *remissio,* repeal, rescindment, revocation, termination, voidance
ASSOCIATED CONCEPTS: abatement by death, abatement of a bequest, abatement of a cause of action, abatement of a freehold, abatement of a legacy, abatement of an action, abatement of debts, abatement of taxes, plea in abatement
FOREIGN PHRASES: ***Cassetur billa.*** That the bill be quashed. ***Cassetur breve.*** That the writ be quashed.

ABATEMENT *(Reduction),* ***noun*** alleviation, curtailment, declination, decline, decrease, decrement, *deminutio,* diminishing, diminution, lessening, lightening, limitation, mitigation, modification, palliation, reduction, relief, *remissio,* suppression, tempering
ASSOCIATED CONCEPTS: abatable nuisance, abatement of a tax

ABDICATE, ***verb*** abandon, back out, be relieved, cede, demit, drop, forgo, forfeit, give the reins to, give up, hand over, hold off, leave, let go, make way for, quit one's hold, relinquish, resign, retire, stand aside, surrender, unclench, vacate office, withdraw, yield

ABDICATION, ***noun*** abandonment, *abdicatio,* abjuration, demission, departure, deposition, dethronement, *eiuratio,* leaving, quitting, relinquishment, renunciation, resignation, surrender, surrender of control, uncrowning, vacating, vacation, withdrawal
FOREIGN PHRASES: ***Cessa regnare, si non vis judicare.*** Cease to reign, if you don't wish to adjudicate.

ABDUCT, ***verb*** carry away, convey away, decamp, denude, deprive, ensnare, impress, kidnap, pirate, purloin, ravish, shanghai, spirit away, subjugate, take away, take by force, take surreptitiously
ASSOCIATED CONCEPTS: kidnapping
FOREIGN PHRASES: ***A piratis aut latronibus capti liberi permanent.*** Persons taken by pirates or robbers remain free.

ABDUCTION, ***noun*** child-stealing, impressment, kidnapping, overmastering, *raptus,* ravishment, shanghaiing, spiriting away, subjugation, taking away

ABEREMURDER, ***noun*** assassination, carnage, dealing death, decimation, destruction of life, elimination, extermination, extinction, homicide, killing, killing with malice aforethought, liquidation, massacre, slaughter, slaying, taking of life, unlawful homicide

ABERRANCE, ***noun*** aberration, abnormality, abnormity, anomaly, change, deviation, difference, distinguishing characteristics, erroneousness, error, individual characteristics, irregularity, out of the ordinary, peculiarity, perversion, unnaturalness

ABERRANCY, ***noun*** aberration, abnormality, abnormity, anomaly, deviation, distinguishing characteristics, erroneousness, error, irregularity, peculiarity, perversion, speciality, unique characteristic, unnaturalness, unusual characteristic

ABERRANT, ***adjective*** abnormal, amorphous, anomalistic, anomalous, astray, changeable, departing, deviative, devious, discursive, disordered, divergent, eccentric, errant, erratic, erroneous, excursive, indirect, irregular, non-uniform, rambling, stray, straying, unnatural, unpredictable, untrue, variable, wandering

ABERRATION *(Abnormality),* ***noun*** alienation, declension, deflection, departure, derailment, deviation, digression, discrepancy, dislocation, disorientation, displacement, divergence, divergency, diversion, irregularity, lapse, misdirection, refraction, wandering, wrong course

ABERRATION *(Insanity),* ***noun*** abnormality, amentia, delirium, delusion, dementedness, derangement, disordered intellect, frenzy, hallucination, loss of reason, lunacy, madness, mental derangement, mental incapacity, mental infirmities, mental instability, mental sickness, paranoia, unsound mind, want of reason

ABET, ***verb*** *adiuvare,* advance, advocate, afford aid, aid, arouse, assist, back, contribute, cooperate with, embolden, encourage, endorse, facilitate, foment, foster, furnish aid, goad, help, incite, instigate, nourish, nurture, prompt, second, serve, spur, stimulate, succor, supply aid, support, urge
ASSOCIATED CONCEPTS: accessory, accomplice, aid and abet, co-conspirator, facilitation

ABETMENT, ***noun*** advocacy, aegis, aid, auspices, backup, collusion, contribution, cooperation, countenance, encouragement, favor, fosterage, guidance, helpfulness, interest, patronage, plying, pressing, sponsorship, urging

ABETTING, ***adjective*** ancillary, coaxing, concerted, conducing, encouraging, expediting, facilitating, fostering, indorsing, inspiring, promoting, prompting, urging
ASSOCIATED CONCEPTS: accessory after the fact, accessory before the fact, accomplice and accessories, aiding and abetting, principals

ABETTOR, *noun* accessory, accomplice, accomplice in crime, actuator, adjutant, advocate, aide, aider, assistant, associate, auxiliary, backer, coadjutor, collaborator, confederate, conspirator, cooperator, encourager, exponent, favorer, fomentor, helper, henchman, impeller, inducer, inspirer, instigator, mainstay, maintainer, motivator, *particeps criminis*, patron, promoter, prompter, protagonist, second, support, supporter, sustainer, upholder
ASSOCIATED CONCEPTS: aiding and abetting, conspiracy, renunciation

ABEYANCE, *noun* arrest, cessation, check, deadlock, delay, desistance, discontinuance, discontinuation, dormancy, halt, immobility, *in dubio esse,* inaction, inactivity, inertion, inertness, interim, interlude, intermission, *intermitti,* interregnum, interruption, interval, lapse, quiescency, recess, recumbency, *rem integram relinquere,* repose, reprieve, respite, rest, stalemate, stay, stillness, stoppage, suspension
ASSOCIATED CONCEPTS: contingency, escrow, fee held in abeyance, held in abeyance, in expectation

ABHOR, *verb* abominate, be appalled by, be repelled by, censure, condemn, consider abhorrent, consider distasteful, contempt, damn, decry, denounce, deplore, deprecate, despise, detest, disdain, disparage, execrate, find heinous, find horrendous, find odious, find offensive, hate, loathe, reprehend, reprobate

ABHORRENT, *adjective* abominable, appalling, awful, contemptible, despicable, detestable, disgusting, distasteful, heinous, horrendous, indictable, loathsome, obnoxious, obscene, odious, offensive, repellent, reprehensible, repugnant, repulsive, revolting, terrible, vile, wretched

ABIDE, *verb* accept, acknowledge, acquiesce, adhere, agree, assent, carry into execution, comply, concur, conform, cooperate, endure, execute, follow, heed, obey, observe, perform, permit, respect, sanction, stare, submit, subscribe to, suffer, tolerate, yield
ASSOCIATED CONCEPTS: abiding conviction

ABIDING, *adjective* changeless, constant, continuing, durable, enduring, eternal, everlasting, fixed, immutable, inherent, lasting, long-lasting, long-lived, long standing, of long duration or standing, perennial, permanent, persistent, persisting, remaining, stable, staying, steadfast, sustained, unaltered, unchanged, unchanging, unshifting, unvaried, unvarying

ABILITY, *noun* ableness, adaptability, adeptness, adequacy, aptitude, aptness, capability, capacity, competence, competency, enablement, *facultas,* faculty, fitness, fittedness, *ingenium,* mastership, mastery, potentiality, *potestas,* proficiency, prowess, skill, versatility, *vires*
ASSOCIATED CONCEPTS: ability to contract, ability to earn, ability to pay, ability to perform, ability to provide, ability to purchase, ability to support, capacity, financial ability, readiness, testamentary ability

ABJECT, *adjective* base, boorish, common, contemptible, corrupt, cowardly, craven, debased, degenerate, degraded, depraved, despicable, discreditable, dishonest, dishonorable, disreputable, ignoble, ignominious, inferior, inglorious, mean, penitent, plebeian, repentant, reproachful, scandalous, scurrilous, servile, sordid, wretched

ABJECTION, *noun* abasement, baseness, debasement, decadence, degeneracy, degradation, demoralization, dishonor, disrepute, humiliation, ignominy, meanness, servility, vileness

ABJECTNESS, *noun* abominableness, baseness, contemptibleness, degradation, despicableness, meanness, obsequiousness, odiousness, pettiness, shabbiness, shoddiness, smallness, sordidness, submissiveness, vileness, worthlessness, wretchedness

ABJUDGE, *verb* adjudicate, appraise, arbitrate, ascertain, assess, award, conclude, consider, decide, declare, decree, deduce, deem, derive, determine, discern, draw a conclusion, examine, find, hold, interpret, judge, prescribe, pronounce formally, rule

ABJURATION, *verb* abandonment, defection, denial, disaffirmation, disallowance, disavowal, disclaimer, disclamation, disownment, forswearing, recall, recantation, rejection, renouncement, renunciation, repudiation, retraction, revocation, revokement
ASSOCIATED CONCEPTS: abjuration of allegiance, law of sanctuary, oath of abjuration

ABJURE, *verb* abandon, abrogate, deny, disaffirm, disavow, discard, disclaim, disown, exclude, forgo, forswear, give up, recant, refuse to admit, reject, relinquish, renounce, repudiate, resign, retract, revoke, surrender, yield

ABLE, *adjective* accomplished, adept, adequate, adroit, apt, bright, clever, competent, deft, dexterous, dynamic, effective, effectual, efficacious, efficient, equal to, experienced, expert, facile, fit, fitted, forward, handy, ingenious, intelligent, inventive, learned, practical, practiced, proficient, qualified, quick, resourceful, sagacious, shrewd, skillful, strong, talented, versed, viable, worthy

ABLENESS, *noun* ability, adequacy, caliber, capability, capacity, competence, efficacy, efficiency, faculty, lucidity, normalcy, normality, normalness, proficiency, quality, rationality, reason, reasonability, saneness, sound mind, soundness of mind, sufficiency

ABNEGATE, *verb* abjure, contravene, decline, deny, disavow, disclaim, disown, drop, forbear, gainsay, let go, negate, quit one's hold, rebuff, recall, refuse, refute, reject, relinquish, renounce, repudiate, repulse, retract, say no, spurn, surrender, unclench

ABNEGATION, *noun* abandonment, abjuration, declination, denial, disallowance, disavowal, disclaimer, forbearance, moderation, negation, nonacceptance, noncompliance, nonconsent, refusal, rejection, renouncement, renunciation, surrender, temperance, unwillingness

ABNORMAL, *adjective* aberrant, amorphous, anomalous, bizarre, curious, deviative, disordered, divergent, eccentric, erratic, exceptional, freakish, frenetic, idiocratic, idiosyncratic, irregular, monstrous, odd, outlandish, peculiar, preternatural, strange, unconformable, unconventional, unheard of, unhinged, unnatural, unusual

ABNORMALITY, *noun* aberration, anomaly, curiosity, deformity, deviation, divergence, erraticism, exception, idiosyncrasy, irregularity, malformation, nonconformity, oddity, peculiarity, perversion, singularity, strangeness, unconformity, unconventionality, unnaturalness, variation

ABNORMITY, *noun* aberrance, aberration, abnormality, anomalism, anomalousness, anomaly, deviation, divergence, erraticism, irregularity, nonconformity, quirk, subnormality, unnaturalness

ABODE, *noun* address, domicile, *domus,* dwelling, dwelling place, fixed residence, *gite,* habitancy, habitat, habitation, home, homestead, house, inhabitancy, inhabitation, living place, place of dwelling, residence, residency
FOREIGN PHRASES: ***Constitutum esse eam domum unicuique nostrum debere existimari, ubi quisque sedes et tabulas haberet, suarumque rerum constitutionem fecisset.*** It is established that the home of each of us is considered to be the place of his abode and books, and where he may have made an establishment of his business.

ABOLISH, *verb* abate, *abolere,* abrogate, annihilate, annul, cancel, declare null and void, *delere,* delete, deprive of force, destroy, disannul, discontinue, disestablish, dispense with, dispose, dissolve, eliminate, eradicate, *exstinguere,* exterminate, extinguish, extirpate, invalidate, negate, nullify, obliterate, override, overrule, overturn, prohibit, quash, raze, render null and void, repeal, repudiate, rescind, retract, revoke, set aside, squelch, *subvertere,* supersede, supplant, suppress, terminate, *tollere,* undo, vacate, vitiate, void, withdraw
ASSOCIATED CONCEPTS: repeal by amendment

ABOLISHMENT, *noun* abatement, annulment, cancellation, cessation, close, completeness, conclusion, culmination, discontinuance, dissolution, elimination, end, expiration, extinguishment, finality, finish, termination

ABOLITION, *noun* abolishment, abrogation, annihilation, annulment, cancellation, defeasance, deposal, destruction, desuetude, discontinuance, *dissolutio,* dissolution, disusage, disuse, elimination, eradication, extermination, extinction, extinguishment, extirpation, invalidation, nonuse, nullification, obliteration, recantation, recision, repeal, repudiation, rescindment, rescission, retraction, revocation, revokement, vacation, voidance
ASSOCIATED CONCEPTS: abolition of a remedy, abolition of an action, abolition of office, abolition of slavery, express abolition, implied abolition
FOREIGN PHRASES: ***Cujus est instituere, ejus est abrogare.*** Whoever may institute, his right it is to abrogate.

ABOMINABLE, *adjective* despicable, diabolical, disgraceful, disgusting, dreadful, evil, foul, heinous, horrendous, horrible, loathsome, nefarious, noisome, odious, reprehensible, repulsive, sickening, sinister, terrible, vile, wicked

ABORT, *verb* abandon, arrest, break off, bring to a close, bring to a standstill, call off, cancel, cease, choke close, conclude, cut off, cut short, deactivate, desist, disable, disallow, discontinue, disengage, drop, expire, extinguish, halt, interrupt, negate, quit, snuff, stop, stymie, suppress, suspend, terminate, thwart
ASSOCIATED CONCEPTS: abandonment of a case, abort litigation, abort the prosecution of a case, failure to prosecute

ABORTION *(Feticide),* ***noun*** aborticide, expulsion of a fetus, termination of a pregnancy

ABORTION *(Fiasco),* ***noun*** blunder, clumsiness, dereliction, disablement, disaster, failure, folly, frustration, inability, incapacity, incompetence, incompetency, ineffectuality, inefficacy, ineptitude, inexpertness, insufficiency, nonfulfilment, quackery, unskillfulness, vain attempt, vain effort, want of success

ABOUND, *verb* brim, bulge, bustle, fill, fill up, flood, flourish, gush, increase, overflow, proliferate, run over, succeed, swarm, swell, teem, thrive, well over

ABOVE *(Before),* ***preposition*** anterior, as contained in an earlier provision, as earlier mentioned, as earlier referred to, as earlier stated, as previously stated, as provided in a previous section, as stated earlier, before mentioned, central, dominant, earlier, first, former, last, preceding, previous, primary, principle, prior

ABOVE *(Higher),* ***preposition*** aloft, beyond, elevated, further, grandest, greatest, largest, most up, overhead, raised, skyward, supreme, top, topmost, up, uplifted, upper, uppermost, upraised, upward
ASSOCIATED CONCEPTS: above reproach, above the law

ABOVE-MENTIONED, *adjective* as contained above, as referred to previously, first, former, precedent, preceding, previous, previously named, previously specified, previously stated, prior

ABOVE-NAMED, *adjective* above-mentioned, as contained above, as referred to previously, first, former, precedent, preceding, previous, previously named, previously specified, previously stated, prior

ABOVE SUSPICION, *adjective* above reproach, absolved, blameless, clean, clear, exculpable, faultless, free from guilt, free from wrong, guilt-free, guiltless, impeccable, incorrupt, inculpable, innocent, irreprehensible, moral, sinless, taintless, unblamable, unblemished, uncensurable, uncorrupted, unreproached, unsoiled, unsullied, upright, vindicated

ABOVE THE LAW, *adjective* above reproach, beyond the reach of the law, capable of exploiting a gray area of the law, exempt from controls, exempt from legal controls, immune from legal responsibility, not subject to oversight, protected from the farthest reaches of the law

ABRIDGE *(Divest),* ***verb*** attach, deprive of, dispossess of, disseise, divest of, expropriate, limit, restrict, seize, strip, take away, usurp, wrest from

ABRIDGE *(Shorten),* ***verb*** abbreviate, bate, boil down, capsulize, *circumcidere,* compress, condense, contract, *contrahere,* curtail, cut down, decrease, diminish, epitomize, foreshorten, give the sum and substance, lessen, *praecidere,* reduce, shrink, sketch, subtract, summarize, synopsize, take away, telescope, trim, whittle

ABRIDGED, *adjective* abbreviated, brief, capsulized, compact, compressed, condensed, contracted, curtailed, decreased, diminished, elliptic, epitomized, foreshortened, laconic, lessened, minimal, reduced, shortened, shrunk, summarized, synopsized, telescoped

ABRIDGMENT *(Condensation),* ***noun*** abbreviation, *abbreviature,* abstract, *aperçu,* brief, capsule, compendium, compression, consolidation, conspectus, contraction, curtailment, digest, epitome, epitomization, extract, précis, reduction, sketch, summary, synopsis
ASSOCIATED CONCEPTS: abridgment of time

ABRIDGMENT *(Disentitlement),* ***noun*** abatement, curtailment, deprivation, deprivement, dispossession, divestiture, limitation, loss, privation, restriction
ASSOCIATED CONCEPTS: abridgment of rights

ABROGATE *(Annul),* ***verb*** abjure, abnegate, abolish, *abrogare,* cancel, contradict, contravene, declare null and void, disannul, disapprove, dissolve, eliminate, impair, invalidate, make void, negate, nullify, obstruct, prohibit, quash, rebuff, refuse, reject, renounce, repudiate, retract, reverse, undo, void
FOREIGN PHRASES: ***Cujus est instituere, ejus est abrogare.*** Whose right it is to institute anything may abrogate it. ***Non impedit clausula derogatoria, quo minus ab eadem potestate res dissolvantur a qua constituuntur.*** A derogatory clause does not prevent things from being dissolved by the same power by which they were originally created.

ABROGATE *(Rescind),* ***verb*** abolish, annul, bar, cancel, countermand, declare null and void, deprive of power, destroy, disannul, eliminate, exclude, invalidate, not accept, nullify, omit, override, overrule, prohibit, recall, recant, repeal, repudiate, *rescindere,* retract, reverse, revoke, set aside, supersede, terminate, vacate, void, waive
ASSOCIATED CONCEPTS: abrogating an appeal, express abrogation
FOREIGN PHRASES: ***Clausula quae abrogationem excludit ab initio non valet.*** A clause which precludes repeal is void from the beginning. ***Perpetua lex est nullam legem humanam ac positivam perpetuam esse, et clausula quae abrogationem excludit ab initio non valet.*** It is a perpetual law that no human and positive law can be perpetual, and a clause which precludes the power of abrogation or repeal is void from the beginning.

ABROGATED, ***adjective*** abolished, annulled, barred, countermanded, declared null and void, defunct, deprived of power, eliminated, excluded, inactive, invalid, invalidated, nullified, overridden, set aside, superseded, terminated, vacated, waived

ABROGATION, ***noun*** abolishment, abolition, annihilation, annulment, canceling, cancellation, countermand, counterorder, defeasance, dissolution, invalidation, nullification, overriding, overruling, recall, recantation, renege, repeal, repudiation, rescission, retraction, reversal, revocation, suppression, undoing, voidance, vacation, vacatur, withdrawal

ABRUPT, ***adjective*** abusive, acrimonious, aggressive, antagonistic, argumentative, arrogant, baneful, bitter, brisk, brusque, calamitous, cantankerous, caustic, combative, contrary, cross, dissentious, factious, gruff, haughty, malevolent, nasty, offensive, oppugnant, peremptory, precipitous, pugnacious, rancorous, rude, sharp, short, surly, terse, unceremonious, wrangling

ABSCIND, ***verb*** amputate, break, cancel, cleave, clip, cut, decapitate, delete, detach, disconnect, disengage, disjoin, dismember, dispart, dissever, dissociate, disunite, divide, erase, excise, extirpate, mutilate, part, partition, rend, rive, rupture, segregate, separate, sever, shear, split, sunder, tear

ABSCOND, ***verb*** absent oneself, avoid, bolt, decamp, *delitescere,* depart, desert, disappear, dodge, elude, emigrate, escape, eschew, evade, expatriate oneself, flee, hide, *latere,* leave, levant, make off, *occultari,* remove, run, run away, steal away, take flight, withdraw, withdraw clandestinely
ASSOCIATED CONCEPTS: abscond on bail, absconding debtor, attachment, fugitive, *quasi in rem jurisdiction*

ABSENCE *(Nonattendance),* ***noun*** abandonment, *absentia,* abstention, avoidance, defection, desertion, nonappearance, nonpresence, removal, truancy, withdrawal
ASSOCIATED CONCEPTS: absence from the state, absent creditors, absent debtor, absent defendant, absent from a jurisdiction, leave of action
FOREIGN PHRASES: ***Absentem accipere debemus eum qui non est eo loci in quo petitur.*** We must consider absent he who is not in that place in which he is sought.

ABSENCE *(Omission),* ***noun*** deficiency, deprivation, disappearance, hiatus, inadequacy, lack, need, negation, nonbeing, nonexistence, shortage, unavailability, void, want
ASSOCIATED CONCEPTS: absence of counsel, absence of fraud, absence of funds, absence of heirs, absence of issue, absence of negligence, absence of notice, absence of wrongdoing

ABSENT, ***adjective*** absorbed, abstracted, astray, away, bare, bemused, blank, deficient, devoid, elsewhere, faraway, flown, gone, heedless, lost, missing, not present, nowhere to be found, null and void, preoccupied, removed, vacant, vacuous, wanting
ASSOCIATED CONCEPTS: absent intent, absent malice, absent the elements of a crime, new trial based on absence of an accused, counsel, evidence, absent witness

ABSOLUTE *(Complete),* ***adjective*** *absolutus,* blanket, comprehensive, downright, entire, exhaustive, final, finished, full, sheer, total, unbounded, unconditional, unconstrained, unlimited, unqualified, unreserved, unrestrained, unrestricted, unstinted, utter, whole, without qualification
ASSOCIATED CONCEPTS: absolute acceptance, absolute admission, absolute assignment, absolute bequest, absolute control, absolute deed, absolute devise, absolute fee, absolute gift, absolute immunity, absolute insuror, absolute owner, absolute power of alienation, absolute power of disposition, absolute sale, absolute transfer, fee simple absolute

ABSOLUTE *(Conclusive),* ***adjective*** accurate, actual, axiomatic, beyond doubt, categorical, certain, clear, clearly defined, decided, decisive, definite, definitive, determinate, exact, explicit, express, final, fixed, inalienable, indisputable, indubitable, obvious, positive, precise, real, settled, straightforward, true, unconditioned, undoubted, unequivocal, unerring, unimpeachable, unmistakable, unmitigated, unmixed, unquestionable, veritable, well-defined
ASSOCIATED CONCEPTS: absolute certainty, absolute conviction, absolute discretion, absolute duty, absolute liability, absolute moral certainty, absolute pardon, absolute privilege, absolute right, absolute title

ABSOLUTE *(Ideal),* ***adjective*** best, beyond compare, champion, consummate, crowning, defectless, excelling, exemplary, faultless, flawless, highest, immaculate, impeccable, incomparable, matchless, model, *ne plus ultra,* paramount, peerless, perfect, preeminent, pure, spotless, stainless, superior, superlative, supreme, taintless, unblemished, unequaled, unexcelled, unrivaled, unsurpassed, untainted, untarnished

ABSOLUTION, ***noun*** acquittal, amnesty, clearance, deliverance, discharge, dismissal, dismissal of an accusation, exculpation, exoneration, forgiveness, forgiveness of sins, grace, liberation, pardon, purgation, release, release from punishment, remission, reprieve, vindication

ABSOLVE, ***verb*** *absolvere,* acquit, adjudge innocent, clear, discharge, exculpate, excuse, exonerate, find not guilty, forgive, free, let off, *liberare,* liberate, pardon, prove innocent, prove not guilty, *purgare,* purge, release from imputation, remit, reprieve, set free, vindicate
ASSOCIATED CONCEPTS: absolve of blame

ABSOLVED, ***adjective*** acquitted, adjudged blameless, clear, cleared, discharged, exculpated, excused, exempt, exonerated, forgiven, found not guilty, free, immune, innocent, let off, liberated, pardoned, proven innocent, reprieved, set free, vindicated

ABSORB *(Assimilate),* ***verb*** accept, acculturate, assimilate, consume, devour, draw, enculturate, gain, habituate, incorporate, integrate, merge, naturalize, soak in, sponge, swallow

ABSORB *(Comprehend),* ***verb*** digest, engage, fathom, grasp, know, perceive, take in, follow, understand

ABSTAIN, ***verb*** avoid, be loath, be neutral, by-pass, cease, decline, defer, desist, discontinue, dispense with, do without, eschew, forebear, forgo, hold back, keep away, keep off, let alone, not use, not vote, refrain voluntarily from, refuse, restrain oneself, shirk, shun, spare, stand aside, take no sides, turn aside from, waive, withhold

ABSTEMIOUS, ***adjective*** careful, cautious, cheap, conservative, economical, economy-minded, frugal, miserly, moderate, parsimonious, penurious, provident, prudent, restrained, self-denying, sparing, Spartan, stinting, temperate, thrifty, unwasteful

ABSTENTION, ***noun*** abstainment, abstemiousness, abstinence, abstinence from action, avoidance, elusion, eschewal, evasion, forbearance, holding off, inaction, nonparticipation, refrainment
ASSOCIATED CONCEPTS: abstention awaiting the state court's decision, abstention based on deferral, abstention based on state issues, doctrine of abstention

ABSTRACT, ***noun*** abbreviation, abbreviature, abridgment, analect, brief, capsule, compendium, compilation, compression, condensation, consolidation, conspectus, contraction, digest, *epitoma,* epitome, extract, pandect, précis, reduction, summary, synopsis
ASSOCIATED CONCEPTS: abstract idea, abstract of a record, abstract of judgment, abstract of title, abstract proposition of law, abstracts of evidence, marketable title acts, title search

ABSTRACT *(Separate),* ***verb*** detach, disengage, disjoin, dissociate, disunite, isolate, remove, take out of context

ABSTRACT *(Summarize),* ***verb*** abbreviate, abridge, capsulize, compact, compress, condense, contract, epitomize, reduce, shorten, synopsize, telescope

ABSTRUSE, ***adjective*** abstract, ambiguous, attenuated, cloudy, complex, difficult to understand, elusive, enigmatic, esoteric, hidden, incomprehensible, indefinable, indefinite, inexplicable, mysterious, nebulous, obscure, profound, puzzling, rarefied, recondite, remote, subtle, technical, unclear, unfathomable, vague

ABSURD, ***adjective*** bizarre, conspicuous, crazy, egregious, extreme, farcical, flagrant, foolish, hysterical, idiotic, implausible, inane, inept, laughable, ludicrous, nonsensical, outrageous, over-the-top, preposterous, rational, ridiculous, unbelievable, unreasonable, unsound, unsuitable, uproarious
ASSOCIATED CONCEPTS: an absurd interpretation of the law, an absurd reading of the law

ABUNDANT, ***adjective*** all that is desired, ample, ample supply, bountiful, comfortable, considerable, copious, cornucopia, extensive, fecund, fertile, fruitful, fulsome, generous, hearty, liberal, overflowing, overly available, plenteous, plentiful, predominant, prolific, replete with, substantial, sufficient, superabundance, surplus, the most wished for, vast

ABUSE *(Corrupt practice),* ***noun*** baseness, breach of trust, deviation from rectitude, dishonesty, distortion, erroneous use, excessive use, exploitation, fraudulency, ill-usage, ill-use, improper usage, improper use, jobbery, malfeasance, malversation, misapplication, misappropriation, misdirection, misemployment, mishandling, mismanagement, misrepresentation, misstatement, misusage, misuse, perversion, *usus perversus,* violation, want of principle, wrong use
ASSOCIATED CONCEPTS: abuse of a mandate, abuse of a proceeding, abuse of authority, abuse of discretion, abuse of executive authority, abuse of legal process, abuse of power, neglect
FOREIGN PHRASES: ***Ab abusu ad usum non valet consequentia.*** A conclusion as to the use of a thing from its abuse is invalid. ***Confirmat usum qui tollit abusum.*** He confirms a use who removes an abuse. ***Omnium rerum quarum usus est, potest esse abusus, virtute sola excepta.*** There may be an abuse of everything of which there is a use, virtue alone excepted.

ABUSE *(Physical misuse),* ***noun*** atrocity, bad treatment, damage, debasement, defilement, dishonor, dishonoring, hurt, ill treatment, ill usage, ill use, impairment, indecent assault, injury, maltreatment, mishandling, mistreatment, misusage, molestation, outrage, persecution, victimization, violation
ASSOCIATED CONCEPTS: abuse of a child, wife-beating

ABUSE *(Misuse),* ***verb*** *abuti,* ill-use, injure, make excessive use of, make improper use of, maltreat, manhandle, misapply, misappropriate, misemploy, mishandle, mistreat, pervert, use improperly, use wrongly
ASSOCIATED CONCEPTS: abuse of a minor

ABUSE *(Victimize),* ***verb*** injure, maltreat, manhandle, mistreat, molest, oppress

ABUSE *(Violate),* ***verb*** debauch, defile, degrade, dishonor, harm, ill-use, persecute, pollute, profane, wrong

ABUSED, ***adjective*** aggrieved, debased, defamed, defiled, degraded, disparaged, execrated, exploited, ill-treated, ill-used, injured, maltreated, mistreated, misused, oppressed, persecuted, victimized, vilified, wronged
ASSOCIATED CONCEPTS: abused children

ABUSIVE, ***adjective*** detracting, insulting, maledictory, menacing, quarreling, reviling, threatening, ungracious
ASSOCIATED CONCEPTS: abusive language, abusive letter, abusive manner

ABUT, ***verb*** *aboutir,* adjoin, attach, be adjacent to, be contiguous, border on, bound, butt, conjoin, connect, end at, extend to, join, lean against, meet, reach, *rei adiacere, rem attingere,* touch, verge on
ASSOCIATED CONCEPTS: abutting land, abutting on the improvement, abutting owner, abutting property owner

ABUTMENT, ***noun*** abutment, abuttal, adhesion, adjacency, adjoinment, appendage, apposition, appurtenance, attachment, buttress, conjunction, connection, contact, contiguity, joint, junction, juxtaposition, union
ASSOCIATED CONCEPTS: abutting owners

ABYSS, ***noun*** absence, black hole, blank, cavity, chasm, emptiness, fissure, gap, hiatus, hole, hollowed-out area, hollowed-out place, lacuna, the unknown, vacuity, vacuum, void

ACADEMIC, ***adjective*** curricular, didactic, educational, erudite, formal, highbrow, intellectual, learned, pedagogical, pedantic, professorial, scholarly, scholastic

ACCEDE *(Concede),* ***verb*** abide by, accept, accord, acknowledge, acquiesce, admit, agree to, approve, assent, back down, capitulate, comply, concur, conform, consent, deign, give assent, give in, grant, obey, permit, submit, subscribe to, succumb, surrender, vouchsafe, yield, yield assent

ACCEDE *(Succeed),* ***verb*** assume, attain, become heir to, come after, come next, displace, follow in order, inherit, reach, replace, supersede, supplant, take the place of

ACCELERATE, ***adjective*** advance, catalyze, ease, expedite, facilitate, fast-track, forward, further, get going, hasten, hurry, increase in speed, precipitate, propel, quicken, rush, step-up, step up the pace, streamline, take to the next level
ASSOCIATED CONCEPTS: accelerated appeal

ACCELERATED JUDGMENT, ***noun*** accelerated decision, expedited determination, expedited judgment, facilitated decision, speeded adjudication

ACCELERATION, ***noun*** dispatch, expedition, expeditious performance, hastening, hurrying, increase of speed, quickening, shortening of time, speedup, spurt, stepping up a pace
ASSOCIATED CONCEPTS: acceleration clause, acceleration doctrine, acceleration of a testamentary gift, acceleration of payments, acceleration of remainders

ACCENTUATE, ***verb*** accent, deepen, emphasize, heighten, highlight, intensify, italicize, make clear, point up, pronounce, punctuate, reaffirm, spearhead, star, strengthen, stress, underline, underscore

ACCEPT *(Admit as sufficient),* ***verb*** accede to, acquiesce, admit as satisfactory, agree to, allow, comply, confirm

ACCEPT *(Assent),* ***verb*** accede to, acquiesce, affirm, agree to, allow, authorize, comply, confirm, endorse, ratify, sanction, tolerate
ASSOCIATED CONCEPTS: accept a contract, ratification

ACCEPT *(Embrace),* ***verb*** adopt, consider as true, embrace, internalize

ACCEPT *(Recognize),* ***verb*** accord recognition to, acknowledge, allow, honor
ASSOCIATED CONCEPTS: accept a bill, accept a check, accept a draft

ACCEPT *(Take),* ***verb*** *accipere,* acquire, obtain, receive, receive with approval, secure, take control of, take hold of, take possession of
ASSOCIATED CONCEPTS: accept a bribe, accept gainful employment

ACCEPTABLE, ***adjective*** adequate, admissible, advisable, agreeable, allowable, applicable, appropriate, attractive, becoming, comfortable, commensurate, conventional, decent, desirable, eligible, entitled, enviable, expedient, fair, felicitous, fit, gratifying, inviting, justifiable, likable, mediocre, moderate, opportune, palatable, passable, pleasant, pleasing, presentable, proper, qualified, respectable, satisfactory, seemly, suitable, tenable, timely, tolerable, unobjectionable, viable, welcome
ASSOCIATED CONCEPTS: acceptable compromise, acceptable contract, acceptable settlement, accord and satisfaction, performance

ACCEPTANCE, ***noun*** accedence, *acceptio,* accession, accordance, acknowledgment, acquiescence, adoption, agreement, allowance, approbation, approval, assent, assurance, compliance, *comprobatio,* concordance, consent, endorsement, ratification, receipt, receptiveness, resignation, sanction, tolerance, toleration
ASSOCIATED CONCEPTS: acceptance by a grantee to a deed, acceptance by conduct, acceptance in a sale, acceptance of a bill of exchange, acceptance of a bribe, acceptance of a check, acceptance of a contract, acceptance of a draft, acceptance of a gift by a donee, acceptance of an insurance application, acceptance of an offer, acceptance of an order, acceptance of benefits, acceptance of employment, acceptance of goods, acceptance of risk, blank acceptance, conditional acceptance, constructive acceptance, conversion by acceptance, implied acceptance
FOREIGN PHRASES: ***Cum in corpore dissentitur, apparet nullam esse acceptionem.*** When there is a disagreement in the substance of a thing, it appears that there is no acceptance.

ACCESS *(Opening),* ***noun*** accessibility, approachability, availability, chance, means, occasion, open position, opportunity, possibility, unfilled place, vacancy

ACCESS *(Right of way),* ***noun*** *accessus,* adit, *aditus,* admission, admittance, approach, course, direct approach, entrance, entrance way, entry, ingress, inlet, means of access, means of approach, opening, passage, passageway, path, right of entry, road, route, way, way in, way of approach, way through

ACCESSIBLE, ***adjective*** achievable, amenable, approachable, assailable, attainable, available, communicative, convenient, obliging, open, open-minded, penetrable, pervious, reachable, receptive, responsive

ACCESSION *(Annexation),* ***noun*** *accessio,* addition, adherence, adhesion, adjoining, affixation, annexing, appendage, attachment, binding, cementation, cohesion, combination, combining, conjoining, consolidation, coupling, fastening, fusion, inclusion, incorporation, joining, merger, putting together, securing, subjoining, subjunction, supplementation, unification, union, uniting
ASSOCIATED CONCEPTS: accession of fixtures, accession of property

ACCESSION *(Enlargement),* ***noun*** accretion, accrual, accumulation, acquisition, addition, advance, aggrandizement,

amplification, appreciation, attainment, augmentation, broadening, burgeoning, development, elaboration, enhancement, expansion, extension, gain, growth, increase, multiplication, progress, progression, supplementation, swelling
ASSOCIATED CONCEPTS: accession of property, accretion, acquisition of title by accession, doctrine of accession, permanent accession, riparian accession

ACCESSORY, ***noun*** abettor, accomplice, accomplice in crime, advisor, aider, assistant, coconspirator, codirector, collaborator, confederate, confrère, *conscius,* consociate, cooperator, copartner, coworker, *culpae socius,* encourager, fellow conspirator, helper, helpmate, partaker, *particeps criminis,* participant, participator, partner, partner in crime, planner, *socius criminis*
ASSOCIATED CONCEPTS: accessory after the fact, accessory before the fact, accessory contract, accessory during the fact, accessory obligation, accessory to a crime, accessory to an offense, aiding and abetting, principal
FOREIGN PHRASES: ***Accessorium non ducit, sed sequitur suum principale.*** That which is the accessory or incident does not lead, but follows its principals. ***Accessorius sequitur naturam sui principales.*** An accessory follows the nature of his principal; thus, an accessory cannot be found guilty of a greater crime than his principal. ***Cujus juris est principale, ejusdem juris erit accessorium.*** He who has jurisdiction of the principal thing also has jurisdiction of the accessory. ***Nullus dicitur accessorius post feloniam, sed ille qui novit principalem feloniam fecisse, et illum receptavit et comfortavit.*** No one is called an "accessory" after the fact but the one who knew the principal had committed a felony, and who received and comforted him. ***Omne principale trahit ad se accessorium.*** Every principal thing draws the accessory to itself. ***Quae accessionum locum obtinent, extinguuntur cum principales res peremp tae fuerint.*** When the principal thing is destroyed, those things which are accessory to it are also destroyed. ***Res accessoria sequitur rem principalem.*** An accessory follows the principal. ***Ubi non est principalis, non potest esse accessorius.*** Where there can be no principal, there cannot be an accessory.

ACCIDENT *(Chance occurrence),* ***noun*** adventitiousness, befalling, blind chance, casus, circumstance, fortuitous event, fortuity, happening, hazard, incident, inevitable occurrence, sudden happening, unanticipated event, undesigned occurrence, unexpected misfortune, unexpected occurrence, unforeseen occurrence
ASSOCIATED CONCEPTS: accidental cause, accidental loss, accidental means
FOREIGN PHRASES: ***Casus fortuitus non est sperandus, et nemo tenetur devinare.*** A fortuitous event is not to be foreseen, and no one is bound to expect it. ***Casus fortuitus non est supponendus.*** A fortuitous happening is not to be presumed.

ACCIDENT *(Misfortune),* ***noun*** adversity, affliction, calamity, casualty, *contretemps,* disaster, injurious occurrence, misadventure, miscarriage, mischance, mishap, unfortunate event
ASSOCIATED CONCEPTS: accident arising out of the course of employment, accidental bodily injury, accidental fires, collision, disability caused by an accident, expectable loss, external, foreseeable loss, violent and accidental means

ACCIDENTAL, ***adjective*** adventitious, casual, chance, coincidental, extrinsic, fortuitous, inadvertent, incidental, indeterminate, undesigned, undetermined, unexpected, unforeseen, unintended, unintentional, unpremeditated, unwitting
ASSOCIATED CONCEPTS: accident and health insurance, accidental loss, accidental means, disability, life insurance, negligence

ACCOMMODATE, ***verb*** accept, *accommodare,* adapt, adjust, administer to, agree, aid, arrange, assist, attune, be capable of holding, benefit, bring into consistency, bring to terms, comfort, compose, contain, convenience, defer, do a favor for, do a service for, favor, fit, furnish, gratify, harmonize, have, have capacity for, help, hold, meet the wants of, minister to, oblige, provide, render a service, serve, settle, settle amicably, suit, supply the wants of, support, yield

ACCOMMODATING, ***adjective*** accepting, adjustable, affable, agreeable, amiable, attentive, benevolent, benignant, charitable, civil, complaisant, compliant, conciliatory, considerate, cordial, courteous, decent, deferential, fair, favorable, friendly, generous, gracious, heedful, helpful, indulgent, kind, kindly, mindful, neighborly, obliging, pliable, polite, solicitous, thoughtful, unselfish, warmhearted, well-intentioned, well-meaning, yielding

ACCOMMODATION *(Adjustment),* ***noun*** accordance, adaptation, agreement, arrangement, *compositio,* composition of differences, compromise, friendly agreement, harmonization, mutual understanding, obliging, provision, readjustment, *reconciliatio,* rectification, settlement

ACCOMMODATION *(Backing),* ***noun*** assistance, assurance, championing, cooperation, endorsement, guarantee, seconding, security, sponsorship, succor, support, surety
ASSOCIATED CONCEPTS: accommodated endorser, accommodated party, accommodated payee, accommodation acceptance, accommodation bill, accommodation endorsement, accommodation guarantor, accommodation maker, accommodation note, accommodation paper, accommodation signer, *cautio fidejussoria*

ACCOMPANY, ***verb*** associate with, coexist, commingle, consort, convoy, join, keep, keep company with

ACCOMPANYING, ***adjective*** accessory, associated, associated with, attendant, attending, coactive, coexistent, collateral, commingled, concomitant, concurrent, co-operant, cooperative, fellow, incidental, joined, joint, synergetic

ACCOMPLICE, ***noun*** abettor, accessory, accessory after the fact, accessory before the fact, advisor, aid, aider, aider and abettor, assistant, associate, associate in crime, associate in guilt, coactor, coconspirator, codefendant, codirector, collaborator, comate, confederate, confrère, *conscius,* consociate, contriver, cooperator, coworker, *culpae socius,* encourager, fellow conspirator, helper, helpmate, partaker, *particeps criminis,* participant, participator, partner, partner in crime, partner in wrongdoing, planner, principal, *socius criminis,* supporter
ASSOCIATED CONCEPTS: accomplice witness, aiding and abetting, complicity, inchoate crimes, mens rea, vicarious liability, Wharton's rule
FOREIGN PHRASES: ***Agentes et consentientes pari poena plectentur.*** Acting and consenting parties are liable to the same punishment.

ACCOMPLISH, ***verb*** achieve, attain, bring about, complete, consummate, discharge, dispatch, effect, enact, execute, finish, fulfill, realize, succeed

ACCOMPLISHMENT *(Achievement),* ***noun*** attainment, conquest, contribution, coup, culmination, deed, enactment, feat, fruition, good deed, good fortune, hit, milestone, performance, positive action, result, success, summit, triumph, victory, win

ACCOMPLISHMENT *(Satisfaction),* ***noun*** completion, consummation, contentedness, contentment, elation, enjoyment, execution, felicity, fulfillment, gratification, happiness, pleasance, pleasure, realization, result, satiation

ACCORD, ***noun*** accommodation, accordance, adjustment, agreement, arrangement, compromise, concession, concord, concordance, mutual understanding, settlement, understanding
ASSOCIATED CONCEPTS: accord and satisfaction, disputed claims, executed accord, executory accord, novation, payment of a debt, release, satisfaction, substituted agreement, unliquidated claim
FOREIGN PHRASES: ***Concordare leges legibus est optimus interpretandi modus.*** To reconcile laws with other laws is the best method of interpreting them.

ACCORDANCE *(Compact),* ***noun*** accommodation, accord, adjustment, agreement, arrangement, conciliation, concord, concordance, concurrence, consonance, contract, *entente cordiale,* pact, reconcilement, reconciliation, settlement, unison, unity

ACCORDANCE *(Understanding),* ***noun*** accommodation, adjustment, agreement, amity, assent, assonance, common view, communion, compatibility, compliance, concinnity, concurrence, conformance, conformity, consensus, consentience, consonance, consonancy, harmonization, harmony, meeting of minds, rapport, reconcilement, reconciliation, unanimity, understanding

ACCORDING TO LAW, ***adjective*** allowable, allowed, authorized by law, conformable to law, conformable with the law, constitutional, de *jure,* due, established, in accordance with the law, in compliance, inviolable, jural, law-abiding, lawful, legal, legalized, legitimate, licit, permissible, proper, rightful, statutory, valid, within the law

ACCORDINGLY, ***adverb*** *a fortiori, a priori,* agreeably, as a matter of course, as a result, because of this, by reason of that, compatibly, compliantly, conformably, consequently, consistently, correspondingly, hence, in due course, inevitably, it follows that, naturally, necessarily, then, thereafter, therefore, thus, wherefore

ACCOST, ***verb*** address, *adoriri,* affront, ambush, approach, assail, assault, assault belligerently, attack, beset, *compellare,* confront, draw near, fall upon, rise in hostility before, set upon, strike at, thrust at, waylay

ACCOUNT *(Evaluation),* ***noun*** appraisal, assessment, *compte rendu,* enumeration, financial statement, ledger, list of receipts and payments, *ratio,* register, statement, statement of debits and credits, statement of pecuniary transactions, tally, valuation
ASSOCIATED CONCEPTS: accounts payable, accounts receivable, account rendered, account stated, bank account, joint account, liquidated account, open account, totten trust account

ACCOUNT *(Report),* ***noun*** brief, description, history, memoir, *memoria, narratio,* narration, presentation, recapitulation, recital, record, review, saga, summary, summation

ACCOUNTABILITY, ***noun*** amenability, blame, burden, charge, commitment, dueness, duty, exposure, incumbency, liability, obligation, onus, responsibility, the decent thing, the proper thing, the right thing, trustworthiness, vulnerability

ACCOUNTABLE *(Explainable),* ***adjective*** construable, deducible, definable, describable, determinable, explicable, inferential, interpretable, renderable, translatable

ACCOUNTABLE *(Responsible),* ***adjective*** answerable, beholden, bound, chargeable, devolving on, liable, obligated, obliged, owing, under obligation
ASSOCIATED CONCEPTS: held accountable for one's actions

ACCOUNTANT, ***noun*** bookkeeper, calculator, certified public accountant, chartered accountant, clerk, reckoner, recorder, registrar, statistician

ACCOUNTING, ***noun*** auditing, bookkeeping, complete report, computation, full report, fully detailed analysis, reckoning
ASSOCIATED CONCEPTS: account stated, accounting officer, accounts receivable

ACCREDIT, ***verb*** accept, affirm, approve, authenticate, authorize, certify, confirm, endorse, ratify, sanction, validate, vouch for
ASSOCIATED CONCEPTS: accredited law school, accredited representative

ACCRETION, ***noun*** addition, advance, annexation, augmentation, enlargement, extension, gain, growth, increment

ACCROACH, ***verb*** appropriate, arrogate, assume, break bounds, encroach, impose upon, infringe, interlope, intrude, invade, obtrude, overstep, presume on, take over, transgress, trespass, usurp

ACCRUE *(Arise),* ***verb*** acquire, be derived, become due, become enforceable, become present, come, develop, emanate, ensue, eventuate, fall due, flow, follow, inure, issue, mature, occur, originate, proceed, progress, result from, rise from, spring, yield
ASSOCIATED CONCEPTS: accrual accounting method, accrual of a cause of action, accrued benefit, accrued claims against a municipal corporation, accrued debt, accrued rights, statute of limitations, tolls
FOREIGN PHRASES: ***Confirmare nemo potest prius quam jus ei acciderit.*** No one can confirm a right before the right accrues to him.

ACCRUE *(Increase),* ***verb*** accumulate, acquire, add on, advance, aggrandize, amass, amplify, annex, appreciate, augment, become added, become greater, become larger, branch out, broaden, build, build up, collect, enlarge, escalate, expand, extend, further, gain, gather, greaten, grow, heighten, improve, intensify, mount, multiply, raise, redouble, supplement, swell, widen
ASSOCIATED CONCEPTS: accrual accounting method, accrual of compensation, accrual of taxes, accrued basis, accrued costs, accrued dividend, accrued earnings, accrued income, accrued interest, accrued overtime, accrued taxes

ACCRUED, ***adjective*** accumulated, added to, annexed, grew, increased, mounted, multiplied
ASSOCIATED CONCEPTS: accrued debts, accrued depreciation, accrued dividends, accrued income, accrued installments, accrued interest, accrued rent, accrued rights, accrued taxes

ACCUMULATE *(Amass),* ***verb*** *accumulare,* agglomerate, aggregate, assemble, bring together, *coacervare,* collect, collect into a mass, collect together, colligate, combine, compile, concentrate, cumulate, garner, gather, gather into a mass, gather together, gather up, hoard, mass, pile up, stockpile, store up, unite
ASSOCIATED CONCEPTS: accumulate dividends, accumulate funds, accumulate income, accumulated damages, accumulated deductions, accumulated earnings, accumulated profits, accumulated reserve, accumulated sick leave, accumulated surplus, accumulation in a trust, accumulative judgment, accumulative sentence, consecutive sentence

ACCUMULATE *(Enlarge),* ***verb*** accrue, add to, aggrandize, amplify, augment, broaden, build up, enlarge in size, expand, extend, gain, greaten, grow, grow larger, increase, make greater, multiply, redouble, reinforce, spread, swell
FOREIGN PHRASES: ***Alienatio rei praefertur juri accrescendi.*** The law prefers the alienation of property rather than accumulation.

ACCUMULATION, ***noun*** abundance, accession, accretion, accruement, agglomeration, aggregation, amassing, amassment, amplification, appreciation, assemblage, augmentation, batch, centralization, collection, compilation, concentration, conglomeration, cumulation, deposit, development, gain, gathering, great quantity, growth, harvest, increase, increment, plenty, plethora, sufficiency
ASSOCIATED CONCEPTS: accumulation of income, accumulation of property, trusts, wills

ACCURATE, ***adjective*** actual, authentic, bona fide, careful, clear-cut, conscientious, correct, defect-free, dependable, direct, errorless, exact, executed with care, explicit, factual, faithful, faultless, free of error, genuine, inerrant, literal, meticulous, minute, particular, perfect, precise, proper, punctilious, realistic, reliable, right, rigorous, scrupulous, thorough, true, trustworthy, truthful, unambiguous, unchallenged, uncolored, undenied, undeviating, undisguised, undisputed, undistorted, unerring, unimpeachable, unmistaken, unperjured, unquestionable, unrefuted, unvarnished, valid, veracious, verbatim, verifiable, well-defined

ACCUSATION, ***noun*** accusal, *accusatio,* allegation, ascription, assertion, attribution, bill of indictment, charge, citation, *crimen, criminatio,* crimination, delation, filing of charges, formal charge, imputation, imputation of blame, incrimination, inculpation, indictment, information, preferring of charges, true bill, true charge
ASSOCIATED CONCEPTS: accusatory instrument, complaint, grand jury report, indictment, information, presentment, warrant
FOREIGN PHRASES: ***Accusare nemo se debet, nisi coram deo.*** No one is bound to accuse himself, except before God.

ACCUSATORY, ***adjective*** contemptuous, decrying, deprecatory, derogative, derogatory, disapproving, disparaging, incriminatory, inculpatory, pejorative
ASSOCIATED CONCEPTS: accusatory instrument, grand jury, indictment, prosecution

ACCUSATORY INSTRUMENT, ***noun*** accusatory document, commencement of a criminal proceeding, criminal complaint, formal accusation, fundamental step in a criminal prosecution, initial step in criminal prosecution
ASSOCIATED CONCEPTS: indictment, prosecution

ACCUSE, ***verb*** *accusare, arguere,* attack, blame, bring a charge, bring accusation, bring in a true bill, charge with, *citare,* cite, complain against, criminate, denounce, expose, fix blame, impeach, implicate, incriminate, inculpate, indict, lodge a complaint, prefer charges, prosecute, report against
ASSOCIATED CONCEPTS: accusatory instrument

ACCUSE OF WRONGDOING, ***verb*** accuse, allege, arraign, bring a charge, charge with, cite, criminate, denounce, expose, fix blame, impeach, implicate, incriminate, inculpate, indict, prefer charges, prosecute
ASSOCIATED CONCEPTS: felony complaint, grand jury, indictment, malicious prosecution

ACCUSED *(Attacked),* ***verb*** attacked, defamed, imputed, maligned, reproached, reproved

ACCUSED *(Charged),* ***verb*** arraigned, brought charges, charged, complained of, filed charges, have charges against, held responsible, impeached, indicted

ACCUSER, ***noun*** accusant, accusatrix, challenger, complainant, delator, denouncer, impeacher, incriminator, indictor, informer, libelant, litigant, party to a suit, petitioner, prosecutor

ACCUSTOMED *(Customary),* ***adjective*** *adsuetus,* common, commonplace, confirmed, consuetudinal, consuetudinary, conventional, established, fixed, habitual, normal, ordinary, prevailing, regular, routine, *solitus,* traditional, usual
ASSOCIATED CONCEPTS: accustomed practice, accustomed use

ACCUSTOMED *(Familiarized),* ***adjective*** acclimated, acclimatized, acquainted, adapted, addicted, adjusted, conditioned, familiar, familiar through use, given to, habituated, in the habit of, ingrained with

ACHIEVE *(Acquire),* ***verb*** acquire, arrive, attain, bring about, build, carry, close, complete, conclude, construct, consummate, decide, determine, discharge, earn, evoke, function, gain, get, implement, obtain, operate, originate, prevail, procure, reach, realize, reap, recover, win

ACHIEVE *(Perform),* ***verb*** accomplish, actualize, carry out, compass, contrive, create, dispatch, effect, effectuate, encompass, execute, finish, fulfill, perfect, perform, produce, succeed, terminate, transact

ACKNOWLEDGE *(Declare),* ***verb*** admit, affirm, ascribe, assert, asseverate, attest to, avow, bear witness, certify, depone, depose, disclose, endorse, express, implicate oneself, state, swear

ACKNOWLEDGE *(Respond),* ***verb*** accede, agree, answer, be responsive, concur, ratify, rejoin, remark, reply, signify assent

ACKNOWLEDGE *(Verify),* ***verb*** admit, admit a right, admit the charge, concede, confess, confirm, defer to, recognize, recognize authority of, testify, yield
ASSOCIATED CONCEPTS: acknowledge a document, acknowledge the signatures on a will

ACKNOWLEDGED, ***adjective*** accepted, acquiesced, admitted, approved, avowed, conceded, confessed, conventional, correct, customary, established, familiar, formal, granted, immemorial, inveterate, longstanding, orthodox, popular, prescriptive, professed, public, putative, received, recognized, rooted, time-honored, traditional, understood, undisputed, unquestioned, usual, warranted

ASSOCIATED CONCEPTS: acknowledged actions, acknowledged certificates, acknowledged consideration, acknowledged debt, acknowledged evidence, acknowledged indebtedness, acknowledged instruments, acknowledged liability, acknowledged parties, acknowledged payments, acknowledged pleadings, acknowledged set-off of a claim, acknowledged signatures, acknowledged statements, authority, false certification, recitals

ACKNOWLEDGMENT *(Acceptance),* ***noun*** accession, acquiescence, admittance, agreement, answer, assent, compliance, concession, concurrence, endorsement, ratification, recognition, replication, reply, response, verification
ASSOCIATED CONCEPTS: acknowledgment to an offer

ACKNOWLEDGMENT *(Avowal),* ***noun*** admission, affirmation, assertion, asseveration, authentication, avowance, certification, *confessio,* confession, confirmation, declaration, formal declaration, statement, validation
ASSOCIATED CONCEPTS: acknowledgment in a deposition, acknowledgment of a conveyance, acknowledgment of a debt, acknowledgment of a deed, acknowledgment of a mortgage, acknowledgment of a will, acknowledgment of an illegitimate child, acknowledgment of indebtedness, acknowledgment of liability, certificate of acknowledgment, public acknowledgment

ACQUAINTANCE, ***noun*** adherent, advocate, affiliate, ally, associate, backer, benefactor, cohort, collaborator, colleague, companion, comrade, confidant, crony, defender, friend, partisan, patron, person, proponent, supporter, sympathizer

ACQUAINTED, ***adjective*** advised, apprised, attuned to, awakened, aware of, briefed, *cognitus,* cognizant of, conscious of, conversant with, enlightened, informed, instructed, introduced to, knowledgeable, notified, *notus, peritus,* posted, primed, told

ACQUIESCE, ***verb*** abide, accede, accept, acknowledge, admit, agree, agree to, allow, assent, be willing, bow to, comply, concede, concur, conform, consent, cooperate, defer to, give in, grant, obey, observe, ratify, receive, recognize, relent, resign oneself, sanction, submit, subscribe to, succumb, suffer, surrender, tolerate, yield

ACQUIESCENCE, ***noun*** accedence, acceptance, accession, accordance, acknowledgment, *adsensus,* agreement, allowance, assent, compliance, concession, concordance, concurrence, consent, grant, implied consent, nonresistance, observance, passive agreement, passive consent, permission, permittance, resignedness, sanction, subjection, submission, submissiveness, submittal, sufferance, tacit assent, willingness
ASSOCIATED CONCEPTS: acquiescence in judgment, acquiescence to a breach of contract, acquiescence to a breach of covenant, acquiescence to boundaries, acquiescence to the terms of a contract, ratification by acquiescence
FOREIGN PHRASES: ***Agentes et consentientes pari poena plectentur.*** Acting and consenting parties are liable to the same punishment. ***Longa patientia trahitur ad consensum.*** Long sufferance is interpreted as consent.

ACQUIRE *(Receive),* ***verb*** accept, achieve, *adipisci,* adopt, be given, come into possession of, derive, gain, glean, obtain, reap, take in, win

ACQUIRE *(Secure),* ***verb*** *adquirere,* annex, appropriate, assume, assume ownership, attain, exact, extort, extract, force from, gain, get, make one's own, obtain by any means, procure, purchase, realize, steal, take, take possession, wrest from
ASSOCIATED CONCEPTS: acquire a business, acquire by fraud, acquire by gift, acquire by inheritance, acquire by will, acquire for resale, acquire ownership
FOREIGN PHRASES: ***Incorporalia bello non adquiruntur.*** Things incorporeal are not acquired in war.

ACQUISITION, ***noun*** acceptance, acceptation, acquirement, appropriation, assumption, attainment, find, gain, gleaning, intaking, obtainment of property, possession, procuration, procurement, realization, receival, receiving, reception, recipience, stealing, taking
ASSOCIATED CONCEPTS: acquisition by purchase, acquisition of assets, acquisition of property, acquisition value
FOREIGN PHRASES: ***Qui acquirit sibi acquirit haeredibus.*** He who acquires for himself acquires for his heirs.

ACQUIT, ***verb*** absolve, *absolvere,* clear, compurgate, declare innocent, discharge, discharge from accusation, exculpate, excuse, exempt, exonerate, find not guilty, give a favorable verdict, grant remission, let off, *liberare,* liberate, make free, pardon, pronounce not guilty, prove innocent, *purgare,* release, remit, reprieve, set at liberty, set free, vindicate
ASSOCIATED CONCEPTS: acquittal in fact, acquittal in law

ACQUITTAL, ***noun*** *absolutio,* absolution, acquitment, acquittance, amnesty, clearance, compurgation, discharge, dismissal, exculpation, exoneration, favorable verdict, letting off, *liberatio,* liberation, pardon, purgation, quittance, release, remission, reprieve, restoration, verdict of not guilty, vindication
ASSOCIATED CONCEPTS: acquittal by a jury
FOREIGN PHRASES: ***Paribus sententiis reus absolvitur.*** When the opinions are equal, where the court is equally divided, the defendant is acquitted.

ACQUITTED, ***adjective*** cleared, exculpated, exonerated, freed of wrongdoing, let go, let off, not guilty, proved innocent, vindicated

ACRIMONIOUS, ***adjective*** acerb, acerbic, acrid, astringent, biting, bitter, blistering, captious, caustic, censorious, choleric, corrosive, cross-tempered, cruel, cutting, cynical, embittered, envenomed, gruff, harsh, hostile, huffy, ill-natured, inimical, irascible, irritable, malevolent, malicious, malignant, negative, peevish, pejorative, petulant, rancorous, resentful, rough, rude, sarcastic, scathing, severe, sharp, snappish, snarling, sour, spiteful, stinging, tart, testy, touchy, vicious, virulent, vitriolic, waspish

ACT *(Enactment),* ***noun*** *acte,* administration, bill, code, deed, dictate, edict, law, legislation, legislative decree, lex, mandate, ordinance, precept, prescript, *règlement,* regulation, resolution, rule, ruling, statute, written law
ASSOCIATED CONCEPTS: Congressional act, legislative act
FOREIGN PHRASES: ***Actus legis nemini est damnosus.*** The act of the law shall prejudice no one.

ACT *(Undertaking),* ***noun*** accomplishment, achievement, action, commission, course, dealing, deed, doing, effectuation, enterprise, execution, feat, implementation, maneuver, manipulation, measure, method, move, operation, performance, perpetration, step, stratagem, task, transaction
ASSOCIATED CONCEPTS: act in official capacity, act of bankruptcy, act of commission, act of cruelty, act of embezzlement, act of flight, act of God, act of infringement, act of

insolvency, act of larceny, act of law, act of misfeasance, act of necessity, act of omission, act of ownership, act of providence, act of reckless disregard, act of violence, act of war, *actus reas,* judicial act, mala prohibita act, overt act
FOREIGN PHRASES: ***Actus me invito factus non est meus actus.*** An act done by me against my will is not my act. ***Actus not facit reum, nisi mens sit rea.*** An act does not render a person guilty, unless the mind is guilty. ***Idem est facere, et non prohibere cum possis.*** It is the same thing to commit an act as not to prohibit it, when it is in your power. ***Facta sunt potentiora verbis.*** Acts or deeds are more powerful than words.

ACT AS AGENT, *verb* act as intermediary, act as substitute, act as surrogate, act for, act in place of, answer for, appear for, designate to represent, front for, intercede, represent, serve in one's stead, stand for, stand in the stead of

ACT ILLEGALLY, *verb* be derelict, be illegal, be perfidious, be recalcitrant, break the law, commit a crime, disobey the law, not comply, refuse to obey, repudiate, resist, transgress, traverse, trespass, violate, violate the law

ACT IN CONCERT, *verb* act jointly, agree, be in collusion with, collude, combine, concur, connive, conspire, cooperate, federate, form a coalition, involve, join, participate, pool, unite

ACT OF GOD, *noun* accident, chance occurrence, fortuitousness, fortuity, random luck

ACT ON *(Complete),* ***verb*** agree, answer, choose, choose a course of action, come to a conclusion, come to an agreement, conclude, decree, determine, draw a conclusion, elect, establish, finalize, find, form a judgment, form a resolution, form an opinion, make a choice, make a decision, make a selection, ok, opt, pronounce, reach a decision, react, reply, resolve, respond

ACT ON *(Rule),* ***verb*** adjudge, adjudicate, arrive at a judgment, ascertain, award, come to a decision, compromise, conclude, decree, determine, finalize, find, judge, make a decision, pronounce, reach a decision, reach a verdict, resolve, rule, sentence, settle
ASSOCIATED CONCEPTS: act on a motion, act on an application, act on case, act on evidence, act on information provided by an informant, act on petition

ACTING, *adjective* adjutant, deputative, deputy, functioning, holding legal rights conferred by another, impermanent, replacing, representative, representing, short-term, speaking by delegated authority, standing in the place of, substituting for, temporary, transient
ASSOCIATED CONCEPTS: acting illegally, acting in a boisterous manner, acting in concert with others, acting in good faith, acting judge, acting mayor, acting officer, acting within the course of employment, acting within the scope of employment

ACTION *(Performance),* ***noun*** accomplishment, achievement, administration, carrying out, concrete results, consummation, course of conduct, discharge, doing, effectuation, enforcement, execution, *factum,* implementation, line of action
FOREIGN PHRASES: ***Non quod dictum est, sed quod factum est inspicitur.*** Not what is said, but what is done, is to be regarded. ***Factum cuique suum, non adversario, nocere debet.*** A man's own acts should prejudice himself, not his adversary. ***Factum infectum fieri nequit.*** A thing which has been done cannot be undone. ***Les lois ne se chargent de punir que les actions exterieures.*** Laws do not assume to punish other than overt acts.

ACTION *(Proceeding),* ***noun*** *actio,* action at law, case, cause, cause in court, court proceeding, formal prosecution, hearing, hearing on the merits, judicial contest, judicial proceeding, lawsuit, legal action, legal contest, legal proceeding, *lis,* litigation, litigation of the charges, prosecution, suit, suit at law, suit in law, trial, trial of a case, trial of the issues
ASSOCIATED CONCEPTS: abatement, action arising under the laws of the United States, action at law, action brought, action by one party against another, action ex delicto, action ex parte, action for a declaratory judgment, action for bodily injury, action for breach of a contract, action for damages, action for deceit, action for disparagement, action for dissolution, action for divorce, action for fraud, action for injury to property, action for liquidated damages, action for misrepresentation, action for money damages, action for recovery of chattel, action for rescission and restitution, action in assumpsit, action in conversion, action in detinue, action in ejectment, action in equity, action in interpleader, action in personam, action in quantum meruit, action in rem, action in replevin, action in tort, action in trespass, action in trover, action of foreclosure, action of garnishment, action on a contract, action on a debt, action on account rendered, action on contract, action quasi in rem, action to quiet title, action to remove a cloud, affirmative action, cause of action, chose in action, civil action, class action, commence an action, consolidation, continuance of action on submitted facts, criminal action, cross action, derivative action, independent actions, joinder of actions, joint action, legal action, local actions, main action, multiplicity of actions, pending action, right of action, severance of actions, stockholders' action, third-party action
FOREIGN PHRASES: ***Ex nudo pacto non oritus nascitur actio.*** No action arises on a contract without a consideration. ***Cum actio fuerit mere criminalis, institui poterit ab initio criminaliter vel civiliter.*** When an action is merely criminal, it can be instituted either criminally or civilly at the outset. ***In rem actio est per quam rem nostram quae ab alio possidetur petimus, et semper adversus eum est qui rem possidet.*** An action in rem is one by means of which we seek our property which is owned by another, and is always against him who possesses the property. ***Actio quaelibet it sua via.*** Every action proceeds in its own course. ***Secta est pugna civilis; sicut actores armantur actionibus, et, quasi, gladiis accinguntur, ita rei muniuntur exceptionibus, et defenduntur, quasi, clypeis.*** A suit is a civil battle; for as the plaintiffs are armed with actions, and as it were, girded with swords, so the defendants are fortified with pleas, and defended, as it were, by shields. ***Remoto impedimento, emergit actio.*** The impediment being removed, the action emerges. ***Omnis quereia et omnis actio injuriarum limita est infra certa tempora.*** Every complaint and every action for injuries is limited within certain times. ***Omnes actiones in mundo infra certa tempora habent limitationem.*** All actions in the world are limited within certain periods of time. ***In haeredes non solent transire actiones quae poenales ex maleficio sunt.*** Penal actions arising from anything of a criminal nature do not pass to heirs. ***Actio personalis moritur cum persona.*** A personal action dies with the person. ***Ex tupi causa non oritur actio.*** No cause of action arises out of an immoral or illegal consideration.

ACTIONABLE, *adjective* accountable, amenable, answerable, bound, causidical, chargeable, controvertible, disputable, justiciable, liable to prosecution, litigable, litigant,

litigious, pertaining to litigation, remediable by an action at law, *res cuius actio est,* responsible, suable, under legal obligation, under obligation, unexempt from
ASSOCIATED CONCEPTS: actionable cause of action, actionable charges, actionable claim, actionable words, actionable wrongdoing

ACTIONS, *noun* bearing, behavior, behavior pattern, comportment, conduct, dealings, demeanor, deportment, doings, guise, manner, mien, mode of action, *modus vivendi,* policy, practice, presence, procedure, ways
ASSOCIATED CONCEPTS: abandonment, abatement, action at law, actions in equity, appeals, arbitrations, bankruptcy, civil actions, collateral estoppel, consolidation, construction, criminal, declaratory judgments, easements, employment, federal actions, fidelity actions, frivolous actions, garnishment, habeas corpus, labor law, landlord and tenant, *lis pendens,* mandamus, marital actions, municipal actions, removal of actions, replevin, res judicata, severance of an action, splitting a cause of action, state actions, summary proceedings, supplemental proceedings, venue

ACTIVATE, *verb* accelerate, actuate, animate, boost, drive, empower, energize, enliven, excite, excite to action, impel, initiate, intensify, launch, maintain, motivate, originate, prompt, quicken, step up, stimulate, stir, urge

ACTIVE, *adjective* assiduous, at work, busily employed, busily engaged, busy, effective, effectual, efficacious, efficient, energetic, enterprising, functioning, *impiger,* in a state of action, in actual process, in operation, in practice, industrious, *industrius, navus,* operant, operating, performing, sedulous, trenchant, vigorous, working
ASSOCIATED CONCEPTS: active concealment, active negligence, active participant, active tort feasor, active trust, active wrongdoing, passive negligence, passive tort feasor

ACTIVITIES, *noun* actions, acts, affairs, arrangements, dealings, deals, doings, exchange, interests, matters, measures, policy, practice, proceedings, relations, transactions, understandings, undertakings

ACTIVITY, *noun* assignment, campaign, cause, crusade, drive, endeavor, enterprise, function, interest, movement, operation, pursuit, undertaking, venture, work

ACTOR, *noun* *actor,* aggrieved party, complainant, intervener, litigant, malcontent, man with a grievance, operator, participant, party, performer, person, petitioner, plaintiff, *qui facit*
ASSOCIATED CONCEPTS: an actor as a witness in a prosecution, an actor in a legal proceeding

ACTS *(Conduct),* ***noun*** actions, bearing, behavior, demeanor, manners, mien, observance, pattern

ACTS *(Legislation),* ***noun*** enactments, laws, provisions of the law, statutes
ASSOCIATED CONCEPTS: acts in emergencies, acts of Congress, acts of insolvency, bills, case law, local ordinances, ordinances, statutes

ACTUAL, *adjective* absolute, accurate, as represented, ascertained, authentic, authenticated, *bona fide,* categorical, categorically true, certain, concrete, correct, *de facto,* decided, defined, definite, demonstrable, demonstrated, determinate, essential, exact, existent, existing, factual, faithful, genuine, honest, in fact, *ipse,* literal, nonabstract, not fictitious, not imaginary, not merely supposed, objective, official, palpable, positive, precise, present, real, realistic, right, rightful, specific, substantial, substantive, tangible, true, true to the facts, true to the letter, truthful, unerring, unerroneous, unfallacious, unfalse, unimagined, unimpeachable, unmistaken, unrefuted, unsupposed, valid, veracious, veritable, *verus,* well-founded, well-grounded
ASSOCIATED CONCEPTS: actual authority, actual bailment, actual book value, actual case or controversy, actual cash receipts, actual cash value, actual damages, actual delivery, actual earnings, actual eviction, actual expense, actual force, actual fraud, actual income, actual intent, actual intent to defraud, actual knowledge, actual loss, actual malice, actual market value, actual notice, actual occupancy, actual possession, actual residence, actual use, actual value, actual waste, actually engaged in business, actually occupied, actually owing, actually owning, actually receive, fair, fair reasonable cash price, reasonable cash price

ACTUARY, *noun* calculator of insurance risks, compiler of tables of mortality, insurance advisor, statistician
ASSOCIATED CONCEPTS: actuarial bureaus, actuarial solvency, actuarial tables

ACTUS REUS, *noun* actions, at fault, bearing, behavior, blamable, blameworthy, censurable, chargeable, condemnable, convicted, criminal, criminous, culpable, delinquent, demeanor, deserving, deserving of blame, deserving reproof, erring, external element of a crime, guilty act, imputable, in error, in the wrong, incriminated, indictable, manners, mien, observance, of punishment, pattern, peccant, reprehensible, reproachable, reprovable, to blame, transgressing

ACUMEN, *noun* acuity, astuteness, caliber, cleverness, common sense, comprehension, discernment, discretion, discrimination, foresightedness, ingenuity, insight, intelligence, intuition, judgment, keenness, mental acuteness, mental capacity, perception, perspicacity, reason, sagacity, sense, sharpness, shrewdness, smartness, subtlety, wisdom

ACUTE, *adjective* *acer,* acuminate, acutus, alert, apt, astute, aware, clear-sighted, critical, crucial, cutting, discerning, fine, foreseeing, intense, intuitive, keen, keenly sensitive, knowledgeable, penetrating, perceptive, perspicacious, *perspicax,* piercing, pointed, prompt, provident, prudent, quick-witted, *sagax,* sapient, sharp, sharp-edged, sharp-witted, *subtilis,* trenchant, vivid

AD DAMNUM CLAUSE, *noun* claim for damages, demanded damages, fixed amount of damages, monetary clause, provision for damages

AD HOC, *adjective* extemporaneous, for the sake of, for this case alone, improvised, in consideration of, on account of, special
ASSOCIATED CONCEPTS: ad hoc appointment, ad hoc committee

AD INFINITUM, *adverb* boundlessly, endlessly, eternally, illimitably, immeasurably, incalculably, incomprehensibly, indefinitely, indeterminately, innumerably, interminably, limitlessly, measurelessly, to infinity, without end

AD INTERIM, *adverb* at the same time, during, during the interval, *en attendant,* for a time, for the time being, in the course of, in the interim, in the intervening time, in the meantime, in the meanwhile, meantime, meanwhile, pending, throughout, till, until, when, while

ASSOCIATED CONCEPTS: ad interim copyright, ad interim restraining order

AD VALOREM, ***adjective*** according to value, appraised, appraisement, assessable, assessment, charge, chargeable, charged, dutiable, duty, evaluated, excisable, imposition, leviable, levy, ratable, taxation, valorization, value added tax, valued at
ASSOCIATED CONCEPTS: ad valorem tax

ADAMANT, ***adjective*** callous, firm, frozen, hard-hearted, immovable, immutable, implacable, inelastic, inexorable, inflexible, intractable, irreconcilable, merciless, obdurate, persistent, pertinacious, resolute, rigid, stationary, stiff, stubborn, tough, unaffected, unalterable, unbending, uncompassionate, uncompromising, unfeeling, unmalleable, unmoved, unpliable, unpliant, unrelenting, unyielding

ADAPT, ***verb*** acclimatize, accommodate oneself, adjust, alter, *aptare,* arrange, change, comply with, conform, convert, correlate, fashion, fit, make conformable, make suitable, modify, modulate, readjust, reconcile, regularize, render accordant, revise, standardize, temper, transform, work a change

ADAPTABLE, ***adjective*** accommodating, accommodative, acquiescent, adaptive, adjustable, adroit, ambidextrous, amenable, applicable, bendable, buoyant, comformable, complaisant, compliant, corrigible, deft, disposable, docile, ductile, elastic, fitting, flexible, governable, idoneous, in accord, in keeping, in line, in step, limber, lissome, lithe, malleable, manageable, moldable, obedient, open to, plastic, pliable, pliant, practical, resilient, sequacious, serviceable, stretchable, submissive, suitable, suited, supple, tractable, tractile, usable, utilizable, versatile

ADAPTED, ***adjective*** able, absorbed, acclimated, acclimatized, accommodating, accordant, accustomed, adaptable, adequate, adjustable, adjusted, agreed, apposite, appropriate, apt, becoming, befitting, capable, centralized, combined, complaisant, compliant, conditioned, conformable, congruous, consonant, correct, correlative, deft, effective, embodied, familiarized, fit, fitting, flexible, harmonious, integrated, malleable, opportune, pertinent, pliant, proper, qualified, seemly, suitable, suited, tempered, unified

ADD *(Calculate),* ***verb*** account, appraise, assess, audit, compute, count, enumerate, estimate, evaluate, figure, measure, modify, reckon, suffix, sum, tally, total, valuate

ADD *(Combine),* ***verb*** adjoin, affix, agglutinate, aject, alter, annex, append, attach, cement, clip to, conjoin, connect, couple, fuse, glue, innovate, match, mix, pair, put with, subjoin, superpose, tack on, unite, weld
ASSOCIATED CONCEPTS: add a paragraph to a complaint, add a party to action

ADD *(Heighten),* ***verb*** broaden, contribute, enhance, expand, extend, greaten, grow, increase, inflate, insert, widen

ADD *(Interject),* ***verb*** express, include, inject, insert, inset, interpose, introduce, intromit, mention, state, supplement

ADDENDUM, ***noun*** additament, addition, adjunct, affix, annex, annexation, *annexe,* appanage, appendage, appendix, attachment, codicil, complement, concomitant, inclusion, insertion, postscript, rider, subscript, supplement, supplementation
ASSOCIATED CONCEPTS: addendum to a contract, pocket part

ADDICT, ***noun*** adherent, ardent admirer, believer, creature of habit, devotee, disciple, enthusiast, fan, fanatic, fancier, follower, frequenter, partisan, practitioner, pursuer, votary, zealot

ADDICTED, ***adjective*** accustomed, attached, fanatic, given over, habituated, imbued with, in the habit, indulgent, obsessed with, prone to, *rei deditus,* surrendered to, under the influence of, wedded to
ASSOCIATED CONCEPTS: addicted to alcohol, addicted to drugs, addicted to pills

ADDITION, ***noun*** *accessio,* accession, accessory, addend, addendum, additament, additive, *adiectio,* adjunct, adjunction, annex, annexation, attachment, augmentation, complement, enlargement, extension, increase, increment, joining, pendant, subjunction, supplement
ASSOCIATED CONCEPTS: addition to a structure

ADDITIONAL, ***adjective*** accessory, added, additive, *additus, adiectus,* another, appended, auxiliary, collateral, extra, further, included, joined, more, other, superadded, supervenient, supplemental, supplementary, ulterior
ASSOCIATED CONCEPTS: additional assured, additional burden, additional charges, additional compensation, additional consideration, additional coverage, additional duties, additional insured, additional relief, additional servitude

ADDITIONALLY, ***adverb*** along with, also, as well as, besides, by the same token, conjointly, ditto, further, furthermore, in addition, in conjunction with, including, more than that, moreover, over and above, plus, similarly, then again, together with, together with that, too

ADDITIVE, ***noun*** accrual, addendum, addition, adjunct, appurtenance, attachment, augmentation, enhancement, extension, increment, supplement

ADDITUR, ***noun*** assessment of damages, increase of damages, increase of jury award

ADDRESS, ***noun*** abode, box number, domicile, dwelling, dwelling place, habitation, headquarters, home, inhabitancy, *inscriptio,* legal residence, *locus,* lodging, lodging place, lodgment, place of business, residence, seat, street number
ASSOCIATED CONCEPTS: business address, last known address, local address, office address, post office address, residence

ADDRESS *(Direct attention to),* ***verb*** apply oneself to, approach, be occupied with, bring to attention, bring to notice, call attention to, call to notice, concern oneself with, devote oneself to, direct to, occupy oneself with

ADDRESS *(Petition),* ***verb*** appeal, call upon, enter a plea, enter a suit for, plead, prepare a complaint, prepare a formal request, prepare a petition, seek redress
ASSOCIATED CONCEPTS: address the court

ADDRESS *(Talk to),* ***verb*** deliver a talk, discourse, discuss, give a speech, harangue, *hominem adloqui,* lecture, orate, preach, *se rei dedere,* sermonize, speak to

ADDUCE, ***verb*** *adducere,* advance, allege, allude, assert, assign, aver, bring to the fore, claim, declare, disclose, divulge, evidence, evince, furnish, give, indicate, introduce, manifest, mention, offer, place in the foreground,

plead, present, produce, *producere, proferre,* proffer, propound, reveal, show, state
ASSOCIATED CONCEPTS: adduce evidence, adduce testimony

ADDUCED, ***adjective*** acknowledged, added, advanced, advocated, alleged, alluded, asserted, averred, avouched, avowed, brought forth, certified, cited, claimed, contended, declared, divulged, enunciated, imparted, insisted, introduced, maintained, presented, proclaimed, stated, supplemented
ASSOCIATED CONCEPTS: evidence adduced at trial

ADEEM, ***verb*** abnegate, abolish, abrogate, annul, avoid, cancel, declare null and void, deny, deprive of, disinherit, disseise, divest, make void, negate, nullify, obliterate, offset, remove, render null and void, render void, repeal, repudiate, rescind, retract, revoke, take away, take back, take from, vacate, void, withdraw
ASSOCIATED CONCEPTS: adeem a bequest, adeem a devise, adeem a gift, adeem a legacy

ADEMPTION, ***noun*** abnegation, abolishment, abolition, abrogation, annulment, cancellation, cancellation of a legacy, contravention, disclamation, discontinuance, disownment, dissolution, extinction, invalidation, negation, nullification, recall, renouncement, renunciation, repeal, repudiation, rescindment, rescission, retraction, revocation, revokement, vacation, *vacatur,* voidance, withdrawal, withdrawment
ASSOCIATED CONCEPTS: ademption of a bequest, ademption of a devise, ademption of a gift, ademption of a legacy, operation of law, satisfaction

ADEPT, ***adjective*** able, accomplished, adroit, apt, artful, capable, clever, competent, deft, dexterous, experienced, expert, gifted, handy, ingenious, masterful, masterly, practiced, professional, proficient, qualified, sharp, skillful, smart, sound, talented, trained, versed, well-skilled

ADEQUACY, ***noun*** ability, ableness, acceptability, admissibility, caliber, capability, capacity, competence, competency, completeness, contentment, deftness, efficacy, efficiency, employability, fitness, proficiency, qualification, satisfaction, satisfactoriness, sufficiency, utility, wherewithal, usefulness
ASSOCIATED CONCEPTS: adequacy of contents of pleadings, adequacy of proof, competency

ADEQUATE, ***adjective*** able, acceptable, *accommodatus,* ample, *aptus,* availing, capable, commensurate, competent, effectual, enough, equal to the need, fair, fit, fully sufficient, *idoneus,* proportionate, reasonable, reasonably sufficient, satisfactory, satisfying, serving, sufficient, sufficient for the purpose, sufficing, suitable, valid
ASSOCIATED CONCEPTS: adequate administrative review, adequate care, adequate cause, adequate consideration, adequate notice, adequate remedy at law, adequate support, fair and adequate consideration

ADEQUATE NOTICE, ***noun*** ample notice, commensurate notice, fair notice, good notice, satisfactory notice, sufficient notice, suitable notice, valid notice
ASSOCIATED CONCEPTS: adequate care, adequate compensation, adequate remedy at law, adequate security

ADEQUATE PROOF, ***noun*** adequate evidence, burden of going forward, burden of proof, legal responsibility, obligation of going forward, sufficient corroboration, sufficient evidence in a case, sufficient evidence to establish a case, sufficient proof, sufficient proof of facts, validation of proof of a case, verification of proof of a case
ASSOCIATED CONCEPTS: cause of action or claim, evidence, evidential burden, failure to sustain, preponderance of the evidence, prima facie case, rebuttal
FOREIGN PHRASES: ***Onus probani.*** Burden of proof.

ADHERE *(Fasten),* ***verb*** agglutinate, anchor, attach, band together, cement, clamp, clasp, cling to, coalesce, cohere, compound, fuse, glue, hold fast, hold firmly, *inhaerere,* join, latch, secure, stick to, stick together, tighten, unite

ADHERE *(Maintain loyalty),* ***verb*** abide by, act in support, advocate, argue for, back, be devoted, be faithful, be loyal, be partisan, be steadfast, be true, champion, comply, conform, *deditum esse,* defend, devote oneself, espouse, follow, give support, keep faith, obey, pay allegiance, preserve, show devotion, stand by, support, uphold

ADHERE *(Persist),* ***verb*** abide, be constant, be devoted, be obstinate, be steadfast, be steady, be unyielding, carry on, cling tenaciously, continue, endure, go to any lengths, go to the limit, have tenacity, hold on, hold tight, *in re stare,* keep going, keep on, maintain, *manere,* persevere, persist in, pursue, show determination, stand firm, stick to, sustain, work unceasingly
ASSOCIATED CONCEPTS: adhere to the Constitution, adhere to the terms of a contract

ADHERE TO, ***verb*** acknowledge, comply, conform, fulfill, have regard to, head, keep, make a practice of, obey, observe, pay attention to, pursue, regard, respect

ADHERENCE *(Adhesion),* ***noun*** attachment, bond, cementation, coherence, cohesion, cohesiveness, concretion, conglutination, connectedness, firmness, fixedness, holding together, sticking together, tenaciousness, tenacity, tie

ADHERENCE *(Devotion),* ***noun*** allegiance, attachment, *bona fide,* bond, compliance, constancy, dedication, devotedness, faithfulness, fealty, fidelity, homage, loyalty, obedience, observance, steadfastness, tenaciousness, tenacity, tie, troth
ASSOCIATED CONCEPTS: adherence to a contract, adherence to the principles of the Constitution

ADHERENT, ***adjective*** adhering, clinging, coherent, cohesive, gluey, glutinous, gummy, mucilaginous, sticking, sticky, tenacious, viscid, viscous

ADHERENT, ***noun*** abettor, accessory, accomplice, acolyte, advocate, aider, ally, approver, backer, champion, companion, confederate, dependent, devotee, disciple, follower, helper, partisan, partner, patron, protégé, satellite, seconder, supporter, upholder

ADHESION *(Affixing),* ***noun*** adherence, adhesiveness, agglomeration, agglutination, aggregation, attachment, cementation, clinging, close contact, coadunation, coagulation, coherence, cohesion, cohesiveness, concretion, condensation, congelation, conglomeration, conglutination, conjunction, connection, consolidation, fusion, glutinosity, gumminess, gummosity, inseparability, inseparableness, iron grip, junction, prehension, solidification, stickiness, union, unity, viscidity, viscosity
ASSOCIATED CONCEPTS: contract of adhesion, unequal bargaining power

ADHESION *(Loyalty),* ***noun*** adherence, adherence to duty, allegiance, alliance, ardor, association, attachment, attention, *bona fide,* bond, close identification, commitment, conscientiousness, consecration, constancy, dependability, devotedness, devotion, devoutness, dutifulness, earnestness, faithfulness, fealty, fidelity, firmness, homage, incorruptibility, integrity, obedience, reliability, resolution, scrupulousness, sense of duty, sense of responsibility, service, servitude, single-mindedness, staunchness, steadfastness, strong connection, submission, submissiveness, subservience, support, tenaciousness, tenacity, tie, troth, trueness, trustiness, trustworthiness, union, unswerving fidelity, vote of confidence, willingness, zeal

ADHESIVENESS, ***noun*** adhesion, coherence, cohesiveness, glutinosity, gumminess, stickiness, stick-to-itiveness, tackiness, toughness, viscidity, viscosity

ADJACENT, ***adjective*** abutting, adjoining, alongside, beside, bordering, conterminous, contiguous, *contiguus,* continuous, convergent, *finitimus,* juxtaposed, meeting, neighboring, next to, proximal, touching, verging on, vicinal, *vicinus*
ASSOCIATED CONCEPTS: adjacent county, adjacent land, adjacent owners, adjacent property

ADJECTIVE LAW, ***noun*** legal course to adhere to, legal methods, procedural law

ADJOIN, ***verb*** abut on, *adiacere,* appose, *attingere,* be adjacent to, be contiguous to, be joined to, border on, cohere, conjoin, connect, converge, juxtapose, juxtaposit, lie beside, lie near to, meet, neighbor, place side by side, reach to, stand by, *tangere,* touch

ADJOINER, ***noun*** addition to, appendage, attachment, conjoiner, connection, convergence, subjoiner

ADJOURN, ***verb*** *ampliare,* continue, defer, delay, hold in abeyance, hold over, intermit, keep pending, postpone, prorogue, put off, recess, reserve, stop, suspend, terminate
ASSOCIATED CONCEPTS: adjourn a case, adjourn a proceeding, adjourn for a session of the court, adjourn for the term of the court, adjourn on consent, adjourned term

ADJOURNMENT, ***noun*** adjournal, break, continuation, deferment, *dilatio,* discontinuation, extension, hold-over, intermission, interruption, moratorium, postponement, prolongation, prorogation, protraction, recess, reservation, respite, stay, suspension, termination
ASSOCIATED CONCEPTS: adjournment for a session, adjournment for the term, adjournment in contemplation of dismissal, adjournment of a hearing, adjournment of a trial, adjournment of the court, *sine die*

ADJUDGE, ***verb*** *addicere, adiudicare,* adjudicate, arbitrate, award, conclude, decide, decree, deem, deliver judgment, determine, dispense, dispense judgment, exercise judgment, find, give an opinion, hold, judge, judicate, judicially determine, make a decision, order, pass judgment, pronounce formally, rule, sentence, settle, sit in judgment
ASSOCIATED CONCEPTS: adjudge bankrupt, adjudge guilt, adjudge incompetent, adjudge innocence, adjudge insolvent, adjudge liability
FOREIGN PHRASES: ***Res judicata pro veritate accipitur.*** A thing which is adjudicated is accepted or received for the truth.

ADJUDICATE, ***verb*** adjudge, arbitrate, award, award judgment, conclude, decide, decree, deem, deliver judgment, determine, determine finally, exercise judicial authority, find, give judgment, hear, hear the case, hold court, judge, make a decision, mediate, order, pass judgment, pass sentence, pronounce, referee, render judgment, rule, rule upon, settle, sit in judgment, try, try the cause
ASSOCIATED CONCEPTS: adjudicate a juvenile delinquent, adjudicate a youthful offender, adjudicate an incompetent, adjudicate bankruptcy, adjudicate guilt, adjudicate innocence, adjudicate insolvency, adjudicate jurisdictional questions, adjudicate liability
FOREIGN PHRASES: ***Cessa regnare, si non vis judicare.*** Cease to reign, if you don't wish to adjudicate. ***In propria causa nemo judex.*** No one can be a judge in his own cause.

ADJUDICATION, ***noun*** act of judgment, adjudgment, arbitrage, arbitrament, arbitration, authoritative decision, award, conclusion, decision, declaration, decree, deliberate determination, determination, determination of issues, disposition, edict, final determination, final judgment, finding, irrevocable decision, judgment, judgment on facts, judicial decision, opinion, order, order of the court, proclamation, pronouncement, reasoned judgment, res judicata, resolution, result, ruling, sentence, settled decision, verdict
ASSOCIATED CONCEPTS: adjudication of a court of competent jurisdiction, adjudication of bankruptcy, adjudication of guilt, adjudication of incompetency, adjudication of innocence, adjudication of insolvency, adjudication of liability, adjudication on the merits, adjudication under law, adjudicative facts, judicial assessment
FOREIGN PHRASES: ***Novum judicium non dat novum jus, sed declarat antiquum; quia judicium est juris dictum et per judicium jus est noviter revelatum quod diu fuit velatum.*** A new adjudication does not promulgate a new law, but declares the old; because adjudication is the utterance of the law, and by adjudication the law is newly revealed which was for a long time hidden. ***Res judicata pro veritate accipitur.*** A thing which is adjudicated is accepted or received for the truth.

ADJUNCT, ***adjective*** accessory, addendum, additament, addition, appanage, appendage, augmentation, auxiliary, branch, complement, component, corollary, extension, subordinate part, supplement
FOREIGN PHRASES: ***Sublato principali, tollitur adjunctum.*** By the removal of the principal thing, the adjunct is taken also.

ADJURATION, ***noun*** affirmation, attestation, averment, avouchment, avowal, avowance, declaration, legal pledge, oath, pledge, solemn avowal, swearing, sworn statement, testimony, vouching, vow

ADJURE, ***verb*** administer an oath, affirm, appeal to, ask, attest, beseech, bid, bind, call, charge, command, conjure, declare, enjoin, entreat, enunciate, exhort, express, formulate, implore, imprecate, petition, plead, pray, prescribe, press, pressure, promise, pronounce, request, require, set down, solicit, state, swear, swear by, swear in, take a pledge, take oath on, urge, witness to

ADJUST *(Regulate),* ***verb*** *accommodare,* accommodate, adapt, *aptare,* attemper, balance, calibrate, coordinate, establish equilibrium, even, methodize, moderate, normalize, reset, restore equilibrium, stabilize, standardize, strike a balance, systematize, temper, tune
ASSOCIATED CONCEPTS: adjust differences, adjusted, adjusted cost basis, adjusted gross income

ADJUST *(Resolve),* ***verb*** accord, amend, arrange, bring to agreement, change, clarify, complete, conclude, conform, correct, curb, emendate, fix, mitigate, rectify, redress, remedy, set, settle, solve, treat
ASSOCIATED CONCEPTS: adjust a claim

ADJUSTER, ***noun*** arbitrater, interagent, interceder, intercessor, interlocutor, intermediary, intermediate, intermediator, intermedium, intervener, mediator, negotiant, negotiator, reconciler

ADJUSTMENT, ***noun*** abatement of differences, *accommodatio,* accommodation, accord, accordance, adaptation, agreement, arrangement, attunement, bargain, binding agreement, coaptation, compact, composition, compromise, concurrence, conformance, conformation, conformity, congruence, congruity, consistency, contract, coordination, correction, covenant, disposition, harmony, mutual concession, mutual understanding, negotiation, pact, reconcilement, reconciliation, rectification, regulating, settlement, stipulation, terms, understanding, uniformity
ASSOCIATED CONCEPTS: adjusted basis, adjusted reserves, adjustment of contracts, adjustment of loss, adjustments in wills

ADJUVANT, ***adjective*** accessory, aiding, ancillary, assistant, assisting, auxiliary, cooperative, helpful, helping, ministerial, obliging, serving, subservient, subsidiary

ADJUVANT, ***noun*** acolyte, adjutant, aid, aide-de-camp, ancillary, assistant, attendant, auxiliary, backer, coactor, coadjutant, colleague, confederate, copartner, help, helper, helpmate, participant, partner, second, servant, subsidiary

ADMEASURE, ***verb*** administer, allocate, allot, apportion, bestrew, broadcast, circulate, classify, diffuse, dispense, dispose, disseminate, distribute, divide, dole, issue, measure, mete, parcel out, partition, propagate, radiate, set apart, share, sow, spread, systematize, tabulate

ADMINISTER *(Conduct),* ***verb*** administrate, carry out, control, direct, dispose of, effect, effectuate, enforce, engineer, govern, guide, handle, have executive charge of, manage, mastermind, minister, officiate, operate, overlook, oversee, pilot, prescribe, preside over, put in force, regulate, *rem administrare, rempublicam gubernare,* settle, steer, superintend, supervise
ASSOCIATED CONCEPTS: administer a bankrupt's assets, administer an estate, administer the law

ADMINISTER *(Tender),* ***verb*** accord, afford, bestow on, confer, deal out, disburse, dispense, disperse, distribute, dole out, extend, give, impart, issue, measure out, mete out, offer, provide with, render
ASSOCIATED CONCEPTS: administer drugs, administer oaths

ADMINISTRATE, ***verb*** administer, captain, command, conduct, control, direct, govern, head, lead, manage, officiate, operate, preside, regulate, render, sit in judgment, stand over, superintend, supervise

ADMINISTRATION, ***noun*** *administratio,* care, conduct, control, direction, dispensation, disposal, disposition, distribution, execution, executive charge, guardianship, guidance, handling, keeping, management, ministration, oversight, performance of executive duties, practical management, *procuratio,* regulation, settlement of an estate, superintendence, supervision
ASSOCIATED CONCEPTS: administration of a bankrupt's estate, administration of an estate, administration of expenses, administration of the laws, fair administration of justice, trust administration
FOREIGN PHRASES: ***Nihil infra regnum subditos magis conservat in tranquilitate et concordia quam debita legum administratio.*** Nothing better preserves in tranquillity and concord those subjected to the same government than the due administration of the laws.

ADMINISTRATION OF JUSTICE *(Dispensation of law),* ***noun*** basic legal mechanism, criminal justice system, dispensation of fairness, dispensing of justice, doling out the law, ensuring propriety, equitableness, guaranty of equity, implementation of law, reasonableness, rectitude, righteousness, rightfulness, sitting in judgment, uprighteousness, uprightness
ASSOCIATED CONCEPTS: appellate courts, county court, federal courts, justice courts, local courts, state courts

ADMINISTRATION OF JUSTICE *(Tribunal),* ***noun*** bar, bench, court system, forum, judicature, judicial forum, judicial tribunal, law court, tribunal

ADMINISTRATIVE, ***adjective*** directorial, guiding, managerial, managing, ministerial, regulative, superintending, supervising, supervisory
ASSOCIATED CONCEPTS: administrative act, administrative action, administrative agency, administrative board, administrative body, administrative capacity, administrative discretion, administrative function, administrative hearings, administrative judges, administrative law, administrative procedures, administrative proceeding, administrative process, administrative regulations, administrative remedy, administrative rulings

ADMINISTRATOR, ***noun*** administrative head, chief executive, curator, custodian, director, executive, guardian, head of affairs, intendant, leader, legal representative, manager, officer of the court, overseer, personal representative, supervisor, supervisor of an estate, trustee
ASSOCIATED CONCEPTS: *administrator cum testamento annexo, administrator de bonis non, administrator de bonis non cum testamento annexo,* administrator executor, administrator general, *administrator pendente lite,* administrator's bond, administratrix, administratrix general, ancillary administrator, *executrix administrator ad prosequendum,* legal representative, supervisor of an estate

ADMIRATION, ***noun*** acclaim, adoration, affection, affinity, appreciation, approbation, approval, attention, awe, commendation, credit, deference, devotion, esteem, estimation, favor, fondness, homage, honor, idolization, lionize, partiality, profound, regard, repute, respect, revere, reverence, tribute, veneration, worship, worth

ADMISSIBILITY, ***noun*** acceptability, adequateness, allowableness, applicability, appositeness, appropriateness, aptness, eligibility, fitness, justifiability, legality, legitimacy, permissibility, presentability, propriety, reasonability, sanctionability, sanctionableness, sufficiency, suitability, tolerability, unexceptionability, unobjectionability, warrantability, warrantableness
ASSOCIATED CONCEPTS: affirmative evidence, confessions, decedent's statements, extrajudicial statements, hearsay, objections, secondary evidence

ADMISSIBLE, ***adjective*** *à propos,* acceptable, *aequus,* allowable, allowed, applicable, appropriate, authorized, eligi-

ble, justifiable, legal, legitimate, licensed, passable, permissible, permitted, presentable, proper, qualified, sanctionable, sanctioned, suitable, tolerable, unexceptionable, unforbidden, unobjectionable, unprohibited, warrantable, warranted
ASSOCIATED CONCEPTS: admissions of party-opponent, confessions, declarations against interest, limited admissibility, McNabb-Mallory rule, Miranda rule, nolo contendere, offer of proof, probative value, requests for admissions, secondary evidence

ADMISSIBLE EVIDENCE, ***noun*** acceptable evidence, creditable evidence, legal evidence, permissible evidence

ADMISSION *(Disclosure),* ***noun*** acknowledgment, assertion, attestation, avowal, communication, *concessio,* concession, confession, declaration, divulgence, enlightenment, exposure, expression, profession, revealment, revelation, statement, testimonial averment, testimony, unmasking, unveiling, voluntary acknowledgment
ASSOCIATED CONCEPTS: acknowledged adversary's claim, admission against interest, admission against pecuniary interest, admission as an exemption to the hearsay rule, admission by conduct, admission by flight, admission implied from silence, admission in a pleading, admission in an answer from a failure to deny, admission of a debt, admission of a fact, admission of a party, admission of guilt, admission of liability, admission to a crime, admission to bail, admissions by a representative, declaration against interest, direct admissions, expression admissions, extrajudicial admissions, implied admission, incidental admissions, inconsistent statement, judicial admissions, oral admissions, plenary admissions, written admissions
FOREIGN PHRASES: ***Qui non negat fatetur.*** He who does not deny admits.

ADMISSION *(Entry),* ***noun*** access, admittance, avenue, course, entrance, entryway, ingress, inlet, opening, passage, passageway, path, road, roadway, route, way
ASSOCIATED CONCEPTS: admission to bail, admission to practice law, admission to the bar

ADMISSION OF GUILT, ***noun*** avowal, concession, confession, confessional, contrition, culpability, disclosure, *mea culpa,* owning up, penance, penitence, remorse, repentance, sinfulness
ASSOCIATED CONCEPTS: admissibility, coerced confession, traditional admissions

ADMIT *(Concede),* ***verb*** accede, accept, acknowledge, acquiesce, affirm, agree, assent, *concedere,* concur, confess, confirm, declare, disclose, divulge, enlighten, expose, *fateri,* grant, recognize, relate, reveal, unmask, unveil
ASSOCIATED CONCEPTS: admit fault, admit in a reply, admit in an answer, admit liability, admit to probate

ADMIT *(Give access),* ***verb*** *adeundi copiam, admittere,* allow entrance, create an opening, give right of entry to, inaugurate, induct, initiate, install, institute, invest, open a passage, open a path, open a road, open a route, open an entryway, open an inlet, throw open, vest, yield passage to
ASSOCIATED CONCEPTS: admit to bail, admit to practice

ADMITTANCE *(Acceptance),* ***noun*** admission, confirmation, designation, entrance, entree, entry, inclusion, induction, initiation, permission

ADMITTANCE *(Means of approach),* ***noun*** access, admission, approach, avenue, course, entrance, entry, entryway, ingress, inlet, liberty of approach, opening, passage, passageway, path, portal, road, route, way

ADMITTED, ***adjective*** accepted, acknowledged, allowed, approved, avowed, believed, conceded, confessed, credited, granted, prescriptive, professed, received, recognized, trusted, undoubted, unquestioned
ASSOCIATED CONCEPTS: admitted and marked as an exhibit, admitted culpability, admitted into evidence, admitted wrongdoing

ADMITTEDLY, ***adverb*** acceptedly, allowedly, assuredly, authentically, authoritatively, avowedly, certainly, concededly, confessedly, doubtlessly, genuinely, incontestably, incontrovertibly, indisputably, indubitably, irrefragably, irrefutably, surely, truly, undeniably, undoubtedly, unquestionably, validly, veritably

ADMIXTURE, ***noun*** amalgam, amalgamation, blend, coalescence, combination, commixture, composite, composition, compound, integration, intermingling, intermixture, melange, mingling, mixture, pastiche
ASSOCIATED CONCEPTS: confusion of goods

ADMONISH *(Advise),* ***verb*** *admonere,* advocate, alert, call attention to, charge, correct, counsel, enjoin, exhort, give advice, give counsel, give notice, inform, instruct, notify, offer counsel, prescribe, propound, recommend, submit, suggest, urge

ADMONISH *(Warn),* ***verb*** address a warning to, administer a rebuke, advise against, caution, censure, *commonere,* counsel against, dehort, deprecate, exhort, expostulate, forebode, forewarn, give warning, *monere,* objurgate, premonish, prewarn, rebuke, remonstrate, reprehend, reprimand, reprove, warn against

ADMONITION, ***noun*** admonishment, advance notice, advice, alarm, animadversion, caution, *caveat,* censure, commonition, contraindication, contrariety, contrary advice, counsel, dehortation, deprecation, dissuasion, exhortation, expostulation, foreboding, forewarning, hindrance, increpation, indication, instruction, intimidation, judicial reprimand, monition, notice, notification, object lesson, objection, protest, rebuke, reminder, remonstrance, reprimand, reproach, reprobation, reproof, signal, stricture, warning

ADOLESCENCE, ***noun*** *adulescentia,* immaturity, juniority, juvenility, minority, nonage, puberty, pubescence, puerility, youth

ADOLESCENT, ***noun*** junior, juvenile, minor, teenager, young person, youngling, youngster, youth

ADOPT, ***verb*** accept, *ad sententiam,* admit, *adoptare,* affiliate, annex, appropriate, arrogate, assimilate, assume, attach oneself to, avail oneself of, borrow, choose, conform to, *constituere,* co-opt, denizenize, elect, embrace, endenizen, espouse, exercise one's option, follow, foster, imitate, make one's own, naturalize, raise, seize, select, select as one's own, take, take on, take possession of, take up, try, usurp, utilize, vote to accept
ASSOCIATED CONCEPTS: adopt a child, adopt a law, adopt a philosophy, legitimation, support

ADOPTION *(Acceptance),* ***noun*** acknowledgment, admission, approbation, approval, assimilation, assumption, attachment to, choice, co-optation, election, embracement,

espousal, favorable reception, ratification, reception, recognition, sanction, selection
ASSOCIATED CONCEPTS: adoption by estoppel, adoption of a contract, adoption of a proposal, adoption of domicile, arrogation

ADOPTION *(Affiliation),* ***noun*** *adoptio,* custody, fosterage, guardianship, parentage, protection, protectorship, wardship
ASSOCIATED CONCEPTS: adoption decree, adoption petition, custody, foster care, foster parent, inheritance by adoption, intestate succession, legitimation, legitimation of child, parental rights, paternity proceedings, support, wards of the juvenile court

ADOPTIVE, ***adjective*** *adoptivus,* appointive, choosing, discretional, elective, preferential, selective
ASSOCIATED CONCEPTS: adoptive father, adoptive mother, adoptive parent, foster care, inheritance by adoptive parents, inheritance from adoptive parents, intestate succession, parental rights, wards of the juvenile court

ADROIT, ***adjective*** adept, apt, artful, capable, clever, competent, deft, efficacious, excellent, experienced, expert, fit, ingenious, practiced, proficient, qualified, resourceful, responsible, skilled, trained, versed
ASSOCIATED CONCEPTS: effective handling of a case, effectiveness of counsel

ADULATE, ***verb*** acclaim, admire, applaud, approbate, approve, celebrate, commend, compliment, eulogize, exalt, express, extol, flatter, glorify, idolize, laud, lionize, overpraise, pay tribute to, praise, salute

ADULATION, ***noun*** admiration for, appreciation, approbation, blandishment, compliment, encomium, eulogy, fawning, flattery, glorification, homage, honor, idolatry, laudation, praise, sycophancy, toadyism

ADULT, ***noun*** *adultus,* elder, fully developed person, fully grown person, grown-up person, mature person, one who has attained legal majority, person of age, person of voting age, *pubes,* senior
ASSOCIATED CONCEPTS: adult male, adult person, adult woman, age of majority

ADULTERATE, ***verb*** abase, *adulterare,* change for the worse, contaminate, *corrumpere,* corrupt, debase, debilitate, defile, degrade, denature, depreciate, deteriorate, devalue, devitalize, impair, infect, lessen, lower the standard, make impure, make lower in quality, mar, pervert, pollute, render spurious, spoil, taint, tamper with, *vitiare,* vitiate, weaken

ADULTERATED, ***adjective*** artificial, contaminated, corrupted, debased, defiled, degraded, deteriorated, devalued, fraudulent, impaired, impure, infected, perverted, polluted, spoiled, spurious, tainted, weakened

ADULTERATION, ***noun*** contamination, corruption, defilement, degradation, deterioration, fraudulence, impairment, infection, perversion, pollution, spuriousness, weakness
ASSOCIATED CONCEPTS: drugs, food, purity of food

ADULTERY, ***noun*** *adulterium,* criminal unchastity, cuckoldry, extramarital promiscuity, extramarital relations, illicit intercourse, illicit love, illicit sexual intercourse, infidelity, marital infidelity, sexual unfaithfulness of a married person, unfaithfulness, unlawful carnal connection, unlawful carnal knowledge, unlawful carnality, violation of the marriage vows
ASSOCIATED CONCEPTS: adultery by collusion, adultery by connivance, condonation of adultery, criminal conversation, dissolution of marriage, recrimination of an action of adultery

ADUMBRATION, ***noun*** blurry image, darkening, dim representation, dimming, faint resemblance, imperfect portrayal, obfuscation, obscuration, uncertainty, vague outline

ADUMBRATIVE, ***adjective*** bleary, blurry, cloudy, dim, foggy, hazy, ill-defined, indefinite, indistinguishable, misty, nebulous, obscure, reflexive, shadowy, shrouded, uncertain, unclear, unknown, unspecified, vague

ADVANCE *(Allowance),* ***noun*** accommodation, anticipated loan, cash payment, compensation, credit, defrayment, disbursement, emolument, expenditure, fee, giving beforehand, installment, investment, pay, payment beforehand, remuneration, subscription
ASSOCIATED CONCEPTS: advance as against profits, advancement from an estate grant, future advances

ADVANCE *(Increase),* ***noun*** amplification, augmentation, elaboration, enhancement, enlargement, enrichment, expansion, extension, improvement, increase, increment, intensification, prolongation, protraction

ADVANCE *(Progression),* ***noun*** elevation, expedition, facilitation, forward motion, forward movement, forwarding, headway, progress, progression, *progressus,* promotion, upsurge
ASSOCIATED CONCEPTS: advance payment, advance sheets, anticipatory repudiation, contract breached in advance

ADVANCED *(Elderly),* ***adjective*** aged, along in years, ancient, old, senior, venerable

ADVANCED *(Progressive),* ***adjective*** contemporary, far ahead, forward-looking, modern, present-day, sophisticated, up-to-date, up-to-the-minute

ADVANCED NOTICE, ***noun*** announcement, declaration, dispatch, forewarning, intelligence, notice, notification, prediction, preliminary, pronouncement, prophecy, prospectus, publication, publicity, warning

ADVANCEMENT *(Improvement),* ***noun*** aggrandizement, amplification, betterment, development, elaboration, elevation, emendation, enlargement, expansion, furtherance, gain, *gradus amplior,* growth, increase, progress, progression, promotion, rise

ADVANCEMENT *(Loan),* ***noun*** accommodation, advance, allowance, anticipation, concession, consideration, investment, realization in advance
ASSOCIATED CONCEPTS: intestate succession, statute of distribution

ADVANTAGE, ***noun*** accommodation, aid, approval, ascendancy, asset, assistance, authority, avail, behoof, benefit, choice, convenience, dominance, easement, edge, eminence, expedience, favor, favorable opportunity, favoring circumstance, gain, good, head start, help, hold, improvement, influence, lead, leverage, mastery, odds, patronage, plus, position, power, precedence, predominance, preeminence, preference, prestige, primacy, privilege, profit, protection, resources, sake, sanction, success, superior situation, superiority, support, supremacy, sway, upper hand, utility, welfare, worth

ADVANTAGEOUS, ***adjective*** advisable, advised, ameliorative, auspicious, beneficial, constructive, effective, effectual, efficacious, expedient, favorable, fine, gainful, good, important, invaluable, opportune, precious, productive, profitable, promising, propitious, rare, rewarding, sensible, superior, treasured, useful, valuable, while, worth

ADVENTITIOUS, ***adjective*** accidental, acquired, casual, circumstantial, external, extraneous, extrinsic, extroverted, foreign, fortuitous, incidental, outward, outward-looking, random, subordinate, subsidiary, transcendent, unintentional, unwitting

ADVENTURE, ***noun*** endeavor, enterprise, episode, exercise, experience, exploit, happening, happenstance, operation, quest, undertaking, venture
ASSOCIATED CONCEPTS: detour and adventure

ADVENTURE, ***verb*** chance, endanger, hazard, imperil, jeopardize, risk, run the risk, stake, take a chance, venture

ADVERSARY, ***adjective*** *adversarius,* adverse party, antagonist, competitor, contender, contestant, contester, corival, disputant, dissentient, enemy, foe, litigant, opponent, opposer, opposing party, oppositionist, oppugnant, resister, rival
ASSOCIATED CONCEPTS: adversary parties, adversary proceeding

ADVERSARY *(Foe),* ***noun*** adverse party, antagonist, arch enemy, arguer, aspirant, assailant, bane, challenger, claimant, combatant, competitor, contender, contestant, enemy, intervener, nemesis

ADVERSARY *(Lawyer),* ***noun*** opposing attorney, opposing attorney-at-law, opposing counsel, opposing counselor, opposing litigator, opposing practitioner, opposite side, opposition, other side
ASSOCIATED CONCEPTS: adversarial proceeding, adversarial setting, opposing party

ADVERSARY *(Litigant),* ***noun*** adverse party, appellant, challenger, claimant, contender, contestant, defendant, disputant, intervener, legal adversary, legal opponent, litigant, litigator, opposing party, opposite disputant, opposite party, opposite side, participant, party, party to a suit, personage, petitioner, plaintiff, pleader, respondent, the defense

ADVERSE *(Hostile),* ***adjective*** antagonistic, antagonistical, deprecatory, disagreeable, discordant, disinclined, disobedient, dissuasive, fractious, inauspicious, indisposed, *infensus,* inimical, intolerant, opposed, recalcitrant, renitent, repugnant, resistive, restive, uncooperative, unfriendly, unpropitious, unreconciled, untoward, unwilling
ASSOCIATED CONCEPTS: adverse claim, adverse effect, adverse enjoyment of property, adverse interest, adverse possession, adverse use, adverse user, adverse witness
FOREIGN PHRASES: ***Longa possessio parit jus possidendi, et tollit actionem vero domino.*** Long possession creates the right of possession, and ripens into a right of action against the real owner.

ADVERSE *(Negative),* ***adjective*** afflictive, calamitous, catastrophic, corrosive, deleterious, destructive, detrimental, dire, disadvantageous, disastrous, disserviceable, dreadful, harmful, hurtful, injurious, insalubrious, malefic, maleficient, prejudicial, ruinous, scatheful, unadvisable, unfavorable, unfortunate
ASSOCIATED CONCEPTS: adverse determination of the court, adverse effect, adverse holding of the court, adverse interest

ADVERSE *(Opposite),* ***adjective*** *adversus,* antipodal, antipodean, antithetical, antonymous, at variance, conflicting, conflictive, contradictory, contradistinct, contrapositive, contrariant, contrarious, *contrarius,* contrary, contrastable, converse, counter, counteractive, diametrically opposite, inverse, irreconcilable, obverse, reverse
ASSOCIATED CONCEPTS: adverse action, adverse party

ADVERSE CIRCUMSTANCE, ***noun*** disadvantage, plight, predicament, regrettable occurrence, unfavorable development, unfortunate situation
ASSOCIATED CONCEPTS: agreements, contracts, impossibility

ADVERSE EVENT, ***noun*** adversity, calamity, casualty, catastrophe, debacle, detriment, infliction, misfortune, plight, tragedy, trouble, unpropitious turn of events

ADVERSE POSSESSION, ***noun*** acquisition, appropriation, assumption, attainment, obtainment, ownership, procurement, proprietorship, recovery, seizure
ASSOCIATED CONCEPTS: adverse claim, adverse holding, adverse interest, adverse party, adverse user, adverse verdict, adverse witness

ADVERSE TO *(Hostile),* ***adjective*** abhorrent to, against, antagonistic to, antipathetic to, at odds with, clashing, conflicting with, contra, contrary to, different, discordant to, hostile to, inimical to, opposed to, repugnant to

ADVERSE TO *(Unfavorable),* ***adjective*** calamitous, catastrophic, disastrous, harmful, inopportune, unfortunate, unlucky, unpropitious

ADVERSELY AFFECTED, ***adjective*** aggrieved, damaged, endamaged, harmed, hurt, ill-treated, impaired, inflicted with injury, injured, wronged

ADVERSITY, ***noun*** adverse circumstances, adverse fortune, affliction, bale, *calamitas,* calamity, catastrophe, *contretemps,* difficulty, disaster, distress, hardship, injuriousness, injury, misadventure, mischance, *miseria,* misfortune, mishap, oppression, perdition, *res adversae,* ruination, ruinousness, setback, suffering, tragedy, visitation

ADVERT, ***verb*** affirm, articulate, assert, asservate, aver, comment, communicate, convey, declare, express, heed, mark, mention, mind, note, notice, recite, recognize, reconsider, remark, review, speak, take cognizance of, take into consideration, tell, utter, verbalize, vocalize, voice

ADVERTENCE, ***noun*** assertion, attention, averment, comment, commentary, declaration, diligence, exclamation, expression, interjection, mention, note, notice, observation, pronouncement, recitation, regard, thought, utterance, word

ADVERTISE, ***verb*** advise, announce, apprise, attract, broadcast, circularize, circulate, communicate, describe, disseminate, divulge, exhibit, expose, feature, flourish, focus the attention, headline, herald, inform, notice, notify, placard, post, proclaim, proffer, promote, promulgate, publish, push, report, rumor, spotlight, spread, throw the spotlight on, transmit, trumpet, warn, whisper

ASSOCIATED CONCEPTS: deceptive advertising practices, false advertisement, unfair trade practices

ADVICE, *noun* advisement, advocacy, communication of knowledge, *consilium,* counsel, direction, guidance, information, instruction, legal counsel, notice, notification, opinion, prompting, proposal, proposition, recommendation, rede, suggestion, view, warning
ASSOCIATED CONCEPTS: advice of counsel, privilege
FOREIGN PHRASES: ***Incivile est, nisi tota lege perspecta, una aliqua particula ejus proposita, judicare, vel respondere.*** Unless the entire law has been examined, it is improper to pass judgment upon a single portion of it. ***Nemo ex consilio obligatur.*** No one is obligated as a consequence of giving advice. ***Simplex commendatio non obligat.*** A mere recommendation is not binding.

ADVICE OF COUNSEL, *noun* advice of legal counsel, communication of legal knowledge, recommendation of counsel, rendering of legal advice, representation
Generally: advisement, consultation, direction, guidance, opinion

ADVISABLE, *adjective* acceptable, advantageous, advisory, appropriate, becoming, befitting, commendable, congruous, desirable, expedient, favorable, feasible, fit, fitting, judicious, opportune, profitable, proper, prudent, recommendable, seemly, sensible, suitable, wise, worthy

ADVISE, *verb* advocate, alert, apprise, *auctorem esse,* caution, coach, communicate, confer with, *consiliari, consilium dare,* consult with, convey, counsel, direct, enlighten, express, familiarize, forewarn, give advice, give an opinion, give counsel, give information, give notice, give one to understand, give suggestions, give warning, guide, *homini suadere,* impart, inform, intimate, make known, mention, notify, offer an opinion, offer counsel, opine, prescribe, propose, recommend, remind, represent, reprove, submit, suggest, warn
ASSOCIATED CONCEPTS: advisory opinion, declaratory judgment
FOREIGN PHRASES: ***Consilia multorum quaeruntur in magnis.*** The advice of many are required in affairs of magnitude.

ADVISOR, *noun* advocate, agent, ally, attorney, backer, cabinet, champion, cohort, confidant, consigliore, consultant, counsel, counselor, defender, espouser, friend, guide, interceder, legal advisor, legal practitioner, mentor, negotiator, patron, promoter, protector, representative, spokesperson, supporter

ADVISORY, *adjective* cautionary, communicatory, consulting, counseling, directing, enlightening, expressive of opinion, guiding, inducive, instructing, recommendatory, suggesting
ASSOCIATED CONCEPTS: advisory board, advisory opinion, advisory referendum

ADVOCACY, *noun* active espousal, advancement, advice, aid, approbation, approval, assistance, auspices, backing, championship, constructive criticism, countenance, defense, encouragement, endorsement, forceful persuasion, furtherance, guidance, help, intercession, interest, patronage, plea, praise, promotion, recommendation, sanction, seconding, sponsorship, subscription, suggestion, support, vindication, vouching, warranting

ADVOCATE *(Counselor),* ***noun*** advisor, apologist, attorney, attorney-at-law, barrister, barrister-at-law, champion, counsel learned in the law, counselor-at-law, defender, friend at court, friend in court, interagent, interceder, intercessor, interlocutor, intermediary, intermediate, intermediate agent, intermediator, intermedium, internuncio, intervener, interventionist, interventor, jurisconsult, jurist, justifier, lawyer, learned counsel, legal advisor, legal practitioner, legal representative, legate, legist, maintainer, man of law, mediator, medium, member of the legal profession, mover, negotiant, negotiator, one called to the bar, paraclete, patron, *patronus,* pleader, proctor, prompter, protector, representative, seconder, solicitor, spokesman, spokeswoman, suasor, upholder, votary

ADVOCATE *(Espouser),* ***noun*** abettor, adherent, apologist, *auctor,* backer, champion, countenancer, defender, encourager, exponent, expounder, favorer, maintainer, partisan, patron, promoter, propagandist, propagator, proponent, seconder, sectary, spokesman, spokeswoman, support, supporter, sympathizer, upholder, votary
ASSOCIATED CONCEPTS: advocate the abolishment of the death sentence, advocate the commission of a crime, advocate the overthrow of government

ADVOCATE, *verb* advise, allege in support, approve, argue for, assert, back, champion, commend, consent, contend for, counsel, defend, endorse, espouse, exhort, favor, give advice, plead for, plead in favor of, plead one's case, plead one's cause, prescribe, promote, prompt, propose, propound, recommend, sanction, second, speak in favor of, *suadere,* subscribe to, suggest, support, uphold, urge
ASSOCIATED CONCEPTS: advocate the commission of a crime, advocate the overthrow of government

AEGIS, *noun* advocacy, aid, auspices, backing, care, championship, countenance, custody, defense, encouragement, fosterage, guaranty, guard, guidance, influence, interest, patronage, protection, safeguard, safekeeping, shelter, shield, sponsorship, support, surety, tutelage

AESTHETIC, *adjective* artistic, cultured, discriminative, ornamental, refined, tasteful

AFFAIR, *noun* activity, adventure, avocation, circumstance, duty, employment, enterprise, event, function, happening, incident, interest, matter, occasion, occupation, occurrence, profession, pursuit, subject, transaction, undertaking, work

AFFAIRS, *noun* activities, concerns, interests, matters, proceedings, pursuits, topics, transactions

AFFECT, *verb* act on, *adficere,* bear upon, cause to alter, cause to vary, change, *commovere,* conduce, exert influence, have an effect upon, have influence, impress, induce, influence, introduce a change, make a change, play a direct part, prevail upon, produce a change, produce an effect, superinduce, *tangere,* transfigure, work a change, work upon
ASSOCIATED CONCEPTS: affect an action, affected with public interest, affecting a substantial right

AFFECTING, *adjective* affected, agitating, altering, changing, emended, exciting, inviting, modifying, moving, potent, provocative, provoking, stirring, touching, transforming

AFFECTION, *noun* admiration, adoration, amorousness, ardor, attachment, closeness, devotion, enchantment, endearment, excitation of feeling, fancy, feeling,

fervency, fervor, firm attachment, fondness, fullness of heart, inclination, infatuation, kindness, love, mutual attraction, partiality, passion, penchant, *pietas,* popular regard, predisposition, proneness, regard, sentiment, sentimental attachment, sentimentality, state of excitement, tender feeling, tender passion, tenderness, understanding, warmth, zealous attachment
ASSOCIATED CONCEPTS: alienation of affection

AFFIANT, ***noun*** attestant, attester, deponent, signer, subscriber, swearer, testifier, voucher

AFFIDAVIT, ***noun*** affirmation under oath, assertory oath, attested statement, averment, avouchment, avowal, avowance, confirmation under oath, declaration under oath, evidence on oath, instrument in proof, solemn affirmation, statement, statement under oath, sworn evidence, sworn statement, testification under oath, *testimonium per tabulas datum,* voluntary attestment under oath, written declaration upon oath, written statement under oath
ASSOCIATED CONCEPTS: affidavit of defense, affidavit of demand, affidavit of judicial power, affidavit of merit, affidavit of service, affidavit to advise the court of a right or on an issue, affidavit to hold to bail, affirmation, verified deposition, verified pleading

AFFILIATE, ***noun*** arm, assistant, associate, auxiliary, branch, branch organization, chapter, colleague, component, division, offshoot, subdivision, subsidiary, wing

AFFILIATE, ***verb*** ally, associate, attach, belong to, bring into close connection, bring into close relation, cement a union, confederate, connect, consociate, embrace, federalize, federate, form a connection, join, join forces, join together, make common cause, pertain to, relate to, unite

AFFILIATED, ***adjective*** allied, associated, closely allied, closely related, confederated, connected, coupled, federated, incorporated, intimately allied, intimately related, joined with, leagued, linked, related, united
ASSOCIATED CONCEPTS: affiliated association, affiliated company, affiliated corporation, affiliated firm, affiliated organization

AFFILIATION *(Amalgamation),* ***noun*** aggregation, alliance, association, centralization, coalition, combination, confederacy, confederation, consortium, corporation, embodiment, federation, fusion, integration, league, merger, unification, union, unity, voluntary association

AFFILIATION *(Bloodline),* ***noun*** agnation, ancestry, apparentation, blood relation, blood relationship, common derivation, consanguinity, descent, family, family connection, family tie, filiality, filiation, heredity, kindred, kinfolk, kinship, kinsmen, line of descent, lineage, next of kin, origin, parentage, relation, relationship, ties of blood, ties of race
ASSOCIATED CONCEPTS: affiliation proceedings, paternity proceedings

AFFILIATION *(Connectedness),* ***noun*** alignment, appositeness, apposition, association, band of union, bond, coaction, coadjuvancy, coalition, colleagueship, combination, concert, conjunction, connection, consociation, copartnership, coworking, friendly association, implication, inclusion, intimate connection, involvement, joint enterprise, link, linkage, membership, participation, partnership, relation, relationship

AFFINITY *(Family ties),* ***noun*** affiliation, ancestry, blood relative, brethren, clan, cognation, common ancestry, connection, *consanguinitas,* consanguinity, family, family connection, filiation, heritage, kindred, kinship, lineage, linkage, *necessitudo,* offspring, parentage, *propinquitas,* relation, relation by blood, relationship, tribe
ASSOCIATED CONCEPTS: challenge to a prospective juror based on affinity
FOREIGN PHRASES: ***Affinis mei affinis non est mihi affinis.*** One who is related by marriage to a person who is related to me by marriage has no affinity to me.

AFFINITY *(Regard),* ***noun*** affection, attachment, attraction, closeness, concern, devotion, fondness, friendliness, friendship, good will, inclination, liking, love, natural liking, partiality, predilection, proclivity, propensity, sympathy, tenderness

AFFIRM *(Claim),* ***verb*** assert, asseverate, aver, declare to be fact, enunciate, establish, express, make a positive statement, make an assertion, proclaim, profess, pronounce, state, state positively, state with conviction

AFFIRM *(Declare solemnly),* ***verb*** asseverate, attest, aver, avouch, avow, depone, depose, give oral evidence, give sworn evidence, give verbal evidence, make a solemn declaration, make an asseveration, make an attestation, make an averment, pronounce, take one's oath, testify, vouch
ASSOCIATED CONCEPTS: affirm a contract
FOREIGN PHRASES: ***Affirmanti, non neganti incumbit probatio.*** The proof is borne by the person who affirms, rather than the person who denies. ***Affirmantis est probare.*** He who is affirming must prove. ***Ei incumbit probatio, qui dicit, non qui negat; cum per rerum naturam factum negantis probatio nulla sit.*** The burden of proof lies upon him who asserts it, not upon him who denies; since by the nature of things, he who denies a fact cannot produce any proof of it.

AFFIRM *(Uphold),* ***verb*** *adfirmare,* approve, authenticate, certify, confirm, *confirmare,* endorse, establish, make firm, ratify, substantiate, support, sustain, validate, verify, vouch for, warrant
ASSOCIATED CONCEPTS: affirm a judicial decision, affirm on appeal, affirmed in part, affirmed in whole

AFFIRMANCE *(Authentication),* ***noun*** acknowledgment, assertion, assurance, attestation, certification, confirmation, countersignature, declaration, endorsement, establishment, predication, pronouncement, ratification, substantiation, validation, verification
ASSOCIATED CONCEPTS: affirmance of a contract, confirmation of a judgment, ratification of a voidable contract
FOREIGN PHRASES: ***Posito uno oppositorum, negatur alterum.*** By the establishment of one of two opposite propositions, the other one is denied.

AFFIRMANCE *(Judicial sanction),* ***noun*** acceptance, acquiescence, assent, concord, concordance, countersignature, endorsement, legal approval, legal authorization, legal ratification, subscription
ASSOCIATED CONCEPTS: affirmed without opinion, en banc affirmance, unanimous affirmance

AFFIRMANCE *(Legal affirmation),* ***noun*** absolute assertion, adjuration, assertory oath, asseveration, attestation, averment, avouchment, avowal, evidence on oath, legal evidence, legal pledge, oral evidence, positive declaration, positive statement, pronouncement, proposition, solemn averment, solemn avowal, statement on oath, sworn

evidence, testimony, verbal evidence, written evidence
ASSOCIATED CONCEPTS: affirmation of a statement

AFFIRMANT, *noun* affirmer, apprizer, attestant, attestator, attester, confirmist, deponent, one who testifies under oath, testifier, voucher
ASSOCIATED CONCEPTS: affidavit, affirmation, deponent, oath, perjury

AFFIRMATION, *noun* absolute assertion, acknowledgment, acquiescence, *adfirmatio,* adjurement, affirmance, approval, assertion, assertory oath, asseveration, attest, attestation, authentication, averment, avouchment, avowal, certification, confirmation, declaration, deposition, endorsement, establishment, factual statement, formal declaration, legal evidence, legal pledge, oath, oath-giving, oath-taking, positive statement, predication, profession, pronouncement, ratification, solemn affirmation, solemn averment, solemn avowal, solemn declaration, statement, statement on oath, substantiation, swearing, sworn evidence, sworn statement, testification, testimonial, testimonium, testimony, validation, verification
ASSOCIATED CONCEPTS: affirmation of fact, affirmation to a will, attorney's affirmation
FOREIGN PHRASES: ***Affirmatio unius exclusio est alterius.*** The affirmance of one thing is the exclusion of the other.

AFFIRMATION UNDER OATH, *noun* affidavit, attestation, authentication, avouchment, certification, declaration, deposition, sworn evidence, verification
ASSOCIATED CONCEPTS: perjury, sworn affidavit

AFFIRMATIVE, *adjective* absolute, affirmatory, categorical, certain, confirmative, confirmatory, convinced, decided, persuaded, positive, sure, undoubting, unqualified
ASSOCIATED CONCEPTS: affirmative action, affirmative action for past discrimination, affirmative action in hiring, affirmative allegation, affirmative authorization, affirmative charge, affirmative covenant, affirmative defense, affirmative easement, affirmative negligence, affirmative plea, affirmative proof, affirmative relief, affirmative showing, affirmative statute, affirmative warranty, affirmative wrongdoing

AFFIRMATIVE ACTION, *noun* effort to correct past injustices, means to right the wrongs of the past, plan to make up for unfairness in the past, positive steps to correct past discrimination
Generally: fairness, just treatment, opportunities, remedial change
Specifically: plan for increased representation for minorities, plan for increased representation for women, racial quotas

AFFIRMATIVE ACTION, *noun* gender, implementation of the means to achieve nondiscrimination, method to address a disparate impact, method to address past injustices, positive discrimination, religion, sexual orientation or national origin, the means to address discrimination with regard to color, the means to address inequality, to provide redress to an underrepresented group, tool to redress historic injustices
ASSOCIATED CONCEPTS: hiring practices, minority rights, past discrimination, promotion, quotas

AFFIX, *verb* add, *adfigere,* adhere, adjoin, *adligare, adnectere,* agglutinate, annex, append, attach, bind, cohere, combine, conjoin, connect, couple, enclose, fasten, fix, incorporate, insert, join, link, put together, secure, subjoin, supplement, unite
ASSOCIATED CONCEPTS: affix a seal to an instrument, affix a signature, affix exhibits to a pleading, affix process to the door

AFFLICT, *verb* agonize, anguish, assault, bruise, burden, chasten, discommode, discompose, disquiet, distress, grate, harm, hurt, impair, infect, inflict, irritate, mistreat, pain, plague, punish, rasp, sicken, smite, strike, victimize

AFFLICTION, *noun* adversity, agony, bereavement, burden, calamity, casualty, catastrophe, curse, destruction, deterioration, disability, disease, disorder, encumbrance, evil, hardship, illness, indisposition, infirmity, misadventure, mischance, misfortune, mishap, ordeal, suffering, tragedy, trouble, unhappiness

AFFORD, *verb* aid, arrange, assist, avail, extend, furnish, give, offer, provide, supply, support, sustain, tender

AFFORDABLE CARE ACT, *noun* federal health care law, health care act, health care coverage, health care reform, HR 3962, insurance reform, medical care laws, "Obamacare"

AFFRAY, *noun* agitation, altercation, battle, brabble, brawl, brush, clash, combat, commotion, conflict, contestation, disturbance, embroilment, encounter, fight, fisticuffs, fracas, fray, free fight, hand-to-hand fight, *melee,* passage at arms, *pugna, rixa,* row, scrimmage, scuffle, set-to, skirmish, sortie, squabble, struggle, tumult, *tumultuous* assault, *tumultus,* turmoil, tussle, violence

AFFRONT, *verb* afflict, aggrieve, antagonize, be offensive, be rude, cause dislike, cause offense, chafe, disconcert, disdain, disoblige, disquiet, distress, disturb, embitter, encounter, gall, give offense to, grieve, hurt the feelings, ill-treat, insult, irritate, make angry, offend, pique, rankle, scorn, slight, snub, sting, vex, wound the feelings, wrong

AFOREDESCRIBED, *adjective* above-mentioned, antecedent, anterior, before-mentioned, inaugural, preceding, precursory, preliminary, prior

AFOREGOING, *adjective* above-mentioned, antecedent, anterior, before-mentioned, earlier, inaugural, last referred to, preceding, precursory, preliminary, previous, prior

AFOREHAND, *adjective* above-mentioned, antecedent, anterior, before-mentioned, inaugural, last referred to, preceding, precursory, preliminary, prior

AFOREMENTIONED, *adjective* above-mentioned, antecedent, anterior, before-mentioned, inaugural, last referred to, last said, preceding, precursory, preliminary, prior

AFORESAID, *adjective* above-mentioned, aforecited, aforedescribed, aforegiven, aforegoing, aforementioned, aforenamed, aforestated, already mentioned, already said, antecedent, anterior, before-mentioned, beforesaid, foregoing, forenamed, former, introductory, mentioned, mentioned previously, named, precedent, preceding, precursive, precursory, preexistent, preluding, prelusory, prevenient, previous, previously specified, prior, recited, said, said in a preceding part, specified

AFORESTATED, *adjective* above-mentioned, antecedent, anterior, before-mentioned, inaugural, last referred to, last said, preceding, precursory, preliminary, prior

AFORETHOUGHT, ***adjective*** beforehand, calculated, contrived, contrived in advance, deliberate, designed, intended, planned, planned beforehand, prearranged, preconceived, preconsidered, predeliberated, predetermined, premeditated, prepared, prepense, preresolved, previously in mind, purposed, purposive, reflective, studied, well-considered, with forethought
ASSOCIATED CONCEPTS: malice aforethought

AFRAID, ***adjective*** affrighted, alarmed, anxious, apprehensive, cautious, distrustful, dreading, fearful, frightened, haunted by fear, leery, nervous, scared, shrinking, terrified, terror-stricken, timid, timorous, uneasy

AFTERMATH, ***noun*** after-effect, aftergrowth, by-product, consequence, development, effect, end, event, gleanings, issue, offshoot, outcome, outgrowth, result, sequel, subsequence, succession, turnout, upshot

AGAIN, ***adverb*** additionally, afresh, anew, consistently, continuously, endlessly, evermore, infinitum, invariably, moreover, often, once again, over again, perpetually, reallege, recurrently, repeatedly, then too
ASSOCIATED CONCEPTS: repeat and reallege each of the allegations contained in a complaint

AGAINST *(On),* ***adjective*** adjoining, alongside, attached to, beside, close to, contiguous, leaning on, lie on, near to, nearby to, next to, right up to

AGAINST *(Opposite),* ***adjective*** conflicting, contra, contradictory, contrary, contrast, diametrical, hostile, on the opposite side, opposed, oppugnant, resistant, versus

AGAINST ONE'S WILL, ***adjective*** against, coerced, commanded, compelled, constrained, enforced, extorted, forced, imperative, imposed, inescapable, inevitable, inexorable, levied, mandatory, obligatory, opposed, preemptory, prescriptive, prescriptory, pressured, required, unavoidable, unconsenting, unwilling

AGE, ***noun*** *aetas,* date, duration of existence, eon, epoch, era, interval of years, longevity, maturity, period, seniority, stage of life, term of life, time of life, vintage, years
ASSOCIATED CONCEPTS: age of consent, age of majority, legal age, statutory age

AGENCY *(Commission),* ***noun*** administration, authority, bureau, charge, command, committee, control, delegation, department, office
ASSOCIATED CONCEPTS: administrative agency, governmental agency

AGENCY *(Legal relationship),* ***noun*** activity, appointment, assignment, authority, care, charge, command, commission, conduct, conduct of affairs, control, delegation, deputation, derivative authority, direction, dominion, duty, employ, employment, function, governance, handling, instrumentality, intermediation, intervention, jurisdiction, management, mandate, mission, procuracy, procuration, proxy, quest, representation, responsibility, role, service, services, superintendence, supervision, task, trust
ASSOCIATED CONCEPTS: actual agency, agency by estoppel, agency coupled with an interest, agency of necessity, deed of agency, exclusive agency, express agency, general agency, implied agency, scope of the agency, undisclosed agency, vicarious liability
FOREIGN PHRASES: ***Actus me invito factus non est meus actus.*** An act done against my will is not my act. ***Qui facit per alium facit per se.*** He who acts through another acts himself. ***Qui mandat ipse fecissi videtur.*** He who orders or commands is deemed to have done the thing himself. ***Quod per me non possum, nec per alium.*** What I cannot do myself, I cannot do through the agency of another. ***Vicarius non habet vicarium.*** A vicar has no deputy.

AGENDA, ***noun*** blueprint, business, business affairs, business on hand, calendar, docket, items of business, legal program, main business, matters to be attended to, order, order of the day, plan, planning, procedure, program of business, program of operation, proposal, proposed action, proposition, schedule, schedule of affairs, scheme

AGENT, ***noun*** alternate, appointee, assistant, delegate, emissary, envoy, functionary, go-between, intermediary, intermediate, intermedium, mediary, medium, middleman, negotiant, negotiator, procurator, proxy, representative, solicitor, substitute
ASSOCIATED CONCEPTS: agent to accept process, authorization of an agent, bailee, common agent, employee, escrow agent, general agent, implied agent, independent contractor, insurance broker, joint venture, managing agent, master-servant relationship, owner-operator relationship, partnership, principal-agent relationship, real estate agent, real estate broker, special agent, subagents, undisclosed agency, warranty of authority
FOREIGN PHRASES: ***Idem agens et patiens esse non potest.*** A person cannot be at the same time the person acting and the person acted upon. ***Delegatus non potest delegare.*** A representative cannot delegate his authority. ***Qui facit per alium facit per se.*** He who acts by or through another acts for himself.

AGGLOMERATION, ***noun*** accumulation, agglomerate, agglutination, aggregate, aggregation, amassment, assemblage, cluster, coagulation, collection, congeries, conglomerate, conglomeration, consolidation, cumulation, glomeration, mass, pile, solidification

AGGRANDIZEMENT, ***noun*** accession, advancement, amplification, augmentation, boom, broadening, deification, dignification, elevation, embellishment, eminence, enablement, enhancement, enlargement, enshrinement, enthronement, exaggeration, exaltation, expansion, extension, gain, glorification, greatness, growth, heightening, honor, inflation, immortalization, largeness, lionizing, magnification, overstatement, preferment, promotion, widening

AGGRAVATE *(Annoy),* ***verb*** acerbate, aggrieve, annoy, bother, cause pain, chafe, dismay, disturb, enrage, envenom, exasperate, excite, give pain, hurt, incense, inflame, infuriate, injure, irk, irritate, madden, miff, nettle, offend, pain, pique, provoke, rankle, ruffle, sour, sting, trouble, vex
ASSOCIATED CONCEPTS: aggravating circumstances

AGGRAVATE *(Exacerbate),* ***verb*** add to, add weight to, amplify, augment, complicate, deepen, deteriorate, further, heighten, impair, increase, intensify, magnify, make more offensive, make more serious, make more severe, make worse, render less excusable, render less tolerable, render worse, worsen
ASSOCIATED CONCEPTS: aggravated assault, aggravating circumstances

AGGRAVATING FACTOR, *noun* a factor that increases the level of an offense, a factor that increases the severity of an offense, a harmful factor, aggravating circumstance, attendant aggravating circumstance
ASSOCIATED CONCEPTS: imposition of a crime

AGGRAVATION *(Annoyance),* ***noun*** complication, difficulty, distress, frustration, grievance, harassment, inconvenience, irritant, irritation, nuisance, ordeal, pressure, provocation, strain, stress

AGGRAVATION *(Exacerbation),* ***noun*** agitation, amplification, augmentation, deepening, enlargement, excitation, fomentation, heightening, increase, inflammation, intensification, magnification, stimulation, worsening
ASSOCIATED CONCEPTS: aggravated assault, aggravation of a crime, aggravation of damages, aggravation of injury, aggravation of the disability
FOREIGN PHRASES: ***Omne crimen ebrietas et incendit et detegit.*** Drunkenness both inflames or aggravates and uncovers every crime.

AGGREGATE, *noun* agglomerate, aggregation, amount, assemblage, assembly, body, collection, conglomeration, entire number, entire quantity, entirety, gross, gross amount, indissoluble entity, indivisible entity, mass, sum, sum total, total, totality, whole
ASSOCIATED CONCEPTS: aggregate corporation, aggregate income, combine

AGGREGATE, *verb* accumulate, acquire, add together, agglomerate, aggroup, amass, amount to, assemble, bring together, build up, clump, cluster, collect, collect into a mass, colligate, compile, conglomerate, cumulate, gather, gather together, group, integrate, join, mass, total, unite
ASSOCIATED CONCEPTS: aggregate claims

AGGREGATION, *noun* accumulation, adhesion, affiliation, agglomeration, aggregate, amassment, body, collection, combination, company, compilation, composite, composition, concentration, conglomeration, congregation, consolidation, corpus, cumulation, force, gathering, group, hoard, incorporation, mass, multitude, organization, selection, totality

AGGRESSION, *noun* aggressiveness, antagonism, assault, attack, beleaguerment, bellicosity, belligerence, belligerency, besiegement, combativeness, contentiousness, drive, enterprise, fight, foray, hostility, hustle, illapse, incursion, infringement, initiative, injury, inroad, intrusion, invasion, irruption, jingoism, martiality, militancy, offense, onset, onslaught, outbreak, provocation, pugnacity, push, pushiness, raid, sally, sortie, storming, transgression, trespass, unprovoked attack, warlikeness

AGGRESSOR, *noun* antagonist, assailant, assailer, assaulter, attacker, belligerent, besieger, combatant, contender, criminal, fighter, foe, initiative seizer, invader, militant, prime mover, provocator, ravager, ruffian, stormer, violator

AGGRIEVED *(Harmed),* ***adjective*** abused, afflicted, anguished, bilked, damnified, deprived of legal rights, distressed, grieved, having suffered invasion of legal rights, hurt, ill-treated, incommoded, injured, misused, pained, preyed upon, provoked, swindled, tyrannized, vexed, wounded
ASSOCIATED CONCEPTS: aggrieved heirs, aggrieved party, aggrieved person

AGGRIEVED *(Victimized),* ***adjective*** adversely affected, cheated, damaged, defrauded, fleeced, harrassed, harried, ill-used, imposed upon, injured, justly complaining, misserved, offended, oppressed, persecuted, taken advantage of, wronged

AGITATE *(Activate),* ***verb*** actuate, arouse, coax, electrify, energize, excite, exhort, ferment, foment, goad, impel, incite, induce, inflame, influence, inspire, inspirit, instigate, irritate, kindle, persuade, prompt, provoke, roil, rouse, spur, stimulate, stir up, urge on

AGITATE *(Perturb),* ***verb*** alarm, concern, discomfort, disconcert, dismay, displease, disquiet, disturb, fluster, fret, jar, perplex, perturbate, shake up, throw into confusion, trouble, unsettle, upset, worry

AGITATE *(Shake up),* ***verb*** convulse, disarrange, dishevel, disorder, impart motion to, mix, mix up, put in motion, ruffle, stir, throw out of order, tousle, tumble

AGONIZE, *verb* anguish, belabor, bemoan, devote painstaking effort, dread, examine painstakingly, fret, labor, labor over, lament, languish, overexert, pour over, slave over, strain, strive, study at great length, study seriously, suffer, take great pains, travail, trouble over, worry over

AGREE *(Comply),* ***verb*** accede, accept, accommodate, accord, acknowledge, acquiesce, adapt, adjust differences, adopt, allow, approve, assent, avow, be accordant, be at one with, be in harmony with, be in unison, be willing, coincide, come to an understanding, come to terms, comply with, *componere,* concede, *concinere,* concord, concur, confirm, *congruere,* consent, cooperate, correspond, fit, give assent, give consent, homologate, ratify, reconcile, settle, subscribe to, suit, understand, unite, yield assent
ASSOCIATED CONCEPTS: agreed case, agreed order, agreed statement of facts

AGREE *(Contract),* ***verb*** adjust differences, arrive at a settlement, bargain, bring into concord, come to an agreement, come to an understanding, come to terms, compromise, consent, *consentire, constituere,* cooperate, covenant, engage, give assurance, make a bargain, make an agreement, make terms, mutually assent, pacisci, pact, pledge, promise, settle, settle by covenant, stipulate, undertake

AGREE TO, *verb* accede, accept, accommodate, acknowledge, acquiesce, adopt, allow, approve, assent, authorize, certify, come to terms, comply, comply with, concur, confirm, cooperate, countenance, covenant, embrace, pass, permit, ratify, sanction, sign, submit, subscribe to, yield
ASSOCIATED CONCEPTS: agreed to contract, agreed to judgment, agreed to stipulation, execution of a contract

AGREEABLE *(Amenable),* ***adjective*** acceptable, accommodating, accordant, acquiescent, amiable, apropos, appropriate, charming, coexistent, compatible, complaisant, compliant, concordant, conformable, congenial, congruous, consensual, consenting, cordial, courteous, delightful, enjoyable, fitting, flexible, friendly, genial, gratifying, likable, malleable, pleasant, pliant, prone, sapid, savory, sociable, suitable, willing

AGREEABLE *(Palatable),* ***adjective*** acceptable, adequate, admissible, allowable, applicable, apposite, appropriate, apt, attractive, becoming, comfortable, commensurate, conventional, desirable, eligible, expedient, fair, felicitous, fit, good, gratifying, inviting, justifiable, likable, opportune, passable, pleasing, proper, qualified, satisfactory, seemly, suitable, tenable, tolerable, unobjectionable, viable

AGREED *(Harmonized),* ***adjective*** accordant, adapted, appeased, arbitrated, arranged, balanced, coherent, compromised, conceded, conciliated, concordant, conforming, correlative, correspondent, counterbalanced, equable, equal, equalized, equivalent, matching, mediated, negotiated, parallel, propitiated, reconciled, settled, suited
ASSOCIATED CONCEPTS: agreed case, agreed price, agreed statement of facts, agreed submission of a case, agreed-upon price, agreed value
FOREIGN PHRASES: ***Ad quod curia concordavit.*** To which the court agreed.

AGREED *(Promised),* ***adjective*** affirmed, approved, arranged, assured, attested, avowed, committed, confirmed, contracted, covenanted, declared, endorsed, guaranteed, insured, pledged, stipulated, sworn, warranted
ASSOCIATED CONCEPTS: agreed price, agreed value

AGREEMENT *(Concurrence),* ***noun*** accord, amity, arrangement, assent, common assent, common consent, common view, community of interests, concord, concordance, conformance, congruence, congruency, congruity, consent, consentaneity, consentaneousness, consentience, consonance, cooperation, good understanding, harmony, meeting of the minds, mutual assent, mutual promise, mutual understanding, oneness, reciprocity of obligation, settlement, unanimity, understanding, uniformity, unison, unity
FOREIGN PHRASES: ***Aggregatio mentium.*** Meeting of the minds. ***Bona fides exigit ut guod convenit fiat.*** Good faith demands that what is agreed upon shall be done. ***Consensus ad idem.*** An agreement of parties for the same thing; a meeting of minds without which no contract exists. ***Conventio privatorum non potest publico juri derogare.*** An agreement of private parties cannot derogate from public right. ***Conventio vincit legem.*** The agreement of parties controls the law. ***Modus et conventio vincunt legem.*** Custom, convention, and agreement of the parties overrule the law. ***Ratihabitio mandato aequiparatur.*** Ratification is equivalent to an express command. ***Quando verba et mens congruunt, non est interpretationi locus.*** When the words and the mind agree, there is no room for interpretation. ***Privatorum conventio juri publico non derogat.*** The agreement of private persons cannot derogate from public law. ***Modus et conventio vincunt legem.*** Custom and agreement control the law. ***Non differunt quae concordant re, tametsi non in verbis iisdem.*** Those matters do not differ which agree in substance, though not in the same words.

AGREEMENT *(Contract),* ***noun*** alliance, arrangement, bargain, binding promise, bond, commitment, compact, concordat, *concordia,* contractual statement, convention, covenant, deal, engagement, legal document, mutual pledge, obliga, obligation, pact, pledge, settlement, stipulation, transaction, understanding, undertaking
ASSOCIATED CONCEPTS: abrogate an agreement, agency agreement, agreement implied in fact, agreement of sale, agreement to answer for the debt of another, agreement to purchase, agreement under seal, agreements in contemplation of marriage, antenuptial agreement, area-wide agreement, articles of agreement, articles of impeachment, articles of incorporation, articles of partnership, articles of war, express agreement, illusory agreement, implied agreement, implied agreement in law, sale agreement, settlement agreement, support agreement
FOREIGN PHRASES: ***Contractus ex turpi causa, vel contra bonds mores nullus est.*** A contract founded on an evil consideration, or against good morals, is void. ***Contractus legem ex conbentione accipiunt.*** Contracts take their law from the agreement of the parties. ***Ex pacto illicito non oritur actio.*** An action will not lie on an agreement to do something unlawful. ***Ex maleficio non oritur contractus.*** No contract is born of wrongdoing. ***Nudum pactum est ubi nulla subest causa praeter conventionem; sed ubi subest causa, fit obligatio, et parit actionem.*** A naked contract is where there is no consideration except the agreement; but where there is a consideration, an obligation is created and gives rise to a right of action. ***In stipulationibus cum quaeritur quid actum sit verba contra stipulatorem interpretanda sunt.*** In the construction of agreements words are interpreted against the person offering them. ***Ea quae dari impossibilia sunt, vel quae in rerum natura non sunt, pro non adjectis habentur.*** Those things which cannot be given, or which are not in existence, are regarded as not included in the contract. ***Conventio facit legem.*** The agreement creates the law (i.e., the parties to a binding contract must keep their promises). ***Ex nudo pacto non oritur actio.*** No action arises on a contract without a consideration. ***Ea quae, commendandi causa, in venditionibus dicuntur, si palam appareant, venditorem non obligant.*** Those things which are said as praise of the things sold, if they are openly apparent, do not bind the seller. ***In contrahenda venditione, ambiguum pactum contravenditorem interpretandum est.*** In a contract of sale, an ambiguous agreement is to be interpreted against the seller. ***In conventionibus, contrahentium voluntas potius quam verba spectari placuit.*** In contracts, it is the rule to regard the intention of the parties rather than the actual words. ***Ome jus aut consensus fecit, aut necessitas constituit aut firmavit consuetudo.*** All right is either made by consent, constituted by necessity, or confirmed by custom. ***Pacta conventa quae neque contra leges neque dolo malo inita sunt omni modo observanda sunt.*** Agreements which are not contrary to the laws nor entered into with a fraudulent design must be observed in all respects. ***Pacta dant legem contractui.*** Stipulations constitute the law for the contract. ***Pacta quae contra leges constitutionesque, vel contra bonos mores fiunt, nullam vim habere, indubitati juris est.*** It is unquestionably the law that contracts which are made contrary to the laws or against good morals, have no force in law. ***Pacta quae turpem causam continent non sunt observanda.*** Contracts which are based on unlawful consideration will not be enforced. ***Quae dubitationis tollendae causa contractibus inseruntur, jus commune non laedunt.*** Those clauses which are inserted in agreements to avoid doubts and ambiguity do not offend the common law. ***Nuda pactio obligationem non parit.*** A naked agreement does not affect an otherwise binding obligation. ***Privatis pactionibus non dubium est non laedi jus caeterorum.*** There is no doubt that private contracts cannot prejudice the rights of others.

AGREEMENT BETWEEN PARTIES, ***noun*** alliance, arrangement, bargain, bilateral contract, binding agreement, compact, contract, covenant, mutual pledge, pact, promise, stipulation, understanding

AID *(Help),* ***noun*** abetment, accommodation, advance, advocacy, aidance, assistance, auspices, backing, benefit,

coadjuvancy, cooperation, countenance, endorsement, espousal, facilitation, furtherance, guidance, help, helpfulness, maintenance, ministration, ministry, patronage, promotion, reinforcement, relief, rescue, service, sponsorship, subscription, subsidy, subsistence, succor, support, sustainment, sustenance, tutelage, willing help
ASSOCIATED CONCEPTS: aid and abet, aid and comfort

AID *(Subsistence)*, ***noun*** benefaction, benefit, charity, compensation, endowment, humanitarianism, maintenance, ministration, ministry, patronage, relief, subsidy, support, sustainment, sustenance

AID, *verb* abet, advance, assist, augment, avail, be auxiliary to, be of service, benefit, collaborate, cooperate with, facilitate, further, give aid, give support, help, minister to, nurture, oblige, promote, provision, reinforce, relieve, render help, rescue, second, serve, service, strengthen, subserve, succor, supplement, support, sustain, uphold
ASSOCIATED CONCEPTS: aid and abet, aid and comfort

AIDE, *noun* abettor, acolyte, adjutant, aider, assistant, attendant, coadjutant, consociate, contributor, helper, helpmate, second, support, supporter, upholder

AILMENT, *noun* affectation, affliction, complaint, complication, condition, difficulty, dilemma, disability, disease, disorder, health problem, illness, inability, indisposition, infirmity, malady, malaise, problem, sickness, trouble

AIM, *verb* aspire, attempt, desire, endeavor, essay, intend, make an effort, make every effort, mean, plan, propose, purport, pursue, pursue a goal, seek, strive, strive to achieve, strive to gain, to accomplish, try, try to do, work to accomplish, work to achieve

AIR, *verb* analyze, bare open, bring into view, circulate, communicate, disclose, discuss, divulge, expose, express, get out in the open, give currency to, impart, leak, post, promulgate, provide sunshine to, republish, reveal, run a concept up the flagpole, share, talk, tell, uncloak, unmask, unveil
ASSOCIATED CONCEPTS: air grievances, air the issues involved in the case, air the terms of a contract

AIR POLLUTION, *noun* contamination, defilement, impure air, unhealthy air

AKIN *(Germane)*, ***adjective*** affiliated, alike, allied, analogous, appertaining, applicable, apropos, associated, closely related, collateral, connected, correlative, correspondent, corresponding, interchangeable, like, linked, parallel, pertinent, related, relating, relevant, resembling, similar

AKIN *(Related by blood)*, ***adjective*** affiliated, connate, consanguine, consanguinean, consanguineous, consanguineus, fraternal, kindred, of the same stock

ALACRITY, *noun* agreeableness, anxiety, briskness, celerity, compliance, dispatch, eagerness, enthusiasm, expedition, facility, haste, immediacy, immediateness, industry, promptitude, promptness, punctuality, quickness, readiness, speed, speediness, spontaneity, swiftness, zeal

ALARM *(Apprehension)*, ***noun*** agitation, anxiety, anxiousness, concern, consternation, dismay, disquiet, disquietude, distress, disturbance, dread, fear, foreboding, fright, horror, misgiving, panic, perturbation, premonition, suspense, trepidation, uncertainty, unease, uneasiness, wariness, worry

ALARM *(Noise)*, ***noun*** beacon, bell, blast, buzzer, loud noise, notice, panic button, safety device, security device, tocsin, tone, warning, whistle

ALCOHOL, *noun* alcoholic beverage, inebriant, intoxicant, intoxicating liquor, liquor, potation, spirits

ALEATORY *(Perilous)*, ***adjective*** adventurous, beset with perils, dangerous, endangered, exposed, exposed to risk, fraught with danger, full of risk, hazardous, imperiled, minatory, ominous, parlous, precarious, riskful, risky, treacherous, unsafe, venturesome, venturous

ALEATORY *(Uncertain)*, ***adjective*** alterable, ambiguous, capricious, changeable, changeful, depending, dubious, equivocal, in question, incalculable, indefinite, mutable, not fixed, open, permutable, protean, undecided, unsettled, unstable, unsure, variable
ASSOCIATED CONCEPTS: aleatory contract

ALERT *(Agile)*, ***adjective*** alive, animated, expeditious, nimble, quick, spirited, sprightly, spry

ALERT *(Vigilant)*, ***adjective*** active, alive, attentive, guarded, observant, on guard, prepared, wary, watchful

ALERT, *verb* advise, alarm, arouse, caution, give notice, notify, put on one's guard, sound the alarm, warn

ALFORD PLEA, *noun* admission of likelihood of conviction, assertion of innocence while pleading guilty, avowing innocence while pleading guilty, denial of act while pleading guilty, guiltlessness while accepting a guilty plea, guilty plea while maintaining innocence, maintenance of innocence while accepting a guilty plea

ALIAS, *adverb* acknowledged elsewhere as, a.k.a., alias dictus, also, also acknowledged as, also acknowledging the name of, also answering to, also called, also known as, also known by, also known under the name of, also recognized as, at other times known as, elsewhere known as, known elsewhere as, known elsewhere by, known elsewhere under the name, known otherwise as, known previously as, known variously as, *nomen alienum,* otherwise called, otherwise known as, otherwise known by, otherwise named, previously called, variously called, variously known as
ASSOCIATED CONCEPTS: alias execution, alias process, alias subpoena, alias summons, alias writ, assumed name

ALIBI, *noun* corroborative excuse, declaration, defense, defensive evidence, defensive plea, exculpatory excuse, excuse, explanation, justifiable excuse, justification, justificatory excuse, plausible excuse, plea in being elsewhere, proof of absence, verifiable excuse, verificative excuse
ASSOCIATED CONCEPTS: affirmative defense, notice of intention to introduce alibi defense, traverse of indictment

ALIEN *(Foreign)*, ***adjective*** coming from another land, external, extrinsic, foreign-born, from abroad, immigrant, imported, not domestic, not indigenous, not native, not naturalized, of foreign origin, outside, unnaturalized

ALIEN *(Unrelated),* ***adjective*** detached, different, digressive, disconnected, disjoined, disrelated, dissociated, from nowhere, inappropriate, independent, insular, irrelated, no relation, not comparable, of external origin, outside, unaffiliated, unallied, unassociated, unconnected, ungermane, unrelated, without context, without relation

ALIEN, ***noun*** *advena, alienigena,* emigrant, *étranger,* expatriate, foreigner, immigrant, interloper, intruder, noncitizen, one excluded from some privilege, outlander, outsider, *peregrinus,* person coming from a foreign country, person from foreign parts, refugee, stranger

ALIENATE *(Estrange),* ***verb*** *abalienare,* aggravate, antagonize, *avertere,* be hateful, be unfriendly, bear malice, break off, cause dislike, cause loathing, come between, destroy goodwill, detach, disaffect, disunite, divide, embitter, enrage, envenom, fall out, harden the heart, incense, make averse, make indifferent, make inimical, make unfriendly, part, pit against, provoke hatred, repel, separate, set against, set at odds, set at variance, sow dissension, take umbrage, turn away, turn off, wean, withdraw the affections of
ASSOCIATED CONCEPTS: alienation of affections, alienation of power

ALIENATE *(Transfer title),* ***verb*** *abalienare,* abalienate, assign, barter, consign, convey, deed, deliver over, demise, devolve, enfeoff, part with, pass, pass over, remise, sign away, sign over, substitute, surrender, transfer ownership, turn over
ASSOCIATED CONCEPTS: alienation of property
FOREIGN PHRASES: ***Regulariter non valet pactum de re mea non alienanda.*** It is a rule that an agreement not to alienate my property is not binding.

ALIENATION *(Estrangement),* ***noun*** abhorrence, abomination, acrimony, *alienatio,* animosity, antagonism, antipathy, aversion, bitterness, breach, break, deflection, disaffection, disfavor, disruption, division, enmity, execration, hostility, implacability, loathing, malevolence, malice, odium, rancor, rift, rupture, schism, separation, split, umbrage, unfriendliness, variance, withdrawal
ASSOCIATED CONCEPTS: alienation of affections, alienation of power
FOREIGN PHRASES: ***Alienatio rei praefertur juri accrescendi.*** Alienation is favored by the law rather than accumulation.

ALIENATION *(Transfer of title),* ***noun*** *abalienatio,* abalienation, assignation, assignment, cession, conferment, conferral, consignation, consignment, conveyance, conveyancing, deeding, deliverance, delivery, demise, enfeoffment, limitation, nonretention, selling, surrender, transference, transmission
ASSOCIATED CONCEPTS: alienation clause, alienation of property

ALIGHT, ***verb*** climb down, depart, descend, *descendere,* disembark, dismount, egress, evacuate, exit, get down, get off, ground oneself, land, leave, part, set down, step down

ALIGN, ***verb*** accommodate, adapt, adjust, ameliorate, amend, attune, change, collimate, conform, correct, cure, improve, level, line up, make uniform, modify, normalize, pattern, perfect, readjust, rectify, regularize, remedy, revise

ALIKE, ***adjective*** accordant, akin, allied, analogous, cognate, comparable, copied, correspondent, corresponding, duplicate, equable, equal, equivalent, even, identical, indistinguishable, interchangeable, kindred, matched, mated, parallel, resemblant, resembling, same, selfsame, similar, synonymous, undiscriminated, uniform

ALIKE, ***adverb*** akin, analogously, both, close to, coincidentally, comparably, correspondently, correspondingly, equally, identically, in common, likewise, similarly, synonymously, together

ALIMONY, ***noun*** allotment, allowance, care, dispensation, emolument, grant, income, maintenance, maintenance allowance, pecuniary aid, pecuniary assistance, personal allowance, provision, recompense, remuneration, separate maintenance, separation money, settlement, stipend, subsidization, subsidy, subvention, support, sustenance, sustentation, upkeep
ASSOCIATED CONCEPTS: alimony award, alimony judgment, alimony penpendente lite, division of property, divorce, necessaries, permanent alimony, separation, support, temporary alimony

ALL, ***adjective*** complete, each and every, full, global, integral, nothing but, only, perfect, the sum of, total, undivided, universal, wholly

ALL, ***noun*** aggregate, all and sundry, allness, assemblage, collectiveness, completeness, complexus, ensemble, entireness, entirety, everyone, everything, fullness, gross amount, indivisibility, intactness, integer, integrality, one and all, sum, sum total, total, totality, undividedness, universality, whole, wholeness

ALLAY, ***verb*** abate, alleviate, appease, assuage, blunt, calm, cause to be still, cause to subside, check, compose, constrain, control, curb, curtail, deaden, decrease, diminish, dull, hush, *lenire,* lessen, lighten, lull, minimize, *mitigare,* mitigate, moderate, mollify, pacify, palliate, qualify, quell, quench, quiet, reduce, reduce in severity, relieve, repress, restrain, silence, slake, smooth, soften, soothe, still, subdue, suppress, temper, tone down, tranquilize

ALLEGATION, ***noun*** *adfirmatio,* assertion, averment, bill of complaint, charge, claim, complaint, crimination, declaration, denunciation, formal averment, imputation, inculpation, *ipse dixit,* plea, positive assertion, positive declaration, positive statement, pronouncement, statement
ASSOCIATED CONCEPTS: allegation of fact, allegation of law, allegation of wrongdoing

ALLEGE, ***verb*** adduce, advance, affirm, announce, annunciate, assert, asseverate, attest, aver, avouch, charge, cite, claim, contend, declare, enunciate, express, maintain, make an assertion, plead, present, profess, pronounce, propound, recite, relate, say, set forth, state, state as true, urge as a reason
ASSOCIATED CONCEPTS: allege a crime

ALLEGE UNDER OATH, ***verb*** adjure, assert as true, attest, authenticate, avouch, avow, bear witness, certify, confirm, declare, declare true, depose, give evidence, guarantee, maintain under oath, make solemn affirmation, state, swear, take an oath, vouch, vow

ALLEGED, ***adjective*** acknowledged, adduced, advanced, advocated, affirmed, announced, argued, asserted, asserted formally, asseverated, assured, averred, avouched, avowed, certified, cited, claimed, contended, declared, divulged, enunciated, imparted, imputed, insisted, introduced, maintained, positively declared, presented, proclaimed, produced, professed, promulgated, pronounced, propounded, put forward, reported, set forth, stated, stressed, testified to, uttered with conviction, vouched

ALLEGIANCE, *noun* adherence, adherence to duty, attachment, bounden duty, call of duty, case of conscience, commitment, constancy, deference, devotedness, devotion, duteousness, dutifulness, faith, faithfulness, fealty, fidelity, *fides,* homage, imperative duty, inescapable duty, loyalty, matter of duty, moral obligation, obedience, obligation, obsequiousness, observance, observance of obligation, onus, pledge, promise, responsibility, sense of duty, steadfastness, subjection, submission, subordination, support, trueness
FOREIGN PHRASES: ***Nemo patriam in qua natus est exuere, nec ligeantiae debitum ejurare possit.*** No man can renounce his native country nor adjure his obligation of allegiance. ***Ligeantia est quasi legis essentia; est vinculum fidei.*** Allegiance is the essence of law; it is the bond of faith.

ALL-ENCOMPASSING, *adjective* all, blanket, broad, compendious, complete, comprehensive, consummate, encyclopedic, entire, everything comprehensible, exhaustive, extensive, far-reaching, full, global, inclusive, massive, maximal, plenary, thorough, total, unabridged, universal, unmitigated, unqualified, vast, whole

ALLEVIATE, *verb* abate, *adlevare,* allay, appease, assuage, attenuate, blunt, calm, check, commute, compose, console, curb, dampen, diminish, disburden, disencumber, divert, dulcify, dull, ease, ease the burden, extenuate, free, help, hush, lessen, lighten, lull, mitigate, moderate, modulate, nullify, obtund, pacify, palliate, qualify, quell, quiet, redress, reduce, relieve, remedy, remit, restrain, salve, slacken, slow down, smooth, soften, solace, soothe, still, subdue, succor, tame, temper, tranquilize, unburden, unload, weaken

ALLIANCE, *noun* accordance, adhesion, affiliation, agreement, alignment, amalgamation, association, band, bloc, cartel, centralization, chain, coalescence, coalition, combination, combine, compact, company, concert, concordant, confederacy, conformity, conjunction, connection, connivance, consolidation, consortium, contract, contribution, convention, cooperative, corporation, covenant, federation, fusion, integration, junction, league, merger, organization, pact, partnership, peace, pool, rapprochement, relationship, sodality, syndicate, treaty, trust, understanding, union

ALLIED, *adjective* affiliated, affinitive, akin, associated, bonded, confederate, connected, federate, kindred, leagued, related

ALLOCATE, *verb* administer, allot, appoint, apportion, appropriate, arrange, assign, assort, cast, class, classify, collocate, consign, deal, deal out, designate, destine, detail, dispense, disperse, dispose, distribute, divide, divide and bestow in shares, dole out, earmark, fix, give out, grant, group, hand out, intend, line up, locate, marshal, mete, parcel out, place, portion off, portion out, prescribe, prorate, ration, render, set apart, set aside, set out, share, situate, specify
ASSOCIATED CONCEPTS: allocate funds, special allocatur

ALLOCATION *(Allotment),* ***noun*** annuity, apportionment, bequest, disbursement, dispensation, distribution, endowment, entitlement, grant, issuance, moiety, percentage, portion due, proportion, quota, ration, share

ALLOCATION *(Apportionment),* ***noun*** appropriation, dispensation, division, fractionation, partition, rationing, reallocation, reckoning, segmentation, separation, split, take
ASSOCIATED CONCEPTS: apportionment, contribution, joint and several liability

ALLONGE, *noun* addendum, additament, addition, adjunct, affix, appendage, appendix, attachment, complement, postscript, rider, supplement

ALLOT, *verb* *addicere,* administer, *adsignare,* allocate, appoint, apportion, assign, deal, delimit, demarcate, designate, dispense, disperse, dispose, *distribuere,* distribute, divide, dole, earmark, indicate, measure, mete, mete out, parcel out, partition, portion out, prorate, ration, share, specify

ALLOTMENT, *noun* *adsignatio,* allocation, annuity, appointment, apportionment, appropriation, arrangement, assignment, assignment by share, designation, dispensation, disposal, disposition, distribution, distribution by lot, dole, ordering, partition, portion, proportion, ration
ASSOCIATED CONCEPTS: allotment certificate, allotment note, allotment system

ALLOW *(Authorize),* ***verb*** accredit, acknowledge, approve, certify, charter, commission, empower, enable, endorse, enfranchise, entitle, give, give authority, give leave, give permission, grant, grant permission, invest, legalize, legitimatize, license, permit, privilege, qualify, sanction, support, sustain, vouchsafe, warrant
ASSOCIATED CONCEPTS: allow to bail, allowable debt, allowable loss, allowed by law, allowed claim
FOREIGN PHRASES: ***Est quiddam perfectius in rebus licitis.*** There is something more perfect in things permitted.

ALLOW *(Endure),* ***verb*** abide, accede, accept, accord, acquiesce, afford, agree, approve, assent, be answerable, be indulgent of, bear, brook, carry on under, concede, consent, countenance, forbear, permit, submit to, suffer, suffer to occur, sustain, take patiently, tolerate, undergo, withstand, yield
FOREIGN PHRASES: ***Tout es que la loi ne defend pas est permis.*** Everything which the law does not forbid is permitted.

ALLOWABLE, *adjective* acceptable, accepted, admissible, approvable, approved, authorized, excusable, granted, justifiable, lawful, legal, legalized, legitimate, licit, not impossible, not improper, not objectionable, pardonable, passable, permissible, proper, right, sanctionable, sanctioned, sufferable, suffered, suitable, tolerable, tolerated, unforbidden, unobjectionable, unprohibited, venial, warrantable
ASSOCIATED CONCEPTS: allowable claims

ALLOWED, *adjective* acceptable, accepted, acknowledged, admissible, admitted, allowable, approvable, approved, authorized, certified, chartered, commissioned, conceded, consented, eligible, empowered, endorsed, enfranchised, granted, justified, lawful, legal, legalized, legitimate, licensed, licit, passed, permissible, permissioned, permitted, ratified, recognized, rightful, sanctioned, sanctioned by the law, suitable, supported by authority, tolerable, tolerated, unforbidden, unprohibited, valid, validated, vouchsafed, warranted, within the law
ASSOCIATED CONCEPTS: allowed claim, allowed into evidence

FOREIGN PHRASES: ***Est quiddam perfectius in rebus licitis.*** There is something more perfect in things permitted.

ALLUDE, ***verb*** advert, *attingere,* bring to mind, cite, connote, convey, *designare,* evince, hint, imply, import, indicate, infer, insinuate, leave an inference, make indirect reference, mention, point to, refer to, relate, *significare,* signify, suggest, touch upon

ALLUSIVE, ***adjective*** allusory, ambiguous, clandestine, connotative, covert, eclipsed, evasive, imperspicuous, implicational, implicative, indicative, indirect, inferential, inferred, notional, obscure, screened, suggestive, tacit, vague, veiled
ASSOCIATED CONCEPTS: evasive contempt

ALLUVION, ***noun*** *batture,* deposit, deposition, residuary, sediment, settlement, settlings
ASSOCIATED CONCEPTS: accretion, alluvial accretion, alluvial land, riparian lands, riparian rights

ALLY, ***noun*** advocate, backer, benefactor, champion, cohort, companion, confederate, contributor, defender, espouser, faithful companion, friend, partisan, proponent, protector, sponsor, supporter, sympathizer

ALMOST, ***adverb*** approximately, close to, nearly, on the brink of, on the verge of, scarcely, within sight of

ALONE *(Solitary),* ***adverb*** apart, detached, in solitude, independently, insular, isolated, privately, removed, separate, solo

ALONE *(Unsupported),* ***adverb*** unabetted, unaccompanied, unaided, unassisted, unattended, unseconded

ALONG, ***adverb*** coupled with, forward, in company with, in conjunction with, lengthwise, side by side, together, with

ALSO, ***adverb*** additionally, as well, besides, extra, furthermore, in addition, including, likewise, moreover, over and above, plus, similarly, then again, together with, too

ALSO KNOWN AS, ***noun*** alias, also called, also identified as, also named, also referred to, assumed name, called, identification, identity, otherwise called, otherwise known, pseudonym

ALTER, ***verb*** adapt, adjust, amend, change, commute, convert, deviate, *immutare,* innovate, invert, make innovations, metamorphose, moderate, modify, modulate, *mutare,* qualify, rearrange, recast, reconstruct, reorganize, temper, transform, transmogrify, transmute, turn, variegate, vary
ASSOCIATED CONCEPTS: alter a document, alter a will, forgery, fraud

ALTER EGO, ***noun*** alternate, counterpart, double, living image, match, other, other half, other person, other self, perfect substitute, second self, shadow, stand-in, twin
ASSOCIATED CONCEPTS: agent, alter ego doctrine, corporate alter ego, piercing the corporate veil, separate corporate entity

ALTERATION, ***noun*** adjustment, conversion, correction, difference, diversity, innovation, modification, modulation, reform, rehabilitation, reorganization, repair, revision, transition, transposition, variability, variance, variation
ASSOCIATED CONCEPTS: alteration of a contract, alteration of a license, alteration of a pleading, alteration of an instrument, restoration of an instrument

ALTERCATION, ***noun*** affray, *altercatio,* angry dispute, argument, bickering, broil, commotion, conflict, contestation, controversy, disaccord, disputation, dispute, disturbance, feud, fight, fracas, heated debate, *iurgium,* jangle, jangling, melee, noisy quarrel, quarrel, *rixa,* row, scuffle, snarl, squabble, strife, wrangle, wrangling
FOREIGN PHRASES: ***Veritas nimium altercando amittitur.*** Truth is lost by too much altercation.

ALTERNATE *(Fluctuate),* ***verb*** be periodic, be unsettled, oscillate, pendulate, show indecision, vacillate, vary, waver

ALTERNATE *(Take turns),* ***verb*** act interchangeably, *alternare, alterner,* change by alternation, follow one another interchangeably, follow one another reciprocally, interchange, interchange regularly, interchange successively, perform by turns, perform reciprocally, perform responsively, permute, substitute, switch
ASSOCIATED CONCEPTS: alternate causes of action, pleading in the alternate

ALTERNATIVE *(Option),* ***noun*** alternate choice, choice, conclusion, decision, determination, discernment, discretion, discrimination, distinction, election, embracement, espousal, free selection, judgment, pick, recourse, remaining course, selection, voluntary decision
ASSOCIATED CONCEPTS: alternative conditions

ALTERNATIVE *(Substitute),* ***noun*** change, other choice, replacement, succedaneum, superseder, supplanter
ASSOCIATED CONCEPTS: alternative conditions, alternative contract, alternative covenant, alternative judgment, alternative legacy, alternative obligation, alternative plea, alternative pleading, alternative relief, alternative remedies, alternative writs

ALTERNATIVE DISPUTE RESOLUTION, ***noun*** alternative litigation resolution, alternative means to litigation, alternative method of resolving a dispute, arbitration, litigation substitute, means to resolve a dispute, mediation, pretrial mediation
Specifically: arbitration, mediation, pretrial mediation

ALWAYS *(Forever),* ***adverb*** all the time, all the while, at all times, for all history

ALWAYS *(Without exception),* ***adverb*** by and large each and every time, invariably, universally

AMALGAMATE, ***verb*** admix, bind, blend, centralize, coadunate, coalesce, combine, commingle, commix, conflate, consolidate, fuse, inosculate, join, meld, merge, mix, solidify, syndicate, unify, unite
ASSOCIATED CONCEPTS: amalgamated labor organizations

AMANUENSIS, ***noun*** clerk, recorder, recording secretary, scribe, scrivener, secretary, writer

AMASS, ***verb*** accrue, accumulate, aggregate, amalgamate, assemble, augment, blend, bond, coalesce, collect, combine, compile, compound, congregate, corral, expand, extend, garner, gather, grow, herd, incorporate, increase, join, link, marry, mix, multiply, optimize, round up, stockpile, swell, unify, unite

AMASSED, ***adjective*** aggregated, amalgamate, amalgamated, blended, collective, compact, complex, composite, compound, compounded, conglomerate, fused, manifold, medley, mingled, mixed, mosaic, multiform, multiple, variegated

AMATEUR, ***adjective*** inept, unaccomplished, unadroit, undextrous, unfit, ungifted, unskilled, untalented

AMATEUR, ***noun*** apprentice, aspirant, beginner, disciple, entrant, fledging, freshman, inexperienced person, initiate, layman, neophyte, novice

AMAZE, ***verb*** affect, astonish, astound, awe, bewilder, blow away, bowl over, captivate, dazzle, dumbfound, enchant, enrapture, enthrall, enthuse, excite, fascinate, flabbergast, floor, impress, influence, inspire, move, mystify, overwhelm, pique, provoke, ravish, shock, startle, stir, strike, stun, stupefy, sway, thrill, touch, wow

AMBIGUITY, ***noun*** abstruseness, *ambiguitas,* bafflement, bewilderment, confounded meaning, confused meaning, confusion, disconcertion, doubtful meaning, doubtfulness, dubiety, dubiousness, duplexity in meaning, equivocalness, equivocation, incertitude, indefinite meaning, indefiniteness, indeterminacy, obscure meaning, obscurity, puzzlement, reconditeness, uncertainty of meaning, unintelligibility, vagueness
ASSOCIATED CONCEPTS: ambiguity upon the factum, latent ambiguity, patent ambiguity
FOREIGN PHRASES: ***Cum in testamento ambigue aut etiam perperam scriptum est benigne interpretari et secundum id quod credibile est cogitatum credendum est.*** Where an ambiguous or even an erroneous expression occurs in a will, it should be interpreted liberally and in accordance with the intention of the testator. ***Ambiguitas verborum latens verificatione suppletur; nam quod ex facto oritur ambiguum verificatione facti tollitur.*** A latent verbal ambiguity may be removed by evidence; for whatever ambiguity arises from an extrinsic fact may be explained by extrinsic evidence. ***Ambiguum placitum interpretari debet contra proferentem.*** An ambiguous plea ought to be interpreted against the party entering it. ***Quae cubitationis tollendae causa contractibus inseruntur, jus commune non laedunt.*** Those clauses which are inserted in agreements to avoid doubts and ambiguity do not offend the common law. ***Quoties in verbis nulla est ambiguitas, ibi nulla expositio contra verba fienda est.*** Whenever there is no ambiguity in the words, then no exposition contrary to the words should be made. ***Quum in testamento ambigue aut etiam perperam scriptum est, benigne interpretari et secundum id quod credibile et cogitatum, credendum est.*** When an ambiguous or even an erroneous expression occurs in a will, it should be construed liberally and in accordance with what is thought the probable meaning of the testator. ***Ubi jus incertum, ibi jus nullum.*** Where the law is uncertain, there is no law. ***Verbis standum ubi nulla ambiguitas.*** Where there is no ambiguity, one must abide by the words.

AMBIGUOUS, ***adjective*** abstruse, *ambiguus,* ambivalent, confused, difficult to comprehend, doubtful, dubious, equivocal, having a double meaning, indefinite, indistinct, inexact, lacking clearness, not clear, not plain, obscure, open to various interpretations, uncertain, unintelligible, vague
ASSOCIATED CONCEPTS: ambiguous language
FOREIGN PHRASES: ***Ambigua responsio contra proferentem est accipienda.*** An ambiguous answer is to be taken against him who offers it. ***In ambigua voce legis ea potius accipienda est significatio quae vitio caret, praesertim cum etiam voluntas legis ex hoc colligi possit.*** In an ambiguous expression of law, that interpretation is to be preferred which is consonant with equity, especially where it is in conformity with the purpose of the law. ***In ambiguis orationibus maxime sententia spectanda est ejus qui eas protulisset.*** In ambiguous expressions, the intent of the person using them is particularly to be regarded. ***In ambiguo sermone non utrumque dicimus sed id duntaxat quod volumus.*** In ambiguous discourse, language is not used in a double sense, but in the sense in which it is meant.

AMBIT, ***noun*** border, boundary, boundary line, bounds, circumference, contour, delineation lines, domain, dominion, furthest extent, furthest point, jurisdiction, limit, lines, orbit, outline, outer limit, pale, perimeter, periphery, province, realm, sphere
ASSOCIATED CONCEPTS: ambit of a statute, within the ambit of the law

AMBIVALENCE, ***noun*** dubiety, dubitancy, equivocalness, hesitation, incertitude, indecision, indecisiveness, indeterminacy, indetermination, irresoluteness, irresolution, mental reservation, prevarication, uncertainty, undecidedness, undetermination, vacillation

AMBULATORY, ***adjective*** able to be altered, alterative, amendable, amendatory, changeable, emendable, emendatory, modifiable, movable, mutable, not fixed, permutable, renunciatory, repudiative, repudiatory, reversible, reversional, revisional, revisory, revocable, revocatory, subject to change, variable
ASSOCIATED CONCEPTS: ambulatory deed, ambulatory patient, ambulatory will
FOREIGN PHRASES: ***Ambulatoria est voluntas defuncti usque ad vitae supremum exitum.*** The will of a deceased person is ambulatory until the latest moment of life.

AMBUSH, ***verb*** assail, assault, attack, attack from a concealed position, bait a trap, catch by perfidy, ensnare, entrap, lay a trap for, lie in wait for, set a trap for, snare, trap, waylay

AMELIORATE, ***verb*** advance, allay, better, change for the better, correct, *corrigere,* cultivate, develop, ease, elevate, enhance, forward, fructify, help, improve, make better, make progress, meliorate, mend, mitigate, palliate, promote, raise, rectify, reform, upgrade
ASSOCIATED CONCEPTS: ameliorating facts and circumstances, ameliorating waste

AMENABILITY, ***noun*** accessibleness, accommodativeness, acquiescence, adaptability, agreeableness, compliance, compliancy, conformability, docility, ductility, flexibility, flexibleness, inclination, influenceability, malleability, manageability, mansuetude, obligingness, persuasibility, placability, plasticity, pliability, pliancy, readiness, receptiveness, responsiveness, servility, submission, submissiveness, tractability, versatility, willingness, yieldingness

AMENABLE, ***adjective*** accessible, acquiescent, agreeable, amiable, available, compliant, *dicto oboediens,* flexible, impressionable, influenceable, movable, obedient, open to suggestions, persuadable, persuasible, pervious, pliable, pliant, reasonable, responsible, suasible, tractable, yielding
ASSOCIATED CONCEPTS: amenable to process

AMEND, ***verb*** add to, adjust, alter, ameliorate, better, change, correct, *corrigere,* edit, emend, *emendare,* emendate, enhance, enrich, improve, mend, modify, perfect, polish, rectify, refashion, refine, reform, remedy, remove faults, renew, revamp, revise, rework, rewrite, upgrade
ASSOCIATED CONCEPTS: amend a certificate of incorporation, amend a law, amend a pleading, amend a statute, amend a will

AMENDMENT *(Correction),* ***noun*** adjustment, amelioration, betterment, change, *correctio,* elaboration, *emendatio,* emendation, enhancement, improvement, melioration, modification, perfection, refinement, reformation, remedy, revampment, revisal, revision, supplement
ASSOCIATED CONCEPTS: amendment in a statute, amendment to a will

AMENDMENT *(Legislation),* ***noun*** act, bill, clause, legislation, legislative act, legislative bill, measure, modification of the law, rider, supplement
ASSOCIATED CONCEPTS: amendment to a charter, amendment to the Constitution, Bill of Rights

AMENITIES, ***noun*** civilities, convention, correctness, decency, decorousness, decorum, elegances, etiquette, formalities, gentilities, manners, prescribed code of conduct, propriety, protocol, seemliness, social code, standards

AMENITY, ***noun*** accommodation, agreeable manner, agreeable way, agreeableness, allure, *amoenitas,* appeal, attractive feature, attractive quality, attractiveness, civility, delightfulness, desirable feature, grace, invitingness, lure, mildness, niceness, pleasantness, pleasingness, refinement

AMERCEMENT, ***noun*** damages, fine, forfeit, forfeiture, pecuniary penalty, penalty

AMICABLE, ***adjective*** affable, amiable, cordial, friendly, genial, harmonious, sociable, unhostile

AMICUS CURIAE, ***noun*** advocate, champion, exponent, friend in court, intercessor, intervening party, intervenor, party, representative, speaker
ASSOCIATED CONCEPTS: amicus brief, amicus motion to intervene

AMMUNITION, ***noun*** *apparatus belli,* armament, armature, arms, ballistics, cartridges, charge, defense, deterrent, explosive, firearms, gunnery, gunpowder, materials of combat, means of attack, muniment, munition, panoply, propellants, provisions, weapons

AMNESTY, ***noun*** absolution, acquittance, act of grace, act of mercy, conciliation, condonation, discharge, disculpation, exculpation, exoneration, forgiveness, general pardon, grace, *ignoscere,* pardon, quittance, release, reprieve, universal forgiveness of past offenses, *venia*
ASSOCIATED CONCEPTS: express amnesty, implied amnesty, presidential pardon

AMONG, ***adverb*** amid, amidst, between, in the middle of, parenthetically

AMORTIZATION, ***noun*** clearance, defrayal, defrayment, disbursement, discharge, extinction of a debt, extinguishment of claim, liquidation of a debt, payment, remittance, satisfaction
ASSOCIATED CONCEPTS: amortization contract, amortization of a mortgage, amortize a loan

AMOUNT *(Quantity),* ***noun*** aggregate, bulk, count, extent, magnitude, mass, measure, measurement, net quantity, number, numeration, strength, substance, sum, summa, total, whole
ASSOCIATED CONCEPTS: amount of evidence, amount of loss
FOREIGN PHRASES: ***Major numerus in se continet minorem.*** The greater number contains in itself the lesser.

AMOUNT *(Result),* ***noun*** conclusion, consequence, effect, end result, full effect, import, net quantity, outcome, outgrowth, product, purport, resultant, sum, sum total, upshot

AMOUNT *(Sum),* ***noun*** account, count, rate, reckoning, statement, summation, tally, value, worth
ASSOCIATED CONCEPTS: amount allowed, amount due, amount in controversy, amount in dispute, amount of loss, amount recovered, jurisdictional amount

AMPLE, ***adjective*** abounding, abundant, adequate, bountiful, broad enough, capacious, commodious, comprehensive, copious, expansive, extensive, generous, large enough, liberal, many, plenteous, satisfactory, sufficient

AMPLIFICATION, ***noun*** accession, accretion, accrual, accumulation, advance, advancement, aggrandizement, aggravation, augmentation, broadening, clarification, deepening, development, dilation, elaboration, enhancement, enlargement, expansion, explanation, extension, furtherance, gain, growth, heightening, increasing, increment, intensification, magnification, progression, restatement, rewording

AMPLIFY, ***verb*** add to, augment, delineate, develop, elaborate, enlarge, expand, extend, increase, specify, specify in greater detail

ANACHRONISTIC, ***adjective*** antedated, antiquated, archaic, archaizing, behind the times, ill-advised, ill-judged, ill-timed, incongruous, misdated, misjudged, noncontemporary, obsolete, outdated, outmoded, previous, untimely, Victorian

ANACOLUTHON, ***noun*** broken thread, disconnectedness, discontinuity, lost connection, non sequitur, unwarranted conclusion

ANALOGOUS, ***adjective*** akin, cognate, commensurate, comparable, congenerous, connatural, correspondent, corresponding, exact, homogenous, interchangeable, kin, kindred, like, matching, proportionate, relatable, related, resemblant, resembling, same, similar, such

ANALOGY, ***noun*** affinity, agreement, close relation, close resemblance, common feature, comparability, comparison, congruity, correlation, correspondence, equivalence, homology, like quality, likeness, logical relation, parallel relation, parallelism, parity, partial similarity, point in common, point of resemblance, points of comparison, relation, relativeness, relativity, resemblance, semblance, similar appearance, similar form, similar relation, similarity, similitude, *similitudo,* symmetry
FOREIGN PHRASES: ***De similibus ad similia eadem ratione procedendum est.*** Proceeding in similar matters we are to proceed by the same rule.

ANALYSIS, *noun* ascertainment, assay, audit, canvassing, close inquiry, consideration, critical examination, critique, delineation, dissection, examination, exhaustive inquiry, *explicatio,* exploration, inquiry, investigation, perusal, probe, research, review, scrutinization, scrutiny, searching inquiry, sifting, strict inquiry, study, survey, treatment
ASSOCIATED CONCEPTS: chemical analysis, lab analysis

ANALYTICAL, *adjective* deductive, demonstrative, diagnostic, experimental, fact-finding, investigative, logical, mathematical, probing, rational, reasoning, resolvent, searching, separative, solvent

ANALYZE, *verb* anatomize, audit, canvass, conduct an inquiry, consider, delineate, delve into, dissect, examine, examine critically, explore, hold an inquiry, inquire into, institute an inquiry, investigate, make an analysis, make an inquiry, probe, question, reason, research, review, scan, scrutinize, set up an inquiry, sift, study, subject to examination, survey

ANARCHY, *noun* absence of authority, breakdown of administration, chaos, confusion, discord, disobedience, disorder, disorderliness, disorganization, disregard, disunion, indiscipline, insubordination, insurgence, insurrection, interregnum, irresponsibility, lawlessness, *licentia,* misgovernment, misrule, mob law, mob rule, nihilism, political disorder, rebellion, revolution, riot, sedition, terrorism, tumult, turmoil, unruliness, uprising
ASSOCIATED CONCEPTS: criminal anarchy

ANCESTOR, *noun* ascendant, *auctor generis, auctor gentis,* forebear, forefather, foregoer, forerunner, genitor, grandsire, parent, patriarch, precursor, predecessor, primogenitor, procreator, progenitor
ASSOCIATED CONCEPTS: ancestral estate, ancestral property, descendant, immediate ancestor, inheritance, lineal ancestor, maternal ancestor, paternal ancestor

ANCESTRY, *noun* affiliation, ascendants, blood, blood relationship, blood tie, bloodline, cognation, connection, consanguinity, derivation, descent, family, family connection, family tree, filiation, forebears, forefathers, former generations, genealogy, genesis, *genus,* heredity, history, kinship, line, lineage, origin, origination, *origo,* parentage, parents, patriarchs, pedigree, predecessors, procreators, stirps, strain
ASSOCIATED CONCEPTS: ancestral estate, ancestral property

ANCILLARY *(Auxiliary),* ***adjective*** abetting, accessory, added, additional, adjunct, adjuvant, advantageous, aidful, aiding, assistant, attendant, beneficial, coadjuvant, collateral, completing, conducive, contributory, cooperative, extra, helpful, in addition, ministrant, more, other, serving as an adjunct, serving as an aid, spare, supernumerary, supplemental, supplementary, supporting
ASSOCIATED CONCEPTS: ancillary acts, ancillary agreements, ancillary attachment, ancillary covenants, ancillary jurisdiction, ancillary proceeding, ancillary relief, ancillary remedies

ANCILLARY *(Subsidiary),* ***adjective*** complementing, dependent, derivational, derivative, ensuing, following, lesser, resultant, resulting, secondary, sequential, subaltern, subordinate

ANCILLARY RELIEF, *noun* accessory relief, additional relief, adjunct relief, an added judgment, attendant relief, beneficial relief, collateral relief, complementing relief, extra relief, other relief, resultant relief, resulting relief, secondary relief, sequential relief, spare relief, subordinate relief, supplemental relief, supplementary relief, supporting relief
ASSOCIATED CONCEPTS: ancillary administration, ancillary attachment, ancillary bill, ancillary jurisdiction, ancillary proceeding

ANEW, *adverb* afresh, again, another time, newly, once more, over again

ANGER, *verb* abrade, aggravate, agitate, alienate, annoy, attack, badger, bait, beleaguer, bother, burn, chafe, create hostility, cross, disquiet, distress, disturb, embitter, enflame, enrage, envenom, exasperate, frazzle, gall, grate, gripe, harass, incense, inflame, infuriate, irk, irritate, madden, nettle, offend, outrage, peeve, perturb, pique, provoke, rankle, rile, roil, trouble, unhinge, unsettle, upset, vex, worry

ANGUISH, *verb* ache, aggrieve, agonize, desolate, disturb, excruciate, grieve, harry, make miserable, pain, prostrate, rack, suffer, torment, torture, trouble, writhe
ASSOCIATED CONCEPTS: mental anguish, noneconomic loss, pain and suffering

ANIMADVERSION, *noun* admonition, adverse comment, aspersion, blame, censorious remark, censure, chiding, condemnation, correction, criticism, deprecation, disapprobation, disapproval, discredit, faultfinding, impeachment, impugnation, imputation, obloquy, rebuke, reflection, remark, remonstrance, reprehension, reprimand, reproach, reprobation, reproof, revilement, stricture

ANIMAL, *noun* *animans,* beast, beast of burden, beast of the field, brute, brute creation, created being, creature, pet, wild being
ASSOCIATED CONCEPTS: animals of a base nature, domestic animals, wild animal
FOREIGN PHRASES: ***Animalia fera, si facta sint mansueta et ex consuetudine eunt et redeunt, volant et revolant, ut cervi, cygni, etc., eo usque nostra sunt, et ita intelliguntur quamdium habuerunt animum revertendi.*** Wild animals, if they are tamed and are accustomed to leave and return, fly away and fly back, as stags, swans, etc., are considered to belong to us so long as they have the intention of returning to us.

ANIMOSITY, *noun* abhorrence, acrimony, aggravation, alienation, anger, antagonism, antipathy, bad blood, bitterness, coldness, difference of opinion, disapproval, discord, disfavor, displeasure, enmity, gall, grudge, hatred, hostility, ignominy, ill will, loathing, malevolence, malice, malignity, prejudice, rancor, resentment, revulsion, strain, tension, venom, vindictiveness, virulence

ANIMUS, *noun* bent, character, decision, deliberateness, design, determination, disposition, fixed purpose, inclination, intendment, intent, intention, intentionality, mind, motive, nature, penchant, predetermination, predilection, predisposition, propensity, purpose, resolution, resolve, set purpose, settled purpose, temper, tendency, volition, will
ASSOCIATED CONCEPTS: *animus derelinquendi, animus et factum, animus furandi, animus revertendi, animus testandi,* antiunion animus

ANNEX *(Add),* ***verb*** affix, append, attach, bind, bring together, combine, conjoin, connect, consolidate, fasten,

fix, hold together, incorporate, interlink, intertwist, join, merge, put together, subjoin, supplement, unite
ASSOCIATED CONCEPTS: annex an exhibit, annex court papers, annex to a pleading, annexed writing, fixtures

ANNEX *(Arrogate),* ***verb*** accroach, appropriate, assume, assume ownership, confiscate, convert, disseise, distrain, expropriate, impound, seize, take over, take possession, take summarily, usurp
ASSOCIATED CONCEPTS: annex a territory

ANNIHILATE, *verb* abolish, annul, blast, cancel, consume, crush, cut down, decimate, demolish, destroy, devour, dismantle, dissolve, efface, eliminate, end, eradicate, expunge, exterminate, extinguish, extirpate, invalidate, kill, liquidate, massacre, negate, nullify, obliterate, overthrow, quench, ravage, remove, render null and void, revoke, ruin, slaughter, slay, snuff out, stifle, subvert, undo, vitiate, wipe out, wreck

ANNOUNCE, *verb* acquaint, advertise, advise, affirm, allege, annunciate, apprise, assert, asservate, aver, broadcast, bruit, bulletin, circulate, communicate, contend, convey, declare, disabuse, disclose, disseminate, enunciate, foretell, give out, herald, inform, maintain, make manifest, mention, notify, observe, post, proclaim, profess, prognosticate, promulgate, pronounce, propound, publish, relate, report, reveal, set forth, signal, speak, specify, state, tell, transmit, trumpet, utter

ANNOUNCEMENT, *noun* broadcast, bulletin, communication, communiqué, declaration, disclosure, dissemination, exposé, exposition, gazette, manifesto, message, news, notice, notification, posting, proclamation, promulgation, pronouncement, publication, release, report, statement, utterance
ASSOCIATED CONCEPTS: legal notice

ANNOY, *verb* acerbate, affront, aggravate, badger, bedevil, bother, chafe, cross, discommode, discompose, displease, disquiet, distress, disturb, enrage, exasperate, fester, fret, gall, get on the nerves of, grate, grieve, harass, harm, harry, heckle, hector, importune, incommode, inconvenience, infest, irk, irritate, nag, needle, offend, pain, pester, pique, plague, provoke, rankle, roil, ruffle, thwart, torment, trouble, upset, vex

ANNUITY, *noun* allotment, allowance, *annua pecunia,* annual allowance, earnings, income, pension, remuneration, retirement income, return, specified income payable for life, stipend, subsidy, subvention, yearly payment
ASSOCIATED CONCEPTS: annuity by a trust, annuity by will, annuity contract, annuity policy, antenuptial annuity, life insurance annuity, verifiable annuity
FOREIGN PHRASES: ***Annua nec debitum judex non separat ipsum.*** A judge does not divide annuities nor debt.

ANNUL, *verb* abnegate, *abolere,* abolish, *abrogare,* abrogate, annihilate, avoid, call back, cancel, cancel out, contradict, contravene, countermand, counterorder, deny, destroy, discontinue, disestablish, efface, end, expunge, exterminate, extinguish, invalidate, make illegal, make void, negate, nullify, obliterate, overrule, put an end to, recall, reduce to nothing, reduce to nought, relinquish, render null and void, render void, renege, repeal, repudiate, rescind, retract, reverse, revoke, set aside, *solvere,* strike out, supersede, terminate, unmake, vitiate, void, withdraw
ASSOCIATED CONCEPTS: annul a marriage, annul a statute, nol-pros

ANNULMENT, *noun* abolishment, abolition, abrogation, cancellation, contravention, decree of nullity, deletion, discontinuance, disestablishment, dissolution, effacement, invalidation, negation, nullification, obliteration, rasure, rescindment, retraction, reversal, revocation, revokement, undoing, vitiation, voidance
ASSOCIATED CONCEPTS: alimony, annulment of a marriage, dissolution of marriage, divorce, separation, voidable marriage

ANNUM, *noun* age, *annus,* continuum of days, cycle, fifty-two weeks, full round of the seasons, period, time, twelve months, year

ANNUNCIATE, *verb* advise, affirm, announce, apprise, assert, aver, communicate, convey, declare, dispatch news, disseminate, enunciate, explain, express, get across, get through, give notice, impart, inform, keep posted, make known, make known publicly, make proclamation, notify, pass on, pass on information, post, proclaim, profess, promulgate, pronounce, propound, publicize, publish, report, specify, state, tell, transmit

ANOMALOUS, *adjective* aberrant, abnormal, anomalistic, atypical, awry, breaking with tradition, deranged, deviating from the common rule, deviative, disarranged, disjunct, dislocated, disordered, disorganized, divergent, eccentric, erratic, in disorder, in the wrong place, inconsistent, irregular, misplaced, nonstandard, nonuniform, not conforming to the usual, out of keeping, out of order, out of the ordinary, peculiar, solecistic, uncommon, unconventional, uncustomary, unnatural, unrepresentative, untypical, unusual

ANOMALY, *noun* aberration, abnormality, amorphism, curiosity, departure, deviation, discrepancy, divergence, eccentricity, exception, incongruity, inconsistency, irregularity, monstrosity, nonconformity, oddity, peculiarity, quirk, singularity, subnormality, unconformity, unnaturalness, variance

ANONYMOUS, *adjective* authorless, bearing no name, having no acknowledged name, incognito, innominate, nameless, of unknown authorship, secret, *sine nomine,* unacknowledged, unclaimed, undesignated, unidentified, unknown, unnamed, unsigned, unspecified, without a name, without the name of the author
ASSOCIATED CONCEPTS: anonymous donor

ANSWER *(Judicial response),* ***noun*** confutation, contradictory evidence, countercharge, counterclaim, counterevidence, counterreply, counterstatement, defense, denial, legal argument, negation, negative evidence, official reply, opposite evidence, plea, plea in rebuttal, rebuttal, rebutting evidence, recrimination, refutation, rejoinder, replication, reply to a charge, surrebuttal, surrebutter, surrejoinder
ASSOCIATED CONCEPTS: amended answer, appearance by an answer, frivolous answer, general appearance, notice of appearance, responsive answer, sham answer, supplemental answer
FOREIGN PHRASES: ***Ambigua responsio contra proferentem est accipienda.*** An ambiguous answer is to be taken against him who offers it.

ANSWER *(Reply),* ***noun*** acknowledgment, denial, negation, reaction, rebuttal, refutal, rejoinder, repartee, replication, respondence, response, retort, return, riposte
ASSOCIATED CONCEPTS: argumentative answer, irrelevant answer, nonresponsive answer, responsive answer

ANSWER *(Solution),* ***noun*** cause, elucidation, explanation, finding, outcome, reason, resolution, result, revelation, verdict

ANSWER *(Be responsible),* ***verb*** be accountable, be answerable, be bound, be chargeable, be compelled, be liable, be obligated, be obliged, be subject, be surety, be under legal obligation, undertake responsibility

ANSWER *(Reply),* ***verb*** acknowledge, act in response to, be responsive, confute, contend, contest, contradict, contravene, controvert, counter, counterclaim, debate, defeat, defend, deny, disclaim, disprove, dispute, forswear, impugn, make a rejoinder, oppose, oppugn, plead, rebut, refute, rejoin, repudiate, *rescribere,* respond, retaliate, retort, return, riposte, say in reply, *se defendere,* traverse
ASSOCIATED CONCEPTS: answer in the alternative, argumentative answer

ANSWER *(Respond legally),* ***verb*** contest, controvert, counterblast, countercharge, counterclaim, defend, plead, rebut, recriminate, rejoin, reply, surrejoin
ASSOCIATED CONCEPTS: appearance by an answer, argumentative answer, supplemental answer

ANSWER FOR *(Act for),* ***verb*** act on behalf of, appear for, be accepted for, be attorney for, be proxy for, be regarded as, be responsible for, be taken as, be the equivalent of, count for, front for, go as, pass as, pass for, represent, serve as, stand for, stand in place for, stand in place of, substitute for, take responsibility for, take the blame

ANSWER FOR *(Sponsor),* ***verb*** champion, commit, contract, defend, endorse, ensure, favor, guarantee, indemnify, insure, promote, protect, support, sustain, undertake, uphold

ANTAGONISM, ***noun*** adversity, animosity, animus, antipathy, bad blood, belligerence, bitterness, combativeness, conflict, contrariness, controversy, disaffection, discord, discordance, dissent, dissonance, estrangement, friction, hatred, hostility, inhospitableness, jaundice, loathing, malice, malignancy, pugnacity, rancor, strife, vendetta, venom, vindictiveness, virulence, vitriol

ANTAGONIZE, ***verb*** act in opposition to, aggress, alienate, cause dislike, cause offense, cause umbrage, compete with, conflict with, contend against, counteract, cross, destroy good will, disaffect, displease, embitter, envenom, estrange, excite hate, go against, incur the hostility of, irritate, make an antagonist of, make unfriendly, offend, oppose, provoke, render inimical, repel, rival, run counter to, set against, set at odds, show ill will, spite, take issue with, take one's stand against, turn against, work against

ANTECEDE, ***verb*** antedate, forerun, go before, have precedence, precede, predate, prevene
ASSOCIATED CONCEPTS: ancestor, antecedent creditor, antecedent debt, antecedent encumbrance, antecedent fraud, antecedent promise

ANTECEDENT, ***adjective*** *antecedens,* anterior, earlier, first, fore, foregoing, forerunning, former, going before in time, inaugural, introductory, precedent, preceding, precursive, precursory, preexistent, prefatory, preliminary, prelusive, preparatory, prevenient, previous, prior
ASSOCIATED CONCEPTS: antecedent creditors, antecedent debt, preexisting debts, preexisting liabilities

ANTECEDENT, ***noun*** ancestor, ancestry, before mentioned, derivation, forerunner, former, last, lineage, original, patriarch, pedigree, pioneer, precedent, precursor, predecessor, preliminary, premise, primogenitor, progenitor, stock

ANTEDATE, ***verb*** affix an earlier date, anachronize, assign to an earlier date, date back, date before the true date, date before the true time, date earlier than the fact, foredate, predate, set an earlier date, transfer to an earlier date

ANTENUPTIAL AGREEMENT, ***noun*** agreement before marriage, concord before marriage, contract before marriage, legal arrangement before marriage, pact before marriage, understanding before marriage

ANTICIPATE *(Expect),* ***verb*** *antevertere,* assume, be ready for, calculate on, consider in advance, contemplate, count on, forearm, get the start on, guard against, have in prospect, hold in view, intuit, make preparations, plan on, preconceive, predispose, prepare for, suppose, surmise, wait for
ASSOCIATED CONCEPTS: anticipated profits, anticipating defenses, anticipation notes, anticipatory breach, anticipatory repudiation, anticipatory warrant, duty to anticipate in negligence

ANTICIPATE *(Prognosticate),* ***verb*** announce in advance, augur, auspicate, betoken, conjecture, divine, forebode, forecast, foreknow, foreshow, forespeak, harbinger, have a presentiment, herald, look forward to, omen, portend, *praevertere,* preannounce, precognize, predetermine, predict, premonish, presage, prophesy, vaticinate

ANTICIPATION *(Expectation),* ***noun*** apprehension, contemplation, divination, forecast, foreseeing, foresight, imminence, insight, intuition, preconception, prediction, preparation, prescience, presentiment, prolepsis, second sight

ANTICIPATION *(Likelihood),* ***noun*** contemplation, expectancy, foreboding, forecast, hope, outlook, possibility, preconception, preoccupation, presumption, prevision, probability, prospect
ASSOCIATED CONCEPTS: anticipation of income, anticipation of injuries

ANTIPATHETIC *(Distasteful),* ***adjective*** abhorrent, bitter, disagreeable, disgusting, displeasing, hateful, loathsome, odious, offensive, repellent, repugnant, repulsive, undesirable, uninviting, unsatisfactory, virulent

ANTIPATHETIC *(Oppositional),* ***adjective*** adverse, alien, alienated, antagonistic, antipodean, antithetic, antithetical, at cross-purposes, averse, conflicting, constitutionally opposed, contradictory, contradistinct, contrapositive, contrary, contrasted, converse, counter, diametrically opposite, having a natural contrariety, inimical, negatory, opposed, opposing, opposite, oppositive, oppugnant, resistant, reverse, unfriendly, unpropitious

ANTIPATHY, ***noun*** abhorrence, abomination, alienation, anathema, animosity, antagonism, antipode, aversion, clashing, collision, conflict, contradiction, contrariness, detestation, deviation, difference, disagreement, disapprobation, disfavor, disgust, disinclination, dislike, enmity, execration, hatred, horror, hostility, ill will, incompatibility, inimicalness, loathing, malice, odium, opposition, rancor, reluctance, repugnance, repulsion, unfriendliness

ANTIPODE, *noun* absolute difference, adverseness, *adversus,* antimony, antipathy, *antipodes,* antipole, antithesis, collision, conflict, contradiction, contradistinction, contraindication, contraposition, contrariety, contrariness, contrary, contrast, converse, counteraction, countermeaning, counterpart, counterpole, direct opposite, disagreement, inconsistency, inverse, inversion, negation, obverse, opposite, opposite extreme, opposite pole, opposite side, oppositeness, opposition, other extreme, polarity, repugnance, reverse, vis-à-vis

ANTIQUATED, *adjective* aged, anachronistic, ancient, antediluvian, antique, archaic, disused, fossilized, moribund, obsolescent, obsolete, old, olden, old-fashioned, ossified, outdated, outmoded, out-of-date, outworn, passé, prehistoric, primitive, quaint, retired, rundown, superannuated, timeworn, unfashionable

ANTIQUE, *adjective* ancient, antedeluvian, archaic, bygone, old, old-fashioned, older, superannuated, timeworn, venerable

ANTITHESIS, *noun* absolute difference, adverseness, antipode, balanced contrast, conflict, *contentio,* contradiction, contradistinction, contraposition, contrariety, *contrarium,* contrary, contrast, converse, counterpart, counterpole, direct opposite, disagreement, divergence, incompatibility, inverse, irreconcilability, mutual exclusiveness, opposite, opposite pole, opposition, other extreme, polarity, reverse, strong contrast

ANTITHETICAL, *adjective* adverse, alien, antipathetic, antipodal, clashing, conflicting, contradictory, contrarian, contrary, controverted, converse, counter, cross, diametric, diametrical, diametrically opposed, disparate, dissident, dissimilar, divergent, inconsistent, inimical, inverse, obverse, opposed, opposite, polar, polarized, unlike

ANTITRUST ACT, *noun* against fair trade, against free commerce, against free mercantilism, against free trade, against open business, against open markets, contrary to good business

ANXIETY, *noun* agitation, alarm, angst, anguish, anxiousness, apprehension, concern, consternation, desperation, discomfort, discomposure, dismay, disquiet, disquietude, distraction, doubt, dread, edginess, fear, hysteria, jitters, jumpiness, misgiving, nervousness, panic, presentiment, restlessness, solicitude, strain, stress, suspense, tension, uncertainty, uneasiness, vexation, worry

ANXIOUS, *adjective* afraid, aggrieved, antsy, apprehensive, bothered, concerned, disquieted, distraught, distressed, disturbed, eager, edgy, expectant, fearful, fluttery, fretful, hypertensive, ill at ease, insecure, jittery, jumpy, nervous, overwrought, panicky, perturbed, restless, shaky, shook-up, skittish, solicitous, stressed, stressed out, tense, troubled, uncomfortable, undone, uneasy, unglued, unnerved, unquiet, unstrung, upset, uptight, vexed, worried

APART, *adjective* alien, alone, asunder, detached, disconnected, disengaged, disjoined, disjoint, disjointed, disjunct, disrelated, dissociated, *distare,* disunited, *diversus,* foreign, having independent qualities, having unique features, having unique qualities, independent, irrelative, isolated, no relation, removed, *separare,* separate, separated, solo, *solus,* unaffiliated, unallied, unassociated, unattached, unconnected, unjoined

ASSOCIATED CONCEPTS: living apart

APARTMENT, *noun* home, place of residence, premises, residence

ASSOCIATED CONCEPTS: condominium, cooperative apartment

APATHETIC, *adjective* aloof, bored, callous, careless, casual, cold, cold-blooded, cursory, disinterested, dragging, dull, frigid, heartless, heedless, impassive, inactive, inattentive, incurious, indifferent, indolent, inert, inexpressive, insensible, insentient, insouciant, lackadaisical, languid, lax, lethargic, lifeless, listless, lukewarm, nonchalant, obtuse, otiose, passionless, passive, perfunctory, phlegmatic, sluggish, soulless, spiritless, stoical, stolid, stony, supine, torpid, unaffected, unanimated, unemotional, unenthusiastic, unfeeling, unimpassioned, uninquisitive, uninterested, unmoved, unsusceptible

APLOMB, *noun* assurance, backbone, balance, boldness, calmness, composure, confidence, constancy, correctness, decorum, demeanor, deportment, dignity, elegance, equanimity, equilibrium, grit, intrepidity, levelheadedness, poise, presence of mind, resolution, restraint, security, self-possession, self-reliance, solidity, stability, stature, steadiness

APOLOGIST, *noun* advocate, arguer in defense, champion, defender, *defensor,* disputant, excuser, exponent, expositer, expounder, favorer, justifier, pleader, proponent, protector, supporter, upholder

APOLOGY, *noun* acknowledgment, admission, amends, atonement, concession, defense, explanation, expression of remorse, mitigation, regret, sorrow

APPALLING, *adjective* abhorrent, abominable, atrocious, beneath contempt, contemptible, deplorable, despicable, detestable, dreadful, foul, frightening, frightful, ghastly, ghoulish, gruesome, harrowing, hateful, heinous, horrendous, horrid, horrifying, loathsome, obnoxious, odious, offensive, outrageous, pathetic, pitiful, repellent, reprehensible, repulsive, revolting, shameful, shocking, terrible, terrifying, unspeakable, vile, villainous

ASSOCIATED CONCEPTS: appalling conduct, contempt of court, harassment

APPARENT *(Perceptible),* ***adjective*** able to be seen, clear, conspicuous, definite, detectable, discernible, distinct, easily seen, evident, explicit, exposed, express, *fictus,* identifiable, in sight, in view, indubitable, known, manifest, *manifestus,* noticeable, notorious, obvious, open, open to view, overt, palpable, patent, perceivable, plain, real, recognizable, self-evident, showing, *species,* tangible, uncovered, undisguised, *videor,* viewable, visible

ASSOCIATED CONCEPTS: apparent ability, apparent agency, apparent authority, apparent cause, apparent danger, apparent defect, apparent easement, apparent from the record, apparent necessity, apparent ownership, apparent partnership, apparent risk, apparent scope of authority, apparent use

APPARENT *(Presumptive),* ***adjective*** appearing, assumptive, conjectural, contemplated, evidential, expected, hopeful, intended, likely, logical, manifest, ostensible, plausible, premised, presumable, probable, proposed,

propositional, prospective, seeming, suggestive, supposable, supposed, suppositional, suppositionary, suppositive, taken for granted, to be supposed
ASSOCIATED CONCEPTS: apparent heir, apparent validity
FOREIGN PHRASES: ***Quod constat clare non debet verificari.*** What is clearly apparent is not required to be proved. ***Quod constat curiae opere testium non indiget.*** That which appears to the court needs not the help of witnesses.

APPEAL, ***noun*** appellate review, *appellatio,* application for retrial, application for review by a higher tribunal, bid, complaint to a superior court, *obtestatio,* petition, reconsideration, recourse to some higher power, reexamination, rehearing, reopening, request for another decision, request for retrial, request for review, resort to superior authority, retrial, review
ASSOCIATED CONCEPTS: appellate courts, appellate jurisdiction, *certiorari*
FOREIGN PHRASES: ***De fide et officio judicis non recipitur quaestio, sed de scientia, sive sit error juris, sive facti.*** The good faith and honesty of a judge are not to be questioned, but his knowledge, whether it be in error of law or fact, may be.

APPEAL, ***verb*** *appelare,* apply for a reexamination of a case, apply for a retrial, apply for a review of a case to a higher tribunal, bid, bring new evidence, claim, consider again with a view to a change or action, contest, contest a case by asking for review, *homini placere, obsecrare,* reconsider, reexamine, refer to, rehear, reopen, request another decision, request reexamination, request reopening of a case, retry, review, seek reexamination, seek reference of a case from one court to another, seek review of a case, sue
ASSOCIATED CONCEPTS: appeal as a matter of right, appeal bond, appeal in forma pauperis, appealable interest, appealable judgment, appealable order, appealed from an order of the court, discretionary appeal, perfect on appeal

APPEAL ON THE MERITS, ***noun*** appeal for reconsideration to a higher court, appeal for review by a higher tribunal, appeal on the law, challenge on the merits to a lower court's decision, challenge to the legal rationale of a lower court, challenge to the legal reasoning of the lower court, remedy for an improper decision, remedy for an improper judgment, request for fairness, request for justice, request for legal redress, request for review, review

APPEAR *(Attend court proceedings),* ***verb*** *adesse,* answer, be in attendance, be manifest, be present, be present to answer, come formally before a tribunal, come into court, *comparere,* enter an appearance, *in iudicium venire,* make an appearance, present an answer, present oneself, put in an appearance, submit oneself to
FOREIGN PHRASES: ***Idem est non esse, et non apparere.*** Not to exist is the same thing as not to appear.

APPEAR *(Materialize),* ***verb*** *apparere,* arise, be in sight, be manifest, become visible, come into sight, come into view, come to light, *conspici,* manifest itself, occur, present to the view

APPEAR *(Seem to be),* ***verb*** be patent, convey the impression, create the impression, give the effect, give the impression, have a certain semblance, have every indication, look, look as if, present the appearance, resemble, seem like, strike one as being, take on the aspect, take on the manner, *videri,* wear the aspect

APPEARANCE *(Coming into court),* ***noun*** answer, entrance in a case, presence in court, response to an action, submission to a court's jurisdiction
ASSOCIATED CONCEPTS: compulsory appearance, general appearance, limited appearance, special appearance, specific appearance, voluntary appearance

APPEARANCE *(Emergence),* ***noun*** *adventus,* arrival into view, coming, evincement, introduction, manifestation, occurrence, rise

APPEARANCE *(Look),* ***noun*** air, aspect, *aspectus,* complexion, demeanor, embodiment, external aspect, face, form, guise, likeness, manner, mien, outward look, outward show, personal presence, physiognomy, posture, pretense, *rem simulare,* show, sight, *species*
ASSOCIATED CONCEPTS: appearance of authority, appearance of validity

APPEASE, ***verb*** allay, alleviate, ameliorate, assuage, calm, capitulate, cater to, coddle, comfort, compose, conciliate, console, content, disarm, give in, gratify, indulge, ingratiate, meliorate, mollify, pacify, placate, please, propitiate, rectify, satiate, soften, soothe, subdue, temper, tranquilize

APPEASEMENT, ***noun*** accommodation, adjustment, allayment, amends, assuagement, calming, conciliation, deadening, détente, dulcification, dulling, mitigation, mollification, pacification, placation, propitiation, rapprochement, reconcilement, reconciliation, salving, satisfaction, softening, soothing, submission, tranquilization

APPELLANT, ***noun*** aggrieved party, appealer, *appellator,* contender, delator, litigant, objector, party, party to a suit, petitioner, suitor
ASSOCIATED CONCEPTS: appellee, respondant

APPELLATE COURT, ***noun*** court of appellate jurisdiction, court of review, higher court, senior court
ASSOCIATED CONCEPTS: appellate division, appellate jurisdiction, appellate term

APPELLATION, ***noun*** alias, appellative, assumed name, call, calling, characterization, cognomen, definition, denomination, description, designation, eponym, identification, label, moniker, name, namesake, nickname, nomenclature, nomination, patronym, pen name, pseudonym, sobriquet, style, surname, term, title

APPEND, ***verb*** add, *addere, adiungere,* affix, annex, attach, augment, conjoin, connect, extend, fasten, include, insert, join, subjoin, supplement

APPENDIX *(Accession),* ***noun*** accessory, additament, *adiungere,* annexation, appendage, attachment, complement, extension, inclusion, insertion, pendant

APPENDIX *(Supplement),* ***noun*** accessio, *addendum, addere,* addition, adjunct, appendage, attachment, codicil, continuation, excursus, rider
ASSOCIATED CONCEPTS: pocket part

APPERCEPTION, ***noun*** acumen, appreciation, astuteness, awareness, cognition, cognizance, conception, discernment, foresight, insight, intellect, judgment, knowledge, mentality, penetration, perception, perspicacity, psyche, realization, reason, reasoning power, recognition, sagacity, sense, understanding

APPERTAIN, *verb* affect, allude to, apply to, associate, be akin, be applicable, be characteristic of, be concerned with, be congruent, be connected with, be dependent upon, be incident to, be intrinsic, be part of, be pertinent, bear on, belong as a part, belong as an attribute, concern, deal with, depend upon, have reference, have relation, inhere, interest, involve, link, pertain, refer, regard, relate, touch

APPLIANCE, *noun* accessory, adjunct, apparatus, appurtenance, attachment, commodity, contrivance, convenience, device, equipment, facility, implement, instrument, *instrumentum,* labor-saving device, machine, means, mechanism, piece of apparatus, precision tool, tool, utensil, utility
ASSOCIATED CONCEPTS: fixtures

APPLICABILITY, *noun* adequacy, application, apposition, aptitude, aptness, availability, efficacy, efficiency, expediency, felicity, pertinence, practicability, propriety, qualification, regard, relativity, relevancy, serviceability, usability, usefulness, utility, utilizability

APPLICABLE, *adjective* à *propos,* acceptable, adaptable, adapted to, appertaining, appliable, appropriate, apt, befit, befitting, belonging, fit, fitting, germane, pertinent, proper, relevant, right, sortable, suitable, to the point, usable, useful, utilizable
ASSOCIATED CONCEPTS: applicable law, applicable local law

APPLICANT *(Candidate),* ***noun*** aspirant, bidder, candidate under consideration, entrant, inquirer

APPLICANT *(Petitioner),* ***noun*** claimant, moveant, party, petitioner, solicitant

APPLICATION, *noun* advancement, bid, motion, *petitio,* petition, presentation, proposal, proposition, request, requisition, requisition to the court, submission
ASSOCIATED CONCEPTS: application duly made, application for a change of venue, application for a discharge, application for a review, application for adjournment, application of payments, application to the court, insurance application, motion
FOREIGN PHRASES: ***Contemporanea expositio est optima et fortissima in lege.*** A contemporaneous construction is the best and strongest in the law.

APPLY *(Pertain),* ***verb*** affect, be applicable, be concerned with, be connected with, be pertinent, be proper to, be relevant, bear upon, belong to, concern, deal with, have a connection to, have bearing on, have reference, have relation, involve, *pertinere ad,* refer, regard, relate, touch

APPLY *(Put in practice),* ***verb*** adapt, adjust, *admovere,* adopt, carry out, convert to use, employ, execute, exercise, exert, put in action, put in operation, put to use, use, utilize

APPLY *(Request),* ***verb*** *ad hominem confugere,* ask, *hominem adire,* make formal request, petition, pray, seek, solicit
ASSOCIATED CONCEPTS: motion

APPOINT, *verb* approve, assign, authorize, charge, charter, choose, commission, confirm, *constituere,* create, delegate, depute, designate, *destinare, dicere,* direct, employ, empower, engage, enlist, entrust, establish, *facere,* give a mandate, license, name, pick, pick out, proclaim, require, sanction, select
ASSOCIATED CONCEPTS: appoint to fill a vacancy, appoint under a will, appointing officer, appointing power, appointive office, public officers

APPOINTED COUNSEL, *noun* appointed attorney, appointed cocounsel, appointed counsel, appointed counsel representing a party, appointed legal adversary, appointed legal counsel, appointed legal opponent, appointed legal representative, appointed litigating attorney, appointed litigating counsel, appointed litigation attorney, appointed litigation counsel, appointed litigator

APPOINTMENT *(Act of designating),* ***noun*** allocation, allotment, assignment, authorization, certification, charter, choice, decree, delegation, deputation, designation to office, dispensation, distribution, installation, naming, nomination, order, ordination, placing in office, requirement, selection
ASSOCIATED CONCEPTS: agency, delegation, limited power of appointment

APPOINTMENT *(Meeting),* ***noun*** agreement as to time and place of meeting, date, engagement, interview, rendezvous, tryst, visit

APPOINTMENT *(Position),* ***noun*** capacity, chargeship, employment, function, incumbency, job, living, occupation, office, post, profession, sphere of occupation, station, undertaking, vocation, work
ASSOCIATED CONCEPTS: agency, authority

APPORTION, *verb* administer, *adsignare,* allocate, allot, assign, assort, award, carve up, classify, deal out, delimit, demarcate, dispense, *dispertire,* disseminate, *distribuere,* distribute, distribute proportionately, divide, divide according to rule, divide into shares, divide proportionately, divide up, dole out, measure out, mete, mete out, parcel out, partition, place in order, portion out, portion out equitably, prorate, set in order, share, split, subdivide

APPORTIONED, *adjective* administered, allocated, allotted, appropriated, assigned, carved up, dealt, dispensed, distributed, divided, divvied up, doled out, measured, meted, parceled out, portioned, proportioned, pro rata, prorated, rationed, split up
ASSOCIATED CONCEPTS: apportioning assessment, apportioning compensation, apportioning damages, apportioning liability, apportioning taxes

APPORTIONMENT, *noun* administration, allocation, allotment, allowance, assignment, assignment in proportion, consignment, disposition, distribution, division, division in proportion, doling out, issuance, just division, measuring out, meting out, partition, partitionment, proportionment
ASSOCIATED CONCEPTS: apportionment of blame, apportionment of damages, apportionment of liability, apportionment of taxes, comparative negligence, doctrine of apportionment, *pro tanto*

APPOSITE, *adjective* accordant, *ad rem,* adapted, affiliated, affinitive, allied, applicable, applying to, appropriate, appurtenant, apropos, apt, associated, associative, bearing upon, befitting, belonging to, cognate, comparable, compatible, congeneric, congenerous, congenial, connatural, connected, consistent, consonant, correlated, correlative, correspondent, corresponding, fit, fitting, germane, in accordance with, in conjunction with, *in loco,* in relation with, pertinent, reconcilable, relating to, relative, relevant, seasonable, suitable, suited, timely, to the point, to the purpose, well-adapted, with reference to

APPOSITION, *noun* abutment, abuttal, adjacency, admissibility, affiliation, applicability, application, appropriateness, aptitude, aptness, bearing, concern, conjunction, connection, contiguity, felicity, fitness, function, interconnection, interest, junction, juxtaposition, mutual relation, nearness, pertinence, placing, propinquity, propriety, proximity, reference, regard, relation, relativeness, relativity, relevance, respect, side by side, state of suitability, union

APPRAISAL, *noun* appraisement, assessment, calculation, computation, determination, estimate, estimated value, estimation, evaluation, examination, fixing a price, measurement, quantification, reckoning, setting a price, setting the value, survey, valuation
ASSOCIATED CONCEPTS: appraisal at actual value, appraisal at estimated value, appraisal at market value, appraisal value

APPRAISE, *verb* appreciate, assess, balance, calculate, compare, conjecture, consider, diagnose, differentiate, discriminate, distinguish, estimate, evaluate, excise, fathom, gauge, judge, measure, opine, ponder, price, rank, rate, reckon, size up, sort out, sound, sum up, survey, take stock, value, weigh
ASSOCIATED CONCEPTS: appraise value of property, criminal record, misconduct

APPRECIABLE, *adjective* appraisable, ascertainable, assessable, calculable, capable of being perceived, cognizable, computable, concrete, considerable, conspicuous, countable, detectable, determinable, discernible, discoverable, distinguishable, estimable, evident, fathomable, gaugeable, knowable, manifest, material, measurable, mensurable, mensural, meterable, notable, noticeable, observable, palpable, patent, perceivable, perceptible, perspicuous, ponderable, prominent, recognizable, seeable, sizable, substantial, substantive, surveyable, tangible, visible, weighable
ASSOCIATED CONCEPTS: appreciable damages, appreciable losses

APPRECIATE *(Comprehend),* ***verb*** acknowledge, apprehend, be aware of, be cognizant of, be conscious of, conceive, discern, know, notice, perceive, realize, recognize, take into consideration, take notice, understand
ASSOCIATED CONCEPTS: appreciate a risk, appreciate the danger

APPRECIATE *(Increase),* ***verb*** advance, become greater, become more numerous, become of greater value, enhance the degree of, gain in worth, grow in value, improve, increase the market price of, make of greater value, rise, rise in value
ASSOCIATED CONCEPTS: appreciate in value

APPRECIATE *(Value),* ***verb*** adequately perceive, *aestimare,* esteem, perceive the worth of, realize the worth of, recognize the worth of

APPRECIATION *(Increased value),* ***noun*** accrual, accruement, accumulation, added monetary worth, addition, advance in worth, gain, gain in worth, growth, growth in value, increase, increased price, increment, realization, rise, rise in value

APPRECIATION *(Perception),* ***noun*** apperception, appraisal, appraisment, assessment, awareness, clear perception, cognition, cognizance, comprehension, consciousness, correct valuation, discernment, estimation, full appraisal, just estimation, measurement, recognition, valuation

APPREHEND *(Arrest),* ***verb*** capture, catch, commit, *comprehendere,* confine, constrain, detain, detain by legal process, fetter, hold, legally restrain, place under arrest, put in restraint, put under arrest, restrain, seize, send to prison, take, take by authority, take captive, take into custody, take prisoner

APPREHEND *(Perceive),* ***verb*** appreciate, be acquainted with, be apprized of, be aware of, be cognizant of, be conscious of, be under the impression, become aware of, cognize, come to know, comprehend, *comprehendere,* conceive of, detect, discern, discover by observation, fathom, have an impression, have an understanding of, have cognizance of, have knowledge of, ken, know entirely, know of, know well, learn, master, realize, recognize, regard as, see, sense, surmise, understand, view

APPREHENSIBLE, *adjective* accountable, cognizable, coherent, comprehensible, conceivable, discoverable, explicable, fathomable, intelligible, knowable, penetrable, perceivable, perceptive, realizable, recognizable, scrutable, understandable, unmistakable

APPREHENSION *(Act of arresting),* ***noun*** arrest, caption, capture, catch, confinement, detention, holding in custody, imprisonment, incarceration, internment, restraint, retention, seizure, taking, taking hold

APPREHENSION *(Fear),* ***noun*** agitation, alarm, anticipation of adversity, anxiety, apprehensiveness, care, concern, consternation, distrust, foreboding, misdoubt, misgiving, mistrust, overanxiety, perturbation, phobia, presentiment, qualm, sense of danger, suspicion, threat, trepidation, uneasiness, worry

APPREHENSION *(Perception),* ***noun*** cognition, cognizance, comprehension, conception, discernment, grasp, idea, image, impression, intellection, judgment, knowledge, mastery, mental capacity, notion, observation, opinion, recognition, reflection, sense, thought, understanding, view

APPREHENSIVE, *adjective* afraid, agitated, alarmed, anticipative of evil, anxious, aware, bothered, cognizant, concerned, conscious, disquieted, distrustful, expectant, fearful, hesitant, leery, mindful, mistrustful, nervous, perceptive, pusillanimous, qualmish, qualmy, sagacious, shrewd, solicitous, suspicious, terrified, timid, tremulous, troubled, uneasy, vigilant, wise, worried

APPRENTICE, *noun* beginner, learner, novice, novitiate, probationer, worker

APPRISE, *verb* acquaint, advise, alert, announce, brief, communicate, convey knowledge, counsel, describe, disclose, divulge, enlighten, familiarize, give information, give notice, impart knowledge, inform, instruct, let know, make aware, make cognizant, make known, notify, orient, point out, publish, report, reveal, tell, warn
ASSOCIATED CONCEPTS: apprise of the facts

APPROACH, *verb* *accedere,* accost, advance, *adventare, appropinquare,* be in proximity, be in sight of, be in the neighborhood of, be in the vicinity of, be near, come forward, come near, confront, converge upon, draw near, edge close to, get near, go near, move near, move toward, pursue, stalk, step up to, verge on

APPROACHES, *noun* accesses, avenues, channels, entrances, entranceways, entryways, gates, highways, ingresses, inlets, intakes, means of access, passages, routes, ways

APPROBATE, *verb* accept, accredit, acquiesce, admire, adopt, advocate, agree with, applaud, approve, assent, authorize, back, commend, concur, confirm, consent, countenance, endorse, esteem, favor, laud, license, pass, praise, prize, ratify, recognize, recommend, salute, sanction, support, validate, value

APPROBATION, *noun* acceptance, acclamation, acquiescence, admiration, adoption, advocacy, agreement, applause, appreciation, approval, assent, attestation, commendation, compliment, concurrence, congratulation, consent, countenance, encomium, encouragement, endorsement, esteem, eulogy, honor, laudation, leave, license, mention, permit, praise, ratification, recognition, recommendation, regard, respect, sanction, satisfaction, support

APPROPRIATE, *adjective* *accommodatus,* accordant, accurate, adapted to, admissible, applicable, apposite, apropos, apt, aptus, befitting, concordant, condign, conformable, *congruens,* congruous, consistent, consonant, correct, correspondent, exact, expedient, fine, fit, fitting, germane, good, harmonious, likely, meet, opportune, pertinent, practicable, precise, proper, relevant, right, rightful, seemly, suitable, suited, timely, well-suited
ASSOCIATED CONCEPTS: appropriate bargaining unit, appropriate cause of action, appropriate remedy

APPROPRIATE, *verb* acquire, adopt, annex, arrogate, assume, assume ownership, borrow, capture, claim, possess, take, take over

APPROPRIATION *(Allotment),* ***noun*** allocation, allowance, apportionment, budget, budgeting, concession, designation of use, dispensation, distribution, setting apart
ASSOCIATED CONCEPTS: appropriation bill, appropriation for public use, appropriation of money, budgetary appropriation

APPROPRIATION *(Donation),* ***noun*** benefaction, bestowal, contribution, disbursement, endowment, funding, gift, grant, guerdon, meed, sponsorship

APPROPRIATION *(Taking),* ***noun*** accroachment, acquisition, adoption, annexation, apprehension, assumption, capture, confiscation, conversion, dispossession, disseisin, divestment, expropriation, impoundment, impropriation, seizure, snatching, taking possession
ASSOCIATED CONCEPTS: appropriation from revenues, appropriation of land, appropriation of payment

APPROVAL, *noun* acceptance, accord, acknowledgment, acquiescence, adoption, affirmance, affirmation, agreement, allowance, *approbatio,* approbation, assent, assurance, authentication, authorization, *comprobatio,* concordance, concurrence, confirmation, consent, countenance, encouragement, endorsement, expression of satisfaction, favor, license, nod of approbation, permit, ratification, recognition, sanction, support, toleration, validation, verification
ASSOCIATED CONCEPTS: acceptance by a bank, approved endorsed note, sale on approval
FOREIGN PHRASES: ***Qui non improbat, approbat.*** He who does not disapprove, approves. ***Quod approbo non reprobo.*** That which I approve I do not later reject.

APPROVE, *verb* accede to, accept, acquiesce in, adopt, advocate, affirm, agree to, allow, *approbare,* approbate, assent to, authenticate, authorize, be in favor of, be satisfied with, certify, *comprobare,* concur in, confirm, consent to, countenance, endorse, favor, make valid, *probare,* ratify, sanction, second, support, sustain, uphold, validate

APPROVED *(Agreed),* ***adjective*** acknowledged, admitted, allowable, allowed, arranged, completed, contracted for, decided, eligible, formal, meritorious, permissible, settled, stipulated

APPROVED *(Authoritative),* ***adjective*** accepted, accredited, authentic, authoritative, conceded, conventional, established, fixed, granted, legal, official, prescriptive, proper, right, standard, unimpeachable, warranted
ASSOCIATED CONCEPTS: approve a claim, approve a public contract, approve a stipulation, approve a transcript, approved adoption, approved the findings of the court, settle on order

APPROXIMATE, *adjective* alike, almost, approaching, close, comparable, estimated, imprecise, in the vicinity of, inexact, like, much the same, nearly accurate, nearly correct, nearly equal, nearly perfect, nearly resembling, nigh, not perfectly accurate, *propinquus,* proximal, proximate, similar, surmised, uncertain, unprecise
ASSOCIATED CONCEPTS: approximate value

APPROXIMATE, *verb* *accedere ad,* advance near to, approach, approach closely, approach in amount, be in the vicinity of, be near, border on, closely resemble, come close in estimation, come close to, come near, come near in position, compare with, draw near, nearly equal, nearly rival, resemble

APPROXIMATION, *noun* approach, calculation, computation, contiguity, correspondence, estimate, estimation, inexactitude, inexactness, interpolation, likeness, measure, nearness, neighborhood, parity, propinquity, proximity, reckoning, resemblance, rough closeness, rough equivalent, sameness, semblance, similitude, tally, unpreciseness, vicinity

APPURTENANCE, *noun* accession, accessory, accompaniment, addendum, additament, addition, adjunct, annex, annexation, *annexe,* appanage, appendage, appendant, appendix, attachment, auxiliary, concomitant, dependency, extension, incidental, pendant, something added, subsidiary, supplement
ASSOCIATED CONCEPTS: accession, appurtenance to realty, appurtenant right, conveyance of property, covenants, deeds of conveyance, easement appurtenant, easements, fixture

APPURTENANT, *adjective* accessory, adjunct, ancillary, annexed, appended, appertaining, attached, auxiliary, belonging, connected, dependent on, incident, necessarily connected, subsidiary, used with another thing
ASSOCIATED CONCEPTS: appurtenant passage of air, appurtenant passage of light, appurtenant to land, appurtenant watercourse, *causa rei,* dominant land, servient land

APROPOS, *adjective* akin, applicable, apposite, appropriate, apt, belonging, concerning, connected, felicitous, fit, germane, linked, pertaining to, pertinent, related, relevant, suitable

APT *(Appropriate),* ***adjective*** applicable, apposite, appropriate, apropos, artful, comely, concordant, congruous, consonant, correct, deft, expedient, expert, felicitous, fit, germane, given to, harmonious, inclined, liable, likely, opportune, pertinent, practiced, presumable, probable, prone, proper, qualified, quick, ready, relative, relevant, resourceful, right, seemly, subject to, subtle, suitable, timely, verisimilar, viable, well-chosen

APT *(Gifted),* ***adjective*** able, accomplished, adroit, alert, bright, clever, competent, dexterous, expert, fitted, gifted, handy, proficient, sharp, skillful, smart

APTITUDE, ***noun*** ability, applicability, bent, endowment, faculty, fitness, flair, gift, inclination, innate ability, intelligence, learning, propensity, propriety, suitability, talent, tendency

ARBITER, ***noun*** adjudicator, advisor, *arbiter,* arbitrator, determiner, *disceptator,* final authority, interagent, interceder, intercessor, intermediary, intermediate, intermediator, intervener, mediator, moderator, negotiant, negotiator, prescriber, recommender, reconciler, referee
ASSOCIATED CONCEPTS: arbitrament, final arbiter

ARBITRARY, ***adjective*** according to desires, capricious, contrary to reason, determined by no principle, done at pleasure, fanciful, illogical, independent of law, independent of rule, *infinitus,* injudicious, irrational, *libidinosus,* nonrational, perverse, unaccountable, unjustified, unreasonable, unreasoned, without adequate determining principle, without consideration, without reason, without substantial cause
ASSOCIATED CONCEPTS: arbitrary act, arbitrary action, arbitrary and capricious, arbitrary classification, arbitrary determination, arbitrary standards, arbitrary verdict

ARBITRARY AND CAPRICIOUS, ***adjective*** absolute, authoritative, baseless, dictatorial, dogmatic, fanciful, groundless, impetuous, motiveless, purposeless, restrictive, unduly, whimsical, willful

ARBITRATE *(Adjudge),* ***verb*** adjudicate, arrange, arrive at a conclusion, ascertain after reasoning, assess, conciliate, decide, decide between opposing parties, decree, decree authoritatively, determine, determine a controversy, determine a point at issue, *dijudicare,* end by a decision, fix conclusively, give judgment, judge, judicate, lead to a decision, make a decision, mete out, order, pass judgment, pronounce formally, pronounce judgment, resolve, rule, settle, settle by authoritative decision, sit in judgment
ASSOCIATED CONCEPTS: mediate

ARBITRATE *(Conciliate),* ***verb*** accord, adjust differences, arrange, bring into agreement, bring into harmony, bring to terms, bring together, *disceptare,* harmonize, intercede, intervene, make compatible, make peace between, moderate, negotiate, prevail with, propitiate, put in accord, reconcile, referee, regulate, render compatible, render concordant, render no longer opposed, restore harmony, settle, settle differences

ARBITRATION, ***noun*** adjudgment, adjustment, apportionment, appraisal, arbitrage, *arbitrium,* assessment, conciliation, decision, decree, determining of a controversy, finding, intercession, interjacence, intermediation, interposition, intervention, judgment, *rapprochement,* resolution, settlement
ASSOCIATED CONCEPTS: advisory arbitration, arbitrability, arbitration agreement, arbitration and award, arbitration award, arbitration clause, arbitration provision, arbitrators, binding arbitration, compulsory arbitration, grievance arbitration, interest arbitration, proceeding to confirm arbitration award, voluntary arbitration

ARBITRATOR, ***noun*** adjudicator, arbiter, determiner, *disceptator,* interagent, interceder, intercessor, intermediary, intermediate, intervenor, interventionist, judicator, moderator, negotiant, negotiator, reconciler, referee, referendary, ruler
ASSOCIATED CONCEPTS: arbitration and award, arbitrator's authority, arbitrator's award, board of arbitrators, scope of arbitrator's authority

ARCANE, ***adjective*** esoteric, incomprehensible, inexplicable, inscrutable, mysterious, recondite, unaccountable, unfathomable, unintelligible, unrecognizable

ARCHAIC, ***adjective*** ancient, antediluvian, antiquated, extinct, fossilized, medieval, obsolescent, obsolete, old, old-fashioned, old-world, outdated, outmoded, passé, prehistoric, primitive, superannuated, timeworn

ARCHITECT, ***noun*** *architectus,* artificer, author, begetter, builder, composer, constructor, contriver, creator, designer, deviser, draftsman, enterpriser, founder, framer, generator, introducer, inventor, maker, organizer, originator, planner, prime mover, projector, schemer

ARDENT, ***adjective*** active, ambitious, animated, aspiring, assiduous, burning, devoted, eager, earnest, enthusiastic, excitable, excited, fanatical, fervent, fervid, feverish, fierce, fiery, glowing, hearty, heated, high-spirited, impassioned, impatient, impetuous, industrious, inflamed, intense, intensive, intent, keen, passionate, ready, sedulous, serious, sincere, spirited, true, vehement, zealous

ARDOR, ***noun*** ardency, *ardor,* drive, eagerness, effusiveness, *élan,* emotion, energy, enthusiasm, excitation of feelings, excitement, exhilaration, fanaticism, fervency, fervidness, fervor, feverishness, fire, force, forcefulness, furor, impassionedness, intense desire, liveliness, magniloquence, passion, passionateness, perfervor, spirit, state of excitability, *studium,* verve, vigor, vigorousness, vitality, vivacity, warmth of feeling, zeal

ARDUOUS, ***adjective*** backbreaking, burdensome, difficult, exhausting, fatiguing, formidable, grueling, hard, hard-earned, hard-fought, intricate, irksome, laborious, lofty, onerous, operose, oppressive, painful, precipitous, punishing, rugged, severe, strenuous, tiresome, toilsome, tough, troublesome, trying, wearisome

AREA *(Province),* ***noun*** *area,* arena, bounds, confines, demesne, domain, expanse, field, jurisdiction, limits, location, orbit, place, premises, purview, range, realm, region, scope, sphere, territory, vicinage, vicinity, zone
ASSOCIATED CONCEPTS: area variance, specific areas of the law

AREA *(Surface),* ***noun*** amount of surface, dimensions, expanse, expansion, extent of surface, measured size, measurements, plane surface, proportions, real size, *superficies,* true dimensions

ARGUABLE, ***adjective*** at issue, contestable, controversial, controvertible, debatable, disputable, in dispute, in question, up for discussion
ASSOCIATED CONCEPTS: arguable claim, arguable contention

ARGUE, ***verb*** advance, affirm, allege, *argumentari,* assert, challenge, claim, confute, *conligere,* contend, contend in argument, contest, controvert, *de re disserere,* debate,

disagree, dispute, elucidate, emphasize, enunciate, establish, explain, expostulate, express, maintain, make an assertion, oppose, present reasons against, present reasons for, proclaim, pronounce, propose, propound, put forth, reason upon, remonstrate, set forth, show, state with conviction, stress, submit, urge
ASSOCIATED CONCEPTS: *a posteriori, a priori, ab inconvenienti, ad hominem, arguendo*

ARGUENDO, ***adverb*** for mere discussion only, for the sake of argument, hypothetically

ARGUMENT *(Contention),* ***noun*** altercation, antagonism, belligerency, bickering, breach, clashing, conflict, contentiousness, controversy, cross-purposes, debate, difference of opinion, disaccord, disagreement, discord, disputatio, disputation, dispute, dissension, dissent, dissidence, disunion, disunity, division, divisiveness, feud, hard feelings, hostility, ill feeling, ill will, lack of concord, misunderstanding, opposition, oral contention, polemics, quarrel, quarreling, strife, variance, verbal conflict, war of words, wrangle, wrangling
ASSOCIATED CONCEPTS: *a posteriori, a priori, apex juris*
FOREIGN PHRASES: ***In rebus manifestis, errat qui auctoritates legum allegat; quia perspicua vera non sunt probanda.*** In clear cases, he errs who cites legal authorities because obvious truths are manifest and do not have to be proved. ***Argumentum ab inconvenienti est validum in lege; quia lex non permittit aliquod inconveniens.*** An argument drawn from what is inconvenient is good in law, because the law will not permit any inconvenience.

ARGUMENT *(Pleading),* ***noun*** argument at the bar, counterstatement, course of reasoning, defense, demonstration, discourse designed to convince, disputation, expression of opinion for or against, plea, pleading, rationale, rebuttal, refutation, statement of defense, statement offered in proof, statement tending to prove a point, submission
ASSOCIATED CONCEPTS: argument submitted to the court, closing argument, equittable argument, legal argument, opening argument, oral argument, preargument statement
FOREIGN PHRASES: ***In rebus manifestis, errat qui auctoritates legum allegat; quia perspicua vera non sunt probanda.*** In clear cases, he errs who cites legal authorities because obvious truths are manifest and do not have to be proved.

ARGUMENTATION, ***noun*** analysis, argument, bickering, conflict, contention, contentiousness, controversy, critical examination, dialectic, dialogue, disaccord, disagreement, disceptation, discord, disputation, dispute, dissension, logical synthesis, pattern of reasoning, polemics, quarrelsomeness, ratiocination, wrangling
ASSOCIATED CONCEPTS: instructions to the jury, reargument, rebuttal, summation, surrebuttal

ARGUMENTATIVE, ***adjective*** belligerent, characterized by argument, combative, contentious, dialectical, discordant, disputatious, dissentient, eristic, eristical, factious, given to controversy, litigious, logomachic, logomachical, petulant, pilpulistic, polemic, polemical, pugnacious, quarrelsome
ASSOCIATED CONCEPTS: argumentative denial

ARISE *(Appear),* ***verb*** become manifest, become noticeable, become visible, come forth, come in sight, come in view, come to light, come to notice, emerge, make an appearance, manifest itself, present itself, reveal itself, show itself
ASSOCIATED CONCEPTS: arise under an obligation, arise under the laws of the United States, arising out of a contract, arising out of and in the course of employment, arising out of employment, arising under federal law, arising under the Constitution, arising upon contract, cause of action arising, counterclaim arising out of the plaintiff's claim

ARISE *(Occur),* ***verb*** become operative, come about, come to pass, eventuate, get under way, happen, proceed, take place, transpire

ARISE *(Originate),* ***verb*** accrue, be born, be derived, become, begin, come from, come into action, come into being, come into existence, come to be, emanate, ensue, eventuate, evolve, flow, follow, grow out of, have origin, initiate, issue forth, proceed from, spring forth, spring up, start, start out, take birth, take origin

ARMED, ***adjective*** *armatus,* bristling with arms, equipped with arms, fortified, furnished with weapons, in arms, issued weapons, panoplied, provided with arms, supplied with arms, under arms, well-armed
ASSOCIATED CONCEPTS: armed burglary, armed felony, armed forces, armed guards
FOREIGN PHRASES: ***Arma in armatos sumere jura sinunt.*** The laws permit the taking up of arms against armed persons. ***Ligna et lapides sub "armorum" appellatione non continentur.*** Sticks and stones are not included within the definition of "arms."

ARMISTICE, ***noun*** alliance, amity, bargain, calm, cease-fire, cessation, cessation of hostilities, charter, compact, concord, convention, covenant, détente, fault, halt to hostility, harmony, order, pact, peace, peacetime, quiet, reconcilement, reconciliation, respite, rest, serenity, settlement, stability, stabilization, standoff, suspension, tranquility, treaty, truce, understanding

ARRAIGN, ***verb*** *accusare,* accuse, accuse of wrong, blame, brand, brand with reproach, bring accusation, bring before a court, bring to trial, bring up for investigation, bring up on charges, call before a court, call to account, charge, *citare,* cite, complain against, criminate, denounce, denunciate, formally accuse, formally charge, formally criminate, formally incriminate, implicate, incriminate, inculpate, *postulare,* prefer charges, prosecute

ARRAIGNMENT, ***noun*** accusation, accusation in court, allegation of criminal wrongdoing, crimination through law enforcement, delation by criminal charges, formal accusal, imputation from criminal proceeding, incrimination, inculpation by prosecution, judicial charge, prosecution
ASSOCIATED CONCEPTS: arrest, bail, felony hearing, indictment

ARRANGE *(Methodize),* ***verb*** adapt, adjust, allocate, apportion, bring into order, bring to terms, collocate, come to an agreement, come to terms, *componere, constituere,* coordinate, determine, devise, *digerere,* direct, fix, fix the order, group, manage, marshal, order, *ordinare,* organize, place in order, program, put in readiness, reduce to order, regulate, resolve, schematize, set in order, settle, size, space, straighten out, systematize

ARRANGE *(Plan),* ***verb*** blueprint, calculate, contrive, design, devise, engineer, formulate, frame, make arrangements, make preparations, mark out a course, prepare, program, project, schedule, shape a course, sketch out

ARRANGED *(Agreed),* ***adjective*** aligned, assorted, classified, contractual, cut and dried, definite, disposed, fixed, formal, graded, grouped, marshaled, orderly, organizational, placed, precise, ranked, regular, settled, stated, systematic, uniform

ARRANGED *(Planned),* ***adjective*** contrived, designed, devised, established, harmonious, organized, plotted, projected, prospective, schematic, set, ready

ARRANGEMENT *(Ordering),* ***noun*** adaption, arraying, collocation, *compositio,* composition, conformation, *conlocatio,* formation, method, regularity, schematism, symmetry, systematization, uniformity

ARRANGEMENT *(Plan),* ***noun*** conception, concoction, contrivance, course of action, ground plan, layout, master plan, method, outline, program of action, schema, scheme, system
ASSOCIATED CONCEPTS: arrangement for the benefit of creditors

ARRANGEMENT *(Understanding),* ***noun*** abatement of differences, accommodation, accord, accordance, adjustment, adjustment by agreement, agreement, compact, compromise, concord, contract, entente, harmonization, mutual agreement, mutual assent, mutual promise, mutual undertaking, pact, proviso, reconciliation, restoration of harmony, settlement, terms
ASSOCIATED CONCEPTS: arrangement through a marital settlement

ARRANT, ***adjective*** clear, complete, confirmed, conspicuous, consummate, definite, identifiable, obvious, palpable, plain, recognizable, salient, striking, through, uncontestable, unmistakable, utter

ARRAY *(Jury),* ***noun*** body of jurors, good men and true, jurors, jurymen, panel, trier, trier of the facts
ASSOCIATED CONCEPTS: challenge to the array, jury panel, venire

ARRAY *(Order),* ***noun*** arrangement, assemblage, classification, collocation, composition, comprehensiveness, course, design, display, disposition, disposure, distribution, due order, fixed order, formation, gamut, good order, gradation, layout, logical order, marshaling, method, methodicalness, methodology, multiplicity, multitude, ordering, organization, parade, pattern, perspective, placing, progression, range of choices, range of view, regularity, rule, schematic arrangement, scope, sequence, series, show, sight, state of order, strict order, subordination, system, systematization, unbroken order, uniformity

ARRAY, ***verb*** accouter, arrange, attire, deploy, display, dispose, draw up, enhance, enrich, file, fix, group, marshal, orchestrate, order, rank, sequence, set in order, sort

ARREARS, ***noun*** arrearage, back payments, balance due, debit, debt, debt unpaid though due, default, deferred payment, deficit, delinquency, indebtedness, indebtment, liability, obligation, outstanding debt, overdue bill, overdue payment, payments past due, *pecuniae residuae,* state of indebtedness, unpaid bill, unpaid debt
ASSOCIATED CONCEPTS: arrears in taxes, arrears of alimony, arrears of assessment, arrears of dues, arrears of interest, arrears of premiums, arrears of rent, arrears of taxes, judgment on arrears

ARREST, ***noun*** apprehension, capture, confinement, custodial detention, imprisonment, incarceration, internment, prehension, restraint, restriction, retention, seizure
ASSOCIATED CONCEPTS: extradition, rendition

ARREST *(Apprehend),* ***verb*** arrêt, capture, cast into prison, catch, commit, commit to an institution, commit to prison, *comprehendere,* confine, constrain, *deprehendere,* deprive of liberty, detain, detain by criminal process, entrammel, give in custody, hold, immure, imprison, *in custodiam dare,* incarcerate, intern, jail, lay under restraint, legally restrain, make captive, make prisoner, place in confinement, put in durance, put in duress, put under restraint, restrain, secure, seize, seize by legal warrant, send to jail, shackle, take by authority, take captive, take charge of, take into custody, take into preventive custody, take into protective custody, take prisoner, throw into prison
ASSOCIATED CONCEPTS: arrest warrant, false arrest, false imprisonment, illegal arrest, prior arrest, probable cause, resisting arrest, search incident to an arrest, warrant of arrest

ARREST *(Stop),* ***verb*** avert, block, bring to a standstill, bring to a stop, check, countercheck, curb, curtail, delay, detain, deter, end, enjoin, foil, foreclose, forestall, frustrate, hinder, hold, hold back, impede, inhibit, interfere, interrupt, keep back, obstruct, prevent, quell, repel, restrain, stall, stay, stifle, subdue, suppress, suspend, thwart, withhold
ASSOCIATED CONCEPTS: arrest of inquest, arrest of judgment

ARRESTED *(Apprehended),* ***adjective*** captured, caught, collared, committed, confined, constrained, detained, held, held in custody, immurred, imprisoned, incarcerated, interned, jailed, kept in custody, legally restrained, made captive, made prisoner, remanded, remanded into custody, restrained, seized, sent to prison, taken by force by the authorities, taken into custody, taken prisoner, under arrest
ASSOCIATED CONCEPTS: arrest warrant, body execution, civil arrest, detention and custody, false arrest, false imprisonment, habeas corpus, imprisonment, malicious prosecution, probable cause to arrest, resisting arrest, restraint of liberty, search incident to an arrest, unlawful arrest

ARRESTED *(Checked),* ***adjective*** adjourned, blocked, bridled, circumscribed, contained, controlled, curbed, deferred, delayed, deterred, discouraged, encumbered, governed, hampered, held back, hindered, impeded, inhibited, interrupted, limited, obstructed, postponed, prescribed, prevented, repressed, restrained, restricted, retarded, slowed down, stayed, stopped, suppressed, suspended, withheld

ARRIVE, ***verb*** accomplish, achieve, advance, alight, appear, approach, attain, befall, betide, come to, consummate, culminate, emerge, enter, eventuate, gain, get to, happen, join, land, make good, occur, reach, show up, supervene, turn up, visit

ARROGANT, ***adjective*** aloof, assertive, assumptive, audacious, autocratic, blunt, bold, bossy, brash, brassy, brazen, bumptious, caustic, cavalier, conceited, contemptuous, cool, curt, despotic, dictatorial, disdainful, disrespectful, domineering, egotistic, forward, haughty, high-and-mighty, imperious, impertinent, impudent, insolent, lofty, obtrusive, oppressive, overbearing, pertinacious, pompous, presumptuous, pretentious, proud, saucy, shameless, smug, supercilious, superior, swaggering, vain

ARROGATE, ***verb*** accroach, adopt, annex, appropriate, ascribe falsely, assume, assume command, attach, collect, commandeer, convert, demand, deprive, expropriate, harass, hijack, impress, infringe, invade, preempt, preoccupy, prepossess, seize, sequester, stake a claim, take, take charge, take command, take over, take possession, usurp, wrest

ARROGATION, *noun* accession, adoption, application, appropriation, ascription, assignation, assignment, assumption, attachment, attribution, impropriation, placement, requisition, seizure, taking, usurpation

ARSENAL, *noun* accumulation, agglomeration, ammassment, conglomeration, depository, garnering, repository, reservoir, storage, treasury

ARSON, *noun* criminal setting of fires, deliberate burning of property, destruction of property by fire, fire-raising, firing, incendiarism, malicious burning of property, pyromania, set conflagration, willful burning of property

ARTFUL, *adjective* able, acute, adept, adroit, apt, artistic, astute, astutus, aware, calculating, *callidus,* canny, capable, characterized by art, clever, contriving, crafty, cunning, deft, devious, dexterous, done with skill, experienced, facile, gifted, imaginative, ingenious, intriguing, knavish, Machiavellian, masterly, plotting, proficient, quick, rascally, ready, resourceful, scheming, serpentine, sharp, sharp-witted, shrewd, skillful, sly, stealthy, subtle, talented, versatile, *versutus,* vulpine, well-planned, wily

ARTICLE *(Commodity),* ***noun*** effect, item, lifeless object, material, material object, matter, object, particular object, *res,* subject, substance, thing

ARTICLE *(Distinct section of a writing),* ***noun*** chapter, clause, contractual clause, division, item, portion, provision, proviso, res, section, subject, term of reference
ASSOCIATED CONCEPTS: article in a statute, paragraph of a statute, subdivision of a statute

ARTICLE *(Precept),* ***noun*** canon, *caput, condicio,* dictated term, dogma, mandate, maxim, principle, requirement, rubric, set of terms, tenet
ASSOCIATED CONCEPTS: articles of incorporation

ARTICULATE, *verb* avow, clarify, communicate, converse, convey, enunciate, express, observe, phrase, pronounce, recite, recount, remark, speak, utter

ARTIFICE, *noun* artful contrivance, artfulness, artificiality, beguilement, charlatanry, cheating, chicanery, circumvention, cleverness, concealment, connivance, contrivance, cover, cozenage, craftiness, crafty device, cunning, cunningness, deceit, deception, delusion, design, device, disguise, distortion, dodgery, duplicity, *espieglerie,* evasion, expediency, fabrication, false claim, false pretensions, falsification, feint, finesse, forgery, fraudulence, guile, hoax, illusion, impersonation, imposture, ingenuity, insidiousness, insubstantiality, intrigue, jobbery, knavery, Machiavellianism, machination, maneuvering, mendacity, misrepresentation, perfidy, pettifoggery, ploy, pretense, pretension, pretext, rascality, ruse, scheme, sham, sharp practice, slyness, snare, stratagem, subterfuge, tactics, trap, trick, trickery, wile, wiliness, wrinkle

ARTIFICIAL, *adjective* adulterine, *artificiosus,* assumed, casuistic, concocted, counterfeited, deceptive, ersatz, faked, false, feigned, fictitious, forged, illusory, imaginary, imagined, imitation, imitative, man-made, not natural, pretended, simulated, simulative, spurious, superficial, unauthentic, ungenuine, unnatural, unreal
ASSOCIATED CONCEPTS: artificial boundaries, artificial ingredients, artificial monuments, artificial person, artificial pond, artificial presumption, artificial watercourse

ARTISAN, *noun* *artifex,* artificer, craftsman, craftworker, faber, handicraftsman, journeyman, laborer, machiner, master craftsman, master workman, mechanic, mechanician, one engaged in a manual enterprise, one skilled in an industrial art, one trained in a mechanic trade, operator, opifex, skilled laborer, skilled worker, technician, tradesman, worker, workingman, workingwoman, workman, workwoman
ASSOCIATED CONCEPTS: artisan lien

AS A CONSEQUENCE, *adverb* *a priori,* accordingly, as a result, as matters stand, because, because of this, by reason of, by the same token, consequently, deductibly, derivatively, doubtlessly, for reasons given, for that reason, hence, in conclusion, in consequence, in that case, in that event, in which case, inferentially, necessarily, on account of, to that end

AS A MATTER OF RIGHT, *adverb* be entitled to, by right, correctly, duly, fitting, properly, rightfully, with authority

AS A RULE, *adverb* as a matter of course, by and large, chiefly, commonly, customarily, for the most part, generally, generally speaking, in general, in most cases, in the main, in the usual course of things, mainly, most frequently, most often, mostly, normally, on the whole, ordinarily, principally, regularly, substantially, to all intents and purposes, usually

AS AGREED UPON, *adverb* according to contract, according to the agreement, according to the bargain, according to the contract, as agreed to, as arranged by the agreement, as contracted for, as negotiated for, as pledged, as promised, as settled upon, consistent with the agreement, corresponding to the contract, in accordance with the contract, in correspondence with the contract, in obedience to the agreement

AS IS, *adjective* as it is, as it stands, as offered, as presented, as represented, as seen, as shown, as things are, in its present condition, in its present form, in its present state, in the same way, just the same, without warranty
ASSOCIATED CONCEPTS: as is contract, caveat emptor, without covenants or warranties

AS PROVIDED BY LAW, *adverb* as contained in the statutes, as set forth by law, as specified in the law, as delineated in the law

AS SET FORTH, *adverb* above-mentioned, antecedently, anteriorly, as contained previously, as determined, as expressed, as specified previously, as stated, as stated preliminarily, as written, before, beforehand, earlier, former, formerly, preceding, preexisting, prior

AS SO DEFINED, *adverb* as contained, as delineated, as explained, as set forth, as specified

AS SOON AS FEASIBLE, *adverb* as soon as possible, as soon as reasonably possible, at the first opportunity, at the first possible moment, expeditiously, forthwith, promptly, without delay

ASCENDANCE, ***noun*** authority, command, dominance, domination, dominion, hegemony, predominance, preponderance, prevalence, primacy, sovereignty, superiority, supremacy, upper hand

ASCENDANT, ***noun*** ancestor, antecedent, forebear, forefather, forerunner, genitor, *praestare,* precursor, predecessor, procreator, progenitor, sire, *summus, superior*

ASCERTAIN, ***verb*** acquire information, acquire intelligence about, adjudge, arrive at a conclusion, assure oneself, become acquainted with, certify, clear from obscurity, clear of doubt, clear of obscurity, *cognoscere,* come to a conclusion, come to know, *comperire,* conclude, confirm, decide, decipher, deduce, derive, descry, determine, discover, disentangle, draw a conclusion, establish, establish with certainty, *explorare,* fathom, ferret out, figure out, find, find out, find out exactly, find the answer, find the solution, learn about, make certain, make oneself acquainted with, make sure, prove, ravel, reassure oneself, remove doubt, render certain, render definite, resolve, satisfy oneself, solve, unearth, unravel, unriddle, unscramble, untangle, verify
ASSOCIATED CONCEPTS: ascertain loss, ascertained by law

ASCERTAINABLE, ***adjective*** answerable, certifiable, cognizable, comprehensible, confirmable, decipherable, definable, demonstrable, determinable, discernible, discoverable, distinguishable, evincible, explainable, fixable, knowable, learnable, perceptible, recognizable, understandable, verifiable
ASSOCIATED CONCEPTS: ascertainable consequences, ascertainable damages, ascertainable debt, ascertainable loss

ASCERTAINED, ***adjective*** absolute, actual, authoritative, axiomatic, certain, clear, cogent, cognizable, common, conclusive, definite, definitive, evident, factual, genuine, incontrovertible, indisputable, indubious, irrefutable, positive, real, reliable, sound, stated, sure, true, trustworthy, unambiguous, unconfuted, undeniable, undoubting, unequivocal, unerring, unmistakable, unqualified, unquestionable, unquestioned

ASCRIBE, ***verb*** accord, accredit, *adsignare,* affiliate, allege to belong, apply, appropriate, *ascribere,* assign, attach, *attribuere,* attribute, charge with, connect with, credit with, derive from, filiate, give, impute, point to, predicate, refer to, trace to
ASSOCIATED CONCEPTS: ascribe a motive

ASCRIPTION, ***noun*** accusal, accusation, alleging, animadversion, appropriation, aspersion, assignment, attribution, blame, citation, complaint, charge, derivation, imputation, innuendo, insinuation, obloquy, reference, reflection, reproach, slur, stigmatization, stricture

ASK, ***verb*** apply, call upon, canvass, challenge, demand, examine, go over, grill, inquire, interrogate, investigate, propose, pry, question, quiz, request
ASSOCIATED CONCEPTS: ask and demand in settling a matter

ASPECT, ***noun*** appearance, *aspectus,* condition, element, facet, factor, feature, *forma,* look, mien, part, peculiar feature, perspective, phase, position, posture, regard, relative position, salient characteristic, situation, slant, state, view, viewpoint, visage, vista

ASPECTS, ***noun*** attributes, character, characteristics, color, difference, features, individual qualities, nature, particularities, parts, peculiarities, perspectives, properties, qualities, segments, traits, unique qualities

ASPERSION, ***noun*** abuse, affront, *calumnia,* calumniation, calumny, censure, condemnation, contumely, defamation, denigration, denunciation, derision, derogatory criticism, detraction, dishonor, disparagement, envenomed tongue, execration, imputation, insult, invective, libel, malediction, objurgation, obloquy, *opprobrium,* railing, rebuke, reproach, reproof, reviling, scurrility, slander, slight, slur, stricture, traducement, vilification, vituperation

ASPORTATION, ***noun*** criminal ablation, criminal remotion, criminal removement, criminal transmission, delocalization, felonious abreption, felonious removal, felonious transference, felonious translocation, furtive removal, illegal amotion, illegal carriage, illegal subduction, illegal transmittance, illegal transplantation, illegal transshipment, wrongful displacement, wrongful removal, wrongful transfer
ASSOCIATED CONCEPTS: burglary, conversion and trover, larceny, robbery

ASSAIL, ***verb*** accost, *adgredi, adoriri,* advance against, advance upon, aggress, assault, assault belligerently, attack, beset, encounter, fall upon, invade, mug, oppugn, *oppugnare,* rush upon, savage, set upon, set upon with violence, storm, thrust at, waylay
ASSOCIATED CONCEPTS: assailant

ASSAILABLE, ***adjective*** accessible, attacked, beatable, censurable, conquerable, criticized, defenseless, exposed, impugnable, indefensible, open to attack, penetrable, pregnable, ridiculed, scorned, sensible, surmountable, vincible, vulnerable, weak

ASSAILANT, ***noun*** accoster, aggressor, antagonist, assailer, assaulter, attacker, bludgeon man, criminal, felon, invader, obstructionist, *qui oppugnat,* ravager, terrorist, thug, violator

ASSASSINATION, ***noun*** annihilation, *caedes,* destruction, dispatching, execution, homicide, killing, liquidation, murder, murder by stealth, slaying, treacherous killing, unlawful homicide
ASSOCIATED CONCEPTS: *aestimatio capitis,* conspiracy, murder, political assassination

ASSAULT, ***noun*** act of hostility, aggression, aggressive action, assailment, attack, besiegement, encounter, *impetus,* incursion, *incursus,* injury, intrusion, irruption, offense, onset, onset with force, onslaught, *oppugnatio,* siege, strike, sudden attack, violation of another's rights
ASSOCIATED CONCEPTS: aggravated assault, assault and battery, assault with a deadly weapon, assault with intent to commit a felony, assault with intent to commit murder, assault with intent to maim, assault with intent to rape, assault with intent to rob, battery, felonious assault, simple assault

ASSAULT, ***verb*** accost, accost bellicosely, *adgredi, addriri,* affront hostilely, aggress, *appetere,* assail, assault belligerently, attack, attack physically, attempt violence to, besiege, deal a blow, harm, oppugn, set upon, set upon with force, set upon with violence, strike, thrust at

ASSAY, *noun* analysis, ascertainment, assessment, breakdown, calculation, computation, diagnosis, examination, experiment, exploration, measurement, probation, probe, test, test case, verification

ASSAY, *verb* analyze, ascertain, assess, calculate, compute, diagnose, endeavor, evaluate, experiment, measure, research, test, try, verify, weigh

ASSEMBLAGE, *noun* accumulation, acervation, agglomeration, aggregation, amassment, array, *assemblage,* assembly, association, audience, bale, band, batch, bevy, body, bolt, bulk, bunch, bundle, caucus, claque, clump, cluster, collection, colligation, combination, committee, company, compilation, concentration, conclave, concourse, confluence, conflux, congeries, conglomerate, conglomeration, congregation, congress, convention, convocation, corps, coven, cumulation, drove, ensemble, flock, flood, gang, gathering, group, heap, horde, ingathering, legion, lot, lump, mass, mass meeting, medley, meeting, miscellany, mob, multitude, outfit, pack, packet, party, pile, queue, rally, réunion, series, set, sheaf, squad, stack, string, swarm, symposium, thicket, throng, tribe, troop, troupe, union
ASSOCIATED CONCEPTS: disorderly assemblage, unlawful assemblage

ASSEMBLY, *noun* aggregation, assemblage, body, caucus, collection, company, conclave, concourse, conference, congregation, *consilium, contio,* convention, conventus, convocation, crowd, gathering, group, mass, meeting, multitude

ASSENT, *noun* acceptance, accord, accordance, acknowledgment, acquiescence, *adsensio, adsensus,* affirmance, affirmation, agreement, approbation, approval, authorization, compliance, concord, concordance, concurrence, confirmation, consent, consentaneity, consonance, endorsement, permission, ratification, recognition, sanction, submission, willing consent, willingness
ASSOCIATED CONCEPTS: legal assent
FOREIGN PHRASES: ***Nemo videtur fraudare eos qui sciunt et consentiunt.*** No one is considered as deceiving those who know and consent to his acts. ***Non refert an quis assensum suum praefert verbis, aut rebus ipsis et factis.*** It is immaterial whether a man gives assent by his words or by his acts and deeds.

ASSENT, *verb* accede, accept, accord, acknowledge, acquiesce, *adnuere, adsentari,* agree, allow, approve, authorize, comply, concede, concur, confirm, conform to, consent, embrace an offer, endorse, express concurrence, favor, give consent, homologate, permit, ratify, recognize, sanction, subscribe to
ASSOCIATED CONCEPTS: assent by acts, assent by gestures, assent by silence, express assent, implied assent, judicial assent, mutual assent
FOREIGN PHRASES: ***Qui non prohibet id quod prohibere potest assentire videtur.*** He who does not forbid what he is able to prevent is deemed to assent. ***Qui tacet consentire videtur, ubi tractatur de ejus commodo.*** He who is silent is deemed to consent.

ASSERT, *verb* *adfirmare,* advance, affirm, allege in support, announce, annunciate, argue for, assever, asseverate, attest, aver, avouch, avow, certify, claim, *confirmare,* contend, declare, depose, *dicere,* emphasize, enunciate, espouse, express, insist upon, maintain, plead one's case, plead one's cause, profess, pronounce, propound, recite, relate, set forth, state, state as true, stress, urge, urge reasons for

ASSERTION, *noun* *adfirmatio,* affirmation, allegation, announcement, asseveration, attestation, averment, avouchment, avowal, declaration, *defensio,* disclosure, enunciation, expression, insistence, insistence on a claim, insistence on a right, *ipse dixit,* positive declaration, positive statement, predication, profession, pronouncement, representation, statement, *vindicatio*
ASSOCIATED CONCEPTS: admission, confession, criminal accusation, false accusation

ASSERTIVE, *adjective* authoritative, confident, dogmatic, influential, potent, powerful, self-assured, strong

ASSESS *(Appraise),* ***verb*** *aestimare,* apprize, ascertain, calculate, calibrate, compute, consider, count, determine, estimate, evaluate, fix the value, gauge, judge, measure, mensurate, mete, rate, reckon, set, valuate, value, weigh
ASSOCIATED CONCEPTS: assess a penalty, assess damages, assessed valuation

ASSESS *(Tax),* ***verb*** affix an impost, charge with one's share, demand a payment, demand toll, exact a charge, exact a toll, excise, fix a valuation, impose a charge, impose a levy, lay an impost, levy
ASSOCIATED CONCEPTS: assess taxes

ASSESSMENT *(Estimation),* ***noun*** *aestimatio,* appraisal, appraisement, calculation, determination, estimate, measure, mensuration, rating, reckoning, survey, valuation
ASSOCIATED CONCEPTS: assessment of damages

ASSESSMENT *(Levy),* ***noun*** amount assessed as payable, capitation, census, cess, charge, charge levied, exaction, exactment, imposition, impost, rate, tallage, tax, toll
ASSOCIATED CONCEPTS: assessed valuation, assessment and collection of taxes, assessment district, assessment for benefits, assessment for special improvements, assessment insurance, assessment lien, assessment of property, assessment roll, assessor, equalized assessment, improvements, municipal improvements, public improvements, special assessment, tax assessment, valuation of property

ASSESSOR, *noun* *censor,* charger, collector, exciseman, official receiver, one who exacts, one who imposes a charge, one who levies, tax collector, tax gatherer, tax man, tax receiver, tax taker, taxer
ASSOCIATED CONCEPTS: tax assessor

ASSETS, *noun* available means, belongings, *bona,* capital, chattels, effects, estate, funds, goods, holdings, inventories, money, pecuniary resources, personal effects, personal resources, possessions, principal, property, reserves, resources, riches, valuables, wealth, wherewithal
ASSOCIATED CONCEPTS: assets of a trust corpus, assets of an estate, capital assets, concealment of assets, contingent assets, corporation's assets, depletion of assets, disposal of assets, equitable assets, fixed assets, foreign assets, fraudulent transfer of assets, liquid assets, partnership assets, personal assets, real assets, sale of assets, testamentary assets

ASSEVERATION, *noun* acknowledgment, adjuration, affirmance, affirmation, assertion, attestation, averment, avouchment, avowal, certification, confirmation, declaration, emphatic assertion, legal pledge, oath, positive declaration, positive statement, profession, pronouncement, solemn averment, solemn avowal, solemn declaration, sworn statement, vow

ASSIDUOUS, *adjective* active, ardent, attentive, busy, committed, conscientious, considerate, constant, determined, devoted, diligent, earnest, employed, enduring, engaged, exacting, fervent, flagging, hard-working, immovable, indefatigable, industrious, laborious, obdurate, persevering, persistent, resolute, scrupulous, sedulous, serious, studious, tenacious, tireless, unflagging, unrelenting, unremitting, unshakable, untiring, zealous

ASSIGN *(Allot),* ***verb*** allocate, apportion, appropriate, deal out, dispense, distribute, divide in portions, dole out, give out, mete out, partition, portion out, *rem homini adsignare,* share
ASSOCIATED CONCEPTS: assign a cause of action, assign a chose in action, assign a lease, assign over, assign without recourse, assignable interest, assigned counsel, assigned risk, sublease

ASSIGN *(Designate),* ***verb*** appoint, ascribe, attribute, authorize, charge, commission, commit powers to another, delegate, depute, detail, empower, entrust, invest, name, prescribe, put in commission, set, specify
FOREIGN PHRASES: ***Assignatus utitur jure auctoris.*** An assignee is clothed with the right of his principal.

ASSIGN *(Transfer ownership),* ***verb*** abalienate, alienate, commit to another's trust, consign, convey, deliver, devolve upon, dispose of, endorse over, entrust, grant, make over to another, negotiate, refer, release, relegate, sign over, surrender to another, transfer to another, transmit

ASSIGNABLE, *adjective* consignable, conveyable, deliverable, devisable, disposable, exchangeable, grantable, negotiable, transferable, transmissible, transmittable
ASSOCIATED CONCEPTS: assignable contract, assignable interest

ASSIGNATION, *noun* application, arrogation, ascription, assignment, attribution, blame, charge, imputation, placement

ASSIGNEE, *noun* accipient, allottee, donee, grantee, receiver, recipient, transferee
ASSOCIATED CONCEPTS: lessee
FOREIGN PHRASES: ***Assignatus utitur jure auctoris.*** An assignee has the rights of his principal.

ASSIGNMENT *(Allotment),* ***noun*** allocation, allowance, apportionment, appropriation, assignation, dispensation, distribution, division, partition, portion
ASSOCIATED CONCEPTS: assignment of choses in action

ASSIGNMENT *(Designation),* ***noun*** appointment, authorization, commission, delegation, deputation, mandate, nomination, placing in office, prescription, selection, signification, specification, stipulation
ASSOCIATED CONCEPTS: assignment of error

ASSIGNMENT *(Task),* ***noun*** business, charge, chore, commission, duty, function, mission, part, pursuit, responsibility, role, stint, work

ASSIGNMENT *(Transfer of ownership),* ***noun*** abalienation, alienation, assignation, cession, conferment, conferral, consignation, consignment, conveyance, conveyancing, delivery, demise, devolvement, disposition, distribution, grant, impropriation, mutual transfer, nonretention, relegation, transfer, transference, transmission, transmittal
ASSOCIATED CONCEPTS: assignment by operation of law, assignment for the benefit of creditors, assignment for value, assignment of a cause of action, assignment of a chose in action, assignment of an account, assignment of claim, assignment of dower, assignment of lease, assignment of rents and profits, assignment of wages, consignment, general assignment, lease, license, partial assignment, promise to make assignment, voluntary assignment
FOREIGN PHRASES: ***Assignatus utitur jure auctoris.*** An assignee is clothed with the right of his principal.

ASSIMILATE, *verb* acculturate, accustom, adopt, amalgamate, associate, blend, combine, commingle, condition, connect, digest, enculturate, fuse, habituate, incorporate, ingest, integrate, intermingle, liken, link, merge, mingle, osmose, subsume, take in, take up

ASSIST, *verb* abet, accommodate, act as assistant to, administer to, afford aid, aid, *auxiliari,* back, be of help, be of use, come to the aid of, cooperate with, do a service, endorse, foster, furnish aid, further, give a hand, give aid, give support, help, help along, intercede for, minister to, nurture, oblige, *opitulari,* participate, promote, reinforce, relieve, second, serve, stand by, subserve, subsidize, *subvenire,* succor, supply aid, support, take part with
ASSOCIATED CONCEPTS: accessory, aiding and abetting, complicity

ASSISTANCE, *noun* accommodation, *adiumentum,* adjuvancy, advocacy, aid, *auxilium,* benefit, benevolence, championship, cooperation, furtherance, help, helpfulness, intercession, participation, reinforcement, subsidy, succor, support
ASSOCIATED CONCEPTS: able assistance of counsel, writ of assistance

ASSISTANT, *noun* abettor, accessory, accomplice, *adiutor, adiutrix,* adjutant, adjuvant, advocate, agent, aide, *aide-de-camp,* aider, apprentice, associate, backer, champion, clerk, coadjutor, coaid, collaborator, colleague, confederate, confrère, cooperator, copartner, coworker, deputy, employee, helper, helpmate, partner, right-hand man, second, seconder, subaltern, subordinate, supporter, underling, underworker
ASSOCIATED CONCEPTS: accessory, accomplice, coconspirator

ASSOCIATE, *noun* adjunct, aid, aide-de-camp, assistant, auxiliary, coadjutant, coadjutor, coadjuvant, cohelper, cohort, collaborator, colleague, comate, companion, compeer, confederate, confidante, confrere, cooperator, copartner, coworker, fellow worker, friend, partner, *socius, sodalis*
ASSOCIATED CONCEPTS: associates in a law office, confederacy, partner, union

ASSOCIATED, *adjective* affiliated, agnate, akin, allied, closely allied, closely related, coactive, coadunate, combined, concerted, confederated, conjoint, conjunct, connate, connected, cooperant, cooperative, coupled, coworking, federate, federated, incorporated, inosculated, interallied, joined, leagued, linked, related, synergetic, united
ASSOCIATED CONCEPTS: associated companies

ASSOCIATION *(Alliance),* ***noun*** affiliation, amalgamation, coalition, combination, combine, company, confederacy, confederation, *conlegium,* corporation, coterie, federation, guild, league, syndicate, union

ASSOCIATED CONCEPTS: articles of association, bar associations, beneficial associations, convenant of associations, joint stock associations, mutual benefit associations, professional associations, unincorporated associations, voluntary associations

ASSOCIATION *(Connection),* ***noun*** bond, coadjuvancy, coalition, colleagueship, combination, conjunction, *conlegium,* connectedness, consociation, copartnership, coworking, involvement, joint enterprise, link, linkage, organization, participation, partnership, relatedness, relation, relationship, societas, working in concert

ASSUAGE, ***verb*** abate, allay, alleviate, appease, attemper, blunt, chasten, check, comfort, compose, curb, diminish, ease, lessen, *levare, mitigare,* mitigate, moderate, mollify, obtund, pacify, palliate, quell, quench, reduce, relieve, remedy, salve, sate, satiate, satisfy, *sedare,* slake, smother, soften, solace, soothe, still, temper, tranquilize

ASSUME *(Seize),* ***verb*** accroach, adeem, adopt, *adsumere,* annex, appropriate, arrogate, commandeer, confiscate, dispossess, distrain, expropriate, help oneself to, make free with, *occupare,* possess oneself of, *rem sibi adrogare,* take as one's own, usurp

ASSUME *(Simulate),* ***verb*** act as, counterfeit, dissemble, dissimulate, don, feign, impersonate, make believe, outwardly seem, pass for, personate, play the part, pose as, pretend to be, profess, put on deceitfully, represent as, take the part of, take the semblance of

ASSUME *(Suppose),* ***verb*** be inclined to think, be of the opinion, conclude, conjecture, consider, deduce, deem true, divine, draw the inference, find probable, gather, have an idea that, hold the opinion, infer, predicate, premise, presume, presuppose, suspect, take for granted, take without proof, theorize, think credible, think likely, think probable

ASSUME *(Undertake),* ***verb*** accept, accept an obligation, attempt, attend to, be willing to bear, become responsible for, begin, broach, commit oneself, contract, contract for, embark upon, engage, enter upon, incur a duty, manage, proceed to, pursue, set about, shoulder, *suscipere,* take care of, take charge, take on oneself, take up, venture upon
ASSOCIATED CONCEPTS: assume a debt, assume a lease, assume a mortgage, assume responsibility, assumed name, assumed risk

ASSUMED *(Feigned),* ***adjective*** adopted, apocryphal, bogus, contrived, counterfeit, deceptive, delusive, disguised, fabricated, factitious, fake, false, fictitious, fraudulent, invented, manufactured, misleading, misrepresented, pretended, pretexted, spurious, synthetic, unauthentic, ungenuine, unreal
ASSOCIATED CONCEPTS: allegation of fact, allegation of law, alleged fact, material allegation, pleading, responsive allegation, specific allegation

ASSUMED *(Inferred),* ***adjective*** accepted, conjectured, connoted, considered true, given, granted, hypothesized, implicit, indicated, insinuated, intimated, posited, postulated, presumed, presupposed, stated, supposed, suppositional, taken for granted, understood

ASSUMPTION *(Adoption),* ***noun*** acceptance, acquisition, receiving, reception, recipience, selection, taking on, undertaking

ASSOCIATED CONCEPTS: *assumpsit on quantum meruit,* assumption agreement, assumption of debt, assumption of facts, assumption of indebtedness, assumption of jurisdiction, assumption of liability, assumption of mortgage, assumption of obligation, assumption of risk

ASSUMPTION *(Seizure),* ***noun*** annexation, appropriation, arrogation, dispossession, encroachment, exaction, expropriation, impropriation, infringement, usurpation

ASSUMPTION *(Supposition),* ***noun*** basis, belief, conjecture, foundation, ground, hypothesis, hypothesization, impression, notion, opinion, personal judgment, postulate, premise, presumption, presupposition, *sumptio,* supposal, surmise, theory, thinking, view

ASSURANCE, ***noun*** adjuration, affirmation, assuredness, attestation, averment, avow, avowal, avowance, commitment, confidence, confidentness, *confirmatio,* covenant, declaration, earnest declaration, engagement, *fiducia,* guaranty, oath, obligation, pact, paction, pledge, promise, reassurance, security, solemn assertion, solemn promise, surety, voucher, vow, warranty
ASSOCIATED CONCEPTS: assurance of title, covenant of future assurances

ASSURE *(Give confidence to),* ***verb*** buoy up, cause to feel certain, cheer, comfort, confirm in conviction, console, convince, deliver from uncertainty, dismiss all doubt, embolden, encourage, enhearten, free from doubt, free from uncertainty, give hope, hearten, inspire, inspire hope, lead to believe, make certain, make confident, offer assurances to, persuade, put at ease, raise expectations, reassure, render certain, restore one's faith, satisfy, set at ease, solace

ASSURE *(Insure),* ***verb*** affirm, agree to indemnify for loss, answer for, asseverate, attest, aver, avouch, avow, certify, confirm, endorse, espouse, give security, guarantee, make a promise, make certain, make sure, pledge, profess, promise, render certain, render safe, secure against loss, solemnly promise, subscribe to, swear, underwrite, verify, vouch for, vow, warrant

ASTONISH, ***verb*** affect, amaze, astound, awe, blow away, captivate, charm, dazzle, electrify, enchant, enrapture, enthrall, enthuse, entrance, excite, fascinate, impress, inspire, interest, move, overawe, overwhelm, pique, stagger, stun, surprise, thrill, wow

ASTRAY, ***adjective*** aberrant, adrift, afield, amiss, awry, circuitous, deviating, errant, erratic, indirect, lost, misguided, misled, off-center, out of one's bearings, out of one's reckoning, random, round-about, straying, undirected, unguided

ASTRINGENT, ***adjective*** acid, acrid, acrimonious, *adstrictorius,* austere, bitter, caustic, dour, exigent, harsh, mordant, rough, severe, stern, strict, stringent, tart

ASTUCIOUS, ***adjective*** acute, adept, adroit, advanced, alert, apt, astute, aware, brilliant, clever, cunning, discerning, educated, erudite, fast on the uptake, genius, informed, ingenious, inventive, keen, knowledgeable, learned, literate, precocious, prudent, quick, quick-witted, resourceful, sagacious, sage, sapient, savvy, scholarly, sharp, shrewd, smart, well-read, wise

ASTUTE, ***adjective*** adroit, agile, alter, apt, artful, bright, brilliant, clear-sighted, clever, cunning, discriminating, discriminative, experienced, informed, ingenious, insightful, intelligent, keen, knowing, knowledgeable, learned, lettered, nimble, perceptive, perspicacious, plugged in, privy, resourceful, sagacious, sage, sapient, savvy, scholarly, sensible, sharp, shrewd, smart, sophisticated, street smart, studious, well-rounded, wise, worldly

ASYLUM *(Hiding place),* ***noun*** covert, exile, haven, inviolable refuge, place of immunity, place of refuge, refuge, retreat, safehold, sanctuary, *sanctum sanctorum,* secure retreat, shelter, temporary refuge

ASYLUM *(Hospital),* ***noun*** lazaretto, mental hospital, mental institution, nursing home, psychiatric hospital, psychiatric ward, sanitorium, shelter for the afflicted, state hospital, state institution

ASYLUM *(Protection),* ***noun*** freedom from danger, refuge, safeguard, safety, sanctuary, security, shelter
ASSOCIATED CONCEPTS: granted asylum

AT FAULT, ***adverb*** culpable, erring, in error, guilty, liable, responsible for, wrong

AT ISSUE, ***adverb*** being analyzed, in contemplation, in dispute, in question, on the agenda, under advisement, under consideration, under examination

AT RISK, ***adverb*** at peril, capable of loss, involved, potentially liable

AT WILL EMPLOYMENT, ***noun*** at the will of the employer, discretionary employment without the necessity of reasons, employment at will, freedom to discharge, freedom to discharge without grounds, freedom to discharge without reasons, freedom to fire
ASSOCIATED CONCEPTS: just cause employees, morally reprehensive reasons, morally wrong reasons

ATMOSPHERE, ***noun*** air, airspace, ambience, aura, background, circumambience, climate, climatic condition, element, environing influence, environment, medium, milieu, mood, setting, space, surroundings, weather
ASSOCIATED CONCEPTS: clouding the atmosphere, polluting the atmosphere

ATROCIOUS, ***adjective*** abhorrent, abominable, appalling, awful, bad, barbaric, beastly, corrupt, deplorable, desperate, diabolical, dire, disgusting, dreadful, errant, evil, fiendish, flagrant, foul, frightening, frightful, ghastly, grisly, grotesque, gruesome, heinous, hideous, horrendous, horrid, horrific, horrifying, jejune, loathsome, lurid, malignant, monstrous, nefarious, noxious, obscene, odious, offensive, onerous, outrageous, perverse, recalcitrant, reprehensible, repugnant, repulsive, revolting, rude, scandalous, terrible, ugly, uncouth, unmannerly, unsightly, unspeakable, vile, villainous, wicked

ATROCITY, ***noun*** abomination, abuse, act of ferocity, atrocious crime, *atrocitas,* barbarity, deed of savagery, ferity, ferocity, fiendishness, flagitious villainy, flagitiousness, flagrancy, gross offense, heinousness, holocaust, infamy, inhumanity, iniquity, malevolence, maltreatment, mercilessness, monstrosity, nefariousness, *nefas, res atrox,* ruthlessness, savagery, truculence, victimization, villainy, wantonly wicked conduct, wickedness

FOREIGN PHRASES: ***Patria potestas in pietate debet, non in atrocitate, consistere.*** Paternal power should consist of affection not of atrocity.

ATTACH *(Join),* ***verb*** add, add as an accessory, *adfigere,* adhere, adjoin, *adligare,* affix, agglutinate, annex, append, assemble, bind, cohere, combine, conjoin, connect, consolidate, couple, embody, embrace, fasten, fasten together, incorporate, insert, link, make one, merge, put together, secure, subjoin, supplement, unite
ASSOCIATED CONCEPTS: attach exhibits

ATTACH *(Seize),* ***verb*** adeem, annex, appropriate, arrogate, confiscate, disseise, distrain, distress, exact, expropriate, garnish, impound, impress, levy, overcome, preempt, press, replevy, retake, secure, seize summarily, sequester, sequestrate, take, take over, take possession of, take summarily, usurp
ASSOCIATED CONCEPTS: attach property, provisional remedy

ATTACHED *(Annexed),* ***adjective*** added, affixed, agglutinated, appendant, appended, *aptus,* bound, conjoined, connected, fastened, fixed, joined, paired, subjoined, united

ATTACHED *(Seized),* ***adjective*** adeemed, annexed, appropriated, arrogated, confiscated, disseised, distrained, expropriated, foreclosed, forfeited, garnisheed, impounded, levied, replevied, sequestered, usurped
ASSOCIATED CONCEPTS: provisional remedy

ATTACHMENT *(Act of affixing),* ***noun*** adjunction, affixation, annexation, annexion, attaching, binding, bond, cohesion, confixation, conjunction, connection, fastening, fixing, insertion, joinder, joining, junction, ligation, nexus, subjunction, that which attaches, tie
ASSOCIATED CONCEPTS: attachment of a security interest, garnishment, in rem jurisdiction, provisional remedy, quasi in rem jurisdiction

ATTACHMENT *(Seizure),* ***noun*** annexation, apprehending, confiscation, deprivation, deprivement, disownment, dispossession, distrainer, distraint, distress, divestment, *embargo,* execution, expropriation, foreclosure, garnishment, impoundage, impoundment, impressment, seizing, sequestration
ASSOCIATED CONCEPTS: ancillary attachment, attachment execution, attachment of persons, attachment of property, attachment proceedings, attachment to obtain jurisdiction, attachment upon mesne process, body attachment, execution, extraordinary remedy, lien or incumbrance, proceeding in rem, property subject to attachment, provisional remedy, sequestration, writ of attachment, wrongful attachment

ATTACHMENT *(Thing affixed),* ***noun*** accessory, addendum, additum, adjunct, affixture, annex, appendage, appendix, appurtenance, fixture, postfix, supplement, supplementary device

ATTACK, ***verb*** abuse, *adgredi, adoriri,* advance upon, aggress, assail, assault, assume the offensive, bear down upon, beat, begin hostilities against, beleaguer, beset, besiege, bombard, charge, combat, commit hostilities, descend on, engage in hostilities, fall upon, fight offensively, fly at, force, hit, impugn, invade, *invehi in,* lay hands on, lay into, make an onset against, open fire upon, oppugn, pitch into, pounce upon, raid, revile, run at, rush upon, set upon with force, shoot at, spring upon, start a fight, start a war,

storm, strike, strike the first blow, tackle, take offensive action, take the initiative, take the offensive, tear into, throw oneself upon, waylay
ASSOCIATED CONCEPTS: assault, attack on credibility, collateral attack, direct attack, impeach, provocation of attack

ATTAIN, ***verb*** accomplish, achieve, acquire, *adsequi,* arrive at, be successful, bring about, bring off successfully, bring to pass, carry through, come by, come to, complete, *consequi,* consummate, earn, effect, effectuate, finish, gain, gain one's end, get, get by effort, get done, get possession of, obtain, perfect, procure, put through, reach, reach one's goal, realize, reap, score a success, secure, succeed, succeed in reaching

ATTAINT, ***noun*** abasement, bad name, bad reputation, bad repute, brand, debasement, defilement, degradation, derogation, deviation from rectitude, disapprobation, discredit, disesteem, disgrace, dishonor, disreputability, disrepute, disrespect, humiliation, ignominy, ill fame, ill favor, ill repute, improbity, imputation, infamy, ingloriousness, loss of reputation, mark, obloquy, odium, opprobrium, reproach, shame, smear, smirch, stain, stigma, taint, tarnish, tarnished honor
ASSOCIATED CONCEPTS: attainder, *autrefois attaint,* bill of attainder, civil death

ATTEMPT, ***verb*** aim at, assay, be at work, be in action, bid for, carry on, *conari,* do one's best, do the needful, drive at, employ oneself, endeavor, essay, exert oneself, go after, go all out for, intend, labor for, make a bid, make a try, make an effort at, make the effort, ply one's task, pursue, put forth an effort, quest, seek to, set out to, strive, take on, *temptare,* test, try, try hard, try one's best, undertake, use one's best endeavors, venture
ASSOCIATED CONCEPTS: attempt to commit a crime, attempt to defraud, attempt to prove, conspiracy, failure of intended act, preparatory acts, renunciation
FOREIGN PHRASES: ***Affectus punitur licet non sequatur effectus.*** The intention is punished although the intended result does not follow. ***Non officit conatus nisi sequatur effectus.*** An attempt does not harm unless a consequence follows. ***In maleficiis voluntas spectatur, non exitus.*** In criminal offenses, the intention and not the result must be regarded. ***Officit conatus si effectus sequatur.*** The attempt becomes of consequence if the effect follows.

ATTEMPTED MONOPOLIZATION, ***verb*** attempt to control competition, conspiracy to monopolize, intent to harm competition, market power inference, market share inference

ATTEND *(Accompany),* ***verb*** be associated with, be connected with, go along with

ATTEND *(Be present at),* ***verb*** frequent, go to, visit

ATTEND *(Heed),* ***verb*** be attentive to, give heed to, listen, mark, mind, note, notice, take notice of

ATTEND *(Take care of),* ***verb*** be attendant on, care for, guard, minister to, see to, serve, wait upon, watch over

ATTENDANCE, ***noun*** accompaniment, ministration, presence

ATTENTION *(Admonition),* ***noun*** admonishment, advice, alarm, announcement, attentiveness, caution, caveat, communication, dehortation, forewarning, formal advice, instruction, intelligence, monition, news, notice, notice of danger, portent, precaution, premonishment, prenotification, presage, threat, warning

ATTENTION *(Care),* ***noun*** absorption, admonition, advice, concentrated focus, concentration, concern to detail, consciousness, consideration, contemplation, deliberation, deterrent, devotion, focus on detail, heed, heedfulness, immersion, introspectiveness, nurturing, reflectiveness, regard, regard for specifics, supervision, support

ATTENUATE, ***verb*** *attenuare,* bate, constrict, constringe, contract, curtail, debilitate, decrease, deflate, devitalize, diminish, diminish in effect, *extenuare,* extenuate, lessen, lighten, make thin, narrow, reduce, reduce in intensity, reduce in strength, render threadlike, taper, weaken, weaken in force
ASSOCIATED CONCEPTS: attenuation between a cause and the result, proximate cause, remote cause

ATTEST, ***verb*** adjure, affirm, assert, authenticate, aver, bear out, bear witness to, certify, confirm, corroborate, declare, declare the truth of, depone, depose, endorse, evince, ratify, *rem testari,* speak on oath, subscribe, substantiate, support, swear, take one's oath, *testem facere, testificari,* testify to, validate, verify, vouch for, witness
ASSOCIATED CONCEPTS: affidavit, interrogatory

ATTESTATION, ***noun*** act of bearing witness, adjuration, affirmation, allegation, assertion, asseveration, attest, attesting declaration, authentication, averment, avouchment, avowal, certification, declaration, endorsement, oath, solemn averment, solemn avowal, solemn declaration, statement, substantiation, swearing, sworn evidence, *testificatio,* testification, *testimonium,* testimony, validification, verification, witnessing
ASSOCIATED CONCEPTS: acknowledgment, attestation clause, attestation of chattel mortgage, attestation of deed, attestation of note, attestation of will, attesting witnesses

ATTITUDE *(Manner),* ***noun*** affectation, air, approach, aspect, behavior, carriage, cast, comportment, composure, conduct, demeanor, deportment, expression, fashion, guise, image, look, mannerism, mode, outlook, posture, presence, presentation, pretense, shape, stance, thinking

ATTITUDE *(Surly approach),* ***adjective*** abrasive, abrupt, acerbic, acidic, acidulous, acrid, acrimonious, bitter, caustic, corrosive, curt, cutting, disagreeable, gruff, harsh, insincere, mordant, nasty, obnoxious, odious, ornery, pungent, resentful, rough, sardonic, satiric, satirical, scalding, scathing, severe, sharp, sharp-tongued, short, smart-alec, snippety, tart, terse, unpleasant, vitriolic, vulgar

ATTORN, ***verb*** allot, assign, cede, confer, confer ownership, consign, convey, deliver, demise, devise, devolve upon, dispose of, give, grant, impart, let, part with, pass down, relinquish, transfer, turn over

ATTORNEY, ***noun*** advocate, attorney-at-law, barrister, counsel, counselor, counselor-at-law, jurisconsult, jurisprudent, jurist, lawyer, learned counsel, legal advisor, legal practitioner, legist, member of the bar, officer of the court, pleader, practitioner, procurator, publicist, solicitor
ASSOCIATED CONCEPTS: attorney of record, staff attorney
FOREIGN PHRASES: ***Consilia multorum quaeruntur in magnis.*** The advice of many is required in affairs of magnitude.

ATTORNEY-CLIENT PRIVILEGE, *noun* confidential relationship, confidentiality, fiduciary privilege, immunity from divulging confidences, nondisclosable relationship, private relationship, privileged relationship
Generally: protected relationship
Specifically: confidential communications
ASSOCIATED CONCEPTS: privileged communications

ATTORNEY IN FACT, *noun* alternate, legal appointee, legal representative, proxy, surrogate

ATTORNEY'S FEES, *noun* compensation for legal services, payment for representation
ASSOCIATED CONCEPTS: alternative fee arrangements, contingent fees, flat fee, hourly fees

ATTORNMENT, *noun* agreement, arrangement, commitment, compact, condition, deal, liability, prerequisite, provision, proviso, requisite, stipulation, understanding

ATTRACT, *verb* bait, beckon, beguile, bewitch, bring, bring in, captivate, charm, draw, draw attention, enchant, enthrall, entice, entrance, entrap, fascinate, interest, knock out, lure, magnetize, motivate, pull, rope in, seduce, spellbind, tempt, wow

ATTRACTIVE, *adjective* adorable, agreeable, alluring, appealing, attracting, attrahent, beauteous, beautiful, beckoning, becoming, beguiling, bewitching, captivating, catching, catchy, charming, comely, delightful, desirable, drawing, elegant, enchanting, engaging, enthralling, enticing, entrancing, exquisite, fair, fascinating, fetching, glamorous, interesting, intriguing, inviting, likeable, luring, magnetic, pleasant, pleasing, prepossessing, pretty, ravishing, seductive, sightly, sweet, tasteful, tempting, titillating, to one's liking
ASSOCIATED CONCEPTS: attractive nuisance doctrine

ATTRACTIVE NUISANCE, *noun* allure, bait, dangerous conditions, draw, endangerment, enticement, inducement, lure, seducement, unprotected
ASSOCIATED CONCEPTS: attractive nuisance doctrine, specific conditions

ATTRIBUTE, *verb* accredit with, *adsignare,* ascribe, assign, charge with, connect with, consider as belonging to, impute, point to, predicate, set down to, *tribuere*
ASSOCIATED CONCEPTS: attribute a cause to an individual

ATTRIBUTION, *noun* accounting, acknowledgment, affirmation, allusion, ascription, assignation, assignment, association, connection, implication, imputation, incrimination, indication, insinuation, mention, quotation, reference, relation

ATTRITION, *noun* decrease, disintegration, dwindling, erosion, fading, falling off, lessening, waning, wearing away

ATTUNE, *verb* acclimatize, accommodate, accord, adapt, adjust, attemper, be harmonious, blend, bring into accord, bring into agreement, fit for a purpose, harmonize, make accordant, make adjustments, make agree, readapt, readjust, rectify, regulate, render accordant, resolve a discord, restore harmony, set right

ATYPICAL, *adjective* aberrant, abnormal, anomalous, dissimilar, diverse, exceptional, never the same, nonuniform, unalike, unrepresentative, variable

AUCTION, *noun* *auctio, auctione vendere,* public sale, public sale of property, sale by bid, sale by outcry, sale to the highest bidder, *sub hasta vendere,* vendue
ASSOCIATED CONCEPTS: auction license, auction sale, auctioneer, highest bidder, public sale

AUDACIOUS, *adjective* assertive, bold, brash, brassy, brazen, bumptious, caustic, curt, dauntless, defiant, disdainful, disrespectful, forward, fresh, impertinent, impudent, insolent, obtrusive, pert, shameless, unabashed

AUDACITY, *noun* audacia, audaciousness, bold front, boldness, bravado, brave face, bravura, confidence in one's powers, daring, defiance of danger, derring-do, hardihood, intrepidity, nerve, overboldness, overdaring, *protervitas,* rashness, recklessness, scorn of the consequences, temerity, undauntedness, want of caution

AUDIENCE *(Assembly),* ***noun*** assemblage, assembly, body, collection, conclave, conference, congregation, convention, conventus, convocation, crowd, encounter, gathering, mass, meeting, multitude

AUDIENCE *(Listeners),* ***noun*** attendees, collection, crowd, group, group of people, guests, hearers, listeners, mass multitude, patrons, public, spectators, viewers

AUDIO RIGHTS, *noun* audiocassette rights, audio reproduction rights, compact disc rights, sound recording rights
Generally: secondary rights, subsidiary rights

AUDIT, *verb* bring into question, certify, check, check on, conduct an inquiry, examine, examine financial accounts, examine the accounts officially, go through the books, hold an inquiry, inspect, inspect accounts officially, investigate, monitor, probe, pursue an inquiry, *rationes dispungere,* reexamine, research, review, scrutinize, search, study, subject to examination
ASSOCIATED CONCEPTS: allowance of claim, audit of account, audited claims, auditor, auditor's report, disallowance of claim, fraudulent audit

AUGMENTATION, *noun* *accessio,* accessory, accrual, accruement, accumulation, adding, advance, advancement, aggrandizement, *amplificatio,* amplification, appreciation, appurtenance, broadening, build-up, cumulative effect, cumulativeness, development, enhancement, enlargement, enlarging, expansion, extension, gain, growth, improvement, increase, increasing, increment, intensification, magnification, progress, proliferation, redoubling, reinforcement, rise, something added, spread, supplement, widening
ASSOCIATED CONCEPTS: augmentation of assets, augmentation of estate

AUGUR, *verb* anticipate, approximate, betoken, connote, divine, envision, estimate, forecast, foresee, foreshadow, foretell, forewarn, harbinger, herald, omen, portend, predict, prefigure, presage, prognosticate, signal, signify, suggest, warn

AUSPICES, *noun* abetment, aegis, assistance, *auspicium,* authority, backing, benign favor, care, charge, countenance, custody, encouragement, favor, favoring influence, fosterage, guardianship, guidance, management, oversight, patronage, protection, protectorship, recommendation, safeguard, sponsorship, superintendence, supervision, support, tutelage, wardenship, wardship
ASSOCIATED CONCEPTS: under governmental auspices

AUSPICIOUS, ***adjective*** betokening success, encouraging, favorable, favored by fortune, favoring, felicitous, *felix,* fortunate, good, hopeful, inspiriting, lucky, of good omen, of promise, opportune, portending happiness, presaging good fortune, promising, propitious, *prosper,* providential, roseate, successful

AUSTERITY, ***noun*** abstemiousness, *austeritas,* bare subsistence, chariness, closed purse, economicalness, economy, frugality, frugalness, good management, husbandry, lack of luxury, meagerness, scantiness, scrimping, self-denial, self-restraint, severe discipline, *severitas,* severity, stinginess, stint, strictness, stringency, subsistence level, temperance, thrift, thriftiness, unwastefulness
ASSOCIATED CONCEPTS: austerity budget

AUTHENTIC, ***adjective*** accordant with the facts, according to the facts, accredited, accurate, actual, as represented, attested, authoritative, bona fide, *certus,* credible, demonstrated, dependable, documented, entitled to acceptance and belief, factual, faithful, founded on fact, from competent sources, from the original data, genuine, genuine in origin, honest, inartificial, legitimate, literal, not apocryphal, not false, not fictitious, not spurious, not tampered with, of the origin reputed, original, positive, pure, real, reliable, solid, sound, true, trusted, trustworthy, unadulterated, uncounterfeited, undisguised, undistorted, unexaggerated, unfabricated, unfaked, unfeigned, unfictitious, unplagiarized, unquestionable, unsimulated, unspecious, unspurious, unsynthetic, valid, verifiable, veritable, *verus,* well-based, well-founded, well-grounded, worthy of belief
ASSOCIATED CONCEPTS: authentic act, authenticate, forgery, notaries

AUTHENTICATE, ***verb*** accredit, affirm, approve, assert, attest, aver, avouch, avow, back up, certify, confirm, corroborate, declare, document, endorse, establish, guarantee, legitimize, profess, prove, reinforce, sanction, substantiate, support, testify to, validate, verify, vouch for, warrant, witness

AUTHOR *(Originator),* ***noun*** architect, *auctor,* begetter, causer, composer, contriver, creator, deviser, discoverer, effecter, fabricator, founder, generator, inaugurator, initiator, innovater, institutor, introducer, inventor, maker, manufacturer, occasioner, organizer, parent, prime mover, producer, sire
ASSOCIATED CONCEPTS: copyright
FOREIGN PHRASES: ***Culpa tenet suos auctores.*** Fault binds its own authors.

AUTHOR *(Writer),* ***noun*** compiler, composer of a literary work, drafter, essayist, literary person, man of letters, person who writes, *scriptor,* verse maker
ASSOCIATED CONCEPTS: copyright, plagiarism

AUTHORITATIVE, ***adjective*** accurate, approved, authentic, circumstantiated, compelling, complete, comprehensive, conclusive, confirmed, correct, decisive, definitive, dependable, exhaustive, important, indisputable, influential, irrefutable, justified, legitimate, masterful, momentous, official, predominant, preeminent, real, reliable, sanctioned, scholarly, sound, supported, thorough, true, trustworthy, truthful, undisputed, unequivocal, verified, veritable

AUTHORITIES, ***noun*** administration, commanders, directors, executives, government, heads, *magistratus,* management, officeholders, officials, persons in office, persons of commanding influence, *potestates,* powers that be, rulers, those holding power, those in command, those in control, those of influence, those who rule
ASSOCIATED CONCEPTS: competent authorities, governmental authorities, lawful authorities, local authorities, municipal authorities, port authorities, turnpike and toll authorities

AUTHORITY *(Documentation),* ***noun*** authoritative example, authoritative rule for future similar cases, court rule, decision, judgment, judicial decision establishing a rule, judicial precedent, legislative precedent, order, precedent, precept, prior instance, *ratio decidendi,* ruling, sanction, statute
ASSOCIATED CONCEPTS: established authority

AUTHORITY *(Legal expert),* ***noun*** able, accomplished, acquainted, adept, adroit, all-knowing, apt, artful, capable, clever, cognizant, competent, conversant, deft, dexterous, effective, efficient, encyclopedic, experienced, facile, finished handy, ingenious, knowing, knowledgeable, learned, masterful, masterly, omniscient, practiced, prepared, professional, proficient, qualified, seasoned, skilled, skillful, trained, tried, versed, veteran, well-qualified, wise
ASSOCIATED CONCEPTS: forensic expert

AUTHORITY *(Power),* ***noun*** *auctoritas,* authoritativeness, control, dominance, domination, force, governance, importance, influence, position of influence, position of power, powers that be, seniority, source, supremacy, sway
ASSOCIATED CONCEPTS: abuse of authority, acting under authority, actual authority, agency, apparent authority, authority by estoppel, authority coupled with an interest, authority of law, authority of the court, colorable authority, constituted authority, de facto authority, delegation of authority, express authority, general authority, implied authority, incidental authority, indicia of authority, lawful authority, legislative authority, limited authority, local authority, municipal authority, naked authority, parental authority, power of attorney, proxy, public authority, real authority, scope of authority, special authority, under cover of authority, unlimited authority, want of authority, written authority
FOREIGN PHRASES: ***Argumentum ab auctoritate est fortissimum in lege.*** An argument drawn from authority is the strongest in the law. ***Majus dignum trahit ad se minus dignum.*** The greater authority appropriates to itself the lesser authority. ***Nihil tam proprium imperio quam legibus vivere.*** Nothing is so becoming to authority as to live in conformity with the laws. ***Non debet cui plus licet, quod minus est non licere.*** He who is given a greater authority ought not to be forbidden that which is less. ***Ubi non est condendi auctoritas, ibi non est parendi necessitas.*** Where there is no authority for establishing a rule, there is no need for obeying it. ***Firmior et potentior est operatio legis quam dispositio hominis.*** The operation of the law is more firm and more powerful than the will of man. ***Fortior et potentior est dispositio legis quam hominis.*** The disposition of the law has greater force and stronger effect than that of man. ***Judici officium suum excedenti non paretur.*** No obedience is to be given to a judge exceeding his office or jurisdiction. ***Legitime imperanti parere necesse est.*** One who commands lawfully must be obeyed. ***In maxima potentia minima licentia.*** In the greatest liberty there is the least freedom. ***Semper praesumitur pro legitimatione puerorum.*** The presumption always is in favor of the legitimacy of children.

AUTHORITY *(Right),* ***noun*** jurisdiction, legal power, legitimacy, prerogative, right to adjudicate, right to command, right to determine, right to settle issues, rightful power

FOREIGN PHRASES: ***Omnis ratihabitio retrotrahitur et mandato priori aequiparatur.*** Every ratification relates back and is taken to be the equal of prior authority. ***Nullius hominis auctoritas apud nos valere debet, ut meliora non sequeremur si quis attulerit.*** No man's influence ought to prevail upon us, that we should not follow better opinions should anyone present them. ***Nemo potest facere per obliquum quod non potest facere per directum.*** No man can do indirectly that which he cannot do directly. ***In rebus manifestis, errat qui auctoritates legum allegat; quia perspicua vera non sunt probanda.*** In clear cases, he errs who cites legal authorities because obvious truths are manifest and do not have to be proved.

AUTHORIZATION, *noun* accreditation, approval, certification, clearance, compliance, consent, credentials, delegation, directive, empowerment, endorsement, go-ahead, granting, leave, legalized, legitimization, license, mandate, order, pass, permission, sanctioned, warrant

AUTHORIZE, *verb* accord, accredit, acquiesce in, admit, advocate, affirm, agree to, allow, appoint, approve, assent to, assign, auctor esse, be favorable to, be in favor of, certify, charge, charter, commission, concede, confer a privilege, confer a right, confirm, confirm officially, consent to, consign, countenance, credit, declare lawful, delegate to, depute, empower, enable, endorse, endow, endow with power, enfranchise, entitle, entrust, establish, formalize, formally sanction, give a right, give authority, give leave, give permission, give power, go along with, grant, grant claims, grant permission, have no objection, homologate, interpose no obstacles, invest with power, legalize, legislate, legitimate, legitimatize, legitimize, license, maintain, make legal, make valid, permit, *potestatem facere,* prescribe, privilege, pronounce legal, put in force, put up with, recognize, recommend, release, restore permission, sanctify, sanction, sanction a claim, sign, subscribe to, suffer to occur, support by authority, sustain, sustain by authority, tolerate, underwrite, validate, vest with a title, vouch for, vouchsafe, warrant
ASSOCIATED CONCEPTS: agency, delegation
FOREIGN PHRASES: ***Semper qui non prohibet pro se intervenire, mandare creditur.*** He who does not prohibit the intervention of another in his behalf is deemed to have authorized it.

AUTOMATIC, *adjective* allowed, authorized, axiomatic, common, customary, everyday, expected, familiar, frequent, habitual, immediate, ingrained, instant, instantaneous, instinctive, natural, perfunctory, permitted, recurrent, reflex, regular, robotic, routine, spontaneous, standard, standard-issue, subliminal, systematic, unconscious, unforced, unplanned, visceral

AUTONOMOUS *(Independent),* ***adjective*** detached, existing as an independent entity, free, free to choose, self-contained, self-reliant, self-sufficient, self-supporting, uncoerced, uncompelled, unconstrained, uncontrolled, unrestricted

AUTONOMOUS *(Self governing),* ***adjective*** at liberty, autarchic, autonomic, enfranchised, free, politically independent, self-determined, self-directing, self-ruling, sovereign

AUXILIARY, *adjective* accessorial, accessory, added, additional, annexed, appurtenant, assistant, backup, contributory, excess, extra, further, peripheral, reinforcement, secondary, subordinate, substitute, supplemental, supplementary, supportive, surplus, tributary

AVAIL *(Be of use),* ***verb*** aid, assist, assist in accomplishing a purpose, be good to, be of service, be of value, be profitable, be useful, benefit, bestead, bring to bear, confer a benefit on, do service, have efficacy, help, perform a function, *prodesse,* promote, serve, service, subserve, succor, suit one's purpose, *valere*

AVAIL *(Bring about),* ***verb*** accomplish, bear fruit, bring forth, cause, conduce, effect, effectuate, engender, evolve, generate, give origin to, give rise to, have force, meet the demand, occasion, produce, profit, provide, *re uti,* realize, render, succeed, suffice

AVAILABLE, *adjective* accessible, approachable, at hand, at one's disposal, attainable, convenient, fit, handy, obtainable, on call, on the market, open, reachable, ready, receptive, securable, suitable, to be had, unfilled, untaken, usable, vacant, willing, within reach
ASSOCIATED CONCEPTS: available remedies

AVENUE *(Means of attainment),* ***noun*** approach, course, course of action, customary way, definite procedure, formula, manner, manner of working, means of access, method, method of attack, mode, mode of operation, procedure, process, scheme, standard procedure, system, tack, technique, way, ways and means

AVENUE *(Route),* ***noun*** approach, boulevard, channel, corridor, course, egress, entrance, entry, ingress, passage, passageway, path, principal thoroughfare, road, roadway, street, way

AVER, *verb* acquainted with, affirm, agree, alert to, attest, avouch, circumspect, cognizant, confirm, conscious of, consent, conversant with, declare, defend, depose, discerning, emphasize, ensure, excellent judgment, familiar with, farsighted, grounded, guarantee, incisive, informed, keen judgment, knowing, knowledgeable, learned, maintain, observant, penetrating, perceptive, perspicuous, present, proclaim, profess, pronounce, prove, reaffirm, reassert, recount, regardful, sagacious, savvy, scholarly, sensitive to the situation, sophisticated, state, stress, support, swear, testify, understanding, understanding of the facts, undertake, well-informed, wise, witting
ASSOCIATED CONCEPTS: acknowledgment, affidavit, perjury

AVERAGE *(Midmost),* ***adjective*** center, centermost, intermediate, mean, mean proportioned, medial, median, mediate, medium, mid, middle, middle class, middle grade, middlemost, middling
ASSOCIATED CONCEPTS: average annual earnings or wages, average capital, average charges, average daily attendance, average daily balance, average daily wage, average price, average speed, average value, average weekly wage, general average, gross average, income averaging, particular average, petty average, simple average

AVERAGE *(Standard),* ***adjective*** common, commonplace, conventional, fair, mediocre, moderate, normal, normative, ordinary, passable, prosaic, stock, typical, unexceptional, unnoteworthy, usual
ASSOCIATED CONCEPTS: average man, average person, average quality

AVERMENT, *noun* adjuration, adjurement, affirmance, affirmation, announcement, assertion, assertment, assertory oath, asseveration, attest, attestation, avouchment, avowal, confirmation, declaration, formulation, instrument

in proof, positive declaration, positive statement, profession, pronouncement, solemn affirmation, statement of facts, statement on oath, swearing, testification, vouching, written statement
ASSOCIATED CONCEPTS: averment of facts, descriptive averment, general averment, material averment, negative averment, particular averments, pleading, unnecessary averments

AVERSE, ***adjective*** adverse, *alienus,* antagonistic, antipathetic, *aversus,* disinclined, disliking, hostile, indisposed, inimical, loath, opposed, reluctant, repelled, repugnant, revolted, undesirous, unfavorable, unwilling

AVERT, ***verb*** *amovere,* arrest, *avertere,* avoid, change the course of, check, counteract, deflect, deter, divert, fend off, forestall, head off, intercept, make possible the avoidance of, parry, prevent, *prohibere,* shove aside, shunt, stave off, thwart, turn, turn aside, turn away, turn to the side, ward off
ASSOCIATED CONCEPTS: averting danger

AVOID *(Cancel),* ***verb*** annul, defeat, destroy the efficacy of, invalidate, make inoperative, make of no effect, make void, make wholly without effect, refute, vacate, void

AVOID *(Evade),* ***verb*** abstain from, avert, balk at, decline, depart from, dodge, elude, escape, eschew, flee from, forbear, forsake, have nothing to do with, hold back, keep at a distance from, keep away from, keep clear of, make off, part company, refrain from, retreat, shun, shy away from, *vitare*

AVOIDANCE *(Cancellation),* ***noun*** abrogation, annulling, annulment, canceling, cessation, discontinuation, dismissal, invalidation, making useless, nullifying, quashing, removal, rendering void, rescission, setting aside, vacating, vacation, voidance
ASSOCIATED CONCEPTS: avoidable preference, avoidance of contract, avoidance of will
FOREIGN PHRASES: ***Falsa demonstratione legatum non perimi.*** A legacy is not nullified by an erroneous description.

AVOIDANCE *(Evasion),* ***noun*** bypass, detour, deviation, dodge, elusion, eschewment, evasion, evasive action, parrying, refraining, retreat, shunning, sidestep
ASSOCIATED CONCEPTS: avoidable consequences, avoidance by the courts of question of constitutionality, avoidance of consequences, avoidance of risk, confession and avoidance, last clear chance, pleading in avoidance

AVOISON, ***noun*** aggressively skirting the law, ahead of the law in tax, avoiding tax liability, ensuring minimum tax liability, exploit a legal ambiguity in tax, exploiting a legal loophole in tax, legal loophole, planning tax avoidance, pursuing a legal gray area in tax

AVOUCH *(Avow),* ***verb*** acknowledge, affirm, affirm with confidence, allege, allege as a fact, assert, assert peremptorily, assert positively, assert under oath, asseverate, attest, aver, bear witness, certify, confirm, confirm by oath, contend, declare, declare openly, declare with positiveness, depose, maintain, make an assertion, make open affirmation, make solemn affirmation, proclaim, profess, pronounce, propound, put in an affidavit, reaffirm, reassert, solemnly affirm, state, state as true, state with conviction, swear, swear an oath, swear the truth, testify, vouch, vow

AVOUCH *(Guarantee),* ***verb*** assume responsibility for, assure, authenticate, back, be answerable for, be surety for, certify, endorse, ensure, give assurance, insure, pledge, pledge one's word, sponsor, underwrite, verify, vouch for, warrant

AVOUCHMENT, ***noun*** acknowledgment, adjuration, affirmance, affirmation, assertion, asseveration, assurance, attest, attestation, averment, avowal, avowance, declaration, formulation, oath, open statement of affirmation, positive assertion, positive statement, proclamation, pronouncement, public declaration, solemn averment, solemn avowal, solemn declaration, statement of facts, swearing, testification, vouch, vow
ASSOCIATED CONCEPTS: affidavit

AVOW, ***verb*** acknowledge, admit, admit frankly, affirm, allege as a fact, articulate, assert, assert on oath, assert peremptorily, assert under oath, asseverate, attest, authenticate, aver, avouch, be bound, bear witness, certify, commit oneself, confess, confirm, *confiteri,* contend, declare, declare openly, declare positively, declare the truth of, depose, enunciate, express, *fateri,* formulate, maintain, make a statement, make an assertion, postulate, predicate, proclaim, profess, *profiteri,* pronounce, propound, protest, set down, speak, state, state as true, state with conviction, swear, take one's oath, testify, vouch, vow, witness
ASSOCIATED CONCEPTS: affidavit, testimony

AVOWAL, ***noun*** acknowledgment, adjurement, affirmance, affirmation, assertion, asseveration, attestation, authentication, averment, *aveu,* avouchment, avowance, *confessio,* confession, confirmation, contention, corroboration, declaration, endorsement, legal pledge, open declaration, positive statement, profession, pronouncement, protestation, statement, statement on oath, testimony, validation, verification

AVULSION, ***noun*** divulsion, evulsion, forcible extraction, plucking out, ripping out, tearing away, tearing off, violent separation, wresting
ASSOCIATED CONCEPTS: accretion, erosion, riparian rights

AWARD, ***noun*** act of judgment, action, adjudgment, adjudication, authoritative decision, decision, decree, determination, edict, finding, grant, judication, judicial decision, judicial sentence, opinion, order, order of the court, pronouncement, pronouncement by a court, recorded expression of a formal judgment, resolution, result, ruling, ruling of the court, verdict, warrant
ASSOCIATED CONCEPTS: arbitration and award, award of damages, compensatory award, confirmation of an award, monetary award, punitive award

AWARD, ***verb*** act on, *addicere, adiudicare,* adjudge, adjudge to be due, adjudicate, bestow by judicial decree, bring in a verdict, conclude, decide, decree, decree by deliberate judgment, decree to be merited, deliver judgment, determine, establish, find, fix, ordain, order, pass judgment, pass sentence, pass upon, pronounce, pronounce judgment, pronounce on, rule, settle

AWARE, ***adjective*** acquainted, alert, apperceptive, apprehensive, apprised, astute, aware, clear-sighted, cognitive, cognizant, comprehending, conscious, conversant, discerning, discriminating, knowing, knowledgeable, familiar, informed, percipient, perspicacious, proficient, sagacious, sensible to, understood, well-posted, well-versed

AWAY, *adjective* at a distance, distant, far, far away, far-off, further away, in the background, in the distance, inaccessible, long distance, long range, out of range, out of reach, out of sight, outlying, remote, removed, separated, unapproachable, uncommunicative, unresponsive

AWE, *verb* affect, amaze, arouse, astonish, astound, blow away, bowl over, bulldoze, electrify, excel, excite, grab, grandstand, impress, inspire, move, outdo, pique, show off, stimulate, stir, strike, stun, succeed, thrill

AWFUL, *adjective* abhorrent, abominable, atrocious, beneath contempt, contemptible, deplorable, despicable, detestable, dreadful, drive, foul, frightening, frightful, ghastly, ghoulish, gruesome, harrowing, hateful, heinous, horrendous, horrid, horrifying, indefensible, loathsome, macabre, obnoxious, odious, offensive, outrageous, pathetic, pitiful, repellent, reprehensible, repulsive, revolting, shameful, shocking, terrible, terrifying, unspeakable, vile, villainous, wholly inadequate
ASSOCIATED CONCEPTS: deplorable conditions

AWKWARD *(Inconsistent)*, ***adjective*** conflicting, cumbersome, discordant, disparate, ill-advised, improper, inapplicable, inapposite, inappropriate, incongruous, inconsistent, maladroit, misdirected, misguided, nonconforming, out of place, painful, peculiar, unfit, unsettling, unsound, unsuitable, wrong

AWKWARD *(Inelegant)*, ***adjective*** abashed, amateurish, boorish, botched, bungling, careless, clumsy, crude, fumbled, graceless, incompetent, inept, inexpert, sloppy, tacky, tactless, uncouth, undiplomatic, ungainly, unpolished, unprofessional, unskilled

AXIOMATIC, *adjective* a priori, absolute, aphoristic, apodictic, apparent, ascertained, assured, beyond all question, beyond dispute, categorical, certain, decided, decisive, definite, determinate, doubtless, incontestable, incontrovertible, indubious, indubitable, irrefutable, manifest, positive, questionless, self-evident, sententious, solid, sure, unambiguous, unchallengeable, uncontested, undeniable, undisputed, undoubted, unequivocal, unimpeachable, unmistakable, unquestionable, unquestioned, well-founded

BABY, *noun* bairn, changeling, child, fledgling, infant, juvenile, kid, minor, toddler, young innocent, youngling
ASSOCIATED CONCEPTS: abortion, adoption, baby act, illegitimacy

BACK *(In arrears)*, ***adjective*** behind, behind time, belated, deferred, delayed, detained, earlier, elapsed, expired, fore, forgotten, former, in abeyance, late, long-delayed, overdue, past, prior, tardy, unpunctual, unready
ASSOCIATED CONCEPTS: back pay, back taxes, back time doctrine, back wages

BACK *(In reverse)*, ***adjective*** backward, hindermost, hindmost, hindward, posterior, rearmost, rearward, retrogressive, retrospective, reversed, turned around
ASSOCIATED CONCEPTS: back lands

BACKBONE, *noun* ardor, audacity, boldness, cornerstone, courage, dependency, determination, earnestness, embodiment, endurance, firmness, fortitude, gist, ground, indefatigability, intestinal fortitude, main point, mainstay, marrow, mettle, nerve, pillar, pith, pluck, quality, resoluteness, resolution, resolve, spine, steadfastness, strength, substance, support, tenacity, underpinning, valor, vigor, will

BACKER, *noun* abettor, adherent, adjunct, adjutant, adjuvant, advocate, aider, ally, assister, auxiliary, benefactor, champion, coadjutant, coadjutor, coadjuvant, defender, endorser, ensurer, exponent, fautor, guarantor, helper, investor, lender, mainstay, maintainer, mortgatee, partisan, patron, promoter, protagonist, protector, reliever, second, seconder, sectary, sponsor, subsidizer, supporter, sustainer, sympathizer, upholder, warrantor

BACKGROUND *(Framework)*, ***noun*** awareness, command of the facts, comprehension, context, familiarity of the facts, insight, knowledge

BACKGROUND *(History)*, ***noun*** abilities, accomplishments, aptitude, biography, capacity, circumstances, credentials, curriculum vitae, CV, deeds, education, endowment, experience, expertise, in-depth experience, knowledge, mastership, past, pedigree, potentiality, preparation, qualifications, record, résumé, specialty, strong suit, suitability, training

BACKGROUND *(Rear Area)*, ***noun*** aft, area in the back, back, behind area, posterior, rear, rear area, rear locale, rear scene, rear scenery, rear surroundings

BACKING, *noun* advocacy, aegis, aid, approval, assistance, auspices, bolstering, championing, charity, comfort, commendation, cooperation, coverage, defense, encouragement, favor, financing, furtherance, guarantee, guidance, help, indorsement, interest, investment, loan, maintenance, patronage, promotion, protection, reinforcement, relief, seconding, security, service, sponsorship, strengthening, subsidy, succor, support, sustenance, warranty

BACKSLIDING, ***verb*** about face, adoption, afterthoughts, change like a chameleon, change of heart, change of mind, conversion, defection, diametrically opposed stance, divergence, diversion, flip-flop, 180 degree about face, qualification, realignment, regression, restructuring, reversal, reversion, temporizer, tergiversation, turn of the tide, turnabout
ASSOCIATED CONCEPTS: flip-flop on a political stance

BACKWARD, ***adjective*** arrested, behindhand, belated, dallying, defected, delayed, delaying, dilatory, impeded, late, mentally deficient, overdue, procrastinating, regressive, retarded, retroactive, retrograde, reversed, slow, subnormal, tardy, untimely

BAD *(Inferior)*, ***adjective*** adultered, base, decaying, defective, degenerative, degraded, deleterious, deplorable, deteriorated, detrimental, dreadful, faulty, foul, fulsome, imperfect, impure, injurious, malignant, *malus,* noxious, objectionable, ruined, undesirable, unfit, unsound, unsuitable
ASSOCIATED CONCEPTS: bad bargain, bad check, bad title

BAD *(Offensive)*, ***adjective*** abhorrent, abominable, accusable, amoral, arrant, atrocious, baleful, baneful, base, contemptible, corrupt, cruel, debauched, degenerate, degraded, demoralized, deplorable, depraved, derogatory, despicable, destructive, detrimental, diabolic, dire, disastrous, disgraced, disgusting, dishonorable, disreputable, evil, execrable, flagitious, flagrant, fulsome, heinous, ignoble, immoral, *improbus,* improper, indecent, infamous, iniquitous, injurious, insidious, loathsome, maleficent, malevolent, malific, *malus,* miscreant, monstrous, nasty, nefarious, *nequam,* nocuous, objectionable, obnoxious, odious, offensive, onerous, oppressive, opprobrious, peccant, perfidious, pernicious, reprehensible, reprobate, repugnant, repulsive, retrogressive, revolting, ruined, ruinous, scandalous, sinful, sinister, treacherous, troublous, turpitudinous, undesirable, unfit, unsuitable, unvirtuous, venal, vicious, vile, villainous, virtueless, wicked
ASSOCIATED CONCEPTS: bad behavior, bad character, bad faith, bad influence, bad motive, bad reputation, bad repute
FOREIGN PHRASES: ***In facto quod se habet ad bonum et malum, magis de bono quam de malo lex intendit.*** In an act or deed which may be considered as both good and bad, the law directs its attention more to the good than the bad.

BAD CHARACTER, ***noun*** bad name, bad reputation, bad repute, baseness, discredit, discreditableness, disesteem, disfavor, disgrace, dishonor, dishonorableness, disreputability, disrepute, ignobility, ignominy, ill favor, ill repute, infamy, lowness, reproachability, undesirability, unrespectability
ASSOCIATED CONCEPTS: character evidence, credibility, impeachment of credibility, imputation of character, reputation, slander

BAD CHECK, ***noun*** deceptive check, defective check, forged check, fraudulent check, inutile check, invalid check, nugatory check, returned check, rubber check, suppositious check, unmarketable check, unserviceable check, unsound check, useless check, valueless check, void check, worthless check
ASSOCIATED CONCEPTS: criminal charge of worthless checkwriting

BAD DEBT, ***noun*** dishonored bill, inconvertible bill, irredeemable bill, irretrievable debt, loss, outstanding debt, protested bill, uncollectible debt, write-off
ASSOCIATED CONCEPTS: bad debt loss, bad debt tax deduction

BAD FAITH, ***noun*** abjection, abjectness, abscondence, apostasy, artifice, base conduct, betrayal, betrayment, breach of faith, broken faith, broken promise, collaboration, collusion, complicity, connivance, cozenage, debasement, deceit, deceitfulness, deception, defalcation, defection, delusion, delusiveness, dereliction, dereliction of duty, deviation from rectitude, deviousness, disaffection, disavowal, dishonesty, dishonor, disingenuousness, disloyalty, disobedience, disrepute, double-dealing, duplicity, fallaciousness, false pretenses, false pretension, false swearing, falseheartedness, falseness, forswearing, fraud, fraudulency, furtiveness, guile, hypocrisy, ignominy, improbity, indiscretion, infidelity, infraction, insidiousness, insincerity, inveracity, lack of conscience, lack of fidelity, lack of principle, lack of probity, *mala fides,* malversation, mendaciousness, mendacity, meretriciousness, misfeasance, misrepresentation, obliquity, peculation, perfidiousness, perfidy, pettifoggery, pretense, pretext, punic faith, recantation, recreancy, reprobacy, sedition, seditiousness, spuriousness, subterfuge, subversion, subversive activity, suppression of truth, surreptitiousness, suspiciousness, traitorousness, treacherousness, treachery, truthlessness, turpitude, unauthenticity, unconscientiousness, underhand dealing, unfairness, unfaith, unfaithfulness, unfaithworthiness, ungenuineness, unloyalty, unscrupulousness, unsteadfastness, untrueness, untrustiness, untrustworthiness, untruthfulness, unveraciousness, unveracity, unverity, venality, violation of allegiance, violation of duty
ASSOCIATED CONCEPTS: fraud

BAD JUDGMENT, ***noun*** aberrancy, aberration, blunder, distortion, errancy, erroneousness, error, fallacy, falseness, faultiness, inattention, indiscretion, inexactness, misapplication, miscalculation, misconception, misestimation, misinterpretation, misjudgment, misreckoning, mistake, perversion, wrong verdict
ASSOCIATED CONCEPTS: bad behavior, bad faith, bad judgment, bad motives

BAD REPUTE, ***noun*** abasement, abjection, abjectness, abomination, allegation, amoralism, amorality, animadversion, antagonism, aspersion, attaint, bad character, bad influence, bad name, betrayal, calumniation, calumny, castigation, censoriousness, censure, charge, condemnation, confutation, contemptibility, contumely, corruption, criminality, crimination, criticism, debasement, decrial, defilement, degeneracy, degradation, delinquency, demoralization, denigration, denunciation, depravity, deprecation, derision, derogation, despicability, despicableness, detraction, deviation from rectitude, deviation from virtue, deviousness, disapprobation, discommendation, discountenance, discredit, disesteem, disfavor, disgrace, disgracefulness, dishonor, dishonorableness, disparagement, displacency, disreputability, disreputableness, disrepute, disrespectability, disrespectfulness, excoriation, exposure, flagitiousness, flagrancy, fraud, fraudulence, ignobility, ignominiousness, ignominy, ill repute, immorality, impaired reputation, improbation, improbity, impropriety, impugnation, increpation, inculpation, indecorum, infamousness, infamy, infidelity, insolence, irreverence, lack of integrity, laxity, loss of honor, loss of reputation, low regard, low standard, maculation, malevolence, malignity, malversation, misbehavior, moral degeneracy, moral turpitude, notoriety, objurgation, obliquity, obloquy, obnoxiousness, obtrectation, odiousness, odium, opprobrium, peccability, peculation,

perfidiousness, perfidy, perversity, prodition, profligacy, public reproach, rapacity, rebuke, reflection, reprehension, reprimand, reproach, reprobation, reproof, revilement, scurrility, sedition, shame, shamefulness, slight, stigma, stricture, suspiciousness, taint, traducement, transgression, turpitude, unacceptableness, unrespectability, unscrupulousness, venality, vice, vilification, vilipendency, want of principle
ASSOCIATED CONCEPTS: character evidence, credibility of witness, moral turpitude, reputation

BADGER, ***verb*** abuse, afflict, aggravate, aggrieve, annoy, annoy excessively, assail, bait, beset, bother, bully, chafe, discomfort, discommode, discompose, disconcert, disquiet, distress, disturb, disturb keenly, exasperate, excruciate, fret, goad, grate, harass, harrow, harry, heckle, hector, hound, importune, incommode, irk, irritate, mortify, nettle, oppress, perplex, persecute, perturb, pester, pique, plague, provoke, rile, roil, ruffle, taunt, tease, torment, torture, trouble, try one's patience, vex, worry

BAFFLE, ***verb*** balk, befog, beguile, bewilder, bluff, bother, check, circumvent, complicate, confound, confuse, cross, defeat, discomfort, disconcert, dismay, disrupt, evade, flummox, fool, frustrate, fuddle, hoax, hinder, impede, incommode, inconvenience, irk, muddle, mystify, nonplus, obfuscate, obstruct, outwit, perplex, perturb, puzzle, stall, stymie, swindle, thwart, trick, upset

BAIL, ***noun*** assurance, bond, caution money, collateral, earnest, gage, guaranty, indemnity, *pignus,* pledge, security, surety, undertaking
ASSOCIATED CONCEPTS: admission to bail, bail bond, bail piece, bonds, cash bail, common bail, excessive bail, execute on bail, forfeiture of bail, *ne exeat,* recognizance, reduction of bail, release on bail, revocation of bail, special bail, straw bail

BAILIWICK, ***noun*** area, arena, authority, circle, department, district, domain, dominion, enclave, field, haunt, jurisdiction, orbit, precinct, province, purlieu, realm, region, specialty, sphere, sway, territory, ward

BAILMENT, ***noun*** giving up, held in pledge, in escrow, transferred, under control

BAILOUT, ***noun*** appropriation, back, bankroll, capitalize, contribution, donation, financial assistance, financial backing, fund, funding, grant, help, investment, rescue, sponsor, subsidization, support, underwrite a grant
ASSOCIATED CONCEPTS: Emergency Economic Stabilization Act, financial bailout, government bailout, Troubled Asset Relief Program

BAIT *(Harass),* ***verb*** afflict, affront, aggravate, aggrieve, agitate, agonize, anger, annoy, arouse, attack, badger, be malevolent, be offensive, beset, besiege, bother, browbeat, cause resentment, chafe, compel, deride, detract, discommode, displease, distract, distress, disturb, dragoon, embitter, enflame, enrage, envenom, exasperate, excite, excite indignation, exhort, give offense to, give umbrage to, goad, grate, harry, haze, heckle, hector, hound, impel, importune, incense, incite, incommode, inconvenience, inflame, inflict, infuriate, instigate, insult, intimidate, irk, irritate, macerate, make wrathful, malign, maltreat, menace, offend, oppress, outrage, peeve, perplex, persecute, perturb, pique, plague, prey upon, provoke, pursue, put out of countenance, put pressure on, raid, rankle, rile, rouse, solicit insistently, spur, taunt, tease, terrorize, threaten, torment, trouble, try one's patience, tyrannize, urge, vex, victimize, worry

BAIT *(Lure),* ***verb*** actuate, allure, appeal to, attract, bamboozle, befool, beguile, bias, chouse, compel, cozen, deceive, decoy, delude, dispose, draw, dupe, enlist, enmesh, ensnare, entangle, entice, entrap, entreat, entreaty, evoke, excite, exert pressure, exhort, forelay, gammon, goad, hold out allurement, impel, importune, incite, induce, influence, inveigle, lead astray, lead into temptation, lobby, persuade, predispose, press, prevail upon, provoke, seduce, snare, solicit, stimulate, suborn, swindle, take advantage of, tantalize, tease, tempt, titillate, trap, trepan, trick, urge
ASSOCIATED CONCEPTS: bait advertising, entrapment

BALANCE *(Amount in excess),* ***noun*** carry-over, excess, extra, leftover, margin, oddments, overflow, overmeasure, overplus, overrun, oversupply, plus, *reliquus,* remainder, remaining portion, remains, remnant, residual, residual portion, residue, residuum, spare, superfluity, superfluousness, superplus, surfeit, surplus, surplusage
ASSOCIATED CONCEPTS: balance due

BALANCE *(Equality),* ***noun*** analagousness, commensurability, comparability, comparableness, comparativeness, correspondence, equalization, equation, equilibration, equilibrium, equipoise, equipollence, equiponderance, equivalence, homeostasis, level, *libro,* neutralization of forces, parity, stabilization, stable equilibrium, state of equilibrium, symmetrical scales, symmetry
ASSOCIATED CONCEPTS: balance account, balance of convenience, balance of hardship, balance sheet, balancing equities

BALANCED, ***adjective*** cadenced, cadent, coextensive, consonant, consistent, constant, equable, equal, equiponderant, equitable, even, evenhanded, fair, firm, fluent, harmonious, just, level, measured, on an even keel, orderly, poised, proportionate, proportioned, rational, regular, sane, square, symmetrical, uniform
ASSOCIATED CONCEPTS: balance of convenience, balance of power, balance of the equities

BALD, ***adjective*** arrant, artless, austere, bare, bawdy, blank, blunt, colorless, disclosed, dull, evident, exact, exposed, factual, flagrant, flat, glaring, insipid, laconic, literal, manifest, mere, obvious, open, outright, overt, plain, raw, revealed, ribald, severe, simple, stark, straightforward, tame, unabstructed, unadorned, undisguised, unembellished, unembroidered, ungarnished, uninteresting, unmistakable, unmitigated, unqualified, unsupported, unvarnished, vapid

BALEFUL, ***adjective*** bad, baneful, calamitous, damaging, dangerous, deadly, deleterious, despiteful, destructive, detrimental, dire, disadvantageous, evil, harmful, heinous, hurtful, ill-omened, inauspicious, insalubrious, lethal, malefic, malevolent, malicious, malignant, mischievous, nocuous, noxious, ominous, pernicious, pestilent, poisonous, portentous, prejudicial, sinister, spiteful, unpropitious, venomous, virulent

BALK, ***verb*** avert, baffle, bar, be obstructive, block, check, counter, counteract, countercheck, curb, defeat, delay, detain, *eludere,* estop, foil, forefend, forestall, *frustrari,* frustrate, give trouble, halt, hamper, hinder, hold in check, hold back, impede, impedite, interlope, interrupt, keep in check, nullify, obstruct, obturate, obviate, occlude, prevent, put in check, restrain, stall, stand in the way, stay, stop, stop short, stultify, stymie, suspend, thwart, traverse

BALLOT, ***noun*** election, election outcome, election results, poll, polling, referendum, vote

BAN, *verb* abrogate, banish, bar, block, censor, check, declare illegal, deny, disallow, disqualify, embargo, enjoin, estop, exclude, forbid, foreclose, forfend, interdict, obstruct, outlaw, prevent, prohibit, proscribe, refuse, refuse permission, repress, restrain, say no to, shut off, shut out, stay, stop, suppress, taboo, veto, withhold permission
ASSOCIATED CONCEPTS: ban on Sunday sales

BANAL, *adjective* colorless, common, commonplace, conventional, deadly, drab, dreary, dull, hackneyed, familiar, flat, insipid, lifeless, matter of fact, mediocre, mundane, ordinary, pedestrian, platitudinous, simple, stale, stereotyped, stuffy, tedious, timeworn, traditional, trite, unimaginative, uninteresting, unoriginal, usual, vapid, worn

BAND, *noun* alliance, army, array, association, bevy, body, cabal, coalition, collection, combination, confederation, congregation, corps, coterie, covey, crew, detail, force, gang, *grex,* group, horde, league, legion, movement, outfit, pack, panel, phalanx, squad, team, tribe, troop, troupe, *turba,* unit

BANEFUL, *adjective* bad, baleful, corrosive, damaging, dangerous, deadly, deleterious, destructive, detrimental, disadvantageous, disastrous, disserviceable, evil, fatal, harmful, heinous, hostile, hurtful, insalubrious, injurious, lethal, malevolent, malignant, mischievous, noisome, noxious, pernicious, pestilent, poisonous, prejudicial, ruinous, sinister, threatening, toxic, unwholesome, venomous, virulent

BANISH, *verb* abandon, ban, bar, cast out, condemn, deport, dismiss, dispel, disperse, displace, drive out, eliminate, exclude, excommunicate, exile, expatriate, expel, export, extradite, isolate, ostracize, oust, outlaw, prohibit, proscribe, reject, remove, renounce, seclude, transport, turn out

BANISHMENT, *noun* deportation, discharge, dismissal, displacement, ejection, eviction, excommunication, exile, exilement, expatriation, expulsion, extradition, *interdictio aquae et ignis,* involuntary exile, ostracism, ostracization, ousting, outlawry, *relegatio,* removal

BANK, *noun* bursary, cash box, coffer, depository, monetary reservoir, money box, pecuniary resource, promptuary, public treasury, repository, reserve, safe, safe-deposit vault, storehouse, strongroom, till, vault
ASSOCIATED CONCEPTS: bank account, bank bill, bank certificate, bank check, bank collections, bank deposit, bank draft, bank examiner, bank money order, bank note, bank of deposit, bank of issue, bank robber, bank stock, bank transaction, bank withdrawal, bankbook, banker's acceptance, banker's lien, banking hours, banking powers, banking privileges, commercial bank, savings bank

BANKRUPT, *adjective* bereft, broke, broken, *decoctor,* defaulting, destitute, failed, impecunious, impoverished, in receivership, in the hands of receivers, incapable of discharging liabilities, indigent, insolvent, left in penury, moneyless, out of funds, out of money, pauperized, penniless, poverty-stricken, ruined, unable to make both ends meet, unable to pay matured debts, unable to satisfy creditors, unmoneyed
ASSOCIATED CONCEPTS: bankruptcy, bankruptcy court, discharge in bankruptcy, estate of the bankrupt

BANKRUPTCY, *noun* defaulting, destituteness, destitution, failure, financial disaster, financial failure, financial ruin, impecuniosity, inability to pay, indigence, insolvency, involuntary liquidation, loss, loss of fortune, pauperism, penury, privation, ruin, ruination
ASSOCIATED CONCEPTS: adverse claims, arrangement for the benefit of creditors, bankruptcy act, bankruptcy assets, bankruptcy court, bankruptcy estate, bankruptcy proceedings, composition in bankruptcy, composition proceedings, discharge in bankruptcy, foreclosure, fraudulent conveyance, fraudulent transfers, involuntary bankruptcy, preferences, priorities, provable debts, receivers in bankruptcy, referees in bankruptcy, reorganization proceedings, sale of assets, schedules, trustee in bankruptcy, valuation, void preference, voidable transfer

BAR *(Body of lawyers),* *noun* advocates, attorneys, attorneys-at-law, barristers, counsel, counselors, counselors-at-law, jurists, lawyers, the legal fraternity, legal profession, legists, solicitors
ASSOCIATED CONCEPTS: bar association, member of the bar

BAR *(Court),* *noun* assize, bench, court of justice, court of law, *curia, forum,* judicature, judiciary, seat of justice, sessions, tribunal
ASSOCIATED CONCEPTS: bar of justice

BAR *(Obstruction),* *noun* balk, ban, barricade, barrier, block, blockage, circumscription, constraint, curb, difficulty, embargo, enjoining, estoppel, exclusion, forbiddance, foreclosure, forestalling, hindrance, hurdle, impediment, impedition, infarction, injunction, interdict, interference, limit, limitation, nonadmission, noninclusion, obstacle, preclusion, prevention, prohibition, proscription, refusal, rejection, restraint, stoppage, stopper, stumbling block, suppression
ASSOCIATED CONCEPTS: bar by former judgment, estoppel

BAR *(Exclude),* *verb* ban, blacklist, circumscribe, debar, deny, disallow, except, exile, forbid, interdict, keep out, leave out, limit, lock out, occlude, omit, ostracize, outlaw, preclude, prevent, prohibit, refuse, reject, relegate, restrict, shut out, spurn, suspend

BAR *(Hinder),* *verb* avert, barricade, block, blockade, bolt, bridle, choke, choke off, curb, embar, enjoin, erect a barrier, estop, fasten, fence, forbid, foreclose, frustrate, hamper, impede, inhibit, interfere with, obstruct, obviate, occlude, preclude, prevent, prohibit, proscribe, put an embargo on, put one's veto upon, repress, restrain, retard, seal, secure, shut off, stand in the way, stay, stop, thwart, trammel

BAR SINISTER, *noun* bastardism, bastardization, bastardy, baton, birth out of wedlock, champain, illegitimacy, illegitimateness, illegitimation, illicit procreation, misbegetting, unlawful begetting

BARE, *verb* admit, air, announce, appear, be disclosed, be public, bring into view, bring out in evidence, bring to light, confess, declare, denude, disclose, display, divulgate, divulge, evince, evulgate, exhibit, expose, expose to view, lay bare, lay open, make apparent, make evident, make known, make manifest, make public, manifest, open, open up, publicize, represent, reveal, set forth evidence, show, surface, tell the truth, uncloak, unclothe, unconceal, uncover, uncurtain, undisguise, undrape, unfold, unfurl, unmask, unscreen, unseal, unsheathe, unshield, unshroud, unveil, unwrap, vent, ventilate

BARGAIN, *noun* accord, accordance, agreement, arrangement, collective agreement, compact, compromise, concord, concordance, concordat, contract, convention, covenant, entente, mutual agreement, mutual pledge, mutual

understanding, mutual undertaking, pact, *pactio,* settlement, stipulation, treaty, understanding
ASSOCIATED CONCEPTS: arm's-length bargain, bargain and sale deed, bargain and sale in a conveyance, bargain collectively, bargain in good faith, bargain in restraint of trade, bargaining agent, bargaining unit, benefit of the bargain rule, collective bargaining, collective bargaining agreement

BARGAIN FOR, *verb* agree to, anticipate, assume, bank on, buy, calculate on, come to terms, contemplate, contract for, count upon, covenant, expect, figure on, foresee, incur, look for, plan on, prepare for, reckon on, specify, stipulate, surmise, think likely

BAROMETER, *noun* climate, conclusion, criterion, feeling, gauge, measure, model, norm, outcome, pattern, result, rule, scale, sounding board, standard, test, touchstone, type, yardstick

BARRAGE, *noun* artillery fire, assault, attack, blare, blast, blitz, bombardment, bombings, boom, broadside, burst, cannonade, clamor, concentration, covering fire, cross fire, explosions, fire, gunfire, protective fire, roar, salvo, shelling, shower, siege, spray, storm, storming, thunder, verbal assault, volley

BARRED, *adjective* banned, debarred, disallowed, excepted, excluded, precluded, prohibited, proscribed, shut out

BARREN, *adjective* arid, bare, childless, desolate, disused, empty, fallow, fruitless, functionless, idle, impotent, inactive, inane, infecund, infertile, insufficient, issueless, nonfertile, nonproducing, nonproductive, profitless, scarce, shallow, sparse, stagnating, sterile, teemless, unable to yield, unfertile, unfruitful, ungerminating, unprocreant, unproductive, unprofitable, unprolific, unrewarded, unrewarding, unsalable, unyielding, vacant, vacuous, valueless, void, void of contents, waste, wasteful, without issue, worthless
ASSOCIATED CONCEPTS: barren land

BARRICADE, *noun* bar, barrier, blockade, bulwark, damper, dike, embankment, fortification, impediment, obstacle, obstruction, protection, rampart, restraint, stockade, wall

BARRICADE *(Hinder),* ***verb*** bar, block, check, deter, enjoin, halt, hamper, impede, lock, obstruct, occlude, shut, stop

BARRICADE *(Protect),* ***verb*** bolt, close, close off, confine, constrict, contain, dam up, defend, dig in, enclose, entrench, fasten, fence in, fortify, lock up, picket, secure, shut out

BARRIER, *noun* bar, barricade, bound, boundary, bulwark, check, confines, enclosure, encumbrance, fence, fortification, hindrance, hurdle, impediment, interference, limit, obstacle, obstruction, partition, prevention, preventive, prohibition, protective device, rampart, restraining device, restraint, restriction, safeguard, stay, stop, stumbling block, termination, wall

BARRISTER, *noun* advocate, attorney, attorney-at-law, counsel, counselor, counselor-at-law, jurisconsult, jurisprudent, jurist, lawyer, learned counsel, legal advisor, legal practitioner, legist, member of the bar, procurator, publicist, solicitor

BARTER, *verb* bargain, buy and sell, deal, dicker, exchange, give and take, give in exchange, haggle, interchange, make exchanges, market, *merces mutare,* merchandise, peddle, *rem pro re pacisci, rem re mutare,* strike a bargain, swap, switch, trade, trade by exchange, trade off, traffic by exchange, vend

BASE *(Bad),* ***adjective*** contemptible, cowardly, despicable, despised, disreputable, heinous, immoral, odious, virtueless, wicked

BASE *(Inferior),* ***adjective*** abject, cheap, common, dilapidated, dirty, lowly, mean, menial, poor

BASE *(Foundation),* ***noun*** basis, cause, pivotal argument, starting point, support

BASE *(Place),* ***noun*** abode, center, central headquarters, headquarters, place, station

BASED ON, *adverb* bear upon, built on, contingent upon, dependent on, founded on, grounded on, relying on, rested on

BASELESS, *adjective* bottomless, empty, erroneous, false, foundationless, gratuitous, groundless, having no foundation, idle, ill-founded, illogical, nonactual, not well-founded, rootless, unbased, uncaused, uncorroborated, unfounded, ungrounded, unjustifiable, unprincipled, unreasonable, unsound, unsubstantial, unsubstantiated, unsupportable, unsupported, unsustainable, unsustained, untenable, unwarranted, vain, without base, without basis, without cause, without reality, without reason

BASIC, *adjective* *a priori,* aboriginal, central, elementary, essential, fundamental, implicit, indispensable, initial, innate, integral, intrinsic, material, monolithic, native, necessary, organic, original, practical, primary, prime, primitive, primordial, requisite, rudimentary, simple, substantial, substantive, ultimate, underlying, virtual, vital
ASSOCIATED CONCEPTS: basic patent, basic understanding of the law

BASIC FACTS, *noun* essentials, the case, the facts in the matter, the facts of the case, the whole story

BASIS, *noun* assumption, authority, background, base, cause, essence, foundation, fulcrum, fundamentals, *fundus,* ground, groundwork, hypothesis, justification, motive, origin, premise, principle, proposition, purpose, *raison d'être,* rationale, reason, root, source, support, underlying principle, warrant
ASSOCIATED CONCEPTS: basis of cost, basis of keeping accounts, basis of the bargain, cash basis, contingency basis, cost-plus basis

BASTARD, *noun* adulterine, bantling, child born before marriage, child born out of wedlock, illegitimate child, nothus, *nullius filius,* spurious issue
ASSOCIATED CONCEPTS: acknowledgment, bastardy proceeding, illegitimate, inheritance, legitimacy support, putative father
FOREIGN PHRASES: ***Bastardus non potest habere haeredem nisi de corpore suo legitime procreatum.*** A bastard cannot have an heir unless he is one lawfully begotten of his own body. ***Bastardus nullius est filius, aut filius populi.*** A bastard is the son of no one, or the son of the people. ***Non est justum aliquem antenatum post mortem facere bastardum qui toto tempore vitae suae pro legitimo habebatur.*** It is not just to make anyone a bastard after his death, who during his lifetime was regarded as legitimate. ***Qui nascitur sine legitimo matrimonio, matrem sequitur.*** He who is born out of lawful matrimony succeeds to the condition

of his mother. ***Partus ex legitimo thoro non certius noscit matrem quam genitorem suum.*** The offspring of a legitimate marriage knows not his mother more certainly than his father. ***Qui ex damnato coitu nascuntur inter liberos non computentur.*** They who are born of an illicit union should not be reckoned among the children.

BASTION, *noun* asylum, bulwark, castle, citadel, defense, fort, fortification, fortress, mainstay, parapet, rampart, sanctuary, security, stronghold, tower

BATTERY, *noun* assault, attack, beating, harmful physical contact, injurious force, offensive action, onslaught, thrashing, unlawful hitting, unlawful striking, unlawful touching
ASSOCIATED CONCEPTS: assault and battery, simple battery

BATTLE *(Dispute),* ***noun*** action, affair, affray, argument, campaign, clash, collision, conflict, confrontation, contention, contest, crusade, discord, dispute, dissension, encounter, engagement, hostilities, ordeal, resistance, row, showdown, strife, struggle

BATTLE *(Fight),* ***noun*** affray, altercation, armed conflict, bout, brawl, combat, conflict, fracas, fray, free-for-all, melee, quarrel, rift, scuffle, skirmish, tussle, war, warfare

BATTLE *(Dispute),* ***verb*** altercate, argue, attack, bicker, campaign, clash, compete, contend, contest, debate, disagree, dissent, encounter, engage, grapple, litigate, oppose, resist, strike at, struggle, take on, wrangle

BATTLE *(Fight),* ***verb*** assault, attack, combat, come to blows, physically assault, pummel, resist, skirmish

BEAR *(Adduce),* ***verb*** acknowledge, acknowledge openly, adjure, admit, affirm, afford proof of, allege, allude to, argue, ascertain, assent, assert, assert absolutely, asseverate, assure, attest, authenticate, aver, avouch, avow, bring forward, bring to light, bring up, call to mind, certify, circumstantiate, cite, claim, contend, corroborate, declare, declare to be fact, demonstrate, denote, depone, depose, display, divulge, document, elucidate, emphasize, endorse, establish, evidence, evince, exemplify, exhibit, expose, express, formulate, furnish evidence, give evidence, give information, give one's word, give witness, guarantee, have evidence, illustrate, imply, indicate, inform, introduce, invoke, involve, maintain, make a statement, make an assertion, make evident, make reference to, make solemn, manifest, name, plead, pledge, point out, point to, present, proclaim, produce, produce the evidence, profess, promulgate, propound, prove, publish, ratify, refer to, represent, show, signify, stand firm, state as fact, state on oath, stipulate, submit, subscribe, substantiate, sustain, swear, take one's oath, testify, validate, verify, vindicate, vouch for, vow, warrant, witness to
ASSOCIATED CONCEPTS: bear false witness, bear witness

BEAR *(Support),* ***verb*** abet, aid, ally, assist, back, back up, bolster, brace, bulwark, buoy up, buttress, carry, champion, contribute to, cradle, cushion, *ferre,* finance, fortify, fortress, foster, furnish assistance, furnish support, furnish sustenance, garrison, *gestare,* give base, give foundation, give ground, give support, hold a brief for, hold up, justify, lend support, maintain, nourish, oblige, plead for, *portare,* promote, prop, provide for, rally to, reinforce, safeguard, sanction, second, shoulder, steady, strengthen, succor, supply aid, supply support, sustain, truss, upbear, uphold, vindicate
ASSOCIATED CONCEPTS: bear the expense, bear weight

BEAR *(Tolerate),* ***verb*** abide, accede to, accept, acquiesce, adhere to, allow, approve, be lenient, be patient, be subjected to, brave, carry on, concede, condone, continue, endure, experience, forbear, go through, keep on, keep one's countenance, labor under, live through, meet with, obey, observe, *pati,* permit, persevere, persist in, plod, put up with, recognize, resign oneself, sanction, show forbearance, spare, stand, stand the strain, submit to, suffer, suffice, support, sustain, *sustinere,* take patiently, *tolerare,* treat with indulgence, undergo, weather

BEAR *(Yield),* ***verb*** accrue, afford, aggrandize, allot, assign, augment, bestow, breed, bring about, bring forth, bring in a supply, cause, confer, contribute, convey, create, deliver, develop, dispense, earn, effectuate, emit, endow, engender, enlarge, equip, evolve, fructify, fund, furnish, gain, generate, give, give increase, grant, impart, make payment, make provision, manifest, minister to, multiply, offer, *parere,* pay back, procreate, produce, profit, proliferate, propagate, provide, provision, purvey, reinforce, remit, render, replenish, reproduce, restore, return, supply, surrender, transfer
ASSOCIATED CONCEPTS: bear interest

BEAR FALSE WITNESS, *verb* abrogate, affirm the contrary, apostatize, be deceitful, be devoid of truth, be dishonest, be erroneous, be faithless, be fallacious, be false, be forsworn, be fraudulent, be insincere, be mendacious, be perfidious, be perjured, be spurious, be untruthful, belie, betray, break faith, contradict, deny, deviate from the truth, distort, falsely testify, falsify, forswear, go back on one's word, impugn, lie, miscite, misreport, perjure oneself, pervert, prevaricate, revoke, speak falsely, swear falsely, take back, tell a lie, utter a falsehood
ASSOCIATED CONCEPTS: false swearing, perjury

BEAR THE EXPENSE, *verb* bear the cost, compensate, defray, defray expenses, defray the cost, discharge, expend, give money, incur costs, incur expenses, indemnify, make compensation, make expenditure, make payment, make restitution, meet the bill, outlay, pay an indemnity, pay compensation, pay damages, pay for, pay in full, pay on demand, pay the bill, pay the costs, pay wages, recompense, refund, reimburse, remit, remunerate, render, repay, restitute, stand the cost

BEAR UPON, *verb* advocate, affect, apply, apply to, cause, coax, concern, connect, have to do with, influence, insist, interest, involve, pertain, pertain to, press, pressure, recommend, refer, regard, relate, relate to, respect, rest on, tie in with, touch, urge
ASSOCIATED CONCEPTS: to bear upon a witness' credibility, to bear upon guilt or innocence, to bear upon the evidence, to bear upon the outcome of a case

BEAR WITNESS, *verb* acknowledge, attest, authenticate, avouch, avow, certify, corroborate, give evidence, inform on, promise, seal, sell out, speak, substantiate, swear, take the stand, tell on, testify, turn informer, turn state's evidence, vouch, witness
ASSOCIATED CONCEPTS: bear witness to a crime, bear witness to an accident, bear witness to an incident

BEARER, *noun* acceptor, carrier, casher, check holder, draft holder, grantee, holder, possessor, receiver, recipient, taker, transferee
ASSOCIATED CONCEPTS: bearer check, bearer instrument, bearer note, bearer paper, negotiable instruments

BEAT *(Defeat),* ***verb*** be superior, be supreme, be victorious over, bring to terms, checkmate, claim a victory, conquer, crush, dash, discomfit, excel, get the best of, get the better of, have the advantage, hold the advantage, lay waste, obtain a victory, outclass, outdo, outflank, outmaneuver, outplay, outpoint, outrange, outrival, overbear, overbid, overcome, overmaster, overmatch, overpower, override, overtake, overthrow, overtrump, overwhelm, predominate, preponderate, prevail over, put to rout, quell, ravage, reduce, repulse, rout, seize the advantage, subdue, subjugate, succeed in winning, *superare,* suppress, surmount, surpass, take precedence, thwart, trample upon, transcend, triumph over, undo, upset, vanquish, *vincere,* win the battle

BEAT *(Pulsate),* ***verb*** alternate, come and go, convulse, ebb and flow, falter, flicker, flitter, fluctuate, flutter, move up and down, oscillate, palpitate, pass and repass, pendulate, pound, pulse, quake, quaver, quiver, reciprocate, seesaw, shake, shiver, shuffle, strike, sway, swing, teeter, throb, thump, toss, tremble, undulate, vacillate, vibrate, wave, waver, writhe

BEAT *(Strike),* ***verb*** abuse, afflict, attack, baste, bastinado, batter, bruise, buffet, *caedere,* club, concuss, contund, contuse, cudgel, cuff, *ferire,* fight, flagellate, flail, flog, fustigate, give a blow, give a thrashing, hit, inflict, kick, knock down, lambaste, land a blow, lash, lunge at, maul, pelt, *percutere,* pound, *pulsare,* pummel, punch, punish, rap, slam, slap, slug, smack, smite, swing, thrash, thresh, trounce, truncheon, *verberare,* whip
ASSOCIATED CONCEPTS: assault, assault and battery, battery

BECAUSE, ***conjunction*** as a consequence, as a result, as long as, by cause of, by reason of, by virtue of, consequently, considering, due to, for the reason that, for the sake of, in that, in the interest of, in view of, now, now that, on behalf of, on the grounds that, over, owing to, since, thanks to, through

BECOME *(Arise),* ***verb*** befall, come about, come into being, come into existence, commence, ensue, germinate, happen, materialize, occur, proceed, result, succeed

BECOME *(Develop),* ***verb*** adorn, alter, arise, befit, behoove, benefit, beseem, change into, come to be, comport, convert, enhance, enrich, evolve, ferment, fit, garnish, harmonize with, heighten, mature, ornament, please, ripen into, satisfy, spring up, suit, take its course, turn into, turn out to be

BEDROCK, ***noun*** anchor, backbone, ballast, basis, bed, brace, bulwark, buttress, center, centerpiece, core, cornerstone, essence, focus, footing, foundation, framework, ground, grounding, groundwork, heart, infrastructure, nucleus, premise, quintessence, root, soul, strength, substructure, sum and substance, support, theory, underpinning

BEFORE, ***adverb*** a priori, above, already, antecedently, anteriorly, beforehand, earlier, early, first, formerly, preceding, preliminarily, prematurely, previous, prior

BEFORE MENTIONED, ***adjective*** above, above-cited, above-mentioned, above-named, above-stated, aforehand, aforestated, antecedent, anterior, earlier, foregoing, forementioned, forenamed, former, latter, named, precedent, preceding, precursive, precursory, preexistent, prefatory, preliminary, prepositive, prevenient, previous, prior

BEFOREHAND, ***adverb*** ahead of, already, antecedent to, as a precursor to, before now, earlier, early, in advance of, in anticipation, on the eve of, preparatory to, previous to, previously, prior to

BEGIN, ***verb*** arise, assume, broach, come into existence, commence, conceive, create, dawn, develop, embark, enter, establish, found, generate, go ahead, inaugurate, incept, initiate, institute, introduce, launch, maintain, open, originate, pave the way, pioneer, preface, prepare, promote, provoke, spring, start, start up, stem, tackle, take on, take shape, undertake, unfold, unveil

BEGINNING, ***noun*** birth, causative, commencement, conception, creation, derivation, early derivation, elementary, embryo, emergence, foundation, fountain, fountainhead, genesis, inauguration, inception, incipience, infancy, initial, kick-off, nascence, onset, opening, origin, origination, overture, preamble, precursor, preface, preliminary, prelude, prime, source, spring, stage, start, starting point

BEHALF, ***noun*** account, advantage, advocacy, aid, aidance, assistance, auspices, avail, behoof, benefaction, benefit, benevolence, betterment, boon, contribution, countenance, defense, endowment, expedience, favor, furtherance, gift, good, help, improvement, increment, interest, ministration, opportunity, preferment, profit, promotion, propriety, protection, sponsorship, stead, support, sustenance, utility, welfare
ASSOCIATED CONCEPTS: agency, representative capacity

BEHAVIOR, ***noun*** actions, air, bearing, beliefs, carriage, character, comportment, conduct, consuetude, course, course of conduct, course of life, decorum, demeanor, deportment, habits, habituation, habitude, inveteracy, line of conduct, manner, manner of life, manners, matter of course, mien, mode of action, *mores,* personal bearing, presence, propriety, ritual, ritualism, routine, way of acting, way of life
ASSOCIATED CONCEPTS: bad behavior, contemptuous behavior, good behavior, indecent behavior
FOREIGN PHRASES: ***Ad vitam aut culpam.*** For life, or until guilty of misbehavior. ***De bono gestu.*** For or during good behavior.

BEHOLD, ***verb*** catch sight of, clap eyes on, consider, descry, detect, discern, discover, distinguish, espy, examine, eye, gaze at, glimpse, heed, inspect, look, look at, look upon, make out, mark, notice, observe, perceive, pierce, recognize, regard, remark, scan, scrutinize, see, see at a glance, sight, spy, stare at, survey, take in, view, watch, witness

BEING *(Core),* ***noun*** actuality, center, character, complexion, constituent, entity, essence, identity, individuality, inherence in, intellect, lifeblood, mind, monad, nature, occurrence, presence, psyche, quiddity, reality, root, spirit, substance, truth, veracity

BEING *(Person),* ***noun*** body, creature, existence, individual, inhabitant, life, living, man, mortal, object, organism, personality, somebody, someone, subsistence, thing, woman

BELAUD, ***verb*** compliment, eulogize, exalt, extol, glorify, laud, make much of, pay tribute, praise, sing the praises of

BELIEF *(Something believed),* ***noun*** canon, conclusion, conviction, credo, creed, doctrinal statement, doctrine, dogma, expectation, maxim, persuasion, precept, principle, rule, tenet
ASSOCIATED CONCEPTS: beyond reasonable doubt, presumption

BELIEF *(State of mind),* ***noun*** absoluteness, assurance, assuredness, certainty, certitude, conclusion, confidence, conviction, credence, credulity, definiteness, expectation, intuition, judgment, *opinio,* opinion, positiveness, sanguineness, understanding, unequivocalness
ASSOCIATED CONCEPTS: good faith belief, suspicion
FOREIGN PHRASES: ***Cuilibet in arte sua perito est credendum.*** Credence should be given to one skilled in his particular art. ***Cuique in sua arte credendum est.*** Everyone is to be believed in reference to his own art or profession. ***Testibus deponentibus in pari numero, dignioribus est credendum.*** When the number of testifying witnesses is equal on both sides, the more worthy are to be believed.

BELIEVABLE, ***adjective*** conceivable, convincing, credential, credible, creditable, dependable, incontestable, incontrovertible, indisputable, indubitable, irrefragable, irrefutable, likely, persuasive, plausible, presumable, probable, reliable, sure, tenable, trustworthy, trusty, undeniable, unimpeachable, unquestionable, verisimilar, well-founded, well-grounded
ASSOCIATED CONCEPTS: evidence of trustworthiness

BELIEVE *(Presume),* ***verb*** admit, apprehend, assert, assume, be assured, be certain, be convinced, conceive, conjecture, consider, declare, deduce, deem, divine, expect, fancy, feel, guess, hold, imagine, infer, judge, know, maintain, opine, perceive, postulate, presuppose, realize, regard, rely on, suppose, surmise, suspect, swallow, theorize, think, trust in, understand

BELIEVE *(Trust),* ***verb*** accept, accredit, acknowledge, be confident of, be sure of, buy, count on, credit, entrust with, give credence to, have confidence in, have faith in, hope, rely upon, swear by
ASSOCIATED CONCEPTS: believe a witness, liable, making a false statement, perjury, slander

BELITTLE, ***verb*** abuse, censure, chastise, condemn, criticize, decry, defame, denigrate, denounce, deprecate, depreciate, derogate, diminish, disapprove of, discommend, discount, discredit, disgrace, dismiss, disparage, downplay, lessen, malign, minimize, play down, put down, reprehend, reprobating, scold, scorn, slander, slur, take down a peg, talk down, tear down, underrate, undervalue, vilify, vilipend

BELLIGERENCY, ***noun*** affray, aggression, aggressiveness, altercation, animosity, antagonism, assault, attack, battling, bellicosity, belligerance, clashing, combat, combativeness, conflict, contentiousness, contestation, controversy, disagreement, discord, disputation, dissension, disturbance, embroilment, encounter, enmity, feud, fighting, fracas, hostility, impugnation, impugnment, inimicality, malevolence, martiality, melee, militancy, opposition, oppugnancy, oppugnation, pugnaciousness, pugnacity, resort to arms, revengefulness, riot, rivalry, scuffle, siege, sparring, state of siege, state of war, strife, time of war, tumult, tussle, unpeacefulness, violence, warfare, warlikeness, wartime, wrangle
ASSOCIATED CONCEPTS: adverse possession, belligerency de facto, international law, national defense

BELOW, ***adverb*** after, beneath, downward, following, lower, subsequent, under, underneath

BENCH, ***noun*** bar, bar of justice, board, cabinet, chamber, circuit, council, court, court of justice, court of law, forum, forum of justice, judge, judgment seat, judicatory, judicature, judicial assembly, judicial forum, judicial tribunal, judiciary, *judicium,* justice, justice seat, law court, legal administration, magistracy, magistrate, magistrature, open court, panel of judges, privy council, seat of judgment, seat of justice, tribunal
ASSOCIATED CONCEPTS: at the bench, bench docket, bench notes, bench warrant

BENCHMARK, ***noun*** bookmark, critical point, crucial point, crux, essence, essential matter, fundamental part, gist, gravamen, heart, key point, linchpin, main point, material point, milestone, pivotal point, prime issue, salient point, substance, substantive point, turning point

BENEATH CONTEMPT, ***adjective*** abhorrent, abominable, appalling, atrocious, contemptible, deplorable, despicable, detestable, dreadful, foul, frightening, frightful, ghastly, ghoulish, gruesome, harrowing, hateful, heinous, horrendous, horrid, horrifying, loathsome, obnoxious, odious, offensive, outrageous, pathetic, pitiful, repellent, reprehensible, repulsive, revolting, shameful, shocking, terrible, terrifying, unspeakable, vile, villainous
ASSOCIATED CONCEPTS: appalling conduct, contempt of court, harassment

BENEFACTOR, ***noun*** abettor, advocate, aid, aider, ally, altruist, assister, backer, beneficent friend, benefiter, champion, contributor, defender, donor, favorer, free giver, friend, giver, Good Samaritan, help, helper, humanitarian, kind person, maintainer, ministrant, patron, philanthropist, promoter, protector, redeemer, rescuer, seconder, succorer, supporter, sustainer, upholder, well-doer

BENEFICIAL, ***adjective*** advantageous, aidful, aiding, anodyne, availing, beneficent, benign, benignant, conducive, constructive, contributive, contributory, convenient, cooperative, edifying, efficacious, favorable, fertile, for one's good, for one's interest, functional, gainful, good for one's advantage, helpful, helping, improving, invaluable, obliging, of general utility, of service, of value, paying, practicable, practical, productive, proficuous, profitable, prolific, promoting, propitious, prosperous, remunerative, salubrious, *salutaris,* salutary, salutiferous, serendipitous, to one's advantage, usable, useful, *utilis,* utilitarian, valuable, worthwhile
ASSOCIATED CONCEPTS: beneficial association, beneficial enjoyment, beneficial estate, beneficial gift, beneficial interest, beneficial owner, beneficial power, beneficial purposes, beneficial use

BENEFICIARY, ***noun*** *bènèficiare,* donee, grantee, heir, heiress, inheritor, legatee, one who receives, payee, receiver, recipient, usufructuary
ASSOCIATED CONCEPTS: beneficiary of a trust, beneficiary under a will, *cestui que trust*

BENEFIT *(Betterment),* ***noun*** accommodation, advantage, assistance, avail, behoof, benefaction, comfort, convenience, enjoyment, expediency, gain, good, gratification, improvement, interest, pleasure, profit, promotion, relief, return, satisfaction, solace, success, succor, usufruct, utility, utilization, welfare, well-being, worth
ASSOCIATED CONCEPTS: beneficial use, benefit of clergy, benefit of counsel, benefit of creditors, benefit of estate, benefit of the bargain, benefit of third person
FOREIGN PHRASES: ***In favorabilibus magis attenditur quod prodest quam quod nocet.*** In things favored, what is beneficial is more regarded than what is harmful. ***Privatum incommodum publico bono pensatur.*** Private inconvenience is compensated for by public benefit.

BENEFIT *(Conferment),* ***noun*** aid, award, benefaction, beneficience, benevolence, bequest, bestowal, bonus, boon, charity, compensation, contribution, courtesy, devise, dispensation, donation, endowment, favor, gift, good turn, gratuity, kindness, largess, legacy, liberality, oblation, offering, offertory, philanthropy, present, presentation, remittance, reward, subsidy, subvention
ASSOCIATED CONCEPTS: benefit certificate
FOREIGN PHRASES: ***Invito beneficium non datur.*** A benefit is not conferred upon a person against his will. ***Privilegium est beneficium personale, et extinguitur cum persona.*** A privilege is a personal benefit, and is extinguished with the death of the person. ***Omnes licentiam habere his quae pro se indulta sunt, renunciare.*** All are free to renounce those privileges which have been allowed for their benefit.

BENEVOLENCE *(Act of kindness),* ***noun*** assistance, benefaction, beneficence, *benevolentia,* boon, charitable effort, charity, favor, good deed, good treatment, good turn, helpfulness, kind office, kind treatment, philanthropy, relief, service, succor, support

BENEVOLENCE *(Disposition to do good),* ***noun*** affection, agreeableness, altruism, amiability, amicableness, beneficence, benignancy, bountifulness, brotherliness, charitableness, charity, clemency, compassion, consideration, cordiality, courtesy, forbearance, friendliness, friendship, generosity, good disposition, good intention, good nature, good will, goodness, goodness and mercy, graciousness, helpfulness, humaneness, humanism, humanity, indulgence, kindheartedness, kindliness, kindness, liberality, mercy, munificence, obligingness, philanthropy, placability, Samaritanism, softheartedness, solicitousness, solicitude, tenderness, thoughtfulness, tolerance, understanding, unselfishness, warmheartedness

BENEVOLENT, ***adjective*** accommodating, affable, agreeable, altruistic, amiable, amicable, bearing good will, beneficient, *benevolus,* benign, big-hearted, bounteous, bountiful, charitable, complacent, condolent, considerate, cooperative, cordial, decent, disposed to good, doing good, eleemosynary, empathetic, freehanded, friendly, full of good will, generous, genial, good-humored, good natured, gracious, helpful, hospitable, humane, humanitarian, indulgent, kind, kindhearted, kindly, kindly disposed, liberal, magnanimous, merciful, munificent, neighborly, obliging, openhanded, philanthropic, softhearted, solicitous, supportive, sweet-tempered, sympathizing, tender, thoughtful, tolerant, understanding, ungrudging, unselfish, unsparing, unstinting, warm, warmhearted, well-intentioned, well-meaning, well-meant
ASSOCIATED CONCEPTS: benevolent and charitable organization, benevolent and charitable purposes, benevolent association, benevolent corporation, benevolent institution, benevolent use, charitable corporation

BENIGN, ***adjective*** anodyne, beneficent, benignant, favorable, gentle, harmless, healthful, healthy, innocent, innocuous, inoffensive, mild, nonabrasive, noncorrosive, nonthreatening, nontoxic, painless, placid, propitious, safe, salubrious, salutary, soft, sound, trustworthy, unobjectionable

BEQUEATH, ***verb*** administer to, afford, allow, assign dower, bestow upon, cede, change hands, contribute, deliver to, demise, devise, devolve upon, dispense, dispose of, distribute, donate, endow with, enfeoff, furnish, give, give away at death, give by will, grant, hand down, hand on, hand over to, interchange, invest, leave, leave a legacy, leave by will, leave to, make a bequest, make a present of, make legacies, pass on to, pass over to, provide, put in possession, remit, render, transfer ownership, vest in, will to
ASSOCIATED CONCEPTS: bequest
FOREIGN PHRASES: ***Da tua dum tua sunt, post mortem tunc tua non sunt.*** Give that which is yours while it is yours; after death it is not yours.

BEQUEST, ***noun*** bequeathal, birthright, demise, devisal, devise, endowment, entail, gift, heirdom, heirloom, hereditament, heritable, heritage, inheritance, legacy, *legatum,* patrimony, testamentary disposition, testamentary gift
ASSOCIATED CONCEPTS: bequest by implication, bequest for life, bequest in trust, devise, gift, inheritance
FOREIGN PHRASES: ***Nemo plus commodi haeredi suo relinquit quam ipse habuit.*** No one leaves a greater advantage for his heir than he himself had.

BERATE, ***verb*** abuse, admonish, assail, attack, belittle, blame, cast aspersions, castigate, censure, chastise, condemn, crucify, denigrate, disparate, flay, hammer, harangue, knock, lace into, lambaste, mock, rail, rake over the coals, rant, rebuke, remonstrate, reprimand, reproach, reprove, revile, ridicule, scorn, scourge, tongue-lash, undermine, upbraid, vituperate

BESEECH, ***verb*** appeal to, ask for, bid, call for, clamor for, demand, desire, enjoin, entreat, exact, implore, importune, insist, invoke, petition, plead, pray, press, pressure, prevail, prevail upon, propose, request, require, requisition, solicit, supplicate, urge, wish for

BESMIRCH, ***verb*** adulterate, befoul, begrime, belittle, bemire, berate, blacken, blot, calumniate, contaminate, corrupt, debase, decry, defame, degrade, denigrate, desecrate, discolor, discredit, disdain, disgrace, dishonor, disparage, foul, hurt, libel, maculate, mire, pollute, profane, revile, slander, smear, soil, stain, sully, taint, tarnish, undermine, violate
ASSOCIATED CONCEPTS: defamation, libel, slander

BESPEAK, ***verb*** argue, attest, call, connote, convey, denote, express, imply, import, indicate, mean, purport, signify, speak of, suggest, tell of, testify

BEST, ***adjective*** above the average, beyond compare, brought to perfection, chief, choice, crowning, distinguished, exceptional, exemplary, extraordinary, faultless, favorite, first-class, first-rate, flawless, foremost, greater, highest, impeccable, incomparable, inimitable, matchless, maximum, most desirable, most excellent, optimal, *optimus,* outstanding, paramount, peerless, perfect, preeminent, quintessential, record-breaking, *sans pareil,* second to none, select, superfine, superior, superlative, supernormal, supreme, surpassing, top-level, top-notch, topmost, transcendent, unapproached, unequaled, unparalleled, unrivaled, uppermost, without comparison
ASSOCIATED CONCEPTS: best ability, best and highest use, best bid, best efforts, best energies, best evidence, best interests, best interests of a child, best interests of the public, best judgment, best quality, best skill and discretion or judgment, best testimony

BEST EVIDENCE RULE, ***noun*** evidentiary procedure, evidentiary rule, exclusion of secondary evidence, original document requirement, original documentation rule, procedural rule requiring original documentation, prohibition against facsimile production
ASSOCIATED CONCEPTS: Federal Rules of Evidence

BESTIALITY, *noun* animalism, barbarity, barbarousness, beastliness, bloodthirstiness, brutality, brutishness, cruelty, ferociousness, ferocity, fiendishness, fierceness, grossness, inhumanity, monstrousness, savagery, unnaturalness, viciousness

BESTOW, *verb* accord, accredit, address, administer, afford, allot, allow, appoint, apportion, *attribuere,* authorize, award, be favorable to, be prodigal, bequeath, cater, cede, charter, commission, communicate, *conferre,* concede, confer, confer a privilege, confer distinction, consent, contribute, convey, deal, deign, deliver, dignify, dispense, dispose of, distribute, dole, donate, empower, endow, enfranchise, enrich, entitle, equip, extend, facilitate, facultate, favor with, finance, foster, fund, furnish, give, give a present, give approval, give assent, give away, give back, give clearance, give consent, give dispensation, give freely, give leave, give one's hand to, give out, give out in shares, give permission, give power, give up, grant, grant a boon, grant a request, grant permission, gratify, hand out, hand over, heap upon, help to, honor with, impart, *impertire,* indulge, install, invest, issue, *largiri,* lavish, lend, let, license, maintain, make a benefaction, make a loan, make a present of, make provision for, mete, minister to, oblige, ordain, part with, pay tribute, permit, philanthropize, present, proffer, promise, provide, provision, ratify, recognize, recommend, reflect honor upon, release, relinguish, remit, render, replenish, restore, sanction, serve, show favor, shower upon, spare, spend, sponsor, submit, supply, tender, transmit, vest, vouchsafe, yield
ASSOCIATED CONCEPTS: bestow a present upon, gifts

BET, *verb* adventure, ante, ante up, cast lots, chance, chance the odds, draw, draw lots, encounter the risk, flip a coin, gamble, game, hazard, incur the risk, lay a wager, lay even money, lay money down, lay odds, leave to chance, parlay, play, play a long shot, play for, punt, put money down, raffle, rely on fortune, risk, run the risk, speculate, sport, stake, stand the hazard, take a chance, take the chances of, toss up, trust to chance, try one's fortune, try one's luck, venture, wager
ASSOCIATED CONCEPTS: betting on horse races, betting on numbers, bettor, gambling, lottery

BETRAY *(Disclose),* ***verb*** acknowledge, admit, air, aperire, avow, bare, bear witness against, bring into the open, bring to light, come clean, confess, declare, divulge, double-cross, expose, give away, give utterance to, impart, inform, inform against, inform on, lay bare, let slip, make a clean breast, make known, make public, own up, report, reveal, sell out, show, tattle, tell, tell on, turn informer, uncover, unearth, unfold, unmask, violate a confidence
ASSOCIATED CONCEPTS: confidences, privileges, professional secrets, trade secrets, trusts, wrongful disclosure

BETRAY *(Lead astray),* ***verb*** abandon, abase, bamboozle, be dishonest, be false to, befool, beguile, bluff, break faith with, break one's promise, cheat, circumvent, corrupt, cozen, debauch, deceive, deceive by treachery, decoy, defile, defraud, deliver up, delude, dupe, enmesh, ensnare, entice, entrap, fleece, forswear, fraud, gammon, give over to the foe, give up treacherously, hoax, hoodwink, inveigle, let down, lure, misinform, mislead, outwit, overreach, play false, prostitute, put on, put something over on, ruin, seduce, sell out, swindle, take in, trick, undo, victimize, violate

BETTER, *verb* abundant, advance, ameliorate, amend, ample, astronomical, beat, best, capacious, cavernous, colossal, commodious, copious, correct, cure, eclipse, enhance, enrich, exceed, excel, excessive, exorbitant, fine-tune, fortify, forward, further, gain strength, gigantic, great, grow, hefty, help, huge, immense, improve, increase, mammoth, massive, meliorate, mend, monstrous, outclass, outdo, outshine, oversize, perfect, polish, promote, propel, raise, rectify, refine, reform, remediate, remedy, retouch, revamp, roomy, sizable, spacious, staggering, strengthen, substantial, surpass, top, transcend, tremendous, trump, update, upgrade, vast, voluminous

BETTERMENT, *noun* accommodation, adjustment, advance, advancement, alteration, amelioration, amendment, bettering, breakthrough, change, change for the better, changeover, constructive change, deviation, difference, divergence, enhancement, enrichment, improvement, increase, lift, melioration, modification, progress, progression, progressive change, redesign, reform, reformation, reshaping, restoration, restructuring, transition, tweaking, upgrade
ASSOCIATED CONCEPTS: financial betterment, improvement in real estate value
FOREIGN PHRASES: ***Nul ne doit s'enrichir aux despens des autres.*** No man should enrich himself at the expense of others.

BETTOR, *noun* better, gambler, gamester, gentleman of fortune, hazarder, piker, player, player for stakes, plunger, punter, risk-taker, sharper, speculatist, speculator, venturer, wagerer

BEWARE, *verb* be careful, be cautious, be chary, be circumspect, be forewarned, be guarded, be on one's guard, be on the alert, be on the lookout, be on the watch, be prepared, be prewarned, be prudent, be warned, be wary, have a care, keep out of harm's way, look about one, look out, mind, receive notice, stop look and listen, take care, take heed, take precautions, take warning, think twice, watch out

BEYOND A REASONABLE DOUBT, *adjective* finding of guilt, no reasonable doubt remains, standard for a determination of guilt, standard for a verdict, standard for guilt, standard to convict, standard to determine criminality, sufficient evidence to convict

BIAS, *noun* bigotry, disinclination, disposition, favoritism, foregone conclusion, *inclinatio,* inclination, intolerance, jaundice, partiality, partisanism, partisanship, penchant, preapprehension, preconceived idea, preconception, predetermination, predilection, predisposition, preference, prejudgment, prejudication, prejudice, prenotion, proclivity, proneness, *propensio animi,* propensity, susceptibility, tendency, trend, undetachment, undispassionateness
ASSOCIATED CONCEPTS: actual bias, bias of mind

BICAMERAL, *adjective* bifurcated, bipartite, bisected, divided, dual chambered, multipartite, separated

BICKER, *verb* agitate, altercate, argue, argue to no purpose, bandy words, battle, be at loggerheads, be at variance, be discordant, brabble, brangle, brawl, cavil, clash, conflict, contend, contest, controvert, differ, disaccord, disagree, dispute, dissent, disunite, embroil, entangle, equivocate, fall foul of, fall out, fence, fight, have an altercation, have it out, have words, jar, join issue, nag, parry, pick a quarrel, pull different ways, quarrel, scrap, spar, spat, split hairs, squabble, take sides, tiff, tilt, wrangle
ASSOCIATED CONCEPTS: bicker over the terms of an agreement, bicker over trivial provisions in a contract

BID, *noun* advance, approach, estimate, *licitatio,* offer, offered price, overture, presentation, price, proffer, proposal, proposition, quotation, quoted price, submission, tender
ASSOCIATED CONCEPTS: auction sale, bid bond, bid in, bid off, bidder, biddings, by-bidding, competitive bidding, proposal, upset bid, with reserve, without reserve

BID-RIGGING, *noun* conspiracy to fix a bid, contrived bidding, criminal act regarding a bid, criminal contrivance in a bid, fixing a bid, fraudulence in a bid, illegal accommodation in a bid, illegal act regarding a bid, illegal action regarding a bid, illegal agreement regarding a bid, illegal arrangement in a bid, illegal contrivances in a bid, illegal consortium, illegal efforts to fix a bid, illegal maneuvering in a bid, illegal means to fix a bid, illegal measures to fix a bid, trumped-up provisions in a bid
ASSOCIATED CONCEPTS: competitive bidding, procurement policies

BIFURCATE, *verb* bisect, branch, branch off, branch out, cleave, cut in two, dichotomize, dimidiate, divaricate, diverge, divide into two, fork, form a fork, furcate, halve, part, partition, ramify, separate, split, sunder
ASSOCIATED CONCEPTS: bifurcated trial

BIFURCATED TRIAL, *noun* bisection of a case, segmentation in a case, segregation in a case, separate liability and damage phases, separate quilt and insanity defense phases, separation in a case, severance in a case, split in a case, split trial, two or more hearings held, two-part trial
ASSOCIATED CONCEPTS: punitive damages

BIG *(Important),* ***adjective*** all-important, central, consequential, considerable, critical, crucial, distinctive, earthshaking, earth-shattering, essential, eventful, exceptional, forceful, grand, grave, high-powered, historic, impressive, meaningful, momentous, monumental, notable, noteworthy, outstanding, remarkable, robust, serious, significant, substantial, superior, weighty, worthwhile, worthy

BIG *(Influential),* ***adjective*** acknowledged, celebrated, distinguished, eminent, great, held in awe, high-level, honored, illustrious, preeminent, prestigious, prominent, recognized, renowned, respected, revered, top

BIG *(Large),* ***noun*** colossal, exceptionally bid, exceptionally large, hefty, huge, humongous, husky, mammoth, massive, oversized, thick, tremendous

BIGAMY, *noun* unlawful marriage, illegal marriage, multiple illegal marriages, multiple spouses, marrying multiple partners, marrying multiple wives, marrying multiple husbands

BIGOT, *noun* diehard, doctrinaire, dogmatic theorist, dogmatist, dogmatizer, energumen, extremist, fanatic, illiberal, infatuate, intolerant, *ipse dixit,* know-all, know-it-all, monomaniac, opinionated person, opinionist, persecutor, ranter, redneck, rigorist, stickler, stubborn person, zealot

BILATERAL, *adjective* bifacial, dual, two-sided
ASSOCIATED CONCEPTS: bilateral contract, bilateral option, bilateral record

BILIOUS, *adjective* bileful, choleric, dyspeptic, jaundiced, spiteful, spleenful

BILK, *verb* appropriate fraudulently, bait, bamboozle, befool, beguile, betray, bluff, cheat, chisel, circumvent, cozen, cully, deceive, defraud, delude, dupe, elude, embezzle, ensnare, entangle, evade, exploit, foist upon, fool, fraud, hoax, hoodwink, humbug, inveigle, levant, misapply, misappropriate, misinform, mulct, peculate, purloin, put something across, put something over, shuffle, swindle, take advantage of, take in, trick, use for one's own needs, utilize for profit, victimize

BILL *(Formal declaration),* ***noun*** allegation of facts, claim, contractual obligation, customs documents, formal petition, indictment, itemized specification, legislative declaration, petition, promissory obligation, specification of details, statement of facts, written certificate, written complaint
ASSOCIATED CONCEPTS: bill for discovery, bill for fraud, bill for new trial, bill in equity, bill in nature of interpleader, bill of attainder, bill of entry, bill of exceptions, bill of health, bill of indictment, bill of instructions, bill of interpleader, bill of particulars, bill of review, Bill of Rights, bill to quiet title, no true bill, true bill

BILL *(Invoice),* ***noun*** account, accounts payable, amount due, audit, balance due, charges, check, cost, deferred payment, demand for payment, expenditures, expenses, figure, itemized account, list, manifest, postponed payment, reckoning, record, report, request for payment, score, statement, statement of indebtedness, *syngrapha,* tally
ASSOCIATED CONCEPTS: bank bill, bill book, bill for account, bill of costs, bill of credit, bill of exchange, bill of lading, bill of sale, bill payable, bill receivable, bond, creditor's bill

BILL *(Proposed act),* ***noun*** draft, legislation, measure, projected law, proposal, proposed enactment, proposed law, proposed regulation, proposed rule, proposed statute, protocol, resolution, *rogatio*
ASSOCIATED CONCEPTS: act of legislature, law, omnibus bill, private bill, revenue bill

BILL OF ATTAINDER, *noun* act of attainder, action prohibited under Article I Section 9 of the U.S. Constitution, improper legislation declaring guilt and punishment without a trial, legislative act declaring criminal guilt and punishment without trial, writ of attainder

BILL OF PARTICULARS, *noun* definite statement, detailed statement of a charge, detailed statement of a claim, formal statement of details of a claim, formal statement of charges, itemized statement, precise specifics of a charge, precise specifics of a claim, specifics of a charge, specifics of a claim, written statement of a charge, written statement of a claim
ASSOCIATED CONCEPTS: demand for a bill of particulars

BIND *(Obligate),* ***verb*** *adstringere,* burden, charge, compel, confirm, conscript, constrain, drive, encumber, exact, force, impose, indent, indenture, *obligare,* oblige, pledge, promise, require, sanction, set a task, warrant
ASSOCIATED CONCEPTS: bind a deal, binding authority, binding instruction, binding receipt, binding transaction
FOREIGN PHRASES: ***Nuda ratio et nuda pactio non ligant aliquem debitorem.*** Naked intention and naked promise do not bind any debtor. ***Quodque dissolvitur eodem modo quo ligatur.*** A thing is unbound in the same manner that it is made binding.

BIND *(Restrain),* ***verb*** block, check, compel, confine, constrain, encumber, fetter, fix, hamper, hinder, immobilize, impede, inhibit, limit, repress, secure, shut in
ASSOCIATED CONCEPTS: bind over

BINDER, *noun* assurance, caution money, collateral, collateral security, deposit, earnest, escrow, expense outlay,

gage, guaranty, handsel, indemnity, installment, investment, payment, pledge, receipt, receipt for payment, recognizance, security, stake, token, token payment
ASSOCIATED CONCEPTS: binder receipt, insurance binder, real estate binder

BINDING, *adjective* coercive, compelling, compulsory, confining, constraining, *de rigueur,* final, hampering, hindering, imperative, incumbent, inhibiting, limiting, mandatory, necessary, obligatory, obliging, required, requisite, restrictive
ASSOCIATED CONCEPTS: binding agreement, binding instruction, binding offer, binding over, binding receipt, binding sale

BIOETHICS, *noun* ethical study of drug research, ethical study of genetic engineering, ideals of genetic engineering and drug research, moral study of drug research, moral study of genetic engineering, morality for genetic engineering, probity for drug research, proper conduct in genetic engineering and drug research, proper moral behavior on genetic engineering, proper moral judgment on drug research, proper moral philosophy on genetic engineering, proper moral principles for drug research, rectitude for genetic engineering, study of ethics in biomedical advances, system of morals for genetic engineering, the ethics of biological medicine, the ethics of biological science
ASSOCIATED CONCEPTS: cloning

BIPARTITE, *adjective* apart, being in two corresponding parts, bicameral, bifurcated, bifurcous, bisected, detached, dichotomous, disconnected, disengaged, disjoined, disjointed, disjunct, disunited, divaricate, divided, furcate, furcular, halved, in two, partitioned, separate, separated, severed, subdivided

BIRTH *(Beginning),* ***noun*** animation, arrival, commencement, creation, debut, embarkation, establishment, *exordium,* genesis, inauguration, inception, incipience, incipiency, incunabula, infancy, introduction, nascency, onset, origin, origination, *ortus,* vitalization
ASSOCIATED CONCEPTS: *ante natus*

BIRTH *(Emergence of young),* ***noun*** arrival, childbirth, delivery, nativity, parturition, vivification
ASSOCIATED CONCEPTS: birth certificate, birth control, issue, pretermission
FOREIGN PHRASES: ***Non nasci, et natum mori, paria sunt.*** Not to be born, and to be born dead, are the same.

BIRTH *(Lineage),* ***noun*** ancestry, bloodline, derivation, descent, extraction, heredity, heritage, inheritance, line, line of descent, parentage, provenance, succession
ASSOCIATED CONCEPTS: birth certificate, legitimacy
FOREIGN PHRASES: ***Qui in utero est pro jam nato habetur, quoties de ejus commodo quaeritur.*** He who is in the womb is regarded as already born, whenever a question arises for his benefit.

BIRTHRIGHT, *noun* absolute right, ancestry, droit, due, entitlement, heritage, heritance, indefeasible right, inheritance, inherited rights, interest, legal right, one's due, *patrimonium,* patrimony, prerogative, primogeniture, privilege, right, rights and privileges, vested interest, vested right

BITTER *(Acrid tasting),* ***adjective*** absinthal, absinthian, acerbate, acerbic, *acerbus,* acid, acidulous, *acidus,* acrid, *asper,* biting, caustic, cutting, disagreeable, distasteful, pungent, sharp, sour, soured, sourish, tart, unappetizing, unpalatable, unpleasant, unsavory, unsweet, vinegarish

BITTER *(Penetrating),* ***adjective*** acrimonious, afflictive, astringent, austere, bilious, biting, brutal, burning, choleric, constringent, corrosive, cutting, double-edged, dyspeptic, harsh, incisive, keen, mordant, nasty, piercing, poignant, pricking, scathing, scorching, severe, smarting, sore, stabbing, stern, stinging, trenchant, venomous, virulent, withering

BITTER *(Reproachful),* ***adjective*** acrimonious, antipathetic, biting, caustic, cross, despiteful, embittered, envenomed, hostile, hurtful, indignant, piqued, provoked, rancorous, resentful, sarcastic, sardonic, scornful, sorrowful, sour-tempered, spiteful, splenetic, unamiable, unhappy, venomous, vexed, vitriolic

BIZARRE, *adjective* aberrant, absurd, anomalistic, atypical, comical, curious, deviant, divergent, eccentric, extraordinary, fanciful, farcical, foolish, implausible, inconceivable, laughable, ludicrous, nonsensical, odd, offbeat, outlandish, outrageous, peculiar, preposterous, ridiculous, strange, surreal, unbelievable, uncanny, uncommon, unexpected, unique, unnatural, unorthodox, unreal, unthinkable, unusual, wacky, weird, wild

BLACKMAIL, *noun* exaction, extortion, hush money, illegal compulsion, oppressive exaction, protection, ransom, shakedown, taking by undue exercise of power

BLAME *(Culpability),* ***noun*** accusal, accusation, blameworthiness, castigation, censurability, censurableness, censure, chargeability, condemnation, crimination, criticism, *culpa,* culpableness, damnation, decrial, delation, delinquency, denouncement, denunciation, dereliction, deviation from rectitude, disapproval, disparagement, dispraise, excoriation, expostulation, exprobation, fault, guilt, guiltiness, incrimination, inculpation, malfeasance, misconduct, neglect, objurgation, obloquy, opprobrium, peccability, rebuke, remonstrance, *reprehensio,* reprehension, reproach, reprobation, reproof, *vituperatio,* wrong
ASSOCIATED CONCEPTS: culpable negligence, *mens rea*
FOREIGN PHRASES: ***Culpa caret qui scit sed prohibere non potest.*** One is clear of blame who knows but cannot prevent.

BLAME *(Responsibility),* ***noun*** accountability, ascription, assignation, assignment, attribution, charge, implication, imputation, liability
ASSOCIATED CONCEPTS: allocation of blame, blameworthy, culpability, placing the blame

BLAME, *verb* abhor, accuse, administer a rebuke, admonish, anathematize, animadvert, arraign, ascribe to, assign to, attribute to, berate, call to account, carp, cast a slur on, castigate, cavil, censure, charge, chastise, chide, cite, complain against, condemn, criminate, criticize, *culpare,* denounce, deplore, deprecate, depreciate, detract, disapprove, discommend, discountenance, disparage, dispraise, execrate, expostulate, fault, find fault, hold no brief for, hold responsible, hold up to reprobation, impeach, implicate, impugn, impute to, incriminate, inculpate, indict, lodge a complaint, objurgate, rebuke, recriminate, remonstrate, reprehend, *reprehendere,* reprimand, reproach, reprobate, reprove, revile, show disapproval, upbraid, vilipend, *vituperare*

BLAMEFUL, *adjective* abject, accusable, at fault, blamable, blameworthy, censorious, censurable, censured, chargeable, compunctious, condemnable, condemned, contemptible, contemptuous, corrupt, criminal, criminous, criticized, culpable, damnatory, decried, delinquent, deplorable, deplored, despicable, disapproved, discommendable, discreditable, discredited, dishonorable, disowned, dispraised, disreputable, disreputed, errant, exceptionable, execrable, faulty, flagitous, found guilty, found wanting, guilty, heinous, held in contempt, ignominious, illaudable, immeritorious, impeachable, imputable, in the wrong, indefensible, indictable, inexcusable, iniquitous, insalubrious, liable, liable to prosecution, nefarious, neglectful, negligent, objectionable, objurgatory, open to criticism, opprobrious, out of favor, peccable, peccant, reprehensible, reprimanded, reproachable, reproachful, reprobate, reprobative, reprovable, responsible, unacceptable, uncommendable, unjustifiable, unpardonable, unpraiseworthy, unworthy, venal, vile, without defense, without excuse, wrongful

BLAMELESS, *adjective* above reproach, above suspicion, absolved, acquitted, clean, clear, condonable, entirely defensible, exculpable, exculpated, exonerated, faultless, free from guilt, free from wrong, guilt-free, guiltless, immaculate, impeccable, incensurable, incorrupt, inculpable, innocent, innocuous, inoffensive, irreprehensible, irreproachable, irreprovable, moral, not guilty, not liable, not tainted, offenseless, perfect, pure, reprieved, rightful, sinless, stainless, taintless, unblamable, unblameworthy, unblemished, uncensurable, uncondemned, uncorrupt, uncorrupted, unculpable, undefiled, unfallen, unguilty, unimpeachable, uniniquitous, unobjectionable, unoffending, unreproachable, unreproached, unreproved, unsoiled, unspotted, unsullied, untainted, upright, vindicated, virtuous, without blame, without fault, without reproach

BLAMEWORTHY, *adjective* abject, accusable, answerable, arrant, at fault, beneath contempt, blamable, blameful, censurable, chargeable, condemnable, condemnatory, condemned, contemned, contemptible, contemptuous, contumelious, convicted, corrupt, criminal, criminous, criticized, culpable, damnatory, delinquent, deplorable, depraved, despicable, devious, discreditable, discredited, disdainful, dishonorable, disreputable, disrespectable, errant, erring, execrable, flagitious, flagrant, *flagrante delicto,* found guilty, guilty, ignominious, illaudable, impeachable, in fault, in the wrong, indefensible, indictable, infernal, inglorious, iniquitous, injurious, insalubrious, irremediable, justiciable, liable, liable to prosecution, nefarious, negligent, not honorable, not respectable, not to be recommended, objectionable, obnoxious, odious, of no repute, open to criticism, opprobrious, peccable, peccant, questionable, reprehensible, reprimanded, reproachable, reprobate, reprobative, reprovable, responsible, ribald, scandalous, sentenced, sinister, tainted, transgressing, uncommendable, unjustifiable, unpraiseworthy, unrespected, unrighteous, unvirtuous, unworthy, venal, without defense, woeful, wrong, wrongful

BLANK *(Emptiness),* ***noun*** absence, barrenness, cipher, hiatus, hollowness, inexistence, insubstantiality, nil, *nonesse,* nonexistence, nonsubsistence, nonentity, nothing, nothingness, nullity, *tabula rasa,* unsubstantiality, vacancy, vacuousness, vacuum, *vacuus,* void, zero
ASSOCIATED CONCEPTS: blank acceptance, blank bond, blank check, blank endorsement, blank instrument, blank verdict, endorsement in blank, signed in blank

BLANK *(Form),* ***noun*** data sheet, document, dossier, instrument, legal document, paper, questionnaire

BLASPHEMY, *noun* apostasy, blasting, cursing, derogation of religion, desecration, disrespect, epithet, execration, expletive, heresy, iconoclasm, impiety, impious utterance, impiousness, imprecation of evil, irreverence, irreverent behavior, lack of piety, lack of reverence, malediction, profanation, profane oath, profaneness, revilement of religion, sacrilege, sacrilegiousness, sanctimoniousness, solemn mockery, swearing, unholiness, unorthodoxy, unsacredness
ASSOCIATED CONCEPTS: freedom of religion, libel and slander
FOREIGN PHRASES: ***Nec veniam, l'aeso numine, casus habet.*** Where the divinity is insulted, the case cannot be pardoned.

BLATANT *(Conspicuous),* ***adjective*** apparent, celebrated, clear, discernible, exposed, famous, manifest, noticeable, notorious, observable, obvious, outstanding, overt, patent, perceivable, plain, prominent, public, sensational, well-known

BLATANT *(Obtrusive),* ***adjective*** bellowing, boisterous, braying, clamorous, coarse, common, crass, crude, crying, flaring, flaunting, gaudy, glaring, gross, harsh, ill-behaved, ill-bred, ill-mannered, improper, indecorous, indelicate, loud, noisy, obstreperous, offensive, offensively assertive, offensively obtrusive, raffish, ribald, rough, rowdy, rude, screaming, scurrilous, tawdry, ululant, uncivil, uncouth, uncultured, undignified, ungenteel, ungentlemanly, ungracious, unladylike, unpolished, unpresentable, unrefined, unseemly, vociferous, vulgar, vulgarian

BLEAK *(Exposed and barren),* ***adjective*** bare, barren, blank, cold, deserted, desolate, exposed, unpopulated, unsheltered, waste

BLEAK *(Not favorable),* ***adjective*** dark, depressing, disheartening, dismal, distressing, forbidding, gloomy, grave, grim, inauspicious, joyless, ominous, somber, sombrous, unfavorable

BLEAK *(Severely simple),* ***adjective*** austere, cheerless, cold, comfortless, depressing, dismal, dour, drear, dreary, dull, gloomy, grim, joyless, somber, sombrous, uninviting

BLEMISH, *verb* abase, attack, begrime, belittle, besmear, besmirch, blacken, blot, cheapen, cloud, compromise, debase, debauch, deface, defame, denigrate, diminish, discolor, disfigure, disgrace, dishonor, flaw, foul, impair, injure, mar, poison, pollute, shame, smear, soil, spoil, stain, stigmatize, sully, taint, tar, tarnish

BLEMISHED, *adjective* besmirched, blistered, bruised, chipped, damaged, defaced, defective, deformed, dented, deteriorated, discolored, discredited, disfigured, disgraced, dishonored, faded, faulty, flawed, imperfect, impure, injured, malformed, marred, misshapen, pitted, pock-marked, soiled, spotted, stained, sullied, tainted, tarnished

BLIGHT, *noun* abnormality, blot, blotch, calamity, damage, defacement, defect, deformity, destruction, disaster, disfigurement, distress, failing, fault, flaw, impairment, irregularity, malformation, mark, scar, spot, stain, taint, weakness
ASSOCIATED CONCEPTS: a blight contained in zoning laws

BLIND *(Concealed),* ***adjective*** buried, camouflaged, covered, covert, dim, disguised, hidden, imperceptible, inconspicuous, indiscernible, latent, masked, obscure, out of view, private, screened, secreted, shadowy, sheltered, shrouded, unapparent, undetected, unexposed, unknown, unobserved, unperceived, unrevealed, unseen, unsuspected

BLIND *(Impassable),* ***adjective*** barred, barricaded, blanked, blockaded, blocked, closed, dead-end, leading nowhere, obstructed, sealed, shut, shut-off, stopped-up, without exit

BLIND *(Not discerning),* ***adjective*** benighted, careless, deluded, headlong, heedless, inadvertent, inattentive, incognizant, inconsiderate, indifferent, indiscriminate, indiscriminating, insensible, insensitive, led astray, mindless, misled by deception, nescient, obtuse, *oculis captus,* rash, thoughtless, unacquainted, unapprised, uncomprehending, unconscious, unconversant, undiscerning, unenlightened, uninformed, unknowing, unlucid, unmindful, unobservant, unobserving, unperceiving, unreflecting, unseeing, unversed, without insight
ASSOCIATED CONCEPTS: blind allegiance, blind amendments

BLIND *(Sightless),* ***adjective*** caecus, deprived of sight, dim-sighted, eyeless, feeble-eyed, groping, in darkness, unseeing, visionless, weak-eyed

BLIND *(Deprive of sight),* ***verb*** blight one's optical powers, destroy one's perception, extinguish visual discernment, make eyeless, make sightless, make unable to see, obstruct one's vision, render eyeless, render sightless, render visionless, ruin one's eyesight, strike sightless, strike visionless

BLIND *(Obscure),* ***verb*** adumbrate, becloud, becurtain, bedim, befog, bemask, benight, blanket, blear, blur, blur the outline, camouflage, cloak, cloud, conceal, conceal from sight, cover, cover up, curtain, dim, eclipse, ensconce, enshroud, envelop, hide, hide away, hide the identity of, hide underground, keep clandestine, keep out of sight, make inconspicuous, make indiscernible, make unapparent, make unperceptible, muddle, obfuscate, occult, overcloud, put in concealment, put out of sight, render dim, render invisible, render uncertain, screen, screen from observation, screen from sight, seclude, secrete, shade, shadow, shield, shroud, veil, veil the brightness

BLOCK, ***verb*** arrest, avert, ban, bar, barricade, blockade, bridle, check, choke, clog, close, cohibit, constrict, cramp, curb, dam, debar, delay, encumber, estop, exclude, fend off, forbid, foreclose, frustrate, halt, hamper, hinder, hobble, impede, intercept, interdict, interfere with, jam, leave out, limit, obstruct, occlude, oppose, parry, plug up, preclude, prevent, prohibit, proscribe, repulse, restrain, restrict, retard, shut off, shut up, snag, stall, stand in the way, stay, stem, stop, stop up, thwart, trammel, wall up

BLOCKADE *(Barrier),* ***noun*** bar, barricade, block, blockage, bottleneck, cordon, curb, impediment, obsessio, *obsidio,* obstacle, obstruction, stop, stumbling block

BLOCKADE *(Enclosure),* ***noun*** circumjacence, circumscription, circumvallation, compass, containment, encincture, encirclement, enclosing, encompassment, envelopment, framing, girdling, sealing off, surrounding
ASSOCIATED CONCEPTS: capture and prize, commercial blockade

BLOCKADE *(Limitation),* ***noun*** compression, confinement, contraction, debarring, exclusion, obturation, occlusion, preclusion, restriction, shutdown, stoppage, strangulation

BLOOD, ***noun*** affinity, agnation, ancestry, breed, brethren, brood, children, clan, cognation, common ancestry, consanguinity, derivation, descent, ethnic group, extraction, family connection, family relationship, family tie, family tree, filiation, genealogical tree, genealogy, gentility, *genus,* heredity, heritage, issue, kind, kindred, kinsfolk, kinship, kinsman, kinsmen, kinswoman, line, lineage, nationality, next of kin, offspring, one's people, parentage, pedigree, propinquity, relations, *sanguis,* stock, strain, ties of family, tribe
ASSOCIATED CONCEPTS: blood heirs, blood issue, blood relatives, full blood, half blood, mixed blood
FOREIGN PHRASES: ***Consanguineus est quasi eodem sanguine natus.*** A person related by consanguinity is, as it were, one born from the same blood. ***Pueri sunt de sanguine parentum, sed pater et mater non sunt de sanguine puerorum.*** Children are of the blood of their parents, but the father and mother are not of the blood of their children.

BLOODLINE, ***noun*** affiliation, ancestry, birth, blood, caste, derivation, descent, dynasty, extraction, family, family tree, genealogy, heredity, history, line, line of ancestors, lineage, origin, parentage, pedigree, progeniture, root, stem, stock, strain, succession
ASSOCIATED CONCEPTS: pedigree

BLUE SKY LAW, ***noun*** canons regarding securities, precepts on securities, securities law, securities oversight, securities rules, securities statutes

BLUEPRINT, ***noun*** design, detailed plan, diagram, draft, ground plan, map, master plan, mechanical drawing, outline, plan, scheme, sketch

BLUNDER, ***noun*** bungle, error, failure, fault, faux pas, foul-up, gaffe, impropriety, inaccuracy, incongruity, indiscretion, lapse, miscalculation, miscue, misdeed, mishap, misperception, misreading, misstep, mistake, misunderstanding, negligence, omission, oversight, slip-up, snafu, solecism, stumble, wrong judgment
ASSOCIATED CONCEPTS: professional malpractice

BLUNT, ***adjective*** abrupt, brusque, candid, curt, direct, forthright, frank, free-spoken, genuine, gruff, guileless, honest, open, openhearted, outspoken, outward, short, straightforward, to the point, truthful, unceremonious, uncolored, undiplomatic, unguarded, unreserved, up-front, vociferous

BLUR, ***verb*** adumbrate, becloud, bedim, belie, block cloud, complicate, confuse, daze, disarrange, disarray, decompose, disguise, dishevel, disorder, fog, hide, jumble, make hazy, make vague, mask, mix up, muddle, muddy, obfuscate, obscure, perplex, screen, shade, shadow, shroud, skew, veil

BLUSTER *(Commotion),* ***noun*** boisterousness, brawl, disturbance, embroilment, eruption, flare-up, fracas, frenzy, hubbub, maelstrom, melee, outbreak, outburst, pandemonium, racket, rampage, riot, row, rumpus, scramble, storm, tempest, temptestuousness, tumult, tumultuousness, turbulence, turmoil, upheaval, uproar

BLUSTER *(Speech),* ***noun*** boast, bragging, *declamatio,* ebullition, ranting, raving, swaggering, talking big

BOARD, ***noun*** bureau, cabinet, commission, *conlegium,* consistory, consultative body, council, court, *curia,* department, directorate, directorship, governing body, judicatory, management, presidium, tribunal
ASSOCIATED CONCEPTS: advisory boards, board of aldermen, board of arbitrators, board of directors, board of education, board of elections, board of equalization, board of examiners,

board of finance, board of health, board of medical examiners, board of public works, board of review, board of special inquiry, board of supervisors, board of trade, board of trustees, de facto boards, draft board, local board, maritime board, qualification board, revenue board, welfare board, zoning board

BODILY, *adjective* carnal, corporal, corporeal, corporeous, *corporeus,* de facto, embodied, existent, existing, human, incarnate, living, manifest, material, materiate, natural, organic, palpable, perceptible, physical, solid, somatic, somatical, tactile, tangible, visible
ASSOCIATED CONCEPTS: bodily condition, bodily contact, bodily function, bodily harm, bodily heirs, bodily infirmity, bodily injury, bodily issue, bodily pain or suffering

BODY *(Collection),* ***noun*** aggregation, assemblage, batch, colligation, community, company, compilation, congeries, conglomeration, entity, gathering, host, mass, multitude, plenum, polity, sodality, troupe, wholeness
ASSOCIATED CONCEPTS: body corporate, body politic, governmental body, reviewing body

BODY *(Main part),* ***noun*** core, *corpus,* essential part, exposition, figure, form, greater part, hub, main part, major part, principal part, shape, structure, substance
ASSOCIATED CONCEPTS: body of an instrument

BODY *(Person),* ***noun*** anatomy, cadaver, carcass, carrion, corporality, corporalness, corporeality, *corpse,* corpus, embodiment, entity, human being, material existence, personage, physical being, physique
ASSOCIATED CONCEPTS: body attachment, body execution, body heirs

BOGUS, *adjective* affected, artificial, counterfeit, false, phony, sham, spurious, unauthentic, ungenuine, unreal, untrue
ASSOCIATED CONCEPTS: bogus ceremony, bogus certificate, bogus check

BOILER PLATE, *adjective* accepted, after the same pattern, common, commonplace, consonant, conventional, customary, dictated, formulary, habitual, homogeneous, patterned, prescribed, regulation, standardized, stereotyped, stock, typical, undeviating, uniform, universal, unvaried, wonted
ASSOCIATED CONCEPTS: boiler plate clause, boiler plate language

BOLD, *adjective* adventurous, audacious, blatant, bodacious, brash, brazen, cocksure, daredevil, daring, dauntless, dramatic, dynamic, emboldened, enterprising, fearless, foolhardy, forceful, forward, gallant, gutsy, heedless, impertinent, impudent, indignant, insolent, intrepid, lionhearted, nervy, reckless, resolute, saucy, stalwart, swashbuckling, unabashed, unblushing, valorous, venturesome

BOLSTER, *verb* aid, back, buoy up, lift, prop, shore up, shoulder, succor, support, sustain, underpin, uphold

BOMB, *noun* ammunition, armament, blockbuster, bombshell, charge, detonator, dynamite, explosive, explosive device, fireball, grenade, gunpowder, hand grenade, high explosive, infernal machine, instrument of warfare, mine, missile, Molotov cocktail, munitions, petard, shell, T.N.T., torpedo, weapon

BOMBAST, *noun* affectation, boastfulness, boasting, braggery, chatter, declamation, diatribe, embellishment, empty talk, enlargement, euphemism, exaggeration, expansion, flatulence, floridness, fustian, garnishing, grandiloquence, grandiosity, harangue, high coloring, high-sounding words, hyperbole, idle speeches, inanity, inflation, loftiness, magnification, magniloquence, oration, ornamentation, orotundity, ostentation, overstatement, polysyllabic profundity, pomposity, pompous prolixity, prate, preciosity, preciousness, pretentiousness, rant, raving, rhetoric, rhetoricalness, rodomontade, sesquipedalian words, sesquipedalism, sesquipedality, superlative, swelling utterance, swollen diction, tirade, tumidity, tumidness, turgescence, turgidity, vainglory, verbiage

BOMBASTIC, *adjective* balderdash, baroque, declamatory, diffuse, extravagant, flashy, flowery, fustian, gaudy, grandiloquent, grandiose, high-flown, histrionic, inflated, magniloquent, orotund, ostentatious, overblown, pompous, prolix, protuberant, rotund, sonorous, swollen, tumid, turgid, vainglorious, verbose, wordy

BOMBSHELL, *noun* astonishment, bewilderment, blow, consternation, eye opener, inexpectation, jolt, nonexpectation, shock, startler, stupefaction, sudden attack, sudden burst, surprisal, surprise, surprise package, thunderbolt, thunderclap, unawaited event, unexpected event, the unforeseen

BONA FIDE, *adjective* aboveboard, accurate, actual, as represented, candid, faithful, forthright, genuine, honest, honorable, in good faith, ingenuous, intended, just, legitimate, meant, open, plain-speaking, principled, real, reliable, rightful, scrupulous, straightforward, trustworthy, unaffected, uncounterfeited, undisguised, undissembling, undistorted, unexaggerated, unfaked, unfeigned, unperfidious, unperjured, unpretended, unpretentious, unreserved, unsimulated, unspecious, unspurious, veracious, veridical
ASSOCIATED CONCEPTS: bona fide assignment, bona fide belief, bona fide business purpose, bona fide claimant, bona fide controversy, bona fide creditors, bona fide domicile, bona fide holder, bona fide holder for value, bona fide holder in due course, bona fide labor dispute, bona fide members, bona fide operation, bona fide purchaser in good faith, bona fide sale, bona fide seller

BOND, *noun* assurance, certificate of debt, certificate of indebtedness, *chirographum,* debenture, evidence of a debt, government paper, guarantee, guaranty, indenture, obligation, promise, promissory note, real security, security, surety, *syngrapha,* voucher, warrant, warranty
ASSOCIATED CONCEPTS: back bond, bearer bond, bond discount, bond for costs, bond for deed, bond for title, bond holder, bond issue, bond of matrimony, bond premium, bonded indebtedness, bondsman, cash bond, construction bond, coupon bond, defense bond, delivery bond, fidelity bond, governmental bond, indemnity bond, interest-free bond, municipal bond, *ne exeat,* serial bond, state bond, supersedeas bond, tax-exempt bond
FOREIGN PHRASES: ***Eodem ligamine quo ligatum est dissolvitur.*** A bond is released by the same formalities by which it was made binding.

BOND *(Hold together),* ***verb*** attach, blend, cement, coagulate, coalesce, cohere, combine, conglutemate, connect, consolidate, couple, fix, fuse, glue, interlock, join, merge, secure, stick, unite

BOND *(Secure a debt),* ***verb*** agree, assure, certify, confirm, contract, covenant, endorse, ensure, give security, guarantee, hypothecate, indenture, insure, pledge, post, promise, secure, stake, underwrite, warrant

BONDAGE, *noun* abject slavery, arrest, bond of slavery, bonds, captivity, chains, coarctation, compulsory service, confinement, constraint, constraint by force, custodianship, custody, detention, durance, enslavement, entombment, fetters, forced confinement, forced labor, forcible restraint of liberty, guardianship, guarding, helotry, immuration, immurement, impoundment, imprisonment, incarceration, internment, involuntary servitude, loss of freedom, manacles, penal restraint, penal servitude, prison, refusal of bail, reins, remand, restraint, restriction, restriction on movement, servitude, slavery, slavishness, subduing, subjection, subjugation, subordination, subservience, surveillance, thralldom, yoke
ASSOCIATED CONCEPTS: involuntary servitude, kidnapping

BONUS, *noun* additive, benefit, *boni,* boon, bounty, dividend, donation, extra, gift, gratuity, honorarium, incentive, perquisites, *pourboire,* premium, *prime,* reward, something over and above, surplus, surplusage, tip
ASSOCIATED CONCEPTS: bonus stock

BOOK, *verb* accuse, arrest, chronicle, docket, engage, enter, enumerate, file, index, inscribe, insert, list, log, make an entry, mark down, note, order, post, prefer charges, record, register, report, schedule, seize legally, tabulate, take into custody, write down

BOOKKEEPING, *verb* accounting, balancing the books, books, compilation of financial records, computation, financial records, fiscal records, preparation of financial records, reckoning, recording, recordkeeping, records, simplification, summarization, synopsis

BOOM *(Increase),* ***noun*** acceleration, accretion, accrual, accruement, accumulation, additament, addition, additory, advance, advancement, amplification, amplitude, annexation, appreciation, appurtenance, attachment, augment, augmentation, boost, broadening, burgeoning, complement, deepening, development, distension, doubling, duplication, enhancement, enlargement, escalation, expansion, extension, gain, growth, heightening, hike, improvement, increasement, increasing, increment, intensification, interest, magnification, production, progress, progression, proliferation, prolongation, protraction, raise, reinforcement, reproduction, rise, spread, spreading, sprouting, strengthening, supplement, swell, swelling, upgrowth, upsurge

BOOM *(Prosperity),* ***noun*** abundance, accomplishment, accumulation, achievement, acquisition, advance, advancement, affluence, aggrandizement, amelioration, amplitude, attainment, augmentation, auspiciousness, avails, benefaction, booming economy, bountifulness, burgeoning, capital gains, copiousness, cornucopia, development, earnings, economic prosperity, escalation, excess, exorbitance, exorbitancy, expansion, expediency, favorable trade balance, flourishing condition, gain, good fortune, great quantity, growth, impetus, improvement, increment, inflation, lucre, mutual profit, opulence, opulency, outgrowth, outpouring, plentifulness, plentitude, prevalence, production, productivity, profit, profit making, profluence, profluency, profuseness, profusion, progress, progression, progressiveness, proliferation, prosperous issue, prosperous outcome, prosperousness, recovery, remuneration, revenue, richness, rising prices, spiral inflation, superabundance, superfluity, surplus, thriving conditions, thriving economy, upgrading, upgrowth, upsurge, upward curve, upward trend, weal, wealth, welfare, well-being

BOOTLEGGER, *noun* black marketeer, contrabandist, gunrunner, illicit dealer, moonshiner, runner, smuggler
ASSOCIATED CONCEPTS: prohibition, sale of intoxicating liquor

BORDER, *noun* ambit, borderland, boundary, bounds, brim, brink, circumference, circumjacence, confine, contiguity, edge, edging, end, enframement, extremity, flange, frame, fringe, frontier, hem, ledge, limit, line of demarcation, marge, margin, outline, outpost, outside, outskirts, pale, perimeter, periphery, purlieus, rim, selvedge, side, skirt, terminal, termination, verge
ASSOCIATED CONCEPTS: border search

BORDER *(Approach),* ***verb*** abut upon, adjoin, align convergently, approximate, be in the vicinity of, be near, close on, come close, come to a point, concentrate, converge, draw near, encroach, gravitate toward, join, juxtapose, juxtaposit, lie near, meet, move toward, near, neighbor, place in juxtaposition, place near, place parallel, proximate, put along side, skim, skirt, unite, verge, verge upon

BORDER *(Bound),* ***verb*** abut upon, adjoin, appose, attach, *attingere,* be adjacent to, be circumjacent to, be conterminous, be contiguous, be in conjunction with, be in contact with, be juxtaposed, butt, cincture, circumpose, circumvalate, circumvent, close in, confine, conjoin, connect, contain, corral, cut off, define, delimit, delimitate, delineate, demarcate, edge, embrace, encase, enchase, encircle, enclose, enclose within bounds, encompass, ensphere, envelop, environ, extend to, flank, frame, gird, hem in, impinge, join, juxtapose, juxtaposit, lean against, lie contiguous to, lie next to, limit, mark off, meet end to end, meet with, outline, place limitations, proscribe, restrain, restrict, shut in, specify limits, stake out, surround

BORN *(Alive),* ***adjective*** animated, begotten, breathing, enlivened, live, living, quick, vital, vitalized

BORN *(Innate),* ***adjective*** congenital, connate, connatural, fundamental, genetic, hereditary, immanent, in the blood, inborn, inbred, incarnate, indigenous, ingrained, inherited, instinctive, instinctual, intrinsic, inwrought, native, natural, organic

BORROW, *verb* accept the loan of, apply for a loan, ask for credit, get on credit, get temporary use of, *mutuari,* obtain a mortgage, obtain the use of, take an advance, take on credit, take on loan
ASSOCIATED CONCEPTS: borrowed capital, borrowed employees, borrowed servant, borrowing statute
FOREIGN PHRASES: ***In satisfactionibus non permittitur amplius fieri quam semel factum est.*** In settlements more must not be received than was received once for all.

BORROWING LIMIT, *noun* breaking point of debt, debt ceiling, debt limit, greatest limit of debt, largest debt, largest loan, maximum amount of debt, maximum debt, maximum funds to be loaned, maximum loan outer limit of debt, outer line of credit
ASSOCIATED CONCEPTS: bankruptcy, fraudulent debt, insolvency, interrogation, solvency

BOUND, *adjective* accountable, answerable, beholden, called by duty, chargeable, committed, compelled, constrained, destined, engaged, forced, having no alternative, impelled, liable, necessitated, obligated, obliged, pledged, pressed by duty, required, responsible, restrained, tied, under a vow, under compulsion, under necessity, under obligation

FOREIGN PHRASES: ***Naturale est quidlibet dissolvi eo modo quo ligatur.*** It is natural for a thing to be unbound in the same way in which it was made binding. ***Nemo tenetur ad impossibile.*** No one is bound to do an impossibility. ***Quo ligatur, eo dissolvitur.*** By the same means by which a thing is bound, it is released.

BOUNDARY, *noun* border, borderline, bound, circumscription, compass, configuration, confine, confinement, contour, delimitation, delineation, division line, edge, enclosure, extremity, finis, limit, limitation, limits, line of circumvallation, line of demarcation, lineaments, lines, outline, perimeter, periphery, radius, rim, *terminus,* verge

ASSOCIATED CONCEPTS: adjoining landowners, boundary line, boundary of a water course, boundary suit, metes and bounds, surveys and surveyors, trespass to try title, zoning

BOUNDS, *noun* borders, boundaries, confines, edge, environs, extent, extremes, farthest limits, frame, fringes, frontier, furthest limits, hem, horizon, limits, line of demarcation, outer boundaries, outer limits, outline, parameters, perimeter, periphery

BOUNTY, *noun* award, benefaction, benevolence, bonanza, bonus, boon, cadeau, conferment, emolument, favor, gift, grant, gratification, gratuity, guerdon, hand sel, honorarium, largess, *largitas, liberalitas,* perquisite, *pourboire,* premium, prize, reward, reward for service, tip, token, tribute

ASSOCIATED CONCEPTS: bounty lands

BOWDLERIZE, *verb* censor, curtail, cut, cut out, delete, edit out, emasculate, eviscerate, excise, expunge, expurgate, extirpate, remove

ASSOCIATED CONCEPTS: censorship, freedom of speech

BOYCOTT, *noun* abstention from buying, abstention from using, avoidance, ban, banning, black-listing, blackballing, debarring, embargo, exclusion, ostracism, proscription, refusal to do business, rejection, shunning, strike, withholding of patronage

ASSOCIATED CONCEPTS: primary boycott, secondary boycott

BRAND, *noun* badge, colophon, copyright label, disgrace, earmark, emblem, hallmark, identification mark, identification tag, impress, imprint, insignia, label, mark, *nota,* owner's mark, owner's sign, *piste,* seal, sigil, sign, signet, smirch, stain, stamp, sticker, stigma, stigmatism, tag, taint, ticket, token, trade name, trademark, watermark

ASSOCIATED CONCEPTS: brand name

BRAND *(Mark),* ***verb*** autograph, blaze, distinguish by mark, earmark, emblaze, emboss, endorse, engrave, identify, impress, imprint, inscribe, label, *notam homini inurere, notare,* print, put a mark on, put an indication on, seal, sign, stamp, tag

BRAND *(Stigmatize),* ***verb*** asperse, attaint, besmear, besmirch, bespatter, blacken, blot, bring into discredit, cast a slur upon, cast aspersions at, corrupt, debase, decry, defame, defile, deride, derogate, dirty, discredit, disgrace, dishonor, disparage, excite disapprobation, hold up to shame, impugn, involve in shame, malign, pillory, put to shame, reflect upon, slur, smear, smirch, smudge, soil, stain, sully, taint, tar, tarnish, throw dishonor upon, vilify, vilipend

ASSOCIATED CONCEPTS: libel, reputation, slander

BRANDISH, *verb* dangle before the eyes, display, draw one's sword, exhibit, flap, flaunt, flourish, gesture, rattle the saber, shake, show, swing, threaten, *vibrare,* wag, waggle, wave, wield

ASSOCIATED CONCEPTS: harassment, menacing

BRAVE, *adjective* adventurous, audacious, bold, bold as a lion, bold-spirited, chivalric, chivalrous, courageous, daring, dauntless, fearless, foolhardy, gallant, heroic, herolike, high-spirited, intrepid, knightly, lionhearted, rash, reckless, soldierly, stalwart, stout, stouthearted, unafraid, unalarmed, undaunted, valiant, valorous, virile

BRAWL, *noun* altercation, brangle, breach of the peace, broil, commotion, deafening row, din, dispute, disturbance, embranglement, embroilment, feud, fight, fisticuffs, fracas, fray, hubbub, imbroglio, jangle, *jurgium, mèlée,* noisiness, outbreak, pandemonium, quarrel, racket, rampage, riot, *rixa,* row, rowdiness, ruction, scramble, scrimmage, scuffle, squabble, tumult, turmoil, uproar, wrangle

ASSOCIATED CONCEPTS: disorderly conduct

BRAWL, *verb* altercate, be noisy, bicker, brangle, break the peace, broil, clamor, create a disturbance, create a riot, dispute angrily, fight, have a row, have words with, jangle, make a commotion, make a racket, make an uproar, quarrel noisily, rampage, riot, *rixari,* row, run riot, scrap, scrimmage, scuffle, set to, spat, squabble, tiff, wrangle

ASSOCIATED CONCEPTS: disorderly conduct

BRAZEN, *adjective* arrogant, assuming, audacious, aweless, barefaced, blatant, bluff, bold, boldfaced, brash, conscienceless, daring, defiant, disrespectful, familiar, flagrant, flaunting, flippant, forward, immodest, immoral, impertinent, *impudens,* impudent, indecent, indecorous, insolent, malapert, obtrusive, of loose morals, outspoken, pert, petulant, presumptuous, *risqué,* rude, saucy, shameless, unabashed, unashamed, unblushing, unembarrassed, unmannerly, unmodest, unreserved, unseemly

BREACH, *noun* break, contravention, default, delinquency, dereliction, *discutere,* disobedience, disregard, dissension, dissentience, encroachment, enmity, failure, illegal evasion, illicitness, impropriety, infidelity, infraction, infringement, inobservance, neglection, nonadherence, noncompletion, nonconformity, nonfulfilment, nonobservance, nonperformance, omission, perfidy, *perfringere,* rejection, repudiation, retraction, shortcoming, tergiversation, transgression, trespass, unconformity, undueness, unduteousness, undutifulness, unfaithfulness, unobservance, violation, violation of law

ASSOCIATED CONCEPTS: anticipatory breach, breach of bond, breach of contract, breach of covenant, breach of duty, breach of faith, breach of lease, breach of marriage promise, breach of promise, breach of the close, breach of the covenant of warranty, breach of the peace, breach of trust, breach of warranty, constructive breach, continuing breach, material breach, partial breach, total breach

BREAK *(Fracture),* ***verb*** burst, cave in, comminute, cut, destroy, fissure, fragment, hew, interpenetrate, *interrumpere,* penetrate, pierce, pulverize, puncture, rend, rupture, scatter, shatter, shiver, smash, splinter, stave in

ASSOCIATED CONCEPTS: breakage, breaking a close, breaking and entering, burglary, forcible entry and detainer

BREAK *(Separate),* ***verb*** cleave, crack, detach, disband, disconnect, disengage, disentangle, disintegrate, disjoin, dislocate, dismantle, dispart, disperse, dissociate, disunite, divaricate, force apart, force open, get free, get loose, incise, lop, open, part, rive, sever, split, split off, subdivide, sunder, take apart, take to pieces, unbind, unchain, unclinch, uncouple, unfetter, unknot, unloose, untie
ASSOCIATED CONCEPTS: break in occupancy, break in the chain of events

BREAK *(Violate),* ***verb*** abscind, be derelict, be guilty of infraction, breach, defy, disobey, disregard, infringe, invade, neglect, trample upon, transgress, trespass

BREAK THE LAW, ***verb*** abuse, breach the law, commit a crime, defy, disobey, disregard the law, flaunt the law, ignore the law, offend, transgress, violate, violate the law, wilfully disregard the law
ASSOCIATED CONCEPTS: criminal law, penal law

BREAKDOWN *(Delineation),* ***noun*** account, analysis, anatomizing, assay, assessment, cataloging, categorization, dissection, division, enumeration, evaluation, examination, inspection, inventory, itemization, reckoning, reduction, report, scrutiny, segmentation, separation, specification, specifics, tabulation

BREAKDOWN *(Deterioration),* ***noun*** atrophy, breakage, damage, debilitation, decadence, decay, declension, decomposition, degeneration, demolition, disintegration, dissolution, enfeeblement, faltering, fermentation, putrefaction, regression, ruin, ruination, spoilage, weakening, wear

BREVET, ***noun*** authorization, charge, charter, declaration, decree, edict, fiat, grant, law, license, mandate, manifesto, ordinance, ordination, *placet,* precept, prescription, rule, sanction, warrant, writ

BRIBE, ***noun*** corrupt money, corrupt offering, graft, hush money, illegal donation, illegal incentive, illegal incitation, illegal inducement, illegal lure, illegal offer, illegal offering, illegal present, illegal reward, offering, *pretium,* protection money, sop, unlawful bait, unlawful compensation, unlawful gift, unlawful gratuity
ASSOCIATED CONCEPTS: acceptance of a bribe, bribe-giving for public office, bribe-receiving, bribery, bribing a witness, corruption, obstructing justice, offer to bribe, official misconduct, rewarding official misconduct, solicitation of a bribe, unlawful gratuities

BRIBERY, ***noun*** allurement, baiting, blandishment, breach of faith, bribing, cajolement, cajolery, collusion, complicity, connivance, corrupt inducement, corrupt payment, corruptibility, corruption, crime, criminality, enticement, illegal incitation, illegal inducement, improbity, inducement, inveiglement, jobbery, lawbreaking, luring, misdealing, opportunism, perfidy, pettifoggery, plying, pressure, prodition, seducement, snaring, tantalization, temptation, tempting, unlawful encouragement, venality
ASSOCIATED CONCEPTS: commercial bribery, obstruction of justice, official misconduct, public bribery

BRIEF, ***adjective*** abbreviated, abridged, aphoristic, bare, brisk, close, cometary, compact, compendious, compressed, concise, condensed, contracted, cursory, curtailed, cut short, elliptical, ephemeral, epigrammatic, epitomized, exact, fading, fleeting, hasty, hurried, laconic, limited, meteoric, momentary, not protracted, passing, pauciloquent, pithy, precise, quick, reduced, sententious, short, short-term, slight, small, sparing of words, speedy, succinct, sudden, summarized, summary, swift, temporary, to the point, transient, transitory, trenchant, unprolonged, volatile
ASSOCIATED CONCEPTS: brief description, brief statement, brief summary

BRIEF, ***noun*** abridgment, account, argument, capsule, compendium, condensation, conspectus, depiction, description, digest, extract, legal abstract, legal document, legal epitome, legal memorandum, memorandum, memorandum of law, outline, outline on the law, profile, representation, résumé, sketch, statement of the case, summary, summary on the law, synopsis, thumbnail sketch, vignette
ASSOCIATED CONCEPTS: *amicus curiae,* appellate brief, brief of evidence, points and authorities, reply brief, responsive brief

BRIGHT *(Intelligent),* ***adjective*** acute, adept, adroit, advanced, alert, apt, astucious, astute, aware, brilliant, clever, cunning, discerning, educated, erudite, fast on the uptake, genius, informed, ingenious, inventive, keen, knowledgeable, learned, literate, precocious, prudent, quick, quick-witted, resourceful, sagacious, sage, sapient, savvy, scholarly, sharp, shrewd, smart, well-read, wise

BRIGHT *(Luminous),* ***adjective*** airy, beaming, blazing, brilliant, burnished, coruscant, coruscating, dazzling, effulgent, flashing, glaring, gleaming, glowing, illumined, incandescent, irradiated, lighted, lightsome, lucent, lucid, luminous, lustrous, open, phosphorescent, polished, radiant, shimmering, shining, sparkling, sunlit, twinkling, vivid

BRILLIANCE, ***noun*** acuity, adeptness, aptitude, brainpower, discernment, erudition, highest IQ, insight, intellect, intelligence, knowledge, luminosity, mastery, mentality, perception, perspicacity, sagacity, sage, sapience, savvy, wisdom

BRING TO LIGHT, ***verb*** disclose, discover, educate, elucidate, enlighten, expose, get out in the open, impart, inform, knowledge, leak out, reveal, shed light on, shed new light, show, take the lid off of, take the wraps off, uncover, unearth, unfold, unmask
ASSOCIATED CONCEPTS: confidentiality, secrecy

BRINK, ***noun*** ambit, apex, barrier, border, borderland, borderline, boundary, brim, confines, cusp, edge, end, environs, frame, fringe, frontier, horizon, limit, line, line of demarcation, lip, margin, perimeter, periphery, proximity, radius, threshold, verge

BROAD, ***adjective*** ample, amplitudinous, *amplus,* blanket, collective, comprehensive, covering all cases, deep, diffuse, encyclopedic, expansive, extended, extending, extensive, far-flung, far-reaching, far-spread, full, general, generalized, generic, immense, inclusive, indefinite, indeterminate, indiscriminate, large, large-scale, latitudinous, *latus,* liberal, liberalistic, nonspecific, outspread, outstretched, pervasive, representative, spacious, spreading, standard, sweeping, synoptic, typical, ubiquitous, unbiased, unconfined, unspecified, vague, wide, widespread
ASSOCIATED CONCEPTS: broad appeal, broad definition, broad interpretation, broad meaning, broad sense, broad spectrum

BROADCAST *(Announce), **verb*** annunciate, circulate, declare, display, disseminate, divulge, drum, edict, endorse, enlighten, exhibit, expose, give currency to, give out, herald, make known, message, promulgate, pronounce, propound, publicize, publish, release, report, reveal, showcase, spread, state, suggest, tell, trumpet, utter, vocalize, voice

BROADCAST *(Televise), **verb*** cover, give air time to, have on a program, have on a show, include on a televised show, perform, prerecorded transmission, put on the air, telecast, transmit, transmit live
ASSOCIATED CONCEPTS: entertainment law

BROADEN, ***verb*** aggrandize, amplify, augment, build, develop, distend, double, drag out, enlarge, expand, extend, fill, fill out, flush out, grow, increase, inflate, magnify, open up, protract, spread, stretch, string out, supplement, swell, unfold, unfurl, unroll, widen
ASSOCIATED CONCEPTS: broaden an investigation

BROKEN *(Fractured), **adjective*** crumbled, damaged, defective, destroyed, disintegrated, dismembered, divided, fractional, fragmentary, injured, lacerated, mangled, mutilated, pulverized, riven, ruptured, sectional, separated, severed, shattered, shivered, slivered, splintered

BROKEN *(Interrupted), **adjective*** checked, deranged, desultory, disarranged, disconnected, discontinuous, disjunct, disordered, divided, erratic, fitful, halting, hindered, incomplete, inconstant, intermittent, irregular, obstructed, spasmodic, sporadic, stopped, suspended, unequal, uneven, unsteady, unsuccessive, variable

BROKEN *(Unfulfilled), **adjective*** contravened, delinquent, derelict, disloyal, disobedient, disregarded, disregardful, dutiless, encroached upon, infringed, infringing, inobservant, insubordinate, lawless, nonadhering, nonobservant, repudiated, transgressed, uncompliant, undutiful, unfaithful, unlawful, unloyal, unobservant, untrue, violated, violative

BROKER, ***noun*** agent, bargaining agent, commission agent, commission merchant, customers' man, dealer, deputy, factor, go-between, intermediary, intermedium, internuncio, *interpres,* link, matchmaker, mediator, medium, middleman, monger, negotiant, negotiator, realtor, regrater, representative, trader
ASSOCIATED CONCEPTS: brokerage, broker's commission, exchange broker, insurance broker, merchandise broker, notebroker, pawnbroker, real estate broker, stockbroker

BROKERAGE, ***noun*** charge, charges, commission, compensation, discount, emolument, factorage, fee, recompense, remuneration
ASSOCIATED CONCEPTS: agents, brokerage business, brokerage commission, brokerage contract, brokers, commissions

BROOD, ***verb*** agonize, be dejected, cogitate, consider, contemplate, deliberate over, despair, despond, dwell upon, fret, grieve, *incubare,* meditate on, mope, morbidly meditate, mull over, muse, ponder, reflect, ruminate, study, sulk, think anxiously, think over, weigh

BROWBEAT, ***verb*** abash, badger, beat down, bully, chide, cow, daunt, deflate, discourage, dishonor, domineer, dress down, drive, exert pressure on, frighten, give one a talking to, goad, harass, humble, humiliate, intimidate, make nervous, make one feel small, nag, overawe, overbear, override, petrify, prevail upon, push into, put in fear, put pressure on, raise apprehensions, reprove, scare, set down, shame into, subdue, trounce

BRUTAL, ***adjective*** atrocious, barbarous, bearish, beastly, bestial, bloody, brutelike, brutish, churlish, coarse, cruel, despotic, domineering, excessive, extreme, fell, ferocious, *ferus,* fierce, flint-hearted, grim, gross, gruff, hardhearted, harsh, *immanis,* inexorable, inhuman, *inhumanus,* mean, merciless, oppressive, over-harsh, overbearing, persecuting, pitiless, primitive, remorseless, rough, rugged, ruthless, sadistic, savage, severe, stonyhearted, truculent, tyrannical, tyrannous, uncivilized, unfeeling, ungentle, unmerciful, unrelenting, untamed, vicious, violent

BRUTALITY, ***noun*** act of inhumanity, barbarity, bestiality, brutalness, brutilization, brutishness, cruelness, cruelty, grossness, hardness, hardness of heart, harshness, heart of stone, heartlessness, *immanitas,* inhumanity, lack of feeling, mercilessness, moral insensibility, pitilessness, ruffianism, ruthlessness, savageness, savagery, truculence, truculency, unfeelingness, violence
ASSOCIATED CONCEPTS: cruel and inhuman treatment, cruel and unusual punishment

BRUTALIZE, ***verb*** barbarize, be pitiless, be vicious to, be wicked to, brutify, bully, corrupt, decivilize, deform one's character, dehumanize, demoralize, hurt, injure, lead astray, make insensitive, make wicked, maltreat, mislead, molest, oppress, persecute, pervert, render evil, run down, seduce, teach wickedness, tyrranize
ASSOCIATED CONCEPTS: assault, cruel and inhuman punishment

BUDGET, ***noun*** accountancy, accounts, allocation, allotment, allowance, appropriation, balance sheet, balance statement, distribution, estimated expenditures, planned disbursement, profit and loss account, provision, ration, statement, statement of account
ASSOCIATED CONCEPTS: appropriations, budget bill, budget notes, itemized budget, municipal budget, public debt limitations

BUFFER ZONE, ***noun*** added protection, bulkhead, bulwark, insulation, medium, rampart, screen, territory for defense

BUILD *(Augment), **verb*** add to, aggrandize, amplify, develop, elevate, enhance, enlarge, expand, extend, grow, heighten, increase, lift, magnify, make higher, make larger, parlay, pyramid, raise, rise, swell

BUILD *(Construct), **verb*** achieve, assemble, carpenter, cast, compile, compose, construct, contrive, create, devise, elevate, engineer, erect, establish, evolve, fabricate, fashion, figure, form, found, frame, lay the foundation, make, manufacture, model, originate, produce, put up, raise, set up, shape, superstruct, upbuild

BUILD UP, ***verb*** accelerate, accrete, accrue, accumulate, aggregate, amass, bulk, concentrate, conglomerate, distend, elevate, enhance, enlarge, enrich, escalate, expand, flesh out, fortify, gain, gather, heighten, inflate, intensify, maximize, multiply, pile up, proliferate, raise, redouble, reinforce, stoke, swell

BUILDING *(Business of assembling), **noun*** *aedificatio,* amalgamation, architecture, arrangement, assembling, causation, collocation, compilation, composition, compounding, conformation, conjunction, constitution, construction,

contriving, craftsmanship, creating, design, development, devising, effectuation, efformation, engineering, establishment, fabrication, fashioning, formation, formulation, foundation, framing, grouping, handiwork, implementation, incorporation, industry, installation, institution, interrelation, making, manufacture, organization, origination, plan, prefabrication, preparation, production, shaping, structuring, synthesis
ASSOCIATED CONCEPTS: building for a particular use
FOREIGN PHRASES: ***Aedificare in tuo proprio solo non licet quod alteri noceat.*** It is not lawful to build upon one's own land what may injure another.

BUILDING *(Structure),* ***noun*** abiding place, abode, address, *aedificium,* boardinghouse, construction, domicile, *domus, dulce domum,* dwelling, dwelling place, edifice, elevation, erection, establishment, fabric, frame, framework, habitat, habitation, headquarters, home, homestead, house, institute, living quarters, lodging, lodging house, lodging place, lodgings, lodgment, piece of architecture, place, place of habitation, premises, quarters, residence, shelter, site, station, superstructure
ASSOCIATED CONCEPTS: building and construction contracts, building code, building contract, building inspector, building laws, building lien, building lines, building loan, building loan mortgage, building material, building or other improvement, building permit, building purposes, building restriction, building site, building superintendent, building trades

BULK, *noun* abundance, accumulation, a commanding portion, amount, *amplitudo,* batch, block, chief part, clump, cluster, corpus, greatest part, heap, lot, magnitude, *magnitudo,* main part, major part, majority, mass, *moles,* overwhelming part, predominant part, principal part, quantity, quantum, size, stack, substance, substantial number, substantial part, substantial quantity, volume
ASSOCIATED CONCEPTS: bulk assignments, bulk cargo, bulk price, bulk property, bulk sale, bulk sales, bulk sales act, bulk sales laws, bulk shipment, bulk storage, bulk transaction, stored in bulk

BULK TRANSFER, *noun* large asset transfer, main asset transfer, major business asset transfer

BULLETIN, *noun* announcement, commentary, communication, communiqué, digest, dispatch, dissemination, edition, gazette, latest news, memorandum, message, news, news flash, newsletter, notification, paper, periodical, promotion, pronouncement, record, release, report, review, scoop, statement, updates

BULWARK, *noun* abutment, asylum, barricade, barrier, bastion, battlement, buffer, bulkhead, buttress, citadel, defense, embankment, fort, fortification, fortress, guard, haven, insulation, insulator, palladium, parapet, preservation, *propugnaculum,* protection, rampart, refuge, safeguard, sanctuary, security, shelter, shield, stockade, stronghold, support

BUMPER CROP, *noun* a sufficiency, affluence, ampleness, amplitude, an ample amount, an ample supple, avalanche, bonanza, bounteousness, bountifulness, copiousness, flood, full measure, fullness, generosity, generousness, glut, great abundance, landslide, lavishness, much, outpouring, overbrim, overbrimming, overburden, overcharge, overflow, overload, plenty, plethora, profuseness, profusion, saturation, superabundance, surfeit

BUMPTIOUS, *adjective* audacious, contumelious, forward, obtrusive, procacious

BUNKO, *noun* bamboozlement, cheating, chicanery, con game, confidence trick, defraudation, double-dealing, dupery, ensnarement, flimflam, gyp, hoax, legal chicanery, pettifogging, racket, ruse, skulduggery, *supercherie,* swindle, trick, victimization, wile
ASSOCIATED CONCEPTS: bunko men, bunko steering, confidence game, fraud, gambling, larceny, wagering

BURDEN, *noun* accountability, adversity, affliction, anxiety, assignment, bother, botheration, bounden duty, brunt, call of duty, care, charge, chore, cumbrance, *devoir,* difficulty, drawback, duty, encumbrance, engagement, errand, handicap, hardship, hindrance, impediment, imposition, job, liability, line of duty, load, mandate, necessity, obligation, onus, oppression, ordeal, pains, requirement, requisite, responsibility, strain, task, tribulation, trouble, undertaking, vexation, weight, work
ASSOCIATED CONCEPTS: burden of covenant, burden of easement, burden of going forward with evidence, burden of loss, burden of persuasion, burden of proof, burden upon commerce, shifting of burden
FOREIGN PHRASES: ***Non debet alteri per alterum iniqua conditio inferri.*** A burdensome condition ought not to be imposed upon one man by the act of another. ***Cum par delictum est duorum, semper oneratur petitor et melior habetur possessoris causa.*** When there is equal fault on both sides, the burden is always placed on the plaintiff and the cause of the possessor is preferred. ***Actus curiae neminem gravabit.*** An act of the court shall prejudice no one. ***Probandi necessitas incumbit illi qui agit.*** The necessity of proving lies with the person who sues. ***Qui sentit onus sentire debet et commodum.*** He who assumes the burden ought to derive the benefit.

BURDEN OF GOING FORWARD, *noun* adequate evidence, adequate proof legally presented at trial, burden of proof, legal responsibility, obligation of going forward, sufficient corroboration, sufficient evidence in a case, sufficient evidence to establish a case, sufficient proof, sufficient proof of facts, validation of proof of a case, verification of proof of a case
ASSOCIATED CONCEPTS: cause of action or claim, evidence, evidentiary burden, failure to sustain, preponderance of the evidence, prima facie case, rebuttal
FOREIGN PHRASES: ***Onus probani.*** Burden of proof.

BURDEN OF PROOF, *noun* adequate evidence, adequate proof legally presented at trial, burden of going forward, legal responsibility, obligation of going forward, sufficient corroboration, sufficient evidence in a case, sufficient evidence to establish a case, sufficient proof, sufficient proof of facts, validation of proof of a case, verification of proof of a case
ASSOCIATED CONCEPTS: cause of action or claim, evidence, evidential burden, failure to sustain, preponderance of the evidence, prima facie case, rebuttal, weight of evidence
FOREIGN PHRASES: ***Onus probani.*** Burden of proof.

BUREAU, *noun* administration, administrative unit, agency, authority, board, branch, commission, committee, department, division, ministry, office, specialized administrative unit, specialized unit

BUREAUCRACY, *noun* administration, agency, authorities, delegated authority, departmentalization, governance, government, government by bureaus, government office, governmental procedure, governmental system for decision making, inflexible routine, management, ministration, official procedure, officialdom, officiation, organization, powers that be, process of governing, red tape, regulation, reins of government, rigid routine, rule, service, sovereignty, state management, strict procedure, system

BURGLAR, *noun* bandit, bank robber, criminal, despoiler, filcher, gangster, holdup man, *homo trium literarum,* housebreaker, larcener, marauder, pilferer, pillager, plunderer, prowler, raider, rifler, robber, safebreaker, safecracker, second-story thief, sneak thief, spoiler, stealer, stickup man, thief
ASSOCIATED CONCEPTS: burglar's tools, criminal trespass

BURGLARY, *noun* breaking and entering, crime, *effractura,* felony, filching, forcible entry, *furtum,* housebreaking, illegality, larceny, lawlessness, looting, marauding, pilfering, pillaging, plunderage, plundering, prowling, purloinment, raiding, robbery, robbing, spoiling, stealing, theft, thievery, unlawful act, unlawful breaking and entering, unlawfulness
ASSOCIATED CONCEPTS: burglar's tools, burglary insurance, common law burglary, receiving stolen goods, robbery, statutory burglary

BURN, *verb* blaze, blister, brand, burn to a cinder, burst into flame, catch fire, cauterize, char, conflagrate, consume, cremate, deflagrate, enkindle, fire, flame up, flare, gut, ignite, incandesce, incendiarize, incinerate, inflame, kindle, light up, melt, overheat, parch, relume, scald, scorch, scorify, sear, seethe, singe, sizzle, smelt, smolder, strike a light, vesicate
ASSOCIATED CONCEPTS: arson, revocation of wills

BURY *(Entomb),* ***verb*** embalm, enshrine, entomb, inhume, inter, inurn, lay to rest, place in a grave, sepulcher, tomb

BURY *(Hide),* ***verb*** camouflage, cloak, conceal, couch, cover, embed, engulf, ensconce, hide, immerse, inter, mask, obscure, plant, secret, shelter, squirrel away, stash away, store away, submerge, to put in a grave, tomb

BUSINESS *(Affair),* ***noun*** activity, concern, duty, interest, matter, mission, proceeding, proposition, responsibility, task, undertaking
FOREIGN PHRASES: ***Aliena negotia exacto officio geruntur.*** The business of another is to be carried out with particular care. ***Constitutum esse eam domum unicuique nostrum debere existimari, ubi quisque sedes et tabulas haberet, suarumque rerum constitutionem fecisset.*** It is established that the home of each of us is considered to be the place of his abode and books, and where he may have made an establishment of his business. ***In suo quisque negotio hebetior est quam in alieno.*** Everyone is more dull in his own business than in that of another.

BUSINESS *(Commerce),* ***noun*** barter, buying and selling, commercial intercourse, dealings, exchange, industry, intercourse, merchandising, merchantry, production, trade, trading, traffic, transaction, ventures
ASSOCIATED CONCEPTS: business address, business agent, business corporation, business crimes, business district, business done in state, business enterprise, business expenses, business hours, business interruption insurance, business invitees, business license, business losses, business name, business paper, business purposes, business records, business restrictions, business secrets, business situs, business trust, business venture, business visitor, doing business, good will of business, in the course of business, interference with business, ordinary course of business, transacting business
FOREIGN PHRASES: ***Ea quae raro accidunt non temere in agendis negotiis computantur.*** Those things which rarely happen are not to be taken into account in the transaction of business without sufficient reason.

BUSINESS *(Commercial enterprise),* ***noun*** cartel, combine, company, concern, corporation, establishment, firm, industry, manufacture, organization, private enterprise, shop, store, syndicate, venture

BUSINESS *(Occupation),* ***noun*** activity, avocation, calling, career, craft, duty, employment, endeavor, following, function, handicraft, job, line, livelihood, living, means of support, mission, office, practice, profession, pursuit, specialty, trade, undertaking, vocation, walk of life, work

BUSINESS JUDGMENT RULE, *noun* corporate director and officer immunity, good faith creating immunity, means to avoid a challenge to the decisions of officers, means to protect officers, means to uphold due care of officers, means to uphold good faith of officers, means to uphold loyalty of officers, reasonable care and prudence to avoid wrongdoing, shield from liability for corporate executives, shield from liability for directors

BUSY, *adjective* active, adroit, assiduous, attentive, brisk, bustling, conscientious, constant, diligent, eager, employed, energetic, engaged, engrossed, enthusiastic, focused, hard-working, indefatigable, industrious, involved, keenly working, laborious, nimble, occupied, operational, operative, persevering, persistent, persisting, preoccupied, purposeful, rapt, sedulous, snowed under, steady, studious, swamped, tied up, unrelenting, untiring, vigorous, vivacious, working copiously, zealous

BUTTRESS, *verb* bolster, boost, brace, bracket, build support, build up, build up the foundation, bulwark, buoy, cantilever, girder, grip, help, increase support, lever, pillow, prop, reinforce, shore up, stave, stirrup, strengthen, strut, support, sustain, truss
ASSOCIATED CONCEPTS: build up of damages, expert testimony

BUY, *verb* acquire by purchase, acquire ownership of, bargain for, complete a purchase, contract, get in exchange, make a purchase, make one's own, *mercari,* obtain, order, pay a price for, pay cash for, pay for, procure, procure title to, purchase, redeem, secure, secure for a consideration, trade
ASSOCIATED CONCEPTS: buy and sell agreement, buy in the ordinary course of business, buy long, buy out, buy short, buyer beware, buyer's needs, buyer's option, buyer's risk, buying a note or a bill, buying and receiving stolen goods, buying broker
FOREIGN PHRASES: ***Caveat emptor, qui ignorare non debuit quod jus alienum emit.*** Let a purchaser beware since he ought not to be ignorant that he is purchasing whatever rights another has. ***Emptor emit quam minimo potest, venditor vendit quam maximo potest.*** The buyer purchases for the least he can; the seller sells for the most he can. ***In pretio emptionis et venditionis, naturaliter licet contrahentibus se circumvenire.*** In respect to the price, in buying and selling, it is naturally permitted to the contracting parties to overreach one another.

BUYER, *noun* client, consumer, customer, end user, patron, prospect, prospective owner, purchaser, regular patron, shopper

BYLAW, *noun* canon, charter, code, municipal regulation, ordinance, prescript, prescription, *reglement,* regulation, rubric, rule, standard
ASSOCIATED CONCEPTS: amendment of bylaws, authorization for bylaws, enactment of bylaws, interpretation of bylaws, repeal of bylaws

BYPASS, *verb* avert, avoid, beguile, circumnavigate, circumvent, deflect, detour, deviate from, disregard, divert, dodge, duck, elude, escape, eschew, evade, flee, ignore, neglect, obviate, omit, overpass, parry, pass over, prevent, shake, shirk, shortcut, shun, sidestep, skirt, stave off, ward off

BYSTANDER, *noun* apprizer, attestant, attester, audience, beholder, corroborator, earwitness, enlightener, eyewitness, indicator, informant, informer, insider, listener, looker, looker-on, monitor, observer, one who bears witness, onlooker, passer-by, reporter, seer, spectator, swearer, teller, testifier, tipster, tout, undercover man, viewer, viewership, watcher, witness, witness, witness as to character, witness to a crime
ASSOCIATED CONCEPTS: accessory, disinterested party, Good Samaritan, innocent bystander, third persons

CABAL, *noun* band, camarilla, clique, coalition, collusion, combination, complicity, complot, confederacy, connivance, conspiracy, council, design, *factio,* faction, gang, intrigue, junta, league, machination, plot, ring, scheme, secret group, secret plot, *societas clandestina,* union

CACHE *(Hiding place),* ***noun*** *abri,* ambuscade, backroom, confinement, hideaway, inmost recesses, place of concealment, protectory, refuge, safe place, safe retreat, secret place, shelter, undercover

CACHE *(Storage place),* ***noun*** depository, place of deposit, place of safety, promptuary, repertory, repository, reservoir, safe, safe place, secret storehouse, stockroom, storage, store of provisions, storehouse, storehouse for safekeeping, storeroom, warehouse

CADAVER, *noun* carcass, corpse, corpus delecti, dead body, victim

CADUCITY, *noun* decadence, decay, decline, decrepitude, degeneracy, deterioration, dotage, feebleness, infirmity of old age, senility, weakness

CAITIFF, *adjective* abject, afraid, base, baseborn, brutish, churlish, craven, currish, dastardly, despicable, fainthearted, fear-stricken, ignoble, ignominious, low, lowborn, mean-spirited, of low extraction, of low origin, of mean extraction, of mean origin, poltroonish, pusillanimous, raffish, recreant, rude, scared, spiritless, uncivilized, uncourageous, unpolished, vile, vulgar, weak-minded

CAJOLE, *verb* allure, bait, coax, entice, importune, lure, ply, pressure, push, tease, tempt, urge

CALAMITY, *noun* act of God, adverse fortune, adversity, affliction, bad fortune, blight, *calamitas,* cataclysm, catastrophe, *clades,* destruction, disaster, evil fortune, evil lot, evil luck, grievous harm, hardship, ill fortune, loss, major misfortune, mischance, misery, misfortune, stroke, tragedy
ASSOCIATED CONCEPTS: calamity bonds

CALCULATE, *verb* account, appraise, ascertain mathematically, assess, average out, cast accounts, cipher, *computare,* compute, consider, count, design, determine, devise, enumerate, estimate, evaluate, figure, figure out, form an estimate, furnish an estimate, gauge, make a computation, make an estimate, measure, mete, number, place a value on, plan, predict, quantify, rank, rate, reckon, score, set a value on, size, suit, take an account of, take into account, take stock, take the dimensions, tally, think out, totalize, valorize, valuate, value, work out

CALCULATION, *noun* analysis, appraisal, arithmetic, assessment, calibration, ciphering, circumspection, computation, deciphering, deliberation, estimate, estimation, evaluation, figures, figuring, forecast, math, mathematics, measurement, number crunching, numbers, planning, prediction, prudence, reckoning, thought, valuation

CALENDAR *(List of cases),* ***noun*** agenda, cases ready for argument, court's log, docket, enumeration of causes arranged for trial, list of cases set down for hearing, list of causes arranged for trial, list of causes instituted in court, list of causes ready for trial, motion docket, order of cases, record, register, register of cases, schedule, systematic arrangement of cases, table of cases, timetable, trial list
ASSOCIATED CONCEPTS: calendar practice, court calendar, *fasti*

CALENDAR *(Record of yearly periods),* ***noun*** agenda, almanac, annals, chronicle, chronology, daybook, diary, docket, established division of time, history, journal, list of

appointments, list of events, log, logbook, memoranda, menology, order of business, plans, program, record, record of yearly periods, register, schedule, schedule of events, sequence of events, system of reckoning time, table, tabular register of the year, timetable
ASSOCIATED CONCEPTS: calendar day, calendar month, calendar week, calendar year, Gregorian calendar

CALIBER *(Measurement),* ***noun*** amount, amplitude, area, breadth, broad gauge, broadness, compass, cross dimension, cross measurement, degree, diameter, diameter of a cylindrical body, dimensions, expanse, extent, full size, gauge, girth, grade, magnitude, mass, measure, measured size, measurement across, proportion, scale, size, thickness, width

CALIBER *(Mental capacity),* ***noun*** ability, ableness, acumen, acuteness, adequacy, aptitude, arguteness, attainment, capability, capableness, capacity, competence, comprehension, depth, discernment, discrimination, efficacy, efficiency, endowment, faculty, genius, gift, good judgment, instinct, intellect, intellectual power, intelligence, judgment, knowledge, mentality, perspicacity, proficiency, qualification, reach of mind, sagacity, sapience, specialty, talent, understanding, wisdom

CALIBER *(Quality),* ***noun*** attribute, capability, character, distinctiveness, eminence, excellence, grade, importance, merit, potency, rate, standing, state, station, status, value, virtue, worth

CALL *(Appeal),* ***noun*** address, adjuration, application, beseechment, bid, cry, earnest request, entreaty, impetration, imploration, importunity, insistent demand, instance, invocation, invocatory plea, invocatory prayer, motion, obsecration, obtestation, petition, plea, prayer, request, requirement, requisition, solemn entreaty, solicitation, suit, supplication, *vox*
ASSOCIATED CONCEPTS: adjournment of a term of the court subject to call, calendar call, call contract, call prior to maturity, calls for more margin, dismissal for failure to answer a call

CALL *(Option),* ***noun*** alternative, choice, decision, demand made on a stock holder, discretion, discretionary order, freedom of choice, liberty of action, opportunity, requirement, requisition, right of put and call, stock agreement
ASSOCIATED CONCEPTS: "call" option on stock or assessments, calls and assessments, "puts" and "calls" as options in a contract

CALL *(Title),* ***noun*** agnomen, alias, antonomasia, appellation, appellative, application, baptism, byword, caption, cognomen, cognomination, compellation, convertible terms, description, designation, epithet, eponym, expression, given name, head, indication, matronymic, name, namesake, naming, nomenclature, patronymic, praenomen, prenomen, proper name, sign, signature, sobriquet, style, surname, synonym, term, trope

CALL *(Appeal to),* ***verb*** address a petition, address a request, address oneself to, adjure, appeal, apply to, ask, ask for, be a suppliant, beg a favor, beg leave, beseech, bespeak, call for aid, call for help, call upon, *clamare,* cry, cry to, entreat, impetrate, implore, importune, invite, invoke, make a petition, make a request, make a requisition, make appeal, make application, make bold to ask, make earnest entreaty, petition, plead for, plead with, prefer a petition, prefer a request, prefer an appeal, press, put to, put up a request, request, solicit, sue, supplicate, turn to, urge

CALL *(Demand),* ***verb*** ask for with authority, assert a right to, claim, claim as a right, clamor for, command, cry for, demand, *deposcere,* exact, *flagitare,* insist on, lay claim to, make a demand, make an authoritative request, make claims upon, make requisition, necessitate, oblige, order, prescribe, present an ultimatum, present one's claim, press, put in a claim for, render necessary, require, require of others, requisition, send an order for

CALL *(Summon),* ***verb*** ask to come, assemble, assemble by summons, beckon, bid come, command to appear, convene, convocate, convoke, desire the presence of, gather, group, invite, invoke, issue an invitation, mobilize, muster, muster up, page, rally, request the presence of, reunite, send for, serve with a writ, subpoena, summon forth, unite
ASSOCIATED CONCEPTS: call as a witness, call for trial, called in question, called to testify, calling the docket

CALL *(Title),* ***verb*** characterize, christen, classify, define, denominate, designate, determine, *dicere,* differentiate, discriminate, distinguish, entitle, give a name, identify, identify by name, individualize, label, name, *nominare,* personalize, provide with nomenclature, specify, supply with an epithet, tag, term, *vocare*

CALLING, ***noun*** activity, business, career, chosen work, concern, craft, employment, endeavor, enterprise, field, function, industry, job, learned profession, lifework, line, line of achievement, line of business, line of work, livelihood, living, means of earning a living, metier, mission, *munus,* occupation, office, operation, position, post, practice, profession, pursuit, specialization, specialty, sphere of activity, task, trade, undertaking, vocation, walk of life, work
ASSOCIATED CONCEPTS: trade or calling, unlawful calling

CALLOUS, ***adjective*** adamant, adamantine, brutal, *callosus,* cold, cold of heart, coldblooded, coldhearted, *durus,* hard, hard of heart, hardened, hard-hearted, heartless, impassive, impenetrable, impenitent, imperturbable, impervious, implacable, inclement, indifferent, indisposed to mercy, indurate, indurated, inexcitable, inexorable, inflexible, infrangible, insensate, insensible, insensitive, insentient, intolerant, obdurate, persecuting, pitiless, relentless, remorseless, rigorous, seared, severe, shock-proof, steeled against, stubborn, tearless, thick-skinned, toughened, unbending, unblushing, uncaring, uncomforting, uncompassionate, uncondoling, unconsoling, unfeeling, unforgiving, unimpressed, unimpressible, unimpressionable, unmelting, unmerciful, unmoved, unpardoning, unpitying, unrelenting, unruffled, unstirred, unsusceptible, unsympathetic, unsympathizing, unyielding

CALM, ***noun*** abeyance, break, cessation, composure, hush, lull, pausation, pause, peace, quiescence, quiet, quietude, respite, serenity, silence, spell, stillness, tranquility

CALUMNIOUS, ***adjective*** abusive, blackening, calumniatory, castigatory, caustic, censorious, comminatory, compromising, condemnatory, contemptuous, contumelious, criminatory, *criminosus,* damaging, damnatory, decrying, defamatory, denigratory, denunciatory, deprecatory, depreciative, depreciatory, derisive, derogatory, detractory, disapproving, discreditable, disparaging, disrespectful, evil-speaking, ignoble, ignominious, imprecative, imprecatory, imputative, injurious, insinuating, insolent, insulting, libelous, maledictory, malevolent, obloquial, obloquious, offensive,

opprobrious, pejorative, scandalous, scurrile, scurrilous, slanderous, slighting, smearing, stigmatizing, unflattering, vilifying, vituperative
ASSOCIATED CONCEPTS: contempt of court, defamation

CAMOUFLAGE, *verb* adumbrate, alter the appearance of, assume a mask, be concealed, becloud, becurtain, bedim, befog, bemask, blanket, blind, bury, change the face of, cloak, close the curtain, cloud, color, conceal, couch, cover, cover up, curtain, deceive, deform, disguise, dissemble, distort, draw the veil, dress up, embellish, embroider, ensconce, enshroud, envelop, fake, gild, give a color to, give a false appearance, give a false coloring, hide, hide away, hide one's identity, keep from sight, keep from view, keep in the dark, keep in the shade, keep out of view, keep secret, make unrecognizable, mask, masquerade, miscolor, obfuscate, obscure, occultate, pervert, put in concealment, reshape, screen, screen from observation, screen from sight, seclude, secrete, shade, shroud, suppress, throw a veil over, twist, twist the meaning of, veil
ASSOCIATED CONCEPTS: fraudulent misrepresentation

CAMPAIGN, *noun* action, activism, activity, cause, course of action, course of conduct, course of proceeding, crusade, design, drive, effort, emprise, endeavor, enterprise, exercise, exertion, expedition, hard task, implementation, large undertaking, line of action, line of conduct, line of proceeding, maneuvering, maneuvers, measures, method, mobilization, motion, movement, operation, organization, plan, plan of offensive, plot, procedure, program, project, proposal, proposition, quest, scheme, self-imposed task, steps, *stipendium,* stratagem, strategy, struggle, tactics, task, undertaking, voluntary work, warfare
ASSOCIATED CONCEPTS: campaign committee, campaign contributions, campaign expenditures, campaign expenses, campaign funds, election campaign, political campaign

CANARD, *noun* deceit, deception, fabrication, false report, false rumor, false statement, falsehood, falsification, fiction, fraud, groundless story, hoax, lie, report intended to delude, roorback, rumor, ruse, trick, unfounded story, untruth, untruthful report

CANCEL, *verb* abolish, abort, abrogate, annihilate, annul, avoid, countermand, counterorder, counterpoise, declare invalid, declare null and void, *delere,* deny, deprive of force, discard, disclaim, discontinue, disestablish, dismiss, dissolve, drop, end, eradicate, excise, expunge, exterminate, extinguish, *inducere,* invalidate, make void, negate, not proceed with, nullify, obliterate, override, overrule, put an end to, quash, quell, quench, recall, recant, remove, render invalid, render useless, render void, renege, repeal, repudiate, rescind, restrain, retract, reverse, revoke, set aside, suspend, terminate, *tollere,* vacate, void, withdraw
ASSOCIATED CONCEPTS: cancel a contract, cancel a debt, cancel an instrument, cancel an order, obsolete, rescission, termination, void

CANCELLATION, *noun* abandoning, abandonment, abolishing, abolishment, abolition, abrogation, abscission, annulling, annulment, cassation, circumduction, countermand, counterorder, deletion, discontinuance, dismissal, dissolution, dissolving, disuse, elimination, eradication, erasure, excision, expunction, extinction, invalidating, invalidation, liquidation, moratorium, negation, nonuse, nullification, nullifying, overruling, rasure, recall, recalling, recantation, relinquishment, renunciation, repeal, repudiation, rescinding, rescindment, rescission, retracting, retraction, reversal, reversing, revocation, revokement, revoking, supersession, surrender, suspension, termination, unmaking, vacation, vacatur, voidance, voiding, waiver, withdrawal, withdrawing
ASSOCIATED CONCEPTS: abatement, cancellation of a contract, cancellation of a lease, cancellation of a mortgage, cancellation of a will, cancellation of an insurance policy, cancellation of bills, cancellation of certificate of registration, cancellation of instruments, cancellation of judgment, cancellation of notes, judicial cancellation

CANDID, *adjective* aboveboard, *apertus sincerus,* apparent, blunt, *candidus,* categorically true, creditworthy, direct, explicit, express, forthright, frank, frankhearted, honest, ingenuous, *liber,* not lying, objective, open, outright, outspoken, overt, realistic, reliable, scrupulous, *simplex,* sincere, straightforward, substantially true, true, true to scale, true to the facts, trustworthy, truthful, unconstrained, undisguised, undissembling, undistorted, uninhibited, unperfidious, unperjured, unreserved, unshaded, untreacherous, veracious, veridical, veritable, verus

CANDIDATE, *noun* applicant, aspirant, aspirer, *candidatus,* challenger, competitor, contender, contestant, designee, desirer, entrant, hopeful, job seeker, nominee, office hunter, office seeker, petitioner, political aspirant, political contestant, runner, seeker, struggler
ASSOCIATED CONCEPTS: candidate for election, candidate for political office, candidate for public office, judicial candidate, legislative candidate, political candidate

CANDOR *(Impartiality),* ***noun*** detachment, disinterestedness, disinterestness, dispassionateness, equitableness, equity, even-handedness, evenness, fair treatment, fairness, justness, liberality, neutrality, nonpartisanship, objectivity, probity, unbias, unprejudicedness

CANDOR *(Straightforwardness),* ***noun*** bluntness, candidness, directness, forthrightness, frankness, genuineness, guilelessness, honesty, ingenuousness, openness, outspokenness, reliability, sincerity, unaffectedness, unpretentiousness, uprightness

CANNABIS, *noun* arouser, bhang, cannabis sativa, drug, grass, hash, hashish, hemp, marijuana, narcotic, opiate, pot, weed
ASSOCIATED CONCEPTS: drug laws

CANON, *noun* act, behest, citation, code, command, commandment, criterion, decree, demand, dictate, dictation, dictum, direction, edict, established principle, fiat, fundamental principle, general rule, imperative, imposition, instruction, interdiction, law, legislation, *lex,* mandate, manifesto, *norma,* order, ordinance, precept, prescript, prescription, proclamation, pronunciamento, public announcement, *regula,* regulation, requirement, requisition, rescript, rule, rule of conduct, ruling, standard, statute, test, ultimatum, warrant, word, writ
ASSOCIATED CONCEPTS: canon law, canons of construction, canons of ethics, canons of judicial ethics, canons of justice, professional canon, rule of construction

CANONS OF ETHICS, *noun* canons governing professional conduct, code of ethics, code of professional responsibility, guidelines of conduct for lawyers, limitations for conduct of attorneys, requirements that govern the conduct of the members of the legal profession, restrictions for conduct of lawyers, rules governing attorney conduct, rules governing lawyers, rules governing the practice of law, rules of professional responsibility

CANTANKEROUS, *adjective* acrimonious, bad-tempered, bilious, captious, caustic, caviling, choleric, churlish, contentious, contrary, critical, cross, demanding, disagreeable, disparaging, fractious, harried, huffy, indignant, irascible, irate, irritable, irritating, nasty, obstinate, offensive, on edge, ornery, peevish, perverse, petulant, quarrelsome, querulous, quick-tempered, rude, severe, testy, uncouth

CANVASS, *verb* *ambire,* analyze, ask, ask earnestly, audit, bring in question, carry on an inquiry, conduct an inquiry, count, delve into, dig into, discuss, dissect, examine, examine searchingly, explore, follow up an inquiry, hold an inquiry, inquire, inquire into, inspect, institute an inquiry, investigate, look about for, look into, make a survey, petition, poll, preexamine, probe, pursue an inquiry, question, report, request, research, review, scan, scrutinize, search, set up an inquiry, study, subject to examination, survey, take up an inquiry, throw open to inquiry
ASSOCIATED CONCEPTS: canvass a jury, canvass the members of a class

CAP, *noun* ceiling, greatest amount, lid, limit, maximum amount

CAP, *verb* complete, conclude, end, finish, finish off, get done, get through with, perfect, terminate

CAP AND TRADE, *noun* economic incentives to control pollution, emission trading scheme, emissions trading, environmental controls, free market emissions trading, means to avoid climate change, means to impose a limit on emissions, means to reduce pollutants, pollution controls, pollution permit trading, trading program to control air pollutants
ASSOCIATED CONCEPTS: environmental conservation, global warming, severe weather

CAPABLE, *adjective* able, accomplished, adept, adequate, adroit, *aptus,* competent, deft, effective, effectual, equal to, expert, facile, fit, fitted, gifted, *idoneus,* masterly, potent, proficient, qualified, skillful, suited, worthy
ASSOCIATED CONCEPTS: capable of assisting with one's defense, capable of contracting, capable of inheriting, capable of taking and holding property, capable to inherit, capable to marry, competence capable of distinguishing right from wrong

CAPACIOUS, *adjective* able to contain a great deal, ample, big, broad, capable of holding much, colossal, commodious, comprehensive, deep, expanded, expansive, extended, extensive, generous, gigantic, great, huge, immense, large, massive, roomy, spacious, substantial, vast, vasty, voluminous, wide

CAPACITY *(Aptitude),* ***noun*** ability, ableness, aptness, capability, capableness, competence, competency, effectuality, faculty, giftedness, potentiality, power, proficiency, qualification, range, reach, scope, skill, talent
ASSOCIATED CONCEPTS: full capacity, lack of capacity, legal capacity, lessened capacity, mental capacity, private capacity, proprietary capacity, quasi-judicial capacity, representative capacity, testamentary capacity, want of capacity
FOREIGN PHRASES: ***Sola ac per se senectus donationem testamentum aut transactionem non vitiat.*** Old age does not alone and of itself vitiate a will, gift, or transaction. ***Furiosus stipulare non potest nec aliquid negotium agere, qui non intelligit quid agit.*** An insane person who knows not what he is doing, cannot contract nor transact any business. ***Furiosus nullum negotium contrahere potest.*** An insane person can make no contract. ***Furiosi nulla voluntas est.*** A madman has no will. ***Homo potest esse habilis et inhabilis diversis temporibus.*** A man is capable and incapable at different times.

CAPACITY *(Authority),* ***noun*** accordance, allowance, authorization, certification, charter, consent, control, dispensation, droit, enablement, jurisdiction, justification, leave, legal capacity, liberty, license, permission, permit, power, prerogative, privilege, qualification, right, sanction, sovereignty, stature, supremacy, warrant
ASSOCIATED CONCEPTS: capacity to sue

CAPACITY *(Job),* ***noun*** assignment, function, occupation, position, role, situation, task

CAPACITY *(Maximum),* ***noun*** ampleness, amplitude, breadth, compass, comprehensiveness, containing power, extent, full complement, full extent, full volume, fullness, greatest amount, greatest extent, greatest size, holding ability, largeness, limit, limit of endurance, limitation, measure, physical limit, plenitude, reach, room, scope, spaciousness, stretch, tankage, upper limit, volume

CAPACITY *(Sphere),* ***noun*** ambit, area, arena, boundaries, bounds, division, domain, extent, field, jurisdiction, limits, orbit, pale, province, reach, realm, region, scope, specialty, stretch, territory

CAPITAL, *noun* assets, available means, balances, bank annuities, belongings, *caput,* cash supplies, credits, economic resources, finances, financial provision, financial resources, funds, funds for investment, funds in hand, holdings, income, investment portfolio, investments, line of credit, liquid assets, money, pecuniary resources, property, ready cash, receipts, reserves, resources, revenue, savings, *sors,* working assets
ASSOCIATED CONCEPTS: authorized capital, capital account, capital assets, capital budget, capital case, capital construction, capital contribution, capital crime, capital expenditure, capital gains, capital gains tax, capital improvement, capital in a corporation, capital investment, capital loss, capital of a state, capital offense, capital outlay, capital paid-in, capital project, capital punishment, capital reserve, capital stock, capital surplus, circulating capital, distribution of capital, equity capital, fixed capital, floating capital, impairment of capital, reduction of capital, return of capital, stated capital, working capital
FOREIGN PHRASES: ***Excusat aut extenuat delictum in capitalibus quod non operatur idem in civilibus.*** That excuses or extenuates a wrong in capital cases which would not have the same effect in civil suits.

CAPITAL PUNISHMENT, *noun* dealing death, death, death sentence, execution, extreme penalty, judicial murder, killing
ASSOCIATED CONCEPTS: cruel and unusual punishment

CAPITALIZE *(Provide capital),* ***verb*** advance, afford aid, afford support, aid, aid with a subsidy, back, back up, bring aid, contribute, extend credit, favor, finance, fund, furnish aid, furnish foundations, furnish support, give aid, give support, help, invest, lend, lend one's aid, lend support, loan, pension, promote, provide capital for, provide for, provide funds for, provide money for, set up, set up in business, sponsor, subsidize, supply aid, supply support, supply with a subsidy, support, venture capital

ASSOCIATED CONCEPTS: capitalization of income, capitalization of net income, capitalization of stabalized income, capitalize earning

CAPITALIZE *(Seize the chance),* ***verb*** avail oneself of, benefit, convert to use, create an opening, employ, exploit, find one's advantage in, make an opening, make the most of, make use of, manipulate, profit, put in operation, put to advantage, put to service, reap the benefit of, render useful, take advantage of, take the opportunity, turn to good account, turn to one's advantage, utilize, utilize for profit

CAPITULATION, ***noun*** abandonment, acquiescence, assent, compliance, consent, docility, giving way, nonresistance, obedience, passiveness, passivity, recedence, recession, relinquishment, resignation, resignedness, self-abnegation, submission, submissiveness, submittal, surrender, unresistingness, yielding
ASSOCIATED CONCEPTS: confession, nolo contendere, plea of guilty

CAPRICIOUS, ***adjective*** apt to change suddenly, changeable, changeful, changing, erratic, everchanging, fanciful, fantasied, fantastical, fickle, flighty, fluctuating, frivolous, giddy, *inconstans,* inconstant, irresolute, irresponsible, *levis,* mercurial, reversible, uncertain, uncontrolled, undisciplined, unmethodical, unreliable, unrestrained, unstable, unsystematic, vacillating, vagarious, variable, wavering, whimsical, without rational basis
ASSOCIATED CONCEPTS: arbitrary and capricious, arbitrary, capricious and unlawful, review of administrative determination

CAPSULE, ***noun*** abbreviation, *abrégé,* abridgment, abstract, analysis, brief, capitulation, compend, compendium, compression, condensation, conspectus, contents, digest, epitome, essence, minute, note, outline, pandect, précis, recapitulation, reduction, résumé, review, skeleton, sketch, substance, sum and substance, summary, syllabus, synopsis

CAPTION, ***noun*** annotation, banner, banner head, banner line, characterization, clause, description, designation, display line, head, heading, headline, headnote, imprint, indication of contents, inscription, legend, mark of identification, notes, preface, rubric, section head, specification, statement, subhead, subheading, subtitle, superscription, title, topic
ASSOCIATED CONCEPTS: caption of a petition, caption of a pleading, caption of indictment

CAPTIOUS, ***adjective*** carping, caviling, critical, demanding, discriminating, exacting, fastidious, faultfinding, finicky, fussy, harsh, hypocritical, judgmental, nit-picking, overcritical, particular, pettifogging, picky, quibbling, rejective, unforgiving

CAPTIVE, ***noun*** bondman, bondsman, *captivus,* captured person, *captus,* convict, felon, helot, hostage, imprisoned person, incarcerated person, inmate, internee, one held in captivity, one held in confinement, one held in subjegation, pawn, person under arrest, prisoner, slave, subject, thrall, victim

CAPTIVITY, ***noun*** bondage, *captivitas,* commitment, committal, confinement, constraint, custody, detention, durance, duress, enslavement, entombment, immuration, immurement, impoundment, imprisonment, incarceration, internment, jail, prison, quarantine, quarantine station, restraint, slavery, subjection, subjugation, term of imprisonment
ASSOCIATED CONCEPTS: domestic animals in captivity

CAPTURE, ***verb*** apprehend, arrest, *capere,* carry away, catch, *comprehendere,* confine, hold captive, hold in captivity, immure, impress, imprison, incarcerate, jail, lock up, make an arrest, make prisoner, net, repress, restrain, restrict, seize, subdue, take by assault, take by force, take captive, take into custody, take possession of, take prisoner
ASSOCIATED CONCEPTS: capture of a criminal defendant, capture of wild animals, captured property

CARDINAL *(Basic),* ***adjective*** apical, basal, capital, central, chief, controlling, elemental, elementary, essential, first, foremost, fundamental, indispensable, key, main, material, necessary, overruling, pivotal, *praecipuus,* preponderant, primal, primary, prime, *primus,* principal, rudimentary, strategic, substantial, substantive, summital, underlying, undermost, uppermost, utmost, vital
ASSOCIATED CONCEPTS: cardinal rule

CARDINAL *(Outstanding),* ***adjective*** absolute, all powerful, best, central, chief, commanding, controlling, crowning, dominant, eventful, excellent, finest, foremost, greatest, greatest possible, highest, incomparable, inimitable, insurmountable, key, leading, major, maximal, momentous, most important, notable, paramount, *praecipuus,* predominant, preeminent, preponderant, prevailing, prime, *primus,* second to none, supereminent, superlative, supreme, top, unequaled, unexcelled, unparalleled, unsurpassed, uppermost, utmost

CARE *(Be cautious),* ***verb*** be cautious, be concerned, bear in mind, beware, consider, *curare,* give heed to, guard, have regard, heed, look out for, mind, pay attention to, protect, take precautions, watch out for, watch over
ASSOCIATED CONCEPTS: care and caution, care and skill, careful, careless, degree of care, due care, extraordinary care, great care, lack of care, ordinary care, slight care, want of care

CARE *(Regard),* ***verb*** administer to, attend, attend to, be concerned, be concerned for, become involved, bother, *curare,* foster, mind, minister to, nurture, pay attention to, protect, serve, supervise, support, sustain, tend, watch over
ASSOCIATED CONCEPTS: care and custody, care and maintenance, custody or control

CAREER, ***noun*** activity, avocation, business, calling, chosen work, craft, *curriculum, cursus,* employment, field, job, lifework, line, livelihood, metier, occupation, office, position, post, profession, pursuit, situation, skilled occupation, specialty, trade, vocation, work

CAREFUL, ***adjective*** *accuratus,* alert, attentive, *attentus,* cautious, circumspect, concerned, *diligens,* discreet, foresighted, guarded, heedful, judicious, meticulous, mindful, on one's guard, on the alert, overcautious, painstaking, precautious, provident, prudent, regardful, scrupulous, thoughtful, unadventurous, unenterprising, vigilant, watchful, wide-awake
ASSOCIATED CONCEPTS: careful and prudent manner, caution, diligence, due care, protection, prudence, reasonable care

CARELESS, ***adjective*** casual, cursory, disregardful, forgetful, hasty, heedless, hurried, impetuous, improvident, imprudent, impulsive, inadvertent, inattentive, incautious, inconsiderate, indifferent, indiscreet, injudicious, insouciant, irresponsible, lackadaisical, lax, loose, neglectful, *neglegens,* negligent, nonchalant, oblivious, overhasty, perfunctory, pococurante, precipitant, precipitate, rash, reckless, regardless, remiss, slack, slipshod, sloppy,

superficial, temerarious, thoughtless, unapprehensive, uncalculating, uncircumspect, unconcerned, unguarded, unmindful, unobservant, unthinking, unwary, wasteful
ASSOCIATED CONCEPTS: careless and imprudent manner, careless and negligent manner, grossly careless, negligence, recklessly careless, standard of care, wantonly careless

CARETAKER *(One caring for property),* ***noun*** archivist, attendant, *concierge,* convoy, curator, custodian, governor, guard, guardian, keeper, lookout, overseer, porter, sentry, sexton, steward, superintendent, supervisor, warden, watchman

CARETAKER *(One fulfilling the function of office),* ***noun*** administrator, collector, commissioner, controller, director, district officer, government servant, grand vizier, high official, key person, magistrate, manager, minister, officeholder, officer, officer in charge, officer of state, overseer, person in charge, public servant, state servant, superintendent

CARGO, ***noun*** baggage, boatload, bulk, capacity, carload, cartload, charge, commodities, consignment, contents, conveyance, freight, freightage, furnishings, goods, haul, impedimenta, lading, lading of a ship, load, luggage, merchandise, *onus,* pack, packages, payload, produce, provisions, shipload, shipment, shipping, stock, tonnage, trainload, transfer, truckload, vanload, ware, wares
ASSOCIATED CONCEPTS: carriers, delivery contract, hot cargo, risk of loss of cargo

CARICATURE, ***noun*** apery, cartoon, characterization, depiction, exaggerated likeness, exaggeration, farce, graphic treatment, grotesque portrayal, grotesque rendition, hyperbole, imitation, lampoon, mimicking, mimicry, mockery, overcoloring, overdrawing, overestimation, parody, personation, portrayal, satire, travesty

CAROUSE, ***verb*** be a drunkard, be convivial, be drunk, be immoderate, be intemperate, carry to excess, celebrate, *comissari,* commit a debauch, debauch, dissipate, drink, drink to excess, enervate oneself, exceed, feast, frolic, go on a spree, imbibe, indulge in dissipation, indulge oneself, lack self-control, live dissolutely, lose control, overindulge, *potare,* quaff, revel, spree, tipple, wallow
ASSOCIATED CONCEPTS: breach of peace, disorderly conduct, disturbing the peace

CARRIAGE, ***noun*** affreightment, airfreight, carrying, cartage, conveyance, drayage, portage, porterage, shipment, shipping, transfer, transference, translocation, transportation, transshipment, truckage, *vehiculum*
ASSOCIATED CONCEPTS: affreightment, carriage of goods, Carriage of Goods by Sea Act

CARRIER, ***noun*** conveyor, dispatcher, express shipper, ferrier, shipper, steamship company, transferor, transport company
ASSOCIATED CONCEPTS: air carriers, baggage, carrier by air, carrier engaged in interstate commerce, carrier for hire, carrier of goods, carrier of passengers, carrier's lien, common carriers, forwarding carriers, initial carriers, motor vehicle carrier, operating carriers, private carriers, public carriers, railroad carriers

CARRY *(Succeed),* ***verb*** accomplish, achieve, attain, be victorious, bring to pass, cause to happen, complete, culminate, effect, effectuate, gain, prevail, score, succeed, triumph, win
ASSOCIATED CONCEPTS: carry a vote

CARRY *(Transport),* ***verb*** bear, bring, cart, convey, convoy, haul, move, take, tote, transport
ASSOCIATED CONCEPTS: carry a concealed weapon, carry a weapon, carry back, carry on a business, carry on trade, carrying charges, carrying on a trade or business, carrying on any trade or business, carrying on business, larceny, take and carry away

CARRY AWAY, ***verb*** abduce, abduct, capture, carry off, commandeer, convey away, drag away, expropriate, kidnap, make off with, overcome, overpower, purloin, ravish, remove, remove bodily, run off with, seize, shanghai, spirit away, steal, take away, take by assault, take by stealth, take captive, take forcibly, take prisoner, thieve, waylay
ASSOCIATED CONCEPTS: abduction, asportation, kidnapping, theft
FOREIGN PHRASES: ***Cepit et asportavit.*** He took and carried away.

CARRY ON, ***verb*** adhere, carry through, continue, develop, endure, go forward, hang on, hold on, hold up, keep up, maintain, perpetrate, persevere, persist, prevail, proceed, remain, résumé, stay, tarry

CARRY OUT, ***verb*** accomplish, achieve, actualize, administer, attain, bring to a conclusion, complete, consummate, effect, effectuate, enforce, execute, finalize, finish, follow through, fulfill, implement, negotiate, perform, perpetrate, practice, prosecute, pull off, put through, realize, reduplicate, reenact

CARTEL, ***noun*** accord, accordance, affiliation, agreement, alliance, amalgamation, association, bloc, body corporate, coadjuvancy, coalition, colleagueship, combination, combine, common consent, community of interest, compact, concert, concord, concordance, concordat, concurrence, confederation, conjunction, consenus, consociation, consonancy, consort, consortium, contract, cooperation, covenant, federation, fusion, group, joint concern, league, merger, mutual understanding, organization, pact, sodality, syndicate, trust, union, unity
ASSOCIATED CONCEPTS: business cartel, international cartel

CASE *(Example),* ***noun*** demonstration, exemplification, illustration, instance, model, occurrence, paradigm, representative, representative selection, sample, specimen, type

CASE *(Lawsuit),* ***noun*** action, cause, claim, contention, controversy, court action, dissension, judicial contest, legal argument, legal dispute, legal issue, legal proceedings, litigation, matter, matter for judgment, proceedings, suit, suit at law
ASSOCIATED CONCEPTS: case arising under laws of the United States, case arising under the Constitution, case at common law, case in equity, case law, case of fraud, case on appeal, case or controversy, criminal case, dismissal of a case, divorce case, equity case, homicide case, injunction case, judicial case, jury case, justiciable case, law case, law of the case, leading case, meritorious case, pending case, prima facie case, sufficient case for jury, trespass on the case
FOREIGN PHRASES: ***Secta est pugna civilis; sicut actores armantur actionibus, et, quasi, a ccinguntur gladiis, ita rei muniuntur exceptionibus, et defenduntur, quasi c lypeis.*** A suit is a civil battle; for as the plaintiffs are armed with actions, and, as it were, girded with swords, so the defendants are fortified with pleas, and are defended, as it were, with shields. ***In consimili casu, consimile debet esse remedium.*** In similar cases, the remedy should be similar. ***Ubi non est directa lex, standum est arbitrio judicis, vel***

procedendum ad similia. Where there is no direct law, the decision of the judge is to be taken, or references to be made to similar cases. ***Certa debet esse intentio, et narratio, et certum fundamentum, et certa res quae deducitur in judicium.*** The intention, declaration, foundation, and matter brought to the court to be tried ought to be certain.

CASE *(Set of circumstances),* ***noun*** affairs, arrangement, background, circumstance, condition, conjuncture, context, course of events, existing state, factors, grounds, juncture, milieu, occurrence, place, plight, point, position, posture, predicament, set of facts, setting, situation, standing, state, state of affairs, status, terms

CASE HISTORY, ***noun*** actions, analysis, archive chronology, background, chronicle, circumstances, documentation, fact sheet, facts, factual background, framework, grounding, history, in-depth analysis, narrative, preparation, record, report, summary, timeline
ASSOCIATED CONCEPTS: criminal rap sheet, priors

CASE IN POINT, ***noun*** another example, as in the instant case, exactly the same case as what is being discussed, example, explanation, for instance, illustration, illustrative case, in this case, instance, instant case, model, occurrence, precedent, prime example, proof, real-life situation, relevant case, representative, the immediate situation
ASSOCIATED CONCEPTS: collateral estoppels, res judicata

CASH, ***noun*** available means, bill, capital, coin, coin of the realm, coinage, currency, dollar currency, finances, funds, hard money, legal tender, medium of exchange, monetary unit, money, moneys, pecunia praesens, pecuniary resources, principal, ready money, reserve, resources, riches, specie, treasure, working assets
ASSOCIATED CONCEPTS: cash and securities, cash assets, cash bail, cash bond, cash dividend, cash down, cash method, cash on delivery, cash on hand, cash surrender value, cash value

CAST *(Register),* ***verb*** assert, ballot, commit oneself, deposit formally, effect, establish, exercise one's choice, exercise one's options, give a vote, go to the polls, hold up one's hand, make a choice, make a decision, make a selection, make an entry, make one's choice, make one's selection, mark down, place on record, poll, put down, put on record, record, register one's vote, select, tabulate, vote
ASSOCIATED CONCEPTS: votes cast

CAST *(Throw),* ***verb*** bestrew, catapult, *conicere,* disseminate, distribute, eject, emit, fling, force, hurl, *iactare,* impart, impel, launch, let off, *mittere,* project, propel, put into motion, radiate, send forth, send off, shed, spread, toss

CAST ASPERSIONS, ***verb*** accuse, asperse, attack, befoul, besmirch, blame, cast slurs, castigate, censure, chide, condemn, decry, defame, denigrate, denounce, deprecate, depreciate, derogate, disesteem, fault, impugn, injure, insult, libel, malign, mudsling, rebuke, reproach, reprobate, reprove, revile, slander, smear, vilify, villainize, vituperate
ASSOCIATED CONCEPTS: defamation, libel, slander

CAST LIGHT ON, ***verb*** illuminate, inform, light, light up, lighten up, radiate, throw light upon, throw sunlight on

CASTIGATE, ***verb*** admonish, be severe, berate, call to account, *castigare,* caution, censure bitterly, chasten, chastise, chide, criticize severely, deal retributive justice, discipline, excoriate, execrate, expostulate, objurgate, rebuke, remonstrate, reprehend, reprimand, reproach, reprove, scold, take to task, upbraid, vituperate
ASSOCIATED CONCEPTS: judicial censure

CASUAL, ***adjective*** aimless, apathetic, blase, causeless, cursory, designless, desultory, fortuitous, haphazard, inattentive, incidental, indeterminate, indifferent, indiscriminate, informal, insouciant, irregular, nonchalant, occasional, orderless, perfunctory, pococurante, purposeless, superficial, thoughtless, unarranged, uncertain, unconcerned, uncritical, undetermined, undirected, unexacting, unfixed, unmethodical, unmeticulous, unmindful, unordered, unorganized, unparticular, unprecise, unpunctilious, unstudied, unsystematic, unweighed
ASSOCIATED CONCEPTS: casual act, casual employment, casual transaction

CASUALTY, ***noun*** accident, adversity, affliction, backset, bad fortune, blight, calamity, catastrophe, contretemps, *débâcle,* disaster, emergency, hardship, ill fortune, ill hap, incident, infliction, injury, misadventure, mischance, misfortune, mishap, serious accident, setback, tragedy, unforeseen accident, unfortunate accident, unfortunate occurence
ASSOCIATED CONCEPTS: casualty insurance, casualty loss

CASUISTRY, ***noun*** behaviorism, deontology, empiricism, ethical philosophy, ethology, idealism, moral science, perfectionism, sophistry, utilitarianism

CATACHRESIS, ***noun*** distortion, exaggeration, false coloring, false construction, false reading, garbling, incorrect usage, misapplication, misapprehension, miscitation, misconception, misconstruction, misexplanation, misexplication, misexposition, misinterpretation, misjudgment, misquotation, misreading, misrendering, misrepresentation, mistake, mistranslation, misunderstanding, misusage, solecism, strained sense, wrong interpretation, wrong usage

CATACLYSM, ***noun*** alluvion, avalanche, convulsion, crash, debacle, deluge, disaster, disturbance, earthquake, eruption, extensive flood, flood, holocaust, inundation, overflow, overflowing, overrunning, quake, storm, temblor, tidal wave, tremor, upheaval, violent upheaval
ASSOCIATED CONCEPTS: act of God, state of emergency

CATALOGUE, ***verb*** analyze, arrange, assort, break down, compile, correlate, distribute, enter, file, group, identify, incorporate, index, label, match, name, number, order, organize, rank, register, segment, sort, tabulate, tally

CATALYST, ***noun*** abettor, activator, active element, active partisan, active reformer, actuator, *agacerie,* agent *provocateur,* agitator, animator, catalytic agent, cause, encouragement, encourager, excitant, exciter, ferment, force, goad, impeller, impetus, impulse, incentive, incitation, incitement, inducement, inspiration, inspirer, instigator, maneuverer, modifying cause, motivating force, motivation, mover, moving spirit, planner, popular ringleader, power, prompter, *provocateur,* provocation, provocative, spur, stimulant, stimulator, strategist, suggester

CATASTROPHE, ***noun*** accident, adversity, affliction, *calamitas,* calamity, cataclysm, collapse, contretemps, *débâcle,* decimation, desolation, destruction, devastation, disaster, downfall, emergency, eradication, extinction, great misfortune, hardship, havoc, holocaust, infliction, misadventure, mischance, misfortune, mishap, notable disaster, obliteration, ravage, ruin, ruination, scourge, serious calamity, tragedy

ASSOCIATED CONCEPTS: act of God, natural catastrophe, state of emergency

CATASTROPHIC, ***adjective*** annihilative, baleful, baneful, cataclysmal, cataclysmic, damaging, deadly, demolishing, deplorable, destroying, destructive, detrimental, devastating, dire, disastrous, eradicative, exterminatory, extirpate, fatal, harmful, horrid, hurtful, injurious, malefic, pernicious, ravaging, ruining, ruinous, sinister, tragic

CATCH, ***verb*** apprehend, arrest, bag, capture, clutch, collar, corner, corral, detain, ensnare, entangle, entrap, fasten, grasp, hold, incarcerate, net, seize, snap up, snare, spirit away, trap

CATCHALL, ***noun*** container, depository, holder, receiver, receptacle, repository
ASSOCIATED CONCEPTS: catchall clause to a contract

CATCHWORD, ***noun*** adage, byword, catch phrase, clew, cliché, clue, colloquialism, common saying, cue word, key, maxim, mot, password, pithy saying, saying, shibboleth, slogan, stock saying, tag, vogue word, watchword
ASSOCIATED CONCEPTS: trademarks

CATEGORICAL, ***adjective*** absolute, apodictic, assured, authoritative, beyond a shadow of doubt, beyond all question, clear-cut, complete, conclusive, confident, convinced, convincing, decided, decisive, definite, definitive, *definitus,* distinct, dogmatic, doubtless, emphatic, evidential, final, forceful, incontestable, incontrovertible, indisputable, indubitable, inevitable, irrefragable, irrefutable, past dispute, positive, settled, *simplex,* strong, total, ultimate, unambiguous, unassailable, unchangeable, unconditional, unconditioned, uncontested, undeniable, undisputed, unequivocal, unhesitating, unmitigated, unqualified, unquestionable, unquestioning, vehement, without a shade of doubt, without appeal, without reserve

CATEGORY, ***noun*** bracket, class, classification, cluster, cubbyhole, department, division, family, genus, grade, group, kind, league, niche, order, organization, rank, section, segment, selection, set, specialty, species, specification, subclass, subdivision, tier, title, type, unit, variety

CATHARSIS, ***noun*** abreaction, acting out, deliverance, detersion, discharge of emotions, emotional release, outlet, purgation, purge, release, riddance, ventilation

CAUCUS, ***noun*** assemblage, *assemblée,* assembly, *attroupement,* body of partisans, committee, conclave, concourse, conference, consultation, convention, convergence, convocation, council, council meeting, discussion, foregathering, gathering, ingathering, mass meeting, meet, meeting, meeting of political leaders, policy-fixing meeting, political confluence, *pourparler,* rally, session, subcommittee, summit, top-level meeting
ASSOCIATED CONCEPTS: congressional caucas, legislative caucus

CAUSAL, ***adjective*** causative, compelling, conductive, constitutive, creative, determinant, determinative, effective, effectual, formative, generating, generative, inception, inducing, influential, institutive, instrumental, originating, originative, productive
ASSOCIATED CONCEPTS: causal connection, causal negligence, causal relationship

CAUSATIVE, ***adjective*** beginning, causal, caused, constitutive, constructive, creative, determinant, directive, dominant, formative, generative, impelling, inceptive, induced, inducing, inductive, influential, inspired, institutive, original, originative, pivotal, predominant, primary, procreative, productive, responsible, stimulating

CAUSE *(Lawsuit),* ***noun*** action, action in court, case, legal action, legal proceedings, litigation, proceedings, subject of dispute, suit, suit at law, trial
ASSOCIATED CONCEPTS: accrual of a cause of action, adversary cause, cause of action, cause pending, meritorious cause, trial of a cause

CAUSE *(Reason),* ***noun*** agent, aim, allurement, base, basis, *causa,* causation, consideration, derivation, design, determinative, end, enticement, factor, foundation, generator, genesis, goal, ground, impulse, incitement, inducement, influence, instigation, intent, intention, mainspring, motivation, motive, object, objective, origin, prompting, purpose, rationale, root, source, spur, stimulant, stimulation, stimulus, temptation, underlying principle
ASSOCIATED CONCEPTS: accidental cause, adequate cause, cause and consequence, cause and effect, cause for removal, cause of death, cause of loss, cause of the injury, cause shown, challenge for cause, compelling cause, concurrent cause, contributing cause, controlling cause, dependent cause, direct cause, discharged for cause, dominant cause, due cause, effective cause, efficient cause, external cause, for cause, good cause, immediate cause, independent cause, initial cause, intervening cause, just cause, justifiable cause, legal cause, meritorious cause, natural cause, nature of the cause, originating cause, primary cause, probable cause, proper cause, proximate cause, reasonable cause, related concepts, remote cause, removal for cause, resulting cause, show cause, sole cause, sufficient cause, superseding intervening cause, supervening cause, unforeseen cause, without cause, without just cause

CAUSE, ***verb*** be responsible, be the author of, breed, bring, bring about, bring down, bring into existence, bring on, bring to pass, causa, compel, conduce to, contribute to, contrive, create, cultivate, develop, direct, effect, effectuate, elicit, engender, engineer, evoke, foment, generate, give occasion for, give origin to, give rise to, inaugurate, incite, induce, influence, initiate, inspire, institute, launch, lay the foundations, lead to, make, motivate, occasion, originate, precipitate, produce, prompt, provoke, sow the seeds of, start, stimulate, superinduce
ASSOCIATED CONCEPTS: causa causans, causa remota, causa *sine qua non*
FOREIGN PHRASES: ***Causa et origo est materia negotii.*** The cause and its origin are the essence of a transaction. ***Causa proxima non remota spectatur.*** The direct and not the remote cause is regarded. ***Causa vaga et incerta non est causa rationabilis.*** A vague and uncertain cause is not a reasonable cause. ***Cessante causa, cessat effectus.*** The cause ceasing, the effect ceases. ***Effectus sequitur causam.*** The effect follows the cause. ***Eventus est qui ex causa sequitur; et dicitur eventus quia ex causis evenit.*** An event is that which follows from the cause, and is called an "event" because it eventuates from causes. ***Malum non habet efficientem, sed deficientem, causam.*** Evil has not an efficient, but a deficient, cause. ***Scire proprie est rem ratione et per causam cognoscere.*** To know properly is to know a thing by its cause and its reason. ***Ubi lex aliquem cogit ostendere causam, necesse est quod causa sit justa et***

legitima. Where the law compels a man to show cause, it is necessary that the cause be just and legal. ***Causae dotis, vitae, libertatis, fisci, sunt inter favorabilia in lege.*** Causes of dower, life, liberty, revenue are among the things favored in law.

CAUSE-IN-FACT, ***noun*** actual cause, causation, derivation, immediate legal basis, sufficiently legal basis, sufficiently legal cause, sufficiently legal factor, sufficiently legal genesis, sufficiently legal inducement, sufficiently legal source

CAUSE OF ACTION, ***noun*** action, action at law, basis for relief, cause, claim, claim for relief, demand, enforceable claim, ground, issue, just claim, lawful cause, legal assertion, reason for legal pursuit, reason for relief, reasonable claim, redressible wrong, right, right of action, right of recovery, right to relief
ASSOCIATED CONCEPTS: accrual of a cause of action, capacity to institute a cause of action, collateral estoppel, derivative cause of action, facts giving rise to a cause of action, facts sufficient to constitute a cause of action, inconsistent claims, joint interest in a cause of action, limitation of actions, meritorious cause of action, relief splitting a cause of action, res judicata, venue

CAUSEWAY, ***noun*** acceleration lane, access road, *agger,* approach road, arterial, arterial highway, artery, avenue, by-passage, causey, concourse, crossroad, drive, driveway, express, express highway, expressway, freeway, highroad, highway, lane, motor road, motorway, parkway, paved road, paved way, post road, raised path, raised road, road, roadway, service road, side road, speed track, speedway, state highway, street, superhighway, thoroughfare, through road, thruway, trunk road, turnpike

CAUSTIC, ***adjective*** abrasive, abrupt, *acerbus,* acrid, acrimonious, acute, astringent, austere, biting, brash, burning, corroding, corrosive, cruel, curt, cutting, derisive, derisory, envenomed, erosive, excorciating, excruciating, harsh, hurtful, insulting, invidious, irritating, lashing, malevolent, malicious, malignant, mocking, mordacious, *mordax,* mordent, piercing, pungent, pyrotic, rancorous, rude, scalding, severe, sharp, short, stinging, tart, tormenting, tortuous, trenchant, ungentle, unkind, venomous, virulent

CAUSTIC, ***adjective*** accusing, acrimonious, argumentative, attacking, belligerent, blaming, cantankerous, captious, caustic, charging, combative, contentious, contrary, contumacious, factious, hostile, implausible, irrational, ludicrous, mean, nasty, nonsensical, obnoxious, odious, offensive, outrageous, perverse, preposterous, pugnacious, recalcitrant, ridiculous, unreasonable, wrangling

CAUTION *(Vigilance),* ***noun*** attention, attentiveness, care, carefulness, *cautio,* circumspection, concern, conscientiousness, consideration, *cura,* diligence, exactitude, exactness, forethought, guardedness, heed, heedfulness, meticulousness, mindfulness, prudence, *prudentia,* regard, thoroughness, wariness, watchfulness
ASSOCIATED CONCEPTS: due caution, ordinary caution

CAUTION *(Warning),* ***noun*** admonition, alarm, alert, augury, caveat, exhortation, foreboding, foretelling, forewarning, monition, notice, omen, portent, precursor, prefiguration, presage, prognosis, prognostic
ASSOCIATED CONCEPTS: cautionary instructions

CAUTION, ***verb*** admonish, advise against, apprise, be vigilant, communicate to, counsel, dissuade, exhort, exhort to take heed, forearm, foreshow, forewarn, give advice, give fair warning, give intimation of impending evil, give notice, give warning, give warning of possible harm, inform, make aware, *monere,* notify of danger, persuade against, precaution, predict, prenotify, prepare for the worst, prescribe, presignify, prewarn, put on guard, remonstrate, serve notice, sound the alarm, spell danger, take precautions, urge, warn
ASSOCIATED CONCEPTS: due caution, ordinary caution, unusual caution
FOREIGN PHRASES: ***Abundans cautela non nocet.*** Extreme caution does no harm.

CAUTIOUS, ***adjective*** advertent, analytical, attentive, calculating, careful, circumspect, concerned, conscientious, conservative, considerate, deliberate, detailed, guarded, heedful, judicious, methodical, painstaking, provident, prudent, regardful, safe, slow, systematic, thoughtful, vigilant, wary, watchful
ASSOCIATED CONCEPTS: criminal intent, malice

CAVEAT, ***noun*** admonishment, admonition, advance notice, advisement, alert, announcement, augury, bodement, caution, communication, direction, foretoken, forewarning, implication, indication, instruction, lesson, monition, notice, notification, order, portendance, portendment, portention, prefiguration, premonition, prewarning, telling, warning, warning sign
ASSOCIATED CONCEPTS: caveat emptor, caveat venditor

CAVEAT EMPTOR, ***noun*** at one's own risk, purchase without a guaranty, purchase without a warranty, purchased at one's risk, unassured purchase, uncovenanted purchase, unendorsed purchase, unguaranteed purchase, unwarranted purchase

CAVIL, ***verb*** attack, belittle, *calumniari,* carp, *carpere,* censure frivolously, complain frivolously, condemn, criticize frivolously, decry, denigrate, denounce, deprecate, deride, disapprove, discredit, disparage frivolously, faultfind, find fault with, haggle, object frivolously, protest frivolously, raise frivolous objection to, raise objections frivolously, raise specious objection to, reprehend, ridicule irresponsibly, upbraid, *vellicare*

CEASE, ***verb*** abate, abrogate, abstain from, adjourn, annul, arrest, be all over, be at an end, be silent, become void, bring to an end, cancel, cause to halt, check, close, come to a close, come to a standstill, come to an end, conclude, consummate, culminate, *desinere,* desist, *desistere,* discontinue, draw to a close, drop, end, expire, extinguish, finish, forbear, get through, give over, halt, hold off, intermit, interrupt, lapse, leave off, make an end of, pause, put a stop to, put an end to, quell, quit, refrain, relinquish, remain, run its course, stanch, stay, stem, stop, stop work, surcease, suspend, terminate, vacate, withdraw
ASSOCIATED CONCEPTS: cease and desist order, cease doing business, cease from occupying, cease to act, cease to do business
FOREIGN PHRASES: ***Cessante causa, cessat effectus.*** When the cause ceases, the effect ceases. ***Cessante ratione legis, cessat et ipsa lex.*** The reason of the law ceasing, the law itself also ceases.

CEDE, ***verb*** abalienate, abandon, abdicate, abjure, accede, alienate, assign, bequeath, concede, *concedere,* confer, consign, convey, deed, deliver, devolve, dismiss, donate, give, give away, give up, give up claim to, grant, part with,

quitclaim, release, relinquish, remise, render, renounce, renounce claim to, resign, sign away, submit, succumb, surrender, tender, transfer, transmit, turn over, vouchsafe, yield
ASSOCIATED CONCEPTS: cede jurisdiction, cede territory

CEILING, *noun* acme, altitude, apex, apogee, climax, culmination, extreme, extremity, farthest point, height, highest degree, highest point, limit, maximum, optimum, peak, pinnacle, record, roof, summit, *tectum,* top, ultimate, utmost, utmost extent, utmost height, uttermost, vertex, zenith
ASSOCIATED CONCEPTS: maximum income ceiling, maximum rent ceiling

CELEBRATE *(Praise),* ***verb*** acclaim, adore, applaud, award, cheer, commemorate, commend, compliment, consecrate, deify, flatter, glorify, hail, honor, idolize, jubilate, laud, memorialize, observe, praise, proclaim, publicize, recognize, recommend, renown, resound, revere, rhapsodize, salute, tout

CELEBRATE *(To have fun),* ***verb*** enjoy, entertain, experience pleasure, give a function, give a party, give an event, hold a function, hold an event, party, rejoice in, relish, revel in, savor, take joy in, take pleasure in, thrill to

CELEBRITY, *noun* acclaim, adoration, character, eminence, esteem, fame, famous distinction, famous status, glory, grandeur, greatness, high regard, idolization, importance, magnanimity, majesty, name, nobility, notability, notoriety, person of notoriety, personality, popularity, preeminence, prestige, prominence, rank, recognition, renown, repute, significance, star status, stardom, status
ASSOCIATED CONCEPTS: entertainment law

CELL *(Enemy combatants),* ***noun*** enemy group, extremist group, extremists, incendiaries, insurgents, rebel organization, revolutionaries, saboteurs, subversives, underground extremists
ASSOCIATED CONCEPTS: enemy combatants, justice courts, military tribunals, Patriotic Act, prison cells, sleeper cell, terrorism, terrorist cell

CELL *(Jail),* ***noun*** cage, *cella,* chamber, compartment, confined room, confinement, cubicle, *cubiculum,* enclosed cage, incarceration, jailhouse, penitentiary, pound, prison, prison house, small cavity, small room, solitary abode

CEMENT, *verb* accouple, adhere, affix, agglomerate, agglutinate, amalgamate, annex, attach, bind, braze, coagulate, coalesce, cohere, combine, concrete, congeal, *conglutinare,* conglutinate, conjoin, connect, consolidate, couple, crystallize, fasten, fix, fix together, fuse, glue, harden, hold together, incorporate, join, make firm, merge, mortar, put together, secure, set, solder, solidify, stick, unite, weld

CENSOR, *verb* ban, bar, blot out, bowdlerize, cancel, *censor,* control, control the flow of news, cut, delete, disallow, disapprove, discountenance, dispense with, disqualify, eject, eliminate, enforce censorship, eradicate, erase, exclude, expunge, expurgate, forbid, impose a ban, inhibit, interfere, judge, keep within bounds, leave out, limit, not include, omit, oversee, pass under review, police, preclude, prevent, prevent publication, prohibit, proscribe, quash, refuse, refuse permission, reject, restrain, restrict, review, rub out, scratch out, sift, submerge, supervise communications, suppress, withhold permission
ASSOCIATED CONCEPTS: censorship, Federal Communications Act

CENSORSHIP, *noun* abolition, abridgment, bar, blackout, block, blockage, blue-penciling, bowdlerization, cancellation, control, curb, deprivation, elimination, expurgation, forbidding, governmental control, hindrance, impediment, imposition of veil of secrecy, inhibition, limitation, news blackout, obliteration, prohibition, repression, restraint, restriction, rigid control, seal of secrecy, stifling, suppression
ASSOCIATED CONCEPTS: censorship of books, censorship of films, censorship of First Amendment rights, censorship of mail, censorship of the theatre

CENSURE, *verb* administer a rebuke, admonish, animadvert upon, assail, attack, berate, blame, bring into discredit, cast a reproach, cast a slur upon, cast blame upon, cast reflection upon, castigate, chastise, chide, condemn, declaim against, decry, denigrate, denounce, denunciate, deprecate, depreciate, descant, disapprove, disparage, dispraise, exclaim against, excoriate, execrate, expostulate, expurgate, find fault with, *fronder,* fulminate against, hold up to execration, hold up to reprobation, impugn, inveigh against, not speak well of, objurgate, raise a hue and cry against, rebuff, rebuke, recriminate, remonstrate, reprehend, *reprehendere,* reprimand, reproach, reprobate, reprove, speak ill of, upbraid, view with disfavor, vilipend, *vituperare*
ASSOCIATED CONCEPTS: censure for improper conduct, censure for prejudicial conduct, letter of admonition, reprimand

CENSUS, *noun* account, calculation, *census,* ciphering, computation, count, counting, demography, enumeration, evaluation, figure-work, figures, figuring, list, listing, measurement, numbering, numeration, official count, official enumeration of inhabitants, official enumeration of the population, official reckoning, official registration, poll, reckoning, recount, registering, registration, score, statement, statistical inquiry, statistics, supputation, tables, tabulation, tally, valuation, vital statistics
ASSOCIATED CONCEPTS: federal census, representation based upon the last census

CENTER *(Central position),* ***noun*** axis, center of gravity, central point, convergence, converging point, core, epicenter, equidistance, eye, focal point, focus, focus of attention, fulcrum, half distance, halfway, media pars, medius, middle, middle distance, middle point, middle position, midmost point, midpoint, midst, point of convergence
ASSOCIATED CONCEPTS: center lane, center line, center of gravity, grouping of contacts doctrine

CENTER *(Essence),* ***noun*** base, basis, bedrock, cardinal point, central nature, chief part, constitutive principle, core, essential part, gist, gravamen, heart, hypostasis, important part, inmost nature, inmost substance, inner reality, main part, main point, nature, nucleus, pith, primary element, prime constituent, prime ingredient, principal part, quid, quiddity, quintessence, *sine qua non,* soul, substance, sum and substance, vital element, vital part

CENTER OF ATTENTION, *noun* arena, center, center of activity, center of attraction, center of focus, center of interest, central point, centrality, converging point, focal point, heart, hub, pivotal point, point of convergence

CENTER OF FOCUS, *noun* arena, center, center of activity, center of attention, center of attraction, center of interest, central point, centrality, converging point, focal point, heart, hub, pivotal point, point of convergence

CENTRAL *(Essential),* ***adjective*** basal, basic, capital, cardinal, chief, crucial, dominant, elemental, first, foremost, foundational, fundamental, highly important, indispensable, intrinsic, intrinsical, key, main, major, necessary, paramount, pivotal, primal, primary, principal, requisite, ruling, significant, supreme, underlying, vital

CENTRAL *(Situated near center),* ***adjective*** center, centermost, centric, centrical, equidistant, focal, halfway, inmost, inner, medial, median, mesial, middle, middlemost, midmost
ASSOCIATED CONCEPTS: central board of appeals, central filing, centralization center of gravity doctrine

CENTRALIZATION, ***noun*** absorption, aggregation, alliance, amalgamation, amassing, assembling, association, bringing together, centering, centralism, coalescence, coalescing, coalition, combination, compacting, compilation, compression, concentralization, concentration, condensation, conglomeration, congregation, consolidation, convergence, converging, coordinate, focalization, fusion, gathering together, grouping, incorporation, massing, merging, narrowing, nucleation, organization, synthesis, systematization, unification, union, unity
ASSOCIATED CONCEPTS: centralization of administration, centralization of government, decentralization

CENTRIST, ***adjective*** central, common, conservative, fair, hands-off, impartial, independent, level-headed, middle ground, middle-of-the-road, moderate, neutral, nonaligned, nonpartisan, nonrevolutionary, rational, reasonable, sensible, traditional, unbiased, uninfluenced, unprejudiced

CEREMONY, ***noun*** *caerimonia,* celebration, commemoration, conventionality, festive occasion, festivity, formal occasion, formality, memorialization, observance, official reception, prescribed procedure, reception, rite, ritual, *ritus,* solemn observance, solemnity, solemnization, state occasion
ASSOCIATED CONCEPTS: ceremonial marriage, marriage ceremonies, testimentary ceremonies

CERTAIN *(Fixed),* ***adjective*** absolute, assured, attested, certified, changeless, conclusive, confident, confirmed, decided, decisive, definite, determinate, determined, firm, guaranteed, incontestable, incontrovertible, indisputable, indubitable, inescapable, inevitable, infallible, irrefragable, irrefutable, official, positive, reliable, settled, stable, static, sure, unambiguous, unanswerable, unappealable, unavoidable, unchanging, undeniable, undisputed, unerring, unfailing, unmistakable, unpreventable, unquestionable, unquestioned
ASSOCIATED CONCEPTS: absolutely certain, capable of being rendered certain, certain powers and privileges, sum certain

CERTAIN *(Particular),* ***adjective*** *certus,* distinct, especial, exact, exclusive, individual, marked, peculiar, precise, singular, special, specific, specified, unique

CERTAIN *(Positive),* ***adjective*** absolute, actual, ascertained, assertive, assured, attested, authoritative, avoidless, axiomatic, beyond a shadow of doubt, beyond all dispute, beyond all question, capable of proof, certified, *certus,* changeless, clear, clear-cut, clearly known, cognizant, conclusive, concrete, confident, consistent, convinced, correct, credulous, decided, decisive, definite, demonstrable, demonstrated, dependable, distinct, doubtless, ensured, established, evident, evidential, existing, factual, final, fully convinced, guaranteed, inalterable, inappealable, incommutable, incontestable, incontrovertible, inconvertible, indefeasible, indestructible, indisputable, indubitable, inerrant, inescapable, inevitable, inexorable, inextinguishable, infallible, inflexible, invariable, inviolate, invulnerable, irreducible, irrefragable, irrefutable, irresistible, irresoluble, irreversible, irrevocable, knowing, past dispute, persuaded, questionless, real, reliable, right, satisfied, secure, self-evident, settled, stated, sure, tangible, true to the facts, unaltered, unambiguous, unassailable, unavoidable, unchangeable, unconfuted, undeniable, undeviating, undisputed, undoubted, undoubtful, undoubting, unequivocal, unerring, unfailing, unhesitating, unimpeachable, unmistakable, unqualified, unquestionable, unquestioned, unrefuted, unshakable, unsusceptible of change, unvarying, unwavering, valid, veracious, verifiable, void of suspicion
ASSOCIATED CONCEPTS: capable of being rendered certain

CERTAIN *(Specific),* ***adjective*** appropriate, ascertained, assigned, bounded, categorical, characteristic, choice, circumscribed, clear-cut, clearly defined, clearly stated, concrete, definite, designated, determinate, distinct, distinguished, esoteric, especial, exact, exclusive, explicit, express, expressed, fixed, individual, limited, marked, noteworthy, particular, peculiar, precise, prescribed, *quidam,* respective, restricted, select, settled, singular, special, specified, stated, well-defined

CERTAINTY, ***noun*** absence of doubt, absolute confidence, absoluteness, assurance, assuredness, authoritativeness, certification, certitude, *certus,* complete conviction, conclusiveness, confidentness, conviction, corroboration, definiteness, firmness, firmness of belief, inability to doubt, incontestability, incontrovertibility, indisputability, indubitability, indubitableness, inerrability, inerrancy, inexorability, infallibility, irrefragability, irrefutability, knowledge, objective certitude, positiveness, quality of being certain, questionlessness, reassurance, reliability, secureness, security, solidity, soundness, stability, substantiality, sure presumption, sureness, surety, unconfutability, undeniability, unequivocalness, unimpeachability, unmistakability, unqualification, unquestionability, unquestionableness, verification, warranty
ASSOCIATED CONCEPTS: absolute certainty, certainty to a common intent, moral certainty, proof to a reasonable certainty, reasonable certainty
FOREIGN PHRASES: ***Certum est quod certum reddi potest.*** That is certain which is capable of being rendered certain. ***Terminus annorum certus debet esse et determinatus.*** A term of years ought to be certain and determinate.

CERTIFICATE, ***noun*** affidavit, attestation, authentication, authorization, certification, charter, covenant, credentials, declaration, endorsement, guarantee, instrument, license, matter of record, muniment, official writing, paper, testament, voucher, warrant, writ, written contract, written evidence
ASSOCIATED CONCEPTS: allotment certificate, certificate of authority, certificate of deposit, certificate of incorporation, certificate of indebtedness, certificate of occupancy, certificate of probable cause, certificate of public convenience and necessity, certificate of reasonable doubt, certificate of stock, certificate under seal, death certificate, demand certificate, land certificate, marriage certificate

CERTIFICATION *(Attested copy),* ***noun*** affirmation, assurance, attestation, attesting declaration, authenticated confirmation, authentification, authoritative attestation, avouchment, confirmation, corroboration, declaration,

documentary evidence, documentation, endorsement, evidence, instrument of proof, legal pledge, proof, ratification, reassurance, reassurement, solemn declaration, statement, substantiation, support, swearing, sworn evidence, testification, testimony, validation, verification, written evidence
ASSOCIATED CONCEPTS: audited and paid, certification of loss reserves, certification of stock, certified, certified according to law, certified check, false certification, fraudulent certification

CERTIFICATION *(Certainness),* ***noun*** absolute certainty, absolute confidence, ascertained fact, ascertainment, assurance, assuredness, authoritativeness, certain knowledge, certainty, certitude, complete conviction, conclusive proof, conclusiveness, confidence, conviction, dependability, freedom from error, incontestability, incontrovertibility, indisputability, indubitability, indubitable fact, inerrancy, inevitableness, infallibility, irrefragability, irrefutability, knowledge, matter of fact, objective certainty, positive fact, positiveness, proof, reliability, reliableness, rigorous proof, sureness, trustworthiness, unambiguity, unimpeachability, unquestionability, unquestionableness, utter reliability

CERTIFICATION *(Certification of proficiency),* ***noun*** affirmance, authority, authorization, citation, confirmation, copy, credential, credentials, declaration, documentation, entitlement, indorsement, letter of recognition, license, recognition
ASSOCIATED CONCEPTS: certification to practice law

CERTIFY *(Approve),* ***verb*** accede to, accept, accord, accord one's approval, accredit, acknowledge, admit, agree, agree to, allow, assent, assent to, authorize, charter, coincide, concur, concur in, confirm, confirm officially, consent, countenance, empower, endorse, entitle, establish, give assent, give clearance, give consent, give permission, indorse, legalize, license, make valid, permit, pronounce legal, ratify, sanction, uphold, validate, yield assent

CERTIFY *(Attest),* ***verb*** acknowledge, advance, advocate, affirm, affirm explicitly, affirm in an official capacity, allege, assert, assert formally, assert oneself, assert positively, assert under oath, asseverate, assure, attest, authenticate, aver, avouch, avow, be sworn, bear out, bear witness, bear witness to, bring forward, claim, confess, confirm, confirm as correct, *confirmare,* convenant, corroborate, countersign, declare the truth of, declare to be true, deliver as one's act and deed, depone, depose, document, endorse, ensure, evidence, evince, execute, fortify, give a guarantee, give one's word, guarantee, guaranty, insist, insure, issue a statement, make absolute, make certain, make one's oath, make sure, proclaim, pronounce, ratify, reaffirm, reassure, reinsure, set one's hand and seal to, solemnly affirm, state emphatically, state with conviction, stress, sustain, swear, swear an affidavit, take one's oath, testify, utter with conviction, validate, verify, vouch, vouch for, vouch for as genuine, warrant
ASSOCIATED CONCEPTS: certification of pleadings

CERTIORARI, ***noun*** appeal to a higher court, application for retrial, course of law, legal procedure, legal process

CERTITUDE, ***noun*** absolute certainty, absoluteness, ascertained fact, assurance, assuredness, attestation, certainness, certainty, certainty of meaning, conclusiveness, confidence, confidentness, conviction, dead certainty, definiteness, freedom from error, incontestability, incontrovertibility, indisputability, indubitability, indubitable fact, indubitableness, inerrability, inerrancy, inevitableness, inexorability, infallibilism, infallibility, infallibleness, irrefragability, irrefutability, irrevocability, moral certainty, objective certainty, positiveness, sure assumption, sure presumption, sureness, surety, unambiguity, undeniability, unequivocalness, unimpeachability, unquestionableness
ASSOCIATED CONCEPTS: proof beyond a reasonable doubt

CESSATION *(Interlude),* ***noun*** abeyance, adjournment, armistice, arrest, break, ceasing, cloture, delay, desistance, discontinuance, discontinuation, dormancy, *embolium,* halt, hiatus, inaction, inactivity, interim, intermediate time, *intermissio,* intermission, interregnum, interruption, interval, intervening episode, intervening period, intervening space, intervening time, lapse, latency, lull, moratorium, pause, pendency, postponement, procrastination, quiescence, remission, respite, rest, standstill, stay, stop, suspension, temporary inaction, truce, wait

CESSATION *(Termination),* ***noun*** abandonment, climax, close, closing, closure, completion, conclusion, consummation, curtain, *dénouement,* determination, dissolution, end, ending, expiration, finale, finis, finish, fulfillment, *intermissio,* issue, outcome, realization, retirement, stoppage, surcease, terminus
ASSOCIATED CONCEPTS: cessation of business, cessation of hostilities, cessation of occupation, cessation of possession, cessation of work

CESSION, ***noun*** abalienation, allowance, assignment, award, bestowal, concession, conveyance, delivery, disposal, disposition, donation, gift, giving up, giving up claim to, grant, handing over, nonretention, parting with, presentation, release, relinquishing claim to, relinquishment, resignation, submittal, surrender, transfer, waiver, yielding

CHAGRIN, ***noun*** acrimony, aggrievement, bitterness, dejection, desolation, despondency, discontent, disgruntlement, dismay, displeasure, disquiet, dissatisfaction, distress, dreariness, enmity, exasperation, frustration, gloom, irritation, melancholy, misery, peevishness, perturbation, remorse, resentment, sadness, sorrow, unease

CHAIN *(Nexus),* ***noun*** act of coming together, act of coupling, act of joining, act of uniting, affiliation, affinity, alliance, association, attachment, attraction, bond, bond of union, bridge, conjunction, connectedness, connecting link, connecting medium, connection, correlation, interconnection, intermedium, interrelation, junction, kinship, liaison, ligament, ligature, link, linkage, privity, relatedness, relation, relationship, relativity, tie, union

CHAIN *(Series),* ***noun*** array, catena, catenation, classification, concatenation, connected series, consecution, constant flow, continuity, cordon, gradation, line, links, order, procession, progression, range, round, row, run, scale, sequence, *series,* set, succession, suit, suite, train, unbroken line, *vinculum*
ASSOCIATED CONCEPTS: chain of causation, chain of circumstances, chain of custody, chain of title

CHAIN OF CUSTODY, ***noun*** complete administration, custodianship, guardianship, preservation, preservation from harm, preservation from injury, proper accounting, proper administration, proper archiving, proper care, proper cataloging, proper documentation, proper recording, proper records and management, proper registration, protection, safe case and control, safeguard, safekeeping, stewardship, trusteeship
ASSOCIATED CONCEPTS: appropriation, care and possession, search and seizure

CHAIN OF EVIDENCE, ***noun*** enemy group, extremist group, extremists, incendiaries, insurgents, rebel organization, revolutionaries, saboteurs, subversives, underground extremists
ASSOCIATED CONCEPTS: enemy combatants, justice courts, military tribunals, Patriotic Act, prison cells, sleeper cell, terrorism, terrorist cell

CHAIRMAN, ***noun*** chair, conductor, director, head, headman, key man, leader, master of ceremonies, moderator, monitor, overseer, person in authority, presider, presiding officer, principal, *qui conventui praeest,* speaker, supervisor, symposiarch
ASSOCIATED CONCEPTS: chairman of a committee, chairman of the board of directors

CHALLENGE, ***noun*** appeal, confront, confute, contradict, controvert, defy, denounce, differ, disagree, disapprove, dispute, dissent, enter an appeal, initiative, menace, negate, object to, oppose, opposition, protest, raise a question, raise objections, reject, remonstrate, repudiate, resist, show reluctance, stand up against, take exception to, threaten, wrangle
ASSOCIATED CONCEPTS: challenge an award of a bid, challenge an opponent, challenge to the law

CHALLENGE, ***verb*** *ad pugnam provocare,* affront, appeal, argue, bid defiance to, call out, call to answer, combat an opinion, confront, confute, contradict, controvert, cry out against, debate, defy, denounce, differ, disagree, disapprove, dispute, dissent, enter a protest, hurl defiance at, invite competition, invite to contest, menace, negate, negative, object to, oppose, protest, quarrel, query, question, raise a question, raise objections, raise one's voice against, reject, remonstrate, repudiate, resist, say no, show reluctance, stand up against, take exception to, threaten, wrangle
ASSOCIATED CONCEPTS: challenge for cause, challenge jurisdiction, challenge of ownership, challenge to a finding of a lower court, challenge to a grand jury's composition, challenge to sufficiency of pleading, challenge to the array, challenge to the panel, challenge to the venire, preemptory challenge

CHAMBER *(Body),* ***noun*** aggregation, *assemblée,* assembly, bench, bench of judges, board, body of judges, cabinet, caucus, collocation, committee, confederacy, confederation, conflux, congress, constituency, convocation, council, court, federation, forum, gathering, group, ingathering, institute, judicial branch, judicial department, judicatory, law-making body, lawmakers, league, legislative body, legislature, mass, meeting, members of the bar, organization, panel, panel of judges, parliament, plenum, representatives, session, society, tribunal, union
ASSOCIATED CONCEPTS: chamber of commerce

CHAMBER *(Compartment),* ***noun*** alcove, antechamber, anteroom, apartment, box, camera, cell, *chambre,* closet, court, cubicle, *cubiculum,* den, division, enclosure, hall, hold, hollow, hollow place, lodging, meeting hall, office, parlor, *pars interior,* partitioned space, reception room, retreat, room, salle, section, separate part, sitting room, stall, stateroom, *thalamus*
ASSOCIATED CONCEPTS: chambers of the court, judicial chambers, legislative chambers

CHAMPION *(Miserly),* ***adjective*** abstemious, avaricious, brummagem, budget, circumspect, economical, frugal, meager, meretricious, miserly, paltry, parsimonious, penurious, provident, prudent, saving, scrimpy, spare, Spartan, stingy, tight, tightfisted

CHAMPION *(Supporter),* ***noun*** abettor, adherent, advocate, apostle, applauder, backer, cheerleader, cohort, confederate, defender, disciple, encourager, enthusiast, espouser, exponent, extremist, friend, loyalist, partisan, proponent, sponsor, stalwart, sympathizer, zealot

CHAMPION *(Winner),* ***noun*** award winner, celebrity, conqueror, finest contender, first, hero, master, medalist, number one, numero uno, popular figure, preeminent figure, prizewinner, recordbreaker, star, titleholder, vanquisher, victor

CHANCE *(Fortuity),* ***noun*** advantage, befalling, casus, circumstance, event, favorable time, fortuitousness, good fortune, happening, occasion, opening, suitable circumstance, time
ASSOCIATED CONCEPTS: arise by chance, last clear chance

CHANCE *(Possibility),* ***noun*** aptitude, attainability, bare possibility, conceivability, conceivableness, contingency, favorable prospect, hope, imaginability, indeterminacy, indeterminateness, liability, likelihood, possibleness, potential, potentiality, probability, prospect, *spes,* uncertainty, unexpectedness, unpredictability
ASSOCIATED CONCEPTS: chance verdict, games of chance
FOREIGN PHRASES: ***Casus fortuitus non est supponendus.*** A chance happening is not to be presumed. ***Casus fortuitus non est sperandus, et nemo tenetur devinare.*** A chance happening is not to be expected, and no one is bound to foresee it.

CHANCE HAPPENING, ***noun*** accident, blunder, bungle, chance good fortune, chance misfortune, chance occurrence, error, fluke, fortuity, lucky situation, miscalculation, misconception, misinterpretation, misjudgment, misreading, misunderstanding, one in a lifetime occurrence, random achievement, random luck, random mistake, random success, stroke of bad luck, stroke of misfortune

CHANGE, ***verb*** adapt, adjust, alter, be converted, be inconstant, be irresolute, convert, convertere *in,* deviate, displace, diverge, evolve, exchange, fluctuate, give in exchange, go through phases, *immutare,* innovate, interchange, make a transition, make different, make over, metamorphose, modify, modulate, permute, put in the place of, recast, recondition, reconstruct, reform, regenerate, remake, reorganize, replace, resolve into, restyle, revise, revive, revolutionize, show phases, subrogate, substitute, switch, switch around, transfigure, transform, transmogrify, transmute, transubstantiate, turn from, turn into, variegate, vary
ASSOCIATED CONCEPTS: additions and alterations, change in circumstances, change in conditions, change in occupancy, change in ownership, change in title, change of address, change of beneficiary, change of domicile, change of duties, change of name, change of ownership, change of parties, change of position, change of possession, change of venue, immaterial change, major change, minor change, permanent change, proposed change

CHANNEL *(Avenue),* ***noun*** arrangement, conduit, course, duct, expedient, facility, forum, instrument, instrumentality, means, medium, method, mode, outlet, passage, path, procedure, process, scheme, set up, strategy, tool, way

CHANNEL *(Navigable water),* ***noun*** body of water, canal, gully, moat, navigable river, navigable stream, stream, trench, trough, water, waterway
ASSOCIATED CONCEPTS: navigable waters of the U.S. Navigation Acts

CHAOS, *noun* agitation, anarchy, bedlam, commotion, confusion, convulsion, disarray, discomposure, discord, disorder, disorderliness, disunion, embroilment, entanglement, ferment, flurry, fracas, furor, havoc, imbroglio, incoherence, irregularity, misrule, mob rule, muddle, pandemonium, panic, perturbation, racket, riot, shambles, stir, storm, tempest, tumult, turbulence, turmoil, unrest, unruliness, upheaval, uproar, upset

CHAOTIC, *adjective* aimless, anarchical, askew, awry, complex, confused, discordant, disordered, disorganized, fermenting, formless, frantic, frenzied, furious, haphazard, mixed-up, muddled, raging, scattered, shapeless, stormy, tempestuous, tumultuous, turbulent, unmethodical, unrestrained, unorganized, unruly, unsystematic, untidy

CHAPTER *(Branch),* ***noun*** affiliate, associate, branch member, branch office, bureau, component, department, division, local, local office, lodge, member, office, organ, section, subdivision, subsidiary

CHAPTER *(Division),* ***noun*** article, *caput,* clause, column, component, fragment, head, heading, paragraph, part, partition, passage, phrase, portion, section, sector, segment, separate part, subdivision, subgroup
ASSOCIATED CONCEPTS: chapter 10 reorganization, paragraphs, sections

CHARACTER *(An individual),* ***noun*** being, body, figure, human, human being, man, mortal, party, person, personage, personality, self-determined being, somebody, someone

CHARACTER *(Personal quality),* ***noun*** *animus,* aspects, attribute, bent, characteristic mood, constitution, description, disposition, dominant quality, essence, essential part, essential quality of one's nature, essentialness, ethos, features, fiber, frame of mind, grain, inclination, individualism, individuality, *ingenium,* inherited characteristics, inner nature, intellect, intrinsicality, intrinsicalness, kind, leaning, makeup, manner, marked traits, mental and spiritual makeup, mettle, mold, moral qualities, *mores, natura,* natural turn of mind, nature, peculiarity, personal traits, personality, predilection, prime ingredients, proclivity, proneness, propension, propensity, *proprietas,* psychological habits, qualities, quiddity, quintessence, slant, striking qualities, style, substantiality, susceptibility, temper, temperament, tendency, tone, trait

CHARACTER *(Reputation),* ***noun*** celebrity, credit, deference, distinction, eminence, esteem, estimation, *existimatio, fama,* fame, grandeur, high reward, honor, *locus standi,* name, nobility, notability, notice, notoriety, notoriousness, *opinio,* place, popular favor, popularity, position, position in society, preeminence, prestige, prominence, public esteem, publicly recognized standing, recognition, regard, renown, reputableness, repute, respect, respectability, standing, station, status
ASSOCIATED CONCEPTS: character evidence, character witness

CHARACTERISTIC, *noun* aspect, attribute, cast, constitution, differentia, differential, distinction, distinctive feature, distinguishing trait, essence, essential part, feature, humor, idiocrasy, idiosyncrasy, immanence, inclination, individuality, inherence, inhersion, leaning, liability, makeup, mannerism, marked feature, marked quality, nature, particularity, peculiar idiom, peculiarity, penchant, personal equation, point of difference, predilection, proclivity, proneness, propensity, property, *proprietas,* quality, quintessence, speciality, specialty, specific quality, tendency, trait, type, uniqueness
ASSOCIATED CONCEPTS: characteristic of and peculiar to business of an employer, characteristic of work performed by an employee

CHARACTERIZE, *verb* classify, construe, delineate, depict, descend to particulars, describe, *designare,* detail, diagram, differentiate, distinguish, draw, elucidate, exemplify, express precisely, formalize, give an account of, give precise meaning to, give the details of, identify, illustrate, individualize, individuate, interpret, make apparent, make clear, make vivid, mark, mark off, *notare,* outline, personify, picture, portray, profile, reflect, render precise, represent, set apart, set forth the character of, specify, specify the peculiarities of

CHARGE *(Accusation),* ***noun*** *accusatio,* allegation, arraignment, attack, blame, castigation, censure, citation, complaint, condemnation, count, countercharge, *crimen,* crimination, delation, denouncement, denunciation, disapprobation, formal complaint, impeachment, imputation, incrimination, inculpation, indictment, information, insinuation, objurgation, plaint, presentment, recrimination, reproach, reproof, summons
ASSOCIATED CONCEPTS: charge of a crime, charges of misconduct, criminal charge, indictment, offense charged, specifically charged

CHARGE *(Command),* ***noun*** call, commandment, commission, dictate, direction, imperative, imposition, injunction, instruction, mandate, *mandatum,* order, precept, proclamation, request, requirement, requisition, subpoena, summons, ultimatum, writ
ASSOCIATED CONCEPTS: charge with responsibility

CHARGE *(Cost),* ***noun*** assessment, debit, disbursement, due, dues, exaction, exactment, expenditure, expense, fee, obligation, outlay, payment, pecuniary burden, *pretium,* price, quotation, rate, rent, tax, toll, valuation, value, worth
ASSOCIATED CONCEPTS: charge against an estate, chargeback, charge-off, charging lien, deferred charges, minimum charge

CHARGE *(Custody),* ***noun*** administration, auspices, care, chaperonage, concern, control, *curare, custodia,* entrusted cause, entrusted object, guardianship, guidance, jurisdiction, keeping, object of responsibility, patronage, protection, safekeeping, superintendence, supervision, trust, trusteeship, *tutela,* tutelage, ward, wardship, watch

CHARGE *(Lien),* ***noun*** accountability, bond, burden, claim on property, commitment, debenture, duty, encumbrance, guarantee, guaranty, hold on property, hypothecation, indebtedness, liability, obligation, pecuniary burden, pignus *judiciale,* pledge, real security, right to dispose of property, security, security on property, tie, *vadium mortuum, vadium vivum*
ASSOCIATED CONCEPTS: charging lien, incumbrance

CHARGE *(Responsibility),* ***noun*** accountability, accountableness, allegiance, appointment, assignment, burden, commitment, engagement, function, imperative duty, inescapable duty, mission, obligation, one's duty, responsibleness, sense of duty, task, undertaking
ASSOCIATED CONCEPTS: public charge

CHARGE *(Statement to the jury),* ***noun*** address to the jury, adjuration, admonition, advice, declamation, definitions on the law, details on the law, direction, discourse, disquisition, exhortation, guidance, instructions, lecture, legal instructions
ASSOCIATED CONCEPTS: charge to the jury

CHARGE *(Accuse),* ***verb*** *accusare, arguere,* arraign, attack, blame, bring accusation, censure, challenge, cite, complain against, condemn, criminate, denounce, denunciate, expostulate, file a claim, hold responsible, impute, incriminate, inculpate, indict, issue a writ, lay responsibility upon, lodge a complaint, put the blame on, recriminate, reprehend, stigmatize
ASSOCIATED CONCEPTS: charged with crime

CHARGE *(Assess),* ***verb*** appraise, assess a tax upon, assess pro rata, assign, assign one's share to, bill, compute, demand payment, dun, estimate, exact, fix a charge, fix the price at, give a final notice, impose, incur a debt, invoice, lay a duty upon, levy, make claims upon, present an ultimatum, present one's claim, pricing, prorate, rate, send a final demand, tax, value

CHARGE *(Empower),* ***verb*** appoint, assign, authorize, authorize formally, commission, confer power on, delegate, delegate authority to, deputize, emper, enable, endow, endow the power, engage, entrust, give authority to, give power to, grant, invest the power, invest with authoritative power, make able, mission, nominate, permit, put in care of, warrant

CHARGE *(Instruct on the law),* ***verb*** admonish, advise, caution, counsel, detail the law, direct, exhort, give advice, give suggestions to, guide, inform, instruct, offer counsel, point out, prepare, prescribe the law, press advice on, propose legal instructions, recommend points of law, suggest, suggest conclusions of law, urge
ASSOCIATED CONCEPTS: charging a jury

CHARITABLE *(Benevolent),* ***adjective*** almsgiving, altruistic, beneficent, *beneficus, benignus,* bounteous, eleemosynary, freehanded, generous, giving, gracious, greathearted, liberal, magnanimous, munificent, openhanded, philanthropic, princely, unselfish, unsparing, unstinting

CHARITABLE *(Lenient),* ***adjective*** accommodating, acquiescent, beneficent, benevolent, benign, benignant, clement, compliant, condoning, considerate, empathetic, exorable, forbearing, forgiving, free from vindictiveness, gracious, helpful, humane, humanitarian, kind, kindhearted, liberal, *liberalis,* merciful, obliging, patient, permitting, sensitive, soft, softhearted, sympathetic, sympathizing, temperate, tolerant, understanding, warm, yielding

CHARITY, ***noun*** active giving, aid, almsgiving, altruism, assistance, backing, benefaction, beneficentia, benevolence, benevolentness, bestowal, bounteousness, bountifulness, clemency, considerateness, consideration, contribution, donation, dotation, endowment, generosity, generous giving, gift, good will, grace, grant, help, hospitality, humaneness, humanitarianism, humanity, kindness, *liberalitas,* liberalness, magnanimity, munificence, patronage, philanthropic gift, philanthropy, relief, support, unselfishness, willing help
ASSOCIATED CONCEPTS: charitable and benevolent institution, charitable association, charitable bequest, charitable contributions, charitable corporation, charitable enterprise, charitable gift, charitable institution, charitable organization, charitable purposes, charitable trusts, charitable use

CHARTER *(Declaration of rights),* ***noun*** announcement, constitution, decree, official announcement, proclamation, promulgation, pronouncement, public announcement, public statement, publication, writing
ASSOCIATED CONCEPTS: amendment of a charter, amendment to a charter, articles of incorporation, charter of a foreign corporation, charter of a municipal corporation, charter of an association, corporate charter, county charter, municipal charter, partnership charter, reform a charter, repeal of a charter, special charter, state charter

CHARTER *(License),* ***noun*** authority, certificate, certificate of permission, dispensation, express permission, grant, imprimatur, instrument, muniment, official document, patent, permit, written permission
ASSOCIATED CONCEPTS: chartered bank, chartered by law, expiration of a charter, renewal of a charter

CHARTER *(Sanction),* ***noun*** acceptance, acknowledgment, acquiescence, admission, allowance, approval, assent, authority, authorization, concurrence, confirmation, consent, countenance, delegation, empowerment, endorsement, enfranchisement, entitlement, franchise, grant, leave, liberty, license, permission, permit, pragmatic sanction, privilege, ratification, recognition, sufferance, support, tolerance, toleration, vested right
ASSOCIATED CONCEPTS: chartered by the law

CHASE, ***verb*** endeavor to overtake, follow, go after, go in pursuit of, go in quest of, hunt, pursue, run after, run in pursuit, search, seek, track, trail, try to overtake

CHATTEL, ***noun*** asset, belonging, commodity, effect, equipment, fortune, holding, movable article of property, movables, personal effect, personalty, possession, property, resource, trapping, valuable
ASSOCIATED CONCEPTS: action to recover a chattel, chattel interest, chattel mortgage, chattel trust, chattels real, conveyance of a chattel, household chattels, lien upon a chattel, personal chattels, personal property
FOREIGN PHRASES: ***Catalla juste possessa amitti non possunt.*** Chattels justly possessed cannot be lost. ***Catalla reputantur inter minima in lege.*** Chattels are considered in law of lesser importance.

CHEAP, ***adjective*** bargain, cut-price, deficient, deplorable, flimsy, imperfect, inadequate, inexpensive, inferior, insubstantial, low-end, poor, shoddy, slipshod, unfavorable, unsatisfactory

CHEAT, ***verb*** act dishonestly, be cunning, be dishonest, befool, beguile, betray, break faith, commit breach of trust, cozen, deceive, defalcate, defraud, deprive of dishonestly, dissemble, dupe, embezzle, *fraudare,* ignore ethics, inveigle, lack honesty, obtain money by false pretenses, peculate, pettifog, play false, practice chicanery, practice fraud, prevaricate, purloin, represent falsely, sharp, swindle
ASSOCIATED CONCEPTS: cheating by false weights and measures, false pretenses, larceny

CHECK *(Bar),* ***noun*** abeyance, arrest, barricade, barrier, block, blockage, cessation, checkmate, control, curb, damper, deadlock, deadstop, delay, detainment, detention, disruption, drawback, embargo, estoppel, foil, frustration, full stop, halt, hindrance, impediment, *impedimentum,* impedition, injunction, interference, interruption, limitation, *mora,* obstacle, obstruction, opposition, preclusion, prohibition, proscription, rebuff, regulation, rejection, restraint, restriction, retardation, retardment, standstill, stop, stoppage, stopper, suspension, trammel

CHECK *(Instrument),* ***noun*** bank paper, banknote, bill, bill of exchange, certificate, commercial instrument, commercial paper, debenture, draft, fiduciary currency, money

order, negotiable paper, note, order on a bank, paper money, security, sight draft, treasury note
ASSOCIATED CONCEPTS: acceptance of a check, altered check, bad check, bank check, bearer check, bill of exchange, cashier's check, certified check, check payable on demand, conditional check, conversion of a check, delivery of a check, deposit of a check, dishonored check, drawee, drawer, endorsed check, endorsement, forged check, holder in due course of a check, insufficient funds, order check, pay check, payee, payment of a check, postdated check, presentment of a check, registered check, time check, unauthorized endorsement, worthless check

CHECK *(Inspect)*, ***verb*** audit, balance accounts, canvass, case, check up, examine, experiment, explore, go over, inquire into, inventory, investigate, keep watch, look for flaws, look into, look over, make a reconnaissance, make a trial run, monitor, observe, overhaul, overlook, oversee, peruse, probe, query, question, quiz, reconnoiter, reexamine, regard carefully, regulate, review, run checks on, run tests on, sample, scan, scrutinize, search into, see about, study, subject to scrutiny, superintend, supervise, survey, take stock, test, try, verify, watch

CHECK *(Restrain)*, ***verb*** abate, adjust, arrest, attemper, bate, block, bring to a standstill, call a halt, cause a stoppage, constrain, control, countercheck, curb, cut off, delay, detain, deter, diminish, discourage, dissuade, draw rein, encumber, estop, freeze, frustrate, halt, head off, hinder, hold in check, impair, impede, impedite, inhibit, intercept, interrupt, intervene, keep back, keep under control, lay under restraint, limit, obstruct, overpower, put a restraint upon, put a stop to, put an end to, put under restraint, restrain, restrict, retard, run counter, set back, slow, slow down, stalemate, stand in the way, stem, stop, stultify, suppress, thwart, undermine

CHICANERY, ***noun*** artifice, craftiness, cunning, deceit, deception, deceptiveness, deviousness, dishonesty, double-dealing, duplicity, fakery, fraud, guile, hoax, insincerity, machination, racket, ruse, scam, sham, stratagem of deception, subterfuge, swindle, tactic, treachery, trick to ensnare, underhandedness, whitewash, wile, wrong
ASSOCIATED CONCEPTS: mayhem

CHIEF, ***noun*** boss, captain, *caput,* chairman, chairperson, chief controller, chieftain, commandant, commander, directing head, director, *dux,* employer, foreman, foreperson, general, head, headman, headperson, highest-ranking person, leader, manager, organizer, overlooker, overseer, person in authority, person in charge, president, primate, *princeps,* principal, principal person, senior, superior, supervising director
ASSOCIATED CONCEPTS: chief agent, chief counsel, chief deputy, chief examiner, chief executive, chief executive officer, chief fiscal officer, chief judge, chief justice, chief of fire department, chief of police, chief officer of a corporation or business, chief place of business

CHILD, ***noun*** adolescent, boy, daughter, *filia, filius,* foster child, girl, grandchild, *infans,* infant, ingenue, issue, juvenile, lineal descendant, minor, newborn, offspring, progeny, *pueri,* scion, young, young boy, young descendant, young girl, youngling, youngster, youth
ASSOCIATED CONCEPTS: abandoned child, abortive child, adopted child, afterborn child, child born out of wedlock, child by future marriage, child custody, child labor, child support, childbirth, childcare, childhood, *en ventre sa mere,* foster child, illegitimate child, legitimate child, minor child, natural child, neglected child, orphan, posthumous child, pretermitted child, stepchild

CHILDREN, ***noun*** babies, brood, descendants, heirs, infants, innocents, issue, lineage, minors, offspring, progeny, *pueri,* rising generation, seed, young people, younger generation, youngsters, youth
ASSOCIATED CONCEPTS: descendants, disinheriting, illegitimate children, legal heirs, legitimate children, limitation, purchase, surviving children

CHILLING EFFECT, ***noun*** damaging effect, deterrence, hindrance, impediment, intimidating impact, menacing effect, obstruction, paralyzing effect, threatening impact, thwarting effect

CHINESE WALL, ***noun*** barrier, detachment, disassociation, disconnection, disunion, dividing wall, division, grouping, impenetrable barrier, isolation, partition, protection, safeguard, secure separation, segmentation, separation, severance, shield, total separation
ASSOCIATED CONCEPTS: Chinese wall between clients, conflict of interest, conflicts of interests

CHIVALRY, ***noun*** accommodation, benevolence, compassion, consideration, courtesy, courtliness, decency, dignity, distinction, fairness, gallantry, generosity, illustriousness, kindness, loftiness, magnanimity, majesty, manners, merit, morality, nobility, politeness, refined manners, righteousness, stately manors, unselfishness, valiance, valor

CHOATE LIEN, ***noun*** according to law, allowed, binding, brought to fruition, compulsory, consummated, enforceable, finished, lawful, legal, legalized, legitimate, legitimized, matured, obligatory, official, perfected, ratified, refined, validated

CHOICE *(Alternatives offered)*, ***noun*** *delectus,* discretion, discrimination, election, opportunities, option, pick, remaining courses, remaining options, selection, substitutes
ASSOCIATED CONCEPTS: alternative causes of action, counsel of one's own choosing, election of remedies, splitting a cause of action

CHOICE *(Decision)*, ***noun*** act of judgment, analysis, appraisal, assessment, conclusion, considered decision, delectus, designation, determination, disposition, election, finding, judgment, order, outcome, predilection, preferability, preference, pronouncement, resolution, resolve, selection, settlement
ASSOCIATED CONCEPTS: domicile of choice, freedom of choice

CHOOSE, ***verb*** act on one's own authority, adopt, appoint, be disposed to, be resolute, be so minded, co-opt, commit oneself to a course, cull, decide, *deligere,* desire, determine, determine upon, discriminate, discriminate between, do of one's own accord, draw, elect, eliminate the alternatives, embrace, excerpt, exercise one's choice, exercise one's discretion, exercise one's option, exercise one's preference, exercise the will, have volition, make a decision, make one's choice, make one's selection, mark out for, opt for, pick, pick out, prefer, put to the vote, resolve, select, set apart, settle, side, support, take a decisive step, take one's choice, take up an option, use one's discretion, use one's option, will
ASSOCIATED CONCEPTS: election of remedies, freedom of choice, voluntary choice

CHRONIC, ***adjective*** ceaseless, confirmed, constant, continual, continuing, continuous, cyclical, deep-rooted, deep-seated, drawn out, endless, enduring, entrenched, established, ever-present, everlasting, extended, forever, frequent, habitual, immedicable, incessant, inextinguished, invariable, lasting, lingering, long-continuing, long-lived, long standing, long-standing, maintained, never-ceasing, never-stopping, not averruncated, not restorable, of long duration, often, ongoing, perdurable, perennial, permanent, perpetual, persevering, persistent, persisting, prolonged, protracted, recurrent, recurring, regular, repeating, repetitious, repetitive, resisting, returning, returning at intervals, serious, set, settled, steadfast, stubborn, sustained, tenacious, unalleviated, unceasing, uncorrectable, undestroyed, undying, unending, unerasable, unfading, unhealable, unintermitting, uninterrupted, unmitigated, unmitigating, unrelievable, unremedied, unremittent, unremitting, unshifting, unslackening, unstopped, unstopping, unsubsiding, unsuppressed, unvarying, unyielding, virulent, wearing

CHRONICLE, ***verb*** characterize, chart, date, declare, delineate, depict, describe, detail, detail in a record, determine, elucidate, enumerate, explicate, interpret, itemize, make a record, narrate, outline, particularize, recite, record, recount, register, relate, render, report, represent, schematize, set down in a record, state, trace, write

CHRONOLOGY, ***noun*** annals, case history, chronicle, commentaries, dates, diary, documentation, genealogy, historical record, history, line, lineage, lineup, list, log, logbook, minutes, narration, narrative, order, recitation, record, register, report

CHURN, ***verb*** convulse, shake up, stir up, whip, work up

CIRCUIT, ***noun*** ambit, area, *arrondissement,* bounds, *circuitus, circulus,* confines, district, domain, dominion, exclusive area, extent, field, hemisphere, jurisdiction, land, *locus, orbis,* orbit, pale, part, place, precinct, province, quarter, range, realm, region, section, site, situs, sphere, territory, zone
ASSOCIATED CONCEPTS: circuit court, circuit court of appeals, circuit judge, circuit officers, judicial circuits, riding circuit

CIRCUITOUS, ***adjective*** ambagious, anfractuous, anguilliform, anguine, circumfluent, circumambulating, circumfluous, circumlocutory, complicated, contorted, convoluted, convolutional, crooked, curved, deviating, deviatory, devious, digressive, discursive, eel-shaped, eellike, excursive, flexuous, helical, helicoid, helicoidal, indirect, intorted, labyrinthine, mazy, meandering, meandrous, oblique, out of the way, rambling, roundabout, roving, serpentiform, serpentile, serpentine, serpentoid, sigmoid, sinuate, sinuous, skirting, snakelike, snaky, spiriferous, tortile, tortuous, turning, twining, twisting, undulate, undulated, undulating, undulative, undulatory, wandering, whorled, winding, zigzag
ASSOCIATED CONCEPTS: circuitous proceedings, circuitous route, circuity of action

CIRCULATE, ***verb*** acquire currency, announce, bandy, be public, be published, become public, bring before the public, bring out, broadcast, bruit abroad, change hands, change places, circuit, circularize, come out, communicate, convey, diffuse, *dispergere,* disperse, disseminate, distribute, *divulgare,* divulgate, divulge, flow, get abroad, give currency to, give forth, give out, give to the world, go forth, have currency, issue, lay before the public, make known, make public, make the round of, noise abroad, pass, pass current, pass from one to another, pass round, print, proclaim, promulgate, propagate, publish, put about, put forward, put into circulation, radiate, reissue, repeat, reveal, rumor, rumor about, send forth, speak of, spread, spread a report, spread abroad, talk of, transmit, trumpet, ventilate, voice

CIRCULATION, ***noun*** allocation, allotment, branching out, *circumagere,* diffusion, dispensation, dispensing, *dispergere,* dispersal, dispersion, dissemination, distribution, divergence, *divulgare,* emanation, flow, flowing, flux, issuance, motion, movement, passage, passing, scattering, spread, spreading, transit, transition, transmigration, transmission

CIRCUMSCRIBE *(Define),* ***verb*** border, *circumscribere, definire,* delimit, delineate, demarcate, demark, determine, distinguish, establish, outline

CIRCUMSCRIBE *(Surround by boundary),* ***verb*** begird, belt, border, bound, circuit, circumvallate, cloister, close around, close in, compass, confine, contain, contour, delineate, determine boundaries, edge, embrace, encircle, enclose, encompass, engird, ensphere, envelop, fence in, fix bounds, fix limits, form a circle round, frame, gird, girdle, hedge in, hem in, include, keep in, mark off, mark out, outline, shut in, surround

CIRCUMSPECT, ***adjective*** alert, assiduous, astute, attending, attentive, careful, cautious, *cautus,* chary, circumspective, cognizant, conscientious, conscious, considerate, contemplative, deliberate, deliberative, diligent, discerning, discreet, discretionary, discriminating, discriminative, exacting, guarded, heedful, intent, introspective, judicious, meditative, meticulous, mindful, observant, observing, on guard, painstaking, particular, percipient, perspicacious, precautionary, precautious, precise, premeditative, prepared, *providus, prudens,* prudent, reflecting, reflective, regardful, scrutinizing, sensitive, thinking, thorough, thoroughgoing, thoughtful, vigilant, wary, watchful, well-considered

CIRCUMSTANCES, ***noun*** accompanying events, attendant conditions, bases, changes, conditions, controlling factors, course of events, details, events, factors, facts, features, full particulars, governing factors, grounds, happenings, incidentals, instances, items, minutiae, occasions, occurrences, particulars, qualifying factors, situations, special points, state of affairs, surrounding facts, surroundings, terms imposed, vicissitudes
ASSOCIATED CONCEPTS: aggravating circumstance, change of circumstances, changed circumstance, circumstances beyond control, exceptional circumstances, extraordinary circumstances, like circumstances, mitigating circumstances, special circumstances, unusual circumstances

CIRCUMSTANTIAL, ***adjective*** accessory, *accuratus,* additional, adscititious, apparent, by inference, collateral, conditional, conjectural, construable, contingent, deduced, extraneous, founded on circumstances, implicational, implicative, implicatory, incidental, inconclusive, indecisive, indicative, indicatory, indirect, inessential, inferential, insinuatory, insubstantial, likely, nonessential, ostensible, presumable, presumptive, probable, second rank, secondary, subsidiary, suggestive, unnecessary, verisimilar
ASSOCIATED CONCEPTS: circumstantial errors, circumstantial evidence, circumstantial inference, corroborating evidence, inference

CIRCUMSTANTIAL EVIDENCE, ***noun*** evidence not leading directly to a conclusion of fact, evidence requiring an inference to form a conclusion, indirect evidence, indirect testimony, inferential evidence, nondirect evidence, proof

CIRCUMVENT, ***verb*** avoid doing, be cunning, be sly, beguile, bypass, *circonvenir, circumscribere, circumvenire,* cloak, conceal, confuse, contravene, contrive, counteract, counterwork, cover, deceive, defeat, defraud, delude, devise, disrupt, elude, escape, evade, foil, hoax, mislead, outmaneuver, outreach, outwit, pettifog, practice chicanery, prevaricate, proceed by stratagem, scheme, swindle, thwart, *tourner la loi,* traverse, trick
ASSOCIATED CONCEPTS: circumvent the law

CITATION *(Attribution),* ***noun*** ascription, assignment, credit, derivation, designation, mention, organization, parentage, quotation, reference, source
ASSOCIATED CONCEPTS: citation of authorities, citation of tables

CITATION *(Charge),* ***noun*** command to appear, decree, dictate, interpellation, legal process, mandate, mittimus, monition, notice, notice to appear, notification, official notice, ordination, precept, prescript, prescription, rescript, subpoena, ukase, warrant, writ, writ of summons
ASSOCIATED CONCEPTS: citation for a crime, citation for a violation, citation for contempt

CITE *(Accuse),* ***verb*** allege, blame, bring a charge, bring an action, call to account, censure, challenge, charge, complain, denounce, discredit, impeach, implicate, impute, incriminate, inform against, lodge a complaint, make a complaint

CITE *(State),* ***verb*** advance, attest, authenticate, bring forward, certify, circumstantiate, document, enunciate, establish, evidence, evince, exemplify, exhibit, express, give as example, illustrate, indicate, introduce as an example, maintain, make evident, make reference to, manifest, mention, name, point to, predicate, present as proof, prove, quote, recite, refer to, refer to legal authorities, set forth, show, show evidence, show proof, specify, substantiate, use in support of propositions of law
ASSOCIATED CONCEPTS: cite a case as precedence

CITIZEN, ***noun*** *civis,* denizen, dweller, habitant, *indigen,* indigene, indweller, inhabitant, inhabiter, inmate, native, occupant, occupier, residencer, resident, resider
ASSOCIATED CONCEPTS: adopted citizens, citizen of a state, citizen of the United States of America, citizens of different states, diversity of citizenship, domicile of a citizen, foreign citizen, native-born citizen, natural-born citizen, naturalized citizen, nonresident citizen, privilege and immunities of citizens, renunciation of citizenship
FOREIGN PHRASES: ***Semel civis semper civis.*** Once a citizen always a citizen.

CITY, ***noun*** megalopolis, metropolis, metropolitan area, municipality, polis, urban district, urban place, urbanization, *urbs*
ASSOCIATED CONCEPTS: city attorney, city council, city court, city districts, city employee, city hall, city limits, city marshal, city officer, city purpose, municipal corporations

CIVIC, ***adjective*** *civicus,* civil, *civilis,* common, communal, community, government, governmental, juridical, lawful, legal, metropolitan, municipal, neighborhood, official, political, public, regulatory, town, urban
ASSOCIATED CONCEPTS: civic affairs, civic enterprise, civic organizations

CIVIL *(Polite),* ***adjective*** accommodating, affable, amiable, chivalric, chivalrous, civilized, cordial, courteous, courtly, cultivated, deferential, dignified, diplomatic, easy-mannered, fine-mannered, genial, genteel, gentlemanlike, gentlemanly, gracious, mannerly, mild, obliging, polished, refined, respectful, urbane, well-behaved, well-bred, well-brought up, well-mannered, well-spoken

CIVIL *(Public),* ***adjective*** civic, civilian, communal, governmental, laic, laical, metropolitan, mundane, municipal, noncriminal, noneccliastical, nonmilitary, oppidan, political, secular, social, societal, temporal, unspiritual, urban, worldly
ASSOCIATED CONCEPTS: civil action, civil aeronautics board, civil arrest, civil authorities, civil case, civil cause, civil ceremony, civil contempt, civil contract, civil courts, civil damages, civil death, civil defense, civil disabilities, civil jurisdiction, civil law, civil liability, civil liberties, civil matters, civil officer, civil proceedings, civil rights, civil service, civil service commission, civil suit, civil unrest, civil war
FOREIGN PHRASES: ***Cum actio fuerit mere criminalis, institui poterit ab initio criminaliter vel civiliter.*** When an action is merely criminal, it can be instituted from the beginning either criminally or civilly.

CIVIL LAW, ***noun*** body of laws, civilian law, code, law of noncriminal disputes, laws, legal restrictions on private citizens, noncommon law, statutes, statutory law, the law governing private citizen relations, the law of private citizen rights, written law
ASSOCIATED CONCEPTS: common law, criminal law, Roman law

CIVIL LIBERTIES, ***noun*** First Amendment guarantees, First Amendment Rights, freedom of expression, freedom of press, freedom of religion, freedom of speech, freedom of thought, fundamental individual rights, guarantees from the Bill of Rights, human rights, individual rights, right to life, right to peacefully assemble, right to petition government for redress, right to privacy, right to property, right to worship
ASSOCIATED CONCEPTS: civil rights, protection against unwarranted governmental interference

CIVILIZATION, ***noun*** accomplishments, acquired knowledge, advancement, advancement of knowledge, civilized life, civilized society, cultivation, culture, enlightenment, evolution, *humanitas,* illumination, level of education, national culture, progress, progression, refinement, social adjustment, social elevation, society, sophistication, state of refinement

CLAIM *(Assertion),* ***noun*** affirmation, allegation, asseveration, averment, avouchment, avowal, declaration, position, predication, presentation, proposition, statement
ASSOCIATED CONCEPTS: claimed use, disputed claims, doubtful claims, false claim, fictitious claims, fraudulent claims
FOREIGN PHRASES: ***Debitorum pactionibus creditorum petitio nec tolli nec minui potest.*** The rights of creditors to sue cannot be prejudiced or diminished by agreements between their debtors.

CLAIM *(Legal demand),* ***noun*** accusation, adjuration, bill of complaint, cause of action, challenge, command, complaint, counterclaim, declaration, exaction, obsecration, plea, postulate, *postulatio,* presentment, requirement, suit, ultimatum
ASSOCIATED CONCEPTS: allowed claim, claim against bankrupt estate, claim against estate, claim and demand, claim arising on contract, claim for alternative relief, claim for support, claim of a creditor, claim of interest, claim or defense

notice of claim, claimed on appeal, claimed use, claims ex delicto, colorable claim, common law claim, compensation claim, conflicting claims, contingent claims, counter claim, court of claims, cross claim, disputed claims, doubtful claims, equitable claims, fictitious claims, fixed claims, fraudulent claims, frivolous claims, illegal claims, indeterminate claims, individual claim, insurance claim, just claim, lawful claim, money claim, moral claims, particular nature of claims, prior claim, proof of claim, provable claim, secured claim, settlement of claim, stale claim, subordination of claim, subsequent claims, undisputed claim, unliquidated claims, unmatured claims
FOREIGN PHRASES: ***Rogationes, quaestiones, et positiones debent esse simplices.*** Demands, questions, and claims ought to be simple.

CLAIM *(Right),* ***noun*** beneficial interest, contingent interest, due, equitable interest, expectancy, heritage, interest, legacy, ownership, privilege, share, stake, title, vested interest
ASSOCIATED CONCEPTS: claim of ownership, claim of right, claim of title

CLAIM *(Demand),* ***verb*** ask for, assert as one's own, assert as one's right, declare one's right, dun, exact as due, have a right, insist upon, make demands on, petition, press, pretend, reclaim, request, require, requisition, seek as due, sue, think one deserves, vindicate a right, vindicate a title
ASSOCIATED CONCEPTS: claim against an estate, claim and demand, claim arising from a contract, claim for relief, claim of right, claim of title, compensation claim, contingent claim, counterclaim, court of claims, fraud claim, insurance claim, money claim, ownership claim, valid claim

CLAIM *(Maintain),* ***verb*** advocate, affirm, allege, assert, asseverate, attest, aver, avouch, avow, certify, charge, contend, declare, hold, insist, make a statement, make an assertion, predicate, profess, propound, put forward, say, stand firm, state, utter with conviction, vow, warrant
ASSOCIATED CONCEPTS: claimed use

CLAIMANT, ***noun*** accusant, accuser, appellant, applicant, asserter, claimer, complainant, libelant, litigant, one who asserts a demand, one who claims a right, party to a suit, person who makes a claim, person with a grievance, petitioner, plaintiff, pleader, postulant, solicitant, solicitor, suitor
ASSOCIATED CONCEPTS: lien claimant, subsequent claimant, suit by claimant
FOREIGN PHRASES: ***Semper necessitas probandi incumbit ei qui agit.*** The burden of proof always lies upon the claimant.

CLAMOR, ***verb*** argue, call for, contend, contest, create a groundswell for, cry out, demand, dispute, espouse, exact, fight, insist, lobby for, muster support for, petition, press for, require, requisition, roar, strive, struggle, wrestle

CLANDESTINE, ***adjective*** arcane, behind the scenes, camouflaged, *clandestinus,* cloaked, collusive, concealed, confidential, conspiring, covert, *cunning,* disguised, ensconced, evasive, furtive, *furtivus,* hidden, in the background, irrevealable, masked, obscure, screened, secluded, secret, secretive, shrouded, sneaking, stealthy, stifled, subterranean, suppressed, surreptitious, undercover, underground, underhand, underhanded, undisclosed, unknown, unrevealed, unseen, veiled, with secret design
ASSOCIATED CONCEPTS: clandestine adultery, clandestine importation, clandestine marriage, clandestine meeting

CLARIFICATION, ***noun*** amplification, apostil, clarification, commentary, deciphering, definition, delineation, demonstration, description, elimination of ambiguousness, elimination of complexity, elimination of complication, elucidation, enlightenment, epexegesis, erasure of ambiguity, exemplification, explanation, explication, exposition, illumination, illustration, increase of clarity, increase of clearness, increase of intelligibility, interpretation, making apparent, making distinct, making evident, making lucid, making perspicuous, making precise, making specific, making trenchant, presentation, refinement, rendering explicit, rendering incisive, rendering unequivocal, rendering unmistakable, scholium, simplification, specification

CLARIFY, ***verb*** articulate, bare, bring to light, clear up, comment upon, construe, decipher, define, delineate, *deliquare,* demonstrate, disentangle, elucidate, enlighten, exemplify, explain, explicate, expose, exposit, expound, free from ambiguity, free from confusion, illuminate, illustrate, interpret, lay open, make clear, make comprehensible, make explicit, make intelligible, make lucid, make understood, refine, render intelligible, shed light on, show, simplify, spell out, subtilize, unfold, unmask, unravel, unscramble, unveil
ASSOCIATED CONCEPTS: clarify and amplify a complaint, clarify the pleadings

CLASH, ***verb*** battle, become hostile to, bicker, brawl, brush with, claim against, collide, combat, concuss, conflict, confront, contend against, contend with, contrast, cross swords, differ, disagree with, discord, disharmonize, duel, feud, fight, grapple, oppose, quarrel, raise Cain, run in with, spar, trade words with, wrangle
ASSOCIATED CONCEPTS: complaint, lawsuit, legal recourse, litigation

CLASS, ***noun*** assortment, bracket, branch, brand, breed, caste, category, classification, *classis,* denomination, designation, division, echelon, genera, genre, *genus,* gradation, grade, group, grouping, hierarchy, ilk, kind, layer of society, order, *ordo,* place, position, rank, rating, sect, set, social rank, social status, sort, standing, station, status, stratum, subdivision, subgroup, suborder, subspecies, type, variety
ASSOCIATED CONCEPTS: class action, class gifts, class interest, class legislation, class suit, definite class, gift to a class
FOREIGN PHRASES: ***Clausula generalis de residuo non ea complectitur quae non ejusdem sint generis cum iis quae speciatim dicta fuerant.*** A general clause of remainder does not include those things which are not of the same kind as those which have been specially mentioned.

CLASS ACTION LAWSUIT, ***noun*** derivative action, directors' and officers' liability, group lawsuit, group litigation, lawsuit by large numbers of litigants with a common grievance, suit by multiple parties with common interest
ASSOCIATED CONCEPTS: representative action

CLASSIFICATION, ***noun*** allocation, allotment, analysis, apportionment, arrangement, assignment, assortment, cataloging, categorization, category, class, codification, denomination, designation, disposition, distribution, division, gradation, group, grouping, identification, methodization, nomenclature, order, ordering, orderly arrangement, ordination, organization, placement, ranking, reducing to order, regulation by a system, specification, subgroup, syntaxis, systematization, taxis, type
ASSOCIATED CONCEPTS: arbitrary classification, illegal classification, unreasonable classification

CLASSIFY, *verb* allocate, allot, analyze, apportion, arrange, assort, brand, break down, cataloge, categorize, class, classify as, codify, collocate, coordinate, correlate, dispose, distinguish, distribute, divide, file, form into classes, grade, group, identify, *in genera describere,* index, introduce a system, label, list, marshal, methodize, name, organize, partition, pigeonhole, place in a category, place in order, put in array, put in order, range, rank, rate, reduce to order, segregate, separate, seriate, set in order, size, sort, specify, subsume, systematize, tag, type
ASSOCIATED CONCEPTS: arbitrary classification, illegal classification, unreasonable classification

CLAUSE, *noun* article, *caput,* condition, *conditiosine qua non,* contract, covenant, exception, exemption, limitation, *membrum,* paragraph, *pars,* passage, phrase, proposition, provision, proviso, qualification, section, sentence, specification, stipulation, term
ASSOCIATED CONCEPTS: commerce clause, commercial clause, enacting clause, escalation clause, forfeiture clause, grandfather clause, incontestable clause, loss payable clause, most favored nation clause, penalty clause, residuary clause, saving clause, specific clause, spendthrift clause, standard mortagagee clause, sunsetting clause
FOREIGN PHRASES: ***Clausula generalis de residuo non ea complectitur quae non ejusdem sint generis cum iis quae speciatim dicta fuerant.*** A general clause concerning the remainder does not include those matters which are not of the same kind with those which have been specially expressed. ***Clausula generalis non refertur ad expressa.*** A general clause does not refer to things expressly mentioned. ***Clausula quae abrogationem excludit ab initio non valet.*** A clause which forbids its abrogation is invalid from the beginning. ***Clausula vel dispositio inutilis per praesumptionem remotam, vel causam ex post facto non fulcitur.*** A useless clause or provision is not supported by a remote presumption, or by a cause that arises afterwards. ***Clausulae inconsuetae semper inducunt suspicionem.*** Unusual clauses always arouse suspicion.

CLEAN, *adjective* above suspicion, acquitted, angelic, blameless, bloodless, cleanhanded, cleanminded, clear, decent, entirely defensible, fair, faultless, free from guilt, free from impurities, free from sin, good, guileless, guiltless, high-minded, high-principled, honest, honorable, immaculate, impeccable, in the clear, incorrupt, incorruptible, innocent, inviolable, inviolate, irreprehensible, irreproachable, irreprovable, law-abiding, lawful, moral, *mundus,* not guilty, not responsible, pure, pure-hearted, pure in heart, *purus,* right-minded, righteous, scrupulous, snowy, spotless, stainless, straight, strictly honest, taintless, unblamable, unblemished, unbribed, uncorrupted, unculpable, unerring, unexceptionable, unguilty, unimpeachable, uninvolved, unmuddied, unobjectionable, unoffending, unsoiled, unspotted, unstained, unsullied, untarnished, unviolated, upright, veracious, virtuous, white, wholesome, without a stain, without reproach
ASSOCIATED CONCEPTS: clean bill of lading, clean credit, clean docket receipt, clean hands doctrine, clean money

CLEAR *(Apparent),* ***adjective*** blunt, clarified, clear-cut, demonstrative, direct, distinct, downright, emphatic, *évident,* evident, exact, explicit, express, expressive, frank, glaring, graphic, identifiable, in bold relief, in evidence, in strong relief, intelligible, limpid, manifest, observable, outspoken, overt, patent, pellucid, perceivable, perceptible, perspicuous, plain, prominent, pronounced, pure, salient, self-evident, showing, shown, straightforward, striking, transparent, unadorned, unambiguous, unblurred, unclouded, uncovered, understood, undisguised, unequivocal, unevasive, unmistakable, visible, vivid, well-defined, well-marked, well-seen
ASSOCIATED CONCEPTS: clear and convincing danger, clear and present danger, clear-cut question of law, clear meaning, clear preponderance, clear proof, clearly ascertainable, last clear chance

CLEAR *(Certain),* ***adjective*** absolute, actual, ascertained, authoritative, beyond a shadow of a doubt, beyond all dispute, categorical, cogent, conclusive, definite, definitive, doubtless, free from doubt, incontestable, incontrovertible, indefeasible, indisputable, indubitable, irrefragable, irrefutable, positive, questionless, settled without appeal, sure, unassailable, unchallengeable, unconfutable, uncontested, uncontroversial, undeniable, undisputed, undoubted, unequivocal, unerring, unhesitating, unimpeachable, unmistakable, unqualified, unquestionable, unquestioned, unrefutable
ASSOCIATED CONCEPTS: clear legal right, clear right, clearly erroneous

CLEAR *(Free from criminal charges),* ***adjective*** absolved, acquitted, at liberty, cleared, condoned, delivered, disburdened, discharged, disculpated, dismissed, exculpated, excused, exempted, exonerated, forgiven, freed, guiltless, immune, justified, manumitted, nonliable, not guilty, pardoned, purged, released, remitted, reprieved, spared, unburdened, uncensurable, unchastised, uncondemned, unpunished, vindicated

CLEAR *(Unencumbered),* ***adjective*** disburdened, disencumbered, exempt, free, free from burden, free from encumbrance, free from hindrance, free from impediment, free from limitation, free from obstruction, not answerable, not responsible, unaccountable, unbound, unbridled, unburdened, unconstrained, uncurbed, unfettered, unhampered, unhindered, unobstructed, unrestrained, untrammeled
ASSOCIATED CONCEPTS: clear title

CLEAR, *verb* absolve, acquit, amnesty, deliver, disburden, discharge, disembroil, disencumber, disentangle, dismiss, exculpate, excuse, exempt, exonerate, *explicare,* extricate, find not guilty, forgive, free, give a reprieve, give absolution, grant a reprieve, grant amnesty, grant remission, let go, let off, liberate, pardon, pronounce not guilty, prove innocent, purge, quash the conviction, release, render free, reprieve, rescue, set at large, set at liberty, set free, shrive, vindicate
ASSOCIATED CONCEPTS: clear and convincing evidence, clear and convincing standard of proof, clear and present danger, clear title, last clear chance doctrine

CLEAR UP, *verb* answer, ascertain, brighten, clarify, complete, construe, consummate, decipher, decode, die away, disentangle, dispatch, dispose of, elucidate, explain, exposit, expound, fathom, figure out, interpret, lift, light, make sense, resolve, settle, simplify, solve, strike, unlock, unravel, unriddle, unscramble, untangle, wind up, work out
ASSOCIATED CONCEPTS: clear up inconsistencies in testimony, clear up misconceptions

CLEARED, *adjective* absolved, acquitted, condoned, disburdened, discharged, dismissed, exculpated, excused, exempted, exonerated, forgiven, freed, guiltless, immune, justified, not guilty, overturned, pardoned, purged, released, reprieved, reversed and overturned, spared, unburdened, vindicated
ASSOCIATED CONCEPTS: Appeals Court, cleared in a probe, DNA, habeas corpus, reversal

CLEARLY DEFINED, *adjective* absolute, blunt, candid, categorical, certain, clear, clearly formulated, comprehensible, decisive, definite, definitive, determinate, direct, distinct, distinctly stated, exact, explanatory, explicit, frank, lucid, obvious, perceptible, plain, pointed, positive, precise, specific, straightforward, unambiguous, unconditional, unequivocal, unmistakable, vivid, well developed

CLEMENCY, *noun* absolution, amnesty, benefaction, beneficence, benevolence, benignity, charity, *clementia,* clementness, commutation, compassion, consideration, decency, disposition to mercy, disposition to pardon, excuse, exemption, extenuation, forbearance, forgiveness, forgivingness, generosity, generousness, gentleness, good will, grace, humaneness, humanity, indemnity, indulgence, kindness, lenience, leniency, lenity, liberality, magnanimity, magnanimousness, *mansuetuda,* mercifulness, mercy, obligingness, pardon, pardoning, purgation, release, reprieve, respite, temperance, tolerance, toleration, willingness to forgive
ASSOCIATED CONCEPTS: clemency by the governor, clemency by the president of the United States, executive clemency

CLERICAL, *adjective* accessory, *ad administrationem pertimens*, administrating, administrative, assistant, assisting, attendant, attending, auxiliary, *ex officio,* helping, instrumental, intermediary
ASSOCIATED CONCEPTS: clerical acts, clerical duties, clerical errors, clerical mistakes, clerical omissions

CLERICAL ERROR, *noun* administrative mistake, clerical mistake, inadvertent negligence of office worker, mistake in preparing a legal document, typographical error
ASSOCIATED CONCEPTS: law office mistake

CLERK, *noun* archivist, chronicler, copyist, court employee, court official, court scribe, judicial administrator, judicial assistant, judicial recorder, judicial secretary, office holder, office worker, official, prothonotary, recorder, record keeper, registrar, *scriba,* scribe, scrivener, secretary
ASSOCIATED CONCEPTS: clerk of the county, clerk of the court, county clerk, papers filed with the clerk, town clerk
FOREIGN PHRASES: ***Errores scribentis nocere non debent.*** An error made by a clerk ought not to prejudice.

CLERK, *verb* aid a judge, assist a judge, help a judge, work for a judge

CLEVER, *adjective* able, adept, adroit, apt, artful, astute, bright, brilliant, canny, creative, cunning, deft, dexterous, discerning, exceptional, gifted, imaginative, ingenious, innovative, insightful, intelligent, intuitive, inventive, keen, knowledgeable, lithe, lithesome, masterly, nimble, original, perspicacious, piercing, politic, proficient, quick-witted, resourceful, sagacious, sapient, savvy, sharp, shrewd, skilled, skillful, sly, smart, spry, versatile, wise

CLIENT, *noun* business contact, buyer of labor, *cliens, consultor,* consumer, customer, employer of legal advice, hirer, offerer, patron, patron of professional services, patronizer, person employing advice, person represented, person represented by counsel, purchaser, retainer of counsel
ASSOCIATED CONCEPTS: attorney-client privilege, attorney-client relationship

CLIMATE, *noun* atmosphere, aura, *caelum,* circumambiency, clime, condition, environment, environmental conditions, feeling, forces of nature, influences, mood, prevailing attitudes, prevailing conditions, prevailing standards, surrounding influence, surroundings

CLIMATE CHANGE, *noun* atmospheric variance, extreme weather, global temperature change, global warming, global weather change, new weather changes, new weather patterns, severe weather, unique changing weather patterns, world weather change

CLINICAL, *adjective* analytical, detached, dispassionate, impersonal, imperturbable, unemotional, unimpressionable

CLOAK, *verb* beguile, belie, blind, bluff, bury, camouflage, cloud, conceal, conceal the truth, construe falsely, couch, cover, cover up, curtain, deceive, decoy, disguise, dissemble, *dissimulare,* dissimulate, distort, divert, dress up, dupe, eclipse, embellish, embroider, ensconce, enshroud, envelop, exaggerate, fake, falsify, feign, forswear, garble, give a false coloring, gloss over, go undercover, hide, hide away, keep a secret, keep hidden, keep in ignorance, keep secret, keep undercover, mask, miscolor, misinform, mislead, misrepresent, muffle, obscure, obstruct the view of, occult, pretend, put out of sight, render invisible, screen, seclude, secrete, shade, shadow, sham, shelter, shroud, sneak, stifle, suppress, swear falsely, veil
ASSOCIATED CONCEPTS: cloaked with authority

CLOG, *verb* arrest, astrict, bar, barricade, be obstructive, block, block up, bridle, burden, checkmate, choke, close, close off, constrict, cumber, dam, deadlock, detain, exclude, forbid, foreclose, forestall, frustrate, hamper, handicap, hinder, hold back, hold in check, hold up, impede, *impedire,* impedite, intercept, interfere, keep out, obstruct, occlude, place limitations, plug, plug up, preclude, prevent, prevent passage, prohibit, put a stop to, repress, restrain, restrict, retard, shut off, stall, stand in the way of, stay, stifle, stop, stop short, stop up, stultify, stymie, suppress

CLONE, *noun* a carbon copy created by genetic engineering, a copy created by genetic engineering, a double created by genetic engineering, a facsimile created through genetic engineering, an exact copy created through genetic engineering, duplication created by genetic engineering, production of a copy, production of a copy through genetic engineering, production of multiple identical copies, propagation asexually, propagation from a clone cell, replication created by genetic engineering, replication through genetic engineering, reproduction asexually
ASSOCIATED CONCEPTS: bioethics, computer clone, embryo splitting, human clone

CLONING, *noun* copy, counterpart, double, duplication, embodiment, exact copy, genetically identical copy, genetically identical individual, genetically identical reproduction, producing, replica, reproduction
Generally: duplicating, manifestation, match

CLOSE *(Intimate),* *adjective* allied, bosom, brotherly, confidential, dear, devoted, faithful, familiar, fast, fraternal, friendly, inseparable, strongly attached
ASSOCIATED CONCEPTS: close corporation, closely held

CLOSE *(Near),* *adjective* adjacent, adjoining, approaching, approximate, at hand, bordering, close at hand, close by, coming, contiguous, forthcoming, handy, imminent, impending, in close proximity, in the area, in the neighborhood, in the vicinity, near at hand, nearby, neighboring, nigh, *propinquus,* proximal, proximate, tangent, touching, vicinal
ASSOCIATED CONCEPTS: close confinement, close proximity

CLOSE *(Rigorous),* ***adjective*** assiduous, attentive, careful, conscientious, diligent, earnest, exact, hard, harsh, intense, keen, meticulous, *parcus,* precise, punctilious, relentless, rigid, scrupulous, severe, sharp, stiff, strict, stringent, *tenax,* uncompromising, unremitting, unsparing

CLOSE *(Conclusion),* ***noun*** adjournment, cessation, closing, closure, completion, *conclusio,* consummation, discontinuance, discontinuation, end, ending, expiration, finale, finis, finish, last part, last stage, omega, peroration, shutdown, stoppage, termination, *terminus,* windup
ASSOCIATED CONCEPTS: the close of a trial, the closing on a real estate transaction

CLOSE *(Enclosed area),* ***noun*** compound, confine, court, courtyard, enclosure, grounds, pen, precinct, square, yard
ASSOCIATED CONCEPTS: breaking the close

CLOSE *(Agree),* ***verb*** accept an offer, arrive at an agreement, bargain, come to an arrangement, come to an understanding, come to terms, consent, endorse, enter into a contractual obligation, establish by agreement, execute, finalize, finalize an agreement, fix by agreement, give assurance, go to contract, guarantee, make a bargain, make an agreement, negotiate, *pacisci,* seek accord, settle, strike a bargain, subscribe, undertake, underwrite
ASSOCIATED CONCEPTS: close a business transaction, close a real estate transaction

CLOSE *(Terminate),* ***verb*** apply the closure, break off, bring to an end, call a halt, cause a stoppage, cease, *claudere,* come to a stop, come to an end, complete, conclude, consummate, discontinue, dispatch, dispose of, eliminate, end, expire, finish, finish up, fulfill, halt, have run its course, interrupt, make an end of, make inactive, *operire,* prosecute to a conclusion, put a stop to, run out, shut down, stop, surcease, suspend, suspend operation, wind up
ASSOCIATED CONCEPTS: close a bank account, close a case, close a grand jury investigation, close an investigation

CLOSE-MINDED, ***adjective*** bigoted, blind, closed, deaf, inflexible, intolerant, narrow-minded, obdurate, obstinate, pigheaded, prejudiced, resistant, rigid, short-sighted, stubborn, unpersuadable

CLOSING ARGUMENTS, ***noun*** closing, closing statements at trial, summation at trial, summing up a case
Generally: recapitulation, reiteration, renumeration, restatement, review

CLOTHE, ***verb*** accouter, *amicire,* appoint, arm, array, attire oneself, bedeck, bedrape, cloak, conceal, costume, cover, cover up, disguise, drape, dress, embroider, empower, enable, encase, endow, endue, enfold, enrobe, envelop, enwrap, equip, fit out, frock, furnish, garb, gear, *induere sibi vestem,* invest, invest with power, outfit, provide, put in uniform, robe, suit, supply, uniform, *vestire,* wrap
ASSOCIATED CONCEPTS: clothe with authority to act, clothe with indicia of ownership

CLOTURE, ***noun*** abandonment, abeyance, adjournal, adjournment, arrest, break, cease, cessation, check, closing, closure, desistance, discontinuance, discontinuation, halt, interruption, lapse, letup, lull, noncontinuance, prorogation, recess, standstill, stay, stop, stoppage, suspension, withdrawal

CLOUD *(Incumbrance),* ***noun*** burden, charge, claim, claim on property, commitment, debt, hold on property, hypothecation, indebtedness, indebtment, liability, mortgage, obligation, obstruction, outstanding debt, *pignus judiciale, pignus legale,* pledge, prescription, real security, restraint, security, security on property, state of indebtedness, *vadium mortuum*
ASSOCIATED CONCEPTS: a cloud on personalty, a cloud on real property

CLOUD *(Suspicion),* ***noun*** apprehension, apprehensiveness, consternation, contestability, controvertibility, deniability, disbelief, disputability, distrust, distrustfulness, doubt, fear, hesitation, incredulity, incredulousness, intimation, lack of certainty, lack of confidence, lack of faith, misdoubt, misgiving, mistrust, mistrustfulness, *onus probandi,* perplexity, puzzlement, questionability, refusal to believe, refutability, reluctance to believe, skepticism, trepidation, unbelief, uncredulousness, want of certainty, want of confidence, want of faith

CLOUT, ***noun*** authoritative power, authority, consequence, controlling power, directing power, dominancy, dominion, eminence, force, hegemony, importance, influence, influentiality, leverage, mastership, notability, potency, power, power of impelling, predominancy, prestige, prominence, puissance, significance, weight

CLUE, ***noun*** data, evidence, finding, guide, hint, idea, index, indication, indicator, information, inkling, insinuation, intimation, key, lead, mark, reason to believe, scent, sign, signal, token

COACH, ***verb*** advise, appraise, counsel, develop, direct, drill, edify, educate, enlighten, foster, give advice, guide, help, improve, inform, instruct, lead, manage, mentor, nurture, oversee, prepare, prompt, provide tutelage, school, shepherd, steer, teach, train, tutor

COACTION, ***noun*** alliance, association, coalition, cohesion, collaboration, colleagueship, collective action, collusion, combined effort, common effort, complicity, concert of action, concourse, concurrence, confederacy, cooperancy, cooperation, cooperativeness, coworking, federation, fellowship, fraternity, fusion, joint effort, joint participation, league, mutual assistance, mutuality, partnership, solidarity, teamwork, union, union of action, united action, working together

COACTOR, ***noun*** abettor, accessory, accessory after the fact, accessory before the fact, accomplice, accomplice in crime, acolyte, adjunct, adjutant, adjuvant, advocate, aid, aide-de-camp, aider, aider and abettor, ally, assistant, associate, attendant, auxiliary, coadjutant, coadjutor, cohelper, collaborationist, collaborator, colleague, colluder, confederate, consociate, consort, conspirator, conspirer, contriver, cooperator, copartner, coworker, deviser, fellow conspirator, helper, henchman, joint-operator, partner, partner in crime, planner, plotter, promoter, promotor, schemer, strategist, supporter

COADJUTANT, ***noun*** abettor, accessory, accomplice, adjutant, adjuvant, aid, aide, aider, ally, apprentice, assistant, associate, attendant, auxiliary, coadjutor, collaborator, colleague, confederate, consociate, cooperator, coworker, deputy, fellow worker, follower, help, helper, henchman, lieutenant, mate, partner, subordinate, supporter, teammate, underling

COADUNATE, ***adjective*** adherent, adhering, adhesive, agglomerate, aggregate, aggregated, allied, amalgamative, assembled, associated, centralized, clinging, coagulated, coagulative, coalesced, coalescent, cohering, cohesive, combined, compact, concerted, confluent, conglomerate, conglomeratic, congregated, conjoined, conjoint, conjugate, conjunct, connected, consolidated, cooperative, fused, incorporated, integrated, interlinked, interlocked, interrelated, joined, leagued, linked, related, unified, united

COALESCENCE, *noun* abutting, accordance, adherence, adhesion, admixture, affiliation, agglomeration, agglutination, alliance, amalgamation, annexation, annexing, assemblage, association, attachment, binding, bond, centralization, closeness, coadunation, coagulation, coalition, coherence, cohesion, cohesiveness, combination, commixture, compound, concrescence, concurrence, confederacy, confederation, confluence, conglomeration, conglutination, conjugation, conjunction, connection, consociation, consolidation, contact, convergence, converging, coupling, federation, fusing, fusion, immixture, incorporation, interconnection, interfusion, joining, junction, league, linkage, merger, merging, mixture, solidification, symbiosis, synthesis, unification, union

COALITION, *noun* affiliation, alliance, amalgamation, association, binding, bond, cartel, combination, combine, coming together, community, concurrence, confluence, conglomerate, congress, conjoining, *conjunctio,* conjunction, conjuncture, connection, consociation, consolidation, consortium, *conspiratio,* convergence, cooperation, federation, fellowship, fusing, fusion, fusion of interests, group, integration, interlocking, joint concern, joint endeavor, junction, league, meeting, merger, merging, mixture, mutual concern, partnership, society, sodality, syndicate, unification, union, union of factions, unity

COARSE, *adjective* awkward, boorish, brash, churlish, classless, cloddish, clumsy, crass, crude, horrendous, ill-bred, impertinent, impolite, irksome, loutish, lowbrow, lubberly, mannerless, noxious, obnoxious, odious, offensive, peccant, pernicious, raffish, recreant, reprehensible, reprovable, rough, rude, rugged, tasteless, uncouth, uncultivated, uncultured, ungraceful, unmannered, unmannerly, unpolished, unrefined, vulgar

COAX, *verb* allure, appeal, attract, bait, blandish, bribe, cajole, captivate, convince, encourage, engage, enlist, ensnare, entice, evoke, exert pressure, exhort, *hominem permulcere, homini blandiri,* impel, incite, induce, influence, insist, inspire, intrigue, inveigle, keep in countenance, lead, lure, manipulate, motivate, offer an inducement, persuade, press, prevail, prevail upon, procure, prod, prompt, provoke, rally, recommend, rouse, spellbind, stimulate, suborn, suggest, sway, tempt, urge

COCONSPIRATOR, *noun* abettor, accessory, accessory after the fact, accessory before the fact, accomplice, adjunct in crime, adjutant in crime, adjuvant in crime, aide in crime, aide in wrongdoing, aider in wrongdoing, ally in crime, ally in wrongdoing, assistant, associate in crime, associate in guilt, auxiliary in crime, coactor in crime, coadjutor, coaider in crime, collaborator, colleague in crime, colluder, companion in crime, comrade in crime, comrade in wrongdoing, confederate, consociate in crime, cooperator in crime, copartner in crime, coworker in crime, fellow conspirator, fellow machinator, fellow plotter, fellow schemer, fellow strategist, fellow traiter, partner, partner in crime, partner in wrongdoing, supporter

CODE, *noun* arrangement of statutes, body of laws, bylaw, canon, capitulary, charter, civil code, codification, codified law, collection, collection of laws, collection of statutes, compilation, compilation of law, compilation of laws, constitution, *corpus juris,* digest, enactment, enactment of rules, established law, established order, firm principle, formulary, formulation, guide, guideline, laws, legal code, legislation, *lex,* maxim, model, norm, ordinance, precedent, precept, precepts, prescript, prescription, principles, regulation by law, regulation by statute, regulations, rubric, rules, ruling, settled law, standard, statute, statute book, statute law, subsidiary law, system of law, system of rules, written constitution, written law
ASSOCIATED CONCEPTS: building code, civil code, code of criminal procedure, code of ethics, code of fair competition, Code of Hammurabi, code of judicial conduct, code of law, code of procedure, code of professional responsibility, code pleading, criminal code, ethics code, Napoleonic code, penal code, probate code
FOREIGN PHRASES: ***Ad ea quae frequentius accidunt jura adaptantur.*** Laws are adapted to those cases which most commonly occur.

CODICIL, *noun* accessory, accompaniment, addendum, additament, addition, addition to a will, additive, additum, adjunct, affixation, affixture, annex, annexation, appanage, appendage, appendix, attachment, augmentation, complement, epilogue, insertion, postscript, sequel, sequela, subscript, suffix, supplement, supplement to a will, testament, will addendum, will supplement
ASSOCIATED CONCEPTS: will

CODIFICATION, *noun* act, arrangement of laws, arrangement of rules, arrangement of statutes, authoritative law, bill, bylaws, canon, capitulary, categorization of laws, collection of statutes, commandment, compendium, compilation, decree, doctrine, enactment, formalization of laws, formulation of laws, lawmaking, legislation, ordinance, precept, prescription, regulation, rule, rules and regulations, rulings, sanctions, scheduling, scheme, set of rules, standardization of laws, statute, statute book, statute law, system, system of laws, system of regulations, systematic arrangement of laws, systematization of laws, tabulation, written law
ASSOCIATED CONCEPTS: codification act, codification of statutes

CODIFY, *verb* accumulate, arrange, assemble, assort, break down, bring into order, catalog, categorize, classify, collect, compile, coordinate, *digerere,* divide, formalize, formulate, group, index, introduce order, list, methodize, organize, rank, reduce to a code, reduce to a digest, reduce to order, regularize, sort, subdivide, systematize, systemize, tabulate
ASSOCIATED CONCEPTS: codifying act

COEQUAL, *adjective* *aequalis,* agreeing, analogous, as great as another, coextensive, coincident, commensurate, comparable, congruent, coordinate, correlative, correspondent, corresponding, equal, equibalanced, equipollent, equiponderant, equivalent, even, homologous, identical in value, interchangeable, level, like in degree, like in quantity, matching, neither more nor less, of equal dignity, of equal power, of like rank, of the same rank, on a footing with, on a level with, on a par, on a par with, on the same footing, parallel, reciprocal, symmetrical, synonymous, tantamount, uniform, up to the mark

COERCE, *verb* apply pressure, bear down, bludgeon, bring pressure to bear, command, compel, conscript, constrain, demand, dictate, dominate, draft, dragoon, drive, elicit by threat, enjoin, enthrall, exact, exhort, extort, foist, force, impel, impose, impose restrictions, impress, induce, insist, interdict, intimidate, issue threats, necessitate, oblige,

oppress, order, press, pressure, prod, push, put pressure on, put under restraint, require, rule, subjugate, suppress, terrorize, threaten, use force upon, wrest from
ASSOCIATED CONCEPTS: duress, harassment
FOREIGN PHRASES: ***Ejus nulla culpa est cui parere necesse sit.*** No guilt attaches to him who is compelled to obey.

COERCION, *noun* blackmail, bondage, brute force, *coercitio,* command, compulsion, constraint, constraint by force, control, dictation, duress, exaction, exigency, extortion, force, forcing, illegal compulsion, impelling, inducement, insistence, intimidation, moral compulsion, necessity, negative compulsion, oppression, oppressive exaction, pressure, prevailing, prohibition, repression, restraint, strong-arm tactics, threat, undue influence, unlawful compulsion
ASSOCIATED CONCEPTS: coercive conduct, duress, extortion, coercion of employees
FOREIGN PHRASES: ***Extortio est crimen quando quis colore, officii extorquet quod non est debitum, vel supra debitum, vel ante tempus quod est debitum.*** Extortion is a crime when, by color of office, any person extorts that which is not due, or more than is due, or before the time when it is due. ***Nihil consensui tam contrarium est quam vis atque metus.*** Nothing is so opposed to consent as force and fear. ***Vis legibus est inimica.*** Force is inimical to the laws.

COERCIVE, *adjective* arm-twisting, browbeating, bulldozing, compelling, compulsory, convincing, drastic, duress-induced, fear-inducing, forceful, harassing, hardheaded, intense, intimidating, mandatory, menacing, militant, ominous, peremptory, persuasive, pressure, severe, strong, terrorizing, threatening, vehement

COEXISTENCE, *noun* coevality, coexisting jointly, coexisting together, coherence, concert, concurrence, conjunction, consonance, coordination, exist together, jointly, living in peace together, living together, living together contemporaneously, living together in harmony, order, pact, rapport, reconciliation, survival, surviving together, sympathy, to be in tune, togetherness, treaty, unanimity, unity

COEXTENSIVE, *adjective* agreeing, aligned, analagous, balanced, coequal, coextending, collateral, comparable, concentric, concurrent, congruent, coordinate, correlative, correspondent, corresponding, equable, equal, equal in scope, equal in space, equal in time, equalized, equidistant, equilateral, equipollent, equiponderant, equipondious, equivalent, even, even-sided, homologous, in equilibrium, lined up, matched, parallel, proportioned, symmetrical, synonymous
ASSOCIATED CONCEPTS: coextensive with rights under the U.S. Constitution

COFFER, *noun* *arca,* bank, *cista,* container, depository, holder, locker, money chest, receptacle, safe, safe-deposit box, storage, strongbox, till, treasury, vault

COGENT, *adjective* appealing conclusively, appealing forcibly, authoritative, commanding, compelling, conclusive, convincing, definite, definitive, demonstrable, demonstrating, determinative, effective, effectual, efficacious, evidential, forceful, forcible, incontestable, incontrovertible, indubitable, inducive, influential, irrefragable, irrefutable, irresistible, logical, meritorious, of consequence, past dispute, persuasive, potent, powerful, proving, puissant, reliable, solid, sound, strong, suasive, substantial, telling, to the point, trenchant, trustworthy, unanswerable, unconfuted, undeniable, undoubtable, undoubted, unequivocal, unquestionable, valid, veridical, weighty, well-founded, well-grounded

COGITATIVE, *adjective* contemplative, deliberate, deliberative, ideative, introspective, meditative, museful, pensive, philosophical, pondering, reflective, ruminant, ruminative, speculative, thinking, thoughtful

COGNATE, *adjective* affiliated, affined, agnate, akin, alike, allied, analogical, analogous, appertaining, appurtenant, associated, bearing upon, belonging, close, closely allied, closely related, coordinate, commensurate, common, comparable, comparative, compared, complementary, concurrent, congeneric, congenerous, congenial, connected, consanguine, consanguineous, correlated, correlative, correspondent, corresponding, entwined, equal, equivalent, germane, homogeneous, homologous, in common with, in the same category, interchangeable, interdependent, interrelated, intimately allied, intimately related, like, linked, mutual, near, of that kind, of that sort, parallel, proportionable, reciprocal, related, relating to, relative, same, serial, sharing, similar, something like, synonymous

COGNITION, *noun* acquaintance, apperception, appreciation, apprehension, awareness, *cognitio,* cognitive process, cognizance, comprehension, conception, consciousness, discernment, enlightenment, familiarity, grasp, illumination, insight, intellection, ken, knowledge, mastery, perception, percipience, realization, recognition, sensibility, understanding, wisdom

COGNIZABLE, *adjective* accountable, apprehensible, ascertainable, ascertained, capable of being examined, capable of being tried in the court, clear, comprehensible, decipherable, definite, discernible, discoverable, distinct, distinguishable, explicable, explicit, familiar, fathomable, intelligible, jurisdictionally sound, knowable, known, lucid, luminous, meaningful, pellucid, penetrable, perceived, perceptible, perspicuous, readable, realizable, realized, recognizable, scrutable, straightforward, unblurred, understandable, understood, unequivocal, unevasive, uninvolved, unmistakable, well-written
ASSOCIATED CONCEPTS: cognizable by the courts

COGNIZANT, *adjective* accomplished, acquainted, alert, apperceptive, apprehensive, apprised, astute, aware, clear-sighted, cognitive, comprehending, conscious, *conscius,* conversant, discerning, discriminating, educated, endowed with consciousness, endowed with reason, enlightened, erudite, expert, familiar, informed, keen, knowing, knowledgeable, learned, lettered, mindful, perceptive, percipient, perspicacious, possessed of knowledge, posted, practiced, proficient, regardful, sagacious, sage, sensible to, sharp, understanding, versed, well-advised, well-educated, well-grounded, well-informed, well-read, well-versed, wise

COGNOMEN, *noun* appelation, appellative, byname, byword, denomination, designation, name, nickname, sobriquet, style

COGNOVIT, *noun* acknowledged judgment, adjudication, admitted judgment, conceded judgment, confessed judgment, confirmed judgment, decision, declaration, decree, determination, disclosed judgment, finding, legal decision

COHABIT, *verb* abide together, be intimate, conjugate, copulate, couple, dwell together, live in sexual intimacy, live together, live with, lodge together, reside together,

room together, share an address, share bed and board, stay together
ASSOCIATED CONCEPTS: cohabit as husband and wife

COHABITATION *(Living together),* ***noun*** abiding together, act of dwelling together, alliance, living together in sexual intimacy, lodging together, lodging together as husband and wife, occupying the same domicile, residing together, rooming together
ASSOCIATED CONCEPTS: cohabiting in a state of adultery, fornication, illicit cohabitation, lewd and lascivious cohabitation
FOREIGN PHRASES: ***Nuptias non concubitus sed consensus facit.*** Not cohabitation but consent makes the valid marriage.

COHABITATION *(Married state),* ***noun*** act of living together as husband and wife, act of pairing, bond of matrimony, conjugal bliss, conjugality, connubiality, coverture, domestication, legal relation of spouses to each other, legal union of a man and a woman, marriage, married status, matrimony, nuptial bond, nuptial tie, state of matrimony, union, *vinculo matrimonii,* wedded state, wedded status, wedlock
ASSOCIATED CONCEPTS: bigamous cohabitation, cohabiting in a state of adultery, matrimonial cohabitation, polygamous cohabitation
FOREIGN PHRASES: ***Nuptias non concubitus sed consensus facit.*** Not cohabitation but consent makes the marriage.

COHERE *(Adhere),* ***verb*** affix, agglomerate, agglutinate, attach, be dense, be tacked together, become solid, cement, clasp, cleave, cling, clot, coagulate, coalesce, *cohaerere,* combine, come together, compress, congeal, conjoin, consolidate, fasten, grasp, grow together, hang on, harden, hold fast, hold on, hold together, hold up, mass, quadrate with, solidify, stay, stick, stick close, stick on to, stick together, unify, unite

COHERE *(Be logically consistent),* ***verb*** accord, agree, be a sound argument, be accordant, be clear, be coherent, be congruous, be intelligible, be logical, be lucid, be rationally connected, be reasonable, be understandable, comport with, conform, correspond, hang together, harmonize, hold together, make sense

COHERENCE, ***noun*** adherence, adhesion, adhesiveness, agreement, apprehensibility, attachment, blending, cleavage, coherency, cohesion, cohesiveness, comprehensibility, concert, congruence, congruity, conjunction, connectedness, connection, consistency, consolidation, consonance, *contextus,* continuity, *convenientia,* correspondence, correspondency, firm hold, fusion, harmony, holding together, intelligibility, interrelation, rationality, sticking together, understandability, union, unity

COHERENT *(Clear),* ***adjective*** adapted to the understanding, apparent, apprehensible, articulate, audible, clear-cut, cogent, cognizable, *cohaerens,* comprehensible, concise, *congruens,* decipherable, defined, definite, direct, discernible, distinct, easily understood, easy to grasp, easy to understand, evident, exact, exoteric, exoterical, explained, explanatory, explicable, explicatory, explicit, express, expressive, fathomable, forthright, graphic, illuminated, in evidence, intelligible, interpreted, knowable, legible, logical, logically appealing, logically consistent, lucid, luminous, making sense, manifest, meaningful, obvious, palpable, pellucid, penetrable, perceivable, perceptible, perspicuous, plain, precise, realizable, recognizable, scrutable, self-evident, simple, straightforward, unambiguous, unblurred, unconfused, understandable, understood, undisguised, unequivocal, unmistakable, visible, vivid, well-defined, well-marked

COHERENT *(Joined),* ***adjective*** accreted, accretive, adherent, adhering, adhesive, agglutinate, agglutinative, allied, amalgamative, cleaving, cleaving together, clinging, close, coadunate, coagulate, coagulated, coalescent, *cohaerens,* cohering, cohesive, combined, composite, compressed, congealed, conglomerate, conglomeratic, *congruens,* conjoined, conjunct, connected, consolidated, *contextus,* coupled, fused, holding together, incorporated, indivisible, inseparable, interlinked, interlocked, interrelated, sticking, sticking together, united, viscous

COHESIVE *(Compact),* ***adjective*** close, compressed, concentrated, concise, concrete, conjacent, conjunct, consolidated, dense, firm, hard, impenetrable, impermeable, indivisible, inseparable, pressed together, solid, strong, substantial, terse, thick, tight, to the point, well-knit

COHESIVE *(Sticking),* ***adjective*** adherent, adhering, adhesive, agglutinate, agglutinative, attached, cementitious, cleaving, clinging, coherent, cohering, conglutinative, connected, consistent, glutinous, holding together, resisting, sticking, tenacious, tied, united

COHORT, ***noun*** abettor, accessory, accomplice, aider and abettor, ally, assistant, associate, attendant, auxiliary, coadjutor, cohelper, *cohors,* collaborator, colleague, comate, companion, comrade, confederate, consociate, cooperator, coworker, faithful companion, fellow, fellow conspirator, follower, friend, helper, particeps *criminis,* partner, socius *criminis,* stalwart, supporter

COINCIDE *(Concur),* ***verb*** accede, accept, accord, acquiesce, agree, approve, arrive at an agreement, arrive at an understanding, arrive at terms, assent, be accordant, be at one with, be of the same mind, be one with, come to an agreement, come to an understanding, come to terms, conform to, consent, correspond, endorse, give assent, go along with, harmonize, meet, merge, nod assent to, subscribe to, synchronize, unite, yield assent

COINCIDE *(Correspond),* ***verb*** accompany, be concomitant, be congruent, be contemporaneous, be identical, be simultaneous, coexist, *concurrere,* conform to, *congruere, convenire,* exist together, fall exactly together, fill identical times, fit exactly, go with, happen together, match

COINCIDENTAL, ***adjective*** accidental, accompanying, at the same time, by circumstance, casual, chance, circumstantial, coexistent, coexisting, coincident, coinciding, coinstantaneous, concomitant, concurrent, conjunctional, contemporaneous, corresponding, fortuitous, *fortuitus,* occurring simultaneously, occurring together, simultaneous, surprising, unexpected, unplanned

COLD *(Callous),* ***adjective*** aloof, antisocial, bleak, brittle, cold-blooded, coldish, cool, cruel, cutting, detached, disinterested, distant, frigid, heartless, ill-tempered, impersonal, inhumane, offish, penetrating, piercing, pitiless, ruthless, uncharitable, unemotional, unfriendly, unsympathetic

COLD *(Freezing),* ***adjective*** arctic, biting, blistering cold, brisk, brumal, chilled, chilly, cool, frigid, frosty, gelid, glacial, icy, numbed, numbing, polar, raw, refrigerated, sharp, wintry, wrenching

COLD-BLOODED, ***adjective*** aloof, barbarous, brutal, brutish, calculated, calculating, callous, cold, cold-hearted, cruel, cruel hearted, deliberate, demoniac, devilish, diabolic,

dispassionate, feelingless, fiendish, frigid, hard, hardhearted, hardened, heartless, imperturbable, impervious, indifferent, indurate, indurated, inhumane, insensitive, malevolent, malicious, malign, obdurate, passionless, pitiless, pococurante, relentless, remorseless, ruthless, savage, soulless, truculent, uncaring, unconcerned, unemotional, unfeeling, unimpressible, uninterested, unkind, unmerciful, unmindful, unmoved, unperturbed, unrelenting, unresponsive, unsolicitous, unsusceptible, unsympathetic, untouched, untroubled, without heart, without warmth
ASSOCIATED CONCEPTS: cold-blooded murder

COLLABORATE, ***verb*** abet, aid, band together, cofunction, collude, combine, concur, conspire, cooperate, coproduce, harmonize, help, interface, involve, join, join forces, join together, league, participate, partner, proceed jointly, succor, take part, team up, unite, work in concert
ASSOCIATED CONCEPTS: coconspirator, felony murder

COLLABORATOR, ***noun*** abettor, affiliate, ally, associate, cohort, colleague, companion, compatriot, comrade, confederate, consultant, coworker, intimate, partner, peer, teammate, workmate
ASSOCIATED CONCEPTS: accomplice, coconspirator

COLLAPSE, ***verb*** atrophy, break, break down, buckle, burst, cave in, crack, crash, crumble, crumple, debilitate, decay, decompose, deflate, degenerate, devolve, die, disintegrate, dissipate, fail, fall, flatten, give out, implode, shatter, smash, snap, splinter, tumble, worsen, yield
ASSOCIATED CONCEPTS: construction cases

COLLATERAL *(Accompanying),* ***adjective*** accessory, additional, affiliated, ancillary, appertaining, associated, attendant, auxiliary, belonging, closely related, concomitant, concurrent, conjoined, connected, correlated, correspondent, corresponding, coupled with, entwined, interrelated, parallel, related, simultaneous, supplemental, supplementary
ASSOCIATED CONCEPTS: collateral action, collateral agreement, collateral attack, collateral contract, collateral estoppel, collateral note, collateral powers, collateral proceeding, collateral promise, collateral source rule, collateral undertaking, collateral warranties

COLLATERAL *(Immaterial),* ***adjective*** being of no importance, extraneous, impertinent, inapplicable, inappropriate, incidental, inconsequential, indifferent, insignificant, insubstantial, irrelevant, meaningless, minor, negligible, nonessential, nugatory, of little moment, peripheral, secondary, trifling, trivial, unconnected, unessential, unimportant
ASSOCIATED CONCEPTS: collateral evidence, collateral facts, collateral fraud, collateral impeachment, collateral inquiry, collateral issue, collateral matter, collateral question, collateral testimony
FOREIGN PHRASES: ***Frustra probatur quod probatum non relevat.*** It is useless to prove that which when proved is irrelevant.

COLLATERAL RELIEF, ***noun*** accessory relief, additional relief, adjunct relief, an added judgment, ancillary relief, attendant relief, beneficial relief, complementing relief, extra relief, other relief, resultant relief, resulting relief, secondary relief, sequential relief, spare relief, subordinate relief, supplemental relief, supplementary relief, supporting relief
ASSOCIATED CONCEPTS: ancillary administration, ancillary attachment, ancillary bill, ancillary jurisdiction, ancillary proceeding

COLLATION, ***noun*** analogical procedure, analogy, appositeness, ascertainment, balance, check, checking, comparability, comparative estimate, comparison, confirmation, *conlatio,* contrast, correlation, cross-check, determination, differentiation, examination, juxtaposition, relation
ASSOCIATED CONCEPTS: collation of seals, collation of the property in an estate

COLLEAGUE, ***noun*** abettor, accessory, accompanier, accomplice, adjunct, adjutant, adjuvant, advocate, aider and abettor, ally, assistant, associate, attendant, auxiliary, backer, brother, champion, coadjutant, coadjutor, coadjutress, coadjutrix, coadjuvant, coaid, codirector, cohelper, collaborator, comate, companion, compeer, comrade, confederate, *confrère, conlega,* consociate, consort, cooperator, coworker, fellow, fellow companion, fellow conspirator, fellow worker, helper, mate, *particeps criminis,* participator, partner, seconder, *socius criminis,* stalwart, stand-by, votary

COLLECT *(Gather),* ***verb*** accumulate, acquire, add to, aggregate, amalgamate, amass, assemble, bring to a common center, bring to a point of union, bring together, compile, concentrate, *conferre, congerere,* conglomerate, consolidate, convene, *convocare,* draw together, embrace, gain, garner, gather together, group, incorporate, join, mass, muster, pile, put together, reunite, roll into one, unify, unite
ASSOCIATED CONCEPTS: collect rent, collect special assessments

COLLECT *(Recover money),* ***verb*** accept, acquire, appropriate, arrogate, assume, be given, be paid, collect payment, demand and obtain payment, exact payment, execute, gain, get back, get money, get possession of, levy, obtain payment, profit, raise, raise contributions, raise funds, reacquire, realize, receive money, receive payment, reclaim, recompense, recoup, recover, redeem, regain, retrieve, secure, secure payment, sequester, settle accounts with, take back again, take possession
ASSOCIATED CONCEPTS: collect a debt, collect on delivery, collect taxes, collecting bank

COLLECTION *(Accumulation),* ***noun*** accession, accretion, acervation, *acervus,* acquisition, addition, agglomeration, aggregate, aggregation, amassment, amount accrued, compilation, concentration, *congestus,* conglomerate, conglomeration, convergence, cumulation, group, growth by addition, heap, hoard, mass, obtainment, pile, stockpile, store
ASSOCIATED CONCEPTS: collection of trust funds

COLLECTION *(Assembly),* ***noun*** aggregation, assemblage, association, audience, colligation, collocation, company, conflux, congregation, conventicle, convention, *conventus,* crowd, forgathering, gathering, group, ingathering, meet, meeting, multitude, muster, rally, reassembly, reunion, throng
ASSOCIATED CONCEPTS: freedom of assembly

COLLECTION *(Payment),* ***noun*** acquittance, adjustment, amends, bearing the cost, cash payment, clearance, compensation, contribution, defrayal, defrayment, disbursement, discharge, enforcement of judgment, expenditure, fulfillment, full satisfaction, guerdon, indemnification, indemnity, installment, making amends, money paid, paying for, payment, price, propitiation, *quid pro quo,* quittance, receipted payment, recompense, rectification, redress, reimbursement, remission, remittance, remuneration, reparation, repayment, requital, restitution, restoration

ASSOCIATED CONCEPTS: collecting bank, collection agencies, collection agent, collection and payment, collection attorney, collection districts, collection of money, collection of taxes, collection officer, for collection only endorsements

COLLECTIVE, ***adjective*** accumulated, accumulative, aggregate, aggregated, amalgamated, amassed, assembled, associated, broad, brought together, combined, compiled, composite, compound, comprehensive, concentrated, concerted, concurrent, confederate, congregate, congregational, congregative, considered together, consolidated, corporate, cumulative, each and every, encyclopedic, entire, every, federative, gathered, general, grouped, integrated, integrative, joined, leagued, massed, mutual, of the same mind, total, unified, united, universal, unspecified, whole, widespread
ASSOCIATED CONCEPTS: collective bargaining, collective bargaining agreement

COLLECTIVE BARGAINING, ***noun*** abatement of differences, adjustment, arbitrage, arbitrament, arbitration, bargaining, compromise, conciliation, conference, intercession, intermediation, interposition, intervention, mediation, mediatorship, negotiation, package bargaining, pattern bargaining, umpirage
ASSOCIATED CONCEPTS: collective bargaining unit

COLLECTIVELY, ***adverb*** altogether, as a group, as a whole, as one, en banc, en bloc, en masse, fully, in a body, in all, in conjunction, in its entirety, integrally, in the aggregate, in toto, mutually, together, totally, unitedly, wholly, withal

COLLIDE *(Clash),* ***verb*** altercate, antagonize, argue, be antagonistic, be at cross-purposes, be at variance, be contrary, be discordant, be in antagonism, be incompatible, be inimical, be mutually opposed, conflict with, confront, contend, contradict, contrast with, contravene, controvert, counter, counteract, countervail, counterwork, differ, differ in opinion, differ violently, disaccord, disagree, dispute, dissent, embroil, encounter, entangle, feud, go contrary to, go in opposition to, hold opposite views, interfere with, join issue, object, oppose, oppugn, quarrel, resist, run afoul of, run against, run at cross-purposes, run counter to, run foul of, show hostility, smash up, take issue, traverse, vary, withstand, work against, wrangle

COLLIDE *(Crash against),* ***verb*** bump, bump into, butt against, come in contact, come into collision, come together, *confligere,* converge, crash into, crash together, drive against, drive into, encounter with a shock, enter into collision, hit, hurtle against, impinge, knock against, knock into, make contact, make impact, meet, run into each other, run together, slam into, smash into, strike, strike against, strike at, strike forcibly against each other

COLLISION *(Accident),* ***noun*** concussion, contact, convergence, crash, encounter, impact, impingement, jar, jolt, meeting, percussion, pileup, shock, striking together, sudden contact, violent contact
ASSOCIATED CONCEPTS: avoidable collision, collision auto insurance, collisions by carriers

COLLISION *(Dispute),* ***noun*** affray, altercation, antagonism, battle, clash, combat, *concursio, concursus,* conflict, contention, contradiction, contrariety, counteraction, disagreement, discord, disputation, embroilment, encounter, fight, fracas, fray, friction, hostility, interference, *mêlée,* opposition, resistence, skirmish

COLLUDE, ***verb*** abet, calculate, combine, conceive, confederate, connive, conspire, contrive, cooperate, design, devise, engineer, foment, frame, incite, intrigue, involve, machinate, maneuver, plan, plot, prearrange, predetermine, scheme
ASSOCIATED CONCEPTS: collusion between husband and wife, collusion to circumvent the law, collusive action, fraudulent conveyances

COLLUSION, ***noun*** abetment, act of working together, agreement, agreement for fraud, alliance, association, cabal, chicanery, coadjuvancy, coagency, collaboration, combination for fraud, combined operation, complicity, complot, concert, concord, concurrence, confederacy, conjunction, *conlusio,* connivance, conspiracy, contrivance, contriving, cooperation, cooperation for fraud, counterplot, covin, deceit, deceitful agreement, deceitful compact, deceitfulness, deception, double-dealing, duplicity, foul play, fraud, fraudulence, guile, hoax, illegal pact, intrigue, intriguery, joint effort, joint planning, junction, knavery, league, liaison, participation, participation in fraud, perfidy, plotting, *praevaricatio,* schemery, scheming, secret association, secret fraudulent understanding, secret understanding, secret understanding for fraud, synergism, synergy, treachery, trickery, underhand dealing, underplot, union
ASSOCIATED CONCEPTS: collusion in divorcing a spouse, collusion in obtaining the grounds of a divorce, collusion in procurement of a judgment, collusion to create diversity of citizenship, collusive action, collusive effort, collusive suit, connivance, conspiracy

COLLUSIVE, ***adjective*** artful, beguiling, calculating, clandestine, confidential, connivant, conniving, conspirational, conspirative, conspiratorial, conspiring, covinous, cunning, deceitful, deceptive, defrauding, designing, fraudulent, furtive, guileful, illicitly covert, indirect, insidious, intriguing, obreptitious, perfidious, plotting, schemeful, scheming, subreptitious, surreptitious, treacherous, undercover, underhanded, wily
ASSOCIATED CONCEPTS: collusion as a divorce defense, collusive claim, collusive suit, conspiracy, fraud and collusion

COLOR *(Complexion),* ***noun*** apparent character, aspects, attribute, bearing, character, characteristics, component, constitution, denomination, description, designation, distinction, endowment, faculty, features, fettle, figure, flavor, form, hue, image, inclination, kind, likeness, lineament, make, manner, mark, nature, particularity, peculiarities, posture, principle, quality, shape, *species,* style, temperament, tendency, tone, trim, type, variety
ASSOCIATED CONCEPTS: the color of a case

COLOR *(Deceptive appearance),* ***noun*** act of dissembling, affectation, allegation, alleged motive, apparent right, appearance, cloak, concealment, cunning, deceit, deception, deceptive covering, device, disingenuousness, display, dissemblance, dissimulation, distortion, equivocalness, equivocation, evasion, exaggeration, external appearance, false appearance, falseness, falsification, feint, gloss, guile, guise, impression, misrepresentation, misstatement, outward appearance, *praetextus,* pretense, pretext, representation, show, *simulacrum,* simulation, subterfuge, *suggestio falsi, suppressio veri*
ASSOCIATED CONCEPTS: color a cause of action, color of authority, color of claim, color of interest, color of jurisdiction, color of law, color of office, color of right, color of state law, color of title, color of title in adverse possession, under color of, under color of law

COLORABLE *(Plausible),* ***adjective*** *ad captandum,* alleged, apparent, apparently right, ben trovato, conceivable,

conjecturable, convincing, credible, feasible, *in posse,* logical, ostensible, persuasive, presumable, presumptive, rational, reasonable, seeming, seemingly fair, seemingly sound, seemingly valid, sensible, supposable, surmisable, tenable, thinkable, *verisimilis,* warrantable
ASSOCIATED CONCEPTS: colorable authority, colorable cause, colorable claim, colorable invocation of jurisdiction, colorable title

COLORABLE *(Specious),* ***adjective*** appearing, artful, crafty, deceitful, deceiving, deceptive, delusive, delusory, factitious, false, feigned, fraudulent, sham, trumped up, untrue

COMAKER, ***noun*** certifier, coapplicant, coborrower, co-obligor, coratifier, cosignatory, cosigner, endorser, party to an instrument

COMBAT, ***noun*** altercation, argument, attack, battle, brawl, clash, conflict, confrontation, contest, controversy, crossfire, disagreement, dispute, duel, face-off, fistfight, fracas, fray, hassle, hostilities, melee, operations, pitched battle, quarrel, ruckus, scrap, scuffle, skirmish, spat, squabble, struggle, warfare

COMBINATION, ***noun*** affiliation, aggregate, aggregation, amalgamation, arrangement, assemblage, bringing together, coadjutorship, coalescence, coalition, collection, composition, compound, *coniunctio,* congregation, conjugation, conjunction, consolidation, fusion, incorporation, joining, junction, merger, pool, *societas,* unification, union
ASSOCIATED CONCEPTS: combination in restraint of trade, combination patent, combination to restrict competition and commerce, combination trademark, combined offense, combined property, illegal combination, patentable combination

COMBINE *(Act in concert),* ***verb*** act as one, act jointly, affiliate with, ally, associate, band together, coact, collaborate, collude, concert, confederate, conspire, cooperate, coordinate, enlist with, enter into partnership with, federate, form a union, harmonize, join forces, join with, league with, make common cause with, marry, pair with, participate with, pool, rally, syncretize, syndicate, take part, team up with, unite, work in unison, work together
ASSOCIATED CONCEPTS: Anti-Monopoly Act, antitrust

COMBINE *(Join together),* ***verb*** admix, affix, agglutinate, amalgamate, annex, append, attach, bind, blend, coalesce, cohere, colligate, commingle, commix, compound, concatenate, conglomerate, conglutinate, *coniungere,* conjoin, connect, *consociare,* consolidate, couple, entwine, fasten, form a union, fuse, glue, group, immix, inosculate, interblend, interfuse, interlink, intermix, intertwine, intertwist, interweave, intwine, link, make a mixture, meld, merge, mingle, *miscere,* mix, paste, piece together, secure, splice, stick together, tack together, tie, unify, unite
ASSOCIATED CONCEPTS: combined offense, combined property

COMFORT, ***verb*** abate, accommodate, allay, alleviate, ameliorate, assist, assuage, assure, bolster, buoy, calm, care for, commiserate, compose, condole, console, ease, elevate, empathize, encourage, enliven, feel for, heal, hearten, help, mitigate, nourish, quiet, reassure, relax, relieve, salve, soften, solace, soothe, support, sustain, sympathize, tranquilize, uplift

COMFORTABLE, ***adjective*** at ease, content, cozy, cushy, easeful, easy, habitable, happy, homelike, hospitable, inviting, laid-back, nice, peaceful, pleasant, relaxed, relaxing, reposeful, restful, resting, snug, soft, suitable, untroubled

COMITY, ***noun*** accommodation, accord, affability, agreeableness, amenity, amiability, amity, benevolence, camaraderie, civility, compliance, concord, considerateness, consideration, cordiality, courtesy, courtly politeness, deference, disposition to please, fellow feeling, friendliness, general reciprocity, gentility, good-fellowship, good will, graciousness, harmony, mansuetude, mutual consideration, mutual respect, neighborliness, obligingness, politeness, *prévenance,* reciprocity, respect, respectfulness
ASSOCIATED CONCEPTS: comity between courts, comity in conflict of laws, comity of nations, comity of states

COMMAND, ***verb*** adjure, authorize, bid, call for, call upon, charge, compel, constrain, decree, demand, direct, direct imperatively, enact, exact, exercise authority, force, give directions, give orders, govern, have control, *hominem iubere facere, homini imperare, homini praecipere ut faciat, imminere,* impose, instruct, issue a command, issue a decree, issue an order, lead, mandate, ordain, order, order with authority, prescribe, proclaim, promulgate an order, require, rule, state authoritatively, take charge, take the lead
FOREIGN PHRASES: ***In maleficio, ratihabitio mandato comparatur.*** In tort, a ratification is regarded as a command. ***Qui mandat ipse fecisse videtur.*** He who gives an order is held to be the doer. ***Ratihabitio mandato aequiparatur.*** Ratification is equivalent to an express command. ***Remissius imperanti melius paretur.*** He who commands more gently is better obeyed.

COMMEMORATE, ***verb*** acclaim, acknowledge, admire, adore, aggrandize, appreciate, bless, celebrate, commend, compliment, consecrate, decorate, dignify, distinguish, ennoble, enshrine, esteem, eulogize, exalt, glorify, honor, immortalize, laud, lionize, magnify, monumentalize, pay homage, pay tribute, perpetuate, praise, recognize, remember, revere, salute, solemnize, treasure, value, venerate

COMMENCE, ***verb*** arise, auspicate, begin, bring, broach, come into existence, come into the world, embark on, engage in, enter upon, inaugurate, incept, *incipere,* initiate, install, institute, introduce, launch, lay the foundations, make one's debut, open, originate, pioneer, put in execution, rise, set forth, set in operation, start, take the initiative, undertake, venture on
ASSOCIATED CONCEPTS: commence a prosecution, commence a suit, commence by filing, commence by summons, commencement of a proceeding, commencement of a suit, commencement of a trial, commencement of action, duly commenced

COMMEND, ***verb*** acclaim, accredit, acknowledge, admire, adore, advocate, applaud, appreciate, approve, boost, build, build up, compliment, endorse, esteem, extol, glorify, hail, honor, idolize, laud, pay homage to, praise, prize, puff up, rate highly, ratify, rave, recognize, recommend, respect, revere, salute, think highly of, treasure, value, venerate

COMMENSURABLE, ***adjective*** analagous, analogical, coequal, coextensive, coherent, commensurate, comparable, concordant, concurrent, conformable, congruous, consistent, consonant, coordinate, correspondent, equal, equivalent, even, identical in size, level, matching, of an equal size, of equal length or volume, parallel, proportional, proportionate, relative, similar

COMMENSURATE, *adjective* acceptable, accordant, adequate, agreeing, analagous, appropriate, coequal, coextensive, commeasurable, commensurable, comparable, concordant, congruent, congruous, consistent, corresponding, equal in extent, equal in measure, equal to, equivalent, fitted, having a common measure, in accord, in agreement, in exact agreement, matching, of equal duration, of equal extent, of equal rank, on a par, on a proper scale, on a suitable scale, on even terms, paralleling, proportional, proportionate, relative, similar, sufficient, sufficing, suitable, synchronal

COMMENT, *noun* animadversion, annotation, assertion, averment, *censeo,* clarification, commentary, dictum, elucidation, enucleation, example, exegesis, exemplification, explanation, explanatory note, explication, exposition, expounding, expression, finding, footnote, gloss, illumination, illustration, interpretation, marginal annotation, mention, notation, note, note of explanation, observation, postulate, reflection, remark, report, scholium, statement, utterance, word of explanation
ASSOCIATED CONCEPTS: comment on defendant's failure to testify, comment on evidence, comment on witness' credibility, comment upon the testimony, comments on the weight of evidence

COMMENT, *verb* allege, animadvert, annotate, assert, bring out, *censere,* clarify, clear, criticize, declare, define, descant, dilate upon, discourse upon, discuss, elucidate, enlighten, enucleate, exemplify, expand on, explain, explicate, exposit on, expound, express, give a sense to, gloss, illuminate, illustrate, interject, interpose, interpret, make clear, make notes, make observations, make remarks, mention, note, notice, observe, opine, pass on, point out, posit, postulate, put a meaning on, rationalize, remark, remark upon, render intelligible, reprove, review, say, *sententiam dicere,* shed light upon, spell out, state, touch upon, treat, utter
ASSOCIATED CONCEPTS: comment on defendant's failure to testify, comment on evidence, comment on witness' credibility, comment upon the testimony, comments on the weight of evidence, prosecutor's comments on evidence

COMMENTARY, *noun* analysis, annotation, clarification, comment, critique, discourse, discussion, dissertation, editorial, elucidation, exegesis, explanation, explication, exposition, illumination, illustration, interpretation, marginalia, notation, note, notice, observation, proposal, remark, report, review, scholium, thesis
ASSOCIATED CONCEPTS: commentaries to the statutes

COMMERCE, *noun* interstate commerce, bargaining, barter, bartering, business, business affairs, business deals, business intercourse, business transactions, buying and selling, chaffering, commercial intercourse, *commercium,* dealing, exchange, fiscal exchange, industry, industry and trade, interchange, interchange of commodities, interchange of goods, intercourse, marketing, mercantile business, mercantile relations, mercantilism, *mercatura,* merchandising, merchantry, monetary exchange, multilateral trade, negotia, negotiation, private enterprise, production and distribution, reciprocal trade, system of exchanges, trade, trading, traffic, traffic of commodities, transportation of commodities, transportation of goods
ASSOCIATED CONCEPTS: affect commerce, affect interstate commerce, arising under a law regulating commerce, commerce among the several states, commerce clause, commerce power, commerce with foreign nations, commercial code, commercial paper, industry affecting commerce, international commerce, intrastate commerce, law regulating commerce, navigation and commerce, regulate commerce, restraint of commerce
FOREIGN PHRASES: ***Commercium jure gentium commune esse debet, et non in monopolium et privatum paucorum quaestum convertendum.*** Commerce, by the law of nations, ought to be common, and not converted into monopoly and the private gain of a few persons. ***Jus accrescendi inter mercatores, pro beneficio commercii, locum non habet.*** The right of survivorship does not exist between merchants for the benefit of commerce.

COMMERCIAL, *adjective* business, businesslike, *commercium,* economic, engaged in commerce, financial, fiscal, in the market, industrial, jobbing, manufactured for sale, mercantile, merchandising, monetary, pecuniary, pertaining to business, pertaining to merchants, pertaining to trade, prepared for sale, skilled in commerce, supplying, trade, trading
ASSOCIATED CONCEPTS: commercial agency, commercial bank, commercial bribery, commercial business, commercial consumption, commercial endorsement, commercial frustration, commercial insolvency, commercial law, commercial letter of credit, commercial loan, commercial mark, commercial partnership, commercial purpose, commercial use, commercial zone

COMMERCIAL ACTIVITY, *noun* activity undertaken as part of commercial enterprise, business activity, business endeavors, mercantile activity

COMMERCIAL RIGHTS, *noun* business rights, economic rights, industrial rights, merchandizing rights, product rights, trade rights

COMMERCIAL SPEECH, *noun* commercial advertising, commercial expression, corporate speech, economic speech, promotional speech, speech for profit, speech on behalf of corporation

COMMINGLE, *verb* admix, alloy, amalgamate, assemble, associate, band, bind together, blend, bring in contact with, coalesce, *commiscere,* combine, commix, compound, conglomerate, conjoin, connect, consolidate, consort with, couple, cross with, embody, entwine, fasten, fuse, harmonize, hybridize, immix, incorporate, interbreed, interlace, interlard, intermingle, intermix, involve together, join, league, link, lump together, merge, mix, mix together, pair with, piece, put together, run together, scramble, stir, unite
ASSOCIATED CONCEPTS: commingling of assets, commingling of funds by an agent, commingling of property

COMMINUQUÉ, *noun* account, announcement, briefing, broadcast, brochure, bulletin, circular, communication, declaration, directive, disclosure, dispatch, document, excerpt, flier, gazette, information, inside story, intelligence, item, letter, memoranda, message, missive, news, note, notice, piece, précis, report, revelation, scoop, skinny, speech, statement, summary, work

COMMISSION *(Act),* ***noun*** accomplishment, achievement, actualization, actuation, attainment, carrying out, completion, consummation, discharge, dispatch, doing, effecting, effectuation, enactment, enforcement, execution, exercise, exercising, fruition, fulfilment, implementation, inflicting, infliction, making, *mandatum,* operation, perpetration, realization, transaction
ASSOCIATED CONCEPTS: commission of crime

COMMISSION *(Agency),* ***noun*** advisory group, appointed group, board, board of inquiry, body of commissioners, body of delegates, body of deputies, bureau, cabinet, consultants, convocation, council, delegation, deliberative group, embassy, executive committee, investigating committee, planning board, representatives, standing committee, trustees
ASSOCIATED CONCEPTS: advisory body, Federal Trade Commission, Municipal Commission, Public Service Commission

COMMISSION *(Fee),* ***noun*** allotment, allowance, bonus, compensation, consideration, defrayment, disbursement, dividend, earnings, emolument, extra compensation, increment, interest, pay, pay-off, payment, percentage, percentage compensation, portion, proceeds, profit, recompense, reimbursement, remuneration, repayment, return, reward, salary, share of profits, stipend, subsidy, wage
ASSOCIATED CONCEPTS: broker's commission, commission merchant, compensation, fees, finder's commission, profits

COMMIT *(Entrust),* ***verb*** allot, assign, authorize, charge, charge with, commission, confer a trust, confide, consign, convey, delegate, employ, empower, engage, grant authority to, invest, invest with power, make responsible for, put an obligation upon, put in the hands of, relegate to, trust, turn over to, vest in
ASSOCIATED CONCEPTS: commit to a writing

COMMIT *(Institutionalize),* ***verb*** arrest, confine, consign, constrain, deliver into custody, enthrall, hold in constraint, hold in restraint, immure, impound, imprison, incarcerate, intern, jail, lock up, place in confinement, put in custody, recommit to custody, remand to custody, remit to custody, restrain, send to an asylum, send to jail, send to prison
ASSOCIATED CONCEPTS: commit to a hospital, commit to a mental institution, commit to prison, committing magistrate

COMMIT *(Perpetrate),* ***verb*** accomplish, achieve, act, act on, administer, apply oneself to, be a participator in, be a party to, be an accomplice, be engaged in, be engrossed in, bring about, bring to pass, carry into execution, carry on, carry out, carry through, complete, consummate, discharge, discharge the duties of, effect, employ oneself, execute, finish, fulfill, go through with, inflict, occupy oneself with, operate, participate in, perform, realize, transact
ASSOCIATED CONCEPTS: commit an offense against the United States

COMMIT TO WRITING, ***verb*** affirm, assert, assure, attest, authenticate, be bound, certify, circumstantiate, commemorate, contract, covenant, document, guarantee, inscribe, insure, make a statement, note, ratify, set down, sign a pact, stipulate, subscribe, underwrite, validate, warrant
ASSOCIATED CONCEPTS: agreements, contracts, holographic will

COMMITMENT *(Confinement),* ***noun*** committal, confining, constraint, detention, durance, handing over into custody, holding in constraint, holding in restraint, immuring, impoundment, imprisonment, incarcerating, incarceration, interning, internment, jailing, legal confinement, legal constraint, locking up, mittimus, placing in confinement, putting in custody, remanding to custody, remitting to custody, restraint, restriction, sending to jail, sentencing
ASSOCIATED CONCEPTS: commitment to an institution, commitment to jail

COMMITMENT *(Responsibility),* ***noun*** accountability, accountableness, agreement, allegiance, assignment, assurance, burden, call of duty, charge, conscience, contract, covenant, devoir, duty, engagement, faithfulness, incumbency, mission, obligation, onus, pledge, promise, sense of duty, solemn declaration, trust, undertaking, vow, warrant

COMMITTEE, ***noun*** advisory group, agency, alliance, appointed group, association, board, body, body of consultants, bureau, cabinet, commission, confederacy, confederation, congregation, *consilium,* council, delegation, federation, fellowship, group of delegates, league, organization, organized group, representatives, staff, syndicate, trustees
ASSOCIATED CONCEPTS: campaign committee, committee of the whole, political committee, standing committee

COMMODITIES, ***noun*** articles, articles of commerce, articles of merchandise, articles of trade, assets, chattels, goods, holdings, items, merchandise, merx, movables, objects, possessions, produce, produced materials, products, properties, raw materials, *res,* specialties, staples, stock, stock in trade, vendibles, wares
ASSOCIATED CONCEPTS: agricultural commodity, commodity rate, horticultural commodity, public utility commodity, stocks and bonds

COMMON *(Customary),* ***adjective*** accepted, ascertained, commonplace, conventional, current, currently perceived, established, everyday, familiar, frequent, generally known, natural, normal, often met with, ordinary, popular, prevailing, prevalent, publicly known, received, recognized, repeatedly recognized, traditional, typical, universally known, usual, usually understood, well-known, widely known, widespread
ASSOCIATED CONCEPTS: common assault, common-law, common-law burglary, common-law contempt, common-law copyright, common-law crime, common-law forgery, common-law jurisdiction, common-law larceny, common-law lien, common-law marriage, common-law misdemeanor, common-law murder, common-law nuisance, common-law remedy, common-law trademark, common-law trust, common-law wife, common liability, common peril, common question of law or fact, common seal, common source of title, common stock, common thief, common use

COMMON *(Shared),* ***adjective*** belonging equally to, belonging to all, belonging to many, collective, communal, *communis,* commutual, conjoint, cooperative, for the use of all, in partnership, joint, mutual, owned jointly, participating, participatory, pertaining to the whole community, pooled, popular, public, *publicus,* reciprocal, shared among several, shared by two or more, universal, used by all
ASSOCIATED CONCEPTS: common adventure, common belief, common boundary line, common carrier, common council, common directors, common disaster, common driveway, common enemy doctrine, common enterprise, common good, common interest, common jurisdiction, common knowledge, common labor, common lands, common necessity, common plan, common plea courts, common property, common recovery, common rights, common scheme, common stock, common wall, common walls

COMMON KNOWLEDGE, ***noun*** accepted fact, acknowledgment, announcement, annunciation, avowance, declaration, disclosure, dissemination, experience, *exposé,* familiarity, general information, history, learning, manifestation, notoriety, *patefactio,* public disclosure, public knowledge, public notice, publicness, state of being public

COMMON SENSE, *noun* acumen, astuteness, balanced judgment, calmness, clear thinking, composure, experience, experienced view, good judgment, good sense, intelligence, intuition, judgment, level-headedness, logic, mental poise, native reason, natural sagacity, ordinary judgment, ordinary sense, plain sense, plausibility, practical discernment, practical knowledge, practicality, presence of mind, prudence, rational faculty, rationality, reason, reasonableness, resourcefulness, sagacity, sapience, *savoir faire,* sensibleness, sober-mindedness, sobriety, solidity, sound perception, sound sense, sound understanding, unbiased impulse, understanding, unemotional consideration, wisdom, worldly wisdom
ASSOCIATED CONCEPTS: commonsense reading of a statute, commonsense ruling

COMMOTION, *noun* affray, *agitatio,* agitation, altercation, brawl, clamor, clash, conflict, confusion, convulsion, disorder, disorderliness, disorganization, disquiet, disquietude, disturbance, ebullition, embroilment, encounter, entanglement, eruption, excitement, ferment, fermentation, fight, fomentation, fracas, fray, furor, imbroglio, inquietude, insurgence, insurrection, maelstrom, mayhem, *mêlée,* moil, *motus,* noisy strife, overthrow, pandemonium, perturbation, public disturbance, quarrel, racket, rampage, rebellion, restlessness, rising insubordination, row, ruction, scuffle, skirmish, stir, struggle, tempest, tumult, *tumultus, turba,* turbulence, turmoil, tussle, unruliness, upheaval, uprising, uproar, violence, welter, whirl

COMMUNICATE, *verb* acquaint, advertise, advise, announce, apprise, articulate, assert, bandy words, breathe, bring word, broadcast, commerce with, commune, *communicare,* confabulate, converse, convey, correspond, deal with, declare, demonstrate, disclose, discourse with, divulge, engage in a conversation, enlighten, enunciate, express, familiarize, find words to express, give an account, give expression, give notice, give notification, give one to understand, give the facts, give tongue, give utterance, give voice, have intercourse, impart, inform, instill, instruct, interchange thoughts, intercommunicate, lay before, let know, let out, make known, mention, narrate, notify, parley, present facts, proclaim, pronounce, publicize, put forth, put in words, relate, reveal, say, send word, serve notice, set forth, signify, sound, speak one's mind, speak, specify, talk, teach, tell, traffic with, transmit, utter, verbalize, vocalize, voice, write

COMMUNICATE EFFECTIVELY, *verb* broadcast, clarify, communicate, convey, decipher, decode, define, deliver, demonstrate, demystify, descramble, disambiguate, disseminate, elucidate, enlighten, enunciate, explain, explain in plain language, explicate, get across, get through to, illuminate, impart, make crystal clear, particularize, simplify, spell out, tell

COMMUNICATION *(Discourse),* ***noun*** collocution, colloquy, *communicatio, communiqué,* conference, conversation, correspondence, dialogue, dissertation, exchange, interchange, intercommunication, intercourse, interlocution
ASSOCIATED CONCEPTS: attorney and client communication, conditionally privileged communication, confidential communication, husband and wife communication, physician and patient communication, privileged communication, telegraph communication, telephonic communication, verbal communication, written communication

COMMUNICATION *(Statement),* ***noun*** announcement, annunciation, declaration, disclosure, dissemination, divulgement, information, message, news, notification, proclamation, report, revelation, utterance, writing

COMMUNITY, *noun* body, body politic, borough, citizenry, city, civilization, *civitas,* commonalty, commonwealth, commune, group, inhabitants, kinship, locality, municipality, neighborhood, partnership, people, polity, populace, population, *respublica,* society, town
ASSOCIATED CONCEPTS: community estate, community interest, community of right or interest, community property

COMMUTE, *verb* abate, abbreviate, abridge, allay, alleviate, alter, ameliorate, bate, change, change penalties, curtail, cut, decrease a punishment, dilute, diminish, ease, exchange, exchange penalties, lessen, lighten, limit, make less extreme, make less harsh, make less intense, make less rigorous, make less rough, make less severe, make lighter, make milder, meliorate, minimize, mitigate, modify sentence, palliate, reduce, reduce a punishment, reduce in asperity, relax severity, relieve, render less difficult, shorten, shrink, slacken, slash, soften, substitute, temper, tone down, trim, truncate
ASSOCIATED CONCEPTS: commute a sentence

COMPACT *(Dense),* ***adjective*** arranged within a small space, bunched, close, close-knit, close-set, close together, closely united, clustered, cohesive, compacted, compressed, concentrated, condensed, consolidated, constricted, constringed, contracted, crammed, crowded, densified, economical of space, firm, firmly united, forced into smaller space, hard, massed, massive, packed, populous, pressed into smaller compass, pressed together, rammed, serried, solid, solidified, space saving, squeezed together, stuffed, thick, tight, tightly knit

COMPACT *(Pithy),* ***adjective*** abbreviated, abbreviatory, abridged, abstracted, aphoristic, aphoristical, apothegmatic, apothegmatical, brief, compendious, concise, condensed, contracted, crisp, curt, digested, direct, epigrammatic, epitomized, expressed concisely, gnomic, gnomical, laconic, meaty, outlined, pointed, recapitulated, sententious, short, shortened, shrunk, straightforward, succinct, summarized, summary, summed up, synoptic, telescoped, terse, tidy, to the point, trim

COMPACT, *noun* agreement, agreement between parties, arrangement, bargain, cartel, commitment, compromise, concord, concordat, contract, contractual obligation, contractual statement, convention, *conventus,* covenant, deal, entente, *entente cordiale,* indenture, mutual pledge, mutual promise, obligation, pact, *pactio, pactum,* pledge, promise, stipulation, treaty, understanding
ASSOCIATED CONCEPTS: interstate compact
FOREIGN PHRASES: ***Pacta privata juri publico derogare non possunt.*** Private compacts cannot derogate from public right. ***Re, verbis, scripto, consensu, traditione, junctura vestes sumere pactasolent.*** Agreements usually take their clothing from the thing itself, from words, from writing, from consent, from delivery.

COMPANION, *noun* abettor, accessory, accomplice, adherent, adjunct, aide, ally, assistant, associate, attendant, auxiliary, buddy, cohort, collaborator, colleague, comate,

compatriot, compeer, comrade, concomitant, consort, cooperator, counterpart, countryman, coworker, crony, deputy, friend, helper, mate, pal, partner, peer, supporter, teammate
ASSOCIATED CONCEPTS: coconspirator, felony murder

COMPANY *(Assemblage)*, ***noun*** aggregation, assembled body, *assemblée,* assembly, *attroupement,* caucas, coalition, conclave, conference, confluence, conflux, congregation, congress, convention, convergence, convocation, crowd, gathering, group, ingathering, league, meeting, mustering, *societas*

COMPANY *(Enterprise)*, ***noun*** association, body corporate, business, business establishment, coetus, combination, commercial enterprise, concern, confederacy, consociation, copartnership, corporate body, corporation, establishment, federation, firm, *grex,* guild, institute, joint concern, organization, partnership
ASSOCIATED CONCEPTS: affiliated company, company union, construction company, corporation, holding company

COMPARABLE *(Capable of comparison)*, ***adjective*** akin, alike, analagous, analogical, approximate, associated, close, cognate, commensurable, *comparabilis,* congeneric, correlative, homogeneous, homologous, kindred, like, much the same, parallel, related, resembling, similar

COMPARABLE *(Equivalent)*, ***adjective*** coequal, commensurate, equable, equal in value, equipollent, even, identical, interchangeable, matched, matching, on par, tantamount, undeviating, uniform, unvarying, without distinction

COMPARATIVE, ***adjective*** analagous to, comparable, comparativus, connected with, contrastive, correlative, corresponding to, estimated by comparison, in connection with, in proportion to, in relation to, in relation with, in respect to, in the same category, judged by comparison, matching, metaphorical, pertaining to, pertinent to, referable to, referential, referring, relating to, relational, relative, rivaling, similar to, similitudinous, vying with, with reference to, with regard to, with relation to
ASSOCIATED CONCEPTS: comparative injury, comparative negligence, comparative rectitude

COMPARE, ***verb*** *aequiperare,* analogize, balance against, bring into comparison, bring into meaningful relation with, bring into relation, *comparare, componere, conferre,* contrast, correlate, differentiate, discriminate between, distinguish between, draw a parallel, equate, estimate relatively, exercise critical judgment, identify with, juxtapose, liken, match, measure, note the similarities and differences, parallel, parallelize, place in juxtaposition, put alongside, relate, represent as resembling, set side by side, show correspondence, show to be analagous, show to be similar, weigh
ASSOCIATED CONCEPTS: comparative negligence, comparing equities

COMPARISON, ***noun*** alikeness, analogical procedure, analogy, association, balance, *comparatio,* comparative estimate, *conlatio,* contrast, correlation, equation, measurement, nearness, parallel, *rapprochement,* relative estimate, relative estimation, resemblance
ASSOCIATED CONCEPTS: comparison of negligence of opposing parties

COMPATIBILITY, ***noun*** acclimation, accommodation, accord, accordance, adjustment, affiliation, agreement, amity, attunement, balance, coexistence, comity, common view, companionship, compliance, concord, concordance, concurrence, conformity, congeniality, congruity, congruousness, *consensus omnium,* consent, consentaneity, consistency, consonance, cooperation, coordination, *entente,* equanimity, harmony, mutual understanding, rapport, reconciliation, unanimity, union, unity
ASSOCIATED CONCEPTS: incompatibility

COMPEL, ***verb*** bear down against, bear hard upon, blackmail, bring pressure to bear upon, burden, cause, coerce, *cogere,* command, *compellere,* constrain, control, decree, demand, dictate, distrain, drive, elicit, employ force, enforce, exact, force, impel, impose, impose a duty, inflict, insist, leave no option, limit, necessitate, obligate, oblige, obtrude on, order, press, pressure, put under obligation, require, restrict, *subigere,* subject, take no denial, threaten, urge, urge forward
ASSOCIATED CONCEPTS: compel accused to give evidence against himself, compel by legal process, compel to testify under a grant of immunity

COMPELLING, ***adjective*** absolute, assertive, authoritative, binding, categorical, coercive, commanding, compulsive, compulsory, constraining, decisive, dominant, driving, emphatic, enforcing, forcible, *gravis,* great, impelling, imperative, incisive, inducive, influential, involuntary, irresistible, necessary, obligatory, obsessing, obsessional, obsessive, of necessity, omnipotent, overpowering, overriding, overruling, overwhelming, peremptory, potent, predominant, preeminent, preponderant, pressing, propulsive, puissant, strong, thrustful, trenchant, unavoidable, *validus, vehemens,* vigorous, weighty
ASSOCIATED CONCEPTS: compelling interest, compelling necessity, compelling need

COMPELLING GOVERNMENT INTEREST, ***noun*** crucial government interest, government interest that is compelling enough to pass the strict scrutiny test, necessary government interest, vital government interest

COMPENDIUM, ***noun*** abbreviation, abridgment, abstract, breviary, brief, capsule, compend, concise treatment, condensation, conspectus, contraction, digest, *epitoma,* epitome, essence, extract, outline, pandect, précis, recapitulation, review, summary, survey, syllabus, synopsis

COMPENSATE *(Counterbalance)*, ***verb*** act against with equal force, allow for, atone, balance, be equivalent, *compensare,* correspond, counteract, counterpoise, countervail, counterweigh, equalize, equate, equilibrate, even, furnish an equivalent, level off, make equal, make level, make steady, make up for, neutralize, offset, oppose, produce equilibrium, restore to equilibrium, set off, square, stabilize, strike a balance

COMPENSATE *(Remunerate)*, ***verb*** allow for, defray, discharge a debt, give equal value, give satisfaction for damage, give satisfaction for injury, honor, indemnify, make payment, make restitution, pay damages, pay for, pay in full, pay the equivalent, pay the value, pay wages, recompense, redress, refund, reimburse, remit, *remunerari,* remunerate for injury, repay, repay for a loss, return, reward, reward for a loss, reward for an injury, salary, satisfy, settle accounts with
ASSOCIATED CONCEPTS: compensation for expenses, compensation for goods sold and delivered, compensation for hospital bills, compensation for injuries, compensation

for out-of-pocket expenses, compensation for pain and suffering, compensation for the negligent acts of another, compensation for wrongdoing, costs, fair and reasonable compensation, fees, penalties, reimbursement, wages, workmen's compensation

COMPENSATION, *noun* amends, atonement, commutation, *compensatio,* consideration, damages, defrayal, defrayment, earnings, emolument, equivalent given for injury, equivalent given for loss sustained, fee, financial remuneration, guerdon, indemnification, indemnity, meed, monetary remuneration, pay, payment, payment of damages, quittance, reclamation, recompensation in value, recompense, recoupment, recovery, rectification, reimbursement, remuneration, remuneration for injury, reparation, repayment, requital, restoration, retainer, retaining fee, retrieval, return, reward, reward for injury, reward for loss, reward for service, salary, satisfaction, satisfaction for damage, satisfaction for injury, settlement, solatium, wages
ASSOCIATED CONCEPTS: adequate compensation, adjusted compensation, agreement for compensation, compensatory damages, fair and reasonable compensation, full compensation, just and adequate compensation, payments of compensation, reasonable compensation
FOREIGN PHRASES: ***Corporalis injuria non recipit aestimationem de futuro.*** A personal injury cannot be compensated for by later acts.

COMPENSATORY, *adjective* atoning, balancing, compensating, compensative, equivalent, expiating, expiatory, in compensation, indemnificatory, paying, propitiating, recompensive, redemptive, refunding, reimbursing, remitting, remunerative, reparative, repaying, restitutive, restitutory, retributive, rewardful, rewarding, satisfying, unindebted
ASSOCIATED CONCEPTS: compensatory damages, compensatory penalties

COMPETE, *verb* battle, be a candidate, be in the running, certare, challenge, clash, combat, contend, contest, *cum homine contendere,* duel, employ stratagem, encounter, engage in a contest, enter, enter competition, joust, match strength with, match wits with, oppose, participate in, rival, spar, strive, struggle, take part, tilt, vie with, wrestle

COMPETENCE *(Ability),* ***noun*** adequacy, adroitness, aptitude, capability, capacity, conversance, dexterity, effectiveness, effectuality, efficacy, eligibility, enablement, endowment, equipment, experience, facility, faculty, fitness, flair, forte, gift, grasp, intelligence, legal competence, legal fitness, mastery, potency, proficiency, qualifications, responsibility, skill, skillfulness, sufficiency, suitability, talent, training
ASSOCIATED CONCEPTS: competency of a witness, competent and intelligent waiver of counsel, competent authority, competent jurisdiction, legally competent
FOREIGN PHRASES: ***Homo potest esse habilis et inhabilis diversis temporibus.*** A man may be capable and incapable at different times. ***Nemo praesens nisi intelligat.*** One is not present unless he understands. ***Nullus idoneus testis in re sua intelligitur.*** No person is deemed to be a competent witness in his own behalf. ***Pupillus pati posse non intelligitur.*** An infant is not considered able to do an act to his own prejudice. ***Sola ac per se senectus donationem testamentum aut transactionem non vitiat.*** Old age alone and of itself will not vitiate a will or gift.

COMPETENCE *(Sanity),* ***noun*** capability, clearmindedness, coherence, healthy mindedness, lucidity, mental balance, mental capacity, mental equilibrium, mental health, normalcy, normality, normalness, rationality, reason, reasonability, sanemindedness, saneness, sense, senses, sound mind, soundmindedness, soundness, soundness of mind
ASSOCIATED CONCEPTS: age of maturity, competency of a witness, competent and intelligent waiver of counsel, age of maturity, infancy, legally competent, mental competence, *non compos mentis*
FOREIGN PHRASES: ***Furiosi nulla voluntas est.*** A madman has no will.

COMPETENCY *(Capacity),* ***noun*** ability, clear-mindedness, coherence, efficiency, faculty, fitness, lucidity, mental capacity, mental equilibrium, qualification, reasonableness
ASSOCIATED CONCEPTS: competency of a guarantor, competency of a guardian, competency of an executive, competency of counsel, competency of jurors to serve on a panel, competency of parties to testify, competency of trustees, competency of witnesses, competency to stand trial, competency to testify, incompetence, objections raised over the competency of a witness, withdrawal from serving in designated capacity due to a lack of competency

COMPETENCY *(Sufficiency),* ***noun*** abundance, adequacy, applicability, capability, craft, dexterity, efficacy, effectiveness, mastery, proficiency, prowess, satisfactoriness, skill
ASSOCIATED CONCEPTS: competency to stand trial, competency to testify, competency of witnesses

COMPETENT, *adjective* able, accomplished, adept, adequate, adroit, artful, capable, *competere,* conversant, credible, deft, dexterous, effective, effectual, efficacious, efficient, enterprising, excellent, experienced, expert, fit, good, ingenious, learned, masterful, masterly, mentally capable, practiced, prepared, proficient, properly qualified, qualified, ready, resourceful, responsible, satisfactory, skilled, skillful, sufficient, suitable, trained, versed, well-fitted
ASSOCIATED CONCEPTS: *capax negotii,* competent and intelligent waiver of counsel, competent authority, competent court, competent evidence, competent jurisdiction, competent witness, legally competent, mentally competent

COMPETITION, *noun* attempt to equal, bout, challenge, combat, conflict, *contentio,* contest, corrivalry, encounter, engagement, open contest, opposition, outrivalry, pitting of strength, pitting of wits, race, rivalry, scramble, strife, striving for superiority, struggle for superiority, trial of superiority, vying for ascendance
ASSOCIATED CONCEPTS: competitive bidding, competitive class, competitive examination, fair competition, free and open competition, unfair competition, unreasonable interference with competition

COMPETITIVE *(Antagonistic),* ***adjective*** adverse, at issue, at variance, challenging, clashing, colliding, combatant, combative, combatting, competing, competitory, conflicting, contending, contentious, contrary, counteractive, decided by competition vying, discordant, disputatious, dissident, emulative, in competition, opposing, oppugnant, rival, rivaling, striving, vying
ASSOCIATED CONCEPTS: competitive bidding, competitive class, competitive examination, unfair competition

COMPETITIVE *(Open),* ***adjective*** accessible to all, common, comprehensive, equal, free, free to all, general, nonexclusive, not partial, not privileged, open to the public, popular, public, unbounded, unclosed, unconfined, universal, unrestrained, unrestricted

ASSOCIATED CONCEPTS: fair competition, free and open competition, unreasonable interference with competition

COMPILATION, ***noun*** accretion, accumulation, agglomeration, aggregation, anthology, arrangement, assemblage, classification, codification, collection, colligation, collocation, combination, conglomeration, consolidation, gathering, incorporation, miscellany, selection
ASSOCIATED CONCEPTS: Official Compilation of Codes, Rules and Regulations

COMPILE, ***verb*** accumulate, agglomerate, aggregate, amass, anthologize, arrange, arrange materials for publication, assemble, bring together, bunch, bunch together, cluster, collect, combine, *componere,* compose, conglomerate, cull, cumulate, draw together, draw up, extract from other works, garner, gather, gather together, glean, group, group together, lump together, make up, mass, prepare, recapitulate, select, select and arrange, unite, write

COMPLACENT, ***adjective*** at ease, carefree, complaisant, compliable, compliant, composed, content, contented, fulfilled, gratified, peaceful of mind, placid, pleased, *qui sibi placet,* reposeful, resigned, satisfied, self-content, self-satisfied, serene, smug, *suffisant,* tranquil, unvexed

COMPLAIN *(Charge),* ***verb*** *accusare,* accuse, arraign, blame, bring a suit, bring an action, bring charges, bring proceedings against, bring up on charges, censure, challenge, charge with, cite, criminate, declaim against, delate, denounce, denunciate, file a charge, file a claim, file a suit, implicate, impute, incriminate, inculpate, inform against, institute a lawsuit, lay an information, lay blame upon, lay responsibility on, lay the blame on, lodge a complaint, make an accusation, prefer charges, prosecute, reprehend, reproach, reprobate, start an action, state a grievance, sue, take action
ASSOCIATED CONCEPTS: complain of a criminal act, complain of a tortious act

COMPLAIN *(Criticize),* ***verb*** accuse, admonish, animadvert, asperse, assail, be critical, be dissatisfied, berate, blame, carp, cast aspersions, castigate, cavil, censure, chastise, chide, condemn, *conqueri de rem,* contravene, decry, defy, denounce, deprecate, differ, disagree, disapprove, disparage, faultfind, find fault, find fault with, malign, object, object to, oppose, protest, rebuke, remonstrate, repine, reprehend, reprimand, reproach, reprove, speak ill of, take exception, take exception to, upbraid

COMPLAINANT, ***noun*** accusant, accuser, aggrieved party, challenger, charger, claimant, complaining party, delator, denouncer, impeacher, incriminator, indicter, indictor, libelant, litigant, one instigating an action, opposing party, party, party to a suit, petitioner, petitioner for legal redress, plaintiff, preferror of charges, prosecution, prosecutor, public prosecutor, relator, suitor
ASSOCIATED CONCEPTS: complainant's costs, complaining witness

COMPLAINT, ***noun*** accusal, accusation, allegation, bill of indictment, case, case for the prosecution, charge, citation, count, crimination, criticism, denouncement, denunciation, expostulation, first pleading, formal allegation, gravamen of a charge, grievance, incrimination, indictment, information, information against, litigation, main charge, objection, particular charge, petition, plaint, plaintiff's initiatory pleading, pleading in a civil action, preferment of charges, prosecution, protest, protestation, *querimonia,* remonstrance, statement of the plaintiff's cause, substance of a charge
ASSOCIATED CONCEPTS: bill of complaint, petition, cross complaint, verified complaint

COMPLAISANT, ***adjective*** acquiescent, agreeable, amenable, amiable, biddable, compliant, conformable, contented, controllable, curbed, disciplinable, docile, duteous, dutiful, easy, easy-going, friendly, generous, good-natured, good-tempered, governable, gracious, happy, indulgent, inhibited, kowtowing, law-abiding, lenient, manageable, obedient, obeisant, obliging, obsequious, permissive, polite, repressed, restrained, satisfied, serene, servile, soft, submissive, subordinate, subservient, surrendering, tractable, unconcerned, yielding

COMPLEMENT, ***noun*** companion, *complementum,* completion, congener, coordinate, correlate, correspondent, corresponding part, counterpart, pendant, reciprocal, remainder, rest, supplement

COMPLETE *(All-embracing),* ***adjective*** absolute, all, all-comprehending, all-comprehensive, all-covering, all-inclusive, all-pervading, all-sufficing, blanket, broad-based, capacious, comprehensive, consummate, developed, encyclopedic, entire, exhaustive, expansive, extensive, full, global, inclusive, of great scope, overall, plenary, sweeping, thorough, thoroughgoing, total, unconditional, undiminished, undivided, unimpaired, unqualified, unreduced, unreserved, unrestricted, unsevered, utter, very thorough, wide-embracing, with no exception, without omissions
ASSOCIATED CONCEPTS: complete abandonment, complete and adequate remedy at law, complete contract, complete coverage, complete delivery, complete jurisdiction, complete liquidation, complete ownership, complete record, complete relief, complete remedy, complete title, completed instrument

COMPLETE *(Ended),* ***adjective*** accomplished, achieved, at an end, brought to a conclusion, carried through, closed, completed, completive, concluded, conclusive, consummated, culminated, decided, definitive, disposed of, done, effected, effectuated, executed, final, finished, over, performed, realized, set at rest, settled, terminated, terminational, terminative, through

COMPLETE, ***verb*** accomplish, achieve, apply a closure, bring to a close, bring to an end, bring to conclusion, bring to maturity, bring to perfection, carry out, carry through, carry to completion, clinch, close, conclude, consummate, determine, discharge, dispatch, dispose of, draw to a close, end, finalize, finish, follow through, fulfill, perfect, polish, realize, seal, succeed, terminate, wind up
FOREIGN PHRASES: ***Extincto subjecto, tollitur adjunctum.*** When the substance is extinguished, the incident ceases.

COMPLETION, ***noun*** accomplishment, achievement, attainment, climax, close, commission, conclusion, consequence, consummation, course, crowning, culmination, denouement, discharge, dissolution, effectuation, end, ending, entirety, execution, expiration, extremity, fait accompli, finale, finality, finish, fulfillment, maturity, outcome, perfection, performance, realization, sequel, settlement, sufficiency, termination, terminus, transaction, windup
ASSOCIATED CONCEPTS: bankruptcy, completion of a trial, dissolution

COMPLEX, *adjective* abstruse, bewildering, chaotic, circuitous, complicated, confused, convoluted, difficult, elaborated, enigmatic, entangled, flexuous, impenetrable, implicated, inextricable, inscrutable, interlaced, interwoven, intricate, involuted, involutional, involved, irreducible, jumbled, kaleidoscopic, knotted, labyrinthine, mingled, muddled, *multiplex,* obscure, perplexing, recondite, sinuous, snarled, tangled, tortuous, unarranged, unclassified, undecipherable, unfathomable, unorganized, varied
ASSOCIATED CONCEPTS: complex issues to be tried

COMPLEX *(Development),* ***noun*** aggregate, aggregation, association, collectivity, compages, composite, compound, conglomerate, conglomeration, group, network, organization, structure, system, totality, unity
ASSOCIATED CONCEPTS: building complex, industrial complex, residential housing complex

COMPLEX *(Entanglement),* ***noun*** clutter, complexus, complication, confusion, convolution, derangement, difficulty, disarrangement, disarray, disorder, disorganization, enmeshment, imbroglio, intricacy, involution, involvement, jumble, labyrinth, maze, muddle, *multiplex,* snag, snarl, tangle, twist

COMPLEXION, *noun* apparent character, apparent state, appearance, aspect, carriage, character, *color,* contour, demeanor, display, disposition, external appearance, facet, fashion, favor, feature, figure, form, guise, image, impression, look, manifestation, manner, mien, nature, outline, outward appearance, port, posture, presence, quality, regard, respect, semblance, shape, slant, spirit, style, temper, tenor, tone, view, visage
ASSOCIATED CONCEPTS: complexion of the case

COMPLIANCE, *noun* accedence, acceptance, accommodation, accord, accordance, acquiescence, adaptability, adherence, agreeability, agreement, assent, bowing, compliancy, concession, concord, concurrence, conformability, conformance, conformity, consent, consonance, consonancy, cooperation, dutifulness, harmony, keeping, nonresistance, obedience, *obsequium,* observance, pliancy, submission, tractability, tractableness, willingness to comply, yielding, yieldingness
ASSOCIATED CONCEPTS: compliance with the law, in compliance with statute, strict compliance, substantial compliance
FOREIGN PHRASES: ***Impotentia excusat legem.*** The impossibility of performing a legal duty is an excuse from the performance. ***Obedientia est legis essentia.*** Obedience is the essence of the law.

COMPLIANT, *adjective* accepting, accommodating, acquiescent, agreeable, amenable, assenting, charitable, collaborative, concordant, concurring, conformable, conforming, consensual, consenting, docile, facile, favorable, indulgent, loyal, malleable, obedient, obeisant, obliging, obsequious, passive, patient, permissive, pliable, pliant, servile, submissive, toadying, tractable, uncomplaining, unreluctant, willing, yielding

COMPLICATE, *verb* aggravate, bedevil, befoul, confound, confuse, dislocate, disorganize, embroil, encumber, entangle, exacerbate, implicate, intensify, involve, jumble, knot, make intricate, make worse, mix up, muddle, obfuscate, obscure, perplex, perturb, snarl, tangle

COMPLICATION, *noun* aggravation, bafflement, barrier, complexity, complexness, complexus, complicated state, confusion, development, difficulty, dilemma, entanglement, hindrance, imbroglio, impediment, *implicatio,* incomprehensibility, inextricability, inscrutability, intricacy, intrigue, involution, involved state, involvement, labyrinth, obscurity, obstacle, obstruction, perplexity, predicament, puzzle, quandary, sinuosity, stumbling block, unforeseen circumstance

COMPLICITY, *noun* abetment, alliance, artifice, association, bad faith, collaboration, collusion, collusiveness, complexity, concert, concurrence, confederacy, connivance, conspiracy, contribution, contrivance, corruption, criminal participation, entanglement, guilt, implication, intricacy, intrigue, mutual assistance, league, plot, scheme
ASSOCIATED CONCEPTS: complicity to commit a crime

COMPLY, *verb* abide by, accede to, accept, accommodate, acknowledge, acquiesce in, adhere to, agree with, assent to, attend to orders, be faithful to, be willing, carry into effect, carry into execution, carry out, cease resistance, complete, *concedere,* concur, conform to, consent to, cooperate with, defer to, fall in with, fit, fulfill, give consent to, go along with, harmonize with, *morem gerere,* not resist, obey, observe, *parere,* perform, relent, resign oneself to, respect, satisfy, stoop, submit to, succumb, yield to
ASSOCIATED CONCEPTS: compliance with statutes

COMPONENT, *noun* aspect, basic substance, complement, component part, constituent, constituent part, content, division, element, elementary unit, factor, feature, fragment, fundamental part, ingredient, installment, integral part, item, material part, one of the contents, part, particular part, physical element, piece, portion, principle part, section, sector, segment, subdivision, unit, unit of composition
ASSOCIATED CONCEPTS: component parts

COMPORT *(Agree with),* ***verb*** accord with, attune, be accordant, be applicable, be apposite, be appropriate, be apt, be consistent, be consonant, be in accordance with, be in keeping, be in tune with, be suitable, become, befit, belong, chime in with, click, cohere, coincide, concur, conform, correspond, fall in with, fit, fit in, fit together, harmonize, jibe, match, mesh with, quadrate, reconcile, render accordant, square with, suit, tally

COMPORT *(Behave),* ***verb*** acquit, act, appear, conduct, demean, deport, discipline, manage, perform, present oneself, quit, represent, seem, show manner, show mien
ASSOCIATED CONCEPTS: demeanor of a witness

COMPOSE, *verb* accomplish, achieve, actualize, arrange, author, be responsible, be the agent, be the cause of, be the reason, bring about, bring into being, bring into effect, bring into existence, build, call into being, call into existence, carry into execution, cause, cause to be, cause to exist, chalk out, compile, *componere,* conceive, construct, contrive, develop, devise, draft, draw out, draw up, effect, *efficere,* efform, engineer, envisage, execute, express, fashion, form, formulate, frame, generate, give rise to, imagine, improvise, invent, orchestrate, organize, originate, pattern, produce, shape, use one's imagination, visualize, work out, work up, write

COMPOSITE, *adjective* accompanied, admixed, agglomerate, aggregate, aggregated, all-embracing, alloyed, amalgamated, amassed, assembled, assorted, blended, clustered, collected, collective, combined, commixed, complex, *compositus,* compound, compounded, conglomerate, conjoint, conjunct, conjunctive, connected, coupled, diversified, fused, gathered, gathered into a whole, glomerate, heterogeneous, incorporated, integrated, intermixed,

joined, medley, miscellaneous, mixed, mosaic, motley, multifarious, multiple, *multiplex,* scrambled, sundry, united, unseparated, varied, variegated, wedded
ASSOCIATED CONCEPTS: composite class, composite facts, composite instrument, composite knowledge, composite statements

COMPOSITION *(Agreement in bankruptcy),* ***noun*** agreement, arrangement, clearance, compact, compromise agreement, contract, discharge, liquidation, mutual agreement, mutual concession, payment in lieu, reciprocal concession, release, settlement, settlement by mutual agreement, settlement on account
ASSOCIATED CONCEPTS: composition agreement, composition in bankruptcy, contract of composition, reorganization

COMPOSITION *(Makeup),* ***noun*** arrangement, array, combination, compilation, *compositio,* compounding, comprisal, concoction, conformation, constitution, construction, contents, creation, design, efformation, embodiment, establishment, fabrication, formation, formulation, inclusion, manufacture, nature, organization, preparation, production, structure, synthesis, union

COMPOSURE, ***noun*** *aequus animus,* aplomb, balance, calm, calmness, command of one's faculties, command of temper, complacence, constraint, content, contentment, control, equability, equanimity, equilibrium, evenness, forbearance, fortitude, harmony, imperturbability, imperturbation, indisturbance, inexcitability, moderation, patience, peace, peace of mind, peacefulness, placidity, placidness, poise, presence of mind, quiescence, quietude, repose, reserve, rest, restraint, sedateness, self-assurance, self-command, self-possession, self-restraint, serenity, stability, tolerance, tranquil mind, *tranquillitas,* tranquillity

COMPOUND, ***adjective*** aggregate, aggregated, amalgamated, assimilated, associated, blended, combined, commixed, complex, complicated, composite, *compositus,* conglomerate, congregated, conjoint, conjugate, conjunct, connected, convoluted, elaborate, embodied, entangled, fused, hybridized, incorporated, infused, inseparable, integrated, interlaced, intermingled, interwoven, intricate, involved, manifold, merged, mingled, mixed, mosaic, motley, multifarious, multiform, multiple, multiplex, solid, tangled, tied, united, varied, variegated, woven
ASSOCIATED CONCEPTS: compound a crime, compound interest, compound larceny, compounding a felony
FOREIGN PHRASES: ***Aestimatid praeteriti delicti ex postremo facto nunquam crescit.*** The weight of an offense committed in the past is never increased by a subsequent fact.

COMPOUND, ***verb*** accrue, add to, advance, aggrandize, aggravate, amount, *ampliare, amplificare,* annex, append, *augere,* be augmented, be numerous, become greater, become larger, branch out, build up, burgeon, contribute to, develop, *dilatare,* dilate, distend, elaborate, enhance, enlarge, enrich, exacerbate, exaggerate, exalt, expand, extend, fill in, fill out, fortify, further, gain ground, gain strength, get ahead, give strength to, glorify, greaten, grow larger, heighten, increase, increase the numbers, inflate, intensify, lend force to, lengthen, magnify, make greater, make larger, multiply, open out, parlay, pile up, prolong, protract, raise, refine, reinforce, restrengthen, spread out, strengthen, subjoin, superadd, supplement, widen
ASSOCIATED CONCEPTS: compounding a crime, compounding a debt, compounding a felony, compounding penalty
FOREIGN PHRASES: ***Aestimatio praeteriti delicti ex postremo facto nunquam crescit.*** The weight of a past crime is never increased by a subsequent fact.

COMPOUNDED, ***adjective*** amalgamated, blended, coalesced, combined, complicated, composite, conglomerate, consolidated, convoluted, elaborate, entangled, fused, incorporated, inextricable, inseparable, integrated, intermingled, intricate, manifold, merged, mingled, mixed, mosaic, motley, multifarious, multiform, solidified, tangled, united, variegated
ASSOCIATED CONCEPTS: compounded crime, compounded larceny, compounded offenses

COMPREHEND *(Include),* ***verb*** be composed of, be comprised of, be made up of, circumscribe, compass, comprise, consist of, constitute, contain, cover, embody, embrace, encircle, encompass, envelop, incorporate, involve, possess, span, take in
ASSOCIATED CONCEPTS: comprehensive zoning

COMPREHEND *(Understand),* ***verb*** absorb, appreciate, apprehend, assimilate, be acquainted, be apprized, be aware, be cognizant, be conscious, be conversant with, be in possession of the facts, be informed, cognize, come to understand, *comprehendere,* conceive, descry, detect, discern, fathom, gain insight, grasp, grow aware, ken, know, master, perceive, realize, recognize, see, take in, understand fully
ASSOCIATED CONCEPTS: comprehend the nature and consequences of an act, intent, scienter

COMPREHENSIBLE, ***adjective*** apprehensible, articulate, ascertainable, clear, clear-cut, cognizable, cognoscible, comprehendable, conceivable, decipherable, defined, disclosed, easily understood, easy to understand, evident, exoteric, explicable, explicit, express, fathomable, graphic, graphical, intelligible, knowable, legible, lucid, luculent, manifest, obvious, overt, palpable, patent, pellucid, penetrable, perceivable, perceptible, perspicuous, *perspicuus,* plain, realizable, recognizable, revealed, self-evident, self-explanatory, simple, unambiguous, unclouded, unconcealed, unconfused, understandable, unhidden, unmistakable, unobscure, unveiled

COMPREHENSION, ***noun*** ability to know, alertness, appreciation, apprehension, attentiveness, awareness, awareness of, capability, capacity to understand, cognition, cognizance, command of thought, *comprehensio,* conception, consciousness, discernment, enlightenment, erudition, expertise, familiarity, grasp, imagination, information, insight, intellect, intellectual power, intellectualism, intellectuality, *intellegentia,* intuition, keeness, knowledge, learning, mastery of thought, mental capacity, mental grasp, mentality, mind, mindfulness, observation, penetration, perception, perspicaciousness, power to grasp ideas, power to understand, rationality, reach of mind, realization, reason, recognition, sagacity, sageness, sense, understanding, wisdom

COMPREHENSIVE, ***adjective*** all-covering, all-embracing, all-inclusive, all-pervading, broad, capacious, compendious, complete, completive, comprising, consummate, containing, copious, discursive, encircling, encyclopedic, exhaustive, expansive, extended, extensive, far-reaching, full, fully realized, having no limit, inclusive, intensive, late patens, overall, panoramic, sweeping, synoptic, thorough, thoroughgoing, total, unconditional, unexclusive, universal,

unmitigated, unqualified, unreserved, unrestricted, wide, wide-reaching, widespread
ASSOCIATED CONCEPTS: comprehensive coverage, comprehensive findings, comprehensive plan, comprehensive police power, comprehensive statute, comprehensive zoning

COMPREHENSIVENESS, *noun* blanket, breadth, capacity, comendiousness, completeness, complex, copiousness, coverage, ensemble, entireness, entirety, exhaustiveness, expansion, extensiveness, full realization, fullness, great scope, inclusiveness, integrality, integrity, omnibus, oneness, substantiality, thoroughness, totality, universality, volumniousness, wholeness, width

COMPRISE, *verb* aggregate, amount to, be composed of, be formed of, be made of, consist of, constitute, contain, embody, embrace, encapsulate, encompass, hold, include, incorporate, involve, subsume, total
ASSOCIATED CONCEPTS: comprising a cause of action

COMPROMISE, *noun* abatement of differences, adaptation, adjustment, agreement, bargain, commutation, composition, concession, deal, happy medium, middle ground, mutual concession, negotiation, peacemaking, settlement, terms
ASSOCIATED CONCEPTS: accord and satisfaction, compromise a claim, compromise agreement, compromise and settlement, compromise of a claim, compromise verdict, discharge or release, novation, offer of compromise
FOREIGN PHRASES: ***Compromissum ad similitudinem judiciorum redigitur.*** A compromise is brought into affinity with judgments.

COMPROMISE *(Endanger),* ***verb*** bring into danger, expose to danger, hazard, imperil, jeopardize, make liable to danger, make vulnerable, place in a dubious position, put at hazard, put in jeopardy, put under suspicion, risk, stake, venture

COMPROMISE *(Settle by mutual agreement),* ***verb*** accommodate, adjust, agree, arrange by mutual concession, bargain, come to an agreement, come to an understanding, come to terms, *compromittere,* concede, conciliate, find a middle ground, harmonize, maintain a middle position, make a compromise, make a deal, make an adjustment, make concessions, mediate, meet halfway, negotiate, reconcile, settle, settle differences, strike a balance
ASSOCIATED CONCEPTS: accord and satisfaction, compromise a claim, compromise agreement, compromise verdict, discharge, discontinuance, negotiation, novation, offer of compromise, quotient verdict, settlement, substitute contract

COMPTROLLER, *noun* accountant, auditor, banker, bookkeeper, bookkeeping expert, bursar, business manager, cashier, chartered accountant, chief accounting officer, depositary, examiner of business accounts, financial officer, inspector of accounts, inventory expert, manager, purser, reckoner, registrar, supervisor of accounts, treasurer, trustee
ASSOCIATED CONCEPTS: city comptroller, state comptroller

COMPULSION *(Coercion),* ***noun*** application of force, constraint, constraint to obedience, constriction, demand, dictation, domination, duress, duty, employment of force, enforcement, force, forcible inducement, forcible urging, forcing, high-pressure methods, imposition, impressment, limitation, *necessitas,* necessity, objective necessity, obligation, oppression, physical force, pressure, requirement, restraint, restriction, spur of necessity, stress, subjection to force, urgency, urging by force, urging by moral constraint, urging by physical constraint, *vis*
ASSOCIATED CONCEPTS: compulsion of law, compulsory act, compulsory contributions, compulsory demand, compulsory liquidation, compulsory nonsuit, compulsory payment, compulsory process, compulsory sale

COMPULSION *(Obsession),* ***noun*** ardor, besetting idea, craze, drive, earnestness, enchantment, engrossment, enthusiasm, fanaticism, fancy, fascination, fervency, fetish, fixation, fixed conviction, fixed idea, infatuation, intentness, irresistible impulse, mania, need, one-track mind, possession, predilection, preoccupation, prepossession, quirk, zeal

COMPULSORY, *adjective* against one's will, authoritative, binding, coactive, coercive, commanded, compelling, constraining, decretive, demanded, enforced, exigent, forced, forcible, imperative, incumbent upon, indefeasible, indispensable, inescapable, irresistible, irrevocable, mandatory, necessary, obligatory, peremptory, prerequisite, prescriptive, pressing, required, requisite, restraining, restrictive, stringent, unable to be evaded, unavoidable, unpreventable, urgent, vital, without choice
ASSOCIATED CONCEPTS: compulsory arbitration, compulsory counterclaim, compulsory education, compulsory insurance, compulsory joinder of parties, compulsory performance of duties, compulsory testimony

COMPURGATION, *noun* absolution, acquittal, acquittance, alibi, benefit of doubt, clearance, defeat of the prosecution, defense, dismissal, exculpation, excuse, exoneration, favorable verdict to the defendant, innocence, just cause, justification, legal defense, liberation, nonprosecution, pardon, reprieve, verdict of not guilty, vindication, withdrawal of the charge

COMPUTATION, *noun* account, accountancy, accounting, adding, amount computed, appraisal, appreciation, assessment, audit, bookkeeping, calculation, count, counting, deduction, enumeration, estimate, estimation, evaluation, figure work, figuring, measurement, numeration, reckoning, score, statistic, sum, summation, tally, total, valuation

CONATUS, *noun* attempt, choice, conation, conative will, desire, determination, direction, disposition, drift, endeavor, fancy, inclination, intention, leaning, mind, natural impulse, natural tendency, nisus, option, penchant, predilection, predisposition, preference, proclivity, proneness, propensity, temperament, tendency, trend, trial, unprompted will, volition, voluntariness, voluntary activity, want, will, wish

CONCEAL, *verb* camouflage, cloak, confine, cover, cover up, curtain, disguise, eclipse, enshroud, entomb, envelop, harbor, hide, keep clandestine, keep from, keep out of sight, keep secret, keep to oneself, keep underground, make inconspicuous, make indiscernible, make unapparent, make unperceptible, mask, not reveal, obscure, *occulere,* protect, render invisible, screen, seclude, secrete, shade, shadow, shield, shroud, store, suppress, throw a veil over, veil, withdraw from observation, withold, withold information

ASSOCIATED CONCEPTS: conceal assets, conceal information, conceal material facts
FOREIGN PHRASES: ***Fraus est celare fraudem.*** It is fraud to conceal a fraud.

CONCEALED *(Confidential),* ***adjective*** abstruse, clandestine, cloaked, covert, cryptic, delitescent, disguised, evasive, furtive, impalpable, latent, lurking, obscure, private, privy, recondite, secret, secreted, shrouded, stealthy, surreptitious, ulterior, unbeknown, undisclosed, unheard, unknown, unrecognized, unsaid, unspoken, untold, veiled
ASSOCIATED CONCEPTS: concealed weapon, concealment of a crime

CONCEALED *(Covered),* ***adjective*** blanketed, buried, camouflaged, disguised, hidden, imperceptible, inconspicuous, invisible, masked, screened, sheltered, unapparent, unexposed, unperceived, unseen
ASSOCIATED CONCEPTS: concealed weapon

CONCEALMENT, ***noun*** camouflage, confinement, cover, deceitfulness, disappearance, disguise, disguisement, duplicity, evasion, furtiveness, hiding, incognito, inconspicuousness, invisibility, nonappearance, obfuscation, obscurity, obsuration, privacy, seclusion, secrecy, secretion, secretiveness, silence, stealthiness, subterfuge, suppression, suppression of the truth
ASSOCIATED CONCEPTS: concealment of assets, concealment of information, concealment of material fact, concealment voiding an insurance policy, concealment with intent to defraud creditors, evasive contempt
FOREIGN PHRASES: ***Aliud est celare, aliud tacere.*** To conceal is one thing; to be silent is another. ***Suppressio veri, suggestio falsi.*** The suppression of truth is equivalent to the suggestion of what is false.

CONCEDE, ***verb*** abide by, accede, accept, acknowledge, acquiesce, affirm, agree, agree in principle, allow, arrive at an agreement, assent, be persuaded, come to terms, comply with, *concedere,* consent, endorse, endure, give in, grant, impart, permit, *permittere,* profess, recognize, respect, sanction, settle, submit, submit to, succumb, tolerate, withdraw one's objections, yield
ASSOCIATED CONCEPTS: conceded facts
FOREIGN PHRASES: ***Qui concedit aliquid, concedere videtur et id sine quo concessio est irrita, sine quo res ipsa esse non potuit.*** He who concedes anything is considered as conceding that without which his concession would be idle, without which the thing itself is worthless.

CONCEIVABLE, ***adjective*** aboveboard, acceptable, apprehensible, authentic, believable, clear, cognitional, coherent, colorable, comprehensible, convincing, credible, doable, earthly, fathomable, graspable, imaginable, intelligible, knowable, likely, likely to happen, likely to occur, logical, lucid, luminous, plain, plausible, possible, practical, presumable, presumptive, probable, rational, reasonable, reliable, sane, sensible, sober, straight, supposable, tenable, thinkable, trustworthy, trusty, up-front

CONCEIVE *(Comprehend),* ***verb*** absorb, accept, appreciate, apprehend, assimilate, conceptualize, conjure up, digest, discern, envisage, envision, fathom, figure out, form a conception, grasp, have an idea, ideate, image, imagine, know, perceive, picture, realize, see, understand, visualize

CONCEIVE *(Invent),* ***verb*** begin, bring into being, bring into existence, coin, compose, *concipere,* concoct, contrive, create, design, develop, devise, draft, dream up, excogitate, fabricate, formulate, frame, generate, give birth to, hatch, inchoate, initiate, innovate, make up, originate, plan, prepare, start
ASSOCIATED CONCEPTS: conceive a criminal plan

CONCENTRATE *(Consolidate),* ***verb*** accumulate, agglomerate, aggregate, amass, assemble, bring into a small compass, bring toward a central point, center, centralize, cluster, coalesce, collect, combine, compact, compress, concenter, condense, congest, conglomerate, congregate, conjoin, *conligere,* constrict, *contrahere,* converge, crowd together, densify, focalize, focus, gather, make firm, make solid, mass, strengthen, unite

CONCENTRATE *(Pay attention),* ***verb*** *animum attendere,* apply the mind, attend, attend minutely, be engrossed in, consider closely, contemplate, direct the mind upon, examine closely, fix one's attention, focus, focus attention on, give attention to, give heed, hearken, listen, meditate, muse, occupy the mind with, occupy the thoughts with, peruse carefully, ponder, put one's mind to, regard carefully, ruminate, scrutinize, study deeply, think intensely

CONCENTRATION *(Centralization),* ***noun*** agglomeration, aggregation, assemblage, collection, combination, compilation, confluence, contemplation, cumulation, density, horde, immersion

CONCENTRATION *(Compression),* ***noun*** absorption, accumulation, agglomeration, amassment, cluster, coagulation, compactness, conflux, congestion, conglomeration, consolidation, convergence, densification, intensification, mass, multitude, press, solidification, throng

CONCENTRATION *(Emphasis),* ***noun*** application, condensation, deepening, devotion, focus, heightening, intensification, interest, observation, regard, strength, strengthening

CONCEPT, ***noun*** abstract idea, abstraction, appraisal, appreciation, apprehension, assessment, assumption, belief, conception, conclusion, conjecture, consideration, deduction, doctrine, estimate, evaluation, fancy, feeling, formative notion, guess, idea, image, impression, intellectualization, judgment, knowledge, mental image, mental impression, mental representation, notion, observation, opinion, percept, perception, persuasion, picture, point of view, postulate, presumption, reflection, representation, supposition, surmise, tenet, theory, thought, understanding, view, visualization
ASSOCIATED CONCEPTS: legal concept

CONCEPTION *(Beginning),* ***noun*** concept, design, idea, ingenuity, invention, notion, original plan, origination, plan, thought

CONCEPTION *(Insemination),* ***noun*** beginning of life, fecundation, fecundity, fertilization, impregnation, inception of pregnancy, pregnancy, superimpregnation

CONCERN *(Business establishment),* ***noun*** business, company, corporation, establishment, firm, house, institution, organization
ASSOCIATED CONCEPTS: partnership, proprietorship

CONCERN *(Interest),* ***noun*** anxiety, attention, care, concernment, consequence, consideration, disquietude, importance, regard, solicitude, *sollicitudo,* uneasiness, worry

CONCERN *(Care),* ***verb*** administer to, attend, attend to, be mindful, be vigilant, be watchful, check, consider, *curare,* devote oneself to, direct the attention to, examine intently, foster, give attention, give one's attention, keep, look after, mind, minister to, pay attention to, regard, respect, safeguard, take care of, take into consideration, take note of, tend, watch

CONCERN *(Involve),* ***verb*** absorb, affect, appertain to, apply, *attinere,* be a factor, be applicable to, be interdependent with, be involved, be one of, be pertinent to, be related to, be relevant, deal with, embody, embrace, enclasp, entail, have a bearing on, have a connection, have a reference, have a relation, have interrelationship with, immerse, influence, interest, pertain to, *pertinere,* refer to, regard, relate to, respect, stand in relation, *versari in re*
ASSOCIATED CONCEPTS: concerned in interest, concerning a matter of law, general state concern, local concern

CONCERT, ***noun*** accord, accordance, agreement, alliance, coaction, coadjument, coadjuvancy, coagency, coalition, coefficiency, collaboration, combination, combined action, combined effort, compatibility, complicity, concord, concordance, concurrence, concurrency, confederation, conjunction, consentaneity, consonance, cooperation, fusion of interests, harmony, joint action, joint operation, merger, mutual assistance, pool, rapport, synergy, teamwork, unanimity, unison, unity
ASSOCIATED CONCEPTS: acting in concert

CONCERTED, ***adjective*** abetting, accordant, agreed, agreeing, aiding and abetting, aligned, amalgamated, assenting, blended, bonded, coacting, coactive, coadjutant, coadjuvant, coalescent, coeval, coexistent, coexisting, cohesive, coincident, coinciding, collaborating, colluding, combined, combining, commixed, composite, concordant, concurrent, concurring, conformable, conforming, congruent, congruous, conjoined, conjoint, conjunct, connective, conniving, consensual, consentaneous, consentient, consenting, consistent with, consolidated, consonant, contributing, converging, cooperating, cooperative, corresponding, coworking, fused, harmonious, harmonized, in accord, in accordance with, in agreement, in alliance, in unison, interactive, joined, joint, merging, mutually agreed, parallel, simultaneous, sympathetic, synergic, united, uniting

CONCESSION *(Authorization),* ***noun*** allowance, authority, authorization, bestowal, clearance, *concessio,* conferment, conferral, endowment, giving, grant, impartment, leave, license, permission, permit, presentation, privilege, sanction, vouchsafement, warrant

CONCESSION *(Compromise),* ***noun*** acceptance, accord, acknowledgment, acquiescence, admission, admitting, agreement, allowance, assent, capitulation, concurrence, giving in, grant, granting, recognition, recognizance, reconciliation, relinquishment, settlement, submission, surrender, yielding

CONCILIATION, ***noun*** abatement of differences, accommodation, accord, accordance, adaptability, adjustment, agreement, appeasement, arrangement, bipartisanship, compact, compliance, compromise, concert, concession, *conciliatio,* concord, concurrence, conformability, conformity, consonance, cooperation, entente, harmony, league, mediation, mutual accord, mutual agreement, mutual concession, mutual understanding, negotiation, pacification, peacemaking, placation, propitiation, reconcilement, reconciliation, reunion, satisfaction, settlement, settlement of differences, solidarity, submission, truce, unanimity, understanding, uniformity, union, unity
ASSOCIATED CONCEPTS: conciliation in a marriage

CONCILIATORY, ***adjective*** accommodative, agreeable, amiable, atoning, bland, civil, compassionate, compatible, concordant, cordial, courteous, deferential, expiatory, forgiving, friendly, gracious, harmonious, magnanimous, mediatory, nonmilitant, obeisant, pacific, pacifying, peacemaking, penitent, persuasive, placable, polite, propitiating, propitiatory, reconcilable, reconciliatory, reconciling, respectful, unresentful

CONCISE, ***adjective*** abbreviated, abridged, abstracted, brief, capsule, capsulized, compact, compacted, compendious, compressed, condensed, contracted, curtailed, curtate, epigrammatic, epitomized, laconic, pithy, short, shortened, succinct, summarized, summary, synoptic, to the point, trenchant

CONCLUDE *(Complete),* ***verb*** abort, adjourn, break off, bring to a close, bring to an end, bring to rest, carry to completion, cease, climax, close, *conficere,* consummate, culminate, discharge, discontinue, dispose of, end, execute, exhaust, finalize, *finire,* finish, fulfill, halt, make an end of, make complete, maturate, prosecute to a conclusion, render complete, seal, set at rest, settle, shut down, stop, surcease, terminate
ASSOCIATED CONCEPTS: conclude a hearing, conclude a trial

CONCLUDE *(Decide),* ***verb*** choose, come to a determination, *conligere,* decide upon, declare, decree, decree by judicial authority, deduce, deem, deliver judgment, determine, end by a decision, find, form a judgment, form a resolution, form an opinion, give a ruling, give an opinion, give judgment, hold, infer, judge, make a decision, make a resolution, make terms, make up one's mind, pass judgment, pronounce a judgment, resolve, rule, seal, settle, settle in one's mind, settle upon, take a decisive step
ASSOCIATED CONCEPTS: conclusion of guilt, findings

CONCLUDED, ***adjective*** abandoned, all over, ceased, closed, completed, conclusive, consummated, crowned, culminated, decided, determinative, discharged, discontinued, dispatched, done, ended, expired, final, finished, fulfilled, halted, lapsed, last, matured, perfected, settled, terminated, through, ultimate

CONCLUSION *(Determination),* ***noun*** adjudication, arbitrament, ascertainment, assessment, authoritative opinion, *conclusio,* consideration, decision, declaration, decree, deduction, derived principle, discernment, estimation, evaluation, final judgment, finding, inference, judgment, observation, opinion, persuasion, pronouncement, realization, reasoned judgment, report, resolution, resolve, result, result ascertained, result of judicial inquest, ruling, settling, solution, surmise, valuation, verdict, view
ASSOCIATED CONCEPTS: conclusion as to intent, conclusion as to motive, conclusion of a trial, conclusion of guilt, conclusion of innocence, conclusion of law, conclusion of mixed law and fact

CONCLUSION *(Outcome),* ***noun*** cessation, close, closure, completeness, completion, *conclusio,* consequence, consequent, consummation, culmination, denouement, effect, effectuation, end, end product, end result, ending, eventuality, final result, finale, finalty, finis,

finish, fulfillment, last stage, outcome, outgrowth, product, repercussion, result, resultance, resultant action, termination, upshot
FOREIGN PHRASES: ***Ab abusu ad usum non valet consequentia.*** A conclusion as to the use of a thing from its abuse is invalid. ***Inclusio unius est exclusio alterius.*** The inclusion of one is the exclusion of another. ***In propria causa nemo judex.*** No one can be judge in his own cause. ***Negatio conclusionis est error in lege.*** The denial of a conclusion is in error in law.

CONCLUSIVE *(Determinative),* ***adjective*** absolute, apparent, ascertained, assured, categorical, certain, conspicuous, definite, demonstrated, evident, final, guaranteed, immutable, incommutable, incontestable, incontrovertible, indefeasible, indisputable, indubitable, infallible, irrefragable, irrefutable, irrepealable, irrevocable, mandatory, obligatory, positive, tested, tried, ultimate, unambiguous, unchallengeable, unchangeable, uncontested, undeniable, undoubted, unequivocal, unimpeachable, unmistakable, unquestionable
ASSOCIATED CONCEPTS: conclusive admission, conclusive beyond a reasonable doubt, conclusive evidence, conclusive judgment, conclusive presumption, conclusive presumption of validity, conclusive proof

CONCLUSIVE *(Settled),* ***adjective*** ascertained, beyond dispute, *certus,* clear, closing, complete, completed, completing, completive, conclusory, confirming, culminating, decided, decisive, definitive, determining, evidential, extreme, final, finished, finishing, terminal, terminative, ultimate
ASSOCIATED CONCEPTS: conclusive adjudification, conclusive as to the facts

CONCOMITANT, ***adjective*** accompanying, aligned, allied, associated, attendant, attending, coincident, complemental, concurrent, conjoint, conjunctional, conjunctive, contemporaneous, contemporary, correlative, correspondent, corresponding, coupled, joint, parallel, simultaneous, synergic
FOREIGN PHRASES: ***Principia data sequuntur concomitantia.*** Given principles are followed by their concomitants.

CONCORDANCE, ***noun*** accord, accordance, agreement, amity, assent, coaction, coincidence, common assent, communion, compact, concert, concord, concurrence, concurrence in opinions, conformance, conformity, congeniality, congruence, congruency, conjunction, consensus, consent, consentaneity, consentaneousness, consistency, consonance, cooperation, correspondence, fraternity, friendship, harmony, likemindedness, neighborliness, oneness, peace, rapport, sympathy, understanding, unity

CONCORDANT, ***adjective*** accommodative, accordant, agreeable, agreeing, aligned, allied, assenting, assentive, at one, banded together, blending, bonded, cemented, coexistent, coexisting, coinciding, combinative, compatible, complementary, compliant, *concors,* concurrent, concurring, conformable, conforming, congruent, congruous, conjoined, conjunctional, consensual, consentaneous, consenting, consistent, consonant, coordinate, correlated, correlative, correspondent, corresponding, fusing, harmonious, in accord, in agreement, in concert, in conjunction, in harmony, in rapport, in unison, joint, merged, merging, mutual, of the same mind, reconcilable, sympathetic, unanimous, uniform, united, uniting

CONCRESCENCE, ***noun*** adherance, amalgamating, blending, coalescence, combining, consolidation, fusion, making one, mingling, mixing, symphysis, uniting

CONCRETE, ***adjective*** bodily, certain, cognizable, definite, demonstrable, determinate, distinct, embodied, existent, existing, explicit, firm, material, palpable, particular, perceptible, physical, real, solid, solidified, *solidus,* specific, substantial, substantive, tangible
ASSOCIATED CONCEPTS: concrete cause of action, concrete idea, concrete interest

CONCUR *(Agree),* ***verb*** accede to, accept, accord, accredit, acknowledge, acquiesce, act in concert, affirm, allow, approbate, approve, assent to, band together, come to an agreement, come to an understanding, come to terms, come together, comply, condone, conform with, consent, cooperate, countenance, defer to, echo, endorse, favor, give credit, go along with, harmonize, hold with, homologate, jibe, join forces, join in, join together, join with, league together, meet, operate jointly, ratify, sanction, say yes, second, side with, signify assent, subscribe to, suit, support, sustain, sympathize with, unite efforts, unite with, uphold, work jointly, yield
ASSOCIATED CONCEPTS: concurring opinion

CONCUR *(Coexist),* ***verb*** accompany, be concomittant, be contemporaneous, be contemporary, be parallel, coincide, exist together, happen at the same time, happen simultaneously, happen together, keep pace with, occur at the same time, occur concurrently
ASSOCIATED CONCEPTS: concurrent acts, concurrent causes, concurrent conditions, concurrent contracts, concurrent covenants, concurrent jurisdiction, concurrent negligence, concurrent power, concurrent sentences, consecutive sentences

CONCURRENT *(At the same time),* ***adjective*** accompanying, associated, at the same instant, attendant, attending, coacting, coactive, coetaneous, coeval, coexistent, coexisting, coincident, coinstantaneous, collateral, concerted, concomitant, conjunctive, contemporaneous, contemporary, convergent, converging, coupled, occurring at the same time, parallel, synchronal, synchronistic, synchronistical, synchronous
ASSOCIATED CONCEPTS: concurrent actions, concurrent findings, concurrent legislation, concurrent remedies, concurrent sentences, concurrent stipulations

CONCURRENT *(United),* ***adjective*** abetting, accordant, acquiescent, acting in conjunction, agreeing, aiding, allied, amalgamated, assenting, associating, assonant, banded together, binding, blended, bonded, cemented, centralized, coacting, coactive, coalitional, cohesive, collaborative, combinative, combined, common, communal, commutual, compatible, complementary, concerted, concordant, concurring, confederated, conforming, conjoined, connected, consentaneous, consolidated, consonant, contributing, cooperative, coupled, coworking, *en rapport,* fused, harmonizing, in accord, in agreement, in unison, interallied, joined, joint, leagued, linked, meeting, merged, of one accord, paired, participating, shared, synergic, undivided, unified, united, wedded, well-matched

CONCURRENT CAUSE, ***noun*** a second legal basis, accompanying legal basis, additional legal basis, another legal basis, another legal basis in concert, coexistent legal basis, coexisting legal basis, coincident legal basis, coinstantaneous legal basis, concomitant legal basis, contemporaneous legal basis

CONCURRENT POWER, ***noun*** joint authority, joint power exercisable by federal and state governments, overhanging authority, overhanging powers, overlapping authority, overlapping jurisdiction of federal and state governments, overlapping powers, overlaying authority, overlaying powers, shared jurisdiction by both federal and state governments

CONDEMN *(Ban),* ***verb*** abhor, abnegate, abrogate, banish, bar, blackball, block, boycott, call a halt, cancel, cast aside, cast out, censor, check, counter, debar, deny, deprive, disallow, disapprove, discommode, discountenance, disfavor, disown, disqualify, embargo, enjoin, exclude, excommunicate, expel, forbid, forestall, frustrate, halt, hamper, impede, interdict, interrupt, keep in bounds, keep out, keep within bounds, lay an embargo on, limit, make impossible, object, obstruct, oppose, ostracize, outlaw, preclude, prevent, prohibit, proscribe, put a stop to, put an embargo on, put an end to, put one's veto to, put under an injunction, put under an interdiction, put under prohibition, quash, quell, refuse, reject, repress, reprobate, restrain, restrict, restrict access, retard, seclude, shut out, stop, suppress, thwart, *vetare,* withhold

CONDEMN *(Blame),* ***verb*** accuse, anathematize, animadvert, asperse, assail with censure, attack, berate, bring into discredit, call to account, cast blame upon, castigate, charge, chide, *condemnare,* criticize, *culpare,* declaim against, decry, denigrate, denounce, deprecate, derogate, disapprove, discountenance, disdain, disparage, dispraise, execrate, find guilty, fulminate against, impeach, implicate, impugn, incriminate, indict, inveigh against, pass censure on, publicly accuse, rebuke, reprehend, reproach, reprove, repudiate, revile, take to task, upbraid, vilify, *vituperare,* vituperate

CONDEMN *(Punish),* ***verb*** adjudge, administer correction, bring to account, carry out a sentence, convict, *damnare,* deal retributive justice, discipline, doom, exact a penalty, exact retribution, execute a sentence, execute justice, impose a penalty, impose penalty, inflict penalty, inflict punishment, pass sentence on, penalize, prescribe punishment, pronounce judgment, pronounce sentence, *punire,* reprimand, reprove, sentence, subject to penalty, take disciplinary action

CONDEMN *(Seize),* ***verb*** accroach, acquire, appropriate, arrogate, assume, assume ownership, attach, compulsorily acquire, confiscate, declare to be forfeited, deprive of corporal possession, deprive of ownership, disentitle, dispossess, disseise, distrain, divest of property, expropriate, foreclose, impound, impropriate, municipalize, nationalize, *publicare,* sequestrate, take for public use, take over, take possession, usurp
ASSOCIATED CONCEPTS: eminent domain

CONDEMNATION *(Blame),* ***noun*** accusation, animadversion, ascription, attack, castigation, censure, charge, chastening, chastisement, chiding, complaint, *condemnatio,* criticism, denigration, denunciation, deprecation, derogation, disapprobation, disapproval, discountenance, discredit, disdain, disfavor, disparagement, dispraise, execration, expostulation, impeachment, implication, imputation, incrimination, inculpation, invective, objection, objurgation, opposition, rebuke, recrimination, reprehension, reprimand, reproach, reprobation, reproof, repudiation, stricture, vilification, vituperation

CONDEMNATION *(Punishment),* ***noun*** conviction, disciplinary action, exaction of penalty, execration, finding of guilty, guilty verdict, infliction, judgment, justice, penalization, penalty, punishing experience, punishment, punition, retribution, retributive justice, sentence

CONDEMNATION *(Seizure),* ***noun*** abrogation, acquisition by right of eminent domain, appropriation, arrogation, assumption, commandeering, compulsory acquisition, confiscation, deprivation, dispossession, distraint, distress, divestment, expropriation, forced sale, forcible seizure, foreclosure, impounding, impropriation, municipalization, nationalization, prehension, takeover, taking of property for public use, taking possession
ASSOCIATED CONCEPTS: condemnation of land for public use, condemnation proceedings, reverse condemnation, title by condemnation

CONDENSE, ***verb*** abbreviate, abridge, abstract, capsulize, compress, consolidate, contract, curtail, cut short, detruncate, digest, epitomize, foreshorten, make brief, make concise, make denser, make terse, outline, précis, reduce, render more compact, shorten, shrink, summarize, sum up, synopsize, truncate

CONDESCEND *(Deign),* ***verb*** accommodate oneself, accord, be courteous, be gracious, descend, *descendere,* disregard prestige, grant, humble oneself, lower oneself, sacrifice pride, *se submittere,* stoop, tolerate, unbend, vouchsafe, waive privilege, yield

CONDESCEND *(Patronize),* ***verb*** assume a patronizing air, be contemptuous, be overbearing, belittle, care nothing for, consider beneath notice, contemn, disdain, disparage, disrespect, hold in contempt, hold in disrespect, look down on, look with scorn upon, spurn, talk down to

CONDIGN, ***adjective*** appropriate, befitting, *debitus,* deserved, due, earned, fit, fitting, just, justified, merited, *meritus,* right, suitable, warranted, well-deserved, well-earned, worthy

CONDITION *(Contingent provision),* ***noun*** article, clause, *condicio,* contractual terms, desideratum, essential provision, exception, final terms, limitation, obligation, pact, postulate, postulation, prerequirement, prerequisite, prescription, presumption, presupposition, promise, provision, proviso, qualification, regulation, requirement, requisite, reservation, restriction, rule, ruling, specification, stated term, stipulation, supposal, supposition, term, ultimatum, uncertain event
ASSOCIATED CONCEPTS: cause, condition implied in law, condition of employment, condition precedent, condition running with the land, condition subsequent, conditions and exceptions, conditions and restrictions, express condition, implied condition, sale on condition, terms and conditions, warranties
FOREIGN PHRASES: ***Ea quae dari impossibilia sunt, vel quae in rerum natura non sunt, pro non adjectis habentur.*** Those things which cannot be given, or which are not in the nature of things, are regarded as not included in the agreement. ***Conditiones quaelibet odiosae; maxime autem contra matrimonium et commercium.*** Any conditions are odious, but especially those which are in restraint of marriage and commerce. ***Proviso est providere praesentia et futura, non praeterita.*** A proviso is to provide for the present and the future, not the past. ***Conditio illicita habetur pro non adjecta.*** An unlawful condition is deemed not to be annexed. ***Conditio praecedens adimpleri debet prius quam sequatur effectus.*** A condition precedent must be fulfilled before the effect can follow. ***Conditio***

dicitur, cum quid in casum incertum qui potest tendere ad esse aut non esse, confertur. It is called a "condition," when something is given on an uncertain event, which may or may not come into existence. ***Conditio beneficialis, quae statum construit, benigne secundum verborum intentionem est interpretanda; odiosa autem quaestatum destruit, stricte secundum berborum proprietatem accipienda.*** A beneficial condition, which creates an estate, ought to be interpreted favorably, according to the intention of the words; but a condition which destroys an estate is odious and ought to be construed strictly according to the letter.

CONDITION *(State),* ***noun*** appearance, aspect, character, circumstance, complexion, *condicio,* crasis, grade, habitude, look, plight, position, posture, predicament, quality, rank, shape, situation, state of being, station, *status,* temperament, tenor
ASSOCIATED CONCEPTS: dangerous condition, emergency condition, financial condition, good operating condition, physical condition

CONDITIONAL, ***adjective*** alterable, changeable, conditioned, containing stipulations, contingent on, dependent on, depending on, depending on a future event, determined by, equivocal, granted on certain terms, hypothetical, imposing a condition, indefinite, indeterminable, indeterminate, liable to, limitative, limited, modified by conditions, negotiable, not absolute, not certain, not sure, pending, possible, provisional, provisionary, provisory, qualified, regulated by, restricted, specified, stipulative, subject to, subject to chance, subject to change, subject to terms, suspenseful, tentative, unassured, uncertain, undecided, under the control of, undetermined, unpositive, unpredictable, unsettled, unsure
ASSOCIATED CONCEPTS: conditional acceptance, conditional agreement, conditional bequest, conditional bill of sale, conditional bond, conditional charge, conditional consent, conditional contract, conditional conveyance, conditional delivery, conditional devise, conditional endorsement, conditional estate, conditional execution, conditional fee, conditional gift, conditional guaranties, conditional judgment, conditional lease, conditional legacy, conditional liability, conditional limitation, conditional obligations, conditional pardon, conditional payment, conditional promise, conditional release, conditional revocation of a will, conditional rights, conditional sale, conditional sales act, conditional sales contract, conditional subscription, conditional will

CONDITIONAL DISCHARGE, ***noun*** absolution, amnesty, atonement, bailout, clearance, clearing, compurgation, deliverance, discharge, emancipation, exculpation, exemption, expiation, extrication, forgiveness, liberation, liberty, pardon, parole, release, remission, reprieve, rescue
ASSOCIATED CONCEPTS: dismissal of criminal charges

CONDITIONAL INTENT, ***noun*** alternative intent, alternative intentions, conditional threat, contingent intent, intent subject to condition, intent with conditions attached, sufficient intent

CONDONATION, ***noun*** absolution, accommodation, acquittal, allowance, amnesty, cancellation, charity, clearance, clemency, compassion, conciliation, concord, discharge, dismissal, disposition to pardon, disregard, excusal, exemption, exoneration, expiation, extenuation, extrication, forgiveness, full pardon, grace, impunity, indemnity, indulgence, lenience, magnanimity, mercy, nonliability, overlooking, pardon, reconcilement, reprieve, sympathy, vindication, willingness to forgive
ASSOCIATED CONCEPTS: condonation as grounds for a dissolution of a marriage

CONDONE, ***verb*** absolve, accept, allow, assoil, be lenient, be merciful, be reconciled, be tolerant, bear with, blot out, clear, countenance, dismiss, disregard, excuse, exempt, exonerate, forbear, forget, forgive, free, give a reprieve, give absolution, give amnesty, grant amnesty, grant immunity, let pass, make allowance, overlook, overlook an offense, palliate, pardon, pass over, permit, recommend to pardon, refrain from punishing, release, relent, remit, reprieve, set free, show mercy, spare, tolerate, vindicate, waive punishment, yield

CONDUCE, ***verb*** abet, advance, aid, assist, augment, bring about, bring on, cause, *conducere,* contribute toward, cooperate, effect, encourage, expedite, favor, foment, foster, incline to, increase the chances, influence, lead to, make probable, predispose to, promote, put ahead, put forward, tend to, work toward

CONDUCIVE, ***adjective*** accessory, accommodating, advantageous, appropriate, beneficial, contributive, convenient, efficacious, facilitative, favorable, fruitful, helpful, leading, obliging, practical, produce, productive, promotive, propitious, salutary, useful

CONDUCT, ***noun*** actions, acts, address, air, aspect, attitude, bearing, behavior, behavior pattern, breeding, carriage, code, compliance, comportment, conformance, correctness, course of behavior, dealings, decorum, deeds, demeanor, deportment, established practice, ethics, etiquette, fashion, guise, habits, management, manner, manners, method, mien, mode of action, mode of behavior, morals, operation, performance, personal bearing, port, posture, practice, presence, procedure, propriety, public manners, role, seemliness, social behavior, social graces, style, way, way of acting, ways, wise
ASSOCIATED CONCEPTS: coercive conduct, course of conduct, disorderly conduct, good conduct, immoral conduct, improper conduct, inequitable conduct, justifiable conduct, reasonable conduct, standard of conduct, unprofessional conduct

CONDUCT, ***verb*** administer, *administrare,* administrate, assume responsibility, carry on, carry out, command, control, deal with, direct, direct affairs, discharge, dispatch, do, enact, execute, *gerere,* guide, handle, have control, lead, look after, manage, officiate at, operate, oversee, *perducere,* pilot, preside over, proceed with, regulate, run, superintend, supervise, take care of, take charge of, transact, usher
ASSOCIATED CONCEPTS: conduct a business, conduct a sale, conducted for profit, conducting business
FOREIGN PHRASES: ***Melius est recurrere quam malo currere.*** It is better to recede than to proceed in error.

CONDUIT *(Channel),* ***noun*** agency, artery, avenue, contrivance, course, device, instrument, machinery, manner, means, medium, method, mode, path, process, route, way
ASSOCIATED CONCEPTS: intermediary and accomplice to a crime

CONDUIT *(Intermediary),* ***noun*** advocate, agent, delegate, deputy, emissary, envoy, functionary, go-between, intermedium, mediary, mediator, medium, middleman, negotiator, proxy, representative, substitute, surrogate

CONFABULATE, ***verb*** advise, bandy, brainstorm, chat, confab, confer, consider, consult, converse, counsel, debate, deliberate, disclose, discuss, dispute, divulge, examine, gossip, groupthink, parley, rehash, review, talk, talk over, treat, ventilate, weigh

CONFEDERACY *(Compact),* ***noun*** affiliation, alignment, alliance, association, body, cartel, coalition, combination, combine, concurrence, confederation, confraternity, consolidation, coterie, federation, fellowship, *foedus,* fusion, guild, league, *pactum,* set, *societas,* society, solidarity, syndicate, trust, unification, union

CONFEDERACY *(Conspiracy),* ***noun*** cabal, collusion, complicity, complot, *coniuratio,* connivance, criminal agreement, illegal agreement, illegal compact, intrigue, plot, schemery, treasonable alliance

CONFEDERATE, ***noun*** abettor, accessory, accomplice, adjunct, adjutant, adjuvant, aid, aider, ally, assistant, associate, auxiliary, coactor, coadjutant, coadjutor, collaborator, colleague, colluder, comate, companion, comrade, confidant, confrere, consociate, conspirator, conspirer, cooperator, coworker, fellow, friend, helper, helpmate, intrigant, participator, partner, support, supporter

CONFER *(Consult),* ***verb*** advise, compare opinions, confide in, consult with, *consultare,* counsel, deliberate, discuss, exchange observations, exhort, give advice, hold a conference, hold a consultation, interchange views, negotiate, palaver, parley, refer, seek advice, take counsel, talk over
ASSOCIATED CONCEPTS: confer with a client, confer with an associate

CONFER *(Give),* ***verb*** accord, adjudge, administer, award, bestow, cede, *conferre,* convey, deliver, dispense, endow, give, grant, hand down, impart, invest, issue, pass down, present, relinquish, tender, transfer, transmit, yield
ASSOCIATED CONCEPTS: confer authority, confer jurisdiction, conferred powers

CONFERENCE, ***noun*** assembly, colloquy, conclave, confabulation, consultation, consultation meeting, convention, conversations, convocation, deliberation, dialogue, discussion, exchange, forum, gathering, interchange of opinions, interlocution, meeting, negotiation, negotiations, palaver, parlance, parley, premeditation, seminar, symposium, talks

CONFESS, ***verb*** acknowledge, acknowledge one's guilt, admit, admit guilt, bare, come forth, compurgate, concede, *confiteri,* declare, disburden one's conscience, disclose, divulge, expose, *fateri,* give evidence, inculpate, lay open, make a confession, make solemn affirmation, own up, purge oneself, reveal, tell all, turn state's evidence, utter, yield
ASSOCIATED CONCEPTS: confess guilt, confess judgment, confess participation
FOREIGN PHRASES: ***Qui tacet non utique fatetur, sed tamen verum est eum non negare.*** He who is silent does not confess, but it is nevertheless true that he does not deny.

CONFESSION, ***noun*** acknowledgment, acknowledgment of guilt, acquiescence, admission, admission of fault, admission of guilt, assertion, avowal of guilt, confirmation, declaration, disclosure, disclosure of fault, divulgement, divulgence, exclamation, exomologesis, incriminating statement, inculpatory statement, pronouncement, purgation, revealment, self-accusation, self-condemnation, statement, utterance
ASSOCIATED CONCEPTS: confessed judgment, confession and avoidance, confession of error, extrajudicial confessions, implied confession, involuntary confession, judgment by confession, judicial confession, voluntary confession, written confession
FOREIGN PHRASES: ***Confessus in judicio pro judicato habetur, et quodammodo sua sententia damnatur.*** A person confessing his guilt in court is deemed to have been found guilty and is, in a manner, condemned by his own sentence. ***Cum confitente sponte mitius est agendum.*** One making a voluntary confession is to be dealt with more leniently.

CONFIDE *(Divulge),* ***verb*** disclose, disclose something secret, discuss private affairs, divulgate, entrust with private information, let know, make known, reveal something private, share secrets, tell a secret, tell with assurance of secrecy, trust to keep secret

CONFIDE *(Trust),* ***verb*** believe in, commit, consign, deliver to the care of, entrust, feel sure of, give in trust, have confidence in, have faith in, hold responsible for, place reliance on, put faith in, put in care of, rely on, rely upon
ASSOCIATED CONCEPTS: attorney-client privilege, confidential creditor, confidential informant, confidential relation, fiduciary relationship, husband-wife privilege, physician-patient privilege, priest-penitant privilege, privileged against self-incrimination, privileged communications

CONFIDENCE *(Faith),* ***noun*** affiance, aplomb, assurance, boldness, certainty, certitude, cocksureness, confidentness, conviction, courage, credence, credulity, fearlessness, *fides, fiducia,* firm belief, heart, intrepidity, morale, nerve, optimism, poise, positiveness, reliance, sanguineness, security, sureness, surety, trust
FOREIGN PHRASES: ***Multa fidem promissa levant.*** Many promises lessen confidence. ***Fides servanda est.*** Good faith must be observed.

CONFIDENCE *(Relation of trust),* ***noun*** assurance of secrecy, classified communication, concealment, confidential communication, confidential matter, intimacy, personal matter, privacy, private, private affair, privileged communication, secrecy, secret, secret communication
ASSOCIATED CONCEPTS: attorney-client confidence, confidential communications, husband-wife confidence, physician-patient confidence, priest-penitent confidence

CONFIDENTIAL, ***adjective*** arcane, *arcanus,* auricular, classified, concealed, *fidus,* hidden, imparted in secret, irrevealable, not for publication, not to be communicated, not to be disclosed, not to be quoted, not to be spoken of, off the record, private, restricted, secret, spoken in confidence, told in confidence, top secret, undercover, unmentionable, unrevealed
ASSOCIATED CONCEPTS: confidential communication, confidential information, confidential proceeding, confidential relationship, fiduciary relationship, privilege

CONFIDENTIAL COMMUNICATION, ***noun*** acquired facts which cannot be revealed, acquired knowledge

which cannot be revealed, compilations which cannot be revealed, concealed documents, knowledge of facts which cannot be revealed, knowledge which cannot be revealed, learning which cannot be revealed, not for publication, not to be communicated, not to be disclosed, not to be quoted, not to be spoken about, private, privileged communication, protected communication, restricted, secret, spoken in confidence, told in confidence, top secret
ASSOCIATED CONCEPTS: attorney-privileged, doctor-patient, priest-penitent, spousal immunity

CONFIDENTIALITY, ***noun*** classified, concealed, hidden, not for publication, not to be communicated, not to be disclosed, not to be quoted, not to be spoken of, privacy, private, protected, restricted, revealed in confidence, secrecy, secret, spoken in confidence, told in confidence, top secret, unmentionable, unrevealed
ASSOCIATED CONCEPTS: affirmative defense, need-to-know principle, nondisclosure agreement, secrecy

CONFIGURATION *(Confines),* ***noun*** borders, boundary, bounds, circumscription, contour, delineation, dimensions, edges, extent, framework, frontiers, limitations, limits, line of demarcation, outline, perimeter

CONFIGURATION *(Form),* ***noun*** anatomy, appearance, arrangement, body, cast, character, composition, conformation, constitution, construction, contour, design, external form, features, figuration, figure, format, formation, frame, framework, *galbe,* layout, lines, look, makeup, outline, outward form, pattern, physique, profile, rough outline, scheme of arrangement, shape, silhouette, skeleton, structural composition, structural design, structure

CONFINE, ***verb*** arrest, barricade, bind, bound, cage, capture, circumscribe, *coercere, cohibere,* commit, commit to prison, constrain, contain, control, detain, enchain, enclose, enthrall, fence in, harness, hold, hold as a hostage, hold back, hold captive, hold in captivity, hold in check, hold in thrall, hold prisoner, immure, impound, imprison, incarcerate, *includere,* institutionalize, intern, jail, keep in custody, keep under control, keep within bounds, limit, lock up, pen in, place in durance, place under protective custody, put into isolation, put under arrest, put under restraint, quarantine, recommit, remand, repress, restrain, restrict, restrict access, seclude, send to jail, shut in, subdue, subjugate, suppress, take into custody, take prisoner, trammel
ASSOCIATED CONCEPTS: actual confinement, confine to an asylum, confinement to a jail, false imprisonment, kidnapping, solitary confinement

CONFINEMENT, ***noun*** apprehension, arrest, bondage, captivity, circumspection, constraint, custody, detainment, enslavement, immurement, impoundment, imprisonment, incarceration, jail, limitation, prison, rein, restraint, restriction, servitude, solitary confinement
ASSOCIATED CONCEPTS: bail pending appeal, bail pending trial

CONFINES, ***noun*** borders, boundaries, boundary lines, bounds, compound, confinements, curbs, curtilages, division lines, edges, enclosures, ends, environs, extents, extremities, fringes, limitations, limits, lines of demarcation, metes, outer edges, outlines, perimeter, precincts, restraints, skirts
ASSOCIATED CONCEPTS: within the confines of the law

CONFIRM, ***verb*** accede, accord, accredit, acknowledge, acquiesce, add strength to, adhere, agree to, agree with, ally, approve, assent, attest, authenticate, authorize, avow, charter, commend, *comprobare,* concede, concur, consent, corroborate, countersign, document, endorse, establish, fortify, give one's word for, give security, guarantee, homologate, join in a compact, legalize, license, make firm, make valid, pass, permit, prove, ratify, recognize, *sancire,* sanction, seal, second, support, sustain, uphold, validate, verify, vote for, vouch for
FOREIGN PHRASES: ***Confirmare nemo potest prius quam jus ei acciderit.*** No one can confirm a right before it accrues to him. ***Confirmare est id firmum facere quod prius infirmum fuit.*** To confirm is to make firm that which had been infirm. ***Confirmat usum qui tollit abusum.*** He confirms a use who removes an abuse.

CONFIRMATION, ***noun*** acceptance, accord, accordance, acknowledgment, acquiescence, admission, affidavit, affirmance, affirmation, approval, assent, assertion, assurance, attestation, authentication, authorization, averment, avouchment, certification, corroboration, corroborative statement, declaration, deposition, documentation, endorsement, legal pledge, oath, proof, ratification, sanction, seal, solemn averment, solemn avowal, solemn declaration, stamp of approval, subscription, substantiation, support, swearing, validation, verification, *visé,* warrant
ASSOCIATED CONCEPTS: confirmation of judgment, confirmation of sale
FOREIGN PHRASES: ***Non valet confirmatio, nisi ille, qui confirmat, sit in possessione rei vel juris unde fieri debet confirmatio; et eodem modo, misi ille cui confirmatio fit sit in possessione.*** Confirmation is not valid unless he who confirms is either in possession of the thing itself or of the right of which confirmation is to be made, and, in like manner, unless he to whom confirmation is made is in possession. ***Confirmatio est nulla ubi donum praecedens est invalidum.*** Confirmation is a nullity where the preceding gift is invalid. ***Confirmatio omnes supplet defectus, licet id quod actum est ab initio non valuit.*** Confirmation supplies all defects, though that which had been done was not valid at the beginning.

CONFISCATE, ***verb*** adeem, annex, appropriate, appropriate to public use, assume, attach, cause to be forfeited, compulsorily acquire, condemn, condemn to public use, deprive, deprive of, disentitle, disinherit, dispossess, disseise, distrain, divest, expropriate, foreclose, forfeit, impound, impress, levy, *publicare,* seize, seize and appropriate, seize as forfeited to the public treasury, seize by authority, sequester, sequestrate, take away from, take over, take possession of, take summarily, wrench away from, wrest away from, wring away from
ASSOCIATED CONCEPTS: condemn, eminent domain, exercise the right of

CONFISCATORY, ***adjective*** acquisitive, appropriating, attaching, capturing, commandeering, conquering, deprivative, depriving, disseizing, distraining, divesting, exacting, expropriatory, extortionary, foreclosing, forfeiting, garnishing, impounding, rapacious, requisitory, seizing, sequestrating, taking, usurpatory
ASSOCIATED CONCEPTS: confiscatory orders, confiscatory rates

CONFLAGRATION, ***noun*** blaze, bonfire, deflagration, destructive fire, devastation, devouring element, fire, general fire, *ignis,* incendiarism, *incendium,* sheet of flame, wall of flame, wholesale destruction, wildfire

CONFLATE, ***verb*** amalgamate, coalesce, combine, commingle, commix, composite, compound, conjoin, converge, fuse, homogenize, incorporate, inmix, integrate, lump together, meld, merge, mingle, mix, unify

CONFLICT, ***noun*** adverseness, affray, altercation, animosity, antagonism, antipathy, argument, argumentation, battle, belligerency, breach, challenge, clash, clash of arms, collision, combat, competition, conflict of opinion, contention, contentiousness, contest, contradiction, contraposition, contrariety, contrariness, contrast, contravention, controversy, corrivalry, counteraction, debate, defiance, difference, disaccord, disagreement, disapprobation, discord, discordance, discrepancy, disharmony, dislike, dispute, disputed point, dissension, dissent, dissidence, dissonance, disunion, disunity, divergence, divergent opinions, division, embroilment, encounter, engagement, enmity, faction, failure to agree, fight, fighting, firm opposition, friction, hatred, hostilities, hostility, incompatibility, incongruence, incongruity, inconsistency, infringement, inharmoniousness, inimicality, interference, irreconcilability, mismatch, misunderstanding, opposing causes, opposition, oppugnancy, polarity, quarrel, quarreling, question at issue, rencounter, renitency, resistance, rivalry, subject of dispute, tension, turmoil, unharmoniousness, variance, want of harmony, wrangle

ASSOCIATED CONCEPTS: center of gravity theory, conflict of interest, conflict of laws, conflicting clauses, conflicting evidence, conflicting findings, conflicting jurisdiction, conflicting provisions, irreconcilable conflict

CONFLICT, ***verb*** abIude, argue, be at cross purposes, be at variance, be contrary, be different, be discordant, be inconsistent, be inharmonious, be opposed, be opposed to, be unwilling, change, clash, collide, combat, come into collision, contend, contest, contradict, contrast, controvert, counteract, cross, debate, defy, depart from, deviate, differ, differ in opinion, disaccord, disagree, disapprove, *discrepare,* dislike, dispute, dissent, *dissentire,* divaricate, diverge from, go contrary to, go in opposition to, have differences, hinder, hold opposite views, interfere with, not abide, not accept, not conform, not have any part of, object, oppose, play at cross purposes, protest, quarrel, refute, *repugnare,* resist, revolt, rival, run against, run at cross purposes, run counter to, run in opposition to, schismatize, set oneself against, strike back, strive against, struggle, take exception, vary, wrangle

ASSOCIATED CONCEPTS: conflicting claim, conflicting clauses, conflicting evidence, conflicting findings, conflicting interests, conflicting jurisdiction, conflicting provisions

CONFLICT OF INTEREST, ***noun*** conflict, divergent interests between clients, ethical breach, prohibiting acceptance or retention of a case, variance of interest between clients

ASSOCIATED CONCEPTS: code of professional responsibility, disqualification

CONFLICT OF OPINION, ***noun*** animosity, antagonism, antipathy, battle, brawl, clash, combat, competition, completely different positions, conflict, conflicting opinions, conflicting views, contention, contest, controversy, difference, differences, disaccord, disagree, discord, disharmony, dishonorable conduct, dispute, disreputable conduct, dissension, dissent, dissention, disunity, division, emulation, enmity, fracas, fray, hostility, ill will, incompatibility, incongruity, not seeing eye to eye, opposition, rancor, rift, rivalry, schism, strife, struggle, tangle, to be at odds, two minds, two ways to look at the same issue, variance

ASSOCIATED CONCEPTS: canons of ethics, Chinese wall, ethical wall, professionalism

CONFLUENCE, ***noun*** amalgamation, combination, combining, conjunction, connecting, connection, consolidation, convergence, coupling, joining, junction, linking, meeting, merging, unification, union

CONFORM, ***verb*** abide by, accede, accept, acclimatize, accommodate, accord, adapt, adhere to, adjust, agree, align, approve, arrive at terms, assimilate, attend to instructions, attune, be at one with, be in harmony, be in keeping, be regulated by, become like, become similar, bend, come round, comply, concede, concur, conventionalize, coordinate, correlate, correspond, equalize, fall in, fall into line, fit, fit in, follow, follow precedent, follow routine, go along with, join the majority, keep to, liken, make uniform, match, measure up to, obey, obey orders, obey regulations, obey rules, observe, observe discipline, *obtemperare,* reconcile, render accordant, side with, stand together, standardize, submit, suit, support, synchronize, systematize, tailor, yield, yield assent

ASSOCIATED CONCEPTS: conformed copies, conformed to the law

CONFORMITY *(Agreement),* ***noun*** accommodation, accord, accordance, acquiescence, adjustment, affinity, agreement, alliance, assent, coincidence, collaboration, combined operation, compatibility, concert, concinnity, concord, concurrence, concurrent opinion, conformance, conformation, congeniality, congruence, congruency, congruity, conjunction, consensus, consent, consonance, *convenientia,* convention, cooperation, correspondence, harmony, joint effort, joint planning, league, likeness, oneness, similarity, uniformity, union

ASSOCIATED CONCEPTS: conformity in pleadings

CONFORMITY *(Obedience),* ***noun*** adherence, assimilation, association, close observance, compliance, conformance, conformation, consent, consistency, conventionality, dutifulness, faithfulness, fidelity, full observance, obeisance, observance, submission, submissiveness, subordination, willingness, yielding

CONFOUND, ***verb*** abash, astonish, astound, baffle, be uncertain, becloud, bewilder, bring into disorder, complicate, *confundere,* confuse, dumbfound, embrangle, embroil, entangle, involve, make havoc, mingle confusedly, mislead, muddle, mystify, nonplus, obfuscate, obscure, *per miscere,* perplex, put into disorder, puzzle, scramble, throw into confusion

CONFRONT *(Encounter),* ***verb*** accost, brave, breast, come across, come face to face with, come in contact, face, meet, stand facing, stand opposite

CONFRONT *(Oppose),* ***verb*** act in opposition to, argue against, assail, be against, be at cross-purposes, be opposite, challenge, come in conflict with, contend against, contend with, contradict, contrapose, contrast with, contravene, controvert, count against, counteract, counterattack, counterwork, cross, defy, deny, disagree with, disapprove, dispute, engage in conflict with, go against, mark against, match against, meet in conflict, object, offer resistance, oppugn, protest, put in opposition, rebuff, recalcitrate, repel, resist, rise against, rival, run counter, run

counter to, *se opponere,* set oneself against, skirmish, stand firm, stem, strike back, struggle, take exception to, turn against, wrangle, wrestle with
ASSOCIATED CONCEPTS: right of cross-examination, right to confront witnesses

CONFRONTATION *(Act of setting face to face),* ***noun*** act of facing, approach, audience, colloquy, coming together, conference, consultation, dialogue, discussion, encounter, engagement, interview, meeting, parley, rencounter
ASSOCIATED CONCEPTS: right of confrontation, right of cross-examination, right to confront witnesses

CONFRONTATION *(Altercation),* ***noun*** affray, argument, battle, bout, brawl, brush, clash, collision, combat, conflict, confrontment, contention, contestation, disagreement, discord, dispute, engagement, fight, fracas, fray, hostile contest, hostile encounter, *mêlée,* opposition, opposure, quarrel, rencounter, row, scuffle, skirmish, squabble, struggle, velitation, wrangle

CONFUSE *(Bewilder),* ***verb*** abash, addle, astonish, baffle, befog, befuddle, bemuddle, confound, *confundere,* daze, discompose, disconcert, distract, embarrass, flurry, fluster, fog, jumble, mislead, mix up, muddle, mystify, nonplus, obfuscate, *permiscere,* perplex, *perturbare,* puzzle, rattle, render uncertain, stump, stupefy, throw into confusion, unhinge, unsettle

CONFUSE *(Create disorder),* ***verb*** clutter, derange, disarrange, disarray, disorder, disorganize, displace, disturb, embroil, entangle, intermingle, jumble, mess, mess up, mingle, mix up, muddle, snarl, throw into confusion, throw into disorder, unsettle
ASSOCIATED CONCEPTS: mistake, mistake of fact, mistake of law

CONFUSION *(Ambiguity),* ***noun*** agitation, amorphousness, astonishment, brouhaha, complex, complexity, complication, confusion, congestion, convulsion, disarrangement, disarray, discomposure, dislocation, disorganization, distraction, doubt, enigma, ferment, fog, fracas, fuzziness, haze, hodgepodge, imbroglio, intricacy, involution, jumble, labyrinth, maze, melee, mix-up, opacity, panic, paraphrenia, patchwork, perplexity, rumpus, scramble, skein, stupefaction, to-do, tumult, turbulence, uncertainty, uproar, vagueness
ASSOCIATED CONCEPTS: confusion of goods, confusion of issues, confusion of rights

CONFUSION *(Commotion),* ***noun*** chaos, dilemma, disorder, disturbance, embroilment, entanglement, havoc, imbroglio, irregularity, medley, muddle, pandemonium, shambles, snarl, tangle, turmoil

CONFUSION *(Consternation),* ***noun*** befuddlement, chagrin, confoundment, disconcertion, disorientation, distress, fear, fluster, fright, mortification, mystification, perturbation, quandary, suffusion, trepidation

CONFUSION *(Turmoil),* ***noun*** anarchy, chaos, clamor, clutter, commotion, complexity, *confusio,* congestion, demoralization, difficulty, disarrangement, disarray, discord, disorder, disorderliness, disorganization, disquiet, disquietude, distraction, disturbance, entanglement, farrago, ferment, frenzy, havoc, imbroglio, inseparable intermixture, muddle, pandemonium, *perturbatio,* rampage, shapelessness, tumult, turbulence, unrest, unsettlement, upheaval, uproar

CONFUTATION, ***noun*** abjurement, challenge, condemnation, contradiction, contrariety, contrary assertion, contravention, countercharge, counterevidence, counterstatement, disavowal, disproof, effective rejoinder, evidence against, evidence on the other side, negation, plea in rebuttal, rebuttal, rebutter, redargution, refutation, rejoinder, renunciation, reply, repudiation, retort, surrejoinder

CONFUTE, ***verb*** answer, argue, challenge, confound, contradict, contravene, controvert, counter, counteract, countercharge, countervail, debate, defeat, demolish, deny, disagree, disavow, disown, disprove, dispute, dissent, fight, gainsay, impeach, impugn, invalidate, negate, oppose, parry, quash, quibble, rebut, refute, reply, repudiate, retort, riposte, set aside, squelch, subvert, upset, vanquish
ASSOCIATED CONCEPTS: confute a witness's testimony

CONGEALMENT, ***noun*** act of hardening, coagulation, cohesion, compactness, concreteness, concretion, condensation, congelation, consistence, consolidation, crystallization, gelatinization, gelling, hardness, impenetrability, impermeability, incompressibility, indivisibility, jellification, petrification, precipitation, solidification, solidity, solidness, thickening, thickness

CONGLOMERATE, ***adjective*** accumulated, agglomerate, aggregate, amalgamated, amassed, assembled, blended, brought together, collected, collectivized, combined, complex, composite, compound, compounded, congregate, congregated, cumulated, gathered into a round mass, glomerate, indiscriminate, inseparable, mass, mingled, miscellaneous, mixed, united, varied

CONGLOMERATION, ***noun*** accumulation, agglomeration, aggregate, aggregation, amassment, array, assembly, assortment, collection, compilation, consolidation, cumulation, forgathering, glomeration, group, ingathering, lot, mass, miscellany, multitude, quantity

CONGREGATE, ***verb*** accumulate, aggregate, aggroup, amass, assemble, bring together, bring together in a crowd, bunch, cluster, collect, collect into a focus, come in contact, come together, compile, concentrate, conglomerate, con*gregari,* convene, converge, convocate, crowd together, gather, get together, group, herd together, ingather, join, mass, meet, meet in a body, rally, receive, throng, unite
ASSOCIATED CONCEPTS: breach of the peace, congregate in a public place

CONGREGATION, ***noun*** aggregate, aggregation, amassment, assemblage, assembly, assembly of persons, association, audience, batch, *coetus,* collection, conclave, conference, congregated body, convention, *conventus,* convergence, convocation, crowd, forgathering, gathering, getting together, horde, ingathering, mass, mass meeting, meeting, multitude, reunion, session

CONGRESS, ***noun*** advisory body, assemblage, assembly, consultive body, council, governmental body, legislative body, legislature, political body

CONGRUENCE, ***noun*** accord, accordance, acquiescence, adjustment, affinity, agreement, coherence, coincidence, common feature, compatibility, compliance, concert, concordance, conformance, conformity, congeniality, congruity, consensus, consistency, correspondence, harmony, identification, likeness, oneness with, parallelism, relevance, resemblance, similarity, understanding, uniformity, unison, unity

CONGRUOUS, ***adjective*** accordant, acquiescent, adapted, agreeable, agreed, akin, analogical, analogous, applicable, apposite, appropriate, assenting, coexistent, coexisting, coincident, coinciding, combining, commendable, commensurate, compatible, concordant, concurrent, conformable, conforming, congruent, consensual, consentaneous, consentient, consistent with, consonant, consubstantial, correlative, correspondent, corresponding, equal, equivalent, fit, fitting, germane, harmonious, harmonized, identified with, in accord, in accordance with, in harmony with, in point, in rapport, in unison with, like, matching, near, parallel, proportional, proportionate, reconcilable, relevant, representative, representing, resembling, similar, similative, suiting, synchronized, synchronous, synonymous

CONJECTURAL, ***adjective*** abstract, allusive, apparent, assumed, circumstantial, debatable, disputable, doubtful, hypothetical, ideal, imagined, impractical, notional, postulated, presumptive, propositional, putative, referential, reputed, speculative, speculatory, suppositional, suppositive, surmised, theoretical, uncertain, undetermined, unsettled
ASSOCIATED CONCEPTS: conjecture as an objection to a witness's testimony

CONJECTURE, ***noun*** assumption, belief, guess, guesswork, hypothesis, imputation, inference, opinion, postulate, postulation, presumption, presupposition, presurmise, speculation, supposal, supposition, surmise, suspicion, theory, thesis, unverified supposition
FOREIGN PHRASES: ***In claris non est locus conjecturis.*** In matters which are obvious, there is no room for conjecture.

CONJOIN, ***verb*** accumulate, add, add to, ally, amass, annex, assemble, attach, be joined, blend, bring together, cement, clap together, clasp together, coalesce, cohere, collect, combine, compound, connect, consolidate, entwine, fuse, gather, hold together, incorporate, interlace, interlock, intertwist, interweave, join together, make one, mass, merge, mix, reunite, unify, unite
ASSOCIATED CONCEPTS: conjoint legacy, conjoint robbery, conjoint wills

CONJOINT, ***adjective*** affiliated, affixed, agreed, allied, amalgamated, assimilated, associated, attached, banded together, blended, bound together, cemented, coalescent, coalitional, cohesive, collective, combined, common, commutual, compact, compatible, composite, concerted, concomitant, concurrent, confederate, confederated, congruent, conjunct, conjunctive, connected, consolidated, corporate, coupled, coworking, *en rapport,* fastened together, federated, federative, fused, in alliance, in common, in conjunction, in league, incorporated, indivisible, inseparable, integrated, interclasped, interdependent, interfused, intermixed, joined, joined together, joint, leagued, linked, locked, merged, mixed, paired, partnered, pieced together, pooled, reciprocally attached, spliced, tied together, together, unified, united, wedded, welded
ASSOCIATED CONCEPTS: conjoint legacy, conjoint robbery, conjoint wills

CONJUGAL, ***adjective*** betrothed, bridal, coniugalis, conjugate connubial, coupled, espoused, marital, married, matched, mated, matrimonial, nuptial, paired, partnered, united, wedded
ASSOCIATED CONCEPTS: conjugal rights

CONJUNCT, ***adjective*** allied, amalgamated, associated, binding, coadunate, coalescent, coherent, cohesive, combined, complex, composite, concerted, conjoint, connected, consensual, consolidated, contiguous, cooperative, correlative, incorporated, indissoluble, indivisible, inextricile, inseparable, integrated, joined, joint, matched, merged, paired, partnered, participant, symbiotic, unified, united
ASSOCIATED CONCEPTS: conjunctive denials, conjunctive obligations, conjunctive of averments, conjunctive relief
FOREIGN PHRASES: ***Conjunctim et divisim.*** Jointly and severally.

CONJUNCTION, ***noun*** adjacency, agreement, alliance, association, compliance, concatenation, concert, concomitance, concord, concurrence, concurrent opinion, conformity, conjoining, connection, cooperation, harmony, joint effort, junction, network, union, united action

CONJURE, ***verb*** call to mind, conceive, conceptualize, contemplate, create, devise, dream up, envisage, *excogitare,* excogitate, fabricate, fancy, *fingere,* form an image, formulate, frame, give play to the imagination, have a vision, imagine, improvise, invent, *machinari,* make up, nurture, originate, perceive, produce, realize, represent to oneself, think of, think up, visualize
ASSOCIATED CONCEPTS: conjure up a cause of action

CONJURE UP, ***verb*** call to mind, conceive, create, devise, dream, envisage, envision, evoke, excogitate, fancy, ideate, imagine, invent, invoke, objectify, occur, picture, recall, recollect, remember, summon, summon up, visualize

CONNECT *(Join together),* ***verb*** *adligare,* amalgamate, annex, append, assemble, attach, band, band together, bind, blend, bridge, bring in contact with, cement, coalesce, cohere, combine, conjoin, *connectere,* consolidate, couple, entwine, fasten together, fuse, gather, graft, harness together, hook, hyphenate, interlink, interlock, intertwine, interweave, *iungere,* join, knit, lace, league, link together, lock, marry, match, meet, merge, pair, partner, put together, solder, subjoin, tie, touch, unite, verge on, wed

CONNECT *(Relate),* ***verb*** affiliate, ally, appertain to, associate, bracket, bridge, cohere, consociate, correlate, draw a parallel, group, integrate, interconnect, interrelate, link together, make relevant, match, pertain to, relate, show a relationship, show affinity, show as cognate, show as kindred, show relation, show resemblance, show similarity, span
ASSOCIATED CONCEPTS: connect the suspect to the crime

CONNECTED *(Affiliated),* ***adjective*** affinitive, allied, amalgamated, apposite, appurtenant, attached, bracketed, coadunate, cognate, coherent, communicating, compact, confederate, congenerous, congenial, conjoint, connatural, consanguineous, consecutive, consolidated, contiguous, continual, continuous, corporate, coupled, federate, germane, homogenous, inseparable, joined, kindred, knit, leagued, related, spliced, unbroken, undivided, united
ASSOCIATED CONCEPTS: connected causes of action, connected counterclaims, connected subjects contained in a bill

CONNECTED *(Apropos),* ***adjective*** akin, applicable, appropriate, associated, collateral, combined, consonant, continued, correlative, linked, pertinent, relevant, uninterrupted

CONNECTION *(Abutment),* ***noun*** abuttal, border, contact, contiguousness, junction, juxtaposition, nearness, tangency, union

CONNECTION *(Fastening),* ***noun*** attachment, binder, bond, bridge, catch, catenation, cohesion, combination, concatenation, conjunction, consolidation, copula, couple, fastener, hitch, holdfast, interconnection, joiner, joint, junction, juncture, knot, liaison, ligature, link, linkage, nexus, splice, tie, unifier, union

CONNECTION *(Relation),* ***noun*** affiliation, alliance, analogy, applicability, application, association, bearing, coalition, coherence, coherency, common denominator, common reference, consanguinity, consociation, correlation, identification, interrelation, kinship, league, liaison, link, linkage, match, parallel, pertinence, propinquity, rapport, reference, relatedness, relationship, relevance, tie
ASSOCIATED CONCEPTS: connection between a suspect and a crime

CONNIVANCE, ***noun*** act of maneuvering, act of scheming, alliance, association, chicanery, coagency, coincidence, collaboration, collusion, combined operation, complicity, complot, concert, concord, concurrence, concurrent opinion, confederacy, conjunction, conspiracy, contrivance, cooperation, corrupt agreement, corrupt collusion, corrupt consent, corrupt consenting, corrupt cooperation, implied assent, *indulgentia,* intrigue, joint effort, joint planning, junction, league, liaison, machination, manipulation, participation, plot, scheme, secret approval, underhand participation, underhanded complicity, underplot, voluntary oversight, working together
ASSOCIATED CONCEPTS: connivance as a defense to a divorce

CONNIVE, ***verb*** act in concert, be a party to, be in collusion with, collude, combine, complot, concert, conspire, cooperate, cooperate with secretly, countermine, counterplot, engineer, *in re connivere,* intrigue, join forces, join with, machinate, make an agreement with, maneuver, participate, participate surreptitiously, plot, *rem dissimulare,* scheme

CONNOTATION, ***noun*** allusion, application, bearing, broad meaning, coloring, comprehension, construction, context, denotation, derivation, drift, essence, essential meaning, expression, force, general meaning, gist, hint, idea, impact, implication, import, inference, information, innuendo, insinuation, intent, intention, interpretation, literal interpretation, literal meaning, literal sense, literality, meaning, natural meaning, object, obvious interpretation, obvious meaning, obvious sense, original meaning, plain meaning, point of, primary meaning, purport, range of meaning, real interpretation, real meaning, real sense, reference, scope, secondary implied meaning, sense, significance, signification, simple meaning, source, spirit, substance, substantial meaning, suggestion, symbolization, tenor, true meaning, unstrained meaning, worth

CONNOTE, ***verb*** allude to, carry a suggestion, communicate, convey, denote, designate, evidence, express, give indirect information, hint, imply, indicate, infer, insinuate, intimate, involve, make indirect suggestion, mean, point to, refer to, represent, signify, speak of, stand for, suggest, symbolize, tell of, touch on

CONQUER, ***verb*** annihilate, beat, best, better, circumvent, control, crush, defeat, discomfit, dominate, foil, humble, master, outdo, outrival, outwit, overcome, overpower, overthrow, prevail, quash, quell, subdue, subject, subjugate, subordinate, surmount, transcend, triumph over, upend, vanquish, whip, win

CONSANGUINEOUS, ***adjective*** affiliated, agnate, akin, allied, ancestral, blood-related, closely allied, closely related, cognate, collateral, congenerous, connatural, consanguine, distantly related, family related, fraternal, hereditary, intimately related, kindred, maternal, matrilineal, nearly allied, nearly related, of the blood, of the same family, of the same kind, paternal, patriarchal, patrilinear, related, relative
ASSOCIATED CONCEPTS: lineal consanguinity

CONSCIENCE, ***noun*** categorical imperative, code of duty, code of honor, compunction, *conscientia,* conscientiousness, ethical judgment, ethical philosophy, ethical self, ethics, high ideals, high standards, honesty, honor, ideals, inner voice, integrity, inward monitor, mind, moral consciousness, moral faculty, moral obligation, moral principles, moral sense, principle, probity, professional ethics, rectitude, scruples, sense of duty, sense of moral right, sense of right and wrong, standards, superego, uprightness
ASSOCIATED CONCEPTS: conscientious objector
FOREIGN PHRASES: ***Fides est obligatio conscientiae alicujus ad intentionem alterius.*** A trust is an obligation of conscience of one to the will of another. ***Judex habere debet duos sales–sales, salem sapientiae, ne sit insipidus; et salem conscientiae, ne sit diabolus*.** A judge ought to have two salts—the salt of wisdom, lest he be insipid; and the salt of conscience, lest he be devilish. ***La conscience est la plus changeante des regles.*** Conscience is the most changeable of rules.

CONSCIENTIOUS, ***adjective*** assiduous, attentive, careful, diligent, duteous, dutiful, exacting, faithful, fastidious, heedful, honest, honorable, incorruptible, just, meritorious, meticulous, minute, moral, observant, painstaking, particular, precise, principled, punctilious, regardful, reliable, *religiosus,* reputable, righteous, *sanctus,* scrupulous, strict, thorough, trustworthy, trusty, uncorrupt, upright, virtuous

CONSCIOUS, ***adjective*** alert, apprehending, aware, calculated, cautious, cognizant, considered, designed, direct, exacting, expected, explicit, heedful, informed, intentional, knowing, meant, mindful, observant, on purpose, open-eyed, perceiving, perceptive, planned, prearranged, predetermined, premeditated, promised, proposed, purposed, purposeful, regardful, sensible, sentient, set, Sophic, studied, supraliminal, vigilant, voluntary, watchful, willful, witting

CONSCIOUS *(Awake),* ***adjective*** able to recognize, active, acute, alert, alive, animate, astir, breathing, endowed with life, enlivened, existent, existing, extant, imbued with life, in existence, inspirited, live, living, mortal, vivified

CONSCIOUS *(Aware),* ***adjective*** acquainted with, apperceptive, appreciative, apprehending, apprised, attentive, cognizant, comprehending, *conscius,* discerning, heedful, informed, knowing, mindful, observant, perceptive, percipient, rational, regardful, sensible, sentient, undeceived, understanding, vigilant, watchful

ASSOCIATED CONCEPTS: conscious act, conscious disregard for others, conscious indifference, conscious reaction

CONSECUTIVE, ***adjective*** chronological, coming after, connected, consequent, *continens,* continual, continuing, continuous, cumulative, ensuing, following in a series, in a line, in a row, in order, in regular order, in sequence, in turn, in unbroken sequence, in uninterrupted succession, nonstop, one after another, one after the other, perennial, recurrent, repeated, repetitive, running, sequent, sequential, serial, serialized, seriate, seriatim, steady, subsequent, succeeding, successive, unbroken, uninterrupted, uninterrupted in course, unremitting

ASSOCIATED CONCEPTS: consecutive sentences

CONSENSUAL, ***adjective*** accordant, acquiesced in, acquiescent, agreeable, agreed upon, approving, assented, at one with, attuned to, carried, coherent, coincident with, collaborating, compatible, compliant, conceded, concomitant, concordant, concurred in, concurrent, confirming, conforming to, congruent, conjunct, consentaneous, consentient, consistent with, cooperative, endorsed, granted, harmonious, harmonized, in agreement, in alliance, joint, like-minded, mutually agreeable, mutually understood, of one accord, of one mind, of the same mind, parallel, popularly believed, reconciled, sympathetic, synergic, unanimous, unchallenged, uncontested, uncontradicted, uncontroversial, uncontroverted, understood, undisputed, united, unopposed, unquestioned, voted

CONSENSUS, ***noun*** acclamation, accord, acknowledgment, affirmance, affirmation, agreement, assonance, attonement, bipartisanship, common consent, compact, compatibility, concent, concentus, concert, concinnity, concord, concordance, concurrence, conformance, conformation, conformity, congruence, consentaneity, consentaneousness, consentience, consistency, consonance, cooperation, correspondence, general agreement, harmony, mutual agreement, mutual sympathy, mutual understanding, reconcilement, solid vote, synchronization, unanimity, uniformity, union, unison

ASSOCIATED CONCEPTS: consensus of opinion, per curiam opinion

CONSENT, ***noun*** accedence, acceptance, accord, acknowledgment, acquiescence, admission, adoption, affirmance, affirmation, agreement, allowance, approbation, approval, assent, assurance, authentication, authority, authorization, certification, commendation, compliance, concession, concord, concordance, concurrence, confirmation, *consensus,* corroboration, countenance, empowering, endorsement, entitlement, grace, grant, guarantee, harmony, indulgence, leave, legalization, license, permission, permit, ratification, sanction, stipulation, subscription, sufferance, support, tolerance, toleration, unison, unity, validation, verification, vouchsafement, warrant, warranty, willingness

ASSOCIATED CONCEPTS: consent decree, consent in writing, consent judgment, consent of adoptive parents, consent of owner, consent of parties, consent to a taking, consent to an act, consent to search, express consent, implied consent, legal consent, limited consent, mutual consent, parental consent, qualified consent, removal of an action by consent, voluntary consent, without consent

FOREIGN PHRASES: ***Consensus non concubitus facit nuptias vel matrimonium et consentire non possunt ante annos nubiles.*** Consent, not cohabitation, constitutes nuptials or marriage, and persons cannot consent before marriageable years. ***Consensus voluntas multorum ad quos res pertinet, simul juncta.*** Consent is the united will of several interested in one subject matter. ***Consentientes et aqentes pari poena plectentur.*** Persons who consent and those who perform are subject to the same penalties. ***Longa patientia trahitur ad consensum.*** Long sufferance is construed as consent. ***Itelius estomnia mala pati quam malo consentire.*** It is better to suffer every ill than to consent to evil. ***Nihil consensui tam controrium est quam vis atque metus.*** Nothing is as much opposed to consent as force and fear. ***Non consentit qui errat.*** He who makes a mistake does not consent. ***Non refert an quis assensum suum praefert verbis aut rebus ipsis et factis.*** It matters not whether a man gives his consent by his words or by his acts and deeds. ***Non videntur qui errant consentire.*** Those who err are not deemed to consent. ***Non videtur consensum retinuisse si quis ex praescripto minantis aliquid immutavit.*** He does not appear to have retained consent who has changed anything through menaces. ***Nuptias non cuncubitus sed consensus facit.*** Not cohabitation but consent makes the marriage. ***Omne jus aut consensus fecit, aut necessitas constituit aut firmavit consuetudo.*** Consent created, necessity established, or custom has confirmed every law. ***Omnis consensus tollit errorem.*** Every consent removes error. ***Qui tacet, consentire videtur.*** He who is silent, is deemed to consent. ***Actus me invito factus non est meus actus.*** An act done against my will is not my act. ***Agentes et consentientes pari poena plectentur.*** Acting and consenting parties are liable to the same punishment. ***Consensus est voluntas plurium ad quos res pertinet, simul juncta.*** Consent is the conjoint will of several persons to whom the thing belongs. ***Consensus facit legem.*** Consent makes the law. ***Consensus tollit errorem.*** Consent removes or obviates mistake. ***Quod meum est sine me auferri non potest.*** What is mine cannot be taken away without my consent. ***Volenti non fit injuria.*** He who consents cannot receive an injury.

CONSENT, ***verb*** accede, accept, accord, acquiesce, *adsentire,* affirm, agree, allow, approve, assent, authorize, be in favor of, be willing, come to terms, comply, concur, *consentire,* endorse, give approval, give consent, give permission, grant, gratify, have no objection, indicate willingness, license, permit, ratify, sanction, suffer, support, tolerate, warrant, yield

ASSOCIATED CONCEPTS: consent to an adjournment, consent to jurisdiction

CONSENT DECREE, ***noun*** an order accepted by the parties, an order acquiesced by the parties, an order agreed to by the parties, an order approved by the parties, an order consented to by the parties, an order endorsed by the parties, an order supported by the parties, an order with the accord of the parties, consent order

ASSOCIATED CONCEPTS: consent rule

CONSENT ORDER, ***noun*** an order accepted by the parties, an order acquiesced by the parties, an order agreed to by the parties, an order approved by the parties, an order consented to by the parties, an order endorsed by the parties, an order supported by the parties, an order with the accord of the parties, consent decree

ASSOCIATED CONCEPTS: consent rule

CONSENTING, ***adjective*** accommodating, accordant, acquiescent, acquiescing, agreeable, agreeing, allowing, approving, assentient, assenting, assentive, compliable,

compliant, concordant, consentaneous, consentient, favorably inclined, in accord, in agreement, in harmony with, inclined to assent, likeminded, marked by consent, of one accord, permitting, voluntary, willing, yielding
ASSOCIATED CONCEPTS: abetting, consenting to be adjudged a bankrupt, permitting, ratifying

CONSEQUENCE *(Conclusion),* ***noun*** aftereffect, aftergrowth, aftermath, climax, completion, conclusion, *consecutio,* consummation, culmination, decision, deduction, denouement, derivation, derivative, determination, development, effect, emanation, ensual, eventuality, execution, final result, finale, finding, finish, fruition, illation, induction, logical result, offshoot, outcome, outgrowth, product, reaction, resolution, response, result, resultant action, settlement, upshot, verdict
ASSOCIATED CONCEPTS: consequential benefits, consequential contempt, consequential contracts, consequential damages, consequential injuries, consequential loss
FOREIGN PHRASES: ***Consuetudo non trahitur in conseqentiam.*** Custom is not drawn into consequence. ***Non officit conatus nisi sequatur effectus.*** An attempt does not harm unless a consequence follows. ***Officit conatus si effectus sequatur.*** The attempt becomes of consequence if the effect follows.

CONSEQUENCE *(Significance),* ***noun*** accent, *auctoritas,* base, basis, core, distinction, effect, essence, essential quality, force, germ, heart, import, importance, influence, magnitude, marrow, materialness, meaning, merit, nature, notable feature, nucleus, point, primary element, principle, prominence, purport, quintessence, relevance, self-consequence, self-importance, seriousness, signification, soul, substance, usefulness, vital part

CONSEQUENTIAL *(Deducible),* ***adjective*** derivative, following, inferential, resultant, sequential
ASSOCIATED CONCEPTS: consequential contempt, consequential damages

CONSEQUENTIAL *(Substantial),* ***adjective*** authoritative, considerable, eminent, great, important, influential, momentous, powerful, self-important, significant, weighty

CONSEQUENTIALISM, ***noun*** an ethical theory, assessment based on the consequences of conduct, assessment based on the impact of conduct, assessment based on the outcome or by-product of conduct, judgment based on the outcome, judgment based on the results of conduct

CONSEQUENTLY, ***adverb*** accordingly, as a consequence, as a matter of course, as a result, as matters stand, as the case may be, because, by reason of, by the same sign, by the same token, *ergo,* finally, for reasons given, for that cause, for that reason, for this reason, for which reason, from that cause, hence, *igitur,* in accordance therefore, in conclusion, in that case, in that event, in which case, it follows that, *itaque,* logically then, naturally, necessarily, of course, of necessity, on account of this, on that account, on this account, such being the case, that being so, that being the case, therefore, thus, thusly, to that end, under the circumstances, wherefore

CONSERVATION, ***noun*** economy, fostering, guarding, harboring, keeping, maintaining, maintenance, nourishing, nursing, preservation, preserving, protecting, protection, providing sanctuary, safeguarding, safekeeping, saving, sheltering, shielding, sparing, storage, support, sustaining, sustentation, upholding, upkeep
ASSOCIATED CONCEPTS: conservation of assets, conservation of property

CONSERVATIVE READING, ***noun*** accurate meaning, correct meaning, defined meaning, definition, distinct meaning, exact meaning, explanation, explicit meaning, express meaning, faithful meaning, inflexible meaning, literal meaning, methodical meaning, meticulous meaning, narrow meaning, not subject to interpretation, ordinary meaning, plain meaning, precise meaning, prescribed meaning, rigid meaning, rigorous meaning, sharply defined, significance, specific meaning, strict meaning, unbending meaning, uncompromising meaning, unequivocal meaning
ASSOCIATED CONCEPTS: construction, literal contract, literal proof plain meaning rule, rules of statutory, soft plain meaning rule, textualism

CONSERVE, ***verb*** avoid using, expend gradually, expend slowly, guard, keep, keep from loss, keep in existence, keep safe, keep unimpaired, maintain, omit using, preserve, prolong, protect, refrain from using, refuse to waste, safeguard, save, save from loss, secure, *servare,* shield, spare, store up, sustain, treasure, use carefully, use frugally, use sparingly, use thriftily

CONSIDER, ***verb*** advert to, analyze, appraise, assess, be attentive, cerebrate, cogitate, confer, *considerare,* consult, contemplate, debate, deliberate, devote attention to, digest, evaluate, examine, *expendere,* gauge, heed, inspect, investigate, mark, meditate on, mull over, muse, notice, observe, pay attention to, ponder, pore over, probe, reckon, reflect upon, regard, *respicere,* ruminate, scrutinize, study, take into account, think about, turn over in one's mind, weigh
ASSOCIATED CONCEPTS: adjudge, consider on its merits

CONSIDERABLE, ***adjective*** abundant, ample, cardinal, commanding, compelling, consequential, dominant, estimable, a good deal of, *gravis,* great, important, impressive, influential, large, *magnus,* marked, material, momentous, not to be overlooked, notable, noteworthy, of importance, of note, overruling, plentiful, potent, powerful, predominant, puissant, reasonable, remarkable, respectable, significant, sizable, special, substantial, tolerable, valuable, worthy of consideration
ASSOCIATED CONCEPTS: considerable damage, considerable provocation, considerable time

CONSIDERATE, ***adjective*** accommodating, affectionate, amiable, attentive, benevolent, caring, charitable, chivalrous, compassionate, complaisant, concerned, cooperate, cordial, decent, discreet, fair, favorable, friendly, generous, humane, keen, kind, kindly, magnanimous, mindful, nice, obliging, patient, philanthropic, polite, responsive, sensitive, solicitous, supportive, sympathetic, tactful, tender, thoughtful, understanding, unselfish, warm-hearted

CONSIDERATION *(Contemplation),* ***noun*** advertency, advisement, attention, attentiveness, cogitation, *consideratio,* examination, forethought, heed, judgment, meditation, pondering, premeditation, reckoning, reflection, review, rumination, serious thought, speculation, study
ASSOCIATED CONCEPTS: due consideration

CONSIDERATION *(Recompense),* ***noun*** accommodation, benefits, bounty, compensation, defrayment, disbursement, emolument, fees, financial assistance, gratuity, guerdon, incentive, indemnification, indemnity, inducement, largess, payment, pecuniary aid, prize, reckoning, refund, reimbursement, remittance, remuneration, reparation, repayment, requital, restitution, return, reward, satisfaction, settlement, solatium, something of value, stipend, subsidy, sum

ASSOCIATED CONCEPTS: adequate consideration, collateral consideration, complete failure of consideration, consideration for a contract, due consideration, failure of consideration, fair and valuable consideration, fictitious consideration, founded on a consideration, fraud in consideration, full and adequate consideration, good and sufficient consideration, illegal consideration, illusory consideration, immoral consideration, lack of consideration, legal consideration, meritorious consideration, moral consideration, mutual consideration, new consideration, nominal consideration, partial failure of consideration, past consideration, pecuniary consideration, present consideration, sufficiency of consideration, valid consideration, want of consideration

FOREIGN PHRASES: ***Ex turpi causa non oritur actio.*** No cause of action arises out of an immoral or illegal consideration. ***In omnibus contractibus, sive nominatis sive innominatis, permutatio continetur.*** In all contracts, whether nominate or innominate, there is implied an exchange. ***L'obligation sans cause, ou sur une fausse cause, ou sur cause illicite, ne peut avoir aucun effet.*** An obligation without consideration, or with a false one, or with an unlawful one, cannot have any effect. ***Nuda pactio obligationem non parit.*** A naked promise does not create a binding obligation. ***Nudum pactum est ubi nulla subest causa praeter conventionem; sed ubi subest causa, fit obligatio, et parit actionem.*** A naked contract is where there is no consideration for the undertaking or agreement; but where there is a consideration, an obligation is created, and an action arises. ***Pacta quae turpem causam continent non sunt observanda.*** Agreements founded upon an immoral consideration are not to be enforced.

CONSIDERATION *(Sympathetic regard),* ***noun*** accommodation, attentiveness, beneficence, benevolence, benignity, care, chivalry, civility, clemency, compassion, complaisance, concern, considerateness, cordiality, courteousness, courtesy, courtliness, deference, delicacy, diplomacy, esteem, estimation, friendliness, gallantry, generosity, geniality, gentleness, good manners, graciousness, helpfulness, humanity, kindheartedness, kindliness, kindness, mercy, neighborliness, obligingness, politeness, regard, respect, solicitousness, solicitude, tact, tenderness, thought, thoughtful regard, thoughtfulness, understanding, unselfishness, willingness to please

CONSIGN, ***verb*** abalienate, assign to, authorize, charge, commit, commit to another's trust, *committere,* convey, deliver, deliver formally, deliver over, deposit with, entrust, give in trust, hand over, have conveyed, send, ship, transfer, transfer for sale, transmit, transplant, transport, turn over

ASSOCIATED CONCEPTS: bailment, conditional sale, consignment contract of goods

CONSIGNMENT, ***noun*** allocation, allotment, appropriation, assignation, assignment, cession, concession, consignation, conveyance, conveyancing, delivering to, dispatchment, distribution, expressage, goods shipped, interchange, merchandise sent, sending, shipment, shipping, transfer, transference, transferring, transmission

ASSOCIATED CONCEPTS: consignment for sale, consignment shipper

CONSIST, ***verb*** add up to, amount to, be composed of, be comprised of, be contained in, be formed of, be made of, be made up of, comprise, *consistere,* constitute, contain, cover, embody, encompass, enfold, entail, envelop, form, has as a component, have as its foundation, hold, in essence is, in nature is, in substance is, include, incorporate, involve, is composed of, is essentially, make up, occupy, synthesize

CONSISTENCY, ***noun*** abidingness, accuracy, adherence, allegiance, certainty, conformity, congruity, constancy, continuous, determination, devotion, doggedness, eagerness, earnestness, evenness, harmony, invariability, one and the same, orderliness, periodicity, precision, predictability, proportion, punctuality, recurrence, regularity, routine, same, smoothness, steadiness, symmetry, systematically, uniformity

CONSISTENT, ***adjective*** accordant, agreeing, alike, coherent, cohering, compatible, compliable, concordant, conformable, congruent with, congruous, consonant, *constans, conveniens,* correspondent, equable, equal, harmonious, logical, not contradictory, regular, self-consistent, unchanging, undeviating, uniform

ASSOCIATED CONCEPTS: consistent cases, consistent causes of action, consistent construction of sales contracts, consistent decisions, consistent defenses, consistent interpretation of the Constitution, consistent precedence, consistent with the public interest

CONSOCIATE, ***noun*** abettor, accessory, accomplice, adherent, adjunct, adjutant, aide, ally, assistant, associate, attendant, auxiliary, coadjutor, cohelper, cohort, collaborator, colleague, comate, companion, comrade, confederate, confidant, confrere, consort, cooperator, copartner, coworker, fellow companion, fellow conspirator, fellow worker, follower, helper, helpmate, intimate, mate, participator, partner, retainer, side-partner

ASSOCIATED CONCEPTS: accomplice

CONSOLIDATE *(Strengthen),* ***verb*** add to, amass, bind, blend, bring together, build up, coalesce, cohere, combine, compact, compound, compress, concatenate, concentrate, condense, congeal, conjoin, conjoint, connect, contract, crystallize, densify, fortify, fuse, harden, intensify, make firm, make solid, mass, mix, put together, render solid, settle firmly, solidify, squeeze together, unify

CONSOLIDATE *(Unite),* ***verb*** accumulate, affiliate, ally, amalgamate, amass, band, become one, bring together, centralize, coact, coadjuvate, coalesce, combine, compound, compress, concentrate, concert, confederate, congeal, conglomerate, conjoin, connect, cooperate, couple, cowork, draw together, federate, fuse, gather together, incorporate, interblend, interfuse, intertwine, join, join forces, join forces with, league, link, lump together, make one, meet, melt into one, merge, mix, mobilize, piece together, put together, roll into one, shade into, solidify, stay together, stick together, synthesize, unionize, work together

ASSOCIATED CONCEPTS: consolidate actions

CONSOLIDATION, ***noun*** affiliation, aggregation, amalgamation, assemblage, association, centralization, coadunation, combination, compact, confederation, conjunction, conjuncture, consortium, federation, fusion, incorporation, integration, junction, league, merger, mixture, pool, solidification, strengthening, unification, union

ASSOCIATED CONCEPTS: consolidated laws, consolidated school district, consolidation of actions, consolidation of stock

CONSONANCE, *noun* accord, accordance, agreement, assent, assonance, attunement, chorus, coherence, coincidence, compatibility, compliance, concert, conciliation, concord, concordance, concurrence, conformity, consensus, consistency, continuity, correspondence, equability, harmony, homogeneity, persistence, rapport, unanimity, uniformity, union, unison, unity

CONSONANT, *adjective* accordant, adapted, agreeing, alike, answerable, appropriate, apt, arranged, at one, attuned, balanced, becoming, coherent, coincident, commensurate, compatible, concerted, concordant, concurrent, conformable, conforming, congenial, *congruens,* congruent, congruous, consentaneous, consentaneus, consentient, consequent, consistent, *conveniens,* cooperating, correspondent, corresponding, equable, equal, fit, fitting, harmonious, in accord, in agreement, in concord, in harmony, in rapport, in unison, logically consistent, parallel, reconcilable, related, self-consistent, similar, suitable, synchronal, synchronized, unchangeable, unchanged, unchanging, undeviating, undiscordant, unified, uniform, unisonant, unisonous

CONSORT, *noun* accompanier, associate, colleague, comate, *comes,* companion, compeer, comrade, *confrère,* conjugal partner, copartner, escort, fellow, fellow companion, helpmate, husband, marital partner, *maritus,* marriage partner, mate, partner, *socius,* spouse, wife
ASSOCIATED CONCEPTS: alienation of affections, criminal conversation, loss of consortium

CONSORTIUM *(Business cartel),* ***noun*** association, business agreement, business combine, business entente, cartel, coalition, combination, combination of financial institutions, confederacy, consolidation, league, merger, monopoly, partnership, pool, syndicate, trust, union

CONSORTIUM *(Marriage companionship),* ***noun*** accommodation, affiliation, affinity, alliance, assistance, association, attachment, closeness, comfort, compact, companionship, compliance, comradeship, concordance, congruity, congruousness, consociation, consortship, correspondence, familiarity, friendship, help, intercommunion, intimacy, league, marriage accord, marriage compatibility, marriage concord, partnership, reciprocal feeling, understanding
ASSOCIATED CONCEPTS: loss of consortium

CONSPICUOUS, *adjective* apparent, *clarus,* clear, clear-*cut, conspicuus,* definite, discernible, discoverable, distinct, distinguishable, distinguished, evident, exposed, exposed to view, flagrant, in bold relief, in evidence, in plain sight, in the foreground, in view, manifest, *manifestus,* marked, notable, noticeable, notorious, observable, obvious, open, overt, patent, perceivable, perceptible, plain, pointed, preeminent, prominent, pronounced, public, recognizable, remarkable, renowned, self-evident, spectacular, standing out, striking, tending to attract attention, unblurred, unclouded, uncovered, undisguised, unhidden, unmistakable, visible, well-defined, well-marked, well-seen
ASSOCIATED CONCEPTS: conspicuous places

CONSPIRACY, *noun* abetment, abetting, acting in combination, acting in concert, acting in harmony, agreeing with another or others, agreement to accomplish an unlawful end, agreement to commit a crime, aiding another or others, an agreement with another or others, associate with another, banded together, coalescence, coalition, colluding together, collusion, combination, combination of operations, combine to perform a crime, combine to plan a crime, combine to plan an unlawful act, combine to plan secretly, combine together, combined operation, combining, combining for a criminal purpose, compact, compliance, complicity, composition, concert, confederacy, connivance, connive jointly, contrivance, contrive jointly, cooperation with, corrupt agreement, countermine, counterplot, criminal arrangement, design jointly, devise jointly, duplicitous agreement, in concert with, intrigue, intriguery, join forces with, join together with, joint effort, joint planning, maneuvering, plan, plot, plot together, proposal, scheme, scheme together, take part in a crime together, take part with another in crime, treasonable alliance, underplot, unlawful combination, unlawful contrivance, unlawful plan, unlawful scheme
ASSOCIATED CONCEPTS: conspiracy charges, conspiracy in restraint of interstate trade, conspiracy in restraint of trade, conspiracy to commit felony, conspiracy to defraud, conspiracy within the Scherman Antitrust Act, continuing conspiracy, criminal conspiracy, entered into a conspiracy, felony murder, furtherance of the conspiracy, overt act

CONSPIRATOR, *noun* abettor, colluder, complotter, confederate, coniuratus, conniver, deceiver, intrigant, intriguer, machinator, plotter, schemer, spy, strategist

CONSPIRE, *verb* abet, act in combination, act in concert, act in harmony, agree, aid, associate, be banded together, be stealthy, cabal, calculate, coact, cohere, collude, combine, combine for some evil design, combine operations, concert, concoct a plot, concur, confederate, confederate for an unlawful purpose, *coniurare,* conjoin, connive, *conspirare,* contribute toward, contrive, cooperate, countermine, counterplot, cowork, design, devise, devise treachery, form a coalition, form plots, frame, hatch a plot, hold together, intrigue, join, join forces, league together, league with, machinate, make an agreement with, make secret arrangements, maneuver, participate in an unlawful scheme, plan, plan a crime, plan an unlawful act, plan secretly, plan to commit a crime, plot, plot an action in advance, plot craftily, plot together, scheme, take part in, take part with, unify, unite
ASSOCIATED CONCEPTS: conspire to commit a crime, conspire to defraud the U.S. government

CONSPIRER, *noun* abettor, accessory, accessory after the fact, accessory before the fact, accomplice, accomplice in crime, adjutant, agent provocateur, aid, aider, aider and abettor, assistant, associate, coactor, coadjutant, coadjutor, cohelper, collaborationist, collaborator, colleague, colluder, confederate, consociate, conspirator, contriver, cooperator, counterpart, fellow conspirator, helper, helpmate, intrigant, intriguer, partner, partner in crime, planner, plotter, promoter, saboteur, schemer, strategist, subversive, traitor
ASSOCIATED CONCEPTS: accomplice

CONSTANCY, *noun* adherence, allegiance, application, attachment, backbone, constance, continuity, decision, determination, devotion, diligence, faithfulness, firmness, fortitude, grit, industry, loyalty, permanence, perpetuity, perseverance, persistence, regularity, reliability, resoluteness, resolution, steadfastness, steadiness, tenacity, uniformity

CONSTANT, *adjective* abiding, aeonian, certain, changeless, chronic, consistent, *constans,* continual, continually recurring, continuing, continuous, dependable, durable, endless, enduring, entrenched, eternal, faithful, firm, *firmus,* fixed, habitual, immortal, immutable, imperishable, inalterable, incessant, inconvertible, indeciduous, indelible, indestructible, indissoluble, inextinguishable, inflexible, invariable, invariant, inveterate, lasting, loyal, perdurable, perennial, permanent, perpetual, regular, reliable, sempiternal, *stabilis,* stable, steadfast, steady, sure, sustained, unchanging, undeviating, undying, unequivocal, uninterrupted, unrelenting, unshaken, unswerving, unvarying, unwavering

CONSTANT, *noun* certainty, conformity, consistency, constancy, *constans,* convention, firmness, *firmus,* fixation, form, immutability, inextricability, invariability, invariable, invariant, inveteracy, maxim, pattern, permanence, prescribed form, procedure, prototype, regularity, reliability, rule, sameness, *stabilis,* stability, standard, standard practice, standard procedure, staunchness, steadfastness, steadiness, symmetry, unchangeableness, uniformity

CONSTERNATION, *noun* affright, agitation, alarm, anxiety, anxious concern, anxiousness, apprehension, apprehensiveness, aversion, boding, despair, dismay, disquiet, disquietude, disturbance, dread, fear, fearfulness, fright, horror, inquietude, *pavor,* perturbation, sudden fear, trepidation

CONSTITUENCY, *noun* affiliates, associates, body of members, chapter, collective members, community, constituents, delegation, district, division, electorate, electors, enrollment, faction, group, interest group, lobby, members, membership, partisanship, party, polity, voters, voting district, voting list

CONSTITUENT *(Member),* ***noun*** associate, colleague, constituency, fellow resident, resident, resident of the same district, resident voter, voter

CONSTITUENT *(Part),* ***noun*** balloter, component, component part, division, element, *elementum,* factor, feature, fraction, fragment, included, ingredient, installment, integral part, integrant, integrant part, one of, *pars,* part, part and parcel, particle, piece, section, sector, segment, subdivision
ASSOCIATED CONCEPTS: constituent elements, constituent members, constituent parts

CONSTITUTE *(Compose),* ***verb*** be a feature, be inherent, be part of, belong, belong intrinsically, classify as, *componere,* comprise, consist of, contain, create, *efficere,* embody, embrace, encompass, form, include, incorporate, inhere in, involve, make up, produce, put together

CONSTITUTE *(Establish),* ***verb*** bring about, bring about by legislation, charter, codify, commission, create, create by law, declare lawful, decree, *designare,* determine, develop, devise, effect, effect by legislation, effectuate, empower, enact, endorse, engender, formulate, formulate by law, give legal form to, inaugurate, install, institute, invest, legalize, legislate, legitimate, legitimatize, legitimize, license, make legal, ordain, organize, originate, pass, prescribe, prescribe by law, put in force, sanction, set up, *statuere,* validate
ASSOCIATED CONCEPTS: constitute a cause of action, constitute a crime, constitute a fraud, constitute an obstruction
FOREIGN PHRASES: ***Eodem modo quo quid constituitur, dissolvitur.*** A thing is discharged in the same way in which it was created.

CONSTITUTION, *noun* act, body of law, body of rules of government, canon, charter, civil law, *civitatis,* code of laws, codification, codified law, collection of laws, compact to govern, compilation of law, dictate, edict, enactment, fundamental law, law, legal code, maxim, organic law, pandect, paramount law, precept, prescription, principles of government, regulation, rubric, statute, supreme law, written law
ASSOCIATED CONCEPTS: action arising under constitution or laws, amendment to the constitution, constitutional amendment, Constitutional Convention, constitutional court, constitutional officer, constitutional question, constitutional right

CONSTRAIN *(Compel),* ***verb*** actuate, apply pressure, assert oneself, bring about by force, bring pressure to bear upon, burden, cause to, charge, coerce, command, command influence, compel, *compellere,* decree, demand, dominate, drive, enforce, enforce obedience, exact, exert influence, force, goad, have influence, impel, impose, impose a duty, induce, insist, insist on, issue a command, leave no option, make necessary, move, move to action, necessitate, obligate, oblige, order, press, pressure, prevail upon, prod, propel, push, put pressure on, put under obligation, require, secure by force, squeeze, subject, take no denial, tell, urge, urge forward, work upon

CONSTRAIN *(Imprison),* ***verb*** arrest, bind, bridle, chain, circumscribe, commit, commit to an institution, commit to prison, confine, confine forcibly, detain, enclose, enthrall, entomb, harness, hold, hold as hostage, hold back by force, hold captive, hold in restraint, immure, impound, incarcerate, institutionalize, intern, isolate, jail, keep as captive, keep in custody, keep in detention, keep prisoner, limit, manacle, put in a cell, put under arrest, put under restraint, restrain, restrict, send to prison, shackle, take captive, take into custody, trammel

CONSTRAIN *(Restrain),* ***verb*** ban, bar, block, bridle, censor, chain, check, control, curb, debar, deny, disallow, forbid, hamper, harness, hinder, hold back, hold back by force, hold down, hold in, hold in check, impede, impose restrictions, inhibit, keep back, keep in check, lay under restraint, limit, obstruct, oppress, preclude, prevent, prohibit, proscribe, put a stop to, put under restraint, refuse, refuse to grant, repress, restrain, restrict, restrict access, subdue, subjugate, suppress, withhold

CONSTRAINT *(Imprisonment),* ***noun*** act of keeping in, apprehension, arrest, bondage, bonds, bounds, captivity, care, charge, commitment, confinement, containment, control, custodianship, custody, detainment, detention, encincture, enclosure, enthrallment, fetter, immuration, immurement, impoundment, incarceration, internment, keeping, legal restraint, preventive custody, preventive detention, prison, prohibition, protective custody, quarantine, remand, restriction

CONSTRAINT *(Restriction),* ***noun*** act of forestalling, act of hampering, act of quelling, act of stifling, act of strangling, act of thwarting, astriction, bar, circumscription, coercion, compulsion, constriction, curb, deprivation, detainment, determent, disallowance, disapprobation, duress, encumbrance, enthrallment, fetter, forbiddance, force, hindrance, impediment, inhibition, interdict, interdiction, limitation, muzzle, obstruction, obstructionism, preclusion, pressure, prevention, prohibition, proscription, rein, repression, restraint, restrictive practice, strangulation, stultification, suppression, temperance, trammel
ASSOCIATED CONCEPTS: estoppel

CONSTRICT *(Compress),* ***verb*** abbreviate, abridge, astringe, bind, capsulize, cause to contract, clench, coarct, compact, concentrate, condense, consolidate, constringe, contract, cram, cramp, crowd, crush, draw together, make brief, make dense, make smaller, narrow, pack tightly, pinch, press, press together, ram, reduce, reduce volume, restrict in area, shorten, shrink, squeeze, telescope, tighten

CONSTRICT *(Inhibit),* ***verb*** arrest, astrict, barricade, be an impediment, be an obstacle, block, check, choke, close, constrain, control, curb, dam, delay, detain, deter, estop, fetter, foil, frustrate, halt, hamper, handicap, hinder, hold back, impede, interfere, keep, keep back, limit, obstruct, occlude, rein in, repress, restrain, restrict, retard, set back, set limitations, set limits, slow, stall, staunch, stay, stem, stifle, stop, strangulate, stymie, suppress, thwart, tie up, withhold

CONSTRUCTION, ***noun*** clarification, comment, commentary, configuration, conformation, constitution, construability, construal, deduction, definability, definition, delineation, description, diagnosis, exegesis, exemplification, explanation, explicability, explication, exposition, expounding, form, formulation, frame, framework, illumination, inference, interpretability, *interpretatio,* interpretation, meaning, rationale, sense, significance, structure, substance, translation, understanding, version

ASSOCIATED CONCEPTS: construction of a contract, construction of a statute, construction of a writing, construction of will, contemporaneous construction, liberal construction, rule of construction, statutory construction, strict construction

FOREIGN PHRASES: ***Contemporanea expositio est optima et fortissima in lege.*** Contemporaneous exposition is the best and most powerful in the law. ***Quum in testamento ambigue aut etiam perperam scriptum est, benigne interpretari et secundum id quod credible et cogitatum, credendum est.*** When an ambiguous or even an erroneous expression occurs in a will, it should be construed liberally and in accordance with what is thought the probable meaning of the testator. ***Copulatio verborum indicat acceptationem in eodem sensu.*** The coupling of words indicates that they are to be taken in the same sense. ***Cum duo inter se pugnantia reperiuntur in testamento, ultimum ratum est.*** When two repugnant matters are found in a will, the last will be confirmed. ***Curiosa et captiosa interpretatio in lege reprobatur.*** A curious and captious interpretation is disapproved. ***Verbis standum ubi nulla ambiguitas.*** Where there is no ambiguity, one must abide by the words. ***Designatio unius est exclusio alterius, et expressum facit cessare tacitum.*** The designation of one is the exclusion of the other, and that which is expressed prevails over that which is implied. ***In ambigua voce legis ea potius accipienda est significatio quae vitio caret, praesertim cum etiam voluntas legis ex hoc colligi possit.*** In an ambiguous expression of law, that interpretation is to be preferred which is consonant with equity, especially where it is in conformity with the purpose of the law. ***Non aliter a significatione verborum recedi oportet quam cum manifestum est, aliud sensisse testatorem.*** The ordinary meaning of the words ought not to be departed from unless it is evident that the testator intended otherwise. ***Non est novum ut priores leges ad posteriores trahantur.*** It is not novel that prior statutes should give place to later ones. ***Non in legendo sed in intelligendo legis consistunt.*** The laws consist not in being read, but in being understood. ***Omnis definitio in lege periculosa.*** All definition in law is dangerous. ***Omnis interpretatio si fieri potest ita fienda est in instrumentis, ut omnes contrarietates amoveantur.*** Every interpretation of instruments is to be made, if they will admit of it, so that all contradictions may be removed. ***In ambiguo sermone non utrumque dicimus sed id duntaxat quod volumus.*** In ambiguous discourse, we do not use language in a double sense, but in the sense in which we mean it. ***Benedicta est expositio quando res redimitur a destructione.*** Blessed is the exposition when a thing is saved from destruction. ***Benignior sententia in verbis generalibus seu dubiis, est praeferenda.*** The more favorable construction is to be placed on general or doubtful expressions. ***Benignius leges interpretandae sunt quo voluntas earum conservetur.*** Laws are to be liberally construed in order that their intent may be preserved. ***Lex non exacte definit, sed arbitrio boni viri permittit.*** The law does not define exactly, but trusts to the judgment of a good man. ***Lex posterior derogat priori.*** A later statute takes away the effect of a prior one. ***Magis de bono quam de malo lex intendit.*** The law favors a good rather than a bad interpretation. ***Maledicta est expositio quae corrumpit textum.*** It is a cursed construction which corrupts the text. ***Mandata licita strictam recipiunt interpretationem, sed illicita latam et extensam.*** Lawful commands receive a strict interpretation, but unlawful commands a broad and extended one. ***Neque leges neque senatus consulta ita scribi possunt ut omnis casus qui quandoque in sediriunt comprehendatur; sed sufficit ea quae plaerumque accidunt contineri.*** Neither laws nor acts of a legislature can be so written as to include all actual or possible cases; it is sufficient if they provide for those things which frequently or ordinarily may happen. ***In stipulationibus cum quaeritur quid actum sit verba contra stipulatorem interpretanda sunt.*** In the construction of agreements words are interpreted against the person offering them. ***Omne majus minus in se complectitur.*** Every greater thing embraces within itself the less. ***Partem aliquam recte intelligere nemo potest, antequam totum, iterum atque iterum, perlegerit.*** No one can rightly understand any part until he has read the whole over again. ***Quamvis lex generaliter loquitur, restringenda tamen est, ut, cessante ratione, ipsa cessat.*** Although a law speaks generally, yet it is to be restrained, so that when its reason fails, it should cease also. ***Quotiens idem sermo duas sententias exprimit, ea potissimum accipiatur, quae rei gerendae aptior est.*** Whenever the same words express two meanings, that is to be adopted which is the better fitted for carrying out the proposed end. ***In ambiguis orationibus maxime sententia spectanda est ejus qui eas protulisset.*** In ambiguous expressions, the intent of the person using them is particularly to be regarded. ***Statutum generaliter est intelligendum quando verba statuti sunt specialia, ratio autem generalis.*** When the words of a statute are special but the reason general, the statute is to be understood generally. ***Tortura legum pessima.*** The torture or wresting of laws is the worst. ***Verba accipienda sunt secundum subjectam materiam.*** Words are to be understood with reference to the subject-matter. ***Verba chartarum fortius accipiuntur contra proferentem.*** The words of a grant are to be taken most strongly against the person offering them. ***Verba generalia generaliter sunt intelligenda.*** General words are to be understood generally. ***Verbis standum ubi nulla ambiguitas.*** Where there is no ambiguity, the words are adhered to. ***Semper sexus masculinus etiam femininum sexum continet.*** The masculine sex of gender always includes the feminine also. ***Semper specialia generalibus insunt.*** Special expressions are always included in general ones. ***Si nulla sit conjectura quae ducat alio, verba intelligenda sunt ex proprietate, non grammatica sed populari ex usu.*** If there be no inference which leads to a different conclusion, words are to be understood according to their proper meaning, not according to a grammatical usage but to a popular and ordinary one. ***Statuta pro publico commodo late interpretantur.*** Statutes enacted for the public good ought to be liberally construed. ***Quando charta continet generalem clausulam, posteaque descendit ad verba specialia quae clausulae generali sunt consentanea, interpretanda est charta secundum verba specialia.*** When a deed contains a general clause, and afterwards descends to special words which are consistent with the general clause, the deed is to be interpreted according to the special words. ***Quando lex est specialis, ratio autem generalis, generaliter lex est intelligenda.*** When the law is special, but its reason is general, the law is to be understood generally. ***Quando licet id quod majus videtur et licere id quod minus.*** When the greater is allowed, the less is to be deemed to be allowed also. ***Quod in minori valet valebit in majori; et quod in majori non valet nec valebit in minori.*** That which is valid in the greater shall be valid in the less; and that which is not valid in the greater shall not be valid in the less. ***Quum in testamento ambigue aut etiam perperam scriptum est, benigne interpretari et secundum id quod credible et cogitatum, credendum est.*** Where an ambiguous or even an erroneous expression occurs in a will, it should be construed liberally and in accordance with what is thought the probable meaning of the testator. ***Semper in dubiis benigniora praeferenda sunt.*** In doubtful cases, the more liberal constructions are always to be preferred. T***ransgressione multiplicata, crescat poenae inflictio.*** Upon the multiplication of the transgression, let the infliction of punishment increase. ***Ex tota materia emergat resolutio.*** The construction should arise out of the whole subject matter. ***Expressio unius est exclusio alterius.*** The expression of one thing is the exclusion of another. ***Generale dictum generaliter est interpretandum.*** A general expression is to be construed generally. ***Generale nihil certum implicat.*** A general expression implies nothing certain. ***In dubio haec legis constructio quam verba ostendunt.*** In a doubtful case, that construction which the words indicate should be adopted. ***In expositione instrumentorum, mala grammatica, quod fieri potest, vitanda est.*** In the drafting of instruments, bad grammar is to be avoided as much as possible. ***In his enim quae sunt favorabilia animae, quamvis sunt damnosa rebus, fiat aliquando extentio statuti.*** In matters that are favorable to the spirit, though injurious to property, an extension of the statute should sometimes be made. ***In rebus quae sunt favorabilia animae, quamvis sunt damnosa rebus, fiat aliquando extensio statuti.*** In matters that are favorable to the spirit, though injurious to things, an extension of a statute should sometimes be made. ***In stipulationibus cum quaeritur quid actum sit verba contra stipulatorem interpretanda sunt.*** In the construction of agreements, terms are interpreted against the person using them. ***In verbis non verba, sed res et ratio, quaerenda est.*** In the construction of words, not the mere words, but the thing and the meaning, are to be inquired into. ***Injustum est, nisi tota lege inspecta, de una aliqua ejus particula proposita judicare vel respondere.*** It is unjust to give judgment or advice concerning any particular clause of a law without having examined the whole law. ***Interpretatio fienda est ut res magis valeat quam pereat.*** Construction should be such that the transaction may be effective rather than fall. ***Interpretare et concordare leges legibus, est optimus interpretandi modus.*** To interpret and harmonize laws with laws is the best mode of interpretation. ***Interpretatio talis in ambiguis semper fienda est ut evitetur inconveniens et absurdum.*** In ambiguous things, such a construction should be always made that the inconvenient and absurd may be avoided. ***Legis constructio non facit injuriam.*** The construction of law does no wrong. ***Generalis clausula non porrigitur ad ea quaeantea specialiter sunt comprehensa.*** A general clause is not extended to include those things that have been previously provided for specially. ***Leges posteriores priores contrarias abrogant.*** Subsequent laws repeal prior laws that are repugnant to them. ***Id quod est magis remotum, non trahit ad se quod est magis junctum, sed e contrario in omni casu.*** That which is more remote does not draw to itself that which is nearer, but the contrary in every case. ***In ambigua voce legis ea potius accipienda est significatio quae vitio caret, praesertim cum etiam voluntas legis ex hoc colligi possit.*** In an ambiguous expression of law, that signification is to be preferred which is consonant with equity, especially when the spirit of the law can be collected from that. ***In obscuris, inspici solere quod verisimiltus est, aut quod plerumque fieri solet.*** In obscure cases, we usually regard what is most probable or what is done. ***In obscuris, quod minimum est sequimur.*** In obscure or doubtful cases, we follow that which is the least. ***In poenalibus causis benignius interpretandum est.*** In penal causes or cases, the more liberal interpretation should be adopted. ***In re dubia, benigniorem interpretationem sequi, non minus justius est quam tutius.*** In a doubtful matter, to follow the more liberal interpretation is no the more just than it is the more safe. ***Generale tantum valet in generalibus, quantum singulare in singulis.*** That which is general prevails in general matters, as that which is particular prevails in particular matters. ***In ambiguo sermone non utrumque dicimus sed id duntaxat quod volumus.*** In ambiguous language, we do not use it in a double sense, but in the sense in which we mean it. ***Generalia specialibus non derogant.*** General words do not derogate from special. ***Generalia sunt praeponenda singularibus.*** General things are to be put before particular things. ***Generalia verba sunt generaliter intelligenda.*** General words are to be understood generally in a general sense. ***Generalibus specialia derogant.*** Special words derogate from the meaning of general ones. ***Verba posteriora propter certitudinem addita, ad priora quae certitudine indigent, sunt referenda.*** Subsequent words, added for the purpose of certainty, are to be referred to the preceding words which are need of certainty. ***Verbis standum ubi nulla ambiguitas.*** One must abide by the words where there is no ambiguity. ***Generalia praecedunt, specialia sequuntur.*** Things general precede, things special follow. ***In ambiguis orationibus maxime sententia spectanda est ejus qui eas protulisset.*** When there are ambiguous expressions, the intentions of the person who uses them is chiefly to be regarded. ***A verbis legis non est recendendum.*** From the words of a statute, there must be no departure. ***Aliud est distinctio, aliud separatio.*** Distinction is one thing; separation is another.

CONSTRUCTIVE *(Creative)*, ***adjective*** advantageous, applicable, causative, contributive, convenient, cooperative, desirable, developmental, effective, effectual, efficient, fabricative, favorable, formative, generative, helpful, important, improving, instrumental, invaluable, operative, originative, practical, productive, profitable, resultant, serviceable, significant, stimulating, suitable, usable, useful, valuable, worthy, yielding

CONSTRUCTIVE *(Inferential),* ***adjective*** apparent, assumable, conceivable, connoted, constructional, implicative, implicatory, implicit, implied, implied in law, in effect, in essence, in practice, indicated, indirect, indirectly meant, inferable, inferred, inferred in law, insinuated, involved, parallel, potential, pragmatic, presumable, presumed, probable, seeming, suggested, supposable, tacit, tacitly assumed, tantamount to, understood, virtual
ASSOCIATED CONCEPTS: constructive contempt, constructive contract, constructive control, constructive conversion, constructive delivery, constructive desertion, constructive escape, constructive eviction, constructive force, constructive fraud, constructive gift, constructive intent, constructive knowledge, constructive malice, constructive mortgage, constructive notice, constructive possession, constructive receipt, constructive total loss, constructive trespass, constructive trust, constructively present

CONSTRUCTIVE NOTICE, ***noun*** assumption of knowledge, constructive knowledge, legal notice, legally sufficient notice, sufficient notice to a party, the legal equivalent of actual notice, to put on notice

CONSTRUE *(Comprehend),* ***verb*** *accipere,* analyze, apprehend, ascertain the meaning of, assimilate, be aware of, be given to understand, cognize, conceive of, conclude, conclude from evidence, consignify, decipher, decode, deduce, deduce by interpretation, deduce the meaning of, deduct, derive by reasoning, determine, determine exactly, discern, disentangle, divine, draw an inference, draw as an implication, explain, fathom, figure out, find out the meaning of, form an opinion, gather, glean, grasp mentally, grow aware, infer, interpret, judge, ken, make deductions, master, opine, perceive, ratiocinate, realize, reason, represent, see through, seize, show the meaning of, solve, take one's meaning, understand, understand by, understand the meaning of

CONSTRUE *(Translate),* ***verb*** analyze, assign a meaning to, characterize, characterize precisely, clarify, clear up, connote, convey, decipher, decode, define, delineate, demonstrate, denote, depict, describe, disclose, elucidate, enlighten, enunciate, explain, explicate, exposit, expound, express, give explanation to, give sense to, illuminate, illustrate, indicate, inform, interpret, *interpretari,* literalize, make intelligible, of, outline, paraphrase, put a meaning on, put an interpretation, put in other words, render, render intelligible, rephrase, restate, retranslate, reveal, reword, signify, transfuse the sense, unfold, unravel
ASSOCIATED CONCEPTS: construe the law

CONSULT *(Ask advice of),* ***verb*** advise with, ask, ask advice, ask an opinion, ask for recommendations, ask for suggestions, call in, confer, *consultare,* deliberate, discuss, exchange observations, interchange views, parley, question, seek counsel, seek guidance, seek the opinion of, take counsel, talk over, turn to, ventilate
ASSOCIATED CONCEPTS: consult with counsel

CONSULT *(Seek information from),* ***verb*** check a reference, check a source, examine a source, inquire of, look up information in, refer to, refer to for information, search for an answer, seek facts from

CONSUME, ***verb*** *absumere,* annihilate, burn up, *consumere,* demolish, destroy, devour, disappear, drain, dwindle, eat, empty, eradicate, evaporate, exhaust, expend, spend, squander, swallow, use up, utilize, waste, wear away, wear out

CONSUMER, ***noun*** buyer, buyer of labor, client, clientele, coemptor, customer, emptor, leaser, lessee, obtainer, patron, procurer, purchaser, purchaser of goods, shopper, transferee, vendee
ASSOCIATED CONCEPTS: consumer action, consumer credit, consumer fraud, consumers sales tax, ultimate consumer

CONSUMMATE, ***verb*** accomplish, achieve, actualize, attain, attain the goal, bring to a close, bring to effect, carry into effect, carry out, carry through, carry to completion, complete, conclude, *conficere, consummare,* do thoroughly, effect, effectuate, end, execute, finalize, finish, follow through, fulfill, implement, leave nothing to be desired, perfect, *perficere,* prosecute to a conclusion, reach the goal, realize, render complete, terminate, to bring to completion
ASSOCIATED CONCEPTS: consummate dower, consummation of a marriage, consummation of an agreement, constructive service
FOREIGN PHRASES: ***Omne testamentum morte consummatum est.*** Every will is consummated by death.

CONSUMPTION, ***noun*** *confectio, consumptio,* decay, decomposition, decrement, depletion, desolation, destruction, devastation, diminishment, diminution, dissipation, exhaustion, expenditure, loss, ravage, ruin, ruination, squandering, usage, use, using up, utilization, wastage, waste, wastefulness, wear, withering
ASSOCIATED CONCEPTS: business consumption, consumption in interstate commerce, consumption of goods, consumption of intoxicating liquors, for use and consumption

CONTACT *(Association),* ***noun*** accord, acquaintanceship, affiliation, alliance, bond, camaraderie, close union, cooperation, coalition, combination, commerce, communication, community, companionship, conjunction, connection, consanguinity, consociation, consortium, cooperation, dealings, exchange, federation, fellowship, interchange, intercommunication, intercommunion, intercourse, interrelation, intimacy, kinship, liaison, link, linkage, mutual intercourse, participation, rapport, relation, relationship, tie, transmission, union
ASSOCIATED CONCEPTS: contacts theory in conflicts of law, grouping of contacts

CONTACT *(Touching),* ***noun*** abutment, abuttal, adhesion, adjacency, coherence, *contactus,* connection, connective, contiguity, contiguousness, contingence, convergence, impact, joining, junction, junction of bodies, juncture, juxtaposition, meeting, nexus, taction, tangency, union

CONTACT *(Communicate),* ***verb*** call, consociate, *contactus,* correspond, establish connection, get through to, get to, have an exchange, have dealings with, inform, interchange, intercommunicate, make connection, meet with, notify, reach, relate, serve notice, signal

CONTACT *(Touch),* ***verb*** abut, adjoin, annex, attach, be contiguous, border, border on, bridge, butt against, cohere, collide with, come together, conjoin, connect, converge, embrace, encounter, establish connection, graze, hit, impinge, inosculate, interconnect, join, lie adjacent to, link, meet, osculate, overlap, reach, rub, strike, unite, verge upon

CONTAGIOUS, ***adjective*** catching, communicable, contaminating, conveyable, epidemic, impartible, infectious, infective, pathogenic, pestiferous, spreading, transferable, transmissible, transmissive

CONTAIN *(Comprise),* ***verb*** be composed of, be compounded of, be constituted of, be formed of, capere, *comprehendere,* consist of, embody, embrace, enfold, envelop, hold, include, incorporate, number, reckon among, subsist of
ASSOCIATED CONCEPTS: containing facts sufficient to constitute a cause of action

CONTAIN *(Enclose),* ***verb*** beleaguer, belt, bind, blockade, border, close in, confine, *continere,* embox, embrace, encapsulate, encase, encincture, encircle, enclasp, encompass, engird, ensphere, envelop, enwrap, fence in, frame, immure, incase, inclose, infold, keep in, quarantine, seal up, shut in, surround

CONTAIN *(Restrain),* ***verb*** arrest, barricade, bind, block, bridle, cage, chain, check, commit to prison, confine, constrain, control, curb, detain, enchain, encumber, enjoin from, fetter, forfend, hinder, hold back, hold in check, hold in custody, impede, impound, imprison, incarcerate, inhibit, jail, keep in captivity, keep in check, keep prisoner, keep under arrest, keep under control, lock up, manacle, obstruct, pinion, place in durance, prohibit, quash, quell, repress, restrict, shackle, stave off, stop, subdue, suppress, thwart, trammel, ward off

CONTAMINATE, ***noun*** abomination, adulteration, befoulment, contagion, defilement, infection, poisoning, pollution, taint, vitiation

CONTAMINATE, ***verb*** adulterate, befoul, corrupt, debase, defile, degenerate, degrade, denaturalize, desecrate, disease, impair, infect, mar, poison, pollute, profane, sully, tamper with, taint, tarnish, vitiate

CONTAMINATION, ***noun*** adulteration, corruption, debauchment, decay, defilement, degradation, despoilment, impureness, impurity, infection, pollution, vitiation

CONTEMN, ***verb*** abhor, abominate, accuse, asperse, be contemptuous of, belittle, besmirch, calumniate, cast aspersions, censure, criticize, debase, debauch, decry, defile, denigrate, denounce, depreciate, deride, derogate, desecrate, despise, detest, disapprove, discredit, disdain, disesteem, dishonor, disparage, disprize, disrate, disregard, disrespect, execrate, expose, exprobate, feel contempt for, flout, hold in contempt, hold in despite, inveigh against, loathe, malign, misprize, not respect, objurgate, oppress, overlook, rebuff, reject, reproach, repudiate, repulse, resent, revile, ridicule, scandalize, scoff at, scorn, slight, slur, smear, spurn, taint, vilify, vilipend, vituperate

CONTEMPLATE, ***verb*** analyze, anticipate, brood, calculate, cogitate, consider, deliberate, discern, dwell upon, entertain, envisage, examine, fixate, fret, meditate, mull over, muse, obsess, opine, perpend, pontificate, pore over, question, reason, reflect, review, revolve, ruminate, scrutinize, speculate, think over, turn, weigh, wrestle

CONTEMPLATION, ***noun*** absorption, aim, attention, brooding, calculation, cerebration, cogitation, concentration, consideration, *contemplatio,* deliberateness, deliberation, design, determination, engrossment, envisagement, envisionment, examination, excogitation, expectance, expectation, forethought, goal, inspection, intellectualization, intent, intention, introspection, musing, observance, pensiveness, plan, pondering, preoccupation, prospect, purpose, ratiocination, reasoning, reflection, resolve, reverie, review, rumination, scrutiny, seriousness, speculation, study, surveillance, thought, thoughtfulness, weighing
ASSOCIATED CONCEPTS: contemplation of assignment, contemplation of bankruptcy, contemplation of insolvency, contemplation of marriage, contemplation of parties, in contemplation of death

CONTEMPORANEOUS, ***adjective*** coeval, coexistent, coexisting, coincident, coinciding, coinstantaneous, concomitant, concurrent, concurring, contemporary, correspondent, corresponding, *quod eodem tempore est,* simultaneous, synchronal, synchronistic, synchronous
ASSOCIATED CONCEPTS: contemporaneous agreement, contemporaneous declaration, contemporaneous exposition, contemporaneous forgeries, contemporaneous memorandum, contemporaneous transaction

CONTEMPORARY, ***adjective*** coexistent, latest, modern, new, present day, up-to-date, up-to-the-minute

CONTEMPT *(Disdain),* ***noun*** abhorrence, abomination, animosity, arrogance, aspersion, aversion, condemnation, contemptuousness, *contemptus,* contumely, debasement, defilement, denigration, denunciation, deprecation, depreciation, derision, derogation, detestation, detraction, disapprobation, disapproval, disdainfulness, disesteem, disfavor, disgust, dislike, disparagement, dispraise, disregard, disrepute, disvaluation, *fastidium,* imprecation, incivility, indignant aversion, infamy, insolence, malediction, misprision, objurgation, obloquy, odium, opposure, opprobrium, rebuff, reproach, reprobation, reproof, reproval, repugnance, revilement, revulsion, ridicule, scorn, scurrility
FOREIGN PHRASES: ***Qui contemnit praeceptum contemnit praecipientem.*** He who contemns a precept contemns the party who gives it.

CONTEMPT *(Disobedience to the court),* ***noun*** audacity, contemptuous resistance, contumaciousness, contumacy, contumely, defiance of orders, deprecation, dereliction, disaffection, disobedience, disposition to resist, disregard of orders, disrespect, disrespectfulness, dissension, encroachment, fractiousness, impertinence, improbity, impudence, indiscipline, indocility, infringement, inobservance, insolence, insubmission, insubordination, intractableness, irreverence, nonadherence, noncompliance, noncooperation, nonobservance, obstinacy, obstructionism, perverseness, recalcitrance, recusancy, refractoriness, refusal to obey orders, reproach, repudiation, repulsion, resistance, resistance to authority, restiveness, rudeness, undutifulness, unobservance, unruliness, unsubmissiveness, unwillingness, violation of orders, willful disregard
ASSOCIATED CONCEPTS: aggravated contempt, civil contempt, common-law contempt, constructive contempt, contempt of court, continuing contempt, criminal contempt, evasive contempt, judicial contempt, obstruction of justice, summary contempt

CONTEMPTIBLE, ***adjective*** abhorrent, *abiectus,* abject, abominable, atrocious, base, blameworthy, censurable, condemnable, condemnatory, contemned, *contemnendus, contemptus,* contumelious, corrupt, culpable, damnable, deplorable, depraved, despicable, despised, detestable, discreditable, disgraceful, disgusting, dishonorable, disreputable, egregious, evil, execrable, foul, fulsome, hateful, heinous, horrendous, horrible, ignominious,

infamous, inglorious, insidious, insufferable, loathsome, nefarious, noxious, objurgatory, odious, offensive, opprobrious, perfidious, repellent, reprehensible, reproachful, reprobative, repugnant, repulsive, shameful, shameless, unworthy, vile, villainous, wicked, worthless
ASSOCIATED CONCEPTS: contemptible criminal act

CONTEMPTUOUS, ***adjective*** abasing, abject, abominable, abusive, accusatory, arbitrary, arrogant, base, brazen, bumptious, calumniating, calumniatory, calumnious, challenging, compromising, contemptible, contumelious, damaging, decrying, defamatory, defiant, defying, denigratory, denunciatory, depreciating, depreciative, derisive, derisory, derogative, derogatory, detestable, detracting, disapproving, discourteous, disdainful, dishonorable, dishonoring, dislikable, disparaging, disregardful, disrespectful, execrable, expressing disdain, flouting, forward, harsh, hateful, ignominious, impertinent, impudent, indignant, infamous, injuring, injurious, insinuating, insolent, insulting, irreverent, libelous, maledicent, malevolent, malicious, malignant, maligning, manifesting contempt, nefarious, objectionable, obnoxious, obtrusive, offensive, opprobrious, repellent, reproachful, reproaching, repugnant, repulsive, reviling, rude, scandalous, scornful, slighting, spiteful, uncivil, vile, vituperative

CONTEND *(Dispute),* ***verb*** altercate, argue, battle, be discordant, bicker, brawl, carry on an argument, challenge, clash, combat, compete, conflict, *contendere,* contest, contradict, *decernere,* differ, disaccord, disagree, discept, discord, dissent, encounter, engage, fight, gainsay, have an altercation, have words with, impugn, litigate, make an issue, oppose, *pugnare,* quarrel, reluct, rival, skirmish, spar, spat, squabble, strike at, strive, struggle, take on, vie with, war, wrangle

CONTEND *(Maintain),* ***verb*** *adfirmare,* advance, affirm, argue, assert, asseverate, assure, attest, aver, avow, claim, claim to know, *confirmare, contendere,* declare, emphasize, express, hold, hold the opinion, insist, make a statement, make an assertion, predicate, profess, say, set forth, state, state emphatically, stress, utter with conviction, vouch, warrant

CONTENDER, ***noun*** adversary, adverse party, antagonist, appellant, applicant, arguer, aspirant, campaigner, candidate, challenger, charger, claimant, combatant, competitor, complainant, contestant, contester, controversialist, corrival, debater, denouncer, disputant, entrant, examinee, feuder, fighter, foe, libelant, litigant, litigator, nominee, office-seeker, opponent, opposer, opposition, oppositionist, party, party to a suit, petitioner, polemist, pugilist, respondent, rival, striver, suitor, the prosecution

CONTENT *(Meaning),* ***noun*** accepted meaning, aim, basis, bearing, cardinal point, chief constituent, chief part, denotation, design, drift, emphasis, essence, essential matter, essential meaning, essential part, exegesis, explanation, explication, exposition, force, general meaning, gist, gravamen, impact, implication, import, intent, intention, interpretation, literal interpretation, literal meaning, literal sense, literality, main point, matter, matter of cognition, meaningfulness, motif, nature, object, obvious interpretation, obvious meaning, obvious sense, plain meaning, point, *prima facie,* primary element, primary meaning, purport, purpose, quiddity, quintessence, salient point, scope, sense, *sensus, sententia,* significance, significant part, signification, *significatio,* spirit, subject, subject matter, substance, substantial meaning, sum, sum and substance, tenor, text, theme
ASSOCIATED CONCEPTS: content contained in an instrument, content of a contract, content of a note

CONTENT *(Structure),* ***noun*** anatomy, arrangement of parts, body, combination, complement, composite, composition, configuration, conformation, constitution, construction, contexture, core, design, form, format, formation, framework, interrelation, makeup, nature, organization, pattern, plan, setup, style of arrangement

CONTENTION *(Argument),* ***noun*** allegation, area of disagreement, argumentation, cause, conflict, contest, controversy, debate, discord, *disputatio,* disputation, dispute, disputed point, ground, issue, legal dispute, legal issue, plea, point, polemic, proposition, reason, root of dissension

CONTENTION *(Opposition),* ***noun*** antagonism, challenge, clashing, combat, competition, competitiveness, conflict, contentiousness, contest, contestation, contrariety, contravention, controversy, counteraction, cross purposes, debate, difference, disaccord, disagreement, discord, disharmony, disputation, dispute, dissension, dissent, dissidence, dissonance, divergence, enmity, faction, factiousness, feud, fight, friction, hostility, inimicality, irreconcilability, protest, protestation, quarrel, quarreling, quarrelsomeness, recrimination, resistance, rivalry, schism, strife, struggle, unappeasability, velitation, wrangling

CONTENTIOUS, ***adjective*** aggressive, argumentative, bellicose, belligerent, cantankerous, captious, caviling, combative, competitive, contrary, contumacious, cross, discordant, disputatious, dissentious, factious, inimical, irascible, litigious, militant, noncooperating, nonpacific, obstinate, perverse, polemical, pugnacious, *pugnax,* quarrelsome, recalcitrant, schismatic, stubborn, uncooperative, unfriendly, unpacific, unpeaceful, wrangling

CONTENTS, ***noun*** components, constituents, details, drift, essence, gist, items, meaning, parts, pith, scope, sense, subject, subject matter, subject of thought, substance, text, themes, thesis, topics
ASSOCIATED CONCEPTS: contents of a chose in action, contents of a note

CONTEST *(Competition),* ***noun*** bout, *certamen, certatio,* challenge, clash, corrivalry, emulation, encounter, engagement, game, match, opposition, pitting of strengths, race, rivalry, rivalship, sport, sporting event, struggle, test of endurance, tournament, tourney, trial
ASSOCIATED CONCEPTS: election contest

CONTEST *(Dispute),* ***noun*** action, altercation, antagonism, argument, battle, bickering, brawl, challenge, clash, combat, contention, controversion, controversy, debate, difference of opinion, disaccord, disagreement, disceptation, discord, disharmony, disputation, dispute, dissension, dissent, dissonance, embroilment, encounter, failure to agree, feud, fight, fracas, fray, impugnation, impugnment, inharmony, litigation, monomachy, noncomformity, obstinacy, opposition, oppugnancy, polemics, quarrel, recalcitrance, recusancy, resistance, revolt, skirmish, squabble, strained relations, strife, variance, verbal contention, verbal engagement, war, war of words, wrangle
ASSOCIATED CONCEPTS: notice of contest, will contest

CONTEST, ***verb*** altercate, argue, battle, call to answer, challenge, combat, conflict, contend, *contendere,* contradict, contravene, controvert, counter, debate, defy, disaffirm, disagree, dispute, fight, gainsay, grapple with, impugn, object, oppose, oppugn, quarrel over, question, refuse to accept, refuse to admit, resist, struggle, take exception to, traverse, vie with
ASSOCIATED CONCEPTS: contest a will, contest an election, contest an insurance policy, contested case

CONTESTABLE, ***adjective*** at issue, close, competing, confutable, controversial, controvertible, debatable, deniable, disputable, questionable, refutable

CONTESTANT, ***noun*** adversary, adverse party, aemulus, antagonist, appellant, battler, belligerent, candidate, challenger, claimant, combatant, complainant, contender, contester, corrival, disputant, foe, libelant, litigant, opponent, opposer, opposing party, opposition, oppositionist, participant, party to a suit, *petitor,* rival, suitor
ASSOCIATED CONCEPTS: contestant to a will

CONTEXT, ***noun*** *argumentum,* background, circumstance, coloring, connection, connotation, extended meaning, force, gist, implication, import, main meaning, meaning, mode of expression, purport, range of meaning, scope, sense, subject matter, sum and substance, surroundings, tenor, text, topic
FOREIGN PHRASES: ***Nemo enim aliquam partem recte intelligere possit antequam totum iterum atque iterum perlegerit.*** No one can rightly understand one part before he has again and again read the whole.

CONTIGUOUS, ***adjective*** abutting, adjacent, adjoining, against, at close quarters, beside, bordering, bounding, close, *confinis,* conjoining, conjunct, connected, conterminous, *continens,* convergent, coupled, edging, end-to-end, fringing, in close proximity, in common boundaries with, in contact, joined, meeting, near, neighboring, next to, on the confines of, on the edge of, proximal, proximate, side-by-side, touching, verging
ASSOCIATED CONCEPTS: contiguous lands, contiguous municipalities, contiguous property, contiguous territory

CONTINENCE, ***noun*** abstainment, abstention, abstinence, asceticism, chastity, conservatism, *continentia,* eschewal, forbearance, moderateness, moderation, prudence, renunciation, restraint, self-command, self-control, self-denial, self-discipline, self-restraint, sobriety, stoicism, temperance, *temperantia,* temperateness
ASSOCIATED CONCEPTS: continuance of a lawsuit

CONTINGENCY, ***noun*** accident, befalling, casus, chance, circumstance, circumstantial event, coincidence, conditional event, contingence, contingent, contingent event, dependent event, doubtful event, fortune, hap, happening, inadvertence, incident, luck, occurrence, possibility, uncertain event, uncertainty, unforeseen occurrence, unintentional happening
ASSOCIATED CONCEPTS: contingency contract, double contingency, unavoidable contingency, unforeseen contingency, unusual or extraordinary contingencies
FOREIGN PHRASES: ***Casus fortuitus non est sperandus, et nemo tenetur devinare.*** A fortuitous event is not to be expected, and no one is bound to foresee it.

CONTINGENT, ***adjective*** attributed to, coincidental, conditioned, consequential, dependent, dependent on, dependent on circumstances, depending, due to, in a state of uncertainty, incident to, possible, provisional, resulting from, subject to, subject to terms, subsidiary
ASSOCIATED CONCEPTS: contingent basis, contingent claim, contingent contract, contingent debt, contingent demand, contingent estate, contingent event, contingent expectancy, contingent fee, contingent fund, contingent gift, contingent interest, contingent legacy, contingent liability, contingent life estate, contingent obligation, contingent remainder, contingent right, contingent use, contingent will

CONTINGENT-FEE AGREEMENT, ***noun*** conditional fee, contingent-fee arrangement, contingency fee, fee conditioned on success, fee dependant on an outcome, outcome-dependant fee, payment conditioned on success, payment contingent on success, payment depending on the recovery

CONTINUAL *(Connected),* ***adjective*** constant, constantly recurring, continued, continuing, *continuus,* nonstop, of regular recurrence, perennial, persistent, proceeding without cessation, proceeding without interruption, regular, steadfast, steady, sustained, unbroken, unceasing, unchanging, unintermitted, uninterrupted, unremitting, unstopped

CONTINUAL *(Perpetual),* ***adjective*** *adsiduus,* boundless, ceaseless, continuous, endless, eternal, everlasting, incessant, infinite, interminable, never-ending, permanent, *perpetuus,* sempiternal, unceasing, unending, unstopped, unvarying

CONTINUANCE, ***noun*** abiding, adjournment of a cause, adjournment of a proceeding, admission of postponement, *adsiduitas, continuatio,* continuation, endurance, extension, lasting, lengthening, perpetuation, *perpetuitas,* perseverance, persistence, postponement, prolongation, protraction, stay, sustained action
ASSOCIATED CONCEPTS: continuance in office, continuance of a nonconforming use, continuance of a partnership, continuance of a proceeding, continuance of criminal case, presumption of continuance

CONTINUATION *(Prolongation),* ***noun*** addition, adherence, *adsiduitas,* augmentation, continuance, *continuatio,* extension, lengthening, maintenance, perpetuation, *perpetuitas,* perseverance, persistence, preservation, protraction, stretching, sustaining, sustenance
ASSOCIATED CONCEPTS: continuation of a business, continuation of a condition, continuation of a fact, continuation of a lien, continuation of an easement, continuation of service

CONTINUATION *(Resumption),* ***noun*** carrying on, continuance, fresh start, new beginning, new start, proceeding, reestablishment, recommencement, recurrence, reinstatement, reinstitution, renewal, reopening, restoration, return, reversion, supplementation
ASSOCIATED CONCEPTS: continuation of a proceeding, continuation of a suit

CONTINUE *(Adjourn),* ***verb*** arrest temporarily, defer, delay, discontinue, hold over, interrupt, keep pending, lay aside, lay over, postpone, prorogue, put over, put over to a future date, recess, respite, restrain, set for a later time, shelve, stall, stay, suspend, table, tide over
ASSOCIATED CONCEPTS: continue an action, grant of a continuance

CONTINUE *(Persevere),* ***verb*** abide, be durable, be permanent, bide, exist, forge ahead, go on, keep, last, linger, maintain, move ahead, persevere, persist, *persistere,* press

onward, prevail, progress, promote, pursue, stay on, subsist, sustain
ASSOCIATED CONCEPTS: continuing application, continuing contracts, continuing nuisance, continuing offer, continuing trespass, continuing wrong

CONTINUE *(Prolong)*, ***verb*** arrange in succession, drag out, draw out, *durare,* extend, extend in duration, lengthen, maintain, maintain continuity, perpetuate, preserve, protract, retain, *stare,* sustain, uphold
ASSOCIATED CONCEPTS: continue in force and effect, continue in office, continue to carry on business, continued and uninterrupted use, continued concealment, continued good health, continued possession, continuing accumulation, continuing affirmative act, continuing and subsisting trust, continuing body, continuing conspiracy, continuing contempt, continuing crime, continuing duty, continuing guaranty, continuing jurisdiction, continuing loan, continuing obligation, continuing offense, continuing offer, continuing proceeding, continuing representation, continuing right, continuing tort, continuing trust

CONTINUE *(Resume)*, ***verb*** begin again, begin over, carry on, carry over, go back to, make a new beginning, proceed, reestablish, rebegin, recommence, reinstate, reinstitute, renew, reopen, restore, return to, take up again

CONTINUITY, ***noun*** coherence, connectedness, connection, consecution, consecutiveness, consistency, constancy, continualness, continuance, *continuatio,* continuation, continuousness, continuum, incessancy, permanence, *perpetuitas,* perpetuity, progression, protraction, sequence, succession, successiveness, unintermittedness, uninterrupted connection, uninterruptedness, uninterruption

CONTINUOUS, ***adjective*** ceaseless, consecutive, constant, continual, continuing, endless, extended, following, incessant, never-ending, perennial, perpetual, progressive, prolonged, repeated, running, sequential, steady, sustained, unbroken, unceasing, unending, unfaltering, unintermittent, unintermitting, uninterrupted, unremitting, unstopped, without cessation, without interruption
ASSOCIATED CONCEPTS: continuous absence, continuous account, continuous activity, continuous adverse possession, continuous and unbroken, continuous and uninterrupted use, continuous course of business, continuous crime, continuous disability, continuous easement, continuous guaranty, continuous injury, continuous nuisance, continuous possession, continuous residence, continuous servitude, continuous tort, continuous use, continuous wrong, continuously carry on, continuously confined, continuously disabled, continuously employed

CONTORT, ***verb*** bend, bend out of shape, deform, *detorquere,* dislocate, *distorquere,* distort, knot, misshape, pervert, turn, twine, twist, twist and turn, wind, wrench, wrest, wrinkle, writhe

CONTOUR *(Outline)*, ***noun*** ambit, bounds, circle, circuit, circumference, circumscription, configuration, delineation, diagram, figuration, figure, form, frame, framework, laterality, *lineamenta,* lines, main features, outside, perimeter, periphery, picture, plan, profile, relief, rough sketch, silhouette, skeleton, sketch, structure, *tournure*

CONTOUR *(Shape)*, ***noun*** configuration, conformation, feature, *figura,* figuration, figure, form, *forma,* formation, frame, lines, profile, relief, sculpture, silhouette, structure, substance, substantial form, turn

CONTRA, ***adverb*** adverse to, against, con, contrarily, contrariwise, contrawise, conversely, counter, in conflict with, in contrast to, in opposition to, inversely, loathe to, on the contrary, on the other hand, opposed to, opposite, oppositely, otherwise, *per contra,* quite the contrary, to the contrary, versus, vice versa

CONTRA, ***noun*** antipode, antithesis, antonym, contrary, converse, counter, extreme, inverse, obverse, offset, opposite, reverse, the other side

CONTRA, ***preposition*** adverse to, against, at cross purposes, athwart, contrariwise, counter, in conflict with, in opposition to, opposed to, opposite to, over against, versus, vis-à-vis

CONTRABAND, ***noun*** banned goods, bootlegged commerce, bootlegged goods, bootlegged trade, bootlegged traffic, captured goods, confiscated goods, confiscated property, embargoed goods, goods exported illegally, goods imported illegally, goods subject to confiscation, goods subject to seizure, illegal property, illegal traffic, illegally exported goods, illegally imported goods, illicit gains, poached trade, poached traffic, prohibited articles, prohibited import, restricted goods, seized articles, seized goods, smuggled commerce, smuggled goods, smuggled trade, smuggled traffic, stolen article, stolen goods, swag
ASSOCIATED CONCEPTS: contraband articles, contraband goods

CONTRACT, ***noun*** accord, accordance, agreement, arrangement, articles of agreement, assurance, avouchment, avowal, bargain, binding agreement, bond, charter, collective agreement, commitment, compact, compromise, concordat, *condicio, conductio,* confirmation, *conventio,* covenant, deal, embodied terms, engagement, *entente,* guarantee, instrument evidencing an agreement, ironclad agreement, legal document, mutual agreement, mutual pledge, mutual promise, mutual undertaking, negotiated agreement, obligation, pact, paction, *pactum,* pledge, pledged word, private understanding, promise, ratified agreement, set terms, settlement, stated terms, stipulation, terms for agreement, understanding, undertaking, warranty, written terms
ASSOCIATED CONCEPTS: acceptance of a contract, accessory contract, action on contract, adhesion contract, aleatory contract, alteration of a contract, alternative contract, anticipatory breach of contract, assent to a contract, assignment of a contract, bilateral contract, breach of a contract, breach of contract, cancellation of a contract, claim arising on contract, collateral contract, collective agreement, commercial contract, concurrent contracts, conditional acceptance of a contract, conditional agreement, conditional contract, consideration in a contract, constructive contract, contingency contract, continuing contract, contract action, contract carrier, contract for an option, contract implied in fact, contract obligation, contract of agency, contract of carriage, contract of employment, contract of guaranty, contract of hire or hiring, contract of indemnity, contract of insurance, contract of record, contract of sale, contract of subscription for stock, contract of suretyship, contract price, contract rights, contract to lease, contract to purchase, contract to sell, contracting out work, de facto contract, divisible contract, endowment contract, enforceable contract, exclusive contract, executed contract, executory contract,

express contract, fictitious contract, fiduciary contract, formal contract, fraudulent contract, future contract, general contract, government contract, gratuitous contract, guaranty contract, illegal contract, illusory contract, immoral contract, impairing the obligation of contract, implied contract, indivisible contract, inequitable contract, installment contract, joint contract, liberty of contract, lump sum contract, marriage contract, material alteration of contract, material breach of contract, obligation of contract, optional contracts, oral contract, parol agreement, parties to a contract, passive breach of contract, performance of a contract, preexisting contracts, private contract, privity of contract, public contract, quasi contract, reformation of a contract, release from a contract, renunciation of a contract, repudiation of a contract, requirements contract, rescission of a contract, restitution on a contract, revival of a contract, right to contract, sealed contract, separable contract, service contract, severable contract, specialty contract, subcontract, surety contract, third-party beneficiary contract, unconditional contract, unconscionable contract, unenforceable contract, unilateral contract, unlawful contract, valid contract, verbal contract, void contract, written contract

FOREIGN PHRASES: ***Vox emissa volat; litera scripta manet.*** Words spoken vanish; the written letter remains. ***Qui cum alio contrahit, vel est, vel debet esse non ignarus conditionis ejus.*** He who contracts with another is not, or ought not to be ignorant of his condition. ***Praescriptio et executio non pertinent advalorem contractus, set ad tempus et modum actionis instituendae.*** Prescription and execution do not affect the validity of the contract, but the time and manner of instituting an action. ***Ex turpi contractu actio non oritur.*** From an immoral contract an action does not arise. ***Dolo malo pactumse non servaturum.*** An agreement induced by fraud is not valid. ***Pacto aliquod licitum est, quid sine pacto non admittitur.*** By agreement, things are allowed which are not otherwise permitted. ***Nulla pactione effici potest ne dolus praestetur.*** By no agreement can it be effected that a fraud shall be maintained. ***In contractibus, benigna, in testamentis, benignior; inrestitutionibus, benignissima interpretatio facienda est.*** In contracts, the interpretations should be liberal; in wills, more liberal; in restitutions, most liberal. ***Scientia utrinque par pares contrahentesfacit.*** Equal knowledge on both sides makes the contracting parties equal. ***Pacta conventa quae neque contra leges, neque dolo malo inita sunt, omni modo observanda sunt.*** Agreements which are not contrary to the laws, nor fraudulently entered into, are in all respects to be observed. ***Pactis privatorum juri publico non derogatur.*** Private contracts do not derogate from public law. ***In stipulationibus cum quaeritur quid actum sit verba contrasti pulatorem interpretanda sunt.*** In agreements, when the question is what was agreed upon, the terms are to be interpreted against the party offering them. ***Privatis pactionibus non dubium est non laedi jus caeterorum.*** There is no doubt that the rights of others cannot be prejudiced by private agreements. ***In omnibus contractibus, sive nominatis sive innominatis, permutatio continetur.*** In all contracts, whether nominate or innominate, an exchange (i.e., a consideration) is implied. ***Pacta quae contra leges constitutionesque vel contra bonos mores fiunt, nullam vim habere, indubitati juris est.*** It is unquestionably the law that contracts which are made contrary to the laws or against good morals have no force in law. ***Nemo tenetur ad impossibile.*** No one is bound to an impossibility. ***Pacta dant legem contractui.*** Stipulations constitute the law for the contract. ***Pacta que turpem causam continent non sunt observanda.*** Contracts which are based on an unlawful consideration will not been forced. ***Conventio vincit legem.*** The agreement of parties controls the law. ***Contractus ex turpi causa, vel contra bonos mores, nullus est.*** A contract founded on a base consideration, or one against good morals, is null. ***Nudum pactum est ubi nulla subest causa praeter conventionem; sed ubi subest causa, fit obligatio, et parit actionem.*** A naked contract is where there is no consideration for the agreement; but where there is a consideration, an obligation is created and gives rise to a right of action. ***Modus et conventio vincunt legem.*** Custom, convention, and an agreement of the parties overrule the law. ***Conventio facit legem.*** An agreement creates the law (i.e. the parties to a binding contract will be held to their promises). ***Ex nudo pacto non oritur actio.*** No action arises on a contract without a consideration. ***Contractus legem ex conventione accipiunt.*** Contracts receive legal sanction from the agreement of the parties. ***Naturale est quidlibet dissolvi eo modo quo ligatur.*** It is natural for a thing to be unbound in the same way in which it was made binding. ***Nihil tam conveniens est naturali aequitati quam unumquodque dissolvi eo ligamine quo ligatum est.*** Nothing is so agreeable to natural equity as that a thing should be dissolved by the same means by which it was bound. ***In conventionibus, contrahentium voluntas potius quam verba spectari placuit.*** In contracts, it is the rule to regard the intention of the parties rather than the actual words. ***Ex maleficio non oritur contractus.*** No contract is born of wrongdoing. ***Ex pacto illicito non oritur actio.*** From an unlawful agreement, no action will lie. ***In contrahenda venditione, ambiguum pactum contra venditorem interpretandum est.*** In the negotiation of a sale, an ambiguous agreement is to be interpreted against the seller. ***In contractibus, rei veritas potius quam scriptura perspici debet.*** In contracts, the truth of the matter ought to be regarded as more important than the writing. ***In contractibus, tacite insunt quae sunt moris et consuetudinis.*** In contracts, matters of custom and usage are tacitly implied. ***Incerta quantitas vitiat actum.*** An uncertain quantity vitiates the act. ***Legem enim contractus dat.*** The contract makes the law. ***Nuda pactio obligationem non parit.*** A naked promise does not create a binding obligation. ***Eisdem modis dissolvitur obligatio quae nascitur ex contractu, vel quasi, quibus contrahitur.*** An obligation which arises in contract, or quasi contract, is dissolved in the same ways in which it is contracted.

CONTRACT, *verb* accept an offer, agree, *contrahere,* covenant, engage, enter into, *locare,* make a bargain, make terms, obligate oneself, pledge, promise, undertake, undertake by contract

ASSOCIATED CONCEPTS: contract to perform services

CONTRACT OBLIGATION, *noun* avowal, bond, commitment, compact, concordant, condition, covenant, guarantee, indenture, issue, liability, pact, pledge, promise, provision, proviso, specific obligation, specific term, term, warranty

CONTRACT PROVISION, *noun* arrangement, article of agreement, clause, condition, limitation, obligation, postulation, prerequisite, proviso, qualification, requisite, restriction, specification, stipulation, term

CONTRACTOR, *noun* architect, artificer, builder, constructor, designer, deviser, engineer, maker, planner, worker

ASSOCIATED CONCEPTS: artisan's lien, independent contractor, general contractor, materials lien, mechanic's lien, subcontractor

CONTRACTUAL, *adjective* accordant, agreed, agreed to, arranged, binding, collectively agreed, committed, consensual, consentient, in accord, in accordance with, in conformity, negotiated, obligated, obligatory, pledged, promised, settled, signed, signed and sealed, stipulated, understood
ASSOCIATED CONCEPTS: contractual agreement, contractual assumption of risk, contractual consideration, contractual liability, contractual obligation, contractual relationship, contractual right, contractual status

CONTRADICT, *verb* *ab re discrepare,* abrogate, affirm the contrary, annul, answer back, argue, assert the contrary, assert the opposite, challenge, clash, come in conflict with, conflict, confute, *contradicere,* contrast, contravene, controvert, counter, counteract, countervail, counterwork, deny, differ, disagree, disclaim, disprove, dispute, dissent, give denial to, go against, go contrary to, go counter to, go in opposition to, impugn, *inter se repugnare,* negate, negative, oppose, oppugn, prove the contrary, quarrel, rebut, refuse to accept, refute, repudiate, reverse, run counter to, take issue with, traverse
ASSOCIATED CONCEPTS: contradiction by a witness on the stand

CONTRADICTION, *noun* adverseness, antipathy, antithesis, assertion of the contrary, assertion of the opposite, conflict, conflicting evidence, confutation, contradistinction, contraindication, contraposition, contraries, contrariety, contrariness, contrary assertion, contrast, contravention, controversion, controversy, counteraccusation, counteraction, counterargument, countercharge, counterevidence, counteroath, counterstatement, defiance, denunciation, difference of opinion, direct opposite, disaccord, disagreement, discord, *discrepantia,* disproof, dispute, dissension, dissent, divergence, divergent opinion, incongruity, inconsistency, negation, negative evidence, opposite extreme, oppositeness, opposites, opposition, other extreme, rebuttal, rebutting evidence, refutal, refutation, rejoinder, *repugnantia,* variance
ASSOCIATED CONCEPTS: contradiction in terms, contradiction of a witness, contradiction of a writing, impeachment of a witness

CONTRADICTORY, *adjective* abjuratory, absonant, adversative, adverse, antagonistic, antithetical, asserting the contrary, asserting the opposite, at odds, at variance, clashing, conflicting, confutative, confuting, contradicting, contradistinct, contraindicating, contrapositive, contrarious, *contrarius,* contrary, contrary to reason, contrasted, contravening, converse, counter, counteractant, countervailing, counterworking, denying, diametrically opposite, disagreeing, disclaiming, discordant, discrepant, dissentient, dissenting, *diversus,* in the opposite scale, inconsistent, inverse, irreconcilable, negating, negatory, obverse, opponent, opposed, opposing, opposite, oppositional, oppositive, rebutting, refutative, refutatory, refuting, *repugnans,* repugnant, reverse, *tout au contraire,* unreconciled
ASSOCIATED CONCEPTS: contradiction of a writing, contradictory evidence, contradictory findings, contradictory instructions, contradictory statement
FOREIGN PHRASES: ***Allegans contraria non est audiendus.*** One making contradictory allegations is not to be heard. ***Cum duo inter se pugnantia reperiuntur in testamento, ultimum ratum est.*** When two things repugnant to each other are found in a will, the last shall be confirmed.

CONTRADISTINCTION, *noun* antagonism, antithesis, clashing, contradiction, contradictoriness, contrariety, contrast, counterpoint, departure from, difference, disparity, dissimilarity, distinction, distinctness, divergence, oppositeness, opposition

CONTRAPOSITION, *noun* antagonism, antithesis, confrontation, confrontment, contradiction, contradistinction, contrariety, contrast, converse, counterpart, disagreement, disparity, dissimilarity, incompatibility, obverse, odds, opposite, opposite side, opposition, otherness, placement against, placement opposite, reverse, unlikeness

CONTRARY, *adjective* abnegative, adversative, adverse, *adversus,* answering, antagonistic to, antipathetic, antithetic, antithetical, at cross purposes, at issue, at variance, averse, captious, conflicting, confutative, confuting, contradicting, contradictory, contradistinct, contraindicating, contrapositive, *contrarius,* contrasted, contrasting, contraway, converse, counter, counteracting, countervailing, denying, diametrically opposite, different, disaffirming, disagreeing, disavowing, discordant, in opposition to, inverse, negative, negatory, obverse, opposed, opposing, opposite, opposite in character, opposite in nature, oppositional, oppugnant, rebutting, refutative, refutatory, refuting, *tout le contraire,* vis-à-vis
ASSOCIATED CONCEPTS: contrary intent, contrary to evidence, contrary to good morals, contrary to law, contrary to public interest, contrary to statute

CONTRARY, *noun* antilogy, antipode, antithesis, conflict, contradiction, contradistinction, contrast, converse, incompatibility, inconsistency, opposite, opposition, other extreme, reverse, vice versa
ASSOCIATED CONCEPTS: contrary to the law

CONTRARY TO FACT, *adjective* aberrant, deceptive, delusory, dishonest, distorted, erroneous, fallacious, false, fraudulent, inexact, questionable, solecistical, specious, unfactual, untrue

CONTRARY TO LAW, *adjective* criminal, false, felonious, illegal, illegitimate, improper, inaccurate, incorrect, inexact, lawless, malefactory, malfeasant, outlawed, prohibited, proscribed, tortious, unauthorized, unlawful, unlicensed, wrong
ASSOCIATED CONCEPTS: contrary to the evidence

CONTRAST, *verb* appose, bring into comparison, *comparare,* compare by observing differences, compare to, compare with, confront, differ, differentiate, *discrepare,* discriminate, distinguish, distinguish between, draw a comparison, exhibit the differences between, institute a comparison, make a comparison, oppose, place against, place in juxtaposition, set in opposition, set off against, set off by opposition, stand out in opposition

CONTRAVENE, *verb* balk, be contrary to, be in conflict with, clash, conflict with, contest, contradict, counteract, cross, defeat, defy, deny, disagree, dispute, disregard, foil, frustrate, gainsay, go against, impugn, infringe, negate, nullify, oppose, rebut, refute, run counter to, thwart, transgress, traverse, violate
ASSOCIATED CONCEPTS: contravene a statute, contravene the law

CONTRAVENTION, *noun* antagonism, argument, breaking an obligation, clash, conflict, confrontation, contention, contest, contradiction, controversion, counteraction,

countervail, debate, denial, disagreement, discord, dissent, dissidence, disunion, disunity, divisiveness, friction, gainsaying, infringement, lack of concord, negation, opposing, opposition, oppugnancy, quarrel, rebuttal, resistance, transgression, traversal, variance, violation, vying with, wrangle
ASSOCIATED CONCEPTS: contravention of a contract, contravention of a statute, contravention of an agreement

CONTRIBUTE *(Assist),* ***verb*** abet, accommodate, *adiuvare,* advance, advise, afford aid, aid, assist, assist substantially, be a party to, be helpful, be of service, bear a part, bring aid, conduce, cooperate, encourage, enter into, furnish aid, give aid, help, intercede for, join in, lend assistance, minister, partake, partake of, participate, *prodesse,* render help, serve, stand by, subscribe to, succor, support, take an active part in, tend
ASSOCIATED CONCEPTS: contributing cause, contributing to delinquency of a minor, contributing to support a dependent

CONTRIBUTE *(Indemnify),* ***verb*** compensate, give back, indemnity, make compensation, make reparation, make restitution, pay back, pay damages, recompense, reimburse, remit, remunerate, restore, return, satisfy, tender

CONTRIBUTE *(Supply),* ***verb*** accord, add, administer, afford, allot, assign, award, bequeath, bequest, bestow, cede, commit, confer, consign, convey, deed, deliver, demise, devote, dispense, dispose of, dole out, donate, endow, enrich, equip, furnish, give, give away, grant, hand over, impart, invest, mete out, pass down, pay, present, proffer, relinquish, remit, render, share, subsidize, supply, tender, transmit, will
ASSOCIATED CONCEPTS: contributed capital, contributing fault, contributing negligence, contributing proximate cause

CONTRIBUTION *(Donation),* ***noun*** alms, assistance, award, benefaction, benefit, bequest, bestowal, bestowment of a share, bonus, boon, bounty, charity, conferment, *conferre, contribuere,* dispensation, endowment, generosity, gift, grant, grant of a share, gratuity, honorarium, lagniappe, largesse, offering, present, presentation, provision, remembrance, subsidy, subvention, succor, sustenance, tribute

CONTRIBUTION *(Indemnification),* ***noun*** compensation, guerdon, indemnity, need, offsetting, paying back, payment, quittance, reckoning, recompense, redress, reimbursement, remuneration, reparation, repayment, requital, requitement, restitution, restoration, return, satisfaction, substitution
ASSOCIATED CONCEPTS: contribution among joint tort feasors, subrogation

CONTRIBUTION *(Participation),* ***noun*** abetment, aid, alliance, assistance, association, coaction, coalition, collaboration, collusion, combination, complicity, comradeship, concert, confederation, consent, cooperation, coordination, encouragement, federation, fellowship, harmony, help, interest, league, partnership, pool, shareholding, sharing, teamwork, union
ASSOCIATED CONCEPTS: accumulated contributions, contributing to the injury, contribution to capital, contributory fault, contributory infringer, contributory negligence, indemnity

CONTRIBUTOR *(Contributor),* ***noun*** abettor, accessory, accomplice, aide, ally, assistant, associate, auxiliary, coadjutor, cohelper, collaborator, colleague, compeer, comrade, confederate, confrere, consort, cooperator, copartner, coworker, fellow, helper, helpmate, mate, participant, participator, partner, party, peer, shareholder, sharer, teammate, teamworker, workfellow

CONTRIBUTOR *(Giver),* ***noun*** almoner, almsgiver, altruist, assignor, benefactor, bestower, donator, donor, granter, grantor, investor, patron, philanthropist, presenter, subscriber, supplier, supporter, testator, vouchsafer

CONTRIBUTORY, ***adjective*** accessory, additional, aiding, assisting, auxiliary, beneficial, conducive, contributing, determining, helpful, helping, influential, instrumental, lending assistance, salutary, secondary, tributary, useful
ASSOCIATED CONCEPTS: contributory cause, contributory negligence

CONTRITE, ***adjective*** apologetic, broken in spirit, chastened, compunctious, conscience-smitten, conscience-stricken, desirous of forgiveness, full of regrets, full of remorse, guilty, humble, humbled, *paenitet,* penitent, penitential, regretful, regretting, remorseful, repentant, rueful, self-accusing, self-condemnatory, self-convicted, self-denunciatory, self-reproachful, sorrowful, sorry, soul-searching

CONTRIVANCE, ***noun*** artifice, collusion, complicity, connivance, craft, deception, design, designing power, device, dodge, engineering, *excogitatio,* intrigue, *inventio,* invention, inventiveness, machination, maneuver, manipulation, means to an end, mechanism, method, plan, plot, scheme, stratagem, strategics, subterfuge, tactics, wile, wily device

CONTRIVE, ***verb*** arrange, cause, collude, compose, conceive, concoct, connive, consider, conspire, counterplot, design, develop a course, devise, draft, effect, *excogitare,* fabricate, fashion, forecast, form, frame, imagine, improvise, induce, intrigue, *invenire,* invent, lay plans, *machinari,* machinate, make up, maneuver, mine, organize, pattern, plan, plot, predesign, preestablish, prepare, procure, project, provoke, scheme, shape out a course, sketch, systematize
ASSOCIATED CONCEPTS: contrive a cause of action

CONTROL *(Restriction),* ***noun*** blockade, brake, check, constraint, curb, deterrence, deterrent, disallowance, exclusion, inhibition, limitation, moderation, prevention, prohibition, qualification, rationing, repression, restraint, restrictive practice, subdual, suppression
ASSOCIATED CONCEPTS: institution of controls, price control

CONTROL *(Supervision),* ***noun*** administration, auspices, authority, care, charge, command, custody, direction, discipline, dominance, domination, dominion, government, guardianship, guidance, jurisdiction, keeping, management, managership, mastery, ministry, *moderatio,* oversight, patronage, power, proctorship, protectorship, *regimen,* regulation, stewardship, superintendence, *temperantia,* ward, wardenship, wardship
ASSOCIATED CONCEPTS: absolute control, circumstances beyond control, complete control, constructive control, exclusive control, immediate control, indirect control, joint control, loss of control, mutuality of control, parental control, reasonable control

CONTROL *(Regulate),* ***verb*** administer, administrate, check, *coercere,* command, conduct, direct, dominate, engineer, govern, guide, handle, have charge of, have in one's charge, have the direction of, have under control, instruct, lead, look after, maintain, manage, manipulate,

moderari, operate, order, overlook, oversee, pilot, preside over, regiment, rule, superintend, supervise, take care of
ASSOCIATED CONCEPTS: Bureau of Control and Accounts, control board, controlled corporation, controlled substance, controlling clause, controlling influence, controlling interest, controlling issues, controlling question of law or fact

CONTROL *(Restrain),* ***verb*** arrest, confine, constrain, *continere,* guard, hamper, hinder, hold back, hold in check, impede, inhibit, keep in check, keep under control, limit, obstruct, prohibit, put under restraint, restrict, retard, subdue, suppress, *temperare,* trammel
ASSOCIATED CONCEPTS: controlled substance

CONTROLLED *(Automatic),* ***adjective*** contrived, devised, machinelike, mechanical, mechanistic

CONTROLLED *(Restrained),* ***adjective*** aloof, calm, conditioned, constrained, cool, detached, disciplined, disengaged, distant, guarded, impassive, imperturbable, in check, inhibited, moderate, obedient, passionless, reflex, restrained, self-controlled, steady, stoical, temperate, unconcerned, undemonstrative, unemotional, unexcitable, unruffled

CONTROLLING *(Authoritative),* ***adjective*** arresting, binding, bridling, coercive, constraining, constrictive, curbing, decisive, dominant, eminent, forceful, holding, impeding, important, in charge, magisterial, measuring, muffling, over, overriding, predominant, regnant, regulating, restraining, smothering, sovereign, stifling, stultifying, ultimate
ASSOCIATED CONCEPTS: a controlling case, controlling caselaw

CONTROLLING *(Dictatorial),* ***adjective*** autocratic, commanding, despotic, dominant, dominating, domineering, executive, harsh, imperious, iron-handed, micromanaging, oppressive, overbearing, pushy, reigning, strict, subjugating, supervising, tyrannical

CONTROVERSIAL, ***adjective*** arguable, at issue, at odds, at variance, confutable, contestable, *controversus,* controvertible, debatable, dialectic, disputable, doubtful, dubious, dubitable, eristic, exhibiting pros and cons, factious, in dispute, in question, not axiomatic, open to discussion, open to doubt, open to question, polemical, problematical, questionable, refutable, speculative, suspect, uncertain, uncertified, undecided, under inquiry, unsure, unverifiable

CONTROVERSY *(Argument),* ***noun*** *altercatio,* altercation, antagonism, argumentation, brawl, break, broil, clashing, conflict, conflict of opinion, contention, contest, contestation, *controversia,* debate, difference of opinion, disaccord, disagreement, *disceptatio,* disceptation, discongruity, discord, discordance, disharmony, disputation, dispute, disputed point, disputed question, dissension, dissidence, dissonance, disunion, disunity, divergence, divergent opinions, embroilment, failure to agree, feud, friction, impugnation, inaccordance, incongruence, inconsistency, inharmoniousness, inharmony, jangle, lack of concord, opposition, polemics, quarrel, question at issue, rupture, set-to, split, squabble, strife, subject of dispute, unconformity, variance, wrangle
ASSOCIATED CONCEPTS: arbitrable controversy, matters in controversy, submission of a controversy

CONTROVERSY *(Lawsuit),* ***noun*** action, case, case at law, cause, contest, judicial contest, legal action, legal argument, legal proceeding, legal process, litigation, matter for judgment, process in law, suit in law
ASSOCIATED CONCEPTS: actual present controversy, amount in controversy, case or controversy, controversies in bankruptcy, controversy arising under Constitution, controversy arising under laws of the United States, controversy at law or in equity, controversy between citizens of a state and a foreign country, controversy between citizens of different states, controversy over claim, justiciable controversy, real controversy, settlement of controversy in bankruptcy, subject of controversy, sum in controversy

CONTROVERT, ***verb*** abjure, abnegate, abrogate, answer, answer conclusively, argue, argue the case, argue the point, attack, confute, contend against in discussion, contest, contradict, contradict absolutely, contravene, counter, debate, defeat, deny, disaffirm, disagree with, disallow, disavow, disclaim, discuss, dismiss, disprove, dispute, give denial to, make a rejoinder, negate, oppose, overwhelm, rebuff, rebut, *refellere, refutare,* refute, repudiate
ASSOCIATED CONCEPTS: controverted question of fact, controverting plea

CONTUMACIOUS, ***adjective*** anarchistic, cantankerous, contemptuous, *contumax,* defiant, defying lawful authority, disobedient, *entêté,* factious, fractious, headstrong, indocile, indomitable, insolent, insolently disobedient, insubordinate, intractable, mutinous, not compliant, obstinate, *pertinax,* perverse, rebellious, recalcitrant, recusant, refractory, refusing to obey, renitant, repulsive, resistant, resisting authority, resisting control, restive, stubbornly disobedient, stubbornly rebellious, uncomplying, ungovernable, unmanageable, unreasonable, unsubmissive, willfully disrespectful
ASSOCIATED CONCEPTS: contumacious conduct, contumacious witness

CONTUMELY, ***noun*** abuse, affront, arrogance, aspersion, berating, castigation, contempt, contemptuous treatment, contemptuousness, *contumelia,* derision, despite, despiteful treatment, discourtesy, disdain, disdainfulness, dishonor, disrespect, effrontery, haughtiness, humiliating rudeness, humiliation, indignity, insolence, insult, invective, objurgation, obloquy, opprobrium, presumptuousness, reproach, revilement, rudeness, scornful insolence, scornful treatment, scornfulness, scurrility, vilification, vituperation

CONVENE, ***verb*** accumulate, aggroup, amass, assemble, bring together, call, call together, call up, collect, congregate, consolidate, converge, convoke, draw together, gather, gather together, group, hold a meeting, hold a session, meet, mobilize, muster, rally, reunite, round up, summon, unite
ASSOCIATED CONCEPTS: convene a session of a court, convene a term of the court

CONVENIENCE, ***noun*** acclimation, accommodation, advancement, advantage, agreeableness, aid, amenity, anodyne, assistance, benefit, betterment, comfort, creature ease, expedience, facility, help, indulgence, luxury, satisfaction, service, shelter, solace

CONVENIENT, ***adjective*** acceptable, accessible, accommodatus, advantageous, agreeable, applicable, appropriate, available, befitting, beneficial, carefree, commodious, conducive, desirable, easily accessible, easily done, easy, effortless, eligible, expedient, fitted, fitting, *habilis,* helpful, *idoneus,* opportune, presenting few difficulties, requiring no effort, serviceable, suitable, suited, useful

ASSOCIATED CONCEPTS: balance of convenience, certificate of public convenience and necessity, convenience and necessity, convenience of parties, enforcement in convenience, greatest convenience, public convenience, reasonably convenient, rule of convenience

FOREIGN PHRASES: ***Non solum quid licet, sed quid est conveniens, est considerandum; quia nihil quod est inconveniens est licitum.*** Not only that which is lawful, but that which is convenient is to be considered, because nothing which is inconvenient is lawful.

CONVENTION *(Assembly),* ***noun*** assembly, cabinet, caucus, clinic, conclave, conference, convocation, discussion, forum, gathering, meeting, panel, parley, rally, retreat, roundtable, seminar, session, summit, symposium, synod

CONVENTION *(Tradition),* ***noun*** birthright, conduct, conservative custom, ethic, form, formality, habit, heritage, inheritance, legacy, manner, mode, norm, officialism, prescription, principle, procedure, protocol, rubric, rule, standard, stereotype, value

CONVENTIONAL, ***adjective*** acceptable, accepted, accustomed, approved, classical, common, conformable, conforming, conforming to accepted standards, customary, established, established by general consent, everyday, familiar, fitting, fixed, general, habitual, in established usage, long-established, natural, normal, of long standing, ordinary, orthodox, permanent, prevalent, regular, routine, standard, time-honored, tradition-bound, traditional, *translaticius,* typical, usual, widely used, wonted

ASSOCIATED CONCEPTS: conventional interest, conventional life estate, conventional mortgage, conventional obligation, conventional sequestration, conventional subrogation, conventional trust

CONVERGE, ***verb*** approach, approach one another, assemble, blend, bring into focus, bring near, bring together, center upon, centralize, close in upon, coalesce, *coire,* come closer, come to a focus, come to a point, come together, concenter, concentralize, concentrate, congregate, consolidate, convene, convocate, draw gradually together, draw in, focalize, focus, gather, *in unum vergere,* incline toward each other, interfuse, join together, meet, merge, taper, unite

CONVERSATION, ***noun*** articulation, *causerie,* chat, collocution, colloquial discourse, colloquy, communication, confabulation, *conloquium,* consultation, conversing, deliberation, dialogue, discourse, discussion, dissertation, exchange, exchange of views, familiar discourse, imparting of thoughts, inquiry, interchange, interchange of information, interchange of opinions, interchange of speech, interchange of thoughts, intercommunication, interlocution, interview, oral communication, parley, questioning, speaking, talk, telling, verbal intercourse

ASSOCIATED CONCEPTS: confidential conversations, criminal conversation, wiretapping conversations

CONVERSE, ***verb*** address, advise, allocute, answer, articulate, attest to, carry on a conversation, comment on, commune with, communicate with, confabulate, confer with, *conferre,* consult with, debate, descant, discourse, discuss, dissertate, exchange ideas, exchange views, have dialogue, have verbal intercourse, hold conference, impart thoughts, inform, interchange ideas, interchange information, interchange opinions, interchange thoughts, interview, make a rebuttal, make a speech, make a statement, parley, perorate, recite, recount, relate, relate ideas, relay ideas, say, speak with, state, talk, utter

CONVERSION *(Change),* ***noun*** alteration, interchange, metamorphosis, passage, reconstruction, shift, switch, transformation, transition, transmutation

ASSOCIATED CONCEPTS: conversion of a security

CONVERSION *(Misappropriation),* ***noun*** appropriation, defraudation, deprivation, embezzlement, fraud, larceny, malfeasance, misapplication, misappropriation of funds, misemployment, misuse, peculation, theft, thievery, unauthorized assumption of property, unlawful appropriation, unlawful use of another's property, wrongful assumption, wrongful exercise of dominion

ASSOCIATED CONCEPTS: action for conversion, attachment, constructive conversion, conversion by assertion of ownership, conversion of goods, conversion of property, conversion of stock, detinue, fraudulent conversion, innocent conversion, involuntary conversion, larceny by conversion, technical conversion, trover, wrongful conversion

CONVERT, ***verb*** actuate, adapt, alter, assimilate, bend, bias, brainwash, budge, change, convince, impel, incline, influence, lead, metamorphose, missionize, modify, move, persuade, prevail, propagate, proselytize, redeem, reform, shift, sway, transform, turn

ASSOCIATED CONCEPTS: conversion of property

CONVERT *(Change use),* ***verb*** alter, amend, become, change, change into, change over, commute, *convertere,* denature, develop, diversify, emend, evolve, exchange, interchange, make into, make over, metabolize, metamorphose, modify, mutate, permute, rearrange, recast, reconstitute, reconstruct, refashion, reform, regenerate, remake, remodel, remold, render different, renovate, reorganize, replace, reshape, restyle, revamp, revise, shift, substitute, switch, transfer, transfigure, transform, transmogrify, transmute, transpose, transshape, transubstantiate, turn, vary

ASSOCIATED CONCEPTS: basic converter, convert bonds, innocent converter

CONVERT *(Misappropriate),* ***verb*** apply dishonestly, appropriate wrongfully, assume unlawful rights of ownership, embezzle, expropriate, misapply, misdirect, misemploy, mismanage, misuse, peculate, put to a wrong use, steal, take illegally

ASSOCIATED CONCEPTS: convert to one's own use, fraudulently convert

CONVERT *(Persuade),* ***verb*** align, brainwash, bring around, convince, enlist, induce, influence, lead to believe, prevail, propagandize, proselytize, reform, sway, talk into, win an argument, win over

CONVERTIBLE, ***adjective*** capable of being exchanged, changeable, commutable, commutative, complementary, compromisable, correlative, counterchangeable, exchangeable, interchangeable, mutable, permutable, reciprocative, reversible, substitutive, transformable, transmutable, transposable

ASSOCIATED CONCEPTS: convertible bond rule, convertible bonds, convertible coupon bonds, convertible securities

CONVEY *(Communicate),* ***verb*** acquaint, advise, affirm, announce, annunciate, apprise, articulate, assert, aver, avow, bare, become known, broadcast, comment, confide, contact, declare, describe, detail, direct the attention to, disclose, disseminate, divulgate, divulge, educate, elucidate, enlighten, evince, explain, expose, express, get across, get in touch, give an account, give notice, impart, indicate, inform, instruct, keep posted, make acquainted, make aware, make known, make public, manifest, mention, narrate, notify, pass on, point out, post, proclaim, promulgate, pronounce, publish, recite, recount, relate, remark, render an account, report, represent, reveal, share, signify, speak, specify, state, suggest, teach, tell, transmit, uncover, vent

CONVEY *(Transfer), **verb*** abalienate, alienate, assign, award, bequeath, carry, cede, consign, contribute, deed, deliver, deliver over, demise, devolve, dispense, donate, endow, enfeoff, give, grant, hand down, hand out, impart, lease, pass, pass down, pass title, present, relinquish, shift, transfer title, transmit, transport, transpose
ASSOCIATED CONCEPTS: lawfully convey, quitclaim and convey

CONVEYANCE, *noun* alienation, alienation of property, assignation, assignment, bestowal, bestowment, conferment, consignation, delivery, demise, devise, devolution, disposal, sale, shift, testamentary disposition, tranmission, transfer, transfer of property, transfer of title, transference, transmission, transmittal
ASSOCIATED CONCEPTS: absolute conveyance, conveyance by deed, encumbrance, fraudulent conveyance, involuntary conveyance, presumptive conveyance
FOREIGN PHRASES: ***Transit terra cum onere.*** Land passes subject to any encumbrances affecting it. ***Nihil tam conveniens est naturali aequitati quam voluntatem domini rem suam in alium transferre ratam habere.*** Nothing is more conformable to natural equity than to confirm the intention of an owner who desires to transfer his property.

CONVICT, *noun* accused, accused person, bad example, captive, condemned person, condemned prisoner, criminal, crook, culprit, defaulter, defendant, delinquent, desperado, desperate criminal, escapee, evildoer, felon, first offender, fugitive, guilty man, guilty person, inmate, internee, jail inmate, lawbreaker, malefactor, malevolent, malfeasant, malfeasor, miscreant, misdemeanant, misfeasor, offender, outlaw, parolee, prisoner, prisoner at the bar, prisoner behind bars, prisoner of state, public enemy, recidivist, recreant, reprobate, rogue, scoundrel, sinner, thief, transgressor, villain, wrongdoer
ASSOCIATED CONCEPTS: certificate of relief from disabilities

CONVICT, *verb* attaint, bring to justice, call to account, cast blame upon, censure, condemn, condemn after judicial investigation, declare guilty of an offense, denounce, denunciate, doom, find against, find guilty, find liable, give a guilty verdict, hold liable, hold responsible, impose a penalty on, inflict a penalty on, inflict punishment, pass censure on, pass sentence on, penalize, prescribe punishment, pronounce judgment, pronounce sentence, punish, put the blame on, sentence, utter judicial sentence against
ASSOCIATED CONCEPTS: convict of a crime, convict of wrongdoing, sentence

CONVICTION *(Finding of guilt),* ***noun*** adjudgment, adjudication, aspersion, avengement, blame, censure, charge, condemnation, criminality, culpability, *damnatio,* damnation, decision, decree, decrial, denouncement, denunciation, determination, exaction of penalty, execution of sentence, final condemnation, finding, hostile verdict, imposition, judgment, passing judgment, penalization, penalty, prescribed punishment, proof of guilt, punishment, punition, reprehension, reprisal, reprobation, reproof, retribution, retributive justice, ruling, sentence, sentencing, unfavorable verdict, verdict
ASSOCIATED CONCEPTS: certificate of conviction, criminal conviction, felony conviction, final conviction, guilty verdict, nolo cotendere plea, record of conviction, sentencing

CONVICTION *(Persuasion),* ***noun*** ascertained principle, assumption, assurance, assured belief, attitude, avowal, certainty, certitude, concept, conception, conclusion, consideration, credence, creed, declaration of faith, doctrine, dogma, faith, firm belief, fixed opinion, impression, inclination, judgment, leaning, mind, *opinio,* opinion, outlook, personal judgment, point of view, position, positiveness, postulation, posture, predilection, predisposition, presupposition, principle, proclivity, profession, propensity, rooted belief, *sententia,* sentiment, settled belief, settled judgment, standpoint, staunch belief, supposition, sureness, tenet, theory, thinking, understanding, unshakable opinion, view, viewpoint, way of thinking, well-founded opinion

CONVINCE, *verb* allure, argue into, assure, bring to reason, carry conviction, clinch an argument, compel, compel belief, convert, dispose, enlist, exert influence, extort belief, gain the confidence of, impel, impress, incline, indoctrinate, induce, influence, inspire, inveigle, lead to believe, make confident, make realize, outweigh, overcome by argument, overweigh, persuade, persuade by argument, *persuadere,* predispose, prevail upon, produce conviction, prompt, propagandize, prove, prove one's point, satisfy, satisfy by evidence, satisfy by proof, suborn, sway, win over

CONVINCING, *adjective* absolute, *ad persuadendum accommodatus,* assured, assuring, attestable, authentic, believable, believed, believing, bona fide, categorical, certain, cogent, coherent, commanding, compelling, conclusive, confirmable, confirmatory, confirming, convictive, corroborating, corroborative, credal, credible, creditable, decisive, deducible, demonstrable, documentary, documented, establishable, established, evident, evincible, forceful, genuine, influential, irrefragable, irrefutable, likely, logical, maintaining, moving, persuasive, plausible, positive, possible, potent, powerful, practiced, prevailing, profound, provable, proving, rational, real, reasonable, reliable, secure, self-evident, stated, strong, suasive, substantial, supportable, sustainable, swaying, tenable, to be believed, tried, true, trusted, trusting, trustworthy, unconfutable, undeniable, undisputed, unrefutable, valid, verifying, well-founded, well-grounded, worthy of credence
ASSOCIATED CONCEPTS: clear and convincing proof, convincing proof

CONVOLUTED, *adjective* baroque, bizarre, byzantine, challenging, complex, complicated, confusing, daedal, detailed, difficult, elaborate, esoteric, extravagant, flamboyant, florid, grotesque, hard-to-grasp, impenetrable, intricate, involute, involved, Kafkaesque, knotty, labyrinthian, manifold, multibranched, multifaceted, multifarious, ornamental, ornate, richly adorned, rococo, sophisticated, unintelligible, varied, variegated
ASSOCIATED CONCEPTS: convoluted caselaw, convoluted facts in a case

COOPERATE, *verb* act in concert, act jointly, act together, *adiuvare,* ally, amalgamate, associate, be a party to, cabal, coact, cofunction, collaborate, collude, combine, combine forces, concert, concord, concur, confederate, conjoin, connive, conspire, contribute, cowork, federate, fraternize, go along with, go into partnership, join forces, join in, join with, league, lend one's support to, lend oneself to, make an agreement with, make common cause with, partake in, participate, pool, pull together, rally round, share in, side with, stand together, take part in, take part with, unite one's efforts, unite with, work as a team, work side by side with, work together

COOPERATION, *noun* affiliation, affinity, aid, alliance, assent, association, coaction, coadjuvancy, coalition, collaboration, combined effort, companionship, confederation, cronyism, esprit de corps, fellowship, fusion, harmony, help, incorporation, integration, liaison, logrolling, merger, mutual help, participation, partisanship, partnership, quid quo pro, rapport, reciprocity, solidarity, support, symbiosis, synergism, synergy, teaming, teamwork, unanimity, unity
ASSOCIATED CONCEPTS: cooperation with the government

COOPERATIVE, *noun* alliance, association, collective, communal business establishment, communal society, commune, concurrent effort, federation, guild, joint action, joint operation, joint possession, partnership, teamwork, union

COORDINATE, *verb* adjust, arrange, assimilate, balance, combine, equalize, harmonize, homologize, integrate, methodize, organize, proportion, regularize, regulate, schematize, set in order, synchronize, systematize

COPARTNER *(Business associate),* ***noun*** adjuvant, associate, auxiliary, coadjutant, cohelper, collaborator, colleague, comate, companion, compeer, *confrère,* consociate, consort, cooperator, coworker, fellow, fellow worker, helper, mate, partner, peer, *personnel,* sharer

COPARTNER *(Coconspirator),* ***noun*** abettor, accessory, accessory after the fact, accessory before the fact, accompanier, accomplice, accomplice in crime, adjunct, adjutant, adjuvant, aid, aide-de-camp, aider and abettor, assistant, associate, attendant, *camarade,* coadjutant, coadjutor, coadjutress, coaid, cohelper, cohort, collaborator, colluder, comate, companion, comrade, confederate, *confrère,* consociate, conspirer, cooperator, copartner in crime, helper, helpmate, *intrigant,* intriguer, machinator, *particeps criminis,* partner in crime, socius criminis, supporter
ASSOCIATED CONCEPTS: joint adventure, joint enterprise, tenant in copartnership

COPIOUS, *adjective* abounding, abundant, ample, bountiful, considerable, *copiosus,* countless, extravagant, exuberant, filled, flowing, full, generous, gigantic, great, in profusion, inexhaustible, innumerable, large, lavish, liberal, luxuriant, massive, more than enough, numerous, of great extent, opulent, overflowing, plenteous, plentiful, populous, producing abundantly, productive, profitable, profuse, profusive, prolific, replete, rich, streaming, superabundant, supernumerary, teeming, unlimited, unmeasured, unrestricted, unsparing, unstinting, voluminous, well-provided, well-stocked, wide, yielding abundantly

COPY, *noun* cast, counterfeit, counterpart, duplicate, duplication, ectype, facsimile, fake, forgery, image, imitation, impress, impression, imprint, likeness, offprint, personation, print, reissue, repetition, replica, representation, reprint, reproduction, simulation, tracing, transcript, transfer
ASSOCIATED CONCEPTS: certified copy, conformed copy, correct copy, true copy

COPY, *verb* adopt, ape, approximate, assume, borrow, caricature, cartoon, cheat, conform, depict, ditto, do like, double, draw, duplicate, echo, emulate, falsify, follow, follow suit, follow the example of, forge, give an encore, *imitari,* imitate, impersonate, infringe copyright, iterate, make a duplicate of, make a transcript of, make a replica, mirror, mock, model, parrot, pattern after, personate, pirate, plagiarize, portray, pretend, print, rebuild, recapitulate, reconstruct, recreate, reduplicate, reecho, reestablish, refashion, rehash, reiterate, remake, repeat, replicate, represent, reprint, reproduce, republish, restate, retell, retrace, revive, rewrite, simulate, take after, trace, transcribe
ASSOCIATED CONCEPTS: counterfeit, impersonate, infringe

COPYCAT KILLING, *noun* carnage, crime, death, destruction, duplicated annihilation, duplicated homicide, duplicated killing, horror, massacre, obliteration, recurring duplicated bloodshed, repeated butchery, reproduced assassination, reproduced murder, shooting, slaying, terrorism, torment

COPYRIGHT, *noun* authority, authorization, certificate of invention, certification, concession, enfranchisement, entitlement for a term of years, exclusive privilege of publication, exclusive privilege of publication and sale, exclusive right of production, grant, license, permit, privilege to publish, privilege to reproduce, right of literary property, sanction
ASSOCIATED CONCEPTS: copyright license, patent

CORDIAL, *adjective* accommodating, affable, affectionate, agreeable, amicable, approachable, attentive, benevolent, benign, benignant, bonhomous, cheerful, collegial, companionable, congenial, convivial, courteous, delightful, devoted, earnest, easygoing, empathetic, engaging, fond, friendly, genial, good-natured, gracious, happy, harmonious, hospitable, jovial, kind, kindly, loving, neighborly, nice, obliging, outgoing, polite, responsive, sincere, sociable, social, sympathetic, tender, tenderhearted, thoughtful, understanding, warm, warmhearted, welcoming

CORE, *noun* backbone, bedrock, body, center, consequence, content, cornerstone, corpus, epitome, essence, fundamentals, gist, gravance, heart, main point, meat, nave, nub, nucleus, prime ingredient, principle, quiddity, quintessence, soul, substance, sum and substance, summary
ASSOCIATED CONCEPTS: core of a case, core of a claim, core of an accusation, core of an allegation, core of testimony

CORE HOLDING, *noun* central holding, critical determination of the court, essential holding of a case, vital portion of decision

CORE POLITICAL SPEECH, *noun* discussion of public issues, First Amendment speech, highly-guarded speech, political expression, position speech, purely expressive speech, words to rally public support for a candidate for public office, words to rally public support for an espoused position, words to rally public support for an issue

CORNERSTONE, *noun* backbone, base, body, cardinal point, core, corpus, critical point, crucial point, crux, essence, essential matter, exigency, foundation, frame of reference, fundamental, gravamen, groundwork, heart, highlight, key, keynote, keystone, landmark, main body, main element, main point, main thing, mainstay, major event, major part, material point, matter of concern, matter of importance, milestone, nucleus, pedestal, pivot, principal part, principle, purport, purpose, quintessence, rudiment, salient point, *sine qua non,* standard, substance, substantiality, support, *terra firma,* threshold

COROLLARY, ***noun*** addition, adjunct, appurtenance, complement, correlation, correspondence, deduction, derivation, derived principle, logical sequence, offshoot, outcome, outgrowth, propinquity, sequent, supplement, syllogism

CORPORAL, ***adjective*** bodily, corporeal, fleshy, incarnate, material, not spiritual, palpable, physical, somatic, substantial, tangible
ASSOCIATED CONCEPTS: corporal imbecility, corporal oath, corporal punishment

CORPORAL PUNISHMENT, ***noun*** beating, branding, caning, capital punishment, conviction, death penalty, death sentence, death warrant, denouncement, denunciation, doom, excommunication, flogging, guilty verdict, hitting, mutilation, punishment, spanking, whipping
FOREIGN PHRASES: ***Corporalis injuna non recipit a estimationem de futuro.*** A personal injury is not satisfied by the outcome of a future proceeding.

CORPORATE *(Associate),* ***adjective*** affiliate, allied, banded, federative, incorporate, leagued, partnered
ASSOCIATED CONCEPTS: corporate act, corporate assets, corporate authorities, corporate body, corporate bonds, corporate commission, corporate conduct, corporate dividends, corporate existence, corporate franchise, corporate name, corporate officer, corporate powers and privileges, corporate property, corporate purpose, corporate rights, corporate seal, corporate securities, corporate stock

CORPORATE *(Joint),* ***adjective*** associated, coincident, compact, concurrent, conjoint, conjunct, correal

CORPORATE GOVERNANCE, ***noun*** code of conduct, corporate canons, corporate dictates, corporate direction, corporate mandates, corporate norms, corporate principles, corporate regulation, corporate restrictions, corporate standards, corporate tenets, directives, guidelines, laws of governance, model of propriety, oversight, rules of conduct, standards, supervision
ASSOCIATED CONCEPTS: affiliated person, audit committee, board committees, board compensation review, board composition, board independence, ethics, executive officers, independent directors, retirement ages selection process, term limits

CORPORATION, ***noun*** affiliate, affiliation, agglomerate, alliance, artificial entity, artificial person, associate, association, body, body corporate, business, business association, business establishment, coalition, combination, combine, commercial enterprise, company, concern, confederacy, conglomerate, *conlegium,* consociation, consolidation, corporate body, enterprise, establishment, federation, firm, foundation, holding company, industry, institute, institution, joint concern, legal body, legal entity, operating company, organization, sodality, stock company, syndicate, union
ASSOCIATED CONCEPTS: alter ego, business trust, cartel, closed corporation, closely held corporation, consolidation, corporate charter, corporate officers dissolution, corporate structure, de facto corporation, de jure corporation, derivative action, directors, dissolution, domestic corporation, fictitious corporations, foreign corporation, joint stock associations, limited partnerships, membership corporation, merger, municipal corporation, officers, parent corporation, public corporation, partnership, proxies, self-dealing, shareholders, sole proprietorship, stockholders, subsidiaries, voting trusts
FOREIGN PHRASES: ***Jus quo universitates utuntur est idem quod habent privati.*** The law which governs corporations is the same as that which governs individuals. ***Corporatio non dicitur aliquid facere nisi id sit collegialiter deliberari, etiamsi major pars id faciat.*** A corporation is not said to do anything unless it be deliberated upon collectively, although the majority should do it.

CORPOREAL, ***adjective*** actual, appreciable, bodily, *bona fide,* certain, concrete, corporal, definite, demonstrable, embodied, existent, firm, fleshly, having substance, in existence, incarnate, material, palpable, physical, real, solid, substantial, substantive, tangible, temporal, unspiritual
ASSOCIATED CONCEPTS: corporeal hereditaments
FOREIGN PHRASES: ***Haereditas, alia corporalis, alia incorporalis; corporalis est, quae tangi potest et videri; incorporalis quae tangi non potest nec videri.*** An inheritance is either corporeal or incorporeal; corporeal is that which can be touched and seen; incorporeal, that which can neither be touched nor seen.

CORPSE, ***noun*** body, *cadaver,* carcass, carrion, casualty, corpus, dead body, dead person, deceased, departed, individual, lifeless body, mortal remains, murder victim, organic remains, remains, victim
ASSOCIATED CONCEPTS: *corpus delicti*

CORPUS, ***noun*** aggregate, aggregation, amassment, assemblage, body, bulk, chief part, collection, collectivity, colligation, compages, compilation, complexus, comprehensiveness, concentration, concretion, confluence, conglomerate, core, cornerstone, corporality, corporeity, cumulation, distillation, embodiment, ensemble, essence, fullness, grand total, gross amount, grouping, import, importance, inclusiveness, integrality, integration, keynote, legal body, legal entity, main body, main part, major part, mass, materiality, materialization, matter, pith, plenum, principal, principle, quantity, quintessence, res, signification, solid substance, solidarity, structure, substance, substantiality, sum, sum and substance, sum total, summation, total, totality, weight, whole, wholeness
ASSOCIATED CONCEPTS: *corpus delicti, corpus juris,* corpus of a trust

CORRECT *(Actual),* ***adjective*** accepted, accurate, appropriate, approved, becoming, certain, comely, conscientious, convenable, convenial, customary, decent, decorous, definite, due, established, exact, exacting, factual, faultless, fitting, flawless, fussy, gracious, impartial, impeccable, in perfect order, infallible, judicious, just right, literal, meticulous, neat, perfect, polite, precise, proper, punctilious, reasonable, redressed, reformed, regulated, remedied, repaired, restored, revised, right, scrupulous, seemly, strict, stylish, suitable, tasteful, tidy, traditional, trim, true, unerring, unmistaken, valid

CORRECT *(Honest),* ***adjective*** equitable, ethical, fair, having a code of conduct, having been brought up properly, having good upbringing, having values, just, moral, official, orthodox, proper, reputable, rightful, scrupulous, true, upright

CORRECT *(Adjust),* ***verb*** alter, ameliorate, amend, appropriate, better, cure, doctor, disabuse, improve, meliorate, mend, reclaim, rectify, redress, reform, remedy, repair, touch up

CORRECT *(Admonish),* ***verb*** berate, castigate, chasten, chastise, chide, disabuse, disenchant, disillusion, enlighten, lecture, objurate, penalize, perfect, punish, put right, rebuke, redress, reprehend, reprimand, reprove, scold, set right, take to task, upbraid

CORRECT *(Review),* ***verb*** amend, change, convert, edit, emend, expostulate, help, regulate, revise

CORRECTION *(Change),* ***noun*** adjustment, alteration, amelioration, amending, amendment, betterment, *correctio,* curative, cure, *emendatio,* emendation, improved version, improvement, melioration, mending, modification, qualification, readjustment, reconstruction, rectification, redaction, reform, reformation, rehabilitation, remedy, removal of errors, renovation, repair, repairing, replacement, rescript, restoration, retraction, revampment, revisal, revised edition, revision, rewrite, righting
ASSOCIATED CONCEPTS: corrective action, corrective procedures

CORRECTION *(Punishment),* ***noun*** amercement, *animadversio,* animadversion, *castigatio,* castigation, censure, chastening, chastisement, condemnation, corrective measure, disciplinary action, discipline, infliction, invective, lesson, payment, penal retribution, penal servitude, penalization, penalty, punition, reprobation, reproval, retribution, retributive justice, scourging, stricture
ASSOCIATED CONCEPTS: board of corrections, correctional facility, house of correction

CORRECTIVE *(Progressive),* ***adjective*** alternative, amendatory, analeptic, antidotal, assuasive, counteractive, curative, emendatory, healing, improving, medicinal, modifying, palliative, progressive, rectifying, reformative, reformatory, remedial, remonstrative, restorative, revisional, salubrious, salutary, sanative, sanatory, therapeutic
ASSOCIATED CONCEPTS: corrective treatment

CORRECTIVE *(Punitive),* ***adjective*** avenging, castigatory, disciplinary, inflictive, medicinal, palliative, penal, penalizing, punishable, punishing, punitory, recriminatory, retaliative, retaliatory, retributive, revengeful, vengeful, vindictive

CORRELATE, ***noun*** affiliate, agnate, ally, analogue, associate, cognate, companion, comparison, complement, complemental term, congener, coordinate, correspondent, counterpart, double, duplicate, equal, equivalent, fellow, like, match, mate, parallel, pendant, reciprocal, reciprocator, relation, similitude, supplement, twin

CORRELATION, ***noun*** analogy, chain, collation, comparison, connection, corollary, correspondence, counterpart, equivalence, functionality, interchange, interconnection, interdependence, likeness, mutual, mutuality, parity, proportion, quid pro quo, reciprocation, reciprocity, relation, relativeness, relativity, resemblance, similarity, similitude, transmutation
ASSOCIATED CONCEPTS: correlation between fact and fiction

CORRELATIVE, ***adjective*** accordant, adapted, affiliate, affiliated, affined, affinitive, agnate, agreeing, akin, allied, amalgamated, analogous, anent, applicable, apposite, appropriate, associated, associative, belonging, cognate, coinciding, collateral, commensurable, commensurate, commutual, comparable, comparative, compatible, complemental, complementary, concerning, concordant, concurrent, conformable, congeneric, congenerous, congruent, congruous, conjoint, conjunct, conjunctive, connate, connatural, connected, connective, consentaneous, consociate, consonant, conspecific, contingent, coordinate, correspondent, corresponding, dependent, equivalent, exchangeable, fellow, fitting, germane, homological, interacting, interdependent, interlinked, interrelated, joined, linked, matched, mutual, mutually related, paired, parallel, pertaining, proportionate, reciprocal, reconcilable, related, relating to, relative, relevant, resembling, similar, suitable, suited
ASSOCIATED CONCEPTS: correlative rights doctrine

CORRESPOND *(Be equivalent),* ***verb*** adapt to, agree, answer the purpose, appertain, approach, approximate, be accordant, be akin, complement, be complemental, be congruent, be related, bear resemblance, belong, border on, bring into relation with, cohere, coincide, compare, comply with, comport with, concur, conform, *congruere,* conjoin, coordinate, copy, correlate, deal with, dovetail, draw a parallel, equal, harmonize, have a comparison, have a connection, have a relation, homologate, homologize, join, liken, match, parallel, pertain, reciprocalize, reconcile, relate, resemble, run parallel to, support an analogy, tie in with, to be similiar, touch, unite
ASSOCIATED CONCEPTS: corresponding tax

CORRESPOND *(Communicate),* ***verb*** acknowledge, contact, disseminate, epistolize, exchange letters, notify, publicize, relate, reply, respond, send a message, transmit, write

CORRESPONDENCE *(Communication by letters),* ***noun*** communication, dispatches, *epistulae,* exchange of letters, letter writing, letters, *litterae,* mail, missives, writings

CORRESPONDENCE *(Similarity),* ***noun*** accord, agreement, analogy, comparability, conformity, congruence, *congruentia,* congruity, correlation, equivalence, harmony, likeness, parity, resemblance, sameness, semblance, similitude, symmetry, uniformity

CORRESPONDENT, ***adjective*** adapted, agreeable, agreed, akin, analogous, answerable, apposite, appropriate, belonging, coequal, coextensive, cognate, coincidental, coinciding, collateral, comfortable, comparable, commensurable, complementary, concomitant, concordant, congruous, consistent, consonant, contemporaneous, correlative, corresponsive, counterpart, counterposed, equal in effect, equal in force, equal in significance, equal in value, equivalent, fit, fitted, germane, harmonious, homologous, mutual, pendent, reciprocal, related, relative, relevant, similar, suitable, suited, synonymous, uniform

CORRESPONDENT, ***noun*** analogue, complement, coordinate, correlative, counterpart, duplicate, equal, equivalent, obverse, pendant, reciprocator, similitude

CORRESPONDING, ***adjective*** accordant, agreeing, akin, analogous, answerable, apposite, coequal, coextensive, cognate, coincidental, coinciding, collateral, commensurate, comparable, compatible, concerted, concomitant, concordant, conformable, congenial, congruous, consonant, contemporaneous, convertible, correlative, equivalent, harmonious, identical, indistinguishable, like-minded, matching, mutual, parallel, pendent, proportionate, reciprocal, reconcilable, relative, similar, synonymous, tantamount

CORRIGIBLE, ***adjective*** able to improve, adaptable, alleviative, alterative, ameliorable, amenable, amendable, beneficial, controllable, correctable, curable, developmental, emendable, extricable, fixable, functional, governable, improvable, manageable, mendable, perfectible, progressive, reclaimable, recoverable, rectifiable, redeemable, reformable, reformational, reformatory, remediable, renewable, repairable, reparable, replaceable, rescuable, resilient, restorable, resurgent, retrievable, revisable, revisional, salvageable, subject to revisal, submissive to correction, tameable, teachable, tractable

CORROBORATE, ***verb*** acknowledge, adduce evidence, advocate, affirm, assent, assure, attest, authenticate, aver, avouch, bear out, bear witness, bolster up, buttress, call to witness, certify, circumstantiate, *comprobare,* confirm, countersign, defend, document, endorse, fortify, guarantee, justify, maintain, manifest, prove, ratify, reassure, reinforce, sanction, strengthen, subscribe, substantiate, support, sustain, testify to, undersign, uphold, uphold in evidence, validate, verify, vouch for, warrant
ASSOCIATED CONCEPTS: corroborating evidence, corroborating witness

CORROBORATION, ***noun*** acknowledgment, affirmation, assurance, attestation, authentication, averment, avouchment, bearing out, certification, circumstantiation, conclusive evidence, conclusive proof, confirmation, demonstrability, demonstration, documentation, endorsement, establishment, establishment of proof, evidence, exemplification, fortification, legal evidence, presentation of evidence, proof, ratification, strengthening, substantiation, support, supportability, supporting evidence, sustaining, testification, testimony, upholding, validation, validification, verifiability, verification, vindication, voucher, witness
ASSOCIATED CONCEPTS: corroborating circumstances, corroborating evidence, corroborative proof, corroborative testimony

CORROBORATIVE, ***adjective*** affirmatory, agreeing, ascertained, assenting, attested, borne out, certified, confirmatory, confirmed, confirming, convincing, corroborating, deductible, determined, established, evidential, evidentiary, prima facie, proved, substantiated, testificatory, valid, validated, verified, vindicatory
ASSOCIATED CONCEPTS: corroborating circumstances, corroborating evidence, corroborating information

CORROSIVE, ***adjective*** acerbic, acidic, acrid, acrimonious, adverse, annihilatory, arrogant, austere, biting, bitter, brusque, captious, carping, caustic, chafing, consuming, corroding, cutting, cynical, deleterious, disrespectful, edacious, erosive, harmful, hostile, incisive, irascible, mean, mordant, offensive, ornery, salty, sarcastic, sardonic, saucy, scorching, scornful, severe, sharp, sharp-tongued, snarling, sour, taunting, trenchant, venomous, vicious, virulent, voracious

CORRUPT, ***verb*** adulterate, befoul, bribe, cause to be dishonest, contaminate, corrode, *corrumpere,* debase, debauch, decay, defraud, degenerate, *depravare,* deprave, devalue, distort, lead astray, misdirect, mislead, pervert, pollute, prostitute, seduce, spoil, suborn, subvert, taint, undermine, *vitiare,* vitiate, vulgarize, warp
ASSOCIATED CONCEPTS: corrupt a minor

CORRUPTION, ***noun*** abuse of public trust, act of bribing, act of profiteering, baseness, breach of faith, breach of trust, bribery, complicity, conduct involving graft, corrupt inducement, *corruptela,* corruptibility, *corruptio,* crime, criminality, debasement, deception, *depravatio,* deviation from rectitude, deviousness, disgrace, dishonesty, dishonor, disloyalty, disrepute, feloniousness, fraudulence, fraudulency, graft, illegality, improbity, indirection, injustice, jobbery, knavery, lack of conscience, lack of principle, lack of probity, malignancy, obliquity, perfidiousness, perfidy, perversion of integrity, scoundrelism, turpitude, unscrupulousness, venality, villainousness, villainy, want of principle, wickedness
ASSOCIATED CONCEPTS: corruption in public office
FOREIGN PHRASES: ***Corruptio optimi est pessima.*** The corruption of the best is worst. ***Maledicta est expositio quae corrumpit textum.*** It is a cursed interpretation which corrupts the text.

COSIGN, ***verb*** accredit, answer for, approve, assure, authorize, back, be surety for, certify, confirm, countersign, endorse, give assurance, give one's signature, guarantee, indorse, insure, promise, ratify, secure, support, undersign, underwrite, validate, vouch for
ASSOCIATED CONCEPTS: accommodation indorser, accommodation party

COST *(Expenses),* ***noun*** business expense, charge, disbursement, expenditure, legal expense, money expended, obligation incurred, outgo, outlay, overhead, payment, running expense
ASSOCIATED CONCEPTS: awarding costs, bill of costs, costs and disbursements

COST *(Penalty),* ***noun*** amercement, bereavement, damage, damages, fine, forfeiture, harm, impairment, injury, loss, penal retribution, penalization, penance, privation, punishment, sacrifice, unfortunate consequence
ASSOCIATED CONCEPTS: court costs, treble costs

COST *(Price),* ***noun*** appraisal, asking price, assessment, carrying charge, charge, consideration, expensiveness, face value, high worth, *impensa,* mark up, marked price, purchase price, quotation, quoted price, reckoning, sum asked for, valuation, value
ASSOCIATED CONCEPTS: accrued costs, actual cost, all costs, cost basis, cost of administration, cost of doing business, cost of materials, cost of repair, cost of replacement, cost-plus contract, costs and expenses, costs of suit, disbursements, fixed costs, full costs, legal costs, legitimate cost, marginal cost, operating costs, sheriff's costs, total cost, wholesale cost

COSTS, ***noun*** burden of expenditure, charges, damages, disbursement, expenditure, expenses, outlay, out-of-pocket expenses, payment, penalty
ASSOCIATED CONCEPTS: award of costs in an action, awards for pain and suffering, bill of costs, certification of costs, damages, fees, fines, payment of costs, penalties, punitive awards, remittiture

COTENANT, ***noun*** another addressee, another denizen, another dweller, another inhabitant, another inhabiter, another leaseholder, another lessee, another lodger, another occupant, another occupier, another paying guest, another possessor, another renter, another resident, another residentiary, coaddressee, codenizen, codweller, cohouseholder, coinhabitant, coinhabiter, coleaseholder, colessee, co-occupant, co-occupier, copossessor, corenter, coresident, coresidentiary

COUNCIL *(Assembly),* ***noun*** advisory board, board, committee, conclave, conference, forum, judicature, palaver, parley, parliament, synod, tribunal

COUNCIL *(Consultant),* ***noun*** advocate, counselor, deliberation

COUNSEL, ***noun*** advisor, advocate, attorney, attorney-at-law, barrister, barrister-at-law, *consilium,* counselor, counselor-at-law, jurisconsult, jurist, lawyer, legal advisor, legal practitioner, legist, member of the bar, member of the legal profession, officer of court, pleader, solicitor
ASSOCIATED CONCEPTS: advice of counsel, aid of counsel, assigned counsel, assistance of counsel, attorney's fees, benefit of counsel, counsel in a cause, counsel of record, denial of counsel, effective counsel, Escobedo Rule, of counsel, opposing counsel, sixth amendment, waiver of counsel
FOREIGN PHRASES: ***Consilia multorum quaeruntur in magnis.*** The advice of many is required in great affairs. ***Praepropera consilia raro sunt prospera.*** Rash counsels are rarely prosperous.

COUNSEL, ***verb*** advise, advocate, caution, coach, commend, confer, consult, direct, discuss, dissuade, encourage, exchange observations, expostulate, forewarn, give a recommendation, give advice, give suggestions to, guide, instruct, offer an opinion to, opine, persuade, prescribe, prompt, propose, reason with, recommend, seek advice, seek to persuade, submit, suggest, suggest a proposed claim, suggest a proposed contention, urge, warn

COUNSELOR, ***noun*** advisor, advocate, attorney, attorney-at-law, barrister, barrister-at-law, counsel, counselor-at-law, individual admitted to the bar, instructor, intercessor, jurisconsult, jurist, lawyer, legal advisor, legal defender, legal practitioner, legal representative, legist, member of the bar, member of the legal profession, officer of court, one called to the bar, solicitor
ASSOCIATED CONCEPTS: counselor at law, of counsel

COUNT, ***noun*** accusation, allegation, assertion, averment, case for the prosecution, charge, citation, claim, comes, condemnation, countercharge, crimination, declaration, delation, denunciation, distinct statement, imputation, inculpation, indictment, item, item in the indictment, main charge, particular charge, statement of a cause of action
ASSOCIATED CONCEPTS: count in an accusatory instrument, omnibus count

COUNTENANCE, ***verb*** abet, accede to, accredit, acquiesce in, adjust oneself to, advocate, affirm, agree to, aid, allow, *approbare,* approbate, approve, approve of, assent to, assist, back, be in favor of, charter, commend, concur in, confirm, consent to, corroborate, empower, endorse, favor, forward, further, give one's blessing, go along with, help, hold with, homologate, license, make allowances for, make valid, *permittere,* ratify, recognize, recommend, sanction, stand by, subscribe to, support, sustain, view with favor

COUNTER, ***verb*** act against, act in opposition to, agitate against, antagonize, avert, be at cross purposes, be contrary, be inimical, be obstructive, bid against, challenge, clash, collide, come in conflict with, compete with, conflict with, confute, contend, contradict, contravene, counteract, countercheck, countermand, countervail, cross, deflect, defy, disapprove, fend, fight against, fight off, foil, frustrate by contrary action, go against, go contrary to, go in opposition to, hinder, hold at bay, hold off, hold out against, impede, inhibit, interfere, make a stand against, militate against, negate, not support, object, obstruct, oppose, pit against, play against, prevent, prohibit, protest, protest against, put in check, raise objections, rebuff, repel, resist, run in opposition to, set against, side against, stand against, strike back, suppress, take a stand against, take evasive action, take issue with, thwart, ward off, work against, work at cross purposes

COUNTERACT, ***verb*** act in opposition to, agitate against, annul, antagonize, be at cross purposes, be contrary, bid against, cancel out, clash, collide, come in conflict with, conflict with, confute, contend, contradict, counter, counterbalance, countermand, countermine, counterpoise, countervail, counterwork, cross, deactivate, defeat, defy, destroy the effect of, disconcert, disrupt, equalize, equiponderate, fight against, find a remedy, foil, frustrate, frustrate by contrary action, go against, go in opposition to, hinder, inhibit, interfere with, make a stand against, match against, militate against, negate, neutralize, nullify, offset, oppose, oppugn, pit against, play against, play at cross purposes, prevent, protest, protest against, rebuff, repress, resist, *resistere,* reverse, rival, run against, run counter, run counter to, run in opposition to, set against, set at naught, side against, squelch, stand against, take issue with, take one's stand against, traverse, undo, withstand, work against

COUNTERARGUMENT, ***noun*** answer, *audi alteram partem,* challenge, confutation, contradiction, contraremonstrance, contravention, controversion, counteraccusation, countercharge, counterclaim, counterprotest, counterreply, counterstatement, defense, denial, disproof, gainsaying, invalidation, negation, opposition, plea, plea in rebuttal, proof, rebuttal, rebutter, *reductio ad absurdum,* refutation, rejoinder, replication, reply, response, retort, subversion, surrebuttal, surrebutter, surrejoinder, traversal, upset

COUNTERATTACK, ***noun*** counteraction, counterassault, counterblast, counterblow, countermeasure, countermovement, counteroffensive, counterplot, counterpush, counterstrike, counterstroke, counterthrust, cross fire, reprisal, retaliation, retort, retortion, revenge, riposte

COUNTERBALANCE, ***verb*** abrogate, acclimatize, accommodate, accustom, adjust, alter, annul, atone for, balance, change, check, checkmate, clash, combat, compensate, conform, confront, contend with, contradict, coordinate, correct, counter, counteract, counterattack, countermand, counterpoise, countervail, cross, debate, defy, deny, disagree, discomfit, dispute, equalize, equate, equipoise, fetter, foil, impugn, integrate, make up for, neutralize, offset, outweigh, reconcile, rectify, redeem, redress, reverse, set off, stabilize, steady, take issue
ASSOCIATED CONCEPTS: balancing of the equities

COUNTERCHARGE, ***verb*** abnegate, answer, answer back, be respondent, be responsive, confute, contradict, counter, defend, negate, oppose by contrary proof, provide the answer, rebut, rebut the charge, recriminate, refute, refute by argument, rejoin, reply, respond, respond conclusively, retort, riposte, say in reply
ASSOCIATED CONCEPTS: counterclaim, cross-claim

COUNTERCLAIM, ***noun*** action to defeat plaintiff's demand, assertion against the plaintiff, cause against an opposing party, cause of action in favor of defendants, claim advanced by defendant, claim for relief by defendant, claim presented by defendant, contraremonstrance, counteraction, counterapplication, countercharge, counterdeclaration,

counterdemand, countermotion, counterpetition, counterpostulation, counterproposal, counterreclamation, counterrequest, countersuit, cross-action, cross-bill, opposing suit, rejoinder, set-off
ASSOCIATED CONCEPTS: compulsory counterclaim, cross-complaint, cross-demand, cross-petition, equitable counterclaim, permissive counterclaim, set-off, sham counterclaim

COUNTERFEIT, ***noun*** act of copying, bogus, copy, criminal imitation, deception, ersatz, fabrication, fake, false copy, false duplication, false representation, false reproduction, falsehood, falseness, falsification, falsity, *falsus,* forged copy, forgery, fradulent copy, fraudulent imitation, imitation, plagiarism, plagiary, pretense, simulation, unauthorized copy
ASSOCIATED CONCEPTS: counterfeit bill, counterfeited written instrument

COUNTERINTELLIGENCE ***noun*** bugging, cloak-and-dagger work, counterespionage, discover, electronic surveillance, espial, espionage, examine, fish out, follow, following, gumshoe, heel, hound, hunt, intelligence, intelligence agency, intelligence work, look for, meddle, military intelligence, observation, observe, peer, pry, scout, scrutinize, search, secret police, secret service, set a watch on, shadowing, sleuth, spot, spy upon, spying, stakeout, tagging, tailing, take note, trail, trailing, turn over, 24-hour surveillance, watch, wiretap, wiretapping

COUNTERMAND, ***noun*** abolishment, abolition, abrogation, annulment, ban, cancellation, counterorder, defeasance, disallowance, invalidation, nullification, prohibition, recall, recantation, repeal, repudiation, rescindment, rescission, retraction, reversal, revocation, revocation of orders, revokement, suppression, vacation, veto, voidance, withdrawal
ASSOCIATED CONCEPTS: countermand an order

COUNTEROFFER, ***noun*** *casus foederis,* contractual terms, counterbid, counterclause, counterconditions, counterexception, counterlimitation, countermeasure, counterplan, counterpresentation, counterproposal, counterproposition, counterprovision, counterqualification, counterrecommendation, counterrequest, counterreservation, counterstipulation, countersuggestion, hard bargaining, negotiation, new offer, part of the bargain, responsive offer, set of terms, terms proposed

COUNTERPART *(Complement),* ***noun*** alter ego, analogue, brother, coequal, congener, coordinate, correlate, correlation, correlative, correspondent, doppelganger, homologue, mate, obverse, pendant, reciprocal, reverse

COUNTERPART *(Parallel),* ***noun*** carbon, carbon copy, copy, corresponding part, double, duplicate, duplication, effigy, equal, equivalent, image, likeness, match, replica, reproduction, *res simillima,* twin

COUNTERPOISE, ***noun*** counteractive force, counterbalance, equal opposition, equaling force, equilibrium, equipoise, of equal importance, of equal weight, offset, offsetting force, state of balance

COUNTERSIGN, ***verb*** certify, confirm, corroborate, endorse, execute, ratify, sanction, second, support

COUNTERTERRORISM, ***noun*** counterespionage, counterintelligence, espionage, intelligence, intelligence agency, intelligence work, spying, surveillance
ASSOCIATED CONCEPTS: enemy combatants, justice courts, military tribunals, national security profiling, Patriot Act, racial profiling, war on terrorism

COUNTERVAIL, ***verb*** abrogate, act against with equal force, agitate against, alter, avail against, balance, be contrary, cancel, cancel out, check, conflict with, confute, contradict, contravene, counter, counteract, counterpoise, cross, damage, destroy, equiponderate, go counter to, hinder, inhibit, interfere, match, militate against, negate, neutralize, offset, oppose, outbalance, prevent, rebut, refute, resist, run counter to, set off, suppress, thwart, traverse, undermine, weaken, weigh against, work against

COUNTLESS, ***adjective*** abounding, beyond a number, bountiful, endless, extensive, horizonless, illimitable, indefinite, inestimable, inexhaustible, infinite, innumerable, innumerate, innumerous, many, measureless, multitudinous, myriad, numberless, numerous, plentiful, slew, uncountable, unfathomable, unlimited, unnumbered, unreckonable, untold, vast

COUPON, ***noun*** allocation, card, certificate, check, cheque, credit, credit check, detachable part of a certificate, detachable portion, dividend, interest certificate, interim dividend, negotiable instrument, note, premium bond, premium certificate, redeemable part, redemption slip, separable part of a certificate, separate ticket, share-out, slip, stub, ticket, token, voucher, written instrument
ASSOCIATED CONCEPTS: coupon bond, coupon book, coupon interest, coupon note

COURAGE, ***noun*** adventurousness, audacity, backbone, boldness, bravery, bravura, brazenness, certitude, confidence, conviction, daring, dash, dauntlessness, determination, endurance, enterprise, fearlessness, fortitude, gallantry, grit, guts, heroism, intrepidity, mettle, moral fiber, nerve, perseverance, persistence, pluckiness, pugnacity, resolution, resolve, spunk, steadfastness, stoutness, temerity, tenacity, valor

COURAGEOUS, ***adjective*** adventuresome, adventurous, assured, audacious, bold, brash, brassy, brave, brazen, cheeky, daring, dauntless, emboldened, enterprising, fearless, forward, gallant, game, gritty, gutsy, hardy, heroic, impetuous, indomitable, intrepid, lionhearted, martial, nervy, plucky, precipitate, resolute, Spartan, stalwart, strong, tenacious, tough, Trojan, unafraid, undaunted, valiant, venturesome, venturous

COURSE, ***noun*** act, act of pursuing, action, activity, advance, approach, arrangment, attack, campaign, completion, conduct, customary manner of procedure, delivery, design, direction, effectuation, effort, employment, endeavor, evolution, execution, exercitation, furtherance, handling, implementation, interaction, *iter,* line of action, line of conduct, management, manner, measures, method, mode, mode of management, mode of procedure, *modus operandi,* motion, movement, operation, order, particular manner of proceeding, performance, perpetration, plan, policy, positive action, practice, praxis, prescribed system, procedure, process, program, pursuance, pursuit, road, route, scheme, succession of acts, system
ASSOCIATED CONCEPTS: arising out of and in course of employment, course of business, course of conduct, course of dealings, course of employment, courses and distances, direct course, general course, water course
FOREIGN PHRASES: ***In dubio, pars mitior est sequenda.*** In doubt, the safer course is to be followed.

COURSE OF ACTION, *noun* action, advance, approach, avenue, case, channels, custom, doctrine, fashion, ideology, logical process, manner, means, measure, method, methodicalness, methodology, mode, modus operandi, movement, operation, plan, policy, position, practice, procedure, proceeding, program, progression, route, routine, schema, scheme, strategy, system, way

COURSE OF CONDUCT, *noun* action, air, attitude, behavior, carriage, comportment, conformance, convention, dealings, decency, decorum, delivery, demeanor, deportment, established practice, manner, method, mien, mode, morals, observance, performance, practice, presence, propriety, routine, rules, savoirfaire, seemliness, social graces, style, tact, taste, time-honored practices, way, ways

COURT, *noun* bar, bar of justice, *basilica,* bench, forum for adjusting disputes, forum of justice, *iudicium,* judgment seat, judicial assembly, judicial forum, judicial tribunal, justice, justice seat, lawcourt, magistrates, place where justice is administered, tribunal
ASSOCIATED CONCEPTS: adjournment of the court, appearance in court, application addressed to the court, civil court, clerk of court, competent court, contempt of court, county court, court-appointed receiver, court below, court calendar, court costs, court in banc, court martial, court of appeals, court of bankruptcy, court of chancery, court of claims, court of common pleas, court of competent jurisdiction, court of first instance, court of general jurisdiction, court of inquest, court of justice, court of last resort, court of limited jurisdiction, court of probate, court of record, court's own motion, court's own witness, criminal court, district court, family court, federal court, fraud upon the court, inferior courts, inherent right of court, jurisdiction of a court, leave of court, legislative courts, local court, municipal courts, opinion of the court, order of the court, power of the court, probate court, proceedings in court, state court, Supreme Court, tax court, term of court, U.S. courts
FOREIGN PHRASES: ***Actus curiae neminem gravabit.*** An act of the court shall prejudice no man. ***Cursus curiae est lex curiae.*** The practice of the court is the law of the court. ***Ea quae in curia nostra rite acta sunt debitae executioni demandari debent.*** Those things which are properly transacted in our court ought to be committed to a due execution. ***Nihil habet forum ex scena.*** The court has nothing to do with what is not before it. ***Nulla curia quae recordum non habet potest imponere finem neque aliquem mandare carceri; quia ista spectant tantummodo ad curias de recordo.*** No court which has not a record can impose a fine or commit any person to prison; because those powers belong only to courts of record.

COURTESY, *noun* affability, amenity, amiability, chivalry, civility, *comitas,* comity, complaisance, consideration, cordiality, courteous conduct, courteousness, courtliness, deference, elegance of manners, etiquette, excellence of behavior, friendliness, gallantry, geniality, gentility, good behavior, good breeding, good manners, graciousness, manners, *officium,* polished manners, polite act, politeness, refinement, respect, reverence, suavity, tact, thoughtfulness, *urbanitas,* urbanity

COURTROOM, *noun* court, lawcourt, part, room in which a court of law is held, room in which a lawcourt is held, room used for the application of the laws, room used for the public administration of justice, room where justice is administered

COVENANT, *noun* agreement, arrangement, avowal, binding agreement, collective agreement, commitment, compact, concordat, contract, contractual obligation, contractual statement, *conventio,* convention, engagement, guarantee, mutual understanding, oath, *pacisci, pact, pactio, pactum,* pledge, promise, stipulation, understanding, undertaking, warranty, written agreement, written pledge
ASSOCIATED CONCEPTS: breach of covenant, collateral covenants, concurrent covenants, covenant against incumbrances, covenant appurtenant to the land, covenant for quiet enjoyment, covenant not to institute suit, covenant in praesenti, covenant not to convey, covenant of future assurrence, covenant of general warranty, covenant of title, covenant of warranty, covenant running with the land, covenant to pay, dependent covenant, doctrine of implied covenants, joint covenant, negative covenants, restrictive covenant

COVER *(Pretext),* ***noun*** alleged reason, camouflage, claim, disguise, excuse, guise, mask, *obtegere, operire,* pretense, profession, screen, sham, subterfuge, *velare*

COVER *(Protection),* ***noun*** blanket, coating, covering, coverture, guard, integument, safeguard, sheath, shelter, shield, veneer

COVER *(Substitute),* ***noun*** alternate, alternative, equivalent item, exchange, replacement, similar item, stand-in, substitution

COVER *(Conceal),* ***verb*** becloud, befog, bury, camouflage, cloak, curtain, disguise, enshroud, hide, keep out of sight, mask, obscure, put out of sight, screen, seclude, secrete, shroud, veil, *velare*
ASSOCIATED CONCEPTS: cover one's assets

COVER *(Guard),* ***verb*** care for, defend, ensure, harbor, insure, keep in safety, keep safe from harm, keep under close watch, make safe, protect, safeguard, secure, sheathe, shelter, shield, take care of, watch over, wrap

COVER *(Provide for),* ***verb*** compensate for, counterbalance, insure, make compensation, make provision for, offset, pay, recompense, replace, substitute, suffice to defray
ASSOCIATED CONCEPTS: buyer's right to cover

COVER UP, *verb* beard, becloud, black out, blanket, bury, cache, camouflage, choke back, cloak, cloud, conceal, couch, deceive, disguise, dissemble, eclipse, ensconce, enshroud, envelop, gag, harbor, hide, hood, keep secret, mask, masquerade, muffle, obscure, obstruct, repress, screen, secret, shelter, shroud, silence, smother, sneak, squash, squelch, stifle, stow, suppress, veil, wrap
ASSOCIATED CONCEPTS: destruction of evidence

COVERAGE *(Insurance),* ***noun*** act of promise-making, amount for which anything is insured, assurance, backing, bond, covenant, guarantee, guaranty, indemnity, obligation, pledge, promise, promise to pay, protection, reassurance, reinsurance, safeguard, security against loss, support, surety, undertaking, underwriting, warrant, warranty
ASSOCIATED CONCEPTS: blanket coverage, casualty coverage, comprehensive coverage, extended coverage, fire coverage, theft coverage

COVERAGE *(Scope),* ***noun*** accommodation, act of compassing, act of comprehending, act of containing, act of embracing, act of encircling, act of encompassing, act of engrossing, act of spanning, act of subsuming, act of surrounding, ambit, bounds, capacity, circulation, circumscription, composition, comprehension, comprehensiveness, comprisal, domain, dominion, embodiment, embrace, enclosure, encompassment, envelopment, expanse, extent of view, fact of comprehending, field, formation, grasp, inclusion, inclusiveness, inclusivity, incorporation, latitude, measure, participation, province, purview, range, range of view, reach, realm, region, room, space, sphere, spread, sweep, that which is comprehended, view, volume, wide currency, zone

COVERT, ***adjective*** clandestine, cloaked, concealed, covered, cryptic, cryptical, dark, delitescent, disguised, furtive, hidden, insidious, invisible, latent, muffled, mysterious, mystic, mystical, nonapparent, occult, out of sight, private, screened, secluded, secret, sheltered, shrouded, sly, sneaky, stealthy, surreptitious, tacit, undercover, underground, underhand, undisclosed, unknown, unobtrusive, unseen, unsuspected, veiled

COVERTURE, ***noun*** condition of a married woman, conjugality, legal status of a married woman, living as man and wife, marriage lines, married state, married tie, matrimony, matronage, matronhood, matronship, nuptial bond, state of a married woman, state of matrimony, union, wedded state, wifedom

CREATE, ***verb*** be responsible, be the agent, be the author, be the cause of, be the reason, beget, bring about, bring into being, bring on, bring out, bring to effect, bring to pass, build, carve, cause, cause to exist, chisel, compose, conceive, concoct, constitute, construct, contribute, contrive, develop, devise, effect, engender, engineer, erect, establish, fabricate, fashion, *fingere,* forge, form, formulate, found, frame, generate, give birth to, give origin to, give rise to, ideate, improvise, inaugurate, induce, initiate, institute, invent, kindle, launch, lay the foundations, make, make up, occasion, organize, originate, pattern, procreate, produce, put together, set going, set up, shape, spawn, start, think up
ASSOCIATED CONCEPTS: create a debt, create a liability, create a lien, created by fraud, created by law

CREATION, ***noun*** arrangement, artistic effort, authorship, beginning, birth, bringing forth, building, causation, composition, concoction, constituting, construction, contriving, defiance of precedent, designing, development, devising, endeavor, engenderment, establishment, expression, fabrication, fashioning, formation, forming, formulation, formulation of a mental image, formulation of a principle, formulation of an idea, foundation, framing, fruition, imagination, *initium,* invention, manufacture, molding, new departure, original work, origination, patterning, preparation, procreation, producing, production, productiveness, productivity, realization, shaping

CREDENCE, ***noun*** acceptance, act of believing, assurance, belief, certainty, complete trust, confidence, conviction, credit, dependence on, faith, firm belief, fixed belief, full assurance, full belief, implicit belief, instinctive belief, persuasion, reliance, subjective belief, sureness, surety, suspension of disbelief, trust, unshaken belief, view
FOREIGN PHRASES: ***Culbet in arte sua perito est credendum.*** Credence should be given to one skilled in his particular profession.

CREDENTIALS, ***noun*** authorization, certificates, certification, documents, identification, papers, passport, proof of authority, recommendations, records, references, testimonials, vouchers

CREDIBILITY, ***noun*** appearance of truth, *auctoritas,* believability, believableness, credibleness, faithfulness, *fides,* integrity, plausibility, probity, rectitude, reliability, tenability, tenableness, trustworthiness, truthfulness, uprightness, veracity, verisimilitude
ASSOCIATED CONCEPTS: credibility of a witness, impeachment of credibility

CREDIBLE, ***adjective*** assured, believable, commanding belief, commanding confidence, convincing, *credibilis,* creditworthy, dependable, deserving belief, deserving of confidence, faithful, faithworthy, frank, honest, incorruptible, indisputable, indubitable, ingenuous, irrefutable, not improbable, of repute, reliable, reputable, scrupulous, sound, straightforward, to be depended on, to be relied upon, true, trusted, trustworthy, truth telling, truthful, uncorrupt, uncorruptible, undeniable, unequivocal, unfailing, unfalse, upright, veracious, verisimilar, void of suspicion, well-grounded, worthy of belief, worthy of confidence, worthy of credence
ASSOCIATED CONCEPTS: attack on credibility, credible evidence, credible person, credible witness

CREDIBLE EVIDENCE, ***noun*** admitted testimony, believable proof, believable testimony, confirmed proof, convincing proof, corroborated proof, credible documents, credible exhibits, credible proof, creditworthy proof, dependable proof, documented proof, honest proof, indisputable proof, indubitable proof, irrefutable proof, legitimate proof, legitimate proof of facts, proof worthy of belief, proof worthy of credence, tested testimony, testimony which is above reproach, trustworthy proof, truthful proof, truthful testimony, validated proof, verified proof
ASSOCIATED CONCEPTS: attack on credibility, credible evidence, credible person, credible witness

CREDIT *(Delayed payment),* ***noun*** advance, chance to borrow money on time, confidence, future payment, installment buying, loan, opportunity to obtain goods on time, permission to defer payment, purchase on time, purchase on trust, reliance
ASSOCIATED CONCEPTS: confirmed credit, consumer credit, contingent creditors, credit agreement, credit association, credit bureau, credit rating, credit union, creditor and debtor, creditor-beneficiary, creditor of bankrupt, creditor of estate, creditor's bill, creditor's committee, creditor's reference, creditor's suits, establishment of credit, extension of credit, general creditors, judgment creditors, junior creditors, letter of credit, line of credit, paper credit, personal credit, preferred creditors, renewal of credit, secured creditors, unconditional credit

CREDIT *(Recognition),* ***noun*** commendation, consideration, distinction, esteem, fame, favorable opinion, good name, high regard, honor, merit, power, prestige, rank, regard, reputableness, reputation, repute, respect, standing, status, worth
FOREIGN PHRASES: ***Judiciis posterioribus fides est adhibenda.*** Faith or credit is to be given to the more recent decisions.

CREDITABLE, ***adjective*** authentic, believable, credible, dependable, effective, honest, legitimate, real, reasonable, reliable, reputable, respected, true, trustworthy, truthful

CREDITOR, ***noun*** backer, debtee, investor, lender, mortgagee, pledgee, seller, sponsor
FOREIGN PHRASES: ***Debitorum pactionibus creditorum petitio nec tolli nec minui potest.*** The rights of creditors to

sue cannot be prejudiced or diminished by agreements between their debtors.

CREDULITY, *noun* belief, blind faith, *credulitas,* credulousness, deceivability, disposition to believe, easiness of belief, foolishness, gullibility, gullibleness, impressibility, innocence, lack of doubt, lack of dubiety, lack of dubiousness, lack of skepticism, lack of sophistication, lack of suspicion, naiveness, naivete, overtrustfulness, persuasibility, pliability, pliancy, readiness to believe, simpleness, simplicity, suggestibility, susceptibility, susceptivity, tractability, trust, trustfulness, uncritical acceptance, unquestioning belief, unsophistication, unsuspectingness, unsuspiciousness

CREDULOUS, *adjective* believing, *credulus,* deceivable, disposed to believe, easily convinced, easily deceived, easily duped, easily taken in, green, gullible, misjudging, naive, overly trustful, persuasible, prone to believe, simple, trusting, undoubting, unquestioning, unsophisticated, unsuspecting, unsuspicious

CRIME, *noun* act prohibited by law, breach of law, contravention, corruption, criminal activity, criminal offense, delict, *delictum,* delinquency, dereliction, deviation from rectitude, encroachment, *facinus,* felony, flagitiousness, fringement, graft, gross offense against law, guilty act, illegality, indictable offense, infringement, jobbery, *maleficium,* malfeasance, malversation, misconduct, misdealing, misdeed, misdemeanor, misdoing, misfeasance, misprision, noncompliance with law, nonobservance of law, nonfeasance, obliquity, offence, offense, offense against the law, offense against the state, official misconduct, omission prohibited by law, public wrong, serious infraction of the law, violation of law, wrong

ASSOCIATED CONCEPTS: accessory to crime, acquittal of crime, antecedent crime, attempted crime, capital crime, commission of a crime, common-law crimes, compounding a crime, concealment of a crime, convicted of a crime, crime against law of nations, crime against nature, crime involving moral turpitude, crime mala in se, crime mala prohibita, crime of violence, *crimen falsi,* element of the crime, guilt, implement a crime, imprisonment, indictable crime, infamous crime, necessarily included crime, pary to crime, proceeds of crime, prosecution for a crime, punishment for a crime, quasi crime, victim

FOREIGN PHRASES: ***Crescente malitia crescere debet et poena.*** Punishment ought to be increased as malice increases. ***Aestimatio praeteriti delicti ex postremo facto nunquam crescit.*** The weight of a past crime is never increased by a subsequent fact. ***Receditur a placitis juris, potius quam injuriae et delicta maneant impunita.*** Settled rules of law will be departed from rather than that crimes should remain unpublished. ***Peccata contra naturam sunt gravissima.*** Crimes against nature are the most heinous. ***Nemo punitur pro alieno delicto.*** No one is to be punished for the crime of another. ***Ubi culpa est, ibi poena subesse debet.*** Where a crime is committed, there punishment should be inflicted. ***Impunities semper ad deteriora invitat.*** Impunity always invites to greater offenses. ***Melior est justitia vere praeveniens quam severe puniens.*** Truly preventive justice is better than severe punishment. ***Multiplicata transgressione crescat poenae inflictio.*** The infliction of punishment should be increased in proportion to the repetition of the offense. ***Poena non potest, culpa perennis erit.*** Punishment cannot be everlasting, but crime will be. ***In atrocioribus delictis punitur affectus licet non sequatur effectus.*** In the more atrocious crimes the intent is punished, although an effect does not follow. ***Crimen laesae majestatis omnia alia crimina excedit quoad poenam.*** The punishment for treason exceeds that for all other crimes. ***Crimen omnia ex se nata vitiat.*** Crime vitiates all which springs from it. ***Crimina morte extinguuntur.*** Crimes are extinguished by death. ***Culpae poena par esto.*** Let the punishment fit to the crime. ***Venia facilitas incentivum est delinquendi.*** Facility of pardon is an incentive to crime. ***Voluntas et propositum distinguunt maleficia.*** The will and purpose distinguish offenses. ***Multiplicata transgressione crescat poenae inflictio.*** The infliction of punishment should be increased in proportion to the repetition of the offense. ***In criminalibus, voluntas reputabitur pro facto.*** In criminal cases, the intent will be taken for the deed. ***In maleficiis voluntas spectatur, non exitus.*** In offenses, the intention is regarded, not the result. ***In omnibus poenalibus judiciis, et aetati et imprudentiae succurritur.*** In all penal judgments, allowance is made for youth and lack of prudence. ***In criminalibus, sufficit generalis malitia intentionis, cum facto paris gradus.*** In crimes, a general malicious intent suffices where there is an act of equal degree. ***Interest reipublicae quod homines conserventur.*** It is in the interest of the state that men be preserved.

CRIME OF VIOLENCE, *noun* crime involving physical force, crime with physical force, offense with substantial risk of force, use of strength to cause harm

CRIMINAL, *noun* bandit, blackguard, buccaneer, burglar, convict, defrauder, evildoer, extortionist, felon, filcher, fugitive, gangster, grafter, guilty person, gunman, hardened offender, juvenile delinquent, kidnapper, killer, knave, lawbreaker, malefactor, malfeasant, manslayer, marauder, misdemeanant, murderer, offender, outlaw, pilferer, pillager, pirate, plunderer, public enemy, recidivist, recreant, reprobate, *reus,* robber, *sceleratus,* smuggler, sneak thief, swindler, terrorist, thief, transgressor, underworld character, villain, worker of iniquity, wrongdoer

ASSOCIATED CONCEPTS: convicted criminal, criminal action, criminal attempt, criminal capacity, criminal case or cause, criminal charge, criminal code, criminal conduct, criminal conspiracy, criminal contempt, criminal conviction, criminal courts, criminal information, criminal intent, criminal judgments, criminal jurisdiction, criminal motive, criminal negligence, criminal offense, criminal procedure, criminal process, criminal prosecution, criminal responsibility, criminal sanctions, criminal solicitation, criminal statute, criminal syndicalism, criminal transaction, criminal trial, habitual criminal, known criminals

FOREIGN PHRASES: ***Frustra legis auxilium invocat qui in legem committit.*** He vainly seeks the aid of the law who transgresses the law.

CRIMINALITY, *noun* blameworthy conduct, corruptness, criminal attitude, criminal conduct, crookedness, culpability, culpable conduct, felonious conduct, feloniousness, fraudulence, guilt, heinous conduct, illegality, illicitness, infamous conduct, infamous misbehavior, lawlessness, malversation, misdoing, official misconduct, outlawry, transgression, unlawfulness, wrongdoing

ASSOCIATED CONCEPTS: criminal culpability, criminal intent

CRIMINOUS, *adjective* blameful, blameworthy, censurable, condemnable, corrupt, criminal, culpable, degenerate, dishonest, errant, evil, felonious, flagitious, flagrant, fraudulent, guilty, illegitimate, illicit, immoral, inexcusable, infamous, iniquitous, irregular, law-breaking, lawless, malefactory, malfeasant, nefarious, peccant, recreant, reprehensible, sinful, unpardonable, vile, villainous, wicked

CRISIS, *noun* breaking point, climax, critical juncture, crossroads, deadlock, difficulty, dire condition, dire strait, emergency, exigency, flash point, hostile situation, impasse, jam, pinch, predicament, problem, stalemate, tinderbox, trauma, turning point, zero hour
ASSOCIATED CONCEPTS: a credible witness

CRITERION, *noun* barometer, basis, code, custom, design, discipline, example, exemplar, form, formula, foundation, frame of reference, gauge, ground rules, guide, ideal, law, measure, model, norm, *obrussa,* pattern, point of comparison, precedent, prescribed form, principle, regulation, rule, rules and regulations, shape, standard, standard of comparison, standard of criticism, standard of judgment, test, test case, type, yardstick

CRITICAL *(Crucial),* ***adjective*** acute, *anceps,* chief, climacteric, climactic, commanding, considerable, deciding, decisive, determining, *dubius,* essential, eventful, exigent, far-reaching, fateful, foremost, grave, imperative, important, imposing, key, major, material, momentous, never to be forgotten, notable, of decisive importance, of great consequence, of importance, of vital importance, outstanding, overruling, overshadowing, paramount, pivotal, pressing, primary, principal, prominent, serious, significant, solemn, strategic, substantial, turning, urgent, vital, weighty
ASSOCIATED CONCEPTS: critical stage of a trial

CRITICAL *(Faultfinding),* ***adjective*** accusing, blaming, captious, carping, castigating, caustic, caviling, censorious, censuring, chiding, choleric, comminatory, condemnatory, condemning, criminative, criminatory, criticizing severely, cynical, damnatory, defamatory, denunciatory, derogatory, disapproving, *elegans,* exacting, hard upon, hard-hitting, hypercritical, inclined to judge with severity, nagging, objecting, objurgatory, overcritical, rebuking, recriminative, reprehensive, reproachful, reprobative, reproving, scarifying, scathing, scolding, severe, taunting, ultracritical, uncomplimentary, upbraiding

CRITICAL JUNCTURE, *noun* boiling point, breaking point, climax, corner, crossroads, deadlock, dilemma, dire strait, emergency, fix, flash point, happening, head, hot, impasse, landmark, milestone, situation, stalemate, turning point, zero hour
ASSOCIATED CONCEPTS: timing to settle a case

CRITICAL POINT, *noun* benchmark, bookmark, critical point, crux, essence, essential matter, fundamental part, gist, gravamen, heart, key point, linchpin, main point, material point, milestone, pivotal point, prime issue, salient point, substance, substantive point, turning point

CRITICISM, *noun* abuse, accusation, admonition, adverse comment, analysis, animadversion, aspersion, blame, carping, caviling, censure, charge, chiding, commentary, complaining, complaint, condemnation, contravention, critical examination, critical remarks, critique, denunciation, deprecation, depreciation, derogation, detraction, disapproval, discommendation, disdain, disparagement, dispraise, disvaluation, exception, expostulation, fault finding, grievance, grumbling, imputation, indictment, insinuation, *iudicium,* lecture, objection, obloquy, odium, opposition, opprobrium, protestation, reflection, rejection, remonstrance, reprehension, reprimand, reproach, reproof, review, revilement, scolding, upbraiding
ASSOCIATED CONCEPTS: fair and honest criticism, freedom of speech, privileged criticism

CRITICIZE *(Evaluate),* ***verb*** adjudge, appraise, assess, consider, examine, gauge, *iudicare,* judge, measure, rank, rate, reckon, review, scrutinize, sum up, take stock of, value, weigh

CRITICIZE *(Find fault with),* ***verb*** animadvert, berate, blame, castigate, censure, chide, complain, condemn, *culpare,* decry, deprecate, depreciate, disapprove, disparage, dispraise, express dissatisfaction, find cause to blame, impugn, object to, objurgate, rebuke, reprehend, *reprehendere,* reprimand, reproach, reprobate, reprove, upbraid

CRITIQUE, *noun* analysis, appraisal, assessment, breakdown, comment, commentary, critical assessment, criticism, discernment, editorial, essay, estimate, evaluation, examination, exposition, inspection, investigation, judgment, observation, opinion, review, revision, scrutiny, study, write-up

CROSS *(Disagree with),* ***verb*** act in opposition to, argue, be opposed to, collide, conflict with, confront, confute, contend, contest, contradict, contravene, controvert, debate, defy, dispute, gainsay, *homini obsistere,* make a stand against, neutralize, oppose, protest, refuse to conform, refute, repudiate, resist, run counter to, speak against, take exception, traverse
ASSOCIATED CONCEPTS: cross action, cross-appeal, cross-claim, cross-complaint, cross-demand, cross-examination, cross-interrogatories, cross libels, cross-motions, cross-petition, cross-remainders, cross section, cross-suit, crosswalk

CROSS *(Intersect),* ***verb*** bisect, braid, crisscross, crosscut, cut across, divide, go across, halve, intercross, interrupt, intersect, lie across, move across, section, segment, separate, split, traverse

CROSS-EXAMINATION, *noun* asking questions, challenge, checking, cross interrogation, cross questioning, enquiry, evidence-seeking, examination, exploration, formulating questions, grilling, inquest, inquiry, inquisition, interpellation, interrogation, investigation, leading inquiry, minute examination, probe, prosecution, query, quest, questioning, reexamination, scrutiny, search, search into facts, searching inquiry, trial
ASSOCIATED CONCEPTS: right to cross-examine, scope of cross-examination

CROSS-EXAMINE, *verb* ask questions, catechize, challenge, check, cross interrogate, cross question, examine, ferret out, grill, inquire of, interpellate, interrogate, petition, probe, query, question, quiz, reexamine, subject to examination
ASSOCIATED CONCEPTS: cross-examination limited to the scope of the direct examination, direct examination, impeachment, right to cross-examine

CROSS-PURPOSES, *noun* adverseness, antonym, at variance, clashing, contention, contradiction, difference of opinion, difficulty, disagreement, discord, disparity, in opposition, misunderstanding, odds, variance

ASSOCIATED CONCEPTS: at cross-purposes with the intent of the law

CROSS-QUESTIONING, ***noun*** close inquiry, cross-examination, cross-interrogation, exploration, inquiry, inspection, interrogation, investigation, probe, query, questioning, reexamination, review, scrutiny

CROSS SECTION, ***noun*** average, characterization, composite representation, embodiment, epitome, example, exemplar, *exempli gratia,* exemplification, *exemplum,* fair sample, *locus classicus,* norm, part exemplifying a mass, part exemplifying a number, profile, random sample, representation, representative sampling, representative section, representative selection, sample

CROSSROAD *(Intersection),* ***noun*** confluence, conjuncture, cross-way, crossing, crossways, four corners, interchange, intercrossing, intersecting road, intersection, joining road, junction, vertex

CROSSROAD *(Turning point),* ***noun*** calm before a storm, climacteric, climax, conjuncture, crisis, critical moment, critical period, critical point, crossways, crowning point, crucial moment, culmination, decisive moment, dividing point, eleventh hour, floodgate, hinge, hour of decision, juncture, landmark, line of demarcation, meeting of events, milestone, pivot, point of no return, relapse, turn, turn of the tide, watershed, well-chosen moment, well-timed initiative

CROWNING *(Best),* ***adjective*** absolute, capping, cardinal, chief, definitive, dominant, foremost, heading, leading, main, master, paramount, preeminent, preponderant, prevailing, prime, principal, stellar, super, superlative, supreme, surmounting, topping, ultimate

CROWNING *(Ending),* ***adjective*** climaxing, closing, concluding, consummatory, culminating, final, finishing, last, terminating

CRUCIAL, ***adjective*** acute, climacteric, conclusive, consequential, critical, deciding, decisive, definitive, determining, essential, exigent, final, grave, imperative, important, influential, instant, material, momentous, of moment, of note, of supreme importance, pivotal, pressing, severe, significant, supreme, urgent, valuable, vital

CRUCIAL POINT, ***noun*** conclusive point, conclusory point, convincing point, cornerstone, crisis, critical moment, crossroads, definitive point, determinative point, determining point, hour of decision, impelling point, juncture, key point, landmark, main point, optimum point, proof positive, turning point

CRUDE, ***adjective*** basic, boorish, homespun, impure, natural, primitive, raw, rough, rude, simple, uncomplicated, undeveloped, undressed, unfiltered, unfinished, unpolished, unprocessed, unrefined, unsophisticated, untreated

CRUEL, ***adjective*** acrimonious, agonizing, atrocious, barbarous, blood-thirsty, brutal, cold, cold-blooded, coldhearted, *crudelis,* demoniacal, devilish, diabolical, distressing, evil-minded, ferocious, fiendish, fierce, hard, hardhearted, harsh, heartless, hellish, ill-intentioned, ill-natured, ill-willed, implacable, indifferent to suffering, inhuman, inhumane, insensitive, malevolent, malicious, malign, malignant, merciless, oppressive, painful, pitiless, punishing, relentless, remorseless, ruthless, sadistic, satanic, savage, severe, spiteful, tortuous, treacherous, tyrannical, unbenevolent, uncompassionate, unfeeling, unkind, unmerciful, unnatural, unpitying, unrelenting, unsympathetic, unsympathizing, vicious
ASSOCIATED CONCEPTS: cruel and abusive treatment, cruel and barbarous treatment, cruel and inhuman punishment, cruel and inhuman treatment, cruel and unusual punishment, cruel disposition, cruel treatment

CRUELTY, ***noun*** atrocity, austerity, barbarity, barbarousness, bloodthirstiness, brutality, brutalness, brutishness, *crudelitas,* cruel act, cruel conduct, deliberate malice, deviltry, enmity, ferity, ferociousness, ferocity, fierceness, harshness, heartlessness, ill nature, ill usage, ill will, infliction of pain, inhumanity, intolerance, malice, malice aforethought, malice prepense, maliciousness, malignance, malignancy, malignity, mercilessness, oppression, outrage, persecution, rancor, relentlessness, remorselessness, ruthlessness, savageness, savagery, severity, spite, sternness, torture, tyranny, uncompassionateness, unkindness, unremorsefulness, viciousness, victimization, violence
ASSOCIATED CONCEPTS: cruelty of treatment, cruelty to animals, cruelty to children, extreme cruelty, habitual cruelty, mental cruelty, unneccessary cruelty

CRY *(Call out),* ***verb*** appeal, call, demand, exclaim want, moan, need, outcry, require, wail, yearn

CRY *(Shed tears),* ***verb*** grieve, howl, lament, mourn, sob, wail, weep, whimper, whine

CRYPTIC, ***adjective*** ambiguous, arcane, befogged, cloudy, dark, deep, Delphic, double-edged, elliptical, enigmatic, fuzzy, impenetrable, imponderable, inscrutable, murky, mysterious, mystic, nebulous, obscure, occult, opaque, shadowy, shrouded, unaccountable, uncertain, vague

CRYSTALLIZE, ***verb*** accumulate, amalgamate, arrange itself, assume a pattern, assume definite characteristics, be solid, become a reality, become definite, become delineated, become firm, become settled, become solid, become visible, bring together, cement, coagulate, cohere, combine, come together, compact, compress, condense, conglomerate, consolidate, develop, eventuate, fall into line, fashion, form, form a core, formulate, set, shape up, solidify, take form, take on character, take order, take shape, thicken, unfold, unify

CUDGEL, ***noun*** arm, *baculum,* bar, bastinado, bat, battering ram, billy, blackjack, bludgeon, cane, club, cosh, deadly device, deadly weapon, deterrent, ferule, *fustis,* instrument for use in combat, instrument of war, lethal instrument, lethal weapon, mallet, means of offense, night stick, pole, shillelagh, staff, stick, truncheon, war hammer, weapon
ASSOCIATED CONCEPTS: deadly weapons

CULL, ***verb*** accumulate, amass, *carpere,* choose, *collect, decerpere,* gather, glean, *legere,* make a selection, pick, pick out, pluck, round up, select, separate, sift, single out, sort out, winnow

CULMINATE, ***verb*** accomplish, cap, climax, close, complete, conclude, consummate, crown, effect, end, execute, finish, reach a peak, reach the highest point, reach the zenith, terminate, top

CULMINATION, *noun* acme, apex, apogee, cap, climax, crest, crown, crowning touch, head, height, highest point, peak, pinnacle, summit, top, topmost point, utmost height, zenith

CULPABILITY, *noun* blame, blameworthiness, censurableness, chargeableness, criminality, delinquency, dereliction, failure in duty, fault, guilt, guiltiness, improbity, misbehavior, misconduct, misdoing, peccability, peccancy, remissness, reprehensibility, reproachableness, transgression, wrongdoing
ASSOCIATED CONCEPTS: culpable recklessness, culpably negligent

CULPABLE, *adjective* accusable, at fault, blamable, blameworthy, censurable, chargeable, condemnable, convictable, criminal, criminous, *culpandus,* delinquent, deserving blame, deserving censure, discreditable, dishonest, disorderly, dissolute, encroaching, felonious, guilty, having violated the law, improper, in error, in the wrong, indictable, indiscreet, lawbreaking, lawless, meriting censure, meriting condemnation, misdemeanant, peccant, punishable, responsible, transgressing, unrighteous, worthy of blame, wrong

CULPRIT. *noun* bad actor, blackhander, convict, criminal, crook, culprit, delinquent, derelict, evildoer, felon, fugitive, guilty party, guilty person, hoodlum, hustler, lawbreaker, malefactor, malfeasant, miscreant, misdoer, misfeasor, offender, outlaw, perpetrator, racketeer, rapscallion, recidivist, reprobate, sinner, transgressor, trespasser, villain, violator, wrongdoer

CULTIVATE, *verb* advance, *colere,* develop, elevate, enrich, farm, forward, foster, further, garden, improve, make better, nourish, nurture, polish, prepare for crops, promote, rarefy, refine, till, train, work

CUMULATION, *noun* accession, accretion, accruement, accumulation, acervation, acquisition, addition, agglomerate, agglomeration, aggregate, aggregation, amassment, ammount accrued, assemblage, assembly, *attroupement,* augmentation, bringing together, build up, bulk, collection, compilation, concentration, conglomerate, conglomeration, congregation, glomeration, growth by addition, mass, pile, reserve, stock, stockpile, storage, store, supply

CUMULATIVE *(Increasing),* ***adjective*** accruing, accumulative, added together, additional, additive, additory, advancing, becoming greater, becoming larger, broadening, continually increasing, enlarging, ever-widening, expanding, flourishing, growing, growing by successive additions, incremental, lengthening, multiplying, on the increase, piling up, strengthening, successively gaining in force, successively waxing in force, swelling, thriving, widening
ASSOCIATED CONCEPTS: cumulative criminal acts, cumulative sentences, cumulative voting

CUMULATIVE *(Intensifying),* ***adjective*** accelerating, aggravative, amplifying, augmentative, becoming more intense, boosting, concentrating, deepening, enhancing, escalating, exaggerating, extending, heightening, intensive, magnifying, maximizing, multiplying, quickening, sharpening, strengthening

CUNNING, *adjective* acute, artful, astute, beguiling, cagey, canny, circular, clandestine, crafty, deceitful, deceiving, deceptive, designing, devious, dexterous, dodgy, double-dealing, evasive, foxy, guileful, ingenious, insidious, insincere, keen, Machiavellian, manipulative, mischievous, roundabout, sharp, shifty, shrewd, slick, slippery, sly, smart, smooth, sneaky, streetwise, subtle, tricky, underhanded, unscrupulous, wily, with guile

CURATIVE, *adjective* analeptic, corrective, emendatory, healing, relieving, remedial, reparative, restorative, therapeutic

CURB, *verb* arrest, brake, check, control, delay, detain, govern, harness, hinder, hold back, hold in check, hold up, impede, inhibit, keep within limits, limit, mitigate, moderate, muzzle, obstruct, prohibit, repress, restrain, retard, snub, stay, suppress, temper, throttle down, trammel, yoke

CURE, *noun* antidote, antipoison, antitoxin, assuager, balm, catholicon, corrective, counteractant, elixir, emollient, healing agent, medical treatment, medicament, medicine, method of treatment, palliative, panacea, recovery, recuperation, redress, relief, remedy, restoration to health, restorative, salve, *sanatio,* successful remedial treatment, therapeutic, tonic

CURE, *verb* ameliorate, apply a remedy, correct, doctor, effect a cure, heal, improve, make well, make whole, mederi, medicate, meliorate, mend, minister to, nurse, palliate, recall to life, reclaim, recover, rectify, recuperate, redeem, redress, regenerate, rehabilitate, rejuvenate, relieve, relieve of something detrimental, remedy, renew, repair, restore, resuscitate, revive, revivify, right, salve, *sanare,* soothe, treat
ASSOCIATED CONCEPTS: cured by verdict, curing defect, curing error, curing title, opportunity to cure

CURIOSITY, *noun* concern, eagerness, eavesdropping, having a probing mind, inquiring mind, inquiry, inquisitiveness, interest, intrusiveness, investigation, meddlesome, meddling, muckraking, newsmongering, nosiness, obtrusiveness, officiousness, probe, questioning, regard, rubbernecking, searching, snooping, thirsty for information, wonderment

CURRENCY, *noun* bank notes, bills, cash, circulating medium, coin, government notes, hard cash, legal tender, medium of exchange, *moneta,* money, money in actual use, notes, paper money, ready money, specie
ASSOCIATED CONCEPTS: lawful currency

CURRENT, *adjective* being done, belonging to the time, concurrent, contemporaneous, contemporary, customary, existent, existing, *hic,* immediate, in fashion, in style, in the fad, in vogue, instant, latest, latter day, new, occurring, of the moment, of the present, of this date, of today's date, popular, present, present day, prevailing, prevalent, recent, revised, stylish, topical, up-to-date, up-to-the-minute, *usitatus,* widespread
ASSOCIATED CONCEPTS: current account, current assets, current basis, current business expenses, current debts, current events, current expenditures, current market value, current obligations, current operating expenses, current rate of exchange, currently distributable

CURRICULUM, *noun* agenda, compendium, course, course of study, discipline, plan, program, prospectus, schedule, seminar, study, syllabus
ASSOCIATED CONCEPTS: continuing legal education

CURSE *(Expletive)*, ***noun*** inappropriate language, obscenity, off-color language, profanity, swear, vulgarism

CURSE *(Imprecation)*, ***noun*** anathema, bad luck, censure, condemnation, denouncement, execration, hex, imprecation, jinx, malediction, malison, spell

CURSORY, ***adjective*** apathetic, brief, careless, casual, desultory, hasty, heedless, hurried, immethodical, inattentive, incautious, indifferent, lax, offhand, passing, perfunctory, quick, rapid, regardless, shallow, short, slapdash, slipshod, speedy, summary, superficial, surface, thoughtless, undiscerning, unmindful, unthorough
ASSOCIATED CONCEPTS: cursory examination

CURTAIL, ***verb*** abate, abbreviate, abridge, clip, cut, cut down, cut short, decrease, diminish, halt, lessen, lop, make smaller, *minuere,* pare, pare down, reduce, retrench, shorten, subtract, trim

CURTAILMENT, ***noun*** abatement, abbreviation, abbreviature, abridgment, compression, condensation, constriction, contraction, cut-back, cutting down, cutting off, declension, decline, decrease, decrescence, depression, deprivation, diminishment, diminution, divestment, elimination, lessening, minimization, modification, privation, reduction, retrenchment, shortening, shrinkage, subduction, subtraction, trimming

CURTILAGE, ***noun*** court, courtyard, enclosure, fenced, garden, land, yard

CUSTODIAL, ***adjective*** cared for, carefully watched, caretaking, keeping, protected, protecting, protective, restraining, safe, screened, sheltering, shielding, tutelary, watched
ASSOCIATED CONCEPTS: custodial interference

CUSTODIAN *(Protector)*, ***noun*** champion, curator, defender, guardian, keeper, manager, overlooker, overseer
ASSOCIATED CONCEPTS: custodian of assets, gratuitous custodian
FOREIGN PHRASES: ***Nemo alienae rei, sine satisdatione, defensor idoneus intelligitur.*** No one is considered a competent defender of another's property, without security.

CUSTODIAN *(Warden)*, ***noun*** caretaker, jailer

CUSTODIANSHIP, ***noun*** captivity, care, charge, confinement, constraint, custody, detention, durance, guardianship, incarceration, restraint, retention, safekeeping

CUSTODY *(Incarceration)*, ***noun*** arrest, arrestment, bondage, bounds, captivity, circumscription, commitment, confinement, constraint, detention, durance, enthrallment, fetter, holding, immuration, immurement, impoundment, imprisonment, limitation, restraint, restriction, safekeeping, thralldom
ASSOCIATED CONCEPTS: arrest, bail, constructive custody, hold in custody, parole, probation
FOREIGN PHRASES: ***Fortior est custodia legis quam hominis.*** The custody of the law is stronger than that of man. ***In custodia legis.*** In the custody of the law.

CUSTODY *(Supervision)*, ***noun*** act of protecting, administration, aegis, auspices, *carcer,* care, charge, control, custodia, custodianship, direction, guardianship, guidance, jurisdiction, keeping, management, preservation, preservation from harm, preservation from injury, protection, regulation, safeguard, safekeeping, stewardship, superintendence, trusteeship, wardship, watch
ASSOCIATED CONCEPTS: custody and control, custody decree, custody of children, custody of property, custody order, custody proceeding, guardianship

CUSTOM, ***noun*** ceremony, characteristic way, common usage, consuetude, convention, conventionalism, conventionality, course of business, dictates of society, established way of doing things, etiquette, familiar way, fashion, fashionableness, formality, habit, habit of a majority, habitual activity, habitual practice, habituation, habitude, institution, manner, matter of course, observance, ordinary manner, practice, prescribed form, prevailing taste, prevalence, rite, ritual, routine, routine procedure, social usage, style, tradition, traditionalism, traditionality, unwritten law, usage, usual manner, vogue, wont, wontedness
ASSOCIATED CONCEPTS: custom of merchants, custom or practice, custom or usage, general custom, local customs, usual course and custom, waiver by custom
FOREIGN PHRASES: ***Servanda est consuetudo loci ubi causa agitur.*** The custom of the place where the action is brought should be observed. ***In contractibus, tacite insunt quae sunt moris et consuetudinis.*** In contracts, matters of custom and usage are tacitly implied. ***Consuetudo tollit communem legem.*** Custom supersedes the common law. ***Consuetudo non trahitur in consequentiam.*** Custom is not drawn into consequence. ***Consuetudo manerii et loci observanda est.*** Custom of a manor and a locality is to be observed. ***Consuetudo est optimus interpres legum.*** Custom is the best interpreter of the laws. ***Consuetudo est altera lex.*** Custom is another law. ***Consuetudo contra rationem introducta potius usurpatio quam consuetudo appellari debet.*** A custom introduced contrary to reason ought rather to be called a usurpation than a custom. ***Ratio est formalis causa consuetudinis.*** Reason is the source and cause of custom. ***Quae praeter consuetudinem et morem majorum fiunt neque placent neque recta videntur.*** Things which are done contrary to the custom and manner of our ancestors neither please nor appear right. ***Optimus interpres rerum usus.*** Usage is the best interpreter of things. ***Optima est legis interpres consuetudo.*** Custom is the best interpreter of the law. ***Omne jus aut consensus fecit, aut necessitas constituit aut firmavit consuetudo.*** Every right is either derived from consent, established by necessity, or confirmed by custom. ***Minime mutanda sunt quae certam habuerunt interpretationem.*** Those matters which have had a certain interpretation are to be altered as little as possible. ***Obtemperandum est consuetudini rationabili tanquam legi.*** A reasonable custom is to be obeyed like law. ***Malus usus abolendus est.*** A bad custom is to be abolished. ***Consuetudo volentes ducit, lex nolentes trahit.*** Custom leads the willing, the law compels the unwilling. ***Consuetudo vincit communem legem.*** Custom overrules the common law. ***In consuetudinibus, non diuturnitas temporis sed soliditas rationis est consideranda.*** In customs, not lapse of time, but the soundness of reason should be considered. ***Consuetudo semel reprobata non potest amplius induci.*** Custom once disallowed cannot again be invoked. ***Consuetudo praescripta et legitima vincit legem.*** A prescriptive and lawful custom prevails over the law. ***Consuetudo neque injuria oriti neque tolli potest.***

Custom can neither arise from nor be abolished by a wrongful act. ***Consuetudo loci observanda est.*** The custom of a locality is to be observed. ***Consuetudo, licet sit magnae auctoritatis, nunquam tamen, praejudicat manifestae veritati.*** A custom, though it be of great authority, should never be prejudicial to manifest truth. ***Consuetudo ex certa causa rationabili usitata privat communem legem.*** A custom, based on a certain and reasonable cause, supersedes the common law. ***Consuetudo et communis assuetudo vincit legem non scriptam, si sit specialis; et interpretatur legem scriptam, si lex sit generalis.*** Custom and common usage override the unwritten law, if it be special; and interprets the written law, if the law be general.

CUSTOMARY, *adjective* accustomed, acknowledged, boilerplate, common, commonplace, consuetudinary, continued, conventional, current, daily, established, everyday, expected, favorite, fixed, formal, frequent, general, habitual, inveterate, longstanding, natural, normal, ordinary, orthodox, popular, prescriptive, prevailing, prevalent, pro forma, recognized, regular, repeated, right, routine, standard, stipulated, stock, systematic, time-honored, traditional, typical, understood, universal, usual, wonted
ASSOCIATED CONCEPTS: customary despatch, customs and usages, customs court

CUSTOMARY USE, *adjective* accepted usage, accustomed use, common use, conventional practice, customary application, established application, established employment, everyday use, general use, habitual use, normal use, ordinary and reasonable use, ordinary use, popular use, prevalent practice, prevailing use, regular use, routine use, standard practice, the norm, ubiquitous use, universal application, usual practice, widespread application

CUSTOMER, *noun* acceptor, bargainer, bidder, business contact, buyer, buyer of labor, client, consumer, *emptor,* investor, leaser, lessee, one of the clientele, one of the purchasing public, patron, prospect, purchaser, purchaser of goods from another, redeemer, share buyer, shopper, taker, user, vendee
ASSOCIATED CONCEPTS: buyer in the ordinary course of business, cash customer, customer in ordinary course of business, duty to customers, interference with customers, loss of customers, occasional customer, solicitation of customers

CUT *(Edit),* ***verb*** abbreviate, cancel, chop, cross out, delete, elide, eliminate, eradicate, erase, excise, expunge, obliterate, reconfigure, redact, redline, remove, rewrite, strike, tear apart, wipe out

CUT *(Injure),* ***verb*** break, cause an abrasion, incise, lacerate, rip, rupture, score, slash, slice, slit, tear, wound

CUT *(Reduce),* ***verb*** abbreviate, abridge, clip, condense, crop, curtail, cut back, decrease, diminish, downgrade, downsize, dwindle, lessen, lower, mark down, minimize, pare, portion, prune, ration, shave, take, trim

CUT *(Stop),* ***verb*** block, discontinue, end, halt, obstruct, pull the plug, repress, sever, silence, suppress

CUT OFF, *verb* annul, arrest, block, blockade, break, break off, break up, can, cease, clamp down, complete, conclude, cut off, cut out, dam, delay, demolish, desist, destroy, discontinue, drop, end, halt, hinder, impede, pack in, quit, rein, rein in, remove, sever, sever ties, shut off, squash, squelch, stop, suspend, take a break, take a respite, terminate
ASSOCIATED CONCEPTS: latches, statute of limitations

CUT OUT, *verb* ban, bar, black out, cut away, debar, delete, divide, edit, eliminate, except, excise, exclude, forbid, omit, rearrange, remove, repress, resist, restrain, rule out, scissor out, separate, sever, stop, toll, truncate

CY PRES, *adverb* as near as may be, as near as practicable, as near as possible

CYBERBULLYING, *noun* e-bullying, electronic harassment, information highway bullying, information superhighway bullying, Internet bullying, intimidator on the web, net bullying, network bullying, online bullying, web bullying, World Wide Web bullying

CYBERCRIME, *noun* a criminal offense on the Web, a criminal offense regarding the Internet, a violation of law on the Internet, an illegality committed with regard to the Internet, breach of law on the Internet, computer crime, contravention through the web, corruption regarding Internet, criminal activity on the Internet, disrupting operations through malevolent programs on the Internet, e-crime, electric crime, Internet crime, sale of contraband on the Internet, stalking victims on the Internet, theft of identify on the Internet
ASSOCIATED CONCEPTS: copyright theft through cybercrime, cyberlaws, cyber-stalking, hacking, privacy

CYBERTERRORISM, *noun* attacks on computer networks, computer terrorism, cybercrime, disruption of computer networks, information highway terrorism, Internet terrorism, massive harm to the information system, online terrorism, terrorism on the net, terrorism through the web, use of viruses to disrupt computer networks, wholesale destruction of computer networks

CYCLE, *noun* age, alternation, circle, circuit, *circulus,* consecution, course, eon, epoch, era, flow, period, progression, recurrence, recurring period, regular return, regularity of recurrence, repetitiveness, revolution, rotation, round, sequence, succession

CYNICAL, *adjective* acrimonious, apt to distrust, arrogant, caustic, cavalier, censorious, condemnatory, contemptuous, contumelious, critical, decrying, defamatory, defeatist, denunciatory, derisive, derogative, derogatory, despising, disapproving, disdainful, disillusioned, disparaging, disposed to doubt, distrustful, distrusting the motives of others, doubtful, doubting, dubious, fault-finding, haughty, holding a low opinion of mankind, inconvincible, indisposed to believe, misanthropic, mistrustful, mocking, *mordax,* pessimistic, questioning, ridiculing, sarcastic, sarcastical, sardonic, scoffing, scornful, skeptical, sneering, supercilious, suspecting, suspicious, unbelieving, untrustful

CYNICISM, *noun* acerbity, acidity, annoyance, antagonism, bitterness, causticity, causticness, censure, chariness, contempt, dark side, dejection, depression, displeasure, distrust, doubt, dubiety, gloom, hopelessness, ill feeling, ill will, incredulity, irony, irritability, jealousy, malice, misanthropy, mockery, nonbelief, peevishness, pessimism, rancor, resentment, rise, sarcasm, scoffing, skepticism, sneering, spite, suspicion, umbrage, uncertainty, vehemence, wariness

DAILY, ***adjective*** accustomed, common, diurnal, established, habitual, ordinary, quotidian, *quotidie,* regular, routine, usual

ASSOCIATED CONCEPTS: daily attendance, daily balance, daily occupation, daily output, daily publication, daily rate of pay, daily wages

DAMAGE, ***noun*** adversity, affliction, aggravation, casualty, declination, decline, decrement, depravation, depreciation, destruction, deterioration, detriment, dilaceration, diminution, disrepair, exacerbation, grievance, hardship, harm, hurt, impairment, infliction, injury, loss, ruin, ruination, spoiling, vexation, vitiation, weakening, wreck, wrong

ASSOCIATED CONCEPTS: actual loss, ad damnum clause, aggravation of damages, business damage, conjectural damages, consequential damages, contingent damages, damages actually sustained, damages by fire, damages by the elements, damages in contemplation of party, damages to land, damages to person, damages to property, damages to realty, *damnum absque injuria,* excessive damages, exemplary damages, future damages, general damages, incidental damages, *injuria absque damno,* limitation of liability, liquidated damages, measure of damages, minimizing damages, nominal damages, personal injury, property damage, punitive damages, remote damages, special damages, treble damages, unliquidated damages, unusual or extraordinary damage

FOREIGN PHRASES: ***Nemo damnum facit, nisi qui id fecit quod facere jus non habet.*** No one is considered as doing damage, except he who does that which he has no right to do. ***Nul sans damage avera error ou attaint.*** No one shall have error or attaint unless he has suffered damage. ***Ubicunque est injuria, ibi damnum sequitur.*** Wherever there is a wrong, there damage follows. ***Quod quis ex culpa sua damnum sentit non intelligitur damnum sentire.*** He who incurs a damage by his own fault is not held to suffer damage. ***Damnum sine injuria esse potest.*** There can be damage or injury inflicted without any act of injustice. ***Actus legis nemini est damnosus.*** An act of the law shall prejudice no one.

DAMAGE, ***verb*** abase, abuse, blemish, blight, break, break down, bruise, cause detriment, cause injury, cause mischief, cheapen, contaminate, corrupt, cripple, crush, debase, deface, defile, deform, degrade, demolish, destroy, devalue, devastate, diminish, disable, disfigure, disparage, disrupt, disserve, do disservice to, do violence to, harm, hurt, impair, incapacitate, injure, lacerate, lay waste, maim, make unsound, malign, maltreat, mangle, mar, mutilate, pervert, pollute, prejudice, ravage, ruin, sabotage, scathe, spoil, stain, taint, tamper with, trample on, traumatize, vandalize, violate, vitiate, weaken, wound, wreck, wrong

ASSOCIATED CONCEPTS: damage from negligence, damage to goods, destruction, estimated damage, latent damage, loss, mitigation of damages, opportunity to repair, patent damage, permanent damage, recovery for damage, water damage

DAMAGES, ***noun*** amends, compensation, costs, expenses, expiation, fine, indemnification, indemnity, injury, just compensation, legal costs, legal liability, loss, penalty, recompense, recovery, reimbursement, remuneration for injury suffered, reparation, repayment for injury sustained, repayment for loss, restitution, restoration

ASSOCIATED CONCEPTS: actual loss, addamnum clause, additur, aggravation of damages, amercement, apportionment of damages, assessment of damages, civil damages, claim for damages, compensatory damages, conjectural damages, consequential damages, contingent damages, continuing damages, damages accrued, damages actually sustained, damages to person, damages to property, damages to realty, *damnum absque injuria,* direct damages, division of damages, duty to minimize damages, estimated damages, excessive damages, exemplary damages, future damages, general damages, incidental damages, intervening damages, irreparable damages, irreparable injury, lawful damages, limitation of liability, liquidated damages, measure of damages, minimizing damages, mitigation of damages, nominal damages, ordinary damages, pecuniary damages, pecuniary loss, permanent damages, presumptive damages, property damage, prospective damages, proximate damages, punitive damages, reasonable certainty of damages, remote damages, special damages, speculative damages, substantial damages, treble damages, unliquidated damages

FOREIGN PHRASES: ***Ubi damna dantur, victus victori in expensis condemnari debet.*** Where damages are given, the losing party ought to be condemned to pay costs to the victor.

DAMAGING, ***adjective*** baneful, calamitous, calumnious, caustic, contemptuous, corrosive, deleterious, destructive, detrimental, disadvantageous, disastrous, grievous, harmful, hurtful, incriminatory, inculpatory, inimical, injurious, insalubrious, malefic, malevolent, malignant, mischievous, mordacious, noisome, noxious, outrageous,

pejorative, pernicious, pestilent, poisonous, prejudicial, ruinous, scathing, unfavorable, virulent, wanton, wasting
ASSOCIATED CONCEPTS: damaging testimony

DAMPEN, *verb* abate, allay, alleviate, assuage, blunt, chasten, chill, constrain, control, cool, cushion, deaden, decrease, deject, depress, deter, diminish, discourage, dishearten, dispirit, dull, lessen, mitigate, moderate, modulate, muffle, mute, palliate, quench, reduce, repress, restrain, smother, sober, soften, stifle, subdue, suppress, tame, temper, weaken

DAMPER *(Depressant),* ***noun*** backset, bleakness, cheerlessness, chill, cloud, crushed spirits, depressing influence, discouragement, disheartener, downheartedness, feeling of dejection, feeling of depression, gloom, glumness, heaviness, heaviness of spirit, joylessness, lack of spirit, lack of warmth, letdown, low spirits, pessimism, sadness, setback, shadow, unhappiness

DAMPER *(Stopper),* ***noun*** bar, barricade, barrier, block, blockage, bridle, check, clog, control, cork, curb, delay, determent, deterrent, difficulty, disadvantage, discouragement, encumbrance, hamper, hindrance, hitch, impediment, impedition, inhibition, interference, interruption, limitation, muffler, obstacle, obstruction, occlusion, oppilation, plug, preclusion, prevention, rein, restraint, restriction, retardation, snag, stoppage, stopper, stopple

DANGER, *noun* assailability, crisis, defenselessness, *discrimen,* exposure to harm, hazard, helplessness, imperilment, jeopardy, lack of protection, lack of safety, liability to injury, menace, nonimmunity, penetrability, *periculum,* peril, perilousness, precariousness, pregnability, risk, susceptibility, threat, unguardedness, vincibility, vincibleness, vulnerability
ASSOCIATED CONCEPTS: apparent danger, appreciation of danger, assumption of risk, avoidance of danger, clear and present danger, danger invites rescue doctrine, danger signal, danger zone, foreseeable dangers, hidden danger, imminent danger, impending danger, inherent danger, intrinsic danger, knowledge of danger, known danger, latent danger, obvious danger, obvious risks, patent danger, unavoidable danger, unnecessary exposure to danger, zone of apprehendable danger
FOREIGN PHRASES: ***Periculosum existimo quod bonorum virorum non comprobatur exemplo.*** I think that dangerous which is not approved by the example of good men.

DANGEROUS, *adjective* alarming, assailable, attended with risk, baleful, baneful, beset with danger, breakneck, causing danger, deadly, destructive, disastrous, explosive, exposed to risk, fearsome, fraught with danger, fraught with peril, full of risk, harmful, hazardous, hurtful, injurious, involving risk, likely to harm, maleficent, malignant, menacing, minatory, ominous, perilous, pestiferous, risky, serious, threatening, treacherous, unprotected, unreliable, unsafe, unsheltered, unstable, unsteady, unstrengthened, untrustworthy, venomous, vicious, viperine, viperous, virulent
ASSOCIATED CONCEPTS: attractive nuisance, danger to the community, dangerous animal, dangerous business, dangerous condition, dangerous contraband, dangerous defect, dangerous drug, dangerous employment, dangerous instrument, dangerous instrumentality, dangerous machinery, dangerous occupation, dangerous or defective condition, dangerous place, dangerous premises, dangerous propensities, dangerous structures, dangerous to health, dangerous to life, dangerous trap, dangerous weapon, deadly weapon

DANGEROUS CONDITION, *noun* crisis, dangerous situation, emergency, endangerment, hazard, imperilment, jeopardy, menace, ominousness, peril, pitfall, precariousness, predicament, razor's edge, threat, unhealthy situation
ASSOCIATED CONCEPTS: dangerous drugs, dangerous instrumentality, dangerous per se, dangerous substance, dangerous weapon, dangers of the sea, known and obvious dangers

DARING, *adjective* adventurous, audacious, blunt, brave, brazen, challenging, chivalrous, courageous, dauntless, defiant, disregardful, doughty, enterprising, fearless, flagrant, foolhardy, forthright, gallant, hardy, heroic, hot-blooded, impulsive, intrepid, lionhearted, mettlesome, outspoken, plucky, presumptuous, rash, reckless, revealing, resolute, self-reliant, shameless, showy, Spartan, spirited, stalwart, unabashed, unblushing, undaunted, unflinching, valiant, valorous, venturesome, virile

DARING, *noun* adventurousness, audaciousness, audacity, backbone, boldness, bravado, bravery, bravura, chivalry, defiance, disregard, élan, enterprise, fearlessness, firmness, foolhardiness, fortitude, gallantry, grit, heart, heroism, mettle, nerve, overboldness, presumption, prowess, rashness, spirit, spunk, valor

DARK, *adjective* angry, black, bleak, clouded, covert, depressing, depressive, dim, evil, gloomy, miserable, moody, murky, mysterious, nasty, occlusive, shadowy, shady, sinister, threatening, unhappy

DARK *(Devoid of light),* ***adjective*** absent of light, bereft of light, black, darkened, darkish, dim, drab, ill-lighted, poorly lit, shaded, somber, sunless, unlighted, without light

DARK *(Dismal),* ***adjective*** cheerless, clouded, dejected, depressed, dim, disconsolate, doleful, dolorous, grim, joyless, melancholy, sad, solemn, somber, sorrowful, sullen

DARK *(Evil),* ***adjective*** base, demoniac, demonic, deplorable, diabolical, immoral, inexorable, infamous, iniquitous, mean, mean spirited, menacing, peccant, pernicious, sinfully malevolent, sinister, terrifying, untoward, vicious, vile, villainous, wicked

DATA, *noun* back-up, documents, evidence, facts, grounds, information, logic, papers, proof, specifics

DATABASE, *noun* catalog, computer base of information, computer file, computer storage, memory
Generally: cyberspace, record, records, registry

DATE, *noun* assigned time, day, day of the week, *dies,* marked time, moment, particular point of time, period, period of time, point of time, specified period of time, *tempus,* time, time during which anything occurs
ASSOCIATED CONCEPTS: antedating, certainty of date, date certain, date of acceptance, date of acknowledgment, date of application, date of appointment, date of availability, date of award, date of birth, date of commencement of action, date of death, date of default, date of enactment, date of execution, date of final judgment, date of injury, date of issue, date of loss, date of maturity, date of notice, date of publication, date of sale, date of taking, date on which a cause of action accrues, delivery date, due date, effective date, expiration date, filing date, future date, publication date, return date, termination date
FOREIGN PHRASES: ***In omnibus obligationibus in quibus dies non ponitur, praesenti die debetur.*** In all obligations in which no time is designated for their payment, the obligation is due immediately.

DATE, *verb* affix a date to, appoint the time of, ascertain the time of, assign a time to, calendar, chronologize, fix the date, fix the time, furnish with a date, mark the time of, note the time of, reckon from some point in time, record, register, *rem tempore tribuere, rem tempori adsignare,* set the date, time
ASSOCIATED CONCEPTS: postdate

DATE RAPE, *noun* acquaintance rape, committing a rape while on a date, forced sexual intercourse on a date, forceful penetration while on a date, forcible rape on a date, sexual assault and rape while on a date
ASSOCIATED CONCEPTS: consent, incapacitation, marital rape, physical resistance, sexual assault

DATED *(Antiquated),* ***adjective*** ancient, antiquated, antique, archaic, discontinued, not modern, obsolete, past, preexisting, stale, superannuated, timeworn, used, vintage, waning, weathered, worn, worn out

DATED *(Date-stamped),* ***adjective*** checked-in, embossed, imprinted, logged-in, marked, recorded, sealed, stamped-in
ASSOCIATED CONCEPTS: a date certain, acknowledgment, date of injury, date of issue
FOREIGN PHRASES: ***Datum.*** A date. ***A datu.*** From the date. ***A die confectionis.*** From the date of the making (action taken). ***A die datus.*** From the day of the actual date.

DAY *(Morning),* ***noun*** broad daylight, daylight, daylight hours, daytime, full day, full sun, light of day, sunlight hours

DAY *(24 Hours),* ***noun*** date, during a 24-hour cycle, period from dawn to dark, solar day, time between sunrise and sunset, 24 hours
ASSOCIATED CONCEPTS: calendar day, day certain, day fixed for trial, day in court, day of trial, day rule, day writ, grace day, judicial day, natural day, work day

DAY IN COURT, *noun* action, case, complete lawsuit, full chance, hearing, legal action, legal contest, legal trial, litigation, occasion, opportunity, proceeding, trial

DE FACTO, *adjective* absolutely, actual, actually, as a matter of fact, authentic, *bona fide,* certain, demonstrable, determinate, existent, existing, existing in fact, factual, genuine, in existence, in fact, in point of fact, in reality, positively, present, real, substantive, tangible, true, truly, unquestionable, valid, veritable, well-founded, well-grounded, with validity
ASSOCIATED CONCEPTS: de facto administrator, de facto admissions, de facto apprenticeship, de facto appropriation, de facto authority, de facto board, de facto board of directors, de facto contract, de facto contract of sale, de facto corporation, de facto court, de facto director, de facto dissolution, de facto districts, de facto domicile, de facto government, de facto guardian, de facto judge, de facto officer, de facto trust, de facto trustee

DE JURE, *adjective* according to law, authorized, authorized by law, by law, by order, by right of law, by statute, in accordance with law, in accordance with the ordinance, in accordance with the statute, in the eyes of the law, lawful, lawfully, legal, legally, legitimate, legitimately, licit, licitly, nomothetical, of right, sanctioned by law, within the law
ASSOCIATED CONCEPTS: de jure board, de jure corporation, de jure director, de jure dissolution, de jure election, de jure judge, de jure marriage, de jure office, de jure officer, de jure sovereignty, de jure title

DE MINIMUS, *adjective* inconsequential, insignificant, meager, moderate, modest, negligible, of minor importance, of no account, paltry, petty, obscure, scanty, slight, trifling, trivial, unworthy of serious consideration

DE NOVO, *adverb* afresh, again, anew, another time, encore, freshly, from the beginning, new, newly, once more, over, over again, revived, second time
ASSOCIATED CONCEPTS: de novo proceeding, hearing de novo, trial de novo

DEACTIVATE, *verb* change, decommission, defuse, demobilize, disarm, disband, disengage, dismantle, fix, undo, withdraw

DEAD, *adjective* at rest, bereft of life, breathless, buried, cadaverous, deceased, defunct, demised, departed, departed this life, deprived of life, destitute of life, devoid of life, dormant, ended, exanimate, expired, extinct, extinguished, inactive, inert, lifeless, long gone, no longer living, not possessing life, passed away, still, terminated, without a sign of life, without life, without the appearance of life
ASSOCIATED CONCEPTS: dead-born, next of kin, presumed dead, surviving spouse, wrongful death
FOREIGN PHRASES: ***Cadaver nullius in bonis.*** A dead body is no one's property.

DEAD, *noun* corpse, the deceased, decedent, the defunct, the departed, *exanimis, exanimus,* fatal casualty, fatality, the late, the late lamented, *mortuus*
ASSOCIATED CONCEPTS: autopsy, dead-born, dead man's statute, decedent's estates, next of kin, presumed dead, surviving spouse, wrongful death
FOREIGN PHRASES: ***Extra legem positus est civiliter mortuus.*** He who is placed outside the law is civilly dead.

DEAD SET, *adjective* ardent, decided, determined, devout, dogged, dutiful, earnest, faithful, fervent, firm, fixed, fixed in purpose, intransigent, obdurate, passionate, purposeful, relentless, resolute, resolved, settled, steadfast, tenacious, uncompromising, unfaltering, unswerving, unyielding, zealous
ASSOCIATED CONCEPTS: dead set against changes in the law

DEADLOCK, *noun* block, blockage, check, checkmate, dead end, dead heat, dilemma, draw, drawn battle, drawn game, frustration, impasse, insoluble difference, no decision, obstruction, paralysis, predicament, quandary, stalemate, stand off, standstill, state of inaction, state of indecision, state of inertia, state of neutralization, stoppage, stumbling block, tie
ASSOCIATED CONCEPTS: deadlock breaking instructions, deadlocked corporation, jury deadlocked, tie vote

DEADLY, *adjective* aiming to destroy, aiming to kill, annihilating, attended with death, baleful, calamitous, capital, cataclysmic, consuming, dangerous, dangerous to life, death-bringing, death-dealing, deathful, deathly, destroying, destructive, disastrous, envenomed, *exitialis,* fatal, feral, grave, homicidal, incurable, internecine, killing, lethal, lethiferous, malignant, mephitic, miasmic, mortal, *mortifer,* mortiferous, murderous, noxious, *perniciosus,* pernicious, pestiferous, poisoned, poisonous, ruinous, sanguinary, seriously dangerous, slaughterous, steeped in poison, stifling, suffocating, tending to cause death, toxic, toxicant, unhealthy, unsafe, venomous
ASSOCIATED CONCEPTS: armed with a deadly weapon, assault with a deadly weapon, deadly attack, deadly force, deadly weapon, possession of a deadly weapon

DEAL, ***noun*** agreement, arrangement, bargain, business transaction, commerce, commercial transaction, compromise, contract, exchange, merchantry, negotiation, operation, pact, pledge, purchase, trade, transaction, understanding

ASSOCIATED CONCEPTS: agreement to sell or exchange, dealer, dealings, lump sum deal, trade deals

DEAL, ***verb*** bargain, barter, buy and sell, carry on negotiations, commercialize, do business, do business with, drive a trade, exchange, export and import, handle, have business relations, have commerce, have dealings with, have to do with, make arrangements, market, merchandise, negotiate, open a trade, open an account with, sell, trade, trade with, traffic, traffic in, turn over

ASSOCIATED CONCEPTS: agreement to sell or exchange, cessation of dealing, dealer, dealing and trading, dealing at arm's length, dealing in, dealing in goods, dealing in property, dealing in securities, dealings, trade deals, transacting business

DEALER, ***noun*** agent, broker, businessman, businessperson, chandler, changer, *colporteur,* commission agent, commission man, conduit, consigner, exporter, factor, hawker, huckster, jobber, local representative, man of business, *mercator,* merchandiser, merchant, middleman, monger, *negotiator,* one engaged in buying and selling, operator, packman, packwoman, peddler, retailer, salesman, salesperson, saleswoman, seller, shipper, shopkeeper, shopman, shopperson, shopwoman, storekeeper, street vendor, trader, tradesman, tradesperson, tradeswoman, trafficker, vendor, wholesale trader, wholesaler

ASSOCIATED CONCEPTS: agent, authorized dealer, broker-dealer, dealer at retail, dealer in goods, dealer in real estate, dealer in securities, dealer's talk, established dealer, merchant, retail vendor or dealer, wares and merchandise, wholesale dealer

DEALINGS, ***noun*** actions, activities, acts, affairs, arrangements, barter, business, business intercourse, business transaction, buying and selling, commerce, commercial enterprise, commercial intercourse, contracts, deals, deeds, doings, exchange, executions, intercourse, interests, manner of conduct, matters, method of business, practice, proceedings, relations, trade, traffic, transactions, understandings, undertakings

ASSOCIATED CONCEPTS: commercial dealings, continuous dealings, direct dealings, mutual dealings, unfair dealings

FOREIGN PHRASES: ***Scire debes cum quo contrahis.*** You ought to know with whom you are dealing.

DEARTH, ***noun*** absence, *caritas,* deficiency, destitution, exiguity, exiguousness, impoverishment, inadequacy, inadequateness, incompleteness, indigence, *inopia,* insufficiency, lack, leanness, littleness, meagerness, need, paucity, *penuria,* penury, pinch, poorness, poverty, privation, rareness, scantiness, scantness, scarceness, scarcity, short supply, shortage, smallness of number, sparsity, want, wantage

DEATH, ***noun*** cessation of life, decease, demise, departure from life, dying, ebb of life, end of life, expiration, extinction, extinguishment, failure of vital functions, fatality, loss of life, mortality, passing away, termination of life

ASSOCIATED CONCEPTS: accidental death, capital punishment, *causa mortis,* cause of death, civil death, Dead Man's Statute, death action, death benefits, death by accidental means, death by natural causes, death by violence, death certificate, death gamble, death penalty, death resulting from accident, death resulting from injury, death sentence, death tax, death trap, death warrant, death without issue, deathbed will, homicide, in contemplation of death, injuries resulting in death, instantaneous death, last illness, life expectancy, likely to produce death, mortality tables, natural death, penalty of death, presumption of death, presumptive death, proof of death, registration of death, right to die, simultaneous death, sudden death, time of death, transfer in contemplation of death, unreasonable risk of death, wrongful death

FOREIGN PHRASES: ***Crimina morte extinguuntur.*** Crimes are extinguished by death. ***Actio personalis moritur cum persona.*** A personal action dies with the person.

DEATH PENALTY, ***verb*** capital punishment, corporal punishment, death sentence, death warrant, punishment by execution, ultimate penalty

ASSOCIATED CONCEPTS: cruel and unusual punishment, death warrant, Eighth Amendment, life in prison

DEATH SENTENCE, ***verb*** capital punishment, condemnation, corporal punishment, death penalty, death warrant, verdict of guilty

ASSOCIATED CONCEPTS: cruel and unusual punishment, death warrant, Eighth Amendment, life in prison

DEBACLE, ***noun*** adversity, blow, breakdown, calamity, cataclysm, catastrophe, collapse, contretemps, crash, defeat, demolishment, demolition, destruction, devastation, disaster, disruption, dissolution, downfall, emergency, failure, fall, fiasco, havoc, misadventure, mischance, misfortune, mishap, overthrow, overturn, ravage, reverse, rout, ruin, ruination, setback, smash, tragedy, upset, wreck

DEBAR, ***verb*** abrogate, arrest, astrict, ban, bar, barricade, block, cancel, check, confine, constrain, countermand, curb, detain, deter, disallow, discourage, dispose of, dissuade, eliminate, embargo, enjoin, estop, exclude, *excludere,* excommunicate, forbid, forestall, gainsay, halt, hamper, hinder, hold back, impede, inhibit, interdict, interfere, limit, obstruct, occlude, outlaw, paralyze, preclude, prevent, *prohibere,* prohibit, proscribe, refuse, remove, restrain, restrict, retard, revoke, shut out, stall, stifle, stop, stymie, suppress, suspend, trammel, veto, ward off, withdraw, withhold

DEBASE, ***verb*** abase, adulterate, bastardize, befoul, cheapen, coarsen, contaminate, *corrumpere,* corrupt, debauch, defile, degrade, dehumanize, demoralize, deprave, depreciate, depress, desecrate, deteriorate, discredit, disgrace, dishonor, downgrade, foul, humble, humiliate, impair, impair in worth, injure, lower, lower in value, pervert, pollute, profane, reduce in quality, soil, stain, taint, tarnish, *vitiare,* vitiate, vulgarize, weaken

DEBATABLE, ***adjective*** admitting of doubt, ambiguous, arguable, at issue, baffling, capable of being debated, changeable, confutable, conjecturable, conjectural, contentious, contestable, controversial, controvertible, cryptic, deniable, disposed to question, disputable, disputatious, doubtable, doubtful, dubious, dubitable, dubitative, enigmatic, eristic, hard to believe, hypothetical, in dispute, in issue, in question, inconceivable, incredible, indecisive, indefinite, indeterminate, nebulous, obscure, open to debate, open to discussion, open to dispute, open to doubt, open to question, open to suspicion, paradoxical, perplexing, possible, precarious, problematic, problematical, puzzling, questionable, refutable, speculative, subject to argument, subject to contention, subject to contravention, subject to controversy, suppositious, suspect, suspicious, theoretical,

unaffirmed, unascertained, unbelievable, uncertain, unconfirmed, undecided, undemonstrable, undemonstrated, under discussion, under examination, undetermined, unfixed, unpredictable, unproven, unreliable, unresolved, unsettled, unsure, unsustainable, unsustained, unverifiable, up for discussion, up in the air, vague
ASSOCIATED CONCEPTS: debatable issue, debatable question

DEBATE, *verb* agitate, altercate, argue, argue pros and cons, attempt to disprove, bandy, battle verbally, canvass, confer with, confute, consider, consult with, contend, contest, controvert, deliberate, disagree, discept, discuss, dispute, engage in oral controversy, examine a question, examine by argument, moot, negotiate, ponder, present reasons for and against, present varied opinions, ratiocinate, reason, refute, weigh, wrangle
ASSOCIATED CONCEPTS: debates of Constitutional Convention, freedom of debate, legislative debate

DEBAUCH, *verb* abuse, be intemperate, *corrumpere,* corrupt, debase, degenerate, degrade, *depravare,* deprave, despoil, dissipate, lead astray, molest, pervert, ruin, stuprate, sully, violate, *vitiare,* vitiate

DEBAUCHERY, *noun* bacchanalia, debauchment, dissipation, dissoluteness, excess, excessiveness, grossness, immoderation, impudicity, incontinence, intemperance, lasciviousness, lechery, lewdness, libertinage, libertinism, licentiousness, lust, obscenity, orgy, profligacy, salacity, seduction, *stuprum,* unrestraint

DEBAUCHMENT, *noun* defilement, defloration, deflowering, perversion, seduction, violation, vitiation

DEBENTURE, *noun* bond, negotiable instrument, paper money, pledge, title deed

DEBILITATE, *verb* cripple, denature, deprive of strength, devitalize, emasculate, enervate, enfeeble, eviscerate, exhaust, impair, incapacitate, injure, lessen, make feeble, make languid, reduce, render weak, sap the strength of, undermine, weaken

DEBIT, *noun* amount due, amount payable, arrears, bills, commitment, debt, deferred payment, *expensum,* indebtedness, liability, obligation, pecuniary due, sum owing, that which is owed
ASSOCIATED CONCEPTS: debit agent, debit and credit system, debit life insurance
FOREIGN PHRASES: ***Perjuri sunt qui servatis verbis juramenti decipiunt aures eorum qui accipiunt.*** They are perjured, who, by preserving the words of an oath, deceive the ears of those who receive it. ***Non decipitur qui scit se decipi.*** A person is not deceived who knows she is being deceived. ***Fraus et dolus nemini patrocinari debent.*** Fraud and deceit should not excuse anyone.

DEBRIEF, *noun* examine, gain information, gain knowledge, get briefing, inquire, interrogate, investigate, question, quiz, scrutinize
ASSOCIATED CONCEPTS: counterintelligence, espionage, interrogation, terrorism

DEBT, *noun* account outstanding, account owing, *aes alienum,* amount due, amount owing, arrearage, arrears, balance owed, balance to pay, bill, debit, deferred payment, deficit, encumbrance, indebtedness, liability, money due, money owed, nonpayment, obligation, sum owed
ASSOCIATED CONCEPTS: action for debt, admission of debt, antecedent debt, bad debt, bad debt loss, bona fide debt, bonded debt, book debt, business debt, common debt, contingent debt, continuing debt, contract debts, corporate debt, creating a debt, creation of a debt, debt against estate, debt arising on contract, debt by contract, debt by loan, debt discharged, debt due, debt founded on contract, debt incurred, debt instruments, debt not yet due, debt of another, debt of bankrupt, debt of municipality, debt of record, debt owed, debt provable in bankruptcy, debt which is to become due, debtor and creditor, debts of deceased, dischargeable debt, equitable debt, evidence of debt, evidence of indebtedness, existing debt, fiduciary debt, fixed debt, floating debt, fraudulent debt, funded debt, holder of debt, imprisonment for debt, inability to pay debts as they mature, just debt, lawful debt, liquidated debt, moral debt, mutual debts, nonpayment of debt, partnership debt, pecuniary debt, preexisting debt, promise to pay, provable debt, public debt, public debt limitations, recovery of debt, secured debt, simple debt, situs of indebtedness, unliquidated debt, unsecured debt, worthless debt
FOREIGN PHRASES: ***Debita sequuntur personam debitoris.*** Debts follow the person of the debtor. ***Debitor non praesumitur donare.*** A debtor is not presumed to make debts. ***Reprobata pecunia liberat solventem.*** Money refused releases the debtor. ***Nemo potest sibi debere.*** No one can be indebted to himself. ***Incendium aere alieno non exuit debitorem.*** A fire does not discharge a debtor from his debt. ***Id solum nostrum quod debitis deductis nostrum est.*** That only is ours which remains to us after deduction of our debts. ***Chirographum non extans praesumitur solutum.*** An evidence of debt not existing is presumed to have been paid. ***Chirographum apud debitorem repertum praesumitur solutum.*** An evidence of debt found in the debtor's hands is presumed to be paid. ***Annua nec debitum judex non separat ipsum.*** A judge does not divide annuities nor debt. ***In satisfactionibus non permittitur amplius fieri quam semel factum est.*** In settlements more must not be received than was received once for all. ***Minus solvit, qui tardius solvit; nam et tempore minus solvitur.*** He does not pay who pays too late; for from the lapse of time, he is judged not to pay. ***In omnibus obligationibus in quibus dies non ponitur, praesenti die debetur.*** In all obligations in which no time is fixed for their fulfillment, the obligation is due immediately.

DEBT LIMIT, *noun* borrowing limit, breaking point of debt, debt ceiling, greatest limit of debt, largest debt, largest loan, maximum amount of debt, maximum debt, maximum funds to be loaned, maximum loan, outer limit of debt, outer line of credit
ASSOCIATED CONCEPTS: bankruptcy, fraudulent debt, insolvency, interrogation, solvency

DEBT SERVICE, *noun* carrying cost, charge, cost of the loan, obligation, overhead payment, repayment
ASSOCIATED CONCEPTS: bankruptcy, fraudulent debt, insolvency, interrogation, solvency, usury

DEBTOR, *noun* borrower, borrowing party, debtor, defaulter, loanee, mortgagor, obligor, pledgor, responsible party
ASSOCIATED CONCEPTS: accord and satisfaction, account stated, assignment, bankruptcy, collection, compromise and settlement, debtor and credit, debtor and creditor relationship, execution, financial transactions, garnishment, reorganization

DEBUNK, ***verb*** cast doubt upon, decry, deflate, derogate, detract, disabuse, disdain, disenchant, disillusion, disparage, expose, puncture, set right, undeceive

DEBUT, ***noun*** admission, appearance, beginning, birth, coming out, disclosure, entrance, entrée, first public appearance, first step, immersion, inauguration, inception, incoming, initial appearance, initiation, introduction, issue, launch, launching, opener, presentation, release, sanctification

DECADENCE, ***noun*** abasement, decay, declension, declination, decomposition, degeneracy, degeneration, degradation, deterioration, devolution, diminution, downfall, downgrade, eclipse, fall, immorality, misconduct, nadir, opulence, spoiling, turpitude

DECADENT, ***adjective*** breaking down, cankered, corrosive, corrupt, crumbling, debauched, decaying, declining, decomposing, decrepit, degenerate, degenerating, depraved, deteriorated, deteriorating, dilapidated, disintegrating, effete, failing, falling, falling into ruin, feeble, immoral, in decadence, in decline, moldering, moribund, on the wane, regressive, retrograde, retrogressive, rotting, shabby, sinking, spoiled, spoiling, unprogressive, wasting, wasting away, weakened, withering, worn out

DECAMP, ***verb*** abandon, become scarce, bolt, break camp, dash, depart, desert, disappear, emigrate, escape, evacuate, flee, fly, get out, hightail, hit the road, leave, make tracks, migrate, move, remove, retire, retreat, run, run away, slip away, vacate, withdraw

DECAY, ***verb*** addle, atrophy, be reduced in worth, become enfeebled, become lower in quality, become putrescent, blight, break down, break up, canker, consume, corrode, corrupt, crumble, decline, decompose, decompound, degenerate, depreciate, deteriorate, dilapidate, disintegrate, fade, fail, fall apart, fall to pieces, grow worse, languish, molder, putrefy, render putrid, retrograde, retrogress, rot, ruin, shrivel, sink, spoil, waste away, wear away, wither, worsen

DECEASE, ***verb*** cease existing, cease living, cease to be, cease to exist, cease to live, come to an end, demise, depart, depart from life, die, end one's life, expire, lose life, meet death, pass away, pass on, perish, succumb
ASSOCIATED CONCEPTS: decedent's estate

DECEASED, ***adjective*** bereft of life, dead, defunct, demised, departed, deprived of life, destitute of life, devoid of life, exanimate, former, late, lifeless, no longer living, passed away, passed on, perished
ASSOCIATED CONCEPTS: Dead Man's Statute, deceased child, deceased debtor, deceased persons, estate of deceased person, transaction or communication with deceased person, transaction with person since deceased
FOREIGN PHRASES: ***Cadaver nullius in bonis.*** A dead body is no one's property.

DECEDENT, ***noun*** dead man, dead person, deceased, deceased person, demised, departed, he who has passed away, intestate individual, she who has expired, testator
ASSOCIATED CONCEPTS: decedent's estate, obligation of the decedent, transaction with decedent

DECEIT, ***noun*** beguilement, camouflage, cheating, collusion, cozenage, craftiness, cunning, deceitfulness, deception, deceptiveness, delusiveness, dissembling, dissimulation, *dolus,* double-dealing, duplicity, equivocation, fabrication, *fallacia,* fallaciousness, falseheartedness, falsehood, falseness, falsification, falsity, forgery, fraud, fraudulence, *fraus,* furtiveness, indirection, insidiousness, insincerity, jugglery, lying, mendacity, misrepresentation, perfidy, perjury, pretense, prevarication, sham, sneakiness, subreption, surreptitiousness, treachery, trickery, underhanded practice, underhandedness, untruth, untruthfulness
ASSOCIATED CONCEPTS: action for fraud or deceit, discovery of the fraud or deceit, fraud or deceit, misrepresentation

DECEITFUL, ***adjective*** artificial, backhanded, beguiling, crafty, cunning, deceiving, deceptive, defrauding, delusive, delusory, devious, dishonest, double-dealing, duplicitous, fallacious, false, feigned, forged, fraudulent, guileful, hypocritical, insincere, knavish, lying, misleading, perfidious, shady, shifty, sneaking, sneaky, specious, treacherous, tricky, two-faced, underhand, underhanded, untrustworthy, untruthful, wily

DECEIVE, ***verb*** befool, beguile, belie, blind, cheat, chicane, circumvent, cog, cozen, decoy, defraud, delude, dissemble, dissimulate, dupe, ensnare, entrap, *fainaigue,* fake, falsify, fool, forswear, gull, hoax, hoodwink, humbug, intrigue, inveigle, lie, misdirect, misguide, misinform, mislead, misrepresent, mulct, practice chicanery, practice deception, prevaricate, snare, sneak, swindle, take advantage, trap, trick, victimize

DECENTRALIZATION, ***noun*** apportionment, branching out, breakdown, delegation, diffusion, disbandment, disintegration, disjoining, disjunction, dispersal, dispersion, dissipation, dissolution, distribution, division, fragmentation, partition, scattering, scission, section, separation, severance, subdivision

DECEPTION, ***noun*** artifice, beguilement, blind, bluff, camouflage, charlatanry, cheat, chicane, chicanery, circumvention, con, counterfeit, cozenage, craft, craftiness, cunning, deceit, decoy, defraudation, defraudment, delusion, device, disguise, dishonesty, dissimulation, dodge, double-dealing, dupery, duplicity, equivocation, fabrication, fake, false appearance, false front, falsehood, falseness, falsification, feint, forgery, fraud, fraudulence, fraudulency, guile, hoax, humbuggery, illusion, imposition, imposture, indirection, indirectness, insincerity, intrigue, knavery, legerdemain, lie, machination, masquerade, mendacity, mirage, misrepresentation, obliquity, pretext, prevarication, rascality, roguery, ruse, sham, simulacrum, snare, stratagem, subterfuge, swindle, trap, trepan, trick, trickery, trickiness, trumpery, untruth, untruthfulness, unveracity, wile
ASSOCIATED CONCEPTS: confusion, deception doctrine
FOREIGN PHRASES: ***Non decipitur qui scit se decipi.*** He is not deceived who knows that he is being deceived. ***Decipi quam fallere est tutius.*** It is safer to be deceived than to deceive.

DECEPTIVE, ***adjective*** artificial, beguiling, bogus, calculated to give a false impression, camouflaged, cheating, collusive, counterfeit, covinous, crafty, cunning, deceitful, deceiving, delusive, delusory, designing, disguised, dishonest, disingenuous, double dealing, fallacious, false, feigned, fraudulent, illusive, illusory, impostrous, indirect, insidious, insincere, knavish, lying, mendacious, misleading, mock, oblique, obliquitous, pretended, prevaricating, scheming, seeming, sham, slippery, sly, sneaky, sophistic, sophistical, specious, spurious, subdolous, tricky, underhanded, untrue, wily

ASSOCIATED CONCEPTS: deceptive acts, deceptive advertising, deceptive practice, deceptively misdescriptive, deceptively similar

DECIDE, ***verb*** adjudge, adjudicate, adjust, agree, arbitrate, arrive at a judgment, ascertain, award, choose, choose a course of action, choose an alternative, choose an option, come to a conclusion, come to an agreement, come to terms, commit oneself, conclude, *constituere, decernere,* decree, determine, diagnose, *diiudicare,* dispose of, elect, end, establish, finalize, find, fix, form a resolution, form an opinion, hold, judge, make a choice, make a decision, make a selection, make up one's mind, opt, ordain, pass, pass judgment, pass sentence, pick, pronounce, reach a decision, reach a verdict, referee, resolve, rule, select, sentence, settle, sit in judgment, terminate, umpire, vote
ASSOCIATED CONCEPTS: decide a case, decide a motion, decided adversely, decided as a matter of law, decided on the merits, decided upon legal principles, jurisdiction to decide

DECIDED, ***adjective*** absolute, categorical, certain, clear, conclusive, decisive, definite, definitive, demonstrated, evident, explicit, indefeasible, indisputable, infallible, irrefutable, manifest, obvious by an overwhelming number, palpable, proven, self-evident, solid, unassailable, undeniable, undisputed, unequivocal, unimpeachable, unmistakable, unqualified, unquestionable, unreserved
ASSOCIATED CONCEPTS: decided litigation advantage

DECISION *(Election),* ***noun*** choosing, judgment, pick, selection, will
ASSOCIATED CONCEPTS: appellate decision, decision upon the merits, lower court decision

DECISION *(Judgment),* ***noun*** choice, decree, determination, placitum, resolution, verdict

DECISIVE, ***adjective*** absolute, assured, authoritative, beyond all dispute, beyond all question, categorical, certain, characterized by decision, clear, clearly defined, commanding, compelling, conclusive, conclusory, consequential, critical, crucial, culminating, definite, definitive, determinant, determinative, determining, effectual, ernest, final, forceful, impelling, imperative, important, incontestable, indubious, inflexible, influential, intent upon, irreversible, irrevocable, momentous, of great consequence, peremptory, pivotal, positive, powerful, purposeful, questionless, resolute, resolved, significant, summary, thrustful, undoubted, unequivocal, unhesitating, unqualified, unquestionable, unquestioned, without doubt, without question
ASSOCIATED CONCEPTS: decisive proof

DECLAIM, ***verb*** address, deliver oratorically, descant, dilate, discourse, dissertate, expand, expatiate, expound, give a formal speech, harangue, hold forth, lecture, make a speech, orate, perorate, preach, prelect, proclaim, rant, recite, rhetorize, sermonize, speak, speak publicly, speak rhetorically, talk

DECLAMATION, ***noun*** address, allocution, art of speaking, *declamatio,* discourse, elocution, grandiloquence, harangue, lecture, oration, oratorical display, oratory, orotundity, *pronuntiatio,* public speaking, reading, recital, recitation, rhetoric, screed, sermon, speech, speechification, talk, tirade

DECLARANT, ***noun*** affiant, affirmant, complainant, one who affirms, one who asserts, one who proclaims, person who makes allegations, proclaimor, witness

DECLARATION, ***noun*** admission, affirmation, announcement, annunciation, assertion, attestation, bulletin, communication of knowledge, *communiqué, declaratio,* decree, decreement, *dictum,* edict, *edictum,* explicit utterance, exposition, expression, fiat, formal assertion, formal notice, *ipse dixit,* notice, notification, official bulletin, positive statement, *praedicatio,* presentation, proclamation, profession, promulgation, pronouncement, public announcement, public notice, publication, recitation, resolution, revelation, solemn averment, solemn avowal, statement, statement of facts, transmission of knowledge, ukase
ASSOCIATED CONCEPTS: declaration against interest, declaration against pecuniary interest, declaration against penal interest, declaration of candidacy, declaration of deceased person, declaration of dividends, declaration of estimated tax, declaration of homestead, declaration of independence, declaration of intent, declaration of intention, declaration of law, declaration of parties, declaration of public necessity, declaration of rights, declaration of trust, declaration of value, declaration of war, dying declarations, extrajudicial declaration, judicial declaration, narrative declaration, *res gestae,* self-serving declaration, spontaneous declaration

DECLARATION UNDER OATH, ***noun*** affirmation under oath, certification under oath, declaration under penalty of perjury, formal declaration, statement under oath, sworn affidavit, verification under oath, written declaration

DECLARATORY, ***adjective*** annuciative, annunciatory, assertative, assertive, communicative, declarative, decretal, decretive, decretory, demonstrative, elucidating, enunciative, enunciatory, explanatory, expository, express, expressive, notificatory, proclamatory, promulgatory, serving to declare
ASSOCIATED CONCEPTS: declaratory act, declaratory action, declaratory decree, declaratory judgment, declaratory order, declaratory statute

DECLARATORY JUDGMENT, ***noun*** affirmation, announcement, declaration, enunciation, judgment of the court, nonexecutionary judgment

DECLARE, ***verb*** advance, affirm, announce, assert, asseverate, assure, aver, avow, bruit, claim, come out, communicate, contend, *declarare,* disclose, divulge, enounce, enunciate, herald, inform, maintain, make a declaration, make a statement, make known, predicate, proclaim, profess, *profiteri,* pronounce, put forward, reveal, say, set forth, state, tell, utter
ASSOCIATED CONCEPTS: declare a nullity, declare insolvent, declare null and void

DECLARER, ***noun*** affiant, author, compiler, composer, declarant, drafter, party, scriptor, sworn declarant, undersigned, writer
ASSOCIATED CONCEPTS: accommodation endorser, accommodation maker, dying declaration

DECLINATION, ***noun*** abnegation, denial, disavowal, disclaimer, negation, nonacceptance, noncompliance, nonconsent, refusal, refusal of consent, rejection, renunciation, repudiation, unwillingness

DECLINE, ***noun*** abatement, act of crumbling, act of dwindling, act of falling away, act of lessening, act of losing ground, act of shrinking, act of slipping back, act of wasting away, act of weakening, act of worsening, atrophy, backward step, cheapening, collapse, consumption, contraction, corrosion, corruption, decadency, decay, decrease,

decrement, decrepitude, decurrence, deflation, degeneracy, degenerateness, degeneration, *deminutio,* depreciation, descension, descent, deterioration, devaluation, dilapidation, diminishing, dissolution, downfall, downgrade, downhill, downtrend, downturn, downward inclination, downward incline, downward trend, drop, ebb, enfeeblement, erosion, failing, fall, falling away, falling-off, gradual crumbling, gradual impairment, lessening, loss, loss of value, lowering, marcescence, pejoration, period of decrease, plunge, recession, regress, regression, relapse, retreat, retroaction, retrocession, retrogradation, retrogression, reversion, ruin, setback, shrinkage, sinkage, sinking, slump, subsidence, wane
ASSOCIATED CONCEPTS: spoilage, waste

DECLINE *(Fall),* ***verb*** come down, decay, degenerate, deteriorate, drop, drop in strength, ebb, fall, lapse, stoop, trend downward, wane, wither
ASSOCIATED CONCEPTS: decline in price

DECLINE *(Reject),* ***verb*** abnegate, abstain, eschew, excuse oneself, hold back, rebuff, *recusare,* refuse, refuse to accept, renounce, *renueve,* repel, repudiate, resist, spurn, turn away, turn down, veto
ASSOCIATED CONCEPTS: decline an appointment, decline to accept an offer

DECOMMISSION, ***verb*** change, deactivate, defuse, demobilize, disarm, disband, disengage, dismantle, fix, undue, withdraw

DECONTAMINATE, ***verb*** absterge, antisepticize, clean, cleanse, depurate, deterge, disinfect, fumigate, hygienize, lustrate, make aseptic, make disease-free, make germ-free, make healthful, make hygienic, make innoxious, make pure, make salubrious, make wholesome, purge, purify, rarefy, refine, remove pollutants, remove unhealthy agents, render harmless, render sanitary, render sterile, sanitize, scour, scrub, sterilize, unadulterate, uncorrupt, unpollute, untaint

DECORUM, ***noun*** act demanded by social custom, amenability, amenableness, amenities, appropriate behavior, appropriateness, best behavior, best of taste, *bienséance,* civility, civilized behavior, code of what is fitting, conduct, conformity, consideration, *convenance,* convention, conventionality, conventions, conventions of society, correctness, courtesy, cultivated taste, custom, decencies, decency, decorousness, *decorum,* delicacy, demeanor, dictates of society, dignity, discrimination, etiquette, fastidiousness, fittingness, form, formalities, formality, gentility, gentlemanliness, good form, good manners, good taste, goodness, grace, mannerliness, manners, modesty, mores, natural courtesy, nice appreciation, nicety, orderliness, point of etiquette, poise, polish, polished manners, politeness, prescribed code of conduct, proper thing to do, properness, propriety, protocol, punctilio, punctiliousness, refined manners, refined taste, refinement, requirement of polite society, respect, respectability, respectful deportment, right note, right thing to do, rules of conduct, sedateness, seemliness, social code, social conduct, social graces, social procedures, social usage, standard, suitability, suitableness, tact, tastefulness, that which is proper

DECOY, ***noun*** allure, allurement, ambush, attraction, bait, blind, camouflage, deception, disguise, diversion, enticement, imitation, inducement, *inlex,* inveiglement, misleader, simulation, trap, trick
ASSOCIATED CONCEPTS: entrapment

DECREASE, ***noun*** abatement, abbreviation, abridgment, alleviation, attenuation, constriction, contraction, curtailment, cut, cutback, deceleration, declension, declination, decline, decline and fall, decrement, decrescence, deduction, deflation, *deminutio,* depreciation, depression, deterioration, devaluation, diminishment, diminution, dissipation, downtrend, downturn, downward trend, drop, dwindling, ebb, fall, falling-off, getting less, *imminutio,* lessening, loss, loss of value, lowering, making less, mitigation, narrowing, reduction, reflux, restriction, retrenchment, shortening, shrinkage, shrinking, sinking, slowing down, slump, subduction, subsidence, subtraction, wane, waning, weakening
ASSOCIATED CONCEPTS: decrease in payment, decrease in price, decrease in value, decreased capacity, decreased cost, decreased earning capacity, decreased or diminished mental capacity

DECREASE, ***verb*** abate, abbreviate, abridge, allay, attenuate, bate, be consumed, become smaller, blunt, cause to diminish, coarctate, compact, compress, concentrate, condense, constrict, constringe, contract, curtail, cut, cut back, cut down, cut off, cut short, dampen, decelerate, decline, deduct, deflate, *deminuere,* depreciate, depress, detract from, die down, diminish, drain, drop, dwindle, ebb, emaciate, extenuate, fall, fall behind, fall below, fall off, go downhill, grow less, *imminuere,* lessen, level off, lower, make brief, make less, make smaller, mark down, melt away, minimize, mitigate, narrow, pare, prune, quell, rake off, recede, reduce, render less, retrench, roll back, run down, scale down, shave, shorten, shrink, sink, slacken, slash, slump, strike off, subduct, subside, subtract, suffer loss, take away, take off, taper, trim, wane
ASSOCIATED CONCEPTS: decrease in payment, decrease in price, decrease in value, decreased capacity, decreased cost, decreased earning capacity, decreased or diminished mental capacity

DECREE, ***noun*** adjudgment, adjudication, authoritative decision, award, command, commandment, decision, declaration, *decretum,* dictate, direction, edict, *edictum,* fiat, final judgment, finding, imperative, interdiction, judgment, judicial decision, mandate, opinion, order, order of the court, *placitum,* proclamation, pronouncement, *pronunciamiento,* resolution, ruling, ruling of the court, *senatus consultum,* sentence, standing order, ukase, verdict
ASSOCIATED CONCEPTS: alimony decree, annulment decree, bankruptcy decree, consent decree, declaratory decree, decree for payment of money, decree for possession of property, decree *nisi,* decree of a court of competent jurisdiction, decree of court of record, decree of dismissal, decree of distribution, decree of nullity, decree of support, decree *pro confesso,* default decree, deficiency decree, divorce decree, entry of decree, final decree, foreclosure decree, foreign decree, interlocutory decree, joint decree, judicial decree, summary decree, supplemental decree

DECREE, ***verb*** adjudge, adjudicate, award, charge, command, deliver judgment, dictate, direct, establish, exact, find, give judgment, give orders, impose, instruct, issue a fiat, issue a proclamation, issue a ukase, issue an edict, judge, order, pass judgment, prescribe, proclaim, promulgate, pronounce, require, rule, sanction
ASSOCIATED CONCEPTS: alimony decree, annulment decree, bankruptcy decree, consent decree, decree by confession, *decree nisi,* decree of dismissal, *decree pro confesso,* default decree, deficiency decree, divorce decree, entry of decree, final decree, foreclosure decree, foreign decree, interlocutory decree, summary decree, supplemental decree

DECREMENT, ***noun*** abatement, abridgment, contraction, curtailment, cut, damage, declension, decrease, decrescence, deduction, deficit, depletion, diminishment, diminution, dissipation, drain, erosion, exhaustion, expenditure, leak, leakage, lessening, loss, shortcoming, shortening, shrinkage, spoilage, subtraction, wastage, waste, wear and tear

DECRETAL, ***adjective*** binding, commanded, commanding, decreed, decretive, decretory, demanded, directive, instructive, jussive, law-giving, mandatory, nomothetic, ordered, preceptive, prescriptive
ASSOCIATED CONCEPTS: decretal paragraph

DECRY, ***verb*** admonish, be unable to respect, belittle, berate, bring discredit on, bring into disrepute, censure, censure as faulty, clamor against, condemn, condemn as worthless, contemn, criticize, cry down, cry out against, declaim against, degrade, denigrate, denounce, deny respect, deprecate, depreciate, depreciate publicly, deride, derogate, despise, detract, detract from, disapprove, disapprove of, discredit, disdain, disesteem, dismiss, disparage, dispraise, disprize, disrespect, fail to appreciate, fault, feel utter contempt for, find fault, find nothing to praise, have no regard for, have no respect for, have no use for, hold cheap, hold in contempt, inveigh against, make little of, malign, not respect, not speak well of, *obtrectare,* protest against, raise a hue and cry against, raise one's voice against, reject, remonstrate against, reprehend, revile, ridicule, scorn, set at nought, set no value on, speak disparagingly of, speak ill of, speak slightingly of, spurn, vilify, vilipend, *vituperare*

DEDICATE, ***verb*** address to, award, bestow, confer, confer honor on, *consecrare,* consecrate, convey, *dedicare,* devote, do honor, donate, endow, enshrine, give, give a prize, give earnestly, give honor, hallow, honor, immortalize, inscribe, offer to give, pay honor, philanthropize, present, reflect honor on, render honor to, set apart, set apart for special use, set aside, vest

DEDICATION, ***noun*** bestowal, celebration, consecration, devotion, endowment, enshrinement, giving, gratuity, honoring, immortalization, inscription, offering, ordination, philanthropy, presentation, presentment, setting apart, setting aside for a particular purpose, solemn appropriation
ASSOCIATED CONCEPTS: act of dedication, actual dedication, appropriation for a public use, appropriation of a charitable use, common-law dedication, constructive dedication, dedication by estoppel, dedication of property for public use, dedication to a charitable use, dedication to a public use, express dedication, implied dedication, irrevocable dedication, manner of dedication, private dedication, public dedication, public easement, revocation of offer of dedication, statutory dedication, unaccepted dedication

DEDUCE, ***verb*** apply reason, arrive at a conclusion, ascertain, assume, calculate, come to a conclusion, conclude, conjecture, consider probable, construe, deduct, deem, derive, determine, divine, draw a conclusion, educe, extract, gather, guess, infer, judge, ratiocinate, rationalize, reason, suppose, surmise, think, think likely, trace, understand

DEDUCT *(Conclude by reasoning),* ***verb*** apply reason, arrive at a conclusion, ascertain, assume, calculate, come to a conclusion, conclude, conjecture, consider probable, construe, deduce, deem, derive, determine, divine, draw a conclusion, educe, extract, gather, guess, infer, judge, rationalize, ratiocinate, reason, suppose, surmise, think, think likely, trace, understand

DEDUCT *(Reduce),* ***verb*** abate, attentuate, bate, cheapen, cut, cut down, decrease, deflate, deplete, depreciate, devaluate, dilute, diminish, discount, downgrade, dwindle, lessen, lower, make less, make smaller, mark down, remove, render few, shrink, slash, strike off, strip, subduct, subtract, take away, take off, trim, truncate, withdraw
ASSOCIATED CONCEPTS: tax credit, tax deduction

DEDUCTIBLE *(Capable of being deducted from taxes),* ***adjective*** able to be subducted, able to be subtracted for tax purposes, allowable, capable of being deducted, capable of being rebated, discountable, likely to decrease taxes, recoupable, removable
ASSOCIATED CONCEPTS: deductible business expense, deductible debt, deductible expense, deductible loss, deductible policy

DEDUCTIBLE *(Provable),* ***adjective*** able to be confirmed, able to be shown, ascertainable, based on evidence, based on proof, capable of being figured out, capable of being proved, conclusible, corroborative, deducible, demonstrable, derivable, documentable, expectable, following, illative, inferable, inferential, likely, presumed, presumptive, probable, ratiocinative, substantiable, supportable, sustainable, testable, traceable, valid, verifiable

DEDUCTION *(Conclusion),* ***noun*** assumption, calculation, divination, hypothesis, illation, implication, logical process, logical sequence, opinion, postulate, postulation, ratiocination, rationalization, reasoned judgment, supposal, supposition, surmise, theory, thesis

DEDUCTION *(Diminution),* ***noun*** abatement, abridgment, attenuation, cut, decline, decrease, decrement, decrescence, *deductio, deminutio,* discount, dwindling, elimination, lessening, lowering, making less, minimization, reduction, removal, shortening, shrinkage, subduction, subtraction, withdrawal
ASSOCIATED CONCEPTS: allowable deduction, business deductions, deduction directed by law, deduction from purchase price, deduction of cost, deduction of expense, deductions from account, deductions from salary, income tax deductions, marital deduction, special deduction

DEDUCTIVE, ***adjective*** analytic, analytical, deducible, evidential, following, inferable, inferential, logical, rational, reasoned, resultant

DEED, ***noun*** assignment, authentication, certificate, charter, conveyance, covenant, document, document which passes a present interest, instrument, instrument which transfers title to realty, muniments, record, release, signed and delivered instrument, transfer, transference
ASSOCIATED CONCEPTS: ancient deed, bargain and sale deed, commissioner of deeds, contract for deed, deed by way of mortgage, deed duly registered, deed for a nominal sum, deed in fee simple, deed in the nature of a mortgage, deed of assignment, deed of conveyance, deed of covenant, deed of gift, deed of land, deed of trust, deed with covenant of warranty, estoppel by deed, executed deed, general warranty deed, gift deed, good and effectual deed, good and sufficient deed, joint deeds, mineral deed, quitclaim deed, recorded deed, registers of deeds, rescission of deed, reservation in a deed, sheriff's deed, simultaneous deeds,

special warranty deed, tax deed, trust deed, void or voidable deeds, warranty deed
FOREIGN PHRASES: ***Interpretatio chartarum benigne facienda est, ut res magis valeat quam pereat.*** The construction of deeds should be liberal in order that the transaction may be effective rather than fail. ***Traditio loqui facit chartam.*** Delivery gives voice to the words of a deed. ***Mala grammatica non vitiat chartam; sed in expositione instrumentorum ma la grammatica quo ad fieri possit evitanda est.*** Bad grammar does not vitiate a deed; but in the drafting of instruments, bad grammar should, as far as possible, be avoided. ***Grammatica falsa non vitiat chartam.*** False grammar does not vitiate a deed. ***Charta de non ente non valet.*** A deed of a thing not in being is invalid. ***Facta tenent multa quae fieri prohibentur.*** Deeds contain many things which are prohibited to be done. ***Allegatio contra factum non est admittenda.*** An allegation contrary to the deed is not admissible.

DEEM, ***verb*** account, adjudge, adopt an opinion, assume, be inclined to think, be of the opinion, be under the impression, believe, believe on consideration, call, conceive, conclude, consider, decide, determine, embrace an opinion, esteem, feel, form a judgment, form an opinion, have an opinion, have the impression, hazard an opinion, hold, hold an opinion, hold in belief, imagine, judge, look upon, opine, perceive, presume, pronounce judgment, regard, suppose, surmise, suspect, take for, take it to be, think, view as
ASSOCIATED CONCEPTS: deemed advisable, deemed to be in the best interests of the child

DEEMPHASIZE, ***verb*** attach little importance to, belittle, declassify, deprecate, depreciate, detract from, disregard, downplay, dwarf, give little weight to, make light of, make little of, marginalize, minify, minimize, moderate, play down, take no account of, think little of, think nothing of, tone down, underplay
ASSOCIATED CONCEPTS: declassification

DEEP *(Down),* ***adjective*** at the lowest point, below, below floor level, below ground level, below the floor, below the ground, beneath, under grade, under the ground, underground, underneath
ASSOCIATED CONCEPTS: declaration against interest, declaration of a dividend, declaration of a trust, in deep trouble with the law, searching deep into the evidence of a case, self-serving declaration

DEEP *(Profound),* ***adjective*** abstruse, astute, complicated, erudite, esoteric, intellectual, intellectually profound, penetrating, perceptive, philosophical, recondite, reflective, sagacious, sage, scholarly, thoughtful, wise
ASSOCIATED CONCEPTS: deep constituted interpretation

DEEP POCKETS, ***noun*** abounding wealth, abundance, abundant wealth, bounteous wealth, bountiful material wealth, riches, source of sufficient funds, substantial assets, substantial support, substantial wealth, wealth, wealthy, well-off, well-provided, well-situated, well-stocked, well-to-do
ASSOCIATED CONCEPTS: insurance, predatory pricing

DEEP-ROOTED, ***adjective*** deeply engrained, deeply implanted, deeply manifest, engrained, ensconced, established, impeded, imprinted, indoctrinated, injected, instilled, manifest
ASSOCIATED CONCEPTS: common law, precedence deep-rooted in the law

DEEP-SEATED, ***adjective*** deep, deeply felt, embedded, engraved, established, fixed, implanted, instilled, manifest
ASSOCIATED CONCEPTS: malicious prosecution, motive

DEFACE, ***verb*** begrime, blacken, blemish, blot, blot out, blotch, blur, cover up, crack, cross out, damage, deform, *deformare,* delete, deprive of form, despoil, destroy, destroy form, disfigure, distort, efface, erase, expunge, flaw, *foedare,* foul, hurt, impair, impair the legibility of, impair the looks of, injure, make illegible, make ugly, make unsightly, mangle, mar, mar the appearance of, mark, misshape, mutilate, obliterate, render illegible, rub off, rub out, scar, scratch, scratch out, smear, smudge, soil, spoil, spoil the look of, spot, stain, strike out, sully, tarnish, unshape, warp, wipe away
ASSOCIATED CONCEPTS: cancellation by defacing, defacing public property

DEFACEMENT, ***noun*** blemish, blot, blotch, blotting out, crack, damage, defect, deformation, deformity, destruction, discoloration, disfiguration, disfigurement, distortion, effacement, erasure, fault, flaw, impairment, injury, injury to outward appearance, marring, mutilation, obliteration, scar, scratch, smear, smudge, soiling, splotch, spot, stain, tarnish, unsightliness, vandalism, wear and tear, wrecking activities
ASSOCIATED CONCEPTS: defacement of ballots, defacement of documents, defacement of labels, defacement of monuments, defacement of public property

DEFALCATE, ***verb*** appropriate to one's own use, cheat, defraud, divert funds, embezzle, falsify accounts, misapply funds, misappropriate money, misemploy funds, misuse entrusted monies, obtain money under false pretenses, peculate, purloin, rob, steal, swindle, take by fraud, thieve

DEFAMATION, ***noun*** abuse, aspersion, calumniation, calumny, denigration, derogation, detraction, discommendation, disparagement, disrepute, false accusation, false publication, false report, imputation, infamy, insinuation, insult, invective, libel, obloquy, scandal, slander, slur, smear, smirch, traducement, untruth
ASSOCIATED CONCEPTS: defamation against title, defamation of business or profession, defamation of character, defamation per quod, defamation per se, defamatory publication, defamatory upon its face, defamatory words, injury to character or reputation, injury to profession or business
FOREIGN PHRASES: ***Inveniens libellum famosum et non corrumpens punitur.*** A person who finds a libel and does not destroy it is punished.

DEFAME, ***verb*** accuse, accuse falsely, anathematize, asperse, assail, belittle, berate, besmear, besmirch, bespatter, blacken, blemish, brand, bring disrepute upon, call names, *calumniari,* calumniate, cast aspersions on, censure, charge, condemn, criticize, damage one's reputation, decry, degrade, denigrate, denounce, depreciate, destroy one's reputation, discredit, disgrace, dishonor, disparage, dispraise, falsify, fulminate, gibbet, give a bad name, impeach, indict, injure the good name of, injure the good reputation of, inveigh against, lessen one's reputation, libel, lower, malign, objurgate, *obtrectare,* ostracize, pillory, put in a bad light, reprehend, revile, run down, scandalize, shame, slander, slur, smear, smirch, spatter, speak evil, speak ill, speak ill of, speak of slightingly, stain the character of, stigmatize, sully, taint, tarnish, traduce, vilify, vilipend, vituperate
ASSOCIATED CONCEPTS: defamation, defamation per quod, defamation per se, defamatory per se, defamatory upon its face, defamatory words, disparagement, injury to character or reputation, injury to profession or business, libel, slander

DEFAULT, *noun* abrogation, ad *vadimonium non venire,* arrear, avoidance, bankruptcy, breach, breach of orders, delinquence, delinquency, dereliction, dereliction of duty, dishonoring, disregard, evasion of duty, failure of credit, failure of duty, failure to answer, failure to appear, failure to meet one's obligations, failure to pay, financial disaster, insolvency, insufficient funds, neglect, nonfulfillment, nonobservance, nonperformance, omission, pretermission, refusal to pay, repudiation, *vadimonium deserere,* violation of duty
ASSOCIATED CONCEPTS: date of default, declaration of default, default decree, default in payment, default of issue, default or misconduct in office, excusable default, failure to pay money due, failure to perform duty, judgment by default, material default, motion for default, motion to open default, motion to vacate default judgment, willful default

DEFAULT, *verb* *ad vadimonium non venire,* avoid, be deficient, be delinquent, be derelict, be faithless, be in arrears, be in debt, be neglectful, be negligent, be remiss, be unfaithful, become unable to meet obligations, breach the agreement, break one's trust, break the contract, desert, dishonor, disregard one's duty, disregard one's obligations, dodge, elude, evade, fail, fail in duty, fail to act, fail to answer, fail to appear, fail to meet financial engagements, fail to pay, fail to perform, forsake, ignore one's obligations, lapse, lose by failure to appear, neglect one's duty, not pay, omit what is due, renege, repudiate, shirk, shirk one's duty, shun, stop payment, *vandimonium* deserere, withhold payment
ASSOCIATED CONCEPTS: date of default, default decree, default in office, default in payment, default of issue, default or misconduct in office, excusable default, judgment by default, motion for default, motion to open default, motion to vacate default judgment, opening of default, willful default

DEFEASANCE, *noun* abolishment, abolition, abrogation, annulment, breakup, canceling, cancellation, cassation, cessation, close, conclusion, deprivation, disallowance, discharge, discontinuance, disendowment, disestablishment, dissolution, end, end of the matter, ending, expiration, finish, invalidation, limit, negation, nullification, ousting, recall, removal, repeal, replacement, rescindment, rescission, retractation, retraction, reversal, reversion, revocation, revokement, stoppage, supersession, suppression, undoing, vacation, voidance, windup, withdrawal
ASSOCIATED CONCEPTS: condition, defeasance clause, defeasance of contract, defeasance of title, defeasible estate

DEFEASIBLE, *adjective* confutable, dismissible, disprovable, dissoluble, *functus officio,* nullifiable, refutable, removable, revocable, subject to being abrogated, subject to being annulled, subject to being canceled, subject to being divested, subject to being invalidated, subject to being repealed, subject to being retracted, subject to being revoked, subject to being taken away, subject to being withdrawn, terminable, voidable
ASSOCIATED CONCEPTS: defeasible deed, defeasible estate, defeasible fee, defeasible interest, defeasible remainder, defeasible title, determinable fee

DEFEAT, *noun* beating, breakdown, collapse, confutation, default, destruction, disappointment, downfall, failure, invalidation, loss, nonfulfillment, overthrow, refutation, *repulsa,* ruin, ruination, setback, thwarting, undoing, vanquishment
ASSOCIATED CONCEPTS: defeat a cause of action, defeat the purpose, defeat the rights, defeated candidate, defeated party

DEFEAT, *verb* beat, block, checkmate, confound, conquer, contravene, crush, demolish, drub, foil, frustrate, gain control over, halt, master, outwit, overcome, overmaster, overpower, overthrow, overwhelm, prevail over, put down, quell, refute, rout, smash, squelch, subdue, subjugate, *superare,* suppress, surmount, thwart, triumph over, trounce, upset, vanquish, *vincere,* victimize
ASSOCIATED CONCEPTS: defeat a cause of action, defeat a will, defeat or impair jurisdiction, defeat the purpose, defeat the rights

DEFEATED, *adjective* beaten, bested, buried, conquered, crippled, crushed, dispatched, dropped, eclipsed, gain a landslide over, mastered, outdone, outshone, outstripped, overcome, overmatched, overpowered, overthrown, pulverized, refuted, run roughshod over, slaughtered, stopped, subdued, subjugated, surmounted, transcended, triumphed over, vanquished

DEFECT, *noun* blemish, blot, damage, deficiency, deformity, demerit, deviation, drawback, failing, fault, faultiness, flaw, foible, frailty, impairment, imperfection, impotency, inadequacy, incompleteness, incompletion, infirmity, insufficiency, lack, *mendum,* mistake, mutilation, shortcoming, weakness
ASSOCIATED CONCEPTS: actionable defect, concealed defect, cure of defects, dangerous defect, defect appearing upon face of record, defect in description, defect in form, defect in material or workmanship, defect in title, defect of parties, defect of substance, hidden defects, immaterial defects, inherent defect, jurisdictional defect, knowledge of defect, latent defect, legal defect, material defect, mental defect, obvious defect, open and obvious defect, patent defect, products liability, structural defects

DEFECT, *verb* abandon allegiance, abdicate, abscond, apostasize, back out, be disloyal, betray, break away, break fealty, break with, cast off, change sides, default, demit, depart, desert, disavow, disobey, disown, forsake, leave, leave unlawfully, mutiny, prove treacherous, quit, rebel, reject, renege, renounce, repudiate, resign, revolt, run away, secede, tergiversate, transfer, violate one's oath, withdraw one's support

DEFECTIVE, *adjective* amiss, awry, below par, below standards, beneath standards, blemished, broken, bruised, crippled, damaged, deficient, deformed, distorted, falling short, faultful, faulty, flawed, impaired, imperfect, *imperfectus,* inadequate, incomplete, incondite, incorrect, infirm, injured, inoperative, insufficient, lacking, lame, marred, mutilated, out of order, unfinished, unsound, wanting, warped, weak
ASSOCIATED CONCEPTS: defective and unsafe condition, defective condition, defective construction, defective in form, defective in substance, defective instrumentality, defective machinery, defective materials, defective or dangerous condition, defective product, defective service of process, defective title, defective workmanship or material, defective writ, mentally defective, products liability

DEFEND, *verb* advocate, allege in support, argue for, champion, espouse, guard, justify, maintain, plead for, plead one's cause, promote a cause, propound, protect, safeguard, shield, stand up for, support, sustain, uphold, urge reasons for
ASSOCIATED CONCEPTS: effectiveness of counsel, opportunity to defend

DEFENDANT, *noun* the accused, accused litigant, accused party, charged party, party against whom a complaint is lodged, party against whom charges are pending, party who is sued, respondent
ASSOCIATED CONCEPTS: codefendant, defendant's rights, indispensable party defendant, necessary party defendant, nominal defendant, party defendant, principal defendant, proper party defendant, third party defendants
FOREIGN PHRASES: ***Favorabiliores rei potius quam actores habentur.*** The condition of the defendant is to be favored rather than that of the plaintiff. ***Reus excipiendo fit actor.*** The defendant by his pleading may make himself a plaintiff. ***Melior est conditio possidentis, et rei quam actoris.*** The condition of the possessor and that of the defendant is better than that of the plaintiff. ***Habemus optimum testem, confitentem reum.*** We have the best witness, a confessing defendant. ***Melior est conditio defendentis.*** The position of the defendant is the better one.

DEFENSE, *noun* confutation, counterargument, espousal, justification, parry, preservation, protection, rebuttal, resistance against attack, support, warding off
ASSOCIATED CONCEPTS: affirmative defense, alibi defense, anticipating a defense, assist in his own defense, coercion as a defense, complete defense, defense of a third person, defense of action, defense of estoppel, defense of insanity, defense on the merits, defensive pleading, equitable defense, frivolous defense, ground of defense, incomplete defense, inconsistent defenses, legal defenses, meritorious defense, motion to strike defense, negative defense, new defense, partial defense, personal defense, self-defense, sham defense, special defense
FOREIGN PHRASES: ***Peccatum peccato addit qui culpae quam facit patrocinium defensionis adjungit.*** He adds one offense to another who connects a wrong which he has committed with his defense. ***Vani timoris justa excusatio non est.*** A frivolous fear is not a lawful excuse. ***Nemo prohibetur pluribus defensionibus uti.*** No one is prohibited from making use of several defenses. ***Impotentia excusat legem.*** Performing a legal duty excuses from the performance. ***Quodcunque aliquis ob tutelam corporis sui fecerit, jure id fecisse videtur.*** Whatever any one does in defense of his person, that he is deemed to have done legally. ***Vim vi repellere licit. modo fiat moderamine inculpatae tutelae, non ad sumendam vindictam, sed ad propulsandam injuriam.*** It is lawful to repel force by force, provided it be done with the moderation of blameless defense, not for the purpose of taking revenge, but to repel injury.

DEFENSIBLE, *adjective* armed, believable, condonable, credible, defendable, exculpatory, excusable, impregnable, invincible, invulnerable, justifiable, justified, maintainable, pardonable, plausible, prepared, sound, supportable, tenable, unassailable, unattackable, vindicable, vindicatory, warrantable

DEFER *(Put off)*, ***verb*** adjourn, arrest, be dilatory, bide, delay, detain, *differre,* discontinue, extend, file, forbear, forestall, gain time, hesitate, hinder, hold back, hold in abeyance, hold off, hold up, impede, interfere, interrupt, intervene, keep pending, lay aside, linger, *obsequi,* obstruct, pause, pigeonhole, postpone, pretermit, procrastinate, prolong, prorogue, put aside, recess, respite, retard, set aside, shelve, stall, stave off, stay, suspend, table, wait, withhold
ASSOCIATED CONCEPTS: deferred charges, deferred compensation, deferred dividend, deferred income, deferred legacy, deferred payments, deferred premiums, deferred sentence, deferred wage

DEFER *(Yield in judgment)*, ***verb*** abide by, abstain, accede, accept, accord, accord superiority to, acknowledge, acquiesce, agree, assent, capitulate, cede, comply, conform to, consent, do honor to, esteem, fall in with, give assent, give consent, give in, give way, go along with, hearken, hold in esteem, honor, *obsequi,* pay respect to, regard, respect, show courtesy, show respect, submit, submit for determination, submit in judgment to, subscribe to, venerate, yield, yield in opinion to
ASSOCIATED CONCEPTS: defer to an administrative agency's decision

DEFERENCE, *noun* acquiescence, assent, complaisance, compliance, consideration, courtesy, esteem, honor, nonresistance, obedience, politeness, regard, respect, respectfulness, submission, submissiveness, submittal, willingness

DEFERMENT, *noun* adjournment, cunctation, dalliance, deferral, delay, dilatoriness, extension, extension of time, interruption, moratorium, postponement, procrastination, prolongation, prorogation, putting off, respite, stoppage, suspension, tabling, tarrying, wait
ASSOCIATED CONCEPTS: deferment of action, draft deferment

DEFIANCE, *noun* affront, challenge, contumacy, dare, daring, disobedience, disregard, disregard of orders, gage, impudence, impudency, insolence, insubmission, insubordination, insurgence, insurgency, insurrection, invitation to combat, mutiny, noncompliance, noncooperation, opposition, oppugnation, *provocatio,* rebellion, rebelliousness, recalcitrance, recalcitrancy, recalcitration, recusancy, resistance, revolt, revolution, sedition, strike, stubbornness, unruliness, uprising
ASSOCIATED CONCEPTS: in defiance of the law

DEFICIENCY, *noun* absence, dearth, defect, deficit, deprivation, destitution, failing, failure to comply, falling short, fault, faultiness, flaw, foible, impairment, imperfection, inadequacy, inadequateness, incompleteness, incompletion, infirmity, insufficiency, lack, loss, meagerness, need, noncompletion, nonfulfillment, nonperformance, omission, paucity, penury, poverty, privation, scarcity, short supply, shortage, shortcoming, sparsity, ullage, want, weakness
ASSOCIATED CONCEPTS: deficiency assessment, deficiency bill, deficiency decree, deficiency judgment, deficiency tax, income tax deficiency, liability for deficiency, mental deficiency, notice of deficiency, recovery of deficiency, tax deficiency

DEFICIENT, *adjective* attenuated, barren, below par, blemished, defective, depleted, devoid, disappointing, discontenting, empty, falling short, faulty, few, flawed, hollow, impaired, imperfect, impoverished, in arrears, inadequate, incompetent, incomplete, inferior, *inops,* insubstantial, insufficient, jejune, lacking, less than necessary, *mancus,* marred, meager, missing, not enough, not satisfying, not up to normal, not up to par, paltry, partial, poor, scant, scanty, scarce, short, shy, sketchy, skimpy, slight, small, sparing, sparse, starved, substandard, thin, too little, unample, uncompleted, undeveloped, unequal to, unfinished, unfulfilled, unfurnished, unnourishing, unprovided, unsatisfactory, unsound, unsufficing, unsupplied, void of, wanting, weak
ASSOCIATED CONCEPTS: deficiency judgment, mentally deficient, totally deficient

DEFICIT, ***noun*** absence, arrears, balance to pay, dearth, default, deficiency, financial shortage, inadequacy, incompleteness, insufficiency, lack, loss, meagerness, omission, overdraft, paucity, scantiness, scarcity, shortage, shortcoming, shortness

DEFILE, ***verb*** abuse, adulterate, afflict, blemish, bloody, compromise, corrupt, cripple, cross, damage, deface, deprave, despoil, destroy, devastate, flaw, harm, hurt, ill-treat, impair, injure, malign, maltreat, mar, mess, mess up, misuse, molest, mutilate, oppress, pollute, ruin, scourge, shake up, shatter, spoil, taint, victimize, violate, vitiate

DEFILEMENT, ***noun*** abomination, adulteration, besmirching, blackening, contamination, corruption, corruption of purity, debasement, debauchment, deflowering, degradation, demoralization, denigration, depravation, desecration, despoilment, devastation, dirtiness, disgrace, dishonor, filthiness, foulness, impairment, indignity, insult, *macula,* outrage, ravagement, ruination, shamefulness, smearing, sullying, turpitude, uncleanliness, uncleanness, violation

DEFINE, ***verb*** characterize, characterize precisely, *circumscribere,* clarify, construe, *definire,* delineate, denominate, depict the essential qualities of, describe, describe the properties of, designate, determine the essential qualities of, determine with precision, differentiate, elucidate, enumerate, establish, exemplify, explain, explain the nature of, expound, fix, fix the meaning, fix with precision, formalize, formulate, give the meaning, identify, illustrate, individualize, individuate, interpret, label, limit, make clear, mark the limits, name, prescribe, render, render precise, specify, spell out, state the meaning of, state the meaning precisely, tell the meaning, term, throw light upon, translate
ASSOCIATED CONCEPTS: defined by law, defined by statute

DEFINED *(Clear),* ***adjective*** clear-cut, coherent, comprehensible, concrete, conditional, confining, conterminable, conterminate, cramped, crystal clear, definite, determinable, determined, distinct, distinguishable, evident, exact, explicit, express, fixed, in focus, manifest, narrow, obvious, patent, perceptible, plain, precise, qualified, quantified, recognizable, specific, straightened, unambiguous, unequivocal, unmistakable

DEFINED *(Determined),* ***adjective*** actual, bound, bounded, determined, finite, fixed, limited, precise, restricted, specific, stated
ASSOCIATED CONCEPTS: defined crime, defined nature of an offense, defined offense, defined within a statute

DEFINED MEANING, ***noun*** accurate meaning, correct meaning, definition, distinct meaning, exact meaning, explanation, explicit meaning, express meaning, faithful meaning, inflexible meaning, literal meaning, methodical meaning, meticulous meaning, narrow meaning, not subject to interpretation, ordinary meaning, plain meaning, precise meaning, prescribed meaning, rigid meaning, rigorous meaning, sharply defined, significance, specific meaning, strict meaning, unbending meaning, uncompromising meaning, unequivocal meaning
ASSOCIATED CONCEPTS: construction, literal contract, literal proof, plain meaning rule, rules of statutory, soft plain meaning rule, textualism

DEFINITE, ***adjective*** absolute, accurate, actual, allowed, ascertained, assured, attested, authoritative, axiomatic, beyond all dispute, beyond all question, bound, bounded with precision, categorical, certain, certified, *certus,* clear, clear-cut, conclusive, confident, *constitutus,* convinced, correct, decided, decisive, *definitus,* demonstrable, determinate, determined, distinct, doubtless, ensured, established, evident, evidential, exact, existing, express, firm, fixed, fully convinced, granted, guaranteed, having fixed limits, immutable, inappealable, incommutable, incontestable, indefeasible, indisputable, indubious, indubitable, inescapable, inevasible, inevitable, inexorable, inflexible, insured, intransmutable, invariable, inviolate, irrefragable, irrefutable, irresistible, irreversible, irrevocable, persuaded, positive, precisely bounded, quantified, questionless, real, reliable, resolute, satisfied, secure, settled, stated, strictly defined, tested, true, unchanging, unconfuted, uncontested, undeniable, undisputed, undoubting, unequivocal, unerring, unfailing, unfaltering, unhesitating, unimpeachable, univocal, unmistakable, unqualified, unquestioned, unrefuted, unshaken, unsuspecting, unsuspicious, unwavering, veritable, well-defined, well-marked
ASSOCIATED CONCEPTS: definite and certain, definite class, definite description, definite failure of issue, definite interest, definite location, definite period, definite quantity, definite sentence, definite term

DEFINITION, ***noun*** clarification, decipherment, decoding, delimitation, delineation, demarcation, description, elucidation, equivalent meaning, exact meaning, exact statement, explanation, explication, expressed meaning, formulation, identification, illumination, interpretation, making intelligible, meaning, representation, simplification, statement of meaning, synonym, translation
FOREIGN PHRASES: ***Omnis definitio in jure civili periculosa est, parum est enim ut non subverti possit.*** Every definition in the law is dangerous, because there is little that cannot be subverted.

DEFINITIVE, ***adjective*** absolute, accurate, ascertained, authentic, authenticated, authoritative, beyond a doubt, beyond all dispute, closing, complete, completed, conclusive, conclusory, confirmative, consummate, crowning, decided, decisive, definite, determinate, determinative, determining, exact, exhaustive, final, fixed, incontestable, incontrovertible, indisputable, indubitable, irrefutable, last, most complete, most precise, perfect, supreme, terminational, terminative, thorough, ultimate, unassailable, uncontested, undeniable, undisputed, undoubted, unimpeachable, unquestionable, without doubt, without question
ASSOCIATED CONCEPTS: definitive decree, definitive judgment, definitive order

DEFLAGRATE, ***verb*** blaze, burn, burn fiercely, burn up, burst into flame, conflagrate, consume, cremate, fire, flame, flame up, flare, flare up, flash, ignite, incandesce, incinerate, inflame, reduce to ashes, scorch, sear, singe, torrefy

DEFLATE, ***verb*** abate, collapse, constrict, cripple, debilitate, decrease, deduct, demote, depreciate, depress, devalue, diminish, disable, disintegrate, dissipate, enfeeble, languish, lessen, minimize, reduce, sap, shrink, squash, subside, succumb, take down, thin, tire, undermine, vitiate, void, weaken, weary, wilt

DEFLECT, ***verb*** avert, bend, curve, deviate, divert, move, pivot, rechannel, redirect, reflect, shift, shunt, sidetrack, sway, swerve, switch, swivel, transfer, twist

DEFRAUD, ***verb*** befool, beguile, bilk, cheat, cheat out of money, *circumscribere,* commit breach of trust, cozen,

deceive, *defraudare,* delude, deprive dishonestly, dupe, embezzle, fleece, fool, hoax, inveigle, levant, mislead, mulct, obtain money on false pretenses, peculate, practice chicanery, practice fraud upon, swindle, take advantage of, take by fraud, take in, trick
ASSOCIATED CONCEPTS: conspiracy to defraud, intent to defraud, use of mails to defraud

DEFRAY, ***verb*** adjust, bear the cost, bear the expense, compensate, contribute, disburse, discharge, expend, foot the bill, give compensation for, honor a bill, indemnify, liquidate, make payment, make repayment, make restitution, meet the bill, pay, pay an indemnity, pay compensation, pay for, pay one's way, pay reparations, pay the costs, redeem, refund, reimburse, remit, remunerate, repay, requite, satisfy a claim, solvere, spend, stand the cost, *suppeditare*
ASSOCIATED CONCEPTS: defraying cost, defraying expenses

DEFRAYAL, ***noun*** collection, compensation, defrayment, disbursement, expenditure, expense, pay, payment, payoff, quittance, recovery, reimbursement, remittance, remuneration, satisfaction, settlement of charges

DEFT, ***adjective*** able, accomplished, adept, adroit, agile, apt, canny, capable, clever, competent, cunning, dexterous, efficient, expert, facile, flexible, gifted, good at, handy, ingenious, light, masterful, masterly, nimble, nimble-fingered, practiced, proficient, qualified, quick, resourceful, sharp, skilled, skillful, slick, smooth, talented

DEFUNCT, ***adjective*** abrogated, all gone, all over with, annulled, canceled, dead, deceased, demised, departed, devoid of life, ended, exanimate, expired, extinct, finished, gone, gone out of existence, inactive, inefficacious, inoperative, lifeless, *mortuus,* no longer living, no more, not endowed with life, not existing, not in action, not in force, obsolete, old-fashioned, out-of-fashion, passed away, past, perished, terminated, unknown, unobserved, unused, vanished, void, without life
ASSOCIATED CONCEPTS: defunct business, defunct corporation

DEFY, ***verb*** affront, assume a fighting attitude, battle, beard, brave, breast, buck, challenge, conflict with, confront, dare, disobey, disregard, flout, front, mutiny, oppose, outface, *provocare,* rebel, resist, resist openly, stand up against, withstand
ASSOCIATED CONCEPTS: defy a court order

DEGENERATE, ***noun*** corrupt person, debased person, debauchee, decadent person, degraded person, depraved person, derelict, disreputable person, immoral person, pervert, rapscallion, recreant, scamp, scapegrace, transgressor, wastrel, worthless person

DEGENERATE, ***verb*** atrophy, be destroyed, be reduced in worth, be worse, become depraved, become deteriorated, become enfeebled, become impaired, become lower in quality, become notably worse, become perverted, become tainted, become worse, break up, canker, come down, consume, corrupt, crumble, debase, debase in quality, debauch, decay, decline, decompose, *degenerare,* degrade, deprave, derange, deteriorate, dilapidate, disband, disintegrate, disorder, dissolve, ebb, erode, fall apart, fall away, fall into decay, fall off, fall to pieces, get worse, go bad, go to pieces, grow weak, grow worse, languish, lapse, lessen in worth, lose morale, make inferior in value, make lower in character, make worse, moulder, poison, pollute, putrefy, render chaotic, retrogress, rot, run down, shrivel, sicken, sink, sink to a lower condition, taint, vitiate, wane, waste, wear, wear away, wither, worsen

DEGRADATION, ***noun*** abasement, abjection, baseness, debasement, decadence, decadency, declension, declination, decline, *dedecus,* degeneratess, degeneration, demotion, deprival of honor, deterioration, discredit, disgrace, dishonor, dismissal from office, disrepute, fall from repute, humiliation, *ignominia,* ignominy, ingloriousness, obloquy, odium, opprobrium, reduction in rank, retrogradation, retrogression, shame

DEGREE *(Academic title),* ***noun*** academic honor, award, certificate, collegiate distinction, credentials, credit, dignification, diploma, distinction, graduation certificate, qualification, title, title of honor

DEGREE *(Kinship),* ***noun*** affiliation, blood relation, blood relationship, cognation, connation, connection, consanguinity, extraction, family connection, family relationship, family tie, filiation, line of descent, proximity of blood, relatedness, relationship between persons, ties of blood
ASSOCIATED CONCEPTS: degree of descent, degree of kindred

DEGREE *(Magnitude),* ***noun*** amount, amplitude, caliber, consequence, dimension, enormity, expanse, extent, greatness, import, importance, intensity, largeness, measure, measurement, might, moment, proportions, range, reach, scope, seriousness, significance, strength, tenor, value, vastness, volume, weight
ASSOCIATED CONCEPTS: degree of care, degree of certainty, degree of crime, degree of disability, degree of offense, degree of proof, degrees of criminality, highest degree of care, lesser included offenses
FOREIGN PHRASES: ***Quae sunt minoris culpae sunt majoris infamiae.*** Those things which are less culpable may be more infamous.

DEGREE *(Station),* ***noun*** classification, echelon, gradation, grade, *gradus,* level of development, manner, mark, *ordo,* plane, point, position, rank, ranking, relative position, rung, situation, stage, stage of advancement, standing, status, step, tier

DEIGN, ***verb*** allow, allow with condescension, be so good as to, condescend, descend, favor, grant, patronize, stoop, vouchsafe

DEJECTED, ***adjective*** brokenhearted, crestfallen, depressed, despondent, disconsolate, doleful, down, downcast, downhearted, forlorn, gloomy, glum, heartsick, heartsore, heavyhearted, inconsolable, joyless, melancholy, miserable, mournful, rejected, unhappy, woeful, wretched

DELAY, ***noun*** *cunctatio,* cunctation, dalliance, deceleration, deferment, demurral, detainment, detention, dilatoriness, impediment, intermission, interruption, lag, lateness, *cessatio, mora,* moratorium, pause, postponement, procrastination, prolongation, prorogation, putting off, retardation, setback, slowness, stall, stay, suspension, tardiness, tarriance, wait
ASSOCIATED CONCEPTS: dilatory motions
FOREIGN PHRASES: ***De morte hominis nulla est cunctatio longa.*** When the death of a human being may be concerned, no delay is considered long. ***Justitia non est neganda non differenda.*** Justice is neither to be denied nor delayed. ***Dilationes in lege sunt odiosae.*** Delays are odious to the law.

DELAY, ***verb*** adjourn, arrest, arrest temporarily, be dilatory, block, bring to a standstill, curb, defer, detain, *detinere,* hamper, hinder, hold, hold back, hold in abeyance, hold over, hold up, impede, impede the progress of, interfere, intermit, keep back, keep from proceeding, keep one waiting, keep pending, lay over, linger, loiter, make inactive, obstruct, postpone, prevent, prolong, protract, put off, remit, retard, set back, shelve, slacken, slow, slow down, slow up, stall, stall for time, stand in the way, stay, stop, stymie, table, *tardare,* tarry, temporize
ASSOCIATED CONCEPTS: accidental delays, damages for delay, delay beyond the seller's control, delay occasioned by the defendant, delayed compensation, dilatory delay, excusable delay, excuse for delay, hinder and delay, inexcusable delay, justifiable delay, laches, unavoidable delay, unreasonable delay, without delay

DELAYED *(Arrested),* ***adjective*** adjourned, belated, contained, deferred, dilatory, late, lingering, overdue, postponed, protracted, remanded, restrained, set back, stopped, suspended, tabled, tardy, unpunctual, untimely

DELAYED *(Lagging),* ***adjective*** arrested, behindhand, delinquent, detained, impeded, in abeyance, in arrears, late, overdue, sluggish
ASSOCIATED CONCEPTS: dilatory action, dismissal due to delay, expedited proceedings, motion to accelerate the proceedings, prejudice due to delay, right to a speedy trial, unusual delay

DELEGATE, ***verb*** accord, accredit, allocate, allot, appoint, appoint as agent, appoint as representative, assign, assign a duty, assign power of attorney to, assign to a position, authorize, authorize formally, authorize to represent, award, bestow, call upon, charge, charge with an errand, charter, choose, commission, commit, commit powers to another, commit to the hands of, *committere,* confer power on, confide, confide for care, confide for use, consign, convey, *credere, delegare,* deliver, deliver in trust, deliver over, deposit with, depute, designate, designate to a post, despatch, detail, devolve on, dispatch, employ, empower, empower to act for another, enable, engage, entitle, entrust, entrust to the care of another, give, give a mandate, give a responsibility to, give authority to, give employment, give in charge, give in trust, give power, give power of attorney, give to, hand over, hire, hold responsible, impose a duty, impower, instate, intitle, intrust, invest, invest with authoritative power, license, make someone a trustee of, make someone guardian of, *mandare,* name, name to fill an appointment, nominate, oblige, offer a job to, offer a post, order, parcel out to, place in an office, place in charge of, place trust in, put in commission, put in one's hands, put in safekeeping, qualify, refer, relegate, sanction, select, send, send as deputy, send on a commission, send on a mission, send on an errand, send out, substitute, swear in, transfer, transmit, trust with, turn over to, vest in, warrant
ASSOCIATED CONCEPTS: delegated legislative function, delegated power, delegated state function, delegation of authority

DELEGATION *(Assignment),* ***noun*** agency, agentship, appointment, authorization, charge, commission, commissioning, consigning, consignment, delegating, deputation, deputization, designation, devolution, entrusting, entrustment, giving over, investing with authority, investiture, license, mandate, ordination, procuration, proxyship, reference, referring, warrant
ASSOCIATED CONCEPTS: delegation of authority, delegation of duty, delegation of governmental power, delegation of judicial power, delegation of legislative functions, delegation of legislative power, delegation of power
FOREIGN PHRASES: ***Vicarius non habet vicarium.*** A deputy cannot have a deputy. ***Quod per me non possum, nec per alium.*** What I cannot do myself, I cannot do through another. ***Delegatas potestas non potest delegari.*** A delegated power cannot be further delegated. ***Delegatus non potest delegare.*** A representative cannot delegate his authority.

DELEGATION *(Envoy),* ***noun*** body of delegates, body of representatives, commission, committee, delegates, deputies, embassy, legation, mission, people delegated, procuracy, representatives

DELETE, ***verb*** blot out, cancel, censor, cross off, cross out, cut, cut out, dele, discard, do away with, drop, edit out, efface, elide, eliminate, eradicate, erase, excise, expel, expunge, extirpate, get rid of, leave out, modify by excisions, obliterate, omit, remove, rub out, rule out, scratch out, strike off, strike out, take out, weed, wipe out

DELETERIOUS, ***adjective*** adverse, bad, baleful, baneful, consuming, corroding, corrosive, damaging, deadly, disadvantageous, disserviceable, envenomed, fatal, foul, harmful, injurious to health, insalubrious, lethal, malefic, maleficent, malignant, miasmal, morbiferous, morbific, nocuous, noisome, noxious, *noxius,* pernicious, pestilential, poisonous, ruinous, septic, toxic, unadvantageous, unfavorable, unhealthful, unhealthy, unsatisfactory, venomous, virulent, wasting
ASSOCIATED CONCEPTS: deleterious drug, deleterious substance

DELIBERATE, ***adjective*** advised, aimed, attentive, calculated, careful, carefully considered, carefully weighed, cautious, characterized by reflection, cogitative, *cogitatus,* conscious, *consideratus,* considered, contemplated, contemplative, controlled, deliberative, designed, determined, dispassionate, done on purpose, excogitative, fixed, full of thought, given due consideration, gradual, intended, intentional, judged, leisurely, maturely considered, measured, meditated, meditative, outlined beforehand, planned, planned in advance, plotted, pondered, prearranged, preconsidered, predeliberated, predesigned, predetermined, premeditated, prepense, *prudens,* prudent, purposed, purposeful, reasoned, reflective, resolved, slow, slow-moving, slow-paced, sober, speculative, studied, thought-out, thoughtful, unhasty, unhurried, volitient, volitional, volitive, voluntary, wary, weighed, well-considered, willed, willful, with forethought
ASSOCIATED CONCEPTS: deliberate act, deliberate and premeditated killing, deliberate and premeditated malice, deliberate and premeditated murder, deliberate and willful misconduct, deliberate assumption of risk, deliberate killing, deliberate or intentional wrongdoing, deliberate speed, deliberately and with premeditation, deliberative body

DELIBERATE, ***verb*** advise together, advise with, analyze, brood, cerebrate, cogitate, confer formally, consider, consider attentively, consider carefully, consider pro and con, *considerare,* consult, *consultare,* contemplate, debate, *deliberare,* discourse about, discuss, examine, examine carefully, excogitate, go into, hold a consultation, hold conclave, investigate, judge, meditate, mull over, negotiate, parley, ponder, ponder over, ponder reasons for and against, ratiocinate, reason, reason out, reason the point, reflect, reflect over, reflect upon, regard upon, review, ruminate, sit in conclave, sit in council, study, take counsel with oneself, take into consideration, take under consideration, think carefully, think over, weigh, weigh in the mind

DELIBERATE OMISSION, ***noun*** abandonment, abnegation, ban, bar, boycott, breach, declination, defalcation, default, delinquency, disregard, elision, exception, exclusion, failure of duty, intentional omission, laches, laxity, leaving out, lockout, neglect, negligence, noncompliance, nonfulfillment, noninclusion, nonperformance, preclusion, relinquishment, renunciation, repudiation, waiver
ASSOCIATED CONCEPTS: obstruction of justice, perjury

DELIBERATION, ***noun*** advisement, analysis, brooding, calculation, careful consideration, carefulness, caution, cautiousness, cerebration, circumspection, close attention, close study, cogitation, conscious purpose, consideration, *consultatio,* contemplation, contemplativeness, counsel, debate, *deliberatio,* determination prepense, discussion, distinct intention, examination, excogitation, forethought, heed, heedfulness, inquiry, inspection, intellection, judgment, level-headedness, logical discussion, mature consideration, mature reflection, meditation, pondering, premeditation, prudence, ratiocination, reflection, rumination, sobriety, study, taking counsel, thinking out, thought, thoughtfulness, unhurriedness, wariness, watchfulness, weighing

DELICATE *(Confidential),* ***adjective*** classified, hush-hush, private, restricted, secret, topsecret

DELICATE *(Sensitive),* ***adjective*** complicated, diplomatic, discreet, politic, ticklish, touchy, tricky

DELICATE *(Tenuous),* ***adjective*** breakable, brittle, crushable, embrittled, feeble, flimsy, fragile, frail, gossamer, infirm, precarious, sensitive, shaky, shivery, sick, slight, soft, susceptible, tender, vulnerable, weak

DELICT, ***noun*** corruption, crime, *delictum,* dereliction of duty, duty unfulfilled, felony, injurious act, injury, malefaction, malfeasance, malversation, misdemeanor, misfeasance, misprision, neglect of duty, negligent act of injury, negligent offense, negligent wrongdoing, nonfeasance, obligation repudiated, offense, official misconduct, tort, violation, violation of a duty, wrong
ASSOCIATED CONCEPTS: quasi delict

DELIMIT, ***verb*** allot, bound, circumscribe, confine, define, demarcate, determine, draw the line, edge, encircle, enclose, encompass, fix, lay out a boundary, mark limits, mark off, mark out, measure, surround

DELINEATE, ***verb*** *adumbrare,* block out, blueprint, circumscribe, construct a figure, contour, convey an impression of, define, depict, *depingere,* describe, *describere,* detail, determine, diagram, draft, draw, draw a picture, engrave, etch, figure, frame, give the details of, illuminate, illustrate, itemize, limn, make a likeness, make apparent, make clear, make vivid, map, mold, outline, paint, paint a picture, particularize, picture, picturize, plot, portray, portray in words, profile, recite, recount, relate, report, represent, represent by diagram, represent by outlines, represent pictorially, set forth, shape, silhouette, sketch, sketch in outline, sketch out, specify, specify the particulars of, survey, tell vividly, trace, trace out, trace the outline of, traverse the outline of

DELINEATION, ***noun*** abstract, account, act of setting forth, the act of tracing, *adumbratio,* blueprint, chart, circumscription, configuration, contour, *débauche,* depiction, depiction of essential features, *descriptio,* description, design, diagram, enumeration of the essential qualities, facsimile, form, framework, graph, line drawn round, map, outline, pattern, plan, plot, portrayal, profile, recital, recitation, relation, rendition, report, representation, representation by words, rough draft, shape, silhouette, skeleton plan, sketch, specification, statements that describe, structure, tracing, verbal portraiture, word picture

DELINQUENCY *(Failure of duty),* ***noun*** breach, breach of a promise, carelessness, default, dereliction of duty, error, failure, failure of obligation, failure to act, incompletion, indifference to act, inobservance, lapse in conduct, malpractice, misprision, neglect, neglect of obligation, negligence, noncompletion, noncompletion of a task, nonfulfillment, nonobservance, nonperformance, omission, omission of duty, omission of obligation, oversight, repudiation of one's duty, slight, slip, unfulfillment of an assignment, unfulfillment of duty

DELINQUENCY *(Misconduct),* ***noun*** atrocity, badness, baseness, breach of the law, corruption, crime, criminality, culpability, decadence, degeneracy, *delictum,* depravity, dereliction, devilishness, dissoluteness, evil, evil behavior, fault, *flagrante delicto,* foulness, heinousness, immorality, improbity, impropriety, indiscretion, infraction, infraction of the law, infringement, iniquity, lawbreaking, lawlessness, malefaction, malfeasance, *malum,* malversation, misbehavior, misdeed, misdoing, misstep, nefariousness, obliquity, offense, outrage, peccability, peccancy, prodigality, profligacy, reprobacy, tort, transgression, trespass, turpitude, unvirtuousness, viciousness, vileness, villainousness, villainy, violation, wantonness, waywardness, wickedness, wrong, wrongdoing
ASSOCIATED CONCEPTS: contributing to delinquency, delinquency proceeding, juvenile delinquency

DELINQUENCY *(Shortage),* ***noun*** arrearage, arrears, dearth, debt, default, deficiency, deficit, depletion, inability to pay, inadequacy, indebtment, insufficiency, lack, late payment, liability, nonfulfillment, nonpayment, obligation, outstanding debt, paucity, scantiness, scarcity, short measure, short supply, shortage, shortness, sparseness, sparsity, unpaid amount
ASSOCIATED CONCEPTS: delinquency assessment, delinquency charges

DELINQUENT *(Guilty of a misdeed),* ***adjective*** accusable, at fault, bad, blamable, blameful, blameworthy, censurable, condemnable, conscienceless, corrupt, criminal, culpable, derelict, dishonest, disreputable, erring, evil, evildoing, evil-minded, flagrant, guilty, *homo maleficus,* immoral, improper, in error, in fault, in the wrong, incorrigible, iniquitous, irredeemable, lawbreaking, maleficent, malevolent, malfeasant, misbehaving, monstrous, nefarious, negligent, offending, peccant, profligate, punishable, remiss, reprehensible, reproachable, reprobate, scandalous, sinful, to blame, transgressing, unjust, unlawful, unprincipled, unscrupulous, unseemly, unvirtuous, unworthy, vicious, villainous, virtueless, wicked, worthless
ASSOCIATED CONCEPTS: delinquent child, delinquent minors

DELINQUENT *(Overdue),* ***adjective*** back, behind, behindhand, chargeable, defaultant, defaulting, deficient, due, failing in duty, in arrears, lacking, missing, neglectful of obligation, not discharged, not met, not paid on time,

outstanding, owed, owing, past due, payable, receivable, remiss, short, to be paid, undefrayed, unliquidated, unpaid, unsatisfied, unsettled, wanting
ASSOCIATED CONCEPTS: delinquent assessments, delinquent debtor, delinquent lands, delinquent payment, delinquent premiums, delinquent property, delinquent taxes, delinquent taxpayer

DELINQUENT, ***noun*** criminal, culprit, dangerous person, evildoer, guilty man, *homo maleficus,* insolvent debtor, lawbreaker, malefactor, malfeasor, mischief-maker, miscreant, misdemeanant, misdoer, misfeasor, neglector of duty, nonpayer, offender, recidivist, recreant, reprobate, rogue, ruffian, scofflaw, swindler, transgressor, trouble maker, undesirable, worker of iniquity, wrongdoer
ASSOCIATED CONCEPTS: delinquent child, delinquent neglected and dependent children, delinquent premiums, delinquent taxes, juvenile delinquent

DELIRIOUS *(Incoherent),* ***adjective*** bereft of reason, crazed, crazy, deranged, hallucinating, insane, lunacy, mad, mentally ill, rabid, ranting, raving, sick, unsound
ASSOCIATED CONCEPTS: criminally insane, insanity defense, involuntary commitment

DELIRIOUS *(Wildly happy),* ***adjective*** ardent, blissful, carried away, ebullient, elated, electrified, enamored, excited, fanatical, feverish, frantic, frenzied, happy, hectic, impassioned, intoxicated, thrilled, tumultuous

DELIVER, ***verb*** carry, cart, commit, communicate, convey, dedere, delegate, entrust, forward, give into another's keeping, give out, hand, hand down, haul, impart, make over, pass on, place in the possession of, *prodere,* put into the hands of, relay, remit, send, ship, surrender, *tradere,* traject, transfer by deed, transfer property, transfer right, transfuse, translate, translocate, transmit, transplant, transport, turn over
ASSOCIATED CONCEPTS: agreement to deliver, constructively delivered, deliver himself up, deliver in trust, deliver possession, deliver up, delivered for shipment, executed and delivered, sold and delivered, writing signed and delivered

DELIVERY, ***noun*** *actio,* conveyance, conveyancing, deliverance, *dictio, elocutio,* impartment, mutual transfer, remittance, rendering, sending, shipment, surrender, transfer, transference, transferral, transmission, transmittal, transmittance, transposal, transposition
ASSOCIATED CONCEPTS: absolute delivery, acceptance, acknowledgment of delivery, actual delivery, complete delivery, conditional delivery, constructive delivery, contingent delivery, delivery and acceptance, delivery bond, delivery f.o.b., delivery in escrow, delivery of a deed, delivery of an instrument, delivery of deed, delivery of freight, delivery of goods, delivery of instrument, delivery of mail, delivery of possession, delivery terms, delivery to a third person, failure of delivery, failure to make delivery, immediate delivery, improper delivery, misdelivery, nondelivery, partial delivery, personal delivery, prompt delivery, proper delivery, sale and delivery, sale for future delivery, substituted delivery, symbolic delivery, tender of delivery, unconditional delivery, valid delivery
FOREIGN PHRASES: ***In traditionibus scriptorum, non quod dictum est, sed quod gestum est, inspicitur.*** In the delivery of writings, not what is said, but what is done, is regarded. ***Periculum rei venditae, nondum traditae, est emptoris.*** The risk of a thing sold, but not yet delivered, is the purchaser's. ***Traditio nihil amplius transferre debet vel potest, ad eum qui accipit, quam est apud eum qui tradit.*** Delivery ought to, and can, transfer nothing more to him who receives than is in possession of him who makes the delivery. ***Traditio loqui facit chartam.*** Delivery makes the deed speak.

DELUDE, ***verb*** be cunning, befool, beguile, bluff, cause error, cheat, cozen, create a false impression, cully, dazzle, deceive, decoy, defraud, *deludere,* dissemble, dupe, falsify, fool, give a false idea, give a false impression, gull, hoax, hoodwink, illude, inveigle, lead astray, lead into error, make a fool of, misdirect, misguide, misinform, mislead, misrepresent, misstate, mystify, persuade to believe error, play a trick on, practice chicanery, practice fraud upon, practice upon one's credulity, swindle, take advantage of, take in, trick

DELUSIVE, ***adjective*** artful, beguiling, bogus, chimerical, crafty, cunning, deceitful, deceiving, deceptive, deluding, delusory, dreamy, elusive, fallacious, *fallax,* false, *falsus,* fancied, fanciful, fantastic, fantastical, feigned, fraudulent, guileful, hallucinative, hallucinatory, illusionary, illusive, illusory, imaginary, imagined, insubstantial, make-believe, misleading, mock, notional, phantasmal, pretended, sham, sleightful, specious, spurious, tricky, unactual, unfounded, unreal, unsubstantial, untrue, *vanus,* visionary, wily

DELVE, ***verb*** ask for, burrow, carry on intensive research, conduct an inquiry, dig down into, dig into, examine, explore, fathom, ferret out, *fodere,* follow the trail, go deep into, go in pursuit of, go in search of, go through, hold an inquiry, hunt for, hunt through, inquire for, inquire into, institute an inquiry, investigate, look around for, look behind the scenes, look for, look into, look through, make inquiry, peer, penetrate, poke, probe, probe to the bottom, prosecute an inquiry, pry, pursue, quest, research, rummage, search, search for, search laboriously, search through, seek, seek a clue, set up an inquiry, track, trail, unearth

DEMAGOGUE, ***noun*** agitator, charismatic leader, declaimer, exciter, factionary, factioneer, factious leader, fanatic, firebrand, fomenter, haranguer, incentor, inciter, inflamer, instigator, leader, mob swayer, *plebicola, plebis dux,* politician, popular agitator, provocator, provoker, rabble-rouser, radical, ranter, rebel, revolutionary, ringleader, rouser, troublemaker, unprincipled politician, unscrupulous agitator, unscrupulous haranguer, urger

DEMAND, ***noun*** asking for what is due, assertion of legal right, authoritative request, behest, bidding, call, claim, command, emphatic inquiry, exigency, imperative request, imposition, legal claim, notice of claim, order, peremptory claim, request to perform, requirement, requisite, statement of claim, ultimatum
ASSOCIATED CONCEPTS: actual demand, cross demand, demand and refusal, demand certificates, demand deposits, demand for payment, demand for relief, demand instruments, demand note, excessive demands, legal demand, notice and demand, on demand, presentment and demand, unreasonable demand
FOREIGN PHRASES: ***Rogationes, quaestiones, et positiones debent esse simplices.*** Demands, questions, and claims ought to be simple.

DEMAND, ***verb*** arrogate, ask, ask for with authority, assert a right to, assert one's rights, call for, claim, claim as one's due, command, direct, enjoin, exact, give notice, impose, insist, make application, order, present one's claim, press, request, require, urge

ASSOCIATED CONCEPTS: actual demand, cross demand, demand and refusal, demand certificates, demand deposits, demand for payment, demand for relief, demand instruments, demand note, excessive demands, legal demand, notice and demand, on demand, presentment and demand, unreasonable demand
FOREIGN PHRASES: ***Nihil peti potest ante id tempus quo per rerum naturam persolvi possit.*** Nothing can be demanded before the time when, in the nature of things, it can be paid. ***Judex non reddit plus quam quod petens ipse requirit.*** A judge should not render judgments for a larger sum than the plaintiff demands.

DEMARCATE, *verb* allocate, allot, apportion, assign, border, bound, circumscribe, compass, confine, contradistinguish, define, delimit, delimitate, demark, determine, determine boundaries, differentiate, discriminate, distinguish, disunite, divide, enclose, encompass, establish boundaries, fence off, fix limits, lay down limits, limit, mark, mark limits, mark out, outline, partition, rope off, segregate, separate, set apart, set bounds to, set off, stake out, zone

DEMEAN *(Deport oneself)*, ***verb*** acquit, act, appear, bear, behave, carry, comport, conduct, convey the impression, create the impression, function, have the mien, leave the impression, look, manage, present oneself, present the appearance, quit, represent oneself, resemble, seem, seem to be, show, take on the manner

DEMEAN *(Make lower)*, ***verb*** abase, belittle, bring down, bring into disrepute, bring low, cheapen, conquer, crush, debase, deflate, degrade, depreciate, derogate, descend, detract from, diminish, discredit, disgrace, dishonor, disparage, humble, humiliate, lower, make ashamed, make lowly, mortify, put down, reduce, shame, stain, take down, tarnish, vanquish

DEMEANOR, *noun* appearance, aspect, attitude, bearing, behavior, carriage, comportment, conduct, countenance, deportment, expression, guise, look, manner, mien, physical appearance, poise, posture, presence, way
ASSOCIATED CONCEPTS: demeanor of witnesses

DEMESNE, *noun* acquest, chattels real, domain, dominion, empire, estate, freehold, hereditament, holding, land, landed estate, landed property, manor, one's own land, property, real estate, real property, realm, realty
ASSOCIATED CONCEPTS: demesne lands

DEMISE *(Conveyance)*, ***noun*** abalienation, alienation, bequeathal, cession, conferment, conferral, conveyancing, deeding, deliverance, delivery, testamentary disposition, transfer, transference, transmission, transmittal

DEMISE *(Death)*, ***noun*** annihilation, cessation of life, decease, departure, end of life, expiration, extinction, extinguishment, loss of life, mortality, necrosis, passing away

DEMISE, *verb* award, bequeath, bestow by will, confer by will, convey, deliver over, devise, devolve upon, endow, give by will, grant by will, hand down, leave, leave a legacy, leave by will, make a bequest, make a legacy, make testamentary disposition, pass by will, pass down, transfer by will, transfer ownership, transmit, will
ASSOCIATED CONCEPTS: demise and grant, demise for a term of years, demise for life, demised premises

DEMIT, *verb* abdicate, give up, go into retirement, hand in one's resignation, lay down one's office, leave, make way for, quit, relinquish, renounce, resign, retire, retire from office, stand aside, stand down, tender one's resignation, vacate office, vacate one's seat, withdraw

DEMOBILIZE, *noun* cure, curtail, deactivate, demilitarize, disarm, disband, disengage, fix, limit, reduce, remedy, sever, stop
ASSOCIATED CONCEPTS: demobilize forces involved in an armed conflict

DEMONSTRABLE, *adjective* absolute, apparent, assured, beyond a question, beyond all doubt, clear, clear-cut, conclusive, decided, definite, dependable, determinate, doubtless, established, evident, incontestable, indisputable, indubitable, not to be disputed, positive, stable, trustworthy, unambiguous, unequivocal, unimpeachable, unmistakable, unqualified, unquestionable, valid, veracious, without doubt, workable

DEMONSTRATE *(Establish)*, ***verb*** authenticate, circumstantiate, clarify, confirm, corroborate, display, elucidate, evince, exemplify, exhibit, illuminate, illustrate, indicate, instruct, lay out, make clear, make evident, make plain, manifest, perform, point out, prove, set forth, show, show by example, substantiate, support, sustain, teach by example, uphold, validate, verify

DEMONSTRATE *(Protest)*, ***verb*** challenge, clamor, complain publicly, contravene, controvert, counter, counteract, cry out against, declare opposition, demur, denounce, dissent, expostulate, express disagreement, express disapproval, express dissatisfaction, impugn, inveigh, march, negate, object, oppose, parade, picket, rail, reject, reluct, remonstrate, resist, show disagreement, show disapproval, show opinion publicly, show opposition, spurn, state opposition, storm, traverse

DEMONSTRATIVE *(Expressive of emotion)*, ***adjective*** communicative, effusive, emotional, emotive, excitable, expressive, fanatical, fervent, feverish, fierce, fiery, free in expression, furious, histrionic, maudlin, overflowing, overwrought, passionate, prone to display of feeling, prone to emotional display, talkative, temperamental, unrestrained, vehement, violent, without reserve

DEMONSTRATIVE *(Illustrative)*, ***adjective*** affording proof, allegorical, analytical, annotative, characteristic, clarifying, confirmative, confirmatory, confirming, connotative, corroborating, declarative, delineatory, depictive, descriptive, elucidative, enlightening, exegetic, exegetical, explanatory, explicative, explicatory, explicit, expository, expressive, graphic, illuminating, illuminative, informative, informing, interpretative, interpretive, representative, revealing, showing, substantiative, suggesting, suggestive, supportive, telling, typical, verificative, verifying
ASSOCIATED CONCEPTS: demonstrative bequest, demonstrative evidence, demonstrative gift, demonstrative legacy, demonstrative words

DEMOTE, *verb* abase, belittle, bring down, bring low, cashier, cause to descend, cause to sink, debase, decrease in importance, dedecorate, deflate, degrade, demean, depose, depreciate, deprive, dethrone, diminish, discrown, dismiss from favor, dispossess, disrate, divest, downgrade, drop, humble, impose a penalty, lessen importance of, lower, lower in rank, make less important, otherwordly, penalize, reduce, reduce to inferior rank, reduce to the ranks, relieve, remove from office, strip, take down, unseat

ASSOCIATED CONCEPTS: demotion in rank, demotion in salary, demotion of employee

DEMUR, ***verb*** beg to differ, challenge, contradict, contravene, controvert, deny, differ, disagree, disapprove, disavow, dissent, enter a demurrer, *exceptionem facere,* not confirm, object, oppose, protest, raise objections, reject, repudiate, scruple, take exception, traverse, withhold assent

DEMURE, ***adjective*** bashful, blushful, blushing, chary, constrained, diffident, humble, introverted, modest, recessive, recoiling, reserved, reticent, sedate, self-conscious, self-effacing, serious, sheepish, shy, silent, sober, staid, timid, timorous, unassertive, unassuming, verecund, withdrawn

DEMURRAGE, ***noun*** compensation for delay, payment for delay, penalty for delay, remittance for delay

DEMURRER, ***noun*** be at variance, challenge, challenge to the sufficiency of the pleading, confutation, denial of the allegations, denial of the pleading, denial of the statements, exception, exception to a pleading, general denial, negation of allegations, objection, objection to a pleading, opposition to allegations, refusal to answer, refutation, repudiation of the allegations, take exception to the allegations, take issue with, traversal
ASSOCIATED CONCEPTS: argumentative demurrer, demurrer to a pleading, demurrer to evidence, demurrer to interrogatories, frivolous demurrer, general demurrer, special demurrer

DENATURE, ***verb*** adulterate, alter, attemper, bemingle, blend, change, cheapen, convert, corrupt, deform, denaturalize, devalue, dilute, disguise, distort, doctor, impair, infuse, intermix, introduce changes, invalidate, make impure, make lower in quality, mask, mix, pervert, pollute, sophisticate, tamper with, transfigure, transform, transmute, vitiate, water down, weaken
ASSOCIATED CONCEPTS: denatured food

DENIAL, ***noun*** abjuration, abnegation, abridgment, challenge, confutation, contradiction, contrary assertion, contravention, deprivement, disaffirmation, disallowance, disavowal, disclaimer, disclamation, disentitlement, dissent, divestment, gainsaying, *negatio,* negation, negative answer, nonacceptance, nonconsent, objection, privation, prohibition, protest, protestation, rebuttal, recantation, refutation, rejection, relinquishment, renouncement, renunciation, *repudiatio,* repudiation, retraction, revocation, spurning, swearing off
ASSOCIATED CONCEPTS: argumentative denial, denial of admittance, denial of civil rights, denial of claim, denial of counsel, denial of due process, denial of equal protection, denial of knowledge or information, denial of liability, denial of motion, denial of relief, general denial, specific denial
FOREIGN PHRASES: ***Per rerum naturam, factum negantis nulla probatio est.*** It is the nature of things that a person who denies a fact is not bound to give proof. ***Justitia non est neganda, non differenda.*** Justice is neither to be denied nor delayed. ***Qui non negat fatetur.*** He who does not deny, admits. ***Posito uno oppositorum negatur alterum.*** One of two opposite positions being established, the other is denied. ***Semper praesumitur pro negante.*** A presumption is always in favor of the person who denies.

DENIGRATE, ***verb*** abase, accuse, asperse, attack, attaint, belittle, besmear, besmirch, bespatter, blacken, blacken one's good name, blemish, brand, call names, calumniate, cast aspersions, charge, compromise, condemn, criticize, decry, defame, degrade, delate, denounce, depreciate, deride, dishonor, expose, gibbet, give a bad name, humiliate, implicate, incriminate, inculpate, insult, libel, lower, malign, pillory, put in a bad light, put to shame, reflect poorly upon, reproach, reprove, revile, run down, shame, slander, smear, smirch, sneer at, soil, speak ill of, stain, stigmatize, sully, tarnish, taunt, traduce, vilify, vilipend, vituperate

DENIZEN, ***noun*** burgher, citizen, dweller, habitant, *incola,* indweller, inhabitant, inmate, occupant, occupier, oppidan, resident, residentiary, sojourner, tenant, townsman

DENOMINATE, ***verb*** call, call by name, christen, classify, coin, *denominare,* denote, designate, distinguish by name, dub, entitle, give a name to, give title to, label, name, phrase, signify, specify, style, term, title

DENOMINATION, ***noun*** appellation, association, band, branch, brotherhood, caption, categorization, category, characterization, class, classification, clique, community, coterie, description, designation, differentiation, distinction, division, faction, genre, group, grouping, heading, identification, kind, label, movement, name, nomenclature, order, organization, party, persuasion, religious order, sect, section, species, subdivision, term, terminology, title, trademark, type, variety
ASSOCIATED CONCEPTS: denomination of money, denominational institution, denominational school, religious denomination

DENOTE, ***verb*** be a name for, be a sign of, be an indication of, bespeak, betoken, convey a meaning, denominate, denotate, depict, depicture, *designare,* designate, express, imply, *indicare,* indicate, label, mark, mean, note, point out, portray, refer to, represent, show, signal, *significare,* signify, stand for, suggest, symbolize, tell the meaning of, token
ASSOCIATED CONCEPTS: denoting ownership, denoting possession

DENOUEMENT, ***noun*** apodosis, climax, close, closing, closure, completion, conclusion, consummation, *dénouement,* determination, development, disclosure, disentanglement, dissolution, end, ending, epilogue, eventuation, *fait accompli,* final happening, final statement, final touch, *finale,* finalization, finis, finish, finishing stroke, fruition, issue, last act, outcome, outgrowth, *quietus,* realization, resolution, result, settlement, solution, summation, termination, *terminus,* unfolding, unraveling, unraveling of plot, unveiling, upshot, windup

DENOUNCE *(Condemn),* ***verb*** anathematize, animadvert, asperse, assail, assail with censure, assault, attack, be censorious, belittle, berate, besmear, besmirch, blackball, blacken, blacklist, brand, bring into discredit, bring to account, call to account, calumniate, cast a slur upon, cast aspersions, cast reflection upon, cast reproach upon, castigate, cavil, censure, challenge, chastise, chide, cite, comminate, condemn openly, contemn, criminate, criticize, criticize severely, cry down, cry out against, declaim against, decry, defame, deflate, degrade, denigrate, denunciate, deprecate, depreciate, derogate, destroy, detract, disapprove, discommend, discountenance, discredit, dishonor, disparage, dispraise, disvalue, dress down, excite disapprobation, exclaim against, excoriate, execrate, find fault with, frown upon, fulminate against, gibbet, impugn, inculpate, inveigh, lash, malign, ostracize, pass censure on, pillory, protest against, publicly accuse, put in a bad light, rebuke, recriminate, reflect upon, remonstrate, reprehend, reprimand, reproach, reprobate, revile, scold, slur, smear, speak ill of, stigmatize, take exception to, take to task, traduce, upbraid, vilify, vilipend, vituperate

DENOUNCE *(Inform against),* ***verb*** accuse, arraign, bear witness against, blame, bring accusation, bring charges, charge, complain against, divulge, hold accountable, hold responsible, impeach, implicate, impute, incriminate, inculpate, incur blame, indict, inform, inform on, involve, lay blame upon, lay charges against, lodge a complaint, make charges against, make formal accusation against, name, point at, publicly accuse, report against, turn informer

DENSITY, ***noun*** closeness, compactness, concentration, concretion, intransparency, opacity, opaqueness, palpability, solidity, thickness

DENUDE, ***verb*** bare, bring to light, defoliate, denudate, disclose, disfurnish, disrobe, divest, doff, exhibit, expose, flay, lay bare, lay open, lay waste, make naked, make public, manifest, open, pare, peel, present to view, publicize, reveal, shed, show, shuck, skin, slough, strip, tear off, uncase, uncloak, unclothe, uncover, uncurtain, undo, undrape, undress, unfold, unfrock, unrobe, unscreen, unsheathe, unshroud, unveil, unwrap, vent

DENUNCIATE, ***verb*** admonish, blame, castigate, censure, charge, chide, complain, condemn, criticize, denounce, disapprove, impute, indict, lambaste, rap, rebuke, reprehend, reproach, reprove, upbraid, vituperate

DENUNCIATION, ***noun*** accusal, *accusatio,* accusation, anathema, aspersion, backbiting, blame, calumny, carping, castigation, censure, charge, chiding, commination, complaint, condemnation, contumely, *coup de bec,* criticism, damnation, decrial, defamation, *delatio,* delation, denigration, denouncement, deprecation, depreciation, derogation, detraction, diatribe, disapprobation, disapproval, discommendation, discountenance, disparagement, dispraise, excoriation, execration, *exposé,* faultfinding, fulmination, incrimination, inculpation, indictment, informing against, invective, malediction, objurgation, obloquy, opprobrium, philippic, plaint, rebuke, recrimination, reprehension, reprimand, reproach, reprobation, reproof, revilement, severe censure, slur, smear, stigmatization, stricture, tirade, tongue-lashing, traducement, upbraiding, utter disapproval, vehement condemnation, vilification, vituperation

DENY *(Contradict),* ***verb*** contravene, controvert, declare to be false, declare to be untrue, disaffirm, disagree, disallow, disavow, disclaim, disown, dispute, dissent, forswear, gainsay, *infitias ire, negare,* negate, refuse to acknowledge, refuse to admit, refuse to allow, reject as erroneous, repudiate, traverse
FOREIGN PHRASES: ***Ei incumbit probatio, qui dicit, non qui negat; cum per rerum naturam factum negantis probatio nulla sit.*** The burden of proof lies upon him who asserts it, not upon him who denies; since by the nature of things, he who denies a fact cannot produce any proof of it.

DENY *(Refuse to grant),* ***verb*** abnegate, forbid, keep from, *negare,* prohibit, refuse to allow, refuse to bestow, refuse to give, refuse to permit, refuse to supply, reject, renege, renounce, withhold
ASSOCIATED CONCEPTS: deny a claim, deny a motion, deny a right, deny due process, deny liability

DEONTOLOGY, ***noun*** an ethical theory, constraint, deontological ethics, following proscribed conduct, following the rule without considering the consequences, obligatory action without considering the consequences

DEPART, ***verb*** abscond, absent oneself, be gone, decamp, desert, deviate, differ, digress, disappear, disassociate, *discedere,* disengage, disjoin, dissociate, diverge, divorce, emigrate, evacuate, exit, expatriate oneself, fade, flee, forsake, issue forth, leave, make an exit, march off, part, recede, resign, retire, set out, start out, swerve, vacate, vanish, vary from, withdraw
ASSOCIATED CONCEPTS: depart from scope of employment, depart from terms of a trust, depart from the state, departure in pleading, material departure

DEPARTMENT, ***noun*** agency, area, assignment, branch, bureau, categorization, category, chapter, class, classification, designation, district, division, domain, field, field of activity, jurisdiction, ministry, *munus, pars,* part, precinct, province, *provincia,* realm, section, sector, specialty, sphere, station, subdivision, subsection, zone
ASSOCIATED CONCEPTS: department of government, department of state, department rules and regulations, executive department, judicial department, legislative department, municipal department

DEPARTURE *(Change),* ***noun*** alteration, amendment, conversion, correction, deformation, deviation, difference, digression, distortion, divergence, diversion, metamorphosis, modification, modulation, rectification, redesign, redoing, refashioning, reform, regulation, remaking, remodeling, replacement, revamping, review, revision, reworking, substitution, tweak, vacation, variation

DEPARTURE *(Leaving),* ***noun*** abandonment, decamping, decampment, disembarkation, egress, egression, embarkation, emigration, evacuation, exit, exiting, exodus, farewell, flight, leave-taking, parting, relinquishment, removal, retreat, running away, withdrawal

DEPENDABILITY, ***noun*** allegiance, ardor, attachment, certainty, constancy, devotedness, devotion, doggedness, eagerness, earnestness, endurance, fealty, fidelity, fixedness, inerrancy, infallibility, loyalty, permanence, perseverance, regularity, reliability, reliance, resolution, responsibility, solidity, solidness, staunchness, steadfastness, true-heartedness, trustworthiness, unfailingness, unflagging devotion, zeal

DEPENDABLE, ***adjective*** assured, certain, conscientious, constant, devoted, faithful, guaranteed, incorrupt, loyal, proved, proven, reliable, reputable, responsible, solid, stable, staunch, steadfast, steady, sure, tested, tried, true, trustable, trusted, trustworthy, trusty, unchanging, unfailing, upright, veracious
ASSOCIATED CONCEPTS: dependable evidence

DEPENDENT, ***adjective*** ancillary, conditional, conditioned, contingent, controlled by, derivative, derived from, due to, evolved from, granted on certain terms, helpless, imposing a condition, incident to, limited, minor, modified by conditions, needing outside support, *obnoxius,* pendent, provisory, qualified, regulated by, reliant, restricted, resulting from, servile, subject, subject to, subordinate, subservient, sustained by, unable to exist without, weak

DEPENDENT, ***noun*** charge, child, helpless person, individual under guardianship, juvenile charge, minor, minor

under guardianship, minor under protectorship, pensioner, person under guardianship, vassal, ward
ASSOCIATED CONCEPTS: actual dependent, dependent and neglected child, dependent person, dependent wife, lawful dependent, legal dependent, minor dependent, partial dependency, total dependency

DEPICT, *verb* characterize, communicate, connote, convey, delineate, *depingere,* describe, *describere,* detail, diagram, draw, *effingere,* embody, enunciate, evince, evoke, exemplify, exhibit, explain, explicate, express, give an account, give expression to, illuminate, illustrate, indicate, limn, manifest, outline, particularize, personify, picture, portray, recite, recount, relate, render an account, report, represent, reveal, set forth, show, signify, sketch, specify, symbolize, tell, tell vividly, typify

DEPICTION, *noun* caricature, delineation, drawing, elucidation, fabrication, illustration, imitation, impersonation, picture, portrait, portraiture, portrayal, rendering, rendition, representation, simulation, sketch, takeoff

DEPLETE, *verb* beggar, bleed, consume, decrease, dissipate, drain, drain of resources, dry up, eliminate, empty, empty out, evacuate, exhaust, expend, finish, impoverish, lessen, lose, pauperize, purge, reduce, render insufficient, run down, spend, unload, use up, void, waste, weaken, wear out

DEPLORABLE, *adjective* afflicted, appalling, atrabilious, atrocious, bad, black, calamitous, catastrophic, demoralizing, depressing, depressive, despicable, dire, disagreeable, disastrous, disheartening, dismal, displeasing, distasteful, distressing, doleful, dolorous, dreadful, dreary, *flebilis,* frightful, ghastly, grievous, horrible, horrid, horrific, horrifying, insufferable, intolerable, lamentable, *miserabilis,* miserable, outrageous, pathetic, piteous, pitiable, pitiful, poor, regrettable, sad, shocking, sorrowful, sorry, terrible, tragic, tragical, unbearable, undesirable, unfortunate, unhappy, unpleasant, unpleasing, unsatisfactory, untoward, vile, wretched

DEPLORE, *verb* be sorry for, bemoan, bewail, brood over, complain, cry over, *deflere, deplorare,* express deep grief for, fret over, grieve for, groan, lament, moan, mourn, regard with sorrow, regret, regret profoundly, repine, rue, shed tears over, show concern for, sigh for, sorrow over, view with regret, weep over

DEPLOY, *verb* assign to battle stations, assign to positions, branch out, broaden, diffuse, *dilatare,* distribute, diverge, expand, *explicare,* extend, fan out, outspread, place, radiate, scatter, splay, spread, spread out in battle formation, stretch out, thin out, unfold, unfurl, widen

DEPONENT, *noun* affiant, apprizer, attestant, attestator, attester, attestor, communicant, communicator, compurgator, enlightener, indicator, informant, informer, one who attests, one who bears witness, one who gives evidence, one who makes an affidavit, one who testifies under oath, party making an affidavit, reporter, swearer, teller, testifier, voucher, witness, witness who gives testimony
ASSOCIATED CONCEPTS: witness

DEPORT *(Banish),* ***verb*** bar, cast out, dislodge, dismiss, displace, drive away, drive out, eject, evict, exclude, exile, expatriate, expel, extradite, force out, oust, outlaw, remove, send away, thrust out, transfer, transport, turn out

DEPORT *(Conduct oneself),* ***verb*** acquit, act, bear oneself, behave, carry oneself, comport oneself

DEPORTATION, *noun* banishment, casting out, dislocation, dismissal, displacement, driving out, ejection, ejectment, elimination, eviction, exclusion, exile, exilement, expatriation, expulsion, extradition, extrusion, forced departure, forced leave taking, ouster, purge, removal, riddance, sending away, thrusting out

DEPORTMENT, *noun* actions, address, air, appearance, aspect, attitude, bearing, behavior, breeding, carriage, comportment, conduct, decorum, demeanor, dignity, guise, *habitus,* look, manner, mien, personal bearing, poise, port, posture, practice, presence, propriety, way, ways

DEPOSE *(Remove),* ***verb*** cast away, cast out, demote, deprive of rank, dethrone, discard, discharge, discharge from office, disemploy, disentitle, disestablish, dislodge, dismiss, displace, dispossess, divest, drive out, drop, eject, evict, exile, expel, fire, impeach, *loco movere,* oust, oust from office, put out, put out of possession, recall, reduce, turn away, turn out, unseat, usurp

DEPOSE *(Testify),* ***verb*** adduce, affirm, affirm under oath, asseverate, attest, aver, avouch, avow, bear witness to, certify, declare under oath, depone, give a solemn declaration, give an account of, give evidence, give proof, give proof by a witness, give sworn testimony, make an affidavit, make deposition, plead, profess, promise, relate, say under oath, swear, swear under oath, *testari, testificari,* verify, vouch, vouch for, witness
ASSOCIATED CONCEPTS: depose a witness

DEPOSIT, *noun* accumulation, collateral, collateral security, *depositum,* down payment, earnest pledge, forfeit, gage, guarantee, installment, money in bank, part payment, pawn, payment, pledge, retainer, security, stake, surety
ASSOCIATED CONCEPTS: binder, certificate of deposit, earnest money, escrow, interpleader, savings deposit, security deposit, time deposit

DEPOSIT *(Place),* ***verb*** *deponere,* dump, install, lay, locate, lodge, place in a receptacle, plant, put, quarter, reposit, rest, set, settle, situate, stash, store, stow

DEPOSIT *(Submit to a bank),* ***verb*** bank, commit, enter into an account, entrust, invest, keep an account, lay by, present money for safekeeping, put at interest, save
ASSOCIATED CONCEPTS: interpleader, stake

DEPOSITION, *noun* compurgation, declaration under oath, disclosure, documentation, oral evidence, oral statement under oath, proof by a witness, solemn declaration, statement on oath, statement under oath, sworn evidence, testification, testimonial, *testimonium,* testimony, transcript of testimony, vouching, written declaration under oath

DEPOSITORY, *noun* *apotheca,* archives, bunker, cache, catchall, coffer, collection, container, depot, hold, holder, magazine, place for safe keeping, place of deposit, receptacle, *receptaculum,* repertory, repository, reservoir, safe, safe-deposit box, storage, store, storehouse, vault, warehouse
ASSOCIATED CONCEPTS: depository box, legal depository, reservoir

DEPRAVED, ***adjective*** abominable, bad, base, base-minded, contemptible, corrupt, debased, debauched, degenerate, degraded, deteriorated, disreputable, dissipated, dissolute, evil, execrable, flagitious, foul, gross, heinous, horrendous, immeritorious, immoral, indecent, iniquitous, lecherous, lewd, licentious, low, low-minded, obscene, perverted, profligate, rank, ruined, salacious, shameful, shameless, sinful, unprincipled, unscrupulous, vile, vitiated, vulgar, warped, wicked
ASSOCIATED CONCEPTS: depraved act, depraved indifference, depraved mind

DEPRECATE, ***verb*** *abominari,* asperse, belittle, berate, cast aspersions, charge, decry, demean, denigrate, denounce, deplore, derogate, detract, disapprove, disclaim, discommend, discredit, disdain, disfavor, dislike, disparage, dispraise, disvalue, excoriate, exprobate, fault, find fault, impugn, inculpate, object, objurgate, oppose, protest, reject, repudiate, traduce, view with disfavor, vilipend

DEPRECIATE, ***verb*** atrophy, attenuate, become deteriorated, become of less worth, belittle, censure, cheapen, contemn, corrode, cut, debase, debilitate, decay, decline, decrease, decry, deduct, defame, deflate, degenerate, degrade, denigrate, denounce, depress, deride, derogate from, deteriorate, detract from, *detrectare,* devaluate, devalue, dilute, diminish the price of, diminish the value of, discount, discredit, disesteem, disgrace, disparage, dispraise, drop, dwindle, ebb, enervate, enfeeble, erode, fall, fault, find fault with, get worse, grow less, grow worse, impoverish, lessen, lessen the price of, lose value, lower, lower in price, lower in reputation, lower in value, lower the value of, make little of, malign, minimize, misprize, *obtrectare,* readjust downward, reduce the purchasing value of, reduce the strength of, retrograde, run down, shrink, sink, slight, slur, soil, spoil, stain, sully, taint, take away, tarnish, traduce, underestimate, underpraise, underprize, underrate, underreckon, undervalue, weaken, wear, worsen
ASSOCIATED CONCEPTS: depreciate a loss, obsolescence

DEPREDATION, ***noun*** foray, havoc, marauding, raid, rapine, ravaging, sack, spoliation

DEPRESS, ***verb*** abase, bring down, bring low, cause to sink, cheapen, dampen, darken, decline, decrease, deflate, deject, depreciate, deteriorate, devaluate, devalue, diminish, discourage, dispirit, drop, ebb, flatten, indent, lessen, lower, make despondent, make sad, plunge, press down, reduce, sadden, shrink, sink, slump, squash, weaken

DEPRESSION, ***noun*** debasement, decline, deflation, dejection, depreciation, despondence, despondency, disheartenment, dispiritedness, dolefulness, economic decline, gloom, lowering, lowness, *maeror,* sinking, slump, *tristitia*
ASSOCIATED CONCEPTS: economic depression

DEPRIVATION, ***noun*** absence, adversity, affliction, bereavement, dearth, deficiency, denial, deprival, detriment, disadvantage, dispossession, distress, divestiture, divestment, expropriation, forfeit, forfeiture, hardship, inadequacy, insufficiency, loss, paucity, penalty, poverty, privation, sacrifice, scarcity, seizure, shortage, suffering, want, withdrawal, withholding

DEPRIVATION OF RIGHTS, ***noun*** absence, adversity, affliction deprival, dearth, deficiency, denial, deprival, detriment, disadvantage, disenfranchisement, dispossession, divestiture, divestment, expropriation, forfeit, forfeiture, forfeiture of benefits, forfeiture of entitlements, forfeiture of liberties, forfeiture of perquisites, forfeiture of prerogatives, forfeiture of privileges, hardship, loss, loss of benefits, loss of entitlements, loss of rights, privation, sacrifice, scarcity, seizure, suffering

DEPRIVE, ***verb*** arrogate, attach, bereave, capture, commandeer, confiscate, convert, denude, despoil, disendow, disentitle, disherit, disinherit, disown, dispossess, disseize, distrain, divest, expropriate, extort, fleece, foreclose, impound, impoverish, leave destitute, mulct, pauperize, purloin, rob, seize, sequester, sequestrate, steal, strip, take away, tear away, usurp, wrench, wrest
ASSOCIATED CONCEPTS: deprivation of liberty, deprivation of property, deprivation of right, deprive of employment, deprive of life, deprived of liberty, deprived of substantial right
FOREIGN PHRASES: ***Privatio praesupponit habitum.*** A deprivation presupposes something possessed.

DEPUTATION *(Delegation),* ***noun*** agents, body of delegates, body of representatives, commissaries, commission, committee, consulate, delegates, delegation, emissaries, envoys, factors, *legati, legatio,* legation, mission, plenipotentiaries, proxies, representation, representatives

DEPUTATION *(Selection of delegates),* ***noun*** appointing, appointment, assignment, authorization, authorizing, commission, conferment, delegation, deputization, designation, devolution, empowering, entrustment, installation, investiture, investment, nomination, procuration

DEPUTY, ***noun*** agent, alternate, ambassador, appointee, assignee, broker, commissary, commissioner, delegate, emissary, envoy, factor, intermediary, *legatus,* lieutenant, minister, plenipotentiary, proctor, procurator, proxy, representative, second, secondary, substitute, surrogate, vicar, vicarius, vicegerent
ASSOCIATED CONCEPTS: de facto deputy, deputy commissioner, deputy marshal, deputy officer, deputy sheriff, general deputy, special deputy
FOREIGN PHRASES: ***Vicarius non habet vicarium.*** A deputy cannot have a deputy.

DERANGED, ***adjective*** bereft of reason, confused, *demens,* demented, disarranged, disconcerted, disjointed, dislocated, disordered, disorganized, displaced, dissonant, distraught, frenetic, frenzied, in disorder, incompetent, inconsistent, insane, *insanus,* insensate, mad, maddened, maniacal, of unsound mind, rabid, reasonless, unbalanced, unsettled

DERELICT *(Abandoned),* ***adjective*** adrift, avoided, cast aside, cast off, castaway, deserted, desolate, discarded, disowned, dispensed with, excluded, forgotten, forlorn, forsaken, friendless, given up, helpless, homeless, ignored, isolated, jettisoned, left, lonely, lonesome, neglected, on the fringe of society, outcast, rejected, relinquished, repudiated, scorned, scrapped, set adrift, shunned, solitary, thrown overboard, uncared for, unclaimed, unfortunate, unfriended, unowned, unpossessed, unwanted, wretched, written off
ASSOCIATED CONCEPTS: derelict property

DERELICT *(Negligent),* ***adjective*** careless, delinquent, disregardful, dutiless, failing in duty, faithless, faulty, heedless, improvident, inattentive, inconsiderate, indifferent, lax, neglectful, neglecting, regardless, remiss, slack, thoughtless, uncircumspect, unconcerned, unfaithful, unheedful, unheeding, uninterested, unmindful, unobservant, unwatchful

DERELICT, *noun* displaced person, drifter, exile, fugitive, ne'er-do-well, outcast, pariah, scamp, tramper, vagrant, wanderer, wastrel

DERELICTION, *noun* abandonment, breach, carelessness, *culpa,* default, defection, delinquency, desertion, disregard, dutilessness, evasion, failure in duty, faithlessness, heedlessness, indifference, laxity, laxness, misprision, neglect, neglectfulness, negligence, noncooperation, nonfeasance, nonobservence, nonperformance, omission, relinquishment, remissness, truancy, unconcern, unfaithfulness
ASSOCIATED CONCEPTS: dereliction of duty, moral dereliction

DERISIVE, *adjective* caustic, contemptuous, crusty, derisory, derogatory, disdainful, impertinent, insolent, mean, mocking, negative, scoffing, scornful, sneering, taunting

DERIVATION, *noun* ancestor, ancestry, antecedent, author, authority, base, basis, begetter, beginning, birth, birthplace, causality, causation, cause, commencement, creator, descent, determinant, extraction, family, first cause, first occasion, foundation, fount, fountainhead, generator, genesis, ground, head, inception, issue, line, lineage, mainspring, origin, origination, parent, parentage, prime motive, primogenitor, producer, progenitor, provenance, provenience, reference, root, source, source material, spring, springhead, starting point, stem, stock, tracing back, ultimate cause

DERIVATIVE, *adjective* ascribable, attributable, caused, coming from, consequent, consequential, derivate, derivational, derived, deriving, descendant, descended, ensuing, evolved, following, hereditary, imitative, resultant, resulting, secondary, sequent, subordinate, subsequent, subsidiary, vicarious
ASSOCIATED CONCEPTS: derivative action, derivative authority, derivative deed, derivative jurisdiction, derivative liabilities, derivative powers, derivative rights, derivative stockholder's suit, derivative title

DERIVATIVE WORK, *noun* consequential work, corollary work, ensuing work, resulting work, secondary work, subsequent work

DERIVE *(Deduce),* ***verb*** conclude, construe, *deducere,* draw a conclusion, draw an inference, extract, infer, make a deduction, obtain by reasoning, reason, theorize, trace

DERIVE *(Receive),* ***verb*** acquire, come into possession, draw from, extract, get, glean, obtain, procure, secure, take, *trahere*

DEROGATE, *verb* abase, asperse, be derogatory, belittle, besmirch, bespatter, blacken, blot, brand, bring down, bring into discredit, bring low, bring shame upon, calumniate, cast a slur upon, cast aspersions, debase, decry, defame, demean, demote, denigrate, depreciate, depress, deprive, *derogare,* detract, *detrahere,* diminish, discredit, disgrace, dishonor, disparage, dispraise, disprize, disrate, humble, incur disgrace, lessen, lessen the reputation of, lower, make ashamed, make little of, make lowly, make smaller, malign, misprize, not do justice to, pull down, put down, reduce, revile, ridicule, run down, scoff, shame, smirch, sneer at, speak evil of, speak ill of, speak slightingly of, stain, subtract from, sully, taint, take something from, tarnish, traduce, underestimate, underrate, underreckon, undervalue, vilify, vilipend, weaken
ASSOCIATED CONCEPTS: derogation of common law, derogation of deed, derogation of right

DEROGATORY, *adjective* belittling, calumniatory, calumnious, censorious, condemnatory, contumelious, defamatory, denunciatory, deprecatory, depreciative, depreciatory, detracting, detractory, disapprobatory, disapproving, discrediting, disdainful, dishonoring, disparaging, faultfinding, injurious, lessening, libelous, objurgatory, pejorative, slanderous, slighting, uncomplimentary, unfavorable, unflattering
ASSOCIATED CONCEPTS: derogatory statements
FOREIGN PHRASES: ***Quae legi communi derogant stricte interpretantur.*** Those things which derogate from the common law are strictly interpreted. ***Quae legi communi derogant non sunt trahenda in exemplum.*** Those things which derogate from the common law are not to be drawn into precedent.

DESCEND, *verb* bequeath, bestow, come down by transmission, come down lineally, deed, demise, *descendere,* endow, entrust, give, give by will, grant, hand down, hand on, leave a legacy, make a bequest, make a legacy, pass by devise, pass by inheritance, pass by operation of law, pass by succession, pass down from generation to generation, pass on, settle upon, transmit, will, will and bequeath

DESCENDANT, *noun* child, family, future generation, heir, issue, kin, lineage, offshoot, offspring, posterity, progeny, scion, succeeding generation, successor
ASSOCIATED CONCEPTS: descendants of the line, direct descendant, lawful descendants, lineal descendant or heir, lineal descendants

DESCENT *(Declination),* ***noun*** change from higher to lower, comedown, coming down, downrush, droop, drop, falling, going down, inclination downward, lapse, settlement, sinking, subsidence

DESCENT *(Lineage),* ***noun*** ancestry, birth, birthright, blood, bloodline, breed, clan, derivation, dynasty, extraction, family tree, filiation, genealogy, heredity, heritage, kin, line, line of ancestors, origin, parentage, paternity, pedigree, race, stock, strain
ASSOCIATED CONCEPTS: ancestors, collateral descent, descendants, line of descent, right and interest by descent, title by descent

DESCRIBE, *verb* annotate, be specific, characterize, clarify, define, delineate, depict, *depingere, describere,* detail, elucidate, explain, *explicare,* expound, give an account, identify, illuminate, illustrate, itemize, make clear, make plain, make vivid, outline, paint, particularize, picture, portray, portray in words, represent by words, specify, spell out
ASSOCIATED CONCEPTS: falsely describe

DESCRIPTION, *noun* account, characterization, definition, delineation, depiction, *descriptio,* details, *enarratio,* explanation, *expositio,* formulation, narrative, outline, particulars, portrayal, profile, sketch, specification
ASSOCIATED CONCEPTS: correct description, description in a will, description of goods, description of land, description of persons, description of property, specific description
FOREIGN PHRASES: ***Veritas demonstrationis tollit errorem nominis.*** In all penal judgments, allowance is made for youth and lack of prudence. ***Falsa demonstratione legatum non perimi.*** A legacy is not nullified by an incorrect description. ***Praesentia corporis tollit errorem nominis; et veritas nominis tollit errorem demonstrationis.***

The presence of the body cures an error in the name; and the accuracy of the name cures an error of description. ***Non accipi debent verba in demonstrationem falsam, quae competunt in limitationem veram.*** Words ought not to be taken to import a false description which may be taken to describe a true limitation.

DESCRIPTIVE, *adjective* characterizing, circumstantial, classificatory, clear, definitional, definitive, delineative, designating, detailed, eloquent, explanatory, explicatory, expositive, expository, graphic, identifying, illuminating, illuminative, illustrative, interpretive, lifelike, narrative, particularized, photographic, pictorial, realistic, representational, representative, revealing, specific, true-to-life, vivid, well-drawn
ASSOCIATED CONCEPTS: descriptive calls, descriptive term, descriptive trade name, descriptive trademark, descriptive word

DESCRIPTIVISM, *noun* a theory of the study of language, accepted usage, accepted use, common interpretation, common usage, common use, customary application, customary use, description, descriptive linguistics, linguistic description, practical use, vernacular

DESEGREGATE, *verb* admix, agglomerate, amalgamate, assimilate, associate, band, be mixed, blend, coalesce, combine racially, combine with, commingle, commix, compound, confederate, conglomerate, conjoin, connect, consolidate, eliminate racial segregation, fuse, incorporate, institute commingling of races, integrate, interblend, interfuse, interlace, interlard, intermingle, intermix, join together, make no racial distinctions, mass, meld, merge, merge in, mingle, mix, promote racial harmony, promote racial mixing, to bring together, unify, unite

DESERTION, *noun* abandonment, abandonment of allegiance, abjuration, absence without leave, act of forsaking, apostasy, AWOL, defection, departure, *derelictio,* disaffection, disloyalty, flight, forsaking, forswearing, leaving, mutiny, quitting, recreancy, renouncement, renunciation, repudiation, resignation, secession, unlawful departure, willful abandonment
ASSOCIATED CONCEPTS: constructive desertion, willful desertion

DESIDERATUM, *noun* aim, ambition, aspiration, desideration, desire, essential object of desire, exigency, goal, necessary, necessity, need, objective, requirement, requisite, requisition, want

DESIGN *(Construction plan),* ***noun*** blueprint, chart, conception, delineation, depiction, *descriptio,* diagram, draft, drawing, *forma,* graph, layout, *lineamenta,* map, model, outline, picture, plan, preliminary drawing, projection, proof, rendering, representation, rough cast, rough copy, rough representation, skeleton, sketch, treatment

DESIGN *(Intent),* ***noun*** aim, ambition, animus, approach, aspiration, bent, *consilium, consulto,* contemplation, course of action, desire, destination, determination, direction, end, end in view, expectation, fixed purpose, forethought, goal, hope, inclination, intention, intentionality, meaning, mission, motive, object, objective, plan, plan of attack, predetermination, projected goal, proposed action, proposed sequence of action, purport, purpose, purpose in view, pursuit, resolve, scheme, set purpose, settled purpose, stratagem, strategy, target, ultimate end, view, way of doing things, will
ASSOCIATED CONCEPTS: common design, formed design, premeditated design

DESIGNATE, *verb* appoint, assign, authorize, be specific, characterize, choose, commission, declare, define, denominate, denote, *designare,* detail, determine, discriminate, earmark, enter into detail, entitle, express, fix, formulate, indicate, itemize, mark, mark out, mention, name, *nominare,* nominate, *notare,* note, particularize, pinpoint, point out, select, set, set apart, set aside, show, signify, specify, stipulate
ASSOCIATED CONCEPTS: designate as a beneficiary, designate as an agent, designate as an executor

DESIGNATED PUBLIC FORUM, *noun* a strict scrutiny forum, area created by government for purpose of fostering political speech, forum designated for public discourse

DESIGNATION *(Naming),* ***noun*** appellation, appointment, approval, assigning, assignment, authorization, calling, categorization, choosing, commissioning, delegating, delegation, denomination, denotation, deputation, description, *designatio,* fixing, identification, indication, installation, label, ordainment, ordination, particularization, placing in office, pointing out, selection, signification, specification, stipulation
ASSOCIATED CONCEPTS: designated agent, designated document, designation of beneficiary

DESIGNATION *(Symbol),* ***noun*** badge, cipher, distinguishing mark, earmark, emblem, hallmark, identification mark, indicator, indicium, initial, insignia, label, mark, name, representation, sign, standard, title, token, totem, trademark, type

DESIRABLE *(Pleasing),* ***adjective*** enjoyable, gratifying, pleasant, pleasurable, pleasureful, welcome

DESIRABLE *(Qualified),* ***adjective*** acceptable, eligible, entitled, qualified, recommendable, suitable, worthy

DESIRE, *noun* ambition, appetency, appetite, *appetitio,* ardent impulse, ardor, aspiration, attraction, avidity, bent, concupiscence, covetousness, craving, *cupiditas,* cupidity, *desiderium,* eagerness, fancy, fondness, hankering, hunger, impulse, inclination, liking, longing, lust, motive, predilection, proclivity, propensity, rapaciousness, thirst, urge, want, will, wish, yearning, yen
ASSOCIATED CONCEPTS: precatory words

DESIRE, *verb* apply for, ask, ask for, aspire, be after, be bent upon, be eager, beg a favor, call for, clamor for, covet, crave, cry out for, desiderate, entreat, *expetere,* express a wish to obtain, have a proclivity, have a yearning, have an appetite, have an impulse, have designs on, have one's heart set on, hope for, incline, like to, long for, make a request for, make application for, press, pursue, put in a claim for, request, solicit, supplicate, urge, want, wish for
ASSOCIATED CONCEPTS: precatory words

DESIST, *verb* abstain, arrest, be quiescent, call off, cease, check, *desinere, desistere,* discontinue, end, finish, forbear, freeze, halt, hold, intermit, interrupt, leave off, make inactive, put a stop to, refrain, repose, rest, stand, stay, stop, surcease, suspend, terminate
ASSOCIATED CONCEPTS: cease and desist order

DESPICABLE, ***adjective*** abhorrent, abominable, condemnable, contemptible, cowardly, craven, dastardly, deplorable, discreditable, disgraceful, highly offensive, ignoble, ignominious, lame, mean, pitiable, pitiful, reprehensible, repugnant, shameful, unethical, unprincipled, unscrupulous

DESPISE, ***verb*** abhor, abominate, be hostile to, be inimical toward, bear malice toward, detest, disfavor, dislike, execrate, feel hostile toward, hate, have an aversion toward, have animus toward, have aversion to, have contempt for, have ill will toward, loathe, resent

DESPOIL, ***verb*** assail, attack, bereave, consume, denude, deplume, depredate, deprive, desolate, devastate, devour, dispossess, divest, forage, foray, impoverish, invade, lay waste, leave destitute, loot, make off with, maraud, overrun, pilfer, pillage, plunder, purloin, raid, ransack, ravage, raven, rifle, rob, ruin, ruinate, sack, seize, spoliate, steal, strip, take, take by force, thieve, wreck

DESPONDENT, ***adjective*** aggrieved, beaten, defeated, defeatist, dejected, depressed, desolate, despairing, disconsolate, dismal, dispirited, dolorous, downcast, dreary, gloomy, hopeless, in despair, inconsolable, joyless, listless, lugubrious, melancholic, melancholy, moody, mournful, pessimistic, rueful, sad, sluggish, somber, sorrowful, sullen, unhappy, unhopeful

DESPOT, ***noun*** autarch, authoritarian, autocrat, captain, dictator, disciplinarian, dominator, magnate, master, mogul, monocrat, oppressive ruler, oppressor, overlord, potentate, sovereign, strongman, taskmaster, totalitarian, tycoon, tyrant

DESTINATION, ***noun*** aim, aspiration, bourn, conclusion, consummation, debarkation point, destiny, end, end result, ending, finish, goal, intent, intention, journey's end, last stop, object, objective, planned place of arrival, point of cessation, point of disembarkation, port, purpose, resting place, result, stop, stopping-place, target, terminal, terminal point, termination, terminus
ASSOCIATED CONCEPTS: destination contracts, final destination, place of destination, point of destination

DESTITUTE, ***adjective*** bankrupt, beggarly, bereft, depleted, deprived, distressed, impecunious, impoverished, indigent, *inops,* insolvent, lacking funds, moneyless, necessitous, needful, needy, out of money, penniless, poor, poverty-stricken, reduced in means, short of money, squalid, unmoneyed, wanting, without resources
ASSOCIATED CONCEPTS: destitute children, destitute of means of support, destitute of property, destitute persons

DESTROY *(Efface),* ***verb*** abort, annihilate, blast, blight, blot out, break to pieces, bring to ruin, burn, consume, corrode, deal destruction, decimate, deface, demolish, desolate, destruct, *destruere,* devastate, devour, *diruere,* disintegrate, dissolve, do away with, eliminate, eradicate, erase, expunge, exterminate, extinguish, extirpate, gut, incinerate, kill, lay waste, level, liquidate, murder, mutilate, obliterate, overthrow, overturn, *perdere,* pulverize, put to death, quell, ravage, raze, reduce to nothing, rend, root out, rub out, ruin, ruinate, scratch out, slay, subvert, uproot, waste, wipe out, wreck
ASSOCIATED CONCEPTS: destroy a will, fraudulently destroyed, lost or destroyed

DESTROY *(Void),* ***verb*** abolish, annul, break up, bring to naught, completely end, dismantle, extinguish, invalidate, make null, nullify, put an end to, render ineffective, terminate, unmake
ASSOCIATED CONCEPTS: destruction of contingent remainders

DESTRUCTIBLE, ***adjective*** accessible, assailable, breakable, delicate, depletable, destroyable, dissolvable, eradicable, exhaustible, extinguishable, ruinable, scissile, unsafe, vulnerable

DESTRUCTION, ***noun*** abolition, annihilation, breaking down, collapse, consumption, decimation, decomposition, demolishment, demolition, devastation, dissolution, eradication, extinction, extirpation, nullification, obliteration, perdition, ruin, ruination, tearing down, undoing, unmaking
ASSOCIATED CONCEPTS: destruction of business, destruction of records, total destruction, willful destruction
FOREIGN PHRASES: ***Res periit domino.*** A thing which has been destroyed is lost to its owner.

DESTRUCTIVE, ***adjective*** annihilating, baleful, damaging, destroying, detrimental, feral, harmful, injurious, internecine, malign, miasmal, miasmatic, miasmic, pernicious

DESUETUDE, ***noun*** abandonment, abeyance, abrogation, absence, abstention, archaism, arrest, cancellation, cessation, desistance, *desuetudo,* discarding, discontinuance, disusage, disuse, dormancy, failure to use, halt, idleness, impotence, inaction, inactivity, inanimation, inertia, inusitation, inutility, neglect, nonavailability, nonobservance, nonretention, nonuse, obsolescence, obsoleteness, omission, relinquishment, stagnation, standstill, state of being unused, stop, stoppage, stoppage of use, surrender, suspension, termination

DESULTORY, ***adjective*** broken, deviating, diffuse, digressive, disarranged, disconnected, discontinuous, discursive, disjoined, disjunct, dispersed, erratic, inconsistent, *inconstans,* inconstant, interrupted, lacking continuity, nonrecurrent, nonuniform, rambling, random, spasmodic, uncohesive, unconnected, unmethodical, unrepeated, unsuccessive, unsystematic, varying

DETACH, ***verb*** break off, cleave, disconnect, disengage, disentangle, *disiungere,* disjoin, dispart, dissever, dissociate, disunite, divide, divorce, part, remove, *seiungere, separare,* separate, sever, split, uncouple, unfasten, unlink, unplug, unstick
ASSOCIATED CONCEPTS: detached dwelling houses, detached pages in a will

DETAIL, ***noun*** aspect, circumstance, circumstantiality, component, component part, division, element, feature, fractional part, fragment, individual part, ingredient, instance, integral part, integrant, item, minor part, minute part, part, particular, particularity, piece, point, portion, section, *singula,* special point, specification, subdivision, technicality, trivia

DETAIL *(Assign),* ***verb*** allocate, appoint, authorize, bid, call, charge, command, commission, compel, consign, decree, delegate, demand, depute, designate, devolve, dictate, distribute, empower, enjoin, entrust, impose, obligate, oblige, order, prescribe, relegate

DETAIL *(Particularize),* ***verb*** amplify, analyze, be precise, catalog, chronicle, circumstantiate, clarify, delineate, depict, describe, draw, elucidate, enumerate, explain, give an account, give details, go into the particulars, illuminate, illustrate, individualize, itemize, make clear, make vivid, narrate, particularize, picture, portray, recite, recount, relate, report, set forth, show, specify, tell, tell details, tell fully, tell particulars

DETAILED, ***adjective*** accounted, accurate, all-inclusive, annotated, complete, comprehensive, delineated, described, descriptive, elaborated, enumerated, exact, exhaustive, explicit, full of details, graphic, inclusive, itemized, meticulous, minute, particular, particularized, plenary, precise, punctilious, replete, representational, specific, thorough, total, vivid, whole
ASSOCIATED CONCEPTS: detailed account, detailed audit, detailed report, detailed statement

DETAILS, ***noun*** circumstances, contents, counts, description, distinct parts, fine points, intelligence, items, minor circumstances, minutiae, niceties, particulars, special points, specifics, trivialities

DETAIN *(Hold in custody),* ***verb*** apprehend, arrest, capture, commit, confine, contain, control, enthrall, guard, hold, hold captive, hold in check, hold in preventive custody, hold in thrall, hold under duress, immure, impound, imprison, incarcerate, intern, isolate, jail, keep in custody, keep in detention, keep under arrest, keep under control, keep within bounds, lock up, mure, pen, place in durance, put under arrest, put under restraint, quarantine, remand, retain, secure, shut in, surround, take captive, take into custody, take prisoner, trammel
ASSOCIATED CONCEPTS: detained in custody, detained in jail

DETAIN *(Restrain),* ***verb*** arrest, bind, bound, chain, check, circumscribe, confine, constrain, contain, control, curb, delay, encumber, fetter, filibuster, forestall, gyve, halt, hamper, hinder, hold back, hold up, impede, inhibit, keep, keep back, keep under control, keep within bounds, lay under restraint, limit, manacle, obstruct, prevent, rein in, restrict, *retinere,* shackle, stall, stay, stop, suppress, *tenere,* trammel
ASSOCIATED CONCEPTS: unlawfully detained

DETAINER, ***noun*** detainment, illegal custody, illegal detention, illegal restraint, illegal withholding, unlawful detention, unlawful restriction, unlawful retention, wrongful impoundment, wrongful keeping

DETECT, ***verb*** be conscious of, become aware of, behold, bring to light, decipher, deduce, descry, determine, diagnose, diagnosticate, discern, discover, disinter, distinguish, divine, educe, espy, expose, extract, feel, ferret out, find, find out, gain knowledge, identify, learn, locate, make out, notice, observe, *patefacere,* perceive, realize, recognize, *rem invenire, reperire,* reveal, see, sense, sight, spot, trace, track, uncover, unearth, unmask, unravel, unveil, view

DETECTION, ***noun*** apprehension, ascertainment, disclosure, discovery, exposure, finding, learning, perception, sighting, spotting, unearthing, unfolding

DETECTIVE, ***noun*** agent, criminologist, espier, examinant, examiner, indagator, inquirer, inquiry agent, inquisitor, inspector, investigator, prober
ASSOCIATED CONCEPTS: police detectives, private detective

DETENTION, ***noun*** arrest, captivity, circumscription, committal, commitment, confinement, constraint, control, *custodia,* custodianship, custody, detainment, durance vile, fetter, guardianship, immuration, immurement, impoundment, imprisonment, incarceration, internment, keeping, keeping back, keeping in, keeping in custody, legal restraint, limitation, preventive custody, prison, protective custody, quarantine, restraint, restriction, restriction on movement, retentio
ASSOCIATED CONCEPTS: detention facility, detention of property, illegal detention, lawful detention, preventive detention
FOREIGN PHRASES: ***Furtum non est ubi initium habet detentionis per dominium rei.*** It is not theft where the commencement of the detention arises through the consent of the owner.

DETER, ***verb*** *absterrere,* avert, avoid, ban, bar, barricade, block, blunt, caution, check, chill, circumscribe, constrict, cow, cramp, cumber, dampen, deflect, deny access, *deterrere,* detour, discommode, discountenance, discourage, disenchant, disencourage, dishearten, disincline, dismay, dissuade, divert, divert from, fend, fend off, fetter, foil, forbid, foreclose, forestall, forfend, frustrate, hamper, hamstring, hinder, hold back, hold up, impede, incommode, indispose, inhibit, interclude, interfere with, intimidate, keep back, keep from, keep off, limit, nip in the bud, obstruct, obturate, obviate, overawe, persuade against, put a stop to, put off, quell, quench, remonstrate, render averse, repel, repress, reprove, restrain, restrict, rule out, set one back, shake one's faith, stave off, stop, stultify, thwart, turn aside, undermine one's belief, ward off, warn
ASSOCIATED CONCEPTS: deter from crime

DETERIORATE, ***verb*** adulterate, aggravate, atrophy, become worse, collapse, corrode, *corrumpere,* corrupt, debase, debauch, debilitate, decay, decline, decompose, decrease, defile, degenerate, degrade, demoralize, denature, *depravare,* depreciate, devalue, dilapidate, downgrade, ebb, lapse, lower, pervert, pollute, prostitute, regress, retrograde, retrogress, spoil, taint, vitiate, wane, waste, weaken, worsen
ASSOCIATED CONCEPTS: deteriorating building, deteriorating goods

DETERIORATION, ***noun*** abasement, abrasion, atrophy, caducity, consumption, corrosion, corruption, debasement, decadence, decay, declension, declination, decomposition, decrepitude, degradation, demission, depreciation, destruction, *deterior condicio,* dilapidation, disintegration, disrepair, emaciation, erosion, gradual decline, gradual impairment, impairment, irrepair, putrefaction, putridity, reduction, retrogradation, retrogression, ruin, ruination, senescence, spoliation, unrepair
ASSOCIATED CONCEPTS: property deterioration

DETERMINABLE *(Ascertainable),* ***adjective*** accountable, admitting of decision, amenable to measurement, appraisable, appreciable, assessable, capable of decision, certifiable, cognizable, computable, construable, countable, decipherable, deducible, definable, detectible, discernible, discoverable, distinguishable, estimable, explainable, explicable, fathomable, fixable, gaugeable, interpretable, judicable, knowable, measurable, mensurable, noticeable, observable, perceivable, perceptible, resolvable, solvable, subject to measurement, surveyable, that may be determined, translatable, verifiable, workable
ASSOCIATED CONCEPTS: determinable period of usefulness
FOREIGN PHRASES: ***Terminus annorum certus debet esse et determinatus.*** A term of years ought to be certain and determinate.

DETERMINABLE *(Liable to be terminated),* ***adjective*** approaching an end, approaching the finish, coming to an end, drawing to a close, having the possibility of termination, liable to be completed, liable to be discontinued, liable to be dropped, liable to be ended, liable to come to an end, liable to expire, nearing completion, subject to be concluded, subject to cancellation, subject to discontinuance, subject to termination, terminable, with the end in sight
ASSOCIATED CONCEPTS: determinable fee, determinable interest, determinable remainder in fee

DETERMINANT, ***noun*** agent, authority, background, base, basis, consideration, constitutive element, contributing force, contributor, decisive factor, determining circumstance, determining element, determining influence, driving force, element, factor, fomentor, generator, genesis, impetus, inducement, instigation, justification, leaven, means, medium, motivation, motive, object, origin, prime mover, producer, root, source, ultimate cause, ultimate motive

DETERMINATION, ***noun*** adjudgment, adjudication, appraisal, appraisement, appreciation, apprisement, apprizement, *arbitrium,* ascertainment, assessment, authoritative estimate, authoritative opinion, award, conclusion, consideration, considered opinion, *consilium,* conviction, court decision, decision, declaration, decree, diagnosis, evaluation, final assessment, finding, *institutum, iudicium,* judgment, judgment on facts, opinion, order, pronouncement, reasoned judgment, reckoning, recommendation, resolution, resolve, result, result ascertained, ruling, sentence, settlement, solution, verdict
ASSOCIATED CONCEPTS: actual determination, determination of a suit, determination of claims, determination of fact, determination of guilt, final determination, judicial determination, official determination, review a determination, self-determination
FOREIGN PHRASES: ***Judicia in deliberationibus crebro maturescunt, in accelerato processu nunquam.*** Judgments frequently mature by deliberations, never by hurried process. ***De audiendo et terminando.*** To hear and determine. ***In propria causa nemo judex.*** No one can be judge in his own case.

DETERMINATION OF DAMAGES, ***noun*** adjudication, assessment, award, award judgment, compensation, finding, grant, inquest, judgment, penalization, penalty, relief, remuneration

DETERMINATIVE, ***adjective*** authoritative, conclusive, convincing, deciding, decisive, decretal, definitive, directing, *ex parte,* final, important, judgmatic, judicious, limiting, limitive, persuasive, shaping, significant, telling, weighty

DETERMINE, ***verb*** adjudge, adjudicate, arrive at a conclusion, ascertain, award, bring in a verdict, bring to an end, bring to justice, choose, come to a conclusion, come to a decision, come to a determination, conclude, confirm, *constituere, decernere,* decide, decide upon, declare, decree, decree by judicial authority, deduce, delimit, deliver judgment, direct, draw a conclusion, end by a decision, estimate, exercise the judgment, find, fix upon, form a judgment, form a resolution, give a ruling, give an opinion, give judgment, hold, infer, interpret, judge, limit, make a decision, make a resolution, make one's choice, make terms, make up one's mind, opine, pass an opinion, pass judgment, pass sentence, prescribe punishment, pronounce, pronounce a judgment, pronounce guilty, reckon, referee, regulate, remain firm, resolve, rule, seal, seal the doom of, settle, settle in one's mind, settle upon, sit in judgment, *statuere,* stipulate, take a decisive step, utter judicial sentence against, weigh, will
ASSOCIATED CONCEPTS: determine the nature of the loss, finally determined, legally determine the rights of the parties to an action

DETERMINED *(Certain),* ***adjective*** ascertained, attested, authenticated, certified, conditioned, confined, confirmed, definite, established, finite, firm, fixed, indomitable, industrious, inexorable, inflexible, intentional, peremptory, positive, prescriptive, qualified, set, settled, substantial, unalterable, uncompromising, validated

DETERMINED *(Strong-willed),* ***adjective*** decided, deliberate, dogged, earnest, obdurate, obstinate, persistent, pertinacious, purposeful, relentless, resolute, resolved, serious, Spartan, staunch, steadfast, stubborn, unfaltering, unflinching, unwavering, unyielding

DETERMINING, ***adjective*** absolute, acute, binding, cardinal, certain, complete, conclusive, contributory, critical, crucial, deciding, decisive, definitive, determinate, fateful, final, important, key, momentous, pivotal, prevailing, primary, ultimate

DETERRENCE, ***noun*** abridgment, active discouragement, admonition, barrier, block, blockade, caveat, check, compulsion, constraint, constriction, contraindication, *contretemps,* control, curb, detainment, deterrent, discouragement, disincentive, dissuasion, extinguishment, forestalling, frustration, halt, hindrance, hurdle, impediment, impedition, inhibition, interference, intimidation, legal restraint, limitation, means of restraint, monition, obstacle, obstruction, opposition, preclusion, prevention, prohibition, prophylaxis, proscription, quashing, repression, resistance, restraint, restriction, stop, striction, stumbling block, suppression, thwarter
ASSOCIATED CONCEPTS: deterrence of crime
FOREIGN PHRASES: ***Nemo prudens punit ut praeterita revocentur, sed ut futura praeveniantur.*** No wise man punishes in order that past things may be revoked, but that future wrongs may be prevented. ***Poena ad paucos, metus ad omnes perveniat.*** If punishment be inflicted on a few, a fear comes to all.

DETERRENT, ***noun*** admonishment, admonition, barrier, barring, block, caution, caveat, constraint, constriction, contraindication, counteraction, counterpressure, curb, damper, deactivation, determent, deterrence, discouragement, disincentive, dissuasion, forestalling, hampering, hinderer, hindrance, hurdle, impedance, impeder, inhibition, inhibitor, insuperable obstacle, interference, interposition, intimidation, legal restraint, limitation, means of restraint, monition, obstacle, obstructer, obstruction, obstructive, obtrusion, occlusion, opposition, preclusion, prevention, proscription, repression, restraint, restriction, retardation, suppression, thwarter, warning

DETEST, ***verb*** abhor, contempt, deplore, deprecate, despise, disapprove of, discountenance, disdain, disfavor, dislike, execrate, hate, loathe, reject, renounce, scorn

DETOUR, ***noun*** alternate route, bypass, bypassage, circuitous route, deflection, departure, deviation, deviation from a direct course, digression, diversion, excursion,

indirect path, loop, roundabout course, temporary route, wrong course
ASSOCIATED CONCEPTS: detour from course of employment, frolic and detour

DETOUR, ***verb*** *aberrare,* alter one's course, avoid, bypass, change direction, change the bearing, circuit, circumambulate, deflect, depart from, depart from one's course, deviate, deviate from a direct course, *digredi,* digress, diverge, divert, divert from its course, drift, encircle, excurse, go around, go out of one's way, go out of the path, go out of the way, go round about, make a circuit, meander, perform a circuit, ramble, sidestep, skirt, stray, swerve, take a circuitous route, take a roundabout course, take a temporary route, take an alternate highway, take an alternate route, take an indirect way, turn aside, vary, veer
ASSOCIATED CONCEPTS: detour from course of employment, frolick and detour

DETRACT, ***verb*** abate, belittle, blacken, blame, decrease, decry, defame, denigrate, depreciate, derogate, deteriorate, diminish, discommend, discount, disparage, distract, divert, draw away, lessen, lower, malign, minimize

DETRIMENT, ***noun*** adulteration, adversity, affliction, aggravation, atrophy, bane, bedevilment, blemish, blow, collapse, contamination, corrosion, corruption, cost, crippling, damage, *damnum,* decadence, decay, deformation, degeneration, demolishment, deprivation, destruction, deterioration, detraction, *detrimentum,* dilapidation, disability, disablement, disadvantage, disintegration, disorder, disturbance, erosion, evil, forfeit, forfeiture, handicap, hardship, harm, hurt, impairment, impotence, inadequacy, inadvisability, *incommodum,* inconvenience, ineffectualness, inefficiency, inexpedience, inexpediency, injuriousness, injury, insufficiency, laming, liability, loss, misfortune, mutilation, obstacle, poisoning, pollution, prejudice, privation, ruin, ruination, undesirability, undoing, unprofitability, weakness
ASSOCIATED CONCEPTS: legal detriment

DETRIMENTAL, ***adjective*** adverse, afflicting, bad, corrupting, crippling, damaging, deleterious, destructive, disadvantageous, disastrous, discommodious, distressing, disturbing, dreadful, extirpative, fulsome, grievous, harmful, hindering, hurtful, ill-advised, ill-contrived, impolitic, inappropriate, inimical, *iniquus,* injurious, inopportune, insalubrious, insidious, internecine, malefic, malignant, noisome, noxious, oppressive, *perniciosus,* pernicious, pestilential, prejudicial, toxic, treacherous, undermining, unfit, unhealthy, unhelpful, unprofitable, unpropitious, unsatisfactory, unsuitable, untoward, unwholesome, unwise
ASSOCIATED CONCEPTS: actively detrimental, detrimental to the best interests of the child, detrimental to the public interest

DEVALUE, ***verb*** adulterate, belittle, cheapen, contaminate, corrupt, damage, debase, debauch, defile, degenerate, degrade, denature, depreciate, depress, deteriorate, dilute, disable, disparage, impair, pollute, reduce, taint

DEVASTATE, ***verb*** demolish, depopulate, depredate, desolate, despoil, destroy, gut, lever, overwhelm, pillage, plunder, raid, ransack, ravage, raze, ruin, sack, wreck

DEVELOP, ***verb*** accrue, *adolescere,* advance, advance in successive gradation, *alere,* amplify, arise from, *augeri,* augment, become, become apparent, begin from, bring forth, bring into being, bring to a complete condition, bring to a more advanced state, bring to light by degrees, broaden, build up, cause to expand, cause to grow, change into, come gradually into existence, come to be, come to maturity, *crescere,* cultivate, derive from, descend from, detail, *educare,* elaborate, emanate, emerge, enlarge, enlarge upon, enter into detail, evolve, *excolere,* expand, expand upon, extend, fill in, fill out, further, germinate, give being to, give forth, give rise to, go into detail, grow, grow better, grow from, improve, increase the strength of, infuse, intensify, invigorate, magnify, make headway, make progress, mature, meliorate, mend, perfect, proceed, produce, progress, promote, raise, reach manhood, refine, reinforce, revive, ripen, shape up, show improvement, stimulate, strengthen, stretch, swell, take form, take shape, unfold, widen, work out in detail

DEVELOPER, ***noun*** builder, building entrepreneur, creator, designer, enterpriser, establisher, land developer, organizer, originator, planner, promoter
ASSOCIATED CONCEPTS: commercial developer, residential developer

DEVELOPMENT *(Building),* ***noun*** commercial building, construction, creation of housing project, development of industrial sites, erection, house-building program, housing, industrial area, industrial building, institution of commercial sites, residential building, urbanization

DEVELOPMENT *(Outgrowth),* ***noun*** accomplishment, achievement, aftergrowth, aftermath, attainment, by-product, conclusion, consequence, consequent, derivation, effect, emanation, ending, ensual, event, eventuality, eventuation, occurrence, offshoot, outcome, product, realization, result, resultant, sequel, side issue, upshot

DEVELOPMENT *(Progression),* ***noun*** accretion, accumulation, advance, advancement, amelioration, ampliation, amplification, anabasis, *auctus,* betterment, change, cultivation, effectuation, elaboration, enhancement, enrichment, evolution, evolvement, expansion, *explicatio,* extension, furtherance, gain, germination, gradual evolution, growth, improvement, increase in size, lengthening, melioration, modernization, progress, progress to maturity, progressive growth, *progressus,* promotion, refinement, reform, reformation, regeneration, remodeling, renovation, reorganization, revision, stimulation, strengthening, supplementation, transfiguration, transformation, unfolding, unravelment, upgrowth, uptrend
ASSOCIATED CONCEPTS: development costs

DEVIANT, ***adjective*** aberrant, abnormal, adverse to, against the rules, atypical, clashing, contrary, counter to, departing from, desultory, deviating, discordant, discrepant, dissident, dissonant, divergent, eccentric, errant, heretical, in violation of, irregular, nonconformist, nonuniform, oblique, out of order, out of step, recalcitrant, stray, unconventional, unfashionable, unorthodox, variant
ASSOCIATED CONCEPTS: deviant behavior

DEVIATE, ***verb*** *aberrare,* alter course, angle off, be at variance, be different, be distinguished from, be oblique, bear no resemblance, bear off, branch out, break bounds, break the pattern, change direction, clash, clash with, conflict with, contrast, *declinare,* deflect, *degredi,* depart from, depart from one's course, differ, digress, disagree, divaricate, diverge, divert from its course, drift, err, fall into error, fly off at a tangent, get off the subject, glance off, go adrift, go amiss, go astray, go awry, go off on a tangent, go out of one's way, go round about, go wrong, infringe a law, infringe custom, make a detour, meander, not conform, perform a circuit, show variety, slip, stand apart, step aside, stray, swerve, take a different course, turn, turn aside, turn out of one's way, vary, veer, wander from the subject

DEVIATE FROM THE TRUTH, ***verb*** alter one's course, deceive, depart from a norm, digress, diverge, drift, fabricate, fake, go astray, lie, maunder, meander, mislead, misrepresent, misstate, prevaricate, skew, stray, struggle, swerve, take a different course, wander

DEVIATING, ***adjective*** aberrant, astray, circuitous, departing, deviative, devious, different, differing, digressive, discursive, disparate, dissimilar, divergent, diverse, diversified, errant, erratic, indirect, labyrinthine, meandering, nonconforming, peculiar, perverse, separate, shifting, sinuous, undirected, vagrant, variant, varying, wandering, widely apart

DEVIATING FROM THE NORM, ***verb*** alter one's course, depart from a norm, digress, diverge, drift, go astray, maunder, meander, skew, slew, straggle, stray, swerve, take a different course, wander

DEVIATION, ***noun*** aberrance, aberrancy, aberration, abnormality, alteration, anomalousness, anomaly, antipathy, antithesis, branching off, breach of practice, change of direction, change of position, contrast, *declinatio,* defiance of custom, departure, departure from usage, detour, difference, *digressio,* disaccord, disaccordance, disagreement, discongruity, discontinuity, discord, discrepancy, disharmony, disparity, dissidence, dissimilarity, dissonance, distinctness, divagation, divergence, diverseness, diversion, incongruity, inconsistency, inconsonance, inharmoniousness, irregularity, nonconformism, nonconformity, nonimitation, nonobservance, nonuniformity, straying, swerve, swerving, unconformity, unlikeness, unorthodoxy, variability, variance, variation
ASSOCIATED CONCEPTS: deviation doctrine, deviation from scope of employment, deviation from the norm

DEVIATION FROM RECTITUDE, ***noun*** abuse, bad faith, bad repute, blame, corruption, crime, disgrace, dishonor, guilt, malfeasance, misconduct, misdoing, misfeasance, misprision

DEVICE *(Contrivance),* ***noun*** artifice, circumvention, craft, design, gimmick, *machina,* machination, maneuver, means to an end, method, plan, program of action, project, resort, ruse, scheme, setup, stratagem, subtle maneuver, system, trick, wile, working plan, working proposition

DEVICE *(Distinguishing mark),* ***noun*** badge of office, design, designation, earmark, emblem, ensign, hallmark, identification mark, indicant, *inscriptio,* insignia, label, mark that designates, sign, symbol, token, trademark

DEVICE *(Mechanism),* ***noun*** apparatus, appliance, equipment, facility, fixture, gadget, gear, implement, instrument, invention, mechanical aid, tool, utensil
ASSOCIATED CONCEPTS: safety device

DEVIOUS, ***adjective*** aberrant, ambagious, artful, circuitous, crafty, crooked, cunning, deceitful, designing, deviating, deviative, *devius,* errant, excursive, foxy, indirect, insidious, labyrinthine, roundabout, scheming, serpentine, sinuous, sly, sneaking, tortuous, tricky, uncandid, unstraightforward, wily

DEVISE *(Give),* ***verb*** allot, assign, bequeath, bestow, confer, convey, endow, give, give and bequeath, give away, give by will, grant, leave, leave by will, make a bequest, make testamentary dispositions, transfer, transmit, transmit by will, will and bequeath, will to
ASSOCIATED CONCEPTS: absolute devise, alienation, bequest, conveyance, demonstrative devise, executory devise, general devise, legacy, testamentary disposition
FOREIGN PHRASES: ***Nemo plus commodi haeredi suo relinguit quam ipse habuit.*** No one leaves a greater benefit to his heir than he had himself. ***Da tua dum tua sunt, post mortem tunc tua non sunt.*** Give that which is yours while it is yours; after death it is not yours. ***Quando aliquis aliquid concedit, concedere videtur et id sine quo res unon potest.*** When anyone grants anything, he is deemed to grant also that without which the thing granted cannot be used.

DEVISE *(Invent),* ***verb*** arrange, calculate, compose, conceive, construct, contrive, create, design, draw up, engineer, erect, evolve, *excogitare,* fabricate, fashion, find a way, form, formulate, frame, have an idea, imagine, improvise, *invenire,* lay down a plan, lay out, make a plan, make arrangements, make up, maneuver, manufacture, map out, piece together, plan, plan out, prearrange, predetermine, prepare, proceed by stratagem, put together, schematize, scheme, set up, shape, sketch out, take steps, work out

DEVISEE, ***noun*** acceptor, beneficiary, donee, grantee, heir, inheritor, legatee, recipient, successor, transferee

DEVOID, ***adjective*** bare, barren, bereft of, blank, bleak, deficient, denuded of, deprived of, deserted, desolate, destitute of, empty, empty of, found wanting, ill-furnished, ill-provided, ill-stored, impotent, in default of, in the absence of, in want of, incomplete, insufficient, lacking, missing, out of, poor, *re vacuus,* scant of, short, short of, sparing, stinted, tenantless, unacquired, unexisting, uninhabited, unmanned, unoccupied, unofficered, unpeopled, unpossessed of, unprovided, unreplenished, unstaffed, unsupplied, untenanted, vacant, vacuous, void of, wanting, without, without content, without resources

DEVOID OF TRUTH, ***adjective*** corrupt, criminal, deceitful, dishonest, disingenuous, fallacious, false, false-hearted, forsworn, fraudulent, immoral, insidious, knavish, lying, mendacious, perfidious, perjured, shameless, unconscientious, unconscionable, unethical, unprincipled, unscrupulous, untruthful, unveracious, wicked

DEVOLUTION, ***noun*** assignment, bequeathal, bequest, change of hands, change-over, conveyance, delegation, delegation of duties, deliverance, delivery, demise, devise, interchange, nonretention, reversion, substitution, succession, succession of property rights, transfer, transfer of property, transference, transmission
ASSOCIATED CONCEPTS: devolution of liability, devolution of property

DEVOLVE, ***verb*** be handed down to, be handed over, be transferred, bequeath, cause to pass to another, cede, change from one to another, change ownership, confer ownership, convey, *deferre,* delegate upon another, deliver, deliver over to a successor, descend by inheritance, descend upon, fall by inheritance, fall by succession, give, grant, interchange, invest with, leave to, make over, *mandare,* pass to, *permittere,* put in possession, sign away, substitute, trade, transfer, transfer ownership, transfer to, transmit, turn over
ASSOCIATED CONCEPTS: devolution of a lease

DEVOTE, ***verb*** allot, apply, apportion, appropriate, assign, attend, be absorbed in, be attentive, be engrossed in, concentrate, concern, *consecrare,* consecrate, contemplate, *dedere,* dedicate, *devovere,* direct attention, focus, give attention, heed, meditate upon, occupy oneself with, pay attention, pay heed, set apart, set aside, think about, turn attention
ASSOCIATED CONCEPTS: devote attention, devote to a public use

DEVOTED *(Faithful),* ***adjective*** affectionate, attached, close, consecrated, constant, dedicated, dependable, devout, earnest, fond, inseparable, loving, loyal, obedient, partisan, passionate, purposeful, reliable, stanch, staunch, steadfast, tender, tried and true, true, unyielding

DEVOTED *(Zealous),* ***adjective*** ardent, assiduous, dutiful, fanatical, fast, fervent, firm, sedulous, serious, sincere

DEVOTION, ***noun*** addiction, adhesion, admiration, affection, affinity, allegiance, application, ardor, attachment, concentration, constancy, dedication, deference, determination, devoutness, diligence, discipline, earnestness, enchantment, engagement, faithfulness, fastness, fealty, fervor, fidelity, firmness, fondness, homage, honor, immersion, inclination, industry, infatuation, involvement, love, loyalty, passion, preoccupation, regard, reverence, sanctity, stanchness, staunchness, yearning, zeal

DIABOLIC, ***adjective*** accursed, amoral, amoralistic, bad-hearted, brutal, brutalized, callous, conscienceless, cruel, cursed, deadly, dehumanized, demoniac, demonic, devil-like, devilish, evil, evil-doing, evil-minded, execrable, fiendish, fiendlike, full of sin, god-forsaken, guilty, heinous, hellish, hopeless, horrible, immoral, impious, infernal, inhuman, iniquitous, irredeemable, irreligious, maleficent, malevolent, malignant, Mephistophelian, merciless, monstrous, murderous, nefarious, outrageous, pitiless, possessed, profane, ruinous, ruthless, sadistic, Satanic, sinladen, sinful, sinister, sinning, transgressing, unnatural, unprincipled, unredeemed, unrighteous, unscrupulous, unvirtuous, vicious, virtueless, wicked

DIABOLICAL, ***adjective*** abominable, baleful, cruel, demoniac, demonic, despicable, devilish, evil, heinous, hellish, horrible, horrid, immoral, infernal, inhuman, iniquitous, Luciferian, malevolent, malicious, malignant, monstrous, nefarious, reprehensible, ruthless, savage, sinister, vicious, vile, villainous, wicked

DIAGNOSE, ***verb*** analyze, appraise, classify, compare critically, discern, distinguish, estimate, examine critically, have insight, identify, judge, make a judgment, recognize, see the difference, sort out, specify, weigh

DIAGNOSIS, ***noun*** analysis, appreciation of differences, assay, breakdown, careful appreciation, categorization, category, classification, classificatory description, conclusion, critical appraisal, critical scrutiny, critique, designation, differentiation, discernment, discretion, discriminating judgment, discrimination, estimation, interpretation, judgment, perception of difference, scientific determination, specification, symptomatology
ASSOCIATED CONCEPTS: faulty diagnosis, malpractice

DIALECTIC, ***noun*** applied logic, apprehension, argumentation, brainwork, cerebration, chain of reasoning, cogitation, concluding, consideration, contemplation, deducing, deduction, deliberation, deriving, discursive reasoning, drawing conclusions, force of argument, induction, inferring, judgment, logic, logic of discursive argument, logical argumentation, logical discussion, logical process, logical sequence, mode of reasoning, ratiocination, rationalism, rationalization, rationalizing, reasoning, reflection, rumination, thinking

DIALOGUE, ***noun*** bull session, causerie, chat, colloquy, communication, communion, confabulation, conference, confrontation, conversation, debate, discourse, disputation, exchange, formal discourse, give and take, interlocution, interview, palaver, parley, powwow, question and answer, script, swapping opinions, symposium, talk, talkfest, verbal intercourse

DIATRIBE, ***noun*** abuse, abusive harangue, abusive language, accusation, act of berating, admonition, adverse comment, animadversion, backbiting, bitter harangue, bitter words, blame, carping, castigation, censure, chiding, complaining, condemnation, countercharge, *coup de bec,* criticism, cutting words, denunciation, deprecation, depreciation, discommendation, disparagement, dispraise, dressing down, faultfinding, gainsaying, harangue, hostile attack, hostile criticism, hostile eloquence, hypercriticism, inculpation, indictment, insult, invective, long vehement speech, objurgation, obloquy, oration, prolonged outburst of denunciation, railing, rebuke, remonstrance, reprehension, reprimand, reproach, reproof, revilement, reviling, sarcasm, scolding, scurrility, sermon, stinging words, strain of invective, stream of abuse, tirade, tongue-lashing, upbraiding, verbal onslaught, vilification, vituperation

DICHOTOMIZE, ***verb*** apportion, bifurcate, bisect, branch, cleave in two, cut in halves, cut in two, detach, disconnect, disjoin, dissect, dissever, disunite, divaricate, diverge, divide, fragment, furcate, halve, keep apart, part, partition, rend, rive, section, sectionalize, segment, separate, separate in two, sever, split, subdivide, transect

DICHOTOMY, ***noun*** bifurcation, bipartition, bisection, dissection, divarication, division, halving, separation, severance, split, subdivision

DICKER, ***verb*** adjust differences, arbitrate terms, argue price, arrange terms, arrive at a price, bargain, barter, bicker, bid for, come to terms, confer on price, contend, deal, drive a bargain, give terms, haggle, have dealings, make terms, negotiate, put through a deal, state one's terms, strike a bargain, trade, transact, wrangle
ASSOCIATED CONCEPTS: dicker over terms of a contract

DICTATE, ***noun*** act, authoritative suggestion, behest, charge, command, commandment, commission, decree, demand, direction, edict, enactment, fiat, imperative, imperious direction, injunction, instruction, judgment, law, mandate, order, ordinance, ordination, precept, prescript, prescription, proclamation, regulation, requirement, rescript, rubric, rule, ruling, ultimatum

DICTATE, ***verb*** bid, charge, command, compel, decree, demand, direct, enjoin, exercise authority, give orders, impose an order, instruct, issue a command, issue an order, oblige, ordain, order, prescribe, require, require authoritatively, rule

DICTATOR, ***noun*** absolute leader, absolute ruler, autarch, autocrat, autocratic master, despot, despotic commander, despotic master, dictatorial mogul, disciplinarian, imperious commandant, inquisitor, martinet, oppressive taskmaster, oppressor, repressive governor, strict disciplinarian, totalitarian, tyrannical leader, tyrant

DICTATORIAL, ***adjective*** absolutistic, arbitrary, arrogant, authoritarian, authoritative, autocratic, censorious, commanding, compelling, controlling, despotic, *dictatorius,* dogmatic, domineering, enslaving, exacting, fanatic, fascist, high-handed, imperative, *imperiosus,* imperious, inexorable, inquisitorial, intimidating, ironhanded, lordly, masterful, monocratic, officious, oppressive, overbearing, peremptory, pompous, power-crazed, power-hungry, power-mad, relentless, repressive, severe, suppressive, supreme, totalitarian, tyrannical, tyrannous, uncompromising, undemocratic, unlimited, unrelenting, unrestricted, with an iron hand

DICTUM, ***noun*** announcement, assertion, authoritative assertion, declaration, extrajudicial opinion, finding, gratuitous remark, illustrative statement, incidental opinion, judicial assertion, judicial comment, judicial remark, observation, opinion, pronouncement, recommendation, remark, statement, statement by way of illustration
ASSOCIATED CONCEPTS: judicial dictum, obiter dictum

DIDACTIC, ***adjective*** academic, adapted to teach, curricular, edifying, educating, educational, educative, enlightening, enriching, erudite, expository, fitted to teach, informational, informative, instructional, instructive, intended for instruction, intended for teaching, learned, pedagogic, propaedeutic, scholarly, scholastic, teaching, tutorial

DIE, ***verb*** be no more, breathe one's last, cease living, cease to exist, decease, demise, depart, end one's life, expire, lose one's life, meet one's death, *mori, mortem obire,* part with life, pass away, pass on, perish, relinquish life, rest in peace, succumb to death, suffer death, *vita decedere*
ASSOCIATED CONCEPTS: die at any time without issue surviving, die by his own hand or act, die in performance of duty, die intestate, die leaving issue, die seised and possessed, die simultaneously, die without children or issue, die without heirs, die without issue, die without lawful issue, testamentary dispositions

DIFFER *(Disagree),* ***verb*** be discordant, be incongruent, be inharmonious, bicker, cavil, clash, conflict with, contend, contradict, dispute, divide on, hold different views, object, oppose, protest, raise objections, reject, repudiate, take exception, take issue, think differently, withhold assent

DIFFER *(Vary),* ***verb*** argue, be at cross purposes, be at variance, be contrary, be dissimilar, be distinct, be distinguished from, be inharmonious, be opposite, be unique, be unlike, bear no resemblance, contrast, depart from, deviate from, digress, disaccord, disaccord with, disagree, discept, *discrepare,* dissent, *dissentire, dissidere,* divaricate from, diverge from, diversify, have a dissimilar opinion, lack resemblance, not agree, not compare with, not conform, not equate, show contrast, show variety, take exception, take issue, think differently, vary, withhold assent
FOREIGN PHRASES: ***Non differunt quae concordant re, tametsi non in verbis iisdem.*** Those matters do not differ which agree in substance, though not in the same words.

DIFFERENCE, ***noun*** adverseness, antipathy, antithesis, antitheticalness, asymmetry, atypicality, breach, change, clash of temperament, clashing, conflict of opinion, contradiction, contradistinction, contraposition, contrariety, contrariness, contrast, controversy, counterpoint, departure, departure from, deviation, differentiation, disaccord, disagreement, discongruity, disconnection, discontinuity, discord, discordance, discrepancy, *discrepantia,* discrimination, disequilibrium, disharmony, disjunction, disparity, disproportion, dissemblance, dissension, dissimilarity, dissimilitude, dissonance, distinction, distinctness, distortion, divergence, diverseness, *diversitas,* diversity, failure to agree, heterogeneity, imbalance, imparity, inaccordance, incommensurability, incongruence, incongruity, incongruousness, inconsistency, inconsonance, individuality, inequality, inharmoniousness, inharmony, irreconcilability, irrelation, lack of connection, lack of resemblance, misunderstanding, multifariousness, mutual exclusiveness, nonconformity, nonimitation, nonuniformity, nuance, oppositeness, opposition, schism, separateness, state of being different, unconformity, unequalness, uniqueness, unlikeness, unrelatedness, variance, variation, variegation, *varietas,* variety
ASSOCIATED CONCEPTS: difference in degree, difference in kind, difference in the nature and elements of a crime, difference in value, difference of opinion, settling of differences

DIFFERENT, ***adjective*** alien, *alius,* altered, antagonistic, antithetic, atypical, changed, clashing, contradictory, contradistinct, contradistinctive, contrary, contrasting, contrastive, deviating, diametric, discordant, *discrepans,* discrepant, disparate, dissimilar, dissonant, distinct, distinctive, divergent, diverse, diversiform, *diversus,* foreign, heterogeneous, idiosyncratic, in disagreement, incommensurable, incomparable, incompatible, incongruous, individual, inharmonious, mismatched, mismated, nonidentical, not the same, novel, opposed, other than, out of the ordinary, peculiar, separate, set apart, singular, unidentical, unique, unlike, unmatched, unrelated, unusual, unwonted, variant, varied, varietal, various, varying
ASSOCIATED CONCEPTS: different causes of action, different offenses

DIFFERENTIAL, ***noun*** attribute, characteristic, constituting a difference, contrasting quality, delicate distinction, difference of degree, differentiating trait, distinction, distinctive feature, distinguishing feature, feature, gradation, grade, graduation, nuance, particularity, peculiarity, property, proportion, quality, rate, ratio, relative quantity, scale, shade of difference, singularity, subtle difference, trait, variant
ASSOCIATED CONCEPTS: wage differential

DIFFERENTIATE, ***verb*** characterize, classify, contrast, demarcate, discern between, discriminate, distinguish, diversify, draw the line, exercise discrimination, make a distinction, make distinctive, mark off by differences, mark out, particularize, perceive clearly, recognize as separate, segregate, separate as different, set apart as different, set off, show a difference, single out, sort out, subtilize, tell apart, tell from

DIFFERENTIATION, ***noun*** contrast, definition, demarcation, denomination, description, despecification, difference, discrepancy, discrimination, disequalization, distinction, distinguishment, diversification, division, individualization, modification, nuance, particularization, segregation, separation, severance, specialization, specification, variation

DIFFERING, ***adjective*** at odds, at variance, clashing, conflicting, deviative, different, disagreeing, discordant, discrepant, discriminatory, disparate, disproportionate, dissenting, dissident, dissimilar, distinct, distinctive, distinguished, divergent, diverse, diversified, incompatible, incongruous, inconsonant, inharmonious, irreconcilable, jarring, nonconforming, peculiar, recusant, separate, unequal, unrelated, variant
ASSOCIATED CONCEPTS: differing accounts, differing claims, differing testimony

DIFFICULT, ***adjective*** arduous, attended by obstacles, awkward, beset with difficulty, beyond one's reach, bothersome, burdensome, complex, complicated, convoluted, *difficile, difficilis,* encompassed with difficulties, enigmatic, entangled by difficulties, fatiguing, grueling, hard, hard to deal with, hard to manage, hard to understand, impassable, *impeditus,* impenetrable, incomprehensible, insoluble, insurmountable, intractable, involved, labored, laborious, labyrinthine, obscure, obstinate, offering a problem, operose, out of reach, painstaking, perplexing, perverse, problematic, puzzling, recondite, refractory, strenuous, stubborn, surrounded by difficulties, too hard, troublesome, unachievable, unapproachable, unavailable, uncertain, unclear
ASSOCIATED CONCEPTS: difficult and extraordinary action, difficult and extraordinary case or proceeding

DIFFICULTY, ***noun*** adversity, affliction, altercation, block, catch, clash, collision, complication, conflict, contestation, convolution, deterrent, dilemma, discomfort, embarrassment, encumbrance, exigency, handicap, hardness, hardship, hindrance, hurdle, impediment, inconvenience, inhibition, interference, misfortune, misgiving, mishap, nuisance, obstacle, obstruction, predicament, quagmire, quandary, rigor, shackle, struggle, tragedy, tribulation, trouble

DIFFIDENT, ***adjective*** abashed, awestricken, awestruck, bashful, blushful, blushing, cautious, demure, deprecating, deprecative, *diffidens,* embarrassed, fainthearted, faltering, hesitating, humble, humbled, lacking self-confidence, modest, overanxious, overapprehensive, overshy, qualmish, quiet, reserved, retiring, self-conscious, self-effacing, shaky, shameful, sheepish, shrinking, shy, timid, timorous, treading warily, tremulous, unambitious, unassuming, unboastful, unheard, unimposing, unobstrusive, unostentatious, unpretentious, unpushing, unsure of oneself, *verecundus,* wary, without vanity

DIFFUSE, ***verb*** bespread, besprinkle, bestrew, break up, broadcast, cast forth, circulate, circumfuse, commingle, deal out, decentralize, *diffundere, diffundi,* disband, disintegrate, disperse, dispread, disseminate, dissipate, distribute, effuse, go in different directions, go in many directions, intermix, intersperse, mix, overspread, *permeare,* permeate, pervade, promulgate, propagate, put into circulation, radiate, scatter, send abroad, send forth, sow, spatter, spread, spread about, spread abroad, spread around, spread far and wide, spread widely, strew, unloose

DIGAMY, ***noun*** finding another mate after the death of the first spouse

DIGEST, ***noun*** abbreviation, abridgment, abstract, analysis, anthology, arrangement, brief, capsule, code, collection, compendium, compilation, condensation, consolidation, conspectus, contraction, epitome, essence, extract, outline, pandect, recapitulation, review, summary, synopsis
ASSOCIATED CONCEPTS: digest of cases, digest of laws

DIGEST *(Comprehend),* ***verb*** absorb, analyze, appreciate, assimilate, cognize, consider, contemplate, fathom, grasp, incorporate, ken, know, muse, register, think about, understand, weigh

DIGEST *(Summarize),* ***verb*** abbreviate, abridge, abstract, capsulize, catalog, classify, codify, condense, cut down, edit, excerpt, make a summary of, make brief, make concise, outline, recapitulate, reduce, select, shorten, sum up, survey

DIGRESS, ***verb*** *aberrare,* alter course, be diffuse, branch out, change direction, depart, detour, deviate, *digredi,* divagate, divaricate, diverge, divert, drift, expatiate, fly off at a tangent, go astray, meander, ramble, rove, shift, sidestep, sidetrack, skirt, stray, swerve, turn, veer, wander

DIGRESSION, ***noun*** aberrancy, aberration, alteration, break, change, circuity, convolution, departure, detour, deviation, *digressio,* divagation, divarication, divergence, diversion, drift, excursus, misdirection, periphrasis, roundabout way, shift in topic, sideslip, sidestep, swerve, variance, variation
ASSOCIATED CONCEPTS: dictum

DILAPIDATED, ***adjective*** altered for the worse, condemned, damaged, decomposed, decrepit, fallen into ruin, far-gone, frayed, friable, impaired, imperfect, marred, mouldering, *obsoletus,* on the wane, ramshackle, ruined, shabby, stale, tabid, timeworn, used, weatherbeaten, wilted, withering, worn, worn out
ASSOCIATED CONCEPTS: depreciation, obsolescence

DILATORY, ***adjective*** after time, behind time, belated, deferring, delayed, delaying, deliberately slow, eleventh hour, inclined to delay, indolent, intended to bring about delay, intended to defer decision, intended to gain time, lackadaisical, last-minute, late, overdue, pausing, procrastinating, procrastinative, procrastinatory, remiss, tardy, unpunctual
ASSOCIATED CONCEPTS: dilatory defense, dilatory exceptions, dilatory motion, dilatory plea, dilatory practice

DILEMMA, ***noun*** awkward predicament, awkward situation, baffle, bafflement, confoundment, confusion, decision, difficult choice, difficulty, imbroglio, impasse, indecision, limited choice, perplexity, predicament, puzzle, puzzlement, puzzling alternative, quandary, uncertainty, unfair choice, vexed question

DILIGENCE *(Care),* ***noun*** absorption of mind, active application, active attention, active study, active thought, *adsiduitas,* advertence, advertency, alertness, application, attention, attention to detail, carefulness, caution, checkup, circumspection, close application, close attention, close study, close thought, concern, consideration, contemplation, deep application, deep attention, deep study, deep thought, deliberate application, deliberate attention, deliberate study, deliberate thought, diligent application, diligent attention, diligent study, diligent thought, *diligentia,* earnestness, exactitude, exactness, exclusive application, exclusive attention, exclusive study, exclusive thought, fastidiousness, foresight, guard, heed, heedfulness, *industria,* inquisitive attention, inspection, intense application, intense study, intense thought, intentness, meticulousness, mindfulness, minute application, minute attention, minute study, minute thought, minuteness, observation, orderliness, painstaking, particularity, pedantry, preparedness,

profound application, profound attention, profound study, profound thought, prudence, rapt attention, readiness, regard, review, scrutiny, seriousness, single-mindedness, studiousness, study, thoroughgoingness, thoroughness, undivided attention, utmost care, vigilance, wakefulness, wariness, watchfulness, whole attention, whole mind
ASSOCIATED CONCEPTS: due diligence, lack of diligence, ordinary diligence, reasonable diligence, utmost diligence

DILIGENCE *(Perseverance),* ***noun*** application, ardor, assiduity, assiduousness, constancy, continuance, determination, devotedness, devotion, doggedness, earnestness, endurance, firmness of purpose, fixity of purpose, habitual devotion, indefatigability, industriousness, insistence, intentness, intrepidity, meticulosity, patience, persistence, persistency, persistent exertion, pertinacity, purposefulness, relentlessness, resolution, restlessness, sedulity, sedulousness, singleness of purpose, staying power, steadfastness, steadiness, steady application, strength of will, stubbornness, tenaciousness, tenacity, tirelessness, undauntedness, undivided attention, vigilence, vigor, zeal, zealousness
ASSOCIATED CONCEPTS: diligence in prosecution

DILIGENT, ***adjective*** assiduous, attentive, busily intent, businesslike, busy, conscientious, constant, dependable, *diligens,* dogged, enduring, exact, faithful, fastidious, hardworking, heedful, indefatigable, industrious, *industrius,* never idle, never tiring, operose, painstaking, perseverant, persevering, persistent, pertinacious, punctilious, relentless, reliable, resolute, responsible, scholarly, sedulous, steadfast, studious, tenacious, thorough, thoroughgoing, tireless, trustworthy, undaunted, unfaltering, unrelenting, unremitting, untiring, unwavering, unwearying, watchful
ASSOCIATED CONCEPTS: diligent creditor, diligent efforts, diligent inquiry, diligent prosecution, diligent search, diligent use, due diligence

DILUTE, ***verb*** abbreviate, add water, attenuate, bate, belittle, cheapen, combine with water, depreciate, detract from, *diluere,* extenuate, lessen the strength of, make less concentrated, make more fluid, make more liquid, make thin, make weak, minimize, mitigate, reduce the strength of, render weak, subtract, take away, thin, thin out, thin with liquid, water, weaken

DIMENSION, ***noun*** area, boundaries, configuration, conformation, measure, outline, proportions, shape, size, square measure, surface, territorial shape

DIMINISH, ***verb*** abate, abbreviate, abrade, abridge, alleviate, assuage, bate, become smaller, belittle, bound, cause to be smaller, cause to taper, cheapen, compress, consume, contract, curb, curtail, cut back, cut down, damp down, dampen, decelerate, decimate, decrease, deduct, deflate, delete, *deminuere,* depopulate, depreciate, depress, deprive, derogate, detract, detract from, dilute, divest, do subtraction, dock, drain, drop off, dull, dwindle, eat away, ebb, economize, empty, erode, excise, expurgate, extenuate, fade away, fall away, grow less, lessen, lighten, limit, lower, make less, make smaller, make thin, minify, minimize, *minuere,* mitigate, pare, prune, quell, quiet, recede, reduce, relieve, remit, render few, render smaller, restrain, retard, retrench, roll back, rub away, run down, run low, scale down, shave off, shorten, shrink, slow down, step down, stifle, subdue, subside, subtract, take away, take from, take off, taper, thin, thin out, tone down, tune down, unload, use up, wane, waste, waste away, weaken, wear away, wear down, wear out, weed out, whittle, withdraw, wither
ASSOCIATED CONCEPTS: diminished responsibility, diminished use, diminishing returns

DIMINUTION, ***noun*** abatement, abbreviation, contraction, decrease, deduction, deflation, diminishment, lessening, let up, lowering, mitigation, reduction, remission, shrinkage

DINT, ***noun*** ableness, authority, control, effectiveness, effectuality, efficacy, force, forcefulness, greatness, influence, might, mightiness, potence, potency, power, powerfulness, prepotency, pressure, puissance, strength, superiority, sway, vigor, weight

DIPLOMATIC, ***adjective*** adept, artful, cautious in dealing, cunning, deft, dexterous, discreet, graceful, polite, politic, prudent, scheming, skillful in handling others, smoothly, strategic, tactful
ASSOCIATED CONCEPTS: diplomatic immunity, diplomatic recognition, diplomatic relations, diplomatic status

DIPSOMANIA, ***noun*** acute alcoholism, addictedness, addiction, alcoholic addiction, alcoholism, bibacity, cacoethes, chronic alcoholism, compulsion, crapulence, craving for drink, drunkenness, ebriosity, excessive drinking, excessiveness, inebriation, inebriety, insobriety, intemperance, intoxication, obsession, potation

DIRE, ***adjective*** annihilative, appalling, awful, baleful, calamitous, cataclysmic, catastrophic, catastrophical, deadly, demolishing, destroying, destructive, devastating, direful, disastrous, dismal, dreaded, dreadful, eradicative, exterminative, extirpative, extirpatory, extreme, fatal, fearful, fell, frightening, grave, grievous, grim, horrible, horrid, horrifying, ill-boding, ill-omened, inauspicious, lethal, ominous, portentous, ruinous, serious, sinister, terrible, tragic, tragical, unfortunate, unlucky, unpropitious, woeful, worst

DIRECT *(Forthright),* ***adjective*** aboveboard, blunt, candid, clear, explicit, face-to-face, forthright, frank, genuine, guileless, honest, ingenuous, open, outspoken, plain, point-blank, pointed, *rectus,* sincere, straightforward, summary, transparent, truthful, unaffected, unambiguous, unassuming, unconstrained, undeceitful, undeceiving, undeceptive, undesigning, undisguising, unfeigning, unpretending, unpretentious, unreserved, unrestrained, veracious, veridical

DIRECT *(Straight),* ***adjective*** aimed, guided, immediate, linear, rectilineal, steered, straightaway, true, unbent, unbroken, undeflected, undeviating, undistorted, unswerving, unturned, unwarped, without a bend, without circumlocution, without divergence
ASSOCIATED CONCEPTS: direct and proximate cause, direct attack, direct benefit, direct cause, direct contempt, direct control, direct damages, direct descendants, direct evidence, direct interest, direct knowledge, direct loss, direct result, direct route, direct tax, direct testimony, direct trust

DIRECT *(Uninterrupted),* ***adjective*** connected, consecutive, continual, continuous, progressive, steady, straight, successive, unbroken, unending, unfaltering, unstopped

DIRECT *(Order),* ***verb*** adjure, bid, call upon, charge, command, decree, demand, dictate, enjoin, give a directive, give an order, give directions, give instructions, give orders, govern, instruct, issue a command, issue a decree, issue an order, ordain, prescribe, rule, set a task, signal, tell
ASSOCIATED CONCEPTS: directed verdict

DIRECT *(Show)*, ***verb*** conduct, designate, guide, *homini viam monstrare,* indicate, instruct, lead, navigate, point, point out, steer

DIRECT *(Supervise)*, ***verb*** administer, *administrare,* administrate, assign, be master, boss, coach, command, conduct, control, *dirigere,* dominate, educate, engineer, exercise authority, exercise supervision, govern, guide, head, lead, look after, manage, mastermind, oversee, preside, preside over, *regere,* regulate, rule, stage, steer, superintend, take command

DIRECT CAUSE, ***noun*** immediate cause, immediate legal basis, immediate legal cause, immediate legal genesis, legitimate legal cause, legitimate legal reason, prime cause, sufficient legal basis, sufficient legal cause, sufficient legal factor, sufficient legal genesis, sufficient legal inducement, sufficient legal source, true justification, true legal basis, true legal cause, true legal inducement, true legal source
ASSOCIATED CONCEPTS: concurrent clause, just cause, sufficient combined causes

DIRECTION *(Course)*, ***noun*** aim, approach, bearing, bent, blueprint, course of action, *cursus,* design, draft, drift, heading, inclination, line, map, master plan, method, outline, plan, policy, procedure, program, range, *regio,* route, scheme, strategy, tactics, tendency, trend, *via,* way

DIRECTION *(Guidance)*, ***noun*** administration, admonition, advice, advocacy, auspices, care, charge, coaching, conduct, *consilium,* counsel, design, directorship, education, enlightenment, exhortation, governorship, *gubernatio,* headship, information, injunction, instruction, jurisdiction, leadership, management, managership, ministration, officiation, oversight, pilotage, preparation, protection, recommendation, regulation, steerage, superintendence, supervision, surveillance, teaching, training, tuition, tutelage, tutoring
ASSOCIATED CONCEPTS: directions of donor, under the direction of

DIRECTION *(Order)*, ***noun*** adjudication, canon, charge, citation, command, commandment, decree, demand, dictate, directive, *edico,* edict, enactment, fiat, imperative, *imperium,* injunction, instructions, *iubeo,* judgment, mandate, ordinance, precept, prescript, prescription, proscription, regulation, rescript, rubric, rule, subpoena, summons, warrant, writ
ASSOCIATED CONCEPTS: direction of verdict, express direction, specific direction of court

DIRECTIVE, ***noun*** behest, bidding, charge, command, commandment, declaration, decree, decretal, demand, dictate, direction, edict, enjoinment, fiat, hest, imperative, instruction, mandate, notification, order, ordinance, precept, prescript, prescription, proclamation, requirement, rescript, ukase, writ

DIRECTOR, ***noun*** administrator, boss, chief, curator, executive, executor, foreman, governor, guide, inspector, intendant, leader, manager, overseer, presiding officer, principal, proctor, procurator, superintendent, supervisor
ASSOCIATED CONCEPTS: board of directors, de facto director, de jure director, director's liability, dummy director, interlocking directorates

DIRECTORY, ***noun*** catalog, guidebook, handbook, index, manual, reference book, reference work

DISABILITY *(Legal disqualification)*, ***noun*** disablement, impairment, invalidation, invalidity, legal incapacity, unfitness, unqualification, unqualifiedness, unsuitability, unsuitableness, unsuitedness, want of legal capacity, want of legal qualification
FOREIGN PHRASES: ***Contra non valentem agere nulla currit praescriptio.*** No prescription runs against a person who is unable to act.

DISABILITY *(Physical inability)*, ***noun*** affliction, ailment, debilitation, debility, deterioration, disablement, disorder, disqualification, feebleness, frailty, handicap, helplessness, illness, impairment, impotence, impotency, inability, inability to work, inadequacy, incapability, incapacitation, incapacity, incompetence, incompetency, indisposition, ineffectiveness, ineffectuality, ineffectualness, inefficacy, inefficiency, infirmity, insufficiency, malady, powerlessness, sickness, unfitness, unsoundness, weakness
ASSOCIATED CONCEPTS: complete disability, continuous disability, disability benefits, disability compensation, disability insurance, general disability, medical disability, mental disability, partial disability, physical disability, proof of disability, temporary disability, total disability

DISABLE, ***verb*** annul, bar, becripple, break, cancel, cripple, crush, damage, deactivate, debar, *debilitare,* debilitate, deflate, deprive of power, deprive of strength, devalue, devitalize, disarm, disassemble, disenable, disenfranchise, disfranchise, dismantle, disqualify, emasculate, endamage, *enervare,* enervate, enfeeble, exhaust, harm, hinder, hurt, impair, inactivate, incapacitate, indispose, injure, invalidate, lame, maim, make inactive, make incapable, make unfit, make useless, mangle, mutilate, neutralize, nullify, paralyze, preclude, prostrate, put out of action, render helpless, render impotent, render incompetent, render powerless, render unfit, ruin, sabotage, scathe, sicken, spoil, stultify, take to pieces, undermine, unnerve, vitiate, weaken, wound, wreck
ASSOCIATED CONCEPTS: disabled from holding office, disabled vehicle, disabled veterans, disabled worker, partially disabled, wholly disabled, workmen's compensation

DISABLED *(Deprived of legal right)*, ***adjective*** disenabled, disqualified, helpless, impotent, incapacitated, ineffectual, inoperative, invalid, invalidated, legally incapable, unable, unendowed, unfit, unqualified, untenable

DISABLED *(Made incapable)*, ***adjective*** bedridden, crippled, debilitated, decrepit, defenseless, deprived of strength, devitalized, disarmed, disenabled, enfeebled, handicapped, helpless, *hors de combat,* impaired, impotent, incapacitated, incompetent, indisposed, ineffective, inefficacious, inept, invalid, maimed, paralytic, paralyzed, pregnable, shattered, unendowed, unfit, unfitted, unfortified, unqualified, useless, vincible
ASSOCIATED CONCEPTS: veterans' rights

DISABLING, ***adjective*** crippling, damaging, debilitating, enfeebling, harming, hurting, impairing, incapacitating, injuring, maiming, paralyzing, weakening

DISABUSE, ***verb*** acquaint, admonish, advise, air, announce, apprise, awaken, brief, clear the mind, communicate, convey, correct, debunk, direct the attention to, disclose, disillusion, divulge, edify, educate, enlarge the mind, enlighten, *eripere,* expose, fill with information, free from a mistaken belief, free from error, give to understand, illumine, impart, indicate, inform, instruct, lay open, let know, make known, manifest, notify, open the mind, point out, prove, put right, put straight, recount, rectify, relate, remedy, remove falsehood, report, reveal, rid of deception, set right, set straight, specify, state, straighten out, teach, tell the truth, unbeguile, unblindfold, uncover, undeceive, unfold, unfool, unmask, unveil, vent

DISACCORD, *noun* affray, animosity, antagonism, argument, argumentation, brawl, broil, caviling, clashing, cleavage, conflict, conflict of opinion, confrontation, contention, contradiction, contrariety, contrariness, controversy, cross-purposes, debate, difference, disaffection, disagreement, discongruity, discord, discordance, discordancy, discrepancy, disharmony, disparity, disputation, dispute, disruption, dissension, dissent, dissidence, dissonance, disunion, disunity, divergence, diversity of opinion, division, embranglement, embroilment, enmity, faction, failure to agree, falling out, feud, fracas, friction, heterodoxy, imbroglio, incompatibility, incongruence, incongruity, inconsistency, inconsonance, inharmoniousness, inharmony, maladjustment, misalliance, nonagreement, nonconformity, noncooperation, odds, opposition, polemics, protest, quarrel, rift, row, schism, skirmish, split, squabble, strained relations, strife, tension, unconformity, variance

DISACCORD, *verb* ablude, altercate, argue, be at variance, bicker, brabble, brangle, break with, challenge, clash, conflict, contend, contradict, contravene, controvert, debate, deny, deviate, differ, differ in opinion, disaffirm, disagree, disapprove, disavow, discept, disclaim, discredit, disharmonize, dispute, dissent, disunite, divaricate, diverge, divide, fall out, gainsay, have differences, have words with, hold opposite views, impugn, join issue, lack harmony, negate, object, oppose, protest, quarrel, rebut, redargue, refuse assent, refuse to accept, refuse to acknowledge, refuse to admit, refuse to consent, refute, reject, remonstrate, repudiate, repugn, resist, run counter to, split, squabble, take exception, traverse, vary, withhold approval, withhold assent, wrangle

DISADVANTAGE, *noun* adverse circumstance, adversity, block, blockade, blockage, burden, check, curb, damage, defect, deficiency, detainment, determent, deterrence, deterrent, detriment, difficulty, disability, disablement, discommodity, discouragement, drawback, embarrassment, encumbrance, failing, fault, frailty, hamper, handicap, harm, hindrance, holdback, impediment, imperfection, imperfectness, imposition, inadequacy, inaptitude, *incommodum,* inconvenience, inexpedience, inferiority, infirmity, inhibition, *iniquitas,* injury, insalubriousness, insufficiency, interference, lack, liability, limitation, loss, nuisance, objection, obstacle, obstruction, penalty, prejudice, prevention, problem, repression, resistance, restraint, restriction, retardation, retardment, setback, shortcoming, stifling, stumbling block, suppression, taint, unfavorable circumstance, unfavorableness, weak point, weakness
FOREIGN PHRASES: ***Cujus est commodum ejus debet esse incommodum.*** He who receives a benefit should also bear the disadvantage.

DISADVANTAGE, *verb* astrict, baffle, balk, bridle, burden, cause problems, check, circumscribe, constrain, cramp, cumber, curb, damage, deprive of advantage, disaccommodate, discommode, encumber, foil, frustrate, hamper, handicap, harm, hinder, hold back, hold in check, impair, impede, impedite, incommode, *incommodum,* inconvenience, inhibit, injure, interfere with, limit, muzzle, obstruct, overburden, overload, prejudice, put out, rein, repress, restrict, retard, saddle, shackle, stall, stymie, suppress, thwart, trammel, weaken, weigh down

DISADVANTAGED, *adjective* burdened, deprived, handicapped, impeded, prejudiced, retarded, weakened

DISADVANTAGEOUS, *adjective* adverse, baleful, baneful, biased, corrosive, counteractant, damaging, deleterious, destructive, detrimental, disapproved, disserviceable, gainless, harmful, hindering, hurtful, impolitic, inadvisable, *incommodus,* injurious, inopportune, insalubrious, malefic, maleficent, malignant, negative, pernicious, prejudicial, profitless, thwarting, unadvisable, unavailing, unfavorable, unfruitful, unhealthy, unhelpful, unprofitable, unpropitious, unwise

DISAFFECT, *verb* alienate, antagonize, cause a rift, cause dislike, cause hostility, come between, destroy the affection of, disenchant, disfavor, disillusion, disoblige, dissatisfy, disunite, divide, envenom, estrange, incense, irritate, make discontented, make disloyal, make hostile, make inimical, make less friendly, make unfaithful, mislike, provoke hatred against, render averse, rile, separate, set against, set at odds, sow dissension, turn away, wean away, withdraw the affections of

DISAFFECTION, *noun* abandonment, alienation, animosity, antagonism, antipathy, aversion, bad blood, bad faith, bitterness, breach, break, contempt, coolness, defection, dereliction, desertion, disagreement, discomfort, discontent, discord, discordance, disfavor, disgust, disillusion, disinclination, dislike, disloyalty, displeasure, dissatisfaction, dissension, dissent, dudgeon, dyspathy, enmity, estrangement, falling-out, falseness, feud, grudge, hatred, hostility, ill will, implacability, infidelity, malaise, malice, mutiny, odium, offense, pique, rancor, rebellion, reluctance, resentment, revenge, schism, secession, sedition, spleen, split, umbrage, unfriendliness, withdrawal

DISAFFIRM, *verb* abjure, abnegate, abolish, challenge, conflict with, contravene, controvert, defy, demur, deny, differ, disaffiliate, disagree, disallow, disavow, disclaim, disown, dispute, disregard, dissent, forswear, gainsay, impugn, negate, object, oppose, oppugn, overrule, overturn, protest, raise objections, rebut, recant, refuse, refute, reject, renounce, repudiate, resist, retract, reverse, run counter to, traverse
ASSOCIATED CONCEPTS: disaffirmance of contract

DISAFFIRMATION, *noun* abjuration, abjurement, contradiction, contravention, contraversion, declination, denial, disallowance, disavowal, disclaimer, disclamation, disowning, disownment, forswearing, negation, refusal, rejection, renunciation, repudiation, traversal

DISAGREE, *verb* argue, battle, be at variance, be contrary, be discordant, be disunited, be in opposition, be of different opinions, be opposed, bicker, break with, cavil, challenge, clash, collide, conflict, confute, contest, contradict, contravene, controvert, create strife, debate, defy, demonstrate, demur, deny, depart, deviate, differ, differ in opinion, disapprove, discord, *discrepare,* dispute, dissent, *dissentire, dissidere,* dissociate oneself, divaricate, diverge, divide, fight, gainsay, have dissension, hold opposite views, lack harmony, not accept, object, oppose, oppugn, protest, quarrel, raise objections, refuse assent, refuse to agree, refute, remonstrate, repudiate, repugn, revolt, split, take a stand against, take exception, take issue, think differently, traverse, vary, wrangle

DISAGREEABLE, ***adjective*** abhorrent, argumentative, arrogant, bellicose, belligerent, bilious, bitter, brusque, cantankerous, choleric, churlish, contentious, contrary, cross, crotchety, dour, glum, grumpy, harsh, ill-natured, indignant, irascible, irate, irritable, melancholic, nasty, obnoxious, offensive, ornery, peevish, petulant, short-tempered, snappish, sour, splenetic, sullen, surly, testy, touchy, uncongenial, unfriendly, ungracious, unpleasant, unsavory

DISAGREEMENT, ***noun*** altercation, argument, argumentation, challenge, conflict, conflict of interest, conflict of opinion, contention, contradiction, contraposition, contrariety, contrariness, contravention, controversy, debate, demurral, difference, difference of opinion, disaccord, discord, discordance, discordancy, discrepancy, *discrepantia,* disharmony, disputation, *dissensio,* dissension, dissent, dissidence, *dissidium,* dissimilitude, dissonance, disunion, disunity, divergent opinions, diversity of opinion, exception, faction, failure to agree, feud, gainsaying, incompatibility, inconsonance, inharmoniousness, negation, nonconsent, objection, odds, opposition, oppugnancy, polemics, quarrel, rebuttal, recusancy, strife, unconformity, variance
FOREIGN PHRASES: ***Cum in corpore dissentitur, apparet nullam esse acceptionem.*** Where there is a disagreement on the substance, it appears that there is no acceptance.

DISALLOW, ***verb*** abjure, abnegate, abrogate, contradict, contravene, controvert, deny, disaffirm, disagree, disapprove, disavow, disclaim, discredit, disown, dispute, dissent, impugn, negate, not accept, not comply, not confirm, object, oppose, protest, rebuff, rebut, refuse, refuse to acknowledge, refuse to allow, refuse to corroborate, refuse to grant, refute, reject, renunciate, repudiate, repulse, resist, spurn, withhold approval
ASSOCIATED CONCEPTS: disallow a claim, notice of disallowance

DISALLOWANCE, ***noun*** abjuration, abjurement, censorship, compliance, contradiction, contravention, countermand, declination, defeasance, denial, disaffirmation, disapproval, disavowal, disclaimer, disownment, embargo, interdiction, nonconsent, nonforbiddance, obstacle, obstruction, prohibition, proscription, refusal, rejection, renunciation, repudiation, restraint, traversal, veto

DISANNUL, ***verb*** abolish, abrogate, annul, cancel, countermand, declare null and void, disclaim, disown, dissolve, invalidate, nullify, overrule, quash, recall, recant, renege, repeal, repudiate, rescind, retract, reverse, revoke, set aside, vacate, vitiate, void, withdraw

DISAPPEAR, ***verb*** *abire,* abscond, be effaced, be erased, be lost to view, become extinct, become imperceptible, decamp, dematerialize, dissipate, dissolve, escape, evanesce, *evanescere,* evaporate, exit, extinguish, fade, fade away, flee, leave, leave no trace, melt away, pass out of sight, recede from view, retreat, take flight, take wing, undergo eclipse, vacate, vanish, vaporize
ASSOCIATED CONCEPTS: unexplained disappearance

DISAPPEARANCE, ***noun*** absence, concealment, dematerialization, departure, desertion, dispersal, dissipation, eclipse, erosion, escape, evanescence, evaporation, exit, exodus, fading, flight, obscuration, occultation, retirement, vanishment, withdrawal
ASSOCIATED CONCEPTS: disappearance of evidence

DISAPPOINT, ***verb*** break one's promise to, cause discontent, dash one's expectation, *deicere,* discourage, disenchant, disgruntle, dishearten, disillusion, disillusionize, displease, dissatisfy, fail, *frustrari,* hinder, let down, make dissatisfied, ruin one's prospects, *spe depellere*

DISAPPOINTED, ***adjective*** crestfallen, dashed, defeated, dejected, despondent, discontented, discouraged, disenchanted, disgruntled, disillusioned, displeased, dissatisfied, distressed, foiled, forlorn, frustrated, let down, put out, successless, thwarted, unsatisfied, unsuccessful

DISAPPROBATION, ***noun*** abhorrence, admonishment, adverse comment, animadversion, aspersion, ban, bar, caviling, censure, chiding, commination, complaint, condemnation, contumely, criticism, damnation, decrial, denouncement, denunciation, deprecation, depreciation, derogation, detraction, diatribe, disagreement, disapproval, discommendation, discontent, discountenance, disdain, disesteem, disfavor, dislike, disparagement, displeasure, dispraise, disrespect, dissatisfaction, dissent, dissidence, exclusion, excoriation, execration, expostulation, gainsaying, imputation, indictment, lamentation, negation, nonapproval, objection, objurgation, opposition, opprobrium, protest, protestation, rating, rebuke, rejection, remonstrance, remonstration, reprehension, reprimand, reproach, reproof, reproval, repudiation, repugnance, repugnancy, revilement, revulsion, scurrility, shunning, vilipendency, vitriol

DISAPPROVAL, ***noun*** abhorrence, adverse comment, animadversion, censure, complaining, complaint, condemnation, contradiction, contravention, criticism, demurrer, demurring, denial, denouncement, denunciation, deprecation, detraction, difference, difference of opinion, disagreement, disallowance, disapprobation, discommendation, discordance, discountenance, disdain, disesteem, disfavor, dislike, disparagement, displeasure, dissatisfaction, dissent, dissentience, dissidence, exception, faultfinding, *improbatio,* low opinion, negation, nonacceptance, nonapproval, nonconsent, objection, opposition, protestation, refusal, rejection, remonstrance, remonstration, reprehension, reproach, repudiation, resistance, shunning, traversal, unacceptance, veto
FOREIGN PHRASES: ***Qui non improbat, approbat.*** He who does not disapprove, approves.

DISAPPROVE *(Condemn),* ***verb*** admonish, animadvert, belittle, berate, brand, call to account, cast aspersions on, cast blame upon, castigate, cavil, censure, chastise, chide, criticize, debase, declaim against, decry, denounce, denunciate, deprecate, discommend, discountenance, discredit, disfavor, dislike, disparage, dispraise, dress down, exclaim against, excoriate, find fault with, fulminate against, hold up to execration, hold up to reprobation, impeach, impugn, malign, muckrake, not take kindly to, object to, objurgate, pass censure upon, pass unfavorable judgment upon, rebuff, rebuke, regard as wrong, regard with blame, remonstrate, reprehend, reprimand, reproach, reprobate, reprove, repudiate, revile, run down, scold, set oneself against, sully, take a dim view of, take exception to, take to task, think ill of, think reprehensible, think wrong, upbraid, view with disfavor, vilipend

DISAPPROVE *(Reject),* ***verb*** abnegate, be against, be contrary, be opposed to, boycott, come in conflict with, *condemnare,* confute, contradict, contravene, controvert, debunk, decline to sanction, demur, deny, deprecate, disaccord with, disagree with, disallow, disavow, disclaim, dispute, gainsay, go against, negate, negative, not abide, not accept, not admit, not approve, not consider, not countenance, not have any part of, not support, object, oppose, pass up, protest, rebuff, refuse, refuse assent to, refuse consent, refuse to confirm, refuse to ratify, refuse to receive, refuse to sanction, reject as inadmissable, renounce, repel, repudiate, resist, scorn, set aside, shun, side against, speak against, spurn, stand against, take exception, take exception to, turn away, turn down, turn from, veto, vote against, vote down, withhold approval from, withhold one's assent, withhold permission

DISARM *(Divest of arms),* ***verb*** *arma homini adimere,* attenuate, cripple, deactivate, debilitate, decimate, deescalate, demilitarize, demobilize, deprive of arms, deprive of means of defense, deprive of power, deprive of strength, deprive of weapons, devitalize, dilute, disable, disenable, disinvigorate, enervate, enfeeble, *hominem armis exuere,* incapacitate, invalidate, make inactive, make useless, muzzle, neutralize, paralyze, put out of combat, reduce forces, reduce in strength, reduce the armament, render harmless, render innocuous, render powerless, render weak, strip, unarm, undermine, weaken

DISARM *(Set at ease),* ***verb*** allay fears, allay mistrust, appease, assuage, assure, beguile, bring around, bring over, conciliate, content, divest of suspicion, gain over, gain the confidence of, make friendly, mollify, pacify, placate, propitiate, quell suspicion, reconcile, remove suspicion, restore harmony, satisfy, smooth over, subdue, touch, tranquilize, win over

DISARRANGE, ***verb*** confuse, derange, discompose, dislocate, disorder, disorganize, disorient, displace, disrupt, disturb, jumble, mismanage, ruffle, scatter, scramble, unsettle, upset

DISASSOCIATE, ***verb*** cut off, detach, disconnect, disengage, disjoin, dissociate, disunite, divide, divorce, isolate, part, remove, seclude, separate, set apart, sever, uncouple, withdraw

DISASSOCIATION, ***noun*** breach, break, breakdown, detachment, dichotomy, discerption, disconnection, discontinuation, disengagement, disjointure, disjunction, dismemberment, disruption, disseverence, dissociation, dissolution, disunion, divarication, divergence, division, divorce, divorcement, interruption, partition, rift, rupture, schism, segmentation, separation, severence, split, sunderance

DISASTER, ***noun*** adversity, affliction, bale, bane, blight, blunder, breakdown, *brutum fulmen, calamitas,* calamity, casualty, cataclysm, catastrophe, *clades,* collapse, *contretemps,* crushing reverse, *déabacle,* devastation, downfall, emergency, extremity, failure, fell stroke, fiasco, great misfortune, great mishap, hard blow, harm, holocaust, misadventure, miscarriage, misery, misfortune, misventure, nasty blow, ravage, ruin, ruination, ruinousness, scourge, setback, sudden misfortune, terrible accident, tragedy, travail, trouble, undoing, unfortunate event, upheaval, upset, woe
ASSOCIATED CONCEPTS: common disaster

DISASTROUS, ***adjective*** all-destroying, annihilative, appalling, bad, baneful, blighting, *calamitosus,* calamitous, cataclysmal, cataclysmic, catastrophic, crushing, damaging, deadly, deleterious, demolishing, desolating, destroying, destructive, detrimental, devastating, dire, disheartening, distressing, dreadful, eradicative, exterminative, exterminatory, extirpative, fell, fraught with harm, frightful, *funestus,* grievous, grim, harmful, harrowing, heartbreaking, horrendous, horrible, horrid, hurtful, ill-omened, injurious, malefic, malign, oppressive, perilous, *perniciosus,* pernicious, ravaging, ruining, ruinous, sinistrous, tragic, tragical, unfavorable

DISAVOW, ***verb*** abnegate, back down, back out, call back, declare not to be true, decline, deny, deny absolutely, deny connection with, deny emphatically, deny entirely, deny peremptorily, deny responsibility for, deny wholly, *diffiteri,* disaffirm, disbelieve, discard, disclaim, discredit, disdain, disown, dispense with, dissent, dissociate oneself, forswear, *infitiari, infitias ire,* invalidate, negate, negative, not accept, not admit, not approve, not confirm, not maintain, not pass, nullify, pass up, protest, recall, recant, refuse, refuse credence, refuse to accept, refuse to acknowledge, refuse to admit, refuse to corroborate, reject, relinquish, renounce, repel, repudiate, repulse, rescind, retract, revoke, scorn, send back, set aside, set at naught, shun, spurn, take back, traverse, turn away from, turn back, turn from, veto, withdraw

DISBAND, ***verb*** break apart, break the association of, break up, cut off, deactivate, demobilize, detach, *dimittere,* discharge, disconnect, disembody, disengage, disjoin, disjoint, dislocate, dismember, dismiss, dismiss from service, disorganize, dispel, disperse, dissever, dissociate, dissolve by dismissal, disunite, divorce, *exauctorare,* go apart, go different ways, go separate ways, let go, let out, part, part company, release, scatter, separate, sever, sunder, unbind, uncouple, withdraw from association

DISBAR, ***verb*** disbench, dismiss from the bar, dismiss from the legal profession, disqualify as an attorney, divest of legal office, drum out of the legal profession, exclude from the profession of law, expel from the bar, expel from the legal profession, invalidate an attorney's license, remove from legal office, remove from the practice of law, remove from the roll of attorneys, render an attorney's license null and void, rescind an attorney's license to practice, revoke one's license to practice law, strike off the roll of lawyers, suspend from the practice of law, suspend from the profession of law, void the license of an attorney
ASSOCIATED CONCEPTS: disbarment proceedings

DISBELIEVE, ***verb*** be doubtful, be incredulous, be skeptical, be unconvinced, challenge, consider implausible, consider not to be true, consider unproven, consider untrue, discredit, dispute, distrust, doubt, give no credence to, give no credit to, harbor doubts, harbor suspicions, have doubts, have qualms, have reservations, hold not to be true, lack faith, mistrust, *non credere,* not accept, not believe, not find tenable, question, refuse credence, refuse to admit, refuse to believe, refuse to credit, reject, reject as untrue, remain unconverted, set no store by, suspect, take no stock in, withhold assent

DISBURSE *(Distribute),* ***verb*** administer, allocate, allot, apportion, assign, circulate, deal out, diffuse, discharge, dispense, disseminate, divide, dole out, give, give away, give out, hand out, make available, make distribution of, mete, parcel out, pass out, prorate, ration, scatter, share, spread

DISBURSE *(Pay out),* ***verb*** bear the cost of, bear the expense of, compensate, defray, defray the cost, *dissolvere,* endure the cost of, expend, *exsolvere,* give money, give out in payment, incur costs, incur expenses, lay out, make expenditure, make payment, meet charges, meet the bill, meet the expense of, outlay, pay, pay off, recompense, reimburse, remunerate, render payment, repay, requite, reward, *solvere,* spend, stand the cost of, support the expense of, tender payment, undergo the cost of, undergo the expense of

DISBURSEMENT *(Act of disbursing),* ***noun*** alloting, allotment, apportioning, apportionment, assigning by lot, compensating, dealing out, dispersal, disposal, disseminating, dissemination, dividing, handing out, laying out, outgo, outlay, parceling out

DISBURSEMENT *(Funds paid out),* ***noun*** allowance, compensation, costs, defrayal, defrayment, emolument, expenditure, expense, fees, money going out, moneys expended, moneys paid out, outgo, outlay, pay, payment, recompense, redress, reimbursement, remittance, remuneration, repayment, restitution, spendings
ASSOCIATED CONCEPTS: disbursements necessarily paid or incurred, legal disbursements, necessary disbursements

DISCARD, ***noun*** castaway, castoff, debris, *déclassé,* derelict, detritus, *évacué,* foundling, leaving, oddment, *proscrit,* reject, remainder, remnant, waste

DISCERN *(Detect with the senses),* ***verb*** appreciate, apprehend, apprehend clearly, ascertain, awake to, become acquainted with, become apprized, become aware of, become informed, behold, cast eyes on, catch sight of, cognize, command a view of, comprehend, descry, detect, discover, espy, examine, experience, fathom, have in sight, inspect, know, lay eyes on, look at, look on, look upon, make out, mentally appreciate, note, notice, observe, perceive, realize, recognize, regard, scrutinize, see, see at a glance, set eyes on, sight, spot, spy, view, visualize, witness

DISCERN *(Discriminate),* ***verb*** detect differences, differentiate, distinguish, exercise discretion, have insight, judge, keep in perspective, make distinctions, note the distinctions, recognize as distinct, see as distinct, see the difference

DISCERNIBLE, ***adjective*** apparent, beholdable, cognizable, detectable, evident, in sight, knowable, manifest, observable, perceivable, perceptible, recognizable, seeable, self-evident, viewable, visible, visual

DISCERNING, ***adjective*** acute, astute, circumspect, clever, cognizant, conscious, critical, discreet, discriminating, discriminative, incisive, intelligent, judicious, juridical, keen-sighted, knowing, lucid, omniscient, penetrating, perceptive, perspicacious, provident, rational, reasonable, responsive, sagacious, sage, sapient, sensible, sensitive, sharp, shrewd, subtle, understanding, wise
ASSOCIATED CONCEPTS: discern right from wrong

DISCERNMENT, ***noun*** acuity, acumen, acuteness, apperception, appreciation, ascertainment, astuteness, clairvoyance, cleverness, cognition, comprehension, conclusion, conspection, diagnosis, discovery, discretion, discrimination, farsightedness, good sense, ingenuity, insight, intelligence, intuition, judgment, ken, knowledge, observance, penetration, perception, perspicacity, profundity, realization, reason, sense, sensibility, sharpness, shrewdness, subtlety, understanding

DISCHARGE *(Annulment),* ***noun*** abolishment, abolition, abrogation, canceling, cancellation, cessation, defeasance, discontinuance, dissolution, invalidation, negation, nullification, recall, repeal, repudiation, rescission, retractation, reversal, revocation, voidance

DISCHARGE *(Dismissal),* ***noun*** *dimissio,* displacement, ejection, elimination, eviction, expulsion, firing, ouster, ousting, removal, removal from employment, replacement, unseating
ASSOCIATED CONCEPTS: cause for discharge, conditional discharge, discharge from army, discharge from employment, discharge of employee, discriminatory discharge, improper discharge

DISCHARGE *(Liberation),* ***noun*** absolution, acquittal, clearance, deliverance, disenthrallment, emancipation, exculpation, exemption, exoneration, extrication, legal release from confinement, loosing, release, release from custody, reprieve, salvation, setting free

DISCHARGE *(Payment),* ***noun*** acquitment, acquittal, acquittance, amortization, amortizement, annulment of debt, clearance, compensation, defrayal, defrayment, full satisfaction, liquidation, paying off, recompense, redemption, refund, reimbursement, remittance, reparation, repayment, restitution, retirement of a debt, return, satisfaction, settlement, settlement on account

DISCHARGE *(Performance),* ***noun*** accomplishment, achievement, attainment, carrying through, commission, completion, conclusion, consummation, culmination, dispatch, effectuation, enforcement, execution, fruition, fulfillment, implementation, observance, perpetration, production, realization, termination
ASSOCIATED CONCEPTS: discharge of duty, faithful discharge of official duties

DISCHARGE *(Release from obligation),* ***noun*** abolition, abrogation, absolution, acquittal, cancellation, defeasance, deliverance, delivery, dismissal, dispensation, emancipation, exception, exculpation, excuse, exemption, exoneration, extrication, invalidation, loosing, nullification, pardon, repeal, reprieve, rescission, revocation, voidance

DISCHARGE *(Shot),* ***noun*** blast, blasting, bombardment, burst, *coniectio, coniectus,* crash, detonation, emanation, *emissio,* emmission, explosion, firing, firing a charge, flare, flash, fulguration, fulmination, fusillade, igniting, salvo, spray, volley

DISCHARGE *(Dismiss),* ***verb*** cashier, cast, cast loose, depose, deprive of office, *dimittere,* disbar, discard, disemploy, displace, drop, eject, exclude, expel, fire, get rid of, give notice, impeach, let go, let loose, *missum facere,* put on the retired list, release, relieve, remove, remove from office, replace, retire, shut out, strike off the roll, suspend, throw out, turn loose, turn out, unseat
ASSOCIATED CONCEPTS: discharged for cause, lawfully discharged, reinstatement

DISCHARGE *(Liberate),* ***verb*** absolve, acquit, bail out, clear, deliver, emancipate, exculpate, excuse, exonerate, extricate, forgive, free, let go, let loose, let out, let out of prison, loose, pardon, parole, purge, release, relieve, render free, set at liberty, set free, turn loose
ASSOCIATED CONCEPTS: discharge from imprisonment, discharge from prison

DISCHARGE *(Pay a debt),* ***verb*** adjust, amortize, clear, hand over, honor, liquidate, make reparation, make restitution, meet, pay in full, pay off, pay up, recompense, redeem, refund, repay, satisfy, satisfy in full, settle, settle accounts, square accounts, strike a balance, take up
ASSOCIATED CONCEPTS: discharge from obligation

DISCHARGE *(Perform),* ***verb*** accomplish, achieve, act on, adjust, administer, attain, bring about, bring to pass, carry into effect, carry into execution, carry out, carry through, complete, comply, concern oneself with, conclude, consummate, culminate, devote oneself to, dispatch, dispose of, do, effect, effectuate, enforce, execute, fulfill, go about, go through with, implement, *munus obire,* proceed with, produce, realize, render, resolve, succeed, transact
ASSOCIATED CONCEPTS: properly discharge one's responsibilities

DISCHARGE *(Release from obligation),* ***verb*** abolish, abrogate, absolve, annul, cancel, declare null and void, discontinue, dismiss, dissolve, excuse, exempt, exonerate, forgive, invalidate, make void, nullify, quash, recall, relieve, relieve of responsibility, remove, render void, repeal, rescind, retract, reverse, revoke, set aside
ASSOCIATED CONCEPTS: discharge of a debt
FOREIGN PHRASES: ***Eodem modo quo oritur, eodem modo dissolvitur.*** It is discharged in the same manner in which it was created.

DISCHARGE *(Shoot),* ***verb*** blast, burst, deliver a charge, detonate, emit, expel, explode, fire, fire at, fulminate, ignite, launch, *mittere,* open fire, send forth
ASSOCIATED CONCEPTS: discharge of a weapon

DISCIPLE, ***noun*** accepter, adherent, admirer, advocate, ally, apostle, apprentice, *auditor,* backer, believer, condisciple, devotee, *discipulus, élève,* favorer, follower, hanger-on, imitator, learner, loyalist, promoter, protegé, pupil, receiver, recruit, scholar, student, supporter, sympathizer, true believer, truster, votary

DISCIPLINARY *(Educational),* ***adjective*** academic, cultural, didactic, didactical, doctrinal, educative, informational, informative, instructional, instructive, paedeutic, pedagogic, pedagogical, preceptive, preceptoral, scholarly, scholastic, training, tuitionary, tutorial

DISCIPLINARY *(Punitory),* ***adjective*** amercing, castigatory, chastening, corrective, inflictive, penal, penological, punishing, punitive, reformational, reformative, reformatory, regulatory, retaliatory, retributive, talionic
ASSOCIATED CONCEPTS: disciplinary action, disciplinary hearing, disciplinary power, disciplinary proceeding

DISCIPLINE *(Field of study),* ***noun*** area of education, area of learning, branch of instruction, branch of knowledge, course, curriculum, doctrine, education, field of interest, field of learning, learning, lore, teaching

DISCIPLINE *(Obedience),* ***noun*** acquiescence, compliance, constancy, constraint, control, curb, deference, devotion, *disciplina,* dutifulness, faithfulness, fidelity, limitation, loyalty, malleability, nonresistance, obsequiousness, observance, pliancy, repression, restraint, self-command, self-conquest, self-denial, self-direction, self-mastery, self-regulation, self-restraint, servility, stoicism, strength of character, strength of will, submission, submissiveness, subordination to rules, will power
ASSOCIATED CONCEPTS: disciplinary proceeding

DISCIPLINE *(Punishment),* ***noun*** amercement, castigation, chastening, chastisement, correction, deprivation, infliction, judgment, just deserts, penal retribution, penalty, penance, penology, reprimand, reproof, retribution, retributive justice, scourge, suffering, trial

DISCIPLINE *(Training),* ***noun*** coaching, conditioning, conduct, cultivation, development, diligent exercise, diligent practice, drill, drilling, exercise, grooming, guidance, inculcation, indoctrination, initiation, instruction, practice, preparation, qualification, readying, regulation, rehearsal, schooling, system of drill, systematic training

DISCIPLINE *(Control),* ***verb*** administer, bridle, bring to a state of obedience, bring under subjection, check, command, curb, direct, dominate, exercise direction over, govern, govern strictly, harness, hold in leash, hold in line, limit, make toe the line, manage, muzzle, oversee, pull in, regulate, rein in, restrain, restrict, stand over, subjugate, superintend, supervise

DISCIPLINE *(Punish),* ***verb*** administer correction, bring to retribution, call to account, carry out a sentence, castigate, chasten, chastise, correct, deal retributive justice, exact a penalty, exact retribution, execute a sentence, execute judgment, execute justice, get even with, give one his deserts, impose a penalty, inflict penalty, inflict penance upon, make an example of, penalize, reprove, scourge, sentence, subject to punishment, take to task, visit punishment
ASSOCIATED CONCEPTS: deterrence, disciplinary proceeding, isolation, rehabilitation, retribution

DISCIPLINE *(Train),* ***verb*** accustom, break in, bring up, coach, condition, cultivate, direct, educate, enlighten, form, foster, give directions, give instructions, give lessons in, groom, guide, habituate, impress upon the mind, inculcate, indoctrinate, infuse, instill, *instituere,* instruct, nurture, prepare, put through paces, qualify, raise, ready, rear, school, show, train by instruction

DISCLAIM, ***verb*** abandon, abnegate, abrogate, annul, cancel, declare null and void, deny, deny any knowledge of, desert, disaffirm, disannul, disavow, disbelieve, discard, discharge, discountenance, disown, dispense with, divest oneself of, forgo, forsake, forswear, give up, not accept, not admit, recant, reject, renounce, *repudiare,* repudiate, rescind, retract, set aside, spurn, take back, take exception to, turn away, unsay

DISCLAIMER, ***noun*** abandonment, abjuration, abjurement, annulment, denial, disaffirmation, disallowance, disavowal, disclamation, disownment, dissociation, negation, nullification, recantation, refusal, rejection, relinquishment, renouncement, renunciation, repudiation, revocation
ASSOCIATED CONCEPTS: disclaimer of interest, disclaimer of knowledge, disclaimer of liability, disclaimer of title, disclaimer of warranties, innocent bystanders, liability to third parties, third parties

DISCLOSE, ***verb*** acknowledge, acquaint, admit, advise, air, allude to, announce, *aperire,* apprise, bare, blazon, bring into the open, bring into view, bring out, bring to light, circulate, communicate, confess, declare, describe, *detegere,* dismask, disseminate, divulge, enlighten, evidence, evince, exhibit, expose, give utterance to, impart, *indicare,* indicate, inform, lay bare, make known, make public,

mention, notify, present, proclaim, promulgate, publish, report, reveal, speak out, speak the truth, tell, uncover, unearth, unfold, unmask, unscreen, unseal, unshroud, unveil, utter, vent, voice
ASSOCIATED CONCEPTS: disclose assets, disclose the location of a debtor's residence, disclose wrongdoing, disclosed principal, disclosure of public information

DISCLOSURE *(Act of disclosing),* ***noun*** admission, advisement, announcement, apprisal, assertion, communication, concession, confession, declaration, disclosing, dissemination, divulgation, divulgement, divulgence, enlightenment, enumeration, exposition, exposure, informing, making aware, making public, mention, notification, presentation to view, proclamation, production, profession, publication, recital, recitation, relation, representation, revealing, revealment, showing, telling, uncovering, uncovery, unfolding, unfoldment, unmasking, unveiling, uttering
ASSOCIATED CONCEPTS: disclosure device, disclosure of assets, disclosure of interest, duty of disclosure, false disclosure, nondisclosure, right to disclosure, voluntary disclosure
FOREIGN PHRASES: ***Suppressio veri, suggestio falsi.*** The supression of truth is equivalent to the suggestion of what is false.

DISCLOSURE *(Something disclosed),* ***noun*** acknowledgment, admission, affirmation, announcement, answer, assertion, averment, avowal, communication, concession, confession, confirmation, declaration, deposition, discovery, divulgence, enunciation, explanation, exposé, exposition, expression, *indicium,* information, inside information, knowledge, manifestation, message, news, notice, notification, presentation, proclamation, profession, publication, recital, remark, report, revealment, revelation, statement, testimony, utterance, word

DISCOMMEND, ***verb*** asperse, attack, belittle, bring into discredit, censure, clamor against, condemn, contemn, criticize, decry, denigrate, denounce, deprecate, depreciate, deride, derogate, detract, disapprove, discredit, disfavor, disparage, dispraise, disvalue, fault, find fault, malign, reflect discredit upon, revile, ridicule, scoff at, slight, slur, sneer at, speak ill of, speak slightingly of, spurn, traduce, underrate, undervalue, view with disfavor, vilify, vilipend

DISCOMMODE, ***verb*** afflict, affront, aggravate, agitate, annoy, arouse, astound, badger, beset, bother, chafe, contravene, counteract, disaccommodate, disadvantage, disconcert, dishearten, disoblige, displease, disquiet, distress, disturb, exasperate, grieve, harry, hinder, impede, impose upon, incommode, inconvenience, irk, irritate, make uneasy, oppress, perplex, perturb, pique, plague, provoke, put to inconvenience, trouble, undermine, unnerve, upset, vex, worry

DISCOMPOSE, ***verb*** addle, afflict, aggravate, agitate, annoy, appall, astound, badger, bedazzle, bedevil, befuddle, bewilder, bring into disorder, browbeat, carp at, chafe, confound, confuse, convulse, cross, daze, dazzle, dement, demoralize, derange, disarrange, discomfit, discomfort, discommode, disconcert, dishevel, dislocate, dismay, disorder, disorganize, displace, disquiet, distemper, disturb, disturb the composure of, embitter, enrage, envenom, exasperate, excite, ferment, fluster, fog, fret, goad, gripe, harass, harry, heckle, hurt the feelings, incense, inflame, infuriate, irk, irritate, jar, jolt, jumble, make uneasy, mix up, mortify, muddle, nettle, nonplus, perplex, perturb, pester, pique, plague, provoke, put out, rattle, rile, roil, ruffle, shake, shake up, shatter, stir, taunt, tease, throw into confusion, torment, tousle, trouble, try the patience, unbalance, unhinge, unsettle, upset, vex, worry

DISCONCERT, ***verb*** abash, agitate, alarm, annoy, appall, astound, bedazzle, bedevil, cause discontent, chagrin, confound, confuse, discomfit, discomfort, discompose, discountenance, dismay, disquiet, disrupt, disturb, fluster, give cause for alarm, *percellere,* perplex, perturb, *perturbare,* puzzle, ruffle, startle, throw into confusion, upset

DISCONNECTED, ***adjective*** abstracted, adrift, apart, asunder, broken, broken off, cut apart, cut in two, detached, disassociated, discontinuous, discrete, disembodied, disjoined, disjointed, disjunct, disjunctive, disparate, disunited, divergent, divorced, incoherent, inconsistent, interrupted, irrational, irrelative, isolated, jumbled, loose, noncohesive, partitioned, put asunder, scattered, separate, separated, set apart, set asunder, severed, sundered, switched off, unaffiliated, unallied, unannexed, unassociated, unattached, uncohesive, unconnected, uncoupled, unintelligible, unjoined, unlinked, unrelated

DISCONSOLATE, ***adjective*** afflicted, anguished, atrabilious, bereaved, brokenhearted, burdened, careworn, cast down, cheerless, comfortless, crestfallen, crushed, dejected, depressed, desolate, despairing, despondent, discouraged, disheartened, dismal, dispirited, distressed, doleful, dolorous, downcast, downhearted, elegiac, encumbered, forlorn, funereal, gloomy, glum, grief-stricken, grieved, grieving, heartbroken, heartsick, heavy-laden, hopeless, hurt, in despair, in heavy spirits, inconsolable, infelicitous, joyless, lachrymose, lamenting, languishing, lost, low-spirited, *maestus,* melancholic, melancholy, miserable, moody, morose, mournful, mourning, overcome, pained, pathetic, pessimistic, plaintive, sad, saturnine, sober, somber, sorrowful, spiritless, stricken, tearful, *triste,* troubled, unconsolable, unhappy, unnerved, wan, weeping, woebegone, woeful, wretched

DISCONTINUANCE, ***noun*** arrest, arrestment, cease, cease-fire, cessation, check, close, closedown, closure, conclusion, cutoff, discontinuation, end, ending, expiration, finish, halt, lapse, letup, moratorium, pause, phaseout, shutdown, stay, stop, stoppage, surcease, suspension, termination
ASSOCIATED CONCEPTS: discontinuance of an action

DISCONTINUANCE *(Act of discontinuing),* ***noun*** abeyance, abolishment, abolition, adjournment, breaking off, cancellation, canceling, cessation, defeasance, desistance, discontinuation, dismissal, disruption, disuse, interruption, interval, invalidation, nonuse, nullification, pause, postponement, recess, remission, stop, stoppage, suspension, termination, withdrawal

DISCONTINUANCE *(Interruption of a legal action),* ***noun*** ampliation, cessation, desistance, discontinuation, dismissal, moratorium, termination, withdrawal

DISCONTINUE *(Abandon),* ***verb*** abolish, abort, abrogate, abstain, annul, apostatize, arrest, break, break off, bring to a close, bring to an end, call off, cancel, cause a discontinuance, cease, cease using, check, close, complete, conclude, consummate, demit, desist, desist from, destroy, discard, disconnect, disjoin, dismiss, dissever, dissolve,

disunite, drop, end, expire, finish, forfeit, forsake, give up, halt, have done with, invalidate, leave, leave off, let lapse, play out, put an end to, quit, relinquish, renounce, repeal, resign, retire, revoke, separate, sever, shut down, stop, sunder, surrender, suspend, terminate, vacate, void, waive, withdraw
ASSOCIATED CONCEPTS: discontinuance of an action, dismissal, judgment of discontinuance, lack of prosecution, nonsuit, voluntary discontinuance

DISCONTINUE *(Break continuity),* ***verb*** adjourn, arrest, balk, break, break off, bring to a standstill, check, cut, cut short, dam up, defer, delay, disconnect, disengage, disjoin, disrupt, dissever, dissolve, disturb, disunite, divide, foil, frustrate, hesitate, hinder, hold in abeyance, intercept, interfere with, interject, intermit, interpose, interrupt, intervene, intrude, leave off, obstruct, part, postpone, punctuate, recess, remit, retard, separate, sever, sunder, suspend, thwart, wait, waive

DISCORD, ***noun*** animosity, antagonism, argumentation, bickering, clashing, conflict, contention, controversy, difference, disaccord, disaccordance, disagreement, discongruity, discordance, *discordia,* discrepancy, disharmony, disparity, dispute, *dissensio,* dissension, dissent, dissentience, dissidence, *dissidium,* dissimilarity, dissonance, disunion, disunity, divergent opinions, diversity, division, divisiveness, enmity, faction, failure to agree, friction, hostility, ill feeling, ill will, incompatibility, incongruence, incongruity, lack of concord, nonagreement, opposition, quarreling, schism, split, strained relations, strife, unharmoniousness, variance, wrangling

DISCORDANT, ***adjective*** adverse, antagonistic, antipathetical, antithetical, antonymous, at cross purposes, at variance, cacophonous, clashing, colliding, conflicting, conflictory, contradictory, contradistinct, contrarious, contrary, counter, differing, disaccordant, disagreeing, *discors, discrepans,* discrepant, dissentient, dissenting, dissident, dissimilar, dissonant, *dissonus,* divergent, diverse, hostile, in disagreement, inaccordant, incompatible, incongruent, incongruous, inconsistent, inconsonant, inharmonious, inimical, inverse, irreconcilable, opposed, opposing, opposite, oppositional, oppugnant, out of accord, strident, unagreeing, variant

DISCOUNT, ***noun*** abatement, allowance, amount deducted, bargain, *decessio,* decrease, decrement, *deductio,* deduction, diminution, lower price, markdown, reduction, special price, subtraction
ASSOCIATED CONCEPTS: discount a loan, discount bills, discount notes, trade discount

DISCOUNT *(Disbelieve),* ***verb*** be indifferent to, belittle, brush aside, *decessio, deductio,* depreciate, discountenance, discredit, disdain, disesteem, disparage, disregard, distrust, doubt, gloss over, harbor suspicions, ignore, make light of, misprize, mistrust, pass over, pay no attention, pay no heed, pay no mind, question, slight, spurn, suspect

DISCOUNT *(Minimize),* ***verb*** abate, abbreviate, abridge, allay, attenuate, condense, curtail, deflate, detract, diminish, lessen, minimalize, pare, reduce, render less, scale down, shorten, underestimate, understate, undervalue

DISCOUNT *(Reduce),* ***verb*** abate, allow a margin, cut, decrease, deduct from, depreciate, detract, lower, lower the sale price, make allowance for, mark down, rebate, reduce the markup, sell below par, slash prices, strike off, subduct, subtract, take from, take off, underprice, undersell, undervalue

DISCOURAGE, ***verb*** advise against, affright, *animum frangere,* argue against, avert, cast down, cause discontent, cause dislike, cause doubt, caution, contraindicate, convince to the contrary, dampen, daunt, deflect, dehort, deject, demoralize, deprecate, depress, deprive of courage, destroy confidence, deter, *deterrere,* disaffect, discountenance, disenchant, disgruntle, dishearten, disillusion, disincline, disinterest, dismay, dispirit, dissuade, divert, expostulate, forestall, frighten away, give one pause, hinder, impose difficulties, indispose, inspire fear, intimidate, keep back, keep from, lessen the self-confidence of, lower the courage of, obstruct by opposition, oppose, persuade against, put a damper on, quench, remonstrate, render averse, repel, reprove, restrain, sadden, scare, set against, thwart, turn aside, turn from, unnerve, upset, warn, weaken the resolution of

DISCOURAGEMENT, ***noun*** cold feet, constraint, curb, damper, defeatism, dejection, demoralization, depression, desolation, despair, despondency, deterrent, disheartenment, disincentive, dismay, dispiritedness, downheartedness, hamper, hindrance, low spirits, obstacle, pessimism, rebuff, resignation, restraint, sadness

DISCOURSE, ***noun*** address, allocution, argument, argumentation, commentary, conference, *conlocutio, conloquium,* conversation, declamation, dialogue, discussion, disquisition, dissertation, elucidation, exchange of views, excursus, exhortation, exposition, expression of views, formal discussion, interchange of views, interlocution, language, lecture, oral communication, oration, prelection, recital, recitation, rhetorical presentation, *sermo,* speech, talk, verbal communication, verbal exposition, verbal intercourse

DISCOURSE, ***verb*** address, comment, commune with, communicate orally, confabulate, confer, *conloqui,* converse, debate, deliver a speech, deliver a talk, deliver an address, dilate, discuss, dissertate, exchange observations, expatiate, explain, expound, give a speech, give a talk, give an address, hold a conference, lecture, make a speech, orate, *orationem facere, orationem habere,* parley, perorate, prelect, recite, sermonize, speak, talk, talk over, talk together

DISCOVER, ***verb*** ascertain, awake to, become informed, behold, bring to light, chance upon, *cognoscere,* collect knowledge, come to know, come upon, *comperire,* deduce, descry, detect, determine, diagnose, discern, divine, elicit, encounter, expose, ferret out, find out, get a glimpse of, identify, *invenire,* investigate, learn, learn for a certainty, learn of, locate, manifest, observe, perceive, pinpoint, realize, see, turn up, uncover, understand, unearth, unravel
ASSOCIATED CONCEPTS: discover facts and information known by an adverse party, discovered negligence, doctrine of discovered peril, proceeding to discover assets

DISCOVERABLE *(Evident),* ***adjective*** accountable, apparent, appreciable, ascertainable, assayable, calculable, clear, computable, conspicuous, countable, detectable, discernible, estimable, evident, manifest, measurable, noticeable, obvious, palpable, patent, perceptible, predictable, recognizable, revealed, seeable, unconcealed, unhidden, unmistakable, viewable, visible

DISCOVERABLE *(Law),* ***adjective*** available evidence, disclosure, evidence release, evidence turned over, obtainable evidence, open evidence, produced evidence, revealed evidence, unconcealed evidence, unhidden evidence, viewable evidence, visible evidence
ASSOCIATED CONCEPTS: evidence, federal rules of procedure, rules of civil procedure

DISCOVERY, ***noun*** acquisition of knowledge, ascertainment, checking, declaration, descrial, detection, discernment, disclosure, disclosure proceedings, distinguishing, divulgence, espial, examination for the purpose of ascertaining facts, exploration, exposition, exposure, finding out, first sight, identification, inquiry, inspection, investigation, investigation to uncover facts, observation, perception, perusal, pretrial examination proceedings, quest, reconnoitering, revealment, revelation, scrutiny, sighting, surveying, uncovering, unearthing
ASSOCIATED CONCEPTS: discovery of deceit, discovery of facts, discovery of fraud, discovery of loss, discovery of mistake, discovery proceeding, discovery which can be patented, doctrine of discovered peril

DISCREDIT, ***noun*** animadversion, aspersion, attaint, baseness, castigation, censure, condemnation, contumely, criticism, debasement, *dedecus,* degradation, denunciation, derogation, disapprobation, disapproval, disbelief, disesteem, disfavor, disgrace, dishonor, disparagement, dispraise, disreputability, disrepute, distrust, *ignominia,* ignominy, impaired reputation, imputation, incredulity, *infamia,* infamy, ingloriousness, lack of confidence, lack of esteem, loss of belief, loss of credence, loss of credit, loss of repute, mistrust, odium, opprobrium, *probrum,* reflection, remonstrance, reprehension, reproach, reprobation, repudiation, revilement, scandal, shame, slur, stain, stigma, stricture, taint, tarnish, turpitude
ASSOCIATED CONCEPTS: discredit a witness

DISCREDIT, ***verb*** *abrogare,* asperse, besmirch, brand, bring disgrace upon, bring into disfavor, bring reproach upon, cast aspersions on, cast shame upon, debase, decry, degrade, denigrate, deprecate, depreciate, deprive of credit, *derogare,* derogate from, discount, disgrace, dishonor, disparage, downgrade, hold up to shame, impair the reputation of, impute shame to, injure the credit of, involve in shame, make distasteful, malign, reflect dishonor upon, reprehend, scandalize, stain, stigmatize, taint, tarnish
ASSOCIATED CONCEPTS: discredit a witness, discredited witness

DISCREET, ***adjective*** astute, calculating, careful, cautious, *cautus,* chary, circumspect, *consideratus,* deliberate, diplomatic, discerning, discretional, discretionary, discriminate, discriminating, discriminative, distinguishing, forethoughtful, guarded, intelligent, judicious, mindful, perceptive, polite, politic, precautious, prepared, *prudens,* prudent, refined, reflecting, regardful, reserved, reticent, sensible, sensitive, subtle, thoughtful, vigilant, watchful, well-advised, wise

DISCREPANCY, ***noun*** aberration, anomaly, asymmetry, clash, conflict, contradiction, contrast, departure, deviation, difference, differential, differentiation, disaccord, disagreement, discongruity, discord, discordance, disharmony, disparity, disputed point, dissimilarity, dissimilitude, dissonance, divergence, failure to correspond, ground of argument, inaccordance, incompatibility, incongruence, incongruency, incongruity, inconsistency, inequality, irreconcilability, lack of accord, lack of agreement, lack of concert, lack of conformity, lack of congruence, lack of congruity, lack of consonance, lack of resemblance, matter of disputation, nonagreement, nonconformity, nonuniformity, split, subject of controversy, subject of dispute, unconformity, unlikeness, variance, variation

DISCREPANT, ***adjective*** at variance, clashing, conflicting, conflictory, contradictory, contrary, deviant, different, differing, disagreeing, discordant, disparate, disproportionate, dissenting, dissident, dissimilar, dissonant, distinct, divergent, diverse, divided, divisive, factious, ill-matched, ill-mated, inapplicable, inapposite, incommensurate, incongruent, incongruous, inconsistent, inconsonant, inimical, jarring, opposite, peculiar, quarreling, schismatic, unconformable, unrelated, variant

DISCRETE, ***adjective*** apart, asunder, cut off, detached, different, disassociated, disconnected, *discontinu,* discontinuous, discretive, disengaged, disjoined, disjoint, disjunct, dissociated, distinct, distinguished, disunited, divided, individual, isolated, noncontinuous, parted, removed, separate, separated, sundered, unannexed, unassimilated, unassociated, unattached, unconnected, unfastened, unjoined

DISCRETION *(Power of choice),* ***noun*** analysis, appraisal, assessment, choice, consideration, contemplation, decision, designation, determination, discrimination, distinction, election, evaluation, examination, free decision, free will, freedom of choice, liberty of choosing, liberty of judgment, license, option, optionality, permission, pick, power of choosing, review, right of choice, sanction, selection, self-determination, suffrage, suo *arbitrio,* volition, will
ASSOCIATED CONCEPTS: absolute discretion, abuse of discretion, administrative discretion, arbitrariness, capriciousness, certiorari, judicial discretion, legal discretion, mandamus, prohibition, unreasonableness
FOREIGN PHRASES: ***Optima est lex quae minimum relinquit arbitrio judicis; optimas judex qui minimum sibi.*** That is the best system of law which leaves the least to the discretion of the judge; that judge is the best who leaves the least to his own discretion. ***Optimam esse legem, quae minimum relinquit arbitrio judicis; id quod certitudo ejus praestat.*** That law is the best which leaves the least discretion to the judge; this is an advantage which results from its certainty. ***Optimus judex, qui minimum sibi.*** He is the best judge who leaves the least to his own discretion. ***Quam longum debet esse rationabile tempus non definitur in lege, sed pendet ex discretione justiciariorum.*** How long a reasonable time ought to be is not defined by law, but is left to the discretion of the judges. ***Quam rationabilis debet esse finis, non definitur, sed omnibus circum stantiis inspectis pendet ex justiciariorum discretione.*** What a reasonable fine ought to be is not defined, but is left to the discretion of the judges, all the circumstances being considered.

DISCRETION *(Quality of being discreet),* ***noun*** ability to get along with others, acuteness, aesthetic judgment, appreciation, appreciativeness, art of negotiating, artful management, artfulness, artistic judgment, attention, care, carefulness, caution, cautiousness, chariness, circumspection, circumspectness, cleverness, competence, concern, considerateness, consideration, craft, deftness, deliberation, delicacy, diplomacy, discernment, discreetness, discriminating taste, discrimination, discriminatory powers, distinction, expertness, facility, finesse, good sense, guardedness, heed, heedfulness, insight, intuition, *iudicium,* judiciousness, mature responsibility, maturity, mindfulness,

nicety, particularness, perception, perspicacity, polish, precaution, presence of mind, providence, prudence, *prudentia,* qualification, quick judgment, refined discrimination, refinement, regardfulness, resourcefulness, safeguard, sagacity, sagesse, *savoir faire,* sensitiveness, sensitivity, sharpness, shrewd diagnosis, shrewdness, skill, sound judgment, sound reasoning, statesmanship, strategy, subtlety, sympathetic perception, tact, tactfulness, taste, technique, thoughtfulness, wariness, watchfulness, wisdom
ASSOCIATED CONCEPTS: absolute discretion, abuse of discretion, administrative discretion, discretion to set aside a judgment, improper exercise of discretion, judicial discretion, prosecutorial discretion, sound discretion
FOREIGN PHRASES: ***Discretio est scire per legem quid sit justum.*** Discretion consists in knowing through the law what is just.

DISCRETIONARY, ***adjective*** conative, discretional, discriminative, elective, left to discretion, left to individual judgment, optional, selective, volitional, volitive
ASSOCIATED CONCEPTS: discretionary authority, discretionary damages, discretionary power of the court, discretionary trusts

DISCRIMINATE *(Distinguish),* ***verb*** characterize, classify, compare, contrast, designate, determine the essentials, differentiate, *diiudicare, discernere, distinguere,* divide, draw the line, individualize, *internoscere,* label, make a choice, make a distinction, make a selection, mark, mark the difference between, note differences, point out, recognize as separate, see the difference, separate, set apart, set off, sift, sort out, tell apart

DISCRIMINATE *(Treat differently),* ***verb*** avoid, be partial, be predisposed, bear a grudge against, bear malice, disapprove of, disfavor, favor, have an affection for, have ill feelings toward, incline toward, lean toward, look down upon, make a distinction, object to, prefer, reject, show an aversion, show bias, show preference, show prejudice, shun, tend toward
ASSOCIATED CONCEPTS: age discrimination, discriminate against an employee, discriminate in price, discriminatory tax, equal protection, invidious discrimination, race discrimination, religious discrimination, sex discrimination, unlawful discrimination

DISCRIMINATING *(Distinguishing),* ***adjective*** contradistinct, contrasting, diacritical, differentiating, differentiative, differing, discriminate, distinctive, inconsistent, individualizing, selective, separative
ASSOCIATED CONCEPTS: discrimination because of race, discrimination in hiring, discriminatory practices, equal protection, illegal discrimination, invidious discrimination, racial discrimination, reverse discrimination

DISCRIMINATING *(Judicious),* ***adjective*** appraising, astute, clear-sighted, critical, discerning, dispassionate, fastidious, impartial, judgmatic, keen, knowing, meticulous, perceptive, perspicacious, rational, reasonable, sagacious, sapient, selective, sober, sound, thoughtful, unbiased, well-advised, wise

DISCRIMINATION *(Bigotry),* ***noun*** bias, blind zeal, class prejudice, favoritism, illiberality, intolerance, opinionativeness, preference, prejudice, race hatred, race prejudice, racialism, racism, unfairness, want of forbearance
ASSOCIATED CONCEPTS: blacklist, civil rights act, compelling state interest, discrimination based on sex, discrimination in hiring and tenure, due process clause, equal protection, illegal discrimination, invidious discrimination, overwhelming state interest, prejudicial discrimination, race discrimination, rational basis, reasonable classification, unjust discrimination

DISCRIMINATION *(Differentiation),* ***noun*** analysis, appraisal, appreciation, assessment, comprehension, consideration, contemplation, contrasting, demarcation, *discrimen,* disequalization, *distinctio,* distinction, distinguishment, division, estimation, examination, evaluation, individualization, segregation, separation, setting apart, weighing
ASSOCIATED CONCEPTS: compelling state interest, equal protection

DISCRIMINATION *(Good judgment),* ***noun*** acumen, acuteness, circumspection, discernment, discreetness, discretion, good sense, insight, *intellegentia,* intelligence, intuition, *iudicium,* judiciousness, knowledge, perception, perspicacity, perspicuity, prudence, *prudentia,* rationality, reason, sagacity, shrewdness, sound reasoning, thoughtfulness, understanding

DISCRIMINATORY, ***adjective*** biased, bigoted, favoring, inequitable, influenced, iniquitous, jaundiced, one-sided, partisan, preconceived, predilected, predisposed, prejudging, prejudiced, selective, separate, slanted, undispassionate, unjust, unjustified, warped
ASSOCIATED CONCEPTS: discriminatory action, discriminatory implementation, discriminatory laws, selective enforcement

DISCURSIVE *(Analytical),* ***adjective*** *a fortiori, a posteriori, a priori,* analytic, argumentative, deductive, dialectic, disquisitional, epagogic, inductive, inferential, interpretative, logical, ratiocinative, ratiocinatory, rational, rationalistic, reasoning

DISCURSIVE *(Digressive),* ***adjective*** aimless, circuitous, desultory, deviating, deviative, devious, disconnected, drifting, errant, indirect, meandering, rambling, random, ranging, roaming, roundabout, roving, shifting, straying, undirected, unsystematic, *vagus, varius,* wandering

DISCUSS, ***verb*** *agitare,* air, analyze, argue for and against, argue the case, argue the point, bandy words, carry on a conversation, comment, comment upon, confabulate, confer, confer with, consider, consult, contend in words, contest, converse, debate, deliberate upon, dialogize, *disceptare,* discourse, discourse about, *disputare, disserere,* dissertate, engage in a conversation, engage in conversation, engage in oral controversy, exchange observations, exchange opinions, explain, have a conference on, hold conclave, hold conference, hold conversations, hold intercourse, indulge in argument, interchange views, join in a conversation, negotiate, parley, partake in a symposium, present varied opinions, reason about, reason with, recite, review, speak of, speak on, take into account, take up in conference, talk about, talk it over, talk of, talk out, talk over, talk together
ASSOCIATED CONCEPTS: confidential information, privileged information

DISCUSSION, ***noun*** analysis, argument, banter, briefing, colloquy, confab, confabulation, conference, consideration, consultation, contention, controversy, debate, deliberation, dialogue, discourse, dispute, dissection of issues, examination, exchange, excursus, forum, huddle, meeting, palaver, parley, prattle, reception, review, roundtable, scrutiny, session, symposium, talk, update, ventilation of issues

ASSOCIATED CONCEPTS: conferencing a case, entering into settlement negotiations

DISDAIN, ***noun*** abhorrence, abjuration, abnegation, act of despising, act of discrediting, act of loathing, act of scorning, act of shunning, act of spurning, act of taunting, airs, arrogance, contempt, *contemptio,* contemptuousness, contumeliousness, declination, denial, derision, detestation, detraction, disapprobation, disapproval, disavowal, disclamation, discountenancing, disesteem, disfavor, dislike, disownment, disregard, disrespect, *fastidium,* haughtiness, haughty contempt, haughty indifference, *hauteur,* icy aloofness, indignant aversion, insolence, nonacceptance, nonrecognition, opprobrium, proud contempt, rebuff, rejection, renunciation, reprobation, repudiation, repulse, repulsion, revilement, scoff, scorn, scornfulness, scorning, sneer, spurning, superciliousness, supreme contempt, unutterable contempt, utter contempt

DISDAIN, ***verb*** abhor, *aspernari,* avoid, be contemptuous of, belittle, brush aside, care nothing for, consider beneath notice, consider beneath oneself, consider unworthy of regard, contemn, decline, decry, deem unbecoming, deem unsuitable, deride, *despicere,* despise, detest, disavow, discard, disclaim, disesteem, disown, disparage, disregard, esteem of no account, esteem of small account, *fastidire,* feel contempt for, feel utter contempt for, flout, gibe, have no use for, hold cheap, hold in contempt, ignore, jeer, laugh at, loathe, look down on, look with scorn on, misprize, mock, not accept, not consider, not respect, pass by, pass over, rebuff, recoil from with pride, regard with proud contempt, reject, renounce, repudiate, repulse, ridicule, scoff, scorn, shun, slight, sneer at, snub, *spernere,* spurn, think nothing of, think unworthy of notice, treat with contempt, turn one's back upon, turn to scorn, view with a scornful eye

DISDAINFUL, ***adjective*** aloof, arrogant, audacious, bumptious, cavalier, cold, condescending, contemptuous, contumelious, cynical, deprecating, derisive, despising, disapproving, discourteous, disrespectful, distant, *fastidiosus,* filled with pride, flouting, full of contempt, haughty, high, icy, imperious, indifferent, indignant, insolent, insulting, intolerant, jeering, lordly, mocking, overbearing, overweening, proud, ridiculing, rude, sardonic, scornful, sneering, snobbish, snobby, snooty, supercilious, superior, unapproachable, uncivil, unmannerly, unsociable

DISEASE, ***noun*** affliction, ailment, attack, bodily deviation from health, bout of sickness, breakdown, chronic disability, collapse, condition, contagion, defect, deterioration, disability, discomfort, disorder, distemper, epidemic, handicap, ill health, illness, indisposition, infection, infirmity, insalubrity, invalidism, loss of health, malady, *morbus,* physical derangement, plague, scourge, sickness, taint, unhealthiness, unsoundness, unwholesome condition, virus, weakness

DISENCUMBER, ***verb*** alleviate, cast off, clear, clear away, deliver from a hindrance, disburden, disembroil, disengage, disentail, disentangle, disjoin, ease, ease the burden, emancipate, exonerate, extract, extricate, free, free from encumbrance, liberate, lighten the labor, loose, loosen, release, relieve, remove, remove a hindrance, remove a restraint, remove an impediment, rescue, save from, set at large, set free, unbar, unbind, unburden, unchain, unclog, unfasten, unfetter, unhamper, unharness, unload, unlock, unloose, unshackle, untie, untrammel, unyoke

DISENDOW, ***verb*** confiscate, cut off, denude, deprive, dethrone, discrown, disentitle, disinherit, disown, dispossess, divest, expropriate, strip, uncrown, unsaddle, unseat, wrest from

DISENGAGE, ***verb*** *avocare,* become detached, break the connection with, cut loose, cut off, decontrol, deliver, detach, disconnect, disembroil, disencumber, disentangle, disenthrall, disjoin, dislodge, dispart, displant, dissever, dissociate, disunite, divorce, draw off, emancipate, expedire, extricate, free, free from engagement, free from pledge, free from vow, let out, *liberare,* liberate, liberate from connection, lift controls, loose, make free, manumit, part, release, release from attachment, relieve of obligation, separate, set at liberty, set free, sever, *solvere,* sunder, unattach, unbar, unbind, unbolt, unbuckle, unchain, unclasp, undo, unfasten, unfetter, unfix, unglue, unhamper, unhitch, unhook, unknot, unlace, unlatch, unlock, unloose, unpin, unravel, unscrew, unshackle, unsnap, unstick, unstrap, untie, withdraw

DISENTANGLE, ***verb*** arrange, clear, detach, disburden, disconnect, disembroil, disencumber, disengage, disinvolve, disjoin, ease, *expedire, explicare, exsolvere,* extricate, free, liberate, loosen, methodize, organize, release, relieve, relieve of complication, separate, set free, straighten out, unfasten, unfetter, unhamper, unknot, unloose, unravel, untie, untwist

DISENTHRALL, ***verb*** bail out, deliver, deliver from bondage, discharge, disengage, emancipate, enfranchise, extricate, free, free from bondage, free from thralldom, give liberty to, let go, let loose, let out, let out of prison, liberate, liberate from oppression, loosen, make free, manumit, redeem, release, release from bondage, release from restraint, render free, rescue, rescue from imprisonment, rescue from oppression, rescue from slavery, set at large, set at liberty, set free, turn loose, unbar, unbind, unchain, unfetter, unlock, unmanacle, unshackle, untie
ASSOCIATED CONCEPTS: Emancipation Proclamation

DISFAVOR, ***verb*** avoid, be loath, deny respect, despise, disaffect, disapprove, discountenance, discredit, disdain, dishonor, dislike, disregard, disrespect, frown on, have no regard for, have no respect for, have no use for, hold cheap, *invidia,* look askance at, look down on, misprize, not care for, not like, not respect, object to, *offensa,* rebuff, regard unfavorably, reject, repel, repulse, turn away, turn from, view with disfavor

DISFRANCHISE, ***verb*** deprive, forfeit, illegalize, limit, make illegitimate, outlaw, prohibit, restrict

DISGRACE, ***noun*** abasement, abjectness, abomination, attaint, bad character, bad name, bad report, bad reputation, bad repute, badge of infamy, baseness, blemish, blot, brand, cause of reproach, cause of shame, comedown, condition of infamy, contempt, debasement, defame, defilement, deflation, degradation, derogation, detestation, deviation from rectitude, disapprobation, disapproval, discredit, disesteem, disfavor, dishonor, disparagement, disreputability, disrepute, disrespect, embarrassment, exclusion from favor, humbled pride, humbling, humiliation, *ignominia,* ignominy, ill favor, ill repute, imputation, indignity, *infamia,* infamy, ingloriousness, loss of honor, loss of reputation, mortification, notoriety, obloquy, odium, opprobrium, reproach, scandal, sense of shame, setdown, shame, shamefacedness, shameful notoriety, slur, smear, smirch, stain, stigma, taint, tarnish, tarnished honor, *turpitudo*
ASSOCIATED CONCEPTS: character evidence, reputation

DISGRACE, ***verb*** abase, abash, affect dishonorably, attaint, be a reproach to, be unable to respect, besmear, blacken, blot, brand, bring down, bring into discredit, bring reproach upon, bring shame upon, cast a slur upon, cast dishonor upon, cast reproach upon, corrupt, debase, debunk, *dedecorare, dedecori esse,* defile, deflate, defrock, degrade, *dehonestare,* demean, demoralize, deny respect, depress, deride, derogate, diminish, disbar, discredit, dishonor, dismiss from favor, disrespect, downgrade, embarrass, fling dishonor upon, have no respect for, hold up to shame, humiliate, impute shame to, involve in shame, lower, make unclean, mock, mortify, pillory, pollute, reflect discredit upon, reflect dishonor upon, reflect shame upon, ridicule, scandalize, shame, slur, smirch, soil, stain, stigmatize, sully, taint, tarnish, throw dishonor upon, treat with disfavor

DISGRACEFUL, ***adjective*** abominable, atrocious, base, beneath one's dignity, blameworthy, censurable, compromising, contemptible, damaging, deflated, degrading, demeaning, demoralizing, deplorable, derogatory, deserving reproach, despicable, detestable, discreditable, dishonest, dishonorable, disreputable, *flagitiosus,* flagitious, flagrant, foul, heinous, horrible, humiliating, humiliative, ignoble, ignominious, improper, indecent, infamous, inglorious, *inhonestus,* iniquitous, odious, opprobrious, outrageous, peccant, *probrosus,* recreant, reprobate, scandalous, shameful, shocking, sinful, tarnished, *turpis,* unseemly, unworthy, vile, worthy of contempt

DISGUISE, ***noun*** artifice, camouflage, caricature, cloak, concealment, counterfeit, cover, covering, deception, deceptive covering, dissimulation, facade, faking, false appearance, false colors, false copy, false front, guise, hiding, imitation, mask, masquerade, pose, posture, pretense, pretension, pretext, representation, screen, semblance, sham, shield, *simulacrum, simulatio,* simulation, smoke screen, veneer, *vestis mutata*

DISGUISE, ***verb*** alter the appearance of, becloud, belie, bemask, camouflage, change the appearance of, change the face of, change the guise of, cloak, conceal, counterfeit, cover, curtain, deceive, dissemble, dissimulate, distort, dress to conceal, dress up, fake, falsify, feign, give a false coloring, give color to, hide, hide one's identity, make unrecognizable, mask, masquerade, misrepresent, muffle, obscure, *occultare,* pass off for, put a false appearance upon, *rem dissimulare,* screen, shield, shroud, simulate, veil

DISGUSTING, ***adjective*** abhorrent, abominable, appalling, atrocious, awful, barbarous, contemptible, despicable, detestable, distasteful, disturbing, dreadful, foul, fulsome, ghastly, grisly, gross, heinous, hideous, horrendous, horrible, horrid, horrific, loathsome, miserable, nasty, nightmarish, noisome, noxious, obnoxious, obscene, odious, offensive, rancid, repellent, repugnant, repulsive, revolting, sick, sickening, terrible, ugly, undesirable, unsavory, unspeakable, unwholesome, upsetting, vile

DISHARMONY, ***noun*** animosity, antagonism, argument, bickering, brawl, clash, conflict, contention, contest, controversy, disaccord, disagreement, discord, discordance, dissension, dissent, dissidence, dissonance, disunion, division, friction, incompatibility, incongruity, infighting, inharmoniousness, schism, strife

DISHONEST, ***adjective*** beguiling, bogus, cheating, conniving, conscienceless, contrary to fact, corrupt, corruptible, counterfeit, cunning, deceitful, deceiving, deceptive, delusive, delusory, designing, destitute of good faith, destitute of integrity, devoid of truth, discreditable, dishonorable, disingenuous, disposed to cheat, disreputable, double-dealing, faithless, fake, faked, fallacious, false, false-hearted, falsified, feigned, fraudulent, *fraudulentus,* guileful, hypocritical, immoral, *improbus,* iniquitous, insidious, insincere, lying, *malus,* meretricious, misleading, nefarious, not honest, not true, perfidious, perjured, scheming, shameless, shifty, spurious, surreptitious, treacherous, truthless, unauthentic, undependable, underhanded, unethical, unfaithful, ungenuine, unprincipled, unreal, unreliable, unscrupulous, untrue, untrustworthy, untruthful, unveracious, unvirtuous, void of truth, wanting in probity, without probity, without truth
ASSOCIATED CONCEPTS: dishonest act, dishonest practice, fraudulent or dishonest acts

DISHONESTY, ***noun*** bad faith, cheating, chicane, chicanery, corruption, corruptness, cozenage, deceit, deceitfulness, deception, deviation from probity, dishonor, disingenuousness, disposition to deceive, disposition to defraud, disposition to lie, duplicity, faithlessness, false swearing, falseheartedness, falsehood, falseness, falsification, falsity, fraudulence, fraudulency, *fraus,* furtiveness, *improbitas,* improbity, infidelity, insincerity, inveracity, knavery, knavishness, lack of conscience, lack of honesty, lack of integrity, lack of principle, lack of probity, lying, mendaciousness, mendacity, perfidiousness, perfidy, perjury, prevarication, surreptitiousness, thievishness, treacherousness, trickiness, truthlessness, undependability, underhand dealing, underhandedness, unreliability, unscrupulousness, unstraightforwardness, untrustworthiness, untruth, untruthfulness, violation of trust, want of integrity, wiliness
ASSOCIATED CONCEPTS: criminal acts, dishonest acts, fraudu-lent acts

DISHONOR *(Nonpayment),* ***noun*** breach of faith, breach of promise, declination, default, delinquency, disregard, failure, improbity, inability to pay, inattention, inobservance, insolvency, nonacceptance, nonadherence, noncompletion, noncompliance, nonfeasance, nonfulfillment, nonobservance, nonpayment at maturity, omission, refusal to accept, refusal to pay, rejection, repudiation of payment
ASSOCIATED CONCEPTS: dishonor of checks, dishonor of negotiated instruments, notice of dishonor

DISHONOR *(Shame),* ***noun*** abasement, abjection, abjectness, aspersion, attaint, bad character, bad favor, bad name, bad reputation, bad repute, badge of infamy, baseness, blemish, blot, brand, calumny, contempt, contumely, debasement, decrial, defamation, defilement, degradation, depravity, derogation, detraction, deviation from rectitude, disapprobation, discredit, disesteem, disfavor, disgrace, disparagement, disreputability, disrepute, disrespect, humiliation, ignobility, *ignominia,* ignominy, ill fame, ill favor, illrepute, improbity, imputation, indignity, *infamia,* infamy, ingloriousness, lack of conscience, lack of honor, lack of principle, lack of probity, loss of reputation, low estimation, mockery, no repute, no standing, notoriety, obloquy, opprobrium, outrage, public disgrace, reproach, ridicule, scandal, scorn, shamefulness, slur, smear, stain, stigma, taint, tarnish, tarnished honor, traducement, turpitude, *turpitudo,* vileness, vilification, wickedness

DISHONOR *(Deprive of honor),* ***verb*** abase, asperse, attaint, besmear, besmirch, blot, brand, bring into discredit, bring shame upon, cast a slur on, cast aspersions, cast reproach upon, contemn, debase, debauch, *dedecorare,* defame, defile, deflower, degrade, *dehonestare,* denigrate, denounce, deride, desecrate, despise, discredit, disgrace, disparage, expose, malign, pillory, reflect discredit upon, reproach, slur, smear, smirch, speak ill of, stain, stigmatize, *stuprare,* taint, tarnish, vilify

DISHONOR *(Refuse to pay),* ***verb*** decline to pay, decline to redeem, disallow payment, disregard, evade, not observe, not pay, refuse payment, refuse to honor, repudiate, stop payment, withhold payment
ASSOCIATED CONCEPTS: dishonor a check, notice of dishonor

DISHONORABLE, ***adjective*** abhorrent, abominable, bad, base, blameworthy, censurable, contemptible, corrupt, cruel, currish, debased, degenerate, despicable, detestable, discreditable, disgraceful, disreputable, disrespectful, execrable, ignominious, immoral, infamous, inglorious, iniquitous, loose, louche, low, low-down, nefarious, offensive, opprobrious, paltry, perverted, reprehensible, reprobate, seamy, shady, shameful, snide, sordid, unsavory, unscrupulous, unworthy, vile, villainous, wicked miscreant, wretched

DISINCENTIVE, ***noun*** averseness, check, constraint, curb, damper, determent, deterrence, deterrent, discouragement, disinclination, dissuasion, hindrance, indisposition, lack of allurement, lack of charm, lack of desire, lack of enticement, lack of impetus, lack of incentive, lack of inducement, lack of motivation, lack of stimulus, lack of temptation, reluctance, restraint, unprovocativeness, unwillingness

DISINCLINED, ***adjective*** adverse, against, antagonistic, antipathetic, antipathetical, averse, *aversus,* balking, contrary, counter, demurring, disaffected, dissenting, dissident, faltering, grudging, hesitant, indisposed, laggard, loath, noncooperating, not in the mood, opposed, qualmish, recalcitrant, refusing, reluctant, restive, shirking, shrinking from, slow to, squeamish, unaccommodating, unconsenting, uncooperative, unenthusiastic, uninclined, unpersuadable, unpersuaded, unreconciled, unwilling, unzealous

DISINGENUOUS, ***adjective*** artful, artificial, conscienceless, counterfeit, crafty, cunning, deceitful, deceiving, deceptive, delusive, delusory, designing, devious, dishonest, dodging, evasive, false, false-hearted, feigned, fraudulent, hypocritical, insidious, insincere, lacking frankness, lying, mendacious, misdealing, misleading, *parum candidus,* perfidious, prevaricating, scheming, shifty, sly, spurious, surreptitious, tricky, truthless, uncandid, underhanded, unethical, ungenuine, unprincipled, unscrupulous, unstraightforward, untrustworthy, untruthful, wanting in candor, wily, without truth

DISINHERIT, ***verb*** abandon, abrogate, annul, cast out, cut off, cut off from inheritance, cut out of one's will, deprive, deprive of hereditary succession, disaffirm, discard, disclaim, disendow, disentitle, disherit, disown, dispossess of hereditary right, divest, exclude from inheritance, *exheredare,* forfeit, forsake, nullify, oust, quash, recall, recant, renounce, replace, repudiate, rescind, retract, revoke, supersede, take away from, turn out, withdraw, withhold
ASSOCIATED CONCEPTS: disinherit a husband, disinherit a wife, disinherit an adopted child, disinherit pretermitted children

DISINTEGRATE, ***verb*** break up, crumble, decay, decompose, diffuse, disband, disperse, dissolve, disunite, fall to pieces, fragment, shatter, split up

DISINTER, ***verb*** bare, bring from obscurity into view, bring out, deracinate, detect, dig out, dig up, dig up out of the earth, discover, disentomb, disinhume, display, draw forth, draw out, educe, *effodere,* elicit, evince, evoke, evulse, excavate, exhibit, exhume, expose, expose to view, extract, extricate, ferret out, find, find out, lay open, make known, manifest, present to view, pull out, pull up, remove, resurrect, reveal, root out, root up, show, take out of the place of interment, turn up, unbury, uncover, unearth, unroot, unsepulcher, untomb, unveil, withdraw

DISINTEREST *(Lack of interest),* ***noun*** aloofness, apathy, boredom, callousness, carelessness, coolness, detachment, disdain, disinterestedness, disregard, heedlessness, inappetance, inappetancy, inattention, inattentiveness, inconsideration, incuriosity, incuriousness, indifference, insensitivity, insouciance, lack of attention, lack of concern, langour, languidness, laxity, listlessness, mindlessness, neglect, neglectfulness, negligence, nonchalance, noninvolvement, obliviousness, perfunctoriness, phlegm, pococurantism, spiritlessness, supineness, tepidity, thoughtlessness, unconcern, unmindfulness, unsolicitousness, want of attention, want of interest

DISINTEREST *(Lack of prejudice),* ***noun*** broadmindedness, candor, catholicity, detachment, dispassion, dispassionateness, equitableness, equity, evenhandedness, fair play, fair treatment, fairness, freedom from bias, freedom from prejudice, freedom from self-interest, impartiality, impartialness, impersonality, indiscrimination, justice, justness, liberality, neutrality, noninvolvement, nonpartisanship, objectivity, open-mindedness, tolerance, toleration, unbiasedness, unprejudice, unselfishness, unslantedness
ASSOCIATED CONCEPTS: disinterested judge, disinterested party, disinterested persons, disinterested witness, without pecuniary interest

DISINVOLVE, ***verb*** clear, disconnect, disembarrass, disentangle, disjoin, extricate, loosen, separate, unbind, unfold, unknot, unravel, unscramble, untangle, untie

DISJOIN, ***verb*** break, cut, cut off, demobilize, depart, detach, dichotomize, disband, disconnect, discontinue, disembody, disencumber, disengage, disentangle, disjoint, dislocate, dismember, dispart, dissect, dissociate, disunite, divide, divorce, excise, extricate, free, insulate, interrupt, isolate, keep apart, loosen, luxate, part, partition, quarter, remove, rend, rive, rupture, segregate, separate, sever, split, subdivide, uncouple, unhitch, unplug

DISJOINT, ***adjective*** apart, detached, disassembled, disassociated, disconnected, disengaged, disjunct, dismantled, displaced, dissected, disunited, divaricated, divided, far between, in two, isolated, removed, rent, riven, sectioned, separate, separated, severed, split, subdivided, sundered, unassociated, unattached, unconnected, unhinged, unjoined, unloosened

DISJOINT, ***verb*** break apart, break up, carve, cleave, cut up, detach, disarticulate, disassemble, disassociate, disband, disconnect, disengage, disjoin, dislocate, dismantle, dismember, dispart, displace, dissect, dissever, dissociate, disunite, divaricate, divide, divorce, luxate, part, quarter, rend, rive, section, segment, separate, sever, split, subdivide, sunder, take apart, tear apart, uncouple, unfasten, unhinge, unjoint, unloosen

DISJOINTED, ***adjective*** aimless, confused, deranged, desultory, disarranged, disassociated, discerpted, discordant, disjunctive, disordered, disorderly, disorganized, erratic, in disarray, in disorder, incoherent, *incompositus,* incongruent, incongruous, indiscriminate, interrupted, jumbled, lacking order, nonuniform, orderless, out of order, spasmodic, unclassified, uncohesive, unsorted, unsuccessive, unsystematic

DISJUNCTIVE *(Alternative),* ***adjective*** alternate, discretional, discretionary, elective, equivalent, having the privilege to choose, interchangeable, noncompulsory, nonobligatory, not compulsory, open to choice, optional, selective, subject to preference, substitute, substitutional, substitutive
ASSOCIATED CONCEPTS: disjunctive allegations, disjunctive covenants, disjunctive relief, disjunctive words of a statute

DISJUNCTIVE *(Tending to disjoin),* ***adjective*** broken, desultory, detached, disarticulated, disconnected, discrete, disjoined, disjoint, disjointed, dismembered, distinct, disunited, divided, divorced, erratic, fitful, inconsistent, individual, insular, intermittent, intermitting, interrupted, irregular, isolated, loose, noncontinuous, not cohesive, not integrated, parted, partitioned, periodic, punctuated, separate, severed, spasmodic, successive, suspended, unannexed, unassociated, unconnected, unjoined, unsuccessive

DISLIKE, ***noun*** abhorrence, abomination, animosity, animus, antagonism, antipathy, aversion, contempt, detestation, disaffection, disapprobation, disapproval, discomfort, disdain, disfavor, disgust, disinclination, disparagement, displeasure, dissatisfaction, distaste, enmity, hatred, hostility, ill will, incompatibility, inimicality, intolerance, loathing, malevolence, malice, objection, odium, prejudice, rancor, rejection, reluctance, renitence, repugnance, repulsion, revulsion, umbrage, unfriendliness, unwillingness

DISLIKE, ***verb*** abhor, abominate, antipathize, condemn, deprecate, detest, disapprove, discountenance, disesteem, disfavor, disrelish, distaste, execrate, loathe, mind, not care for, not like, object to, resent, scorn

DISLOCATE, ***verb*** agitate, cast out, complicate, confound, confuse, derail, derange, disarrange, disconnect, disjoin, disjoint, dislodge, disorder, disorganize, disorient, displace, disturb, disunite, eject, evacuate, evict, expel, luxate, mislay, misplace, move, oust, remove, scatter, throw into confusion, throw out of joint, throw out of order, unseat, unsettle, upset

DISLOCATION, ***noun*** change, derangement, disarticulation, disjunction, disorder, disorganization, displacement, disruption, disturbance, inconvenience, nonlocation, unsettledness, unsettlement, upheaval

DISLODGE, ***verb*** banish, carry off, cart away, cashier, cast out, *deicere,* delocalize, demote, *depellere,* deport, depose, deracinate, dethrone, detrude, disbar, discharge, disemploy, disenthrone, disestablish, dislocate, dismiss, displace, displant, dispossess, disturb, divest of office, eject, eliminate, evacuate, evict, exclude, exile, expatriate, expel, *expellere,* expropriate, extract, force out, lay off, oust, overthrow, push out, put out, relegate, remove, retire, rid, send away, supersede, supplant, take away, throw away, throw out, thrust out, turn out, unload, unseat, uproot, usurp

DISLOYAL, ***adjective*** anarchistic, apostate, canting, cheating, corrupt, crooked, deceitful, deceptive, defiant, disaffected, disobedient, double-crossing, faithless, false, faltering, fickle, inconstant, irresolute, irresponsible, misleading, perfidious, recreant, seditious, snaky, subversive, traitorous, treacherous, treasonable untrue, trustless, uncertain, undependable, unfaithful, unreliable, unscrupulous, untrue, untrustworthy, venal

DISLOYALTY, ***noun*** apostasy, barratry, betrayal, betrayal of trust, breach, breach of faith, breach of promise, breach of trust, broken promise, contumacy, defection, dereliction of allegiance, desertion, disobedience, faithlessness, falseness, falsity, fickleness, improbity, inconstancy, *infidelitas,* infidelity, insincerity, insubordination, insurgency, insurrection, lack of fidelity, lack of loyalty, malfeasance, mutineering, mutinousness, mutiny, perfidiousness, perfidy, rebellion, recreancy, revolt, sabotage, sedition, seditiousness, subversion, subversive activity, traitoriousness, treachery, treason, treasonable activities, unfaithfulness, unsteadfastness, venality, violation of allegiance, violation of trust, want of loyalty

DISMAL, ***adjective*** black, bleak, cheerless, cloudy, comfortless, dark, deplorable, depressing, despairing, despondent, dim, dingy, dire, disagreeable, disconsolate, dreary, dull, dusky, flat, foggy, gloomy, gray, joyless, lamentable, lifeless, lowering, lugubrious, obscure, overcast, pessimistic, sad, saturnine, shadowy, solemn, somber, sombrous, tedious, umbrageous, uncomfortable, unconsoling, unhappy, unilluminated, uninviting, unpleasant, unrelieved

DISMANTLE, ***verb*** annihilate, break down, break up, crush, decimate, demolish, demount, denude, destroy, detach, disaggregate, disconnect, disjoin, disjoint, dismember, dissemble, dissever, disunite, divide, extinguish, knock down, raze, ruin, separate, strike, strip, take apart, take down, undo

DISMAY, ***noun*** affright, agitation, alarm, anxiety, apprehension, chagrin, consternation, discomfort, discomposure, discouragement, disheartenment, disquiet, doubt, dread, fret, inquietude, intimidation, misgiving, mistrust, perturbation, pique, qualm, scare, shock, trepidation, uneasiness, worry

DISMAY, ***verb*** abash, aggravate, agitate, alarm, appall, bewilder, bother, confound, daunt, deter, discomfort, discompose, disconcert, discourage, disquiet, disturb, embarrass, harrow, horrify, intimidate, panic, perturb, startle, take aback, unnerve

DISMISS *(Discharge),* ***verb*** cashier, cast out, demobilize, depose, deprive of force, disemploy, dispatch, dispense with, displace, dispossess, eject, expel, fire, lay off, oust, purge, release, remove, remove from office, send away, send off, set free, suspend, turn away, turn out, unseat, vacate
ASSOCIATED CONCEPTS: dismiss a cause of action, dismissal because of laches, dismissed for cause, dismissed with prejudice, dismissed without prejudice, motion to dismiss, motion to dismiss for failure to state a claim, motion to dismiss for lack of jurisdiction, nonsuit

DISMISS *(Put out of consideration),* ***verb*** brush aside, decline, deny, disallow, disavow, discountenance, disregard, ignore, lay aside, not hear of, pass over, pay no regard to, put out of mind, refuse, reject, rule out, set aside, take no notice, think no more of

DISMISS CHARGES, ***verb*** absolve, acquit, clear, discharge, exculpate, exonerate, forgive, grant amnesty to, palliate, pardon, prove innocent, release, reprieve, restitute, vindicate

DISMISSAL *(Discharge),* ***noun*** cashiering, deposition, *dimissio,* discharge from employment, disemployment, dislodgment, displacement, ejection, elimination, exclusion, expulsion, firing, layoff, ouster, release from employment, removal from a job, removal from a position, removal from office, severance

DISMISSAL *(Termination of a proceeding),* ***noun*** annulment, cancellation, conclusion of a proceeding, conclusion of an action, discontinuance, disposal, ending of a proceeding, ending of an action, invalidation, nonsuit, quashing, rejection, removal of a cause out of court, termination of an action

ASSOCIATED CONCEPTS: dismissal for cause, dismissal for failure to prosecute, dismissal for want of jurisdiction, dismissal for want of substantial federal question, dismissal of a cause for want of prosecution, dismissal of a charge, dismissal of an action with prejudice, dismissal of an appeal, dismissal of an employee, dismissal of proceedings, dismissal on the merits, dismissal without prejudice

DISMISSED, ***adjective*** acquitted, clear, discarded, discharged, dispensed, exculpated, forgiven, free, obsolete, pardoned, rejected, released, vindicated

ASSOCIATED CONCEPTS: automatic dismissal, dismiss due to improper venue, dismiss for failure to answer, dismiss for improper parties, dismiss for insufficient evidence, dismiss for want of jurisdiction, dismiss for want of prosecution, dismissal with prejudice, dismissed case, dismissed case due to delay, dismissed charges, failure to prosecute, harmless error, involuntary dismissal, irregularities, judgment of dismissal, voluntary dismissal

DISOBEDIENT, ***adjective*** apostatizing, arbitrary, averse, contrary, contumacious, culpable, defiant, delinquent, derelict, disloyal, disorderly, disregarding, disrespectful, fractious, froward, headstrong, hostile, ill-behaved, incorrigible, indisposed, insubordinate, insurgent, insurrectional, intractable, irascible, irresponsible, lawbreaking, lawless, licentious, loath, misbehaving, mutinous, neglectful, negligent, *non obsequi,* noncompliant, obdurate, objecting, obstinate, obstreperous, opposed, opposing, perfidious, perverse, rebellious, recalcitrant, recusant, refractory, reluctant, remiss, renitent, resistant, resistive, restive, riotous, stubborn, traitorous, transgressive, treasonous, trespassing, truant, uncompliant, uncomplying, unconsenting, uncooperative, undependable, undisciplined, undutiful, unfaithful, ungovernable, unmanageable, unmindful, unreliable, unruly, unsubmissive, unwilling, unyielding, violating, violative, wayward, wild, willful

ASSOCIATED CONCEPTS: disobedience to lawful mandate of court, lawful disobedience, willful disobedience

DISOBEY, ***verb*** act illegally, arise, be derelict, be disloyal, be insubordinate, be mutinous, be negligent, be perfidious, be recalcitrant, be recusant, be treasonous, be undisciplined, be unruly, betray, break a law, break a rule, break the law, commit a crime, contravene, cross, defy, deviate, disregard, fail to comply, go counter to, ignore, infringe, insurrect, misbehave, mutiny, negate, neglect, not comply, not cooperate, not heed, not listen, not mind, not obey, oppose, pay no attention to, rebel, recalcitrate, refuse, refuse to obey, reject, repudiate, resist, revolt, revolutionize, rise, shirk, transgress, traverse, trespass, violate

ASSOCIATED CONCEPTS: disobedience, disobedience to a lawful mandate of the court, failure to comply, willful disobedience

DISOBLIGE, ***verb*** act contrary, affront, antagonize, balk, be unaccommodating, be unwilling, cause displeasure, debase, decline, degrade, demur, denigrate, denounce, deprecate, disaccommodate, discommode, disdain, dishonor, disparage, disregard, fail to accommodate, fail to comply with, give offense to, ignore, incommode, incur disapproval, insult, malign, maltreat, neglect to obey, not accept, not comply with, not obey, offend, *offendere,* put out, rebuff, refuse, refuse to oblige, reject, repel, repudiate, scorn, shrink, slight, spite, spurn, traduce, treat with indignity, turn down, vilipend, withhold consent

DISORDER *(Abnormal condition),* ***noun*** affliction, ailment, complaint, condition, disability, disease, distemper, handicap, illness, indisposition, infirmity, malady, malfunction, sickness

DISORDER *(Lack of order),* ***noun*** anarchism, anarchy, breach of peace, chaos, commotion, confusion, derangement, disarrangement, disarray, discomposure, disharmony, dishevelment, disorderly conduct, disorganization, disturbance, fracas, irregularity, lack of regular order, lawlessness, muddle, pandemonium, racket, riot, slipshodness, tumult, tumultuousness, turbulence, turmoil, unrest, uproar

ASSOCIATED CONCEPTS: breach of the peace, disorderly conduct

DISORDERED, ***adjective*** aberrant, abnormal, agitated, amiss, anarchical, anomalous, askew, atypical, awry, bedraggled, bemuddled, capricious, changeable, changeful, chaotic, confused, deviating, disarranged, discomposed, discontinuous, disheveled, disjunct, dislocated, disorganized, divergent, diverse, entangled, heterogeneous, illogical, immethodical, impetuous, in chaos, in disarray, in hysterics, incoherent, inconsistent, incontrollable, inverted, involved, jumbled, lawless, messy, nonuniform, not belonging, orderless, out of order, out of place, patternless, random, raveled, shapeless, tangled, tumultuary, tumultuous, turbulent, twisted, unarranged, unassembled, unclassified, uncoordinated, undisciplined, uneven, unkempt, unmanageable, unmethodical, unorganized, unpatterned, unruly, unsystematic, untidy, without method

DISORDERLY, ***adjective*** aberrant, aggressive, agitated, anarchic, anarchical, anarchistic, barbaric, barbarous, bellicose, blustering, blustery, boisterous, brutal, careless, churlish, confused, contumacious, defiant, deranged, destructive, disagreeable, disarranged, discomposed, discontinuous, discourteous, disgraceful, disheveled, disjointed, disobedient, disorganized, dissolute, disturbed, explosive, fitful, fluctuating, froward, heinous, ill-mannered, immethodical, immoderate, impolite, improper, incendiary, incorrigible, indecorous, inflammatory, insolent, insurrectionary, intemperate, irregular, lawbreaking, lawless, licentious, loud, mannerless, misbehaved, misbehaving, mutinous, nihilistic, nonobservant, obstreperous, orderless, out of order, outrageous, quarrelsome, rackety, raging, rampant, random, rebellious, recalcitrant, refractory, resisting, restive, revolutionary, riotous, rough, rowdy, rude, ruffianly, savage, scampish, scandalous, slovenly, stormy, strong, tangled, tempestuous, tumultuary, tumultuous, turbulent, unauthorized, unbridled, uncivil, uncivilized, uncommendable, uncontrolled, uncourtly, uncurbed, undisciplined, uneven,

ungenteel, ungentle, ungentlemanlike, ungentlemanly, ungoverned, unladylike, unmanageable, unmannered, unmannerly, unmethodical, unmitigated, unquelled, unregulated, unrepressed, unruly, unseemly, unsettled, unsteady, unsubmissive, unsystematic, untidy, untrained, uprisen, uproarious, violent, warlike, wayward, wild
ASSOCIATED CONCEPTS: breach of the peace, disorderly conduct, disorderly houses, disorderly persons, disturbance of the public peace

DISORGANIZE, ***verb*** abolish the organization of, agitate, bedevil, befog, befuddle, bewilder, bother, clutter, come to pieces, complicate, confound, *confundere,* confuse, daze, deactivate, decompose, deform, demobilize, deprive of organization, derange, destroy the form of, deteriorate, disarrange, disband, discompose, disconcert, dishevel, disintegrate, disjoin, dismantle, disorder, disorientate, dispel, disperse, disrupt, dissipate, dissolve, distract, disturb, embrangle, entangle, interrupt, invert, liquidate, make havoc, misarrange, *miscere,* misplace, muddle, obfuscate, obscure, perplex, perturb, *perturbare,* play havoc with, put out of order, ravel, render uncertain, revert, scatter, scramble, separate, tangle, tear up, throw into confusion, throw into disorder, throw out of order, tumble, twist, unbalance, undo, unmake, unsettle, upset

DISORIENT, ***verb*** abash, baffle, befuddle, bewilder, confound, dement, derange, disarrange, discompose, disconcert, dislocate, dislodge, disorder, disorganize, distract, disturb, fluster, impair, invert, make havoc, misdirect, mislay, mislead, misplace, muddle, mystify, nonplus, obfuscate, obscure, overturn, perturb, render uncertain, ruffle, scramble, throw into confusion, throw into disorder, throw out of order, trouble, unbalance, unsettle, upset

DISOWN *(Deny the validity),* ***verb*** abjure, abnegate, affirm the contrary, annul, call in question, challenge, confute, contest, contradict, contravene, controvert, countermand, demur, deny, deny absolutely, deny peremptorily, deny the possibility, deny wholly, disaffirm, disagree, disallow, disannul, disavow, disbelieve, disclaim, disprove, disregard, dissent, forswear, hold no brief for, impugn, *infitiari,* invalidate, negate, negative, not accept, not admit, not confirm, not maintain, nullify, object, oppose, overrule, protest, rebut, recant, refuse credence, refuse to accept, refuse to admit, refuse to corroborate, refute, reject, render null and void, *repudiare, repudiate,* rescind, retract, reverse, revoke, set aside, set at nought, stand up to, take issue with, traverse, undo, vacate, void

DISOWN *(Refuse to acknowledge),* ***verb*** abandon, abjure, alienate, cast away, cast off, cede, cut off, cut out of one's will, deprive of hereditary succession, deprive of the right to inherit, disaffiliate, disallow, disclaim, disclaim the responsibility for, disdain, disendow, disinherit, dispense with, dispossess, dispossess of hereditary right, dissociate oneself, divest, divorce, forsake, get rid of, give up, have nothing to do with, *infitiari,* jettison, let go, not maintain, oust, part with, rebuff, refuse to recognize, relinquish, renounce, *repudiare,* repudiate, repulse, scorn, spurn
ASSOCIATED CONCEPTS: disown a child

DISPARAGE, ***verb*** affront, asperse, be insolent, be rude, belittle, bemock, besmear, bespatter, blacken, blot, bring reproach upon, calumniate, cavil, censure, cheapen, condemn, contemn, criticize, debase, decry, defame, deflate, degrade, denigrate, depreciate, deride, derogate, detract, discount, discredit, disesteem, disfavor, disgrace, dishonor, disregard, disrespect, downgrade, *elevare, extenuare,* find fault with, frown upon, gibe, humiliate, imitate insultingly, insult, jeer, lampoon, laugh at, look down on, lower the estimation of, make fun of, make light of, make sport of, malign, minimize, misprize, mock, play down, reflect poorly upon, ridicule, run down, scoff, scorn, shame, slander, slight, slur, smear, sneer, speak ill of, stain, stigmatize, sully, taint, tarnish, taunt, think little of, traduce, underrate, undervalue, vilify, vilipend
ASSOCIATED CONCEPTS: disparage a name, disparage a product

DISPARAGEMENT, ***noun*** accusation, act of berating, act of running down, admonishment, adverse criticism, aspersion, bad review, belittlement, belittling, blame, brand, castigation, complaint, condemnation, confutation, contempt, criticism, damnation, decrial, denigration, *dénigrement,* denouncement, denunciation, deprecation, depreciation, derogation, destructive criticism, detraction, disapprobation, disapproval, discontent, discourtesy, disesteem, disfavor, dishonor, disillusionment, dislike, displeasure, disrepute, disrespect, disrespectfulness, exception, faultfinding, hostile criticism, hypercriticism, impeachment, impugnation, imputation, indignation, insinuation, invective, irreverence, low estimation, low opinion, low valuation, mockery, muckraking, nonapproval, objection, objuration, obloquy, *obtrectatio,* outcry, overcriticalness, poor opinion, protest, rebuke, rejection, reprehension, reprimand, reproach, reprobation, reproof, revilement, ridicule, rude reproach, rudeness, scant respect, scolding, scorn, slighting language, stigma, tirade, uncomplimentary remark, vilification, vilipendency, vituperation, want of respect
ASSOCIATED CONCEPTS: disparagement of goods, disparagement of property, disparagement of title

DISPARAGING, ***adjective*** abusive, blameful, calumnious, censorious, condemnatory, contemptuous, contumelious, damnatory, defamatory, denunciatory, deprecative, derogatory, detractory, disrespectful, incriminatory, inculpatory, injurious, invective, inveighing, libelous, maledictory, objurgatory, pejorative, reproachful, reprobative, reviling, scandalous, scurrile, scurrilous, slanderous, unfavorable, vilifying, vituperative
ASSOCIATED CONCEPTS: disparagement of goods, disparagement of name, disparagement of products, libel, slander

DISPARATE, ***adjective*** aberrant, atypical, clashing, conflicting, contradictory, contrasting, departing from, deviating, different, differentiated, differing, digressive, disagreeing, discordant, discrepant, disproportionate, dissimilar, distinct, distinguished, divaricating, divergent, essentially different, ill-matched, incommensurable, incongruent, incongruous, inconsistent, inconsonant, independent, irreconcilable, irregular, nonuniform, not comparable, not the same, out of proportion, separate, unconformable, unequal, uneven, unlike, unmatched, varied
ASSOCIATED CONCEPTS: disparate award, disparate relief

DISPARITY, ***noun*** argument, asymmetry, conflict of opinion, contradiction, contradistinction, contraposition, contrast, controversy, deviation, difference, disaccord, disagreement, discord, discordance, discrepancy, disequilibrium, disharmony, dissimilitude, *dissimilitudo,* dissonance, disunity, divergence, diversity, failure to agree, imbalance, incommensurability, incompatibility, incongruence, incongruity, inequality, inharmoniousness, irreconcilability, irrelation, lack of relation, lack of symmetry, nonagreement, nonconformity, nonuniformity, unconformity, unlikeness, variance, variation

DISPASSIONATE, *adjective* aloof, ascetic, *blasé,* calm, *calme,* cold, cold-blooded, cold-hearted, collected, composed, controlled, cool-headed, detached, disengaged, disinterested, even-handed, even-tempered, fair, heartless, immovable, impartial, impassive, impersonal, imperturbable, indifferent, inexcitable, inscrutable, neutral, nonchalant, objective, open-minded, passionless, peaceful, phlegmatic, placatus, placidus, sangfroid, self-controlled, selfless, steady, stoical, stolid, subdued, temperate, tolerant, tranquil, *tranquillus,* unaffected, unbiased, uncorrupted, undemonstrative, undisturbed, unemotional, unexcited, unfeeling, ungrudging, unimpassioned, unimpressible, unimpressionable, uninfluenced, uninvolved, unirritable, unjealous, unmindful, unnervous, unoffended, unpassionate, unperturbed, unprejudiced, unprepossessed, unresponsive, unruffled, unsentimental, unshaken, unstirred, unsusceptible, unswayed, untouchable, without nerves, without warmth

DISPATCH *(Act of putting to death),* ***noun*** act of killing, act of slaying, assassination, bloodshed, death by violence, deathblow, destruction, disposal, doing away with, execution, extermination, homicide, killing, liquidation, massacre, murder

DISPATCH *(Message),* ***noun*** aviso, bulletin, circular, communication, *communiqué,* correspondence, enlightenment, epistle, *epistula,* information, instruction, letter, *litterae,* mail, missive, monition, news, note, notice, notification, official correspondence, postal communication, report, statement, stream of correspondence, telegram

DISPATCH *(Promptness),* ***noun*** alacrity, briskness, bustle, celerity, dash, *dépêche, diligence,* excitation, expeditiousness, expedition, expeditious performance, fast rate, fastness, *festinatio,* feverish haste, flurry, haste, hastiness, hurry, immediateness, impetuosity, inability to wait, instantaneity, liveliness, lively pace, movement, nimbleness, precipitance, precipitancy, precipitation, precipitousness, *promptitude, properatio,* punctuality, punctualness, quick discharge, quick riddance, quickness, rapidity, readiness, rush, scramble, scurry, speed, speediness, speedy completion, speedy disposition, speedy transaction, spurt, suddenness, summariness, swift execution, swift rate, timeliness, urgency
ASSOCIATED CONCEPTS: with all possible dispatch

DISPATCH *(Dispose of),* ***verb*** accomplish, achieve, attain, bring about, bring off, bring to a conclusion, bring to an end, bring to pass, carry out, carry through, carry to completion, close, complete, conclude, *conficere,* consummate, deal with definitely, do the deed, effect, effectuate, execute, finish, fulfill, implement, make an end of, make final disposition of, *perficere,* perform, realize, see through, set at rest, succeed, work out

DISPATCH *(Put to death),* ***verb*** assassinate, bring down, commit murder, *coup de grâce,* cut down, deal a deathblow, deprive of life, destroy, dispose of, do away with, end, end life, execute, exterminate, give the deathblow, hasten one's end, *interficere, interimere,* kill, liquidate, make away with, massacre, murder, put an end to, put down, put out of the way, put to death, remove from life, slaughter, slay, take life, take one's life away

DISPATCH *(Send off),* ***verb*** address, detail, direct, expedite, fling, forward, get under way, hasten, hasten on, have conveyed, hurry, hurry along, hurry on, impart motion, impel, *mittere,* mobilize, move on, post, propel, push, push through, put in motion, remit, rush, rush off, send, send away, send forth, send through the mail, set going, ship, speed, speed along, speed on its way, transfer, transmit
ASSOCIATED CONCEPTS: with all due dispatch

DISPEL, *verb* banish, bestow, bestrew, break up, broadcast, cast adrift, cast off, cast out, deal out, diffuse, discharge, *discutere,* disintegrate, dismiss, *dispellere,* disperse, disperse completely, disseminate, *dissipare,* dissipate, dissolve, do away with, drive away, drive away by scattering, drive off in various directions, eject, expel, fling off, get rid of, loose, push away, put into circulation, radiate, release, remove, rout, scatter, send, send flying, send home, set abroach, set aside, set asunder, shake off, spread, strew, string out, throw away, throw off, turn adrift, utterly disperse
ASSOCIATED CONCEPTS: dispel an inference

DISPENSABLE, *adjective* disposable, excusable, expendable, extraneous, futile, gratuitous, in excess, inconsequential, ineffectual, minor, needless, negligible, nonessential, of no avail, otiose, pardonable, petty, redundant, replaceable, severable, sparable, spendable, superfluous, supernumerary, unavailing, unessential, unimportant, unnecessary, unrequired

DISPENSATION *(Act of dispensing),* ***noun*** accommodation, administration, allocation, allotment, appointment, apportionment, assignment, bestowal, bestowment, conferment, conferral, dispersal, dispersion, disposal, disposition, dissemination, distribution, division, fair sharing, impartation, impartment, issuance, partition, presentation, presentment, provision, repartition, share, subvention, transfer

DISPENSATION *(Exception),* ***noun*** absolution, acquiescence, allowance, amnesty, approval, authorization, *carte blanche,* certificate of exemption, clearance, *congé,* consent, deliberate omission, escape clause, exception, exception in favor of, exclusion, exculpation, excuse, exemption, exemption from law, exoneration, forgiveness, freedom, grace, grant, immunity, indulgence, leave, liberty, license, noninclusion, nonliability, nonresponsibility, omission, pardon, permission, permit, privilege, relaxation of law, release from obligation, sanction, special privilege, sufferance, tolerance, toleration, warrant
ASSOCIATED CONCEPTS: concession, franchise, special dispensation

DISPENSE, *verb* administer, allocate, allot, appoint, apportion, appropriate, assign, bestow, bestow upon, confer, deal, deal to, detail, *dimittere,* dispense, disperse, dispose of, disseminate, *distribuere,* distribute, divide in portions, do away with, do without, dole out, donate, give out, grant, hand out, issue, mete, parcel out, portion out, proportionate, provide, ration, *re carere,* render, scatter, serve, share, tender
ASSOCIATED CONCEPTS: dispense with

DISPENSE WITH, *verb* abandon, abjure, abolish, abstain, cede, censor, disavow, disclaim, dismiss, disown, dispose of, do without, except, exclude, excuse, exempt, extinguish, forbear, forgo, forswear, give up, jettison, not use, pass over, refrain, refuse, relinquish, renounce, sell off, set aside, spare, waive, yield
ASSOCIATED CONCEPTS: dispense with the testimony

DISPERSE *(Disseminate),* ***verb*** administer, allocate, apportion, assign, bestow in shares, bestrew, cast forth, cast

off, circulate, consign, convey, deal, deal out, dispense, dispose, distribute, divide, dole, dole out, give away, give out among a number, issue, mete out, parcel out, partition, pass out, pay dividends, pay out, portion out, propagate, scatter abroad, spread, spread abroad, spread out, strew
ASSOCIATED CONCEPTS: disperse public information

DISPERSE *(Scatter),* ***verb*** asunder, decentralize, depart, diffuse, disband, disintegrate, disjoin, dispart, dispel, *dispellere, dispergere, dissipare,* dissipate, dissolve, disunite, divide, go different ways, go in different directions, go separate ways, part, partition, rend, rive, scatter abroad, separate, split up, spread widely

DISPERSION, ***noun*** allocation, decentralization, diffraction, diffusion, disjunction, dispensation, dispersal, dissemination, dissipation, distribution, divergence, division, emanation, parting, radiation, refraction, scattering, separation, spread

DISPLACE *(Remove),* ***verb*** banish, carry away, cart away, cast out, change the place of, clear away, convey, delocalize, deport, detach, discard, discharge, dislocate, dislodge, dismiss, dispatch, disperse, dispossess, disturb, eject, evict, exclude, exile, expatriate, expel, export, expropriate, *loco suo movere,* move, not retain, oust, purge, put out, send, send away, shift from its place, take away, throw out, transfer, turn out, unhouse, unjoint, unseat
ASSOCIATED CONCEPTS: displaced person, displaced worker

DISPLACE *(Replace),* ***verb*** act for, act the part of, answer for, change for, count for, double for, exchange, fill another's position, fill in for, interchange, make a shift with, make way for, offer in exchange, pass for, put in the place of, replace with, stand in for, substitute, succeed, supersede, supplant, switch, take another's place, take in exchange, take over another's duties, take the place of, transfer, transpose, understudy for

DISPLAY, ***verb*** brandish, bring to light, demonstrate, disclose, divulge, evidence, evince, exhibit, express, flaunt, flourish, illustrate, indicate, parade, present, reveal, show, wave

DISPLEASE, ***verb*** affront, agitate, anger, annoy, antagonize, bait, chafe, chagrin, disaffect, disappoint, discommode, discontent, disenchant, disgruntle, dishearten, dislike, disoblige, dissatisfy, disturb, embitter, exasperate, excite, fret, grate, harrow, harry, inflame, irritate, offend, pique, plague, provoke, repel, rile, sour, vex, worry

DISPLEASURE, ***noun*** antagonism, antipathy, censure, condemnation, criticism, denunciation, deprecation, disapprobation, discountenance, disesteem, disfavor, dislike, dispraise, distaste, objection, opposition, opprobrium, rejection, reprehension, reproach, reprobation

DISPOSABLE, ***adjective*** adaptable, advantageous, available, consumable, dispensable, employable, expendable, exploitable, fit for use, free for use, helpful, movable, of service, of use, on call, open to, pervious, procurable, reachable, ready for use, realizable, salable, securable, serviceable, spendable, suitable, to be had, usable, useful, utilitarian, utilizable, within reach
ASSOCIATED CONCEPTS: disposable assets

DISPOSE *(Apportion),* ***verb*** deal out, distribute, dole out, fix, mete out, parcel out, place

DISPOSE *(Incline),* ***verb*** affect, arrange, bend, bias, decide, determine, incline, induce, influence, put, sway, tend, verge
ASSOCIATED CONCEPTS: disposing mind and memory

DISPOSITION *(Determination),* ***noun*** adjustment, conclusion, decision, disposal, final settlement of a matter, finding, order, pronouncement, putting in order, resolution, settlement, solution
ASSOCIATED CONCEPTS: disposition of a case

DISPOSITION *(Final arrangement),* ***noun*** adjustment, administration, arrangement, array, *conlocatio,* control, direction, dispensation, disposal, *dispositio,* distribution, grouping, management, marshaling, method, order, ordering, *ordinatio,* organization, placement, regulation, settlement
ASSOCIATED CONCEPTS: conditional disposition, final disposition, fraudulent disposition, power of disposition, testimentary disposition
FOREIGN PHRASES: ***Cujus est dare, ejus est disponere.*** Whoever has the right of giving a thing, has the right of any disposition of it.

DISPOSITION *(Inclination),* ***noun*** aptitude, bent, bias, cast, character, characteristic, characteristic mood, constitution, frame of mind, grain, humor, idiosyncrasy, inclination, individualism, *indoles, ingenium,* leaning, liking, makeup, mental constitution, mold, mood, native character, *natura,* natural fitness, natural tendency, nature, penchant, personality, predilection, predisposition, preference, proclivity, proneness, propensity, spirit, temper, temperament, tendency, turn of mind
FOREIGN PHRASES: ***Impunitas continuum affectum tribuit delinquendi.*** Impunity confirms the disposition of a delinquent.

DISPOSITION *(Transfer of property),* ***noun*** alienation, arrangement for disposal, assignment, conveyance, conveyancing, deliverance, delivery, dispensation, disposal, distribution, giving, manner of disposal, release, relinquishment, relinquishment by gift, sale, surrender, transfer, transference, vouchsafement, yielding
ASSOCIATED CONCEPTS: dispose of and convey, disposition by will, final disposition, fraudulent disposition, power of disposition, sale or other disposition, testamentary disposition
FOREIGN PHRASES: ***Cujus est dare, ejus est disponere.*** He who has a right to give, has the right to dispose of the gift.

DISPOSSESS, ***verb*** cause to forfeit, declare forfeit, depose, deprive, deprive of occupancy, *deturbare,* disendow, disentitle, dislodge, displace, disseise, disseize, divest, eject from possession, evict, expel, expropriate, foreclose, oust, *possessione depellere,* relieve of, remove, turn out
ASSOCIATED CONCEPTS: dispossess a tenant, eviction, foreclosure, summary proceedings

DISPOSSESSION, ***noun*** abridgment, assumption, bereavement, condemnation, confiscation, dislodgment, disownment, disqualification, distrust, divestment, ejection, eviction, expropriation, expulsion, foreclosure, forfeiture, ouster, privation, removal, taking, usurpation
ASSOCIATED CONCEPTS: adverse possession, ejection, landlord-tenant, wrongful dispossession, wrongful eviction

DISPRAISE, ***noun*** blame, castigation, censure, condemnation, criticism, decrial, denunciation, depreciation, detraction, disapprobation, disapproval, discommendation, discredit, disgrace, dishonor, disparagement, dissatisfaction, disvaluation, ignominy, malediction, obloquy, onus, opprobrium, rebuke, reprimand, reprisal

DISPRAISE, ***verb*** blame, castigate, censure, condemn, criticize, damn, decry, defame, denounce, deprecate, depreciate, derogate, disapprove, discommend, discountenance, discredit, dishonor, disparage, disvalue, fault, inveigh, lessen, malign, reprimand, rebuke

DISPROPORTIONATE, ***adjective*** assymetrical, at odds, at variance, conflicting, contrary to reason, disaccordant, discordant, discrepant, disparate, divergent, excessive, ill-adapted, ill-matched, ill-proportioned, ill-sorted, ill-suited, illogical, *impar,* improperly proportioned, *inaequalis,* inapplicable, inapposite, inappropriate, incommensurable, incommensurate, incompatible, inconformable, incongruent, incongruous, inconsequent, inconsistent, inconsonant, infelicitous, inharmonious, inordinate, irrational, irreconcilable, lacking proportion, mismatched, not following, not in keeping, out of joint, out of keeping, out of place, out of proportion, overcharged, overmuch, poorly adapted, superfluous, too much, unapt, unbalanced, unbefitting, uncalled for, unconformable, undeserved, undeserving, undue, unequal, uneven, unfitting, unjustifiable, unreasonable, unseemly, unsuitable, unsymmetrical, untoward, unwarrantable, unwarranted, wanting in proportion
ASSOCIATED CONCEPTS: disproportionate penalty, disproportionate to the value, punishment disproportionate to the crime

DISPROVE, ***verb*** belie, confute, contravene, controvert, counteract, countervail, deny, discredit, dispel, find unfounded, invalidate, negate, nullify, oppugn, prove false, prove the contrary, prove to be wrong, prove to the contrary, rebut, *redarguere, refellere,* refute, show the fallacy of, show to be false, traverse

DISPUTABLE, ***adjective*** admitting of doubt, ambiguous, apocryphal, appealing to reason, arguable, arguing, argumentative, at issue, confutable, conjectural, contestable, controversial, controvertible, cryptic, debatable, deniable, disputatious, doubtable, doubtful, doubting, dubious, dubitable, dubitative, enigmatic, equivocal, eristic, fallible, hard to believe, hypothetical, improbable, in dispute, in doubt, in issue, in question, incredible, indefinite, indeterminate, *infamis,* not axiomatic, not to be believed, of doubtful certainty, open to debate, open to discussion, open to doubt, open to question, open to suspicion, paradoxical, perplexing, polemic, problematic, questionable, refutable, speculative, subject to argument, subject to controversy, suppositional, suspect, suspicious, theoretical, to be decided, unaffirmed, unascertained, unbelievable, uncertain, unconfirmed, undecided, undemonstrable, undemonstrated, under discussion, undetermined, unfixed, unknown, unlikely, unproven, unreliable, unresolved, unsettled, unsure, unsustainable, unsustained, unverifiable, vague
ASSOCIATED CONCEPTS: disputable presumption

DISPUTANT, ***noun*** adversary, adverse party, antagonist, argumentative person, assailant, belligerent, caviler, combatant, contender, contestant, controversialist, controvertist, discussant, dissenter, litigant, objector, obstructionist, opponent, opposer, oppositionist, polemicist, resister, rival, wrangler

DISPUTATIOUS, ***adjective*** argumentative, bickering, cantankerous, captious, competitive, contentious, contrary, controversial, debatable, dialectic, discordant, discrepant, disputable, disputative, dissenting, dissentious, divided, fractious, hostile, litigious, logomachical, moot, petulant, polemic, pugnacious, quarrelsome, querulous, remonstrative, schismatic, testy

DISPUTE, ***noun*** aggressive argument, *altercatio,* altercation, argument, bickering, challenge, clash of opinions, conflict, conflict of opinion, contention, *controversia,* controversy, debate, *démêlé,* difference, difference of opinion, disaccord, disagreement, *disceptatio,* discord, dissension, dissentience, dissidence, disturbance, disunity, divergence, divergent opinions, embranglement, embroilment, failure to agree, feud, imbroglio, impugnation, legal battle, litigation, nonagreement, opposition, polemic, remonstrance, remonstration, strife, variance, verbal contention, verbal controversy, verbal engagement, wrangle
ASSOCIATED CONCEPTS: amount in dispute, dispute as to the amount, dispute concerning terms or conditions of employment, jurisdictional dispute, labor dispute, matter in dispute, undisputed claim

DISPUTE *(Contest),* ***verb*** *altercari,* altercate, argue against, argue vehemently, be at cross purposes, be at variance, bring in question, call in question, challenge, clash, collide, combat, compete, conflict, confute, contend, contend for, contradict, contravene, controvert, deny, deny absolutely, deny emphatically, deny entirely, deny flatly, deny peremptorily, deny the genuineness of, differ, disagree with, dissent from, doubt, gainsay, give denial to, have a feud with, have an altercation, have differences, have words with, impugn, negative, not agree, object to, oppose by argument, quarrel over, query, question the truth of, recriminate, refute, *rixari,* strive against, struggle against, take exception, take issue with, traverse
ASSOCIATED CONCEPTS: disputed claim, disputed demand, disputed issue, disputed question of fact, disputed writing, labor dispute
FOREIGN PHRASES: ***Non est certandum de regulis juris.*** There is no disputing about rules of the law.

DISPUTE *(Debate),* ***verb*** *ambigere,* argue, argue a case, argue a point, argue in opposition, argufy, bandy words, be contrary, bicker, carry on an argument, confute, contend in argument, contradict, controvert, differ, disagree, discept, *disceptare, disputare,* dissent, divide on, have a verbal controversy over, hold an argument, indulge in argument, make a rejoinder, not agree, parry, rebut, refute, wrangle

DISPUTE RESOLUTION, ***noun*** alternative dispute resolution, judicial alternative, means to conclude an action, means to gain a decision, means to gain a determination, means to gain an outcome, means to obtain findings, means to resolve an action
ASSOCIATED CONCEPTS: alternative dispute resolution

DISPUTED POINT OF LAW, ***noun*** at issue, bone of contention, contention, debatable point, desideratum, development, difficulty, in question, issue, issue under consideration, matter in dispute, outgrowth, point, point in question, problem, question at issue, sticking point, under advisement, under examination

DISQUALIFICATION *(Factor that disqualifies),* ***noun*** defect, disability, disablement, failure, handicap, inability, inadequacy, inaptitude, incapability, incapacitation, incapacity, incompetence, incompetency, ineptitude, inexpertness, insufficiency, invalidation, invalidity, lack of dexterity, lack of proficiency, lack of qualification, shortcoming, unaptness, undeftness, undesirability, unfitness, unfittedness, unpreparedness, unproficiency, unqualifiedness, unskillfulness, unsuitability, want of ability, want of skill

DISQUALIFICATION *(Rejection),* ***noun*** banishment, deposal, deprivation, dethronement, disapprobation, disbarment, discharge, disentitlement, disfavor, disfranchisement, dislodgment, dismissal, displacement, dispossession, ejection, elimination, eviction, exclusion, expulsion, forfeiture, inadmissibility, ineligibility, invalidation, loss of right, nonadmission, noninclusion, ouster, preclusion, rejecting, rejection, repudiation, throwing out
ASSOCIATED CONCEPTS: disqualification to hold office, legal disqualification

DISQUALIFY, ***verb*** bar, block, check, counteract, debar, deny, deprive of power, disable, disarm, disenable, disentitle, disfranchise, dispossess of right, divest of right, *excipere,* exclude, incapacitate, inhibit, interfere, invalidate, make impossible, make useless, neutralize, preclude, prevent, prohibit, reject, render impotent, render unfit, restrain, restrict, rule out, stop, strip of right, undermine, unfit
ASSOCIATED CONCEPTS: disqualified for interest, disqualified to act, disqualifying interest, disqualifying opinion, permanently disqualified

DISQUIET, ***noun*** agitation, anarchy, anxiety, chaos, commotion, disconcert, disease, disorder, disruption, excitement, ferment, fermentation, inquietude, perturbation, restiveness, restlessness, tension, trouble, tumult, turbulence, turmoil, uneasiness, unsettlement, upheaval, uproar

DISREGARD *(Lack of respect),* ***noun*** affront, aloofness, bad manners, belittlement, callousness, contempt, contemptousness, contumely, depreciation, discourtesy, disdain, disesteem, disfavor, dishonor, disobedience, disregardfulness, disrespect, heedlessness, impoliteness, impudence, inappreciation, inattentiveness, incivility, inconsiderateness, inconsideration, indifference, insensitivity, insolence, insult, low estimation, outrage, regardlessness, rudeness, scoffing, scorn, slight, snub, thoughtlessness, underestimation, undervaluation, unheedfulness, unmindfulness, want of thought

DISREGARD *(Omission),* ***noun*** breach of orders, default, delinquency, dereliction of duty, disregardfulness, failure to carry out, infraction, infringement, malefaction, malpractice, misbehavior, misconduct, neglect, neglectfulness, noncompliance, nonobservance, preterition, pretermission, refusal to obey, regardlessness, remissness, transgression, trespass, violation

DISREGARD *(Unconcern),* ***noun*** carelessness, disinterest, disinterestedness, disregardfulness, exclusion, heedlessness, improvidence, imprudence, inattention, inattentiveness, incaution, inconsideration, indifference, inobservance, insouciance, lack of care, lack of consideration, lack of interest, lack of observation, leaving out, mindlessness, neglect, neglectfulness, negligence, nonobservance, oblivion, obliviousness, overlooking, oversight, regardlessness, unconsciousness, unheedfulness, unmindfulness, unthinkingness, unwariness, unwatchfulness, want of notice, want of thought

DISREGARD, ***verb*** be incurious, be indifferent, be insensitive, dismiss, fail to notice, fail to observe, feel no concern, give no heed, ignore, leave out, leave out of consideration, neglect, *neglegere,* not bother with, not consider, not hear, not heed, not include, not listen, not think about, not think of, not trouble oneself, *omittere,* overlook, *parvi facere,* pass by, pay no attention, pay no regard to, pretermit, refuse to hear, refuse to know, refuse to regard, snub, spurn, take no account of, take no interest, take no note of, take no notice of, think little of, think nothing of, treat without due respect
ASSOCIATED CONCEPTS: disregard for the law, instruct the jury to disregard testimony, reckless disregard

DISREPAIR, ***noun*** collapse, corrosion, damage, decadence, decadency, decay, decrepitude, degeneration, deterioration, dilapidation, impaired condition, impairment, lack of maintenance, neglect, ruination

DISREPUTABLE, ***adjective*** abominable, arrant, bad, base, beastly, being in ill repute, characterless, cheap, coarse, conscienceless, contemptible, corrupt, crass, degraded, demoralizing, deplorable, despicable, despised, detestable, devious, discreditable, discredited, disgraced, disgraceful, dishonest, dishonorable, disliked, disrespectable, dissolute, dreadful, foul, hateful, having a bad reputation, heinous, held in contempt, horrendous, horrid, ignoble, ignominious, immoral, improper, impure, in disgrace, indecent, indecorous, indelicate, inelegant, *infamis,* infamous, inglorious, iniquitous, insincere, knavish, licentious, loathsome, meretricious, misdealing, nefarious, not reputable, not respectable, not thought much of, notorious, objectionable, obnoxious, odious, of bad character, of ill fame, opprobrious, prevaricating, profligate, recreant, rejected, reprehensible, reproached, ribald, shameful, shameless, spurious, suspicious, tasteless, undignified, unethical, unprincipled, unrefined, unrespectable, unsavory, unscrupulous, untrustworthy, untruthful, unworthy

DISREPUTE, ***noun*** abasement, abjectness, abominableness, bad character, bad reputation, bad repute, baseness, beastliness, brand, contemptibility, debasement, degradation, despicability, despicableness, discreditableness, disesteem, disgracefulness, dishonor, dishonorableness, disparagement, disreputability, disreputableness, disrespect, execrableness, heinousness, ignobility, ignominiousness, ignominy, ill fame, ill favor, ill repute, *infamia,* infamousness, infamy, ingloriousness, loathsomeness, loss of honor, loss of reputation, monstrousness, nefariousness, no reputation, no repute, obloquy, obnoxiousness, odiousness, odium, opprobrium, shady reputation, shame, shamefulness, shoddiness, stain, taint, turpitude, vileness, want of esteem, wickedness, wretchedness

DISRESPECT, ***noun*** abruptness, affront, arrogance, audacity, bluntness, brashness, brazenness, brusqueness, cavalierness, condescension, contempt, contemptuousness, contumacy, contumely, curtness, defiance, depreciation, derision, derisiveness, detraction, discourteousness, discourtesy, disdain, disesteem, dishonor, disobedience, disparagement, disregard, disrespectfulness, effrontery, flippancy, flout, impertinence, impoliteness, impudence, incivility, indecorum, insolence, *insolentia,* insubordination, insult, inurbanity, irreverence, lack of consideration, lack of courteousness, lack of courtesy, lack of politeness, lack of respect, mockery, offense, pertness, presumption, presumptuousness, rebuff, ridicule, rude behavior, rudeness, sauciness, scoffing, scorn, shortness, slight, sneer, snub, spurn, superciliousness, tactlessness, uncourtliness, ungallantness, ungentlemanliness, ungraciousness, unmannerliness, unmannerly conduct, unpoliteness, vilification, vilipendency, want of esteem
ASSOCIATED CONCEPTS: disrespect to flag

DISRUPT, ***verb*** agitate, annoy, break apart, cause chaos, cause confusion, cause scission, confuse, create a disturbance, create disorder, derange, disarrange, discompose, discontinue, dishevel, disjoin, disorder, disorganize, disquiet, dissociate, distract, disturb, embroil, fluster, get in the way, hinder, impede, infringe, intercept, interfere, intermit, interrupt, intervene, intrude, meddle, mess up, mix up, obstruct, overturn, perturb, prevent, rend asunder, ruffle, rupture, split up, stir up, stop, sunder, suspend, thwart, unsettle, upset

DISSATISFACTION, ***noun*** annoyance, chagrin, complaint, dejection, disaffection, disagreement, disappointment, disapprobation, disapproval, discomfort, discontent, discontentedness, discontentment, discouragement, disesteem, disfavor, disgruntlement, disgust, dislike, displeasure, disquiet, dissatisfiedness, dissent, distaste, fault finding, grievance, grudge, inquietude, irritation, *molestia,* nonapproval, nonfulfillment of one's hopes, *offensa, offensio,* opposition, pique, querulousness, regret, state of not being satisfied, umbrage, uncomfortableness, uneasiness of mind, unhappiness, unhappiness with one's lot, unsatisfaction, vexation
ASSOCIATED CONCEPTS: express dissatisfaction

DISSECT, ***verb*** analyze, anatomize, assay, assess, break down, classify, cut, deconstruct, diagnose, divide, evaluate, examine, inspect, investigate, schematize, scrutinize, segment, separate, sort, study, subdivide

DISSEISIN, ***noun*** arrogation, assuming ownership, attachment, capture, commandeering, compulsory acquisition, confiscation, deprivation, deprivation of possession, disendowment, displacement of rightful owner, dispossession, distraint, distress, divestment, exclusion of entitled owner, expropriation, forcible seizure, foreclosure, impropriation, ouster, prehension, privation of seisin, seizure, sequestration, take over, taking, taking possession, taking without compensation, wrongful dispossession
ASSOCIATED CONCEPTS: adverse possession, disseisin by election

DISSEMINATE, ***verb*** announce, annunciate, apprise, broadcast, bruit, carry a report, circulate, communicate, convey, deal out, diffuse, dispatch news, dispense, disperse, *disseminare,* distribute, impart, inform, issue, make public, notify, promulgate, propagate, publicize, publish, publish abroad, radiate, relay, report, *spargere,* spread a report, spread far and wide, strew, transmit, utter
ASSOCIATED CONCEPTS: publication of a libel

DISSENSION, ***noun*** angry disagreement, argumentation, bickering, *brouillerie,* caviling, clashing, conflict, conflict of opinion, contention, controversy, difference of opinion, differences, disaccord, disaffection, disagreement, discord, discordance, *discordia,* disharmony, dispute, dissent, dissentience, dissidence, dissonance, disunion, disunity, divergence, divergent opinions, diversity of opinion, division, friction, lack of harmony, nonagreement, nonassent, nonconcurrence, protest, protestation, quarrel, refusal of agreement, remonstrance, resentment, rift, schism, strife, strong dissension, violent disagreement, wrangling

DISSENT *(Difference of opinion),* ***noun*** apostasy, argument, caviling, challenge, clash, confirmed opposition, conflict, conflict of opinion, contraposition, demur, disaccord, disagreement, discord, discordance, disharmony, disparity, dissension, dissentience, dissidence, dissonance, divergence, diversity of opinion, expostulation, failure to agree, friction, lack of harmony, nonagreement, noncompliance, objection, oppositeness, opposition, schism, unconformity, variance

DISSENT *(Nonconcurrence),* ***noun*** contrariety, disagreement, disapproval, disavowal, disclaimer, discontent, dissatisfaction, dissension, dissentient voice, disunity, nonagreement, nonassent, nonconformity, nonconsent, nonobservance, objection, opposition, repudiation, variance
ASSOCIATED CONCEPTS: dissenting opinion, dissenting vote

DISSENT *(Differ in opinion),* ***verb*** argue, be at variance, be contrary, be of contrary sentiment, bicker, clash, collide, conflict, confute, contradict, differ, differ in sentiment, disagree, disagree in opinion, dispute, *dissentire, dissidere,* not agree, oppose, quarrel, take exception, take issue with
ASSOCIATED CONCEPTS: dissenting fiduciary, dissenting stockholders

DISSENT *(Withhold assent),* ***verb*** be unwilling, challenge, decline, decline to agree, defy, demur, disallow, disapprove, negate, negative, nonconsent, not accept, not approve, not consider, not defend, not hold with, object, oppose, prohibit, protest, raise objections, raise one's voice against, rebuff, refuse, refuse assent, refuse to admit, reject, repudiate, repulse, resist, spurn
ASSOCIATED CONCEPTS: dissent from the majority opinion

DISSENTER, ***noun*** agitator, apostate, boycotter, contrarian, defector, disbeliever, disputant, disruptor, dissident, extremist, heresiarch, heretic, individualist, infidel, malcontent, misbeliever, nonconformist, objector, picketer, protester, radical, rebel, recusant, renegade, revolutionary, rioter, schismatist, sectarian, separationist, separatist, skeptic
ASSOCIATED CONCEPTS: a minority opinion, the Supreme Court decision

DISSENTING, ***adjective*** arguing, argumentative, at cross-purposes, at issue, at loggerheads, at odds, at variance, caviling, clashing, conflicting, conflictive, conflictory, contentious, contradicting, controverting, debating, declining to agree, demurring, denying, differing, disaccordant, disagreeing, disapproving, discordant, discrepant, disharmonious, disputatious, disputative, disputing, dissentient, dissentious, dissident, dissonant, disunited, divergent, divided on, factious, going contrary to, in conflict, in disagreement, incongruous, inconsistent, inharmonious, irreconcilable, not abiding, not accepting, not agreeing, not conforming, objecting, opposing, polemical, protesting, quarreling, quarrelsome, questioning, recusant, refusing to admit, refusing to agree, refuting, repudiating, repugning, resisting, running counter to, taking exception, taking issue with, unconsenting, varying, withholding approval, withholding assent, wrangling
ASSOCIATED CONCEPTS: dissenting judges, dissenting opinion, dissenting shareholders

DISSERVICE, ***noun*** bad turn, damage, detriment, *detrimentum,* harm, ill turn, *incommodum,* injury, injustice, malfeasance, mischief, misdeed, misdoing, mistreatment, outrage, unkindness, wrong

DISSIDENCE, ***noun*** argument, bickering, clashing, conflict, contradiction, contrariety, controversy, contumaciousness, difference, disaccord, disagreement, discongruity, discord, discordance, discordancy, disharmony, dissension, dissent, dissonance, disunion, disunity, divergence, faction, incongruence, incongruity, inharmoniousness, noncompliance, nonconcurrence, nonconformity, opposition, quarrel, recusancy, schism, strife, unconformity, variance, wrangle

DISSIDENT, *adjective* antagonistic, at odds with, at variance with, challenging, clashing, contrary, differing, disagreeing, discontented, discordant, discrepant, disinclined, disobedient, dissatisfied, dissentient, dissenting, dissentious, divergent, divided, factious, inaccordant, inacquiescent, incompatible, inconsistent with, irreconcilable, loath, malcontent, noncompliant, nonconforming, nonconformist, nonobservant, not consenting, objecting, opposing, protestant, protesting, quarreling, rebellious, recalcitrant, recusant, refusing, resistant, unassenting, unconformable, unconsenting, unwilling

DISSIMILAR, *adjective* aberrant, asymmetrical, atypical, clashing, contrary, contrasted, contrasting, deviating, different, differing, disagreeing, discordant, discrepant, *dispar,* disparate, *dissimilis,* divergent, divers, diverse, diversified, heterogeneous, incongruent, irregular, irrelative, mismatched, mixed, multiform, nonidentical, nonuniform, not comparable, not similar, odd, of a different kind, of all sorts, of many kinds, unalike, unconformable, unidentical, unlike, unmatched, unpaired, unrelated, unresembling, unsame, unsimilar, untypical, varied, variegated, variform, various
ASSOCIATED CONCEPTS: dissimilar condition

DISSIPATE *(Expend foolishly),* ***verb*** abuse, be extravagant, be immoderate, be intemperate, be prodigal, burn up, consume, consume one's substance, deny oneself nothing, deplete, drain, empty, exhaust, expend, indulge in extravagance, indulge oneself, live idly, misspend, misuse, overdraw, overspend, overstrain, practice extravagance, prodigalize, spend, spend lavishly, spend wastefully, use up, waste
ASSOCIATED CONCEPTS: dissipation of assets, dissipation of property, waste

DISSIPATE *(Spread out),* ***verb*** bestrew, break up, cast forth, cease, cease to be, dematerialize, diffuse, disappear, disintegrate, disperse, disseminate, *dissipare,* dissolve, diverge, evanesce, fade, fade away, overspread, radiate, scatter, scatter thinly, scatter to the winds, scatter widely, sow, spread, spread over, sprinkle, strew, vanish

DISSOCIATE, *verb* break up, cut adrift, cut off, demobilize, detach, disassociate, disband, disconnect, disencumber, disengage, disjoin, dispart, disperse, displace, dissever, disunite, divide, divorce, free, have no concern with, isolate, keep apart, liberate, loosen, part, release, remove, scatter, segregate, separate, set free, sever, sunder, take leave, unbind, unchain, uncouple, undo, unlock, unloose, unyoke, withdraw

DISSOLUTE, *adjective* abandoned, base-minded, carnal, concupiscent, corrupt, corrupted, debased, debauched, decadent, degenerate, degraded, depraved, dissipated, *dissolutus,* evil-minded, free-living, graceless, immoderate, immoral, impure, incontinent, incorrigible, indecent, indulgent, iniquitous, intemperate, lascivious, libertine, libidinous, licentious, low-minded, lustful, *luxuriosus,* perverted, polluted, prodigal, profligate, prurient, rakish, reprobate, salacious, satyric, sensual, shameless, unashamed, unbridled, unchaste, uncurbed, unprincipaled, unrestrained, unvirtuous, warped, wayward
ASSOCIATED CONCEPTS: dissolute person

DISSOLUTION *(Disintegration),* ***noun*** adulteration, atomization, atrophy, breaking up, corrosion, corruption, crumbling, decay, decomposition, demolition, deterioration, dilapidation, disassembly, disbanding, dismantlement, disorganization, dispersal, disruption, dissipation, erosion, rotting, separation, spoilage, spoliation, undoing

DISSOLUTION *(Termination),* ***noun*** abolishment, abolition, abrogation, annihilation, annulment, breaking up, cancellation, canceling, cessation, close, closing, completion, conclusion, death, defeasance, demise, destruction, discontinuance, dismissal, *dissolutio,* disuse, effacement, elimination, end, ending, eradication, erasure, expiration, expunction, extinction, extinguishment, extirpation, finis, finish, invalidation, liquidation, nullification, obliteration, overthrow, prorogation, repeal, rescission, revocation, revokement, ruin, ruination, suppression, voidance
ASSOCIATED CONCEPTS: corporate dissolution, de facto dissolution, de jure dissolution, dissolution of marriage, dissolution of partnership, dissolution proceeding
FOREIGN PHRASES: ***Nihil tam naturale est, quam eo genere quidque dissolvere, quo colligatum est.*** Nothing is so natural as to dissolve anything in the way in which it was made binding. ***Nihil tam conveniens est naturali aequitati quam unumquodque dissolvi eo ligamine quo ligatum est.*** Nothing is so agreeable to natural equity as that a thing should be dissolved by the same means by which it was bound. ***Nihil est magis rationi consentaneum quam eodem modo quodque dissolvere quo conflatum est.*** Nothing is more consonant to reason than that a thing should be dissolved in the same way in which it was created.

DISSOLVE *(Disperse),* ***verb*** atomize, decompose, diffuse, disintegrate, dispel, dissipate, *dissolvere,* evanesce, intersperse, *liquefacere,* melt away, radiate, scatter, spread

DISSOLVE *(Separate),* ***verb*** break apart, break up, decentralize, demobilize, detach, disband, disconnect, disengage, disjoin, dismantle, dispart, dissever, dissociate, disunite, divide, divorce, part, set asunder, sever, split up, sunder, take apart, uncouple, undo

DISSOLVE *(Terminate),* ***verb*** abort, abrogate, break up, bring to an end, bring to conclusion, call off, cancel, cease, conclude, desist, destroy, disband, discontinue, dispose of, draw to a close, efface, effect a dissolution, end, erase, expire, finish, halt, neutralize, nullify, obliterate, quash, render inert, revoke, split up, stop, undo, vitiate, wipe out
ASSOCIATED CONCEPTS: dissolving an injunction
FOREIGN PHRASES: ***Eddem modo quo quid constituitur, dissolvitur.*** Anything is dissolved in the same manner in which it is made binding.

DISSONANCE, *noun* altercation, animosity, antipathy, argument, clash, collision, competition, conflict, contention, contrariety, controversy, disaccord, disagreement, discord, discordance, discrepancy, disharmony, dispute, dissention, dissidence, dissimilarity, disunion, division, enmity, friction, hostility, ill-will, incongruence, inconsistency, infighting, misbeliever, nonconformist, protester, quarrel, rancor, rebel, recusant, row, run-in, schism, scrape, separation, spat, strife, warfare

DISSONANT, *adjective* at variance, atonal, blaring difference, cacophonous, clangorous, clashing, contrariant, contrary, contrasting, diametrically opposed, different, disconsonant, discordant, discrepant, displeasing, divisive, grating, harsh, heterogeneous, incompatible, inconsistent, inharmonious, jarring, off-beat, off-key, oppositional, paradoxical, raucous, strident, tuneless, unmelodious, unmixable, unpleasant, uproarious

DISSUADE, ***verb*** abash, advise against, argue against, attempt to divert, attempt to prevent, cause doubt, caution, convince to the contrary, daunt, *dehortari,* deter from one's purpose, *deterrere,* discourage, disenchant, dishearten, disillusion, dispirit, *dissuadere,* divert by appeal, divert from, exhort against, frighten away, raise apprehension, remonstrate, render averse, stave off, talk out of, turn from a purpose, urge not to

DISTANCE, ***noun*** area, berth, breadth, cast, clearance, depth, extension, extent, gamut, height, lead, length, measurement, perspective, range, reach, remove, scale, scope, space, spacing, spectrum, sphere, spread, stretch, territory, volume

DISTANT *(Detached),* ***adjective*** afar, far, far away, far-off, in the distance, out of distance, out of range, out of reach, out of sight, outlying, remote, removed
ASSOCIATED CONCEPTS: distant relative, trust and estates, wills

DISTANT *(Far),* ***adjective*** aloof, coif, remote, removed, standoffish, unapproachable, uncommunicative, unfriendly, unresponsive, unsociable, withdrawn

DISTASTEFUL, ***adjective*** abhorrent, abominable, an affront, appalling, awful, causing anger, causing displeasure, causing resentment, disagreeable, foul, insipid, invidious, loathsome, nauseating, noisome, noxious, obnoxious, odious, offensive, repellent, repugnant, repulsive, savorless, shocking, sickening, tactless, tasteless, unacceptable, unappetizing, uncongenial, uninviting, unpalatable, unsavory

DISTILL, ***verb*** boil down, clarify, concentrate, condense, decoct, *destillare,* draw forth, draw out, draw out the essence, drop, expel, extract, filtrate, filter, free from extraneous matter, press out, purify by removing the foreign and nonessential, reduce to extreme purity and strength, separate, squeeze out, *stillare,* strain, strain out, take out, trickle, vaporize and condense, wring
ASSOCIATED CONCEPTS: distilled liquor, distilled spirits, distilling apparatus, distilling the essence out of a case

DISTINCT *(Clear),* ***adjective*** apparent, *clarus,* clear-cut, clear to the mind, clear to the senses, clearly defined, concrete, conspicuous, crystal clear, definite, *distinctus,* distinguishable, easily perceived, easily understood, eidetic, evident, explicit, exposed to view, express, for all to see, glaring, graphic, in full view, indubitable, intelligible, lucid, manifest, noticeable, obvious, palpable, particular, pellucid, perceivable, perceptible, *perspicuus,* positive, precise, pronounced, recognizable, self-evident, sharp, striking, unambiguous, unclouded, uncovered, undisguised, undistorted, unequivocal, unhidden, visible, visualized, vivid, well-defined, well-drawn, well-marked
ASSOCIATED CONCEPTS: clear and distinct, distinct action

DISTINCT *(Distinguished from others),* ***adjective*** characteristic, contrasted, contrasting, decidedly different, departing from, different, differing, disassociated, discrepant, discrete, discriminate, dissimilar, distant, distinctive, *distinctus,* distinguished by nature, distinguished by station, divergent, diverse, divorced, idiosyncratic, incongruent, incongruous, individual, marked, nonuniform, not identical, not the same, observably different, out of the ordinary, particular, peculiar, poles apart, removed, separate, *separatus,* set apart, singular, special, standing apart, uncommon, unconfused, unimitated, unique, unlike, unlike others, unusual
ASSOCIATED CONCEPTS: distinct entity, distinct interests

DISTINCT MEANING, ***noun*** accurate meaning, correct meaning, defined meaning, definition, exact meaning, explanation, explicit meaning, express meaning, faithful meaning, inflexible meaning, literal meaning, methodical meaning, meticulous meaning, narrow meaning, not subject to interpretation, ordinary meaning, plain meaning, precise meaning, prescribed meaning, rigid meaning, rigorous meaning, sharply defined, significance, specific meaning, strict meaning, unbending meaning, uncompromising meaning, unequivocal meaning
ASSOCIATED CONCEPTS: construction, literal contract, literal proof, plain meaning rule, rules of statutory, soft plain meaning rule, textualism

DISTINCTION *(Difference),* ***noun*** antithesis, characteristic difference, contrariety, contrast, differentia, differential, differentiation, disaccord, disagreement, discongruity, discrepancy, *discrimen,* discrimination, disharmony, disparity, dissension, dissonance, *distinctio,* distinguishing characteristic, distinguishing quality, diverseness, earmark, individuality, irrelation, nonuniformity, peculiarity, perceivable dissimilarity, point of difference, special marking, unconformity, unique feature, uniqueness, unlikeness, variance, variant, variation
ASSOCIATED CONCEPTS: substantial distinction

DISTINCTION *(Reputation),* ***noun*** account, *aura popularis,* brilliance, celebrity, credit, *dignitas,* dignity, eminence, exaltation, fame, grandeur, greatness, honor, illustriousness, immortality, importance, loftiness, marked superiority, name, nobility, notability, note, noteworthiness, popular favor, prestige, prominence, public esteem, renown, reputability, repute, respectability, significance, special favor, superiority

DISTINCTIVE, ***adjective*** characteristic, conspicuous, contrasting, diacritical, different, differentiating, differentiative, differing, discriminating, distinct, distinguishing, exclusive, idiomatic, idiosyncratic, indicating difference, indicative, individualistic, individualizing, marked, noteworthy, noticeable, particular, peculiar, *proprius,* salient, separative, serving to distinguish, singular, special, uncommon, unimitated, unique, unlike
ASSOCIATED CONCEPTS: distinctive characteristic, distinctive name

DISTINGUISH, ***verb*** ascertain, characterize, classify, contradistinguish, define, demarcate, differentiate, discern, discriminate, *distinguere,* divide, draw a distinction, exercise discretion, exercise discrimination, individualize, *internoscere,* judge, make distinctions, mark out, note differences, particularize, perceive clearly, point out an essential difference, recognize as different, *secernere,* separate, set apart, specify, winnow
ASSOCIATED CONCEPTS: distinguish between right and wrong, distinguishing cases, distinguishing characteristics, distinguishing mark
FOREIGN PHRASES: ***Ubi lex non distinguit, nec nos distinguere debemus.*** Where the law does not distinguish, we ought not to distinguish. ***Qui bene distinguit bene docet.*** He who distinguishes well teaches well.

DISTINGUISHABLE, ***adjective*** able to draw a distinction, able to exercise discretion, ascertainable, capable of being judged, capable of making distinctions, classifiable, definable, demarcation, differentiation, discernment, essentially different, individualized, particularized, recognized as different, separated, set apart, specified
ASSOCIATED CONCEPTS: distinguishable case law, distinguishable mark, distinguishable precedence

DISTINGUISHED *(Renowned),* ***adjective*** acclaimed, aristocratic, august, celebrated, decorous, dignified, elegant, elevated, eminent, exalted, famed, famous, glorious, honored, illustrious, important, luminous, magisterial, majestic, noble, notable, noteworthy, outstanding, paramount, predominant, preeminent, prominent, redoubtable, reputable, seemly, signal, star, stately, superior, venerable

DISTINGUISHED *(Unique),* ***adjective*** anomalous, characteristic, contrasting, custom, customized, different, distinct, distinctive, especial, extraordinaire, extraordinary, idiosyncratic, matchless, memorable, particular, peculiar, peerless, phenomenal, preternatural, separate, special, specialized, uncommon, unique, unparalleled, unrivaled, unusual

DISTORT, ***verb*** bend, camouflage, caricature, change out of recognition, change the face of, conceal, contort, corrupt, deform, disguise, disproportion, dissemble, *distorquere,* exaggerate, falsify, give a false idea, give a false impression, give a strained meaning, give a turn, give twist, inflate, make unlike, miscite, miscolor, misconstrue, misdescribe, misdirect, miseducate, misestimate, misexplain, misexpress, misinform, misinstruct, misinterpret, mislead, misquote, misread, misreckon, misreport, misrepresent, misshape, misteach, mistranslate, overdo, overdramatize, overstate, palter with the truth, paralogize, parody, pervert, play upon words, put a false construction on, put a false sense on, put an erroneous construction on, reshape, strain, strain the meaning, strain the sense, strain the truth, stretch, stretch the meaning, transfigure, transform, turn awry, twist, twist the meaning, twist the sense, twist the words, understate, warp, wrench, wrench the meaning, wrench the sense
ASSOCIATED CONCEPTS: distort the truth

DISTORT THE MEANING, ***verb*** belie, bias, contort, deform, distort, falsify, garble, interpret incorrectly, manipulate, misapply, misapprehend, miscolor, misconceive, misconstrue, misdirect, misinterpret, misjudge, misread, misrender, misreport, misstate, mistranslate, misuse, pervert, put a false construction on, twist, warp
ASSOCIATED CONCEPTS: distort the meaning of a decision, distort the meaning of a statute, distort the truth

DISTORTION, ***noun*** anamorphosis, camouflage, caricature, contortion, convolution, deception, deformation, deformity, disguise, disparity, disproportion, dissemblance, dissimilarity, dissimilitude, *distortio,* embroidery, enlargement, exaggeration, expansion, false coloring, false construction, false copy, false reading, falsification, gloss, hyperbole, illusion, imbalance, irrelation, magnification, misapplication, misconstruction, misdirection, misexplanation, misinformation, misinstruction, misinterpretation, misquotation, misrendering, misrepresentation, mistranslation, misusage, misuse of words, one-sided conception, one-sided view, over coloring, overstatement, perversion, *pravitas,* satire, simulacrum, strained sense, stretch, travesty, twist, unlikeness, warped judgment, wrong interpretation

DISTORTION OF THE TRUTH, ***noun*** deceitfulness, deception, exaggeration, fabrication, faking, falsehood, falsification, falsity, garbling, lie, lying, mendacity, misconception, misconstruction, misinterpretation, misrepresentation, mythomania, perfidy, perversion, sophistry, spuriousness, untruthfulness
ASSOCIATED CONCEPTS: perjury, uttering a false statement

DISTRACTION, ***noun*** agitation, ambiguity, befuddlement, complication, confoundment, confusion, daze, disarray, disorder, disorganization, disorientation, disruption, disturbance, divergency, diversion, engrossment, fluster, interference, interruption, mystification, preoccupation, shambles, turmoil

DISTRAIN, ***verb*** annex, appropriate, assume ownership, attach, bear away, carry away, carry off, compulsorily acquire, confiscate, deprive of, divest, garnish, *hominis bona vendere,* hurry off with, impound, impress, lay hold of, levy, levy a distress, make away with, possess oneself of, preempt, replevy, seize, sequester, sequestrate, take away, take into custody, take over, take possession of

DISTRAINT, ***noun*** annexation, appropriation, attachment, capture, confiscation, dispossession, distress, divestment, execution, expropriation, forcible seizure, garnishment, impoundage, impoundment, levy, obtainment, securement, seizure and appropriation, seizure to procure satisfaction of a debt, sequestration
ASSOCIATED CONCEPTS: distraint for rent, process of distraint

DISTRESS *(Anguish),* ***noun*** agitation, agony, anxiety, anxiousness, blight, depression, desolation, despair, despondency, difficulty, discomfort, discomposure, disquiet, disquietude, dissatisfaction, infelicity, inquietude, mental agony, misery, pain, perturbation, sadness, sorrow, suffering, torment, trial, tribulation, trouble, uneasiness, unhappiness, vexation, woe, worry, wretchedness
ASSOCIATED CONCEPTS: distress for rent, distress warrant, mental distress, unreasonable distress, warrant of distress

DISTRESS *(Seizure),* ***noun*** acquirement, acquisition, adoption, annexation, appropriation, arrogation, assumption, attachment, capture, confiscation, deprivation, deprivement, dispossession, disseisin, distraint, divestment, expropriation, impoundage, impoundment, impress, impressment, impropriation, levy, removal, seizing, sequestration, snatching, taking, usurpation

DISTRESS, ***verb*** afflict, aggravate, aggrieve, agitate, agonize, annoy, bedevil, bother, cause suffering, chagrin, discompose, disgust, disquiet, disturb, exacerbate, grieve, harass, harrow, harry, hurt, irk, irritate, make miserable, make sorrowful, make unhappy, molest, offend, pain, perturb, sadden, subject to strain, torment, trouble, upset, vex, worry

DISTRIBUTE, ***verb*** admeasure, administer, allocate, allot, appropriate, arrange, array, assign, assign places to, assort, class, classify, deal, decentralize, dispense, *dispertire,* disseminate, *distribuere,* divide, *dividere,* dole, file, give out, mete, parcel out, portion out, prorate, ration, scatter, set in order, share, sort, sow, space, spread, sprinkle, systematize
ASSOCIATED CONCEPTS: distributed among creditors, distributed because of liquidation, distribution of an estate

DISTRIBUTION *(Apportionment),* ***noun*** allocation, allotment, appropriation, assignment, dealing out, dispensation,

disposal, dissemination, division, dole, handing out, issuance, parceling out, partition, placement, proporting, rationing, repartition, sharing
ASSOCIATED CONCEPTS: capital distribution, distribution by operation of law, distribution of assets, distribution of capital, distribution of corporate assets, distribution of earnings or profits, distribution of powers and functions, distribution of proceeds, distribution points, just and equal distribution, partial distribution, per capita distribution, per stirpes distribution, pro rata distribution, ratable distribution

DISTRIBUTION *(Arrangement),* ***noun*** assemblage, categorization, classification, collocation, disposition, disposure, formation, gradation, graduation, grouping, management, marshaling, ordering, organization, placement, regimentation, serialization, systematization

DISTRICT, *noun* *ager,* area, circuit, constituency, department, domain, locale, locality, neighborhood, pale, precinct, province, quarter, realm, *regio,* region, section, sphere, *terra,* territorial division, territory, tract, ward, zone
ASSOCIATED CONCEPTS: business district, collection district, election district, federal district, improvement district, judicial district, school district, tax district

DISTRICT ATTORNEY, *noun* accuser, attorney for the people, attorney representing the state's interest, law enforcement agent, the people, prosecuting attorney, the prosecution, prosecutor, public attorney, public pleader, public prosecutor, the state, state's attorney
ASSOCIATED CONCEPTS: attorney general, county attorney, prosecuting attorney, state's attorney

DISTRUST, *verb* challenge, deny, disbelieve, discount, disfavor, doubt, eschew, give no credence to, mistrust, question, reject, repudiate, scoff at, scorn, scout, suspect
ASSOCIATED CONCEPTS: credibility of a witness

DISTURB, *verb* agitate, alarm, annoy, arouse, badger, bedevil, befuddle, bewilder, bother, churn, *commovere,* confound, confuse, *conturbare,* derange, disarrange, discomfit, discompose, disconcert, dishevel, dislocate, dislodge, dismay, disorder, disorganize, disorientate, displace, displant, displease, disquiet, distemper, distract, distress, enrage, exasperate, ferment, fluster, havoc, incommode, interfere, interrupt, intrude, irk, make uneasy, meddle, molest, nettle, nonplus, outrage, overturn, perplex, perturb, *perturbare,* pique, plague, puzzle, rearrange, roil, rouse, ruffle, shake, shake up, startle, stir up, subvert, tamper, trouble, unbalance, unnerve, unseat, unsettle, upset, vex, worry
ASSOCIATED CONCEPTS: disturbing the peace, right to quiet enjoyment

DISTURBANCE, *noun* affray, agitation, annoyance, anxietude, anxiety, anxiousness, commotion, confusion, disarrangement, discomfiture, discomposure, disconcertion, discontinuity, dishevelment, dislocation, disorder, disorganization, displacement, disquiet, disquietude, embroilment, eruption, faction, ferment, fomentation, fracas, fuss, hindrance, inquietude, interruption, intrusion, maelstrom, misarrangement, misgiving, molestation, *motus,* perturbation, quandary, rebellion, restiveness, restlessness, revolt, revolution, state of disorder, trepidation, tumult, *tumultus, turbatio,* turbulence, turmoil, unrest, unruliness, unsettlement, uprising, uproar
ASSOCIATED CONCEPTS: creating a disturbance, disorderly conduct, disturbance of court, disturbance of possession, disturbance of quiet possession, disturbing the peace, nuisance

DISUSE, *noun* abandonment, abolishment, abolition, abstinence, archaism, cessation of use, decay, desuetude, discontinuance, discontinuation, disregard, disusage, failure to use, ignorement, inattention, inusitation, neglect, nonemployment, nonuse, obsolescence, staleness, suspension, unemployment

DIVERGE, *verb* avoid, bifurcate, branch off, branch out, deflect, depart, detour, deviate, digress, disperse, divaricate, diversify, divide, excurse, extend, fork, part, proliferate, scatter, separate, sheer, split, spread, stray, swerve, veer, wander

DIVERGENT, *adjective* aberrant, bifurcate, bifurcated, branching, departing, deviating, deviative, deviatory, different, differing, discrepant, disharmonious, disparate, dissimilar, divaricating, diverging, diverse, diversified, eccentric, factional, factious, forking, furcate, furcated, incompatible, inconsistent, nonuniform, parting, radiating, ramified, separating, straying, taking different courses, unconventional, untraditional, variant, varying
ASSOCIATED CONCEPTS: divergent interests

DIVERSE, *adjective* *alius,* assorted, contrastive, deviative, different, differing, disagreeing, discrepant, *dispar,* disparate, dissimilar, distinct, distinguishable, divergent, divers, diversified, diversiform, *diversus,* heterogeneous, incomparable, manifold, miscellaneous, mixed, motley, multifarious, multiform, several, sundry, unidentical, unlike, unmatched, variant, varied, variegated, various, varying
ASSOCIATED CONCEPTS: diverse citizenship, diverse interests, diversity jurisdiction

DIVERSIFICATION, *noun* alteration, assortment, change, contrast, deviation, difference, differentiation, heterogeneity, multifariousness, multiformity, separation, shift, variation
ASSOCIATED CONCEPTS: diversification of investments

DIVERSIFY, *verb* accommodate, adapt, adjust, alter, branch out, build, change, develop, diverge, embrace, encompass, evolve, expand, extend, grow, include, increase, involve, metamorphose, mix, modify, modulate, multiply, proliferate, ramify, regenerate, revolutionize, shift, spread out, subsume, take in, temper, transform, variegate, vary
ASSOCIATED CONCEPTS: race-based admission programs

DIVERSION *(Detour),* ***noun*** aberration, alteration, aviation, curve, deflection, departure, deviation, digression, divagation, divergency, inconsistency, irregularity, loop, modification, obfuscation, reversion, shift, straying, transgression, turn, twist, variance, variation, veering, wandering

DIVERSION *(Distraction),* ***noun*** aberration, agitation, befuddlement, bewilderment, complication, confoundment, confusion, daze, disarray, disconcertion, disorder, disorganization, disorientation, divertissement, engrossment, fluster, interference, interruption, mystification, preoccupation, shambles, turmoil

DIVERSITY, *noun* assortment, discongruity, *discrepantia,* dissimilarity, dissimilitude, diverseness, *diversitas,* heterogeneity, inconformity, irregularity, manifoldness, medley, miscellany, mixture, multifariousness, multiformity, multiplicity, nonuniformity, unconformity, unevenness, unlikeness, variability, variation, variegation, variety, variousness
ASSOCIATED CONCEPTS: diversity jurisdiction, diversity of citizenship

DIVERT, ***verb*** cause to bend, cause to curve, cause to deviate, cause to turn from, change the course of, deflect, *derivare,* deter, deviate, distract, draw aside, draw away, misappropriate, misdirect, mislead, parry, pull aside, push aside, put off the track, redirect, shift, shunt, sidetrack, swerve, turn aside, veer
ASSOCIATED CONCEPTS: diversion of assets, diversion of corporate funds, diversion of proceeds, diversion of public funds to a private purpose, diversion of trust funds, illegal diversion, unlawful diversion

DIVEST, ***verb*** attach, confiscate, depose, deprive, despoil, discharge, disendow, disentitle, dislodge, displace, dispossess, disrobe, disseize, distrain, drive out, evict, expel, expropriate, forfeit, lay bare, lay open, oust, reduce, relieve, remove, seize, strip, take away, uncover, unseat
ASSOCIATED CONCEPTS: divesting of title, divestiture of rights

DIVIDE *(Distribute),* ***verb*** admeasure, administer, allocate, allot, apportion, appropriate, assign, carve, consign, dispense, disperse, dispose, *distribuere, dividere,* dole, dole out, endow, give out, issue, mete, mete out, parcel out, pass out, pay out, portion out, prorate, ration, serve, share

DIVIDE *(Separate),* ***verb*** bisect, cleave, cut, demarcate, detach, disconnect, disengage, *disiungere,* disjoin, dismember, dispart, dissever, dissociate, disunite, *dividere,* divorce, fractionize, fragment, halve, part, partition, section, sectionalize, segment, segregate, *separare,* separate, sever, split, sunder, tear, unbind, uncouple
ASSOCIATED CONCEPTS: divide and distribute, divided according to law, divided court, divided equally, divided share and share alike

DIVIDEND, ***noun*** advantage, allotment, benefit, distribution of earnings, distribution of profits, gain, increment, interest, net profit, profit, return, share
ASSOCIATED CONCEPTS: cumulative dividends, dividend accumulations, dividend additions, dividend earned or declared, dividend in liquidation, dividend in scrip, dividend payable in stock, dividend-paying corporation, dividends paid, guaranteed dividends, life insurance dividend, liquidation dividend, participating dividend, preferential dividend, preferred dividend, regular dividend, stock dividend, taxable dividend, unauthorized dividends, unpaid dividends

DIVISIBLE, ***adjective*** apportionable, bisectable, breakable, capable of being divided, cleavable, detachable, disconnectable, dissectible, disseverable, dividable, dividual, fissile, fissionable, partible, scissile, separable, severable, subdivisible, susceptible of apportionment, susceptible of division, tearable
ASSOCIATED CONCEPTS: divisible contract, divisible covenant, divisible divorce, divisible guaranty, divisible offense

DIVISION *(Act of dividing),* ***noun*** allocation, allotment, apportionment, breaking, breakup, cleavage, cut, cutting, departmentalization, detachment, disaccord, disagreement, disassociation, disbandment, disconnection, discord, disengagement, disharmony, disjunction, disjuncture, dismemberment, dispersal, dispersion, dissemination, dissension, disseverance, dissipation, dissociation, dissonance, distribution, disunion, disuniting, disunity, *divisio,* divorce, faction, noncooperation, opposition, parceling, parting, *partitio,* partition, portioning, rationing, schism, scission, section, segmentation, segregation, sejunction, separation, severance, sharing, split, splitting, spread, sunderance, tearing, uncoupling, untying
ASSOCIATED CONCEPTS: division of costs, division of damages, division of governmental powers, division of property, equitable division, final division and distribution, political subdivision

DIVISION *(Administrative unit),* ***noun*** area, branch, cadre, canton, category, chapter, class, classification, department, district, group, grouping, province, region, ward, zone

DIVISIVE, ***adjective*** bisected, causing disagreement, causing disassociation, causing disjunction, causing separation, cleavable, creating dissension, creating disunity, creating hostility, discordant, discrepant, disengaging, disjoined, disjunctive, dissentient, dissident, dissonant, diverging, dividing, divisible, factious, fragmentable, inharmonious, partible, schismatic, separable, severable, split, subdivisive

DIVORCE, ***noun*** annulment of marriage, broken marriage, conclusion, decree of nullity, *discidium,* dissolution of marriage, dissolution of the marriage bond, disunion, *divortium,* finality, judgment dissolving a marriage, judicial separation of a husband and wife, legal dissolution of marriage, legal nullification of marriage, legal termination of marriage, repudiation of a marriage, *repudium*
ASSOCIATED CONCEPTS: absolute divorce, alimony, annulment of marriage, comparative rectitude, custody of children, decree for divorce, divisible divorce, divorce action, divorce proceeding, divorce suit, foreign divorce, grounds for divorce, judgment of divorce, legal separation, limited divorce

DIVORCE, ***verb*** annul, annul a marriage, detach, disjoin, dissociate, dissolve of the bonds of matrimony, dissolve the marriage of, disunite, legally discard a spouse, nullify a marriage, part, put asunder, put out of matrimony, put out of wedlock, release from matrimonial status, release from matrimony, release from wedlock, sever, split up, sunder, uncouple, unmarry, unyoke
ASSOCIATED CONCEPTS: separation

DIVULGATION, ***noun*** disclosure, dissemination, divulgement, divulgence, evulgation, making public, proclamation, promulgation, spreading abroad

DIVULGE, ***verb*** acquaint, advertise, air, apprise, bare, blurt out, break news, breathe, bring to light, broadcast, communicate, confide, disclose, divulgate, enlighten, evince, expose, impart, inform, lay bare, lay open, leak, let drop, let slip, make known, make public, manifest, noise abroad, proclaim, promulgate, publicize, publish, relate, report, reveal, spread abroad, squeal, tattle, tell, unbosom, uncover, unmask, unveil, voice
ASSOCIATED CONCEPTS: divulge or publish

DNA, ***noun*** authentication, certification, confirmation of identity, proof of identity, scientific evidence, scientific means of designation, scientific means of identity, scientific means to distinguish a person, scientific method to reveal identity, substantiation, validation of identity, verification of identity, deoxyribonucleic acid
ASSOCIATED CONCEPTS: appeal of a case, DNA fingerprint, DNA polymerase, forensics, overturning a case, reversal of a case

DNA SAMPLING, ***noun*** Combined DNA Index System (CODIS), compiling DNA, DNA evidence, DNA profiling, using a reference sample with DNA

DO, ***verb*** accomplish, achieve, act, actualize, arrange, attain, bring about, carry into effect, commit, complete, create, determine, discharge, effect, effectuate, end, execute, finish, follow through, fulfill, implement, interpret, make, make happen, negotiate, occur, operate, perform, pull off, realize, render, solve, succeed, transact, transpose, undertake, wind up, work, wrap up

DOCKET, ***noun*** agenda, calendar, catalog, entry book, enumeration, list, list of cases, listing, order of the day, program, record, record of proceedings, register, registry, roll, schedule, slate
ASSOCIATED CONCEPTS: bench docket, court docket, docket book, docket entry, docketing a judgment, docketing cases

DOCTOR-ASSISTED SUICIDE, ***noun*** active euthanasia, euthanasia, medically assisted suicide, mercy killing, physician-assisted suicide
ASSOCIATED CONCEPTS: passive euthanasia

DOCTRINE, ***noun*** belief, canon, credendum, credo, creed, dogma, formulated belief, gospel, maxim, orthodoxy, philosophy, precept, principle, professed belief, rule, system, system of belief, teaching, teachings, tenet, universal principle
ASSOCIATED CONCEPTS: added risk doctrine, avoidable consequences doctrine, beneficial consideration doctrine, collateral source doctrine, cy pres doctrine, de facto doctrine, doctrine of abstention, doctrine of assumed risk, doctrine of avoidable consequences, doctrine of last clear chance, doctrine of recrimination, doctrine of relation back, doctrine of res judicata, doctrine of subrogation, doctrine of the law of the case, doctrine of unclean hands, doctrine of unjust enrichment, emergency doctrine, exclusive control doctrine, exhaustion of remedies doctrine, humanitarian doctrine, imminent peril doctrine, last clear chance, main purpose doctrine, res ipsa loquitur doctrine, rescue doctrine

DOCUMENT, ***noun*** book, certificate, confirmation, diploma, evidence, evidentiary record, instrument, *instrumentum, litterae,* official publication, paper, proof, record, recorded material, register, report, *tabula,* verification, writ, written material
ASSOCIATED CONCEPTS: allograph, ancient documents, cancellation of document, document of a public nature, document of title, integrated document, legal documents, public document

DOCUMENT, ***verb*** assemble the facts, authenticate, back, bear out, buttress, circumstantiate, collect evidence, confirm, corroborate, demonstrate, establish, evidence, exhibit, fortify, give references, justify, make certain, make evident, manifest, prove, provide with documents, provide with proof, show, strengthen, substantiate, support, sustain, uphold, validate, verify

DOCUMENTARY, ***adjective*** accredited, accurate, actual, attested, authentic, authoritative, certified, chronicled, correct, described, documental, documented, evidential, factual, founded on fact, genuine, in writing, not fictitious, on record, real, recorded, reported, true, valid, veracious, veritable, written
ASSOCIATED CONCEPTS: defense based upon documentary evidence, documentary evidence, documentary stamp

DOCUMENTATION, ***noun*** annals, authentication, authority, basis, certification, circumstantiation, confirmation, corroboration, data, evidence, evidential record, evidentiary record, exhibit, factual basis, grounds, grounds for belief, medium of proof, proof, record, recorded material, reference, source, substantiation, support, supporting evidence, validation, verification

DOCUMENTS, ***noun*** case history, chronicle, credentials, data, documentation, evidence, exhibits, file, instruments, legal instruments, manuscript, moving papers, official writing, papers
ASSOCIATED CONCEPTS: ancient documents, attorney-client privilege, attorney's work product, documentary evidence, production of documents, public documents, subpoena, traditional documents

DOGMA, ***noun*** article of faith, axiom, belief, canon, conviction, credendum, credo, creed, declaration of faith, dictum, doctrinaire opinion, doctrine, *dogma,* doxy, maxim, orthodoxy, persuasion, *placitum,* precept, principle, professed belief, rule, tenet

DOGMATIC, ***adjective*** absolute, arrogant, assertive, assertory, assured, authoritarian, authoritative, canonical, categorical, certain, confident, creedal, decided, definite, definitive, dictatorial, doctrinaire, doctrinal, domineering, emphatic, fanatical, forceful, imperious, insistent, intolerant, magisterial, narrow-minded, opinionated, opinionative, orthodox, overbearing, pedantic, peremptory, positive, positivistic, sure, tenacious, unequivocal, unshakable, unyielding

DOLE, ***verb*** admeasure, allocate, allot, allow, apportion, appropriate, assign, award, bestow, contribute, deal, deliver, dispense, distribute, divide, furnish, give, give away, give out, grant, hand out, hand over, issue, measure out, mete, mete out, parcel out, pay out, portion, present, ration, share, spare, supply

DOMAIN *(Land owned),* ***noun*** alodium, demesne, estate, freehold, hereditament, holding, land, manor, possession, property, real estate, real property, realty, seigniory, tenure
ASSOCIATED CONCEPTS: eminent domain

DOMAIN *(Sphere of influence),* ***noun*** bailiwick, department, dominion, jurisdiction, kingdom, province, realm, region, seigniory, territory
ASSOCIATED CONCEPTS: private domain, public domain

DOMESTIC *(Household),* ***adjective*** belonging to the house, domiciliary, family, home, homemaking, household, housekeeping, internal, pertaining to one's household, pertaining to the family, pertaining to the home, relating to the family, relating to the home
ASSOCIATED CONCEPTS: domestic animals, domestic duties, domestic employment, domestic fixtures, domestic purposes, domestic relations, domestic servants, domestic service, domestic status, domestic use

DOMESTIC *(Indigenous),* ***adjective*** endemic, home, homemade, local, national, native, native grown, not foreign, not imported
ASSOCIATED CONCEPTS: domestic commerce, domestic corporation, domestic judgment

DOMICILE, ***noun*** abiding place, abode, accommodations, address, billet, *domicilium, domus,* dwelling, habitance, habitancy, habitat, habitation, home, house, inhabitance, inhabitancy, living quarters, lodging, lodgment, place of occupancy, place of residence, quarters, residence, residency, tabernacle

ASSOCIATED CONCEPTS: abandonment of domicile, acquisition of domicile, bona fide domicile, change of domicile, de facto domicile, family domicile, legal domicile, matrimonial domicile, plural domiciles
FOREIGN PHRASES: ***Uxor sequitur domicilium viri.*** The wife follows the domicile of her husband. ***Domus sua cuique est tutissimum refugium.*** Everyone's home is his safest refuge.

DOMICILIARY, *noun* citizen, denizen, dweller, habitant, indweller, inhabitant, inhabiter, native, occupant, occupier, resident, settler

DOMINANCE, *noun* ascendance, ascendancy, authority, control, dominancy, domination, dominion, eminence, force, governance, hold, importance, influence, mastery, mightiness, power, predominance, predominancy, prepollence, prepollency, preponderance, prepotency, primacy, sovereignty, supremacy, sway, weight

DOMINANT, *adjective* ascendant, authoritative, cardinal, chief, commanding, controlling, eminent, first, foremost, governing, hegemonical, influential, leading, main, master, overshadowing, paramount, predominant, predominating, preeminent, preponderant, prepotent, prevailing, prevalent, primary, prime, principal, regnant, ruling, sovereign, superior, supreme, unsurpassed, weighty
ASSOCIATED CONCEPTS: dominant aspect rule, dominant estate, dominant land, dominant party, dominant right, dominant tenant, serviant land

DOMINATE, *verb* administer, carry authority, command, compel, control, dictate, domineer, govern, have power, hold down, influence, keep subjugated, lead, manage, master, oppress, overrule, predominate, preponderate, preside over, prevail, reign over, repress, rule, rule over, subdue, subject, subjugate, sway, tame, tyrannize

DOMINATION, *noun* administration, ascendancy, authority, command, control, dictation, dictatorship, dominance, dominion, force, hegemony, hold, influence, jurisdiction, mastery, monopoly, oppression, potency, power, predominance, preponderance, prevalence, primacy, reign, rule, sovereignty, superiority, supremacy, suzerainty, transcendence

DOMINION *(Absolute ownership),* ***noun*** claim, control, deed, demesne, domain, freehold, holding, interest, lawful possession, manor, ownership, possession, possessorship, power of disposal, property, proprietorship, right, right of possession, right to property, rightful possession, seignorage, seisin, stake, territory, title
ASSOCIATED CONCEPTS: act of dominion

DOMINION *(Supreme authority),* ***noun*** ascendancy, authority, command, control, *dicio,* dominance, dominancy, domination, eminent domain, empery, government, grip, hegemony, hold, *imperium,* jurisdiction, lordship, management, mastery, *potestas,* power, primacy, regency, reign, rule, sovereignty, supremacy, sway

DONATE, *verb* accord, administer, aid, assist, award, bequeath, bestow, comp, confer, contribute, devote, dispense, endow, endue, favor, furnish, gift, give, give away, grant, help, impart, lavish, mete out, pay, present, proffer, provide, provide as a courtesy, render, tender, volunteer

DONATION, *noun* alms, benefaction, bequest, bestowment, bounty, charity, contribution, dispensation, *donum,* dotation, endowment, gift, grant, gratuity, handout, impartation, impartment, largess, munificence, offering, philanthropy, present, presentation, provision, subsidy, subvention
ASSOCIATED CONCEPTS: charitable donation, donation *causa mortis,* donation deed, donation of land, gratuitous donation, special donation

DONATIVE, *adjective* aiding, awarding, beneficent, benevolent, bestowing, bountiful, charitable, conferring, contributing, contributory, conveying, dispensing, eleemosynary, endowing, freehanded, furnishing, generous, given away, giving, granting, gratuitous, imparting, openhanded, philanthropic, presenting, providing, supplying
ASSOCIATED CONCEPTS: donative intent, donative trust

DONEE, *noun* acceptor, beneficiary, devisee, grantee, legatee, recipient

DONOR, *noun* aider, almsgiver, altruist, assignor, backer, benefactor, benefactress, bequeather, bestower, cheerful giver, conferrer, consignor, contributor, deliverer, devisor, distributor of largess, donator, free giver, generous giver, giver, Good Samaritan, grantor, helper, humanitarian, patron, patroness, philanthropist, presenter, rewarder, subscriber, vouchsafer
FOREIGN PHRASES: ***Voluntas donatoris in charta doni sui manifeste expressa observetur.*** The will of the donor which is clearly expressed in his deed of gift should be observed.

DORMANT, *adjective* abeyant, asleep, at rest, becalmed, deactivated, hibernating, *iacere,* in abeyance, in suspense, inactive, inert, inoperative, latent, passive, quiescent, quiet, resting, sleeping, slumbering, smoldering, static, still, suspended, torpid, unaroused, unawakened, undeveloped, unwakened
ASSOCIATED CONCEPTS: dormant case, dormant corporation, dormant judgment, dormant partner, dormant powers, dormant season

DOSSIER, *noun* archive, brief, case history, data, document, documentation, facts, file, journal, papers, portfolio, record, recorded information, recorded material, résumé

DOUBLE, *noun* alterego, carbon copy, clone, copy, counterpart, duplicate, duplication, facsimile, imitation, likeness, look-alike, match, mimic, mirror image, picture, replica, spitting image, twin

DOUBLE DEALING, *noun* artfulness, bad faith, cheating, chicanery, covertness, cozenage, craft, craftiness, crookedness, cunning, deceit, deception, deviousness, dishonesty, dissimulation, duplicity, equivocation, fakery, falsehood, forgery, guile, guilefulness, lie, mendacity, mountebankery, prevarication, sanctimoniousness, secrecy, shadiness, slyness, sneakiness, treacherousness, treachery, trickery, unscrupulousness, untrustworthiness, untruth, wile, wiliness

DOUBLE JEOPARDY, *noun* double prosecution, double punishment, recharged, relitigated, reprosecuted, retried, tried for the same crime

DOUBT *(Indecision),* ***noun*** ambiguity, anxiety, apprehension, apprehensiveness, confusion, *dubitatio, dubito,* faltering, feeling of uncertainty, hesitancy, improbability, inability to decide, incertitude, indefiniteness, indeterminateness, indetermination, infirmity of purpose, insecurity, instability, irresolution, lack of certitude, lack of confidence, lack of conviction, lack of faith, matter of dubitation, misgiving, perplexity, precariousness, qualification, qualm,

qualmishness, quandary, question, reluctance, reservation, reserve, self-doubt, state of suspense, suspended judgment, suspense, uncertain state, uncertainness, uncertainty, undecidedness, undeterminedness, unsettled opinion, unsettlement, unsteadiness, unsureness, vacillation, vagueness, want of confidence, want of faith, wavering
ASSOCIATED CONCEPTS: beyond a reasonable doubt standard, rational doubt, reasonable doubt
FOREIGN PHRASES: ***Nobiliores et benigniores praesumptiones in dubiis sunt praeferendae.*** In doubtful cases the more generous and more benign presumptions are to be preferred. ***Ambiguitas verborum latens verificatione suppletur; nam quod ex facto oritur ambiguum verificatione facti tollitur.*** A latent verbal ambiguity may be removed by evidence; for whatever ambiguity arises from an extrinsic fact may be explained by extrinsic evidence. ***Quae dubitationis tollendae causa contractibus inseruntur, jus commune non laedunt.*** Those clauses which are inserted in agreements to avoid doubts and ambiguity do not offend the common law.

DOUBT *(Suspicion),* ***noun*** apprehension, chariness, consternation, critical attitude, disbelief, discredit, dismay, distrust, distrustfulness, doubtfulness, dubiety, dubiousness, dubitation, faithlessness, hesitation, improbability, incredibility, incredulity, incredulousness, lack of confidence, lack of faith, lack of trust, matter of dubitation, misdoubt, misgiving, mistrust, mistrustfulness, qualm, qualmishness, question in one's mind, refusal to believe, reluctance to believe, skepticalness, skepticism, *suspicio,* suspiciousness, unbelief, uncredulousness, want of confidence, want of faith, want of trust, wariness

DOUBT *(Distrust),* ***verb*** awake a suspicion, be apprehensive, be doubtful, be dubious, be incredulous, be nervous, be skeptical, be suspicious, be uncertain, challenge, disbelieve, discredit, dispute, entertain doubts, entertain suspicions, feel distrust, find hard to believe, give no credence to, greet with skepticism, half believe, harbor doubts, harbor suspicions, have doubts, have fears, have misgivings, have questions, have suspicions, impugn, lack confidence in, misbelieve, misdoubt, misgive, mistrust, not admit, not believe, object, query, question, raise a question, raise a suspicion, refuse to believe, refuse to trust, regard with suspicion, suspect, withhold reliance
ASSOCIATED CONCEPTS: doubt the credibility of a witness

DOUBT *(Hesitate),* ***verb*** be in a quandary, be irresolute, be puzzled, be uncertain, be undecided, be undetermined, debate, delay, deliberate, demur, dubitate, equivocate, falter, feel unsure, fluctuate, have qualms, have reservations, hold off, pause, ponder, push aside, put off a decision, puzzle over, scruple, stop to consider, table, think it over, vacillate, waver, withhold judgment
ASSOCIATED CONCEPTS: beyond a reasonable doubt, beyond a shadow of a doubt, free from all doubt

DOUBTFUL, ***adjective*** arguable, at issue, conditional, conjectural, contestable, controvertible, debatable, disbelieving, disposed to question, disputable, distrustful, doubtable, doubting, dubious, dubitable, *dubius,* equivocal, implausible, improbable, in a dilemma, in a quandary, in dispute, in doubt, in question, in suspense, inconceivable, inconvincible, incredible, indecisive, indistinct in character or meaning, irresolute, misbelieving, mistrustful, mistrusting, of uncertain issue, open to doubt, open to question, open to suspicion, problematic, questionable, questioning, speculative, suppositional, unbelievable, unconvincing, unlikely, unresolved, unsettled in opinion, unsolved, unsure, unsustainable, untenable
ASSOCIATED CONCEPTS: doubtful cases, doubtful credit, doubtful debts, doubtful title

DOUBTING, ***adjective*** cynical, disbelieving, disputable, distrustful, doubtful, dubious, hesitant, inconvincible, incredulous, indecisive, irresolute, jealous, leery, misbelieving, mistrustful, mistrusting, questioning, skeptical, suspicious, uncertain, unconvinced, undetermined, unresolved, unsure, vacillating, wary

DOWER, ***noun*** allotment, allowance, appanage, award, bequest, bestowal, bestowment, dos, dotation, effects, endowment, estate, inheritance, jointure, legacy, remainder, settlement, widow's estate, widow's portion
ASSOCIATED CONCEPTS: consummated right of dower, curtesy, dower interest, dower right, election of dower, estate in dower, inchoate right of dower, right of dower, widow's dower
FOREIGN PHRASES: ***Favorabilia in lege sunt fiscus, dos, vita, libertas.*** Favorites of the law are the treasury, dower, life, and liberty.

DOWN *(Dejected),* ***adjective*** depressed, despondent, disconsolate, discouraged, downcast, gloomy, glum, somber sorrowful, sullen, unhappy, upset, weary
ASSOCIATED CONCEPTS: capacity, incompetency, mental illness,

DOWN *(Lowest point),* ***adjective*** below, beneath, depressed, far below, lower, lowest, rock-bottom, under, underground, underneath
ASSOCIATED CONCEPTS: interest rates down, trip and fall, slip and fall

DOWN PAYMENT, ***noun*** collateral, deposit, installment, payment, retainer, stake, surety

DOWNFALL, ***noun*** abasement, adversity, breakdown, calamity, casualty, cataclysm, catastrophe, collapse, debacle, decline, defeat, demotion, destruction, disaster, disgrace, failure, fall, fatality, humiliation, miscarriage, misfortune, perdition, prostration, reverse, ruin, ruination, setback, slump, undoing

DOWNGRADE, ***verb*** debase, decline, deduct, deflate, defrock, degrade, demote, depreciate, deprive, deteriorate, discredit, disgrace, disparage, humiliate, mock, pillory, reduce, supersede, suspend, unfrock

DOXOLOGY, ***noun*** adulation, compliment, glorification, hero worship, idolatry, laudation, overpraise, paean, praise

DRACONIAN, ***adjective*** austere, exacting, extreme, fanatical, formalistic, harsh, inflexible, insensitive, intolerant, precise, punctilious, puritanical, relentless, rigid, rigorous, ruthless, severe, Spartan, stiff, strict, stringent, unbending, uncompassionate, uncompromising
ASSOCIATED CONCEPTS: Draconian laws

DRAFT, ***noun*** acceptance bill, bank check, bank note, bank paper, bill, bill of exchange, cashier's check, check, commercial paper, debenture, letter of credit, *lettre de change,* money order, negotiable instrument, negotiable paper, note, order, order for payment, promissory note, voucher, warrant
ASSOCIATED CONCEPTS: bill of exchange, check, overdraft, sight draft

DRAFT A BRIEF, ***noun*** draft a synopsis of the salient legal points, draft support for the position espoused, pen an explanation of the law, prepare a legal document, prepare a summary on the law, prepare justification, write a legal memorandum, write a memorandum of law

DRAFT A DOCUMENT, *noun* complete a contract, complete an agreement, finish an instrument, prepare a negotiable instrument, prepare materials, write an instrument

DRAFT A WILL, *noun* pen a testamentary instrument, prepare a last will and testament, prepare a testamentary document, prepare a will for a testator, write a testamentary disposition

DRAMATIC RIGHTS, *noun* dramatizing rights, live stage rights, performance rights, stage presentation rights, stage rights, theatrical rights

DRAMATICALLY OPPOSED, *verb* about face, adoption, afterthoughts, change like a chameleon, change of heart, change of mind, conversion, defection, divergence, diversion, flip-flop, 180-degree about face, qualification, realignment, regression, restructuring, reversal, reversion, temporizer, tergiversation, turn of the tide, turnabout
ASSOCIATED CONCEPTS: flip-flop on a political stance

DRASTIC, *adjective* acting with force, desperate, dire, exceeding, excessive, extreme, fanatic, fanatical, forceful, harsh, immoderate, improper, inordinate, intemperate, intense, outrageous, powerful, radical, severe, strict, strong, undue, unmitigated, unreasonable, vigorously effective, violent
ASSOCIATED CONCEPTS: drastic remedy, extraordinary remedy

DRAW *(Attendance),* ***noun*** frequence, level of attendance

DRAW *(Attraction),* ***noun*** attractiveness, enticement, force, gravity, influence, magnetism, pull

DRAW *(Tie),* ***noun*** dead heat, deadlock, impasse, stalemate, standoff

DRAW *(Depict),* ***verb*** delineate, describe, picture, portray, represent, sketch

DRAW *(Extract),* ***verb*** concentrate, condense, derive, pull, receive

DRAW THE LINE, *noun* ascertained boundary, bound, boundary, delineate the boundary, determination, fix the boundary, fix the guideline, guideline, limit, limitation, outer limit, outer perimeter, perimeter, prescribed limit, prescribed limitation, restriction, set the parameter

DRAWBACK, *noun* damage, decremental, defect, disadvantage, discount, fault, flaw, harm, hurt, impediment, inconvenience, injury, liability, objection, obstacle, prejudice, protest, protestation, qualification, set-off

DRIVE *(Cause),* ***noun*** action, activity, charitable cause, charitable effort, charity, commitment to a cause, contribution to promote a cause, crusade, dedicated effort for a charitable effort, enterprise, fund-raising, initiative, maneuver, march, mission, movement, organization, perseverance for a cause, project, pursuit, push, undertaking

DRIVE *(Effort),* ***noun*** animation, appetency, appetite, application, ardor, avidity, caring, commitment, desire, devotion, emotionalism, energy, enterprise, enthusiasm, fervor, frenzy, hunger, industriousness, initiative, intensity, keenness, mission, ownership, passion, push, undertaking, yearning, yen, zeal

DRIVE *(Travel),* ***verb*** commute, cruise, errand, excursion, expedition, flight, hop, jaunt, journey, journey by car, junket, outing, passage, peregrination, progress, quest, ramble, ride, sail, spin, tour, transportation, travels, trek, trip, voyage

DROIT, *noun* appurtenance, authority, authorization, birthright, certification, claim, due, dueness, easement, eligibility, empowerment, entitlement, faculty, franchise, just claim, legal power, legal right, legal title, license, licitness, power, prerogative, prescriptive right, pretension, privilege, right, sanction, vested right, warrant
ASSOCIATED CONCEPTS: right

DROP, *verb* abandon, abate, check, decline, desert, diminish, discard, discontinue, disregard, fade, flag, forbear, forget, forgo, forsake, give up, ignore, inhibit, jettison, maroon, neglect, quit, recede, relent, relinquish, remit, renounce, restrain, scrap, shed, slacken, stop, subside, surrender, taper, taper off, throw away, vacate, vanish, wane, yield
ASSOCIATED CONCEPTS: drop a case

DROP A CASE, *verb* bring to a close a case, bring to an end a case, cancel an action, cause a discontinuance, cease litigation by a plaintiff, conclude litigation by a plaintiff, discontinue an action, end prosecutor by a prosecutor, stop litigating by a plaintiff, stop prosecuting by a prosecutor, terminate a case by a plaintiff, terminate a case by a prosecutor

DRUG, *noun* alterant, analgesic, anesthetic, anesthetic agent, anodyne, antibiotic, chemical substance, curative preparation, medical preparation, medicament, *medicamentum,* medication, medicinal component, medicinal ingredient, narcotic preparation, narcotic substance, nepenthe, opiate, painkiller, palliative, physic, prescription, remedy, sedative, soporific, stimulant, stupefacient
ASSOCIATED CONCEPTS: adulterated drugs, dangerous drugs, drug addiction, habit-forming drug, influence of drugs, labeling of drugs, poisonous drugs or chemicals, possession of drugs, preparation of drugs, prescription drugs, regulation of drugs, sale of drugs

DRUG, *verb* administer, anesthetize, anoint, apply a remedy, benumb, cure, deaden, desensitize, dose, dull, heal, inject, *medicare,* medicate, narcotize, numb, palliate, physic, poultice, prescribe, put to sleep, stun, stupefy, treat
ASSOCIATED CONCEPTS: drug addicts

DRUNK, *adjective* *ebrius,* inebriated, intemperate, intoxicated, overcome, overcome by liquor, riotous, saturated, sottish, *temulentus,* uncontrolled, under the influence of liquor, unsober
ASSOCIATED CONCEPTS: alcoholism, delirium tremens, driving while intoxicated, drunkometer test, intoxication, voluntary intoxication

DUBIOUS, *adjective* ambiguous, *anceps,* arguable, chancy, conditional, confusing, confutable, contestable, contingent, controversial, controvertible, debatable, dependent, disputable, doubtful, dubitative, *dubius,* equivocal, fallible, hazy, in dispute, in doubt, in question, *incertus,* insecure, moot, perplexing, provisional, questionable, refutable, shadowy, skeptical, speculative, suppositional, unascertained, unassured, unauthentic, unauthenticated, unauthoritative, uncertain, uncertified, unconfident, unconfirmed, undemonstrated, undetermined, unexplained, unlikely, unreliable, unresolved, unsound, unsure, unverifiable, vacillating, vague, wavering

DUBITATIVE, *adjective* contestable, controversial, controvertible, deniable, disputable, doubtable, doubtful, dubious, dubitable, in doubt, open to question, questionable, refutable, suspect, unsustainable

DUE *(Owed),* ***adjective*** chargeable, claimable, collectable, condign, *debitus,* delinquent, deserved, earned, in arrears, merited, outstanding, owing, to be paid, uncompensated, unpaid, unrewarded, unsettled
ASSOCIATED CONCEPTS: amount due, balance due, debt due, due bills, due date, due on demand, indebtedness due, justly due and owing, legally due, money due, payment due, rent due, taxes due
FOREIGN PHRASES: ***Nihil peti potest ante id tempus, quo per rerum naturam persolvi possit.*** Nothing can be demanded before the time when, in the nature of things, it can be paid.

DUE *(Regular),* ***adjective*** according to law, allowable, appropriate, authorized, befitting, correct, expedient, fit, lawful, legal, legislated, legitimate, licit, nomothetic, permitted, proper, rightful, sanctioned, statutory
ASSOCIATED CONCEPTS: due acknowledgment, due administration of justice, due and proper care, due and reasonable care, due care, due compensation, due consideration, due course, due course of business, due course of law, due diligence, due execution, due exercise of discretion, due process of law, due proof, due proof of death, due proof of loss, due regard, holder in due course

DUE, *noun* accounts collectable, accounts outstanding, arrears, balance to pay, charge, claim, compensation owed, deberi, debit, debt, deficit, droit, entitlement, favor owed, fee, indebtedness, lawful claim, liability, obligation accrued, outstanding debt, overdue payment, pledge, right, something owed, that which is owing, vested right
ASSOCIATED CONCEPTS: due and payable, due in full, due on demand, having become due, payable upon sight

DUE DATE, *noun* absolute outside date due, appointed hour, bottom line, boundary line, crunch time, cutoff, cutoff point, deadline, drop dead outside date, exact date due, limit, limitation, maximum, pivotal moment, precise date due, restriction, specific time due, submission date, time due, time limit, zero hour
ASSOCIATED CONCEPTS: appearance date, return date

DUE PROCESS, *noun* due process of law, legal fairness, legal safeguards, protection against deprivations, protection guarantees, protection of deprivation of accepted legal principles
Generally: fundamental fairness
Specifically: Fifth Amendment, Fourteenth Amendment
ASSOCIATED CONCEPTS: procedural due process, right to confront accuser, substantive due process

DULL, *adjective* arid, blank, blunt, colorless, desolate, dispiriting, drab, dreary, dry, flat, gloomy, glum, insipid, jejune, languid, leaden, lumbering, lusterless, monotonous, numbing, obtuse, palling, pedantic, pedestrian, ponderous, prosaic, retiring, soggy, somber, spiritless, stale, sterile, subdued, sullen, tedious, unexciting, uninteresting, unspectacular, vapid, wearisome

DULY, *adverb* accurately, as required, correctly, deservedly, fairly, legitimately, rightfully
ASSOCIATED CONCEPTS: duly adjudged, duly allowed, duly appointed, duly assigned, duly awarded, duly certified, duly commenced, duly commissioned, duly completed, duly convened, duly directed, duly enacted, duly entered into, duly established, duly executed, duly filled, duly found, duly given, duly issued, duly made, duly organized, duly presented, duly prosecuted, duly qualified, duly recorded, duly rendered, duly served, duly shown, duly summoned, duly sworn, duly verified

DUN, *noun* bill of accounts, bill of costs, claim, demand, entreaty, exaction, final demand, final notice, forcible demand, *fuscus,* impetration, importunity, insistence, insistent demand, levy, notice, obsecration, obtestation, peremptory demand, reckoning, request, requisition, solicitation, statement, strong request, *suffuscus,* threat, ultimatum, warning notice

DUN, *verb* beseige, beset, clamor for payment, demand, demand payment, demand with threats, exact, *exposcere, flagitare,* give final notice, importune, insist, make claims upon, make demands on, plague, press a claim, request, require

DUPE, *verb* befool, beguile, bilk, cheat, circumvent, counterfeit, cozen, create a false impression, cully, deceive, defraud, delude, ensnare, entrap, fleece, fool, gull, hoax, inveigle, *lactare,* make a fool of, misdirect, misguide, mislead, mulct, outmaneuver, outsmart, outwit, play a trick, play upon, practice chicanery, put something over, set a trap for, sport with, swindle, take advantage of, take by fraud, take in, trap, trick, victimize

DUPLICATE, *noun* carbon, carbon copy, copy, ditto, double, ectype, *exemplar, exemplum,* facsimile, gemination, imitation, likeness, match, photostat, reenactment, repetition, replica, representation, reproduction, twin
ASSOCIATED CONCEPTS: duplicate copy, duplicate original

DUPLICATION, *noun* approximation, carbon copy, clone, copy, counterfeit, counterpart, dead ringer, double, dupe, duplicate, extra, facsimile, fake, forgery, imitation, impression, likeness, look-alike, match, mirror, mock, print, redundancy, replica, replication, reproduction, reserve, semblance, sham, spare, spitting image, twin, version

DUPLICITY, *noun* artifice, casuistry, chicanery, deceitfulness, deception, dissimulation, double-dealing, duality, duplexity, equivocation, evasion, false conduct, falseheartedness, falseness, fraud, guile, hypocrisy, insincerity, perfidy, sham, trickery, two-facedness

DURABLE, *adjective* abiding, aeonian, ageless, amaranthine, ceaseless, changeless, chronic, constant, continual, continuing, endless, enduring, established, eternal, everlasting, firm, *firmus,* fixed, hard, hardy, holding up well, immortal, immovable, immutable, imperishable, impervious to change, incessant, indeciduous, indelible, ineradicable, inerasable, inexhaustible, inexpungeable, interminable, intransmutable, invariable, inveterate, inviolate, irremovable, lasting, lifelong, living, long-continuing, long-enduring, long-lasting, long-lived, long standing, longevous, maintained, never-ending, not easily worn out, of long duration, of long standing, perdurable, permanent, perpetual, persevering, persistent, persisting, remaining, resistant, robust, rocklike, sempiternal, settled, *solidus,* sound, *stabilis,* stable, staying, steadfast, strong, sturdy, substantial, surviving, sustained, tenacious, timeless, tough, unaltered, unceasing, unchangeable, undying, unending, unfading, unfailing, unintermitting, uninterrupted, unyielding, without end

DURANCE, *noun* arrest, bondage, bonds, captivity, commitment, confinement, custody, detention, forced confinement, forcible detention, immurement, incarceration, internment, legal restraint, *lettre de cachet,* quarantine, restraint, restriction on movement, thrall, thralldom

DURATION, *noun* age, continuance, continuance in time, continuation in time, course, epoch, era, extension in time, extent, interregnum, interval, lasting period, length of time, limit, period, period of time, phase, season, space of time, span, spell, stage, stretch, *temporis spatium,* tenancy, tenure, term, time, while
ASSOCIATED CONCEPTS: duration of any office, duration of contract, duration of emergency, duration of liability, duration of possession, duration of use, duration of war

DURESS, *noun* bondage, captivity, coaction, coercion, compulsion, confinement, constraint, control, dominance, enforcement, exaction, force, high pressure, impressment, necessitation, obligation, press, pressure, repression, requirement, restriction, stress, subjection, subjugation, threat
ASSOCIATED CONCEPTS: actionable duress, business compulsion, defense of duress, duress of goods, duress of property, legal duress, moral duress, payment under duress, undue influence
FOREIGN PHRASES: ***Vani timores sunt aestimandi, qui non cadunt in constantem virum.*** Those fears are to be regarded as groundless which do not affect an ordinary man. ***Nihil consensui tam contrarium est quam vis atque metus.*** Nothing is so contrary to consent as force and fear. ***Vani timoris justa excusatio non est.*** A frivolous fear is not a lawful excuse.

DURING, *preposition* all along, all the while, as, at the same time as, at the time, for the time being, in the course of, in the interim, in the meanwhile, in the middle of, meanwhile, through, throughout, throughout the course, throughout the duration, when, while, while pending, while waiting
ASSOCIATED CONCEPTS: during good behavior, during normal work hours, during the heat of passion, during the trial

DUTY *(Obligation),* ***noun*** accountability, allegiance, answerability, assignment, burden, charge, chore, commission, commitment, debt, dictate of conscience, engagement, *fides,* function, indebtedness, liability, moral necessity, moral obligation, *munus,* obedience, office, *officium,* pledge, promise, responsibility, role, task, work
ASSOCIATED CONCEPTS: absolute duty, breach of duty, conditional duty, continuing duty, delegation of duty, duty enjoined by law, duty of support, equitable duty, imperative duty, in performance of duty, in the line of duty, lawful duty, legal duty, ministerial duty, moral duty, neglect of duty, nondelegatable duty, nondiscretionary duty, official duty, on duty, private duty, public duty, relief from duty, scope of servant's duties, statutory duty, unfit for duty, violation of duty
FOREIGN PHRASES: ***Qui jussu judicis aliquod fecerit non videtur dolo malo fecisse, quia parere necesse est.*** He who does anything by command of a judge will not be deemed to have acted from an improper motive, because it was necessary to obey. ***Judicis officium est opus diei in die suo perficere.*** It is the duty of a judge to finish the day's work within that day. ***Judicis est judicare secundum allegata et probata.*** It is the duty of a judge to decide according to the allegations and proofs.

DUTY *(Tax),* ***noun*** assessment, burden, capitation, charge, exaction, exactment, excise, imposition, impost, levy, onus, rate, revenue, tallage, tariff, task, tax on demand, taxation, toll, tribute, *vectigal*
ASSOCIATED CONCEPTS: duty on exports, duty on imports

DWARF, *verb* control, dominate, minimize, overshadow, rise above, stunt, tower over
ASSOCIATED CONCEPTS: federal government's laws dwarfing state laws, supremacy clause

DWELL *(Linger over),* ***verb*** accent, accentuate, brood over, continue, emphasize, extend, harp upon, impress, *in re commorari,* insist, intensify, point up, prolong, prolongate, reiterate, *rem longius prosequi,* stress

DWELL *(Reside),* ***verb*** abide, be located, be present, be settled, be situated, be stationed, billet, bunk, denizen, domicile, domiciliate, *domicilium, habere, habitare,* have a habitation, have one's address at, indwell, inhabit, live, lodge, make one's home, occupy, populate, quarter, remain, reside, room, settle, sojourn, stay, stop, take up one's abode, take up residence, tarry, tenant
ASSOCIATED CONCEPTS: citizenship

DWELLING, *noun* abode, camp, domicile, *domicilium, domus,* dormitory, edifice, habitation, homestead, house, living quarters, lodging, lodging place, lodgment, place of residence, quarters, residence, *sedes,* shelter, tabernacle
ASSOCIATED CONCEPTS: dwelling house purposes, inhabited dwelling house, multiple dwelling, principal dwelling place, private dwelling

DYNAMIC, *adjective* animated, assertive, athletic, charismatic, delightful, electric, electrifying, energetic, enlivened, enterprising, excellent, exceptional, exciting, forceful, hearty, impelling, impressive, incredible, intense, kinetic, lively, magnetic, masterful, peppy, potent, powerful, power-packed, productive, progressive, puissant, punchy, refreshed, rejuvenated, resounding, robust, spectacular, spirited, strong, unambiguous, vehement, vigorous, vigorously effective, vivacious, wonderful, wowing, zealous

DYNAMITE CHARGE, *noun* Allen charge, command to arrive at findings, dynamite admonition, dynamite instruction, order to arrive at findings, shotgun charge, shotgun instruction, third-degree charge

DYNASTY (*Descent*), ancestors, ancestry, blood, bloodline, brood, clan, class, classification, descendants, family tree, genealogy, generations, genre, group, heirs, in-laws, kin, kind, kindred, line, lineage, network, offspring, origin, parentage, pedigree, progeny, race, relations, relatives, siblings, stock, system, tribe

DYNASTY *(Tradition),* accepted tradition, acknowledged pedigree, administration, ancestry, custom, dominion, empire, established tradition, line, regime, respected place, respected tradition, sovereignty, unique place, well-steeped tradition

DYSEPTIC, *adjective* bilious, bitter, choleric, embittered, jaundiced, sour, sour-tempered, spiteful

E

EACH, ***adverb*** apart, exclusively, independently, individually, particularly, per, per capita, personally, respectively, separately, singly, specifically, uniquely, variously
ASSOCIATED CONCEPTS: realleging prior facts

EACH, ***pronoun*** each one, each other, every last one, every one, individually, one, one after another, one and all, one another, one by one, the individual one, the particular one
ASSOCIATED CONCEPTS: each ground of a complaint, joint and several liability

EAGER, ***adjective*** agressive, alacritous, ambitious, anxious, appetent, ardent, aspiring, assiduous, athirst, avid, *avidus,* bent upon, covetous, craving, desirous, diligent, disposed, earnest, enthusiastic, excited, fanatic, fanatical, fervent, *fervidus,* forward, full of enterprise, full of enthusiasm, full of initiative, impassioned, impatient, inclined, industrious, intense, interested, keen, longing, passionate, perfervid, pushy, ravenous, ready, spirited, tantalized, tempted, unable to resist, vehement, voracious, willing, wishful, yearning, zealous, zestful

EARLIER, ***adjective*** advance, ancient, antecedent, anterior, back, beforehand, budding, earliest, embryonic, erstwhile, first, foregoing, foremost, former, inaugural, initial, introductory, leading, maiden, original, pioneer, precedent, preceding, preexisting, preliminary, previous, primal, primitive, prior

EARLY, ***adjective*** antecedent, earlier, first, former, introductory, past, precedent, preceding, precursory, preexistent, prefatory, preliminary, preparatory, previous, seminal
ASSOCIATED CONCEPTS: early payment of principle

EARMARK, ***noun*** brand, cachet, designation, distinguishing mark, emblem, identification, indication, label, mark, mark of identification, mark of identity, sign, symbol

EARN, ***verb*** achieve, achieve by continued effort, acquire by service, attain, be deserving, be entitled to, be successful, be worthy, clear, deserve, gain, gain by labor, gain by service, get a profit, get by effort, have a right to, *merere,* merit, merit as compensation, net, obtain a victory, procure by effort, profit, prosper, realize, reap, receive compensation, secure, succeed in reaching, win
ASSOCIATED CONCEPTS: ability to earn, earned commissions, earned income, earned premiums, earned surplus, earned wages, a sum earned and unpaid

EARN OUT, ***verb*** bring to a zero balance, bring up to date, defray the expenses, lend, loan, paid back, pay back after an advance, repayment, used up
Generally: indemnify, recoupment, reimburse, remit, remunerate

EARNEST, ***adjective*** assiduous, bent upon, concentrating, conscientious, determined, devoted, diligent, eager, *enixus,* enthusiastic, fervent, firm, grave, *gravis,* impassioned, intent, *intentus,* purposeful, resolute, serious, set upon, sincere, sober, solemn, staid, strong-willed, thoughtful, zealous

EARNEST MONEY, ***noun*** binder, collateral, collateral security, deposit, down payment, earnest, earnest money deposit, earnest payment, earnest pledge, escrow funds, front money, funds, good faith binder, good faith deposit, guarantee, installment, part payment, pledge, security, security deposit, stake

EARNINGS, ***noun*** balance, commission, compensation, earned income, emolument, fruit of labor, gains, income, *lucrum,* money earned, pay, payment, personal gain, proceeds, profit, profits, profits from employment, *quaestus,* rate, receipts, recompense, remuneration, returns, revenue, reward, reward of labor, reward of office, salary, takings, wages, winnings
ASSOCIATED CONCEPTS: accrued earnings, annual earnings, corporate earnings, earning capacity, future earnings, gross earnings, individual earnings, loss of earnings, net earnings, profits, rents, surplus earnings, total earnings

EASE, ***verb*** abate, alleviate, ameliorate, bate, calm, comfort, console, cushion, disburden, disencumber, ease the burden, expedite, extenuate, facilitate, free from anxiety, give repose, give rest, help along, lessen, let up, lighten, loosen, make comfortable, make easy, mitigate, moderate, *otium,* pacify, *quies,* quiet, reduce tension, relax, release from pressure, relieve, render less difficult, slacken, soften, *tranquillitas,* unburden, unload, unstrain

EASEMENT, ***noun*** advantage in land, convenience, gateway, interest in land, liberty of use, privilege, right of passage, right of use, right of way, serviceway, way over land

ASSOCIATED CONCEPTS: affirmative easement, apparent easement, appurtenance, appurtenant easement, discontinuing easement, dominant and servient estates, easement by grant, easement by necessary implication, easement by prescription, easement in gross, easement of access, easement of convenience, easement of necessity, equitable easement, implied easement, implied reservation of easement, incorporeal hereditament, incumbrance, intermittent easement, irrevocable license, license in nature of easement, natural easement, necessary easement, negative easement, noncontinuous easement, prescription, private easement, profit a prendre, public easement, quasi easement, right of way, right of way in gross, secondary easement, servitude, visible easement
FOREIGN PHRASES: ***Iter est jus eundi, ambulandi hominis; non etiam jumentum agendi vel vehiculum.*** A way is the right of going or walking by man, and does not include the right of driving a beast of burden or a vehicle.

EASILY *(By far),* ***adverb*** beyond question, certainly, definitely, doubtlessly, easy, far and away, indisputably, indubitably, naturally, obviously, unquestionably, without a doubt, without any question
ASSOCIATED CONCEPTS: claims easily preventable, laws easily circumvented

EASILY *(Without trouble),* ***adverb*** accessible, adroitly, apparent, dexterously, effortless, effortlessly, elementary, facilely, handily, manageable, not burdensome, nothing to it, obvious, requiring no effort, simply, skillfully, smoothly, uncomplicated, undemanding, with ease, with no trouble at all, without even trying

EASY *(Effortless),* ***adjective*** effortless, facile, not burdensome, not complicated, not difficult, push over, quick and easy, simple, soft, straightforward, uncomplicated
ASSOCIATED CONCEPTS: easy access to the courts, simple contract

EASY *(Lenient),* ***adjective*** accommodating, benevolent, easy, forbearing, indulgent, lax, loose, permissive, pushover, relaxed, soft, unburdensome, undemanding, understanding, unexacting, unoppressive

EASY *(Obvious),* ***adjective*** apparent, axiomatic, clear, distinct, evident, indisputable, manifest, obvious, plain, readily comprehensible, readily learnable, simple, straightforward, totally comprehensible, totally learnable, uncomplicated, undemanding
ASSOCIATED CONCEPTS: easy construction of a legal document

EAVESDROP, ***verb*** hearken, intercept, listen, listen stealthily, overhear, tap the lines, wiretap
ASSOCIATED CONCEPTS: eavesdropping device, search warrant, suppression hearing, wiretapping

EBB, ***verb*** crumble, decay, decline, decrease, degenerate, deteriorate, drop, drop off, dwindle, fade away, fail, fall, fall away, fall off, move back, recede, *recedere,* retire, retreat, shrink, sink, slide, slip, slip back, subside, wane, waste away, withdraw

EBULLIENT, ***adjective*** bubbling, bubbly, effervescent, filled with personality, outward, sparkling

ECCENTRIC, ***adjective*** aberrant, anomalous, bizarre, contrary, curious, departing from the usual course, deviant, deviating, deviative, different, differing, divergent, erratic, extraordinary, idiosyncratic, independent, individual, *inusitatus,* irregular, *mirus,* nonconforming, nonconformist, *novus,* odd, out of the common run, out of the ordinary, outlandish, peculiar, quaint, queer, singular, strange, uncommon, unconforming, unconventional, unfashionable, unimitative, unique, unorthodox, unusual, wayward

ECHO, ***verb*** copying, duplication, imitation, reecho, reflect, repeat, repetition, resound, return, reverberate, reverberation
ASSOCIATED CONCEPTS: a circuit court decision echoing another circuit of the U.S. Court of Appeals

ECLIPSE, ***verb*** adumbrate, becloud, block, by far exceed, by far outweigh, cloak, cloud, conceal, cover, dwarf, enshroud, exceed, far exceed, far outweigh, hide, obfuscate, overshadow, shade, shadow, surpass

ECOLOGY, ***noun*** antipollution project, bioecology, bionomics, conservation, environmental science, environmental studies, human environment, maintenance, management of natural resources, natural science, nature study, pollution control, preservation, protection, study of ecosystems, study of environs, study of surroundings, support, survival studies, sustainment, sustenance

ECONOMIC, ***adjective*** cost-effective, cost-reducing, economical, labor-saving, money-saving, time-saving, thrifty
ASSOCIATED CONCEPTS: economic activity, economic conditions, economic depression, economic groups, economic factors, economic interest, economic policy, economic segregation, economic status, economic value

ECONOMIC LIBERTIES, ***noun*** economic freedom, free markets, freedom of economic initiative, open markets

ECONOMICAL, ***adjective*** *attentus,* avoiding extravagance, careful, chary of expense, cheap, cost-reducing, *diligens,* economizing, efficient, financially prudent, forehanded, free from waste, frugal, *frugi,* inexpensive, labor-saving, money-conscious, money-saving, niggardly, parsimonious, provident, prudent, saving, sparing, thrifty, time-saving, unlavish, unwasteful

ECONOMY *(Economic system),* ***noun*** administration, administration of economics, administration of resources, economic science, management, management of resources, regulation of finances, system of distributing wealth, wealth

ECONOMY *(Frugality),* ***noun*** avoidance of waste, careful management, carefulness, carefulness in outlay, chariness, cheapness of operation, economicalness, forehandedness, freedom from extravagance, frugalness, good management, husbanding of resources, management, paring, *parsimonia,* prevention of waste, providence, prudence, restriction, saving, scheduling, sound stewardship, sparing, thrift, thriftiness

ECSTATIC, ***adjective*** approving, beatific, beside oneself, blissful, carried away, delighted, delirious with joy, dithyrambic, elated, elevated, emotional, enchanted, enraptured, enthusiastic, entranced, excited, exultant, felicitous, full of feeling, glad, happy, heartfelt, joyful, joyous, jubilant, overjoyed, overpowered with emotion, passionate, radiant, rapt, rapturous, rhapsodical, thrilled, tingling, transported

EDGE *(Advantage),* ***noun*** advantageous position, benefit, favorable position, head start, jump, lead, odds, superiority, upper hand, vantage

EDGE *(Border),* ***noun*** bank, boundary, bounds, brim, brink, confines, corner, demarcation line, dividing line, edging, extremity, *fimbriae,* frame, fringe, frontier, limit, lip, margin, *margo,* molding, *ora,* outer edge, outline, outskirts, periphery, point, rim, side, skirts, tip, verge

EDICT, ***noun*** authoritative command, canon, command, *consultum,* declaration, decree, *decretum,* dictate, *edictum,* enactment, fiat, judgment, law, legislation, mandate, order, ordinance, precept, pronouncement, regulation, regulation by law, regulation by statute, rule, ruling, statute

EDIFICATION, ***noun*** acquirement, advancement, advantage, attainment, avail, benefit, betterment, direction, education, educational clarification, educational knowledge, enlightenment, gain, guidance, improvement, information, instruction, knowledge, learning, mental cultivation, preparation, profit, progress, schooling, spiritual upbuilding, teaching, training, tuition, tutelage, uplifting

EDIFICE, ***noun*** architectural monument, building, building of imposing appearance, construction, high structure, imposing building, piece of architecture, public building, skyscraper, structure, tower

EDIFY, ***verb*** brief, coach, direct, discipline, *docere,* educate, enlarge the mind, enlighten, guide, improve, inform, instruct, prime, school, show, strengthen, teach, train, tutor, upbuild, uplift

EDIT, ***verb*** alter, amend, annotate, arrange, choose, comment on, correct, cross out, cut, dele, delete, emend, emendate, erase, expunge, improve, *librum edere,* make corrections, make improvements, make ready for publication, modify by excisions, polish, prepare for publication, put right, rearrange, rectify, redact, redraft, refine, remove errors, revamp, revise, rework, rewrite, select, strike out, trim, weed, write notes for

EDITORIAL, ***adjective*** analytical, critical, editing, elucidative, elucidatory, enlightening, explaining, explanatory, explicatively, explicatory, expositive, expository, illuminative, illustrative, journalistic, reportorial, technical
ASSOCIATED CONCEPTS: law review, plain language

EDITORIALIZE, ***verb*** articulate a personal position, elucidate on, examine an issue, issue a policy statement, issue a position statement, opine on, personal analysis, prepare critical analysis, present a perspective, write a column, write a commentary, write an analytical piece, write an article, write an opinion piece
ASSOCIATED CONCEPTS: broadcasting law, free speech, First Amendment

EDUCATE, ***verb*** brief, bring up, civilize, coach, cultivate, direct, discipline, drill, edify, *educare,* enlighten, *erudire,* explain, familiarize, give lessons, guide, implant, inculcate, indoctrinate, inform, initiate, *instituere,* instruct, interpret, nurture, preach, prepare, prime, rear, school, show, teach, train, tutor, wipe out illiteracy

EDUCATION, ***noun*** accomplishments, acquirements, acquisition of knowledge, body of knowledge, coaching, cultivation, culture, direction, edification, elucidation, enlightenment, erudition, explanation, general information, guidance, imparting of skill, improvement of the mind, inculcation, indoctrination, instruction, intellectuality, knowledge, learning, letters, literacy, pedagogy, preparation, propaedeutics, qualification, scholarship, schooling, science of teaching, store of knowledge, studies, system of knowledge, systematic training, teaching, training, tuition, tutelage, tutoring, upbringing
ASSOCIATED CONCEPTS: board of education, educational corporation, educational facilities, educational institution, educational purposes, educational trust, educational uses

EDUCE, ***verb*** bring forth, bring out, bring to light, call forth, deduce, derive, discover, draw, draw forth, draw out, elicit, evoke, evolve, extract, extricate, ferret out, infer, lay open, make obvious, obtain, procure, pull, pull out, secure, summon forth, unearth, unfold, unveil
ASSOCIATED CONCEPTS: educe evidence

EFFACE, ***verb*** abolish, annihilate, black out, blot out, cancel, decimate, delete, demolish, destroy, destruct, devour, discontinue, disintegrate, dissolve, do away with, eliminate, end, eradicate, erase, expel, expunge, exterminate, extinguish, liquidate, obliterate, quell, ravage, raze, remove, root out, ruin, scratch out, stop, terminate

EFFECT, ***noun*** accomplishment, achievement, aftermath, *consecutio,* consequence, development, effectuation, *effectus,* end product, end result, eventuation, eventus, final result, fruit, fruition, impact, issue, outcome, outgrowth, payoff, product, reaction, repercussion, response, result, resultant, resultant action, sequel, termination, upshot
ASSOCIATED CONCEPTS: cause and effect, chilling effect, effective procuring cause, force and effect, natural effect, personal effects
FOREIGN PHRASES: ***Effectus sequitur causam.*** The effect follows the cause. ***Verba accipienda sunt cum effectu, ut sortiantur effectum.*** Words are to be received with effect, so that they may be productive of effect. ***Cessante causa, cessat effectus.*** The cause ceasing, the effect must cease. ***Cum quod ago non valet ut ago, valeat quantum valere potest.*** When that which I do is of no effect as I do it, it shall be as effective as it can (otherwise) be made. ***Nova constitutio futuris formam imponere debet non praeteritis.*** A new law ought to affect the future, not what is past. ***Non efficit affectus nisi sequatur effectus.*** The intention amounts to nothing unless some effect follows. ***Verba accipienda ut sortiantur effectum.*** Words should be taken so that they may have some effect. ***Cuicunque aliquis quid concedit concedere videtur et id, sine quo res ipsa esse non potuit.*** Whoever grants anything to another is supposed to grant that also without which the grant itself would be of no effect. ***Juris affectus in executione consistit.*** The effectiveness of a law lies in its execution. ***Quando quod ago non valet ut ago, valeat quantum valere potest.*** When that which I do does not have effect as I do it, let it have as much effect as it can. ***Cessante ratione legis, cessat et ipsa lex.*** Where the reason for a law ceases, the law itself also ceases. ***Officit conatus si effectus sequatur.*** The attempt becomes of consequence if the effect follows.

EFFECTIVE *(Efficient),* ***adjective*** able, adapted, adequate, advantageous, capable, competent, convenient, effectual, efficacious, *efficax,* equal to, expedient, fit, functional, handy, helpful, implemental, instrumental, of service, of use, practicable, practical, pragmatic, productive, proficient, profitable, serviceable, skillful, successful, to the purpose, unerring, up to, useful, utilitarian, valid

EFFECTIVE *(Operative),* ***adjective*** active, at work, effectual, fit for use, having legal force, in action, in effect, in force, in operation, operational, ready for use, usable, valid, working

ASSOCIATED CONCEPTS: effective assignment, effective at death, effective date, effective dissolution

EFFECTS, *noun* assets, belongings, *bona,* chattel property, chattels, contents, estate, goods, holdings, legal estate, means, movable property, paraphernalia, personal property, personalty, possessions, property, *res,* resources, things, wealth, worldly substance
ASSOCIATED CONCEPTS: household effects, personal effects, personal property, personalty

EFFECTUAL, *adjective* achieved, authoritative, binding, effective, efficacious, efficient, end result, eventuation, final result, impact, outcome, outgrowth, response, result, resultant, resultant action, rewarding, upshot, valuable, worthwhile

EFFECTUATE, *verb* accomplish, achieve, attain, bring to maturity, bring to pass, carry into effect, carry into execution, carry through, cause, cause to happen, complete, effect, enact, enforce, execute, fulfill, manage, perform, produce, put in force, realize, succeed, work

EFFECTUATION, *noun* accomplishment, achievement, act, action, arrangement, bequest, bestowal, carrying out an action, commission, completion, conclusion, consignment, conveyance, culmination, determination, discharge, disposal, distribution, enactment, end, execution, finalization, fulfillment, goal, implementation, order, performance, provision, realization, result, sequence, settlement, success, ultimate conclusion, upshot, winding up

EFFICACIOUS, *adjective* adept, adequate, beneficial, capable, compelling, competent, consummate, effective, effectual, efficient, emphatic, fruitful, functional, impressive, operative, potent, powerful, powerful sound, practical, productive, puissant, serviceable, striking, strong, successful, sufficient, usable, useful, valid, virtuous, workable

EFFICIENCY, *noun* ability, ableness, adeptness, adroitness, capability, capableness, command, competence, competency, deftness, dexterity, dexterousness, effectiveness, efficacy, *efficientia,* excellence, expertness, handiness, helpfulness, mastery, potency, productiveness, proficiency, prowess, quickness, resourcefulness, skill, skillfulness, vis

EFFICIENT, *adjective* able, adroit, capable, competent, deft, dexterous, effective, effectual, expedient, expeditious, expert, functional, *habilis,* mighty, potent, powerful, practical, productive, proficient, puissant, skilled, skillful
ASSOCIATED CONCEPTS: efficient cause, efficient intervening cause

EFFORT, *noun* applied energy, arduousness, assiduity, assiduousness, attempt, *conatus, contentio,* endeavor, essay, exertion, expenditure of energy, hard work, industry, laboriousness, *opera,* pains, strain, strenuousness, struggle, toil, travail, trial, vigor, vigorousness

EFFORTLESS *(Accomplished),* ***adjective*** a natural, deft, dexterous, docile, practiced, skilled, skillful, talented

EFFORTLESS *(Easy),* ***adjective*** deft, dexterous, easily done, easy, nothing to it, readily mastered, simple
ASSOCIATED CONCEPTS: simplified court system, simplified procedures for uncontested divorce

EFFUSE, *verb* deal out, diffuse, disperse, disseminate, distribute, exude, flow, flow out, give clemency to, issue, notify, outpouring, pour out, promulgate, publicize, publish, radiate, spill, transmit

EFFUSIVE, *adjective* building up, complimentary, complimenting, delighted with, demonstrative, ebullient, emotional, emotive, enthusiastic, exuberant, fervent, gushing with compliments, gushy, heaping praise, overflowing, praising, profuse

EGO, *noun* character, conceit, egoism, egotism, feelings, identity, image of oneself, individuality, person, personality, pride, pride in administration by others, pride in place in society, pride in reputation, pride in status, self, self-concept, self-esteem, self-identity, self-image
ASSOCIATED CONCEPTS: alter ego

EGREGIOUS, *adjective* absurd, appalling, arrant, bizarre, excessive, extravagant, flagrant, glaring, immoderate, inordinate, intemperate, outrageous, outré, remarkable, uncomfortable

EGRESS, *noun* departure, discharge, doorway, egression, *egressus,* emergence, emersion, emigration, escape, evacuation, exit, *exitus,* exodus, gate, gateway, leavetaking, means of exit, opening, outlet, parting, passage out, place of exit, way out, withdrawal

EITHER, *adjective* alternative, both, choice, each, either alternate, either item, either one, either or, either particular one, either possibility, either potentiality, on the one hand, one, one of two, one or the other, the one and the other
ASSOCIATED CONCEPTS: either case law or common law, either party to a marriage, either state law or federal, pleading in the alternative

EJECT *(Evict),* ***verb*** cast out, *deicere,* dislodge, displace, dispossess, divest, expel, get rid of, oust, put out, put out of possession, remove, remove from premises, rid, summarily dispossess, throw out, thrust out, turn out, turn out of possession

EJECT *(Expel),* ***verb*** cast forth, cast out, detrude, discard, discharge, disgorge, dismiss, *eicere,* eliminate, eruct, eructate, exclude, *expellere, extrudere,* force out, jettison, oust, push away, push out, remove, throw out, thrust out

ELABORATE, *adjective* baroque, beautified, bedecked, complex, complicated, daedal, decorated, deluxe, detailed, developed minutely, done with thoroughness, *elaboratus,* embellished, executed with exactness, fancy, festooned, flamboyant, flashy, garnished, grandiose, highly wrought, intricate, intricately wrought, involute, involved, labored, marked by excessive effort, ornamented, ornate, ostentatious, painstaking, palatial, perfected, rich, showy, studied, sumptuous, wrought with labor

ELABORATE, *verb* add to, amplify, augment, be more specific, detail, develop, enlarge upon, enrich, expand, give additional information, go into detail, improve upon, magnify, perfect, refine, state something in detail

ELABORATION, *noun* addition, adornment, amplification, augmentation, blossoming, coloring, details, elucidation, embellishment, emergence, enhancement, evolution, evolvement, expansion, explication, flourishing, flowering, further delineation, garnish, hyperbole, improvement, incubation, magnification, maturation, metamorphosis, ornamentation, perfection, progress, progression, refinement, specification, specifics, statement, supplementation

ELAPSE, *verb* cease, cease to be, close, come to an end, conclude, disappear, discontinue, draw to a close, end, expire, finish, go, go by, happen, lapse, occur, pass, pass by, run out, slip away, stop, succumb, take place, terminate, transpire, vanish
ASSOCIATED CONCEPTS: time elapsing for an appeal, time elapsed to challenge a ruling

ELATED, *adjective* blissful, delighted, ecstatic, euphoric, exalted, excited, exhilarated, exultant, happy, in paradise, joyful, jubilant, overjoyed, pleased, rejoicing, thrilled, triumphant

ELDER, *noun* adult, advanced in years, ancestor, ancient, antiquated, antique, archaic, early, elderly, matured, older man, older woman, one of the older generation, original, senior, senior citizen, superannuated, veteran, vintage
ASSOCIATED CONCEPTS: elder care, medicare, social security

ELDERLY, *adjective* advanced in years, aetate *provectus,* aged, along in years, hoary, matured, old, seasoned, senescent

ELECT *(Choose),* ***verb*** *creare,* decide, *deligere,* determine in favor of, distinguish by special selection, *eligere,* eliminate the alternatives, exercise an option, exercise discretion, make a choice, make a selection, name, opt for, pick, select, settle on, will
ASSOCIATED CONCEPTS: election of remedies, election of rights, election under a will, equitable election, right of election

ELECT *(Select by a vote),* ***verb*** appoint by vote, cast the majority of ballots for, choose for office, designate for office by vote, place in office, select for office, vote into office
ASSOCIATED CONCEPTS: election by ballot, election contest, election day, election district, election laws, election returns, electioneering, elective office, general election, notice of election, popular election, primary election, public election, regular election, special election

ELECTION *(Choice),* ***noun*** appointment, choice between alternatives, cooptation, decision, deliberate choice, designation, determination, *electio,* option, pick, preference, selection, *suffragia,* volition
ASSOCIATED CONCEPTS: election between inconsistent remedies, election of remedies, election of rights, election under a will, equitable election, estoppel by election
FOREIGN PHRASES: ***Consecratio est periodus electionis; electio est praeambula consecration is.*** Consecration is the termination of election; election is the preamble of consecration. ***Electio est interna libera et spontanea separatio unius rei ab alia sine compulsione, consistens in animo et voluntate.*** Election is an internal, free, and spontaneous separation of one thing from another, without compulsion, consisting of intention and will. ***Electio semel facta, et placitum testatum non patitur regressum.*** An election once made, and the intent shown, cannot be recalled. ***Electiones fiant rite et libere sine interruptione aliqua.*** Elections should be made in due form and freely, without any interruption.

ELECTION *(Selection by vote),* ***noun*** appointment by vote, balloting, choosing by vote, plebiscite, poll, referendum, representation, selection for office by vote, vote-casting
ASSOCIATED CONCEPTS: ballots, caucus, election contest, election district, election law, election petitions, election returns, general election, primary election, referendum, regular election, special election

ELECTIVE *(Selective),* ***adjective*** alternative, bestowed by ballot, by vote, choosing, cooptive, disjunctive, on approval, open to choice
ASSOCIATED CONCEPTS: elective franchise, elective office

ELECTIVE *(Voluntary),* ***adjective*** appointive, discretionary, gratuitous, not required, optional, spontaneous

ELECTORATE, *noun* American voters, body politic, constituency, constituents, general election voters, registered voters, voters
ASSOCIATED CONCEPTS: electoral college, elector

ELECTROCUTION, *noun* capital punishment, condemnation by death, conviction of death sentence, death penalty, death sentence, death warrant, execution, first-degree murder with death sentence, give the chair, judgment of death, put to death, ultimate sentence
ASSOCIATED CONCEPTS: death by legal injection, Eighth Amendment, gas chamber

ELECTRONIC MONITORING, *noun* electronic surveillance, e-monitoring, mass acquisitions of electronic files, mass electronic monitoring, monitoring pursuant to the Foreign Intelligence Surveillance Law, spying on terrorists, targeting foreign nationals
ASSOCIATED CONCEPTS: terrorism, terrorist cell

ELECTRONIC RIGHTS, *noun* all media and technology rights, electronic data, electronic product rights, electronic publishing rights, interactive media rights, multimedia rights, non linear display rights

ELEGANT, *adjective* aesthetic, beautiful, chic, deluxe, dignified, distinguished, *elegans,* exquisite, fashionable, gorgeous, graceful, grand, handsome, in good taste, lovely, magnificent, proportioned, refined, sophisticated, splendid, stately, stylish, tasteful, unmeretricious

ELEMENT, *noun* cantle, component, component part, constituent, content, detail, *elementum,* essential part, factor, feature, fraction, fragment, fundamental part, ingredient, integral part, item, member, part, particle, piece, portion, rudiment, section, segment, substance
ASSOCIATED CONCEPTS: elements of a cause of action, elements of a crime, elements of recovery

ELEMENTAL, *adjective* basic, beginning, crude, delineated in basic terms, easy, easy to understand, foundational, fundamental, inceptive, initiatory, introductory, obvious, plain, precursory, prefatory, primal, primary, primitive, rudimental, rudimentary, simple, simplified, sophomoric, starting, uncomplicated, understandable, unsophisticated

ELEMENTARY, *adjective* abecedarian, apparent, basal, basic, beginning, crude, easy, easy to understand, elemental, foundational, fundamental, inceptive, initiatory, introductory, obvious, plain, precursory, prefatory, primary, primitive, *primus,* proemial, rudimental, rudimentary, simple, simplified, starting, uncomplex, uncomplicated, understandable, unraveled, unsophisticated
ASSOCIATED CONCEPTS: elementary canon of interpretation

ELEVATE, *verb* advance, aggrandize, *attollere,* beatify, boost, build up, canonize, cause to rise, confer an honor, consecrate, deify, dignify, distinguish, erect, exalt, glorify, heave up, heft, heighten, hoist, hold aloft, hold up, honor, improve, jack up, *levare,* lift, make higher, pick up, pitch, promote, prop, put on a pedestal, raise, raise aloft, raise to a higher position, sanctify, sublimate, upgrade, uplift, upraise

ELEVATION, *noun* advancement, aggrandizement, altitude, canonization, consecration, coronation, deification, dignification, *elatio,* elevated place, eminence, eminency, erection, exaltation, height, high land, highness, lift, loftiness, promotion, rise, sanctification, stature, steepness, tallness, uplift, upright distance

ELICIT, *verb* arouse, author, awaken, beget, bring about, bring forth, bring forward, bring out, call forth, cause, draw forth, draw out, *eblandiri,* educe, effect, effectuate, *elicere, evocare,* evoke, extract, generate, initiate, make manifest, stimulate, summon forth

ELIDE, *verb* abate, abolish, annul, cancel, countermand, declare null and void, delete, discard, dismiss, dispel, dissolve, end, eradicate, extinguish, extirpate, invalidate, leave out, nullify, obliterate, omit, overrule, overturn, put an end to, quell, quench, repeal, repress, rescind, reverse, stop, subdue, suppress, terminate, vacate, withdraw

ELIGIBLE, *adjective* acceptable, appropriate, approved, befitting, capable, desirable, *dignus,* employable, fit, fit for appointment, fit for election, fit for selection, fit to be chosen, fitting, *idoneus,* legally qualified, *opportunus,* proper, qualified, right, satisfactory, suitable, usable
ASSOCIATED CONCEPTS: eligible to hold public office

ELIMINATE *(Eradicate),* ***verb*** abolish, annihilate, blot out, cancel, clear out, consume, cut out, decimate, delete, demolish, deracinate, desolate, destroy, devour, dispatch, dispose of, dissolve, do away with, efface, end, erase, evacuate, expunge, expurgate, exterminate, extirpate, get rid of, kill, lay waste, liquidate, nullify, obliterate, overthrow, purge, put a stop to, put an end to, quash, quell, raze, remove, render useless, slaughter, stamp out, strike out, suppress, sweep away, tear out, terminate, uproot, void, weed out, wipe out

ELIMINATE *(Exclude),* ***verb*** ban, banish, bar, blockade, cashier, cast out, censor, count out, debar, deport, disallow, disbar, discard, disdain, dismiss, disqualify, disregard, do away with, eject, elide, evacuate, evict, except, exclude, excommunicate, exempt, exile, expatriate, expel, keep out, leave out, lock out, omit, ostracize, oust, outlaw, preclude, prevent, prohibit, proscribe, put aside, rebuff, reject, remove, renounce, repulse, rule out, set aside, shed, shut out, spurn, throw out, thrust out, turn out, weed

ELIMINATION, *noun* abatement, abolition, annihilation, cancellation, curtailment, depletion, destruction, discardment, discharge, disposal, disposition, disqualification, dissolution, ejection, emptying, end, eradication, evulsion, exclusion, excretion, exhaustion, expulsion, extermination, extinction, extinguishment, extirpation, extrusion, exudation, nullification, obliteration, omission, prohibition, proscription, purge, rejection, removal, renunciation, riddance, separation, voidance
ASSOCIATED CONCEPTS: censorship, elimination of rights

ELITE, *noun* aristocracy, best part, best people, choice group, chosen few, cream of society, fashionable society, gentry, high society, most carefully selected group, nobility, optimates, privileged class, select body, select few, superior group, top people, upper circles, upper classes

ELONGATION, *verb* add to, aggrandize, amplify, augment, compound, continue, continuing, drag out, draw out, enlarge, enlarge upon, expand, extend, grow longer, increase, lengthen, linger, make larger, meandering, neverending, prolong, protract, spread, stretch, supplement, sustain

ELOQUENT, *adjective* articulate, calculated to stir, communicative, compelling, convincing, *disertus,* effective, *eloquens,* expressive, flowing, fluent, forceful, full of feeling, full of meaning, full of substance, graceful, impassioned, impressive, incisive, informative, meaningful, mellifluous, moving, movingly expressive, persuasive, pithy, pointed, powerful, powerfully expressive, pregnant, rich, spellbinding, striking, telling, trenchant, vivid

ELSEWHERE, *adverb* absent, another place, away, further away, gone, in a distant place, in a foreign location, in a foreign place, in a foreign setting, in another place, in some other place, not present, not under consideration, outside, remote, removed

ELUCIDATE, *verb* annotate, ascertain, bring out more clearly, cast light upon, clarify, clear of obscurity, clear up, comment upon, commentate, construe, decipher, decode, define, demonstrate, describe, detail, determine, disentangle, enlighten, enucleate, exemplify, explain, *explanare,* explicate, *exponere,* exposit, expound, find a clue, give an explanation, give an interpretation, illuminate, illustrate, interpret, *interpretari,* lay open, make apparent, make clear, make intelligible, make less confusing, make lucid, make plain, make sense of, make simple, make understandable, manifest, paraphrase, popularize, put in other words, ravel, rephrase, restate, shed light upon, simplify, solve, spell out, teach, throw light upon, translate, unfold, unravel, unriddle, unscramble, untangle

ELUCIDATION, *noun* analysis, annotation, annunciation, clarification, comment, commentary, construction, deciphering, decoding, demonstration, details, disentanglement, edification, enlightenment, exegesis, explanation, explication, exposition, gloss, illumination, illustration, interpretation, justification, rationale, rationalization, reasoning, restatement, specifications, translation, unscrambling

ELUDE, *verb* abscond, avoid, baffle, be concealed, break away, break loose, dodge, *eludere,* escape, escape by artifice, escape detection, escape notice, evade, *evitare,* flee, get away, hide, keep aloof, keep out of sight, make an escape, mystify, outmaneuver, outwit, parry, remain hidden, remain undiscovered, shun, slip away, slip out, steal away, take evasive action

ELUSIVE, *adjective* abstruse, apt to flee, baffling, difficult, difficult to catch, difficult to comprehend, difficult to understand, eluding clear perception, elusory, enigmatic, equivocal, escaping, evanescent, evasive, fleeting, fugitive, hard to define, hard to express, hard to grasp, hard to maintain, hard to understand, impalpable, intangible, liable to disappear, mysterious, nebulous, obscure, occult, puzzling, runaway, shadowy, shunning, slippery, tending to elude, tending to escape, tending to slip away, uncertain, unclear, vanishing

ELUSORY, ***adjective*** abstract, complex, convex, deceptive, elusive, enigmatic, evanescent, evasive, fleeting, furtive, hard to grasp, hazy, illusive, impalpable, imponderable, intangible, mysterious, oblique, obtruse, recondite, transient
ASSOCIATED CONCEPTS: illusory agreements, illusory statutes

EMANATE, ***verb*** arise from, come forth, come from, debouch, derive from, descend from, *effundi,* effuse, eject, *emanare,* emerge, emit, ensue from, exude, fall out, flow forth, *fluere,* follow from, go out of, grow from, grow out of, issue, originate in, pour out of, proceed, project, radiate, result, spring from, stream out

EMANCIPATION, ***noun*** acquittal, deliverance, deliverance from bondage, discharge, enfranchisement, extrication, freedom, *liberatio,* liberation, liberty, *manumissio,* manumission, pardon, possession of full rights, release, release from custody, reprieve, salvation, setting free, unshackling
ASSOCIATED CONCEPTS: complete emancipation, emancipation of minors, Emancipation Proclamation, express emancipation, implied emancipation, partial emancipation

EMASCULATION, ***noun*** castration, debilitation, debility, decrepitude, depleted, enervation, expurgation, fault, helplessness, infirmity, impotence, languor, unmanning, weakness

EMBARGO, ***noun*** authoritative stoppage of trade, ban, bar, control of trade, debarment, denial, detention of ships, disallowance of trade, exclusion from commerce, forbiddance, freeze, governmental order of prohibition, halt, interference, legal restraint, preclusion, prohibition, restraint, restriction, stop, stoppage
ASSOCIATED CONCEPTS: embargo of commerce, embargo of goods, embargo of products

EMBARK, ***verb*** auspicate, begin, commence, engage in an enterprise, enter, enter upon, get under way, go into, inaugurate, initiate, institute, launch, make a beginning, originate, plunge into, *rationem inire,* set out, start, start out, take on, take the first step, take up, undertake, venture

EMBARRASS, ***verb*** abash, annoy, baffle, bedevil, beset, bewilder, bother, burden, cause confusion, cause discomfort, cause to feel ill at ease, chagrin, confuse, *conturbare,* discomfit, discomfort, discompose, disconcert, disquiet, distress, disturb, encumber, fluster, *impedire,* incommode, make self-conscious, make uncomfortable, mortify, nonplus, perturb, plague, put at a disadvantage, render flustered, render ill at ease, shame, trouble, upset, vex, worry

EMBARRASSMENT, ***noun*** abashment, awkward situation, awkwardness, bafflement, chagrin, confusion, constraint, discomfiture, discomfort, discomposure, disturbance, fluster, humiliation, *implicatio,* mortification, perturbation, pudency, *scrupulus,* self-consciousness, shame, uneasiness

EMBASSY, ***noun*** ambassadorial function, ambassadorial office, ambassadorial residence, commission, consulate, delegation, deputation, diplomatic corps, embassage, establishment of an ambassador, legateship, *legatio,* legation, mission, mission of the ambassador, official headquarters of an ambassador, official mission
ASSOCIATED CONCEPTS: consular and diplomatic officers

EMBED, ***verb*** bury, deposit, engraft, entrench, fix, fix firmly, implant, impress, imprint, infix, ingrain, insert, lodge, plant, press in, root, seat, set, set firmly, settle, stamp

EMBELLISH, ***verb*** add details, adorn, array, beautify, bedeck, bedizen, bejewel, beribbon, bespangle, better, blazon, chase, dandify, deck, *decorare,* decorate, dizen, dress up, elaborate, emblazon, emboss, embroider, encrust, enhance, enrich, *exornare,* fix up, frill, garnish, gild, glamorize, grace, illuminate, illustrate, improve, make beautiful, make elaborate, make improvements, make resplendent, meliorate, ornament, polish, rubricate, smarten, spangle, spruce up, stretch, tool, touch up, trim, varnish

EMBEZZLE, ***verb*** appropriate fraudulently, appropriate to one's own use, *avertere,* commit larceny, defalcate, defraud, divert to one's own use, filch, *intercipere, intervertere,* misapply, misappropriate, misappropriate funds, misappropriate intrusted funds, misuse, pilfer, purloin, swindle, take by fraud, take feloniously, thieve
ASSOCIATED CONCEPTS: convert

EMBEZZLEMENT, ***noun*** appropriation, breach of trust, cheating, defalcation, fraud, fraudulent appropriation, fraudulent appropriation of money, fraudulent conversion, larceny, malversation, misappropriation, peculation, pilfering, purloining, stealing, swindle, theft, theft of money entrusted to one's care, theft of money entrusted to one's management, thievery, wrongful appropriation
ASSOCIATED CONCEPTS: conversion, corporate embezzlement, embezzlement of public funds, larceny, misappropriation, theft by means of embezzlement

EMBEZZLER, ***noun*** cheater, criminal, crook, culprit, defalcator, defrauder, evildoer, *interceptor,* lawbreaker, malefactor, one who commits larceny, peculator, *pecuniae aversor,* pilferer, purloiner, swindler, thief

EMBLEM, ***noun*** allusion, badge, banner, chevron, coat of arms, colors, crest, crown, escutcheon, figure, flag, hallmark, identification, image, indicium, insignia, keepsake, logo, mark, medal, monogram, motto, pennant, regalia, seal, sign, signet, standard, symbol, token
ASSOCIATED CONCEPTS: brand, emblem law, logo, mark, registration, trademark

EMBLEMATIC, ***adjective*** allusive, denotative, indicant, indicative, representational, representative, suggestive, symbolic, typical

EMBODIMENT, ***noun*** actualization, bodily presentation, bodily representation, concrete expression, corporeity, definite form, *effigies,* form, formation, incarnation, manifestation, material figuration, material representation, materialization, personification, realization, representation, *simulacrum,* substantiality, synthesis, tangibility, tangible form, visible form
ASSOCIATED CONCEPTS: embodied in a contract, embodied in the instrument

EMBODY, ***verb*** actualize, constitute, corporealize, exhibit in visible form, express in concrete form, form, give concrete form to, give definite form to, give tangible form to, incarnate, *includere,* incorporate, integrate, interblend, interfuse, intermix, invest with a body, invest with matter, make corporeal, make visible, manifest, materialize, personify, put into bodily form, substantialize, syncretize, synthesize

EMBOLDEN, ***verb*** abet, animate, assure, bolster, buoy, cheer, encourage, enhearten, foment, give confidence, hearten, impel, incite, inspire, inspirit, instigate, invigorate, nerve, press, promise, rally, reassure, rouse, stimulate, strengthen, urge

EMBRACE *(Accept),* ***verb*** adopt, advocate, affiliate, agree to, assume, be in favor of, concur in, consent to, countenance, endorse, espouse, favor, make one's own, ratify, sanction, seize, subscribe to, support, take to oneself, take up, welcome

EMBRACE *(Encircle),* ***verb*** begird, belt, cincture, circumscribe, compass, *complecti, comprehendere,* contain, cover, encincture, enclose, encompass, enfold, engird, envelop, gird, girdle, hold, include, incorporate, integrate, invest, involve, lap, receive, skirt, surround, take in

EMBROILMENT, ***noun*** affray, agitation, brawl, breach, broil, chaos, clash, combat, commotion, complication, conflict, confusion, contention, contest, derangement, difference of opinion, disarrangement, disorder, disquiet, dissension, dissentience, disturbance, embranglement, encounter, engagement, entanglement, ferment, fracas, fray, imbroglio, involvement, mix-up, muddle, odds, outbreak, pandemonium, quarrel, riot, row, rupture, squabble, strife, struggle, tumult, turbulence, turmoil, unrest, uproar, violence

EMBRYO, ***noun*** basis for development, beginning, bud, commencement, earliest stage, fetus, first stage, genesis, germ, immature stage, inchoation, incipience, incipient organism, origin, origination, partus, rudiment, rudimentary state, seed, source, start, starting point, undeveloped stage
ASSOCIATED CONCEPTS: abortion

EMBRYONIC, ***adjective*** amorphous, antecedent, basic, beginning, commencing, developing, developmental, early, elementary, evolving, first, formless, fundamental, germinal, immature, imperfect, inceptive, inchoate, incipient, initial, initiative, introductory, nascent, older, originating, preliminary, primitive, rudimentary, shapeless, undeveloped, unfinished, unformed, unshaped

EMEND, ***verb*** adjust, alter, ameliorate, amend, better, change, correct, *corrigere,* do over, *emendare,* emendate, fix, help, improve, make better, make corrections, make improvements, make repairs, meliorate, mend, put in order, put right, reconstruct, rectify, redo, refine, reform, remedy, remodel, remove errors, render better, reorganize, repair, restore, retouch, revamp, revise, rework, rewrite, rid of defects, right, set right, set straight, touch up, work over

EMERGE, ***verb*** appear, arise, arrive, become apparent, become manifest, become plain, become visible, break through, burst forth, come forth, come forward, come into notice, come into view, come out, come out of hiding, come to light, crop up, dawn, emanate, *emergere,* enter the picture, exit, expose, issue, loom, make an appearance, manifest, materialize, put in an appearance, rise, show, show up, surface, turn up

EMERGENCE, ***noun*** appearance, arrival, commencement, development, evidence, initiation, issue, manifestation, materialization, notice, now apparent, show, start, viewed
ASSOCIATED CONCEPTS: emergent law, the emergence of law

EMERGENCY, ***noun*** accident, *casus,* climacteric, condition of insufficiency, crisis, critical point, crucial period, difficulty, dilemma, *discrimen,* exigency, extremity, insufficiency of service, last-minute need, necessitousness, need, need for action, needfulness, plight, predicament, pressing necessity, pressing need, strait, sudden peril, *tempus,* trouble, unexpected happening, unforeseen condition, unforeseen occurrence, urgency
ASSOCIATED CONCEPTS: Emergency Court of Appeals, Emergency Defense Act, emergency employment doctrine, Emergency Price Control Act, private necessity, public emergency, public necessity

EMERGENCY AID, ***noun*** assistance in the face of immediate danger, crisis intervention, intervention to prevent harm, split-second intervention, warrantless entry in exigent circumstances, warrantless entry to provide immediate aid
ASSOCIATED CONCEPTS: exception to Fourth Amendment Warrant Requirement

EMINENCE, ***noun*** aggrandizement, *amplissimus gradus,* authority, celebrity, consequence, dignity, distinction, elevated rank, elevation, esteem, exaltation, fame, *fastigium,* glory, grandeur, great station, greatness, height, high position, high rank, high station, honor, importance, important station, influence, loftiness, majesty, mark, mightiness, nobility, notability, note, noteworthiness, *praestantia,* preeminence, prestige, prominence, renown, repute, standing, supereminence, superiority, supremacy, weight

EMINENT DOMAIN, ***noun*** annex for public use, assume for public use, take possession for public use, usurp for public use

EMIT, ***verb*** beam, cast out, discharge, eject, *emittere,* eructate, erupt, exhale, exhaust, expel, expend, exude, give forth, give off, give out, gush, hurl, issue, jet, let out, pour forth, pour out, put forth, radiate, secrete, send forth, send out, shed, shoot, spurt, squirt, throw, throw off, throw out

EMOLUMENT, ***noun*** advance, allowance, benefit, bonus, commission, compensation, consideration, disbursement, earnings, fee, income, indemnification, pay, payment, profit, recompense, remuneration, requital, restitution, return, revenue, reward, salary, stipend, tribute, wage

EMOTION, ***noun*** affect, agitation, *animi motus,* ardor, eagerness, ebullition, enthusiasm, ferment, fervor, furor, great feeling, mood, passion, reaction, response, sensation, sensitiveness, sentiment, spirit, stir, turmoil, verve, zeal

EMPANEL, ***verb*** calendar, docket, enlist jurors, enroll, enter those names designated as jurors, insert names on a register, list for jury duty, list jurors, place upon a list, register, schedule, select jurors, sign in
ASSOCIATED CONCEPTS: empanel a jury

EMPATHIZE, ***verb*** be compassionate, be in tune, be sorry for, be understanding, comfort, commiserate, condole, express sympathy, feel for, grieve for, have pity for, identify with, pity, project, react, relate to, respond, share grief, share sorrow, show solace, show tenderness, soothe, sympathize, understand

EMPATHY, ***noun*** affinity, communion, compassion, comprehension, congeniality, decency, insight, pity, rapport, sympathy, understanding, warmth

EMPHASIS, ***noun*** accent, accentuation, affirmation, attention, concentration, consequence, consideration, distinction, distinctness, eminence, *emphasis,* energy, exclamation, force, force of expression, force of voice, forcibleness, highlight, ictus, importance, impressiveness, inflection, insistence, intensity of expression, moment, most important point, notability, note, outstanding feature, positiveness, pressure, primacy, prominence, salience, saliency, significance, special attention, special concern, special intonation, special significance, strength, stress, thrust, underlining, underscoring, value, vigorous enunciation, vociferation, weight, worth

EMPHASIZE, *verb* accent, accentuate, affirm, argue, articulate, assert, bear, contend, dwell, enforce, enhance, feature, heighten, highlight, insist, intensify, iterate, magnify, mark, plead, point up, pronounce, protest, punctuate, reaffirm, repeat, spearhead, spotlight, stress, underline, underscore, vociferate

EMPHATIC, *adjective* absolute, categorical, clear, compelling, decided, dogmatic, energetic, explicit, express, forceful, forcible, graphic, insistent, overt, positive, reiterative, resounding, strong, telling, vehement, vivid

EMPIRICAL, *adjective* analytical, based on evidence of the senses, based on observation, derived from experience, diagnostic, guided by experiment, provisional

EMPLOY *(Engage services)*, ***verb*** add to the payroll, appoint, assign, authorize, commission, contract, delegate, *detineri,* empower, engage, enlist, enroll, entrust with a task, entrust with management, fill a position, fill a vacancy, fill an opening, find help, furnish occupation for, give a job to, give a position to, give a post to, give employment, give work to, hire, keep in service, *occupatum,* place, put to work, recruit, retain, retain the services of, secure, set to work, sign up, staff, take into employ, take into service, use another's services, use as an agent, *versari*
ASSOCIATED CONCEPTS: actual employment, customarily employed, dangerous employment, employed in hazardous work, employed in interstate commerce, lawfully employed, legally employed, permanently employed

EMPLOY *(Make use of)*, ***verb*** apply, avail oneself of, capitalize upon, exercise, exploit, have recourse to, manipulate, mobilize, operate, ply, practice, profit by, put in action, put in operation, put to service, put to use, resort to, take advantage of, turn to account, turn to use, use, utilize, wield, work

EMPLOYEE, *noun* agent, apprentice, assistant, attaché, factotum, hand, help, helper, hired hand, hireling, jobholder, laborer, mercenary, personnel, representative, salaried worker, servant, staff person, subordinate, toiler, wage earner, worker, workman
ASSOCIATED CONCEPTS: agent, bona fide employee, borrowed employee, casual employee, de facto employee, independent contractor, joint adventurer, loaned employee, part-time employee, permanent employee, provisional employee, servant, subcontractor

EMPLOYEE-NUMEROSTY REQUIREMENT, *noun* criteria for lawsuit under Title VII of the Civil Rights Act of 1964, requisite number of employees required for liability purpose, threshold number of employees necessary for employer coverage

EMPLOYER, *noun* administrator, boss, chief, controller, director, executive, head, leader, management, manager, master, overseer, owner, patron, proprietor, superintendent, superior, supervisor, taskmaster
ASSOCIATED CONCEPTS: employers' liability acts

EMPLOYMENT, *noun* activity, appointment, assignment, avocation, berth, billet, business, calling, capacity, career, commission, craft, duty, employ, engagement, enterprise, field, function, incumbency, industry, job, labor, lifework, line, livelihood, living, means of livelihood, means of support, *negotium,* occupation, office, position, post, practice, profession, pursuit, retainment, service, situation, specialty, task, trade, vocation, work
ASSOCIATED CONCEPTS: abandonment of employment, arising out of and in course of employment, available for employment, casual employment, conditions of employment, contract of employment, course of employment, covered employment, dangerous employment, duration of employment, during term of employment, engaged in employment, exempt employment, extrahazardous employment, extraordinary employment, general employment, grade of employment, injury arising in course of employment, permanent employment, place of employment, private employment, professional employment, public employment, scope of employment, seasonal employment, temporary employment, tenure of employment

EMPLOYMENT DISCRIMINATION, *noun* bias in the workplace, prejudice in an employment environment
Generally: differentiation, disequalization, inequality, injustice, unfairness

EMPOWER, *verb* accredit, activate, aggrandize, allow, appoint, arm, assign, authorize, capacitate, commission, confer power on, delegate, depute, deputize, enable, endow, energize, entrust, franchise, give ability, give authority, give permission, give power, give right, grant, grant authority, grant power, *homini rei,* impart power to, implement, invest, license, make able, make capable, make potent, permit, potentiate, *potestatem facere,* privilege, qualify, render competent, sanction, strengthen, train, vest, warrant

EMPTY *(Nothing left)*, ***adjective*** all gone, bare, blank, depleted, devoid, drained, exhausted, hollow, nothing left inside, unfilled, vacuous, void, without contents
ASSOCIATED CONCEPTS: empty judgment, empty law

EMPTY *(Vacant)*, ***adjective*** abandoned, available, barren, deserted, fruitless, idle, no one home, not inhabited, unclaimed, uninhabited, unoccupied, untenanted, up for grabs
ASSOCIATED CONCEPTS: empty premises

EMPTY *(Without substance)*, ***adjective*** devoid of merit, inconsequential, ineffective, ineffectual, insignificant, insubstantial, meaningless, meritless, unavailing, unimportant, unreal, unsatisfying, useless, vain, valueless, without substance, worthless
ASSOCIATED CONCEPTS: an empty threat, veiled threat of law suit

EMULATE, *verb* copy, ditto, echo, follow, imitate, impersonate, mimic, mirror, repeat, rival, strive

EMULOUS, *adjective* admiring, competing, competitive, contending, copying, envious, follow the example of, following, imitative, jealous, rival

EN BANC, *adverb* all together, as a unit, as a whole, collectively, *en bloc, en masse,* entirely, in a body, in a mass, in sum, *in toto,* one and all

EN MASSE, *adverb* all together, as a body, as a group, as a whole, as one, at the same time, collectively, *en bloc,* ensemble, in assembly, in mass, in the aggregate, together

EN ROUTE, ***adverb*** along the way, bound, during the journey, during travel, in passage, in progress, in transit, midway, on the journey, on the road, on the way

ENABLE, ***verb*** abet, aid, allow, approve, arm, assist, authorize, capacitate, confer, consent, emancipate, empower, endow, facilitate, *facultatem facere,* give ability, give authority, give means, give permission, give power, grant, help, *homini rei,* implement, indulge, invest, let, liberate, license, make able, make capable, make possible, make practicable, permit, privilege, provide, provide means, qualify, release, remove a disability, render assistance, render competent, sanction, strengthen, supply with means, support
ASSOCIATED CONCEPTS: enabling act, enabling legislation, enabling statute

ENABLING LEGISLATION, ***noun*** establishing legislation, first initiative, law giving authority, law giving power, law granting authority, law granting license, law investing power, original ordinance, seminal measure, underlying act, underlying legislative pronouncement
ASSOCIATED CONCEPTS: enacting clause

ENACT, ***verb*** adopt a measure, appoint by act, codify, command, declare, decree, dictate, enjoin, establish, establish by law, give legislative sanction, institute by law, issue a command, legislate, make into a statute, make laws, ordain by law, order, pass, *perferre,* prescribe, put in force, put into effect
ASSOCIATED CONCEPTS: enacting clause
FOREIGN PHRASES: ***Non obligat lex nisi promulgata.*** A law is not obligatory unless it is promulgated. ***Ejus est interpretari cujus est condere.*** It is for him who enacts anything to give it interpretation.

ENACTMENT, ***noun*** act, bill, charter, codification, decree, dictate, edict, establishment, fiat, law, legislation, *lex,* measure, ordinance, *plebiscitum,* regulation, rule, ruling, *sanctio,* statute, statutory law
FOREIGN PHRASES: ***Leges suum ligent latorem.*** Laws should bind their own proposer. ***Jus constitui oportet in his quae ut plurimum accidunt non quae ex inopi nato.*** Laws ought to be made with a view to those cases which occur most frequently and not to those which are of rare or accidental occurrence. ***Leges figendi et refigendi consuetudo est periculosissima.*** The practice of making and remaking the laws is a most dangerous one. ***Quod populus postremum jussit, id jus ratum esto.*** What the people have last enacted, let that be the settled law.

ENCHANTING, ***adjective*** adorable, alluring, appealing, arresting, attractive, beguiling, bewitching, captivating, darling, delightful, engrossing, entrancing, fetching, haunting, hypnotic, interesting, mesmerizing, moving, pleasant, pleasing, riveting, spellbinding, tantalizing, tempting, terrific, winning

ENCLOSE, ***verb*** blockade, bound, bracket, capture, *cingere,* circumscribe, circumvallate, close in, compass, confine, contain, embrace, encase, encincture, encircle, encompass, enfold, envelop, environ, fence in, gird, girdle, hem in, immure, impound, imprison, incarcerate, *includere,* insert in a wrapper, insert in an envelope, keep behind bars, keep in, keep in custody, limit, pen, put a barrier around, put into a receptacle, restrain, restrict, retain, ring, *saepire,* shut in, surround, take into custody, trammel, wall in

ENCLOSURE, ***noun*** arena, barrier, blockade, border, boundary, bracket, cincture, circle, circumjacence, circumscription, circumvallation, confine, confinement, container, containment, custody, edge, embrace, encasement, encirclement, enclosed space, encompassment, enfoldment, envelopment, fence, fenced in area, girdle, immurement, impoundment, imprisonment, incarceration, insertion, limit, limitation, perimeter, pound, receptacle, restriction, trammel, walled-in area, wrapper, zone

ENCOMPASS *(Include),* ***verb*** *adscribere, complecti,* comprise, consist of, contain, *continere,* cover, embrace, hold, incorporate, span, subsume, take in
ASSOCIATED CONCEPTS: encompass a broad cross section of the law

ENCOMPASS *(Surround),* ***verb*** be circumjacent, begird, belt, border, bound, cincture, *cingere,* circle, circuit, *circumcludere, circumplecti,* circumscribe, compass, corral, edge, encase, encincture, encircle, enclose, enclose on all sides, engird, enring, ensphere, envelop, enwrap, fence in, form a circle round, gird, girdle, hem in, immure, keep in, pen in, ring, shut in, wall in, wrap

ENCOUNTER, ***verb*** catch, chance upon, collide, come face to face, come together, confront, converge, crash into, cross, engage, face, gather together, greet, happen upon, hold a meeting, hold convocation, huddle, join, mass, meet, meet by chance, meet by happenstance, meet coincidentally, pass, reencounter, reunite, salute, see, stumble upon, unite

ENCOURAGE, ***verb*** back, back up, boost, embolden, endorse, hearten, inspire, support

ENCROACH, ***verb*** breach, commit an infraction, enter by stealth, enter upon the domain of another, enter wrongfully, impinge, infiltrate, infringe, ingress wrongfully, interfere, interlope, intrude, intrude illegally, invade, invade unlawfully, *invadere,* irrupt, make an incursion, make inroads, obtrude, *occupare,* overstep, penetrate, raid, transgress, trespass, violate

ENCROACHMENT, ***noun*** breach, entrance by stealth, entrance upon the domain of another, illegal intrusion, impingement, imposition, incursion, infiltration, infraction, infringement, *iniuria,* inroad, interference, interloping, intrusion, invasion, irruption, obtrusion, overlap, overstepping, penetration, prying, raid, real estate trespass, transgression, trespass, unlawful invasion, violation, wrongful entry, wrongful ingress
ASSOCIATED CONCEPTS: adverse possession, common nuissance, easements, public nuissance

ENCUMBER *(Financially obligate),* ***verb*** assess, burden, charge, hold liable, *impedire,* impose a charge, impose a lien, make accountable for, make responsible for, mortgage, obligate, *onerare,* place a cloud on, *praegravare,* subject to a charge, subject to a liability
ASSOCIATED CONCEPTS: mortgage

ENCUMBER *(Hinder),* ***verb*** block, block up, burden, charge, cramp, cumber, disadvantage, discommode, entangle, entrammel, frustrate, hamper, hinder movement, hold back action, hold up, impede, impose, incommode, inconvenience, inflict, inhibit, interfere, interrupt, keep back, lade, limit, obstruct action, render difficult, retard, saddle, shackle, slow down, strain, tax, thwart, tie up, trammel, trouble, weaken, weigh down

ENCUMBRANCE, *noun* burden, charge, claim, curb, difficulty, disadvantage, drawback, hampering, hindering, hindrance, hitch, hurdle, impediment, *impedimentum,* imposition, inconvenience, infliction, interference, liability, lien, lien on an estate, load, mortgage, obstacle, obstruction, *onus,* oppression, pressure, restriction, retardation, stay, stop, stoppage
ASSOCIATED CONCEPTS: easements, mortgage
FOREIGN PHRASES: ***Transit terra cum onere.*** Land passes subject to any encumbrances affecting it.

END *(Intent),* ***noun*** aim, ambition, aspiration, bourn, *consilium,* desideration, desideratum, design, desire, desired result, destination, dream, expectation, goal, guiding principle, hope, idea, intended result, intendment, intention, mission, motivating idea, motivation, motive, object, objective, purpose, reason, target, wish
ASSOCIATED CONCEPTS: ends of justice

END *(Termination),* ***noun*** accomplishment, achievement, adjournment, attainment, border, borderline, bound, boundary, cessation, close, closing piece, closure, completion, concluding part, conclusion, consummation, culmination, curtain, death, decease, decline, demise, denouement, departure, destination, destiny, determination, dissolution, edge, elimination, ending, estoppage, *exitus,* expiration, expiry, extinction, extinguishment, extreme, extreme point, extremity, fate, final event, final state, finale, finality, finis, finish, fulfillment, furthermost part, halt, last of a series, last part, limit, limitation, omega, outcome, point, pole, realization, remnant, result, resultant, retirement, stop, stoppage, tail, terminal, terminal point, termination, terminus, tip, upshot, wane

ENDANGER, *verb* abuse, be careless with, be malevolent, bring into peril, bully, compromise, damage, dare, expose, expose to danger, expose to injury, expose to loss, harm, hazard, hurt, impair, imperil, *in discrimen, in periculum,* injure, jeopardize, leave defenseless, leave unprotected, make insecure, make liable to danger, make liable to injury, make unsafe, make vulnerable, maltreat, menace, misuse, molest, peril, persecute, prey upon, put in hazard, put in jeopardy, risk, risk exposure to harm, speculate with, stake, subject to loss, terrify, terrorize, threaten, torment, torture, victimize, violate
ASSOCIATED CONCEPTS: endanger life, endanger safety

ENDEAVOR, *noun* achievement, aim, application, assiduity, attempt, bid, campaign, cause, *conatus, contentio,* deed, effort, emprise, enterprise, essay, exercise, exertion, experiment, exploit, feat, labor, *nisus,* pains, project, pursuance, pursuit, quest, scheme, search, strain, strenuous effort, struggle, sustained trial, task, toil, travail, trial, try, undertaking, venture, work

ENDEAVOR, *verb* address oneself to, aim, apply oneself to, aspire, assay, assume, attempt, attempt strenuously, be resolute, bestir oneself, bid, compete for, *conari, contendere,* do all one can, do one's best, do one's utmost, engage in, *eniti,* essay, exert effort, exert oneself, experiment, labor, make a bid, make an attempt, make an effort, persevere, pursue, put oneself out, resolve, risk, seek, set about, spare no effort, spare no pains, strain, strive, struggle, tackle, take a crack at, take action, take on, take pains, take up, take upon oneself, test, toil, trouble oneself, try, undertake, venture, vie for, work at

ENDEMIC *(Contagious),* ***adjective*** catching, communicable, dangerous, epidemic, epizootic, infectious, pestiferous, transmittable

ENDEMIC *(Native),* ***adjective*** autochthonal, autochthonous, born, domestic, indigenous, local, original, regional

ENDLESS, *adjective* boundless, ceaseless, continual, continuous, countless, endless, enduring, eternal, everlasting, illimitable, immeasurable, incalculable, incessant, indefinite, indeterminable, inexhaustible, infinite, innumerable, interminable, limitless, measureless, never-ending, nonstop, perpetual, recurring, unbounded, unceasing, unchecked, unconditional, unconfined, uncontrolled, undying, unending, unfathomable, uninterrupted, universal, unlimited, unmeasured, unremitting, unrestrained, unrestricted, untold, vast, without end, without number
ASSOCIATED CONCEPTS: endless case law, endless punishment, endless torments, endless violence

ENDORSE, *verb* approve, attest, authenticate, back, certify, commend, confirm, ratify, sanction, second, support, validate

ENDORSEMENT *(Backing),* ***noun*** advertisement, advocacy, approval, assistance, assurance, attestation, authorization, commendation, encouragement, imprimatur, license, patronage, recommendation, sanction, signature, stamp of approval, support, testimonial, testimony, vouch, word
ASSOCIATED CONCEPTS: political endorsement

ENDORSEMENT *(Signature),* ***noun*** acceptance, approval, authorization, autograph, confirmation, countersignature, execution, go-ahead, passage, permission, ratification, sanction, seal, signet, signing, sponsorship, stamp of approval, support, underwriting, warrant
ASSOCIATED CONCEPTS: endorsement to an insurance policy

ENDORSER, *noun* attestant, attester, backer, certifier, confirmer, cosigner, countersigner, guarantor, proponent, ratifier, signatory, sponsor, subscriber, surety, undersigned, underwriter

ENDOW, *verb* aid, allot, allow, award, bequeath, bestow, contribute, donate, endue, enrich, fund, furnish, give, grant, hand down, hand out, hand over, help, *hominem, instruere,* make pecuniary provision, pass down, present, provide, put in the hands of, subsidize, supply, supply with means

ENDOWMENT, *noun* aid, allotment, allowance, appropriation, assistance, award, benefaction, benefit, bequeathal, bequest, bestowal, bestowment, boon, bounty, contribution, donation, dowry, enrichment, fund, funding, gift, grant, present, presentation, presentment, provision, stipend, subsidy
ASSOCIATED CONCEPTS: annuity, endowment fund, endowment policy in insurance

ENDUE, *verb* accord, allot, allow, apportion, arm, assign, award, bestow, confer, dispense, donate, empower, enable, endow, enrich, entrust, fortify, furnish, give, grant, hand out, invest, invigorate, make provision for, present, provide, strengthen, supply

ENDURE *(Last),* ***verb*** abide, be constant, be durable, be firm, be permanent, be preserved, be prolonged, be protracted, be timeless, carry on, continue, continue to be, continue to exist, *durare,* exist, exist uninterruptedly, exist without break, extend, forge ahead, go on, hang on, have duration, have no end, hold one's ground, hold out, keep, linger on, live on, maintain, move ahead, outlast, outlive, perdure, *permanere,* persevere, persist, press onward, prevail, progress, refuse to give up, refuse to yield, remain, remain alive, remain valid, stand, stand fast, stay, subsist, survive, sustain, wear, weather, withstand

ENDURE *(Suffer),* ***verb*** accustom oneself to, be subjected to, bear, bear pain, bear up under, bear without resistance, bide, brave, brook, continue under pain, countenance, encounter, experience, experience unpleasantly, face, feel, forbear, go through, make the best of, meet, pass through, *perferre,* put up with, receive, resign oneself to, stand, stomach, submit to, suffer pain, sustain, *sustinere,* swallow, take, take patiently, tolerate, undergo, weather, withstand

ENEMY, ***noun*** adversary, antagonist, arch rival, assailant, betrayer, foe, nemesis, opponent, opposer, opposition, rival, sworn opponent, the other side
ASSOCIATED CONCEPTS: alien enemy, tending to aid a public enemy

ENEMY ALIEN, ***noun*** adventitious, adversary, adverse, antagonist, antagonistic, assailant, attacker, barbarian, competitor, conflicting, contender, contestant, contradictory, contrary, contrasting, counteracting, differing, dissimilar, distant, emigrant, exotic, external, extrinsic, faraway, foe, foeman, foreign, foreigner, hostile, hostile nation *or* state, hostile party, immigrant, inimical, newcomer, nonterrestrial, opponent, opposed, opposer, opposite, outlander, outlandish, outsider, outward, remote, rival, Satan, strange, stranger, the adversary, the archenemy, the devil, the enemy, the opposition, the other side, them, tramontane, transalpine, transatlantic, transmarine, transmontane, transpacific, ultramarine, ultramontane, ultramundane, unearthly, unlike, unnaturalized, unnaturalized citizen, vier, wetback

ENEMY COMBATANT, ***noun*** active combatant in the foreign theater of conflict, an enemy force, anarchist, assailant, assassin, attacker, combatant, demoniac force, destroyer, detainee, enemy alien, enemy operation, faction at war, fanatic, foreign assailant, hostile force, insurgent, internees, murderer, opponent, radical, rebel, revolutionary, revolutionist, rival force, subversive force, terrorist
ASSOCIATED CONCEPTS: alien enemies, detainees, justice courts, military tribunals, Patriotic Act, prisoners of war, public enemies, terrorism, treason

ENERGETIC, ***adjective*** active, aggressive, alive, ambitious, animated, brisk, busy, chipper, committed, determined, devoted, diligent, driving, dynamic, eager, effective, effectual, efficacious, efficient, electric, emphatic, enterprising, enthusiastic, excited, exerting effort, exertive, forceful, forcible, full of energy, full of life, hardworking, industrious, jumping, laborious, lively, mighty, physical, potent, powerful, pushing, ready to go, robust, snappy, spirited, vibrant, vigorous, vital, wholeheartedly supporting, zealous

ENERGIZE, ***verb*** activate, agitate, animate, augment, boost, charge, dynamize, elate, electrify, empower, encourage, enliven, excite to action, exhilarate, galvanize, give life to, goad, imbue with life, incite, inflame, inspire, intensify, invigorate, kindle, labor, liven, magnetize, pep up, quicken, reinforce, restore, spur, stimulate, strain, strengthen, struggle, toil, vitalize, vivify

ENERGY, ***noun*** activation, activity, animation, ardor, brawn, dash, drive, dynamism, enterprise, ferment, fervor, fire, force, forcefulness, go, hustle, impetus, industry, intensity, labor, life, liveliness, lustiness, main force, might, mightiness, momentum, muscle, potency, potentiality, power, pressure, puissance, punch, push, sinew, spirit, stamina, steam, stir, strength, strenuousness, verve, vigor, virility, vitality, vivacity, zeal

ENERVATE, ***verb*** adulterate, attenuate, debase, debilitate, defeat, deplete, deprive of strength, devitalize, dilute, diminish, disable, drain, enfeeble, fatigue, handicap, impair, incapacitate, invalidate, lessen, lower, minimize, paralyze, reduce, sap, strain, thin, tire, undermine, water down, weaken

ENFORCE, ***verb*** administer, bring to pass, carry into effect, carry into execution, carry out, carry through, coerce, compel, compel obedience, *confirmare,* dictate, drive, effect, effectuate, employ force, exact, execute, *exsequi,* force, have executed, impel, implement, impose, insist on, insist upon, make compulsory, make effective, necessitate, obtain by compulsion, obtain by force, press, put in action, put in force, put in operation, put into effect, put into execution, put pressure on, require, strengthen, subject to pressure
ASSOCIATED CONCEPTS: enforce a contract, enforce a judgment, enforce a lien, enforce provisions of the law, enforce sanctions, enforcement proceedings

ENFORCEMENT, ***noun*** administration, carrying into effect, carrying out, coaction, compulsion, compulsory execution, constraint, dictation, effectuation, exaction, execution, force, forcible urging, implementation, imposition, insistence, insistence upon, necessitation, necessity, obligation, obligement, pressure, requirement, strengthening, support
ASSOCIATED CONCEPTS: enforcement of a contract, enforcement of a judgment, enforcement of a lien, enforcement of a right, enforcement proceeding
FOREIGN PHRASES: ***Pacta conventa quae neque contra leges neque dolo malo inita sunt omni modo observanda sunt.*** Agreements which are not contrary to the laws nor entered into with a fraudulent design must be observed in all respects. ***Executio juris non habet injuriam.*** The execution of law does no injury. ***Scire leges non hoc est verba earum tenere, sed vim ac potestatem.*** To know the laws is not to observe their words alone, but their force and power. ***Interest reipublicae ne maleficia remaneant impunita.*** It concerns the state that crimes do not go unpunished. ***Ex nudo pacto non oritur nascitur actio.*** No action arises on a contract without a consideration. ***Nemo jus sibi dicere potest.*** No one can declare the law for himself.

ENFRANCHISE, ***verb*** *accipere,* admit to citizenship, *adsciscere,* affranchise, allow, authorize, disenthrall, emancipate, empower, endow with political privilege, franchise, free, free from political disabilities, give liberty to, give political privileges to, give the right to vote, grant, liberate, license, manumit, permit, permit to vote, qualify, *recipere,* release, restore to liberty, sanction, set at liberty, set free

ENGAGE *(Hire),* ***verb*** appoint, arrange for the services of, arrange for the use of, bind, book, charter, commission, *conducere,* contract for, employ, enlist, enlist in one's service, fill a position, give a job to, give a situation to, give employment to, lease, let, obtain, procure, put to work, put under contract, reserve, retain, secure, set to work, staff with, take into one's employ, take into service
ASSOCIATED CONCEPTS: engage the services of an employee

ENGAGE *(Involve),* ***verb*** absorb, assail, associate, attack, battle, become involved, bring into conflict, busy, carry on hostilities, combat, compete, connect, contend, contest,

draw in, encounter, engross, enmesh, entangle, enter into, enter into conflict with, entertain, fight with, fill one's time, gear with, hold the interest of, *incipere,* interest, interlock, join battle with, link, meet, mesh together, occupy, oppose, partake, participate, share, struggle, take on, take part, tangle, undertake, wage war, war with
ASSOCIATED CONCEPTS: doing business, engaged in agriculture, engaged in commerce, engaged in doing business, engaged in interstate commerce, engaged in manufacture, engaged in transacting business, primarily engaged, principally engaged

ENGAGE IN, ***verb*** accept, apply oneself to, assume, be occupied with, carry on, commence, commit to, concern oneself with, conduct, contract, devote oneself to, embark on, employ, endeavor, execute, exercise, follow, labor, manage, operate, participate, ply, practice, prosecute, pursue, take up, touch, undertake, use, venture on, work

ENGAGEMENT *(Appointment),* ***noun*** adventure, application, assignation, assurance, commitment, competition, contract, covenant, duty, encounter, enlistment, enterprise, interaction, interaffiliation, interplay, interview, involvement, meeting, obligation, pursuit, responsibility, undertaking

ENGAGEMENT *(Confrontation),* ***noun*** altercation, argument, battle, brawl, clash, collision, combat, conflict, confrontation, contention, disagreement, discord, dispute, embroilment, fight, fracas, fray, skirmish, squabble, struggle, wrangle

ENGENDER, ***verb*** arouse, author, be the cause of, bear, beget, begin, breed, bring about, bring forth, bring into being, bring into existence, call forth, call into being, cause, cause to exist, create, develop, effect, effectuate, excite, execute, furnish, *generare,* generate, *gignere,* give rise to, hatch, help, induce, incite, induce, initiate, institute, lead to, manufacture, occasion, originate, plant, produce, provoke, spawn, start, stir up, take birth, yield
ASSOCIATED CONCEPTS: engender a settlement

ENGINE, ***noun*** apparatus, appliance, contraption, contrivance, convenience, device, facility, generator, implementation, locomotive, machine, machinery, means, mechanical aid, mechanical device, mechanism, method, motor, muscle power, power plant, powerhouse, source of power, tool, transducer, transformer, turbine, utensil, utility

ENGINEER, ***noun*** architect, artificer, contractor, contriver, creator, framer, instigator, inventor, machinist, maker, manager, mechanic, originator, producer

ENGINEER, ***verb*** arrange, assemble, brew, build, cause, collude, compose, conspire, construct, contrive, control, create, devise, direct, erect, finagle, handle, hatch, intrigue, jockey, machinate, manage, maneuver, manipulate, manufacture, militate, negotiate, operate, originate, oversee, pioneer, plan, plot, produce, program, raise, regulate, run, scheme, wangle

ENGROSS *(Copy),* ***verb*** address, assimilate, inscribe, inscroll, record, scribe, scroll, superscribe, transcribe, write, write out

ENGROSS *(Monopolize),* ***verb*** absorb, busy, obsess, consume, corner, devour, drink in, employ, engage, haunt, have all to oneself, immerse, impropriate, occupy, preoccupy, take up

ENGULF, ***verb*** absorb, annihilate, bury, consume, deluge, destroy, devour, drown, entomb, exterminate, immerse, inundate, liquidate, overcome, overwhelm, submerge, submerse, swallow up

ENHANCE, ***verb*** add to, advance in value, aggrandize, *amplificare,* amplify, appreciate, *augere,* augment, better, boost, brighten, cultivate, deepen, develop, elaborate, elevate, emphasize, enlarge, enrich, escalate, exaggerate, expand, extend, heighten, improve, increase the value of, intensify, lift, magnify, make better, make improvements, make more attractive, make more valuable, maximize, perfect, polish, promote, raise, refine, reinforce, retouch, sharpen, strengthen, touch up, upgrade, uplift, upraise
ASSOCIATED CONCEPTS: enhanced in value

ENHANCED SENTENCING, ***noun*** aggravating factors involved in sentencing, enhancement fact involved in sentencing, higher-level classification involved in sentencing, increased penalties in the sentencing process
ASSOCIATED CONCEPTS: prior history enhancement used in sentencing

ENHANCEMENT *(Exaggeration),* ***noun*** aggrandizement, elaboration, embellishment, exaggeration, exaltation, hyperbole, magnification, overstatement, superlative

ENHANCEMENT *(Increase),* ***noun*** accession, advance, aggrandizement, amelioration, amendment, amplification, augmentation, betterment, boom, deepening, development, enlargement, enrichment, exaltation, heightening, improvement, intensification, melioration, progress, raising, reform, renewal, revaluation, strengthening

ENIGMA, ***noun*** *aenigma, ambages,* ambiguous saying, arcanum, bewilderment, braintwister, complexity, confusing statement, confusion, difficulty, inexplicable statement, inscrutable person, knotty point, mystery, obscure question, obscure statement, paradox, perplexity, poser, problem, puzzle, puzzling problem, question, riddle, secret, stumper, teaser

ENIGMATIC, ***adjective*** ambiguous, baffling, bewildering, bothering, confounding, confusing, conjectural, cryptic, disconcerting, esoteric, hard to understand, hidden, inexplicable, mysterious, mystifying, nebulous, obscure, of hidden meaning, perplexing, perturbing, puzzling, secret, veiled

ENJOIN, ***verb*** abate, ban, bar, barricade, bid, block, blockade, bring to a standstill, cause to halt, charge, command, constrain, curb, decree, dictate, direct, disallow, disapprove, discountenance, embargo, exact, exhort, foil, forbid, forbid by law, forestall, frustrate, give orders, hamper, hinder, hold in check, impede, impose, impose a ban, impose a duty, impose a task, impose with authority, inhibit, insist on, instruct, interdict, issue an order, keep from happening, keep in bounds, lay under embargo, limit, make unlawful, not countenance, not permit, oblige, order, place under interdiction, place under the ban, positively direct, preclude, prevent, prohibit, prohibit by legal injunction, prompt, proscribe, put a stop to, put an end to, put under an injunction, put under an interdiction, put under embargo, put under the ban, quash, quell, repress, require, restrain, restrain by injunction, restrict, retard, rule, stem, stop, suppress, thwart
ASSOCIATED CONCEPTS: permanent injunction, preliminary injunction, temporary injunction

ENJOY *(Take pleasure in),* ***verb*** admire, adore, appreciate, apprise, cherish, delight in, dote on, esteem, extol, fancy, favor, find satisfaction in, honor, idolize, indulge in, like, love, luxuriate in, prefer, prize, rejoice in, relish, respect, revel in, revere, savor, treasure, value, venerate, wallow in, worship

ENJOY *(Use)*, ***verb*** acquire, appropriate, assume ownership in, claim, command, conserve, control, dwell, dwell in, hold, inhabit, keep, live in, manage, occupy, own, possess, preserve, procure, rent, reserve, retain, take up residence in, use, utilize, withhold

ENJOYMENT *(Pleasure)*, ***noun*** amusement, bliss, delectation, delight, diversion, ecstasy, entertainment, exhilaration, *fructus,* gaiety, *gaudium,* gratification, gusto, merriment, recreation, refreshment, rejoicing, relaxation, relish, satisfaction, thrill, treat, zest
FOREIGN PHRASES: ***Omnis privatio praesupponit habitum.*** Every privation presupposes a former enjoyment.

ENJOYMENT *(Use)*, ***noun*** avail, disposal, employment, habitation, occupancy, occupation, ownership, possession, prerogative, proprietorship, retention, seisin, tenancy, tenure, usuage, utilization
ASSOCIATED CONCEPTS: adverse enjoyment, covenant of quiet enjoyment

ENLARGE, ***verb*** add to, aggrandize, *amplificare,* amplify, annex, *augere,* augment, broaden, build, build up, develop, *dilatare,* dilate, distend, elaborate, enhance, escalate, exaggerate, expatiate, extend, fatten, fill out, grow, increase, inflate, intensify, lengthen, magnify, make greater, make larger, multiply, progress, protract, raise, spread, stretch, supplement, swell, widen
ASSOCIATED CONCEPTS: materially alter, repair

ENLARGEMENT *(Addition)*, ***noun*** accession, advance, advancement, aggrandizement, aggravation, augmentation, broadening, expatiation, explication, extension, fullness, growth, increment, intensification, multiplication, proliferation, spreading, tumefaction, widening

ENLARGEMENT *(Exaggeration)*, ***noun*** amplification, blow-up, development, distortion, enhancement, expansion, increase, inflation, magnification, overstatement

ENLIGHTEN, ***verb*** account for, acquaint, apprise, clarify, disclose, divulge, edify, educate, elucidate, enable to comprehend, enable to see, enucleate, explain, explicate, expound, free from ignorance, free from prejudice, free from superstition, give reason for, illuminate, illumine, illustrate, impart, inform, *inluminare, inlustrare,* instruct, interpret, make aware, make clear, make known, notify, report, reveal, shed light upon, simplify, spell out, teach, tutor

ENLIGHTENMENT, ***noun*** appreciation, awakening, clarification, cognition, cognizance, comprehension, direction, disabusal, disclosure, edification, education, elucidation, enucleation, experience, explication, explanation, familiarity, illumination, insight, instruction, intelligence, knowledge, learning, mention, monition, objectivity, perception, publication, rationalism, realization, recongition, refinement, sense, teaching, tip, understanding

ENLIST, ***verb*** activate, admit, attract, call up, conscript, draft, employ, engage, enroll, get, impress, induce, induct, initiate, inscribe, join, mobilize, muster, procure, recruit, register, retain, sign up
ASSOCIATED CONCEPTS: conscription, enlist into a voluntary army, enlist support of witnesses, enlistment

ENMESH, ***verb*** box in, capture, complicate, confuse, draw in, embroil, engage, ensnare, ensnarl, entangle, entoil, entrap, envelop, hook, implicate, incriminate, involve, lure, mesh, mire, net, rope in, snare, tangle, trammel, trap, twist

ENMITY, ***adjective*** acrimony, alienation, anger, animosity, animus, antagonism, antipathy, aversion, bitterness, contention, despise, dislike, estrangement, hard feelings, hate, hatred, hostility, ill will, invidiousness, loathe, malevolence, malice, malignity, odium, opposition, rancor, repugnance, venom

ENMITY, ***noun*** animosity, animus, antagonism, antipathy, bad blood, bitterness, blood feud, conflict, coolness, disaffection, discord, estrangement, feud, friction, grudge, hate, hatred, hostility, ill-will, inhospitableness, jaundice, loathing, malice, malignancy, malignity, rancor, score, spite, spitefulness, strain, tension, unfriendliness, vendetta, venom, vindictiveness, virulence, vitriol alienation

ENNOBLE, ***verb*** a higher position, adorn, advance, aggrandize, bestow honor upon, boost, build up, canonize, confer an honor, consecrate, deify, dignify, distinguish, elevate, erect, exalt, glorify, grace, heighten, hold aloft, honor, knight, lift, lionize, look up to, magnify, praise, promote, prop, put on a pedestal, raise, sanctify, uplift

ENORMITY, ***noun*** complexity, enormous size, enormousness, immense scope, immensity, vast size
ASSOCIATED CONCEPTS: enormity of a crime

ENORMOUS, ***adjective*** colossal, excessive, gigantic, huge, immense, large, mammoth, massive, tremendous, vast
ASSOCIATED CONCEPTS: enormous burden of proof to overcome

ENOUGH, ***noun*** a satisfactory amount, a substantial amount, a sufficient amount, a suitable amount, abundance, acceptable amount, adequacy, adequate amount, ample amount, complete amount, copious amount, full amount, just amount, minimal amount, plenteous amount, plenty
ASSOCIATED CONCEPTS: enough evidence, imprisonment, tough enough laws

ENRAGE, ***verb*** acerbate, agitate, anger, enflame, exacerbate, exasperate, fire up, incense, inflame, infuriate, irk, irritate, lash into, madden, provoke, rile
ASSOCIATED CONCEPTS: provocation, self-defense

ENRICHMENT, ***noun*** adornment, advancement, aggrandizement, appreciation, beautification, betterment, cultivation, decoration, development, embellishment, endowment, enhancement, furtherance, improvement, ornamentation, refinement, reward
ASSOCIATED CONCEPTS: unjust enrichment, unlawful enrichment

ENROLL, ***verb*** accept as a member, *adscribere,* book, catalog, docket, draft, enlist, enter, enter on a list, enter on a record, enter on a register, file, induct, initiate, inscribe, join, list, make a member, make a record, record, recruit, register, sign up, subscribe

ENSCONCE, ***verb*** blanket, camouflage, cloak, cloud, conceal, cover, cover up, curtain, disguise, eclipse, encase, enclose, enshield, enshroud, envelop, enwrap, guard, hide, hide away, hide from view, hide securely, keep from danger, keep guarded, keep hidden, keep safe, keep secret, keep under cover, mask, obscure, preserve, protect, safeguard, screen, seclude, secrete, secure, shade, shadow, sheathe, shelter, shield, shroud, suppress, veil, watch over, wrap

ENSCONCED, ***adjective*** deep-rooted, deeply engrained, deeply implanted, deeply manifest, engrained, established, impeded, imprinted, indoctrinated, injected, instilled, manifest
ASSOCIATED CONCEPTS: precedence deep-rooted in the law, common law

ENSHROUD, ***verb*** blanket, camouflage, case, cloak, cloud, conceal, cover, curtain, disguise, eclipse, encase, enclose, ensconce, envelop, enwrap, guard, hide, hood, invest, keep clandestine, keep from notice, keep from view, keep hidden, keep out of sight, keep under cover, mantle, mask, obscure, obstruct the view of, prevent from being discovered, prevent from being seen, protect, render invisible, screen, seclude, secrete, shade, sheathe, shelter, shield, shroud, surround, swathe, veil, visor, wrap

ENSNARE, ***verb*** allure, ambuscade, ambush, apprehend, bait, bamboozle, beguile, bilk, bluff, capture, catch, catch unprepared, cheat, cozen, deceive, decoy, defraud, delude, dupe, enmesh, entangle, entice, entrap, fool, gull, hoax, hoodwink, hook, *inlicere, inretire,* lay a trap for, lead astray, lead on by artifice, lure, misdirect, misguide, mislead, net, outmaneuver, outwit, play one false, set a trap for, snare, take advantage of, take by craft, take by stratagem, trap, trepan, trick, victimize, waylay
ASSOCIATED CONCEPTS: entrapment

ENSUE, ***verb*** arise, attend as consequence, be caused by, be due to, be subsequent, be the effect of, come after, come afterward, come next, derive, develop, eventuate, flow, follow, follow as a consequence, follow in a train of events, grow out of, issue, occur, proceed, result, spring, succeed, supervene, transpire

ENSUING, ***adjective*** after, following, later, next, posterior, resultant, resulting, subsequent, succeeding, successive, sequential

ENSURE, ***verb*** ascertain, assure, certify, check, clinch, confirm, corroborate, dismiss doubt, endorse, give security, give surety, guarantee, indemnify against loss, insure, keep from harm, keep safe, make certain, make sure, offer collateral, promise, protect, safeguard, secure, underwrite, verify, warrant

ENTAIL, ***verb*** *adferre,* call for, demand, force, impel, include as a necessary consequence, *inferre,* involve, make essential, make incumbent, make inescapable, make necessary, make requisite, make unavoidable, necessitate, need, obligate, occasion, require

ENTANGLEMENT *(Confusion),* ***noun*** agitation, chaos, commotion, complexity, complication, confusedness, derangement, disarrangement, disarry, disorder, disorganization, embroilment, enmeshment, ferment, imbroglio, intricacy, irregularity, jumble, maze, mix-up, snag, snarl, tumult

ENTANGLEMENT *(Involvement),* ***noun*** dilemma, entrapment, fix, *implicatio,* implication, incrimination, inculpation, predicament, scrape, strait

ENTER *(Go in),* ***verb*** arrive, board, come in, cross the threshold, effect an entrance, gain admittance, gain entry, go into, *inire, intrare, introire,* make an entrance, pass into, set foot in, step in, walk in
ASSOCIATED CONCEPTS: breaking and entering, forcible entry, immigration, lawful entry, open and peaceable entry, trespass

ENTER *(Insert),* ***verb*** implant, infuse, inject, intercalate, interject, interpose, introduce, intromit, place into, put in, stick in

ENTER *(Penetrate),* ***verb*** bore, cut into, cut through, drill, empierce, gore, impale, infiltrate, interpenetrate, invade, lance, perforate, pervade, pierce, prick, puncture, sink into, stab, transpierce

ENTER *(Record),* ***verb*** catalog, check in, chronicle, enroll, file, inscribe, inscroll, jot down, list, log, make an entry, mark down, note, place in the record, post, put down, put in writing, put on record, *referre,* register, report, set down, tabulate, take down, transcribe, write down, write in
ASSOCIATED CONCEPTS: entered on the record, entry of a judgment

ENTER AN APPEARANCE, ***verb*** appear as a counselor at law, appear as an attorney, appear as counsel, arrive, attend, check in, defend, disclose representation, disclosure, entry of an appearance, official disclosure, register as an attorney in court, represent, show, show up in court, turn up

ENTERPRISE *(Economic organization),* ***noun*** business, business establishment, commercial establishment, company, concern, corporate body, corporation, firm, house, industry, syndicate
ASSOCIATED CONCEPTS: commercial enterprise, free enterprise, private enterprise

ENTERPRISE *(Undertaking),* ***noun*** activity, adventure, attempt, campaign, cause, effort, endeavor, engagement, *inceptum,* job, occupation, operation, opus, plan, program, project, pursuit, scheme, task, undertaking, venture
ASSOCIATED CONCEPTS: mutual enterprise

ENTERTAIN *(Consider),* ***verb*** analyze, assimilate, chew over, cogitate, consider, contemplate, debate, deliberate, digest, dwell, examine, eye, fixate, fret, mull over, muse, obsess, opine, pore over, propend, question, reason, reflect, reminisce, review, revolve, ruminate, speculate, study, think over, turn, weigh, wrestle with

ENTERTAIN *(Host),* ***verb*** amuse, bewitch, captivate, comfort, disport, divert, enchant, engage, engross, enjoy, enthrall, excite, gratify, have fun, indulge, interest, intrigue, occupy, pique, please, regale, satisfy, solace, stimulate

ENTERTAIN *(Perform),* ***verb*** act, amuse, captivate, delight, divert, enact, headline, imitate, impersonate, inspire, inspirit, masquerade, mime, mimic, pantomime, play, play-act, portray, recreate, regale, role-play, showcase, star

ENTERTAINMENT, ***noun*** amusement, cabaret, carnival, celebration, cheer, concert, delight, enjoyment, exhibition, extravaganza, festival, firm industry, frolic, fun, gaiety, gala, gratification, jollity, joviality, lark, merriment, merrymaking, movie industry, party, pastime, performance, pleasure, presentation, production, reception, recreation, regalement, relaxation, show, spectacle, treat
ASSOCIATED CONCEPTS: entertainment law

ENTHRALL, ***verb*** absorb, arrest, bedazzle, beguile, bewitch, captivate, catch up, charm, delight, elate, enchant, engage, engross, enrapture, entrance, excite, exhilarate, fascinate, gladden, gratify, grip, hypnotize, involve, mesmerize, monopolize, please, satisfy, spellbind, stir, thrill

ENTHUSIASM, ***noun*** animation, bounce, buoyancy, delight, determination, devotedness, devotion, eagerness, ebullience, ecstasy, elation, emotion, energy, excitement, exhilaration, exuberance, feeling, fervor, fever, fire, force, frenzy, furor, fury, glow, gusto, heat, intensity, intentness, interest, joy, keenness, liveliness, mania, passion, rage, rapture, relish, snap, spirit, vehemence, verve, vigor, vim, vitality, zeal, zealousness, zest, zip

ENTHUSIAST, ***verb*** addict, adherent, admirer, aficionado, angel, backer, believer, booster, champion, collector, devotee, disciple, fan, fanatic, fiend, follower, hound, lover, maniac, partisan, promoter, supporter, zealot

ENTHUSIASTIC, ***adjective*** absorbed, all fired up, all worked up, animated, anxious, ardent, attracted, avid, burning, chomping at the bit, charged up, crazed, delighted, demonstrative, desiring, desirous, dying to, eager, earnest, ebullient, ecstatic, effervescent, effusive, emotive, energetic, enraptured, enthused, excited, exhilarated, expressive, exuberant, fanatical, fascinated, fervent, fervid, fevered, feverish, fiery, gushing, impassioned, impatient, intent, interested, keen, keen about, longing, passionate, spirited, thrilled, vehement, vigorous, vivacious, wholehearted, zealous

ENTICE, ***verb*** allure, bait, cajole, coax, decoy, divert, induce, inveigh, lure, seduce, tempt

ENTICEMENT, ***noun*** allurement, appeal, attraction, bait, beckoning, call, charm, decoy, enchantment, encouragement, entrapment, impetus, impulse, incentive, inducement, influence, invitation, lure, motivation, persuasion, power, seducement, seduction, snare, stimulus, sway, temptation, trap, wrongful allure, wrongful allurement, wrongful appeal, wrongful attraction, wrongful attractiveness, wrongful bait, wrongful decoy, wrongful draw, wrongful glamour, wrongful inducement, wrongful invitation, wrongful lure, wrongful seduction, wrongful solicitation, wrongful temptation
ASSOCIATED CONCEPTS: coercion and enticement, illegal enticement

ENTIRE, ***adjective*** absolute, across the boards, aggregate, all-inclusive, complete, complete gamut, complete universe, comprehensive, entire universe, exhaustive, extensive, full, full-fledged, gross, inclusive, in-depth, integral, plenary, sound, sweeping, thorough, total, unabated, unabridged, unalloyed, unbounded, undiminished, undividable, unequivocal, unimpaired, unimpeded, unitary, universal, unlimited, unmitigated, unmodified, unqualified, unrestricted, whole, widesweeping
ASSOCIATED CONCEPTS: entire act, entire benefit, entire contract, entire estate, entire use

ENTIRETY, ***noun*** accumulation, aggregate, all, amount, assemblage, collectiveness, collectivity, completeness, completion, comprehensiveness, congeries, ensemble, entire amount, entireness, everything, exhaustiveness, fullness, gross, gross amount, inclusiveness, indiscerptibility, indiscerptibleness, intactness, lot, lump, mass, sum, total, totality, totalness, *totus,* undiminished quantity, undividedness, whole, wholeness
ASSOCIATED CONCEPTS: entirety clause, tenants by the entirety, tenants in common

ENTITLED, ***adjective*** allowed, authorized, deserved, deserving, desirable, due, earned, eligible, empowered, fit, having the right, justified, labeled, legalized, licensed, merited, ordained, permitted, privileged, qualified, sanctioned, suitable, warranted, worthy

ENTITLEMENTS, ***noun*** advance, advantages, aid, allocations, allowance, annuities, assistance, benefits, benefits provided to the public, bequests, birthrights, concessions, endowments, exemptions, favors, funds, government programs, grant-in-aid, grants, guaranteed benefits, help, legacies, liberties, personal financial benefits, privilege, relief, rights, social programs, state aid, stipends, subsidies, subsistence, subventions, support
ASSOCIATED CONCEPTS: Medicaid, Medicare, Social Security, unemployment insurance

ENTITY, ***noun*** actuality, being, body, character, corpus, creature, embodiment, existence, individual, item, life, living thing, matter, module, object, oneness, organism, separate existence, single item, single piece, specimen, tangible object, unit, unit of being
ASSOCIATED CONCEPTS: corporate entity, distinct entity, legal entity, separate entity

ENTRANCE, ***noun*** access, adit, *aditus,* admission, anteroom, approach, door, entry, entryway, foyer, gangway, gate, gateway, illapse, infiltration, influx, ingress, inlet, inroad, insertion, introgression, *introitus,* invasion, lobby, means of access, means of entering, mouth, opening, *ostium,* passage, passageway, penetration, place of entry, portal, reception, threshold, vestibule, way in
ASSOCIATED CONCEPTS: forcible entrance, public entrance

ENTRAP, ***verb*** allure, bait, beckon, befool, beguile, bring unawares into danger, bring unawares into evil, catch, catch by artifice, deceive, decoy, draw as by a lure, draw by artful inducements, draw in, dupe, enmesh, ensnare, entangle, entice, fool, hold out allurement, hold out temptation, *inlicere, inretire,* inveigle, lay a snare for, lay a trap for, lead astray, lead by inducement, lead into danger by artifice, lead into temptation, lead on, lure, lure into a compromising act, set a snare for, set a trap for, snare, take in, tempt, trap, trip up
ASSOCIATED CONCEPTS: predisposition to commit a crime

ENTREATY, ***noun*** adjuration, appeal, beseechment, call, cry, earnest request, impetration, imploration, importunity, invocation, *obsecratio,* obsecration, *obtestatio,* petition, plea, prayer, *preces,* request, solicitation, suit, supplication

ENTRENCH, ***verb*** advance, barricade, brace, bulwark, buttress, defend, embattle, embed, encroach, establish, fortify, immerse in, immersed in, infiltrate, invade, make inroads, overrun, protect, reinforce, shore up, solidify, surround, wall
ASSOCIATED CONCEPTS: entrench leadership, entrench power

ENTREPRENEUR, ***noun*** administrator, baron, business leader, businessman, businessperson, businesswoman, director, employer, enterpriser, exec, executive, financier, industrialist, magnate, man of commerce, owner, producer, top executive, tycoon
ASSOCIATED CONCEPTS: entrepreneur law, free trade

ENTRUST, ***verb*** appoint, assign, assign the care of, authorize, charge with a duty, charge with a trust, commit, *committere, concredere,* consign, delegate, depute, deputize, devolve, elect, empower, give a mandate, give a responsibility to, invest empower, license, make someone guardian of, *mandare,* place in the protection of, put in charge, trust, turn over for safekeeping
ASSOCIATED CONCEPTS: entrust goods, entrust personal property
FOREIGN PHRASES: ***Securius expediuntur negotia commissa pluribus, et plus vident oculi quam oculus.*** Matters which are entrusted to several persons are executed more surely, because eyes see more than an eye.

ENTRY *(Entrance),* ***noun*** access, adit, admission, entrance, immigration, ingress, ingression, passage
ASSOCIATED CONCEPTS: entry on land, forcible entry, lawful entry, trespass

ENTRY *(Record),* ***noun*** account, bulletin, chronicle, deposition, file, information preserved in writing, inscription, item, memo, memorandum, minute, *nomen,* note, recorded item, registration, report, statement recorded in a book, writing, written record
ASSOCIATED CONCEPTS: entry by court, entry in regular course of business, entry of an appeal, entry of an appearance, entry of an order, entry of judgment, writ of entry

ENUMERATE, ***verb*** be specific, catalog, count, designate, detail, differentiate, enroll, *enumerare,* index, inventory, itemize, keep count, list, make a list, mention, mention one by one, mention specifically, name expressly, name one by one, number, numerate, point out, specify, tabulate
ASSOCIATED CONCEPTS: descriptive enumeration, enumerated counts, enumerated motions
FOREIGN PHRASES: ***Enumeratio infirmat regulam in casibus non enumeratis.*** Enumeration disaffirms the rule in cases which are not enumerated.

ENUMERATION, ***noun*** ascertainment, breviary, brief, budget, cache, capsule, cataloging, completion, declaration, demographics, demography, enunciation, evaluation, fund, hoard, implementation, inventory, mine, nest egg, numeration, ordering, outline, pool, pot, précis, purse, recap, recapitulation, repertoire, reserve, reservoir, resource, roundup, rundown, run-through, source, statistics, stats, stock, stockpile, sum, summarization, summing-up, synopsis, tally, well, wrap-up
ASSOCIATED CONCEPTS: enumeration of the paragraphs in a complaint

ENUNCIATE, ***verb*** accent, affirm, announce, annunciate, apprise, articulate, assert, asseverate, aver, declaim, declare, *edicere,* emit, enounce, explain, express, give expression, give utterance, *indicare,* inform, intonate, intone, make an announcement, mouth, notify, phonate, proclaim, profess, promulgate, pronounce, pronounce distinctly, pronounce in a distinct manner, *pronuntiare,* publish, put in words, say, speak, speak clearly, state, stress, tell, utter, verbalize, vocalize, voice

ENUNCIATION *(Articulation),* ***noun*** articulation, delivery, diction, elocution, expression, fluency, phonation, precise grammar, precise pronunciation, saying, speaking, specific style of speaking, speech, utterance, vocalization, voicing, wording

ENUNCIATION *(Declaration),* ***noun*** amplification, announcement, attestation, communication, disclosure, enumeration, explanation, exposition, presentation, proclamation, statement, talking, verbalization

ENVELOP, ***verb*** beleaguer, beseige, beset, blanket, box, cage, case, *circumfundere,* circumscribe, cloak, cloister, close in, clothe, compass, completely cover, conceal, confine, corral, cover, curtain, edge, embox, embrace, encapsulate, encase, encircle, enclose, encompass, enfold, enshroud, ensphere, environ, enwrap, fence in, frame, go around, hedge in, hem in, hide, hood, *involvere,* mask, *obducere,* obscure, overlay, protect, screen, sheathe, shelter, shield, shroud, surround, swaddle, swathe, veil, wall in, wrap, wrap around, wrap up

ENVELOPMENT, ***noun*** clothe, concealment, cover, embracement, encasement, enclosement, hood, overlay, protection, screen, sheathe, shelter, shield, shroud, surroundings

ENVIABLE, ***adjective*** advantageous, appropriate, apt, auspicious, befitting, beneficial, best, better, correct, covetable, desirable, effective, efficacious, excellent, exceptional, exemplary, favored, fitting, fortunate, lucky, meritorious, opportune, positive, privileged, promising, propitious, providential, right, satisfactory, suitable, superior, timely, welcome, well-timed

ENVIRONMENT, ***noun*** atmosphere, aura, circumstances, context, environs, locality, milieu, situation, surroundings

ENVIRONMENTAL CONSERVATION, ***noun*** maintenance of the environment, maintenance of the habitat, preservation of the environs, protection of the environment

ENVISION, ***verb*** conceive, conceptualize, concoct, conjure, contemplate, create, daydream, dream, duplicate, envisage, expect, fabricate, fancy, fantasize, fantasy, foresee, hallucinate, ideate, image, imagine, invent, make up, manufacture, materialize, meditate, muse, picture, predict, prefigure, project, re-create, reflect, regard, relive, reminisce, see, theorize, think up, view, vision, visualize

EPHEMERAL, ***adjective*** *brevis,* brief, caducous, *caducus,* continuing for a short time, deciduous, disappearing, elusive, enduring only a very short time, ephemerous, evanescent, existing for a short time, fleeting, fugacious, fugitive, hurried, impermanent, lasting a very short time, meteoric, meteorical, momentary, mortal, nondurable, not lasting, passing, perishable, short, short-lived, temporal, temporary, transient, transitory, unenduring, *unius diei,* unstable, vanishing, volatile

EPHEMERALLY, ***adverb*** a condition of short duration, a passing condition, a situation of finite duration, brief condition, evanescence, fading condition, fleeting condition, fluffiness, insubstantiality, light overview, momentary condition, nonsubstantial perspective, short-lived condition, temporary situation, transience, transitory situation

EPIC, ***adjective*** chronicle, classic, colossal, descriptive, detailed, elevated, exalted, fabulous, fantastic, grand, grandiose, great, heroic, high-flown, high-sounding, historic, historical, history, impressive, inflated, legend, legendary, lofty, majestic, major, momentous, monumental, narrative, on a grand scale, saga, significant, story, superhuman, tremendous, vast

EPIDEMIC *(Disease),* ***noun*** ailment, contagion, disease, endemic, illness, infection, malady, pandemic, plague, scourge, sickness

ASSOCIATED CONCEPTS: antiepidemic law, epidemic law, pandemic

EPIDEMIC *(Large scale),* ***noun*** a far-reaching occurrence, a rampant situation, a universal situation, a widespread situation, acceleration, an omnibus situation, burgeoning number, comprehensiveness, extensiveness, flurry, increasing number, mounting number, upsurge, upswing, upturn
ASSOCIATED CONCEPTS: class action

EPIPHANY, ***noun*** comprehension, contemplation, creation, disclosure, divine inspiration, divine revelation, expression, innovation, manifestation, meaning, mystical experience, mystical intuition, prophecy, prophetic, remarkable idea, revelation, revolutionary idea, revolutionary solution, understanding

EPISODE, ***noun*** chapter, circumstance, event, experience, happening, incident, occasion, occurrence, sequel, short-lived event, sudden event

EPITOME, ***noun*** characteristic part, core, embodiment, essence, exemplification, model, representative, standard, *summarium,* typical component, typical part, typification

EPITOMIZE, ***verb*** abstract, actualize, boil down, brief, characterize, concretize, digest, duplicate, embody, encapsulate, exemplify, express, externalize, illustrate, image, incarnate, incorporate, instantiate, manifest, mean, model, objectify, personify, represent, resemble, substantiate, symbolize, translate into, typify

EQUAL, ***adjective*** abreast, *aequalis, aequus,* alike, balanced, coequal, coextensive, coordinate, democratic, equable, equalized, equally divided, equidistant, equilateral, equipollent, equitable, even, evenhanded, fair, fair-minded, homologous, identical in amount, identical in quantity, identical in size, identical in value, impartial, just, like, like in degree, like in quantity, matched, of the same degree, of the same rank, on a par, on even terms, on the same level, same, similar, symmetric, symmetrical, tantamount, tied, to the same degree, unbiased, unchanging, undeviating, unfluctuating, uniform, unprejudiced, unvaried, unvarying
ASSOCIATED CONCEPTS: equal before the law, equal in degree, equal in value, equal protection of laws, equal taxation, equally divided, separate but equal

EQUALITY, ***noun*** balance, equal in quality, equal opportunity, equal rights, equal status, equivalence, evenhandedness, evenness, fairness, fairness in opportunity, righteousness

EQUALIZE, ***verb*** accommodate, adjust, balance, compensate, counteract, counterbalance, equate, equilibrate, equipoise, even, homogenize, level, normalize, regularize, standardize

EQUATE, ***verb*** analyze, assess, balance, compare, coordinate, counterbalance, determine, equalize, judge, match, measure against
ASSOCIATED CONCEPTS: equate law with morality, equating law with justice

EQUIPMENT, ***noun*** accouterment, apparatus, appointment, material, provisioning, supplies
ASSOCIATED CONCEPTS: equipment trust agreement, equipment trust certificate

EQUIPOISE, ***noun*** balance, counterbalance, counterpoise, counterweight, equal distribution of weight, equality of force, equality of weight, equilibration, equilibrium, equiponderance, even balance, evenness, match, offset, parity, stability, symmetry

EQUIPPED, ***adjective*** able, accoutered, accustomed, adapted, adjusted, all set, allotted, armed, arrayed, authorized, bedecked, clothed, conditioned, educated, empowered, enabled, entitled, fit, fitted, fitted out, furnished, girded, groomed, habituated, indoctrinated, instructed, loaded, outfitted, prepared, readied, ready, ready to go, rigged, schooled, seasoned, set up, shaped, steeled, stocked, suited, supplied, tailored, trained

EQUITABLE, ***adjective*** *aequus,* deserved, detached, disinterested, dispassionate, distributing justice, equal, evenhanded, exhibiting equity, existing in equity, fair, fair-minded, giving each his due, honest, honorable, impartial, incorrupt, incorruptible, *iustus,* just, merited, *meritus,* neutral, objective, principled, proper, reasonable, right, righteous, scrupulous, unbiased, unbigoted, unchallengeable, unprejudiced, upright
ASSOCIATED CONCEPTS: equitable assignment, equitable charge, equitable claim, equitable conversion, equitable counterclaim, equitable defenses, equitable estate, equitable estoppel, equitable interest, equitable lien, equitable life estate, equitable mortgage, equitable rate of interest, equitable recission, equitable recoupment, equitable relief, equitable remedy, equitable rights, equitable set-off, equitable title, fair and equitable value

EQUITABLE ESTOPPEL, ***noun*** bar, equity, fairness, justice, legal argument barred by a party's prior conduct, legal bar, principle that denies legal relief to a wrongdoer, prohibition, relief barred by the misrepresentations of a party

EQUITY *(Justice),* ***noun*** *aequitas, aequum,* chancery, evenhandedness, fair-mindedness, fair treatment, fairness, honesty, ideal justice, impartial justice, *iustitia,* justice, justice as distinguished from conformity to enactments or statutes, justice ascertained by natural reason, justice under the law, justness, natural right, quality of being equal and fair, reasonableness, recourse to the principles of natural justice, redress, remedial justice, right dealing, righteousness, rightfulness, spirit of the law, unwritten law, uprightness
ASSOCIATED CONCEPTS: balance of equities, chancery, equitable right, equity action, equity jurisdiction, existing equities, suit in equity
FOREIGN PHRASES: ***Nihil tam conveniens est naturali aequitati quam unumquodque dissolvi eo ligamine quo ligatum est.*** Nothing is so agreeable to natural equity as that a thing should be dissolved by the same means by which it was bound. ***Lex aequitate gaudet; appetit perfectum; est norma recti.*** The law delights in equity; it grasps at perfection; it is a rule of right. ***In fictione juris semper aequitas existit.*** In a fiction of law, equity is always present. ***Equitas sequitur legem.*** Equity follows the law. ***Lex respicit aequitatem.*** The law regards equity. ***Ratio in jure aequitas integra.*** Reason in law is impartial equity. ***Nulli vendemus, nulli negabimus, aut differemus rectum vel justitian.*** We will sell to none, we will deny to none, we will delay to none, either equity or justice. ***Judex ante oculos aequitatem semper habere debet.*** A judge ought always to have equity before his eyes. ***Aequitas supervacua odit.*** Equity abhors superfluous things. ***Aequitas uxoribus, liberis, creditoribus maxime favet.*** Equity favors wives and

children, creditors most of all. ***Aequitas est quasi aequalitas.*** Equity is as it were equality. ***Aequum et bonum est lex legum.*** That which is equitable and right is the law of laws. ***In omnibus quidem, maxime tamen injure, aequitas spectanda sit.*** In all matters, but especially in law, equity should be regarded. ***Prima pars aequitatis aequalitas.*** The prime element of equity is equality. ***Nemo allegans suam turpitudinem audien dus est.*** No one should be permitted to testify as a witness to his own baseness or wickedness. ***Nemo ex suo delicto meliorem suam conditionem facere potest.*** No one can improve his condition by his own misdeed. ***Jure naturae aequum est neminem cum alterius detrimento et injuria fieri locupletiorem.*** According to the laws of nature, it is just that no one should be enriched by the detriment and injury of another. ***Nihil iniquius quam aequitatem nimis intendere.*** Nothing is more unjust than to extend equity too far. ***Judex aequitatem semper spectare debet.*** A judge ought always to regard equity. ***Bonus judex secundum aequum et bonum judicat, et aequitatem stricto juri praefert.*** Good judges decide according to what is just and right, and prefer equity to strict law. ***Si aliquid ex solemnibus deficiat, cum aequitas poscit, subveniendum est.*** If anything is deficient in formal requisites, where equity requires it, it should be supplied. ***Aequitas nunquam contravenit legis.*** Equity never counteracts the laws. ***Aequitas non facit jus, sed juri auxiliatur.*** Equity does not make law, but assists law. ***Aequitas ignorantiae opitulatur, oscitantiae non item.*** Equity assists ignorance, but not carelessness. ***Vigilantibus et non dormientibus jura subveniunt.*** The laws aid the vigilant and not those who slumber. ***Aequitas agit in personam.*** Equity acts upon the person. ***Jure naturae aequum est neminem cum alterius detrimento et injuria fieri locupletiorem.*** By natural law it is not just that any one should be enriched by the detriment or injury of another. ***Hoc quidem perquam durum est, sed ita lex scripta est.*** This indeed is exceedingly hard, but such is the written law. ***Nemo debet aliena jactura locupletari.*** No one ought to gain by another's loss. ***Frustra legis auxilium quaerit qui in legem committit.*** He vainly seeks the aid of the law who transgresses the law. ***Commodum ex injuria sua non habere debet.*** No person ought to derive any advantage by his own wrong. ***Nemo ex proprio dolo consequitur actionem.*** No one acquires a right of action from his own fraud.

EQUITY *(Share of ownership),* ***noun*** allotment, apportionment, claim, division, interest, investment, part, portion, right, stake, vested interest

EQUIVALENCE, ***noun*** accord, alikeness, coequality, coherence, comparability, compatibility, correlation, correspondence, counterbalance, equality, equivalency, exact equivalent, exchangeability, harmony, interchangeability, like, likeness, match, par, parallelism, parity, resemblance, sameness, similarity, similitude, stasis, symmetry, synchronicity, synonymy

EQUIVALENT, ***adjective*** alike, as good as, balancing, coequal, comparable, compensatory, equal, equal in effect, equal in force, equal in power, equal in significance, equal in value, equalized, equipollent, even, identical, identical in size, identical in value, interchangeable, like, of equal force, of equal value, of equal weight, on a par with, parallel, *pro re valere,* reciprocal, same, similar, substitutable, synonymous, tantamount, without difference

ASSOCIATED CONCEPTS: equivalent acts, fair equivalent, substantially equivalent

EQUIVOCAL, ***adjective*** ambiguous, *ambiguus,* ambivalent, amphibological, amphibolous, *anceps,* bewildering, cloudy, confusing, controversial, debatable, deceptive, dim, disputable, doubtful, dubious, enigmatic, enigmatical, equivocating, equivocatory, hard to understand, hazy, imperspicuous, imprecise, indecisive, indefinite, indeterminate, misleading, moot, nebulous, obscure, of doubtful meaning, of uncertain significance, open, open to question, perplexing, possessing double meaning, prevaricating, puzzling, questionable, recondite, shadowy, uncertain, unclarified, unclear, undecided, undefined, undetermined, unexplained, unintelligible, unplain, unresolved, unsolved, unsure, untransparent, vague, veiled

FOREIGN PHRASES: ***Verba aequivoca, ac in dubio sensu posita, intelliguntur digniori et potentiori sensu.*** Equivocal words and those which are used in a doubtful sense are to be understood in their more worthy and effective sense.

EQUIVOCATE, ***verb*** avoid a straight answer, be ambiguous, be false, be unclear, be untruthful, be vague, deceive, disguise, dissemble, dissimulate, dodge, elude, evade, fence, hedge, lie, misguide, misinform, mislead, misrepresent, misstate, mystify, palter, parry, prevaricate, quibble, shift, shuffle, *tergiversari,* tergiversate

ERADICATE, ***verb*** abolish, annihilate, annul, black out, blot out, cause to cease, deal destruction, delete, demolish, deracinate, destroy, destroy thoroughly, displace, dispose of, dissolve, do away with, do away with completely, efface, eject, eliminate, *eradere,* erase, *evellere, excidere,* expunge, expurgate, exterminate, extinguish, extirpate, extract, lay waste, leave no trace of, leave no vestige of, liquidate, obliterate, purge, remove, remove utterly, stamp out, strike out, subtract, sweep away, unroot, uproot, void, weed out

ERASE, ***verb*** abolish, annihilate, annul, black out, blot out, cancel, clean up, cut, deal destruction, decimate, delete, demolish, destroy, discard, dismantle, dispose of, dissolve, do away with completely, edit, efface, eliminate, eradicate, exceed the record, excise, expel, expunge, exterminate, extinguish, extirpate, jettison, kill, leave no vestige of, liquidate, obliterate, negate, nullify, obliterate, oust, purge, remove, rescind, rewrite the records, snuff, stamp out, strike, strike out, terminate, throw out, uproot, void, wipe out, withdraw

ERODE, ***verb*** abrade, break down, consume, decay, decrease, deteriorate, diminish, disintegrate, dissolve, file, gradually eat away, grind, lessen, lose, make thin, rasp, recede, reduce, rub away, scrape, shrink, strip, waste, weaken, wear, wear away, wear down, wear down by friction, weather

ASSOCIATED CONCEPTS: erode the credibility of a witness

EROSION, ***noun*** abrasion, attrition, breakdown, consumption, crumbling, decay, decrease, decrement, deterioration, detrition, diminishment, diminution, disappearance, disintegration, dissolution, gradual eating away, gradual wearing away, grinding, lessening, loss, recession, reduction, rubbing away, shrinkage, thinning out, waste, wear, wearing away, wearing down by friction

ERR, ***verb*** be deceived, be erroneous, be in the wrong, be misguided, be misled, be mistaken, blunder, cause error, commit an error, delude oneself, *errare,* fall into error, *falli,* go amiss, go astray, go wrong, labor under a misapprehension, make a mistake, misapprehend, miscalculate, miscompute, misconstrue, misinterpret, misjudge, misreckon, mistake, misunderstand, receive a false impression, slip, *vagari*

ERRANT, ***adjective*** aberrant, amiss, astray, at fault, awry, deviant, deviating, deviatory, erring, erroneous, fallacious, faultful, faulty, imperfect, incorrect, misdirected, mistaken, not right, peccant, wrong

ERRATIC, ***adjective*** aberrant, abnormal, bizarre, capricious, changeable, changeful, eccentric, extraordinary, inconsistent, inconstant, intermittent, irregular, mercurial, not consistent, odd, outlandish, peculiar, random, sporadic, strange, unconventional, unfixed, unique, unorthodox, unpredictable, unsettled, unsteady, unusual, volatile, wandering
ASSOCIATED CONCEPTS: erratic behavior, erratic law enforcement, insanity

ERRONEOUS, ***adjective*** aberrant, amiss, blundering, containing error, counterfeit, devoid of truth, erring, fallacious, false, *falsus,* faulty, fictitious, groundless, illogical, inaccurate, incorrect, inexact, mistaken, spurious, unfounded, ungrounded, unreal, unsound, unsubstantial, unsustainable, untrue, wrong
ASSOCIATED CONCEPTS: erroneous assessment, erroneous decision, erroneous judgment, erroneous law, erroneous order, erroneous tax

ERROR, ***noun*** aberrance, aberrancy, aberration, *corrigendum,* delusion, deviation, distorted conception, distortion, *erratum,* erroneous statement, *error,* false conception, false impression, fault, flaw, inaccuracy, incorrect belief, inexactness, injustice, lapse, malapropism, misbelief, miscalculation, miscarriage of justice, miscomputation, misconception, misconjecture, miscount, misguidance, misinterpretation, misjudgment, misprint, misreckoning, misstatement, mistake, mistaken belief, mistaken judgment, mistranslation, misunderstanding, misuse of words, oversight, *peccatum,* poor judgment, slip, unfactualness, wrong course, wrong impression, wrongness
ASSOCIATED CONCEPTS: assignment of error, clerical error, confession of error, coram nobis, cross-errors, error apparent on the record, error of fact, error of judgment, error of law, fatal errors, fundamental error, harmful error, immaterial error, judicial error, legal error, manifest error, obvious error, plain error, prejudicial error, presentation of error, reversible error, substantial error, technical error, writ of error
FOREIGN PHRASES: ***De fide et officio judicis non recipitur quaestio, sed de scientia, sive sit error juris, sive facti.*** The good faith and honesty of a judge are not to be questioned, but his knowledge, whether it be in error of law or fact, may be. ***Praesentia corporis tollit errorem nominis; et veritas nominis tollit er rorem demonstrationis.*** The presence of the body cures an error in the name; and the accuracy of the name cures an error of description. ***Veritas nominis tollit errorem demonstrationis.*** Correctness of the name cures error in the description. ***Veritas demonstrationis tollit errorem nominis.*** Correctness of the description cures the error of the name. ***Error qui non resistitur approbatur.*** An error which is not resisted or opposed is waived. ***Error fucatus nuda veritate in multis est probabilior; et saepenumero rationibus vincit veritatem error.*** Error artfully disguised is, in many instances, more probable than naked truth; and frequently error overwhelms truth by argumentation. ***Non videntur qui errant consentire.*** Those who err are not deemed to consent. ***Falsa orthographia, sive falsa grammatica, non vitiat concessionem.*** Bad spelling or grammar does not vitiate a deed. ***Vitium clerici nocere non debet.*** Clerical errors ought not to prejudice. ***Communis error facit jus.*** Common error makes the law. ***Tutius erratur ex parte mitiori.*** It is safer to err on the side of leniency. ***In generalibus versatur error.*** Error thrives on generalities. ***Error juris nocet.*** An error of law works an injury. ***Nihil facit error nominis cum de corpore constat.*** An error in the name is of no consequence when there is certainty as to the person. ***Tutius semper est errare acquietando, quam in puniendo; ex parte miseric ordiae quam ex parte justitiae.*** It is always safer to err in acquitting than in punishing; on the side of mercy rather than on the side of justice. ***Negatio conclusionis est error in lege.*** The denial of a conclusion is error in law. ***Errores ad sua principia referre, est refellere.*** To refer errors to their sources is to refute them.

ERUDITE, ***adjective*** academic, bookish, cerebral, cultivated, cultured, educated, elevated, enlightened, highbrow, highly analytical, informed, intellectual, intelligent, knowing, knowledgeable, learned, lettered, literate, mentally acute, polished, professorial, refined, scholarly, sharp, smart, well-bred, well-read, well-versed

ESCALATION, ***noun*** acceleration, accumulation, addition, aggrandizement, ascension, augmentation, boost, building, burgeoning, climb, development, elaboration, enlargement, escalation, expansion, gain, growth, improvement, increase, intensification, jump, magnification, maximization, multiplication, optimization, raise, rise, spread, surge, upsurge, zenith

ESCAPE, ***verb*** abscond, achieve liberty, avoid, avoid arrest, avoid capture, avoid peril, become free, bolt, break from prison, break loose, break out, circumvent, decamp, depart custody, depart unlawfully, desert, disappear, *elabi,* elude, evade, *evadere,* find freedom, flee, *fugere,* gain liberty, get to safety, levant, make a getaway, run away, slip away, sneak off, steal away, take flight
ASSOCIATED CONCEPTS: extradition, flight, forcible escape

ESCAPE HATCH, ***noun*** alternative, choice, clause, condition, contingency, contrivance, definition, device, escape clause, escape valve, evasion, exception, excuse, expedient, given, grounds, loophole, means of escape, means to escape, mechanism for evasion, opening, outlet, saving clause, technicality, vehicle of escape, way of escape, way out
ASSOCIATED CONCEPTS: contracts

ESCHEAT, ***verb*** be forfeited back, cede back, go back, *hereditas caduca,* obstruct the course of descent, recede, regress, relapse, retrocede, retrovert, return, reverse, revert, revert to the state, slip back, turn back
ASSOCIATED CONCEPTS: forfeiture

ESCHEATMENT, ***noun*** act of reverting, confiscation, conversion to the government, deprivation, descent by forfeiture, forfeiture, reversion to the government, reversion to the state

ESCHEW, ***verb*** abstain, avoid, back away from, boycott, bypass, deny oneself, do without, elude, evade, flee from, forbear, forswear, give a wide berth, have nothing to do with, keep at a distance, keep away, keep clear of, keep out of the way, make unwelcome, neglect, recoil from, refrain, reject, shrink from, shun, stand aloof, stand clear, turn aside, turn away from, *vitare,* withdraw from

ESCROW, *noun* conditional deed held in trust, conditional instrument, contingent deed held in trust, entrustment, instrument held until the performance of a condition, written instrument of contingency

E-SIGNATURE, *noun* cryptographic signature, digital signature, electronic approval, electronic authorization, electronic confirmation, electronic seal, electronic signature, encrypted digital signature, e-signing, legally binding electronic authorization, signature via e-mail

ESOTERIC, *adjective* abstruse, acroamatic, acroamatical, acroatic, arcane, cabalistic, cabalistical, concealed, confidential, confined to a select circle, covert, cryptic, deep, designed for the initiated, difficult to comprehend, enigmatic, enigmatical, esoterical, for a select few, hidden, involved, mysterious, mystic, mystical, obscure, occult, private, profound, puzzling, recondite, secret, shrouded, shrouded in mystery, understood by a select few, understood by the initiated, undisclosed, undivulged, untold, veiled

ESPIONAGE, *noun* espial, intelligence, obtaining national defense secrets, obtaining of classified information, practice of spying on others, search made for useful military information, secret observation, secret watching, spying, subversive activity, surveillance, systematic secret observation of the words and conduct of others, undercover work
ASSOCIATED CONCEPTS: espionage act, treason

ESPOUSE, *verb* abet, accept, adopt, advocate, aid, ally, argue for, assist, associate with, back, become a participator, become a partisan, champion, choose, contribute to, cooperate, defend, embrace, endorse, enter into, favor, help, join, lend oneself to, opt, participate, side with, sponsor, stand behind, stand up for, subscribe to, support, take part in, take up, uphold

ESQUIRE, *noun* advisor, advocate, *armiger,* attorney, attorney-at-law, barrister, counsel, counselor, counselor-at-law, jurisconsult, jurisprudent, jurist, lawyer, legal advisor, legal practitioner, legist, member of the bar, member of the legal profession, officer of the court, practitioner, solicitor
ASSOCIATED CONCEPTS: advice of counsel, assigned counsel, assistance of counsel, attorney of record, attorney's fees, benefit of counsel, Code of Professional Responsibility, counsel of record, denial of counsel, effective counsel, of counsel, Sixth Amendment, waiver of counsel

ESSENCE, *noun* basic part, core, embodiment, essential part, fundamental part, gist, heart, hypostasis, inmost nature, inner being, meaning, *natura,* nature, pith, quiddity, quintessence, soul, substance, *vis*
ASSOCIATED CONCEPTS: essence of a contract, essence of testimony by a witness

ESSENTIAL *(Inherent),* ***adjective*** basal, basic, basilar, basilary, elemental, fundamental, immanent, implicit, integral, intrinsic, intrinsical, main, primary

ESSENTIAL *(Required),* ***adjective*** basic, binding, called for, chief, compulsory, critical, crucial, demanded, exigent, fundamental, important, incumbent upon, indispensable, lacking, mandatory, material, necessary, needed, needful, obligatory, of vital importance, pressing, primary, *proprius,* requisite, urgent, *verus*
ASSOCIATED CONCEPTS: essential duties, essential governmental duties, essential parties, essential services, essential terms of a contract

ESTABLISH *(Entrench),* ***verb*** cause to endure, *confirmare,* fix deeply, fix permanently, implant firmly, ingrain, make durable, make firm, make lasting, make permanent, make stable, make steadfast, perpetuate, plant, put on a firm basis, root, situate, solidify, *stabilire,* stabilitate, stabilize, steady, strengthen

ESTABLISH *(Launch),* ***verb*** begin, bring about, bring into being, bring into existence, build, charter, *constituere,* constitute, construct, create, develop, form, found, give rise to, inaugurate, inchoate, initiate, *instituere,* institute, introduce, lay the foundations, open, organize, originate, prepare, put in motion, set going, set in operation, set up, start, *statuere*
FOREIGN PHRASES: ***Cujus est instituere, ejus est abrogare.*** Whoever may institute, his right it is to abrogate.

ESTABLISH *(Show),* ***verb*** ascertain, attest, authenticate, certify, circumstantiate, cite evidence, confirm, corroborate, demonstrate, document, manifest, *probare,* prove, substantiate, testify to, uphold, uphold in evidence, validate, verify, *vincere*
ASSOCIATED CONCEPTS: conclusively establish, establish beyond a reasonable doubt, establish by a fair preponderance of the credible evidence, establish to a clear certainty, established by law, legally established

ESTABLISHED *(Created),* ***adjective*** approved, commenced, created, established, filed, formed, founded, inaugural, inaugurate, incorporated, initial, initiated, innovate, institutional, organized, original, originated, pioneer, set-up, started
ASSOCIATED CONCEPTS: incorporation

ESTABLISHED *(Traditional),* ***adjective*** accepted, approved, authentic, authenticated, confirmed, conventional, deep-rooted, demonstrated, dominant, endorsed, entrenched, guaranteed, identifiable, identified, ingrained, orthodox, permanent, predominant, preeminent, regular, secure, set, settled, stable, substantiated, sure, undeniable, undisputed, unshakable, unsinkable, upheld, verified, vested

ESTATE *(Hereditament),* ***noun*** bequest, birthright, devise, gift by succession, heritage, heritance, inheritance, legacy, patrimony
ASSOCIATED CONCEPTS: beneficial estate, charge against an estate, claim against an estate, distribution, estate tax, residue

ESTATE *(Property),* ***noun*** acres, *ager,* assets, assets and liabilities, belongings, chattels, chattels real, chose in action, collective assets, earthly possessions, effects, equity, freehold, goods, grounds, hereditament, holdings, intangible assets, interest in land, land and buildings, lands, liquid assets, material assets, material things which are owned, personalty, piece of landed property, *possessio,* possessions, real estate, realty, resources, right, title and interest in land, tangible assets, tangibles, tenement, territory, valuables, *villa*
ASSOCIATED CONCEPTS: absolute estate, conditional estate, defeasible estate, equitable estate, estate at sufferance, estate at will, estate by entirety, estate by purchase, estate for life, estate for years, estate from period to period, estate from year to year, estate in common, estate in expectancy, estate in land, estate in remainder, estate in reversion, estate

lands, estate on a conditional limitation, estate pur autre vie, estate tail, estate upon a limitation, executory estate, fee-simple estate, fee-tail estate, forfeiture of an estate, freehold, joint estate, landed estate, life estate, limited estate, next eventual estate, qualified estate, vested estate
FOREIGN PHRASES: ***Post executionem status lex non patitur possibilitatem.*** After the execution of the estate, the law suffers not a possibility.

ESTATE PLANNING, *noun* arrangements for succession, proper testamentary scheme, testamentary planning, will planning
Generally: tax planning

ESTEEM, *noun* acclamation, account, admiration, adoration, adulation, affection, applause, appreciation, approval, attachment, bias, confidence, deference, devotion, eminence, enthusiasm, estimation, favor, fondness, glorification, homage, honor, interest, like, love, obeisance, partiality, praise, preference, prize, recognition, regard, respect, reverence, satisfaction, value, veneration, worth

ESTIMATE *(Approximate cost),* ***noun*** admeasurement, *aestimatio,* appraisal, appraisement, approximate calculation, approximate judgment of value, approximate value, approximation, assessment, calculation, charge, computation, considered guess, educated guess, estimation, evaluation, gauge, market price, measurement, quotation, rate, rating, reckoning, rough calculation, rough guess, statement of the costs, valuation, value, worth
ASSOCIATED CONCEPTS: fraudulent estimates

ESTIMATE *(Idea),* ***noun*** assumption, belief, conjecture, consideration, deduction, determination, guess, guesswork, impression, *iudicium,* judgment, observation, opinion, perception, personal judgment, reaction, reckoning, speculation, supposal, supposition, surmisal, surmise, understanding, view

ESTIMATE, *verb* *aestimare,* appraise, budget, calculate approximately, *censere,* conjecture, evaluate, figure, figure costs, form an opinion, gauge, give an approximate value, guess, judge, place a value on, put an approximate price on, rank, rate, reckon, set a price on, set a value on, suppose, survey, value, weigh
ASSOCIATED CONCEPTS: estimated tax, estimated cash value, estimated cost, estimated revenue, final estimate

ESTIMATION *(Calculation),* ***noun*** admeasurement, appraisal, appraisement, approximate calculation, approximate judgment of value, approximation, assessment, assumption, computation, conjecture, considered guess, deduction, educated guess, estimate, evaluation, gauge, guess, guesswork, judgment, measurement, mensuration, opinion, rating, reckoning, rough calculation, rough guess, speculation, supposal, supposition, surmisal, surmise, valuation, weighing

ESTIMATION *(Esteem),* ***noun*** admiration, appreciation, approbation, approval, commendation, credit, deference, favor, favorable opinion, favorable recognition, favorable repute, fondness, good opinion, good reputation, good standing, high opinion, high regard, homage, honor, praise, regard, respect, reverence, veneration

ESTOP, *verb* avert, ban, bar, barricade, bind, block the way, block up, blockade, bring to a stop, create a stoppage, cut off, encumber, fend off, forbid, forestall, halt, hamper, handicap, hinder, impede, inhibit, interfere, interrupt, intervene, not allow, obstruct, obviate, preclude, prevent, prohibit, put a stop to, put an end to, restrain, restrict, shackle, stand in the way, stay, stop, stop the progress of, stop the way, stymie, thwart, turn aside, ward off
ASSOCIATED CONCEPTS: change in position

ESTOPPEL, *noun* ban, bar, bar to an allegation, barrier, barring, blockage, disallowance, forbiddance, hindrance, impediment, inhibition, legal restraint, obstruction, preclusion, preclusion by act, preclusion by conduct, prohibition, restraint, restriction
ASSOCIATED CONCEPTS: agency by estoppel, collateral estoppel, equitable estoppel, estoppel by concealment, estoppel by conduct, estoppel by deed, estoppel by judgment, estoppel by laches, estoppel by matter in pais, estoppel by matter of accord, estoppel by recital, estoppel by record, estoppel by silence, estoppel by suppression, estoppel by verdict, estoppel letter, judicial estoppel, partnership by estoppel, ratification, stare decisis, waiver
FOREIGN PHRASES: ***Nemo contra factum suum venire potest.*** No man can contradict his own act or deed. ***Un ne doit prise advantage de son tort demesne.*** One ought not to take advantage of his own wrong.

ESTRANGE, *verb* *abalienare,* alienate, avoid, be disjoined, break with, cut off, disaffect, disband, disconnect, dispart, dissever, dissociate, disunite, divert from original use, divert from the original possessor, divide, draw apart, drive apart, exclude, fall out, isolate, keep aloof, keep apart, keep at a distance, leave out, offend, part, part company, segregate, separate, set against, set apart, set at variance, sever, sunder
ASSOCIATED CONCEPTS: separation of spouses

ESTRANGEMENT, *noun* abalienation, abandonment, *alienatio,* alienation, alienation of affection, breach, break, cleavage, conflict, detachment, difference, disaffection, disagreement, disassociation, *discidium,* disconnection, discord, disengagement, disfavor, disharmony, disjunction, disloyalty, disruption, dissevering, dissociation, dissonance, disunion, disunity, division, divorce, divorcement, dudgeon, enmity, hostility, ill will, incompatibility, loss of affection, parting, riddance, rift, rupture, schism, segregation, separate maintenance, separation, severance, severance of relations, split, sundering, termination of cohabitation, unfriendliness, variance, withdrawal

ET AL., *adverb* and all, and everyone, and more of the same, and other parties, and other things, and others, and the rest

ETERNITY, *noun* aeon, age, all time, an everlasting time period, beyond, boundlessness, ceaselessness, endlessness, eon, forever, future, hereafter, history, immeasurable amount of time, immortality, indefinite long time period, infinity, interminableness, kingdom come, lifetime, limitlessness, nonstop time, now and forever, permanence, permanency, perpetuity, protracted time period, spanning time, time without end, timelessness

ETHICAL, *adjective* above board, conforming to moral standards, conforming to professional conduct, decent, good, honest, honorable, idealistic, in accord with ethics, in accordance with the rules for right conduct, in accordance with the standards of a profession, just, law-abiding, legitimate, moral, *moralis,* principled, professional, relating to moral action, respectable, right, righteous, straight, uncorrupt, uncorrupted, unimpeachable, upright, virtuous

ASSOCIATED CONCEPTS: Code of Judicial Conduct, Code of Professional Responsibility

ETHICS, *noun* casuistry, code, code of morals, code of right and wrong, conduct, good conduct, goodness, honesty, honor, ideals, integrity, justice, laws of a profession, moral behavior, moral conduct, moral judgment, moral obligation, moral philosophy, moral practice, moral principles, moral rectitude, moral strength, moral tone, morality, morals, *philosophia moralis,* principles, principles of morality, probity, professional standards, rectitude, righteousness, sense of right and wrong, standards, standards of conduct, standards of professional behavior, system of morals, uprightness, values, virtue, virtuous conduct, virtuousness
ASSOCIATED CONCEPTS: legal ethics, professional delinquency, professional ethics

EUTHANASIA, *noun* assisted dying, authorization to end life for humane reasons, early death for humane reasons, grant permission to terminate life for humane reasons, grant to terminate life for humane reasons, legalized killing for humane reasons, legalized taking of life for humane reasons, license to take life for humane reasons, loss of life for humane reasons, means to die sanctioned, permission to terminate life for humane reasons, permit to terminate life for humane reasons, permitting to die for humane reasons
ASSOCIATED CONCEPTS: involuntary euthanasia, physician-assisted suicide, voluntary euthanasia

EVACUATE, *verb* abscond, absent oneself, break camp, clear out, decamp, depart, disappear, empty, escape, exit, flee, leave, leave empty, *locum vacuefacere,* make a departure, march out, move out, quit, remove, retreat, run away, send away, take flight, vacate, vanish, withdraw

EVACUATION, *noun* abandonment, clearing, decampment, desertion, egress, egression, embarkation, emigration, escape, exit, exodus, expatriation, expulsion, farewell, flight, getaway, leaving, migration, passage, quitting, recession, removal, retreat, setting forth, takeoff, taking leave, vanishing, withdrawal, withdrawing

EVADE *(Deceive),* ***verb*** avoid, be evasive, beguile, circumvent, defraud, delude, dissemble, dodge, equivocate, falsify, fool, hedge, hoax, lie, mislead, misrepresent, outwit, palter, pretend, prevaricate, shuffle, sophisticate, trick

EVADE *(Elude),* ***verb*** avoid, dodge, escape, escape notice, flee, get away from, hide from, keep clear of, slip out
ASSOCIATED CONCEPTS: evade execution of a judgment, evade the law

EVALUATE, *verb* appraise, ascertain the amount of, assess, calculate, class, criticize, determine the worth of, estimate, express an opinion, figure costs, find the value of, form an opinion, gauge, give an estimate, give an opinion, judge, measure, place a value on, prepare an estimate, price, rank, rate, reckon, review, set a figure, set a price on, set a value on, value
ASSOCIATED CONCEPTS: evaluate the evidence

EVALUATION, *noun* analysis, appraisal, appraisement, assessment, audit, belief, calculation, check, checkup, computation, conjecture, consideration, conviction, determination, estimate, estimation, examination, hypothesis, impression, inspection, judgment, measurement, notion, opinion, perception, rating, reassessment, reckoning, review, scan, scrutiny, sentiment, stock, study, survey, theory, view

EVAPORATE, *verb* abate, cease to be, constrict, consume, decrease, deflate, dematerialize, desiccate, disappear, dispel, disperse, dissipate, dissolve, evanesce, evanish, fade, fizz, foam, froth, lessen, lose, melt, parch, pass, reduce, vanish, vaporize, weaken

EVASION, *noun* *ambages,* artful dodge, artifice, avoidance, camouflage, chicane, chicanery, circumvention, concealment, covering up, craftiness, cunningness, deceit, deceitfulness, deception, device, disingenuousness, distortion, dodge, elusiveness, equivocation, escape by cleverness, escape by trickery, fabrication, flight, guile, knavery, *latebra,* maneuver, masquerade, misrepresentation, obfuscation, partial truth, perversion of the truth, pretext, prevarication, ruse, secrecy, secretiveness, secretness, sham, slyness, sophistical excuse, stealth, stealthiness, subterfuge, subtlety, *tergiversatio,* tergiversation, trick, underhand dealing
ASSOCIATED CONCEPTS: evasion of taxation, evasive contempt, evasive pleading

EVASIVE, *adjective* *ambiguus,* ambivalent, artful, avoiding, beguiling, clandestine, concealed, covert, covinous, crafty, deceitful, deceiving, deceptive, delusive, eluding, elusive, elusory, equivocating, feigned, fictitious, fictive, furtive, guileful, hedging, hypocritical, in disguise, misleading, misrepresentative, mysterious, perfidious, pretended, scheming, secluded, secretive, seeking to avoid, seeking to elude, seeking to evade, shifty, sleightful, slippery, sneaky, stealthy, surreptitious, tending to evade, tricky, truthless, untruthful, unveracious, unwilling, using evasion, vague
ASSOCIATED CONCEPTS: evasive argument, evasive contempt, evasive pleading, evasive witness

EVEN, *verb* abate, cease to be, constrict, consume, decrease, deflate, dematerialize, desiccate, disappear, dispel, disperse, dissipate, dissolve, evanesce, evanish, fade, fizz, foam, froth, lessen, lose, melt, parch, pass, reduce, vanish, vaporize, weaken

EVENHANDED, *adjective* balanced, befitted, candid, considerate, deserved, deservedly, deserving, detached, disinterested, dispassionate, equal, equitable, exact, fair, fair-minded, forthright, frank, impartial, indifferent, just, neutral, nondiscriminating, nondiscriminatory, nonpartisan, objective, open, precise, principled, proper, rational, reasonable, scrupulous, spare, square, straight, straightforward, unbiased, unbigoted, unchallengeable, uncolored, uncorrupt, uncorrupted, unprejudiced, unslanted, upright, virtuous, without favor
ASSOCIATED CONCEPTS: the just administration of law

EVENT, *noun* adventure, affair, development, episode, *eventus, exitus,* experience, *factum,* hap, happening, incident, marked occurrence, milestone, occasion, occurrence, proceeding, transaction
ASSOCIATED CONCEPTS: contingent event, fortuitous event, future event, person interested in the event, unforseen event, witness to an event
FOREIGN PHRASES: ***Casus fortuitus non est sperandus, et nemo tenetur devinare.*** A fortuitous event is not to be forseen, and no one is bound to expect it. ***Casus fortuitus non est supponendus.*** A fortuitous happening is not to be presumed.

EVENTUALLY, *adverb* anon, directly, finally, forthwith, immediately, imminently, in time, momentarily, one of these days, presently, promptly, right away, shortly, someday, sometime, sometime soon, soon, sooner or later, straightaway, subsequently, ultimately

EVERYDAY *(Normal),* ***adjective*** accustomed, average, boring, common, customary, familiar, garden-variety, habitual, homely, plain, prosaic, regular, run-of-the-mill, standard, standard-issue, typical, unexceptional, unremarkable, usual, wonted, workaday

EVERYDAY *(Unimportant),* ***adjective*** anemic, banal, bland, boring, commonplace, dreary, dry, dull, expected, generic, humdrum, insignificant, insipid, jejune, minor, monotonous, mundane, normative, ordinary, plain, predictable, quotidian, regular, routine, spiritedness, tedious, tiresome, traditional, trivial, ubiquitous, unimportant, uninspiring, uninteresting

EVERYTHING, *noun* accumulation, aggregate, aggregation, all inclusive, all-inclusive package, built in, collection, collectiveness, collectivity, complete, complex, comprehensiveness, ensemble, entirety, from soup to nuts, gross, group, intactness, lock stock and barrel, mass, omnitude, plenitude, quantity, sum, totality, unity, universality, universe, whole

EVICT, *verb* *depellere,* deprive of possession, *detrudere, deturbare,* dislodge, displace, dispossess, disturb, eject, expel, jettison, kick out, oust, put out of house by legal process, recover property, remove, take possession, thrust out, turn adrift, turn out, turn out of doors, turn out of house and home, uproot, wrest property from
ASSOCIATED CONCEPTS: actual eviction, constrictive eviction, partial eviction, total eviction, unlawful eviction

EVICTION, *noun* act of driving out, act of throwing out, deprivation of possession, dislodgment, dispossession, divestment, ejection, ejectment, entry under paramount title, *evictio,* expulsion, extrusion, forcible expulsion from property, intentional exclusion of lessee, ouster, ouster by paramount title, recovery of property from another's possession, removal, takeover of property
ASSOCIATED CONCEPTS: abandonment of possession, actual eviction, breach of covenant of quiet enjoyment, constructive eviction, eviction by paramount title, partial eviction, total eviction, unlawful eviction
FOREIGN PHRASES: ***Sive tota res evincatur, sive pars, habet regressum emptor in venditorem.*** The purchaser who has been evicted totally or in part has an action against the vendor.

EVIDENCE, *noun* admitted testimony, body of facts on which belief is based, circumstances in a case, confirmation, corroboration, document, documentation, documents, exhibit, exhibits, exhibits submitted to jury, facts, facts admitted at trial, facts judicially noted, facts which bear on the point in question, facts which establish the point in issue, factual matter, ground of proof, grounds for belief, *indicium,* instrument of proof, matter legally submitted to the jury, matters of fact, means of proof, means of proving a fact, medium of proof, persuasive facts, probative matter, proof, proof legally presented at trial, proof of facts, record, relevant fact, relevant material, species of proof, substantiation, *testimonium,* that which furnishes proof, that which tends to prove, validation, verification
ASSOCIATED CONCEPTS: acceptance of evidence, admission of evidence, affirmative evidence, after-discovered evidence, against the weight of the evidence, all the evidence favorable to the plaintiff, best evidence, burden of going forward, burden of persuasion, burden of proof, character evidence, circumstantial evidence, clear and convincing evidence, clear preponderance of the evidence, collateral evidence, competent evidence, conclusive evidence, conflicting evidence, corroborating evidence, credible evidence, cumulative evidence, demonstrative evidence, destruction of evidence, direct evidence, documentary evidence, evidence of title, exclusion of evidence, expert evidence, extrinsic evidence, fabricated evidence, fair preponderance of evidence, favorable evidence, foundation for evidence, hearsay evidence, immaterial evidence, impeaching evidence, incompetent evidence, incredible evidence, inculpatory evidence, independent evidence, indispensable evidence, insufficient evidence, intrinsic evidence, introduction of evidence, irrelevant evidence, judicial evidence, legal evidence, material evidence, newly discovered evidence, objection to evidence, offering in evidence, opinion evidence, parol evidence, persuasive evidence, positive evidence, preponderance of evidence, presumptive evidence, prima facie evidence, primary evidence, probative evidence, real evidence, rebutting evidence, receiving evidence into the record, record evidence, reliable evidence, res gestae, rules of evidence, satisfactory evidence, scintilla of evidence, secondary evidence, state's evidence, substantial evidence, substantive evidence, sufficient evidence, sufficient evidence to support the verdict, supporting evidence, suppression of evidence, sworn evidence, taking evidence, testimony, visible evidence, weight of evidence, written evidence
FOREIGN PHRASES: ***Ponderantur testes, non numerantur.*** Witnesses are weighed, not counted. ***Principia probant, non probantur.*** Principles prove, they are not proved. ***Praesumptiones sunt conjecturae ex signo verisimili ad probandum assumptae.*** Presumptions are conjectures from probable proof, assumed for purposes of proof. ***Testimonia ponderanda sunt, non numeranda.*** Evidence is to be weighed, not counted. ***De non apparentibus, et non existentibus, eadem est ratio.*** The law is the same respecting things which do not appear and those which do not exist. ***Non potest probari quod probatum non relevat.*** That may not be proved which, if proved, is irrelevant.

EVIDENCE, *verb* attest, authenticate, avouch, bear out, bear witness to, bring to light, bring to view, certify, circumstantiate, confirm, declare to be genuine, declare to be true, demonstrate, denote, disclose, display, establish, evince, exemplify, expose, give indication of, illustrate, imply, indicate, *indicium,* infer, instance, lay bare, make obvious, make plain, manifest, reveal, signify, suggest, swear, tell of, tend to show, *testimonium,* uncover, unsheathe, verify
ASSOCIATED CONCEPTS: proof evidencing a crime occurred

EVIDENT, *adjective* *apertus,* apparent, appearing, axiomatic, axiomatical, bald, clear, conspicuous, discernible, disclosed, distinct, easily seen, easy to perceive, easy to see, *evidens,* explicit, exposed, express, glaring, in evidence, in full view, in sight, in view, indisputable, indubitable, lucid, manifest, *manifestus,* noticeable, obvious, open, open to the vision, open to view, ostensible, overt, palpable, patent, perceivable, perceptible, perspicuous, plain, pronounced, revealed, salient, showing, standing out, standing out clearly, transparent, unconcealed, undeniable, undisguised, unequivocal, unhidden, unmistakable, unquestionable, visible
ASSOCIATED CONCEPTS: evident mistake, proof of guilt being evident

EVIDENTIARY, ***adjective*** admissible circumstances in a case, admitted testimony, corroboration, documentation with evidentiary value, documents which play a role in a trial, documents which tend to prove the outcome, exhibits, exhibits submitted to jury, facts admitted, facts judicially noted, facts proving the outcome of a trial, facts which bear on the point in question, facts which establish the point in issue, grounds for belief, having confirmatory effect, information which furnishes proof, instrument of proof, means of proof in a case, means of proving a fact at trial, medium of proof, proof, proof legally presented at trial, proof of facts, relevant documents, relevant information, relevant matters, substantiation, validation, verification
ASSOCIATED CONCEPTS: evidentiary facts, evidentiary importance, evidentiary law, rules of evidence, the law of evidence

EVIDENTIARY PRIVILEGE, ***noun*** confidentiality, evidentiary bar, immunity from testifying, privileged evidence, right to refuse testimony
ASSOCIATED CONCEPTS: accountant-client privilege, attorney-client privilege, executive privilege, physician-patient privilege, priest-penitent privilege, spousal privilege, voter privilege

EVIL, adjective adverse, bad, baleful, baneful, contemptible, corrupt, damaging, dangerous, dark, debased, debauched, degenerate, deleterious, despicable, destructive, detrimental, diabolic, diabolical, disreputable, fatal, harmful, horrible, hostile, hurtful, ignoble, ill, immoral, infernal, inimical, iniquitous, injurious, insidious, lethal, malignant, menacing, mischievous, nefarious, nocuous, noisome, noxious, ominous, onerous, perilous, pernicious, prejudicial, reprehensible, ruinous, sinister, unethical, unfriendly, unlawful, unrighteous, unsafe, venomous, vicious, vile, villainous, wicked, wrong

EVINCE, ***verb*** bespeak, betoken, bring into view, demonstrate, denote, display, evidence, exhibit, furnish evidence, illustrate, indicate, make clear, make evident, make manifest, make plain, manifest, *ostendere,* point to, *praestare, probare,* prove, show, show signs

EVISCERATE, ***verb*** cut out, damage, debilitate, deprive of essential parts, deprive of force, deprive of vital parts, devitalize, dig out, disembowel, dismantle, embowel, enervate, enfeeble, exenterate, exsect, extract, gut, harm, impair, injure, mar, pick out, pluck, pull out, remove an essential part, rip out, sap, spoil, take away an essential part, tear out, weaken

EVOKE, ***verb*** accomplish, achieve, arouse, be the cause of, bring about, bring forth, bring out, bring to pass, call forth, call up, cause, cause to happen, draw forth, draw out, educe, effect, effectuate, *elicere,* elicit, *evocare,* excite, *excitare,* extract, generate, give rise to, hasten, incite, induce, initiate, inspire, instigate, motivate, obtain, occasion, precipitate, procure, produce, prompt, provoke, rouse, secure, stimulate, summon, summon forth, summon up

EVOLVE, ***verb*** advance, arise from, become, change into, come from, come to be, derive from, descend from, develop, emerge, *evolvere, explicare,* follow, grow from, have a common origin, issue, originate from, progress, result, spring from, take form, take shape, turn into, undergo evolution, unfold

EVULSION, ***noun*** avulsion, deracination, disengagement, displacement, drawing out, ejection, elicitation, elimination, eradication, excavation, exsection, extirpation, extraction, extrication, plucking out, pull, pulling out, removal, ripping out, separation, unravelment, unrooting, uprooting, withdrawal

EX OFFICIO, ***adverb*** authoritarian, by divine right, by law, by right, de jure, duly, empowered, in authority, in charge, in control, in office, official

EX PARTE, ***adjective*** by one party, done by one person, for one party, in behalf of one party, on one side only, on the application of one party, one-sided, unilateral
ASSOCIATED CONCEPTS: ex parte application, ex parte decree, ex parte hearing, ex parte motion, ex parte proceeding

EX PARTE, ***adverb*** biased, in the interest of one party, one sided, partial, partisan, prejudiced, relating to one side only, unilateral
ASSOCIATED CONCEPTS: ex parte affidavit, ex parte appointment, ex parte certificate, ex parte commission, ex parte declaration, ex parte experiment, ex parte investigation, ex parte motion and order, ex parte petition, ex parte presentment, ex parte proceedings, ex parte settlement, ex parte statement

EX POST FACTO, ***adjective*** affecting a previous act, after, after the act is committed, after the fact, afterward, at a later period, at a later time, at a subsequent period, at a succeeding time, directly after, following in time, later, later in time, retroactive, thereafter
ASSOCIATED CONCEPTS: ex post facto law

EXACERBATE, ***verb*** aggravate, arouse, augment, deteriorate, enrage, *exacerbare,* excite, heighten, incense, incite, increase, inflame, infuriate, intensify, irritate, make more severe, make worse, provoke, render worse, worsen

EXACT, ***adjective*** accurate, admitting of no deviation, allowing no departure from the standard, careful, clear cut, close, correct, defined, detailed, *diligens, exactus,* explicit, express, faithful, literal, meticulous, minute, particular, plain, precise, punctilious, punctual, right, rigid, scrupulous, specific, strict, *subtilis,* true to fact, undeviating, unerring, unexaggerated, verbatim, with no mistake, without error
ASSOCIATED CONCEPTS: exact copy

EXACT, ***verb*** ask for, assess, call for, charge, claim, clamor for, coerce, compel, constrain, cry for, demand, demand payment, demand toll, draw from, dun, elicit, enforce, enjoin, extort, force, force payment, impel, impose, impose a duty, impose a tax, insist upon, lay a duty on, lay claim to, levy, make an authoritative request, make demands, make obligatory, make pay, make requisition, mulct, necessitate, obligate, oblige, order, press, require, require authoritatively, requisition, squeeze, task, tax, threaten, toll, urge, wrench, wrest, wring
ASSOCIATED CONCEPTS: certified copy, exact copy

EXAGGERATE, ***verb*** amplify, augment, blow up, boost, broaden, build up, caricature, color, develop, elaborate, embellish, enhance, enlarge, exalt, expand, extend, fabricate, flesh out, fudge, hedge, heighten, hyperbolize, inflate, invent, magnify, melodramatize, misinform, misreport, misrepresent, overdo, overemphasize, overstate, pad, play up, romanticize, satirize, sensationalize, stress, stretch, supplement

EXAGGERATION, ***noun*** addition, aggrandizement, augmentation, boast, brag, caricature, disproportion,

distortion, embellishment, embroidery, enlargement, excess, excessiveness, exorbitance, exorbitancy, expansion, extravagance, extravagant statement, extremes, gasconade, histrionics, hyperbole, immoderacy, immoderateness, immoderation, inaccuracy, inexactitude, inexactness, inflation, inordinacy, inordinateness, intemperance, intemperateness, intensification, magnification, misleading enlargement, outrageousness, overassessment, overemphasis, overenthusiasm, overpraise, overstatement, overvaluation, rodomontade, sensationalism, stretch, superfluity, superfluousness, *superlatio,* superlative, *traiectio,* undueness, unreasonable amplification
ASSOCIATED CONCEPTS: deceit, fraud, misrepresentation

EXALTED, ***adjective*** aggrandized, boosted, canonized, deified, dignified, elevated, ennobled, enshrined, glorified, heightened, idealized, idolized, intense, lifted, magnified, outstanding, prominent, raised, romanticized, supreme, uplifted

EXAMINATION *(Study),* ***noun*** active study, analysis, audit, careful noting of details, check, close inquiry, close observation, consideration, deliberation, diligent attention, exhaustive inquiry, exploration, inquest, *inquisitio,* inquisition, inspection, *investigatio,* investigation, observation, perquisition, perusal, reconnaissance, research, review, scrutiny, search, strict inquiry, survey
ASSOCIATED CONCEPTS: cross-examination, direct examination of a witness, examination before trial, examination in chief, examination of records, examination of title

EXAMINATION *(Test),* ***noun*** interrogation, interview, probation, questioning under oath, quiz, set of questions
ASSOCIATED CONCEPTS: blood tests, board of examiners, civil service examination, entrance examination, health examination, medical examiners, mental examination, motor vehicle examination, physical examination, professional examinations, title examination

EXAMINE *(Interrogate),* ***verb*** catechize, challenge, inquire, *inquirere, inspicere,* interpellate, interview, *investigare,* probe, put questions to, query, question, question under oath, quiz, subject to questioning
ASSOCIATED CONCEPTS: examine a witness

EXAMINE *(Study),* ***verb*** analyze, anatomize, audit, canvass, check, conduct research on, contemplate, delve into, dissect, explore, go over, inquire into, inspect, investigate, keep under surveillance, look for flaws, look into, look over, look through, make an analysis, monitor, observe, peer at, peruse, probe, pry into, reconnoiter, regard carefully, research, review, scrutinize, study systematically, subject to analysis, subject to scrutiny, survey, take stock of, watch closely
ASSOCIATED CONCEPTS: examine books and records

EXAMPLE, ***noun*** archetype, case, case in point, demonstration, *documentum,* exemplar, exemplification, *exemplum,* exponent, guide, ideal, illustration, instance, metaphor, model, norm, paradigm, pattern, point of comparison, representation, representative, representative selection, sample, simile, something to be imitated, specimen, standard, standard of comparison, typical instance
FOREIGN PHRASES: ***Nil agit exemplum litem quod lite resolvit.*** A precedent which settles a controversy with a question does no good. ***Plus exempla quam peccata nocent.*** Examples do more harm than crimes.

EXASPERATE, ***verb*** affront, aggravate, alienate, anger, annoy, antagonize, badger, bait, bother, bristle, bug, craze, cross, displease, disturb, enflame, enrage, frustrate, gall, get, goad, grate, gripe, harass, incense, infuriate, insult, irk, madden, miff, nettle, offend, peeve, perturb, pester, pique, plague, rankle, rattle, rile, roil, rouse, ruffle, spite, tease, unnerve, vex

EXCEED, ***verb*** best, conquer, crush, defeat, distance, dwarf, eclipse, exceed, lick, master, outcompete, outpace, outperform, outrun, outshine, outstrip, overpass, overreach, overstep, pass, subdue, surmount, surpass, tower over, transcend, triumph, trump

EXCEL, ***verb*** accomplish, achieve, advance, beat, best, better, cap, conquer, correct, cream, eclipse, enhance, floor, flourish, fulfill, further meliorate, gain, master, meet with success, one-up, outclass, outdistance, outdo, outperform, outrace, outshine, outstrip, outweigh, pass, prevail, realize, refine, reform, revamp, surmount, surpass, triumph, trounce, whip, win

EXCELLENCE, ***noun*** arete, balance, celebrity, class, consequence, credit, decoration, distinction, distinguishment, éclat, efficiency, eminence, fame, fineness, flair, goodness, greatness, illustriousness, importance, lauded, majesty, merit, nobility, perfection, polish, preeminence, prestige, quality, rank, recognition, refinement, renown, repute, significance, stellar, sterling, style, superiority, supremacy, virtue, worth

EXCELLENT, ***adjective*** accomplished, admirable, attractive, awesome, bang-up, banner, capital, choice, classic, distinguished, exceptional, fantastic, heavenly, high-class, in a league of its own, incomparable, incredible, laudable, noted, outstanding, preferable, premium, prize, proficient, select, sensational, special, standard, sterling, striking, superfine, superior, superlative, supernal, terrific, top-shelf, transcendent, unsurpassed, wonderful, world-class

EXCEPT *(Exclude),* ***verb*** count out, deduct, delete, differentiate, discount, discriminate, dismiss, disregard, eliminate, *excipere,* exempt, *eximere,* extract, leave out, make an exception, omit, pick out, put aside, remove, separate, set apart, single out, subduct, subtract, take out, treat as a special case

EXCEPT *(Object),* ***verb*** be at variance, call in question, challenge, come in conflict with, contradict, contravene, cry out against, decry, demur, denounce, deplore, differ, disapprove, discountenance, dispute, dissent, entreat against, express disapproval, feel disapproval, find fault, gainsay, go contrary to, impeach, impugn, make objection, object to, oppose, protest, refuse to accept, repudiate, run counter to, take exception

EXCEPTION *(Exclusion),* ***noun*** apartness, breach of practice, contrariety, defiance of custom, departure from usual, detachment, deviation, disconformity, disruption, exemption, expulsion, inconsistency, infraction of rule, irregularity, nonconformity, noninclusion, nonuniformity, oddity, omission, preclusion, rarity, removal, segregation, separation, severance, special case, subtraction, unconformity, unconventionality, withdrawal
ASSOCIATED CONCEPTS: exception in a deed, proviso, reservation, statutory exception

EXCEPTION *(Objection),* ***noun*** adverse criticism, challenge, charge, clamor, complaint, contradiction, contravention,

criticism, demurrer, disapprobation, disapproval, discommendation, discontent, dislike, disparagement, displeasure, dispraise, dispute, dissatisfaction, dissent, grievance, improbation, impugnation, lack of agreement, lack of conformity, nonagreement, nonapproval, offense, opposition, outcry, protest, protest against a ruling, protestation, rebuke, rejection, remonstrance
ASSOCIATED CONCEPTS: bill of exceptions, formal objection, general exception, peremptory exception, special exception
FOREIGN PHRASES: ***Exceptio firmat regulam in contrarium.*** An exception affirms the rule to be the contrary. ***Omnis regula suas patitur exceptiones.*** Every rule is subject to its own exception. ***Exceptio semper ultima ponenda est.*** An exception is always to be placed last. ***Exceptio quoque regulam declarat.*** An exception also declares the rule. ***Exceptio quae firmat legem, exponit legem.*** An exception which confirms the law expounds the law. ***Omnis exceptio est ipsa quoque regula.*** Every exception is itself also a rule. ***Ubi quid generaliter conceditur, inest haec exceptio, si non aliquid sit contra jus fasque.*** Where anything is granted generally, this exception is implied: that nothing shall be contrary to law and right. ***Exceptio firmat regulam in casibus non exceptis.*** An exception confirms the rule in cases not excepted. ***Exceptio probat regulam de rebus non exceptis.*** The exception proves the rule concerning things not excepted.

EXCERPT, *noun* citation, clipping, excerption, extract, part, passage, passage taken from a book, portion, quotation, quote, quoted passage, reference, representative selection, select passage, selection
ASSOCIATED CONCEPTS: redact portions of a confession

EXCESS, *adjective* excessive, exorbitant, extra, extravagant, extreme, immoderate, inordinate, lavish, more than enough, needless, *nimium,* overabundant, overflowing, overmuch, profuse, recremental, recrementitial, recrementitious, redundant, spare, superabundant, supererogative, supererogatory, superfluous, supernumerary, surplus, undue, unnecessary, unneeded
ASSOCIATED CONCEPTS: excess fees, excess of jurisdiction, excess profits tax

EXCESSIVE, *adjective* characterized by excess, disproportionate, exaggerated, exceeding, exceeding what is usual, exorbitant, extra, extravagant, extreme, fanatical, fulsome, gross, immoderate, *immoderatus, immodicus,* inordinate, intemperate, needless, *nimius,* nonessential, out of bounds, outrageous, overflowing, overmuch, plethoric, preposterous, profuse, rank, redundant, spare, superabundant, supererogatory, superfluous, supernumerary, surplus, unbounded, uncalled for, unconscionable, undue, unnecessary, unneeded, unreasonable
ASSOCIATED CONCEPTS: excessive assessment, excessive bail, excessive damages, excessive sentence, excessive tax, excessive verdict

EXCHANGE, *noun* bargain, barter, bazaar, bourse, business intercourse, buying and selling, change, commerce, commutation, conversion, deal, interchange, intercourse, market, mart, merchantry, *permutatio,* permutation, rearrangement, reciprocation, reciprocity, replacement, reprisal, requital, retaliation, shift, shuffle, stock market, substitute, substitution, supplanting, swap, trade, traffic, transaction, transfer, transposal, transposition
ASSOCIATED CONCEPTS: bill of exchange, exchange of property, reciprocal exchange, reciprocal transfers

EXCISE, *noun* assessment, capitation, charge, custom, demand, duty, exaction, exactment, fee, imposition, impost, levy, liability, obligation, tariff, tax, taxation, toll
ASSOCIATED CONCEPTS: direct tax, excise tax, fee, gift tax, license tax, privilege tax

EXCISE *(Cut away),* ***verb*** abscind, clip, cut, cut out, deduct, delete, detruncate, diminish, disjoin, dissever, divest, eradicate, expunge, expurgate, extract, pare, pluck out, remove, separate, sever, subduct, subtract, take away, take out, tear out, thin, truncate, weed, withdraw

EXCISE *(Levy a tax),* ***verb*** appraise, assess, charge, charge duty, claim, collect, compel payment, demand, demand payment, demand toll, enforce payment, exact, force payment, impose a duty on, impost, lay a duty on, lay claim to, levy, levy an excise on, oblige, raise, require a tax, requisition, take, tax
ASSOCIATED CONCEPTS: direct tax, franchise tax, gift tax, indirect tax, privilege tax, succession tax

EXCITE *(Aggravate),* ***verb*** agitate, annoy, arouse, bother, enflame, enrage, exasperate, gall, get the best of, harass, induce, irritate, jeer, madden, move, pique, prod, propel, provoke, set off, stir, taunt, tease, trigger, upset, vex, vitalize

EXCITE *(Thrill),* ***verb*** arouse, delight, drive, electrify, fire up, get going, ignite, impassion, instigate, instill exciting feelings, interest, intrigue, key up, motivate, move, pique, provoke, pump up, rivet, spark, start, stimulate, titillate, trigger, vitalize
ASSOCIATED CONCEPTS: in the heat of passion

EXCITEMENT, *noun* appetite, ardor, avidity, avidness, desirousness, electricity, encouragement, energy, enthusiasm, enticement, galvanization, impatience, incentive, incitation, incitement, inducement, inspiration, instigation, interest, jest, keenness, lure, lust, motivation, nervousness, passion, spur, stimulant, stimulation, stimulus, thirst

EXCLAMATION, *noun* cry, emphasis, holler, howl, interjection, proclamation, remark, scream, screech, shout, shriek, squeak, squeal, statement, yell, yowl

EXCLUDE, *verb* avoid, ban, banish, bar, block, blockade, boycott, cast out, censor, count out, debar, deny entry, deport, deprive, disallow, disbar, discount, disdain, dismiss, disown, displace, disqualify, disregard, eject, eliminate, eradicate, except, *excludere,* excommunicate, excuse, exempt, exile, *eximere,* expatriate, expel, force out, forswear, have nothing to do with, ignore, impose a ban, isolate, keep from entering, keep out, lay aside, leave out, leave unregarded, liberate, make an exception, neglect, omit, ostracize, oust, outlaw, overlook, pass over, place out of bounds, preclude, prevent, *prohibere,* prohibit, proscribe, put aside, put out, quarantine, rebuff, refuse to admit, refuse to consider, refuse to include, refuse to see, reject, remove, renounce, repel, repudiate, repulse, restrict, rule out, scorn, segregate, sequester, set apart, set aside, shut out, spurn, taboo, take out, throw out, thrust out, treat as a special case, turn away, turn out, uproot, veto, weed
ASSOCIATED CONCEPTS: exclude from a will, exclude from employment

EXCLUSION, *noun* apartheid, avoidance, ban, bar, blackball, boycott, debarment, denial, denial of entry,

deportation, disbarment, discard, dislodgment, dismissal, disownment, displacement, ejection, *exclusio,* exemption, exile, expatriation, expulsion, immunity, intolerance, isolation, monopoly, nonacceptance, nonadmission, nonconsideration, noninclusion, omission, ostracism, preclusion, prejudice, privilege, prohibition, purge, refusal, rejection, removal, repudiation, riddance, seclusion, segregation, separation, voidance
ASSOCIATED CONCEPTS: Escobedo rule, exception, exclusion from a will, exclusion of a juror, exclusionary clause, exclusionary rule, Miranda rule, systematic exclusion
FOREIGN PHRASES: ***Inclusio unius est exclusio alterius.*** The inclusion of one is the exclusion of another. ***Expressio unius est exclusio alterius.*** The expression of one thing is the exclusion of another.

EXCLUSIONARY RULE, ***noun*** exclusion of evidence resulting from illegal search and seizure, exclusion of evidence resulting from wrongful search, exclusion of illegally recovered evidence, fruit of the poisonous tree, illegally obtained evidence, inadmissible evidence

EXCLUSIVE *(Limited),* ***adjective*** biased, bigoted, choice, clannish, cliquish, esoteric, exclusionary, exclusory, illiberal, preclusive, prejudiced, prohibitive, restricted, restrictive, select, selective, snobbish, snobby, uncharitable
ASSOCIATED CONCEPTS: exclusive agency, exclusive control, exclusive franchise, exclusive immunity, exclusive jurisdiction, exclusive license, exclusive ownership, exclusive possession, exclusive remedy, exclusive right, exclusive use

EXCLUSIVE *(Singular),* ***adjective*** distinct, especial, isolated, lone, one, only, separate, single, sole, solitary, special, unique

EXCLUSIVE CONTROL, ***noun*** cornered market, domination, exclusive care, exclusive dominance, monopoly, ownership, single use, sole accountability, sole control, sole liability, sole liability for, sole responsibility, under the sole and exclusive care and control
ASSOCIATED CONCEPTS: medical malpractice

EXCLUSIVE RIGHTS, ***noun*** distinctiveness, exclusive right, limited territory, restrictive territory, restrictiveness, selectiveness, singularity, sole and undivided right, specialization, uniqueness
ASSOCIATED CONCEPTS: covenant not to compete

EXCULPABLE, ***adjective*** absolved, acquitted, blameless, clear, clear of blame, clear of fault, cleared, devoid of wrongdoing, exemplary, exonerated, faultless, free and clear of wrongdoing, free from blame, free of guilt, guiltless, immaculate, impeccable, inculpable, innocent, irreprehensible, irreproachable, law-abiding, not guilty, palliative, pure, scott-free, unblemished, unimpeachable, unspotted, unsullied, untarnished, upright, upstanding, vindicated, virtuous

EXCULPATE, ***verb*** absolve, absolve of fault, absolve of wrongdoing, acquit, clear, clear from a charge, clear from alleged guilt, clear from imputation of fault, declare guiltless, declare not guilty, dismiss, *excusare,* excuse, exonerate, free, free from blame, give absolution to, justify, liberate, pardon, prove guiltless, prove not guilty, set free, vindicate, vindicate from unjust reproach
ASSOCIATED CONCEPTS: exculpatory clause, exculpatory evidence, exculpatory statement, mitigation of damages

EXCULPATORY, ***adjective*** absolve, absolve of fault, absolve of liability, absolve of wrongdoing, acquit, clear, clear from, clear from a charge, clear from imputation of fault, clear from liability, clear of blame, clear of guilt, clearing, declare not guilty, excuse, exonerate, free, free from blame, justify, liberate, tending to absolve, tending to clear, tending to pardon, tending to prove guiltless, tending to prove not guilty, tending to set free, tending to vindicate
ASSOCIATED CONCEPTS: exculpatory clause, exculpatory evidence

EXCULPATORY CLAUSE, ***noun*** absolution from liability, clear from a charge, clear from alleged guilt, clear from imputation of fault, condition to clear of liability, contract to clear of liability, covenant to clear of liability, declaration to clear of liability, exception to liability, excuse against the imposition of liability, exemption from liability, exemption from liability, means to absolve of liability, means to clear of liability, out clause, provision to absolve of liability, proviso to absolve of liability, vindication from liability
ASSOCIATED CONCEPTS: contracts, trusts and estates, wills

EXCUSE, ***noun*** alibi, allowance, defense, dispensation, exculpation, *excusatio,* exemption, exoneration, explanation for some delinquency, extenuation, justification, mitigation, ostensible reason, pretense, pretext, rationalization, reason, subterfuge
ASSOCIATED CONCEPTS: excusable assault, excusable homicide, excusable neglect, legal excuse
FOREIGN PHRASES: ***Impotentia excusat legem.*** The impossibility of performing a legal duty is an excuse from the performance. ***A l'impossible nul n'est tenu.*** No one is bound to do what is impossible.

EXCUSE, ***verb*** absolve, acquit, allow for, bear with, clear, condone, discharge, exculpate, exempt, exonerate, *expurgare,* extenuate, forgive, free, give absolution to, give dispensation, grant amnesty to, judge with indulgence, justify, let off, liberate, make allowances for, overlook, pardon, pass over, pronounce innocent of wrong, provide with an alibi, regard indulgently, release, release from obligation, relieve, remit, reprieve, shrive, vindicate
ASSOCIATED CONCEPTS: affirmative defense, alibi, defense, just cause, justification, lawful excuse, legitimate excuse, reasonable excuse
FOREIGN PHRASES: ***Impotentia excusat legem.*** The impossibility of performing a legal duty is an excuse from the performance. ***Injuria non excusat injuriam.*** One wrong does not excuse another. ***Ignorantia excusator, non juris sed facti.*** Ignorance of fact may excuse, but not ignorance of law. ***Ignorantia eorum quae quis scire tenetur non excusat.*** Ignorance of those things which a person is deemed to know is no excuse. ***Vani timoris justa excusatio non est.*** A frivolous fear is not a lawful excuse. ***Ignorantia juris non excusat.*** Ignorance of the law is no excuse. ***Regula est, juris quidem ignorantiam cuique nocere, facti vero ignorantiam non nocere.*** The rule is that a person's ignorance of the law may prejudice him, but that his ignorance of fact will not.

EXECUTE *(Accomplish),* ***verb*** achieve, act, act upon, attain, bring about, bring to pass, carry into effect, carry into execution, carry out, commit, complete, discharge, do, effect, effectuate, *efficere,* enact, fulfill, manage, perform, perpetrate, put in action, put in force, realize, see through, succeed, take action, transact
ASSOCIATED CONCEPTS: execute a contract, execute a note, execute a promise, execute a warrant, execute after entry

of a judgment, execute an agreement, execute an instrument, execute an obligation, execute an order, execute the laws, executed consideration, executed contract, executed estate, executed fine, executed remainder, executed trust, execution creditor, execution debtor, execution lien, execution sales, garnishment, tax execution

EXECUTE *(Sentence to death),* ***verb*** condemn, condemn to death, deprive of life, dispatch, end life, inflict capital punishment, kill, punish with death, put to death, put to death according to law, slay, *supplicium*
ASSOCIATED CONCEPTS: execute pursuant to a death sentence, execution of a sentence, sentence

EXECUTION *(Completion),* ***noun*** accomplishment, achievement, act, action, administration, application, art, completion, conquest, consummation, contrivance, denouement, discharge, doing, effectuation, effort, enactment, expedition, feat, finalization, following, fulfillment, handling, implementation, oration, performance, perpetration, practice, production, proficiency, prosecution, pursuance, realization, triumph

EXECUTION *(Collection on a judgment),* ***noun*** annihilation, defrayal, defrayment, discharge, enforcement, payment, recompense, remittance, remuneration, resolution, satisfaction

EXECUTION *(Killing),* ***noun*** capital punishment, corporal punishment, death penalty, decapitation, electrocution, gassing, guillotining, hanging, impalement, lethal injection, lynching, punishment of death sentence

EXECUTIVE, ***adjective*** administrative, directing, high-level, legislative, managing, ministerial, officiating, presiding
ASSOCIATED CONCEPTS: executive acts, executive branch, executive clemency, executive committee, executive council, executive department, executive director, executive duties, executive officer, executive order, executive powers, executive records, executive session

EXECUTIVE, ***noun*** administrator, employer, industrialist, key man, key person, key woman, manager

EXECUTIVE PRIVILEGE, ***noun*** classified, concealed, confidential, confidentiality with other branches of government, confidential relationship, executive department's immunity, executive department's privilege, executive immunity, hidden, imparted in secret, not for publication, not to be communicated, not to be disclosed to other branches of government, president's staff's nondisclosures, private with other branches of government, protected communication from other branches of government, protected relationship, restricted from other branches of government, secret, spoken in confidence, told in confidence, top secret, unmentionable, unrevealed
Generally: freedom from testifying, nondisclosable information, nondisclosure, refusal to disclose
ASSOCIATED CONCEPTS: invoking executive privilege

EXECUTOR, ***noun*** administrator, administrator of a will, administrator of the decedent's estate, administratrix, custodian, delegate, fiduciary, legal representative, person in charge, person in responsibility, person named to carry out the provisions of a will, personal representative, representative of the decedent, trustee
ASSOCIATED CONCEPTS: administor, administrix, ancillary executor, custodian, executor named in a will, executorship expenses, executrix, guardian, independent executors, probate court, surrogate's court

EXECUTORY, ***adjective*** contingent, *imperfectus, infectus,* not yet carried into operation, unaccomplished, unadministered, uncompleted, unexecuted, unfinished, unfulfilled, unperformed
ASSOCIATED CONCEPTS: executory accord, executory bequest, executory consideration, executory contract, executory devise, executory estate, executory gift, executory instrument, executory interest, executory limitation, executory remainder, executory treaty, executory trust

EXEMPLAR, ***noun*** apotheosis, archetype, example, *exemplum,* exponent, frame of reference, good example, guide, height of perfection, hero, ideal, model, model of virtue, nonesuch, nonpareil, paradigm, paragon, pattern, person of repute, prize, prototype, replica, shining example, specimen, standard, standard for comparison, standard for imitation, standard of perfection, superior individual, the epitome of virtue, the finest example, the paragon of virtue, the perfect example, the prime example, the summit

EXEMPLARY, ***adjective*** excellent, honorable, ideal, illustrative, in point, laudable, meritorious, model, normal, normative, paradigmatic, personifying, praiseworthy, precedential, representative, sample, serving as a deterrent, serving as a model, serving as a pattern, serving as a sample, serving as a warning, serving as an instance, typifying, used as a deterrent, used as a model, used as a specimen, worthy, worthy of imitation
ASSOCIATED CONCEPTS: exemplary damages

EXEMPLIFY, ***verb*** act the part of, actualize, be taken for, be the equivalent of, betoken, cite, connote, convey an impression, delineate, demonstrate, denote, depict, display, elucidate, embody, enucleate, evidence, evince, exhibit, explicate, express, give an example, give an instance, give concrete form to, illuminate, illustrate, indicate, instance, make clear by examples, make evident, make manifest, make obvious, make plain, manifest, picture, point to, portray, portray by example, produce an instance, render manifest, represent, show by example, signify, stand for, symbolize, typify
ASSOCIATED CONCEPTS: exemplified copies

EXEMPT, ***adjective*** absolved, at liberty, cleared, discharged, excluded, excused, exempted, favored, free, free of binding obligation, freed from, immune, *immunis, liber,* liberated, not answerable, not liable, not responsible, not restricted, not subject to, outside, possessed of immunity, privileged, protected, released, relieved from liability, set apart, shielded, *solutus,* unaffected, unbound, unchecked, unconfined, uncontrolled, unencumbered, unimpeded, unrestrained, unrestricted, waived
ASSOCIATED CONCEPTS: exempt from attachment, exempt from execution, exempt from sale, exempt from taxation, exempt property

EXEMPTION, ***noun*** allowance, discharge, disengagement, exception, freedom, freedom from duty, freedom from liability, freedom from obligation, freedom from requirements, freedom from service, *immunitas,* immunity, liberation, liberty, license, permit, privilege, release, release from liability, release from obligation, special privilege
ASSOCIATED CONCEPTS: exemption from jury service, exemption from sale, exemption statute, homestead exemption, personal exemption, tax exemption

EXERCISE *(Discharge a function),* ***verb*** act, administer, carry into execution, carry on, carry out, conduct, do duty, *efficere,* engage in, execute, *exercere, facere,* officiate, perform, practice, pursue, put in motion, put into action, put into effect, put into practice, serve as, translate into action, wage
ASSOCIATED CONCEPTS: authority exercised under the U.S. Constitution, exercise an option, exercise jurisdiction, exercise of judicial discretion
FOREIGN PHRASES: ***Cui jurisdictio data est, ea quoque concessa esse videntur, sine quibus jurisdictio explicari non potest.*** To whomsoever jurisdiction is given, those things also are supposed to be granted, without which the jurisdiction cannot be exercised. ***Frustra est potentia quae nunquam venit in actum.*** A power is a vain one if it is never exercised.

EXERCISE *(Use),* ***verb*** apply, avail oneself of, bring into play, bring to bear, draw on, employ, make use of, manipulate, operate, practice, put in action, put in practice, put to use, put to work, turn to account, utilize, wield
ASSOCIATED CONCEPTS: exercise a right to vote, exercise an option, exercise discretion, exercise dominion, exercise due care, exercise of power

EXERT, ***verb*** apply, bring into operation, bring into play, bring to bear, *contendere,* employ, exercise, expend, make use of, manipulate, operate, put forth, put in action, set to work, spend, strain, strive, try, use, utilize, wield, work

EXHAUST *(Deplete),* ***verb*** *absumere, conficere,* consume, consume completely, *consumere,* debilitate, deflate, deprive of strength, devitalize, dissipate, drain, draw, draw out, empty, enervate, enfeeble, expend, fatigue, overtire, reach the end of, run through, sap, spend, strain, tax, tire, use, use up, waste, weaken, wear out, weary
ASSOCIATED CONCEPTS: exhaust all available assets

EXHAUST *(Try all possibilities),* ***verb*** carry to completion, complete, *exhaurire,* finish, follow through, litigate completely, treat thoroughly, use up available remedies
ASSOCIATED CONCEPTS: exhaustion of administrative remedies, exhaustion of remedies, exhaustion of state remedies

EXHAUSTIVE, ***adjective*** absolute, across-the-board, all-embracing, all-encompassing, all-out, broad, compendious, complete, comprehensive, covered completely, embracing, embracive, encyclopedic, expansive, extensive, far-reaching, general, global, inclusive, in-depth, infinite, intensive, methodical, panoramic, profound, sweeping, systematic, thorough, total, umbrella, unhampered, universal, unrestrained, wide-ranging

EXHIBIT, ***noun*** disclosure, display, document produced as evidence, evidence, exhibition, exposition, item of evidence, object produced as evidence, object submitted in proof of facts, presentation, revelation, showing

EXHIBIT, ***verb*** bring forward, bring to light, bring to notice, bring to view, demonstrate, disclose, display, evidence, evince, *exhibere, exponere,* expose, express, feature, illustrate, indicate, lay bare, lay open, make clear, make known, make obvious, make plain, manifest, offer for inspection, open up, point out, present, present for consideration, present to view, produce, *proponere,* reveal, reveal to public notice, set forth, show, submit in evidence, uncover, unveil
ASSOCIATED CONCEPTS: exhibit in evidence

EXHORT, ***verb*** *adhortari,* adjure, admonish, advise, advocate, animate, arouse, beg, beseech, caution, charge, coax, command, counsel, encourage, enjoin, entreat, goad, impel, implore, importune, incite, induce, influence, inspire, inspirit, instigate, instruct, offer advice, persuade, plead, press, prevail upon, prompt, push, recommend, rouse, spur, stimulate, talk into, urge, warn

EXIGENCY, ***noun*** crisis, critical situation, difficulty, exigence, imperativeness, necessity, need, press, pressing necessity, pressure, requirement, urgency, urgent need, want
ASSOCIATED CONCEPTS: public exigency

EXIGENT, ***adjective*** acute, badly needed, clamant, compelling, compulsory, critical, crucial, crying, demanding, essential, grave, high priority, imperative, important, indispensable, inescapable, insistent, mandatory, necessary, necessitous, needed, needful, not to be delayed, not to be overlooked, pressing, required, requiring immediate attention, requiring immediate care, requiring prompt action, serious, unavoidable, urgent, vital
ASSOCIATED CONCEPTS: exigent circumstances

EXILE, ***verb*** banish, cast out, deport, dismiss, displace, dispossess, eject, eliminate, evict, exclude, excommunicate, exile, expatriate, expel, expulse, kick out, ostracize, oust, reject, relegate, repudiate, run out, spurn, throw out, transport

EXIST, ***verb*** be, be alive, be in effect, be in present force, breathe, come into existence, continue, continue to be, continue to live, endure, *esse, exsistere, exstare,* go on, have being, have existence, have life, inhere, last, live, live on, persist, remain, remain alive, stay, stay alive, subsist, survive
ASSOCIATED CONCEPTS: corporate existence, existing creditors, existing debt, existing estate, existing law, existing liability, existing lien, existing rights, existing use

EXISTENCE, ***noun*** activity, actuality, animation, being, breath, continuance, continuation, corporality, duration, endurance, essence, genuineness, life, living, physical existence, presence, quintessence, reality, realness, subsistence, substance, survival

EXIT, ***verb*** abandon, abscond, decamp, depart, desert, disappear, emigrate, escape, evacuate, find a passage, find a way out, forsake, get away, go, leave, move, part, perish, pull out, quit, remove, retire, retreat, take off, vacate, walk out, withdraw

EXONERATE, ***verb*** absolve, absolve of a charge, acquit, clear, clear of an imputation of guilt, declare blameless, declare innocent, declare not guilty, discharge, discharge of responsibility, exculpate, excuse, forgive, free from accusation, free from blame, give absolution, grant a reprieve, grant amnesty, liberate, pardon, pronounce free from guilt, prove blameless, prove not guilty, purge, release from an obligation, release from liability, relieve, relieve from accusation, relieve of blame, relieve of liability, remit a penalty, set free, vindicate
ASSOCIATED CONCEPTS: indemnify

EXONERATION, ***noun*** absolution, absolution of a charge, acquittal, acquittance, act of indemnity, amnesty, bill of indemnity, clearance, clearing, discharge, dismissal of charges, dispensation, exculpation, excuse, forgiveness,

freedom, freedom from accusation, freedom from guilt, freeing from blame, liberation, pardon, release, relief from, remission, reprieve, vindication, withdrawal of the charge
ASSOCIATED CONCEPTS: exoneration clause in a will, exoneration of bail, pardon

EXORBITANT, ***adjective*** dear, enormous, excessive, expensive, extortionate, extravagant, extreme, fabulous, greedy, gross, high-priced, huge, immense, immoderate, *immodicus,* inordinate, intemperate, outrageous, overmuch, preposterous, uncalled-for, unconscionable, undue, unreasonable, unwarranted

EXPAND, ***verb*** accumulate, add to, advance, aggrandize, aggravate, amplify, ascend, augment, balloon, be augmented, be distended, become broad, become greater, become larger, blow up, branch out, broaden, build up, burgeon, deepen, develop, develop in greater detail, *dilatare,* dilate, distend, elaborate, elevate, enhance, enlarge, enlarge on, enter into detail, escalate, exacerbate, exaggerate, expatiate on, express in fuller form, extend, *extendere,* fan out, fatten, fill out, further, gain, gain strength, go into detail, greaten, grow, grow larger, heighten, increase, increase in bulk, increase in extent, increase the capacity of, inflate, intensify, *lazare,* lengthen, magnify, make greater, make larger, make more comprehensive, maximize, multiply, outspread, outstretch, progress, prolong, raise, redouble, render broad, render larger, shoot upward, sprawl, spread, spread out, spread over, step up, stretch, stretch out, supplement, swell, unfold, wax, widen

EXPANSION, ***noun*** accession, accretion, accrual, addendum, addition, appendix, assemblage, augmentation, blossoming, boost, collection, continuation, development, elaboration, emergence, evolvement, extension, flowering, gain, growth, improvement, increase, increment, maturation, metamorphosis, progress, progression, proliferation, raise, ripening, rise, step-up, supplement

EXPATRIATE, ***verb*** abandon nationality, banish, cast out, change national allegiance, deport, drive from one's native land, eject, exclude, exile, expel, leave one's country, outlaw, renounce citizenship, renounce rights of citizenship, send away, transport, withdraw from one's native land
ASSOCIATED CONCEPTS: aliens, citizenship, deportation

EXPECT *(Anticipate),* ***verb*** await, bargain for, be certain, be confident, be prepared, calculate upon, count on, *expectare,* have in prospect, look for, look forward to, plan on, prepare for, provide for, reckon on, *sperare,* wait for, watch for
ASSOCIATED CONCEPTS: contingent expectancy, expectancy of heir, expectant estate, expectant interest, expectant right, life expectancy

EXPECT *(Consider probable),* ***verb*** apprehend, assume, believe, conclude, conjecture, consider likely, divine, envision, fancy, forecast, foresee, gather, guess, have a hunch, have a presentiment, imagine, infer, judge, predict, presume, prognosticate, prophesy, regard likely, suppose, surmise, suspect, think, think likely

EXPECTANT, ***adjective*** alert, anticipant, anticipatory, antsy, anxious, breathless, brooding, eager, enthusiastic, excited, imminent, impatient, nervous, open-eyed, open-mouthed, pending, raring, restive, restless, vigilant, watchful

EXPECTATION, ***noun*** anticipation, assurance, awaiting, calculation, contemplation, expectance, expectancy, *exspectatio,* foreboding, forefeeling, foreknowledge, foresight, hope, intention, misgiving, *opinio,* preconception, presentiment, presumption, presurmise, prevenience, probability, promise, prospect, prospection, prospicience, *spes,* suspense, trust, waiting
ASSOCIATED CONCEPTS: expectant estates, expectant heir, expectant right, reasonable expectation

EXPEDIENCE, ***noun*** acceptability, advantageousness, appropriateness, aptness, commendableness, convenience, discrimination, expediency, favorableness, feasibility, felicitousness, fitness, fittingness, meetness, opportuneness, practicality, pragmatism, profitableness, propitiousness, propriety, prudence, reasonableness, rightness, seemliness, sense, sensibleness, sound judgment, suitability, suitableness, timeliness, usefulness, *utilitas,* utility, worthiness

EXPEDIENT, ***noun*** agency, alternative, apparatus, appliance, arrangement, artifice, auxiliary, campaign, *consilium,* contributing force, contrivance, convenience, course, design, device, equipment, formula, implement, instrument, invention, *machina,* machination, machine, makeshift, maneuver, material, means, means to an end, measure, mechanism, medium, method, mode of procedure, plan, practice, procedure, proceeding, process, *ratio,* resort, resource, ruse, scheme, shift, step, stopgap, stratagem, strategy, stroke, subterfuge, suggestion, tactic, technique, tool, treatment, trick, undertaking, utensil, vehicle, way, wherewithal

EXPEDITE, ***verb*** accelerate, accomplish promptly, advance, aid, assist, clear the way, dispatch, drive on, ease, encourage, *expedire,* facilitate, forward, foster, further, give a start, hasten, help, hurry, move up, pave the way, precipitate, promote, push ahead, push forward, push through, put into action, quicken, rush, set in motion, smooth, speed, speed up, stimulate, support, urge forward, urge on

EXPEDITIOUS, ***adjective*** accelerated, accomplished efficiently, active, alacritious, brisk, *celer,* done quickly, done with expedition, efficient, express, fast, fleet, hasty, immediate, instant, *maturus,* prompt, *promptus,* punctual, quick, rapid, ready, snappy, speedy, spirited, swift, with alacrity, with dispatch, with speed

EXPEL, ***verb*** banish, cut out, deport, discard, discharge, dislodge, dismiss, disown, dispose of, dispossess, drive out, *eicere,* eject, eliminate, emit, evict, exclude, excommunicate, *exigere,* exile, expatriate, *expellere,* extrude, force away, force out, get rid of, kick out, ostracize, oust, outlaw, purge, put out, reject, remove, rout out, throw out, thrust out, turn out, weed out

EXPEND *(Consume),* ***verb*** apply, avail oneself of, burn, deplete, devour, dissipate, employ, exert, exhaust, finish, lessen, reduce, spend, turn to account, use, use up, waste

EXPEND *(Disburse),* ***verb*** allocate, allot, apportion, assign, bear the cost of, bear the expense of, distribute, *erogare, expendere,* give money, *impendere,* incur an expense, incur costs, make an expenditure, make payment, meet the expense of, pay, pay out, render payment, spend, support the expense of

EXPENDABLE, ***adjective*** accessory, added, additional, auxiliary, dispensable, disposable, duplicate, excess, excessive, expletive, extra, extraneous, functionless, futile, gratuitous, impotent, inapplicable, inconsequential, ineffectual, inessential, inoperative, insignificant, inutile, irrelevant, leftover, needless, negligible, nonessential, nonfunctional, nugatory, of no account, overplus, peripheral, purposeless, redundant, replaceable, spare, substitutable, superabundant, supererogatory, superfluous, supernumerary, supplemental, supplementary, surplus, trifling, unavailing, uncalled-for, unessential, unimportant, unnecessary, unneeded, unprofitable, unrequired, unusable, unused, useless, valueless, worthless

EXPENDITURE, *noun* amount, cash paid, charge, cost, cost incurred, defrayal, defrayment, disbursement, discharge, expense, expenses, funds paid out, investment, money expended, outgo, outlay, payment, price, remittance, spendings, sum
ASSOCIATED CONCEPTS: actual expenditure, capital expenditure, extraordinary expenditure, good faith expenditure, lawful expenditure, legitimate expenditure, ordinary expenditure

EXPENSE *(Cost),* ***noun*** amount, appraisal, appraisement, assessment, budgeted items, buying price, charge, consideration, cost incurred, costliness, debit, defrayal, defrayment, discharge of a debt, *dispendium,* drain on resources, due, exaction, exactment, expenditure, fair value, fee, *impendium, impensa,* market price, monetary value, money expended, obligation, outgo, outlay, overhead, payment, price, rate, remittance, sum, sum charged, valuation, value, worth
ASSOCIATED CONCEPTS: accrued business expense, actual expenses, capital expense, collection expense, contingent expense, current expenses, deductible expense, disbursements, expenditures of an estate, expenses in bringing an action, expenses incurred, expenses of administration, expenses of condemnation, expenses of receivership, extraordinary expenses, general operating expense, incidental expenses, legitimate expense, maintenance expense, mandatory expense, necessary and regular expense, necessary business expense, nonbusiness expense, office expenses, operating expenses, ordinary expenses, personal expenses, proper expenses, reasonable expenses, unusual expenses, witness expenses

EXPENSE *(Sacrifice),* ***noun*** abandonment, casualty, cession, concession, consumption, costliness, damage, decline, deprival, deprivation, deterioration, detriment, disadvantage, disposal, dissipation, dissolution, drain, drain on resources, erosion, forfeit, forfeiture, harm, hurt, ill fortune, impairment, injury, loss, penalty, privation, relinquishment, renunciation, surrender

EXPENSIVE, *adjective* absonant, big-ticket, costly, excessive, exorbitant, extortionate, extravagant, extreme, fancy, high-end, lavish, luxurious, overpriced, plush, posh, premium, pricey, prohibitive, rich, sky-high, spendy, steep, stiff, sumptuous, swank, unaffordable, uneconomic, uneconomical, unreasonable

EXPERIENCE *(Background),* ***noun*** acquaintance, adroitness, apprenticeship, cognizance, competence, competency, cosmopolitanism, education, empiricism, enlightenment, *experientia,* expertise, expertness, familiarity, instruction, judgment, ken, know-how, knowledge, learning, mastery, maturity, *peritia,* perspicaciousness, practical knowledge, practical wisdom, practice, preparation, proficiency, qualification, schooling, seasoning, skill, skillfulness, sophistication, teaching, training, tuition, understanding, wisdom, worldliness
FOREIGN PHRASES: ***Experientia per varios actus legem facit. Magistra rerum experientia.*** Experience by various acts makes law. Experience is the mistress of things. ***Per varios actus legem experientia facit.*** By various acts experience makes the law.

EXPERIENCE *(Encounter),* ***noun*** adventure, befalling, circumstance, confrontation, episode, escapade, event, happening, incident, occasion, occurrence, pass, phenomenon, presentation, proceeding, situation, transpiration, venture

EXPERIMENT, *noun* assay, attempt, dry run, endeavor, essay, examination, *experimentum,* first attempt, investigation, organized observation, *periculum,* research, search, test, testing program, trial, tryout, venture, verification

EXPERT, *adjective* able, accomplished, acquainted, adept, adroit, all-knowing, apt, artful, *callidus,* capable, clever, cognizant, competent, conversant, deft, dexterous, effective, efficient, encyclopedic, experienced, facile, finished, handy, ingenious, knowing, knowledgeable, learned, masterful, masterly, omniscient, practiced, prepared, professional, proficient, qualified, *sciens,* seasoned, skilled, skillful, trained, tried, versed, veteran, well-qualified, wise
ASSOCIATED CONCEPTS: expert evidence, expert opinion, expert witness, handwriting expert

EXPERT, *noun* authority, connoisseur, experienced hand, experienced person, experienced personnel, genius, knowing person, man of erudition, man of learning, master, master hand, mastermind, paragon, practiced hand, practitioner, professional, proficient person, qualified person, sage, savant, scholar, skilled hand, skilled practitioner, sophisticate, specialist, specializer, specially trained person, strategist, technician, trained person, trained personnel, veteran, virtuoso
ASSOCIATED CONCEPTS: expert testimony, expert witness

EXPERTISE, *noun* ability, acquaintance, adroitness, aptness, art, artfulness, background, capability, cleverness, command, conversance, dexterity, experience, facility, faculty, familiarity, finesse, fluency, genius, gift, ingenuity, judgment, knack, know-how, mastery, proficiency, prowess, savvy, sharpness, skill set, skills, specialty, strength, talent
ASSOCIATED CONCEPTS: expert testimony

EXPIATION, *noun* acknowledgment, adjustment, amends, apology, atonement, compensation, damages, *expiatio,* full satisfaction, guerdon, indemnification, indemnity, pacification, paying back, payment, *piaculum, poena,* propitiation, punishment, quittance, reckoning, recompense, reconciliation, recoupment, recovery, repayment, requital, restitution, satisfaction, settlement, solatium

EXPIRATION, *noun* cessation, close, closing, closure, completion, conclusion, consummation, death, discontinuance, discontinuation, dissolution, dying, end, ending, expiry, *exspiratio,* finish, limit, period, retirement, running out, stop, stoppage, term, termination
ASSOCIATED CONCEPTS: expiration of a charter, expiration of a contract, expiration of a franchise, expiration of a grant, expiration of a lease, expiration of a license, expiration of a patent, expiration of a period of redemption, expiration of a sentence, expiration of a term of office, expiration of a trademark, expiration of an insurance policy, expiration of an option to buy, expiration of credit

EXPIRE, *verb* *animam edere,* become void, cease, cease to be, close, come to a close, come to an end, conclude, decease, depart, die, die away, die out, disappear, discontinue, draw to a close, elapse, end, *exspirare,* fade away, finish, go, lapse, pass, pass away, perish, run out, stop, succumb, surcease, terminate, vanish, wear away, wind up

EXPLAIN, ***verb*** account for, annotate, assign a meaning to, cause to be understood, clarify, clear of obscurity, clear up, decipher, define, demonstrate, describe, disentangle, elucidate, enlighten, enucleate, exemplify, *expedire, explanare,* explicate, *exponere,* expound, give reason for, illuminate, illustrate, increase clarity, interpret, make clear, make evident, make explicit, make manifest, make plain, manifest, offer an explanation, paraphrase, point out, popularize, put across, put in other words, rephrase, restate, reveal, shed light upon, show, simplify, solve, specify, spell out, teach, tell how, throw light upon, translate, unfold, unravel, unscramble, untangle

EXPLANATION, ***noun*** amplification, annotation, clarification, commentary, deciphering, defense, definition, delineation, demonstration, description, elucidation, enucleation, exegesis, exemplification, *explanatio, explicatio,* explication, exposition, expounding, illumination, illustration, *interpretatio,* interpretation, justification, key, meaning, plain interpretation, rationale, rendering, rendition, showing, simplification, solution, strict interpretation, translation, unfolding
ASSOCIATED CONCEPTS: commentary to a statute, explanatory expressions in a will

EXPLANATORY, ***adjective*** annotative, apodictal, clarifying, commentarial, demonstrational, demonstrative, descriptive, elucidative, enlightening, evincive, exegetic, exegetical, exemplificative, explicative, explicatory, explicit, expository, expressive, illustrative, informative, informatory, interpretative, justificatory, revealing, revelatory

EXPLETIVE, ***noun*** addition, anathema, bad language, blaspheming, curse, denunciation, ecphonesis, embellishment, execration, foul invective, foul language, imprecation, injection, insertion, interjection, interpolation, irreverence, malediction, outcry, profane interjection, rhetorical phrase, rhetorical word, scurrility, strong language, swearing, unnecessary addition, unnecessary inclusion

EXPLICABLE, ***adjective*** accountable, apprehensible, ascribable, cognizable, coherent, comprehensible, conceivable, constructable, deducible, determinable, discoverable, easily understood, explainable, fathomable, intelligible, interpretable, knowable, penetrable, scrutable, understandable

EXPLICATE, ***verb*** clarify, define, describe, detail, develop, elucidate, enlighten, *enodare,* enucleate, explain, *explicare,* expound, give a detailed explanation, illuminate, illustrate, interpret, *interpretari,* make clear, make explicit, make plain, render clear, reveal, shed light upon, simplify, spell out, throw light upon, translate, unfold, unfold the meaning of, unfold the sense of, unriddle, untangle

EXPLICATORY, ***adjective*** analytical, clarifying, coherent, commentarial, demonstrative, descriptive, elucidative, enlightening, evincive, exegetic, exemplificative, explanatory, explicative, expository, illustrative, informative, informatory, interpretative, revealing, revelatory

EXPLICIT, ***adjective*** absolute, accurate, *apertus,* beyond doubt, categorical, certain, clear, clearly defined, clearly expressed, clearly formulated, clearly stated, comprehensible, crystal-clear, decided, definite, *definitus,* determinate, direct, distinct, distinctly expressed, distinctly stated, easy to understand, evident, evincive, exact, explanatory, express, expressed outright, forthright, indisputable, intelligible, lucid, manifest, obvious, open, outspoken, patent, perspicuous, plain, pointed, positive, precise, recognizable, specific, straightforward, strict, sure, to the point, transparent, unambiguous, unconfusing, understandable, undisguised, unequivocal, unmistakable, well-developed
ASSOCIATED CONCEPTS: explicit notice, explicit power

EXPLOIT *(Make use of),* ***verb*** apply, avail oneself of, bring into play, capitalize on, consume, employ, exercise, fall back on, find useful, implement, make the most of, manipulate, operate, profit by, put in practice, put into action, put into operation, put to service, put to use, put to work, resort to, set in motion, set to work, take advantage of, turn to account, use, utilize, wield, work

EXPLOIT *(Take advantage of),* ***verb*** abuse, do an injustice to, ill-treat, ill-use, maltreat, manipulate, milk, misapply, misappropriate, misdirect, misemploy, misgovern, mishandle, mismanage, mistreat, misuse, oppress, overburden, overtask, overtax, overuse, overwork, persecute, put to wrong use, turn selfishly to one's own account, use badly, use improperly, use selfishly, use wrongly, victimize

EXPLOITATION, ***noun*** employ, misapplication, misuse, overcharge, profiteering, turning to account, unethical use, use, usury, utilization, utilization for profit

EXPLORE *(Analyze),* ***verb*** anatomize, appraise, ascertain, assay, break down, consider, criticize, delve into, develop, dig into, dissect, examine, hunt, inquire, inspect, investigate, peruse, ponder, pour over, probe, prospect, question, *reconnoître,* research, scope, scout, screen, scrutinize, search, seek, study, survey, test, weigh

EXPLORE *(Search),* ***verb*** browse, come across, cruise, detect, dig up, discover, espy, examine, hunt, identify, inspect, investigate, locate, look for, notice, observe, perceive, peruse, probe, prospect, research, reveal, scan, scout, search, seek, skim, skirt, surf, thumb through, tour, travel, traverse, unearth

EXPLOSION *(Detonation),* ***noun*** blast, bombing, charge, detonation of a weapon detonated, detonation of an incendiary device, detonation of bomb, detonator, discharge, proponent

EXPLOSION *(Outcry),* ***noun*** agitation, clamor, clangor, commotion, complaint, cri de coeur, cry, din, excitement, fury, howl, impassioned protest, insurgence, insurrection, opposition, outburst, protest, racket, repercussion, revolution, road, tumult, uproar, vociferation

EXPLOSIVE *(Detonative),* ***adjective*** blast, capable of being detonated, capable of exploding, combustible device, dangerous, detonating, discharge, incendiary device, violent

EXPLOSIVE *(Violent),* ***adjective*** acute, aggravating, aggressive, almighty, antagonistic, belligerent, blistering, combative, combustible, convulsive, cyclonic, destructive, dreadful, excruciating, fearsome, ferocious, fierce, frightful, furious, harsh, hellacious, hostile, hot, intense, magnified, paroxysmal, profound, rigorous, ruinous, severe, stormy, stressed, tempestuous, terrible, truculent, tumultuous, vehement, vexing, vicious, violent, volatile

EXPONENT *(Explainer),* ***noun*** definer, exegete, explicator, expositor, expounder, interpreter

EXPONENT *(Representative),* ***noun*** abettor, advocate, apologist, backer, demonstration, emblem, embodiment, example, exemplar, exemplifier, illustration, indicant, indication, proponent, proxy, sample, specimen, substitute, symbol, token, type

EXPOSE *(Disclose),* ***verb*** abandon, advertise, air, bare, bring into the open, bring to light, cast out, *coarguere,* defame, denounce, denude, deprive of protection, descry, detect, *detegere,* dig up, disclose, discover, display, divest, divulge, emerge, endanger, evince, exhibit, *exponere,* feature, find, give away, hazard, hold up to public ridicule, hunt down, imperil, indicate, inform on, issue, jeopardize, lay bare, lay open, lay open to harm, locate, make liable, make visible, manifest, muckrake, open to view, present, produce, publish, put in a conspicuous place, put in danger, put in peril, put in view, report, reveal, risk, shame, show, show off, smoke out, strip, strip of disguise, subject, turn out, uncloak, unconceal, uncover, undrape, undress, unearth, unfold, unmask, unsheathe, unveil, unwrap, vent
ASSOCIATED CONCEPTS: expose to disease, expose to harm, expose to obloquy, expose to ridicule, expose to the elements

EXPOSE *(Incriminate),* ***verb*** abase, accuse, betray, brand, denounce, dishonor, endanger, hazard, impeach, imperil, implicate, impugn, inform, jeopardize, refute, stigmatize

EXPOSIT, ***verb*** account for, clarify, clear up, elucidate, enlighten, enucleate, explain, explicate, expound, give a lesson, give reason for, hold forth, illuminate, make clear, make lucid, make plain, make simple, make understandable, present, set forth, shed light upon, simplify, spell out, state, throw light upon, unfold

EXPOSITORY, ***adjective*** clarifying, commentarial, declarative, declaratory, demonstrative, descriptive, didactic, discursive, discursory, disquisitional, dissertational, divulgatory, elucidative, enlightening, exegetical, exemplary, exemplificative, explanatory, explicative, explicatory, graphic, illuminating, illuminative, illustrative, informative, informatory, instructive, narrative, realistic

EXPOSTULATE, ***verb*** admonish, advise against, animadvert upon, appeal against, argue, attempt to divert, cast reproach upon, castigate, caution, chastise, chide, convince to the contrary, correct, declaim against, dehort, deter, disapprove, discourage, disincline, dissuade, divert by appeal, divert by persuasion, enjoin, exclaim against, exhort against, find fault with, gainsay, give advice against, object, objurgate, oppose, premonish, protest, reason earnestly against, recommend against, remonstrate, repugn, take exception, talk out of, turn aside, urge against, view with disfavor, withhold assent

EXPOSTULATION, ***noun*** admonition, altercation, blame, caution, complaint, condemnation, confirmed opposition, contention, contrary advice, criticism, dehortation, deprecation, difference, disapprobation, disapproval, dissidence, dissent, dissuasion, expostulation, guidance, objection, objuration, protest, protestation, rebuke, remonstrance, remonstration, reproach, reproof

EXPOSURE, ***noun*** danger, discernibility, discovery, divulgation, exposé, exposition, hazard, jeopardy, laying open, liability, manifestation, openness, perceptibility, peril, presentation, publication, publicity, revelation, risk, susceptibility, susceptivity, unfolding, unmasking, unveiling, visibility, vulnerability
ASSOCIATED CONCEPTS: exposure to asbestos, exposure to toxic chemical, insurance coverage and exposure

EXPOUND, ***verb*** clarify, clear of obscurity, clear up, comment upon, commentate, construe, define, delineate, develop, elucidate, enucleate, explain, explicate, exposit, illustrate, interpret, make clear, make plain, present the meaning of, reveal, set forth, simplify, solve, spell out, state fully, state in detail, unfold, unriddle
ASSOCIATED CONCEPTS: expound the law

EXPRESS, ***adjective*** advised, aforethought, calculated, categorical, certain, clear, clearly indicated, clearly stated, conscious, decided, defined, definite, deliberate, determinate, direct, distinct, distinctly indicated, distinctly stated, emphatic, especially prepared, exact, explicit, fixed, intended, intended for a specific purpose, intentional, meant, not accidental, not by chance, outlined beforehand, outspoken, particular, peculiar, plain, planned, planned in advance, positive, prearranged, precise, predetermined, premeditated, purposeful, purposive, single, specially prepared, specific, specified, unambiguous, unequivocal, willful, with forethought
ASSOCIATED CONCEPTS: express abrogation, express agreement, express authority, express condition, express contract, express covenant, express malice, express notice, express permission, express promise, express terms, express trust, express warranty

EXPRESS, ***verb*** affirm, air, allege, articulate, assert, asseverate, aver, breathe, comment, communicate, convey, couch in terms, *declarare,* declare, denote, describe, disclose, enumerate, enunciate, *exprimere,* find words for, formulate, give expression to, give vent to, give voice to, impart, indicate, make a statement, make an assertion, make explicit, make known, make plain, manifest directly, mouth, observe, phrase, predicate, present, proclaim, pronounce, put in words, remark, say, set down, set forth, set forth in words, show, *significare,* speak, state, state directly, state with conviction, tell, utter, vent, verbalize, voice
FOREIGN PHRASES: ***Quoties in verbis nulla est ambiguitas, ibi nulla expositio contra verba fienda est.*** Whenever there is no ambiguity in the words, then no exposition contrary to the words should be made. ***Tacita quaedam habentur pro expressis.*** Certain things, though unexpressed, are considered as explicit. ***Expressio unius est exclusio alterius.*** Expression of one thing is the exclusion of another. ***Expressio eorum quae tacite insunt nihil operatur.*** The expression of those things which are tacitly implied has no effect.

EXPRESSION *(Comment),* ***noun*** articulation, assertion, asseveration, cliché, communication, declaration, expressed opinion, formula, formulation, idiom, indication, locution, maxim, mention, motto, profession, remark, representation in language, saying, *sententia,* set phrase, setting forth in words, statement, verbalism, verbum, vocal embodiment of thought, voicing, *vox*
ASSOCIATED CONCEPTS: construction, interpretation
FOREIGN PHRASES: ***Expressio unius est exclusio alterius.*** The expression of one thing is the exclusion of another.

EXPRESSION *(Manifestation),* ***noun*** appearance, demonstration, disclosure, display, emergence, evidence, evincement, exhibit, exhibition, exposition, exposure, illustration, indication, instance, mark, presentation, presentment, revealment, revelation, show, showing, sign, token, uncovering

EXPRESSIVE, *adjective* animated, artistic, clear, coherent, declaratory, demonstrative, depictive, descriptive, ebullient, effervescent, eloquent, emphatic, exhibitive, expositive, expository, forceful, forcible, fraught with meaning, graphic, imaginative, indicative, informative, irrepressible, lively, meaningful, momentous, moving, natural, pithy, significant, spirited, strong, substantial, suggestive, telling, unaffected, vital, vivacious, vivid, weighty

EXPROPRIATE, *verb* abridge, annex, appropriate, arrogate, assume, carry away, commandeer, confiscate, convert, deprive, dislodge, displace, dispossess, divest, hijack, impress, occupy, plagiarize, seize, take over, take possession of, transfer, usurp

EXPROPRIATION *(Divestiture),* ***noun*** attachment, confiscation, deprivation, dislodgment, dispossession, disseisin, distraint, distress, divestment, ejection, eviction, expulsion, forcible seizure, foreclosure, removal, sequestration

EXPROPRIATION *(Right of eminent domain),* ***noun*** compulsory purchase, condemnation, condemnation for public use, government appropriation of private land, seizure of private property for public use, seizure of property by the government, seizure of property in the public interest, taking for public use, taking of private land by the government

EXPULSION, *noun* ban, banishment, debarment, deportation, deprivation, detrusion, disbarment, discharge, disgorgement, dislodgment, dismissal, displacement, dispossession, disqualification, driving out, effusion, ejection, ejectment, elimination, enforced withdrawal, eruption, eviction, *exactio,* excision, exclusion, excommunication, exile, expatriation, expelling, *expulsio,* extradition, extrusion, isolation, ostracism, ouster, outlawing, permanent exclusion, purge, putting out, rejection, removal, segregation, separation, suspension, termination of membership, throwing out

EXPUNGE, *verb* abrade, annul, black out, blot out, cancel, cause to disappear, censor, cross off, cross out, *delere,* delete, destroy, dispose of, do away with, edit out, efface, eradicate, erase, excise, extinguish, extirpate, *inducere,* leave no trace, nullify, obliterate, *oblitterare,* put an end to, quash, quell, raze, remove, remove all sign of, remove all trace of, render illegible, rub out, scratch out, strike out, take out, wipe away, wipe off, wipe out
ASSOCIATED CONCEPTS: expunge the record

EXPURGATE, *verb* abridge, amend by removing, blue-pencil, bowdlerize, cancel, censor, clean up, cleanse, conceal, cross out, cut, cut out, delete, depurate, efface, eliminate, enforce censorship, erase, expunge, *expurgare,* free from objectionable content, make better, purge, purify, refine, strike out, suppress, weed

EXPURGATED, *adjective* bowdlerized, censored, clarified, cleansed, diminished, disinfected, edited, emasculated, excised, excluded, pure, purged, purified, refined

EXQUISITE, *adjective* better, classic, dainty, delicate, elegant, elite, excellent, exceptional, exclusive, exquisite, fabulous, fancy, fine, first-class, first-rate, gorgeous, grand, great, high-grade, impeccable, jewel-like, marvelous, noble, outstanding, par excellence, premium, prime, rare, select, sensational, special, spectacular, splendid, stellar, sterling, superb, superior, superlative, supernal, supreme, terrific, top, top-notch, transcendent, ultra rare, unsurpassed, wonderful

EXTANT, *adjective* alive, current, currently existing, existent, existing, in being, in current use, in existence, living, not extinct, not lost, present, standing, still existing, still to be found, subsistent, surviving, undestroyed, visible

EXTEMPORANEOUS, *adjective* ad hoc, ad lib, automatic, casual, extemporary, extempore, immediate, impromptu, improvisational, improvised, impulsive, informal, instinctive, offhand, offhanded, off-the-cuff, snap, spontaneous, spur-of-the-moment, unauthorized, unplanned, unpracticed, unprepared, unrehearsed, unscripted, unstudied
ASSOCIATED CONCEPTS: evidence, extemporaneous utterance

EXTEND *(Enlarge),* ***verb*** add, aggrandize, amplify, *augere,* augment, broaden, build up, carry beyond the limit, carry further, cause to grow, continue, deepen, develop, dilate, distend, draw out, elongate, enlarge the scope of, expand, increase, increase the length of, inflate, lengthen, magnify, make larger, make more comprehensive, *propagare,* protract, spread out in area, stretch, stretch out, supplement, swell, widen
ASSOCIATED CONCEPTS: extended lease, extension of a contract, extension of credit, extension of time for good cause

EXTEND *(Offer),* ***verb*** advance, give, hold out, introduce, place at one's disposal, present, present an opportunity, present for acceptance or rejection, proffer, propose, provide an opportunity, put forth, put forward, put forward for consideration, submit, tender

EXTENSION *(Expansion),* ***noun*** addition, aggrandizement, amplification, augmentation, broadening, dilatation, dilation, distention, enlargement, growth, increase, increase of size, increment, magnification, *prolatio, propagatio,* spreading, stretching, supplementation, widening

EXTENSION *(Postponement),* ***noun*** abeyance, added time, additional time, adjournment, break, continuance, continuation, deferment, deferral, delay, extra time, further time, intermission, moratorium, more time, pause, prolongation, recess, respite, rest, stall, stay, suspension, suspension of activity, temporary stop, temporary suspension
ASSOCIATED CONCEPTS: extension for good cause, extension of payment, extension of renewal of note, extension of time

EXTENSIVE, *adjective* ample, *amplus,* big, branching, broad, broad-based, capacious, commodious, comprehensive, considerable, covering a wide area, deep, diffuse, diffusive, embracing a large area, encompassing a wide area, expanded, expansive, extended, extending, far-flung, far-ranging, far-reaching, great, inclusive, large, large-scale, latus, liberal, *magnus,* prevalent, spread-out, spreading, sweeping, vast, wide, wide-reaching, widely extended, widespread
ASSOCIATED CONCEPTS: extensive damage

EXTENT, *noun* amount, area, borders, bounds, breadth, circuit, compass, comprehensiveness, coverage, degree, dimensions, distance, expanse, gauge, *hactenus,* length, limit, limitation, magnitude, measure, quantity, range, reach,

scope, size, space, spaciousness, span, stretch, sweep, width
ASSOCIATED CONCEPTS: extent of injury, extent of loss

EXTENUATE, ***verb*** absolve, acquit, allow for, attemper, attenuate, clear, condone, debilitate, deprive of strength, dilute, diminish, enervate, enfeeble, exculpate, excuse, exonerate, forgive, justify, lessen, *levare,* lighten, make allowance for, make excuses for, make less serious, *minuere, mitigare,* mitigate, moderate, palliate, pardon, qualify, reduce, reduce in strength, soften, temper, thin, vindicate, weaken

EXTENUATING CIRCUMSTANCES, ***noun*** alleviating circumstances, consideration, exception, extenuation, mitigating circumstances, mitigation, palliation, palliative circumstances, partial excuse, qualification, qualifying reasons, softening circumstances

EXTERNAL, ***adjective*** cover, covering, exterior, extraneous, extrinsic, facade, face, finish, foreign, outdoor, outer, outer side, outermost, outlying, outmost, outside, outward, peripheral, shell, skin, surface

EXTINCT, ***adjective*** antiquated, away, bygone, bypassed, dated, dead, defunct, departed, disappeared, disintegrated, done, ended, expired, extinguished, faded, fallen, finished, gone, knowing, lapsed, lost, missing, nonextant, obsolete, passé, terminated, vanished, void

EXTINGUISH, ***verb*** abolish, abort, annihilate, annul, assassinate, blot out, bring to an end, butcher, cancel, choke, crush, cut out, deaden, deal destruction, demolish, deracinate, destroy, devastate, dismantle, dispel, dispense with, do away with, drown out, efface, end, eradicate, erase, expunge, exterminate, *extinguere,* extirpate, finish off, hold down, keep down, kill, kill by suffocation, lay waste to, liquidate, murder, nullify, obliterate, put an end to, put out, put to death, quash, quell, quench, raze, reduce to nothing, repress, *restinguere,* ruin, shatter, slaughter, slay, smother, squash, squelch, stifle, strangle, subdue, suffocate, suppress, terminate, wipe out
ASSOCIATED CONCEPTS: extinguish a debt, extinguish a legacy, extinguish a right
FOREIGN PHRASES: ***Resoluto jure concedentis resolvitur jus concessum.*** When the right of the grantor is extinguished, the right granted is extinguished. ***Extincto subjecto, tollitur adjunctum.*** When the substance is extinguished, the incident ceases.

EXTIRPATE, ***verb*** abolish, annihilate, annul, blast, blot out, bring to ruin, cancel, consume, cut down, deal destruction, demolish, deracinate, desolate, destroy, devastate, devour, dissolve, do away with, efface, eliminate, end, *eradicare,* eradicate, erase, *excidere, exstirpare,* exterminate, extinguish, get rid of, gut, lay waste, level, liquidate, nullify, obliterate, overturn, pluck out, pull out, pull up by the roots, purge, put an end to, quash, quell, ravage, raze, remove, render null, rid, root out, rub out, sacrifice, shatter, smash, stamp out, tear out, tear to pieces, unmake, uproot, weed out, wipe out

EXTORT, ***verb*** blackmail, coerce, compel, compel by intimidation, compel by threat, constrain by force, draw out by compulsion, draw out by force, elicit by threat, exact, exact by force, *exprimere, extorquere,* force, gain by wrongful methods, gain wrongfully, obtain by compulsion, obtain in an unlawful manner, obtain unlawfully, victimize, wrest, wring
ASSOCIATED CONCEPTS: kidnapping
FOREIGN PHRASES: ***Accipere quid ut justitiam facias, non est tam accipere quam extorquere.*** The acceptance of anything as a reward for doing justice is extorting rather than accepting.

EXTORTION, ***noun*** blackmail, coercion, compulsion, corrupt demanding, exaction, exaction by oppression, illegal compulsion, obtaining by force, obtaining by threat, oppression, oppressive exaction, rapaciousness, rapacity, *res repetundae,* taking by undue exercise of power, unlawful taking, wrenching, wresting, wresting money by force, wringing, wrongful exaction
ASSOCIATED CONCEPTS: kidnapping
FOREIGN PHRASES: ***Extortio est crimen quando quis colore officii extorquet quod non est debitum, vel supra debitum, vel ante tempus quod est debitum.*** Extortion is a crime when anyone under color of office extorts that which is not due, or more than is due, or before the time when it is due.

EXTORTIONIST, ***noun*** blackmailer, compeller, corrupt demander, demander, exacter, illegal exacter, illegal taker, taker, unlawful obtainer, wrester
ASSOCIATED CONCEPTS: coercion, kidnapping, larceny

EXTRA, ***adjective*** abundant, accessory, additional, ample, bountiful, copious, de trop, dispensable, excess, excessive, extraneous, gratuitous, needless, nonessential, plenteous, plentiful, redundant, supererogatory, superfluous, supplemental, supplementary, surplus, uncalled-for, unnecessary

EXTRACT, ***verb*** abridge, abstract, bring forth, choose, cite, collect, cull, deduce, derive, dig out, distill, draw, draw forth, draw out, educe, elicit, epitomize, *evellere,* eviscerate, evoke, excavate, *excerpere,* excerpt, *extrahere,* gather, glean, make a selection, mine, obtain, pick, pick out, pull, pull out, quarry, quote, remove, select, separate, single out, summarize, take out, withdraw

EXTRADITION, ***noun*** apprehension and transfer, capture and deportation, change of place, deportation, seizure and transference, sending to another state for trial, surrender of an individual, transfer to another authority, transference, translocation, turning over to a foreign state
ASSOCIATED CONCEPTS: habeas corpus, rendition

EXTRANEOUS, ***adjective*** additional, alien, *alienus,* aside from the point, coming from without, derived from without, dispensable, extra, extraneus, extrinsic, extrinsical, foreign, impertinent, inapplicable, inapposite, incidental, inconsequent, inconsequential, irrelative, irrelevant, needless, noncompulsory, nonessential, nonpertinent, optional, peripheral, pleonastic, redundant, strange, subsidiary, superfluous, supervenient, supplementary, unaffiliated, unallied, unassociated, uncalled for, unessential, unnecessary, unneeded, unrelated
ASSOCIATED CONCEPTS: extraneous evidence

EXTRAORDINARY, ***adjective*** above-average, amazing, beyond the ordinary, curious, different, especial, exceeding the usual, exceptional, *extraordinarius,* infrequent, *inusitatus,* irregular, notable, noteworthy, *novus,* out of the ordinary, out of the regular order, outstanding, peculiar, phenomenal, rare, remarkable, singular, special, supernormal, unaccustomed, uncommon, uncustomary, unequaled, unexampled, unfamiliar, unheard of, unique, unordinary, unparalleled, unprecedented, unusual, worthy of attention, worthy of regard
ASSOCIATED CONCEPTS: extraordinary care, extraordinary circumstances, extraordinary expenses, extraordinary grand jury, extraordinary peril, extraordinary prerogative writ, extraordinary purpose, extraordinary remedy, extraordinary risks, extraordinary services, extraordinary session

FOREIGN PHRASES: ***Ubi cessat remedium ordinarium, ibi decurritur ad extraordinarium.*** Where an ordinary remedy fails, then resort must be made to an extraordinary one. ***Recurrendum est ad extraordinarium quando non valet ordinarium.*** Resort must be made to the extraordinary when the ordinary does not succeed. ***Nunquam decurritur ad extraordinarium sed ubi deficit ordinarium.*** Resort is never made to the extraordinary until the ordinary fails.

EXTREME *(Exaggerated),* ***adjective*** aggrandized, amplified, beyond the limit, drastic, enlarged, exceeding, exceeding the bounds of moderation, excessive, exorbitant, fanatical, flagrant, going to the utmost lengths, going too far, gross, hyperbolic, immoderate, inordinate, intemperate, magnified, out of bounds, out of proportion, outrageous, overboard, overdone, overstated, overzealous, rabid, radical, undue, unreasonable, unwarranted, violent

EXTREME *(Last),* ***adjective*** at the edge, at the utmost point, concluding, conclusive, definitive, determinative, ending, endmost, *extremus,* farthest, farthest removed, final, finishing, furthest, hindermost, hindmost, last, most distant, most remote, outermost, situated at the farthest limit, *summus,* terminal, terminative, ultimate, *ultimus,* utmost, uttermost
ASSOCIATED CONCEPTS: extreme cases
FOREIGN PHRASES: ***Probatis extremis, praesumuntur media.*** The extremes having been proved, those things which lie between are presumed.

EXTREMITY *(Death),* ***noun*** cessation of being, cessation of existence, cessation of life, close, completion, conclusion, demise, departure, discontinuance, discontinuation, dissolution, end, end of life, expiration, extinction, extinguishment, finish, passing, quietus, stoppage, termination

EXTREMITY *(Furthest point),* ***noun*** border, borderline, boundary, brink, edge, end, extreme limit, *extremitas,* farthest end, farthest point, farthest reach, final point, fringe, frontier, limit, margin, outer edge, outside, pole, tail end, terminal point, termination, terminus, tip, ultimate point, utmost point, verge

EXTRICATE, ***verb*** clear, cut loose, deliver, deobstruct, detach, disburden, discharge, disembarrass, disembroil, disencumber, disengage, disentangle, disenthrall, disjoin, dislodge, disprison, enlarge, exonerate, *expedire,* free, let loose, *liberare,* liberate, loosen, make free, ransom, redeem, release, release from restraint, relieve, rescue, save, set at large, set at liberty, set free, tear loose, unbind, unfetter, unhamper, unharness, unknot, unloose, unloosen, unravel, unshackle, untie

EXTRINSIC, ***adjective*** accessory, added, additional, alien, apart, applied from without, collateral, contingent, derived from without, exterior, external, extra, extraneous, extrinsical, foreign, incidental, irrelevant, nonessential, outside, peripheral, secondary, separate, strange, subordinate, subsidiary, supplemental, unessential
ASSOCIATED CONCEPTS: extrinsic agreements, extrinsic ambiguity, extrinsic circumstances, extrinsic evidence, extrinsic facts, extrinsic fraud, extrinsic mistake

EXUDE, ***verb*** bleed, discharge, disembogue, drain, drip, drop, effuse, eliminate, emit, escape, excrete, find outlet, find passage, find vent, flow out, give off, gush, issue, leak, *manare,* ooze, pass, release, run, secrete, seep, spout, trickle, vent, weep

EYEWITNESS, ***noun*** *arbiter,* attestant, attester, bystander, compurgator, corroborator, giver of evidence, identifier, informant, informer, looker-on, observer, one who obtains evidence first hand, one who personally observes an occurrence, one who testifies to what he has seen, onlooker, seer, spectator, spectator et *testis,* testifier, viewer, watcher

FABRICATE *(Construct),* ***verb*** assemble parts, bring into being, bring into existence, build, call into being, cast, cause to be, cause to exist, complete, compose, create, devise, erect, establish, execute, *fabricari,* fashion, form, generate, make, manufacture, mold, organize, piece together, produce, put together, set up, shape, structure, turn out

FABRICATE *(Make up),* ***verb*** be untruthful, beguile, counterfeit, deceive, delude, devise falsely, dissemble, dissimulate, distort, fake, falsify, feign, fictionalize, forswear, invent, lie, misguide, misinform, mislead, misrepresent, misstate, palter, perjure oneself, pretend, prevaricate, sham, stretch the truth, tell a falsehood, tell a lie, trump up
ASSOCIATED CONCEPTS: fabricated evidence

FABRICATION, ***noun*** canard, deceit, dishonesty, distortion, equivocation, exaggeration, fable, fairy tale, fake, fallacy, falsehood, falsification, fiction, fraudulence, invention, libel, lie, make-believe, mendacity, misconception, misstatement, myth, narrative, nonsense, perjury, pose, pretense, prevarication, story, tale, untruth, yarn

FACE *(Image)*, ***noun*** appearance, aspect, being, delineation, depiction, features, feel, guise, impression, likeness, look, mien, portrayal, replica

FACE *(Physical appearance)*, ***noun*** affectation, appearance, aspect, cast, countenance, cover, covering, demeanor, expression, exterior, facade, features, guise, image, imitation, likeness, lineaments, looks, mask, mien, mug, outside, presence, resemblance, skin, surface, veneer, visage

FACE AMOUNT, ***noun*** exact amount, precise amount, sum, sum shown, sum stated, total

FACE VALUE *(First blush)*, ***noun*** appearance, emanation, manifestation, semblance, visual impact

FACE VALUE *(Price)*, ***noun*** price charged, quoted price, sum, total, worth

FACILE, ***adjective*** accomplished, amenable, attainable, compliable, compliant, conquerable, deft, dexterous, docile, easily done, easily influenced, easily persuaded, easy, easygoing, effortless, *facilis,* flexible, flowing, fluent, impressionable, malleable, manageable, moldable, performable, pliable, pliant, practiced, quick, readily mastered, ready, simple, skilled, skillful, smooth, tractable, undemanding, within reach, yielding

FACILITATE, ***verb*** accelerate, advance, aid, assist, assist the progress, clear, clear the way, deobstruct, disburden, disencumber, disentangle, ease, enable, encourage, *expedire,* expedite, forward, foster, free from difficulty, free from hindrance, free from impediment, free from obstruction, further, give clearance, hasten, help, lend a hand, lessen the labor, lift a ban, lighten, make a path for, make easy, make possible, open the way for, pave the way, promote, push forward, quicken, render a task easier, render assistance, render less difficult, simplify, smooth, speed up
ASSOCIATED CONCEPTS: accomplice, aiding and abetting, facilitation

FACILITATION, ***noun*** advancement, aid, assistance, cleared the way, ease, encouragement, expedience, expedition, furtherance, help, involvement, lubrication, open the doors, play a positive role, promotion, quickening, support
ASSOCIATED CONCEPTS: criminal facilitation, facilitation of a crime, facilitation of a felony

FACILITY *(Easiness)*, ***noun*** ability, adeptness, adroitness, capability, competence, deftness, dexterity, ease, effortlessness, expertise, expertness, *facilitas,* flexibility, fluency, freedom from difficulty, grace, gracefulness, proficiency, quickness, readiness, ready ability, skill, smoothness

FACILITY *(Institution)*, ***noun*** agency, bureau, *conlegium,* establishment, foundation, institute, organization, organized society, *sodalitas*
ASSOCIATED CONCEPTS: reinsurance facility

FACILITY *(Instrumentality)*, ***noun*** agency, apparatus, appliance, channel, *consilium,* contrivance, device, *facultas,* implement, instrument, machinery, manner, means, mechanism, medium, method, technique, tool, *via,* way

FACSIMILE, ***noun*** copy, duplicate, exact copy, mold, molding, oneness, replica, reproduction, sameness, semblance

FACT, ***noun*** absolute certainty, absolute reality, actual occurrence, actual reality, actuality, authenticated incident, certainty, documented event, established matter, established phenomenon, event, existent thing, experience, *factum,* incontrovertible incident, indisputable event, palpable episode, perceived happening, real episode, real experience, reality, *res,* substantiated incident, tangible proof, true incident, truth, verifiable happening
ASSOCIATED CONCEPTS: conceded facts, established fact, facts in issue, facts of a case, facts pleaded, facts presented, facts which constitute a cause of action, question of fact, stipulated facts, uncontroverted facts, undisputed facts
FOREIGN PHRASES: ***Ubi factum nullum, ibi fortia nulla.*** Where there is no principal in fact, there can be no accessory. ***Regula est, juris quidem ignorantiam cuique nocere, facti vero ignorantiam non nocere.*** The rule is that a person's ignorance of the law may prejudice him, but that his ignorance of fact will not. ***Ex facto jus oritur.*** Law arises out of facts. ***Ad quaestionem facti non respondent judices; ad quaestionem juris non respondent juratores.*** Judges do not answer to a question of fact; jurors do not answer to a question of law. ***Facta sunt potentiora verbis.*** Facts are more powerful than words.

FACT FINDING, ***noun*** ascertainment of facts, authentication of facts, certification of facts, conclusion based on facts, confirmation of facts, decision based on facts, declaration based on facts, decree based on facts, determination based on facts, draw a conclusion on the facts, evidence based on facts, finding on facts, form a resolution on facts, incontrovertible determination based on facts, investigation of the facts, resolution based on facts, substantiation of the facts, tangible proof of the facts, verification based on facts

FACTION, ***noun*** cabal, camarilla, clique, conspiracy, contentious group, disaccord, disagreeing party, discord, dissension, dissent, division, *factio, pars,* partisan conflict, partisanship, pressure group, side, splinter party, united body

FACTIOUS, ***adjective*** argumentative, at loggerheads, at odds, bellicose, cantankerous, combative, contentious, controversial, contumacious, disagreeing, discordant, disputatious, dissenting, dissident, divergent, divided, divisive, hostile, implacable, inimical, insubordinate, irascible, militant, mutinous, negative, polemic, pugnacious, quarrelsome, schismatic, turbulent, uncooperative, unilateral

FACTITIOUS, ***adjective*** assumed, contrived, counterfeited, faked, false, feigned, fictitious, forged, imaginary, imagined, imitative, pretended, simulated, simulative, unauthentic

FACTOR *(Commission merchant)*, ***noun*** agent, broker, commercial agent, delegate, deputy, envoy, interagent, intermediary, manager, medium, middleman, one who sells for factorage, proctor, *procurator,* representative
ASSOCIATED CONCEPTS: consignee, factors' lien

FACTOR *(Ingredient)*, ***noun*** additive, agent, aid, aspect, cause, component, constituent, constitutive element, content, contributing force, determinant, element, elementary unit, feature, integral part, part, portion, segment, unit

FACTUAL, ***adjective*** accurate, actual, ascertained, attested, authentic, authoritative, correct, definite, definitive, dependable, disinterested, errorless, exact, faithful, genuine, honest, incontestable, incontrovertible, infallible, irrefutable, literal, objective, official, precise, real, realistic, reliable, right, rigid, scrupulous, strict, true, trustworthy, unbiased, uncolored, undeniable, undeviating, undisguised, undisputed, undistorted, unerring, unerroneous, unexaggerated, unfabricated, unimagined, unimpeachable, unmistakable, unprejudiced, unquestionable, unrefuted, unspurious, valid, veracious, veridical

FACULTY *(Ability),* ***noun*** ableness, adroitness, aptitude, capability, capacity, cleverness, competence, competency, cunning, deftness, dexterity, enablement, endowment, equipment, expertise, expertness, fitness, flair, gift, handiness, knack, know-how, potency, power, proficiency, qualification, readiness, skill, skillfulness, strength, talent, *vis*
ASSOCIATED CONCEPTS: the faculty to comprehend

FACULTY *(Teaching staff),* ***noun*** body of professors, instructional corps, instructional personnel, instructors, lecturers, literati, mentors, officers of instruction, professorate, professors, teachers, teaching body, teaching personnel, tutors

FADE, ***verb*** abate, becoming, blanch, bleach, blench, cease, cloud, decay, decline, decrease, degenerate, deliquesce, deteriorate, die, die out, dim, diminish, disappear, discolor, dissolve, drop off, ebb, etiolate, evaporate, fail, faint, falloff, flag, flicker, grow dimmer, grow duller, languish, lessen, let up, lose brightness, lose luster, neutralize, obsolesce, pale, perish, reduce, sag, shrivel, sink, slacken, subside, taper off, tarnish, tone down, turn colorless, turn dull, vanish, wane, wash out, waste away, weaken, wilt, wither

FAIL *(Lose),* ***verb*** be defeated, be demoted, be unsuccessful, become bankrupt, become insolvent, botch, bungle, *cadere,* collapse, come short, come to naught, come to nothing, *concidere,* crash, decline, *deficere,* deteriorate, disappoint, dishonor, err, fall short, flunk, fold, go out of business, go under, lose, miscarry, miss the mark, not succeed, prove inadequate, prove unsatisfactory, prove useless, succumb

FAIL *(Neglect),* ***verb*** abandon, avoid, break one's promise, break one's word, desert, evade, forsake, ignore, leave, let one down, mismanage, miss, miss an opportunity, omit, prove unreliable, shirk
ASSOCIATED CONCEPTS: fail to act, fail to appear, fail to comply

FAILING, ***noun*** asthenia, atony, blemish, cachexia, collapse, debilitation, decadence, decay, decline, decrepitude, defeat, deficiency, delinquency, disadvantage, failure, fallibility, fault, fiasco, flaw, foible, frailty, imperfection, inadequacy, infirmity, insufficiency, misconduct, perfunctoriness, nonfulfillment, shortcoming, unworthiness, vice, weakness, weak point

FAILURE *(Bankruptcy),* ***noun*** commercial failure, default, discontinuance of business, economic downfall, failure to maintain solvency, financial disaster, financial loss, financial ruin, inability to maintain solvency, inability to meet financial obligations, insolvency, insufficiency of funds, lack of funds, suspension of business
ASSOCIATED CONCEPTS: failure to meet one's obligations, insolvency

FAILURE *(Falling short),* ***noun*** *defectio,* defectiveness, deficiency, delinquency, dereliction, inability, insufficiency, lack, loss of strength, noncompletion, nonfulfillment, nonobservance, nonperformance, omission, oversight, pretermission, shortcoming, slip, want
ASSOCIATED CONCEPTS: failure of consideration, failure of evidence, failure of heirs, failure of issue, failure of proof, failure of purpose, failure of title, failure of trust, failure to act, failure to bargain collectively, failure to comply, failure to file a return, failure to give notice, failure to make delivery, failure to perform, failure to prosecute, law office failures, partial failure

FAILURE *(Lack of success),* ***noun*** aborted attempt, beating, botch, breakdown, collapse, debacle, defeat, disappointment, downfall, drubbing, error, fall, fiasco, fruitless effort, frustration, ineffectualness, labor in vain, loss, miscarriage, misfortune, mistake, ruin, unsuccessful attempt, vain attempt

FAILURE TO COMPLY, ***noun*** contravention, default, defiance, deficiency, deliquency, dereliction, disobedience, disregard, evasion, ignoring, inexecution, infringement, laxity, mutiny, neglect, neglect to obey, negligence, nonfeasance, nonfulfillment, nonobservance, omission, rebellion, recalcitrance, refusal to obey, resistance, revolt, transgression, violation

FAILURE TO UNDERSTAND, ***noun*** error, laboring under a misapprehension, misapprehension, miscalculation, misconception, misconstruance, miscount, misguidance, misinterpretation, misjudgment, misread, misreckon, mistake, misunderstanding

FAIR *(Just),* ***adjective*** *aequus,* affording no undue advantage, appropriate, balanced, deserved, detached, dispassionate, equal, equitable, evenhanded, fair-minded, fitting, honest, honorable, impartial, merited, objective, scrupulous, sporting, sportsmanlike, square, suitable, unbiased, uncolored, uncorrupted, uninfluenced, unprejudiced, unswayed, upright
ASSOCIATED CONCEPTS: fair and impartial trial, fair hearing, fair on its face, fair preponderance of evidence, fair representation, fair trade, fair trial, fair wages

FAIR *(Satisfactory),* ***adjective*** acceptable, adequate, bearable, decent, good enough, mediocre, medium, middling, moderate, moderately good, passable, reasonable, reasonably good, respectable, *secundus,* sufficient, suitable, tolerable, unexceptional, unobjectionable
ASSOCIATED CONCEPTS: fair aggregate value, fair and equitable value, fair and reasonable compensation, fair and reasonable market value, fair and reasonable value, fair cash value, fair consideration, fair equivalent, fair market value, fair preponderance, fair return on investment, fair use, fair valuation, fair value

FAIR TRADE AGREEMENT, ***noun*** trade agreement on set prices, trade alliance on set prices, trade binding promise on set prices, trade commitment on set price, trade compact on set prices, trade concordat on set prices, trade deal on set prices, trade obligation on set prices, trade pact on set prices, trade pledge on set prices, trade understanding on set prices

FAIR USE, ***noun*** exception to copyright holders' exclusivity, exclusion to permissions, fairness abridgement, limitation of an author's exclusive right over creative work, permissions not required for incorporation, use without infringement

FAIRLY *(Clearly),* ***adverb*** absolutely, *aperte,* certainly, *clare,* completely, conspicuously, decidedly, decisively, definitely, discernibly, *distincte,* distinctively, distinctly, distinguishably, doubtlessly, evidently, explicitly, fully, indubitably, intelligibly, irrefragably, irrefutably, legibly, lucidly, manifestly, markedly, noticeably, obviously, openly, palpably, perceptibly, plainly, pointedly, positively, prominently, recognizably, surely, tangibly, unambiguously, unconfusedly, undeniably, understandably, undoubtedly, unequivocally, unmistakably, unquestionably, visibly, vividly, with assurance, with certainty, with confidence

FAIRLY *(Impartially),* ***adverb*** *aeque,* benevolently, disinterestedly, dispassionately, equably, equally, equitably, evenhandedly, evenly, free from prejudice, honestly, honorably, impersonally, in a fair manner, *iuste,* justly, lawfully, legally, morally, properly, righteously, rightfully, rightly, scrupulously, tolerantly, unbiasedly, with justice, without bias, without distinction, without favor, without prejudice
ASSOCIATED CONCEPTS: adjudicate a case fairly

FAIRLY *(Moderately),* ***adverb*** acceptably, adequately, decently, *mediocriter,* mildly, modestly, not badly, passably, presentably, pretty well, rather well, satisfactorily, somewhat, to a degree, to a limited extent, to some extent, tolerably, up to standard, well enough, within bounds, within reason

FAIRNESS, ***noun*** *aequitas,* appropriateness, balance, detachment, disinterestedness, dispassionateness, equality, equitable treatment, equitableness, equity, evenhanded justice, evenhandedness, fair-mindedness, fair play, fair treatment, honesty, impartiality, integrity, *iustitia,* just dealing, justice, justness, lack of corruption, lack of prejudice, objectivity, open-mindedness, probity, reasonableness, rectitude, right, rightfulness, rightness, scrupulousness, unbiasedness, uprightness

FAIT ACCOMPLI, ***noun*** accomplished fact, accomplishment, achievement, actuality, actualization, attainment, carrying through, certainty, completeness, completion, consummation, deed done, effectuation, execution, fact, finished product, fruition, fulfillment, implementation, matter of fact, reality, realization, undeniable fact, work done

FAITH, ***noun*** acceptance, allegiance, assurance, assured expectation, belief, certainty, certitude, confidence, constancy, conviction, credence, deep-rooted belief, dependence, fidelity, *fides,* firm belief, freedom from doubt, hope, implicit belief, implicit confidence, loyalty, *opinio,* optimism, *persuasio,* reliance, sanguine expectation, sanguineness, staunch belief, staunch loyalty, steadfast belief, steadfastness, sureness, surety, troth, trust, unquestioning acceptance, unshakable trust
FOREIGN PHRASES: ***Fides servanda est.*** Faith must be observed. ***Judiciis posterioribus fides est adhibenda.*** Credit should be given to the more recent decisions. ***Ligeantia est quasi legis essentia; est vinculum fidei.*** Allegiance is the essence of law; it is the bond of faith.

FAITHFUL *(Diligent),* ***adjective*** assiduous, attentive, careful, conscientious, constant, dogged, exacting, *fidelis, fidus,* indefatigable, industrious, laborious, meticulous, mindful, painstaking, particular, persevering, persistent, pertinacious, relentless, sedulous, thorough, tireless, unflagging, unrelenting, unremitting, untiring, unwavering
ASSOCIATED CONCEPTS: faithful discharge of duty, faithful performance bond, faithful service

FAITHFUL *(Loyal),* ***adjective*** constant, dependable, devoted, devout, duteous, dutiful, firm, incorruptible, obedient, patriotic, reliable, resolute, sincere, single-hearted, staunch, steadfast, true, trustworthy, unfailing, unwavering, zealous

FAITHFUL *(True to fact),* ***adjective*** accurate, adhering to an original, close, conformable, correct, corresponding, equivalent, exact, faultless, genuine, honest, like, literal, perfect, precise, real, realistic, strict, true

FAITHFULLY, ***adverb*** absolutely, accurately, acquiescently, closely, compliantly, conscientiously, consistently, constantly, devotedly, diligently, duteously, dutifully, earnestly, exactly, expressly, *fideliter,* firmly, honestly, honorably, in every respect, in good faith, incorruptibly, literally, loyally, meticulously, obediently, observantly, precisely, punctiliously, reliably, religiously, resolutely, responsibly, rigidly, scrupulously, sincerely, stanchly, steadfastly, steadily, strictly, submissively, to the letter, truly, trustingly, trustworthily, truthfully, undeviatingly, unerringly, unswervingly, uprightly, veraciously, verbatim, virtuously, with allegiance, with constancy, with fealty, with fidelity, with good faith, word for word
ASSOCIATED CONCEPTS: faithfully discharge the duties of office, faithfully perform, perform duties faithfully, serve faithfully

FAITHFULNESS, ***noun*** adherence, allegiance, attachment, commitment, conformity, constancy, credibility, deference, devotion, discipline, fidelity, firmness, homage, integrity, loyalty, meticulousness, rectitude, responsibility, trustworthiness, veracity

FAITHLESS, ***adjective*** apostatizing, changeable, corrupt, corruptible, deceitful, derelict, disaffected, dishonest, dishonorable, disloyal, double-dealing, false, falsehearted, fickle, fluctuating, hypocritical, inconstant, indifferent, *infidelis,* insincere, mutable, *perfidiosus,* perfidious, *perfidus,* recreant, shifting, traitorous, treacherous, treasonable, treasonous, trothless, two-faced, undependable, unfaithful, unloyal, unpatriotic, unreliable, unscrupulous, unstable, unsteadfast, untrue, untrustworthy, vacillating, variable, wavering
ASSOCIATED CONCEPTS: divorce

FAKE, ***noun*** charlatan, copy, counterfeit copy, emulation, fabrication, facsimile, false representation, falsehood, falsification, feigned copy, forged duplicate, forgery, fraud, fraudulent replica, hoax, imitation, imposter, pretender, quack, replica, reproduction, ruse, simulation, unauthorized reproduction
ASSOCIATED CONCEPTS: counterfeit, forgery

FAKE, ***verb*** act, act falsely, adulterate, affect, alter with intent to deceive, be deceitful, beguile, belie, bluff, cheat, claim falsely, counterfeit, cover up, cozen, deceive, decoy, defraud, delude, disguise, dissemble, dissimulate, distort, dupe, fabricate, falsify, feign, foist off, forge, go through the motions, hoax, hoodwink, imitate, lie, make a show of, make believe, malinger, mislead, misrepresent, pass off, plagiarize, portray falsely, pose as, prepare something specious, pretend, put on an act, put up a front, render spurious, sham, simulate, swindle, trick
ASSOCIATED CONCEPTS: false pretenses

FALL *(Decline),* ***noun*** abatement, bottom, burnout, decadence, declension, decrease, decrement, defeat, degeneracy, degeneration, depletion, depression, descent, deterioration, devolution, dive, downfall, downgrade, downturn, drop, ebb, eclipse, loss, plummet, plunge, reduction, reversal, ruin, setback, sunset, undoing

FALL *(Decline),* ***noun*** accident, calamity, casualty, disaster, incident, liability, misadventure, misfortune, mishap, slip, stumble
ASSOCIATED CONCEPTS: negligence, trip and fall

FALLACIOUS, ***adjective*** abounding in error, beguiling, contrary to fact, deceitful, deceiving, deceptive, delusive, delusory, devoid of truth, distorted, erroneous, *fallax,* false, faultful, faulty, faulty in logic, fraudulent, groundless, guileful, illusive, illusory, in error, inaccurate, incorrect, invalid, miscalculated, misconstructed, misfigured, misleading, misrepresentative, mistaken, paralogistic, sophistical, truthless, unfounded, ungrounded, unsound, untrue, *vanus,* wrong

FALLACIOUSNESS, ***noun*** aberrancy, aberration, bad faith, casuistry, deceit, deception, deceptiveness, defectiveness, delusion, deviation, distortion, equivocation, erroneousness, fallacy, falseness, faultiness, faulty reasoning, fraudulence, illogic, illogicalness, illusion, inaccuracy, misapplication, self-contradiction, sophism, sophistry, speciousness

FALLACY, ***noun*** *captio,* deception, deceptive belief, delusion, deviation from truth, distortion, erroneous reasoning, erroneousness, error, fallacious argument, false appearance, falseness, falsity, faultiness, faulty reasoning, flaw in reasoning, illusion, inaccuracy, misapprehension, misbelief, miscalculation, misconception, misconstruction, misinterpretation, misjudgment, misleading notion, mistake, mistaken idea, paralogism, sophism, sophistry, unsound argument, *vitium,* worthless argument

FALLIBLE, ***adjective*** deficient, errable, errant, erring, *errori obnoxius,* faulty, flawed, imperfect, liable to be erroneous, liable to mistake, not perfect, prone to error, prone to inaccuracy, uncertain, undependable, unpredictable, unreliable, unstable, unsure, untrustworthy, weak

FALLOUT, ***noun*** a bleak outcome, a deleterious outcome, a deleterious outgrowth, a malignant scenario, an extremely unfortunate sequence of events, deleterious aftermath, deleterious developments, deleterious effects, deleterious results, grave consequences, important and significant effects

FALSE *(Disloyal),* ***adjective*** apostatizing, corrupt, deceitful, disaffected, dishonest, dishonorable, double-dealing, double-tongued, faithless, false hearted, fickle, hypocritical, inconstant, insincere, knavish, perfidious, *perfidus,* recreant, roguish, tergiversating, traitorous, treacherous, treasonable, treasonous, trothless, two-faced, undependable, underhanded, unfaithful, unprincipled, unreliable, unscrupulous, unsteadfast, untrue, untrustworthy

FALSE *(Inaccurate),* ***adjective*** abounding in error, concocted, contrary to fact, deceiving, deceptive, delusive, devoid of truth, distorted, erroneous, fallacious, faulty, fictitious, groundless, improper, in error, incorrect, invalid, mendacious, misleading, mistaken, truthless, unfounded, ungrounded, unreliable, unsound, untrue, unveracious, wrong
ASSOCIATED CONCEPTS: altered, false advertising, false and malicious, false and misleading, false arrest, false check, false entry, false imprisonment, false information, false instrument, false oath, false personation, false pretense, false reports, false representation, false statement, false swearing, false testimony, false writing, knowingly false, materially false

FALSE *(Not genuine),* ***adjective*** artificial, assumed, beguiling, bogus, copied, counterfeit, deceitful, deceptive, delusory, designed to deceive, factitious, fake, feigned, *fictus,* forged, fraudulent, given to deceit, imitation, intentionally untrue, make believe, misrepresentative, mock, pretend, pseudo, sham, simulated, spurious, *subditus,* substitute, synthetic, unreal
ASSOCIATED CONCEPTS: false checks, false claim, false pretenses, false representation, false statement, false swearing, false witness

FALSE ALARM, ***noun*** deception, fabrication, fake, false alert, false arrest, false danger signal, false notice, false notification, false signal, false warning, fraud, misrepresentation, sham

FALSE ARREST, ***noun*** bogus arrest, illegal detainment, illegal placement in confinement, improper arrest, improper captivity, improper commitment to prison, improper confinement, improper constraint, improper deprivation of liberty, improper imprisonment improper incarceration, improper legal restraint, improper placement into protective custody, improper restraint, improper seizure, wrong capture, wrongful placement into custody

FALSE PRETENSE, ***noun*** act, affectation, affectedness, artifice, artificiality, assumed basis, bogus purpose, bogus reason, chicane, chicanery, circumvention, circumvention of truth, cozenage, deceit, deceitful purpose, deceitfulness, deceptive reason, deceptive representation of fact, delusion, designed misrepresentation, device, disguise, dishonesty, dissemblance, dissimulation, dupery, duplicity, evasion of truth, fabrication, facade, factitious reasons, fake, fake reasons, fakery, false representation of fact, falsehood, falseness, falsification, falsity, *falsus,* feigned basis, feint, *fictus,* forgery, fraud, fraudulence, fraudulency, guise, hoax, impetus, imposture, improper, improper basis, improper intent, improper intention, improper motivation, improper motive, improper pretensions, intentional untruths, invention, lie, mask, masquerade, mendacity, misinformation, misrepresentation, misstatement, perfidy, perversion of truth, pettifoggery, pretense, pretext, prevarication, ruse, sham, simulated basis, simulation, *simulatus,* sleight, spurious reasons, spuriousness, stratagem, subterfuge, suppression of truth, surreptitiousness, swindle, treacherousness, treachery, trick, trumped-up basis, trumped-up reasons, underhandedness, unnaturalness, untruth, untruthfulness, unveracity, wile, wrong foundation, wrong incentive
ASSOCIATED CONCEPTS: cheating by false pretenses, false representation, larceny, obtaining property by false pretenses, under false pretenses

FALSE STATEMENT, ***noun*** delusion, distortion, error, fabrication, fallacy, falsehood, falsity, fiction, half-truth, hallucination, illusion, inaccuracy, lie, misbelief, miscomprehension, misconception, misinterpretation, misrepresentation, mistruth, myth, perjury, pretense, sophism, story, tale, untruth
ASSOCIATED CONCEPTS: perjury

FALSEHOOD, ***noun*** canard, *commentum,* deception, dissimulation, distortion, distortion of truth, equivocation, evasion, fabrication, false assertion, false statement, falsification, falsity, *falsum,* fiction, flam, fraud, fraudulence, inaccuracy, intentional misstatement, invention, inveracity, lie, *mendacium,* misrepresentation, misstatement, nonconformity to fact, perversion of truth, pretense, pretext, prevarication, story, tale, untrue declaration, untruth
FOREIGN PHRASES: ***Lex punit mendacium.*** The law punishes mendacity.

FALSIFICATION, *noun* beguilement, *corrumpere,* counterfeit, deceit, deceitfulness, deception, disguise, dissimulation, distortion, dupery, duplicity, exaggeration, fabrication, fake, fibbing, flimflam, forgery, forswearing, fraud, hoax, imposture, indirection, insincerity, *interpolare,* invention, lying, mendacity, misconstruction, misquotation, misrepresentation, misstatement, mockery, perjury, phoniness, pretense, prevarication, trickery, trumpery, untruthfulness, *vitiare*
ASSOCIATED CONCEPTS: falsification of evidence, falsification of records, falsification of testimony, perjury

FALSIFY, *noun* deceive, disguise, distort, dupe, duplicity, fabricate, fake, forge, fraudulent, invent, lie, misrepresent, misstate, prevaricate
ASSOCIATED CONCEPTS: falsify a record, falsify reports, falsify tax returns
FOREIGN PHRASES: ***Falsus in uno, falsus in omnibus.*** False in one thing, false in everything.

FALSIFY, *verb* adulterate, alter, alter fraudulently, belie, camouflage, color, *corrumpere,* dissemble, distort, doctor, embellish, embroider, exaggerate, fabricate, fake, feign, garble, *interpolare,* lie, make false statements, miscite, miscolor, misquote, misreport, misrepresent, misstate, pervert, represent falsely, stretch, tamper with, tell a falsehood, twist, violate the truth, *vitiare*
ASSOCIATED CONCEPTS: falsify records

FAME, *noun* acclaim, accolade, acknowledgment, cachet, celebrity, character, distinction, eminence, esteem, glory, greatness, honor, illustriousness, mark, name, note, notoriety, place, popularity, position, preeminence, prestige, prominence, rank, recognition, renown, reputability, reputation, repute, respect, standing, stardom, stature, status, superstardom, visibility

FAMILIAR *(Customary),* ***adjective*** accepted, accustomed, acknowledged, clichéd, common, commonplace, consuetudinary, conventional, current, established, everyday, *familiaris,* frequent, general, generally seen, habitual, hackneyed, homely, household, humble, inveterate, natural, normal, *notus,* ordinary, popular, prevailing, prevalent, recognized, regular, regulation, routine, standard, stereotyped, stock, time-honored, traditional, typical, understood, unexceptional, universal, universally recognized, unoriginal, usual, well-known, well-trodden, widespread, wonted
ASSOCIATED CONCEPTS: custom and usage

FAMILIAR *(Informed),* ***adjective*** accomplished, acquainted, advised, apprised, aware of, briefed, capable, certified, closely acquainted, cognitive, cognizant, competent, conscious, conversant, counseled, deft, dexterous, educated, enlightened, erudite, experienced, expert, fit, fitted, *gnarus,* instructed, intimate, knowing, knowledgeable, learned, lettered, literate, mindful, on intimate terms, *peritus,* practiced, prepared, privy to, proficient, qualified, schooled, *sciens,* sensible, skilled, skillful, trained, tutored, used to, versed, well-acquainted, well-educated, well-versed
ASSOCIATED CONCEPTS: familiar with the facts sufficient to sign an affidavit

FAMILY *(Common ancestry),* ***noun*** ancestry, antecedents, birth, blood connection, clan, common extraction, common forebears, common lineage, common parentage, consanguinity, descent, dynasty, ethnic group, ethnicity, extraction, filiation, folk, genealogy, house, kin, kindred, kinship, kinsmen, line, line of ancestors, line of descent, lineage, origin, parentage, people, same line of descent, same strain, sept, stirps, stock, strain, tribe

FAMILY *(Household),* ***noun*** brood, domestic circle, domestic establishment, *familia,* family unit, home circle, issue, offspring, progeny
ASSOCIATED CONCEPTS: adoption, curtesy, dependent, domestic relation, dower, family court, family law, family purpose doctrine, head of household, heirs, next of kin, surviving spouse

FAMOUS, *adjective* acclaimed, applauded, *celeber,* celebrated, celebrated in public, conspicuous, distinguished, elevated, eminent, esteemed, exalted, fabled, famed, foremost, glorified, glorious, held in high esteem, highly reputed, holding public interest, honored, illustrious, important, in the limelight, in the public eye, in the spotlight, *inlustris,* known, leading, legendary, memorable, notable, noted, noteworthy, notorious, outstanding, popular, preeminent, prominent, public, recognized, remarkable, renowned, sung, talked of, universally recognized, well-known
ASSOCIATED CONCEPTS: libel, public figure, right to privacy, slander

FANATICAL, *adjective* ardent, burning, devoted, dogmatic, enthusiastic, excessive, extreme, fanatic, *fanaticus,* fervent, immoderate, impassioned, inordinate, obsessed, obsessive, overemotional, overenthusiastic, overzealous, passionate, phrenetic, phrenetical, possessed, rabid, radical, resolute, ultrareligious, unreasonable, unreasonably resolute, unyielding, zealous

FANTASTIC, *adjective* beyond anything ever experienced, celebrated, clever, colossal, compelling, dignified, distinguished, elevated, eminent, enormous, esteemed, exalted, excellent, expert, extensive, extraordinary, far-reaching, first-rate, glorious, grand, huge, immense, important, in another dimension, inconceivable, incredible, inexplicable, leading, lofty, major, massive, mastered, mighty, momentous, monstrous, noted, outrageous, outstanding, paramount, perfect, potent, powerful, preeminent, remarkable, renowned, skillful, splendid, strong, substantial, superior, supreme, unequaled, unparalleled

FAR, *adjective* back, beyond the eye, beyond the horizon, distant, far away, far back, far off, further, in the distance, inaccessible, miles away, out of reach, out of sight, out of the way, outlying, remote, removed, too distant, too far, too far away, too far removed, unapproachable
ASSOCIATED CONCEPTS: far apart for purposes of settlement

FAR-FETCHED, *adjective* concocted, doubtable, doubtful, implausible, impossible, improbable, inconceivable, incredible, long odds against being correct, not probably correct, only remotely possible, poor prospect of truth, questionable, remote, small chance, unbelievable, unimaginable, unlikely

FAR-REACHING, *adjective* boundless, comprehensive, considerable, endless, enormous, epidemic, extended, extensive, far-flung, far-ranging, great, having a significant impact, huge, immeasurable, immense, infinite, large scale, limitless, of great extent, of great scope, prodigious, spread out, substantial, sweeping, tremendous, uncircumscribed, unending, unlimited, vast, wide, widespread

FARCE, *noun* absurdity, burlesque, comedy, dry humor, dry wit, humor, imitation, jest, joke, lampoon, mockery,

nimble wit, nonsense, parody, pleasantry, pretense, quick wit, satire, slapstick, spoof, wit
ASSOCIATED CONCEPTS: judgment a farce, travesty of justice, verdict a farce

FARE, ***noun*** carfare, charge, charge for carriage of passengers, charge for conveyance of a person, cost of commutation, cost of conveyance, cost of transportation, expense, expense of transportation, fee, hire, money paid for passage, *naulum,* passage, passage money, payment for the right of carriage, portage fee, price, price of a ticket, price of passage, sum paid for carrying a passenger, tariff, ticket, toll, transportation charge, transportation fee, *vectura*
ASSOCIATED CONCEPTS: rates, fares, and charges of carrier

FASCINATE, ***verb*** allure, appeal to, attract, beguile, bewitch, captivate, capture, charm, coax, compel, delight, enamor, enchant, engage, engross, enrapture, enthrall, excite, grab, grip, hold attraction for, hold interest, hold spellbound, hypnotize, infatuate, influence, interest, intoxicate, intrigue, invite, kindle, mesmerize, overpower, overwhelm, pique, please, provoke, seize, stimulate, stir, transfix, win over

FASCINATION, ***noun*** allure, animal magnetism, appeal, attractiveness, captivation, charisma, compulsion, enchantment, fascination, force field, glamour, magic, magnetism, obsession, preoccupation, seductiveness

FASHION, ***noun*** buzz, caprice, chic, craze, crush, dernier cri, enthusiasm, fancy, fashion, fervor, flavor, furor, fuss, go, hot ticket, infatuation, last word, latest, mode, new wave, novelty, passion, rage, sensation, style, trend, uproar, vogue

FAST, ***adjective*** accelerated, active, agile, alactricious, at once, blistering, blue streak, breakneck, breathless, brisk, expeditious, expeditiously, fleet, flying, galloping, haste, hastened, high-speed, hurried, on the double, posthaste, prompt, pronto, quick, racing, rapid, rushed, snappy, speedily, speedy, straightaway, supersonic, swift, swiftly, velocious, vigorous, whirlwind

FASTIDIOUS, ***adjective*** choosy, conscientious, dainty, delicate, demanding, discerning, discriminating, exacting, finical, finicky, fussy, meticulous, nice, overdemanding, painstaking, particular, pernickety, persnickety, picky, prim, prissy, selective

FAT CAT, ***noun*** affluent contributor, contributor with deep pockets, moneyed contributor, rich backer, rich contributor, wealthy campaign contributor, wealthy contributor, wealthy donor, wealthy supporter
ASSOCIATED CONCEPTS: campaign finance laws, election laws, limits on campaign contributions, publicly funded campaigns

FATAL, ***adjective*** annihilative, calamitous, catastrophic, causing death, causing destruction, consumptive, deadly, death-dealing, deathly, deleterious, demolishing, destroying, destructive, devastating, dire, disastrous, eradicative, *exitialis,* exterminative, extirpative, fateful, fell, feral, *funestus,* harmful, hurtful, injurious, involving death, involving ruin, killing, lethal, lethiferous, malignant, mortiferous, murderous, noisome, noxious, *perniciosus,* pernicious, poisonous, ruining, ruinous, slaughterous, toxic, tragic, venomous, virulent, wasting
ASSOCIATED CONCEPTS: fatal consequences, fatal defect, fatal errors, fatal injury, fatal to a cause of action, fatal variance

FATALITY, ***noun*** accidental death, calamity, casualty, *casus,* cataclysm, catastrophe, deadliness, deadly accident, death, death by accident, destruction, disaster, downfall, fatal accident, fatal casualty, fatal mishap, lethality, liability to disaster, malignance, malignancy, malignity, mischance, misfortune, mortality, perniciousness, ruin, subjection to fate, sudden death, tragedy, violent death, virulence, virulency

FATE *(Destiny),* ***noun*** certainty, destination, destined lot, fate-to-be-predetermined events, fortune, future, future course of events, future state, inevitability, inevitableness, lot, luck, outcome, power to predetermine events, predestination, predetermination, sureness, ultimate future, what is destined to happen, what is doomed to occur, what is fated to occur, what is written, what looms
ASSOCIATED CONCEPTS: fortuitous event, insurance, the defendant's fate is with the jury
FOREIGN PHRASES: ***Fatum.*** Fate.

FATE *(Termination),* ***noun*** apocalypse, bad luck, bane, bitter end, catastrophe, collapse, conclusion, curtain, cutoff, death, death knell, death warrant, deathblow, debacle, destruction, disaster, doom, downfall, end, end of the world, final blow, final event, final curtain, final result, finale, finis, finish, ill luck, last act, misfortune, payoff, quietus, ruin, ruination, terminus, tough luck, undoing, windup

FATED, ***adjective*** certain, destined, determined, doomed, foredoomed, in the cards, inescapable, inevitable, ordained, predestinated, predestined, predetermined, preordained, sure, unavoidable, written

FATUOUS, ***adjective*** absurd, absurdly foolish, addled, asinine, brainless, deficient in reason, destitute of reason, dumb, fatuitous, *fatuus,* foolish, idiotic, ill-advised, illogical, imbecilic, inane, incapable of managing one's own affairs, inept, *ineptus,* irrational, ludicrous, moronic, nonsensical, obtuse, ridiculous, scatterbrained, senseless, shallow, silly, simple, stupid, thoughtless, unintelligent, unreasoning, unthinking, unwise, vacuous, witless
ASSOCIATED CONCEPTS: fatuous claim

FAULT *(Mistake),* ***noun*** aberration, blunder, bungling, erratum, error, error of judgment, failing, false step, flaw, impropriety, inaccuracy, miscalculation, misjudgment, misstep, misunderstanding, omission, oversight, slip
FOREIGN PHRASES: ***Imperitia culpae adnumeratur.*** Unskillfulness is considered as negligence. ***Quod quis ex culpa sua damnum sentit non intelligitur damnum sentire.*** He who suffers a damage by his own fault is not considered to have suffered damage. ***Culpa tenet suos auctores.*** A fault binds its own authors. ***Magna negligentia culpa est; magna culpa dolus est.*** Gross negligence is fault; gross fault is equivalent to a fraud.

FAULT *(Responsibility),* ***noun*** accountability, answerability, blame, cause for blame, *culpa,* culpability, *delictum,* delinquency, dereliction, liability, malefaction, misbehavior, misconduct, misdeed, misfeasance, negligence, *peccatum,* transgression
ASSOCIATED CONCEPTS: comparative fault, contributory fault, contributory negligence, gross fault, with all faults, without fault
FOREIGN PHRASES: ***Culpa est immiscere se rel ad se non pertinenti.*** A person is at fault who intermeddles in matters not concerning him. ***Ejus nulla culpa est, cui parere necesse sit.***

No guilt attaches to a person who is compelled to obey. ***In pari delicto potior est conditio possidentis, defendentis.*** Where the parties are equally guilty of wrongdoing, the defendant holds the stronger position.

FAULT *(Weakness),* ***noun*** debility, defect, deficiency, delicacy, devitalization, drawback, emasculation, failing, feebleness, flaw, foible, frailty, impairment, imperfection, impotence, impuissance, inadequacy, incapacity, infirmity, instability, insufficiency, lack of strength, loss of strength, powerlessness, shortcoming, vitiation, vulnerable point, weak point

FAULT, ***verb*** *accusare,* accuse, admonish, animadvert, attack, berate, blame, bring into discredit, cast a slur upon, cast blame upon, castigate, censure, charge, chastise, chide, condemn, criticize, *culpare,* declaim against, decry, denigrate, denounce, deprecate, depreciate, disapprove, discommend, discountenance, disparage, dispraise, dress down, hold to blame, impeach, impugn, impute, remonstrate, reprehend, reprimand, reprove, scold, take to task, upbraid

FAULTLESS *(Infallible),* ***adjective*** above suspicion, absolute, accurate, best, chaste, correct, finished, flawless, ideal, immaculate, impeccable, incorruptible, indefectible, intact, irreproachable, letter-perfect, literal, irreprehensible, perfect, precise, pure, sinless, stainless, unadulterated, unblemished, uncontaminated, unimpeachable, untainted, virtuous, whole, without reproach

FAULTLESS *(Not guilty),* ***adjective*** blameless, free from guilt, free from moral wrong, guiltless, inculpable, innocent, lawful, legitimate, pardonable, sinless, unblamable, unoffending, upright, virtuous, without harm, without offense

FAULTY, ***adjective*** aberrant, amiss, awry, below par, blemished, damaged, defective, deficient, distorted, errant, erroneous, fallacious, false, flawed, found wanting, full of faults, impaired, imperfect, imprecise, improper, inaccurate, inadequate, incorrect, inferior, injured, invalid, lacking, less than perfect, malformed, *mendosus,* mistaken, not ideal, out of order, solecistic, solecistical, unfit, unprecise, unsatisfactory, unsound, *vitiosus,* wanting, warped, wrong

FAVOR *(Act of kindness),* ***noun*** accommodation, act of generosity, act of grace, benefaction, *beneficium,* benefit, benevolence, benignity, boon, bounty, charity, courtesy, friendly turn, good deed, good service, good turn, grace, indulgence, kind act, philanthropy

FAVOR *(Partiality),* ***noun*** approval, attachment, attraction, bent, bias, disposition, favoritism, fondness, inclination, kind regard, leaning, liking, partisanship, penchant, predilection, preference, preferential treatment, prejudice, proclivity, proneness, propensity
ASSOCIATED CONCEPTS: challenge to the favor, favored legislation, favored treatment

FAVOR *(Sanction),* ***noun*** abetment, advancement, advocacy, aegis, aid, approbation, approval, assistance, auspices, backing, benefaction, championship, cooperation, countenance, encouragement, endorsement, espousal, fosterage, furtherance, good opinion, help, leave, patronage, permission, sponsorship, subscription, support

FAVOR, ***verb*** advance, advocate, afford advantages, aid, approve, assist, back, be biased, be favorable to, be indulgent toward, be partial to, be prejudiced, befriend, benefit, bolster, boost, champion, countenance, deal with gently, ease, encourage, endorse, facilitate, fancy, *favere,* further, grant favors to, gratify, help, make easier, prefer, promote, regard with favor, regard with kindness, sanction, show consideration for, show favor to, show unfair bias, *studere,* succor, *suffragari,* support, treat differently, treat with partiality
ASSOCIATED CONCEPTS: favored beneficiary

FAVORABLE *(Advantageous),* ***adjective*** advisable, appropriate, auspicious, becoming, befitting, beneficial, *commodus,* conducive, convenient, desirable, encouraging, expedient, felicitous, fit, fitting, fortunate, full of promise, good, helpful, opportune, politic, profitable, promising, propitious, *prosperus,* providential, salutary, seasonable, suitable, timely, useful, wise
ASSOCIATED CONCEPTS: favorable decision

FAVORABLE *(Expressing approval),* ***adjective*** acclamatory, acquiescent, admiring, agreeable, approbative, approving, assenting, benign, commending, compliant, cooperative, encomiastic, encouraging, eulogistic, eulogistical, favorably prejudiced, favoring, generous, gracious, helpful, kind, laudatory, obliging, panegyrical, praising, reassuring, recommendatory, responsive, uncritical, willing

FAVORABLE DECISION, ***noun*** advisable outcome, an outcome which followed precedence, appropriate determination, auspicious determination, becoming outcome, befitting outcome, beneficial outcome, correct decree, desirable outcome, fair result, fit determination, fitting outcome, fortunate result, good result, impartial determination, judicious determination, just resolution, just result, just verdict, opportune determination, propitious result, providential result, reasonable outcome, right choice, salutary solution, Solomon-like determination, suitable result, the correct decision, the right decision, the right pronouncement, victory, win, wise resolution
FOREIGN PHRASES: ***Favorabilia in lege sunt fiscus, dos, vita, libertas.*** Things favorable considered within the law are the treasury, dower, life, and liberty.

FAVORABLE POSITION, ***noun*** advantage, edge, favorable opportunity, handicap, head start, high road, inside track, point of vantage, strategic advantage, superior situation, upper hand, winning position
FOREIGN PHRASES: ***Favorabilia in lege sunt, fiscus, dos, vita, libertas.*** Things which are favorably considered in law are the treasury, dower, life, and liberty. ***Favorabiliores rei, potius quam actores, habentur.*** The condition of the defendant shall be favored, rather than that of the plaintiff.

FAVORITE, ***adjective*** admired, adored, appreciated, beloved, best, cherished, choice, chosen, dear, desirable, elect, esteemed, fashionable, favored, handpicked, important, legendary, loved, notable, outstanding, pet, precious, preferable, preferred, prized, prominent, relished, remarkable, revered, select, selected, significant, special, treasured

FAVORITISM, ***noun*** attachment, bias, discrimination, fondness, inequality, inequity, leaning, one-sidedness, partialism, partiality, partisanship, penchant, preference, prejudice, proclivity, proneness, slant

FEALTY, ***noun*** allegiance, compliance, constancy, deference, devotion, duteousness, duty, faith, faithfulness, fidelity, homage, humble service, loyalty, obedience, respect, reverence, servility, steadfastness, support, veneration

FEAR, *noun* affright, alarm, anxiety, apprehension, apprehension of danger, apprehension of harm, apprehension of injury, apprehension of punishment, apprehensiveness, awe, concern, consternation, cowardice, cowardliness, cravenness, diffidence, dismay, disquietude, dread, faint-heartedness, fearfulness, foreboding, fright, horror, intimidation, *metus,* misgiving, panic, *pavor,* phobia, presentiment, pusillanimity, qualm, scare, state of anxiety, terror, timidity, *timor,* timorousness, trepidation, uneasiness, want of confidence
ASSOCIATED CONCEPTS: duress, mental anguish
FOREIGN PHRASES: ***Nihil consensui tam contrarium est quam vis atque metus.*** Nothing is so opposed to consent as force and fear. ***Vani timoris justa excusatio non est.*** A frivolous fear is not a lawful excuse. ***Vani timores sunt aestimandi, qui non cadunt in constantem virum.*** Those fears are to be regarded as groundless which do not affect an ordinary, steady man.

FEAR, *verb* anticipate danger, anticipate injury, apprehend, apprehend danger, apprehend harm, apprehend punishment, be a coward, be afraid, be alarmed, be anxious, be apprehensive, be concerned, be cowardly, be daunted, be fearful, be frightened, be horrified, be in awe, be intimidated, be nervous, be overawed, be petrified, be scared, be startled, be terrified, be timid, cower, dare not, dread, feel terror, fret, have qualms, live in terror, lose courage, *metuere,* stand aghast, stand in awe, take alarm, take fright, *timere, vereri,* worry

FEARFULNESS, *noun* affright, agitation, alarm, anxiousness, apprehension, consternation, distrust, faint-heartedness, fear, fright, intimidation, misgiving, nervousness, pusillanimousness, shyness, stress, suspicion, superstition, terror, timidity, timorousness, tremulousness, trepidation, unease

FEARLESS, *adjective* adventurous, audacious, bold, brave, confident, courageous, daring, dauntless, gallant, heroic, indomitable, intrepid, resolute, self-reliant, Spartan, spirited, stout-hearted, unabashed, unafraid, unawed, undaunted, unfearing, unflinching, unfrightened, unscared, unshakable, unterrified, valiant

FEASIBLE, *adjective* acceptable, achievable, appropriate, attainable, available, believable, comprehensible, conceivable, contingent, credible, doable, imaginable, likely, maintainable, plausible, possible, practicable, probably, realizable, reasonable, sensible, supportable, sustainable, thinkable, usable, viable, workable

FEASIBILITY, *noun* achievability, advantageousness, attainability, expedience, expediency, feasibleness, likelihood, opportuneness, performability, possibility, potentiality, practicability, practicableness, practicality, profitableness, reasonableness, usefulness, utility, viability, workability, workableness
ASSOCIATED CONCEPTS: feasibility study

FEATURE *(Appearance),* ***noun*** aspect, countenance, external appearance, form, lineament, *lineamentum,* lines, look, outward appearance, physiognomy, shape, visage

FEATURE *(Characteristic),* ***noun*** aspect, attribute, component, constituent, detail, distinction, distinctive trait, element, factor, idiosyncrasy, individuality, ingredient, mark, notability, outstanding property, part, particular, peculiarity, point, *proprietas,* quality, salient point, salient quality, singularity, trait

FEATURE *(Special attraction),* ***noun*** featured attraction, highlight, lead item, main attraction, main item, outstanding item, principal item, special attraction, specialty, star

FECKLESS, *adjective* abortive, aimless, careless, counterproductive, feeble, foolhardy, negligent, fruitless, futile, good-for-nothing, ineffective, ineffectual, inefficacious, inefficient, inexpedient, irresponsible, meaningless, nonproductive, pointless, profitless, reckless, sustainable, unavailing, unmindful, unproductive, unsuccessful, usable, useless, viable, weak, workable, worthless,

FEDERAL, *adjective* allied, associated, banded, central, combined, confederate, federate, federative, *foederatus, foedere sociatus,* governmental, joined in a union, joint, leagued, merged, national, united
ASSOCIATED CONCEPTS: federal aid, federal common law, federal Constitution, federal courts, federal government, federal jurisdiction, federal law, federal offense, federal question, federal regulation, federal rights

FEDERALIZE *(Associate),* ***verb*** act in concert, affiliate, ally, amalgamate, associate, band in a federation, band together, centralize, collaborate, combine, confederate, consociate, consolidate, cooperate, federate, form a cartel, form a union, go into partnership, incorporate, join, join forces, league, make a common cause with, merge, organize, participate, pool, syncretize, team up, unify, unionize, unite, unite in a league, work as a team, work together

FEDERALIZE *(Place under federal control),* ***verb*** assume authority, exercise federal authority over, exert authority, exert federal control, place under federal administration, place under federal rule, seize from private control, seize from state control, seize power, take command, take control

FEDERATE, *verb* act in concert, affiliate, ally, amalgamate, assemble, associate, band, collaborate, combine, concert, confederate, conjoin, consociate, join, join forces, league, merge, organize, participate, pool one's interests, unify, unionize, unite, unite by compact, unite in a federation, unite in a league

FEDERATION, *noun* affiliation, alliance, amalgamation, association, centralization, coalition, combination, combine, concert, confederacy, confederation, cooperation, federal union, integration, league, merger, organized body, pool, syndicate, unification, union
ASSOCIATED CONCEPTS: labor federation, unincorporated association

FEE *(Charge),* ***noun*** charge for services, compensation, compensation for labor, compensation for professional service, consideration, cost, disbursement, dues, emolument, exactment, expenditure, expense, fare, fixed charge, *merces,* payment, price, recompense, remuneration, reward, toll, wage
ASSOCIATED CONCEPTS: attorney's fee, counsel fees, reasonable fee, splitting a fee

FEE *(Estate),* ***noun*** absolute inheritance, absolute interest in realty, corporal hereditament, feod, feud, fief, freehold, hereditament, holding, interest, land, landed estate, landed property, lands, legal estate, property, real estate, real property, realty, right of possession, title, unconditional inheritance, unlimited inheritance, unrestricted inheritance, vested interest in land

ASSOCIATED CONCEPTS: absolute fee, base fee, conditional fee, contingent fee, defeasible estate, determinable fee, fee simple, fee tail, limited fee, qualified fee
FOREIGN PHRASES: ***Feodum est quod quis tenet ex quacunque causa sive sit tenementum sive redditus.*** A fee is that which any one holds from whatever cause, whether it be tenement or rent.

FEE FOR SERVICES, ***noun*** direct-bill the patient, direct payment, direct payment to a doctor for care provided, entire payment, full payment, independent rates, nondiscounted rate, payment by a patient to a doctor for medical services, payment for medical services to a practitioner, payment in full for services provided, payment of the entire bill, payment without accepting any insurance, payment without insurance, payment without regard to health insurance payments
ASSOCIATED CONCEPTS: health care, HMOs, PPOs

FEE SIMPLE, ***noun*** absolute interest in realty, estate in fee simple, estate in land, fee simple absolute, holding, legal estate, ownership in property, ownership in real estate, ownership in real property, ownership in realty, ownership interest, real estate ownership, right in real property, title to property, title to real property, unlimited right to property ownership, unrestricted right to property ownership, vested interest in land
ASSOCIATED CONCEPTS: allodial title, concurrent estate, defeasible estate, fee simple determinable, fee tail, future estate, leasehold estate, life estate

FEEBLE, ***adjective*** asthenic, breakable, broken-down, damaged, debilitated, delicate, disabled, drained, effete, enfeebled, exhausted, faint, feckless, flagging, flimsy, fragile, frail, helpless, impaired, impotent, incapable, incapacitated, ineffective, infirm, injured, invalid, lame, languid, powerless, sapped, slight, soft, softened, susceptible, tender, tired, vulnerable, weakened, weary, worn-out

FEEDBACK, ***noun*** acknowledgment, alternative view, answer, clarification, comments, criticism, elucidation, explanation, illumination, input, interpretation, positive input, reaction, reply, response, sense, sentiment, translation
ASSOCIATED CONCEPTS: negative feedback, polling, positive feedback

FEEL, ***verb*** appreciate, be informed of, believe, comprehend, conceive, conclude, deduce, glean, grasp, internalize, know, labor under, learn, note, observe, perceive, sense, share, sustain, sympathize, understand
ASSOCIATED CONCEPTS: feel positive about the outcome of a case, feel the defendant is guilty or innocent

FEELING *(Compassion),* ***noun*** aesthetic sense, affect, affection, appreciation, ardor, capacity, chord vibration, commiseration, delicacy, discernment, discrimination, echo, emotion, empathy, faculty, fellow feeling, fervor, heart, identification, intuition, judgment, keenness, passion, pathos, pity, refinement, response, sensibility, sentiment, sentimentality, sharpness, soul, spirit, susceptivity, sympathy, taste, tenderheartedness, tenderness, vibe, warmth

FEELING *(Consciousness),* ***noun*** activity, awareness, consideration, contractibility, discrimination, enjoyment, excitability, excitation, excitement, feel, feeling in one's bones, flash, foreboding, forefeeling, funny feeling, galvanism, gut feeling, hunch, impressibility, impression, innervation, intimation, intuition, intuitive impression, motility, motor response, perception, perceptiveness, perceptivity, preapprehension, premonition, presentiment, reaction, receptivity, reflex, responsiveness, sensation, sense, sensibility, sensitiveness, sensitivity, sensory response, sensuality, sentience, shrinking, susceptibility, suspicion, synesthesia, tact, tactfulness, titillation, vague feeling, voluptuousness

FEELING *(Premonition),* ***noun*** attitude, conception, emotions, estimation, feeling sensibilities, foreboding, gut reaction, hunch, idea, inkling, notion, opinion, outlook, passions, point of view, position, posture, sentiment, stance, susceptibilities, sympathies, theory, thought, viewpoint, way of thinking

FEELING *(Suspicion),* ***noun*** assumption, belief, common belief, concept, conclusion, conjecture, consideration, estimation, hunch, idea, impression, inkling, intuition, judgment, notion, observation, opinion, premonition, presumption, prevailing belief, prevailing sentiment, reaction, response, sensation, sense, sentiment, stance, supposition, theory, thinking, thought, vague feeling, view, viewpoint

FEELING *(View),* ***noun*** air, atmosphere, attitude, belief, character, characteristic, conception, emotions, estimation, feeling sensibilities, idea, mood, notion, opinion, outlook, passions, point of view, position, posture, sentiment, stance, susceptibilities, sympathies, theory, thought, viewpoint, way of thinking
ASSOCIATED CONCEPTS: feeling about the outcome of a case

FEIGN, ***verb*** affect, beguile, belie, cheat, concoct, counterfeit, create a false appearance, deceive, delude, disguise, dissemble, dissimulate, distort the truth, fabricate, falsify, *fingere,* imagine, imitate deceptively, impersonate, lack candor, lie about, make a false show of, make believe, make up, mislead, misreport, misrepresent, misstate, palter, personate, pretend, prevaricate, represent fictitiously, sham, *simulare,* simulate, speak falsely
ASSOCIATED CONCEPTS: feigned accomplice, feigned disability, feigned dispute, feigned issue

FEIGNED, ***adjective*** apocryphal, artificial, assumed, bogus, colorable, counterfeit, deceptive, delusive, disguised, dishonest, disingenuous, evasive, fabricated, factitious, faked, false, fictitious, forged, fraudulent, hypocritical, illusory, imaginary, insincere, lying, make-believe, mendacious, mock, mythical, pretended, pseudo, sham, simulated, spurious, supposititious, trumped up, unauthentic, untrue, ungenuine
ASSOCIATED CONCEPTS: feigned accomplice, feigned action, feigned issue

FEINT, ***noun*** ambush, artifice, camouflage, chicanery, counterfeit, deception, device, disguise, dodge, dupery, duplicity, fakery, false appearance, false pretense, gimmick, illusion, legerdemain, maneuver, mask, masquerade, pass, ploy, prestidigitation, pretext, ruse, sham, sleight, stratagem, subterfuge, swindling, trap, trick, trickery, wile

FELICITOUS, ***adjective*** accordant, adapted, agreeing, applicable, apposite, appropriate, apropos, apt, becoming, befitting, concinnous, concordant, conformable, congruous, consonant, desirable, effective, excellent, fit, fitting, fortunate, germane, happy, harmonious, ideal, in place, inspired, joyful, joyous, meet, opportune, perfect, pertinent, relevant, rightful, seemly, successful, suitable, suiting, tasteful, timely, to the point, to the purpose, *venustus,* well-chosen, well-expressed, well-timed

FELLOW *(Cohort)*, ***noun*** adjunct, attendant, colleague, companion, comrade, confederate, consort, contributor, copartner, correlative, individual, mate, member, participant, partner, peer, person

FELLOW *(Complement)*, ***noun*** associate, coequal, counterpart, equal, equipollent, like, match, obverse, parallel, reciprocal, similitude

FELLOW SERVANT, ***noun*** associate worker, employee, fellow employee, participatory employee, worker
ASSOCIATED CONCEPTS: common service, concurrent negligence, delegation of duty, invitees, master and fellow servant, superintending, superior servant, vice principal, workers' compensation

FELON, ***noun*** convict, criminal, culprit, delinquent, evildoer, guilty person, lawbreaker, malefactor, *nefarius,* offender, outlaw, recidivist, recreant, reprobate, *sceleratus, scelestus,* transgressor, wrongdoer
ASSOCIATED CONCEPTS: convicted felon
FOREIGN PHRASES: ***Nullus dicitur felo principalis nisi actor, aut qui praesens est, abettans aut auxilians ad feloniam faciendam.*** No one is called a principal felon except the party actually committing the felony, or the person who is present, aiding and abetting in its commission.

FELONIOUS, ***adjective*** against the admonition of law, against the law, against the rules, base, condemnable, contrary to law, criminal, criminous, culpable, dishonest, dissolute, done with intent to commit crime, evildoing, extralegal, fraudulent, illegal, illegitimate, immoral, in violation of law, *inlicitus,* lawbreaking, lawless, malfeasant, malicious, nefarious, *non legitimus,* nonlegal, of the quality of a felon, offending, outlawed, outside the law, perfidious, transgressing, unallowed, unauthorized, unlawful, unlicensed, unpardonable, unwarrantable, *vetitus,* villainous, wicked, wrong, wrongful
ASSOCIATED CONCEPTS: felonious act, felonious arson, felonious assault, felonious homicide, felonious intent, felonious purpose, feloniously taking

FELONY, ***noun*** capital crime, crime graver than a misdemeanor, criminal activity, criminal offense, gross offense, heinous crime, heinous misconduct, illegality, indictable offense, misdeed punishable by imprisonment, offense, offense punishable by imprisonment, transgression, violation of law, wrongdoing
ASSOCIATED CONCEPTS: assault with intent to commit felony, capital felony, common law felony, compounding a felony, felonious intent, felony conviction, felony murder, substantive felony
FOREIGN PHRASES: ***Felonia, ex vi termini significat quodlibet capitale crimen felleo animo perpetratum.*** Felony by force of the term, signifies any capital crime perpetrated with a criminal mind. ***Felonia implicatur in qualibet proditione.*** Felony is implied in every treason.

FEMALE, ***noun*** female being, female gender, female sex, gender, girl, her, herself, lady, Miss, Mrs., Ms., she, woman
ASSOCIATED CONCEPTS: women's rights
FOREIGN PHRASES: ***Feme, Femme.*** A woman. ***Feme covert.*** A married woman. ***Feme sole.*** A single woman.

FENCE, ***noun*** buyer of stolen goods, buyer of stolen property, disposer of stolen goods, purchaser of stolen goods, purchaser of stolen property, receiver, receiver of stolen goods, receiver of stolen property, recipient of stolen goods, recipient of stolen property, vendor of stolen goods, vendor of stolen property
ASSOCIATED CONCEPTS: burglary, robbery, theft

FEOFFEE, ***noun*** acceptor, assignee, devisee, donee, donee of a corporeal hereditament, grantee, legatee, one to whom a fee is conveyed, one to whom seisin passes, one to whom title is passed, one who is enfeoffed, receiver, recipient of a fee, transferee

FEOFFMENT, ***noun*** assignation of title, cession of a fee, conferral of a fee, conferment of title, conveyance of realty, conveyancing, conveying title, delivery of title, gift of a freehold interest, investiture of title, livery of seisin, passing of seisin, transfer of property, transmission of title

FEOFFOR, ***noun*** assignor, bequeather, bestower, devisor, donor, giver, grantor, one who enfeoffs another, one who gives a corporeal hereditament, one who transfers property by deed, one who transfers real property to another, person making a feoffment, person who conveys a fee, transferor

FERMENT, ***verb*** agitate, arouse, create a disturbance, create turbulence, excite, fervid, flame, foment, impassion, incense, incite, inflame, instigate, kindle, pique, stir, stir up

FEROCIOUS, ***adjective*** agitated, antagonistic, belligerent, brutal, cataclysmic, combative, combustible, contentious, cruel, destructive, dreadful, explosive, fearsome, frightening, frightful, furious, hard, hellacious, mad, malicious, mean, pugnacious, quarrelsome, rabid, rough, ruinous, savage, tempestuous, terrible, truculent, tumultuous, turbulent, vehement, vicious, violent, volcanic

FEROCITY, ***noun*** agitation, commitment, excitement, extreme emotion, ferociousness, fierceness, raging, ranting, raving, ravished, roaring, viciousness, violence, zealousness

FERRET, ***verb*** bring to light, dig out, discover, disinter, elicit, find, fish out, hunt, look for, *rimari,* root out, search, seek, trace, track down, unearth
ASSOCIATED CONCEPTS: ferret out a crime

FERRET OUT, ***verb*** announce, bare, bring about, bring out, debunk, disclose, discover, divulge, enquire about, expose, find, investigate into, locate, reveal, uncloak, unclothe, uncover, unmask, unveil
ASSOCIATED CONCEPTS: ferret out crime

FERTILE, ***adjective*** arable, bearing offspring freely, creative, fecund, *fecundus,* feracious, *ferax, fertilis,* flowering, fructiferous, fructuous, fruitful, imaginative, ingenious, inventive, lush, luxuriant, original, originative, parturient, philoprogenitive, procreant, procreative, productive, profitable, progenerative, prolific, rank, rich, yielding
ASSOCIATED CONCEPTS: fertile octogenarian rule, presumption of fertility

FERVENT, ***adjective*** active, all out, animated, *ardens,* ardent, avid, committed, dedicated, devoted, devout, eager, earnest, enthusiastic, excited, feeling, *fervens,* fervid, *fervidus,* feverish, fierce, fiery, hearty, hectic, impassioned, in earnest, intense, keen, passionate, perfervid, resolute, serious, sincere, spirited, vehement, zealous, zestful
ASSOCIATED CONCEPTS: testator's fervent desire

FERVID, *adjective* agitate, ardent, create a disturbance, create a turbulence, devoted, devout, earnest, earnestly, excite, faithful, fervent, impassioned, instigate, intense, intent, passionate, perfervid, serious, sincere, spirited, stir, stirred-up, zealous

FERVOR, *noun* abandon, animation, ardency, ardor, eagerness, earnestness, emotion, enthusiasm, excitement, fanaticism, fervency, fervor, fire, gusto, heat, histrionics, hot-bloodedness, intensity, keenness, mania, obsession, oomph, passion, torridity, torridness, vehemence, warmth, zeal, zest

FETTER, *noun* bond, bridle, catena, chain, check, *compes,* confinement, constraint, control, curb, detention, deterrence, deterrent, disadvantage, encumbrance, gyve, hamper, handicap, hindrance, impediment, imprisonment, incarceration, inhibition, interference, iron, limitation, lock, manacle, means of restraint, obstacle, obstruction, prevention, prohibition, rein, repression, restraint, restriction, shackle, strap, suppression, tie, trammel, *vinculum,* yoke

FETTER, *verb* bind, *catenas,* chain, check, confine, curb, enchain, enclose, entrammel, gyve, hamper, handcuff, handicap, hinder, immobilize, impede, *impedire,* impose restraint, inhibit motion, inhibit movement, keep in check, lock up, make captive, make prisoner, manacle, paralyze, prohibit, put in irons, put under restraint, restrain, restrain motion, restrain movement, restrict, secure, secure with chains, shackle, shut in, suppress, tie, tie down, trammel, *vincula*

FETUS, *noun* baby, embryo, genesis, immature stage, life, origination, seed, source, starting point, unborn young

FEUD, *noun* alienation, altercation, animosity, animus, antagonism, bitterness, breach, clash, conflict, contention, controversy, difference, disaccord, disagreement, discord, dispute, dissension, enmity, estrangement, faction, grudge, hereditary enmity, hostility, ill will, incompatability, inimicality, *inimicitia,* intolerance, inveterate hatred, inveterate strife, malevolence, mutual aversion, odds, open breach, open quarrel, opposition, private war, quarrel, rancor, rupture, *simultas,* split, strain, strife, tension, variance, vendetta

FEVER *(Excitement),* ***noun*** agitation, ardor, arousing, delirium, desire, disquiet, eagerness, enthusiasm, excitation, exhilaration, fervency, fever pitch, feverish excitement, feverishness, fire, fomentation, frenzy, galvanization, heat, intensity, panic, passion, provocation, stimulation, stirring up, tizzy, turmoil, upset, working up, zeal, zealousness, zest
ASSOCIATED CONCEPTS: proceedings reaching a fever pitch

FEVER *(Illness),* ***noun*** affliction, ailment, burning-up, elevated temperature, feverishness, has a disorder, has a malady, has an affliction, has an ailment, ill health, illness, in poor health, infirmity, not healthy, sickness, temperature
ASSOCIATED CONCEPTS: fee services, health care, HMO

FEVER PITCH, *noun* boil, boiling point, crescendo, excitement, extreme enthusiasm, fermentation, fervency, fever of excitement, feverishness, fire, flap, flurry, fluster, frenzy, fuming, furor, fuss, heat, intensity, maelstrom, nervousness, passion, rage, restlessness, roil, turbulence, turmoil, unrest, upset, zeal, zealousness

FEW, *adjective* a few, a handful of, a small number of, a sprinkling of, excess of two, few and far between, hardly any, inconsequential, inconsiderable, infrequent, insignificant, least, less, little, littlest, low, lowest, meager, minimal, minimum, more than two, negligible, not many, not too many, occasional, of small number, petty, picayune, precious few, rare, scant, scarce, scarcely any, seldom, several, slightest, small, smallest, some, sparse, straggling, superficial, too few, trifling, unimportant

FEW AND FAR BETWEEN, *adjective* an inconsiderable amount, few, hard to come by, hardly any, infrequent, less, meager, negligible, not many, not much, not too many, one-shot, one-time, piddling, scant, scanty, scarce, scarcely any, seldom, seldom met with, seldom seen, slim, slow, small number of, some, sparse, sporadic, spotty, unique, unprecedented, unusual

FIAT, *noun* authoritative order, authorization, command, decree, decree having the force of law, dictate, direction, directive, edict, enactment, hest, *imperium,* imposition, injunction, instruction, *iussum,* judgment, mandamus, *mandatum,* order, prescript, prescription, pronouncement, regulation, rescript, rule, sanction, ukase, warrant

FICTION, *noun* canard, *commentum,* concoction, fable, fabrication, *fabula,* false statement, falsehood, falsification, fancy, fantasy, feigned story, figment, invention, legend, lie, myth, perjury, prevarication, product of imagination, *res ficta,* untruth, untruthful report
FOREIGN PHRASES: ***Fictio legis inique operatur alieni damnum vel injuriam.*** Fiction of law is wrongful if it works loss or harm to anyone. ***Fictio juris non est ubi veritas.*** A fiction of law will not exist where the fact appears. ***Les fictions naissent de la loi, et non la loi des fictions.*** Fictions arise from the law, and not law from fictions. ***Fictio cedit veritati. Fictio juris non est ubi veritas.*** Fiction yields to truth. Where truth is, fiction of law does not exist.

FICTITIOUS, *adjective* apocryphal, arbitrarily invented, artificial, chimerical, *commenticius,* concocted, counterfeit, deceiving, delusive, erroneous, fabled, fabricated, fake, faked, false, fancied, fanciful, feigned, fictional, fictive, *fictus,* figmental, forged, founded on fiction, illusive, illusory, imaginary, imagined, invented, legendary, make-believe, mendacious, misleading, misrepresentative, mythic, mythical, mythological, nonexistent, notional, phony, pretended, sham, spurious, trumped-up, unfounded, unhistorical, unreal, untrue
ASSOCIATED CONCEPTS: fictitious address, fictitious claims, fictitious corporation, fictitious debts, fictitious name, fictitious parties, fictitious payee, fictitious person, fictitious statements

FIDELITY, *noun* allegiance, conscientiousness, constancy, *constantia,* devotedness, devotion, dutiful adherence, dutifulness, faith, faithfulness, fealty, *fidelitas, fides,* good faith, homage, loyalty, stanchness, steadfastness, trueness, trustiness, trustworthiness
ASSOCIATED CONCEPTS: fidelity bond, fidelity guaranty, fidelity insurance

FIDUCIARY, *adjective* commanding belief, commanding confidence, confidential, deserving belief, fiducial, founded in confidence, reliable, sound, trusted, trustworthy, worthy of belief, worthy of credence
ASSOCIATED CONCEPTS: fiduciary bequest, fiduciary bond, fiduciary capacity, fiduciary relation

FIDUCIARY, *noun* agent, caretaker, custodian, executor, guardian, one who handles property for another, one who

transacts business for another, person entrusted with property of another, trustee
ASSOCIATED CONCEPTS: escrow, trust

FIELD *(Land)*, ***noun*** area, clearing, flatland, grass area, ground, lot, open area, parcel, tract, plain, property, space

FIELD *(Place for sports)*, ***noun*** athletic field, ball field, center, game field, grounds, park, playing field, sports field, stadium

FIELD *(Specialty)*, ***noun*** appointment, area, art, assignment, bailiwick, billet, business, call, calling, craft, employment, engagement, enterprise, handcraft, handicraft, line, livelihood, living, métier, mission, office, place, position, post, profession, racket, specialty, trade, vocation

FIEND *(Addict)*, ***noun*** abuser, drug abuser, drug addict, drug user, narcotics addict, person hooked on something, user

FIEND *(Enthusiast)*, ***noun*** admirer, adorer, buff, crazed fan, devotee, disciple, fan, fanatic, idolizer, individual with a one-track mind, individual with a single minded dogma, infatuate, lover, worshiper, zealot

FIERCE *(Ferocious)*, ***adjective*** battling, blustering, blusterous, blustery, by force, clamorous, contentions, destructive, devastating, distracted, feral, fighting, frantic, frenzied, frightening, furious, gladiatorial, militant, possessed, rabid, raging, rampant, ranting, raving, ravished, rip-roaring, roaring, tempestuous, thunderous, torrential, truculent, turbulent, uncontrollable, uncontrolled, unrestrained, warlike, warring
ASSOCIATED CONCEPTS: fierce criticism, fierce debate, fierce fight

FIERCE *(Intense)*, ***adjective*** abandoned, acute, aggressive, amok, angry, animal, animated, ardent, avid, awful, barbarous, bellowing, berserk, beside oneself, bestial, bloodthirsty, bloody, blue in the face, bold, brutal, brutish, carried away, cruel, dangerous, deep, delirious, demoniacal, demonic, desperate, distracted, eager, earnest, ecstatic, enraged, enraptured, enthusiastic, fanatical, fearsome, feral, ferocious, fervent, fervid, fiery, frantic, frenzied, frightening, frothing, fulminating, furious, grim, haggard, hard, hardboiled, hearty, high-spirited, hog-wild, hostile, howling, hysterical, impassioned, impetuous, in a transport or ecstasy, in hysterics, insane, intoxicated, irate, keen, mad, madding, malevolent, malign, maniac, maniacal, menacing, merciless, monstrous, mouth, murderous, orgasmic, orgiastic, out of one's wits, passionate, possessed, primitive, rabid, raging, ramping, ranting, ravening, raving, ravished, roaring, rough, running mad, ruthless, sanguinary, savage, sense, spirited, storming, terrible, tigerish, tough, transported, truculent, unbridled, unchecked, uncivilized, uncontrollable, uncontrolled, uncurbed, unrestrained, untamed, venomous, vicious, violent, virulent, wild, wild-eyed, wild-looking, wrathful, zealous

FIERI FACIAS, ***noun*** authorization to seize, authorization to seize chattels, authorization to take, execution on property, judicial authorization to remove chattels, judicial authorization to remove goods, levy on goods to pay a judgment, means to pay a judgment, order to seize, permission to seize, remedy, writ of execution, writ to seize

FIFTH AMENDMENT *(Double jeopardy)*, ***noun*** protection against being tried twice for the same offense, protection against multiple punishment, protection against multiple punishment for the same offense

FIFTH AMENDMENT *(Self-incrimination)*, ***noun*** protection against exposing one's self to prosecution, protection against incriminating one's self, protection against testifying against one's self
Generally: due process protection
Specifically: right to remain silent
ASSOCIATED CONCEPTS: full immunity, Miranda Warnings, transactional immunity, use and derivative immunity, use immunity

FIGHT *(Argument)*, ***noun*** altercation, bickering, broil, *certamen,* clash, conflict, confrontation, contest, controversy, debate, difference, disagreement, discord, disputation, dispute, dissension, embroilment, estrangement, expression of contrary opinions, imbroglio, logomachy, oral contention, polemics, *pugna,* quarrel, row, schism, squabble, strife, variance, verbal contest, war of words, wrangle

FIGHT *(Battle)*, ***noun*** action, affray, appeal to arms, armed action, assault, attack, bloodshed, bout, brawl, clash of arms, combat, contest, encounter, engagement, exchange of blows, fracas, fray, hostile encounter, *pugilatio,* rencounter, resistance, scuffle, skirmish, struggle, tussle, war, warfare

FIGHT *(Battle)*, ***verb*** act in opposition, altercate, appeal to arms, assail, assault, assume the offensive, attack, bandy with, be violent, break the peace, campaign, carry on war, challenge, close with, combat, come to blows, commit hostilities, compete with, confront, contend, contest, declare war, dispute, duel, engage, exchange blows, exchange fisticuffs, face danger, go to war, grapple with, have words with, joust, make war, oppose, *proelium committere,* pummel, rebel, reluct, resist, resort to arms, revolt, scrimmage, scuffle, set to, skirmish, spar, squabble, stand up to, strike, struggle against, take on, take the offensive, take up arms, tourney, tussle, vie with, wage war, wrestle with

FIGHT *(Counteract)*, ***verb*** act in opposition to, be at cross-purposes, be contrary, be obstructive, confound, confute, contradict, counter, countermine, counterpose, counterwork, cross, debar, defy, disapprove, foil, frustrate, hinder, impede, inhibit, interfere, make a stand against, negate, object, obstruct, oppose, preclude, prevent, protest, rebuff, reject, repulse, resist, run against, run counter to, side against, spurn, stand against, stand up to, thwart, traverse, vote down, work against
ASSOCIATED CONCEPTS: fight passage

FIGMENT, ***noun*** canard, chimera, concoction, creation of the mind, deception, delusion, fabrication, falsehood, falsification, fancy, fantasy, feigned story, fiction, fiction of the mind, flight of fancy, hallucination, idle fancy, illusion, imagined thought, inaccuracy, invention, lie, mirage, myth, product of the imagination, reverie, romance, story, unreality, untruth

FIGURATIVE, ***adjective*** allegoric, allegorical, anagogic, anagogical, depictive, descriptive, emblematic, emblematical, evidential, exhibitive, expressive, figural, illustrating, illustrational, illustrative, imagistic, imitative, implicative, indicative, indicatory, metaphoric, metaphorical, pictographic, pictorial, portraying, representational, representative, representing, satirical, signifying, simulative, standing for, suggestive, symbolic, symbolical, symbolizing, symptomatic, typical, typifying, vivid

FIGURE *(Form)*, ***noun*** art form, configuration, conformation, design, device, diagram, drawing, figuration, formation, illustration, layout, model, picture, prototype, representation, representation in art, representative, shape, symbol

FIGURE *(Individual),* ***noun*** head, human being, leader, mortal, official, overseer, person, somebody, someone, supervisor

FIGURE *(Numeral),* ***noun*** aggregate, amount, Arabic numerals, charge, expenditure, expense, number, price, quotation, rate, Roman numerals, sales price, sum, total, value

FIGURE, ***verb*** ascertain, conclude, decide, determine, estimate, infer, opine, suppose, think

FIGURE OUT, ***verb*** answer, ascertain, break, clear up, comprehend, conclude, conjecture, crack, decide, decipher, decode, deduce, gather, infer, interpret, iron out, judge, rationalize, reason, resolve, solve, speculate, straighten out, understand, unravel, unscramble, untangle, untie, work out

FILE, ***noun*** archive, card index, catalog, classified index, docket, dossier, entry, folder, information, list, notebook, orderly arrangement of papers, record, record of the court, recorded information, register, registry, report, roll
ASSOCIATED CONCEPTS: duly filed, file a brief, file a complaint, file a lien, file a mortgage, file a reply, file a reply brief, file a summons, file papers, filed in open court, filing fee, filing of a claim, reporting act

FILE *(Arrange),* ***verb*** align, arrange methodically, array, assign places to, bring into order, catalog, categorize, class, classify, codify, collocate, coordinate, distribute, fix the order, grade, graduate, group, *limare,* line up, make orderly, marshal, organize, pigeonhole, place in order, position, put in array, put in order, range, rank, reduce to order, regulate, set in order, set to rights, sort, subdivide, systematize

FILE *(Place among official records),* ***verb*** book, calendar, chronicle, deliver an instrument, deposit among records of the court, docket, document, enroll, enter, inscribe, list, place an instrument in a place of deposit, place in official custody of the clerk, place on record, preserve permanently as a public record, put on record, receive an instrument officially, register, store in the archives
ASSOCIATED CONCEPTS: docket, filing fee, filing of a deed, filing of a suit, filing of claims, filing of papers, filing of pleadings, late filing, time to file

FILIATION, ***noun*** affiliation, assignment of paternity, blood relationship, cognation, determination of a child's paternity, family connection, fatherhood, fathership, kinship, lineage, parentage, paternity, relationship, ties of blood
ASSOCIATED CONCEPTS: filiation proceeding
FOREIGN PHRASES: ***Semper praesumitur pro legitimatione puerorum.*** The presumption always is in favor of the legitimacy of children. ***Filiatio non potest probari.*** Filiation cannot be proved. ***Pater est quem nuptiae demonstrant.*** He is the father whom the marriage points out.

FILIBUSTER, ***noun*** attempt to obstruct legislation, blockage, cunctation, delay, delay in legislation, dilatory obstruction, hindrance, impediment, interference, obstruction, obstruction to congressional action, prevention of congressional action, protraction, retardation, retardment, stalling, stoppage

FILL *(Pervade),* ***verb*** diffuse, extend throughout, imbue, infuse, leave no void, occupy, penetrate, perfuse, permeate, saturate, spread throughout

FILL *(Sell out),* ***verb*** bulged, fill to capacity, fill to overflowing, fill to the brim, fill up, jam in, overfill, pack in, stuff in, supply, swell with a crowd

FILL *(Supply),* ***verb*** appoint, choose, elect, furnish, lay in or by, name, outfit, provide, refill, renew, replenish, restock, stock, store
ASSOCIATED CONCEPTS: fill an order under the Uniform Commercial Code

FILTER, ***noun*** classification, means to rectify, means to refine, purification, purifier, refinery, screen, sieve, sifter, strainer

FILTER, ***verb*** clarify, clean, clear, distill, filtrate, find, leach, pass through, percolate, purify, rectify, refine, screen, strain
ASSOCIATED CONCEPTS: filter the evidence through the jury

FINAL, ***adjective*** closing, completing, concluding, conclusive, conclusory, crowning, decisive, definitive, determinative, end, ending, extreme, *extremus,* finishing, irrevocable, last, rearmost, supreme, terminal, terminating, terminational, terminative, ultimate, *ultimus,* unappealable, without appeal
ASSOCIATED CONCEPTS: final accounting, final adjudication, final and conclusive, final award, final conviction, final decision, final decree, final determination, final disposition, final finding, final hearing, final judgment, final offer, final order, final settlement, final submission

FINAL APPEAL, ***noun*** appeal of last resort, appeal to the ultimate power, appeal to U.S. Supreme Court or Court of Appeals, application for concluding appeal, conclusive appeal, decisive appeal, definitive appeal, determinative appeal, extreme appeal, finishing appeal, irrevocable decision, last appeal, last appellate stage, last decision, last hearing, last recourse, last reexamination, resort to the highest tribunal, review by a highest tribunal, review by highest authority, review by the highest court
ASSOCIATED CONCEPTS: Court of final appeal, final adjudification

FINALE, ***noun*** apex, capstone, climax, close, closing, conclusion, consummation, coup de grace, crescendo, crown, culmination, end, endgame, ending, epilogue, finish, grand finale, home stretch, inclusion, outcome, peak, pinnacle, summit, termination, ultimate outcome, upshot, wind-up, wrap-up, zenith

FINALITY, ***noun*** accomplishment, achievement, cessation, close, closure, completeness, completion, conclusion, consummation, definitiveness, denouement, determination, end, ending, entireness, entirety, execution, expiration, expiry, extremity, finish, fulfillment, fullness, halt, implementation, maturation, maturity, performance, stop, stoppage, term, terminal, termination, terminus, totality, wholeness

FINALITY OF JUDGMENT, ***noun*** final decision, final decree, final disposition, final judgment of the court, judgment disposing of case before the court
ASSOCIATED CONCEPTS: noninterlocutory decree, res judicata

FINALIZE, ***verb*** achieve, cap, clinch, close, complete, conclude, consummate, crown, decide, draw to a close, effect, end, finish, get done, get it over with, perfect, perfect in detail, put the finishing touches on, seal, settle, terminate, wind up

FINALLY *(Conclusively),* ***adverb*** absolutely, assuredly, beyond the shadow of a doubt, certainly, convincingly, decisively, definitely, in the end, in the long run, irrevocably, permanently, ultimately, when all is said and done

FINALLY *(Ultimately),* ***adverb*** after a time, after all, at the end, at the final point, at the last moment, belatedly, eventually, in conclusion, in consequence, in the end, inevitably, lastly, necessarily, therefore, when all is said and done

FINANCE, ***noun*** accounts, *aerarium,* art of monetary relations, budget, business science, commercial theory, economics, exchange, expenditure, financial affairs, financial resources, *fiscus,* funds, income, investments, management of money, monetary theory, money, money dealings, money-making, money matters, *pecuniaria,* pecuniary management, public economy, public revenue, resources, revenue, science of monetary relations, science of wealth, theory of business, theory of fiscal relations, wealth, working capital

FINANCE, ***verb*** advance, aid, assist, back, capitalize, float, fund, invest, lend, loan, patronize, pay for, provide capital, provide funds, provide money, provide subvention, put up the money, set up in business, sponsor, subsidize, supply money, support, sustain

FINANCIAL, ***adjective*** *ad aerarium pertinens,* budgetary, bursal, fiscal, monetary, nummary, pecuniary, sumptuary
ASSOCIATED CONCEPTS: financial institution, financial loss, financial responsibility, financial worth

FIND *(Adjudge),* ***verb*** adjudicate, ascertain, award, conclude, confirm, decide, declare a verdict, decree, detect, determine, encounter, experience, hear of, hold, judge, learn, observe, perceive, pronounce, rule, sentence, settle, sit in judgment

FIND *(Determine),* ***verb*** adjudge, adjudicate, announce a conclusion, arrive at a conclusion, arrive at a verdict, ascertain, ascertain and declare, ascertain by judicial inquiry, calculate, come to a conclusion, compromise, conclude, decide, decide a question of fact, decide upon, declare a verdict, deduce, deliver judgment, determine a controversy, determine after judicial inquiry, determine an issue, draw a conclusion, establish as facts, give an opinion, give judgment, hold, judge, make a decision, pass an opinion, pass judgment, pronounce as an official act, resolve, rule, set a question at rest, sit in judgment
ASSOCIATED CONCEPTS: findings of fact

FIND *(Discover),* ***verb*** acquire information about, answer, apprehend, ascertain, attain by effort, bare, become acquainted with, become apprised of, become informed, bring into the open, catch a glimpse of, chance upon, *cognoscere,* come upon, create, decipher, decode, detect, discern, disclose, disentangle, disinter, divine, divulge, elicit, encounter, explore, expose, fathom, ferret out, figure out, gather knowledge, get to the bottom of, glimpse, happen upon, hit upon, identify, *invenire,* invent, ken, know, learn, light upon, locate, make certain, meet with, notice, observe, obtain by search, perceive, realize, recognize, reveal, run across, solve, strike, stumble on, trace, uncloak, unconceal, uncover, understand, unearth, unfold, unlock, unmask, unravel, unscramble, unscreen, unshroud, unveil, verify

FIND *(Locate),* ***verb*** achieve, attain, collect, descry, dig up, discover, disinter, espy, expose, furnish, gain, gather, procure, provide the wherewithal, recover, repossess, resolve, retrieve, spot, supply, uncover, unearth

FINDING, ***noun*** ascertainment, award, conclusion, decision, decree, determination, judgment, judicial conclusion, judicial outcome, judicial verdict, opinion, opinion of the court, order, outcome, precedent, pronouncement, report, resolution, resolution of the court, result, ruling, sentence, solution, verdict, verdict after judicial inquiry
ASSOCIATED CONCEPTS: administrative finding, erroneous finding, evidence sufficient to support a finding, evidentiary finding, finding of a referee, finding of fact, finding of guilt, general findings, implied findings, inconsistent findings, special finding, supplemental findings

FINDING OF GUILT, ***noun*** adjudication, award, censure, condemnation, conviction, conviction of guilt, criminal conviction, decision, decree, decrial, denunciation, determination, judgment, judgment of guilt, pronouncement, ruling, sentence, unfavorable verdict, verdict

FINE, ***noun*** amercement, compulsory payment, forfeit, forfeiture, legal liability, liability, mulct, *multa,* payment for misconduct, pecuniary penalty, pecuniary punishment, penalty, prescribed punishment, sconce
ASSOCIATED CONCEPTS: excessive fine, forfeitures, penalties
FOREIGN PHRASES: ***Quam rationabilis debet esse finis, non definitur, sed omnibus circumstantiis inspectis pendet ex justiciariorum discretione.*** What a reasonable fine ought to be is not defined, but is left to the discretion of the judges, all the circumstances being considered. ***Mulcta damnum famae non irrogat.*** A fine does not impose a loss of reputation.

FINE, ***verb*** amerce, exact a penalty, exact retribution, impose a forfeiture, impose a mulct, impose a penalty, impose payment for misconduct, impose pecuniary punishment, inflict a penalty upon, mulct, *multare,* penalize, punish, punish by pecuniary penalty, subject to a pecuniary penalty, tax

FINE PRINT, ***noun*** boilerplate, detailed clauses, detailed conditions, detailed contingencies, detailed grounds, express conditions, intricate notice of conditions, limitations, limiting conditions, precise conditions, prerequisites, provisions, provisos, requisites, small pica font, small print, specific warnings, specification, specified warnings, terms
ASSOCIATED CONCEPTS: contract

FINESSE, ***noun*** acuteness, adeptness, adroitness, artful management, artfulness, artifice, astuteness, canniness, cunning, deception, deftness, delicacy, elegance, grace, guile, maneuver, nicety, polish, prowess, refined discrimination, refinement, ruse, *savoir faire,* science, shrewdness, skill, slyness, stratagem, subterfuge, subtleness, tact, taste, trickery, wile, wiliness, worldly wisdom

FINESSE, ***adjective*** ability, acuteness, adeptness, adroitness, astuteness, brilliance, cageyness, canniness, capability, capacity, cleverness, competence, craftiness, cunningness, deftness, dexterousness, expertness, facility, faculty, foxiness, handiness, ingeniousness, ingenuity, judiciousness, know-how, marksmanship, mastership, mastery, proficiency, prowess, resourcefulness, savvy, sharpness, shrewdness, skill, skillfulness, technical mastery, technical skill, technique, virtuosity, workmanship

FINGERPRINTS, ***noun*** identification, identification records, impression, impression of fingers, imprint, marks, marks left by a person's finger, means of identification, prints

FINISH, *verb* accomplish, achieve, arrive at the end of, bring to a close, bring to an end, bring to completion, cap, carry out, carry through, cease, close, come to a close, come to an end, complete, conclude, *conficere, consummare,* consummate, discontinue, end, finalize, halt, perfect, put a stop to, put an end to, stop, *terminare,* terminate, wind up
FOREIGN PHRASES: ***Extincto subjecto, tollitur adjunctum.*** When the substance is extinguished, the incident ceases.

FINISHED *(Complete),* ***adjective*** absolute, choice, classic, complete, completed, concluded, conclusive, consummated, defunct, elegant, ended, entire, extinct, faultless, final, flawless, full, ideal, immaculate, impeccable, irredeemable, perfect, perfected, prime, primed, refined, shapely, skilled, sound, thoroughgoing, trained, whole

FINISHED *(Gone),* ***adjective*** consumed, decided, defunct, done with, elapsed, irrecoverable, lapsed, no more, obsolete, passé, passed, settled, through, used up

FIRE *(Burn),* ***verb*** conflagrate, deflagrate, heat, ignite, incandesce, inflame, kindle, light, scorch, singe, warm
ASSOCIATED CONCEPTS: Fire Act, Firefighter's Rule, Fireman's Rule, invitees

FIRE *(Discharge),* ***verb*** depose, dismiss, expel, lay off, remove, stimulate, terminate, torrefy

FIRE *(Stimulate),* ***verb*** animate, arouse, electrify, enliven, excite, foster, goad, incite, inspirit, quicken, rouse, spur, stir

FIRM, *adjective* anchored, balanced, confirmed, durable, established, fast, fastened, *firmus,* fixed, immobile, immotile, immovable, indissoluble, inflexible, irremovable, moored, motionless, rigid, rooted, secure, secured, securely fixed, set, settled, solid, *solidus,* sound, *stabilis,* stable, stanch, stationary, steadfast, steady, stout, strong, sturdy, substantial, taut, unalterable, unbending, unmovable, unmoving, unyielding
ASSOCIATED CONCEPTS: firm offer

FIRM, *noun* association, bureau, business, business establishment, business house, commercial enterprise, commercial house, company, concern, enterprise, establishment, holding company, house, industry, institution, joint concern, office, organization, partnership
ASSOCIATED CONCEPTS: corporation, law firm, professional corporation

FIRMNESS, *noun* adherence, assurance, backbone, callosity, certainty, compactness, confidence, constancy, courage, determination, durability, endurance, fixedness, force, fortitude, hardness, high morale, immutability, inexorability, inflexibility, intransigence, intrepidity, obdurateness, obstinacy, pertinacity, prowess, purpose, reliability, renitence, resoluteness, resolution, resolve, rigidity, rigor, secureness, security, solidity, soundness, spirit, stability, stanchness, staunchness, steadfastness, steadiness, stiffness, stoutness of heart, strength, substantiality, surety, temper, tenacity, toughness, unyieldingness
FOREIGN PHRASES: ***Firmior et potentior, est operatio, legis quam dispositio hominis.*** The operation of law is firmer and more powerful than the will of man.

FIRST *(Earlier),* ***adjective*** aboriginal, anterior, earlier, earliest, embryonic, inaugural, incipient, introductory, previous, primeval, primitive, prior
ASSOCIATED CONCEPTS: at first impression, first lien, first reading, first stages of litigation, on first blush

FIRST *(Superior),* ***adjective*** antecedent, authentic, capital, cardinal, central, chief, crowning, dominant, foremost, highest, important, initial, leading, maiden, main, original, paramount, precessional, precursory, preeminent, preferred, premier, primary, prime, primordial, principal, second to none, starting, stellar, superior, supreme, unprecedented, vital
ASSOCIATED CONCEPTS: first-degree offense

FIRST, *adverb* *ab initio,* at first, at the outset, before, chiefly, first and foremost, firstly, formerly, from the beginning, initially, in the beginning, in the front, originally, primarily, principally

FIRST AMENDMENT *(Free speech),* ***noun*** freedom of expression, freedom of right to assemble, freedom of speech, freedom of the right to petition, freedom to amass, freedom to express an opinion, right of free speech
ASSOCIATED CONCEPTS: Bill of Rights, slander

FIRST AMENDMENT *(Freedom of right to assemble),* ***noun*** freedom to amass, freedom to collect, freedom to gather

FIRST AMENDMENT *(Freedom of the press),* ***noun*** freedom to express an opinion, freedom to print, freedom to publish, freedom to write
ASSOCIATED CONCEPTS: libel

FIRST AMENDMENT *(Freedom of the right to petition),* ***noun*** freedom of the right to challenge, freedom of the right to oppose, freedom of the right to speak out

FIRST APPEARANCE, *noun* appearance, debut, inauguration, initial, gambit, opening

FIRST IMPRESSION, *noun* earliest reaction, early reaction, first blush reaction, first ever impression, first reaction, first sight impression, first stage, initial reaction, original reaction, primary reaction, prime reactive
ASSOCIATED CONCEPTS: case of first impression, first impression of the defendant on the jury

FIRST OFFENSE, *noun* first charge, first crime, first criminal violation, first violation

FIRST POSITION, *adjective* antecedent place, anterior place, beginning place, best place, cardinal place, crowning place, earliest place, first-class place, first-rate place, foremost place, grade a place, greatest place, highest place, leading place, main place, major place, original place, paramount place, precedent place, preceding place, predominant place, preeminent place, premier place, prevailing place, primal place, primary place, prime place, primeval place, principal place, supreme place, uppermost place
ASSOCIATED CONCEPTS: bankruptcy, filings, recording statutes

FIRST SALE DOCTRINE, *noun* exception to copyright holder's distribution right, exhaustion rule, first sale rule, right of first sale

FIRST STEP, *noun* beginning, birth, commencement, debut, embarkment, embryo, genesis, inauguration, inception, inchoation, incipiency, initiation, introduction, nascency, onset, opener, opening, origin, origination, outset, point of departure, start, starting point, unveiling

FIRSTHAND, ***adjective*** absolute, admissible, attestative, authentic, certain, conclusive, decisive, determinative, documented, empirical, eyewitness, factual, incontrovertible, indisputable, irrefutable, overwhelming, reliable, sure, valid
ASSOCIATED CONCEPTS: firsthand knowledge of a crime

FISCAL, ***adjective*** budgetary, bursal, economic, financial, *fiscalis,* monetary, pecuniary, pertaining to financial matters, pertaining to government finances, pertaining to monetary receipts and expenditures, pertaining to the public revenues, pertaining to the public treasury, relating to accounts, relating to money matters, relating to the management of revenue
ASSOCIATED CONCEPTS: fiscal affairs, fiscal year

FISCAL CLIFF, ***noun*** appointed hour, bankruptcy, brink of disaster, budgetary crisis, call to action, climax, crisis point, critical juncture, critical point, crossroad, crucial point, day of decision, D-day, drop-dead date, economic crisis, final date before disaster, financial precipice, fiscal emergency, moment of truth, outside date, precipice fiscal dilemma, turning point, urgency, vital moment, zero hour
ASSOCIATED CONCEPTS: budget cuts, deficit, sequestration

FISHING EXPEDITION, ***noun*** careless inquisition, careless probe, comprehensive research, comprehensive study, comprehensive survey, fundamental research, investigation with reckless abandon, reckless inquiry, reckless investigation, reckless pursuit, wanton examination, wanton exploration, wanton inquest, widespread scrutiny, widespread search, wild inquest
ASSOCIATED CONCEPTS: prosecutorial misconduct

FIT, ***adjective*** able, acceptable, accommodated, adapted, adequate, adjusted, advantageous, advisable, applicable, apposite, appropriate, apropos, apt, *aptus,* becoming, befitting, capable, *commodus,* compatible, competent, concordant, conformable, congruous, consistent, consonant, correspondent, eligible, fitted, fitting, harmonious, *idoneus,* in keeping, in place, legitimate, matched, opportune, pertinent, prepared, primed, proper, qualified, ready, relevant, right, seasonable, seemly, sortable, suitable, suited, tailor-made, tasteful, to the purpose, well-fitted, well-qualified, well-suited, well-timed, wise, workable, worthy
ASSOCIATED CONCEPTS: fit for use, fitness for a particular purpose, implied warranty of fitness, reasonably fit for the purpose intended

FITNESS *(Ability),* ***noun*** admissibility, applicability, appositiveness, appropriateness, aptitude, aptness, competence, expedience, faculty, felicity, instinct, propriety, seemliness, skill, suitableness

FITNESS *(Relevancy),* ***noun*** acceptability, admissibility, advisability, capability, capacity, compatibility, competency, congruity, correctness, correspondence, desirability, due, efficiency, eligibility, expedience, pertinence, propriety, qualification, worthiness
ASSOCIATED CONCEPTS: fitness for a particular purpose under product liability theories

FITTING, ***adjective*** adapted, appropriate, auspicious, becoming, convenient, correct, desirable, expedient, favorable, geared to, likely, opportune, proper, propitious, providential, seasonable, seemly, suitable, suited, relevant, timely

FIX *(Arrange),* ***verb*** adjust, align, array, assign places to, assort, bring into order, catalog, class, classify, codify, collocate, *constituere,* coordinate, distribute, divide, establish, file, form, grade, graduate, group, index, introduce order into, line up, list, marshal, methodize, *ordinare,* organize, place, place in order, prepare, put in order, put in proper order, range, rank, regulate, set in order, sort, sort out, sort systematically, straighten out, systematize, tabulate
ASSOCIATED CONCEPTS: fix prices

FIX *(Make firm),* ***verb*** attach, confirm, consolidate, embed, entrench, establish, fasten in position securely, fasten securely, ground, harden, implant, infix, ingraft, ingrain, lock, lodge, make fast, make rigid, pin, place permanently, plant, ratify, render solid, root, secure, set, solidify, stabilize, stiffen, tether
ASSOCIATED CONCEPTS: fix compensation, fix rates

FIX *(Repair),* ***verb*** adjust, alter, ameliorate, amend, correct, do repairs, emend, freshen, freshen up, heal, improve, improve upon, invigorate, make corrections, make over, make restoration, make sound, make whole, meliorate, mend, overhaul, patch, patch up, purify, put in condition, put in good condition, put in order, put in repair, put in shape, rebuild, reclaim, recondition, reconstruct, rectify, redintegrate, redress, refashion, *reficere,* refit, reform, refurbish, regenerate, rehabilitate, reinvigorate, rejuvenate, remake, remedy, remove the errors, renew, renovate, *reparare, restituere,* restore, retouch, return to the original state, revamp, revive, revivify, right, service, set aright, set right, straighten, touch up

FIX *(Settle),* ***verb*** agree, arrange, arrive at a conclusion, arrive at an agreement, ascertain, come to a determination, come to a resolution, come to an agreement, conclude, *constituere,* decide, *definire,* determine, establish, make a decision, resolve, seal, set, *statuere,* straighten out, work out

FIXATION, ***noun*** compulsion, delusion, fascination, fixedness, fixity, infatuation, intoxication, lodgment, monomania, obsession, predilection, preoccupation, prepossession

FIXED *(Securely placed),* ***adjective*** anchored, *certus,* fast, fastened, firm, firmly established, firmly implanted, firmly seated, firmly set, immovable, irremovable, made fast, permanent, rendered stable, rigid, secure, set, solid, sound, stable, steadfast, steady, tethered, tight

FIXED *(Settled),* ***adjective*** arranged, changeless, closed, decided, definite, determined, entrenched, established, not fluctuating, not varying, permanent, predetermined, prescribed, rooted, unchangeable, unchanging, unshifting, unvarying, unwavering, well-established
ASSOCIATED CONCEPTS: fixed asset, fixed by law, fixed capital, fixed costs, fixed income, fixed liability, fixed salary, fixed term, fixed time

FIXING A BID, ***verb*** bid-rigging, conspiracy to fix a bid, contrived bidding, criminal act regarding a bid, criminal contrivance in a bid, fraudulence in a bid, illegal accommodation in a bid, illegal act regarding a bid, illegal action regarding a bid, illegal agreement regarding a bid, illegal arrangement in a bid, illegal contrivances in a bid, illegal consortium, illegal efforts to fix a bid, illegal maneuvering in a bid, illegal means to fix a bid, illegal measures to fix a bid, trumped-up provisions in a bid

FIXTURE, ***noun*** addition to realty, affixed to realty, attachment to realty, permanent attachment to real property, something constructively affixed to real property,

something immovable from realty, something physically annexed to realty
ASSOCIATED CONCEPTS: appurtenance, domestic fixtures, equipment, irremovable fixtures, machinery, permanent fixtures, removal of fixtures, trade fixtures

FLAGITIOUS, ***adjective*** abominable, accursed, amoralistic, arrant, atrocious, bad, base, blameworthy, criminal, decadent, degenerate, depraved, diabolical, disgraceful, dissolute, egregious, evil, execrable, facinorous, felonious, flagrant, grievous, heinous, ignominious, immoral, impious, incarnate, inexcusable, inexpiable, infernal, iniquitous, monstrous, nefarious, outrageous, profligate, reprehensible, reprobate, scandalous, shameful, shocking, sinister, unprincipled, unrighteous, unscrupulous, vile, villainous, wicked

FLAGRANT, ***adjective*** aiming for effect, apparent, arrant, audacious, blatant, bold, brazen, clear, conspicuous, daring, done for effect, enormous, flagitious, flaming into notice, flashy, flaunting, glaring, gross, immodest, *impudens,* infamous, loud, manifest, *manifestus,* monstrous, nefarious, noticeable, notorious, obtrusive, obvious, open, outrageous, outstanding, plain, prominent, pronounced, scandalizing, scandalous, screaming, shameless, shocking, showy, striking, striving for effect, visible, wanton
ASSOCIATED CONCEPTS: flagrant abuse of the law

FLAIR, ***noun*** a way with, ability, acuity, acumen, acuteness, adequacy, adroitness, aptitude, aptness, astuteness, caliber, capability, capableness, capacity, competence, competency, deftness, dexterity, discernment, efficacy, efficiency, endowment, enthusiasm, equipment, expertness, facility, faculty, felicity, fitness, flamboyance, gift, inclination, innate ability, innate aptitude, instinct, keenness, knack, leaning, liveliness, long suit, natural gift, panache, perception, percipience, perspicacity, potential, potentiality, power, proclivity, proficiency, propensity, qualification, qualities, sagaciousness, sagacity, savvy, sharpness, showiness, shrewdness, skill, skillfulness, smartness, spirit, strength, strong flair, strong point, strong suit, style, sufficiency, susceptibility, talent, talents, tendency

FLAMBOYANT, ***adjective*** affected, baroque, brave, braw, bright, colorful, dazzling, elaborate, extravagant, fancy, flaming, flashy, flowery, frilled, frilly, fussy, garish, gaudy, glitzy, grandiose, high-flown, high-flying, lofty, ornate, orotund, ostentatious, overdone, pompous, pretentious, sensational, sensationalistic, showy

FLATULENT, ***adjective*** bombastic, bombastical, declamatory, fustian, garrulous, grandiloquent, high-flown, inflated, long-winded, mouthy, oratorical, orotund, pompous, pretentious, prolix, rhetorical, talkative, tumid, turgid, verbose, wordy

FLAUNT, ***verb*** air, be conspicuous, be ostentatious, be showy, boast, brag, brandish, display, display oneself boldly, display with effrontery, exhibit, exhibit boastfully, flash, flourish, gloat, *lactare,* make a gaudy display, make a show of, make a showy appearance, make a spectacle, make a splash, make a splurge, *ostentare,* parade, parade conspicuously, put forth, put forward, shake, show, show off, sport, spotlight, strut, swagger, vaunt, wave, wave brazenly, wave conspicuously, wave ostentatiously, wear

FLAVOR *(Essence),* ***noun*** attributes, character, characteristic, configuration, core, distinctive features, essential meaning, expertise, feature, figure, gist, good point, heart, impression, mannerism, mark, material issues, meaning, mold, nature, particularity, peculiarity, point of character, property, quality, quintessence, redeeming feature, savor, shape, signature, singularity, sole, substance, sum and substance, taste, trait
ASSOCIATED CONCEPTS: the flavor of a holding, the flavor of an argument, the flavor of an issue

FLAVOR *(Taste),* ***noun*** appreciation, deliciousness, favor, like, palate, salty taste, savor, sense of taste, sharp taste, sour taste, sourness, spicy taste, sweet taste, sweetness, taste in the mouth

FLAW, ***noun*** blemish, blot, breach, crack, defacement, defect, deficiency, deformity, demerit, disfigurement, error, failing, failure, fault, foible, frailty, gap, imperfection, imperfectness, inferiority, infirmity, injury, limitation, loophole, maculation, marring feature, *mendum,* omission, patch, rift, shortcoming, stain, unevenness, vice, *vitium,* weak point, weak spot, weakness
ASSOCIATED CONCEPTS: latent defect

FLAWED, ***adjective*** below par, blemished, damaged, defective, deficient, fallible, faulty, impaired, imperfect, inadequate, incomplete, incorrect, inexact, insufficient, lacking, marred, peccable, sinister, soiled, vicious, deformed, defaced, scarred, unfinished, unsound, vulnerable, wanting
ASSOCIATED CONCEPTS: flawed argument

FLAWLESS, ***adjective*** absolute, best, complete, consummate, defectless, faultless, immaculate, impeccable, infallible, intact, irreproachable, 100 percent, perfect, precise, pure, sound, spotless, unblemished, untainted, without blemish

FLEE, ***verb*** abandon, abscond, absent oneself, clear out, decamp, desert, disappear, *effugere,* escape, evacuate, evade, fly, *fugam petere,* hasten away, hide, make an escape, make off, play truant, remove oneself, retire, retreat, run, run away, run off, take flight, take to one's heels, withdraw
ASSOCIATED CONCEPTS: flee from creditors, flee from justice, unlawful flight to avoid prosecution

FLEETING EXPLETIVES, ***noun*** ephemeral indecency, nonscripted verbal profanity, obscenity broadcast unintentionally, single inadvertent indecency, single indiscretion

FLEXIBLE, ***adjective*** adaptable, adjustable, bendable, bending, capable of conforming to new situations, capable of responding to changing situations, disposed to yield, ductile, easily bent, easily managed, elastic, *facilis, flexibilis,* flexile, formable, *lentus,* limber, lissome, lithe, malleable, manageable, moldable, plastic, pliable, pliant, responsive, responsive to change, soft, stretchable, supple, tractable, unexacting, unstrict, waxen, wieldy, willing to yield to influence of others, willowy, yielding

FLIGHT, ***noun*** absconding, avoidance, decampment, departing, departure, desertion, disappearance, *effugium,* elusion, escaping, evacuation, evasion, exodus, fleeing, *fuga,* hasty departure, hegira, leaving, removal, retreat, running away
ASSOCIATED CONCEPTS: flight from justice, fugitive from justice, unlawful flight to avoid prosecution

FLIMFLAM, ***noun*** a pack of lies, artifice, bamboozlement, befooling, bluffing, calculated deception, circumven-

tion, conning, deceiving, deception, deceptiveness, defrauding, delusion, delusiveness, dupery, empty talk, enmeshment, ensnarement, fallaciousness, falseness, falsity, fiction, fooling, fraud, illusion, legal fiction, mirage, pretense, prevarication, trickery, trumped-up story, willful misconception
ASSOCIATED CONCEPTS: bunco, confidence games, fraud

FLIP-FLOP, *verb* about face, adoption, afterthoughts, backsliding, change like a chameleon, change of heart, change of mind, conversion, defection, diametrically opposed stance, divergence, diversion, 180-degree about face, qualification, realignment, regression, restructuring, reversal, reversion, temporizer, tergiversation, turn of the tide, turnabout
ASSOCIATED CONCEPTS: flip-flop on a political stance

FLOAT, *verb* announce, attempt, buoy, buoy up, instigate, issue, launch, offer, present, project, promote, propel, sell, set in motion, try
ASSOCIATED CONCEPTS: float a bond, float an idea or a concept

FLOOD *(Abundance)*, ***noun*** a sufficiency, affluence, ampleness, amplitude, an ample amount, an ample supple, avalanche, bonanza, bounteousness, bountifulness, bumper crop, copiousness, full measure, fullness, generosity, generousness, glut, great abundance, landslide, lavishness, much, outpouring, overbrim, overbrimming, overburden, overcharge, overflow, overload, plenty, plethora, profuseness, profusion, saturation, superabundance, surfeit

FLOOD *(Deluge)*, ***noun*** avalanche, burst of rain, catastrophe, cloudburst, downfall, downpour, drenching rain, driving rain, groundwater, heavy rain, heavy shower, inundation, massive amounts of rain, massive amounts of raising groundwater, pelting rain, pouring rain, rainfall, rainstorm, rainwater, raising water, sheets of rain, spurt of rain, storm, streams of rain, thundershower, thunderstorm, torrent of rain, torrential downpour, torrential rain
ASSOCIATED CONCEPTS: FEMA, National Flood Insurance Program

FLOOD *(Overabundance)*, ***noun*** barrage, cataclysm, engulfment, excess, flux, glut, influx, inundation, landslide, overabundance, overage, overflow, overkill, superfluity, surfeit, surplus, torrent
ASSOCIATED CONCEPTS: a flood of cases

FLOOD *(Water)*, ***noun*** appointed hour, bankruptcy, brink of disaster, budgetary crisis, call to action, climax, crisis point, critical juncture, critical point, crossroad, crucial point, day of decision, D-day, drop-dead date, economic crisis, final date before disaster, financial precipice, fiscal emergency, moment of truth, outside date, precipice fiscal dilemma, turning point, urgency, vital moment, zero hour
ASSOCIATED CONCEPTS: budget cuts, deficit, sequestration

FLOODGATE, *noun* allow in massive problems, avoidance, circumvention, colossal opening, door, escape, evasion, exhaust, exit, inundation, means, moat, open faucet, open flood hatch, open gate, opening, outlet, overflow, provide a wide opening, release, safety valve, spout, vent
ASSOCIATED CONCEPTS: immigration, open the floodgates

FLOOR, *noun* base, basis, bedrock, bottom, flooring, foundation, fundamental basis, girder, ground, groundwork, jumping off point, premise, principle, rudiment, starting point, support, supporting structure, underlying principle, underpinning basis
ASSOCIATED CONCEPTS: floor plan in zoning and construction laws, hacking the floor in parliamentary procedure, minimum wage

FLOUT, *verb* affront, be contemptuous of, be disrespectful, be scornful, care nothing for, *cavillari*, contemn, defy, deride, despise, disdain, disregard, esteem slightly, feel contempt for, fleer, gibe, hold in contempt, hold in derision, hold in disrespect, hold up to scorn, insult, jeer, laugh at, *ludificari*, mock, outrage, rail at, revile, ridicule, scoff, scorn, set no store by, show contempt for, slight, sneer, spurn, take no account of, treat with contempt, treat with disdain, view with a scornful eye

FLOW, *verb* become, develop, go, journey, meander, move, pass, proceed, progress, roam, run, travel, turn into, voyage

FLUCTUATE, *verb* alter, alternate, be changeful, be intermittent, be periodic, be unsteady, change, change continuously, *fluctuare*, intermit, move in waves, pendulate, rise and fall, shift, show variety, swing, vary, wave, waver

FLUFF, *noun* elusive support, ephemeral content, fleeting analysis, immaterial substance, inadequate analysis, momentary analysis, no substance, passing consideration, smoke and mirrors, support that is vaporizing, temporal consideration, thin content, trifle, triviality

FLUID, *adjective* able to adapt, adaptable, adjustable, alterable, alterative, continuous, flexible, fluent, impermanent, inconstant, liquid, malleable, mobile, modifiable, movable, ongoing, resilient, solvent, transient, transitory
ASSOCIATED CONCEPTS: cash flow

FLUKE, *noun* accident, blunder, bungle, chance good fortune, chance happening, chance misfortune, chance occurrence, error, fortuity, lucky situation, miscalculation, misconception, misinterpretation, misjudgment, misreading, misunderstanding, once in a lifetime occurrence, random achievement, random luck, random mistake, random success, stroke of bad luck, stroke of misfortune

FLUVIAL, *adjective* along the river banks, coursing, diffluent, eddying, flowing, fluent, fluid, fluidic, fluviatic, fluviatile, fluvicoline, from the river, riparian, riverine, rivery, rolling, running, streaming, streamy, surging

FOCAL POINT, *noun* arena, attraction, axis, base, capital, center, center of activity, center of attention, center of attraction, center of focus, center of interest, central, central point, centrality, converging point, core, cynosure, epicenter, essence, eye, focus, ground zero, heart, highlight, hot spot, hotbed, hub, locus, mecca, nerve center, nexus, nucleus, point, point of convergence, quintessence, seat, soul, vortex

FOCUS, *noun* arena, center, center of activity, center of attention, center of attraction, center of consciousness, center of interest, central point, centrality, convergence, converging point, focal point, gathering place, goal, heart, hub, objective, point of concentration, point of convergence
ASSOCIATED CONCEPTS: target of an investigation

FOCUS, *verb* attend, attend minutely, bring into focus, bring the mind to bear upon, bring together, center, centralize, come to a point, concenter, concentrate on, concentrate the mind, concentrate the thoughts, direct one's

thoughts to, direct toward one object, examine closely, fix on, fix the thoughts upon, give attention, give the mind to, look to, meditate upon, occupy the thoughts with, regard carefully, render central
ASSOCIATED CONCEPTS: focus an investigation on a suspect

FOE, *noun* *adversarius,* adversary, adverse party, antagonist, armed enemy, assailant, attacker, belligerent, bitter enemy, combatant, competitor, contender, contestant, detractor, disputant, enemy, fighter, foeman, hostile person, *hostis, inimicus,* one who is unfriendly, one who opposes, open enemy, opponent, opposer, opposing party, opposite camp, opposite side, other side, outlaw, public enemy, public opponent, rival, sworn enemy

FOIBLE, *noun* blemish, defect, deficiency, demerit, failing, failure, fault, flaw, frailty, frailty of character, human weakness, imperfection, lack, limitation, moral weakness, need, problem, room for improvement, shortcoming, vice, *vitium,* want, weak point, weak side, weakness, weakness of character

FOIL, *verb* baffle, balk, be obstructive, bring to naught, cause to be nugatory, check, confound, counter, counteract, countermine, cripple, crush, dash, dash one's hopes, defeat, disable, disappoint, disrupt, *eludere,* frustrate, get in the way of, hamper, hinder, impede, intercept, keep from being successful, nip, obstruct, override, prevent, render vain, restrain, retard, ruin, spoil, stultify, subdue, thwart, undermine, upset, vanquish
ASSOCIATED CONCEPTS: foil a crime

FOIST, *verb* apply pressure, beguile, coerce, compel, compel to accept, constrain, deceive, fob off on, force, force upon, gull, impose, impose by fraud, inflict, insert surreptitiously, palm off, palm off fraudulently, pass off as genuine, put in slyly, put in stealthily, *subdere, supponere,* thrust upon surreptitiously, trick

FOLLOW *(Be behind),* ***verb*** be after, bring up the rear, chase, come after, fall back, fall behind, fall behind, follow after, follow up, get behind, go after, go behind, harass, hound, hunt, lag behind, on the footsteps of, on the heels of, pursue, search, seek, shadow, straggle, succeed, track, trail
ASSOCIATED CONCEPTS: follows the property, priorities in bankruptcy, recording statutes

FOLLOW *(Conform),* ***verb*** abide by, accept as an authority, accord, adhere to, adopt, ape, attend to, be consistent with, be guided by, be in keeping, comply, comply with, copy, copy after, copycat, do as, do like, echo, emulate, follow in the footsteps of, follow in the steps of, follow in the wake of, follow like sheep, follow suit, follow the example of, give allegiance to, harmonize, heed, hold fast, imitate, jump on the bandwagon, match, mimic, mind, mirror, model after, model on, note, obey, observe, pattern after, pattern on, play follow the leader, put oneself in another's shoes, reflect, regard, shape after, simulate, string along, take a leaf out of one's book, take after, take as a model, walk in the shoes of, yield to
ASSOCIATED CONCEPTS: follow precedence, follow the dictates of the court

FOLLOW THROUGH, *verb* accomplish, achieve, act, attain, be instrumental, bring to fruition, conclude, decide, determine, discharge, effectuate, enforce, execute, find a method, find the means, find the way, fulfill, gain, gain results, get, obtain, perform, produce, realize, take the necessary measures
ASSOCIATED CONCEPTS: attach, contempt, execution, filing a judgment, filing an appeal, order of the court

FOLLOW-UP, *noun* by-product, completion, consequence, result, sequel

FOLLOW UP, *verb* accomplished, be thorough, carry through, complete, conduct, develop, discharge, end, execute, finalize, finish, follow through, gain a determination, gain finality, gain results, go through with, handle, manage, oversee, perform, prosecute to a conclusion, pursue, scrutinize closely, see through, supervise, transact

FOLLOWING, *adjective* ensuing, next, resulting, subsequent, succeeding, successive
ASSOCIATED CONCEPTS: following form doctrine

FOLLY, *noun* absurdity, absurdness, act of folly, blooper, blunder, eccentricity, excessiveness, extravagance, foolery, foolishness, frivolity, frivolousness, gaffe, humor, humorousness, indiscretion, ineptitude, insanity, laughableness, ludicrousness, lunacy, madness, mindlessness, nonsense, nonsensicality, nonsensicalness, oddity, oddness, senselessness, shallowness, strangeness, stupidity, thoughtlessness, triviality

FOMENT, *verb* abet, agitate, aid, arouse, awaken, call forth, encourage, engender, enkindle, excite, ferment, fire, foster, *fovere,* galvanize, goad, impassion, incite, infect, inflame, infuse life into, inspirit, instigate, kindle, promote, provoke, rouse, set astir, stimulate, stir, stir up, urge, wake up, waken, work up

FONDNESS, *noun* adoration, adulation, affection, affinity, allegiance, appetite, appreciation, ardor, attachment, craving, crush, deification, desire, devotedness, devotion, eagerness, enthusiasm, esteem, estimation, faithfulness, fancy, favor, fealty, fervor, fidelity, fondness, idolatry, idolization, infatuation, like, liking, longing, loyalty, lust, partiality, passion, preference, regard, relish, respect, steadfastness, taste, worship, yearning, zeal

FOOD, *noun* bread, comestibles, diet, dish, edibles, feast, feed, foodstuffs, meal, nourishment, nurture, nutriment, plate, platter, provender, provisions, refreshments, repast, serving, spread, supplies, sustenance, viands, victuals, vittles

FOOL, *verb* bamboozle, beguile, bluff, buffalo, cheat, con, cozen, delude, dupe, fake out, fleece, hoax, hoodwink, hustle, misguide, misinform, mislead, play a joke, scam, shortchange, snow, stint, string along, sucker, swindle, take in, tease, trick

FOOLISH, *adjective* absurd, beyond belief, bizarre, crazy, illogical, improper, inappropriate, incorrect, incredible, ludicrous, monstrous, not advisable, not smart, outlandish, outrageous, preposterous, ridiculous, senseless, unfitting, unseemly, unsuitable, unwise, weird, wrong

FOOTNOTE, *noun* additional information, afterthought, annotation, citation, comment, commentary, definition, elucidation, exegesis, explanation, explication, gloss, illustration, interpretation, notation, note, observation, reference, remark, reminder, statement

FOR, *conjunction* as, as a result of, associated with, because of, by reason of, caused by, concerning, due to, for the sake of, in consideration of, in contemplation of, in favor of, in furtherance of, in pursuance of, in spite of, in support of, in the direction of, in the interest of, instead of, on account of, on behalf of, on the part of, to the extent of, toward, with a view to, with regard to, with respect to

FOR CAUSE, *adverb* for legitimate reason, for just reason, with cause, with justification

FORAY, *noun* aggression, armed attack, attack, brigandage, depredation, drive, hostile invasion, incursion, inimical descent, inroad, invasion, looting, maraud, offense, offensive, pillaging, plundering, predatory incursion, push, raid, ransack, razzia, sack, sudden attack, thrust

FORBEAR, *verb* abstain, be patient, be temperate, be tolerant, bear with, break off, cease, decline, delay enforcing rights, deny oneself, desist from, dispense with, do without, endure, forgo, hold back, hold in abeyance, hold off, keep back, keep from, leave off, not proceed with, put up with, refrain, refrain from action, renounce, restrain, sacrifice, stop, submit, submit without complaint, suffer, *supersedere, temperare,* tolerate, treat with indulgence, wait, waive, withhold, withhold action
ASSOCIATED CONCEPTS: forbearance as consideration

FORBEARANCE, *noun* absolution, abstention, acceptance, amenability, benevolence, charity, clemency, empathy, favor, forgiving, grace, lenience, leniency, lenity, mercifulness, passivity, quarter, restraint, settlement, sufferance, tolerance

FORBID, *verb* ban, bar, block, check, command not to do, debar, declare illegal, deny, deny permission, deprive, deter, disallow, disapprove, discountenance, discourage, enjoin, exclude, forfend, hinder, impede, inhibit, *interdicere,* interdict, make forbidden, not allow, obstruct, oppose, order not to do, outlaw, preclude, prevent, prohibit, proscribe, put under an injunction, refuse, refuse approval, refuse consent, refuse to allow, refuse to authorize, refuse to give permission, refuse to permit, render impossible, restrain, restrict, stop, taboo, veto, withhold consent, withhold permission
ASSOCIATED CONCEPTS: disallow a claim, mala prohibita, prohibit by an administrative agency, prohibition
FOREIGN PHRASES: ***Qui non prohibet id quod prohibere potest assentire videtur.*** He who does not forbid what he is able to prevent is deemed to assent.

FORCE *(Compulsion),* ***noun*** arbitrary power, authority, coaction, coercion, command, compulsion, constraining power, constraint, constriction, control, demand, dictation, discipline, drive, duress, enforcement, exaction, impelling, imposition, impressment, inducement, insistence, martial law, necessitation, necessitude, necessity, need, oppression, persuasion, pressure, prevailing, repression, restraint, restriction, sanction, spur of necessity, stress, strict control, subjection, subjugation, urgency, vehemence
ASSOCIATED CONCEPTS: ejectment by force, forced merger, forced payment, forced sale
FOREIGN PHRASES: ***Vis legibus est inimica.*** Force is inimical to the laws. ***Quod alias bonum et justum est, si per vim vel fraudem petatur, malum et injustum efficitur.*** What otherwise is good and just, becomes bad and unjust if it is sought by force and fraud. ***Non videtur vim facere, qui jure suo utitur et ordinaria actione experitur.*** He is not considered to use force who exercises his own right, and proceeds by ordinary action. ***Ejus nulla culpa est, cui parere necesse sit.*** No guilt attaches to a person who is compelled to obey. ***Nihil consensui tam contrarium est quam vis atque metus.*** Nothing is so opposed to consent as force and fear.

FORCE *(Legal efficacy),* ***noun*** authorized might, lawful power, lawful vigor, legal vitality, legitimate puissance, rightful strength, sanctioned effectiveness, sanctioned potency, statutory cogency, valid potentiality

FORCE *(Strength),* ***noun*** ability, ableness, ascendancy, authoritativeness, brawn, capability, cogency, command, competence, consequence, control, domination, dominion, effectiveness, effectuality, efficacy, empowerment, enablement, endurance, energy, firmness, forcefulness, hardiness, impact, *impetus,* importance, influence, influentiality, intensity, *manus,* mastery, might, mightiness, omnipotence, physical power, potence, potency, power, powerfulness, predominance, pressure, primacy, proficiency, stamina, supremacy, sway, vigor, vigorousness, virulence, *vis,* vitality
ASSOCIATED CONCEPTS: armed force, constructive force, excessive force, intervening force, physical force, superior force, threats of force, unnecessary force, unreasonable force
FOREIGN PHRASES: ***Vim vi repellere licet, modo fiat moderamine inculpatae tutelae, non ad sumendam vindictam, sed ad propulsandam injuriam.*** It is lawful to repel force by force, provided it be done with the moderation of blameless defense, not for the purpose of taking revenge, but to repel injury.

FORCE *(Break),* ***verb*** batter, breach, crack, disjoint, fissure, *inrumpere,* invade, pry, rend, rive, rupture, shatter, smash, split, strain, tear asunder, wrench

FORCE *(Coerce),* ***verb*** apply pressure, cause to yield, command, compel, constrain, control, demand, enforce, enforce obedience, enjoin, enslave, enthrall, exercise power over, *exprimere, extorquere,* extort, impose, insist, make obligatory, necessitate, obligate, oblige, order, overpower, overwhelm, press, push, put under obligation, require, tax, urge, use violence

FORCEFUL *(Persuasive),* ***adjective*** absolute, arresting, authoritative, categorical, compelling, conclusive, controlling, convincing, decided, decisive, definitive, determined, dominating, domineering, dynamic, effective, energetic, firm, fixed, formidable, important, insistent, intransigent, marked, obdurate, pertinent, pointed, potent, resolute, resounding, satisfying, significant, sound, stable, stalwart, staunch, striking, substantial, telling, tenacious, tough, trenchant, unambiguous, unyielding, valid, vehement, vigorous, weighty, well-founded

FORCEFUL *(Strong),* ***adjective*** able, capable, enduring, full-blooded, hard, hearty, heavy, heavy-duty, immovable, ironclad, muscular, overpowering, powerful, secure, solid, strong, sturdy, vigorous, vivacious

FORCIBLE, *adjective* aggressive, authoritative, binding, brought about by force, coercive, commanding, compelling, compulsory, controlling, convincing, dominant, done by force, drastic, emphatic, energetic, enforced, forceful, full of power, full of strength, having a strong effect, having force, having great strength, impelling, impressive, incumbent, influential, intense, invincible, oppressive, *per vim factus,* powerful, predominant, prepotent, prevailing, producing a powerful effect, required, resistless, strong, vehement, vigorous, violent, wielding power

ASSOCIATED CONCEPTS: defilement, forcible detainer, forcible dispossession, forcible entry, forcible repossession, forcible trespass, rape, sodomy

FOREBODE, *verb* admonish, allude, anticipate, augur, betoken, connote, divine, forecast, foresee, foreshadow, foretell, forewarn, harbinger, hint, imply, indicate, insinuate, intimate, portend, predict, prefigure, presage, presignify, prognosticate, promise, prophesy, signify, suggest, warn

FOREBODING, *adjective* anxiety filled, anxiousness, apprehension, apprehensiveness, concerning, dark, disquieting, disquietude, distressing, disturbing, dreading, fearful, foreshadowed, ill-omened, inauspicious, intimidating, menacing, nervous, ominous, perturbing, portentous, premonitory, tension provoking, threatening, troubling, unfavorable, unpropitious, upsetting, vexatious, warning

FOREBODING, *noun* alarm, anticipation, anxiety, apprehensive, augury, care, caution, concern, disquiet, doubt, dread, fear, forecast, foreknowledge, foreshadowing, foresight, hint, impression, inkling, misgiving, nervousness, omen, perturbation, portent, prediction, presage, prescience, presentiment, prognosis, prophecy, sign, suspicion, threat, unease, warning, worry

FORECAST, *noun* actuarial prediction, all beforehand, anticipation, augur, augury, conjecture, consideration, contemplation, design, determine, discretion, divination, envisagement, envisionment, estimate, estimation, farseeingness, farsightedness, feeling, figure out, forebode, foreboding, forecasting, foreglance, foregleam, foreglimpse, forehandedness, foreknowing, foreseeing, foresight, foresightedness, foretelling, forewarn, fortunetelling, gauge, guess, guesswork, guestimation, hunch, improbability, inference, longsightedness, looking ahead, omen, plan, plan ahead, portend, prediction, prefiguration, prefigurement, prefiguring, preparation, prepublication, presage, presaging, presentiment, preshowing, presignifying, presigning, preview, prevision, probability, prognosis, prognostication, prophesy, prophesying, prospect, prospection, sagacity, soothsaying, statistical prediction

FORECLOSE *(Action to seize property),* ***verb*** enforcement of a lien through the judiciary, extinguish rights through the judiciary, extinguish the equity of redemption through the judiciary, remove rights through the judiciary, seize by judicial process, transfer ownership by judicial process, transfer ownership rights by judicial process, transfer title by judicial process
ASSOCIATED CONCEPTS: deed in lieu of foreclosure

FORECLOSE *(Extinguish),* ***verb*** bar, deprive, destroy equity of redemption, disentitle, divest, forfeit, halt, remove, shut out, stop, terminating rights
ASSOCIATED CONCEPTS: foreclosure opportunity, statute of limitations, statutory foreclosure, strict foreclosure

FORECLOSURE, *noun* confiscation, deprivation, disentitlement, dislodgment, dispossession, distraint, distress, divestment, enforcement of mortgage, eviction, expropriation, expulsion, forfeiture, legal enforcement of a lien, privation, process of extinguishment of rights, removal, suit to extinguish the equity of redemption
ASSOCIATED CONCEPTS: ejectment, foreclosure decree, foreclosure of a lien, foreclosure of a mortgage, foreclosure of collateral, foreclosure proceedings, foreclosure sale, redemption by purchaser

FOREGOING, *adjective* above, above-mentioned, aforementioned, antecedent, before-mentioned, earlier, early, first, former, last, latter, named, older, precedent, preceding, preexistent, preliminary, previously referred to, previously stated, prior, referred to above, referred to earlier, referred to previously, senior

FOREGONE CONCLUSION, *noun* forejudgment, foreordination, inevitable result, onesidedness, partiality, preconceived idea, preconclusion, predecision, predesigned conclusion, predetermination, predetermined conclusion, predilection, predisposition, prejudged conclusion, prejudgment, prejudice, prejudiced view, prenotion, preordination, prepossession, presentiment, presupposal, presupposition, presurmise

FOREIGN, *adjective* *adventicius,* alien, attached to another jurisdiction, belonging to another country, detached, different, disconnected, dissociated, distant, *externus,* extraneous, extrinsic, independent, nonresident, not indigenous, not native, outside, peregrine, *peregrinus,* remote, separate, strange, subject to another jurisdiction, unaffiliated, unallied, unassociated, unconnected, unfamiliar, unrelated, unusual, without connection
ASSOCIATED CONCEPTS: foreign bills, foreign commerce, foreign corporation, foreign divorce, foreign judgment, foreign jurisdiction, foreign laws, foreign notes, foreign patents, foreign state

FOREIGN LANGUAGE RIGHTS, *noun* foreign interpretation rights, foreign translation rights, nonresidential translation rights

FOREJUDGE, *verb* assume, be prejudiced, be rash, decide in advance, determine in advance, have a bias, have a prejudice, have a prepossession, judge beforehand, judge in advance, jump to a conclusion, preconceive, preconclude, predecide, predetermine, prejudge, prejudicate, prepossess, presume, presuppose, presurmise

FOREMAN, *noun* chairman of a jury, chief, commander, director, head, leader, manager of the jury, master, member of the jury, overseer, presiding juryman, superintendent, supervisor
ASSOCIATED CONCEPTS: grand jury foreman, petit jury foreman, trial jury foreman

FOREMOST, *adjective* best, cardinal, central, chief, commanding, critical, crowning, dominant, eminent, essential, famous, first, important, in the forefront, influential, initial, leading, main, major, notable, noteworthy, original, outstanding, paramount, preceding, predominant, preeminent, premier, preponderant, prevailing, primal, primary, prime, principal, professional, prominent, rated, renowned, ruling, salient, stellar, superior, superlative, uppermost, vital

FORENSIC, *adjective* adapted to argumentation, arguable, argumentative, barristerial, belonging to courts of justice, belonging to debate, capable of being debated, concerning the law, contentious, contestable, controversial, controvertible, discursive, disputable, disputative, fitted for legal argumentation, fitted for public *argumentation, forensis, iudicialis, iuridicialis,* judicatory, judicial, jural, juridic, juridical, jurisdictional, jurisprudential, juristic, lawful, learned in the law, legal, legalistic, litigious, open to discussion, pertaining to the courts, pertaining to the law, polemical, proper to public debate, solicitorial, statutory, subject to contention, subject to controversy
ASSOCIATED CONCEPTS: forensic medicine

FORERUNNER, *noun* ancestor, antecedent, antecessor, auspice, forebear, harbinger, herald, leader, messenger, omen, pioneer, portent, *praenuntius,* precedent, precursor, predecessor, preface, prefigurement, presage, progenitor, scout, sign, vanguard, warning

FORESEE, *verb* anticipate, augur, await, be clairvoyant, be provident, conjecture, contemplate, divine, envisage, envision, expect, forecast, forebode, foretell, look ahead, look forward, preconceive, predict, presage, prognosticate, promise, prophesy, show foresight, surmise, vaticinate
ASSOCIATED CONCEPTS: foreseeability as proximate cause

FORESEEABLE, *adjective* anticipatable, anticipated, calculable, contemplated, counted upon, expected, forecasted, foreknowable, foreseen, foretellable, known in advance, looked for, perceived, planned, *praesciens,* predictable, predicted, probable, prophesied, reasonably anticipated, to be expected, vaticinal
ASSOCIATED CONCEPTS: duty to anticipate, forseeability in considering proximate cause, forseeable dangers, forseeable injury, forseeable risk, last clear chance
FOREIGN PHRASES: ***Nemo tenetur divinare.*** No man is bound to foretell or to have foreknowledge of a future event. ***Rerum progressus ostendunt multa, quae in initio praecaveri seu praevide ri non possunt.*** In the course of events, many problems arise which at the beginning could not be guarded against or foreseen.

FORESEEN, *adjective* anticipated, awaited, expected, forecast, foretold, looked for, predicted, presaged, presumed, promised, prophesied

FORESHADOW, *verb* adumbrate, augur, auspicate, betoken, bode, divine, forebode, forecast, forewarn, herald, point to, portend, precurse, predestine, predict, prefigure, premonstrate, presage, preshow, presignify, prognosticate, promise, prophesy, threaten, vaticinate, warn

FORESIGHT, *noun* acumen, anticipation, astuteness, boding, clairvoyance, diligence, discernment, discretion, expectation, forecast, forethought, insight, omen, perception, perspicacity, portent, precaution, precognition, preconception, prediction, premeditation, premonition, prenotion, preparation, presagement, prescience, presentiment, prevision, prognosis, prognostication, prospect, providence, prudence, sagacity, second sight, sense, shrewdness, vaticination, vision, wisdom

FORESTALL, *verb* act in advance, *antevertere,* anticipate, arrest, avert, avoid, await, be armed, be forewarned, bring to a standstill, cancel, censor, check, counteract, deter, disallow, enjoin, estop, filibuster, forbid, forfend, frustrate, halt, hinder, hold back, impede, inhibit, intercept, interfere, intervene, look forward to, make provisions, obstruct, obviate, *praecipere, praevenire,* preclude, prepare for, prevent, prohibit, provide against, stave off, stay, stifle, stop, stymie, suppress, suspend, take precautions, thwart, veto, wait for, ward off
ASSOCIATED CONCEPTS: forestall an action

FORETHOUGHT, *noun* advance planning, aim, anticipation, calculation, circumspection, consideration, consideration in advance, contemplation, deliberate intention, deliberation, design, direction, distinct purpose, fixed purpose, intent, intention, plan, planned course of action, planning ahead, plot, preconsideration, predeliberation, predetermination, premeditation, previous consideration, previous design, previous reflection, prior planning, prior thought, *providentia,* provision, purpose, resolution, resolve, scheme, shrewdness, strategy, thought beforehand, thoughtfulness, volition, will, willfulness
ASSOCIATED CONCEPTS: malice

FOREWARN, *verb* admonish beforehand, advise, advise against, advise beforehand, alarm, alert, alert to danger, augur, caution, caution against danger, caution beforehand, caution in advance, counsel, deter, discourage, dissuade, exhort, expostulate, forbid, forebode, forecast, foreshadow, foreshow, give fair warning, give intimation of impending evil, give notice, give previous notice to, give previous warning to, give warning of possible harm, inform, make acquainted with, make aware, notify, offer a word of caution, ominate, portend, *praemonere,* predict, prefigure, premonish, prepare, presage, preshow, prewarn, prognosticate, prophesy, put on guard, signal, threaten, urge against, urge to take heed, vaticinate, warn, warn beforehand, warn in advance
ASSOCIATED CONCEPTS: abandon a crime, forseeability, notice

FORFEIT, *verb* abandon, abdicate, abjure, alienate by breach of condition, be deprived of, capitulate, cede, concede, default, deliver up, demit, disgorge, escheat, fail to keep, fail to retain, forgo, forswear, give away, give up, give up claim to, give up the argument, give up the point, incur a loss, let go, let slip, lose, lose an opportunity, lose by breach of condition, lose by default, lose by failure to appear, meet with a loss, part with, put aside, quit, *re multari,* relinquish, *rem amittere,* renounce, repudiate, sacrifice, surrender, waive, withdraw, yield
ASSOCIATED CONCEPTS: forfeit a bond, forfeit a deposit, forfeit bail

FORFEITURE *(Act of forfeiting),* ***noun*** confiscation, deprivation, deprivation of a right, destruction of a right, disenfranchisement, disentitlement, dispossession, divestiture of property, divestment, eviction, exaction, expropriation, forcible seizure, foreclosure, involuntary loss of right, loss of right, punishment, seizure, seizure of a privilege
ASSOCIATED CONCEPTS: action for forfeiture, forfeiture clause, forfeiture of bail, forfeiture of bond, forfeiture of deposit, forfeiture of office, forfeiture provision, redemption of property forfeitured, relief from forfeiture, right of forfeiture, tax forfeiture
FOREIGN PHRASES: ***Nullus jus alienum forisfacere potest.*** No man can forfeit the right of another.

FORFEITURE *(Thing forfeited),* ***noun*** amercement, cost, fine, loss, loss consequent to a default, mulct, pecuniary penalty, penal retribution, penalization, penalty, punishment

FORFEITURE BY WRONGDOING, *noun* defendant's responsibility for witness unavailability, forfeiture of hearsay objection due to intentional unavailability of witness
ASSOCIATED CONCEPTS: exception to the Sixth Amendment Confrontation Clause

FORGE *(Counterfeit),* ***verb*** commit forgery, copy fraudulently, fake, falsify, feign, imitate, imitate falsely, imitate fraudulently, issue counterfeit money, make a spurious copy of, produce counterfeit money, reproduce fraudulently, simulate, *subicere, supponere*
ASSOCIATED CONCEPTS: forged check, forged instrument

FORGE *(Produce),* ***verb*** actualize, bring into being, bring into existence, build, cause, compose, concoct, construct, contrive, create, develop, devise, efform, evolve, fabricate, fashion, form, formulate, frame, hammer out, invent, make, manufacture, model, mold, originate, put together, shape

FORGERY, *noun* copy, counterfeit, counterfeiting, deception, fake, false fabrication, falsification, fraud, fraudulence, fraudulent document, imitation, imposition, imposture, misrepresentation, sham, *subiectio*
ASSOCIATED CONCEPTS: alteration of instruments, false entry, forged check, forged instrument, fraud

FORGET *(Forgive)*, ***verb*** absolve, acquit, allow, clear, condone, disregard, exculpate, excuse, exempt, exonerate, give amnesty, ignore, misremember, overpass, pardon, pass over, release, remit, reprieve, settle, turn a blind eye, unlearn

FORGET *(Neglect)*, ***verb*** abandon, blank, brush, desert, disappoint, dismiss, drop, fail, fail to recall, fail to remember, leave, let down, lose, miss, misremember, neglect, omit, overlook, shirk, slack, slight, snub, unable to recall

FORGIVE, *verb* absolve, acquit, bear no malice, cancel, clear, *condonare*, condone, exculpate, excuse, exempt, exonerate, forget, give absolution, grant amnesty, grant pardon, *ignoscere*, overlook, palliate, pardon, reprieve, shrive, vindicate
ASSOCIATED CONCEPTS: executive pardon, forgiveness of debt

FORGO, *verb* abandon, abdicate, abjure, abnegate, abstain from, avoid, bypass, cast aside, cast off, cease, cede, decline, deny oneself, desist from, *dimittere*, discard, discontinue, dismiss, dispense with, dispose of, do without, drop, eliminate, eschew, forbear, forfeit, forsake, forswear, give up, give up claim to, give up the right to, go without, hold back, hold off, keep aloof from, keep away from, keep from, lay aside, lay down, leave, leave off, let alone let pass, make do without, not use, omit, part with, pass, quit, refrain from, refuse, reject, release, relinquish, renounce, renounce claim to, reserve, resign, rid oneself of, sacrifice, shun, sign away, stop, surrender, swear off, throw aside, waive, withdraw from, withhold, write off, yield, yeild up
ASSOCIATED CONCEPTS: forgo interest owed, forgo opportunity

FORM *(Arrangement)*, ***noun*** array, ceremony, class, classification, custom, design, distribution, efformation, established practice, *facies*, fashion, *figura*, *forma*, formality, format, formation, formula, formulary, grouping, kind, manner, method, mode, model, order, organization, outline, pattern, plan, procedure, regimentation, regularity, rite, ritual, scheme, shape, sort, style, system, systematization, type, way
ASSOCIATED CONCEPTS: form of action, objections to form
FOREIGN PHRASES: ***Si aliquid ex solemnibus deficiat, cum aequitas poscit, subveniendum est.*** If anything is deficient in formal requisites, where equity requires it, it should be supplied. ***Forma legalis forma essentialis.*** Legal form is essential form. ***Forma non observata, infertur adnullatio actus.*** If form is not observed, it is inferred that the act is a nullity.

FORM *(Document)*, ***noun*** blank, card, copy, data sheet, information blank, instrument, muniment, questionary, questionnaire, record, reference form, register, registry, report, standard letter, written document
ASSOCIATED CONCEPTS: legal forms, standard form

FORM, *verb* arrange, assemble, build, compose, *conformare*, construct, contrive, create, design, devise, embody, establish, *fabricari*, fabricate, fashion, *figurare*, forge, formulate, frame, give shape to, initiate, make, manufacture, materialize, mold, organize, produce, put together, shape, structure
ASSOCIATED CONCEPTS: form a corporation

FORM AN OPINION, *verb* adjudge, adjudicate, arbitrate, come to a conclusion, conclude, construe, decide, decree, deduce, derive, extrapolate, finalize, find, gather, hammer out, interpret, philosophize, rationalize, read, reason, rule, select, settle, understand, work out

FORMAL, *adjective* accepted, according to established form, affected, approved, businesslike, ceremonial, ceremonious, confirmed, conventional, customary, decorous, fixed, following established custom, following established form, following established rules, *formalis*, formalistic, in accordance with conventional requirements, inflexible, mannered, observant of form, official, polite, pompous, prescriptive, prim, proper, reserved, rigid, ritual, ritualistic, set, starched, stiff, stilted, systematic, traditional, unbending, uncompromising
ASSOCIATED CONCEPTS: formal acceptance, formal charges, formal defect, formal party

FORMALITY, *noun* ceremonial rite, ceremoniousness, ceremony, convention, conventionality, correctness, custom, decorum, established mode, etiquette, formalness, observance of form, outward form, prescribed form, propriety, punctilio, rigidity, rigidness, rite, ritual, *ritus*, rule of proceeding, set form, settled method, solemnity, stiffness, stiltedness
ASSOCIATED CONCEPTS: formalities in executing a will

FORMALIZE, *verb* conventionalize, form, give form to, give formal approval to, give formal status to, legalize, legitimate, legitimatize, make formal, make official, make valid, ritualize, shape, solemnize, validate
ASSOCIATED CONCEPTS: formalize an agreement

FORMAT, *noun* anatomy, appearance, arrangement, blueprint, completed form, composition, configuration, conformation, contents, contour, creation, design, figuration, finished form, form, layout, look, makeup, mode, model, plan, shape, sketch, structure, structuring, style, type, variety

FORMATION, *noun* arrangement, array, coinage, composition, concoction, configuration, *conformatio*, conformation, construction, creation, efformation, establishment, fabrication, figuration, *forma*, format, foundation, generation, genesis, institution, invention, layout, manufacture, order, organization, origination, production, structure, synthesis, systematization

FORMER, *adjective* antecedent, bygone, earlier, erstwhile, foregoing, late, past, preceding, preexistent, previous, prior, *pristinus*, quondam, retired, whilom
ASSOCIATED CONCEPTS: former adjudication, former conviction, former jeopardy, former marriage, former trial, former will

FORMIDABLE, *adjective* alarming, appalling, arduous, awe-inspiring, awesome, dangerous, deterring, difficult, disturbing, dreadful, exciting fear, fear-inspiring, fearful, fierce, *formidolosus*, frightening, frightful, hard to overcome, horrible, horrifying, huge, indomitable, menacing, overpowering, overwhelming, redoubtable, terrible, terrifying, threatening, unconquerable, unnerving, unyielding

FORMULA, *noun* avenue, axiom, canon, code, criterion, expedient, fixed expression, form, formulary, maxim, method, mode, model, phrase, postulate, prescribed procedure, prescription, principle, proposition, recipe, rubric, rule, standard, theorem, usage
ASSOCIATED CONCEPTS: formula instruction

FORMULATE, *verb* arrange, compose, devise, draft, draw up, efform, express in a formula, express in a systematic way, express in precise form, fabricate, fashion, forge, form, formularize, formulize, frame, give form to, hammer out, indite, produce, put into shape, put together, redact, reduce to a formula, set down, shape, state systematically, turn out

FORMULATION, *noun* composition, construction, creation, definition, delineation, description, determination, elaboration, expression, fashioning, formation, forming, framing, preparation, rule

FORSAKE, *verb* abandon, abdicate, abjure, cut off, desert, discard, disclaim, disown, disregard, distance, drop, dump, forget, forgo, give up, ignore, jettison, leave, maroon, neglect, quit, recant, reject, relinquish, renounce, repudiate, resign, retract, retreat, sacrifice, scrap, shed, shuck off, spurn, strand, surrender, throw away, vacate, withdraw, yield

FORSWEAR, *verb* abandon, abhor, abjure, abnegate, avoid, break off, cast aside, cast away, cast off, decline, deny, desert, disaccustom, discard, disclaim, discontinue, discountenance, disdain, dispense with, divest oneself, do without, drop, eschew, forgo, forsake, give up, lay aside, leave, let alone, omit, part with, proscribe, quit, refrain from, refuse, reject, relinquish, renounce, repel, repudiate, sacrifice, scorn, shun, spurn, toss aside, waive, withdraw from, yield

FORTHCOMING, *adjective* about to happen, advancing, anticipated, approaching, at hand, awaited, close at hand, coming, coming soon, destined, drawing near, due, ensuing, eventual, expected, fated, following, foreseeable, future, imminent, impending, inescapable, inevitable, in store, looming, near, nearing, nigh, on the agenda, on the docket, on the horizon, oncoming, pending, planned, predestined, predicted, projected, promised, prospective, scheduled, to come, ultimate, unavoidable, upcoming, yet to be
ASSOCIATED CONCEPTS: expectancy under a will

FORTHRIGHT, *adjective* blunt, bona fide, candid, direct, downright, emphatic, exact, explicit, factual, frank, genuine, honest, ingenuous, outspoken, plain-spoken, positive, scrupulous, simple, sincere, straight, straightforward, unadorned, unaffected, unambiguous, unembroidered, unequivocal, unmistakable, unvarnished, upright

FORTHWITH, *adverb* as soon as can be reasonably expected, at once, immediately, instantaneously, instantly, promptly, quickly, straightaway, with all reasonable speed, with reasonable dispatch

FORTIFY, *verb* assure, augment, authenticate, bolster, brace, buoy, buttress, cheer, confirm, comfort, document, embolden, encourage, endue, entrench, harden, hearten, help, inspirit, invigorate, make safe, nurture, protect, prop, ratify, reaffirm, reassure, reinforce, secure, shore up, stand by, stiffen, stimulate, strengthen, supplement, sustain, uphold

FORTUITOUS, *adjective* accidental, adventitious, casual, chance, circumstantial, coincidental, designless, *forte oblatus, fortuitus,* haphazard, happening by chance, involuntary, lucky, occurring by chance, providential, random, spontaneous, surprise, surprising, uncalculated, undesigned, undirected, unexpected, unforeseen, unintended, unintentional, unlooked for, unmeant, unmotivated, unplanned, unpredicted, unpremeditated, unrehearsed
ASSOCIATED CONCEPTS: fortuitous event

FORTUITY, *noun* accident, accidentalness, adventitiousness, adventure, casualness, casualty, chance, chance occurrence, coincidence, contingence, fluke, fortuitousness, happenstance, hazard, occurrence, opportunity, quirk, random luck, randomness, speculation, uncertainty
ASSOCIATED CONCEPTS: fortuitous collision, fortuitous event

FORTUNATE *(Accomplished),* ***adjective*** booming, doing quite well, flourishing, fortuitous, halcyon, happy, moneyed, of adequate means, on top of the world, prosperous, successful, thriving, triumphant, wealthy, well-heard, well-off

FORTUNATE *(Opportune),* ***adjective*** advantageous, auspicious, encouraging, favorable, fortuitous, hopeful, just in time, lucky, of promise, optimistic, perfect timing, prevailing, promising, propitious, providential, timely, triumphant, victorious, well-timed, winning

FORTUNE, *noun* abundance, accession, acquisitions, affluence, assets, bankroll, belongings, boon, capital, chattels, currency, effects, finances, funds, holdings, kismet, means, money, opulence, personal property, possessions, prosperity, reserve, resources, riches, savings, substance, substantial wherewithal, success, treasure, valuables, wealth, wherewithal, worth

FORUM *(Court),* ***noun*** assize, the bench, court of justice, court of law, courtroom, *forum,* judicatory, judicature, judicial tribunal, panel of judges, session of the court, tribunal
ASSOCIATED CONCEPTS: *forum non conveniens,* law of the forum

FORUM *(Medium),* ***noun*** agency, agent, channel, instrument, intermediary, means, means of expression, mechanism, method of communication, method of expression, mode of communication, vehicle

FORUM NON CONVENIENS, *noun* better alternative forum available, better choice of jurisdictions, in appropriate forum, inconvenient forum, more appropriate court, more convenient court
ASSOCIATED CONCEPTS: forum shopping, *lex fori, lis alibi pendens*

FORUM SHOPPING, *noun* forum picking, forum selection, litigant seeking the most favorable court, search for a better venue, search for a more favorable court, search for a more sympathetic court, selecting a court because it is likely to provide a more favorable judgment
ASSOCIATED CONCEPTS: forum selection clause

FORWARD, *verb* abet, accelerate, actuate, adjuvate, advance, aid, assist, drive, encourage, expedite, facilitate, favor, foster, further, hasten, help, impel, influence, inure, meliorate, move, nurture, precipitate, promote, propel, put in motion, quicken, subserve, succor, support

FOSTER, *verb* abet, advance, advocate, aid, *alere,* assist, befriend, breed, bring up, care for, cherish, coach, countenance, cultivate, encourage, favor, forward, further, harbor, help, hold dear, indulge, look after, minister to, nourish, nurse, nurture, *nutrire,* patronize, promote, protect, raise, rear, safeguard, stimulate, subserve, succor, support, sustain, take care of, tend, train, treasure, watch over, work for

FOUL PLAY, *noun* artifice, attack, chicanery, collusion, connivance, crime, deception, dishonesty, double-dealing, duplicity, fraud, guile, improper conduct, injustice, knavery, machination, misconduct, misdoing, perfidiousness, perfidy, transgression, treacherousness, treachery, trickery, underhanded dealing, unfair conduct, unfairness, violation

FOUND *(Decided),* ***adjective*** adjudged, agreed, approved, ascertained, command, confirmed, decreed, determined, determined on its merits, dictated, finalized, held, judged, mandated, mandatory, opined, ordained, ordered, prescribed, propounded, required, resolved, ruled, specified

FOUND *(Recovered),* ***adjective*** apparent, appeared, disclosed, discovered, dug-up, exposed, furnished, gained, gathered, procured, retrieved, revealed, seen, spotted, supplied, surfaced, uncovered, unearthed
ASSOCIATED CONCEPTS: bailment

FOUNDATION *(Basis),* ***noun*** base, bedrock, beginning, cornerstone, frame, framework, *fundamenta,* fundamental principle, groundwork, keystone, origin, premise, root, rudiment, *sedes,* skeleton, substructure, support, supporting structure, underlying principle, underpinning
ASSOCIATED CONCEPTS: foundation for evidence, foundation of a claim, foundation of a lien, laying a foundation for a document

FOUNDATION *(Organization),* ***noun*** association, charitable institution, charity, *conlegium,* eleemosynary corporation, endowed institution, endowment, establishment, fund invested for a charitable purpose, institute, institution, organization to aid the needy, organized body for charity, philanthropic institution, *sodalitas*
ASSOCIATED CONCEPTS: charitable foundation, not-for-profit organization

FOURTEENTH AMENDMENT, ***noun*** due process of law, legal fairness, legal safeguards, protection against deprivations, protection guarantees, protection of deprivation of accepted legal principles
ASSOCIATED CONCEPTS: procedural due process, right to confront accuser, substantive due process

FRACAS, ***noun*** affray, altercation, battle, bickering, blows, brawl, breach of the peace, broil, clash, commotion, conflict, contention, disagreement, discord, dispute, dissension, disturbance, fight, fray, fuss, jangle, jar, melee, noisy quarrel, outbreak, quarrel, riot, row, rowdiness, ruction, scramble, scuffle, set-to, squabble, squall, trouble, tumult, turmoil, tussle, uproar, wrangle
ASSOCIATED CONCEPTS: disorderly conduct, disturbing the peace

FRACKING, ***verb*** breaking, breaking up, cracking, disambiguation, dismembering, extracting, fracturing, fragmenting, hydraulic fracking, induced hydraulic fracking, injecting, injections in fractures in rocks, means to extract hydrocarbons, means to withdraw gases or petroleum, obtaining from the ear, ruining, splintering, splitting, withdrawing, wrecking

FRACTIOUS, ***adjective*** apt to quarrel, bad-tempered, bearish, bickering, cantankerous, captious, carping, caviling, choleric, churlish, complaining, contentious, contrary, crabby, cranky, cross, cross-grained, crusty, *difficilis,* difficult, disposed to cavil, disputatious, exceptious, excitable, faultfinding, fretful, grouchy, hot-tempered, ill-tempered, impatient, inclined to anger, indocile, inflammable, irascible, irritable, moodish, moody, *morosus,* peevish, perverse, pettish, petulant, quarrelsome, querulous, rebellious, recalcitrant, refractory, restive, sharp-tempered, short-tempered, shrewish, snappish, spleenful, spleeny, splenetic, stubborn, surly, temperamental, testy, touchy, unmanageable, unruly, untractable, waspish

FRAGMENT, ***verb*** atomize, blast, break, break off, break up, burst, bust, crack, crush, destroy, detonate, disintegrate, dismember, disrupt, explode, fracture, grind, pop, pulverize, reduce, rive, ruin, shatter, shiver, sliver, smash, splinter, split

FRAILTY, ***noun*** blemish, breakability, brittleness, debility, defect, defectiveness, deficiency, delicacy, demerit, destructibility, enervation, failing, failure, failure of strength, fallibility, fault, feebleness, flaw, flimsiness, foible, *fragilitas,* fragility, human weakness, imperfection, imperfectness, impotence, inadequacy, *infirmitas,* infirmity, instability, liability to err, loss of strength, peccability, proneness to error, shortcoming, unsoundness, unworthiness, vulnerability, vulnerableness, want of moral strength, weak point, weak side, weakness
ASSOCIATED CONCEPTS: human frailty

FRAME *(Mood),* ***noun*** animus, attitude, bent, character, condition, constitution, cue, disposition, fiber, grain, heart, makeup, mental constitution, mettle, mind, nature, proclivity, proneness, propensity, spirit, state of feeling, state of mind, streak, temper, temperament

FRAME *(Structure),* ***noun*** build, building, chassis, *compages,* construction, fabric, framework, groundwork, shell, skeleton, support

FRAME *(Charge falsely),* ***verb*** accuse falsely, accuse unfairly, accuse unjustly, bear false witness, blame falsely, blame unfairly, blame unjustly, charge unfairly, charge unjustly, conspire against, criminate falsely, criminate unfairly, criminate unjustly, denounce falsely, denounce unfairly, denounce unjustly, fabricate evidence, fake charges against, falsely call to account, hatch a plot against, impeach falsely, impeach unfairly, impeach unjustly, implicate falsely, implicate unfairly, implicate unjustly, incriminate unjustly, inculpate falsely, inculpate unfairly, inculpate unjustly, lay a plot, lie against, make false statements, perjure oneself, prearrange fraudulently, swear falsely, tell falsehoods about, tell lies about, trump up a charge, unfairly call to account, unjustly call to account, unjustly involve

FRAME *(Construct),* ***verb*** block out, build, carpenter, coin, compose, concoct, constitute, contrive, create, design, devise, draft, draw up, enframe, erect, fabricate, fashion, fit together, forge, form, formulate, hammer together, make, manufacture, map out, mold, organize, originate, piece together, plan, prepare, produce, put together, raise, set up, shape, sketch, systematize, write
ASSOCIATED CONCEPTS: frame an issue

FRAME *(Formulate),* ***verb*** arrange, cast, *componere,* conceive, *concipere,* concoct, contrive, create, design, devise, draft, draw up, excogitate, express, fashion, forge, form, formalize, hatch, invent, lay plans, make arrangements, map out, organize, originate, plan, produce, pull into shape, put into shape, scheme, set up, shape, sketch, take measures, take steps, think up, work up
ASSOCIATED CONCEPTS: frame a complaint

FRAME *(Prearrange),* ***verb*** arrange, charge falsely, conspire against, contrive, contrive a result, ensure a result, fake,

fake the evidence, incriminate unjustly, lie against, plan, plant the evidence, prearrange, prearrange fraudulently, predesign, predetermine, trump up, use false evidence
ASSOCIATED CONCEPTS: framed evidence, framed testimony, perjury

FRAME-UP, ***noun*** baseless charge, cabal, conspiracy, counterfeit evidence, faked charge, false charge, false evidence, false information, foul play, frame, hoax, intrigue, machination, perjured testimony, plant, trap, trickery, trumped-up charge, trumped-up story
ASSOCIATED CONCEPTS: perjury

FRAMEWORK, ***noun*** architecture, borderlines, boundaries, bounds, cap, ceiling, configuration, confines, delineation, design, edges, figure, foundation, fringe, infrastructure, limitations, lines, outline, parameters, perimeter, periphery, plan, plans, profile, schema, schematic, scheme, shape, shell, skeleton, structure

FRANCHISE *(License),* ***noun*** allowance, assent, authorization, charter, concession, consent, dispensation, droit, exemption, favor, grace, grant, immunity, indulgence, leave, monopoly, pass, permission, permit, prerogative, privilege, recognition, right, sanction, sufferance, tolerance
ASSOCIATED CONCEPTS: corporate franchise, federal franchise, franchise tax, grant of a franchise, irrevocable franchise, license, municipal franchise, perpetual franchises, personal franchise, public franchise, secondary franchise, special franchise

FRANCHISE *(Right to vote),* ***noun*** ballot, choice, discretion, enfranchisement, freedom of choice, liberty of choice, liberty to vote, option, prerogative, privilege, right of choice, right of representation, suffrage, vote, voting power

FRANK, ***adjective*** aboveboard, blunt, candid, clear, clear-cut, crystal clear, decent, direct, distinct, evident, explicit, express, forthright, honest, ingenuous, manifest, obvious, on the up and up, open, open and aboveboard, open and sincere, open and genuine, sincere, straight, straightforward, straight-out, unequivocal, unreserved, upfront
ASSOCIATED CONCEPTS: franking privilege

FRAUD, ***noun*** artfulness, artifice, beguilement, charlatanism, charlatanry, cheating, chicane, chicanery, *circumscriptio,* collusion, covin, cozenage, craftiness, crookedness, cunning, deceit, deceitful practice, deceitfulness, deception, deceptiveness, delusiveness, dishonesty, dissembling, dissimulation, double-dealing, dupery, duplicity, fabrication, *fallacia,* fallaciousness, false conduct, false representation, falseness, falsification, falsity, fraudulence, *fraus,* furtiveness, guile, improbity, insidiousness, intentional deception, intrigue, lack of probity, mendacity, misrepresentation, outwitting, perfidy, pretense, prevarication, quackery, ruse, sham, sneakiness, subreption, surreptitiousness, swindling, treachery, trickery, trickiness, underhandedness, unscrupulousness, untruthfulness, wiliness
ASSOCIATED CONCEPTS: action for fraud, actionable fraud, bad faith, collateral fraud, collusion, constructive fraud, debt created by fraud, deceit, discovery of fraud, extrinsic fraud, false representation, fraudulent misrepresentation, fraudulent representation, implied fraud, intrinsic fraud, mail fraud, material fraud, misrepresentation, positive fraud, presumptive fraud, public fraud, statute of frauds
FOREIGN PHRASES: ***Qui per fraudem agit frustra agit.*** What a man does fraudulently he does vainly. ***Vendens eandem rem duobus falsarius est.*** He is fraudulent who sells the same thing to two persons. ***Dolus auctoris non nocet successori.*** The fraud of a predecessor does not prejudice the successor. ***Fraus latet in generalibus.*** Fraud lies hidden in general expressions. ***Fraus est odiosa et non praesumenda.*** Fraud is odious and will not be presumed. ***Fraus et jus nunquam cohabitant.*** Fraud and justice never dwell together. ***Nulla pactione effici potest ut dolus praestetur.*** It cannot be provided in any contract that fraud can be practiced. ***Nemo ex dolo suo proprio relevetur, aut auxilium capiat.*** No one is relieved or gains an advantage by his own fraud. ***Nemo videtur fraudare eos qui sciunt et consentiunt.*** No one is considered as deceiving those who know and consent to his acts. ***Lata culpa dolo aequiparatur.*** Gross fault or negligence is equivalent to fraud. ***Ex dolo malo non oritur actio.*** No right of action can arise out of fraud. ***Non decipitur qui scit se decipi.*** A person is not deceived who knows he is being deceived. ***Fraus et dolus nemini patrocinari debent.*** Fraud and deceit should not excuse anyone. ***Dolus et fraus nemini patrocinentur; patrocinari debent.*** Deceit and fraud shall excuse or benefit no man; they themselves need to be excused. ***Dolum ex indiciis perspicuis probari convenit.*** Fraud should be established by clear showings of proof. ***Aliud est celare, aliud tacere.*** To conceal is one thing, to be silent is another. ***Dolus circuitu non pergator.*** Fraud is not purged by circuity. ***Quod alias bonum et justum est, si per vim vel fraudem petatur, malum et injustum efficitur.*** What otherwise is good and just, becomes bad and unjust if it is sought by force and fraud. ***Megna negligentia culpa est; magna culpa dolus est.*** Gross negligence is fault; gross fault is equivalent to a fraud. ***Dolo malo pactumse non servaturum.*** An agreement induced by fraud is not valid. ***Fraus est celare fraudem.*** It is fraud to conceal a fraud.

FRAUDULENT, ***adjective*** beguiling, bogus, cheating, conniving, contrary to fact, corrupt, counterfeited, crafty, crooked, cunning, deceitful, deceiving, deceptive, delusive, delusory, designing, destitute of good faith, destitute of integrity, devoid of truth, discreditable, dishonest, dishonorable, disingenuous, disreputable, *dolosus,* double-dealing, fake, faked, fallacious, false, falsified, feigned, finagling, forsworn, *fraudulentus,* furtive, guileful, iniquitous, insidious, meretricious, misleading, not honest, not true, perfidious, perjured, phony, scheming, sham, shifty, sneaky, spurious, surreptitious, treacherous, trickish, tricky, truthless, unauthentic, underhanded, unethical, unfaithful, ungenuine, unreal, unreliable, unscrupulous, untrue, untrustworthy, untruthful, unveracious, unvirtuous, void of truth, wanting in probity, wily, without probity, without truth
ASSOCIATED CONCEPTS: fraudulent concealment, fraudulent conveyance, fraudulent intent, fraudulent misrepresentation, fraudulent practice, fraudulent preferences, fraudulent representation, fraudulent transfer
FOREIGN PHRASES: ***Dolosus versatur in generalibus.*** A fraudulent person takes refuge in generalities.

FRAY, ***noun*** affray, battle, brabble, brawl, broil, clash, combat, commotion, contention, contest, disagreement, dispute, dissension, disturbance, fight, fracas, jangle, melee, *pugna,* quarrel, row, ruction, rumpus, scramble, scrimmage, scuffle, skirmish, strife, tumult, turmoil, uproar

FREE *(At no charge),* ***adjective*** complimentary, costing nothing, costless, expenseless, for nothing, given, given away, gratis, gratuitous, *gratuitus,* not charged for, provided without charge, unbought, uncharged, unpaid, untaxed, without cost
ASSOCIATED CONCEPTS: free on board

FREE *(Enjoying civil liberty),* ***adjective*** autonomic, autonomical, autonomous, democratic, emancipated, enfranchised, enjoying liberty, exempt from external authority, franchised, freed, independent, liberated, manumitted, not enslaved, not in bondage, not subject to regulation, removed from bondage, saved from bondage, self-directing, self-governing, self-ruling, sovereign, *sua sponte, sua voluntate,* unenslaved, unenthralled, unsubjected
ASSOCIATED CONCEPTS: free access, free press, free speech
FOREIGN PHRASES: ***A piratis aut latronibus capti liberi permanent.*** Persons taken by robbers remain free.

FREE *(Not restricted),* ***adjective*** at large, at liberty, cast loose, clear from, disengaged, immune from restriction, independent, let out, *liber,* liberated, loose, privileged, *solutus,* unattached, unbound, unbridled, uncaught, unchained, unchecked, uncoerced, unconfined, uncurbed, unentangled, unfastened, unfettered, unfixed, unhampered, unhindered, unimpeded, unobstructed, unpent, unprevented, unqualified, unreined, unrestrained, unshackled, unstopped, untied, untrammeled
ASSOCIATED CONCEPTS: free and voluntary, free enterprise, free from encumbrances, free press, free speech

FREE *(Relieved from a burden),* ***adjective*** absolved, acquitted, clear, cleared, delivered, disburdened, discharged, disembarrassed, disencumbered, disengaged, disentangled, dismissed, excused, exempted, exonerated, *immunis,* liberated, pardoned, paroled, quit of, ransomed, *re liber,* released, relieved, reprieved, rescued, rid, saved, set free, spared, unburdened, unencumbered, unimpeded, *vacuus*
ASSOCIATED CONCEPTS: free and clear, free from fault

FREE, ***verb*** absolve, acquit, affranchise, clear, come to the rescue, deliver, deliver from bondage, disburden, discharge, disembroil, disencumber, disengage, disentangle, disenthrall, dismiss, emancipate, enfranchise, exculpate, excuse, exempt, *eximere,* exonerate, extricate, forgive, franchise, give a reprieve, give absolution, grant a reprieve, grant amnesty, grant pardon, let escape, let go, let loose, let out, let out of prison, *liberare,* liberate, manumit, pardon, parole, privilege, purge, ransom, redeem, release, release from restraint, relieve, remit, rescue, save, set at large, set at liberty, set free, *solvere,* turn loose, unbind, unburden, unchain, unfasten, unfetter, unfix, unimprison, unleash, unmanacle, unshackle, untie, vindicate

FREE ENTERPRISE, ***noun*** at liberty, business enterprise, business immune from restriction, capitalism, capitalistic policies, capitalistic system, deregulation of business enterprise, free competition, free economy, free enterprise economy, free enterprise system, free trade, *laissez-faire* public policy, laissez-fairism, noninterference, nonintervention, noninvolvement, open market, private enterprise, private ownership, self-regulating market, unbound economic policy, unimpeded free competition, unobstructed free competition

FREE HAND, ***noun*** absolute discretion, authority, blank check, carte blanche, complete liberty, discretion, every option, freedom, full authority, full delegated authority, full power, full range, latitude, leeway, maneuvering space, total discretion, unbridled authority, unbridled discretion, unhampered authority

FREE TRADE, ***noun*** absence of government control, autonomous business, business at liberty, capitalism, decontrolled marketplace, democratic business environment, deregulated business, deregulation, economic autonomy, emancipated business place, fair trade, free business dealings, free commercial enterprise, free competition, free enterprise, free interchange of goods, free intercourse of goods, free market, free mercantile business, free mercantile relations, free movement of goods, free multilateral trade, immune from restriction, independent, *laissez-faire,* noninterference in trade, nonintervention in trade, noninvolvement in trade, open market, reciprocal trade, trade liberalism, unbounded trade, unbridled trade, unconstrained trade, uncurbed trade, unfettered commerce, unfettered commercial affairs, unfettered merchandising, unhampered trade, unhindered trade, unimpeded trade, unobstructed trade, unregimented trade, unregulated trade, unrestrained business intercourse, unrestrained trade, unrestricted trade, unshackled trade, without trade barriers
ASSOCIATED CONCEPTS: balanced trade, comparative advantage, international barter, protectionism

FREEDOM, ***noun*** affranchisement, *arbitrium,* autonomy, civil liberty, decontrol, deliverance, discharge, disengagement, disenthrallment, disimprisonment, emancipation, empowerment, enfranchisement, entitlement, exemption, exemption from external control, exemption from restraint, extrication, franchise, franchisement, independence, latitude, leave, leeway, legal right, liberation, *libertas,* liberty, license, *licentia,* noninterference, permit, political independence, prerogative, privilege, redemption, relaxation of control, release, right to decide, room, self-determination, self-government, self-rule, unconstraint, unfettering, uninhibitedness, unrestraint
ASSOCIATED CONCEPTS: freedom from fault, freedom of action, freedom of assembly, freedom of conscience, freedom of contract, freedom of press, freedom of religion, freedom of speech, freedom of thought, freedom of trade, freedom of worship
FOREIGN PHRASES: ***Impius et crudelis judicandus est qui libertati non favet.*** He should be adjudged impious and cruel who does not favor liberty. ***Libertas non recipit aestimationem.*** Freedom does not admit a valuation. ***Libertas est naturalis facultas ejus quod cuique facere libet, nisi quod de jure aut vi prohibetur.*** Liberty is a person's natural power which permits one to do as he pleases. ***Libertas inestimabilis res est.*** Liberty is a thing of inestimable value.

FREEDOM OF ASSOCIATION, ***noun*** authority, authorization, autonomy, blanket permission, choice, civil liberty, constitutional freedom, decontrol, emancipation, free will, freedom of affiliation, freedom of alignment, freedom of alliance, inclusion, incorporation, independence, *laissez-faire,* latitude, liberation, liberty, license, openness, participation, privilege, self-determination, self-direction, unconditional authority, unconstrained use, unrestrained use, unrestricted use
ASSOCIATED CONCEPTS: First Amendment protection, individual freedoms, individual liberties

FREEDOM OF CHOICE, ***noun*** alternatives, artistic license, authority, blanket permission, call, carte blanche, civil liberty, decontrols, deregulation, discretion, emancipation, franchise, free choice, free will, lack of censorship, *laissez-faire,* latitude, liberation, liberty, license, noninterference, nonintervention, openness, option, permission, prerogative, privilege, pre abortion, pre choice, right of choice, right of selection, rights, self-determination, self-direction, unbridled discretion, unconditional authority, unconstraint, unrestraint, unrestricted use

FREEDOM OF INFORMATION REQUEST, *noun* ask for information, communication requesting information, disclosure request, elicit information, FOIL request, formal demand for information, request for data, request for documents, request for information, request for records, request for specifics

FREEDOM OF PRESS, *noun* authority of the press, autonomy of the press, blanket permission for the press, broadcast freedom, civil liberty, commentators, communications, communications industry, constitutional freedom, contributors, correspondents, First Amendment rights, free commentary, free journalism, free public communication, freedom of expression, freedom to publish, freedom to write, full franchise of expression, lack of censorship, liberty, license, noninterference, nonintervention, openness, privilege, self-determination of the press, unbridled freedom to publish, unrestricted freedom of expression, unrestricted freedom of the press

FREEDOM TO DISCHARGE, *noun* at the will of the employer, at will employment, discretionary employment without the necessity of reasons, employment at will, freedom to discharge without grounds, freedom to discharge without reasons, freedom to fire
ASSOCIATED CONCEPTS: just cause employees, morally reprehensive reasons, morally wrong reasons

FREEHOLD, *noun* acres, domain, estate, estate for life, estate in fee, fee simple, feud, fief, hereditament, *immune,* interest in real property, land, landed estate, landed property, life estate, *praedium liberum,* property, real property, realty, territory, vested interest in land

FREIGHT, *noun* article of commerce, cargo, carload, consignment, freightage, goods, lading, load, merchandise, *onus,* packages, pay load, shipment

FRENETIC, *adjective* berserk, crazed, crazy, deranged, excited, feverish, frantic, frenzied, *furens,* furibund, hysterical, *insanus,* maniacal, overwrought, perturbed, possessed, raving, restless, unsettled, *vesanus,* worked up, wrought up

FREQUENCY, *noun* common occurrence, commonness, continuity, *crebritas,* cycle, frequence, *frequentia,* periodicity, prevalence, rate, recurrence, regularity, regularity of recurrence, repetition, repetitiveness, succession, usualness

FREQUENT, *adjective* accustomed, common, consuetudinal, consuetudinary, *creber,* customary, familiar, *frequens,* habitual, numberless, numerous, oft-repeated, often done, persistent, prevalent, reiterative, repeated, repetitive, usual

FRICTION, *noun* abrasion, antagonism, antipathy, attrition, chafing, clash, clashing, collision, conflict, contention, contravention, controversy, counteraction, disaccord, disagreement, discord, disharmony, dissension, dissent, dissonance, erosion, fretting, friction, grating, grinding, hostility, inflammation, interference, irritation, jangle, lack of harmony, opposition, polarity, quarrel, renitency, resistance, strained relations, strife, tension, ulceration, unharmoniousness

FRIEND, *noun* acquaintance, adherent, advocate, ally, associate, backer, benefactor, cohort, colleague, companion, comrade, confidant, confederate, confrère, crony, defender, faithful companion, favorer, friend-in-need, partisan, partner, patron, proponent, supporter, sympathizer
ASSOCIATED CONCEPTS: ***Amicus curiae.*** Friend of the court.

FRIENDLY, *adjective* accessible, affable, affectionate, agreeable, amiable, amicable, auspicious, benevolent, close, companionable, compatible, congenial, cooperative, cordial, devoted, empathetic, encouraging, familiar, fast, favorable, favorably disposed, firm, fond, fraternal, generous, genial, gracious, harmonious, hearty, helpful, homey, hospitable, kind, kind-hearted, loyal, obliging, openhearted, peaceable, pleasant, receptive, sociable, staunch, sympathetic, warm hearted, welcoming

FRIGHT, *noun* affright, agitation, alarm, anxiety, apprehension, consternation, cowardice, dismay, disquietude, dread, extreme fear, fear, fear of danger, horror, intimidation, misgiving, panic, *pavor,* phobia, scare, sudden terror, *terror,* trepidation

FRIGHTEN, *verb* affright, alarm, browbeat, bully, bullyrag, cow, daunt, deter, disquiet, *exterrere,* fright, give cause for alarm, horrify, intimidate, menace, panic, petrify, raise apprehension, scare, shock, shock with sudden fear, startle, strike with overwhelming fear, terrify, terrorize, threaten, unnerve

FRIGHTFUL, *adjective* abhorrent, abominable, appalling, atrocious, awful, contemptible, deplorable, despicable, detestable, disastrous, dreadful, foul, frightening, ghastly, ghoulish, harrowing, heinous, hideous, horrendous, horrid, horrifying, loathsome, macabre, monstrous, nauseating, obnoxious, odious, offensive, outrageous, regrettable, repellent, reprehensible, repulsive, revolting, shameful, shocking, terrible, terrifying, vile, villainous

FRINGE, *noun* border, brink, edge, extremity, fimbriation, frontier, furthest point, furthest reach, limit, margin, outskirt, parameter, penumbra, periphery, skirt, verge

FRISK, *verb* check, conduct a search, examine, examine closely, examine intently, explore, hunt, hunt through, inspect, investigate, *lascivire,* look into, look over, look through, peer into, poke into, probe, pry into, rake through, review, *salire,* scan, scour, scrutinize, search one's pockets, search through, seek, subject to scrutiny
ASSOCIATED CONCEPTS: reasonable belief that safety requires a patting down, search, stop, and frisk

FRIVOLOUS, *adjective* childish, flighty, flimsy, flippant, giddy, immaterial, *inanis,* insignificant, *levis,* light, light-minded, meaningless, minor, *nugax,* of little weight, of no account, paltry, petty, senseless, shallow, silly, slight, superficial, trifling, trivial, unimportant, unserious, unworthy of serious notice, worthless
ASSOCIATED CONCEPTS: frivolous answer, frivolous appeal, frivolous cause of action, frivolous claims, frivolous pleading

FROLIC, *noun* amusement, antic, caper, carousal, drollery, entertainment, escapade, fun, gaiety, gambol, jocoseness, jollity, joviality, lark, merriment, merrymaking, mirth, play, pleasantry, recreation, rollick, romp, vagary
ASSOCIATED CONCEPTS: detour and frolic

FROLIC, *verb* act up, amuse oneself, caper, carouse, cavort, dance, disport, enjoy oneself, frisk, gambol, have a good time, have fun, joke, paint the town red, play, revel, rollick, romp, sport

FRONT *(Anterior),* ***noun*** area in foreground, beginning, closest area, designated area in the foreground, exterior, facade, face, foreground, forepart, frontage, frontal area, head
ASSOCIATED CONCEPTS: road frontage, street frontage

FRONT *(Concealed criminal operation),* ***noun*** alter ego, concealed business, cover, cover up, criminal operation, disguise, felonious operation, fraudulent operation, illegitimate operation, illicit operation, lawless operation, masked operation, pretense, sham, sham device, sham means, sham vehicle, unlawful operation, unlicensed operation, untoward operation
ASSOCIATED CONCEPTS: illegal fencing operation

FRONTAGE, ***noun*** border along the road, border of the property, edge of the property, front boundary of the land, front of a lot, front of a tract of land, front of the land, front of the property, land at the street, outer limits of a property, outskirts of the property, periphery of a property, property at the curb, side of a property along the periphery, side of a property at the front, the outer line of a tract of land
ASSOCIATED CONCEPTS: zoning

FRONTIER, ***noun*** ambit, border, borderland, bound, boundary, boundary line, circumjacencies, compass, *confinium,* demarcation line, edge, *faubourg, finis,* fringe, limit, limitations, line of demarcation, march, outer district, outer edge, outer part, outlines, outlying area, outlying borders, outlying districts, outpost, outskirts, perimeter, periphery, remote district, rim, termination

FROWARD, ***adjective*** cantankerous, captious, contrary, contumacious, *contumax,* cross, crusty, *difficilis,* difficult, disobedient, fractious, headstrong, indocile, insubmissive, insubordinate, intractable, irascible, irritable, moody, obstinate, peevish, *pertinax,* perverse, petulant, querulous, rebellious, refractory, restive, splenetic, stubborn, surly, troublesome, unaccommodating, uncooperative, ungovernable, unmanageable, unruly, unyielding, wayward, willful, willfully contrary

FRUCTIFY, ***verb*** ameliorate, bear, bear fruit, beget, blossom, bring forth, conceive, cultivate, enrich, fatten, fecundate, fertilize, flourish, generate, impregnate, inseminate, irrigate, make fruitful, make productive, pollinate, procreate, produce, proliferate, propagate, reproduce, spermatize, thrive

FRUGAL, ***adjective*** abstemious, careful, cautious, chary, cheap, conservative, economical, economy-minded, *frugi, parcus,* parsimonious, penny-conscious, provident, prudent, restrained, sparing, spartan, stinting, thrifty, unwasteful

FRUGALITY, ***noun*** abstention, abstinence, austerity, carefulness, chariness, economizing, economy, frugalness, moderation, parsimoniousness, parsimony, plain living, prudence, retrenchment, scrimping, skimping, sparingness, temperance, thrift, thriftiness, unwastefulness

FRUITION, ***noun*** accomplishment, achievement, attainment, consummation, effectuation, execution, flowering, *fructus,* fulfillment, gratification, implementation, performance, production, realization, satisfaction, success
ASSOCIATED CONCEPTS: accrual of a cause of action, maturity of a debt

FRUSTRATE, ***verb*** abort, *ad inritum redigere, ad vanum,* annul, baffle, balk, be obstructive, bring to nought, cancel, check, checkmate, confound, counter, counteract, cripple, defeat, disappoint, disconcert, discourage, foil, forestall, hinder, invalidate, let down, mar, neutralize, nullify, obstruct, oppose, outwit, override, prevent, render invalid, render null and void, spoil, stultify, stymie, thwart, undermine, undo
ASSOCIATED CONCEPTS: frustrate performance of a contract, frustration of purpose

FRUSTRATION, ***noun*** abortive attempt, defeat, failure, foil, futile effort, hindrance, impediment, inability of performance, inability to be completed, incapacity, interference, interruption, noncompletion, nonfulfillment, nonperformance, obstruction, prevention, prevention of accomplishment, thwarted expectation, thwarting, unsatisfied hopes, unsuccessfulness
ASSOCIATED CONCEPTS: commercial frustration, frustration of purpose, frustration under a contract, impossibility of performance

FUGITIVE, ***noun*** absconder, avoider, defaulter, deserter, escaped prisoner, escapee, escaper, evader, fleer, *fugitivus,* hunted person, levanter, one who flees, person who flees justice, prisonbreaker, *profugus,* refugee prisoner, renegade, runagate, runaway
ASSOCIATED CONCEPTS: fugitive from justice, fugitive warrant

FULFILL, ***verb*** abide by, accomplish, achieve, adhere to, answer, be faithful to, be sufficient, bring about, bring to completion, bring to pass, carry into effect, complete, comply with, consummate, discharge, do, effect, effectuate, *efficere,* execute, *explere,* fill, finish, follow, heed, *implere,* keep, live up to, make good, meet, obey, observe, perfect, perform, realize, redeem, satisfy, serve, suffice
ASSOCIATED CONCEPTS: fulfillment of trust purpose

FULL, ***adjective*** abounding, abundant, affluent, baggy, brimful, brimming over, charged, chock-full, cloyed, complete, comprehensive, crammed, detailed, entire, entirely occupied, exhaustive, filled, filled to utmost capacity, flowing, flush, fraught, glutted, gorged, imbued, *integer,* laden, loaded, mature, maximum, occupied, overflowing, packed, plenary, *plenus,* plethoric, replete, *repletus,* resonant, rich, sated, satiated, satisfied, saturated, soaked, stuffed, surfeited, swollen, teeming, total, unabridged, unstinted, well-provided, well-stocked, well-supplied, whole
ASSOCIATED CONCEPTS: full amount, full and true value, full cash value, full consideration, full control, full faith and credit, full hearing, full opportunity to be heard, full payment, full performance, full satisfaction, full settlement, full-time employment

FULL-FLEDGED, ***adjective*** all-encompassing, all-inclusive, all-out, broad, complete, comprehensive, entire, every possible combination, extensive, liberal, maximum, thorough, total, unabridged, unbridled, unrestrained, vast, voluminous, whole, without abridgment, without limitation, without reduction, without restraint

FULL-SCALE, ***adjective*** all-encompassing, all-inclusive, broad, complete, entire, extensive, jealously, maximum, total, unbridled, unrestrained, vigorously, whole, with every concentrated effort, with every effort, with force, without control, without reduction, without restraint

FULL THROTTLE, ***adjective*** act on, all out, as fast as possible, at full speed, commence, continued at maximum, flow, following at full throttle, forging ahead, gathering steam, get in high gear, going forward, in full gear, in high gear, making headway, making progress, maximum strength, moving ahead, pressing on, progressing, pushing on, rolling on, springing from, streaming

FULLY EXECUTED *(Consummated),* ***adjective*** completed, discharged, fulfilled, realized

FULLY EXECUTED *(Signed),* ***adjective*** authenticated, authorized, binding, completed, executed, legitimized

FULLY SECURED, ***adjective*** backed-up, bonded, certified, covered, guaranteed, hypothecated, insured, pledged, mortgaged, warranted

FULMINATE, ***verb*** blame, blast, bluster, burst, cast blame, censure, condemn, criticize harshly, decry, denounce, denunciate, detonate, disapprove of, discharge, disfavor, erupt, explode, go off, not approve, object to, oppose, potent, reprehend, thunder, trigger, upbraid

FUN, ***noun*** amusement, carousing, conviviality, dalliance, delight, distraction, diversion, enjoyment, entertainment, festivity, fling, frolic, gaiety, gambol, hobby, jest, joy, lark, laugh, merriment, merrymaking, pastime, play, pleasance, pleasure, recreation, relaxation, revel, reveling, rollick, romp, sport, spree

FUNCTION, ***noun*** appropriate activity, assignment, business, chore, design, duty, employment, exploitation, mission, *munus,* occupation, office, *officium,* performance, purpose, pursuit, responsibility, role, task, usage, use, utility, work
ASSOCIATED CONCEPTS: discretionary function, executive function, government function, judicial function, legislative function, political function, quasi-judicial function

FUNCTION, ***verb*** achieve, act, act effectively, answer a purpose, avail, be effective, be in operation, be useful, benefit, carry on, carry out, effectuate, execute, have effect, manage, operate, perform, render a service, run, serve, work

FUNCTIONAL, ***adjective*** adequate, advantageous, applicable, applied, convenient, effective, effectual, efficacious, efficient, employable, expedient, fit for use, gainful, handy, helpful, in action, in operation, in order, instrumental, invaluable, operable, operant, operational, operative, practicable, practical, pragmatic, profitable, sensible, serviceable, suitable for use, usable, useful, utile, utilitarian, utilizable, valuable, workable, working
ASSOCIATED CONCEPTS: functional claim, functional depreciation, functional disability

FUNCTIONARY, ***noun*** administrator, bureaucrat, commissary, commissioner, delegate, dignitary, office holder, officer, official, representative, syndic

FUND, ***noun*** accumulation, assets, capital, *copia,* endowment, foundation, fount, hoard, investment, mine, nest egg, *pecunia,* pool, reserve, reservoir, resources, savings, spring, stock, store, sum of money, supply, well
ASSOCIATED CONCEPTS: available fund, cash funds, commingling of funds, contingent fund, endowment fund, escrow fund, guaranty fund, insurance fund, joint fund, misapplication of funds, misappropriation of funds, permanent funds, reserve fund, residuary fund, trust fund

FUND, ***verb*** accommodate, accumulate, afford, allot, amass, apportion, bank, be a benefactor, bestow, cache, collect, conserve, contribute, deposit, dispense, dole, donate, endow, endue, equip, finance, furnish, garner, give, give money, grant, hand out, hoard, invest money, keep, keep in reserve, lay in store, lay up, maintain, pay, pay for, present, present money, preserve, provide, provide for, provide money, provide the wherewithal, provision, purvey, reserve, retain, save, save up, settle upon, spare, stock, stockpile, store, subsidize, supply, sustain, treasure, yield

FUNDAMENTAL, ***adjective*** basal, basic, basilar, basilary, cardinal, central, constitutional, elemental, elementary, essential, inchoative, indispensable, key, necessary, needed, organic, primary, *primus,* principal, *principalis,* required, requisite, rudimentary, structural, underlying, vital
ASSOCIATED CONCEPTS: fundamental change, fundamental error, fundamental issue, fundamental law, fundamental question, fundamental right

FUNDING, ***noun*** aid, allotment, appropriation, award, backing, bankroll, capital, charity, endowment, establishment, financing, foundation, gift, grant, infusion, inheritance, investment, means, nourishment, patronization, promotion, settlement, sponsorship, stakes, subsidy, support, underwriting

FUNDS, ***noun*** assets, bank account, capital, cash, currency, economic success, finance, income, liquid assets, lucre, means, money, pecuniary resources, pelf, personalty, possessions, principal, proceeds, property, revenue, specie, stocks and bonds, substance, treasure, wealth, wherewithal
ASSOCIATED CONCEPTS: Social Security Fund, Unemployment Compensation Fund, Welfare Fund, Workers' Compensation Fund

FUNNY, ***adjective*** amusing, bizarre, blithesome, campy, comedic, comic, comical, crazy, diverting, droll, farcical, hilarious, humorous, hysterical, incredibly comical, jocose, jocular, jocund, jokey, jolly, jovial, kooky, laughable, ludicrous, merry, outrageous, peculiar, ridiculous, riotous, risible, screaming, sidesplitting, uproarious, whimsical, witty, wonderfully amusing, wry

FURIOUS, ***adjective*** concentrated, crazed, crazy, delirious, demented, emotional, excessive, exorbitant, extravagant, extreme, ferocious, feverish, fierce, frantic, frenetic, frenzied, high-pressured, hostile, immoderate, inordinate, intense, intensive, irrational, lavish, lunatic, mad, maniacal, overmuch, rabid, severe, unconscionable, undue, upset, vehement, violent, wild

FURLOUGH, ***noun*** absence, *commeatus,* holiday, leave, leave of absence, leisure, liberty, recess, respite, rest, suspension of work, time off, vacation

FURNISH, ***verb*** accommodate, accouter, afford, appoint, apportion, arm, bestow, contribute, enable, endow, endue, equip, fit out, gear, give, grant, indulge, *instruere,* lavish, outfit, present, produce, provide, provision, purvey, rig, stock, *suppeditare,* supply, yield
ASSOCIATED CONCEPTS: furnish proof, labor furnished, material furnished, work furnished

FUROR, ***noun*** ado, agitation, broil, clamor, commotion, craze, disruption, disturbance, eruption, excitement, ferment, ferocity, fervency, fever, flare-up, fracas, fray, frenzy, fury, fuss, hysteria, madness, maelstrom, mania, outbreak, outburst, pandemonium, passion, pother, rabidity, rage, rumpus, stir, storm, tempest, tumult, turbulence, turmoil, upheaval, uproar, wildness

FURTHER, ***adverb*** a greater extent, additionally, at a further point, at a more distant point, besides, beyond, else, extra, farther, furthermore, in addition, more, plus, supplementary, to a greater extent
ASSOCIATED CONCEPTS: continuance, further consideration, further conveyance, further hearing, further notice, further proceeding, further security, further waste, furtherance

FURTHER, *verb* advance, contribute to, facilitate, favor, forward, foster, impel, motivate, move, promote

FURTHERANCE, *noun* advancement, advocacy, aid, amelioration, assistance, behalf, betterment, championship, change for better, cooperation, course, defense, development, favor, gain, growth, headway, help, improvement, lift, longevity, preferment, progress, progression, promotion, reinforcement, raise, rise, succor, uptrend
ASSOCIATED CONCEPTS: furtherance of a crime, in the furtherance of the business of the employer, in the furtherance of the discharge of duties

FURTHERMORE, *adverb* additionally, along with, also, at the same time, besides, beyond, by the same token, in addition, in conjunction with, likewise, moreover, over and above, then again, together with, too, what's more

FURTIVE, *adjective* backstair, catlike, clandestine, cloaked, concealed, covert, crafty, cunning, deceitful, evasive, feline, *furtivus,* hangdog, hidden, indirect, insidious, masked, mysterious, private, secret, secretive, shady, shifty, shrouded, sly, sneaking, sneaky, stealthy, subtle, surreptitious, thievish, undercover, underground, underhand, undisclosed, unobtrusive, unrevealed, unseen, veiled

FUSE, *verb* adhere, admix, agglutinate, amalgamate, assimilate, band together, blend, blend together, bond, cement, coadunate, coalesce, combine, combine together, commingle, compile, compound, condense, confederate, conglomerate, conjoin, connect, consolidate, embody, federate, flux, galvanize, incorporate, interfuse, intermix, join, league, lock, lump together, meld, melt together, merge, mingle, mix, refine, run, smelt, solder, unify, unite, weld

FUSTIAN, *adjective* bombastic, declamatory, flatulent, *gausape,* grandiloquent, grandiose, high-flown, high-sounding, inflated, mouthy, orotund, pompous, pretentious, ranting, swollen, tumid, turgid

FUSTIAN, *noun* affectation, altiloquence, bombast, bombastic language, bombastry, declamation, empty talk, euphuism, *gausape,* high-sounding words, idle speech, inflated language, inflated speech, inflated style, magniloquence, orotundity, pomposity, pretentious speech, rant, rhetoric, rodomontade, sesquipedalianism, swollen language, turgid language, verbiage, verbosity, wordiness

FUTILE, *adjective* abortive, barren, bootless, feckless, fruitless, *futilis,* gainless, hopeless, *inanis,* ineffective, ineffectual, inefficacious, insignificant, inutile, nugatory, otiose, profitless, resultless, unavailing, unfruitful, unimportant, unproductive, unprofitable, unsubstantial, unsuccessful, useless, vain, valueless, *vanus,* wasted, worthless
ASSOCIATED CONCEPTS: failure to exhaust a futile remedy
FOREIGN PHRASES: ***Lex neminem cogit ad vana seu inutilia peragenda.*** The law compels no one to do futile or useless things. ***Lex nil facit frustra, nil jubet frustra.*** The law does not do anything nor commands anyone to do anything which would be futile.

FUTILITY, *noun* barrenness, counterproductivity, emptiness, foolishness, fruitlessness, impossibility, ineffectiveness, ineffectualness, insufficiency, lack, profitlessness, thoughtlessness, unproductivity, uselessness, want, wastefulness, witlessness

FUTURE, *adjective* advancing, anticipated, approaching, arriving, close, close at hand, coming, designate, destined, ensuing, eventual, expected, fated, following, foreseeable, forthcoming, *futurus,* imminent, impending, inevitable, later, likely, looked toward, looming, near, near at hand, next, nigh, pending, planned, planned for, possible, *posterus,* predestined, predicted, probable, prospective, scheduled, sequent, subsequent, succeeding, to be, to come, ultimate, upcoming
ASSOCIATED CONCEPTS: after acquired property, future acquired property, future advances, future contingency, future damages, future debt, future earnings, future estates, future expectancy, future interests, future loss of earnings, future payments, future profits, future services

GAG RULE, *noun* judicial bar of communication, judicial cessation of communication, judicial preclusion of communication, judicial prevention of communication, judicial prohibition of communication, judicial prohibition of expression, judicial suspension of communication, judicial termination of communication, order of silence

GAIN, *noun* accomplishment, accretion, accrual, achievement, advancement, amplification, appreciation, attainment, augmentation benefit, betterment, enlargement, expansion, growth, heightening, improvement, increase, increment, master, obtainment, procurement, productiveness, profit, success, upturn, winning

ASSOCIATED CONCEPTS: gain derived from capital, gain derived from profits, net gain

GAIN, ***verb*** accept, accomplish, achieve, acquire, adopt, advance, assume, attain, avail, bag, be better for, be improved by, benefit, *capere,* capture, cash in on, clear, collect, come by, come into, *consequi,* derive, draw, earn, extract, flourish, gather, get, get possession of, glean, grasp, harvest, improve, learn, *lucrari,* make, make a profit, make capital, make money, master, move forward, net, obtain, pick up, procure, profit, prosper, realize, reap, reap profits, reap rewards, reap the benefit of, receive, secure, succeed, take, thrive, turn to account, win, yield returns
ASSOCIATED CONCEPTS: accrued gain, activity for gain, annual gain, business gain, capital gains, economic gain, gainful employment, long-term capital gain, net gain, pecuniary gain, private gain, short-term capital gain
FOREIGN PHRASES: ***Nemo debet aliena jactura locupletari.*** No one ought to gain by another's loss.

GAINFUL, ***adjective*** advantageous, beneficial, fertile, fruitful, lucrative, *lucrosus,* money-making, paying, productive, profitable, *quaestuosus,* remunerative, rewarding, useful, valuable, well-paying, worthwhile
ASSOCIATED CONCEPTS: gainful employment

GAINSAY, ***verb*** act against, be contrary, conflict with, contest, contradict, contravene, controvert, counter, deny, disaffirm, disagree, disallow, disavow, disclaim, dispute, dissent, forbid, impugn, negate, oppose, oppugn, protest, rebut, refuse to admit, refute, reject, repudiate, speak against, take exception to, take issue with, traverse

GALVANIZE, ***verb*** animate, arouse, astonish, astound, confound, dumbfound, electrify, enkindle, excite, fluster, foment, impress, infuse new life into, inspire, inspirit, overwhelm, petrify, put about, quicken, shock, spur on, stagger, startle, stimulate, stir, strike dumb, stun, stupefy, thrill, turn one's head, wake

GAMBLE, ***verb*** *alea ludere,* bet, chance, lay a wager, lay money on, play for money, play for stakes, practice gaming, risk, speculate, stake, take a chance, try one's luck, wager
ASSOCIATED CONCEPTS: bookmaking, gambling apparatus, gambling device, gambling houses

GAME CHANGE, ***noun*** adjustment, alteration, amendment, c-change, change in direction, change in focus, changeover, conversion, entire makeover, major alteration, major change, major difference, major modification, major transformation, metamorphosis, modulation, monumental difference, refashioning, reform, remodel, revamp, review, revision, revolutionary change, shift, supplantation, transformation, transition

GAMUT, ***noun*** breadth, circuit, compass, complete sequence, complete series, extent, length, limit, progression, range, reach, scope, span, stretch, sweep, vastness, whole range, width

GARBLE, ***verb*** bewilder, befuddle, blur, cloud, complicate, confound, confuse, discombobulate, fog, jumble, mix up, muddle, mystify, nonplus, obfuscate, obscure, perplex, scramble
ASSOCIATED CONCEPTS: plain language

GARISH, ***adjective*** bedizened, blatant, blinding, cheap, cheaply magnificent, coarse, crude, dazzling, flamboyant, flashy, flaunting, gaudy, glaring, glittering, in bad taste, indelicate, loud, obtrusive, ostentatious, pompous, pretentious, showy, spangled, tawdry, vivid, vulgar

GARNER, ***verb*** accumulate, acquire, aggregate, amass, assemble, bank, bring together, cache, collect, compile, *condere,* deposit, fund, gather, group, hoard, keep in reserve, muster, reserve, save, stock, stockpile, store, stow, treasure

GARNISH, ***verb*** appropriate, attach, commandeer, confiscate, *decorare,* distrain, execute, *exornare,* impound, *instruere,* levy upon, seize, seize and appropriate, sequester, sequestrate

GARNISHMENT, ***noun*** annexation, appropriation, confiscation, dispossession, distraint, distress, divestiture, execution, expropriation, impoundment, levy, seizure
ASSOCIATED CONCEPTS: attachment, enforcement of judgments, equitable garnishment, execution, garnishment of a debt, lien

GARRULOUS, ***adjective*** babbling, chattering, chatty, communicative, declamatory, effusive, eloquent, gabby, glib, gossiping, gossipy, indiscreet, leaky, long-winded, loquacious, prattling, talkative, tattling, verbose, wordy

GATHER *(Accumulate),* ***verb*** accrue, aggregate, assume, batch, collect, compile, concentrate, congregate, conjoin, connect, convene, cull, deduce, deduct, extract, gain, garner, gather, harvest, hold, join, mass, obtain, pick, pluck, procure, read, reap, secure, store

GATHER *(Compile),* ***verb*** amass, assemble, bring together, cluster, glean, group, harvest, hoard, marshal, meet, mobilize, muster, pick, pluck, rally, secure, stockpile

GATHERING, ***noun*** accumulation, aggregate, aggregation, amassment, assemblage, assembly, caucus, chamber, collection, company, compilation, concentration, conclave, conference, confluence, conflux, congregation, convention, convergence, convocation, cumulation, forgathering, gang, ingathering, mass, meet, meeting, mob, mobilization, multitude, muster, pack, rendezvous, selection, throng, turnout

GAUGE, ***verb*** adjudge, appraise, appreciate, arrive at a conclusion, ascertain, assess, calculate, calibrate, class, compute, consider, decide, deduce, determine, draw an inference, estimate, evaluate, exercise judgment, fathom, form an estimate, form an opinion, imagine, judge, make an estimation, measure, *metiri,* opine, rank, rate, set a value on, size up, suppose, surmise, survey, valorize, valuate, value, weigh

GAVEL, ***noun*** club, device to gain order, hammer, instrument of control, means of control, symbol of office, mallet, wooden mallet
ASSOCIATED CONCEPTS: parliamentary procedure

GAY, ***noun*** homoerotic, homophile, homosexual, lesbian, life partner, same sex partner
ASSOCIATED CONCEPTS: gay marriage

GAY MARRIAGE, ***adjective*** homosexual, homosexually bonded, homosexually joined, homosexually married, lesbian bonded, lesbian joined, lesbian married, same sex, same sex wedded
ASSOCIATED CONCEPTS: gay rights

GENDER, *noun* female, category, class, classification, delineation, kind, male, neuter, sex, sexuality, type
ASSOCIATED CONCEPTS: gender law

GENDER BIAS, *noun* gender prejudice, one-sidedness, partiality, partisanship, prejudice, sexual discrimination, unequal treatment, unfair treatment, unfairness, unlawful treatment of a protected class
ASSOCIATED CONCEPTS: employment law

GENDER DISCRIMINATION, *noun* favoritism, gender bias, gender prejudice
Generally: intolerance, one-sidedness, partiality, partisanship, sexual discrimination, unfairness

GENE PATENT, *noun* biotech patenting of genes, ownership of gene design, owning a gene patent, patenting a gene and its characteristics, protecting genetic research

GENERAL, *adjective* accepted, average, broad, catholic, characteristic, common, common to many, *communis,* customary, ecumenical, epidemic, extensive, *generalis,* habitual, illustrative, inclusive, not partial, not select, open to all, ordinary, pandemic, popular, prevailing, prevalent, regular, relevant to all, representative, rife, standard, sweeping, typical, undisputed, universal, unrestricted, usual, vast, widespread
ASSOCIATED CONCEPTS: general agency, general agent, general appearance, general applicability, general assignment for the benefit of creditors, general bequest, general brokerage, general circulation, general creditor, general damages, general denial, general election, general issue, general jurisdiction, general legacy, general lien, general obligation, general power of appointment, general release, general statute, general strike, general verdict, general welfare
FOREIGN PHRASES: ***Generale tantum valet in generalibus, quantum singulare in singulis.*** That which is general prevails in general matters, as that which is particular prevails in particular matters. ***Generalibus specialia derogant.*** Special words derogate from the meaning of general ones. ***Generalis regula generaliter est intelligenda.*** A general rule is to be understood generally. ***Generalis clausula non porrigitur adea quaeantea specialiter sunt comprehensa.*** A general clause is not extended to include those things that have been previously provided for specially. ***Statutum generaliter est intelligendum quando verba statuti sunt specialia, ratio autem generalis.*** When the words of a statute are special but the reason general, the statute is to be understood generally. ***Generalia praecedunt, specialia sequuntur.*** General matters precede, special matters follow. ***In generalibus versatur error.*** Error thrives in generalities. ***Fraus latet in generalibus.*** Fraud lies hidden in general expressions.

GENERAL AGREEMENT, *noun* acclamation, accord, acquiescence, affirmance, affirmation, common consent, concord, concordance, concurrence, consensus, consent, consentaneity, consentience, harmony, like-mindedness, meeting of minds, unanimousness, understanding, union, universal agreement
ASSOCIATED CONCEPTS: bilateral agreement, conditioned agreement, executory agreement, express agreement, implied agreement, parole agreement

GENERAL MEANING, *noun* connotation, content, cornerstone, drift, essence, essential matter, essential part, gist, idea, implication, import, important part, main point, marrow, meat, principle, purport, quintessence, sense, significance, substance, sum and substance, tenor

GENERAL PRINCIPLES, *noun* approach, course of action, line of action, mode of management, *modus operandi,* overall approach, policy, procedure, strategy

GENERAL RELEASE, *noun* absolute resolution, all-encompassing release, clearance, complete discharge, complete release from liability, comprehensive release, disculpation, disposal, excusal, exemption, full extrication, relinquishment, solution

GENERALITY *(Bulk),* *noun* better part, biggest part, body, common run, greater part, greatest number, largest part, main body, main part, majority, mass, predominant part, preponderance, preponderancy, preponderation, principal part, universality

GENERALITY *(Vague statement),* *noun* abstraction, broad statement, general law, general principle, general rule, general statement, generalization, imprecision, inexactitude, inexactness, loose statement, principle, simplistic statement

GENERALIZATION, *noun* appraisal, assumption, attitude, broad statement, conclusion, estimate, estimation, general statement, generality, guide, hypothesis, illation, imprecise statement, inexact statement, inference, observation, postulate, postulation, premise, presumption, presupposition, supposal, supposition, theorization, theory

GENERALIZE, *verb* assume, conclude, deal in generalities, discuss in the abstract, draw inferences, *generatim,* hypothesize, ignore distinctions, *loqui,* make a generalization, suppose, surmise, theorize, universalize, *universe*

GENERALLY, *adverb* as a rule, chiefly, commonly, customarily, extensively, for the most part, habitually, in general, in most cases, in the main, in the usual course of things, mainly, most frequently, most often, naturally, normally, on the whole, ordinarily, principally, regularly, usually, without particularizing

GENERALSHIP, *noun* administration, administratorship, authority, captainship, care, charge, command, direction, directorate, directorship, *ductus,* guidance, headship, intendance, intendancy, jurisdiction, lead, leadership, management, managership, mastership, stewardship, superintendency, supervision, supervisorship

GENERATE, *verb* animate, author, be the cause, beget, begin, breed, bring about, bring forth, bring into being, bring into existence, call into being, call into existence, cause, cause to be, conduce, construct, contrive, create, develop, do, effect, effectuate, elicit, engender, evoke, execute, fabricate, father, form, formulate, found, frame, *generare, gignere,* give life to, give rise to, inaugurate, induce, initiate, institute, invent, kindle, launch, lay the foundation of, make, manufacture, occasion, open, originate, *parere,* produce, provoke, set in motion, sire, start, undertake, vitalize, vivify

GENERIC, *adjective* applicable to a class, blanket, broad, collective, common, comprehensive, general, indeterminate, inexact, nonexclusive, nonspecific, not particular, not special, sweeping, universal, unspecified, wide
ASSOCIATED CONCEPTS: generic name, trade name, trademark

GENEROUS, *adjective* altruistic, beneficent, benevolent, big-hearted, bountiful, capacious, charitable, chivalrous, copious, decent, donative, gracious, humane, kind, kindly, magnanimous, meritorious, munificent, noble, philanthropic, unselfish, warmhearted

GENESIS, *noun* beginning, birth, commencement, cradle, creation, dawn, derivation, exordium, formation, foundation, inception, inchoation, incipience, incipiency, incunabula, initiation, introduction, launching, nativity, onset, origin, origination, outset, provenance, rise, root, source, start

GENETIC, *adjective* atavistic, congenital, hereditary, incarnate, ingrained, inherited, innate

GENETIC ENGINEERING, *noun* a carbon copy created by genetic engineering, a copy created by genetic engineering, a double created by genetic engineering, a facsimile created through genetic engineering, an exact copy created through genetic engineering, clone, duplication created by genetic engineering, production of a copy, production of a copy through genetic engineering, production of multiple identical copies, propagation asexually, propagation from a clone cell, replication created by genetic engineering, replication through genetic engineering, reproduction asexually
ASSOCIATED CONCEPTS: bioethics, computer clone, embryo splitting, human clone

GENIUS, *noun* aptitude, brilliant intellect, cognition, creative power, endowment, expert, gift, ingenuity, insight, inspiration, intellect, intelligence, mastermind, natural gift, perception, percipience, prodigy, propensity, sagacity, science, sense, specialty, talent, wisdom

GENOCIDE, *noun* annihilation, bloodbath, butchery, carnage, decimation, extermination, liquidation, mass destruction, mass execution, mass extermination, mass murder, mass slaying, slaughter, wholesale murder
ASSOCIATED CONCEPTS: Geneva Convention, War Crimes Commission

GENRE, *noun* breed, category, character, class, classification, denomination, description, designation, division, form, generic class, genus, group, nature, species, specific category, specific class, specific type, type, variety

GENUINE, *adjective* accurate, actual, ascertained, authentic, authenticated, bona fide, demonstrable, exact, factual, forthright, frank, *germanus,* guileless, honest, inartificial, legitimate, *merus,* natural, official, original, plain, pure, purebred, real, rightful, simple, sincere, *sincerus,* sterling, tested, true, unadulterated, unaffected, unalloyed, uncolored, uncounterfeited, undisguised, undistorted, unfabricated, unfaked, unfeigned, unfeigning, unfictitious, unimitated, unimpeachable, uninvented, unpretended, unpretending, unpretentious, unquestionable, unsimulated, unspurious, unsynthetic, unvarnished, valid, veridical, veritable
ASSOCIATED CONCEPTS: genuine issue

GERMANE, *adjective* accordant, *adfinis,* affinitive, allied, applicable, applying to, apposite, appropriate, appurtenant, apropos, apt, associated, bearing upon, belonging to, cognate, concerning, congruent, congruous, connected, correlated, correspondent, fitting, important, pertaining to, pertinent, referring, related, relating, relative, relevant, to the point

GERMINATE, *verb* become, bud, burgeon, develop, emerge, evolve, flourish, gemmate, generate, *germinare,* grow, produce, progress, pullulate, sprout, thrive, vegetate, yield

GERRYMANDER, *verb* arrange beneficial political boundaries, create new political boundaries, devise new political boundaries, doctor redistricting, engineer new political boundaries, engineer new political lines, finagle, finesse new political districts, manipulate political districts, mastermind, new political boundaries, tamper with drawing political districts, use machinations to draw new boundaries

GESTURE, *noun* characterization, connotation, delineation, enunciation, expression, illustration, image, indication, indicator, manifestation, mark, means of expression, picture, portrayal, representation, sign, signal, signification, symbolization, waive

GET, *verb* accumulate, achieve, acquire, appropriate, attain, capture, collect, earn, elicit, gain, gain possession of, gather, harvest, obtain, possess, procure, realize, receive, recover, secure, seize, take, take over, take possession of
ASSOCIATED CONCEPTS: devices and bequests under a will, laws of intestacy

GET ACROSS, *verb* broadcast, clarify, communicate, communicate effectively, convey, decipher, decode, define, deliver, demonstrate, demystify, descramble, disambiguate, disseminate, elucidate, enlighten, enunciate, explain, explain in plain language, explicate, get through to, illuminate, impart, make crystal clear, particularize, simplify, spell out, tell

GET AWAY WITH *(Let off),* ***verb*** absolved, be under the radar, escape, escape punishment, escape without any penalty, found not guilty, get off, get off easy, get off lightly, get off with a slap on the wrist, go free, lack evidence to accuse, lack proof to accuse, let loose, pardon, walk away unscathed
ASSOCIATED CONCEPTS: getting away with murder

GET AWAY WITH *(Put over on),* ***verb*** accomplish without difficulty, carry off, escape notice, get by without any downside, succeed without a problem

GET EVEN WITH, *verb* avenge, even the score, exact a price, exact revenge, get back, get justice, get revenge, make reprisals, pay back, reciprocate, reckon with, repay, requite, respond in kind, retaliate, revenge, settle a score, strike back at

GHOST, *noun* apparition, bogey, familiar, ghoul, haunt, imp, incubus, materialization, mystical figure, phantasm, phantom, poltergeist, shadow, specter, spirit, spook, sprite, vision, visitant

GIFT *(Flair),* ***noun*** ability, adeptness, adroitness, aptitude, capability, capacity, cleverness, competence, cunning, deftness, dexterity, dextrousness, endowment, expertise, expertness, facility, faculty, felicity, forte, genius, handiness, inborn aptitude, ingeniousness, ingenuity, innate ability, innate quality, instinct, knack, mastery, *natura et ingenium,* natural ability, natural quality, proficiency, qualification, quality, readiness, skill, skillfulness, special ability, special endowment, talent, turn

GIFT *(Present),* ***noun*** allowance, award, benefaction, bestowment, contribution, dispensation, donation, donative, *donum,* endowment, favor, grant, gratuity, legacy, *munus,* present, presentation, tribute

ASSOCIATED CONCEPTS: absolute gift, acceptance of a gift, bequest, charitable gift, class gift, conditional gift, contingent gift, delivery of a gift, devise, donative intent for a gift, executory gift, expectation of a gift, future gift, gift causa mortis, gift for a public purpose, gift in contemplation of death, gift in praesenti, gift to take effect at death, illusory gift, incomplete gift, intervivos gift, qualified gift, revocable gift, testamentary gift, unconditional gift, verbal gift
FOREIGN PHRASES: ***Invito beneficium non datur.*** A benefit is not conferred upon a person against his will. ***Modus legem dat donationi.*** Custom gives validity to the gift. ***Ubi et dantis et accipientis turpitudo versatur, non posse repeti dicimus; quotiens autem accipientis turpitudo versatur, repeti posse.*** Where there is turpitude by both the giver and receiver, we say it cannot be recovered back; but whenever the turpitude is in the receiver only, it can be recovered. ***Non valet donatio nisi subsequatur traditio.*** A gift is invalid unless accompanied by possession. ***Nemo dare potest quod non habet.*** No one is able to give that which he has not. ***Nemo praesumitur donare.*** No one is presumed to have made a gift. ***Inter alias causas acquisitionis, magna, celebris, et famosa est causa donationis.*** Among other methods of acquiring property, there is a great, frequently used, and famous means, that of gift. ***Cujus per errorem dati repetitio est, ejus consulto dati donatio est.*** That which when given through mistake can be recovered back, when given deliberately is a gift. ***Cujus est dare, ejus est disponere.*** He who has a right to give, has the right to dispose of the gift. ***Nul charter, nul vente, ne nul done vault perpetualment, si le donor n'est seise al temps de contracts de deux droits, sc. del droit de possession et del droit de propertie.*** No grant, no sale, no gift, is valid forever, unless the donor, at the time of contract, has two rights, namely, the right of possession and the right of property. ***Sola ac per se senectus donationem testamentum aut transactionem non vitiat.*** Old age alone and of itself will not vitiate a will or gift. ***Qui sciens solvit indebitum donandi consilio id videtur fecisse.*** One who knowingly pays what is not due is deemed to have done it with the intention of making a gift. ***Legatum morte testatoris tantum confirmatur, sicut donatio inter vivos traditione sola.*** A legacy is confirmed by the death of a testator, in the same manner as a gift, as between living persons is confirmed by delivery alone. ***Donatio perficitur possessione accipientis.*** A gift is perfected by the possession of the receiver. ***Confirmatio est nulla ubi donum praecedens est invalidum.*** A confirmation is a nullity where the preceding gift is invalid. ***Dans et retinens, nihil dat.*** A person who gives and retains possession, gives nothing. ***Donari videtur, quod nullo jure cogente conceditur.*** That is considered to be given which is transferred under no legal compulsions. ***Donator nunquam desinit possidere, antequam donatorius incipiat possidere.*** A donor never ceases to possess until the donee begins to possess. ***Donatio non praesumitur.*** A gift is not presumed to have been made. ***Dona clandestina sunt semper suspiciosa.*** Clandestine gifts are always open to suspicion.

GIMMICK, *noun* artifice, contrivance, deception, design, device, flimflam, gadget, invention, maneuver, method, plan, ploy, ruse, scheme, secret device, snag, stratagem, strategy, subterfuge, trap, trick
ASSOCIATED CONCEPTS: false advertising

GIST *(Ground for a suit),* ***noun*** alleged reason, base, basis, basis of argument, basis of litigation, cardinal point, cause, cause of action, essential ground, essential matter, essential part, focal point of the complaint, foundation of a suit, gravamen, gravamen of a charge, gravamen of the complaint, great point, ground, important point, keystone, main charge, main point, object of the action, outstanding feature, pith of a matter, point, principal part, principal point, reason, reason for which suit is commenced, salient point, substance, substantial part of a complaint, sum and substance, ultimate cause
ASSOCIATED CONCEPTS: gist of a cause of action, gist of an offense, gist of the complaint

GIST *(Substance),* ***noun*** backbone, basis, broad meaning, connotation, core, drift, essence, essential meaning, essential part, fundamentals, general meaning, idea conveyed, implication, import, *index,* intrinsic nature, marrow, matter, meaning, pith, primary meaning, purport, quiddity, quintessence, real content, reality, root, sense, spirit, substantial meaning, sum and substance, tenor, true meaning, vital principle

GIVE *(Grant),* ***verb*** accord, adminster, afford, allot, assign, award, bequeath, bestow, cede, commit, concede, confer, consign, contribute, deal, deed, deliver, devise, devote, dispense, dispose of, distribute, donate, endow, entrust, equip, furnish, impart, indulge, leave, make a gift, make a presentation, pass, present, *prodere,* proffer, provide, remit, submit, supply, surrender, transfer, transmit, turn over, vouchsafe, will
ASSOCIATED CONCEPTS: bequeath, convey, deliver, devise, dispose, give judgment, give notice
FOREIGN PHRASES: ***Praesentare nihil aliud est quam praesto dare seu offere.*** To present is no more than to give or offer forthwith.

GIVE *(Yield),* ***verb*** abate, become flexible, become less rigid, become pliant, collapse, compromise, concede, crumble, *deponere,* ease, loosen, retreat, sag, soften, surrender

GIVE AND TAKE, *noun* accommodation, an exchange of ideas, arguments, banter, barter, bicker, collaboration, communication, compromise, contention, conversation, dialogue, disagreement, discussion, discussion of positions, ideas bandied about, interaction, interchange, negotiation, back and forth, quibbling, repartee, sparring, squabbling, thrashing out of ideas
ASSOCIATED CONCEPTS: collective bargaining

GIVE IN, *verb* abandon, abjure, abnegate, accede, allow, authorize, capitulate, cede, commit, concede, consign, deliver, demit, demur, deny, desert, disavow, discard, forsake, give up, leave, permit, quit, relinquish, render, renounce, resign, shed, step aside, step down, surrender, turn over, vacate, waive, yield

GIVE NOTICE, *verb* air, announce, assert, blazon, brief, broadcast, caution, declare, disclose, divulge, enlighten, express, fill in, herald, hint, inform, make known, mention, notify, post, publicize, report, reveal, state, warn
ASSOCIATED CONCEPTS: public notice

GIVEN *(Certain),* ***adjective*** absolute, accustomed, agreed, assured, automatic, committed, customary, definite, disposed, guaranteed, habituated, indubious, linded, pledged, practiced, predisposed, seasoned, solid, standard, sure, used, willing

GIVEN *(Donated),* ***adjective*** administered, afforded, aided, allocated, allotted, assisted, benefited, bestowed, committed, conferred, contributed, departed with, dispensed, doled out, endowed, extended, furnished, gifted, granted, guaranteed, handed out, helped, imparted, issued, lavished, meted out, presented, proffered, promised, provided, rendered, sacrificed, tendered

GLANCE, *verb* behold, briefly observe, catch a brief look at, catch a glimpse of, glimpse, look, peek, picture, scan, see, skim, snatch a glimpse, sneak a look at, sneak a peek at, view quickly, watch, witness

GLARING, *adjective* apparent, blatant, bright, brilliant, clear, conspicuous, crude, distinct, downright, egregious, evident, extreme, flagrant, flamboyant, flashy, flaunting, garish, glittering, intense, loud, manifest, noticeable, notorious, obtrusive, obvious, open, ostentatious, outrageous, outright, overt, patent, penetrating, perceivable, perceptible, piercing, prominent, pronounced, salient, self-evident, sensational, spectacular, stark, striking, unequivocal, vivid, vulgar

GLEAN, *verb* accumulate, aggregate, amass, assemble, batch together, bring together, collect, cull, cumulate, draw together, extract, *facere,* garner, gather, harvest, lay in store, obtain, pick up, procure, save, scrape together

GLIMPSE, *verb* blink, browse, catch, glance at, look over, notice, peek, peep, peruse, rake, scan, see, skim, squint, view

GLOBAL, *adjective* all-embracing, all-inclusive, complete, comprehensive, extensive, far-reaching, international, nonsectarian, omnipresent, overall, pandemic, prevailing, prevalent, total, universal, widespread, world-wide

GLOBAL WARMING, *noun* adamantine, austere forecasts, callous, extreme weather, fierce weather, foreboding weather patterns, hard weather, harsh weather, intractable weather conditions, merciless climate changes, obstinate weather, rigorous weather patterns, rough weather, severe weather, stark climate changes, tough conditions, unforgiving conditions, unrelenting climate change, unyielding weather
ASSOCIATED CONCEPTS: cap and trade, reducing the use of carbon fuels

GLOOM, *noun* affliction, anguish, apprehension, bitterness, blackness, chagrin, cheerlessness, cloud over, darkness, dejection, depression, desolation, despair, despondency, dimness, distress, doldrums, dolor, dullness, dumps, foreboding, gloominess, grief, heaviness, low spirits, malaise, melancholia, melancholy, misery, misgiving, morbidity, moroseness, mortification, mourning, obscurity, oppression, overcast, pensiveness, pessimism, sadness, shade, shadow, sorrow, sullenness, the blues, the doldrums, vexation, weariness, woe

GLOOMY, *adjective* bleak, cheerless, chill, Cimmerian, cloudy, cold, comfortless, dark, darkening, depressing, depressive, desolate, dire, disconsolate, dismal, doleful, drear, dreary, elegiac, forlorn, funereal, glum, lonesome, lugubrious, melancholy, miserable, morbid, morose, mournful, ominous, saturnine, solemn, somber, sullen

GLORIFY, *verb* acclaim, adore, aggrandize, apotheosize, applaud, beatify, belaud, bless, boost, brighten, canonize, celebrate, cherish, compliment, consecrate, deify, dignify, elevate, ennoble, enshrine, enthrone, exalt, extol, flatter, glamorize, gratify, hail, honor, idealize, idolatrize, idolize, immortalize, increase, laud, lift, lionize, magnify, make illustrious, overestimate, panegyrize, praise, praise highly, promote, raise, recognize, recommend, regard, renown, revere, rhapsodize, romanticize, tout, treasure, trumpet, uplift, worship

GLORIOUS, *adjective* admirable, august, awe inspiring, beautiful, blissful, brilliant, captivating, celebrated, celestial, charming, commanding, conspicuous, delectable, delightful, dignified, distinguished, ebullient, ecstatic, elated, elevated, eminent, enchanting, enjoyable, enraptured, entranced, esteemed, estimable, exalted, excellent, exemplary, exultant, fabulous, famed, famous, far-famed, festive, glorified, grand, gratifying, grave, great, halcyon, heavenly, heroic, honorable, honored, illustrious, immortal, immortalized, imperial, impressive, jubilant, lofty, magnificent, majestic, marked, marvelous, memorable, meritorious, named, noble, notable, noted, notorious, overjoyed, peerless, praiseworthy, preeminent, prestigious, princely, regal, remarkable, renowned, royal, serene, spectacular, splendid, stately, striking, sublime, successful, superb, superior, supreme, surpassing, surprising, time-honored, towering, transcendent, triumphant, unique, unrivaled, victorious, well-known, winning, wonderful, wondrous, worthy

GLORY, *verb* acclaim, adore, aggrandize, apotheosize, applaud, belaud, boost, canonize, celebrate, cherish, compliment, consecrate, deify, dignify, elevate, ennoble, enshrine, extol, flatter, gratify, hail, honor, idealize, idolize, increase, laud, lift, lionize, magnify, praise, promote, raise, recognize, recommend, renown, rhapsodize, romanticize, tout, treasure, trumpet, worship

GLUTTONOUS, *adjective* crapulent, crapulous, debauched, edacious, excessive, greedy, immoderate, inabstinent, incontinent, indulgent, inordinate, insatiable, intemperate, omnivorous, orgiastic, ravenous, unrestrained, voracious

GO, *verb* abandon, advance, amble, budge, decamp, decease, demise, depart, disappear, emigrate, evacuate, flit, gain ground, hie, hike, journey, leave, make a journey, make off, make progress, march, meander, migrate, move, pace, part, part company, pass away, peregrinate, perish, proceed, promenade, quit, retreat, ride, roam, rove, set out, slip away, steal off, stride, strut, succumb, take flight, take wing, traipse, travel, tread, trek, trudge, walk, wander, wend, withdraw

GO *(Start)*, *verb* begin, carry on, commence, continue, embark upon, inaugurate, initiate, keep going, maintain, originate, persist, proceed

GO *(Travel)*, *verb* get away, go to, jet to, journey, journey to, leave, take a cruise to, take a plane to, tour, travel by car to, travel to, vacation to

GO-AHEAD, *noun* acceptance, accord, affirmance, affirmation, agreement, approval, assent, authorization, compliance, confirmation, consent, endorsement, green light, imprimatur, leave, liberty, license, nod, okay, permission, ratification, sanction, say-so, sign-off, special permission, validation, willingness

GO ALONG WITH, *verb* accede to, acquiesce to, affiliate with, agree to, agree in opinion, agree on, agree with, allow, amalgamate with, approve, arrive at an agreement, assent, associate, band, coadunate, cohere, collaborate, collude, combine, come to an agreement, come to an understanding, come to terms, comply, concur, confederate, conform,

conform to, conjoin, consent, consolidate, conspire, cooperate, correspond, countenance, echo, give in to, go with, grant, harmonize, join forces with, league with, merge with, pull together, ratify, sanction, side with, stand together, submit to, unite efforts with, work together with, yield to
ASSOCIATED CONCEPTS: settlement

GO-BETWEEN, *noun* agent, appeaser, arbiter, arbitrator, broker, buffer, *conciliator,* connecting link, connection, contact, contractor, dealer, delegate, diplomat, interagent, interceder, intercessor, intermediary, intermediate, intermediate agent, intermediator, *interpres,* judge, liaison, link, mediary, mediator, middleman, moderator, negotiator, ombudsman, pacifier, peacemaker, procurer, propitiator, reconciler, referee, representative, spokesman, umpire, vehicle
ASSOCIATED CONCEPTS: arbitration, conduit, court system, mediation

GO TO CONTRACT, *verb* close, come to an agreement, conclude, covenant, enter into an agreement, make terms, obligate oneself, pledge, settle with

GO UP AGAINST, *verb* act in opposition to, argue against, attack, battle, be at cross purposes, be contrary to, be on the opposite side of, be on the other side of, challenge, collide, combat, confront, confute, contend, contest, contradict, contravene, controvert, counter, counteract, counterattack, counterbalance, countermine, counterpoise, countervail, counterweigh, counterwork, debate, defy, demur, deny, disaffirm, disagree, disapprove, dispute, encounter, go contrary to, join issue, land into, negate, object, obstruct, offer resistance, oppose, oppugn, prevent, prohibit, protest, put in opposition, rebut, refute, reject, remonstrate, repel, resist, set against, stand firm against, stand on the other side of, take a stand against, take exception to, take issue with
ASSOCIATED CONCEPTS: litigation

GOAD, *noun* catalyst, encouragement, fillip, impetus, incentive, incitement, inducement, instigation, lash, pique, pressure, prick, prod, provocation, spur, stimulant, stimulus, thorn, tickler

GOAD, *verb* abet, agitate, annoy, arouse, badger, bait, bring pressure to bear on, browbeat, constrain, discompose, egg on, exhort, foment, harass, hector, hustle, impel, incite, inflame, instigate, invite a quarrel, irritate, jab, lash, motivate, needle, nudge, pique, poke, press, pressure, push, prod, prompt, propel, shove, spur, stimulate, sting, stir up, taunt, tease, torment, urge, vex, whip, worry

GOAL, *noun* aim, ambition, aspiration, design, destination, determination, end, fixed purpose, hope, intent, intention, mark, mission, object, objective, plan, predeliberation, predetermination, premeditation, purpose, resolution, resolve, scheme, set purpose, target

GONE *(Dead),* ***adjective*** bygone, deceased, defunct, demised, exanimate, expired, extinct, lifeless, passed, passed on

GONE *(Finished),* ***adjective*** accomplished, achieved, at an end, brought to a conclusion, completed, concluded, consumed, consummated, culminated, disposed of, done, done with, ended, executed, final, over with, past, realized, settled, spent, terminated, through

GONE *(Irretrievable),* ***adjective*** abrogated, absent, annulled, away, canceled, departed, disappeared, flown, gone away, inefficacious, irrecoverable, irredeemable, irretrievable, irreversible, left, lost, no more, not present, null, over, used up, vanished, void

GONE *(Unremembered),* ***adjective*** ancient, distant, elapsed, forgotten, lapsed, not recalled, not remembered, old, out of sight, over, unrecalled, unrecollected

GOOD *(Favorable),* ***adjective*** admirable, ample, apt, auspicious, beneficial, capital, choice, clean, cordial, correct, estimable, ethical, excellent, fair, favorable, fine, first-rate, genial, healthful, innocent, legitimate, palatable, praiseworthy, preferable, proper, propitious, reliable, replete, responsible, right, rightful, salubrious, salutary, savory, select, seemly, serviceable, solid, sound, sterling, sufficient, unsullied, untainted, wholesome, worthy

GOOD *(Nice),* ***adjective*** apt, agreeable, bona fide, chaste, commendable, conscientious, cordial, decent, decorous, devout, dutiful, estimable, ethical, exemplary, genial, genuine, honest, honorable, human, just, kind, likeable, meritorious, moral, pious, proper, pure, reliable, righteous, sapid, seemly, sincere, solid, sufficient, toothsome, upright, valid, valuable, virtuous, well-behaved, wholesome, worthy
ASSOCIATED CONCEPTS: Good Samaritan

GOOD *(Skilled),* ***adjective*** competent, correct, first-rate, fit, proficient, right, select, skilled, tiptop
ASSOCIATED CONCEPTS: a licensed practitioner in good standing

GOOD *(Benefit),* ***noun*** advantage, benefit, blessing, enjoyment, excellence, favor, gain, happiness, improvement, item, kindness, prize, profit, prosperity, service, weal, well-being, windfall

GOOD *(Virtue),* ***noun*** caliber, character, ethics, honesty, integrity, merit, probity, rectitude, righteousness, value, veracity, weal, worth

GOOD BEHAVIOR, *noun* character, correctness, decency, decorum, ethics, etiquette, fitness, good conduct, goodness, high-mindedness, honesty, honor, incorruptibility, integrity, irreproachability, moral rectitude, morals, propriety, rectitude, righteousness, right-mindedness, scrupulosity, seemliness, uprightness, virtue, virtuousness
ASSOCIATED CONCEPTS: time off for good behavior as a prisoner

GOOD CAUSE SHOWN, *noun* legitimate basis proven, proper cause demonstrated, reasonable basis shown, substantial cause shown, substantial factors proven, sufficient foundation shown, sufficient grounds
ASSOCIATED CONCEPTS: temporary restraining orders

GOOD FAITH, *noun* bona fide, goodness, honest effort, probity, rectitude, sanctity, uprightness
ASSOCIATED CONCEPTS: good faith attempt, good faith estimate, good faith purchaser, offer in good faith

GOOD FAITH RELIANCE *(Constitutional law),* ***noun*** bona fide reliance, detrimental reliance, genuine belief, good faith doctrine, honest belief, honest reliance, reasonable reliance

GOOD FAITH RELIANCE *(Contract),* ***noun*** bona fide reliance, exemption for reliance on a defective warrant under the exclusionary rule, genuine belief actions are legal, good faith exception to exclusionary rule, reasonable person test

GOOD SAMARITAN, ***noun*** aide, aider, altruist, assistant, assister, befriender, benefactor, deliverer, donor, giver, helper, helping hand, humanitarian, kind person, one who gives assistance, one who helps another, one who renders aid, patron, philanthropist, redeemer, rescuer, succorer, unselfish person
ASSOCIATED CONCEPTS: Good Samaritan law

GOOD STANDING, ***noun*** admiration, appreciation, approbation, approval, enviable reputation, esteem, estimation, favorable repute, high regard, prestige, respect, reverence, veneration

GOODWILL, ***noun*** altruism, amity, benefaction, beneficence, benevolence, brotherhood, charity, cheerful consent, cheerful willingness, commercial advantage, cordiality, countenance, customer approval, customer encouragement, earnestness, established patronage, established popularity, established reputation, favor, favorable disposition, favorable regard, friendly disposition, geniality, good name, good nature, good reputation, helpfulness, humanity, kindness, known name, munificence, patronage, philanthropy, proven name, public favor, public support, sponsorship, support, sympathy, tolerance, willingness
ASSOCIATED CONCEPTS: impairment of good will, sale and transfer of good will

GOODS, ***noun*** appurtenances, articles of commerce, assets, belongings, chattels, commodities, consumer durables, durables, effects, items, materials, paraphernalia, personal estate, possessions, produce, products, property, resources, staples, stock, stock-in-trade, supplies, things for sale, vendibles
ASSOCIATED CONCEPTS: bulk sale, chattels, foreign goods, goods and chattels, goods sold and delivered, personalty, sale of goods, special goods, tangible goods

GOVERN, ***verb*** administer, administrate, assume command, be in power, *coercere,* command, conduct, control, dictate, direct, dominate, enact, exercise authority, exercise power over, exert authority, give orders, guide, have authority, have executive charge of, have jurisdiction over, head, hold authority, hold office, hold sway, lead, legislate, manage, officiate, order, oversee, pilot, prescribe, preside over, prevail on, *regere,* regulate, reign, restrain, rule, steer, superintend, supervise, take charge, take command, wield authority
ASSOCIATED CONCEPTS: governing authority, governing body, governing law
FOREIGN PHRASES: ***Minor minorem custodire non debet, alios enim praesumitur male regere qui seipsum regere nescit.*** A minor ought not to be guardian to a minor, for a person who knows not how to govern himself is presumed to be unfit to govern others. ***Mitius imperanti melius paretur.*** The more gently a person commands, the better he is obeyed.

GOVERNANCE, ***noun*** administration, agency, authority, bureaucracy, control, dictation, dominance, domination, dominion, executive power, government, hegemony, influence, jurisdiction, management, mightiness, power, regime, reins of government, rule, supremacy, sway
ASSOCIATED CONCEPTS: corporate governance

GOVERNING, ***verb*** administering, bossing, bridling, captaining, conducting, conquering, controlling, curbing, dictating, directing, domineering, heading, inhibiting, leading, lording, managing, measuring, micromanaging, overseeing, presiding, regulating, reigning, restraining, ruling, subduing, supervising, swaying, taming, tyrannizing

GOVERNING PRINCIPLE, ***noun*** allowance, autarky, freedom, doctrine, dogma, guideline, limitation, maxim, mode of management, permission, policy, precepts, procedure, prohibition, protocol, restraint, rule, strategy, tactics, tenet

GOVERNMENT *(Administration),* ***noun*** *administratio,* authorization, command, control, decision making, direction, dominion, governance, *gubernatio,* guidance, jurisdiction, management, power, *procuratio,* regnancy, regulation, reign, rule, rulership, state management, statecraft, statesmanship, stewardship, superintendence, sway

GOVERNMENT *(Political administration),* ***noun*** administration, agency of the state, authority, body of office holders, congress, delegates, *ii qui reipublicae praesunt,* lawgivers, lawmakers, legislators, ministers, *penes quos est reipublica,* political community, political leaders, political regime, politicians, politicos, polity, public servants, representatives, ruling power, sovereign, state managers, statemongers, statesmen
ASSOCIATED CONCEPTS: de facto government, de jure government, democratic government, federal government, governmental agency, governmental body, governmental function, governmental immunity, powers of government, provisional government
FOREIGN PHRASES: ***Privilegium non valet contra rempublicam.*** A privilege is of no avail against the state.

GOVERNOR, ***noun*** caretaker, director, elected official, executive, executive leader, government official, highest state official, politician, potentate, public official, statesman
ASSOCIATED CONCEPTS: executive branch of government

GRACE, ***noun*** absolution, clemency, concession, excuse, favor, forbearance, forgiveness, indulgence, pardon, reprieve

GRACE PERIOD, ***noun*** concession, exemption, leniency, pardon, period of allowance, period of indulgence, period of tolerance, reprieve

GRACIOUS, ***adjective*** accommodating, affable, agreeable, amiable, approachable, attentive, benign, benignant, character, charming, congenial, considerate, convivial, cordial, correctness, courteous, decency, decorum, ethics, etiquette, fitness, friendly, genial, good conduct, goodness, high-mindedness, honesty, honor, hospitable, incorruptibility, integrity, irreproachability, kind, kindly, moral rectitude, morals, neighborly, obliging, outgoing, polite, propriety, rectitude, righteousness, right-mindedness, scrupulosity, seemliness, sociable, sweet, thoughtful, uprightness, virtue, virtuousness

GRADATION, ***noun*** class, classification, continuity, continuum, course, degree, differential, grade, gradual advance, gradualism, graduation, hierarchy, intensity, measure, order, rank, rate, regular progression, sequence, step, succession, series, stage, standard, variation

GRADE *(Accomplishment),* ***noun*** achievement, acquirement, attainment, conquest, cut, fulfillment, measurement, pass muster, pass scrutiny, stand the test, success

GRADE *(Rating),* ***noun*** achievement, marks, category, evaluation, measurement, merit, performance, rank, ratio, results, standing, station, status, success, value

GRADUAL, ***adjective*** by degrees, continuous, creeping, gradational, graduated, in steps, leisurely, measured, methodical, orderly, paced, progressive, regular, slow, step-by-step, systematic

GRAFT, ***noun*** blackmail, bribery, corruption, exploitation, fraudulent income, hush money, illegal profit, illicit profit, illicit revenue, *inserere,* kickback, money illegally acquired, political corruption, profiteering, property illegally acquired, unjust acquisition, unlawful gain
ASSOCIATED CONCEPTS: bribery, corruption, official misconduct

GRAND, ***adjective*** august, capacious, compendious, comprehensive, dignified, distinguished, elegant, elevated, eminent, exalted, excellent, famous, first-rate, glorious, good, grandiose, great, illustrious, imperial, important, impressive, leading, lofty, magnificent, majestic, mighty, momentous, noble, palatial, paramount, pompous, preeminent, princely, prodigious, prominent, proud, renowned, splendid, stately, stellar, sublime, superb, superior, supreme, very magisterial, wide-reaching

GRAND LARCENY, ***noun*** crime, crime graver than a misdemeanor, crime greater in value than petit larceny, criminal offense, felony, gross offense, illegality, larceny of property which exceeds petit larceny, misdeed, offense, theft, transgression, violation of law, wrongdoing

GRANDILOQUENCE, ***noun*** abstruse language, bloated wording, bombastic wording, complex legalese, convoluted wording, inflated wording, legal jargon complexities, legalese, legalism, long winded jargon, orotund language, ostentatious wording, pedantic verbiage, pompous wording, sophisticated legal term, sophisticated legal verbiage, swollen wording, technical language, technical term, technical wording, turgid wording

GRANDIOSE, ***adjective*** affected, boastful, bombastic, enormous, exorbitant, flamboyant, flashy, flaunting, fustian, grandiloquent, high-sounding, huge, immense, inflated, lofty, magniloquent, mighty, ornate, orotund, ostentatious, pompous, pretentious, showy, stupendous, theatrical, tumid, turgid, vainglorious

GRANT, ***noun*** acknowledgment, allotment, allowance, appanage, award, benefaction, benefit, bequeathal, bequest, bestowal, boon, bounty, concession, devise, dispensation, donation, *donum,* douceur, endowment, favor, gift, gratuity, handsel, indulgence, lagniappe, largess, largesse, legacy, legal cession, libation, oblation, present, reward, subscription, subsidy, subvention
ASSOCIATED CONCEPTS: express grant, grant and convey, grant by implication, grant of power, legislative grant, license, private land grant, public grant
FOREIGN PHRASES: ***Resoluto jure concedentis resolvitur jus concessum.*** When the right of the grantor is extinguished the right granted is extinguished. ***Ubi aliquid conceditur, conceditur et id sine quo res ipsa esse non potest.*** When anything is granted, that also is granted without which it could not exist. ***Quando aliquis aliquid concedit, concedere videtur et id sine quo res uti non potest.*** When anyone grants anything, he is deemed to grant also that without which the thing cannot be used. ***Quod sub certa forma concessum vel reservatum est non trahitur ad valorem vel compensationem.*** That which is granted or reserved under a certain form cannot be twisted into a valuation or compensation. ***Qui concedit aliquid concedit omne id sine quo concessio est irrita.*** He who grants anything is considered to grant everything without which the grant is worthless. ***A gratia.*** By grace, not by right. ***Cuicunque aliquis quid concedit concedere videtur et id, sine quo res ipsa esse non potuit.*** Whoever grants a thing is presumed also to grant that without which the grant of the thing itself would be of no use. ***Quaelibet concessio fortissime contra donatorem interpretanda est.*** Every grant is to be interpreted most strictly against the grantor. ***Concessio versus concedentem latam interpretationem habere debet.*** A grant ought to have a liberal interpretation against the grantor. ***Nul charter, nul vente, ne nul done vault perpetualment, si le donor n'est seise al temps de contracts de deux droits, sc. del droit de possession et del droit de propertie.*** No grant, no sale, no gift is valid forever unless the donor, at the time of the contract, has two rights, namely, the right of possession and the right of property.

GRANT *(Concede),* ***verb*** accede, accept, accord, acknowledge, acquiesce, admit, agree, allow, approve, assent, authorize, be persuaded, cede, *concedere,* concur, confer a privilege, consent, *dare,* empower, enable, express concurrence, favor, give, give authority, give clearance, give consent, give leave, give permission, gratify, have no objection, indulge, let, license, permit, *permittere,* privilege, recognize, sanction, support, vouchsafe, warrant, yield, yield assent
ASSOCIATED CONCEPTS: grant a franchise, grant a mistrial, grant a motion, grant a right of way, grant a right to a jury trial, grant an adjournment, grant an easement, grant an injunction, grant or allowance, granting clause
FOREIGN PHRASES: ***Cui jus est donandi, eidem et vendendi et concedendi jus est.*** One who has a right to give has also a right to sell and to grant.

GRANT *(Transfer formally),* ***verb*** assign, award, bequeath, bestow, bestow voluntarily, cede, change ownership, *concedere,* confer, confer formally, confer ownership, consign, convey, convey by deed, deed, deliver, demise, devise, devolve upon, give, give away, give over to, impart, make a present, make conveyance of, make over, pass, pass over, *permittere,* present, put in possession, sign over, transfer, transfer by writing, transfer ownership, transmit
ASSOCIATED CONCEPTS: grant a license, grant a privilege, grant a right of way, grant of easement, grant by implication, grant by necessity, grant in gross, grant in praesenti, land grant, proprietary grant
FOREIGN PHRASES: ***Quaelibet concessio fortissime contra donatorem interpretanda est.*** Every grant is to be interpreted most strictly against the grantor.

GRANT AUTHORITY TO, ***verb*** accredit, allow, appoint, assign, authorize, commission, confer a right, consent, delegate, depute, deputize, empower, endow, enfranchise, entrust, give a mandate to, give permission, give power, invest, invest with power, license, nominate, ordain, sanction, vest, warrant
ASSOCIATED CONCEPTS: agent

GRANT OF RIGHTS, ***noun*** authorization, bestowal of authority, ceding of authority, conveyance of authority, conveyance of rights, grant of authority, transfer of rights

GRANTEE, ***noun*** acceptor, beneficiary, devisee, donee, recipient, taker
ASSOCIATED CONCEPTS: grantee of power

GRANTOR, ***noun*** assignor, bequeather, bestower, conferrer, contributor, devisor, donator, giver, investor, presenter, rewarder, testator
ASSOCIATED CONCEPTS: grantor of a power

GRAPHIC, ***adjective*** clear, cogent, coherent, comprehensible, decorative, delineatory, demonstrative, descriptive, detailed, distinct, effective, energetic, explicatory, explicit, expressive, illustrative, imaginative, lively, lucid, lurid, pictorial, precise, realistic, representing, scenic, sharp, striking, strong, suggestive, telling, unequivocal, vivid, well-delineated

GRAPPLE, ***verb*** attack, battle, clasp, clinch, close, close with, clutch, combat, come in conflict with, compete with, confront, contest, do battle with, encounter, engage with, fasten upon, fight, get hold of, grasp, grip, hang on, hold, hold fast, oppose, seize, struggle, tackle, take hold of, take on, tussle, vie with, wrestle

GRASP *(Mastery),* ***noun*** ability, apprehension, clasp, cognition, compass, competence, comprehension, conception, embrace, grip, handle, hold, judgment, ken, knowledge, mastery, perception, purchase, range, reach, retention, savvy, scope, seizure, sense, stretch, sweep, thorough understanding, understanding

GRASP *(Possession),* ***noun*** clench, clutch, de facto possession, embracement, grip, hold, purchase, taking hold

GRASP, ***verb*** apprehend, capture, clasp, clinch, clutch, cohere, comprehend, conceive, digest, discern, fathom, gain, get to the bottom of, grab, grapple, grip, hold, hold firmly, ken, penetrate, realize, recognize, retain, seize, seize the meaning, sense, snatch, take, understand

GRASSROOTS, ***adjective*** basic elements, collective, common, comprehensive, extensive, far-reaching, from the bottom up, general, general public, global, groundswell, large-scale, omnibus, ordinary, popular, prevalent, rank and file, substantial, sweeping, the masses, total, universal
ASSOCIATED CONCEPTS: grassroots political support

GRATIFICATION, ***noun*** beatitude, benefit, bliss, cheer, comfort, delectation, delight, elation, enchantment, enjoyment, exhilaration, felicity, fruition, gladness, glee, happiness, indulgence, joy, jubilation, merriment, pleasure, rapture, relish, satisfaction, savor, stimulus, thrill, titillation, transport, well-being

GRATIFY, ***verb*** amuse, appease, assuage, calm, captivate, cater to, charm, coddle, comfort, delight, gladden, humor, indulge, ingratiate, mollify, mollycoddle, pacify, pamper, placate, please, pleasure, quench, rejoice, sate, satiate, satisfy, soothe, spoil, titillate, warm

GRATIS, ***adjective*** as a favor, complimentary, costless, expenseless, for nothing, free, free of charge, free of cost, free of expense, *gratiis, gratuito,* unbought, unpaid for, unrecompensed, voluntary, without charge, without consideration, without monetary inducement, without monetary reward, without pecuniary gain, without recompense, without reward

GRATITUDE, ***noun*** acknowledgment, appreciation, appreciativeness, deepest appreciation, expression of appreciation, genuine appreciation, grace, gratefulness, praise, recognition, responsiveness, sense of indebtedness, sense of obligation, sincere appreciation, thankfulness, thanks

GRATUITOUS *(Given without recompense),* ***adjective*** bestowed, by way of gift, chargeless, charitable, complimentary, contributory, costless, donated, expenseless, for nothing, free, free of cost, free of expense, given, given away, gratis, not charged, not charged for, not subject to a payment, provided without charge, unbought, unpaid, unpaid for, unrecompensed, voluntary, without charge, without compensation, without consideration
ASSOCIATED CONCEPTS: gratuitous agency, gratuitous allowance, gratuitous bailment, gratuitous contract, gratuitous guest, gratuitous invitee, gratuitous licensee, gratuitous service, gratuitous undertaking, gratuitous use

GRATUITOUS *(Unwarranted),* ***adjective*** additional, baseless, causeless, dispensable, excessive, extraneous, *gratuitus,* groundless, inapposite, inappropriate, inessential, irrelative, irrelevant, needless, nonpertinent, not fitting, not following, not necessitated, not pertinent, superfluous, uncalled for, unconnected, undesirable, undue, unessential, unfounded, unjustified, unnecessary, unneeded, unprovoked, unrelated, unsuitable, unsuited, without basis, without foundation
ASSOCIATED CONCEPTS: gratuitous remarks during an examination of a witness

GRATUITY *(Bribe),* ***noun*** corrupting gift, corruption, graft, hush money, illegal gain, influence by a gift, jobbery, kickback, price, price of corruption, protection, rakeoff, sop, subornation
ASSOCIATED CONCEPTS: bribe receiving, emolument, illegal gratuity, official misconduct, tampering with a witness

GRATUITY *(Present),* ***noun*** award, benefaction, bonus, charity, contribution, dispensation, dole, donative, extra, favor, gift, grant, handout, offering, perquisite, premium, presentation, reward, tip, unearned increment

GRAVAMEN, ***noun*** burden of a charge, cardinal point, center, central point, content, core, cornerstone, crux, essence, essence of a grievance, essential matter, essential part, essential point, focal point, gist, gist of a charge, grievance, key, keystone, main point, material part, material point, nucleus, pith, pivotal point, principal part, root, salient point, *sine qua non,* spirit, substance, substantial cause, substantial part of a complaint, sum and substance, thrust
ASSOCIATED CONCEPTS: gravamen of a complaint

GRAVE *(Important),* ***adjective*** chief, consequential, critical, essential, exigent, *gravis,* imperative, indispensable, pressing, serious, *serius,* substantial, *tristis,* urgent, weighty

GRAVE *(Solemn),* ***adjective*** cheerless, dolorous, frowning, grim, heavy, humorless, joyless, pensive, sad, saturnine, serious, sober, somber, sorrowful, spiritless, uncheerful, uncheery, unlively
ASSOCIATED CONCEPTS: grave consequences for illegal acts

GRAVE CONSEQUENCES, ***noun*** a bleak outcome, a deleterious outcome, a deleterious outgrowth, a malignant scenario, an extremely unfortunate sequence of events, deleterious aftermath, deleterious developments, deleterious effects, deleterious results, important and significant effects, severe fallout
ASSOCIATED CONCEPTS: punishment

GRAVITATE, ***verb*** approach, be attracted, be prone to, draw near, draw toward, have a proclivity for, have a propensity for, head toward, incline, lean, move toward, tend, tend toward, trend
ASSOCIATED CONCEPTS: gravitate to a life of crime

GRAVITY, *noun* attraction, attractiveness, concern, consideration, draw, enormity, greatness, heaviness, heft, import, importance, interest, magnetism, magnitude, materiality, momentousness, ponderosity, ponderousness, pull, pulling power, severity, significance, solemnity, weight
ASSOCIATED CONCEPTS: gravity of a crime

GRAY AREA, *noun* ambiguous, blind, borderline, chance, complex, cryptic, contingent, dark, enigmatic, equivocal, esoteric, foreign, gamble, hidden, indeterminate, mysterious, never experienced before, new, novel, obscure, open question, puzzling, questionable, secret, strange, unascertained, uncalculated, uncertain, undecided, undefined, undesignated, undetermined, undisclosed, undiscovered, unexplored, unfamiliar, unfixed, unidentified, uninvestigated, unknown, unset, unsettled, unstudied, untold, untraced
ASSOCIATED CONCEPTS: statutory construction

GREAT *(Major),* ***adjective*** able, absolute, adroit, august, big, bulky, capacious, celebrated, chief, clever, colossal, commanding, compelling, complete, consequential, crackerjack, critical, dandy, dignified, distinguished, elevated, eminent, enormous, esteemed, exalted, excellent, expert, extensive, extraordinary, extreme, fabulous, famous, far-reaching, fine, first-rate, gigantic, glorious, grand, high-minded, huge, illustrious, immense, important, influential, inordinate, large, leading, lofty, magnanimous, main, majestic, major, massive, master, maximum, meritorious, mighty, momentous, monstrous, noble, notable, noted, outstanding, paramount, perfect, potent, powerful, preeminent, prime, principal, prodigious, proficient, profound, puissant, remarkable, renowned, respectable, serious, sizable, skillful, solid, splendid, strong, sublime, substantial, superior, supreme, topflight, unconditional, vast, very good, weighty

GREAT *(Many),* ***adjective*** abundant, ample, boundless, considerable, copious, countless, excessive, generous, illimitable, inexhaustible, manifold, many, multitudinous, numerous, unlimited, voluminous

GREED, *noun* acquisitiveness, appetency, avarice, avariciousness, *avaritia, aviditas,* avidity, covetousness, crapulence, *cupiditas,* cupidity, desire to hoard wealth, eagerness, edacity, excess, gluttonous appetite, gluttony, greediness, gulosity, incontinence, indulgence, inordinate desire, inordinate desire to gain, insatiability, insatiableness, intemperance, intense desire, lust for money, omnivorousness, overindulgence, possessiveness, ravenousness, selfishness, voraciousness, voracity

GRIEF, *noun* adversity, affliction, agony, anguish, anxiety, bereavement, bitterness, broken heart, burden, calamity, casualty, catastrophe, chagrin, concern, contrition, desolation, despair, despondency, disaster, discomfort, discontent, displeasure, dole, dolor, failure, gloom, grievance, hardship, heartache, heavy heart, ill-fortune, malaise, melancholy, misadventure, mischance, misery, misfortune, mishap, ordeal, pain, remorse, reverse, ruin, sadness, sorrow, sorrowfulness, strain, tension, tragedy, tribulation, trouble, vexation, woe, worry

GRIEVANCE, *noun* affliction, annoyance, burden, cause of sorrow, charge, complaint, criticism, discontent, disservice, foul play, grounds for complaint, hardship, iniquity, *iniuria,* injury, injustice, objection, oppression, problem, *querela, querimonia,* reason to complain, trial, trouble, unfairness, vexation, wrong
ASSOCIATED CONCEPTS: arbitration, exhaustion of contractual remedies, grievance committee

GRIEVE, *verb* ache, aggrieve, anguish, be anguished, be sad, bemoan, bewail, complain, cry, cut to the quick, desolate, discommode, distress, feel regret, fret, groan, harass, lament, languish, moan, mourn, pain, pine, repine, rue, sadden, sorrow, suffer, take to heart, torment, wail, weep

GRIEVOUS, *adjective* afflicting, afflictive, agonizing, appalling, arrant, atrocious, bad, base, bitter, burdensome, cataclysmic, catastrophic, crushing, cutting, deplorable, detrimental, dire, disastrous, distressing, doleful, dolorous, dreadful, execrable, glaring, grave, grim, gross, horrible, iniquitous, insufferable, intense, intolerable, lamentable, mournful, nefarious, oppressive, outrageous, pitiable, piteous, plaintive, raw, rueful, ruinous, sad, severe, shameful, sharp, sorrowful, terrible, torturous, tragical, unbearable, vile, violent, woeful
ASSOCIATED CONCEPTS: grievous crime

GROSS *(Flagrant),* ***adjective*** absolute, aggravated, atrocious, big, colossal, considerable, deplorable, dire, disgusting, dreadful, easily seen, egregious, enormous, evident, extreme, fulsome, gigantic, glaring, grave, great, grievous, heinous, horrible, huge, immense, indelicate, lamentable, large, manifest, massive, monstrous, obvious, odious, offensive, outrageous, reprehensible, shameful, shocking, terrible, unmitigated, utter
ASSOCIATED CONCEPTS: gross fraud, gross inadequacy, gross misconduct, gross neglect, gross negligence, gross unfairness

GROSS *(Total),* ***adjective*** aggregate, all-inclusive, complete, comprehensive, entire, exhaustive, full, inclusive, *incredibilis,* intact, inviolate, lacking nothing, *magnus, nimius,* plenary, unabridged, unbroken, uncut, undeducted from, undeleted, undiminished, undivided, unexpurgated, unreduced, unshorn, unshortened, whole, without deductions
ASSOCIATED CONCEPTS: easement in gross, gross earnings, gross estate, gross income, gross profit, gross receipts, gross sales, gross value

GROSS REVENUES, *noun* aggregate income, all encompassing revenues, comprehensive earnings, gross income, income without deductions, total proceeds

GROUND, *noun* assumption, backbone, base, basis, *causa,* cause, cause for complaint, cause for protest, complaint, criticism, data, evidence, fact, footing, foundation, grave injustice, gross wrong, inequity, infliction, iniquity, injury, injustice, justification, motive, objection, oppression, oppressive act, origin, outrage, premise, principle, proof, purpose, *ratio,* rationale, reason, resentment, root, support, supposition, unjust deed, unjustness, wrong
ASSOCIATED CONCEPTS: cause of action, general grounds, good and sufficient grounds, ground for complaint, ground of action, grounds of belief, meritorious grounds, reasonable grounds

GROUNDLESS, *adjective* baseless, empty, erroneous, fallacious, false, ill-founded, inaccurate, paralogistic, unfounded, unjustifiable, unreal, unreasonable, unsound, unsubstantiated, unsupported, unsustainable, unsustained, untenable, untrue, unwarranted, vain, without foundation, without reality

GROUNDS *(Cause),* ***noun*** arguments, base, basis, case, circumstances, data, determinant, documentation, elements, evidence, factors, facts, foundation, fundament, justification,

medium of proof, motive, occasion, principles, proof, pros and cons, provisions, rationale, reason to believe, terms
ASSOCIATED CONCEPTS: grounds to convict of a crime, grounds to impeach, grounds to indict

GROUNDS *(Property),* ***noun*** area, estate, land, lot, premises, parcel, parcel of land, property, real property, realty, section

GROUP, ***noun*** affiliation, aggregate, array, assemblage, assembly, association, band, bracket, branch, category, circle, class, classification, clique, cluster, coalition, collection, community, conglomeration, constituency, corps, crowd, denomination, faction, family, force, galaxy, gathering, genus, guild, horde, league, membership, nomination, order, organization, representation, sect, section, segment, sodality, species, subdivision, team, throng, troupe, sector, unit, variety

GROUP, ***verb*** adjust, align, allocate, arrange, array, assemble, catalog, categorize, class, classify, cluster, codify, collect, combine, compile, compose, congregate, connect, convene, coordinate, form into ranks, gather, index, intertwine, line up, marshal, match, organize, place, put together, rank, register, screen, size, sort, subdivide

GROW *(Enlarge),* ***verb*** accrue, accumulate, advance, amplify, appreciate, augment, burgeon, dilate, earn interest, expand, gain, increase, inflate, intensify, magnify, mellow, multiply, progress, propagate, pullulate, spread, stem, strengthen, swell, thrive, wax, widen

GROW *(Mature),* ***verb*** blossom, build, develop, engender, evolve, expand, germinate, increase, maturate, nurture, progress, pullulate, ripen

GROWTH *(Evolution),* ***noun*** advancement, development, evolvement, expansion, flowering, fruition, germination, improvement, maturation, movement toward adulthood, movement toward maturity, progress, ripening, sprouting, unfolding

GROWTH *(Increase),* ***noun*** accumulation, addition, advancement, aggrandizement, amplification, *auctus,* augmentation, distention, enlargement, escalation, expansion, extension, heightening, increment, *incrementum,* inflation, intensification, multiplication, rise, spread, surge, swell, swelling

GRUELING *(Difficult),* ***adjective*** complex, complicated, difficult, extreme, formidable, hard, harsh, involved, labyrinthine, obscure, onerous, opaque, operose, trying

GRUELING *(Weakening),* ***adjective*** debilitating, devitalizing, enervating, enfeebling, exhausting, fatiguing, onerous, operose, painful, punishing, sapping, tiresome, tiring, weakening, wearying

GUARANTEE, ***verb*** answer for, assume responsibility, assure, back, be responsible for, become liable, become surety for, certify, commit oneself, ensure, *fides,* give assurance, give one's word, guard, hypothecate, impignorate, insure, make oneself answerable for, obligate, pledge, promise, safeguard, secure, *sponsio,* sponsor, stake, support, underwrite, *vadimonium,* vouch for, warrant
ASSOCIATED CONCEPTS: guarantee a title, guarantee against breakage, guarantee payment

GUARANTEED *(Definite),* ***adjective*** agreed, assured, attested, certain, certified, committed, conclusive, definite, dependable, ensured, indubious, inevitable, pledged, promised, reliable, safe, secure, secured, solid, sure

GUARANTEED *(Insured),* ***adjective*** assured, covenanted, ensured, promissory, warranteed

GUARANTOR, ***noun*** approver, attester, backer, co-signatory, cosigner, endorser, guarantee, guaranty, insurer, obligator, sponsor, subscriber, supporter, surety, warrantor
ASSOCIATED CONCEPTS: commercial transactions

GUARANTY, ***noun*** assurance, backing, bond, certification, commitment, endorsement, gage, guard, hypothecation, indemnity, insurance, pact, pledge, promise to pay another's debt, recognizance, safeguard, security, stake, support, surety, token, voucher, warrant, warranty
ASSOCIATED CONCEPTS: absolute guaranty, collateral guaranty, continuing guaranty, fidelity guaranty, guaranty company, guaranty fund, guaranty insurance, guaranty of payment, indemnity bond, limited guaranty, special guaranty, suretyship

GUARD *(Guardian),* ***noun*** bodyguard, custodian, defender, defense, keeper, monitor, palladium, panoply, peace officer, protector, security, sentinel, sentry, surveillance, ward, warden, watchman

GUARD *(Safeguard),* ***noun*** palladium, protection, protector, refuge, safe conduct, safeguard, safekeeping, shield, veil

GUARD, ***verb*** be vigilant, beware, care, conserve, control, cover, defend, detain, ensconce, enshroud, ensure, escort, harbor, keep, keep under surveillance, maintain, make safe, monitor, patrol, preserve, protect, safeguard, save, secure, shelter, shield, supervise, sustain, uphold

GUARD AGAINST, ***verb*** be on the vigil for, be there for, champion, defend, insulate, look out for, overlook, oversee, preserve, protect, safeguard, secure, shield, stand by the side of, stand guard over, superintend, take care of, take measures for, take steps for, watch over
ASSOCIATED CONCEPTS: guard against crime, guard against fraud

GUARDED, ***adjective*** alert, attentive, awake, aware, careful, cautious, *cautus,* chary, circumspect, *circumspectus,* conservative, defended, discreet, fenced, heedful, in custody, noncommittal, protected, prudent, reserved, reticent, safe, safeguarded, secured, sheltered, shielded, shy, suspicious, under surveillance, vigilant, wary, watched over, watchful

GUARDIAN, ***noun*** argus, attendant, bodyguard, caretaker, champion, chaperon, conductor, conservator, curator, custodian, *custos,* defender, *defensor,* escort, gatekeeper, guard, keeper, overseer, patron, *praeses,* preserver, protector, safeguard, safekeeper, sentinel, sentry, sponsor, superintendent, supervisor, trustee, tutelar, warden, warder, watchman
ASSOCIATED CONCEPTS: de facto guardian, domestic guardian, general guardian, guardian ad litem, guardian by statute, guardian de son tort, guardian of the person, legal guardian, special guardian, testamentary guardian
FOREIGN PHRASES: ***Tuta est custodia quae sibimet creditur.*** That guardianship is secure which trusts to itself alone. ***Lucrum facere ex pupilli tutela tutor non debet.*** A guardian ought not to make money out of the guardianship of his ward. ***Custos statum haeredis in custodia existentis meliorem, non deteriorem, facere potest.*** A guardian can make the estate of an existing heir under his guardianship better, but not worse. ***Minor minorem custodire non debet, alios enim praesumitur male regere qui seipsum***

regere nescit. A minor ought not to be guardian to a minor, for a person who knows not how to govern himself is presumed to be unfit to govern others.

GUARDIANSHIP, *noun* adoption, auspices, care, charge, control, custody, patronage, preservation, protection, protectorship, safekeeping, trust

GUESS, *verb* assume, *augurari,* be of the opinion, believe, conjecture, deem, *divinare,* divine, estimate, forejudge, form an estimation, gather, have a hunch, hypothesize, imagine, infer, judge, judge at random, judge with uncertainty, *opinari,* opine, postulate, presume, presuppose, reckon, speculate, suppose, surmise, suspect, take for granted, theorize, think, think likely
ASSOCIATED CONCEPTS: speculative testimony

GUEST, *noun* boarder, confidante, friend, frequenter, houseguest, inmate, lodger, patron, regular, renter, sharer, traveler, visitor
ASSOCIATED CONCEPTS: guest statute

GUIDANCE, *noun* admonition, advice, advisement, advocacy, backing, bidding, briefing, coaching, consilium, consultation, counsel, criticism, cue, direction, directive, *ductus,* edification, education, encouragement, enlightenment, exhortation, expostulation, fosterage, help, hint, inculcation, indoctrination, information, instruction, lead, leadership, lesson, management, monition, opinion, orientation, patronage, pedagogy, persuasion, precept, prescription, prompting, recommendation, reference, schooling, sponsorship, steering, suggestion, supervision, teaching, training, tuition, tutelage, tutoring
ASSOCIATED CONCEPTS: advisory opinion, assistance of counsel, declaratory judgment

GUIDE, *noun* advisor, archetype, bellwether, code, conductor, criterion, director, educator, example, exemplar, generalization, indication, instructor, marshal, master, maxim, mentor, model, monitor, paradigm, paragon, pattern, pedagogue, pilot, precedent, precept, preceptor, precursor, prototype, rule, sample, specimen, standard, symptom, teacher

GUIDE, *verb* advise, attend, command, conduct, control, convoy, counsel, direct, dispose, engineer, escort, familiarize with, go ahead, go in the van, inculcate, indicate, indoctrinate, inform, instill, instruct, lead, light the way, manage, maneuver, marshal, motivate, officiate, orientate, overlook, oversee, predominate, prescribe, preside, prevail, rear, recommend, regulate, rule, shepherd, show, steer, superintend, teach

GUIDELINE, *noun* advisory limitation, aspect, bench mark, borderline indication, boundary, confinement, dictate, dimension, direction, formula, gauge, general guideline, guide, idea, instruction, key, limitation, margin, marker, measure, outer limits, parameter, perimeter, restraint, restriction, rule, specific, standard, yardstick

GUILT, *noun* blame, blameworthiness, breach of law, censurability, corruption, crime, criminal activity, criminal deed, criminal offense, criminality, criminousness, *culpa,* culpability, delict, delinquency, deviation from rectitude, dishonesty, fault, felonious conduct, ill conduct, immorality, impeachability, improbity, improper conduct, iniquity, lawbreaking, malefaction, malfeasance, malpractice, malversation, misbehavior, misconduct, misdeed, misdemeanor, misdoing, misfeasance, misprision, *noxia,* offense, offense against the law, offensiveness, official misconduct, peccadillo, peccancy, reprehensibility, reproach, sin, sinfulness, transgression, turpitude, unlawful practice, unrighteousness, vice, viciousness, violation, violation of law, *vitium,* wrong, wrongdoing
ASSOCIATED CONCEPTS: admission of guilt, finding of guilt, guilt beyond a reasonable doubt, guilt by association, *nolo contendre,* presumption of innocence
FOREIGN PHRASES: ***Cum par delictum est duorum, semper oneratur petitor et melior habetur possessoris causa.*** When there is equal fault on both sides, the burden is always placed on the plaintiff, and the cause of the possessor is preferred. ***Quae sunt minoris culpae sunt majoris infamiae.*** Those things which are less culpable may be more infamous. ***Poenae suos tenere debet actores et non alios.*** Punishment belongs to the guilty and not others. ***Excusat aut extenuat delictum in capitalibus quod non operatur idem in civilibus.*** That excuses or extenuates a wrong in capital cases which would not have the same effect in civil suits.

GUILTY, *adjective* at fault, blamable, blameworthy, censurable, chargeable, condemnable, convicted, criminal, criminous, culpable, delinquent, deserving of blame, deserving of punishment, deserving reproof, erring, imputable, in error, in the wrong, incriminated, indictable, peccant, reprehensible, reproachable, reprovable, *sceleratus,* to blame, transgressing
ASSOCIATED CONCEPTS: bail, conviction, find the defendant guilty, guilty as charged, guilty knowledge, guilty of the crime charged, guilty of wrongdoing, innocence, insanity, parole, plea of guilty, qualified plea of guilty, sentencing, verdict

GUILTY ACT, *noun* blameworthy action, blameworthy conduct, contemptuous action, contrite, culpable act, culpable action, culpable feat, culpable undertaking, culpable wrongdoing, guilty action, guilty behavior, guilty conduction, onerous act, onerous action
ASSOCIATED CONCEPTS: ability to stand trial, conviction, guilty plea

GUILTY PLEA, *noun* acceptance of criminal wrongdoing, admission of blame, admission of guilt, admission of punishment, admission of the charges as read, at fault, blameworthiness, conviction, culpable plea, plea of guilt
ASSOCIATED CONCEPTS: Fifth Amendment, plea of nolo contendere, right against self-incrimination torture

GUISE, *noun* act, affectation, airs, appearance, camouflage, charade, cloak, color, costume, deceit, deception, disguise, dissembling, dissimulation, double-dealing, duplicity, excuse, facade, fakery, falseness, falsity, fraud, front, gloss, guise, image, impersonation, infidelity, perfidy, performance, persona, portrayal, pose, pretense, pretext, semblance, show, treachery, treason, unfaithfulness

GUN, *noun* armament, arms, carbine, firearm, lethal instrument, munition, piece, pistol, repeater, revolver, rifle, shotgun, *tormentum,* weapon
ASSOCIATED CONCEPTS: concealed weapon, deadly weapon

GUN CONTROL, *noun* check on the sale of guns, control of armaments, control of arms, control of firearms, control over weapons, limitations on gun sales, limits on owning weapons, private citizen firearm restrictions, prohibition on green sales, prohibition on sale of firearms, prohibition on the ownership of arms, regulation on gun sales, regulation on use of weapons, restrictions on sale of arms, restrictions on weapon sales
ASSOCIATED CONCEPTS: background checks, Brady Law, civil right to gun possession, gun control, mandatory waiting periods, National Rifle Association, right to bear arms, Second Amendment, trigger locks

HABEAS CORPUS, *noun* appeal, application for discharge, application for liberty, collateral review of detention, collateral review, complaint to a higher court, examination, extraordinary remedy, extraordinary writ, judicial reexamination, petition for release, redress, remedy, review, writ, writ for deliverance from illegal confinement, writ to gain freedom
ASSOCIATED CONCEPTS: coram nobis, exhaustion of state remedies, federal writ of habeas corpus, prerogative writ, special proceeding, state writ of habeas corpus, writ of inquiry

HABIT, *noun* acquired mode of behavior, attitude, characteristic behavior, characteristically repeated action, common practice, confirmed way, consuetude, *consuetudo,* convention, conventionality, course of conduct, custom, customary action, customary conduct, disposition, fashion, frequently repeated act, *habitus,* inclination, inveterate practice, leaning, mannerism, mode, *mos,* observance, particularity, pattern, peculiarity, practice, predisposition, proclivity, propensity, recurrence, repetition, routine, rule, second nature, style, tendency, tradition, trait, usual procedure, way
ASSOCIATED CONCEPTS: confirmed habits, continued habits, custom and usage, temperate habits

HABITABLE, *adjective* adequate, appropriate for residence, capable of being inhabited, comfortable, fit for dwelling, fit for habitation, fit to be occupied, fit to live in, *habitabilis,* inhabitable, livable, occupiable, residential, suitable, suitable for living in, tenantable
ASSOCIATED CONCEPTS: warranty of habitability

HABITANT, *noun* abider, boarder, denizen, domiciliary, dweller, *habitator, incola,* indweller, inhabitant, inhabiter, inmate, lodger, occupant, occupier, resident, residentiary, resider, settler, sojourner, squatter, tenant, townsman, villager
ASSOCIATED CONCEPTS: residency laws

HABITATION *(Act of inhabiting),* ***noun*** abiding, continuance, dwelling, habitancy, inhabitance, inhabitancy, inhabitation, lodgment, occupancy, occupation, possession, remaining, residence, residing, settlement, sojourn, sojournment, tenancy

HABITATION *(Dwelling place),* ***noun*** abiding place, abode, accommodations, address, domicile, *domicilium, domus,* dwelling, habitat, headquarters, home, homestead, house, housing, living quarters, lodging, lodgment, nest, place, place of abode, place of residence, quarters, residence, settlement, site, tabernacle, *tectum*

HABITUAL, *adjective* according to habit, accustomary, accustomed, automatic, chronic, common, commonplace, confirmed, constant, consuetudinary, continual, customary, daily, established, expected, familiar, fixed, frequent, general, ingrained, inveterate, *inveteratus,* natural, normal, ordinary, periodic, periodical, perpetual, prevalent, recurrent, recurring, regular, repeated, rooted, routine, set, standard, sustained, traditional, typical, *usitatus,* usual, wonted
ASSOCIATED CONCEPTS: habitual cohabitation, habitual criminal, habitual cruel and inhuman treatment, habitual insanity, habitual intemperance, habitual intoxication, habitual offender, habitual use, habitual violator, predicate felon, recidivist

HABITUATION, *noun* acclimation, acclimatization, accustoming, adaptation, adjustment, conditioning, confirmed habit, customariness, familiarization, inurement, inveteracy, inveterate habit, inveterateness

HACKING, *verb* barging in, breaking into, encroaching, infringing, interceding, interfering, interloping, intermeddling, interposing, intervening, intruding, invading, meddling, nosing, obtruding, prying, tampering, trespassing
ASSOCIATED CONCEPTS: cyberterrorism

HACKING INTO, *verb* breaking in on, breaking into, breaching, cut in on, force into, gaining access, gaining by force, interfere, interlope, interrupt, intervene, intrude on, penetrate
ASSOCIATED CONCEPTS: cybercrime, identity theft

HAGGLE, *verb* argue, bargain, beat down, bid for, chaffer, deal, dicker, dispute, drive a bargain, higgle, make terms, negotiate, palter, quibble, stickle, underbid, wrangle
ASSOCIATED CONCEPTS: arm's-length bargaining, bickering over price

HALLMARK, *noun* champion, example, exemplar, good example, height of perfection, ideal, model, model of virtue, paramount example, specimen, standard, standard for comparison, summit, the best
ASSOCIATED CONCEPTS: hallmark law

HALLOWED, *adjective* adored, blessed, consecrated, divine, glorified, holy, honored, regarded as holy,

respected, revered, sacred, sanctified, venerated, worshiped
ASSOCIATED CONCEPTS: hallowed law

HALT, *noun* abandonment, abeyance, armistice, arrest, block, break, breathing spell, cessation, check, close, closing, deadlock, delay, desistance, detention, deterrent, discontinuance, discontinuation, end, ending, estoppage, estoppel, hesitation, impasse, impediment, inactivity, *intermissio,* intermission, interruption, lapse, lull, obstruction, pause, prevention, prohibition, recess, remission, respite, rest, shutdown, stalemate, standstill, stay, stop, stopover, stoppage, suspension, termination, time out, truce, wait
ASSOCIATED CONCEPTS: freeze, injunction, restraining order

HALT, *verb* adjourn, arrest, balk, bar, bar someone's way, barricade, block, blockade, break, break off, bring to a standstill, call a halt, cease, check, come to a stop, *consistere,* counteract, curb, cut short, dam, deadlock, debar, defeat, desist, deter, disallow, discontinue, end, estop, foil, forbid, frustrate, hamper, hinder, hold, impede, inhibit, interrupt, make inactive, obstruct, pause, preclude, prevent, prohibit, put an end to, quell, quit, remain, rest, restrain, restrict, stand, stand still, stay, stem, stop, stop an advance, stop short, subdue, *subsistere,* suspend, terminate, thwart, wait
ASSOCIATED CONCEPTS: abandon a crime, discontinue an action, injunction, stop and frisk laws

HAMPER, *verb* arrest, balk, bar, barricade, bind, block, brake, bridle, burden, check, choke, clog, confine, counteract, cramp, curb, debar, delay, deter, encumber, estop, fetter, foil, frustrate, handicap, hinder, hold back, impede, *impedire,* impedite, *implicare,* inhibit, intercept, interfere, interrupt, limit, manacle, muzzle, obstruct, oppose, preclude, prevent, rein, repress, resist, restrain, restrict, retard, shackle, smother, stymie, suppress, thwart, trammel, undermine, withhold
ASSOCIATED CONCEPTS: hamper a prosecution

HAND DOWN AN OPINION, *verb* adjudge, adjudicate, allow, arbitrate, articulate, comment, commentate, conclude, decide, determine, editorialize, express, judge, moderate, note, observe, opine, prosecute, referee, reflect, resolve, rule, settle, speak, specify, state, umpire, weigh in
ASSOCIATED CONCEPTS: directed verdict, final judgment, summary judgment

HAND OVER, *verb* abandon, abjure, abnegate, accede, capitulate, cede, commit, concede, consign, deliver, demit, deny, desert, disavow, discard, disclaim, disown, entrust, forfeit, forsake, give up, issue, lay down, part with, present, release, relinquish, renounce, resign, shed, surrender, transfer, turn in, turn over, vacate, yield
ASSOCIATED CONCEPTS: disclosure, hand over a defendant, hand over evidence

HANDCUFF, *noun* bond, bridle, chain, collar, fastener, fetter, harness, manacle, *manicae,* padlock, pinion, shackle, trammel

HANDCUFF, *verb* belay, bind, bridle, chain, enchain, entrammel, fasten, fetter, gyve, hamper, hold, lash, leash, make fast, manacle, pinion, put in irons, render powerless, rope, secure, shackle, strap, string, tether, tie, tie one's hands, tie the hands of, tie up, trammel

HANDICAP, *noun* affliction, barrier, blemish, bridle, burden, defect, deficiency, detriment, difficulty, disability, disadvantage, discommodity, drawback, encumbrance, faultiness, hindrance, hurdle, impairment, impediment, *impedimentum,* imperfection, inconvenience, inferiority, insufficiency, interference, limitation, obstacle, obstruction, onus, remora, restraint, shortcoming, stumbling block

HANDLE *(Manage),* ***verb*** administer, be master of, command, conduct, control, deal with, direct, dominate, execute, exercise authority, exercise direction over, exercise power over, exert authority, govern, guide, have authority, have charge of, have the care of, have the direction of, have under control, hold authority, keep in order, keep order, keep under control, look after, manipulate, officiate, operate, possess authority, preside over, regulate, reign over, rule, see to, superintend, supervise, use, wield, wield authority

HANDLE *(Trade),* ***verb*** auction, barter, bring to market, carry, carry on a trade, carry on business, carry on commerce, carry on negotiations, chaffer, conduct business, deal in, do business, drive a bargain, effect a sale, exchange, exchange in commerce, have commerce, have for sale, hawk, interchange, make a bargain, make a sale, market, merchandise, offer for sale, peddle, put up for sale, sell, sell at the market, trade, trade in, traffic in, transact business, vend

HANDLING, *noun* administration, carrying out, conduct, control, direction, discipline, disposition of, effective management, effectuation, enforcement, governing, guidance, have charge of, management, mastermind, oversight, pilot the project, preside over, regulation, rule over, superintendence over, supervision over
ASSOCIATED CONCEPTS: handling of a case, handling of an issue, handling of litigation, handling stolen goods, safe patient handling law

HANDSEL, *noun* deposit, down payment, earnest money, first installment, first payment, first receipts, installment, payment, security, stake money

HANDWRITING, *noun* autography, calligraphy, *chirographum,* chirography, cursive writing, hand, longhand, *manus,* pencraft, penmanship, script, scription, style of penmanship, writing
ASSOCIATED CONCEPTS: forgery, handwriting expert, handwriting sample, holographic wills

HANG, *verb* condemn to death, corporal punishment, deprive of life, dispose of by death, end the life of a condemned, inflict capital punishment, inflict mortal punishment, kill, murder, punish by death, punish with death, put to death, put to death according to law, slay, snuff out the life of, terminate the life of
ASSOCIATED CONCEPTS: death by lethal injection, death penalty, electric chair, gas chamber, right to life

HAPHAZARD, *adjective* accidental, adventitious, arbitrary, capricious, casual, chance, chaotic, confused, designless, desultory, determined by chance, disordered, disorderly, fitful, immethodical, indiscriminate, irregular, nonsystematic, orderless, planless, promiscuous, random, systemless, unaimed, unarranged, unconsidered, undirected, unforeseen, unguided, unintended, unintentional, unmethodical, unorganized, unplanned, unpredictable, unpremeditated, unsorted, unsystematic, without order

HAPPEN, *verb* appear, arise, arrive, become, become a fact, become known, befall, bring to light, come into being, come into existence, crop up, develop, emerge, ensue, eventuate, issue, materialize, occur, proceed, recur, result, take effect, take its course, take place, transpire, turn up, uncover, unearth

HAPPENING, *noun* action, affair, *casus,* chance event, course of events, development, episode, event, experience, incident, matter, occasion, occurrence, phenomenon, proceeding, transpiration, unfolding
ASSOCIATED CONCEPTS: unforeseen happening

HAPPENSTANCE, *noun* accident, accidental occurrence, casualty, chance, chance happening, circumstance, coincidence, fate, fortuitousness, fortuity, inexpectation, involuntariness, random luck, serendipity, unexpected occurrence, unforeseen occurrence, unpredictability

HAPPY, *adjective* animated, at peace, blissful, bright, bubbling over, buoyant, carefree, celebrating, cheerful, cheery, chipper, contented, convivial, delighted, delirious, ecstatic, elated, enchanted, enraptured, euphoric, exhilarated, exuberant, exultant, favorable, felicitous, festive, flourishing, full of cheer, fun-loving, genial, glad, good-humored, intoxicated, jocund, joking, jovial, joyful, jubilant, laughing, merry, of good cheer, on top of the world, overjoyed, peaceful, pleased as punch, positive, prosperous, radiant, rapturous, rejoicing, smiling, sparkling, spirited, thrilled, thriving, untroubled, upbeat, vivacious, zestful
ASSOCIATED CONCEPTS: happy outcome to litigation

HARANGUE, *noun* abusive speech, bombast, *contio,* declamation, declamatory speech, diatribe, disquisition, effusion, exhortation, expatiation, invective, lecture, prelection, tirade, vehement speech
ASSOCIATED CONCEPTS: harassment

HARASS, *verb* acerbate, afflict, aggrieve, agitate, agonize, alarm, alienate, anger, annoy, arose, arrogate, assail, badger, bagger, be malevolent, bedevil, beset, besiege, bludgeon, bother, browbeat, burden, coerce, confound, convulse, discomfort, discompose, disconcert, dismay, dispirit, disquiet, distress, disturb, enrage, envenom, *exagitare,* exasperate, excite, excruciate, fret, goad, grieve, harbor a grudge, harrow, harry, haunt, heckle, hurt, ill-treat, ill-use, importance, incense, incommode, infest, inflame, infuriate, injure persistently, intimidate, intrude upon, irk, irritate, malign, maltreat, miff, misuse, mock, obsess, offend, oppress, outrage, overburden, overdrive, overrun, overstrain, overtax, overwork, perplex, pester, pique, plague, prey upon, provoke, rankle, shake up, *sollicitare,* spite, strain, terrorize, torment, trouble, tyrannize, unsettle, upbraid, upset, vex, *vexare,* victimize, wear down, weigh on
ASSOCIATED CONCEPTS: barratry, employment law, harassing a witness, workplace sexual harassment

HARASSMENT, *noun* alarm, annoyance, bother, discomfort, disconcertedness, dismay, disregard, disturbance, enragement, excitement, injury, offense, outrageous behavior, outrageous conduct pain, provocation, rankle
ASSOCIATED CONCEPTS: employment law, sexual harassment, workplace violation

HARBINGER, *noun* announcer, annunciator, *antecursor,* augur, augury, auspice, courier, crier, forerunner, foretoken, forewarning, herald, informer, intelligencer, messenger, omen, portent, *praenuntius,* precursor, premonitory sign, presage, proclaimer, prognostic, publicizer, sign, teller, usher, warning

HARBOR, *verb* afford sanctuary, aid, cache, care for, cloak, conceal, cover, defend, ensconce, give refuge, grant asylum, guard, haven, hide, insure, keep, keep out of sight, keep safe, keep secret, lodge, look after, maintain, preserve, protect, provide refuge, provide safety, provide sanctuary, quarter, safeguard, screen, seclude, secrete, secure, shelter, shield, shroud, stow away, sustain, watch
ASSOCIATED CONCEPTS: accessory after the fact, alienation of affections, assisting escape, harbor and secrete, harboring a criminal, harboring a fugitive, harboring an animal

HARD, *adjective* arduous, beyond one's reach, bothersome, burdensome, complex, complicated, convoluted, demanding, difficult, enigmatic, grueling, impassable, impenetrable, incomprehensible, insoluble, insurmountable, involved, involving obstacles, overwhelming, perplexing, problematic, puzzling, vigorous, strenuous, stubborn, troublesome, unachievable, unavailable
ASSOCIATED CONCEPTS: hard-and-fast law, hard choices, hard lessons learned from law

HARD-CORE, *adjective* adamant, constant, decided, dedicated, determined, devoted, enduring, firm, fixed, hard, immobile, immovable, inexorable, inflexible, intractable, intransigent, invariable, obdurate, obstinate, opinionated, persevering, persistent, recalcitrant, relentless, resolute, rigid, set, settled, solid, stanch, steadfast, steady, stern, stiff, strong, stubborn, tenacious, unbending, unchangeable, uncompromising, uncontrollable, undeviating, unwavering, zealous
ASSOCIATED CONCEPTS: pornography

HARDENED, *adjective* calculated, calculating, callous, cold, cold-hearted, cruel, cruel-hearted, deliberate, diabolic, dispassionate, fiendish, hard, imperturbable, impervious, indifferent, insensitive, passionless, remorseless, ruthless, uncaring, unconcerned, unemotional, unfeeling, uninterested, unkind, unmerciful, unmoved, unperturbed, unrelenting, unresponsive, unsympathetic, untouched
ASSOCIATED CONCEPTS: hardened criminal

HARDLY, *adverb* almost, almost all, barely, deficient, few, inadequately, incomplete, inconsiderably, insufficiently, limited, little, meagerly, not abundant, not plentiful, not quite, paltry, rarely, scantly, scarcely, seldomly, sparingly, sparsely, thinly scattered

HARDSHIP, *noun* adversity, affliction, misfortune, suffering, travail

HARM, *noun* aggravation, balefulness, bedevilment, damage, *damnum,* deadliness, detriment, *detrimentum,* disablement, disservice, evil, hurt, hurtfulness, ill consequence, ill-treatment, impairment, injury, malignance, malignancy, malignity, mischief, misfortune, mutilation, noxiousness, perniciousness, ruin, scathe, scourge, virulence
ASSOCIATED CONCEPTS: accidental harm, bodily harm, forseeable harm, irreparable harm, unreasonable risk of harm

HARM, *verb* abuse, adulterate, afflict, aggravate, attack, be malevolent, bruise, cause pain, corrode, corrupt, cripple, damage, debase, deface, demolish, devastate, disadvantage, disfigure, disserve, do evil, do mischief, do violence, endamage, exacerbate, hurt, ill-treat, ill-use, impair, incapacitate, infect, inflict injury, injure, *laedere,* maim, maltreat, mar, misuse, mutilate, *nocere,* pervert, plague, pollute, ravage, ruin, scathe, scourge, smite, spoil, subvert, worsen, wound, wrong

ASSOCIATED CONCEPTS: accidental harm, bodily harm, forseeable harm, irreparable harm, unreasonable harm

FOREIGN PHRASES: ***Error scribentis nocere non debit.*** An error made by a clerk ought not to prejudice. ***Qui jure suo utitur, nemini facit injuriam.*** One who exercises his legal rights, injures no one.

HARMFUL, ***adjective*** afflicting, bad, baleful, baneful, calamitous, cataclysmic, catastrophic, consuming, consumptive, corrosive, costly, crippling, cruel, crushing, damaging, dangerous, deleterious, destructive, detracting, detrimental, devouring, dire, disadvantageous, disastrous, disserviceable, evil, fell, fiendish, foul, hurtful, illintentioned, inexpedient, infectious, injurious, insalubrious, insidious, internecine, malefic, maleficent, malicious, malign, mephitic, merciless, miasmal, mischievous, morbific, nasty, *nocens,* nocent, nocuous, noisome, noxious, *noxius,* pernicious, pestiferous, pestilential, pitiless, poisonous, polluted, ruinous, spiteful, subversionary, subversive, toxic, treacherous, troublous, unfavorable, unfortunate, unhealthy, unlucky, unpropitious, unsafe, unwholesome, venomous, vicious, wicked, wounding

ASSOCIATED CONCEPTS: harmful consequences from an overt act, harmful products

HARMLESS, ***adjective*** benign, blunt, gentle, hurtless, impotent, *innocens,* innocent, innocuous, *innocuus,* innoxious, *innoxius,* inoffensive, nonmalignant, nonpoisonous, nontoxic, nonvenomous, nonviolent, nonvirulent, powerless, tame, trustworthy, unaggressive, unhazardous, uninjurious, unmilitant, unthreatening, weak, without risk

ASSOCIATED CONCEPTS: harmless beyond a reasonable doubt, harmless error, hold harmless

HARMONIOUS, ***adjective*** accordant, acquiescent, adapted, adjusted, agreeable, agreeing, allied, amicable, apposite, apt, arranged, assenting, becoming, blended, bonded, *canorus,* coexistent, coexisting, combined, compatible, concinnous, concordant, *concors,* conforming, congenial, *congruens,* congruent, congruous, consentaneous, consentient, consistent, consonant, cooperative, coordinated, correlative, correspondent, corresponding, equable, fraternal, frictionless, friendly, halcyon, joint, leagued, matching, pacific, peaceful, pleasant, pleasing, proportional, proportionate, sociable, suitable, suiting, unanimous, united, unstrained, untroubled

HARNESS, ***verb*** control, command, constraint, curb, direct, dominate, get one's hands around, get the entire picture on, govern, guide, handle, instruct, lead, limit, maintain, manage, operate, overlook, oversee, pilot, rule, superintend, supervise

ASSOCIATED CONCEPTS: harness and control energy, seat belt harness laws

HARP, ***verb*** accentuation, attention, beat into the ground, drill into someone's head, bother, disturb, dwell on, emphasize, force, go over and over, hammer into someone's head, harass, harp on, hassle, persist in, pester, pound into someone's head, push, reiterate, repeat, state repeatedly

HARROW, ***verb*** aggrieve, agitate, alarm, annoy, appall, assail, badger, bedevil, beset, besiege, bother, browbeat, bully, chafe, chagrin, cross, discompose, disconcert, dismay, displease, disquiet, disturb, *excruciare,* fret, give pain, harass, harm, harry, hurt, ill-treat, ill-use, inflict pain, injure, irritate, lacerate, lancinate, maltreat, misuse, molest, needle, outrage, persecute, perturb, pique, plague, provoke, spite, tease, torment, *torquere,* try, upset, vex, *vexare,* wrong

HARRY *(Harass),* ***verb*** aggrieve, annoy, badger, bait, be offensive, be rude, beleaguer, beset, bother, browbeat, bully, *cruciare,* deride, discompose, disconcert, displease, distress, disturb, fluster, fret, haze, heckle, hound, importune, irritate, needle, offend, oppress, persecute, pester, pique, plague, provoke, rile, ruffle, tease, torment, *torquere,* try, vex, *vexare,* worry

HARRY *(Plunder),* ***verb*** assail, attack, create havoc, despoil, forage, foray, invade, lay waste, maraud, pillage, raid, ransack, ravage, rob, sack, seize, spoliate, strip

HARSH, ***adjective*** acerb, acerbic, acid, acrid, acrimonious, ascetic, astringent, austere, biting, bitter, brusque, brutal, burning, caustic, corrosive, crude, cruel, despiteful, discordant, disrespectful, draconian, drastic, excessive, extreme, feral, ferine, ferocious, grating, grim, grueling, gruff, ill-natured, incisive, inclement, inharmonious, inhuman, inhumane, intense, merciless, mordacious, mordant, noisome, noxious, oppressive, piercing, pitiless, punishing, rancorous, rigorous, rough, ruthless, savage, scathing, severe, sharp, stern, stinging, strident, stridulous, stringent, surly, truculent, uncomforting, unconsoling, unfeeling, unflattering, ungentle, ungracious, unkind, unkindly, unmerciful, unmitigated, unpitying, unsympathetic, untender, virulent, vituperative, withering

ASSOCIATED CONCEPTS: cruel and unusual punishment, harsh penalty, harsh rule

HASTE, ***noun*** acceleration, alacrity, briskness, celerity, dash, dispatch, eagerness to act quickly, expedition, expeditiousness, *festinatio,* flurry, frenzy, hurriedness, hurry, hustle, inability to wait, precipitance, precipitancy, precipitation, precipitousness, *properantia, properatio,* quickness, rapidity, rashness, rush, speed, swiftness, urgency, velocity

ASSOCIATED CONCEPTS: speedy trial

FOREIGN PHRASES: ***Festinatio justitiae est noverca infortunii.*** The hastening of justice is the stepmother of misfortune.

HASTEN, ***verb*** accelerate, advance, *contendere,* dash, dispatch, drive forward, expedite, facilitate, forward, help along, hurry, hurry along, hustle, incite, lose no time, make haste, *maturare,* move fast, move quickly, move speedily, precipitate, press, pressure, promote, *properare,* push on, put on speed, race, rouse, rush, rush through, speed along, spur, urge on

HATE, ***noun*** abhorrence, abomination, anger, animosity, animus, antagonism, antipathy, aversion, bias, bitterness, contempt, detestation, disdain, disgust, dislike, distaste, enmity, execration, grudge, hatred, horror, hostility, ill feeling, ill will, intolerance, loathing, malevolence, malice, malignancy, meanness, odium, prejudice, rancor, repugnance, repulsion, resentment, revulsion, scorn, spite, umbrage, venom, virulence, vitriol

ASSOCIATED CONCEPTS: hate crimes

HATE CRIME, ***noun*** offense involving animosity toward others, offense involving antagonism toward others, offense involving discrimination, offense involving enmity toward others, offense involving hate, offense involving hatred, offense involving intolerance, offense involving malevolence toward others, offense involving prejudice, offense involving victim's color of skin, offense involving victim's ethnicity, offense involving victim's gender, offense involving victim's national origin, offense involving victim's race, offense involving victim's religion, offense involving victim's sexual orientation

HATRED, *noun* abhorrence, abomination, animosity, animus, antagonism, antipathy, aversion, defamation, detestation, dislike, enmity, hostility, ill feeling, ill will, intolerance, loathing, malevolence, odium, prejudice, revulsion

HAVEN, *noun* anchorage, asylum, citadel, cove, harbor, hideout, landing, place of safety, port, *portus,* protection, refuge, resting place, retreat, sanctuary, shelter
ASSOCIATED CONCEPTS: diplomatic immunity

HAVING NO FOUNDATION, *adjective* baseless, empty, erroneous, false, foundationless, gratuitous, groundless, idle, ill-founded, illogical, nonactual, rootless, unbased, uncorroborated, unfounded, ungrounded, unjustifiable, unreasonable, unsound, unsubstantial, unsubstantiated, unsupportable, unsustainable, untenable, unwarranted, without basis, without cause, without foundation, without reality, without reason

HAVOC, *noun* anarchy, carnage, cataclysm, chaos, chaotic state, confusion, depredation, derangement, desolation, destruction, devastation, disorder, disorganization, dispersion, disruption, holocaust, overturning, pillage, plundering, ravage, ruin, ruination, sack, scattering, shambles, spoliation, *strages,* turmoil, upheaval, *vastatio,* violence, waste
ASSOCIATED CONCEPTS: disorderly conduct, disturbing the peace

HAZARD, *noun* *casus,* cause for alarm, chance, danger, dangerous course, dangerous situation, endangerment, *fors,* gamble, imperilment, insecurity, jeopardy, liability to injury, menace, *periculum,* peril, pitfall, precariousness, risk, source of risk, threat, uncertainty, unsafe object, unsureness
ASSOCIATED CONCEPTS: dangerous hazard, extreme hazard, hazardous business, hazardous condition, hazardous employment, hazardous undertaking, inherent hazard, latent hazard, moral hazard, patent hazard, private hazard, public hazard, undue hazard

HAZARDOUS *(Dangerous),* ***adjective*** adverse, chancy, dangerous, fraught with danger, full of danger, insalubrious, insecure, noxious, ominous, perilous, precarious, risky, shaky, threatening, toxic, unprotected, unreliable, unsafe, unsound, unsteady
ASSOCIATED CONCEPTS: hazardous materials, hazardous substances, hazardous waste

HAZARDOUS *(Imprudent),* ***adjective*** aleatory, chancy, full of risk, menacing, riskful, speculative, threatening, venturesome, venturous
ASSOCIATED CONCEPTS: aleatory contract

HEAD *(Chairperson),* ***noun*** acme, apex, beginning, cap, capital, chairman, chief, commandant, commencement, conclusion, crest, crisis, crown, crowning event, director, employer, end, flowering, fructification, fruition, heading, height, inception, issue, leader, manager, master, overseer, person in control, prime, principal, realization, ruler, section, superior, supervisor, top, ultimate, upper part, windup, zenith

HEAD *(Culmination),* ***noun*** conclusion, consummation, finality, finish, paramount, pinnacle, summit

HEAD *(Initiate),* ***verb*** incept, instigate, introduce, lead, lead the way, originate, pioneer, precurse, set in motion, spearhead, take the lead

HEAD *(Oversee),* ***verb*** command, control, determine, direct, govern, guide, inaugurate, incept, introduce, manage, officiate, originate, preside, preside over, regulate, spearhead, superintend, supervise

HEADLINE, *noun* banner, caption, communication, head, header, heading, lead to a story, lead to an article, lead to written copy, major announcement, major development, major news, news, news headline, post, reportage, reporting, running head, significant disclosure, superscription, title

HEAD-ON, *adjective* contrary to in direct opposition, convergence in direct opposition, crash, encounter, impact, meeting, percussion, striking together, sudden contact, violent contact

HEADING, *noun* banner, caption, head, headline, label, proper title, section, superscription, title, topic

HEADQUARTERS, *noun* base, base camp, base of authority, base of operations, center, center of authority, center of operations, central station, chief office, distributing center, home base, home office, main office, manager's office, *praetorium,* residence, seat, supply base
ASSOCIATED CONCEPTS: nerve center of a corporation

HEADSTRONG, *adjective* audacious, bullheaded, cantankerous, contrary, contumacious, disobedient, foolhardy, forward, headlong, hot-blooded, impetuous, incautious, inexorable, inflexible, intractable, irresponsible, obdurate, obstinate, pertinacious, perverse, pigheaded, precipitate, rash, recalcitrant, reckless, resolute, restive, self-assured, self-willed, strong-willed, stubborn, uncontrollable, ungovernable, unhesitating, unmanageable, unruly, untoward, unyielding, vehement, wanton

HEADWAY, *noun* advance, ascent, betterment, climb, development, forward motion, furtherance, gain, ground gained, growth, improvement, momentum, progress, progression, promotion, upswing

HEAL, *verb* alleviate, ameliorate, attend to, be on the mend, convalesce, cure, cure medically, disinfect, doctor, effect a cure, fix, fix up, get better, get well, grow better, help to get well, improve, make better, make right, make well, make whole, meliorate, mend, minister to, mitigate, nurse, on tract, palliate, rebuild, reconstruct, recover, recuperate, regenerate, rehabilitate, reinvigorate, rejuvenate, relieve, remedy, renew, repair, restore, restore to health, resuscitate, revitalize, revive, set straight, set right, show improvement, take care of, treat, work a cure

HEALTH, *noun* condition, fitness, freedom from ailment, freedom from disease, haleness, hardiness, heartiness, physical condition, robustness, ruggedness, salubriousness, salubrity, *salus, sanitas,* soundness, soundness of body, stamina, state of health, strength, sturdiness, *valetudo,* vigor, vitality, well-being, wholesomeness
ASSOCIATED CONCEPTS: bill of health, board of health, dangerous to health, department of health, health care, health

education and welfare, health insurance, impairment of health, mental health, public health and safety, public health law, sanitary code

HEALTH CARE, *noun* coverage, health coverage, health insurance, health protection, medical coverage, medical insurance, medical plan, plan

HEALTH MAINTENANCE ORGANIZATION, *noun* closed medical organization, closed medical panel, controlled medical coverage, HMO, supervised medical care
Generally: group health care coverage, health maintenance coverage

HEAR *(Give a legal hearing),* ***verb*** adjudicate, *causam, cognoscere,* conduct a trial, decide, examine judicially, examine the witnesses, give a formal hearing to, give a judicial hearing to, give an official hearing to, hold court, inquire into, investigate judicially, judge, preside over, put on trial, referee, sit in judgment, try, try a case, try the cause
ASSOCIATED CONCEPTS: arbitrate, hear and report, mediate

HEAR *(Give attention to),* ***verb*** accept advice, acknowledge, advert, attend to, audition, ausculate, be attentive, be guided by, *cognoscere,* comply, defer to, give audience, give way, heed, listen, mind, note, obey, pay attention, regard, submit, subscribe, succumb, yield

HEAR *(Perceive by ear),* ***verb*** *auribus,* become aware of, become conscious of, detect, discern something audible, make out, notice, perceive something audible, *percipere,* receive information aurally, recognize, take cognizance of

HEAR A CASE, *verb* consider the merits of a case, determine the outcome of litigation, hear opposing sides in a case, hear the evidence presented, hear the testimony presented, listen to the evidence, listen to the merits of a case, listen to the testimony submitted, try a case, weigh the evidence in a case
ASSOCIATED CONCEPTS: judgment, litigation

HEARING, *noun* action, case at law, close inquiry, *cognitio,* contest, examination, exhaustive inquiry, formal proceeding, formal questioning, inquest, inquiry, inquisition, interrogation, investigation, judicial examination, judicial investigation, legal proceedings, legal trial, litigation, presentation of arguments and evidence, presentation of testimony, probe, public inquest, public proceeding, searching inquiry, strict inquiry, trial, trial at the bar, trial by jury, trial in court
ASSOCIATED CONCEPTS: adjudicative hearing, adversary hearing, de novo hearing, default hearing, due process, fair and impartial hearing, fair hearing, final hearing, formal hearing, full hearing, hearing on damages, hearing on the merits, interlocutory hearing, judicial hearing, notice of hearing, preliminary hearing, public hearing, statutory hearing, suppression hearing, traverse
FOREIGN PHRASES: ***Qui aliquid statuerit, parte inaudita altera, aequum licet dixerit, haud aequum fecerit.*** He who decides anything without hearing both sides, although he may decide correctly, has by no means acted justly.

HEARING OFFICER, *noun* adjudicator, arbitrator, administrative officer, final authority, hearing examiner, intermediary, intervener, mediator, moderator, negotiator, reconciler
ASSOCIATED CONCEPTS: administrative law judge, chief administrator hearing officer, staff hearing officer

HEARSAY, *noun* *auditio,* evidence from impersonal knowledge, gossip, groundless rumor, indirect evidence, popular report, report, *rumor,* secondary evidence, secondhand evidence, unconfirmed account, unconfirmed report, unverified comments, unverified news
ASSOCIATED CONCEPTS: admission, ancient writings, business records, declarations against pecuniary interest, declarations against penal interest, dying declarations, exceptions to hearsay rules, hearsay evidence, records of past recollection, reputation as to pedigree, res gestae, spontaneous declarations

HEART *(Essential part),* ***noun*** core, essence, fundamental, marrow, nerve, nucleus, pith, sum and substance
ASSOCIATED CONCEPTS: heart of the case, heart of the pleadings

HEART *(Fortitude),* ***noun*** ardor, backbone, doughtiness, fearlessness, fervor, focus, gallantry, intestinal fortitude, mettle, spirit, substance, toleration, valor

HEART *(Kindness),* ***noun*** altruism, benevolence, charity, clemency, compassion, gentleness, grace, humanity, kind offices, kind treatment, leniency, magnanimity, mercifulness, mercy, pity, sympathy, temperament, tenderness

HEARTENING, *adjective* assuring, auspicious, bright, cheerful, comforting, consoling, encouraging, favorable, felicitous, fortunate, full of promise, halcyonian, halcyonic, hopeful, opportune, optimistic, promising, propitious, providential, reassuring, roseate, salubrious, salutary

HEARTLESS, *adjective* apathetic, brutal, callous, cold, cold-blooded, cruel, disdainful, disinterested, dispassionate, hardened, hard-hearted, impervious, indifferent, insensible, insensitive, insouciant, insusceptible, iron-hearted, obdurate, passionless, pitiless, remorseless, ruthless, sinister, soulless, spiritless, stony, unaffected, uncaring, unconcerned, unemotional, unfeeling, unforgiving, unmoved, unpitying, unrelenting, unresponsive, unsusceptible, unsympathetic, untouched, without compunction

HEAVEN, *noun* abode of God, abode of God and angels, abode of spirits, abode of the saints, aerosphere, afterworld, bliss, canopy of heaven, celestial city, celestial sphere, city of God, divine abode, ecstasy, eternal home, Garden of Eden, glory, God's kingdom, great beyond, heavenly city, heavenly home, heavenly kingdom, hereafter, holy city, home of the Gods, kingdom of God, kingdom of heaven, life everlasting, next world, paradise, rapture, supreme happiness, the abode of saints, the hereafter, throne of God, utopia, Valhalla, world to come

HEAVY *(Burdened),* ***adjective*** benumbing, careworn, clumsy, dejected, depressed with sorrow, dull, dulled, gloomy, languid, leaden, serious, sluggish, somber, stolid, tempestuous, tiresome, torpid, violent, weary
ASSOCIATED CONCEPTS: heavy burden to fulfill in order to prove a case

HEAVY *(Important),* ***adjective*** commanding, eventful, immense, noteworthy, overwhelming, prominent, significant, solemn, vast

HEAVY *(Onerous),* ***adjective*** afflictive, burdensome, consequential, critical, cumbersome, difficult, excessive, grave, grievous, hard, imposing, intense, intolerable, momentous, notable, oppressive, striking, severe, substantial, trying, unbearable, unpleasant, unwieldy, wearying

HEAVY *(Ponderous),* ***adjective*** careful, deliberate, ominous, profound, serious, weighty

HEAVY-HANDED, ***adjective*** crushing, determined, firm, forceful, forcible, hard, harsh, inflexible, intense, perseverant, persevering, persistent, persuasive, potent, powerful, puissant, resolute, rugged, staunch, steadfast, steady, tenacious, unremitting, unyielding, vigorous

HECTOR, ***verb*** badger, bait, beset, bluster, bother, browbeat, bully, cow, distress, disturb, fret, gibe, goad, harass, harrow, harry, heckle, hound, insult, intimidate, irritate, jeer, menace, molest, nag, nettle, offend, persecute, pester, plague, pother, provoke, roil, tease, threaten, torment, treat with insolence, trouble, vex, worry

HEDGE, ***noun*** caution, circumspection, course of protection, equivocation, hesitancy, hesitation, instrumentality of protection, means of protection, method of protection, prevention against loss, prevention of downside, protection, protection against loss, safeguard
ASSOCIATED CONCEPTS: hedge laws, hedges encroaching on another, hedge against inflation, notice of appeal as hedge against loss, person's property

HEDGE, ***verb*** be careful, be cautious, border, bound, circle, circumscribe, compass, conceal, cover, delimit, delimitate, delineate, demarcate, divide, dodge, edge, encircle, enclose, encompass, ensphere, evade, fence, flank, girdle, guard, hide, limit, mark off, outline, play safe, protect, render safe, ring, safeguard, screen, shelter, shield, surround

HEED, ***verb*** attend to, be attentive, be aware, be careful, be cautious, be conscious of, be guided by, check, comply, consider, *curare,* follow, hark, hear, hearken to, listen to, look to, mark, mind, note, notice, obey, *observare,* observe, *parere,* pay attention, recognize, regard, respect, take care, take cognizance of, take into account, take note, take notice, watch
ASSOCIATED CONCEPTS: heed counsel's advice

HEEDLESS, ***adjective*** blind, careless, deaf, disregardful, hasty, improvident, imprudent, impulsive, inattentive, incautious, *incautus,* insouciant, irresponsible, mindless, neglectful, *neglegens,* negligent, nonobservant, oblivious, off guard, precipitate, rash, reckless, *temerarius,* thoughtless, unaware, uncaring, unconcerned, undiscerning, unhearing, unheedful, unheeding, unmindful, unnoticing, unobservant, unperceiving, unseeing, unsolicitous, unthinking, unwary, unwatchful, without consideration
ASSOCIATED CONCEPTS: recklessness

HEGEMONY, ***noun*** ascendance, ascendancy, authority, command, control, directorship, dominance, domination, dominion, governance, headship, importance, influence, lawful authority, leadership, lordship, mastery, paramountcy, power, predominance, predominating influence, prepollence, regency, reign, rule, superiority, supremacy, sway

HEIGHT *(Maximum),* ***noun*** culmination, end, extreme, extremity, high point, limit, maximum, perfection, supremacy, top, utmost, zenith

HEIGHT *(Measurement),* ***noun*** altitude, angular measurement, ceiling, distance upward, elevation, expanse, extent, extent upward, highest part, length, tallness, upright distance, vertex
ASSOCIATED CONCEPTS: height restrictions in construction

HEIGHTEN *(Augment),* ***verb*** add, advance, aggravate, *amplificare,* amplify, *augere,* build up, enhance, enlarge, exacerbate, *exaggerare,* expand, greaten, improve, increase, intensify, magnify, make higher, make larger, multiply, promote, raise, reinforce, strengthen, vivify

HEIGHTEN *(Elevate),* ***verb*** *altior,* build up, hold up, lift up, make higher, pick up, raise, raise aloft, uplift, upraise

HEINOUS, ***adjective*** abhorrent, abominable, arrant, atrocious, awful, bad, baleful, baneful, base, beastly, black, confounded, contemptible, damnable, deplorable, despicable, *detestabilis,* detestable, devilish, diabolic, dire, disgraceful, disgusting, distasteful, dreadful, egregious, evil, execrable, facinorous, flagitious, flagrant, foul, fulsome, ghastly, gross, hateful, hellish, horrendous, horrible, horrid, infamous, infernal, iniquitous, invidious, loathsome, low, malefic, mean, monstrous, *nafarius,* nasty, *nefandus,* nefarious, noisome, objectionable, obnoxious, odious, offensive, opprobrious, outrageous, pernicious, reprehensible, reptilian, repugnant, revolting, rotten, satanic, shameful, shocking, sickening, sinister, terrible, unprincipled, vicious, vile, villainous, wicked, wretched, wrong
ASSOCIATED CONCEPTS: heinous crime

HEIR, ***noun*** acceptor, after-comer, after-generations, allottee, *bénéficiaire,* beneficiary, consignee, descendant, devisee, donee, inheritor, inheritrix, legatee, one who inherits, parcener, payee, possessor of descent, posterity, receiver, recipient, scion, successor, survivor, transferee
ASSOCIATED CONCEPTS: adopted heir, aggrieved heir, bodily heir, coheir, collateral heir, distributee, eligible heir, expectant heir, heir apparent, heirs at law, heirs in fee simple, illegitimate heir, immediate heir, intestate succession, issue, legal heir, legitimate heir, lineal heir, living heir, natural heir, natural offspring, next of kin, presumptive heir, pretermitted heir, Rule in Shelley's Case, surviving heir, unknown heir
FOREIGN PHRASES: ***Haeres est aut jure proprietatis aut jure representationis.*** A person is an heir either by right of property or by right of representation. ***Haeredum appellatione veniunt haeredes haeredum in infinitum.*** Under the name heirs come the heirs of heirs without limit. ***Cohaeredes una persona censentur, propter unitatem juris quod habent.*** Coheirs are regarded as one person because they own under unity of right. ***In haeredes non solent transire actiones quae poenales ex maleficio sunt.*** Actions which are penal and which arise out of anything of a criminal nature do not pass to the heirs. ***Posthumus pro nato habetur.*** A posthumous child is regarded as born before the death of the parent. ***Nemo est haeres viventis.*** No one can be the heir of a living person. ***Haeres minor uno et viginti annis non respondebit, nisi in casu dotis.*** A minor heir under 21 years of age is not answerable, except in the matter of dower. ***Filius est nomen naturae, sed haeres nomen juris.*** Son is the natural name, but heir is a name of law. ***Nemo potest esse dominus et haeres.*** No one can be both owner and heir. ***Haeres est pars antecessoris.*** An heir is a part of his ancestor.

HELM, ***noun*** administration, auspices, authority, care, charge, command, custody, direction, discipline, dominance, domination, dominion, government, guardianship, guidance, jurisdiction, keeping, leadership, management, oversight, power, regulation, stewardship, superintendence, ward

HELP, *noun* abetment, accommodation, advantage, advice, aid, assist, assistance, *auxilium,* avail, backing, benefaction, benefit, benevolence, boon, care, charity, contribution, cooperation, cure, deliverance, encouragement, expedient, facilitation, favor, fosterage, furtherance, good turn, guidance, hand, helpfulness, humanitarianism, kindness, ministration, patronage, philanthropy, redress, reinforcement, relief, remedy, rescue, resource, seconding, service, stead, strengthening, *subsidium,* subvention, succor, support, sustenance, use, utility
ASSOCIATED CONCEPTS: Good Samaritan

HELP, *verb* abet, accommodate, advance, advise, aid, alleviate, ameliorate, apply a remedy, assist, avail, back, be benevolent, be of use, benefit, better, boost, come to the aid of, contribute, cooperate, correct, cure, do a service, ease, encourage, expedite, facilitate, fix, fortify, forward, furnish assistance, further, heal, improve, intercede for, lend a hand, lend aid, lend support, make easy, oblige, patronize, promote, prop, put right, rally, reinforce, relieve, remedy, render assistance, second, serve, smooth, speed, stand by, stead, strengthen, *subvenire,* succor, *succurrere,* support, sustain, work for
ASSOCIATED CONCEPTS: aid and abet, facilitation, rescue doctrine

HELPLESS *(Defenseless),* ***adjective*** abandoned, aidless, conquerable, deserted, exposed, expugnable, forsaken, friendless, guardless, in danger, *inermis, inops,* open to attack, pregnable, resourceless, shelterless, unaided, unarmed, unarmored, unbefriended, uncovered, undefended, unfortified, unguarded, unprotected, unsheltered, unshielded, unstrengthened, unsupported, untenable, vincible, vulnerable, without aid, without succor
ASSOCIATED CONCEPTS: last clear chance

HELPLESS *(Powerless),* ***adjective*** crippled, debilitated, dependent, disabled, enervated, feeble, impotent, incapable, incompetent, invalid, paralyzed, prostrate, strengthless, unable, weak, without force
ASSOCIATED CONCEPTS: disability, incompetency

HENCE, *adverb* accordingly, as a consequence, as a result, before, consequently, earlier, finally, formerly, in consequence, in that event, necessarily, previous to, prior to, then too, therefore

HENCEFORTH, *adverb* from here on in, from now on, from this day forward, from this day on, from this moment in time on, from this point forward, from this point in time forward, hereafter, immediately, in the future, starting tomorrow, subsequently, thereafter
ASSOCIATED CONCEPTS: plain language

HENCHMAN, *noun* aide, ally, assassin, backer, champion, colleague, confidante, enforcer, follower, hatchet man, heavy, hired gun, hit man, right-hand man, supporter, thug, tool, trigger-man

HERALD, *verb* advertise, air, announce, apprise, augur, betoken, blazon, circulate, communicate, cry, disseminate, enlighten, enunciate, forecast, forerun, foreshow, foretell, foretoken, gazette, give tidings, harbinger, inform, introduce, make known, notify, omen, presage, proclaim, prognosticate, promulgate, publicize, publish, report, spread, tell, tip, trumpet, usher in, warn
ASSOCIATED CONCEPTS: *nuntiare*

HERE, *adverb* at a specific point, this juncture, at this place, at this point, at this point in time, at this spot, at this time, at this very moment, now, now precisely at this point, precisely at a point, quickly, right away, right here, within reach, without delay

HEREABOUTS, *adverb* around here, here, in the area, in the direction of, in the general vicinity, in the locale, in the vicinity, near here, somewhere close, somewhere near
ASSOCIATED CONCEPTS: plain language

HEREAFTER *(Eventually),* ***adverb*** at a fixed time, later, ultimately
ASSOCIATED CONCEPTS: hereafter acquired, hereafter built

HEREAFTER *(Henceforth),* ***adverb*** afterwards, from here on, from now on, from this time on

HEREBY, *adverb* by means of, by the aid of, by virtue of, through, through the medium of, whereby

HEREDITAMENT, *noun* bequest, devise, heirloom, heritable, heritage, heritance, inheritable property, inheritance, patrimony, personal property capable of being inherited, property which may descend to an heir, real property capable of being inherited
ASSOCIATED CONCEPTS: corporeal hereditament, easement, incorporeal hereditament

HEREDITARY, *adjective* ancestorial, ancestral, ancient, congenital, connatal, connate, constitutional, genealogical, genetic, hereditable, *hereditarius,* heritable, inborn, inbred, indigenous, ingenerate, inherited, innate, instinctive, instinctual, lineal, native, passed down, *paternus,* traditional, transmissible
ASSOCIATED CONCEPTS: hereditary disease, hereditary insanity, hereditary succession

HEREIN, *adverb* in, inside, inwardly, therein, wherein, within

HEREINAFTER, *adverb* after this, after today, afterwards, beginning now, commencing immediately, from here on in, from here on out, from now on, from now on in, from this day forward, from this day on, from this moment on, from this point on, from this time forward, from this time on, hereafter, immediately, immediately following today, in a subsequent part of the statement, in a subsequent part of this document, in future, in the future, looking ahead, subsequently
ASSOCIATED CONCEPTS: plain language

HEREOF, *adverb* about this, concerning this, in this regard, on this subject, regarding this, relating to this, with reference to, with specific reference to, with specific regard to
ASSOCIATED CONCEPTS: plain language

HERETIC, *noun* apostate, dissenter, dissentient, dissident, *haereticus,* iconoclast, infidel, misbeliever, nonconformist, protestant, schismatic, sectarian, separatist, skeptic, unbeliever

HERETOFORE, *adverb* before now, earlier, formerly, from the start, historically speaking, in the past, previous to, previously, prior to, retrospectively, up to this time

HEREWITH, ***adverb*** added to, along with this, appended to, attached to, by these means, connected to, enclosed with, fastened to, inside with, joined with, together with
ASSOCIATED CONCEPTS: plain language

HERITABLE, ***adjective*** alienable, assignable, bequeathable, bestowable, consignable, conveyable, devisable, exchangeable, givable, hereditable, hereditary, inheritable, negotiable, testamentary, transferable, transmissible
ASSOCIATED CONCEPTS: bequest, curtesy, devise, dower, intestate succession laws, legacy, testamentary gift

HERITAGE, ***noun*** ancestry, bequest, birthright, descent, expectations, future possession, hereditament, *hereditas, heredium,* heritance, incorporeal hereditament, inheritance, inherited lot, inherited portion, legacy, lineage, *patrimonium,* patrimony, portion, reversion
ASSOCIATED CONCEPTS: descendants

HERO, ***noun*** brave person, celebrity, champion, combatant, conquering hero, conqueror, decorated hero, deity, demigod, fearless soldier, fighter, folk hero, god, goddess, great man, great woman, guardian, heroine, highest type, ideal type, idol, immortal, luminary, man of courage, man of valor, martyr, master, megastar, model, notable, paragon, perfect type, person who serves as a shining example, phoenix, pillar of the community, protector, soldier, stalwart, star, superhero, superstar, tiger, valiant knight, warrior
ASSOCIATED CONCEPTS: Good Samaritan laws

HEROIC, ***adjective*** bold, brave, courageous, daring, dauntless, doughty, fearless, *fortis, fortis et invictus,* gallant, herolike, intrepid, lionhearted, noble, resolute, soldierly, stalwart, stout, stouthearted, unblenching, undaunted, unflinching, unshrinking, valiant, valorous
ASSOCIATED CONCEPTS: Good Samaritan

HESITANT, ***adjective*** averse, balking, balky, cautious, dallying, debating, deliberate, demurring, diffident, doubtful, doubting, equivocal, faltering, fluctuating, groping, halfhearted, hesitating, hesitative, indecisive, irresolute, lacking confidence, loath, pausing, qualmish, reluctant, shrinking, shy, slow, tentative, timid, unassured, uncertain, unconfident, undecided, unresolved, unsettled, unsure, vacillating, wavering
ASSOCIATED CONCEPTS: hestitant buyer, hestitant reluctant seller

HESITATE, ***verb*** balk, be dilatory, be dubious, be irresolute, be tentative, be uncertain, *cunctari,* dally, debate, delay, deliberate, demur, doubt, *dubitare,* equivocate, falter, fluctuate, *haerere,* have reservations, hold back, oscillate, pause, ponder, procrastinate, question, quibble, reluctant, scruple, shift, slow, stop, think twice, vacillate, wait, waver

HESITATION, ***noun*** caution, *cunctatio,* delay, diffidence, doubt, dubiety, *dubitatio,* dubitation, equivocation, faltering, fluctuation, *haesitatio,* hesitancy, holding back, incertitude, indecision, irresolution, nervousness, oscillation, overcaution, qualm, reluctance, scruple, second thoughts, slowness, tentativeness, uncertainness, uncertainty, unsureness, unwillingness, vacillation, wavering

HETEROGENEOUS, ***adjective*** assorted, different, disparate, dissimilar, *dissimilis,* diverse, diversified, diversiform, *diversus,* incongruous, irrelative, miscellaneous, mixed, motley, multiform, nonuniform, unalike, unequal, unlike, unmatched, unrelated, variant, varied, variegated, variform, various, varying, without relation

HIATUS, ***noun*** abeyance, adjournment, break, cessation, chasm, delay, disconnection, discontinuity, disjunction, disunion, fracture, gap, gulf, halt, *hiatus,* incompleteness, interference, interim, interlude, intermission, interregnum, interruption, interstice, interval, intervening period, lacuna, lapse, lull, moratorium, opening, pause, recess, respite, rest, rift, separation, spell, standstill, stop, stoppage, suspension, temporary stop

HIDDEN, ***adjective*** *absconditus,* abstruse, ambushed, arcane, blind, buried, camouflaged, clandestine, cloaked, close, clouded, concealed, covered, covert, cryptic, dark, delitescent, disguised, eclipsed, enigmatical, enshrouded, esoteric, hieroglyphic, indiscernable, invisible, latent, lurking, masked, mysterious, mystic, mystical, obscure, obscured, occult, *occultus,* out of sight, out of view, perdu, puzzling, recondite, screened, secluded, secret, secreted, shrouded, suppressed, surreptitious, unapparent, uncomprehended, undeciphered, undercover, underground, underhanded, undetected, undisclosed, undivulged, unexplained, unexposed, unknown, unobserved, unperceived, unrevealed, unseen, untold, veiled
ASSOCIATED CONCEPTS: attractive nuisance, duty to discover, hidden assets, hidden danger, hidden defects, hidden traps, latent defects, patent defects

HIDE, ***verb*** *abdere,* abscond, *abscondere,* be clandestine, become indiscernible, become unapparent, bury, cache, camouflage, *celare,* cloak, closet, cloud, conceal, conceal from knowledge, conceal from sight, cover, cover up, curtain, deceive, disguise, dissemble, eclipse, ensconce, enshroud, envelop, fail to reveal, harbor, hush up, keep out of sight, keep out of view, keep secret, keep to oneself, keep under cover, mask, obscure, protect, put out of sight, render invisible, screen, seclude, secrete, shade, shadow, shelter, shield, shroud, smuggle, store, stow away, suppress, veil, withhold, wrap
ASSOCIATED CONCEPTS: hide assets, hide behind the law, hide fraud, terrorist cells

HIDEOUS, ***adjective*** abhorrent, abominable, appalling, atrocious, contemptible, deplorable, despicable, detestable, dreadful, foul, frightening, frightful, ghastly, gruesome, heinous, horrendous, horrid, horrifying, macabre, monstrous, obnoxious, odious, offensive, pathetic, pitiful, regrettable, repellent, reprehensible, repulsive, revolting, scary, shameful, shocking, terrible, terrifying, unspeakable, vile

HIERARCHY *(Arrangement in a series),* ***noun*** arrangement, categorization, chain, classification, collocation, distribution, gradation, grouping, order, order of succession, progression, range, run, seriation, series, succession, system

HIERARCHY *(Persons in authority),* ***noun*** administrators, authorities, bureaucracy, commanders, controllers, dictators, directors, government, heads, leadership power, management, managers, masters, officials, persons in power, powers, regency, regime, rulers, sovereignty

HIGH DEGREE OF PROBABILITY, ***adjective*** all but guaranteed, almost a certainty, almost certain, great likelihood, having a high degree of certainty, high degree of belief, in all likelihood, most assuredly, most certainly, substantial likelihood, substantial possibility, substantial potential, substantial potentiality
ASSOCIATED CONCEPTS: mathematical degree of probability

HIGH-MINDED, ***adjective*** admirable, conscientious, estimable, ethical, fair, firm in principle, high-principled, honest, honorable, incorrupt, incorruptible, meritorious, moral, noble, principled, reputable, respectable, right-minded, righteous, scrupulous, sterling, trustworthy, uncorrupt, uncorrupted, upright, upstanding, virtuous, worthy

HIGH-POWERED, ***adjective*** aggressive, all-powerful, authoritative, commanding, compelling, connected, dominant, dynamic, effective, efficient, forceful, highest, important, in control, indomitable, influential, mighty, omnipotent, overpowering, potent, powerful, ruling, supreme
ASSOCIATED CONCEPTS: high-powered law firm, high-powered lobbyist

HIGH PROBABILITY, ***noun*** almost certainly, favorable prospect, in all likelihood, in most instances, with a high degree of certainty
ASSOCIATED CONCEPTS: high probability of chance, high probability of risk, high probability of success

HIGH TECHNOLOGY, ***noun*** best scientific advancement, highest standard of technology, most advanced discipline, most advanced technology, most developed technology, most perfected design, most up-to-date technology, newest advancement, newest design, newest development, newest invention

HIGHEST *(Gravest),* ***adjective*** apical, best, capital, chief, critical, crown, crucial, crying, deep, desperate, earnest, essential, far-reaching, forcible, head, heavy, intense, intensified, maximal, maximum, momentous, most, of great force, of great number, overmost, paramount, potent, preeminent, pressing, principal, serious, sharp, strong, superlative, supreme, telling, tiptop, top, topmost, top-notch, urgent, vigorous, violent, vital, weighty, zenithal
ASSOCIATED CONCEPTS: highest degree of care, highest proved value

HIGHEST *(Most Important),* ***adjective*** best, capital, cardinal, chief, crowning, distinguished, eminent, exalted, first, foremost, greatest, important, leading, main, major, maximal, maximum, most, most august, most celebrated, most consequential, most considerable, most dominant, most influential, most memorable, most momentous, most notable, most prominent, most remarkable, most significant, noble, notable, paramount, preeminent, primary, prime, principal, superlative, supreme, uppermost
ASSOCIATED CONCEPTS: highest court, highest decision, highest law in the land

HIGHEST *(Tallest),* ***adjective*** best, biggest, colossus-sized, giant-sized, grandest, greatest, largest, lofty, mammoth-sized, maximal, maximum, most considerable, most elevated, most sizable, most substantial, most towering, paramount, preeminent, soaring, steepest, supreme

HIGHLIGHT, ***noun*** central point, cynosure, distinctive feature, focal point, high spot, important event, keynote, memorable part, outstanding feature, prominent detail, prominent part, salient point, significant feature, striking part

HIGHLY, ***adverb*** abundantly, appreciatively, certainly, chiefly, clearly, considerably, decidedly, enormously, entirely, exceedingly, extraordinarily, extremely, greatly, hugely, immensely, in great measure, largely, mostly, noticeably, obviously, overwhelmingly, predominantly, prominently, significantly, substantially, vastly
ASSOCIATED CONCEPTS: highly immoral, highly qualified, highly specialized area of the law

HIJACK, ***verb*** abduct, appropriate, arrogate, assume command, bear away, capture, carry away, carry off, commandeer, convey away, dispossess, expropriate, force, help oneself to, impress, intercept, lay hold of, make off with, make prisoner, overcome, overpower, overwhelm, pirate, plunder, secure, seize, snatch, take, take away, take by assault, take by force, take captive, take prisoner
ASSOCIATED CONCEPTS: air piracy

HINDER, ***verb*** annoy, arrest, barricade, be an impediment, be an obstacle, block, bother, check, clog, constrain, cramp, cripple, curb, detain, discommode, discourage, encumber, fetter, get in the way, halt, hamper, hamstring, handicap, hold back, impair, impede, *impedire,* incommode, inconvenience, inhibit, intercept, interfere, interrupt, keep back, obstruct, occlude, prevent temporarily, *prohibere,* render difficult, restrain, restrict, retard, *retardare,* set back, shackle, slow down, stand in the way, trammel, traverse, work against
ASSOCIATED CONCEPTS: interference with a contract, interference with a lawful order, obstructing justice

HINDRANCE, ***noun*** annoyance, arrest, barrier, blockade, bother, check, complication, constriction, detention, deterrent, detriment, difficulty, disadvantage, discouragement, drawback, embargo, encumbrance, hamper, handicap, holdback, impediment, *impedimentum,* inconvenience, inexpedience, inhibition, interference, interposition, interruption, obstacle, obstruction, preclusion, problem, restraint, restriction, retardation, retardment, setback, shackle, striction

HINDSIGHT, ***noun*** act of looking backward, afterthought, consideration, contemplation, contemplation of past events, contemplation of the past, deliberation, later meditation, later thought, looking back, meditation, memory, musing, recall, recollection, reconsideration, reexamination, reflection, remembrance, retrospect, retrospection, review, review of things past, rumination, second thoughts, second view, subsequent meditation, subsequent reflection, survey of time past, thoughts of the past

HINGE, ***verb*** arise from, around, center, center on, critical moment, critical period, critical point, crossways, crowning point, crucial moment, culmination, decisive moment, depend on, derive from, emanate from, ensue from, evolve from, generate from, hang, issue from, juncture, pivot, turn out
ASSOCIATED CONCEPTS: case hinging on circumstances, outcome hinges on the evidence

HINT, ***noun*** adumbration, allusion, clue, connotation, covert allusion, cue, faint outline, faint suggestion, foreshadowing, idea, implication, indication, indirect suggestion, inference, inkling, insinuation, intimation, *significatio,* slight indication, slight mention, suggestion, trace, vague impression, vague suggestion

HINT, ***verb*** adumbrate, advert, allude, clue, connote, cue, give an inkling, imply, indicate, infer, insinuate, intimate, make an allusion, prompt, refer, *significare,* signify, *subicere,* suggest
ASSOCIATED CONCEPTS: disclosure

HIRE, ***verb*** add to the payroll, appoint, assign to a position, authorize, commission, *conducere,* contract for, delegate, depute, designate to a post, employ, engage, enlist, fill a position, fill a vacancy, furnish occupation for, give a job to, give employment to, give work to, induct, install, place in office, procure, put on payroll, put to work, recruit, retain, secure the

services of, set to work, staff, take into service, take on
ASSOCIATED CONCEPTS: bailee for hire, carriage, contract for hiring, discrimination in hiring, employment contract

HISTORY *(Background),* ***noun*** account, adventures, all aspects, all sides, delineation, depiction, each and every detail, entire universe, epic, episodes, events, experiences, explanation, exposition, facts, information, intelligence, narration, narrative, recapitulation, recital, record, representation, retelling, review, saga, series of incidents, story, summary

HISTORY *(Past),* ***noun*** annals, archives, bygone era, chronicle, days of old, earlier point in time, historical times, old days, prior point in time, prior time, record, schedule, the past, times gone by, tradition, yesterday
ASSOCIATED CONCEPTS: legal history

HISTRIONIC, ***adjective*** affected, aiming for effect, artificial, dramatic, embroidered, exaggerated, exhibitionistic, insincere, mannered, melodramatic, orotund, ostentatious, overacted, pretentious, *scaenicus,* self-conscious, showy, stagy, stilted, striving for effect, theatric, theatrical, unnatural

HISTRIONICS, ***noun*** acting, affectation, affectedness, airs, *ars ludicra,* artificial behavior for effect, display, dramatic art, dramatic representation, dramaturgy, emotional display for effect, exaggeration, false show, fanfaronade, melodramatics, orotundity, ostentation, overacting, overemphasis, parade, performance, pretense, *scaenicus,* show, showmanship, stagecraft, theatrecraft, theatricalism, theatricality, theatricalness

HIT, ***verb*** accost, assail, assault, attack, batter, beat, besiege, damage, deal a blow, harm, hurt, inflict harm, inflict injury
ASSOCIATED CONCEPTS: battery, hit and run

HIT AND RUN, ***noun*** accident, breaking the law, commission prohibited by law, crime, criminal matter, departure, felony, flight, hasty departure, illegality, knockdown, leaving the scene of an accident, malfeasance, motor vehicle matter, nonobservance of law, offense, offense against the law, serious infraction of the law, wrong, wrongdoing

HOARD, ***noun*** accumulation, *acervus,* aggregation, amassment, cache, collection, *copia,* cumulation, fund, heap, mass, repository, reserves, riches, saving, stack, stock, stockpile, store, supply, treasure

HOARD, ***verb*** accrue, accumulate, acquire, agglomerate, aggregate, aggroup, amalgamate, amass, augment, bank, batch together, bring together, build up, bunch, cache, cluster, *coacervare,* collect, *conligere,* cumulate, deposit, draw together, garner, garner up, gather for oneself, gather in, gather up, get together, group, hang on to, have in store, heap, hide, hide away, hive, hold back, husband, husband one's resources, keep, keep back, keep in reserve, lay by, lay in store, lay up, load up, lump together, pack away, pile, pile up, preserve, provide, put aside, reposit, reserve, retain, save up, set apart, set aside, set by, stock up, stockpile, store, store secretly, store up, stow, stow away, treasure up, withhold

HOAX, ***noun*** artifice, beguilement, canard, cheat, chicanery, circumvention, counterfeit, cozenage, deceit, deception, defraudation, delusion, device, dupery, duplicity, fabrication, fake, false alarm, false report, falsification, fraud, fraudulence, fraudulency, guile, imposition, imposture, knavery, lie, *ludificatio,* machination, masquerade, misrepresentation, pettifogging, practical joke, pretense, ruse, scheme, sham, shift, stratagem, subterfuge, swindle, trick, trickery, wile
ASSOCIATED CONCEPTS: false representation, forgery, fraud, impersonation

HOIST, ***noun*** burglary, felonious taking, fraudulent taking, larceny, misappropriation, pilferage, pilfering, purloining, robbery, stealing, swindling, theft, thievery, wrongful taking

HOLD *(Decide),* ***verb*** abjudge, abjudicate, ascertain, come to a conclusion, conclude, decide legally, decree, determine, find, fix, judge, make a decision, pass judgment, propound, resolve, rule, settle

HOLD *(Possess),* ***verb*** assume authority, assume command, be accorded, be heir to, be in possession of, be master of, be offered, be possessed of, be proffered, be vouchsafed, bear the responsibility of, care for, cling to, collect, command, conserve, control, devolve upon, direct, dominate, exercise direction over, fill a post, gather, get control, get possession of, grasp, *habere,* have, have a firm grip on, have a title to, have absolute disposal of, have as property, have by inheritance, have by tenure, have claim upon, have in hand, have in one's possession, have inherited, have rights to, have the care of, have the charge of, have the direction of, have title to, have under control, hold fast, hold in one's grasp, impropriate, inherit, keep, keep as one's own, keep for, keep in hand, keep in readiness, keep in reserve, keep on, keep prepared, lay aside, lay away, not dispose of, not part with, occupy, own, *possidere,* preserve, receive, recover, retain, save, secure, set apart, set aside, take authority, take command, takeover, *tenere,* wield restraint over
ASSOCIATED CONCEPTS: adverse holding, hold in due course, hostile holding

HOLD ACCOUNTABLE, ***verb*** accuse, blame, brand, bring to account, castigate, charge, condemn openly, convict, criminate, denounce, expose, incriminate, implicate, impugn, inculpate, inveigh against, rebuke, reprehend, reprimand, reproach, reprobate, revile, take to task, upbraid, vilify, vituperate

HOLD IN ABEYANCE, ***verb*** adjourn, defer, delay, discontinue, forbear, give ground, give way, hold up, lay over, postpone, procrastinate, prolong, protract, retard, shelve, suspend, table, temporize

HOLD OFF, ***verb*** abandon, abdicate, abjure, abstain, avoid, cease, cede, deny oneself, desist from, dispense with, disposed of, do without, drop, eschew, fast, forbear, forfeit, forgo, forswear, give up, give up on, go without, hold back, lay down, leave off, let alone, make do without, not use, pass up, refrain, release, relinquish, renounce, reserve, resign, sacrifice, shun, surrender, waive, withhold, write off, yield, yield up
ASSOCIATED CONCEPTS: forego interest owed, forego opportunity

HOLD OUT *(Deliberate on an offer),* ***verb*** make overtures, offer, place at ones disposal, present, proffer, *promittere,* propone, propose, put forward, submit, suggest, urge, volunteer

HOLD OUT *(Resist),* ***verb*** balk, be unwilling, hold fast, hold one's own, make a resolute stand, not budge, not compromise, not give up, not submit, not weaken, not yield, offer resistance, oppugn, persevere, persist, refuse, refuse consent, remain firm, repel, *resistere,* stand fast, stand firm, withhold assent, withhold consent, withstand

HOLD RESPONSIBLE FOR, ***verb*** accuse, ascribe to, attribute to, blame, call to account, censure, charge, charge with, cite, convict, criticize, denounce, deprecate, execrate, fix the responsibility for, impeach, implicate, impugn, impute to, incriminate, inculpate, indict, reprehend, upbraid

HOLD UP *(Delay),* ***verb*** adjourn, arrest, arrest temporarily, be dilatory, block, brake, bring to a standstill, call a halt, call off, cause a stoppage, cause to arrive late, cause to move with undue slowness, cause to put off to a later time, check, contain, control, cumber, curb, decelerate, defer, detain, deter, *detinere,* encumber, filibuster, gain time, halt, hamper, hinder, hold in abeyance, impede, impede the progress of, incommode, inconvenience, inhibit, interfere, interrupt, intervene, keep one waiting, keep pending, lay aside, lay under restraint, obstruct, pigeonhole, postpone, procrastinate, prolong, protract, push aside, put a stop to, put aside, put off, put off to a future time, put under restraint, repress, reserve, resist, restrain, retard, *retinere,* set aside, set one back, shelve, slacken, slow up, stall, stand in the way, stave off, stop, suppress, suspend, table, *tardare,* thwart, undermine, upset, withhold

HOLD UP *(Rob),* ***verb*** abscond with, abstract, appropriate, carry away, carry off, commit robbery, *compilare,* depredate, despoil, divert, *eripere, expilare,* impress, make off with, maraud, misappropriate, pickeer, pilfer, pillage, pirate, plunder, poach, purloin, reave, reive, remove, rob, run off with, sack, spirit away, spoil, stick up, take away, take by theft, take dishonestly, take feloniously, take possession of, take wrongfully, thieve, walk off with, withdraw

HOLD UP TO SCORN, ***verb*** belittle, condemn, deride, disdain, disesteem, disparage, feel contempt for, flout, hold in contempt, hold in derision, hold up to obloquy, insult, jape, jeer, laugh at, mock, rail at, revile, ridicule, scoff, scorn, slight, sneer at, taunt

HOLDBACK, ***noun*** kept in reserve, reservation, reserved rights, withheld, withholding

HOLDBACK, ***verb*** check, constrain, contain, control, curb, curtail, desist, detain, enjoin, forbear, hesitate, hinder, hold, hold at bay, hold fast, hold up, impede, inhibit, keep back, keep from, keep in check, not proceed, not use, obstruct, prevent, prohibit, proscribe, put the brakes on, refuse, regress, repress, restrain, restrict oneself, retain, retard, slow down, smother, stay, stop, suppress, withhold
ASSOCIATED CONCEPTS: holdback in construction law, retention on construction contracts

HOLDER, ***noun*** endorsee, individual in possession, keeper, owner, payee, person in possession, possessor, receiver, recipient
ASSOCIATED CONCEPTS: bona fide holder, holder for value, holder in due course, holder in good faith, holder of a lien, joint holder, legal holder, license holder, negotiable instruments, original holder, policyholder, property holder, shareholder, stockholder

HOLDING *(Property owned),* ***noun*** asset, belonging, chattel, domain, effect, estate, exclusive possession, interest, land, landed estate, legal estate, *possessio,* possession, property, real estate, real property, realty, resource, seisin, share, stake
ASSOCIATED CONCEPTS: holding a lien, holding a position of authority, holding company, holding for value, holding in due course, holding office, holding over

HOLDING *(Ruling of a court),* ***noun*** act of judgment, action, adjudication, ascertainment, conclusion, conclusion of the matter, considered opinion, decision, decree, *decretum,* deduction, deliverance, determination, dictate, final judgment, finding, *iudicium,* judgment, judgment on facts, judicial decision, law, law of the case, maxim, opinion, order, order of the court, outcome, precedent, precept, professional advice, professional decision, pronouncement, pronouncement by a court, recommendation, recorded expression of a formal judgment, report, resolution, result, sentence, *sententia,* settled decision, settlement by authoritative decision, that which is decided, upshot, verdict, written order
ASSOCIATED CONCEPTS: decision en banc, holding of the court, opinion per curiam

HOLDOVER, ***noun*** carry over, individual who stays on, one who remains, one who stays on, relic, remainder, remaining portion
ASSOCIATED CONCEPTS: eviction, holdover tenant

HOLE ***noun*** absence, abyss, aperture, cave, cavern, cavity, chamber, chasm, cleft, depression, depth, excavation, fracture, hollow, incision, indentation, opening, orifice, pit, rupture, shaft, tunnel, vacuum, void

HOLIDAY, ***noun*** celebration, day of festivities, day off, *dies festus, feriae,* festival, fête, furlough, gala, jubilee, leave, leisure, lull, recess, rest, time off, vacation
ASSOCIATED CONCEPTS: general holiday, legal holiday

HOLLOW, ***noun*** bare, bereft of, carved out, clear, deficient, deprived, destitute of, devoid, devoid of, empty, lacking, short of, vacant, vacuous, void, wanting, without
ASSOCIATED CONCEPTS: hollow victory

HOLOGRAPHIC, ***adjective*** cursive, graphic, handwritten, in black and white, in longhand, in print, in writing, inscribed, inscriptional, longhand, manuscript, on paper, penned, printed, scribbled, scriptorial, scriptural, under one's hand, written
ASSOCIATED CONCEPTS: execution of a will, nuncapative will, probate court, surrogate court, will formalities

HOMAGE, ***noun*** allegiance, attention, compliance, consideration, constancy, court, *cultus,* deference, devotedness, devotion, esteem, estimation, exaltation, faithfulness, fidelity, glorification, high regard, honor, humility, loyalty, obedience, obeisance, *observantia,* regard, respect, reverence, service, servility, servitude, subjection, submission, submissiveness, subservience, veneration, *verecundia*

HOME *(Domicile),* ***noun*** abode, apartment, cottage, *domicilium, domus,* dormitory, dwelling, dwelling place, fireside, fixed residence, habitat, habitation, haven, homeland, homestead, house, household, living quarters, locality, lodging, lodging place, native environment, permanent legal address, place of abode, place of dwelling, place of existence, place of one's domestic affections, place of refuge, place of residence, place of rest, place to live in, place where one lives, quarters, refuge, residence, resting place

ASSOCIATED CONCEPTS: home office, home rule domicile, homesite
FOREIGN PHRASES: ***Constitutum esse eam domum unicuique nostrum debere existimari, ubi quisque sedes et tabulas haberet, suarumque rerum constitutionem fecisset.*** It is established that the home of each of us is considered to be the place of his abode and books, and where he may have made an establishment of his business.

HOME *(Place of origin),* ***noun*** birthplace, country, country of origin, fatherland, homeland, mother country, motherland, native ground, native hearth, native land, native soil, place of birth

HOME INVASION, ***noun*** act prohibited by law, breach of law, contravention, crime, criminal activity, criminal offense, encroachment, felony, illegality, infringement, offense, offense against the law, robbery, serious infraction of the law
ASSOCIATED CONCEPTS: break in, breaking and entering, burglary, housebreaking, robbery, trespassing

HOME RULE, ***noun*** autonomy, enfranchisement, franchise, freedom from domination, freedom from interference, freedom of action, freedom of choice, independence, individualism, noninterference, nonintervention, political independence, self-containment, self-derived power, self-determination, self-direction, self-government, self-legislation, self-reliance, self-subsistence, self-sufficiency, self-support, sovereignty, unlimited sovereignty

HOMEMADE, ***adjective*** amateurish, coarse, crude, do-it-yourself, domestic, domestically manufactured, handcrafted, home-born, homegrown, home-manufactured, home-produced, home-raised, homespun, home-woven, indigenous, internal, locally made, locally manufactured, locally produced, made at home, made locally, manufactured, native-grown, native-raised, natural, personally made, produced domestically, self-made, simple, unskilled
ASSOCIATED CONCEPTS: homemade law, homemade wills

HOMESTEAD, ***noun*** abode, acreage, acres, country house, domicile, dwelling, dwelling place, edifice, estate, farm, farm land, farmplace, farmstead, grounds, habitation, home, house, household, living quarters, lodging, lodging place, manor, messuage, place of residence, place of settlement, quarters, residence
ASSOCIATED CONCEPTS: homestead laws

HOMICIDE, ***noun*** annihilation, assassination, butchery, *caedes,* capital crime, capital murder, carnage, crime, destruction of life, elimination, extermination, felony, felony murder, killing, liquidation, manslaughter, massacre, murder, removal, slaughter, slaying, termination of life, violent death
ASSOCIATED CONCEPTS: assault with intent to murder, *corpus delicti,* criminally negligent homicide, culpable homicide, excusable homicide, felonious homicide, felony murder, infanticide, involuntary manslaughter, justifiable homicide, manslaughter, premeditated homicide, voluntary homicide
FOREIGN PHRASES: ***Maihemium est homicidium inchoatum.*** Mayhem is unfinished homicide.

HOMOSEXUAL, ***adjective*** gay, gay person, homoerotic, homophile, lesbian
ASSOCIATED CONCEPTS: gay marriage, gay rights

HONEST, ***adjective*** aboveboard, accurate, actual, artless, as represented, authentic, bald, blunt, candid, clean, conscientious, correct, creditable, decent, downright, earnest, equitable, erect, estimable, ethical, evenhanded, exact, factual, fair, fair-dealing, forthright, frank, free from fraud, genuine, guileless, historical, honorable, impartial, impeccable, inartificial, incapable of deceit, incorrupt, incorruptible, ingenuous, innocent, inviolate, irrepoachable, just, laudable, law-abiding, legal, legitimate, licit, literal, moral, open, outspoken, plain-speaking, principled, *probus,* proper, pure, reliable, reputable, respectable, right, scrupulous, *simplex,* sincere, *sincerus,* sound, stainless, sterling, straightforward, true, true to the facts, truehearted, trustworthy, truthful, unadulterated, unaffected, unassumed, unassuming, unbiased, unbribable, uncolored, uncopied, uncounterfeited, undiluted, undisguised, undisguising, undissembling, undissimulating, undistorted, unembroidered, unexaggerated, unfabricated, unfaked, unfeigned, unfeigning, unfictitious, ungarbled, uninvented, unperjured, unpretended, unpretending, unpretentious, unsimulated, unsophisticated, unspecious, unspurious, unsynthetic, unvarnished, valid, veracious, veridical, veritable, well-principled
ASSOCIATED CONCEPTS: honest belief, honest claim, honest dispute

HONESTY, ***noun*** accuracy, artlessness, authenticity, baldness, bluntness, candidness, candor, conscientiousness, estimableness, exactitude, factualness, fairness, fidelity, *fides,* frankness, genuineness, guilelessness, high character, high-mindedness, high principles, honorableness, impartiality, inartificiality, incorruptibility, ingenuousness, integrity, legitimacy, openness, plainness, plainspeaking, principles, *probitas,* probity, reality, realness, reputability, repute, respectability, rightness, sanctity, scrupulosity, scrupulousness, simplicity, *sinceritas,* sincerity, soundness, stainlessness, trustworthiness, truth, truthfulness, unadulteration, unaffectedness, unconstraint, undeceitfulness, undeceptiveness, unreserve, unrestraint, unspeciousness, unspuriousness, unvarnished truth, uprightness, upstandingness, validity, veraciousness, veracity, veridicality, verity, virtue, worthiness
ASSOCIATED CONCEPTS: character evidence, reputation for honesty

HONOR *(Good reputation),* ***noun*** character, *dignitas, existimatio, fama,* good name, good opinion, goodness, high regard, incorruptibility, integrity, moral rectitude, principle, probity, purity, rectitude, regard, reliability, reputability, repute, respectability, righteousness, scrupulousness, sense of responsibility, standing, status, trustiness, trustworthiness, uprightness, virtue
ASSOCIATED CONCEPTS: reputation evidence

HONOR *(Outward respect),* ***noun*** acclaim, admiration, adulation, aggrandizement, appreciation, approbation, approval, commendation, consideration, courtesy, credit, deference, devotion, distinction, esteem, estimation, exaltation, favor, glorification, glory, high regard, homage, laud, laudation, obeisance, praise, prominence, regard, reverence, tribute, veneration, worship

HONOR, ***verb*** acclaim, accredit, advance, aggrandize, applaud, belaud, bepraise, canonize, *celebrare,* celebrate, cheer, cite, commemorate, commend, compliment, confer distinction on, congratulate, consecrate, crown, *decorare,* decorate, defer to, distinguish, elevate, ennoble, esteem, eulogize, exalt, extol, glorify, hail, hold in esteem, idolize, laud, lionize, look up to, make important, memorialize, pay deference, pay homage, pay respects, pay tribute, praise, prize, promote, put on a pedestal, raise, raise to distinction,

regard, respect, revere, reverence, salute, set store by, show respect, toast, value, venerate
ASSOCIATED CONCEPTS: honorary trust

HONORABLE *(Honest),* ***adjective*** beyond reproach, blameless, chaste, Christian, clean, creditable, decent, erect, esteemed, estimable, ethical, excellent reputation, fair, full of integrity, good, held in esteem, high-minded, high-principled, highly regarded, highly reputed, highly respectable, honored, immaculate, in favor, in good order, in high favor, in one's good books, inviolate, irreproachable, just, law-abiding, law-loving, law-revering, manly, meritorious, moral, much esteemed, noble, of repute, prestigious, principled, pure, reputable, respectable, respected, revered, reverend, right, right-minded, righteous, sinless, spotless, squeaky-clean, stainless, sterling, straight-arrow, true-blue, true-dealing, true-devoted, true-disposing, truehearted, true-souled, true-spirited, unblemished, uncorrupt, uncorrupted, undefiled, unimpeachable, unsmirched, unspotted, unstained, unsullied, untarnished, upright, uprighteous, upstanding, venerable, venerated, virtuous, well-thought-of, worshipful, worth one's salt, worthy, yeomanly

HONORABLE *(Judge),* ***adjective*** acclaimed, adjudger, adjudicator, administrator of justice, admired, applauded, arbiter, arbitrator, assessor, celebrated, chancellor, distinguished, elected, eminent, esteem, esteemed, exalted, eximious, favor, held, held in esteem or high, held in respect, her honor, high, highly considered, highly regarded, highly reputed, his honor, honorable justice, honorary, honored, honorific, illustrious, in favor, in high, in high regard, intercessor, interpreter, jurist, justice, justicer, magistrate, marked, moderator, much admired, negotiator, noble, notable, noted, of mark, of note, one who dispenses justice, praetor, preeminent, prestigious, prominent, quaestor, referee, respected, revered, surrogate, the court, umpire, venerable, well-thought-of, widely acclaimed, your honor

HONORABLE *(Upright),* ***adjective*** august, awe-inspiring, dignified, estimable, ethical, high-minded, high-principled, honest, incorruptible, legitimate, moral, noble-minded, principled, respected, time-honored, to be trusted, tried and true, true, trustworthy, truth-loving, uncorrupted, upstanding, venerable

HONORARIUM, ***noun*** acknowledgment, arrangement, compensation, consideration, earnings, emolument, fee, financial remuneration, gratuity, guerdon, income, indemnity, installment, meed, payment, quittance, recompense, reimbursement, remuneration, requital, retainer, reward for service, salary, settlement, stipend

HONORARY, ***adjective*** commemorative, commendatory, dedicatory, enshrining, hallowing, honorific, honorifical, in memory of, in tribute, kept in remembrance, memorial, perpetuating, recalling to mind, serving to commemorate
ASSOCIATED CONCEPTS: honorary degree, honorary officer, honorary trust

HONORED, ***adjective*** acclaimed, admired, adored, applauded, appreciated, approved, celebrated, cheered, commended, complimented, considered, distinguished, ennobled, esteemed, eulogized, exalted, extolled, fabled, famed, famous, far-famed, glorified, hailed, held in highest esteem, held in highest regard, held in highest respect, highly regarded, honored, idolized, lauded, lionized, much-acclaimed, much-admired, mythical, notable, noted, notorious, of mark, praised, prized, renowned, respected, revered, saluted, sought-after, time-honored, valued, well-considered, well-known, well-thought-of, world-class, worshiped

HOODLUM, ***noun*** agitator, bandit, blackguard, brigand, burglar, convict, criminal, embezzler, evildoer, felon, firebrand, gunman, holdup man, knave, larcener, larcenist, lawbreaker, malefactor, malevolent, malfeasant, malfeasor, miscreant, mobster, oppressor, outlaw, peculator, pickpocket, purloiner, rogue, roisterer, rough, ruffian, scoundrel, stealer, thief, villain, wrongdoer
ASSOCIATED CONCEPTS: juvenile delinquent, multiple offender, predicate felon, youthful offender

HOODWINK, ***verb*** be dishonest, befool, beguile, blind, blindfold, cheat, cozen, deceive, defraud, delude, dupe, *fallere,* hoax, *inludere,* inveigle, *ludificari,* make a fool of, misinform, mislead, mystify, outwit, puzzle, swindle, trick
ASSOCIATED CONCEPTS: deception, fraud, misrepresentation

HOPE, ***verb*** assume, expect, feel sure, give credence to, have faith in, have no doubt, have no reservations, look forward to, place reliance in, pray for, presume, put confidence in, rely on
ASSOCIATED CONCEPTS: hopelessly insolvent

HOPELESS, ***adjective*** comfortless, depressing, desolate, desperate, dismal, doubtable, dreary, futile, grim, impossible, inauspicious, incorrigible, incurable, insoluble, irrecoverable, irredeemable, irreparable, irretrievable, irreversible, unachievable, unattainable, uncorrectable, undoable, unfavorable, unobtainable, unpromising, unrealizable, useless

HORIZON, ***noun*** border, boundary, field of view, field of vision, prospect, range, range of vision, realm, skyline, view, vista

HORNBOOK, ***noun*** abstract on the law, analysis, analyzation, annotated text, capitulation, capsule, commentary, compendium, condensation, desk book, digest of the law, discourse on the law, dissection, dissertation on the law, encyclopedia, excursus, exposition, manual, manual of instruction, pandect, primer, recapitulation, review, runthrough, study, study book, text, textbook, topical outline, treatise, treatise on the law

HORRENDOUS, ***adjective*** abominable, appalling, atrocious, awful, contemptible, deplorable, despicable, detestable, disgusting, dreadful, foul, frightening, frightful, ghastly, ghoulish, gruesome, harrowing, heinous, hideous, horrible, horrid, horrifying, loathsome, macabre, monstrous, obnoxious, odious, offensive, pathetic, pitiful, reprehensible, repulsive, revolting, shameful, shocking, terrible, terrifying, unspeakable, vile, villainous

HORRIBLE, ***adjective*** abhorrent, abominable, appalling, atrocious, awful, contemptible, deplorable, despicable, detestable, disgusting, dreadful, foul, frightening, frightful, ghastly, ghoulish, gruesome, harrowing, heinous, hideous, horrendous, horrid, horrifying, loathsome, macabre, monstrous, obnoxious, odious, offensive, pathetic, pitiful, reprehensible, repulsive, revolting, shameful, shocking, terrible, terrifying, unspeakable, vile, villainous

HORRID, ***adjective*** abhorrent, abominable, appalling, atrocious, awful, despicable, dire, disastrous, disgusting, distasteful, dreadful, foul, ghastly, grim, gross, heinous, hideous, horrendous, horrible, horrific, loathsome, nasty, noisome, noxious, obnoxious, obscene, odious, repellent, repugnant, repulsive, revolting, terrible, undesirable, unpleasant, unspeakable, vile

HORRIFY, ***verb*** abash, alarm, appall, become reprehensible, consternate, disgust, dismay, distress, disturb, frighten, intimidate, nauseate, offend, outrage, petrify, repel, repulse, scare, scare to death, shock, sicken, startle, stun, stupefy, terrify
ASSOCIATED CONCEPTS: horrifying a jury to evoke a desired response

HORROR, ***noun*** abhorrence, abomination, anguish, aversion, awfulness, detestation, disgust, fright, frightfulness, ghastliness, gruesomeness, hideousness, horribleness, horridness, loathing, loathsomeness, lunacy, odiousness, offense, outrage, rancor, repugnance, repulsion, revulsion

HORTATIVE, ***adjective*** admonitory, advising, advisory, consultative, didactic, exhortative, exhortatory, expostulative, expostulatory, full of exhortation, full of urgency, *hortans,* hortatory, *monens,* monitorial, persuading, persuasive, remonstrative, suasive, warning

HOST *(Multitude),* ***noun*** a many, a mass of, aggregation, an abundance of, army, array, assembly, body, cloud, cluster, company, congregation, crowd, crush, flood, galaxy, group, herd, horde, jam, large amount, litter, nest, no end of, numbers, pack, panoply, quantities, school, scores, slew, storm

HOST *(Owner),* ***noun*** barkeeper, bartender, hostess, hotel keeper, innkeeper, inviter, owner, owner of an establishment, party-giver, proprietor, restaurant owner, restaurateur, saloon keeper, serving liquor, tavern keeper
ASSOCIATED CONCEPTS: host liability statute

HOSTAGE, ***noun*** bond, captive, collateral, guarantee, internee, *obses,* pledge, political prisoner, prisoner, real security, security
ASSOCIATED CONCEPTS: false imprisonment, kidnapping, ransom

HOSTILE, ***adjective*** abusive, acrimonious, actively opposed, adverse, aggressive, alienated, antagonistic, antipathetic, antipodal, antithetic, antithetical, antonymous, arguing, argumentative, assaulting, at odds, at variance, baneful, battling, besetting, bitter, bristling, calamitous, cantankerous, challenging, clashing, combative, competitive, conflicting, contentious, contesting, contradictory, contrariant, contrarious, contrary, counteracting, counteractive, destructive, disaffected, disagreeing, disastrous, discordant, disdainful, disloyal, disputatious, dissentient, dissenting, dissentious, dissident, divided, dreadful, embittered, estranged, factious, frictional, full of hate, full of malice, harmful, harsh, ill-disposed, ill-willed, in opposition, inacquiescent, incompatible, inconsistent with, *infensus, infestus,* inimical, *inimicus,* irreconcilable, malevolent, noncooperating, opposed, opposing, opposite, oppositional, oppugnant, polarized, pugnacious, rancorous, reactionary, refractory, renitent, reverse, schismatic, spiteful, truculent, unapproving, unconsonant, uncooperative, unharmonious, vicious, vis-à-vis, wrangling
ASSOCIATED CONCEPTS: hostile fire, hostile intent, hostile party, hostile possession of property, hostile witness

HOSTILE WITNESS, ***noun*** adverse testifier, adverse witness, antithetical witness, challenger, contrary witness, disagreeing witness, dissenting witness, dissentious witness, dissident, harmful witness, opposing witness, traitor, turncoat, witness in opposition
ASSOCIATED CONCEPTS: cross examination, leading questions

HOSTILITY, ***noun*** alienation, animosity, animus, antagonism, antipathy, bad blood, bitterness, blood feud, conflict, contention, coolness, disaffection, discord, estrangement, feud, friction, grudge, hate, hatred, hostility, inhospitableness, jaundice, loathing, malice, malignancy, malignity, opposition, rancor, score, spite, spitefulness, strain, tension, unfriendliness, vendetta, venom, vindictiveness, virulence, vitriol
ASSOCIATED CONCEPTS: hostile workplace

HOT-BLOODED, ***adjective*** aggressive, amorous, athirst, avid, barbarous, bold, brutal, burning, careless, danger-loving, daredevil, daring, desirous, desperate, eager, excessive, excitable, extreme, febrile, fervent, fervid, feverish, fiery, flaming, foolhardy, frantic, hasty, headstrong, heated, heedless, high-spirited, high-strung, hot-headed, hot-tempered, immoderate, impatient, impractical, imprudent, inattentive, incautious, inflamed, inflammatory, insuppressible, intemperate, intense, intent, irrepressible, lustful, madcap, oversensitive, passionate, piquant, quenchless, quick-tempered, rampant, rash, reckless, risk-taking, savage, sensitive, short-tempered, strong-willed, temerarious, thoughtless, torrid, turbulent, unadvised, unbridled, uncircumspect, uncontrollable, ungentle, ungovernable, unmitigable, unquelled, unquenched, unrepressed, unwary, vehement, venturesome, violent, wanton, willful, zealous
ASSOCIATED CONCEPTS: heat of passion, manslaughter, temporary insanity

HOUSE, ***noun*** abode, accommodations, *aedes,* business establishment, business firm, clan, commercial establishment, company, concern, domicile, *domicilium, domus,* dwelling, dwelling place, family, firm, habitation, home, homestead, household, kin, kindred, lineage, living place, living quarters, lodging, place of habitation, quarters, residence, shelter, tribe
ASSOCIATED CONCEPTS: House of Representatives

HOUSE ARREST, ***noun*** confinement at home, confinement to a residence, custodial detention, domestic restraint, house confinement, imprisonment, punishment at home, restraint at home, restriction at home, retention at home, serving a sentence at home, serving time at home

HOUSEBREAKING, ***noun*** appropriation, breaking and entering, burglarizing, burglary, felony, filching, forcible entry, larceny, looting, pilfering, plundering, raiding, robbery, stealing, theft, thievery, trespassing

HOUSEHOLD *(Domestic),* ***adjective*** at home, *domesticus,* domiciled, domiciliary, domiciliated, family, fond of home, having home interests, home, home-loving, home-owning, homemaking, housekeeping, in residence, *lares, penates,* pertaining to home, pertaining to the family, residential, residentiary
ASSOCIATED CONCEPTS: household articles, household effects, household goods, household member, household servant

HOUSEHOLD *(Familiar),* ***adjective*** accustomed, celebrated, cognized, common, commonly known, commonplace, conventional, customary, everyday, famous, habitual, ordinary, plain, popular, prevalent, recognized, regular, renowned, simple, standard, stock, talked-about, talked-of, universally recognized, usual, well-known, well-recognized, widely known, widespread, workaday

HOUSEHOLD, *noun* domestic circle, domestic domicile, domestic establishment, domus, establishment, *familia,* family, family abode, family circle, family dwelling place, habitation, home, homestead, lodging, parents and children, place of abode, residence
ASSOCIATED CONCEPTS: homestead
FOREIGN PHRASES: ***Domus sua cuique est tutissimum refugium.*** Everyone's home is his safest refuge. ***Debet sua cuique domus esse perfugium tutissimum.*** Every man's home should be a perfectly safe refuge.

HUMAN, *noun* being, body, character, human being, individual, living soul, man, member of the human race, one, particular one, party, person, woman
ASSOCIATED CONCEPTS: human rights law, United Nations Declaration of Human Rights

HUMANE, *adjective* altruistic, beneficent, benevolent, benign, bounteous, brotherly, charitable, *clemens,* clement, considerate, decent, fraternal, generous, helpful, hospitable, humanitarian, *humanus,* kind, kindhearted, kindly, merciful, *misericors,* philanthropic, unselfish, warmhearted
ASSOCIATED CONCEPTS: gift for a humane purpose

HUMANITY *(Humaneness),* ***noun*** altruism, beneficence, benevolence, benignancy, benignity, charitableness, clemency, *clementia,* compassion, feeling, gentleness, good will, *humanitas,* kindheartedness, kindness, lenience, leniency, lenity, mercifulness, mercy, mildness, *misericordia,* sympathy, understanding, unselfishness
ASSOCIATED CONCEPTS: crimes against humanity, humanitarian doctrine, humanitarian laws, last clear chance

HUMANITY *(Mankind),* ***noun*** generations of man, *gens humana, hominum generis,* homo sapiens, human beings, humankind, *humanum genus,* man, mortals, people, peoples of the earth, persons
ASSOCIATED CONCEPTS: crimes against humanity

HUMBLE, *adjective* acquiescent, base, common, compliant, decent, deferential, demure, meek, menial, modest, plain, plebian, prole, proletarian, reserved, resigned, retiring, self-deprecating, self-effacing, servile, sheepish, shy, subdued, submissive, sycophantic, timid, unaffected, unaggressive, unassertive, unobtrusive

HUMILIATE, *verb* abase, abash, affront, befool, bespatter, blackball, blacken, brand, bring shame upon, cast a slur upon, cast down, contemn, cow, crush, debase, defame, deflate, degrade, demean, demote, depreciate, deride, derogate, discredit, disgrace, dishonor, disparage, disrank, disrate, downgrade, embarrass, expose to infamy, fill with shame, give offense to, hold in derision, hold in disrespect, humble, incur blame, insult, laugh at, lower, make a fool of, make lowly, malign, misprize, mock, mortify, offend, put down, put out of countenance, put to shame, reduce to the ranks, render humble, ridicule, scoff, scorn, shame, show disrespect, slight, sneer, snub, spurn, stain, stigmatize, sully, taint, tarnish, treat with disrespect, treat with indignity, undervalue, vanquish, vilify
ASSOCIATED CONCEPTS: mental anguish

HUMILIATION, *noun* chagrin, defamation, degradation, disgrace, dishonor, disparagement, disrespect, embarrassment, ignominy, insult, malign, mortification, obloquy, ridicule, scoff, scorn, shame, shame, slander, slight, sneer, snub, spurn, taint, treat with indignity
ASSOCIATED CONCEPTS: defamation, frivolous lawsuit with sanctions, libel, slander

HUMOR, *adjective* amusement, burlesque, cheer, comedy, comic, drollery, enjoyment, farce, foolery, fun, funniness, hilariousness, humorousness, improv, jest, jocularity, lampoon, parody, playfulness, pleasure, richness, satire, slapstick, uproariousness, whimsical comical, whimsy, wit, witty

HUNT, *verb* burrow, chase, chase after, conduct a search, *consectari,* delve for, ensnare, explore, fasten oneself upon, ferret, follow, follow close upon, follow the trail, forage, give chase, go after, go in pursuit of, go in search of, grope for, gun for, hawk, hound, inquire for, look for, probe, prowl after, pry, pursue, quest, root, run after, search for, search out, seek, set a trap for, snare, stalk, trace, track down, trail, trap, try to find, venari
ASSOCIATED CONCEPTS: extradition, hunt for a fugitive, rendition, search and seizure, search warrant

HURDLE, *noun* barricade, barrier, block, constraint, curb, detainment, difficulty, drawback, hamper, handicap, hindrance, impediment, inconvenience, limitation, obstacle, obstruction, prohibition, restraint, restriction, stumbling block, wall

HURRICANE, *noun* adversity, calamity, catastrophe, disaster, flood, natural disaster, rain, rain and wind storm, rainstorm, serious calamity, storm, tragedy, upheaval
ASSOCIATED CONCEPTS: FEMA

HURRY, *verb* accelerate, conclude, create, demand more, develop, drive faster, drive harder, engender, expedite, get more productivity, go faster, hasten, in high gear, pick up the pace, precipitate, press, press forward, push, quicken, quicken the pace, speed up, spur, to go full throttle
ASSOCIATED CONCEPTS: expedited trial, speedy trial

HURT, *noun* abuse, affliction, affront, batter, bruise, clobber, contuse, cripple, cut, damage, deface, defacement, destroy, detriment, disfigure, disfigurement, disservice, flaw, gash, gore, hamstring, harm physically, hit, impair, impairment, indignity, inequity, injure, injustice, laceration, lame, maim, mangle, physical damage, pulverize, raze, scar, vitiate, wound, wrong
ASSOCIATED CONCEPTS: damages contained in a complaint

HURT *(Harm),* ***verb*** afflict, aggrieve, blemish, break, cause damages, compromise, cross, damage, decimate, devastate, disadvantage, impair, maltreat, mar, mutilate, scrape, spoil, torment, torture

HURT *(Offend),* ***verb*** abuse, affront, breach, break, denigrate, deny, disparage, disregard, disrespect, distress, disturb, infringe, insult, interfere, malign, miff, neglect, oppress, outrage, pain, prevent, revile, slap, slight, snub, stray, torment, traduce, transgress, trespass, upset, violate, wound
ASSOCIATED CONCEPTS: hurt the chances of success in a lower court, hurt the chances on appeal

HUSH MONEY, *noun* blackmail, blood money, bribe, bribe money, corrupt money, cover-up, criminal payoff, enticement, graft, gratuity, illegal bribe, illegal funds, illegal gratuity,

illegal money, illegal payoff, illegal payout, inducement, payoff, payoff for corruption, payoff for silence, payoff to quash testimony, prize, slush fund, suppression of evidence
ASSOCIATED CONCEPTS: bribery, public officials' code of conduct

HYPERBOLE, *noun* aggrandizement, amplification, enhancement, enlargement, exaggeration, extravagance, magnification, overemphasis, overenlargement, overstatement

HYPERBOLIC, *adjective* blown-up, distorted, elaborated, embellished, enhanced, enlarged, exaggerated, expanded, expressed to an excess, expressed to an extreme, grandiloquent, heightening, inflated, intensified, magnified, maximization, over amplified, overdoing, overemphasized, puffing up, sensationalized, stretched, stretched to the imagination, swelled

HYPOCRISY, *noun* artfulness, charlatanism, charlatanry, deceit, deceitfulness, deception, dishonesty, dissembling, *dissimulatio,* double-dealing, duplicity, false profession, falsification, fraud, fraudulence, *fraus,* front, guile, hollow pretense, imposture, improbity, insincerity, perjury, pharisaism, pretense, pretense of virtue, pretension, quackery, sanctimoniousness, sanctimony, show, trickery

HYPOTHECATION, *noun* collateral, contract of mortgage, contract of pledge, creation of a lien, guarantee, lien, mortgage, pledge, security
ASSOCIATED CONCEPTS: hypothecated property

HYPOTHESIS, *noun* assertion, assignment of cause, assumption, conclusion drawn from accepted truths, *coniectura,* conjecture, deduction, guess, inference, postulate, postulation, speculation, suggestion, supposal, supposition, surmise, tentative explanation, tentative law, theory, thesis, unproved theory

HYPOTHETICAL, *adjective* assumed, conjectural, hypothetic, imaginary, make-believe, *opinabilis,* pretended, speculative, supposed, suppositional, suppositive, unreal, unverifiable
ASSOCIATED CONCEPTS: hypothetical controversy, hypothetical facts, hypothetical issue, hypothetical pleading, hypothetical question, speculation

IDEA, *noun* abstraction, aim, appraisal, apprehension, assessment, belief, calculation, *cogitatio,* conceit, concept, conception, conjecture, conviction, doctrine, dogma, estimate, estimation, evaluation, excogitation, fancy, guess, hypothesis, impression, inference, intent, intention, judgment, *notio,* notion, object, opinion, percept, perception, persuasion, plan, point of view, presupposition, product of imagination, purpose, reflection, sentiment, supposition, surmise, suspicion, tenet, theory, thought, train of thought, valuation, view, viewpoint

IDEAL, *adjective* absolute, abstract, advantageous, archetypical, best, complete, consummate, dreamy, excellent, exemplary, fancied, fantastic, faultless, fictitious, idealistic, legendary, optimum, supreme, utopian

IDENTICAL, *adjective* alike, coequal, comparable, congeneric, congenerous, consimilar, consubstantial, duplicate, equal, equivalent, exact, exactly alike, exactly the same, faithful, homogeneous, *idem,* indistinguishable, interchangeable, like, matching, resembling, similar, synonymous, tantamount, twin, uniform, without distinction
ASSOCIATED CONCEPTS: identical issue, identical real estate

IDENTIFICATION, *noun* appellation, ascertainment, association, certification, characterization, classification, cognizance, comparison, corroboration, definition, delineation, denomination, description, designation, detection, discernment, disclosure, ID, identity classification, identity comparison, identity verification, label, proof of domicile, proof of identity, proof of residency, recognition, recognizance, recollection, signature, signification, substantiation, verification
ASSOCIATED CONCEPTS: extrajudicial identification, laws, national identification cards, lineup, voter identification
FOREIGN PHRASES: ***Ex multitudine signorum, colligitur identitas vera.*** The true identity of a thing is shown from a number of signs. ***Nihil facit error nominis cum de corpore constat.*** An error in the name is of no consequence when there is certainty as to the person.

IDENTIFY, *verb* analyze, ascertain, attest, authenticate, call, catalog, certify, classify, confirm, corroborate, delineate, denominate, denote, describe, descry, designate, detect, determine, discriminate, distinguish, espy, establish, give a name to, give an appellation to, know, label, locate, name, perceive, pick out, pinpoint, place, point a finger to, prove, provide with nomenclature, recognize, recollect, select, specify, spot, style, substantiate, term, uncover, verify
ASSOCIATED CONCEPTS: DNA, identity theft

IDENTIFY WITH, ***verb*** associate with, compare, connect with, empathize with, equate with, relate to, understand, look up to, hold in highest regard

IDENTITY *(Individuality),* ***noun*** being, characteristic, difference, dissimilarity, distinction, distinctive feature, distinctiveness, distinctness, distinguishing characteristic, distinguishing quality, idiosyncrasy, individualism, mannerism, oneness, originality, particularity, peculiarity, perceivable dissimilarity, personal characteristic, personality, personship, quality of being singular, self, selfhood, selfness, singleness, singularity, speciality, specialty, specific quality, specificity, uniqueness, unlikeness
ASSOCIATED CONCEPTS: duty to ascertain identity, proof of identity
FOREIGN PHRASES: ***Nihil facit error nominis cum de corpore constat.*** An error in the name is of no consequence when there is certainty as to the person. ***Ex multitudine signorum, colligitur identitas vera.*** The true identity of a thing is shown from a number of signs. ***Nomina sunt mutabilia, res autem immobiles.*** Names are mutable, but things are immutable.

IDENTITY *(Similarity),* ***noun*** agreement, alikeness, closeness, coequality, comparability, conformability, consimilarity, consimilitude, consimility, duplication, equality, equipollence, equipollency, equivalence, homogeneity, identicalness, interchangeability, likeness, match, oneness, parallelism, parity, resemblance, sameness, semblance, similarity, similitude, synonymity, uniformity, unity

IDENTITY THEFT, ***noun*** crime through impersonation, criminal theft through impersonation, embezzlement through impersonation, felonious deception, felonious taking through impersonation, fraudulent deception, fraudulent taking through impersonation, grand larceny by impersonation, illegal deception, larcenous deception, larceny by impersonation, misappropriation through impersonation, petit larceny by impersonation, pilferage by impersonation, pilfering by impersonation, stealing by deception, stealing through impersonation, swindling by deception, swindling through impersonation, taking illegally through impersonation, theft by impersonation, thievery by impersonation, thievery by imposed deception, wrongful deception

IDEOLOGICAL, ***adjective*** analytical, cerebral, clairvoyant, conjectural, devout, having a strong bent, having strong beliefs, hopeful, idealistic, imaginative, intellectual, logical, metaphysical, pedantic, principled, quixotic, rational, reasoning, spiritual, subjective, thoughtful

IDIOSYNCRASY, ***noun*** curiosity, eccentricity, erraticism, individualism, irregularity, kink, mannerism, oddity, peculiarity, predilection, predisposition, proclivity, quiddity, quirk, singularity, trick

IDLE, ***adjective*** disengaged, fallow, fruitless, futile, *ignavus,* inactive, indolent, inert, jobless, lazy, listless, motionless, *otiosus,* shiftless, slothful, still, uncultivated, unemployed, unoccupied, unprofitable, unused, vacant, *vacuus,* workless

IDLE THREAT, ***noun*** deficient threat, empty threat, harmless threat, ineffectual threat, meaningless threat, menacing, mere notice, mere talking, mere warning, only words, saber-rattling, subtle intimidation, testing, trial balloon, veiled threat

IGNOBLE, ***adjective*** abject, base, baseborn, beggarly, below par, boorish, common, contemptible, corrupt, cowardly, craven, debased, degenerate, degraded, depraved, despicable, discreditable, disgraceful, dishonest, dishonorable, disreputable, humble, *humilis,* ignominious, indecent, infamous, inferior, inglorious, *inhonestus, inliberalis,* insignificant, low, lowborn, lowly, mean, menial, of humble birth, of low character, of low extraction, of low station, peasant, plebian, proletarian, raffish, reproachful, scandalous, scrubby, scurrilous, servile, shameful, sorry, subaltern, unchivalrous, uncouth, uncultivated, underbred, ungenteel, unmanly, unrespectable, untitled, unworthy, vile, vulgar, wicked, worthless

IGNOMINIOUS, ***adjective*** base, blameworthy, contemptible, contemptuous, corrupt, criminal, debased, debauched, degenerate, depraved, despicable, discreditable, disgraceful, dishonorable, ignoble, immoral, inglorious, low, mean, miserable, notorious, opprobrious, reprehensible, seamy, shady, shameful, sordid, unethical, unrespectable, unsavory, villainous, wretched, wrong

IGNOMINY, ***noun*** abasement, abjection, abjectness, attaint, bad name, bad reputation, bad repute, badge of infamy, blot, brand, chagrin, condemnation, contempt, contemptibility, contemptibleness, culpability, culpableness, debasement, dedecoration, degradation, demotion, denunciation, derision, derogation, despisedness, disapprobation, disapproval, discommendation, discredit, discreditableness, disesteem, disfavor, disgrace, dishonor, dishonorableness, dislike, disparagement, dispraise, disreputability, disreputableness, disreputation, disrepute, disvaluation, embarrassment, faded reputation, humiliation, ignobility, *ignominia,* ignomy, ill favor, ill repute, imputation, *infamia,* infamy, ingloriousness, irreverence, lack of respect, loss of honor, loss of reputation, loss of respect, low standing, mortification, obloquy, odium, opprobrium, ostracism, poor reputation, reproach, scandal, sense of disgrace, sense of shame, shame, slur, smirch, stain, stigma, taint, tarnish, tarnished honor, *turpitudo,* unrespectability

IGNORANCE, ***noun*** benightedness, bewilderment, blindness, darkness, denseness, fog, foolishness, greenness, haze, illiteracy, illiterateness, *imprudentia,* incapacity, incognizance, incomprehension, ineptitude, inerudition, inexperience, innocence, *inscientia, inscitia,* insensibility, lack of education, lack of knowledge, lack of learning, maze, nescience, obtuseness, perplexity, rawness, simpleness, simplicity, unacquaintance, unawareness, unconsciousness, unenlightenment, unfamiliarity, unintellectuality, unintelligence, unknowingness, unlearnedness, unscholarliness, untaught state, unworldliness, vagueness, want of knowledge
ASSOCIATED CONCEPTS: culpable ignorance, essential ignorance, ignorance of law, involuntary ignorance, plead ignorance, voluntary ignorance
FOREIGN PHRASES: ***Ignorantia praesumitur ubi scientia non probatur.*** Ignorance is presumed where knowledge is not proved. ***Ignorantia legis neminem excusat.*** Ignorance of the law excuses no one. ***Regula est, juris quidem ignorantiam cuique nocere, facti vero ignorantiam non nocere.*** The rule is that a person's ignorance of the law may prejudice him, but that his ignorance of fact will not. ***Ignorantia juris sui non praejudicat juri.*** Ignorance of one's right does not prejudice the right. ***Ignorantia excusator, non juris sed facti.*** Ignorance of fact may excuse, but not ignorance of

law. ***Ignorantia juris quod quisque tenetur scire, neminem excusat.*** Ignorance of law, which everyone is bound to know, excuses no one. ***Nemo tenetus informare qui nescit, sed quisquis scire quod informat.*** No one who is ignorant of a thing is bound to give information about it, but everyone is bound to know that concerning which he gives information.

IGNORANCE OF LAW, ***adjective*** blindness, devoid of knowledge of the law, have no idea of the specifics of the law, incognizance, incomprehension, ineptitude, lack of knowledge of legal requirements, lack of learning of legal requirements, no knowledge of legal constraints, not schooled in the law, obtuseness, unawareness of rules, unawareness of rules of conduct, unawareness of standards which are imposed, unawareness of statutory requirements, unfamiliarity, unfamiliarity with established rule of law, unfamiliarity with laws, unfamiliarity with legal requirements, vagueness on the specifics in the law
ASSOCIATED CONCEPTS: defenses, due process, notice
FOREIGN PHRASES: ***Ignorantia, legis neminem, excusat.*** Ignorance of the law excuses no one. ***Ignorantia, praesumitur, ubi scientia non probatur.*** Ignorance is presumed where knowledge has not been proven.

IGNORANT, ***adjective*** analphabetic, benighted, dark, dense, devoid of knowledge, devoid of learning, devoid of understanding, failing to comprehend, illiterate, in a daze, in a fog, incapable, incompetent, inept, inexperienced, lacking education, lacking knowledge, lacking learning, lacking the ability to comprehend, lacking understanding, nonliterate, not being aware, not capable of comprehending, not capable of learning, obtuse, perplexed, raw, rude, simple, unaware, unconscious, uneducated, unenlightened, uninstructed, unknowing, unlearned, unlettered, unprepreпared, unread, unschooled, untaught, untutored
ASSOCIATED CONCEPTS: ignorance of the law, ignorance of the law is not an excuse for actions, ignorant of the rule of law

IGNORE *(Disbelieve),* ***verb*** be indifferent to, brush aside, discountenance, disregard, gloss over, make light of, pass over, pay no attention to, pay no heed to, pay no mind to, turn a deaf ear to

IGNORE *(Disregard),* ***verb*** be indifferent to, belittle, brush aside, depreciate, discountenance, discredit, disesteem, disparage, disregard, distain, distrust, doubt, gloss over, harbor suspicions, make light of, misprize, mistrust, pass over, pay no attention, pay no heed, pay no mind, question, slight, spurn, suspect

ILL *(Bad),* ***adjective*** adverse, antagonistic, baleful, bellicose, belligerent, calamitous, cantankerous, corrupt, crabbed, crabby, cross, damaging, degenerate, deleterious, depraved, destructive, detrimental, evil, fell, fractious, harm, harmful, hostile, hurtful, immoral, inauspicious, infelicitous, iniquitous, injurious, insult, irascible, irritable, low, mean, mischief, misfortune, nefarious, nocuous, pernicious, ruinous, sinful, snappish, snappy, sullen, trouble, unfavorable, unfriendly, unkind, unkindly, unlucky, unpromising, unpropitious, wicked, wrong

ILL *(Sick),* ***adjective*** afflicted, ailing, bedridden, confined, diseased, feeble, feverish, has a medical condition, in the hospital, indisposed, infirm, laid up, malady, not feeling well, not up to snuff, not well, on the sick list, out of commission, under the weather, weak
ASSOCIATED CONCEPTS: fee for service, health care, HMO

ILL-ADVISED, ***adjective*** counterproductive, disadvantageous, falsely construed, foolish, hasty, ill-considered, ill-contrived, ill-judged, impolitic, imprudent, inadvisable, inappropriate, inconsiderate, *inconsultus,* inconvenient, inexpedient, infelicitous, injudicious, inopportune, interpreted incorrectly, irresponsible, labored over under a misapprehension, misadvised, miscalculated, misconstrued, miscounseled, misestimated, misguided, misinformed, misinterpreted, misjudged, misled, mistaken, misunderstood, rash, reckless, senseless, shortsighted, *temerarius,* unconsidered, undesirable, unfit, unpolitical, unreasonable, unseemly, unsuitable, unwise

ILL-CONCEIVED, ***adjective*** deceived, distorted, estimated incorrectly, failed to understand, impolitic, inexpedient, laboring under a misapprehension, misapprehended, miscalculated, misconstrued, misestimated, misguided, misinformed, misinterpreted, misjudged, misled, mistake, mistaken, misunderstood, perverted the meaning of, reasonless, received a false impression of, received a wrong impression of, senseless, thoughtless, valued incorrectly
ASSOCIATED CONCEPTS: ill-conceived decision by the count

ILL-CONSIDERED, ***adjective*** adverse, against, antagonistic, antipathetic, averse, badly assessed, contrary, disadvantageous, discordant, disturbing, fractious, hasty, hostile, ill-advised, ill-judged, impolitic, imprudent, inadvisable, inappropriate, infelicitous, inhospitable, injudicious, misadvised, misguided, offensive, opposed, pugnacious, reckless, senseless, shortsighted, unconsidered, undesirable, unfit, unfriendly, unpleasant, unreasonable, unseemly, unsuitable, unsympathetic, unwise
ASSOCIATED CONCEPTS: ill-considered opinion or course of action

ILL-CONTRIVED, ***adjective*** counterproductive, falsely construed, foolish, ill-advised, imprudent, inadvisable, inexpedient, injudicious, interpreted incorrectly, misadvised, miscalculated, misconstrued, misestimated, misguided, misinformed misinterpreted, misjudged, misled, mistaken, misunderstood, to labor under a misapprehension, unpolitical

ILL-DISPOSED, ***adjective*** acrimonious, against, antagonistic, anti, antipathetic, apprehensive, averse, belligerent, considering, contentious, contra, contrary, crusty, discordant, disdainful, disputatious, epugnant to, fractious, hostile, hostile to, ill-intentioned, ill-natured, ill-willed, inhospitable, inimical, malevolent, malicious, mean, on the fence, opposed to, opposing, quarreling, rancorous, reluctant, repellent, resentful, resistant, resistive, sinister, spiteful, testy, unaligned, unfavorable, unfriendly to, unpropitious, unsympathetic, unsympathetic to

ILL-FOUNDED, ***adjective*** apocryphal, baseless, empty, erroneous, fallacious, false, fanciful, groundless, inaccurate, incorrect, insubstantial, sophistic, sophistical, suppositional, trumped up, unbased, unconfirmed, unfounded, ungrounded, unsubstantial, unsupportable, unsupported, unsustainable, untenable, unwarranted, without basis, without foundation, without sound basis, without substance

ILL-JUDGED, ***adjective*** acting without due consideration, against reason, blind, careless, hasty, headstrong, heedless, ill-advised, ill-chosen, ill-considered, ill-contrived, illogical, impatient, imprudent, inconsiderate, inept, inexact, inexpedient, injudicious, irrational, lacking discretion, misadvised, miscalculated, rash, reckless, shortsighted, showing poor judgment, thoughtless, unconsidered, undiscerning, unenlightened, unguided, unreasonable, unreasoning, unsensible, unsound, unthinking, unthoughtful, unwise, wild

ILL-NATURED, ***adjective*** abject, acrimonious, antipathetic, arrant, base, cantankerous, coarse, contemptible, contentious, contrary, crusty, despicable, disobliging, disputatious, froward, hostile, ignoble, ignominious, ill-disposed, ill-tempered, inhospitable, knavish, mean, nervous, objectionable, pusillanimous, scandalous, servile, snappish, testy, unaccommodating, vicious, vile, villainous, virulent

ILL REPUTE, ***noun*** bad name, bad repute, baseness, contemptibility, contemptibleness, degradation, disapproval, disesteem, disfavor, disgrace, dishonor, dislike, disreputability, disreputation, disrespectability, improperness, impropriety, infamy, notoriety, questionability, questionableness, rascality, shadiness, shame, unpopularity

ILL-REPUTE, ***adjective*** berated, censured, contemptible, debased, defamed, degraded, denunciated, discredited, disesteemed, disfavored, disgraced, dishonored, disparaged, disrespected, has a bad reputation, having a stigma, lewd, reviled, scorned, shamed, vilified
ASSOCIATED CONCEPTS: discrediting a witness

ILL TREATMENT *(Misuse),* ***noun*** ill usage, ill use, maltreatment, mishandling, mistreatment, misusage

ILL TREATMENT *(Oppression),* ***noun*** abuse, bullying, intimidation, malice, outrage, persecution, tyranny, viciousness, victimization
ASSOCIATED CONCEPTS: ill treatment of prisoners

ILL-USE, ***verb*** abuse, *abuti,* afflict, be hurtful, be malevolent, bruise, buffet, castigate, cause evil, damage, deal hard measure to, do an injustice to, do evil, do harm to, do violence, do wrong, flagellate, grind, harm, hurt, ill-treat, injure, knock about, malign, maltreat, manhandle, manipulate, mishandle, mistreat, misuse, oppress, overdrive, persecute, plague, show ill will, torment, torture, treat cruelly, treat unfairly, treat unkindly, use badly, use wrongly, vicitimize
ASSOCIATED CONCEPTS: contributory negligence, misuse of a product

ILL WILL, ***noun*** acerbity, acute dissatisfaction, adverseness, alienation, animosity, animus, antagonism, antipathy, aversion, bad intent, belligerency, bitter feelings, bitterness, chagrin, conflict, contrariety, coolness, deliberate malice, detestation, disaffection, discontent, dislike, disquiet, dissatisfaction, enmity, hard feelings, hostility, ill disposition, ill feeling, ill intent, incompatibility, inimicality, intolerance, malevolence, *malevolentia,* malice, maliciousness, malignance, malignancy, odium, opposition, rancor, resentment, spite, spitefulness, strain, tension, unfriendliness, unfriendly feeling, unkindness, unpopularity, wrath

ILLEGAL, ***adjective*** actionable, against the law, banned, contrary to law, criminal, exceeding the law, felonious, forbidden, illegitimate, illicit, impermissible, improper, *inlicitus,* invalid, lawless, not according to law, not allowed, not approved, not authorized by law, not covered by law, not permitted, not valid, outlawed, outside the law, prohibited, prohibited by law, proscribed, punishable, *quod contra leges fit,* unauthorized, unchartered, unconstitutional, unjustified, unlawful, unsanctioned, unwarrantable, unwarranted, *vetitus,* without authority, wrongful
ASSOCIATED CONCEPTS: illegal acts, illegal business, illegal combination, illegal contract, illegal detention, illegal discrimination, illegal force, illegal operation, illegal picketing, illegal possession, illegal practice, illegal purpose, illegal restraint, illegal sale, illegal search and seizure, illegal statute, illegal taking, illegal tax, illegal trade, illegal transaction, illegal use, mala in se, mala prohibita

ILLEGALITY, ***noun*** corruptness, criminality, illegitimacy, impropriety, infraction, infringement, lawlessness, malefaction, misdeed, transgression, unauthorization, underhandedness, unfitness, unlawfulness, violation of the law
ASSOCIATED CONCEPTS: *ultra vires*
FOREIGN PHRASES: ***Pacta quae contra leges constitutionesque vel contra bonos mores fiunt nullam vim habere, indubitati juris est.*** It is unquestionably the law that contracts which are made contrary to the laws or against good morals, have no force in law.

ILLEGALLY, ***adverb*** contrary to law, criminally, feloniously, illegitimately, illicitly, impermissibly, improperly, in violation of law, tortiously, unlawfully, without legal authority, without legal sanction, wrongfully
ASSOCIATED CONCEPTS: acting illegally, illegally assessed, illegally obtained, illegally procured, illegally sold

ILLEGITIMATE *(Born out of wedlock),* ***adjective*** adulterine, base-born, bastard, misbegot, misbegotten, *nothus,* of illicit union, unlawfully begotten, unnatural
ASSOCIATED CONCEPTS: illegitimate children, legitimation, paternity proceeding, presumption of legitimacy
FOREIGN PHRASES: ***Parentum est liberos alere atiam nothos.*** It is the duty of parents to support their children even when illegitmate. ***Qui nascitur sine legitimo matrimonio, matrem sequitur.*** He who is born out of lawful matrimony succeeds to the condition of his mother. ***Non est justum aliquem antenatum post mortem facere bastardum qui toto tempore vitae suae pro legitimo habebatur.*** It is not just to make anyone a bastard after his death, who during his lifetime was regarded as legitimate. ***Justum non est aliquem antenatum mortuum facere bastardum, qui pro tota vita sua pro legitimo habetur.*** It is not just to make a bastard after his death one elder born who all his life has been accounted legitimate. ***Qui ex damnato coitu nascuntur inter liberos non computentur.*** They who are born of an illicit union should not be reckoned among the children.

ILLEGITIMATE *(Illegal),* ***adjective*** against the law, banned, contrary to law, criminal, forbidden, illicit, impermissible, improper, interdicted, lawbreaking, malfeasant, *non legitimus,* not according to law, not permitted, outlawed, outside the law, prohibited, prohibited by law, proscribed, unallowed, unauthorized, unlawful, unlicensed, unsanctioned, wrongful

ILLIBERAL, ***adjective*** avaricious, *avarus,* biased, bigoted, churlish, close, close-fisted, conservative, covetous, dogmatic, fanatical, grasping, greedy, grudging, hidebound, inhospitable, *inliberalis,* intolerant, mean, mercenary, miserly, narrow, narrow-minded, niggardly, onesided, opinionated, parochial, parsimonious, partial, penurious, persecuting, petty, prejudiced, reactionary, selfish, *sordidus,* sparing, stingy, stinting, tight, tightfisted, uncharitable, unchivalrous, ungenerous, ungentlemanly

ILLICIT, *adjective* accusable, actionable, against the law, banned, censored, contrary to law, criminal, exceeding the law, felonious, forbidden, forbidden by law, guilty, illegal, illegitimate, immoral, impermissible, improper, infamous, iniquitous, injudicial, *inlicitus,* interdicted, lawless, nonconstitutional, nonlegal, not according to law, not allowed, not approved, not covered by law, not permitted, out of bounds, outlawed, outside the law, prohibited, proscribed, punishable by law, *quod contra leges fit,* taboo, tortious, triable, unallowed, unauthorized, unconstitutional, under ban, unlawful, unlegalized, unlegislated, unprincipled, unsanctioned, unseemly, unwarrantable, unwarranted, *vetitus,* wicked, without authority, wrong, wrongful
ASSOCIATED CONCEPTS: illicit cohabitation, illicit relations, illicit relationship, illicit trade

ILLITERACY, *noun* ineducation, inerudition, unintellectualism, unlearnedness, unscholarliness

ILLNESS, *noun* affliction, ailing, ailment, complaint, defect, disability, disease, disorder, infirmity, malady, prostration, sickness
ASSOCIATED CONCEPTS: mental illness, terminal illness, unemployment compensation, Workers' Compensation Law

ILLOGICAL, *adjective* *absurdus,* contradictory, contrary to reason, contrary to the rules of logic, fallacious, faulty, groundless, inconsistent, indefensible, irrational, logically unsound, mistaken, nonscientific, paralogistic, self-contradictory, sophistic, sophistical, unfounded, ungrounded, unscientific, unsound, unsustainable, untenable, without basis, without foundation
ASSOCIATED CONCEPTS: arbitrary and capricious

ILLUDE, *verb* be cunning, befool, beguile, cheat, chouse, circumvent, cozen, deceive, decoy, defraud, delude, deride, dupe, ensnare, fool, gerrymander, gull, hoax, inveigle, lead astray, lead into error, make a fool of, misdirect, misguide, misinform, mislead, mock, outmaneuver, outwit, play false, practice chicanery, put something over, ridicule, scorn, swindle, take advantage of, take in, trick, victimize

ILLUMINATE *(Brighten),* ***verb*** cast light upon, light, light up, lighten up, radiate, throw light upon, throw sunlight on

ILLUMINATE *(Inform),* ***verb*** acquaint, advise, apprise, cast light upon, clarify, clear up, convince, counsel, define, delineate, demonstrate, disabuse, edify, elaborate, elucidate, embellish, enlighten, enucleate, explain, expound, familiarize with, give insight to, illustrate, impart, inspire, instill, instruct, lecture, make aware, make clear, make explicit, notify, stimulate, unfold

ILLUMINATION, *noun* clarification, cognition, cognizance, comment, construction, definition, education, elucidation, explanation, explication, illustration, information, instruction, intellectual enlightenment, learning, realization, recognition, simplification, solution

ILLUSION *(Deception),* ***noun*** aberration, distortion, fallacy, false impression, misbelief, misconception, prestidigitation

ILLUSION *(Impression),* ***noun*** apparition, artifice, chimera, daydream, deception, delusion, dream, figment, hallucination, masquerade, mirage, myth, optical illusion, phantasm, phantasmagoria, phantom, semblance, specter, spirit, unreality, vision, wraith

ILLUSORY, *adjective* casuistic, casuistical, chimerical, conjuring, counterfeit, deceiving, deceptive, deluding, delusive, fabricated, fallacious, false, *falsus,* fancied, fanciful, fatuitous, feigned, fictitious, hatched, illusive, imaginary, imagined, insidious, insubstantial, invented, make-believe, misleading, mythic, mythological, not true, notional, phantasmal, pretended, sophistic, sophistical, suppositional, tenuous, tricky, unactual, unauthentic, unreal, unsubstantial, unsupportable, *vanus,* visionary
ASSOCIATED CONCEPTS: illusory agreement, illusory appointment, illusory contract, illusory promise, illusory transfer, illusory trust
FOREIGN PHRASES: ***Judicium non debet esse illusorium; suum effectum habere debet.*** A judgment ought not to be illusory; it ought to have its proper effect.

ILLUSTRATE, *verb* cite, clarify, define, demonstrate, display, elucidate, enlighten, exemplify, exhibit, explain, expound, furnish an example, give an instance, illuminate, *inlustrare,* instance, interpret, make evident, make plain, make vivid, manifest, produce an example, represent, show, show by example, teach by examples
ASSOCIATED CONCEPTS: illustrative questions

ILLUSTRATION, *noun* case in point, clarification, depiction, depictment, display, elucidation, enucleation, example, exemplar, exemplification, *exemplum,* explanation, explication, exponent, exposition, illumination, instance, manifestation, model, practical demonstration, relevant instance, representation, sample, showing, simplification, specimen

ILLUSTRATIVE, *adjective* annotative, clarifying, definitive, delineatory, depictive, descriptive, elucidative, evincive, exemplary, explanatory, expository, figurative, general, graphic, illuminative, indicative, inferential, interpretative, narrative, picaresque, representative, symbolic, typical

ILLUSTRIOUS, *adjective* acclaimed, *amplus,* applauded, bright, brilliant, celebrated, conspicuous, distinguished, eminent, excellent, eximious, famed, famous, glorious, grand, great, heroic, honored, important, *inlustris,* known, memorable, noble, notable, noted, popular, prominent, radiant, remarkable, renowned, resplendent, shining, signal, splendid, *splendidus,* splendorous, sublime, talked of, time-honored, transplendent, well-known, widely known

IMAGE, *noun* appearance, apprehension, aspect, color, complexion, concept, conception, copy, counterpart, duplicate, embodiment, fancy, fantasy, form, guise, impression, likeness, living picture, look, material representation, mental image, model, percept, perception, phase, phenomenon, physiognomy, picture, portrait, presence, reflection, reproduction, resemblance, semblance, symbol, vision

IMAGINARY, *adjective* abstract, artificial, chimerical, contrive, contrived, delusional, delusive, fabled, fabricated, fanciful, fantasied, fantastic, feigned, fictional, fictitious, fictive, hypothetical, ideal, idealized, illusory, invented, made-up, make-believe, mythical, nonexistent, notional, phantasmagoric, phantasmal, phantasmic, phantom, pretend, theoretical, unreal, whimsical

IMAGINATION, *noun* conceive, concept, conception, conceptualization, creation, creative power, creativity,

formulation, idea, illusion, image, imaginative faculty, imaginativeness, innovativeness, inventiveness, perception, presumption, vision
ASSOCIATED CONCEPTS: perjury, trumped-up charges

IMAGINATIVE, ***adjective*** clever, constructive, creative, ingenious, innovative, inventive, original, productive, resourceful, visionary

IMAGINE, ***verb*** apprehend, assume, believe, compose, conceive, conclude, conjure, conjure up, contrive, create, deduce, delineate, depict, devise, dream, envision, expect, fabricate, fancy, gather, guess, ideate, improvise, infer, invent, judge, make up, opine, originate, picture, plan, presume, pretend, profess, regard, scheme, speculate, suppose, surmise, suspect, think, visualize

IMBALANCE, ***noun*** difference, disequilibrium, disparity, disproportion, dissimilarity, distortion, diversity, inconstancy, inequality, irregularity, unevenness, unjust distribution, variableness

IMBROGLIO, ***noun*** babel, bedlam, broil, chaos, commotion, complexity, complicated misunderstanding, complication, confusing situation, confusion, difficult situation, difficulty, dilemma, disagreement, disorder, disturbance, embarrassing situation, embranglement, embroilment, entanglement, fracas, impasse, intricate involvement, intricate plot, involved situation, jam, jungle, labyrinth, maze, melee, mess, muddle, perplexing state of affairs, pickle, plight, predicament, quandary, riot, row, rumpus, scrape, stew, stymie, tight spot, tumult, turmoil, uproar, welter

IMBUE, ***verb*** bathe, drench, fill, *imbuere,* implant, impress upon the mind, inculcate, indoctrinate, *inficere,* influence, infuse, inject, inspire, instill, leaven, permeate, pervade, pour in, saturate, soak, *tingere*

IMITATE, ***verb*** adopt, be like, caricature, clone, copy, counterfeit, duplicate, echo, emulate, fabricate, fake, follow, follow as an example, follow suit, forge, impersonate, look like, make a copy, match, mimic, mirror, model after, pattern after, parrot, plagiarize, portray, pose, pretend, reflect, repeat, replicate, represent, reproduce, simulate
ASSOCIATED CONCEPTS: counterfeit, identity theft

IMITATION, ***adjective*** artificial, bogus, burlesque, copied, counterfeit, deceptive, dummy, *effigies,* ersatz, factitious, faked, false, feigned, imitated, imitative, make-believe, mock, phony, pretended, pseudo, quasi, sham, simulacrum, simulated, spurious, substitute, synthetic, unauthentic, ungenuine
ASSOCIATED CONCEPTS: forgery

IMMACULATE, ***adjective*** above suspicion, blameless, chaste, clean, faultless, flawless, impeccable, incorrupt, inculpable, innocent, irreproachable, perfect, pure, refined, sinless, spotless, spotlessly clean, unblemished, undefiled, unflawed, unimpeachable, unpolluted, unsoiled, unstained, unsullied, untainted, untarnished, virginal, virtuous

IMMANENT, ***adjective*** basic, characteristic, congenital, deep-rooted, elemental, fundamental, habitual, hereditary, ingrained, inherited, innate, integral, intrinsic, inveterate, natural, subjective

IMMATERIAL, ***adjective*** baseless, beside the point, beside the question, bodiless, chimerical, diminutive, ethereal, *expers corporis,* extraneous, groundless, impertinent, inapplicable, inappreciable, inappropriate, inconsequential, incorporeal, inessential, insignificant, insubstantial, intangible, irrelevant, lightweight, meaningless, minor, nominal, nonessential, nonphysical, not connected with, not important, not pertaining to, not pertinent, *nullius momenti,* of little account, of no consequence, of no essential consequence, of no importance, of no moment, of no significance, off the point, off the topic, other wordly, out of place, out-of-the-way, outside the question, pointless, remote, sine corpore, spectral, trivial, unessential, unimportant, unrelated, unsubstantial, vaporous, without depth, without substance, without weight, worthless
ASSOCIATED CONCEPTS: immaterial allegations, immaterial alteration, immaterial averment, immaterial breach, immaterial facts, immaterial issues, immaterial testimony, immaterial variance, incompetent evidence, irrelevant evidence

IMMATERIALITY, ***noun*** inconsequence, incorporeality, inessentiality, insignificance, insubstantiality, insufficiency, intangibility, irrelevance, irrelevancy, lack of depth, lack of substance, lightness, meagerness, nonessentiality, otherworldliness, paltriness, pettiness, pointlessness, shallowness, spirituality, spiritualness, thinness, triviality, unimportance, unnoteworthiness, unsubstantiality, worthlessness

IMMATURE, ***adjective*** callow, crude, green, gullible, ignorant, inexperienced, jejune, juvenile, naive, puerile, raw, rudimental, rudimentary, undeveloped, unfinished, unfledged, unformed, unmellowed, unprepared, unripe, unseasoned, unsophisticated, young, youthful

IMMEASURABLE, ***adjective*** boundless, countless, endless, extending forever, extensive, great, illimitable, immerse, indeterminate, inexhaustible, infinite, innumerable, interminable, large, limitless, measureless, never-ending, unbounded, undeterminable, undetermined, unfathomable, unlimited, untold, vast
ASSOCIATED CONCEPTS: immeasurable harm

IMMEDIACY, ***noun*** availability, closeness, confines, convenience, environs, hear, immediateness, instantaneousness, nearness, simultaneousness, neighborhood, now, occurrence, occurring at the present time, precinct, presence, propinquity, proximity, simultaneity, vicinage, vicinity
ASSOCIATED CONCEPTS: statute of limitations

IMMEDIATE *(At once),* ***adjective*** flash, instant, instantaneous, *praesens,* prompt, quick, speedy, sudden, unhesitating, with reasonable dispatch, without delay

IMMEDIATE *(Imminent),* ***adjective*** about to happen, anticipated, approaching, at hand, close, close at hand, coming, drawing near, expected, following, foreseen, forthcoming, impendent, impending, in the offing, in view, looked for, momentary, near at hand, nearing, next, nigh, prospective, to come, upcoming

IMMEDIATE *(Not distant),* ***adjective*** abutting, adjacent, adjoining, at hand, bordering, bounding, close, close at hand, conjoining, conterminous, contiguous, handy, juxtapositional, near, near by, neighboring, next to, proximate, verging
ASSOCIATED CONCEPTS: immediate beneficiaries, immediate benefit, immediate cause, immediate consequences, immediate control, immediate damage, immediate delivery, immediate irreparable harm, immediate legatees, immediate need, immediate transferor

IMMEDIATELY *(In the proximity),* ***adverb*** alongside, around, at close quarters, at close range, close by, close to, closely, directly, in the area of, in the neighborhood of, in the vicinity of, near, nearby, next door, promptly, proximately, without an interval of time
ASSOCIATED CONCEPTS: proximate cause

IMMEDIATELY *(Instantly),* ***adverb*** at once, at the same time, at this moment, concurrently, in a moment, in an instant, instaneously, instantly, now, posthaste, promptly, pronto, quickly, rapidly, right away, shortly, simultaneously, speedily, straight off, suddenly, this very moment

IMMENSE, ***adjective*** boundless, broad, bulky, capacious, colossal, endless, enormous, exorbitant, extremely large, far-reaching, gigantic, grandiose, gross, huge, illimitable, immeasurable, innumerable, mammoth, massive, monumental, mountainous, myriad, outrageous, prodigious, stupendous, titanic, tremendous, vast

IMMERSE *(Engross),* ***verb*** absorb, attend, be attentive, bury, engage, enthrall, fascinate, grip, hold, hold spellbound, interest, involve, monopolize, occupy, overwhelm, preoccupy, submerge, take up

IMMERSE *(Plunge into),* ***verb*** bathe, cover with water, deluge, dip, douse, drench, drown, duck, dunk, engulf, flood, insert, inundate, place under a liquid, plunge into a liquid, put under water, send to the bottom, sink, soak, souse, steep, submerge, submerse, swamp, thrust under

IMMIGRANT, ***noun*** alien, expatriate, foreigner, incomer, migrant, naturalized citizen, newcomer, resident alien, settler
ASSOCIATED CONCEPTS: immigration law

IMMIGRATION, ***noun*** admission of foreigners, *adventus,* change of national location, colonization, entry of aliens, establishment of foreign residence, expatriation, foreign influx, incoming population, ingress, migration, movement of population, transmigration
ASSOCIATED CONCEPTS: issuance of visas, passports

IMMINENT, ***adjective*** about to be, about to happen, alarming, approaching, at hand, brewing, closing in, coming, destined, drawing near, expected, following, forecasted, forthcoming, future, *imminere,* impendent, *impendere,* impending, in store, in the offing, in the wind, in view, instant, likely to happen, looming, menacing, minatorial, minatory, near, near at hand, nearing, next, ominous, on the way, oncoming, overhanging, portentous, *praesens,* predicted, prospective, threatening, threatening harm, upcoming
ASSOCIATED CONCEPTS: imminent danger, imminent irreparable harm, imminent peril

IMMOBILIZE, ***adjective*** fixed, have no freedom, have no mobility, immovable, impassive, inactive, inexpressive, inflexible, like a statue, motionless, paralyzed, rigid, riveted, rooted, stationary, staunch, steadfast, still, transfixed, unmoving

IMMODERATE, ***adjective*** exaggerated, excessive, exorbitant, extravagant, extreme, inordinate, intemperate, not balanced, not fair, overblown, preposterous, self-indulgent, squandering, unbalanced, unconscionable, uncontrolled, uncurbed, unlimited, unreasonable, unrestrained, unwarranted
ASSOCIATED CONCEPTS: immoderate punishment, immoderate use

IMMORAL, ***adjective*** amoral, arrant, bad, base, conscienceless, corrupt, criminal, debauched, degenerate, depraved, dishonest, dishonorable, disreputable, dissipated, dissolute, evil, exploitative, false, flagitious, graceless, heinous, ignoble, illaudable, illegal, illicit, improper, impure, indecent, iniquitous, knavish, lacking morals, lecherous, lewd, libidinous, licentious, *male moratus,* miscreant, nefarious, objectionable, *perditus,* pernicious, perverted, pettifogging, *pravus,* profligate, promiscuous, prurient, reprobate, roguish, salacious, shameless, shocking, sinful, unchaste, unconscionable, unethical, unjustifiable, unlawful, unmoral, unprincipled, unrighteous, unscrupulous, unvirtuous, unwholesome, wicked, without integrity, wrong
ASSOCIATED CONCEPTS: immoral act, immoral agreement, immoral conduct, immoral consideration, immoral contract, obscenity
FOREIGN PHRASES: ***Ex turpi causa non oritur actio.*** No cause of action arises out of an immoral or illegal consideration.

IMMORALITY, ***noun*** atrocity, bad repute, carnality, concupiscence, contamination, corruption, criminality, delinquency, demoralization, depravity, dissoluteness, evil, indecency, iniquity, knavery, lechery, lewdness, licentiousness, loose morals, misdoing, obscenity, perversion, profligacy, salacity, sexual promiscuity, sin, turpitude, vice, wantonness, wickedness, wrong
ASSOCIATED CONCEPTS: adultery, bribery, criminal conversation, immoral conduct, immoral contracts, lewdness

IMMORTAL, ***adjective*** always, canonizing, commemorating, continuity, continuous, endless, endlessness, eternal, everlasting, forever, imperishable, indestructible, lasting, never dying, permanent, perennial, undying, unfading

IMMORTALITY *(Deathlessness),* ***noun*** athanasy, canonization, commemoration, continuity, deathlessness, endless life, endlessness, eternal continuance, eternity, everlastingness, imperishability, indestructibility, infinity, perpetuation, perpetuity, undying repute, unlimited existence

IMMORTALITY *(Distinction),* ***noun*** commemoration, enshrinement, immortal name, imperishability, lasting fame

IMMOVABLE, ***noun*** affixed property, fixed assets, fixed chattel, fixed property, fixture, *immobilis, immotus,* land, property permanently affixed to the realty, real estate, real property, *stabilis*

IMMUNE, ***adjective*** absolved, armored, clear, excused, exempt, free, granted amnesty, *immunis,* immunized, impregnable, inaccessible, inexpugnable, inviolable, invulnerable, not accountable, not answerable, not liable, not responsible, not subject, possessed of immunity, privileged, protected, released, safe, screened, sheltered, shielded, spared, unaccountable, unaffected by, unanswerable, unassailable, unattackable, under shelter, unencumbered, unexposed, unliable, unpunishable, unrestrained, unrestricted, unsubject, unsusceptible, unthreatened, untouchable, untouched, without risk
ASSOCIATED CONCEPTS: immune from prosecution

IMMUNITY, ***noun*** absolution, acquittal, charter, commutation, discharge, exception, exculpation, exemption, exemption from punishment, franchise, freedom, freedom from exemption, freedom from obligation, freedom from prosecution, *immunitas,* liberation, liberty, license, nonliability, privilege, protection, release, release from charge, release from duty, relief, reprieve, respite, safety from prosecution, special privilege, *vacatio*

ASSOCIATED CONCEPTS: absolute immunity, complete immunity, derivative immunity, full transactional immunity, full waiver, governmental immunity, immunity from arrest, immunity from prosecution, immunity from service of process, limited immunity, limited waiver, partial immunity, privileges and immunities, qualified immunity, state immunity, transactional immunity, use and derivative immunity, use immunity, waiver of immunity

IMMUNIZE, ***verb*** counterbalance, countervail, free, grant immunity, guard against, inoculate, make safe, neutralize, not affected by, offset, preserve, privileged, protect, resist, safeguard, shield, shield from damage, shield from danger, shield from injury, unsusceptible to, vaccinate against

IMMURE, ***verb*** cast into prison, commit to an institution, commit to prison, confine, constrain, detain, encage, enclose, enclose within walls, entomb, gate, hold, hold captive, hold in captivity, hold in check, hold within bounds, impound, imprison, incarcerate, *includere,* isolate, keep in, keep in captivity, keep in check, keep in custody, keep in detention, keep prisoner, keep under arrest, keep within bounds, lay under restraint, lead into captivity, lock in, lock up, make captive, put under arrest, quarantine, restrain, seal up, seclude, send to prison, shelter, shut up, take captive, take into custody, throw into prison, wall up

IMMUTABLE, ***adjective*** adamant, ageless, confirmed, constans, constant, continual, continuous, durable, eternal, firm, fixed, immovable, *immutabilis,* implacable, incontrovertible, indestructible, inexorable, inflexible, intractable, invariable, irremovable, irrevocable, never changing, never varying, nonelastic, not to be changed, not to be moved, obstinate, perennial, permanent, perpetual, persistent, relentless, riveted, rooted, settled, *stabilis,* static, steadfast, steady, stiff, unaging, unalterable, unbending, unchangeable, unchanging, uncompromising, undeviating, undying, unending, unmalleable, unpliable, unrelenting, untractable, unyielding, vested
ASSOCIATED CONCEPTS: immutable principle of law
FOREIGN PHRASES: ***Nomina sunt mutabilia, res autem immobiles.*** Names are mutable, but things are immutable.

IMPACT *(Effect),* ***noun*** aftermath, bearing, cogency, concern, conclusion, consequence, deduction, full effect, germaneness, import, interest, materiality, meaning, outcome, outgrowth, pertinency, preference, reaction, relevance, repercussion, result, reverberation, upshot, value

IMPACT *(Importance),* ***noun*** consequence, end result, force, gravity, greatness, import, magnitude, mark, merit, meaning, moment, net result, noted value, portent, pronounced impression, reaction, result, significance, signification, substance, value, weightiness
ASSOCIATED CONCEPTS: impact from a landmark decision of the court

IMPACT, ***verb*** compress, cram, crowd, drive, drive firmly in, fill, fill to capacity, force, force together, hammer in, inject, insert, jam, load, overburden, overcrowd, overload, pack, pack close, pack in, pack together, press, press together, push, push together, ram, shove, squeeze, strike, thrust in, wedge

IMPAIR, ***verb*** adulterate, affect injuriously, blight, blunt, contaminate, cripple, crumble, damage, *debilitare,* debilitate, decrease in excellence, demolish, deplete, deprive of power, desecrate, devalue, dilapidate, diminish, diminish in quality, dissipate, disturb, dull, enervate, enfeeble, erode, *frangere,* harm, hinder, hurt, *imminuere,* injure, lessen in power, lessen in value, make inroads on, make worse, mar, obtund, paralyze, pollute, put out of commission, reduce, relax, render feeble, ruin, sap, stifle, taint, undermine, unhinge, waste, weaken, wear out, worsen
ASSOCIATED CONCEPTS: impairing the obligation of contracts, impairment of capital, impairment of good will, impairment of memory, impairment of powers, impairment of security

IMPAIRED CONDITION, ***noun*** atrophy, caducity, collapse, corrosion, damage, decadence, decadency, decay, decrepitude, degeneration, deterioration, detriment, dilapidation, disrepair, fault, impairment, impediment, injury, lack of maintenance, neglect, ruination, weakness, wear and tear
ASSOCIATED CONCEPTS: driving while impaired, impairing the rights of contract

IMPAIRMENT *(Damage),* ***noun*** detriment, disrepair, harm, hurt, injury, loss
ASSOCIATED CONCEPTS: impairment of vision

IMPAIRMENT *(Disability),* ***noun*** affliction, ailment, debilitation, debility, deterioration, disablement, disorder, disqualification, feebleness, frailty, handicap, helplessness, illness, impairment, impotence, impotency, inability, inability to work, inadequacy, incapability, incapacitation, incapacity, incompetence, incompetency, indisposition, ineffectiveness, ineffectuality, ineffectualness, inefficacy, inefficiency, infirmity, insufficiency, malady, powerlessness, sickness, unfitness, unsoundness, weakness
ASSOCIATED CONCEPTS: complete disability, continuous disability, disability benefits, disability compensation, disability insurance, general disability, medical disability, mental disability, partial disability, proof of disability, temporary disability, total disability

IMPAIRMENT *(Drawback),* ***noun*** detriment, disadvantage, inability, liability, limitation
ASSOCIATED CONCEPTS: impairment of funds, impairment of security

IMPALPABILITY, ***noun*** abstraction, bodilessness, flimsiness, immateriality, immaterialness, imperceptibility, inappreciability, incorporality, incorporealism, incorporeality, incorporeity, insubstantiality, intangibility, lack of substance, unconcreteness, unsolidity, unsubstantialness

IMPALPABLE, ***adjective*** attenuated, barely seen, concealed, covered, covert, delicate, difficult to feel, difficult to perceive, difficult to see, doubtable, dubitable, equivocal, fine, hidden, immateriate, imperceptible, inappreciable, inapprehensible, incapable of being perceived, inconspicuous, incorporeal, indefinite, indistinct, infinitesimal, intangible, invisible, little, microscopic, minute, nonmaterial, not manifest, not readily discerned, obscure, *quod tangi non potest,* screened, shaded, shadowy, shrouded, slight, small, subtle, tiny, unapparent, unclear, undiscernable, unevident, unexplicit, unnoticeable, unobservable, unobvious, unpatent, unperceivable, unplain, unpronounced, unreal, unrecognizable, unrevealed, unsubstantial, untouchable, vague, veiled, very fine

IMPANEL, ***verb*** catalog, enter, enumerate, itemize, list, record, register, schedule
ASSOCIATED CONCEPTS: impanel a jury

IMPART, ***verb*** accord, acquaint, advise, apprise, be indiscreet, bestow, brief, *communicare,* communicate, confer, confide, convey, deliver, disclose, dispense, educate, endow, enlighten, enrich, favor with, *impertire,* inform, instruct, issue, make known, mention, point out, present, provide, relate, reveal, teach, tell, transfer, transmit

IMPARTIAL, ***adjective*** *aequabilis, aequus,* broadminded, detached, disinterested, dispassionate, equitable, even, evenhanded, evenly balanced, fair, fair-minded, free from bias, free to choose, honest, honorable, impersonal, incorrupt, *incorruptus,* independent, indifferent, *integer,* judicious, just, lacking prejudice, neutral, nonpartisan, not biased, not partial, objective, open, open-minded, reasonable, scrupulous, unaffected, unbiased, unbigoted, unbought, unbribed, uncolored, uncommitted, uncompelled, uncorrupt, uncorrupted, undecided, uninfluenced, unjaundiced, unopinionated, unopinioned, unprejudiced, unprepossessed, unswayed, untouched, without a preference, without favoritism
ASSOCIATED CONCEPTS: fair and impartial, impartial hearing officer, impartial judge, impartial jury, impartial trial
FOREIGN PHRASES: ***Nemo potest esse simul actor et judex.*** No one can be at the same time judge and suitor. ***Judex non potest injuriam sibi datam punire.*** A judge cannot punish a wrong done to himself. ***Judex non potest esse testis in propria causa.*** A judge cannot be a witness in his own case.

IMPASSE, ***noun*** abruption, bar, block, blockade, blockage, cessation, check, complete standstill, complexity, dead end, dead stop, deadlock, desistance, deterrence, difficulty, dilemma, discontinuance, discontinuance of activity, discontinuation, end, halt, hopelessness, impediment, impossibility, impossible task, inextricability, insoluble difference, insuperability, insuperable obstacle, nonresumption, obstacle, obstruction, perplexity, preclusion, predicament, problem, quagmire, quandary, stalemate, stall, standstill, state of inaction, state of no progress, stop
ASSOCIATED CONCEPTS: impasse in negotiations

IMPASSION, ***verb*** affect, agitate, arouse the emotions, electrify, encourage, enkindle, excite, incite, infect, inspire, kindle, move, provoke, rouse, spirit, spur, stir, stir the feelings, stir up

IMPATIENCE, ***adjective*** agitation, anger, annoyance, anxiety, disquiet, eager, excitable, excited, have a short temper, hotheadedness, in impetuosity, intolerance, irascibility, nervousness, possess a quick temper, prickly, quick-tempered, short, snappish

IMPEACH, ***verb*** *accusare,* accuse, accuse of maladministration, accuse of misconduct, admonish, animadvert, attack, attaint, blame, bring a charge, bring charges, bring into discredit, bring to account, bring to justice, bring up for investigation, call in question, call to account, cast an imputation upon, cast blame upon, castigate, censure, challenge, challenge the credibility of, charge, charge to, charge with, complain against, condemn, confute, criticize, declaim against, decry, denigrate, denounce, denunciate, disapprove, discredit, disparage, dispute, expose, fault, file a claim, find an indictment against, hold at fault, implicate, impugn, impute fault to, inculpate, incur blame, indict, indict for maladministration, prefer a claim, prefer charges, put on trial, put the blame on, rebuff, recriminate, reprimand, reproach, reprove, ridicule, take to account, upbraid, vituperate
ASSOCIATED CONCEPTS: impeach a government official, impeach a witness

IMPEACHABILITY, ***noun*** blame, blameworthiness, censurability, chargeability, culpability, discredit, dishonor, disrepute, grave culpability, guiltiness, liability, peccability

IMPEACHMENT, ***noun*** accusal, *accusatio,* accusation, act of discrediting, admonition, animadversion, arraignment, attack, blame, castigation, censure, challenge, charge, complaint, condemnation, countercharge, criminal proceeding, crimination, criticism, denigration, denouncement, denunciation, disapproval, discommendation, exposure, hostile criticism, imputation of dereliction, imputation of fault, indictment, questioning integrity, questioning witness's veracity, rebuke, reprimand, reproach, reproof, vilification
ASSOCIATED CONCEPTS: articles of impeachment, character evidence, collateral impeachment, impeachment of a governmental officer, impeachment of a verdict, impeachment of a witness, impeachment of credibility, moral terpitude, prior inconsistent statement, reputation evidence

IMPECCABLE, ***adjective*** above reproach, absolutely ravishing, absolutely the finest, beautiful, complete, delightful, excellent, exemplary, faultless, finished, flawless, glorious, ideal, immaculate, incredible, irreproachable, perfect, refined, spotless, stylish, superb, unblemished, virtuous

IMPECUNIOUS, ***adjective*** bankrupt, beggared, beggarly, broke, cleaned out, destitute, distressed, embarrassed, flat, flat broke, hard up, impoverished, in need, in straitened circumstances, in the red, in want, indigent, insolvent, necessitous, needy, not well off, out of money, pauperized, penniless, penurious, pinched, poor, poorly off, poverty-stricken, short, short of cash, short of funds, short of money, strapped, unable to make ends meet, unmoneyed, unprosperous, without funds, without money

IMPEDE, ***verb*** annul, arrest, barricade, be a drag on, be an obstacle to, be in the way, block, blockade, bolt, bother, brake, bring to a standstill, burden, cause to delay, check, circumscribe, confine, cramp, cumber, curb, dam up, deadlock, decelerate, delay, detain, deter, disable, drag, embarrass, encumber, erect a barrier, estop, fetter, foreclose, frustrate, hamper, handicap, hinder, hold back, hold in check, hold up, impair, *impedire,* incommode, inconvenience, inhibit, interfere, interrupt, keep back, keep in check, limit, load, mar, obstruct, paralyze, postpone, preclude, press, prevent, quell, restrain, restrict, retard, set one back, shackle, slacken, slow down, stalemate, stand in the way, stay, stop, stop in progress by hindrances, suffocate, suspend, thwart, trammel, turn aside
ASSOCIATED CONCEPTS: impede negotiations
FOREIGN PHRASES: ***Ubi aliquid impeditur propter unum, eo remoto, tollitur impedimentum.*** Where anything is impeded by one single cause, with the removal of it, the impediment is removed.

IMPEDIMENT, ***noun*** bar, barrier, block, blockade, blockage, brake, burden, censorship, check, clog, complication, constraint, counteraction, damper, delay, deterrent, deterrence, difficulty, disability, disadvantage, discouragement, drawback, encumbrance, estoppel, fetter, frustration, hamper, hampering, handicap, hindrance, holdback, *impedimentum,* impasse, imposition, inconvenience, inhibition, interference, interruption, limitation, load, objection, obstacle, obstruction, obtrusion, opposition, preclusion,

predicament, prevention, prohibition, resistance, restraint, restriction, retardation, retardment, setback, shackle, snag, stop, stoppage, stumbling block, trammel
ASSOCIATED CONCEPTS: absolute impediment, detrimental impediment, impediment to a legal remedy, legal impediment, prohibitive impediments, relative impediments
FOREIGN PHRASES: ***Non valet impedimentum quod de jure non sortitur effectum.*** An impediment which has no effect in law is of no force. ***Remoto impedimento, emergit actio.*** The impediment being removed, the action comes to life.

IMPEDITIVE, ***adjective*** burdensome, conditional, cumbrous, deterrent, difficult, hindering, inhibitive, inhibitory, labyrinthine, limitative, limiting, onerous, preclusive, preventive, prohibitive, proscriptive, repressive, restrictive, suppressive

IMPEL, ***verb*** actuate, agitate, arouse, catapult, cause, drive forward, drive onward, encourage, fling, give an impetus, heave, hurl, impart momentum, impart motion, *incitare,* incite, incite to action, induce, instigate, jaculate, launch, mobilize, motivate, move forward, precipitate, press on, prod, project, prompt, propel, push, put in motion, rouse, send headlong, set going, set in motion, set moving, shove, spur, start, stimulate, throw, urge, urge forward, *urgere*

IMPEND, ***verb*** approach, be at hand, be forthcoming, be imminent, be in store, be near, be near at hand, draw near, *imminere, impendere,* loom, menace, promise ill, threaten
ASSOCIATED CONCEPTS: impending danger, impending death, impending peril

IMPENDING, ***adjective*** about to happen, approaching, brewing, close, forthcoming, future, hanging, immediate, inevitable, in prospect, instant, in the offing, looming, near at hand, necessary, oncoming, pending, projecting, prospective, proximate, suspended, threatening, unavoidable
ASSOCIATED CONCEPTS: impending indictment

IMPENETRABLE, ***adjective*** adamantine, closed, complex, crass, difficult, dull, enigmatic, hidden, impassable, impermeable, imperviable, impervious, inaccessible, inapprehensible, incomprehensible, indefinable, inexplicable, inexpressive, inexpugnable, insoluble, insurmountable, mysterious, obscure, obtuse, opaque, past comprehension, pathless, recondite, shut, snug, solid, stolid, tight, unfathomable, unopened, unreachable, untrodden

IMPERATIVE, ***adjective*** compulsory, critical, crucial, demanding, essential, exigent, *impero,* indispensable, mandatory, necessary, needful, obligatory, pressing, required, requiring immediate attention, requisite, unavoidable, urgent
ASSOCIATED CONCEPTS: imperative power, imperative statute, imperative trust

IMPERCEPTIBLE, ***adjective*** blurred, concealed, dim, enshrouded, faint, hazy, hidden, ill-defined, impalpable, inappreciable, inaudible, indiscernible, indistinct, inscrutable, intangible, invisible, minuscule, minute, nebulous, obscure, scant, screened, shadowy, unapparent, unappreciable, undiscernible, unnoticeable, unseeable, unseen, vague, veiled, very slight, very subtle

IMPERFECT, ***adjective*** abortive, average, bad, below par, blemished, broken, corrupt, crippled, crude, damaged, decrepit, defective, deficient, deteriorated, disfigured, failing, fair, faulty, feeble, flawed, fragmentary, frail, garbled, harmed, hurt, impaired, *imperfectus,* inadequate, incomplete, indifferent, inelegant, inexact, inferior, infirm, injured, insufficient, lacking, lame, limited, marred, mediocre, middling, moderate, mutilated, ordinary, out of order, partial, passable, peccable, poor, raw, rickety, rough, ruined, scanty, short, tainted, tolerable, uncompleted, uncultured, undeveloped, unfinished, unpolished, unsatisfactory, unsound, unsuitable, wanting, warped, weak
ASSOCIATED CONCEPTS: imperfect description, imperfect grant, imperfect performance, imperfect title

IMPERFECTION, ***noun*** blemish, defect, defectiveness, deficiency, deformity, disfigurement, drawback, error, failing, fault, faultiness, flaw, foible, frailty, imperfectness, inadequacy, incompleteness, infirmity, liability, limitation, malformation, misdeed, offense, omission, shortcoming, taint, transgression, vice, weak point, weakness
ASSOCIATED CONCEPTS: allergic user

IMPERIAL, ***adjective*** arbitrary, august, authoritarian, authoritative, chief, commanding, despotic, dictatorial, dogmatic, dominant, domineering, grand, imperatorial, imperious, imposing, kinglike, kingly, lofty, lordly, magisterial, magnificent, majestic, mandating, masterful, monarchal, paramount, peremptory, predominant, preeminent, princely, regal, royal, ruling, sovereign, splendid, stately, supreme, tyrannical
ASSOCIATED CONCEPTS: imperial law

IMPERIL, ***verb*** compromise, endanger, expose, expose to danger, hazard, jeopardize, put in danger, put in peril, risk, stake

IMPERIOUS, ***adjective*** arbitrary, assertive, authoritative, autocratic, bumptious, commanding, compelling, critical, despotic, dictatorial, dogmatic, domineering, haughty, heavy-handed, high-and-mighty, high-handed, imperative, overbearing, peremptory, powerful, requisite, tyrannical
ASSOCIATED CONCEPTS: imperious law

IMPERMEABLE, ***adjective*** airtight, close, compact, dense, hermetic, impassable, impenetrable, impervious, imporous, incompressible, nonporous, shut, solid, unpenetrable, unpierced

IMPERMISSIBLE, ***adjective*** actionable, against the law, banned, black-market, contraband, contrary to law, criminal, disallowed, disapproved, felonious, forbidden, illegal, illegitimate, illicit, iniquitous, irregular, nonlegal, objectionable, out of bounds, outlawed, outside the law, prohibited, proscribed, punishable, unallowable, unauthorized, unchartered, unconstitutional, under ban, unentitled, unlawful, unlicensed, unsanctioned, vetoed, wicked, wrong, wrongful
ASSOCIATED CONCEPTS: impermissible grounds for divorce

IMPERSONAL *(Dispassionate),* ***adjective*** candid, cold, cold-blooded, detached, disinterested, dispassionate, frigid, general, impartial, indefinite, insensible, neuter, nonsubjective, objective, passionless, undetermined, unfeeling, unforthcoming, unjaundiced, unselfish, unspecified, without warmth

IMPERSONAL *(Unbiased),* ***adjective*** uninfluenced, unprejudiced, unswayed

IMPERSONATE, ***verb*** act a part, act out, act the part of, ape, assume a character, copy, double for, dress as, enact, *hominem imitari,* imitate, masquerade as, mime, mimic, mirror, parrot, *partes hominis agere,* pass for, personate, personify, portray, pose as, pretend to be, represent, represent oneself to be, take the part of

ASSOCIATED CONCEPTS: fraud, impersonation of a governmental officer

IMPERTINENT *(Insolent),* ***adjective*** abusive, arrogant, assuming, audacious, bellicose, bold, brash, brazen, cavalier, churlish, coarse, contempt, contemptuous, contumacious, contumelious, defiant, derisive, discourteous, disdainful, disrespectful, flippant, forward, fresh, haughty, hostile, ill-mannered, impolite, improper, impudent, *insolens,* insubordinate, insulting, intrusive, irreverent, malapert, offensive, pert, presumptuous, procacious, provocative, rebellious, rough, rude, saucy, scoffing, shameless, surly, unabashed, uncivil, uncouth, ungracious, unmannerly, unpolished, unrefined, vulgar

IMPERTINENT *(Irrelevant),* ***adjective*** alien, beside the mark, beside the point, beside the question, disconnected, extraneous, gratuitous, immaterial, inadmissible, inapplicable, inapposite, inappropriate, inapropos, incidental, incongruous, inconsequent, independent, irrelative, malapropos, off the subject, out of place, *quod nihil ad rem est,* remote, separate, unallied, unapt, unconnected, unrelated, without connection

ASSOCIATED CONCEPTS: impertinent questioning

IMPERTURBABLE, ***adjective*** callous, calm, cold-blooded, collected, composed, cool, dispassionate, even-tempered, impassive, impervious, inexcitable, inexpressive, inured, levelheaded, nonchalant, patient, peaceable, philosophical, placid, resolute, sedate, serene, stable, steady, stoic, tranquil, unflappable, unmoved, unruffled, unworried, unworrying

IMPERVIOUS, ***adjective*** *adrogans,* airtight, blind to, blocked, buffered, callous, closed, deaf to, dense, detached, hard, hard to convince, hardened, hermetic, impassable, impassive, *impeditus, impenetrabilis,* impenetrable, imperforate, *imperiosus,* impermeable, impersuadable, impersuasible, imperturbable, imperviable, *impervious,* imporous, inaccessible, incapable of being affected, incapable of being impaired, incapable of being influenced, incapable of being injured, indifferent, indurate, indurated, insensate, insensitive, inured, invious, locked, not permitting passage, not permitting penetration, obstinate, obstructed, obtuse, opaque, pachydermatous, pathless, protected, safe, sealed, seared, shielded, shut, steeled, stubborn, thick, thick-skinned, tight, unaffected, unamenable, uninfluenceable, uninfluenced, unmovable, unmoved, unnavigable, unopened, unpassable, unperforated, unpierceable, unreachable, unreceptive, unresponsive, unswayable, unventilated, unyielding, waterproof, watertight

IMPETUOUS, ***adjective*** abrupt, capricious, careless, changeable, dashing, disordered, emotional, excitable, fervid, fickle, foolhardy, hasty, headstrong, heedless, hot-blooded, hotheaded, ill-conceived, impatient, impulsive, incautious, intense, mercurial, overhasty, overzealous, precipitate, quick, rash, reckless, slapdash, spirited, spontaneous, spur-of-the-moment, stormy, stubborn, sudden, swift, thoughtless, uncontrollable, uncontrolled, unexpected, ungovernable, ungoverned, unstable, vehement, volatile, zealous

ASSOCIATED CONCEPTS: impetuous employee

IMPETUS, ***noun*** actuation, boost, call, drive, encouragement, energy, force, goad, impellent, impelling force, impulse, impulsion, incentive, influence, instigation, jog, jolt, kick, momentum, motive, moving force, pressure, propellant, propulsion, propulsive force, purpose, push, reason, shove, spur, start, stimulus, thrust, urge, *vis*

IMPIETY, ***noun*** apostasy, backsliding, desecration, disregard, disrespect, iniquity, irreligion, irreverence, malediction, noncomformity, offense, profaneness, profanity, recusancy, reprobation, sacrilege, sacrilegiousness, sinfulness, transgression, undutifulness, unrighteousness, unspirituality, violation, wickedness

IMPINGE, ***verb*** advance upon, aggress, attack, bang, barge in, break bounds, break in on, bump, butt against, collide, come into collision, contact, dash against, encroach, entrench on, fall against, foray, force oneself in, hit, *impingi,* impose, *incidere,* infringe, interlope, intrude, invade, knock, knock against, make impact, make inroads, obtrude, overrun, overstep, overstep boundaries, pommel, raid, run into, strike, tap, thrust, touch, transgress established bounds, trench upon, trespass, violate

IMPIOUS, ***adjective*** amoral, blasphemous, desecrative, diabolic, heretical, immoral, iniquitous, irreligious, irreverent, nefarious, offensive, peccant, perverted, profane, recusant, reprobate, sacrilegious, satanic, sinful, sinister, undevout, undutiful, unethical, ungodly, unrighteous

FOREIGN PHRASES: ***Impius et crudelis judicandus est qui libertati non favet.*** He is judged to be impious and cruel who does not favor liberty.

IMPLACABLE, ***adjective*** adamant, immovable, *implacabilis, inexorabilis,* inexorable, inexpiable, inflexible, intransigent, irreconcilable, obdurate, obstinate, pitiless, relentless, unappeasable, unbending, uncompromising, unforgiving, unpacifiable, unpropitiating, unrelenting, unyielding, vindictive

IMPLANTED, ***adjective*** deep-rooted, deep-seated, embedded, engraved, entrenched, established, etched, impressed, inculcated, indoctrinated, ingrained, injected, well-established, well-founded

IMPLAUSIBLE, ***adjective*** beyond belief, contrary to experience, doubtable, doubtful, dubitable, hard to believe, hardly possible, improbable, inconceivable, incredible, open to doubt, open to suspicion, questionable, suspicious, unbelievable, unconvincing, unheard of, unimaginable, unlikely, unsubstantiated, untenable, unthinkable

IMPLEAD, ***verb*** add as a third party, bring in as a third party, commence proceedings against a third party, *in ius vocare,* institute an action against a third party, join as a third party, make one a third party, plead a cause against a third party, sue a third party

ASSOCIATED CONCEPTS: counterclaim, crossclaim, third-party defendant, third-party plaintiff, third-party practice

IMPLEMENT, ***verb*** accomplish, achieve, actualize, bring about, bring off, bring to pass, carry into effect, carry into execution, carry out, carry through, complete, consummate, discharge, do, effect, effectuate, enact, enforce, execute, fulfill, give force to, give validity to, make a reality, make active, make valid, perform, provide the means, put in force, put in practice, put into effect, realize, see through, set in motion, succeed, take action, work out

ASSOCIATED CONCEPTS: implement the agreement of the parties, implement the order of the court

IMPLEMENTATION, *noun* accomplishment, achievement, act, action, attainment, commission, consummation, course, discharge, effectuation, enforcement, execution, *fait accompli,* finality, fruition, fulfillment, instrumentation, means, mechanism, method, performance, procedures, production, realization, result, rules, upshot

IMPLICATE, *verb* accuse, *admiscere,* allege to be guilty, associate, brand, bring into connection with, charge, connect, criminate, delate, denounce, draw in, embroil, engage, enmesh, entangle, expose, hold responsible, *implicare,* impute, include, incriminate, inculpate, infer, inform against, *inligare,* interlace, intertwine, involve, link, lodge a complaint, make a party to, point to, suggest, tangle
ASSOCIATED CONCEPTS: implicate a codefendant, implicate an accomplice, implicate in a crime

IMPLICATION *(Incriminating involvement),* ***noun*** complicity, connection, crimination, culpability, enmeshment, entanglement, inculpation, link
ASSOCIATED CONCEPTS: implication of a codefendant

IMPLICATION *(Inference),* ***noun*** allusion, broad meaning, coloring, connotation, hidden meaning, hint, import, indication, innuendo, insinuation, intimation, overtone, signification, suggested meaning, suggestion, tacit inference
ASSOCIATED CONCEPTS: easement by implication, gift by implication, grant by implication, necessary implication
FOREIGN PHRASES: ***Omissio eorum quae tacite insunt nihil operatur.*** The omission of those things which are tacitly expressed is unimportant.

IMPLICATIVE, *adjective* allusive, assumed, circumstantial, hinting, implicational, implicatory, incriminatory, inculpatory, indicative, inferential, inferring, leading, presumed, provocative, provoking, referential, suggestive, supposed

IMPLICIT, *adjective* absolute, allusive, basic, implied, implied rather than expressly stated, inherent, innate, intrinsic, not declared openly, not expressed, not plainly apparent, suggested, suggestive, tacit, *tacitus,* understood, unexpressed, unpronounced, unsaid, unspoken, unvoiced
ASSOCIATED CONCEPTS: implicit in the facts of a case, implicit powers

IMPLIED, *adjective* alluded to, allusive, assumed, connoted, expressed indirectly, implicit, indicated, inferential, inferred, insinuated, meant, signified, suggested, tacit, undeclared, understood, unspoken
ASSOCIATED CONCEPTS: implied acceptance, implied acquiescence, implied admission, implied agency, implied agreement, implied authority, implied contract, implied covenant, implied dedication, implied malice, implied notice, implied powers, implied promise, implied ratification, implied trust, implied warranty

IMPLODE, *verb* bankrupt, blow up, cave, cave in, close, collapse, deflate, decommissioned, disintegrate, dismantled, end, ended abruptly, fold, fold up, terminate

IMPLORE, *verb* appeal to, beseech, besiege, call, call upon, entreat, evoke, exhort, importune, invoke, obsecrate, obtest, petition, plead, pray, press, pressure, request, solicit, solicitate, supplicate, urge

IMPLY, *verb* advert, allude to, carry a suggestion, connote, denote, drop a hint, give a hint, give indirect information, hint at, include by implication, *indicare,* indicate, indirectly state, infer, insinuate, intimate, involve, leave an inference, make an allusion to, point to, show indirectly, *significare,* state in nonexplicit terms, suggest, whisper
ASSOCIATED CONCEPTS: implied acceptance, implied agency, implied authority, implied consent, implied contract, implied dedication, implied easement, implied in law, implied knowledge, implied license, implied malice, implied notice, implied permission, implied power, implied promise, implied ratification, implied trust, implied warranty
FOREIGN PHRASES: ***In omnibus contractibus, sive nominatis sive innominatis, permutatio continetur.*** In all contracts, whether nominate or innominate, there is implied an exchange. ***Expressio eorum quae tacite insunt nihil operatur.*** The expression of those things which are tacitly implied has no effect.

IMPOLITIC, *adjective* careless, foolish, harebrained, hasty, headlong, heedless, ill-advised, ill-considered, ill-judged, *imprudens,* imprudent, inadvisable, incautious, inconsiderate, *inconsultus,* indiscreet, inexpedient, injudicious, rash, reckless, senseless, stupid, temerarious, thoughtless, undiplomatic, unreasonable, unsensible, unsound, untactful, unthinking, unwary, unwise

IMPONDERABLE, *adjective* immaterial, immateriate, impalpable, imponderous, impossible to calculate, impossible to measure, impossible to weigh, incalculable, incapable of being evaluated, incomputable, inestimable, intangible, subtile, unsubstantial, unweighable, vague

IMPORT, *noun* connotation, consequence, drift, essence, gist, gravity, idea, importance, matter, meaning, meaningfulness, moment, pith, point, purport, sense, seriousness, significance, *significatio,* signification, substance, sum, tenor, *vis,* weight, weightiness

IMPORTANCE, *noun* concern, concernment, consequence, distinction, eminence, emphasis, essentiality, fame, grandeur, gravity, greatness, import, influence, irreplaceability, magnitude, mark, materiality, materialness, memorability, memorableness, merit, moment, momentousness, *momentum,* notability, note, noteworthiness, outstanding quality, paramountcy, *pondus,* precedence, prestige, primacy, priority, prominence, relevance, repute, salience, seriousness, significance, solemnity, substance, substantiality, superiority, supremacy, urgency, usefulness, value, *vis,* weight, weightiness

IMPORTANT *(Significant),* ***adjective*** big, capital, chief, commanding, consequential, considerable, crucial, dignified, distinguished, esteemed, famous, far-reaching, first, foremost, formidable, grand, grave, *gravis,* high-level, illustrious, imposing, impressive, influential, leading, *magnus,* main, majestic, major, marked, material, mattering much, memorable, mighty, momentous, notable, noteworthy, of great consequence, of great magnitude, of great weight, of high standing, of high station, of importance, outstanding, overshadowing, paramount, portentous, powerful, preeminent, primary, prime, principal, prominent, relevant, remarkable, salient, serious, signal, solemn, substantial, superior, supreme, valuable, weighty, well-known

IMPORTANT *(Urgent),* ***adjective*** acute, called for, clamant, clamorous, cogent, compelling, critical, crucial, crying, demanding attention, driving, essential, exigent, high-priority, impelling, imperative, importunate, in demand, indispensable, inescapable, instant, necessary, necessitous, needed, prerequisite, pressing, requested, required, requisite, unavoidable, vital, wanted

IMPORTUNE, *verb* adjure, appeal, apply to, ask urgently, badger, beg, beseech, beset, besiege, bother, cajole, call upon, clamor for, coax, cry to, demand, dun, entreat persistently, *fatigare,* harass, hound, impetrate, implore, insist, inveigle, make bold to ask, nag, obsecrate, obtest, pester, petition, plague, plead, ply, pray, press, press by entreaty, push, *rem hominem flagitare,* request, requisition, solicit, solicit earnestly, solicit insistently, sue, supplicate, urge

IMPOSE *(Enforce),* ***verb*** bid, bind, burden, charge, coerce, command, compel, conscript, constrain, decree, demand, dictate, direct, drive, enact, encumber, enjoin, exact, execute, extort, force upon, impel, *imponere, iniungere,* insist upon, lay upon, leave no option, make, make obligatory, necessitate, oblige, obtain by force, ordain, order, prescribe, press, put in force, require, require compliance, tax
ASSOCIATED CONCEPTS: impose by law

IMPOSE *(Intrude),* ***verb*** encroach, enter unlawfully, entrench, force an entrance, force oneself in, impose, infringe, insinuate, intercede, interfere, interlope, interpose, intervene, invade, obtrude, overreach, overstep, poach, thrust oneself in, transgress, trespass, violate

IMPOSE *(Subject),* ***verb*** bring under rule, coerce, compel, constrain, control, domineer, effect, enslave, force, make submissive, master, oblige, overcome, require, subdue, subject to authority, subject to control, subject to dependence, subject to influence, subjugate, subordinate

IMPOSE A BAN, *verb* bridle, censor, check, condemn, curb, deny, deter, dictate, disallow, discourage, dissuade, edict, embargo, enjoin, halt, interdict, limit, mandate, negate, outlaw, preclude, prevent, prohibit, proscribe, protest, refuse, reject, repress, restrain, silence, stop, suppress, veto
ASSOCIATED CONCEPTS: injunction, temporary restraining order, writ of prohibition

IMPOSE A PENALTY, *verb* bring to account, discipline, exact a penalty, execute a sentence, fine, inflict punishment, levy, penalize, punish, rebuke, reprimand, subject to penalty, subject to punishment
ASSOCIATED CONCEPTS: judgment, sentence

IMPOSITION *(Excessive burden),* ***noun*** encroachment, encumbrance, excessive demand, extraordinarily burdensome requirement, hindrance, impediment, infliction, infringement, interference, onus, unjust burden, unjust requirement

IMPOSITION *(Tax),* ***noun*** charge, duty, excise, levy, penalty, tariff, toll

IMPOSSIBILITY, *noun* difficulty, failure, futility, hopelessness, impossibleness, impracticability, impracticality, inaccessibility, inconceivability, infeasibility, inoperability, insuperability, insuperableness, insurmountability, lack of possibility, lack of potentiality, unachievability, unattainability, unattainable, unavailability, unfeasibility, unobtainability, unobtainableness, unperformability, unpracticability, unthinkability, unworkability

ASSOCIATED CONCEPTS: frustration of purpose, impossibility of performance, legal impossibility, rescission, supervening impossibility
FOREIGN PHRASES: ***Lex non intendit aliquid impossibile.*** The law does not intend anything impossible. ***Lex non cogit ad impossibilia.*** The law does not require the performance of the impossible. ***Impotentia excusat legem.*** The impossibility of performing a legal duty excuses from the performance. ***A l'impossible nul n'est tenu.*** No one is bound to do what is impossible. ***Argumentum ab impossibili valet in lege.*** The argument from impossibility is of great force in law. ***Impossibilium nulla obligatio est.*** One cannot be obliged to perform impossible tasks.

IMPOSSIBLE, *adjective* absurd, contrary to reason, hopeless, impassable, impracticable, improbable, inaccessible, incapable of being done, incapable of existing, incapable of happening, inconceivable, incredible, infeasible, innavigable, insuperable, insurmountable, *nullo modo fieri potest,* out of the question, paradoxical, preposterous, *quod fieri non potest,* self-contradictory, unachievable, unattainable, unbelievable, unfeasible, unimaginable, unlikely, unmanageable, unobtainable, unreasonable, unthinkable, unworkable, unyielding, visionary

IMPOSTURE, *noun* cheat, chicane, counterfeit, craft, cunning, deceit, deception, dodge, duplicity, fake, *fallacia,* false conduct, forgery, fraud, fraudulence, *fraus,* guile, hoax, hollow pretense, imitation, knavery, pretense, ruse, sham, sleight, subterfuge, swindle, swindling, trap, trick, trickery, wile

IMPOTENCE, *noun* debilitation, debility, defenselessness, failure, feebleness, forcelessness, helplessness, *imbecillitas,* impotency, impuissance, inability, inadequacy, incapability, incapacitation, incapacity, incompetence, incompetency, ineffectiveness, ineffectuality, ineffectualness, inefficaciousness, inefficacy, inefficiency, ineptitude, *infirmitas,* insufficiency, lack of power, lack of strength, powerlessness, strengthlessness, unfitness, weakness

IMPOTENT, *adjective* barren, disabled, inadequate, ineffective, inept, infertile, innocuous, powerless, spent, sterile, unproductive, unprofitable, unsuccessful, useless, vain, valueless, weak, without power, worthless

IMPOUND, *verb* appropriate, attach, confiscate, deprive of, distrain, hold in legal custody, remove, retain in custody, seize, sequester, sequestrate, take, take into custody, take into legal custody, take over, take possession of
ASSOCIATED CONCEPTS: impounding a jury, impounding property

IMPRACTICABLE, *adjective* beyond control, difficult, hard to deal with, hopeless, impassable, impossible, impractical, inapplicable, incapable of being accomplished, inconceivable, inoperable, insuperable, insurmountable, out of the question, *quod fiere non potest,* thorny, too hard, unachievable, undoable, unemployable, unfeasible, unfunctional, unhandy, unmanageable, unperformable, unrealizable, unreasonable, unserviceable, unsuitable for practical use, unusable, unviable, unwieldy, unworkable, useless

IMPRECATION, *noun* abuse, anathema, aspersion, bad wishes, blasphemy, commination, curse, damnation, denunciation, execration, expletive, *exsecratio,* foul language, fulmination, ill wishes, invocation of evil, malediction, malison, objuration, obsecration, *preces,* profanity, swearing, vilification, vindictive oath, vituperation

IMPRECISE, ***adjective*** approximate, approximated, ballpark, debatable, disputable, dubious, erroneous, estimated, eyeballed, false, faulty, flawed, inaccurate, inconclusive, incorrect, indefinite, indeterminate, inexact, loose, mistaken, off, questionable, rough idea, specious, uncertain, unconfirmed, undefined, unsubstantiated, unsupported, vague, wrong
ASSOCIATED CONCEPTS: dismissal of a complaint for failure to state a cause of action

IMPREGNABLE, ***adjective*** armored, bulletproof, defended, guarded, immune, implacable, indomitable, insuperable, insurmountable, inviolable, invulnerable, protected, safe, safeguarded, secure, shielded, unassailable, unbeatable, unbeaten, unbowed, unbreachable, unconquerable, unconquered, undefeated, unstoppable, unsubdued, untouchable

IMPRESS *(Affect deeply),* ***verb*** absorb, amaze, arouse, astound, awe, electrify, galvanize, have a strong effect, hit, influence, inspire, intrigue, make an impact upon, make an impression on, move, move strongly, *movere,* penetrate, pierce, reach, rouse, smite, stir, strike, strike hard, strike home, stun, touch

IMPRESS *(Procure by force),* ***verb*** acquire, appropriate, arrogate, attach, deprive, disentitle, disseise, expropriate, garnish, impound, impropriate, levy, seize, sequester, sequestrate, take, take possession of

IMPRESSION, ***noun*** *animi motus,* apprehension, belief, concept, conception, consciousness, consideration, effect, feeling, general notion, guiding conception, image, image in the mind, impact, imprint, indirect influence, influence, inward perception, mark, mental attitude, mental image, mental view, notion, *opinio,* opinion, organizing conception, outward perception, perception, print, *putare,* reaction, reflection, remembrance, response, sensation, sense, sense perception, sensory perception, subconscious perception, trace, visible effect
ASSOCIATED CONCEPTS: case of first impression, impression on the minds of the jurors

IMPRESSIVE, ***adjective*** absorbing, assuring, awe-inspiring, commanding, considerable, electrifying, eloquent, enthusiastic, exciting, fervent, formidable, grand, important, imposing, influential, magnificent, majestic, major, memorable, momentous, moving, notable, noteworthy, outstanding, overpowering, paramount, persuasive, pervading, potent, prodigious, profound, prominent, proud, rapturous, remarkable, sapid, satisfactory, satisfying, sensational, solemn, spectacular, stellar, striking, strong, telling, weighty

IMPRIMATUR, ***noun*** accession, agreement, approbation, approval, assent, authority, authorization, backing, benediction, blessing, cache, consent, countenance, endorsement, goodwill, license, OK, ratification, sanction, support, vote

IMPRISON, ***verb*** bring into custody, cast into prison, circumscribe, commit to an institution, commit to prison, confine, constrain, deprive of freedom of movement, deprive of liberty, detain, detain in custody, enclose, entomb, hold captive, hold in captivity, hold in restraint, immure, *in carcerem, in custodiam,* incarcerate, *includere,* intern, jail, keep as captive, keep behind bars, keep in captivity, keep in custody, keep in detention, keep under arrest, lock in, lock up, mew, place in confinement, put behind bars, put in a cell, put in irons, put into a cage, put under lock and key, put under restraint, refuse bail, restrain, send to jail, send to prison
ASSOCIATED CONCEPTS: false imprisonment, habeas corpus, imprison at hard work, imprison for a term of years, parole, term of imprisonment

IMPRISONMENT, ***noun*** commitment to an institution, commitment to prison, confinement, custody, detainment, detainment in custody, held in captivity, held in restraint, in captivity, in custody, in jail, incarceration, internment, keep behind bars, kept as captive, kept in captivity, kept in custody, kept in detention, kept under arrest, locked up, put behind bars, put in a cell, put under restraint, sent to jail, sent to prison
ASSOCIATED CONCEPTS: false imprisonment, habeas corpus

IMPROBABILITY, ***noun*** bare possibility, doubt, doubtfulness, implausibility, impossibility, inexpectation, infrequency, little chance, long odds, *non verisimilis,* nonexpectation, poor chance, poor prospect, questionability, rare occurrence, rarity, small chance, small hope, uncertainty, unlikelihood, unlikeliness
ASSOCIATED CONCEPTS: inherently improbable evidence, inherently improbable testimony

IMPROBABLE, ***adjective*** a distant chance, barely a possibility, defying logic, doubtful, dubious, hardly possible, implausible, little chance, little hope, little likelihood, long odds, not likely, not likely to occur, not probable, poor chance, poor prospect, questionable, rare, remote possibility, uncertainty, unexpected, unlikelihood, unlikely

IMPROBITY, ***noun*** artfulness, breach of trust, corruption, craftiness, crookedness, deceit, deceitfulness, deviousness, dishonesty, disingenuity, disingenuousness, duplicity, falsehood, falseness, falsity, fraud, fraudulence, fraudulency, furtiveness, graft, guile, indirection, insidiousness, insincerity, inveracity, jobbery, knavery, lack of conscience, lack of integrity, lack of principle, lying, mendaciousness, mendacity, obliquity, rascality, roguery, shadiness, surreptitiousness, treacherousness, trickiness, truthlessness, undependability, underhandedness, unreliability, unscrupulousness, unstraightforwardness, untrustworthiness, untruthfulness

IMPROMPTU, ***adjective*** ad-lib, extemporaneous, extemporary, extemporized, immediate, improvised, makeshift, not arranged, not planned, offhand, off-the-cuff, spontaneous, spur-of the-moment, unprompted, unrehearsed

IMPROPER, ***adjective*** amiss, awkward, contrary to decency, contrary to good taste, discordant, discrepant, erroneous, false, forbidden, gross, ill-adapted, ill-founded, ill-timed, illicit, illogical, immodest, immoral, inaccurate, inadmissible, inapplicable, inapposite, inappropriate, inapt, incongruous, incorrect, indecent, *indecorous,* indecorus, indelicate, *indignus,* inept, inexact, infelicitous, inharmonious, inopportune, irrelevant, mistaken, naughty, not pertinent, not right, not suitable, objectionable, off-color, off the mark, out of place, prohibited, risque, unadapted, unallowable, unauthorized, unbecoming, unbefitting, uncharacteristic, undesirable, undue, unfit, unfitting, unmeet, unreasonable, unrefined, unseasonable, unseemly, unsound, unsuitable, unsuited, untimely, unwarrantable, wide of the mark, wrong, wrongful

ASSOCIATED CONCEPTS: improper act, improper conduct, improper discharge, improper influence, improper joinder of actions, improper motive, improper performance, improper practice, improper use

IMPROPER VENUE, ***noun*** improper court location, improper location, incorrect court location, incorrect location, not suitable location, unauthorized location, unsuitable location, wrong judicial location
ASSOCIATED CONCEPTS: local venue, waiver of venue

IMPROPRIATE, ***verb*** accroach, adopt, annex, apply to one's own uses, appropriate, arrogate, assume, assume ownership, avail oneself of, bear away, carry away, claim, claim unduly, confer ownership on oneself, convert, disseise, embezzle, employ, help oneself to, lay hold of, make one's own, make use of, misappropriate, peculate, pirate, possess, purloin, rob, seize, steal, take as one's own, take for oneself, take over, take possession of, take to oneself, thieve, use, usurp

IMPROPRIETY, ***noun*** bad taste, improper action, improper behavior, imprudence, inappropriate behavior, inappropriateness, incongruousness, incorrectness, indecency, indecorousness, indecorum, indelicacy, indiscretion, inelegance, inexpedience, inexpediency, inopportuneness, lack of good taste, misbehavior, peccadillo, *quod indecorum est,* tactlessness, unaptness, unfitness, unfittingness, unseemliness, unsuitability, unsuitable action, unsuitableness, untimeliness, want of caution, want of circumspection
ASSOCIATED CONCEPTS: crime, violation

IMPROVE, ***verb*** advance, ameliorate, amend, appreciate, beautify, correct, cultivate, cure, develop, doctor, edify, edit, elaborate, elevate, embellish, emend, enhance, ennoble, enrich, fix, flourish, gain, gain strength, heighten, help, increase, modernize, modify, mollify, nurture, perfect, progress, promote, prosper, rectify, recuperate, redeem, redress, refine, reform, rehabilitate, relieve, remedy, repair, restore, retouch, revise, supplement

IMPROVEMENT, ***noun*** amelioration, betterment, change for the better, melioration, recovery, rehabilitation
ASSOCIATED CONCEPTS: improvement bond, improvement district

IMPROVIDENT, ***adjective*** brash, careless, dissipated, extravagant, happy-go-lucky, hasty, headlong, heedless, *improvidus, imprudens,* imprudent, impulsive, incautious, incautus, indiscreet, injudicious, lacking foresight, lax, losel, neglectful, negligent, prodigal, profligate, rash, reckless, remiss, shiftless, spendthrift, squandering, temerarious, thoughtless, thriftless, uneconomical, unfrugal, unguarded, unpreparing, unproviding, unthrifty, unwary, wasteful, without foresight

IMPROVISE, ***verb*** adept, ad-lib, compose, concoct, create, devise, extemporize, fabricate, invent, invent offhand, make up, originate, play by ear, ride with the waves, utilize, without preparation

IMPRUDENCE, ***noun*** blunder, carelessness, heedlessness, impetuosity, impolicy, improvidence, inadvisability, incautiousness, inconsiderateness, inconsideration, indiscreetness, indiscretion, injudiciousness, irrationality, irresponsibility, neglect, negligence, recklessness, senselessness, temerity, thoughtlessness, unreasonableness, unwiseness, witlessness
ASSOCIATED CONCEPTS: imprudent act, imprudent advice

IMPRUDENT, ***adjective*** adventurous, brash, careless, foolhardy, foolish, hasty, hazardous, heedless, hot-headed, ill-advised, ill-considered, ill-judged, impolitic, improvident, impulsive, inadvisable, incautious, inconsiderate, *inconsultus,* indiscreet, inexpedient, injudicious, inopportune, lacking caution, lacking judgment, lacking prudence, neglectful, overhasty, precipitate, rash, reckless, shortsighted, temerarious, *temerarius,* thoughtless, unadvised, uncalculated, uncircumspect, undesirable, unguarded, unwary, unwise, venturesome, venturous, wanting discretion, wanton
ASSOCIATED CONCEPTS: negligence

IMPUDENCE, ***noun*** arrogance, audacity, boldness, brashness, brazenness, contempt, defiance, disdain, disregard, disrespect, disrespectfulness, effrontery, flippancy, forwardness, gall, impertinence, insolence, nerve, overbearance, pertness, rudeness, temerity

IMPUGN, ***verb*** assail, assail by argument, attack, attack by words, be skeptical, call in question, cast doubt, cast reflection upon, challenge as false, confute, contest, contradict, controvert, criticize, denounce, disbelieve, discredit, disprove, dispute, doubt the truth of, find fault with, impeach, *improbare, impugnare,* inveigh against, involve in suspicion, negate, oppose, oppose as false, *oppugnare,* overcome by argument, query, question, raise a hue and cry against, raise a question as to, raise one's voice against, raise questions, rebut, refuse credence, refute, render suspect, take issue with, throw doubt upon, undermine one's belief
ASSOCIATED CONCEPTS: defamation, impugn the integrity of a witness

IMPUGN A WITNESS, ***verb*** assail, attack, call in question, cast doubt, cast doubt on testimony of a witness, cast doubt on the integrity of a witness, challenge, confute, contest, contradict, controvert, criticize, denounce, discredit, disprove, dispute, find fault with, impeach, involve in suspicion, oppose as false, question a witness, raise questions regarding the integrity of a witness, rebut, refute, reveal, undermine confidence in a witness, undermine the credibility of
ASSOCIATED CONCEPTS: discrepancies, impeachment, impugn a witness's competency or credibility, rules of evidence

IMPUGNATION, ***noun*** adverse comment, adverse criticism, animadversion, antagonism, attack, censure, challenge, condemnation, conflict, confrontation, contradiction, contrariety, contrariness, contravention, counteraction, counterwork, criticism, decrial, defiance, difference, disagreement, disapprobation, disapproval, discord, disfavor, disputation, dispute, dissent, faultfinding, gravamen, grievance, hostile attack, hostility, impugnment, lack of harmony, nonacceptance, nonagreement, noncompliance, nonconsent, noncooperation, obstruction, opposition, oppugnancy, protest, protestation, rejection, reprehension, reprobation, repudiation, resistance, rivalry, traversal, want of harmony

IMPUISSANCE, ***noun*** caducity, debility, decrepitude, disability, disablement, exhaustion, failure, feebleness, frailty, helplessness, impotence, inability, inaptitude, incapability, incapacity, incompetence, inefficacy, inefficiency, ineptitude, infirmity, invalidity, lack of force, lack of might, lack of power, lack of strength, lack of vigor, powerlessness, prostration, strengthlessness, weakness

IMPULSE, *noun* actuation, drive, encouragement, impelling force, *impetus, impulsio,* impulsion, *impulsus,* incentive, motivation, motive, pressure, push, spontaneity, spontaneous inclination, stimulant, sudden desire, sudden force, thrust
ASSOCIATED CONCEPTS: heat of passion, impulsive acts, irresistible impulse, uncontrollable impulse

IMPULSIVE *(Impelling),* ***adjective*** activating, actuating, animating, compelling, driving, dynamic, dynamical, energizing, impellent, kinetic, moving, prompting, propulsive, pushing, stimulating, urging

IMPULSIVE *(Rash),* ***adjective*** abrupt, adventurous, bold, breakneck, careless, daring, emotional, extemporaneous, extemporary, foolhardy, hasty, heedless, hotheaded, hurried, ill-considered, impetuous, impromptu, improvised, imprudent, incautious, indeliberate, injudicious, offhand, passionate, precipitant, precipitate, precipitous, quick, rapid, reckless, risk-taking, risky, snap, spontaneous, sudden, swift, temerarious, thoughtless, unadvised, unanticipated, uncalculating, unchary, uncircumspect, unconsidered, uncontrolled, unexpected, unmindful, unpremeditated, unprepared, unprompted, unthinking, venturesome, venturous, without prudence, without thought

IMPUNITY, *noun* absolution, acquittal, amnesty, condonation, dispensation, escape, exemption, exemption from judgment, exemption from penalty, exemption from punishment, freedom, freedom from judgment, freedom from penalty, freedom from punishment, immunity, *impunitas,* liberation, license, nonliability, nonprosecution, pardon, prerogative, privilege, protection, reprieve

IMPURE *(Adulterated),* ***adjective*** alloyed, contaminated, degraded, diluted, hybrid, mixed, perverted, polluted, sullied, tainted, tampered with, unclean, unrefined, watered down

IMPURE *(Debased),* ***verb*** amoral, base, contaminated, defiled, degenerate, degraded, depraved, immodest, immoral, improper, indecent, lascivious, licentious, passionate, poisoned, profligate, promiscuous, shameless, sinful, sullied, unchaste

IMPUTATION, *noun* abuse, accusal, accusation, adverse criticism, allegation, animadversion, arrogation, ascription, aspersion, attaint, attribution, blame, brand, calumny, censure, challenge, charge, condemnation, criticism, defamation, denouncement, detraction, disapprobation, discredit, disgrace, dishonor, disparagement, disrepute, exprobration, faultfinding, ignominy, ignomy, incrimination, inculpation, insinuation, obloquy, onus, opprobrium, reference, reproach, slur, stain, stigma, stigmatization, stricture, traducement, vilification
ASSOCIATED CONCEPTS: imputation of a crime, imputation of negligence, imputation of payment

IMPUTE, *verb* *adsignare,* apply, ascribe, *ascribere,* assign, attach, *attribuere,* attribute, attribute vicariously, blame, charge to, charge upon, credit, fix the burden of, fix the responsibility for, fix upon, place the blame on, place the responsibility for, put
ASSOCIATED CONCEPTS: imputed consent, imputed guilt, imputed intent, imputed knowledge, imputed liability, imputed negligence, imputed notice

IN ACCORDANCE WITH, *adjective* accordant, affiliated, affinitive, allied, applicable, apposite, appropriate, appurtenant, apropos, apt
ASSOCIATED CONCEPTS: bearing upon, befitting, belonging to, cognate, comparable, congeneric, congruous, connected, correspondent, germane, in conjunction with, pertinent, pursuant to, relevant, with reference to

IN ADDITION, *adverb* added to, additionally, also, as well, besides, furthermore, moreover, over and above, plus, taken together with, then again, then too, too
ASSOCIATED CONCEPTS: alternative relief

IN AGREEMENT, *adjective* affirmed, approved, arranged, assented, assured, attested, avowed, committed, concurred, confirmed, consented, contracted, covenanted, declared, endorsed, guaranteed, having a meeting of the minds, in consonance with, pledged, promised, stipulated, subscribed, sworn, understood, undertaken, warranted

IN ALL LIKELIHOOD, *preposition* apparently, conceivably, expectedly, feasibly, for the most part, indubitably, likely, logically, ostensibly, plausibly, possibly, practicably, predominately, presumably, presumptively, promisingly, reasonably, seemingly, supposedly, unquestionably, with considerable certainty, with direct certainty, with realistic certainty

IN ALL RESPECTS, *preposition* absolutely, all-comprehensively, all-inclusively, broad-based, capaciously, comprehensively, consummately, developed, encyclopedically, entirely, exhaustively, expansively, extensively, fully, globally, in all regards, inclusively, overall, sweepingly, thoroughly, totally, unconditionally, undividedly, universally, unreduced, utterly, very thoroughly, with every aspect considered, with no exception, without omissions,
ASSOCIATED CONCEPTS: inadequate in all respects, insufficient in all respects

IN ARREARS, *adjective* behind, belated, dawdling, deficient, delayed, delinquent, detained, dilatory, dragging, lagging, latish, outstanding, overdue, overmuch, owed, owing, past due, payable, postponed, slow, sluggish, unconscionable, unhurried, unpaid, unsettled, untimely
ASSOCIATED CONCEPTS: bankruptcy laws, outstanding judgment

IN BETWEEN, *adjective* affiliated with, allying with, amid, amidst, among, around, associating with, at intervals, between, bounded by, centrally located, coached in between, enclosed by, halfway, halfway from both, in the middle, in the middle of, in the midst of, inserted between, intermediate to, intervening, linking, located in the area of, located in the proximity of, lodged between, mid, midst, midway, nestled between, situated between, within
ASSOCIATED CONCEPTS: distinctions in law

IN CAMERA, *noun* confidential, confidentially, in antechambers, in chambers, in judge's chamber, in judicial chamber, in private, in secrecy, out of public view

IN CONCLUSION, *adverb* as a completion, as closure, as the finale, as the outcome, finally, at the outgrowth, in closing, in consequence, in culmination, in ending, in finishing, in fulfillment, in the final result, lastly, the result, the upshot is
ASSOCIATED CONCEPTS: conclusion to a memorandum, summation to the jury

IN CONSPIRACY WITH, *preposition* abet with, act in combination with, act in concert with, act in harmony with,

agree with, aid with, associate with, be banded together with, collude with, combine for some evil design with, combine operations with, combine with, concert with, concoct a plot with, conjoin with, connive with, contrive with, cooperate with, design with, devise treachery with, devise with, form a coalition with, form a plot with, in complicity with, join forces with, join with, participate for an unlawful purpose with, plan a crime with, plan secretly with, plan to commit a crime, plan to perform an unlawful act with, plan with, plot an action in advance with, plot craftily with, plot together with, plot with, scheme with, take part with
ASSOCIATED CONCEPTS: conspiracy theory

IN CUSTODY, ***adverb*** behind bars, captive, confined, detained, held, imprisoned, in prison, incarcerated, jailed, kept in prison, maintained in prison, under arrest, under lock and key

IN DUE COURSE, ***adverb*** eventually, in good time, in the long run, in time, presently, shortly, soon, ultimately

IN EFFECT, ***adverb*** actually, basically, effectively, elementary, essentially, for all practical purposes, for the most part, in reality, intrinsically, materially, necessarily, originally, practically, primarily, really, vitally

IN EXTREMIS, ***adjective*** approaching death, at one's end, at the conclusion of life, at the last stage, at the point of death, at the termination of life, during the last moments of life, dying, expiring, in one's last moments, in the final moments of life, in the jaws of death, moribund, near death, near one's end, on one's deathbed, passing away, terminally ill, under a sense of impending death
ASSOCIATED CONCEPTS: dying declaration, gift causa mortis

IN FULL FORCE, ***adjective*** functioning, high-powered, in full effect, mighty, omnipotent, operating, overpowering, potent, puissant, strong, with full effect, with full force

IN FULL GEAR, ***adjective*** act on, all out, as fast as possible, at full speed, at full throttle, commence, continued at maximum, flow, following at full throttle, forging ahead, gathering steam, get in high gear, going forward, in high gear, making headway, making progress, maximum strength, moving ahead, pressing on, progressing, pushing on, rolling on, springing from, streaming

IN FURTHERANCE, ***preposition*** for, for the sake of, in favor of, in the name of, in the service of, on account of, on behalf of

IN GENERAL, ***adverb*** accepted, average, broad, common to many, customary, extensive, generally, habitual, in common, inclusive, most of the time, overall, popular, prevailing, prevalent, representative, sweeping traditionally, typical, universal, usually, widespread
ASSOCIATED CONCEPTS: summation before a jury

IN GOOD FAITH, ***adverb*** bona fide, constantly, devotedly, fairly, faithfully, honestly, legitimately, steadily, truly
ASSOCIATED CONCEPTS: good faith effort, presented in good faith, written in good faith

IN HARMONY, ***adjective*** accordant, adapted, agreeing, alike, appropriate, apt, arranged, at one with, attuned, balanced, becoming, coincident, commensurate, compatible, concerted, concordant, concurrent, conformable, conforming, congruent, congruous, consentient, consistent, cooperating, correspondent, corresponding, equable, equal, fit, fitting, harmonious, in accord, in agreement, in concert, in tandem with, in unison, parallel, related, similar, suitable, synchronized, unchanged, unchanging, undeviating, unified, uniform
ASSOCIATED CONCEPTS: conspiracy, contractual obligations

IN HARMONY WITH, ***preposition*** accordant with, agreeing with, alike with, at one with, attuned to, balanced with, coincident with, commensurate with, compatible with, concerted with, concordant to, concurrent with, conforming to, congruent with, congruous with, consistent with, cooperating with, correspondent with, corresponding to, equably with, equally with, fitting with, harmoniously with, in accordance with, in agreement with, in concord with, in rapport with, in unison with, logically consistent with, parallel with, reconcilably, related to, similarly with, suitably with, uniformly with
ASSOCIATED CONCEPTS: coconspirators

IN LIEU OF, ***preposition*** as a substitute for, as an alternative, as proxy for, by proxy, for, in place of, instead of, on behalf of, rather than, representing
ASSOCIATED CONCEPTS: in lieu of payment

IN LIGHT OF, ***preposition*** because of, by way of explanation, considering, even considering, in consideration of, in view of, taken in relation to, taken together with, taken with regard to, to clarify, to clear up, to simplify, with knowledge of, with regard to, with specific reference to
ASSOCIATED CONCEPTS: in light of precedence, in light of the circumstances

IN PART, ***adverb*** in installments, in some measure, incompletely, not wholly, partially, partly, somewhat, to a certain extent, to a degree, to a limited extent

IN PERSON, ***adverb*** bodily, in one's own person, individually, personally, privately

IN PLAIN VIEW, ***adjective*** freely seen, immediately apparent, in plain sight, lawful observation, openly seen, rule of evidentiary admissibility, within plain sight
ASSOCIATED CONCEPTS: inadvertent discovery, plain feel, plain hearing, plain smell, probable cause, search and seizure

IN SOLIDO, ***noun*** aggregate, each and every, in whole, joint and several, one and all, sum total, the entirety, total, totality

IN STRICT CONFORMITY, ***adverb*** in accordance with, in keeping with, in line with, in obedience with, in strict compliance with, predominantly the same

IN TERROREM, ***adjective*** alarmed, apprehensive, concerned, filled with anxiety, fraught with apprehension, frightened, horrified, in a state of anxiety, in fear, intimidated, mortified, scared, timorous, uneasy, with an apprehension of danger, with an apprehension of harm, with an apprehension of injury, with an apprehension of punishment, with consternation, with fright, with panic, with timidity, with trepidation
ASSOCIATED CONCEPTS: *in terrorem* clauses, *in terrorem* letters

IN THE HEAT OF, ***verb*** during extreme emotion, in the emotion of, in the excitement of, in the fervor of, in the fury of, in the passion of, while caught up in emotion, while caught up in the moment, while excited, while extremely

emotional, while overcome with emotion, while passionately involved, without thinking
ASSOCIATED CONCEPTS: in the heat of the commission of a crime

IN TOTO, ***adverb*** absolutely, all in all, altogether, as a whole, collectively, completely, comprehensively, entirely, fully, in all, in all respects, in full, in its entirety, in the aggregate, in the whole, *omnino,* on all counts, *plane, prorsus,* thoroughly, totally, unabridgedly, unanimously, undividedly, unreservedly, utterly, wholly, without omission

IN TRUST, ***adverb*** held in pledge, held in trust, in escrow, under fiduciary control

IN WRITING, ***adverb*** expressed in writing, in black and white, on paper, recorded, reduced to a writing, scriptory, stated in a writing, stated in writing

INABILITY, ***adjective*** defect, disability, disablement, failure, feebleness, frailty, handicap, helplessness, inadequacy, inaptitude, inaptness, incapability, incapableness, incapacitation, incapacity, incompetence, incompetency incomprehension, ineligibility, ineptitude, ineptness, infirmity, insufficiency, lack of ability, shortcoming, unfitness, unsuitability, unsuitableness
ASSOCIATED CONCEPTS: disability and inability to serve under the Twenty-Fifth Amendment

INABILITY, ***noun*** disability, disablement, disqualification, failure, helplessness, impotence, impuissance, inadequacy, incapability, incapacitation, incapacity, incompetence, incompetency, ineffectualness, inefficacy, inefficiency, ineptitude, ineptness, *infirmitas,* infirmity, *inopia,* insufficiency, lack of ability, lack of competence, lack of power, powerlessness, shortcoming, undeftness, unfitness, unproficiency, unskillfulness, want of ability, want of capacity, want of power, want of skill
ASSOCIATED CONCEPTS: inability to meet an obligation, inability to pay a debt as it matures, inability to pay arrears, inability to work

INACCESSIBLE, ***adjective*** beyond reach, distant, elusive, far, far away, far off, impossible to reach, *inaccessus,* inapproachable, out of reach, out of touch, *rari aditus,* remote, removed, separated, unaccessible, unachievable, unacquirable, unapproachable, unattainable, unavailable, unobtainable, unprocurable, unreachable, unrealizable, unsecurable
ASSOCIATED CONCEPTS: inaccessibility of property, inaccessible to service of process, inaccessible witness

INACCURACY, ***noun*** aberration, blunder, canard, deception, delusion, erratum, erroneousness, error, exaggeration, fallacy, falsehood, falsification, fault, illusion, imprecision, impropriety, incorrectness, inexactitude, inexactness, miscalculation, misconstruction, misestimation, misinterpretation, misjudgment, misprint, misrepresentation, misstatement, mistake, obliquity, oversight, unpreciseness

INACCURATE, ***adjective*** amiss, approximate, blundering, broad, careless, erring, erroneous, fallacious, false, *falsus,* faulty, garbled, general, generalized, groundless, imprecise, improper, incorrect, *indiligens,* inexact, loose, misreported, misstated, mistaken, slipshod, unconscientious, unfactual, unfounded, unfussy, unpainstaking, unreal, unsound, unstrict, untrue, untrustworthy, wrong

INACTION, ***noun*** abeyance, abrogation, abstinence from action, *cessatio,* cessation, dormancy, failure to act, idleness, immobility, impotence, indolence, inertness, inoccupation, languor, latency, motionlessness, *otium,* paralysis, passiveness, passivity, *quies,* quiescence, rest, sloth, sluggishness, stagnation, stillness, suspended animation, suspension, torpidity, torpor, unemployment, unprogressiveness, vegetation

INACTIVE, ***adjective*** abeyant, abolished, abrogated, apathetic, canceled, comatose, destroyed, disabled, dormant, idle, *ignavus,* inanimate, indifferent, indolent, *iners,* inert, inoperative, insentient, invalid, languid, latent, lazy, lethargic, lethargical, listless, motionless, nugatory, null, obsolete, otiose, pococurante, powerless, *quietus,* recumbent, reposing, resting, sedentary, slothful, sluggish, spiritless, stagnant, static, supine, suspended, torpid, unbusied, unemployed, unexercised, unmoving, unspirited, unstirred, vegetative, void, weak
ASSOCIATED CONCEPTS: inactive account, inactive trust

INADEPT, ***adjective*** artless, awkward, feckless, feeble, impotent, incapable, incompetent, ineffective, ineffectual, inefficacious, inefficient, inept, inexpert, insufficient, lacking, lame, poor, unable, unaccomplished, unadroit, unapt, unclever, undeft, undexterous, unendowed, unequal to, unfacile, unfit, unfitted, ungifted, unproficient, unqualified, unskillful, unsuccessful, untalented, wanting, without dexterity

INADEQUATE, ***adjective*** assailable, deficient, depleted, disabled, disappointing, displeasing, emasculate, exhausted, feckless, feeble, helpless, impaired, *impar,* impotent, incapable, incompetent, incomplete, indefensible, ineffective, ineffectual, inefficacious, inept, inferior, inoperative, insubstantial, insufficient, lacking, not enough, not up to expectation, nugatory, perfunctory, poor, powerless, scant, short, unable, unapt, undeveloped, unempowered, unequal to, unfit, unfitted, unreplenished, unsatisfactory, unsufficing, untenable, useless, vincible, vulnerable, wanting, weak
ASSOCIATED CONCEPTS: inadequate consideration, inadequate damages, inadequate remedy at law, inadequate representation

INADMISSIBILITY, ***noun*** debarment, disqualification, exclusion, impropriety, inappositeness, inappropriateness, inaptitude, inaptness, ineligibility, misalliance, nonadmission, objectionability, preclusion, rejection, unacceptability, undesirability, unfitness, unqualification, unsuitability
ASSOCIATED CONCEPTS: challenges, inadmissibility of evidence

INADMISSIBLE, ***adjective*** banned, barred, disallowed, disapproved, excepted, excluded, improper, inapplicable, inapposite, inappropriate, incompetent, ineligible, *inlicitus,* irrelevant, not admitted, not allowed, not capable of being introduced as evidence, not included, not receivable as evidence, not receivable in evidence, not to be admitted, not to be allowed, not wanted, objectionable, prohibited, refused, rejected, suppressed, undue, unfit, unfitted, unqualified, unreceivable, unsuitable, wrong
ASSOCIATED CONCEPTS: inadmissible evidence, inadmissible statement, inadmissible testimony, incompetent testimony

INADVERTENCY, ***noun*** carelessness, dereliction, disregard, inattention, inattentiveness, indifference, laxity, miscue, mistake, neglect, negligence, nonobservance, omission, oversight, thoughtlessness, unmindfulness

INADVERTENT, ***adjective*** accidental, blind, careless, disregardful, heedless, *imprudens,* inattentive, neglectful,

negligent, oblivious, regardless, thoughtless, undesigned, undiscerning, unheedful, unheeding, unintended, unintentional, unmeant, unmindful, unnoticing, unobservant, unperceptive, unpremeditated, unseeing, unthinking
ASSOCIATED CONCEPTS: neglect, negligence

INADVISABLE, ***adjective*** adverse, deleterious, detrimental, disadvantageous, disapproved, harmful, hurtful, ill-advised, ill-considered, ill-judged, impolitic, imprudent, inappropriate, inexpedient, infelicitous, injudicious, injurious, inopportune, insalubrious, misadvised, misguided, nocuous, objectionable, pernicious, undesirable, unfavorable, unfitting, unhealthy, unhelpful, unprofitable, unsatisfactory, unsensible, unsound, unsuitable, untoward, unwise, wrong

INAFFABLE, ***adjective*** bad-natured, bad-tempered, bellicose, belligerent, cantankerous, contrary, difficult, discourteous, disrespectful, fractious, impolite, intractable, obstreperous, offensive, perverse, petulant, pugnacious, rude, touchy, troublesome, truculent, unaccommodating, unapproachable, uncivil, uncomplaisant, uncooperative, uncourtly, ungallant, ungracious, unmannerly, untoward, unyielding, vexatious

INALIENABLE, ***adjective*** incapable of being conveyed, incapable of being sold, incapable of being transferred, nontransferable, not able to be conveyed, *quod abalienari non potest,* secured by law, unable to be bought, unable to be disposed of, unforfeitable, untouchable
ASSOCIATED CONCEPTS: inalienable lands, inalienable rights

INANE, ***adjective*** absurd, asinine, fatuous, foolish, imbecile, incogitant, inept, insipid, irrational, ludicrous, nonsensical, ridiculous, senseless, shallow, thought-free, thoughtless, unintelligent, unreasoning, unthinking, vacuous, vain

INAPPEALABLE, ***adjective*** absolute, beyond all dispute, beyond all question, beyond question, clear, conclusive, decided, decisive, definite, definitive, established, final, finally settled, fixed, impregnable, incapable of being reviewed, incontestable, incontrovertible, indisputable, irrefutable, irrevocable, not to be disputed, past dispute, peremptory, *quod refutari non potest,* unassailable, unchangeable, uncontroversial, unimpeachable, unrefutable, without power of appeal

INAPPLICABLE, ***adjective*** alien, at variance, clashing, disagreeing, discordant, discrepant, divergent, foreign, ill-adapted, impertinent, improper, inadmissible, inapposite, inappropriate, inapt, incommensurable, incompatible, incongruent, incongruous, inconsistent, infelicitous, irrelevant, jarring, malapropos, misapplied, mismatched, misplaced, *non valere,* out of keeping, out of place, unapt, uncalled for, unconformable, unconsonant, unfit, unfitted, unfitting, ungermane, unharmonious, unqualified, unsuitable, unsuited, unusable, wrong

INAPPOSITE, ***adjective*** alien, aside from the point, at variance, beside the mark, beside the point, clashing, disagreeing, discordant, discrepant, disproportionate, dissonant, extraneous, far-fetched, foreign, ill-adapted, ill-timed, illogical, immaterial, impertinent, improper, inaccordant, inadmissible, inapplicable, inappropriate, inapt, incidental, incompatible, incongruent, incongruous, inconsequent, inconsequential, inconsistent, inept, inessential, infelicitous, inharmonious, inopportune, insignificant, irreconcilable, irrelative, irrelevant, isolated, jarring, lacking importance, lacking relevance, malapropos, negligible, *non idoneus,* of little importance, pointless, remote, trivial, unallied, unapt, unbecoming, unbefitting, unconformable, uncongenial, unconnected, unconsonant, undue, unessential, unfavorable, unfit, unfitting, ungermane, unharmonious, unimportant, unnoteworthy, unrelated, unseasonable, unsuitable, unsuited, untimely, untoward, wrong

INAPPRECIABLE, ***adjective*** beneath consideration, beneath notice, disregarded, impalpable, imperceptible, inconsequential, inconsiderable, infinitesimal, insignificant, insubstantial, intangible, irrelevant, little, marginal, meager, mean, *minimus,* minor, negligible, of little account, of little importance, paltry, petty, scant, scanty, slight, small, trifling, unimportant, unworthy of consideration, unworthy of notice

INAPPREHENSIBLE, ***adjective*** abstruse, acroamatic, acroamatical, acroatic, ambiguous, beyond comprehension, beyond understanding, enigmatic, enigmatical, hidden, impenetrable, impossible to understand, incognizable, incomprehensible, indistinct, inexplicable, inexpressible, inscrutable, mysterious, mystic, mystical, obscure, opaque, past comprehension, puzzling, recondite, unaccountable, undecipherable, undefinable, undiscoverable, unexplainable, unfathomable, unintelligible, unknowable, unreadable, unrecognizable, vague

INAPPROPRIATE, ***adjective*** alien, amiss, clashing, disagreeing, discordant, discrepant, disproportionate, dissonant, divergent, forced, gratuitous, impertinent, impolitic, improper, in bad taste, inadmissible, inapplicable, inapposite, inapt, incompatible, incongruent, incongruous, inconsistent, indecorous, ineligible, inessential, inexpedient, infelicitous, inopportune, irrelevant, maladjusted, malapropos, misapplied, misbecoming, misdirected, misplaced, *non idoneus,* objectionable, odd, out of character, out of keeping, out of place, remote, unadvisable, unapt, unbecoming, unbefitting, uncalled for, uncommendable, unconformable, unconsonant, undesirable, undignified, undue, unfit, unfitted, unfitting, ungermane, unharmonious, unmeet, unseasonable, unseemly, unsuitable, unsuited, untimely, untoward, wrongly timed

INAPT, ***adjective*** at variance, clashing, discordant, discrepant, disproportionate, dissonant, ill-adapted, ill-suited, ill-timed, impolitic, improper, inaccordant, inadmissible, inadvisable, inapplicable, inapposite, inappropriate, incompatible, incongruent, incongruous, inconsistent, inexpedient, infelicitous, inharmonious, inopportune, irreconcilable, jarring, malapropos, mismatched, misplaced, objectionable, out of character, out of keeping, out of place, out of proportion, unapt, unbecoming, unbefitting, uncongenial, unconsonant, undesirable, undue, unfit, unfitting, unmeet, unqualified, unseasonable, unseemly, unsuitable, untimely, untoward, unwise

INARTICULATE, ***adjective*** abstruse, abysmal, close, defective, deficient, deprived of speech, fumbling, garbled, guarded, inadequate, inaudible, incommunicative, incomprehensible, inconversable, indiscernible, indistinct, indistinguishable, ineffective, inelegant, inferior, laconic, monosyllabic, muffled, mute, nebulous, not able to vocalize a position, not fluent, not glib, not polished, not smooth, opaque, *parum distinctus,* poor, reserved, reticent, silent, sparing of words, taciturn, tongue-tied, unclear, unfathomable, unintelligible, unplain, unrefined, untrained, unvocal, vague, withdrawn

INATTENTIVE, ***adjective*** absent-minded, absorbed, apathetic, blind, careless, casual, cursory, dazed, derelict, disregardful, distracted, forgetful, heedless, inadvertent, incogitant, inconsiderate, indifferent, lax, mercurial, neglectful, negligent, oblivious, off guard, perfunctory, preoccupied, reckless, remiss, thoughtless, unaware, undiscerning, unguarded, unmindful, unobservant, unresponsive, unsuspecting, wandering

INAUDIBLE, ***noun*** abstruse, acroamatic, acroamatical, acroatic, ambiguous, beyond comprehension, concealed, dark, deep, difficult to comprehend, dim, dull, enigmatic, enigmatical, esoteric, faint, fathomless, gentle, hard to hear, hard to make out, hard to understand, hidden, impenetrable, imperceptible, impossible to hear, impossible to understand, inapprehensible, incalculable, incogniscible, incoherent, inconceivable, indefinite, indistinct, inexplicable, inscrutable, insoluble, insolvable, intricate, low, meaningless, metaphysical, miraculous, muffled, mumbled, murmured, mute, muted, muttered, mysterious, mystic, mystical, nebulousness, noiseless, not heard, obscure, occult, out of earshot, puzzling, quiet, recondite, silent, soft, stifled, still, unaccountable, unclear, unfathomable, unimaginable, unintelligible, unknowable, unrecognizable, unthinkable, vague, whispered

INAUGURAL, ***adjective*** commencing, embryonic, exploratory, foundational, inceptive, incipient, initial, initiative, initiatory, introductory, nascent, original, precursory, prefatory, preliminary, premier, preparatory, primal, primary, prime, prior, rudimentary

INAUSPICIOUS, ***adjective*** adverse, boding, disadvantageous, ill-timed, inadvisable, inexpedient, *infelix,* inopportune, mistimed, *nefastus,* ominous, presageful, problematic, problematical, unfavorable, unlucky, unpromising, unpropitious, untimely, untoward

INBRED, ***adjective*** absorbed, acquired, born, congenital, connate, deep-rooted, engrafted, genetic, hereditary, implicit, inborn, inculcated, indigenous, ingenerate, ingrained, inherent, inherited, innate, instilled, integral, intrinsic, native, natural

INCALCULABLE, ***adjective*** aleatory, boundless, countless, endless, enormous, equivocal, illimitable, immeasurable, immense, imponderable, incomprehensible, incomputable, indefinite, indeterminate, inestimable, inexhaustible, infinite, innumerable, innumerous, interminable, limitless, measureless, multitudinous, myriad, numberless, unaccountable, unbounded, uncertain, uncountable, unfathomable, unlimited, unmeasured, unnumbered, unpredictable

INCAPABLE, ***adjective*** crippled, disabled, feeble, impuissant, inadequate, incompetent, ineffective, ineffectual, inept, *inhabilis,* insufficient, not equal to, unable, unempowered, unequipped, unfit, unpowerful, unqualified, unskillful, unsuitable, unsuited, useless, weak
ASSOCIATED CONCEPTS: incapable of conducting his own affairs, incapable of intended use, incapable party, legal incapacity, physically incapable, total incapacity
FOREIGN PHRASES: ***Contra non valentem agere nulla currit praescriptio.*** No prescription runs against a person who is unable to act. ***Nemo admittendus est inhabilitare seipsum.*** No one is allowed to incapacitate himself.

INCAPABLE OF KNOWING RIGHT FROM WRONG, ***adjective*** bereft of reason, crazy, defective, demented, insensate, legally insane, mentally deficient, mentally deranged, mentally ill, *non compos mentis,* not of sound mind, unsound

INCAPACITATION, ***noun*** affliction, caducity, calamity, debility, disability, disablement, handicap, inability to work, incapacity for work, infirmity, misfortune, sickness

INCAPACITY, ***noun*** adynamy, anility, caducity, disability, disablement, disenablement, disqualification, dotage, failure, feebleness, helplessness, impotence, impuissance, inability, inadequacy, inaptitude, incapability, incapacitation, incompetence, incompetency, incomprehension, inefficacy, inefficiency, ineptitude, infirmity, *inscitia,* lack of capacity, lack of fitness, lack of power, morosis, unfitness, unproficiency, unskillfulness, weakness
ASSOCIATED CONCEPTS: disability, incapacity for work, incapacity to sue, legal incapacity, mental incapacity, permanent incapacity, physical incapacity, total incapacity

INCARCERATE, ***verb*** cast into prison, commit to prison, confine, constrain, hold in captivity, hold in custody, immune, imprison, institutionalize, intern, jail, lock in, lock up, place in confinement, put behind bars, put under lock and key, put under restraint, remand, restrain, restrict, send to prison, shut in, take into custody, throw in the brig
ASSOCIATED CONCEPTS: incarcerate an inmate, penal reform, prison conditions, prisoners' rights

INCARCERATED PERSON, ***noun*** captive, convict, convicted person, criminal, felon, hostage, inmate, internee, lawbreaker, prisoner, transgressor, wrongdoer

INCARCERATION, ***noun*** arrest, bondage, captivity, carcer, commitment, confinement, confinement by public authority, confinement in a jail, confinement in a penitentiary, confinement under legal process, constraint, *custodia,* custodianship, custody, detention, immurement, impoundment, imprisonment, internment, legal restraint, restraint, restriction, restriction on personal liberty, *vincula*
ASSOCIATED CONCEPTS: deterrence, habeas corpus, isolation, parole, rehabilitation, retribution, sentencing

INCENDIARY *(Aggravating),* ***adjective*** accelerant, agitating, angering, arousing, distressing, disturbing, enraging, fomenting, ignition, inciter, inciting, inflaming, inflammatory, infuriating, instigating, instigator, irking, provoking, stirring, turbulent, vexing

INCENDIARY *(Burning),* ***adjective*** aggravating, agitator, angering, ardent, arousing, arsonist, blazing, building-burner, burnable, combustible, criminal, electrifying, enraging, exasperating, exciting, fiery, firebrand, firebug, fire-setter, flammable, fomenting, hot, ignitable, incensing, inciter, inciting, inflaming, inflammatory, infuriating, instigating, instigator, insurgent, maddening, mischief-maker, mutineer, organizer, outraging, piquing, provocative, pyromaniac, rabble-rouser, rebel, revolutionary, ringleader, smoldering, stimulating, stirring, thrilling, torch, troublemaker
ASSOCIATED CONCEPTS: incendiary bomb, incendiary device, incendiary explosive

INCENSE, ***verb*** *accendere,* aggravate, agitate, anger, antagonize, arouse, arouse ire, arouse resentment, cause dislike, cause loathing, cause resentment, chafe, discompose, disquiet, embitter, embroil, enkindle, enrage, envenom, exacerbate, exasperate, excite, excite hatred, excite indignation, harass, *incendere,* inflame, inflame with

wrath, infuriate, irritate, kindle one's wrath, madden, make one lose one's temper, nettle, pique, provoke, provoke hatred, provoke ire, push too far, put into a temper, raise anger, rile, ruffle, vex, work into a passion
ASSOCIATED CONCEPTS: heat of passion, incense the jury, mistrial, prejudice, provocation

INCENTIVE, ***noun*** actuation, allure, allurement, appeal, attraction, bait, causality, causation, cause, cause of action, consideration, driving force, encouragement, enticement, goad, impetus, impulse, impulsion, *incitamentum,* incitement, inducement, influence, *inritamentum,* inspiration, instigation, lure, motivation, motive, persuasion, prompting, provocation, provocative, reason, spur, stimulant, stimulus, tantalization, temptation
ASSOCIATED CONCEPTS: incentive contract

INCEPTION, ***noun*** beginning, birth, commencement, dawn, debut, derivation, embarkation, exordium, genesis, inauguration, *inceptum,* inchoation, incipience, incipiency, initiation, *initium,* onset, opening, origin, origination, outbreak, outset, rise, source, start, starting point

INCERTITUDE, ***noun*** ambiguity, bewilderment, changeableness, dilemma, doubt, doubtfulness, dubiety, dubiosity, dubiousness, dubitancy, dubitation, fog, haze, hesitancy, hesitation, indecision, indetermination, insecurity, irresolution, misgiving, perplexity, quandary, question, uncertainness, uncertainty, unsureness, vacillation, vagueness

INCESSANT, ***adjective*** *adsiduus,* ceaseless, constant, continual, continuous, continuus, endless, eternal, everlasting, frequent, indefatigable, infinite, interminable, interminate, iterative, long-lasting, never-ending, nonstop, perennial, perpetual, *perpetuus,* persistent, recurrent, reiterative, repeated, repetitious, returning, steady, sustained, timeless, unbroken, unceasing, undying, unending, unintermittent, unintermitting, uninterrupted, unremitting, untiring, unwearying, without ceasing, without interruption, without stopping

INCEST, ***noun*** abnormal cohabitation, abnormal relationship, brother-sister relationship, carnal abuse, degenerate behavior, degenerative behavior, depraved, father-daughter relationship, illegal relationship, illicit relationship, immoral family relationship, immoral relationship, inbreeding, incestuous relationship, interbreeding, lewdness, mother-son relationship, perversion, sex crime, sexual abnormality, sexual abuse, sexual deviance, sexual deviation, sexual offense, sexual perversion, unlawful sexual intercourse
ASSOCIATED CONCEPTS: incest laws

INCESTUOUS, ***adjective*** banned family relationships, criminal family relationships, forbidden family relationships, illegal family relationships, immoral family relationships, improper family relationships, inbred, interbred, perversion, prohibited relationship, sexual abnormality, sexual deviance, sexual deviation, sexual offense, sexual perversion, unlawful family relationships
FOREIGN PHRASES: ***Incestuosi.*** Those offspring of incestuous relationships.

INCHOATE, ***adjective*** anticipatory, basic, beginning, budding, commencing, developing, early, elemental, elementary, embryonic, fragmentary, fundamental, half-begun, half-done, hardly begun, immature, imperfect, in its infancy, inaugural, inceptive, incipient, *incohatus,* incomplete, infant, infant stage, initial, initiatory, introductory, just begun, maiden, nascent, newborn, not completely formed, not fully executed, not fully formed, original, out of order, partial, prefatory, preliminary, preparatory, primal, primary, prime, primeval, primitive, primordial, rudimental, rudimentary, semiprocessed, sketchy, starting, uncompleted, undeveloped, unexecuted, unfinalized, unfinished, unprocessed
ASSOCIATED CONCEPTS: attempt, conspiracy and solicitation, inchoate contract, inchoate crimes, inchoate gift, inchoate interest, inchoate lien, inchoate right, inchoate title, inchoate will

INCIDENCE, ***noun*** amount, degree, embodiment, experience, exposure, extent, frequency, measure, number, number of times occurred, prevalence, range of occurrence, rate, representative number, representative selection, sample, scope
ASSOCIATED CONCEPTS: causation, incidence of a crime, incidence of drug abuse, incidence rate

INCIDENT, ***adjective*** accessory, affiliated, allied, appertaining to, apropos, associated, bearing upon, belonging, circumstantial, collateral, connected, contextual, contingent, correlative, dependent on, following upon, implicated, in connection with, in relation to, inherent in, pertaining to, related to, relating to, relative to, subject to, subsidiary
ASSOCIATED CONCEPTS: customarily incident, necessary and incident to

INCIDENT, ***noun*** affair, case, *casus,* contingency, episode, event, experience, happening, occasion, occurrence, pass, proceeding

INCIDENTAL, ***adjective*** accessory, accidental, accompanying, added, additional, allied, associated, attendant, extrinsic, *forte oblatus,* minor, not vital, parenthetic, secondary, subordinate, subsidiary, supervenient, supplemental, supplementary
ASSOCIATED CONCEPTS: incidental authority, incidental benefits, incidental consequence, incidental damages, incidental expenses, incidental jurisdiction, incidental power, incidental relief, incidental to employment, incidental use, incidental work

INCINERATE, ***verb*** blaze, burn, burn to a cinder, burn up, burning to ashes, catch fire, conflagrate, deflagrate, fire, ignite, incandesce, inflame, kindle, light up, melt down, roast, scald, scorch, sear, singe, smolder, strike a light
ASSOCIATED CONCEPTS: EPA

INCIPIENT, ***adjective*** aboriginal, beginning, budding, commencing, elemental, elementary, embryonic, foundational, fundamental, immature, inceptive, inchoate, inchoative, incunabular, infant, initial, initiatory, introductory, maiden, nascent, original, precursory, prefatory, primal, primary, primeval, primitive, proemial, rudimental, rudimentary, starting, uncompleted

INCISIVE, ***adjective*** acute, biting, brisk, caustic, cutting, discerning, effective, electric, galvanic, harsh, keen, mordacious, mordant, *mordax,* moving, penetrating, piercing, piquant, pointed, powerful, pungent, sarcastic, sarcastical, satiric, satirical, scathing, sententious, severe, sharp, slashing, stinging, telling, trenchant, vehement

INCITE, ***verb*** advise, advocate, agitate, animate, arouse, arouse to action, awaken, bring about, bring on, call

forth, cause, counsel, drive, encourage, energize, enthuse, excite, exert influence, exert pressure, exhort, foment, give advice, give impetus, goad, impart momentum, impassion, *incitare,* induce, influence, initiate, inspire, inspirit, *instigare,* instigate, kindle, launch, move, persuade, press, prevail upon, prompt, provoke, push, rally, recommend, rouse, set in motion, spur on, start, stimulate, stir, stir up, urge, wake
ASSOCIATED CONCEPTS: incite a riot

INCIVILITY, ***noun*** acerbity, acrimony, boorishness, discourteousness, discourtesy, disrespect, ill breeding, impertinence, impoliteness, impropriety, inappropriateness, indecency, indecorum, indelicacy, inelegance, insult, misbehavior, provocation, rudeness of manner, slight, snub, tactlessness, unbecoming conduct, uncouthness, uncultivation, unrefinement, urbane, vulgarity
ASSOCIATED CONCEPTS: professionalism

INCLEMENT, ***adjective*** arctic, astringent, austere, biting, bitter, bleak, blustery, cold, crisp, cruel, freezing, frigid, glacial, grim, gusty, harsh, icy, inexorable, merciless, nasty, nipping, penetrating, piercing, rainy, rigorous, rough, rugged, ruthless, severe, sharp, stone-cold, stormy, stringent, tempestuous, unrelenting, unsparing, violent, wintry

INCLINATION, ***noun*** affinity, aptitude, aptness, bent, bias, cast, direction, fondness, *inclinatio,* leaning, liking, partiality, penchant, predilection, predisposition, preference, prejudice, proclivity, proneness, propensity, readiness, slant, *studium,* tendency, *voluntas*
FOREIGN PHRASES: ***Judicium redditur in invitum, in praesumptione legis.*** In presumption of law, a judgment is given against one's inclination. ***Favores ampliandi sunt; odia restringenda.*** Favorable inclinations should be encouraged; animosities should be restrained.

INCLINED, ***adjective*** acquiescent, affected, agreeable, amenable, apt, assenting, bent, consenting, content, delighted, desirous, disposed, dispositioned, eager, favorable, glad, happy, leaning, liable, moved, partial to, pleased, predisposed, prepared, *proclivis,* prompted, prone, *propensus,* ready, receptive, slanted, stimulated, tending, trending, well-disposed, willing

INCLUDE, ***verb*** absorb, *adscribere,* be composed of, be formed of, be made up of, begird, boast, bound, bracket, circumscribe, classify, close in, combine, compass, *complecti,* comprehend, *comprehendere,* consist of, consolidate, contain, cover, embody, embrace, encircle, encompass, engird, envelop, girdle, hold, incorporate, involve, merge, put a barrier around, span, subsume, surround, take in, unify, unite
FOREIGN PHRASES: ***In eo quod plus sit semper inest et minus.*** The less is always included in the greater. ***Inclusio unius est exclusio alterius.*** The inclusion of one thing is the exclusion of another.

INCLUSION, ***noun*** all acceptance, all-embracing universe, all-encompassing universe, all facets, blanket analysis, broad analysis, compendious amount, comprehensive number, diverse mix, diverse mixture, every facet, every side, exhaustive approach, extensive analysis, full vision, mainstreaming everyone, sweeping analysis, total number, total scope, umbrella, universe, unlimited acceptance
ASSOCIATED CONCEPTS: inclusion of children with disabilities, inclusionary approach

INCLUSIVE, ***adjective*** all-embracing, broad, comprehensive, comprising, consisting of, containing, embodying, embracing, encircling, enclosing, exhaustive, extensive, full, general, inclusory, sweeping, total, vast, wide

INCOGNITO, ***adjective*** alias, anonymous, assumed name, camouflaged, charade, clandestine, concealed, confidential agent, confidentially, cover, discreetly, disguise, disguised, false identity, isolated, mask, masked, masquerade, mysterious, mysteriously, mystery man, nameless, privacy, private, privately, privileged, protected, quietly, recluse, retired, screen, secluded, seclusion, secrecy, secret, secret agent, secreted, secretive, secretiveness, secretly, sheltered, shielded, under an assumed name, under cover, undisclosed, unidentified, unknown, unnamed, unrecognized, unrevealed, unspecified, veiled, with circumspection, without a name, without fanfare

INCOGNIZANT, ***adjective*** benighted, blind, clueless, deaf, heedless, ignorant, insensible, mystified, nescient, oblivious, unacquainted, unadvised, unapprized, unaware, unconscious, unenlightened, unfamiliar, uninformed, uninstructed, unknowing, unmindful, unrealizing, unseeing, unsuspecting, unwitting

INCOHERENCE, ***noun*** absence of meaning, chaos, disconnection, discontinuity, disjunction, disorder, illegibility, imperspicuity, inapprehensibility, incomprehensibility, lack of clarity, meaninglessness, randomness, ranting, raving, unclearness, undecipherability, unevenness, unintelligibility, wandering
ASSOCIATED CONCEPTS: commitment to an institution, guardian, insanity, lack of capacity

INCOHERENT, ***adjective*** babble, confused, deranged, deviating, digressive, disconnected, discontinuity, discordant, disjointed, illogical, inarticulate, irrational, jumbled, lacking clarity and cohesion, mixed-up, muddled, scrambled, unfit, unintelligible, variant, wandering
ASSOCIATED CONCEPTS: chromatic coherence, experience incoherence, insanity defense, intent and coherence, polarization coherence, rehabilitations, spatial coherence, temporal coherence, waive equation

INCOME, ***noun*** allowance, annuity, business profits, commercial profits, compensation, consideration, earnings, emoluments, fees, financial remuneration, financial resources, fringe benefits, gain derived from capital, gain derived from labor, gains, gross, gross income, gross return, increase in amount of wealth, livelihood, means, money coming in, net return, pay, payment, *pecunia,* pension, periodic returns from property or labor, proceeds, profit from conversion of assets, profit from sale, profits, profits of commerce, *quaestus,* receipts, recompense, remuneration, return in money, return on capital, returns, revenue, salary, sale proceeds, something produced by capital, stipend, subsidy, value received, *vectigal,* wage, wages, wealth
ASSOCIATED CONCEPTS: accumulated income, actual income, affordable housing, aggregate income, annual net income, current income, deferred income, division of income, employment law, estimated income, garnishment of income, gross income, income-bearing property, income execution, income tax, income tax evasion, income yield, legacy, life income, low income, minimum wage, net income, retirement income, social security income

INCOMING, ***adjective*** about to be received, approaching, arriving, coming, entering, homeward, homeward-bound, in transit, inbound, incoming, mailed, receiving, sent, shipped, soon to be received

INCOMMENSURABLE, ***adjective*** at variance, cannot be compared to, cannot be weighed against, discordant, discrepant, disproportionate, dissimilar, greatly dissimilar, illbalanced, incomparable, incongruent, inconsistent, inconsonant, inharmonious, lopsided, mismatched, out of proportion, unbalanced, unequal
ASSOCIATED CONCEPTS: incommensurable goods, incommensurable values

INCOMMENSURATE, ***adjective*** at variance, discordant, discrepant, disproportionate, inaccordant, incommensurable, inconsistent, mismatched, out of keeping, out of proportion, short, unconformable, unequal

INCOMMUNICABLE, ***adjective*** be silent, confidential, immutable, inexpressible, keep quiet, keep silent, not speak, not speaking, not talking, silent, top secret

INCOMPARABLE, ***adjective*** beyond, beyond comparison, beyond imitation, beyond words, excellent, exceptional, exquisite, extraordinary, incredible, matchless, peerless, perfect, rare, superior, superlative, supreme, unapproachable, unequaled, unique, unmatchable, unparalleled, unrivaled, unsurpassed, unusual, without equal

INCOMPATIBLE, ***adjective*** antipathetical, clash, conflict, contradictoriness, contrariety, contrast, controversy, disaccord, disagreement, discord, discordance, dispute, dissension, dissent, dissidence, disunion, disunity, divergence, faction, fight, hatred, hostility, incongruous, inimicality, intolerance, not agreeing, not compatible, not harmonizing, opposition, repelling, repugnance, variance
ASSOCIATED CONCEPTS: doctrine of incompatibility, incompatibility, incompatibility of public offices

INCOMPATIBILITY *(Difference),* ***noun*** animosity, antagonism, antipathy, clash, conflict, contradictoriness, contrariety, contrast, controversy, disaccord, disagreement, discord, discordance, dislike, dispute, dissension, dissent, dissidence, disunion, disunity, divergence, division, faction, fight, hatred, hostility, inimicality, intolerance, intransigence, intransigency, irreconcilability, irreconcilable difference, irreconcilableness, lack of agreement, misunderstanding, nonagreement, opposition, quarrel, repugnance, unfriendliness, variance, want of adaptation, want of agreement
ASSOCIATED CONCEPTS: divorce for incompatibility

INCOMPATIBILITY *(Inconsistency),* ***noun*** antithesis, clash, conflict, contrast, disagreement, disconformity, discongruity, discord, discordance, discordancy, discrepancy, disharmony, disparity, dissimilarity, dissimilitude, dissonance, divergence, incongruity, inconsonance, inequality, inharmoniousness, inharmony, lack of agreement, lack of harmony, nonconformity, nonuniformity, unconformity, unlikeness, unsuitableness, variance, want of agreement
ASSOCIATED CONCEPTS: incompatible use of land

INCOMPETENCE, ***noun*** illegitimacy, inadequacy, incapability, incapacity, inefficiency, inexpertness, insufficiency, mismanagement, negligence, undeftness, unendowment, unfitness, unprofessional conduct, unproficiency, unqualifiedness
ASSOCIATED CONCEPTS: incompetence of counsel, incompetence of representation, incompetent evidence

INCOMPETENCY, ***noun*** awkwardness, deficiency, deranged, disqualification, failure, frailty, impotence, inability, inadequacy, inaptitude, incapabability, incapacitation, incapacity, ineffectiveness, inefficiency, ineptitude, insufficiency, inutility, lack, mental defect, mental disease, powerlessness, shortcoming, unfitness, weakness
ASSOCIATED CONCEPTS: not guilty by reason of insanity

INCOMPETENT, ***adjective*** amateurish, awkward, bungling, clumsy, deficient, disqualified, floundering, gauche, gawky, ignorant, improficient, inadequate, incapable, incapacitated, ineffective, ineffectual, inefficient, inept, inexperienced, inexpert, *inhabilis, inscitus,* insufficient, *inutilis,* lacking qualification, maladroit, raw, stumbling, stupid, unable, unadapted, unapt, unequal, unequipped, unfit, unfitted, ungainly, unhandy, uninitiated, unqualified, unskilled, unskillful, unsuitable, untrained, useless, without adequate ability
ASSOCIATED CONCEPTS: incompetence of counsel, incompetent evidence, incompetent witness

INCOMPLETE, ***adjective*** defective, deficient, devoid, disappointing, failing, faulty, fragmentary, half-done, imperfect, imperfected, inaccurate, inadequate, inchoate, insufficient, lacking, left undone, less than perfect, not completed, outstanding, partial, perfunctory, rough, sketchy, truncated, unaccomplished, uncompleted, undeveloped, unexecuted, unfinished, unsatisfactory, wanting

INCOMPREHENSIBLE, ***adjective*** abstruse, acroamatic, acroamatical, acroatic, ambiguous, beyond comprehension, concealed, dark, deep, difficult to comprehend, dim, enigmatic, enigmatical, esoteric, fathomless, hard to understand, hidden, impenetrable, impossible to understand, inapprehensible, incalculable, incognoscible, incoherent, inconceivable, indefinite, inexplicable, inscrutable, insoluble, insolvable, *intellegi non potest,* intricate, meaningless, metaphysical, miraculous, mysterious, mystic, mystical, nebulousness, obscure, occult, puzzling, *quod comprehendi,* recondite, unaccountable, unclear, unfathomable, unimaginable, unintelligible, unknowable, unrecognizable, unthinkable, vague

INCOMPREHENSIVE, ***adjective*** abstract, abstruse, ambiguous, beyond comprehension, beyond understanding, complex, complicated, deep, difficult, difficult to comprehend, enigmatic, esoteric, hard to understand, impenetrable, impossible to understand, inapprehensible, incoherent, indecipherable, inexplicable, intricate, involved, jumbled, metaphysical, muddled, mysterious, mystic, mystical, nebulous, oblique, obscure, perplexed, profound, recondite, unclear, undecipherable, unexplainable, unfathomable, unimaginable, unintelligible, vague

INCONCEIVABLE, ***adjective*** disputable, doubtful, excluded, extraordinary, hard to believe, implausible, impossible, impracticable, inapprehensible, incogitable, incomprehensible, incredible, inexplicable, infeasible, marvelous, miraculous, not understandable, out of the question, overwhelming, portentous, prodigious, questionable, rare, staggering, stupendous, surprising, suspect, suspicious, unbelievable, uncanny, unconsidered, undreamed, unexplainable, unimaginable, unreasonable, unthinkable, unthought of, unusual

INCONCLUSIVE, ***adjective*** doubtful, flimsy, indecisive, ineffective, not final, *quo nihil efficitur,* subject to verification, unascertained, uncertain, unconfirmed, uncorroborated,

undemonstrated, unestablished, unproved, unproven, unsettled, unsubstantiated, unsupported, unsupported by evidence, unsure, untested, untried, unverified, weak
ASSOCIATED CONCEPTS: inconclusive account, inconclusive evidence

INCONGRUENT, ***adjective*** contradictory, different, disagreeing, discordant, discrepant, disjointed, disparate, disproportionate, dissimilar, distinct, diverse, ill-assorted, ill-matched, improper, inapplicable, inapposite, inappropriate, inapt, incompatible, incongruous, inconsistent, inconsonant, inept, inharmonious, inopportune, malapropos, peculiar, unalike, unconformable, unequal, unfortunate, unmatched

INCONGRUITY, ***noun*** abnormality, absurdity, absurdness, contradiction, contradictoriness, contrariety, contrariness, deviation, difference, disagreement, discordance, discordancy, discrepancy, disharmony, disparity, dissimilarity, dissimilitude, dissonance, impropriety, inapplicability, inappropriateness, incompatibility, incongruousness, inconsistency, inconsonance, inharmoniousness, lack of consonance, lack of harmony, ludicrousness, misalliance, mismatch, nonconformity, *repugnantia,* ridiculousness, unconformity, unfitness, unfittingness, unlikeness, unsuitability, variance

INCONGRUOUS, ***adjective*** alien, *alienus,* at odds, at variance, clashing, conflicting, contradictory, contrary, disaccordant, disagreeing, discordant, discrepant, disharmonious, disproportionate, dissonant, divergent, ill-matched, illogical, improper, inaccordant, inapplicable, inapposite, inappropriate, incompatible, inconformable, *incongruens,* incongruent, inconsequent, inconsistent, inconsonant, inharmonious, irreconcilable, irregular, jarring, lacking agreement, lacking harmony, misjoined, mismatched, mismated, *non aptus,* out of character, out of keeping, out of place, strange, unbecoming, uncongenial, uncoordinated, unfit, unfitting, unsuitable

INCONSEQUENCE, ***noun*** disassociation, disconnection, disjunction, dissociation, immateriality, impertinence, impertinency, inapplicability, inappositeness, inconsequentiality, inconsiderableness, inconsistence, inconsistency, insignificance, irrelevance, irrelevancy, negligibility, paltriness, smallness, triviality, unimportance, unnoteworthiness, unrelatedness

INCONSEQUENTIAL, ***adjective*** dispensable, flimsy, frivolous, immaterial, impertinent, inapplicable, inappreciable, inappropriate, inconsequent, inconsiderable, inessential, insignificant, invalid, irrelevant, minor, niggling, nonessential, not vital, nugatory, of minor importance, of no account, of no consequence, paltry, petty, picayune, remote, slight, superficial, trifling, trivial, unconnected, unessential, ungermane, unimportant, unnecessary, unrelated, unsound, unwarranted, worthless
ASSOCIATED CONCEPTS: irrelevant evidence

INCONSIDERABLE, ***adjective*** beneath notice, *exiguus,* immaterial, inappreciable, inconsequential, insignificant, insubstantial, irrelevant, *levis,* meager, mean, minor, minute, modest, negligible, nominal, nonessential, not worth considering, not worthy of notice, nugatory, of no consequence, of no moment, paltry, petty, piddling, slight, small, *tenuis,* trifling, trivial, unessential, unimportant, unworthy of consideration, unworthy of notice, worthless

INCONSIDERATE, ***adjective*** blind, blunt, brusque, careless, cavalier, censorious, churlish, derelict, disobliging, disregardful, flippant, harsh, heedless, ill-advised, ill-judged, impolitic, imprudent, inattentive, incautious, indifferent, indiscreet, injudicious, intolerant, neglectful, negligent, oblivious, reasonless, reckless, remiss, rude, self-centered, selfish, severe, tactless, thoughtless, uncharitable, unconsidered, ungracious, unheeding, unkind, unmindful, unobliging, unobservant, unpolitic, unthoughtful, unwary

INCONSIDERATION, ***noun*** carelessness, cruelty, disregard, disrespect, disrespectfulness, foolhardiness, forgetfulness, hastiness, heedlessness, impetuosity, improvidence, imprudence, impulsiveness, inadvertence, inadvertency, inattention, inattention to consequences, incaution, incautiousness, incircumspection, inconsiderateness, indiscretion, injudiciousness, irresponsibility, lack of care, lack of caution, lack of consideration, lack of respect, lack of reverence, meanness, neglect, negligence, oversight, precipitance, precipitancy, prodigality, rashness, recklessness, regardlessness, thoughtlessness, unkindness, unpremeditation, unwariness

INCONSISTENCY, ***noun*** antilogy, antinomy, capriciousness, changeableness, contradiction, contradictoriness, contrariety, deviation, difference, disaccord, disagreement, discord, discordance, discordancy, discrepancy, disparity, dissimilarity, dissimilitude, dissonance, divergence, diversity, fitfulness, flightiness, inapplicability, inappropriateness, incompatibility, incongruity, incongruousness, inconsonance, inconstancy, *inconstantia,* inequality, inharmony, instability, lack of accord, mercurialness, *mutabilitas,* nonconformity, unconformity, unlikeness, unsteadiness, unsuitableness, vacillation, variance, volatility, want of harmony

INCONSISTENT, ***adjective*** at variance, capricious, changeable, conflicting, contradictory, *contrarius,* contrary, different, disagreeing, discordant, discrepant, dissonant, divergent, erratic, fickle, fitful, flighty, illogical, incompatible, incongruous, inconsonant, *inconstans,* inconstant, irreconcilable, jarring, lacking accord, lacking harmony, mercurial, moody, mutable, notional, paradoxical, unstable, unsteady, unsuitable, vacillating, variable, volatile
ASSOCIATED CONCEPTS: alternative pleadings, inconsistent causes of action, inconsistent defenses, inconsistent statements, inconsistent verdict

INCONSPICUOUS, ***adjective*** barely seen, blurred, concealed, covert, dim, faint, feeble, fuzzy, half-seen, half-visible, hazy, hidden, ill-defined, ill-marked, imperceptible, indefinite, indiscernible, indistinct, indistinguishable, invisible, merely visible, misty, modest, nebulous, obscure, *obscurus,* out of sight, *parum insignis,* poorly defined, poorly seen, quiet, retiring, shadowy, shrouded, subtle, suppressed, unapparent, unclear, undefined, undiscernible, unevident, unnoticeable, unnoticed, unobserved, unobtrusive, unobvious, unostentatious, unperceivable, unpretentious, unpronounced, unrecognizable, unseeable, unseen, vague, veiled, viewless

INCONTESTABILITY, ***noun*** impregnability, incontrovertibility, indefeasibility, indisputability, indubitableness, irrefragibility, irrefutability, unassailability, undeniability, unequivocalness, unimpeachability, unquestionability, unrefutability
ASSOCIATED CONCEPTS: incontestability clause, incontestable policy

INCONTESTABLE, ***adjective*** absolutely clear, beyond all question, clear, conclusive, impregnable, inappealable,

incontrovertible, indefeasible, indisputable, indubious, indubitable, irrefragable, irrefutable, noncontroversial, past dispute, unambiguous, unassailable, uncontradictable, undeniable, unequivocal, unimpeachable, unquestionable
ASSOCIATED CONCEPTS: incontestable claim

INCONTESTABLY, *adverb* admittedly, assuredly, authoritatively, certainly, clearly, conclusively, incontrovertibly, indisputably, indubiously, indubitably, infallibly, irrefutably, irresistibly, obviously, palpably, patently, plainly, reliably, self-evidently, unambiguously, unassailably, uncontradictably, uncontroversially, undeniably, unequivocally, unimpeachably, unmistakably, unquestionably

INCONTROVERTIBLE, *adjective* absolute, apodictic, ascertained, assured, authoritative, beyond a shadow of a doubt, beyond contradiction, capable of proof, certain, clear-cut, conclusive, definite, demonstrable, established, factual, inappealable, incontestable, indisputable, indubious, indubitable, irrefragable, irrefutable, noncontroversial, past dispute, positive, questionless, *quod refutari non potest,* settled, sure, testable, true, unambiguous, unanswerable, unchallengeable, unconfutable, uncontradictable, undeniable, unequivocal, unimpeachable, unmistakable, unquestionable, unshakable, veracious
ASSOCIATED CONCEPTS: incontrovertible fact, incontrovertible proof

INCONVENIENCE, *verb* annoy, be obstructive, be uncooperative, bother, disadvantage, discommode, displace, disturb, encumber, give trouble, hamper, hinder, impede, impose hardship, incommode, irritate, obstruct, stall, stand in the way, stymie, thwart, trouble, unsettle, vex
ASSOCIATED CONCEPTS: forum non conveniens, public inconvenience
FOREIGN PHRASES: ***Privatum incommodum publico bono pensatur.*** Private inconvenience is compensated by public benefit. ***Argumentum ab inconvenienti est validum in lege, quia lex non permittit aliquod inconveniens.*** An argument drawn from what is inconvenient is good in law, because the law will not permit any inconvenience. ***Quod est inconveniens aut contra rationem non permissum est in lege.*** What is inconvenient or contrary to reason is not permitted in the law.

INCONVENIENT, *adjective* bother, disadvantage, discommode, displace, disturbance, encumbering, hamper, hinder, impede, impose hardship, incommode, irritate, obstruct, stand in the way, stymie, thwart, trouble, unsettle, vex
ASSOCIATED CONCEPTS: forum non conveniens

INCONVINCIBLE, *adjective* cynical, disbelieving, disposed to doubt, distrustful, doubtful, doubting, dubious, given to suspicion, hard to convince, inclined to suspect, incredulous, indisposed to believe, questioning, skeptical, slow to believe, suspecting, suspicious, unbelieving, uncertain, unwilling to accept, wary, without faith

INCORPORATE *(Form a corporation),* ***verb*** affiliate, begin a corporation, charter, confer a corporate franchise upon, confer corporate status upon, create a corporation, establish a corporation, form a company, initiate a corporation, *inserere,* organize a corporation, start a corporation
ASSOCIATED CONCEPTS: certificate of incorporation

INCORPORATE *(Include),* ***verb*** absorb, alloy, become a component, become an ingredient, bring together, centralize, coalesce, combine, compound, consolidate, contain, couple, cover, embody, embrace, encircle, encompass, fuse, interblend, interfuse, interlace, intermix, involve, join, meld, merge, mix, put together, take in, unite, weave, yoke
ASSOCIATED CONCEPTS: incorporate by reference

INCORPORATION *(Blend),* ***noun*** aggregation, amalgamation, assimilation, centralization, coalescence, combination, commixation, compound, consolidation, fusion, infusion, interfusion, interlacement, intermixture, minglement, mixture, unification, union
ASSOCIATED CONCEPTS: incorporation by reference
FOREIGN PHRASES: ***Verba relata hoc maxime operantur per referentiam, ut in eis inesse videntur.*** Words incorporated by reference have as great an effect through reference, as they are deemed to be inserted.

INCORPORATION *(Formation of a business entity),* ***noun*** association, chartering, coalition, *coniunctio, cooptatio,* establishment of a firm, formation of a company, formation of a corporation, formation of an organization, organization of a commercial concern, organization of a company, unification, union
ASSOCIATED CONCEPTS: certificate of incorporation, dissolution of a corporation

INCORPOREAL, *adjective* asomatous, bodiless, ethereal, immaterial, immateriate, impalpable, incorporal, intangible, nonphysical, not of material nature, spiritual, unbodied, unembodied, unfleshly, unsubstantial, unworldly, without body, without substance
ASSOCIATED CONCEPTS: incorporeal chattels, incorporeal hereditament
FOREIGN PHRASES: ***Haereditas, alia corporalis, alia incorporalis; corporalis est, quae tan gi potest et videri; incorporalis quae tangi non potest nec videri.*** An inheritance is either corporeal or incorporeal; corporeal is that which can be touched and seen; incorporeal is that which can neither be touched nor seen.

INCORRECT, *adjective* amiss, awry, erring, erroneous, fallacious, false, *falsus,* faulty, flawed, imperfect, imprecise, *improbus,* improper, inaccurate, inappropriate, inexact, miscalculated, misconstrued, misfigured, misjudged, misleading, mistaken, *perversus,* solecistic, solecistical, sophistic, sophistical, unfactual, ungrounded, unsound, untrue, unveracious, wrong

INCORRIGIBLE, *adjective* beyond help, beyond reform, chronic, cureless, hardened, hopeless, impenitent, incapable of correction, incurable, intractable, intransigent, inveterate, irreclaimable, irrecoverable, irredeemable, irreformable, irremediable, irreparable, lost, obdurate, obstinate, past cure, past hope, *perditus,* recalcitrant, recidivous, refractory, remorseless, reprobate, stubborn, toughened, unapologizing, uncontrite, uncontrollable, ungovernable, unmanageable, unreformable, unregretful, unregretting, unrepentant, unsubmissive, wicked
ASSOCIATED CONCEPTS: incorrigible child, incorrigible juvenile delinquent, multiple offender

INCORRUPTIBLE, *adjective* above suspicion, blameless, dependable, ethical, faultless, guiltless, having integrity, high-principled, honest, honorable, impeccable, *incorruptus,* inculpable, *integer,* irreproachable, just, meritorious, moral, reliable, reputable, respectable, *sanctus,* scrupulous, sinless, stanch, trustable, trustworthy, trusty, unable to be bought, unblemished, unbribable, uncorrupt, unerring, unimpeachable, untarnishable, untreacherous, unvenal, upright, virtuous

INCREASE, ***verb*** abound, accrue, accumulate, add on, add to, aggrandize, *amplificare,* amplify, annex, appreciate, augment, become larger, become greater, boost, branch out, broaden, build, burgeon, *crescere,* develop, *dilatare,* dilate, enlarge, escalate, expand, extend, flourish, gain, gain ground, *gliscere,* greaten, grow, inflate, lengthen, make greater, make larger, maximize, mount, multiply, progress, proliferate, prolong, protract, pullulate, raise, rise, skyrocket, spread, step up, stretch, supplement, surge, swell, thrive, widen
ASSOCIATED CONCEPTS: increase in value, increased cost, increased hazard, increased risk, increased valuation

INCREDIBLE, ***adjective*** absurd, beyond belief, doubtful, hard to believe, hardly credible, implausible, impossible, improbable, inconceivable, *incredibilis,* nonsensical, open to doubt, open to suspicion, preposterous, ridiculous, staggering, suspect, suspicious, unbelievable, unconvincing, unimaginable, unlikely, unthinkable
ASSOCIATED CONCEPTS: incredible statements, incredible testimony

INCREDULITY, ***noun*** amazement, denial, disbelief, discredit, distrust, distrustfulness, doubt, doubtfulness, dubiety, dubiousness, faithlessness, inability to accept, inability to believe, inconvincability, incredulousness, indisposition to admit, indisposition to believe, lack of belief, lack of faith, mistrust, mistrustfulness, question, reluctance to believe, skepticalness, skepticism, suspicion, suspiciousness, uncertainty, unwillingness to believe, want of faith

INCREDULOUS, ***adjective*** disposed to doubt, distrustful, doubtful, doubting, dubious, hard to convince, *incredulus,* indisposed to believe, mistrustful, questioning, skeptical, slow to believe, suspecting, suspicious, unbelieving, unconvinced, untrusting, unwilling to accept, without belief, without faith, wondering

INCREMENT, ***noun*** accretion, addition, augmentation, boost, enlargement, expansion, extension, gain, growth, increase, *incrementum,* raise, rise, supplement, surge
ASSOCIATED CONCEPTS: unearned increment

INCRIMINATE, ***verb*** accuse, allege, ascribe, ascribe blame, assign, attribute, blame, bring accusation, bring charges against, bring proceedings against, bring up on charges, cast blame upon, charge, charge with a crime, charge with an offense, complaint against, condemn, connect with a crime, criminate, denounce, draw in, enmesh, entangle, expose, find fault with, hold accountable, hold responsible, impeach, *impedire, implicare,* implicate, impute, impute guilt to, inculpate, indict, inform against, insinuate, involve, involve in criminal proceedings, involve in guilt, lay blame upon, lodge a complaint, make a party to, place the blame on, point the finger at, prefer charges, prosecute, providing evidence, providing information of a crime, proving, proving guilt, recriminate, stigmatize, *suspectum reddere*
ASSOCIATED CONCEPTS: Fifth Amendment, incriminating admission, incriminating circumstance, incriminatory statement, Miranda warnings, self-incrimination

INCRIMINATION, ***noun*** accusal, accusation, assignation, attribution, blame, calling to account, censure, charge, complaint, crimination, decrial, denouncement, impeachment, implication, imputation, imputation of wrongdoing, inculpation, indictment, recrimination, reproach, reproachful accusation
ASSOCIATED CONCEPTS: Fifth Amendment, incriminating admission, incriminating circumstance, incriminating statement, privilege against self-incrimination, privileges and immunities, self-incrimination
FOREIGN PHRASES: ***Accusare nemo se debet.*** No one is bound to accuse himself.

INCRIMINATORY, ***adjective*** accusatory, accusing, blaming, charging with guilt, condemnatory, condemning, convicting, criminative, criminatory, damaging, damnatory, damning, defamatory, denunciatory, disparaging, establishing guilt, harming, implicating, implicative, implicatory, imputative, imputing blame, inculpatory, involving in guilt
ASSOCIATED CONCEPTS: incriminatory admission, incriminatory statement, incriminatory testimony

INCUBATE, ***verb*** appear, arise, become distinct, breed, develop, give form to, grow, materialize, mature, nurture, produce, take form, transforming

INCULCATE, ***verb*** convince, direct, discipline, educate, guide, imbue, implant, impress, impress by repeated statement, impress upon the mind, imprint, *inculcare,* indoctrinate, infix, infuse, inspire, instill, instruct, lecture, plant, preach, prelect, press, propagandize, sermonize, teach, train, urge

INCULPABLE, ***adjective*** above suspicion, blameless, entirely defensible, exculpable, faultless, free from fault, free from guilt, guiltless, impeccable, *innocens,* innocent, *integer,* irreprehensible, irreproachable, not blamable, not guilty, pure, *sanctus,* sinless, unblamable, unblameworthy, uncorrupt, unerring, unimpeached, unreproached, unreproved, virtuous

INCULPATE, ***verb*** accuse, arraign, blame, bring to justice, charge, cite, criminate, impeach, implead, implicate, imply guilt, impute, incriminate, indict, institute proceedings, involve in blame, lodge a complaint, press charges, prosecute, recriminate

INCULPATION, ***noun*** accusation, blame, charging with fault, charging with guilt, condemnation, crimination, denunciation, faultfinding, implication, imputation, incrimination
ASSOCIATED CONCEPTS: confessions, exculpatory statements, inculpatory statements

INCULPATORY, ***adjective*** accusative, accusatory, accusing, blaming, charging with guilt, condemnatory, condemning, convicting, criminative, criminatory, damaging, damnatory, damning, denouncing, denunciatory, disparaging, establishing guilt, implicating, implicative, implicatory, imputative, imputing blame, incriminating, incriminatory, inculpating, injuring, involving in guilt
ASSOCIATED CONCEPTS: inculpatory admission, inculpatory evidence, inculpatory facts, inculpatory statements

INCUMBENT, ***noun*** bureaucrat, commissioner, dignitary, functionary, holder of an office, job holder, minister, occupant of an office, officebearer, officeholder, officer, official, person in authority
ASSOCIATED CONCEPTS: de facto incumbent, incumbent officer

INCUMBRANCE *(Burden),* ***noun*** deadweight, disadvantage, handicap, impediment, load, millstone, onus, oppression, weight

INCUMBRANCE *(Lien),* ***noun*** commitment, liability, imposition, obligation, restraint, title impairment
ASSOCIATED CONCEPTS: artisan's lien, encumbrance upon property, materialman's lien

INCUR, ***verb*** acquire, assume, bargain for, become liable for, become responsible for, bring on, bring upon oneself, contract, enter into, expose onself to, fall into, get, *incurrere,* lay oneself open to, meet with, run the chance, undertake
ASSOCIATED CONCEPTS: claim incurred, incur a debt, incur a liability, incur an obligation, incurred risk, incurring indebtedness, penalty incurred

INCUR COSTS, ***verb*** acknowledge the costs, answer for, assume liability for, be answerable for, be liable for, be responsible for, bear the expense, disburse, expend, lay out for, outlay, pay the costs
ASSOCIATED CONCEPTS: assessment of costs, bill of costs, inquest

INCUR EXPENSES, ***verb*** assume liability for, be responsible for, bear the expense, disburse, expend, outlay, pay for, pay the costs, pick up the tab

INCURABLE, ***adjective*** beyond hope, beyond remedy, deadly, difficult, fatal, grave, hopeless, inoperable, irredeemable, irremediable, irreparable, irretrievable, irreversible, little hope, malignant, no hope, past hope, serious, terminal, terminal case, unsalvageable

INCURSION, ***noun*** advancement, aggression, assault, attack, breach, encroachment, entrance, foray, forced entry, hostile entrance, *incursio,* infiltration, influx, infringement, ingress, ingression, inroad, introgression, intrusion, invasion, irruption, onslaught, overrun, overstepping, penetration, raid, rushing in, sortie, storm, violation

INDAGATION, ***noun*** analysis, audit, careful search, careful study, challenge, check, close inquiry, dissection, examination, exhaustive inquiry, exhaustive study, exploration, exploratory examination, inquest, inquiry, inquisition, inspection, interrogation, investigation, minute investigation, narrow search, observation, perquisition, perscrutation, perusal, probe, quest, questioning, research, review, rigorous search, scrutation, scrutiny, search, searching investigation, strict examination, strict inquiry, strict search, study, systematic search, test, trial

INDEBTED, ***adjective*** beholden, bound, bounden, devoted, encumbered, in arrears, in debt, legally obliged to repay, obaeratus, obligated, *obligatus,* obliged, owing, short of funds, thankful, unable to pay, under obligation
ASSOCIATED CONCEPTS: involuntary indebtedness, voluntary indebtedness

INDEBTEDNESS, ***noun*** arrearage, arrears, balance due outstanding debt, debt, delinquency, liability, obligation, outstanding balance, outstanding indebtedness, unpaid debt, unpaid indebtedness
ASSOCIATED CONCEPTS: bankruptcy laws, outstanding judgment

INDECENCY, ***noun*** impropriety, indecorousness, indelicacy, obnoxiousness, tastelessness, unseemingliness, untastefulness, vulgarity
ASSOCIATED CONCEPTS: indecent assault, indecent exposure, indecent liberties, indecent publications, lewd and lascivious conduct

INDECENT, ***adjective*** abusive, atrocious, bawdy, censurable, coarse, crude, debauched, degenerate, depraved, disreputable, dissolute, distasteful, embarrassing, foul, gross, immodest, immoral, improper, impure, inappropriate, indecorous, inelegant, lascivious, lecherous, lewd, libertine, libidinous, licentious, lickerish, loose, lubricous, lurid, lustful, noxious, objectionable, obnoxious, off-color, offensive, outrageous, perverted, pornographic, profane, profligate, promiscuous, racy, reprehensible, repulsive, ribald, risqué, salacious, salty, scandalous, scatological, scurrilous, shameful, shameless, suggestive, tawdry, unacceptable, unapt, unbecoming, unbefitting, unfitting, unseemly, unsuitable, vile, vulgar, wanton, X-rated

INDECIPHERABLE, ***adjective*** abstract, abstruse, arcane, baffling, blurred, complex, complicated, concealed, cryptic, difficult, effaced, enigmatic, erased, esoteric, illegible, impenetrable, incomprehensible, indistinct, indistinguishable, inexplicable, inextricable, inscrutable, intricate, involved, mysterious, nebulous, oblique, obscure, puzzling, recondite, tangled, unclear, undecipherable, undistinguishable, unexplainable, unfathomable, unrecognizable, vague, veiled

INDECISION, ***noun*** changeableness, dilemma, doubt, doubtfulness, dubiety, dubiousness, dubitancy, *dubitatio,* dubitation, equivocalness, fickleness, fluctuation, *haesitatio,* hesitancy, hesitation, inability to decide, incertitude, *inconstantia,* indetermination, infirmity of purpose, instability, irresoluteness, irresolution, lack of certainty, lack of decision, oscillation, quandary, tendency to change the mind, tendency to waver, uncertainty, unsettled opinion, unsteadiness, unsureness, vacillation

INDECISIVE, ***adjective*** careful, cautious, changeable, circumspect, dubious, equivocal, fickle, hesitant, irresolute, lacking leadership, noncommitted, oscillating, prudent, unable to act, unable to decide, uncertain, uncertainty, uncommitted, unsure, vacillating

INDEED, ***adverb*** above all, absolutely, actually, admittedly, affirmative, all the more, as a matter of fact, assuredly, by all manner of means, by all means, certainly, chiefly, clearly, decidedly, decisively, definitely, demonstrably, distinctly, dominantly, especially, first of all, for certain, for the most part, in chief, in effect, in fact, in point of fact, in reality, in the first place, in the main, in truth, indeed, mainly, manifestly, most assuredly, most certainly, mostly, noticeably, observably, obviously, particularly, positively, precisely, predominantly, primarily, principally, surely, to be sure, truly, unequivocally, unmistakably, unquestionably, without a doubt

INDEFATIGABLE, ***adjective*** active, assiduous, avidity, busy, conscientious, determined, diligent, dogged, energetic, industrious, inexhaustible, intense, laborious, meticulous, painstaking, patient, persevering, persistent, pertinacious, relentless, sedulous, slavish, spirited, steadfast, steady, strenuous, stubborn, tenacious, unabating, unfaltering, unflagging, unflinching, unremitting, untiring, unwavering, vigorous, weariless

INDEFEASIBLE, ***adjective*** binding, confirmed, entrenched, established, immutable, imperishable, imprescriptible, *in perpetuum ratus,* inalienable, incapable of being defeated, incapable of being revoked, incontestable, incontrovertible, indestructible, indissoluble, indubitable, ineradicable, inextinguishable, insusceptible of change, intransmutable, invariable, inviolable, irrefragable, irremovable, irreversible, irrevocable, nonreversible, not forfeitable, not to be abrogated, not to be annulled, not to be made void, permanent, reverseless, settled, unalterable, unchallengeable, unchangeable, undefeatable, undeniable, undisputable, unquestionable

ASSOCIATED CONCEPTS: indefeasible estate, indefeasible interest, indefeasible title, indefeasibly vested

INDEFENSIBLE, *adjective* accessible, assailable, capable of being conquered, capable of being overcome, conquerable, defenseless, exposed, helpless, inexcusable, inexpiable, insupportable, pregnable, *quod defendi non potest,* unfortified, unguarded, unjustifiable, unprotected, untenable, unwarrantable, vincible, vulnerable

INDEFINABLE, *adjective* abstruse, beyond expression, confusing, cryptic, difficult to explain, difficult to translate, difficult to understand, enigmatic, enigmatical, hard to explain, hard to translate, hard to understand, impenetrable, impossible to explain, impossible to translate, impossible to understand, incomprehensible, indescribable, inexplicable, inexpressible, inscrutable, mysterious, obscure, opaque, perplexing, puzzling, unaccountable, unclear, unfathomable, unplain, untranslatable

INDEFINITE, *adjective* alterable, ambiguous, *ambiguus,* amorphic, amorphous, barely seen, blurred, blurry, boundless, broad, changeable, cloudy, controvertible, cryptic, debatable, dim, doubtful, dubious, *dubius,* enigmatic, enigmatical, equivocal, evasive, faint, formless, ill-defined, imperspicuous, imprecise, in doubt, *incertus,* indecisive, indeterminate, indistinct, indistinguishable, inexact, inexplicit, mysterious, nondescript, nonspecific, not positive, not sharp, obscure, opaque, open to question, oracular, questionable, shapeless, subject to change, suppositional, theoretical, unascertained, unbounded, uncertain, unclear, undecided, undefined, undetermined, undiscernible, unexact, unintelligible, unlimited, unresolved, unsettled, unspecified, unstable, unsure, untold, vague

ASSOCIATED CONCEPTS: indefinite contract, indefinite failure of issue, indefinite liability, indefinite sentence

INDELIBLE, *adjective* changeless, deep, deep-felt, durable, enduring, fadeless, fast, firm, fixed, fixed in the mind, haunting, immovable, immutable, imperishable, impressed on the mind, incapable of being deleted, indefeasible, *indelibilis,* indestructible, indissoluble, ineffaceable, ineradicable, inerasable, inextinguishable, ingrained, insoluble, irremovable, irreversible, irrevocable, keen, lasting, memorable, nagging, never to be erased from the mind, never to be forgotten, nonperishable, penetrating, permanent, persevering, persistent, persisting, pervading, pervasive, piercing, plaguing, poignant, profound, recurrent, reverseless, rooted, *sempiternus,* stable, stamped on one's memory, steadfast, unalterable, unchangeable, undestroyable, unerasable, unfading, unforgettable, unforgotten, unyielding, vivid

ASSOCIATED CONCEPTS: indeligible public interests in property, indeligible ruse

INDEMNIFICATION, *noun* amends, compensation, indemnity, monetary remuneration, payment, recompense, redemption, reimbursement, remuneration, reparation, repayment, requital, requitement, restitution, restoration, return, satisfaction

INDEMNIFY, *verb* answer for, compensate, compensate for injury, compensate for loss, compensate for loss sustained, *damnum restituere, damnum sarcire,* give back, give satisfaction, grant monetary compensation, guarantee, insure, make good, make good against anticipated loss, make reparation, make restitution, make up, offer compensation, offer reparation, offer satisfaction, pay, pay back, pay compensation, pay reparations, recompense, recompense for past loss, redeem, refund, reimburse, remunerate, repay, requite, restore, return money paid out, save harmless, secure against damage, secure against loss

ASSOCIATED CONCEPTS: subrogate

INDEMNITY, *noun* act of holding harmless, amends, assurance against loss, compensation, full satisfaction, indemnification, *lex oblivionis,* payment, protection against loss, recompense, recoupment, redemption, refund, reimbursement, remuneration, repayment, requitement, restitution, restoration, return, security, security against damage, security against loss, setoff, vindication

ASSOCIATED CONCEPTS: contract of indemnity, covenant of indemnity, indemnity against liability, indemnity against loss, indemnity agreement, indemnity bond, indemnity insurance, indemnity mortgage, indemnity policy, indemnity reinsurance, limitation of indemnity, subrogation

INDEMONSTRABLE, *adjective* containing variables, doubting, equivocal, incalculable, indecisive, inexplicit, irresolute, irresponsible, not ascertainable, not provable, skeptical, uncertain, unconfirmable, unconvinced, uncountable, unprovable, unsure, unverifiable

ASSOCIATED CONCEPTS: indemonstrable principles

INDENTURE, *noun* agreement, agreement to work, apprenticeship agreement, arrangement, commitment, compact, contract, contract to work, contractual obligation, contractual statement, covenant, deed of agreement, instrument, mutual agreement, mutual undertaking, pact, *pactum,* stipulation, undertaking

INDENTURED, *adjective* apprenticed, articled, bound by agreement, bound by contract, contracted, engaged, enslaved, obligated, obliged, promised, tied down, under obligation

ASSOCIATED CONCEPTS: indentured apprentice

INDEPENDENCE, *noun* authority, authorization, autonomy, delegation, disassociation, disconnection, emancipation, freedom, liberty, license, not controlled, prerogative, privilege, self-determination, self-direction, sovereignty, unencumbered, unrestraint, unshackled

INDEPENDENT, *adjective* autarkic, autonomous, detached, disconnected, dissociated, free, freelance, irrelative, *liber,* masterless, neutral, nonpartisan, self-governing, self-reliant, self-subsistent, self-supporting, *solutus,* sovereign, unaffiliated, unallied, unassociated, unattached, unbound, unbridled, unchecked, uncommitted, unconnected, unconquered, uncontrolled, uncurbed, unencumbered, unenslaved, unenthralled, unfettered, unhindered, uninfluenced, unreined, unshackled, unsubjected, unvanquished

ASSOCIATED CONCEPTS: independent advice, independent agreement, independent cause, independent contractor, independent covenant, independent duty, independent negligence, independent tortfeasor, independently established

FOREIGN PHRASES: ***Illud quod alteri unitur extinguitur neque amplius per se vacare licet.*** That which is united to another is extinguished, nor can it be independent.

INDESCRIBABLE, *adjective* astonishing, astronomical, beyond words, dazzling, delightful, extraordinary, incommunicable, inconceivable, incredible, indefinite, inexpressible, miraculous, nondescript, off the charts, remarkable, striking, stunning, unheard of, unspeakable, unusual, wonderful, wondrous

INDESTRUCTIBILITY, *noun* *aplomb,* ceaselessness, changelessness, constancy, continuance, continuity, durability, durableness, endlessness, endurance, eternalness, everlastingness, immortality, immutability, imperishability, indefeasibility, indelibility, indissolubility, ineradicableness, inerasableness, insusceptibility to change, interminability, lastingness, permanence, perpetuity, stability, steadiness, unalterability, unchangeability
ASSOCIATED CONCEPTS: indestructible trust

INDESTRUCTIBLE, *adjective* abiding, durable, endless, enduring, everlasting, fadeless, hardy, imperishable, indefeasible, indelible, indissoluble, ineffaceable, inerasable, inextinguishable, insusceptible, invulnerable, irrevocable, lasting, nonperishable, perennial, permanent, perpetual, *perpetuus,* persevering, persisting, *quod everti non potest,* reliable, sturdy, tenacious, tough, undestroyable, undying, unfading, unyielding
ASSOCIATED CONCEPTS: indestructible trust

INDETERMINATE, *adjective* ambiguous, *anceps,* boundless, cryptic, *dubius,* endless, equivocal, featureless, fluctuant, fluid, formless, hazy, ill-defined, immeasurable, in a state of uncertainty, in doubt, inarticulated, incalculable, *incertus,* inconclusive, indefinite, indistinct, infinite, interminable, limitless, measureless, nonspecific, not ascertained, not designated, not fixed, not fixed in extent, not made certain, not particularly designated, not precise, not settled, obscure, open, open to question, shapeless, speculative, termless, unbounded, uncertain, unclear, undecided, undefined, unfathomable, unfixed, unlimited, unmeasured, unordered, unresolved, unsettled, unspecified, vague, without bound, without end, without limit, without measure
ASSOCIATED CONCEPTS: indeterminate damages, indeterminate penalty, indeterminate punishment, indeterminate sentence

INDETERMINATION, *noun* ambiguousness, blurred line, blurry line, borderline decision, boundless variables, clouded choices, confusion, doubtfulness, equivocalness, immeasurable choices, imprecise, in a state of uncertainty, in doubt, inconclusiveness, indefiniteness, indefinity, indeterminateness, indistinctness, inexactness, inexplicitness, infiniteness, interminableness, lacking specificity, limitlessness, nebulousness, obscurity, speculation, uncertainness

INDEX *(Catalog),* ***noun*** earmark, enumeration, indicant, indicator, list, listing, listing of contents, mark, sign

INDEX *(Docket),* ***verb*** categorize, codify, file, submit

INDEX *(Gauge),* ***noun*** measure, guide, scale

INDEX *(Relate),* ***verb*** catalog, class, classify, document, enumerate, group, inventory, itemize, list, specify, record, supply or furnish with reference

INDICANT, *noun* augury, auspice, badge, beacon, brand, caution, characteristic, cipher, clue, cue, diagnostic, emblem, ensign, example, exponent, figure, flag, foretoken, hint, implication, index, indication, indicator, landmark, manifestation, mark, note, omen, pointer, portent, presage, prognostic, representation, representative, sign, signal, signature, signboard, stamp, suggestion, symbol, symptom, token, trademark, visible token, watchword

INDICATE, *verb* advert to, allude to, augur, be a sign of, be a token of, bespeak, betoken, brief, call attention to, connote, convey, direct, direct attention to, evidence, evince, express briefly, express generally, foretoken, give a signal, guide, highlight, hint, imply, index, *indicare,* insinuate, intimate, make necessary, make needed, mark out, point out, point to, portend, presage, show, signal, signalize, *significare,* signify, sketch, stand for, suggest, touch on

INDICATION, *noun* allusion, augury, auspice, badge, brand, clue, connotation, cue, emblem, evidence, evincement, exponent, foretoken, guide, hint, implication, index, indicant, indicator, *indicium,* innuendo, insinuation, intimation, mark, marker, mention, monition, note, omen, pointer, portent, premonitor, premonitory sign, presage, prognostic, prompt, reference, sign, signal, *significatio,* signpost, suggestion, symbol, symptom, token, trace, *vestigium,* warning

INDICATOR, *noun* attestant, attester, augury, auspice, badge, beacon, clue, cue, emblem, ensign, flag, foreshadowing, harbinger, herald, hint, index, informant, informer, landmark, mark, note, pointer, precursor, prognostic, semaphore, sign, stamp, symbol, symptom, token, warning, witness

INDICIA, *noun* characteristic marks, characteristics, evidence, expressions, features, hints, indications, manifestations, marks, means of recognition, signs, symbols, tokens
ASSOCIATED CONCEPTS: indicia of ownership

INDICT, *verb* accuse, blame, bring a formal accusation against, call to account, charge, charge with offense, charge with the commission of a crime, formally charge, formally charge with a crime, implicate, incriminate, inculpate, lodge a complaint, make formal accusation against, *nomen deferre,* prefer charges

INDICTMENT, *noun* accusal, *accusatio,* accusation, allegation, castigation, charge, complaint, *crimen,* delation, denunciation, formal accusation, grand jury's accusation, *libellus,* main charge, presentment, reproach, written accusation
ASSOCIATED CONCEPTS: arraignment, counts of an indictment, felony complaint, felony information, grand jury, indictable offense, motion to quash, no true bill, plea, presentment, true bill

INDIFFERENCE, *noun* aloofness, apathy, blankness, coldness, coolness, detachment, disinterestedness, disregard, impassiveness, imperturbability, inattention, inconsideration, insouciance, laxity, lukewarmness, neglect, negligence, nonchalance, nonobservance, unconcern

INDIFFERENT, *adjective* aloof, callous, casual, derelict, disinterested, dispassionate, distant, fair, faithless, heedless, impartial, impassible, imperfect, impervious, inactive, inappreciable, inattentive, inconsequential, incurious, insensate, insignificant, insipid, insouciant, languid, lax, listless, marginal, mediocre, middling, moderate, negligent, neutral, nonchalant, not caring, obdurate, oblivious, ordinary, otiose, passable, passive, perfunctory, phlegmatic, poor, reckless, remiss, slipshod, thoughtless, tolerable, unbiased, unconcerned, uninquisitive, uninterested, unjaundiced, unmindful, unprejudiced, unresponsive, usual, vapid
ASSOCIATED CONCEPTS: disinterested party, impartiality

INDIGENCE, ***noun*** bare subsistence, dearth, destitution, egestas, embarrassment, impecuniosity, impoverishment, *inopia,* insolvency, insufficiency, insufficient income, *mendicitas,* narrow means, necessitousness, need, neediness, needy circumstances, pauperism, pennilessness, penury, poor circumstances, poorness, poverty, privation, scarcity, want

INDIGNATION, ***adjective*** adversarial, adverse, antithetical, at odds, averse, dead set against, differing, disagreeing, disinclined, fractious, hesitant, hostile, not feeling like, not in favor of, not in the mood, not inclined, obdurate, opposed, queasy, recalcitrant, reluctant, resistant, righteousness, squeamish, unwilling
ASSOCIATED CONCEPTS: inequality and indignation, moral indignation, righteous indignation

INDIRECT, ***adjective*** allusive, ambagious, backhanded, circuitous, circumambulating, circumlocutory, covert, crooked, desultory, deviating, deviatory, devious, *devius,* digressing, digressive, excursive, hidden, implicit, labyrinthine, meandering, *non rectus,* oblique, *obliquus,* out of the way, periphrastic, periphrastical, rambling, roundabout, serpentine, sidelong, sinuous, tacit, tortuose, turning, twisting, understood, unexpressed, vagrant, wandering, winding, zigzag
ASSOCIATED CONCEPTS: indirect benefit, indirect evidence, indirect interest, indirect notice, indirect result, indirect tax, indirect testimony

INDIRECTION *(Deceitfulness),* ***noun*** concealment of truth, cozenage, craft, craftiness, cunning, deceit, deception, deviousness, dishonesty, disingenuity, disingenuousness, dissimulation, duplicity, falsehood, falseness, fraud, fraudulency, guile, hypocrisy, improbity, insincerity, intrigue, lack of candidness, lack of conscience, lack of probity, mendaciousness, mendacity, obliqueness, obliquity, perfidiousness, perfidy, perversion of truth, pretense, prevarication, slyness, underhandedness, unstraightforwardness, untrustworthiness, untruthfulness

INDIRECTION *(Indirect action),* ***noun*** aberrance, aberrancy, circuitous action, circuitous route, circuitousness, circuity, circumflexion, circumlocution, crookedness, departure, deviation, deviousness, digression, divagation, obliquation, obliqueness, obliquity, periphrasis, roundabout action, roundaboutness, straying, swerve, unstraightforward action, zigzag

INDISCERNIBLE, ***adjective*** camouflaged, concealed, delitescent, disguised, evanescent, hidden, impalpable, imperceptible, inconspicuous, indistinguishable, invisible, screened, unapparent, unbeholdable, undiscoverable, unnoticeable, unperceivable, unrecognizable, unregarded, unseeable, veiled

INDISCREET, ***adjective*** careless, culpable, hasty, heedless, ill-judged, impetuous, impolitic, improvident, imprudent, impulsive, incautious, inconsiderate, indiscriminating, inexpedient, injudicious, inopportune, lacking prudence, misadvised, precipitate, thoughtless, uncritical, undiscerning, unpolitic, unprofessional, unreflecting, unselective, unsensible, unsound, unthinking, unwise

INDISCRETION, ***noun*** blunder, carelessness, error, ill judgment, impoliticness, imprudence, *impudentia,* incaution, incautiousness, incircumspection, injudiciousness, lack of circumspection, lack of consideration, lack of judgment, misconduct, misjudgment, misstep, mistake, offense, *os impudens,* poor judgment, rashness, recklessness, slip, tactlessness, thoughtlessness, uncircumspection, unwariness, unwiseness

INDISCRIMINATE, ***adjective*** blanket, broad, comprehensive, designless, haphazard, immethodical, not choosy, not selective, orderless, promiscuous, *promiscuus,* random, systemless, unaimed, uncritical, undifferentiating, undirected, unmethodical, unorganized, unparticular, unspecific, unsystematic

INDISPENSABLE, ***adjective*** basic, called for, cardinal, central, compulsory, critical, crucial, dictated, essential, exigent, fundamental, high-priority, imperative, important, imposed, integral, irreplaceable, key, main, major, mandatory, *necessarius,* necessary, necessitated, needed, obligatory, of importance, pivotal, pressing, primary, required, requisite, significant, unavoidable, urgent, vital, wanted
ASSOCIATED CONCEPTS: indispensable evidence, indispensable parties

INDISPENSABLE PARTY, ***noun*** added party, compulsory defendant, compulsory party, critical added party, essential party, imperative party, mandatory party, obligatory party, required party, requisite party, vital party
ASSOCIATED CONCEPTS: indispensable party to an action, motion to dismiss for failure to join an indispensable party

INDISPOSED, ***adjective*** adverse, antipathetic to, at loggerheads to, at odds, averse, dead set against, differing, disagreeing, disinclined, fractious, hesitant, hostile, loath, obdurate, opposed, out of commission, out of order, out of sorts, recalcitrant, reluctant, resistant

INDISPUTABLE, ***adjective*** absolute, apodictic, assured, authoritative, axiomatic, believable, beyond a shadow of a doubt, beyond dispute, categorical, certain, clear, conclusive, decided, decisive, definite, definitive, demonstrable, demonstrated, determinate, evident, explicit, factual, impregnable, inappealable, incontestable, incontrovertible, indefeasible, indisputable, indubious, indubitable, infallible, irrefutable, manifest, obvious, official, palpable, positive, proven, real, reliable, self-evident, solid, unassailable, unconditional, undeniable, undisputed, undoubting, unequivocal, unimpeachable, unmistakable, unmitigated, unqualified, unquestionable, unrefutable, unreserved, unshakable, well-founded

INDISTINCT, ***adjective*** ambiguous, blurred, blurry, cryptic, delitescent, dim, dusky, enigmatic, enigmatical, faded, faint, filmy, foggy, half-seen, hazy, ill-defined, illegible, imperceptible, inaudible, incomprehensible, indistinguishable, lacking clarity, lacking precision, misty, muffled, mysterious, nebulous, nubilous, *obscurus,* out of focus, *parum clarus, perplexus,* smoky, unclear, undecipherable, undefined, unintelligible, unplain, unrecognizable, vague, weak

INDISTINCTNESS, ***noun*** blur, blurriness, delitescence, delitescency, dimness, dullness, faintness, filminess, fog, fogginess, fuzziness, gloom, grayness, haziness, imperceptibility, inaudibility, indefiniteness, indistinguishability, mistiness, murkiness, mysteriousness, nebulosity, obscuration, obscurity, opacity, paleness, poor visiblity, shadow, shadowiness, smokiness, unclearness, unplainness, vagueness

INDISTINGUISHABLE, ***adjective*** alike, balanced, coequal, coincident, coinciding, collateral, comparable, corresponding, duplicate, equal, equivalent, exact, exactly alike, exactly the same, hard to make out, homogeneous, identical, indiscernible, interchangeable, like, matching, similar, uniform, without distinction

INDIVIDUAL, *adjective* detached, deviating, different, differentiated, discrete, disjoined, disjunct, distinct, distinctive, distinguishable, exceptional, extracted, extraordinary, independent, individualized, isolated, nonconforming, nonuniform, particular, *proprius,* rare, separate, separated, single, singular, *singularis,* sole, solitary, special, unallied, unannexed, unassimilated, unassociated, unattached, unclassifiable, uncommon, unconnected, unconventional, unimitated, unique, unjoined, unrelated, unusual
ASSOCIATED CONCEPTS: individual capacity, individual causes of action, individual damages, individual debts, individual liability

INDIVIDUAL, *noun* autonomous being, being, body, character, distinct indivisible entity, human being, individuality, integer, monad, monas, one, organism, particular one, party, person, person full of character, personage, personality
ASSOCIATED CONCEPTS: individual capacity, individual liability, individual property, individual rights

INDIVIDUAL RIGHTS, *noun* authority, authorization, basic rights, civil rights, constitutional rights, fundamental rights, inalienable rights, just claims, justification, legal power, power, privilege, right, sanction, vested interest
ASSOCIATED CONCEPTS: freedom, individualism, Libertarianism

INDIVIDUALISM, *noun* attribute, badge, brand, character, characteristic, credentials, differential, disposition, distinctive feature, earmark, feature, identity, idiosyncrasy, independence, individuality, leaning, lineament, mark, nature, originality, particularity, peculiarity, personality, property, quality, self-determination, self-identity, singularity, specialty, temperament, tendency, trait, type

INDIVIDUALITY, *noun* being, character, characteristic, curiosity, definiteness, diagnostic, difference, distinction, eccentricity, entity, feature, identity, idiosyncrasy, individual, integrality, mannerism, nonconformity, oneness, originality, particularity, peculiarity, person, personality, property, quirk, singleness, singularity, specialty, specific quality, temperament, trait, uniqueness

INDIVISIBLE, *adjective* close, impartible, incapable of being divided, incapable of being separated, indiscerptible, *individuus,* inseparable, inseverable, nondivisible, one, tenacious, unbreakable, undividable, united, unsunderable
ASSOCIATED CONCEPTS: indivisible contract, indivisible injury, indivisible ownership of property

INDOCTRINATE, *verb* beat into, beat into the head, brainwash, brainwash with propaganda, convert, convince, drill into, drum into, get into the head of, imbue, implant, impregnate, impress upon the mind, inculcate, indoctrinate, infect, infix, influence, infuse, ingrain, instill, persuade, pound into head, program, subvert, train, urge, win over
ASSOCIATED CONCEPTS: indoctrinating jurors

INDOLENT, *adjective* apathetic, cunctative, *deses,* dilatory, idle, *ignavus,* inactive, indifferent, indisposed to action, *iners,* lackadaisical, lacking vigor, laggard, languid, lax, lazy, leaden, lethargic, listless, loafing, motionless, negligent, otiose, passive, phlegmatic, procrastinative, shiftless, slack, slothful, sluggish, stagnant, supine, torpid, unenterprising

INDOMITABLE, *adjective* bold, brave, courageous, dauntless, defiant, determined, doughty, energetic, fearless, firm, forceful, forcible, formidable, hardy, impregnable, incapable of being subdued, indefatigable, indocile, *indomitus,* inextinguishable, insuperable, insurmountable, intractable, *invictus,* invincible, irrepressible, irresistible, masterful, omnipotent, overpowering, overwhelming, persevering, plucky, potent, powerful, puissant, quenchless, recalcitrant, redoubtable, refractory, resisting, resistless, resolute, resolved, solid, sound, stable, stalwart, stanch, stiff, stout, strong, stubborn, tough, unbeatable, unconquerable, undaunted, unflinching, ungovernable, unmanageable, unquenchable, unruly, unshrinking, unsubduable, unsubmissive, unwavering, unyielding, valiant, vigorous

INDORSE, *verb* accredit, acquiesce in, advocate, affirm, allow, assent to, assist, authenticate, authorize, certify, commend, concur in, confirm, confirm officially, consent to, *consignare,* cosign, countenance, countersign, encourage, guarantee, initial, inscribe one's signature, lend one's name to, make valid, *praestare,* ratify, recommend, sanction, second, sign, sign one's name on, stand by, subscribe to, support, sustain, undersign, underwrite, uphold, validate, vouch for
ASSOCIATED CONCEPTS: indorse a check, indorse a note, indorse a warrant, indorse an instrument

INDORSEMENT, *noun* acceptance, accord, acquiescence, *adfirmatio,* affirmance, agreement, approbation, approval, assent, authorization, backing, certification, championship, compliance, *comprobatio,* concurrence, *confrmatio,* confirmation, consent, encouragement, esteem, favor, liking, partisanship, permission, ratification, sanction, sponsorship, stamp of approval, support, warrant
ASSOCIATED CONCEPTS: conditional indorsement, indorsement for collection, indorsement in blank, indorsement in due course, indorsement of an instrument, indorsement without recourse, subsequent indorsement

INDUBIOUS, *adjective* absolute, ascertained, assured, attested, certain, confident, convinced, definite, demonstrable, demonstrated, doubtless, factual, foolproof, guaranteed, incontestable, irrefutable, official, past dispute, positive, safe, satisfied, sure, tested, tried, uncontested, undeniable, undoubtful, unequivocal, unshakable, verifiable, without doubt, without question

INDUCE, *verb* actuate, *adducere,* affect, be responsible, begin, bring, bring about, bring on, bring to pass, call forth, cause, coax, conduce, convince, create, develop, drive, effect, effectuate, encourage, enlist, entice, exercise influence over, generate, goad, hasten, impel, *impellere,* incite, *inducere,* influence, inspire, instigate, inveigle, kindle, lead one to, lure, motivate, move, obtain, occasion, originate, persuade, precipitate, prevail on, prevail upon, produce, prompt, propel, provoke, rouse, spur, stimulate, sway, talk into, urge
ASSOCIATED CONCEPTS: fraud in inducement, induce to sign a contract, inducement, inducing a breach of contract, inducing perjury, inducing trade, libel, material inducement, undue influence

INDUCEMENT, *noun* allurement, attraction, blandishment, *causa,* cause, consideration, drive, encouragement, enticement, exhortation, fillip, goad, *incitamentum*, incitation, incitement, influence, *inlecebra,* inspiration, instigation, persuasion, persuasiveness, pressure, prompting, provocation, provocative, stimulant, stimulater, stimulation, stimulative, stimulus, urging
ASSOCIATED CONCEPTS: fraud in the inducement, inducement to purchase, material inducement

INDUCT, *verb* admit, appoint, assign, bring in, call up, commission, conscript, delegate, employ, engage, give entrance to, impress, *inaugurare,* inaugurate, initiate, install, instate, introduce, introduce into office, invest, license, name, nominate, ordain, place in office, post, prepare, recruit, start up, usher in

INDULGE, *verb* accommodate, acquiesce, allow, bear with, do a favor, do service for, endure, entertain, favor, flatter, fulfill, give in to, give license to, go along with, humor, jumps into, minister to, pamper, pander to, permit, satiate, satisfy, spoil, tolerate, yield to

INDULGENCE, *noun* accordance, acquiescence, allowance, approval, benevolence, *benignitas,* clearance, clemency, compassion, favor, forgiveness, generosity, generousness, grant, gratification, gratification of desire, humoring, inabstinence, *indulgentia,* leave, lenience, leniency, lenity, license, magnanimity, obligingness, pampering, pardon, patience, permission, quarter, sanction, sufferance, tolerance, toleration, *venia,* vouchsafement

INDURATE, *adjective* become fixed, become hardened, calcify, callous, chilled, cold, concrete, conditioned, hard, harden, hardened, ossified, petrified, rigid, toughen, unyielding, vitreous, vitrify

INDUSTRIAL, *adjective* automated, commercial, engaged in business, engaged in traffic, factory-made, industrialized, machine-made, manufactural, manufactured, manufactured for sale, mass-produced, mechanical, mechanized, mercantile, relating to traffic, standardized, technical, technological
ASSOCIATED CONCEPTS: industrial accident, industrial board, industrial commission, industrial disease, industrial dispute, industrial insurance, industrial uses

INDUSTRIOUS, *adjective* active, *adsiduus,* aggressive, ardent, assiduous, busily engaged, busy, dedicated, determined, devoted, diligent, eager, earnest, energetic, enthusiastic, hard working, indefatigable, *industrius,* intent, laborious, never idle, operose, painstaking, persevering, persistent, purposeful, sedulous, *sedulus,* sleepless, steadfast, steady, studious, tenacious, thorough, tireless, unceasing, undeviating, unfaltering, unflagging, unrelaxing, unremitting, unsleeping, unswerving, untiring, unwavering, unyielding, zealous

INDUSTRY *(Activity),* ***noun*** *adsiduitas,* alacrity, application, ardor, assiduity, assiduousness, attention, bustle, busyness, constancy, determination, devotedness, devotion, diligence, *diligentia,* drive, dynamism, eagerness, earnestness, effort, employment, endeavor, endurance, energy, enterprise, enthusiasm, exertion, hard work, indefatigability, *industria,* intentness, labor, laboriousness, occupation, perseverance, persistence, pursuance, pursuit, sedulity, sedulousness, steadfastness, stir, strenuousness, tenacity, toil, vigor, vim, work, zeal, zealousness

INDUSTRY *(Business),* ***noun*** enterprise, establishment, manufacture, mercantile business, métier, production, profession, pursuit, trade, undertaking, work
ASSOCIATED CONCEPTS: engage in industry, industrywide contract

INEBRIATION, *noun* alcoholism, bacchanalianism, bibulosity, bibulousness, dipsomania, drunkenness, ebrietas, inebriety, influence of liquor, insobriety, intemperance, intoxication, potation
ASSOCIATED CONCEPTS: driving while intoxicated, drunken driving, under the influence of alcohol

INEFFABLE, *adjective* amazing, astounding, awe-inspiring, awesome, beyond expression, beyond words, fearful, great, impossible to describe, impossible to express, incommunicable, inconceivable, incredible, *incredibilis,* indefinable, indescribable, inexpressible, *infandus,* marvelous, miraculous, mysterious, nameless, not explainable, not expressible, not to be spoken, overwhelming, sacred, splendid, staggering, strange, terrific, unable to be expressed, unable to be spoken, undefinable, unheard, unimaginable, unmentionable, unnamable, unpronounceable, unspeakable, untranslatable, unutterable
ASSOCIATED CONCEPTS: ineffable accident

INEFFECTIVE, *adjective* abortive, barren, disabled, effete, emasculated, feckless, feeble, figurehead, fruitless, futile, gainless, good for nothing, impotent, inadequate, incompetent, indecisive, ineffectual, inefficacious, inept, inoperative, insufficient, inutile, *inutilis,* invalid, *invalidus,* lame, neutralized, nugatory, null, powerless, profitless, sterile, unauthoritative, unavailing, unfruitful, uninfluential, unoperative, unproductive, unprofitable, unserviceable, unsuccessful, useless, vain, void, weak, withered, without effect, without weight, worthless
ASSOCIATED CONCEPTS: ineffective restriction

INEFFECTIVE ASSISTANCE OF COUNSEL, *noun* deficient performance by counsel resulting in prejudice, incompetent representation, ineffective representation, legally insufficient representation, representation below acceptable standards, unreasonably poor legal representation
ASSOCIATED CONCEPTS: Sixth Amendment Assistance of Counsel Clause, legal malpractice

INEFFECTUAL, *adjective* abortive, barren, effete, emasculated, feckless, feeble, figurehead, fruitless, futile, gainless, good for nothing, idle, impotent, inadequate, incompetent, indecisive, ineffective, inefficacious, inept, inoperative, insufficient, inutile, *inutilis,* invalid, *invalidus,* lame, neutralized, nugatory, null, powerless, profitless, sterile, unauthoritative, unavailing, unempowered, unfruitful, uninfluential, unoperative, unproductive, unprofitable, unserviceable, unsuccessful, useless, vain, void, weak, withered, without effect, without weight, worthless

INEFFICACIOUS, *adjective* barren, feeble, for naught, futile, idle, impotent, inadequate, incapable, incompetent, ineffective, ineffectual, inefficient, inept, infertile, inutile, profitless, sterile, to no avail, to no purpose, unavailing, unproductive, unprofitable, unrewarding, unsuccessful, unyielding, valueless, weak, worthless

INEFFICACY, *noun* disability, disablement, failure, feebleness, forcelessness, helplessness, impotence, inability, inadequacy, incapability, incapacitation, incapacity, incompetence, incompetency, ineffectiveness, ineffectuality, ineffectualness, inefficaciousness, inefficiency, insufficiency, lack of power, lack of strength, powerlessness, unfruitfulness, unskillfulness, weakness

INEFFICIENT, ***adjective*** abortive, careless, counterproductive, disorganized, feckless, fruitless, futile, hamstrung, improvident, incompetent, ineffectual, inefficacious, inefficient, inept, inexpedient, limited, pointless, prodigal, profitless, unavailing, unproductive, unprofitable, unqualified, unsuccessful, useless, weak, worthless

INELEGANT, ***adjective*** awkward, base, boorish, churlish, cloddish, coarse, common, crass, crude, earthy, graceless, gross, homely, homespun, ill-bred, ill-mannered, improper, in bad taste, indecorous, indelicate, *inelegans, inurbanus, invenustus,* lacking elegance, lacking good taste, lacking grace, lacking refinement, low, offensive, ribald, rough, rude, rustic, tasteless, uncourtly, uncouth, uncultivated, uncultured, undignified, ungainly, ungenteel, ungraceful, unkempt, unmannerly, unpolished, unrefined, unseemly, untasteful, vulgar, without taste

INELIGIBLE, ***adjective*** cast out, disallowed, disapproved, disentitled, disqualified, eliminated, excluded, expelled, improper, inadmissible, inappropriate, inapt, *inopportunus,* kept out, not considered, not eligible, objectionable, out of the question, outcast, rejected, unacceptable, unadapted, unchosen, undesirable, unentitled, unequipped, unfit, unfitted, unfitting, unqualified, unsuitable, unsuited, unwanted
ASSOCIATED CONCEPTS: disability, ineligible to run for political office

INEPT *(Inappropriate),* ***adjective*** absurd, at variance, bizarre, clashing, discordant, discrepant, disproportionate, dissonant, ill-adapted, ill-advised, ill-suited, ill-timed, illogical, impolitic, improper, imprudent, inaccordant, inadmissible, inadvisable, inapplicable, inapposite, inapt, incompatible, incongruent, incongruous, inconsistent, indecorous, inexpedient, infelicitous, inharmonious, injudicious, inopportune, insagacious, irreconcilable, jarring, ludicrous, malapropos, mismatched, misplaced, objectionable, out of character, out of keeping, out of place, out of proportion, outrageous, preposterous, ridiculous, silly, unapt, unbecoming, unbefitting, uncongenial, unconsonant, undesirable, undue, unfit, unfitting, unmeet, unqualified, unseasonable, unseemly, unsuitable, unsuited, untimely, untoward, unwise

INEPT *(Incompetent),* ***adjective*** awkward, blundering, bungling, clumsy, disqualified, foolish, ignorant, ill-qualified, impotent, inadept, inadequate, inapt, incapable, incompetent, ineffective, ineffectual, inefficacious, inefficient, *ineptus,* inexpert, lacking dexterity, lacking dexterousness, lacking skill, maladroit, powerless, puerile, raw, unable, unadroit, unapt, unclever, undeft, unfacile, ungainly, unhandy, unproductive, unproficient, unqualified, unskillful, useless
ASSOCIATED CONCEPTS: incompetency of counsel, incompetent to contract, insanity, under the age of majority

INEPTITUDE, ***noun*** fatuity, futility, impotence, impropriety, impuissance, inability, inadequacy, inanity, inaptitude, inappropriateness, incapacity, incompetence, inefficacy, inefficiency, inutility, stupidity, unfitness, uselessness, worthlessness
ASSOCIATED CONCEPTS: inadequacy of counsel, ineffective counsel

INEQUALITY, ***noun*** asymmetry, bias, contrast, deviation, difference, disaccord, disagreement, discrepance, discrepancy, disparity, disproportion, disproportionateness, dissimilarity, dissimilitude, *dissimilitudo,* dissonance, distinction, divergence, diversity, imbalance, imparity, *inaequalitas,* incompatibility, incongruity, incongruousness, inconsistency, inconsonance, injustice, irregularity, lack of equality, lack of symmetry, nonconformity, nonuniformity, partiality, prejudice, unbalance, unconformity, unevenness, unfairness, unlikeness, ununiformity, variance, variation

INEQUITABLE, ***adjective*** discriminatory, favoring, one-sided, partial, partisan, prejudiced, unbalanced, uneven, unfair, unjust, weighted

INEQUITY, ***noun*** bias, biased judgment, bigotry, discrimination, disproportion, favor, favoritism, foregone conclusion, foul play, inequitableness, injustice, intolerance, leaning, miscarriage of justice, one-sidedness, partiality, partisanism, partisanship, preapprehension, preconceived idea, preconceived notion, preconception, predilection, preference, preferential treatment, prejudgment, prejudice, prenotion, prepossession, presentiment, presumption, undetachment, undispassionateness, undueness, unfairness, unjust decision, unjustness

INERTIA, ***noun*** apathy, dormancy, dullness, firmness, immobility, immobilization, immovability, inability to act, inaction, inactivity, indecision, indisposition to move, indolence, inertness, inexcitability, irresolution, lack of activity, lack of motion, lack of movement, languor, lassitude, laziness, lethargy, lifelessness, motionlessness, negligence, oscitancy, paralysis, passiveness, passivity, quiescence, resistance to change, rest, sloth, sluggishness, stagnation, stupor, supineness, torpor, vegetation, want of activity, weariness

INESCAPABLE, ***adjective*** absolute, cannot be avoided, certain, destined, fated, fateful, for sure, inevasible, inexorable, necessary, predestined, sure, unalterable, unavoidable, uncontrollable, uneluctable, unpreventable, unstoppable, unyielding
ASSOCIATED CONCEPTS: inescapable law, inescapable truths

INESTIMABLE, ***adjective*** above all price, above all value, above appraisal, beyond price, choice, costly, immeasurable, immensurable, *inaestimabilis,* incalculable, infinite, inimitable, invaluable, irreplaceable, matchless, measureless, peerless, precious, priceless, rare, select, unequalled, unique, unmatched, unparalleled, unsurpassable, valuable, without equal, without price

INEVITABLE, ***adjective*** about to happen, approaching, assured, at hand, brewing, certain, decided, definite, destined, determined, fated, fixed, following, foreordained, forthcoming, guaranteed, imminent, impending, in store, in the offing, ineluctable, ineludible, inescapable, inevasible, *inevitabilis,* looming, near, *necessarius,* next, ordained, predestined, preordained, sure, sure to happen, to come, unalterable, unavoidable, unchangeable, unfailing, unpreventable, unquestionable
ASSOCIATED CONCEPTS: inevitable accident, inevitable casualty, inevitable occurrence

INEXACT, ***adjective*** ambiguous, approximate, approximative, broad, careless, crude, erroneous, estimated, faulty, flawed, general, guessed, *haud accuratus,* hazy, imperfect, imprecise, inaccurate, incorrect, loose, miscalculated, misfigured, misinterpreted, misreported, misstated, mistranslated, more or less, nearly accurate, nearly correct, rough, surmised, unclear, unmeticulous, unrevised, unscientific, unspecified, vague, without precision

INEXCUSABLE, ***adjective*** atrocious, blameworthy, brutal, condemnable, cruel, disgraceful, flagitious, heinous, immoral, incapable of being justified, incorrigible, indefensible, inexpiable, irremissible, monstrous, objectionable, outrageous, *quod nihil excusationis habet,* reprehensible, reprobate, shameful, unallowable, unatonable, unforgivable, unjustifiable, unpardonable, unprincipled, unreasonable, unwarrantable, unwarranted, vicious, without defense, without excuse
ASSOCIATED CONCEPTS: inexcusable conduct, inexcusable delay, inexcusable neglect

INEXCUSABLE DELAY, ***noun*** default, dereliction, dilatoriness, disregard, failure of duty, indifference, inobservance, lack of diligence, laggardness, laxity, laxness, malfeasance, neglect, neglectfulness, negligence, noncompliance, nonfeasance, nonobservance, nonperformance, prejudicial delay, procrastination, remissness, unconscionable delay, undue delay, unexplained delay, unnecessary prolongation, unreasonable delay
ASSOCIATED CONCEPTS: failure to litigate, laches

INEXCUSABLE NEGLECT, ***noun*** breach of trust, careless abandon, carelessness, delinquency, dereliction, disregard, failure to care, heedlessness, idleness, inaction, inattention, inattentiveness, indifference, inexcusable carelessness, malfeasance, malignant oversight, nonfeasance, nonperformance, omission, reckless absentmindedness, recklessness, severe laxity, severe laxness, thoughtlessness, unforgivable abandonment
ASSOCIATED CONCEPTS: inexcusable neglect of duty, latches, malpractice

INEXORABLE, ***adjective*** adamant, convinced, decided, determined, dogged, firm, headstrong, immovable, immutable, implacable, indomitable, *inexorabilis,* inflexible, intractable, merciless, obdurate, obstinate, opinionated, opinionative, persevering, persistent, persisting, pertinacious, pitiless, positive, relentless, resistant, resolute, resolved, set, severe, steadfast, steady, sternly just, strong-minded, strong-willed, stubborn, tenacious, unalterable, unbending, unchanging, uncompassionate, uncompromising, uncontrollable, unfaltering, unimpressible, unmanageable, unmerciful, unmovable, unmoved by entreaties, unpersuadable, unrelenting, unshaken, unwavering, unyielding, willful

INEXPEDIENCE, ***noun*** disadvantage, disadvantageousness, folly, foolishness, imprudence, inadvisability, inappropriateness, inexpediency, infelicity, injudiciousness, inopportuneness, *inutilitas,* ludicrousness, rashness, senselessness, undesirability, undesirableness, unfitness, unfittingness, unprofitability, unsensibleness, unsoundness, unsuitability, unthoughtfulness, untimeliness, unwiseness

INEXPEDIENT, ***adjective*** confused, detrimental, foolhardy, foolish, half-baked, ill-advised, ill-conceived, ill-considered, ill-contrived, ill-thought-out, impolitic, imprudent, inadvisable, inconsiderate, injudicious, inopportune, madcap, misguided, misjudged, rash, reckless, thoughtless, unreasonable, unseemly, unwise, wrong

INEXPERIENCED, ***adjective*** amateur, artless, beardless, callow, green, *ignarus,* ignorant, ill-qualified, immature, *imperitus,* inapt, inept, inexpert, innocent, lacking experience, lacking proficiency, lacking skill, naive, new, poorly qualified, raw, *rudis,* sophomoric, unaccustomed, unacquainted, unadapted, unbusinesslike, unconversant, undeveloped, undisciplined, undrilled, unfamiliar, unfledged, unhabituated, uninformed, uninitiated, unlicensed, unpracticed, unqualified, unripe, unschooled, unseasoned, unskilled, unsophisticated, untrained, untried, untutored, unused, unversed, unworldly, verdant, without experience, without knowledge, young, youthful

INEXPIABLE, ***adjective*** base, blameworthy, censurable, condemnable, disgraceful, evil, facinorous, flagitious, heinous, indefensible, inexcusable, *inexplicabilis,* infamous, nefarious, reprehensible, scandalous, shameful, unallowable, unatonable, unforgivable, unjustifiable, unpardonable, unreasonable, vicious, villainous, virtueless, wicked, without defense, without excuse

INEXPLICABLE, ***adjective*** abstruse, acroamatic, acroamatical, acroatic, baffling, concealed, enigmatic, enigmatical, esoteric, hard to understand, hidden, impenetrable, inapprehensible, incapable of being explained, incomprehensible, indefinable, *inexplicabilis,* inscrutable, insoluble, insolvable, mysterious, mystic, mystical, obscure, occult, paradoxical, puzzling, recondite, shrouded in mystery, strange, unaccountable, undecipherable, undiscoverable, unexplainable, unfamiliar, unintelligible, unknowable, unknown, unrecognizable

INEXPRESSIVE, ***adjective*** apathetic, blank, characterless, cold, deadpan, devoid of expression, dim, dull, empty, enigmatic, enigmatical, expressionless, hardened, impassive, impenetrable, imperturbable, impervious, incomprehensible, inexplicable, inscrutable, lackluster, listless, meaningless, nebulous, nonsensical, obtuse, poker-faced, puzzling, senseless, spiritless, stupid, trite, unaffected, unanimated, undecipherable, unemotional, unfathomable, unintelligible, unmoved, vacant, vacuous, vague, void

INEXPUGNABLE, ***adjective*** defensible, formidable, hardy, immune, impenetrable, imperdible, impregnable, indomitable, *inexpugnabilis,* inextinguishable, insuperable, insurmountable, invincible, inviolable, invulnerable, irresistible, mighty, potent, powerful, protected, puissant, redoubtable, resistless, safe, secure, secure from capture, strong, sturdy, tenable, unassailable, unattackable, unbeatable, unbreakable, unchallengeable, unconquerable, unsubduable, unyielding

INEXTRICABLE, ***adjective*** adhering, attached, bound, cohesive, combined, complex, complicated, compounded, confused, conjunct, connected, convoluted, embrangled, entangled, fast, fixed, immovable, impacted, indissoluble, indivisible, *inexplicabilis, inextricabilis,* inseparable, inseverable, insoluble, intricate, involute, involuted, involved, irreducible, irremovable, jammed, joined, knotted, labyrinthine, matted, mazy, mixed, raveled, snarled, stuck, tangled, tangly, tied, turbid, twisted, wedged

INFALLIBLE, ***adjective*** assured, *certus,* continuing, defectless, dependable, enduring, errorless, everlasting, exhaustless, faithful, faultless, flawless, foolproof, free from imperfection, free from mistake, *haud dubius,* imperishable, incapable of error, incontestable, incontrovertible, indefatigable, indefectible, indefective, indomitable, inerrable, inerrant, inexhaustible, irrefragable, irreproachable, lasting, never-failing, perfect, reliable, secure, stable, stainless, stanch, staying, steady, sure, tenacious, trustworthy, trusty, unassailable, unbeatable, unchanged, unchanging, unconquerable, undestroyable, undying, unerring, unfading, unfailing, unfaltering, unflagging, unimpeachable, unquestionable, unquestioned, unspotted, unstoppable, unsurpassed, untainted, unwavering, unyielding, without blemish

INFAMOUS, *adjective* abominable, arrant, atrocious, bad, base, contemptible, contemptuous, despicable, detestable, discreditable, disgraceful, dishonorable, disreputable, egregious, execrable, felonious, flagitious, flagrant, heinous, ignoble, ignominious, illicit, inexpiable, inglorious, iniquitous, Machiavellian, malevolent, maleficent, monstrous, nefarious, notorious, odious, opprobrious, outrageous, peccant, perfidious, profligate, reprehensible, reprobate, scandalous, scurrilous, shameful, shameless, shocking, sinister, unprincipled, unrespectable, villainous

INFAMY, *noun* abasement, aspersion, bad name, bad reputation, baseness, blot, brand, contempt, defamation, degradation, derision, detestableness, disapprobation, disapproval, discredit, disesteem, disfavor, disgrace, dishonor, disrepute, disrespect, evil fame, humiliation, ignobility, *ignominia,* ignominiousness, ignominy, ill repute, *infamia,* infamousness, ingloriousness, loss of reputation, notoriety, obloquy, odium, opprobrium, probrum, public reproach, reproach, scandal, scorn, shame, stain, stigma, taint, tarnish
ASSOCIATED CONCEPTS: infamous acts, infamous crime, infamous offense, infamous punishment, infamy from conviction of a crime
FOREIGN PHRASES: ***Quae sunt minoris culpae sunt majoris infamiae.*** Those things which are less culpable may be more infamous.

INFANT, *noun* baby, child, *infans,* innocent, juvenile, little one, minor, nursling, one who has not come of age, one who has not reached his majority, person under the age of majority, person under 18 years old, person who is not of full age, toddler, tot, young person, youngster, youth
ASSOCIATED CONCEPTS: adoption, after-born child, age of minority, best interests of the child, child abuse, child labor, child support, custody, delinquent child, emancipation, filiation proceeding, foster child, guardian, guardian ad litem, illegitimate children, incompetency to contract, infanticide, juvenile delinquency, neglected child, pretermitted child, ratification of an infant's contract, visitation
FOREIGN PHRASES: ***In omnibus poenalibus judiciis, et aetati et imprudentiae succurritur.*** In all penal judgments, allowance is made for youth and lack of prudence. ***Infans non multum a furioso distat.*** An infant does not differ much from an insane person. ***In judiciis, minori aetati succurritur.*** In judicial proceedings, infancy is aided. ***Qui in utero est pro jam nato habetur, quoties de ejus commodo quaeritur.*** He who is in the womb is regarded as already born, whenever a question arises for his benefit. ***Pupillus pati posse non intelligitur.*** An infant is not considered able to do an act to his own prejudice.

INFEASIBLE, *adjective* absurd, impossible, impracticable, inaccessible, inconceivable, out of reach, out of the question, unachievable, unattainable, unimaginable, unlikely, unobtainable, unrealistic, unreasonable, unthinkable, unworkable, visionary

INFECT, *verb* adulterate, befoul, besmirch, blight, canker, cause illness, *contaminare,* contaminate, corrupt, debase, defile, dirty, empoison, envenom, foul, harm, impair, make ill, make impure, pervert, poison, pollute, putrefy, render unclean, smirch, soil, spoil, stain, sully, taint, tarnish, transmit disease, vitiate, *vitiis* inficere

INFER, *verb* conclude, conclude from evidence, conjecture, *conligere,* consider probable, construe, deduce, derive, derive by reasoning, draw a conclusion, draw an inference, extract, gather, glean, guess, hint, imply, indicate, insinuate, intimate, judge from premises, posit, postulate, presume, reach a conclusion, reason, reckon, suppose, surmise, suspect, understand
ASSOCIATED CONCEPTS: infer guilt from the evidence

INFERABLE HARM, *noun* aggravation, balefulness, bedevilment, damage, deadliness, detriment, disablement, disservice, evil, hurt, hurtfulness, ill consequence, ill-treatment, impairment, injury, malignance, malignancy, malignity, mischief, misfortune, mutilation, noxiousness, perniciousness, ruin, scathe, scourge, virulence

INFERENCE, *noun* allusion, assumption, *conclusio,* conclusion, *coniectura,* conjecture, deduction, guess, guesswork, hint, hypothesis, illation, implication, impression, inkling, judgment, observation, postulate, postulation, postulatum, premise, presupposal, presupposition, speculation, supposal, supposition, surmise, suspicion, theorem, theory, thesis, understanding
ASSOCIATED CONCEPTS: evidentiary inference, favorable inference, legal inference, legitimate inference, presumption
FOREIGN PHRASES: ***Expressa nocent, non expressa non nocent.*** Things expressed may be prejudicial; that which is not expressed will not.

INFERIOR *(Lower in position),* ***adjective*** accessory, auxiliary, *deterior,* governed by, in the power of, insignificant, junior, less powerful, lesser, lower, lower in authority, lower in rank, lower in the scale, lowly, menial, minor, of less importance, puisne, reduced, secondary, subaltern, subject, subjugated to, subordinate, subservient, subsidiary, tributary, under, unimportant
ASSOCIATED CONCEPTS: inferior courts

INFERIOR *(Lower in quality),* ***adjective*** adulterated, amateurish, awful, bad, badly made, base, below, below par, blemished, bush, bush-league, cheap, contemptible, crude, damaged, defective, deficient, displeasing, faulty, flimsy, imperfect, inadequate, incompetent, indifferent, inelegant, inferior grade, inferior to, insignificant, insipid, insufficient, junior, less than, less valuable, lesser, lousy, low, low-grade, lower, lower than, lowly, malformed, mediocre, menial, middling, minor, miserable, not as good as, not the quality of, not up to par, paltry, passable, pedestrian, petty, poor, rank, second-class, second fiddle, second-rate, secondary, servile, shabby, shoddy, slipshod, subordinate, subordinate to, subservient, subsidiary, substandard, trashy, unacceptable, undesirable, unsatisfactory
ASSOCIATED CONCEPTS: in bankruptcy, inferior bargaining position, inferior position, inferior products, inferior quality, inferior services

INFERRED IN LAW, *adjective* apparent, conceivable, connoted, constructive, implicative, implicatory, implied, implied in law, in effect, in essence, in practice, indirectly meant, inferable, insinuated, presumable, presumed, tantamount to, understood, virtual

INFEST, *verb* abound, assail, attack, beleaguer, beset, contaminate, crowd, defile, fill, fill up, flock, flood, infect, invade, overrun, overspread, overwhelm, pack, penetrate, plague, ravage, swarm, teem

INFIDELITY, *noun* abandonment of allegiance, apostasy, bad faith, betrayal, betrayal of oath, betrayal of trust, breach of faith, breach of promise, breach of trust, broken faith, broken word, cuckoldry, deceitfulness, defection, desertion, disaffection, dishonor, disloyalty, double-dealing, dutilessness, evasion of duty, faithlessness, falseheartedness, falsity, fickleness, inconstancy, *infidelitas,* lack of faith, lack of loyalty, mutiny, *perfidia,* perfidiousness, perfidy, rebellion, recreancy, revolt, sedition, seditiousness, traitorousness, treachery, treason, undutifulness, unfaithfulness, violation of oath
ASSOCIATED CONCEPTS: adultery

INFILTRATE, *verb* access, advance, assail, assault, bombard, enter, foist, impregnate, insinuate, invade, lay siege to, light into, overwhelm, penetrate, percolate, permeate, pervade, raid, riddle, rush, saturate, storm, strike, suffuse, transfuse, work into

INFINITE, *adjective* boundless, ceaseless, countless, endless, enduring, eternal, everlasting, exhaustless, illimitable, immeasurable, imperishable, incalculable, indestructible, inexhaustible, *infinitus,* innumerable, interminable, lasting, limitless, measureless, numberless, perdurable, permanent, perpetual, persistent, sempiternal, termless, timeless, unbounded, unceasing, undying, unending, unlimited, unmeasured, unnumbered, without end, without limit, without measure, without number

INFINITY, *adjective* boundless, ceaseless, complete, continual, continually, endless, enormous, eternal, everlasting, expansively, great, huge, immense, immortal, indefinite, infinite, innumerable, interminable, perfect, permanent, perpetual, unbounded, unceasing, undeterminable, uninterrupted, unlimited

INFIRM *(Irresolute),* ***adjective*** changeable, easily led, faint-hearted, faltering, fickle, inconstant, indecisive, insecure, pliable, precarious, undecided, undetermined, unreliable, unresolved, unstable, unsteady, untrustworthy, vacillating, wavering

INFIRM *(Weak),* ***adjective*** ailing, debilitated, defective, deteriorated, enfeebled, failing, feeble, flimsy, fragile, frail, frangible, helpless, imperfect, impotent, insecure, insubstantial, languid, nonsubstantial, powerless, sickly, unsound, wasted, weakened, withered, worn

INFLAME, *verb* aggravate, agitate, anger, arouse, convulse, deflagrate, discompose, electrify, embitter, energize, enliven, enrage, envenom, exacerbate, exasperate, excite, foment, galvanize, goad, harass, ignite, impassion, incense, incite, infuriate, intensify, invigorate, irritate, kindle, madden, nettle, offend, perturb, pester, pique, provoke, rouse, stimulate, stir up, taunt, vex
ASSOCIATED CONCEPTS: inflame the jury

INFLAMMATORY, *adjective* combustible, dissentious, explosive, fomenting, heated, immoderate, incendiary, incitive, inciting, inflammable, intemperate, offensive, provocative, scorching, unbridled, volcanic
ASSOCIATED CONCEPTS: inflammatory statements, inflammatory testimony

INFLATE, *verb* aggrandize, amplify, balloon, bloat, blow up, broaden, cause to bulge, dilate, distend, enlarge, escalate, exaggerate, expand, extend, fatten, fill out, fill with air, grow, increase, increase dimensions, *inflare,* magnify, make greater, make larger, make swollen, make tumid, pad, puff up, pump up, raise above the proper value, rise, spread, stretch, sufflate, surge, swell, upsurge, wax

INFLATED *(Bombastic),* ***adjective*** altiloquent, altisonant, artificial, declamatory, flatulent, fustian, grandiloquent, high-flown, high-sounding, *inflatus,* magniloquent, mouthy, oratorical, ostentatious, overblown, pedantic, pompous, pretentious, rhetorical, stilted, tumid, *tumidus,* turgid, vainglorious, verbose

INFLATED *(Enlarged),* ***adjective*** amplified, augmented, ballooned, bloated, blown up, dilated, distended, enlarged by swelling, expanded, extended, filled, *inflatus,* puffed, puffed up, puffy, spread, stretched, swelled, swollen, tumid, *tumidus,* turgid, *turgidus*

INFLATED *(Overestimated),* ***adjective*** aggrandized, amplified, embellished, enlarged, exaggerated, exaggerative, excessive, heightened, hyperbolic, magnified, miscalculated, overdrawn, overpraised, overpriced, overprized, overrated, overstated, overstressed, overvalued

INFLATED *(Vain),* ***adjective*** arrogant, boastful, braggart, bumptious, conceited, condescending, contemptuous, disdainful, egocentric, egoistic, egoistical, egotistic, egotistical, grandiose, haughty, immodest, impressed with oneself, lordly, overbearing, overproud, overweening, patronizing, pleased with oneself, pompous, pretentious, prideful, proud, scornful, self-applauding, self-centered, self-glorifying, self-important, self-lauding, self-satisfied, showy, strutting, superior, swaggering, vaporing, vauntful

INFLATION *(Decrease in value of currency),* ***noun*** boost in prices, currency devaluation, decrease in purchasing power, high prices, hike in prices, jump in prices, price increase, substantial rise of prices, undue expansion of currency, upturn in prices

INFLATION *(Increase),* ***noun*** aggrandizement, amplification, bloatedness, blowing up, dilation, distension, elevation, enlargement, escalation, exaggeration, expansion, extension, growth, increase, *inflatio,* rise, spread, sufflation, surge, swell, swelling, turgescence, turgidity, turgidness, upsurge, waxing
ASSOCIATED CONCEPTS: inflation of damages, inflation of value

INFLECTION, *noun* accent, accentuation, cadence, emphasis, expression, intonation, modulation, pitch, stress, tone, voice change
ASSOCIATED CONCEPTS: demeanor of a witness, polygraph test

INFLEXIBLE, *adjective* adamant, cantankerous, changeless, contumacious, decided, determined, dogged, firm, fixed, hard, hardened, headstrong, immobile, immovable, immutable, impersuadible, impersuasible, indocile, indomitable, inelastic, inexorable, intractable, intransigent, invariable, mulish, nonelastic, obdurate, obstinate, obstinatus, opinionated, opinionative, persevering, pertinacious, *pertinax,* refractory, relentless, resolute, resolved, rigid, rigidus, rigorous, solid, steadfast, stiff, strict, stringent, strong-willed, stubborn, tenacious, unalterable, unamenable, unbending, unchangeable, uncompromising, unmalleable, unmanageable, unmovable, unpliable, unpliant, unrelenting, unswayable, unyielding, willful
ASSOCIATED CONCEPTS: inflexible bargaining position

INFLICT, *verb* administer a penalty, administer punishment, agitate, agonize, apply, beset, bring about, bring upon, burden, cause, cause to suffer, coerce, commit, deal, disquiet, distress, enforce, force, force upon, give pain, harass, harm, hurt, *imponere,* impose, impose punishment, *inferre, infligere,* injure, maltreat, mete out, perform, produce injury, punish, put into force, strike, torment, torture, wound, wreak
ASSOCIATED CONCEPTS: inflict pain and suffering, inflict punishment

INFLICTION, *noun* abuse, application, blow, castigation, commission, commitment, execution, force, harassment, imposition, *incommodum,* injury, maltreatment, misfortune, oppression, ordeal, penalty, performance, perpetration, persecution, plague, punishment, torment, torture, trial, violence, wound

INFLOW, *noun* approach, arrival, coming in, entrance, entry, immigration, importation, incoming, incursion, induction, infiltration, influx, ingoing, ingress, ingression, initiation, inpour, inpouring, inroad, inrush, insertion, introduction, introgression, inundation, invasion, irruption, penetration, progress

INFLUENCE, *noun* ascendance, ascendancy, authority, command, consequence, control, dominance, domination, dominion, effect, effectiveness, effectuality, eminence, encouragement, forcefulness, governance, hegemony, hold, importance, incitation, incitement, inspiration, instigation, leadership, leverage, masterfulness, mastery, might, mightiness, omnipotence, paramountcy, *pondus,* potency, *potentia,* power, powerfulness, predominance, predominancy, prepollence, prepollency, prepotency, prestige, provocation, puissance, reign, rule, sovereignty, superiority, supremacy, sway, urging, vis, weight
ASSOCIATED CONCEPTS: coercion controlling influence, improper influence, influence peddling, political influence, undue influence

INFLUENCE, *verb* actuate, arouse, brainwash, bring pressure to bear, cajole, carry weight, convince, direct, form, guide, impel, *impellere,* impress, incite, induce, inspire, inveigle, lead, militate, modify, mold, motivate, move, *movere,* persuade, prejudice, pressure, prevail upon, prompt, pull strings, shape, stimulate, sway, talk into, urge, work upon
ASSOCIATED CONCEPTS: bribery, control, duress, improper influence, under the influence of alcohol, undue influence, wrong influence

INFLUENCED, *adjective* biased, decided, induced, inequitable, interested, one-sided, partial, partisan, persuaded, prejudiced, prepossessed, swayed, undetached, undispassionate, unfair
ASSOCIATED CONCEPTS: unduly influenced

INFLUENTIAL, *adjective* authoritative, cogent, commanding, consequential, controlling, convincing, determinative, distinguished, dominant, domineering, effective, effectual, efficacious, eminent, empowered, esteemed, foremost, governing, *gravis,* hegemonic, hegemonical, honored, illustrious, imperious, important, impressive, leading, mighty, multipotent, notable, noteworthy, omnipotent, paramount, potens, potent, powerful, predominant, preeminent, prepollent, preponderant, prepotent, prevailing, prevalent, prominent, puissant, recognized, reigning, renowned, reputable, respectable, respected, ruling, strong, supreme, well-known, well-recognized, well-regarded, worthy of notice

INFORM *(Betray),* ***verb*** accuse, announce, bear witness against, betray the secret, break faith, break trust, charge, communicate, confess, declare, denounce, disclose, disclose intentionally, disclose secrets, divulge, expose, give over to the foe, *hominis nomen deferre,* impart, impeach, implicate, incriminate, inculpate, lay bare, lay open, make known, report against, reveal, tell secrets, testify against, uncover, unmask, violate a confidence, violate the confidence of

INFORM *(Notify),* ***verb*** acquaint, advertise, advise, announce, annunciate, apprise, blazon, brief, carry tales, communicate, confide, describe, detail, disabuse, disclose, divulge, *docere,* educate, enlighten, explain, familiarize, give a report, give an account, give notice, give out information, give the facts, give tidings, herald, impart, instruct, keep posted, let know, level with, make known, mention, narrate, notify, *nuntiare,* orient, outline, point out, post, present information, proclaim, promulgate, publish, recite, recount, relate, report, reveal, send word, set right, set straight, signify, state, tattle, teach, tell, testify, tip, tout, trumpet, undeceive, warn

INFORMAL, *adjective* casual, common, congenial, cursory, extemporaneous, extempore, familiar, natural, nonchalant, offhand, ordinary, perfunctory, relaxed, spontaneous, unceremonial, unceremonious, unconventional, uncustomary, unmethodical, unofficial, unorthodox, unrestrained, unstereotyped, unstrict, without ceremony, without formality
ASSOCIATED CONCEPTS: informal charges, informal contract, informal hearing, informal proceeding

INFORMALITY, *noun* absence of ceremony, affability, casualness, ease, easiness, easygoingness, extemporaneousness, familiarity, fellowship, flexibility, freedom, freedom from affectation, friendliness, inexactitude, inexactness, informalness, ingenuousness, inobservance, irregularity, latitude, laxity, liberty, license, lightness, looseness, naturalness, noncompliance, nonconformity, nonobservance, offhandedness, plainness, relaxation, simplicity, slackness, unaffectedness, unassumingness, unceremoniousness, unconstraint, unconventionality, unorthodoxy, unrigorousness, want of formality

INFORMANT, *noun* accuser, advisor, announcer, annunciator, appriser, *auctor,* communicant, communicator, delator, dispatcher, divulger, enlightener, envoy, harbinger, herald, information giver, informer, intelligencer, narrator, notifier, proclaimer, relator, reporter, source, spy, stool pigeon, talebearer, tipper, tipster, witness
ASSOCIATED CONCEPTS: paid informant, reliable informants, undercover informant

INFORMATION *(Charge),* ***noun*** accusal, accusation, allegation, charge, criminal accusal, formal accusation, formal averment, formal charge, formal criminal charge, formal criminal complaint, official criminal charge, prosecutorial complaint, written accusation
ASSOCIATED CONCEPTS: felony information, misdemeanor information

INFORMATION *(Facts),* ***noun*** communiqué, data, exact data, figures, news, notice, notification, specifics, statistics

INFORMATION *(Knowledge),* ***noun*** acquired facts, acquired knowledge, available facts, book learning, collected writings, communication, communiqué, compilations, comprehension, education, enlightenment, erudition, experience, familiarity, grasp, intelligence, intelligent

grip, knowledge, knowledge of facts, known facts, learning, lore, mental grasp, revelation, understanding, wisdom
ASSOCIATED CONCEPTS: duty to ascertain information, privileged information, upon information and belief, withholding information
FOREIGN PHRASES: ***Nemo tenetur informare qui nescit, sed quisquis scire quod informat.*** No one who is ignorant of a thing is bound to give information about it, but everyone is bound to know that concerning which he gives information.

INFORMATIONAL, ***adjective*** advisory, communicative, documentary, edifying, educational, educative, enlightening, enriching, explanatory, explicative, illuminating, informatory, instructional, instructive, narrative, revealing, revelatory, telling

INFORMATIVE, ***adjective*** advisory, communicative, communicatory, didactic, disclosing, edifying, educational, educative, enlightening, enriching, explanatory, explicative, explicatory, explicit, expositive, expository, expressive, homiletic, homiletical, hortative, hortatory, illuminating, instructional, instructive, newsy, pedogogic, preceptive, propaedeutic, propaedeutical, revealing, scholastic

INFORMATORY, ***adjective*** acquainting, admonitory, advising, advisory, chatty, clarifying, communicative, descriptive, disclosing, doctrinal, documentary, educational, elucidatory, enlightening, explanatory, explicative, explicatory, expositive, expository, gossipy, hortative, hortatory, illuminating, informational, informative, instructive, monitory, newsy, notifying, presenting information, reporting, revealing, revelatory, teaching, telling

INFORMED *(Educated),* ***adjective*** accomplished, conversant with, cultured, enlightened, erudite, expert, instructed, knowledgeable, learned, lettered, literate, prepared, proficient, schooled, taught, trained, versed, well-educated, well-grounded, well-read, well-rounded, well-versed, widely read

INFORMED *(Having information),* ***adjective*** abreast, acquainted, advised, apprized, briefed, enlightened, familiar, familiarized, forewarned, notified, posted, primed, set straight, tipped, told, undeceived, warned
ASSOCIATED CONCEPTS: informed decision, informed opinion

INFORMER *(A person who provides information),* ***noun*** advisor, announcer, annunciator, communicant, communicator, courier, crier, *delator,* divulger, envoy, harbinger, herald, intelligencer, messenger, notifier, proclaimer, relater, reporter, source, spokesman, teller, tipper, tipster, warner

INFORMER *(One providing criminal information),* ***noun*** accuser, auctor, complainant, criminal information supplier, impeacher, indicter, informant, information supplier, one who supplies criminal information to the police, police tipper, squealer, tipster, witness against
ASSOCIATED CONCEPTS: corroboration, reliable informer

INFRACTION, ***noun*** breach, breach of faith, breach of law, breach of orders, breach of privilege, breach of promise, breach of the peace, breach of trust, breaking, contravention, crime, default, defiance, defiance of orders, disobedience, encroachment, evasion of duty, failure, failure of duty, *immunitio,* infringement, inobservance, noncompliance, nonobservance, nonobservance of rules, offense, omission, overstepping, refusal to obey, transgression, trespass, *violatio,* violation, violation of law, violation of orders, wrong
ASSOCIATED CONCEPTS: infraction of rules, infraction of the law, traffic infraction

INFRANGIBLE, ***adjective*** cohesive, durable, everlasting, firm, hallowed, holy, indestructible, indiscerptible, indissoluble, indissolvable, indivisible, inseparable, insoluble, inviolable, invulnerable, lasting, perdurable, resistant, sacred, sacrosanct, secure, solid, strong, unbreakable, unchangeable, united, unshakeable, unshatterable

INFREQUENT, ***adjective*** atypical, discontinuous, erratic, exceptional, extraordinary, few, inconstant, inhabitual, intermittent, irregular, limited, occasional, outstanding, periodic, phenomenal, rare, *rarus,* scarce, seldom happening, seldom occurring, seldom seen, singular, sparse, sporadic, uncommon, uncustomary, unfrequent, unsteady, untypical, unusual

INFRINGE, ***verb*** abuse a privilege, abuse one's rights, advance stealthily, aggress, arrogate, breach, break, break bounds, break in upon, break into, commit a breach, *frangere,* impinge, impose, infract, interfere, interlope, intrude, invade, meddle, overstep, *rumpere,* seize wrongfully, take liberties, transgress, trespass, use wrongfully, usurp, *violare,* violate, violate a contract, violate a law, violate a privilege, violate a regulation
ASSOCIATED CONCEPTS: infringe on a copyright, infringe on a trademark

INFRINGEMENT, ***noun*** abuse of privilege, aggression, arrogation, breach, contravention, disfranchisement, disobedience, dispossession, entrance upon domain of another, force, illegality, *immunitio,* incursion, infraction, injustice, interference, intrusion, invasion, invasion of a right, misdoing, misfeasance, nonobservance, repudiation, seizure, surpassing, trangression, transcendence, transcending, trespass, trespassing, usurpation, *violatio,* violation, violation of a contract, violation of a law, violation of a privilege, violation of a regulation, violence, wrong, wrongdoing, wrongfulness
ASSOCIATED CONCEPTS: copyright infringement, license infringement, patent infringement, trademark infringement

INFUSE, ***verb*** imbrue, imbue, implant, impregnate, inculcate, *incutere, infundere,* ingrain, *inicere,* inject, insert, inspire, inspirit, instill, introduce

INFUSION, ***noun*** imbruement, imbuement, implantation, impregnation, inculcation, infiltration, *infusio,* injection, insertion, instillation, introduction, penetration, permeation

INGENIOUS, ***adjective*** adroit, artful, brilliant, clever, creative, dexterous, fecund, fresh, fruitful, generative, germinal, gifted, groundbreaking, imaginative, innovative, inspired, inventive, masterful, novel, original, productive, prolific, Promethean, resourceful, sharp, smart, sophisticated, talented, visionary

INGENUOUS, ***adjective*** aboveboard, *apertus,* artless, blunt, candid, childlike, devoid of dissimulation, downright, forthright, frank, free from reserve, genuine, guileless, honest, honorable, inartificial, innocent, *liber,* naive, natural, open, outspoken, plain, rustic, simple, *simplex,* sincere, spontaneous, straightforward, transparent, trustworthy, truthful, unaffected, unconstrained, undesigning, undisguised, unforced, unreserved, unrestrained, unself-conscious, unsophisticated, unstudied, unsuspicious, veracious, with simplicity, without guile

INGLORIOUS, ***adjective*** arch, audacious, blameworthy, bold-faced, boorish, brash, churlish, contemptible, discourteous, disgraceful, disrespectful, ignoble, ill-bred, ill-mannered, impertinent, inconsiderate, insolent, loutish, offensive, rude, shameful, thoughtless, uncalled-for, uncivil, ungracious, unmannered, unmannerly, vulgar

INGRAIN, ***verb*** embed, engrave, establish, fix, imbue, implant, impregnate, impress, imprint, inculcate, indoctrinate, infix, influence, infuse, inject, inspire, instill, introduce, invest, permeate, train

INGRAINED, ***adjective*** confirmed, deep, deep-seated, embedded, engrafted, entrenched, essential, established, firmly established, firmly fixed, fixed, habitual, implanted, inborn, inbred, indelible, indwelling, ineffaceable, infixed, ingrown, inherent, innate, *insitus,* intrinsic, inveterate, *inveteratus,* inwrought, permanent, rooted, set, settled, thorough, well-established

INGRATITUDE, ***adjective*** animus *ingratus,* heedlessness, inappreciation, inconsiderateness, inconsideration, insensibility, lack of appreciation, lack of consideration, lack of gratitude, respectlessness, rudeness, thanklessness, thoughtlessness, unappreciativeness, unfeelingness, ungratefulness, unthankfulness, want of consideration

INGREDIENT, ***noun*** aspect, component, component part, constituent, constituent part, content, element, essential part, factor, feature, fragment, fundamental part, integral part, member, *membrum,* pars, part, section, sector, unit, unit of composition, vital part

INGRESS, ***noun*** access, admission, admittance, approach, entrance, entry, incoming, incursion, ingoing, ingression, *ingressus,* inlet, inroad, liberty to enter, means of access, means of entry, passage, power of entrance, right of entry, right to enter, way in, way to

ASSOCIATED CONCEPTS: easement, license, right of access

INHABIT, ***verb*** abide, be established in, be resident in, board, colonize, domicile, dwell in, dwell permanently, have quarters, *incolere,* keep house, live, lodge, occupy, remain, reside in, room, sojourn, squat, stay, take up residence, tenant, visit

INHABITANT, ***noun*** abider, addressee, boarder, citizen, cohabitant, denizen, dweller, habitant, *habitator, homo,* householder, *incola,* indweller, inhabiter, inmate, lodger, native, occupant, occupier, permanent resident, resident, residentiary, settler, sojourner, tenant

ASSOCIATED CONCEPTS: citizenry, residency

INHABITATION *(Act of dwelling in),* ***noun*** dwelling, habitancy, habitation, inhabitancy, living, lodging, lodgment, occupancy, occupation, sojourn, stay, tenancy, tenantry

INHABITATION *(Place of dwelling),* ***noun*** abode, asylum, domicile, *domicilium,* dwelling, dwelling place, edifice, establishment, home, house, living quarters, living space, lodging, lodging place, lodgment, place, place of abode, place of residence, quarters, refuge, residence, residency, sedes, *tectum*

INHARMONIOUS, ***adjective*** at odds, clashing, conflicting, contradictory, derived at variance, differing, disagreeable, discordant, disharmonious, dissonant, factious, harsh, incompatible, inharmonic, irreconcilable, opposing, unharmonious

INHERENT, ***adjective*** connate, deep-rooted, essential, fixed, immanent, implicit, inborn, inbred, ineffaceable, ingrained, ingredient, innate, *innatus, insitus,* instinctive, integral, internal, intrinsic, native, natural, subsistent

ASSOCIATED CONCEPTS: inherent defect, inherent power, inherently dangerous

INHERIT, ***verb*** accede to, acquire, acquire from ancestors, be granted a legacy, be the heir of, come into possession as an heir, derive from, fall heir to, gain, have succession as an heir, obtain, receive, receive a legacy, receive an endowment, receive as right, receive by bequest, receive by devise, receive by law of descent, receive by succession, receive property as an heir, *rem hereditate accipere,* succeed to, take, take as an heir, take by descent, take by inheritance, take by succession

INHERITANCE, ***noun*** appanage, benefaction, bequest, devise, dispensation, endowment, gift, *hereditas,* heritage, inherited property, legacy, presentation, property obtained by descent, property obtained by devise, provision, seisin, succession of property

ASSOCIATED CONCEPTS: coparcenary, curtesy, descent, distribution, dower, inheritance estate, inheritance tax, intestate succession, patrimony, wills

FOREIGN PHRASES: ***Haereditas, alia corporalis, alia incorporalis; corporalis est, quae tangi potest et videri; incorporalis quae tangi non potest nec videri.*** An inheritance is either corporeal or incorporeal; corporeal is that which can be touched and seen; incorporeal is that which can neither be touched nor seen. ***Feodum simplex quia feodum idem est quod haereditas, et simplex idem est quod legitimum vel purum; et sic feodum simplex idem est quod haereditas legitima vel haereditas pura.*** A fee simple is so called because fee is the same as inheritance, and simple is the same as lawful or pure; and so fee simple is the same as a lawful inheritance or pure inheritance. ***Filius est nomen naturae, sed haeres nomen juris.*** Son is the natural name, but heir is a name of law. ***Haeredum appellatione veniunt haeredes haeredumin infinitum.*** Under the name heirs come the heirs of heirs without limit. ***Haereditas est successio in universum jus quod defunctus habuerit.*** Inheritance is the succession to every right which the deceased had possessed. ***Haereditas nihil aliud est, quam successio in universum jus, quod defunctus habuerit.*** An inheritance is nothing other than the succession to all the rights which the deceased had. ***Si quis praegnantem uxorem reliquit, non videtur sine liberis decessisse.*** If a man dies leaving his wife pregnant, he is considered as having died childless. ***Major haereditas venit unicuique nostrum a jure et legibus quam a parentibus.*** A greater inheritance comes to each one of us from justice and the laws than from our parents.

INHIBIT, ***verb*** arrest, ban, bar, bridle, check, choke, constrain, control, curb, debar, delay, disallow, enjoin, estop, extinguish, forbid, frustrate, gag, govern, harness, hinder, hold back, hold in, impede, intercept, *interdicere,* interdict, interrupt, keep in, leash, muzzle, obstruct, paralyze, prevent, prohibit, proscribe, pull in, quench, refuse to allow, rein in, repress, restrain, restrict, retard, smother, stifle, stop, strangle, suppress, suspend, taboo, veto, withhold

INHIBITED, ***adjective*** arrested, barricaded, blocked, bogged down, bound, chained, checked, conservative, constrained, controlled, cramped, curbed, delayed, encumbered, fettered, haltered, handicapped, held back, hindered, hobbled, impeded, leashed, manacled, mired, obstructed, reigned, restrained, retarded, shackled, short-circuited, stymied, tethered, thwarted, tied down, tied up, trammeled

INIMICAL, *adjective* adverse, alienated, antagonistic, antipathetic, antipathetical, at variance, at war with, bellicose, belligerent, contrary, cool, cross, disaffected, estranged, harmful, hostile, hurtful, *inimicus,* irreconcilable, malevolent, mean, noxious, on bad terms, opposed, opposing, pernicious, repugnant, unfavorable, unfriendly, unpropitious, up in arms, warlike

INIMITABLE, *adjective* banner, classic, divine, dynamite, excellent, exceptional, extraordinary, fabulous, famous, fantastic, grand, high-grade, immense, incomparable, incredibly unique, marvelous, marvelously unique, matchless, nonpareil, one-of-a-kind, peerless, rare, sensational, singular, special, splendid, uncommon, unequaled, unique, unmatched, unparalleled, unrivaled, unsurpassable, unusual

INIQUITOUS, *adjective* accursed, atrocious, bad, base, black, corrupt, criminal, culpable, depraved, dishonest, disreputable, dissolute, evil, facinorous, felonious, flagitious, foul, gross, heinous, immoral, *improbus,* improper, incorrigible, inequitable, infamous, *iniquus, iniustus,* irreclaimable, knavish, lawless, malevolent, miscreant, naughty, nefarious, objectionable, peccant, pernicious, profligate, recreant, reprehensible, reprobate, scandalous, scurvy, shameful, sinful, sinning, unfair, unjust, unjustifiable, unprincipled, unrighteous, vicious, vile, villainous, wicked, wrong
FOREIGN PHRASES: ***Nullum iniquum est praesumendum in jure.*** Nothing iniquitous is to be presumed in law.

INITIAL, *adjective* basic, beginning, commencing, early, elementary, embryonic, first, fundamental, inaugural, inceptive, inchoate, incipient, initiative, initiatory, introductory, leading, maiden, nascent, opening, original, prefatory, premier, primal, primary, *primus,* pristine, rudimentary, starting
ASSOCIATED CONCEPTS: initial carrier, initial fault, initial license, initial loss, initial payment, initial pleading, initial stage of a proceeding

INITIATE, *verb* admit, begin, break ground, bring into use, broach, commence, conceive, direct, discover, enlighten, enter upon, familiarize, found, give entrance to, *imbuere,* implant, inaugurate, inchoate, *incipere,* inculculate, indoctrinate, induct, inform, *initiare,* install, instill, institute, instruct, introduce, invent, launch, lay the foundation, lead, lead the way, open, originate, pioneer, plant, preinstruct, prepare, present, prime, prompt, propose, set afoot, set going, set up, start, take the initiative, take the lead, teach, think of, train, undertake, usher in
ASSOCIATED CONCEPTS: initiate an action

INJECT, *verb* drive in, force in, imbed, imbue, implant, impregnate, infix, *infundere,* infuse, inoculate, insert, instill, interjaculate, interject, interpolate, interpose, introduce, intromit, pierce, place into, press in, put into, ram in, saturate, shoot, thrust in, transfuse, vaccinate

INJUDICIOUS, *adjective* blind, disadvantageous, hasty, heedless, ill-advised, ill-judged, impolitic, impolitical, improvident, imprudent, inappropriate, incautious, inconsiderate, *inconsideratus, inconsultus,* indiscreet, inexpedient, inopportune, insufficiently considered, irrational, lacking discretion, misguided, needless, negligent, objectionable, precipitate, reckless, showing lack of judgment, showing poor judgment, temerarious, thoughtless, unadvisable, uncalculating, unconsidered, undesirable, undiscerning, unfit, unprofitable, unreasoned, unsound, unsuitable, unwary, unwise

INJUNCTION, *noun* ban, bidding, command, command to undo wrong, denial, enjoinder, imperative, *imperium,* interdiction, *iussum,* judicial order to refrain from an act, *mandatum,* order, precept, prescript, prohibition, proscription, restraining order, restraint, restriction, stay order, warrant
ASSOCIATED CONCEPTS: cease and desist order, dissolution of an injunction, interlocutory injunction, modification of injunction, order to show cause, permanent injunction, preliminary injunction, temporary injunction, temporary restraining order

INJURE *(Harm),* ***verb*** abuse, aggravate, blemish, bruise, brutalize, cripple, damage, debase, debilitate, deface, disable, disfigure, do harm to, endanger, eviscerate, harrow, hit, hurt, ill-treat, ill-use, impair, inflict, inflict pain, lacerate, maim, maltreat, mangle, mar, mishandle, mistreat, misuse, molest, mutilate, spoil, violate, vitiate, wound

INJURE *(Persecute),* ***verb*** affront, annoy, asperse, blacken, calumniate, defame, denigrate, disadvantage, disparage, insult, libel, malign, offend, oppress, prejudice, slander, subvert, traduce, vilify, wrong

INJURIOUS *(Derogatory),* ***adjective*** abusive, calumnious, contemptuous, contumelious, corrupt, defamatory, detractory, detrimental, disadvantageous, inadvisable, insulting, invidious, libelous, malevolent, mischievous, pejorative, pernicious, prejudicial, scurrilous, slanderous, unfavorable

INJURIOUS *(Harmful),* ***adjective*** abusive, adverse, bad, baneful, calamitous, corrosive, corrupt, damaging, dangerous, deleterious, destructive, depraved, destructive, detrimental, disadvantageous, disastrous, facinorous, fatal, felonious, grievous, harmful, hurtful, inequitable, iniquitous, insalubrious, insidious, lethal, malefic, malignant, nefarious, noisome, noxious, offensive, outrageous, peccant, pernicious, perverse, pestiferous, pestilent, ruinous, sinister, unjust, vicious, virulent, wrongful

INJURY, *noun* abuse, adversity, bane, breakage, damage, *damnum,* deprivation, detriment, *detrimentum,* disservice, harm, harmful act, hurt, ill-treatment, impairment, *incommodum,* invasion of a legal right, loss, offense, physical hurt, prejudice, privation, violence, wrong
ASSOCIATED CONCEPTS: accidental injury, cause of injury, comparative injury, compensable injury, contributory negligence, direct injury, efficient cause, future injury, indirect injury, indivisible injury, injury to business, injury to property, injury to reputation, intentional injury, irreparable injury, malicious injury, permanent injury, personal injury, previous injury, proof of injury, *res ipsa loquitur,* serious injury suffered, wanton injury
FOREIGN PHRASES: ***Quid sit jus, et in quo consistit injuria, legis est definire.*** What constitutes right, and what injury, it is the business of the law to define. ***Non omne damnum inducit injuriam.*** Not every loss produces an injury. ***Neminem laedit qui jure suo utitur.*** He who stands on his own rights injures no one. ***Jus est norma recti; et quicquid est contra normam recti est injuria.*** Law is the rule of right; and whatever is contrary to the rule of right is an injury. ***Melius est in tempore occurrere, quam post causam***

vulneratum remedium quaerere. It is better to meet a thing in time, than to seek a remedy after an injury has been inflicted. ***Prohibetur ne quis faciat in suo quod nocere possit alieno.*** It is forbidden for anyone to do on his own property what may injure another's. ***Lex nemini facit injuriam.*** The law works injury to no one. ***Paci sunt maxime contraria vis et injuria.*** Violence and injury are especially hostile to peace. ***Res inter alios judicatae nullum aliis praejudicium faciunt.*** Transactions between strangers ought not to injure those who are not parties to them. ***Volenti non fit injuria.*** No injury is done where the person injured consents. ***Corporalis injuria non recipit aestimationem de futuro.*** A personal injury cannot be compensated for by later acts. ***Fictio legis inique operatur alieni damnum vel injuriam.*** Fiction of law is wrongful if it works loss or harm to anyone. ***Privatis pactionibus non dubium est non laedi jus caeterorum.*** There is no doubt that private contracts cannot prejudice the rights of others. ***Damnum sine injuria esse potest.*** There can be damage or injury inflicted without any act of injustice. ***Ab assuetis non fit injuria.*** No injury is done by things long acquiesced in. ***Consuetudo neque injuria oriti neque tolli potest.*** A custom can neither arise nor be abolished by an injury. ***Aedificare in tuo proprio solo non licet quod alteri noceat.*** It is not lawful to build upon one's own land what may injure another. ***Factum unius alteri nocere non debet.*** The act of one person should not prejudice another. ***Injuria non praesumitur.*** A wrong is not presumed. ***Lex nemini operatur iniquum, nemini facit injuriam.*** The law never works an injury, or does a wrong.

INJUSTICE, ***noun*** abuse, bias, bigotry, breach, crime, damage, denial of justice, discrimination, disparity, encroachment, error of the court, evil, fault of the court, favoritism, illegality, imposition, improbity, inequality, inequitable action, inequity, infraction, infringement, infringement on one's rights, iniquity, *iniuria, iniustitia,* injury, malfeasance, maltreatment, miscarriage, miscarriage of justice, misfeasance, mistake of the court, mistreatment, offense, omission of a court, oppression, outrage, partiality, partisanship, persecution, prejudice, transgression, tyranny, unevenness, unfair action, unfairness, unjust treatment, unjustness, unlawfulness, unrighteousness, violation, violation of right, wrong, wrong verdict, wrongdoing
ASSOCIATED CONCEPTS: social injustice
FOREIGN PHRASES: ***Fictio legis inique operatur alicui damnum vel injuriam.*** Fiction of law is wrongful if it works loss or harm to anyone. ***Lex nemini operatur iniquum, nemini facit injuriam.*** The law never works an injury, or does a wrong.

INMATE, ***noun*** captive, *captus,* convict, dweller, habitant, inhabitant, lawbreaker, occupant, occupier, prisoner, resident, roomer
ASSOCIATED CONCEPTS: inmate at a correctional institution

INNATE, ***adjective*** basic, congenital, constitutional, derived from within, essential, existing from birth, fundamental, hereditary, immanent, inborn, inbred, indigenous, infixed, ingrained, inherent, inherited, *innatus, insitus,* instinctive, intrinsic, intuitive, involuntary, native, natural, *proprius*

INNOCENCE, ***noun*** absence of guilt, blamelessness, exculpation, exoneration, freedom from blame, freedom from guilt, freedom from illegality, guiltlessness, incorruption, innocency, *innocentia, integritas,* sinlessness
ASSOCIATED CONCEPTS: presumption of innocence
FOREIGN PHRASES: ***Omnis indemnatus pro innoxis legibus habetur.*** Every uncondemned person is regarded by the law as innocent. ***Quisquis praesumitur bonus; et semper in dubiis pro reo respondendum.*** Everyone is presumed to be good; and in doubtful cases it should be resolved in favor of the accused. ***In favorem vitae, libertatis, et innocentiae, omnia praesumuntur.*** Every presumption is made in favor of life, liberty, and innocence.

INNOCENT, ***adjective*** blameless, *culpa vacuus,* faultless, free from guilt, guiltless, *innocens, insons,* sinless, unblamable, unoffending, upright, virtuous, without harm, without offense
ASSOCIATED CONCEPTS: innocent holder for value, innocent misrepresentation, innocent mistake, innocent purchaser, innocent third party, innocent trespass
FOREIGN PHRASES: ***Minatur innocentibus qui parcit nocentibus.*** He who spares the guilty threatens those who are innocent.

INNOCENT BYSTANDER, ***noun*** attester, beholder, blameless witness, chance looker-on, corroborator, eyewitness, faultless witness, guiltless witness, informant, informer, observer, onlooker, passer-by, perceiver, spectator, testifier, viewer, watcher, witness, witness free from guilt

INNOCENT OWNER, ***noun*** affirmative defense to forfeiture allegation, innocent owner defense, property owner not involved in offense
ASSOCIATED CONCEPTS: 18 USCS § 983—General Rules for Civil Forfeiture Proceedings

INNOCUOUS, ***adjective*** harmless, hurtless, innocent, innoxious, inoffensive, mild, nonirritating, nonmalignant, nontoxic, painless, safe, simple, uninjurious, unlikely to cause harm, unlikely to cause injury, unobjectionable, unobnoxious, unoffending, virtuous, without power to harm, without tendency to harm

INNOVATE, ***verb*** author, begin, bring about, bring forward, conceive, concoct, construct, contrive, create, develop, devise, establish, inaugurate, induct, initiate, institute, introduce, invent, launch, organize, originate, pioneer, present, produce, set up, start, think up, unveil, usher in

INNOVATION, ***noun*** adaptation, alteration, breaking of precedent, change, change in method, departure, digression, divergence, diversification, exchange of obligations, invention, modernization, modification, neoterism, new device, new idea, new method, new phase, *novare,* novelty, radically new measure, revision, revolution, shift, variation

INNUENDO, ***noun*** accusation, allusion, aside, aspersion, charge, connotation, *denuntiatio,* hint, implication, implied indication, imputation, incrimination, indication, indirect allusion, inference, insinuation, mention, *nuntius,* oblique allusion, overtone, reference, reflection, *significatio,* suggestion
ASSOCIATED CONCEPTS: defamation, disparagement, libel, slander

INNUMERABLE, ***adjective*** boundless, countless, endless, exhaustless, frequent, immeasurable, immense, incalculable, incapable of being counted, incomprehensible, incomputable, inexhaustible, infinite, *innumerabilis, innumerus,* interminable, legionary, limitless, many, more than one can tell, much, multitudinous, myriad, numberless, sumless, uncountable, uncounted, unfathomable, unlimited, unmeasured, unnumbered, untold

INNUMEROUS, *adjective* bottomless, boundless, countless, endless, extensive, fathomless, horizonless, illimitable, immeasurable, immense, incalculable, incomputable, indefinite, inestimable, inexhaustible, infinite, limitless, many, multifold, multiple, multitudinous, numerous, plenty, too many to count, unbounded, unmeasured, vast

INOCULATE, *verb* endue, fill, flood, imbed, imbue, implant, inculcate, infuse, inject, insert, instill, interpose, introduce, inundate, invest, invigorate, pierce, protect, put into, saturate, shoot, steep, suffuse, thrust in, vaccinate

INOPERABLE *(Impracticable),* ***adjective*** undoable, unfeasible, unworkable

INOPERABLE *(Incurable),* ***adjective*** cureless, hopeless, immedicable, remediless

INOPERATIVE, *adjective* abeyant, asleep, broken, comatose, deactivated, dead, deadlocked, dormant, dull, fallow, ineffective, ineffectual, inert, latent, lifeless, moribund, not functional, off, quiescent, sleepy, slow, suspended, unproductive, unusable, unused, unworkable, useless, vacant

INOPPORTUNE, *adjective* at the wrong time, badly calculated, badly timed, ill-chosen, ill-seasoned, ill-timed, inadvisable, inappropriate, inauspicious, inconvenient, inexpedient, *inopportunus,* malapropos, misjudged, mistimed, undesirable, unfavorable, unfit, unfortunate, unpropitious, unseasonable, unsuitable, unsuited, untimely, wrong

INORDINATE, *adjective* crammed, exaggerated, exceeding, excessive, exorbitant, extortionate, extraordinary, extravagant, extreme, fanatical, gluttonous, great, immoderate, *immoderatus, immodicus,* inabstinent, intemperate, lavish, monstrous, needless, nimious, out of bounds, out of limits, outrageous, overcharged, overflowing, overmuch, preposterous, prodigal, profuse, prohibitive, redundant, superabundant, supererogatory, superfluous, supersaturated, unbridled, uncalled-for, unconscionable, uncurbed, undue, unlimited, unnecessary, unreasonable, unrestrained, wasteful, without restraint

INPUT *(Data),* ***noun*** capture of information, communications, enumerated facts, facts, figures, files, information, numbers, raw data, specifics, statistics

INPUT *(Thinking),* ***noun*** analysis, communication, contribution, enlightenment, expression, imparting knowledge, impartment of wisdom, involvement, partaking, participation, provide a prospective, provide expertise, provide information, provide knowledge, sharing thoughts, weigh-in

INQUEST, *noun* determination of damages, examination, hearing, inquiry, interrogation, investigation, judicial inquiry, legal investigation, *quaestio,* quest, questioning, review, search, search into facts
ASSOCIATED CONCEPTS: assessment of damages, civil inquest, coroner's inquest

INQUIRE, *verb* ask, catechize, conduct research, cross-examine, delve into, examine, explore, interrogate, investigate, look into, probe, propose a question, pry into, pursue, query, question, quiz, research, scrutinize, search, search into, seek information, solicit, sound out, study, subject to scrutiny, survey

INQUIRE INTO, *verb* analyze, canvass, check, conduct an inquiry, consider, delve into, examine, explore, ferret out, hear, hold an inquiry, institute an inquiry, interrogate, investigate, monitor, probe, pry, pursue, query, question, reconnoiter, research, review, scrutinize, search, set up an inquiry, sound, study, unearth, want to know
ASSOCIATED CONCEPTS: grand jury inquiry, special investigation

INQUIRY *(Request for information),* ***noun*** examination, examination into facts or principles, exploration, hearing, inquisition, *interrogatio,* interrogation, investigation, *percontatio,* poll, probe, query, question, scrutiny, search, search for information, survey
ASSOCIATED CONCEPTS: duty to inquire, inquiry into title, reasonable inquiry, speculative inquiry
FOREIGN PHRASES: ***Quaerere dat sapere quae sunt legitima vere.*** Inquiry is the way to know what things are truly lawful. ***Quaeras de dubiis legem bene discere si vis.*** Inquire into doubtful matters if you wish to understand the law well. ***Quaere de dubiis, quia per rationes pervenitur ad legitimam rationem.*** Inquire into doubtful matters, because by reasoning we arrive at legal reason.

INQUIRY *(Systematic investigation),* ***noun*** analyzation, asking, assay, canvassing, *cognitio,* conference, delving into evidence, disquisition, examination, exploration, fundamental research, hearing, hearing of evidence, inquest, *inquisitio,* inquisition, interrogation, investigation, legal trial, narrow search, overview, perusal, probe, pursuit, *quaestio,* question, research, scrutiny, search, study, survey, trial
ASSOCIATED CONCEPTS: grand jury inquiry, judicial inquiry, public inquiry

INQUISITION, *noun* examination, harassment, infliction, inquest, inquiry, interrogation, oppression, persecution, scrutiny, unfair inquiry

INQUISITIVE, *adjective* *audiendi, cupidus, curiosus,* curious, eager for knowledge, fond of investigation, given to research, inquiring, interested, interrogative, investigative, questioning, quizzical, scrutinizing, searching, seeking, speculative

INROAD, *noun* access, advancement, aggression, assault, attack, charge, consumption, damage, detriment, entrance, havoc, impairment, incursion, infiltration, inflow, infraction, infringement, ingress, interference, interloping, intervention, invasion, intrusion, introgression, irruption, loss, offensive, onslaught, outrage, overrunning, overstepping, ravage, sally, transgression, trespass

INSALUBRIOUS, *adjective* baleful, baneful, calamitous, damaging, dangerous, deleterious, destructive, detrimental, disadvantageous, disastrous, fraught with danger, gravis, harmful, hazardous, hurtful, injurious, *insalubris,* lethal, lethiferous, malefic, maleficent, menacing, mephitic, miasmal, miasmatic, miasmatical, miasmic, morbific, morbifical, mortiferous, noisome, noxious, ominous, pathogenic, perilous, pernicious, pestiferous, *pestilens,* pestilent, pestilential, poisonous, risky, ruinous, threatening, toxic, unclean, unfavorable to health, unhealthful, unhealthy, unhygienic, unsafe, unsanitary, unwholesome, venomous, virulent

INSANE, ***adjective*** bereft of reason, certifiable, crazed, crazy, defected, delirious, demented, deranged, disordered, frenetic, frenzied, hysterical, incoherent, insensate, lunatic, mad, maniacal, manic, mental, mentally deranged, *non compos mentis,* of unsound mind, paranoiac, psychotic, raving, unsound, wandering, wild

ASSOCIATED CONCEPTS: insanity defense, insanity plea

INSANITY, ***noun*** aberration, aberration of mind, abnormality, alienation, alienation of mind, amentia, brain damage, craziness, daftness, delirium, delusion, dementedness, deranged intellect, derangement, diseased mind, disordered intellect, disordered mind, disordered reason, disorientation, frenzy, hallucination, *insania,* loss of reason, lunacy, madness, mental abnormality, mental alienation, mental decay, mental deficiency, mental derangement, mental disease, mental incapacity, mental infirmities, mental instability, mental sickness, mental unsoundness, paranoia, raving, unbalanced mind, unsound mind, unsoundness of mind, *vecordia,* want of comprehension, want of reason

ASSOCIATED CONCEPTS: adjudication of insanity, diminished capacity, habitual insanity, incompetency, insane delusion, insane impulse to act, insanity defense, insanity plea, irresistible impulse

FOREIGN PHRASES: ***Furiosus nullum negotium contrahere potest.*** An insane person can make no contract. ***Furiosus stipulare non potest nec aliquid negotium agere, qui non intelligit quid agit.*** An insane person who knows not what he is doing, cannot contract nor transact any business. ***Furiosi nulla voluntas est.*** A madman has no will. ***Furiosus solo furore punitur.*** A madman is punished by his madness alone. ***Furor contrahi matrimonium non sinit, quia consensu opus est.*** Insanity prevents a marriage from being contracted, because consent is required. ***Ira furor brevis est.*** Anger is short insanity. ***Furiosus absentis loco est.*** A madman is considered as a person who is absent. ***Insanus est qui, abjecta ratione, omnia cum impetu et furore facit.*** A person is insane who, deprived of reason, does everything with violence and rage.

INSATIABLE, ***adjective*** acquisitive, avaricious, covetous, craving, discontented, gluttonous, grasping, greedy, hoggish, incapable of being satisfied, *inexplebilis, insatiabilis,* intemperate, piggish, quenchless, rapacious, selfish, unappeasable, unfilled, unquenchable, unsated, unsatisfied

INSCRIBE, ***verb*** *ascribere,* commit to writing, *consignare,* engrave, enroll, enscroll, enter, imprint, *inscribere,* insert, letter, list, make an entry, mark, post, put in writing, put upon record, record, register, scribe, write

INSCRIPTION, ***noun*** autograph, caption, dedication, engraving, entry, *index, inscriptio,* legend, mark, record, superscription, *titulus,* written matter

ASSOCIATED CONCEPTS: inscribed securities, registration of a deed

INSCRUTABLE, ***adjective*** ambiguous, baffling, blank, cloudy, concealed, deadpan, enigmatic, expressionless, hidden, impassive, impenetrable, impossible to understand, inapprehensible, incognizable, incomprehensible, indiscernible, inexplicable, insoluble, mysterious, obscure, *obscurus,* occult, *occultus,* past comprehension, poker-faced, puzzling, secret, *tectus,* unable to be investigated, unaccountable, unclear, undiscoverable, unfathomable, unintelligible, unknowable, unrevealed, unsearchable, vague

INSECURE, ***adjective*** adrift, borderline, changeable, changeful, dangerous, defenseless, dependent, endangered, exposed, exposed to risk, fragile, frail, fraught with danger, harborless, hazardous, helpless, *incertus,* infirm, *instabilis,* lacking stability, perilous, precarious, risky, shaky, slippery, speculative, subject to chance, subject to change, ticklish, tottering, treacherous, unassured, unbalanced, uncertain, unconfident, undependable, unfastened, unprotected, unreliable, unsafe, unsettled, unsheltered, unshielded, unsound, unstable, unsteadfast, unsteady, unsure, untrustworthy, venturesome, venturous, vulnerable

ASSOCIATED CONCEPTS: insecure obligation, insecurity clause

INSECURITY, ***noun*** ambiguity, bewilderment, danger, dilemma, doubt, doubtfulness, dubiousness, endangerment, exposure, fallibility, hazard, haziness, hesitation, incertitude, indecision, infirmity, instability, jeopardy, obscurity, peril, perplexity, precariousness, quandary, risk, suspicion, threat, uncertainty, undependability, unreliability, unsoundness, unsteadiness, unsureness, untrustworthiness, vacillation, vagueness, vulnerability

INSEMINATE, ***verb*** embed, implant, impregnate, inject, insert, introduce, plant, pollinate, pollinize, seed, sow

INSENSATE, ***adjective*** affectless, callous, callow, case-hardened, cold-blooded, compassionless, desensitized, hard-boiled, hard-hearted, heartless, impervious, indurate, inhuman, inhumane, insensate, insensitive, iron-hearted, merciless, obdurate, pachydermatous, pitiless, remorseless, ruthless, soulless, stony, uncaring

INSENSIBLE, ***adjective*** apathetic, benumbed, bewildered, blind, callous, clueless, comatose, dazed, deaf, deprived of sensation, dormant, drugged, dull, emotionless, exanimate, frigid, heedless, ignorant, imperceptive, impercipient, inanimate, incapable of feeling, incapable of perceiving, inexcitable, insensate, insensitive, insentient, *obdurescere,* passive, senseless, spiritless, stony, stupefied, supine, torporific, unacquainted, unaffected, unaroused, unaware, unconscious, undiscerning, unenlightened, unfeeling, unhearing, unknowing, unmindful, unmoved, unperceptive, unrealizing, unresponsive, unseeing, unsuspecting, untouched, unwitting, vegetating, void of feeling

INSENSITIVE, ***adjective*** blind, callous, cold-blooded, cruel, draconian, hard, impervious, indiscreet, insensate, insensible, insentient, numb, obtuse, ponderous, relentless, remorseless, ruthless, thick-skinned, unaffected, unfeeling, unimpressionable, unresponsive, unsusceptible

INSENTIENCE, ***noun*** absence of feeling, absence of sensation, blackout, blankness, immobility, inability to act, inability to perceive, inaction, inactivity, inanimateness, inanimation, incognizance, incomprehension, indifference, *inertia,* inertness, insensateness, insensibility, insensibleness, insensitivity, lack of awareness, lack of comprehension, lack of knowledge, lack of perception, lifelessness, nonrecognition, powerlessness, senselessness, stillness, stupor, suspension of consciousness, trance, unawareness, unconsciousness, unfamiliarity, unfeelingness, want of sensibility

INSEPARABLE, ***adjective*** attached, blended, cemented, close, combined, consolidated, constantly together, devoted, fast, firm, fused, glued, impartible, incapable of being parted, indiscerptible, indissoluble, indivisible, inextricable, infrangible, inseverable, insoluble, integrated, interdependent, intertwined, intimate, joined, locked, molded together,

nondivisible, *perpetuo comitari,* tenacious, undissolvable, undividable, united, unsunderable, welded
ASSOCIATED CONCEPTS: inseparability of easement, inseparability of statutory provisions

INSERT, ***verb*** affix, append, attach, book, embed, enter, file, graft, imbed, imbue, immerse, implant, infuse, inject, inlay, inscribe, inscroll, inset, instill, interject, interpolate, interpose, intersperse, intervene, intrude, obtrude, penetrate, pierce, plant, set in, splice, thrust in

INSERTION, ***noun*** addendum, additament, addition, appendix, entry, extension, inclusion, inset, intercalation, interjection, interpolation, *interpositio,* introduction, parenthesis, penetration, plant, postscript, supplement, supplementation, transplantation
ASSOCIATED CONCEPTS: codicil, insertion of a clause to a contract, rider

INSEVERABLE, ***adjective*** bound up with, impartible, indiscerptible, indivisible, inextricable, infrangible, infusible, inseparable, insoluble, insunderable, irresolvable, joined, one, unbreakable, undividable, united

INSIDE, ***adjective*** backstage, behind, behind-the-scenes, clandestine, classified, closeted, confidential, hushed, in behind, in the back of, indoors, interior, internal, inward, nonpublic, personal, private, privy, restricted, secret, unadvertised, undercover, undisclosed, untold

INSIDE INFORMATION, ***noun*** clandestine, closeted, collusive, concealed information, confidential facts, covert, nonpublic, private information, private materials, secret correspondence, undisclosed information, unmentioned
ASSOCIATED CONCEPTS: corporate law, insider trading, securities cases

INSIDER TRADING, ***noun*** criminality, disclosure of confidential information, illegal disclosure, illegal use, illegal use of secret information, illegality, impropriety, infraction, infringement, misappropriate nonpublic information and material, prohibited use of confidential information, SEC violation, use of restricted information, violation of law
ASSOCIATED CONCEPTS: insiders, Rule 10b-5, Securities Exchange Act

INSIDIOUS, ***adjective*** artful, beguiling, cheating, conniving, covinous, crafty, cunning, deceitful, deceiving, deceptive, designing, devious, dishonest, disloyal, *dolosus,* ensnaring, *fallax,* false, false-hearted, foxy, fraudulent, furtive, guileful, hypocritical, inconstant, indirect, *insidiosus,* intriguing, lying, perfidious, plotting, scheming, serpentine, sly, stealthy, subtle, surreptitious, treacherous, tricky, underhanded, unscrupulous, vulpine, wily

INSIGHT, ***noun*** ability to understand, acuity, acumen, acuteness, apperception, astuteness, awareness, cleverness, cognition, cognizance, comprehension, consciousness, discernment, discrimination, enlightenment, *intellegentia,* intuition, intuitiveness, *iudicium,* keenness, ken, noesis, penetration, perception, percipience, percipiency, perspicacity, realization, sagaciousness, sagacity, sensitivity, sharpness, shrewdness, understanding, wisdom

INSIGNIFICANCE, ***noun*** *exiguitas,* immateriality, inconsequence, inconsequentiality, inessentiality, insubstantiality, irrelevance, irrelevancy, momentariness, nominalness, paltriness, paucity, scantiness, scarceness, shallowness, smallness, sparseness, transientness, triviality, unimportance, unnoteworthiness

INSIGNIFICANT, ***adjective*** beneath consideration, collateral, expendable, frivolous, futile, ignoble, immaterial, inapposite, inappreciable, incidental, inconsequential, inconsiderable, indifferent, inferior, irrelevant, meager, meaningless, mediocre, minor, minute, moderate, modest, negligible, niggling, nominal, nonessential, nonsubstantial, nugatory, of little account, paltry, petty, picayune, remote, senseless, slight, small, tenuous, trifling, trivial, unessential, unimportant, unnoteworthy, usual, worthless

INSINCERE, ***adjective*** artificial, deceitful, deceptive, dishonest, disingenuous, disreputable, dissembling, dissimulating, evasive, faithless, false, false league, fraudulent, guileful, hollow, hypocritical, illegitimate, illusive, lying, mendacious, perfidious, shallow, specious, superficial, treacherous, uncandid, unfrank, unnatural, untrue, untruthful

INSINUATE, ***verb*** add, advert, allude to, append, curry favor with, describe, hint, implant, imply, impose, impress, incriminate, indicate, infer, infiltrate, infuse, inject, inlay, insert, instill, interject, interpolate, interpose, intimate, introduce, involve, mention, point to indirectly, presume, refer, signal, suggest, weave
ASSOCIATED CONCEPTS: sexual harassment

INSINUATION, ***noun*** allusion, aspersion, clue, hint, implication, indirect allusion, indirect comment, indirect implication, inference, innuendo, intimation, oblique hint, reference, *significatio,* suggestion, veiled observation, veiled remark

INSIPID, ***adjective*** banal, bloodless, boring, colorless, diluted, dreary, dull, feeble, flat, flavorless, *frigidus,* half-hearted, impotent, inactive, ineffective, *ineptus,* insubstantial, *insulsus,* irresolute, languid, limp, pointless, powerless, savorless, spiritless, tame, tasteless, torpid, unanimated, uncaptivating, undramatic, unelevated, unemphatic, unentertaining, unexciting, unimpassioned, uninspired, uninspiring, uninteresting, unsavory, unscintillating, unsparkling, unspiced, unspirited, unstrengthened, unvivid, vapid, void of taste, weak, without force, without taste

INSIST, ***verb*** accent, accentuate, argue, be obstinate, be peremptory, be resolute, bid, brook no denial, command, contend, demand, dictate, *efflagitare,* emphasize, enforce, enjoin, exact, exert pressure, exhort, *exposcere,* force upon, importune, impose, impress on, *instare,* lay stress on, order, override, persevere, persist, press, press earnestly, put pressure on, repeat, require, stand firm, stress, take no denial, underline, urge
ASSOCIATED CONCEPTS: insist on legal protections, insist on one's rights

INSISTENT, ***adjective*** argumentative, assertive, bent upon, clamorous, coactive, coercive, commanding, compelling, crying, demanding, disposed to insist, dogmatic, driving, emphatic, exigent, forceful, harping, impelling, imperative, importunate, incessant, insisting on notice, instant, intent upon, iterative, monotonous, peremptory, perseverant, persevering, persistent, persisting, pertinacious, pressing, recurrent, reiterative, repeated, repetitional, repetitionary, requesting, serious, striking, tenacious, urgent, vehement
ASSOCIATED CONCEPTS: coercion, improper influence, intimidation

INSOLENCE, ***noun*** abruptness, audaciousness, audacity, brusqueness, churlishness, contempt, crudity, curtness, disagreeableness, discourtesy, disrespect, gruffness, impertinence, impoliteness, impudence, incivility, inconsideration, obnoxiousness, presumption, pretense, retort, rudeness, sass, sullenness, surliness, tactlessness, ungraciousness, vulgarity

INSOLENT, ***adjective*** abusive, arrogant, assuming, audacious, bellicose, bold, brazen, bumptious, contemptuous, contumacious, *contumax,* contumelious, defiant, derisive, discourteous, disdainful, disobedient, disobliging, disregardful, disrespectful, flippant, fresh, froward, haughty, hectoring, imperious, impertinent, impolite, *impudens,* impudent, *insolens,* insulting, intolerant, magisterial, malapert, nervy, offensive, opprobrious, outrageous, overbearing, pert, presumptuous, procacious, rude, sarcastic, saucy, shameless, supercilious, swaggering, toplofty, unabashed, unmannerly
ASSOCIATED CONCEPTS: contempt

INSOLUBLE, ***adjective*** disputable, doubtable, doubtful, dubious, futile, hopeless, implausible, impracticable, incomprehensible, inconceivable, inextricable, infeasible, insolvable, insuperable, outlandish, preposterous, shaky, suspect, unattainable, undoable, unexplainable, unlikely, unrealizable, unworkable

INSOLVENT, ***adjective*** bankrupt, broke, defaulting, destitute, failed, impecunious, impoverished, in arrears, indebted, lacking funds, moneyless, out of funds, out of money, penniless, reduced, ruined, unable to pay

INSPECT, ***verb*** analyze, audit, check, check out, check over, comb, delve into, examine, explore, investigate, look into, monitor, observe, oversee, peruse, pick over, plumb, pore over, probe, research, review, scan, scrutinize, study, survey, view, watch
ASSOCIATED CONCEPTS: depositions, disclosure, discovery, document production, interrogatories, notice to produce guilty, subpoenas

INSPECTION, ***noun*** appraisal, ascertainment, assessment, careful scrutiny, critical examination, critical viewing, critique, evaluation, examination, exploration, inquest, inquiry, inventory, observation, perusal, reconnaissance, review, scrutiny, study, surveillance, survey, trial, visual examination
ASSOCIATED CONCEPTS: audit, authority to inspect, inspection for patent or latent defects, inspection of premises, inspection of records, on sight inspection, subject to inspection

INSPIRATION, ***noun*** animus, arousal, artistry, awakening, brainchild, catalyst, creativity, encouragement, example, flash, hero, idea, illumination, incentive, influence, ingenuity, insight, motivation, motive, muse, resource, spark, spur, stimulation, stimulus, talent, vision

INSPIRE, ***verb*** actuate, animate, arouse, awaken, bring about, cause, convince, effect, effectuate, elicit, encourage, enkindle, enliven, evoke, *excitare,* exert influence, fill with enthusiasm, generate, give an impetus, imbue, impassion, impel, *incendere, incitare,* incite, induce, influence, instigate, kindle, launch, motivate, move, occasion, originate, persuade, precipitate, prevail upon, produce, prompt, provoke, set astir, stimulate, sway, underlie, urge, wake

INSTALL *(Build In),* ***verb*** construct, embed, emplace, ensconce, fit, fix, lodge, place, put in

INSTALL *(Induct),* ***verb*** consecrate, crown, embed, emplace, ensconce, enthrone, establish, inaugurate, initiate, instate, invest, ordain, put in, usher in

INSTALLATION, ***noun*** admission, ceremony of induction into an office, establishment, inauguration, induction, initiation, installment, instatement, institution, introduction, investiture, launching, ordination, placement, presentation

INSTALLMENT, ***noun*** advance, allotment, contract payment, deposit, disbursement, dividend, division, down payment, fraction, one of several parts, one of several payments, one of successive parts, parcel, part payment, part payment of a debt, partial payment, *pensio,* periodic payment, *portio,* portion, remittance, section, segment, successive portion, token payment
ASSOCIATED CONCEPTS: installment contract, installment note, installment payments, installment plan, installment sale

INSTANCE, ***noun*** case, case in point, clarification, demonstration, elucidation, embodiment, ensample, example, exemplar, exemplification, *exemplum,* frame of reference, illustration, model, paradigm, representative, representative selection, sample, specimen, type
ASSOCIATED CONCEPTS: first instance, special instance, specific instance

INSTANT, ***adjective*** approaching, at once, at the present time, at this moment, close, close at hand, current, early, existent, forthcoming, forthwith, imminent, impending, in process, looming, near, near at hand, punctual, *punctum temporis,* ready, simultaneous, speedy, upcoming, without delay
ASSOCIATED CONCEPTS: instant case, instant motion

INSTANTANEOUS, ***adjective*** abrupt, expeditious, hasty, hurried, immediate, instant, occurring in an instant, *praesens,* prompt, quick, rapid, simultaneous, speedy, subitus, swift, without delay, without perceptible time lapse

INSTANTLY, ***adverb*** anon, at once, directly, expeditiously, *extemplo,* fast, forthwith, hastily, hurriedly, immediately, instantaneously, now, presently, promptly, quickly, rapidly, right away, right now, shortly, soon, speedily, straightway, swiftly, with speed, without a wait, without any lapse of time, without delay, without hesitation, without notice

INSTATE, ***verb*** admit, appoint, *confirmare, constituere,* designate, endow, enlist, enroll, ensconce, entrust, establish, establish in an office, found, give admittance to, give entrance to, *inaugurare,* inaugurate, induct, *initiare,* initiate, install, *instituere,* introduce, introduce into office, invest, launch, lay the foundations, lead the way, name, nominate, place, place in office, plant, put in possession, receive, seat, set, *stabilire, statuere,* take in

INSTIGATE, ***verb*** abet, actuate, agitate, coax, embolden, encourage, enflame, enkindle, excite, fire, fire up, foment, generate, goad, impel, incite, induce, inflame, influence, initiate, inspire, inspirit, invigorate, lure, motivate, move, persuade, prevail upon, prod, prompt, provoke, push, spur, start, stimulate, stir up, thrust, urge
ASSOCIATED CONCEPTS: code of conduct for law enforcement officials, entrapment

INSTIGATION, ***noun*** actuation, agitation, animation, cajolery, causation, coaxing, easement, encouragement,

excitation, exhortation, fomentation, goading, helpfulness, hortation, impetus, impulsion, incentive, incitation, incitement, inducement, influence, initiation, insistance, insistence, inspiration, invigoration, invitation, irritation, motivation, persuasion, perturbation, piquancy, pressure, prompting, provocation, solicitation, stimulation, *stimulus,* suasion, supporting, taunting, urging
ASSOCIATED CONCEPTS: accomplice, aiding and abetting a crime, instigation of a crime, promoting a crime
FOREIGN PHRASES: ***Plus peccat author quam actor.*** The originator or instigator of a crime is a worse offender than the actual perpetrator of it.

INSTILL, *verb* direct, educate, familiarize with, ground, guide, impart, impart gradually, implant, impress upon the mind, inculcate, indoctrinate, infix, inform, infuse, inject, *instillare,* instruct, prepare, propagandize, qualify, school, teach, train, tutor

INSTINCT, *noun* affinity, *appetitus,* aptitude, aptness, automatic reaction, bent, fitness, inborn proclivity, inclination, innate inclination, innate proclivity, intuition, involuntariness, native tendency, natural sense, natural tendency, predisposition, proclivity, proneness, propensity, reflex action, tendency, untutored intelligence

INSTINCTIVE, *adjective* abrupt, automatic, chance, conditioned, hereditary, inadvertent, innate, instantaneous, instinctive, involuntary, mechanic, mechanical, natural, offhand, Pavlovian, quick, random, rash, reactionary, reactive, reflect, simple, spontaneous, subconscious, subliminal, sudden, unconscious, unintended, unplanned, unpremeditated, unwitting, visceral

INSTITUTE, *noun* academy, alliance, association, board, body, brotherhood, cadre, chamber, clan, clique, club, coalition, collective, college, community, concern, congress, conlegium, consortium, cooperative, coterie, council, educational institution, establishment, fellowship, firm, foundation, fraternity, group, guild, house, institution, institution of learning, league, lyceum, order, organization, place of education, school, society, *sodalitas,* syndicate, system, union, university
ASSOCIATED CONCEPTS: business institution, charitable institution, educational institution, financial institution, lending institution, literary institution, penal institution, philanthropic institution, private institution, public institution

INSTITUTE A LAWSUIT, *verb* bring suit, bring to litigation, commence an action, file a claim, institute an action at law, litigate, sue, take action

INSTITUTION *(Commencement),* ***noun*** beginning, inauguration, inception, initiation, installation, installment, open introduction

INSTITUTION *(Custom),* ***noun*** academy, alliance, association, bylaw, canon, code, custom, established usage, establishment, familiar practice, fraternity, institute, law, league, ordinance, organization, permanent rule, place of education, prevalent practice, regulation, union

INSTRUCT *(Direct),* ***verb*** advise, advocate, bid, brief, call upon, charge, coach, command, compel, counsel, decree, demand, dictate, enact, exact, give a directive, give a mandate, give an order, give authoritative instructions to, give the signal, give the word, give the word of command, guide, impose a duty, impose a task, issue a command, issue a decree, issue an order, lay down the law, make a decree, make an order, *mandare,* order, pass orders, *praescribere,* prescribe, prescribe a task, prompt, promulgate a decree, promulgate an order, recommend, require, send an order, suggest, tell
ASSOCIATED CONCEPTS: instruct the jury

INSTRUCT *(Teach),* ***verb*** acquaint, comment upon, convey information, direct one's attention, edify, educate, elucidate, enlighten, *erudire,* explain, expound, familiarize, fill with information, give by way of information, give lessons in, give to understand, guide, guide the studies of, illumine, impart, implant, impress upon the memory, impress upon the mind, inculcate, indoctrinate, inform, instill, *instituere,* lecture, make known, point out, prepare, present, prime, provide with information, put before, qualify, school, show, train, tutor

INSTRUCTION *(Direction),* ***noun*** advice, authoritative statement, bidding, categorical imperative, caveat, charge, command, commandment, commission, decree, edification, firm advice, guidance, jury charge, mandate, *mandatum,* order, *praescriptum,* precept, regulation, requirement, rule, word of command, written order
ASSOCIATED CONCEPTS: instruction to a jury, peremptory instruction, special instructions
FOREIGN PHRASES: ***Matter en ley ne serra mise in bouche del jurors.*** A matter of law shall not be put into the mouth of jurors.

INSTRUCTION *(Teaching),* ***noun*** detailed statement, discourse, *doctrina,* edification, education, *eruditio,* explanation, exposition, guidance, inculcation, indoctrination, *institutio,* lecture, pedagogy, preaching, preparation, recital, recitation, schooling, sermon, training, tutelage, tutoring, upbringing

INSTRUMENT *(Document),* ***noun*** bill, certificate, charter, deed, draft, evidential writing, executed and delivered writing, formal writing, official record, official writing, paper, record, solemn writing, *syngrapha, tabula,* writing, writing delivered as the evidence of an agreement, writing which gives formal expression to a legal act, written formal expression
ASSOCIATED CONCEPTS: allonge, instrument evidencing a debt, instrument of writing, negotiable instrument
FOREIGN PHRASES: ***Mala grammatica non vitiat chartam, sed in expositione instrumentorum mala grammatica quoad fieri possit evitanda est.*** Bad grammar does not vitiate a deed, but in the drafting of instruments, bad grammar should, as far as possible, be avoided. ***Ubi nulla est conjectura quae ducat alio, verba intelligenda sunt ex proprietate, non grammatica, sed populari ex usu.*** Where there is nothing which calls for another construction, words are to be understood according to their proper sense, not according to their strict grammatical meaning, but according to their popular sense. ***Qui haeret in litera haeret in cortice.*** He who adheres to the letter of an instrument goes but skin deep into its meaning.

INSTRUMENT *(Tool),* ***noun*** agency, agent, aid, apparatus, appliance, article, channel, contributing force, contrivance, device, equipment, facility, implement, *instrumentum,* machine, machinery, means, mechanical construction, mechanism, medium, utensil, utility, vehicle
ASSOCIATED CONCEPTS: instrument of fraud

INSTRUMENTAL, *adjective* advantageous, aiding, assisting, auxiliary, beneficial, conducive, contributory, helpful, indispensable, serviceable, useful, valuable

INSTRUMENTALITY, *noun* channel, device, equipment, expedient, implement, instrument, interagent, intermediary, intermediate, intermedium, machinery, manner, means, medium, method, mode, operation, process, resource, stratagem, technic, technique, tool, vehicle, way, wherewithal
ASSOCIATED CONCEPTS: dangerous instrumentality

INSUBORDINATE, *adjective* contumacious, defiant, disloyal, disobedient, dissident, fractious, froward, indocile, insubmissive, insurgent, insurrectionary, intractable, lawless, mutinous, noncompliant, rebellious, recalcitrant, recusant, refractory, resistive, restive, revolutionary, sansculottic, *seditiosus,* treacherous, treasonous, *turbulentus,* uncomplying, ungovernable, unruly, wayward
ASSOCIATED CONCEPTS: contempt, discharge

INSUBSTANTIAL, *adjective* airy, baseless, bodiless, chimerical, ephemeral, fanciful, feeble, flimsy, fragile, frail, groundless, hallucinatory, illusive, illusory, imaginary, imagined, immaterial, impalpable, inadequate, inconsequential, inconsiderable, incorporeal, infirm, insignificant, lacking firmness, lacking substance, lame, made poorly, modest, nonexistent, notional, of no consequence, paltry, petty, picayune, poor, powerless, scant, slender, slight, slim, spectral, superficial, tenuous, thin, trifling, trivial, unbased, unfirm, unfounded, ungrounded, unimportant, unreal, unsolid, unsound, unsubstantial, unsupportable, unsustainable, untenable, vague, visionary, weak, without basis, without foundation, without plausibility, without reality, wobbly, worthless

INSUFFERABLE, *adjective* acute, agonizing, crushing, distressing, dreadful, excruciating, extreme, frightful, harrowing, harsh, hurtful, impossible, insupportable, *intolerabilis,* intolerable, *intolerandus,* painful, past bearing, past enduring, racking, searing, severe, torturous, unbearable, unendurable

INSUFFERABLE HARM, *noun* disablement, evil, malignance, malignancy, malignity, massive injury, not corrected by monetary compensation, noxiousness, permanent harm, perniciousness, ruin, serious damage, serious ill-treatment, significant detriment, significant ill-consequence, significant impairment, unbearable aggravation, unbearable harm, virulence
ASSOCIATED CONCEPTS: Latham Act, Patent Act, permanent injunctions, preliminary injunctions, temporary restraining orders, Uniform Trade Secrets Act

INSUFFICIENCY, *noun* absence, dearth, deficiency, deficit, depletion, emptiness, exhaustion, exiguity, exiguousness, falling short, fewness, inadequacy, inadequateness, incompetence, incompleteness, *inopia,* lack, meagerness, need, not enough, paucity, *penuria,* scantiness, scantness, scarcity, short fall, short measure, short supply, shortage, shortcoming, sparseness, stint, too few, want
ASSOCIATED CONCEPTS: insufficiency of evidence, insufficiency of law to support a verdict

INSUFFICIENT, *adjective* bereft of, defective, deficient, denuded of, destitute of, devoid of, drained, failing, faint, feeble, *haud sufficiens, impar,* imperfect, in default, inadequate, incapable, incommensurate, incompetent, incomplete, inconsiderable, lacking, lean, meager, missing, negligible, not enough, not sufficient, paltry, poor, scant, scanty, scarce, short, shy, slender, slight, slim, spare, sparse, thin, too little, uncompleted, unequal, unfinished, unfit, unfitted, unqualified, unsound, unsufficing, unsuited, wanting, weak
ASSOCIATED CONCEPTS: insufficient evidence, insufficient funds, insufficient service, insufficient verdict

INSUFFICIENT EVIDENCE, *noun* a negligible amount of evidence, absence of sufficient evidence, bereft of evidence, deficient amount of evidence, devoid of sufficient proof, failing proof, inadequate amount of persuasive facts, inadequate confirmation, inadequate facts to prove the point in question, inadequate means of proof, inadequate proof, inadequate proof of facts, inadequate substantiation, incomplete evidence, insufficient admitted testimony, insufficient body of facts, insufficient corroboration, insufficient facts to establish the point in issue, insufficient means of proving a fact, insufficient proof at trial, insufficient verification, lacking proof, lean on evidence, meager degree of evidence, paltry amount of evidence, scant testimony, slim proof, sparse proof, thin evidence, weak on evidence
ASSOCIATED CONCEPTS: dismissal of an action, woefully insufficient evidence

INSULAR, *adjective* alone, apart, confined, detached, discrete, distinct, enisled, isolated, removed, self-sufficient, separate, solitary

INSULATE, *verb* compartmentalize, cut off, detach, isolate, keep apart, quarantine, screen off, seclude, segregate, separate, sequester, set apart, zone

INSULT, *noun* abuse, affront, aspersion, atrocity, defamation, defilement, derision, diatribe, disparagement, enormity, impertinence, incivility, indignity, insolence, mockery, offense, offensive remark, open disrespect, outrage, provocation, rebuff, revilement, ridicule, rudeness, slap in the face, slight, snub, uncomplimentary remarks, vulgarity

INSULT, *verb* affront, be rude to, denigrate, deride, disoblige, disparage, display insolence toward, disregard, disrespect, flout, hector, hold in derision, humiliate, jeer, mock, offend, pique, provoke, raise one's dander, rebuff, ridicule, treat with contemptuousness, treat with discourtesy, treat with indignity

INSUPERABLE, *adjective* beyond control, difficult, formidable, impassible, impervious, impossible, impracticable, impregnable, inaccessible, incapable of being overcome, incapable of being surmounted, indomitable, innavigable, insurmountable, *invictus,* invincible, invulnerable, out of reach, out of the question, unachievable, unassailable, unattackable, unattainable, unbeatable, unbridgeable, unconquerable, undefeatable, unfeasable, unmasterable, unobtainable, unovercomable

INSURABLE INTEREST, *noun* acceptable insured, acceptable risk, capable of being insured, insurable ownership, insurable risk, insurable stake, legitimate interest, stake, sufficiently close relationships, vested interest
ASSOCIATED CONCEPTS: life insurance

INSURANCE, *noun* agreement to pay, assurance against loss, bond against risk, compensation for injury, compensation for loss, contract against future loss, contract against unknown contingencies, guarantee against loss, indemnification, indemnity against loss, pledge, promise, protection against loss, security against loss, stipulation to compensate for loss, warranty against loss
ASSOCIATED CONCEPTS: accident insurance, binder, casualty insurance, claim, coinsurance, contract of insurance, contributing insurance, controlled insurance, endowment

insurance, excess insurance, fidelity insurance, fire insurance, group insurance, guaranty insurance, health insurance, insurance agent, insurance application, insurance broker, insurance carrier, insured, insurer, liability insurance, life insurance, loss, marine insurance, nonforfeitable insurance, occupational disability insurance, ordinary insurance, paid-up insurance, policy of insurance, premium, property insurance, reinsurance, surety insurance, term insurance, title insurance, valued insurance, vehicle insurance, whole life insurance

INSURE, ***verb*** cover against loss, gain indemnity against loss, guarantee against loss, have underwritten, obtain insurance, protect against loss, reassure, secure against loss, underwrite against loss

INSURER, ***noun*** assurer, compensator, guarantee, guarantor, indemnifier, indemnitor, insurance company, recompenser, remunerator, surety, underwriter
ASSOCIATED CONCEPTS: absolute insurer, accident and health insurer, agent, broker, casualty insurer, liability insurer, life insurer

INSURGENCY, ***noun*** agitators, criminals, exciters, guerrillas, incendiaries, inducers, inspirers, insurrection, prompters, provokers, rebellion, rebels, revolutionaries, stimulators, uprising
ASSOCIATED CONCEPTS: counter insurgency strategy, global insurgency, quelling insurgency

INSURGENT, ***noun*** agitator, anarchist, demagogue, disrupter, insubordinate, insurrectionary, insurrectionist, mutineer, nihilist, radical, rebel, *rebellis,* reformer, renegade, revolter, revolutionary, revolutionist, rioter, seditionary, subverter, traitor

INSURMOUNTABLE, ***adjective*** beyond one's power, beyond one's reach, beyond the bounds of possibility, formidable, hardly possible, impassable, impenetrable, impossible, impracticable, impregnable, inaccessible, incapable of being done, incapable of being overcome, incapable of success, indomitable, inexpugnable, insoluble, insuperable, invincible, out of reach, out of the question, too difficult, too hard, unachievable, unassailable, unattackable, unattainable, unbeatable, unconquerable, undefeatable, unfeasible, unmasterable, unperformable, unrealizable, unsolvable, unsubduable, unsurmountable, unvanquishable, unviable, unworkable

INSURRECTION, ***noun*** anarchy, defiance, disobedience, disorder, disturbance, insubordination, insurgence, insurgency, *motus,* mutineering, mutiny, noncompliance, outbreak, overthrow, political upheaval, *rebellio,* rebellion, resistance to government, revolt, revolution, riot, rising, *seditio,* sedition, uprising

INSUSCEPTIBLE *(Resistant),* ***adjective*** able to withstand, capable of resisting, defended, fortified, having immunity, having resistance, immune, immunized, not sensitive to, protected, repellent, strengthened, strong, tough, unyielding

INSUSCEPTIBLE *(Uncaring),* ***adjective*** aloof, apathetic, blind, callous, capable of resisting, capable of withstanding, cold, cool, deaf, detached, devoid of feeling, distant, frigid, hard, hardened, heartless, impassive, impervious, incapable of caring, indifferent, indurate, indurated, inflexible, insensate, insensible, insensitive, insolicitous, insouciant, *insusceptire,* lacking feeling, numb, obdurate, obstinate, pachydermatous, pococurante, recalcitrant, regardless, removed, renitent, *sensu carere,* stubborn, tough, toughened, unaffected, unaroused, unbending, unconcerned, unemotional, unfeeling, ungiving, unimpassioned, unimpressible, uninterested, unmoved, unresponsive, unstirred, unsympathetic, untouched, unwilling to care, unyielding, without regard

INTACT, ***adjective*** all-embracing, all in one, all-inclusive, complete, comprehensive, entire, faultless, flawless, free from imperfection, full, in good order, in its original form, in one piece, in perfect condition, inclusive, *intactus, integer,* integral, inviolate, perfect, preserved, replete, safe, *salvus,* solid, sound, together, unabated, unabridged, unaffected by injury, unalloyed, unaltered, unblemished, unbroken, unbruised, uncensored, unchanged, uncut, undamaged, undecayed, undefaced, undemolished, undestroyed, undiminished, undivided, unedited, unexpurgated, unfaded, unharmed, unhurt, unified, unimpaired, uninjured, unmarked, unmarred, unreduced, unscarred, unscathed, unscratched, unsevered, unshattered, unspoiled, unsullied, untainted, untorn, untouched, unworn, whole, with nothing missing, without loss
ASSOCIATED CONCEPTS: keeping a law intact

INTANGIBLE, ***adjective*** abstract, aerial, airy, amorphous, asomatous, bodiless, difficult to appraise, dim, discarnate, disembodied, ethereal, immaterial, impalpable, imperceptible, imponderable, inappreciable, inconspicuous, incorporal, incorporate, incorporeal, indefinite, indiscernible, infinitesimal, insensible, insubstantial, intactile, *intactilis,* invisible, nonphysical, nonsubstantial, not clear to the mind, not definite, shadowy, spiritual, theoretical, unapparent, unbeholdable, uncertain, unconcrete, undiscernible, unearthly, unfleshly, unperceivable, unphysical, unseeable, unsolid, unsubstantial, untouchable, vague, weightless, without form, without physical substance
ASSOCIATED CONCEPTS: intangible assets, intangible personalty, intangible property

INTANGIBLE, ***noun*** assignable rights of action, chose in action, incorporeal entity, *intactilis,* personal chattels which are not in possession, personal right not reduced to possession, right, right to personal things, right to recovery
ASSOCIATED CONCEPTS: intangible assets, intangible personalty, intangible property, intangible trust property

INTEGRAL, ***adjective*** basic, cardinal, central, component, constituent, elemental, essential, essential to completeness, fundamental, indispensable, integrant, irreplaceable, *necessarius,* necessary, needed, needful, prerequisite, primary, required, requisite, vital
ASSOCIATED CONCEPTS: integral part of a case

INTEGRATE, ***verb*** accommodate, adjust, aggregate, amass, assimilate, combine, complete, connect, constitute a whole, coordinate, desegregate, embody, embrace, fit, harmonize, join, make into a whole, proportion, relate, synchronize, systematize, unify

INTEGRATION *(Amalgamation),* ***noun*** admixture, affiliation, alliance, association, blend, blending, coadunation, coalition, coexistence, combination, confederation, consolidation, federalization, fusion, incorporation, intermixture, medley, merger, mingling, mix, unification, union
ASSOCIATED CONCEPTS: integration of the terms into a contract

INTEGRATION *(Assimilation),* ***noun*** agreement, alliance, association, coalition, coexistence, combination,

confederation, consociation, cooperation, federation, fellowship, merger, mingling, participation, partnership, racial balance, racial harmonization, racial harmony, removal of discrimination, solidarity, togetherness, undividedness
ASSOCIATED CONCEPTS: equal protection, segregation

INTEGRITY, *noun* character, estimableness, fairness, faithfulness, fidelity, good faith, goodness, high character, high-mindedness, honesty, honor, honorableness, incorruptibility, *innocentia, integritas,* justness, moral soundness, moral strength, morality, nobleness, principle, *probitas,* probity, propriety, purity, rectitude, reputability, responsibility, righteousness, scruples, scrupulousness, self-respect, sincerity, sound moral principle, strict honesty, trustworthiness, truthfulness, upright moral character, uprightness, uprightness of character, upstandingness, veridicality, virtue, virtuousness, worthiness
ASSOCIATED CONCEPTS: character evidence, impugning the integrity of a witness, want of integrity

INTELLECT, *noun* ability to perceive, ability to reason, ability to understand, brain, brilliance, cerebration, cognition, cognitive faculty, comprehension, genius, intellectual powers, intellectuality, *intellegentia,* intelligence, *mens,* mental ability, mental acuteness, mental capacity, mental faculty, mentality, mind, power to reason, rational faculty, rationality, reach of mind, reason, reasoning faculty, reasoning power, sense, understanding

INTELLECTUAL GILL-NETTING, *noun* gaining intellectual rights through burying the language in an agreement, purchase of all intellectual rights in boilerplate language, purchase of intellectual rights, purchasing perpetual and universal multimedia rights in hidden contractual language

INTELLECTUAL PROPERTY RIGHTS, *noun* creative product protection, creative thinking protection, protection, protection of creativity, protection of writings
ASSOCIATED CONCEPTS: copyrights, patent trademarks

INTELLIGENCE *(Intellect),* ***noun*** acumen, aptitude, astuteness, brains, brilliance, cleverness, cognition, cognitive faculty, comprehension, genius, insight, intellectional faculty, intellectual power, intellectuality, *intellegentia,* keenness, *mens,* mental ability, mental acuteness, mental capacity, mental faculty, mentality, mind, power to reason, quickness of perception, rational faculty, rationality, reach of mind, reason, reasoning faculty, reasoning power, sagacity, sense, understanding, wisdom

INTELLIGENCE *(News),* ***noun*** account, acquired facts, aviso, communication, communiqué, data, details, dispatch, enlightenment, information, knowledge, known facts, message, monition, notice, *nuntius,* report, tidings, tip, warning, word

INTELLIGENT, *adjective* able, acute, astute, brainy, bright, capable, clever, discerning, enlightened, gifted, intellectual, judicious, knowing, knowledgeable, perspicacious, perceptive, percipient, sagacious, sapient, sciential, sensible, sharp-witted, shrewd, talented, understanding, well-informed, wise

INTELLIGIBLE, *adjective* apprehensible, articulate, clear, cognizable, cognizant, coherent, comprehensible, definite, descriptive, distinct, easily understood, evident, explicable, explicit, fathomable, graphic, knowable, lucid, manifest, obvious, palpable, pellucid, plain, plain-spoken, precise, realizable, scrutable, simple, solvable, unambiguous, understandable, unequivocal, unmistakable

INTEMPERATE, *adjective* exceeding, excessive, exorbitant, extravagant, extreme, immoderate, inabstinent, indulgent, inordinate, unbridled, unchecked, uncontrolled, uncurbed, uninhibited, unlimited, unmeasured, unreined, unrestrained, unruly, unsuppressed, untempered, wasteful

INTEND, *verb* aim, aspire to, be determined to, calculate, *cogitare,* design, desire, determine upon, drive at, elect, endeavor, expect, fix the mind upon, harbor a design, have in mind, have in view, *intendere,* mean, plan, premeditate, presume, propose, purpose, resolve, scheme, set as a goal
ASSOCIATED CONCEPTS: intended design, intended destination, intended purpose, intended to take effect upon death, precatory words

INTENSE, *adjective* *acer,* acrimonious, active, acute, aggressive, agonizing, all-consuming, ambitious, angry, animated, anxiety ridden, *ardens,* ardent, aspiring, assiduous, brisk, burning, close, concentrated, consuming, cutting, deep, determined, diligent, distressing, drastic, dynamic, earnest, emotional, emotive, energetic, enthusiastic, excessive, excitable, excited, extraordinary, extreme, fervent, fervid, feverish, fierce, fiery, flaming, flaring, forceful, frantic, frenzied, grave, harrowing, harsh, head-strong, heated, heightened, high-pressure, hostile, hot-heated, hysterical, impassioned, impatient, impetuous, impulsive, industrious, inflamed, injurious, intensified, intensive, intent, *intentus,* keen, malicious, nervous, passionate, perfervid, powerful, profound, pungent, purposeful, rancorous, resolved, rigorous, serious, severe, sharp, single-minded, stinging, strenuous, strict, strong, tense, testy, undeviating, unwavering, vehement, vigorous, vivid, zealous
ASSOCIATED CONCEPTS: intense law enforcement focus, intense scrutiny

INTENSIFY, *verb* add to, aggravate, *amplificare, augere,* augment, boost, concentrate, deepen, emphasize, enhance, escalate, exacerbate, exaggerate, heighten, increase, inflame, magnify, redouble, sharpen, step up, strengthen

INTENSITY, *noun* acuteness, amplitude, ardor, brightness, brilliance, degree, devotion, eagerness, earnestness, energy, enthusiasm, extent, extreme degree, fervency, fervor, force, furiousness, high degree, high pressure, loudness, magnitude, main force, mightiness, passion, potency, power, pressure, puissance, rigor, severity, sharpness, spirit, strength, vehemence, vigor, vividness, warmth, zeal

INTENSIVE, *adjective* acute, ardent, concentrated, exhaustive, fervent, forceful, intense, *intentivus,* powerful, sharp, strenuous, strong, thorough, thoroughgoing, unmitigated, vehement, vigorous, zealous

INTENT, *noun* aim, *attentus,* choice, contemplation, design, determination, end, *erectus, intentus,* meaning, mind, motive, object, objective, plan, point, predetermination, purport, purpose, resolution, resolve, scheme, scope, view, volition
ASSOCIATED CONCEPTS: charitable intent, corrupt intent, criminal intent, felonious intent, fraudulent intent, general intent, implied intent, intent of parties to contract, intent of testator, intent to defraud, larcenous intent, malice, mutual intent, premeditation, presumed intent, specific intent, testamentary intent, transferred intent

FOREIGN PHRASES: ***Quod factum est, cum in obscuro sit, ex affectione cujusque capit interpretationem.*** When there is doubt about an act, it receives interpretation from the feelings or disposition of the actor. ***Impunitas continuum affectum tribuit delinquendi.*** Impunity confirms the disposition of a delinquent. ***Intentio mea imponit nomen operi meo.*** My intent gives a name to my act. ***Non aliter a significatione verborum recedi oportet quam cum manifestum est, aliud sensisse testatorem.*** The ordinary meaning of the words ought not to be departed from unless it is evident that the testator intended otherwise. ***Quicunque jussu judicis aliquid fecerit non videtur dolo malo fecisse, quia parere necesse est.*** Whoever does anything by the command of a judge is not deemed to have done it with an evil intent, because it is necessary to obey. ***Voluntas et propositum distinguunt maleficia.*** The will and purpose distinguish offenses. ***In criminalibus, sufficit generalis malitia intentionis, cum facto paris gradus.*** In crimes, a general malicious intent suffices where there is an act of equal degree. ***In criminalibus, voluntas reputabitur pro facto.*** In criminal cases, the intent will be taken for the deed. ***Voluntas facit quod in testamento scriptum valeat.*** The will of the testator gives validity to what is written in the will. ***Actus non facit reum, nisi mens sit rea.*** An act does not render a person guilty, unless the mind is guilty. ***Impunitas continuum affectum tribuit delinquendi.*** Impunity confirms the disposition of a delinquent. ***In atrocioribus delictis punitur affectus licet non sequatur effectus.*** In the more atrocious crimes the intent is punished, although an effect does not follow. ***Malitia est acida; est mali animi affectus.*** Malice is sour; it is the quality of an evil mind. ***Voluntas in delictis, non exitus spectatur.*** In crimes, the intent, and not the result, is regarded.

INTENTION, *noun* aim, ambition, *consilium,* design, desire, destination, determination, direction, earnestness, end in view, end intended, fixed direction, fixed purpose, goal, *institutum,* mark, object, objective, plan, *propositum,* purpose, resolution, resolve, set purpose, settled determination, target, ultimate purpose
ASSOCIATED CONCEPTS: donative intention, implied intention, the intention of the parties, malicious intention
FOREIGN PHRASES: ***In testamentis plenius voluntates testantium interpretantur.*** In wills, the intentions of the testators should be fully regarded. ***Non efficit affectus nisi sequatur effectus.*** The intention amounts to nothing unless some effect follows. ***In conventionibus, contrahentium voluntas potius quam verba spectari placuit.*** In contracts, it is the rule to regard the intention of the parties rather than the actual words. ***Culpa lata dolo aequiparatur.*** Gross negligence is held equivalent to malice. ***In maleficiis voluntas spectatur, non exitus.*** In offenses, the intention is regarded, not the result. ***Intentio inservire debet legibus, non leges intentioni.*** The intention of a party ought to be subservient to the laws, not the laws to intentions. ***Benigne faciendae sunt interpretationes, propter simplicitatem laicorum, ut res magis valeat quam pereat; et verba intentioni, non e contra, debent inservire.*** Interpretations should be liberal, because of the lack of training of laymen, so that the subject matter should be valid rather than void; and words should be subject to the intention, not the intention to the words.

INTENTIONAL, *adjective* by design, calculated, *cogitatus,* conscious, *consideratus,* considered, contemplated, decided, deliberate, designed, determined, intended, knowing, *lentus,* meditated, outlined before hand, planned, pondered, prearranged, preconsidered, predesigned, predetermined, premeditated, purposed, purposeful, reasoned, resolved, studied, thought out, thoughtful, willful
ASSOCIATED CONCEPTS: intentional act, intentional homicide, intentional neglect, intentional tort

INTER VIVOS, *noun* conferment between the living, conveyance between the living, transfer among the living
ASSOCIATED CONCEPTS: inter vivos will

INTERAGENT, *noun* agent, broker, go-between, instrument, intermediary, intermediate, intermediate agent, intermediator, intervener, intervening agent, mediating agency, mediator, medium, middleman, negotiator, spokesman, vehicle

INTERCEDE, *verb* act as agent, act as go-between, act as mediator, arbitrate, bring into harmony, bring to an understanding, bring to terms, bring together, compose differences, conciliate, *deprecari,* interfere, intermeddle, intermediate, interpose, intervene, judge, make peace between, meddle, mediate, moderate, negotiate, petition for, plead, referee, settle, stand between, step in, umpire

INTERCEPT, *verb* avert, block, check, close with, come between, commandeer, confiscate, debar, detain, dispossess, disrupt, foil, forestall, hamper, hinder, impede, impound, inhibit, interfere, interpose, interrupt, obstruct, occlude, parry, preclude, prevent, restrain, retard, stave, stay, stem, stop, thwart, wrest from
ASSOCIATED CONCEPTS: intercept criminal activity

INTERCESSION, *noun* arbitrage, arbitration, conciliation, *deprecatio,* diplomacy, instrumentality, interference, interjection, intermeddling, intermediation, interposition, intervention, mediation, negotiation, peacemaking, reconcilement, reconciliation, supplication

INTERCHANGE, *noun* alternation, barter, change, exchange, give and take, intercourse, *permutatio,* rearrangement, reciprocal exchange, reciprocation, requital, retaliation, swap, trade, transaction

INTERDICT, *verb* arrest, bar, block, check, debar, declare illegal, deny, deter, disallow, embargo, enjoin, forbid, halt, hinder, impede, inhibit, *interdicere,* obstruct, preclude, prevent, prohibit, proscribe, refuse permission, repress, restrain, restrict, stop, thwart, veto

INTEREST *(Concern),* ***noun*** absorption, admiration, anxiety, application, assiduity, attention, attention to detail, awe, care, close attention, concentration, conscientiousness, consequence, consideration, curiosity, curiousness, desire to know, diligent attention, disposition to inquire, eagerness, enthusiasm, esteem, excitement, gravity, heed, heedfulness, import, importance, inclination to ask questions, intentiveness, intentness, mark, meddling, meticulosity, mindfulness, minute attention, minuteness, moment, note, pertinence, preoccupation, prying, questioning, regard, regardfulness, relevance, reverence, salience, significance, solicitude, studiousness, *studium,* thoughtfulness, undivided attention, veneration, weight, weightiness, worry
ASSOCIATED CONCEPTS: conflict of interest, declaration against interest, direct interest, insurable interest, interest in the controversy, interested witness, legal interest, material interest, real party in interest, united in interest

INTEREST *(Ownership),* ***noun*** assets, belongings, claim, dominion, droit, holding, lawful possession, part,

participation, percentage of ownership, portion, possession, property, proprietorship, right, right of ownership, rightful possession, seisin, share, stake, title
ASSOCIATED CONCEPTS: accounts bearing interest, assignable interest, beneficial interest, common interest, contingent interest, continuity of interest, controlling interest, future interest, interest in land, joint interest, legal interest, legal rate of interest, life interest, person interested in a will, property interest, qualified interest, remainder interest, remaining interest, transfer of interest, undivided interest
FOREIGN PHRASES: ***Nemo plus juris ad alienum transferre potest quam ipse habet.*** No one can transfer to another any greater right than he himself has.

INTEREST *(Profit),* ***noun*** accrual, advantage, dividend, earnings, *faenus,* gain, increment, monetary benefit, monetary gain, premium for the use of money, profit from money loaned, *usura*
ASSOCIATED CONCEPTS: legal rate of interest, usury

INTEREST, ***verb*** absorb, affect, arouse, arouse notice, arouse one's enthusiasm, attract, attract notice, beguile, catch the eye, concern, *delectare,* divert one's attention, engage the attention, engage the mind, engage the thoughts, engross, engross the mind, engross the thoughts, entangle, entertain, enthrall, entice, excite, fascinate, grip, hold the attention, inspire, involve, move, occupy, occupy the attention, pique, *placere,* rouse, stir, tantalize, tempt, titillate, touch, whet one's interest

INTERESTED, ***adjective*** affected, affiliated, associated, biased, concerned, connected, directly affected by the outcome of a controversy, having investments in, influenced, involved, one-sided, partial, partisan, prejudiced, prepossessed, solicitous, undetached
ASSOCIATED CONCEPTS: interested juror, interested party, interested witness

INTERFERE, ***verb*** arrest, bar, be an obstacle, block, break in, burden, check, clog, counteract, countervail, cramp, cripple, cross, curb, deter, disallow, disturb, encroach, encumber, entrammel, fetter, foil, forbid, hamper, handicap, hinder, impede, infringe, inhibit, intercede, intercept, interject, intermeddle, intermit, *interpellare,* interpose, interrupt, intervene, *intervenire,* intrude, invade, meddle, obstruct, preclude, prevent, prohibit, retard, stop, thwart, work against
ASSOCIATED CONCEPTS: interference with business relations, interference with contract rights, interference with interstate commerce, unreasonable interference
FOREIGN PHRASES: ***Forstellarius est pauperum depressor et totius communitatis et patriae publicus inimicus.*** A forestaller is an enemy of the poor and a public enemy of the country. ***Nemo debet immiscere se rei ad se nihil pertinenti.*** No one should interfere with a thing that in no respect concerns him.

INTERFERE WITH THE LAW, ***verb*** bar to investigation, become an obstacle to prosecutors, block prosecution, counteract the smooth prosecution of the law, countervail instructions, disturb a prosecution, hamper prosecution, handicap prosecution, hinder prosecution, impede prosecution, infringe on a prosecution, inhibit prosecution, interrupt a prosecution, meddle in a prosecution, obstruct a prosecution, prevent a prosecution, prohibit an ongoing prosecution, retard an investigation, stop an investigation, thwart a criminal investigation, work at cross-purposes with an investigation
ASSOCIATED CONCEPTS: consent necessity, law enforcement, self defense, torts

INTERFERENCE, ***noun*** antagonism, antipathy, bar, barrier, censure, check, collision, conflict, contravention, damper, disapproval, disturbance, encumbrance, fetter, friction, frustration, hindrance, impediment, imposition, infringement, interception, intercession, intermediacy, interposition, interruption, intervention, intrusion, invasion, meddling, nuisance, obstruction, onus, opposition, prohibition, resistance, restraint, setback, stricture, stumbling block
ASSOCIATED CONCEPTS: contempt, frustration of contract, interference with contractual relations

INTERIM, ***adjective*** impermanent, intermediate, makeshift, provisional, provisory, temporary, *temporis intervallum,* tentative, transient, unfinished, unofficial
ASSOCIATED CONCEPTS: interim relief, interim stay, provisional remedies

INTERIOR, ***adjective*** inherent, innate, inner, innermost, internal, inward, private, secret

INTERIOR, ***noun*** center, core, essence, inland, inner part, inside, middle

INTERJECT, ***verb*** add, blurt, comment, exclaim, explain, express, force in, implant, include, incorporate, infiltrate, inject, insert, intercalate, *intericere,* interjaculate, intermingle, interpolate, *interponere,* interpose, interrupt, intervene, interweave, introduce, intromit, place into, put between, set forth, specify, state, thrust in, vociferate, work in

INTERLOCKING, ***adjective*** connective, correlative, interacting, interlinking, meshing
ASSOCIATED CONCEPTS: interlocking defenses, interlocking instruments, interlocking signal systems

INTERLOCUTORY, ***adjective*** interim, intermedial, intermediary, intervening, interventional, nonfinal, nonpermanent, not final, provisional, provisory, temporary, tentative, transient, transitory
ASSOCIATED CONCEPTS: interlocutory appeal, interlocutory costs, interlocutory decree, interlocutory injunction, interlocutory order, interlocutory rulings

INTERMEDIARY, ***noun*** agent, *arbiter,* arbitrator, buffer, *conciliator,* connecting link, connection, delegate, *deprecator,* diplomat, emissary, go-between, interceder, intercessor, link, mediary, mediator, medium, middleman, moderator, negotiant, negotiator, peacemaker, pleader, propitiator, reconciler, referee, representative, vehicle

INTERMEDIATE, ***adjective*** average, between, central, compromising, equidistant, halfway, inserted, instrumental, intercurrent, interjacent, intermediary, interposed, intervenient, intervening, mean, medial, median, mediatorial, mediatory, medium, *medius,* mesial, mesne, mid, middle, midmost, moderate, neutral, transitional
ASSOCIATED CONCEPTS: interlocutory order, intermediate appellate court, intermediate order
FOREIGN PHRASES: ***Extremis probatis, praesumuntur media.*** When the extremes have been proved, those things which are between them are presumed.

INTERMINABLE, ***adjective*** boundless, ceaseless, constant, continual, continuous, drawn-out, durable, endless, eternal, everlasting, extended, extensive, illimitable, immeasurable, incessant, indeterminate, inexhaustible, infinite, innumerable, limitless, long-drawn, long-winded, measureless, olamic, open-headed, permanent, perpetual, profuse, prolonged, protracted, stretched, tediously long, termless, unbounded, unending, unceasing, uninterrupted, unlimited, unremitting, wearisome, without limit or end

INTERMISSION, *noun* abeyance, adjournment, break, cessation, delay, discontinuance, discontinuity, halt, hiatus, interim, interlude, intermittence, interregnum, interruption, interval, intervention, leave, lull, pause, pendency, recess, remission, respite, rest, stoppage, suspense, suspension

INTERMITTENT, *adjective* alternate, broken, cyclic, cyclical, desultory, discontinuous, fitful, flickering, fluctuating, infrequent, intermitting, interrupted, irregular, nonuniform, occasional, periodic, recurrent, recurring, remittent, rhythmic, seasonal, serial, spasmodic, sporadic, termly, unregular, unsuccessive, wavering

INTERNAL, *adjective* absorbed, domestic, domesticus, enclosed, implanted, infixed, ingrained, inmost, innate, inner, innermost, inside, *interior, intestinus,* private, under the surface, within boundary lines
ASSOCIATED CONCEPTS: internal affairs, Internal Revenue Service

INTERNMENT, *noun* apprehension, arrest, bondage, captivity, confinement, constraint, custody, detention, durance, immuration, immurement, impoundment, imprisonment, imprisonment term, incarceration, preventive custody

INTERPOSE, *verb* be an obstacle to, block, break into, come between, force in, hinder, impede, infiltrate, infringe, inject, insert, intercalate, intercede, intercept, interfere, *intericere,* interject, intermeddle, intermediate, *interponere,* interrupt, intervene, introduce, intrude, mediate, obstruct, obtrude, parenthesize, penetrate, place between, prevent, put in, stand in the way, thrust in
ASSOCIATED CONCEPTS: interpose a claim, interpose a defense, interpose an objection

INTERPOSITION, *noun* arbitration, insertion, intercalation, intercession, intercurrence, interjacence, interjection, interlocation, intermediation, interpenetration, interposure, interruption, intervention, introduction, negotiation

INTERPRET, *verb* annotate, characterize, clarify, clear up, *conicere,* construe, convey the meaning of, decipher, decode, deduce, define, delineate, depict, describe, diagnose, explain, explain the meaning, *explanare,* explicate, expound, figure out, give one an idea of, give one an impression of, illuminate, illustrate, *interpretari,* make clear, make plain, make sense of, offer an explanation of, reveal, set forth the meaning, simplify, solve, throw light upon, translate, translate orally, understand, unfold, unravel, unscramble
ASSOCIATED CONCEPTS: construction, interpret a contract, interpret a will

INTERPRETATION, *noun* analysis, annotation, application, clarification, comment, commentary, connotation, construction, content, decipherment, definition, depiction, description, diagnosis, elucidation, exegesis, exemplification, explanation, explication, exposition, illustration, implication, inference, meaning, portrayal, prognosis, reading, rendering, rendition, resolution, revelation, scholium, sense, significance, signification, solution, translation, understanding, version
ASSOCIATED CONCEPTS: authentic interpretation, close interpretation, customary interpretation, exact interpretation, free and unrestricted interpretation, genuine interpretation, incorrect interpretation, legal interpretation, liberal interpretation, limited interpretation, predestined interpretation, restricted interpretation, rightful interpretation, unfair interpretation

INTERPRETIVE, *adjective* annotative, clarifying, constructive, definitive, elucidative, enlightening, explanatory, explicative, illuminating, interpretational

INTERRELATED, *adjective* affiliated, affinitive, agnate, akin, allied, analogous, associated, cognate, conjugate, connatural, connected, consanguineous, consociate, correlated, correlative, enmeshed, fraternal, germane, interaffiliated, interallied, interassociated, interconnected, interlinked, interwoven, joined, kindred, linked, of the same family, pertinent, related, relevant, sib, tied, united

INTERRELATION, *noun* chain, coherence, connection, contact, correlation, interaffiliation, interassociation, interconnection, interdependence, interrelationship, mutual dependence, mutuality, nexus, proportion, relationship

INTERROGATE, *verb* ask, badger, catechize, conduct an inquiry, cross-examine, delve into, grill, heckle, inquire, interpellate, investigate, pose, probe, prosecute an inquiry of, put questions to, question, quiz, require an answer

INTERROGATION, *noun* catechization, cross-examination, examination, exploration, formal questioning, grilling, inquest, inquiry, inquisition, inspection, *interrogatio,* investigation, *percontatio,* probe, *quaestio,* query, questioning, scrutiny, search, taking information
ASSOCIATED CONCEPTS: grand jury inquiry, interrogation of a party to an action, interrogation of a witness

INTERROGATIVE, *adjective* all-searching, diagnostic, exploratory, fact-finding, inquisitional, inquisitive, inquisitorial, interested, interrogational, *interrogativus,* investigative, penetrating, piercing, probing, prying, questioning, quizzical, scrutinizing, searching

INTERROGATORIES, *noun* demands, inquiries, pretrial inquiries, questioning, questions, written requests for information

INTERRUPT, *verb* arrest, balk, barge in, break, break in, butt in, cause to cease, cause to delay, cease, check, chime in, clog, come between, cut, delay, desist, disconnect, discontinue, disjoin, dissever, dissolve, distract, disturb, disunite, divide, foil, frustrate, get in the way, hinder, inhibit, intercept, interfere, intermit, *intermittere, interpellare,* interpose, intrude, leave off, meddle, obstruct, punctuate, put a stop to, put an end to, retard, separate, sever, stop, sunder, suspend, thwart
ASSOCIATED CONCEPTS: interrupt a separation, interrupt possession

INTERRUPTION, *noun* abeyance, armistice, arrest, bar, block, break, cessation, check, clog, deadlock, delay, disconnection, discontinuance, disjunction, dissolution, disunion, gap, halt, hiatus, hindrance, impediment, *intercapedo,* interception, interference, interim, interlude, *intermissio,* intermission, interstice, *intervallum,* intrusion, lull, obstacle, obstruction, pause, recess, respite, severance, standstill, stop, stoppage, sunderance, suspension, truce

ASSOCIATED CONCEPTS: business interruption insurance, interruption of adverse possession, interruption of service

INTERSECTION, *noun* *bivium,* concourse, conjunction, connection, crossing, crossing point, crosspoint, crossroad, crosswalk, cruciation, *decussatio,* decussation, interconnection, intercrossing, joining place, joint, junction, juncture, meeting place, meeting point, traversal, union

INTERSPERSE, *verb* diffuse, disseminate, distribute, *immiscere,* interfuse, interlard, intermingle, interpenetrate, interpolate, interpose, interweave, mix, pepper, put between, scatter, shake, sprinkle, work in

INTERTWINE, *verb* braid, crisscross, cross, enlace, enmesh, entangle, entwine, form a network, *innectere,* inosculate, interknit, interlace, interlink, intermix, interthread, intertwist, interweave, inweave, knot, lace, mesh, plait, plat, *redimire,* reticulate, splice, tangle, tie together, twine together, twist, web, wreathe

INTERVAL, *noun* abeyance, break, gap, halt, hiatus, interim, interlude, intermission, interregnum, interruption, interstice, *intervallum,* intervening time, lapse, lull, pause, recess, respite, rest, *spatium interiectum,* spell, truce

INTERVENE, *verb* become a party to an action, break in, come between, encroach, infringe, intercede, *intercedere,* interfere, intermeddle, interpose, interrupt, *intervenire,* intrude, meddle, obtrude, step in, *supervenire*
ASSOCIATED CONCEPTS: intervening act, intervening agency, intervening cause, intervening efficient cause, intervening estate, intervening force, intervening parties, intervening sufficient cause, intervening superceding cause, intervenor, intervention as of right, intervention by leave of court

INTERVENING CAUSE, *noun* act which breaks the chain of events, break in causation, break in liability, break in proximate cause, independent act, interceding cause, interfering cause, interrupting cause, intervening act, intruding cause, nullifying act or action, overriding act or action, overruling act or action, preclusion, superseding intervening cause
ASSOCIATED CONCEPTS: duty of care, intervening damages, intervening force, negligence, proximate cause, standard care, superseding cause, torts

INTERVENTION *(Imposition into a lawsuit),* ***noun*** entrance into a lawsuit, entrance of a third party, insertion, interference, interjection, interjection into a lawsuit, interposition, intrusion
ASSOCIATED CONCEPTS: intervention by leave of the court, intervention by right

INTERVENTION *(Interference),* ***noun*** intercalation, interception, intercession, interjacence, interjection, interloping, intermeddling, intermediation, interpolation, interposition, interruption, *interventus,* intrusion

INTERVIEW, *noun* audience, audition, colloquy, conference, *congressio, conloquium,* consultation, conversation, dialogue, discussion, exchange of views, hearing, meeting, mutual exchange, oral examination, question and answer, talk, verbal intercourse

INTIMATE, *adjective* allied, associated with, brotherly, close, closely acquainted, closely associated, confidential, confiding, *coniunctus,* consociated, faithful, familiar, *familiaris,* federate, fraternal, friendly, guarded, inmost, innermost, *intimus,* linked, on familiar terms, personal, private, secret, strongly attached, trusted
ASSOCIATED CONCEPTS: confidentiality, fiduciary relationship

INTIMATION, *noun* allusion, *denuntiatio,* hint, idea, implication, inference, inkling, innuendo, insinuation, mention, *nuntius,* overtone, reference, suggestion

INTIMIDATE, *verb* abash, affright, alarm, badger, browbeat, bully, coerce, cow, daunt, dismay, dispirit, disquiet, duress, frighten, harass, hector, *incutere, inicere,* menace, overawe, petrify, put in fear, scare, shock, terrify, terrorize, threaten, unnerve
ASSOCIATED CONCEPTS: unlawful intimidation

INTOLERABLE, *adjective* impossible, insufferable, insupportable, unbearable, unendurable
ASSOCIATED CONCEPTS: intolerable cruelty, intolerable severity

INTOLERANCE, *noun* *acerbitas, adrogantia,* aversion, bias, bigotry, chauvinism, discrimination, dislike, hatred, illiberality, incapacity to endure, jaundice, jingoism, lack of toleration, narrow-mindedness, narrowness, one-sidedness, partiality, persecution, preconception, prejudgment, prejudice, racism, rejection, sectarianism, sectionalism, segregation, slant, subjectivity, *superbia,* want of forbearance, want of toleration
ASSOCIATED CONCEPTS: intolerable cruelty

INTOLERANT, *adjective* biased, bigoted, close-minded, closed, disobliging, dogmatic, fanatical, illiberal, inconsiderate, inhospitable, insensitive, insular, jaundiced, mean spirited, narrow, narrow-minded, not open, one-sided, opinionated, partial, prejudiced, racist, sexist, small-minded, uncharitable, unfriendly, ungenerousness, unreasonable, unsympathetic
ASSOCIATED CONCEPTS: bias crimes

INTONATION, *noun* accentuation, cadence, delivery, inflection, phonation, pitch, quality, resonance, sound, timbre, tonality, tone, tone of voice, vocalism, voice
ASSOCIATED CONCEPTS: demeanor

INTOXICATION, *noun* carousing, consuming alcohol to an excess, consuming an overabundance of alcohol, downing excessive alcohol, drinking to an excess, exorbitant drinking, imbibing to an excess, insobriety, intemperance, reveling, superfluity
ASSOCIATED CONCEPTS: driving while under the influence, drunken driving

INTRACTABLE, *adjective* adamant, balky, beyond control, contrary, contumacious, defiant, *difficilis,* disobedient, dogged, firm, froward, headstrong, heedless, incorrigible, indocile, *indocilis,* indomitable, inflexible, insubordinate, insuppressible, irrepressible, mulish, not easily governed, not pliable, obdurate, obstinate, obstreperous, pertinacious, perverse, pervicacious, rebellious, recalcitrant, refractory, resistive, restive, stubborn, tenacious, unbending, uncontrollable, uncurbed, undisciplined, ungovernable, unmalleable, unmanageable, unruly, unsubmissive, unwilling, unyielding, wayward, willful

INTRANSIGENT, *adjective* adamant, adamantine, bullheaded, determined, dogged, firm, hard, hardened, inconvincible, inexorable, obdurate, obsessive, obstinate, opinionated, ossified, pat, persistent, pertinacious, pigheaded, relentless, resolute, resolved, set, severe, single-minded, steadfast, stern, strict, stubborn, tenacious, unbending, uncompromising, unflinching, unrelenting, unyielding, willful

INTRICATE, ***adjective*** complex, complicated, delicate, difficult, elaborate, involved, tangled, tricky

INTRIGUE, ***noun*** artifice, collusion, connivance, conniving, conspiracy, contrivance, counterplot, cover-up, design, frame-up, imbroglio, machination, maneuver, manipulation, plot, scheme, series of events, stratagem, strategy, subterfuge, trickery, web of intrigue

INTRINSIC *(Belonging),* ***adjective*** implicit, inherent, native, pertinent
ASSOCIATED CONCEPTS: intrinsic fraud, intrinsic jury, intrinsic value

INTRINSIC *(Deep down),* ***adjective*** deep-seated, inner, internal, inward

INTRODUCE, ***verb*** bring in, enter, *inducere,* induct, inject, insert, interpose, *introducere, invehere,* offer, offer as an exhibit, place before, present, present formally, present to the court for acceptance, proffer, put, put forward, put forward for consideration, put in, submit, surrender, tender, usher in

INTRODUCE INTO EVIDENCE, ***verb*** offer as an exhibit, offer evidence, place into evidence, present evidence, present formally, put forward for consideration, submit as evidence, submit to the court
ASSOCIATED CONCEPTS: introduce into evidence exhibits, introduce into evidence prior testimony

INTRODUCTION, ***noun*** act of bringing in, admittance, formal presentation, *inductio,* induction, interposition, *introductio, invectio,* offering, offering as an exhibit, placing, presentation
ASSOCIATED CONCEPTS: introduction of evidence

INTROSPECTION, ***noun*** contemplation, innermost thoughts, introversion, *ipsum se inspicere,* looking within, meditation, musing, pensiveness, reflection, reverie, self-absorption, self-communion, self-counsel, self-examination, self-inspection, self-knowledge, self-scrutiny, self-study, thoughtfulness

INTRUDE, ***verb*** come uninvited, crash, encroach, enter uninvited, enter unlawfully, foist oneself, force oneself, horn in, impose, infringe, interfere, interlope, interrupt, invade, irrupt, obtrude, se *interponere,* thrust in, thrust oneself, trench on, trespass
ASSOCIATED CONCEPTS: invade privacy, trespass

INTRUSION, ***noun*** aggression, attack, encroachment, forced entrance, *importunitas,* imposition, incursion, infiltration, infringement, interference, interloping, interruption, invasion, irruption, meddling, obtrusion, overrunning, trespass, uninvited attendance, uninvited entry, unlawful entry, unwelcome suggestion
ASSOCIATED CONCEPTS: intrusion of rights, right of privacy, trespass

INTRUSIVE, ***adjective*** hindering, infringing, interfering, interloping, interruptive, invading, invasive, obtrusive, trespassing

INTUITION, ***noun*** apprehension, awareness, belief, clairvoyance, discernment, divination, extrasensory insights, feeling, foreboding, forecast, foreknowledge, forethought, gut reaction, hunch, inkling, insight, inspiration, instinct, intuitiveness, perception, preconception, prediction, premonition, prescience, presentiment, prevision, readiness, realization, sagacity, second sight, sixth sense, thinking, visceral reaction

INUNDATE, ***verb*** bury, deluge, drench, engulf, fill to superfluity, flood, flow over, glut, immerse, overflood, overflow, overspread, overwhelm, pour over, run over, rush upon, saturate, spill over, surge, swamp

INURE *(Accustom),* ***verb*** acclimate, acclimatize, accustom, acquaint, adjust, *adsuefacere,* condition, domesticate, familiarize, get used to, habituate, harden, make routine, naturalize, sanctify by custom, season, toughen

INURE *(Benefit),* ***verb*** accumulate, advance, advantage, aid, assist, avail, be of use, be profitable, bolster, contribute, enhance, enrich, forward, furnish aid, further, gain, help, improve, pay, profit, promote, render useful, serve, subserve, supply aid, turn to account, upgrade, yield gain, yield profit

INVADE, ***verb*** aggress, arrogate, assail, assault, attack, break in, encroach, enter hostilely, impinge, *incurrere, incursionem,* infringe, intrude, *invadere,* obtrude, overrun, overtake, penetrate, raid, run over, trespass, usurp, violate
ASSOCIATED CONCEPTS: invade the corpus of a trust, invade the province of the jury, invasion of privacy, invasion of property rights, invasion of rights

INVALID, ***adjective*** abrogated, baseless, canceled, fallacious, faulty, futile, having no force, inadequate, ineffective, ineffectual, inefficacious, *infirmus,* inoperative, *inritus,* lacking authority, lacking force, lacking strength, not binding, *nugatorius,* nugatory, null, quashed, unauthentic, untenable, untrue, useless, vain, void, weak, without legal efficacy
ASSOCIATED CONCEPTS: invalid delegation, invalid gift, invalid transfer, invalid will
FOREIGN PHRASES: ***Ab abusu ad usum non valet consequentia.*** A conclusion as to the use of a thing from its abuse is invalid.

INVALIDATE, ***verb*** abolish, abort, abrogate, annul, cancel, confute, deprive of legal effect, disannul, disprove, disqualify, erase, *inritum facere, labefactare,* make void, nullify, override, overrule, overthrow, quash, refute, repeal, repudiate, rescind, *rescindere,* retract, reverse, revoke, undermine, undo, vitiate, withdraw
ASSOCIATED CONCEPTS: invalidate a transfer, invalidate a will, invalidate an election

INVALIDITY, ***noun*** annulment, cancellation, disqualification, erroneousness, fallaciousness, fallacy, falseness, falsity, inadequacy, incompetence, ineffectiveness, nullity, unsoundness, untenableness, vitiation, voidness
ASSOCIATED CONCEPTS: declaration of invalidity
FOREIGN PHRASES: ***Pacta quae turpem causam continent non sunt observanda.*** Contracts which are based on an unlawful consideration will not be enforced. ***Pacta quae contra leges constitutionesque, vel contra bonos mores fiunt, nullam vim habere, indubitati juris est.*** It is unquestionably the law that contracts which are made contrary to the laws or against good morals, have no force in

law. ***Quae ab initio non valent, ex post facto convalescere non possunt.*** Things invalid from the beginning cannot be made valid by a subsequent act.

INVALUABLE, *adjective* beyond price, costly, expensive, *inaestimabilis,* incalculable, incapable of being appraised, inestimable, matchless, of inestimable value, peerless, precious, *pretiosissimus,* priceless, unequaled, unparalleled, valuable, without price

INVARIABLE, *adjective* certain, changeless, constant, definite, determinate, durable, enduring, established, fixed, hard-and-fast, immovable, immutable, inalterable, incommutable, inflexible, lasting, permanent, set, settled, stable, stationary, steadfast, steady, sure, unalterable, unchangeable, unchanging, unvarying

INVARIABLY, *adverb* always, as a rule, changelessly, commonly, constantly, conventionally, customarily, faithfully, fixedly, frequently, generally, habitually, immutably, in all cases, in every instance, normally, ordinarily, perpetually, regularly, repeatedly, rigidly, routinely, steadily, systematically, traditionally, unalterably, unchangeably, undeviatingly, uniformly, unvarying, usually, without exception

INVASION, *noun* aggression, assault, attack, attack on rights, breach, disobedience, encroachment, foray, hostile entry, *incursio,* incursion, infiltration, infraction, infringement, inroad, *inruptio,* interference, interloping, intervention, intrusion, overstepping, raid, siege, transgression, trespass, violation
ASSOCIATED CONCEPTS: invasion of a corpus, invasion of principal, invasion of privacy, invasion of rights, wrongful invasion

INVEIGH, *verb* attack, blast, cry out against, denounce, dispraise, exclaim against, fulminate, impugn, *incessere, increpare, insectari,* lash, protest against, rage against, rail, raise one's voice against, rate, revile, scold, score, storm against, thunder against, utter invective, vilify, vituperate

INVEIGLE, *verb* allure, attract, bait, bamboozle, befool, beguile, blandish, cajole, cheat, chouse, coax, cozen, deceive, decoy, defraud, delude, draw, ensnare, entangle, entice, entrap, fool, gull, illaqueate, importune, induce, influence, lay a trap, lead astray, lead on, lure, maneuver, mislead, persuade, seduce, snare, suborn, sway, tempt, trap, trick, urge, victimize, wheedle, win

INVENT *(Falsify),* ***verb*** *comminisci,* counterfeit, distort, embroider, exaggerate, fabricate, fake, falsify, feign, fib, fictionalize, humbug, lie, make believe, make up, misrepresent, misstate, pervert, pretend, prevaricate, sham, trump up, varnish

INVENT *(Produce for the first time),* ***verb*** author, bring into being, build, coin, come upon, compose, conceive, concoct, construct, contrive, create, design, devise, discover, draft, dream up, envisage, *excogitare,* excogitate, fabricate, fashion, find, forge, form, imagine, improvise, initiate, introduce, *invenire,* manufacture, originate, produce, realize, *reperire,* think of, think up, visualize

INVENTION, *noun* brainchild, coinage, composition, concoction, contraption, contrivance, creation, creative effort, creative fabrication, discovery, fabrication, finding, formation, handiwork, improvisation, innovation, *inventum,* origination, product, *reperta*

INVENTORY, *noun* catalog, checklist, contents, enumeration, index, itemization, itemized list, list, list of properties, manifest, merchandise list, record, register, schedule of articles, stock book, stock list, stock sheet, *tabula,* tally sheet
ASSOCIATED CONCEPTS: inventory of assets

INVERSE, *adjective* antipodal, antipodean, antithetical, contrary, converse, *conversus,* diametrically opposite, *inversus,* inverted, opposite, reverse, reversed, transposed, turned about
ASSOCIATED CONCEPTS: inverse condemnation, inverse discrimination

INVEST *(Fund),* ***verb*** advance, back, buy into, buy stock, deal in futures, employ capital, finance, gamble, infuse funds, lay out, lend, lend on security, loan, make an investment, *occupare,* outlay, play the market, *ponere,* provide capital, provide money, put out at interest, put up, risk, risk one's money, sink, speculate, sponsor, support, venture
ASSOCIATED CONCEPTS: invest capital

INVEST *(Vest),* ***verb*** appoint, authorize, charge, charter, commission, confer power, deferre, delegate, depute, empower, enable, endow with authority, entrust, furnish with rank, give a mandate, give authority, give power, grant authority, grant power, inaugurate, induct, install, instate, institute, license, *mandare,* name, nominate, ordain, permit, privilege, put in commission, sanction

INVESTIGATE, *verb* analyze, ask, collect facts, conduct an inquiry, consider, deliberate upon, delve into, dig into, discuss, dissect, examine, examine in detail, examine the particulars, examine with care and accuracy, explore, go into, hold an inquiry, inquire into, inquire into systematically, inspect, interrogate, look into, peer into, *perscrutari,* probe, pursue an inquiry, *quaerere,* question, reconnoiter, review, scan, scrutinize, search into, seek information regarding, study in detail, survey, take evidence, track, track mentally
ASSOCIATED CONCEPTS: investigate a crime, investigate charges, investigate the merits of a case

INVESTIGATION, *noun* careful search, careful study, close inquiry, collection of facts, detailed examination, examination, exhaustive study, exploration, formal scrutiny, *indagatio,* inquire to ascertain facts, inquiry, *inquisitio,* interrogation, *investigatio,* legal inquiry, official inquiry, probe, questioning, research, scrutinization, scrutiny, search, searching inquiry, statistical inquiry, strict inquiry, systematic search
ASSOCIATED CONCEPTS: blanket investigation, criminal investigation, governmental investigation, judicial investigation, legislative investigation

INVESTMENT, *noun* backing, capital invested, capital outlay, employment of capital, endowment, financial backing, financing, invested capital, invested money, invested property, loan, loan at interest, outlay, speculation, venture
ASSOCIATED CONCEPTS: investment broker, investment contract, investment security, investment trust

INVETERATE, *adjective* accustomed, addicted, chronic, chronical, confirmed, customary, deep-rooted, entrenched, established, firmly established, fixed, frequent, habitual, habituated, hardened, ingrained, inured, *inveteratus,* long-standing, *penitus defixus, penitus insitus,* rooted, set, time-honored, wonted

INVIDIOUS, *adjective* abominable, calculated to provoke resentment, disagreeable, disliked, disobliging, harmful, hateful, hurtful, injurious, *invidiosus,* irksome, likely to excite ill will, loathsome, malicious, objectionable, obnoxious, odious, offensive, plaguesome, rancorous, spiteful, troublesome, unacceptable, unaccommodating, ungracious, unkind, unpleasant, unwelcome, vexatious
ASSOCIATED CONCEPTS: invidious discrimination

INVIGORATE, *verb* activate, amp up, arouse, awaken, charge, encourage, energize, enliven, enthuse, excite, fire, inspire, jump-start, kindle, lift, liven up, motivate, move, pep up, propel, quicken, raise, rally, recharge, rejuvenate, rekindle, renew, revitalize, rouse, spark, spike, stimulate, stir, strengthen, vitalize, vivify, wake

INVIGORATING, *adjective* analeptic, animating, bracing, energizing, enlivening, exhilarating, healthful, invigorative, medicinal, nourishing, quickening, refreshing, remedial, reparative, restorative, salubrious, salutary, stimulating, vitalizing

INVINCIBLE, *adjective* all-powerful, ever-victorious, impossible to defeat, impossible to vanquish, incapable of being overcome, indestructible, indomitable, ineradicable, inexpugnable, *inexsuperabilis,* inextinguishable, inpermeable, insuperable, insurmountable, *invictus,* inviolable, invulnerable, irresistible, overpowering, overwhelming, resistless, secure from capture, unable to be overcome, unable to be quelled, unable to be subjugated, unassailable, unbeatable, unconquerable, unsubduable, unvanquishable, unyielding

INVIOLABILITY, *noun* immunity from assault, impenetrability, impregnability, incorruptibility, indestructibility, inexpugnability, inviolableness, invulnerability, protection, safety, sanctitas, security, security against violence, unassailability
ASSOCIATED CONCEPTS: inviolability of constitutional rights, inviolability of contracts

INVIOLABLE, *adjective* absolute, consecrated, exempt, hallowed, holy, honored, immune, inalienable, invincible, inviolate, privileged, protected, pure, recognized, respected, revered, ritual, sacred, sacrosanct, sanctified, secure, shielded, time-honored, unassailable, unchangeable, uncontested, untouchable, venerated

INVIOLATE, *adjective* complete, consecrated, free from desecration, free from impairment, hallowed, intact, *intactus, integer, inviolatus,* pure, sacred, sanctified, scatheless, secure, sound, spotless, stainless, unaffected by injury, unaltered, unblemished, unbroken, uncorrupted, undefiled, undestroyed, undisturbed, unharmed, unhurt, unimpaired, uninjured, unpolluted, unprofaned, unscathed, unspotted, unstained, untouched, unviolated, whole

INVISIBLE *(Small),* ***adjective*** diminutive, imperceptible, inappreciable, inconspicuous, infinitesimal, microbic, microscopic, minuscule

INVISIBLE *(Veiled),* ***adjective*** cloaked, concealed, covert, enshrouded, evanescent, hidden, impalpable, indiscernible, intangible, latent, lost to view, masked, obscure, screened, suppressed, unapparent, undetected, undisclosed, undiscovered, undivulged, unexplained, unexposed, unnoticeable, unperceived, unrevealed, unseeable, unseen, untraced, veiled

INVITATION, *noun* advance, allurement, appeal, approach, attraction, bid, bidding, call, challenge, encouragement, enticement, incitement, inducement, *invitatio,* offer, overture, petition, plea, proffer, prompting, proposal, proposition, provocative, request, solicitation, summons, tender, urging
ASSOCIATED CONCEPTS: business invitation, invitation to bid, license by invitation

INVOICE *(Bill),* ***noun*** account, account rendered, note, reckoning, statement, statement of account, statement of obligations, statement particularizing debts due, tab

INVOICE *(Itemized list),* ***noun*** account of goods shipped, account of merchandise, bill of lading, check list, enumeration, inventory, itemized account, *libellus,* list of goods, list of items, list of items shipped, list of mercantile goods, merchandise specification, schedule, schedule of items and their respective prices
ASSOCIATED CONCEPTS: Uniform Commercial Code

INVOKE, *verb* ask solemnly for, beg for, bid, call on for a blessing, call on for help, call up, conjure, entreat, *implorare,* implore, *invocare,* invocate, raise spirits, recite a spell, recite an incantation, summon, summon by incantation
ASSOCIATED CONCEPTS: invoke the authority of the court, invoke the Fifth Amendment

INVOLUNTARY, *adjective* against one's will, averse, coactus, coercive, compulsory, forced, independent of volition, *invitus,* mandatory, obligatory, unassenting, unconscious, unintended, unintentional, unmeditated, unpremeditated, unthinking, unwilled, unwilling, without consent, without power of choice, without will
ASSOCIATED CONCEPTS: involuntary bailment, involuntary bankruptcy, involuntary confession, involuntary dismissal, involuntary manslaughter, involuntary payment, involuntary sale, involuntary servitude, involuntary statements, involuntary suretyship, involuntary trust, involuntary unemployment

INVOLUNTARY MANSLAUGHTER, *noun* accidental homicide, accidental killing, accidental murder, killing with criminal negligence, killing with reckless disregard, killing without caution, killing without circumspection, unintentional homicide, unintentional killing, unpremeditated killing
ASSOCIATED CONCEPTS: corporate manslaughter, murder

INVOLUTION, *noun* complexity, complication, confusion, convolution, embroilment, entanglement, imbroglio, *implicatio,* intricacy, involvement, knot, labyrinth, maze, puzzle, sinuation, sinuosity, sleave, snarl, tangle, torsion, tortility, tortuosity, tortuousness, twist, web

INVOLVE *(Implicate),* ***verb*** accuse, ally, associate, blame, brand, bring accusation, bring charges, cast a slur on, charge, connect, consociate, *continere,* criminate, delate, denounce, draw in, entangle, incriminate, inculpate, interconnect, interrelate, lay the blame on, link together, lodge a complaint, make a party to, make participator, prefer charges, prove to be a participant in, relate, show to be an abettor, stigmatize, tie in with
ASSOCIATED CONCEPTS: involve a codefendant

INVOLVE *(Participate),* ***verb*** act in concert, associate, be a part of, be a party to, be in league with, collaborate, collude, confederate, connect, contribute, cooperate, enter into, have a hand in, join forces, join in, lend oneself to, make common cause with, partake, play a part, relate,

share, side with, strike in with, support, take part, take sides, team up, unite, work together
ASSOCIATED CONCEPTS: involve a case or controversy, involve a constitutional question, involve life or liberty, involve the merits of a case, involve title to real property, involve wrongdoing

INVOLVED *(A party to),* ***adjective*** absorbed, absorbed with, added as a defendant, added as a party, caught up in, contributing, devoted to, engaged, engrossed in, immersed in, implied, intent, intent on, occupied, sued, taken up with

INVOLVED *(Complex),* ***adjective*** a party to, cloudy, complexed, complicated, compound, concerned, confounded, confused, constructive, convoluted, difficult, disordered, elaborate, esoteric, implicated, inextricable, interested, intricate, involute, involutional, labyrinthine, obscure, problematic, recondite, sinuous, tortuous, unclear

INVOLVEMENT *(Association),* ***noun*** incrimination, inculpation

INVOLVEMENT *(Complex),* ***noun*** affiliation, complex, complexness, complication, complicity, dilemma, embroilment, engagement, engrossment, enmeshment, entailment, entanglement, implication, inextricability, involution, participation, perplexity, personal involvement, quagmire, quandary, relation, relationship, sympathy, tanglement

INVOLVEMENT *(Concentration),* ***noun*** absorption, application, devotion, engagement, intentness, occupation, preoccupation

INVULNERABLE, ***adjective*** certain, defensible, entrenched, fortified, immune, impenetrable, impregnable, indestructible, indomitable, inexpugnable, infrangible, insuperable, invincible, inviolable, permanent, safe, scatheless, secure, tenable, unassailable, unattackable, unbreakable, unchallengeable, unconquerable, unsurmountable

IOTA, ***noun*** bit, crumb, dab, dash, drop, fragment, grain, jot, minute quantity, morsel, particle, scintilla, shred, small amount, small quantity, spark, tittle, trace, whit

IPSO FACTO, ***adverb*** absolutely, by the act itself, by the fact itself, by the mere fact, by the very fact, essentially, positively, truly

IRASCIBLE, ***adjective*** bad-tempered, belligerent, cantankerous, captious, choleric, churlish, contentious, cranky, cross, disobedient, disputatious, dissentious, easily riled, edgy, fiery, fractious, froward, hostile, huffy, ill-humored, ill-natured, impatient, ireful, irritable, moody, nettlesome, perverse, petulant, pugnacious, quarrelsome, querulous, quick-tempered, snappish, testy, thin-skinned, unamiable

IRK, ***verb*** aggravate, aggrieve, annoy, badger, chafe, discommode, discompose, distress, disturb, exasperate, exercise, harass, incommode, irritate, jade, nettle, offend, perturb, pique, plague, provoke, rile, roil, ruffle, trouble, try one's patience, wear upon

IRKSOME, ***adjective*** annoying, boresome, boring, bothersome, distressing, *gravis,* irritating, jejune, *molestus, odiosus,* tiresome, tiring, troublesome, weariful, wearing, wearisome, wearying

IRONCLAD, ***adjective*** covered, defended, difficult to alter, difficult to break, difficult to change, exacting, firm, immutable, impossible to alter, impossible to break, impossible to change, inexorable, inflexible, ironbound, irreversible, irrevocable, relentless, rigid, rigorous, strict, stringent, unalterable, unbending, unbreakable, unchangeable, unchanging, uncompromising, unmalleable, unpliant, unrelenting, unshakeable, unyielding

IRONCLAD AGREEMENT, ***noun*** binding contract, binding legal document, concrete provisions, definite commitment, exact and binding agreement, precise covenants, solid protections, strong provisions, substantial understanding

IRONIC, ***adjective*** cynical, ironical, paradoxical, quizzical, sarcastic, sarcastical, sardonic, satiric, satirical

IRONY, ***noun*** cynicism, *dissimulatio, ironia,* mockery, sarcasm, satire

IRRATIONAL, ***adjective*** absurd, *absurdus,* bizarre, brainless, contrary to reason, crazy, foolish, heedless, ill-advised, ill-considered, ill-judged, illogical, imprudent, injudicious, insensate, ludicrous, mindless, nonsensical, outrageous, preposterous, reasonless, ridiculous, senseless, *stultus,* stupid, thoughtless, unconsidered, unintelligent, unreasonable, unreasoned, unreasoning, unreflecting, unsensible, unsound, unthinking, unthoughtful, unwise, utterly illogical, void of reason, without judgment, without reason, without rhyme or reason, witless
ASSOCIATED CONCEPTS: irrational behavior

IRREBUTTABLE, ***adjective*** incontestable, indisputable, indubitable, irrefutable, unchallengeable, unimpeachable, unquestionable
ASSOCIATED CONCEPTS: irrebuttable evidence

IRRECLAIMABLE, ***adjective*** abandoned, beyond cure, beyond hope, hopeless, incurable, irredeemable, irremediable, irreparable, irretrievable, irreversible, irrevocable, lost, ruined, undone, unredeemed

IRRECONCILABILITY, ***noun*** absolute difference, conflict, contention, contrariety, difference, disagreement, discongruity, discrepancy, disinclination, disparity, enmity, hostility, implacability, incommensurability, incompatibility, incongruity, inconsistency, inconsonance, intransigence, irrelation

IRRECONCILABLE, ***adjective*** adamant, alienated, antagonized, at variance, *contrariae,* estranged, firm, hostile, immovable, immutable, *implacabilis,* implacable, implacably opposed, *inexorabilis,* inexorable, inexpiable, inflexible, inimical, intransigent, refusing to agree, refusing to harmonize, rigid, unable to be pacified, unadjustable, unaffected, unalterable, unappeasable, unbending, unchangeable, uncompromising, unconformable, unforgiving, unmoved, unreconciled, unyielding
ASSOCIATED CONCEPTS: irreconcilable conflict, irreconcilable differences

IRRECONCILABLE DIFFERENCES, ***noun*** adamantness, complete alienation, complete intractability, immovability, immovable resolution, immutability, incurableness, inexorable positions, intransigence, irreparableness, irreversibility, irrevocability, obduracy, rigidity, rigorism, ruined relationship, total inflexibility, unbendingness, unmoved positions, unyieldingness

ASSOCIATED CONCEPTS: divorce, no fault divorce

IRRECOVERABLE, *adjective* beyond recall, incorrigible, irredeemable, irreparable, irretrievable, irreversible, past hope

IRREDEEMABLE, *adjective* beyond remedy, consumed, cureless, dissipated, expended, finished, gone, gone to waste, hopeless, immitigable, incapable of being bought back, inconvertible, incorrigible, incurable, irreclaimable, irrecoverable, irreformable, irreparable, irretrievable, irreversible, irrevocable, lost, past cure, past hope, past mending, past recall, remediless, ruined, spent, squandered, unchangeable, undone, unpayable, used up, wasted, without hope

IRREFUTABLE, *adjective* axiomatic, axiomatical, beyond doubt, certain, *certus,* demonstrable, *firmus,* inappealable, incontestable, incontrovertible, indisputable, indubious, indubitable, irrefragable, past dispute, positive, proven, questionless, sure, testable, unanswerable, unchallengeable, unconfutable, uncontestable, uncontroversial, undeniable, undoubtable, unequivocal, unimpeachable, unmistakable, unquestionable
ASSOCIATED CONCEPTS: irrebuttable presumption

IRREGULAR *(Improper),* ***adjective*** against the rules, condemnable, criminal, criminous, dishonest, foul, illegal, illegitimate, illicit, immoral, nefarious, open to objection, out of place, prohibited, unauthorized, unwarranted, wicked, wrong, wrongful
ASSOCIATED CONCEPTS: irregular conduct, irregular indorsement, irregularity in proceeding, jurisdictional irregularity

IRREGULAR *(Not usual),* ***adjective*** aberrant, abnormal, anomalistic, anomalous, asymmetric, asymmetrical, atypical, deviating from the general rule, deviating from the norm, deviating from the standard, deviative, divergent, eccentric, erratic, exceptional, extraordinary, freakish, heteroclite, *inaequabilis, inusitatus,* odd, out of order, out of place, out of the ordinary, peculiar, queer, singular, strange, unconformable, unconventional, unique, unnatural, unsymmetric, unsymmetrical, unusual
ASSOCIATED CONCEPTS: irregular incorporation, irregular judgment

IRREGULARITY, *noun* aberrance, aberrancy, aberration, abnormality, abnormity, anomaly, asymmetry, breach, changeableness, confusion, crookedness, desultoriness, deviation, disarrangement, discontinuity, disorder, disorderliness, distortion, divergence, eccentricity, exception, fitfulness, idiosyncrasy, illegality, imperfection, improperness, inconsistency, infringement, intermittence, jaggedness, lack of order, lack of propriety, lack of symmetry, lawlessness, lumpiness, malformation, malfunction, mutability, nonconformity, oddity, oddness, peculiarity, rarity, roughness, singularity, solecism, strangeness, turbulence, unconformity, unevenness, uniqueness, unnaturalness, unorthodoxy, unpunctuality, unruliness, unsmoothness, unsteadiness, ununiformity, unusualness, variability, variableness, variation, violation, want of method, wildness

IRRELATIVE, *adjective* alien, apart, detached, impertinent, inapplicable, inapposite, independent, irrelevant, removed, separate, separated, strange, unaffiliated, unallied, unassociated, unattached, unconnected, unrelated, without connection, without relation

IRRELEVANT, *adjective* alien, *alienus,* aside from the point, beside the mark, beside the point, beside the question, deviating, extraneous, far from the point, foreign, gratuitous, immaterial, impertinent, inapplicable, inapposite, inappropos, inappropriate, inapt, incongruous, inconsequent, inconsequential, inessential, insignificant, irrelative, malapropos, *nihil ad rem pertinet,* not applicable, not on point, not pertaining to, not pertinent, not significant, not to the point, not to the purpose, not vital, off the subject, off the topic, out of order, out of place, out of the way, remote, unallied, unapt, unconnected, unessential, unimportant, unrelated, unsuitable, unwarranted, without reference to
ASSOCIATED CONCEPTS: irrelevant evidence, irrelevant pleading, irrelevant statement, irrelevant testimony

IRREMEDIABLE, *adjective* beyond correction, beyond cure, beyond hope, beyond recall, beyond redress, beyond remedy, cureless, deadly, hopeless, immedicable, immitigable, impossible to better, incurable, inevitable, inexpiable, irrecoverable, irredeemable, irreparable, irretrievable, irreversible, irrevocable, past cure, past help, past mending, remediless, ruined, unable to be corrected, unable to be fixed, unable to be remedied, unfixable, unimprovable

IRREPARABLE, *adjective* incurable, irrecoverable, irredeemable, irreversible, remediless, ruined, undone
ASSOCIATED CONCEPTS: irreparable damage, irreparable harm, irreparable injury

IRREPARABLE HARM, *adjective* beyond recall, incurable effect, irreclaimable damage, irrecoverable effect, irredeemable impairment, irretrievable effect, irretrievable injury, irreversible effect, irrevocable damage
ASSOCIATED CONCEPTS: Lanham Act, Patent Act, permanent injunctions, preliminary injunctions, temporary restraining orders, Uniform Trade Secrets Act

IRREPREHENSIBLE, *adjective* above suspicion, aboveboard, blameless, circumspect, exalted, faultless, free from fault, free of guilt, guiltless, honest, impeccable, incorruptible, inculpable, *innocens,* innocent, innoxious, inoffensive, irreproachable, irreprovable, not guilty, *sanctus,* sinless, spotless, stainless, straightforward, unassailable, unblamable, unblameworthy, unblemished, uncensurable, unchallengeable, undeserving of censure, unerring, unexceptionable, unfallen, unimpeachable, uninvolved, unobjectionable, unoffending, unsullied, upright, virtuous

IRRESISTIBLE, *adjective* cogent, compelling, forceful, forcible, formidable, impossible to overcome, impossible to resist, impossible to withstand, indomitable, *insuperabilis, invictus,* invincible, mighty, omnipotent, overpowering, overwhelming, potent, powerful, puissant, resistless, strong, superior, unbeatable, unconquerable, vigorous
ASSOCIATED CONCEPTS: irresistible force, irresistible impulse

IRRESOLUTE, *adjective* capricious, changeable, changeful, doubtful, doubting, *dubius,* erratic, faltering, fickle, fluctuating, frivolous, hesitant, hesitating, *incertus,* indecisive, infirm of purpose, lukewarm, mercurial, mutable, oscillating, spineless, timid, uncertain, undecided, undetermined, unfixed, unresolved, unsettled, unsteadfast, unsteady, vacillant, vacillating, vacillatory, volatile, wavering

IRRESPECTIVE, *adjective* despite, in spite of, regardless of, without reference, without respect or regard to

IRRESPONSIBLE, *adjective* arbitrary, capricious, changeable, disloyal, disobedient, dutiless, flighty,

fluctuating, frivolous, inconstant, infirm of purpose, lawless, mutinous, perfidious, rash, rebellious, shiftless, thoughtless, treacherous, trustless, uncontrolled, uncurbed, undependable, undisciplined, undutiful, unfaithworthy, unreliable, unrestrained, unstable, unsteady, untrustworthy, untrusty, vacillating, wavering
ASSOCIATED CONCEPTS: incompetence, irresponsible actions

IRRETRIEVABLE, ***adjective*** dissipated, dissolved, forfeited, given up, gone, hopelessly lost, *inreparabilis,* irreclaimable, irrecoverable, irredeemable, irreparable, lost, past recall, spent, unrecoverable, untraceable, vanished

IRREVERENT, ***adjective*** arch, assertive, audacious, belligerent, blasphemous, bluff, blunt, bold-faced, brash, brazen, curt, defiant, disobedient, disrespectful, forward, heathen, heretical, impertinent, impious, impudent, insolent, miscreant, obtrusive, pagan, profane, reprobate, sacrilegious, supercilious, unblushing, ungodly, unholy

IRREVERSIBLE, ***adjective*** beyond remedy, cureless, entrenched, hopeless, immutable, impossible to change, impossible to reverse, incommutable, incurable, indefeasible, indissoluble, indissolvable, ineradicable, inextinguishable, irreclaimable, irrecoverable, irredeemable, irreformable, irremedial, irremovable, irreparable, irrepealable, irretrievable, irrevocable, lasting, nonreversible, not capable of annulment, permanent, remediless, reverseless, unalterable, unchangeable, unrestorable, unreturnable
ASSOCIATED CONCEPTS: irreversible damage, irreversible detriment

IRREVOCABLE, ***adjective*** beyond recall, binding, changeless, definite, final, firm, fixed, immitigable, immovable, immutable, impossible to change, incapable of revocation, incommutable, indefeasible, indelible, indestructible, indissoluble, indissolvable, ineluctable, ineradicable, inescapable, inevasible, inevitable, inextinguishable, inflexible, *inrevocabilis,* intransmutable, irreclaimable, irredeemable, irremediable, irremovable, irreparable, irrepealable, irretrievable, irreversible, lasting, nonreversible, permanent, persisting, remediless, reverseless, settled, stable, unable to be annulled, unalterable, unavoidable, unchangeable, unmodifiable, unrepealable, unrestorable, without appeal
ASSOCIATED CONCEPTS: irrevocable dedication, irrevocable gift, irrevocable grant, irrevocable license, irrevocable option, irrevocable pledge, irrevocable transfer, irrevocable trust

IRRITATE, ***verb*** affront, aggravate, agitate, anger, annoy, badger, bother, bully, chafe, discompose, displease, disturb, enrage, exacerbate, exasperate, excite anger, excite impatience, fret, gall, give offense, grate, harass, hector, incense, inflame, infuriate, *inritare,* irk, jar, madden, molest, nag, needle, nettle, offend, pain, peeve, persecute, pester, pique, plague, provoke, put out of humor, rankle, rasp, rile, rub the wrong way, ruffle, sting, stir to anger, tease, torment, torture, vex

ISOLATE, ***verb*** banish, blacklist, confine, cut off, detach, disconnect, disengage, disjoin, dislocate, dissever, dissociate, disunite, enisle, exclude, excommunicate, exile, insulate, island, keep apart, keep from contact with others, keep in solitude, maroon, ostracize, outlaw, part, place by itself, put aside, quarantine, refuse to associate with, rope off, seclude, segregate, *seiungere,* separate, sequester, set apart, set aside, sever, split, sunder
ASSOCIATED CONCEPTS: isolated occurrence, isolated transaction

ISOLATION, ***noun*** aloneness, confinement, ghettoization, incarceration, insulation, loneliness, lonesomeness, privacy, quarantine, removal, retirement, secludedness, seclusion, segregation, separation, sequestration, solitariness, solitary confinement, solitude, vacuum, withdrawal

ISSUANCE, ***noun*** announcement, broadcast, bulletin, communication, communiqué, culmination, debouchment, decree, delivery, discharge, dispatch, effluence, effluency, effusion, egress, egression, emanation, emergence, emission, escape, exit, final result, fruit, gush, issue, manifesto, message, notice, notification, outcome, outflow, outgo, outlet, outpour, proclamation, promulgation, pronouncement, pronunciamento, prospectus, public announcement, publication, publicity, release, report, rescript, result, statement, ultimate result, upshot
ASSOCIATED CONCEPTS: issuance of an insurance policy, issuance of execution, issuance of order, issuance of process, issuance of subpoena, issuance of summons

ISSUE *(Matter in dispute),* ***noun*** *causa,* cause, debatable point, disputed point of law, disputed question, fact put in controversy by the pleadings, field of inquiry, item on the agenda, material point, material point deduced by the pleadings, matter, matter in hand, matter in question, matter of contention, point, point in question, problem, proposition, question, question at issue, *res,* subject for inquiry, topic under consideration
ASSOCIATED CONCEPTS: bond issue, collateral issue, fundamental issue, genuine issue, immaterial issue, joining of issue, justiciable issue, labor issue, material issue, moot issue, note of issue, triable issue
FOREIGN PHRASES: ***Placita negativa duo exitum non faciunt.*** Two negative pleas do not make an issue.

ISSUE *(Progeny),* ***noun*** child, children, descendants, family, heirs, *liberi,* lineage, lineal descendants, offspring, *progenies, stirps*
ASSOCIATED CONCEPTS: adopted children, die without issue, failure of issue, last issue, legitimate issue
FOREIGN PHRASES: ***Si quis praegnantem uxorem reliquit, non videtur sine liberis decessisse.*** If a man dies leaving his wife pregnant, he is considered as having died childless.

ISSUE *(Publish),* ***verb*** air, announce, assert formally, bring into the open, broadcast, call public attention to, circulate, communicate, declare, disclose, dispense, disperse, disseminate, distribute, divulge, *edere,* enunciate, expose, give out, give public notice of, inform, lay before the public, make a public announcement, make known, notify, notify publicly, offer to the public, post, print, proclaim, promulgate, pronounce, *pronuntiare,* propound, publicize, put forth, put forward, put into circulation, put out, release, reveal, send out, set forth, spread, state, utter with conviction
ASSOCIATED CONCEPTS: issue a decision of the court, issue a judgment, issue an order

ISSUE *(Send forth),* ***verb*** break forth, burst forth, come forward, come onto the horizon, come out, come out in the open, *egredi,* egress, emanate, emerge, *erumpere, exire,* exit, exude, flow, flow out, make its appearance, manifest itself, pour forth, pour out, put in an appearance, spring up, stream, surface, surge, transmit
ASSOCIATED CONCEPTS: issue stock

ISSUE AN ORDER, ***verb*** command, declare, decree, determine, dictate, direct, find, hand down a judicial command, hand down a judicial instruction, instruct, make an authoritative command, mandate, prescribe, proclaim, pronounce, publish an order, rule

ISSUE OF FACT, *noun* debatable issue, disputed factual point, disputed question, inquiry into the truth, issue to be addressed, material disputed point, material point, matter in question, matter of contention, point at issue, point in question, point to be determined, question at issue, question for inquiry, question to be addressed, question to be determined, questionable issue
ASSOCIATED CONCEPTS: affidavit, disputed fact a law, evidence, issue of material fact, issues of disputed fact

ITEM, *noun* article, asset, commodity, component, constituent, count, detail, effect, element, entity, entry, feature, gadget, good, ingredient, merchandise, object, pars, part, particular, piece, piece of information, piece of news, point, possession, product, *res,* salable commodity, separate paragraph, singleton, specification, staple, story, unit, vendible, ware
ASSOCIATED CONCEPTS: item of appropriation, item on deposit, itemization of damages, itemized account

ITEMIZE, *verb* be specific, catalog, circumstantiate, count, designate, detail, document, enter into detail, enumerate, index, inventory, list, mention, mention in detail, note, number, particularize, point out, post, recapitulate, recount, register, set down, specify, state by items, tabulate
ASSOCIATED CONCEPTS: itemize an account, itemize damages, itemize expenses

ITERATION, *noun* adaptation, carbon copy, copy, duplication, interpretation, latest draft, new draft, print, reduplication, reiteration, rendition, renewal, repeat, repetition, replay, replication, reprint, reprise, rerun, reworking, variation, version

ITERATIVE, *adjective* duplicative, echoing, harping, recurrent, recurring, redundant, reiterant, repeated, repetitious, repetitive, tautological

ITINERANT, *adjective* ambulant, ambulatory, passing, peripatetic, journeying, moving, traveling, wandering, wayfaring
ASSOCIATED CONCEPTS: itinerant dealer, itinerant merchant, itinerant trader, itinerant vendor

ITINERANT, *noun* drifter, peripatetic, traveler, rambler, roamer, rover, runabout, voyager, wanderer

JACTATION, *noun* boast, boastfulness, brag, braggadocio, braggardism, conceit, fanfaronade, gasconade, jactitation, ostentation, pretension, rodomontade, self-glorification, swagger, swank, vainglory, vanity, vaunt, venditation

JAIL, *noun* *carcer,* cell, detention cell, detention center, detention station, house of correction, house of detention, inclosure, keep, penal institution, penitentiary, place of confinement, prison, prisonhouse, reformatory, stockade

JAIL, *verb* apprehend, capture, cast into prison, commit to an institution, commit to prison, confine, constrain, detain, hold captive, hold in captivity, hold in custody, immure, impound, imprison, *in carcerem, in custodiam,* incarcerate, institutionalize, isolate, lock in, lock up, place inconfinement, put behind bars, put under restraint, restrain, restrict, send to prison, shut in, shut up, subjugate, take into custody

JAILBREAK, *noun* break, breakout by inmates, escape by inmates, flight by inmates, forcible escape by inmates, liberation, planned escape by inmates, prison break, revolt
ASSOCIATED CONCEPTS: overcrowding

JAPE, *verb* bemock, burlesque, caricature, chaff, flout, fool, gibe at, imitate insultingly, jeer, jest, joke, lampoon, laugh at, make fun of, mimic, mock, parody, play tricks upon, poke fun at, ridicule, satirize, scoff, taunt, tease, travesty, twit

JARGON *(Technical language),* ***noun*** argot, cant, code, coined words, language of a particular profession, legalese, neologism, neology, private language, professional language, professional vocabulary, specialized language, specialized terminology, specialized vocabulary
ASSOCIATED CONCEPTS: legal jargon

JARGON *(Unintelligible language),* ***noun*** babble, blabber, blather, confused language, confused talk, confusion, double talk, empty talk, foolishness, gibberish, inanity, incoherence, incoherent discourse, jabber, jumble, nonsense, nonsensical language, nonsensical talk, nonsensicalness, prattle, rambling talk, senseless talk, silly talk, unintelligible talk

JEALOUS, *adjective* begrudging, competitive, covetous, desiring, desirous, discontented, disposed to envy, dissatisfied, distrustful, doubting, envious, greedy, grudging, *invidus, lividus,* longing, possessive, rival, suspicious

JEER, ***verb*** *cavillari,* deprecate, depreciate, deride, disparage, disregard, disrespect, gibe, have no regard for, hold in derision, *inridere,* insult, laugh at, make fun of, mock, ridicule, scoff, sneer, speak derisively, speak slightingly, taunt, treat with insolence, twit

JEJUNE *(Dull),* ***adjective*** bleak, boresome, boring, colorless, common, commonplace, drearisome, dreary, dry, flat, flavorless, hollow, indifferent, insipid, monotonous, ordinary, plain, ponderous, prosaic, prosy, stolid, tame, tasteless, tedious, thin, tiresome, torpid, undramatic, unenlivened, unentertaining, unexciting, unimpassioned, uninspired, uninspiring, unlively, unpointed, unspirited, usual, vacuous, vapid, weak, wearisome

JEJUNE *(Lacking maturity),* ***adjective*** adolescent, apathetic, arid, babyish, banal, bland, blank, boring, callow, childish, childlike, colorless, dull, empty, flat, foolish, frivolous, green, immature, inane, inert, inexperienced, infantile, infantine, insipid, juvenile, languid, naïve, plain, puerile, spiritless, stagnant, stolid, trite, unexciting, unfledged, uninteresting, unlearned, unsophisticated, unspirited, vacuous, vapid, with no energy, with no zip, young

JEOPARDIZE, ***verb*** endanger, expose to danger, imperil, in *periculum,* leave unprotected, menace, peril, place in danger, risk, stake, threaten

JEOPARDY, ***noun*** crisis, danger, dangerous situation, dangerousness, endangerment, hazard, imperilment, insecurity, instability, menace, peril, perilousness, precariousness, risk, threat, uncertainty, unsafety, vulnerability
ASSOCIATED CONCEPTS: double jeopardy, former jeopardy, placed in jeopardy
FOREIGN PHRASES: ***Nemo bis punitur pro eodem delicto.*** No one can be punished twice for the same offense.

JETTISON, ***verb*** cast overboard, discard, dispense with, dispose of, eject, eliminate, expel, get rid of, part with, rid oneself of, slough, throw away, throw overboard, toss out, toss overboard

JOB, ***noun*** assignment, avocation, billet, business, calling, chore, duty, employment, function, labor, mission, obligation, occupation, position, profession, responsibility, role, task, trade, undertaking, vocation, work

JOBBERY, ***noun*** baseness, corruption, crime in public office, criminality, debasement, debauchery, decadence, degeneracy, demoralization, depravity, dishonesty, immorality, impropriety, iniquitousness, iniquity, licentiousness, meanness, misuse of the public trust, profligacy, public rebuke, public censor, public reproof, reprehensible conduct, reprehensibleness, unscrupulousness, wrong, wrongdoing

JOCULAR, ***adjective*** amusing, arch, comic, diverting, facetious, frisky, frivolous, frolicsome, full of fun, funny, gamesome, gay, given to joking, gleeful, gleesome, hilarious, humorous, *iocosus, iocularis,* jesting, jocose, jocund, joking, jolly, joshing, jovial, joyful, joyous, laughing, light, merry, merrymaking, mirth-loving, mirthful, playful, pleasant, *ridiculus,* roguish, rollicking, rompish, sportive, sprightly, tricksy, waggish, witty

JOIN *(Associate oneself with),* ***verb*** act in concert, affiliate, align, ally, associate, band together, be united, become a member, become connected with, belong to, combine, confederate, consociate, consort, cooperate, enlist, enroll, enter, fraternize, league together, make an agreement with, mingle, participate, pool, register, *se coniungere,* side with, sign on, subscribe, take part, take up membership, team up with, unite

JOIN *(Bring together),* ***verb*** accouple, accumulate, adhere, aggregate, aggroup, alloy, amalgamate, amass, annex, append, assemble, attach, band, bind, blend, bridge, bring in contact, coact, collect, colligate, collocate, combine, commingle, compound, concatenate, *conectere,* conglomerate, conglutinate, *coniungere,* conjoin, connect, consolidate, convene, *copulare,* couple, entwine, federalize, federate, fit together, fuse, gather, glue, group, harness, incorporate, inosculate, interlink, interlock, intertwine, intertwist, interweave, knit, link, marry, mass, match, meld, merge, mix, pair, piece together, pool, put together, rally, splice, subjoin, unify, unite, wed, weld, yoke
ASSOCIATED CONCEPTS: issue joined, joinder of parties

JOINDER, ***adjective*** assemblage, bringing together, coalescence, combination, concatenation, conjugation, conjunction, connection, coupling, joining, junction, linkage, linking, unification, union
ASSOCIATED CONCEPTS: fraudulent joinder, improper joinder, joinder of issue, joinder of parties, misjoinder, permissive joinder, severance

JOINDER OF A PARTY, ***noun*** adding a claimant, adding a complainant, adding a defendant, adding a party, adding a plaintiff, enlisting a party, joining a party, joining an opposing party, joining a petitioner, joining a plaintiff
ASSOCIATED CONCEPTS: compulsory joinder, indispensable party, joinder of additional defendants, joinder of an interested party, joinder of third parties, misjoinder, necessary joinder, nonjoinder, notice of joinder, permissive joinder

JOINT, ***adjective*** allied, amalgamated, associated, coadunate, coalitional, collaborative, collective, combined, common, communal, *communis,* community, concerted, concordant, concurrent, confederate, conjoint, conjugate, conjunct, consolidated, cooperative, coordinated, corporate, correal, harmonious, inseparable, joined, leagued, merged, mixed, mutual, shared, synergetic, unified, united
ASSOCIATED CONCEPTS: joint account, joint action, joint adventure, joint and several liability, joint enterprise, joint interest, joint liability, joint negligence, joint ownership, joint resolution, joint tenancy, joint tort feasors

JOINT AND SEVERAL, ***adjective*** absolute and individual, all-encompassing and individual, blanket and individual, complete, comprehensive and individual, each and every and individual, entire and individual, full and individual, global and individual, omnibus and individual, the sum of total and individual, undivided and individual, universal and individual, wholly and individual
ASSOCIATED CONCEPTS: tortfeasors

JOINT AND SEVERAL LIABILITY, ***noun*** absolute, abstruse, across-the-board, aggregate, all-embracing, all inclusive, all-out, bewildering, chaotic, circuitous, clear, collective, combined, complete, complicated, composite, comprehensive, confused, convoluted, difficult, downright, dyed-in-the-wool, elaborated, enigmatic, entangled, entire, exhaustive, explicit, express, extended, extensive, flexuous, full, full-fledged, gradely, gross, impenetrable, implicated, inclusive, in-depth, individually and collectively liable, individually and mutually liable, inextricable, inscrutable, integral, interlaced, interwoven, intricate, involuted, involutional, involved, irreducible, jumbled, kaleidoscopic, knotted,

labyrinthine, mingled, muddied, multiplex, obscure, out-and-out, outright, perplexing, plenary, radical, rank, recondite, sheer, sinuous, snarled, straight-out, sweeping, tangled, teetotal, thorough, together or separate, tortuous, unambiguous, unarranged, unclassified, uncompromised, unconditional, undecipherable, unequivocal, unfathomable, universal, unmitigated, unmodified, unorganized, unqualified, unreserved, utter, varied, whole, widespread
ASSOCIATED CONCEPTS: ostensible principal, torts

JOINT CUSTODY, ***noun*** custody shared equally by both parents, equal custody, joint care, joint guardianship, shared custody
Generally: cooperative care, shared responsibility

JOSTLE *(Bump into),* ***verb*** bang into, buffet, bump, bump against, butt, collide, crash into, crowd, elbow, *fodicare,* graze against, hit against, hustle, jab, jar, jolt, knock, knock against, nudge, poke, press, prod, push, run against, shake, shove, strike against, strike together
ASSOCIATED CONCEPTS: disorderly conduct

JOSTLE *(Pickpocket),* ***verb*** abscond with, convey away, lift, loot, misappropriate, pick one's pockets, pilfer, purloin, run away with, run off with, steal, take away, walk off with, waylay
ASSOCIATED CONCEPTS: larceny

JOURNAL, ***noun*** *acta diurna,* biographical record, cashbook, chronicle, chronology, contemporary account, daily paper, daily register, daybook, diary, *ephemeris,* gazette, historical record, ledger, log, logbook, magazine, narrative, periodical, record, register, serial

JUDGE, ***noun*** adjudger, adjudicator, administrator of justice, arbiter, arbitrator, assessor, chancellor, the court, her honor, his honor, honorable justice, intercessor, interpreter, *iudex,* jurist, justice, justicer, magistrate, moderator, negotiator, one who dispenses justice, *praetor, quaesitor,* referee, surrogate, umpire, your honor
ASSOCIATED CONCEPTS: administrative judge, appellate judge, chief judge, County Court Judge, Court of Appeals Judge, Court of Claims Judge, District Court Judge, Family Court Judge, inferior court judge, judge de facto, judge of a court of record, justice of the peace, Justice of the Supreme Court, law clerk, lay judge, magistrates, presiding judge, removal of a judge, superior court judge, Surrogate, town judge
FOREIGN PHRASES: ***In propria causa nemo judex.*** No one can be a judge in his own case. ***Ignorantia judicis est calamitas innocentis.*** The ignorance of a judge is the misfortune of the innocent. ***Judex bonus nihil ex arbitrio suo faciat, nec propositione domesticae voluntatis, sed juxta leges et jura pronunciet.*** A good judge should do nothing of his own arbitrary will, nor on the dictate of his personal wishes, but should decide according to law and justice. ***Veritas habenda est in juratore; justitia et judicium in judice.*** Truth should be possessed by a juror; justice and judgment by a judge. ***Judicium a non suo judice datum nullius est momenti.*** A judgment rendered by one who is not the proper judge is of no force. ***Quicquid judicis auctoritati subjicitur, novitati non subjicitur.*** Whatever is subject to the authority of a judge is not subject to innovation. ***Sententia a non judice lata nemini debet nocere.*** A sentence or judgment rendered by a person who is not a judge ought not to harm anyone. ***Respiciendum est judicanti ne quid aut durius aut remissius constituatur quam causa deposcit; nec enim aut severitatis aut clementiae gloria affectan da est.*** It is a matter of import to a judge that nothing should be either more leniently or more severely construed than the cause itself demands; for the glory neither of severity nor clemency should be affected. ***Judicis est in pronuntiando sequi regulam, exceptione non probata.*** The judge in his decision ought to follow the rule, the exception not having been proved. ***Nemo potest esse simul actor et judex.*** No one can be at the same time judge and suitor. ***Praxis judicum est interpres legum.*** The practice of judges is the interpreter of the laws. ***Judex non potest injuriam sibi datam punire.*** A judge cannot punish a wrong done to himself. ***Boni judicis est ampliare justitiam.*** It is the duty of a good judge to make precedents which amplify justice. ***Quemadmodum ad quaestionem facti non respondent judices, ita ad quaestionem juris non respondent juratores.*** Just as judges do not answer questions of fact, so jurors do not answer questions of law. ***Boni judicis est judicium sine dilatione mandare executioni.*** It is the duty of a good judge to issue judgments without delay. ***De jure judices, de facto juratores, respondent.*** Judges decide questions of law; jurors, questions of fact. ***Ubi non est manifesta injustitia, judices habentur pro bonis viris, et judicatum pro veritate.*** Where there is no manifest injustice, judges are to be regarded as honest men, and their judgment as truth. ***Judex damnatur cum nocens absolvitur.*** A judge is condemned when a guilty person is acquitted. ***Nemo sibi esse judex vel suis jus dicere debet.*** No man ought to be his own judge or to administer the law in cases involving his family. ***Judici officium suum excedenti non paretur.*** No obedience is to be given to a judge exceeding his office or jurisdiction. ***Non refert quid notum sit judici, si notum non sit in forma judicii.*** It matters not what is known to a judge, if it be not known in a judicial form. ***Judex debet judicare secundum allegata et probata.*** A judge ought to decide according to the allegations and the proofs. ***Judex non potest esse testis in propria causa.*** A judge cannot be a witness in his own case. ***In re propria iniquum admodum est alicui licentiam tribuere sententiae.*** It is unjust for anyone to assign to himself the privilege of deciding his own case. ***De fide et officio judicis non recipitur quaestio, sed de scientia, sive sit error juris, sive facti.*** The good faith and honesty of a judge are not to be questioned, but his knowledge, whether it be in error of law or fact, may be. ***Judex ante oculos aequitatem semper habere debet.*** A judge ought always to have equity before his eyes. ***Judices non tenentur exprimere causam sententiae suae.*** Judges are not bound to explain the reason for their sentences. ***Judex aequitatem semper spectare debet.*** A judge ought always to regard equity. ***Bonus judex secundum aequum et bonum judicat, et aequitatem stricto juri praefert.*** Good judges decide according to what is just and right, and prefer equity to strict law. ***Ad questiones facti non respondent judices; ad questiones legis non respondent juratores.*** Judges do not answer to a question of fact; jurors do not answer to a question of law. ***Qui aliquid statuerit, parte inaudita altera, aequum licet dixerit, haud aequum fecerit.*** He who decides anything without hearing both sides, although he may decide correctly, has by no means acted justly. ***Judex habere debet duos sales–salem sapientiae, ne sit insipidus; et salem conscientiae, ne sit diabolus.*** A judge ought to have two salts—the salt of wisdom, lest he be insipid; and the salt of conscience, lest he be devilish. ***Optimam esse legem, quae minimum relinquit arbitrio judicis; id quod cer titudo ejus praestat.*** That law is the best which leaves the least discretion to the judge; this is an advantage which results from its certainty. ***Optima est lex quae minimum relinquit arbitrio judicis; optimus judex qui minimum sibi.*** That is the best system of law which leaves the least to the discretion of the judge; that judge is the best who leaves the least

to his own discretion. ***Optimus judex, qui minimum sibi.*** He is the best judge who leaves the least to his own discretion. ***Judicis officium est opus diei in die suo perficere.*** It is the duty of a judge to finish the day's work within that day. ***Judicis est judicare secundum allegata et probata.*** It is the duty of a judge to decide according to the allegations and proofs. ***Quam rationabilis debet esse finis, non definitur, sed omnibus circumstantiis inspectis pendet ex justiciariorum discretione.*** What a reasonable fine ought to be is not defined, but is left to the discretion of the judges, all the circumstances being considered.

JUDGE, *verb* adjudge, adjudicate, appraise, arbitrate, ascertain, assess, conclude, condemn, consider, criticize, decide, decree, deduce, deem, derive, determine, discern, draw a conclusion, estimate, examine, find, hold, infer, interpret, *iudicare, iudicium exercere,* moderate, negotiate, pass sentence upon, pass under review, perceive, pronounce, reckon, referee, reprobate, resolve, review, rule on, sentence, settle, sit in judgment, try, try a case, umpire, value, weigh
FOREIGN PHRASES: ***Judicis est jus dicere, non dare.*** It is the duty of a judge to declare the law, not to make it. ***Judex est lex loquens.*** The judge is the law speaking; that is, he is the mouthpiece of the law. ***Boni judicis est ampliare jurisdictionem.*** It is the duty of a good judge to enlarge his remedial authority.

JUDGE'S CHAMBER, *noun* judge's antechamber, judge's anteroom, judge's court chamber, judge's private office, judicial chamber, judicial office, judicial room

JUDGMATIC, *adjective* calculating, circumspect, considerate, determinative, discriminating, discriminative, enlightened, fair-minded, impartial, judicative, judicatory, judicial, judicious, juridical, juristic, just, magisterial, nonpartisan, percipient, perspicacious, politic, provident, prudent, reflecting, sagacious, thoughtful, tolerant, unbiased, unbigoted, unprejudiced, well-advised, well-judged

JUDGMENT *(Discernment),* ***noun*** ability to distinguish, acumen, acuteness, analysis, apperception, appraisal, assessment, astuteness, awareness, circumspection, close observation, cognitive faculties, cognitive powers, comprehension, conclusion, consideration, *consilium,* contemplation, critical faculty, critical spirit, criticalness, critique, decision, diagnosis, discrimination, discursive faculties, estimate, estimation, evaluation, examination, exhaustive inquiry, grasp, incisiveness, inquiry, insight, inspection, intellectual faculties, intellectual powers, intuition, *iudicium,* judiciousness, keenness, mental faculty, observation, opinion, penetration, perception, perceptiveness, percipience, perspicacity, perspicuousness, probing, quickness, ratiocination, rational faculty, rationality, reasoning, reasoning faculties, reasoning power, review, sagacity, sapience, sharpness of mind, understanding, weighing
ASSOCIATED CONCEPTS: failure to exercise reasonable judgment
FOREIGN PHRASES: ***Incivile est, nisi tota lege perspecta, una aliqua particula ejus proposita, judicare, vel respondere.*** Unless the entire law has been examined, it is improper to pass judgment upon a portion of it. ***Judicia in deliberationibus crebro maturescunt, in accelerato processu nunquam.*** Judgments frequently mature by deliberations, never by hurried process.

JUDGMENT *(Formal court decree),* ***noun*** adjudgment, adjudication, announcement, arbitrament, assessment, censure, conclusion, condemnation, consideration, decision, declaration, decree, determination, evaluation, finding, *iudicium,* judicature, judicial assertion, legal decision, opinion, order, precedent, pronouncement, recommendation, report, resolution, result, ruling, sentence
ASSOCIATED CONCEPTS: advisory judgment, collateral attack on a judgment, conditional judgment, confession by judgment, consent judgment, declaratory judgment, default judgment, deficiency judgment, docketing a judgment, enforcement of a judgment, execution of judgment, final judgment, foreign judgment, full faith and credit, interlocutory judgment, judgment by confession, judgment creditor, judgment debtor, judgment in rem, judgment lien, judgment non obstante veredicto, judgment roll, money judgment, opening a default judgment, personal judgment, relief from judgment, res judicata, satisfaction of a judgment, vacating a judgment
FOREIGN PHRASES: ***Ubi eadem ratio ibi, idem jus; et de similibus idem est judicium.*** Where there is the same reason, there is the same law; and where there are similar situations, the judgment is the same. ***Respiciendum est judicanti ne quid aut durius aut remissius constituatur quam causa deposcit; nec enim aut severitatis aut clementiae gloria affectanda est.*** It is a matter of import to a judge that nothing should be either more leniently or more severely construed than the cause itself demands; for the glory neither of severity nor clemency should be affected. ***Non exemplis sed legibus judicandum est.*** Judgment should not be rendered from examples, but by the law. ***Res judicata pro veritate accipitur.*** A thing which is adjudicated is accepted or received for the truth. ***Judicium non debet esse illusorium; suum effectum habere debet.*** A judgment ought not to be illusory; it ought to have its proper effect. ***Judicium a non suo judice datum nullius est momenti.*** A judgment by one who is not the proper judge is of no force. ***Omnis conclusio boni et veri judicii sequitur ex bonis et veris praemissis et dictis juratorum.*** Every conclusion of a good and true judgment arises from good and true premises and the verdicts of jurors. ***In praeparatoriis ad judicium favetur actori.*** In those matters preceding judgment the plaintiff is favored. ***Frustra agit qui judicium prosequi nequit cum effectu.*** He sues vainly who cannot prosecute his judgment with effect. ***Sacramentum habet in se tres comites–veritatem, justitiam, et judicium; veritus habenda est in jurato; justitia et justicium in judice.*** An oath has in it three components—truth, justice, and judgment; truth in the party swearing; justice and judgment in the judge administering the oath. ***Veredictum, quasi dictum veritatis; ut judicium, quasi juris dictum.*** A verdict is, as it were, the expression of the truth; as a judgment is the expression of the law. ***Judicium semper pro veritate accipitur.*** A judgment is always taken for truth. ***Judiciis posterioribus fides est adhibenda.*** Credit should be given in the more recent decisions. ***Judex non reddit plus quam quod petens ipse requirit.*** A judge should not render judgments for a larger sum than the plaintiff demands. ***Parum est latam esse sententiam nisi mandetur executioni.*** It is not enough that sentence should be given unless it be reduced to execution.

JUDGMENT ON THE FACTS, *noun* act of judgment, adjudication, authoritative decision, decision, deliberative determination, determination, disposition, final judgment, findings, holding, irrevocable decision, judicature, judicial decision, opinion, pronouncement, resolution, ruling, settled decision, verdict
ASSOCIATED CONCEPTS: a judgment or decree, appeals, directed verdict, pleadings, setting aside, summary judgment, supplementary proceedings

JUDICATORY, *noun* bar of justice, bench, court, court of justice, court of law, forum, institution where justice is

rendered, judicature, judiciary, law court, place where justice is administered, *ratio iudiciorum,* tribunal
ASSOCIATED CONCEPTS: inferior judicatory

JUDICATURE, ***noun*** administration of justice, authority, bench, court, court of law, court's jurisdiction, extent of the court's authority, forum, *iurisdictio,* judicatory, jurisdiction, jurisdiction of the court, legal authority, legal power, tribunal

JUDICIAL, ***adjective*** considerate, disinterested, equitable, fair, forensis, impartial, *iudicialis,* judgelike, judgmatic, judicative, judicious, juridical, juristic, juristical, just, knowing, politic, prudent, prudential, rational, reasonable, reasoned, sagacious, sage, sapient, sensible, thoughtful, unbiased, unbigoted, uninfluenced, unprejudiced, unswayed, wise
ASSOCIATED CONCEPTS: critical state in a judicial proceeding, judicial act, judicial business, judicial circuit, judicial decision, judicial district, judicial function, judicial inquiry, judicial notice, judicial office, judicial opinion, judicial power, judicial proceeding, judicial review, judicial separation, judicial sequestration, judicial tribunal
FOREIGN PHRASES: ***Officia judicialia non concedantur antequam vacent.*** Judicial offices are not to be granted or appointed before they become vacant.

JUDICIAL CONTEST, ***noun*** action, case, lawsuit, legal action, legal dispute, legal matter, legal proceedings, legal recourse, litigation, judicial proceeding, judicial recourse, proceedings, suit, trial

JUDICIAL DETERMINATION, ***noun*** action, award, court resolution, court's finding, declaration, decree, decretal, findings of fact and conclusions of law, holding, opinion judgment, judicial fiat, judicial pronouncement, order, order of the court, pronouncement, ruling, sentence

JUDICIAL PROCEEDING, ***noun*** action, case, cause in court, court proceeding, hearing, hearing on the merits, judicial contest, judicial recourse, lawsuit, legal action, legal dispute, legal proceeding, legal recourse, legal remedy, litigation, prosecution, suit, suit at law, suit in law, trial, trial of a case, trial of the issues

JUDICIAL REVIEW, ***noun*** *certirari,* judicial analysis, judicial review, judicial scrutiny, legal analysis, legal review, legal scrutiny
Specifically: judicial scrutiny
ASSOCIATED CONCEPTS: appellate system, basis to appeal, grounds to appeal, judicial issue, jurisdiction, trial de novo

JUDICIARY, ***noun*** administration of justice, arm of the law, bar, bench, body of judges, courts, courts of justice, department of justice, explicators of the law, forum of justice, interpreters of the law, judicatory, judicature, judicial branch, judicial branch of government, judicial department, judicial forum, justices, law courts, legal forum, magistracy, tribunal
ASSOCIATED CONCEPTS: judiciary powers

JUDICIOUS, ***adjective*** apperceptive, astute, calculating, careful, cautious, considerate, considered, deliberate, diplomatic, discerning, discreet, discretionary, discriminating, enlightened, heedful, judgmatic, mindful, moderate, perceptive, percipient, perspicacious, politic, provident, *prudens,* prudent, prudential, rational, reasonable, reflecting, regardful, sagacious, sagax, sage, *sapiens,* sapient, sensible, shrewd, sound, tactful, temperate, thorough, thoughtful, undaring, well-considered, wise

JUDICIOUSNESS, ***noun*** astuteness, cautiousness, deliberation, diplomacy, discernment, discretion, discriminating judgment, discrimination, enlightenment, expedience, good judgment, judgment, moderation, perception, perspicacity, prudence, rationality, reason, reasonableness, restraint, sagaciousness, sagacity, sense, sensibility, shrewdness, soundness, tactfulness, temperance, thoughtfulness

JUMPING OFF POINT, ***noun*** base, basis, bedrock, bottom, floor, flooring, foundation, fundamental basis, girder, ground, groundwork, premise, principle, rudiment, starting point, support, supporting structure, underlying principle, underpinning basis
ASSOCIATED CONCEPTS: floor plan in zoning and construction laws, hacking the floor in parliamentary procedure, minimum wage

JUNCTION, ***noun*** accompaniment, adhesion, alliance, association, attachment, chain, coalescence, coalition, collusion, combination, concentration, concomitance, concourse, concurrence, confluence, conflux, conjugation, conjunction, connection, connivance, consolidation, contact, convergence, correlation, crossroad, coupling, encounter, focalization, hinge, intersection, joining, liaison, meeting, union

JUNCTURE *(Crisis),* ***noun*** contingency, critical moment, critical point, crux, dilemma, emergency, exigency, extremity, plight, predicament, quandary, strait

JUNCTURE *(Eventuality),* ***noun*** advent, assemblage, coadunation, coalescence, coincidence, concentration, concourse, concurrence, confluence, conflux, congregation, conjuncture, contingency, convergence, correlation, crisis, crossroad, event, eventuality, incident, intersection, meeting, moment, occasion, period, point, posture, situation, stage, union

JUNCTURE *(Stage),* ***noun*** correlation, eventuality, moment, opportunity, period, turning point

JUNIOR, ***adjective*** associate, auxiliary, inferior, little, lower, low-level, minor, minute, petty, secondary, second-class, second-rate, slight, small, smaller, small-time, subordinate, subsidiary, two-bit

JURAL, ***adjective*** according to law, de jure, founded in law, judicatory, judicial, judiciary, juridical, juristic, legal, of law, pertaining to law, recognized by law, sanctioned by law, within the law

JURAT, ***noun*** accreditation, affirmation, asseveration, attestation, attesting statement, authentication, avouchment, avowal, certification, confirmation, documentation, endorsement, ratification, solemn declaration, statement which confirms information on an affidavit, substantiation, verification, verifying statement
ASSOCIATED CONCEPTS: affidavit, affirmation, notary public, oath

JURIDICAL, ***adjective*** according to law, adjudged, advising, advisory, authoritative, authorized, concerning the law, conformable with the law, discerning, discretionary, discriminating, discriminative, enlightened, equitable, fair, forensic, impartial, in accordance with the law, in conformity to the law, *iuridicialis,* judgelike, judgmatic, judicative, judicatorial, judicatory, judicial, judiciary, judicious, jural, juridic, jurisprudential, juristic, just, justifiable, justified, lawful, legal, legalistic, legalized, magisterial, perceptive, percipient, perspicacious, politic, prescribed, principled, proper, provident, prudent, prudential, rational, reflecting, right, rightful, sagacious, sage, sanctioned, sapient, solicitorial, sound, unbiased, understanding, unprejudiced, warranted, well-advised, within the law

JURISDICTION, ***noun*** authority, authority to hear and decide a case, capacity to decide the matter in issue, capacity to hear the controversy, command, control, decision-making power over the case, domain, domination, dominion, extent of authority, grasp, *iurisdictio,* legal authority, legal power, legal power to decide a case, legal right, power, province, purview, range, reach, realm, reign, sovereignty, sphere, superintendence, supervision, territorial range of authority, territory

ASSOCIATED CONCEPTS: basis jurisdiction, civil jurisdiction, concurrent jurisdiction, court of competent jurisdiction, equity jurisdiction, exclusive jurisdiction, *forum non conveniens*, in personam jurisdiction, in rem jurisdiction, inherent jurisdiction, jurisdiction of the court, jurisdiction over the person, jurisdictional amount, jurisdictional defect, jurisdictional dispute, jurisdictional facts, jurisdictional plea, jurisdictional requirement, jurisdictional statement, lack of jurisdiction, limited jurisdiction, original jurisdiction, pendent jurisdiction, primary jurisdiction, quasi in rem jurisdiction, subject matter jurisdiction, submission to jurisdiction, venue, want of jurisdiction

FOREIGN PHRASES: ***Est boni judicis ampliare jurisdictionem.*** It is the duty of a good judge to extend the jurisdiction. ***Extra territorium jus dicenti impune non paretur.*** One exercising jurisdiction outside of his territorial limits cannot be obeyed with impunity. ***Jurisdictio est potestas de publico introducta, cum necessitate juris dicendi.*** Jurisdiction is a power introduced for the public good, on account of the necessity of administering justice. ***Quaelibet jurisdictio cancellos suos habet.*** Every jurisdiction has its own bounds. ***Qui habet jurisdictionem absolvendi, habet jurisdictionem ligandi.*** He who has jurisdiction to release, has jurisdiction to bind. ***Rerum ordo confunditur si unicuique jurisdictio non servetur.*** The order of things is confused if everyone does not give heed to his own jurisdiction. ***Ubi est forum, ibi ergo est jus.*** Where the forum is, there the law is accordingly. ***Judici officium suum excedenti non paretur.*** No obedience is to be given to a judge exceeding his office or jurisdiction. ***Est boni judicis ampliare jurisdictionem.*** It is the duty of a good judge to interpret his jurisdiction liberally. ***In personam actio est, qua cum eo agimus qui obligatus est nobis ad faciendum aliquid vel dandum.*** The action in personam is that in which we sue him who is under obligation to us to do something or give something. ***In omni actione ubi duae concurrunt districtiones, videlicet, in rem et in personam, illa districtio tenenda est quae magis timetur et magis ligat.*** In every action where two distresses concur, that is to say, in rem and in personam, that is to be chosen which is most dreaded and which binds more firmly. ***Cui jurisdictio data est, ea quoque concessa esse videntur, sine quibus jurisdictio explicari non potest.*** Those things without which jurisdiction could not be exercised are held to be given to each to whom jurisdiction has been granted. ***Debet quis juri subjacere ubi delinquit.*** Everyone ought to be subject to the law of the place where he commits an offense. ***Nihil habet forum ex scena.*** The court has nothing to do with what is not before it. ***Judicium a non suo judice datum nullius est momenti.*** A judgment rendered by one who is not the proper judge is of no force.

JURISDICTIONAL AMOUNT, ***noun*** amount involved in a case, domain, extent of authority, jurisdiction, jurisdictional authority, jurisdictional boundary, jurisdictional legal authority, jurisdictional legal power, jurisdictional monetary limit, jurisdictional monetary threshold, jurisdictional outer edge, jurisdictional perimeter, jurisdictional power, monetary amount that can be heard by a court, province, purview, range, sphere, territorial authority, territorial range, territory

ASSOCIATED CONCEPTS: amount in controversy, subject matter jurisdiction

JURISPRUDENCE, ***noun*** body of laws, corpus juris, doctrines of lawmaking, *iuris prudentia,* knowledge of law, legal code, legal learning, legal philosophy, legal practice, legal precedent, legal science, nomography, nomology, philosophy of law, science of law, science of legal relations, system of laws

FOREIGN PHRASES: ***Scire leges non hoc est verba earum tenere, sed vim ac potestatem.*** To know the laws is not to observe their words alone, but their force and power. ***Cessante ratione legis, cessat et ipsa lex.*** Where the reason for a law ceases, the law itself also ceases. ***Jurisprudentia est divinarum atque humanarum rerum notitia, justi atque injusti scientia.*** Jurisprudence is the knowledge of things divine and human, the science of what is just and unjust.

JURIST, ***noun*** advocate, attorney, attorney-at-law, barrister, bencher, counsel, counselor, counselor-at-law, intercessor, iuris consultus, *iuris peritus,* judge, jurisconsult, jurisprudent, justice, lawyer, learned counsel, legal advisor, legal expert, legal practitioner, legal representative, legalist, legist, magistrate, master of jurisprudence, member of the bar, member of the legal profession, one called to the bar, pleader, practicing lawyer, practitioner of the law, procurator, prosecutor, public attorney, solicitor

FOREIGN PHRASES: ***Natura appetit perfectum, ita et lex.*** Nature seeks perfection, and so does the law. ***Non verbis sed ipsis rebus. leges imponimus.*** We do not impose laws upon words, but upon the things themselves. ***Leges naturae perfectissimae sunt et immutabiles, humani vero juris conditio semper in infinitum decurrit, et nihil est in eo quod perpetuo stare possit.*** The laws of nature are the most perfect and immutable, but the condition of human law is unending, and there is nothing in it which can continue perpetually.

JUROR, ***noun*** adjudger, adjudicator, appraiser, arbiter, assessor, assessor of liability and damages, estimator, evaluator, examiner, hearer, individual selected for jury service, *iudex,* jurat, juryman, member of a jury, one authorized to deliver a verdict, one of an adjudgment body, one sworn to deliver a verdict, reviewer, swearer, trier of fact

ASSOCIATED CONCEPTS: challenge for cause, competent juror, foreman, grand juror, peremptory challenge to the selection of a juror, petit juror

FOREIGN PHRASES: ***Veritas habenda est in juratore; justitia et judicium in judice.*** Truth should be possessed by a juror; justice and judgment by a judge. ***Omnis conclusio boni et veri judicii sequitur ex bonis et veris praemissis et dictis juratorum.*** Every conclusion of a good and true judgment arises from good and true premises and the verdicts of jurors. ***Triatio ibi semper debet fieri, ubi juratores meliorem possunt habere notitiam.*** Trial ought always to be had where the jurors can have the best information. ***Quemadmodum ad quaestionem facti non respondent judices, ita ad quaestionem juris non respondent juratores.*** Just as judges do not answer questions of fact, so jurors do not answer questions of law.

JURY, ***noun*** adjudgment body, adjudicators, arbiters, arbitrators, array, assessors, body of jurors, determiners, *iudices,* judges of the facts, jurymen, panel, reviewers of fact, talesmen, tribunal, triers of fact

ASSOCIATED CONCEPTS: acquittal by a jury, advisory jury, challenges, charge to the jury, empaneling a jury, fair and impartial jury, foreman of the jury, grand jury, hung jury, impartial jury, instructing the jury, invading the province of the jury, petit jury, polling a jury, right to trial by jury, special grand jury, swearing of the jury
FOREIGN PHRASES: ***Matter en ley ne serra mise in boutche del jurors.*** A matter of law shall not be put into the mouth of jurors. ***Paribus sententiis reus absolvitur.*** When the opinions are equal, where the court is equally divided, the defendant is acquitted. ***Nemo qui condemnare potest, absolvere non potest.*** No one who can convict is unable to acquit. ***Patria laboribus et expensis non debet fatigari.*** A jury ought not to be troubled by labors and expenses. ***De jure judices, de facto juratores, respondent.*** Judges decide questions of law, jurors, questions of fact.

JURY DELIBERATIONS, ***noun*** chance verdict, common jury, compromised verdict, consideration by the jury, contemplation by the jury, jury analysis, jury review, panel determination
ASSOCIATED CONCEPTS: grand jury, jury verdict, petit jury, quotient verdict, special jury, special verdict, trial jury

JURY NULLIFICATION, ***noun*** commonsense judgment, disregard of the law by a body of jurors, improper verdict, independence by judges of the facts, independence by jurymen, independence by reviewers of fact, independence of the law by jurors, juror activism, jurors' disregard of the law, jurors' independence, jury independence, paid jurors, prejudicial verdict, professional jurors, refusal to convict even after the jury believes the defendant is guilty, turning back the evidence, unwillingness to convict by a jury, verdict of acquittal contrary to the law, wrongful determination
ASSOCIATED CONCEPTS: new trial, retrial, reversal

JURY-RIGGING, ***verb*** accompany, adjudgment body, adjudicators, agree, alternative, arbiters, arbitrators, array, assessors, be in time, body of jurors, coexist, coextend, coincide, concur, contemporize, co-occur, determiners, emergency, expedient, fixing a jury, go along with, go hand in hand, impermanent, improvised, isochronize, judges of the facts, jurymen, keep in, keep pace with, keep time, makeshift, match, panel, provisional, put or be in phase, reviewers of fact, step, stopgap, substitute, succedaneous, sync, synchronize, talesmen, temporary, time, tribunal, triers of fact
ASSOCIATED CONCEPTS: mistrial, peremptory challenges

JUST, ***adjective*** aboveboard, according to law, admissible, *aequus,* affording no undue advantage, appropriate, as it should be, authoritative, awarded deservedly, balanced, befitting, bona fide, cogent, condign, conscientious, constitutional, deserved, deserving, detached, direct, disinterested, dispassionate, due, equable, equitable, ethical, even-handed, exact, expected, express, fair, fair and square, fair-minded, fit, fitting, forceful, honest, honorable, impartial, incorruptible, *iustus,* judicious, juridical, justifiable, justified, lawful, legal, legitimate, licit, logical, merited, meritorious, *meritus,* moral, objective, open-minded, open to reason, owed, owing, precise, principled, proper, rational, reasonable, reputable, right, righteous, rightful, scrupulous, sincere, solid, sound, square, straight, straightforward, sufficient, suitable, unbiased, unbigoted, unbought, unbribable, unbribed, unchallengeable, uncolored, uncorrupt, uncorrupted, unimpeachable, uninfluenced, unprejudiced, unswayed, upright, upstanding, veracious, virtuous, weighty, wise, worthy
ASSOCIATED CONCEPTS: just and reasonable grounds, just cause, just claim, just compensation, just debts, just decision, just terms, just value in a case, without just cause
FOREIGN PHRASES: ***Ubi lex aliquem cogit ostendere causam, necesse est quod causa sit justa et legitima.*** Where the law compels a man to show cause, it is necessary that the cause be just and legal.

JUST CLAIM, ***noun*** contingent interest, in accordance with legal provisions, legitimate cause of action, legitimate legal issues, overwhelming proof, proper issues, strong basis, substantiated complaint, verifiable complaint

JUSTICE, ***noun*** *aequitas,* equitableness, equity, fair-mindedness, fair play, fair treatment, fairness, freedom from bias, impartiality, *iustitia,* justness, objectivity, probity, propriety, reason, reasonableness, rectitude, reparation, retribution, right, righteousness, rightfulness, uprighteousness
ASSOCIATED CONCEPTS: due administration of justice, ends of justice, equity, fleeing from justice, fugitive from justice, in furtherance of justice, in the interests of justice, miscarriage of justice, obstructing justice, preventive justice, speedy justice, substantial justice
FOREIGN PHRASES: ***Melior est justitia vere praeveniens quam severe puniens.*** Truly preventive justice is better than severe punishment. ***Justitia non est neganda non differenda.*** Justice is neither to be denied nor delayed. ***In re propria iniquum admodum est alicui licentiam tribuere sententiae.*** It is unjust for anyone to assign to himself the privilege of deciding his own case. ***Sacramentum habet in se tres comites–veritatem, justitiam, et judicium; veritus habenda est in jurato; justitia et justicium in judice.*** An oath has in it three components—truth, justice, and judgment; truth in the party swearing; justice and judgment in the judge administering the oath. ***Justitia est constans et perpetua voluntas jus suum cuique tribuendi.*** Justice is the constant and perpetual means to render to each one his rights. ***Lex dilationes semper exhorret.*** The law always abhors delays. ***Boni judicis est ampliare justitiam.*** It is the duty of a good judge to make precedents which amplify justice. ***Discretio est scire per legem quid sit justum.*** Discretion consists in knowing through the law what is just. ***Justitia est duplex, viz., severe puniens et vere praeveniens.*** Justice is double, that is to say punishing severely and truly preventing. ***Nulli vendemus, nulli negabimus, aut differemus rectum vel justitian.*** We will sell to none, we will deny to none, we will delay to none, either equity or justice. ***Justitia non novit patrem nec matrem; solum veritatem spectat justitia.*** Justice knows neither father nor mother; justice looks to the truth alone. ***Quod ad jus naturale attinet omnes homines aequales sunt.*** All men are equal as far as the natural law is concerned. ***Accipere quid ut justitiam facias, non est tam accipere quam extorquere.*** The acceptance of a reward for doing justice is not so much an acceptance as an extortion. ***Justitia nemini neganda est.*** Justice is to be denied to no one. ***Plena et celeris justitia fiat partibus.*** Let full and speedy justice be done to the parties. ***Jure naturae aequum est neminem cum alterius detrimento et injuria fieri locupletiorem.*** According to the laws of nature, it is just that no one should be enriched by the detriment and injury of another. ***Fiat justitia, ruat coelum.*** Let right be done, though the heavens fall. ***Nihil magis justum est quam quod necessarium est.*** Nothing is more just than what is necessary. ***Lex non deficit in justitia exhibenda.*** The law does not fail in dispensing justice. ***Bonus judex secundum aequum et bonum judicat, et aequitatem stricto juri***

praefert. Good judges decide according to what is just and right, and prefer equity to strict law. ***Lex plus laudatur quando ratione probatur.*** The law is most praiseworthy when it is consistent with reason. ***Vigilantibus et non dormientibus jura subveniunt.*** The laws aid the vigilant and not those who slumber. ***Judex bonus nihil ex arbitrio suo faciat, nec propositione domesticae voluntatis, sed juxta leges et jura pronunciet.*** A good judge should do nothing of his own arbitrary will, nor on the dictate of his personal wishes, but should decide according to law and justice. ***Qui aliquid statuerit, parte inaudita altera, aequum licet dixerit, haud aequum fecerit.*** He who decides anything without hearing both sides, although he may decide correctly, has by no means acted justly. ***Fraus et jus nunquam cohabitant.*** Fraud and justice never dwell together. ***Festinatio justitiae est noverca infortunii.*** The hastening of justice is the stepmother of misfortune. ***Commodum ex injuria sua non habere debet.*** No person ought to derive any advantage by his own wrong. ***Veritas habenda est in juratore; justitia et judicium in judice.*** Truth should be possessed by a juror; justice and judgment by a judge. ***Jus est ars boni et aequi.*** Law is the science of what is good and just. ***Lex est dictamen rationis.*** Law is the dictate of reason. ***Lex est ratio summa, quae jubet quae sunt utilia et necessaria et contraria prohibet.*** That which is law is the consummation of reason, which commands those things useful and necessary while prohibiting the contrary. ***Sequi debet potentia justitiam, non praecedere.*** Power ought to follow justice, not precede it. ***Summa caritas est facere justitiam singulis, et omni tempore quando necesse fuerit.*** The greatest charity is to do justice to everyone, and at all times when it is necessary.

JUSTICE COURT, ***noun*** bar, bar of justice, bench, for adjusting disputes, forum, forum of justice, judgment seat, judicial assembly, judicial forum, judicial tribunal, justice, justice seat, lawcourt, magistrates, place where justice is administered, tribunal

JUSTICIABLE, ***adjective*** actionable, amenable to law, appropriate for a trial, arguable, capable of being decided by a court, capable of being litigated, capable of being tried, cognizable, disputable, enforceable, jurisdictional, legally enforceable, liable to prosecution, litigable, proper for judicial examination, proper for judicial review, proper to be examined in courts of justice, ripe to submit for judicial review, subject to a court case, subject to action of a court of justice, subject to being resolved in court, triable
ASSOCIATED CONCEPTS: justiciable controversy, justiciable disputes

JUSTIFIABLE, ***adjective*** acceptable, admissible, allowable, condonable, defendable, defensible, excusable, exemptible, expiable, forgivable, inculpable, *iustus,* justified, lawful, legal, legalized, legitimate, *legitimus,* licit, maintainable, merited, meritorious, pardonable, permitted, plausible, practicable, proper, rational, reasonable, sanctioned, sensible, sound, suitable, vindicable, warrantable, warranted, well-grounded, worthy
ASSOCIATED CONCEPTS: defense of justification, justifiable controversy, justifiable homicide

JUSTIFICATION, ***noun*** adjustment, allowance, clarifying statement, clearance, compurgation, defense, exculpation, *excusatio,* excuse, exonerating circumstance, exonerating fact, exoneration, explanation, exposition, extenuation, good excuse, ground for excusing, legal defense, mitigating circumstance, mitigation, palliation, *purgatio,* rationalization, reason, reasonable excuse, reasoning, statement of defense, vindication
ASSOCIATED CONCEPTS: justification for committing an unlawful act, legal cause

JUSTIFIED, ***verb*** accounted for, championed, condoned, countenanced, defended, endorsed, espoused, exculpated, excused, exonerated, explained, forgiven, legitimatized, maintained, made excuses for, made legitimate, mitigated, offered in defense, plead one's cause, proven as warranted, proven the truth of, seconded, shown to be just, spoken in favor of, stood up for, supported, sustained, upheld, urged as reasons for, vindicated, warranted, with adequate reasons, with sufficient reasons
ASSOCIATED CONCEPTS: family court, justification, juvenile delinquency court, juvenile justice system, Megan's Law, moral justification, termination from employment, torture

JUSTIFY, ***verb*** absolve, account for, allege in support, allege in vindication, answer for, argue for, back, be answerable for, be apologist for, bear out, bolster, champion, condone, contend for, countenance, declare guiltless, defend, defend as conformable to law, defend as conformable to right, endorse, espouse, espouse the cause of, exculpate, *excusare,* excuse, exonerate, explain, forgive, give as an excuse, legitimate, maintain, maintain as conformable to duty, maintain as conformable to justice, make defense for, make excuses for, make explanation of, make legitimate, mitigate, offer in defense, palliate, plead for, plead one's cause, pragmatize, prove the truth of, prove warranted, *purgare,* second, show to be just, speak in favor of, stand up for, strengthen, support, sustain, uphold, urge reasons for, vindicate, warrant

JUVENILE, ***adjective*** callow, childish, childlike, immature, inexperienced, infantine, intended for youth, *iuvenilis,* minor, pubescent, *puerilis,* suited to youth, unadult, underage, undeveloped, unfledged, unseasoned, vernal, young, youthful
ASSOCIATED CONCEPTS: juvenile court, juvenile delinquent, Person in Need of Supervision, youthful offender

JUVENILE, ***noun*** adolescent, child, fledgling, immature person, inexperienced person, *iuvenilis,* junior, juvenal, minor, person under legal age, puerile person, *puerilis,* stripling, teen, teenager, ward, young person, youngling, youngster, youth
ASSOCIATED CONCEPTS: juvenile court, juvenile delinquent

JUVENILE DELINQUENT, ***noun*** blameworthy child, blameworthy minor, culpable youth, derelict adolescent, derelict inexperienced person, derelict junior, immature youngster, misbehaving teenager, miscreant, misguided teen, misguided young person, neglectful fledgling, offending immature person, violator under age, young wrongdoer

JUXTAPOSE, ***verb*** abut, adjoin, align, annex, appose, arrange side by side, border, bring near, bring together, connect, coordinate, interconnect, join, line up, make contiguous, make even, make uniform, neighbor, osculate, place close together, place near, place next to, place side by side, position together, put alongside, put beside, put close together, put side by side, range together, set side by side

JUXTAPOSITION, ***noun*** adjacency, apposition, collation, collocation, connection, contact, contiguity, contiguousness, propinquity

KEEN, *adjective* acute, aggressive, all fired-up, all out, ambitious, animated, anxious, ardent, assiduous, avid, brisk, burning, committed, deep, deep-felt, desirous, diligent, disposed, dynamic, eager, earnest, ebullient, energetic, enterprising, enthused, enthusiastic, excited, extreme, exuberant, fervent, fervid, feverish, fiery, flaming, full of enthusiasm, heartfelt, hearty, heated, intense, intent, obsessed, passionate, pliant, proactive, profound, prompt, quick, raring to, ready, receptive, responsive, robust, spirited, vibrant, vigorous, vital, vivacious, vivid, zealous, zestful

KEEP *(Continue),* ***verb*** be constant, be steadfast, carry forward, carry on, endure, extend, forge ahead, go on, keep going, last, lengthen, live on, maintain, move ahead, never cease, perpetuate, *perseverare,* persevere, persist, press onward, progress, prolong, pursue, remain, run on, stay, stick to, support, survive, sustain, wear

KEEP *(Fulfill),* ***verb*** abide by, acknowledge, adhere to, be faithful to, be true to, carry out, celebrate, commemorate, complete, comply with, conform to, discharge, follow, heed, honor, live up to, make good, meet, *observare, observe,* perform, regard, respect, *retinere,* satisfy, solemnize, stand by

KEEP *(Restrain),* ***verb*** arrest, bar, block, cage, check, *cohibere,* confine, constrain, contain, control, curb, delay, deprive, detain, deter, enclose, foil, frustrate, halt, hamper, hinder, hold, hold back, hold in, hold up, impede, inhibit, obstruct, prevent, prohibit, restrict, retard, *retinere,* shut in, shut up, stay, stifle, stop, stymie, suppress, thwart, withhold

KEEP *(Shelter),* ***verb*** accumulate, amass, bank, cache, care for, cause to endure, cause to last, cherish, cling to, *condere,* conserve, deposit, embrace, foster, guard, have, hold, husband, keep alive, keep safe, lay aside, lay away, look after, maintain, nurture, pile up, possess, preserve, protect, put aside, put away, reserve, retain, retard decay, safeguard, save, secure, shelter, spare, store, support, sustain, take care of, tend, treasure, watch over

KEEP GOING, *verb* carry on for, continue, don't give up, don't let up, endure, extend, fulfill, further keep administering to, keep advancing, keep at, keep attending to, keep on, maintain, maintain a course, manage, minister to, perpetuate, persevere, persist, press on, proceed, pursue, resume, retain, stay on top of, steadfastly persevere, stick to, stick with, support, sustain
ASSOCIATED CONCEPTS: tolling statute of limitations or appeals

KEEP IN CUSTODY, *verb* capture, cast into prison, catch, under lock and key, commit to a prison, commit to jail, confine, constrain, deprive of liberty, detain, encage, hold, hold captive, imprison, imprison by authority, incarcerate, jail, legally restrain, lock up, make a captive, make a prisoner, place in confinement, place in custody, place in preventive custody, place in protective custody, put under restraint, remain in confinement, restrain, restrict, secure, seize, seize by legal warrant, take captive, take prisoner
ASSOCIATED CONCEPTS: chain of custody, child custody, speedy trial, visitation

KEEP IN PERSPECTIVE, *noun* analyze correctly, correctly perceive, judiciousness keep as the center, keep as the center of attention, keep as the center of interest, keep as the central point, keep as the converging point, keep as the focal point, keep as the goal, keep as the heart of the matter, keep as the objective, organize, the law of perspective

KEEP THE PEACE, *verb* agreement not to disturb, alliance not to disturb, armistice, calm, calmness, coexistence, concord, cooperation, end of hostilities, end of unrest, end of violence, harmony, hush, lull, maintain quiet, neutrality, pact, quiet, quietness, rapport, reconciliation, serenity, silence, stillness, suspension of hostilities, tranquility, treaty, truce, unanimity, unity
ASSOCIATED CONCEPTS: curfews, law enforcement

KEN, *noun* 20/20 vision, appreciation, apprehension, awareness, comprehension, discernment, discrimination, farsightedness, field of view, field of vision, foresight, intelligence, know-how, knowledge, perception, percipience, peripheral field of vision, practical knowledge, range of vision, recognition, scope, sentience, understanding, vision, wisdom

KEY, *adjective* critical, crucial, decisive, fateful, important, influential, major, momentous, significant, weighty

KEY *(Passport),* ***noun*** bar, pass, permit, ticket

KEY *(Solution),* ***noun*** answer, method, resolution, way

KEY MAN, *noun* indispensable person, man of mark, officer, person of importance, person of repute, president, top person

KEYNOTE, *noun* anchorage, basis, bedrock, body, bottom line, bull's-eye, centerpiece, central focus, chief focus, core, cornerstone, essence, foundation, framework, groundwork, heart, highlight, main, main point, major focus, nucleus, pith, pivot, point, predominant focus, root, substance, sum, theme, thesis, underpinning

KICK THE CAN DOWN THE ROAD, *verb* arrest, bottleneck, check, dally, dam, dawdle, delay, detain, drag, drag one's feet, give the run around, goldbrick, hinder, hold back, impede, linger, logjam, obstruct, pause, play a waiting game, postpone, procrastinate, prolong, protract, shirk, stall, wait
ASSOCIATED CONCEPTS: budgetary cuts, continuing resolution

KICKBACK, *noun* bribe, criminal gift, criminal share, graft, hush money, illegal commission, illegal compensation, illegal cut, illegal payment, illegal percentage paid, illlegal recompense, illegal remuneration, payoff, payola, protection money
ASSOCIATED CONCEPTS: anti-kickback law, illegal kickback scheme, official corruption

KIDNAP, *verb* abduct, bear off, capture, carry off, convey away, ensnare, hold for ransom, impress, put under duress, run away with, run off with, seize, shanghai, snatch, spirit away, steal away, take away, take by force, unlawfully seize, waylay
ASSOCIATED CONCEPTS: false imprisonment
FOREIGN PHRASES: ***A piratis aut latronibus capti liberi permanent.*** Persons captured by pirates or robbers remain free.

KILL *(Defeat),* ***verb*** abolish, abrogate, annul, arrest, beat, block, cancel, check, *conficere,* counteract, crush, destroy, devitalize, dispatch, extinguish, *interficere,* invalidate, nullify, overthrow, overturn, prevail over, put down, quash, quell, repress, repulse, revoke, squash, stop, surmount, thwart, triumph, *trucidare,* upset, vanquish
ASSOCIATED CONCEPTS: kill a legislative bill

KILL *(Murder),* ***verb*** assassinate, *conficere,* deprive of life, destroy, dispatch, execute, exterminate, injure fatally, *interficere,* liquidate, massacre, *occidere,* put to death, slaughter, slay, smite
ASSOCIATED CONCEPTS: deliberate killing, intent to kill, justifiable killing, malicious killing, premeditated killing

KILLER, *noun* annihilator, assassin, assassinator, butcher, criminal, decapitator, destroyer, exterminator, gunman, hit man, liquidator, manslayer, mass murderer, mass slayer, murderer, serial murderer, shooter, slayer, triggerman, villain
ASSOCIATED CONCEPTS: cop killer law, serial killer

KILLING, *noun* annihilation, assassination, bloody murder, decimation, destruction, elimination, execution, extermination, homicide, liquidation, massacre, murder, murderous assault, slaughter, slaughtering, slaying, violent death
ASSOCIATED CONCEPTS: criminally negligent homicide, intent to kill, justifiable killing, malicious killing, premeditation, self-defense, wrongful death

KIN, *noun* affiliation, blood relation, blood relative, descendant, distant relative, family, family ties, ilk, kindred, kinship, line, lineage, near relation, next of kin, relation, relation through ties of blood, relationship through consanguinity, relative, sibling, stock
ASSOCIATED CONCEPTS: next of kin

KIND, *adjective* accommodating, affable, affectionate, agreeable, amiable, amicable, assisting, beneficent, benevolent, benign, benignant, brotherly, charitable, chivalrous, class, compassionate, compliant, considerate, cordial, courteous, decent, delicate, diplomatic, easy-going, forbearing, forgiving, fraternal, friendly, gallant, generous, genial, gentle, giving, good, good-natured, gracious, grade, heedful, helpful, hospitable, humane, humanitarian, kindhearted, kindly, lenient, merciful, mild, nice, noble, noble-minded, obliging, patient, philanthropic, pleasant, sensitive, softhearted, solicitous, sort, sympathetic, sympathizing, tactful, temperate, thoughtful, tolerant, understanding, well-intentioned, well-meaning

KIND, *noun* breed, category, character, class, classification, denomination, designation, division, form, *forma,* generic class, *generis,* genre, genus, group, ilk, modus, nature, sort, species, type, variety
ASSOCIATED CONCEPTS: payment in kind

KINDHEARTEDNESS, *noun* act of kindness, affection, agreeableness, altruism, amiability, amicableness, benefaction, benefit, benevolence, blessing, charity, clemency, compassion, consideration, cordiality, courteousness, courtesy, decency, generosity, gentleness, goodness, good disposition, good intentions, good-heartedness, good nature, good-natured disposition, graciousness, heartfelt sympathy, humane, humanity, id, kindheartedness, kindliness, kindly disposed, kindness, loving, merciful, mildness, nice, philanthropic, softheartedness, sympathy, thoughtfulness, understanding, virtuous, warmheartedness

KINDLE, *verb* affect, begin, commence, create, embark, emerge, engender, enkindle, establish, evolve, give birth, inaugurate, incept, incite, induce, initiate, instigate, led, motivate, nourish, nurture, occasion, originate, procure, start, stoke

KINDNESS, *noun* act of charity, act of grace, act of humanity, advantageous, affability, affectionate, agreeableness, aid, altruism, amiability, amicability, amicableness, assistance, beneficence, beneficial, benevolence, big-heartedness, brotherhood, charitableness, chivalry, clemency, compassion, consideration, cordiality, courteousness, decency, delicacy, diplomacy, fair, favorable, fellowship, fraternal, friendliness, friendship, gallantry, generosity, good intentions, good nature, goodheartedness, goodness, goodwill, graciousness, helpfulness, hospitality, humaneness, kindheartedness, lovingness, magnanimous, mindfulness, niceness, philanthropy, solicitousness, succor, sympathy, thoughtfulness, understanding, warmheartedness, warmth

KINDRED, *noun* ancestor, ancestral relation, blood relations, blood relatives, brethren, clan, clansmen, *cognati, consanguinei,* descendant, family, folk, kin, kinsfolk, kinsmen, kinspeople, lineage, *necessarii,* next of kin, relation by birth, relation by blood, relation by consanguinity, relations, relatives, stock
ASSOCIATED CONCEPTS: collateral kindred, degree of kindred

KING, *noun* authority, bigwig, boss, chief, chieftain, commander, czar, dictator, director, emperor, executive, governor, head, head honcho, high chief, imperator, leader, lord, magnate, majesty, master, monarch, overlord, paramount lord, patriarch, person who is reported to, potentate, power, royal personage, ruler, superior

KINGDOM, *noun* area of control, country, demesne, domain, holding, interest, land, manor, nation, ownership, possession, private domain, property, proprietorship, province, right of possession, rightful possession, seisin, territory

KINSHIP, *noun* affiliation, affinity, association, bond, brotherhood, closeness, cognation, connection, consanguinity, family, family connection, kindredship, link, propinquity, relation, relationship, tie

KLEPTOMANIAC, *noun* criminal, lawbreaker, lifter, offender, petty thief, pilferer, pillager, purloiner, stealer, thief, wrongdoer
ASSOCIATED CONCEPTS: shoplifting

KNAVERY, *noun* artfulness, artifice, beguilement, cheat, cheating, chicanery, circumvention, corruption, cozenage, craft, craftiness, criminality, cunning, cunningness, deceit, deceitfulness, deception, defraudation, deviousness, dishonesty, double-dealing, dupery, duplicity, foul play, fraud, fraudulence, *fraus,* guile, hoax, humbuggery, insincerity, knavishness, lack of principle, lack of probity, legerdemain, malfeasance, *malitia, nequitia,* pettifoggery, rascality, roguery, roguishness, scampishness, scoundrelism, shadiness, sharp practice, skulduggery, slyness, treachery, trick, trickery, trickiness, turpitude, underhand dealing, unreliability, untrustworthiness, villainousness, villainy, wiles, wrongdoing

KNOCK DOWN, *verb* accost, assault, attack, batter, be reckless in harming a person, beat, besiege, damage, deal a blow, harm, hit, hurt, inflict harm, inflict injury, injure, shruck off
ASSOCIATED CONCEPTS: assault, battery, dart out case, hit and run

KNOCK-AND-ANNOUNCE RULE, *noun* knocking and announcing requirement before entry, requirement that police officers announce their presence, requirement that police officers knock prior to entering premises to execute search

KNOW, *verb* absorb, apperceive, appreciate, apprehend, assimilate, be apprised of, be informed, cognize, comprehend, conceive, conclude, conjecture, deduce, digest, discern, fathom, find, gather, glean, grasp, identify, infer, internalize, learn, master, perceive, pierce, read, realize, recognize, retain, understand

KNOW-HOW, *noun* ability, adeptness, adroitness, artfulness, artisanship, artistry, background, brilliance, capability, capableness, capacity, cleverness, command, competence, craft, craftsmanship, deftness, dexterity, execution, experience, expertise, expertness, faculty, flair, gift, grace, ingeniousness, ingenuity, intellect, knack, knowledge, mastery, proficiency, prowess, resourcefulness, savoir faire, skill, skillfulness, style, tactfulness, talent, technical mastery, technique, touch, workmanship
ASSOCIATED CONCEPTS: specialization in law

KNOWING, *adjective* acquainted, acute, apperceptive, apprehending, apprised, astute, aware, cognitive, cognizant, comprehending, conscious, deliberate, designed, educated, heedful, informed, instructed, intended, intentional, knowledgeable, meant, mindful, perceptive, percipient, planned, posted, *prudens,* purposeful, schooled, *sciens,* taught, understanding, well-informed, well-posted, well-versed
ASSOCIATED CONCEPTS: knowing or conscious, knowingly aid, knowingly and willfully, knowingly possess, knowingly receive, knowingly suffer or permit

KNOWINGLY, *adverb* advisedly, deliberately, designedly, intentionally, learnedly, pointedly, purposefully, with knowledge, wittingly
ASSOCIATED CONCEPTS: knowingly and willfully, knowingly permit, knowingly suffer

KNOWLEDGE *(Awareness),* ***noun*** acquaintance, apperception, appreciation, appreciativeness, cognition, cognizance, comprehension, consciousness, discernment, enlightenment, familiarity, grasp, information, intellection, intelligence, ken, know-how, mindfulness, perception, perceptiveness, percipience, realization, recognition, understanding
ASSOCIATED CONCEPTS: actual knowledge, actual notice, common knowledge, constructive knowledge, discovery, full knowledge, guilty knowledge, implied knowledge, imputed knowledge, judicial notice, knowledge sufficient to form a belief, scienter

KNOWLEDGE *(Learning),* ***noun*** *cognitio,* command, *doctrina,* education, enlightenment, erudition, expertise, familiarity, familiarization, information, ken, know-how, mastery, proficiency, scholarship, *scientia,* skill, study, wisdom
FOREIGN PHRASES: ***Idem est scire aut scire debet aut potuisse.*** To be bound to know or to be able to know is the same as to know. ***Lex neminem cogit ostendere quod nescire praesumitur.*** The law compels no one to divulge that which he is presumed not to know. ***Scienti et volenti non fit injuria.*** A wrong is not done to a person who understands and consents. ***Ignorantia praesumitur ubi scientia non probatur.*** Ignorance is presumed where knowledge is not proved. ***Ignorantia facti.*** Ignorance of facts excuses; ignorance of law does not excuse. ***Scientia utrimque par pares contrahentes facit.*** Equal knowledge on both sides makes the contracting parties equal.

KNOWLEDGEABLE, *adjective* apperception, cognition, cognizance, comprehension, discernment, enlightenment, familiarity, grasp, intellection, intelligence, ken, know-how, understanding
ASSOCIATED CONCEPTS: knowledgeable experts

KNOWN *(Established),* ***adjective*** appreciated, ascertained, catch on, celebrated, comprehended, computed, conceived, discerned, disclosed, discovered, established, familiar, famous, known, noted, notorious, popular, prevalent, prominent, prominently known, recognized, revered, well-known, well-received
ASSOCIATED CONCEPTS: earliest known uses, little known laws, nationally known

KNOWN *(Obvious),* ***adjective*** accepted, acknowledged, admitted, advertised, aired, clear, come to light, confessed, declared, disclosed, discovered, established, evident, exposed, familiar, identified, manifest, obvious, patently known, proclaimed, publicized, published, realized, recognized, revealed, uncloaked, unconcealed, uncovered, undisguised, unmasked, well-known

KUDOS, *noun* acclaim, acclamation, accolade, applause, approbation, approval, commendation, compliment, congratulation, credit, distinction, endorsement, flattery, glory, honor, laudation, magnification, plaudits, popular favor, popularity, praise, prestige, recognition, renown, tribute

LABEL, *noun* brand, cachet, classification, description, docket, emblem, hallmark, identification, identification tag, insignia, mark, mark of identification, marker, sign, slip, stamp, sticker, superscription, tag, ticket
ASSOCIATED CONCEPTS: disclaimer on a label, misleading labels, trademark for a brand on a label, warning on a label

LABEL, *verb* betoken, brand, call, call by a distinctive title, characterize, classify, define, demarcate, denominate, denote, describe, designate, differentiate, distinguish by a mark, docket, earmark, entitle, identify, imprint, indicate, mark, name, provide with nomenclature, put a mark upon, set apart, single out, specify, stamp, tag, term, ticket, title

LABOR *(Exertion),* ***noun*** discipline, effort, endeavor, energy, enterprise, industry, mental toil, pains, strain, strife

LABOR *(Work),* ***noun*** advocation, assignment, calling, craft, duty, employ, employment, job, line of business, line of work, occupation, profession, pursuit, responsibility, task, toil, trade, undertaking, vocation
ASSOCIATED CONCEPTS: boycotts, closed shop, collective bargaining, labor arbitration, labor dispute, labor organization, labor relations, labor union, lockout, open shop, scope of employment, skilled labor, strikes, terms and conditions of employment, union labor, union shop, wildcat strike, workmen's compensation

LABOR, *verb* apply oneself, attend to business, be diligent, be employed, be industrious, *contendere,* devote oneself to, do a job, do work, drudge, endeavor, engage in, exercise, exert energy, exert oneself, follow one's vocation, *laborare,* plod, plug away, ply, ply one's trade, strain, strive, struggle, toil, travail, work, work hard

LABOR UNDER A MISAPPREHENSION, *verb* be deceived, be misguided, be misinformed, be misled, be mistaken, blunder, deceive oneself, delude oneself, estimate incorrectly, fail to understand, interpret incorrectly, make a mistake, misapprehend, miscalculate, misconstrue, misestimate, misinterpret, misjudge, misunderstand, put a false interpretation to, receive a false impression, receive a wrong impression

LABORIOUS, *adjective* active, arduous, assiduous, Augean, backbreaking, brutal, burdensome, bustling, busy, challenging, demanding, difficult, diligent, effortful, employed, engaged, exacting, exertive, exhausting, fatiguing, formidable, grueling, heavy, hellacious, Herculean, industrious, intensive, intricate, involved, murderous, occupied, onerous, oppressive, painstaking, relentless, rigorous, rough, rugged, sedulous, severe, stiff, strenuous, tied-up, tiresome, toilsome, tough, troublesome, uphill, vigorous, working

LABYRINTH *(Complex),* ***noun*** complexity, complication, confused situation, difficulty, enigma, involvement, intricacy, intricate state, knotty problem, maze, mystery, problem, puzzle, riddle, tangle

LABYRINTH *(Winding course),* ***noun*** circuitous course, complex course, complexity, complicated arrangement, complication, convolution, involvement, maze, meander, meanderings, problem, puzzle, tanglement, tortuousness course, winding path, windings and turnings

LABYRINTHINE, *adjective* baroque, byzantine, complex, complicate, complicated, confusing, convoluted, daedal, elaborate, intricate, involute, involved, knotty, sophisticated, tangled

LACHES, *noun* delay, delay attended by change of position, delay that results in disadvantage, dereliction, dereliction of duty, failure of duty, failure to litigate within reasonable period, improvidence, inattention, inexcusable delay, inexcusable delay in assertion of rights, inobservance, lack of diligence, laggardness, laxity, laxness, laziness, neglect, neglectfulness, negligence, nonfeasance, nonperformance, omission, prejudicial delay, procrastination, remissness, unconscionable delay, undue delay, unexcused delay, unexplained delay, unnecessary prolongation, unreasonable delay, want of duty
ASSOCIATED CONCEPTS: equity, estoppel by laches, statute of limitations
FOREIGN PHRASES: ***Tempus enim modus tollendi obligationes et actiones, quia tempus currit contra desides et sui juris contemptores.*** For time is a means of dissipating obligations and actions, because time runs against the slothful and careless of their own rights. ***Vigilantibus et non dormientibus jura subveniunt.*** The laws relieve the vigilant and not those who sleep on their rights.

LACK, *verb* be bereft of, be deficient, be deprived of, be desirous, be destitute, be in need, be in want, be inadequate, be inferior, be insufficient, be needy, be poor, be wanting, be without, crave, desiderate, desire, fall short,

feel a dearth, hunger for, long for, miss, need, require, suffer privation, want, wish for, yearn for
ASSOCIATED CONCEPTS: lack of capacity, lack of consideration, lack of due care, lack of good faith, lack of intent, lack of jurisdiction, lack of knowledge, lack of mutuality, lack of probable cause, lack of prosecution, lack of trustworthiness

LACK ABILITY, *adjective* forceless, helpless, ill-qualified, impotent, inadequate, inapt, incapable, ineffective, ineffectual, inept, inferior, not able, not equal to, not up to the task, outgunned, outmanned, outmatched, powerless, unable, unequipped, unfit, unqualified, unsuitable, untalented
ASSOCIATED CONCEPTS: capacity, lack of legal ability to act

LACK AGREEMENT, *adjective* at an impasse, at cross purposes, contrary, discord, discordance, disharmonious, disputing, dissenting, failed to agree, far apart, feuding, fixed, holding divergent opinions, intransigent, not arriving at a consensus, not gaining conformity, unable to reach a resolution, warring
ASSOCIATED CONCEPTS: meeting of the minds, spirit of an agreement

LACK CONFIDENCE IN, *noun* doubtful thoughts, doubting feelings, equivocal feelings, hesitancy, hold a dubious belief, insecurity, lack assurance, lack certitude, lack faith, lack sureness, lack trust, problematic, skeptical conclusion, suspiciousness, tentativeness, uncertain of, uncertainty, unconvinced of the outcome, undecided in ascertaining the results, unsettledness, unsure of feelings, wavering in a determination
ASSOCIATED CONCEPTS: confidentiality, encryption

LACK CONVICTION, *adjective* considering, have no opinion, have no view, hold no belief, lack assurance, lack belief, lack certainty, lack certitude, lack faith, lack of direction, mulling it over, not convinced, not resolute, not sold on, pondering, unable to persuade, undecided

LACK HONESTY, *adjective* beguiling, bogus, cheating, conscienceless, corrupt, deceitful, deceiving, deceptive, devoid of honesty, dishonorable, disingenuous, faked, fallacious, false, false-hearted, fraudulent, guileful, immoral, iniquitous, insidious, insincere, lying, meretricious, nefarious, not honest, perfidious, shameless, treacherous, unauthentic, underhanded, unethical, unprincipled, unscrupulous, untrustworthy, untruthful, void of truth, without probity
ASSOCIATED CONCEPTS: lack of civility and honesty

LACK OF AWARENESS, *adjective* blinded, heedless, ignorant, inattentive, incognizant, not heeding, off guard, surprised, unadvised, unapprised, unconscious, undiscerning, unenlightened, unfamiliar with, uninformed, unknowing, unmindful, unprepared, unsuspecting, unwarned, without any notice

LACK OF CAPACITY, *noun* disease, impotence, inadequacy, inaptitude, incapability, incapacity, incompetence, ineffectiveness, ineffectuality, ineffectualness, inefficaciousness, ineptitude, insanity, insufficiency, mental defect, mental disease, mental disorder, mental effeteness, mentally incapacitated, powerlessness
ASSOCIATED CONCEPTS: ability to stand trial, incapacity, intent

LACK OF CARE, *adjective* careless, casual, cavalier, disregardful, flippant, forgetful, heedless, inadvertence, inattention, inattentive, inconsiderate, indifferent, lackadaisical, lacking awareness, lacking concern, lax, neglectful, negligent, not affording protection, not attending to, not consciousness, not heeding, not looking after, reckless, unattended, uncaring, unconcerned, unheeding, unmindful, without heed, without prudence, without regard
ASSOCIATED CONCEPTS: manslaughter, negligence

LACK OF CERTAINTY, *noun* ambiguity, ambivalence, confusion, contingency, darkness, dimness, doubt, doubtfulness, dubiousness, equivocation, hesitancy, hesitation, incertitude, indecision, indefiniteness, indetermination, irresolution, perplexity, precariousness, quandary, reluctance, undependability, unpredictability, unreliability, unsteadiness, vacillation, wavering

LACK OF CONTROL, *adjective* disobedient, disorderly, fractious, frenzied, headstrong, hysterical, impetuous, incorrigible, indocile, insubordinate, insuppressible, insurgent, irrepressible, lawless, obstreperous, out of control, recalcitrant, refractory, riotous, tempestuous, uncontrollable, ungovernable, unmanageable, unruly, untoward, violent, wild

LACK OF PERSONAL JURISDICTION, *noun* bereft of authority, deficient personal jurisdiction, inadequate personal jurisdiction, insufficient personal jurisdiction, lack of authority to hear and decide a case, lack of capacity to decide the matter in issue, lack of capacity to hear the controversy, lack of decision-making power over the case, lack of legal authority, lack of legal power to decide a case, lack of purview, want of personal jurisdiction, without personal jurisdiction

LACK OF SUBJECT MATTER, *noun* bereft of authority, deficient subject matter jurisdiction, inadequate subject matter jurisdiction, insufficient subject matter jurisdiction, lack of authority to hear and decide a case, lack of capacity to decide the matter in issue, lack of capacity to hear the controversy, lack of decision-making power over the case, lack of legal authority, lack of legal power to decide a case, lack of purview, want of subject matter jurisdiction, without subject matter jurisdiction

LACKLUSTER, *adjective* acceptable, adequate, all right, average, common, decent, fair, fine, indifferent, mediocre, medium, middling, moderate, modest, ordinary, passable, run-of-the-mill, second-class, second-rate, sufficient, sufficing, unexceptional, unimpressive

LACONIC, *adjective* abbreviated, abridged, *adstrictus, brevis*, brief, brusque, closemouthed, compendious, compressed, concise, condensed, contracted, curt, economical of words, epigrammatic, exact, mum, pauciloquent, pithy, pointed, precise, quiet, reserved, reticent, secretive, sententious, short, sparing of words, succinct, summarized, taciturn, telegraphic, terse, to the point, uncommunicative, ungarrulous, unloquacious, untalkative

LAG, *verb* dally, dawdle, decelerate, decrease, delay, diminish in pace, ebb, fail, fall back, fall behind, get behind, go leisurely, hold back, idle, lag behind, linger, lose strength, move slowly, procrastinate, put off, saunter, slow up, take one's time, trail, wane
ASSOCIATED CONCEPTS: implementation date

LAISSEZ FAIRE, *noun* abstinence from action, hands-off policy, nonhampering, noninfringement, noninterference, nonintermeddling, noninterruption, nonintervention, nonintrusion, nontampering, refraining from involvement, refusal to become involved

LAMENT, *verb* bemoan, bewail, commiserate, feel concern for, feel emotions for, feel for, feel remorse for, feel sensitive to, fret, grieve, grieve for, mourn, mourn for, pine, pity, regret, sympathize

LAMENTABLE, *adjective* awful, comfortless, deplorable, depressing, depressive, disheartening, dismal, distressful, distressing, doleful, dreadful, *flebilis,* grave, grievous, horrible, horrid, joyless, *lamentabilis,* low, lugubrious, melancholy, miserable, mournful, painful, pathetic, piteous, pitiable, pitiful, poor, regrettable, rueful, sad, saddening, sorrowful, sorry, terrible, tragic, uncomfortable, unfavorable, unfortunate, unhappy, woeful, wretched

LANCINATE, *verb* break through, cleave, cut, cut into, discerp, divide, empierce, fractionalize, fragment, gash, gore, impale, incise, knife, lacerate, lance, make an incision, penetrate, perforate, pierce, prick, puncture, rend, rip, rive, slash, slit, stab, stick, sunder, tear, transpierce

LAND, *noun* property, real estate, seisin, terrain, tract
ASSOCIATED CONCEPTS: abutting land, adjacent land, agreement to sell land, alienation of land, appurtenance to land, common lands, condemnation of land, contiguous land, contract of sale of land, convey an interest in land, covenants running with the land, easement, easement running with the land, equitable interest in land, high land, improvements upon land, interest in land, land contract, land grant, land tax, lease of land, lien on land, raw land, right of way, subdivision of land, suit to recover land, survey of land, title in land, title in fee, trespass on land tract, undivided land, unimproved land, vacant land, wastelands

LANDHOLDER, *noun* estate owner, freeholder, holder of legal title, landlord, landowner, leaseholder, one who has land, owner of an estate in land, owner of the fee, owner of the fee simple absolute, property holder, property owner, proprietor, real property holder, real property owner, titleholder

LANDLOCKED, *adjective* buried, completely surrounded, confined, contained, embedded, encased, encompassed, hemmed in, implanted, locked in, wedged in
ASSOCIATED CONCEPTS: easements, egress, landlocked states

LANDLORD, *noun* *agrorum possessor,* lessor, owner of an estate in land, owner of lands, owner of tenements, propietory owner, proprietor
ASSOCIATED CONCEPTS: ejectment proceeding, landlord's lien

LANDMARK *(Conspicuous object),* ***noun*** boundary marker, cairn, cynosure, direction post, familiar object, guidepost, *lapis,* marker, monument, prominent object, signpost, waymark
ASSOCIATED CONCEPTS: preservation of landmarks

LANDMARK *(Significant change),* ***noun*** cardinal point, critical happening, critical juncture, critical occasion, crucial point, decisive turn, event, high point, key point, material point, milestone, moment of change, salient point, significant event, significant occurrence
ASSOCIATED CONCEPTS: landmark decision

LANDOWNER, *noun* *agrorum possessor,* estate owner, freeholder, holder of legal title, landed proprietor, landholder, landlord, owner of an estate in land, owner of land, owner of real estate, owner of real property, owner of the fee, property holder, property owner, proprietor, real property holder, real property owner, titleholder
ASSOCIATED CONCEPTS: landowner's liability

LANDSLIDE *(Avalanche),* ***noun*** accident, adversity, affliction, bad luck, calamity, casualty, catastrophe, devastation, disaster, emergency, hardship, infliction, misery, misfortune, ravage, tragedy, trouble
ASSOCIATED CONCEPTS: catastrophe insurance

LANDSLIDE *(Overwhelming support),* ***noun*** conclusive, decisive, large, lopsided, many, overwhelming
ASSOCIATED CONCEPTS: landslide political victory

LANGUAGE, *noun* communication, composition, dialect, expression, faculty of speech, folk speech, form of expression, formulation, idiom, jargon, *lingua,* linguistics, means of communication, oral, *oratio,* parlance, phrasing, phraseology, rhetoric, *sermo,* speech, spoken expression, spoken word, talk, terminology, tongue, verbal intercourse, verbiage, vernacular, vocabulary, wordage, wording, written expression, written word
ASSOCIATED CONCEPTS: abusive language, ambiguous language, obscene language, precatory language

LANGUID, *adjective* adynamic, anemic, apathetic, apathetical, asthenic, drooping, dry, dull, empty, exanimate, exhausted, faint, fatigued, feeble, flagging, hebetudinous, impotent, inactive, indifferent, ineffective, inert, lackadaisical, *languens,* languorous, *lassus,* leaden, lethargic, lethargical, lifeless, limp, listless, lukewarm, lustless, lymphatic, passionless, passive, phlegmatic, phlegmatical, pithless, pluckless, powerless, prosaic, remissus, sapless, sickly, sinewless, slack, slow, sluggish, spunkless, stagnant, stale, strengthless, supine, tired, torpid, unagressive, unanimated, unimpassioned, uninspired, uninterested, unrefreshed, unrestored, unspirited, unstrengthened, vapid, wan, weak, without animation, without force, without spirit

LANGUISH, *verb* ail, become disheartened, become ill, become weak, collapse, decay, decline, despair, despond, deteriorate, droop, drop, ebb, fade, fail, fail in health, fall ill, fall sick, flag, fret, go into a decline, grieve, grow weak, lament, *languere, languescere,* live under unfavorable conditions, lose heart, lose spirit, lose strength, pine, pine away, repine, sag, sicken, sink, slump, stagnate, succumb, suffer, *tabescere,* vegetate, waste away, weaken, wear away, wilt, wither

LANGUOR, *noun* apathy, debility, drowsiness, dullness, emasculation, enervation, fatigue, feebleness, heaviness, hebetude, helplessness, idleness, immobility, impotence, inaction, inactivity, indifference, indolence, inertness, inexcitability, lack of strength, *languor,* lassitude, laziness, lethargy, lifelessness, listlessness, oscitancy, passivity, phlegm, quiescence, sloth, slow motion, slow pace, slowness, sluggishness, somnolence, somnolency, stagnation, supineness, tiredness, torpidity, torpidness, torpor, vegetation, weakness, weariness

LANGUOROUS, *adjective* apathetic, careless, dull, enervated, exhausted, feeble, frail, heedless, impassive, inactive, indifferent, indolent, inert, lackadaisical, languid, languishing, lazy, lethargic, limp, passive, phlegmatic, slothful, sluggish, spiritless, stolid, tired, torpid, weak, weary

LAPSE *(Break),* ***noun*** *fuga,* hiatus, interlude, interruption, lull, pause, recess
ASSOCIATED CONCEPTS: devise, lapsed, legacy

LAPSE *(Expiration),* ***noun*** decline, default, delinquency, dereliction, *error,* error, expiry, failure, inconstancy, *lapsus,* misdeed, misstep, mistake, negligence, *peccatum,* recreancy, regression, relapse, retrogradation, retrogression, reversion, secession, shortcoming, slip, termination
ASSOCIATED CONCEPTS: lapsed bequest, lapsed devise, lapsed legacy, lapsed license, lapsed policy

LAPSE *(Cease),* ***verb*** abate, become forfeit, become void, come to an end, complete, conclude, discontinue, end, expire, pass to another, relinquish, reverti, run out, stop, terminate
FOREIGN PHRASES: ***Accusator post rationabile tempus non est audiendus, nisi se bene de omissione excusaverit.*** An accuser ought not to be heard after the lapse of a reasonable time, unless he can account satisfactorily for his delay.

LAPSE *(Fall into error),* ***verb*** be at fault, commit an error, deviate from the proper path, deviate from virtue, do wrong, err, *errare,* fail, fall from grace, go astray, go awry, misbehave, misstep, *peccare,* slip, slip from virtue, stray, transgress, trespass, weaken

LAPSE IN JUDGMENT, ***noun*** be at fault, commit an error, deviation from the proper path, deviation from virtue, error, failure to act properly, fated moment, gone astray, gone awry, improper action, improper decision, improper judgment, misbehavior, misstep, negligent determination, negligent interval, slip, transgression, wrong decision, wrong evaluation, wrongdoing
ASSOCIATED CONCEPTS: negligence, reckless

LAPSE IN TIME, ***noun*** loss of age, loss of chronology, loss of computation of time, loss of duration, loss of end of the matter, loss of era, loss of interim, loss of interlude, loss of interval, loss of period, loss of tenure, loss of term
ASSOCIATED CONCEPTS: latches

LARCENOUS, ***adjective*** brigandish, burglarious, criminal, dishonest, felonious, fraudulent, lawbreaking, piratic, piratical, plundering, plunderous, predaceous, predatory, privateering, rapacious, ravaging, thieving, thievish
ASSOCIATED CONCEPTS: larcenous intent

LARCENY, ***noun*** abstraction, appropriation, brigandage, embezzlement, felonious stealing, fraudulent taking, *furtum,* misappropriation, peculation, pickpocketing, pilferage, rapacity, rapine, swindle, swindling, theft, thievery, unlawful acquisition, unlawful conversion, unlawful taking, wrongful taking
ASSOCIATED CONCEPTS: compound larceny, conversion, embezzlement, fraud, grand larceny, larceny by device, larceny by false pretenses, larceny by fraud, larceny by trick, petit larceny, receiving stolen goods, simple larceny

LARGE, ***adjective*** abundant, all-embracing, all-inclusive, big, broad, capacious, colossal, comprehensive, considerable, endless, enlarged, enormous, excessive, exhaustive, expansive, extensive, gargantuan, giant, giant-size, grand, great, great big, huge, immeasurable, immense, infinite, king-size, lavish, limitless, lofty, massive, monstrous, of great scope, oversized, sizable, substantial, tremendous, unbounded, unlimited, vast, wide-ranging, wide-reaching
ASSOCIATED CONCEPTS: large law firms

LARGESS *(Generosity),* ***noun*** aid, almsgiving, altruism, assistance, benefaction, beneficence, benignancy, benignity, bounteousness, bountifulness, bounty, charitableness, charity, *congiarium,* free giving, freehandedness, freeness, generosity, generousness, graciousness, help, helpfulness, hospitableness, hospitality, indulgence, kindliness, kindness, *largitio,* lavishment, lavishness, liberality, liberalness, magnanimity, magnanimousness, munificence, openhandedness, philanthropy, prodigality, readiness to give, selflessness, thoughtfulness, unselfishness

LARGESS *(Gift),* ***noun*** alms, assistance, award, benefaction, benefit, bestowment, bonus, boon, bounty, charity, contribution, dole, donation, donative, dotation, endowment, favor, grant, gratuity, handout, handsel, help, offering, present, presentation, presentment, vail, voluntary conveyance

LASCIVIOUS, ***adjective*** bawdy, carnal, coarse, concupiscent, corrupt, debauched, depraved, dissipated, dissolute, erotic, fleshly, goatish, immodest, immoral, improper, *impurus,* indecent, *lascivus,* lecherous, lewd, libertine, *libidinosus,* libidinous, lickerish, lubric, lubricous, lustful, obscene, Paphian, pornographic, promiscuous, prurient, ribald, salacious, satyric, satyrical, sensuous, sex-ridden, shameless, unblushing, unchaste, unregenerate, wanton
ASSOCIATED CONCEPTS: indecent and lascivious, lewd and lascivious cohabitation, obscenity

LASH *(Attack verbally),* ***verb*** admonish, animadvert upon, assail, berate, betongue, blackguard, cast reproach upon, castigate, chastise, chide, criticize severely, decry, excoriate, exprobrate, flay, fulminate against, impugn, increpate, inveigh, objurgate, rave against, rebuke, reprehend, reprimand, reproach, reprove, revile, scarify, scathe, slate, take to task, upbraid, vilify, vilipend, vituperate

LASH *(Strike),* ***verb*** bastinado, batter, beat, birch, bruise, cudgel, deal a blow to, deal a stroke, drub, *flagellare,* flagellate, flay, flog, fustigate, give a beating, give a thrashing, hit, larrup, maul, pelt, pound, pummel, scourge, slap, smite, switch, thrash, trounce, truncheon, whack

LAST *(Final),* ***adjective*** aftermost, climactic, climactical, closing, completive, completory, concluding, conclusive, conclusory, crowning, decisive, definitive, determinative, end, ending, endmost, extreme, farthest, final, finishing, furthest, hindermost, hindmost, outermost, permanent, rear, terminal, terminating, terminational, terminative, ultimate
ASSOCIATED CONCEPTS: last clear chance, last known address, last residence, last will and testament

LAST *(Preceding),* ***adjective*** above, above-cited, above-mentioned, above-named, above-stated, aforegoing, aforementioned, aforesaid, *antecedens,* antecedent, anterior, before mentioned, earlier, fore, foregoing, former, freshest, introductory, most recent, newest, past, precedent, precursory, prefatory, preliminary, preludial, preludious, prelusive, prelusory, previous, *prior*

LAST, ***verb*** be long-lived, be stable, be timeless, be unconsumed, be unexhausted, bide, carry on, continue, *durare,* endure, exist, hang on, hold on, hold out, hold up, keep up, linger, live on, outlive, perdure, *permanere,* persevere, persist, prevail, prolong, protract, remain, stand firm, stay, stay on, subsist, survive, sustain, wait, withstand

LASTING, ***adjective*** abiding, continuing, enduring, lingering, maintained, perpetuated, perseverant, persistent, persisting, preserved, remaining, standing, staying, surviving, sustained, undestroyed, uneradicated, unerased, unfailing, unremoved, unrepealed

LATE *(Defunct),* ***adjective*** dead, deceased, demised, demortuus, departed, erstwhile, former, once, one-time, passed on, perished, previous, then

LATE *(Tardy),* ***adjective*** after time, behind time, belated, deferred, delayed, detained, held up, lagging, moratory, overdue, past due, postponed, retarded, slow, unpunctual, unready
ASSOCIATED CONCEPTS: late filing

LATENCY, ***noun*** behind the scenes, below the surface, camouflaged, concealed, covered, hidden from view, not manifested, screened, submerged, unapparent, under the surface, underlying, undetected, undeveloped, undiscovered, unexposed, unnoticed, unrevealed, unseen, unsuspected, veiled
ASSOCIATED CONCEPTS: toll the statute of limitations

LATENT, ***adjective*** *abditus, absconditus,* arcane, behind the scenes, below the surface, camouflaged, concealed, covered, covert, delitescent, hidden from view, imperceptible, indiscernible, *occultus,* screened, submerged, unapparent, under the surface, underlying, undetected, undeveloped, undiscovered, unexposed, unmanifested, unnoticed, unrevealed, unseen, unspied, unsuspected, veiled
ASSOCIATED CONCEPTS: latent ambiguity, latent danger, latent defect, latent injury, latent liability

LATER, ***adverb*** after, after a time, after a while, after that, afterwards, at a future time, at a later date, at a later point in time, at a subsequent time, at some point in the future, before long, before too long, imminently, in days to come, in the aftermath, in the course of time, in the future, in the immediate future, in the sequel, later on, next, sequentially, subsequently, succeeding, successively, then, tomorrow

LATEST, ***adjective*** current, final, just completed, just done, just finished, last, most current, most recent, newest, recent, up-to-date, up-to-the-minute

LATITUDE, ***noun*** absence of restraint, accommodation, amplitude, autonomy, carte blanche, choice, discretion, ease of movement, exemption from control, expanse, expansion, extension, field, free course, free decision, free hand, free play, free thought, free will, freedom, freedom of action, full play, independence, indiscipline, largeness, leverage, liberalism, *libertas,* liberty, license, *licentia,* maneuverability, margin, noninterference, nonintervention, openness, opportunity, option, play, power of choice, power to choose, range, range of choice, right of choice, room, scope, space, unconstraint, uninhibitedness, unrestraint, unstrictness, will

LAUD, ***verb*** accredit, acknowledge, adulate, applaud, cheer, commend, crack up, deify, extol, flatter, glorify, hail, honor, idolize, laud, magnify, overpraise, praise, recognize, recommend, salute

LAUDABLE, ***adjective*** admirable, approvable, commendable, creditable, deserving, estimable, excellent, exemplary, hallowed, *laudabilis, laudatus, laude dignus,* matchless, meritorious, model, noble, peerless, praiseworthy, saintly, sterling, uncensurable, unimpeachable, virtuous, worthwhile, worthy, worthy of estimation

LAUDATION, ***noun*** benediction, blessing, doxology, encomium, eulogy, exaltation, glorification, honor, idolatry, invocation, magnification, praise

LAUGH AT, ***verb*** abase, be amused by, belittle, bully, burn, caricature, chaff, corn, debase, decry, degrade, demean, denigrate, deride, discredit, gibe, harass, harry, hassle, heckle, humiliate, jibe, jive, josh, kid, lampoon, mock, needle, parody, pester, pillory, put down, rag, razz, rib, ride, roast, satirize, shoot down, skewer, smirch, sneer, spoof, target, taunt, tease

LAUNCH *(Initiate),* ***verb*** activate, begin, embark, establish, found, generate, handsel, inaugurate, induce, institute, introduce, lay the foundations, make active, open, originate, put in motion, set going, set in motion, start, take the first step, take the lead, touch off, trigger, undertake

LAUNCH *(Project),* ***verb*** cast, catapult, *contorquere,* eject, fling, heave, hurl, *immittere,* impel forward, jaculate, lance, pitch, precipitate, propel, push, send flying, send forth, send headlong, send off, set in motion, shoot, throw, thrust, toss

LAUNCH AN INQUIRY, ***verb*** conduct an investigation into, delve into, dig into, examinate, explore, fact-find, go into, inquire, investigate, look into, nose into, probe, pry into, scrutinize, search, search for information, search into
ASSOCIATED CONCEPTS: launch a public inquiry, launch an independent inquiry

LAVISH *(Opulent),* ***adjective*** abounding, abundant, affluent, ample, bounteous, bountiful, copious, costly, effusive, excess, extravagant, generous, immoderate, inordinate, liberal, luxuriant, munificent, open-handed, opulent, overabundant, overflowing, overlavish, overluxuriant, oversufficient, plenteous, plentiful, profuse, rich, sumptuous, superabundant

LAVISH *(Wasteful),* ***adjective*** extravagant, immoderate, improvident, intemperate, overflowing, overlavish, overluxuriant, oversufficient, squandering, thriftless, unthrifty

LAVISH, ***verb*** being generous, being extravagant, be liberal, bestow, be thriftless, be wasteful, carry to excess, furnish, luxuriate, pour on, spare no expense, spend, spend freely, spend recklessly, squander

LAW, ***noun*** act, article, body of rules, canon, charter, code, command, decree, decree absolute, dictum, enactment, established rule, expressed command, fiat, firm principle, instruction, *ius,* jurisprudence, legal code, *lex,* mandate, maxim, norm, order, ordinance, precedent, precept, prescribed form, prescription, principle, pronouncement, *regula,* regulation, rescript, rubric, rule, rule of conduct, set of rules, settled principle, standard, standing order, statute, tenet
ASSOCIATED CONCEPTS: action at law, adequate remedy at law, adjective law, administrative law, allowed by law, amendatory law, antitrust laws, application of the law, appropriation law, arising under laws of the united states, at law and in equity, attorney-at-law, authorized by law, aviation law, bankruptcy law, blue sky law, breach of the law, by operation of law, change in the law, civil law, civil rights law, civil service law, color of law, color of state law, commercial law, common law, common-law marriage, common-law trust, compliance with laws, conclusion of law, constitutional law, contrary to law, controversy arising under the laws of the United States, corporate law, court of law, criminal law, declare the law, domestic relations law, due process of law, duties and liabilities imposed by law, election law, enjoined by law, entertainment law, environmental law, equal protection of the law, error of law, established by law, ex post facto, executed in accordance with law, existing laws, federal law, fixed by law, foreign laws,

fundamental law, general law, governed by law, homestead law, ignorance of law, implied by law, inconsistent with law, instructions on the law, insufficient in law, insurance law, international law, issue of law, judgment founded upon a matter of law, knowledge of the law, labor law, law and equity, law enforcement, law of the case, law of the land, limited by law, local law, maritime law, martial law, matter of law, military law, mistake of law, municipal law, natural heirs at law, not in accordance with law, obligation imposed by law, omnibus law, operation of law, ordinary course of law, organic law, patent and trademark law, penal law, practice of law, preexisting law, prescribed by law, presumption of law, procedural law, process of law, prospective law, provided by law, provided by state law, question of law, question of local law, question of state law, real estate law, regulated by law, remedy at law, securities law, session laws, special law, specially prescribed by law, specific law, standing laws, state law, substantive law, sufficient as a matter of law, suits at law, supreme law, surrender by operation of law, tax law, terminate by limitation of law, under color of law, unemployment compensation law, uniform operation of laws, unwritten law, without due process of law

FOREIGN PHRASES: ***Ubi lex est specialis, et ratio ejus generalis, generaliter accipienda est.*** Where the law is special, and the reason of it general, it ought to be construed generally. ***Praxis judicum est interpres legum.*** The practice of the judges is the interpreter of the laws. ***Lex nemini operatur iniquum, nemini facit injuriam.*** The law never works an injury, or does a wrong. ***Lex est norma recti.*** Law is the rule of right. ***Lex est sanctio sancta, jubens honesta, et prohibens contraria.*** Law is a sacred santion, commanding that which is right, and prohibiting the contrary. ***Lex est tutissima cassis; sub clypeo legis nemo decipitur.*** Law is the safest helmet; under the shield of the law no one is deceived. ***Lex fingit ubi subsistit aequitas.*** The laws feigns where equity subsists. ***Lex intendit vicinum vicini facta scire.*** The law presumes that one neighbor is cognizant of the acts of his neighbor. ***Non est certandum de regulis juris.*** There is no disputing about rules of the law. ***Receditur a placitis juris, potius quam injuriae et delictamaneant impunita.*** In order that crimes not go unpunished, the law will be departed from. ***Res est misera ubi jus est vagum et incertum.*** It is a sorry state of affairs when law is vague and mutable. ***Salus populi est suprema lex.*** The welfare of the people is the supreme object of the law. ***Si a jure discedas, vagus eris, et erunt omniaomnibus incerta.*** If you depart from the law, you will go astray, and everything will be in a state of uncertainty to everyone. ***Ubi lex non distinguit, nec nos distinguere debemus.*** Where the law does not distinguish, we ought not to distinguish. ***Ubi non est lex, ibi non est transgressio, quo ad mundum.*** Where there is no law, there is no transgression, so far as worldly concerns and matters. ***Firmior et potentior est operatio legis quam dispositio hominis.*** The operation of the law is more firm and more powerful than the will of man. ***Non jus ex regula, sed regula ex jure.*** The law does not arise from the rule, but the rule comes from the law. ***Non verbis sed ipsis rebus, leges imponimus.*** We do not impose laws upon words, but upon the things themselves. ***Quando abest provisio partis, adest provisio legis.*** When a provision of the party is lacking, the provision of the law supplies it. ***Quod naturalis ratio inter omnes homines constituit, vocatur jus gentium.*** The rule which natural reason has established among all men is called the law of nations. ***Ratio est legis anima; mutata legis ratione mutatur et lex.*** Reason is the soul of law; the reason of law being changed, the law is also changed. ***Ratio potest allegari deficiente lege; sed ratio vera et legaliset non apparens.*** Where the law is deficient, the reason can be alleged, but it must be true and lawful and not merely apparent. ***Non in legendo sed in intelligendo legis consistunt.*** The laws consist not in being read, but in being understood. ***Lex semper intendit quod convenit rationi.*** The law always intends what is agreeable to reason. ***Lex spectat naturae ordinem.*** The law regards the order of nature. ***Lex succurrit ignoranti.*** The laws assist the ignorant. ***Lex succurrit minoribus.*** The law assists minors. ***Melius est jus deficiens quam jus incertum.*** A deficient law is better than an uncertain one. ***Multa in jure communi contra rationem disputandi, procommuni utilitate introducta sunt.*** Many things have been introduced into the common law which are contrary to the public good, which are inconsistent with sound reason. ***Non exemplis sed legibus judicandum est.*** Judgment should not be rendered from examples, but by the law. ***Id possumus quod de jure possumus.*** We may do only that which we are able to do lawfully. ***Idem est non probari et non esse; non deficit jus, sed probatio.*** What is not proved and what is not are the same; it is not a defect of the law, but a want of proof. ***Jus civile et quod sibi populus constituit.*** The civil law is that law which the people establish for themselves. ***Lex prospicit, non respicit.*** The law looks forward, not backward. ***Lex rejicit superflua, pugnantia, incongrua.*** The law rejects those matters which are superfluous, repugnant, or incongruous. ***Lex semper dabit remedium.*** The law always furnishes a remedy. ***Contra legem facit qui id facit quod lex prohibit; in fraudem vero qui, salvis verbis legis, sententiam ejus circumvenit.*** He who does what the law prohibits, acts in fraud of the law; the letter of the law being inviolate, cheats the spirit of it. ***Les fictions naissent de la loi, et non la loi des fictions.*** Fictions arise from the law, and not law from fictions. ***Legem enim contractus dat.*** The contract makes the law. ***Ubi non est directa lex, standum est arbitrio judicis, vel procedendum ad similia.*** Where there is no direct law, the decision of the judge is to be taken, or references to be made to similar cases. ***Consuetudo ex certa causa rationabili usitata privatcommunem legem.*** A custom, based on a certain and reasonable cause, supersedes the common law. ***Jus vendit quod usus approbavit.*** The law recommends what use or custom has approved. ***La ley favour la vie d'un homme.*** The law favors human life. ***Actus legis nemini est damnosus.*** The act of the law shall prejudice no one. ***Matter en ley ne serra mise in bouche del jurors.*** A matter of law shall not be put into the mouth of jurors. ***Equitas sequitur legem.*** Equity follows the law. ***Non obligat lex nisi promulgata.*** A law is not obligatory unless it is promulgated. ***Lex respicit aequitatem.*** The law regards equity. ***Ignorantia juris non excusat.*** Ignorance of the law is no excuse. ***Executio juris non habet injuriam.*** The execution of law does no injury. ***Ignorantia excusatur, non juris sed facti.*** Ignorance of fact may excuse, but not ignorance of law. ***Scire leges non hoc est verba earum tenere, sed vim ac potestatem.*** To know the laws is not to observe their words alone, but their force and power. ***Perpetua lex est nullam legem humanam ab positivam perpetuamesse, et clausula quae abrogationem excludit ab initio non valet.*** It is a perpetual law that no human and positive law can be perpetual, and a clause in a law which precludes the power of abrogationor repeal is void from the beginning. ***Experientia per varios actus legem facit. magistra rerum experientia.*** Experience by various acts makes law. Experience is the mistress of things. ***Nemo jus sibi dicere potest.*** No one can declare the law for himself. ***Lex aequitate gaudet; appetit perfectum; est norma recti.*** The law delights in equity; it grasps at perfection; it is a rule of right. ***In fictione juris semper aequitas existit.*** In a fiction of law, equity is always present. ***Optima est lex quae minimum relinquit arbitrio judicis; optimus judex qui minimum sibi.*** That is the best system of law which leaves the least to the discretion of the judge; that judge is the best who leaves the least to his own discretion. ***Jus quo universitates utuntur est idem quod habent privati.*** The law which governs corporations is the same as that which governs individuals. ***Ignorantia facti excusat, ignorantia juris non excusat.*** Ignorance of fact excuses; ignorance of the law does not excuse. ***Regula est, juris quidem ignorantiam cuique nocere, facti vero ignorantiam non nocere.*** The rule is that a person's ignorance of the law may prejudice him, but that his ignorance of fact will not. ***Per varios actus legem experientia facit.*** By various acts experience makes the law. ***Juris affectus in executione consistit.*** The effectiveness of a law lies in its execution. ***Cessante ratione legis, cessat et ipsa lex.*** Where the reason for a law ceases, the law itself also ceases. ***Fortior et potentior est dispositio legis quam hominis.*** The disposition of the law has greater force and stronger effect than that of man. ***Lex non curat de minimis.*** The law does not regard small matters. ***Hominum causa jus constitutum est.*** Law is established for the benefit of mankind. ***Judicis est jus dicere, non dare.*** It is the duty of a judge to declare the law, not to make it. ***Lex est dictamen rationis.*** Law is the dictate of reason. ***Lex est ratio summa, quae jubet quae sunt utilia et necessaria et contraria prohibet.*** That which is law is the consummation of reason, which commands those things useful and necessary while prohibiting the contrary. ***Nemo est supra leges.*** No one is above the law. ***Ubi jus incertum, ibi jus nullum.*** Where the law is uncertain, there is no law. ***Lex neminem cogit ad vana seu inutilia peragenda.*** The law compels no one to do futile or useless things. ***Ex facto jus oritur.*** Law arises out of facts. ***Ad quaestionem facti non respondent judicis; ad quaestionem juris non respondent juratores.*** Judges do not answer to a question of fact; jurors do not answer to a question of law. ***Constructio legis non facit injuriam.*** A law properly interpreted creates no wrong. ***Argumentum ab inconvenienti est validum in lege, quia lex non permittit aliquod inconveniens.*** An argument drawn from what is inconvenient is good in law, because the law will not permit any inconvenience. ***Injustum est, nisi tota lege inspecta, de una aliqua ejus particula proposita judicare vel respondere.*** It is unjust to give judgment or advice concerning any particular clause of a law without having examined the whole law. ***Cuilibet licet juri pro se introducto renunciare.*** Any one may waive or renounce the benefit of a principle or rule of law that exists only for his protection. ***Ignorantia legis neminem excusat.*** Ignorance of law excuses no one. ***Ipsae leges cupiunt ut jure regantur.*** The laws themselves are desirous of being governed by what is right. ***Exempla illustrant non restringunt legem.*** Examples illustrate but do not restrain the law. ***Obedientia est legis essentia.*** Obedience is the essence of the law. ***Consuetudo est altera lex.*** Custom is another law. ***Consuetudo vincit communem legem.*** Custom overrules common law. ***Consuetudo praescripta et legitima vincit legem.*** A prescriptive and legitimate custom prevails over the law. ***Consuetudo et communis assue tudo vincit legem non scriptam, si sitspecialis; et interpretatur legem scriptam, si lex sit generalis.*** Custom and common usage override the unwritten law, if it be special; and interpret the written law, if the law be general. ***Consuetudo est optimus interpres legum.*** Custom is the best interpreter of the laws. ***Conventio privatorum non potest publico juri derogare.*** The agreement of private persons cannot derogate from public right. ***Conventio vincit legem.*** The express agreement of parties overcomes the law. ***Quamvis lex generaliter loquitur, restringenda tamen est, ut, cessante ratione, ipsa cessat.*** Although a law speaks generally, yet it is to be restrained, so that when its reason fails, it should cease also. ***Processus legis est gravis vexatio, executio legis coronat opus.*** The process of the law is a grave vexation; the execution of the law crowns the work. ***Ubi eadem ratio, ibi idem jus; et de similibus idem est judicium.*** Where there is the same reason, there is the same law; and where there are similar situations, the judgment is the same. ***Lex nil frustra facit.*** The law does nothing in vain. ***Lex non deficit in justitia exhibenda.*** The law does not fail in dispensing justice. ***Lex plus laudatur quando ratione probatur.*** The law is most praiseworthy when it is consistent with reason. ***Ubi lex aliquem cogit ostendere causam, necesse est quod causa sit justa et legitima.*** Where the law compels a man to show cause, it is necessary that the cause be just and legal. ***Ita semper fiat relatio ut valeat dispositio.*** Let the interpretation be so made that the disposition stands. ***Judex est lex loquens.*** The judge is the law speaking; that is, he is the mouthpiece of the law. ***Natura appetit perfectum; ita et lex.*** Nature seeks perfection, and so does the law. ***A verbis legis non est recedendum.*** The words of the law must not be departed from. ***Apices juris non sunt jura.*** Legal niceties are not law. ***Communis error facit jus.*** A common error makes law. ***Casus omissus et oblivioni datus dispositioni communis juris relinquitur.*** A case omitted and forgotten is left to the disposal of the common law. ***Contemporanea expositio est optima et fortissima in lege.*** Contemporaneous exposition is the best and most powerful in the law. ***Neque leges neque senatus consulta ita scribi possunt ut omnis casus qui quandoque in sediriunt comprehendatur; sed sufficit ea quae plaerumque accidunt contineri.*** Neither laws nor acts of a legislature can be so written as to include all actual or possible cases; it is sufficient if they provide for those things which frequently or ordinarily may happen. ***Jura eodem modo destituuntur quo constituuntur.*** Laws are abrogated by the same means by which they are enacted. ***Jura naturae sunt immutabilia.*** The laws of nature are unchangeable. ***Leges humanae nascuntur, vivunt, et moriuntur.*** Human laws are born, live, and die. ***Legibus sumptis desinentibus, lege naturae utendum est.*** When laws imposed by the state fail, the laws of nature must be invoked. ***Tortura legum pessima.*** The torture or wresting of laws is the worst kind of torture. ***Leges suum ligent latorem.*** Laws should bind their own proposer. ***Jus constitui oportet in his quae ut plurimum accidunt non quae ex inopinato.*** Laws ought to be made with a view to those cases which occur most frequently and not to those which are of rare or accidental occurrence. ***Nova constitutio futuris formam imponere debet, non praeteritis.*** A new law ought to affect the future, not what is past. ***Ad ea quae frequentius accidunt jura adaptantur.*** Laws are adapted to those cases which most commonly occur. ***Inde datae leges ne fortior omnia posset.*** Laws were made lest the stronger might become all-powerful. ***Ex malis moribus bonae leges natae sunt.*** Good laws arise from evil morals. ***Quando lex est specialis, ratio autem generalis, generaliter lex est intelligenda.*** When a law is special, but its reason general, the law is to be understood generally. ***Intentio inservire debet legibus, non legesintentioni.*** The intention ought to be subservient to the laws, not the laws to intentions. ***Legislatorum est viva vox, rebus etnon verbis, legem imponere.*** The voice of the legislators is the living voice, to impose laws upon things, and not on words. ***Optimam esse legem, quae minimum relinquit arbitrio judicis; id quod certitudo ejus praestat.***

That law is best which leaves the least to the decision of the judge; this being an advantage which results from its certainty. ***Leges posteriores priores contrariasabrogant.*** Subsequent laws repeal prior laws that are repugnant to them. ***Jus est ars boni et aequi.*** Law is the science of what is good and just. ***Nihil infra regnum subditos magis conservatin tranquillitate et concordia quam debitalegum administratio.*** Nothing better preserves in tranquillity and concord those subjected to the same government better than one due administration of the laws. ***Aequum et bonum est lex legum.*** That which is equitable and good is the law of laws.

LAW-ABIDING, *adjective* according to law, acquiescent, *bene moratus,* careful to follow the law, complying, conforming, conforming to the laws, descent, dutiful, ethical, evenhanded, follows the law, follows the prescribed laws, high-minded, high-principled, honest, honorable, in conformity with the law, incorrupt, incorruptible, inviolate, irreproachable, law-revering, legal, legitimate, licit, moral, noble, not illegitimate, obedient, obsequious, observant, on the up-and-up, principled, proper, reputable, respectable, right-minded, righteous, scrupulous, statutable, statutory, sticks to the law, sticks to the letter of the law, straight, straightforward, trustworthy, trusty, unbribable, uncorrupted, unimpeachable, upright, upstanding, valid, virtuous, well-principled, within the law, within the limits of the law
ASSOCIATED CONCEPTS: law-abiding citizens

LAW COURT, *noun* bench, court of justice, forum for adjusting disputes, forum of justice, judicial forum, judicial tribunal, judiciary, justice court, place where justice is administered, tribunal

LAW FIRM, *noun* attorneys-at-law, business company, counselors-at-law, law office(s), legal practitioners, LLC, partnership, PLC
ASSOCIATED CONCEPTS: prominent law firm, white glove law firms

LAW OF THE CASE, *noun* conclusion, conclusion of the matter, decision, decree, determination, dictate, final judgment, finding, holding, judicial decision, maxim, opinion, order, order of the court, outcome, precedence, precedent, precept, principle, pronouncement, pronouncement by a court, resolution, result, settled holding, underlying basis, upshot, written order

LAWBREAKER, *noun* arsonist, convict, convicted felon, criminal, crook, defrauder, delinquent, embezzler, felon, fugitive, guilty person, hoodlum, *legis violator,* malefactor, malfeasor, miscreant, misdemeanant, misfeasor, murderer, offender, outlaw, racketeer, recidivist, thief, transgressor, vandal, violator, wrongdoer

LAWBREAKING, *adjective* anarchic, anarchical, corrupt, criminal, culpable, defiant, dirty, disobedient, disorderly, felonious, forward, fraudulent, illegal, illegitimate, illicit, insubordinate, intractable, lawless, mutinous, offensive, rebellious, recalcitrant, refractory, riotous, tricky, undisciplined, unlawful, unruly, wrong, wrongful
ASSOCIATED CONCEPTS: penal law, prosecution

LAWFUL, *adjective* according to fiat, according to law, allowable, allowed, authorized by law, conformable to law, conformable with the law, constitutional, established, in accordance with the law, in conformity to the law, inviolable, juridic, law-abiding, legal, legalized, legitimate, *legitimus,* licit, nomothetic, obedient, permissible, permitted, prescribed by law, proper, sanctioned, sanctioned by law, statutable, statutory, unprohibited, valid, warranted by law, within the law
ASSOCIATED CONCEPTS: lawful act, lawful age, lawful beneficiary, lawful business, lawful command, lawful custody, lawful damages, lawful entry, lawful heirs, lawful interest, lawful issue, lawful order, lawful possession, lawful process, lawful purpose, lawful representative, lawful use

LAWFUL AUTHORITY, *noun* agency of the law, authorized agent of the law, authorized officer, established authority, legitimate member of law enforcement, member of a law enforcement agency, member of the police force, officer sanctioned by law, officer with credentials, police, proper authority, rightful authority, sanctioned authority, security, valid member of law enforcement

LAWFUL POSSESSION, *noun* allowable retention, authorized proprietorship, authorized retention, lawful retention, legal retention, legitimate control over, legitimate ownership, legitimate retention, permissible control, permitted control, possession in accordance with the law, possession in conformity to the law, possession prescribed by law, proper bailment, proper ownership, proper title, retention sanctioned by law, retention warranted by law, right of retention, rightful control, rightful retention, sanctioned retention, valid retention
ASSOCIATED CONCEPTS: governmental authority, marshal law, rule of law

LAWFUL POWER, *noun* allowed authority, authority authorized by law, constitutional power, established power, force in power, lawful right, legal power, legalized authority, legitimate authority, legitimized power, permitted authority, power according to law, proper power, rightful authority, sanctioned power, valid power, warranted power
ASSOCIATED CONCEPTS: carrying of weapons

LAWFULLY, *adverb* absolutely according to law, absolutely within conformity to the law, allowably, conforming to the law, definitely reflected in statute, entirely established, entirely in accordance with the law, entirely sanctioned, entirely sanctioned by law, entirely warranted by law, entirely within the law, entirely within the prescriptions of the law, law-abidingly, legally, legitimately, obediently, permissibly, properly, validly
ASSOCIATED CONCEPTS: lawfully authorized electronic surveillance, lawfully engaged in an investigation

LAWLESS, *adjective* against the law, anarchic, anarchical, arrant, *audax,* capricious, contrarious, contumacious, corrupt, criminal, degenerate, difficult, disobedient, disobeyed, disobeying, disorderly, disreputable, *effrenatus,* felonious, heedless, ill-disciplined, illegal, immoral, in defiance of the law, incorrigible, insidious, insolent, insubordinate, intemperate, intractable, irresponsible, knavish, lawbreaking, licensed, mutinous, nonconformist, nonlegal, nonobservant, not observant of the law, outlaw, profligate, rascally, rebellious, recalcitrant, recreant, recusant, refractory, reinless, restive, revolutionary, riotous, seditious, subversive, transgressive, unaccountable, unbidden, uncompliant, uncomplying, unconformable, unconstrained, uncontrolled, uncurbed, undisciplined, unfettered, ungovernable, ungoverned, unprincipled, unreined, unrighteous, unscrupulous, unsubmissive, unsuppressed, untamed, untoward, unwarrantable, unwarranted, venal, violative, wayward, without law, wrongful

LAWLESSNESS, ***noun*** actions in defiance of the law, anarchy, criminal anarchy, disreputable conduct, felonious conduct, havoc, illegal conduct, insidious behavior, insubordination to the rule of law, irresponsible conduct, lawbreaking activity, mutinous conduct, outlawed conduct, rebellious conduct, recalcitrant conduct, revolutionary conduct, riotous behavior, seditious activity, subversive actions, uncontrolled actions, ungovernable actions, unlicensed behavior, unsuppressed conduct, untoward behavior, unwarrantable behavior, wrongful action
ASSOCIATED CONCEPTS: international law, rule of law

LAWMAKER, ***noun*** alderman, alderwoman, assemblyman, assemblywoman, bill drafter, congressman, congresswoman, councilman, councilwoman, formulator of laws, lawgiver, legislative draftsman, legislator, member of a legislature, member of Congress, member of the Assembly, member of the House, member of the Senate, politician, politico, proposer of a law, proposer of legistation, representative, representative in Congress, senator
ASSOCIATED CONCEPTS: Assembly, Congress, House of Representatives, Senate

LAWSUIT, ***noun*** action, action at law, case, case for decision, cause in court, claim, contention, contest, controversia, controversy, controversy before a court, court action, dispute, judicial contest, legal action, legal argument, legal contest, legal controversy, legal dispute, legal proceedings, *lis,* litigation, matter for judgment, proceeding, suit at law, suit in equity, trial

LAWYER, ***noun*** *avocat,* advocate, attorney, attorney-at-law, barrister, barrister-at-law, counsel, counselor, counselor-at-law, iurisconsultus, *iurisperitus, jurisconsult,* jurisprudent, jurist, legal advisor, legal advocate, legal consultant, legal practitioner, legist, member of the legal profession, solicitor
ASSOCIATED CONCEPTS: admission to bar, attorney-client privilege, bar association, character and fitness committee, code of professional conduct, grievance committee, work product

LAX, ***adjective*** absentminded, apathetic, careless, casual, derelict, disorganized, disregarding, *dissolutus,* feckless, forgetful, halfhearted, heedless, idle, imprecise, improvident, imprudent, inaccurate, inadvertent, inattentive, incautious, indifferent, indolent, inexact, lackadaisical, lazy, loose, mindless, neglectful, *neglegens*, negligent, nonaggressive, oblivious, perfunctory, pococurante, regardless, remiss, remissus, slack, slipshod, slothful, slovenly, sluggish, temerarious, thoughtless, unambitious, unapprehensive, unaspiring, unaware, uncaring, uncircumspect, unconcerned, undemanding, unenterprising, unguarded, unheeding, uninterested, unmindful, unobservant, unobserving, unprepared, unstrict, unthinking, unthorough, unthoughtful, untidy, unwary, unwatchful

LAXITY, ***noun*** amorality, apathy, carelessness, dereliction, disregard, heedlessness, imprecision, improvidence, inaccuracy, inadvertence, inadvertency, inattention, inattentiveness, indifference, indolence, inexactitude, inexactness, inobservance, lack of control, lack of interest, lack of thoroughness, laziness, looseness, neglect, neglectfulness, *neglegentia,* negligence, noncompletion, nonfeasance, nonfulfillment, nonperformance, oversight, perfunctoriness, remissness, slackness, sloppiness, sloth, slovenliness, thoughtlessness, unconcern, unpreparedness, unrigorousness, untidiness, unwatchfulness

LAY ASIDE, ***verb*** abandon, adjourn, cancel, continue, defer, delay, detain, discard, disclaim, discount, dismiss, disregard, drop, exclude, extend, forestall, forgo, hold, hold in abeyance, hold off, hold up, ignore, isolate, keep, keep pending, lay away, lay by, lay in a stock, not decide, over rule, pass over, pause, pick out, place on hold, postpone, preserve, pretermit, procrastinate, prolong, put aside, put in suspension, put off, put on hold, recess, reject, relinquish, remove, renounce, repudiate, retain, retard, scrap, segregate, select, separate, set apart, set aside, set by, shelve, shut out, spurn, stall, stave off, stay, stockpile, store away, store up, suspend, table, turn over, wait, weed out, winnow, withdraw, withhold

LAY DOWN *(Dictate the Law),* ***noun*** ascertain, assert, declare, delineate, determine, maintain, proclaim, report, specify, state, state categorically
ASSOCIATED CONCEPTS: lay down the law

LAY DOWN *(Give up),* ***noun*** cede, declare defeat, quit, relinquish, submit, surrender, turn over, yield

LAY DOWN THE LAW, ***verb*** administer the law, carry into effect the law, carry into execution the law, carry out the law, compel obedience with the law, effectuate the law, enforce the law, enforce to the letter of the law, ensure compliance, execute the law, implement the law, impose the law, insist upon, make compulsory, mandate, necessitate, obtain by force, put into effect, put into execution, put pressure on, read the riot act, require, strictly regulate, subject to pressure

LAY THE BLAME ON, ***verb*** accuse, ascribe blame, blame, bring up on charges, cast blame upon, charge, charge with an offense, complain against, condemn, connect with a crime, criminate, denounce, expose, find fault with, hold accountable, implicate, impute guilt to, inculpate, indict, inform on, insinuate, involve, involve in criminal proceeding, lodge a complaint, place the blame on, prefer charges, prosecute

LAY WASTE, ***verb*** abolish, annihilate, deal destruction, deracinate, desolate, destroy, destroy thoroughly, devastate, efface, obliterate, ravage

LAYER, ***noun*** amount, band, belt, blanket, cloak, cover, coverage, covering, curtain, level, shell, stratum, thickness, tier, zone

LAYMAN, ***noun*** amateur, civilian, laic, nonprofessional, nonspecialist, one who has no specialized training, unskilled practitioner, untrained person
ASSOCIATED CONCEPTS: lay witness

LAYOFF, ***noun*** banishment, cashiering, cessation, desistance, discarding, discharge, discontinuance, discontinuation, disemployment, dismissal, displacement, ejection, ejectment, elimination, expulsion, firing, halt, idling, interruption, letting go, ouster, rejection, release, removal, retirement, riddance, stoppage, suspension of employment, temporary deprivation, temporary discharge, temporary suspension, termination, termination of employment
ASSOCIATED CONCEPTS: suspension, temporary layoff

LAZY, ***adjective*** apathetic, careless, derelict, disinterested, disregardful, drowsy, dull, forgetful, heedless, idle, inattentive, indifferent, indolent, inert, lackluster, languorous, lax, lethargic, listless, neglectful, oblivious, phlegmatic, quiescent, remiss, shiftless, slack, sleepy, slothful, sluggish, supine, thoughtless, torpid, unambitious, unconcerned, unenergetic, unimpressive, unmindful

LEAD *(Introduction),* ***noun*** connection, foreword, opening, preamble, preface, prelude, prologue, prompt

LEAD *(Predominant),* ***noun*** clue, direction, example, generalship, guidance, headline, indication, influence, leading role, leadership, precedence, precedent, predominance, primacy, priority, protagonist, sign

LEAD, ***verb*** assume mastery over, coax, command, conduct, control, direct, dominate, drive, gain ascendancy, govern, guide, handle, head, hold the reins, influence, initiate, introduce, manage, manipulate, marshal, motivate, officiate, originate, oversee, persuade, pilot, pioneer, precede, predominate, preside, prevail upon, prompt, regulate, rule, run, show the way, steer, superintend
ASSOCIATED CONCEPTS: leading questions, leading the witness

LEAD COUNSEL, ***noun*** advocate in charge, commanding counsel, controlling counsel, counsel in charge, first counsel, supervising and controlling counsel

LEADER, ***noun*** administrator, antecedent, captain, chairman, chief, commander, controller, demagogue, director, employer, forerunner, manager, mastermind, official, overseer, pathfinder, pioneer, precursor, predecessor, principal, protagonist, ruler, shepherd, supervisor

LEADERSHIP, ***noun*** ascendancy, authority, captaincy, chieftainship, direction, directorate, directorship, domination, first place, generalship, governorship, guidance, influence, legal power, management, mastery, paramountcy, potency, primacy, predominance, premiership, prerogative, presidency, proctorship, puissance, reign, right, seigniory, sovereignty, statesmanship, steering, superintendency, superiority, supremacy, suzerainty, sway

LEADING *(Guiding),* ***adjective*** controlling, directing, implicational, implicative, implicatory, inferential, insinuating, insinuative, instructional, instructive, referential, regulating, steering, suggestive, supervising, supervisory
ASSOCIATED CONCEPTS: leading a witness, leading question

LEADING *(Ranking first),* ***adjective*** beyond compare, capital, cardinal, central, chief, dominant, dominating, finest, first, foremost, greatest, main, most influential, outstanding, paramount, predominant, preeminent, prevailing, *primarius,* primary, prime, *princeps,* principal, prominent, stellar, supreme, top, topmost, unequaled, unexcelled, unmatched, unparalleled, unrivalled, unsurpassed

LEADING CASE, ***noun*** case dispositive on a salient point, case which is dispositive of an issue, decisive case in point, greatest precedence, highest case in a circuit, highest case of precedence, milestone, most critical case in a subject area, most major case in point, number one case in the area

LEAGUE, ***noun*** accord, affiliation, agreement, alignment, alliance, association, axis, band, bloc, cartel, club, coalition, collaboration, combination, combine, compact, complicity, concord, concordat, concurrence, confederacy, confederation, conjunction, cooperation, copartnership, corporation, covenant, deal, federation, fellowship, foedus, fusion, gang, group, guild, mutual undertaking, network, organization, pact, *pactum,* participation, partnership, pool, ring, *societas,* society, sodality, treaty, trust, understanding, unification, union

LEANING, ***noun*** attitude, bent, bias, conviction, disposition, favor, favorable predisposition toward, favoritism, feeling, gravitation, habit, idiosyncrasy, in disequilibrium, inclination, liking, partiality, penchant, predisposition, predisposition toward, prejudgment, prejudice, prepossession, proclivity, proneness, propensity, readiness, stand, standpoint, susceptibility, temperament, tendency, trend, unbalanced
ASSOCIATED CONCEPTS: judge's leaning toward issuing a decision

LEAP OF FAITH, ***verb*** blind acceptance, blind accession, blind belief, blind confidence, blind intentions, misguided trust, quantum confidence in, unjustified belief, unjustified confidence, unjustified freedom from doubt, unquestioning acceptance, unshakable trust, unwarranted conviction, unwarranted credence, unwarranted loyalty, unwarranted progression, unwarranted reliance, unwarranted trust

LEARN, ***verb*** acquire knowledge, analyze, become knowledgeable, comprehend, concentrate on, edify, educate, enlighten, experience, gain erudition, gain information, gain knowledge, pursue knowledge, study, understand

LEARNED, ***adjective*** accomplished, acquainted with, acroatic, apprised of, aware, bibliophilic, bookish, cognizant, conversant, *doctus,* educated, enlightened, erudite, eruditus, experienced, expert, familiar, informed, instructed, knowing, knowledgeable, lettered, literate, *litteratus,* omniscient, pansophic, pedantic, pedantical, professional, professorial, proficient, profound, recondite, sagacious, sage, sapient, scholarly, schooled, skilled, studious, versant, versed, well-educated, well-informed, well-read, well-rounded, well-taught, well-trained, widely read, wise

LEARNING, ***noun*** acquired knowledge, acquirements, acquisition of knowledge, analysis, attainment, body of knowledge, common knowledge, comprehension, discipline, edification, education, enlightenment, erudition, experience, extensive knowledge, information, instruction, mental cultivation, pedantry, practical learning, proficiency, pursuit of knowledge, quest, recall, recalling, recollection, remembering, remembrance, sagaciousness, sagacity, science, search, study

LEASE, ***noun*** agreement, *conductio,* contract, contract for exclusive possession of lands, contract for possession and profits, conveyance in consideration of recompense, conveyance of interest in real property, conveyance of land for a designated period, grant, grant of realty, grant of use and possession, instrument, instrument granting possession of premises, legal agreement, permission to rent, tenant-landlord agreement, written agreement
ASSOCIATED CONCEPTS: assignment of lease, building lease, cancellation of a lease, concurrent lease, divisible lease, forfeiture of lease, implied lease, let premises, long-term lease, option to lease, parol lease, perpetual lease, renewal of lease, rent, sublease, term of lease, termination of lease, voidable lease

LEASE, ***verb*** allow the use of, charter, contract for exclusive possession, contract for possession of land, contract for use and occupation, convey for a designated period, convey real property for a specified period, demise, engage, engage premises for a designated period, grant exclusive possession for a designated period, grant use and

possession, lend on security, let, let premises for a designated period, *locare,* rent, rent out, sublet, subrent
ASSOCIATED CONCEPTS: assignment of a lease, cancellation of a lease, commencement of a lease, extension of a lease, forfeiture of a lease, joint lease, lease at will, lease for years, lease of premises, month-to-month tenacy, perpetual lease, renewable lease, sublease, tenacy, tenacy at sufferance, tenacy at will, term of a lease, termination of a lease, voidable lease

LEASEHOLD, *noun* estate for a fixed term, estate for a fixed term of years, estate in realty, freehold, interest in real estate, interest of a lessee, land held by lease, land leased, property leased, real property subject to a lease, tenure by lease

LEAST *(Inadequate),* ***adjective*** beneath, deficient, imperfect, incompetent, inferior, insufficient, lowest, mediocre, poorest

LEAST *(Insignificant),* ***adjective*** bottom number of, fewest, infinitesimally low, littlest, lowest, microscopically small, minimal, minute, minutest, most trivial, next to nothing, slightest, small, smallest, trivial

LEAST RESTRICTIVE MEANS, *noun* least restricted means to achieve interest, least restrictive way to effectively achieve government interest

LEAVE *(Absence),* ***noun*** absentation, break, *commeatus,* departure, freedom from duty, furlough, holiday, inactivity, interlude, intermission, interval of rest, leisure, liberty, nonappearance, nonattendance, parting, pause, recess, recreation time, relaxation, removal, repose, respite, rest, retirement, retreat, suspension of work, vacation
ASSOCIATED CONCEPTS: leave of absence, sick leave

LEAVE *(Permission),* ***noun*** accordance, acquiescence, agreement, allowance, approbation, approval, assent, authorization, certification, concurrence, consent, countenance, dispensation, endorsement, exemption, favor, grace, grant, imprimatur, indorsement, indulgence, legalization, liberty, license, *licentia, permissio,* permittance, sanction, sufferance, tolerance, vouchsafement, warrant
ASSOCIATED CONCEPTS: leave of court

LEAVE *(Allow to remain),* ***verb*** cease, deposit, desist, discard, disuse, drop, forbear, forget, give up, let be, let continue, let go, let stand, neglect, permit, relinquish, renounce, repudiate, set aside, shun, stop, supersede, surrender, suspend, waive
ASSOCIATED CONCEPTS: leave no issue, leave the scene of an accident

LEAVE *(Depart),* ***verb*** abandon, abdicate, abjure, abscond, be off, bid farewell, break away, decamp, defect, desert, disappear, *discedere,* drop out, embark, emigrate, escape, evacuate, *excedere,* exit, flee, fly, forsake, go, go away, go forth, migrate, move on, part, *proficisci,* pull out, quit, resign, retire, retreat, run away, secede, set out, slip away, take leave, tergiversate, vacate, vanish, withdraw

LEAVE *(Give),* ***verb*** accord, allot, apportion, assign, award, bequeath, bestow, confer, consign, demise, devise, donate, endow, entrust, give by will, grant, hand down, impart, *legare,* make a bequest, make a testamentary disposition, present, *relinquere,* settle upon, transmit, will

LEAVE A LEGACY *(Accomplish),* ***verb*** bring about, consummate, dedicate, enrich, fulfill, make a contribution to society, minister, pass down, realize, redound to, succeed

LEAVE A LEGACY *(Bequeath),* ***verb*** allot, assign, bestow, demise, descend, devise, dispense, donate, endow, entrust, give, hand down, leave, leave by will, make a bequest, pass on, transmit by will, will, will to
ASSOCIATED CONCEPTS: bequeaths and devises, estates, gifts, wills

LEAVE A WILL, *verb* compose a will, draw up a testament, prepare a last will and testament, prepare a testament, prepare an instrument, produce an instrument, write a document, write a testament

LEAVE OUT, *verb* ban, banish, bar, blackball, blacklist, block, count out, debar, deport, disregard, eliminate, exclude, excommunicate, exile, expel, forget, freeze out, impede, not include, obstruct, obviate, omit, ostracize, oust, overlook, pass over, prohibit, remove, rule out, shut out, skip, slight, suspend, throw out

LECHEROUS, *adjective* addicted to lewdness, bawdy, concupiscent, corrupt, debauched, depraved, desirous, dissipated, dissolute, erotic, erotical, fleshly, gluttonous, goatish, immoral, inclined to lewdness, lascivious, lewd, libertine, libidinous, licentious, lickerish, loose, lubric, lubricous, lustful, profligate, prurient, rakish, reprobate, ruttish, salacious, sexually indulgent, unbridled, unchaste, unregenerate, unrestrained, unspiritual, wanton

LECTURE, *(Admonish),* ***verb*** berate, chide, correction, discipline, dress down, excoriate, harangue, rebuke, remonstrate, reprimand, reproach, scold, teach, teach an example to, tear into, tongue-lash, upbraid

LECTURE *(Speak),* ***verb*** address, comment, deliver an address, discuss, elucidate, give a talk on, instruction, prepare comments, prepare a disclosure on, present, present information on, remonstrate, speak on, talk on, teach
ASSOCIATED CONCEPTS: continuing legal education

LEDGER, *noun* account book, account of transactions, accounts, balance sheet, bankbook, book of accounts, book of records, books, calculation, cashbook, *codex accepti et expensi,* computation, daybook, diary, entries, file, index, log, logbook, passbook, profit and loss statement, record, record book, record of credits and debits, record of money transactions, register, registry, running account, statement

LEERY, *adjective* afraid, apprehensive, careful, cautious, chary, circumspect, distrustful, doubtful, doubting, dubious, entertaining suspicion, frightened, guarded, heedful, hesitant, hesitating, in doubt, mistrustful, questioning, shy of, skeptical, suspect, suspecting, suspicious, unbelieving, uncertain, unconvinced, unsure, vigilant, wary, watchful, without belief, without faith

LEEWAY, *noun* allowance, breathing room, breathing space, deviation, elbowroom, extra room, freedom, headroom, indulgence, latitude, liberty, license, margin, room to maneuver, room to move, room to operate, room to spare, slack, some play, space
ASSOCIATED CONCEPTS: federal sentencing guidelines, mandates

LEFT *(Direction),* ***adjective*** left hand, left-hand side, left side, leftward, near, on the other side, over there, port, portside

LEFT *(Liberal),* ***adjective*** communalistic, communistic, leftist leanings, leftwing, liberal, progressive, radical, revolutionary, socialistic

LEFT *(Remaining),* ***adjective*** balance, continuing, extra, leftover, over, spare, staying, surplus, surplusage
ASSOCIATED CONCEPTS: no child left behind, remainder

LEFTOVER, ***noun*** balance, carry-over, excess, extra, overage, remainder, remaining, remnants, residual, residue, residuum, rest, surplus, unused

LEGACY, ***noun*** bequeathal, bequest, bestowal, conferment, dispensation, disposition, disposition of personalty, dotation, endowment, gift by will, gift of property by will, grant, heritance, impartment, inheritance, *legatum,* testamentary gift
ASSOCIATED CONCEPTS: absolute legacy, alternate legacy, charitable legacy, conditional legacy, contingent legacy, cumulative legacy, demonstrative legacy, general legacy, indefinite legacy, lapsed legacy, pecuniary legacy, residuary legacy, special legacy, specific legacy

LEGAL, ***adjective*** according to the law, allowable, allowed, approved, authorized, authorized by law, cognizable in courts of law, constitutional, decreed, enforceable in a court of law, established by law, good and effectual in law, governed by law, in conformity with law, lawful, legalized, legitimate, *legitimus,* licit, permissible, permitted by law, prescribed, prescribed by law, proper, *quod* ex *lege,* recognized by the law, required by law, rightful, sanctioned, *secundum leges fit,* statutory, sufficient in law, valid, warranted, within the law
ASSOCIATED CONCEPTS: legal action, legal age, legal arrest, legal beneficiaries, legal capacity to sue, legal cause, legal claim, legal consideration, legal damages, legal detriment, legal disability, legal duty, legal entity, legal heir, legal notice, legal obligation, legal presumption, legal proceedings, legal process, legal remedy, legal representative, legal tender, legal title
FOREIGN PHRASES: ***Id possumus quod de jure possumus.*** We may do only that which we are able to do lawfully.

LEGAL ACTION, ***noun*** action, action at law, cause, controversy, instituted proceedings, judicial proceedings, judicial recourse, lawsuit, legal process, legal recourse, litigation, matter, proceeding, process, prosecution, suit, suit in law

LEGAL ADVISOR, ***noun*** advocate, attorney-at-law, barrister, counsel, counselor, counselor-at-law, lawyer, legal practitioner, legist, member of the bar, member of the legal profession, officer of the court, pleader, solicitor
ASSOCIATED CONCEPTS: appointment of counsel, retention of counsel

LEGAL AGREEMENT, ***noun*** binding agreement, binding compact, binding contract, formal conveyance of interest, formal document, understanding

LEGAL ARGUMENT, ***noun*** affirmation, allegation, argument, asseveration, attestation, belief, cause of action, claim, counter argument, course of reasoning, declaration, defending of a cause by argument, defense, defensive measures, doctrine, insistence on a right or claim, issue, justification, philosophy, pleading, position, positive declaration or statement, statement, statement offered in proof

LEGAL ASSISTANT, ***noun*** assistant, contract paralegal, freelance paralegal, independent paralegal, law assistant, legal document assistant, legal technician, paralegal, traditional paralegal

LEGAL AUTHORITY *(Legal ability),* ***noun*** agent under the law, authorization, authorized legal permission to act, lawful power to act, lawful right to act, legal permission, proper legal power, statutory authority

LEGAL AUTHORITY *(Legal support),* ***noun*** backup to support a position, case law, cases on point to back up a contention, cases to prove an issue of law, cases which support a contention, legal research, statutes to prove an issue, support for a legal argument, support for a theory

LEGAL CLAIM, ***noun*** action, allegation, bill of complaint, complaint, declaration, demand, lawsuit, legal process, right, suit, summons
ASSOCIATED CONCEPTS: affirmative defenses, counterclaim, cross-claims, defenses

LEGAL DISCOURSE, ***noun*** analysis of legal language, examination of legal language, legal conversation, legal expression, precise expression of legal concepts, technical analysis of legal language, verbal exchange

LEGAL DISPUTE, ***noun*** action, action at law, action in court, aggressive argument, case, challenge in the courts, claim, conflict, confutation, contention, controversy, court action, disputation, field action, judicial contest, lawsuit, legal action, legal challenge, legal clash, legal contest, legal disagreement, legal feud, legal proceeding, litigation, proceeding, suit at law, suit in law, trial
ASSOCIATED CONCEPTS: dispute resolution

LEGAL DOCUMENTS, ***noun*** evidentiary records, exhibits, legal evidence, legal instruments, legal materials, legal papers, legal proof, legal record, legal reports, legally written materials, papers, recorded material, verifications
ASSOCIATED CONCEPTS: discovery, document management, legal forms, legal research

LEGAL EVIDENCE, ***noun*** admitted testimony, body of facts on which belief is based, circumstances in a case, confirmation, corroboration, document, documentation, documents, documents which tends to prove, exhibit, exhibits submitted to jury, facts, facts admitted at trial, facts judicially noted, facts which bear on the point in question, facts which establish the point in issue, factual matter, ground of proof, grounds for belief, instrument of proof, legal proof, legal validation, legal verification, matter legally submitted to the jury, matters of fact, means of proof, means of proving a fact, medium of proof, persuasive facts, proof legally presented at trial, proof of facts, record, relevant fact, relevant material, substantiation, testimony which furnishes proof
ASSOCIATED CONCEPTS: demonstrative evidence, digital evidence, documentary evidence, exculpatory evidence, physical evidence, rules of evidence, scientific evidence, testimony

LEGAL EXPERT, ***noun*** authority, experienced, expert witness, highly qualified individual, highly technical

specialist, leading authority in the field, legal scholar, professional authority, qualified professional, scholar, specialist, specially trained person, technician, well-known authority
ASSOCIATED CONCEPTS: forensic witness, legal consultant

LEGAL ISSUE, *noun* affirmation, allegation, argument, asseveration, cause, concern arising from law, counterargument, debatable point, declaration, disputed point of law, disputed question, fact put in controversy by the pleadings, field of inquiry, finer legal pint, finer point of law, item, insistence on a right or claim, justification, legal contention, legal question, legality, material point, material point educed from the pleadings, matter, matter in hand, matter in question, matter of contention, overriding question to be researched, overriding question to be resolved, point, point in question, point of contention, position, positive declaration, positive statement, problem, question at issue, question of law, sticking point, subject for inquiry
ASSOCIATED CONCEPTS: issue named in a will

LEGAL PRACTITIONER, *noun* advocate, attorney, attorney-at-law, barrister, counsel, counselor, counselor-at-law, Juris Doctor, lawyer, legal professional, member of the bar, practitioner, professional, solicitor, specialist

LEGAL PRECEDENT, *noun* authoritative decision, authoritative principle of law, case law, controlling law, decree, established doctrine, legal doctrine, model, paradigm, ruling, standard

LEGAL PROCEEDING, *noun* action, action at law, case, cause, contest, controversy, instituted proceeding, judicial dispute, judicial recourse, lawsuit, legal dispute, legal process, legal recourse, litigation, matter, proceeding, prosecution of a claim, suit, trial
ASSOCIATED CONCEPTS: commencement of an action, enforcement of judgments, judgment, prosecution of a case, verdict

LEGAL PROCESS, *noun* summons, summons for a case, summons for a cause in court, summons for a controversy before a court, summons for a court action, summons for a judicial contest, summons for a legal action, summons for a legal contest, summons for a legal controversy, summons for a legal dispute, summons for a trial, summons for an action, summons for an action at law, summons for legal proceedings, summons for litigation, summons for suit at law, writ
ASSOCIATED CONCEPTS: means to compel attendance

LEGAL PROFESSION, *noun* admitted attorneys, legal community, practicing attorneys, the bar, the profession of law

LEGAL RECOURSE, *noun* action, action at law, case, case for decision, cause in court, claim, contention, contest, controversy, controversy before a court, court action, court proceedings, dispute, judicial contest, legal action, legal argument, legal contest, legal controversy, legal dispute, legal proceedings, litigation, matter for judgment, proceeding, suit at law, suit in equity, trial

LEGAL REPRESENTATIVE, *noun* administrator, adminstratrix, appointed representative, attorney-at-law, authorized individual, authorized representative, executor, executrix, legal agent, legal proxy, legal spokesman, legal substitute, professional representative
ASSOCIATED CONCEPTS: personal representative

LEGAL RIGHT, *noun* authority, authorization, cause, claim, empowerment, entitlement, freedom, inalienable right, just claim, legitimate right, license, power, prerogative, vested right or interest
ASSOCIATED CONCEPTS: due process, freedom of the press, free speech, right against self-incrimination, right to assemble, right to petition

LEGALESE, *noun* language of the law, lawyer's language, legal language, legal parlance, legal usage, legal writing, the legal profession's language

LEGALISM *(Conservative meaning of the law)*, ***noun*** according to the letter of the law, by the strict letter of the law, chapter and verse of, conforming precisely to the law, conservative interpretation, exactly according to the law, literal interpretation of the law, orthodox interpretation of the law, precise interpretation of the law, strict interpretation of the law

LEGALISM *(Legalese)*, ***noun*** abstruse language, bloated wording, bombastic wording, complex legalese, convoluted wording, grandiloquent language, inflated wording, legal jargon complexities, long-winded jargon, orotund language, ostentatious wording, pedantic verbiage, pompous wording, sophisticated legal term, sophisticated legal verbiage, swollen wording, technical language, technical term, technical wording, turgid wording
ASSOCIATED CONCEPTS: legal term, legal verbiage, technical language, technical term

LEGALISTIC, *adjective* absolute adherence with the letter of the law, absolute compliance with words contained on the page, strict adherence with the law, strict compliance with the text of the law, strict respect for language in a law

LEGALITY, *noun* accordance with law, allowableness, authorization, conformity to law, conformity with the law, constitutionality, lawfulness, legalism, legitimacy, legitimateness, permissibleness, rightfulness, sanction, sanctionableness, validity, warrantableness
ASSOCIATED CONCEPTS: legality of consideration, legality of contract, legality of obligation, legality of purpose

LEGALIZATION, *noun* affirmation, approval, authorization, codification, confirmation, legislative sanction, legitimatization, passing into law, ratification, regulation by statute, sanction, validation

LEGALIZE, *verb* approve, authorize, bring into conformity with law, confirm, confirm by law, decree by law, enact by law, *ferre,* legislate, legitimate, legitimatize, make lawful, make legal, order by law, permit by law, pronounce legal, sanction, sanction by law, validate

LEGALLY BINDING, *adjective* compulsory, controlled for, controlling, effective, enforceable, final, fully executed, governing, has legal effect, has legal force, imperative, in effect, legally adopted, legally committed, legally compelled, legitimate, mandatory, necessary, obligated for, obligatory, operative, prescribed, required, signed, valid, validated
ASSOCIATED CONCEPTS: contracts, instrument, marriage

LEGALLY ENFORCEABLE, *adjective* authoritative, authorized, binding, compelling, compulsory, decreed valid, effective, established, formulate, has legal effect, has legal force, imposed, in effect, legally binding, legitimate, legitimatized, licensed, mandated, mandatory, necessary,

operative, ordained, prescribed, put into force, put into operation, put into practice, required, sanctioned, valid, validated, warranted
ASSOCIATED CONCEPTS: legally enforceable rights

LEGALLY IN FORCE, *adjective* compulsory, controlled for, controlling, effective, enforceable, final, fully executed, governing, has legal effect, has legal force, imperative, in effect, legally adopted, legally binding, legally committed, legally compelled, legitimate, mandatory, necessary, obligated for, obligatory, operative, prescribed, required, signed, valid, validated
ASSOCIATED CONCEPTS: contracts, instrument, marriage

LEGATEE, *noun* beneficiary, devisee, distributee, donee, feoffee, grantee, heir apparent, heir at law, heiress, inheritor, legal heir, legatary, one who inherits, recipient, transferee
ASSOCIATED CONCEPTS: pecuniary legatee, remainderman, residuary legatee, sole legatee, specific legatee

LEGEND *(Fable),* ***noun*** adventure, chronicle, epic, epos, fable, fantasy, fiction, folklore, lore, myth, mythology, odyssey, romance, saga, story, tale, tradition, yarn

LEGEND *(Inscription),* ***noun*** abstract, annotation, brief, caption, chronicle, cipher, compendium, device, epitaph, heading, imprint, impression, narrative, record, rubric, superscription

LEGENDARY *(Famous),* ***adjective*** acclaimed, celebrated, distinguished, eminent, epic, esteemed, exalted, fabled, famed, famous, heroic, illustrious, memorable, notable, outstanding, renowned

LEGENDARY *(Fictitious),* ***adjective*** apocryphal, fabled, fanciful, fictional, figmental, idealistic, imagined, mythological, storied, uncanonical, unhistorical, unwritten

LEGISLATE, *verb* authorize, codify, *constituere,* create by law, decree, dictate, effect, enact, enact laws, establish, establish by law, exercise the function of legislation, formulate, institute, *leges facere,* make into law, make laws, make legal, order, originate, pass, pass laws, prescribe laws, put in force, rule, sanction, *scribere,* vote in

LEGISLATION *(Enactments),* ***noun*** acts, bills, body of laws enacted, canon, canons, codes, dictates, laws, measures, ordinances, prescripts, provisions of a law, regulations, rulings, statutes

LEGISLATION *(Lawmaking),* ***noun*** codification of laws, enacting laws, formulating rules for the future, legislative process, preparation of laws
FOREIGN PHRASES: ***Leges figendi et refigendi consuetudo est periculosissima.*** The practice of making and remaking the laws is a most dangerous one. ***Jura eodem modo destituuntur quo constituuntur.*** Laws are abrogated by the same means by which they are enacted. ***Legislatorum est viva vox, rebus et non verbis, legem imponere.*** The voice of the legislators is the living voice, to impose laws upon things, and not on words. ***Neque leges neque senatus consulta ita scribi possunt ut omnis casus qui quandoque in sediriunt comprehendatur; sed sufficit ea quae plaerumque accidunt contineri.*** Neither laws nor acts of a legislature can be so written as to include all actual or possible cases; it is sufficient if they provide for those things which frequently or ordinarily may happen.

LEGISLATIVE, *adjective* congressional, decreeing, enacting, lawgiving, lawmaking, legislating, ordained by legislation, ordaining, prescriptive, statutory
ASSOCIATED CONCEPTS: legislative enactment

LEGISLATIVE DECREE, *noun* act, article, canon, chapter of law, code, legislative command, legislative enactment, legislative established law, legislative fiat, legislative initiative, legislative law, legislative legal code, legislative mandate, legislative maxim, legislative order, legislative ordinance, legislative precedent, legislative precept, legislative prescription, legislative principle, legislative pronouncement, legislative rule, legislative sanction, legislative set of rules, legislative standard, legislative statute, legislative tenet

LEGISLATIVE ENACTMENT, *noun* canon, code, codification, codified law, dictate, edict, enactment, law, legal code, legislation, mandate, measure, order, ordinance, provision of the law, regulation, rubric, statute, written law

LEGISLATIVE INTENT, *noun* background on a law, intent by lawmakers, intent of the government, jurisdictive, legislative interpretation, legislative meaning, purpose of a law, reason and rationale for a law, the concepts behind a law, the construction of a law, the intent of a law, the intent of a legislative enactment, the intent of the lawmakers in passing a law, the legislative initial for a law, the meaning of the law, the need for a law, the object of the law, the objective of a law, the origin of a law, the reach of a law

LEGISLATIVE MANDATE, *noun* legislative command, legislative decree, legislative directive, legislative fiat, legislative forced imperatives, legislative imposed standards, legislative order, legislative pronouncement, legislative rule, legislative tenet
ASSOCIATED CONCEPTS: unfunded mandates

LEGISLATOR, *noun* congressman, lawgiver, lawmaker, member of a governmental body, member of a legislative body, member of parliament, officer of state, official representative, one who formulates laws, one who gives or makes laws, one who helps to pass laws, parliamentarian, politician, public servant, representative, senator

LEGISLATURE, *noun* assembly, body of persons who formulate laws, congress, house of representatives, lawmaking body, law-making branch of government, lawgivers, lawmakers, legislative body, parliament, senate

LEGITIMACY, *noun* authorization, conformity to law, genuineness, justifiability, lawfulness, legality, legitimateness, legitimation, legitimization, licitness, originality, permissibility, realness, rightfulness, soundness, validity
ASSOCIATED CONCEPTS: illegitimacy, paternity proceeding
FOREIGN PHRASES: ***Semper praesumitur pro legitimatione puerorum.*** The presumption always is in favor of the legitimacy of children. ***Cum legitimae nuptiae factae sunt, patrem liberi sequuntur.*** Children of a lawful marriage follow the condition of the father. ***Praesumitur pro legitimatione.*** There is a presumption in favor of legitimacy. ***Non est justum aliquem antenatum post mortem facere bastardum qui toto tempore vitae suae pro legitimo habebatur.*** It is not just to make anyone a bastard after death who during his lifetime was regarded as legitimate. ***Pater est quem nuptiae demonstrant.*** He is the father whom the marriage points out.

LEGITIMATE *(Lawfully conceived),* ***adjective*** born in wedlock, born of parents legally married, conceived of

parents legally married, natural, of lawful parentage, sired in wedlock
ASSOCIATED CONCEPTS: legitimate issue

LEGITIMATE *(Rightful),* ***adjective*** according to law, allowed, authorized, constitutional, enacted, genuine, in accordance with law, in accordance with legal provisions, juristic, law-abiding, lawful, legal, legalized, legislated, licensed, licit, mandated, official, real, recognized by law, rightful, sanctioned, sanctioned by custom, sanctioned by law, sanctioned by legal authority, sound, statutable, statutory, valid, well-founded, well-grounded, within the law
ASSOCIATED CONCEPTS: legitimate business, legitimate heirs, legitimate purpose, legitimate title

LEGITIMATE, ***verb*** approve, authorize, certify, declare lawful, legalize, legitimatize, make lawful, make legal, make legitimate, sanction, validate

LEGITIMIZE, ***verb*** authorize, confirm, constitute, declare lawful, enact, legalize, legitimate, make legal, make legitimate, make proper, pass, ratify, sanction, validate

LEND, ***verb*** accommodate with, advance, afford, aid, allow credit, assist, *commodare,* entrust, extend credit, finance, furnish, furnish credit, give, give credit, give money over, grant, invest, loan, permit to borrow, provide, provide with, put up the money, sign over, supply, supply aid, turn over
ASSOCIATED CONCEPTS: lend credit, lend funds

LENGTH, ***noun*** breadth, continuance, dimension, distance, distance lengthwise, elongation, expanse, expansion, extensiveness, extent, lengthiness, limit, long-windedness, magnitude, measure, measurement, proportion, range, reach, size, span, stretch
ASSOCIATED CONCEPTS: length of memoranda of law, term limit

LENGTHEN, ***verb*** add to, aggrandize, amplify, augment, compound, continue, draw out, elongate, enlarge, enlarge upon, expand, extend, increase, keep, make larger, project, prolong, prolongate, protract, spin out, spread, stretch, supplement, sustain, temporize

LENGTHY *(Prolix),* ***adjective*** digressive, discursive, garrulous, long-winded, loquacious, talky, verbose

LENGTHY *(Prolonged),* ***adjective*** elongated, extensive, far-reaching, gaunt, lengthened, made to last, prosy, protracted, rangy, sesquipedalian, spare, sustained

LENGTHY *(Tedious),* ***adjective*** accented, boring, desultory, diffuse, drawn-out, elongated, endless, errant, extended, interminable, long-spun, roving, spun out, tiresome, wearisome, wordy

LENIENCE, ***noun*** acceptance, benevolence, charity, clemency, compassion, condonation, consideration, disposition to mercy, endurance, favor, flexibility, forbearance, forgiveness, forgivingness, freedom from vindictiveness, generousness, gentleness, grace, humanity, indulgence, kindness, lack of strictness, leniency, lenity, liberality, longanimity, mercifulness, mercy, mildness, moderation, pampering, patience, pity, placability, placableness, quarter, ruth, softheartedness, softness, sympathy, tolerance, toleration, understanding

LENIENCY, ***noun*** allowance, benevolence, charitableness, compassion, compassionateness, condonation, condoning, considerateness, easiness, easygoingness, endurance, forbearance, forgiveness, generosity, generousness, humaneness, humanity, indulgence, kindheartedness, kindness, lenience, liberality, liberalness, mercifulness, mercy, mildness, moderateness, moderation, pardon, patience, permissiveness, sympathy, temperance, temperateness, tolerance, willingness to forgive, yielding
ASSOCIATED CONCEPTS: leniency delays, leniency law, leniency policies, sentencing

LENIENT, ***noun*** allowing, benevolent, charitable, *clemens,* clement, compassionate, condoning, considerate, easy, easygoing, enduring, exorable, favoring, forbearing, forgiving, free from vindictiveness, generous, gentle, humane, humoring, indulgent, indulging, kind, kindhearted, *lenis,* liberal, long-suffering, longanimous, magnanimous, merciful, mild, *mitis,* moderate, pampering, pardoning, patient, pitying, placable, soft, softhearted, sparing, sympathetic, tolerant, undemanding, unstrict, willing to forgive, yielding
FOREIGN PHRASES: ***Cum confitente sponte mitius est agendum.*** One confessing voluntarily should be dealt with more leniently.

LESS *(Fewer),* ***adjective*** a decreased number, a limited number, a reduced number, a restricted number of, a smaller number, curtailed, cutback, diluted, diminished, fewer, hardly any, in decline, lessened, lesser, limited, little, minus, not as many, not as much, pared down, reduced, slighter, smaller
ASSOCIATED CONCEPTS: concise legal writing, plain language

LESS *(Inferior),* ***adjective*** attenuated, belittled, beneath, circumscribed, curtailed, cutback, declined, decreased, deemphasized, deficient, deflated, depressed, diluted, diminished, dissipated, downplayed, dropped, eroded, fallen, in decline, inferior, insignificant, junior, lessened, lesser, limited, lower, lowered, mediocre, minimized, minor, pared down, reduced, retrenched, scaled-down, secondary, second-rate, subordinate, watered-down, weakened

LESSEE, ***noun*** boarder, *conductor,* holder of an estate by virtue of a lease, leaseholder, lodger, occupant, occupier, person in possession, possessor, property holder, rent payer, rentee, renter, resident, roomer, tenant

LESSEN, ***verb*** abate, abbreviate, abridge, abstract, adulterate, allay, alleviate, assuage, attenuate, bate, belittle, boil down, calumniate, censure, check, compress, condense, contract, curb, curtail, cut, cut down, decimate, decline, decrease, decry, deduct, defame, deflate, degenerate, deliquesce, *deminuere,* deplete, depreciate, dequantitate, deride, derogate, deteriorate, detract, devaluate, die away, dilute, diminish, discommend, discount, discredit, disparage, dispraise, disvalue, dock, drop off, dull, dwarf, dwindle, ease, ebb, erode, evaporate, extenuate, *imminuere,* let up, lighten, lower, malign, melt away, minify, minimize, mitigate, moderate, modulate, palliate, pare, qualify, reduce, remit, run down, set at naught, shorten, shrink, slacken, slight, soothe, speak slightingly, stigmatize, stunt, subdue, subside, subtract, summarize, take away, taper, temper, thin, thin out, traduce, trim, underestimate, underrate, undervalue, vilify, vilipend, wane, waste away, water down, weaken, wear away, weed out

LESSEN IN VALUE, ***verb*** abate, curtail, cut, decline, decrease, deflate, depreciate, depress, diminish, dropping, dwindling, eroding, lower, reduce, shrink, subside, wane
ASSOCIATED CONCEPTS: depreciation, residual value insurance

LESSER, ***adjective*** ancillary, baser, diminished, humbler, inferior, junior, less considerable, lower, mediocre, minor, more modest, secondary, second-rate, shorter, simpler, slighter, smaller, subaltern, subordinate, subservient, under, unimportant
ASSOCIATED CONCEPTS: lesser charge, lesser included offense

LESSER INCLUDED OFFENSE, ***noun*** decreased charge, inferior charge, lower charge within the crimes charged, reduced charge, smaller charge, subordinate charge
ASSOCIATED CONCEPTS: acceptance of guilt, guilty plea, verdict

LESSON *(Castigation),* ***noun*** admonishment, censure, chastening, chastisement, chiding, correction, denunciation, disciplinary measure, discipline, infliction, punishment, punition, rebuke, reprimand, reproach, reproof, scolding, tongue-lashing, upbraiding

LESSON *(Example),* ***noun*** advice, archetype, education, exemplary, gold standard, good example, ideal, illustration, instruction, learning experience, lecture, maxim, model, moral fable, noble action, paragon, preachment, precedent, precept, prototype, schooling, sermon, shining example, standard, teaching

LESSOR, ***noun*** business owner, landlord, owner, property owner

LET *(Lease),* ***verb*** allow the use of, charter, contract, convey, demise, grant, grant the occupancy of, hire, hire out, lend, loan, make available, rent, rent out

LET *(Permit),* ***verb*** affranchise, allow, approve, assent, authorize, certify, commission, concede, *concedere,* consent, empower, enable, endorse, enfranchise, entitle, entrust, favor, franchise, give leave, give permission, grant, have no objection, indulge, liberate, license, make possible, oblige, *pati,* privilege, release, sanction, *sinere,* suffer, support, tolerate, vouchsafe, warrant, yield

LET DOWN *(Disappointing outcome),* ***noun*** dash one's hopes, defeat one's expectations, disappointment, disconcertedness, disenchantment, disgruntlement, disheartenment, disillusionment, dissatisfaction, failure, failure to live up to expectations, fall, fallen short, feelings of failure, frustration, thwarted hopes

LET DOWN *(Rest),* ***noun*** abatement, allayment, alleviation, diminution, drugging, easing, lessening, let up, lightening, loosening, mitigation, reduction, relaxation, relenting, slackening, slacking off

LET GO, ***verb*** abandon, cede, clear, disband, discharge, do away with, free, give up, leave, leave hold of, liberate, release, relinquish, remit, surrender, terminate, yield, yield control of
ASSOCIATED CONCEPTS: release from bailment, release from custody

LET OFF, ***verb*** absolve, acquit, clear, discharge, excuse, exempt, exonerate, expiate, forgive, free, let go, liberate, loose, pardon, release, relieve, remit, spare, unburden, vindicate, whitewash
ASSOCIATED CONCEPTS: finding of innocence, finding of not guilty, reversal

LET OUT *(Disclose),* ***verb*** air, bare, break the news, communicated, divulge, expose, express audibly, impart, leak, let slip out, make known, remove the veil, reveal, shine light on, slip, take the lid off, take the wraps off, tell, uncloak, uncover, unfold, unfurl, unmask, unveil, unwrap, utter sounds
ASSOCIATED CONCEPTS: confidentiality, off officials, privilege

LET OUT *(Release),* ***verb*** deliver, demobilize, discharge, dismiss, free, let go, let go free, let loose, let off, let out on bail, pardon, parole, release from custody, release from prison, unbridle, unchain, unfetter, unharness, unlatch, unleash, unlock, unshackle
ASSOCIATED CONCEPTS: appeal, habeas corpus

LET STAND, ***verb*** affirm, approve, assent to, back, certify, confirm, consent to, corroborate, defend, endorse, establish, fortify, ratify, reaffirm, reinforce, sanction, substantiate, support, sustain, uphold, validate, verify, vindicate
ASSOCIATED CONCEPTS: let stand a ruling, let stand a verdict, let stand an award

LETHAL, ***adjective*** annihilative, baleful, baneful, dangerous, deadly, death-bringing, death-dealing, deathly, destructive, evil, *exitialis,* fatal, fell, feral, *funestus,* harmful, hurtful, injurious, internecine, internecive, killing, lethiferous, malefic, maleficent, maleficial, malign, malignant, mortal, *mortifer,* mortiferous, murderous, nocent, nocuous, noxious, pernicious, pestiferous, pestilent, pestilential, poisonous, slaughtering, toxic, toxiferous, unhealthy, venomous, virulent
ASSOCIATED CONCEPTS: lethal weapon

LETHARGY, ***noun*** apathy, boredom, disinterest, dullness, ennui, fatigue, heedlessness, idleness, inaction, inactivity, inanition, incuriosity, indifference, indolence, inertia, languor, lassitude, laziness, listlessness, passiveness, sleepiness, sloth, slowness, sluggishness, stupor, torpidity, torpidness, unconcern, unmindfulness, weariness

LETTER, ***noun*** account, announcement, bulletin, card, communication, communiqué, correspondence, dispatch, document, e-mail, epistle, item, mail, memo, memorandum, message, missive, note, piece, release, report, transmittal
ASSOCIATED CONCEPTS: enforcement to the letter of the law

LETTER OF CREDIT, ***noun*** credit account, credit note, guaranty, negotiable instrument, paper credit, security
ASSOCIATED CONCEPTS: financial guarantee, letter of delegation, letter of exchange, letter of introduction, letter of license, letters testamentary

LETTER OF THE LAW, ***noun*** according to the letter, an orthodox interpretation, by chapter and verse, conservative interpretation, exact words of the law, exactly as written, literal interpretation, literally interpreted, perfectly as written, precise interpretation, precisely as written, strict construction, strict interpretation
ASSOCIATED CONCEPTS: respecting the spirit and letter of the law

LEVEL *(Balance),* ***noun*** aligned, equal, equal on a plane, even, exact, in the same plane, matched, of the same height, same, standard, straight, uniform

LEVEL *(Grade),* ***noun*** advanced status, class, freshman, graduate, junior, lowerclassman, program, senior, seniority, sophomore, status, underclassman, undergraduate, upperclassman, year, year of graduation, year of studies

LEVEL *(Plane),* ***noun*** bank, deep slope, distance upward, easy slope, elevation, equal, exact, flat, flat surface, flattened, flush, grade, gradient, inclination, incline, inclined plane, on a line, parallel, pitch, slope, steep slope

LEVERAGE, *noun* advantage, force, influence, potency, pressure, purchase, vantage

LEVIED, *adjective* assessed, attached, collected, commandeered, confiscated, conscripted, drafted, exacted, excised, extorted, imposed as an assessment, put a duty on, recruited, seized, taken by force, take possession of, taxed, tolled

LEVY, *noun* assessment, attachment, collection, confiscation, duty, exaction, exactment, excise, gathering, impost, impressment, seizure, setting aside of specific property, tariff, tax, taxation, toll

LEVY, *verb* affix, assess, attach, charge, collect, confiscate, conscript, demand, disseise, distrain, divest, enlist, exact, execute, force, garnish, gather, impose, inflict, lay on, muster, place, put on, raise, require, seize, set, take by force, take up, tax, usurp, wrest
ASSOCIATED CONCEPTS: levy a tax, levy an assessment, wrongful levy

LEWD, *adjective* bawdy, carnal, concupiscent, corrupt, depraved, dissolute, exhibiting lust, immodest, immoral, *impudicus,* impure, *impurus, incestus,* indecent, indelicate, lascivious, lecherous, libertine, libidinous, licentious, lubricous, lustful, morally impure, morally unrestrained, obscene, offensive, pornographic, profligate, prurient, publicly indecent, questionable, reprobate, ribald, risque, ruttish, rutty, salacious, scandalous, scarlet, scurrilous, sexually impure, sexually indecent, shameless, suggestive, unchaste, unclean, unvirtuous, vulgar, wanton
ASSOCIATED CONCEPTS: lewd and lascivious cohabitation, obscenity

LEX LOCI, *noun* enactment in the area, firm principles in the area, law of the locale, law of the locality, law of the region, legal code in the local area, local law, settled principles in the area, the law in the area, the law of the circuit, the law of the judicial circuit, the law of the place, the law of the site, the law of the territory, the law of the vicinity, the law of the zone
ASSOCIATED CONCEPTS: choice of law, domicile, forum selection, lex domicilii, lex loci arbitri, lex loci celebrations in marriage, lex loci contractus, lex loci delicti commissi, lex situs, lex tori
FOREIGN PHRASES: ***Lex loci actus.*** The law of the location where the act was done.

LIABILITY, *noun* accountability, accountableness, amenability, amenableness, answerability, aptness, bounden duty, burden, contract obligation, debit, debt, disadvantage, drawback, due, duty, duty to pay, encumbrance, handicap, hindrance, indebtedness, legal obligation, legal responsibility, obligation, onus, proclivity, proneness, responsibility, unliquidated claim, vulnerability
ASSOCIATED CONCEPTS: absolute liability, admission of liability, civil liability, contingent liability, criminal liability, denial of liability, existing liability, fixed liability, incurring a liability, joint liability, known liability, legal liability, liability imposed by law, liability insurance, liability without fault, limited liability, manufacturer's liability, original liability, pecuniary liability, potential liability, primary liability, secondary liability, several liability, statutory liability, strict liability, tort liability
FOREIGN PHRASES: ***Quando de una et eadem re duo onerabiles existunt, unus pro insufficientia alterius, de integro, onerabitur.*** When two persons are chargeable with one and the same thing, one of them is chargeable with the whole thing, upon the failure of the other.

LIABLE, *adjective* accountable, amenable, answerable, bound in equity, bound in law, bound to, bound to respond, chargeable, exposed to, exposed to penalty, in danger, justly responsible, legally bound, legally responsible, obligated, obliged, obliged in law, *obnoxius,* responsible, subject to, susceptible, under legal obligation, under obligation, vulnerable
ASSOCIATED CONCEPTS: jointly liable, liable for debts, liable in tort, liable to forfeiture, liable to penalty, liable to prosecution, liable to punishment, party liable, personally liable, secondarily liable

LIAISON, *noun* administrator, agent, bond, connection, contact, delegate, deputy, emissary, envoy, go-between, interagent, intercessor, intermediary, intermedium, lieutenant, link, linkage, manger, mediating agency, mediator, messenger, negotiant, negotiator, nexus, representative, spokesman, spokesperson, substitute, tie

LIBEL, *noun* accusation, aspersion, calumny, *carmen famosum,* censorious writing, defamation, defamatory writing, degradation, denigration, denunciation, disparagement, false accusation, false publication, false statement, falsehood, falseness, falsification, impairment of reputation, impeachment of virtue, injury to character, injury to one's reputation, invective, *libellus famosus,* malicious defamation, malicious falsehood, malicious publication, revilement, slur, smear, vilification, writing that discredits, written accusation
ASSOCIATED CONCEPTS: actionable libel, libel per quod, libel per se, publication of libel, slander

LIBEL, *verb* accuse falsely, accuse in writing, asperse, besmirch, calumniate, censure, condemn, debase, decry, defame, defame by a published writing, degrade, denigrate, denounce, derogate, discredit, discredit in writing, disparage, expose to public contempt, impair one's reputation, incriminate, injure another's reputation, injure by a published writing, injure one's reputation, maliciously defame, malign, publish a falsehood, revile, ridicule, scandalize, slander, slur, smear, traduce, vilify
ASSOCIATED CONCEPTS: absolute privilege, actionable libel, actual malice, criminal libel, defamation, defense of truth, disparagement, First Amendment, libel per quod, libel per se, privileged communication, publication, qualified privileged, republication, slander, trade libel

LIBELOUS, *adjective* abusive, acrimonious, aspersive, calumnious, condemnatory, contemptuous, damaging, damnatory, defamatory, denunciatory, derogatory, detracting, detractive, discreditable, discrediting, disgracing, dishonorable, dishonoring, disparaging, false and injurious, humiliating, ignominious, ill-willed, improficient, injurious, insulting, malevolent, malicious, malignant, odious, pejorative, scandalous, scurrile, scurrilous, traducing, vilifying, vituperative

LIBERAL *(Broad-minded),* ***adjective*** adaptable to change, advanced, emancipated, fair-minded, flexible, freethinking, impartial, *liberalis,* liberated, neutral, nonpartisan, not narrow-minded, objective, open, open-minded, progressive, receptive, tolerant, unbiased, unbigoted, uninfluenced, unopinionated, unprejudiced, unswayed

LIBERAL *(Generous),* ***adjective*** abundant, almsgiving, altruistic, ample, beneficent, benevolent, bounteous, bountiful, charitable, copious, free, freely giving, generous, handsome, hospitable, humane, humanitarian, lavish, magnanimous, munificent, *munificus,* openhanded, openhearted, philanthropic, plentiful, princely, prodigal, profuse, selfless, stintless, ungrudging, unselfish, unsparing, unstinting

LIBERAL *(Not literal),* ***adjective*** broad, enlarged, extended, free from narrowness, general, imprecise, inexact, loose, open, unprecise, unrigorous, unstrict, wide, with license

ASSOCIATED CONCEPTS: liberal construction, liberal interpretation

LIBERALITY, ***noun*** benefaction, beneficence, benefit, benevolence, charitableness, chivalry, clemency, generosity, generous giving, generous offering, generousness, gratuity, habit of giving, kindness, lavishness, lenience, liberal-mindedness, magnanimity, munificence, open-heartedness, philanthropy, reward, tolerance, unselfishness

LIBERATE, ***verb*** acquit, affranchise, bail out, deliver, discharge, disembroil, disengage, disenthrall, disimprison, dislodge, dismiss, emancipate, enfranchise, exculpate, exonerate, extract, franchise, free, give freedom, give liberty to, let go, let loose, let out, *liberare,* loose, manumit, *manumittere,* open up, pardon, parole, redeem, release, release from custody, rescue, separate, set at large, set at liberty, set free, turn loose, unbind, unchain, undo, unfasten, unfetter, unloose, unshackle, untie, vindicate

LIBERATED, ***adjective*** absolved, acquitted, affranchised, cleared, delivered, discharged, disengaged, emancipated, exculpated, exonerated, extricated, free, freed, liberal, pardoned, paroled, redeemed, released, sovereign, unbound, vindicated

LIBERATION, ***noun*** absolution, achievement of liberty, acquittal, acquittance, affranchisement, deliverance, delivery, discharge, disembroiling, disengagement, disenthrallment, disimprisonment, dislodgment, dismissal, emancipation, enfranchisement, exculpation, exoneration, franchisement, freedom, freeing, *liberatio, manumissio,* manumission, pardon, parole, redemption, release, releasing from custody, rescue, separation, unbinding, unchaining, unfettering, unshacking, untying, vindication

LIBERTY, ***noun*** absence of foreign rule, absence of restraint, absence of servitude, affranchisement, autonomy, choice, clearance, deliverance, emancipation, enfranchisement, exemption from control, exemption from external control, exemption from restraint, franchise, free will, freedom, freedom from captivity, freedom of action, freedom of choice, grant, independence, latitude, leave, *liber,* liberation from foreign restraint, *libertas,* license, *licentia,* noninterference, permission, political independence, power of choice, power to choose, prerogative, privilege, right, right of choice, sanction, self-determination, self-direction, self-government, unconstraint, uninhibitedness

ASSOCIATED CONCEPTS: abuse of liberty, civil liberty, deprivation of liberty, individual liberties, liberty of contract, liberty of free press, liberty of speech, personal liberty, political liberty, religious liberty

FOREIGN PHRASES: ***Favorabilia in lege sunt fiscus, dos, vita, libertas.*** Favorites of the law are the treasury, dower, life, and liberty. ***Libertas inaestimabilis res est.*** Liberty is a thing of inestimable value. ***Libertas est naturalis facultas ejus quod, cuique facere libet, nisi quod de jure aut vi prohibetur.*** Liberty is a person's natural power which permits one to do as he pleases. ***Libertas non recipit aestimationem.*** Freedom does not admit a valuation.

LICENSE, ***noun*** accordance, allowance, approbation, approval, assurance, authority, authorization, canation, certification, charter, clearance, confirmation, consent, *copia,* empowerment, endorsement, enfranchisement, entitlement, exception, fiat, formal permission, franchise, freedom, grant, imprimatur, leave, liberty, permission, permit, *potestas,* power, prerogative, privilege, right, sanction, special privilege, vouchsafement, warrant, written permission

ASSOCIATED CONCEPTS: assignment of a license, cancellation of license, easement, issuance of license, patent license, permanent license, renewal of a license, revocation of license, suspension of license

LICENSE, ***verb*** allow, approve, authorize, certify, charter, clothe with authority, clothe with power, confirm, empower, enable, endow, enfranchise, entitle, grant, invest, permit, sanction, strengthen warrant

ASSOCIATED CONCEPTS: license fee, license tax, licensed to practice law, professional licenses

LICENSEE, ***noun*** appointee, assignee, assignee in fact, consignee, donee, nominee, selectee, transferee

LICENSING OF RIGHTS, ***noun*** approval of rights, authority, formal authorization, formal permission, granting of rights, sanctioning of use, warranted use

LICENSOR, ***noun*** appointer, assignor, consignor, nominator, releasor, selector, transferor

LICENTIOUS, ***adjective*** abandoned, aberrant, bawdy, concupiscent, debauched, disorderly, dissipated, dissolute, *dissolutus,* free, freethinking, immoral, *impudicus,* impure, indecent, indelicate, lascivious, lewd, libertine, *libidinosus,* loose, lubricous, lurid, nonconforming, obscene, profligate, promiscuous, rakish, riotous, ruttish, scandalous, scarlet, unchaste, uncontrolled, unconventional, uncurbed, undisciplined, ungoverned, unreined, unrestrained, unruly, vulgar, wanton, wild

LICIT, ***adjective*** according to edict, according to law, admissible, allowable, allowed, authorized, chartered, constitutional, in accordance with the law, judicatory, judicial, juridic, jurisprudent, jurisprudential, just, law-abiding, lawful, lawlike, legal, legalized, legislated, legitimate, *legitimus,* licensed, mandated, obedient, permissible, permitted, prescribed, proper, *quod ex lege,* right, rightful, sanctionable, sanctioned, sound, statutable, statutory, unprohibited, upright, valid, warrantable, warranted, within the law

LID, ***noun*** cap, ceiling, cover, greatest number, limit, maximum, most quantity, outer limit, outer restriction, roof, stop, top, top number

ASSOCIATED CONCEPTS: caps on awards

LIE, ***noun*** calumny, deceit, deception, distortion, fabrication, false statement, falsehood, falsification, falsity, *falsum,* fiction, fraud, intentional distortion, intentional exaggeration, intentional misstatement, intentional untruth, invention, mendacity, *mendacium,* misrepresentation, misstatement, perversion, prevarication, untruth

ASSOCIATED CONCEPTS: defamation, libel, perjury, polygraph test, slander

LIE *(Be sustainable),* ***verb*** be allowable, be appropriate, be available, be established, be evident, be fitting, be permissible, be permitted, be possible, be proper, be suitable, be suited, be supportable, be warranted, exist, extend, stand

LIE *(Falsify),* ***verb*** be dishonest, be untruthful, bear false witness, belie, commit perjury, concoct, counterfeit, deceive, delude, deviate from the truth, dissimulate, equivocate, fable, fabricate, falsify, fib, fool, forswear, invent, *mentiri,* misguide, misinform, mislead, misrepresent, misstate, palter, perjure oneself, pervert, pretend, prevaricate, represent falsely, swear falsely, tell a falsehood, tell an untruth

ASSOCIATED CONCEPTS: false testimony, lie detector, perjury

LIEN, ***noun*** charge, charge imposed on specific property, claim, claim on property, debt, hold on property, hold upon the property of another, incumbrance, indebtedness, indebtment, liability, obligation, pledge, property right, real security, right to enforce charge upon property, security, security on property, stake

ASSOCIATED CONCEPTS: agricultural lien, artisan's lien, attorney's lien, builder's lien, carrier's lien, common-law lien, concurrent lien, contractor's lien, discharge of lien, equitable lien, factor's lien, general lien, judgment lien, junior lien, landlord's lien, mechanic's lien, possessory lien, prior lien, priority of a lien, statutory lien, superior lien, vendor's lien

LIFE *(Period of existence),* ***noun*** *anima,* continuance, cycle, duration, endurance, existence, lastingness, lifetime, period, period of survival, span, survival, term, term of activity, term of effectiveness, time, time from birth to death, *vita*

ASSOCIATED CONCEPTS: life annuity, life estate, life expectancy, life imprisonment, life insurance company, life interest, life tenant

FOREIGN PHRASES: ***Non nasci, et natum mori, paria sunt.*** Not to be born, and to be born dead, are the same. ***La ley favour la vie d'un homme.*** The law favors human life.

LIFE *(Vitality),* ***noun*** activeness, activity, *alacritas,* alertness, animation, ardor, breeziness, briskness, drive, dynamic quality, dynamism, eagerness, effervescence, energy, enthusiasm, exuberance, fieriness, fire, impassionedness, intensity, jocularity, jocundity, joviality, liveliness, lustiness, spirit, spiritedness, sprightliness, verve, vigor, vim, vis, vivacity, zeal, zest, zestfulness

LIFE SUPPORT, ***noun*** artificial maintenance of life, continuance of life through medical equipment, extension of life by technological means, sustenance of life by artificial means *Generally:* being kept alive, fostering of life, life retention, preservation of life, prolongation of existence

LIFEBLOOD, ***noun*** animus, arterial blood, basic, basic nutrition, driving force, essence of life, essential ingredient, force of life, foundation, fundamental, inspiration, inspiriting force, inspiriting power, life essence, moving force, raison d'etre, spirit, vital energy, vital flame, vital fluid, vital force, vital principle, vital spark, vital spirit

LIFELESS *(Dead),* ***adjective*** abrogated, annihilated, annulled, at rest, bereft of life, breathless, cadaveric, cadaverous, canceled, deceased, defunct, demised, departed, destitute of life, devoid of life, ended, exanimate, *exanimus,* expired, extinct, gone, impercipient, inanimate, insensate, insensient, irrecoverable, late, null, passed away, passed on, perished, pulseless, quashed, repealed, unanimated, unfeeling, unrevived, void, without life

LIFELESS *(Dull),* ***adjective*** apathetic, arid, banal, barren, benumbing, boring, characterless, colorless, commonplace, deactivated, deadened, debilitated, dismal, dormant, drearisome, dreary, dronish, dry, empty, *exsanguis,* feeble, flat, *frigidus,* hebetudinous, inactive, indolent, inert, inexcitable, insensible, insipid, insulse, lackadaisical, lackluster, laggard, languid, languourness, lazy, leaden, lethargic, lethargical, listless, lumpish, lusterless, monotonous, oscitant, passionless, passive, phlegmatic, pococurante, producing boredom, producing ennui, prosaic, quiescent, quiet, slothful, sluggish, somber, spiritless, stagnant, stale, stodgy, stupefied, supine, tame, tedious, tired, tiresome, torpescent, torpid, trite, unactivated, unaroused, uncaptivating, unenlivened, unenterprising, unentertaining, unenthusiastic, unfeeling, unfertile, unimaginative, unimpassioned, uninspired, uninspiring, uninteresting, uninventive, unlively, unoriginal, unresponsive, unsparkling, unspirited, unvivid, usual, vapid, vegatating, vegetative, weak, wearisome, wearying

LIFETIME, ***noun*** *aetas, aevum,* age, duration of life, epoch, era, generation, life, life span, life's duration, period of existence, period of life, period of survival, season, span, span of years, term, time, years of existence

ASSOCIATED CONCEPTS: life estate, pur autre vie, rule against perpetuities

LIFT *(Boost),* ***noun*** accommodation, advancement, aid, assist, assistance, auspices, backing, betterment, bliss, elation, encouragement, enhancement, exaltation, furtherance, good turn, guidance, help, improvement, inspiration, maintenance, ministration, nurture, patronage, preferment, promotion, rapture, relief, succor, support, sustenance, transport

LIFT *(Elevation),* ***noun*** acclivity, advance, ascension, ascent, climb, crane, derrick, elevator, eminence, erection, escalator, heave, height, hill, hoist, pickup, promotion, raise, raising, rise, rising, slope, sphere, upgrade, upheaval, uplift, vantage point, winch

LIFT *(Boost),* ***verb*** advance, aggrandize, ameliorate, benefit, buoy, elate, ennoble, exalt, give one a lift, heighten, improve, inspire, inspirit, promote, soar, support, take the load off one's mind, uplift

LIFT *(Decontrol),* ***verb*** free, liberate, lighten, release, take off, unburden

LIFT *(Raise),* ***verb*** acquit oneself of, appropriate, ascend, build, clear, come up or off, dignify, do a good turn, elevate, enhance, erect, flush, grow, heave, help, hoist, leaven, liquidate, mount, pick up, pull, raise, rear, set on its feet, take, take off, take up, transport, tug, upraise, uprear

LIFT *(Steal),* ***verb*** pilfer, purloin, snatch, swipe, thieve

LIFT A BAN, ***verb*** abate, abolish, alleviate, annihilate, cancel, clear, delete, eliminate, eradicate, free, obliterate, obviate, omit, release, relieve, remove, suspend, take away, withdraw

ASSOCIATED CONCEPTS: lift a ban on abortions, lift a ban on arms, lift a ban on funding, lift a ban on immigration

LIGHT *(Easy),* ***adjective*** breezy, carefree, cushy, debonair, effortless, facile, lighthearted, manageable, not burdensome, not complex, not complicated, not difficult, not involved, nothing to it, painless, plain, simple, smooth, straightforward, uncomplicated

LIGHT *(Entertaining),* ***adjective*** amusing, animated, beamish, bird-witted, blithe, blithesome, breezy, capricious, carefree, changeable, cheerful, cheery, comical, debonair, delighted, distracting, diverting, easygoing, elated, erratic, fickle, flighty, flyaway, free and easy, frivolous, gay, glad, gleeful, happy, happy as a lark, happy-go-lucky, humorous, impulsive, in good or high spirits, inconsequential, inconsiderable, inconstant, insouciant, irresponsible, jaunty, jocund, jolly, jovial, joyful, jubilant, laughing, lighthearted, lively, mercurial, merry, mirthful, optimistic, out in left field, out to lunch, petty, pleasing, pleasurable, positive, recreative, riant, scatterbrained, skittish, smiling, sportive, sunny, superficial, trifling, trivial, unimportant, untroubled, upbeat, volatile, whimsical, witty

LIGHT *(Weightless),* ***adjective*** airy, buoyant, diluted, feathery, floatable, floating, fluffy, light as a feather, light as air, lighter than air, slender, slight, superficial, thin, thin-bodied, unsubstantial, watered down

LIGHT *(Daylight),* ***noun*** crack of dawn, dawn, day, daybreak, daylight hours, daytime, starlight, sunbeam, sunlight, sunrise, sunshine, sunup, visibility

LIGHT *(Illumination),* ***noun*** beaming, brightness, brilliance, brilliancy, clearness, comprehension, effulgence, emanation, flood of light, fluorescence, glare, gleam, gleaming, glimmer, glitter, glow, glowing, incandescence, irradiation, knowledge, lambency, lightness, luminescence, luminosity, luminous energy, luminousness, luster, openness, publicity, radiance, radiation, sheen, shine, shining, sparkle, sunlight, understanding
ASSOCIATED CONCEPTS: evidence coming to light, shine the light of law

LIGHTEN, ***verb*** allay, alleviate, assuage, cut down, decrease, disburden, disencumber, ease, ease up, have less weight, lessen, lessen the load, lessen the weight of, make less burdensome, make lighter, mitigate, reduce, reduce the load of, reduce weight of, relieve, remove, temper, unburden, unload

LIKE, ***adjective*** akin, alike, allied to, analogous, approaching, approximate, close, cognate, common to, comparable, comparative, congeneric, congruous, equal, equivalent, identical, illustrative, imitative, implicatory, implying, inferential, near, not unlike, parallel, probable, related, relative, relevant, similar, resembling, suggestive of, symbolic, uniform, unique with

LIKE, ***verb*** admire, affect, appreciate, be attracted to, be fond of, be partial to, befriend, care, care for, care to, choose, correlate, delight in, desiderate, desire, enjoy, esteem, fancy, feel inclined, find agreeable to one's taste, find convenient, have a mind to, hold in regard or affection, please, regard with favor, relish, savor, take a fancy to, take pleasure in, think fit, want, welcome, wish

LIKE-KIND, ***adjective*** alike, analogous, another of similar quality, close copy, close imitation, close match, close reproduction, commensurable, comparable, comparative, comparison, correlative, correspondent, equal, equivalent, identical, like, near, of equal quality, parallel, related, relive, replicate, similar, sister, twin
ASSOCIATED CONCEPTS: exchanges of like-kind properties, property of like-kind, quality of like-kind

LIKELIHOOD, ***noun*** anticipation, chance, conceivability, conceivableness, confident expectation, excellent prospect, expectance, expectancy, expectation, fair chance, fair prospect, favorable chance, favorable prospect, good chance, good prospect, likeliness, plausibility, possibility, possibleness, potential, potentiality, *probabilitas,* probability, prospect, reasonable chance, reasonable ground, reasonable presumption, reasonable prospect, *veri similitudo,* well-grounded hope, well-grounded possibility

LIKELY, ***adverb*** by all odds, doubtless, doubtlessly, in all likelihood, in all probability, indubitably, more likely than not, most likely, no doubt, presumably, presumptively, probably, undoubtedly, very likely, with almost a certainty
ASSOCIATED CONCEPTS: likely to be reversed on appeal, likely to prevail, likely to uphold the law, likely violates the law

LIKE-MINDED, ***adjective*** agreeing, akin, allied, analogous, cogeneric, coincident, commensurate, congenial, connate, connatural, consonant, correspondent, corresponding, equivalent, homogenous, indistinguishable, kin, kindred, like, matching, of the same bent, of the same persuasion, parallel, relatable, resembling, same, similar, synonymous, twin, uniform
ASSOCIATED CONCEPTS: conspiracy, joint tortfeasors

LIKENESS, ***noun*** analogy, carbon copy, caricature, clone, cloneness, comparability, conformity, counterpart, depiction, doppelganger, double, duplicate, duplication, facsimile, illustration, image, look-alike, match, mirror image, parallel, parallelism, parity, photograph, portrait, replica, representation, resemblance, ringer, semblance, silhouette, similitude, sketch, spitting image, twin, two of a kind

LIMIT, ***noun*** ambit, border, bound, boundary, boundary line, *circumscriptio,* circumscription, extreme boundary, final point, finis, fringe, frontier, furthest point, line of demarcation, outer edge, outer line, outer point, perimeter, rim, *terminus,* verge
ASSOCIATED CONCEPTS: jurisdictional limit, territorial limit

LIMIT, ***verb*** bind, bridle, check, circumscribe, *circumscribere,* confine, constrain, constrict, contain, curb, deter, enclose, *finire,* hamper, hem in, hinder, hold back, impede, leash, modulate, narrow, proscribe, repress, restrain, restrict, set bounds, suppress, *terminare*

LIMITATION, ***noun*** barrier, block, *circumscriptio,* circumscription, clause, condition, constraint, curb, demarcation, *determinatio,* disallowance, prohibition, proscription, provision, qualification, reservation, restraint, restriction, specific confinement, specific curtailment, specification
ASSOCIATED CONCEPTS: alternative limitations, collateral limitation, conditional limitation, contingent limitation, conveyance upon a limitation, estate upon a limitation, executory limitation, limitation of actions, limitation of damages, limitation of liability, limitation of time, limitation of warranties, limitation over, public debt limitation, special limitation, statute of limitations, tax limitation, words of limitation

LIMITED, ***adjective*** *angustus,* bounded, *brevis,* checked, circumscribed, circumscriptive, confined, confining, constricted, controlled, cramped, curbed, definite, enclosed, fixed, hampered, impeded, insular, narrow, *parvus,* prescribed, restrained, restricted, stinted
ASSOCIATED CONCEPTS: limited agency, limited by law, limited guaranty, limited jurisdiction, limited partnership, limited waiver of immunity, limited warranty

LIMITING, *adjective* checking, circumscribing, close fitting, confining, constricting, containing, curbing, hampering, hindering, impeding, repressing, restraining, restricting, restrictive, stinting, suppressing

LIMITS, *noun* amplitude, area, boundary, bounds, capacity, configuration, confines, dimensions, extremity, frontiers, limitations, metes and bounds, outlines, perimeters, premises, purview, range, reach, scope
ASSOCIATED CONCEPTS: basis jurisdiction, jurisdiction of the courts, limited jurisdiction, monetary jurisdiction

LINE *(Ancestry),* ***noun*** arrangement, avenue, beat, birth, blood, bloodline, channel, communication, course, derivation, descent, direction, dispatch, drift, epistle, family, stock, genealogy, heredity, idea, lane, letter, lineage, method, missive, nature, note, origin, parentage, path, progeny, race, railroad, road, route, scheme, sort, succession, system, tendency, track, trail, transportation, way
ASSOCIATED CONCEPTS: descendant, direct line, maternal line, paternal line

LINE *(Business),* ***noun*** activity, airline, avocation, bus line, calling, career, chain, employment, livelihood, merchandise, occupation, profession, pursuit, specialization, specialty, stock in trade, undertaking, vocation, work

LINEAGE, *noun* ancestors, ancestry, antecedents, blood relatives, bloodline, clan, descent, extraction, family, folk, forebears, forefathers, genealogy, gens, *genus,* line, line of descent, origin, *origo,* parentage, progenitors, *stirps*

LINEUP, *noun* arrangement, arrangement with a potential defendant, configuration with the defendant, file, formation with the defendant, grouping, line to identify the criminal, line with a potential defendant, line with the likely suspect, order, parade, police lineup, queue, showing, showing of criminal defendants, showing of criminals for inspection and identification, showing of possible suspects, showing of suspected criminals, stage arrangement containing the guilty party
ASSOCIATED CONCEPTS: double-blind lineup, prejudicial and overly suggestive lineup, show-up

LINK, *noun* affiliation, alliance, association, bond, bridge, chain, connection, connective, contact, coupler, coupling, go-between, interconnection, intermediary, intermedium, intersection, joint, juncture, kinship, liaison, linkage, medium, member, nexus, privity, propinquity, relation, relationship, tie, union, vinculum, weld

LINK, *verb* ally, anastomose, appertain, associate, attach, band, bind, bridge, combine, commingle, conjoin, connect, consolidate, contact, couple, engage, fasten, fuse, fix, identify with, implicate, inosculate, interconnect, join, knot, marry, merge, relate, unite, span, tie, touch, yoke

LINKAGE, *noun* affiliation, affinity, alliance, association, bond, coalescence, combination, concatenation, confluence, conjugation, conjunction, connection, coupling, hookup, interconnection, intersection, joinder, joining, junction, juncture, linking, marriage, meeting, relationship, tie, tie-up, union, weld
ASSOCIATED CONCEPTS: evidence, link to a crime

LINKED, *adjective* affiliated, associated, cemented, coalesced, combined, compared, concatenated, conjugated, connected, corded together, coupled, equated, fused, grouped, hitched, hooked, identified, integrated, interconnected, interlinked, interlocked, intermeshed, joined, likened, lumped together, related, strung together, tied together, united, welded, yoked

LIQUID *(Changeableness),* ***noun*** convertibleness, fluency, fluidity, fluidness, liquidness, ready to be converted
ASSOCIATED CONCEPTS: liquid debt, liquid funds

LIQUID *(Fluid),* ***noun*** damp solution, fluid, fluidic solution, liquefied solution, moist solution, solvent, watery substance, wet substance

LIQUIDATE *(Convert into cash),* ***verb*** cash in, change into cash, change into money, conclude, distribute assets, exchange for money, finish, realize in cash, redeem, sell, sell assets, terminate, terminate business affairs, turn into money
ASSOCIATED CONCEPTS: liquidated account, liquidating trust, liquidation of assets, trustees in liquidation

LIQUIDATE *(Determine liability),* ***verb*** adjust, ascertain liability, ascertain the amount of indebtedness, ascertain the balance due, assemble and apportion assets, cancel debts, determine the amount of indebtedness, discharge, discharge a liability, discharge debts, dispose of, extinguish indebtedness, make restitution, meet payments, pay, pay and settle, pay debts, satisfy, settle, settle accounts with the debtors and creditors
ASSOCIATED CONCEPTS: liquidated claim, liquidated damages, liquidated debt, liquidated demand

LIS PENDENS, *noun* filed notice, notice of an action, notice of pending suit, notice of right, notice on file

LIST, *noun* accounting, an account, archive, arrangement, catalog, directory, docket, enumeration, file, index, inventory, itemization, listing, manifest, overview, record, register, specific delineation, specific listing, summary, tally
ASSOCIATED CONCEPTS: court calendar, docket

LISTEN, *verb* ausculate, be attentive, concentrate on, give one's attention to, hark, hear, hearken, heed, intercept, listen in, monitor, obey, overhear, pick up

LISTLESS, *adjective* absent, abstracted, apathetic, benumbed, careless, despondent, disinterested, distant, dormant, dreamy, dull, exanimate, faineant, faint, heedless, idle, impassive, inactive, inanimate, inattentive, incurious, indifferent, indolent, inert, inexpressive, insipid, insouciant, lacking zest, lackadaisical, lackluster, laggard, languid, lethargic, lifeless, nonchalant, oblivious, otiose, pepless, phlegmatic, slack, sluggish, spiritless, stagnant, supine, torpid, unconcerned, uninterested

LITERACY, *noun* education, bookishness, culture, edification, enlightenment, erudition, intelligence, knowledge, learning, literacy, reading, scholarship, wisdom
ASSOCIATED CONCEPTS: literacy laws

LITERAL, *adjective* accurate, authentic, careful, close, correct, exact, factual, faithful, faultless, meticulous, precise, rigid, scrupulous, strict, textual, to the letter, true, true to fact, truthful, unchanged, uncorrupted, undeviating, undistorted, unembroidered, unerring, unexaggerated, unfigurative, ungarbled, unmetaphorical, unvaried, unvarnished, veracious, verbatim, without exaggeration, word-for-word
ASSOCIATED CONCEPTS: literal interpretation

LITERAL MEANING, *noun* accurate meaning, correct meaning, defined meaning, definition, distinct meaning, exact meaning, explanation, explicit meaning, express meaning, faithful meaning, inflexible meaning, methodical meaning, meticulous meaning, narrow meaning, not subject to interpretation, ordinary meaning, plain meaning, precise meaning, prescribed meaning, rigid meaning, rigorous meaning, sharply defined, significance, specific meaning, strict meaning, unbending meaning, uncompromising meaning, unequivocal meaning
ASSOCIATED CONCEPTS: construction, literal contract, literal proof plain meaning rule, rules of statutory, soft plain meaning rule, textualism

LITERALLY, *adverb* correctly, definitely, distinctly, exactly, explicitly, expressly, precisely, rigidly, rigorous, similarly, specifically, unambiguously, uncompromisingly, unequivocally, unerringly
ASSOCIATED CONCEPTS: laws read literally, strict construction

LITERATE, *adjective* accomplished, apprised, aware, conversant, cultivated, cultured, disciplined, educated, enlightened, enriched, erudite, having formal education, informed, intellectual, knowing, knowledgeable, learned, lettered, literary, polished, practiced, proficient, qualified, sapient, scholarly, scholastic, schooled, skilled, studied, studious, trained, well-educated, well-informed, well-read, well-taught, widely read

LITERATURE, *noun* *belles lettres,* books, classics, information, letters, literary output, papers, printed word, publication, reading matter, store of knowledge, treatises, work, works, writings, written language, written word

LITIGABLE, *adjective* actionable, appealable, arguable, argumentative, capable of being debated, confutable, contestable, controversial, controvertible, disputable, in dispute, justiciable, refutable

LITIGANT, *noun* adversary, adverse party, appellant, appellee, claimant, complainant, contender, contestant, controversialist, correspondent, cross-complainant, cross-defendant, defendant, disputant, intervenor, legal adversary, legal opponent, litigationist, litigator, opponent, opponent in a lawsuit, party, party to a lawsuit, party to a legal action, party to a proceeding, party to a suit, party to an action, party to legal proceeding, petitioner, plaintiff, respondent, suitor, the defense
ASSOCIATED CONCEPTS: public interest litigant law, vexatious litigant law
FOREIGN PHRASES: ***Litigare.*** To litigate.

LITIGATE, *verb* altercate, appeal to the law, assert in court, bring action against, bring an action, bring suit, bring to the bar, bring to trial, carry on a lawsuit, contend, contest in court, contest in law, go into litigation, institute legal proceedings, *litigare,* prefer a claim, press in court, pursue in court, seek legal redress, start a lawsuit, start an action, sue, take to court, urge in court

LITIGATING COUNSEL, *noun* appointed counsel, attorney, cocounsel, counsel, counsel representing a party, legal adversary, legal counsel, legal opponent, legal representative, litigating attorney, litigation attorney, litigation counsel, litigator, retained counsel
ASSOCIATED CONCEPTS: vexatious litigation laws

LITIGATION, *noun* action, case, cause, controversy, disputation, dispute, judicial contest, lawsuit, legal action, legal battle, legal contest, legal dispute, legal matter, legal proceeding, legal remedy, matter, proceeding, suit, suit at law, trial, wrangling
ASSOCIATED CONCEPTS: appellate proceedings, civil proceedings, collateral proceedings, common-law proceedings, criminal proceedings, frivolous litigation, plenary proceedings, special proceedings, summary proceedings, supplemental proceedings

LITIGATOR, *noun* appointed counsel, attorney, cocounsel, counsel, counsel representing a party, lead counsel, legal adversary, legal opponent, litigating attorney, litigation counsel, of counsel, opposing counsel, retained counsel

LITIGIOUS, *adjective* actionable, aggressive, antagonistic, arguing, argumental, argumentative, at variance, bellicose, belligerent, combative, conflicting, contentious, contested, contrary, controversial, controvertible, debatable, disagreeing, discordant, disposed to controversy, disputable, disputatious, disputative, dissentious, eristic, eristical, exceptious, fighting, given to disputation, hostile, inimical, irreconcilable, litigatory, *litigiosus,* militant, offensive, open to debate, open to question, opposing, polemic, polemical, pugnacious, quarrelsome, querulous, unpeaceful, warlike
ASSOCIATED CONCEPTS: barratry

LITTLE, *adjective* abbreviated, cursory, diminutive, few, fleeting, immaterial, inadequate, inappreciable, inconsequential, inconsiderable, inessential, inferior, insignificant, insubstantial, insufficient, Lilliputian, limited, meager, minor, minute, negligible, nonessential, paltry, petty, scant, slight, slim, sparse, superficial, trivial, unessential, unimportant, unimpressive
ASSOCIATED CONCEPTS: little-known law, little law

LITTLE-KNOWN, *adjective* abstract, abstruse, arcane, concealed, cryptic, dark, enigmatic, esoteric, hidden, mysterious, mystic, mystical, nebulous, obscure, perplexing, profound, puzzling, recondite, secret, shrouded in mystery

LITTORAL, *adjective* beach, beachfront, coastal, coastland, lakeside, riparian, seaboard, seacoast, seashore, seaside, tidewater, waterfront, waterside

LIVE *(Conscious),* ***adjective*** animate, animated, breathing, endowed with life, existent, existing, full of life, growing, imbued with life, incarnate, living, mortal, quick, viable, vital

LIVE *(Existing),* ***adjective*** abiding, continued, continuing, enduring, existent, extant, intact, lasting, ongoing, perduring, persevering, persisting, progressing, remaining, staying, surviving, sustained, unceasing, unchecked, undestroyed, unended, unfading, unfailing, unreversed, unrevoked, unstopped
ASSOCIATED CONCEPTS: live cause of action

LIVELIHOOD, *noun* business, calling, career, craft, employment, enterprise, job, keep, line of work, living, maintenance, means, occupation, position, profession, pursuit, resources, situation, source of income, subsistence, support, sustainment, sustenance, trade, undertaking, venture, *victus,* vocation, work

LIVID, *adjective* angry, disgusted, enraged, frantic, frenzied, fuming, furious, hostile, inflamed, infuriated, ireful, offended, offensive, outraged, raging, storming, tempestuous, tumultuous, turbulent

LIVING *(Alive),* ***noun*** activity, animal existence, animation, being alive, breathing, existence, existing, having life, respiring, subsisting, surviving, vitality
ASSOCIATED CONCEPTS: assisted living laws, living and cohabitating together, living trust, living will

LIVING *(Occupation),* ***noun*** area, career, discipline, domain, field, livelihood, maintenance, means of living, niche, profession, province, realm, specialty sphere, subsistence, trade

LIVING QUARTERS, ***noun*** abode, accommodations, address of residency, apartment, domicile, dwelling, habitation, home, house, housing, location of residency, lodging, lodgment, place, place of residency, residence, residency, shelter
ASSOCIATED CONCEPTS: closing, commercial leases, recording, residential leases

LIVING WILL, ***noun*** an instrument prescribing care in life-threatening situations, an instrument preventing medical life support to sustain life, an instrument to refuse care through medical life support, instructions for care when the patient has a terminal illness, instructions for care when the patient has an incurable disease, instructions for care when the patient has an incurable illness, instructions for care when the patient has an incurable injury
ASSOCIATED CONCEPTS: durable power of attorney, euthanasia

LOAD, ***verb*** burden, cram, cumber, fill, fill up, flood, freight, inundate, lade, make heavy, mass, *onerare,* onus *imponere,* pack, pile, put aboard, put goods in, put on board, saddle, shower upon, stack, steeve, store, stow, stuff, take on cargo, weigh down, weight

LOAN, ***noun*** accommodation, advance, advancement, aid, allotment, assistance, backing, *commodare,* credit, dole, entrustment, extension of credit, financing, funding, grant, imprest, moneys borrowed, *mutuum,* pledge, res *commodata,* stake, stipend, subsidy, sum entrusted, sum of money borrowed, sum of money lent, temporary accommodation, time payment, trust
ASSOCIATED CONCEPTS: bond, building loan, construction loan, continuing loan, discount, excessive loan, forbearance, gratuitous loan, loan association, loan broker, loan value of a policy, mortgage, secured loan, simple loan, stock loan, temporary loan, unpaid loan, usurious loan, usury laws
FOREIGN PHRASES: ***Creditorum appellatione non hi tantum accipiuntur qui pecuniam crediderunt, sed omnes quibus ex qualibet causa debetur.*** Under the head of "creditors" are included, not only those who have lent money, but all to whom from any cause a debt is owing.

LOAN, ***verb*** accommodate, advance, allow, extend credit, furnish funds, give, lend, permit to borrow, supply funds

LOATHE, ***verb*** abhor, be repulsed by, detest, dislike, dislike intensely, harbor hostility toward, harbor ill will toward, hate, have a strong distaste toward, have animus toward, have antagonism toward, have antipathy toward, have aversion to, have enmity toward, have ill feeling toward, have malevolence toward, possess hostility toward

LOATHSOME, ***adjective*** abhorrent, abject, abominable, accursed, annoying, appalling, atrocious, base, below contempt, beneath contempt, blameworthy, contemptible, deplorable, despicable, detestable, disagreeable, disgusting, disliked, dissatisfactory, distasteful, distressing, dreadful, execrable, *foedus,* forbidding, foul, frightful, fulsome, ghastly, hateful, heinous, hellish, hideous, horrible, horrid, insufferable, intolerable, invidious, irritating, loathful, mean, nasty, nauseating, nauseous, objectionable, obnoxious, odious, offensive, opprobrious, painful, putrid, rancid, rank, repellent, repelling, reprehensible, repugnant, repulsive, revolting, shocking, sickening, *taeter,* terrible, ugly, unbearable, undesirable, unendurable, unpalatable, unpleasant, unsavory, vile

LOBBY, ***noun*** active partisans, active reformers, active supporters, activists, advocates, agitators, influencers, influential persons, persuaders, petitioners, pressure group, reformers, special interest group, special interests, zealous advocates

LOBBY, ***verb*** actively represent, actuate, advance, arouse, bring pressure to bear, defend, effect, encourage, enlist, espouse, exercise influence, exert influence, exert pressure, incline, induce, influence, inspirit, instigate, motivate, negotiate, personally solicit, persuade, press, pressure, procure, promote, provoke, pull strings, put pressure on, represent, request, solicit, solicit votes, sway, urge, use one's influence, work on
ASSOCIATED CONCEPTS: lobbyists, registration laws, special interest groups

LOBBYIST, ***noun*** active partisan for, active supporter, activist, advocate, agent, government affairs executive, government affairs representative, influencer, influential agent, legislative representative, peddler of influence, persuader, reformer, representative, retained agent, special interest representative
ASSOCIATED CONCEPTS: disclosure ethics, law disclosure, lobbyist law, lobbyist registration

LOCAL, ***adjective*** adjacent, adjoining, civic, close, district, divisional, domestic, limited, localized, municipal, native, near, nearby, neighborhood, provincial, regional, restricted, sectional, subdivisional, surrounding, territorial
ASSOCIATED CONCEPTS: local act, local action, local agent, local application, local assessment, local authorities, local bill, local concern, local improvement, local law, local rules

LOCALE, ***noun*** address, area, district, domain, domicile, environs, exact location, geographic location, geographic place, habitat, home, location, neighborhood, place, precise location, region, scene, seat, sector, site, spot, territory, venue

LOCALITY, ***noun*** address, area, bearings, demesne, district, domain, environment, environs, habitat, locale, location, *locus,* neighborhood, pale, place, position, province, purlieus, quarter, region, scene, seat, section, sector, site, situation, *situs,* spot, station, surroundings, terrain, territory, venue, vicinage, vicinity, whereabouts, zone

LOCATE, ***verb*** ascertain a position, assign to a place, bring to light, come upon, define limits, define location, delineate, demarcate, deposit, designate a place, detect, discern, discover, discover by search, discover by survey, discover the location of, discover the place of, establish, expose, ferret out, find, fix the position, house, install, lodge, make a place for, map out, move to, park, pinpoint, place, position, put, put in place, quarter, reveal, search out, select boundaries, set, set in place, settle, situate, station, stumble on, take up abode, trace, track down, uncover, unearth

LOCATION, *noun* area, demesne, district, environment, fixation, locale, locality, locus, neighborhood, place, placement, plot, point, position, post, purlieus, quarter, region, scene, section, site, spot, station, territory, vicinage, vicinity, zone
ASSOCIATED CONCEPTS: domicile, residency, venue

LOCK, *verb* arrest, attach, band, bar, barricade, block, blockade, bolt, cage, catch, cement, check, cinch, clasp, close, close fast, *concludere,* confine, connect, couple, curb, cut off, dam, encircle, enclose, enthrall, entwine, fasten, fuse, glue, grapple, hamper, hinder, hold, immobilize, immure, impede, impound, imprison, incarcerate, inhibit, intern, jail, join, link, lock up, make fast, make insaperable, *obserere,* obstruct, occlude, padlock, pen, prohibit, put behind bars, restrain, restrict, seal, secure, shackle, shut out, shut up, stop, trap, unite, weld, yoke
ASSOCIATED CONCEPTS: lockout

LOCK UP, *verb* apprehend, arrest, bar, bind, capture, catch, commit, confine, constrict, detain, gate, hamper, hinder, immure, impede, impound, imprison, incarcerate, jail, remand to jail, repress, restrain, restrict, shut, suppress
ASSOCIATED CONCEPTS: sentencing, sentencing guidelines

LOCKOUT, *noun* barring out, cessation of employment, cessation of the furnishing of work, close-out, coercive refusal to furnish work, employer work stoppage, exclusion of workers, nonadmission of employees, preclusion of work, refusal to furnish work, repudiation of employment, stoppage of work, temporary closing, work stoppage
ASSOCIATED CONCEPTS: strike

LOCO PARENTIS, *adverb* as a substitute for a parent, as an alternative for a parent, in place of a parent, instead of a parent

***LOCUS,* noun** bailiwick, demesne, emplacement, environment, ground, locale, locality, location, place, placement, position, region, site, *situs,* territory
FOREIGN PHRASES: ***Locus crontractus, locus criminis.*** The place of the crime. ***Locus delecti.*** The place of the offense. ***Locus partitus.*** A place divided. ***Locus reisitae.*** A place where something is situated.

LODGE *(Bring a complaint),* ***verb*** accuse, bring a case, bring a suit, bring accusation, bring an action against, bring charges against, bring proceedings against, bring to justice, bring to the bar, bring to trial, bring up on charges, call to account, cast blame upon, charge with, file a claim, file a suit, fix the blame for, incriminate, inculpate, place the blame for, prefer charges, prosecute
ASSOCIATED CONCEPTS: lodge a criminal complaint

LODGE *(House),* ***verb*** afford sanctuary, assign to lodgings, bed, berth, domicile, find a place for, find room for, furnish room for, furnish with quarters, garrison, harbor, *hospitio excipere,* hostel, install, locate, make a place for, park, place, put, quarter, screen, shield, situate, station, supply accommodations for

LODGE *(Reside),* ***verb*** abide, board, camp, *deversari, devertere,* domicile, dwell, encamp, establish oneself, inhabit, live, locate oneself, make one's home at, place, quarter, remain, reside, rest, set up housekeeping, settle, sleep at, sojourn, squat, station, stay, stop, take lodgings, take rooms, take up quarters, take up residence in, tarry, tenant

LODGE A COMPLAINT, *noun* accuse, blame, bring a suit, bring an action, bring charges, bring proceedings against, bring up on charges, challenge, charge with, cite, complain of, criminate, file a charge, file a claim, file a suit, implicate, impose blame upon, impose responsibility on, impute, incriminate, inculpate, inform against, institute a lawsuit, make an accusation, prefer charges

LODGER, *noun* addressee, boarder, denizen, *deversor,* dweller, habitant, indweller, inhabitant, inhabiter, inmate, *inquilinus,* leaseholder, lessee, occupant, occupier, possessor, rent payer, renter, resident, residentiary, resider, roomer, sojourner, tenant, termor, transient

LODGING, *noun* abode, accommodation, address, apartment, asylum, berth, billet, chambers, *deversorium, deverticulum,* domicile, dormitory, dwelling, dwelling place, habitat, habitation, harbor, home, housing, inhabitance, inhabitancy, living place, lodging place, lodgment, *meritoria,* place of residence, place of rest, protection, quarters, refuge, residence, rooms, shelter

LOFTY, *adjective* august, cavalier, celebrated, celestial, dignified, distinguished, elevated, eminent, enhanced, esteemed, exalted, exalted ideal, fabled, famous, far-reaching, heavenly, heightened, high, high intellectual values, high score value, honorable, illustrious, immortal, kingly, leading, legendary, lordly, magisterial, magnificent, majestic, noble, notable, noted, predominant, preeminent, princely, prominent, raised, renowned, respected, revered, soaring, venerable
ASSOCIATED CONCEPTS: lofty goals, lofty ideals, lofty plans

LOGIC, *noun* analytic, analytical, argument, argumentation, art of controversy, art of disputation a, chain of reasoning, cogent, common sense, course of argument, course of thought, deduction, dialectic, dialectical, dialectics, explanation, good sense, inference, line of reasoning, logical reasoning, method of reasoning, philosophical, philosophy, polemics, process of reasoning, ratiocination, rational, rationalization, reason, reasoned, reasoning, science of reasoning, sense, sound judgment, sound reasoning, thought process, wisdom
ASSOCIATED CONCEPTS: laws of logic, logical relevancy

LOGICAL, *adjective* analytic, analytical, cogent, coherent, consistent, deductive, dialectic, dialectical, inductional, inductive, philosophical, ratiocinative, ratiocinatory, rational, reasonable, reasoned, sound

LOITER, *verb* be idle, be vagrant, hang around, idle, linger, move aimlessly, pass time in idleness, poke, stand around, tarry, wander aimlessly
ASSOCIATED CONCEPTS: vagrancy

LONE, *adjective* alone, deserted, exclusive, first and last, individual, isolated, lonesome, one and only, only, single, singular, sole, solitary, unique
ASSOCIATED CONCEPTS: lone dissenter

LONG *(Delayed),* ***adjective*** continued, day after day, dilatory, dragged out, drawn out, endless, enduring, eternal, forever and a day, hour after hour, interminable, long drawn-out, marathon, overlong, perpetual, prolonged, protracted, sustained delay, unending delay, without end
FOREIGN PHRASES: ***Longa possession jus parit.*** Long possessions begets what is right.

LONG *(Lengthy),* ***adjective*** boundless, broad, continued, day after day, deep, distant, elongate, elongated, endless, enduring, eternal, expanded, expansive, extended, extensive, faraway, far-off, far-reaching, far-seeing, forever and a day, great, hour after hour, interminable, large, lasting, lengthened, limitless, lofty, outstretched, perpetual, remote, spread out, stretched out, stretching, sustained, unending, widespread, without end
ASSOCIATED CONCEPTS: long arm of the law, long-term

LONG AND SHORT OF IT, ***noun*** analysis, assessment bottom line, conclusion, essence, essential parts, evaluation, immediate answer, immediate assessment, pro or con, professional opinion, quick answer, quick assessment, quick determination, result, solution, upshot

LONG-ARM JURISDICTION, ***noun*** jurisdiction of the court, jurisdiction over foreigners, jurisdiction over out-of-state defendants, personal jurisdiction over nondomiciliaries, personal jurisdiction over nonresident defendant, sufficient jurisdiction
ASSOCIATED CONCEPTS: long-arm statute

LONG-DRAWN *(Protracted),* ***adjective*** delayed, dilatory, enduring, eternal, forever and a day, lengthy, lingering, long, long-lived, long-winded, meandering, overlong, perpetual, prolonged, roundabout, tedious, unending, without end
ASSOCIATED CONCEPTS: long-drawn-out trials

LONG-DRAWN *(Verbose),* ***adjective*** garrulous, lengthy, lingering, long-winded, loquacious, meandering, orotund, overlong, prolix, prolonged, repetitious, roundabout, tedious, unending
ASSOCIATED CONCEPTS: plain language

LONG-LASTING, ***adjective*** abiding, anchored, constant, dependable, durable, enduring, established, fastened, firm, fixed, immovable, impervious, lasting, perdurable, perduring, permanent, persistent, riveted, robust, rooted, secure, soldered, sound, stable, stationary, steady, stout, strong, substantial, tenacious, tough, unshakable

LONGANIMITY, ***noun*** composure, control, endurance, forbearance, forgiveness, forgivingness, fortitude, imperturbation, indulgence, inexcitability, lenience, leniency, magnanimity, optimism, pardon, patience, patient endurance, perseverance, placability, placidity, refusal to be provoked, resignation, self-control, stamina, steadiness, stoicism, submission, sufferance, temperance, tenacity, tolerance, toleration, tranquility, understanding

LONGEVITY, ***noun*** advancement, age, continuance, continuation, durability, durableness, duration, elderliness, endurance, furtherance, great span of life, lastingness, length of life, long life, longlivedness, maintenance, old age, oldness, perpetuation, persistence, prolongation, protraction, seniority, surviorship, survival, survivance, years

LONGSTANDING, ***adjective*** abiding, acknowledged, admitted, aged, ancient, antique, chronic, constant, continuing, continous, customary, deep-rooted, deep-seated, durable, enduring, established, fixed, habitual, hallowed, handed down, immemorial, immutable, inborn, inbred, ingrained, inveterate, lasting, legendary, lingering, long-established, long-lasting, long-lived, long-term, of long duration, of long standing, perennial, perpetual, persistent, persisting, prolonged, protracted, recognized, recurring, remaining, rooted, steadfast, sustained, time-honored, traditional, tried-and-true, true-blue, unabating, unfading, venerable
ASSOCIATED CONCEPTS: longstanding law, longstanding policy

LOOK *(Complexion),* ***noun*** appearance, aspect, bearing, cast, color, complexion, condition, configuration, countenance, demeanor, deportment, fashion, feature, figure, front, general aspect, guise, idea, impression, manner, mien, presence, quality, seeming, semblance, shape, show, thought
ASSOCIATED CONCEPTS: first look

LOOK *(Sight),* ***noun*** contemplation, gaze, glimpse, glower, inspection, observance, reconnaissance, regard, survey, view, vision

LOOK, ***verb*** attend, be a spectator, be cautious of, be closely observant, be on guard, be on the lookout for, behold, contemplate, examine, explore, eye, gaze at, inspect, keep under observation, look at, monitor, note, notice, observe, pay attention to, peer, perceive, regard, scrutinize, see, sport, stare, stare at, study, superinted, survey, tend, view, visualize, watch, witness
ASSOCIATED CONCEPTS: a free look, cancellation in insurance

LOOK INTO, ***verb*** ask about, check, delve into, dig into, evaluate, examine, explore, inquire, inquire into, inspect, investigate, look up, observe, poke into, probe, pursue, research, review, scrutinize, search, search into, study
ASSOCIATED CONCEPTS: criminal investigation, grand jury investigation

LOOK OVER, ***verb*** analyze, check thoroughly, edit, examine, go over, inspect, make corrections, make improvements, provide suggested changes, provide suggested edits, recheck, reexamine, review, revise, reword, rewrite, scrutinize, to examine in a cursory way, to examine swiftly

LOOK UP, ***verb*** delve into, explore, ferret through, find, gain, go to see, inquire into, look into, pry, pursue, research, scrutinize, search for, search thoroughly, seek out, study, track down
ASSOCIATED CONCEPTS: legal research

LOOMING *(Becoming visible),* ***adjective*** appearing, ascending, ascertainable, becoming clear, coming into view, coming to light, coming to the fore, emerging, impending, materializing, menacing, mounting, noticeable, revealing itself, rising, showing itself, surfacing, threatening, towering, visible

LOOMING *(Menacing),* ***adjective*** admonitory, brewing, dangerously, foreboding, hanging over, hovering over, ill-omened, impending, ominous, portentous, precariously lingering, threatening, with a black cloud overhead
ASSOCIATED CONCEPTS: looming battle in Congress, looming lawsuits

LOOPHOLE, ***noun*** alternative, aperture, contrivance, device, escape clause, escape hatch, escape valve, evasion, exception, excuse, expedient, *foramen,* means of escape, mechanism for evasion, opening, outlet, saving clause, uncommunicativeness, vehicle for escape, way of escape, way out

LOOSE *(Disconnected),* ***adjective*** detached, free, freed, liberated, separate, suggestive, unattached, unbound, unchained, unclasped, unconnected, unfastened, unlatched, unlocked, unrestrained, untethered, untied

LOOSE *(Inexact),* ***adjective*** abstruse, careless, circuitous, confused, cursory, decumbent, deviative, disconnected, discursive, disjointed, erratic, free, heedless, inaccurate, indefinite, inexact, lax, lecherous, liberal, licentious, muddled, obscure, open-ended, perfunctory, promiscuous, rambling, salacious, unexacting, vague, weak

LOOSEN *(Ease up),* ***verb*** abate, allay, alleviate, assuage, decrease tension, diminish, ease, ease off, extricate, free, lessen, let loose, let up, lighten, mitigate, moderate, palliate, reduce, relax, release, relieve, soften, soften up, weaken
ASSOCIATED CONCEPTS: loosen a monopoly, loosen rules, loosen the law

LOOSEN *(Release),* ***verb*** cut loose, detach, disjoin, ease, free, let go, let loose, let up, loosen, relax, relieve tension, unbind, unbolt, unbridle, unbuckle, undo, unfasten, unfetter, unlatch, unlock, unloosen, unshackle, untie

LOOT, ***verb*** abscond with, appropriate, break into, burglarize, carry off, defalcate, depredate, despoil, embezzle, forage, harry, lay waste, make off with, maraud, peculate, pilfer, pillage, pirate, plunder, prey upon, purloin, raid, ransack, ravage, rifle, rob, sack, seize, spoil, spoliate, steal, strip, take, thieve

LOQUACIOUS, ***adjective*** babbling, blabbing, chattering, chatty, communicative, copious in speech, disposed to talk freely, effusive, exuberant, flatulent, fluent, gabby, garrulous, *garrulus,* glib, gushy, informative, jabbering, longwinded, longiloquent, *loquax,* noisy, prattling, profuse, prolix, rambling, talkative, talking, tonguey, verbal, verbose, *verbosus,* vociferous, voluble, windy, wordy

LOSE *(Be deprived of),* ***verb*** *amittere,* be deprived of, be impoverished, be without, become poorer by, experience a loss, fail to find, fail to keep, forfeit, forget, incur a loss, meet with a loss, mislay, misplace, miss, part with, sacrifice, squander, suffer a deprivation, suffer loss, waste

LOSE *(Undergo defeat),* ***verb*** be confounded, be defeated, be destroyed, be disappointed, be foiled, be frustrated, be humbled, be left behind, be outdistanced, be outvoted, be overthrown, be ruined, be thwarted, be unsuccessful, come in last, fail, fail to win, forfeit, go down in defeat, succumb, suffer by comparison, suffer defeat, take a beating, yield
ASSOCIATED CONCEPTS: lose a case

LOSE BY DEFAULT, ***verb*** abrogate responsibilities, be delinquent, be derelict, fail to answer, fail to appear, fail to meet one's obligations, neglect, never answer the docket call, omission, violation of duty

LOSE GROUND, ***verb*** backsliding, backtrack, fail, fail to keep up, fail to make progress, fail to progress, fall behind, lose footing, regression, return, reverse, slip, weaken a position

LOSS, ***noun*** calamity, catastrophe, cost, *damnum,* decline, decrement, deprivation, *detrimentum,* disaster, failure, forfeit, forfeiture, *iactura,* ill fortune, ill luck, misfortune, privation, removal, ruin, sacrifice, waste
ASSOCIATED CONCEPTS: actual loss, allowable loss, business loss, capital loss, cause of loss, consequential loss, constructive total loss, damages, deductible, direct loss, financial loss, guaranty funds, indemnification, involuntary losses, irreparable loss, loss of bargain, loss of earnings, loss of life, loss of profits, loss of services, loss payable clause, loss reserves, measure of damages, net loss, operating loss, out-of-pocket loss, pecuniary loss, permanent loss, profit and loss, recovery of losses from bad debts, salvage loss
FOREIGN PHRASES: ***Nemo debet locupletari ex alterius incommodo.*** No one ought to gain by another's loss. ***Fictio legis inique operatur alieni damnum vel injuriam.*** Fiction of law is wrongful if it works loss or harm to anyone. ***Non omne damnum inducit injuriam.*** Not every loss produces an injury. ***Lex citius tolerare vult privatum damnum quam publicum malum.*** The law would rather tolerate a private loss than a public evil. ***Officium nemini debet esse damnosum.*** An office ought to be injurious to no one. ***Non videntur rem amittere quibus propria non fuit.*** Persons to whom a thing did not belong are not considered to have lost it.

LOSS OF AFFECTION, ***noun*** cause of action, damages, deprivation of companionship, forfeiture of companionship, loss of care, loss of companionship, loss of consortium, loss of passion
ASSOCIATED CONCEPTS: alienation of affection

LOSS OF OPPORTUNITY, ***noun*** cost of removing from use, deprivation, forfeiture, loss of availability, loss of productivity, loss of prospective benefit, loss of readiness, loss of use, privation, removal, sacrifice
ASSOCIATED CONCEPTS: interference with contractual relations, loss of opportunity doctrine

LOSS OF REPUTATION, ***noun*** abasement, attaint, badge of infamy, bad reputation, bad repute, baseness, black eye, black mark, blemish, debasement, defilement, degradation, derogation, discredit, disesteem, disfavor, disgrace, dishonor, disparagement, disrepute, exclusion from favor, humiliation, ignominy, ill repute, infamy, ingloriousness, obloquy, odium, opprobrium, reproach, scandal, shame, shameful notoriety, stain, stigma, tarnish, turpitude
ASSOCIATED CONCEPTS: libel, slander

LOSS OF VALUE, ***noun*** contraction, debasement, declension, declination, decline, declivity, decrease, deflation, degeneration, depreciation, deterioration, devaluation, diminution, dwindling, losing ground, recession, regression, retrenchment, retrogression, shrinking
ASSOCIATED CONCEPTS: diminishment, inquest

LOST *(Disoriented),* ***adjective*** adrift, astray, baffled, befogged, befuddled, bemuddled, bewildered, confused, mystified, obfuscated, perplexed, puzzled, strayed, unable to find the way, wandering, without bearings

LOST *(Taken away),* ***adjective*** absent, annihilated, confiscated, depleted, destroyed, dissipated, effaced, eliminated, eradicated, exhausted, exterminated, extinguished, extirpated, forfeited, gone, gone to waste, hidden, irreclaimable, irrecoverable, irredeemable, irretrievable, irrevocable, mislaid, misplaced, missing, nowhere to be found, obliterated, obscured, out of sight, perished, sacrificed, squandered, taken, thrown away, vanished, wasted

LOST CAUSE, *noun* a defeated cause, abortion, bankruptcy, bomb, defeat, dereliction, downfall, flop, frustration, hopeless situation, insolvency, losing game, malfunction, misadventure, miscarriage, misstep, nonperformance, nonstarter, nonsuccess, omission, terminal case, total loss, waste of energies, waste of time

LOT, *noun* parcel, part, piece, piece of ground, plot, portion, small parcel of land, subdivision, tract
ASSOCIATED CONCEPTS: adjacent lots, block, building lot, contiguous lots, partition of lots, vacant lot

LOTTERY, *noun* allotment by chance, bet, chance, draw, drawing, gamble, game of chance, lot, raffle, *sors, sortitio,* sweepstake, wager

LOUD *(Deafening),* ***adjective*** big-voiced, blaring, blatting, blustering, boisterous, booming, brawling, clattery, crashing, ear-piercing, ear-rending, ear-splitting, earthshaking, emphatic, fulminating, grinding, head-splitting, howling, intense, jarring, loud-sounding, noisy, obstreperous, penetrating, piercing, powerful, pulsating, pulsing, raucous, rebounding, reechoing, repercussive, resonant, resounding, roaring, roiling, roistering, rollicking, shouting, shrill, sounding, throbbing, thundering, thunderous, tumultuous, vociferous

LOUD *(Ostentatious),* ***adjective*** blinding, brash, conspicuous, extravagant, flagrant, flaring, flashy, flaunting, garish, gaudy, glaring, intrusive, jazzy, loudmouthed, lurid, meretricious, obtrusive, offensive, ornate, outlandish, out-of-place, outstanding, pronounced, rude, showy, snazzy, spectacular, splashy, striking, tasteless, tawdry, vulgar

LOVE *(Affection),* ***noun*** adoration, ardor, attachment, attraction, cherishing, closeness, craving, crush, desire, devotedness, devotion, emotion, enchantment, enjoyment, esteem, fancy, fervor, flame, fondness, friendship, infatuation, intimacy, like, liking, longing, mutual attraction, passion, rapture, regard, sentiment, tender passion, tenderness, true love, wanting, warmth, weakness, yearning
ASSOCIATED CONCEPTS: marriage ceremonies, same-sex marriages

LOVE *(Penchant),* ***noun*** affection, avocation, consuming interest, dedication, devotion, effort, inclination, interest, likening for an interest, passion, predilection, pursuit, relished interest, vocation, zest for an effort

LOW *(Ignoble),* ***adjective*** deep, depraved, depressed, flat, heinous, ignoble, inelegant, lamentable, minimal, nominal, odious, offensive, outrageous, poor, prone, scandalous, scarce, scurrilous, servile, subaltern, tainted, unelevated

LOW *(Nominal),* ***adjective*** inconsiderable, inferior, insignificant, meager, minimal, minimum, minute, modest, negligible, nonsubstantial, reduced, unimportant, unsubstantial

LOWER *(Below),* ***verb*** bring down, bring low, decrease, de-escalate, demote, descend, detrude, down further, drop, go down, go under, immerse, incline, less, lessen, lesser, let down, lower level, push down

LOWER *(Reduce),* ***verb*** cutback, declass, decrease, deflate, defrock, demote, depose, depreciate, devaluate, dilute, diminish, disbar, discount, dissipated, downgrade, downplay, dropped, lessen, lesser, lowered, modify, palliate, pared down, play down, quell, relieve, remove, retrench, scale down, smaller, soften, soothe, strip, subtract, take away

LOWEST *(Far below),* ***adjective*** all the way down, entirely under, extremely far under, furthest down, inferior in position, rock-bottom, under, way down, way under

LOWEST *(Least),* ***adjective*** fewest, littlest, minimal, shortest, slightest, smallest

LOYAL, *adjective* allegiant, beholden, biddable, bound, bounden, committed, compliant, conscientious, constant, dedicated, dependable, devoted, duteous, dutiful, faithful, fast, *fidelis, fidus, filial,* firm, honorable, incorrupt, incorruptible, indebted, obedient, patriotic, pledged, reliable, resolute, slavish, staunch, steadfast, steady, tried, true, truehearted, trustworthy, trusty, unbetraying, unbought, unbribed, unchangeable, unchanging, undeviating, unfailing, unimpeachable, uninfluenced, unperfidious, unswayed, unswerving, untreacherous, unwavering, worthy of confidence
ASSOCIATED CONCEPTS: duty of loyalty, faithful performance, loyalty oath, undivided loyalty

LOYALTY, *noun* adherence, adherency, allegiance, attachment, bond, compliance, constancy, dedication, dependability, devotedness, devotion, duty, faithfulness, fealty, *fidelitas,* fidelity, *fides,* good faith, group feeling, incorruptibility, obedience, reliability, single-mindedness, singleness of heart, stanchness, steadfastness, submissiveness, support, troth, trueness, trustworthiness, zeal

LUCID, *adjective* apparent, articulate, certain, clear, clear-cut, clear-minded, clear-thinking, clear-witted, clearheaded, comprehending, comprehensible, crystalline, diaphanous, discerning, discriminating, distinct, effulgent, evident, explicit, express, fulgid, illuminated, illumined, indisputable, intelligible, limpid, lucent, *lucidus,* luculent, manifest, nitid, obvious, overt, palpable, patent, pellucid, *pellucidus,* perceptive, perspicacious, perspicuous, *perspicuus,* plain, pronounced, rational, refulgent, responsible, sagacious, sage, sane, sensible, simple, sober, sound, straightforward, transparent, unambiguous, undeniable, understandable, understood, undisguised, unequivocal, unmistakable, unquestionable

LUCK, *noun* advantageous outcome, chance, coincidence, destiny, fate, fortuity, gamble, good break, good fortune, good luck, opportunity, positive results, serendipity
ASSOCIATED CONCEPTS: gaming laws, moral luck

LUCRATIVE, *adjective* accumulative, advantageous, bearing revenue, beneficial, compensating, compensatory, contributive, fertile, fruitful, gainful, high-paying, invaluable, *lucrosus,* moneymaking, paying, productive, profitable, *quaestuosus,* remunerative, rewardful, rewarding, successful, useful, valuable, well-paying, worthwhile

LUDICROUS, *adjective* absurd, amusing, asinine, at variance with the facts, barely possible, beyond belief, bizarre, comical, contrary to common sense, contrary to reason, crazy, derisible, doubtable, dubitable, eccentric, fallacious, fantastic, fantastical, farcical, fatuous, foolish, funny, hard to believe, humorous, idiotic, implausible, impossible, inane, incongruous, inconsistent, incredible, irrational, laugh-provoking, laughable, nonsensical, odd, open to doubt, outlandish, peculiar, preposterous, queer, questionable, ridiculous, risible, senseless, silly, staggering belief, strange, suspect, unbelievable, unconvincing, unheard of, unreasonable, untenable, unthinkable, wild, without reason

LUGUBRIOUS, ***adjective*** cheerless, crestfallen, dark, dejected, depressing, despondent, disconsolate, discouraged, disheartened, dismal, dispirited, doleful, dolorous, downcast, dreary, elegiac, *flebilis,* forbidding, forlorn, funereal, gloomy, glum, grieving, heavyhearted, joyless, low-spirited, *lugubris,* melancholy, miserable, morose, mournful, piteous, plaintive, sad, saturnine, somber, sorrowful, tearful, unhappy, weary, woebegone, woeful, wretched

LULL, ***noun*** abatement, armistice, break, breather, breathing spell, breathing time, brief silence, calm, calmness, cessation, cessation of activity, cessation of sound, desistance, discontinuance, discontinuation, halt, hush, idleness, inactivity, interlude, intermission, interregnum, interruption, pause, peace, period of rest, quiescence, quiescency, quiet, recess, remission, repose, respite, rest, silence, soundlessness, standstill, stay, stillness, stop, stoppage, subsidence, suspension, temporary quiet, temporary stillness, tranquillity, truce

LULL, ***verb*** allay, alleviate, assuage, calm, cause to relax, compose, cradle, dulcify, ease, encourage repose, hush, induce forgetfulness, make calm, mitigate, pacify, palliate, placate, put to rest, put to sleep, quell, quiet, quiet down, quieten, relax, remit, remove one's anxieties, remove one's fears, rock, *sedare,* settle, silence, soothe, still, stupefy, subdue, tranquilize

LUMP SUM PAYMENT, ***noun*** aggregate, bulk payment, conglomerate, congregate, entire funds due, payment at once, payment for all due, payment in bulk, payment in mass, total outstanding payment, total payment
ASSOCIATED CONCEPTS: awards, disability, divorce, employment termination, lump sum settlement

LUMP TOGETHER, ***verb*** admix, amalgamate, annex, append, attach, bind, blend, coalesce, cohere, commingle, commix, compound, conglomerate, conglutinate, conjoin, connect, consolidate, couple, entwine, fasten, form a union, fuse, glue, group, interblend, interfuse, interlink, intermix, link, meld, merge, mingle, mix, paste, piece together, put together indiscriminately, splice, tie, unify, unite
ASSOCIATED CONCEPTS: classifications, drawing new congressional lines, gerrymandering, lumping sale, reapportionment, redistricting

LUNACY, ***noun*** craziness, delusion, dementia, derangement, disordered mind, folly, foolishness, frenzy, impairment of mental faculties, insaneness, insanity, instability of mental powers, madness, mania, mental aberration, mental abnormality, mental dissociation, mental illness, mental imbalance, mental sickness, unsoundness of mind

LUNATIC, ***adjective*** absurd, bereft of reason, crazed, crazy, daft, dementate, demented, deranged, disordered, foolish, frenetic, frenzied, insane, insensate, irrational, mad, maniacal, manic, mentally aberrant, mentally ill, mentally unbalanced, nonsensical, obsessed, of unsound mind, out of one's mind, out of one's senses, possessed, raging, ranting, raving, reasonless, senseless, touched, unhinged, unsettled, wandering, wild

LURE, ***noun*** allure, attractive nuisance, bait, dangerous conditions, draw, endangerment, enticement, inducement, seducement, unprotected
ASSOCIATED CONCEPTS: attractive nuisance doctrine, specific conditions

LURE, ***verb*** *adlicere,* allure, attract, bait, beguile, bewitch, bribe, cajole, captivate, charm, coax, court, decoy, draw on, entice, hold out allurement, hold out temptation, induce, *inlicere,* inveigle, *pellicere,* provoke desire, seduce, tantalize, tempt

LURID, ***adjective*** appalling, *caliginosus,* coarse, disgusting, exaggerated, extreme, fulsome, ghastly, glaringly vivid, graphic, gross, gruesome, harsh, horrible, horrifying, indelicate, *luridus, obscurus,* offensive, overwhelming, racy, repulsive, revolting, risque, salacious, scabrous, scrofulous, sensational, shocking, startling, uncensored, unexpurgated, unusual, vulgar

LURK, ***verb*** ambuscade, be stealthy, be unseen, conceal oneself, crouch, *delitescere,* ensconce oneself, escape detection, escape notice, escape observation, escape recognition, hide, keep out of sight, *latere, latitare,* lie concealed, lie hidden, lie in ambush, lie in wait, lie low, move furtively, prowl, seclude oneself, secrete oneself, skulk, slink, sneak, steal

LUXURY, ***noun*** accessory, added comfort, added convenience, added creature toy, added enjoyment, added pleasure, added state-of-the-art edition, added technological advancement, advantage, delight, delightfulness, ease of comfort, extra, extravagance, frill, gadgetry, newest product, nicety, nonessential, option, physical pleasure
ASSOCIATED CONCEPTS: luxury tax

LUXATE, ***verb*** break, detach, disconnect, disengage, disjoin, disjoint, dislocate, dispart, displace, dissever, dissociate, disunite, eject, expel, part, put out of joint, put out of place, rend, rive, separate, sever, sunder, throw out of gear, unhinge, unjoint, wrench

LYING, ***adjective*** bluffing, covinous, cunning, deceitful, deceptive, delusive, delusory, devoid of truth, dishonest, disingenuous, dissembling, double-dealing, equivocating, fabricating, faithless, faked, false, feigned, fictitious, forsworn, fraudulent, mendacious, misleading, misrepresentative, perfidious, perjured, sneaky, spurious, treacherous, tricky, trumped up, truthless, uncandid, unfactual, untrue, untruthful, unveracious
ASSOCIATED CONCEPTS: perjury

LYNCH LAW, ***noun*** anarchy, blatant violation of law, breakdown of administration, disorderliness, flagrant abuse of the law, illegal infliction of punishment, lack of due process, lack of justice, lack of legal sanction, lawlessness, misgovernment, misrule, mob rule, mobocracy, nihilism, ochlocracy, outlawry, paralysis of authority, punishment without trial, reign of terror, summary punishment by mob, taking the law in one's own hands, terrorism, unruliness

MACABRE, ***adjective*** abhorrent, abominable, atrocious, awful, beneath contempt, contemptible, deplorable, despicable, detestable, dreadful, drive, foul, frightening, frightful, ghastly, ghoulish, gruesome, harrowing, hateful, heinous, horrendous, horrid, horrifying, indefensible, loathsome, obnoxious, odious, offensive, outrageous, pathetic, pitiful, repellent, reprehensible, repulsive, revolting, shameful, shocking, terrible, terrifying, unspeakable, vile, villainous, wholly inadequate
ASSOCIATED CONCEPTS: deplorable conditions

MACHIAVELLIAN, ***adjective*** arch, artful, base, cagey, calculating, canny, cheating, clever, collusive, collusory, conniving, conscienceless, contriving, corrupt, covinous, crafty, crooked, cunning, deceitful, deceiving, deceptive, delusive, designing, devious, dirty, dishonest, dishonorable, disingenuous, double-crossing, double-dealing, double-tongued, evasive, faithless, falsehearted, feline, foxy, fraudulent, guileful, hypocritical, ignoble, immoral, infamous, insidious, insincere, intriguing, knavish, mean, misdealing, opportunist, perfidious, plotting, rascally, roguish, scheming, shady, shameless, sharp, shifty, shrewd, slick, slippery, sly, smooth, sneaking, sneaky, stealthy, subdolous, tortuous, treacherous, trickish, tricky, two-faced, undependable, underhand, underhanded, unethical, unprincipled, unscrupulous, untrustworthy, untruthful, venal, vile, vulpine, wily

MACHINATION, ***noun*** artful dodge, artifice, cabal, collusion, conspiracy, contrivance, covin, crafty design, crafty device, crafty plan, design, dodge, *dolus,* foul play, intrigue, jugglery, *machina,* maneuver, manipulation, plot, ploy, ruse, scheme, stratagem, strategy, subterfuge, tactic, treachery, trick, underplot, wile, wily device

MACHINE, ***noun*** accessory, accoutrement, apparatus, appliance, automation, contraption, contrivance, device, engine, expedient, gear, implement, instrument, means, mechanism, piece of equipment, system, tool, utensil

MACHINERY *(Equipment),* ***noun*** apparatus, appurtenances, effects, equipment, facilities, heavy equipment, mechanism, products

MACHINERY *(Means),* ***noun*** contrivance, devices, guns, inner workings, instruments, means to implement, mechanism, mechanization, methods, organization, power, system, tools, vehicle, wherewithal, workings

MAD *(Absurd),* ***adjective*** absent-minded, anserine, apish, asinine, befooled, beguiled, bemused, besotted, bird-brained, brainless, buffoonish, careless, childish, clueless, confused, crackbrained, crazy, credulous, daft, dangerous, dazed, derisible, dizzy, doting, driveling, dull-witted, dumb, excessive, extravagant, fatuitous, fatuous, feebleminded, fond, fool, fool headed, foolish, for the birds, fuddled, futile, gaga, giddy, groundless, gulled, harebrained, harum-scarum, idiotic, ill-advised, ill-considered, illogical, ill-suited, imbecile, imbecilic, immature, impractical, improper, imprudent, inane, inappropriate, incoherent, incongruous, inconsistent, indiscreet, inept, infatuated, injudicious, insane, insensate, irrational, irresponsible, laughable, light-headed, light-minded, ludicrous, maudlin, moronic, muddled, muddlepated, nonsensical, perilous, pointless, preposterous, puerile, rambling, rash, reckless, ridiculous, risible, scatterbrained, senseless, sentimental, short-sighted, silly, simple-minded, spastic, stupid, thoughtless, unfounded, unreasonable, unsafe, unsensible, unsound, unwary, unwise, wandering, wet, wild-eyed, witless

MAD *(Insane),* ***adjective*** bereft of reason, deluded, demented, deprived of reason, deranged, idiosyncratic, insane, irrational, lunatic, manic, mentally deficient, non compos mentis, not of a sound mind, reasonless, senseless, unbalanced, unsound

MAD *(Irritated),* ***adjective*** abandoned, amok, angry, annoyed, at the end of one's rope, bellowing, berserk, beside oneself, blue in the face, carried away, chafed, delirious, demoniacal, demonic, displeased, distracted, drive one mad, ecstatic, enrage, enraged, enraptured, fed up, feral, ferocious, fierce, fiery, flaming, flared up, flaring, flushed with anger, frantic, frenzied, frenzy, frothing at the mouth, fulminating, fuming, furious, galled, haggard, hog-wild, howling, hysterical, in a huff, in a transport *or* ecstasy, in high dudgeon, in hysterics, incensed, indignant, inflamed, infuriate, infuriated, intoxicated, irate, ireful, lash into fury, madden, madding, make one's blood boil, maniac, maniacal, nettled, orgasmic, orgiastic, out of one's wits, peeved, piqued, possessed, rabid, raging, ramping, ranting, raving, ravished, ready to burst, red-hot, riled, roaring, running mad, storming, transported, uncontrollable, up in arms, vexed, violent, white-hot, wild, wild-eyed, wild-looking, work up into a passion, wrathful, wroth

MAELSTROM, ***noun*** bluster, bouleversement, cataclysm, commotion, disturbance, fervor, furor, fury, gulf, outbreak, outburst, pandemonium, paroxysm, squall, storm, tempest, tumult, upheaval, uproar, upset, vortex, whirlwind

MAGIC, ***adjective*** by chance occurrence, coincidental, fortunate, lucky, out of the ordinary, magical, miraculous, mystic, mystical, mysterious, occult, sorcery, supernatural, uncanny, under a charm, under a spell, unusual, wizardly, wonderful

MAGISTRATE, ***noun*** arbitrator, assessor, judge, jurist, justice, legist, *magistratus,* moderator, officer, official

MAGNANIMITY, ***noun*** altruism, beneficence, benevolence, charitable contributions, charity, chivalry, civility, community, compassion, cordiality, courtesy, dispensation, eleemosynary interests, empathy, fellowship, friendliness, generosity, grace, greatheartedness, honor, humaneness, kindliness, kindness, magnificence, mercy, neighborliness, nobility, philanthropy, selflessness, service, valor, worthiness

MAGNANIMOUS, ***adjective*** altruistic, benevolent, bighearted, brotherly, charitable, chivalrous, compassionate, exalted, fraternal, generous, generous to a fault, giving, great hearted, great spirited, high-minded, idealistic, kind, magnificent, noble, noble-minded, overly generous, philanthropic, princely, stately, sympathetic, unselfish
ASSOCIATED CONCEPTS: charitable organizations

MAGNATE, ***noun*** aristocrat, aristocratic, baron, big businessman, big gun, big name, bigwig, capitalist, captain of industry, celebrity, dignitary, director, distinguished person, enterpriser, entrepreneur, financier, giant, industrialist, leading figure, lion, lord, luminary, man of distinction, man of eminence, manager, name, noble, nobleman, person of eminence, person of importance, person of influence, personality, pillar of society, power, power elite, star, superstar, top executive, tycoon, very important person
ASSOCIATED CONCEPTS: industrial magnate

MAGNETIC, ***adjective*** absorbing, alluring, appealing, arresting, attracting, attractive, beguiling, bewitching, captivating, charismatic, charming, compelling, dynamic, effective, electric, electrical, enchanting, engaging, engrossing, enthralling, enticing, entrancing, exciting, fascinating, glamorous, grabbing, gripping, hypnotic, interesting, intriguing, inviting, irresistible, magnetized, mesmeric, mesmerizing, persuasive, potent, powerful, provocative, spellbinding, tantalizing, tempting, winning

MAGNIFICATION *(Enlargement),* ***noun*** amplification, augmentation, blowup, boost, buildup, elaboration, enhancement, enlargement, exaggeration, expansion, greatening, heighten, increase the size of, intensification, maximization, raising
ASSOCIATED CONCEPTS: magnification of damages

MAGNIFICATION *(Exaggeration),* ***noun*** amplification, augmentation, broadening, elaboration, enhancement, enlargement, expansion, extension, extremism, glorification, heightening, hyperbole, hyperbolism, inflation, overstatement, superlative

MAGNIFICENT, ***adjective*** august, awe-inspiring, beauteous, beautiful, brilliant, distinguished, elegant, exalted, excellent, exceptional, glorious, gorgeous, grand, great, handsome, imposing, impressive, lovely, luxurious, majestic, nice-looking, out of this world, outrageous, plush, posh, pretty, princely, radiant, regal, resplendent, royal, splendid, splendiferous, stately, sublime, superb, terrific

MAGNIFY, ***verb*** add to, aggrandize, *amplificare,* amplify, *augere,* augment, balloon, boost, broaden, build up, cause growth, deepen, emphasize, enhance, enlarge, *exaggerare,* exaggerate, exalt, expand, extend, glorify, heighten, idealize, increase, increase the size of, inflate, intensify, make great, make larger, make more important, maximize, overestimate, overprize, overrate, overstate, overstress, overvalue, play up, raise, spread, strengthen, stretch, stretch a point, swell, widen

MAGNITUDE, ***noun*** amplitude, *amplitudo,* bearing, concern, consequence, consideration, degree, dimension, effect, eminence, enormity, essentiality, extension, extent, gauge, gravity, immensity, import, importance, *magnitudo,* mark, materiality, materialness, measure, measurement, momentousness, precedence, primacy, priority, proportions, range, reach, scale, scope, seriousness, significance, size, span, *spatium,* stature, stretch, value, vastness, volume, weight, weightiness, worth

MAIL, ***noun*** envelope sent, formal communication sent, item sent, letter sent for delivery, message sent, note sent, package sent, package which is posted, postal matter, sent communication, sent correspondence, sent letter, sent packages, sent through regular means, sent through U.S. mail
ASSOCIATED CONCEPTS: mail matter

MAIM, ***verb*** cripple, damage, deface, disable, hobble, hurt, impair, incapacitate, injure, lame, make useless, mutilate, wound

MAIN FOCUS, ***noun*** cardinal feature, cardinal point, center, central idea, chief feature, chief issue, chief part, chief point, core, critical feature, critical point, crucial feature, crucial point, crux, essence, essential matter, essential part, essential point, essentialness, fundamental feature, fundamental part, fundamental point, gravamen, heart, implication, import, important feature, important part, important point, main force, main idea, major part, major portion, material point, meaning, nucleus, pivotal point, prime basis, prime ingredient, principal point, prominent aspect, prominent point, purport, quintessence, salient feature, salient point, significance, substance

MAIN FORCE, ***noun*** aggressiveness, brute force, compulsion, controlling force, controlling power, dominant strength, duress, effort, energy, forcefulness, full force, intensity, matchless effort, maxim effort, might, potence, potency, power, powerfulness, pressure, puissance, push, sheer force, sheer power, strength, toughness, unrivaled effort, utter force, vigor

MAIN POINT, ***noun*** backbone, base, basis, benchmark, *caput,* cardinal feature, cardinal point, center, central idea, chief feature, chief idea, chief issue, chief part, chief point, core, cornerstone, cream, crisis, critical feature, critical point, crucial feature, crucial point, crux, drift, elixir, essence, essential matter, essential part, essential point, essentialness, focal point, focus, force, fundamental feature, fundamental part, fundamental point, gist, gravamen, great point, heart, heart of the matter, implication, import, important feature, important part, important point, inner core, kernel, key, key point, keynote, keystone, lifeblood, main idea, main thing,

major part, marrow, material point, meaning, nub, nucleus, outstanding feature, pith, pivotal point, prime constituent, prime ingredient, prime issue, principal point, prominent aspect, prominent point, purport, quiddity, quintessence, real issue, *res summa,* root, salient feature, salient point, sense, significance, substance, tenor, vital concern
ASSOCIATED CONCEPTS: the main point in a legal argument

MAINLY, *adverb* above all, all in all, all things considered, chiefly, cardinally, consequentially, dominantly, effectively, essentially, exhaustive, first, foremost, in general, in the main, on balance, on the whole, overall, particularly, predominantly, preponderantly, prevailing, primarily, principally, usually

MAINSTAY, *noun* anchor, assurance, backbone, backer, bastion, brace, bulwark, buttress, champion, chief reliance, cornerstone, crutch, deliverance, dependence, foundation, help, keystone, maintainer, nucleus, pillar, principal backer, principal maintainer, principal support, principal supporter, principal sustainer, prop, rampart, reinforcement, reliance, right arm, right hand, salvation, security, staff, stay, strength, stronghold, support, sustainer, sustenance, tower of strength, upholder

MAINTAIN *(Carry on),* ***verb*** *adfirmare, confirmare, contendere,* continue, follow up, go on, keep alive, keep going, keep on, keep up, perpetuate, persevere, persist, proceed with, prolong, pursue, shore up, stick to

MAINTAIN *(Commence),* ***verb*** activate, begin, embark upon, initiate, institute, introduce, launch, originate, set in motion, set in operation, start, undertake
ASSOCIATED CONCEPTS: maintain an action

MAINTAIN *(Sustain),* ***verb*** abet, adhere, advocate, aid, assist, attend, be firm, be firmly fixed, bear up against, bolster, buttress, care for, champion, come to the defense of, conserve, countenance, cover, defend, espouse the cause of, feed, finance, guard, hold up, justify, look after, make provision, make safe, nourish, nurse, nurture, oversee, preserve, protect, provide for, rally to, safeguard, save, screen, secure, see to, service, shelter, shield, shoulder, side with, stand by, stand firm, stand one's ground, stick to, subscribe to, subsidize, substantiate, supply, support, take care of, take charge of, uphold, vindicate, watch over, weather

MAINTENANCE *(Support of spouse),* ***noun*** aid, alimony, allowance, assistance, financial backing, financing, legal assistance, legal support, means of subsistence, monetary help, necessaries, necessities of life, preservation, provisions, subsidy, subsistence, sustenance, upkeep, *victus*
ASSOCIATED CONCEPTS: separate maintenance, support and maintenance

MAINTENANCE *(Upkeep),* ***noun*** care, carrying charge, *conservatio,* conservation, cost, disbursement, drain on resources, expenditure, expense, outlay, overhead, repair, running expenses, *salus,* service
ASSOCIATED CONCEPTS: ordinary maintenance and repair, reasonable maintenance

MAJESTIC, *adjective* aristocratic, august, awe-inspiring, baronial, classic, courtly, exquisite, fine, gallant, genteel, glorious, graceful, grand, grandeur, grandiose, handsome, inspiring, lavish, luxurious, magnificent, noble, ornate, ostentatious, patrician, prominent, refined, rich, royal, significant, sophisticated, splendid, stately, tasteful

MAJOR, *adjective* big, chief, comprehensive, consequential, considerable, crucial, decisive, distinguished, enormous, essential, extensive, extraordinary, far-reaching, fateful, goodly, grave, great, high-level, important, imposing, impressive, intense, key, large, leading, massive, matchless, material, memorable, meritorious, moderately large, momentous, notable, noteworthy, outstanding, paramount, ponderous, pressing, prime, principal, remarkable, serious, significant, sizable, sober, solemn, substantial, supreme, top, top-level, tremendous, unparalleled, vital, weighty, worthy of consideration, worthy of remark

MAJORITY *(Adulthood),* ***noun*** age of discretion, age of majority, age of responsibility, full age, full legal age, legal age, legal competence, legal maturity, manhood, matureness, maturity, voting age, womanhood
FOREIGN PHRASES: ***Minor ante tempus agere non potest in casu proprietatis nec etiam convenire.*** A minor under age cannot act in a case of property.

MAJORITY *(Greater part),* ***noun*** better part, biggest share, body, bulk, generality, greater number, larger number, larger part, lion's share, main body, main part, *maior numerus, maior pars,* major part, mass, more than half, most, plurality, predominance, predominant part, preponderance, preponderation, principal part, weight of numbers
ASSOCIATED CONCEPTS: majority rule, majority vote, plurality, quorum, requisite majority

MAKE, *verb* accomplish, achieve, actualize, assemble, attain, author, beget, bring about, bring forth, bring into being, bring into existence, bring to effect, bring to pass, build, call into being, call into existence, carry into effect, carry into execution, cast, cause, cause to exist, coin, compel, complete, compose, compound, concoct, constitute, constrain, construct, contrive, *creare,* create, develop, devise, draft, draw up, effect, effectuate, efform, enact, enforce, engender, erect, establish, evolve, execute, *fabricari,* fabricate, *facere,* fashion, force, forge, form, formulate, frame, generate, give birth to, give origin to, give rise to, hammer out, hatch, have in production, improvise, initiate, institute, invent, kindle, machine, manufacture, model, mold, organize, originate, pattern, perform, piece together, prepare, produce, provide, put together, set up, shape, synthesize, think up, turn out, yield results
ASSOCIATED CONCEPTS: make a decision, make a demand, make a motion, make an agreement, make an offer

MAKE A DEMAND, *verb* announce a sum demanded, ask for recompense, assert a legal right for damages, conduct negotiations, demand compensation, impose a claim, impose a peremptory claim, impose a requirement, make a financial claim, make an authoritative request for damages, request compensation, serve an ultimatum, state a claim, state a requisite sum as damages, state an amount in question, state an imperative

MAKE A FINDING, *verb* adjudge, adjudicate, announce a conclusion, arrive at a conclusion, ascertain, ascertain by judicial inquiry, calculate, come to a conclusion, conclude, decide, deduce, deliver, determine, draw a conclusion, establish, hold, judge, make a decision, pass judgment, pronounce, resolve, rule

MAKE A MOTION, *verb* apply, ask for, make a formal application, make a request, make application, move, offer for more consideration, petition, propose formally, put forth, put forward, request, requisition, submit

MAKE A REBUTTAL, ***verb*** answer, argue, argue against, confute, contradict, contravene, controvert, countercharge, counterclaim, deny, disagree, disprove, dispute, join issue, negate, oppose, present arguments against, rebuff, rebut, refute, rejoin, reply, repudiate, respond, retaliate, retort, submit arguments against, surrebut, surrejoin, take a stand against
ASSOCIATED CONCEPTS: rebut an argument, rebuttal case, surrebuttal.

MAKE A STATEMENT, ***verb*** affirm, allege, argue, assert positively, asseverate, attest, authenticate, aver, avouch, avow, bear, certify, claim, confirm, contend, converse, declare, explain, express, formulate, maintain, present, proclaim, profess, pronounce, propose, purport, report, speak, state, validate, verify, warrant
ASSOCIATED CONCEPTS: closing statement, statement to the jury

MAKE AN ARGUMENT, ***verb*** advance, allege, argue, assert, challenge, claim, confute, contend, contest, controvert, debate, disagree, dispute, elucidate, emphasize, enunciate, establish, explain, expostulate, express, maintain, oppose, present arguments against, present arguments for, proclaim, pronounce, propose, propound, put forth, put forward, remonstrate, set forth, show, state with conviction, stress, submit, urge
ASSOCIATED CONCEPTS: arguments contained in a submission, oral argument

MAKE APPLICATION, ***verb*** appeal, appeal for, apply, bid, bid for, call for, demand, file for, make formal request, move, obsecrate, petition, petition for, put in for, request, seek, solicit
ASSOCIATED CONCEPTS: make application for a directed verdict, make application for costs, make application for substitution of counsel, make application for summary judgment

MAKE CERTAIN, ***verb*** accomplish, achieve, acquire, affect, attain, complete, conclude, consummate, determine, earn, effectuate, end, ensure, execute, finish, get done, get it over with, guarantee, influence, leave no stone unturned, make absolutely certain, make absolutely definite, make definite, make unequivocal, perfect in detail, procure, put the finishing touches on, realize, reap, seal, secure, settle, take every step necessary, take no conceivable chance, win

MAKE CLEAR, ***verb*** articulate, bare, bring to light, clear up, comment upon, construe, decipher, define, delineate, demonstrate, disentangle, elucidate, enlighten, exemplify, explain, explicate, expose, exposit, expound, free from ambiguity, free from confusion, illuminate, illustrate, interpret, lay open, make comprehensible, make explicit, make intelligible, make lucid, make understood, refine, render intelligible, shed light on, show, simplify, spell out, subtilize, unfold, unmask, unravel, unscramble, unveil
ASSOCIATED CONCEPTS: plain language

MAKE INROADS, ***verb*** ameliorate a situation, be light years ahead, become better, develop, enhance, enrich, expand, forge ahead, gain, gain ground, get strides ahead, go forward, grow, improve, increase, make advancements, make headway, make progress, make quantum leaps, meliorate, mend, move ahead, move onward, press on, proceed, prosper, push on, progress
ASSOCIATED CONCEPTS: investigations

MAKE KNOWN, ***verb*** acknowledge, admit, advise, affirm, announce, apprise, bare, blurt out, break the news, bring to light, circulate, communicate, concede, confess, confide, confirm, declare, describe, disabuse, disclose, display, disseminate, divulge, enlighten, evince, explain, expose, give currency to, give inside information, impart, indicate, inform, make public, make publicly known, manifest, mention, notify, off, open, promulgate, publish, set right, tell, uncloak, uncover, unearth, unfold, unmask, unseal, unveil, utter, vent, verify, voice
ASSOCIATED CONCEPTS: confidentiality, grand jury secrecy, privilege

MAKE LEGAL, ***verb*** approve by law, authorize by law, bring into conformity with the law, confirm by law, decree by law, enact by statute, enact into law, legalize, legislate, legitimatize by law, make lawful, order by law, pass into law, permit by law, pronounce by statute, ratify, sanction by common law, sanction by law, sanction by the judiciary, validate

MAKE NULL AND VOID, ***verb*** abolish, abrogate, annul, cancel, declare not binding, declare of no effect, declare of no legal authority, declare of no legal effect, declare of no legal force, declare of no validity, declare without legal authority, defeat, disestablish, end, eradicate, extinguish, fail to consummate, make defunct, negate, nullify, obliterate, omit, overrule, overturn, quash, render forceless, render impotent, render ineffective, render inefficacious, render inoperative, render invalid, repeal, rescind, reverse, revoke, set aside, supersede, suspend, terminate, vacate, void, withdraw
ASSOCIATED CONCEPTS: annulment, declare a marriage null and void, law superseded and null and void

MAKE PROGRESS, ***verb*** advance, ameliorate, approach, ascend, climb, complete, continue onward, develop, enhance, enrich, expand, finish, forge ahead, gain, gain ground, get ahead, get results, go forward, go on, grow, improve, increase, keep going, keep moving, make headway, meliorate, mend, mount, move on, press on, proceed, prosper, ripen, rise

MAKE RESTITUTION, ***verb*** atone, compensate, indemnify, make amends, make whole, pay, pay back, pay damages, provide legal redress, recompense, refund, reimburse, remit, remunerate, repay, return, reward, satisfy an obligation, settle
ASSOCIATED CONCEPTS: criminal restitution law, law of restitution, legal remedies

MAKE VOID, ***verb*** annul, cancel, declare not binding, declare null and void, declare of no force, declare useless, declare without legal force, determine not in force, extinguish, make ineffective, make ineffectual, make inoperative, make meaningless, nullify
ASSOCIATED CONCEPTS: void for vagueness, void where prohibited by law, voidable

MAKER, ***noun*** author, devisor, donor, initiator, producer
ASSOCIATED CONCEPTS: maker of a note, maker of an instrument

MALADMINISTRATION, ***noun*** bad job, blunder, botchery, bungling, default, dereliction of duty, evasion of duty, failure of duty, incompetency, inefficiency, inefficient management, malfeasance, malversation, misadministration, misapplication, misconduct, misdirection, misfeasance, misgovernment, misguidance, mishandling, mismanagement, misrule, neglect, negligence, poor administration, *prava rerum administratio,* unproficiency, want of duty

MALADROIT, *adjective* awkward, botched, bungling, callow, clumsy, fumbled, gauche, graceless, handless, heavy-hand, ill-equipped, inapt, incapable, incompetent, inept, inexpert, uncoordinated, unfit, unhandy, unprepared, unqualified, unskilled, unskillful, untrained, useless

MALADY, *noun* abnormality, affliction, ailment, defect, deformity, desperate condition, disability, disease, disorder, handicap, health difficulty, health problem, illness, impairment, infirmity, medical condition, sickness, syndrome, weakness

MALAPROPOS, *adjective* amiss, awkward, clumsy, graceless, improper, inapposite, inappropriate, inapt, incongruous, incorrect, indecorous, infelicitous, malapropos, out of place, perverse, unbecoming, unfit, unhappy, unseemly, unsuitable, untoward, wrong

MALCONTENT, *noun* agitator, anarchist, ardent champion of change, brawler, caviler, censurer, complainant, complainer, critic, crusader, demonstrator, detractor, diehard, disputer, dissenter, dissentient, dissident, extremist, fanatic, faultfinder, fighter, fretter, griper, grumbler, heretic, *homo rerum novarum cupidus,* instigator, insubordinate, insurgent, insurrectionist, kicker, mutineer, nihilist, nonconformist, noncooperator, objector, obstructionist, petitioner, political agitator, protester, rabble-rouser, radical, reactionary, reactionist, rebel, recusant, reformer, renegade, repiner, resister, revisionist, revolter, revolutionary, revolutionist, rioter, seditionary, seditionist, traitor, troublemaker, whiner, wrangler

MALEDICTION, *noun* abusive speech, anathema, curse, damnation, defamation, denunciation, *dirae,* dispraise, evil-speaking, execration, *exsecratio,* foul language, fulmination, ill wishes, imprecation, invective, malevolence, malison, obloquy, revilement, tongue-lashing, verbal abuse, verbal assault, verbal attack, vilification, vituperation

MALEFACTION, *noun* abomination, atrocity, breach, contravention, crime, encroachment, evil deed, felony, harm, horror, hurt, illegal act, infringement, malfeasance, malpractice, misdeed, offense, outrage, tort, transgression, violation, wrong, wrongdoing

MALEFACTOR, *noun* bandit, brigand, convict, criminal, culprit, delinquent, desperado, evildoer, felon, gangster, hardened criminal, *homo maleficus, homo sceleratus,* hoodlum, hooligan, lawbreaker, lawless individual, mischief-maker, miscreant, misdemeanant, offender, offender against the law, outlaw, racketeer, rapscallion, rascal, recidivist, reprobate, rogue, ruffian, scamp, scoundrel, transgressor, trespasser, villain, violator of laws, wrongdoer

MALEFIC, *adjective* antagonistic, antipathetic, bad, baleful, calamitous, corrupt, deadly, deleterious, destructive, incompetent, inept, inimical, injurious, malicious, malignant, noxious, pernicious, pestilential, poisonous, ruinous, venomous, wicked

MALEFICENT, *adjective* antagonistic, baleful, baneful, deleterious, detrimental, diabolic, evil, evil-disposed, evil-intentioned, evil-minded, harmful, heinous, hostile, hurtful, ill-natured, inimical, injurious, invidious, lethal, malefic, malevolent, malicious, malignant, merciless, noxious, obnoxious, odious, offensive, oppressive, perfidious, pernicious, ruthless, surly, vicious
FOREIGN PHRASES: ***Maleficia propositis distinguuntur.*** Evil deeds are to be distinguished from evil purposes.

MALEVOLENCE, *noun* abomination, acerbity, acrimony, actively opposed, adverse, aggressive, animosity, antagonism, antagonistic, antipathetical, belligerence, bitterness, contempt, cruelty, devilishness, diabolicalness, disdain, embitterment, enmity, evil, evil-mindedness, full of hate, full of malice, grudge, harshness, hate, hatefulness, hostility, hurtfulness, ill will, iniquitousness, injuriousness, invidiousness, ire, lethalness, malice, maliciousness, malignance, malignity, meanness, mercilessness, odium, perfidiousness, perniciousness, pique, pitilessness, rancor, repugnance, resentfulness, resentment, spite, treacherousness, vengeance, venom, venomousness, viciousness, virulence, vitriol

MALEVOLENT, *adjective* acrimonious, actively opposed, adverse, aggressive, antagonistic, antipathetic, antipathetical, baleful, baneful, barbarous, bellicose, belligerent, bilious, bitter, bloodthirsty, brutal, churlish, cold, cold-blooded, conspiratorial, cruel, damaging, deadly, deleterious, demoniac, demoniacal, demonial, despiteful, devilish, diabolic, diabolical, disaffected, disobliging, embittered, envenomed, evil, evil-minded, faithless, ferocious, feuding, fiendish, full of hate, full of malice, full of revenge, full of spite, galling, grim, grudgeful, grudging, hard-hearted, harmful, harsh, hateful, heinous, hellish, hostile, hurtful, ill-disposed, ill-intentioned, ill-natured, ill-wishing, implacable, infamous, infernal, iniquitous, injurious, invidious, lethal, malefic, maleficent, *malevolus,* malicious, malign, malignant, mean, merciless, mischievous, oppugnant, perfidious, pernicious, pitiless, plotting, poisonous, rancorous, repugnant, resentful, retaliative, retaliatory, revengeful, ruinous, ruthless, satanic, savage, scatheful, sinister, snaky, spiteful, spleenful, treacherous, truculent, unamicable, unfeeling, unfriendly, unkind, venomous, vicious, villainous, vindictive, viperous, virulent, vitriolic, warlike, wicked

MALFEASANCE, *noun* bad conduct, corruption, dereliction, deviation from rectitude, ill conduct, illegal action, infringement, injurious action, misbehavior, misdeed, misdoing, misgovernment, mismanagement, overstepping, peccadillo, peccancy, transgression, unjust performance, unlawful action, wrongful action, wrongful conduct
ASSOCIATED CONCEPTS: malfeasance in office, malfeasance of a public officer, misconduct, misfeasance, nonfeasance

MALFEASANT, *noun* a corrupt person, a derelict person, a person with wrongful actions, a person with wrongful conduct, an actor with ill conduct, an individual whose conduct deviates from rectitude, an individual with bad conduct, an individual with illegal actions, an individual with misbehavior, an individual with unjust actions, an individual with unlawful actions, a person with misdeeds, a person with transgressions, criminal, defendant, felon, lawbreaker, malefactor, miscreant, offender, reprobate, rogue, transgressor, wrongdoer
ASSOCIATED CONCEPTS: impeachment, malfeasance in office

MALFEASOR, *noun* accused, bad actor, convict, corrupter, criminal, culprit, delinquent, felon, immoralist, lawbreaker, miscreant, misdemeanant, misdoer, offender, outlaw, perpetrator, racketeer, reprobate, sinner, suspect, transgressor, trespasser, villain, wrongdoer

MALFUNCTION, *noun* abnormality, anomaly, breakdown, bug, defect, deviation, disorder, error, failure, fault, flaw, glitch, hitch, impairment, irregularity, malformation, misfire, mishap, miss, mistake, problem, technological problem

MALICE, *noun* acrimony, active ill will, animosity, animus, antagonism, antipathy, aversion, bad intent, bad intention, bitter animosity, conscious violation of law, contempt, culpable recklessness, detestation, disaffection, dislike, enmity, evil disposition, evil intent, hard feelings, hard-heartedness, harmful desire, hate, hatred, hostility, ill feeling, ill will, intentional wrongdoing, *invidia,* invidiousness, loathing, malevolence, *malevolentia,* maliciousness, *malignitas,* malignity, odium, personal hatred, pique, pitilessness, rancor, rankling, repugnance, repulsion, resentment, spite, spitefulness, umbrage, venom, viciousness, violent animosity, wanton disregard, wrath
ASSOCIATED CONCEPTS: actual malice, constructive malice, implied malice, legal malice, malice aforethought, malice in fact, malice in law, malicious abandonment, malicious abuse of process, malicious arrest, malicious injury, malicious intent, malicious mischief, malicious prosecution, malicious use, malicious wrong, universal malice
FOREIGN PHRASES: ***In criminalibus, sufficit generalis malitia intentionis, cum facto paris gradus.*** In crimes, a general malicious intent suffices where there is an act of equal degree. ***Malitia est acida; est mali animi affectus.*** Malice is sour; it is the quality of an evil mind. ***Maleficia propositis distinguuntur.*** Evil deeds are distinguished by their evil purposes. ***Malitiis hominum est obviandum.*** The malicious designs of men must be thwarted. ***Eum qui nocentem infamat, non est aequum et bonum ob eam rem condemnari; delicta enim nocentium nota esse oportet et expedit.*** It is not just and proper that he who speaks ill of a bad man should be condemned on that account; for it is fitting and expedient that the crimes of bad men be made known. ***Malum non praesumitur.*** Evil is not presumed.

MALICE AFTERTHOUGHT, *noun* bent, criminal intent, devices, intention, objective, plan, plot, preconceived action, preconceived plan, predetermination, preplanned action, pretension, purpose, resolution, resolve, scheme
ASSOCIATED CONCEPTS: commission of a crime, intent

MALICIOUS, *adjective* acrimonious, antagonistic, brutal, cruel, demoniac, demoniacal, destructive, diabolic, diabolical, evil, evil-minded, feral, ferocious, harmful, hateful, hostile, ill-disposed, ill-natured, invidious, *invidus,* malefic, maleficent, maleficial, malevolent, *malevolus,* malignant, merciless, mischievous, ornery, pernicious, relentless, resentful, ruthless, savage, spiteful, treacherous, truculent, unfeeling, venemous, vicious, vindictive, virulent, wanton, wicked
ASSOCIATED CONCEPTS: malicious mischief, malicious prosecution
FOREIGN PHRASES: ***Malitiis hominum est obviandum.*** The malicious designs of men must be thwarted.

MALICIOUS PROSECUTION, *noun* indefensible prosecution, Kafka-like prosecution, malicious charges instituted by a prosecutor, malicious criminal enforcement, malicious pursuit by a law enforcement agency, prosecution maintained with venal intentions, prosecution without proper procedures, reprehensible prosecution, unconscionable prosecution, unconstitutional prosecution, underhanded prosecution, unfair prosecution, unjust and unfair pursuit of criminal charges, unjustifiable prosecution, unmerited prosecution, unprincipled prosecution, unscrupulous prosecution, unwarrantable prosecution, wrongful prosecution

MALIGN, *verb* abuse, anathematize, asperse, attack, attack the reputation of, besmirch, blaspheme, bring into discredit, calumniate, cast a slur upon, cast aspersions, curse, decry, defame, defile, denigrate, denounce, deprecate, derogate, disesteem, dishonor, dishonor by false reports, disparage, dispraise, falsify, fulminate against, impugn, libel, revile, ridicule, slander, slur, smear, smirch, speak evil of, speak ill of, spread an evil report, stain one's reputation, traduce, vilify, vilipend, vituperate

MALIGNANT, *adjective* atrocious, baleful, baneful, barbarous, bitter, blackhearted, bloodthirsty, brutal, brutish, cancerous, caustic, cold-blooded, coldhearted, consuming, corrosive, cruel, damaging, dangerous, deadly, death-bringing, death-dealing, deathly, deleterious, demoniacal, despiteful, destructive, detrimental, devilish, diabolical, envenomed, evil, evil-minded, execrable, fatal, fell, feral, ferocious, fiendish, fiendlike, flint-hearted, foul, hard of heart, harmful, hateful, heinous, hellish, hostile, hurtful, ill-intentioned, infernal, inhuman, iniquitous, injurious, insalubrious, invidious, lethal, malefic, maleficent, malevolent, malicious, malign, marble-hearted, mephitic, miasmal, miasmatic, miasmatical, monstrous, morbid, morbiferous, morbific, morbifical, mordacious, murderous, nasty, nefarious, nocuous, noisome, noxious, oppressive, peccant, pernicious, persecuting, pestiferous, pestilential, poisonous, rancorous, resentful, revengeful, ruinous, ruthless, satanic, savage, scatheful, scurrilous, sinful, sinister, spiteful, spleenful, stonyhearted, tending to cause death, toxic, toxiferous, treacherous, truculent, unmerciful, venomous, vicious, vile, villainous, vindictive, violent, virulent, virulently inimical, vitriolic, wicked

MALLEABLE, *adjective* accommodating, acquiescent, adaptable, adjustable, agreeable, amenable, amiable, bendable, compliant, conformable, conforming, controllable, deferential, docile, ductile, *ductilis,* easily bent, easily influenced, easily persuaded, easy, easygoing, elastic, flexible, flexile, following, formable, governable, impressionable, *lentus,* limber, lissome, lithe, lithesome, manageable, meek, moldable, moldable like putty, moldable like wax, *mollis,* obliging, plastic, pliable, pliant, soft, softened, spineless, stretchable, submissive, tame, teachable, tractable, twistable, usable, weak like putty, weak-minded, weak-willed, well-behaved, willing, yielding

MALPRACTICE, *noun* breach of practice, breach of profession, carelessness, culpable professional neglect, dereliction of duty, improper professional action, improper professional conduct, injudicious treatment, injurious treatment by a professional, misconduct, professional error of judgment, professional laxness, professional misconduct, professional neglect, professional negligence, unprofessional conduct, unprofessional treatment, violation of professional code, violation of professional duty
ASSOCIATED CONCEPTS: legal malpractice, medical malpractice, professional malpractice

MALTREAT, *verb* abuse, assail, ill-treat, ill-use, mishandle, mistreat, oppress, persecute

MALVERSATION, *noun* abuse, bad repute, crime, criminality, delinquency, dereliction, evil, immorality, impropriety, malfeasance, malpractice, misbehavior, mischief, misconduct, misdemeanor, naughtiness, offense, transgression, wrongdoing

MAMMOTH, *adjective* as high as the sky, astronomical, colossal, enormous, gargantuan, gigantic, great, huge, immense, large, massive, monstrous, mountainous, thundering, towering, tremendous, up to the sky, vast, walloping

MANAGE, *verb* administer, *administrare,* administrate, be in power, boss, care for, carry on, command, conduct, control, cope with, dictate, direct, disburse, dominate, engineer, execute, exercise authority, govern, guide, handle, have control, have under command, head, keep in order, lead, look after, maneuver, manipulate, master, mastermind, occupy the chair, officiate, operate, order, oversee, pilot, preside, preside over, *regere,* regiment, regulate, rule, run, see to, steer, subjugate, superintend, supervise, sway, take charge of, take over, *tractare,* transact, treat, wield authority, work

MANAGEABLE, *adjective* able to be completed, able to be finished, controllable, capable of completing, capable of finishing, doable, operable, performable, under control, workable
ASSOCIATED CONCEPTS: judicially manageable standards

MANAGED CARE, *noun* controlled medical panel, supervised medical care, supervised medical panel
Generally: health care system

MANAGEMENT *(Directorate),* ***noun*** administration, administrators, advisors, authority, board, board of directors, bureau, bureaucracy, caretakers, central office, chair, chairmen, command, committee, controllers, custodians, decision-making body, directors, directorship, executive committee, executive office, executives, front office, generals, governing body, government, headmen, headquarters, leaders, leadership, officers, officials, party in power, power, presidency, presidium, regime, steering committee, stewards, strategists, superintendents, supervisors

MANAGEMENT *(Judicious use),* ***noun*** conduct, cunning practice, dealing, disposal, economic use, employment, finesse, frugality, handling, manipulation, operation, prudent conduct, running, skillful treatment, steerage, thrifty use, treatment, usage, utilization

MANAGEMENT *(Supervision),* ***noun*** *administratio,* administration, administrators, authority, board of directors, care, charge, command, control, controllers, *cura,* direction, directorate, directors, directorship, executive arm, executives, generalship, governance, guidance, leadership, managers, managership, oversight, pilotage, protectorship, regulation, steering, stewardship, superintendence, surveillance, *tractatio,* wardship
ASSOCIATED CONCEPTS: exclusive management, fraud in management, general management, management of one's affairs, management of property

MANDAMUS, *noun* charge, command, decree, dictate, direct, legislate, order, rule
ASSOCIATED CONCEPTS: writ of mandamus

MANDATE, *noun* authoritative command, authoritative order, behest, bid, canon, charge, command, command by the court, commandment, decree, decretal, dictate, dictation, direction, directive, edict, enactment, fiat, imperative, instruction, judicial command, judicial decree, judicial order, *mandatum,* order, precept, prescript, prescription, proscription, regulation, request, requirement, requisition, rule, ruling, ultimatum, written order
ASSOCIATED CONCEPTS: judicial mandate, legislative mandate, mandate of the court
FOREIGN PHRASES: ***Rei turpis nullum mandatum est.*** The mandate of an immoral thing is void. ***Cui jurisdictio data est, ea quoque concessa esse videntur, sine quibus jurisdictio explicari non potest.*** To whom jurisdiction is given, those things also are held to be granted, without which the jurisdiction cannot be exercised.

MANDATORY, *adjective* binding, bounden, called for, coercive, commanded, commanding, compulsory, crucial, decreed, demanded, essential, exigent, imperative, incumbent on, indispensable, involuntary, necessary, necessitated, necessitous, obligatory, ordained, peremptory, prerequisite, prescribed, pressing, required, requisite, unavoidable, urgent, vital, without appeal, without choice
ASSOCIATED CONCEPTS: mandatory injunction, mandatory relief, mandatory sentence, mandatory statutory provisions

MANDATORY MINIMUM SENTENCE, *noun* mandatory minimum, mandatory sentencing laws, minimum jail term, minimum number of years in prison, nondiscretionary minimum, obligatory minimum term of imprisonment, set sentencing requirements
ASSOCIATED CONCEPTS: fixed sentence, forced sentence

MANEUVER *(Tactic),* ***noun*** approach, course of conduct, *decursio, decursus,* device, line of action, management, manipulation, mode of procedure, move, operation, plan of attack, planned campaign, procedure, scheme, stratagem, strategy, stroke, undertaking

MANEUVER *(Trick),* ***noun*** artful dodge, artifice, *artificium,* chicanery, circumvention, cozenage, crafty device, cunning contrivance, deception, decoy, design, device, dodge, *dolus,* feint, fraud, fraudulent expedient, hoax, legerdemain, machination, plot, ruse, scheme, sharp practice, sleight, stratagem, subterfuge, trap, underhanded act, wile

MANEUVER, *verb* arrange, be in collusion, brew, cabal, cheat, collude, complot, concoct, connive, conspire, contrive, countermine, counterplot, deploy, design, devise, engineer, *evagari,* form a plot, frame, intrigue, jockey, lay plans, machinate, make a plan, make arrangements, manage, move, plan, plan strategy, plot, prearrange, proceed by stratagem, scheme, shift, take steps, trick, work out

MANIC, *adjective* agitated, aroused, enraged, excited, frantic, frenzied, hyped-up, hyper, hyperactive, hysterical, incensed, inflamed, nervous, out of control, perturbed, stirred-up, worked-up, wrought-up
ASSOCIATED CONCEPTS: insanity defense

MANIFEST, *adjective* *apertus,* apparent, avowed, bald, bare, beholdable, blatant, clear, clear-cut, conspicuous, crying, crystal clear, defined, discernible, disclosed, distinct, easy to see, *evidens,* evident, explicit, exposed, express, eye-catching, flagrant, glaring, gross, identifiable, in bold relief, in evidence, in focus, in full view, in sight, in the foreground, in view, indisputable, indubitable, insuppressible, lucid, marked, naked, not concealed, not obscure, notable, noticeable, observable, obvious, open, ostensible, overt, palpable, patent, perceivable, perceptible, perspicuous, *perspicuus,* plain, prominent, pronounced, public, recognizable, revealed, salient, seeable, showable, standing out, sticking out, striking, tangible, transparent, unclouded, unconcealed, uncontestable, undisguised, unhidden, unmistakable, unquestionable, visible, well-defined, well-marked, well-seen
ASSOCIATED CONCEPTS: manifest danger, manifest error, manifest necessity, manifest peril

MANIFEST, *verb* air, *aperire,* attest, bare, be evidence of, bespeak, betoken, bring forth, bring forward, bring into the

open, bring out, bring to light, bring to notice, bring to the front, bring to view, certify, *declarare,* declare, demonstrate, denote, designate, disclose, discover, display, divulge, evidence, evince, exhibit, explain, expose, expose to view, express, hold up, hold up to view, illuminate, illustrate, impart, indicate, lay bare, lay open, lay out, make clear, make conspicuous, make evident, make known, make obvious, make plain, make visible, mark, open, open up, point out, present, proclaim, prove, publish, represent, reveal, set forth, set out, show, signify, speak out, testify, throw open, unconceal, uncover, uncurtain, undrape, unearth, unfold, unmask, unscreen, unshroud, unveil
FOREIGN PHRASES: ***In rebus manifestis, errat qui auctoritates legum allegat; quia perspicua vera non sunt probanda.*** In clear cases, he mistakes who cites legal authorities; for obvious truths are not to be proved. ***Manifesta probatione non indigent.*** Manifest facts do not require proof.

MANIFESTATION, *noun* appearance, badge, *declaratio, demonstratio,* demonstration, disclosure, discovery, display, divulgence, emblem, emergence, evidence, evincement, exhibit, exhibition, expose, exposition, exposure, expression, indication, *indicium,* mark, materialization, production, representation, revelation, show, showing, sign, signal, signification, symbol, symptom, uncovering, unfolding, unmasking, unveiling
ASSOCIATED CONCEPTS: manifestation of intent

MANIFOLD, *adjective* assorted, considerable, divers, diverse, diversified, innumerable, many, miscellaneous, multifarious, multifold, multiform, multiple, *multiplex,* multiplicate, multitudinous, myriad, numerous, populous, profuse, several, sundry, teeming, variegated, various, *varius*

MANIPULATE *(Control unfairly),* ***verb*** dominate, exploit, influence, manage, misuse, pull strings, pull wires, rig, rule, take advantage of, use

MANIPULATE *(Utilize skillfully),* ***verb*** apply, command, conduct, control, direct, drive, employ, engineer, govern, guide, handle, lead, make use of, maneuver, operate, pilot, ply, put in action, put into operation, regulate, run, set in motion, set to work, steer, *tractare,* use, utilize, wield, work

MANIPULATION, *noun* change, control, dominate, employment, execution, exercise, exploitation, finagling, governance, handling, influence, machination, management, maneuvering, maneuvers, plotting, ploy, regulation, scheming, take advantage of
ASSOCIATED CONCEPTS: manipulation of security prices, market manipulation law

MANNER *(Behavior),* ***noun*** actions, acts, address, air, appearance, approach, aspect, attitude, bearing, behavior pattern, carriage, comportment, conduct, consuetude, course of action, course of conduct, custom, customary procedure, decorum, demeanor, deportment, distinctive social attitude, etiquette, fashion, guise, habit, habitual practice, line of action, line of conduct, look, method, method of action, mien, mode, mode of proceeding, observance, operation, pattern, personal bearing, personal style, port, posture, practice, praxis, presence, procedure, proceeding, routine, stance, style, tactics, tone, usage, way, wise, wont

MANNER *(Kind),* ***noun*** brand, categorization, category, class, classification, denomination, description, designation, division, fashion, form, grouping, ilk, kind, make, order, selection, sort, species, style, type, variety

MANNERISM, *noun* affectation, attitude, attribute, characteristic, custom, disposition, distinct quality, eccentricity, habit, inclination, individualism, mark, nature, oddity, pattern, peculiarity, practice, quirk, singularity, tendency, tic, trait

MANNERS, *noun* bearing, behavior, civilities, conduct, convention, courtesy, custom, decorum, delicateness, demeanor, deportment, etiquette, fashion, form, formalities, mien, mode, pleasantries, poise, politeness, politesse, proprieties, protocol, style, ways

MANSLAUGHTER, *noun* accidental homicide, homicide, *homicidium, hominis caedes,* killing, murder, reckless homicide, unintentional homicide, unintentional murder, unpremeditated murder
ASSOCIATED CONCEPTS: involuntary manslaughter, killing in the heat of passion, second-degree manslaughter, voluntary manslaughter

MANUAL, *adjective* by hand, by use of the hands, each one, hand-operated, not automated, not automatic, old-fashioned, one-at-a-time, one-by-one, without technology
ASSOCIATED CONCEPTS: manual labor, manual rates

MANUAL, *noun* comprehensive book, exercise book, guidebook, handbook, how-to book, reference book, standard, step-by-step analysis, text, textbook
ASSOCIATED CONCEPTS: buyer's manual

MANUFACTURE, *noun* assemblage, assembly, composition, construction, creation, development, execution, *fabrica,* fabrication, fashioning, forging, formation, forming, making, molding, origination, preparation, production, synthesis

MANUFACTURE, *verb* assemble, build, compose, construct, contrive, create, devise, engineer, evolve, *fabricari,* fabricate, fashion, forge, form, formulate, generate, invent, make, make by mechanical industry, make up, mass produce, mold, originate, process, produce, put in production, put together, turn out, turn out by industrial process
ASSOCIATED CONCEPTS: manufacture goods, products liability involved in manufactured goods

MANY *(Ample),* ***adjective*** abundant, adequate, aplenty, bounteous, bountiful, considerable, copious, filled, fulsome, lavish, luxuriant, plenteous, profuse, rich, rife, sufficient, surplus

MANY *(Multiple),* ***adjective*** countless, diverse, innumerable, manifold, miscellaneous, mixed, multifold, multitudinous, myriad, numberless, numerous, several, some, sundry, uncountable
ASSOCIATED CONCEPTS: multiple causes of action

MAR, *verb* abase, begrime, besmear, besmirch, blemish, blight, cloud, color, damage, darken, debauch, deface, demoralize, dirty, dishonor, distort, harm, pervert, pollute, spoil, stain, subvert, tar, tarnish, touch, twist

MARATHON, *adjective* extended, forever, interminable, lasting, lengthened, lingering, long, long-continued, long-continuing, long-drawn, long-drawn-out, long-winded, never-ending, overlong, prolonged, protracted, taking forever, time-consuming, unending

MARGIN *(Outside limit),* ***noun*** bank, border, boundary, bounds, brim, brink, circumference, curb, edge, frame, fringe, hem, ledge, limit, lip, outskirt, perimeter, periphery, portal, rim, shore, skirt, threshold, verge

MARGIN *(Spare amount),* ***noun*** amount reserved, clearance, elbowroom, extra amount for contingencies, extra amount for emergencies, headway, latitude, leeway, opening, reserve, reserved amount, room, room to spare, space
ASSOCIATED CONCEPTS: margin of profit

MARGINAL, ***adjective*** average, bare, barely acceptable, barely adequate, below par, borderline, fair, humble, *in margine positus, in margine scriptus,* inappreciable, indifferent, low-quality, meager, mediocre, mere, middling, moderate, modest, passable, poor, scant, scanty, skimpy, tenuous, tolerable, trifling, undistinguished, wanting, weak

MARGINALIA, ***noun*** commentary, entry, footnote, inscription, notation, note, memorandum, record, register

MARK, ***noun*** autograph, badge, characteristic, check, cipher, countermark, emblem, identification, idiosyncrasy, imprint, indication, initials, manifestation, marker, particularity, proof, record, representation, sign, signature, stamp, symbol, token, trace, trademark, vestige

MARK, ***verb*** brand, check, customize, designate, differentiate, earmark, hallmark, identify, impress, imprint, inscribe, label, letter, name, particularize, stamp, tag, ticket

MARKED OFF THE CALENDAR, ***verb*** deferred, delayed, extended, halted temporarily, held in abeyance, held off, in suspense, not heard, placed in oblivion, prolonged, put off indefinitely, shelved, stalled, stricken from the calendar, suspended, suspended until restored, tabled, unsettled

MARKET *(Business),* ***noun*** agora, bazaar, bourse, concern, department store, emporium, establishment, exchange, fair, financial center, general store, house, *macellum,* mart, *mercatus, nundinae,* open mart, place of business, place of buying and selling, place of commerce, place of trade, place of traffic, retail store, rialto, shop, shopping center, store, trade fair, trading house, trading post, variety store
ASSOCIATED CONCEPTS: actual market value, fair market price, market conditions, market place, market price, market value

MARKET *(Demand),* ***noun*** call, call for, consumer demand, desire, desire to buy, desire to obtain, earnest seeking, essentiality, heavy demand, indispensability, inquiry, insufficiency, interest, lack, mania, necessity, need, outlet, pressing requirement, pursuit, request, requirement, requisition, run, search, steady demand, strong demand, vogue, want, willingness to purchase, wish

MARKETABLE, ***adjective*** commercial, exchangeable, fit for sale, merchantable, salable, tradable, *venalis,* vendible
ASSOCIATED CONCEPTS: marketable title

MARKETPLACE, ***noun*** agora, emporium, exchange, exposition, financial center, *forum,* open market, place of business, place of business traffic, place of buying and selling, place of commerce, place of trade, plaza, shopping center, square, trading place
ASSOCIATED CONCEPTS: public markets

MARRED, ***adjective*** blemished, blighted, bruised, cankered, contaminated, corrupted, crippled, damaged, defaced, defective, deformed, despoiled, disabled, discolored, disfigured, faulty, flawed, fouled, garbled, hamstrung, harmed, hurt, impaired, imperfect, impure, infected, injured, lamed, maimed, mangled, marked, mutilated, no longer in perfect condition, pitted, rotten, ruined, scarred, scathed, scratched, speckled, spoiled, spotted, stained, sullied, tainted, tarnished, wounded

MARRIAGE *(Intimate relationship),* ***noun*** accouplement, alliance, bond, close relationship, closeness, cohabitation, couplement, coupling, intimacy, joining, linkage, linking, tie, union
ASSOCIATED CONCEPTS: common-law marriage

MARRIAGE *(Wedlock),* ***noun*** bond of matrimony, cohabitation, *coniugium,* conjugal union, conjugality, connubiality, espousal, espousement, marriage tie, married life, married state, married status, *matrimonium,* matrimony, *nuptiae,* nuptial bond, nuptial tie, spousal, wedded state, wedding
ASSOCIATED CONCEPTS: adultery, annulment, bigamous marriage, consensual marriage, consummation of marriage, contract of marriage, coverture, curtesy, divorce, dower, marriage ceremony, marriage license, marriage promise, polygamous marriage, solemnize a marriage, void marriage, voidable marriage
FOREIGN PHRASES: ***Nuptias non concubitus sed consensus facit.*** Not cohabitation but consent makes the valid marriage. ***Pater est quem nuptioe demonstrant.*** He is the father whom the marriage points out. ***Semper praesumitur pro matrimonio.*** The presumption is always in favor of the validity of a marriage. ***Subsequens matrimonium tollit peccatum praecedens.*** A subsequent marriage removes a previous fault.

MARRY, ***verb*** affiance, coalesce, combine, commit, compound, conjoin, conjugate, connect, couple, engage, espouse, fuse, hitch, join, link, match, mate, pair off, unify, unite, wed
ASSOCIATED CONCEPTS: Defense of Marriage Act, gay marriage

MARSHAL, ***noun*** arm of the law, bailiff, county officer, court officer, *dux,* federal officer, law enforcement agent, minor officer of the law, officer, officer of the law, officer who carries out orders of the court, peace officer

MARSHAL, ***verb*** allocate, allot, apportion, arrange, array, assign, bring to order, collocate, compose, coordinate, deal out, *disponere,* distribute, fix, form into ranks, group, guide, index, *instruere,* introduce order, lead, line up, manage, muster, organize, parcel out, place, place in order, position, put in order, rank, regiment, regulate, set in order, set up, systematize
ASSOCIATED CONCEPTS: marshaling assets, marshaling liens, marshaling remedies, marshaling securities

MARVELOUS, ***adjective*** amazing, animating, astonishing, astounding, awesome, awful, conspicuous, energizing, enlightening, enlivening, excellent, extraordinary, eye-opening, fabulous, impressive, incomprehensible, inconceivable, incredible, meritorious, mind-boggling, miraculous, notable, noticeable, outstanding, phenomenal, portentous, prodigious, rare, remarkable, sensational, singular, smashing, spectacular, staggering, striking, stunning, stupendous, sublime, surprising, terrific, unbelievable, uncommon, unimaginable, unique, unthinkable, unusual, unwonted, wonderful, wondrous

MASK *(Cover),* ***noun*** camouflage, cloak, cover-up, deflection, device, disguise, excuse, facade, false front, feint, front, guise, lame excuse, masquerade, mere cosmetics, obscuration, pretense, pretension, pretext, professed motive, refuge, screen, sham, smoke screen, stalking horse, stratagem, subterfuge, varnish, whitewash

MASK *(Shield),* ***noun*** camouflage, deflection, disguise, false front, false identity, incognito, masquerade, pretense, shield, veil

MASS *(Body of persons),* ***noun*** aggregate, assemblage, body, cluster, congregation, crowd, drove, flock, gathering, host, mob, multitude, *multitudo,* phalanx, plurality, swarm, throng, *vulgus*
ASSOCIATED CONCEPTS: mass market, mass picketing

MASS *(Weight),* ***noun*** amplitude, bigness, body, bulk, density, dimension, extent, fullness, gauge, greatness, immensity, largeness, magnitude, measure, measurement, sizableness, size

MASSACRE, ***verb*** annihilate, assassinate, blow away, blow up, butcher, decimate, demolish, destroy, devastate, eradicate, exterminate, kill, mow down, murder, purge, silence, slaughter, slay, snuff out, waste, wipe out
ASSOCIATED CONCEPTS: assault guns, background checks, murder in the first degree

MASSIVE, ***adjective*** august, Brobdingnagian, burdensome, colossal, elephantine, enormous, giant, gigantic, gross, hefty, Himalayan, huge, immense, infinite, large, major, mammoth, mega, monstrous, monumental, outsize, overweight, planetary, ponderous, prodigious, solid, substantial, tremendous, unlimited, vast, weighty, whopping

MASTER, ***adjective*** arch, authoritative, capital, central, chief, commanding, controlling, crowning, dictating, dominant, eminent, foremost, governing, great, head, hegemonic, hegemonical, incomparable, influential, leading, main, most important, outstanding, paramount, predominating, preeminent, prepotent, prevailing, prevalent, primary, prime, ranking, recognized, regnant, reigning, ruling, sovereign, star, stellar, supereminent, supreme, top-flight, well-known
ASSOCIATED CONCEPTS: agency, master and servant

MASTERFUL, ***adjective*** ace, adept, adroit, apt, artistic, authoritarian, authoritative, brilliant, clever, crackerjack, cunning, slick, deft, dexterous, diplomatic, excellent, exemplary, expert, first-rate, ingenious, lordly, magical, model, polished, powerful, preeminent, professional, proficient, quintessential, refined, resourceful, statesmanlike, stylish, technically brilliant, the complete professional, the consummate professional, virtuoso
ASSOCIATED CONCEPTS: masterful arguments in court

MASTERMIND, ***noun*** authority, creative genius, creator, expert, genius, intellect, intellectual, intellectual prodigy, leader, learned person, luminary, master, mental giant, mentor, person of intellect, prodigy, pundit, qualified person, sage, savant, specialist, strategist, tactician, thinker, wise man

MASTERY, ***noun*** ability, accomplishment, achievement, acquirement, acquisition, adeptness, adroitness, artisanship, artistry, attainment, brilliance, chieftainship, cleverness, cognizance, command, competence, comprehension, craftsmanship, cunning, expertise, expertness, extensive knowledge, facility, finesse, grace, grasp, in-depth knowledge, influence, ingeniousness, ingenuity, knowledge, nobility, perfection, polish, practical ability, preeminence, premiership, proficiency, profound knowledge, skill, skillfulness, specialized knowledge, style, success, superiority, tact, tactfulness, technical brilliance, technical mastery, technical skill, technique, timing, total command, unique knowledge, victory over, virtuosity, wizardry

MATCH *(Contest),* ***noun*** bout, championship, competition, fight, final game, game, games, joust, matching, meet, playoff game, test, tournament, tourney

MATCH *(Duplicate),* ***noun*** clone, companion, copy, equal, exact copy, exact duplicate, exact likeness, facsimile, likeness, mate, mirror, mirror copy, model, perfect likeness, reflection, replica, resemblance, semblance, the image, twin

MATCH *(Marriage),* ***noun*** alliance, arranged marriage, bed, bond, bridal bed, bridebed, cohabitation, common-law marriage, conjugal bliss, conjugal bond, conjugality, coverture, getting hitched, holy matrimony, holy wedlock, homosexual marriage, husbandhood, ill-assorted marriage, interfaith marriage, intermarriage, interracial marriage, lesbian, living as man and wife, marriage bed, marriage sacrament, married state or status, married status, matching, match-up, matrimonial union, matrimony, misalliance, miscegenation, mixed marriage, nuptial bond, one flesh, remarriage, sacrament of matrimony or marriage, splicing, spousehood, tying the knot, union, wedded bliss, wedded state, weddedness, wedding knot, wedlock, wifehood

MATERIAL *(Important),* ***adjective*** basic, capital, cardinal, central, compelling, consequential, considerable, critical, crucial, decisive, effective, essential, extensive, far-reaching, fundamental, indispensable, influential, key, leading, main, major, memorable, momentous, necessary, paramount, pertinent, pivotal, prevalent, primary, principal, relevant, remarkable, salient, signal, significant, substantial, valuable, vital, weighty, worth considering
ASSOCIATED CONCEPTS: material allegation, material alteration, material amendment, material change in circumstances, material defect, material defendant, material departure from the truth, material error, material evidence, material fact, material false representation, material misrepresentation, material witness

MATERIAL *(Physical),* ***adjective*** actual, bodily, concrete, corporeal, *corporeus, de facto,* earthly, mundane, nonspiritual, palpable, real, secular, solid, substantial, tactile, tangible, temporal, unspiritual, worldly
ASSOCIATED CONCEPTS: material furnished

MATERIAL POINT, ***noun*** benchmark, cardinal point, center, central idea, chief point, core, cornerstone, critical point, crucial point, crux, essence, essential matter, essential part, essential point, focal point, focus, fundamental point, gist, gravamen, heart, heart of the matter, important issue, important part, inner core, kernel, linchpin, main idea, marrow, material point, meat, nitty-gritty, nucleus, pivotal point, prime feature, prime issue, quintessence, root, salient point, substance, substantive point
ASSOCIATED CONCEPTS: material point in an argument

MATERIALITY *(Consequence),* ***noun*** caliber, distinction, eminence, gravity, greatness, import, importance, magnitude, materialness, matter, memorability, momentousness, notability, notableness, priority, prominence, purport, rank, relevance, salience, significance, substantiality, sum and substance, value, weight, weightiness, worth

MATERIALITY *(Physical existence),* ***noun*** bodiliness, bodily existence, body, concreteness, corporality, corporeity, embodiment, entity, essential nature, existence, mass, material existence, materialness, matter, palpability, physical being, physical nature, physicalness, reality, solidity, substance, substantiality, substantialness, tangibility

MATERIALMAN, ***noun*** artificer, builder, constructor, contractor, designer, deviser, engineer, outfitter, provider, supplier
ASSOCIATED CONCEPTS: materialman's lien

MATERNITY, ***noun*** fertility, motherhood, motherliness, parenthood, propagation, reproduction

MATRIMONY, ***noun*** alliance, cohabitation, conjugality, connubiality, consortium, espousal, espousement, joining, marriage, marriage tie, married life, married state, married status, match, mating, *matrimonium,* nuptial bond, nuptial state, nuptial tie, partnership, sacrament of marriage, spousal, union, wedded state, wedlock
ASSOCIATED CONCEPTS: matrimonial action, matrimonial cohabitation, matrimonial domicile, matrimonial res

MATTER *(Case),* ***noun*** action, *causa,* cause, cause in court, claim, court action, dispute, inquiry, lawsuit, legal action, legal proceedings, litigation, pleadings, proceedings, suit, suit at law, trial
ASSOCIATED CONCEPTS: matter of record

MATTER *(Subject),* ***noun*** business on hand, case, case in question, claim, concern, debatable point, dispute, field of inquiry, *institutum,* issue, item on the agenda, point, point at issue, point in question, problem, proposition, *propositum,* question, *res,* subject for inquiry, subject matter, topic, topic for discussion
ASSOCIATED CONCEPTS: immaterial matter, matter in controversy, matter in dispute, matter in issue, matter in pais, matter of fact, matter of form, matter of law, matter of record, matter of substance, matters pending
FOREIGN PHRASES: ***Certa debet esse intentio, et narratio, et certum fundamentum, et certa res quae deducitur in judicium.*** The intention, declaration, foundation, and matter brought to judgment ought to be certain. ***Eventus varios res nova semper habet.*** A new matter always holds the possibility of a different result. ***Culpa est immiscere se rel ad se non pertinenti.*** It is a fault for anyone to meddle in matters which do not concern him.

MATTER IN DISPUTE, ***noun*** argument, bone of contention, case, concern, conclusion, conflict, contention, contentiousness, contestation, controversy, crux, debate, dialogue, disputation, disputatiousness, dispute, embroilment, essence of the dispute, feud, fight, fighting, focus of attention, formal argument, fracas, hostility, imbroglio, infighting, issue, item for the agenda, litigation, matter, matter being examined in depth, matter in hand, matter under investigation, open controversy, open quarrel, plot, point, point at issue, point in question, polemic, position, premise, pretext, problem, purport, quarrel, quarreling, question, question at issue, point at issue, rationale, reason, reasoning, refutation, result, stance, subject, subject matter, substance, text, thesis
ASSOCIATED CONCEPTS: subject matter of dispute

MATTER IN QUESTION, ***noun*** argument, concern, conclusion, controversy, crux, dialogue, dispute, embroilment, focus of attention, formal argument, imbroglio, issue, item for the agenda, litigation, matter, matter being examined in depth, matter in controversy, matter in dispute, matter in hand, matter under investigation, plot, point, point at issue, point in question, polemic, position, premise, pretext, problem, purport, question, question at issue, rationale, reason, reasoning, refutation, result, stance, subject, subject matter, substance, text, thesis, underlying issue

MATTER OF COURSE, ***noun*** common practice, common run, common state of affairs, customary procedure, general run, natural state, ordinary run of things, ordinary state, prescribed form, procedure, regular procedure, routine, routine event, routine happening, rule, set form, usual custom, usual occurrence, usual practice, usual procedure, usual thing

MATTER OF RECORD, ***noun*** a material part of the record, a point in question, accounted for on the record, chronicled, documented on the record, entered into evidence, entered into testimony, entered into the record, introduced into evidence, introduced into testimony, on the record, part of the record, part of the recorded proceedings, part of the text of the record, part of the transcript, part of the transcription
ASSOCIATED CONCEPTS: court testimony, estoppel by matter of record

MATURE, ***verb*** accrue, advance toward perfection, age, attain majority, attain maturity, become due, become fully developed, become payable, become perfected, become prime, become ripe, bring to full development, bring to its peak, bring to maturity, bring to perfection, come of age, consummate, culminate, develop, evolve, fall due, finish, grow up, *maturare,* maturate, nurture, perfect, ripen, season
ASSOCIATED CONCEPTS: matured account

MATURITY, ***noun*** adulthood, completion, consummation, culmination, due date, evolution, falling due, fulfillment, full age, full development, full growth, majority, matureness, *maturitas,* perfected condition, perfection, preparedness, readiness
ASSOCIATED CONCEPTS: maturity of a debt, maturity of an obligation

MAXIM, ***noun*** adage, aphorism, aphoristic expression, axiom, byword, canon, established principle, expression, gnomic saying, moralism, pithy saying, postulate, *praeceptum,* precept, principium, principle, proverb, proverbial saying, *regula,* rule, sage reflection, saw, saying, sententious saying, sententious utterance, statement of general truth, teaching, truth, wise saying

MAXIMIZE, ***verb*** add, aggrandize, amplify, augment, balloon, blow up, broaden, build up, distend, enhance, enlarge, escalate, exaggerate, extend, increase, inflate, loosen, magnify, pad, puff, push, spread, stretch, well, widen

MAXIMUM *(Amplitude),* ***noun*** ampleness, capacity, fullness, greatest, peak, plentitude, saturation, size, total, utmost

MAXIMUM *(Pinnacle),* ***noun*** crown, culmination, limit, most, ne plus ultra, upper extremity

MAYHEM, ***noun*** agitation, anarchy, brawl, bustle, chaos, clamor, commotion, complication, confusion, discombobulation, discord, disorder, fracas, havoc, hullabaloo,

imbroglio, insurrection, mischief, pandemonium, quarrel, rebellion, revolution, riot, ruckus, trouble
ASSOCIATED CONCEPTS: crime of mayhem

MAZE *(Confusion),* ***noun*** complexity, confusion, convolution, intricacy, labyrinth, meandering, network, puzzle, snarl, tangle, twist, winding

MAZE *(Winding course),* ***noun*** bafflement, befuddlement, bewilderment, complex, convolution, disorientation, entanglement, incomprehensibility, intricacy, labyrinth, meandering, morass, network, perplexity, puzzle, tangle, torsion, twist, winding

MEAGER, ***adjective*** a cosmetic measure, a drop in the bucket, bare, bare-boned, cursory, deficient, depthless, inadequacy, inadequate, inconsequential, inconsiderable, infrequent, insignificant, insufficient, lacking, lean, measly, miserly, negligible, niggardly, not enough, not much, not plentiful, paltry, petty, picayune, piddling, pittance, rare, scant, scanty, scarce, seldom seen, shabby, shallow, skeletal, skimping, slender, slight, slim, small, spare, sparing, sparse, sprinkled, superficial, tenuous, too little, trifling, trivial, underfed, undernourished, undersized, underweight, unimportant, unsuitability, wanting

MEAN *(Average),* ***adjective*** central, grouping, intermediary, medial, median, medium, mesial, middle, midmost, statistical average

MEAN *(Base),* ***adjective*** abject, brutal, contemptible, degrading, despicable, disgraceful, dishonorable, heinous, ignoble, ignominious, inappreciable, inconsiderate, inimical, intermediate, loathsome, low-grade, low-minded, Machiavellian, malevolent, mediocre, mercenary, miserly, nasty, niggardly, odious, paltry, penurious, perverse, petulant, questionable, servile, shady, shameful, spiteful, tightfisted, vicious, vile, villainous, wretched

MEAN, ***noun*** average, balance, center, heart, mean proportion, median, mediocrity, medium, middle ground, middle state, normal, rule

MEAN, ***verb*** affirm, allude to, bespeak, betoken, connote, convey, declare, denote, express, imply, import, indicate, intend, intimate, manifest, propose, purport, represent, signify

MEANING, ***noun*** acceptation, connotation, content, definition, denotation, drift, explanation, idea, import, interpretation, purport, semantics, semasiology, sense, *sententia,* significance, *significatio,* signification, substance, tenor, text, *vis*
ASSOCIATED CONCEPTS: plain meaning, secondary meaning
FOREIGN PHRASES: ***Primo excutienda est verbi vis, ne sermonis vitio obstruatur oratio, sive lex sine argumentis.*** The force of a word should be ascertained in the beginning, lest the sentence be destroyed by the fault of expression, or the law be without reason. ***Sensus verborum est anima legis.*** The meaning of words is the spirit of the law. ***In testamentis ratio tacita non debet considerari, sed verba solum spectari debent; adeo per divinationem mentis a verbis recedere durum est.*** In wills an unexpressed intention ought not to be considered, but the words alone ought to be regarded; for it is difficult to recede from the words by guessing at their intention.

MEANINGLESS, ***adjective*** absurd, asinine, empty, failed, failing, farcical, fatuous, foolish, frivolous, fruitless, futile, hollow, immaterial, inane, inapplicable, incomprehensible, inconsequential, inconsiderable, ineffective, ineffectual, inefficacious, insignificant, insubstantial, irrational, irrelevant, malfunctioning, minor, miscarried, miscarrying, negligible, nonsensical, not worth mentioning, of little account, of little consequence, of little effect, of little import, of little importance, of no concern, of no great weight, paltry, petty, picayune, piddling, pointless, purposeless, senseless, small, trivial, unessential, unfortunate, unimportant, unintelligible, unreasonable, unsubstantial, unsuccessful, useless, worthless
ASSOCIATED CONCEPTS: jury nullification, meaningless law, meaningless utterances, rendered meaningless

MEANS *(Funds),* ***noun*** assets, finances, resource, resources, wealth, wherewithal
ASSOCIATED CONCEPTS: means doctrine, means of knowledge, means of satisfaction, means of support

MEANS *(Opportunity),* ***noun*** application, capacity, devices, employment, fashion, form, guise, handiness, manner, measures, method, mode, serviceability, style, system, tone, usage, use, ways, wherewithal

MEASURE, ***noun*** act, bill, caveat, declaration, decree, dictate, edict, enactment, law, legislation, legislative enactment, legislative mandate, legislative proclamation, mandate, piece of legislation, prescript, prescription, proposal, proposed act, proposition, regulation, rubric, rule, ruling, statute
ASSOCIATED CONCEPTS: appropriate measures, measure of benefit, measure of damages, measure of value, regulatory measure, remedial measures

MEASURE, ***verb*** admeasure, appraise, ascertain dimensions, ascertain size, assess, bring into comparison, calculate, calibrate, compare, compute, correlate, *demetiri,* determine size, determine value, estimate, evaluate, fathom, form an estimate, form an opinion, gauge, grade, graduate, graph, judge, liken, make a comparison, make an estimate, mark off, match, *metari,* mete, meter, pace off, *permetiri,* portion out, quantify, rank, rate, reckon, rule, set a value on, size, span, survey, value, weigh
ASSOCIATED CONCEPTS: appropriate measure of damages

MEASURABLE, ***adjective*** appraisable, appreciable, ascertainable, calculable, capable of being delineated, capable of being quantified, computable, considerable, determinable, estimable, fathomable, measured, numerable, perceptible, quantifiable, ratable
ASSOCIATED CONCEPTS: measurable pollutants

MEASUREMENT, ***noun*** admeasurement, amount, analysis, appraisal, appraisement, assessment, bulk, calculation, capaciousness, capacity, computation, dimensions, estimate, estimation, extent, gauge, girth, greatness, largeness, limit, magnitude, mass, measure, *mensio, mensura,* mensuration, metage, meterage, quantification, quantity, rating, reckoning, size, span, survey, valuation, vastness
ASSOCIATED CONCEPTS: measurement of damages, measurement of liability

MECHANICS LIEN, ***noun*** charge, charge imposed on specific property, claim on property, hold on property, right to enforce charge on property, security on property

MECHANISM, ***noun*** apparatus, appliance, avenue, components, contrivance, device, force, gadget, implement, innards, instrument, instrumentality, machinery,

means, medium, method, operation, route, source, structure, system, tool, workings
ASSOCIATED CONCEPTS: finding a mechanism to enforce the law

MEDDLE, *noun* barge in, be curious, be officious, break in on, bust in, chime in, crash the gates of, dabble in, encroach, encumber, horn in, impose, infringe, inject into, inquire, insert yourself into, interfere, interlope, intermeddle, interpose, interrupt, intervene, intrude, muscle into, obstruct, provide your two cents, pry, push in, tamper with, trespass
ASSOCIATED CONCEPTS: tampering with evidence

MEDIATE, *verb* adjust, adjust difficulties, arbitrate, arrange differences, bring to an understanding, bring to terms, bring together, compromise, conciliate, effect an agreement, intercede, interfere, intervene, moderate, negotiate, *pacem conciliare,* parley, reconcile, referee, restore harmony, *se interponere,* settle, settle a dispute, settle by conciliation, settle differences, umpire, work out differences
ASSOCIATED CONCEPTS: arbitrate

MEDIATION, *noun* adjustment, adjustment of difficulties, arbitration, conciliation, finding a middle course, intercession, interference, intervention, intervention to facilitate a compromise, negotiation, negotiation process, parley, reconciliation, settlement of difficulties, settlement of dispute
ASSOCIATED CONCEPTS: fact finding, mediation board

MEDICAID, *noun* government-provided health insurance for the uninsured, health care for the underprivileged, health coverage for low income persons
Generally: health insurance, medical assistance, medical coverage, national health insurance, supplemental medical program

MEDICAL CONFIDENTIALITY, *noun* doctor-patient confidentiality, health care provider confidentiality, patient confidentiality, protection of personal identifiable medical information

MEDICARE, *noun* government health insurance coverage, government program for hospitalization of persons 65 years of age, government-provided health insurance for senior citizens
Generally: health care, health protection, national health insurance, supplemental medical program

MEDICINAL, *adjective* Aesculapian, alexipharmic, alleviative, analeptic, anodyne, antidotal, antifebrile, assuasive, balmy, beneficial, cleansing, corrective, curative, demulcent, depurative, emollient, febrifugal, healing, health-giving, helpful, invigorating, lenitive, medical, medicative, palliative, purifying, recuperative, recuperatory, reformative, remedial, restitutive, restorative, roborant, salubrious, salutary, salutiferous, sanative, sanatory, soothing, therapeutic, therapeutical, tonic, vulnerary

MEDIOCRE, *adjective* acceptable, adequate, all right, average, banal, colorless, common, commonplace, decent, everyday, fair, fairish, good enough, inconsequential, indifferent, inferior, inglorious, insignificant, lesser, lifeless, low-class, low-grade, low-quality, meager, mean, *mediocris,* medium, middle, middling, moderate, modest, normal, ordinary, passable, poor, prosaic, prosaical, run-of-the mill, satisfactory, second-rate, so-so, standard, tolerable, trite, trivial, typical, undistinguished, unexceptionable, unexciting, unimportant, uninspiring, uninteresting, unnoteworthy, unobjectionable, unremarkable, usual

MEDIOCRITY, *noun* acceptability, adequateness, average, averageness, baseness, common lot, commonness, commonplaceness, deficiency, fairness, inconsiderableness, inferiority, inferiorness, insignificance, low grade, low quality, mean, meanness, *mediocritas,* middle state, ordinariness, passableness, poorness, satisfactoriness, standardness, tolerability, tolerableness, triviality, unexceptionality, unimportance, unnoteworthiness, unremarkableness, unsatisfactoriness

MEDIUM, *noun* agency, agent, broker, channel, delegate, deputy, emissary, envoy, expedient, go-between, instrument, instrumentality, interagency, interagent, intermediary, intermediate, intermediate agent, intervener, link, machinery, means, mechanism, mediating agency, mediator, middleman, mouthpiece, negotiant, negotiator, spokesperson, tool, vehicle

MEET, *verb* amass, assemble, associate, band together, center around, cluster, collect, collide, come face to face, come together, concur, *concurrere, confluere,* congregate, convene, converge, convoke, encounter, flock, forgather, gather together, get together, group, hold a convocation, hold a meeting, hold a session, huddle, *inter se congredi,* join, mass, muster, parley, rally, rejoin, reunite, swarm, throng, unite

MEETING *(Conference),* ***noun*** assembly, caucus, colloquy, conclave, *concursus, congressio,* consistory, consultation, convention, *conventus,* convocation, discussion, encounter, exchange of views, forum, gathering, interchange of views, negotiation, open discussion, panel, parley, plenum, reunion, seminar, session, summit, symposium, synod
ASSOCIATED CONCEPTS: annual meeting of shareholders, meeting of creditors, organizational meeting, public meeting, regular meeting, special meeting

MEETING *(Encounter),* ***noun*** appulsion, clash, collision, concours, confrontation, contact, convergence, convergency, engagement, fusion, intersection, joining, junction, juncture, merger, rendezvous, unification, union
ASSOCIATED CONCEPTS: meeting of minds

MEETING OF THE MINDS, *noun* accordance, agreement, common assent, compatibility, complete accord, compliance, concert, concord, concordance, concurrence, consensus, consentaneity, harmony, like-mindedness, mutual understanding, rapport, unanimity, unanimousness, understanding, uniformity, unison, unity
ASSOCIATED CONCEPTS: bilateral contract, rescission of an agreement

MELANGE, *noun* admixture, amalgam, assortment, blend, cento, combination, commixture, composition, compound, confused mass, conglomeration, farrago, gallimaufry, hash, hodgepodge, intermixture, jumble, medley, minglement, miscellaneous collection, miscellany, mixture, olio, pastiche, patchwork, potpourri, union

MELIORATE, *verb* adorn, advance, ameliorate, amend, assuage, beautify, better, correct, cultivate, cure, doctor, elaborate, elevate, embellish, emend, enhance, enrich, forward, have a good influence, improve, invigorate, lard, make better, make improvements, mend, mitigate, modernize, palliate, polish, purify, raise, reclaim, rectify, reface, refine, reform, refresh, refurbish, regenerate, rehabilitate, reinvigorate, relieve, render better, renew, renovate, reorganize, repair, restore, revive, touch up, transfigure, transform, upgrade, uplift

MELTDOWN, *noun* agitation, alarum, anxiety, apprehension, breakdown, destruction, discomposure, disquiet, disturbance, episode, incident, perturbation, tailspin
ASSOCIATED CONCEPTS: fiscal meltdown, global fiscal crisis, recession

MEMBER *(Constituent part),* ***noun*** article, branch, category, component, department, division, element, factor, feature, fraction, ingredient, integral part, item, link, part, piece, portion, section, segment, share, small part, subdivision, subordinate part, unit

MEMBER *(Individual in a group),* ***noun*** affiliate, associate, belonger, cardholder, committeeperson, comrade, confederate, constituent, cooperator, copartner, cosharer, enlistee, enrolled person, fellow, follower, guildsman, insider, participator, partner, patron, registered person, shareholder, sharer, stockholder, teammate

MEMBER OF THE LEGAL PROFESSION, *noun* advocate, attorney, attorney at-law, barrister, barrister-at-law, counsel, counselor, counselor-at-law, esquire, lawyer, legal advisor, legal advocate, legal consultant, legal practitioner, practitioner, solicitor

MEMORABLE, *adjective* celebrated, classic, consequential, descent, distinguishable, doable, dramatic, electrifying, elevated, eminent, esteemed, estimable, eventful, excellent, exceptional, exciting, extraordinary, famous, fantastic, favorable, fine, first-rate, formidable, historic, illustrious, important, inspiring, makes the cutoff, marked, momentous, notable, noteworthy, of mark, ordinary, outstanding, passes muster, passes the grade, prestigious, prominent, reasonably notable, remarkable, special, sublime, telling, thrilling, top-notch, top ten, unique, unusual
ASSOCIATED CONCEPTS: memorable decision

MEMORANDUM, *noun* aide-memoir, annotation, brief, chronicle, memoir, notation, note, postnote, record, report
ASSOCIATED CONCEPTS: memorandum of law

MEMORANDUM OF LAW, *noun* brief, brief containing legal arguments, brief containing legal justification, compendium of law justifying a case, condensation of law supporting a case, extract of body of law justifying a position, legal abstract of law supporting a case, legal document, legal memorandum, memorandum, summary of case law supporting an action, summary of law supporting positions, summary on the law, supporting legal issues, supporting positions, synopsis of law, the legal arguments in favor of a case, the legal basis supporting the outcome of a case
ASSOCIATED CONCEPTS: memorandum of law in support, motion for a directed verdict, motion to dismiss

MEMORY *(Commemoration),* ***noun*** celebration, remembrance, writing

MEMORY *(Retention),* ***noun*** mind, recalling, recollection, reflection

MEN, *noun* chaps, fellows, gentlemen, gents, guys, lads, males, members of the male sex

MENACE, *noun* commination, danger, dangerous situation, hazard, imminent danger, imperilment, intimidating force, intimidation, minacious force, minacity, peril, prognostic, threat

MENACE, *verb* affright, alarm, cause alarm, comminate, direct a threat against, disconcert, disquiet, disturb, exhibit hostile intentions, frighten, impend, inspire fear, intimidate, put in bodily fear, put in fear, raise apprehensions, scare, show hostility, startle, strike with overwhelming fear, terrify, threaten, unnerve

MENDACIOUS, *adjective* artful, clever in deception, collusive, concocted, counterfeit, covinous, cunning, deceitful, deceiving, devoid of truth, dishonest, distorted, embroidered, fabricated, false, falsified, feigned, fictitious, fraudulent, given to lying, incorrect, insincere, invented, lacking truth, lying, made up, make-believe, *mendax,* misrepresentative, misrepresented, misstated, not straightforward, perfidious, perjured, perverted, pretended, prevaricating, sham, sly, spurious, truthless, uncandid, ungenuine, untrue, untruthful, unveracious, unveridical, varnished, void of truth, wrong

MENDACITY, *noun* deception, dishonesty, disingenuousness, distortion, exaggeration, fabrication, falsehood, falsification, guilefulness, inaccuracy, legal fiction, lie, lying, mendaciousness, misrepresentation, misstatement, not credible, overstatement, partial truth, prevarication, sketch, tale, untruth, untruthfulness

MENIAL, *adjective* base, basic, beginning, crude, elemental, fundamental, humble, introductory, lamblike, lowly, modest, mundane, ordinary, preliminary, preparatory, primal, primary, primitive, rudimental, rudimentary, servile, simple, slavish, tedious, trivial, unassuming, uncomplicated, unpretentious

MENS REA, *noun* criminal design, criminal guilt, criminal intent, criminal purpose, criminality, culpability, vice, wrong, wrongdoing

MENTAL ABILITY, *noun* acuity, acumen, alertness, aptitude, astuteness, braininess, brainpower, brilliance, canniness, capacity, common sense, discernment, discriminability, insight, intellect, intellectualism, intelligence, judgment, keenness, mentality, mind, perception, reason, sense, talent, understanding, wisdom, wit

MENTAL CAPACITY, *noun* ability, adequacy, adroitness, aptitude, capability, clearheadedness, competence, effectiveness, facility, faculty, fitness, health, lucidity, normalcy, normality, rationality, reason, sanity, soundness, understanding, wherewithal
ASSOCIATED CONCEPTS: criminal insanity, intent, mens rea, not guilty by reason of insanity

MENTALLY ILL, *adjective* bereft of reason, certifiable, delirious, demented, deranged, disabled, disordered, frenetic, frenzied, hysterical, incoherent, maniacal, manic, mental, mentally deranged, neurotic, of unsound mind, paranoiac, phobic, psychotic, raving, suffering with schizophrenia, unsound
ASSOCIATED CONCEPTS: insanity

MENTION *(Reference),* ***noun*** allegation, allusion, assertion, comment, communication, enlightenment, expression, hint, implication, indication, indirect hint, inference, insinuation, intimation, *mentio,* note, passing word, recital, recitation, referent, relation, remark, report, statement, suggestion

MENTION *(Tribute),* ***noun*** acclaim, acclamation, adulation, applause, appreciation, approbation, approval, blandishment, celebration, citation, commendation, compliment, credit, decoration, esteem, eulogistic speech, eulogy, exaltation, expression of merit, flattery, glorification, high opinion, homage, honor, laud, laudation, mark of honor, official recognition, panegyric, plaudit, praise, public recognition, regard, respect

MENTION, ***verb*** acquaint, adduce, advert to, affirm, allude to, announce, annunciate, apprise, assert, bring word, broach, cite, comment upon, communicate, confide to, convey information, convey knowledge, declare incidentally, denominate, direct the attention to, disclose, discuss, divulge, enlighten, enumerate, express, give a hint, give notice, give utterance, hint at, impart, indicate, inform, insinuate, intimate, let know, make allusion to, make known, name, note, notify, observe, point out, point to, recite, recount, refer to, remark on, report, reveal, speak of, specify, state, stipulate, suggest, talk about, tell, touch upon, utter, voice

MERCANTILE, ***adjective*** business, commercial, economic, exchange, financial, fiscal, industrial, market, merchandising, monetary, trade
ASSOCIATED CONCEPTS: mercantile law, mercantile paper

MERCENARY, ***adjective*** accessible to bribery, acquisitive, avaricious, bribable, *conductus,* corrupt, corruptible, covetous, exacting, exploitative, grasping, greedy, hired, hireling, leased, materialistic, *mercenarius,* money conscious, money hungry, motivated by a desire for money, motivated by greed, opportunistic, paid, possessive, profiteering, purchasable, rapacious, selfish, simoniacal, unidealistic, usurious, venal, *venalis*

MERCHANDISE, ***noun*** articles, articles of commerce, assets, belongings, capital goods, cargo, chattel, commodities, consumer durables, consumer goods, contents, effects, freight, goods, goods for sale, items for sale, line, line of goods, manufactured goods, material assets, materials, *merx,* movables, possessions, produce, property, provisions, *res venales,* salable commodities, shop goods, specialty, staples, stock, stock in trade, store, supplies, tangible assets, vendibles, wares

MERCHANT, ***noun*** businessperson, chandler, consigner, dealer, distributer, distributor, entrepreneur, handler, hawker, huckster, *mercator,* merchandiser, middleman, monger, peddler, retailer, salesperson, seller, shopkeeper, shopman, storekeeper, trader, tradesperson, vendor
FOREIGN PHRASES: ***Jus accrescendi inter mercatores, pro beneficio commercii, locum non habet.*** The right of survivorship does not exist between merchants for the benefit of commerce.

MERCILESS, ***noun*** barbaric, barbarous, bestial, brutal, callous, cold-blooded, cold-hearted, cruel, ferocious, fierce, harsh, heartless, indifferent, inhuman, monstrous, murderous, pitiless, relentless, remorseless, ruthless, sanguinary, savage, severe, stony-hearted, unappeasable, uncaring, uncivilized, uncompassionate, unconcerned, unfeeling, unforgiving, unmerciful, unremorseful, unsparing, unsympathetic, untamed, unyielding, vicious, vindictive, without mercy
ASSOCIATED CONCEPTS: merciless law

MERCURIAL, ***adjective*** adaptable, capricious, changeable, changeful, erratic, finicky, fluctuating, fluid, inconsistent, inconstant, irregular, mutable, temperamental, uncertain, undependable, unpredictable, unreliable, unstable, unsteady, vacillating, variable, versatile, volatile, wavering

MERE, ***adjective*** bare, just, nothing but, only, plain, sheer, simple
ASSOCIATED CONCEPTS: mere assumption of title, mere glimmering of reason, mere license, mere possibility

MERETRICIOUS, ***adjective*** artificial, bedizened, brummagem, cheap, counterfeit, deceitful, deceptive, delusive, fake, false, fraudulent, garish, gaudy, imitation, misleading, mock, ornate, sham, showy, speciously attractive, spurious, tawdry, theatrical, tinsel, vulgar
ASSOCIATED CONCEPTS: adultery, meretricious relationship

MERGE, ***noun*** alliance, amalgamation, amassing, association, blending, bringing together, buildup, coalescence, combination, coming together, compact, compound, compression, concentration, condensation, congealing, congealment, congelation, conglomeratization, conjoining, conjunction, conjuncture, connection, consolidation, contract, contraction, crystallization, fortification, fusion, hardening, intensification, joining, melding, mixing, mixture, solidification, supplement, unification, uniting
ASSOCIATED CONCEPTS: doctrine of merger in copyright law, doctrine of merger in estates, merge companies, merger doctrine

MERGE, ***verb*** absorb, ally, amalgamate, associate, band together, be one with, be swallowed up, blend, cement, combine, compound, conglomerate, conjoin, consolidate, entwine, fuse, harmonize, incorporate, intermingle, intermix, intertwine, join, join forces, lose identity, lose individuality, melt into one, mix, piece together, unify, unite, weld

MERGER, ***noun*** absorption, affiliation, alliance, amalgamation, assimilation, association, centralization, coalescence, coalition, combination, confederation, conflation, consolidation, federation, fellowship, fusion, incorporation, integration, joinder, joint concern, loss of identity, mixture, partnership, solidarity, syndicate, unification, union, united front, voluntary association
ASSOCIATED CONCEPTS: compulsory merger, conglomerate merger, consolidation, forced merger, horizontal merger, merger of estates, vertical merger

MERIT, ***noun*** character, concern, concernment, consequence, consideration, credit, desert, deservedness, *dignitas,* distinction, excellence, emphasis, good actions, good behavior, goodness, greatness, honor, import, importance, interest, meritoriousness, *meritum,* note, praiseworthy quality, quality, rectitude, richly deserving, righteousness, self-importance, significance, superiority, uprightness, value, virtue, *virtus,* worth, worthness
ASSOCIATED CONCEPTS: affidavit of merits, dismissal on the merits, merit system

MERIT, ***verb*** be deserving, be entitled to, be worthy of, deserve, due, earn, justify, richly deserve

MERITORIOUS, ***adjective*** above par, acceptable, admirable, approvable, approved, august, benevolent, better, charitable, chivalric, chivalrous, choice, commendable, commendatory, conscientious, creditworthy, creditable, dazzling, decent, deserving, deserving of commendation,

deserving of compliment, deserving of praise, deserving of reward, desirable, dignified, distinctive, distinguished, duteous, dutiful, edifying, elevated, eminent, entitled, enviable, estimable, ethical, excellent, exemplary, extraordinary, fine, first-rate, generous, glorious, good, good-quality, gracious, great, greathearted, guiltless, heroic, high-minded, high-principled, honest, honorable, idealistic, impeccable, incorrupt, incorruptible, irreproachable, just, *laudabilis,* laudable, laudatory, *laude dignus,* lofty, magnanimous, magnificent, marvelous, moral, noble, perfect, philanthropic, popular, possessing merit, praiseworthy, preeminent, prime, princely, principled, proper, quality, rare, refined, reliable, remarkable, reputable, right-minded, righteous, select, solid, sound, splendid, stainless, sterling, sublime, substantial, superb, superior, superlative, supreme, terrifc, tested, uncensurable, unimpeachable, unselfish, upright, valuable, virtuous, well-done, well-intentioned, wonderful, worth imitating, worthwhile, worthy, worthy of fame, worthy of praise
ASSOCIATED CONCEPTS: meritorious cause, meritorious cause of action, meritorious claim, meritorious defense, meritorious grounds

MESNE, ***adjective*** coming between, interfering, interjacent, intermediary, intermediate, intervenient, intervening, mean, median, middle, transitional
ASSOCIATED CONCEPTS: mesne attachment, mesne grant, mesne process, mesne profits

MESSAGE, ***noun*** account, billet, bulletin, cable, communication, disclosure, dispatch, intelligence, issuance, letter, missive, note, notice, notification, report, signal, statement, telegram, wire

METAMORPHOSES, ***noun*** adjustment, alteration, change, development, disfigurement, distortion, emerging reformation, modification, mutation, refashioning, reformation, remodeling, revamping, revision, reworking, shift, transfiguration, transformation, transition, transmutation

METE, ***noun*** barrier, border, borderland, borderline, bound, boundary, boundary line, boundary mark, bounds, circumscription, confine, division line, end, limit, limitation, line of circumvallation, line of demarcation, margin, measure, outline, perimeter, periphery, rim, terminal, terminus
ASSOCIATED CONCEPTS: legal description, metes and bounds

METE, ***verb*** admeasure, administer, allocate, allot, apportion, apportion by measure, appropriate, assess, assign, bestow, consign, deal out, dispense, distribute, divide, dole out, give, give out, hand out, issue, measure, measure out, parcel out, pay out, present, ration, share out, split, weigh out

METEORIC RISE, ***noun*** ascension, ascension to stardom, ascension to the top, ascent, augmentation, blastoff, boost, change, elevation, expansion, gain, hike, increase, levitation, liftoff, promotion, soaring, upgrade, upheaval, upsurge, upsweep, upturn

METHOD, ***noun*** arrangement, blueprint, classification, consistency, course, course of action, custom, discipline, established order, fixed order, formula, habit, layout, logical order, manner, master plan, means, mode, *modus,* operation, order, orderliness, orderly arrangement, orderly disposition, organization, plan, practice, procedure, process, program, program of action, *ratio,* reduction to order, regular arrangement, regularity, regularity of action, routine, rule, scheme of arrangement, sequence, settled procedure, setup, system, tactic, technique, uniformity, *via,* way, working plan
ASSOCIATED CONCEPTS: business methods, method of operations

METHODICAL, ***adjective*** carefully designed, carefully planned, clocklike, correct, detailed, detail-oriented, exact, ordered, orderly, organized, precise, regular, specific, standardized, structured, systematic, systematized, thorough, thoughtful

METICULOUS, ***adjective*** alert, assiduous, attentive, careful, circumspect, clean, conscientious, considered, correct, *diligens,* diligent, exact, exacting, faithful, fastidious, finical, finicking, finicky, fussy, gingerly, heedful, industrious, mindful, minute, minutely careful, neat, orderly, overcareful, painstaking, particular, precise, punctilious, regardful, rigid, rigorous, scrupulous, strict, thorough, thoroughgoing, tidy, vigilant, watchful

MIDDLE, ***adjective*** average, axial, centermost, central, centric, centroidal, equidistant, halfway, interjacent, intermediary, intermediate, mean, medial, median, mediate, mediocre, medium, mid, midmost, midway, pivotal

MIDDLE, ***noun*** average, axis, center, centrality, central part, central point, central position, centrum, core, focal point, heart, hub, kernel, mean, medium, mesne, mid-point, midst, nucleus

MIGHT, ***noun*** authoritativeness, brawn, durability, efficacy, energy, force, greatness, influence, intensity, main force, mightiness, muscle, potency, potential, powerfulness, prowess, puissance, robustness, severity, sinew, strength, sturdiness, toughness, vigor, vitality

MIGRANT, ***noun*** colonist, gypsy, nomad, ranger, rover, settler, trekker, wanderer

MILD *(Affable),* ***noun*** amiable, calm, civil, compassionate, conciliatory, considerate, docile, easy, easy to get along with, easy-going, easy-natured, fair, forbearing, forgiving, genial, good-natured, good-tempered, gracious, halcyon, humane, inane, indulgent, insipid, judicious, kind, lenient, lukewarm, meek, mellow, merciful, moderate, mollifying, nonviolent, pacific, passive, peaceful, placid, pleasant, pretty, prudent, sensitive, serene, sober, subdued, submissive, sympathetic, tactful, tame, tepid, tractable, tranquil, unassertive, unassuming, uncomplaining

MILD *(Temperature),* ***noun*** bland, easy, flat, gentle, insipid, jejune, moderate, middle ground, neutral, passive, placid, pleasant, pretty, soft, subdued, tame, tasteless, temperate, tepid, tranquil, unexcessive, unflavored, weak

MILESTONE, ***noun*** boiling point, break, breaking point, climax, crossroad, crucial point, event, flash point, happening, highlight, juncture, landmark, major development, major point, milepost, significant development, turnabout, turnaround, watershed

MILITANT AGGRESSOR, ***noun*** adversary, agitator, antagonist, assailant, attacker, belligerent, brawler, bruiser, combatant, contender, disputant, duelist, enemy, fighter, foe, offensive, opponent, pugilist

MILITARY TRIBUNAL, ***noun*** armed services court, armed services court of law, armed services judiciary, army

tribunal, judiciary of the army, military court, military court of law, military judiciary, military trial
ASSOCIATED CONCEPTS: Patriot Act

MILITATE, ***verb*** act on, affect, agitate, bring about change, carry on, *contra rem facere,* contrive, control, deal with, direct, engineer, handle, have effect on, have influence on, influence, interfere, manage, maneuver, manipulate, meddle, mold, operate, perform on, *rei adversari, rei obstare,* shape, steer, take action, wield, work

MIND, ***noun*** animus, attitude, brain, brains, comprehension, *conatus,* concept, conception, concern, conscience, consideration, contemplation, conviction, desire, estimation, expectation, frame, gray matter, intellect, intelligence, intent, judgment, memory, mentality, observation, personal judgment, pleasure, position, propensity, psyche, reason, theory, thinking, understanding, will, wish

MINDFUL, ***adjective*** aware, be reminded of, bear in mind, call to mind, conjure up, do not forget, fix in the mind, have at your fingertips, heed, keep in mind, know, know once again, master, memorize, preserve, recall, recognize, recollect, remind oneself, retain, summon up, think back
ASSOCIATED CONCEPTS: mitigating factors in sentencing

MINIMAL, ***adjective*** abbreviated, abridged, below the mark, brief, cut, deficient, diminished, diminutive, exiguous, fragmentary, impalpable, inappreciable, inconsiderable, infinitesimal, insufficient, lean, least, lesser, light, Lilliputian, limited, little, low, meager, minimum, minor, minute, moderate, modest, narrow, paltry, reduced, rudimentary, scant, scanty, scarce, short, shortened, slender, slight, slim, small, smallest, thin, tiny, under par, under the mark, undersized, unimportant
ASSOCIATED CONCEPTS: minimal jurisdictional contacts, minimal standards

MINIMIZE, ***verb*** abbreviate, abridge, attach little importance to, attenuate, bedwarf, belittle, cheapen, clip, criticize, curtail, cut down, cut down to size, cut short, decimate, decrease, decry, deduct, deflate, degrade, demote, depreciate, derogate, detract, diminish, discount, disparage, disprize, dwarf, lessen, lower, make brief, make less, make little of, make smaller, make thin, misprize, overshadow, pare, pay little attention to, pay little heed to, prune, reduce, render less, ridicule, run down, scale down, scorn, set at naught, shave, shorten, show no respect, shrink, slash, slight, slur over, sneer at, strip, subtract, thin, think little of, think nothing of, underestimate, underpraise, underprice, underrate, underreckon, understate, undervalue
ASSOCIATED CONCEPTS: minimize damage

MINIMUM, ***noun*** bit, dash, drop, fragment, iota, jot, least amount, least part, least quantity, lowest quantity, minim, modicum, morsel, mote, *pars minima,* particle, piece, quorum, scantling, scintilla, shade, sliver, small amount, small quantity, sprinkling, sufficiency, sufficient amount, tincture, tinge, tittle, touch, trace, whit
ASSOCIATED CONCEPTS: minimum age, minimum charge, minimum fee schedule, minimum price, minimum wage

MINIMUM WAGE, ***noun*** bare minimum wage, barely adequate income, least recompense, lowest acceptable wage, lowest lawful pay, lowest legal hourly rate of compensation, lowest permissible wage, lowest possible remuneration

MINISTERIAL, ***adjective*** administrative, agential, attendant, attending, auxiliary, bureaucratic, effectual, functional, helpful, helping, implemental, instrumental, intermedial, intermediary, intermediate, intervening, managing, officiating, operative, practical, serviceable, useful
ASSOCIATED CONCEPTS: ministerial act, ministerial duty, ministerial officer

MINOR, ***adjective*** accessory, cursory, dispensable, expendable, futile, immaterial, inappreciable, inconsequential, inconsiderable, ineffectual, inessential, inferior, insignificant, insubstantial, irrelevant, junior, less important, lesser, little, low-level, lower, meaningless, mere, minimal, minimum, minute, modest, negligible, nonessential, not vital, not worth mentioning, nugatory, obscure, of no account, of second rank, paltry, peripheral, petty, picayune, scant, secondary, slight, small, smaller, subaltern, subordinate, subsidiary, superficial, trifling, trivial, unessential, unimportant, uninfluential, unnecessary, unnoteworthy, unnoticeable
ASSOCIATED CONCEPTS: minor breach, minor defect, minor dispute, minor subdivision

MINOR, ***noun*** adolescent, baby, child, dependent, *filius familias,* individual under age, individual under the age of majority, infant, junior, juvenile, one not legally competent, person under legal age, person under 18 years of age, person who is not of full age, pubescent, teenager, underage person, ward, young person, youngling, youngster, youth
ASSOCIATED CONCEPTS: emancipation of a minor, minor dependent, unemancipated minor
FOREIGN PHRASES: ***Minor minorem custodire non debet, alios enim praesumitur male regere qui seipsum regere nescit.*** A minor ought not to be guardian to a minor, for a person who knows not how to govern himself is presumed to be unfit to govern others. ***Meliorem conditionem suam facere potest minor, deteriorem nequaquam.*** A minor can make his own condition better, but by no means worse. ***Succurritur minori; facilis est lapsus juventutis.*** A minor is to be favored; youth errs easily. ***Minor non tenetur respondere durante minori aetati, nisi, in causa dotis, propter favorem.*** A minor is not held responsible during his minority, unless, by reason of favor, in the matter of dower.

MINORITY *(Infancy),* ***noun*** childhood, immaturity, inexperience, infant status, legal immaturity, legal incapacity, legal incompetence, nonage, period of being under legal age, period of being under statutory age, puerility, unripeness, youth, youthfulness
ASSOCIATED CONCEPTS: age of minority, incapacity to contract, voidable contracts
FOREIGN PHRASES: ***Haeres minor uno et viginti annis non respondebit, nisi in casu dotis.*** A minor heir under 21 years of age is not answerable, except in the matter of dower. ***Minor ante tempus agere non potest in casu proprietatis nec etiam convenire.*** A minor under age cannot act in a case of property.

MINORITY *(Outnumbered group),* ***noun*** insignificant number, lesser group, lesser part, the outvoted, paltry few, peripheral group, powerless group, secondary group, small group, small number, small percentage, small proportion, small quantity, smaller group, smaller part, subordinate group, subsidiary group, uninfluential group, weak group
ASSOCIATED CONCEPTS: minority group, minority member, minority party, minority stockholders

MINUTE, ***adjective*** fiddling, foolish, frivolous, incidental, inconsequential, inconsiderable, insignificant, little, minimal, minor, negligible, nugatory, slight, small, tiny, trifling, trivial

MIRACLE, ***noun*** accomplishment, beauty, curiosity, delight, event, good fortune, happening, inconceivable marvel, incredible wonder, inspiring development, marvel, occurrence, phenomenon, portent, revelation, sensation, sight, spectacle, spectacular development, splendor, surprise, wonder, wow

MISADVISED, ***adjective*** badly advised, fatuous, ill-advised, ill-considered, ill-judged, illogical, impolitic, imprudent, in error, inadvisable, incautious, indiscreet, inexpedient, infelicitous, injudicious, irrational, irresponsible, misconducted, misdirected, misguided, misinformed, misinstructed, misled, mistaken, poorly advised, reasonless, reckless, senseless, shortsighted, thoughtless, unconsidered, unreasonable, unreflecting, unsensible, unsound, unthinking, unthoughtful, unwary, unwise, wrongly advised

MISAPPLICATION, ***noun*** abuse, corrupt use, dishonest application, dishonest use, distortion, errancy, error, extravagance, false construction, fraudulent application, idle expenditure, illegal application, improper use, impropriety, incorrect application, incorrect usage, incorrect use, irregularity, malapropism, malpractice, misappropriation, misconception, misconstruction, misemployment, misexplanation, misexplication, mishandling, misinterpretation, misjudgment, mismanagement, mistake, mistranslation, misunderstanding, misusage, misuse, misuse of funds, misuse of words, perversion, poor usage, prodigality, reckless expenditure, squandering, useless expenditure, usus perversus, waste, wasteful expenditure, wastefulness, wrong application, wrong interpretation, wrong usage, wrong use, wrongful use
ASSOCIATED CONCEPTS: misapplication of funds

MISAPPREHEND, ***verb*** be deceived, be in error, be misled, be mistaken, blunder, confuse, distort, err, fail to understand, have the wrong impression, miscalculate, miscomprehend, misconceive, misconstrue, misdeem, misinterpret, misjudge, misreckon, mistake, misunderstand, receive a false impression, take amiss, take wrongly

MISAPPROPRIATE, ***verb*** bilk, cheat, commit breach of trust, divert, embezzle, exploit, expropriate, misapply, misdirect, misemploy, mismanage, peculate, pilfer, purloin, rob, steal, swindle

MISAPPROPRIATION, ***noun*** abuse, appropriation for a dishonest use, appropriation for a wrongful use, arrogation, breach of trust, conversion, defalcation, defraudation, diversion, embezzlement, fraud, fraudulent conversion, illegal use of property, larceny, malversation, misapplication, misemployment, misusage, misuse, peculation, pilferage, stealing, swindle, theft, thievery, wrongful conversion of property, wrongful use
ASSOCIATED CONCEPTS: conversion, misappropriation of funds

MISCALCULATE, ***verb*** be erroneous, be in error, be misguided, be misled, be mistaken, be wrong, blunder, calculate wrongly, commit an error, deceive oneself, deviate, err, *errare,* estimate incorrectly, fall into error, *falli,* go amiss, go astray, go awry, have the wrong impression, labor under a misapprehension, labor under an error, make a mistake, *male computare,* miscompute, misconceive, misconjecture, misconstrue, miscount, misdeem, misestimate, misjudge, misreckon, mistake, receive a false impression, slip, slip up, stray, stumble, understand incorrectly

MISCARRIAGE, ***noun*** abortion, abortive attempt, abortive effort, bad behavior, breakdown, *cadere,* collapse, default, defeat, disappointment, downfall, failure, fiasco, frustration, futile effort, hopeless failure, ineffectiveness, ineffectual attempt, loss, lost labor, misadventure, misbehavior, mischance, misconduct, misfire, mistake, negative result, noncompletion, nonfulfillment, nonperformance, nonsuccess, overthrow, *parum procedere,* perdition, rout, ruin, *secus procedere,* stoppage, successlessness, total loss, unlawful act, unproductivity, vain attempt, vain effort
ASSOCIATED CONCEPTS: miscarriage of justice

MISCELLANEOUS, ***adjective*** admixed, aggregated, amalgamated, assorted, blended, collected, combined, commingled, commixed, composite, disparate, diverse, diversified, diversiform, *diversus,* eclectic, heterogeneous, inconsistent, indiscriminate, intermixed, jumbled, manifold, many, medley, merged, mixed, mosaic, motley, multifarious, multiform, multiplex, nonuniform, of every description, of mixed character, of various kinds, *promiscuus,* scrambled, sundry, unclassified, unselected, unsorted, varied, variegated, variform, various, *varius*

MISCHIEF, ***noun*** annoyance, criminality, cruelty, damage, *damnum,* danger, detriment, devilment, deviltry, disservice, evil, evil conduct, fault, foul play, frolicsomeness, harm, harmful action, hurt, ill consequence, impishness, *incommodum,* infliction, injurious conduct, injuriousness, injury, injustice, knavery, maleficium, malicious action, malignity, maltreatment, meanness, misbehavior, misconduct, misdoing, misusage, molestation, nastiness, naughtiness, nuisance, outrage, playfulness, prankishness, puckishness, rascality, roguery, roguishness, ruin, transgression, trouble, vice, villainy, waggery, waggishness, wickedness, wrong, wrongdoing
ASSOCIATED CONCEPTS: malicious mischief

MISCONCEIVE, ***verb*** be deceived, be misguided, be misinformed, be misled, be mistaken, blunder, deceive oneself, delude oneself, distort the meaning, err, estimate incorrectly, fail to understand, fall into error, guess wrong, interpret incorrectly, labor under a misapprehension, make a mistake, misapprehend, miscalculate, misconjecture, misconstrue, misdeem, misestimate, misinterpret, misjudge, misreckon, misunderstand, *perperam accipere,* pervert, put a false construction on, receive a false impression, receive a wrong impression, value incorrectly

MISCONCEPTION, ***noun*** blunder, confusion, deception, delusion, distortion, error, fallacy, false assumption, false impression, falsity, illogical conclusion, incorrect assumption, incorrect conclusion, misapplication, misapprehension, misconjecture, misestimation, misguided conclusion, misinformation, misjudgment, mistake, misunderstanding, wrong impression

MISCONDUCT, ***noun*** bad conduct, bad management, crime, *delictum,* delinquency, dereliction, deviation from rectitude, dishonest management, disorderly conduct, error, failing, failure, fault, guilty act, ill management, illegality, improper conduct, impropriety, indiscretion, infamous conduct, maladministration, malfeasance, malpractice, malversation, misadministration, misbehavior, misdeed, misdemeanor, misdoing, misfeasance, misgovernment,

misguidance, mismanagement, misprision, negligence, nonfeasance, offense, peccadillo, *peccatum,* tort, transgression, turpitude, unprofessional conduct, wrong, wrongdoing
ASSOCIATED CONCEPTS: discharge for misconduct, gross misconduct, misconduct in office, official misconduct

MISCONSTRUE, *verb* be confused, be in error, be misled, be wrong, blunder, confuse, construe wrongly, distort, fail to understand, garble, get wrong, have an incorrect impression, make a mistake, misapprehend, misconceive, misinterpret, misjudge, misread, mistake, misunderstand, pervert, put a false sense on, receive a false idea, receive a false impression, twist the words, understand improperly

MISCUE, *noun* bad idea, blunder, botch, bungle, clumsy performance, corrigendum, deviation, erratum, error, flaw, fumble, impropriety, inadvertence, inadvertency, irregularity, miscalculation, misjudgment, miss, misstatement, misstep, mistake, misunderstanding, omission, oversight, slip, stumble

MISDEED, *noun* abomination, atrocity, bad behavior, blunder, crime, cruel act, culpable omission, delict, *delictum,* delinquency, dereliction, dutilessness, evil deed, fault, felony, guilty act, illegality, improper behavior, impropriety, infamous conduct, infraction, infringement, iniquity, injury, injustice, lapse, lawlessness, malefaction, *maleficium,* malfeasance, malpractice, malversation, misbehavior, misconduct, misdemeanor, misdoing, misfeasance, mistake, offense, outrageous act, peccadillo, peccancy, *peccatum,* scrape, sin, slip, transgression, trespass, villainy, violation, wicked action, wicked deed, wrong, wrongdoing

MISDEMEANOR, *noun* act committed in violation of law, act of lawbreaking, breach of law, crime committed, criminal act, criminal activity, criminal offense, *delictum,* dereliction, guilty act, illegality, improbity, impropriety, indiscretion, infamous conduct, malfeasance, malversation, misdeed, misdoing, misfeasance, offense, offense against the law, peccadillo, punishable offense, transgression, violation of law, wicked deed, wrong
ASSOCIATED CONCEPTS: felony, high crimes and misdemeanors, misdemeanor complaint, petit misdemeanor, violation

MISDIRECT, *verb* confound, confuse, create a false impression, give a false impression, instruct badly, involve in error, lead astray, lead into error, misaddress, misadvise, miseducate, misguide, misinform, misinstruct, mislead, misteach, put off the scent, throw into confusion

MISDOING, *noun* badness, blunder, bungle, crime, cruel act, culpability, delinquency, deviation from rectitude, dishonesty, disorderly conduct, dutilessness, error, evildoing, fault, foul play, guilty act, illegality, immorality, improbity, impropriety, incorrectness, indiscretion, inexcusability, infamous conduct, injustice, irregularity, knavery, lawlessness, maladministration, malefaction, malpractice, malversation, misapplication, misbehavior, mischief, misconduct, misdeed, misdemeanor, misfeasance, mismanagement, misprision, offense, outrage, peccadillo, rascality, roguery, ruffianism, scrape, sharp practice, slip, transgression, trespass, turpitude, unrighteousness, unsuitability, vice, villainy, violation, wicked deed, wickedness, wrong, wrongfulness

MISDOUBT, *verb* be apprehensive, be doubtful, be irresolute, be nervous, be skeptical, be uncertain, be undetermined, challenge, cherish doubts, disbelieve, distrust, doubt, entertain doubts, entertain suspicions, give no credence to, give no credit to, harbor suspicions, have doubts about, have fears, have no confidence in, have no faith in, have questions, have reservations, have suspicions, hesitate, hold questionable, lack confidence, lack conviction, lack faith, misbelieve, misgive, mistrust, pause, question, scruple, suspect, waver, withhold judgment

MISEMPLOY, *verb* abuse, *abuti,* corrupt, defile, desecrate, dissipate, distort, divert, employ improperly, ill-treat, ill-use, maltreat, manipulate improperly, misapply, misappropriate, misconduct, misdirect, misdo, mishandle, mismanage, misrule, misspend, mistreat, misuse, molest, overtax, overwork, pervert, pollute, prostitute, ruin, spoil, squander, taint, use wrongly, violate, waste, wear out

MISERABLE *(Deplorable),* ***adjective*** awful, bad, disconcerting, disgusting, lousy, low, morbid, poor, terrible, unacceptable, unpleasant, upsetting, wretched
ASSOCIATED CONCEPTS: deplorable prison conditions

MISERABLE *(Unhappy),* ***adjective*** bleak, brokenhearted, cheerless, crestfallen, depressed, depressing, depressive, desolate, despondent, disconsolate, dismal, distressed, downcast, dreary, elegiac, forlorn, funereal, gloomy, glum, hopeless, inconsolable, melancholic, melancholy, morose, pessimistic, sad, sepulchral, sorrowful, woeful

MISERY, *noun* ache, affliction, agony, asperity, calamity, crucible, curse, depths of despair, difficulty, disaster, distress, drag, gall, hardship, heartache, heartbreak, horror, joylessness, misfortune, nightmare, ordeal, pain, rigor, soreness, straits, torment, torture, tragedy, trial, tribulation, unhappiness

MISESTIMATION, *noun* bad judgment, distorted idea, distorted impression, erroneousness, error, fallaciousness, false idea, false impression, inaccuracy, inaccurateness, incorrect appraisal, incorrect evaluation, incorrect valuation, inexactitude, inexactness, misapprehension, miscalculation, miscomputation, misconception, misconjecture, misinterpretation, misjudgment, misreckoning, misstatement, mistake, misunderstanding, poor judgment, uncorrectness, unpreciseness, warped idea, warped impression, warped judgment, wrong impression

MISFEASANCE, *noun* breach of law, civil wrong, dereliction, deviation from rectitude, improper action, improper performance, infringement, injurious exercise of lawful authority, injurious exercise of authority, misconduct, misdeed, misdoing, offense, offense against the law, official misconduct, peccadillo, transgression, unlawful use of power, violation of law, wrong, wrong arising from affirmative action, wrongdoing, wrongful performance of a normally legal act, wrongfulness
ASSOCIATED CONCEPTS: malfeasance, negligence, nonfeasance

MISFORTUNE, *noun* accident, adverse event, adverse fortune, adverse lot, adverse luck, adversity, affliction, backset, bad fortune, bad luck, bale, blow, *calamitas,* calamity, casualty, cataclysm, catastrophe, comedown, destruction, disadvantage, disappointment, disaster, evil fortune, *fortuna adversa,* hardship, ill fortune, ill luck, *incommodum,* infelicity, misadventure, mischance, mishap, problem, reverse, ruin, setback, suffering, tragedy, trial, tribulation, trouble, unforeseen adversity, unfortunate occurrence, unlucky accident, unlucky happening, visitation
FOREIGN PHRASES: ***Festinatio justitiae est noverca infortunii.*** The hastening of justice is the stepmother of misfortune.

Negligentia semper habet infortunium comitem. Negligence always has misfortune for a companion.

MISGIVING, *noun* anxietude, anxiety, anxious concern, anxiousness, apprehension, apprehensiveness, concern, critical attitude, disquiet, distrust, doubt, doubtfulness, dubiety, fear, fearfulness, forbodement, foreboding, gaingiving, hesitation, inquietude, lack of certainty, lack of confidence, *metus timor,* mistrust, mistrustfulness, nervousness, objection, perturbation, *praesagium,* prediction of misfortune, premonition, presage, presentiment, qualm, reluctance, reservation, reserve, skepticalness, skepticism, *sollicitudo,* trepidation, uncertainty, uneasiness

MISGOVERN, *verb* administer badly, administer improperly, administer poorly, govern badly, maladminister, male *administrare, male regere,* manage badly, misadminister, misdirect, misguide, mismanage, misrule, rule dishonestly

MISGUIDE, *verb* befool, beguile, bewilder, cause a mistake, cause error, conceal, corrupt, create a false impression, deceive, delude, dissemble, distort, falsify, fool, *in errorum inducere,* lead astray, lead into error, lie, maladminister, misadvise, misconduct, misdirect, miseducate, mishandle, misinform, misinstruct, mislead, mismanage, misrepresent, misstate, misteach, pervert, tell a falsehood, tell a lie, tell an untruth, trip

MISHANDLE *(Maltreat),* ***verb*** abuse, assail, assault, batter, defile, handle badly, ill-treat, ill-use, impose upon, injure, manhandle, maul, misemploy, misuse, molest, overburden, persecute, ravish, rough, treat abusively, treat ill, treat improperly, tyrannize, use dispiteously, use wrongly, victimize, violate, wrong

MISHANDLE *(Mismanage),* ***verb*** abuse, administer improperly, conduct dishonestly, conduct without efficiency, conduct without honesty, handle badly, maladminister, manage badly, misconduct, misdirect, misuse, squander, use wrongly, waste

MISHAP, *noun* accident, adversity, affliction, bump, calamity, casualty, cataclysm, catastrophe, challenge, collision, deathblow, dilemma, disaster, failure, glitch, hardship, interference, letdown, malfunction, misadventure, mischance, misfortune, obstacle, obstruction, roadblock, tragedy, trial, wall, wreck

MISINFORM, *verb* conceal, create a false impression, deceive, delude, distort, exaggerate, falsify, give a false impression, misadvise, miscolor, misdirect, miseducate, misguide, misinstruct, mislead, misrepresent, misstate, misteach, propagandize, report inaccurately

MISINTERPRET, *verb* be misled, blunder, confuse, distort, err, explain incorrectly, fail to understand, garble, jumble, make a mistake, make an error, *male interpretari,* misapprehend, miscalculate, misconceive, misconjecture, misconstrue, misdeem, misjudge, misread, misreckon, misrepresent, mistake, mistranslate, misunderstand, place a false construction on, place a wrong construction on, place an erroneous construction on, receive a false impression, receive a wrong idea, receive an incorrect impression, twist the meaning, understand incorrectly
ASSOCIATED CONCEPTS: bilateral mistake, mistake of fact, mistake of law, recission, reformation, unilateral mistake

MISINTERPRETATION, *noun* distortion, incomprehension, misapplication, misapprehension, misconception, misconstruction, misconstruing, misestimation, misimpression, misinterpretation, misknowledge, misperception, misprison, misreading, mistake
ASSOCIATED CONCEPTS: professional malpractice

MISJOINDER, *noun* bad match, incongruity, misalliance, misfit, mismatch
ASSOCIATED CONCEPTS: misjoinder of causes, misjoinder of parties

MISJUDGE, *verb* be bewildered, be perplexed, blunder, err, err in judgment, estimate incorrectly, fail to recognize, have a wrong impression, judge erroneously, judge inaccurately, judge wrongly, make a mistake, make an error, male *iudicare,* misapprehend, miscalculate, miscompute, misconceive, misconstrue, misdeem, misesteem, misestimate, misinterpret, misread, misreckon, mistake, misthink, misunderstand, rate incorrectly

MISJUDGMENT, *noun* bad judgment, error, fallacy, grave injustice, gross injustice, imposition, inaccuracy, inaccurateness, inequitableness, inequity, inexactitude, inexactness, injustice, misapprehension, miscalculation, miscarriage of justice, miscomputation, misconception, misconstruction, misestimation, misinterpretation, mistake, misunderstanding, poor judgment, unfair judgment, unfairness, unjust opinion, unpreciseness, wrong estimation

MISLABEL, *verb* brand incorrectly, classify incorrectly, deceive, defraud, describe incorrectly, designate incorrectly, docket incorrectly, falsely characterize, identify incorrectly, label incorrectly, lead astray, lead into error, mark incorrectly, misbrand, mischaracterize, misclassify, misdenominate, misdescribe, misdesignate, misdirect, misguide, misidentify, misinform, mislead, mismark, misname, misrepresent, misstate, misticket, mistitle, name incorrectly, represent incorrectly, stamp incorrectly, tag incorrectly, ticket incorrectly, title incorrectly
ASSOCIATED CONCEPTS: fraud

MISLEAD, *verb* bait, be dishonest, befool, beguile, cause error, cheat, corrupt, counterfeit, cozen, create a false impression, cully, deceive, *decipere,* decoy, defraud, delude, dissemble, distort, double-cross, dupe, ensnare, entrap, *fallere,* falsify, fib, fool, give a false idea, give a false impression, guide astray, guide into error, guide wrongly, *in errorem inducere,* lead astray, lead into error, lie, misadvise, misdescribe, misdirect, miseducate, misguide, misinform, misinstruct, misrepresent, misstate, misteach, pervert, practice deception, prevaricate, seduce, snare, sophisticate, swindle, take advantage of, take in, tell a falsehood, tell an untruth, trap, trick, varnish

MISMANAGE, *verb* act foolishly, act improperly, administer improperly, administer inefficiently, administer poorly, blunder, boggle, botch, bungle, confound, derange, disarrange, fail, flounder, fumble, ill-manage, maladminister, manage poorly, manage unskillfully, misadminister, misapply, misappropriate, misconduct, misdirect, misdo, misemploy, misgovern, misguide, mishandle, misrule, missend, misuse, neglect, pervert, reduce to chaos, spoil, violate rules
ASSOCIATED CONCEPTS: mismanage trust assets

MISNOMER, *noun* error in naming, misapplied name, miscalling, misnaming, misterm, wrong designation, wrong name

MISPRISION, *noun* contempt, delinquency, deviation from rectitude, malefaction, malfeasance, malpractice, malversation, misconduct, misdeed, misfeasance, neglect, negligence, obstruction of justice, offense, transgression, violation, wrongful action of a public official
ASSOCIATED CONCEPTS: clerical misprision, misprision of felony, misprision of treason

MISPRIZE, *verb* be contemptuous of, belittle, contemn, deprecate, depreciate, despise, disdain, disesteem, disparage, disprize, disregard, feel contempt for, hold cheap, hold in contempt, look down upon, make little of, make nothing of, minimize, misjudge, overlook, push aside, ridicule, run down, scorn, set at naught, slight, sneer at, speak slightingly of, underestimate, underprize, underrate, underreckon, undervalue

MISREAD, *verb* be deceived, be erroneous, be mistaken, blunder, confuse, distort, err, fall into error, garble, interpret incorrectly, make a mistake, misapprehend, misconstrue, misdeem, misidentify, misinterpret, mistake, mistranslate, misunderstand, pervert, put a false construction on, put a wrong construction on, read incorrectly, receive a false impression, receive a wrong impression, receive an incorrect impression, translate incorrectly, twist the meaning of, understand incorrectly

MISREPRESENT, *verb* assert incorrectly, be false, bear false witness, beguile, belie, betray, break faith, *calumniari,* camouflage, color, contort, deceive, defraud, delude, *depravare,* disguise, dissemble, dissimulate, distort, distort intentionally, dupe, embroider, equivocate, exaggerate, explain wrongly, fabricate, fake, falsify, feign, fool, give a false coloring, give a false representation, hoax, lie, malign, miscite, miscolor, misdescribe, misexplain, misguide, mislead, misquote, misreport, misrepresent, misstate, misteach, mock, overstate, palter, pass off for, perjure oneself, pervert, pretend, prevaricate, put a false appearance on, put a false construction on, represent falsely, represent fraudulently, represent incorrectly, sham, simulate, slant, speak falsely, state an untruth, state falsely, tell a falsehood, tell lies, trick, trump up, twist the meaning of, understate, utter a falsehood
ASSOCIATED CONCEPTS: fraud, knowingly misrepresent, misrepresent a material fact

MISREPRESENTATION, *noun* deceitfulness, deception, deceptive statement, deceptiveness, distortion, exaggeration, fabrication, false representation, false statement, falsehood, falsification, falsity, fraud, inaccuracy, incorrect assertion, intentional misstatement, lie, misapplication, misconstruction, misguidance, misquotation, misreport, misstatement, misstatement of fact, overstatement, untrue statement, untruth, untruthfulness, unveracity
ASSOCIATED CONCEPTS: actionable misrepresentation, deceit, false misrepresentation, fraudulent misrepresentation, innocent misrepresentation, material misrepresentation, misrepresentation of a material fact, negligent misrepresentation

MISRULE, *noun* anarchism, anarchy, breakdown of administration, chaos, confusion, disorder, disorganization, impolicy, lawlessness, maladministration, malfeasance, misconduct, misdirection, misgovernment, misguidance, mishandling, mismanagement, turmoil, unruliness

MISS *(Long for),* ***verb*** desiderate, desire, pine for, regret the loss

MISS *(Overlook),* ***verb*** disregard, fail to accomplish, fail to attain, fail to catch, fail to hear, fail to perform, fail to receive, fail to see, fail to understand, fall short, gloss over, go amiss, go astray, ignore, lack, let slip, let the moment pass, lose, lose an opportunity, miscarry, miscue, misfire, miss a chance, miss the mark, not succeed, omit, overlook, pretermit, prove unsuccessful, skip

MISS THE MARK *(Not convey properly),* ***verb*** be off the mark, cause error, close to, commit an error, get an incorrect assessment, give a false impression, gloss over the significance, go amiss, go astray, go wrong, labor under a misapprehension, make a mistake, miss the importance, miss the most important issue, not be clear, not be germane

MISS THE MARK *(Not on point),* ***verb*** be deceived, be erroneous, be misguided, be misled, be mistaken, be wrong, commit an error, delude oneself, fall into error, labor under a misapprehension, make a mistake, misapprehend, miscalculate, miscompute, misconstrue, misinterpret, misjudge, misunderstand, receive a false impression
ASSOCIATED CONCEPTS: directed verdict, motion to dismiss

MISSION, *noun* aim, appointment, assignment, business, calling, charge, commission, concern, delegation, design, duty, embassy, errand, goal, job, legation, mandate, objective, office, profession, purpose, pursuit, task, trust, undertaking, venture, vocation, work

MISSTATE, *verb* be deceptive, be erroneous, deceive, delude, dissemble, distort, falsify, give a false impression, give a wrong idea, lead astray, lead into error, lie, misguide, misinform, mislead, misreport, misrepresent, pervert, prevaricate, state incorrectly, state misleadingly, tell a falsehood, tell a lie, tell an untruth, twist the meaning

MISSTATEMENT, *noun* bad reporting, blunder, deceit, deception, deviation from truth, distortion, duplicity, erratum, error, false statement, falsehood, falsification, fiction, imprecision, inaccuracy, incorrect statement, inexactitude, inexactness, insincerity, lie, mendacity, *mendacium,* misinformation, misrepresentation, mistake, perjury, perversion, pretense, slip, subreption, suppression of truth, untruth, untruthfulness, wrong statement
ASSOCIATED CONCEPTS: misstatement of fact

MISSTATEMENT OF FACT, *noun* distortion, exaggeration, fabrication, false coloring, false statement, falsification, garbled version, misconstruction, misinformation, misinterpretation, misrepresentation, misstatement, perversion, untruth
ASSOCIATED CONCEPTS: perjury, subornation of perjury

MISSTEP, *noun* accident, blunder, challenge, dilemma, errancy, error, fault, fumble, gaffe, inaccuracy, inconvenience, interference, lapse, misapprehension, miscalculation, miscue, misimpression, misinterpretation, misjudgment, mistake, obstacle, obstruction, omission, oversight, problem, slip, slipup, stumble, trip

MISTAKE, *verb* be deceived, be erroneous, be in the wrong, be misguided, be misled, be mistaken, blunder, bungle, commit an error, confuse, err, fall into error, get wrong, go amiss, go astray, go wrong, identify incorrectly, *ignorare,* labor under a misapprehension, misapprehend, miscalculate, misconceive, misconstrue, misidentify, misinterpret, misjudge, misread, misunderstand, name inaccurately, put a false sense on, receive a false impression, receive a wrong impression, slip up, stumble

ASSOCIATED CONCEPTS: excusable mistake, harmless error, mistake of fact, mistake of law, mistaken identity, mutual mistake, unilateral mistake

MISTAKEN, ***adjective*** beguiled, confused, cozened, deceived, deluded, duped, errant, erroneous, fallacious, false, fooled, hoaxed, hoodwinked, ill-advised, inaccurate, inexact, misadvised, misguided, snowed, strung along, tricked, untrue, wrong
ASSOCIATED CONCEPTS: case of mistaken identity

MISTREAT, ***verb*** abuse, afflict, aggrieve, annoy, assail, assault, attack, badger, be hurtful, be malevolent, be offensive, be pitiless, be rude, be violent, bear malice, berate, bother, bruise, bully, burden, cause evil, cause pain, create havoc, debase, desecrate, destroy, disoblige, distress, disturb, do an injustice to, do violence to, do wrong, force, give pain, harass, harm, harrow, harry, heckle, hurt, ill-treat, ill-use, impair, induce pain, inflict evil, inflict pain, injure, lay waste, lead into trouble, make mischief, malign, maltreat, manhandle, maul, misemploy, misgovern, mishandle, mismanage, misrule, misuse, molest, offend, oppress, overburden, overtask, overtax, overwork, persecute, pervert, plague, pollute, prostitute, provoke, run down, savage, show ill will, spite, strain, strike, torment, torture, trample on, tread on, treat badly, tyrannize, use dispiteously, use hard, use wrongly, vex, victimize, violate, waste, wear out, work evil, worry, wound, wrong

MISTRIAL, ***noun*** abrogation, annulment, cancellation, collapse, disannulment, erroneous trial, failure, fruitless trial, ineffective trial, invalid trial, nonfulfillment, nonsuccess, nugatory trial, nullification, nullity, revocation, terminated trial, unproductive trial, unsuccessful trial, useless trial, void trial, worthless trial
ASSOCIATED CONCEPTS: deadlocked jury, declaration of a mistrial, prejudicial error

MISTRUST, ***verb*** apprehend, be anxious, be apprehensive, be cautious, be doubtful, be dubious, be loath, be nervous, be skeptical, be uncertain, cherish doubts, distrust, doubt, dread, entertain doubts, entertain suspicions, fear, give no credit to, harbor doubts, harbor suspicions, have anxiety, have doubts, have fears, have misgivings, have no faith in, have no trust in, have qualms, have reservations, have suspicions, hesitate, hold back, lack belief in, lack confidence in, lack faith in, lack trust in, misdoubt, misgive, question, regard with suspicion, shrink from, shy from, suspect, treat with reserve

MISUNDERSTAND, ***verb*** be confused, be ignorant, be in the wrong, be misguided, be misled, be mistaken, blunder, commit an error, confuse, delude oneself, distort, err, fail to understand, fall into error, jumble, labor under a misapprehension, lack information, make a mistake, misapprehend, miscalculate, misconceive, misconstrue, misdeem, misinterpret, misjudge, misperceive, misread, misreckon, mistake, *perperam,* pervert, put a false construction on, put a wrong construction on, put an erroneous construction on, receive a wrong impression, twist the meaning, understand wrongly

MISUSAGE, ***noun*** abuse, bad treatment, corruption, debasement, defilement, degradation, desecration, distortion, diversion, exploitation, force, ill treatment, ill usage, improper usage, improper use, impropriety, maladministration, malapropism, malpractice, malversation, misapplication, misappropriation, misemployment, mismanagement, mispronunciation, misuse, peculation, perversion, pollution, prostitution, violation, wrong use

MISUSE, ***noun*** abuse, degradation, erroneous use, ill treatment, ill usage, ill use, improper usage, improper use, incorrect usage, incorrect use, maladministration, malpractice, maltreatment, misapplication, misappropriation, misemployment, mishandling, mismanagement, mistreatment, misusage, perversion, solecism, *usus,* violation, wrong use
ASSOCIATED CONCEPTS: misuse of a product, misuse of an easement, misuse of funds, misuse of powers, misuse of property, patent misuse
FOREIGN PHRASES: ***Expedit reipublicae ne sua re quis male utatur.*** It is for the interest of the state that no one should make ill use of his property.

MITIGATE, ***verb*** abate, abate in intensity, adjust, allay, alleviate, ameliorate, appease, assuage, check, control, curb, cushion, decrease, diminish, ease, give relief, *lenire,* lessen, lessen in force, lighten, make less severe, meliorate, *mitigare, mitiorem facere,* moderate, moderate in severity, mollify, palliate, reduce, regulate, relieve, restrain, soften, temper, unburden
ASSOCIATED CONCEPTS: duty to mitigate

MITIGATING, ***adjective*** abating, alleviating, ameliorative, assuaging, calmative, diminishing, discounting, easing, exculpatory, excusing, extenuating, lessening, limiting, meliorative, modifying, palliative, qualifying, reducing, relieving, softening, subduing, tempering
ASSOCIATED CONCEPTS: duty to mitigate damages, mitigating circumstances

MITIGATING FACTOR, ***noun*** diminution of sentence, extenuating circumstance, factor that decreases the severity of an offense, favorable sentencing consideration, helpful factor, lower-level classification, mitigating circumstance

MITIGATION, ***noun*** abatement, abridgment, adjustment, alleviation, assuagement, attenuation, comforting, decrease, diminishment, diminution, easing, lessening, *levamentum, levatio,* lightening, *mitigatio,* moderation, palliation, reduction, relaxation, relief, softening, soothing, weakening
ASSOCIATED CONCEPTS: mitigation of damages, mitigation of sentence

MITTIMUS, ***noun*** authorization, command, command to incarcerate, court order of imprisonment, decree, decretal, direction to imprison, edict, legal order, mandate, official order, order, transcript of minutes of commitment, warrant of commitment, written precept of imprisonment
ASSOCIATED CONCEPTS: commitment

MIX, ***verb*** amalgamate, associate, blend, combine, commingle, commix, compound, conjoin, consolidate, denature, desegregate, diffuse, fuse, incorporate, interfuse, intermingle, interpolate, intersperse, interweave, join, merge, mingle, pool, put together, unite

MIXED, ***adjective*** amalgamated, assorted, bound, brought together, combined, commixed, composite, conglomerate, cross-bred, disparate, divergent, diverse, eclectic, heterogeneous, hybrid, incorporated, indiscriminate, intermingled, intermixed, joint, merged, motley, multiple, multitudinous, myriad, sundry, unsorted, various
ASSOCIATED CONCEPTS: single-purpose bills

MOCK *(Deride),* ***verb*** chaff, *deridere,* disparage, fleer, flout, gibe, heckle, hold in derision, hold up to ridicule, hoot, *inridere,* insult, jeer, joke about, lampoon, laugh at, *ludibrio,* make a butt of, make a fool of, make fun of, poke fun at, rag, ridicule, satirize, scoff, scorn, sneer, snicker, snigger, spurn, taunt, tease, treat with contempt, treat with derision, treat with disrespect, treat with scorn, trifle with, twit

MOCK *(Imitate),* ***verb*** act, ape, assume the appearance of, burlesque, caricature, copy, counterfeit, do likewise, duplicate, echo, emulate, fake, feign, follow, follow suit, follow the example of, impersonate, mime, mimic, mirror, model after, pantomine, parody, parrot, pattern after, personate, play a part, portray, pretend, repeat, reproduce, satirize, simulate, take after, take off on, travesty

MODE, ***noun*** convention, course, craze, custom, design, fad, fashion, form, formula, guise, habit, manner, means, method, *modus,* outline, practice, precedent, prevailing style, prevailing taste, prevalence, procedure, process, protocol, rage, *ratio,* regulations, routine, rule, rules, scheme, shape, style, system, taste, technique, tendency, tenor, trend, usage, *via,* vogue, way

MODE OF OPERATION, ***noun*** approach, avenue, behavior, conduct, course, course of conduct, definite procedure, fashion, form, guise, line of action, manner of operating, means, method, methodology, mode, *modus operandi,* plan of action, practice, procedure, process, standard procedure, strategy, style, system, tactics, technique, usage, way, ways and means

MODEL, ***noun*** antetype, archetype, copy, copy in miniature, design, example, *exemplar, exemplum,* facsimile, gauge, guide, ideal, image, imitation, miniature, mold, paradigm, paragon, pattern, plan, precedent, prototype, replica, representation, sample, specimen, standard
ASSOCIATED CONCEPTS: Model Code

MODERATE *(Preside over),* ***verb*** act as chairman, act as moderator, act as president, administer, be at the head of, be in authority, chair, command, control, direct, discipline, govern, have charge of, head, hold in check, hold sway over, hold the chair, lead, manage, master, officiate, oversee, pilot, police, regulate, run, stand over, steer, supervise, take charge of

MODERATE *(Temper),* ***verb*** abate, allay, alleviate, appease, assuage, attemper, blunt, calm, chasten, check, constrain, cool, curb, dampen, decelerate, decrease, diminish, dull, ease, hush, keep within bounds, lessen, lighten, limit, make less, mitigate, modify, mollify, mute, narrow, pacify, palliate, qualify, quell, quiet, reduce, repress, restrain, season, slacken, slow down, smooth, sober, soften, soothe, still, subdue, suppress, tame, tone down, tranquilize, weaken

MODERATION, ***noun*** abstemiousness, abstinence, alleviation, assuagement, avoidance of extremes, balance, calmness, composure, conservatism, constraint, continence, *continentia,* control, coolness, deliberateness, diminution, dispassionateness, economy, equanimity, fairness, forbearance, frugality, gentleness, innocuousness, justice, lack of excess, lenience, leniency, lenity, limitation, mean, mildness, mitigation, moderateness, moderatism, modus, nonviolence, palliation, patience, quiet, reasonableness, reduction, regulation, restraint, restriction, sedateness, self-control, sobriety, steadiness, temperance, *temperantia,* temperateness, thrift, thriftiness

MODERN, ***adjective*** au courant, contemporary, current, fashionable, futuristic, happening, high-tech, in modish, latest, modernistic, modernized, new, new age, newest, nouvelle, now, present, recent, relevant, stylish, updated, up-to-date
ASSOCIATED CONCEPTS: a modern interpretation of the Constitution, a modern reading of the construction of a statute

MODEST *(Insubstantial),* ***adjective*** average, intermediate, little, middling, midsize, minimal, moderate, nominal, slight, small

MODEST *(Unassuming),* ***adjective*** acquiescent, bashful, cowering, cringing, demure, diffident, down-to-earth, meek, mousy, overmodest, passive, quiet, reserved, retiring, self-effacing, sheepish, shrinking, subdued, timid, unaffected, unaggressive, unassertive, unobtrusive, unpretentious, yielding

MODICUM, ***noun*** fraction, fragment, grain, insignificant amount, iota, minimum, minor amount, mite, particle, *paululum, paulum,* small amount, small quantity, trifle amount

MODIFICATION, ***noun*** adaptation, adjustment, alteration, change, correction, exception, limitation, partial change, qualification, reservation, restriction, slight change, variation
ASSOCIATED CONCEPTS: amendment, material modification, modification of a contract, modification of a decree, modification of a will, modification of an order, modification of judgment, reformation

MODIFY *(Alter),* ***verb*** adapt, adjust, affect, ameliorate, amend, change, *commutare,* convert, correct, effect a change, emend, emendate, give a new form to, improve, improve upon, introduce changes, make adjustments, make corrections, make improvements, meliorate, metamorphose, modernize, *mutare,* overhaul, qualify, readjust, rearrange, recast, reconstruct, rectify, refine, reform, regularize, remodel, remold, render in a better form, reshape, revamp, revise, rework, rewrite, touch up, transfigure, transform, transmute, transubstantiate, vamp, vary, work over
ASSOCIATED CONCEPTS: modify a contract, modify a decision, modify an order

MODIFY *(Moderate),* ***verb*** abate, allay, assuage, blunt, check, condition, curb, cushion, decrease, ease, extenuate, lessen, lighten, limit, lower, make less extreme, make less intense, make less severe, mitigate, *moderari,* mollify, qualify, reduce, regulate, restrict, soften, subdue, temper, *temperare,* tone down

MODUS OPERANDI, ***noun*** approach, behavior, conduct, course, course of conduct, definite procedure, line of conduct, manner, manner of operating, means, method, methodology, mode, mode of operation, mode of procedure, operation, order, pattern, procedure, process, routine, standard procedure, style, system, tactics, technique, way, ways and means

MODUS VIVENDI, ***noun*** interim agreement, manner of living, method of living, mode of living, nonpermanent agreement, nonpermanent arrangement, provisional settlement, temporary agreement, temporary arrangement, temporary settlement, transient arrangement, way of life, way of living, working arrangement

MOIETY, ***noun*** allotment, division, equal part, equal share, 50 percent, fraction, fragment, half, indefinite portion, indefinite share, measure, parcel, part, percentage, piece, portion, ration, section, segment, share

MOLD, *verb* alter, break down, change, coach, commute, convert, corrupt, develop, disintegrate, encourage, form, influence, inspire, make over, metamorphose, modify, mutate, recast, redo, refashion, remake, retool, revise, revolutionize, rework, serve as a role model, shape, transfigure, transform

MOLEST *(Annoy),* ***verb*** anger, arouse, badger, bother, discommode, disquiet, disturb, harass, harm, harry, hound, hurt, incense, incommode, inconvenience, inflame, injure, interfere with, interrupt, irk, irritate, misuse, perturb, pester, pique, plague, provoke, ruffle, *sollicitare,* tease, torment, trouble, vex, *vexare,* worry

MOLEST *(Subject to indecent advances),* ***verb*** abuse, assault, attack, defile, rape, ravish, sexually abuse, sexually assault, violate

MOLESTATION, *noun* abuse, aggravation, annoyance, bother, disturbance, ill treatment, ill usage, inconvenience, interference, interruption, intrusion, irritation, maltreatment, meddling, mistreatment, nuisance, oppression, persecution, *vexatio,* vexation

MOLLIFICATION, *noun* abatement, allayment, alleviation, amelioration, appeasement, assuagement, calmness, check, conciliation, curb, deadening, decrease, diminishment, diminution, dulcification, easement, easing, lessening, lightening, lull, mediation, melioration, mitigation, pacification, palliation, placation, propitiation, reconciliation, reduction, relaxation, relief, slackening, softening, softness, soothing, tranquilization

MOLLIFY, *verb* abate, allay, alleviate, ameliorate, appease, assuage, attemper, blunt, calm, check, compose, conciliate, cool, curb, deaden, decrease, diminish, dulcify, dull, ease, give relief, hush, improve, *lenire,* lessen, lull, make better, mediate, meliorate, mellow, milden, *mitigare,* mitigate, moderate, *mollire,* pacificate, pacify, palliate, placate, propitiate, quell, quiet, reconcile, reduce, relax, relieve, restrain, smooth, soften, soothe, still, subdue, temper, tone down, tranquilize, weaken

MOMENT, *noun* a mere split second, beat, eyeblink, flash, heartbeat, instant, minute, nanosecond, period, phase, second, space, spell, split second, stretch, time, while

MOMENTOUS, *adjective* big, consequential, critical, crucial, earthshaking, far-reaching, fateful, grand, grave, great, important, impressive, *magni momenti,* major, marked, material, memorable, notable, noteworthy, outstanding, prominent, remarkable, serious, signal, significant, special, stirring, substantial, uncommon, unordinary, unusual, weighty

MOMENTUM, *noun* antecedent, boost, catalyst, cause, encouragement, goad, headway, impetus, incentive, incitation, incitement, inducement, instigation, motivation, motive, occasion, reason, spark, spur, stimulant, stimulus, success

MONETARY, *adjective* capital, financial, fiscal, minted, numismatical, nummulary, pecuniary, stamped
ASSOCIATED CONCEPTS: monetary damages, monetary relief

MONEY, *noun* affluence, assets, bank note, bankroll, buying power, capital, cash, change, coin, coinage, currency, finances, fortune, funds, greenback, hard cash, income, legal tender, means, measure of value, medium of exchange, mintage, *nummus, pecunia,* property, resources, revenue, riches, specie, standard of value, substance, token, treasure, wealth, wherewithal, working capital
ASSOCIATED CONCEPTS: money award, money damages, money decree, money demand, money due and owing, money had and received, money judgment, money paid into court, moneyed corporation

MONITION *(Legal summons),* ***noun*** authoritative citation to appear, authoritative command, bidding, call, citation, command, commandment, decree, dictate, direction, edict, fiat, invitation, legal notice, mandate, notice to appear, notification, official call, official notice, order, requisition, rescript, subpoena, summons, summons to appear and answer, warrant, writ

MONITION *(Warning),* ***noun*** admonishment, admonition, advice, alarm, alert, caution, caveat, dehortation, enlightenment, exhortation, forewarning, hint, indication, information, notice, notification, prediction of danger

MONITOR, *verb* *admonitor,* attend, audit, check, conduct an inquiry, control, eavesdrop, examine, guard, inquire into, inspect, investigate, keep in sight, keep in view, listen, observe, overlook, oversee, review, scan, scrutinize, study, subject to examination, subject to scrutiny, survey, watch

MONOPOLIZE, *verb* absorb, appropriate, control, control market supply, control prices, control trade, corner, corner the market, dominate, engage, engross, enthrall, exercise exclusive rights, grip, have all to oneself, hold spellbound, hold the interest of, involve, keep entirely to oneself, obtain exclusive possession, occupy, own exclusively, retain exclusive control, retain exclusive possession, secure exclusive control, secure exclusive possession, stifle competition, suppress competition
ASSOCIATED CONCEPTS: conspiracy to monopolize, restraint of trade

MONOPOLY, *noun* control, control of the market, control of trade, domination, exclusive control, exclusive possession, exclusive privilege to carry on a traffic, exclusive right, *monopolium,* oligopoly, sole control of a commodity
ASSOCIATED CONCEPTS: antitrust laws, combination in restraint of trade, exemptions from antitrust laws, price fixing, trust
FOREIGN PHRASES: ***Commercium jure gentium commune esse debet, et non in monopolium et privatum paucorum quaestum convertendum.*** By the law of nations, commerce ought to be common and not converted into a monopoly and the private gain of a few persons. ***Monopolia dicitur, cum unus solus aliquod genus mercaturae universum emit, pretium ad suum libitum statuens.*** A monopoly is said to exist when one person alone buys up the whole of one kind of commodity, fixing a price at his own pleasure.

MONSTROUS, *adjective* aberrant, abnormal, abominable, awful, bad, bloodcurdling, defaced, deformed, dire, distorted, fearsome, forbidding, formidable, frightening, grotesque, heart-stopping, heinous, horrible, horrific, horrifying, irregular, misshapen, nightmarish, noxious, obscene, offensive, onerous, repulsive, revolting, shocking, terrible, ugly, unspeakable, vile

MONUMENT, ***noun*** achievement, cairn, cenotaph, cromlech, dolmen, lasting reminder, mark, memorial, *monumentum,* permanent structure, remembrance, reminder, shrine, testimonial

MONUMENTAL, ***adjective*** august, awesome, baronial, colossal, cosmic, enormous, epic, extraordinary, huge, imposing, impressive, incredible, magnific, magnificent, majestic, major, massive, noteworthy, operatic, opulent, palatial, regal, remarkable, royal, sensational, splendid, stately, titanic, tremendous

MOOT, ***adjective*** abstract, academic, actionable, arguable, contentious, contestable, contested, controversial, controvertible, debatable, disputable, disputatious, disputed, doubtful, dubious, hypothetical, in dispute, in issue, in question, open to discussion, open to question, problematical, questionable, questioned, speculative, subject to controversy, suppositional, theoretical, uncertain, undecided, under discussion, undetermined, unsettled, untried
ASSOCIATED CONCEPTS: academic question, moot appeal, moot case, moot controversy, moot court, moot question

MORAL, ***adjective*** aboveboard, *bene moratus,* bound by duty, commendable, conscientious, correct, creditable, decent, deserving, duteous, dutiful, estimable, ethical, exemplary, good, high-minded, high-principled, honest, *honestus,* honorable, idealistic, incorrupt, incorruptible, innocent, just, laudable, law-abiding, meritorious, noble, praiseworthy, principled, *probus,* proper, pure, reputable, respectable, responsible, right-minded, righteous, *sanctus,* scrupulous, spotless, truehearted, trustworthy, uncorrupt, uncorrupted, unerring, upright, upstanding, virtuous, well-conducted, worthy
ASSOCIATED CONCEPTS: moral certainty, moral character, moral consideration, moral dereliction, moral duty, moral obligation, moral turpitude

MORAL RECTITUDE, ***noun*** character, decency, decorousness, decorum, ethics, ethos, etiquette, fitness, honesty, incorruptibility, integrity, irreproachability, moral fortitude, principles, propriety, righteousness, right-mindedness, seemliness, standards, uprightness, virtue, virtuousness
ASSOCIATED CONCEPTS: character and fitness committee, professional conduct

MORALITY, ***noun*** authenticity, candor, character, correctness, decency, decorousness, decorum, etiquette, forthrightness, frankness, genuineness, good faith, guilelessness, honesty, honor, integrity, irreproachableness, propriety, rectitude, rightness, scrupulosity, seemliness, sincerity, trustworthiness, truth, uprightness, virtue

MORATORIUM, ***noun*** abeyance, break, cessation, close, deferral, delay, desistance, discontinuance, end, ending, halt, hold, interim, interval, leaving off, lull, pause, period, period of obligatory delay, postponement, recess, respite, rest, standstill, stop, stoppage, suspension, temporary halt, temporary relief, termination, wait, waiting period
ASSOCIATED CONCEPTS: moratorium acts, moratorium on repayment of debt

MORDACIOUS, ***adjective*** acerbic, acid, acrid, acrimonious, acute, biting, bitter, caustic, corrosive, cutting, harsh, incisive, knifelike, malicious, mordant, penetrating, piercing, pointed, pungent, rancorous, raw, rough, scathing, severe, sharp, slashing, spiteful, stinging, trenchant, uncharitable, unkind, virulent, vitriolic

MORTAL, ***adjective*** a living being, alive, animate, anthropoid, awake, being, bodily, corporeal, creatural, earthborn, existent, fleshly, hominid, human, humanlike, individual, living, material, natural, person, physical, temporal, terrestrial, worldly

MORTALITY, ***noun*** *condicio mortalis,* death, destruction, evanescence, extinction, fatality, fugaciousness, fugacity, human race, humanity, humanness, impermanence, man, mankind, *mortalitas,* mortalness, subjection to death, temporary existence, transientness, transitoriness
ASSOCIATED CONCEPTS: mortality tables

MORTGAGE, ***noun*** charge, collateral security, conditional conveyance of land, conditional property transfer, contractual obligation, encumbrance, engagement, indebtedness, loan transaction, obligation, *pignus,* pledge, pledge for the payment of a debt, pledge of security, real security, security, security for a debt, something owing, state of indebtedness, transfer of property as security for a debt, transfer of security
ASSOCIATED CONCEPTS: amortization of a mortgage, assignment of a mortgage, assumption of a mortgage, chattel mortgage, constructive mortgage, equitable mortgage, first mortgage, foreclosure of a mortgage, holder of a mortgage, lien, maturity of a mortgage, mortgage commitment, mortgagee in possession, mortgagee of record, mortgagor, purchase money mortgage, recording of a mortgage, redemption of a mortgage, second mortgage, subject to a mortgage

MORTIFY, ***verb*** abash, affront, besmirch, castigate, censure, cheapen, condemn, confound, debase, depreciate, discomfit, disconcert, discountenance, discredit, disgrace, disgust, dishonor, disparage, embarrass, fluster, humiliate, insult, lower, nonplus, offend, rattle, shame, smirch

MOST *(Biggest),* ***adjective*** best, biggest, greatest, highest, hugest, largest, topmost, unparalleled, unrivaled, unsurpassed, uppermost

MOST *(More),* ***adjective*** a lot, abundance, ample, innumerable, manifold, many, maximum, multitudinous, numerous, quite a lot

MOTIF, ***noun*** adornment, arrangement, beautification, composition, construction, decoration, design, detail, dominant theme, embellishment, figuration, figure, form, format, garnishment, illumination, main feature, ornament, ornamentation, overall theme, pattern, plan, prevailing idea, recurring theme, shape, structure, style, theme

MOTION, ***noun*** application, application for a ruling, application for an order, application for proposed relief, claim, demand, petition, proposal, proposed measure, proposition, request, *rogatio, sententia*
ASSOCIATED CONCEPTS: alternative motions, costs of a motion, ex parte motion, interlocutory motion, motion for a more definite statement, motion for a new trial, motion for a nonsuit, motion for a decree, motion for judgment, motion for judgment notwithstanding verdict, motion for reargument, motion for summary judgment, motion papers, motion to dismiss, motion to quash, motion to set aside judgment, motion to strike, motion to vacate a judgment, omnibus motion, premature motion, renewal of a motion, withdrawal of a motion

MOTION IN LIMINE, ***noun*** motion to exclude as evidence, preliminary motion, pretrial motion on admissibility, threshold motion

MOTIVATE, *verb* activate, actuate, adjure, advise, affect, allure, animate, appeal, arouse desire, attract, captivate, carry weight, cause, challenge, charge, command, compel, convince, direct, draw, encourage, exert influence, exhort, fill with longing, fire up, goad, guide, impel, incite, incline, induce, infect, inflame, influence, inspire, inspirit, instigate, interest, invite, lead, move, move to action, persuade, press, prevail upon, promote, prompt, provide with a motive, provoke desire, rouse, set in motion, spirit, spur, stimulate, stir up, sway, talk into, tempt, urge, work upon

MOTIVE, *noun* aim, causa, causation, compulsion, consideration, design, determination, driving force, encouragement, end, goal, impelling power, impulse, incentive, inducement, influence, inner drive, inspiration, moving cause, moving power, moving spirit, object, objective, personal reasons, persuasion, plan, point, proposal, prospect, provocation, purpose, *ratio,* rationale, reason, reason for action, stimulant, stimulation, stimulus
ASSOCIATED CONCEPTS: corrupt motive, intent

MOUTHPIECE, *noun* advocate, agent, ambassador, attorney, barrister, delegate, emissary, envoy, face, figurehead, hired gun, instrument, lawyer, negotiator, pleader, professional, protagonist, representative, solicitor, speaker, spokesman

MOVABLE, *noun* *agilis,* chattels personal, effects, goods, *mobilis,* personal effects, personal property, personalty, possessions, transportables, transportable property
ASSOCIATED CONCEPTS: fixtures, movable goods, movable machinery
FOREIGN PHRASES: ***Mobilia non habent situm.*** Movables have no situs or local habitation.

MOVE *(Alter position),* ***verb*** abscond, alter the position, break camp, carry, change an abode, change place, change residence, come away, *commovere,* convey, depart, disperse, emigrate, exit, flee, go, go away, go forth, go from home, go on, go one's way, journey, leave, leave a place, migrate, move out, part company, progress, propel, push on, put in motion, remove, slip away, slip off, take flight, transfer, translocate, transport, transpose, vacate, walk away, walk off

MOVE *(Judicially request),* ***verb*** apply, ask for, introduce, make a demand, make a motion, make a petition, make a request, make a requisition, make application, make formal application, make one's submission, offer for consideration, petition, propose, propose a motion, propose an action formally, put forth, put forward, put up a petition, referre, request, requisition, submit, submit a formal request
ASSOCIATED CONCEPTS: motion practice, move the court

MOVEMENT *(Activity),* ***noun*** campaign, cause, crusade, mass movement, motion, operation, principle, series of actions directed toward a particular end, undertaking

MOVEMENT *(Progress),* ***noun*** action, agitation, campaign, circulation, course, denomination, effort, great cause, interest, issue, measure, outflow, performance, removal, shift, step, stir, stride, transition, transmittal, traveling

MOVEMENT *(Shipment),* ***noun*** cartage, conveyance, transit, transportation

MOVING *(Evoking emotion),* ***adjective*** absorbing, affecting, agitating, animating, arousing, arresting, astonishing, awakening, breathtaking, captivating, charming, impelling, imposing, impressive, inciting, inflaming, influencing, inspiriting, instigating, interesting, *miserabilis,* overpowering, overwhelming, persuading, piquant, poignant, prompting, provocative, provoking, rousing, sensational, sensitive, stimulating, stimulative, stirring, thrilling, touching, warm

MOVING *(In motion),* ***adjective*** active, ambulant, ambulative, ambulatory, changing, conveyable, detachable, drifting, fugitive, itinerant, journeying, kinetic, locomotive, meandering, mercurial, migratory, mobile, motile, motive, mundivagant, nomadic, passing, peripatetic, removable, restless, roaming, roving, separable, shifting, touring, transient, transitional, transmigratory, traveling, unattached, unfastened, unsettled, unstaid, unstationary, vacillating, vagabond, vagrant, voyaging, wandering, wavering, wayfaring
ASSOCIATED CONCEPTS: moving papers, moving party, moving violation

MUCH, *adjective* a lot, abounding, adequate, ample, beaucoup, bountiful, comfortable, countless, generous, innumerable, legion, liberal, many, multifold, multiple, multitudinous, numberless, numerous, plenteous, plentiful, plenty, replete, rich, rife, significant, sufficient, surplus, wealthy

MUCKRAKE, *verb* aggravate, agitate, anger, antagonize, bother, cause distress through an investigation, change, condemn, enquire, enrage, exasperate, expose, get, inflame, investigate, offend, outrage, perturb, rankle, rile, unhinge, unsettle, upset through inquiry

MUDDLE, *verb* addle, baffle, becloud, befog, befuddle, bewilder, botch, bungle, cloud, complicate, confound, *confundere,* confuse, daze, derange, disarrange, discompose, disconcert, disorder, disorganize, disturb, embrangle, entangle, fluster, fog, fuddle, ignore distinctions, jumble, make a mess of, make havoc, mismanage, mix up, obfuscate, *permiscere,* puzzle, scramble, stupefy, throw into confusion, throw out of order, *turbare,* unsettle, upset

MULCT *(Defraud),* ***verb*** cheat, deceive, embezzle, fudge, peculate, practice fraud, sharp, steal, swindle, trick

MULCT *(Fine),* ***verb*** amerce, deprive, distrain, exact a fine, impose a fine, penalize, punish

MULL OVER, *verb* analyze, brood, chew over, cogitate, consider, contemplate, deliberate, entertain, examine, fixate on, kick around, meditate, muse, obsess, opine, question, reflect, reminisce, review, ruminate, speculate, study, think through

MULTIFARIOUS, *adjective* different, disparate, dissimilar, diverse, diversified, heterogeneous, irregular, manifold, many, miscellaneous, mixed, motley, multiform, multigenerous, multiplex, nonuniform, numerous, varied, variegated, various, *varius*

MULTIFOLD, *adjective* diversified, diversiform, manifold, many, multifarious, multiform, multigenerous, multiple, multiplex, multiplicate, multitudinous, numerous, varied, variegated, variform

MULTIPLE, *adjective* abundant, aggregate, ample, assorted, composed of several elements, considerable, different, divergent, diverse, diversified, generous, innumerable,

many, miscellaneous, mixed, more than one, multifarious, multifold, multiplex, multitudinous, myriad, numerous, plenteous, plural, profuse, several, sundry, superabundant, uncounted, unnumbered, untold, varied, various
ASSOCIATED CONCEPTS: multiple claims, multiple damages, multiple dwelling, multiple offender, multiplicity of suits

MULTIPLICITY, ***noun*** many sidedness, multitudinous, numerousness, plurality

MULTIPLY, ***verb*** accelerate, accumulate, add to, aggrandize, amplify, augment, bear, beget, boom, boost, breed, build up, bump, compound, engender, enlarge, escalate, expand, extend, flesh out, generate, heighten, increase, inflate, intensify, produce, propagate, reproduce, spike, stoke, supersize, swell

MULTITUDE, ***noun*** abundance, accumulation, aggregation, amassment, army, array, assemblage, assembly, band, bevy, body, cluster, collection, conglomeration, congregation, covey, crowd, cumulation, drove, flock, force, gathering, herd, horde, host, legion, magnitude, many-sidedness, mass, masses, multiplicity, numbers, numerosity, numerousness, plurality, populace, profusion, quantities, quantity, scores, swarm, throng, troupe, volume

MUNDANE, ***adjective*** accustomary, average, banal, bodily, carnal, common, commonplace, conventional, corporeal, customary, earthly, everyday, familiar, fleshly, frequent, habitual, hackneyed, homespun, irreligious, material, nonsacred, nonspiritual, ordinary, pedestrian, physical, plain, profane, prosaic, prosy, regular, routine, secular, sensual, simple, stale, standard, stereotyped, sublunar, sublunary, tedious, tellurian, telluric, temporal, terrene, terrestrial, trite, typical, undistinguished, uneventful, unexalted, ungodly, unhallowed, unholy, unimaginative, uninspired, uninteresting, unpoetical, unsacred, unsanctified, unspiritual, usual, wearisome, well-known, well-trodden, workday, worldly, worldly minded

MUNIFICENT, ***adjective*** altruistic, beneficent, benevolent, bighearted, bountiful, charitable, compassionate, freehearted, generous, hospitable, humanitarian, kindly, lavish, liberal, openhanded, philanthropic, Samaritan, sympathetic, unselfish

MURDER, ***noun*** act of killing, act of slaying, act of taking life, assassination, *caedes,* destruction, destruction of human life, destruction of life, destructiveness, elimination, genocide, homicide, intentional killing, killing, liquidation, massacre, *occisio,* taking of human life, unlawful killing, violent death
ASSOCIATED CONCEPTS: assault with intent to murder, attempted murder, felonious homicide, felony murder, first-degree murder, premeditated murder, second-degree murder, voluntary manslaughter, willful murder

MURDERER, ***noun*** annihilator, assassin, assassinator, butcher, contract killer, criminal, destroyer, eradicator, executioner, exterminator, gunman, hired gun, hired killer, hit man, killer, liquidator, slaughterer, slayer, sniper

MUSE, ***verb*** be abstracted, be distracted, be in a reverie, be inattentive, be occupied in concentration, be occupied in study, bestow thought upon, brood, cerebrate, cogitate, comment, commune with oneself, concentrate, consider, contemplate, daydream, debate, deliberate, digest, disregard, examine, intellectualize, introspect, meditate, mull, note, ponder, reflect, remark, review, revolve, ruminate, speculate, study in silence, study quietly, take into consideration, take stock of, think, think about, think over, turn over, weigh

MUST-CARRY RULES, ***noun*** cable provider requirement, digital must-carry, local TV station requirement, requirement to carry locally licensed television stations, signal carriage obligation, television station mandate

MUTABLE, ***adjective*** alterable, capricious, changeable, changeful, commutable, fickle, fluctuating, inconstans, inconstant, irresolute, *mutabilis,* protean, subject to change, transient, uncertain, undecided, unreliable, unsettled, unstable, unsteadfast, unsteady, vacillating, variable, versatile, volatile, wavering
FOREIGN PHRASES: ***Nomina sunt mutabilia, res autem immobiles.*** Names are mutable, but things are immutable. ***Res est misera ubi jus est vagum et incertum.*** It is a sorry state of affairs when law is vague and mutable.

MUTE, ***adjective*** close-lipped, closemouthed, dumb, hushed, inarticulate, incapable of speech, incommunicative, indisposed to talk, *mutus,* noiseless, pauciloquent, quiescent, quiet, refraining from utterance, reserved, reticent, silent, soundless, speechless, still, taciturn, tight-lipped, tongue-tied, unable to speak, unable to utter articulate sound, uncommunicative, unexpressive, unloquacious, untalkative, unvocal, unvocalizing, voiceless, wordless

MUTILATE, ***verb*** amputate, batter, blemish, bruise, butcher, cripple, cut, damage, debilitate, deface, deform, deprive of an important part, disable, disfigure, dismantle, dismember, distort, gash, impair, incapacitate, injure, knock out of shape, lacerate, maim, mangle, mar, *mutilare,* render a document imperfect, render imperfect, tear, tear apart, truncate, twist, unshape, warp, wound, wreck

MUTINY, ***noun*** defiance, disloyalty, disobedience, insubordination, insurgence, insurgency, insurrection, *motus,* opposition, oppugnancy, outbreak, rebellion, refusal to comply, resistance, revolt, revolution, *seditio,* sedition, subversion, treason, upheaval, uprising

MUTUAL *(Collective),* ***adjective*** coadjutant, coadjutive, coadjuvant, coadunate, coalitional, collaborated, collaborative, combined, common, communal, communalistic, commutual, confederated, conjoint, cooperant, cooperative, federal, federate, federated, federative, general, in common, interdependent, joint, leagued, participatory, shared, unified, united
ASSOCIATED CONCEPTS: mutual benefit association, mutual enterprise, mutual insurance company, mutual savings bank

MUTUAL *(Reciprocal),* ***adjective*** bilateral, commutative, complemental, complementary, concurrent, correlative, correspondent, corresponding, done reciprocally, equivalent, interactive, interchanged, interrelated, *mutuus,* parallel, reciprocating, reciprocative, two-sided, two-way
ASSOCIATED CONCEPTS: mutual consent, mutual covenants, mutual easements, mutual mistake, mutual promise, mutual wills

MUTUAL AGREEMENT, ***noun*** acclamation, accord, accordance, affirmation, common consent, concord, concordance, concurrent agreement, consensus, consentaneity, consentience, contract, general agreement, likemindedness, meeting of the minds, mutual arrangement, mutual bargain, pact, unanimity, unison, universal agreement

MUTUAL UNDERSTANDING, *noun* accord, agreement, alliance, amity, bilateral contract, common agreement, common understanding, communion, compact, concordance, concurrence, contract, correlative agreement, entente, interchangeable commitment, joint agreement, joint pact, meeting of minds, mutual promise, pact, reciprocal agreement, reciprocal commitment, treaty

MUTUALITY, *noun* coequality, commonality, commutability, commutation, correlation, correlativeness, correlativity, correspondence, dependence, exchange, interaffiliation, interassociation, interchange, interchangeability, interconnection, interdependence, intermutation, interplay, interrelation, mutual dependence, mutual relation, permutation, reciprocality, reciprocalness, reciprocation, reciprocity
ASSOCIATED CONCEPTS: mutuality of consent, mutuality of contract, mutuality of obligation, mutuality of remedy

MYRIAD, *adjective* boundless, countless, endless, illimitable, immense, incalculable, inexhaustible, infinite, innumerable, innumerous, limitless, manifold, many, measureless, multitudinous, numberless, numerous, sumless, uncountable, uncounted, unending, unfathomable, unlimited, unnumberable, unnumbered, untold, without number

MYSTERIOUS, *adjective* abstruse, arcane, *arcanus,* baffling, cabalistic, clandestine, cloaked, coded, concealed, covert, cryptic, dark, disguised, enigmatic, enigmatical, esoteric, furtive, hidden, impenetrable, incomprehensible, ineffable, inexplicable, inscrutable, magical, masked, mystic, mystical, mystifying, obscure, occult, *occultus,* oracular, perplexing, preternatural, privy, puzzling, recondite, runic, screened, secret, secretive, *secretus,* shadowy, sphinxian, sphinxlike, stealthy, strange, supernatural, supernormal, surreptitious, transcendental, umbrageous, unaccountable, uncanny, undeciphered, undercover, underhand, undisclosed, unexplainable, unexplained, unfathomable, unintelligible, unknown, unrevealed, untold, veiled, weird

MYSTERY, *noun* abstruseness, arcanum, cabala, cabalism, concealment, enigma, hidden meaning, inexplicableness, inscrutability, inscrutableness, mysticism, obscurity, occultism, occultness, puzzle, *res occulta,* riddle, secrecy, secret, secretiveness, thaumaturgy, undiscoverability, unexplored ground, unfathomability, unfathomableness

MYSTICAL, *adjective* abstruse, ambiguous, apocryphal, arcane, cabalistic, cryptic, dark, difficult to ascertain, enigmatic, esoteric, hermetic, incomprehensible, magical, mysterious, obscure, occult, opaque, orphic, perplexing, recondite, secret, strange, tenebrous, uncertain, unclear, unfathomable, vague

MYTH, *noun* absurd story, concoction, doubtful narrative, fable, fabrication, *fabula,* false story, falsehood, fantasy, fiction, fictitious story, figment, folklore, folktale, invention, legend, legendary story, story, tale, tall story, tradition, trumped-up story, unreality, untrue story, untruth, yarn
ASSOCIATED CONCEPTS: legal fiction

MYTHICAL, *adjective* allegorical, chimerical, contrived, fabled, fabulous, fake, fanciful, fantastic, fictional, fictitious, ideal, imaginary, imagined, invented, legendary, made up, make-believe, phantasmal, phantasmic, phantom, pretend, romanticized, storied, unreal, visionary, whimsical

NAïVE, *adjective* believing, callow, childish, childlike, credulous, deceivable, deludable, dupable, exploitable, foolable, green, gullible, immature, inexperienced, innocent, natural, open, plain, provincial, simple, *simplex,* trusting, unaffected, unfeigned, unschooled, unsophisticated, unsuspecting, unsuspicious, unworldly, void of suspicion

NAKED *(Lacking embellishment),* ***adjective*** bare, basal, basic, devoid of consideration, elementary, fundamental, laid bare, mere, plain, sheer, simple, stark, straight, unadorned, unadulterated, uncomplicated, undecorated, undisguised, unembellished, unexaggerated, unmasked, unornamented, unvarnished, unveiled
ASSOCIATED CONCEPTS: naked promise

NAKED *(Perceptible),* ***adjective*** apparent, brought to light, clear, cognizable, conspicuous, discernible, disclosed, discoverable, distinct, distinguishable, easy to see, evident, explicit, exposed, express, in plain view, made public, manifest, not obscure, noticeable, observable, obvious, open, ostensible, overt, patent, perceivable, plain, prominent, recognizable, revealed, unconcealed, unmistakable, visible

NAME, *noun* being, characteristic, difference, distinction, distinctiveness, distinctness, identifier, identifying characteristic, identity, individualism, oneness, originality,

particularity, personage, personal characteristic, personality, quality of being singular, self, selfness, singleness, singularity, specialty, uniqueness
ASSOCIATED CONCEPTS: distinctive name, trade name

NAMED, *adjective* called, classified, delineated, denoted as, described as, designate as, determined as, discriminated as, distinguished as, identified as, known as, recognized as, referred to as, specified as
ASSOCIATED CONCEPTS: named in a caption

NARCOTIC, *adjective* anesthetic, anodyne, anodynous, assuaging, assuasive, calmant, calmative, deadening, depressant, dulling, hypnotic, mitigating, narcotical, opiate, pain-killing, palliative, paregoric, sedative, slumberous, somniferous, somnific, soothing, soporiferous, soporific, stupefactive, torporifc, tranquilizing

NARCOTIC, *noun* alleviative, alleviator, anesthetic, anodyne, assuasive drug, barbiturate, calmative, depressant, dope, drug, hypnotic, lenitive, medication, medicine, mitigative, opiate, pain reliever, painkiller, palliative, sedative, somnifacient, soother, soporific, stupefacient, tranquilizer

NARRATION, *noun* account, chronicle, delineation, depiction, depictment, description, descriptive account, discourse, disquisition, *expositio,* exposition, iteration, *narratio,* narrative, portrayal, recapitulation, recital, recitation, recountal, recounting, reiteration, relation, rendition, repetition, report, representation, restatement, retelling, review, setting forth, sketch, storytelling, summarization, summary, tale, tale telling

NARRATIVE, *adjective* anecdotal, communicative, declarative, declaratory, descriptive, detailed, disquisitional, epic, exegetic, exegetical, explanatory, explicative, explicatory, expositive, expository, graphic, illuminating, illuminative, illustrative, informational, informative, *narrare,* recounted, reported, sequential, storylike, told
ASSOCIATED CONCEPTS: narrative testimony

NARROW, *adjective* attenuated, bigoted, circumscribed, compressed, confined, constricted, contracted, *contractus,* cramped, crowded, defined, dogmatic, exact, fanatical, fine, illiberal, incapacious, inhibiting, intolerant, limited, literal, narrow-minded, opinionated, parochial, pinched, precise, prescribed, protected, provincial, qualified, registered, restricted, rigid, scant, scanty, simple, slender, strict, tapering, thin, tight
ASSOCIATED CONCEPTS: a narrowly written decision, narrow interpretation

NARROW MEANING, *noun* accurate meaning, correct meaning, defined meaning, definition, distinct meaning, exact meaning, explanation, explicit meaning, express meaning, faithful meaning, inflexible meaning, literal meaning, methodical meaning, meticulous meaning, not subject to interpretation, ordinary meaning, plain meaning, precise meaning, prescribed meaning, rigid meaning, rigorous meaning, sharply defined, significance, specific meaning, strict meaning, unbending meaning, uncompromising meaning, unequivocal meaning
ASSOCIATED CONCEPTS: construction, literal contract, literal proof, plain meaning rule, rules of statutory, soft plain meaning rule, textualism

NARROWLY TAILORED, *noun* government action that addresses essential elements of government interest, government action that goes no further than necessary, government action that is appropriate, government action that is not overbroad, government action that utilizes the least restrictive means

NASCENCY, *noun* beginning, birth, commencement, creation, debut, development, emergence, entrance, entry, evolution, evolvement, first appearance, first stage, first step, formation, foundation, founding, genesis, inauguration, inception, inchoation, incipience, incipiency, incunabula, induction, infancy, initiation, introduction, invention, launching, nascence, nativity, onset, origin, origination, outset, rise, start, starting

NASCENT, *adjective* beginning, blossoming, budding, burgeoning, developing, earlier, early, elemental, elementary, embryonic, first, first ever, first of all, fledgling, flowering, formative, foundational, fundamental, germinal, in its infancy, inaugural, inceptive, inchoate, incipient, incunabular, infant, infantile, infantine, initial, initiatory, introductory, inventive, original, originating, potential, prenatal, primal, primary, prime, primeval, primitive, promising, rudimental, rudimentary, seminal, youthful

NATION, *noun* captive nation, commonweal, commonwealth, confederation, county, developed nation, domain, dominion, kingdom, land, nationality, possession, power, province, realm, territory
ASSOCIATED CONCEPTS: comity, free trade, international law

NATIONAL, *adjective* affecting the nation as a whole, common, country-wide, domestic, established by the federal government, federal, general, government, government-owned, governmental, public, publicly owned, societal, sovereign

NATIONALITY, *noun* allegiance, birth, body politic, citizenry, commonwealth, country, fatherland, habitancy, homeland, inhabitancy, inhabitation, nation, national group, national status, native land, nativity, origin, people, polity, populace, society, sovereign state, statehood, stock
ASSOCIATED CONCEPTS: immigration and naturalization

NATIONALIZE, *verb* appropriate for federal use, appropriate for government use, make national, make national in character, place under government control, remove from private ownership, seize for public use, seize for the government, socialize, transfer control to the government, transfer ownership to the government

NATIVE *(Domestic),* ***adjective*** aboriginal, autochthonal, autochthonic, autochthonous, domestic, enchorial, enchoric, endemic, endemical, home-grown, indigenous, local, locally born, not alien, not foreign, original, regional, unborrowed, vernacular

NATIVE *(Inborn),* ***adjective*** basic, born, congenital, connate, connatural, essential, fundamental, genetic, hereditary, inbred, indigenous, ingenerate, ingenit, ingrained, inherent, inherited, innate, instinctive, instinctual, intrinsic, natal, natural, organic, original

NATIVE RIGHTS, *noun* Aboriginal American rights, indigenous rights, Native American civil rights, Native American rights, tribal sovereignty

NATURAL, *adjective* artless, authentic, characteristic, connate, consistent, crude, free from affectation,

fundamental, genuine, inborn, inbred, indigenous, ingenerate, ingrained, innate, *innatus,* instinctive, instinctual, lifelike, native, nativus, normal, organic, original, pure, real, realistic, regular, true to life, typical, unadulterated, unartificial, uncultivated, unsynthetic, untouched
ASSOCIATED CONCEPTS: natural law

NATURALIZE *(Acclimate),* ***verb*** accommodate, accustom, adapt, adjust, assimilate, become habituated, cultivate a habit, familiarize, fit the pattern, get used to, habituate, harmonize, inure, learn a habit, make easy, make natural, normalize, regularize

NATURALIZE *(Make a citizen),* ***verb*** accept as a citizen, admit citizenship, adopt, adopt as a citizen, adopt into a nation, assimilate, citizenize, confer privileges of a native citizen, confer rights of citizenship, denizenize, endow with rights of citizenship, extend citizenship to an alien, *homini civitatem dare,* nationalize, place in the condition of natural born subjects

NATURE *(Kind),* ***noun*** attribute, brand, breed, character, characteristic, description, designation, differentia, differential, distinctive feature, domain, feature, ilk, individualism, label, make, manner, mannerism, mark, model, mold, particularity, peculiarity, persuasion, quality, quirk, specialty, species, sphere, strain, style, taint, tang, taste, the like or likes of, token, trait, tribe, trick, type, variety
ASSOCIATED CONCEPTS: nature of an action, the nature of a case

NATURE *(Naturalness),* ***noun*** artlessness, inartificiality, intactness, natural man, natural state, nature in the raw, pristineness, state of nature, virginity
ASSOCIATED CONCEPTS: environmental law

NEAR, ***adjective*** adjacent, adjoining, approaching, approximate, bordering, close, close by, contiguous, imminent, impending, in close proximity, in the area, in the neighborhood, in the vicinity, nearby, neighboring, next, next to, proximal, proximate to, surrounding, tangent, touching, vicinal
ASSOCIATED CONCEPTS: case near to being put on the trial calendar, case nearly ready for trial, cases near trial, completion, near competition, substantial completion

NEARBY, ***adjective*** abutting, accessible, adjacent, adjoining, approaching, bordering, close, close-up, coming, contiguous, convenient, handy, immediate, local, near, neighboring, next-door, nigh, proximate

NEAREST, ***adjective*** almost, approximate, closer, closest, close-up, immediate, most immediate, near, nearby, neighboring, next-door, proximate, relative

NEBULOUS, ***adjective*** abstruse, ambiguous, bleared, blurred, blurry, clouded, cloudy, confused, dim, dusky, faint, foggy, hazy, ill-defined, imperspicuous, indeterminate, indistinct, lacking clarity, nebulose, *nebulosus,* not clear, obfuscated, obscure, out of focus, pale, recondite, shadowed, shadowy, uncertain, unclear, undefined, undiscernible, unintelligible, vague
ASSOCIATED CONCEPTS: nebulous contract

NECESSARY *(Inescapable),* ***adjective*** avoidless, certain, choiceless, compelling, constraining, decided, decreed, designated, destined, expected, fated, fateful, fixed, foreordained, imminent, impending, ineluctable, ineludible, inevitable, inexorable, irresistible, irrevocable, ordained, sealed, settled, sure, unalterable, unavoidable, uncontrollable, undeniable, unevasible, unpreventable
ASSOCIATED CONCEPTS: necessary damages, necessary expenses, necessary implication, necessary inference, necessary injury

NECESSARY *(Required),* ***adjective*** all-important, basic, binding, bounden, chief, coercive, compelling, compulsory, critical, crucial, demanded, dictated, essential, exigent, expedient, fundamental, imperative, important, imposed, incumbent, indispensable, integral, key, mandatory, necessitated, necessitous, needed, obligatory, paramount, prerequisite, prescribed, prime, principal, requisite, requisitioned, significant, strategic, strategical, substantive, urgent, vital
ASSOCIATED CONCEPTS: necessary parties

NECESSARY, ***noun*** essence, essential, essentiality, indispensable thing, *necessitas,* necessities, necessitousness, necessitude, necessity, need, prerequirement, prerequisite, qualification, requirement, requisite, vitals
ASSOCIATED CONCEPTS: duty to provide necessaries, necessaries of life

NECESSARY PARTY, ***noun*** critical party who cannot be joined, crucial party who cannot be joined, integral defendant who cannot be joined, integral disputant who cannot be joined, integral party who cannot be joined, integral petitioner who cannot be joined, integral plaintiff who cannot be joined, integral respondent who cannot be joined, needed party who cannot be joined, party whose interests will be affected, prescribed party whose cannot be joined, significant party who cannot be joined, strategic party who cannot be joined, vital party who cannot be joined
ASSOCIATED CONCEPTS: indispensable party, proper party

NECESSITATE, ***verb*** call for, clamor for, coerce, *cogere,* compel, concuss, create a need, decree, demand, dictate, enjoin, exact, force, impel, impose, insist upon, leave no choice, leave no option, make indispensable, make inevitable, make necessary, make unavoidable, obligate, oblige, ordain, predetermine, raise a demand, render necessary, require

NECESSITY, ***noun*** absolute requisite, basic ingredient, central element, characteristic feature, compelling quality, compulsory detail, crucial part, *egestas,* elementary detail, essential, essential element, exigency, fundamental, fundamental principle, fundamental unit, highly important detail, imperative, indispensable, indispensable provision, inevitable, integral part, irreplaceable feature, irresistible compulsion, main ingredient, mandatory factor, necessary attribute, necessary component, *necessitas,* need, precondition, prerequirement, prerequisite, primary constituent, qualification, recognized condition, required item, requirement, requisite, rudiment, significant detail, strategic item, urgency, urgent requirement, vital part, vitals
ASSOCIATED CONCEPTS: compelling necessity, economic necessity, finding of necessity, prescription by necessity, public necessity, strict necessity
FOREIGN PHRASES: ***Quod est necessarium est licitum.*** That which is necessary is lawful. ***Necessitas excusat aut extenuat delictum in capitalibus, quod non operatur idem in civilibus.*** Necessity excuses or extenuates an offense in capital cases, but not in civil cases. ***Necessitas est lex temporis et loci.*** Necessity is the law of a particular time and place. ***Lex judicat de rebus necessario faciendis quasi re ipsa factis.*** The law judges of things which must necessarily be done as if they were actually done. ***Necessitas***

inducit privilegium quoad jura privata. Necessity gives a privilege with reference to private rights. ***Necessitas publica major est quam privata.*** Public necessity is greater than private.

NECTAROUS, *adjective* candied, cloying, delectable, delicious, dulcet, honeyed, luscious, melliferous, oversweet, rich, saccharine, sugary, sweet, tasty

NEED *(Deprivation)*, ***noun*** absence, dearth, deficiency, deficit, demand, exigency, extremity, inadequacy, incompleteness, indigence, insufficiency, lack, necessitousness, necessitude, necessity, paucity, penury, privation, scantiness, scarcity, shortage, shortness of supply, thirst, vacuum, want, wantage

NEED *(Requirement)*, ***noun*** compulsion, compulsory detail, crucial part, demand, desideration, desideratum, essential element, essentiality, essentialness, fundamental, highly important detail, indispensability, indispensable provision, integral part, irreplaceability, irreplaceable feature, mandatory factor, necessary, necessary attribute, necessary component, necessity, obligation, precondition, preliminary condition, prequisiteness, prerequirement, proviso, required item, requisite, requisiteness, strategic item, urgency, urgent requirement, vital part, vitalness

NEED, *verb* claim, clamor for, crave, cry for, demand, desire, exact, feel the necessity for, feel the want of, find indispensable, find necessary, have an urge for, have need for, have occasion for, have use of, hunger for, long for, lust for, miss, require, thirst for, want, yearn for

NEEDLESS, *adjective* avoidable, beside the point, causeless, dispensable, excess, excessive, exorbitant, expendable, expletive, extra, extraneous, fruitless, futile, gratuitous, groundless, inordinate, irrelevant, *non necessarius*, noncompulsory, nonessential, optional, overabundant, overmuch, overplentiful, oversufficient, pleonastic, prodigal, redundant, spare, superabundant, supererogatory, superfluous, supernumerary, supervenient, surplus, unavailing, uncalled-for, undesirable, unessential, unnecessary, unneeded, unprofitable, unrequired, unrewarding, unwanted, useless, valueless, wanton, wasteful, worthless

NEFARIOUS, *adjective* abominable, arrant, bad, base, confounded, contemptible, corrupt, criminal, degenerate, deplorable, depraved, despicable, detestable, devilish, diabolical, discreditable, disgraceful, dishonorable, dissolute, dreadful, evil, execrable, felonious, flagitious, flagrant, foul, gross, hateful, heinous, horrible, ignoble, immoral, impious, improper, indecent, infamous, infernal, iniquitous, malignant, miscreant, monstrous, *nefarius*, obnoxious, odious, outrageous, peccant, pernicious, profligate, reprehensible, reprobate, scandalous, shameful, sinful, sinister, terrible, treacherous, unrighteous, vile, villainous, wicked, wrong

NEGATE, *verb* abnegate, abolish, abort, abrogate, annihilate, annul, cancel, confound, confute, contradict, contravene, controvert, counter, counteract, countermand, counterpoise, declare invalid, declare null and void, defeat, demur, deny, deprive of force, destroy, disaffirm, disallow, disavow, disclaim, discontinue, discredit, disprove, dispute, disregard, explain away, falsify, impugn, invalidate, negative, neutralize, nullify, object, obliterate, offset, oppose, override, overrule, overthrow, prohibit, protest, prove the contrary, quash, rebut, recant, refute, render null and void, renounce, repeal, repudiate, rescind, retract, reverse, revoke, rule out, set aside, suppress, suspend, traverse, vacate, veto

NEGATION, *noun* abjuration, abnegation, abolishment, abolition, abrogation, annulment, cancellation, cassation, confutation, contradiction, contravention, declination, declinature, defiance, denial, disaffirmation, disagreement, disapprobation, disapproval, disavowal, disclaimer, disproof, dissent, forswearing, gainsay, gainsaying, *infitiatio*, invalidation, *negatio*, nonacceptance, nonagreement, noncompliance, nonconsent, noncorroboration, nullification, objection, opposition, protest, protestation, recantation, refusal, refutation, rejection, repeal, repudiation, rescission, resistance, retractation, retraction, reversal, revocation, revokement, traversal
ASSOCIATED CONCEPTS: negation of warranty

NEGATIVE, *adjective* acrimonious, antagonistic, antipathetic, antipathetical, argumentative, at odds with, attacking, averse, belligerent, bickering, cantankerous, clashing, conflicting, confutative, contentious, contesting, contradictory, contrary, contrasted, contrasting, contravening, converse, counteractive, countering, demurring, denying, disaccordant, disavowing, discordant, disobliging, disputing, dissentient, dissident, factious, fractious, gainsaying, hostile, ill-willed, impugning, incompatible, inimical, inverse, *negans*, negatory, opposed, opposing, opposite, quarrelsome, rancorous, rebuffing, rebutting, refuting, rejecting, repudiating, repugnant, resistive, reverse, spurning, traversing, unaffirmative, unconverted, unconvinced
ASSOCIATED CONCEPTS: negative covenant, negative easement, negative evidence, negative testimony

NEGATIVE ADVERTISING, *noun* blemishing political ads, derogative political ads, derogatory commercials, immoral ads, malicious political ads, marring political ads, mean commercials, nasty political spots, negative commercials, offensive election commercials, smearing political ads
ASSOCIATED CONCEPTS: election law, Federal Election Commission

NEGLECT, *noun* abandonment, absentmindedness, breach, bungling, careless abandon, carelessness, default, delinquency, dereliction, disregard, failure, heedlessness, idleness, improvidence, imprudence, inaction, inadvertence, inattention, inattentiveness, *incuria*, indifference, indiligence, *indiligentia*, inexecution, inexertion, laches, laxity, laxness, misprision, *neglegentia*, negligence, noncompletion, noncompliance, nonfeasance, nonfulfillment, nonobservance, nonperformance, omission, oversight, procrastination, prodigality, rashness, recklessness, remissness, slackness, slight, sloth, slovenliness, thoughtlessness, unactivity, unalertness, unconcern, unconscientiousness, unheedfulness, unmindfulness, unobservance, unwariness, unwatchfulness
ASSOCIATED CONCEPTS: culpable neglect, neglect of duty, neglect to act, neglect to prosecute, willful neglect
FOREIGN PHRASES: ***Magna culpa dolus est.*** Gross neglect is the equivalent of fraud.

NEGLECT, *verb* be careless, be inattentive, be lax, *deserere*, disdain, disregard, fail, forget, gloss over, ignore, *intermittere*, lay aside, leave alone, lose sight of, *neglegere*, not care for, not use, omit, overlook, pass by, pass over, pay no attention, pay no heed to, pay no regard to, pretermit, procrastinate, refuse to recognize, shirk, shun, skip, slight, take no note, take no notice

NEGLECTFUL, ***adjective*** careless, delinquent, derelict, disregardful, forgetful, heedless, inadvertent, inattentive, incautious, injudicious, inobservant, irresponsible, lax, mindless, neglectful, not diligent, not heedful, oblivious, reckless, remiss, thoughtless, unconcerned, unheeding, unmindful, unthinking, unwatchful
ASSOCIATED CONCEPTS: defendants neglectful of their duty, neglectful parents

NEGLIGENCE, ***noun*** abandonment, breach of duty, carelessness, culpa, delinquency, dereliction, disregard, failure, heedlessness, improvidence, imprudence, inadvertence, inadvertency, inattention, inattentiveness, incautiousness, incircumspection, inconsideration, *incuria,* indifference, *indiligentia,* inobservance, irresponsibility, lack of attention, lack of diligence, laxity, laxness, neglectfulness, *neglegentia,* obliviousness, omission, oversight, recklessness, regardlessness, remissness, slackness, unalertness, unconcern, unmindfulness, unobservance, unwariness, unwatchfulness, want of thought
ASSOCIATED CONCEPTS: actionable negligence, active negligence, assumption of risk, causal negligence, comparative negligence, concurrent negligence, contributory negligence, criminal negligence, culpable negligence, estoppel by negligence, gross negligence, imputed negligence, last clear chance doctrine, malpractice, negligence per se, ordinary negligence, passive negligence, *res ipsa loquitur,* standard of care, supervening negligence, wanton negligence, willful negligence
FOREIGN PHRASES: ***Magna negligentia culpa est; magna culpa dolus est.*** Gross negligence is fault; gross fault is equivalent to a fraud. ***Culpa lata dolo aequiparatur.*** Gross negligence is equivalent to intentional wrong.

NEGLIGENCE PER SE, ***idiom*** absolute delinquency, absolute fault, breach, breach of a standard of conduct, contravention, crime, disobedience, failure, infraction, lapse, misbehavior, misconduct, misdeed, misdemeanor, neglect, noncompliance, offense, oversight, pure dereliction, strict imposition of liability, transgression, trespass, violation, wrongdoing
ASSOCIATED CONCEPTS: negligence per quod

NEGLIGENT, ***adjective*** bungling, careless, delinquent, derelict, disregardant, disregardful, heedless, ill-considered, improvident, imprudent, inadvertent, inattentive, incautious, indifferent, *indiligens,* injudicious, inobservant, irresponsible, lax, mindless, neglectful, *neglegens,* oblivious, off guard, rash, reckless, regardless, remiss, *remissus,* slack, slipshod, slothful, slovenly, temerarious, temerous, thoughtless, unalert, uncalculating, uncircumspect, unconcerned, undiligent, unheedful, unheeding, unmindful, unthinking, unthorough, unwary, unwatchful
ASSOCIATED CONCEPTS: negligent act, negligent conduct, negligent injury

NEGLIGIBLE, ***adjective*** beneath notice, dispensable, expendable, immaterial, imperceptible, inappreciable, inconsequential, inconsiderable, insignificant, insubstantial, irrelevant, *levis,* light, little, meager, minor, minute, moderate, modest, nominal, nugatory, of little account, of little consequence, of little importance, of no moment, of no significance, paltry, picayune, poor, puny, scant, scanty, slight, small, *tenuis,* trifling, trivial, unessential, unimportant, unnoteworthy, unsubstantial, unworthy of regard, valueless
FOREIGN PHRASES: ***De minimis non curat lex.*** The law pays no attention to insignificant things.

NEGOTIABLE, ***adjective*** alienable, assignable, capable of being transferred, consignable, conveyable, exchangeable, interchangeable, maneuverable, marketable, salable, transferable, transmissible, transmittible, vendible
ASSOCIATED CONCEPTS: commercial paper, negotiable contract, negotiable instruments, promissory note

NEGOTIABLE INSTRUMENT, ***noun*** bank check, bank note, bank paper, bill, bill of exchange, cashier's check, check, commercial instrument, commercial paper, commercial transition, debenture, draft, negotiable paper, note, personal check, promissory note, secured
ASSOCIATED CONCEPTS: dishonor, named payee presentment

NEGOTIATE, ***verb*** accommodate, arbitrate, arrange for, bargain, bid for, bring to terms, come to terms, dicker, haggle, hurdle, intercede, intermediate, make peace, make terms, mediate, meet halfway, parley, referee, settle, settle disputes, straighten out, surmount, transact, umpire, work out

NEGOTIATION, ***noun*** arbitrament, arbitration, bargaining, compromise, conference, *conloquium,* consultation, contract talks, deliberation, dickering, diplomacy, discussion, exchange of views, haggling, mediation, parley, summitry, treaty-making
ASSOCIATED CONCEPTS: collective bargaining, preliminary negotiation

NEGOTIATOR, ***noun*** adjudicator, adjuster, agent, arbiter, bargainer, broker, consul, dealer, delegate, diplomat, emissary, envoy, financier, go-between, intermediary, mediator, merchant, middleman, moderator, plenipotentiary, politician, representative, tactician
ASSOCIATED CONCEPTS: arbitration, litigation, mediation

NEIGHBORHOOD, ***noun*** area, citizenry, city, commune, community, hamlet, locale, locale enclave, locality, place, populous, public, region, town, vicinity, village

NEOPHYTE, ***noun*** abecedarian, amateur, apprentice, beginner, catechumen, debutant, entrant, fledgling, freshman, learner, newcomer, novice, prentice, pupil, student, tenderfoot, trainee, tyro

NEPOTISM, ***noun*** bias, corruptibility, corruption, family patronage, favor, favoritism, inequitableness, inequity, injustice, interest, leaning, partiality, partisanism, partisanship, patronage, preferential treatment, undetachment, unfairness, unjustness

NESCIENCE, ***noun*** blindness, darkness, greenness, ignorance, ignoration, incognizance, inexperience, lack of awareness, lack of knowledge, lack of learning, naïveté, rawness, unawareness, uncomprehension, unenlightenment, uninformedness, unintelligence, unknowingness, unlearnedness

NET, ***adjective*** clear, irreducible, leftover, remaining, residual, residuary, surplus, surviving, unexpended, unspent
ASSOCIATED CONCEPTS: net assets, net balance, net capital stock, net earnings, net estate, net income, net loss, net premium, net price, net proceeds, net profit, net rents, net revenues, net value, net worth

NETTLE, ***verb*** acerbate, affront, aggravate, agitate, anger, annoy, antagonize, badger, chafe, disquiet, disturb, exasperate, excite, fret, gall, goad, harass, incense, insult, ire, irritate, miff, pester, pique, provoke, rankle, sting, tease, upset, vex

NETWORK, *noun* body, combined system, complicated system, interface, intertwining system, laced system, systematic web, weave, weaving, web, webbing

NEUTRAL, *adjective* disengaged, disinterested, dispassionate, equitable, fair, fair-minded, impartial, impersonal, independent, indifferent, isolationist, nonaligned, nonbelligerent, noncombatant, noncommittal, noninterfering, noninterventionist, nonparticipant, nonparticipating, nonpartisan, objective, pacific, pacifistic, peaceable, peaceful, unaffected, unbiased, unbigoted, uncommitted, unconcerned, uninfluenced, uninvolved, unjaundiced, unprejudiced, unprepossessed, unswayed
ASSOCIATED CONCEPTS: neutral property

NEUTRALITY, *noun* aloofness, detachment, disinterest, disinterestedness, dispassionateness, impartiality, indifference, moderateness, neutralism, nonbelligerence, noncombatance, noninterference, nonintervention, nonparticipance, nonparticipation, nonpartisanship

NEUTRALIZE, *verb* annul, balance, cancel, cancel out, counterbalance, counterpoise, countervail, deactivate, deaden, demagnetize, destroy the effect of, disable, disenable, equalize, incapacitate, invalidate, make ineffective, negate, nullify, offset, render inert, render inoperative, render neutral, vitiate

NEW *(Creative)*, ***adjective*** causative, conceived, conceptive, conceptual, constructive, created with a different approach, created with a different look, created with a fresh approach, created with a fresh look, effectuated, formative, imagined, ingenious, innovative, inventive, original, originated by, originative, produced, produced by someone blessed with talent, produced by someone capable, produced by someone talented, resourceful, talented, unique
ASSOCIATED CONCEPTS: patents

NEW *(Initial)*, ***adjective*** beginning, chief, elementary, first, first ever, foremost, fundamental, inaugural, inceptive, inchoate, incipient, introductory, nascent, original, preliminary, primary, primary original, rudimentary, seminal, unique
ASSOCIATED CONCEPTS: new law

NEWS, *noun* broadcast news, coverage, current affairs, daily news, developments, happenings, hard news, information, intelligence, media, news gathering, news medium, news service, press, reportage, reporting, television, the fourth estate, the press, the press corps, word

NEWSWORTHY, *adjective* acclaimed, consequential, contemporary, crucial, essential, far-reaching, front-page, great, important, influential, meaningful, momentous, notable, noteworthy, paramount, relevant, significant, substantive, timely, topical, urgent, vital

NEXT *(Near)*, ***adjective*** abutting, adjacent, adjoining, bordering, connecting, contiguous, immediate, in the neighborhood, in the vicinity, joined, juxtaposed, neighboring, tangential

NEXT *(Noted)*, ***adjective*** acclaimed, applauded, celebrated, consequential, conspicuous, distinguished, eminent, exalted, extraordinary, famed, famous, foremost, great, honored, illustrious, important, known, leading, matchless, much touted, notable, noteworthy, notorious, outstanding, popular, preeminent, prominent, recognized, remarkable, reputable, singular, unexampled, unique, unparalleled, unprecedented, well-known

NEXT *(Succeeding)*, ***adjective*** additional, consequent, ensuing, following, progressive, sequent, sequential, serial, subsequent, successive
ASSOCIATED CONCEPTS: next devisee, next estate, next of kin

NEXT OF KIN, *noun* blood kindred, blood relation, blood relative, close relative, collateral relative, consanguineal relations, family, family connection, family tie, individual's nearest relative, kin, kindred, kinsman, kinspeople, near relation, nearest blood relation, nearest relative by blood, related by affinity, relation by blood, relations, relatives
ASSOCIATED CONCEPTS: decedent's estate, heirs

NEXUS, *noun* affiliation, alliance, association, attachment, bond, bridge, connecting link, connection, connective, coupling, interconnection, intermedium, interrelation, kinship, liaison, link, privity, relation, relationship, thread, tie, union, vinculum

NICE, *adjective* affable, agreeable, befitting, correct, decent, decorous, delicate, exact, finespun, genial, genteel, good-natured, good-tempered, gracious, hospitable, mellow, nice, nuanced, palatable, pleasant, polite, refined, respectable, seemly, subtle, sweet, well-disposed

NOBLE, *adjective* aristocratic, august, courtly, dignified, distinguished, elevated, eminent, esteemed, estimable, exalted, famous, glorious, grand, held in esteem, heroic, highly esteemed, honorable, honored, inspiring, kingly, lauded, lofty, magisterial, magnificent, majestic, meritorious, outstanding, prestigious, princely, prominent, regal, renowned, reputable, respectable, respected, revered, royal, soaring, stately, superb, worthy

NOISE, *noun* ado, blare, blatancy, cacophony, charivari, clamor, clamorousness, clangor, clatter, cry, detonation, din, discord, fanfare, fracas, harsh sound, hubbub, hullabaloo, jangle, loudness, outcry, pandemonium, racket, ruckus, ruction, *sonitus,* sound, stir, *strepitus,* tumult, unpleasant sound, uproar, uproariousness, vociferance, vociferation
ASSOCIATED CONCEPTS: disturbing the peace, noise pollution, nuisance

NOISOME, *adjective* abhorrent, abominable, arrant, atrocious, awful, base, blameworthy, brutal, coarse, contemptible, crude, deplorable, despicable, detestable, disgusting, dreadful, egregious, execrable, fetid, foul, grievous, heinous, horrible, horrid, ignoble, infamous, monstrous, nefarious, noxious, objectionable, obnoxious, odious, offensive, repellent, reprehensible, repugnant, repulsive, revolting, rude, sad, shameful, shocking, sickening, terrible, vile, woeful, wretched

NOLLO CONTENDERE, *noun* acceptance of penalty, admission of the facts, plea, settlement

NOLLO PROSEQUI, *noun* abrogation, cancellation, counter order, countermand, reversal, reversion

NOMINAL, *adjective* cheap, cut-rate, hardly worth mention, honorary, in name only, inconsiderable, inexpensive, insignificant, little, low, low-priced, meager, meaningless,

minimum, minute, moderate, modest, negligible, *nomine,* petty, reduced, scanty, simple, slight, small, superficial, symbolic, titular, titulary, token, trifling, trivial, unactual, unimportant, unsubstantial
ASSOCIATED CONCEPTS: nominal capital, nominal consideration, nominal damages, nominal defendant, nominal owner, nominal parties, nominal plaintiff, nominal value

NOMINATE, ***verb*** appoint, assign, call, choose, commission, constitute, denominate, *designare,* designate for appointment, designate for election, *dicere,* draft, engage, entitle, install, label, name, name for office, *nominare,* ordain, ordinate, place in authority, place in command, place in office, propose, propose as a candidate, put up, select, specify, style, suggest, tag, title, vote into office

NOMINATION, ***noun*** appointment, assignment, authorization, choice, choosing, delegation, denomination, deputization, *designatio,* designation, election, naming, *nominatio,* ordainment, ordination, proposal, selection

NOMINEE *(Candidate),* ***noun*** chosen representative, flag bearer, named representative, political representative, selection

NOMINEE *(Delegate),* ***noun*** appointee, consignee, licensee, representative, selectee, trustee

NON COMPOS MENTIS, ***adjective*** abnormal, bereft of reason, crazed, crazy, declared insane, defective, demented, deprived of one's wits, deranged, dim-witted, diseased in mind, disoriented, distraught, dull-witted, feeble-minded, idiotic, insane, insanely deluded, lunatic, mad, maddened, manic, maniacal, mental, mentally deficient, mentally diseased, mentally ill, mentally sick, mentally unsound, mindless, moronic, of unsound mind, out of one's mind, out of one's senses, out of one's wits, psychologically abnormal, psychopathic, psychotic, raving, senseless, simple-minded, unbalanced, unsettled, unsettled in one's mind, unsound, unstable, utterly senseless
ASSOCIATED CONCEPTS: insanity, lack of capacity

NON SEQUITUR, ***noun*** anacoluthon, bad logic, circular reasoning, contradiction of terms, disconnectedness, discontinuity, fallacious argument, fallacious reasoning, fallacy, false reasoning, flaw in the argument, illogical conclusion, illogical deduction, illogical result, inconsequence, irrational conclusion, irrelevancy, loose thinking, lost connection, nonsensicality, nonsensicalness, paralogism, sophism, sophistry, specious argument, specious reasoning, unfounded conclusion, unwarranted conclusion, wrong reasoning

NONACCEPTANCE, ***noun*** abnegation, abridgment, at an impasse, confutation, contradiction, contrary assertion, contravention, disaffirmation, disallowance, disavowal, disclamation, dissent, negation, no agreement, no meeting of the minds, objection, protest, rebuttal, recantation, refutation, rejection, renouncement, renunciation, retraction
ASSOCIATED CONCEPTS: presentment

NONAGE, ***noun*** adolescence, childhood, early stage, immaturity, infancy, legal immaturity, legal minority, minority, period of legal immaturity, period of legal minority, tender age, youth

NONAPPEARANCE, ***noun*** absence without leave, absentation, absenteeism, concealment, default, failure to appear, hiding, imperceptibility, indiscernibility, inexistence, invisibility, invisibleness, nonattendance, nonpresence, obscurity, truancy, unperceivability, unseeableness, vanishment

NONCANCELABLE, ***adjective*** abiding, durable, indelible, ineffaceable, irrepealable, irreversible, lasting, nonabolishable, nonannullable, nonerasable, nonrescindable, nonretractable, nonreversible, permanent, unchangeable, undestroyable, unquashable, unvoidable
ASSOCIATED CONCEPTS: noncancelable clause

NONCHALANT, ***adjective*** *aequo animo,* apathetic, blase, calm, carefree, casual, collected, composed, cool, dispassionate, easygoing, impassive, imperturbable, indifferent, insouciant, inured, lacking enthusiasm, lacking interest, lacking warmth, lukewarm, offhand, passionless, pococurante, self-controlled, spiritless, studied, unaffected, unaroused, unblushing, uncaring, unconcerned, unenthusiastic, unexcited, unfeeling, unflappable, unimpassioned, unimpressed, uninterested, unmindful, unmoved, unruffled, unshocked, unspirited, unstirred, untouched, unworried

NONCOMMITTAL, ***adjective*** careful, cautious, changeable, close, discreet, evasive, faltering, guarded, hedging, heedful, hesitant, hesitating, incommunicative, inconstant, indecisive, infirm of purpose, irresolute, irresolved, laconic, lukewarm, mutable, neutral, on guard, precautionary, precautious, prudent, reserved, reticent, secretive, silent, taciturn, unassured, uncertain, uncommitted, uncommunicative, undaring, undecided, unforthcoming, uninvolved, unresolved, unresponsive, unsettled, unsteadfast, unsteady, unsure, vacillating, vague, wary, watchful, wavering

NONCOMPETE CLAUSE, ***noun*** agreement not to compete, contract against competing, covenant not to compete, express promise not to compete, noncompete agreement, prohibition against competition, restrictive covenant not to compete, restrictive provisions against competing
ASSOCIATED CONCEPTS: golden handcuffs, per se violations of law, restrictive covenants, scope of geographical area, time period

NONCOMPLIANCE *(Improper completion),* ***noun*** deficient work, faulty work, inadequate final work, poor quality work, shabby work, wrong implementation
ASSOCIATED CONCEPTS: noncompliance with a judicial order

NONCOMPLIANCE *(Nonobservance),* ***noun*** defiance, disloyalty, disregard of orders, non occurrence, nonconformity, refusal

NONCONFORMING, ***adjective*** aberrant, alien, at odds with, at variance with, Bohemian, contrary, defiant, deviating, different, differing, disagreeing, disapproved, discordant, disobedient, dissentient, dissenting, dissident, dissimilar, distinct, distinguished, diversified, eccentric, exotic, heretical, incongruous, independent, irregular, lawless, nonadhering, noncompliant, nonobservant, nonuniform, original, out of line, out of step, peculiar, quaint, rare, remarkable, singular, solitary, special, unaccountable, unaccustomed, unadaptable, unadjustable, unclassifiable, uncommon, unconformable, unconventional, uncustomary, unexpected, unfashionable, unique, unordinary, unorthodox, unparalleled, unprecedented, unsubmissive, unusual, unwonted
ASSOCIATED CONCEPTS: nonconforming use

NONCONFORMITY, ***noun*** aberration, abnormality, abnormity, anomalousness, anomaly, apostasy, bizarreness, Bohemianism, change, contrast, defiance, departure, deviation, difference, disagreement, disconformity, disobedience, disparity, dispute, dissent, dissidence, dissimilarity, distinctness, divergence, diverseness, diversity, eccentricity, exception, exceptionality, heresy, heterodoxy, heterogeneity, idiosyncrasy, incongruity, inconsistency, independence, individuality, irregularity, lack of agreement, nonagreement, nonconcurrence, nonuniformity, objection, originality, otherness, peculiarity, protest, protestation, recusancy, rejection, separateness, separatism, singularity, strangeness, unconformity, unconventionality, uniqueness, unlikeness, unorthodoxness, unorthodoxy, variance, variation, variety, veto

NONCONSENTING, ***adjective*** critical, declinatory, defiant, disapproving, discontented, disobedient, disparaging, dissentient, dissenting, dissident, faultfinding, hostile, inacquiescent, insubordinate, intractable, nonconformant, noncontent, objecting, overcritical, protesting, recalcitrant, recusant, refusing, resistant, seditious, unapproving, uncomplying, unconsenting, unsubmissive, unwilling

NONCONTESTABLE, ***adjective*** nonchallengeable, noncontrovertible, nondebatable, nondisputable, nonproblematical, nonquestionable, nonrefutable, undeniable, undoubtable, unquestionable
ASSOCIATED CONCEPTS: noncontestable clause

NONDESCRIPT, ***adjective*** average, boring, characteristic, common, commonplace, conventional, difficult to classify, difficult to describe, dull, everyday, familiar, hackneyed, homely, indescribable, insipid, mediocre, middling, not extraordinary, not odd, not singular, not special, not unique, ordinary, pedestrian, plain, prosaic, stock, trite, typical, unadorned, unclassifiable, undistinguished, unenlivened, unexceptional, unexciting, unidentifiable, uninteresting, unremarkable, usual

NONENTITY, ***noun*** blank, cipher, existenceless, figurehead, inexistence, insignificance, insignificancy, insubstantiality, matter of no consequence, matter of no importance, *nihil,* no one, nobody, nonbeing, nonexistence, nothing, nothingness, nought, nullity, *terrae filius,* unsubstantiality, unsubstantialness

NONESSENTIAL, ***adjective*** accessory, added, additional, adscititious, auxiliary, avoidable, beside the point, beside the question, dispensable, excess, expendable, extra, extraneous, extrinsic, extrinsical, frivolous, gratuitous, incidental, inconsequential, inessential, insignificant, minor, needless, negligible, of little consequence, of little importance, of no account, of no concern, of no consequence, of no importance, of no significance, of small importance, optional, parenthetic, parenthetical, peripheral, redundant, spare, supererogatory, superfluous, supervenient, supplemental, supplementary, trifling, trivial, uncalled for, unessential, ungermane, unimportant, unnecessary, unneeded, unnoteworthy, unrequired, unwarranted
ASSOCIATED CONCEPTS: nonessential services

NONEXISTENT, ***adjective*** chimerical, fancied, fantastic, fantastical, hallucinatory, hypothetical, ideal, illusory, imaginary, imagined, inexistent, legendary, notional, theoretical, unborn, uncreated, unexisting, unreal, visionary

NONFEASANCE, ***noun*** delinquency, dereliction, disregard, disregard of duty, failure, inattention, indifference, laxity, misprision, neglect of duty, negligence, nonfulfillment, nonperformance, omission

NONMILITANT, ***adjective*** accommodative, agreeable, amicable, appeasable, conciliable, conciliative, conciliatory, concordant, forgiving, gentle, halcyon, irenic, irenical, meek, neutral, nonaggresive, noncombatant, noncombative, nonviolent, pacificatory, pacifistic, peace-loving, peaceable, peaceful, placable, placative, propitiable, propitiatory, tolerant, unaggressive, unbellicose, unbelligerent, uncontentious, unhostile, unmilitant, unpugnacious, unwarlike

NONOBSERVANCE, ***noun*** arbitrary, averse, contrary, contumacious, defiant, delinquent, derelict, disloyal, disregarding, disrespectful, fractious, hostile, incorrigible, independent, indisposed, insubordinate, insurgent, intractable, irascible, irresponsible, lawbreaking, lawless, licentious, loath, mind of his or her own, misbehaving, mutinous, neglectful, negligent, noncompliant, nonconforming, obdurate, objecting, obstinate, obstreperous, opposed, opposing, perfidious, rebellious, recalcitrant, refractory, reluctant, remiss, resistant, resistive, restive, stubborn, uncooperative, undependable, undisciplined, undutiful, unfaithful, ungovernable, unmanageable, unmindful, unreliable, unruly, unwilling, unyielding, violating, wayward, wild, willful
FOREIGN PHRASES: ***Non observata forma, interftur adnullatio actus.*** Where form is not observed, the annulling of the act is implied or follows.

NONOBVIOUSNESS, ***noun*** invention which is not an obvious combination of preexisting work, invention which is not an obvious development of a preexisting work, invention which is not an obvious variation of a preexisting work, patent for invention unexpected by a person with ordinary skill in the art, requirement for patentability

NONPARTISAN, ***adjective*** autonomous, broad-minded, detached, disengaged, equitable, evenhanded, fair, fair-minded, impartial, independent, judicious, latitudinarian, moderate, neutral, nonaligned, objective, self-determined, self-directing, self-governing, sovereign, unbiased, unbigoted, uncommitted, uncompelled, unforced, uninduced, uninfluenced, unprejudiced, unswayed, unwarped

NONPAYMENT, ***noun*** bad debt, balance due, default, deferred payment, delinquency, dishonor, dishonored bill, evasion, failure, failure to pay, lapse, neglect, outstanding debt, oversight, refusal to pay, repudiation, unpaid dues
ASSOCIATED CONCEPTS: nonpayment of rent

NONPERFORMANCE, ***noun*** avoidance, breach of promise, default, delinquency, dereliction of duty, disregard, dutilessness, evasion, evasion of duty, failure to perform, idleness, inactivity, inexecution, laxity, neglect, negligence, noncompletion, noncompliance, noncooperation, nonfeasance, nonfulfillment, nonpractice, omission, truancy, unduteousness, undutifulness, unfulfillment
ASSOCIATED CONCEPTS: nonperformance of a contract, nonperformance of a duty

NONPHASED, ***adjective*** addled, at a loss, at a nonplus, at a stand *or* standstill, at an impasse, at one's wit's end, baffled, bamboozled, bewildered, buffaloed, confounded, dazed, deadlocked, fuddled, in a dilemma, in suspense, muddled, mystified, nonplussed, on tenterhooks, on the horns of a dilemma, perplexed, puzzled, stuck *and* stumped, stymied

NONPROFIT, ***adjective*** altruistic, beneficent, benevolent, charitable, eleemosynary, humanitarian, munificent, philanthropic, public service
ASSOCIATED CONCEPTS: nonprofit corporation

NONRESIDENCE, ***noun*** absence, nondomicile, nonhabitancy, nonhabitation, noninhabitance, noninhabitancy, nonoccupance, nonoccupancy, nonoccupation, nonpresence, nontenancy

NONSECTARIAN, ***adjective*** all-comprehensive, all-embracing, all-including, all-inclusive, broad, broad-based, collective, comprehensive, ecumenical, general, global, interdenominational, mixed, undenominational, universal, unspecified, worldwide

NONSUBSTANTIAL *(Not sturdy),* ***adjective*** adynamic, asthenic, attenuated, below par, breakable, brittle, defective, deficient, delicate, destructible, enervated, ephemeral, fallacious, feeble, flimsy, fragile, frail, frangible, ghostly, illogical, inadequate, infirm, intangible, lame, limp, mediocre, perishable, powerless, slight, sorry, strengthless, tenuous, unearthly, ungrounded, unsolid, unsound, unstable, unsturdy, unsubstantial, untenable, weak, weakly, without force, without foundation, wobbly

NONSUBSTANTIAL *(Not sufficient),* ***adjective*** deficient, depleted, deprived, disappointing, drained, inadequate, incomplete, insignificant, insubstantial, lacking, low, meager, niggardly, paltry, scant, scanty, scarce, stingy, thin, too little, too small, unacceptable, ungratifying, unsatisfactory, unsatisfying, unsufficing, wanting

NONSUIT, ***noun*** defeat, directed verdict, failure to establish a cause of action, failure to make a case, failure to meet the burden of proof, failure to present sufficient evidence, hostile verdict, insufficiency as a matter of law, insufficient evidence, judgment for the defendant as a matter of law, termination of a case by inaction, termination of a judicial contest, termination of a lawsuit, termination of a lawsuit by failing to proceed, termination of a legal action, termination of a legal proceeding, termination of a proceeding, termination of a suit in law, termination of an action, termination of an action at law by failure to proceed, termination of an action by neglect, termination of litigation
ASSOCIATED CONCEPTS: compulsory nonsuit, demurrer, discontinuance, dismissal, involuntary nonsuit, motion for nonsuit, peremptory nonsuit, voluntary nonsuit

NONTOXIC, ***adjective*** benign, harmless, hurtless, innocent, innocuous, innoxious, inoffensive, nonfatal, nonirritating, nonlethal, nonmalignant, nonpoisonous, nonvenomous, nonvirulent, not baneful, not dangerous, not deadly, not deleterious, not pernicious, not toxiferous, safe, undestructive, unhazardous, uninjurious, unobjectionable, without risk

NONUSE, ***noun*** abeyance, absence, abstinence, desuetude, disusage, disuse, forebearance, neglect, nonemployment, nonutilization, suspension

NORM, ***noun*** average, general performance, generality, habit, median, midpoint, model, mold, ordinary run, pattern, point of comparison, regular performance, rule, standard, typical performance

NORMAL *(Regular),* ***adjective*** according to rule, average, common, commonplace, conforming, conventional, customary, established, everyday, habitual, natural, orderly, ordinary, representative, routine, standard, standardized, true to form, typical, unexceptional, unvarying, usual
ASSOCIATED CONCEPTS: normal conditions, normal course of business, normal use

NORMAL *(Sane),* ***adjective*** fit, logical, lucid, mentally sound, of sound judgment, rational, reasonable, responsible, sensible, sound, temperate

NOSCITUR A SOCIIS, ***adverb*** comprehended from accompanying words, perceived from accompanying words, realized from accompanying words, recognized from accompanying words, understood from accompanying words

NOT ADMISSIBLE, ***adjective*** banned, barred, deemed improper, deemed inapplicable, disallowed, disapproved, excepted, excluded, inadmissible, inapposite, inappropriate, ineligible, irrelevant, not admitted in, not allowed as evidence, not allowed in, not allowed in evidence, not allowed to be admitted as evidence, not capable of being introduced as evidence, objectionable, prohibited, refused, rejected, suppressed, unfit, unqualified, unsuitable, wrong
ASSOCIATED CONCEPTS: evidence obtained by torture, hearsay, impeachment, not admissible into evidence

NOT COUNTENANCED, ***adjective*** disallowed, forbidden, illegitimate, improper, inappropriate, incorrect, not allowed, not approved, not blessed, not permitted, not proper, prohibited, proscribed, unapproved, uncertified, undue, unendorsed, unlawful, unlicensed, unsanctioned, unsuitable, unwarranted
ASSOCIATED CONCEPTS: a deception not countenanced, a substantial departure not countenanced by law, mistake not countenanced, not countenanced by the courts, practices not countenanced by the courts

NOT EQUITABLE, ***adjective*** biased, fraudulent, improper, inequitable, jaundiced, not balanced, not fair, not just, not proper, one-sided, prejudiced, unequal, uneven, unfair, unjust, unprincipled, unreasonable
ASSOCIATED CONCEPTS: not equitable process

NOT GUILTY, ***adjective*** above suspicion, blameless, clean-handed, exculpable, faultless, free from guilt, guilt-free, guiltless, impeccable, incorrupt, inculpable, innocent, not responsible, sinless, unblemished, unimpeachable, uninvolved
ASSOCIATED CONCEPTS: plea of not guilty

NOT HONORABLE, ***adjective*** conniving, conscienceless, corrupt, deceitful, deceiving, deceptive, delusive, delusory, discreditable, dishonorable, disingenuous, disreputable, faithless, fake, faked, false, false-hearted, falsified, fraudulent, guileful, immoral, iniquitous, insidious, insincere, lying, meretricious, misleading, nefarious, not fair, not honest, not just, not legitimate, not proper, not true, perfidious, shameless, shifty, spurious, surreptitious, treacherous, underhanded, unethical, unfaithful, unprincipled, unprofessional, unscrupulous, untrue, untrustworthy, untruthful, worthy of disbarment

NOT PERMITTED, ***adjective*** banished, banned, barred, blocked, checked, curbed, debarred, denied, disallowed, disqualified, enjoined, excluded, forbid, foreclosed, halted, hampered, hindered, illegal, impeded, inhibited, interdicted, interfered, limited, negated, obstructed, omitted, opposed, ordered stopped, precluded, prevented, proscribed, quashed, quelled, refused, refused permission, regulated, rejected, repressed, repudiated, restrained, restricted, revoked, shut out, smothered, stayed, stopped, suppressed, suspended, thwarted, vetoed
ASSOCIATED CONCEPTS: motion practice, not permitted to disclose confidences, not permitted to many, punitive damages in private lawsuits

NOT PERTINENT, ***adjective*** alien, discordant, discrepant, dissonant, gratuitous, improper, inadmissible, inapplicable, inapposite, incongruent, incongruous, inconsistent, ineligible, inessential, inopportune, irrelevant, misapplied, misdirected, misplaced, not appropriate, not germane, not related, objectionable, undue, unfit, unfitting, unharmonious, unsuitable, unsuited
ASSOCIATED CONCEPTS: evidence presented that is not pertinent, information requested that is not pertinent, not pertinent trait or character, objections

NOT SUBSTANTIATED, ***adjective*** baseless, controvertible, empty, flimsy, groundless, ill-conceived, ill-founded, inconclusive, insubstantial, not proven, poorly argued, unfounded, ungrounded, unproved, unsound, unsubstantial, unsupportable, unsupported, unsustainable, unverifiable, without a sound basis, without basis, without foundation
ASSOCIATED CONCEPTS: allegations not substantiated, arguments not substantiated, claims not substantiated, complaints not substantiated, motions not substantiated

NOT VALID, ***adjective*** abrogated, baseless, canceled, fallacious, faulty, futile, having no force, inadequate, ineffective, ineffectual, inefficacious, inoperative, invalid, lacking authority, lacking force, lacking strength, not binding, nugatory, null, quashed, spurious, unauthentic, untenable, untrue, useless, vain, void, without legal basis, without legal efficacy, without legal justification
ASSOCIATED CONCEPTS: objections, patents, recordation in copyright office, validity of claims, wills

NOTABLE, ***adjective*** above par, acclaimed, astonishing, atypical, awe-inspiring, awesome, celebrated, conspicuous, distinguished, eminent, exceptional, extraordinary, famed, famous, foremost, illustrious, important, impressive, leading, luminous, marked, memorable, momentous, momumental, newsworthy, *notabilis,* noted, noteworthy, outstanding, preeminent, prime, prominent, rare, remarkable, rememberable, renowned, salient, signal, significant, singular, special, striking, superior, talked of, top-rank, transcendent, unforgettable, worthy of notice, worthy of remark

NOTARIZE, ***verb*** accord one's approval, accredit, affirm, affix a legal signature, affix one's signature to, approve, attach a legal signature, attest to, authenticate, authorize, bear witness, certify, confirm, confirm officially, evidence, legalize, make valid, pronounce legal, seal, set one's hand and seal, sign, sign and seal, sign legally, subscribe, undersign, validate, witness

NOTARY PUBLIC, ***noun*** attestor of documents, clerk of the court, commissioner of oaths, functionary, indorser, notary, official, recorder, register, registerer, registrar, *scriba,* scribe, scrivener, subscriber

NOTATION, ***noun*** annotation, chronicle, comment, commentary, entry, footnote, inscription, marginalia, memorandum, minute, note, record, register

NOTE *(Brief comment),* ***noun*** abstract, *adnotatio,* annotation, billet, brief, *codicilli,* comment, commentary, communication, dispatch, entry, *epistula,* exegesis, explanatory comment, explanatory remark, footnote, gloss, marginal annotation, memorandum, message, minute, missive, record, reminder, scholium, short letter, statement, word of explanation
ASSOCIATED CONCEPTS: note of issue

NOTE *(Written promise to pay),* ***noun*** bond, check, debenture, draft, money order, negotiable instrument, negotiable paper, voucher
ASSOCIATED CONCEPTS: accommodation note, bank note, bearer notes, cognovit note, commercial paper, negotiable note, promissory note, treasury note

NOTE *(Notice),* ***verb*** acknowledge, advert to, apperceive, appreciate, attend, be attentive, become aware, become conscious, cognize, direct attention to, discern, discover, fix attention on, give attention to, hearken to, heed, look at, make out, mark, mind, observe, pay attention to, pay heed to, perceive, realize, regard, see, take account of, take cognizance of, take notice, turn attention to, watch, witness

NOTE *(Record),* ***verb*** *adnotare,* annotate, calendar, catalog, chronicle, commit to writing, docket, document, enregister, enter, jot down, keep accounts, log, make a memorandum, make an entry, mark, mark down, pen, put in writing, put on paper, put on record, scribe, set down, take down, write, write down

NOTED *(Acknowledged),* ***adjective*** accepted, admitted, cleared, declared, disclosed, discovered, established, evident, exposed, familiar, identified, manifest, obvious, patently known, proclaimed, realized, recognized, revealed, well-known
ASSOCIATED CONCEPTS: as noted, briefly noted, judicial notice

NOTED *(Well-known),* ***adjective*** acclaimed, applauded, celebrated, consequential, conspicuous, distinguished, eminent, exalted, extraordinary, famed, famous, foremost, great, honored, illustrious, important, known, leading, matchless, much touted, notable, noteworthy, notorious, outstanding, popular, preeminent, prominent, recognized, remarkable, reputable, singular, unexampled, unique, unparalleled, unprecedented
ASSOCIATED CONCEPTS: a noted authority

NOTEWORTHY, ***adjective*** above par, amazing, anomalous, astonishing, astounding, atypical, bizarre, breathtaking, celebrated, choice, commanding, considerable, conspicuous, curious, different, distinctive, distinguished, egregious, eminent, especial, excellent, exceptional, extraordinary, extreme, famous, fantastic, foremost, idiosyncratic, illustrious, important, impressive, incredible, individual, individualistic, infrequent, leading, main, marked, material, memorable, momentous, monumental, newsworthy, notable, noticeable, novel, odd, original, out of the ordinary, outstanding, paramount, peculiar, peerless, pertinent, phenomenal, preeminent, principal, prodigious, prominent, queer, rare, remarkable, renowned, salient, signal, significant, singular, special, standing out, stirring, strange, surprising, telling, uncommon, uncustomary, unequaled, unfamiliar, unforgettable, unheard of, unimitated, unique, unparalleled, unprecedented, unusual, wonderful, wondrous, worthy of notice, worthy of remark

NOTHING *(Void),* ***noun*** blank, clean slate, emptiness, empty feeling, empty space, inanity, nothingness, vacuity, vacuum
ASSOCIATED CONCEPTS: nothing but the truth, nothing to hide

NOTHING *(Zero),* ***noun*** naught, nil, none, not one iota, nothing at all, nothing whatever

NOTICE *(Announcement),* ***noun*** bulletin, circular, communication, communique, declaration, decree, *denuntiatio,*

disclosure, dispatch, enlightenment, enunciation, flier, information, memorandum, mention, message, news, note, notification, presentation, proclamation, *promulgatio,* pronouncement, publicity, release, reminder, report, revelation, statement
ASSOCIATED CONCEPTS: legal notice, notice of appeal, notice of appearance, notice of claim, notice of motion, notice of protest, public notice
FOREIGN PHRASES: ***Notitia dicitur a noscendo; et notitia non debet claudicare.*** Notice is named from a knowledge being had; and notice ought not to be imperfect.

NOTICE *(Heed),* ***noun*** absorption, advertence, advertency, alertness, *animadversio,* attention, attentiveness, care, careful attention, carefulness, cautel, caution, cautiousness, circumspection, cognizance, consideration, discernment, engrossment, guard, heedfulness, mindfulness, *notatio,* observance, observation, recognition, regard, regardfulness, scrutiny, surveillance, thought, vigil, vigilance, wariness, watch, watchfulness
ASSOCIATED CONCEPTS: judicial notice
FOREIGN PHRASES: ***De minimis non curat lex.*** The law is not concerned with trifling matters.

NOTICE *(Warning),* ***noun*** admonishment, admonition, caution, caveat, commination, communication, counsel, dehortation, *denuntiatio,* forewarning, monition, premonishment, prenotification, ultimatum
ASSOCIATED CONCEPTS: absence of notice, actual notice, adequate notice, constructive notice, due notice, explicit notice, express notice, implied notice, imputed notice, notice of disallowance, notice to appear, notice to vacate, proper notice, reasonable notice, requisite notice, timely notice, verified notice, written notice

NOTICE *(Give formal warning),* ***verb*** address a warning to, advise, apprise, communicate, convey knowledge to, *denuntiatio,* direct attention to, disclose, divulge, entrust with information, forewarn, formally advise, give fair warning, give information, give warning, impart knowledge of, impart to, inform, instruct, make a formal proclamation, make acquainted with, make an announcement, make known, make mention of, make public, notify, offer a word of caution, pass on information, *promulgatio,* publish, put on one's guard, reveal, warn
ASSOCIATED CONCEPTS: notice a deposition, notice a hearing

NOTICE *(Observe),* ***verb*** acknowledge, *animadvertere,* appreciate, ascertain, assess, attend to, be attentive, be conscious of, become aware of, become conscious of, behold, call attention to, cognize, comment, detect, discern, discover, distinguish, elucidate, examine closely, examine intently, give heed to, glance at, hear, heed, inspect, investigate, look, look at, mark, mention, *notatio,* note, observe, occupy oneself with, pass under review, pay attention, perceive, pore over, realize, recognize, regard, review, scrutinize, see, sight, spot, take cognizance, take into account, take into consideration, take stock of, view, watch, witness

NOTICE OF APPEARANCE, ***noun*** announcement of the lawyer in a case, entrance by counsel in a case, formal notification of counsel's presence, noted presence in court, notice of entry, notification of representation, notification of the entry of counsel to a case, official acknowledgment of counsel's presence, official appearance by counsel, official statement of representation, statement of counsel's appearance
ASSOCIATED CONCEPTS: attorney of record, court proceeding, notice of limited appearance

NOTIFICATION, ***noun*** announcement, annunciation, aviso, bulletin, caution, communication, communiqué, declaration, *denuntiatio,* disclosure, dispatch, dissemination, divulgation, enlightenment, enunciation, evulgation, information, intelligence, intercommunication, knowledge, legal notice, mention, message, monition, news, notice, proclamation, *promulgatio,* promulgation, pronouncement, publicity, release, report, revelation, statement, transmission of knowledge, warning
ASSOCIATED CONCEPTS: due process, process of service, proper notification

NOTIFY, ***verb*** acquaint, advertise, advise, alert, announce, annunciate, apprise, break the news, brief, bring word, call attention to, caution, communicate, confide, contact, convey, counsel, declare, disclose, disseminate, divulge, enlighten, enunciate, exhort, forewarn, give notice, give the facts, give to understand, give warning, herald, impart, indicate, inform, instruct, issue a proclamation, issue a pronouncement, let know, make an announcement, make known, make public, mention, post, proclaim, promote, promulgate, propagate, publicize, publish, recount, relate, remind, report, reveal, serve notice, signal, signify, state, tell, tip off, transmit, warn
ASSOCIATED CONCEPTS: notify a defendant of charges pending, notify of an action pending

NOTION, ***noun*** abstraction, apprehension, belief, caprice, concept, conception, conviction, desire, estimation, fancy, feeling, humor, idea, impression, inclination, inkling, judgment, mental image, *notio,* opinion, sentiment, suggestion, supposition, *suspicio,* thought, understanding, vagary, view, whim

NOTORIETY, ***noun*** attaint, bad report, bad reputation, bad repute, bruit, celebrity, censure, conspicuousness, dedecoration, degradation, denunciation, disapprobation, discredit, disesteem, disfavor, disgrace, dishonor, disparagement, disreputability, disreputableness, disrepute, disrespect, distinction, eclat, eminence, *fama,* fame, famousness, flagrancy, ignominy, ignomy, ill repute, imputation, indignity, *infamia,* infamousness, infamy, ingloriousness, loss of honor, loss of reputation, name, notability, notedness, obloquy, odium, opprobrium, popular repute, popularity, prominence, public notice, publicity, recognition, renown, reproach, reputation, repute, scandal, shame, significance, slur, stigma, stigmatization, taint, unrespectability

NOTORIOUS, ***adjective*** arrant, blameworthy, celebrated, conspicuous, contemptible, degraded, deplorable, despised, discreditable, disgraceful, dishonorable, disreputable, disrespectable, egregious, famed, famous, flagrant, generally known, glaring, held in contempt, ignoble, ignominious, infamous, inglorious, *nobilis,* noted, *notus,* odious, of ill fame, of ill repute, opprobrious, outcast, outrageous, prominent, publicized, renowned, scandalous, shameful, shameless, shocking, unfavorably known, unrespectable, unseemly, unworthy of respect, villainous, without repute
ASSOCIATED CONCEPTS: notorious easement, notorious possession, open and notorious use

NOTWITHSTANDING, ***preposition*** all the same, although, despite, even, however, in any case, in any event, in spite of, nevertheless, none the less, still, yet

NOVATION, ***noun*** complete substitution, exchange, replacement, substitution
ASSOCIATED CONCEPTS: novation of a contract

NOVEL, ***adjective*** alien, anomalous, bizarre, different, distinctive, eccentric, exceptional, extraordinary, foreign, fresh, innovative, inusitate, irregular, modern, neoteric, neoterical, new, newly come, nonconformist, *novus,* odd, original, peculiar, quaint, rare, recent, singular, strange, uncharacteristic, uncommon, unconventional, uncustomary, unfamiliar, unheard of, unique, unordinary, unorthodox, unprecedented, untested, untried, unused, unusual, up-to-date, up-to-the-minute
ASSOCIATED CONCEPTS: novel question of law

NOVICE, ***noun*** amateur, apprentice, aspirant, beginner, catechumen, disciple, entrant, fledgling, freshman, hopeful, inexperienced person, initiate, learner, neophyte, new arrival, newcomer, probationer, pupil, recruit, rookie, *rudis,* student, trainee, tyro, unskilled person, untrained individual

NOW AND FOREVER, ***adverb*** evermore, for ever and ever, forever, forevermore

NOXIOUS, ***adjective*** adverse, bad, baleful, baneful, brutal, causing danger, contaminated, corrupting, damaging, dangerous, deleterious, destructive, detrimental, disadvantageous, fatal, fraught with danger, harmful, hazardous, hurtful, impairing, injurious, insalubrious, internecine, jeopardous, lethal, malefic, malicious, malignant, menacing, mischievous, nocent, noisome, offensive, perilous, pernicious, pestiferous, pestilent, poisonous, precarious, risky, ruinous, scatheful, threatening, toxic, unfavorable, unhealthy, unsafe, unwholesome, vicious, virulent

NUANCE, ***noun*** cast, degree, delicacy, difference, differentiation, discrimination, distinction, hidden meaning, implication, nicety, shade, shade of difference, shade of meaning, shadow, subtle difference, subtlety, suggestion, touch, variance

NUCLEUS, ***noun*** apex, axis, base, capital, center, central, core, cornerstone, cynosure, epicenter, eye, focus, ground zero, heart, hub, locus, mecca, nerve center, nexus, nucleus, omphalos, seat, vortex

NUGATORY, ***adjective*** fatuous, frivolous, frothy, futile, immaterial, inadequate, inane, inapt, incompetent, inconsequential, ineffective, ineffectual, inefficacious, inept, inoperative, insignificant, insubstantial, inutile, invalid, irrelevant, jejune, *nugatorius,* null, null and void, otiose, paltry, petty, purposeless, slight, superficial, trifling, trivial, unavailing, unfruitful, unimportant, unproductive, unprofitable, unserviceable, useless, vain, valueless, void, worthless

NUISANCE, ***noun*** affliction, aggravation, annoyance, anxiety, bedevilment, bother, burden, cause of distress, devilment, difficult situation, difficulty, discomfort, displeasure, disturbance, grievance, handicap, harassment, hardship, hindrance, imposition, inconvenience, infliction, infringement, injurious interference, interference, intrusion, irritation, molestation, obstacle, ordeal, pain, pest, pestilence, plague, problem, scourge, trial, trouble, unlawful obstruction, unwarrantable intrusion, vexation, worry
ASSOCIATED CONCEPTS: abatement of a nuisance, attractive nuisance, common nuisance, continuing nuisance, nuisance at law, nuisance in fact, nuisance per se, public nuisance
FOREIGN PHRASES: ***Aedificare in tuo proprio solo non licet quod alteri noceat.*** It is not lawful to build upon one's own land what may injure another.

NUISANCE VALUE, ***noun*** cost to resolve a frivolous action, disposal value, number to dispose of a frivolous case, number to get rid of a frivolous action, number to make a case go away, price to resolve a frivolous case, quick settlement amount for a frivolous case, value to dispose of a frivolous lawsuit, walking money
ASSOCIATED CONCEPTS: frivolous lawsuit

NULL *(Insignificant),* ***adjective*** beneath notice, dispensable, disregarded, empty, expendable, immaterial, impuissant, inappreciable, inconsequential, inconsiderable, inessential, inferior, insubstantial, insufficient, irrelevant, meaningless, minor, negligible, nominal, nugatory, of no account, of no effect, of no moment, of no value, paltry, peripheral, petty, pointless, powerless, puny, secondary, small, superficial, tenuous, token, trifling, trivial, unavailing, unessential, unimportant, uninfluential, unmeaningful, unnecessary, unsubstantial, useless, valueless, without consequence, without meaning, without significance, without substance, worthless

NULL *(Invalid),* ***adjective*** abolished, abrogated, annulled, canceled, dead, defeated, defunct, deleted, disannulled, disestablished, effectless, extinct, extinguished, forceless, gone, impotent, ineffective, ineffectual, inefficacious, inoperative, *inritus,* negated, no longer law, not valid, nugatory, nullified, obliterated, of no binding force, of no effect, of no validity, of no weight, omitted, overruled, powerless, quashed, repealed, rescinded, reversed, revoked, set aside, strengthless, superseded, suspended, unauthorized, unsanctioned, useless, vacated, valueless, void, withdrawn, without authority, without legal effect, without legal force, without potency, without value, worthless

NULL AND VOID, ***adjective*** abolished, abrogated, annulled, canceled, defeated, defunct, disannulled, disestablished, effectless, extinct, extinguished, forceless, impotent, ineffective, ineffectual, inefficacious, inoperative, invalid, negated, no longer law, not valid, nugatory, nullified, obliterated, of no binding force, of no effect, of no legal weight, of no validity, omitted, overruled, quashed, repealed, rescinded, reversed, revoked, set aside, strengthless, superseded, suspended, unauthorized, unsanctioned, useless, vacated, valueless, void, withdrawn, without authority, without legal effect, without legal force, without potency, without value, worthless

NULLIFICATION, ***noun*** abolishment, absolute contradiction, annulment, cancel, cancellation, canceling, contradiction, contrary assertion, contravention, countering, disaffirmation, disallowance, disavowal, disclaimer, disclamation, disproof, emphatic denial, flat denial, invalidation, recantation, refutation, renunciation, repeal, repudiation, rescinding, rescission, retraction, reversal, revocation, revoke, setting aside, striking down, suspension, voidance
ASSOCIATED CONCEPTS: antinullification, Constitution, state's rights, ultimate sovereign

NULLIFY, ***verb*** abolish, abrogate, *ad inritum redigere,* annul, cancel, cast aside, counteract, countermand, declare null and void, deprive of efficacy, deprive of legal force, disannul, dissolve, invalidate, make useless, make valueless, make void, negate, neutralize, obliterate, offset, outweigh, override, overrule, overturn, quash, recall, recant, render invalid, renege, repeal, repudiate, rescind, retract, reverse, revoke, suspend, vacate, vitiate, void

NULLITY, *noun* blankness, *inanitas,* inefficacy, inexistence, insignificance, invalidity, naught, nihility, nonbeing, nonentity, nonexistence, nothing, nothingness, oblivion, vacuity, *vanitas,* void
ASSOCIATED CONCEPTS: decision to overrule decision

NUMBER, *noun* account, accounting, aggregate, calculation, collection, complement, count, decimal, degree, estimate, exponent, figure, integer, integral, multitude, overall amount, overall quantity, quantity, score, sum, symbol, tally, total
ASSOCIATED CONCEPTS: gaming

NUMEROUS, *adjective* abundance, ample, an excessive amount, bounteous, bountiful, copious, countless, ever so many, exhaustless, generous, lavish, liberal, many, much, multiple, myriad, not a few, overflowing, plentiful, plentious, plenty, rampant, too many

NUNC PRO TUNC, *noun* acknowledged, operative with respect to the past, ratified, reaffirmed, reconfirmed, reendorsed, reestablished, retroactive effect, retrospective effect, revalidated
ASSOCIATED CONCEPTS: nunc pro tunc order

NUNCUPATIVE, *adjective* articulated, conversational, conveyed orally, declared, dictated, enunciated, expressed in words, not written, oral, oral declaration, oral testimony, oratorical, parol, phonic, pronounced, spoken, stated, unwritten, uttered, verbal, vocal, voiced
ASSOCIATED CONCEPTS: nuncupative will

NUPTIAL, *adjective* allied, betrothed, bridal, conjugal, connubial, coupled, espoused, *genialis,* marital, married, mated, matrimonial, *nuptialis,* united, wedded
ASSOCIATED CONCEPTS: antenuptial agreement

NUPTIAL AGREEMENTS, *noun* contract regarding a marriage arrangement, contract regarding the bonds of matrimony, marriage agreement, marriage compact, marriage concordat, marriage understanding, marriage undertaking, matrimonial contract, pact, pledge, postnuptial agreement, prenuptial agreement, spousal agreement
ASSOCIATED CONCEPTS: domestic relations, family law, postnuptial agreements, prenuptial agreement

NURTURE, *verb* advance, aid, assist, back, bolster, bring to maturity, bring up, care for, cherish, coach, cultivate, develop, direct, educate, encourage, enrich, feed, fortify, forward, foster, further, give aid, harbor, help, improve, instruct, invigorate, maintain, make provisions for, make strong, mold, nourish, nurse, *nutrire,* patronize, prepare, promote, provide for, rear, render better, render strong, sponsor, strengthen, succor, supply aid, support, sustain, teach, train, tutor, victual

OATH, *noun* adjuration, affirmation, affirmation of truth, affirmation of truth of a statement, asseveration, attestation, avouchment, avowal, avowance, guarantee, *iusiurandum,* open declaration, pledge, promise, solemn affirmation, solemn avowal, solemn declaration, solemn invocation, swearing, sworn pledge, sworn promise, sworn statement, vow
FOREIGN PHRASES: ***Repellitur a sacramento infamis.*** An infamous person is denied the right to make an oath. ***Sacramentum habet in se tres comites-veritatem, justitiam, et judicium; veritus habenda est in jurato; justitia et justicium in judice.*** An oath has in it three components—truth, justice, and judgment; truth in the party swearing; justice and judgment in the judge administering the oath. ***Juramentum est indivisibile; et non est admittendum in parte verum et in parte falsam.*** An oath is indivisible; it is not to be held as partly true and partly false. ***Jusjurandum inter alios factum nec nocere nec prodesse debet.*** An oath made between other parties ought neither to hurt nor profit. ***Non est arctius vinculum inter homines quam jusjurandum.*** There is no stronger bond between men than an oath. ***Jurato creditur in judicio.*** He who makes an oath is to be believed in a judicial proceeding. ***Jusjurandi forma verbis differt, re convenit; hunc enim sensum habere debet: ut Deus invocetur.*** The form of taking an oath differs in language, agrees in meaning; for it ought to have this meaning: that the deity is invoked. ***Perjuri sunt qui servatis verbis juramenti decipiunt aures eorum qui accipiunt.*** They are perjured, who, preserving the words of an oath, deceive the ears of those who receive it. ***Omne sacramentum debet esse de certa scientia.*** Every oath ought to be founded on certain knowledge. ***Sacramentum si fatuum fuerit, licet falsum, tamen non committit perjurium.*** A foolish oath, although false, does not give rise to perjury.

OBDURATE, ***adjective*** callous, cold, decided, determined, dogged, dogmatic, dogmatical, firm, hard, hard-bitten, hardened, hard-hearted, harsh, headstrong, heartless, immovable, immutable, impervious, impossible to influence, incorrigible, indifferent, indurate, indurated, inexorable, inflexible, insensitive, intractable, intransigent, invariable, iron-hearted, irreclaimable, merciless, mulish, obstinate, opinionated, opinionative, pertinacious, pervicacious, pig-headed, positive, recalcitrant, refractory, relentless, remorseless, resolute, stony, strong-minded, strong-willed, stubborn, tenacious, unalterable, unbending, uncaring, unchangeable, uncompassionate, uncompromising, unconcerned, uncontrollable, unfeeling, unforgiving, ungovernable, unmalleable, unmanageable, unmerciful, unpitying, unrelenting, unresponsive, unstirred, unsusceptible, unsympathetic, untouched, unyielding, willful

OBEDIENT, ***adjective*** acquiescent, amenable, attentive, behaved, biddable, complaisant, compliable, compliant, complying, conformable, conforming, controllable, dedicated, deferential, devoted, *dicto audiens,* docile, ductile, duteous, dutiful, faithful, governable, honoring, law-abiding, loyal, manageable, meek, obeisant, obliging, *oboediens,* observant, *obtemperans,* passive, pliant, regardful, respectful, reverential, rule-abiding, servile, submissive, subservient, supple, tame, tractable, unresisting, venerating, well-behaved, willing, yielding
FOREIGN PHRASES: ***Ubi non est condendi auctoritas, ibi non est parendi necessitas.*** Where there is no authority for establishing a rule, there is no need of obeying it. ***Ejus nulla culpa est cui parere necesse sit.*** No guilt attaches to a person who is compelled to obey. ***Quicunque jussu judicis aliquid fecerit non videtur dolo malo fecisse, quia parere necesse est.*** Whoever does anything by the command of a judge is not deemed to have done it with an evil intent, because it is necessary to obey. ***Prudenter agit qui praecepto legis obtemperat.*** He acts prudently who obeys the precept of the law. ***Obedientia est legis essentia.*** Obedience is the essence of the law. ***Legitime imperanti parere necesse est.*** One who commands lawfully must be obeyed.

OBEISANT, ***adjective*** affable, amiable, civil, complaisant, compliant, conciliatory, courteous, decorous, deferential, deferring, duteous, dutiful, eager to please, good-humored, good-natured, gracious, helpful, honorable, humble, meek, nonresisting, obedient, obliging, pliant, polite, respectful, reverent, reverential, self-abasing, showing homage, submissive, subservient, surrendering, unresisting, willing, yielding

OBEY, ***verb*** abide by, accede, accept, accommodate, acquiesce, act in accordance with orders, act on, adhere to, agree, answer to, assent, attend to, attend to orders, be devoted to, be faithful to, be governed by, be guided by, be loyal to, be obedient, be regulated by, be subject, behave, bend to, be ruled by, bow to, carry out, come at call, comply, conform, consent, defer to, do the will of, execute, fall in with, follow, follow orders, fulfill, fulfill the commands of, give allegiance to, give way, heed, humble oneself to, keep, kneel to, listen, live by, mind, *oboedire, obsequi,* observe, *parere,* perform, please, respect, respond, satisfy, serve, submit, succumb, surrender, take orders, yield
FOREIGN PHRASES: ***Ejus nulla culpa est cui parere necesse sit.*** No guilt attaches to a person who is compelled to obey.

OBFUSCATE, ***verb*** addle, adumbrate, baffle, becloud, bedim, befuddle, begloom, bemist, bewilder, blacken, blind, blur, cloak, cloud, complicate, conceal, confound, confuse, cover, curtain, darken, daze, dim, disconcert, disturb, dull, eclipse, fluster, fog, hide, keep one guessing, mist, mix up, muddle, mystify, nonplus, obscure, obumbrate, occult, overshadow, perplex, perturb, put off the track, puzzle, screen, shade, shield, shroud, stupefy, throw into confusion, throw off the scent, unsettle, upset, veil

OBJECT, ***noun*** aim, butt, commodity, concern, *consilium,* corporeal body, design, destination, end, final cause, finis, goal, item, material product, material substance, matter, point, *propositum,* purpose, subject, substance, target, ultimate purpose

OBJECT, ***verb*** attack, be at variance, be averse, call in question, challenge, complain, *contra dicere recusare,* contravene, controvert, criticize, demur, disagree, disapprove, dispute, dissent, enter a demurrer, enter a protest, except, express an objection, express disapproval, find fault, oppose, protest, put forward in opposition, quarrel, *repugnare,* resist, state by way of objection, state opposition, take exception

OBJECT LESSON, ***noun*** case in point, crowning example, demonstration, embodiment, epitome, example, exemplar, exemplification, explanation, heinous example, illustration, instance, most wretched instance, paragon, quintessence, relevant instance, representative, specimen, symbol, terrible, worst

OBJECT TO, ***verb*** absolutely differ with, be at variance with, be averse to, be diametrically opposed to, be on all fours with, call in question, challenge, complain, contravene, controvert, counter, criticize, deny, disagree with, disapprove, dispute, dissent, express an objection, express disapproval, find fault, oppose, protest, put forward in opposition, resist, state by way of objection, state opposition, take exception, undermine
ASSOCIATED CONCEPTS: evidence, rules of procedure

OBJECTION, ***noun*** adverse argument, adverse charge, adverse comment, adverse reason, challenge, *contradictio,* counterargument, countercharge, criticism, denunciation, difference, disagreement, disapprobation, disapproval, dissatisfaction, dissent, exception, expostulation, grievance, opposition, protest, *quod contra dicitur,* reason for disapproval, rebuke, rejection, remonstrance, reservation
ASSOCIATED CONCEPTS: frivolous objection, general objection, grounds for an objection, oral objection, overrule an objection, preservation of an objection, specific objection, sustain an objection, technical objection, waiver, written objection

OBJECTIONABLE, ***adjective*** abhorrent, abominable, annoying, antipathetic, base, deplorable, despicable, detestable, disagreeable, disgusting, dislikable, displeasing, distasteful, evil, exceptionable, execrable, filthy, foul, fulsome, gross, hateful, heinous, horrid, illaudable, impalatable, improper, inadvisable, inappropriate, inexpedient, insufferable, intolerable, invidious, loathsome, nasty, nefarious, noisome, noxious, obnoxious, obscene, odious, offensive, opprobrious, peccant, pernicious, repugnant, repulsive, revolting, scurvy, sickening, unacceptable, unappealing, unbearable, unbecoming, uncommendable, undesirable, unendurable, uninviting, unlikable, unpalatable, unpleasant, unpleasing, unsatisfactory, unsavory, unseemly, unsuitable, vile, wrong
ASSOCIATED CONCEPTS: objectionable conduct, objectionable material, objectionable question

OBJECTIVE, ***adjective*** actual, broad-minded, candid, concrete, corporeal, desired, detached, disinterested, dispassionate, equitable, factual, fair, fair-minded, impartial, impersonal, judicial, just, material, neutral, nonpartisan, nonsubjective, open-minded, real, reasonable, scientific, sober, unbiased, unbigoted, uncolored, uninfluenced, unjaundiced, unprejudiced, unslanted, unswayed, unwarped

OBJECTIVE, ***noun*** achievement, aim, ambition, aspiration, design, desire, desired object, destination, dream, end, expectation, final point, fixed purpose, formulated intention, goal, height of one's ambition, hope, idea, intent, intention, *locus qui petitur,* mark, mission, point, purpose, pursuit, set purpose, settled purpose, target, terminal point
ASSOCIATED CONCEPTS: lawful objectives

OBJECTIVITY, ***noun*** *aequitas,* broadmindedness, detachment, disinterest, disinterestedness, dispassion, dispassionateness, equitableness, equity, fair-mindedness, fair play, fairness, immovability, impartiality, impersonality, justice, justness, lack of bias, lack of jaundice, lack of prejudice, neutrality, noninvolvement, nonpartisanship, nonsubjectivity, open-mindedness

OBJURGATE, ***verb*** abase, admonish, berate, blame, call down, castigate, censure, chasten, chastise, chide, humble, humiliate, penalize, punish, rake over the coal, rebuke, reprehend, reprimand, reproach, scold, scourge, upbraid

OBJURGATION, ***noun*** accusation, admonishment, admonition, berating, castigation, chiding, denunciation, expostulation, lecture, rebuke, reprehension, reprimand, reproach, reproof, reproval, scolding, sermon, upbraiding

OBLIGATE, ***verb*** agree to perform, agree to be burdened with, assume a duty, assume a moral responsibility for, assume responsibility for, assume the performance of, become legally responsible for, become obliged, charged with, committed to accomplish, compel, contracted, covenanted, indebted to, promise to do
ASSOCIATED CONCEPTS: contractual duties, implied obligations

OBLIGATION *(Duty),* ***noun*** agreement, burden, charge, commitment, compulsion, contract, covenant, debt, duty owed, *homini gratiam debere,* legal responsibility, moral responsibility, necessity, oath, obligement, *officium,* pact, performance owed, promise, responsibility, social responsibility, that which a person owes to another, that which is due from a person
ASSOCIATED CONCEPTS: alternative obligation, antecedent obligation, community obligation, conditional obligation, contingent obligation, contractual obligation, existing obligation, fiduciary obligation, impairment of obligation, joint obligation, legal obligation, moral obligation, mutual obligations, parental obligation, pecuniary obligation, personal obligation, privity of obligation, secured obligation, several obligations, statutory obligations, voluntary obligation
FOREIGN PHRASES: ***Fides est obligatio conscientiae alicujus ad intentionem alterius.*** A truth is an obligation of conscience of one to the wishes of another. ***Nihil tam naturale est, quam eo genere quidque dissolvere, quo colligatum est; ideo verborum obligatio verbis tollitur; nudi consensus obligatio contrario consensu dissolvitur.*** Nothing is so natural as to dissolve anything in the way in which it was made binding. ***In omnibus obligationibus in quibus dies non ponitur, praesenti die debetur.*** In all obligations in which no time is fixed for their fulfillment, the obligation is due immediately. ***Eisdem modis dissolvitur obligatio quae nascitur ex contractu, vel quasi, quibus contrahitur.*** An obligation which arises in contract, or quasi contract, is dissolved in the same ways in which it is con-tracted. ***Idem est scire aut scire debet aut potuisse.*** To be bound to know or to be able to know is the same as to know. ***Nuda pactio obligationem non parit.*** A naked agreement does not affect an otherwise binding obligation. ***Impossibilium nulla obligatio est.*** One cannot be obliged to perform impossible tasks. ***Unumquodque dissolvitur eodem ligamine quo ligatur.*** Every obligation is dissolved by the same manner with which it is created. ***Omnia quae jure contrahuntur, contrario jure pereunt.*** All contracts which are entered into under a law, become void under a contrary law. ***Ignorantia eorum quae quis scire tenetur non excusat.*** Ignorance of those things which a person is deemed to know is no excuse. ***L'obligation sans cause, ou sur une fausse cause, ou sur cause illicite, ne peut avoir aucun effet.*** An obligation without consideration, or upon a false consideration, or upon unlawful consideration, cannot have any effect. ***Nudum pactum est ubi nulla subest causa praeter conventionem; sed ubi subest causa, fit obligatio, et parit actionem.*** A naked contract is where there is no consideration except the agreement; but where there is a consideration, an obligation is created and gives rise to a right of action.

OBLIGATION *(Liability),* ***noun*** accountability, amount due, charge, debit, debt, duty to pay money, indebtedness, indenture, outstanding debt, that which is owing, unliquidated claim, unpaid debt

OBLIGATION OF GOING FORWARD, ***noun*** adequate evidence, adequate proof legally presented at trial, burden of going forward, burden of proof, legal responsibility, sufficient corroboration, sufficient evidence in a case, sufficient evidence to establish a case, sufficient proof, sufficient proof of facts, validation of proof of a case, verification of proof of a case
ASSOCIATED CONCEPTS: cause of action or claim, evidence, evidential burden, failure to sustain, preponderance of the evidence, prima facie case, rebuttal
FOREIGN PHRASES: ***Onus probani.*** Burden of proof.

OBLIGATORY, ***adjective*** binding, coactive, coercive, commanded, compelling, compulsatory, compulsive, compulsory, constrained, dictated, enforced, essential, exigent, forced, forcible, imperative, importunate, imposed, incumbent on, indispensable, inescapable, involuntary, leaving no choice, mandatory, necessary, necessitated, not to be avoided, not to be evaded, prerequisite, pressing, required, requisite, unavoidable, unforgoable, urgent, vital, with force of law, without appeal, without choice
ASSOCIATED CONCEPTS: obligatory advance, obligatory payment, obligatory writing

OBLIGE, ***verb*** bind, coerce, compel, dragoon, elicit, exact, force, impel, impose, make another accept a role, make another accept responsibility for, make another party perform, obligate, require

OBLIGEE, ***noun*** bestower, financier, grantor, lender, lessor, mortgage holder, mortgagee

OBLIGOR, ***noun*** borrower, debtor, drawee, loan applicant, loanee, mortgagor, pledgor
ASSOCIATED CONCEPTS: obligor on a note

OBLIQUE *(Evasive)*, ***adjective*** ambivalent, backhanded, circuitous, circumlocutory, cloaked, concealed, devious, disingenuous, elusive, elusory, equivocal, equivocating, furtive, indeterminate, indirect, inexact, lacking clarity, prevaricating, recondite, roundabout, secretive, sinuous, unclear, underhand, underhanded, unstraightforward, vague, veiled

OBLIQUE *(Slanted)*, ***adjective*** angled, askew, aslant, awry, diagonal, inclined, inclining, leaning, *obliquus*, slanting, sloping, steep, tilted, tipped, tipping

OBLITERATE, ***verb*** *abolere*, abolish, annihilate, annul, blot out, bring to nothing, cancel, conceal, consume, cover, cover up, defeat, *delere*, delete, demolish, deracinate, desolate, destroy, devastate, devour, disintegrate, dispel, dissipate, dissolve, efface, eliminate, erase, expunge, exterminate, extinguish, extirpate, gut, invalidate, level, liquidate, mask, mow down, nullify, obscure, omit, pull up by the roots, quash, quell, ravage, raze, remove, remove the traces, render illegible, render imperceptible, rub off, rub out, ruin, rule out, scratch out, screen, shroud, smash, snuff out, squash, stamp out, strike out, suppress, swallow up, sweep away, tear down, topple, unmake, wipe out, wreck, write off

OBLIVIOUS, ***adjective*** absent, absentminded, absorbed, abstracted, blank, careless, distracted, dreamy, faraway, forgetful, heedless, *immemor*, inattentive, inconsiderate, indifferent, insensible, mindless, neglectful, negligent, *obliviosus*, overlooking, preoccupied, remiss, thoughtless, unaware, uncaring, unconscious, undiscerning, unheeding, unmindful, unnoticing, unobservant, unrecognizing, without consideration

OBLOQUY, ***noun*** abasement, abuse, abusive language, accusation, animadversion, aspersion, berating, blame, castigation, censure, chastisement, chiding, contempt, criticism, debasement, defamation, degradation, denunciation, derision, derogation, diatribe, disapprobation, discredit, disesteem, disfavor, disgrace, dishonor, disparagement, disrepute, disrespect, dressing down, execration, exprobration, faultfinding, humiliation, ignominy, ill favor, ill repute, infamy, ingloriousness, invective, lashing, *maledictum*, objurgation, odium, opprobrium, reproach, revilement, scolding, shame, slur, stigma, stricture, tirade, tongue-lashing, traducement, verbal abuse, vilification, *vituperatio*, vituperation
ASSOCIATED CONCEPTS: defamation

OBNOXIOUS, ***adjective*** abhorrent, abominable, annoying, antagonizing, antipathetic, base, beastly, blameworthy, censurable, contemptible, deplorable, despicable, detestable, disagreeable, disgusting, displeasing, execrable, faulty, foul, fulsome, gross, hateful, heinous, hellish, horrible, horrid, impalatable, insufferable, intolerable, invidious, *invisus*, loathful, loathsome, nasty, nauseating, nefarious, noisome, noxious, *noxius*, objectionable, odious, offensive, opprobrious, pernicious, poisonous, rank, repellent, reprehensible, repugnant, repulsive, revolting, unbearable, unendurable, unpleasant, unpleasing, unwholesome, vile, villainous, vulgar, wretched

OBNUBILATE, ***verb*** adumbrate, becloud, bedim, blacken, blind, blur, cast a shadow, cloak, cloud, cloud over, conceal, cover, cover up, curtain, darken, dim, disguise, dull, eclipse, encompass with gloom, enshroud, fog, haze, hide, make indistinct, mask, obfuscate, obscure, occult, overcast, overcloud, overshadow, screen, shade, shadow, shroud, veil, wrap

OBSCENE, ***adjective*** bawdy, broad, debauched, foul, immodest, immoral, impure, indecent, indelicate, *inquinatus*, lascivious, lecherous, lewd, libidinous, licentious, lubricous, lurid, lustful, obscenus, offensive, offensive to decency, offensive to modesty, patently offensive, pornographic, profane, profligate, ribald, risque, salacious, scabrous, sensual, sexy, shameful, shameless, spicy, tending to excite lustful desires, *turpis*, unchaste, unwholesome, vile, vulgar, wanton

OBSCENITY, ***noun*** bawdiness, coarseness, dirtiness, immodesty, immorality, impropriety, indecency, indecorum, indelicacy, lechery, lewdness, lubricity, *obscenitas*, offensiveness, pornography, ribaldry, salaciousness, salacity, scurrillity, smut, smuttiness, *turpitudo*, unchastity, vileness, vulgarity

OBSCURATION, ***noun*** adumbration, blackout, blur, cloud, concealment, darkening, darkness, dimming, dimness, disappearance, faintness, fogginess, fuzziness, gloom, gloominess, indistinctness, obfuscation, obliteration, obscurity, occultation, opacity, opaqueness, overshadowing, privacy, retirement, seclusion, secrecy, shade, shading, shadowing, unclearness, unintelligibleness, vagueness

OBSCURE *(Abstruse)*, ***adjective*** complex, cryptic, cryptical, deep, difficult, difficult to understand, enigmatic, enigmatical, esoteric, hidden, impalpable, incomprehensible, intricate, involved, mysterious, profound, recondite, transcendental, unapparent, unintelligible

OBSCURE *(Faint)*, ***adjective*** blurred, blurry, concealed, dim, hard to see, hidden, impalpable, imperceptible, inconspicuous, indefinite, indiscernible, indistinct, invisible, murky, nebulous, pale, shadowy, subtle, unapparent, unclear, undistinguished, unplain, vague, veiled, weak

OBSCURE *(Remote)*, ***adjective*** alien, distant, far, foreign, isolated, private, rare, removed, secluded, strange, unconnected, unknown, unrenowned
ASSOCIATED CONCEPTS: obscure meaning

OBSCURE, ***verb*** adumbrate, becloud, bedim, befog, begloom, benight, blacken, blind, blur, cast a shadow, cloak, cloud, conceal, cover, cover up, curtain, darken, darkle, dim, disguise, dull, dusk, eclipse, encloud, enshroud, fog, haze, hide, keep in the dark, make dim, make indistinct, mask, mislead, obfuscate, occult, overcast, overcloud, overshadow, screen, shade, shroud, suppress, veil, wrap
FOREIGN PHRASES: ***Semper in obscuris quod minimum est sequimur.*** In obscure matters the construction which is least obscure should always be applied.

OBSEQUIOUS, ***adjective*** compliable, compliant, concessive, crawling, cringing, crouching, deferential, docile, enslaved, fawning, flattering, groveling, humble, ingratiating, obedient, scraping, servile, slavish, spineless, submissive, subordinate, subservient, sycophantic, toadying, unassertive, yielding

OBSERVANCE, ***noun*** abidance, acquiescence, adherence, allegiance, attention, compliance, conformance, cooperation, faithful adherence, honor, performance, respect, satisfaction, regard, submission, submissiveness
ASSOCIATED CONCEPTS: freedom of religion

OBSERVATION, ***noun*** advertence, advertency, annotation, ascertainment, assertion, attention, attentiveness, check, cognition, cognizance, comment, commentary, concentration, conclusion, consideration, declaration, detection, *dictum*, discovery, espial, espionage, estimation, examination, expression of opinion, finding, heed, heedfulness,

inspection, intentness, investigation, look, mention, mindfulness, *notatio,* note, notice, *observatio,* opinion, pronouncement, reconnaissance, reflection, regard, remark, report, scrutiny, statement, study, supervision, surveillance, survey, utterance, view, watch, watchfulness, witnessing
ASSOCIATED CONCEPTS: observation of the demeanor of a witness

OBSERVE *(Obey),* ***verb*** abide by, acquiesce, adhere to, attend, be faithful to, be guided by, be regulated by, be submissive to, bow to, carry out, cling to, comply with, conform, *conservare,* cooperate, discharge, do the will of, execute, follow, fulfill, heed, honor, keep, obey, *observare,* pay attention to, perform, respect, satisfy, show regard for, yield to
ASSOCIATED CONCEPTS: observe the laws

OBSERVE *(Remark),* ***verb*** announce, articulate, assert, aver, comment, communicate, couch in terms, declare, exclaim, express, give expression to, give tongue to, give utterance to, give voice to, impart, make a remark, make mention of, mention, muse, phrase, proclaim, put into words, say, state, tell, utter, vocalize, voice

OBSERVE *(Watch),* ***verb*** *animadvertere,* attend, be a spectator, be a witness, be attentive, be aware, be conscious, be vigilant, behold, command a view, descry, devote attention to, direct the eyes to, espy, examine, eye, follow, gaze at, give attention to, give heed to, have in sight, heed, hold in view, inspect, keep an eye on, keep in sight, keep in view, lay eyes on, look, look at, mark, mind, note, notice, *observare,* pay attention, pay heed, peer at, perceive, peruse, reconnoiter, regard, review, scan, scout, scrutinize, see, *spectare,* spy, survey, take cognizance of, take note, take notice, take stock, turn the attention to, turn the eyes on, view
ASSOCIATED CONCEPTS: eyewitness

OBSESS, ***verb*** agitate, annoy, bedevil, beset, besiege, bewitch, compel, control, craze, dement, derange, discompose, disconcert, distress, dominate, drive, enthrall, gnaw, haunt, hold captive, hound, infatuate, madden, nag, overpower, pervade, plague, possess, preoccupy, prey on the mind, seize, torment, trouble, unbalance, unhinge, vex, weigh on the mind

OBSESSION, ***noun*** absorption, application, attraction, compulsion, craze, crotchet, dominating action, engrossment, exclusive attention, fanaticism, fancy, fascination, fetish, fixation, fixed idea, immersion, infatuation, irresistible impulse, mania, monomania, passion, preoccupation, rapt attention, ruling passion, ruling whim, single-mindedness, undivided attention, whole attention

OBSOLETE, ***adjective*** abandoned, anachronistic, anachronous, ancient, antediluvian, antiquated, antique, archaic, archaistic, bygone, dated, dead, discarded, discontinued, dismissed, disused, early, expired, extinct, fallen into desuetude, fallen into disuse, no longer in use, obsolescent, *obsoletus,* old, old-fashioned, out-of-date, out of use, outdated, outmoded, outworn, past, primitive, rejected, retired, stale, timeworn, unfashionable, unmodern
ASSOCIATED CONCEPTS: obsolete covenant, obsolete records, obsolete restrictions

OBSTACLE, ***noun*** arrest, balk, barricade, barrier, block, bridle, catch, check, constraint, curb, dam, delay, detainment, difficulty, disallowance, drawback, embargo, enjoining, estoppel, fence, forbiddance, hamper, handicap, hindrance, hurdle, impediment, *impedimentum,* inconvenience, inhibition, injunction, limitation, obstruction, preclusion, prohibition, proscription, remora, restraint, restriction, snag, stop, stoppage, stopper, stumbling block, suppression, trammel

OBSTRUCT, ***verb*** bar, barricade, block, brake, bridle, bring to a standstill, check, choke, circumscribe, congest, countervail, cramp, cripple, curb, debar, delay, disable, embar, encumber, estop, forbid, frustrate, halt, hamper, hamstring, handicap, hinder, impede, impedite, inhibit, interfere with, interrupt, intervene, limit, occlude, oppilate, preclude, prevent, prohibit, restrain, retard, slow down, snag, stall, stand in the way, stay, stem, stop, stop up, stymie, suppress, suspend, terminate, thwart, trammel, trap
ASSOCIATED CONCEPTS: obstruct a lawful authority, obstruct an investigation, obstruct justice, obstructing governmental administration

OBSTRUCTION, ***noun*** balk, ban, bar, barricade, barrier, block, blockade, blockage, bridle, catch, check, clog, closure, congestion, constraint, constriction, cork, curb, dam, difficulty, disallowance, embargo, embarrassment, enjoining, fence, forbiddance, hamper, hindrance, hitch, hurdle, impediment, *impedimentum,* impedition, injunction, interference, interruption, limitation, obstacle, *obstructio,* obstruent, obturation, occlusion, plug, preclusion, prevention, prohibition, proscription, remora, restraint, restriction, shackle, snag, stop, stopper, stricture, trammel
FOREIGN PHRASES: ***Forstellarius est pauperum depressor, et totius communitatis et patriae publicus inimicus.*** A forestaller is an enemy of the poor, and a public enemy of the county.

OBSTRUCTIONIST, ***noun*** assailant, extremist, firebrand, hellion, incendiary, inciter, inflamer, initiator, instigator, intruder, invader, meddler, mischievous person, provocateur, provoker, raider, ringleader, rowdy person, sparkplug, trespasser, troublesome person, unruly person

OBTAIN, ***verb*** accumulate, achieve, acquire, *adipisci,* appropriate, arrive at, attain, be in receipt of, capture, collect, come into possession, *consequi,* earn, enter into possession, gain, gain possession, gather, get, get hold of, get possession of, grab, hold, lay hands upon, *nancisci,* pick up, pocket, possess, procure, reach, realize, receive, recover, secure, seize, take, take over, take possession, win
ASSOCIATED CONCEPTS: obtain a judgment, obtain a search warrant

OBTRUDE, ***verb*** accroach, break in, burst in, butt in, encroach, force, impose, *inculcare,* infringe, *ingerere,* interfere, interlope, intermeddle, interpose, interrupt, intervene, intrude, invade, meddle, trespass

OBTRUSIVE, ***adjective*** aggressive, assuming, bold, brash, brazen, encroaching, forward, impertinent, insolent, interfering, interrupting, interruptive, intruding, intrusive, invasive, malapert, meddlesome, meddling, officious, presuming, presumptuous, prominent, protruding, protrusive, protuberant, prying, pushy, rude, saucy, self-assertive, unmannerly

OBTUND, ***verb*** abate, allay, alleviate, anesthetize, assuage, benumb, blunt, calm, deaden, desensitize, dull, ease, impair the force of, make blunt, make less violent, mitigate, moderate, modulate, numb, palliate, quell, quiet, reduce the edge, reduce the violence, soften, take the edge off, weaken

OBTURATE, ***verb*** block, clog, close, cork, hinder, interfere, obstruct, prevent, shut, stop up, stopper

OBTUSE, ***adjective*** asinine, blockish, blunt, blunt-witted, callous, dense, doltish, dronish, dull, dull-witted, hebes, idiotic, ignorant, imbecilic, imperceptive, impercipient, insensitive, lumpish, moronic, oafish, obtusus, opaque, phlegmatic, retusus, senseless, simple, simple-minded, slow, stupid, thick, thickheaded, torporific, uncaring, uncomprehending, undiscerning, unfeeling, unimaginative, unintelligent, witless

OBVIATE, ***verb*** abolish, annihilate, crush, decimate, defeat, demolish, destroy, eliminate, foil, invert, obliterate, overcome, overpower, overset, overthrow, overturn, overwhelm, quell, repress, reverse, ruin, subdue, subvert, suppress, topple, upend, uproot, upset, vanquish
ASSOCIATED CONCEPTS: obviate the terms of a contract

OBVIATION, ***noun*** abolition, abrogation, arresting, bar, blockage, cancellation, check, deterrent, elimination, forestalling, interdiction, prevention, removal, stoppage, turning aside

OBVIOUS, ***adjective*** accessible, *apertus,* apparent, axiomatic, axiomatical, bald, bright, clear, comprehensible, conspicuous, discernible, discoverable, distinct, distinguishable, evident, exoteric, exoterical, explicit, exposed, glaring, in evidence, in view, indisputable, intelligible, lucid, manifest, *manifestus,* notable, noticeable, observable, open, overt, palpable, patent, perceivable, perceptible, perspicuous, *perspicuus,* plain, prominent, pronounced, recognizable, revealed, standing out, striking, transparent, uncamouflaged, unconcealed, undeniable, understandable, undisguised, unhidden, unmasked, unmistakable, unquestionable, unscreened, visible, well-defined
ASSOCIATED CONCEPTS: obvious danger, obvious defect, obvious error, obvious risks

OCCASION, ***noun*** advent, affair, chance, conjuncture, episode, event, experience, happening, incident, instance, juncture, moment, *occasio,* occurrence, opening, opportunity, point, situation, suitable time, *tempus,* time

OCCASION, ***verb*** breed, bring about, cause, create, effect, generate, give cause for, induce, make, produce, provoke

OCCLUDE, ***verb*** arrest, bar, barricade, block, blockade, check, choke off, close, cork, cover, dam up, debar, deter, fasten, hamper, hedge in, hem in, hinder, impede, inhibit, intercept, interclude, interrupt, lock, obstruct, obturate, oppilate, plug, preclude, prevent, prohibit, restrain, restrict, retard, seal, shut, shut in, shut off, stanch, stop, stop up, throttle, thwart, trammel, trap

OCCUPANCY, ***noun*** actual possession, control, dominion, enjoyment, habitation, holding, inhabitancy, occupation, ownership, *possessio,* possession, proprietorship, residence, retention, temporary possession, tenure
ASSOCIATED CONCEPTS: certificate of occupancy, continuous occupancy, illegal occupancy, partial occupancy, physical occupancy, principal occupation, residency laws, right of occupancy

OCCUPANT, ***noun*** addressee, denizen, dweller, freeholder, habitant, householder, inhabitant, inmate, leaseholder, lessee, lodger, occupier, possessor, renter, resident, residentiary, resider, roomer, sojourner, tenant
ASSOCIATED CONCEPTS: bona fide occupant, illegal occupancy, lawful occupant, right of occupancy, tenant in occupancy

OCCUPATION *(Possession),* ***noun*** ascendancy, authority, charge, command, control, direction, domination, dominion, influence, inhabitation, jurisdiction, mastery, occupancy, *occupatio,* ownership, power, predominance, predominancy, proprietary rights, proprietorship, residence, retention, right to retain, rule, seizure, superintendence, tenure

OCCUPATION *(Vocation),* ***noun*** activity, avocation, business, calling, capacity, career, chosen work, craft, employment, enterprise, field, industry, job, line, livelihood, mission, *negotium,* office, position, profession, pursuit, situation, specialty, trade, undertaking, venture, work

OCCUPY *(Engage),* ***verb*** absorb, absorb the attention, absorb the mind, absorb the thoughts, address oneself to, amuse, apply oneself to, apply the attention to, apply the mind to, arrest the attention, attract the attention, attract the mind, attract the thoughts, be active with, be at work on, be concerned with, be employed, busy oneself with, captivate, catch the attention, claim one's thoughts, concentrate on, concern oneself with, devote, direct the attention to, direct the mind to, engage the attention, engage the mind, engage the thoughts, engross, engross the mind, engross the thoughts, entertain, enthrall, entrance, excite the attention, fascinate, go about, immerse, *in re versari,* interest, invite the attention, involve, keep busy, monopolize, monopolize the thoughts, obsess, *occupare,* plunge into, ply, preoccupy, rivet the attention, rivet the mind, rivet the thoughts, set about, set to work, specialize in, spend one's time in, tackle, take employment, take on, take part, take up, *tenere,* turn the attention to, turn the mind to, undertake, work at

OCCUPY *(Take possession),* ***verb*** abide, acquire, annex, appropriate, assume, assume ownership, be possessed of, *capere,* capture, claim, colonize, command, conquer, control, denizen, dominate, dwell, dwell in, expropriate, have possession of, have rights to, have title to, help oneself to, hold, indwell, inhabit, invade, keep, keep hold of, keep house, live, live in, lodge, make one's home at, move into, obtain, *occupare,* own, possess, procure, recover, reside in, retain, seize, settle in, stay, take from, take over, take up residence in
ASSOCIATED CONCEPTS: actually occupy, lawfully occupy

OCCUR *(Come to mind),* ***verb*** be uppermost in the mind, become aware, become visible, come into view, conjure up, crop up, cross one's mind, emerge, enter the mind, enter the picture, manifest itself, pass in the mind, present itself, present itself to the mind, remember, reveal itself, show itself, *subit,* suggest itself

OCCUR *(Happen),* ***verb*** arise, become a fact, become known, come about, come into being, come into existence, come to pass, develop, emerge, *fieri, incidere,* materialize, proceed, recur, result, take effect, take its course, take place, transpire

OCCURRENCE, ***noun*** affair, *casus,* circumstance, contingency, episode, event, eventuality, experience, fortuity, happening, happenstance, incident, instance, occasion, phenomenon, predicament, proceeding, realization, *res,* situation, transaction, turn, venture
FOREIGN PHRASES: ***Casus fortuitus.*** A chance occurrence.

ODD *(Numeral),* ***adjective*** alternating number, every other number, symbol, uneven digit, uneven figure, uneven integer, uneven number

ODD *(Strange),* ***adjective*** alien, antagonistic, antithetic, atypical, changed, contradictory, contradistinctive, contrary, contrasting, contrastive, deviating, diametrically opposed, different, discordant, discrepant, disparate, dissimilar, dissonant, distinct, distinctive, divergent, diverse, foreign, idiosyncratic, in disagreement, incommensurable, incomparable, incompatible, incongruous, individual, inharmonious, mismatched, opposed, out of the ordinary, peculiar, set apart, unique, unlike, unmatched, unrelated, unusual, variant, varied, varying

ODDITY, ***noun*** aberrance, aberrancy, aberration, abnormality, anomalism, anomaly, bizarreness, caprice, capriciousness, curiosity, curiousness, deformity, deviancy, deviation, distinctiveness, divergence, eccentric, exception, fancifulness, fantasticality, grotesqueness, idiosyncrasy, incongruousness, individuality, irregularity, malformation, mannerism, maverick, misfit, oddness, original, peculiarity, quaintness, rarity, strangeness, uniqueness

ODIOUS, ***adjective*** abject, abominable, accursed, annoying, base, beastly, blameworthy, coarse, confounded, contemptible, corrupt, cursed, damnable, despicable, detestable, diabolic, dirty, disagreeable, disgraceful, disgusting, displeasing, evil, execrable, forbidding, foul, frightening, fulsome, grotesque, hateful, heinous, hideous, horrible, horrid, ignoble, ignominious, infamous, infernal, insufferable, intolerable, *invidiosus,* invidious, *invisus,* loathsome, low, mean, monstrous, nasty, objectionable, obnoxious, *odiosus,* offensive, rank, repellent, reprehensible, repugnant, repulsive, revolting, rotten, scurvy, shocking, sickening, sinister, tainted, ugly, unbearable, unendurable, unlovable, unpalatable, unpleasant, unpopular, unworthy, vile, vulgar

ODIUM, ***noun*** abhorrence, alienation, animosity, animus, antipathy, aversion, avoidance, bad feeling, blame, censure, contempt, criticism, debasement, degradation, derision, despite, detestation, disaffection, disapproval, disesteem, disfavor, disgrace, disgust, dishonor, dislike, displeasure, disrepute, distaste, dudgeon, enmity, execration, hate, hatred, horror, hostility, humiliation, ignobility, ignominy, ill will, infamy, inimicalness, loathing, malevolence, malice, maliciousness, obloquy, odiousness, opprobrium, rancor, rebuke, reproach, repugnance, repulsiveness, resentment, revulsion, scandal, scorn, shame, strong aversion, unpopularity, venom

OF COURSE, ***adverb*** absolutely, agreeable, as expected, by all means, certainly, definitely, exactly, for a fact, for sure, indeed, indubitably, naturally, okay, positively, surely, undoubtedly, unquestionably, with every degree of certainty, without a doubt, without fail, yes

OF GREAT IMPORT, ***adjective*** of major significance, of overwhelming significance, of serious import, of significant consequence, of significant importance, of significant meaning, of vast importance

OFF THE CHARTS, ***adjective*** amazing, astonishing, beyond words, exceptional, great, incredible, marvelous, masterful, mind-blowing, prodigious, spectacular, successful, terrific, wonderful

OFFEND *(Insult),* ***verb*** abuse, affront, anger, annoy, be discourteous, be impolite, chagrin, displease, distress, disturb, embarrass, enrage, gall, horrify, hurt, incense, inflame, infuriate, injure, irk, irritate, *laedere,* madden, make angry, mortify, nettle, *offendere,* outrage, pain, pique, provoke, ridicule, rile, slight, snub, taunt, tease, treat with discourtesy, treat with indignity, vex, wound

OFFEND *(Violate the law),* ***verb*** break a law, break the law, commit a breach of the law, commit a crime, commit a fault, commit an infraction, commit offense, commit sin, contravene, disobey the law, disregard the law, err, infringe, infringe a law, misconduct oneself, *peccare,* transgress, trespass, *violare*

OFFENDER, ***noun*** aggressor, assailant, criminal, delinquent, evildoer, felon, lawbreaker, malefactor, malfeasant, one implicated in the commission of a crime, one who breaks the law, one who commits a crime, *peccans,* sinner, transgressor, violator, wrongdoer
ASSOCIATED CONCEPTS: first offender, multiple offender, youthful offender

OFFENDING, ***adjective*** aberrant, annoying, blameworthy, condemned, culpable, delinquent, devious, disobedient, displeasing, erratic, exasperating, galling, guilty, in error, irritating, miscreant, naughty, noncompliant, offensive, provoking, repellant, repugnant, stray, transgressing, unorthodox, vexing, wandering, wayward

OFFENSE, ***noun*** aggression, assault, attack, breach, breach of the law, breaking of the law, crime, criminal act, criminal deed, criminality, delict, *delictum,* delinquency, disobedience, encroachment, evil behavior, evil deed, failure, felony, illegal act, illegal conduct, illegality, impropriety, infraction, infringement, injury, inobservance, lawbreaking, lawlessness, malefaction, malfeasance, malpractice, malversation, misconduct, misdeed, misdemeanor, misdoing, misfeasance, misprision, noncompliance, nonobservance, *offensio,* official misconduct, omission, outrage, pecability, *peccatum,* transgression, umbrage, unlawful act, unrighteousness, violation, violation of law, violation of orders, wrong, wrongdoing, wrongfulness
ASSOCIATED CONCEPTS: bailable offense, capital offense, charged with an offense, compound offense, continuing offense, degree of offense, grave offense, lesser offense, minor offense, offense against public decency, offense at common law, petty offense, prior offense, public offense
FOREIGN PHRASES: ***Peccata contra naturam sunt gravissima.*** Crimes against nature are the most heinous.

OFFENSE SPECIFIC RIGHT, ***noun*** limitation on extension to factually related offenses, right limited to specific offense, right limited to the offense at issue
ASSOCIATED CONCEPTS: Sixth Amendment Right to Counsel

OFFENSIVE *(Offending),* ***adjective*** abhorrent, abominable, abusive, annoying, antipathetic, beneath contempt, biting, blasphemous, coarse, contemptible, contumelious, detestable, disagreeable, discourteous, disdainful, disgusting, displeasing, disrespectful, distasteful, execrable, foul, gravis, harsh, hateful, heinous, hideous, horrible, horrid, ignoble, ill-bred, impertinent, impious, impudent, inaffable, indecent, inharmonious, insolent, insulting, intolerable, invidious, irritating, loathsome, low, malignant, monstrous, nasty, nauseating, noxious, objectionable, obnoxious, *odiosus molestus,* odious, offending, opprobrious, outrageous, peccant, putrid, reeking, repellent, repelling, reprehensible, repugnant, repulsive, revolting, ribald, rude, sarcastic, saucy, shocking, sickening, stinging, truculent, unbearable, uncivil, uncongenial, unendurable, ungracious, unmannered, unmannerly, unpalatable, unpleasant, unpleasing, unsavory, unspeakable, vile, wounding

OFFENSIVE *(Taking the initiative),* ***adjective*** aggressive, agitational, antagonistic, assailant, assailing, attacking, battling, bellicose, combative, contentious, disruptive, exciting, fighting, hostile, inciting, incursive, inflammatory, instigating, instigative, invading, invasive, militant, militaristic, provocative, provoking, unpacific, unpeaceful, warlike

OFFENSIVE WORK ENVIRONMENT, ***noun*** abhorrent workplace, abominable job environment at work, actionable workplace, execrable milieu at work, hostile workplace, repulsive workplace, unacceptable workplace

OFFER *(Propose),* ***verb*** bid, bring forward, hold forth, hold out, invite, lay before, make a bid, make a proposition, make an overture, *offerre,* pose, proffer, *profiteri,* propound, put forth, put forth for acceptance, put forth for consideration, put forward, put forward for consideration, recommend, submit, suggest, urge upon, venture

OFFER *(Tender),* ***verb*** advance, cede, extend, offer performance, pay, present, present for acceptance, produce, proffer, proffer payment, remit, render, submit, tender performance

FOREIGN PHRASES: ***Praesentare nihil aliud est quam praesto dare seu offere.*** To present is no more than to give or offer forthwith.

OFFICE, ***noun*** appointment, assigned task, berth, billet, bureau, business, capacity, charge, duty, employment, function, incumbency, job, *munus,* occupation, *officium, partes,* place of business, place of employment, position, post, profession, role, service, situation, station, trade, trust, work, workplace

ASSOCIATED CONCEPTS: impeachment from public office, malfeasance in office, misconduct in office, misfeasance in office, neglect of duty, nonfeasance in office, removal from office, vacancy in office

FOREIGN PHRASES: ***Officium nemini debet esse damnosum.*** An office ought to be injurious to no one. ***Nemo duobus utatur officiis.*** No one should hold two offices at the same time. ***Officia judicialia non concedantur antequam vacent.*** Judicial offices are not to be granted or appointed before they become vacant.

OFFICER, ***noun*** elected representative, functionary, named representative, officeholder, official

ASSOCIATED CONCEPTS: officer of the court, officer of the law

OFFICER OF THE COURT, ***noun*** advocate, appointed official of the court system, attorney, attorney-at-law, barrister, barrister-at-law, counsel, counselor, counselor-at-law, designated official of the court system, judicial designate, judicial officer, judicial official, legal advisor, legal advocate, legal consultant, legal practitioner, member of the legal profession, official of the court

OFFICIAL, ***adjective*** accredited, approved, assured, attested, authenticated, authoritative, ceremonious, certain, certified, conclusive, correct, decided, definite, dependable, endorsed, established, formal, guaranteed, indisputable, insured, legitimate, licensed, magisterial, officiary, proper, proven, *publicus,* reliable, sanctioned, to be depended on, to be trusted, trustworthy, undeniable, unequivocal, unimpeachable, valid, verified, worthy of confidence

ASSOCIATED CONCEPTS: official act, official bond, official business, official misconduct, official notice, official proceeding, official record

OFFICIAL, ***noun*** administrative head, administrator, bureaucrat, executive, executive officer, functionary, head of government, leader, leader of affairs, office bearer, officeholder, officer, overseer, person in authority, person responsible, *praefectus,* public officeholder, superintendent, supervisor

ASSOCIATED CONCEPTS: public official

OFFICIAL MISCONDUCT, ***noun*** criminal conduct by a public official, criminal conduct by an administration's member, dereliction of performance in office, deviation from rectitude, dishonest management, failing to uphold a sworn oath of office, failure in office, guilty act while a public official, illegal act, illegality by a public official, improper conduct by a public official, impropriety by a public official, maladministration by a public servant, malfeasance by a public servant, misadministration by a public servant, misconduct by a public official, misdeeds by a public official, misfeasance by a public official, misgovernment, misguidance by a public official, mismanagement by an officeholder, misprision by an officeholder, nonfeasance by an officeholder, offenses while in office, transgressions by an officeholder, turpitude by an officeholder, wrongdoing, by a public official

ASSOCIATED CONCEPTS: unlawful gratuities

OFFICIATE, ***verb*** act, administer, carry out, command, conduct, direct, discharge a function, do duty, execute, exercise, fill an office, function, govern, guide, head, hold an office, lead, manage, minister, moderate, occupy the chair, *officio fungi,* oversee, perform, pilot, preside, regulate, run, serve, steer, superintend, supervise, take the chair

OFFSET, ***noun*** allowance, balance, compensation, contrast, counter, counteractant, counteragent, counterbalance, counterblast, counterpoise, counterweight, equalization, equivalent, hedge, impedance, neutralizer, nullifier, opposite, opposition, preventative, satisfaction, set off, substitute

OFFSHOOT, ***noun*** addition, annex, branch, by-product, derivative, descendant, development, division, extension, issue, member, offspring, outgrowth, satellite, scion, subdivision, subsidiary, supplement

OFFSPRING, ***noun*** brood, cadet, child, children, descendants, family, heir, issue, lineage, next generation, offshoots, posterity, *progenies,* progeny, *proles,* scion, spawn, *stirps,* successor, younger generation

ASSOCIATED CONCEPTS: illegitimate offspring, natural offspring

OFTEN, ***adjective*** accustomed, common, consistently, customary, familiar, frequent, habitual, numerous, occurring over again, often done, often repeated, over and over again, persistent, prevalent, repeated, repetitive, same, usual

OLD, ***adjective*** advanced in years, ancient, antiquated, antique, archaic, crumbling, decadent, decayed, declining, decrepit, deteriorated, dilapidated, discontinued, disintegrated, early, elderly, enfeebled, hoary, *inveteratus,* matured, no longer young, not modern, obsolete, olden, original, past, preceding, preexisting, run down, rusty, stale, superannuated, timeworn, used, *vetus, vetustus,* vintage, waning, weakened, weathered, worn, worn out

ASSOCIATED CONCEPTS: ancient records doctrine

OMINOUS, ***adjective*** adverse, alarming, augurial, auspicial, baleful, bodeful, dangerous, dark, depressing, dire, direful, disastrous, dismaying, dispiriting, disquieting, disturbing, divinatory, fatidic, fatidical, fear-inspiring, fearful, forbidding, foreboding, frightful, gloomy, grim, hapless, haunting, hopeless, ill-boding, ill-fated, ill-omened, ill-starred, inauspicious, luckless, menacing, minacious, minatory, monitory, morbid, perilous, pessimistic, portending evil, portentous, precursive, precursory, premonitory, presageful, presaging, presentient, pythonic, sinister, somber, threatening, threatful, unfortunate, unlucky, unpromising, unpropitious, vatic, vaticinal

OMISSION, ***noun*** breach, carelessness, default, default in performance, delinquency, dereliction, disregard, excluding, exclusion, failure, failure to perform, inadvertence, laxity, laxness, leaving out, neglect, neglect to perform, negligence, nonfeasance, noninclusion, oversight, passing over, *praetermissio,* pretermission, remissness, slip
ASSOCIATED CONCEPTS: material omission, negligent omission, omission of duty, omission to act, willful omission
FOREIGN PHRASES: ***Omissio eorum quae tacite insunt nihil operatur.*** The omission of those things which are tacitly expressed is unimportant.

OMIT, ***verb*** abstain from inserting, bypass, cast aside, count out, cut out, delete, discard, dodge, drop, exclude, fail to do, fail to include, fail to insert, fail to mention, leave out, leave undone, let go, let pass, let slip, miss, neglect, *omittere,* pass by, pass over, *praetermittere,* skip, slight, transire
FOREIGN PHRASES: ***Casus omissus et oblivioni datus dispositioni communis juris relinquitur.*** A case omitted and forgotten is left to the disposal of the common law.

OMNIBUS, ***adjective*** all-embracing, all-inclusive, blanket, broad, catholic, collective, compendious, complete, composite, comprehensive, encyclopedic, encyclopedical, exhaustive, expansive, extensive, general, generic, generical, inclusive, inclusory, indiscriminate, limitless, miscellaneous, of great scope, overall, pandemic, sweeping, unlimited, unqualified, unrestricted, wide-reaching, widespread
ASSOCIATED CONCEPTS: omnibus law

OMNIPOTENT, ***adjective*** able, all-powerful, almighty, capable, dominant, dominating, effective, effectual, godlike, Herculean, illimitable, infinitely powerful, irresistible, mighty, *omnipotens,* overwhelming, plenipotent, plenipotentiary, possessing unlimited power, potent, powerful, predominant, prepotent, puissant, ruling, sovereign, strong, supreme, uncircumscribed, unlimited in power

OMNISCIENT, ***adjective*** all-knowing, all-seeing, allwise, apperceptive, comprehending, deific, deifical, discerning, encyclopedic, farseeing, foreseeing, godlike, infinitely wise, informed, knowing, knowledgeable, oracular, Palladian, pansophic, pansophical, perceptive, percipient, predicting, prescient, sagacious, sapient, smart, understanding, well-informed, wise

ON BEHALF OF, ***verb*** act for, act vicariously, appearing for, as agent for, be deputy for, be envoy for, be spokesman for, be the authorized agent for, be the authorized representative for, by proxy, in behalf of, representing, stand in for, substitute for
ASSOCIATED CONCEPTS: notice of appearance, representation

ON OR ABOUT, ***adverb*** approximately, in the general time frame, in the immediate vicinity of, in the neighborhood of, more or less, somewhere about

ON POINT, ***adjective*** compliant, conclusive, consummate, decisive, definite, exact, explicit, fixed, infallible, literal, narrow, particular, perceptive, positive, precise, rational, rigid, rigorous, solid, sound, specific, strict, stringent, sure, systematic, unambiguous, undeniable, unequivocal, unmitigated, well-defined
ASSOCIATED CONCEPTS: a case on point, research is on point

ON PURPOSE, ***adjective*** by design, deliberately, having a mission, having an intended result, intended, purposeful, to a particular goal, to a specific end, to gain a desired result, with a plan, with a singleness of purpose, with an intended motive, with an intended objective, with intent, with perserverance, with persistence, with specific intent, with tenacity, with the will to gain an intended result
ASSOCIATED CONCEPTS: malice, public purpose

ON THE DOCKET, ***noun*** anticipated, approaching, arranged, case which is calendared, due, expected, filed with the court, forthcoming, high on the agenda, imminent, impending, listed on the calendar, litigation docket, on the calendar, pending, planned, projected, prospective, put down on the docket, scheduled, scheduled case, set, slated, upcoming
ASSOCIATED CONCEPTS: case ready for trial

ON THE GROUNDS, ***adjective*** argued, arising from, based on, brought as a result of, brought on account of, built on, contingent upon, dependent on, established by, founded on, grounded on, justified by, rationalized by, relying on, rested on, rooted in, settled upon
ASSOCIATED CONCEPTS: charges brought on the grounds that, grounds for divorce, legal grounds, on the grounds for appeal, on the grounds of prejudice, predicted on the grounds for dismissal

ON THE LEVEL, ***adjective*** aboveboard, credible, decent, dependable, fair, honest, legitimate, on the up-and-up, open, sincere, square, straight, trustworthy, truthful, up front

ON THE OTHER HAND, ***adverb*** alternatively, by way of opposition, contrarily, contrariwise, conversely, counter, in direct contraposition, in opposition, interchangeably, inversely, just the opposite, just the other way around, just the reverse, oppositely, otherwise, quite to other contrary, rather, to the contrary, to the other extreme, vice versa

ON THE RECORD, ***noun*** capable of being released, capable of being reported, documented, for attribution, for public consumption, for the record, not discrete but open, not private, not secret, officially, out in the open, preserved for the record, put in the minutes, recorded, reported to the public

ON THE WHOLE, ***adverb*** all considering, all in all, all things considered, by and large, chiefly, essentially, everything being equal, for all intents and purposes, for all practical purposes, for the most part, generally, having said that, in the long run, in the main, mainly, mostly, nearly, on balance, on the average, overall, substantially, taking all things into consideration, taking everything into account, that being so, uncharacterized
ASSOCIATED CONCEPTS: the record taken as a whole

ONEROUS, ***adjective*** arduous, backbreaking, burdensome, crushing, cumbersome, difficult, exacting, excessive, fatiguing, formidable, *gravis,* grinding, grueling, hard, harrowing, harsh, heavy, Herculean, intolerable, laborious, oppressive, overbearing, overpowering, overtaxing, pressing, rigorous, severe, strenuous, taxing, tedious, toilsome, trying, unbearable, unwieldy, wearisome, weighty

ONE-SIDED, *adjective* biased, colored, discriminatory, exparte, *impar, inaequalis,* influenced, *iniquus,* interested, jaundiced, narrow, narrow-minded, partial, partisan, prejudiced, prepossessed, sectarian, slanted, swayed, undetached, undispassionate, uneven, unfair, unjust, warped
ASSOCIATED CONCEPTS: one-sided contract

ONGOING, *adjective* abiding, adjourned, continuous, enduring, extension, lasting, lengthening, perpetuating, persevering, persisting, postponed, prolonged, protracted, stayed, successively continued
ASSOCIATED CONCEPTS: labor law, ongoing negotiations

ONLY *(No more than),* ***adjective*** bare, mere, plain, simple

ONLY *(Sole),* ***adjective*** exclusive, first and last, individual, lone, singular, solitary, unique

ONLY *(Unrepeated),* ***adjective*** unmatched, unparalleled

ONLY, *adverb* alone, apart, at least, at the very least, exclusively, merely, plainly, purely, simply, singly, solely

ONLY, *conjunction* but, but for the fact that, excepting that, if it were not that

ONSET *(Assault),* ***noun*** advance, aggression, assailment, attack, barrage, blitzkrieg, bombardment, charge, dragonnade, encounter, foray, forced entrance, fusillade, incursion, intrusion, invasion, maraud, offense, offensive, onrush, onslaught, raid, seizure, siege, storm, strike, thrust

ONSET *(Commencement),* ***noun*** aurora, beginning, birth, coming, dawn, embarkation, entrance, establishment, exordium, fashioning, first appearance, first move, first step, forging, forming, foundation, genesis, inauguration, inception, inchoation, incipience, incunabula, infancy, initiation, introduction, launching, making, oncoming, opening, origin, origination, outbreak, outset, rise, source, start, starting point, threshold

ONUS *(Blame),* ***noun*** accusation, blameworthiness, charge, culpability, error, fault, flaw, guiltiness, misdeed, reprehension, responsibility, shortcoming, transgression

ONUS *(Burden),* ***noun*** affliction, burdensome requirement, charge, drawback, encumbrance, handicap, hindrance, impediment, inescapable duty, interference, load, obstruction, responsibility, struggle, unusual task, weary load, weight

ONUS *(Stigma),* ***noun*** badge, blemish, blot, blotch, brand, censure, condemnation, degradation, denunciation, discredit, disgrace, dishonor, dispraise, imputation, infamy, mark of Cain, reproach, scar, shame, slur, smirch, smudge, smutch, soil, spot, stain, taint, tarnish

OPACITY, *noun* asininity, blockishness, confusion, darkness, denseness, density, dimness, doltishness, dull-wittedness, dullness, fatuity, hebetude, impenetrability, imperceptibility, inapprehensibility, incomprehensibility, indiscernibility, indistinctness, indistinguishability, inscrutability, lack of understanding, lumpishness, nebulosity, oafishness, obfuscation, obscuration, obscurity, obtuseness, opaqueness, simplicity, slow-wittedness, slowness, stolidity, stolidness, stupidity, stupidness, thickheadedness, thick-wittedness, thickness, unclarity, unclearness, unfathomableness, unintelligibility, unplainness, unsearchableness, vacuity, vagueness, vapidity, want of transparency

OPAQUE, *adjective* addlebrained, addleheaded, addlepated, ambiguous, asinine, benighted, bewildering, birdbrained, blind, blockish, boeotian, brainless, cloddish, clouded, cloudy, concealed, confused, confusing, cryptic, dark, dense, difficult, difficult to comprehend, difficult to understand, dim, dimwitted, doltish, dull, dull-witted, duncelike, duncical, enigmatic, fatuitous, fatuous, featherbrained, foggy, hard to comprehend, hard to understand, hazy, ignorant, ill-defined, imbecilic, impenetrable, imperceptive, imperspicuous, impervious, incomprehensible, indistinct, inscrutable, lacking clarity, loutish, lumpish, mindless, misty, moronic, muddleheaded, muddy, nebulous, nescient, nontranslucent, oafish, obfuscated, obscure, obtuse, purblind, puzzling, recondite, senseless, shadowy, simple, simple-minded, slow in understanding, stolid, stupid, thick, thick-headed, thick-witted, turbid, unclarified, unclear, uncomprehending, unenlightened, unfathomable, unintelligent, unintelligible, unplain, unreasoning, unthinking, untransparent, vacuous, vague, witless

OPEN *(Accessible),* ***adjective*** allowable, allowed, approachable, attainable, available, defenseless, fit for travel, free of access, free to all, insecure, navigable, obtainable, *patere,* permitted, pregnable, procurable, public, reachable, securable, susceptible, unbarred, unblocked, undefended, unenclosed, unfenced, unfortified, unguarded, unlocked, unobstructed, unoccupied, unrestricted, unsealed, unshielded, vacated, vulnerable, within reach
ASSOCIATED CONCEPTS: open account, open market, open shop

OPEN *(In sight),* ***adjective*** *aspertus,* apparent, bare, beholdable, blatant, *clarus,* clear, conspicuous, discernible, discoverable, distinct, evident, exposed, exposed to view, eye-catching, glaring, in full view, manifest, *manifestus,* marked, noticeable, observable, obvious, outstanding, overt, patent, perceivable, perceptible, perspicuous, plain, prominent, pronounced, recognizable, revealed, salient, seeable, striking, transparent, unclouded, unconcealed, uncovered, undisguised, unhidden, unmistakable, unobstructed, unprotected, unsecluded, unsheltered, unshielded, visible
ASSOCIATED CONCEPTS: open and notorious possession, open court

OPEN *(Persuasible),* ***adjective*** acquiescent, amenable, *apertus, candidus,* flexible, impressible, impressionable, inducible, influenceable, malleable, movable, open-minded, persuadable, pervious, receptive, respondent, responsive, sensitive, *simplex,* suasible, suggestible, susceptible, swayable, sympathetic, tractable

OPEN *(Unclosed),* ***adjective*** *adapertus,* agape, ajar, coverless, dehiscent, gaping, lidless, *patens,* patulous, *patulus,* spacious, spread out, unclogged, uncorked, uncovered, unfastened, unfurled, unlatched, unlocked, unsealed, unshut, unstoppered, wide, yawning

OPEN AND OVERBOARD, *adjective* aboveboard, blunt, candid, clear, clear-cut, crystal clear, decent, direct, distinct, evident, explicit, express, forthright, frank, honest, ingenuous, manifest, obvious, on the up and up, open, open and genuine, open and sincere, sincere, straight, straightforward, straight-out, unequivocal, unreserved, upfront
ASSOCIATED CONCEPTS: franking privilege

OPEN TO QUESTION, *verb* allowed to ask questions, free to address issues, free to inquire, free to question, freely permitted to inquire into issues, not restrained from asking questions, permitted to ask questions

OPEN-ENDED, *adjective* boundless, ceaseless, changing, continued, continuing, expansive, going on, illimitable, illimited, indecisive, indefinite, indeterminable, inexact, infinite, interminable, limitless, loose, measureless, modifiable, not particular, not specific, ongoing, termless, unbounded, unbridled, unceasing, unconfined, unconstrained, uncontrolled, undefined, unending, unlimited, unmeasured, unrestricted, vague, variable, wide-open, without limits, without specified limits

OPENING *(Initial presentation of a case),* ***noun*** beginning of a case, commencement of a case, counsel's initial statement, counsel's introductory statement, counsel's overview of a case, inception of litigation, initiation of a legal case, introduction of a case, introductory, presentation, start of a case
ASSOCIATED CONCEPTS: litigation, opening statement

OPENING *(Opportunity),* ***noun*** availability, chance, means, moment, occasion, once-in-a-lifetime chance, place, possibility, presented with an opportunity

OPENING STATEMENT, *noun* opening argument, presentation of basics, presentation of data, presentation of essentials, presentation of the documentation, presentation of the evidence, presentation of the facts

OPEN-MINDED, *adjective* accessible, amenable, broadminded, detached, disinterested, dispassionate, equitable, evenhanded, fair, fair-minded, impartial, independent, indifferent, judicial, just, latitudinarian, liberal, neutral, objective, open, persuadable, persuasible, reasonable, receptive, responsive, tolerant, unbiased, unbigoted, uncolored, undogmatic, unimpassioned, uninfluenced, unjaundiced, unprepossessed, unswayed, unwarped

OPERATE, *verb* accomplish, achieve, act, act upon, administer, administrate, assume responsibility, attain, bring about, caretake, carry into execution, carry on, carry out, cause, command, conduct, control, deal with, direct, discharge, do, drive, effect, effectuate, enforce, engage in, engineer, execute, exercise, exercise power over, exert, fulfill, function, govern, handle, have charge of, impel, implement, lead, look after, manage, maneuver, manipulate, mastermind, militate, minister, move, officiate, oversee, perform, perpetrate, pilot, practice, preside over, prevail over, put into effect, put into practice, regulate, rule, run, steer, superintend, supervise, take care of, take charge of, work
ASSOCIATED CONCEPTS: operate to the detriment of a party

OPERATION, *noun* act, action, campaign, course of action, crusade, *effectio,* enterprise, execution, exploit, function, handling, management, move, movement, performance, practice, procedure, proceeding, process, production, pursuit, routine, step, stratagem, stroke, task, thrust, transaction, undertaking, venture

OPERATIVE, *adjective* acting, active, adequate, advantageous, ample, applicable, at work, beneficial, capable, competent, effective, effectual, *efficax,* efficient, employed, fruitful, functional, functioning, helpful, in action, in effect, in force, in harness, in operation, in play, instrumental, on duty, operational, performing, potent, productive, serviceable, successful, sufficient, usable, useful, valid, workable, working, yielding

OPEROSE, *adjective* arduous, backbreaking, bothersome, burdensome, crushing, demanding, difficult, effortful, emasculating, embittering, enervating, exacting, exhausting, fagging, fatiguing, formidable, grinding, grueling, hard, hard to cope with, Herculean, irksome, laborious, onerous, painstaking, plodding, pressing, Sisyphean, straining, strenuous, tiresome, tiring, toilsome, troublesome, trying, uphill, vexatious, weakening, wearing, wearisome, wearying

OPINE, *verb* adjudge, appraise, *arbitrari,* assume, be convinced, be persuaded, be satisfied, believe, cherish a belief, conclude, conjecture, consider, dare say, deem, determine, diagnose, esteem, estimate, express an opinion, fancy, feel, guess, have a hunch, have an idea, have an opinion, have faith, have no doubt, hold, hypothesize, imagine, infer, judge, look upon, nurture a belief, *opinari,* postulate, preconceive, prejudge, presume, presuppose, pronounce judgment, reckon, regard, rest assured, speculate, stand, suppose, surmise, suspect, theorize, think, view, ween

OPINION *(Belief),* ***noun*** assumption, attitude, conclusion, conjecture, consideration, conviction, determination, estimate, estimation, evaluation, fancy, feeling, guess, hypothesis, idea, impression, *iudicium,* judgment, notion, outlook, perspective, persuasion, point of view, position, posture, preconception, presumption, presupposition, reaction, reflection, sentiment, speculation, stance, stand, supposition, surmise, suspicion, theory, thesis, thinking, thought, view, viewpoint
FOREIGN PHRASES: ***Incivile est, nisi tota lege perspecta, una aliqua particula ejus proposita, judicare, vel respondere.*** Unless the entire law has been examined, it is improper to pass judgment upon a portion of it. ***Incivile est, nisi tota sententia inspecta, de aliqua parte judicare.*** It is improper to pass an opinion on any part without examining the entire sentence. ***Nullius hominis auctoritas apud nos valere debet, ut meliora non sequeremur si quis attulerit.*** No man's influence ought to prevail upon us, that we should not follow better opinions, should any one present them. ***Opinio est duplex, scilicet, opinio vulgaris, orta inter graves et discretos, et quae vultum veritatis habet et opinio tantum orta inter leves et vulgares homines absque specie veritatis.*** Opinion is of two fold, namely, common opinion, which springs up among grave and discreet persons and which has the appearance of truth, and opinion which arises among foolish and ordinary men. ***Opinio quae favet testamento est tenenda.*** An opinion which favors a will is to be followed.

OPINION *(Judicial decision),* ***noun*** adjudication, ascertainment, assessment, authoritative statement, conclusion, conclusion of the matter, consideration, decision, declaration, decree, decreement, determination, final judgment, finding, formal statement, judgment, judgment on facts, order, position, pronouncement, report, resolution, rule, ruling, sentence, *sententia,* settlement by authoritative decision, solution
ASSOCIATED CONCEPTS: advisory opinion, concurring opinion, dissenting opinion, expert opinion, judicial opinion, legal opinion, majority opinion, memorandum opinion, minority opinion, opinion evidence, opinion of the court, per curiam opinion, professional opinion, written opinion
FOREIGN PHRASES: ***Ubi non est directa lex, standum est arbitrio judicis, vel procedendum ad similia.*** Where there

is no direct law, the decision of the judge is to be taken, or references to be made to similar cases. ***Judices non tenentur exprimere causam sententiae suae.*** Judges are not bound to explain the reason for their sentences.

OPPONENT, ***noun*** *adversarius,* adversary, adverse party, challenger, combatant, contender, corrival, disputant, one who opposes, opposer, opposing litigant, opposing party, opposite, opposite side, opposition, other side

OPPORTUNE, ***adjective*** advantageous, appropriate, apt, auspicious, befitting, *commodus,* convenient, due, expedient, fit, fitting, *idoneus, opportunus,* propitious, providential, seasonable, suitable, suited, timely, well-timed

OPPORTUNITY, ***noun*** auspiciousness, chance, convenience, *copia,* fair chance, favorable chance, favorable time, fit time, fitting occasion, fitting time, fortuity, good chance, good fortune, hap, liberty, luck, *occasio,* occasion, opening, opportune moment, opportune time, possibility, *potestas,* proper occasion, proper time, propitiousness, prospect, readiness, reasonable chance, right time, ripeness, scope, suitable circumstance, suitable occasion, suitable time, time, turn
ASSOCIATED CONCEPTS: earliest practicable opportunity, opportunity to appear, opportunity to be heard

OPPOSE, ***verb*** act in opposition to, argue against, balk, battle, be at cross purposes, be contrary to, block, buck, challenge, collide, combat, come in conflict with, confront, confute, contend, contest, contradict, contravene, controvert, counter, counteract, counterattack, counterbalance, countermine, counterpoise, countervail, counterweigh, counterwork, debate, defy, demur, deny, disaffirm, disagree, disapprove, dispute, encounter, fight, go against, go contrary to, join issue, negate, not submit, not yield, object, obstruct, offer resistance, oppugn, prevent, prohibit, protest, put in opposition, rebut, recalcitrate, refute, reject, remonstrate, repel, repugn, repulse, resist, set against, stand firm against, strive, strive against, take a stand against, take exception to, take issue with, tourney
ASSOCIATED CONCEPTS: oppose a motion, opposing counsel, opposing interest, opposing parties
FOREIGN PHRASES: ***Error qui non resistitur approbatur.*** An error which is not resisted or opposed is waived.

OPPOSED TO, ***verb*** act in opposition to, argue against, balk, battle, be at cross purposes, be contrary to, block, challenge, collide, combat, come in conflict with, confront, confute, contend, contest, contradict, contravene, controvert, counter, counteract, counterattack, counterbalance, countermine, counterpoise, countervail, counterweigh, counterwork, debate, defend, defy, deny, disaffirm, disagree, disapprove, dispute, fight, go against, go contrary to, go up against, negate, not yield, object, obstruct, offer resistance, oppugn, prevent, prohibit, protest, put in opposition, rebut, refute, reject, remonstrate, repel, repulse, resist, stand firm against, take a stand against, take exception to, take issue with
ASSOCIATED CONCEPTS: picketing

OPPOSING, ***adjective*** adverse, against the grain, antagonistic, anti, antithetical, autonomous, averse, conflicting, confrontational, contending, contradictory, contrary, contrasting, controverting, counterbalancing, defensive, differing, disputing, dissentient, enemy, incendiary, objecting, on the other side, opposite, polar contrast, rival
ASSOCIATED CONCEPTS: opposing counsel

OPPOSING COUNSEL, ***noun*** competitor's counsel, defendant's or plaintiff's counsel, disputant's attorney, opponent' attorney, opposing litigant's attorney, opposite counsel, the adversary's counsel, the appellant's or appellee's counsel, the opponent's lawyer, the other party's lawyer, the other side's counsel, the petitioner's or respondent's attorney

OPPOSING PARTY, ***noun*** adversary, appellant, appellee, challenger, claimant, complainant, contender, defendant, disputant, petitioner, plaintiff, respondent, the other party, the other side
ASSOCIATED CONCEPTS: adversarial system, litigation

OPPOSITE, ***adjective*** absonant, *adversarius,* adverse, antagonistic, antipodal, antipodean, antithetic, antithetical, clashing, conflicting, contradictive, contradictory, *contrarius,* contrary, contrasted, contrasting, converse, counter, diametrically opposed, disagreeing, discordant, facing, hostile, incompatible, inconsistent, inharmonious, inimical, inverse, inverted, mismated, mutually opposed, negative, opposed, opposing, oppugnant, perverse, resisting, resistive, reverse, reversed, wayward

OPPOSITION, ***noun*** antinomy, challenge, conflict, confutation, contention, contrariety, contrary action, contravention, counteraction, counterattack, counterplot, counterworking, denial, disagreement, disapprobation, disapproval, dissension, enmity, impugnation, impugnment, interference, objection, oppugnancy, oppugnation, protest, protestation, recalcitration, refutation, remonstrance, remonstration, resistance, running counter to, struggle, traversal, want of harmony

OPPRESS, ***verb*** abuse, afflict, aggrieve, annoy, berate, burden, crush, dishearten, dispirit, distress, encumber, handicap, harass, maltreat, overpower, overthrow, overwhelm, persecute, plague, pray, press, pressure, prey on, smother, strain, subdue, subjugate, suppress, tax, torment, trample, trouble, tyrannize, vex, weigh heavy upon, worry, wrong

OPPRESSION, ***noun*** abuse, abusiveness, brutality, brute force, coercion, compulsion, cruelty, despotism, dictatorship, domination, enslavement, force, harassment, harshness, ill treatment, inhumanity, *iniuria,* injustice, iron rule, liberticide, maltreatment, misrule, mistreatment, misuse of power, persecution, reign of terror, repression, rule of might, ruthlessness, severity, subjection, subjugation, suppression, torment, totalitarianism, tyranny, *vexatio,* victimization

OPPRESSIVE, ***adjective*** afflictive, arduous, burdensome, confining, cruel, crushing, cumbersome, cumbrous, depressing, detrimental, devouring, difficult, difficult to bear, distressing, engulfing, exacting, exhausting, fatiguing, formidable, galling, grievous, grinding, hard, harmful, harsh, heavy, hurtful, imperious, inhuman, *iniquus,* intolerable, irksome, laborious, *molestus,* onerous, operose, overbearing, overpowering, overwhelming, painful, pernicious, ponderous, rigorous, severe, stifling, strenuous, suffocating, taxing, tiring, toilsome, troublesome, trying, tyrannical, unbearable, uncomfortable, unendurable, unreasonable, unyielding, upsetting, vexatious, wearing, wearisome, weighty

OPPROBRIUM, ***noun*** abasement, attaint, bad light, bad name, blot, brand, contempt, culpability, debasement, *dedecus,* defamation, degradation, derogation, disapprobation, discredit, disesteem, disgrace, dishonor, disrepute, disrespect, humiliation, ignobility, ignominiousness, ignominy, ill fame, ill repute, imputation, indignity, infamousness, infamy, ingloriousness, loss of honor, loss of reputation, loss of standing, notoriety, obloquy, odium, reproach, scandal, shady reputation, shame, slur, smirch, stain, stigma, taint, tarnish, vilification

OPPUGN, ***verb*** aggress, assault, attack, be contrary, buck, call in question, challenge, clash, combat, conflict, confront, contend, contradict, contravene, controvert, counter, countervail, counterwork, criticize adversely, cross, deal a blow, defy, denounce, descend upon, disagree, dispute, dissent, fall upon, fight, foil, gainsay, go against, hinder, hold out against, interfere with, militate against, object, obstruct, oppose, outface, pounce upon, protest, reason against, recalcitrate, refute, reluct, reluctate, remonstrate, resist, run against, run counter to, set upon, side against, stand against, stand up to, strike at, strive against, take exception, take the offensive, thrust at, thwart, traverse, wrangle

OPT FOR, ***verb*** ascertain, choose, decide on, determine, elect, favor, lean toward, make a choice, pick, prefer, select, take

OPTION *(Choice),* ***noun*** alternate choice, alternative, choice, discretion, election, free decision, free selection, free will, freedom, freedom of choice, leave, liberty, opportunity, pick, power to choose, preference, right of choice, selection
ASSOCIATED CONCEPTS: election between options, exercise of option, options after default

OPTION *(Contractual provision),* ***noun*** acquired right, agreement, allowance, approval, authorization, consent, continuing offer, continuing offer to buy, favor, grant, guaranty, license, power, prerogative, privilege, proviso, right, right to buy or sell, sanction, stipulation, term, understanding
ASSOCIATED CONCEPTS: conditional option, continuing option, exercise of an option, first option, irrevocable option, option to buy, option to lease, option to purchase, option to renew, option to sell

OPTIONALLY, ***adverb*** alternatively, at the option of, discretionally, electively, preferably, selectively

OPULENT, ***adjective*** abounding in riches, affluent, comfortable, flourishing, flush, moneyed, opulentus, pecunious, propertied, prosperous, rich, richly endowed, rolling in riches, substantial, well-fixed, well-off, well provided for, well-situated, well-to-do, with means, worth a great deal

ORACULAR, ***adjective*** cryptic, divinatory, enigmatic, fatidic, fatidical, foreknowing, foretelling, knowing, mysterious, mystical, obscure, ominous, portentous, precursive, precursory, predicting, predictive, presaging, prognostic, prophetic, sage, sapient, sibylline, vatic, vaticinal, wise

ORAL, ***adjective*** announced, articulated, audible, by word of mouth, communicated, enunciated, expressed, expressed in words, phonic, said, said aloud, sounded, spoken, spoken aloud, told, unwritten, uttered, verbal, vocal, vocalized, voiced
ASSOCIATED CONCEPTS: nuncupative will, oral contract, oral testimony, statute of frauds

ORAL COMMUNICATION, ***noun*** dissemination, divulgement, information, message, news, notification, proclamation, report, revelation, utterance, verbal announcement, verbal annunciation, verbal declaration, verbal disclosure, writing
ASSOCIATED CONCEPTS: defamation, public official, right to privacy, slander

ORAL EVIDENCE, ***noun*** corroboration, document, documentary evidence, documentation, species of proof, substantiation, validation, verbal confirmation, verbal explanation of facts admitted at trial, verbal proof, verbal proof of facts, verbal proof presented at trial, verbal testimony, verbal testimony which is part of the record, verification
ASSOCIATED CONCEPTS: independent experts, transcripts, wiretaps

ORCHESTRATE, ***verb*** adapt, adjust, allot the parts, arrange, assemble, assign the parts, bring into order, bring together, compose, concert, conduct, construct, coordinate, harmonize, lay out, methodize, order, organize, preconcert, predetermine, put in order, put into a systematic form, reduce to order, regiment, regulate, set in order, set to music, standardize, symphonize, systematize

ORDEAL, ***noun*** affliction, agony, anguish, annoyance, burden, calamity, cross, difficulty, dilemma, distress, hurdle to surmount, nightmare, obstacle to overcome, pain, plague, scourge, suffering, test, torment, torture, trial, tribulation, trouble, wall

ORDER *(Arrangement),* ***noun*** adjustment, allocation, allotment, apportionment, array, catalog, categorization, chronology, classification, composition, design, disposal, distribution, form, formation, gradation, grouping, layout, lineup, methodology, *ordo,* organization, pattern, placement, plan, procession, progression, rotation, sequence, setup, stratification, structure, system, systematization
ASSOCIATED CONCEPTS: order of creditors, order of priorities, order of proof

ORDER *(Judicial directive),* ***noun*** authoritative command, behest, command, commandment, court commandment, court instruction, declaration, decree, dictate, direction, directive, edict, *edictum,* fiat, imperative, instruction, *iussum,* judicial command, judicial instruction, mandate, *mandatum,* precept, prescript, prescription, proclamation, pronouncement, rescript, rule, ruling, ukase
ASSOCIATED CONCEPTS: appealable order, charging order, confinement order, decision, decretal order, entry of order, final order, interlocutory order, motion, nonappealable order, nunc pro tunc order, order granting a new trial, order of dismissal, order of the court, order staying execution, order to show cause, preliminary order, restraining order, self-executing order, settle order, suspension order

ORDER, ***verb*** adjure, call forth, call upon, cite, command, compel, decree, demand, dictate, direct, *edicere, imperare,* impose, impose a duty, impose a task, insist on, instruct, issue a decree, issue one's fiat, *iubere,* make a requisition, make demands on, oblige, ordain, prescribe, proscribe, require, rule, serve, tell, warrant
ASSOCIATED CONCEPTS: administrative order, amended order, appealable order, charging order, confinement order, contempt order, entry of judgment and order of the court, ex parte order, final order, interlocutory order, nunc pro tunc order, order granting a new trial, order of discontinuance, order of probate, order of proof, order of the court, order to show cause, restraining order, reviewable order, special order, stay order, suspension order, vacation of an order

FOREIGN PHRASES: ***Quando aliquid mandatur, mandatur et omne per quod pervenitur ad illud.*** When something is commanded, everything by which it can be accomplished is also ordered.

ORDER OF THE COURT, *noun* authoritative pronouncement, authoritative ruling, binding order, command, court command, declaration by the court, edict, fiat, imperative, judicial command, judicial decree, judicial dictate, judicial direction, judicial directive, judicial mandate, pronouncement
ASSOCIATED CONCEPTS: entered order

ORDINANCE, *noun* authoritative rule, canon, charter, code, command, decree, decretum, direction, edict, *edictum,* enactment, fiat, imperative, law, legal command, legislation, legislative decree, legislative edict, local law, local legislation, local rule, mandate, maxim, municipal code, municipal regulation, ordainment, order, ordination, prescript, proclamation, regulation, requirement, rule, statute
ASSOCIATED CONCEPTS: city ordinance, criminal ordinance, local ordinance, municipal ordinance, regulatory ordinance, traffic ordinance, violation of an ordinance, zoning ordinance

ORDINARY, *adjective* accepted, accustomary, accustomed, average, banal, boring, bourgeois, bromidic, characteristic, colloquial, commonplace, *communis,* consuetudinary, conventional, customary, daily, drab, established, expected, familiar, fixed, frequent, general, generally practiced, habitual, hackneyed, homely, homespun, household, humdrum, insipid, known, mediocre, middling, normal, oft-repeated, pedestrian, philistine, platitudinous, plebeian, plentiful, popular, prevailing, prevalent, prosaic, prosaical, *quotidianus,* recognized, regular, regulation, repeated, representative, rife, simple, stale, standard, stereotyped, stock, taken for granted, traditional, *translaticius,* trite, typical, unassuming, undistinguished, unexceptional, unexciting, unimaginative, unoriginal, unvaried, usual, vernacular, wearisome, well-trodden, well-worn, widespread, wonted, workaday
ASSOCIATED CONCEPTS: necessary expenses, ordinary care and skill, ordinary course of business, ordinary course of trade, ordinary duty, ordinary expenses, ordinary income, ordinary loss, ordinary meaning, ordinary negligence, ordinary prudent person, ordinary reasonable man, ordinary risk, ordinary standard of care, ordinary use, ordinary wear and tear
FOREIGN PHRASES: ***Recurrendum est ad extraordinarium quando non valet ordinarium.*** Resort must be made to the extraordinary when the ordinary does not succeed.

ORDINARY WEAR AND TEAR, *noun* diminution, disrepair, normal damage, normal decline in value, normal deterioration, normal detriment, normal harm, normal impairment, normal loss
ASSOCIATED CONCEPTS: depreciation, residual value insurance

ORGAN, *noun* affiliate, agency, annex, appendage, arm, associate, branch, branch office, bureau, chapter, component, department, division, extension, instrument, instrumentality, local, lodge, means, member, newspaper, office, offshoot, part, periodical, post, ramification, section, subdivision, subsidiary, unit, wing

ORGANIC, *adjective* anatomical, basal, basic, constitutional, deep-rooted, derived from within, elemental, fundamental, implanted, inborn, inbred, indigenous, ingrained, inherent, innate, instinctive, intrinsic, intrinsical, native, natural, original, primary, primitive, rooted, rudimentary, structural, substantial, substantive, underlying

ORGANIZATION *(Association),* ***noun*** affiliation, aggregation, alliance, bloc, club, coalition, combination, community, company, corps, coterie, establishment, faction, federation, foundation, group, institute, institution, joint concern, league, *reipublicae forma,* school, sodality, syndicate, troupe
ASSOCIATED CONCEPTS: charitable organization, de facto organization, domestic organization, labor organization, nonprofit organization, political organization

ORGANIZATION *(Structure),* ***noun*** arrangement, build, classification, composition, configuration, conformation, constitution, construction, *descriptio,* design, figuration, figure, form, formation, framework, grouping, interrelation of parts, makeup, manner of construction, order, placement, plan, regularity, scheme, shape, style of arrangement, systematization, temperatio

ORGANIZE *(Arrange),* ***verb*** adjust, align, assort, catalog, categorize, class, classify, combine, *componere,* correlate, establish guide lines, establish parameters, file, form into classes, get in formation, grade, group, introduce a system, introduce order, lay down guide lines, list, marshal, methodize, order, *ordinare,* place, place in order, put in array, put in order, put into shape, rank, rate, reduce to order, regiment, regulate, separate into categories, set guidelines, set in array, set in order, sort, standardize, straighten, systematize
ASSOCIATED CONCEPTS: organize a corporation, organized labor

ORGANIZE *(Unionize),* ***verb*** affiliate, amalgamate, associate, band together, cement a union, centralize, collaborate, combine, confederate, consolidate, create, enlist employees in a labor union, enlist in a labor union, enter into a league, establish, federate, form, form a labor union, form into a body, formulate, incorporate, institute, join, join together, merge, mold, set up, unify, unite, unite for a common purpose
ASSOCIATED CONCEPTS: organized labor

ORGANIZED LABOR UNION, *noun* brotherhood, craft union, guild, industrial union, industry, labor association, labor organization, labor union, trade, trade union, trades union
ASSOCIATED CONCEPTS: employment law

ORGULOUS, *adjective* affected, aloof, arrogant, assuming, blustering, boastful, boasting, bragging, conceited, condescending, contemptuous, disdainful, egocentric, egoistic, egoistical, egotistic, egotistical, fanfaronading, flaunting, gasconading, grand, grandiose, haughty, immodest, imperious, inflated, insolent, intolerant, lofty, lordly, narcissistic, overbearing, overproud, overweening, patronizing, pompous, presumptuous, prideful, scornful, self-applauding, self-centred, self-flattering, self-glorifying, self-important, self-lauding, self-magnifying, self-praising, self-satisfied, supercilious, thrasonical, vain, vainglorious, vaunting

ORIGIN *(Ancestry),* ***noun*** ancestral descent, birth, bloodline, derivation, descent, dynasty, extraction, family, filiation, genealogical tree, genealogy, heritage, kith and kin, line, line of ancestors, line of descent, lineage, *origo,* parentage, parenthood, pedigree, race, stock, tribe
FOREIGN PHRASES: ***Origine propria neminem posse voluntate sua eximi manifestum est.*** It is evident that no one by his own will can renounce his own origin.

ORIGIN *(Source),* ***noun*** beginning, birth, birthplace, cause, commencement, cradle, creation, dawn, derivation, *fons,* font, foundation, fountainhead, genesis, inception, initiation, nascency, nativity, onset, *origo, principium,* root, starting point, wellspring
FOREIGN PHRASES: ***Ex facto jus oritur.*** Law arises out of facts. ***Causa et origo est materia negotii.*** The cause and origin are the substance of the transaction.

ORIGINAL *(Creative),* ***adjective*** artful, clever, daring, demiurgic, demiurgical, different, eccentric, envisioning, exceptional, fanciful, fecund, fertile, fictive, fresh, gifted, imaginal, imaginative, individual, ingenious, inimitable, inspired, inventive, nonconformist, novel, odd, originative, out of the ordinary, poetic, productive, rare, resourceful, singular, unborrowed, uncommon, unconformable, unconventional, uncopied, uncustomary, underived, unexampled, unexpected, unfashionable, unheard of, unimitated, unique, unmatched, unordinary, unorthodox, unparalleled, unusual, unwonted, visioned, visualizing, whimsical

ORIGINAL *(Initial),* ***adjective*** antecedent, authentic, basal, basic, basilar, beginning, commencing, earliest, elemental, elementary, embryonic, first, formative, foundational, fundamental, germinal, inaugural, inauguratory, inchoate, inchoative, incipient, incunabular, infant, initial, initiative, initiatory, introductory, maiden, nascent, natal, native, nonimitative, opening, precursory, preliminary, prelusive, prelusory, primal, primary, prime, primeval, primigenial, primitive, primordial, pristine, proemial, pure, rudimental, rudimentary, seminal, starting, underlying
ASSOCIATED CONCEPTS: best evidence rule, original action, original decree, original evidence, original holder, original issue, original jurisdiction, original stock, original undertaking, original writing

ORIGINALITY, *noun* boldness, brilliance, cleverness, creativity, daring, entry, freshness, imagination, ingeniousness, ingenuity, innovation, interpretation, invention, modernity, novelty, resourcefulness, spirit, unorthodoxy

ORIGINATE, *verb* activate, arouse, author, awaken, beget, begin, break ground, breed, bring about, bring into existence, bring on, bring to pass, cause, coin, commence, compose, conceive, concoct, contrive, create, devise, draft, effect, elicit, engender, engineer, establish, evoke, fabricate, father, forge, form, formulate, found, frame, generate, get going, get up, give birth to, give impulse to, give origin to, give rise to, handsel, improvise, inaugurate, induce, initiate, inspire, institute, introduce, invent, kindle, launch, lay the foundation for, lead, make, make up, manufacture, motivate, mount, open, pioneer, plan, precipitate, prepare, produce, promote, prompt, propagate, provoke, raise, set afloat, set going, set in motion, set up, sire, start, stimulate, take the first step, take the initiative, take the lead, think up, trigger, undertake, usher in

ORIGINATION, *noun* ancestry, beginning, birth, causation, cause, coinage, commencement, composition, cradle, creation, dawn, derivation, discovery, emergence, etymology, exordium, fabrication, fomentation, font, foundation, fountain, fountainhead, genesis, inauguration, inception, inchoation, incipience, incipiency, incunabula, infancy, initiation, instigation, introduction, invention, motivation, motive, nascency, nativity, onset, opening, outset, parentage, production, provenance, provenience, rise, root, source, spring, start, starting point, stimulation, stimulus, wellspring

ORIGINATOR, *noun* author, beginner, commencer, composer, conceiver, concocter, contriver, creator, deviser, engineer, establisher, father, formulator, founder, framer, generator, improviser, inaugurator, inducer, initiator, inspirer, introducer, inventor, leader, maker, manufacturer, motivator, pioneer, precipitator, preparer, producer, propagator, provoker, starter, stimulator, the first one to bring into existence, the one who broke ground, undertaker
ASSOCIATED CONCEPTS: origination on loan

OROTUND, *adjective* affected, artificial, blustering, bombastic, clear, declamatory, elocutionary, flatulent, forceful, full, fustian, grandiloquent, grandiose, high-flown, histrionic, inflated, magniloquent, mellow, oratorical, pompous, presumptuous, pretentious, resonant, rhetorical, showy, sonorous, stilted, strong, stuffy, swelling, swollen, theatrical, tumid, turgescent, turgid, vainglorious, windy

ORPHAN, *noun* abandoned child, abandoned infant, bereaved child, castaway, child without parents, foundling, homeless child, *orbus,* orphaned child, orphaned infant, parentless child, twice-bereaved child, waif, ward

ORTHODOX, *adjective* accepting, according to custom, according to regulation, according to rule, according to the book, accustomed, acknowledged, approved, believing, bound by convention, canonical, common, commonplace, compliant, conformable, conforming, conservative, conventional, correct, customary, devoted to convention, doctrinal, established, formal, habitual, inflexible, literal, ordinary, *orthodoxus,* prescriptive, prevailing, proper, recognized, rigid, scrupulous, strict, traditional, typical, unbending, unchangeable, uncompromising, unheterodox, usual, wonted

OSCILLATE, *verb* *agitari,* agitate, alternate, be doubtful, be indecisive, be irresolute, be uncertain, be undecided, be undetermined, be unresolved, be unsteady, be unsure, beat, bounce, debate, deliberate, falter, flap, fluctuate, flutter, fret, hesitate, librate, lurch, move in waves, move to and fro, pendulate, rock, rotate, seesaw, shift, sway, swerve, swing, turn, undulate, vacillate, vary, waver

OSMOSIS, *noun* absorption, assimilation, diffusion, digestion, engulfment, infiltration, ingress, interpenetration, introgression, passage, penetration, permeation, saturation, seepage, transmission

OSSIFIED, *adjective* bony, calcified, calloused, congealed, crystallized, dense, firm, fossilized, hard, hardened, incrassate, incrassated, indurated, lapidified, petrified, solid, solidified, stiff, stiffened, stony, thick, thickened, tough, toughened, turned to bone

OSTENSIBLE, *adjective* able to be seen, apparent, appearing, assumable, assumed, avowed, believable, claimed, clear, colorable, conjecturable, credible, deceiving, deceptive, declared, deluding, delusional, delusive, delusory, discernible, evident, explicit, express, *fictus,* illusional, illusionary, illusive, illusory, indubitable, likely, manifest, misleading, noticeable, observable, obvious, outward, overt, patent, perceivable, perceptible, perspicuous, plain, plausible, presumable, pretended, professed, purported, reasonable, seeable, seeming, self-evident, shown, *simulatus,* so-called, specious, supposable, supposed, surface, surmisable, visible

OSTENTATIOUS, *adjective* conspicuous, elaborate, exhibitionistic, extravagant, flagrant, flashy, garish, gaudy, grandiose, loud, obtrusive, offensive, peacocky, pompous, pretentious, showy, spectacular, theatrical, vain

OSTRACISM, ***noun*** avoidance, ban, banishment, blackball, blacklist, blame, blockade, censure, condemnation, coventry, criticism, decrial, deportation, disbarment, dislodgment, dismissal, displacement, dissociability, distance, ejection, elimination, eviction, exclusion, excommunication, exile, exilement, expatriation, expulsion, extrusion, hostility, inhospitality, intolerance, isolation, lockout, nonadmission, noninclusion, obloquy, omission, preclusion, prejudice, prohibition, proscription, quarantine, refusal, rejection, reprobation, reproof, segregation, separation, shame, snub, stricture, suspension, unfriendliness, unsociableness

OTHERWISE, ***adverb*** apart from this, besides, by way of opposition, contrarily, contrariwise, conversely, counter, excepting that, excluding that, in a different circumstance, in a different manner, in a different way, in opposition, in other respects, in other ways, on the other hand, oppositely, quite to the contrary, rather, regardless, the other way around, to just the opposite, to just the reverse, to the contrary, with this as an exception
ASSOCIATED CONCEPTS: otherwise law abiding

OTIOSE, ***adjective*** abortive, apathetic, arid, barren, bootless, dallying, dilatory, disengaged, dispensable, disused, dormant, dried up, effete, exhausted, expendable, faineant, fallow, feckless, fruitless, futile, idle, impotent, impracticable, impractical, inactive, indolent, ineffective, ineffectual, inefficacious, inefficient, inert, infertile, inoperative, invalid, issueless, jejune, jobless, lackadaisical, laggard, lagging, lame, languorous, lazy, leaden, lethargic, lethargical, lifeless, listless, lymphatic, motionless, neglectful, nonfunctional, nonfunctioning, nonparticipating, nugatory, null and void, oscitant, passive, phlegmatic, powerless, resultless, slack, slothful, slow, sluggish, spiritless, stagnating, sterile, supine, torpescent, torpid, unable, unadaptable, unavailing, uncalled-for, unemployed, unfertile, unfruitful, unnecessary, unneeded, unoccupied, unpersevering, unproductive, unprofitable, unprolific, unserviceable, unsubstantial, unsuccessful, unusable, unwanted, unworkable, useless, vain, valueless, wasted, weary, worthless

OUST, ***verb*** banish, cast out, chase out, depose, deprive of office, dislodge, dismiss, displace, dispossess, divest of office, drive out, eject, expel, force out, purge, put out, remove, remove from office, repudiate, throw out, thrust out, turn out, unseat
ASSOCIATED CONCEPTS: impeachment, removal from public office

OUSTER, ***noun*** deprivation, dislodgment, dispossession, ejection, elimination, eviction, exclusion, permanent exclusion, removal, repudiation

OUT-OF-BOUNDS, ***adjective*** banned, barred, disallowed, forbidden, illegal, impermissible, improper, nonpermissible, not acceptable, not allowed, not appropriate, not proper, off limits, prohibited, ruled out, unauthorized, unlawful, unlicensed, unsanctioned

OUT-OF-ORDER, ***adjective*** discordant, egregious, improper, indecent, indecorous, inharmonious, objectionable, out of place, outrageous, prohibited, shocking, unallowable, unauthorized, unbecoming, unbefitting, uncharacteristic, undesirable, unreasonable, unrefined, unruly, unseemly, unsound, wrong

OUT OF POCKET, ***adverb*** compensation, costs, damages, expenses, just compensation, payment, recovery, remuneration, reparation for loss, repayment, restitution, restoration, retrieval, satisfaction
ASSOCIATED CONCEPTS: pocket expenses

OUT-OF-POCKET EXPENSES, ***noun*** administrative reimbursable expenses, defrayal, defrayment, disbursement, entertainment expenses, expenses, individual expenses, itemized expenses, payments, recompense, recoupment, reimbursables, remittance, remuneration, repayment, travel expenses
ASSOCIATED CONCEPTS: out-of-pocket rule

OUT OF THE ORDINARY, ***adjective*** aberrant, aberrated, abnormal, anomalous, atypical, especial, exceeding, extraordinaire, extraordinary, irregular, odd, peculiar, rare, singular, uncommon, uncustomary, unique, unusual, unwonted

OUT OF THE QUESTION, ***adjective*** doubtable, hopeless, implausible, impossible, impractical, inconceivable, infeasible, insoluble, insolvable, insuperable, insurmountable, ridiculous, unattainable, unbelievable, undoable, unimaginable, unrealizable, unsolvable

OUTBALANCE, ***verb*** be greater in value, be greater in weight, be superior, better, compensate, counteract, counterbalance, counterpoise, countervail, counterweigh, cover, dominate, eclipse, equalize, equiponderate, exceed, gain the ascendancy, get ahead of, have the advantage, have the edge on, hedge, indemnify, make compensation, make leeway, make up for, neutralize, offset, outdo, outpoint, outrival, outstrip, outvie, outweigh, overbalance, overcome, overmatch, overtop, overweigh, pass, predominate, preponderate, prevail, recoup, redeem, rise above, rival, set off, surpass, top, transcend, trump

OUTBREAK, ***noun*** affray, aggression, agitation, assault, attack, bloodshed, blow up, brawl, breach, breach of the peace, burst, cataclysm, commotion, conflict, convulsion, declaration of war, disruption, disturbance, ebullition, eruption, explosion, ferocity, fit, flare-up, foment, fomentation, fracas, fray, fury, insurgence, insurrection, invasion, irruption, mayhem, mutinousness, mutiny, onslaught, outburst, overthrow of authority, paroxysm, proruption, quarrel, rage, raid, rebellion, revolt, revolution, riot, rising, rush, siege, spasm, strife, throe, thunder, torrent, unruliness, uprising, uproar, violent behavior, warfare

OUTBURST, ***noun*** affray, agitation, attack, blast, blaze, blowout, blowup, bluster, breach of the peace, burst, clamor, commotion, convulsion, detonation, discharge, disgorgement, disquiet, disquietude, disruption, disturbance, ebullition, ejaculation, emission, eruption, explosion, expulsion, fit, flare up, flurry, foment, fomentation, fray, frenzy, furor, fury, fuss, gush, hysteria, hysterical state, hysterics, impetuosity, insurgence, insurrection, irascibility, irascibleness, irruption, jet, mayhem, outbreak, outpour, paroxysm, proruption, rage, rampage, rebellion, restlessness, revolt, revolution, rising, rush, sally, spasm, spurt, stir, strife, sudden excursion, tempest, throe, thunder, torrent, unruliness, upheaval, uproar, vehemence, violence, volcano

OUTCOME, ***noun*** achievement, aftereffect, aftermath, answer, attainment, close, completion, consequence, consummation, creation, culmination, decision, denouement, development, effect, end, end product, ending, eventuality, eventuation, finding, finish, fruit, fruition, fulfillment,

issue, judgment, offspring, outgrowth, product, production, realization, resolution, result, resultant, sequence, sequent, settlement, solution, upshot, yield
ASSOCIATED CONCEPTS: outcome-determinative test

OUTCRY, *noun* accusation, blame, brawl, broken silence, bruit, burst of sound, castigation, censure, charge, chiding, chorus, clamor, clamorousness, complaint, condemnation, *convicium,* criticism, cry, denunciation, diatribe, din, disapprobation, disapproval, discontent, dislike, dissatisfaction, dissent, disturbance, execration, explosion, fracas, furor, grievance, howl, hullabaloo, invective, lament, loud noise, loud protest, noise, objection, opposition, pandemonium, philippic, plaint, protest, protestation, racket, raised voice, rebuke, reprimand, reproach, reprobation, revilement, scolding, scream, shout, stricture, tumult, turmoil, upbraiding, uproar, vilification, vituperation, *voces, vociferatio,* vociferation, wail, weeping, yell

OUTDATED, *adjective* anachronistic, anachronous, ancient, antediluvian, antiquated, antique, archaic, behind the age, behind the times, bygone, dated, defunct, demode, discarded, disused, expired, extinct, fallen into desuetude, fallen into disuse, forgotten, former, gone by, gone out, grown old, no longer customary, no longer fashionable, no longer in style, no longer prevailing, no longer prevalent, no longer stylish, not current, not in vogue, not modern, obsolescent, obsolete, of a previous fashion, of a previous style, of great age, of old, of the old order, of the old school, old, old-fashioned, old-time, old-world, olden, out-of-date, out-of-fashion, out-of-use, outmoded, outworn, passe, past, primitive, quaint, rejected, stale, styleless, superannuated, superseded, unaccepted, uncontemporary, uncurrent, unfashionable, unpracticed, unstylish

OUTED, *verb* betrayed, confidentiality announced, confidentiality revealed, cover blown off, identity declared, identity disclosed, identity divulged, identity exposed, identity revealed, inform on the identity, leak the identity, make known, make public, promulgation, publication, release confidential information, reveal confidential information, secret identity brought out into the open, secret identity brought to light, tell everything, tell the identity, unburden the identity of, uncover, unmask, unveil

OUTFLOW, *noun* abatement, current, defluxion, discharge, disemboguement, drain, drainage, ebb, effluence, efflux, effusion, egression, emanation, emergence, emersion, emigration, eruption, escape, evacuation, exodus, expenditure, expense, export, exportation, expulsion, extravasation, extrusion, exudation, flood, flux, gush, issue, jet, leakage, movement, ooze, outburst, outgush, outpour, outstream, outward flow, outward sweep, overflow, recession, refluence, reflux, runoff, seep, shipments, spill, spout, spurt, stream, tide, transudation, wane, withdrawal

OUTGROWTH, *noun* aftereffect, aftermath, development, effect, end result, eventuality, eventuation, excrescence, fruit, issue, offshoot, offspring, repercussion, result, resultance, resultant, sequel, sprout, yield

OUTLAW, *noun* bandit, brigand, convict, criminal, delinquent, evildoer, felon, fugitive, fugitive from the law, habitual criminal, habitual offender, hardened criminal, lawbreaker, lawless individual, malefactor, miscreant, notorious criminal, offender, offender against society, *proscriptus,* public enemy, racketeer, recidivist, robber, swindler, thief, transgressor, underworld character, violator of the law

OUTLAW, *verb* *aqua et igni interdicere,* banish, bar, declare illegal, declare unlawful, exclude, expel, forbid by law, make unlawful, place outside the protection of the law, proscribe, *proscribere,* put beyond the protection of the law, reject, repel

OUTLAY, *noun* amount expended, budgeted items, charge, cost, disbursement, expenditure, expense, *impensa,* outgo, payment, spending, *sumptus*

OUTLET, *noun* access, aperture, avenue, channel, chute, conduit, demand, door, egress, *egressus, emissarium,* exhaust, exit, *exitus,* floodgate, gate, gateway, hatch, hole, market, means of escape, opening, passage out, path, portal, spout, vent, way out

OUTLINE *(Boundary),* *noun* ambit, border, bounds, bourn, brink, circuit, circumference, circumscription, compass, confine, contour, demarcation, edge, edging, external form, *extrema lineamenta,* extremity, frame, fringes, frontier, limitations, limits, line of demarcation, lineaments, margin, metes, pale, perimeter, periphery, profile, rim, skirt, threshold, tracing, verge

OUTLINE *(Synopsis),* *noun* abbreviation, abridgment, abstract, *adumbratio,* agenda, brief, compend, compendium, compression, condensation, conspectus, contents, contraction, core, digest, epitome, essence, minute, note, pandect, recapitulation, report, skeleton, sketch, summation, syllabus

OUTLOOK, *noun* angle, aspect, attitude, emotional tone, field of view, frame of mind, frame of reference, observation, perspective, point of observation, point of view, position, posture, regard, slant, stand, standpoint, viewpoint, way of thinking

OUTMODED, *adjective* anachronistic, anachronous, ancient, antediluvian, antiquated, antique, archaic, behind the age, behind the times, bygone, dated, demoded, desuete, disapproved, discarded, disused, expired, extinct, fallen into desuetude, fallen into disuse, forgotten, former, gone out, grown old, neglected, no longer conventional, no longer customary, no longer prevailing, not in vogue, obsolescent, obsolete, of a previous fashion, of a previous style, of the old school, old, old-fashioned, old-world, outdated, out-of-date, out-of-fashion, out-of-use, outworn, passe, past, primitive, quaint, rejected, retired, stale, styleless, superannuated, superseded, unaccepted, uncurrent, unfashionable, unpracticed, unstylish

OUTPOUR, *verb* be effusive, be prolix, cascade, cast forth, decant, detrude, discharge, discourse at length, disembogue, disgorge, drain, effuse, eject, emit, empty, enlarge upon, eruct, eructate, evacuate, exhaust, expel, extravasate, harangue, inundate, let fall, pour forth, pour out, rant, send forth, send out, shed, spill, spout, spurt, stream, vent

OUTPUT, *noun* accomplishment, achievement, amount produced, avail, benefit, creation, crop, discharge, earnings, effectuation, emanation, end, end product, fruit, gain, harvest, issuance, issue, manufactured product, merchandise, outcome, proceeds, produce, product, production, profit, quantity produced, result, return, yield
ASSOCIATED CONCEPTS: output contract

OUTRAGE, *noun* abomination, absurdity, abuse, affront, atrocity, contempt, contumacious, cruelty, disgracefulness, dishonorableness, disrespect, harmfulness,

hatefulness, horribleness, ignobleness, iniquitousness, injuriousness, intolerableness, malevolence, maliciousness, nefariousness, odiousness, offensiveness, perfidiousness, unreasonableness, wickedness
ASSOCIATED CONCEPTS: moral outrage

OUTRAGEOUS, ***adjective*** abominable, absurd, abusive, acrimonious, affronting, arrant, atrocious, barefaced, base, black, brazen, conspicuous, contemptible, *contumeliosus,* contumelious, corrupt, cruel, deplorable, despicable, despiteful, dire, disgraceful, dishonorable, disobliging, disrespectful, drastic, egregious, enormous, exaggerated, excessive, execrable, exorbitant, extreme, fanatic, fanatical, ferocious, flagitious, flagrant, foul, fulsome, galling, glaring, gross, grossly offensive, harmful, hateful, heinous, horrifying, hot-headed, hyperbolical, ignoble, *immanis,* immense, immoderate, *immoderatus,* infamous, infuriating, iniquitous, injurious, inordinate, insolent, insulting, intolerable, low, mad, madcap, malevolent, malicious, malign, malignant, maniacal, monstrous, nefarious, notorious, odious, offensive, opprobrious, overdone, perfidious, preposterous, questionable, rabid, radical, raging, reprehensible, scandalous, shameless, shocking, sinful, spiteful, tempestuous, unconscionable, undue, unpleasant, unreasonable, unwarranted, villainous, wanton, wicked, wild, wrongful
ASSOCIATED CONCEPTS: outrageous conduct

OUTRIGHT, ***adjective*** absolute, all-out, altogether, complete, comprehensive, consummate, downright, entire, exhaustive, flagrant, full, full-fledged, obvious, out-and-out, sheer, straightforward, straight out, sweeping, thorough, through and through, total, unconditional, undiminished, undivided, unequivocal, unmitigated, unqualified, utter
ASSOCIATED CONCEPTS: outright grant

OUTRUN, ***verb*** beat, catch up, catch up with, come up to, edge out, gain on, leave behind, leave standing, outdo, outmaneuver, outpace, outperform, outrange, outreach, outrival, outstrip, overtake, pass, prevail over, win

OUTSET, ***noun*** beginning, birth, commencement, dawn, embarkation, entrance, exordium, first move, first step, foundation, genesis, inauguration, inception, inchoation, incipience, incipiency, induction, infancy, initiation, *initium,* introduction, launching, onset, opening, origin, origination, outbreak, rise, start, starting point, threshold

OUTSIDE *(Exterior),* ***adjective*** aways, back, exterior, external, front, not within, outermost, outlying, outmost, outside, outward, side

OUTSIDE *(Foreign),* ***adjective*** alien, extraneous, external, foreign, immaterial, inapplicable, insignificant, irrelevant, nonessential, supervenient, unessential, unnecessary

OUTSOURCING, ***verb*** contracting with outside sources, disposing of, eliminating work, eliminating workers, going outside, hiring outside sources, retaining others, retaining outside sources, subcontracting

OUTSPOKEN, ***adjective*** abrupt, blunt, brazen, brusque, candid, direct, earnest, forthcoming, forthright, guileless, honest, natural, open, plain, plainspoken, real, rude, straightforward, undiplomatic, unguarded, uninhibited, unrestrained, unsubtle, up-front, vocal, vociferous

OUTSTANDING *(Prominent),* ***adjective*** august, celebrated, chief, consequential, conspicuous, distinctive, distinguished, elevated, eminent, especial, esteemed, exalted, excellent, excelling, exceptional, eximious, extraordinary, famed, famous, far-famed, foremost, great, honorable, honored, illustrious, important, imposing, impressive, incomparable, influential, known, luminous, lustrous, majestic, marked, memorable, nonpareil, notable, noted, noteworthy, paramount, peerless, preeminent, prestigious, princely, principal, ranking, recognized, remarkable, renowned, reputable, respected, revered, royal, salient, significant, special, starring, sublime, substantial, supereminent, superior, superlative, supreme, transcendent, unforgettable, unparalleled, venerable

OUTSTANDING *(Unpaid),* ***adjective*** delinquent, due, in arrears, overdue, owing, past due, payable, surviving, uncollected, ungathered, unliquidated, unrecompensed, unrequited, unsatisfied, unsettled

OUTSTANDING *(Unresolved),* ***adjective*** in suspense, incomplete, indefinite, irresolved, open, pending, unadjusted, unascertained, unconcluded, undecided, undetermined, unfinished, unsettled

OUTWEIGH, ***verb*** be of greater significance, beat, better, come first, dominate, eclipse, exceed, exceed in importance, exceed in value, excel, get ahead of, go beyond, outbalance, outdo, outrank, outrival, overbalance, overpoise, overpower, overshadow, overtop, overweigh, *potiorem,* predominate, preponderate, prevail, rise above, *superare,* surpass, take precedence over, top, transcend, *vincere,* weigh more than

OVER AGAIN, ***adjective*** do over, duplicate, give an encore, perform multiple times, re-create, recur, redo, reduplicate, reenact, remake, renew, repeat, replicate, reproduce, resume, retrace
ASSOCIATED CONCEPTS: concurrent sentences, consecutive sentences

OVERABUNDANCE, ***noun*** abundance, bellyful, bounty, excess, overage, overflow, overkill, overstock, oversupply, plenitude, plenty, plethora, plus, profusion, stock, sufficiency, superfluity, supply, surfeit, surplus, too much

OVERABUNDANT, ***adjective*** abundant, ample, baroque, devilish, excessive, exorbitant, extravagant, extreme, fancy, immoderate, inordinate, insane, intolerable, lavish, overdue, overextravagant, overmuch, steep, stiff, towering, unconscionable, undue, unmerciful

OVERAGE, ***noun*** avalanche, balance, deluge, excess, extra, glut, inundation, leftover, overabundance, overflow, overmeasure, overplus, oversupply, plenty, profusion, redundance, redundancy, remainder, remnant, repletion, residue, spare, supersaturation, surfeit, surplus, surplusage, too many, too much, undue amount

OVERALL, ***adjective*** all-in-one, all-embracing, all-encompassing, all-inclusive, blanket, complete, comprehensive, entire, extended, extensive, general, globally, inclusive, panoramic, sweeping, total, undivided, universal, whole, wholesale, with all sides considered, with every aspect

OVERBEARING, ***adjective*** aggressive, arrogant, assumptive, authoritarian, authoritative, autocratic, belligerent, despotic, dictatorial, domineering, huffy, imperious, lofty, lordly, magisterial, narcissistic, onerous, pompous, strong-handed, tyrannical, tyrannous, unreasonable

OVERCOME *(Overwhelm),* ***verb*** astonish, bewilder, bowl over, break down, burden, confound, crush, daze, deluge, discomfit, drown, encumber, engulf, flood, get the upper hand, glut, hamper, immerse, inundate, overlay, overload, overpower, overtax, prostrate, saddle, shatter, stagger, stun, submerge, swallow up, swamp, weigh down, whelm

OVERCOME *(Surmount),* ***verb*** beat, command, conquer, defeat, destroy, dominate, drub, eclipse, get the better of, get the upper hand, master, outdo, outrival, outshine, outstrip, overmatch, overpower, overshadow, overthrow, prevail over, quash, quell, rise above, rout, subdue, subjugate, tower above, transcend, triumph over, vanquish
ASSOCIATED CONCEPTS: overcome a presumption

OVERDRAW, ***verb*** aes *alienum contrahere,* be debited with, be in debt, be prodigal, become bankrupt, become insolvent, deplete, dissipate, exhaust, incur a debt, overcharge, overextend, overspend, overstrain, overstretch, owe, owe money, run into debt, spend more than one has, squander
ASSOCIATED CONCEPTS: overdraw an account

OVERDUE, ***adjective*** behind time, belated, *debitus,* delayed, delinquent, due, in arrears, late, long-delayed, more than due, not on time, outstanding, past due, past the time for payment, remiss, tardy, unpaid, untimely

OVERESTIMATE, ***verb*** adulate, aggrandize, attach too much importance to, enlarge, estimate too highly, exaggerate, exalt, exceed, expand, extol, flatter, glorify, inflate, magnify, make too much of, maximize, misestimate, misjudge, misrepresent, overassess, overcalculate, overcount, overdo, overjudge, overlaud, overmeasure, overpraise, overprize, overrate, overstate, overvalue, set too high an estimate

OVEREXTEND, ***verb*** develop too fast, develop too much, distend, go too far, grow too fast, grow too much, overcommit, overdevelop, overexpand, spread too far, spread too thin, strain, stretch, stretch too far

OVERHEAD, ***noun*** budget, business expenses, charges, cost, cost incurred, cost of living, current expenses, disbursement, drain on resources, expenditures, expense, general expenses, liabilities, living expenses, money expended, operating expenses, outlay, payments, spendings, upkeep
ASSOCIATED CONCEPTS: overhead expenses

OVERHEAR, ***verb*** attend, become aware of, catch, detect, eavesdrop, *exaudire, excipere,* find out, glean knowledge of, hear, intercept, listen in on, listen stealthily, monitor, obtain knowledge of, pick up, receive information, receive knowledge of, *subauscultare*
ASSOCIATED CONCEPTS: eavesdropping, wiretapping

OVERINDULGE, ***verb*** be gluttonous, be greedy, be intemperate, be selfish, be voracious, carry to excess, carry too far, cater to excessively, coddle excessively, eat excessively, favor excessively, gratify to excess, humor excessively, lack self-control, overdo, overeat, overgorge, overgratify, pamper excessively, satiate to excess, satisfy to excess, spoil excessively

OVERLAP, ***verb*** adjoin, cover, encroach, exceed, extend beyond, go beyond, imbricate, *imminere, impendere,* impinge, infringe, invade, lap over, lie over, make contact, overgrow, overhang, overlay, overlie, override, overrun, overspread, project, protrude, reach over, run over, spread over, superimpose, touch

OVERLOAD, ***verb*** burden, choke, congest, cram, crowd, cumber, deluge, drench, encumber, flood, force, glut, gorge, inundate, load to excess, make heavy, oppress, overabound, overburden, overdo, overdose, overexert, overfeed, overfill, overstrain, overstuff, overtask, overtax, overuse, overweigh, overwhelm, overwork, pack, saddle, saturate, soak, strain, supercharge, supersaturate, surcharge, surfeit, weigh down, work to excess

OVERLOOK *(Disregard),* ***verb*** fail to appreciate, fail to observe, fail to see, forget, leave out, leave undone, let ride, miss, neglect, omit, pass over, take no notice

OVERLOOK *(Excuse),* ***verb*** condone, disregard, excuse, forgive, pardon

OVERLOOK *(Superintend),* ***verb*** administer, be at the helm, be inattentive to, command, command a view of, *condonare,* conduct, control, direct, examine, govern, guide, have charge of, hold the reins, ignore, *ignoscere,* inspect, look after, look out, look over, oversee, pilot, *praeterire,* preside, review, scrutinize, steer, study, supervise, survey, watch over

OVERLY, ***adverb*** abnormally, excessively, exorbitantly, extortionately, extraordinarily, extravagantly, immoderately, improperly, inappropriately, inexcusably, inordinately, intemperately, intolerably, monstrously, overly, overmuch, singularly, unacceptably, unbearably, uncommonly, unconscionably, uncustomarily, unduly, unreasonably, unruly, unusually

OVERPOWER *(Defeat),* ***verb*** attack, conquer, crush, get the upper hand, master, outmaneuver, overcome, overwhelm, prevail, rout, stun, stupefy, subdue, subjugate, surmount, vanquish

OVERPOWER *(Overtake),* ***verb*** beat, finish first, master, outmaneuver, outrace, overmaster, overmatch, overset, prevail over, trounce, upset, win

OVERREACH, ***verb*** accroach, annul, cheat, *circumscribere, circumvenire,* circumvent, deceive, defeat one's own purpose, defeat oneself by overdoing matters, defraud, dupe, encroach, exceed, extend beyond, extend over, fool, get the better of, have one's plans backfire, mislead, nullify one's gains, offset, outsmart, outwit, overact, overdo, overextend, overshoot, reach beyond, reach over, reach too far, thwart, trick, trip, undermine, undo
ASSOCIATED CONCEPTS: undue influence

OVERRIDE, ***verb*** act despite, annul, cancel, counteract, countermand, crush, defeat, discard, dismiss, disregard, do away with, dominate, flout, fly in the face of, ignore, invalidate, make ineffectual, make null and void, make void, neglect, nullify, outweigh, overcome, overpower, overrule, overturn, pass over, prevail over, quell, reverse, revoke, set aside, subdue, supersede, surpass, take no account of, take precedence, thwart, upset
ASSOCIATED CONCEPTS: override a veto, overriding state in terest

OVERRULE, ***verb*** abrogate, annul, cancel, countermand, decide against, *gubernare,* invalidate, make null, make void, nullify, obviate, override, overturn, refuse to sustain, reject, reject by subsequent action, reject by subsequent decision, renounce, repeal, repudiate, rescind, retract, reverse, revoke, rule against, rule out, set aside, supersede, undo, upset, *vincere,* void
ASSOCIATED CONCEPTS: overrule a decision, overrule a motion, overrule an objection

OVERSEE, ***verb*** administer, attend to, be at the helm, be the guiding force, carry on, coach, command, conduct,

control, dictate, direct, dominate, engineer, examine, execute, govern, guide, handle, have authority over, have charge of, have the direction of, head, instruct, lead, look after, manage, master, mastermind, navigate, officiate, pay attention to, pilot, *procurare,* reconnoiter, regiment, regulate, rein, rule, scrutinize, steer, superintend, supervise, watch, watch over
ASSOCIATED CONCEPTS: master servant relationship, principal agent relationship, respondeat superior

OVERSHADOW, ***verb*** cast into the shade, dominate, dwarf, eclipse, extinguish, obscure, outshine, overshadow, prevail over, reduce, rise above, run circles around, shroud, steal the spotlight from, surmount, take the glory out of, top, tower above, tower over, upstage

OVERSIGHT *(Carelessness),* ***noun*** blunder, careless mistake, careless omission, *erratum,* error, failure, failure to notice, heedlessness, inadvertency, inattention, *incuria,* lapse, laxity, laxness, mistake, neglect, negligence, nonobservance, remissness, slip, supervision, thoughtlessness, unintentional mistake, unintentional omission
ASSOCIATED CONCEPTS: negligence

OVERSIGHT *(Control),* ***noun*** management, overlooking, superintendence, supervision, watchful care, watchfulness

OVERSTATEMENT, ***noun*** aggrandizement, amplification, boasting, coloring, distortion, elaboration, embroidery, enlargement, exaggerated statement, exaggeration, expansion, extravagance, extravagancy, falsification, hyperbole, hyperbolism, inflated statement, inflation, magnification, magniloquence, misjudgment, misrepresentation, misstatement, overestimation, puffery

OVERSTEP, ***verb*** accroach, advance beyond proper limits, break in upon, encroach, entrench, exceed, go beyond, go over, go too far, impinge, infringe, interfere, intrude, invade, meddle, not observe, obtrude, overpass, overrun, run over, strain, stretch, transcend, transgress, trench on, trespass, usurp, violate

OVERT, ***adjective*** *apertus,* apparent, clear, definite, disclosed, distinct, easily seen, evident, explicit, exposed, express, glaring, in full view, in plain sight, manifest, *manifestus,* noticeable, notorious, obvious, open, ostensible, palpable, patent, perceptible, perspicuous, plain, public, revealed, unconcealed, uncovered, undisguised, unhidden, visible

OVERT ACT, ***noun*** action, beginnings, commencement, criminal act, dealings, deed, doings, intentional act, maneuver, manifest act, open act, outward act, start
ASSOCIATED CONCEPTS: conspiracy

OVERTHROW, ***verb*** abolish, *adfligere,* be victorious over, break up, bring down, cast down, conquer, defeat, *deicere,* dethrone, *diruere,* disrupt, eradicate, exterminate, extirpate, fell, invert, master, nullify, obliterate, obviate, overmaster, overpower, overrun, overset, overturn, overwhelm, prostrate, quash, quell, ravage, refute, remove, reverse, revolt, revolutionize, shatter, subdue, subjugate, subvert, suppress, surmount, terminate, throw down, throw over, topple, turn upside down, uncrown, unseat, upend, uproot, upset

OVERTURE, ***noun*** advance, approach, beginning, bid, *condicio,* exordium, foreword, initiative, introduction, invitation, motion, offer, opening of negotiations, preamble, preface, preliminary, preliminary negotiation, prelude, presentation, proem, proffer, proposal, proposition, tender

OVERTURN, ***verb*** abolish, annihilate, conquer, crush, defeat, demolish, destroy, *evertere,* foil, invert, obliterate, overcome, overpower, overset, overthrow, overwhelm, quell, repress, reverse, ruin, subdue, subvert, *subvertere,* suppress, topple, upend, uproot, upset, vanquish
ASSOCIATED CONCEPTS: overturn a decision

OVERVIEW, ***noun*** analysis, comprehensive analysis, detailed summary, examination, general outlook, introduction, iteration, outline, recap, recapitulation, recount, recounting, reiteration, statement, summary, summation, survey
ASSOCIATED CONCEPTS: law firm profile

OVERWHELM, ***verb*** astonish, beat, besiege, bewilder, bury, confound, confuse, conquer, daze, defeat, deluge, *demergere,* destroy, discomfit, immerse, impress, inundate, master, obruere, *opprimere,* overcome, overpower, overrun, overthrow, quash, quell, shock, stun, subdue, subjugate, submerge, suppress, surmount, surprise, triumph over, vanquish, weigh down

OVERWHELMING, ***adverb*** absolutely, astonishingly, astronomically, comfortably, completely, decisively, definitively, distinctly, dramatically, emphatically, immensely, overpoweringly, popularly, radically, significantly, strongly
ASSOCIATED CONCEPTS: overwhelmingly approved, overwhelming passing the legislature, overwhelmingly rejected, overwhelmingly supported

OWE, ***verb*** be beholden, be bound, be due, be in debt, be indebted, be liable, be obligated, be under obligation, contract a debt, debere, have a loan, have an obligation, incur a debt
ASSOCIATED CONCEPTS: debt owed, debtor-creditor laws, legally owed, taxes owed

OWN, ***verb*** be in possession of, be in receipt of, be master of, be possessed of, claim, command, contain, control, dominate, enjoy, *habere,* have, have a deed for, have a title to, have claim upon, have hold of, have in hand, have rights to, have to one's name, hold, keep, maintain, occupy, possess, *possidere,* retain, *tenere*
FOREIGN PHRASES: ***Id solum nostrum quod debitis deductis nostrum est.*** That only is ours which remains to us after deduction of our debts.

OWNER, ***noun*** claimer, controller, holder, homeowner, householder, land owner, landlord, lessor, legitimate person entitled to, master, occupier, person holding ownership on record, possessor, property owner, proprietor, receiver, record holder, retainer, title holder
ASSOCIATED CONCEPTS: beneficial owner, co-owner, equitable owner, general owner, gun owner, joint owners, owner of copyright, part owners, record owner, repeated owner

OWNERSHIP, ***noun*** claim, control, dominion, *dominium,* holding, mastery, occupancy, possessorship, proprietary, proprietorship, right of possession, seisin, tenancy, tenure, title, use
ASSOCIATED CONCEPTS: absolute ownership, apparent ownership, certificate of ownership, change of ownership, exclusive ownership, incident of ownership, individual ownership, joint ownership, occupation, ownership rights, possession, proprietary interest, qualified ownership, silent partner, sole ownership, sole proprietor, tenancy by the entirety, transfer of ownership, unconditional ownership, undisclosed interest, unqualified ownership

P

PACHYDERMATOUS, *adjective* coldblooded, coldhearted, difficult to change, immovable, impassive, impenetrable, impenitent, impervious, implacable, insensitive, intransigent, indurate, obdurate, stubborn, thick-skinned, tough, unsympathetic, unyielding

PACIFY, *verb* accommodate, alleviate, appease, assuage, becalm, bring to terms, calm, *componere,* conciliate, dulcify, ease, *lenire,* make peace, mediate, mellow, mollify, pacificate, placate, please, propitiate, quell, quiet, reconcile, relieve, restore harmony, restore to a state of peace, restore to a state of tranquillity, reunite, salve, satiate, satisfy, settle, settle differences, smooth, soothe, still, subdue, tranquilize

PACT, *noun* agreement, alliance, arrangement, assurance, bargain, bond, charter, coalition, compact, compromise, concord, concordance, concordat, consentaneity, consortium, contract, convention, cooperation, covenant, deal, entente, *foedus,* guarantee, indenture, league, mutual agreement, mutual pledge, mutual promise, *pactio,* paction, *pactum,* pledge, promise, reconciliation, settlement, stipulation, treaty, understanding, union, warranty

PAIN, *noun* ache, adversity, affliction, aggravation, agony, ailment, anguish, blight, calamity, disability, discomfort, disease, displeasure, distress, *dolor,* grief, grievous trouble, hurt, ill, infliction, injury, malady, malaise, misery, ordeal, pang, sickness, sore, soreness, sorrow, strong discomfort, suffering, torment, unease, woe, worry
ASSOCIATED CONCEPTS: pain and suffering

PAIN AND SUFFERING, *noun* award for permanent damage, award for serious damage, award for sustained damage, damages, damages for an injured party, damages for emotional distress, damages for mental distress, damages for physical distress, damages for the afflicted, damages for the impaired, grant for damages sustained, noneconomic damages
ASSOCIATED CONCEPTS: general damages, special damages

PAINFUL, *adjective* aching, afflictive, agonizing, anguishing, arduous, beset with difficulties, difficult, difficult to endure, discomforting, distressful, distressing, disturbing, excruciating, grievous, grueling, hard to endure, harmful, harrowing, hurtful, hurting, inflamed, insufferable, intolerable, irksome, irritating, laborious, smarting, sore, throbbing, tiresome, tormenting, torturous, troublesome, troubling, trying, unbearable, uncomfortable, unendurable, unpleasant, unsufferable, wearisome

PAINSTAKING, *adjective* assiduous, attentive, careful, conscientious, diligent, earnest, elaborate, energetic, exacting, hardworking, heedful, industrious, labored, laborious, meticulous, never-tiring, operose, *operosus,* particular, persevering, plodding, precise, punctilious, regardful, scrupulous, sedulous, *sedulus,* sparing no pains, strenuous, strict, thorough, untiring, zealous

PALATABLE, *adjective* acceptable, agreeable, ambrosial, ambrosian, amenable, appetizing, becoming, causing pleasure, cibarious, comestible, congenial, delectable, delicate, delicious, delightful, drinkable, dulcet, *dulcis,* eatable, edible, enjoyable, epicurean, esculent, flavorful, flavorous, flavorsome, good, good-tasting, good to eat, gratifying, inviting, iucundus, likable, *luscious,* meeting standards, nectareous, nice, piquant, pleasant, pleasing, pleasurable, potable, prepossessing, refreshing, relishable, sapid, satisfactory, savory, scrumptious, *suavis,* succulent, tangy, tasteful, tasty, tempting, toothsome, unobjectionable, up to par, welcome

PALAVER, *noun* babble, balderdash, blather, chatter, empty words, foolishness, gab, idle chatter, idle talk, mere chatter, nonsense, prattle, twaddle, words

PALE, *adjective* anemic in comparison, become impotent, become tarnished, colorless in comparison, contrast, dim, dismal, drab, drained of color, dreary in comparison, fails in comparison, feeble in comparison, flat in comparison, flimsy in comparison, frail in comparison, ghastly, impotent, inadequate, incompetent, ineffective, insufficient, lackluster, languishing, lose their luster, lusterless, obfuscated, obscured, pallid

PALIMONY, *noun* alimony for a longtime relationship, alimony to a live-in companion, award of support, cohabitation with an obligation for alimony, divorce allowance, divorce payments, domestic-partner alimony, nonmarital alimony, out of wedlock with an award of alimony, support for an out-of-wedlock companion, support for unmarried cohabitants
ASSOCIATED CONCEPTS: divorce laws, palimony agreements

PALLIATE *(Abate),* *verb* allay, alleviate, appease, arrest, assuage, attemper, bate, bound, bring to a standstill, cease, check, circumscribe, curb, curtail, deactivate, decelerate, decrease, desist, diminish, discontinue, ease, eliminate, lenify, lessen, limit, make less severe, make mild, minimize, mitigate, moderate, modulate, obtund, pacify, qualify, quell, quiet, reduce, regulate, relieve, soften, still, stop, subdue, suppress, suspend, temper, terminate

PALLIATE *(Excuse)*, ***verb*** absolve, acquit, adjudge innocent, allow for, assoil, be lenient, clear, condone, declare guiltless, defend, discharge, disculpate, dismiss charges, exculpate, exempt, exonerate, extenuate, forbear, forgive, give amnesty, give dispensation, grant absolution, grant amnesty, grant exemption, grant immunity, judge innocent, justify, let go, let off, liberate, license, make allowance for, overlook, pardon, permit, privilege, provide justification, release, release from obligation, remit the penalty, reprieve, rescue, set free, show mercy, shrive, spare, support, tolerate, vindicate

PALLIATIVE *(Abating)*, ***adjective*** allaying, alleviating, alleviative, assuaging, assuasive, beneficial, calmative, consolatory, corrective, curative, easeful, helpful, lenient, drudge, mitigating, mitigative, modifying, modulatory, mollifying, pacifying, quelling, quieting, relieving, restorative, sedative, softening, soothing, stilling, subduing, tempering, therapeutic, tranquilizing

PALLIATIVE *(Excusing)*, ***adjective*** apologetic, condonable, condoning, excepting, exculpable, exculpating, excusatory, exempting, expiating, extenuating, extenuative, forgiving, justificatory, justifying, pardoning, qualifying, vindicating, vindicative, vindicatory

PALPABLE, ***adjective*** able to be felt, able to be handled, able to be touched, apparent, bold, certain, clear, clear-cut, conspicuous, crystal clear, definite, detectable, discernible, disclosed, discoverable, distinct, easily perceived, easily seen, *evidens*, evident, exhibited, explicit, glaring, identifiable, in evidence, indisputable, indubitable, lucid, manifest, *manifestus*, marked, notable, noticeable, observable, obvious, overt, patent, perceivable, perceptible, perspicuous, plain, prominent, pronounced, readily perceived, readily seen, recognizable, revealed, salient, seeable, self-evident, stark, striking, tactile, tangible, touchable, *tractabilis*, unconcealed, uncontestable, uncovered, uncurtained, undisguised, undoubtable, unequivocal, unhidden, unmasked, unmistakable, unobscure, unobscured, unquestionable, unscreened, unshrouded, unveiled, visible

PALTER, ***verb*** act, act insincerely, be deceitful, be deceptive, be dishonest, be evasive, be false, be fraudulent, be hypocritical, be inconstant, be insincere, be mendacious, be perfidious, be uncandid, be untruthful, bear false witness, beguile, betray, bluff, break faith, cant, cheat, concoct, counterfeit, cozen, deal crookedly, deceive, defraud, delude, deviate, disguise, dissemble, dissimulate, distort, doctor, dodge, dupe, equivocate, evade, evade the truth, fabricate, fake, falsify, feign, fence, fool, forswear, gammon, hoax, inveigle, invent, lack candor, lead astray, lie, make false pretenses, make false statements, manufacture, masquerade, misdirect, misguide, misinform, mislead, misrender, misreport, misrepresent, misstate, perjure, pervert, playact, pose, pretend, prevaricate, profess, render lip service, represent falsely, shift, shuffle, talk insincerely, tergiversate, trifle, trump up, twist, use trickery, utter a falsehood, victimize

PALTRY, ***adjective*** below par, beneath contempt, beneath notice, cheap, contemptible, deficient, despicable, diminutive, humble, inadequate, incomplete, inconsequential, inconsiderable, insignificant, irrelevant, lacking, little, meager, mean, measly, mediocre, minute, *minutus*, miserable, modest, negligible, niggardly, nugatory, of little consequence, of little value, of no account, of small value, pathetic, petty, piddling, pitiful, poor, puny, *pusillus*, scant, scanty, scarce, shameful, slight, small, sorry, trifling, trivial, unappreciable, unimportant, unsatisfactory, unworthy of serious consideration, useless, valueless, vile, *vilis*, wanting, worthless, wretched

PANACEA, ***noun*** answer, assistance, balm, catholicon, correction, corrective, curative, cure, cure-all, cure for all ills, healing agent, improvement, medicament, medicine, palliative, relief, remedy, restorative, restorative agent, solution, solution to difficulties, tonic, universal cure, universal remedy

PANDECT *(Code of laws)*, ***noun*** body of law, canon, canon of laws, charter, code, codification, codified law, collection of laws, complete body of laws, digest, digest of law, enactment, legal code, principles, statute book

PANDECT *(Treatise)*, ***noun*** analysis, article, commentary, compendium, complete digest, comprehensive digest, conspectus, data paper, digest, discourse, discussion, disquisition, dissertation, essay, excursus, exhaustive tract, explanation, exposition, formal discourse, formal essay, handbook, lucubration, manual, outline, paper, position paper, publication, study, summary, survey, syllabus, synopsis, tract, tractate, treatment

PANADEMIC, ***noun*** all-embracing epidemic, far-reaching disease, global epidemic, international dispose, universal disease, widespread disease, worldwide epidemic

PANDEMONIUM, ***noun*** affray, agitation, anarchy, bedlam, chaos, clamor, commotion, confusedness, confusion, convulsion, derangement, din, disarrangement, disarray, discomposure, disharmony, disorder, disorganization, disquietude, disruption, disturbance, embroilment, entanglement, ferment, fracas, frenzy, imbroglio, inquietude, jumble, lack of order, melee, mix-up, noise, outcry, panic, racket, rampage, riot, roar, row, ruction, rumpus, stir, storm, trouble, tumult, turbulence, turmoil, unruliness, uproar, uproariousness, vociferation, want of method, wild uproar, wildness

PANDER, ***verb*** assist, attend, be instrumental, be of service, be servile, be subservient, be useful, cater, court favor, do service, furnish, give, gratify, help, humor, indulge, ingratiate oneself, make contented, make oneself useful, minister, obey, oblige, pamper, please, procure, provide, purvey, render service, satisfy, satisfy desires, serve, subserve, supply, tend, toady, truckle to, wait on, work in the service of

PANEL *(Discussion group)*, ***noun*** advisory body, caucus, conference, *consilium*, council, deliberative body, exchange of views, forum, joint discussion, open discussion, open forum, roundtable, seminar, summit, symposium

PANEL *(Jurors)*, ***noun*** body of jurors, body of persons summoned as jurors, body of persons sworn to render a verdict, group of jurors, jury, list of jurors, persons summoned to attend the court as jurymen, triers of fact
ASSOCIATED CONCEPTS: grand jury, panel en banc, petit jury

PANIC, ***noun*** affright, agitation, alarm, anxiety, awe, confusedness, confusion, consternation, cowardice, despair, discomposure, disorder, disquietude, disturbance, dread, fear, fearfulness, flutter, frenzy, fright, great fear,

horror, hysteria, hystericalness, inquietude, irrational terror, nervousness, outcry, overpowering fright, pandemonium, pavor, perturbance, perturbation, phobia, sheer terror, stampede, state of terror, sudden fear, terror, trepidation, turmoil, unreasoning fear
ASSOCIATED CONCEPTS: heat of passion, manslaughter, temporary insanity

PANOPLY, *noun* armature, armor, armored protection, barrier, brigandine, buffer, covering, cuirass, defense, defensive arms, defensive clothing, defensive equipment, deterrent, envelopment, fender, fortification, full array, guard, means of protection, precaution, preservation, preventive measure, protection, protective covering, protective outfit, safeguard, screen, shelter, shield, targe

PAR *(Equality),* ***noun*** *aequalis, aequus,* balance, equal footing, equal value, equal worth, equality, equalness, equipollence, equivalence, evenness, identicalness, identity, interchangeableness, likeness, sameness, similarity
ASSOCIATED CONCEPTS: above par value, at par value, par value of stock

PAR *(Face amount),* ***noun*** amount, appraisal, appraisement, evaluation, face value, market price, price, rate, valuation, value, value in exchange, worth

PARADE, *noun* caravan, cavalcade, column, display, exhibit, exhibition, gala, grandeur, honorary march, honorary procession, march, motorcade, presentation, public procession, salute to, show, spectacle, stream of marchers, throngs of marchers, walk of marchers
ASSOCIATED CONCEPTS: parade law, permits

PARADIGM, *noun* archetype, example, exemplar, guide, ideal, model, norm, original, paradigma, pattern, prototype, sample, standard

PARADOX, *noun* antilogy, antinomy, contradiction, contrariety, disagreement, discrepancy, dissonance, enigma, incompatibility, incongruity, inconsistency, inconsonance, irreconcilability, lack of agreement, lack of harmony, perplexity, puzzle, *quod est admirabile contraque opinionem omnium,* seeming contradiction, self-contradiction

PARADOXICAL, *adjective* abnormal but true, absurd but true, ambiguous but true, bewildering, conflicting but true, confounding but true, contradictory but true, enigmatic but true, incompatible but true, incongruous but true, inconsistent but true, inconsonant but true

PARAGON, *noun* acme of perfection, champion, eminent person, example, exceller, exemplar, good example, great person, height of perfection, hero, ideal, man of mark, model, model of virtue, nonesuch, nonpareil, person of repute, prize, standard, standard for comparison, summit, superior individual

PARALEGAL, *noun* assistant, law assistant, legal administrative assistant, legal document assistant, legal assistant, legal technician

PARALLEL, *adjective* abreast, agreed, akin, aligned, analogous, coequal, coextending, coextensive, cognate, coincident, collateral, commensurable, comparable, comparing, comparison, concerted, concomitant, concurrent, congeneric, congenerous, congruous, consensual, consonant, correlative, correspondent, corresponding, equal, equidistant, equivalent, even, matched, matching, mutual, of a kind, opposite, proportioned, resembling, similar, symmetrical, tantamount, tied, uniform

PARALLEL, *noun* analogue, coequal, companion, compeer, complement, correspondent, counterpart, double, equal, equivalent, fellow, like, match, mate, peer, resemblance, same, twin

PARALLEL, *verb* associate, be comparable to, be equal with, be equivalent to, be parallel, coextend, compare, compare with, copy, correlate, correspond to, double, draw a parallel, duplicate, follow, go alongside, imitate, match, relate, run parallel to

PARAMOUNT, *adjective* arch, beyond compare, beyond comparison, cardinal, champion, chief, crowning, distinguished, extraordinary, first, foremost, grand, great, greatest, head, hegemonic, hegemonical, highest, incomparable, inimitable, leading, main, master, matchless, memorable, model, notable, peerless, preeminent, prepollent, prepotent, primary, prime, principal, prominent, regnant, reigning, remarkable, salient, second to none, significant, sovereign, *summus,* supereminent, superior, superlative, supreme, top, transcendent, transcendental, unapproached, unequaled, unexcelled, unmatched, unparalleled, unrivaled, unsurpassed, without parallel, worthy of notice, worthy of remark

PARANOIA, *noun* delusional insanity, delusions, diseased mind, disordered reason, insanity, lunacy, madness, mania, mental aberration, mental disease, phobia, unreasonable fear, unreasonable fright

PARAPHERNALIA *(Apparatus),* ***noun*** accessories, accompaniments, accouterments, apparatus, appliances, articles, attachments, contrivances, conveniences, equipage, equipment, gear, impedimenta, implements, instruments, material, supplies, tools, utensils

PARAPHERNALIA *(Personal belongings),* ***noun*** accessories, appointments, assets, chattels, effects, estate, goods, holdings, merchandise, movables, parcels, perquisites, personal effects, personal estate, personal property, personalty, possessions, property, resources, seisin, trappings

PARAPHRASE, *noun* abridgment, brief, citation, condensation, description, elucidation, enucleation, equivalent meaning, explanation, explication, free translation, free wording, indirect quotation, *interpretatio,* interpretation, loose rendering, loose translation, meaning, minute, nonliteral translation, paraphrasis, recapitulation, rendering, rendition, representation, restatement, rewording, simplification, summary, synopsis, translation, version

PARASITE, *noun* *adsecula,* barnacle, beggar, bloodsucker, borrower, burden, cadger, destructive agency, follower, leech, loafer, mendicant, nonworker, panhandler, scrounger, sponge, sycophant

PARCEL, *noun* acreage, area, block, district, enclave, enclosure, estate, field, ground, land, lot, property, patch, piece, piece of land, plot, plot of ground, plot of land, portion, real estate, region, section, sector, segment, square, terrain, territory, tract
ASSOCIATED CONCEPTS: conveyance, partition

PARCEL, *verb* administer, allocate, allot, appoint, apportion, appropriate, assign, award, bestow, carve, deal out, dispense, dispose of, *distribuere,* distribute, divide, divide into shares, *dividere,* dole out, give away, give out, grant, measure, mete, part with, *partiri,* partition, pass out, portion out, prorate, ration, sectionalize, segment, split up, subdivide

PARCEL OUT, ***verb*** allocate, allot, allow, apportion, appropriate, assign, award, bestow, contribute, dispense, distribute, divide, dole out, furnish, give, give away, give out, grant, hand out, hand over, issue, measure out, mete out, pay out, portion, present, ration, share, spare, supply

PARDON, ***noun*** absolution, acquittal, amnesty, clearance, clemency, compurgation, discharge, dismissal, dispensation, exemption from punishment, exoneration, forgiveness, leniency, obliteration of grievances, release, release from penalty, release from punishment, relinquishment, reprieve, *venia,* vindication
ASSOCIATED CONCEPTS: amnesty, commutation, conditional pardon, parole, relief from disabilities, suspended sentence, unconditional pardon
FOREIGN PHRASES: ***Veniae facilitas incentivum est delinquendi.*** Facility of pardon is an encouragement to crime.

PARDON, ***verb*** acquit, cancel a punishment, cancel an offense, condone, deliver, discharge, emancipate, excuse, exonerate, expunge the record of, fail to exact a penalty, forgive, give absolution, grant amnesty, grant clemency, grant forgiveness, grant remission, let loose, liberate, overlook, purge, redeem, release, release from punishment, remission of guilt, reprieve, set at liberty, set free, suspend charges, vindicate

PARDONABLE, ***adjective*** admissible, allowable, blameless, condonable, defensible, *excusabilis,* excusable, expiable, faultless, forgivable, guiltless, innocent, inoffensive, justifiable, justified, passable, permitted, slight, unblamable, unculpable, understandable, unobjectionable, vindicable

PARENT, ***noun*** ancestor, author, author of one's existence, derivation, father, generator, mother, mover, originator, precursor, predecessor, primogenitor, procreator, progenitor, source
ASSOCIATED CONCEPTS: abusive parent, child welfare, neglect

PARENTAGE, ***noun*** ancestry, antecedents, birth, bloodline, derivation, descent, extraction, family, family connection, family tree, filiation, forebears, forefathers, foreparents, former generations, genealogical tree, genealogy, genesis, *genus,* house, line, line of ancestors, lineage, origin, paternity, pedigree, primogenitors, progenitors, source, stem, *stirps,* stock, tribe
ASSOCIATED CONCEPTS: determination of parentage, illegitimacy, legitimacy, paternity proceeding

PARENTHETICAL, ***adjective*** beside the mark, beside the point, beside the question, explanatory, explicative, expressive, external, extraneous, extrinsic, illustrative, incidental, inconsequent, inconsequential, inessential, inserted, intervening, nonessential, not at issue, not to the purpose, of interest, also an issue, also material, also on point

PARENTS, ***noun*** ancestor, begetter, creator, father, forebear, founder of the family, genitor, head of the household, immediate forebear, matriarch, mother, parens, patriarch, precursor, predecessor, procreator, progenitor
ASSOCIATED CONCEPTS: abandonment of child, adoptive parent, custody of children, duty to support, fitness of parent, foster parent, in loco parentis, natural parent, paternity proceeding, sole surviving parent
FOREIGN PHRASES: ***Parentum est liberos alere etiam nothos.*** It is the duty of parents to support their children even when illegitimate.

PARI MATERIA, ***noun*** in consonance, in harmony, on the same matter, read as one, read in tandem, read with respect of another, read together

PARIAH, ***noun*** castaway, deportee, derelict, exile, expatriate, fugitive, heretic, offender, outcast, outlaw, outsider, proscribed person, rebel, renegade, scab, sectarist, sectary, tergiversator

PARITY, ***noun*** alikeness, analogy, approximation, balance, close correspondence, coequality, comparability, comparison, correlation, correspondence, equability, equality, equation, equilibrium, equipoise, equivalence, equivalency, identical value, identicalness, likeness, parallelism, resemblance, sameness, semblance, similarity, similitude, state of being equal, symmetry, uniformity
ASSOCIATED CONCEPTS: wage parity

PARLANCE, ***noun*** address, allocution, choice of words, command of idiom, command of language, command of words, conference, conversation, delivery, diction, discourse, elocution, eloquence, expression, fashion, flow of language, flow of words, fluency, formulation, idiom, interlocution, locution, manner, manner of speaking, mode, oral communication, oratory, phraseology, recitation, rhetoric, sense of language, speech, spoken word, style, talk, terminology, tone, use of words, utterance, verbal intercourse, vocabulary, vocalization, wordage

PARLAY *(Bet),* ***verb*** ante, back, bet on, gamble, hazard, lay a wager, lay money on, make a bet, make book, play, risk, speculate, stake, take a chance, trust to chance, venture, wager

PARLAY *(Exploit successfully),* ***verb*** boost, broaden, build up, develop, elevate, escalate, exalt, expand, further, maximize, pyramid, raise, use

PARLEY, ***noun*** assembly, collocution, colloquy, communication, conclave, conference, congress, *conloqui,* consultation, convention, conversation, council, debate, deliberation, dialogue, diplomacy, *disceptare,* discussion, exchange of views, hearing, intercommunication, interlocution, interview, meeting, negotiation, oral communication, seminar, summit, summit conference, summit talk, symposiac, symposium, talk, verbal intercourse

PAROCHIAL, ***adjective*** biased, dogmatic, fanatical, hidebound, illiberal, insular, intolerant, jaundiced, limited, literal, narrow, narrow-minded, one-sided, opinionated, opinionative, orthodox, *parochialis,* partial, partisan, predisposed, prejudiced, prepossessed, provincial, regional, restricted to a small area, restricted to a small scope, sectarian, small-minded, unbending, uncatholic, unimaginative, unliberal, untolerating

PARODY, ***noun*** amphigory, apery, buffoonery, burlesque, caricature, cartoon, comical representation, distortion, exaggeration, farce, imitation, lampoon, ludicrous imitation, mime, mimicry, mockery, mummery, pasquinade, ridicula *imitatio,* ridicule, satire, squib, travesty

PAROL, ***adjective*** evidenced solely by speech, expressed, expressed solely by speech, lingual, not committed

to writing, not expressed by writing, not written, nuncupative, oral, outspoken, told, unwritten, uttered, verbal, vocal, voiced
ASSOCIATED CONCEPTS: extrinsic evidence, parol agreement, parol assignment, parol contract, parol evidence rule, parol gift, parol lease

PAROLE, *noun* affirmation, conditional deliverance, conditional discharge, conditional disenthrallment, conditional disimprisonment, conditional emancipation, conditional freedom, conditional freedom from confinement, conditional independence, conditional liberation, conditional liberty, conditional release, conditional reprieve, declaration, deliverance, discharge, emancipation, freedom, freeing from prison, granting freedom, liberation, liberty, release, release from prison, reprieve, setting free
ASSOCIATED CONCEPTS: commutation of sentence, conditions of parole, pardon, parole board, probation, release from dissabilities

PAROLE, *verb* cast loose, conditionally release, conditionally release from imprisonment, deliver, discharge, disimprison, emancipate, free, let go free, let out of jail, let out of prison, liberate, make free, release, release conditionally, release from imprisonment, set at liberty, set free, turn loose, unbolt, uncage, unchain, unfetter, unharness, unshackle
ASSOCIATED CONCEPTS: commutation, commute, pardon, parole board, probation

PAROLE EVIDENCE RULE, *noun* controlling writing, inadmissible verbal evidence to contradict an agreement between the parties, prohibition against injecting extrinsic terms into an agreement, prohibition against oral evidence in interpreting a contract, prohibition on extrinsic evidence
ASSOCIATED CONCEPTS: completely integrated contract

PARRY, *verb* avert, avoid, beat off, block, brush off, chase away, chase off, confute, counter, *defendere,* deflect, dodge, drive away, drive back, elude, escape, evade, fence, fend off, fight off, foil, force back, hedge, hold at bay, hold back, hold off, intercept, interfere, intervene, keep at bay, keep away, keep clear of, keep off, offer resistance, oppose, outface, prevent, *propulsare,* push away, put up a struggle, rebuff, refute, reluct, reluctate, repel, *repellere,* repulse, resist, sidestep, stave off, stop, stymie, take evasive action, thwart, turn aside, turn away, turn back, ward off, withstand

PARSIMONIOUS, *adjective* acquisitive, avaricious, chary, cheap, close, closefisted, curmudgeonly, economical, excessively frugal, frugal, grasping, grudging, illiberal, mean, mercenary, miserly, niggardly, *parcus,* penny-pinching, penurious, petty, *restrictus,* scrimping, selfish, small-minded, sparing, stingy, stinting, tenax, thrifty, tight, uncharitable, ungenerous, unwilling to give, unyielding

PART *(Place),* ***noun*** area, division, locale, location, premises, purlieus, quarter, room, section, site, spot
ASSOCIATED CONCEPTS: part in a courthouse

PART *(Portion),* ***noun*** allocation, allowance, amount, bit, chip, chunk, collop, component, constituent, cutting, detachment, detail, division, excerpt, factor, fraction, fragment, helping, ingredient, interest, lump, measure, particle, percentage, piece, quantity, section, segment, serving, share, slab, slice, subdivision, subgroup
ASSOCIATED CONCEPTS: principal part

PART *(Role),* ***noun*** burden, character, charge, chore, concern, function, impersonation, job, mimesis, *partes,* performance, portrayal, province, realm, representation, responsibility, task, undertaking

PART *(Leave),* ***verb*** be gone, break away, defect, depart, escape, evacuate, get away from, go, go away, go forth, march off, migrate, move away, move out, quit, remove, retire, retreat, separate oneself from, set off, set out, take leave, take one's departure, tear oneself away, withdraw

PART *(Separate),* ***verb*** be severed, be sundered, bifurcate, break, carve, compartmentalize, cut in two, detach, disassociate, disconnect, disengage, disentangle, disjoin, dismember, dissever, dissociate, dissolve, disunite, divide, *dividere,* fissure, halve, isolate, keep apart, parcel, *partiri,* partition, portion, section, *separare,* sever, sort out, split, stand between, subdivide, sunder, tear assunder, undo, unloose

PART WITH, *verb* award, bequeath, bestow, cede, contribute, confer, depart, dispense with, dispose of, donate, get away from, gift, give away, give up, grant, impart with, leave, separate from, pass, transfer, turn over, will

PARTAKE, *verb* accept, be a party to, experience, have a hand in, have a portion of, have a share of, lend oneself to, participate, receive, sample, savor, share, share in, take, take a share of, take an active part in, take part in, taste

PARTIAL *(Biased),* ***adjective*** bigoted, *cupidus,* discriminatory, favorably disposed, inclined, influenced, *iniquus,* interested, jaundiced, narrow-minded, one-sided, partisan, predisposed, prejudiced, prepossessed, prone, restricted, *studiosus,* subjective, swayed, unbalanced, unequal, uneven, unfair, unjust, unjustified, unreasonable
ASSOCIATED CONCEPTS: partial acceptance, partial delivery, partial performance, partial restraint, partial summary judgment

PARTIAL *(Part),* ***adjective*** apart, confined, divided, divisible, factional, fragmentary, incomplete, limited, narrow, not complete, not completed, *partim,* sectional, split, uncompleted, unfinished, unperformed, wanting

PARTIAL *(Relating to a part),* ***adjective*** abridged, deficient, divided, divisible, fractional, fragmentary, imperfect, incomplete, inexact, insufficient, limited, *partim,* scanty, sectional, segmental, sketchy, uncompleted, undeveloped, unfinalized, unfinished, unperfected, unthorough, wanting
ASSOCIATED CONCEPTS: partial payment, partial summary judgment

PARTIALITY, *noun* affinity, attachment, attraction, bent, bias, biased judgment, discrimination, favor, favoritism, fondness, inclination, *iniquitas,* injustice, intolerance, leaning, liking, one-sidedness, partisanship, penchant, preconception, predilection, predisposition, preference, preferential treatment, prejudgment, prejudice, prepossession, proclivity, propensity, taste

PARTICIPANT, *noun* abettor, accessory, accomplice, adjuvant, aid, ally, assistant, associate, attendant, auxiliary, coadjutor, collaborator, colleague, comate, companion, comrade, confederate, cooperator, copartner, coworker, fellow, fellow worker, helper, mate, partaker, *particeps,* participator, partner, party, shareholder, sharer
ASSOCIATED CONCEPTS: participant in a crime

PARTICIPATE, *verb* act in concert, act together, affiliate with, aid, associate, be a party to, be in league with, be involved, become involved with, collaborate, compete, confederate, *consortem,* contribute, cooperate, engage, engage in, enter into, *esse participem,* get in the act, go along with, have a hand in, have a part in, have a part of, have a share of, join, join forces, join in, join in partnership with, partake, play a part in, share, share in, take a part in, take a part of, take an active part in, take an interest in, take part, undertake, unite efforts with, unite with, work together
ASSOCIATED CONCEPTS: participate in a business venture, participate in a conspiracy, participate in a crime, participate in a labor dispute

PARTICIPATION, *noun* assistance, association, attendance, camaraderie, companionship, concurrence, conjunction, connection, cooperation, fellowship, help, kinship, league, membership, partnership, relation, support, union

PARTICLE, *noun* atom, bit, component part, crumb, cutting, fragment, grain, granule, hint, mite, modicum, moiety, molecule, morsel, piece, pittance, point, scintilla, snippet, speck, spot, suggestion, trace

PARTICULAR *(Exacting),* ***adjective*** accurate, astringent, attentive, attentive to detail, careful, choosy, conscientious, critical, *delicatus,* demanding, difficult to please, discriminating, discriminative, *elegans,* epicurean, excessively critical, exigent, fastidious, faultfinding, finical, finicky, fussy, hairsplitting, hard to please, heedful, hypercritical, inflexible, meticulous, mindful, overconscientious, overcritical, overfastidious, overmeticulous, painstaking, persnickety, picky, precise, punctilious, quality-minded, querulous, regardful, rigid, rigorous, scrupulous, selective, stern, strict, stringent, thorough, thoroughgoing, uncompromising, unyielding

PARTICULAR *(Individual),* ***adjective*** characteristic, definite, distinct, distinctive, distinguished, especial, exclusive, original, own, peculiar, personal, respective, separate, single, singular, special, specific, unique, unusual
ASSOCIATED CONCEPTS: particular gift, particular purpose
FOREIGN PHRASES: ***Generale tantum valet in generalibus, quantum singulare in singulis.*** That which is general prevails in general matters, as that which is particular prevails in particular matters.

PARTICULAR *(Specific),* ***adjective*** characteristic, chosen, differential, differentiated, distinct, distinctive, distinguishable, distinguished, eccentric, especial, exceptional, express, extraordinary, idiosyncratic, individual, marked, noteworthy, odd, outstanding, peculiar, prominent, *proprius,* select, selected, separate, *separatus,* signal, single, singular, special, striking, uncommon, unique, unmistakable, unusual

PARTICULAR, *noun* article, aspect, case, circumstance, detail, event, experience, fact, feature, incident, incidental, instance, item, item of information, matter, minutia, occasion, occurrence, particularity, piece of information, point, punctilio, respect, single case, special point, specific, specification
ASSOCIATED CONCEPTS: bill of particulars

PARTICULARITY, *noun* care, carefulness, characteristic, characteristic quality, circumstantiality, conscientiousness, criticalness, detail, discriminatingness, discrimination, distinctive feature, exactingness, exactitude, exactness, fastidiousness, feature, finicality, finicalness, fussiness, individuality, item, lineament, mark, meticulousness, minute circumstance, minuteness, particularness, perfectionism, preciseness, precision, punctiliousness, rigidness, scrupulosity, scrupulousness, selectiveness, singleness, singularity, special point, specific quality, strictness, trait, uniqueness

PARTICULARLY, *adverb* above all, chiefly, distinctly, eminently, especially, expressly, extraordinally, individually, inordinately, mainly, markedly, *maxime,* notably, observably, peculiarly, *praecipue, praesertim,* preeminently, primarily, principally, prominently, remarkably, signally, singularly, specially, specifically, strikingly, supremely, uncommonly, uncustomarily, unfamiliarly, uniquely, unusually

PARTISAN, *adjective* biased, clannish, cliquish, denominational, devoted, factional, factionary, fanatic, *fautor, homo studiosus,* influenced, leagued, partial, predisposed, sectarian, swayed, undetached, undispassionate

PARTISAN, *noun* adherent, advocate, ally, apostle, backer, believer, champion, comrade, confederate, copartner, coworker, defender, devotee, disciple, encourager, enthusiast, favorer, fellow worker, follower, friend, hanger-on, mainstay, maintainer, participant, partner, party-liner, party member, patron, promoter, proselyte, satellite, seconder, sectarian, sectary, sponsor, support, supporter, sustainer, sympathizer, upholder, votary, zealot, zealotist
ASSOCIATED CONCEPTS: discrimination, partisan motives

PARTISANSHIP, *noun* advocacy, blind allegiance, blind sponsor, blind support, blind sympathy, proselytism, sectarian allegiance, unfair allegiance, unjust allegiance, zealotry
ASSOCIATED CONCEPTS: election law

PARTITION, *verb* allocate, allot, apportion, break up, carve, compartmentalize, cut up, dissect, distribute, divide, divide into distinct portions, divide into portions, divide into shares, divide proportionately, divide up, dole out, form into classes, group, mete, mete out, parcel out, pigeonhole, place in a category, portion, portion out, prorate, section, sectionalize, segment, sever, sever the unity of possession, share, split up, subdivide
ASSOCIATED CONCEPTS: partition property

PARTNER, *noun* abettor, accessory, accomplice, adjutant, adjutor, adjuvant, aid, aider, ally, assistant, associate, coadjutant, coadjutor, cohelper, collaborator, colluder, comate, companion, compeer, confederate, consociate, cooperator, coowner, copartner, coworker, fellow worker, helper, member of a partnership, partaker, *particeps,* participant, participator, sharer, teammate, teamworker, workfellow
ASSOCIATED CONCEPTS: equal partner, general partner, limited partner, managing partner, nominal partner, partner in crime, silent partner, surviving partner
FOREIGN PHRASES: ***Cum aliquis renunciaverit societati, solvitur societas.*** When any partner renounces the partnership, the partnership is dissolved. ***Socii mei socius meus socius non est.*** The partner of my partner is not my partner.

PARTNERSHIP, *noun* alliance, association, coalition, combination, concord, confederacy, confederation, conjunction, connection, consociation, *consortio,* consortium, cooperation, cooperative society, copartnership, federation, fellowship, firm, guild, joint interest, league, legal entity, mutual company, participation, pool, *societas,* sodality, syndicate
ASSOCIATED CONCEPTS: commercial partnership, copartnership, corporation, dissolution of partnership, general

partnership, joint enterprise, joint venture, limited partnership, partnership agreement, partnership assets, partnership at will, partnership debts, partnership for a single transaction, partnership property, professional partnership, silent partner, special partnership, voluntary association
FOREIGN PHRASES: ***Nemo debet in communione invitus teneri.*** No one should be retained in a partnership against his will. ***Si alicujus rei societas sit et finis negotio impositus est, finitus societas.*** If there is a partnership in any matter and the business is concluded, the partnership is ended.

PARTY *(Litigant),* ***noun*** adversary, appellant, appellee, challenger, charger, claimant, complainant, contender, contestant, controversialist, defendant, disputant, intervener, libelant, opposing party, petitioner, plaintiff, respondent, suitor
ASSOCIATED CONCEPTS: adverse party, defect in parties, disinterested party, indispensable party, jurisdiction of parties, material party, mutuality of parties, necessary parties, nominal party, nonjoinder of parties, opposing party, party in practice, prevailing party, proper party, real party in interest, substantial party
FOREIGN PHRASES: ***Saepe constitutum est, res inter alios judicatas aliis non praejudicare.*** It has often been decided that matters adjudged between others ought not to prejudice those who are not parties.

PARTY *(Participant),* ***noun*** attendant, cooperator, member, partaker, participator, partisan, partner, sharer
ASSOCIATED CONCEPTS: accommodation party, competent party, guilty party, injured party, innocent party, real party in interest, third party

PARTY *(Political organization),* ***noun*** association, body, caucus, club, coalition, combine, confederation, faction, group, league, lobby, organized group, party machine, political machine

PASS *(Advance),* ***verb*** *abalienatio,* award, bequeath, cede, change, change ownership, communicate, confer ownership, continue, convey, cross, deliver over, devolve, endow, flow, go, go by, go on, go past, proceed, progress, relay, remise, transfer ownership, transfer title, *transgredi, transire,* transmit, transpire
ASSOCIATED CONCEPTS: pass by will, pass title

PASS *(Approve),* ***verb*** accede to, accept, acquiesce, adopt, advocate, affirm, agree to, allow, approbate, assent, authorize, be in favor of, carry, confirm, consent, declare lawful, decree, dictate, enact, endorse, establish, establish by law, favor, give approval, give legislative sanction to, institute, institute by law, legalize, legislate, legitimize, make into law, make legal, ordain, ordain by law, prescribe, put in force, put into effect, put through, ratify, sanction, support, sustain, uphold, validate, vote favorably, vote in
ASSOCIATED CONCEPTS: pass a law

PASS *(Determine),* ***verb*** announce, decide, declare, decree, deliver, deliver a judgment, determine, enunciate, give an opinion, impart, ordain, present, pronounce, pronounce judgment, put forth, render a decision, render a judgment, rule, set forth
ASSOCIATED CONCEPTS: pass judgment

PASS *(Satisfy requirements),* ***verb*** accomplish, achieve, *approbare,* attain, be accepted, be graduated, be promoted, be successful, be victorious, come up to the standard, conform to, conquer, do well, earn, finish, fulfill, get by, get through, make one's mark, master, meet requirements, prevail, qualify, reach, realize, satisfy requirements, stand the test, succeed, triumph

PASS AWAY, ***verb*** break down, decease, demise, depart, die, end, expire, fade, fall, flatline, give out, part, pass on, perish, quit, succumb

PASS JUDGMENT, ***verb*** adjudge, adjudicate, administrator, arbitrate, ascertain, assess, compromise, conclude, decide, decree, declare, deliver, determine, dispense justice, draw a conclusion, establish, find, hold, interpret, judge, moderate, negotiate, officially act, order, referee, resolve, rule, umpire

PASS UP, ***verb*** abandon, abdicate, abjure, abstain, avoid, cease, cede, deny oneself, desist from, dispense with, disposed of, do without, drop, eschew, fast, forbear, forfeit, forgo, forswear, give up, give up on, go without, hold back, hold off, lay down, leave off, let alone, make do without, not use, refrain, release, relinquish, renounce, reserve, resign, sacrifice, shun, surrender, waive, withhold, write off, yield, yield up
ASSOCIATED CONCEPTS: forgo interest owed, forgo opportunity

PASSABLE, ***adjective*** acceptable, accessible, achievable, admissible, allowable, approachable, bearable, beaten, broad, capable of passing, clear, crossable, easy, fair, fit for travel, fordable, free, mediocre, middling, moderate, navigable, open, ordinary, penetrable, pervious, presentable, pretty good, reachable, realizable, receivable, serviceable, tolerable, travelable, traveled, traversable, unimpeded, unobstructed, usable, within reach

PASSION, ***noun*** agitation, anger, ardency, ardor, avidity, craze, desire, eagerness, ecstasy, emotion, eruption, excitability, excitement, explosion, fanaticism, feeling, ferment, fervency, fervor, fierceness, fire, frenzy, furor, fury, glow, gusto, heat, hunger, impetuosity, impulse, infatuation, intensity, intoxication, ire, irresistible urge, itch, lust, mania, rabidity, rage, rampage, rampancy, rapture, storm, strong feeling, temper, thrill, transport, vehemence, vehement desire, verve, violence, violent anger, wrath, zeal
ASSOCIATED CONCEPTS: heat of passion

PASSIVE, ***adjective*** acquiescent, amenable, apathetic, calm, compliable, compliant, complying, concessive, conformable, docile, dormant, duteous, dutiful, enduring, feeble, flexible, forbearant, heedless, indifferent, indolent, influenced, irresolute, lamblike, languorous, malleable, nonresistant, nonresisting, obedient, obeisant, obsequious, otiose, phlegmatic, pliable, pliant, quiescent, receptive, recumbent, resigned, resistless, restrained, sequacious, servile, subdued, subject, submissive, subordinate, subservient, supine, supple, tame, tractable, unassertive, undemonstrative, unopposing, unresistant, unresisting, yielding
ASSOCIATED CONCEPTS: passive negligence, passive tortfeasor

PAST, ***adjective*** ancient, antediluvian, antiquated, archaic, back, defunct, departed, elapsed, expired, forgotten, former, gone, gone by, historical, irrecoverable, lapsed, last, late, lost, no longer functioning, obsolete, old, outdated, outmoded, over, passed, previous, prior, quondam, retired, unrecollected, unremembered
ASSOCIATED CONCEPTS: past consideration, past recollection

PAST, ***noun*** ancient times, antecedence, anteriority, antiquity, history, former time, former times, long ago, past times, preexistence, previous time, previousness, retrospection, the past, times past

PAST DUE, *adverb* in arrears, in debt, in default, outstanding, overdrawn, overdue

PATENT, *adjective* *apertus,* apparent, *clarus,* clear, conspicuous, disclosed, discoverable, easy to be seen, evident, exposed, exposed to view, free to all, glaring, in full view, in view, individual, manifest, *manifestus,* noticeable, observable, obvious, open, ostensible, overt, perceivable, perceptible, perspicuous, plain, plain to be seen, prominent, public, published, revealed, standing out, uncamouflaged, unconcealed, undisguised, unhidden, unmasked, unobstructed, unshaded, unusual, visible, wide-open
ASSOCIATED CONCEPTS: patent ambiguity, patent danger, patent defect, patent error

PATENT, *noun* certificate of invention, *diplomatis,* exclusive license, exclusive privilege, exclusive right, exclusive title, governmental grant, grant, grant of authority, legal right, license, permit, privilege, right, right to profits accruing, use and title
ASSOCIATED CONCEPTS: assignment of a patent, infringement of a patent, patent license, patent right

PATERNAL, *adjective* ancestral, benevolent, benign, family, fatherlike, fatherly, kindly, parental, patriarchal, patrimonial, protective

PATERNITY, *noun* ancestry, derivation, descent, fatherhood, fathership, lineage, male parentage, origin, parentage, paternal parentage, progenitorship
ASSOCIATED CONCEPTS: paternity proceeding
FOREIGN PHRASES: ***Filiatio non potest probari.*** Filiation cannot be proved. ***Pater est quem nuptiae demonstrant.*** He is the father whom the marriage points out.

PATH, *noun* access, access path, access road, approach, avenue, channel, course, device, entrance, easement, footpath, ingress, means, method, passage, passageway, pathway, right of way, road, roadway, route, street, trail, walkway, way

PATIENCE *(Composure),* ***noun*** acceptance, calm, composure, condonation, ease, equanimity, even temper, forbearance, forgiveness, imperturbability, indulgence, lenience, leniency, longanimity, moderation, passiveness, passivity, placidity, poise, refusal to be provoked, resignation, self-control, self-possession, serenity, stoicism, sufferance, temperament, temperance, tolerance, tranquility, understanding

PATIENCE *(Indefatigability),* ***noun*** assiduousness, determination, diligence, firmness, persistence, pertinacity, quiet perseverance, sedulity, staying power, tenacity of purpose

PATIENT, *adjective* acquiescent, agreeable, assiduous, calm, compliant, composed, constant, continuing, controlled, decided, determined, diligent, docile, dogged, dutiful, easygoing, enduring, firm, forbearing, forgiving, hard working, imperturbable, indefatigable, indulgent, lamblike, levelheaded, long-suffering, longanimous, meek, mild, mild-tempered, nonresisting, pacific, passive, *patiens,* peaceable, perseverant, persevering, persistent, persisting, pertinacious, philosophic, placid, pliant, plodding, quiescent, quiet, quietly persevering, reconciled, relentless, resigned, resolute, resolved, restrained, sedulous, self-controlled, serene, steadfast, steady, stoic, stoical, submissive, sympathetic, tenacious, *tolerans,* tolerant, tractable, tranquil, unceasing, unchangeable, uncomplaining, uncompromising, undaunted, understanding, undeviating, undiscouraged, undisturbed, unfaltering, unflagging, unflinching, unmurmuring, unperturbed, unrelaxing, unrelenting, unremitting, unresisting, unruffled, unshaken, unswerving, untiring, unvexed, unwavering, unwearied, unwearying, unyielding, yielding

PATIENT, *noun* *aeger, aegrotus,* case, convalescent, convalescent case, hospital case, hospitalized person, ill individual, inmate, invalid, medical case, one seeking cure, one seeking relief, one undergoing therapy, one undergoing treatment, shut-in, sick individual, sick person, sickling, victim
ASSOCIATED CONCEPTS: doctor-patient privilege

PATROL, *verb* attend, be on the alert, be on the lookout, be on the watch, *circumire,* cover, cover a beat, go the rounds, guard, inspect, keep an eye on, keep guard, keep in view, keep vigil, keep watch, look out, march, monitor, observe, overlook, pace, perform sentry duty, police, protect, reconnoiter, safeguard, scan, scout, stand guard, stand sentinel, superintend, sweep through, traverse, walk, walk a beat, watch

PATRON *(Influential supporter),* ***noun*** advocate, backer, benefactor, champion, defender, endorser, favorer, financer, friend, guardian, helper, influential sponsor, investor, leader, patronus, philanthropist, promoter, sponsor, supporter, upholder

PATRON *(Regular customer),* ***noun*** business contact, buyer, client, *consultor,* consumer, customer, *emptor,* frequenter, patronizer, prospective buyer, purchaser, shopper, supporter, vendee

PATRONAGE *(Power to appoint jobs),* ***noun*** advantage, assistance, *auctoritas,* authority, backing, choice, control, controlling power, directing agency, dominance, domination, *favor,* good offices, *gratia, indulgentia,* influence, influentiality, *patrocinium,* persuasion, position of influence, power, *praesidium,* predominance, preference, right of choice, selection, sway

PATRONAGE *(Support),* ***noun*** aid, assistance, backing, care, commendation, commercial backing, cordial assistance, countenance, encouragement, favor, friendly interest, friendship, guardianship, guidance, help, influence, interest, protection, protectorship, recommendation, special privileges, sponsorship, support, tutelage

PATRONIZE *(Condescend toward),* ***verb*** assume a lofty bearing, deign, favor, grant, indulge, look down on, lower oneself, oblige, talk down to, treat in a condescending way, vouchsafe

PATRONIZE *(Trade with),* ***verb*** be a customer of, buy from, deal with, do business with, *favere,* favor with one's patronage, frequent, frequent as a customer, have dealings with, purchase from, shop at, shop with, support, traffic with, transact business with, transact with, use

PATTERN, *noun* antetype, archetype, basis, criterion, design, die, draft, example, *exemplar, exemplum,* form, guide, ideal, impression, layout, matrix, model, mold, norm, original, outline, paradigm, paragon, plan, precedent, prototype, rule, sample, shape, specifications, *specimen,* standard, standard of criticism, standard of judgment, template, tracing
ASSOCIATED CONCEPTS: pattern jury instructions

PAUCITY, *noun* absence, bare subsistence, dearth, deficiency, deprivation, destitution, drought, exigency, exiguity, famine, fewness, finite quantity, fraction, inadequacy, infrequency, insufficiency, lack, limited amount, minimum, minority, modicum, need, *paucitas,* pittance, poverty, privation, rareness, scantiness, scantness, scarceness, scarcity, shortage, small number, small quantity, sparseness, sparsity, thinness, trickle, trifle, uncommonness, want

PAUSE, *noun* abeyance, armistice, break, breather, breathing spell, cessation, deferment, delay, demur, demurral, disconnection, gap, halt, hesitance, hesitancy, hesitation, *intercapedo,* interim, interlude, *intermissio,* intermission, interruption, interval, *intervallum,* intervening period, lag, letup, lull, moratorium, procrastination, recess, relaxation, remission, respite, rest, rest period, space, standstill, stay, stillness, stoppage, suspension, time out, truce, vacation

PAUSE, *verb* be dubious, be irresolute, be uncertain, bide time, break, breathe, cast anchor, cease, come to a standstill, consider, dally, dawdle, delay, deliberate, demur, desist, discontinue, dwell, forbear, halt, hang back, hesitate, hold back, hold off, intermit, *intermittere,* interrupt, linger, loiter, mark time, *morari,* put off, reflect, repose, rest, slacken, stall, stand still, stay, stop and consider, straddle, suspend, take a breather, take time out, tarry, think over, think twice, vacillate, wait, waver, weigh

PAWN, *verb* bond, deposit, deposit as collateral, deposit as security, give as security, give in earnest, guarantee, hypothecate, impignorate, mortgage, offer collateral, *pignerare,* pledge, post, put at hazard, put at stake, put in pledge, risk, stake, wager

PAY, *noun* allowance, award, compensation, consideration, defrayal, defrayment, earnings, emolument, fee, grant, hire, income, indemnity, meed, *merces,* monetary return, payment, perquisite, profit, reckoning, recompense, reimbursement, remittance, remuneration, repayment, return, revenue, reward, salary, settlement, solatium, stipend, *stipendium,* support, wages

PAY, *verb* acquit, adjust, award, be a good investment, be profitable, bear the cost, clear, compensate, contribute, defray, deposit, disburse, discharge a debt, expend, finance, foot, give payment, hand over, honor, indemnify, liquidate, make a good return, make compensation, make good, make payment, make restitution, meet, *numerare, pendere,* present, quit, ransom, reckon with, recompense, reimburse, remunerate, render, reward, satisfy, settle, spend, square, square accounts, subsidize, support, tender

PAY DAMAGES, *verb* award damages, conclude, finalize, indemnify, make restitution, make whole, pay for injuries sustained, pay for losses sustained, pay for the losses, pay just compensation, pay the value of a case, recompense, remunerate, resolve, restitution, restoration, settle
ASSOCIATED CONCEPTS: pay damages for defrauding investors

PAYABLE, *adjective* collectable, due, justly claimable, mature, maturing, outstanding, owing, redeemable, uncollected, unpaid, unsatisfied, unsettled
ASSOCIATED CONCEPTS: accounts payable, bills payable, due and payable, payable to bearer, payable upon demand, sum payable

PAYEE, *noun* acceptor, assignee, consignee, devisee, donee, drawer, endorsee, grantee, recipient, taker, transferee

PAYMENT *(Act of paying),* ***noun*** acquittal, acquittance, amortization, amortizement, clearance, compensation, defrayal, defrayment, disbursement, discharge of a debt, expenditure, liquidation, outlay, quittance, receipt in full, reckoning, recompense, reimbursement, remittance, restitution, return, satisfaction, settlement, spending, subsidy

PAYMENT *(Remittance),* ***noun*** allotment, allowance, amount, charge, compensation, consideration, earnings, emolument, expenditure, expense, fee, gratuity, guerdon, honorarium, indemnification, indemnity, money, pay, premium, quittance, recompense, reimbursement, remittance, remuneration, reparation, restitution, salary, solatium, stipend, tribute, wage
FOREIGN PHRASES: ***In satisfactionibus non permittitur amplius fieri quam semel factum est.*** In settlements, more must not be received than was received once for all. ***Reprobata pecunia liberat solventem.*** Money refused releases the debtor. ***Quicquid solvitur, solvitur secundum modum solventis; quicquid recipitur, recipitur secundum modum recipientis.*** Whatever money is paid, is paid according to the direction of the payor; whatever money is received, is received according to that of the recipient. ***Qui ignorat quantum solvere debeat, non potest improbus videre.*** He who does not know how much he ought to pay, cannot seem dishonest. ***Jus non patitur ut idem bis solvatur.*** Law does not suffer the same thing to be twice paid. ***Bona fides non patitur ut bis idem exigatur.*** Good faith does not allow us to demand the payment of the same thing twice.

PAYOFF *(Payment in full),* ***noun*** discharge, payout, satisfaction in full, settlement

PAYOFF *(Result),* ***noun*** closure, conclusion, consummation, determination, end, finale, finish

PAYROLL, *noun* allowance, compensation, disbursement of salary, employees' earnings, employees' salaries, labor expense, list of paid employees, list of salaried employees, list of wages to be paid out, payment, payment for services, recompense, remuneration, salary, stipend, wages
ASSOCIATED CONCEPTS: certification payroll, payroll check-off system, payroll deduction, payroll tax

PEACE, *noun* accord, adjustment of differences, agreement, alliance, amity, armistice, brotherhood, calm, calmness, coexistence, community of interests, conciliation, concord, concordance, concordancy, *concordia,* consentaneity, consentaneousness, cooperation, end of hostilities, fellowship, fraternalism, freedom from war, friendliness, friendship, good will, harmoniousness, harmony, hush, law and order, lull, neutrality, oneness, order, orderliness, *otium,* pacification, pact, *pax,* quiescence, quiet, quietness, rapport, reconciliation, repose, serenity, silence, stillness, suspension of hostilities, tranquility, treaty, truce, unanimity, unity
ASSOCIATED CONCEPTS: breach of the peace, disturbing the peace, peace officer
FOREIGN PHRASES: ***Paci sunt maxime contraria vis et injuria.*** Violence and injury are especially hostile to peace.

PEACE OFFICER, *noun* arm of the law, civil officer, constable, custodian of the law, detective, guard, guardian of the peace, law enforcement agent, law officer, member of the police force, officer, officer of the law, patrolman, police, police constable, police officer, policeman, policewoman, protector, security officer, sheriff

PEACEABLE, ***adjective*** agreeable, amiable, amicable, bloodless, calm, composed, contented, disposed to peace, easygoing, equable, forgiving, free from war, friendly, gentle, good-tempered, halcyon, halcyonian, imperturbable, inoffensive, kindly, lamblike, mild, moderate, neutral, noncombative, orderly, pacific, pacificatory, pacifistic, patient, peace-loving, peaceful, peacelike, *placabilis,* placid, *placidus,* quiescent, quiet, reasonable, restrained, satisfied, sedate, serene, slow to take offense, sober, still, tame, temperate, tolerant, tranquil, unagitated, unanxious, unbellicose, unbelligerent, uncontentious, undisturbed, unexcitable, unexcited, unmilitant, unmoved, unpugnacious, unresisting, unruffled, untroubled, well-disposed

PECCABLE, ***adjective*** bad, below par, blamable, blameworthy, censurable, culpable, defective, erring, exceptionable, fallen, fallible, faulty, flawed, guilty, illaudable, imperfect, inadequate, iniquitous, lacking, lax, less than perfect, liable to err, liable to sin, objectionable, recreant, reprehensible, reprobate, tainted, twisted, unchaste, uncommendable, unheroic, unprincipled, unrighteous, unsound, unstable, unvirtuous, virtueless, warped, wayward

PECCANT *(Culpable),* ***adjective*** aberrant, accursed, accusable, amoral, astray, bad, base, blameful, blameworthy, censurable, chargeable, criminal, criminous, debauched, dishonest, erroneous, evil, execrable, faultful, fiendish, foul, full of mischief, guilty, guilty of transgression, heinous, illegal, immoral, impious, incorrigible, inexcusable, inexpiable, infamous, iniquitous, intolerable, maleficent, maleficial, meriting blame, mischievous, naughty, nefarious, offensive, *peccans,* reprehensible, reprobate, scandalous, shameful, sinful, transgressing, trespassing, unforgivable, unjust, unjustifiable, unpardonable, unprincipled, unrighteous, unscrupulous, unvirtuous, unworthy, vicious, vile, villainous, wicked, without excuse, wretched, wrong, wrongful

PECCANT *(Unhealthy),* ***adjective*** afflicting, contaminated, corroding, corrosive, dangerous, deadly, deleterious, detrimental, disadvantageous, diseased, disserviceable, envenomed, *gravis,* harmful, injurious, insalubrious, *insalubris,* lethal, malefic, maleficent, malignant, miasmal, morbid, morbific, nocuous, noisome, noxious, perilous, pestilent, poisoned, poisonous, septic, tainted, toxic, unfavorable to health, unhygienic, unwholesome, venomous, virulent

PECULATE, ***verb*** appropriate criminally, appropriate dishonestly, appropriate illegally, appropriate wrongfully, bilk, cheat, cozen, deceive, defraud, divert, embezzle, misappropriate, mulct, obtain money on false pretenses, obtain under false pretenses, pilfer, purloin, rob, steal, swindle

PECULATION, ***noun*** bad repute, defalcation, embezzlement, fraud, larceny, misapplication, misappropriation, misuse, pilferage, pilfering, purloining, skimming, theft, thieving

PECULIAR *(Curious),* ***adjective*** aberrant, abnormal, abnormous, alien, anomalistic, anomalistical, anomalous, astonishing, bizarre, breaking with tradition, eccentric, foreign, inexplicable, irregular, little-known, mysterious, mystifying, odd, out of place, out of the ordinary, out of the way, outlandish, perplexing, preternatural, puzzling, queer, rare, remarkable, signal, singular, startling, strange, supernatural, surprising, unaccountable, unaccustomed, unclassified, unconformable, unconventional, uncustomary, unexampled, unexpected, unfamiliar, unheard of, unimaginable, unnatural, unorthodox, weird

PECULIAR *(Distinctive),* ***adjective*** atypical, characteristic, contrasted, contrasting, contrastive, deviating, different, differentiated, differing, disagreeing, discordant, discrepant, disparate, dissimilar, dissonant, distinct, distinguishable, distinguished, divergent, exceptional, extraordinary, idiosyncratic, in a different class, inconformable, incongruent, incongruous, individual, marked, noteworthy, original, out of the ordinary, particular, separated, singular, special, uncommon, unconformable, unconforming, unequal, unimitated, unique, unlike, unusual, variant

PECULIARITY, ***adjective*** atypical, characteristic, contrasted, contrasting, contrastive, deviating, different, differentiated, differing, disagreeing, discordant, discrepant, disparate, dissimilar, dissonant, distinct, distinctive, distinguishable, distinguished, divergent, exceptional, extraordinary, idiosyncratic, in a different class, incongruent, incongruous, individual, marked, one-of-a-kind, original, particular, singular, special, uncommon, unconformable, unequal, unique, unlike all others, unusual, variant
ASSOCIATED CONCEPTS: peculiar susceptibilities

PECUNIARY, ***adjective*** budgetary, economic, economical, fiducial, fiduciary, financial, fiscal, monetary, numismatical, nummary, *pecuniarius,* sumptuary
ASSOCIATED CONCEPTS: pecuniary advantage, pecuniary damages, pecuniary gain, pecuniary injury, pecuniary interest, pecuniary legacy, pecuniary loss, pecuniary profit

PEDAGOGIC, ***adjective*** admonishing, admonitory, advisory, cautionary, didactic, dogmatic, educational, enlightening, holier-than-thou, instructive, moralistic, moralizing, preachy, prescriptive, self-righteous, sententious

PEDAGOGUE, ***noun*** academician, advisor, classmaster, don, educator, expounder, faculty member, governor, guide, headmaster, inculcator, instructor, learned man, lecturer, *magister,* man of letters, master, preceptor, professor, sage, scholar, schoolman, schoolmaster, schoolteacher, teacher, trainer, tutor

PEDANT, ***noun*** affecter, bluffer, closed-minded person, dogmatist, narrow-minded person, opinionated person, philosophaster, pretender, sciolist

PEDANTIC, ***adjective*** abstruse, academic, affected, arid, bombastic, didactic, doctrinaire, donnish, egotistic, erudite, excessive moralizing, formal, fussy, grandiloquent, inflated, magniloquent, pompous, punctilious, recondite, rhetorical, stilted

PEDESTRIAN, ***adjective*** arid, banal, barren, boresome, boring, characterless, cold, colorless, commonplace, dead, deadly, diffuse, drab, drearisome, dreary, dry, dull, flat, graceless, hackneyed, heavy, humorless, inelegant, inferior, insipid, jejune, lifeless, meaningless, mediocre, monotonous, ordinary, plain, platitudinous, plodding, pointless, ponderous, prosaic, prosy, soporific, spiritless, stale, stodgy, stuffy, tame, tasteless, tedious, tiresome, trite, unamusing, uncaptivating, uncharming, unenlivened, unentertaining, unimaginative, uninspiring, uninteresting, uninventive, unlively, unoriginal, unpoetical, unreadable, unscintillating, unsparkling, unvaried, unvivid, unwitty, usual, wearisome

PEDESTRIAN, ***noun*** ambulator, foot passenger, foot traveler, marcher, peripatetic, roamer, rover, traveler afoot, walker

PEER, *noun* associate, coequal, companion, compeer, competitor, comrade, contemporary, contender, corrival, equal, equivalent, fellow, likeness, match, mate, opposite number, *par,* parallel, rival

PEJORATIVE, *adjective* abusive, acrimonious, belittling, blackening, calumnious, castigatory, censorious, critical, cynical, damaging, decrying, defamatory, denigrating, denunciatory, depreciative, depreciatory, derisive, derogative, derogatory, detracting, disapproving, discourteous, disdainful, disparaging, disrespectful, faultfinding, harsh, injurious, insulting, irreverent, scornful, severe, slighting, smearing, spiteful, uncomplimentary, underestimating, unflattering, venomous, vilifying, vituperative

PELLUCID, *adjective* apparent, clear, clear-cut, comprehensible, crystalline, diaphanous, disclosed, easy to understand, exoteric, explicit, express, hyaline, intelligible, limpid, lucid, manifest, obvious, overt, palpable, patent, *pellucidus,* plain, pure, recognizable, revealed, simple, straightforward, transparent, unambiguous, unconcealed, understandable, undisguised, unhidden, unquestionable

PENAL, *adjective* castigatory, containing a penalty, corrective, disciplinary, enacting punishment, inflictive, mulctuary, *poenalis,* prohibiting, punishing, punitive, punitory, relating to a penalty, retaliatory, retributive
ASSOCIATED CONCEPTS: penal action, penal bond, penal law, penal ordinances, penal statute
FOREIGN PHRASES: ***In haeredes non solent transire actiones quae poenales ex maleficio sunt.*** Actions which are penal and which arise out of anything of criminal nature do not pass to the heirs.

PENALIZE, *verb* amerce, avenge, bring to account, call to account, carry out a sentence, castigate, chastise, confiscate, correct, discipline, exact a penalty, exact retribution, execute a sentence, execute judgment, fine, forfeit, harm, hurt, impose a penalty, inflict a penalty, inflict punishment, mulct, punish, put at a disadvantage, rebuke, reprimand, reprove, retaliate, revenge, sentence, subject to a handicap, subject to penalty, subject to punishment, visit punishment

PENALTY, *noun* amercement, castigation, compulsory payment, cost, deprivation, disadvantage, disciplinary action, fine, forefeiture, forfeit, handicap, infliction, liability, loss, *multa,* onus, penal retribution, penance, *poena,* prescribed punishment, punishment, punishment fixed by law, punishment prescribed by law, reprisal, retributive justice, sconce, sentence
ASSOCIATED CONCEPTS: action for penalty, civil penalty, confiscatory penalty, criminal penalty, excessive penalty, penalty clause, penalty for forfeiture, subject to penalty
FOREIGN PHRASES: ***Quod a quoque poenae nomine exactum est id eidem restituere nemo cogitur.*** No one is compelled to restore that which has been exacted as a penalty.

PENALTY PHASE, *noun* postjudgment phase, postliability phase of trial, posttrial sentencing, punishment phase, sentencing in bifurcated trial

PENCHANT, *noun* affinity, appetite, ardor, attachment, attraction, bent, bias, capacity, competence, direction, disposition, eagerness, enthusiasm, fancy, fondness, gravitation, inborn ability, *inclinatio,* inclination, innate ability, leaning, liking, partiality, particular aptitude, passion, polarity, predilection, predisposition, preference, prejudice, proclivity, proneness, *propensio,* propension, propensity, relish, specialty, specific aptness, specific quality, talent, tendency, weakness

PENDENCY, *noun* abeyance, adjournment, break, cessation, continuance, discontinuity, halt, hiatus, interim, interlude, intermediate time, intermission, interregnum, interruption, interval, intervening period, lapse, lull, moratorium, pause, postponement, recess, respite, suspense, suspension, temporary stop
ASSOCIATED CONCEPTS: pendency of an action, pendency of an appeal

PENDENT, *adjective* additional, adjunct, adscititious, affinitive, allied to, ancillary, appurtenant, auxiliary, close, closely connected, cognate, collateral, complementary, congeneric, congenerical, congenerous, connatural, correspondent, corresponding, equivalent, *instar omnium,* matching, much the same, quasi, secondary, similar, something like, subsidiary, supplemental
ASSOCIATED CONCEPTS: pendent claim, pendent jurisdiction

PENDING *(Imminent),* ***adjective*** about to happen, anticipated, approaching, at hand, close, close at hand, coming, eventual, expectant, fearful, foreseen, foreshadowing, forthcoming, immediate, impending, instant, looming, minacious, momentary, near, ominous, on the horizon, oncoming, overhanging, prospective, threatening, upcoming
ASSOCIATED CONCEPTS: pending action, pending case, pending cause, pending claim, pending proceeding

PENDING *(Unresolved),* ***adjective*** in a state of uncertainty, in abeyance, in question, indefinite, indeterminate, open to discussion, open to question, still in debate, suspenseful, unascertained, uncertain, unclear, unconcluded, undecided, under consideration, undetermined, unfixed, unsettled, unsolved

PENETRABLE, *adjective* able to be pierced, absorbent, accessible, agape, ajar, assailable, attackable, conquerable, dehiscent, foraminated, foraminous, gaping, open, opened, passable, *penetrabilis,* perforable, perforated, permeable, pervious, *pervius,* porous, pregnable, receptive, riddled, susceptible, unclosed, vincible, vulnerable, wide open, yawning

PENETRATE, *verb* absorb, bore, break into, burst in upon, cut through, empierce, enter, erupt, fill, filter in, flow in, force a passage, give entrance to, go through, gore, imbrue, impale, impregnate, infiltrate, inflow, inject, insert, interfuse, lance, leak into, leaven, make a passage, osmose, overspread, pass, *penetrare,* perforate, permeate, pervade, *pervadere,* pierce, pour in, prick, probe, puncture, riddle, run through, saturate, seep in, sink in, skewer, slip into, soak through, spear, spike, stab, suffuse, tincture, transpierce, tunnel

PENITENT, *adjective* apologetic, atoning, awakened, chastened, compunctious, conciliatory, conscience-smitten, conscience-stricken, contrite, expiatory, full of regrets, humble, making amends, penitential, piacular, plagued by conscience, propiatory, purgatorial, reformed, regenerate, regretful, remorseful, repentant, rueful, self-accusing, self-condemned, self-convicted, self-reproachful, sobered, sorrowful, sorry

PENITENT, *noun* confessor, conscience-smitten person, conscience-stricken person, contrite person, penance

doer, reformed character, remorseful person, repentant person, shriver
ASSOCIATED CONCEPTS: priest-penitent privilege

PENITENTIARY, ***noun*** cell, detention camp, detention center, house of correction, house of detention, jail, jailhouse, lockup, penal colony, penal institution, penal settlement, place of confinement, place of detention, place of imprisonment, prison, prisonhouse, reformatory

PENSION, ***noun*** allotment, allowance, *annua,* annual allowance, annuity, compensation, emolument, endowment, fee, financial remuneration, grant, grant for support, grant in aid, payment, pecuniary aid, remittance, remuneration, retirement benefits, retirement income, specified income payable for life, stated maintenance, stipend, subsidization, subsidy, subvention, support
ASSOCIATED CONCEPTS: pension act, pension and benefit fund, pension benefits

PENSIVE, ***adjective*** absorbed, abstracted, attentive, calculating, concentrating, contemplative, deliberative, dreaming, dreamy, engrossed, full of thought, given to thought, *in cogitatione* defixus, introspective, meditative, museful, musing, obsessed, occupied, rapt, ratiocinative, ratiocinatory, reasoning, reflective, ruminant, ruminative, self-communing, serious, sober, speculative, studious, thoughtful, wistful

PENUMBRA, ***noun*** brink, cover, edge, fringe, margin, outskirt, reflection, shade, shadow
ASSOCIATED CONCEPTS: penumbra of a constitutional amendment

PENURIOUS, ***adjective*** chary, cheap, churlish, close, close-fisted, close-handed, frugal, greedy, grudging, illiberal, impoverished, in distress, in need, in want, indigent, mean, mercenary, miserly, needy, niggard, niggardly, nonpaying, parsimonious, penniless, petty, poverty-stricken, saving, selfish, shabby, sordid, sparing, stingy, tenax, ungenerous, unwilling to pay, venal

PEOPLE, ***noun*** citizenry, commonality, community, community at large, country, cultures, general public, humanity, inhabitants, multitude, nation, national group, nationality, persons, populace, population, race, society, state

PER ANNUM, ***adverb*** annually, at a fixed interval, on the anniversary, on the basis of a year, yearly

PER CAPITA, ad***verb*** allocated, an equal percentage, each to each, per head, percentage, pro rata, proportionately, respectively, share and share alike, to each according to his share

PER DIEM, ***preposition*** per day, for each and every day, for each day, for every day

PERAMBULATE, ***verb*** amble, circle, circumambulate, course, cover, cross, go around, go for a walk, go on an outing, go on foot, hike, jaunt, journey, make rounds, march, meander, pace, pass, pass through, patrol, pedestrianize, *peragrare,* peregrinate, *perlustrare, pervagari,* promenade, prowl, ramble, range, reconnoiter, roam, rove, saunter, scour, stalk, step, stride, stroll, strut, sweep through, take a constitutional, take a walk, take an airing, tour, tramp, travel, traverse, tread, trek, trudge, walk, walk through, wander

PERCEIVABLE, ***adjective*** apparent, appearing, appreciable, apprehensible, before one's eyes, beholdable, bold, clear, cognizable, detectable, discernible, disclosed, discoverable, distinct, distinguishable, easy to see, evident, exoteric, explicit, exposed, exposed to view, express, glaring, in evidence, in full view, in plain sight, in sight, in view, knowable, macroscopic, manifest, naked, notable, noticeable, observable, obvious, open, open to view, overt, palpable, patent, perceptible, perspicuous, plain, plain to be seen, prominent, recognizable, remarkable, revealed, salient, seeable, showing, sighted, tangible, transparent, unclouded, unconcealed, unhidden, unmistakable, viewable, visible, visual, well-defined, well-marked
ASSOCIATED CONCEPTS: last clear chance, latent defect, patent defect

PERCEIVE, ***verb*** apperceive, appreciate, apprehend, awaken, be acquainted with, be apprised of, be attentive to, be aware of, be cognizant of, be conscious of, be informed of, be sensitive to, become aware of, become conscious of, cognize, *cognoscere,* come to know, comprehend, detect, discern, discover, discriminate, distinguish, espy, experience, externalize, familiarize oneself, feel, gain insight into, give attention to, have cognizance of, have knowledge of, ken, know, learn, make out, mark, note, notice, observe, *percipere,* react, realize, recognize, regard, see, sense, *sentire,* take notice, understand, witness
ASSOCIATED CONCEPTS: perceive a product defect, perceive danger

PERCENTAGE, ***noun*** allotment, commission, contingent, factorage, fraction, interest, moiety, part, percent, portion, proportion, quota, rate per hundred, ratio, ration, share

PERCEPTIBLE, ***adjective*** apparent, apprehensible, ascertainable, beholdable, clear, clearly defined, clearly marked, cognizable, comprehensible, defined, detectable, discernible, disclosed, discoverable, distinct, distinguishable, easy to be seen, evident, explicit, exposed, exposed to view, express, glaring, in bold relief, in evidence, in full view, in plain sight, in sight, in view, indubitable, knowable, macroscopic, manifest, *manifestus,* marked, naked, notable, noticeable, observable, obvious, open, open to view, overt, palpable, patent, perceivable, perspicuous, plain, prominent, recognizable, revealed, salient, seeable, showing, shown, sighted, tangible, unconcealed, understandable, unhidden, unmistakable, viewable, visible, visual, well-defined, well-marked

PERCEPTION, ***noun*** ability to make distinctions, acuity, acumen, acuteness, apperception, appraisal, appreciation, apprehension, ascertainment, assessment, astuteness, attention, awareness, clear sight, cleverness, cognition, cognizance, comprehension, consciousness, deduction, detection, determination, discernment, discovery, discriminating judgment, discrimination, espial, estimate, evaluation, field of vision, finding, grasp, idea, image, impression, inkling, insight, *iudicium,* judgment, keen sight, keeness, mental image, mental impression, *mentis acies,* mindfulness, noesis, note, notice, notion, observation, penetration, percipience, perspicaciousness, perspicacity, point of view, quick sense, realization, recognition, regard, sagaciousness, sagacitas, sagacity, scrutiny, sense, sensibility, sensory experience, sharp sight, sharpness, shrewdness, sight, smartness, supposition, surmise, theory, understanding, view, viewpoint, visualization

PERCEPTIVE, ***adjective*** acute, apperceptive, apprehensive, astute, aware, cognitive, cognizant, comprehending, conscious, discerning, discriminating, discriminative, easily affected, feeling, impressible, impressionable, keen, knowing, mindful, percipient, perspicacious, quick of apprehension, receptive, responsive, sagax, sensible, sensitive, sentient, sharp, shrewd, understanding, wise

PERCIPIENT, ***adjective*** acquainted, acute, apperceptive, astute, au courant, bright, brilliant, circumspect, cognizant, conscious, discerning, discriminating, informed, keen, knowing, knowledgeable, perceptive, reasonable, supraliminal, understanding, vigilant, watchful

PEREMPTORY *(Absolute),* ***adjective*** actual, axiomatic, certain, complete, decided, decisive, definite, determinate, determined, express, final, imperious, implicit, incontrovertible, independent, overbearing, perfect, positive, real, resolute, resolved, self-existent, total, unalterable, unconditional, unconditioned, unequivocal, unlimited, unqualified, unquestionable, unrestricted, without limitation
ASSOCIATED CONCEPTS: peremptory adjournment, peremptory challenge, peremptory exception, peremptory plea, peremptory writ

PEREMPTORY *(Imperative),* ***adjective*** assertive, authoritative, commanding, compulsory, crucial, decisive, demanding, despotic, dictatorial, domineering, essential, exigent, firm, imperious, important, inexorable, inflexible, iron-handed, mandatory, necessary, obligatory, paramount, pressing, unavoidable, urgent
ASSOCIATED CONCEPTS: peremptory instruction

PEREMPTORY CHALLENGE, ***noun*** absolute challenge, arbitrary challenge, axiomatic challenge, certain challenge, challenge as of right, challenge within prerogative, conclusive challenge, decision challenge, discretionary challenge, final determining challenge, guaranteed challenge, objection as of right, positive challenge, rejection as of right, right to eliminate jurors, self-determined challenge, unperative challenge, unrestricted challenge
ASSOCIATED CONCEPTS: challenge for cause

PERFECT, ***adjective*** absolute, best, classic, consummate, excellent, exception, extraordinary, fabulous, faultless, fine, flawless, great, ideal, immaculate, impeccable, inerrant, infallible, irreproachable, masterly, prime, seamless, superb, ultimate, unblemished, uninjured

PERFECT, ***verb*** *absolvere,* accomplish, bring to a conclusion, bring to an end, bring to completion, bring to fullness, carry out, complete, conclude, consummate, correct, culminate, *cumulare,* effectuate, execute, finish, follow to a conclusion, *perficere,* refine
ASSOCIATED CONCEPTS: perfect a security interest, perfect an appeal, perfect a title

PERFECT STORM, ***noun*** apocalypse, Armageddon, calamity, cataclysm, catastrophe, disaster, eradication, extinction, great downfall, great misfortune, hardship, havoc, infliction, obliteration, upheaval, worst-case scenario

PERFECTION, ***noun*** accomplishment, achievement, attainment, climax, completeness, completion, consummation, correctness, crown, crowning point, culmination, development, effectuation, elaboration, entireness, exactitude, exactness, excellence, faultlessness, finish, flawlessness, fulfillment, fullness, goodness, height, highest degree of proficiency, idealization, impeccability, paragon, peak, pinnacle, pinpoint precision, preeminence, quintessence, realization, refinement, summit, superiority, transcendence, ultimate, wholeness
ASSOCIATED CONCEPTS: perfection of a lien

PERFERVID, ***adjective*** burning, exceedingly ardent, impassioned, on fire, overly passionate, too zealous

PERFIDIOUS, ***adjective*** base, betraying, cheating, conniving, corrupt, deceitful, deceiving, designing, dishonest, dishonorable, disloyal, disobedient, dissembling, double-crossing, double-dealing, faithless, false, falsehearted, fraudulent, guileful, hypocritical, inconstant, insidious, intriguing, knavish, lying, *perfidiosus, perfidus,* perjured, plotting, scheming, shifty, slippery, sneaking, sneaky, traitorous, treacherous, treasonable, treasonous, tricky, trothless, unconscionable, undependable, unfaithful, unprincipled, unreliable, unscrupulous, untrue, untrustworthy, untruthful, without honor

PERFIDY, ***noun*** adultery, betrayal, deceit, deception, disloyalty, double-crossing, double-dealing, faithlessness, falseness, falsity, inconstancy, lying, treachery, treason, unfaithfulness, unreliability, wickedness

PERFORM *(Adhere to),* ***verb*** abide by, achieve, be faithful to, carry into execution, carry out, cling to, complete, comply with, conclude, consummate, enact, end, enforce, execute, finish, fulfill, keep, keep one's word, observe, obtain, practice, put in force, put in practice, respect, satisfy, transact
ASSOCIATED CONCEPTS: perform a contract

PERFORM *(Execute),* ***verb*** accomplish, achieve, bring into operation, bring to pass, carry into execution, complete, discharge, discharge a duty, do, effect, effectuate, employ oneself, enact, function, *perficere,* perpetrate, pursue a course, put in force, serve, serve in the capacity of, take action, take steps, work

PERFORMANCE *(Execution),* ***noun*** accomplished fact, accomplishment, achievement, act, action, attainment, carrying into effect, carrying through, commission, completion, consummation, culmination, deed, enactment, finished product, fulfilment, implementation, operation, perpetration, production, realization, rendition, work
ASSOCIATED CONCEPTS: full performance, impossibility of performance, partial performance, performance bond, prevention of performance
FOREIGN PHRASES: ***Non quod dictum est, sed quod factum est inspicitur.*** Not what is said, but what is done, is to be regarded. ***Lex non cogit ad impossibilia.*** The law does not require the performance of the impossible.

PERFORMANCE *(Workmanship),* ***noun*** ability, accomplishment, achievement, action, aptitude, aptness, *ars,* art, artfulness, *artificium,* attainment, caliber, capability, capacity, competence, competency, composition, construction, craft, craftsmanship, creation, dexterity, effort, endowment, exhibition, expertness, faculty, finesse, formation, forte, handicraft, handiness, handiwork, ingenuity, manipulation, manufacture, mastership, mastery, operation, opus, play, preparation, production, proficiency, qualification, quality of execution, quality of work, representation, show, skill, skillfulness, talent, technique, virtuosity, work, working ability

PERFUNCTORY, ***adjective*** absent-minded, abstracted, apathetic, below par, careless, casual, cursory, deficient, disinterested, dispassionate, disregardful, failing, formal, half-hearted, hasty, heedless, hollow, hurried, ill-done, imperfect, inadequate, inattentive, incautious, incomplete, indifferent, inexact, insubstantial, lacking, lax, lenient, lukewarm, mechanical, mindless, needing, neglectful, negligent, offhand, omitting, passionless, poor, poorly done, quick, regardless, remiss, requiring, routine, rushed, short, sketchy, speedy, substandard, superficial, thoughtless, unattended to, uncaring, unconcerned, undiscerning, unenthusiastic, unexamined, unfeeling, unguarded, unheeded, unheedful, unheeding, uninspired, uninterested, uninvolved, unmindful, unobservant, unregarded, unresponsive, unstudied, unthinking, unthorough, unthought of, unwatchful, unweighed, wanting, without concern, without enthusiasm

PERIL, *noun* approach of danger, crisis, danger, dangerous situation, desperate situation, emergency, endangerment, exposure to danger, exposure to destruction, exposure to harm, exposure to injury, exposure to loss, hazard, helplessness, hopelessness, imperilment, insecurity, jeopardy, liability to injury, parlous state, precariousness, predicament, risk, source of danger, source of risk, susceptibility, susceptibleness, susceptivity, threat, uncertainty, unhealthy situation, unsafety, unsureness, vulnerability, vulnerable point
ASSOCIATED CONCEPTS: common peril, discovered peril, doctrine of discovered peril, doctrine of last clear chance, manifest peril, unforeseen peril

PERIMETER, *noun* ambit, border, borderline, boundary, bounds, brink, circuit, circumference, compass, configuration, confines, contour, curb, delineation, edge, enclosure, frontier, girdle, limit, limitations, margin, outline, outside edge, pale, periphery, purview, range, zone
ASSOCIATED CONCEPTS: adverse possession, constructive eviction, metes and bounds, trespassing

PERIOD, *noun* age, bout, continuance, course, diuturnity, duration, eon, epoch, era, hitch, interval, juncture, length of time, limited time, point, season, shift, span, spell, stage, stint, stretch, tenure, term, time, time interval, time stretch, tour, while
ASSOCIATED CONCEPTS: period of redemption

PERIODIC, *adjective* cadenced, cadent, continual, cyclic, cyclical, erratic, fluctuating, frequent, habitual, intermittent, measured, occasional, occurring again, oft-repeated, oftentime, patterned, perpetual, reappearing, recurrent, recurring, regular, regulated, remittent, repeated, returning, returning at intervals, rhythmic, rhythmical, seasonal, serial, *sollemnis,* spasmodic, sporadic, successive, systematic, variable

PERIPHERAL, *adjective* beside the point, circumferential, collateral, exterior, external, extraneous, farthest, fringe, impertinent, inconsequential, inessential, irrelevant, on the edge, outer, outermost, outland, outlying, outmost, outside, perimetric, perimetrical, secondary, trivial, ungermane, unimportant, without

PERIPHERY, *noun* ambit, border, borderland, bound, boundary line, circuit, circumambiency, circumference, circumscription, compass, confine, contour, delimitation, demarcation, edge, end, exterior, extreme edge, fringe, frontier, limit, limitation, line of demarcation, march, margin, mete, outer boundary, outer part, outline, outpost, outside, outside surface, outskirts, pale, perimeter, *perimetros,* purlieu, rim, skirts, surrounding area, surrounding space, terminus, verge

PERISH, *verb* be annihilated, be destroyed, be eradicated, be extinguished, be null and void, be ruined, become extinct, cease, cease living, cease to be, cease to exist, cease to live, come to an end, come to naught, come to ruin, crumble, depart, die, die away, die out, disappear, evanesce, evaporate, expire, fade, fade away, fade out, fail, go, *interire,* leave no trace, lose life, meet death, melt away, pass, pass away, pass on, *perire,* peter out, relinquish life, render null, sink away, succumb, surrender, vanish, wilt, wither

PERJURE, *verb* be false, be untruthful, bear false witness, break one's oath, break one's word, deviate from the truth, falsify, falsify testimony, feign, forswear, hide the truth, lie, misrepresent, palter, *periurare, periurium facere,* put a false construction upon, say less than the truth, speak falsely, strain the truth, stretch the truth, swear falsely, tell a falsehood, tell a lie, trump up, utter a falsehood

PERJURY, *noun* act of oath-breaking, distortion of the truth, false statement, false swearing, falsehood, falseness, falsification, intentional misstatement, invention of lies, misrepresentation, misstatement, *periurium,* perversion of truth, prevarication, untruth, violation of an oath, willful distortion of the truth, willful falsehood, willful telling of a falsehood, willful telling of a lie
ASSOCIATED CONCEPTS: subornation of perjury
FOREIGN PHRASES: ***Lex punit mendacium.*** The law punishes mendacity. ***Perjuri sunt qui servatis verbis juramenti decipiunt aures eorum qui accipiunt.*** They are perjured, who, preserving the words of an oath, deceive the ears of those who receive it. ***Sacramentum si fatuum fuerit, licet falsum, tamen non committit perjurium.*** A foolish oath, although false, does not give rise to perjury. ***Qui non libere veritatem pronunciat proditor est veritatis.*** He who does not freely speak the truth is a betrayer of the truth.

PERMANENT, *adjective* abiding, ageless, ceaseless, changeless, chronic, confirmed, constant, continued, continuing, dateless, deep-seated, durable, endless, enduring, engrafted, entrenched, established, eternal, everlasting, fast, fixed, immortal, immutable, imperishable, incommutable, indefatigable, indefeasible, indelible, indestructible, ineradicable, inextinguishable, infinite, ingrained, insusceptible to change, interminable, intransient, intransmutable, invulnerable, irremovable, irreversible, irrevocable, lasting, long-lasting, never-ceasing, never-ending, never-stopping, nonreversible, perdurable, perduring, perennial, *perennis,* perpetual, perpetuated, persevering, persistent, persisting, preserved, radicated, remaining, reverseless, rooted, secure, sempiternal, set, *stabilis,* stable, static, stationary, staying, steadfast, steady, surviving, sustained, tenacious, unalterable, unceasing, unchangeable, unchanging, unchecked, undestroyable, undying, unending, unerasable, unfading, unfailing, unflagging, uninterrupted, unmodifiable, unmovable, unrepealable, unshifting, unvarying, unwavering, unyielding, without end

PERMEATE, *verb* bathe, diffuse, drench, fill, go through, imbue, impregnate, infiltrate, infuse, inject, interpenetrate, leaven, osmose, overrun, overspread, pass through, penetrate, percolate, pervade, run through, saturate, seep, soak, souse, spread through, steep, suffuse, transfuse, wash, waterlog

PERMISSIBLE, *adjective* according to law, admissible, allowable, allowed, amenable to law, approvable, approved, authorized, constitutional, empowered, fitting, franchised, granted, lawful, legal, legally sound, legitimate, licensed, *licet,* licit, *licitus,* permitted, proper, sanctioned, sanctioned by law, stamped with approval, sufferable, tolerable, unchallenged, unforbidden, unprohibited, viable, warrantable, within the law

PERMISSION, *noun* acquiescence, allowance, approval, assent, authority, authorization, blessing, concurrence, consent, *copia,* countenance, *facultas,* formal consent, full authority, grace, leave, license, *potestas,* sanction, tolerance, visa
ASSOCIATED CONCEPTS: explicit permission, implied permission, permission of the court
FOREIGN PHRASES: ***Tout ce que la loi ne defend pas est permis.*** Everything which the law does not prohibit is allowed.

PERMISSIVE, *adjective* acquiescent, allowing, broadminded, complaisant, discretional, granting, indulgent, lenient, liberal, mild, nonprohibitive, tolerant, tolerating, volitive, yielding
ASSOCIATED CONCEPTS: permissive counterclaim, permissive joinder, permissive statute, permissive use

PERMIT, *noun* affirmation, approbation, approval, authority, authorization, *carte blanche,* certificate, charter, confirmation, document granting permission, fiat, grant, leave, legalization, license, pass, passport, patent, permission, privilege, sanction, ticket of leave, visa, voucher, warrant
ASSOCIATED CONCEPTS: license

PERMIT, *verb* accord one's approval, agree to, allow, approve, approve of, assent, authorize, award assent, be in favor of, be indulgent of, confer a privilege, consent, empower, enable, entitle, facilitate, give clearance, give consent, give leave, give opportunity for, give permission, give power, grant permission, have no objection, let, license, make possible, remove the obstacles, sanction, suffer, tolerate, warrant, yield assent

PERNICIOUS, *adjective* adverse, affliciting, baleful, baneful, brutal, calamitous, catastrophic, corrosive, crippling, cruel, damaging, deadly, death-bringing, death-dealing, deathful, deathly, deleterious, destructive, detrimental, devouring, diabolic, dire, disadvantageous, disastrous, disserviceable, distressing, envenomed, evil, *exitiosus,* extirpative, fatal, fell, fiendish, fraught with evil, fraught with harm, harmful, hurtful, inimical, injurious, insalubrious, insidious, killing, lethal, malefic, maleficent, maleficial, malevolent, malign, malignant, menacing, mephitic, mischievous, morbiferous, morbific, mortal, murderous, nocent, noisome, painful, *perniciosus,* pestiferous, pestilential, poisonous, ruinous, serious, sinister, tending to cause death, toxic, toxicant, toxiferous, treacherous, unhealthful, unhealthy, unkind, unpropitious, unwholesome, venomous, vicious, violent, virulent, wicked

PERORATION, *noun* address, bombast, declamation, discourse, *epilogus,* formal speech, grandiloquence, homily, lecture, magniloquence, monologue, oration, oratorical display, orotundity, *peroratio,* prelection, prepared speech, public address, recitation, rhetorical discourse, sermon, soliloquy, speech, talk

PERPETRATE, *verb* accomplish, achieve, be guilty of, bring about, bring to pass, carry into execution, carry off, carry on, carry out, carry through, commit, *committere,* do, effect, effectuate, execute, follow through, fulfill, implement, impose, inflict, maneuver, manipulate, perform, produce, put into action, put into effect, take measures, transact, work, work out
ASSOCIATED CONCEPTS: perpetrate a crime

PERPETUAL, *adjective* *adsiduus,* amaranthine, ceaseless, chronic, constant, continuous, deathless, endless, enduring, eternal, ever-abiding, everlasting, fixed, having no limit, immortal, imperishable, impossible to stop, incessant, indelible, indestructible, ineradicable, inexhaustible, infinite, interminable, intransient, lasting, never-ceasing, never-dying, never-fading, never-failing, never-stopping, perdurable, *perennis,* permanent, perpetuated, persistent, sempiternal, *sempiternus,* stable, surviving, unceasing, undestroyable, unending, unerasable, unfading, unfailing, uninterrupted, unlimited, unrepealable, without end
ASSOCIATED CONCEPTS: perpetual easement, perpetual franchise, perpetual injunction, perpetual lease, perpetual lien, perpetual succession
FOREIGN PHRASES: ***Perpetua lex est nullam legem humanam ac positivam perpetuam esse, et clausula quae abrogationem excludit ab initio non valet.*** It is a perpetual law that no human and positive law can be perpetual, and a clause in a law which precludes the power of abrogation or repeal is void from the beginning.

PERPETUATE, *verb* carry forward, carry on, cause to be continued, cause to endure, cause to last, eternize, immortalize, keep alive, keep in existence, maintain, make eternal, make everlasting, make last, make permanent, make perpetual, preserve, prolong, render deathless, retain, save, sustain
ASSOCIATED CONCEPTS: perpetuate testimony

PERPETUITY, *noun* boundlessness, ceaselessness, constancy, constant progression, continualness, continuance, continuation, continued existence, continuous time, continuousness, endless duration, endless time, endlessness, eternalness, eternity, everlasting, forever, incessancy, indefiniteness, infinite duration, infiniteness, infinity, interminability, never-endingness, perenniality, permanence, perpetualness, perpetuation, *perpetuitas,* time without end, timelessness, unintermitted continuance, uninterrupted existence, uninterruptedness
ASSOCIATED CONCEPTS: after-born children, in perpetuity, lives in being, period of perpetuities, restraint on alienation, rule against perpetuities

PERPLEX, *verb* baffle, bedevil, bemuse, beset, bewilder, bother, complicate, confound, confuse, corner, discompose, disconcert, disorient, disquiet, *distrahere,* disturb, embarrass, encumber, entangle, fill with doubt, fog, involve, make difficult, make intricate, mix up, muddle, mystify, nonplus, perturb, pose, pother, puzzle, rattle, render uncertain, snarl, *sollicitare,* tangle, tease, trouble, unsettle, upset, vex, worry

PERQUISITE, *noun* allowance, annuity, benefaction, bonus, compensation, consideration, donation, emolument, endowment, fee, financial remuneration, financial reward, gain, gift, gratuity, incidental profits, payment, premium, present, profit, recompense, remuneration, return, revenue, reward, reward for service, stipend, subsidy, tip, token, wage

PERSECUTE, *verb* abuse, afflict, aggrieve, agonize, annoy, assail, attack, badger, be intolerant, be malevolent, be malicious, be offensive, be ruthless, bedevil, beset, bother, browbeat, bully, carp at, chevy, crucify, damage, distress, disturb, do an injustice to, do harm, do mischief, do violence, do wrong to, dragoon, endamage, enrage, harass, ill-treat, ill-use, inflict evil, injure, maltreat, manhandle, misemploy, mishandle, mistreat, misuse, offend, oppress, outrage, overburden, overtax, overwork, plague, provoke, refuse to tolerate, scathe, scourge, show no mercy, show no pity, torment, treat poorly, trouble, use dispiteously, *vexare,* victimize, wrong

PERSECUTOR BAR, *noun* bar to asylum for a persecutor, prohibition on asylum for a persecutor, prohibition on asylum when persecution on account of belonging to a social group occurred, prohibition on asylum when persecution on account of national origin occurred, prohibition on asylum when persecution on account of political opinion occurred, prohibition on asylum when persecution on account of race occurred, prohibition on asylum when persecution on account of religion occurred

PERSEVERANCE, *noun* application, backbone, constancy, continuance, continuation, determination, devotion, diligence, doggedness, endurance, firmness of purpose, indefatigableness, industry, intransigency, obduracy, obduration, obstinacy, patience, persistence, pertinacity, purpose, resoluteness, resolve, single-mindedness, singleness of purpose, stamina, steadfastness, steadiness, stubbornness, tenacity, tolerance, will, zeal

PERSEVERE, *verb* adhere, apply oneself, be constant, be determined, be obstinate, be resolute, be steadfast, be steady, be stubborn, be tenacious, be unyielding, carry on, cling, cling tenaciously, *constare,* continue, endure, exert oneself, follow up, go forward, go on, hang on, hold fast, hold on, hold out, keep driving, keep going, keep on, keep up, labor, last, maintain, maintain a course, outlast, perpetuate, persist, *persistere, perstare,* plod, plug away, prevail, prolong, pursue, refuse to give up, refuse to yield, remain, resist change, run on, spare no effort, stand fast, stand firm, stay, stick to, stop at nothing, struggle, survive, sustain, take no denial, toil, work unceasingly, work unflaggingly

PERSIST, *verb* abide, be determined, be obstinate, be resolute, be steadfast, be steady, be tenacious, be unyielding, bide, carry on, cling to, continue, drag on, endure, go forward, go on, hold fast, hold on, hold out, insist, keep at, keep on, last, linger, live on, maintain, make headway, never cease, outlast, perdure, persevere, *persistere, perstare,* plod, plug away, prevail, progress, pursue relentlessly, refuse to give up, remain, remain unchanged, stay, stick to, survive, sustain, take no denial, toil unceasingly, work unceasingly, work unflaggingly

PERSISTENT, *adjective* abiding, adamant, assiduous, chronic, continued, continuing, continuous, determined, diligent, dogged, durable, enduring, everlasting, faithful, indefatigable, insistent, lasting, obstinate, patient, perdurable, perseverant, persevering, pertinacious, purposeful, refusing to relent, relentless, remaining, repeated, resolute, resolved, sedulous, serious, set upon, staying, steadfast, steady, strong-willed, stubborn, sustained, tenacious, tireless, unallayed, unceasing, unchanging, unchecked, undaunted, undeviating, undiscouraged, undying, unfailing, unfaltering, unflagging, unrelaxing, unremitting, unstopping, unswerving, untiring, unvarying, unwavering, unwearying, unyielding

PERSON, *noun* autonomous being, being, caput, chap, character, fellow, *homo,* human, human being, human creature, individual, living being, living soul, member of the human race, mortal, mortal body, *mortalis,* party, personage, somebody, someone, soul

ASSOCIATED CONCEPTS: adult person, artificial person, competent person, credible person, disorderly person, fictitious person, injured person, natural person, person aggrieved, person in need of supervision, poor person, third person, unauthorized person

PERSON OF INTEREST, *noun* an individual the subject of investigation, individual under investigation, potential suspect, suspicious person not arrested, suspicious person not charged

PERSONAL *(Individual),* ***adjective*** characteristic, differentiating, discriminative, distinct, distinguishing, idiosyncratic, own, particular, peculiar, private, select, specific

ASSOCIATED CONCEPTS: personal action, personal appearance, personal communication, personal covenant, personal effects, personal estate, personal exemption, personal expenses, personal goods, personal injury, personal judgment, personal jurisdiction, personal liability, personal obligation, personal privilege, personal property, personal representative, personal rights, personal safety, personal service of process, personal services, personal transaction, personally responsible

PERSONAL *(Private),* ***adjective*** buried, clandestine, closed, concealed, confidential, covert, cryptic, hidden, intimate, *privatus,* privy, restricted, secret, singular, subjective, undisclosed, unrevealed, unshared, untold, veiled

ASSOCIATED CONCEPTS: personal articles, personal belongings

PERSONALITY, *noun* attributes, being, character, characteristics, disposition, distinction, distinctiveness, egohood, identity, individualism, individuality, *ingenium,* makeup, nature, oneness, originality, particularity, peculiarities, personal identity, personal mark, predisposition, selfhood, selfness, singularity, soul, style, temperament, traits, type, uniqueness

PERSONALTY, *noun* assets, available means, belongings, chattels, effects, funds, holdings, investments, personal property, personal resources, possessions, property, resources, wealth

PERSONHOOD LAWS, *noun* abortion ban, fetal protection, fetal right-to-life statute, laws championing pregnancy from the time of implantation, laws protecting human embryos, laws protecting life beginning at conception, legal protection of preborn humans, right to life laws

ASSOCIATED CONCEPTS: abortion rights, prochoice advocacy, right to life

PERSONIFY, *verb* ascribe personal qualities to, be the embodiment, characterize, copy, embody, embrace, exemplify, humanize, incarnate, manifest, *orationem attribuere,* symbolize, treat as human, typify

PERSONNEL, *noun* assistants, band of employees, body of employees, cast, clerical staff, company, corps of employees, coworkers, crew, employees, factotums, fellow workers, help, labor supply, laborers, laboring force, manpower, members, office force, servantry, servants, staff, team of employees, work force, work party, workers, working people

PERSPECTIVE, *noun* angle of vision, attitude, conception, distance, eyereach, feeling, field of view, field of vision, framework, impression, inclination, leaning, line of sight, mental view, orientation, outlook, point of observation, point of view, position, range of view, range of vision, scope of vision, sense of proportion, situation, slant, standpoint, thought, vantage point, view, viewpoint, way of thinking

PERSPICACIOUS, *adjective* *acutus,* alert, apperceptive, argute, artful, astute, bright, canny, clear-sighted, clear-headed, clever, crafty, cunning, dioristic, discerning, discriminating, discriminative, farseeing, farsighted, foresighted, forethoughtful, hardheaded, informed, intelligent, judicious, keen, keen-eyed, keen-sighted, keen-witted, knowing, long-sighted, nimble-witted, observant, penetrating, perceptive, percipient, *perspicax,* piercing, quick, quick-witted, sagacious, *sagax,* sage, sapient, sensible, sharp, sharp-sighted, sharp-witted, shrewd, understanding, wise

PERSPICACITY, *noun* acuity, acumen, acute discernment, acuteness, astuteness, capacity, clear thinking, clear thought, clear vision, discernment, discretion, discrimination, farsightedness, insight, judgment, ken, perception, perceptiveness, sagacity, sense, sensitivity, sharpness of mind, shrewdness, tact, understanding

PERSPICUOUS, *adjective* accurate, apparent, appreciable, apprehensible, clear, cognizable, coherent, comprehensible, conceivable, definite, distinct, evident, exact, explicable, explicit, factual, forceful, genuine, intelligible, manifest, obvious, overt, palpable, patent, pellucid, perceivable, perceptible, real, transparent, truthful, unambiguous, understandable, unmistakable

PERSUADE, *verb* actuate, advise, align, bend to one's will, blandish, bring a person to his senses, bring around, bring over, bring to reason, cajole, coax, compel, convert, convince, counsel, enlist, exercise influence, exert influence, exhort, gain the confidence of, impel, importune, impress, indoctrinate, induce, influence, inveigle, lead, lead to believe, lure, make one's point, make oneself felt, motivate, move, prevail upon, prompt, propagandize, proselyte, proselytize, rouse, satisfy by evidence, satisfy by proof, seduce, sell, suborn, sway, urge, win over, woo

PERSUASION, *noun* actuation, advocacy, alignment, argument, blandishment, cajolement, cajolery, cajoling, coaxing, conversion, dissuasion, encouragement, enlistment, enticement, exhortation, incitation, incitement, inducement, influence, insistence, inveiglement, motivation, pleading, pressure, prompting, propaganda, proselytism, salesmanship, solicitation, suasion, winning over

PERSUASIVE, *adjective* actuating, arousing, authoritative, coaxing, cogent, compelling, convictive, convincing, credible, effective, eloquent, forceful, hortative, hortatory, impelling, impressive, inductive, influential, inspiring, inviting, logical, moving, persuasory, plausible, pointed, potent, powerful, propagandistic, provocative, provoking, rousing, sound, strong, suasive, subornative, swaying, telling, tempting, tenable, touching, valid, weighty
ASSOCIATED CONCEPTS: persuasive arguments, persuasive authority, persuasive legal testimony

PERTAIN, *verb* appertain, be appropriate, be associated with, be concerned with, be connected to, be suitable, bear upon, befit, behoove, belong, concern, have implications for, have interrelationship with, have reference to, have relation to, have relevance, have significance for, refer, relate, stand in relation to, tie in with, touch upon

PERTINACIOUS, *adjective* adamant, adhering to a purpose, assidous, bent, bullheaded, certain, continuing, decided, determined, diligent, dogged, earnest, enduring, exhibiting purpose, faithful, firm, hard to get rid of, headstrong, holding to a purpose, immovable, immutable, implacable, indefatigable, indomitable, industrious, inexorable, inflexible, insistent, intent, intractable, inveterate, mulish, never-tiring, never-wearying, obdurate, obstinate, *obstinatus,* painstaking, patient, persevering, persistent, persisting, *pertinax,* pervicacious, *pervicax,* pigheaded, plodding, purposeful, relentless, resolute, resolved, rigid, sedulous, self-willed, serious, set, single-minded, stalwart, stanch, steadfast, steady, strong-willed, stubborn, sure, tough, unbending, uncompromising, undaunted, undeviating, undistracted, undoubting, unfaltering, unflagging, unflinching, unmovable, unrelaxing, unrelenting, unremitting, unshakable, unshaken, unshrinking, unswerving, untiring, unwavering, unwearying, unyielding, willful, zealous

PERTINACITY, *noun* adamancy, bullheadedness, diligence, doggedness, firmness, hardheadedness, hardness, immovability, inflexibility, intransigence, inveteracy, obduracy, obstinacy, perseverance, recalcitrance, rigidity, rigor, stubbornness, willfulness

PERTINENT, *adjective* adapted, affinitive, appertaining, applicable, apposite, appropriate, appurtenant, apropos, apt, associated, associative, bearing on the question, belonging, concerning, connected, fit, fitting, germane, having direct bearing, having to do with, material, opposite, pertaining, referential, referring, regarding, related, relating, relational, relevant, suitable, to the point, to the purpose, with reference to
ASSOCIATED CONCEPTS: pertinent testimony, relevant evidence

PERTURB, *verb* abash, agitate, alarm, annoy, arouse, badger, baffle, bewilder, bother, bring into disorder, cause a fuss, cause agitation, cause alarm, cause confusion, cause disorder, cause upset, churn, complicate, confound, confuse, derange, disarrange, discomfit, discompose, disconcert, dismay, disorder, disquiet, distract, distress, disturb, embarrass, entangle, exasperate, excite, ferment, flurry, fluster, fret, frustrate, gall, give cause for alarm, grieve, harass, harry, inflame, infuriate, irk, irritate, jar, jolt, madden, make havoc, make uneasy, nonplus, outrage, pain, perplex, perturbate, *perturbo,* pester, pique, plague, pother, provoke, put out, rouse, ruffle, shake, shake up, shock, snarl, stir, stir up, throw into confusion, trouble, unnerve, unsettle, upset, vex, work up, worry

PERUSAL, *noun* analysis, attention, close reading, contemplation, discovery, examination, inquiry, inspection, investigation, reading, review, scrutiny, study, survey

PERUSE, *verb* analyze, browse, check, con, conduct research on, consider, contemplate, delve into, devote oneself to, examine, explore, feel out, glance over, glean information, go over, inquire into, inspect, investigate, look over, observe, overlook, pass under review, peer into, pore over, probe, pry into, read, regard studiously, research, review, scan, scrutinize, search, study, subject to scrutiny, survey, take note of, take stock of, thumb, turn one's gaze upon, turn the leaves of, watch

PERVADE, *verb* affect entirely, bathe, be rife, diffuse, disseminated, drench, enter, extend through, fill, filter through, flow into, force a passage, go through, imbrue, imbue, implant, impregnate, infiltrate, infuse, inject, instill, interfuse, interpenetrate, intrude, invade, make an entrance, overspread, pass through, penetrate, perforate, permeate, pierce, radiate, run into, run through, saturate, seep in, soak, spread, spread through, steep, suffuse, transfuse

PERVERSE, *adjective* bad, bad-natured, bad-tempered, base, bellicose, belligerent, boorish, bumptious, cantankerous, captious, churlish, contemptible, contrary, contumacious, contumelious, corrupt, corrupted, crabbed, cranky, cross, crusty, debauched, degenerate, depraved, deviating, difficult, discourteous, disobedient, disorderly, evil, evil-minded, fractious, froward, hard to deal with, hard to manage, headstrong, ill-behaved, ill-natured, ill-tempered, impolite, improper, impudent, inaffable, incorrigible, inimical, insubordinate, insulting, intractable, irascible, mean, nasty, naughty, negative, negativistic, noncompliant, obstinate, obstreperous, peevish, persisting in error, persisting in fault, *perversus,* perverted, petulant, pugnacious, refractory, reprobate, resistive, rude, self-willed, snappish, snarling, spiteful, spleenful, spleeny, splenetic, stubborn, surly, testy, thoughtless, touchy, troublesome, truculent, unaccommodating, uncivil, uncomplaisant, uncompliant, uncooperative, unfriendly, ungallant, ungovernable, ungracious, unhelpful, unmanageable, unmannerly, unpolite, unreasonable, unruly, untoward, unyielding, venomous, vexatious, waspish, wayward, wicked, wrong, wrongheaded

PERVERSION, *noun* abasement, aberrance, aberrancy, aberration, abnormality, abomination, abuse, baseness, contamination, *corruptio,* corruption, debasement, debauchery, defilement, degradation, demoralization, *depravatio,* depravation, depravity, evil behavior, foulness, immorality, infraction, lewdness, looseness of morals, malefaction, misuse, pollution, prostitution, sophistication, turpitude, unnatural habit, violation, vitiation, want of principle, wickedness
ASSOCIATED CONCEPTS: deviant sexual behavior

PERVERT, *verb* abuse, canker, contaminate, *corrumpere,* corrupt, debauch, degenerate, demoralize, *depravare,* deprave, divert, falsify, infect, lead astray, lower, make corrupt, misapply, mislead, misrepresent, misuse, poison, pollute, prostitute, render evil, ruin, soil, sophisticate, spoil, stain, subvert, taint, tamper with, teach wickedness, vitiate, warp
FOREIGN PHRASES: ***Quae ad unum finem loquuta sunt, non debent ad alium detorqueri.*** Those words which are spoken to one end ought not to be perverted to another.

PESSIMISM, *noun* blighted hope, cheerlessness, cynicism, dashed hopes, defeatism, dejectedness, dejection, depression, despair, desperation, despondence, despondency, disconsolation, discouragement, disheartenment, dispiritedness, dolefulness, downcastness, downheartedness, faint hope, forlorn hope, gloom, gloominess, gloomy outlook, glumness, heaviness of heart, heaviness of spirit, hopelessness, joylessness, lack of enthusiasm, lack of expectation, low-spiritedness, low spirits, melancholia, melancholy, misery, sorrowfulness, uncheerfulness, unhappiness, wretchedness

PESSIMISTIC, *adjective* cheerless, crushed, cynical, defeatist, dejected, depressed, despairing, desperate, despondent, disconsolate, discouraged, disheartened, dismayed, dispirited, distrustful, downcast, downhearted, foreboding, forlorn, gloomy, glum, grieved, heavyhearted, hopeless, joyless, low-spirited, melancholic, melancholy, miserable, morbid, morose, sad, sorrowful, troubled, uncheerful, uncheery, unhappy, unjoyful, unpromising, wretched

PESTILENT, *adjective* baleful, baneful, contagious, damaging, dangerous, deadly, death-dealing, deathly, deleterious, destructive, disastrous, disease-ridden, diseased, epidemic, evil, fatal, feral, foul, harmful, hurtful, infectious, injurious, insalubrious, killing, lethal, lethiferous, malefic, maleficent, malign, malignant, mephitic, morbid, morbiferous, morbific, morbifical, mortal, murderous, nocent, nocuous, noisome, noxious, pernicious, *pestilens,* pestilential, plagueful, poisonous, tending to cause death, terrible, threatening, toxic, toxicant, toxiferous, unhealthful, unhealthy, venomous, violent, virulent

PETITION, *noun* adjuration, application, bid, call for aid, demand, earnest request, entreaty, formal writing embodying a request, formal written plea, formal written request, invocation, *libellus,* motion, plea, prayer, request, request for relief, requisition, solemn request, written application for relief
ASSOCIATED CONCEPTS: affidavit, cross-petition, ex parte petition, filing of petition, order dismissing a petition, petition for a name change, petition for divorce, verified petition, voluntary petition in bankruptcy

PETITION, *verb* adjure, advocate, appeal for, apply for, apply to, ask for, beseech, bid, call upon, clamor for, entreat, entreat earnestly, file for, formally urge, *implorare,* implore, make a requisition, make application, make demands, make written application, obtest, plead, pray for, prefer a request to, request, requisition, *rogare,* seek, solemnly request, solicit, urge
ASSOCIATED CONCEPTS: petition for a rehearing, petition for a writ of certiorari, petition for a writ of mandamus, petition for a writ of prohibition, petition for redress, petition for removal, petition for review

PETITIONER, *noun* applicant, asker, litigant, movant, one who applies for relief, one who files an application for relief, one who requests relief, party, pleader, solicitant, solicitor, *supplex,* supplicant
ASSOCIATED CONCEPTS: aggrieved party

PETTIFOG, *verb* beguile, bluff, cavil, circumvent, connive, deceive, dodge, dupe, ensnare, evade, fence, mislead, outmaneuver, palter, prevaricate, split hairs, trick, trifle

PETTIFOGGER, *noun* beguiler, bluffer, charlatan, cheat, con artist, deceiver, dishonest lawyer, disreputable lawyer, empiric, fake, faker, fraud, hypocrite, imitator, impersonator, masquerader, mimic, mocker, phony, pretender, quack, sham, trickster, unscrupulous lawyer
ASSOCIATED CONCEPTS: code of professional conduct, criminal law

PETTIFOGGERY, *noun* artfulness, artifice, bamboozlement, cheating, chicane, chicanery, circumvention, corruption, cozenage, craft, craftiness, cunning, deceit, deception, dishonesty, dodgery, duplicity, equivocation, evasion, foul play, fraud, fraudulence, fraudulency, fraudulent practice, guile, humbug, indirection, intrigue, jobbery, jugglery, juggling, knavery, petty dishonesty, sharp practice, treachery, trickery, trickiness, underhand dealing, underhand practice

PETTY, *adjective* beggarly, contemptible, diminutive, dispensable, expendable, fribble, frivolous, inappreciable,

inconsequential, inconsiderable, insignificant, limited, little, marginal, meager, mean, minor, minute, *minutus,* negligible, nonessential, nugatory, of small account, of small moment, paltry, petit, picayune, piddling, puny, scant, scanty, skimpy, slight, small, sparse, *tenuis,* trifling, trivial, unessential, unimportant, unnotable, unworthy of regard, worthless
ASSOCIATED CONCEPTS: petty larceny, petty misdemeanor, petty offense

PETULANT, ***adjective*** acrimonious, annoyed, argumentative, bad-tempered, bearish, cantankerous, captious, carping, cavilling, censorious, choleric, churlish, contentious, crabbed, crabby, cranky, cross, cross-tempered, crusty, curmudgeonly, difficult, disagreeable, disputatious, fractious, fretful, froward, grouchy, growling, grumbling, grumbly, grumpy, hot-headed, hot-tempered, huffy, ill-humored, ill-tempered, impatient, indocile, iracund, irascible, irritable, liverish, mean, mean-tempered, moody, nagging, out of humor, out of sorts, peevish, perverse, pettish, *petulans,* piqued, pugnacious, quarrelsome, querulous, short, short-tempered, shrewish, snappish, snappy, snarling, sour, sour-tempered, spiteful, spleenful, splenetic, splenetical, surly, testy, touchy, vixenish, waspish, whiny

PHANTOM, ***noun*** airy spirit, apparition, appearance, banshee, chimera, creation of the imagination, creation of the mind, delusion, disembodied spirit, dream, eidolon, fiction, fictive creation, figment, figment of the imagination, ghost, ghostly form, hallucination, illusion, image, *imago,* incorporeal being, mental image, mirage, phantasm, poltergeist, revenant, shade, specter, spirit, sprite, unreality, vapor, vision, wraith

PHASE *(Aspect),* ***noun*** angle, consideration, facet, feature, part, point, portion, *ratio,* section, side, *status*

PHASE *(Period),* ***noun*** age, continuance, duration, epoch, era, measured time, moment, period of time, point, point of time, season, session, shift, space of time, span, spell, stage, state, step, stretch, tenure, term, time, tour

PHENOMENAL, ***adjective*** amazing, exceptional, extraordinary, fantastic, great, incredible, magical, marvelous, noticeable, outstanding, preternatural, prodigious, rare, superhuman, transcendent, transcendental, uncanny, uncommon, unearthly, unique, with a wow factor, wonderful

PHENOMENON *(Manifestation),* ***noun*** apparition, appearance, display, feature, figure, form, image, materialization, presence, realization, shape, show, sight, sign, spectacle, vision

PHENOMENON *(Unusual occurrence),* ***noun*** amazement, amazing thing, astonishing thing, astonishment, curiosity, exception, experience, freak occurrence, marvel, miracle, nonesuch, nonpareil, *ostentum,* portent, *prodigium,* rare occurrence, rarity, *res mira,* sight, special occurrence, spectacle, unusual circumstance, unusual happening, unusual incident, wonder, wonderment, wonderwork

PHILANTHROPIC, ***adjective*** accommodating, almsgiving, altruistic, beneficent, benevolent, benign, benignant, bighearted, bounteous, bountiful, brotherly, charitable, civic-minded, considerate, devoted to others, eleemosynary, free, freehanded, generous, giving, good-natured, good-hearted, gracious, helpful, hospitable, humane, humanitarian, *humanus,* indulgent, kind, kindhearted, kindly, lavish, liberal, magnanimous, munificent, obliging, open-handed, princely, public-spirited, selfless, ungrudging, unselfish, unsparing, unstinting

PHILANTHROPIST, ***noun*** almsgiver, altruist, backer, benefactor, bestower, conferrer, contributor, donor, Good Samaritan, grantor, helper, humanitarian, patron, supporter, volunteer

PHILANTHROPY, ***noun*** almsgiving, altruism, beneficence, benevolence, *benevolentia,* benignancy, benignity, bounteousness, bountifulness, bounty, brotherhood, brotherliness, brotherly love, charitableness, charity, considerateness, consideration, devotion to others, fellow feeling, free giving, free-handedness, generosity, good-heartedness, good nature, good will, good works, graciousness, helpfulness, hospitableness, hospitality, humaneness, humanitarianism, *humanitas,* indulgence, kindliness, kindness, largess, lavishness, liberality, love of mankind, magnanimity, munificence, open-handedness, princeliness, public spirit, self-sacrifice, selflessness, ungrudgingness, unselfishness, unsparingness

PHILISTINE, ***noun*** artless person, conformist, conventionalist, nouveau riche, social climber, traditionalist

PHILLIPIC, ***noun*** abusive language, acrimony, aspersion, bitter language, bitter words, castigation, censure, chastisement, commination, contumely, defamation, denunciation, detraction, diatribe, disparagement, execration, harangue, invective, malediction, obloquy, reprobation, revilement, screed, tirade, tongue-lashing, verbal abuse, vilification, vituperation

PHILOSOPHY, ***noun*** axiom, belief, belief system, doctrine, dogma, explanation, gospel, ideology, manifesto, principle, rationale, tenet, testament, theory

PHLEGMATIC, ***adjective*** aloof, apathetic, bloodless, bovine, callous, calm, cold, cold-blooded, comatose, cool, detached, disinterested, dispassionate, distant, dull, frigid, halfhearted, hebetudinous, impassive, imperturbable, indifferent, inert, insensible, lackadaisical, languid, languorous, lazy, *lentus,* lethargic, lethargical, lifeless, listless, lymphatic, oscitant, passionless, passive, *patiens,* phlegmatical, pluckless, sedate, serene, slow, sluggish, sober, spiritless, spunkless, staid, stoical, stolid, stony, stupefied, supine, tame, *tardus,* torpid, unagitated, unanxious, unapprehensive, uncaring, uncommunicative, unconcerned, undemonstrative, undisturbed, unemotional, unexcitable, unexcited, unfeeling, unflustered, unimpassioned, unperturbed, unresponsive, unruffled, unsusceptible, untroubled, unworried

PHOBIA, ***noun*** abhorrence, abject fear, alarm, antipathy, anxiety, apprehension, aversion, awe, detestation, dislike, distaste, disturbance, dread, fear, fright, horror, loathing, obsession, panic, repugnance, terror, trepidation, unreasoned alarm, unreasoned fear

PHRASE, ***noun*** adage, aphorism, apothegm, byword, caption, clause, dictum, figure of speech, formula, idiom, inscription, motto, peculiar expression, proverb, saw, saying, slogan, trite expression, turn of expression, utterance, watchword, word group

PHRASE, ***verb*** articulate, call, clothe in words, come out with, comment, communicate, convey, couch, declare, deliver, denominate, describe, designate, dub, entitle, enunciate, express, find words to express, formulate, give expression to, give tongue to, give utterance, give voice to, give words to, impart, make known, mouth, name, observe, present, pronounce, put, put into language, put into words, recite, relate, remark, say, sound, speak, state, style, talk, tell, term, utter, verbalize, vocalize, voice, word

PHRASEOLOGY, *noun* argot, cant, choice of language, choice of words, command of idiom, command of language, composition, dialect, *dicendi genus,* diction, expression, expression of ideas, formulation, idiom, jargon, language, lingo, literary artistry, literary style, locution, manner of expression, mode of expression, mode of speech, oratory, parlance, patois, pattern of words, peculiarity of phrasing, phrasing, rhetoric, selection of words, speech, style, terminology, text, tone, turn of expression, usage, use of words, vein, vocabulary, wording

PHYSICAL, *adjective* actual, bodily, carnal, concrete, corporal, corporeal, corporeous, earthly, embodied, external, flesh and blood, fleshly, human, incarnate, material, materiate, mundane, natural, nonspiritual, organic, palpable, real, sensible, sensual, sensuous, somatic, substantial, substantive, systemic, tangible, temporal, unspiritual, worldly
ASSOCIATED CONCEPTS: physical assets, physical condition, physical contact, physical control, physical damage, physical delivery, physical depreciation, physical disability, physical force, physical impairment, physical injury, physical loss, physical property

PICK UP *(Acquire),* ***verb*** absorb, accumulate, achieve, adopt, amass, annex, appreciative, attain, become cognizant, become conscious of, become conversant with, capture, catch, come by, comprehend, cultivate, detect, discern, draw, embrace, form, gain, garner, get, grasp, learn, master, obtain, procure, rack up, recognize, secure, take on, understand

PICK UP *(Overhear),* ***verb*** detect, discern, find out, hear, heed, intercept, learn, listen, listen in, listen into, listen stealthily, monitor, notice, realize, receive, spy, surveil

PICKET, *verb* avoid, blackball, blockade, boycott, demonstrate, demonstrate against, demonstrate protest, dissuade from entering, persuade not to work, protest, repudiate, restrict access, take part in a demonstration
ASSOCIATED CONCEPTS: informational picketing, lawful picketing, mass picketing, organizational picketing, peaceful picketing, primary picketing, recognitional picketing, retaliatory picketing, secondary boycotts, situs picketing, sympathy strikes, unlawful picketing, violent picketing

PICTURE, *verb* caricature, characterize, conceive, conceptualize, conjure up, delineate, depict, diagram, document, envisage, envision, fantasize, ideate, illustrate, imagine, outline, portray, render, represent, silhouette, sketch, visualize

PIECE, *noun* aspect, atom, bit, chip, clipping, component, crumb, flake, fraction, grain, granule, molecule, morsel, oddment, paring, part, particle, portion, remainder, scrap, section, segment, shard, shaving, sliver, snip, snippet, splinter

PIECEMEAL, *adverb* by degrees, drop by drop, gradually, in installments, in small doses, in small quantities, inch by inch, little by little, partially
ASSOCIATED CONCEPTS: piecemeal zoning

PIERCE *(Discern),* ***verb*** appreciate, apprehend, be acquainted with, be apprised of, be aware of, be conscious of, be informed, behold, cognize, comprehend, descry, detect, discover, distinguish, fathom, glimpse, grasp, have in sight, have knowledge of, know, lay eyes on, make out, make sensible, note, notice, observe, perceive, realize, recognize, see, understand, view, witness

PIERCE *(Lance),* ***verb*** bore, *confodere,* cut through, drive into, empierce, gore, impale, insert, knife, penetrate, perforate, plunge in, poniard, prick, puncture, run through, skewer, spear, spike, spit, stab, stick, *transfigere,* transfix, transpierce
ASSOCIATED CONCEPTS: pierce the corporate veil

PIERCING OF THE CORPORATE VEIL, *noun* alter ego, finding of additional liability in a subsidiary, finding of additional liability in shareholders, finding of personal liability, lancing of the corporate veil, lifting of the corporate veil, piercing of a body corporate's liability, piercing of a corporate body's liability, piercing of an artificial entity's liability, piecing of limited liability

PIERCING THE CORPORATE VEIL, *noun* breaking the corporate facade, exposure of shareholders' personal assets, lifting the corporate veil, mechanism to create shareholder liability, nonlimited liability
ASSOCIATED CONCEPTS: alter ego liability, alter ego theory, cloak, exposure as an alter ego, fraud, instrumentality rule, legitimate corporate purpose, limited liability, prevent unfairness or injustice, sham, unity of interest and ownership

PIGEONHOLE, *verb* allocate, allot, arrange, assort, bracket, break down, catalog, categorize, class, collocate, divide, docket, file, form into classes, grade, group, index, label, list, methodize, name, order, organize, place, place in a category, put in order, rank, rate, reduce to order, section, sort, subdivide, subsume, systematize, tabulate, tag, ticket, type

PILFER, *verb* abscond with, appropriate illegally, bilk, commit larceny, convert, deprive illegally, embezzle, filch, *furari,* loot, make off with, misappropriate, pillage, poach, purloin, rob, seize, steal, *surripere,* take, thieve

PILLAGE, *noun* appropriation, booty, brigandage, depredation, deprivation, despoilment, despoliation, destruction, devastation, *direptio, expilatio,* foray, havoc, maraud, piracy, plunder, plunderage, prey, raid, ransack, rapacity, *rapina,* rapine, ravage, razzia, sack, spoliation, vandalism

PILLAGE, *verb* bring to ruin, burglarize, damage, depopulate, depredate, desolate, despoil, destroy, devastate, lay in ashes, lay in ruins, lay waste, level, loot, make a shambles, make havoc, maraud, pirate, plunder, raid, ransack, reave, rob, ruin, ruinate, sabotage, sack, spoil, spoliate, steal, strip, thieve, waste, wreck
ASSOCIATED CONCEPTS: larceny

PILLORY, *verb* accuse, asperse, attaint, befoul, belittle, berate, besmear, besmirch, bespatter, blacken, blot, brand, bring shame upon, calumniate, cast a slur upon, cast aspersions on, cause a scandal, damage a reputation, debase, defame, defile, degrade, denigrate, denounce, destroy a reputation, discredit, disgrace, dishonor, disparage, expose, expose to infamy, gibbet, give a bad name, hold up to ridicule, hold up to shame, impute shame to, lampoon, laugh at, lower, make fun of, malign, mock, put in a bad light, put to shame, ridicule, run down, scandalize, scorn, smear, smirch, soil, spatter, speak ill of, stain, stigmatize, sully, taint, tarnish, traduce, vilify, vituperate

PINNACLE, *noun* acme, apex, apogee, cap, ceiling, climax, consummation, crest, crown, crowning point, culmination, extremity, head, height, highest degree, highest point, meridian, peak, point, summit, tip, top, upper extremity, utmost extent, utmost height, zenith

PINPOINT, *verb* be specific, enumerate, fix in, focus, locate, place, quantify, site, situate, specify
ASSOCIATED CONCEPTS: pinpoint rule

PIONEER, *noun* adventurer, colonist, colonizer, discoverer, establisher, explorer, forerunner, founder, founding father, frontiersman, innovator, inventor, lead, leader, modernist, pacesetter, pathfinder, precursor, predecessor, ringleader, scout, settler, trail blazer, vanguard

PIQUE, *verb* affront, agitate, anger, annoy, arouse resentment, bait, bedevil, beset, bother, bully, bullyrag, cause resentment, discompose, disgust, dismay, displease, disquiet, distemper, disturb, enrage, exasperate, fret, gall, give offense, give umbrage, gnaw, goad, harass, harry, heckle, hurt, incense, incite, incommode, inflame, infuriate, instigate, insult, irk, irritate, kindle wrath, madden, make wrathful, molest, needle, nettle, offend, pain, persecute, perturb, pester, plague, pother, provoke, put out of countenance, rile, roil, rouse, ruffle, *sollicitare,* sting, stir up, taunt, tease, torment, torture, trouble, try the patience, upset, vex, work up, worry

PIRATE *(Reproduce without authorization),* ***verb*** adopt and pass off as one's own, appropriate, borrow dishonestly, copy, counterfeit, crib, help oneself to, make use of without permission, plagiarize, purloin, steal, take illegally

PIRATE *(Take by violence),* ***verb*** commit piracy, commit robbery, despoil, lay hold of, loot, pillage, plunder, ransack, rifle, rob, sack, seize, spoil, spoilate, steal, take by force, thieve

PITEOUS, *adjective* awful, deplorable, despicable, disgusting, distressing, emotional, grievous, heartbreaking, heartrending, lamentable, miserable, mournful, pitiable, pitiful, poor, regrettable, reprehensible, rueful, sad, sorrowful, sorry, terrible, touching, upsetting, woeful, wretched

PITFALL, *noun* abyss, catch, chasm, danger, dangerous spot, exposure to danger, exposure to harm, *fovea,* hazard, imminent danger, obstacle, peril, predicament, problem, quagmire, risk, risks, snare, threat, trap

PITHY, *adjective* brief, compact, compendious, compressed, concise, condensed, epigrammatic, full of meaning, gnomic, incisive, juicy, laconic, meaningful, meaty, *medullosus,* packed, pointed, sententious, substantial, succinct, summary, terse, trenchant

PITTED AGAINST, *verb* act in opposition to, argue against, attack, battle, be at cross purposes, be contrary to, be on the opposite side of, be on the other side of, challenge, collide, combat, confront, confute, contend, contest, contradict, contravene, controvert, counter, counteract, counterattack, counterbalance, countermine, counterpoise, countervail, counterweigh, counterwork, debate, defy, demur, deny, disaffirm, disagree, disapprove, dispute, encounter, go contrary to, go up against, join issue, land into, negate, object, obstruct, offer resistance, oppose, oppugn, prevent, prohibit, protest, put in opposition, rebut, refute, reject, remonstrate, repel, resist, set against, stand firm against, stand on the other side of, take a stand against, take exception to, take issue with
ASSOCIATED CONCEPTS: litigation

PITY, *noun* commiseration, compassion, condolement, condolence, consolation, feeling, fellow feeling, fellow suffering, fellowship in sorrow, kindliness, lenience, leniency, lenity, mercifulness, mercy, *misericordia,* quarter, ruth, sympathy
ASSOCIATED CONCEPTS: amnesty, clemency, pardon

PIVOTAL, *adjective* basic, critical, crucial, decisive, elementary, essential, fundamental, indispensable, life-and-death, material, necessary, pressing, requisite, urgent, weighty
ASSOCIATED CONCEPTS: pivotal juncture in settling a case

PIVOTAL POINT, *noun* center, center of activity, center of attention, center of attraction, center of interest, central point, centrality, converging point, critical point, crux, essence, focal point, gravamen, heart, hub, key issue, main issue, most important part, point of convergence

PLACABLE, *adjective* appeasable, benevolent, capable of being appeased, capable of being pacified, charitable, clement, compassionate, conciliatory, disposed to mercy, *exorabilis,* exorable, forbearant, forbearing, forgiving, generous, gracious, indulgent, lenient, longanimous, magnanimous, merciful, mild, pacifiable, *placabilis,* reasonable, reconcilable, reluctant to punish, ruthful, satisfiable, softhearted, sparing, understanding, unresentful, unrevengeful, unvindictive, willing to forgive

PLACATE, *verb* allay, appease, assuage, bring to terms, calm, conciliate, disarm, dulcify, heal the breach, humor, hush, make peace, mollify, pacificate, pacify, patch up a quarrel, *placare,* please, propitiate, quiet, reconcile, restore harmony, salve, satisfy, silence, smooth, soothe, still, tranquilize, win over

PLACE, *noun* area, city, community, country, district, division, environment, locale, locality, location, neighborhood, point, region, scene, section, site, spot, state, territory, town, vicinity, village, zone
ASSOCIATED CONCEPTS: jurisdiction, long-arm jurisdiction, place of domicile, place of employment, place of residence, place to be named with particularity in searches and seizures, short-arm jurisdiction, venue

PLACID, *adjective* at peace, balmy, calm, calmative, collected, composed, cool, easeful, easygoing, equable, even, gentle, halcyon, halcyonian, imperturable, irenic, irenical, meek, mild, motionless, pacific, paradisiacal, pastoral, patient, peaceable, peaceful, *placidus,* quiescent, quiet, quietus, reposeful, restful, serene, smooth, soothing, still, stormless, subdued, tame, tranquil, *tranquillus,* unagitated, undemonstrative, undisturbed, unexcited, unimpassioned, unmoved, unruffled, unstirring, untroubled

PLAGIARISM, *noun* appropriation, appropriation of a literary composition, copying, copyright infringement, duplication, forgery, imitation, imitation of an original, infringement, literary forgery, literary piracy, literary theft, misappropriation, pilfering, reproducing, reproduction, simulation, stealing, taking, thievery, unauthorized borrowing
ASSOCIATED CONCEPTS: copyright

PLAGIARIZE, *verb* adopt as one's own, apply to one's own uses, appropriate, avail oneself of, borrow dishonestly, copy from, counterfeit, duplicate, expropriate, fabricate, falsify, follow as a model, forge, imitate, infringe, misappropriate, paraphrase, pass off another's ideas as one's own, pass off another's writings as one's own, pirate, reduplicate, steal

PLAGUE, *verb* afflict, aggravate, aggrieve, annoy, badger, bait, bedevil, beset, bother, browbeat, bullyrag, cross, devil, discommode, discompose, displease, disquiet, distress, disturb, *exagitare,* exasperate, *exercere,* fret, gall, gibe, grate, harry, haunt, heckle, hector, incommode, inflict pain on, irk, irritate, macerate, molest, mortify, nag, needle, nettle, offend, oppress, pain, persecute, pester, pique, pother, prey on, provoke, rack, roil, ruffle, scourge, smite, spite, taunt, tease, torment, torture, trouble, try the patience, vex, worry

PLAIN LANGUAGE, *noun* accepted language, clear language, cogent writing, concise writing, conventional language, correct English, exact writing, plain English, plain speaking, plain speech, precise expression, precise writing, specific writing, unambiguous legalese, understandable language
Generally: plain language laws
ASSOCIATED CONCEPTS: comprehensible writing, correct writing, effective writing, proper writing

PLAINT, *noun* agony, anguish, complaint, cry, dirge, discontent, displeasure, dissatisfaction, distress, expression of discontent, expression of grief, expression of pain, grief, grieving, groan, lament, *lamenta,* lamentation, moan, outcry, *querela, querimonia,* sigh, sorrow, wail, whine, woe

PLAINTIFF, *noun* accuser, adversary, claimant, complainant, individual who brings a lawsuit, litigant, one who brings an action, opponent, party to the suit, party who sues, petitioner, *petitor,* suitor
ASSOCIATED CONCEPTS: indispensable party plaintiff, nominal plaintiff, proper plaintiff, real plaintiff, third-party plaintiff
FOREIGN PHRASES: ***Reus excipiendo fit actor.*** The defendant by pleading may make himself a plaintiff. ***Melior est conditio possidentis ubi neuter jus habet.*** The condition of the possessor and that of the defendant is better than that of the plaintiff. ***Cum par delictum est duorum, semper oneratur petitor, et melior habetur possessoris causa.*** When there is equal fault on both sides, the burden is always placed on the plaintiff, and the cause of the possessor is preferred. ***In praeparatoriis ad judicium, favetur actori.*** In those matters preceding judgment, the plaintiff is favored.

PLAN, *noun* agenda, alternative, ambition, arrangement, cabal, campaign, complot, conspiracy, course of action, curriculum, design, draft, expedient, forethought, hope, intendment, intent, intention, itinerary, plot, predeliberation, preparation, program, projection, proposal, proposed action, proposition, prospectus, readiness, resolve, schedule, scheme, strategem, strategy, suggestion, syllabus, tactic, undertaking
ASSOCIATED CONCEPTS: ecological plan, feasibility plan, plan for reorganization, planning board

PLAN, *verb* aim, arrange, block out, cabal, calculate, collude, complot, concoct, connive, conspire, contrive, counterplot, design, determine upon, devise, engineer, establish guidelines for, expect, figure, frame, harbor a design, have a policy, intend, intrigue, lay out, lay the foundation, look ahead, machinate, make arrangements, make preparations, make ready, map out, mark out a course, organize, outline, plot, prearrange, preconcert, precontrive, predesign, predetermine, premeditate, prepare, project, propose, provide for, purpose, resolve, schedule, scheme, set up, shape a course, take measures, think ahead, work out

PLANT *(Covertly place),* ***verb*** bury, cache, camouflage, cloak, cover up, disguise, hide away, keep clandestine, keep hidden, keep secret, mantle, mask, obscure, put in concealment, put out of sight, render invisible, screen, secrete, shade, shroud, veil, wrap
ASSOCIATED CONCEPTS: entrapment

PLANT *(Place firmly),* ***verb*** base, bed, deposit, embed, engraft, ensconce, establish, fix, ground, implant, impregnate, infix, inject, inlay, insert, inset, install, instill, lay the foundation, locate, make a place for, place, put, root, set, set firmly, set up, settle, situate, sow, station, stick in, thrust in

PLATFORM, *noun* assumed position, attitude, body of principles, campaign promises, course, course of action, declaration, declaration of policy, doctrine, line of conduct, outlook, party line, party planks, plan, plan of action, point of view, policy, position, precepts, principles, program, proposal, proposed action, proposition, rule of action, scheme, tenets, view

PLATITUDE, *noun* absence of meaning, banality, cliche, commonplace expression, commonplace idea, commonplace phrase, dearth of ideas, dull comment, flat saying, hackneyed expression, hackneyed idea, hackneyed phrase, hackneyed saying, inanity, insipid remark, meaningless saying, nonsense, reiteration, senseless prate, stale comment, stereotyped saying, threadbare phrase, trite expression, trite phrase, trite remark, trite saying, triviality, truism, vapid expression, want of originality

PLAUSIBILITY, *noun* believability, capability, chance, contingency, credibility, eventuality, feasibility, liability, likelihood, possibility, potentiality, probability, prospect, sense, viability

PLAUSIBLE, *adjective* accepted, apparent, arguable, believable, cogitable, colorable, commanding belief, conceivable, conjecturable, convincing, credible, defensible, demanding belief, deserving belief, feasible, grantable, imaginable, justifiable, legitimate, logical, maintained, ostensible, possible, presumable, *probabilis,* putative, rational, reasonable, seeming, seemingly worthy of acceptance, sensible, sound, supposed, suppositional, thinkable, *verisimilis,* within the realm of possibility, worthy of credence

PLEA, *noun* allegation, answer, arguments at the bar, assertion, claim, counterstatement, defendant's answer to charges, defense, *exceptio, excusatio,* legal argument, legal defense, *petitio,* pleading, pleadings, rebuttal, refutation, reply, response, retort, statement alleged in defense, statement alleged in justification, statement of defense, statement which answers the charges, statements on behalf of the defense
ASSOCIATED CONCEPTS: entering a plea, plea in abatement, plea in bar, plea in equity, plea of estoppel, plea of guilty, plea of insanity, plea of nolo contendere, plea of not guilty, plea of payment, plea of recoupment, plea of release, plea of self-defense, plea of setoff
FOREIGN PHRASES: ***Ambiguum placitum interpretari debet contra proferentem.*** An ambiguous plea ought to be interpreted against the party entering it. ***Exceptio falsi omnium***

ultima. A false plea is the worst of all. ***Interdum evenit ut exceptio quae prima facie justa videtur, tamen inique noceat.*** It sometimes happens that a plea which on its face seems just, nevertheless is injurious and inequitable.

PLEAD *(Allege in a legal action),* ***verb*** advance, affirm, affirm explicitly, allege, assert, assert formally, assert positively, attest to, bring forward, contend, emphasize, enunciate, maintain, make an affidavit, make an assertion, present, proclaim, put forth, put forward, put in an affidavit, reaffirm, reassert, set forth, state, state emphatically, stress, swear
ASSOCIATED CONCEPTS: plead a cause of action, responsive pleading

PLEAD *(Argue a case),* ***verb*** advocate, argue at the bar, argue the point, bring into court, *causam agere,* contend for, defend a case, maintain by arguments, prosecute one's case, put one's case, speak for, speak up for, stand up for, state one's case, urge reasons for, use arguments

PLEAD *(Implore),* ***verb*** address a request, beseech, call upon, charge, clamor for, entreat, importune, make a request, *obsecrare, orare,* petition, prefer a request, press, put up a request, request, solicit, supplicate, urge

PLEAD GUILTY, ***verb*** accept guilt, acknowledge guilt, admit guilt, concede fault, confess guilt, declare guilt
ASSOCIATED CONCEPTS: prosecution of a criminal case

PLEAD INNOCENT, ***verb*** contradict charges of guilt, disaffirm guilt, disavow guilt, disclaim any wrongdoing, refute charges, reject charges, repudiate guilt
ASSOCIATED CONCEPTS: prosecution of a criminal case

PLEADING, ***noun*** accusation, allegation, allegation of facts, answer, argument, claim, complaint, counterstatement, defendant's answer to charges, defense, denial, formal assertion, formal averment, plaintiff's allegations, plea, rebuttal, reply, responsive allegations, statement of defense, written statement of defense, written statements of accusation
ASSOCIATED CONCEPTS: alternative pleading, amendment to a pleading, amplication of the pleadings, argumentative pleading, blind pleading, clarification of the pleading, defect in the pleading, demurrer, failure to state a cause of action, failure to state a claim, formal pleading, frivolous pleading, inconsistent pleadings, liberal construction of pleadings, motion to correct pleadings, motion to dismiss the pleading, petition, prejudicial pleading, privileged pleadings, responsive pleading, scandalous pleading, sham pleading, supplemental pleading, verified pleading
FOREIGN PHRASES: ***Placita negativa duo exitum non faciunt.*** Two negative pleas do not make an issue. ***Qui non negat fatetur.*** He who does not deny admits. ***Ambigua responsio contra proferentem est accipienda.*** An ambiguous answer is to be taken against him who offers it.

PLEASANT, ***adjective*** affable, agreeable, amiable, attractive, congenial, darling, delightful, desirable, dulcet, enjoyable, felicific, felicitous, good, good-natured, harmonious, inviting, kindly, nice, palatable, personable, pleasing, pleasurable, pretty, satisfying, sweet, welcome

PLEASE, ***verb*** amuse, appease, assuage, captivate, cater to, charm, coddle, comfort, content, delight, divert, entertain, fulfill, gladden, gratify, humor, indulge, ingratiate, mollify, pamper, placate, pleasure, quench, sate, satiate, satisfy, spoil, suit, titillate, treat

PLEASURE, ***noun*** benefit, bliss, comfort, content, contentedness, delectation, delight, diversion, ease, elation, enjoyment, excitement, felicity, fulfillment, gaiety, gladness, glee, gratification, happiness, intoxication, jollity, joy, jubilation, pleasance, relish, satisfaction, thrill

PLEBISCITE, ***noun*** ballot, choice, election, mandate, poll, referendum, vote

PLEDGE *(Binding promise),* ***noun*** act of giving one's word, agreement, assurance, attestation, avowal, avowance, commitment, compact, contract, covenant, guarantee, oath, obligation, promise, promissory oath, *promissum,* solemn declaration, solemn word, statement on oath, undertaking, vow, warranty, word, word of honor

PLEDGE *(Security),* ***noun*** collateral, deposit, earnest, earnest payment, guarantee, installment, personal security, *pignus,* real security, security, stake, stake money, token payment
ASSOCIATED CONCEPTS: assignment, collateral security, pledge of securities, pledged personalty, pledged property, secured transactions

PLEDGE *(Deposit),* ***verb*** bond, give as a guarantee, give as security for a debt, give as security for an obligation, give as surety, give one's signature, give security, guarantee, hypothecate, impignorate, indorse, insure, offer collateral, post, put in pawn, put up, stake

PLEDGE *(Promise the performance of),* ***verb*** assert solemnly, assure, avow, be answerable for, become bound to, bind, bind oneself, commit oneself, contract an obligation, covenant, engage solemnly, engage to give, give a guarantee, give assurance, give one's word, guarantee, make a promise, *obligare, oppignerare,* promise solemnly, take upon oneself, undertake, warrant, vow

PLENARY, ***adjective*** absolute, complete, comprehensive, entire, exhaustive, full, full-blown, full-charged, fully constituted, fully furnished, limitless, thorough, total, unconfined, undiminished, unlimited, unqualified, unrestricted, whole
ASSOCIATED CONCEPTS: plenary action

PLENIPOTENTIARY, ***noun*** advocate, agent, ambassador, assistant, broker, chancellor, coagent, consul, delegate, deputy, diplomat, diplomatic agent, emissary, envoy, factor, legate, lieutenant, messenger, official representative, proctor, provost, proxy, regent, representative, secondary, speaker, spokesman, spokesperson, substitute, surrogate, viceroy

PLENITUDE, ***noun*** abundance, affluence, ampleness, amplitude, avalanche, bounteousness, capacity, copiousness, deluge, enough, fruitfulness, luxury, mass, opulence, piles, plethora, profusion, prosperity, quantity, sufficiency, torrent, volume, wealth

PLETHORA, ***noun*** abundance, accumulation, amplitude, congestion, deluge, engorgement, excess, exorbitance, exorbitancy, flood, full measure, fullness, glut, great quantity, heap, impletion, inundation, load, margin, nimiety, overabundance, overflow, overload, overplus, oversupply, plentifulness, plenty, profuseness, profusion, repleteness, repletion, richness, satiation, satiety, saturation, spate, superabundance, superfluity, superfluousness, supersaturation, surfeit, surplus, surplusage, swelling, turgescence, undue amount

PLIABLE, ***adjective*** accommodating, acquiescent, adaptable, adaptive, adjustable, alterable, amenable, assenting, bendable, biddable, changeable, compliant, conformable, conforming, controllable, docile, ductile, easily bent, easily influenced, easily persuaded, easygoing, elastic, facile, fictile, *flexibilis,* flexible, flexile, formable, formative, governable, impressionable, inclined, lamblike, *lentus,* limber, lissome, lithe, lithesome, malleable, manageable, manipulable, meek, modifiable, moldable, mutable, nonresisting, obedient, obliging, persuadable, persuasible, pervious, plastic, pliant, protean, proteiform, receptive, responsive, sequacious, servile, slavish, stretchable, suasible, submissive, supple, swayable, teachable, tractable, tractile, variable, versatile, willing, yielding

PLIANT, ***adjective*** accommodating, acquiescent, adaptable, agreeable, bendable, compliable, compliant, concessive, conformable, conforming, deferential, docile, ductile, easily bent, easily persuaded, elastic, flexible, formable, impressible, impressionable, indecisive, indulgent, influenceable, irresolute, *lentus,* limber, lithe, malleable, manageable, meek, moldable, *mollis,* movable, nonresisting, obedient, obeisant, passive, plastic, pliable, readily influenced, receptive, responsive, sequacious, servile, slavish, soft, submissive, subordinate, subservient, suggestible, supple, susceptible, susceptive, swayable, tractable, tractile, unassertive, undecided, willing, yielding

PLIGHT, ***noun*** adverse circumstance, adversity, awkward situation, case, circumstance, condition, corner, crisis, critical situation, difficulty, dilemma, embarrassing position, embarrassing situation, emergency, footing, hardship, imbroglio, lot, misfortune, muddle, pass, pinch, position, predicament, problem, quagmire, quandary, reverse, scrape, setback, situation, state, state of affairs, station, strait, trial, trouble

PLOT *(Land),* ***noun*** acreage, *agellus,* block, division, field, ground, lot, parcel of land, patch, piece of land, plat, property, tract

PLOT *(Secret plan),* ***noun*** cabal, chicane, collusion, complicity, complot, *coniuratio,* conspiracy, *conspiratio,* counterplot, deception, design, intrigue, manipulation, ploy, ruse, scheme, stratagem, tactic, trick

PLOT, ***verb*** act in collusion, arrange, be in collusion, cabal, collude, connive, conspire, deal secretly, devise, engineer, form a plan, frame, have designs, intrigue, machinate, make a plan, make arrangements, make preparations, maneuver, organize, outline, plan mischief, plan secretly, prearrange, preconcert, premeditate, prepare, scheme, take measures, take steps, undermine, work out

PLOY, ***noun*** action, artifice, contrivance, device, maneuver, mechanism, plan, ruse, scheme, stratagem, trick, way, wile

PLUNDER, ***noun*** booty, depredation, devastation, foray, haul, ill-gotten goods, illicit gains, loot, maraud, pillage, *praeda,* raid, *rapina,* rapine, ravin, razzia, robbery, sack, seizure, spoils, spoliation, stolen articles, stolen goods, take, theft

PLUNDER, ***verb*** buccaneer, carry off, *compilare,* deplume, depredate, desolate, despoil, displume, divest, *expilare,* flay, impoverish, lay in ruins, lay waste, loot, maraud, overthrow, pillage, pirate, *praedari,* prey on, purloin, raid, ransack, ravage, raze, reave, rifle, rob, ruin, sack, seize, spoliate, steal, strip, take away, thieve

PLURALITY, ***noun*** advantage in votes cast, bulk, great number, host, large amount, large number, large quantity, lead, main part, majority, multitude, preponderance, preponderancy, shoal, superiority in number, weight of numbers
ASSOCIATED CONCEPTS: majority, quorum

PLY, ***verb*** busy oneself with, carry on, devote oneself to, do work with, employ, engage in, *exercere,* exercise, exploit, handle, make use of, manipulate, occupy oneself with, operate, persevere at, practice, pursue, put in practice, put into effect, tackle, take up, undertake, use, utilize, wage, wield, work

POACH, ***verb*** appropriate, carry off, filch, *furtim feras intercipere,* make off with, misappropriate, peculate, pilfer, pirate, plunder by stealth, purloin, rifle, run off with, snatch, steal, take by illegal methods, take by unfair methods, take illegally, walk off with

POIGNANT, ***adjective*** acute, affecting, arresting, bitter, eloquent, emotional, engaging, engrossing, expressive, impactful, impressive, inspirational, moving, passionate, penetrating, pert, piquing, provoking, sensitive, stirring, touching

POINT *(Item),* ***noun*** argument, *caput,* consideration, designated ground, detail, feature, ground, issue, matter, particular, reason, *res,* specific, thought
ASSOCIATED CONCEPTS: point of law, point of order

POINT *(Period of time),* ***noun*** conjuncture, exact moment, hour, instant, interval, juncture, moment, occasion, precise moment, second, specific moment, stage, time

POINT *(Purpose),* ***noun*** aim, core, design, end, essence, goal, import, intent, intention, motive, object, objective, purport, reason, significance, substance

POINT OF VIEW, ***noun*** angle, angle of vision, apprehension, attitude, belief, concept, conception, conviction, estimate, idea, opinion, outlook, perception, perspective, platform, position, posture, private opinion, respect, side, slant, stand, standpoint, viewpoint

POINTLESS, ***adjective*** aimless, brainless, empty, frivolous, fruitless, haphazard, hopeless, illogical, immature, inane, inconsequential, insignificant, mindless, minor, negligible, nonsensical, purposeless, senseless, slight, trifling, trivial, unimportant, unreasonable, wasteful

POISE, ***noun*** air, aspect, attitude, bearing, behavior, breeding, carriage, class, composure, conduct, counterpoise, decorum, demeanor, deportment, elegance, exceptional pedigree, finest breeding, look, mannerisms, manners, mien, presence, refinement, stance, station

POISON, ***noun*** agent that kills, bane, contagion, substance that kills, toxic, toxicant, toxin, venom

POLARIZE, ***verb*** break up into opposing factions, contrapose, contrast, oppose, pit against one another, put in opposition

POLEMIC, ***adjective*** argumental, argumentative, conflicting, contentious, contestable, contradictory, controversial, debatable, dialectic, dialectical, discordant, discrepant, disputatious, dissentient, dissonant, divided, eristic, eristical, factious, inharmonious, open to debate, open to discussion, open to question, polemical, pugnacious, quarrelsome, schismatic, subject to controversy, unreconciled

POLEMICAL, *adjective* acidic, aggressive, argumentative, bearish, bellicose, belligerent, bilious, cantankerous, combative, contentious, contrary, controversial, disputatious, feisty, fractious, intractable, militant, obdurate, obstinate, pugnacious, quarrelsome, querulous, recalcitrant, scrappy, testy, truculent

POLICE, *noun* arm of the law, constabulary, custodians of the law, detective force, forces of law and order, government officers, law enforcement agency, law enforcement agents, law enforcement body, officers, officers of the law, peace officers, police force, police officers
ASSOCIATED CONCEPTS: police action, police brutality, police power

POLICE, *verb* care for, check, control, exercise authority, exert authority, have authority, have charge of, invigilate, keep guard, keep in order, keep in view, keep order, keep orderly, keep under control, keep vigil, keep watch, observe, overlook, oversee, patrol, preserve public order, preserve public tranquility, prevent crime, prevent offenses against the state, promote public health and safety, protect, regulate, render safe, restrain, restrict access, rule, safeguard, secure, stand guard, stand sentinel, superintend, supervise, systematize, use one's authority, watch, watch diligently

POLICY *(Contract),* ***noun*** agreement, arrangement, contractual obligation, contractual statement, insurance contract, legal document, mutual agreement, mutual undertaking, obligation, pact, schedule, understanding
ASSOCIATED CONCEPTS: insurance policy

POLICY *(Plan of action),* ***noun*** approach, *consilium,* course, course of action, course of conduct, doctrine, established order, fundamental principles, general guidelines, general principles, governing course of action, governing plan, governing principle, line, line of action, line of conduct, management, manner of proceeding, method, mode of management, party line, plan, plan of campaign, platform, polity, prescribed form, principles, procedure, program, proposal, proposed action, proposition, rule of action, scheme, stratagem, ways
ASSOCIATED CONCEPTS: public policy

POLITIC, *adjective* acute, artful, artfully contrived, astute, *astutus,* brilliant, calculating, canny, careful, cautious, circumspect, clever, considerate, contemplative, crafty, cunning, deceitful, diplomatic, discreet, effective, efficacious, enlightened, expedient, farsighted, feline, foxy, guarded, heedful, ingenious, judicial, judicious, knowing, mindful, perceptive, practical, provident, *prudens,* prudent, prudential, prudently contrived, regardful, sagacious, sensible, sharp, shrewd, subtle, tactful, thoughtful, well-adapted, well-advised, well-devised, well-informed, well-judged, wily, wise

POLITICAL, *adjective* administrative, bureaucratic, civic, *civilis,* governmental, partisan, public, *publicus*
ASSOCIATED CONCEPTS: political question

POLITICAL QUESTION, *noun* controversy that is nonjusticiable, declination to rule on a case, doctrine that prevents encroachment by judiciary on legislative and executive branches, nonjudicial matter to be determined by the legislative or executive branch, nonjusticiable controversy, nonjusticiable question, nonlegal issue of politics over which a court lacks jurisdiction

POLITICAL SPIN, *noun* appropriate fashion, comfortable alibi, comfortable approach, comfortable form, defensive methodology, exculpable approach, exculpatory approach, explanatory manner, move, nicety, normal approach, perfect answer, political blueprint, political design, political explanation, political game plan, political program, political scheme, political tactic, political tactics, reasonable solution, right strategy, shift, smooth political technique, style, understandable modus operandi

POLITICAL THEATER, *noun* crafty scheme, political antics, political artifice, political contrivance, political display, political exhibit, political exhibition, political intrigue, political machinations, political means, political methods, political plot, political scheme, political show, political showmanship

POLITICIAN, *noun* campaigner, candidate, governmental leader, lawgiver, lawmaker, legislator, office seeker, officeholder, officer of state, official, partisan, party member, politico, public servant, representative, statesman

POLITICS, *noun* campaigning, *civilis ratio,* electioneering, governance, government, matters of state, partisanism, party leadership, party politics, party system, political affairs, political influence, political involvement, political maneuvers, political methods, political partisanship, political process, political strategy, public service, state affairs, statesmanship
ASSOCIATED CONCEPTS: campaign financing laws, disclosure laws, election laws, lobbying laws, reporting laws
FOREIGN PHRASES: ***Politiae legibus non leges, politiis adaptandae.*** Politics should be adapted to the laws, not the laws to politics.

POLITY, *noun* body politic, civil constitution, commonwealth, constitution, country, course, form of government, fundamental principles of government, line, nation, nationality, plan of action, platform, policy, principles, procedure, program, recognized principles, *reipublicae forma,* republic, sovereignty, state, system of government

POLL *(Canvass),* ***noun*** capitation, catalog of persons, census, census report, census return, count, enumeration, evaluation, inquiry, numbering, numeration, public opinion, questionary, questionnaire, register, registration, return, statistic, survey, tabulation, tally

POLL *(Casting of votes),* ***noun*** ballot, casting of ballots, choice, consensus, decision, determination, election, elective privilege, expression of will, formal expression of choice, plebiscite, popular decision, preference, referendum, selection, voice, vote
ASSOCIATED CONCEPTS: electioneering at poll, polling place

POLL, *verb* ballot, call the roll, canvass, collect the vote, compute, conduct research on, count, enumerate, keep count of, keep score, list, make a survey, record the vote, register, run checks on, sample, score, survey, tabulate, take a census, take a roll call, tally, total

POLLUTE, *verb* adulterate, alloy, befoul, begrime, bemire, besmirch, bespatter, contaminate, corrupt, debase, debauch,

defile, degrade, denaturalize, deprave, desecrate, destroy, dirty, dishonor, filthify, foul, grime, impair, infect, maculate, make foul, mess, mire, muck, muddy, pervert, poison, profane, prostitute, render filthy, smirch, soil, spatter, spoil, stain, sully, taint, tarnish, undermine, unhallow, violate, vitiate
ASSOCIATED CONCEPTS: ecology, environmental conservation, environmental protection, nuissance

POLLUTION, *noun* affliction, contamination, corruption, decay, decomposition, desecration, deterioration, dirtiness, fouling, greenhouse effect, illness, impurity, plague, rot, ruination, scourge, spoiling, withering

POLYGAMOUS, *adjective* engaging in bigamy, engaging in unlawful marriage, having multiple husbands, having multiple wives, having plurality of wives or husbands, practicing plural marriage
ASSOCIATED CONCEPTS: bigamy, monogamy

POMPOUS, *adjective* arrant, arrogant, assumptive, audacious, authoritarian, barefaced, belligerent, bombastic, bossy, bumptious, cavalier, chesty, conceited, condescending, contentious, dictatorial, domineering, haughty, high-and-mighty, high-handed, huffy, imperious, important, lofty, lordly, masterful, peremptory, pompous, presuming, presumptuous, pretentious, self-asserting, self-assertive, self-important, supercilious, superior

PONDER, *verb* analyze, apply the mind, appraise, brood over, cerebrate, cogitate, commune with oneself, concentrate upon, consider, *considerare,* contemplate, debate, deliberate, devote thought to, digest, evaluate, examine, excogitate, give thought to, intellectualize, introspect, meditate, mull over, muse, occupy the thoughts with, *ponderare,* premeditate, puzzle over, rack the brains, ratiocinate, rationalize, reason, reflect upon, review, revolve in the mind, ruminate, speculate, study, take account of, take under consideration, theorize, think deeply, think on, turn over in the mind, view from all sides, view with deliberation, weigh, wonder about

PONDERABLE, *adjective* appreciable, ascertainable, cognizable, comprehensible, considerable, discernible, discoverable, distinguishable, knowable, palpable, perceptible, real, recognizable, substantive, understandable, weighable

PONDEROUS, *adjective* awkward, big, boring, bulky, burdensome, clumsy, corpulent, cumbersome, cumbrous, dense, drearisome, dreary, droning, dull, elephantine, enormous, forced, *gravis,* hard to lift, heavy, hulking, labored, large, leaden, lifeless, lumbering, lumpish, lusterless, lymphatic, massive, monotonous, onerous, oppressive, overweight, *ponderosus,* prosaic, slow-moving, sluggish, stiff, stolid, stout, supine, tedious, unlively, unmanageable, unwieldy, wearisome, wearying, weighty

PONZI SCHEME, *noun* fraud, fraudulent investment operation, fraudulent transfer scheme, illegal scam, illusory profit scheme, investment fraud, pyramid scheme, scam, unlawful investment activity, unlawful scam, unregistered investment

POOL, *noun* alliance, amalgamation, bank, cartel, coalition, collaboration, collective, collectivism, combination, combination of funds, combine, common fund, common ownership, community of possession, confederacy, confederation, consolidation, consortium, cooperation, copartnership, cosharing, federation, joint concern, joint ownership, joint possession, league, mutual ownership, partnership, syndicate, trust, unification, union
ASSOCIATED CONCEPTS: insolvency pool, involuntary market pool, mortgage pool, stock pool

POOL, *verb* affiliate with, ally, amalgamate, associate, band together, blend, collaborate, combine, confederate, conjoin, connect, consolidate, coordinate, enter into partnership with, federate, involve together, league, merge, mix, share, unify, unite
ASSOCIATED CONCEPTS: pooling of assets

POOR *(Inferior in quality),* ***adjective*** bad, badly made, barely passable, base, beggarly, below par, below standard, cheap, coarse, common, contemptible, crude, defective, deficient, dubious, faulty, flimsy, gimcrack, imperfect, inadequate, inartistic, indifferent, inferior, lacking in quality, low, low-grade, marred, meager, mean, mediocre, *mediocris,* miserable, ordinary, paltry, pitiful, rejected, scant, scrub, scrubby, scurvy, second best, second-rate, seedy, shabby, shoddy, sleazy, sordid, sorry, subgrade, substandard, tawdry, *tenuis,* trashy, under average, undergrade, unimpressive, unsatisfactory, unsightly, unworthy, valueless, vulgar, wanting, weak, worthless, wretched
ASSOCIATED CONCEPTS: poor condition

POOR *(Underprivileged),* ***adjective*** bankrupt, beggared, bereft of funds, depleted, deprived, destitute, dispossessed, distressed, drained, *egens,* embarrassed, empty-handed, fortuneless, hard up, ill-provided for, impecunious, impoverished, in distress, in embarrassed circumstances, in narrow circumstances, in need, in penury, in pinched circumstances, in reduced circumstances, in straitened circumstances, in want, indigent, *inops,* insolvent, *mendicus,* moneyless, necessitous, needful, needy, out of cash, out of money, pauperized, penniless, penurious, poverty-stricken, reduced, reduced to beggary, ruined, short, short of money, starved, straitened, strapped, suffering privation, unable to make ends meet, unmoneyed, unprosperous, unprovided for, with meager funds, with scanty funds, without a penny
ASSOCIATED CONCEPTS: petition to proceed as a poor person

POPULACE, *noun* body politic, canaille, citizenry, common folk, common people, commonage, commonalty, commoners, community, crowd, folk, folks, general public, habitants, humanity, individuals, inhabitants, masses, multitude, nation, people, persons, *plebs,* population, proletariat, public, residents, society

POPULAR, *adjective* accepted, accredited, admired, asked for, attractive, beloved, celebrated, conventional, coveted, current, customary, demanded, desirable, desired, doted on, enjoyed, esteemed, estimable, fair-haired, famous, fashionable, favored, favorite, highly thought of, in demand, in favor, in high esteem, in high favor, in vogue, liked, loved, noted, orthodox, palatable, pet, pleasing, praised, preferred, prevailing, prevalent, received, requested, respected, sought after, stamped with approval, standard, stylish, venerable, wanted, well-liked, well-received, well thought of, winning
ASSOCIATED CONCEPTS: popular election, popular name, popular name for a statute, popular sense

POPULATION, *noun* body politic, citizenry, citizens, *civium,* commonalty, community, dwellers, folk, general public, habitancy, habitants, humanity, *incolarum numerus,* inhabitants, masses, nation, natives, number of people, people, persons, populace, populacy, public, residents, society

POPULOUS, ***adjective*** *celeber,* close, closely packed, compact, crammed, crawling with people, crowded, dense, *frequens,* full, inhabited, massed, multitudinous, numerous, occupied, packed, peopled, populated, rife, swarming, teeming, tenanted, thick, thickly settled, thronged, well-populated

PORNOGRAPHY, ***noun*** bawdiness, curiosa, erotica, filth, indecency, lewdness, lubricity, obscene art, obscene literature, obscenity, prurience, salaciousness, salacity, smut, vulgarity
ASSOCIATED CONCEPTS: censorship, First Amendment rights

PORTAL, ***noun*** access, aperture, approach, corridor, door, doorway, entrance, entranceway, entry, gate, gateway, ingress, inlet, means of access, opening, passageway, postern, pylon

PORTEND, ***verb*** adumbrate, announce, augur, augurate, auspicate, be an omen, be harbinger, betoken, bode, caution, divine, forebode, forecast, foreshadow, foreshow, foretell, foretoken, forewarn, give token, herald, indicate, indicate beforehand, menace, notify, omen, ominate, precurse, predict, prefigurate, prefigure, preindicate, premonish, premonstrate, presage, preshow, presignify, prognosticate, prophesy, put on guard, show promise, *significare,* signify, threaten, vaticinate, warn

PORTENT, ***noun*** augury, auspice, boding, caution, foreboding, forecast, foreshadowing, foretelling, harbinger, herald, note, precursor, prediction, prefiguring, presage, prognosis, prophecy, token, warning

PORTENTOUS *(Eliciting amazement),* ***adjective*** amazing, astonishing, breathtaking, exceptional, extraordinary, great, inconceivable, incredible, indescribable, marvelous, memorable, miraculous, notable, noteworthy, novel, out of the ordinary, outstanding, phenomenal, prodigal, prodigious, rare, remarkable, shocking, singular, staggering, startling, stirring, striking, stupendous, superb, superlative, surprising, tremendous, uncustomary, unexampled, unheard of, unique, unparalleled, unprecedented, unusual, wonderful, wondrous

PORTENTOUS *(Ominous),* ***adjective*** alarming, augural, augurous, baleful, black, bodeful, boding, cautionary, dark, dire, direful, divinatory, doomful, dread, dreadful, dreary, fateful, fatiloquent, fearful, forbidding, foreboding, foretelling, forewarning, forthcoming, frightening, frightful, gloomy, grim, haunting, heralding, ill-boding, ill-fated, ill-starred, inauspicious, indicative, intimidating, mantic, menacing, minacious, minatorial, minatory, monitory, ominous, oracular, perilous, portending evil, premonitive, premonitory, presageful, presaging, presentient, prophetic, prophetical, pythonic, sibylline, sinister, somber, suggestive, threatening, unpropitious

PORTFOLIO, ***noun*** futures, holdings, investments, negotiables, *scrinium,* securities, stocks, stocks and bonds

PORTION, ***noun*** allotment, amount, component, element, excerpt, fair share, fragment, installment, measure, moiety, part, percentage, piece, portion, quantity, quota, ration, section, sector, segment, share

PORTION, ***verb*** allocate, allot, apportion, bequeath, bequest, break down into portions, break up into units, budget, disperse, divide into shares, dole, dole out, parcel, partition, prorate, ration, section, segment, separate, split up, split up into units, subdivide

PORTRAY, ***verb*** act, adumbrate, characterize, convey a verbal image, convey an impression, delineate, depict, depicture, *depingere,* describe, detail, draw, express, give words to, illustrate, limn, outline, paint, particularize, picture, present, recreate, report, represent, represent in words, reproduce, set forth, show, sketch, specify, stage, tell vividly

POSE *(Impersonate),* ***verb*** act as, act the part of, ape, assume the character of, assume the role of, copy, counterfeit, double for, emulate, imitate, masquerade as, mimic, mock, model oneself after, parody, pass for, personate, play a part, portray, pretend to be, simulate, take the part of

POSE *(Propound),* ***verb*** advance, ask, assert, broach, declare, interrogate, introduce, lay before, lay down, make a motion, moot, move, offer, posit, postulate, predicate, present, proffer, propose, put forward, put to, puzzle, query, question, set before, state, submit, suggest, tender, throw out, volunteer
ASSOCIATED CONCEPTS: pose a question

POSIT, ***verb*** acknowledge, advance, advocate, affirm, allege, announce, argue, assert, asseverate, assume, attest, aver, avouch, avow, bring forward, certify, cite, claim, contend, declare, enunciate, express, hypothesize, inform, insist, issue a statement, lay down, maintain, moot, pose, postulate, predicate, proclaim, profess, promulgate, pronounce, propose, propound, put forth, put forward, say, set forth, state, stipulate, submit, take a stand, tell, testify, utter with conviction, vouch

POSITION *(Business status),* ***noun*** appointment, assignment, avocation, business, calling, career, concern, duty, echelon, employment, function, incumbency, job, line of business, line of work, means of livelihood, occupation, office, post, practice, profession, pursuit, responsibility, role, situation, specialty, sphere, station, trade, vocation, walk of life, work

POSITION *(Point of view),* ***noun*** apprehension, attitude, bearing, bent, bias, conclusion, feeling, frame of mind, inclination, judgment, leaning, mental outlook, mind set, opinion, outlook, pose, posture, predilection, predisposition, preference, presumption, proclivity, proneness, propensity, sentiment, slant, standpoint, tendency, turn of mind, view, viewpoint, way of thinking

POSITION *(Situation),* ***noun*** circumstances, condition, footing, ground, *locus,* place, plight, posture, predicament, spot, state, station, status

POSITIVE *(Confident),* ***adjective*** assured, believing, certain, *certus,* convinced, decided, decisive, definite, determined, fully convinced, insistent, perfectly sure, persuaded, reassured, satisfied, secure, self-assured, self-confident, sure, trusting, undoubting, unhesitating, unquestioning, unshaken, untroubled, unwavering
ASSOCIATED CONCEPTS: positive identification

POSITIVE *(Incontestable),* ***adjective*** absolute, ascertained, authentic, axiomatic, axiomatical, beyond all question, beyond doubt, categorical, certain, clear, conclusive, decided, definite, determinate, evident, explicit, final, inappealable, incontestable, incontrovertible, indisputable, indubitable, inescapable, infallible, irrefragable, irrefutable,

past dispute, precise, reliable, sound, sure, true, trustworthy, unanswerable, unchallengeable, unconfutable, undeniable, unequivocal, unerring, unimpeachable, unmistakable, unqualified, unquestionable, unrefutable
ASSOCIATED CONCEPTS: positive proof

POSITIVE *(Prescribed),* ***adjective*** assigned, binding, commanded, compulsory, decreed, demanded, dictated, enacted, enjoined, established, exacted, fixed, imperative, imposed, instituted, issued, laid down, legislated, mandatory, obligatory, ordained, required, requisite, ruled, set, stated authoritatively
ASSOCIATED CONCEPTS: positive law

POSSE, ***noun*** arm of the law, armed band, band, band of armed men, band of men armed with legal authority, body of men armed with legal process, body of men summoned by a sheriff, civilian police, custodians of the law, detachment of police, detail, force armed with legal authority, group of deputies, group of persons organized with legal authorization, law enforcement body

POSSESS, ***verb*** acquire, *adfirmatio,* assume ownership, be in possession of, be in receipt of, be seized of, come into possession of, command, control, devolve upon, enjoy, enter into possession, gain, gain for oneself, get, get as one's own, *habere,* have, have a deed for, have a title to, have absolute disposal of, have as property, have at one's command, have at one's disposal, have for one's own, have in hand, have rights to, hold, keep, maintain, monopolize, obtain, occupy, own, receive, retain, secure, seize, take possession, tenere
ASSOCIATED CONCEPTS: lawfully possess, seized or possessed
FOREIGN PHRASES: ***Aliud est possidere, aliud esse in possessione.*** It is one thing to possess; it is another to be in possession.

POSSESSION *(Ownership),* ***noun*** authority, custody, demesne, domination, dominion, exclusive right, lordship, occupancy, *possessio,* proprietorship, right, right of retention, seisin, supremacy, tenancy, title
ASSOCIATED CONCEPTS: action to recover possession, actual possession, adverse possession, chain of possession, constructive possession, continuity of possession, continuous possession, debtor in possession, estate in possession, holder in possession, hostile possession, lawful possession, mortgagee in possession, naked possession, notorious possession, open and notorious possession, party in possession, peaceable possession, person in possession, physical possession, purchaser in possession, quiet possession, right of possession, tenant in possession, undisturbed possession, uninterrupted possession, unlawful possession, wrongful possession
FOREIGN PHRASES: ***Traditio nihil amplius transferre debet vel potest, ad eum qui accipit, quam est apud eum qui tradit.*** Delivery ought to, and can, transfer nothing more to him who receives than is in possession of him who makes the delivery. ***Jus triplex est–propietatis, possessionis, et possibilitatis.*** Right is threefold—of property, of possession, and of possibility. ***In aequali jure melior est conditio possidentis.*** In a case of equal right the condition of the party in possession is the better. ***Pro possessione praesumitur de jure.*** A presumption of law arises from possession. ***Nihil praescribitur nisi quod possidetur.*** There is no prescription for that which is not possessed. ***Privatio praesupponit habitum.*** A deprivation presupposes something held or possessed. ***Duorum in solidum dominium vel possessio esse non potest.*** Sole ownership or possession cannot be in two persons. ***Cum de lucro duorum quaeritur, melior est causa possidentis.*** When the question of gain lies between two persons, the cause of the possessor is the better. ***Longa possessio parit jus possidendi, et tollit actionem vero domino.*** Long possession creates the right of possession, and deprives the true owner of his right of action. ***Aliud est possidere, aliud esse in possessione.*** It is one thing to possess; it is another to be in possession. ***Quod meum est sine facto meo vel defectu meo amitti vel in alium transferri non potest.*** That which is mine cannot be transferred to another without my act or my default. ***Quod meum est sine me auferri non potest.*** What is mine cannot be taken away without my consent. ***Nul charter, nul vente, ne nul done vault perpetualment, si le donor n'est seise al temps de contracts de deux droits, sc. del droit de possession et del droit de propertie.*** No grant, no sale, no gift, is valid forever, unless the donor, at the time of the contract, has two rights, namely, the right of possession and the right of property. ***Donatio perficitur possessione accipientis.*** A gift is perfected by the possession of the receiver. ***Melior est conditio possidentis, et rei quam actoris.*** The condition of the possessor and that of the defendant is better than that of the plaintiff. ***In pari delicto melior est conditio possidentis.*** When the parties are equally in the wrong, the condition of the possessor is the preferable one. ***Longa possessio jus parit.*** Long possession begets right. ***Donator nunquam desinit possidere, antequam donatorius incipiat possidere.*** A donor never ceases to possess until the donee begins to possess. ***Non valet donatio nisi subsequatur traditio.*** A gift is invalid unless accompanied by possession. ***Nemo dare potest quod non habet.*** No one is able to give that which he has not. ***Terra manens vacua occupanti conceditur.*** Land remaining vacant is given to the occupant. ***Non potest videri desisse habere qui nunquam habuit.*** A person who has never had cannot be deemed to have ceased to have it. ***In pari causa possessor potior haberi debet.*** In an equal cause he who has the possession has the advantage. ***Cum par delictum est duorum, semper oneratur petitor et melior habetur possessoris causa.*** When there is equal fault on both sides, the burden is always placed on the plaintiff and the cause of the possessor is preferred.

POSSESSION *(Property),* ***noun*** asset, belonging, bona, chattel, effect, goods, holding, item, item of personalty, money, movable, *possessio,* resource, treasure, valuable
FOREIGN PHRASES: ***Non possessori incumbit necessitas probandi possessiones ad se pertinere.*** It is not incumbent on the possessor of property to prove that his possessions belong to him.

POSSESSIONS, ***noun*** assets, belongings, *bonorum,* capital, chattels, colonies, domain, dominions, earnings, effects, equity, estate, fortune, funds, goods, holdings, items of personalty, material wealth, movables, pecuniary resources, personal property, personalty, *possessio,* private property, property, *res,* resources, stock, stock in trade, territory, treasure, wealth, worldly belongings

POSSIBILITY, ***noun*** achievability, anticipation, attainability, availability, chance, conceivability, conceivableness, expectance, expectancy, expectation, *facultas,* favorable opportunity, favorable prospect, feasibility, gamble, hope, likelihood, opportunity, plausibility, *posse,* potential, potentiality, *potestas,* probability, promise, prospect, suggestion, uncertainty, viability, viableness
FOREIGN PHRASES: ***Jus triplex est–propietatis, possessionis, et possibilitatis.*** Right is threefold—of property, of possession, and of possibility. ***Ultra posse non potest***

esse, et vice versa. What is beyond possibility cannot exist, and the reverse, what cannot exist is not possible.

POSSIBLE, *adjective* achievable, anticipated, apt, attainable, believable, capable, cogitable, conceivable, credible, feasible, grantable, imaginable, liable, likely, obtainable, performable, plausible, potential, probable, promising, rational, realizable, reasonable, superable, supposable, surmountable, thinkable, unrealized, viable, within reach, within the range of possibility, within the realm of possibility, workable

POST, *noun* appointment, berth, billet, business, capacity, career, charge, commission, department, employment, field, function, incumbency, job, line, *locus,* means of livelihood, *munus,* occupation, office, place, position, profession, pursuit, service, situation, station, task, undertaking, vocation, work

POST, *verb* advertise, announce publicly, bestow, call public attention to, circulate, communicate, convey, deliver, dispose of, distribute, give away, give forth, give out, give public notice of, impart, issue, issue a statement, make known, make public, offer to the public, pay, present, print, proclaim, publish, put up a sign, report, spread, spread abroad
ASSOCIATED CONCEPTS: post a notice, post bail

POSTERITY, *noun* bloodline, children, descendants, descent, family, future relatives, heirs, issue, later generations, line, lineage, offspring, *posteritas,* progeny, scion, seed, stock, succeeding generations, successors

POSTHUMOUS, *adjective* after death, continuing after death, following death, occurring after death, postmortem
ASSOCIATED CONCEPTS: posthumous child

POSTPONE, *verb* adjourn, arrest temporarily, defer, delay, *differre,* extend, gain more time, hold off, keep for future action, lay aside, pigeonhole, *proferre,* prorogate, prorogue, push aside, put aside, put off, reprieve, set aside, shelve, stall, stave off, stay, suspend, table
ASSOCIATED CONCEPTS: postpone a case

POSTULATE, *noun* assertion, assumed truth, assumption, axiom, conjecture, foundation, hypothesis, premise, speculation, starting point, statement, suggestion, *sumptio,* supposal, supposition, surmise, theorem, thesis, truism

POSTULATE, *verb* advance, assume, conjecture, consider, contend, determine, guess, hazard a supposition, hypothesize, infer, posit, predicate, premise, presume, presuppose, propound, put forth, put forward, reason, regard as axiomatic, specify, speculate, start, suggest, surmise, take as an axiom, take for granted, theorize, venture a conjecture, venture a supposition

POSTURE *(Attitude),* ***noun*** air, aspect, bearing, bent, cast, demeanor, disposition, disposition of mind, feeling, inclination, leaning, lie, manner, nature, opinion, outlook, partisan outlook, philosophy, point of view, pose, position, presence, sentiment, standpoint, temper, temperament, view, viewpoint, way of thinking

POSTURE *(Situation),* ***noun*** circumstance, *condicio,* condition, conjuncture, context, existing state, footing, juncture, lot, pass, plight, point, position, predicament, setting, shape, standing, state, state of affairs, station, *status,* terms, turn

POTENCY, *noun* ability, authoritativeness, authority, brawn, caliber, capability, clout, command, competence, control, effect, effectiveness, efficacy, energy, faculty, force, function, influence, intensity, main force, might, mightiness, muscle, omnipotence, potential, potentiality, power, powerfulness, predominance, pressure, prestige, puissance, quality, stamina, strength, sway, validity, vigor, virility, virtue, weight

POTENT, *adjective* able, active, affecting, capable, cogent, commanding, compelling, convincing, dominant, dramatic, dynamic, effective, effectual, efficacious, efficient, energetic, forceful, forcible, formidable, generative, impelling, important, impressive, indefatigable, indomitable, influential, inspiring, inspiriting, intense, invincible, manly, masterful, mighty, moving, operative, penetrating, powerful, predominant, prepotent, prevailing, productive, puissant, ruling, stiff, strong, telling, trenchant, useful, valid, vigorous, virile, weighty

POTENTIAL, *adjective* accessible, achievable, allowable, allowed, anticipated, attainable, concealed, conceivable, covert, doable, dormant, expected, feasible, future, imaginable, latent, likely, obtainable, performable, permissible, permitted, possible, *potentialis,* practicable, realizable, thinkable, unapparent, undetected, undisclosed, undiscovered, unexposed, unexpressed, unmanifested, unrealized, unseen, workable
ASSOCIATED CONCEPTS: potential existence, potential interest

POTENTIAL, *noun* ability, aptitude, capability, capacity, chance, competence, dormant energy, endowment, feasibility, force, latent power, might, mightiness, possibility, possibleness, potency, *potentialis,* power, powerfulness, practicability, proficiency, promise, prospect, puissance, qualification, skill, strength, talent, workability
ASSOCIATED CONCEPTS: potential damages, potential loss

POVERTY, *noun* absence, bare subsistence, beggarliness, beggary, dearth, deficiency, deficit, depletion, destitution, difficulty, distress, embarrassed circumstances, exigency, famine, humbleness, impecuniosity, impecuniousness, impoverishment, indigence, insolvency, lack, leanness, loss of fortune, meagerness, mendicancy, mendicity, moneylessness, narrow means, necessitousness, necessity, need, neediness, needy circumstances, paucity, pauperism, pennilessness, penury, poor circumstances, poorness, privation, reduced circumstances, scantiness, scantity, scantness, scarceness, scarcity, shortage, slender means, sparseness, starvation, straitened circumstances, straits, subsistence level, *tenuitas,* unprosperousness, want
ASSOCIATED CONCEPTS: proceed in forma pauperus

POWER, *noun* auspices, authority, command, competence, control, controlment, dominance, domination, dominion, eminence, facility, force, hold, importance, influence, jurisdiction, mastership, mastery, potency, predominance, prepollence, prepollency, pressure, prestige, primacy, puissance, reign, rule, supremacy, supremeness, sway, vis, warrant, weight
ASSOCIATED CONCEPTS: apparent power, appointing power, arbitrary power, capacity, concurrent power, contingent power, continuing power, delegated power, discretionary power, equitable power, exercise of power, extinguishment of power, extraordinary power, general power, implicit power, implied power, inchoate power, incidental power, inherent power, legislative power, limited power, mandatory power, necessary power, nonexclusive power of

appointment, power coupled with an interest, power of alienation, power of appointment, power of attorney, power of disposition, power of sale, power of termination, release of power, retention of power, revocation of power, special power, taxing power, testamentary power
FOREIGN PHRASES: ***Nemo potest facere per obliquum quod non potest facere per directum.*** No man can do indirectly that which he cannot do directly. ***Sequi debet potentia justitiam, non praecedere.*** Power ought to follow justice, not precede it. ***Potentia non est nisi ad bonum.*** Power is not conferred but for the good. ***Fortior et potentior est dispositio legis quam hominis.*** The disposition of the law has greater force and stronger effect than that of man. ***Frustra est potentia quae nunquam venit in actum.*** A power is a vain one if it is never exercised. ***Potestas stricte interpretatur.*** Power should be strictly interpreted. ***Delegatus non potest delegare.*** A representative cannot delegate his authority.

POWERFUL, *adjective* able, able-bodied, armipotent, authoritative, autocratic, autocratical, brawny, cogent, commanding, compelling, consequential, controlling, deafening, dominant, dominating, dynamic, effective, effectual, efficacious, empowered, forceful, forcible, great, hard, hearty, hegemonic, hegemonical, Herculean, high-potency, impelling, imperious, important, impregnable, indomitable, influential, intense, invincible, irresistible, leonine, loud, lusty, magisterial, mighty, multipotent, muscular, obeyed, omnipotent, overpowering, overwhelming, physically strong, plenipotent, potent, powerpacked, prevailing, puissant, regnant, reigning, resounding, rugged, ruling, sinewy, sovereign, stalwart, stentorian, stout, strapping, striking, strong, telling, trenchant, unconquerable, unquenchable, unweakened, vehement, vigorous, weighty

POWERLESS, *adjective* abrogated, adynamic, asthenic, canceled, crippled, debilitated, decrepit, defenseless, deposed, disabled, disqualified, drooping, droopy, effete, emasculated, exhausted, faint, faintish, feeble, figurehead, flaccid, forceless, fragile, frail, futile, harmless, helpless, *impotens,* impotent, impuissant, inactive, inadequate, inapt, incapable, incapacitated, incompetent, indefensible, ineffective, ineffectual, inefficacious, inept, infirm, *infirmus,* inoperative, *invalidus,* languid, languishing, listless, lustless, marrowless, mightless, nerveless, nugatory, null and void, palsied, paralytic, paralyzed, pithless, pregnable, sapless, sickly, sinewless, spent, spineless, strengthless, submissive, superannuated, torpid, unable, unapt, unarmed, unavailing, unempowered, unendowed, unequipped, unfit, unfortified, uninfluential, unnerved, unqualified, unsteady, unstrengthened, unstrung, unsupported, useless, vigorless, vincible, weak, weaponless, without authority, without force, without vitality, yielding

PRACTICABLE, *adjective* achievable, attainable, capable of being done, doable, effectible, feasible, not too difficult, obtainable, operable, performable, possible, practical, realizable, reasonable, within reach, within the bounds of possibility, workable
ASSOCIATED CONCEPTS: as soon as practicable

PRACTICAL, *noun* adaptable, advantageous, aiding, all-purpose, applicable, assisting, beneficial, commodious, conducive, convenient, effective, effectual, efficacious, efficient, employable, expedient, expediential, fitting, functional, handy, helpful, implemental, instrumental, invaluable, of general utility, operational, operative, practicable, profitable, serviceable, suitable, to the purpose, useful, utilitarian, utilizable, valuable, workable

PRACTICE *(Custom),* ***noun*** behavior, common course, confirmed habit, consuetude, conventionality, course of action, course of conduct, customary course, established order, fixed ways, frequent repetition, general course, habit, habitual course, habituation, habitude, inveterate habit, line of action, line of proceeding, manner, matter of course, method, mode, mode of procedure, natural course, order of the day, ordinary course, pattern, prescription, procedure, routine, settled disposition, style, usage, use, usual custom, usual method, way
ASSOCIATED CONCEPTS: custom and usage, practice in the industry
FOREIGN PHRASES: ***Cursus curiae est lex curiae.*** The practice of the court is the law of the court. ***Multa multo exercitatione facilius quam regulis percipies.*** You will perceive many things much more easily by practice than by rule.

PRACTICE *(Procedure),* ***noun*** approach, arrangement, conduct, *consuetudo,* course, course of action, course of conduct, established order, *exercitatio,* form, general guidelines, governing course of action, governing plan, line of action, line of conduct, manner of proceeding, method, mode, mode of management, *mos,* observance, operation, order of the day, organization, outline, plan of action, policy, prescribed form, prescribed usage, process, program, protocol, required manner, routine, rule, rules of business, scheme, stratagem, strategy, system, tactics, treatment, usual way, *usus,* way, way of doing things
ASSOCIATED CONCEPTS: civil practice, criminal practice

PRACTICE *(Professional business),* ***noun*** avocation, business, calling, career, chosen career, chosen field, chosen profession, employment, life, life's work, line of business, line of work, occupation, pursuit, specialty, trade, undertaking, vocation
ASSOCIATED CONCEPTS: practice of law, practice of profession

PRACTICE *(Engage in),* ***verb*** be employed, carry on business, devote oneself to, employ, employ one's professional skill, employ oneself in, engage in, *exercere, facere, factitare,* follow a calling, follow a profession, follow as an occupation, labor at one's vocation, perform the duties of, perform the functions of, pursue, specialize, specialize in, undertake, work at
ASSOCIATED CONCEPTS: practice law

PRACTICE *(Train by repetition),* ***verb*** acquire the habit, apply one's self to, become familiar with, condition, cultivate a habit, discipline, do repeatedly, drill, exercise, familiarize with, learn a habit, *meditari,* perfect a routine, perform repeatedly, prepare, rehearse, school, take training, work at

PRACTICED, *adjective* able, accomplished, adept, adroit, apt, artful, canny, capable, clever, competent, conversant, crafty, deft, dextrous, efficient, effortless, equipped, experienced, expert, facile, gifted, habituated, handy, informed, initiated, knowing, learned, masterful, masterly, panurgic, prepared, proficient, qualified, resourceful, seasoned, shrewd, skilled, skillful, smooth, sophisticated, talented, trained, veteran, well-qualified

PRACTITIONER, *noun* artificer, artisan, artist, attorney, counselor, craftsman, creative worker, journeyman, lawyer, master worker, professional, solicitor, specialist, trained person
ASSOCIATED CONCEPTS: legal practitioner, single practitioner, sole practitioner

PRAGMATIC, *adjective* clear-thinking, expedient, feasible, matter-of-fact, practical, rational, realistic, reasonable, sensible, serviceable, sound, straight-thinking, unidealistic, unromantic, unsentimental, useful, utilitarian

PRAGMATISM, *noun* expedience, expediency, matter of factness, practical attitude, practicality, practicalness, rationality, realism, realistic attitude, realisticness, reasonableness, sensibility, sensibleness, sound thinking, unidealism, unsentimentality

PRAISE, *noun* acclaim, acclamation, accolade, admiration, adulation, advocacy, applause, appreciation, approbation, approval, celebration, commendation, compliment, congratulation, credit, deserved tribute, distinction, encomium, estimation, exaltation, fame, glorification, glory, homage, honor, kudos, laud, laudation, mention, panegyric, plaudit, prestige, recommendation, regard, remembrance, renown, repute, respect, testimonial, tribute

PRAISE, *verb* admire, adore, adulate, applaud, approbate, approve, celebrate, commend, compliment, congratulate, express admiration of, extol, flatter, glorify, hold in esteem, honor, idolize, indorse, laud, panegyrize, pay tribute, pay tribute to, recommend, regard, value, venerate

PRATTLE, *noun* blather, gabble, nonsensical talk, twaddle, verbiage

PRATTLE, *verb* babble, blather, chatter, gab, jabber, prate, prattle, talk nonsense

PRAY, *verb* address a request, adjure, appeal to, apply to, ask earnestly, beseech, bid, call upon, clamor for, cry for help, entreat, entreat persistently, impetrate, implore, importune, make a request, make earnest petition for, make supplication, obtest, *orare,* petition, plead, *precari,* prefer a petition, prefer a request, press, put up petitions, raise up one's voice, requisition, *rogare,* solicit, supplicate, urge, urge persistently, urge repeatedly
ASSOCIATED CONCEPTS: pray for relief in a complaint

PRAYER, *noun* application, application for relief, beseechment, call, claim, earnest entreaty, earnest request, entreaty, humble entreaty, *imploratio,* imploration, importunity, invocation, motion, petition, plea, *precatio,* request, request for relief, request for the aid of the court, requisition, solemn entreaty, supplication, urgent request, *votum*
ASSOCIATED CONCEPTS: prayer for relief

PREAMBLE, *noun* beginning, *exordium,* foreword, foundation, introduction, introductory part, introductory statement, lead, opening, preface, prefatory note, prelude, prelusion, proem, prolegomenon, prologue
ASSOCIATED CONCEPTS: preamble to a constitution

PREARRANGE, *verb* agree to beforehand, arrange beforehand, arrange in advance, concoct, consider beforehand, ensure a result, forearm, foreordain, lay down a plan, map out, plan, plot, preconcert, precontrive, predesign, predestinate, predestine, predetermine, preestablish, premeditate, preorder, prepare, preresolve, project, resolve beforehand

PRECARIOUS, *adjective* alarming, chancy, changeable, critical, crumbling, dangerous, defenseless, delicate, doubtful, dubious, *dubius,* equivocal, exposed, fraught with danger, full of risk, guardless, hazardous, impermanent, *incertus,* infirm, insecure, jeopardous, menacing, perilous, riskful, risky, shaky, slippery, thorny, threatening, ticklish, tottering, treacherous, unassured, uncertain, undependable, unfaithworthy, unprotected, unreliable, unsafe, unsettled, unsheltered, unshielded, unsound, unstable, unsteadfast, unsteady, unsubstantial, unsure, untrustworthy, vulnerable

PRECATORY, *adjective* advisory, appealing, asking, beseeching, entreating, expressing entreaty, imploratory, imploring, importunate, pleading, suggesting, suggestive
ASSOCIATED CONCEPTS: precatory words

PRECAUTION, *noun* alertness, anticipation, attention, care, carefulness, caution, circumspection, forearming, foresight, forethought, guarantee, guardedness, heed, heedfulness, premunition, preventive measures, prior measure, protection, providence, provision, prudence, safeguard, security, solicitude, surveillance, timely care, vigil, vigilance, wariness, warning, watch, watchfulness
ASSOCIATED CONCEPTS: last clear chance doctrine, precautions to guard against injury, standard of care

PRECEDE, *verb* antecede, *antecedere,* antedate, *antegredi, anteire,* anticipate, be ahead of, come before, come first, forerun, go ahead of, go before, go in advance, go in front of, harbinger, herald, introduce, lead, lead the way, pave the way, pioneer, preexist, prepare the ground, scout, take the lead, usher in

PRECEDENCE, *noun* advantage, antecedence, authority, elevation, exaltation, importance, predominance, preeminence, preference, prestige, primacy, priority, rank, seniority, status, superiority, supremacy
ASSOCIATED CONCEPTS: recording statute

PRECEDENT, *noun* archetype, authoritative decision, authoritative example, authoritative principle of law, authoritative rule, authority, basis, criterion, example, *exemplum,* foundation, frame of reference, guide, judicial antecedent, justification, maxim, model, model instance, point of comparison, preceding instance, precept, precursor, predecessor, prior instance, rule, rule for future determinations, rule for future guidance, standard
ASSOCIATED CONCEPTS: collateral estoppel, condition precedent, controlling authority, precedent sub silentio, res judicata, stare decisis

PRECEDING, *adjective* above-mentioned, abovenamed, antecedent, anterior, before mentioned, earlier, first-named, former, inaugural, introductory, precedent, precessional, precursive, precursory, preexistent, prefatory, preliminary, preludial, prelusive, prelusory, preparatory, prevenient, previous, prior, superior

PRECEPT, *noun* axiom, canon, charge, code, command, commandment, decree, dictate, direction, doctrine, dogma, edict, fiat, guide, injunction, instruction, law, legal order, mandate, order, ordinance, *praeceptum, praescriptum,* prescript, principle, regulation, requirement, rubric, rule, statute, teaching, tenet, warrant, writ
ASSOCIATED CONCEPTS: legal precept

PRECIOUS, *adjective* adorable, beloved, cherished, darling, dear, disarming, endearing, favored, favorite, fond, invaluable, loved, pet, precious, priceless, rare, special, sweet, winning, winsome

PRECIPITATE, *adjective* abrupt, breakneck, foolhardy, harebrained, hasty, headlong, headstrong, heady, hellbent, hot-headed, hurried, immediate, impetuous, imprudent, impulsive, *inconsultus,* indiscreet, injudicious, madcap, overconfident, overly hasty, *praeceps,* precipitant, precipitous, quick, rapid, rash, reckless, rushed, speedy, sudden, swift, *temerarius,* thoughtless, uncalculating, unexpected, unprepared for, violent, wild

PRECIPITATE *(Hasten),* ***verb*** *accelerare,* accelerate, advance, bring on, expedite, forward, further, hurry, make haste, *maturare, praecipitare,* quicken, rush, speed, speed up, spur, urge forward

PRECIPITATE *(Throw down violently),* ***verb*** catapult, chuck, *deicere,* discharge, drop, ejaculate, expel, fell, fling, fling downward, heave, hurl headlong, jaculate, launch, let fall, let fly, pitch, *praecipitare,* project, propel, send flying, send forth, send headlong, shoot, shy, throw down, throw headlong, toss

PRECISE, ***adjective*** accurate, careful, clean-cut, clear-cut, close, correct, critical, defined, definite, detailed, determinate, *diligens,* distinct, *elegans,* even, exact, explicit, express, faithful, fastidious, faultless, finical, finicky, flawless, fussy, inflexible, literal, methodical, meticulous, narrow, painstaking, particular, precisian, proper, punctilious, punctual, rigid, rigorous, scientific, scrupulous, severe, sharply defined, specific, stiff, strict, thorough, truthful, unambiguous, unbending, uncompromising, unequivocal, unerring, watchful, well-defined

PRECLUDE, ***verb*** ban, bar, bar from access, block, check, choke, control, cramp, cripple, curb, cut off, debar, defeat, detain, deter, discourage, encumber, estop, exclude, foil, forbid, foreclose, frustrate, handicap, hinder, impede, interfere with, interrupt, make impossible, obstruct, oppose, override, preempt, prevent, *prohibere,* prohibit, regulate, restrain, restrict, retard, stay, stop, thwart
ASSOCIATED CONCEPTS: estoppel, preclude from introducing into evidence

PRECLUSION, ***noun*** ban, bar, curb, exclusion, forestalling, interference, obstruction, obviation, opposition, override, preemption, prevention, prohibition, regulation, restraint, restriction
ASSOCIATED CONCEPTS: claim preclusion, issue preclusion, preclusion order, statutory preclusion

PRECOGNITION, ***noun*** clairvoyance, foreboding, foreknowledge, foresight, forethought, perception, prenotion, presage, prescience, presentiment

PRECONCEIVE, ***verb*** anticipate, assume, be biased, be jaundiced, be prejudiced, forejudge, foresee, have a bias, have foreknowledge, incline, intuit, judge beforehand, jump to a conclusion, *praeiudicare,* preapprehend, precognize, preconclude, predecide, predetermine, predict, predispose, prejudge, prepossess, presume, presuppose, presurmise, surmise

PRECONCEPTION, ***noun*** anticipation, assumption, bent, bias, fixed idea, foregone conclusion, forejudgment, inclination, leaning, partiality, *praeiudicata opinio,* preapprehension, preconceived idea, preconclusion, predetermination, preestimate, prejudgment, prejudication, prejudice, prejudiced view, prenotion, prepossession, presentiment, presumption, presupposal, presupposition, presurmise

PRECONDITION, ***noun*** contingency, demand, fundamentals, meat and potatoes, must, necessity, need, nuts and bolts, prerequisite, principle, provision, qualification, quintessence, requirement, requisite, reservation, rudiments, rule, *sine qua non,* stipulation, strings, terms

PRECURSOR, ***noun*** advance guard, ancestor, announcer, antecedent, augury, avant-courier, forebearer, forefather, foregoer, forerunner, guide, harbinger, herald, omen, parent, pathfinder, patriarch, pioneer, portent, *praecursor, praenuntius,* precedent, predecessor, preparation, preparer, presage, preview, prodrome, prognostic, scout, sign, token, usher, vanguard, warning

PRECURSORY, ***adjective*** advance, antecedent, beginning, earlier, exploratory, first, foregoing, forerunning, foreshadowing, forewarning, foundational, inaugural, inauguratory, initiatory, introductory, leading, *praecurrentia,* precedent, preceding, precursive, prefatory, preliminary, preludial, preludious, prelusive, prelusory, preparatory, prevenient, previous, prior, prognosticative

PREDATORY, ***adjective*** bloodthirsty, carnivorous, depredatory, devouring, greedy, living by prey, lupine, pillaging, plundering, *praedabundus, praedatorius,* predacious, predative, raiding, rapacious, raptorial, ravaging, ravening, ravenous, spoliatory, voracious, vulturine, vulturish, vulturous, wolfish

PREDECESSOR, ***noun*** ancestor, antecedent, antecessor, elder, forebearer, forefather, foregoer, foreparent, forerunner, former incumbent, former officeholder, founder, originator, patriarch, precursor, procreator, progenitor

PREDETERMINATION, ***noun*** aim, bias, closed-mindedness, conclusion beforehand, conclusion in advance, decision beforehand, decision in advance, destined lot, destiny, fate, fixed future, force of circumstances, foredoom, foregone conclusion, forejudgment, foreordainment, forethought, fortune, goal, inevitability, inevitableness, inexorable fate, intention, jaundice, kismet, lot, object, objective, one-sidedness, partiality, preapprehension, preconception, preconclusion, predecision, predeliberation, predestination, predetermined course of events, prejudgment, prejudice, premeditation, prenotion, prepossession, preresolution, presumption, presupposal, presupposition, presurmise, purpose, resolve, undetachment, will

PREDETERMINE, ***verb*** agree beforehand, be biased, be influenced, be jaundiced, be prejudiced, be prepossessed, be swayed, contrive a result, decide beforehand, decide in advance, destinate, destine, determine beforehand, determine in advance, doom, fate, forecast, forejudge, foreordain, foreordinate, intend, jump to a conclusion, map out, ordain, plan, *praefinire, praestituere,* prearrange, preconceive, preconclude, preconsider, predecide, predestinate, predestine, predispose, preestablish, prejudge, premeditate, preordain, preresolve, presume, presuppose, presurmise, project, reserve, resolve beforehand

PREDICAMENT, ***noun*** adverse circumstances, adversity, *angustiae,* barrier, case, circumstance, complication, condition, conjuncture, corner, crisis, critical situation, danger, dangerous condition, *difficultas,* difficulty, dilemma, embarrassing position, embarrassment, emergency, entanglement, exigency, fix, hole, imbroglio, impasse, impediment, intricacy, jeopardy, mess, misfortune, obstacle, obstruction, occurrence, pass, perplexity, pinch, plight, position, posture, precariousness, pressure, quandary, scrape, situation, sorry plight, state, straits, tight situation, tight spot, trial, trouble, trying situation

PREDICATE, *adjective* assume, base, contend, establish, found, ground, hang a hat on, maintain, postulate, premise, presume, presuppose, rest, suppose
ASSOCIATED CONCEPTS: a predicate to pleading a case, a predicate to charging a crime

PREDICATE, *verb* assume, base, believe, conceive, conclude, conjecture, establish, figure, found, ground, guess, hang, imagine, perceive, postulate, premise, presume, presuppose, rest, suppose

PREDICT, *verb* adumbrate, advise, announce in advance, anticipate, augur, auspicate, betoken, bode, divine, envision, forebode, forecast, foreknow, foresee, foreshadow, foreshow, forespeak, foretell, foretoken, forewarn, give notice, herald, indicate, indicate beforehand, make a prediction, make a prognosis, notify, omen, ominate, point to, portend, *praedicere,* preannounce, preindicate, premonish, premonstrate, presage, presignify, prognose, prognosticate, promise, prophesy, read, read the future, signify, soothsay, tell fortunes, tell the future, *vaticinari,* vaticinate, warn

PREDILECTION, *noun* affection, affinity, appetence, appetency, appetite, attachment, bent, bias, choice, desire, disposition, fancy, favor, fondness, inclination, infatuation, leaning, liking, love, partiality, partisanship, penchant, predisposition, preference, prejudgment, prejudice, prepossession, proneness, propensity, *studium,* taste, tendency

PREDISPOSITION, *noun* affection, appetence, appetency, appetite, aptitude, aptness, ardor, attachment, attraction, bent, bias, cast, character, desire, disposition, fancy, favor, favoritism, fondness, foregone conclusion, *inclinatio,* inclination, keenness, leaning, liking, longing, natural tendency, nature, partiality, penchant, preapprehension, preconception, preconclusion, preconsideration, predecision, predetermination, predilection, preference, prejudice, prepossession, *proclivitas,* proclivity, proneness, propenseness, propension, propensity, readiness, *studium,* susceptibility, taste, temperament, tendency, turn, warp, weakness, willingness, wish, yearning, zeal

PREDOMINANCE, *noun* almightiness, ascendency, authority, command, control, controlling influence, dominance, domination, dominion, influence, jurisdiction, lead, leadership, mastery, mightiness, omnipotence, paramountcy, *potentia,* power, predominancy, predomination, prepollence, prepollency, prepotency, *principatus,* puissance, pull, regency, reign, rule, seniority, sovereignty, strength, superiority, supremacy, supreme authority, sway, upper hand, weight

PREDOMINANT, *adjective* abundant, all-powerful, almighty, ascendant, authoritative, cogent, commanding, common, controlling, dominant, dominating, effective, efficacious, epidemic, extensive, forceful, foremost, general, governing, important, influential, mighty, omnipotent, overpowering, overruling, pandemic, paramount, potent, powerful, *praepollens,* preponderant, prevailing, prevalent, principal, puissant, rampant, recognized, regnant, reigning, rife, ruling, sovereign, strong, superior, supervisory, supreme, weighty, widely recognized, widespread

PREDOMINATE *(Command),* ***verb*** administer, be sovereign, be supreme, carry weight, command, determine, direct, dominate, gain the upper hand, govern, guide, have influence, have sway, have the upper hand, hold dominion, hold office, influence, lead, manage, master, mastermind, override, overrule, oversee, overshadow, play a leading part, *praepollere,* prevail, pull the strings, reign, rule, rule over, supervise, sway, take the lead, *vincere*

PREDOMINATE *(Outnumber),* ***verb*** be in the majority, be rife, be superior in number, eclipse, exceed, go beyond, outrank, outrival, outstrip, outweigh, overtop, *plures esse,* preponderate, rise above, surpass

PREEMINENT, *adjective* best, capital, cardinal, central, chief, distinguished, dominant, eminent, grandest, greatest, highest, illustrious, leading, master, matchless, mighty, noble, notable, noteworthy, number one, paramount, predominant, premier, primary, prominent, unequaled, unparalleled

PREEMPT, *verb* acquire beforehand, annex, appropriate, appropriate for use, arrogate to oneself, assume, capture, catch, exclude, force from, gain possession, impropriate, invade, obtain, occupy, preclude, preoccupy, seize, take, take over, take possession of, usurp
ASSOCIATED CONCEPTS: doctrine of federal preemption, preemption in filing, preemptive right, preemptive right of shareholders, right of preemption

PREEMPTION, *noun* appropriation, displacement, exclusion, preclusion, replacement, substitution, supersedence, supersession, supervention, supplanting
ASSOCIATED CONCEPTS: federal preemption, preemption doctrine

PREEXISTING, *adjective* antecedent, anterior, earlier, preexistent, previous, prior
ASSOCIATED CONCEPTS: preexisting condition, preexisting debt

PREFACE, *noun* beginning, commencement, exordium, foreword, introduction, introductory part, opening, overture, *praefatio,* preamble, prefatory note, preliminary comment, preliminary statement, prelude, prelusion, proem, prolegomenon, prolusion, *prooemium*

PREFACE, *verb* advance, begin, commence, head, herald, inaugurate, initiate, institute, introduce, launch, lead in, lead the way, make a start, open, place before, *praefari,* preamble, precede, prelude, put first, say in advance, set in motion, start, usher in

PREFER, *verb* adopt, advance, *anteponere,* approve, be fond of, be partial to, bring forward, choose, cling to, dignify, elect, elevate, embrace, espouse, fancy, favor, fix upon, further, graduate, grant favors to, have a fancy for, indulge one's fancy, lean toward, like better, move up, patronize, pick, pick out, play favorites, *praeoptare, praeponere,* prize, promote, pull strings for, put forward, raise, recommend, sanction, select, set above others, show preference, single out, take a fancy to, take to, tend, think better, treat with partiality, value

PREFERABLE, *adjective* above par, better, choice, chosen, deserving of preference, enjoyable, excellent, excelling, favorite, good, likable, *melior,* more advantageous, more desirable, more in demand, more pleasing, more popular, more select, picked, *potior,* preferred, relishable, selected, superior, surpassing, worthy of choice

PREFERENCE (Choice), *noun* bias, discretion, disposition, election, fancy, favorite, inclination, leaning, liking, option, partiality, preconceived liking, predilection, prejudice, proclivity, proneness, propensity, selection
ASSOCIATED CONCEPTS: preferred risk

PREFERENCE *(Priority), **noun*** advancement, advantage, benefit, favored treatment, front position, *praepositio,* precedence, preeminence, preferment, preferred standing, seniority
ASSOCIATED CONCEPTS: calendar preference, fraudulent conveyances, fraudulent preference, preferred stock, unlawful preference, voidable preference
FOREIGN PHRASES: ***Qui prior est tempore potior est jure.*** He who is first in time is first in right. ***Prior tempore potior jure.*** First in time, superior in right.

PREFERENTIAL, *adjective* advantageous, better, biased, choice, desired, discriminating, discriminative, distinguished, elite, exceptional, exclusive, extraordinary, favored, first-rate, high-grade, marked, outstanding, paramount, partial, partisan, preferred, priority, privileged, prize, recommended, select, selected, selective, special, superb, superior
ASSOCIATED CONCEPTS: preferential treatment

PREFERRED *(Favored), **adjective*** adopted, approved, choice, chosen, decided upon, elected, endorsed, especially liked, fancied, favorite, handpicked, liked, picked out, preferable, preferential, selected, set apart, settled upon, singled out, special, taken

PREFERRED *(Given priority), **adjective*** first, given preference, having priority, having seniority, placed in advance, preceding, prior
ASSOCIATED CONCEPTS: preferred stock, voidable preference

PREFERRED PROVIDER ORGANIZATION, *noun* care plan, comprehensive health plan, controlled medical coverage, discounted health membership group, discounted provider network, network of medical care providers, organization of medical providers, PPO
Generally: supervised medical services, plan organization
Specifically: employer-sponsored plan

PREJUDGE, *verb* condemn beforehand, forejudge, judge before hearing, judge beforehand, judge in advance, jump to a conclusion, *praeiudicare,* preconceive, preconclude, precondemn, preconsider, predecide, predetermine, preestimate, prejudicate, presume, presuppose, presurmise, resolve beforehand, rush to conclusion

PREJUDICE *(Injury), **noun*** damage, detriment, *detrimentum,* disadvantage, harm, hurt, impairment, injustice, irreversible damage, loss, unfairness, wrong
ASSOCIATED CONCEPTS: absence of prejudice, dismissal with prejudice, dismissal without prejudice, prejudice to a party's rights, prejudicial error

PREJUDICE *(Preconception), **noun*** bent, bias, discrimination, favoritism, forejudgment, inclination, intolerance, leaning, narrow-mindedness, one-sidedness, *opinio praeiudicata,* partiality, partisanship, personal bias, preconceived idea, preconceived notion, preconception, predetermination, predilection, predisposition, preference, prejudgment, prepossession, provincialism, slant, subjectivity, unreasonable bias
ASSOCIATED CONCEPTS: disqualification for bias

PREJUDICE *(Influence), **verb*** affect, bear upon, bend to one's will, bias, bring pressure to bear, carry weight, color, convince, distort, exercise influence over, exercise influence upon, exert influence, gain over, give an inclination, have influence over, have influence upon, influence against, jaundice, persuade, predetermine, predispose, prejudge, prepossess unfavorably, present with bias, prevail over, slant, sway, turn, twist, warp, win over
ASSOCIATED CONCEPTS: prejudice the trier of fact

PREJUDICE *(Injure), **verb*** affect detrimentally, cause damage to, cause detriment, cause pain, damage, demolish, destroy, devastate, disadvantage, disservice, exacerbate, harm, hurt, impair, inflict injury, maim, mar, play havoc with, ravage, ruin, spoil, taint, weaken, wound, wreck, wrong
ASSOCIATED CONCEPTS: prejudicial error

PREJUDICIAL, *adjective* biased, colored, damaging, *damnosus,* deleterious, destructive, detrimental, directed against, disadvantageous, disserviceable, harmful, hostile, hurtful, inimical, injurious, *nocens, noxius,* opinionated, partisan, pernicious, preconceived, preconceptual, predecisive, predispositional, prepossessed, slanted, tending to impair, tending to obstruct, unfavorable, unjust
ASSOCIATED CONCEPTS: prejudicial error

PRELIMINARY, *adjective* aforementioned, antecedent, anterior, beginning, coming before, early, exordial, foregoing, former, inaugural, incipient, initial, initiatory, introductory, opening, original, preceding, precursive, precursory, preexisting, prefatory, preludial, prelusive, prelusory, preparative, preparatory, prevenient, previous, primary, prior, proemial, starting, trial
ASSOCIATED CONCEPTS: preliminary agreement, preliminary hearing, preliminary injunction, preliminary notice, preliminary plea, preliminary relief, preliminary restraining order

PRELUDE, *noun* beginning, commencement, exordium, foreword, inauguration, inception, induction, initiation, introduction, opening, outset, overture, preamble, preface, preliminary part, prelusion, preparation, proem, prologue, *prooemium,* start

PREMATURE, *adjective* ahead of time, anticipatory, before time, embryonic, green, hasty, ill-considered, ill-timed, *immaturus,* inchoate, inopportune, mistimed, overhasty, *praematurus,* precipitate, rash, raw, sooner than due, sooner than intended, too early, too soon, unanticipated, underripe, undeveloped, unformed, unmatured, unprepared, unready, unripe, unseasonable, untimely
ASSOCIATED CONCEPTS: exhaustion of remedies, premature action

PREMEDITATED, *adjective* aforethought, calculated, conscious, considered, deliberate, deliberately intended, foreordained, intended, intentional, maturely considered, outlined beforehand, planned, planned beforehand, planned in advance, plotted, prearranged, preconsidered, precontrived, predeliberated, predesigned, predeterminated, predetermined, predevised, preresolved, reasoned, studied, thought out, well-considered, well-devised, willful, with forethought
ASSOCIATED CONCEPTS: intent, malice aforethought, premeditated crime, premeditated murder

PREMEDITATION, *noun* advance planning, aforethought, deliberate intent, deliberate intention, design, distinct purpose, forethought, machination, *praemeditatio,* prearrangement, preconsideration, predeliberation, predetermination, preresolution, previous deliberation, previous reflection, prior determination
ASSOCIATED CONCEPTS: intent

PREMISE, ***noun*** assumption, axiom, basis, belief, conclusion, foundation, given, ground, hypothesis, hypothetical, postulate, precept, presumption, presupposition, principle, rule, standard, supposition, tenet, theory, thesis, truism, verity

PREMISE, ***verb*** accept, affirm, assume, base, believe, claim, conceive, conclude, conjecture, contend, credit, declare, deduce, figure, gather, hypothesize, infer, judge, postulate, presume, presuppose, profess, reckon, say, suppose, surmise, suspect, take, theorize, think

PREMISES *(Buildings),* ***noun*** *aedificium,* bounds, domiciles, *domus,* dwellings, edifices, grounds, homes, house with the grounds belonging to it, land, limits, lodgings, piece of land, place, property, quarters, real estate, residences, structures, tract of land
ASSOCIATED CONCEPTS: premises liability

PREMISES *(Hypotheses),* ***noun*** affirmations, assertions, assumed positions, axioms, bases, foundations, grounds, positions, postulates, *principia,* terms, theorems, theses

PREMIUM, ***adjective*** best, capital, choice, desirable, elect, estimable, excellent, fine, finest, first-class, first-rate, grade A, high-grade, high-quality, incomparable, inimitable, matchless, peerless, precious, prime, quality, second to none, select, specially selected, splendid, superb, superfine, superior, superlative, top-notch, unbeatable, unequaled, unmatched, unparalleled, unrivaled, unsurpassed, very fine, worthy

PREMIUM *(Excess value),* ***noun*** amount over par, bonus, bounty, charge beyond normal, charge to excess, excessive charge, extra, incentive, increased value, overcharge, prize

PREMIUM *(Insurance payment),* ***noun*** amount paid periodically, annual commitment, annual encumbrance, annual fee, annual installment, annual liability, annual obligation, annual payment, annual rate of insurance, annual remittance, contract payment, periodic payment, yearly payment
ASSOCIATED CONCEPTS: assessment of a premium, earned premiums, gross premium, net premium, reduction of premium

PREMONITION, ***noun*** augury, auspice, boding, caution, divination, evil adumbration, feeling, foreboding, forefeeling, foreshadowing, foretoken, forewarning, hunch, intimation, misgiving, *monitio, monitum,* omen, portent, prediction, premonishment, prenotification, presage, presentiment, presurmise, prevision, prewarning, sign, warning

PREOCCUPATION, ***noun*** absorbed interest, absorption, abstraction, attentiveness, concentration, daydreaming, deep study, depth of thought, devotion, distraction, dreaminess, engrossment, enthrallment, fascination, fixation, fixed idea, *idée fixe,* immersion, intentness, involvement, musing, obsession, pensiveness, *praeoccupatio,* prepossession, profound thought, rapt attention, reverie, study, trance

PREORDAIN, ***verb*** appoint beforehand, appoint in advance, decide in advance, decree beforehand, destine, determine beforehand, enact beforehand, establish beforehand, fix beforehand, foredoom, forejudge, foreshadow, preconceive, preconclude, preconsider, predecide, predeliberate, predestine, predetermine, preestablish, prejudge, preresolve, resolve beforehand

PREPARATION, ***noun*** anticipation, apprenticeship, arrangement, background, basis, building, development, education, equipment, establishment, evolution, foresight, forethought, foundation, groundwork, initiation, instruction, making ready, neophytism, novitiate, plan, precaution, preliminaries, preliminary step, premunition, prior measure, probation, providence, provision, prudence, qualification, readiness, readying, rehearsal, safeguard, teaching, training
ASSOCIATED CONCEPTS: preparation for trial, preparation of a crime

PREPARATORY, ***adjective*** anticipatory, beginning, early, expectant, foundational, inaugural, inceptive, incipient, initial, initiative, initiatory, introductory, opening, precautionary, precedent, preceding, precursory, prefatory, preliminary, preludial, prelusive, prelusory, preparative, prepositional, prior, proemial, provident, qualifying, starting
ASSOCIATED CONCEPTS: preparatory acts

PREPAY, ***verb*** defray in advance, discharge in advance, give compensation for in advance, make payment in advance, meet the bill ahead of time, pay in advance, presettle, satisfy in advance, settle in advance, tender in advance
ASSOCIATED CONCEPTS: prepayment clause

PREPONDERANCE, ***noun*** dominance, domination, majority, outweighing, paramountcy, plurality, predominance, predomination, preeminence, prepollence, prepollency, preponderancy, preponderation, prevalence, superiority
ASSOCIATED CONCEPTS: preponderance of the credible evidence

PREPOSTEROUS, ***adjective*** absurd, bizarre, crazy, extravagant, fanciful, foolish, implausible, inconceivable, incredible, insane, nonsensical, outrageous, ridiculous, unbelievable, unimaginable, unreal, unthinkable, wild

PREREQUISITE, ***noun*** condition, demand, essential desideratum, exigency, fundamental, groundwork, indispensable item, necessary condition, necessary item, necessity, need, needed item, precondition, preliminary condition, pressing need, prior condition, proviso, requirement, requisite, specification, stipulation, vital part
ASSOCIATED CONCEPTS: condition precedent, jurisdictional prerequisite

PREROGATIVE, ***noun*** advantage, authority, authorization, benefit, charter, claim, droit, due, exclusive privilege, exclusive right, franchise, freedom, grant, inalienable right, legal power, liberty, license, perquisite, power, preference, prior right, priority, privilege, right, rightful power, sanction, special right, title, vested right, warrant
ASSOCIATED CONCEPTS: managerial prerogative, prerogative writ

PRESAGE, ***verb*** adumbrate, advise, announce in advance, anticipate, augur, *augurari,* augurate, auspicate, betoken, bode, divine, envision, forebode, forecast, foreknow, foresee, foreshadow, foreshow, foretell, foretoken, forewarn, have a presentiment, impend, indicate beforehand, indicate in advance, judge the future, make a prediction, omen, ominate, point to, portend, *portendere, praesagire,* predict, prefigurate, prefigure, preindicate, premonstrate, preshow, presignify, prewarn, prognosticate, promise, prophesy, signify, soothsay, threaten, vaticinate, warn

PRESAGEFUL, ***adjective*** augural, augurial, auspicial, foreboding, monitory, ominous, portentous

PRESCRIBE, *verb* administer, advocate, bid, charge, command, conduct, control, decide, decree, demand, designate, dictate, direct, enjoin, exact, exercise authority, give a directive, give a mandate, give an order, give directions, guide, impose, instruct, issue an order, lay out, lead, mandate, mark out, ordain, order, pilot, *praescribere,* prevail over, proclaim, regulate, require, set, steer, superintend, write a prescription
ASSOCIATED CONCEPTS: prescribe remedies, prescribed by law

PRESCRIPTION *(Claim of title),* ***noun*** authority, claim, inalienable right, interest, license, prerogative, right, vested interest, vested right
ASSOCIATED CONCEPTS: adverse possession, easement by prescription, right by prescription, title by prescription
FOREIGN PHRASES: ***Praescriptio et executio non pertinent ad valorem contractus, set ad tempus et modum actionis instituendae.*** Prescription and execution do not affect the validity of the contract, but the time and manner of instituting an action. ***Usucapio constituta est ut aliquis litium finis esset.*** Prescription was established so that there be an end to lawsuits. ***Nihil praescribitur nisi quod possidetur.*** There is no prescription for that which is not possessed. ***Interruptio multiplex non tollit praescriptionem semel obtentam.*** Frequent interruptions do not defeat a prescription once obtained. ***Praescriptio est titulus ex usu et tempore substantiam capiens ab auctoritate legis.*** Prescription is a title by authority of law, deriving its force from use and time.

PRESCRIPTION *(Custom),* ***noun*** convention, conventional usage, fashion, habit, institution, observance, practice, precedent, tradition, usage, use

PRESCRIPTION *(Directive),* ***noun*** act, authority, axiom, canon, charge, command, decree, dictate, direction, doctrine, edict, enactment, formula, formulary, injunction, instruction, law, maxim, measure, order, ordinance, precept, prescript, principle, proposal, regulation, rubric, rule, ruling, statute, theorem

PRESCRIPTIVE, *adjective* accepted, acknowledge, acknowledge through possession, acknowledge through use, admitted, binding, commanded by long use, commanding, compulsory, customary, decretal, determined, dictated, established, fixed, legalized, long-established, longstanding, obligatory, ordained by custom, popular, preceptive, prescribed, recognized, recognized because of continued possession, recognized through use, required by custom, rooted, set, settled, time-honored, traditional, traditive, understood, unwritten, usual, vested, wonted
ASSOCIATED CONCEPTS: prescriptive rights

PRESCRIPTIVISM, *noun* a theory of the study of language, linguistic prescription, prescription, rules of grammar, rules of language, standard usage, standard use

PRESENCE *(Attendance),* ***noun*** being, nearness, *praesentia,* proximity, sojournment, visitation

PRESENCE *(Poise),* ***noun*** air, appearance, aspect, bearing, behavior, carriage, comportment, conduct, decorum, demeanor, deportment, gentility, guise, image, look, manner, mien, ostent, outward show, personality, posture, presentation, refinement, semblance, style, visage, way, ways
ASSOCIATED CONCEPTS: demeanor of a witness

PRESENT *(Attendant),* ***adjective*** accessible, accounted for, adjacent, at close quarters, at hand, available, close, close at hand, close by, convenient, handy, in attendance, in the company of, in the presence of, in the vicinity, in view, near at hand, nearby, nigh, on hand, on the spot, *praesens,* proximate, unremoved, vicinal, within reach

PRESENT *(Current),* ***adjective*** at hand, at this moment, at this time, attendant, available, contemporaneous, contemporary, current, existent, existing, extant, going on, here, immediate, in view, instant, latest, living, modern, near, near in time, nigh, on the spot, *praesens,* present-day, present-time, prevalent, ready, recent, topical, ubiquitary, ubiquitous, unremoved, up-to-date, up-to-the-minute
ASSOCIATED CONCEPTS: clear and present danger, present ability, present consideration, present controversy, present enjoyment, present gift, present interest, present transfer

PRESENT *(Introduce),* ***verb*** demonstrate, disclose, display, exhibit, expose to view, give an introduction, *introducere,* make acquainted, make an introduction, make known, offer, offer evidence, open to view, propose, put forth, set forth, show, suggest, uncover, unveil
ASSOCIATED CONCEPTS: present a case, present evidence

PRESENT *(Make a gift),* ***verb*** accord, allot, award, bequeath, bestow, confer, contribute, convey, deed, deliver, dispense, dole out, *donare,* donate, endow, extend, furnish, give, give as a gift, give over, grant, hand, hand over, impart, let have, make over, mete out, *munerari,* offer, place at one's disposal, proffer, provide, remit, render, supply, tender, vouchsafe

PRESENT *(Prefer charges),* ***verb*** accuse, blame, charge, cite, criminate, fix the responsibility, implicate, impute, incriminate, lodge a complaint, prefer charges
ASSOCIATED CONCEPTS: present an indictment

PRESENTMENT, *noun* accusation, arraignment, charge, citation, imputation, indictment, information

PRESERVATION, *noun* care, cherishing, conservation, curing, custody, defense, eternization, freedom from danger, guardianship, guarding, immortalization, maintenance, nourishment, nurture, perpetuation, protection, protective custody, safeguarding, safekeeping, safety, salvation, sanctuary, saving, security, shielding, storage, support, *tuitio,* upkeep, ward, wardship

PRESERVE, *verb* attend to, bolster, care for, champion, cherish, *condire,* conserve, continue, cure, defend, economize, ensconce, ensure, favor, foster, give support, guard, harbor, haven, hoard, house, husband, insure, keep, keep alive, keep from harm, keep intact, keep safe, keep sound, keep under cover, keep up, keep watch over, lend support, look after, maintain, mind, minister to, nourish, patronize, perpetuate, prolong, promote, protect, protect from injury, provide for, provide sanctuary, put away, reinforce, rescue, safeguard, save, screen, secure, *servare,* shelter, shield, shield from danger, shield from injury, spare, stand behind, support, sustain, *sustinere,* take care of, tend, treasure, *tueri,* uphold, watch, watch over
ASSOCIATED CONCEPTS: preserve one's rights, preserve records, preserve the peace

PRESIDE, *verb* act as chairman, act as president, administer, administrate, assume command, be at the head of, be in authority, be in charge, be in the chair, be the chairman, chair, command, control, direct, exercise supervision, govern, guide, have authority over, have control, head, hold a

position of authority, hold authority, hold sway, hold the chair, keep order, lead, manage, occupy the chair, officiate, overlook, oversee, pilot, *praesidere,* regulate, reign, rule, steer, superintend, supervise, sway, take care of, take charge, take over, wield authority
ASSOCIATED CONCEPTS: preside over a hearing, preside over court, presiding justice, presiding officer

PRESS, ***noun*** authors, columnists, commentators, contributors, correspondents, editors, interviewers, journalistic writers, journalists, literary publications, media, members of the media, members of the press, news business, news gatherers, newsmen, newspaper world, newspaperman, newspapers, newswriters, publicists, publishers, reporters
ASSOCIATED CONCEPTS: censorship, First Amendment, freedom of speech, freedom of the press

PRESS *(Beseech),* ***verb*** adjure, appeal, ask earnestly, beg, call upon, enjoin, entreat, exhort, impetrate, implore, importune, petition, plead, request, supplicate, urge, *urgere*

PRESS *(Constrain),* ***verb*** bear down on, bind, bring pressure to bear, coerce, command, compel, decree, demand, drive, enforce, exact, extort, force, impel, impose, insist, make, make necessary, necessitate, obligate, oblige, order, put pressure on, put under obligation, require, take no denial, urge forward, wring

PRESS *(Goad),* ***verb*** aggravate, agonize, annoy, badger, beset, bother, browbeat, carp at, disquiet, drive, harry, heckle, hector, hound, incite, *instigare,* instigate, irritate, molest, persecute, pester, plague, prod, provoke, put pressure on, stir up, taunt, tease, torment, trouble, vex, worry

PRESSING, ***adjective*** acute, cogent, compelling, compulsory, constraining, critical, crucial, demanded, demanding, driving, essential, exacting, exigent, forceful, grave, high priority, impelling, imperative, important, importunate, indispensable, major, mandatory, necessary, needed, obligatory, operose, peremptory, prerequisite, relentless, required, requisite, serious, urgent, vital

PRESSURE, ***noun*** anxiety, anxiousness, brunt, brute force, burden, coercion, compulsion, constraining force, constraint, controlling power, crisis, drive, duress, encumbrance, exertion, exhortation, exigency, force, hardship, heaviness, hindrance, imperativeness, importunateness, influence, influentiality, insistence, intensity, intimidation, load, necessity, need, obligation, oppression, persuasion, *pondus,* power, power of directing, power of impelling, press, pull, push, strain, stress, sway, tension, undue influence, urgency, *vis,* weight
ASSOCIATED CONCEPTS: undue influence

PRESSURE, ***verb*** adjure, advocate, bear down, beg, beseech, blandish, cajole, coax, coerce, command, compel, constrain, drive, entreat, exhort, force, goad, implore, induce, influence, insist, intimidate, oppress, persuade, plead, press, prod, push, request, solicit, stress, urge
ASSOCIATED CONCEPTS: coercion, duress, intimidation, undue influence

PRESTIDIGITATION, ***noun*** conjuring, deluding, illusion, juggling, legerdemain, magic, palming, sleight of hand, sorcery, trickery

PRESTIGE, ***noun*** ascendance, ascendency, aura, authority, celebrity, consequence, control, credit, dazzle, degree, dignity, distinction, *éclat,* eminence, esteem, estimation, exaltation, *fama,* fame, famousness, favor, force, glamor, *gloria,* glory, good repute, grandeur, greatness, high honor, high repute, honor, illustriousness, import, importance, influence, influentiality, luster, majesty, mark, name, nobility, *nomen,* notability, note, noteworthiness, notoriety, paramountcy, place, position, potency, power, precedence, predominance, predomination, preeminence, primacy, prominence, public favor, rank, regard, renown, reputation, repute, respect, significance, splendor, standing, station, status, superiority, sway, weight, worth

PRESUME, ***verb*** anticipate, apprehend, assume, believe, come to a hasty conclusion, conceive, conclude, conjecture, consider as true, consider probable, contemplate, count upon, dare say, deduce, deem, derive, divine, estimate, expect, forejudge, form an opinion, gather, guess, hazard a guess, hypothesize, infer, judge, jump to conclusions, opine, perceive as true, posit, postulate, preconceive, prejudge, presuppose, presurmise, regard as axiomatic, speculate, *sumere,* suppose, surmise, suspect, take for granted, take without proof, theorize, think, think likely, understand, venture
ASSOCIATED CONCEPTS: presume innocence

PRESUMPTION, ***noun*** anticipation, assumption, belief, conception, *coniectura,* conjecture, deduction, ground for believing, hypothesis, inference, likelihood, *opinio,* opinion, postulate, predilection, predisposition, premise, presupposition, probability, reasonable supposition, required assumption, required legal assumption, speculation, strong probability, supposition, surmise
ASSOCIATED CONCEPTS: conclusive presumption, disputable presumption, presumption against suicide, presumption of authority, presumption of constitutionality, presumption of continuance, presumption of death, presumption of delivery, presumption of innocence, presumption of knowledge, presumption of law, presumption of legitimacy, presumption of regularity, rebuttable presumption, statutory presumption
FOREIGN PHRASES: ***Cuicunque aliquis quid concedit concedere videtur et id, sine quo res ipsa esse non potuit.*** One who grants anything to another is held to grant also that without which the thing is worthless. ***Lex judicat de rebus necessario faciendis quasi re ipsa factis.*** The law judges of things which must necessarily be done as if they were actually done. ***Novatio non praesumitur.*** A novation is not presumed. ***Nemo praesumitur malus.*** No one is presumed to be wicked. ***Nemo praesumitur ludere in extremis.*** No one is presumed to be jesting while at the point of death. ***Nihil nequam est praesumendum.*** Nothing wicked should be presumed. ***Semper praesumitur pro legitimatione puerorum.*** The presumption always is in favor of the legitimacy of children. ***Stabit praesumptio donec probetur in contrarium.*** A presumption stands until the contrary is proven. ***Praesumptiones sunt conjecturae exsigno verisimili ad probandum assumptae.*** Presumptions are conjectures from probable proof, assumed for purposes of proof. ***Fraus est odiosa et non praesumenda.*** Fraud is odious and will not be presumed. ***Donatio non praesumitur.*** A gift is not presumed to have been made. ***Nemo praesumitur donare.*** No one is presumed to have made a gift. ***Favorabiliores rei, potius quam actores, habentur.*** The condition of the defendant is to be favored rather than that of the plaintiff. ***Nobiliores et benigniores praesumptiones in dubiis sunt praeferendae.*** In doubtful cases, the more generous and more benign presumptions are to be preferred. ***Nullum iniquum est praesumendum in jure.*** Nothing iniquitous is to

be presumed in law. ***Quisquis praesumitur bonus; et semper in dubiis pro reo respondendum.*** Everyone is presumed to be good; and in doubtful cases it should be resolved in favor of the accused. ***Praesumitur pro legitimatione.*** There is a presumption in favor of legitimacy. ***Semper praesumitur pro matrimonio.*** The presumption is always in favor of the validity of a marriage. ***Malum non praesumitur.*** Evil is not presumed. ***Pro possessione praesumitur de jure.*** A presumption of law arises from possession. ***Praesumptio violenta, plena probatio.*** Strong presumption is full proof. ***Semper qui non prohibet pro se intervenire, mandare creditur.*** He who does not prohibit the intervention of another in his behalf is deemed to have authorized it. ***Probatis extremis, praesumuntur media.*** The extremes having been proved, those things which lie between are presumed. ***In favorem vitae, libertatis, et innocentiae, omnia praesumuntur.*** Every presumption is made in favor of life, liberty, and innocence. ***Nulla impossibilia aut inhonesta sunt praesumenda, vera autem et honesta et possibilia.*** No things that are impossible or dishonorable are to be presumed, but things that are true and honorable and possible. ***Omnia praesumuntur legitime facta donec probetur in contrarium.*** All things are presumed to be lawfully done until the contrary is proven. ***Lex neminem cogit ostendere quod nescire praesumitur.*** The law compels no one to divulge that which he is presumed not to know. ***Injuria non praesumitur.*** A wrong is not presumed.

PRESUMPTION OF INNOCENCE, ***noun*** assumption of innocence, belief of innocence, criminal standard of guilt, innocent until proven guilty, predisposition of innocence, premise rested on innocence, presupposition toward innocence, reasonable supposition of innocence, required assumption of innocence, required legal assumption of innocence, supposition of innocence
ASSOCIATED CONCEPTS: fundamental rights

PRESUMPTIVE, ***adjective*** anticipated, apparent, assumed, assumptive, believable, circumstantial, conceivable, conjecturable, conjectural, conjectured, credible, easy to believe, evidential, feasible, hypothesized, imagined, inferable, inferred, likely, plausible, possible, postulated, postulational, presumable, presumed, presupposed, probable, putative, seeming, speculative, speculatory, supposed, suppositional, supposititious, suppositive, surmisable, suspect, theoretical, well-founded, well-grounded
ASSOCIATED CONCEPTS: presumptive damages, presumptive evidence, presumptive grant, presumptive notice, presumptive ownership, presumptive possession

PRESUMPTUOUS, ***adjective*** *adrogans,* arrogant, assuming, audacious, bold, brash, brazen, cavalier, conceited, contumelious, daring, dictatorial, discourteous, disdainful, disrespectful, domineering, egoistic, egotistic, egotistical, excessively bold, excessively confident, familiar, flippant, foolhardy, forward, haughty, ill-bred, ill-mannered, imperious, impertinent, impolite, impudent, insolent, insulting, intrusive, irreverent, lacking respect, lofty, lordly, magisterial, malapert, offensive, outrageous, overbearing, overconfident, overfamiliar, overly bold, overly confident, overweening, pert, pompous, presuming, provocative, rash, rude, saucy, shameless, supercilious, unabashed, unceremonious, uncourtly, ungenteel, vain

PRESUPPOSE, ***verb*** assume, be biased, be inclined to think, be jaundiced, be prejudiced, believe, conjecture, count upon, decide beforehand, decide in advance, deduce, deem, determine beforehand, determine in advance, divine, draw an inference, estimate, expect, forejudge, gather, guess, have a bias, hypothesize, imagine, infer, intuit, judge, judge in advance, jump to a conclusion, opine, persuade oneself, posit, postulate, preconceive, preconclude, predecide, predetermine, preestimate, prefigurate, prefigure, prejudge, presume, presurmise, reckon, regard, rush to a conclusion, speculate, suppose, surmise, suspect, take for granted, theorize, think, trow, understand
ASSOCIATED CONCEPTS: presuppose a fact not in evidence

PRETEND, ***verb*** act, affect, assume, be deceitful, be hypocritical, beguile, bemask, bluff, cheat, claim falsely, counterfeit, cozen, deceive, delude, disguise, dissemble, *dissimulare,* dissimulate, dupe, fake, falsify, feign, *fingere,* fool, give a false appearance, hide under a mask, hoodwink, imagine, imitate, impersonate, lie, make a pretext of, make a show, make believe, malinger, mask, masquerade, mimic, mislead, misrepresent, pass off, perform, play, play act, play false, portray, present falsely, prevaricate, profess, purport, put on, put on a false front, seem, sham, *simulare,* simulate, twist the truth

PRETENSE *(Ostentation),* ***noun*** affectation, affectedness, airs, artificiality, blatancy, bravado, demonstration, display, empty show, false appearance, false show, fanfaronade, flagrancy, flashiness, flourish, fuss, garishness, gaudiness, glare, glitter, grandiosity, histrionics, impressive effect, inflation, insincerity, loftiness, mockery, obtrusiveness, *ostentatio,* ostentatiousness, outward show, panache, parade, pomp, pomposity, pompousness, pose, pretension, pretentiousness, sham, show, showiness, splash, splurge, theatricality, unnaturalness, window dressing

PRETENSE *(Pretext),* ***noun*** appearance, beguilement, bluff, camouflage, cheat, claim, cloak, color, cover, deceit, deception, disguise, duplicity, empty words, excuse, fabrication, false appearance, false plea, false show, falsehood, falseness, falsification, feint, forgery, fraud, fraudulence, guise, hoax, hypocrisy, imitation, invention, lie, mask, mendacity, misrepresentation, ostensible purpose, ostensible reason, plea, *postulatio,* professed purpose, ruse, semblance, sham, show, simulation, *simulatione,* subterfuge, trick, trickery, untruth
ASSOCIATED CONCEPTS: false pretnese, fraudulent pretense, larceny by false pretense

PRETENTIOUS *(Ostentatious),* ***adjective*** adorned, artificial, bespangled, brassy, conspicuous, decorated, embellished, flamboyant, flashy, fulgent, fulgid, garish, gaudy, meretricious, ornamented, ornate, *ornatus,* overly decorated, showy, superficial, tawdry

PRETENTIOUS *(Pompous),* ***adjective*** affected, arrogant, boastful, boasting, bombastic, braggardly, braggart, conceited, extravagant, full of affectation, *gloriosus,* grandiloquent, grandiose, haughty, *iactans,* immodest, inflated, *inflatus,* opinionated, overdramatized, prideful, prim, self-admiring, self-applauding, self-esteeming, self-glorifying, self-important, self-satisfied, smug, snobbish, stilted, swollen, *theatralis,* tumid, *tumidus,* turgescent, turgid, vain, vainglorious

PRETERMIT, ***verb*** abandon, avoid, bypass, cast aside, disregard, forget, gloss over, ignore, lay aside, leave, leave out, leave undone, let pass, miss, neglect, not care for, omit, overlook, pass, pass over, pay no attention to, pay no regard to, put aside, put off, shelve, skip, slight, suspend
ASSOCIATED CONCEPTS: pretermitted heir

PRETEXT, *noun* affectation, alibi, alleged purpose, alleged reason, camouflage, charade, claim, cover, deception, defense, disguise, evasion, excuse, fabrication, false appearance, false ground, false motive, false pretense, false reason, false show, falsification, feint, fraud, guise, insincerity, invention, justification, lie, make-believe, mask, misrepresentation, misstatement, obfuscation, ostensible motive, ostensible purpose, ostensible reason, *praetextum,* pretense, pretension, professed purpose, profession, ruse, semblance, sham, shift, show, *simulatio,* simulation, *species,* stratagem, subterfuge, trick, trickery, untruth, wile
FOREIGN PHRASES: ***Praetextu liciti non debet admitti illicitum.*** That which is illegal ought not to be permitted under a pretext of legality.

PREVAIL *(Be in force),* ***verb*** be in general use, control, dictate, direct, dominate, domineer, exist widely, govern, guide, have authority over, have charge of, have dominion over, have force, have superiority over, predominate, preponderate
ASSOCIATED CONCEPTS: prevailing rate of interest, prevailing rate of wages

PREVAIL *(Persuade),* ***verb*** actuate, argue into, bring around, cajole, carry weight with, coax, convert, convince, enlist, gain the confidence of, guide, have effect, impel, incite, indoctrinate, induce, influence, inspire, inveigle, lure, motivate, move, *persuadere,* prompt, propagandize, seduce, sway, urge, wear down, win over, woo

PREVAIL *(Triumph),* ***verb*** be a winner, be effective, be efficacious, be in control, be in general use, be in the ascendant, be prevalent, be successful, be the victor, be triumphant, be victorious, carry authority, command, conquer, control, dominate, exceed, excel, gain a victory, gain the advantage, gain the upper hand, get the upper hand, have mastery, have superiority, lead, master, meet with success, overcome, predominate, preponderate, prosper, quell, reign, rule, subdue, succeed, *superare,* suppress, surmount, surpass, take over, thrive, transcend, *vincere,* win
ASSOCIATED CONCEPTS: prevail in a court of law, prevailing party

PREVAIL UPON, *verb* affect, be influential, beseech, bring over, bring to reason, carry weight with, coax, convince, encourage, enlist, entice, entreat, exercise influence over, exercise influence upon, exercise influence with, exhort, *exorare,* have influence over, have influence upon, have influence with, impel, importune, induce, influence, lead, motivate, move, move by persuasion, overcome another's resistence, persuade, *persuadere,* predispose, spur, sway, talk into, urge, wield influence, win over

PREVAILING *(Current),* ***adjective*** abundant, accepted, accustomary, accustomed, all-embracing, bourgeois, catholic, characteristic, colloquial, common, commonplace, comprehensive, conformable, contemporary, conventional, current, customary, diffuse, dominant, epidemic, established, everyday, extensive, familiar, frequent, general, generally accepted, global, habitual, in vogue, latest, natural, normal, pandemic, popular, predominant, prevalent, rampant, regular, rife, stock, sweeping, typical, universal, up-to-date, usual, vernacular, well-known, widely accepted, widespread, wonted, workaday, worldwide
ASSOCIATED CONCEPTS: prevailing conditions, prevailing rate, prevailing rate of interest

PREVAILING *(Having superior force),* ***adjective*** ascendant, authoritative, chief, commanding, conquering, controlling, defeating, determining, directing, dominant, dominating, effective, effectual, efficacious, forceful, governing, heading, hegemonic, hegemonical, influential, leading, mighty, moving, operative, overcoming, overruling, paramount, persuasive, potent, powerful, predominant, predominating, preponderant, preponderating, *puissant, régnant,* ruling, strong, successful, supreme, triumphal, triumphant, unvanquished, victorious, weighty, winning
ASSOCIATED CONCEPTS: prevailing party

PREVALENT, *adjective* abundant, accepted, accustomary, accustomed, all-embracing, ascendant, catholic, characteristic, chief, colloquial, common, commonplace, conformable, conventional, current, customary, dominant, epidemic, established, everyday, extensive, familiar, frequent, frequently met, general, generally accepted, global, habitual, household, normal, ordinary, pandemic, pedestrian, *pervulgatus,* popular, predominant, preponderant, prevailing, rampant, regular, rife, run of-the-mill, set, standard, stock, sweeping, typical, universal, vernacular, well-known, widely accepted, widely known, widespread, worldwide

PREVARICATE, *verb* be dishonest, be evasive, be untruthful, bear false witness, beg the question, belie, conceal the truth, concoct, counterfeit, deceive, defraud, delude, deviate, deviate from the truth, dissemble, dissimulate, distort, dodge, dupe, elude, equivocate, evade, evade the truth, fabricate, falsify, feign, fence, fergiversate, fib, forswear, gloss over, hedge, hoodwink, invent, lie, make believe, mince the truth, misguide, misinform, mislead, misrepresent, misstate, palter, parry, perjure, pervert, pretend, put on, quibble, sham, shift, shuffle, sophisticate, speak falsely, stretch the truth, tell a falsehood, tell a lie, tell an untruth, *tergiversari,* tergiversate, twist the truth
ASSOCIATED CONCEPTS: false swearing, perjury

PREVENT, *verb* arrest, avert, avoid, baffle, balk, bar, block, check, checkmate, circumvent, contest, counter, counteract, countercheck, cut off, debar, defeat, deflect, delay, detain, deter, discourage, estop, fend off, foil, forbid, foreclose, forestall, forfend, frustrate, halt, hamper, handicap, hinder, hold back, impede, *impedire,* inhibit, intercept, interfere, interrupt, keep from, keep from happening, limit, muzzle, neutralize, *obstare,* obstruct, obviate, oppose, override, overrule, paralyze, parry, preclude, *prohibere,* prohibit, repress, restrain, restrict, retard, rule out, stave off, stay, stop, thwart, tie, turn aside, turn away, veto, ward off
ASSOCIATED CONCEPTS: prevent competition, prevent waste, prevented by law, prevention of performance
FOREIGN PHRASES: ***Qui non prohibet id quod prohibere potest assentire videtur.*** He who does not forbid what he is able to prevent is deemed to assent.

PREVENTION, *noun* bar, barrier, constraint, constriction, control, damper, determent, deterrence, deterrent, disadvantage, fetter, hindrance, impediment, inhibition, interference, obstacle, obstruction, obtrusion, obviation, preclusion, predisposition, presumption, prohibition, restraint, restriction, retardation, stoppage, thwarting

PREVENTIVE, *adjective* alert, antidotal, antiseptic, arresting, aseptic, averting, blocking, careful, cautious, checking, counteractant, counteracting, defensive, deterrent, deterring, disinfectant, forestalling, germicidal, guarded, guarding, hindering, hygienic, impedimental, impeding, impeditive, inhibitive, inhibitory, interfering, judicious, neutralizing, obstructive, opposing, precautionary, preclusive, preservative, preventative, prohibitive, prophylactic, protecting, protective, provident, regardful, resistive, restraining, restrictive, retardant, safeguarding, shielding, thwarting, warding off, watchful

PREVENTIVE MEASURE, *noun* adequate plans, adequate procedures, adequate steps, buffer, defense, forearming, immunization, inoculation, precaution, preservation, protection, safeguard, screen, security, shield
ASSOCIATED CONCEPTS: preventive justice

PREVIOUS, *adjective* above-cited, above-mentioned, above-named, aforementioned, aforesaid, already indicated, antecedent, anterior, earlier, early, erstwhile, first, fore, foregoing, foregone, forementioned, forerunning, former, initial, initiatory, introductory, one-time, past, precedent, preceding, precursive, precursory, preexistent, prefatorial, prefatory, preliminary, prelusive, prelusory, preparatory, prevenient, previously mentioned, prior
ASSOCIATED CONCEPTS: previous conviction, previous disability, previous injury, previous order, previously considered, previously determined, prior conduct, prior conviction, prior injury

PREVIOUSLY NAMED, *adjective* above-mentioned, as stated earlier, as stated earlier in this document, beforementioned, forenamed, former, previously referred to

PREY, *verb* commit violence, consume, depredate, despoil, destroy, devour, eat, extort, fatten upon, feast upon, feed upon, fleece, forage, foray, grab, gut, harass, harrow, hunt, kill, loot, maraud, oppress, parasitize, pillage, pirate, plague, plunder, *praedari,* profit by cheating, profit by swindling, raid, ransack, ravage, raven, ravish, rob, seize, spoil, spoliate, strip, torment, torture, victimize, waste

PRICE, *noun* amount, appraisal, appraisement, charge, compensation, cost, disbursement, due, estimate, estimation, exaction, exchange value, expenditure, expense, fare, fee, figure, outlay, payment, premium, *pretium,* purchase money, quotation, rate, recompense, selling price, toll, valuation, value, worth
ASSOCIATED CONCEPTS: abatement of price, contract price, established price, fair price, inadequacy of price, market price, market value, price adjustment, price control fee schedules, price discrimination, price fixing, reasonable price, retail price, stipulated price
FOREIGN PHRASES: ***Emptor emit quam minimo potest; venditor vendit quam maximo potest.*** The buyer purchases for the least he can; the seller sells for the most he can.

PRICELESS, *adjective* beyond price, commanding a high price, costly, dear, expensive, extraordinary, high, high-priced, *inaestimabilis,* incalculable, incomparable, inestimable, invaluable, irreplaceable, matchless, peerless, precious, *pretiosissimus,* rare, sterling, unequaled, valuable, without price

PRIDE, *noun* affectation, affected manner, affectedness, airs, boastfulness, braggadocio, braggartism, cockiness, condescension, coxcombry, dandyism, egoism, egotism, foppishness, haughtiness, hubris, immodesty, lordliness, narcissism, pomposity, satisfaction, self-admiration, self-applause, self-approval, self-esteem, self-exaltation, self-glorification, self-importance, self-satisfaction, smugness, snobbery, superciliousness, superiority, swagger, toploftiness, vain pretensions, vainglory, vanity

PRIMA FACIE *(Legally sufficient),* ***adjective*** adequate, lawfully sufficient, legally adequate, satisfactory, sufficient on its face, sufficient on the pleadings, sufficient to make out a case, sufficiently strong, suitable
ASSOCIATED CONCEPTS: prima facie case, prima facie claim, prima facie evidence, prima facie negligence, prima facie nuisance, prima facie proof, prima facie tort

PRIMA FACIE *(Self-evident),* ***adjective*** apparently, at first glance, at first sight, at first view, at sight, before further examination, by all appearances, on presentation, on the face of the matter, on the first view, ostensibly, presumably, seemingly, to all appearances

PRIMACY, *noun* ascendancy, authority, command, consequence, control, domination, dominion, eminence, excellency, first place, greatness, headship, hegemony, height, high position, hold, importance, influence, jurisdiction, lead, leadership, paramountcy, power, predominancy, predomination, preeminence, prestige, rule, seniority, sovereignty, supereminence, superiority, supremacy, supremeness, sway, weight

PRIMARY, *adjective* basal, basic, central, chief, constitutive, determining, dominant, earliest, elemental, elementary, essential, first, formative, fundamental, greatest, highest, important, inaugural, initial, key, leading, main, nascent, necessary, nonpareil, original, overriding, overruling, paramount, predominant, preeminent, prime, *primus,* principal, *principalis,* prominent, requisite, ruling, second to none, supereminent, supreme, topmost, transcendent, underlying, unsurpassed, uppermost, utmost, vital
ASSOCIATED CONCEPTS: primary boycott, primary evidence, primary insurance, primary jurisdiction, primary liability, primary picketing, primary purpose, primary right, primary surety, primary tort feasor

PRIMARY, *noun* ballot, choice, contest, contestation, election, election contest, exclusive competition, exclusive contest, exclusive election, exclusive political competition, exclusive political contest, first competition, first contest, first election, first political competition, first political contest, inaugural competition, inaugural contest, inaugural election, inaugural political competition, inaugural political contest, nomination contest, nominative competition, nominative contest, nominative election, partisan competition, partisan contest, partisan election, party competition, party contest, party election, political competition, political contention, political election, political rivalry, poll, preference, selection, vote
ASSOCIATED CONCEPTS: primary evidence, primary responsibility

PRIMARY CARE, *noun* chief medical practitioners, first-contact doctors, first response medical care, main doctors, main health care physicians, main medical providers, main physicians, preliminary health care providers, preliminary medical office, primary doctors, primary medical office, primary providers, prime doctors, principal doctors

PRIMARY RIGHTS, *noun* direct rights, first publication rights, first rights, original rights, print publication rights, printing rights, publishing rights

PRIME *(Most valuable),* ***adjective*** best, beyond all praise, beyond compare, capital, cardinal, champion, chief, choice, crowning, dominant, eminent, excelling, exceptional, exemplary, exquisite, finest, first-class, first in quality, first-rate, foremost, front, greatest, head, highest, important, leading, matchless, nonpareil, of highest excellence, of the best quality, optimas, paramount, peerless, predominant, preeminent, preponderant, prevailing, priceless, principal, prize, prominent, remarkable, select, specially selected, splendid, superb, supereminent, superior, superlative, supreme, top, transcendant, unequaled, unmatched, unparalleled, unrivaled, unsurpassable, unsurpassed, utmost, without comparison

PRIME *(Original),* ***adjective*** aboriginal, authentic, basal, basic, beginning, dawning, earliest, early, elemental, elementary, embryonic, first, formative, fossil, fundamental, generative, genuine, germinal, inaugural, inceptive, incipient, initial, institutive, introductory, native, oldest, originative, primal, primary, primeval, primitive, primordial, *primus,* rudimentary, starting

PRIMITIVE, ***adjective*** aged, ancient, antediluvian, antiquated, antique, backward, basic, crude, dated, early, elementary, embryonic, homely, low, musty, obsolete, old, old-fashioned, old-time, organic, original, out-of-date, outworn, passé, past, prime, primeval, primordial, quaint, rudimentary, simple, uncomplicated, underdeveloped, undeveloped, unmodernized, unsophisticated

PRIMOGENITOR, ***noun*** ancestor, ancestral relation, ancestral relative, antecedent, ascendant, elder, father, forebear, forefather, forerunner, founder of the family, grandsire, *origo,* parent, patriarch, precursor, predecessor, procreator

PRIMORDIAL, ***adjective*** aboriginal, archetypal, basal, basic, beginning, creative, elemental, elementary, first, fundamental, original, primal, primary, prime, primeval, primigenial, primitive, pristine, protogenic, prototypal, rudimentary, underived

PRINCIPAL, ***adjective*** cardinal, chief, controlling, dominant, essential, first, foremost, hegemonic, hegemonical, highest, leading, main, most considerable, most important, most powerful, outstanding, paramount, predominant, preeminent, prevailing, primal, primary, prime, *primus, princeps, principalis,* prominent, ruling, stellar, supereminent, supreme
ASSOCIATED CONCEPTS: principal activity, principal contract, principal contractor, principal obligation, principal place of business, principal sum, principal wrongdoing
FOREIGN PHRASES: ***Omne principale trahit ad se accessorium.*** Every principal thing draws the accessory to itself. ***Quae accessionum locum obtinent, extinguuntur cum principales res peremptae fuerint.*** When the principal thing is destroyed, those things which are accessory to it are also destroyed. ***Sublato principali, tollitur adjunctum.*** By the removal of the principal thing, the adjunct is also taken.

PRINCIPAL *(Capital sum),* ***noun*** assets, assets in hand, capital, caput, circulating capital, economic resources, fixed capital, fund, funds, gross amount, holdings, invested sum, main body, material assets, money, *nummi,* original sum, principal part, property, resources, sors, sum, sum total, tangible assets, totality, wealth, whole, working capital

PRINCIPAL *(Director),* ***noun*** boss, chief, chief actor, chief authority, chief executive, chief party, chieftain, commandant, commander, controller, directing head, director, employer, engager of services, executive, executive officer, foreperson, governor, head, headperson, *magister,* manager, master, overlooker, overseer, owner, person in authority, person in charge, proprietor, senior, superintendent, superior, supervisor, taskmaster
ASSOCIATED CONCEPTS: partially disclosed principal, principal in the first degree, undisclosed principal

FOREIGN PHRASES: ***Nullus dicitur accessorius post feloniam, sed ille qui novit principalem feloniam fecisse, et illum receptavit et comfortavit.*** No one is called an accessory after the fact but the one who knew the principal had committed a felony, and who received and comforted him. ***Nullus dicitur felo principalis nisi actor, aut qui praesens est, abettans aut auxilians ad feloniam faciendam.*** No one is called a principal felon except the party actually committing the felony, or the person who is present, aiding and abetting in its commission. ***Res accessoria sequitur rem principalem.*** An accessory follows the principal. ***Qui per alium facit per seipsum facere videtur.*** He who acts through another is deemed as having acted himself. ***Ubi non est principalis, non potest esse accessorius.*** Where there can be no principal, there cannot be an accessory.

PRINCIPLE *(Axiom),* ***noun*** accepted belief, adage, admitted maxim, article of belief, article of faith, assertion, assurance, basic doctrine, basic law, basic rule, basic truth, belief, canon, conviction, credo, declaration of faith, *decretum,* doctrine, dogma, established rule, form, formula, formulated belief, foundation, fundamental doctrine, fundamental law, fundamental rule, gospel, *institutum,* instruction, intuitive truth, law, law of conduct, maxim, model, philosophy, policy, position, postulate, postulate of reason, precept, professed belief, profession of faith, proposition, provision, received maxim, recognized maxim, regula, regulation, reliance on, rubric, rule, rule of action, sage maxim, self-evident proposition, self-evident truth, settled principle, standard, statement of belief, statement of position, tenet, theorem, truism, way of thinking
ASSOCIATED CONCEPTS: equitable principle, legal principle
FOREIGN PHRASES: ***Principia data sequuntur concomitantia.*** Given principles are followed by their concomitants. ***Principia probant, non probantur.*** Principles prove, they are not proved. ***Unumquodque principiorum est sibimetipsi fides; et perspicua vera non sunt probanda.*** Every general principle is its own evidence, and plain truths need not be proved.

PRINCIPLE *(Virtue),* ***noun*** character, conviction, ethics, goodness, honesty, honor, honorableness, incorruptibility, *integritas,* integrity, justice, moral excellence, moral rectitude, morality, nobleness, probity, rectitude, righteousness, rightfulness, scrupulousness, trustworthiness, truth, uprightness, virtuousness

PRIOR, ***adjective*** antecedent, anterior, earlier, first, foregoing, former, inaugural, introductory, late, lead, leading, old, past, precedent, preceding, precursory, preexistent, prefatory, preliminary, preludial, prelusive, preparatory, prevenient, previous, quondam, *superior*
ASSOCIATED CONCEPTS: prior approval, prior conviction, prior lien, prior restraint

PRIORITY, ***noun*** advantage, antecedence, commanding position, essential status, exigency, first place, importance, necessity, needfulness, precedence, preeminence, preference, primacy, prior right, requisiteness, right-of-way, right to precedence, right to preference, seniority, superiority, supremacy, urgency, vitalness
ASSOCIATED CONCEPTS: priority of claim, priority of lien, priority statute
FOREIGN PHRASES: ***Qui prior est tempore potior est jure.*** He who is first in time is first in right. ***Prior tempore potior jure.*** First in time, superior in right.

PRISON, ***noun*** bastille, *carcer,* cell, facility, house of correction, house of detention, house of reform, incarcera-

tion facility, jail, penal colony, penal institution, penitentiary, prison house, reformatory
ASSOCIATED CONCEPTS: prison term
FOREIGN PHRASES: ***Carcer ad homines custodiendos, non ad puniendos, dari debet.*** A prison should be used for the custody of men, and not for their punishment.

PRISONER, ***noun*** captive, confined individual, convict, criminal, detainee, felon, hostage, incarcerated person, individual held in custody, individual jailed, inmate, internee, jailed person, person under arrest

PRIVACY, ***noun*** concealment, confidentiality, confidentialness, delitescence, disassociation, dissociation, evasion, evasiveness, intimacy, isolation, obscurity, penetralia, privateness, quietude, retirement, retreat, seclusion, secrecy, secretiveness, separateness, separation, solitariness, solitude, *solitudo,* voluntary exile, withdrawal
ASSOCIATED CONCEPTS: invasion of privacy, right of privacy

PRIVATE *(Confidential),* ***adjective*** abstruse, arcane, arcanus, clandestine, closet, concealed, covert, cryptic, cryptical, dark, esoteric, esoterical, hidden, intimate, inviolable, mysterious, off the record, personal, privy, recondite, secret, undercover, undisclosable, undivulgable, unrevealable
ASSOCIATED CONCEPTS: private papers, private writings

PRIVATE *(Not public),* ***adjective*** closed, confined, exclusive, individual, individualized, limited, nonofficial, nonpublic, not open, personalized, *privatus,* reserved, restricted, select, unofficial
ASSOCIATED CONCEPTS: private action, private agreement, private bill, private carrier, private corporation, private detective, private dwelling, private employment, private enterprise, private grant, private institution, private investigator, private nuissance, private property, private purposes, private sale, private statute, private trust, private use
FOREIGN PHRASES: ***Privatum incommodum publico bono pensatur.*** Private inconvenience is compensated for by public benefit. ***Pactis privatorum juri publico non derogatur.*** Private contracts do not derogate from public law. ***Jura publica anteferenda privatis.*** Public rights are to be preferred to private rights.

PRIVATE *(Secluded),* ***adjective*** apart, cloistered, hidden, inaccessible, insular, isolated, out-of-the-way, quiet, remote, removed, seclusive, separate, solitary, unfrequented

PRIVATE RIGHT OF ACTION, ***noun*** civil cause of action, individual right to sue, private cause of action, private right to bring a lawsuit, private right to maintain an action

PRIVATION, ***noun*** absence, attachment, bad fortune, bad luck, bankruptcy, beggary, bereavement, confiscation, dearth, deprivation, deprivement, destitution, dispossession, dissipation, distress, divestment, exhaustion, famine, financial straits, hardship, impecuniosity, impecuniousness, indigence, *inopia,* insufficiency, lack, loss, loss of fortune, mendicancy, mendicity, narrow means, necessitude, necessity, need, neediness, pauperism, penury, pinch, poverty, reduced circumstances, riddance, sequestration, starvation, straitened means, want

PRIVILEGE, ***noun*** advantage, affranchisement, allowance, authority, authorization, *beneficium,* benefit, chance, charter, dispensation, enfranchisement, entitlement, exemption, favor, franchise, freedom, grant, honor, *immunitas,* immunity, indulgence, liberty, license, opportunity, permission, perquisite, prerogative, priority, release, right, sanction, title, tolerance, vouchsafement, warrant
ASSOCIATED CONCEPTS: executive privilege, immunity, privilege against self-incrimination, privileged communications, privileged statement, privileges and immunities, qualified privilege
FOREIGN PHRASES: ***Privilegium est beneficium personale, et extinguitur cum persona.*** A privilege is a personal benefit, and is extinguished with the death of the person. ***Privilegium non valet contra rempublicam.*** A privilege is of no avail against the state. ***Necessitas inducit privilegium quo ad jura privata.*** Necessity gives a privilege with reference to private rights.

PRIVILEGED, ***adjective*** allowed, authorized, chartered, empowered, entitled, excepted, excluded, excused, exempt, exempted, favored, franchised, free of, immune, *immunis,* immunized, licensed, not accountable, not subject, permitted, sanctioned, specially provided for, unrestrained
ASSOCIATED CONCEPTS: privileged communications, privileged information, privileged matter

PRIVILEGED COMMUNICATION, ***noun*** attorney's work product, closed conversation, confidential communication, confidential discussion, nondisclosable communication, private communication, private interchange, privileged discussion, privileged writing
ASSOCIATED CONCEPTS: attorney-client relationship, doctor-patient privilege, husband-wife privilege, physician-patient privilege, priest-penitent privilege, waiver

PRIVITY, ***noun*** affiliation, attachment, connecting medium, connection, contractual bond, derivative interest, interconnection, legal relationship, link, mutual relationship, mutuality of interest, nexus, relation, relationship, successive relationship, tie
ASSOCIATED CONCEPTS: privity of contract, privity of estate, privity of possession

PRIVY, ***adjective*** acquainted with, arcane, auricular, buried, clandestine, cognizant of, concealed, confidential, covert, cryptic, cryptical, dark, exclusive, furtive, hidden, inmost, limited, murky, mysterious, nonpublic, obscure, personal, private, recondite, reserved, restricted, secret, sequestered, stealthy, surreptitious, undisclosed, unrevealed

PRIVY, ***noun*** contracting party, interested party, partaken, participant, party
ASSOCIATED CONCEPTS: parties and privies

PRIZE, ***noun*** accolade, advantage, award, blue ribbon, bonus, booty, bounty, capture, catch, cordon, cup, decoration, distinction, find, first place, gain, guerdon, honor, inducement, jackpot, loot, medal, meed, payment, pillage, plum, plunder, *praemium,* premium, prey, privilege, recompense, reward, spoil, title, token, trophy, winning

PRO FORMA, ***adjective*** as a matter of form, by course of conduct, by custom, by habit, by past practice, by trade and usage, by usage, ceremoniously, common, customary, for the sake of appearances, for the sake of form, formally, in due form, in set form, ritualistically, ritually, standard, superficially, usual
ASSOCIATED CONCEPTS: pro forma decree, pro forma judgment, pro forma order

PRO HOC VICI, ***idiom*** allowed to practice, permitted to practice for one time only, practice for a particular purpose, unadmitted temporarily
ASSOCIATED CONCEPTS: jurisdiction, practice of law

PRO RATA, ***adjective*** alloted, apportioned, appropriately, distributed, equivalently, in proportion, on even terms, proportionate
ASSOCIATED CONCEPTS: apportionment, pro rata share

PRO RATA, ***adverb*** each to each, in equal shares, proportionately, respectively, to each according to his share

PRO TEMPORE, ***adverb*** briefly, for a time, for the moment, for the present occasion, for the time being, momentarily, pro tem, provisionally, temporarily, transitorily

PROBABILITY, ***noun*** anticipation, appearance of truth, believability, chance, conceivability, credibility, credibleness, expectation, fair chance, fair expectation, favorable chance, liability, liableness, likelihood, likeliness, odds, ostensibility, plausibility, possibility, presumption, promise, prospect, reasonable chance, reasonableness, susceptibility, tendency, *veri similitudo,* verisimilitude

PROBABLE, ***adjective*** apparent, apt, believable, conceivable, conjecturable, credible, feasible, foreseeable, full of promise, indubitable, liable, likely, logical, ostensible, plausible, possible, practicable, presumable, presumptive, promising, reasonable, seeming, supposed, surmisable, to be expected, unquestionable, *veri similis,* verisimilar, verisimilous
ASSOCIATED CONCEPTS: probable cause

PROBABLE CAUSE, ***noun*** adequate legal basis, ample legal basis to pursue, just and adequate basis, just evidence, just meritorious evidence, just qualified evidence, legally adequate basis to proceed, legally compelling basis, legally competent evidence, legally sufficient cause, satisfactory legal basis, sufficient evidence, sufficient legal basis
ASSOCIATED CONCEPTS: plain view doctrine, reasonable suspicion

PROBATE, ***noun*** authentication of a will, authentication proceeding, judicial validation of a will, proof of the validity of a will, proof of the will, validation of a testament, validity proceedings, will validation proceeding, will verification proceeding

PROBATE, ***verb*** adjudge the validity of a will, adjudicate the validity of a will, authenticate a will, certify a will, confirm the validity of a will, establish the authenticity of a will, establish the genuineness of a will, establish the validity of a will, prove the validity of a will, substantiate, validate a will, verify a testament
ASSOCIATED CONCEPTS: probate a will, probate court, probate proceeding

PROBATION, ***noun*** conditional suspension of sentence, exemption, freedom, liberation, parole, period of testing, period of trial, *probatio,* release
ASSOCIATED CONCEPTS: parole, probation term, probationary employee, revocation of probation

PROBATIONER *(One being tested),* ***noun*** apprentice, beginner, candidate, entrant, initiate, learner, neophyte, newcomer, novice, novitiate

PROBATIONER *(Released offender),* ***noun*** criminal released at large, criminal under suspension of sentence, lawbreaker under suspension of sentence, malefactor under suspension of sentence, offender under suspension of sentence, parolee, released convict, released criminal, released felon, released lawbreaker, released malefactor, released prisoner, released transgressor, released wrongdoer, wrongdoer released from prison

PROBATIVE, ***adjective*** demonstrative, empiric, empirical, evidential, evidentiary, experimental, exploratory, offering evidence, probatory, providing evidence, providing proof, verificative
ASSOCIATED CONCEPTS: probative evidence, probative facts, probative value, probative weight

PROBE, ***noun*** analysis, careful search, critical examination, deep study, examination, exhaustive study, exploration, exploratory examination, indagation, inquiry, inspection, investigation, perquisition, perscrutation, pursuit, quest, research, review, rigorous search, *rimari, scrutari,* scrutiny, search, searching examination, strict examination

PROBE, ***verb*** check over, conduct an inquiry, conduct research on, consider attentively, delve into, dig into, dissect, examine, explore, follow up, indagate, inquire into, inspect, institute an inquiry, interrogate, investigate, look into, make an examination, make inquiries, observe, peruse, plumb, poke into, pry into, pursue an inquiry, put to the test, question, review, *rimari,* run checks on, scan, *scrutari,* scrutinize, search into, seek, seek information regarding, study, study in detail, subject to scrutiny, take up an inquiry, unearth

PROBITY, ***noun*** candidness, candor, conscience, dependability, deservingness, equitableness, equity, fair play, fairness, faith, frankness, good faith, goodness, guilelessness, high principles, honesty, honor, honorableness, impartiality, incorruptibility, ingenuousness, integrity, justice, merit, moral excellence, morality, morals, principle, *probitas,* rectitude, reputability, righteousness, scrupulousness, sincerity, straightforwardness, trustiness, trustworthiness, truth, truthfulness, undeceptiveness, uprightness, veraciousness, veracity, virtue

PROBLEM, ***noun*** anxiety, bafflement, bone of contention, care, cause for concern, complexity, complication, crisis, difficulty, dilemma, enigma, exercise, matter in dispute, moot point, mystery, obstacle, plight, point in dispute, point to be settled, predicament, puzzle, quandary, question, riddle, source of perplexity, stumper, subject of dispute, tight situation, trouble, vexed question

PROBLEMATIC, ***adjective*** ambiguous, complex, complicated, contestable, controversial, controvertible, cryptic, cryptical, debatable, difficult, disputable, doubtful, dubious, *dubius,* enigmatic, enigmatical, equivocal, imperspicuous, *incertus,* insoluble, involved, knotty, moot, mysterious, open to doubt, paradoxical, perplexing, problematical, puzzling, questionable, raveled, shrouded in mystery, snarled, tangled, tentative, troublesome, uncertain, unconvincing, undecided, undemonstrable, undetermined, unsettled, vague, worrisome

PROCACIOUS, ***adjective*** aloof, annoyed, apathetic, bumptuous, cool, disapproving, distant, frigid, forward, impertinent, impudent, incurious, indifferent, insolent, lukewarm, offhand, petulant, reserved, solitary, unenthusiastic, uninterested, unresponsible, unresponsive, unsociable, unwelcoming

PROCEDURAL, *adjective* adjective, directive, functional, methodical, operative, relating to method, relating to the mechanics of a lawsuit, relative to the manner of proceeding, systematic
ASSOCIATED CONCEPTS: procedural defect, procedural due process, procedural law, procedural matter, procedural question, procedural right, procedural rule of law, procedural statute

PROCEDURAL DUE PROCESS, *noun* due process in civil and criminal proceedings, due process of law, fundamental fairness in procedure, individual protections in legal procedure, nonsubstantive due process, procedures that safeguard individual legal rights
ASSOCIATED CONCEPTS: Fifth and Fourteenth Amendments

PROCEDURE, *noun* act, action, adjective law, behavior, common practice, conduct, course, course of action, custom, established method, habit, line of action, manner of proceeding, manner of working, matter of course, measure, method, methodology, mode, mode of operation, mode of use, modus operandi, motion, order, particular course of action, plan, plan of action, policy, practice, proceeding, process, program, proscribed form, routine, rule, scheme, set form, set format, step, strategy, system, tactics, usage, way, way of operation
ASSOCIATED CONCEPTS: civil procedure, criminal procedure, judicial procedure, pretrial procedure, rule of procedure
FOREIGN PHRASES: ***Cursus curiae est lex curiae.*** The practice of the court is the law of the court.

PROCEED *(Continue),* *verb* begin again, begin where one left off, carry on, get back to work, get on, recommence, reinstate, renew, resume, return, take up again

PROCEED *(Go forward),* *verb* act, advance, arise, emanate, ensue, extend, flow, follow, follow a course, gain ground, get ahead, get on, go, go ahead, go forth, issue, keep going, keep moving, make headway, make progress, make rapid strides, move ahead, move forward, pass on, press on, progress, propel oneself, push ahead, push on, roll on, spring, take steps
ASSOCIATED CONCEPTS: proceed with a case, proceed with due diligence

PROCEEDING, *noun* *actio,* action, action at law, case, cause, conduct of a lawsuit, course of an action at law, dispute, hearing, lawsuit, legal action, legal procedure, litigation, matter, performance, prescribed method of action, prescribed mode of action, procedure, process, prosecution, series of events, step, steps in the prosecution of an action, suit, suit at law, transaction, trial, undertaking
ASSOCIATED CONCEPTS: abandonment of a proceeding, annulment proceeding, arbitration proceeding, bankruptcy proceeding, bastardy proceeding, certiorari proceeding, commencement of a proceeding, condemnation proceeding, contempt proceeding, criminal proceeding, custody proceeding, discontinuance of a proceeding, enforcement proceeding, equitable proceeding, extraordinary proceeding, filiation proceeding, garnishment proceeding, guardianship proceeding, habeas corpus proceeding, in personam proceeding, in rem proceeding, judicial proceeding, lawful proceeding, legal proceeding, liquidation proceeding, mandamus proceeding, official proceeding, partition proceeding, pending proceeding, plenary proceeding, probate proceeding, public proceeding, quasi in rem proceeding, special proceeding, supplementary proceeding, testamentary proceeding, void proceeding

PROCEEDS, *noun* avails, balance, benefit, earnings, effect, end result, gain, gross profit, income, money coming in, net profit, produce, product, profit, receipts, *reditus,* renumeration, result, returns, revenue, sum derived from a sale, value received, yield
ASSOCIATED CONCEPTS: proceeds of a crime, proceeds of a sale, proceeds of an insurance policy

PROCESS *(Course),* *noun* action, conduct, continued movement, continuing development, handling, line of action, manner, means, method, methodology, mode of operation, operation, performance, plan, policy, procedure, progressive course, *ratio,* regular proceeding, ritual, routine, scheme, series of measures, strategy, system, tactics, transaction, treatment, way, ways and means
ASSOCIATED CONCEPTS: due process, judicial process

PROCESS *(Summons),* *noun* authoritative citation to appear before a court, authoritative command, behest, bidding, citation, command, direction, instruction to appear, legal call, *lis,* official call, official notice, requirement to appear, signal by which one is summoned, subpoena, writ
ASSOCIATED CONCEPTS: abuse of process, compulsory process, defective process, irregular process, return of process, service of process

PRO-CHOICE, *noun* abortion advocate, accepting abortion, approving abortion, endorsing abortion, in favor of abortion, pro-abortion, sanctioning abortion, supporting legalized abortion, supportive of abortion
Generally: self-determination
ASSOCIATED CONCEPTS: abortion on demand, legalized abortion, spontaneous abortion, voluntary abortion

PROCLAIM, *verb* advertise, air, announce, annunciate, assert, asseverate, blare, blaze abroad, broach, broadcast, bruit, call out, circulate, communicate, cry, *declarare,* declare, disseminate, divulge, enounce, exclaim, gazette, give notice of, give out, hawk about, herald, inform, make a proclamation, make known, make public, noise abroad, *praedicare,* promulgate, *pronuntiare,* propagate, publicize, publish, release, report, set forth, sing out, sound forth, spread abroad, state, tell, thunder forth, trumpet, utter, ventilate

PROCLAMATION, *noun* announcement, annunciation, declaration, decree, decretal, edict, *edictum,* exclamation, fiat, mandate, manifesto, message, notification, official publication, promulgation, pronouncement, public announcement, public avowal, public notice, publication, recitation, rescript, statement

PROCLIVITY, *noun* ability, appetence, appetency, aptitude, aptness, bent, bias, disposition, facility, gift, gravitation, inclination, inherent ability, innate disposition, innate sense, instinct, leaning, liking, natural sense, partiality, penchant, predilection, predisposition, prejudice, *proclivitas,* proneness, propensity, readiness, talent, tendency, turn

PROCRASTINATE, *verb* adjourn, be dilatory, be idle, be inert, be neglectful, block, dally, dawdle, defer, delay, *differre,* dilly dally, do nothing, filibuster, gain time, hang back, hesitate, hold back, hold up, idle, keep one waiting, kill time, lag, let slide, let slip, let the matter stand, linger, loaf, loiter, neglect, pause, pigeonhole, play for time, postpone, *procrastinare,* prolong, prorogue, protract, push aside, put off, retard, shelve, stall, stave off, suspend, table, tarry, wait, waste time

PROCRASTINATION, *noun* deferment, delay, frivoling, hindrance, idling, interference, loitering, pause, playing around, postponement, puttering, stonewalling, toying, trifling

PROCTOR, *noun* advocate, agent, appointee, broker, caretaker, delegate, deputy, functionary, instrument, lawyer, lieutenant, manager, minister, monitor, officer, procurator, proxy, representative, second, steward, surrogate, vicar

PROCURATOR, *noun* administrator, advisor, agent, appointee, assistant, broker, business representative, caretaker, conductor, *curator,* delegate, deputy, director, emissary, envoy, executor, factor, go-between, intendant, intermediary, intermediate, intermedium, *legatus,* lieutenant, manager, middleman, *moderator,* monitor, overseer, proctor, prolocutor, proxy, representative, solicitor, spokesman, steward, substitute, superintendent, supervisor, syndic, viceregent

PROCURE, *verb* accomplish, accumulate, achieve, acquire, appropriate, attain, bag, bring, buy, capture, cause, come by, commandeer, *comparare,* dig up, earn, effect, enlist, fetch, find, force from, gain, gather, get, glean, help oneself to, hire, lay hands on, make a purchase, obtain, pick up, provide, purchase, realize, reap, receive, secure, seize, take, take possession of

PRODIGAL, *adjective* careless, dissipated, dissipative, excessive, extravagant, heedless, immoderate, improvident, imprudent, intemperate, lavish, liberal, profligate, reckless, spendthrift, squandering, thriftless, unbridled, uncurbed, uneconomical, unfrugal, unrestrained, unthrifty, wanton, wasteful

PRODIGIOUS *(Amazing),* ***adjective*** abnormal, anomalous, astonishing, astounding, bizarre, curious, dumbfounding, exceptional, extraordinary, fantastic, freakish, grotesque, impressive, inconceivable, incredible, indescribable, marvelous, miraculous, noteworthy, out of the common run, out of the ordinary, outlandish, overwhelming, peculiar, phenomenal, queer, remarkable, renowned, singular, startling, strange, striking, supernormal, surprising, unaccountable, unaccustomed, uncommon, unconventional, uncustomary, unexampled, unfamiliar, unheard of, unimaginable, unique, unprecedented, unthinkable, weird, wonderful, wondrous

PRODIGIOUS *(Enormous),* ***adjective*** astronomical, big, colossal, cyclopean, elephantine, gargantuan, giant, gigantic, grand, great, Herculean, huge, *immanis,* immense, *ingens,* large, leviathan, mammoth, massive, mighty, monster, monstrous, monumental, sizable, stupendous, substantial, terrific, thumping, titanic, towering, tremendous, vast, whopping

PRODUCE *(Manufacture),* ***verb*** accomplish, achieve, assemble, bear, beget, breed, bring about, bring forth, bring into being, bring into existence, bring to pass, build, coin, compose, conceive, concoct, construct, contrive, create, devise, draw up, effect, effectuate, engender, erect, execute, fabricate, fashion, form, formulate, furnish, generate, give birth to, give rise to, hatch, institute, invent, make, make up, originate, prepare, procreate, propagate, provide, raise, realize, result in, turn out, yield
ASSOCIATED CONCEPTS: producing cause

PRODUCE *(Offer to view),* ***verb*** air, bring forward, bring into view, bring out, bring to light, bring to the fore, bring to the front, demonstrate, disclose, display, divulge, dramatize, evidence, evince, exhibit, expose, give a performance, hold up to view, impart, lay bare, lay out, make known, make visible, manifest, parade, present, put on display, put on the stage, reveal, set out, show, uncover, unfold, unmask, unscreen, unveil
ASSOCIATED CONCEPTS: failure to produce, notice to produce, produce a witness, produce evidence

PRODUCT, *noun* accomplishment, article, article of merchandise, article of trade, commodity, creation, crop, effect, emanation, end result, final outcome, fruit, handiwork, harvest, invention, issue, item, merchandise, offspring, *opus,* outcome, output, proceeds, produce, result, salable commodity, stock in trade, yield
ASSOCIATED CONCEPTS: product defect, product patent, products liability

PRODUCTION *(Operation),* ***noun*** execution, industry, manifestation, manufacture

PRODUCTION *(Output),* ***noun*** accomplishment, attainment, business, compilation, composition, constitution, construction, consummation, creation, discharge, disclosure, dispatch, effectuation, establishment, fabrication, formation, fruition, fulfillment, implementation, lengthening, manifestation, organization, origination, outcome, output, performance, preparation, presentation, realization, work
ASSOCIATED CONCEPTS: production of a witness, production of documents, production of evidence

PRODUCTIVE, *adjective* advantageous, causative, constructive, creational, creative, demiurgic, demiurgical, efficient, fecund, ferax, fertile, formative, fructiferous, fructuous, fruitful, gainful, imaginative, industrial, inventive, life-giving, luxuriant, manufacturing, original, originative, paying, potent, pregnant, profitable, proliferative, proliferous, prolific, rank, remunerative, resourceful, rich, teeming, *uber,* useful, valuable, worthwhile, yielding

PRODUCTS, *noun* articles of commerce, assets, chattels, commodities, consumer durable, durables, effects, goods, holdings, items, line of goods, manufactured goods, merchandise, produce, produced materials, resources, staples, stock in trade, supplies, vendibles
ASSOCIATED CONCEPTS: products liability insurance

PROFANE, *adjective* bad, blasphemous, coarse, common, damnatory, dirty, disrespectful, evil, execrative, faithless, foul-spoken, foulmouthed, godless, impious, *impius,* imprecative, imprecatory, improper, impure, indelicate, irreligious, irreverant, laic, laical, lay, maledictive, maledictory, miscreant, mundane, peccable, peccant, polluted, *profanus,* sacrilegious, secular, shameless, sinful, smutty, temporal, transient, transitory, unblest, unconsecrated, undevout, ungodly, unhallowed, unholy, unprintable, unreligious, unsacred, unsaintly, unsanctified, unspeakable, unvirtuous, vice-ridden, virtueless, vulgar, wicked, worldly

PROFANITY, *noun* billingsgate, blasphemy, cursing, denunciation, derisive language, desecration, disparagement,

disrespect, execration, foul language, foul talk, *impietas,* invective, malediction, obloquy, profanation, profane language, profaneness, swearing, vilification, vituperation, vulgarity
ASSOCIATED CONCEPTS: censorship, obscenity

PROFESS *(Avow),* ***verb*** acknowledge, admit, advocate, affirm, announce, assert, asseverate, assure, attest, aver, avouch, contend, declare, disclose, divulge, hold out, lay bare, lay open, maintain, make a statement, make an assertion, make clear, make evident, make known, own, pledge, proclaim, pronounce, put forth, put forward, reveal, set forth, state, subscribe to, tell, utter

PROFESS *(Pretend),* ***verb*** affect, claim, concoct, counterfeit, create a false impression, disguise, dissemble, dissimulate, fabricate, feign, give a false impression, imagine, make a show of, make believe, pass for, posture, practice chicanery, put a false construction upon, represent fictitiously, sham, simulate

PROFESSION *(Declaration),* ***noun*** affirmation, announcement, assertion, assurance, attestation, averment, avowal, claim, confession, declaration of faith, disclosure, enunciation, notification, oath, pledge, presentation, *professio,* pronouncement, representation, statement, troth, vow, word, word of honor

PROFESSION *(Vocation),* ***noun*** association, avocation, business, calling, career, chosen work, concern, craft, employment, endeavor, engagement, field, job, learned profession, lifework, line of work, manus, occupation, office, position, practice, pursuit, role, specialty, trade, undertaking, vocation, walk of life, work
ASSOCIATED CONCEPTS: professional corporation

PROFESSIONAL *(Stellar),* ***adjective*** admirable, businesslike, choice, commendable, excellent, exemplary, foremost, highest quality, illustrious, incomparable, laudable, model, paramount, praiseworthy, preeminent, prime, principal, sterling, superb, superior, unequaled, unexcelled, unrivaled, unsurpassed, well done

PROFESSIONAL *(Trained),* ***adjective*** able, adept, career, competent, established, experienced, expert, learned, proficient, qualified, skilled, skillful, specialized, trained, well-qualified
ASSOCIATED CONCEPTS: professional capacity, professional corporation, professional ethics, professional misconduct, professional opinion, professional skill and judgment

PROFESSIONAL, ***noun*** accomplished practitioner, adept practitioner, adroit practitioner, authority, competent practitioner, experienced person, expert, master, practiced individual, practitioner, proficient practitioner, qualified practitioner, skilled practitioner, skilled technician, specialist, trained person
ASSOCIATED CONCEPTS: professional opinion

PROFESSIONALISM, ***noun*** ability, businesslike, ethics, excellence, experience, expert, mastery, poise, professional demeanor, recognition, skill, specialization, style, talent, technique

PROFFER, ***verb*** adduce, advance, advertise, bid, bring forward, donate, extend, give, hold out, invite, lay before, make a bid, make a motion, make an offer, make an overture, make possible, move, offer, prefer, present, promise, *promittere,* propose, propound, put forward, put up, render, set forth, submit, suggest, tender, volunteer

PROFICIENCY, ***noun*** ability, aptitude, background, capability, chops, command, experience, expertise, facility, familiarity, fluency, know-how, knowledge, literacy, mastery, moxie, savvy, skill, training, virtuosity

PROFICIENT, ***adjective*** able, accomplished, adept, adequate, adroit, advanced, capable, clever, competent, conversant, cunning, deft, dexterous, effective, efficacious, efficient, equal to, excellent, experienced, expert, facile, good, habilitated, handy, ingenious, knowing, masterful, *peritus,* practiced, qualified, quick, ready, *sciens,* skilled, skillful, talented, trained, up to, well-qualified, well-versed

PROFIT, ***noun*** accruance, accumulation, acquisition, advancement, advantage, augmentation, avails, benefaction, benefit, clearance, compensation, dividend, earnings, emolument, financial reward, *fructus,* fruits, gain, growth, harvest, improvement, incentive, income, increase, increment, interest, *lucrum,* meed, output, pay, payment, premium, prize, proceeds, produce, *quaestus,* realization, receipts, remuneration, return, revenue, reward, service, take, utility, value received, windfall, winnings, yield
ASSOCIATED CONCEPTS: accumulated profits, anticipated profits, capital, carrying on business for profit, distributable profits, excessive profits, excess profits tax, gross profit, loss of profits, margin of profit, net profit, not for profit, pecuniary profits, profit a prendre, profit sharing, prospective profit, remote profits, secret profits, speculative profits, surplus profits, underwriting profits, undistributed profits
FOREIGN PHRASES: ***Ubi periculum, ibi et lucrum collocatur.*** He who risks a thing, should receive the profits arising from it.

PROFIT, ***verb*** acquire, advance, assist, avail, be better for, be improved by, be of use, benefit, cash in on, clear, confer a benefit on, contribute, draw profit from, edify, gain, gain advantage, harvest, help, improve, learn a lesson from, make capital out of, make good use of, make improvement, make money by, make use of, obtain a return, produce a good effect, produce a good result, *proficere,* put to use, realize, reap, reap the fruits, turn to account, use, utilize, yield returns

PROFITABLE, ***adjective*** advantageous, advisable, aiding, assisting, beneficial, desirable, edifying, emolumental, expedient, favorable, *fructuosus, frugifer,* fruitful, gainful, helpful, invaluable, lucrative, money-making, paying, productive, remunerative, rewarding, salutary, serviceable, successful, useful, *utilis,* valuable, well-paying, worthwhile

PROFLIGATE *(Corrupt),* ***adjective*** abandoned to vice, base, corrupted, debauched, degenerate, depraved, disgraceful, disreputable, dissipated, dissipative, dissolute, evil, evil-minded, fallen, flagitious, foul, heinous, immoral, indecent, infamous, iniquitous, lacking decency, lacking principle, lacking shame, lawless, lost to principle, lost to virtue, morally evil, nefarious, offensive, peccant, *perditus,* rascally, rotten, scampish, shameful, shameless, sinful, unethical, unprincipled, unredeemable, unregenerate, unrepentant, vice-ridden, vicious, vile, vitiated, wicked

PROFLIGATE *(Extravagant),* ***adjective*** economically imprudent, immoderate, improvident, intemperate, overly liberal, prodigal, *profligatus,* reckless, spendthrift, squandering, thriftless, unrestrained, unthrifty, wasteful

PROFOUND *(Esoteric),* ***adjective*** abstruse, acroamatic, acroamatical, acroatic, astute, complicated, erudite, esoteric, gnostic, intellectual, intellectually deep, knowing, learned, oracular, penetrating, perceptive, philosophical, recondite, reflective, sagacious, sage, scholarly, thoughtful, wise

PROFOUND *(Intense),* ***adjective*** abysmal, acute, bottomless, deep, deeply felt, fathomless, great, heart-stirring, heartfelt, heavy, impressive, indelible, intense, moving, penetrating, piercing, sharp, soul-stirring, strong, touching, unfathomable, vivid

PROFUSE, ***adjective*** abounding, abundant, affluent, ample, boundless, bounteous, bountiful, copious, countless, crowded, diffuse, discursive, *effusus,* endless, excessive, exorbitant, extravagant, exuberant, flush, full, garrulous, generous, illimitable, immeasurable, immoderate, improvident, incalculable, inexhaustible, infinite, innumerable, inordinate, intemperate, interminable, lavish, liberal, limitless, long-winded, loquacious, luxuriant, measureless, multitudinary, multitudinous, munificent, myriad, numberless, numerous, overabounding, overflowing, overgenerous, padded, plentiful, prodigal, profligate, *profusus,* prolific, prolix, protracted, rambling, reckless, redundant, replete, rich, rife, spendthrift, squandering, sumptious, superfluous, surplus, swarming, teeming, thriftless, unbridled, uncurbed, unnumbered, unsparing, unstinted, unstinting, unthrifty, unwarranted, verbose, wanton, wasteful, without bound, without end, without limit, without stint, wordy

PROGENITOR, ***noun*** ancestor, antecedent, antecessor, begettor, forebear, forefather, foregoer, forerunner, genitor, origin, *parens,* parent, precursor, predecessor, primogenitor, procreator, sire, source

PROGENY, ***noun*** bloodline, brood, children, descendants, family, fruit, heirs, issue, line, lineage, offspring, posterity, *progenies,* scions, seed, sons, stock, succeeding generations, tribe, young

PROGNOSIS, ***noun*** conjecture, estimate, foreboding, forecast, foreknowledge, foresight, foretelling, guess, opinion, preannouncement, prediction, prefiguration, prefigurement, premonition, prenotice, presage, presagement, presumption, prognostication, promise, prophesy, supposition, vaticination

PROGNOSTICATE, ***verb*** advise, augur, augurate, auspicate, betoken, bode, conjecture, counsel, divine, forebode, forecast, foresee, foresee the future, foreshadow, foreshow, foretell, foretoken, herald, indicate beforehand, indicate in advance, look ahead to, look forward to, make a prediction, ominate, portend, preannounce, predict, premonish, premonstrate, presage, presignify, presume, promise, prophesy, signify, soothsay, speculate, spell, surmise, tell fortunes, theorize, vaticinate

PROGRAM, ***noun*** agenda, arrangement, blueprint, calendar, campaign, catalog, course, curriculum, design, docket, draft, list, order, outline, plan, policy, presentation, project, proposal, prospectus, schedule, series of events, set of tactics, strategy, syllabus, system

PROGRAM, ***verb*** arrange, block out, book, budget, calendar, design, determine, devise, direct, docket, draft, engineer, *excogitare,* form a plan, frame, lay a plan, lay out, list, make an agenda, make arrangements, manage, map out, organize, outline, plan, plot, preconcert, predetermine, preestablish, project, register, schedule, scheme, sketch, slate, work out

PROGRESS, ***noun*** accomplishment, achievement, advance, advancement, amelioration, augmentation, betterment, change, development, emendation, enhancement, enrichment, flow, furtherance, gain, growth, headway, improvement, increase, increment, march, melioration, movement, movement forward, onward motion, passage, perfection, preferment, progression, *progressus,* promotion, reclamation, recovery, redemption, reform, rehabilitation, reorganization, restoration, rise, steady advance, success

PROGRESS, ***verb*** advance, ameliorate, approach, ascend, become better, climb, continue onward, convalesce, develop, enhance, enrich, expand, forge ahead, gain, gain ground, get ahead, go ahead, go forward, go on, grow, grow better, grow up, improve, increase, keep going, keep moving, make headway, make progress, maturate, mature, meliorate, mend, mount, move ahead, move on, move onward, press on, press onward, proceed, *proficere, progredi,* prosper, push on, recuperate, ripen, rise

PROGRESSIVE *(Advocating change),* ***adjective*** advanced, corrective, emendatory, enterprising, forward looking, improvement-minded, liberal, modern, open-minded, reformational, reformative, reformatory, remedial, up-to-date

PROGRESSIVE *(Going forward),* ***adjective*** advancing, consecutive, continuous, dynamic, endless, forward, forward moving, growing, moving, ongoing, proceeding, profluent, rising, serial, successive, transitional, traveling, uninterrupted

PROHIBIT, ***verb*** ban, banish, bar, block, check, circumscribe, control, counteract, curb, debar, deny, disallow, disqualify, embargo, enjoin, exclude, forbid, foreclose, forfend, gainsay, halt, hamper, hinder, impede, inhibit, interdict, interfere, limit, make illegal, negate, negative, obstruct, omit, oppose, preclude, prevent, proscribe, protest, quash, quell, refuse, refuse permission, regulate, reject, repress, repudiate, restrain, restrict, revoke, shut out, smother, stay, stop, suppress, suspend, thwart, traverse, veto

ASSOCIATED CONCEPTS: prohibited action, prohibited by law, prohibited form, prohibited practice

FOREIGN PHRASES: ***Contra legem facit qui id facit quod lex prohibit; in fraudem vero qui, salvis verbis legis, sententiam ejus circumvenit.*** He who does what the law prohibits acts in fraud of the law; the letter of the law being inviolate, cheats the spirit of it. ***Cui licet guod majus, non debet quod minus est non licere.*** He who is allowed to do the greater ought not to be prohibited from doing the less. ***Idem est facere, et nolle prohibere cum possis.*** It is the same thing to commit an act as not to prohibit it when it is in your power.

PROHIBITION, ***noun*** ban, banishment, bar, barrier, block, check, circumscription, constraint, counterorder, curb, debarment, denial, determent, deterrence, deterrent, disallowance, discouragement, disqualification, elimination, embargo, enforced abstention, enjoining, eradication, estoppel, exclusion, forbiddance, hindrance, illegality, illegitimacy, impediment, inhibition, injunction, interdict, interdiction, *interdictum,* interference, limit, limitation, negation, nonadmission, noninclusion, obstacle,

obstruction, ostracism, outlawry, preclusion, prevention, proscription, refusal, rejection, repression, repudiation, restraint, restriction, stay, stop, stoppage, suppression, taboo, traversal, unconstitutionality, unlawfulness, veto
ASSOCIATED CONCEPTS: injunctions, restraining orders, statutory prohibition, writ of prohibition
FOREIGN PHRASES: ***Semper qui non prohibet pro se intervenire, mandare creditur.*** He who does not prohibit the intervention of another in his behalf is deemed to have authorized it. ***Quando aliquid prohibetur ex directo, prohibetur et per obliquum.*** When anything is prohibited directly, it is also prohibited indirectly.

PROHIBITIVE *(Costly),* ***adjective*** exorbitant, expensive, extortionate, extravagant, high-priced, immoderate, inordinate, preposterous, unconscionable, undue, unreasonable, unwarranted

PROHIBITIVE *(Restrictive),* ***adjective*** deterrent, disallowing, disqualifying, exclusive, exclusory, hindering, impeding, impossible, inhibitive, inhibitory, injunctive, interdictive, interdictory, interfering, limitative, limiting, obstructive, preclusive, preventing, preventive, prohibitory, proscriptive, repressive, restraining, suppressive

PROJECT, *noun* activity, aim, ambition, assignment, attempt, *consilium,* contrivance, deal, design, determination, device, employment, end, endeavor, engagement, enterprise, essay, fixed intention, goal, idea, *inceptum,* intent, intention, job, object, objective, occupation, outline, plan, projected campaign, projected scheme, proposal, proposition, *propositum,* purpose, pursuit, resolution, scheme, set purpose, task, undertaking, venture

PROJECT *(Extend beyond),* ***verb*** arch, bulge, hang over, jut, jut out, lengthen, overhang, protrude, protuberate, stand out, stick out, widen

PROJECT *(Impel forward),* ***verb*** cast, discharge, drive, eject, emit, expel, fling, hurl, launch, let fly, propel, push, send, send off, shoot forward, sling, throw, thrust, traject

PROLEPSIS, *noun* apriorism, assumption, hypothesis, postulation, presupposition

PRO-LIFE, *noun* against abortion, antiabortion, antithetic to abortion, diametrically opposed to abortion, hostile to abortion, in favor of barring abortion, in favor of life, in favor of prohibiting abortion, in opposition to abortion, inimical to abortion, opposed to abortion, pro-human life, right-to-life advocate
ASSOCIATED CONCEPTS: consistent life ethic, human rights, partial birth abortions, pro-choice, pro-life movement, unborn child

PROLIFERATE, *verb* abound, be fruitful, be numerous, be plentiful, blossom, breed, bud, burgeon, fecundate, fecundify, flourish, flower, grow, grow in number, have offspring, have progeny, increase the number of, make manifold, *multiplicare,* multiply, mushroom, produce rapidly, propagate, reproduce, reproduce in kind, reproduce rapidly, spawn, spread, sprout, swell, thrive, wax

PROLIFIC, *adjective* abundant, breedy, copious, creative, fecund, feracious, fertile, fruitbearing, fruitful, generative, philoprogenitive, procreative, productive, profuse, progenitive, proliferative, proliferous, rich, teeming, verbose, wordy, yielding

PROLIX, *adjective* bombastic, boresome, boring, circumlocutory, copious, diffuse, discursive, drearisome, extended, full of verbiage, lengthy, long, long-spun, long-winded, *longus,* maundering, monotonous, padded, pleonastic, pleonastical, prolonged, prosy, protracted, rambling, redundant, repetitive, spread out, spun out, tedious, tiresome, unconcise, uneconomical, verbose, *verbosus,* wandering, wearisome, wordy

PROLIXITY, *noun* effusion, long-windedness, loquacity, redundancy, verbiage, verbosity, wordiness

PROLONG, *verb* be steadfast, continue, drag out, draw out, extend, *extendere,* hold over, increase, keep, lengthen, linger, maintain, make longer, perpetuate, persevere, preserve, *prorogare,* protract, retain, slow down, spin out, stretch, sustain, tarry, *trahere*

PROMINENCE, *noun* brilliancy, celebrity, character, clout, consequence, consideration, conspicuousness, cedit, distinction, eminence, emphasis, honor, fame, grandeur, greatness, height, illustriousness, import, importance, influence, majesty, notability, notoriety, paramountcy, popularity, prestige, projection, protuberance, reputation, respectability, significance, splendor, status, superiority, weight

PROMINENT, *adjective* apparent, bold, brilliant, celebrated, consequential, conspicuous, credited, dignified, discernible, distinct, distinctive, distinguished, elevated, eminent, evident, exalted, extended, famous, flagrant, foremost, glaring, honored, illustrious, important, imposing, influential, jutting, known, leading, lofty, main, manifest, marked, memorable, noble, notable, noticeable, notorious, obtrusive, obvious, outstanding, powerful, predominent, preeminent, principal, projecting, *prominens,* pronounced, protruding, protrusive, protuberant, raised, recognizable, relieved, remarkable, renowned, respected, rising, salient, showy, significant, striking, upmost, visible, weighty, well-known, well-marked, well-seen

PROMISCUOUS, *adjective* alloyed, amalgamated, blended, carnal, casual, chaotic, commingled, composite, confused, conjoined, crossbred, crossed, debauched, dissolute, diverse, easy, free, fused, heterogeneous, immodest, immoral, incontinent, indiscriminate, indiscriminative, indistinguishable, intemperate, interlarded, intermixed, interwoven, joined, jumbled, lax, lewd, licentious, loose, mingled, miscellaneous, mixed, profligate, *promiscuus,* scrambled, unchaste, uncritical, undiscerning, undiscriminating, unselective, unvirtuous, variegated, wanton, wild

PROMISE, *noun* affirmation, agreement, asseveration, assurance, avowal, bond, commitment, compact, consent, contract, covenant, declaration, engagement, *fides,* guarantee, oath, obligation, pact, paction, pledge, *promissum,* stipulation, treaty, understanding, vadium, vow, warranty, word
ASSOCIATED CONCEPTS: bilateral promises, consideration, contract, gift, unilateral promise
FOREIGN PHRASES: ***Ea quae, commendandi causa, in venditionibus dicuntur, si palam appareant, venditorem non obligant.*** Those things which are said as praise of the things sold, if they are openly apparent do not bind the seller. ***Nudum pactum est ubi nulla subest causa praeter conventionem; sed ubi subest causa, fit obligatio, et parit actionem.*** A naked contract is where there is no consideration except the agreement; but where there is a consideration, an obligation is created and gives rise to a

right of action. ***Nuda pactio obligationem non parit.*** A naked agreement does not affect an otherwise binding obligation. ***Nuda ratio et nuda pactio non ligant aliquem debitorem.*** Naked intention and naked promise do not bind any debtor.

PROMISE *(Raise expectations),* ***verb*** augur well, betoken, bid fair, cheer, embolden, encourage, enhearten, excite expectation, forebode, forecast, foreshadow, foreshow, foretell, forewarn, foster hope, give expectation, give hope, inspirit, lead one to expect, make a prediction, portend, predict, presage, prognosticate, prophesy, quicken, raise hopes, set astir, show signs of, signify, stimulate, suggest, threaten

PROMISE *(Vow),* ***verb*** accept a liability, accept an obligation, accept responsibility, adjure, affirm, affirm positively, agree, assert, assert an oath, assert positively, assert solemnly, assert under oath, asseverate, assure, attest, aver, avouch, avow, be answerable for, bear witness, become bound, bind, bind by a pledge, bind oneself, bind oneself by oath, certify, commit oneself, consent, contract, contract an obligation, covenant, declare, engage, engage in solemn manner, give assurance, give one's honor, give one's word, give one's word of honor, give security, guarantee, hypothecate, incur a duty, insure, make a solemn resolution, make an avowal, make an engagement, make an oath, make oneself answerable, obligate oneself, pledge, pledge one's credit, pledge one's honor, pledge one's word, pledge oneself, plight, plight one's honor, plight one's word, *polliceri,* stake one's credit, stipulate, swear, swear an oath, take a vow, take an oath, take upon oneself, testify, undertake, underwrite, vouch, vow, warrant
ASSOCIATED CONCEPTS: breach of promise, nude promise, promise to answer for the debt of another, promise to pay

PROMISSORY, ***adjective*** committed to payment, consisting of a guarantee, consisting of a pledge, containing a pledge, containing an assurance, guaranteed, on oath, on one's word, on one's word of honor, promising, promising to underwrite, under oath, vouched for
ASSOCIATED CONCEPTS: promissory estoppel, promissory note

PROMOTE *(Advance),* ***verb*** advocate, advance in rank, aggrandize, better, dignify, elevate, encourage, exalt, favor, forward, further, graduate, help, magnify, move up, pass, prefer, *promovere, provehere,* push up, raise, upgrade

PROMOTE *(Organize),* ***verb*** abet, advertise, advocate, aid in organizing, assist, avail, back, befriend, benefit, bestead, bolster, build up, carry on, champion, come to the aid of, contribute to, cooperate, cultivate, develop, encourage, facilitate, foster, further, help, hold up, lend a hand, maintain, nourish, nurse, nurture, patronize, propagandize, push, render a service to, sanction, second, serve, speak for, speed, sponsor, stir up, subscribe to, subserve, support, sustain, uphold, urge

PROMOTER, ***noun*** *adiutor,* advocate, aider, auctor, backer, benefactor, encourager, enterpriser, *fautor,* financial backer, financier, founder, organizer, organizer of business enterprises, organizer of commercial enterprises, patron, planner, prime mover, publicist, sponsor, supporter

PROMOTION *(Advancement),* ***noun*** advance, amelioration, betterment, elevation, elevation in rank, exaltation, forwarding, graduation, headway, improvement, increase, lift, passing, preferment, progress, progression, raise, rise, uplift

PROMOTION *(Encouragement),* ***noun*** abetting, advertising, aid, *amplificatio,* assistance, backing, benefit, boosting, campaign, cultivation, fostering, furtherance, help, maintenance, publicity, service, sponsorship, upkeep

PROMPT, ***adjective*** businesslike, eager, early, efficient, expeditious, immediate, instant, instantaneous, on time, precise, *promptus,* punctual, quick, ready, seasonable, speedy, spontaneous, summary, swift, timely, unhesitating, without delay
ASSOCIATED CONCEPTS: prompt judicial action

PROMPT, ***verb*** activate, actuate, advise, alert, animate, arouse, cause, dispose, encourage, excite, exhort, goad, hint, hound, impel, incite, incline, induce, influence, initiate, inspire, instigate, lead, motivate, move, occasion, persuade, press, prod, promote, provoke, push, recommend, remind, rouse, spur on, stimulate, stir, suggest, tempt, urge
ASSOCIATED CONCEPTS: leading a witness, subornation

PROMULGATE, ***verb*** air, announce, annunciate, blaze, blazon, bring into the open, broadcast, bruit, circulate, communicate, declare, disclose, disseminate, divulge, emit, enounce, give currency, give notice of, give publicity to, hawk about, herald, issue, make known, notify, proclaim, *promulgare,* propagate, publicize, publish, report, reveal, set forth, spread, spread abroad, vent
ASSOCIATED CONCEPTS: promulgate a law, promulgate a rule
FOREIGN PHRASES: ***Non obligat lex nisi promulgata.*** A law is not obligatory unless it is promulgated.

PRONE, ***adjective*** agreeable, apt, bent, biased, compliant, disposed, eager, easily persuaded, favorable, given, inclined, liable, likely, minded, partial, predisposed, *proclivis, pronus,* propense, ready, tending, well-disposed, willing

PRONOUNCE *(Pass judgment),* ***verb*** adjudge, adjudicate, announce authoritatively, conclude, decide, declare to be, decree, deliver judgment, determine, find, give a ruling, give an opinion, give judgment, judge, officially utter, pass sentence upon, prescribe punishment, *pronuntiare,* rule, utter formally, utter judicial sentence

PRONOUNCE *(Speak),* ***verb*** accent, accentuate, announce, announce authoritatively, announce officially, articulate, assert, break silence, communicate, declare, deliver, deliver an address, deliver formally, *dicere,* emit, emphasize, enounce, enunciate, *enuntiare,* express, form, frame, present, proclaim, recite, say, sound, speak formally, state, stress, tell, utter, utter formally, utter forth, verbalize, vocalize, voice

PRONOUNCE A JUDGMENT, ***verb*** adjudge, adjudicate, arbitrate, cogitate, conclude, decide, declare, decree, deem, deliberate, determine, find, impose justice, judge, mediate, opine, pronounce justice, prosecute, referee, resolve, rule, settle

PRONOUNCEMENT, ***noun*** affirmation, announcement, annunciation, assertion, asseveration, authoritative statement, averment, comment, decision, declaration, decree, deliverance, dictum, edict, enunciation, expression, fiat, formal statement, imperative, judgment, manifesto, notice, notification, observation, opinion, predication, profession, promulgation, pronunciamento, publication, remark, report, ruling, statement, utterance

PROOF, ***noun*** argumentum, assurance, attestation, averment, certainty, certification, clear demonstration, clear indication, conclusiveness, confirmation, data, demonstration, documentation, establishment, evidence, evident demonstration, facts, *indicium,* manifestation, process of proving, proved strength, ratification, records, satisfaction, satisfactory evidence, showing, substantiation, sufficient evidence, *testimonium,* testimony, verification, warrant

ASSOCIATED CONCEPTS: adequate proof, affirmative proof, burden of proof, clear and convincing proof, collateral proof, failure of proof, final proof, furnish proof, legal proof, positive proof, proof beyond a reasonable doubt, proof evident, proof of claim, proof of death, proof of disability, proof of payment, proof positive, quantum of proof, satisfactory proof

FOREIGN PHRASES: ***Semper necessitas probandi incumbit ei qui agit.*** The burden of proof always lies upon the claimant. ***Non possessori incumbit necessitas probandi possessiones ad se pertinere.*** It is not incumbent on the possessor of property to prove that his possessions belong to him. ***Affirmanti, non neganti incumbit probatio.*** The burden of proof is on the party who affirms, not upon one who denies. ***Facultas probationum non est angustanda.*** The right of offering proof is not to be narrowed. ***In criminalibus, probationes debent esse luce clariores.*** In criminal cases, the proofs ought to be clearer than light. ***Quod per recordum probatum, non debet esse negatum.*** That which is proved by record ought not to be denied. ***Quod constat curiae opere testium non indiget.*** That which is clear to the court needs not the help of witnesses. ***Qui melius probat melius habet.*** He who proves most recovers most. ***Praesumptio violenta, plena probatio.*** Strong presumption is full proof. ***Perspicua vera non sunt probanda.*** Evident facts need not be proved. ***Per rerum naturam factum negantis nulla probatio est.*** It is in the nature of things that a person who denies a fact is not bound to give proof. ***Probandi necessitas incumbit illi qui agit.*** The necessity of proving lies with the person who sues. ***Frustra probatur quod probatum non relevat.*** It is useless to prove that which when proved is irrelevant. ***Principia probant, non probantur.*** Principles prove, they are not proved. ***Praesumptiones sunt conjecturae ex signo verisimili ad probandum assumptae.*** Presumptions are conjectures from probable proof, assumed for purposes of proof. ***Reus excipiendo fit actor.*** The defendant by pleading may make himself a plaintiff. ***Idem est non probari et non esse; non deficit jus, sedprobatio.*** What is not proved and what is not are the same; it is not a defect of the law, but a want of proof. ***Factum negantis nulla probatio sit.*** No proof is required of him who denies a fact. ***Quod constat clare non debet verificari.*** What is clearly apparent is not required to be proved. ***Semper necessitas probandi incumbit ei qui agit.*** The claimant is always bound to prove; the burden of proof lies on the actor. ***Ei incumbit probatio, qui dicit, non qui negat; cum per rerum naturam factum negantis probatio nulla sit.*** The burden of proof lies upon him who asserts it, not upon him who denies; since, by the nature of things, he who denies a fact cannot produce any proof of it.

PROPAGANDA, ***noun*** *arrière pensée,* brainwashing, conditioning, conversion, distortion, false teaching, implantation, inculcation, indoctrination, initiation, inoculation, misinstruction, misleading, persuasion, preaching, promotion, teaching

PROPAGATE *(Increase),* ***verb*** be fruitful, bear, beget, breed, bring into being, continue, create, engender, father, fecundate, generate, *gignere,* give birth, multiply, originate, procreate, produce, progenerate, proliferate, pullulate, reproduce, sire, spawn, teem

PROPAGATE *(Spread),* ***verb*** advertise, air, blaze, blazon, broadcast, circulate, diffuse, disseminate, enunciate, evulgate, hawk about, herald, issue, make known, make public, noise abroad, notify, proclaim, promote, promulgate, publicize, publish, repeat, report, spread abroad, tell, transmit, trumpet, vent, ventilate, *vulgare*

PROPEL, ***verb*** actuate, cast, catapult, constrain, discharge, dispatch, drive, drive forward, eject, emit, force, goad, heave, hurl, impel, launch, move, pitch, precipitate, prod, project, provoke, push, push forward, send, set in motion, spirit, start, stimulate, thrust, urge

PROPENSITY, ***noun*** ability, affinity, aptitude, aptness, art, attraction, bent, bias, capacity, deftness, dexterity, disposition, facility, fancy, favor, felicity, fondness, forte, genius, gift, inclination, knack, leaning, liking, mind, partiality, passion, penchant, ply, predilection, predisposition, preference, *proclivitas,* proclivity, proneness, *pronus,* propenseness, propension, *propensus,* qualification, readiness, relish, sharpness, skill, talent, taste, tendency, warp, weakness

ASSOCIATED CONCEPTS: propensity to commit a crime, viscous propensities

PROPER, ***adjective*** acceptable, accurate, adapted, apposite, appropriate, apt, *aptus,* becoming, befitting, condign, conventional, correct, decorous, ethical, fitting, formal, free of error, honest, *idoneus,* legitimate, moral, opportune, orthodox, particular, precise, *rectus,* relevant, respectable, right, righteous, seasonable, seemly, suitable, suited, tasteful, true, unmistaken, virtuous, well-bred

ASSOCIATED CONCEPTS: proper party

FOREIGN PHRASES: ***Non solum quid licet, sed quid est conveniens est considerandum, quia nihil quod est inconveniens est licitum.*** Not only that which is lawful, but that which is convenient is to be considered, because nothing which is inconvenient is lawful.

PROPERTY *(Distinctive attribute),* ***noun*** aspect, attitude, attribute, character, characteristic, disposition, distinction, distinguishing quality, distinguishing trait, earmark, feature, individuality, mark, marked feature, marked quality, particularity, peculiarity, personality, point, *proprietas,* quality, singularity, specific quality, style, temperament, tone, trait

PROPERTY *(Land),* ***noun*** acreage, acres, demesne, domain, dominions, estate, freehold, ground, grounds, holding, homestead, household, land, landed interests, landed property, leasehold, lot, parcel, plot, premises, real estate, real property, realty, territory, tract

ASSOCIATED CONCEPTS: abandoned property, absolute property, accretions to property, acquisition of property, after-acquired property, assessable property, assessed valuation of taxable property, base property, commercial property, community property, corporate property, damage to property, devising property, distributable property, encumbrance on property, estate, execution against property, freehold, homestead, individual property, joint property, lien on property, market value, property tax, public property, purchase of property, separate and distinct properties, similar property, special property, specific property, suit affecting property, suit concerning property, taking of property for private purposes, taking of property for public use without just compensation, taxable property, title to real property, transfer of interest in property, transfer of property intended to take effect at death, unplatted land, urban property, value of the property

FOREIGN PHRASES: ***Transit terra cum onere.*** Land passes subject to any encumbrances affecting it. ***Jus descendit, et non terra.*** The right descends, not the land. ***Regulariter non valet pactum de re mea non alienanda.*** It is a rule that an agreement not to alienate my property is not binding. ***Cujus est solum, ejus est usque ad coelum et ad inferos.*** He who owns the soil owns also up to the sky above it, and to the center of the earth beneath it.

PROPERTY *(Possessions),* ***noun*** accessories, appointments, assets, available means, belongings, *bona,* chattels, effects, estate, financial resources, funds, goods, hereditaments, holdings, immovables, investments, material assets, movables, ownership, pecuniary resources, personal effects, personal resources, possessions, resources, substance, tangible assets, tangibles, valuables
ASSOCIATED CONCEPTS: appurtenance, articles of personalty, bequeathing property, fixtures, intangibles, movables, proceeds of property, receiving stolen property, tangible property, trust property
FOREIGN PHRASES: ***Nemo cogitur rem suam vendere, etiam justo pretio.*** No one is compelled to sell his own property, even for a just price. ***Quae ab hostibus capiuntur, statim capientium fiunt.*** Things taken from enemies immediately become the property of the captors. ***Duorum in solidum dominium vel possessio esse non potest.*** Sole ownership of possessions cannot be in two persons. ***Jus triplex est–propietatis, possessionis, et possibilitatis.*** Right is threefold—of property, of possession, and of possibility. ***Nemo alienae rei, sine satisdatione, defensor idoneus intelligitur.*** No one is considered a competent defender of another's property, without security. ***Nul charter, nul vente, ne nul done vault perpetualment, si le donor n'est seise al temps de contracts de deux droits, sc. del droit de possession et del droit de propertie.*** No grant, no sale, no gift, is valid forever, unless the donor, at the time of the contract, has two rights, namely, the right of possession and the right of property. ***Prohibetur ne quis faciat in suo quod nocere possit alieno.*** It is forbidden for any one to do on his own property what may injure another's. ***Proprietas verborum est salus proprietatum.*** Propriety of words is the salvation of property. ***In re communi neminem dominorum jure facere quicquam, invito altero posse.*** One of the owners of common property may not exercise any authority over it against the will of another of them. ***Expedit reipublicae ne sua re quis male utatur.*** It is for the interest of the state no one should make ill use of his property. ***Mobilia non habent situm.*** Movables have no situs or local habitation. ***Catalla juste possessa amitti non possunt.*** Chattels cannot be deprived of when they are lawfully possessed. ***Interest reipublicae ne sua quis male utatur.*** It concerns the state that people do not misuse their property. ***Rerum suarum quilibet est moderator et arbiter.*** Every one is the manager and master of his own affairs or his property. ***In re pari potiorem causam esse prohibentis constat.*** Where a thing is owned in common, it is clear that the cause of the party prohibiting its use is the stronger. ***In re communi potior est conditio prohibentis.*** In relation to property held in common, the position of the one who prohibits is the more favorable.

PROPHETIC, ***adjective*** alarming, augural, bodeful, clairvoyant, divinatory, *divinus,* farseeing, farsighted, fateful, fatidic, fatidical, *fatidicus,* fatiloquent, foreboding, forecasting, foreknowing, foreseeing, foresighted, foretelling, forewarning, haruspical, indicative, mantic, menacing, minacious, minatorial, minatory, monitorial, monitory, ominous, oracular, portentous, precognitive, precursive, predictive, predictory, prefigurative, preindicative, premonitory, presageful, presaging, prescient, presentient, prognostic, prognosticative, prophetical, pythonic, sibylic, sibylline, vatic, vaticinal

PROPHYLACTIC, ***adjective*** preservative, preventative, preventive, protective, safeguarding, salutary
ASSOCIATED CONCEPTS: prophylactic rule

PROPINQUITY *(Kinship),* ***noun*** affiliation, affinity, agnation, alliance, association, bond, close association, cognation, common ancestry, connection, consanguinity, family connection, filiation, kindred, link, nearness of blood, nearness of relation, relationship, tie

PROPINQUITY *(Proximity),* ***noun*** adjacency, apposition, closeness, contiguity, juxtaposition, nearness, vicinage

PROPINQUITY *(Similarity),* ***noun*** accord, affinity, affinity of nature, alikeness, comparison, compatibility, concert, concord, congeniality, correspondence, equivalence, harmony, homogeneity, likeness, parallelism, proximity, resemblance, semblance, similitude, synonymity, unity

PROPITIATE, ***verb*** accommodate, appeal to, appease, beguile, calm, conciliate, content, disarm, gain the favor of, humor, ingratiate, make amends, make favorably inclined, make peace, mollify, offer sacrifice, pacificate, pacify, placate, please, *propitiare,* reconcile, satisfy, soften, soothe, tranquilize, win over

PROPITIOUS, ***adjective*** accommodating, advantageous, approving, auspicious, beneficial, benevolent, benign, benignant, cheering, clear, clement, cloudless, conducive, disposed to bestow favors, encouraging, expedient, favorable, favorably inclined, felicitous, fortunate, friendly, full of promise, generous, golden, gracious, happy, heartening, heaven sent, helpful, helping, hopeful, indulgent, inspiriting, kind, kindhearted, kindly, lucky, merciful, obliging, opportune, presenting favorable conditions, promising, *propitius,* providential, reassuring, roseate, seasonable, supporting, sympathetic, timely, unhostile, well-disposed, well-intentioned, well-meaning

PROPONENT, ***noun*** abettor, advocate, ally, apologist, backer, benefactor, champion, defender, endorser, enthusiast, espouser, exponent, friend, justifier, partisan, patron, pleader, protector, seconder, spokesman, sponsor, subscriber, supporter, sympathizer, upholder, vindicator, votary, well-wisher
ASSOCIATED CONCEPTS: proponent of a will

PROPORTION, ***noun*** allotment, apportionment, commensuration, comparative size, comparison, concinnity, correlation, distribution, eurhythmy, factional part, fraction, grace, harmony, interrelation, measure, *pars,* part, percent, percentage, portion, quantum, quotum, ratio, relation, relationship, relative estimate, relativity, share, symmetry

PROPORTIONATE, ***adjective*** agreeing, analogous, balanced, commeasurable, commensurate, comparable, comparative, compatible, consistent, correlative, corresponding, distributional, equivalent, even, harmonious, proportionable, proportional, relative, scaled, uniform, well-balanced
ASSOCIATED CONCEPTS: per capita, per stirpes, pro rata

PROPOSAL *(Report),* ***noun*** analysis, appraisal, commentary, critical analysis, examination, in-depth analysis, plan, summary, writing

PROPOSAL *(Suggestion),* ***noun*** design, draft, exhortation, idea, measure, motion, offer, overture, plan, possibility, presentation, proffer, proposition, recommendation, scheme, submission, suggestion, tender, thought

PROPOSE, ***verb*** advance, advise, advocate, contend, counsel, declare, introduce, lay before, make a motion, make a suggestion, move, nominate, offer, plan, *ponere,* pose, postulate, present, proffer, propound, put forward, recommend, set forth, submit, suggest, tender, voice

PROPOSITION, ***noun*** approach, arrangement, assertion, assumption, bid, *condicio,* conjecture, course of action, declaration, declared intention, design, formulated intention, hypothesis, idea, offer, overture, plan, position, postulate, premise, presentation, program of action, project, proposal, *propositio,* prospectus, provisional hypothesis, recommendation, resolution, *rogatio,* scheme, strategy, submission, suggestion, supposition, tender, tentative approach, tentative statement, terms proposed, theory, thesis

PROPOUND, ***verb*** advance, advocate, allege, argue, aver, contend, exhibit, hypothesize, introduce, lay before, maintain, make a motion, moot, move, offer, pose, posit, postulate, predicate, present, proffer, project, propose, put forth, put forward, recommend, set forth, submit, suggest, tender, throw out, voice
ASSOCIATED CONCEPTS: propound the law

PROPRIETARY, ***adjective*** entailed, exclusive, holding property, landed, pertaining to ownership, pertaining to property, praedial, restrictive
ASSOCIATED CONCEPTS: proprietary function, proprietary interest, proprietary lease, proprietary right

PROPRIETOR, ***noun*** *dominus,* householder, landlord, landowner, manager, master, owner, possessor, proprietary

PROPRIETY *(Appropriateness),* ***noun*** accordance, adaptation, admissibility, advisability, agreeableness, applicability, aptitude, aptness, becomingness, compatibility, conformity, congruity, consonance, correspondence, dueness, equity, expedience, expediency, felicity, fitness, harmony, justness, pertinence, properness, reasonableness, relevance, right, rightness, seemliness, suitability, suitableness, utility

PROPRIETY *(Correctness),* ***noun*** convention, conventional conduct, conventionalities, correctitude, correctness, courteousness, courtesy, decency, decorousness, decorum, delicacy, demureness, dignity, discrimination, elegance, ethicality, etiquette, good behavior, good breeding, good manners, grace, manners, modesty, morality, politeness, proper formality, properness, rectitude, refinement, respectability, restraint, ritual, taste, tradition
FOREIGN PHRASES: ***Proprietates verborum observandae sunt.*** The proper meanings of words are to be observed.

PRORATE, ***verb*** allocate, allot, apportion, apportion pro rata, assess pro rata, assess proportionally, distribute, distribute proportionally, divide, divide proportionally, dole, mete out, parcel out, portion, split up
ASSOCIATED CONCEPTS: prorate taxes

PROSAIC, ***adjective*** boresome, boring, colorless, common, commonplace, dry, dull, everyday, flat, *frigidus,* hackneyed, humdrum, *ieiunus,* jejune, matter of fact, mediocre, monotone, monotonous, mundane, ordinary, pedestrian, plain, platitudinous, prolix, prosaical, prosy, spiritless, stale, stock, tame, tedious, tiresome, trite, unentertaining, unimaginative, unimpassioned, uninspiring, uninteresting, unoriginal, unpoetic, unpoetical, unvaried, usual, vapid, wearisome

PROSCRIBE *(Denounce),* ***verb*** accuse, anathematize, banish, blame, castigate, censure, charge, condemn, criticize, curse, damn, denunciate, execrate, incriminate, ostracize, outlaw, reject

PROSCRIBE *(Prohibit),* ***verb*** abrogate, ban, bar, circumscribe, disallow, embargo, enjoin, exclude, forbid, halt, oppose, outlaw, prevent, *proscribere,* refuse, refuse permission, repudiate, restrain, restrict, revoke, taboo

PROSCRIPTION, ***noun*** ban, banishment, boycott, censure, condemnation, countermand, denial, denunciation, disallowance, disfavor, elimination, embargo, eviction, exclusion, forbiddance, inhibition, injunction, interdict, interdiction, intolerance, prohibition, *proscriptio,* rejection, relegation

PROSECUTE *(Carry forward),* ***verb*** advance, be resolute in, be steadfast, bring about, bring to pass, carry on, carry out, conduct, continue, follow up, go after, maintain, *persequi,* persevere in, persist, proceed with, pursue, put through
ASSOCIATED CONCEPTS: dismissal for want of prosecution, failure to prosecute, prosecute a claim, prosecute an action

PROSECUTE *(Charge),* ***verb*** *accusare,* arraign, bring action against, bring before a court, bring suit, bring to justice, file a charge, file a claim, prefer a claim, prefer charges, proceed against civilly, proceed against criminally, sue, summon, take one to court
ASSOCIATED CONCEPTS: prosecute for a criminal offense, prosecuting attorney

PROSECUTING ATTORNEY, ***noun*** attorney general, district attorney, government attorney, people's attorney, prosecution, prosecutor, public prosecutor, state's attorney, U.S. attorney
ASSOCIATED CONCEPTS: criminal law

PROSECUTION *(Criminal trial),* ***noun*** action, bringing to trial, legal action, legal process, legal trial, litigation, pursuit by a law enforcement agency, suit, trial, undertaking
ASSOCIATED CONCEPTS: criminal prosecution, lawful prosecution, pending prosecution, want of prosecution

PROSECUTION *(Government agency),* ***noun*** the government, the people, the prosecuting attorney, the state, state's attorney
ASSOCIATED CONCEPTS: the prosecution

PROSECUTION HISTORY ESTOPPEL, ***noun*** bar to resurrection of surrendered elements of patent, equitable tool for determining proper scope of patents, file-wrapper estoppel, limitations imposed due to applicant's history of narrowing a patent
ASSOCIATED CONCEPTS: preclusion to doctrine of equivalents in patent law

PROSECUTOR, ***noun*** *accusator,* attorney general, criminal trial lawyer for the people, district attorney, government attorney, prosecuting attorney, prosecution, public prosecutor, state's attorney
ASSOCIATED CONCEPTS: public prosecutor, special prosecutor

PROSPECT *(Outlook)*, ***noun*** ambition, anticipation, assurance, calculation, certainty, chance, coming events, confidence, contemplation, destiny, expectance, expectancy, expectation, fair chance, faith, fate, forecast, fortune, futurity, good chance, hope, intention, likelihood, likeliness, plan, possibility, prediction, presumption, probability, promise, reasonable chance, reliance, speculation, time ahead, trust, well-grounded hope

PROSPECT *(Prospective patron)*, ***noun*** applicant, candidate, interested party, likely client, likely customer, likely patron, likely person, possibility, possible client, possible customer, possible patron, prospective client, prospective customer, recruit

PROSPECTIVE, ***adjective*** abeyant, about to be, anticipated, approaching, arranged, awaited, close at hand, coming, conceivable, considered, destined, earmarked, eventual, expectant, expected, foreseen, forthcoming, future, *futurus,* hoped for, imaginable, immediate, imminent, impending, in prospect, in store, in view, intended, likely, looked for, looming, on the horizon, planned, possible, potential, preparing, projected, promised, scheduled, soon to be, soon to happen, subsequent, to be, to come, ultimate, upcoming
ASSOCIATED CONCEPTS: prospective contract, prospective liabilities, prospective relief, prospective rights
FOREIGN PHRASES: ***Nova constitutio futuris formam imponere debet non praeteritis.*** A new law ought to affect the future, not what is past. ***Lex prospicit, non respicit.*** The law looks forward, not backward.

PROSPECTUS, ***noun*** analysis, announcement, blueprint, bulletin, catalog, description, outline, plan, platform, program, scheme, sketch, statement, summary, syllabus, synopsis

PROSPERITY, ***noun*** abundance, achievement, affluence, blessings, boom, booming economy, comfort, comfortable circumstances, ease, expansion, felicity, fortunate condition, full purse, good fortune, good luck, good times, heyday, luck, luxury, opulence, palmy days, plenty, profit, *prosperitas,* prosperousness, *res secundae,* riches, richness, run of luck, success, successfulness, thriving condition, weal, wealth, well-being

PROSPEROUS, ***adjective*** abounding in riches, affluent, ascendant, blooming, booming, comfortable, established, *florens,* flourishing, flush, fortunate, happy, in clover, in easy circumstances, lucky, moneyed, palmy, pecunious, profiting, *prosperus,* providential, rich, rising, *secundus,* successful, thriving, unbeaten, undefeated, wealthy, well off, well-situated, well-to-do

PROSTRATION, ***noun*** abasement, bow, breakdown, cataclysm, collapse, consumption, debility, decay, decrepitude, defeat, dejection, demolition, depression, desolation, despair, despondency, destruction, distress, downfall, downthrow, enervation, exhaustion, extinction, extremity, faint, fall, fatigue, feebleness, genuflection, helplessness, horizontality, illness, impotence, kneeling, lassitude, loss of power, lowliness, misery, obeisance, overset, overthrow, overturn, ravage, recumbency, repose, rout, ruin, ruination, sickness, stupor, subjection, submission, suffering, surrender, swoon, tiredness, undoing, upset, vanquishment, waste, weakness, weariness, wrack, wreck, wretchedness

PROTAGONIST, ***noun*** agent, champion, hero, lead, leader, leading character, main character, most important character, mouthpiece, prime mover, principal, principal character

PROTEAN, ***adjective*** alterable, assuming different forms, changeable, changeful, everchanging, fluid, kaleidoscopic, metamorphic, mobile, modifiable, movable, multiform, multiphase, mutable, nonuniform, omniform, permutable, polymorphic, polymorphous, proteiform, transformable, unsettled, variable, varying, versatile

PROTECT, ***verb*** arm, armor, attend, barricade, bulwark, care for, champion, chaperone, cherish, conduct, conserve, convoy, cover, cushion, *custodire,* defend, *defendere,* ensure, escort, fight for, flank, fortify, foster, garrison, guard, harbor, haven, house, immunize, inoculate, insulate, keep, look after, maintain, mount guard, nurse, patrol, patronize, preserve, safeguard, save, screen, seclude, secure, sentinel, shade, sheathe, shelter, shepherd, shield, shroud, shutter, sponsor, support, sustain, take care of, treasure, *tutari,* veil, ward, watch over
ASSOCIATED CONCEPTS: self-defense

PROTECTION, ***noun*** aegis, armor, asylum, barricade, buckler, bulwark, citadel, conservation, covering, covert, coverture, custody, defense, fortification, freedom from danger, guarantee, guard, guardianship, haven, hedge, immunity, invulnerability, oversight, palladium, panoply, patronage, *praesidium,* preservation, preserve, refuge, safe conduct, safeguard, safekeeping, safety, salvation, sanctuary, security, shelter, shield, strength, stronghold, supervision, support, *tutela,* tutelage, wardship, wing
FOREIGN PHRASES: ***Inde datae leges ne fortior omnia posset.*** Laws were made lest the stronger might become all-powerful.

PROTECTIVE, ***adjective*** armored, conservational, conservative, conservatory, covering, custodial, defensive, fortified, guardian, heedful, preservative, preventive, prophylactic, safeguarding, screening, sheltering, shielding, solicitous, strengthened, tutelary, vigilant, watchful
ASSOCIATED CONCEPTS: protective custody, protective order

PROTECTIVE ORDER, ***noun*** defense, guard against danger, order of protection, order to ensure safety, protection, protection against a danger, refuge, safeguard, safekeeping, safety, sanctuary, security, shelter, shield, temporary restraining order
ASSOCIATED CONCEPTS: family law and domestic violence protective orders, restraining order

PROTÉGÉ, ***noun*** adherent, apprentice, charge, dependent, disciple, follower, initiate, learner, novice, pensioner, pupil, student, trainee, trust, ward

PROTEST, ***noun*** challenge, clamor, complaint, counteraction, criticism, declaration of disapproval, declaration of dissent, declaration of opposition, defiance, demonstration, disapproval, dissent, dissidence, formal criticism, formal declaration, formal declaration of dissent, hostile demonstration, opposition, outcry, *recusatio,* remonstrance, remonstration, repudiation, resistance
ASSOCIATED CONCEPTS: file a protest

PROTEST, ***verb*** announce, attack, challenge, complain, contradict, contravene, cry out against, dehort, demur, denounce, deny, disaffirm, disagree, disapprove, disclaim, discountenance, dispute, dissent, exclaim against, exhort against, express opposition, go contrary to, impugn, *intercedere,* inveigh, negate, oppose, raise objections,

recusare, refuse, remonstrate, reprehend, repudiate, revolt, speak against, take exception, traverse, veto, vote against
ASSOCIATED CONCEPTS: payment under protest, protest a will, protest an election, written notice of protest

PROTOCOL *(Agreement),* ***noun*** arrangement, charter, compact, concord, concordat, contract, covenant, diplomatic agreement, pact, stipulation, treaty, understanding

PROTOCOL *(Etiquette),* ***noun*** behavior, ceremony, code, code of behavior, conventional practice, conventionalities, correct behavior, correctitude, correctness, courtesy, customs, decorum, dictates, diplomatic code, form, formalities, good behavior, good form, good manners, manners, politeness, practice, prevailing form, proper behavior, proprieties, punctilio, regulations, rules, set of rules, set of standards, system of rules

PROTOTYPE, ***noun*** archetype, example, exemplar, first, guide, ideal, model, mold, original, paradigm, paragon, pattern, precedent, protoplast, sample, source, standard

PROTRACT *(Prolong),* ***verb*** delay, drag out, filibuster, gain time, hold up, procrastinate, retard

PROTRACT *(Stall),* ***verb*** continue, elongate, extend, lengthen out, shelve, string out

PROTRACTED, ***adjective*** continuing, dragged out, drawn out, elongated, extended, lengthened, lengthy, lingering, long, long-continued, long-drawn, meandering, never-ending, ongoing, prolix, prolonged, unending

PROUD *(Conceited),* ***adjective*** affected, aloof, arrogant, assuming, boastful, braggart, condescending, contemptuous, defiant, disdainful, egoistic, egoistical, flaunting, haughty, imperious, insolent, lordly, obstinate, orgulous, overweening, overbearing, patronizing, pompous, presumptuous, prideful, puffed up, self-applauding, self-important, self-satisfied, supercilious, swollen, turgescent, turgid, uppish, uppity, vain, vainglorious, without modesty

PROUD *(Self-respecting),* ***adjective*** content, contented, delighted, dignified, grand, gratified, happy, honored, imposing, impressive, lofty, magnificent, majestic, noble, pleased, satisfied, splendid, stately, thrilled, well-pleased, well-satisfied

PROVABLE, ***adjective*** ascertainable, capable of being demonstrated, capable of being proven, capable of being shown, capable of positive proof, capable of proof, confirmable, deducible, demonstrable, determinable, discoverable, establishable, incontestable, indisputable, inferable, irrefutable, supportable, susceptible of proof, sustainable, unimpeachable, verifiable, verificatory, well-founded, well-grounded
ASSOCIATED CONCEPTS: provable claim

PROVE, ***verb*** ascertain, ascertain as truth, authenticate, confirm, corroborate, *declarare,* demonstrate, establish, establish as truth, establish the genuineness of, establish the validity of, evince, manifest, *probare,* put to the proof, put to the test, show, show clearly, substantiate, support, uphold, validate, verify
FOREIGN PHRASES: ***In rebus manifestis, errat qui auctoritates legum allegat; quia perspicua vera non sunt probanda.*** In clear cases, he makes mistakes who cites legal authorities; for obvious truths are not to be proved.

PROVERBIAL, ***adjective*** acknowledged, aphoristic, axiomatic, common, commonly known, commonplace, epigrammatic, familiar, general, known, legendary, notorious, oft repeated, popular, prevalent, recognized, sententious, succinct, traditional, universal, unquestioned, well-known, widely known

PROVIDE *(Arrange for),* ***verb*** anticipate needs, appoint, care for, *consulere,* contract, direct, engage, get ready, look after, make allowance for, make preparations, make provision, make ready, manage, organize, pave the way, plan, prepare, *providere,* ready, serve, take into account, take measures, take steps

PROVIDE *(Supply),* ***verb*** accommodate, accord, administer, afford, allow, award, bestow, confer, contribute, deliver, donate, endow, equip, feed, fund, furnish, give, grant, impart, maintain, *ornare, praebere,* present, produce, purvey, replenish, stock, *suppeditare,* sustain

PROVIDED, ***adverb*** assuming that, on condition that, provisionally, subject to, with the understanding, with the stipulation, with this proviso
ASSOCIATED CONCEPTS: as provided by law

PROVIDENT *(Frugal),* ***adjective*** careful, economical, money conscious, parsimonious, penurious, prudent, saving, sparing, stingy, thrifty, unlavish

PROVIDENT *(Showing foresight),* ***adjective*** alert, anticipating, calculating, careful, cautious, chary, circumspect, discerning, discreet, equipped, farseeing, forecasting, forehanded, foreseeing, heedful, judicious, on guard, politic, precautionary, precautious, predictive, prepared, prognostic, prudent, prudential, ready, thoughtful, vigilant, wary, watchful

PROVINCE, ***noun*** appointment, area, assigned task, assignment, business, canton, capacity, charge, circuit, colony, compass, county, demesne, department, district, division, domain, dominion, duty, field, function, job, jurisdiction, occupation, office, orbit, part, precinct, *provincia,* realm, region, scope, section, specialty, sphere, subdivision, territory, tract

PROVINCIAL, ***adjective*** annexed, backwood, boorish, bucolic, churlish, closed-minded, colonial, divisional, dogmatic, fanatical, gauche, gawky, hayseed, ill-mannered, illiberal, inflexible, ingrown, insular, intolerant, inurbane, local, loutish, narrow, narrow-minded, oafish, outlying, parochial, petty, regional, rigid, rough, rude, sectional, small-minded, straitlaced, unbroadened, uncourtly, uncouth, ungraceful, unpolished, unrefined, unsophisticated, untraveled

PROVISION *(Act of supplying),* ***noun*** accommodation, arrangement, catering, donation, endowment, furnishing, preparation, procurement, providence, purveyance, servicing, serving

PROVISION *(Clause),* ***noun*** article of agreement, *condicio,* condition, limitation, obligation, proviso, qualification, requirement, reservation, restriction, specification, stipulation, term
ASSOCIATED CONCEPTS: damages provision, express provision, forfeiture provision, mandatory provision, penal provision, procedural provision, restrictive provision, self-executing provision, statutory provision, substantive provision, technical provision

FOREIGN PHRASES: ***Quando abest provisio partis, adest provisio legis.*** When a provision of the party is lacking, the provision of the law supplies it.

PROVISION *(Something provided),* ***noun*** cache, cumulation, fund, hoard, maintenance, ration, reserve, resources, staples, stock, stockpile, store, supply

PROVISIONAL, ***adjective*** alterable, conditional, contingent, dependent on circumstances, equivocal, for a time, in a state of uncertainty, *in tempus,* indefinite, indeterminate, interim, limited, makeshift, modifiable, nonpermanent, of short duration, passing, provisory, subject to change, subject to terms, substitute, temporarily established, temporary, tentative, transient, transitional, transitory, unascertained, unassured, unconfirmed, undecided, undetermined, unsettled
ASSOCIATED CONCEPTS: provisional appointment, provisional court, provisional employee, provisional government, provisional receiver, provisional remedy

PROVISIONAL REMEDY, ***noun*** interim relief, preservation of the status quo, pretrial relief, temporary order, temporary relief
ASSOCIATED CONCEPTS: prejudgment order, pretrial order, injunctive relief, irrefutable harm, irreparable harm

PROVISO, ***noun*** condition, contingency, demand, essential, limitation, modification, must, necessity, need, paragraph, precondition, prerequisite, provision, qualification, requirement, reservation, restriction, section, stipulation, terms

PROVOCATION, ***noun*** abuse, actuation, affront, aggression, agitation, angering, annoyance, causation, cause, defiance, exasperation, excitation, excitement, fomentation, goad, grievance, impulsion, incentive, incitement, inducement, inflammation, inspiration, instigation, insult, invitation, irritation, motivation, motive, offense, pressure, prick, prodding, prompting, provocative, spur, stimulant, stimulation, stimulus, taunt, temptation, urge, vexation
ASSOCIATED CONCEPTS: defense of provocation, extreme provocation, just provocation, legal provocation

PROVOCATIVE, ***adjective*** aggravating, alluring, annoying, arousing, attractive, bellicose, captivating, challenging, defiant, desirable, electric, electrifying, enchanting, entrancing, exasperating, exciting, galling, galvanic, galvanical, grating, inciting, inflaming, inflammatory, influential, inspirational, interesting, intoxicating, intriguing, invidious, inviting, irksome, irresistible, irritating, motivating, persuasive, piquant, provoking, ravishing, seductive, stimulating, stimulative, stirring, suggestive, tantalizing, tempting, thrilling, titillating, urgent, vexatious, vexing

PROVOKE, ***verb*** actuate, affront, aggravate, agitate, anger, animate, annoy, antagonize, arouse, awaken, badger, bait, begin, beset, bother, bring about, call forth, cause, challenge, defy, discompose, displease, disquiet, distress, drive, effect, egg on, elicit, enkindle, enrage, envenom, evoke, exacerbate, exasperate, excite, fire, fret, gall, generate, give offense, give origin, give rise, grate, harass, heckle, hector, hound, impel, incense, incite, induce, inflame, infuriate, instigate, insult, irk, irritate, kindle, madden, motivate, move, move to anger, nettle, occasion, offend, originate, persecute, perturb, pique, plague, promote, prompt, propel, push, put out, put out of humor, rally, roil, rouse, spur, stimulate, sting, stir, stir up, taunt, tease, torment, try one's patience, vex, work into a passion, work up, wound

PROWESS *(Ability),* ***noun*** adeptness, adroitness, cleverness, competence, competency, craft, deftness, dexterity, excellence, expertise, expertness, facility, finesse, know-how, mastership, mastery, proficiency, skill, skillfulness, virtuosity, wizardry

PROWESS *(Bravery),* ***noun*** absence of fear, backbone, boldness, braveness, constancy, contempt of danger, courage, courageous deeds, courageousness, daring, dauntlessness, defiance of danger, derring-do, doggedness, doughtiness, fearlessness, fiber, firmness, gallant acts, gallantness, gallantry, grit, hardihood, hardiness, heroic achievement, heroism, intrepidity, lustiness, manliness, mettle, might, nerve, perseverence, pluck, resoluteness, sinew, spirit, stability, stamina, stout heart, strength, sturdiness, valiancy, valor, valorousness, vigor, *virtus,* vitality

PROWL, ***verb*** be stealthy, creep, cruise, drift, gad, go about stealthily, gumshoe, hover, lie in ambush, lie in wait, loiter, lurk, meander, move secretly, move under cover, peregrinate, ramble, range, roam, rove, scavenge, skulk, slink, sneak, stay incognito, steal, stray, stroll, tramp, *vagari,* wander about

PROXIMATE, ***adjective*** about to happen, abutting, adjacent, adjoining, approaching, at hand, attached, bordering, bordering upon, close, close at hand, close by, closest, connected, connecting, contactual, conterminal, conterminous, contiguous, edging, expected, following, forthcoming, fringing, immediate, imminent, impendent, impending, in close proximity, juxtaposed, near, nearest, neighboring, next, nigh, prospective, proximal, *proximus,* sequent, subsequent, succeeding, tangent, tangential, touching, upcoming, verging, vicinal
ASSOCIATED CONCEPTS: proximate cause

PROXIMATE CAUSE, ***noun*** causation, derivation, immediate legal basis, immediate legal cause, immediate legal genesis, proper cause, proximate causation, sufficient legal basis, sufficient legal causation, sufficient legal cause, sufficient legal factor, sufficient legal genesis, sufficient legal inducement, sufficient legal source
ASSOCIATED CONCEPTS: contribution-efficient cause, contributory negligence, immediate cause, intervening cause, negligence, proximate consequence, proximate result, torts

PROXY, ***noun*** agency, agent, authority to act for another, broker, delegate, deputy, dummy, emissary, envoy, lieutenant, messenger, *procurator,* representation, representative, substitute, substitution, surrogate, *vicarius,* written authorization
ASSOCIATED CONCEPTS: proxy statement, solicitation of proxy

PRUDENCE, ***noun*** attention, calculation, care, careful budgeting, carefulness, *cautio,* caution, *circumspectio,* circumspection, close watch, common sense, concern, conservation, conservatism, considerateness, consideration, cunning, deliberation, discretion, discrimination, economy, forethought, foresight, frugality, heed, heedfulness, husbandry, judgment, judiciousness, precaution, preparedness, presence of mind, providence, *prudentia,* regard, sense, shrewdness, tact, temperance, thrift, vigilance, watchfulness

PRUDENT, ***adjective*** advertent, calculating, canny, careful, cautious, cautus, chary, circumspect, *circumspectus,*

considerate, discreet, discriminating, economical, farsighted, forearmed, foreseeing, foresighted, frugal, guarded, heedful, judicious, levelheaded, mindful, politic, precautionary, precautious, prepared, provident, prudential, regardful, sagacious, sage, sapient, saving, sensible, shrewd, sober, sparing, thoughtful, thrifty, wary, well-advised, wise
ASSOCIATED CONCEPTS: prudent person, reasonable man
FOREIGN PHRASES: ***Prudenter agit qui praecepto legis obtemperat.*** He acts prudently who obeys the precept of the law. ***Sapiens omnia agit cum consilio.*** A wise man does everything deliberately.

PRURIENT, *adjective* bawdy, carnal, coarse, concupiscent, cyprian, debauched, dirty, dissipated, dissolute, erotic, fleshly, foul, immodest, impure, indecent, lascivious, lecherous, lewd, *libidinosus,* libidinous, licentious, lickerish, lubricious, lustful, obscene, pornographic, ribald, salacious, satyric, shameless, smutty, suggestive, unchaste, unclean, unvirtuous, wanton
ASSOCIATED CONCEPTS: pornography, prurient interests

PUBLIC *(Affecting people),* ***adjective*** civic, civil, collective, common, communal, countrywide, federal, general, government, governmental, municipal, national, nationwide, social, societal, state
ASSOCIATED CONCEPTS: public authorities, public benefit, public benefit corporation, public business, public charge, public charity, public convenience, public corporation, public document, public function, public funds, public good, public improvements, public interest, public necessity, public notice, public nuisance, public office, public policy, public purpose, public safety, public sector, public service commission, public use, public utilities, public welfare, public works
FOREIGN PHRASES: ***Pacta privata juri publico derogare non possunt.*** Private contracts cannot derogate from public right. ***Necessitas publica major est quam privata.*** Public necessity is greater than private. ***Jura publica anteferenda privatis.*** Public rights are to be preferred to private parts. ***Privatum commodum publico cedit.*** Private good yields to public good. ***Privatum incommodum publico bono pensatur.*** Private inconvenience is compensated for by public benefit. ***Lex citius tolerare vult privatum damnum quam publicum malum.*** The law would rather tolerate a private loss than a public evil.

PUBLIC *(Known),* ***adjective*** acknowledged, aired, announced, apparent, broadcast, bruited about, circulated, commonly known, disclosed, disseminated, divulged, encyclic, encyclical, evident, exoteric, familiar, manifest, notorious, obvious, overt, popular, proclaimed, promulgated, propagated, *publicus,* published, recognized, released, renowned, reported, revealed, spread abroad, ventilated, well-known, widely known

PUBLIC *(Open),* ***adjective*** accessible, approachable, attainable, available, community, free to all, not private, permitted, reachable, unbarred, unprohibited, unreserved, unrestricted
ASSOCIATED CONCEPTS: public accommodations, public documents, public domain, public hearing, public institutions, public place, public property, public records, public sale

PUBLIC, *noun* body politic, citizenry, commonalty, commonwealth, community, folk, general public, *homines,* laymen, nation, persons, polity, populace, population, *populus,* social group, society
ASSOCIATED CONCEPTS: public good, public use, public utility, public welfare

PUBLIC DOMAIN, *noun* available for use by the public, creative work freely usable, dominion to use, free to all, freely used by the community, invention freely usable, logo freely usable, not private, open for the community, permitted, publicly accessible, publicly obtainable, publicly usable, unreserved, unrestricted, within the province of the public
ASSOCIATED CONCEPTS: copyrights, patents, proprietary rights

PUBLIC ENTWINEMENT, *noun* action which is fairly attributable to the state, acts that are entangled with state action, private organization that exercises state power, public involvement in management and control of organizations, state actor, sufficient government involvement to qualify as state action

PUBLIC FORUM, *noun* forum where the public congregates and can speak, government-owned property open to public discussion, open forum for public discourse, public arena for public discussion, public place for discussion, public property open to public discussion

PUBLIC OPTION, *noun* federal health insurance plan, government carrier, government insurance company, government-run health insurance, public health insurance option, public insurance option
ASSOCIATED CONCEPTS: Affordable Care Act, free market, Obamacare

PUBLIC SERVICE *(Government service),* ***noun*** appointment, civil service, government employment, member of the public sector, public life

PUBLIC SERVICE *(Performance for the public benefit),* ***noun*** common good, performed for greater good, performed for public benevolence, performed for the benefit of society, performed for the public benefit, performed for the public good

PUBLICATION *(Disclosure),* ***noun*** advertisement, announcement, broadcast, circulation, communication, currency, dissemination, enlightenment, *expositio,* issuance, notice, notification, *praedicatio,* presentation to the public, proclamation, promulgation, pronouncement, *pronuntiatio,* propagation, public announcement, release, report, revealment, revelation, statement, transmission
ASSOCIATED CONCEPTS: defamation, libel, slander

PUBLICATION *(Printed matter),* ***noun*** book, *editio libri,* edition, folio, issue, literary magazine, literature, magazine, organ, periodical, printing, reading matter, tome, volume, work, writing, written discourse

PUBLICITY, *noun* advertisement, advertising, airing, announcement, billing, broadcast, bulletin, common knowledge, disclosure, dissemination, divulgation, divulgement, divulgence, enunciation, evulgation, exposure, fame, famousness, information, issuance, limelight, news, notice, notification, notoriety, presentation, press agentry, press notice, proclamation, promotion, promulgation, propagation, public distribution, public notice, public relations, publication, release, report, revealment, revelation, spotlight, utterance, ventilation, write-up

PUBLICIZE, *verb* acclaim, advertise, announce, annunciate, bear, blazon, broadcast, endorse, give currency to, hail, herald, laud, merchandise, post, praise, proclaim, promote, promulgate, publish, push, recommend, release, review, sell, talk up, tout, trumpet

PUBLISH, ***verb*** advertise, air, announce, blazon, bring before the public, bring out, broadcast, call public attention to, circulate, communicate, cover, declare, deliver, diffuse, disclose, disseminate, distribute, *divulgare,* divulge, emit, expose, express, give out, give public notice of, go to press, have printed, herald, impart, inform, issue, issue a statement, issue for distribution, issue for public sale, lay before the public, make known, make public, print, proclaim, *proferre,* publicize, put forth, put into circulation, put out, put to press, report, reveal, run off, spread, state, tell, trumpet, utter, ventilate
ASSOCIATED CONCEPTS: publish libel, publish slander

PUERILE, ***adjective*** asinine, callow, childish, childishly foolish, fatuous, foolish, green, immature, inadequate, inane, infantile, infantine, injudicious, jejune, juvenile, kiddish, naïve, nonsensical, petty, piddling, *puerilis,* raw, senseless, shallow, silly, simple, unwise, unworthy of serious consideration

PUERILITY, ***noun*** babyishness, boyishness, childishness, childlike, girlishness, infantilism

PUGNACIOUS, ***adjective*** aggressive, antagonistic, argumentative, bellicose, belligerent, bickering, combative, contentious, defiant, disposed to fight, disputatious, dissentious, factious, fighting, fractious, given to fighting, hostile, inimical, militant, militaristic, offensive, quarrelsome, rebellious, rowdy, stubborn, threatening, unfriendly, unpacific, unpeaceful, warlike

PUISSANCE, ***noun*** authoritativeness, brawn, dint, dominance, energy, force, lustiness, masterfulness, might, mightiness, potence, potency, power, predominance, robustness, stamina, stoutness, strength, vigor, vitality

PULLULATE, ***verb*** be fruitful, be productive, bloom, blossom, breed, bud, burgeon, burst forth, come forth, develop, flourish, flower, generate, germinate, increase, luxuriate, multiply, open, procreate, produce, proliferate, put forth, reproduce, rise, shoot forth, spring up, sprout, teem, vegetate, wax

PUNCTILIOUS, ***adjective*** accurate, attentive, careful, ceremonious, conscientious, correct, *diligens,* dutiful, exact, exacting, faithful, fastidious, finical, finicking, finicky, formal, fussy, methodical, meticulous, minutely correct, observant, observant of decorum, particular, precise, refined, rigid, rigorous, scrupulous, starched, stiff, strict, systematic, thorough, uncompromising

PUNCTUAL, ***adjective*** accurate, attentive, conscientious, dependable, diligent, early, exact, exacting, expeditious, fussy, meticulous, minutely correct, never late, on schedule, on time, precise, prompt, properly timed, ready, regular, scrupulous, seasonable, steady, strict, systematic, timed, timely, well-timed

PUNDIT, ***noun*** analyst, annotator, authority, brain, champion, columnist, commentator, enthusiast, evaluator, genius, guru, intellectual, master, mastermind, mentor, observer, polymath, Renaissance man, savant, scholar, seer, teacher, thinker, wise one

PUNISH, ***verb*** amerce, bring to retribution, call to account, *castigare,* castigate, chasten, chastise, condemn, correct, discipline, exact retribution, flog, inflict penalty, lash, penalize, reprimand, retaliate, scourge, sentence, slate, smite, subject to penalty, take to task, take vengeance on, teach a lesson to, torture, trounce, *ulcisci,* whip
ASSOCIATED CONCEPTS: cruel and excessive punishment, cruel and inhuman punishment, cruel and unusual punishment, excessive punishment
FOREIGN PHRASES: ***In quo quis delinquit, in eo de jure est puniendus.*** In whatever the offense, he is to be punished by the law.

PUNISHMENT, ***noun*** amercement, avengement, *castigatio,* castigation, censure, chastening, chastisement, compulsory payment, correction, damages, deprivation, disciplinary action, discipline, forfeiture, infliction, mulct, nemesis, penal retribution, penalization, penalty, penalty imposed on an offender, penance, *poena,* punition, reprimand, retribution, retributive justice, talion, vengeance
ASSOCIATED CONCEPTS: capital punishment, corporal punishment, cruel and inhuman punishment, excessive punishment
FOREIGN PHRASES: ***Nulla curia quae recordum non habet potest imponere finem neque aliquem mandare carceri; quia ista spectant tantummodo ad curias de recordo.*** No court which has not a record can impose a fine nor commit any person to prison; because those powers belong only to courts of record. ***Poena ad paucos, metus ad omnes perveniat.*** If punishment is inflicted on a few, a fear comes to all. ***Nemo prudens punit ut praeterita revocentur, sed ut futura praeveniantur.*** No wise man punishes in order that past things may be revoked, but that future wrongs may be prevented. ***Ubi damna dantur, victus victori in expensis condemnari debet.*** Where damages are given, the losing party ought to be condemned to pay costs to the victor. ***Interest reipublicae ne maleficia remaneant impunita.*** It concerns the state that crimes do not go unpunished. ***Tutius semper est errare acquietando, quam in puniendo, ex parte misericordiae quam ex parte justitiae.*** It is always safer to err in acquitting than in punishing, on the side of mercy rather than on the side of justice. ***In omnibus poenalis judiciis, et aetati et imprudentiae succurritur.*** In all penal judgments, allowance is made for youth and lack of prudence. ***Qui peccat ebrius luat sobrius.*** He who offends when drunk shall be punished when sober. ***Melior est justitia vere praeveniens quam severe puniens.*** Truly preventative justice is better than severe punishment. ***Justitia est duplex, viz., severe puniens et vere praeveniens.*** Justice is double, that is to say punishing severely, and truly preventing. ***Qui parcit nocentibus innocentes punit.*** He who spares those who are guilty punishes those who are innocent. ***Reus laesae majestatis punitur ut pereat unus ne pereant omnes.*** A traitor is punished that one may die lest all perish. ***Poena non potest, culpa perennis erit.*** Punishment cannot be everlasting, but error or sin will be. ***Judex damnatur cum nocens absolvitur.*** The judge is condemned when a guilty person is acquitted. ***Lubricum linguae non facile trahendum est in poenam.*** A slip of the tongue ought not readily be subjected to punishment. ***In atrocioribus delictis punitur affectus licet non sequatur effectus.*** In the more atrocious crimes the intent is punished, although an effect does not follow. ***Judex non potest injuriam sibi datam punire.*** A judge cannot punish a wrong done to himself. ***Nemo bis punitur pro eodem delicto.*** No one can be punished twice for the same offense. ***Transgressione multiplicata, crescat poenae inflictio.*** Upon the multiplication of transgression, let the infliction of punishment be increased. ***Poena suos tenere debet***

actores et non alios. Punishment belongs to the guilty and not others. ***Nemo cogitationis poenam patitur.*** No one suffers punishment on account of his thoughts. ***Receditur a placitis juris, potius quam injuriae et delicta maneant impunita.*** In order that crimes not go unpunished, the law will be departed from.

PUNITIVE, ***adjective*** avenging, castigatory, disciplinary, mulctuary, penal, penalizing, punishing, punitory, retaliatory, retributive, talionic, vindictive
ASSOCIATED CONCEPTS: punitive action, punitive damages

PUNITIVE DAMAGES, ***noun*** award for wrongdoing, award to deter similar conduct, award to punish the defendant, compensation for wrongdoing, penalty for wrongdoing, recovery for highly offensive conduct, recovery for improper action, retributive damages
ASSOCIATED CONCEPTS: compensatory damages restitution, due process, Fifth Amendment, Fourth Amendment, irreparable damages, malicious conduct, nominal damages, reckless disregard, restitution, statutory damages

PURCHASE, ***verb*** acquire, acquire ownership of, assume ownership, buy, buy up, collect, gain, invest in, make payment for, obtain, order, pay for, pick up, procure, procure title to, redeem, secure, secure for a consideration
ASSOCIATED CONCEPTS: words of purchase

PURCHASER, ***noun*** acquirer, buyer, client, clientele, consumer, customer, end user, enjoyer, owner, patron, person conducting business, person conducting transactions, possessor, procurer, prospect, retail client, retail customer, shopper, user

PURE, ***adjective*** absolute, chaste, clean, clear, complete, disinfected, entire, expurgated, faultless, flawless, guileless, guiltless, homogeneous, honorable, immaculate, incorrupt, innocent, *integer,* perfect, positive, *purus,* real, righteous, sheer, simple, sincere, sinless, spotless, stainless, sterilized, taintless, total, true, unadulterated, unblemished, unclouded, uncontaminated, uncorrupt, uncorrupted, undefiled, unmarred, unmingled, unmitigated, unmixed, unpolluted, unspotted, unstained, unsullied, untainted, untarnished, untouched, upright, utter, virtuous, whole
ASSOCIATED CONCEPTS: pure comparative negligence

PURELY *(Positively),* ***adverb*** absolutely, decidedly, downright, entirely, essentially, fundamentally, in all respects, in truth, perfectly, really, seriously, thoroughly, totally, unconditionally, unequivocally, utterly
ASSOCIATED CONCEPTS: purely charitable institution, purely charitable purpose, purely manufacturing purposes, purely public charity

PURELY *(Simply),* ***adverb*** barely, essentially, merely, mostly, plainly

PURGE *(Purify),* ***verb*** clarify, clean, cleanse, clear, depurate, deterge, discharge, edulcorate, eliminate, elutriate, empty, eradicate, evacuate, excrete, expel, expurgate, filter, free from impurity, get rid of, rectify, refine, rout out, sanctify, scour, separate, strain, sublimate, sweep out, wash away

PURGE *(Wipe out by atonement),* ***verb*** absolve, acquit, clear, exculpate, excuse, exempt, forgive, grant absolution, pardon, reclaim, redeem, shrive
ASSOCIATED CONCEPTS: purge of contempt

PURIFY, ***verb*** absolve, acquit, amend, cleanse, clear, distill, elevate, ennoble, exonerate, filter, heal, honor, improve, purge, refine, regenerate, restore, sanctify, uplift, vindicate

PURLOIN, ***verb*** appropriate dishonestly, appropriate fraudulently, *avertere,* burglarize, cheat, commit larceny, defalcate, defraud, embezzle, filch, *furari,* misapply, misappropriate, misuse, peculate, pilfer, poach, rob, seize, snatch, spirit away, steal, *surripere,* swindle, take, take by fraud, take dishonestly, take feloniously, take wrongfully, thieve, unlawfully deprive

PURPORT, ***verb*** allege, allude, claim, connote, convey, declare, declare with positiveness, denote, express, imply, *indicare,* indicate, infer, insinuate, intend, intimate, mean, pose as, pretend, profess, represent, say, show, *significare,* signify, state, suggest

PURPORTED, ***adjective*** alleged, assumed, avowedly, claimed, in name only, ostensible, pretended, pretexed, professed, specious, so-called

PURPOSE, ***noun*** aim, ambition, application, aspiration, avail, basis, constancy, deliberation, design, desire, desired result, destination, determination, direction, doggedness, drive, eagerness, end, expectation, final cause, firmness, force, function, goal, guiding principle, hope, idea, *institutum,* intended result, intent, intention, *mens,* mission, motivating idea, motive, object, objective, perseverance, persistence, plan, point, *propositum,* resolution, resolve, service, significance, singleness, target, tenacity, use, volition, voluntariness, will, wish, zeal
ASSOCIATED CONCEPTS: business purpose, charitable purpose, intent, malice, unlawful purpose
FOREIGN PHRASES: ***Lex neminem cogit ad vana seu inutilia peragenda.*** The law compels no one to do futile or useless things. ***Lex nil facit frustra, nil jubet frustra.*** The law does not do anything nor commands anyone to do anything which would be futile. ***Impunitas continuum affectum tribuit delinquendi.*** Impunity confirms the disposition of a delinquent. ***Benigne faciendae sunt interpretationes, propter simplicitatem laicorum, ut res magis valeat quam pereat; et verba intentioni, non e contra, debent inservire.*** Interpretations should be liberal, because of the lack of training of laymen, so that the subject matter should be valid rather than void; and words should be subject to the intention, not the intention to the words. ***Frustra fit per plura, quod fieri potest per pauciora.*** That is needlessly done by many which can be done by fewer. ***Potentia inutilis frustra est.*** Useless power is vain.

PURPOSEFUL, ***adjective*** advantageous, beneficial, bound, calculated, contributory, decided, dedicated, deliberate, designed, determined, devoted, dogged, earnest, firm, helpful, inexorable, intended, intense, intent, intentional, intransigent, meant, obstinate, persevering, persistent, pertinacious, planned, practical, productive, purposive, resolute, resolved, sedulous, serious, single-minded, stalwart, staunch, steadfast, steady, strong-minded, strong-willed, stubborn, studied, telic, tenacious, uncompromising, undeviating, unfaltering, unflagging, unflinching, unhesitating, unshrinking, unswerring, unwavering, usable, useful, utilitarian, valuable, willful, worthwhile, zealous

PURPOSELY, ***adverb*** according to plan, by choice, by design, by will, calculatedly, consciously, deliberately,

designedly, expressly, intentionally, knowingly, on purpose, pointedly, purposefully, studiously, volitionally, voluntarily, willfully, willingly, with forethought, with free will, with intent, with premeditation, wittingly
ASSOCIATED CONCEPTS: intent, malice

PURSUANT TO, *preposition* according to, agreeable to, agreeing to, commensurate with, compatible to, conforming to, consistent with, consonant with, in accord with, in accordance with, in harmony with
ASSOCIATED CONCEPTS: pursuant to the law

PURSUE *(Carry on)*, ***verb*** adhere to, cling to, conduct, continue, cultivate, enact, engage, execute, follow, go in for, keep on, keep up, maintain, perform, *permanere,* persevere, persist, *persistere,* practice, proceed, prosecute, stick to

PURSUE *(Chase)*, ***verb*** *consectari,* ferret out, follow, follow a trail, go after, go in pursuit of, hunt, *prosequi,* prowl, quest, run after, run down, search, seek, *sequi,* trace, track, trail

PURSUE *(Strive to gain)*, ***verb*** aim, aspire to, attempt, be bent upon, be determined to get, be intent upon, bid for, *consectari,* contrive to gain, court, covet, desire, endeavor to gain, exert oneself for, intend, labor for, progress, push toward, seek, seek to attain, *sequi,* set as a goal, solicit, steer for, strive for, struggle for, try for, try one's best, try to obtain, work for

PURSUIT *(Chase)*, ***noun*** chase, *consectatio,* effort to secure, hunt, inquest, inquiry, inquisition, investigation, probe, prosecution, quest, search, stalk, *studium*
ASSOCIATED CONCEPTS: hot pursuit doctrine

PURSUIT *(Effort to secure)*, ***noun*** attempt, campaign, effort, endeavor, exertion, hunt, investigation, laborious application, probe, quest, search, strenuous effort, struggle, sustained trial, try, undertaking, venture
ASSOCIATED CONCEPTS: hot pursuit doctrine

PURSUIT *(Goal)*, ***noun*** aim, ambition, destination, end, object, objective, purpose, target

PURSUIT *(Occupation)*, ***noun*** activity, appointment, avocation, business, calling, capacity, career, chosen work, concern, craft, department, employment, endeavor, engagement, enterprise, field, function, job, lifework, line, living, means of livelihood, metier, *negotium,* office, position, post, practice, profession, project, province, regular employment, situation, specialization, specialty, sphere, task, trade, undertaking, venture, vocation, work

PURVIEW, *noun* ambit, area, arena, borderline, boundary, bounds, breadth, circumscription, compass, concern, confine, contemplation, delimitation, department, design, extent, latitude, *latitudo,* limit, limitation, limits, *locus,* magnitude, meaning, orbit, perimeter, plan, province, purpose, range, reach, scope, span, sphere, stretch, term, territory, view, zone
ASSOCIATED CONCEPTS: purview of a statute

PUSH, *noun* acceleration, assault, attack, boost, foray, impact, impetus, impulse, impulsion, incursion, main force, pressure, propulsion, shove, stimulus, thrust

PUSH, *verb* advocate, animate, back, be resolute, boost, carry to a conclusion, coerce, constrain, dispatch, drive, drive on, endeavor, endure, exert one's self, exhort, expedite, facilitate, follow up, foray, force, forge ahead, get behind, give impetus to, goad, grind, impact, impel, importune, incite, induce, instigate, jostle, launch, motivate, nudge, persevere, persist, plod, plug away, press, press forward, press on, pressure, prod, project, promote, provoke, quicken, see it through, set in motion, shove, speed, spur, stimulate, strive, struggle, struggle on, support, thrust, urge, urge to action

PUSILLANIMOUS, *adjective* afraid, bashful, careful, cautious, cowardly, coy, diffident, fainthearted, fearful, feeble, frightened, scared, shy, soft, timid, timorous, unmanly, wary, weak

PUT *(Phrase)*, ***verb*** ascribe, attribute, cast, describe, express, impute, pose, posit, postulate, present, propound, say, set forth, state, throw

PUT *(Place)*, ***verb*** apply, assign a place, attach, base, deposit, dispense, fix, give, imbed, implant, infuse, inject, install, instill, introduce, lodge, park, place, plant, position, raise, repose, seat, set, site, situate, station, submit, tender
ASSOCIATED CONCEPTS: constructive bailment, involuntary bailment

PUT FORTH, *verb* advance, advise, air, argue, communicate, display, emit, employ, exert, exhibit, extend, go forth, issue, make a suggestion, move, offer, parade, pass, plead, posit, postulate, present, profess, proffer, propose, proposition, propound, publish, pullulate, put forward, raise, reach forth, set forth, start, start out, submit, use, venture to say
ASSOCIATED CONCEPTS: examine a witness, introduce into evidence, proffer into evidence, put allegations in a complaint, put forth pleadings

PUT IN AN APPEARANCE, *verb* actualize, appear, arise, arrive, come out, emerge, record the representation of a client, register as an attorney, represent, represent as counsel, resurface, show up, turn up

PUT INTO MOTION, *verb* actualize, begin, cause, commence, create, effectuate, engender, establish, father, found, generate, give birth to, inaugurate, initiate, institute, kick off, launch, lead off, organize, originate, pioneer, set up, spawn, springboard, start

PUTATIVE, *adjective* acknowledged, alleged, assumed, attributed, avowed, believed, claimed, commonly considered, conjectured, deemed, *falsus,* ostensible, presumed, presumptive, professed, purported, recognized, reported, reputed, speculative, supposed
ASSOCIATED CONCEPTS: putative father, putative parent

PUZZLE, *verb* addle, baffle, befog, befuddle, bemuse, bewilder, buffalo, complicate, confound, confuse, discombobulate, disorient, fox, fuddle, maze, muddle, muddy, mystify, obfuscate, perplex, pose, vex

PYRAMID SCHEME, *noun* artifice, cheating, chicanery, cozenage, crookery, cunning, deception, device, fraud, hoax, play, plot, ploy, Ponzi scheme, sham, skulduggery, stratagem, swindling, trickery

QUAGMIRE, *noun* complication, crisis, critical situation, dead end, deadlock, difficulty, dilemma, distress, emergency, entanglement, exigency, imbroglio, impasse, involvement, mess, misfortune, muddle, nonplus, perplexity, pinch, plight, predicament, problem, quandary, scrape, spot, state, strait, tight situation, trial, tribulation, trouble

QUALIFICATION *(Condition),* ***noun*** *condicio, exceptio,* exception, exemption, limitation, modification, provision, proviso, requirement, requisite, reservation, restriction, specification, stipulation, term

QUALIFICATION *(Fitness),* ***noun*** ability, acceptability, admissibility, applicability, appositeness, appropriateness, aptitude, aptness, capability, capacity, compatibility, competency, correctness, desirability, efficiency, eligibility, endowment, entitlement, expedience, fittingness, occasion, pertinence, preparation, preparedness, propriety, readiness, relevance, right, rightness, skill, suitability, suitableness, suitedness, worthiness

QUALIFIED *(Competent),* ***adjective*** able, acceptable, accomplished, adapted, adept, adequate, apt, capable, deft, efficacious, eligible, entitled, equal to, equipped, experienced, expert, fit, knowing, licensed, practiced, proficient, skilled, skillful, suitable, trained, versed, well-suited, worthy, worthy of choice
ASSOCIATED CONCEPTS: qualified applicant, qualified elector

QUALIFIED *(Conditioned),* ***adjective*** *accommodatus,* checked, circumscribed, circumstanced, conditional, contingent upon, controlled, curbed, decreased, defined, delimited, dependent, diminished, *idoneus,* limitary, limited, moderated, modified, not absolute, prerequisite, prescribed, provisional, provisionary, provisory, restricted, stipulatory, subject to terms
ASSOCIATED CONCEPTS: qualified acceptance, qualified endorsement, qualified privilege, qualified right

QUALIFIED IMMUNITY, *noun* immunity for public officials except for violation of a clearly established right, immunity for public officials when performing duties responsibly, protection for public officials from lawsuits, shield for government officials reasonably performing duties
ASSOCIATED CONCEPTS: 42 USC §1983

QUALIFY *(Condition),* ***verb*** alter, attemper, bound, confine, control, correct, *extenuare,* govern, introduce changes, introduce new conditions, keep within limits, limit, modify, narrow, regulate, restrict, revise, specify, temper
ASSOCIATED CONCEPTS: qualified acceptance, qualified fee, qualified gift, qualified endorsement, qualified privilege

QUALIFY *(Meet standards),* ***verb*** accredit, allow, *aptum,* authorize, certify, confer a right, empower, enable, endorse, entitle, give a permit, give a warrant, have the qualifications, have the requisites, license, make capable, make competent, make suitable, measure up, meet the demands, meet the specifications, permit, practice, prepare, sanction
ASSOCIATED CONCEPTS: failure to qualify, qualify for appointment

QUALITY *(Attribute),* ***noun*** characteristic, endowment, feature, idiocrasy, idiosyncrasy, individualism, nature, particularity, peculiarity, property, singularity, trait

QUALITY *(Excellence),* ***noun*** ability, ableness, aptness, caliber, character, class, competency, fineness, goodness, grade, merit, might, potency, potentiality, power, puissance, rank, soundness, standing, status, superiority, validity, value, worth

QUALITY *(Grade),* ***noun*** ability, ableness, aptness, character, condition, distinction, earmark, endowment, feature, merit, nature, particularity, property, standing, tendency, worth
ASSOCIATED CONCEPTS: inferior quality, warranty as to quality

QUALM, *noun* anxiety, apprehension, apprehensiveness, compunction, concern, diffidence, disquiet, distrust, doubt, doubtfulness, dubiety, dubiousness, equivocalness, feeling of uncertainty, foreboding, hesitance, hesitancy, hesitation, incertitude, lack of certainty, lack of confidence, lack of conviction, misgiving, mistrust, nervousness, pause, question, scruple, skepticism, suspicion, twinge of conscience, uncertainty, undecidedness, uneasiness, want of confidence, worry

QUANDARY, *noun* bafflement, bewilderment, confoundment, confusedness, confusion, difficulty, dilemma, disconcertion, doubt, doubtfulness, dubiety, dubiosity, dubiousness, dubitation, incertitude, indecision, indetermination, irresolution, nonplus, perplexity, perturbation, plight, predicament, puzzlement, quagmire, state of doubt, uncertainness, uncertainty

QUANTIFY, *verb* analyze, appraise, ascertain, assess, compute, count, delineate, demarcate, determine, estimate, evaluate, explain, figure, gauge, measure, rank, rate, scale, size, specify, survey, understand, value, weigh

QUANTITY, *noun* abundance, aggregate, allotment, amount, amplitude, apportionment, batch, bulk, bunch, crowd, fullness, heap, host, large number, legion, lot, mass, measure, measurement, mess, muchness, multiplicity, multitude, multitudinousness, myriads, number, *numerus,* pack, plenty, portion, profusion, *quantitas,* quantum, store, sum, sum total, supply, totality, volume

QUANTUM MERUIT, *noun* compensation for value received, contractual obligation to pay for value received, indemnification for value received, payment, payment for as much as deserved, payment for benefit received, payment for value obtained, payment for value provided, payment for value received, recompense, recovery, redress, remuneration for value received

QUANTUM OF PROOF, *noun* level of proof required, proper measure of proof required, standard of proof required
ASSOCIATED CONCEPTS: beyond a reasonable doubt standard in criminal cases, preponderance of the evidence standard in most civil cases

QUARANTINE, *noun* confinement, custody, detachment, medical segregation, period of detention, period of isolation, restraint of movement, sanitary cordon, seclusion, segregation, separation, strict isolation

QUARREL, *verb* altercate, argue, bicker, brawl, challenge, clash, contend, contest, controvert, dare, debate, discuss, dispute, fall out, fight, hassle, jar, object, protest, quibble, row, scrap, spat, squabble, tangle, tiff, wrangle

QUASH, *verb* abate, abolish, annul, cancel, countermand, declare null and void, destroy, disannul, discard, disestablish, dismiss, dispel, dissolve, end, eradicate, extinguish, extirpate, invalidate, make void, nullify, obliterate, overrule, overthrow, overturn, overwelm, put an end to, put down, quell, quench, repeal, repress, rescind, *rescindere,* reverse, squelch, stop, subdue, suppress, terminate, vacate, withdraw
ASSOCIATED CONCEPTS: motion to quash, quash a subpoena

QUASI, *adjective* almost, imitation, mock, mostly, near, not entirely, pseudo, pseudonymous
ASSOCIATED CONCEPTS: quasi civil action, quasi contract, quasi corporation, quasi crime, quasi criminal, quasi criminal proceeding, quasi derelict, quasi easement, quasi estoppel, quasi fee, quasi guardian, quasi in rem, quasi individual, quasi judicial officer, quasi jurisdictional facts, quasi legislative agency, quasi lien, quasi municipal corporation, quasi partnership, quasi party, quasi powers, quasi proceedings, quasi public corporation, quasi remainder, quasi trustee

QUASI, *adverb* almost as, apparently, as if, as though, as though it were, in a certain sense, in a manner, in name only, just as, seemingly but not actually, to a certain extent

QUELL, *verb* abate, clamp down, crack down, crush, douse, exterminate, extinguish, obliterate, put down, put out, quash, quench, repress, silence, smother, snuff out, squelch, stop, subdue, subjugate, suppress, vanquish

QUERULOUS, *adjective* bewailing, canting, captious, carping, censorious, clamorous, complaining, contentious, cross, difficult, difficult to please, discontented, disputatious, dissatisfied, exceptious, faultfinding, fractious, fretful, grouchy, grumbling, hard to please, hypercritical, hypersensitive, irritable, lamentative, lamenting, maledicent, mournful, nagging, overcritical, peevish, pettish, petulant, plaintful, plaintive, pugnacious, puling, quarrelsome, *queribundus,* querimonious, *querulus,* shrewish, splenetic, tearful, testy, touchy, vixenish, wailful, waspish, whimpering, whining, whiny

QUERY, *noun* call, examination, exploration, inquiry, inquisition, interrogation, interrogatory, investigation, issue, poll, probe, probing, question, questionnaire, request, research, study, survey

QUEST, *noun* chase, crusade, expedition, exploration, hunt, inquiry, journey, perquisition, pursuit, research, search, searching, seeking

QUESTION *(Inquiry),* ***noun*** asking, essay, examination, exploration, inquisition, interpellation, interrogation, interrogatory, investigation, probe, *quaestio,* query, *rogatio,* scrutiny, search, subject of inquiry, survey, test, theme of inquiry
ASSOCIATED CONCEPTS: leading question
FOREIGN PHRASES: ***Rogationes, quaestiones, et positiones debent esse simplices.*** Demands, questions, and claims ought to be simple. ***Multiplex et indistinctum parit confusionem; et quaestiones quo simpliciores, eo lucidiores.*** Multiplicity and indistinctness produce confusion; and the more simple the questions, the more lucid they are.

QUESTION *(Issue),* ***noun*** bone of contention, case, enigma, mystery, point in dispute, problem, proposition, puzzle, subject, theme, topic
ASSOCIATED CONCEPTS: mixed question of law and fact, political question, question of fact, question of law

QUESTION THE VERACITY OF, *verb* be doubtful, be dubious, be skeptical, be suspicious, be uncertain, challenge, disbelieve, discredit, dispute, distrust, doubt, doubt the truth of, entertain doubts, find hard to believe, give no credence to, greet with skepticism, harbor certain doubts, harbor suspicions, have misgivings about, have one's doubts, have questions over, have reservations, hesitate to accept as true, impugn, lack confidence in, misbelieve, mistrust, question, suspect, withhold reliance
ASSOCIATED CONCEPTS: cross examination, examination of a witness, interrogation, question under oath

QUESTION UNDER OATH, *verb* ask, conduct questioning, cross-examine, examine, examine judicially, examine on direct, examine while on trial, grill, inquire, interrogate, investigate, probe, put to the question, question, request, rest, subject to intense cross-examination, subject to questioning

QUESTIONABLE *(Dubious),* ***adjective*** ambiguous, arguable, at issue, contestable, controversial, controvertible, debatable, disputable, doubtable, doubtful, dubious, dubitable, enigmatical, equivocal, experimental, fallible, hard to believe, hardly possible, improbable, inconceivable, incredible, indefinite, indeterminate, in dispute, in question, moot, more than doubtful, not axiomatic, objectionable, open to doubt, open to question, perplexing, puzzling, speculative, suspect, suspicious, tentative, unauthentic, uncertain, unconvincing, undecided, undetermined, unlikely, unreliable, unsettled, unsound, unsure, unsustainable, untenable, untrustworthy, vague

QUESTIONABLE *(Unethical),* ***adjective*** corrupt, dishonest, dishonorable, disreputable, ill-gotten, immoral, perfidious, shady, unconscionable, underhanded, unprincipled, unscrupulous, untrustworthy

QUESTIONNAIRE, ***noun*** blank, canvas, census, examination, examination paper, form, form to be completed, form to be filled in, inquiry, poll, public opinion poll, question list, request for information, statement, study, survey
ASSOCIATED CONCEPTS: questionable testimony

QUEUE, ***noun*** assemblage, chain, file, lineup, order, progression, range, rank, retinue, row of people, sequence, series, single file, string, succession, tier, train

QUIBBLE, ***verb*** bicker, cavil, contend with, differ, disagree, dispute, dissent, equivocate, fence, haggle, join issue, oppose, palter, quarrel, tergiversate, wrangle

QUICK *(Discerning),* ***adjective*** acute, adept, adroit, agile, aggressive, astute, brainy, bright, brilliant, clever, deft, dexterous, discerning, educable, educatable, fiery, instructable, intelligent, irascible, irritable, keen, nimble-fingered, of ready intelligence, peppery, sagacious, schoolable, sharp, skillful, snappish, teachable, trainable

QUICK *(Fleeting),* ***adjective*** active, artful, born, brief, caducous, cursory, deft, elusive, ephemeral, evanescent, expeditious, express, facile, fast, fleet, fleeting, frisky, hasty, hurried, immediate, impermanent, impulsive, instant, instantaneous, meteoric, momentary, nimble, passing, perfunctory, perishable, perspicacious, precipitate, proficient, prompt, rapid, ready, short-lived, speedy, spirited, sudden, summary, swift, temporary, transient, transitory, vivacious, volatile, wide-awake

QUID PRO QUO, ***noun*** agreement, counterbalance, counterpoise, equipoise, exchange, express agreement, give and take, interchange, measure for measure, mutual agreement, mutual consideration, mutual understanding, one thing in return for another, reciprocality, reciprocation, reciprocity, something equivalent, something for something, substitute, understanding

QUIESCENCE, ***noun*** abeyance, calm, calmness, cessation, composure, dead calm, dead stop, dormancy, dying down, hush, immobility, inaction, inactivity, inertia, inertness, intermission, latency, lethargy, lull, motionlessness, passivity, pause, peace, peacefulness, placidity, quiet, quietness, quietude, remission, repose, rest, restfulness, serenity, silence, sleep, stagnation, standstill, stillness, subsidence, suspense, tranquility

QUIET *(Low-key),* ***adjective*** at rest, collected, contented, cool, cool-headed, decent, demure, diffident, dispassionate, dormant, easygoing, gentle, humble, imperturbable, inconspicuous, inexcitable, laconic, lifeless, meek, mild, moderate, modest, orderly, patient, peaceable, placid, private, resting, restrained, retiring, sedate, serene, sober, solemn, stagnant, static, subdued, taciturn, unassuming, undemonstrative, unemphatic, unobtrusive, unostentatious, unperturbed, unpresumptuous, unpretentious, unresisting, vegetating

QUIET *(Soundless),* ***adjective*** calm, glassy, halcyon, hushed, inarticulate, latent, lethargic, mum, mute, noiseless, passive, peaceful, quiescent, reserved, reticent, speechless, silent, still, tranquil, uncommunicative, unmoved, voiceless
ASSOCIATED CONCEPTS: covenant of quiet enjoyment, quieting title

QUIET, ***noun*** calm, calmness, cessation, composure, dormancy, ease, freedom from disturbance, gentleness, hush, immobility, intermission, latency, lull, moderation, muteness, noiselessness, passivity, patience, pause, peace, peacefulness, placidity, quiescence, quietness, quietude, relaxation, repose, reserve, rest, restfulness, reticence, serenity, silence, soundlessness, stagnation, still, stillness, tranquility, uncommunicativeness

QUIET, ***verb*** alleviate, appease, assuage, blunt, calm, close, comfort, compose, conclude, cut short, decrease, dulcify, dull, lull, mitigate, moderate, mollify, mute, pacify, palliate, placate, put a stop to, quell, relieve, remit, repress, silence, sober, soften, soothe, stifle, strangle, subdue, subside, temper, terminate, tranquilize, wind up

QUIETUDE, ***noun*** calm, comity, concord, harmony, hush, lull, mildness, peace, peacefulness, placidity, quietness, relaxedness, repose, respite, restfulness, sereneness, serenity, silence, stillness, tranquility

QUINTESSENCE, ***noun*** acme, acme of perfection, center, character, characteristic, consequence, consummation, content, core, cornerstone, corpus, culmination, distilled essence, elixir, essence, essentialness, essential part, gist, heart, height, kernel, lifeblood, main point, marrow, *ne plus ultra,* optimum, prime, quiddity, soul, spirit, substance, summit, superlative, ultimate

QUIRK *(Accident),* ***noun*** accidental occurrence, casualty, chance, circumstance, fate, fortuitous event, fortuity, freak, hap, inadvertence, luck, misadventure, mischance, mishap, nonintentional occurrence, turn, twist, undesigned occurrence, unforeseen event, unforeseen occurrence, unintentionality, unplanned happening, unpremeditation

QUIRK *(Idiosyncrasy),* ***noun*** aberration, abnormality, abnormity, anomaly, bizarreness, defiance of custom, departure, deviation, divergence, eccentricity, exception, fancy, habit, idiocrasy, individuality, infringement of custom, irregularity, kink, mannerism, nonconformity, oddity, outlandishness, particularity, peculiarity, queerness, singularity, strange behavior, strange occurrence, strangeness, twist, unconformity, unconventionality, unorthodoxy, unusualness, vagary

QUIT *(Discontinue),* ***verb*** abandon, abdicate, abjure, abort, acknowledge defeat, admit defeat, apostatize, arrest, back out, become inactive, break off, bring to an end, call a halt, capitulate, cause a stoppage, cause to halt, cease, cease progress, cease to use, cease work, check, come to a standstill, cut out, desist from, drop, finish, forgo, forsake, forswear, give up, go into retirement, go out of business, halt, have done with, intermit, lay aside, leave off, leave unfinished, make an end of, nol-pros, put a stop to, put an end to, relinquish, renounce, resign, retire, secede, stand aside, step down, stop, succumb, suffer defeat, surcease, surrender, suspend, tergiversate, terminate, withdraw, yield

QUIT *(Evacuate)*, ***verb*** abandon, abscond, beat a retreat, decamp, defect, depart from, desert, disappear, egress, emigrate, escape, exit, flee, forsake, get out, go, go away, go forth, go out, hurry away, leave, make a departure, make an exit, move away, part, pull out, remove oneself, retire, retreat, run away, separate from, set forth, set out, take flight, take leave, take leave of, take oneself away, turn one's back on, vacate, vanish, walk away, walk out, withdraw
ASSOCIATED CONCEPTS: notice to quit, quit

QUIT *(Free of)*, ***verb*** absolve, acquit, clear, deliver, discharge, disembroil, disencumber, disengage, disentangle, emancipate, exonerate, extricate, grant amnesty to, liberate, lift controls, manumit, pardon, release, render free, rescue, set at liberty, set free

QUIT *(Repay)*, ***verb*** balance accounts, be even with, clear a debt, clear accounts, compensate, discharge a debt, indemnify, make compensation, make payment, make reparation, make restitution, pay a debt, pay an indemnity, pay back, pay in full, pay off, pay old debts, recompense, refund, reimburse, remunerate, restore, return, settle a debt, settle an account

QUITCLAIM, ***noun*** acquittance, deed exculpating the transferor, deed of release, quittance, receipt, waiver
ASSOCIATED CONCEPTS: quitclaim and convey, quitclaim deed, quitclaim sales

QUIXOTIC, ***adjective*** chimerical, dreamy, fanciful, idealistic, illusory, impracticable, impractical, mad, notional, quixotical, romantic, unrealistic, utopian, visionary

QUIZ, ***noun*** catechism, examination, inquest, inquiry, inquisition, investigation, interrogation, quest, questioning, quizzing, request, review, test

QUIZ, ***verb*** ask, catechize, check, cross-examine, cross-question, examine, grill, inquire, interrogate, investigate, probe, query, question, question under oath, test

QUORUM, ***noun*** abundance, adequacy, adequateness, ampleness, completeness, enough, full measure, legal minimum, plentifulness, plenty, plenum, quota, sufficience, sufficiency, sufficient number, sufficient quantity
ASSOCIATED CONCEPTS: absence of quorum, full quorum

QUOTA, ***noun*** allocation, allotment, allowance, apportionment, appropriation, assignment, check, circumscription, constraint, containment, contingent, control, curb, dispensation, extent, inhibition, limit, limitation, measure, number, percentage, portion, proportion, quantity, quantum, ratio, ration, regulation, restraint, restriction, share, suppression
ASSOCIATED CONCEPTS: quota system, racial quota

QUOTATION *(Estimate)*, ***noun*** appraisal, appraisement, assessment, calculation, check, computation, cost, estimation, evaluation, measurement, price, reassessment, reckoning, valuation

QUOTATION *(Statement)*, ***noun*** allusion, citation, exact quote from a source, excerpt, extract, line, reference, saying, section, snippet, statement, words said

QUOTE, ***verb*** adduce, *adferre,* circumstantiate, cite, cite a holding of a case, corroborate, detail, document, duplicate, establish, excerpt, extract, give word for word, go into detail, instance, make reference, paraphrase, point out, produce an instance, *proferre,* recapitulate, recite, recount, refer, reiterate, repeat, rephrase, report, reproduce, restate, retell, reword, specify, substantiate, support, validate, verify

RACE, ***noun*** ancestry, birth, breed, class, cultural group, culture, descent, ethnic group, ethnic stock, extraction, family, folk, genealogy, genus, group, kind, line, parentage, people, phylum, stem, stirps, stock, strain
ASSOCIATED CONCEPTS: discrimination, race, creed, and color

RACE, ***verb*** accelerate, bolt, chase, compete, dart, dash, engage in a contest of speed, enter a competition, fly, gallop, hasten, hie, hurry, hustle, move at an accelerated rate of speed, plunge ahead, pursue, run, run a race, run swiftly, rush, scamper, scramble, scud, speed, sprint, spurt, tear, whiz
ASSOCIATED CONCEPTS: assumption of risk, race to the recording office, racing commission

RACE-CONSCIOUS ADMISSIONS PROCESS, ***noun*** deferential treatment for minorities in the admissions process, giving minority students a preference through the admissions procedures, quota alternative, race criteria to ensure minority representation, use of racial criteria in admissions, using race to admit students for diversity

RACKET, *noun* conspiracy, corruption, criminal activity, criminality, dishonesty, fraud, fraudulence, illegitimate undertaking, illicit business, illicit scheme, improbity, lawbreaking, lawlessness, misdealing, organized illegal activity, scheme, thievery, trick, underworld activity

RACKETEER, *noun* contrabandist, criminal, dealer in illicit goods, extorter, gangleader, gangster, illicit dealer, malefactor, member of organized crime, miscreant, mobster, offender, underworld character, underworld gangster

RADIATE, *verb* beam, branch out, coruscate, diffuse, disperse, emanate in rays, emit heat, emit rays, exude, *fulgere,* irradiate, issue rays, overspread, *radiare,* ramify, reflect, scatter, send, send forth, shed, splay, spread, throw off heat, throw out, transmit

RADICAL *(Extreme),* ***adjective*** absolute, altogether, complete, comprehensive, entire, exhaustive, intensive, maximal, plenary, sweeping, thorough, thoroughgoing, total, whole

RADICAL *(Favoring drastic change),* ***adjective*** advocating change, fanatical, freethinking, iconoclastic, insurgent, insurrectionary, militant, mutinous, progressive, rebellious, recusant, revolutionary, ultraist, uncompromising

RAID, *verb* assail, assault, attack, charge, conquer, crush, despoil, dominate, invade, loot, maraud, overcome, overpower, overwhelm, pillage, plunder, ransack, ravage, rush, sack, storm, strike, strip, subdue, subject, subjugate, vanquish

RAINMAKER, *noun* activity to develop business, bringing in a case flow, bringing in cases, bringing in new business, bringing in new clients, bringing in new files, bringing in new matters, bringing in work, client development, producing business, producing new clients, producing new work
ASSOCIATED CONCEPTS: business development, client development, marketing

RAISE *(Advance),* ***verb*** aggrandize, augment, boost, bring up, dignify, elevate, enhance, enlarge, ennoble, exalt, further, glorify, heighten, honor, increase, lift, move up, prize, promote, propose, *provehere,* put, suggest, uplift, upraise
ASSOCIATED CONCEPTS: raise an objection

RAISE *(Collect),* ***verb*** accumulate, assemble, bring together, *conligere,* gather together, get, levy, muster, obtain, procure

RAISON D'ETRE, *noun* animus, arterial blood, basic, basic nutrition, driving force, essence of life, essential ingredient, force of life, foundation, fundamental, inspiration, inspiriting force, inspiriting power, life essence, lifeblood, moving force, spirit, vital energy, vital flame, vital fluid, vital force, vital principle, vital spark, vital spirit

RAMBLING, *adjective* circuitous, circular, circumlocutory, crooked, curvy, indirect, long-winded, meandering, prolix, rambling, roundabout, serpentine, sinuous, tortuous, twisting, verbose, wandering, winding

RAMPANT, *adjective* dominant, everywhere, excessive, extravagant, exuberant, *ferox,* flourishing, growing, irrepressible, overabundant, prevalent, prolific, rife, spreading, *superbire,* unchecked, uncontrolled, unrestrained, unstopped, widespread, wild

RANCOR, *noun* acerbity, acrimony, animosity, antagonism, antipathy, aversion, bitter feelings, bitterness, enmity, grudge, harshness, hate, hatred, hostility, ill feeling, ill will, *invidia,* malevolence, malice, malignity, *odium,* resentment, revenge, revengefulness, ruthlessness, spite, spitefulness, uncharitableness, unfriendliness, vendetta, vengeance, vengefulness, venom, venomousness, vindictiveness, virulence

RANDOM, *adjective* accidental, aimless, blind, casual, chance, cursory, designless, desultory, done without reason, fortuitous, haphazard, immethodical, incidental, indiscriminate, irregular, orderless, promiscuous, purposeless, stray, unaimed, unarranged, uncoordinated, undesigned, undirected, unguided, unorganized, unpremeditated

RANGE, *noun* ambit, area, arena, boundaries, bounds, breadth, compass, distance, earshot, extent, field, gamut, *genus,* hearing, limit, line, perimeter, power, reach, scope, space, span, sphere, stretch, sweep

RANK, *noun* caste, class, degree, dignity, echelon, evaluation, fashion, footing, level, measure, place, position, preeminence, preferment, quality, run, situation, standing, state, station, status, stratum

RANSOM, *noun* cost of reclamation, cost of recovery, deliverance, extrication, *pretium,* price of redemption, price of retaking, price of retrieval, redemption, rescue

RANSOM FACTOR, *noun* disposal value, harassment value, means to avoid protracted litigation, means to get out of a case, nuisance value, practical means to cut losses, settlement after cost-benefit analysis is conducted, settlement to avoid litigation, settlement to dispose of a case, settlement value regardless of the merits

RAPACIOUS, *adjective* avaricious, *avidus,* cormorant, depredatory, devouring, grasping, greedy, insatiable, insatiate, living on prey, lupine, marauding, pillaging, piratical, plundering, predacious, predatory, preying, *rapax,* ravening, ravenous, voracious, vulturine, vulturous, wolfish

RAPE, *noun* abuse, assault, constupration, defilement, defloration, depredation, despoliation, forcible violation, pillage, plunder, plunderage, *rapere,* rapine, ravage, ravishment, seduction, sexual assault, spoliation, stupration, violation
ASSOCIATED CONCEPTS: criminal assault, statutory rape

RAPID, *adjective* accelerated, active, bustling, expeditious, express, fast, feverish, fleet, galloping, hasty, hurried, instant, light-footed, lively, nimble, posthaste, quick, *rapidus,* rushing, smart, speedy, swift, *velox,* winged

RAPPORT, *noun* accord, accordance, affinity, agreement, alliance, closeness, compatibility, concord, concordance, concurrence, congruity, consonance, empathy, harmonious relation, harmony, intimacy, mutual appreciation, mutuality, relationship, understanding

RAPPROCHEMENT, *noun* accord, accordance, agreement, alliance, amiability, amicability, amity, concord, concordance, cordial relations, cordiality, fellow feeling, fellowship, fraternization, friendliness, friendship, harmony, improved relations, mutual friendliness, mutuality, neighborliness, rapport, reciprocity, reconcilement, reconciliation, reunion, unanimity, understanding, unison, unity

RARE, ***adjective*** choice, curious, different, excellent, exceptional, exquisite, extraordinary, fine, incomparable, inconceivable, infrequent, *inusitatus,* matchless, noteworthy, out of circulation, out of the ordinary, peerless, precious, priceless, *rarus,* scarce, seldom seen, select, singular, *singularis,* special, strange, superlative, uncommon, uncustomary, unequaled, unexampled, unfamiliar, unique, unparalleled, unusual

RATE, ***noun*** amount, assessment, charge, cost, expense, fare, fee, hire, *magno,* obligation, pace, *parvo emere,* payment, price, quotation, standard, tempo, valuation, value, velocity, worth
ASSOCIATED CONCEPTS: legal rate of interest, rate of exchange

RATE, ***verb*** *aestimare,* appraise, apprize, assess, calculate, class, classify, compute, determine, esteem, estimate, evaluate, figure, fix the price of, gauge, grade, judge, measure, merit, price, quantify, rank, reckon, set a value on, tag, value, weigh

RATIFICATION, ***noun*** acceptance, acknowledgment, approbation, approval, assent, certification, confirmation, consent, corroboration, endorsement, *sanctio,* sanction, stamp of approval, substantiation, validation
ASSOCIATED CONCEPTS: implied ratification, ratification of a contract, ratification of unauthorized acts
FOREIGN PHRASES: ***Ratihabitio mandato aequiparatur.*** Ratification is equivalent to an express command. ***Omnis ratihabitio retrotrahitur et mandato priori aequiparatur.*** Every ratification relates back and is taken to be the equal of prior authority. ***In maleficio, ratihabitio mandato comparatur.*** In tort, a ratification is regarded as a command.

RATIFY, ***verb*** accept, accredit, acknowledge, affirm, agree to, approve, assent, assure, attest, authenticate, back, bear out, buttress, certify, circumstantiate, concur, confirm, consent, corroborate, countenance, countersign, embrace, endorse, establish, guarantee, indorse, insure, make valid, pass, sanction, seal, sign, subscribe, substantiate, support, sustain, uphold, validate, verify, warrant
ASSOCIATED CONCEPTS: estoppel, express ratification, principal and agent

RATING, ***noun*** analysis, appraisal, assessment, classification, determination, estate, estimation, evaluation, grade, grading, grouping, measurement, placement, quantification, rank, ranking, status, valorization, valuation

RATIO, ***noun*** amount, balance, correlation, degree, differential, fixed relation, measure, percentage, perspective, proportion, proportional relation, proportionality, quota, range, relative estimate, relative quantity, scale, share, standard

RATIOCINATION, ***noun*** analysis, argumentation, cerebration, cogitation, deduction, dialectics, intellection, intellectualization, logic, *ratiocinatio,* rationality, rationalization, reasoning, thinking, thought

RATION, ***noun*** allotment, allowance, apportionment, appropriation, assignment, *demensum,* dispensation, distribution, division, dole, helping, measure, parcel, part, percentage, piece, pittance, portion, proportion, provision, quantity, quota, serving, share, slice

RATIONAL, ***adjective*** agreeable to reason, analytical, balanced, cerebral, clearheaded, cognitive, *consentaneus,* discerning, discriminating, endowed with reason, enlightened, exercising reason, intelligent, judicious, justifiable, knowing, legitimate, levelheaded, logical, lucid, objective, plausible, ratiocinative, *ratione praeditus,* reasonable, reasoning, reflective, sagacious, sage, sane, sensible, sober, sound, stable, thinking, thoughtful, understanding, well-grounded, wise
ASSOCIATED CONCEPTS: rational basis

RATIONALE, ***noun*** account, basis, cause, elucidation, explanation, explication, exposition, fundamental reason, ground, logical reasoning, motivation, motive, presumption, proposition, reason, reasoning, speculation, surmise, theory

RATIONALIZE, ***verb*** account for, adduce, analyze, cogitate, construe, excogitate, excuse, explain, explain away, justify, make acceptable, make allowances, make excuses, reason, reconcile, reflect, theorize, think, think logically, vindicate

RAVAGE, ***verb*** annihilate, beat, crush, decimate, defeat, demolish, desolate, despoil, destroy, devastate, eradicate, expunge, extinguish, extirpate, foray, harry, loot, maraud, obliterate, overpower, overrun, overthrow, overwhelm, pillage, plunder, raze, rub out, ruin, sack, scourge, shatter, smash, strip, total, vaporize, wipe out, wreck

REACH, ***verb*** accomplish, achieve, amount to, approach, arrive, attain, catch up, come to, communicate with, contact, equal, extend to, gain, get, get at, get in touch with, get through to, impress, influence, keep pace with, meet, move, obtain, overtake, strike, succeed, touch, triumph
ASSOCIATED CONCEPTS: overreaching

REACT, ***verb*** acknowledge, act, answer, answer back, be affected, behave, boomerang, bounce back, counter, echo, feel, proceed, rebound, reciprocate, recoil, reply, respond, retaliate, return, take action

REACTION *(Opposition),* ***noun*** backfire, backlash, challenge, clash, conflict, contradiction, contrariety, countertendency, differences, disagreement, disapprobation, discountenance, expression of disapproval, objection, offset, polarity, protest, rebound, rebuff, recalcitration, renitence, renitency, reprisal, resistance, retaliation, retroaction

REACTION *(Response),* ***noun*** answer, attitude, effect, emotion, feeling, impact, impression, perception, reciprocal action, rejoinder, repercussion, reply, return, reverberation, sensation, sense, sentiment, view
ASSOCIATED CONCEPTS: allergic reaction

READ, ***verb*** apprehend, collect, con, conclude, consider probable, decipher, deduce, derive, digest, discern, draw a conclusion, gather, glean, grasp, guess, infer, interpret, know, leaf through, make out, perceive, peruse, pore over, presume, reason, scan, skim, study, thumb through, understand

READILY, ***adverb*** eagerly, easily, effortlessly, enthusiastically, freely, gladly, graciously, heartily, lief, *prompte,* promptly, quickly, smoothly, voluntarily, willingly

READY *(Prepared),* ***adjective*** able, accessible, armed, arranged, at hand, available, equipped, expectant, fit, groomed, in harness, in order, in position, in readiness, in working order, loaded, mature, mobilized, on call, *paratus,* primed, prompt, *promptus,* quick, ripe, set, speedy, standing by, swift, waiting

READY *(Willing),* ***adjective*** acquiescent, agreeable, alacritous, alert, animated, anxious, ardent, assenting, available, avid, cheerful, compliant, consenting, delighted, disposed, eager, enthusiastic, expeditious, favorably minded, fervent, given, glad, happy, inclined, keen, predisposed, prone, propense, zealous, zestful

REAFFIRM, ***verb*** accent, accentuate, buttress, confirm, emphasize, fortify, go over, insist, iterate, punctuate, reassert, reiterate, repeat, restate, retell, stress, sustain, underline

REAFFIRMATION, ***noun*** absolute assertion, acknowledgment, affirmance, approval, authentication, certification, confirmation, declaration, formal declaration in support or against, pronouncement, ratification, statement, substantiation, swearing, validation, verification
ASSOCIATED CONCEPTS: bankruptcy, reaffirmation agreement

REAL, ***adjective*** accurate, actual, ascertained, authentic, bonafide, conformable to fact, correct, dependable, factual, genuine, *germanus,* inartificial, incontestable, indisputable, irrefutable, legitimate, natural, right, scientific, *sincerus,* sure, true, trustworthy, truthful, undeniable, undoubtable, unerroneous, unfallacious, unfeigned, unimagined, unimpeachable, unmistaken, unquestionable, unsimulated, unspurious, unsynthetic, valid, veracious, veritable, verus
ASSOCIATED CONCEPTS: real estate, real party interest, real property, real servitude

REAL ESTATE, ***noun*** acreage, block, chattels real, domain, estate, fee, freehold, ground, hereditament, land, landed estate, lot, parcel, plot, property, real property, realty

REAL PROPERTY, ***noun*** development, domain, frontage, land, lease, patch, plot, property, real estate, territory, tract, zone

REALISTIC, ***adjective*** actual, authentic, depictive, exact, faithful, genuine, graphic, lifelike, natural, naturalistic, practical, pragmatic, real, representational, representative, truthful, undisguised, undistorted, unidealistic, unromantic, veracious

REALITY, ***noun*** actual existence, actuality, authenticity, being, existence, factualness, genuineness, legitimacy, realness, substance, substantiality, substantialness, truth, veracity, *veritas,* verity

REALIZATION, ***noun*** accomplishment, achievement, acquirement, acquisition, actualization, apperception, appreciation, apprehension, attainment, awareness, cognition, cognizance, completion, comprehension, consciousness, consummation, discernment, discovery, effectuation, *effectus,* execution, fruition, fulfilment, illumination, implementation, ken, knowledge, materialization, mindfulness, perception, performance, production, profit, receipt, recognition, sensibility, substantiation, understanding

REALIZE *(Make real),* ***verb*** accomplish, achieve, actualize, bring about, bring to pass, carry into effect, carry out, carry through, complete, consummate, do, effect, effectuate, *efficere,* engineer, *facere,* implement, materialize, perform, produce, substantiate

REALIZE *(Obtain as a profit),* ***verb*** achieve, acquire, attain, benefit, clear, come by, earn, enjoy, gain, get, make, net, obtain, obtain a return, *pecuniam redigere,* procure, produce, profit, reap, receive, turn into cash, turn into money

REALIZE *(Understand),* ***verb*** absorb, appreciate, apprehend, assimilate, become aware, become conscious, cognize, comprehend, *comprehendere,* digest, discern, fathom, grasp, *intellegere,* know, learn, make out, perceive, recognize, see, take in

REALM, ***noun*** area, authority, bailiwick, country, demesne, department, domain, dominion, empire, field, jurisdiction, kingdom, land, monarchy, orbit, perimeters, power, province, region, *respublica,* sphere, territory

REALTY, ***noun*** acres, estate, grounds, holdings, land, land owned, property, real estate, real property
ASSOCIATED CONCEPTS: conveyance of realty, description of realty, interest in realty, sale of realty, title to realty

REAP, ***verb*** achieve, acquire, attain, be rewarded, benefit, clear, collect, cull, cut, *demetere,* derive, draw, earn, gain, gather, get, glean, harvest, obtain, pick, pick up, procure, profit, realize, receive, recover, retrieve, secure, take, take in, take the yield, win

REAPPORTION, ***verb*** allot again, apportion anew, deal out anew, dispense, distribute again, distribute anew, dole out, parcel, portion out, ration, reallocate, reallot, reappoint, rearrange, reassign, reassort, reclassify, redisperse, redistribute, redistrict, redivide, remeasure, repartition, rezone, split again
ASSOCIATED CONCEPTS: reapportion a legislature

REARRANGE, ***verb*** adapt, alter, change, fine-tune, modify, put together, readjust, reconstruct, redistribute, rehash, reorganize, rephrase, replace, reposition, reset, reshuffle, revamp, revise, rework, shift, tighten

REARREST, ***verb*** catch again, constrain again, legally restrain again, make captive again, place in custody again, recapture, recommit, reconfine, redetain, reimprison, rejail, seize again, take prisoner again

REASON *(Basis),* ***noun*** account, actuation, aim, argument, *causa,* causation, cause, consideration, defense, derivation, design, end, excuse, explanation, extenuation, foundation, genesis, goal, ground, impetus, incentive, incitation, inducement, inspiration, instigation, intent, intention, mainspring, motivation, motive, object, origin, prime mover, principle, provocation, purpose, *ratio,* rationale, root, sake, source, spring, stimulation, vindication, wherefore
ASSOCIATED CONCEPTS: reason for classification
FOREIGN PHRASES: ***Causa patet.*** The reason is apparent. ***Eadem est ratio, eadem est lex.*** The reason being the same, the law is the same. ***Vitium est quod fugi debet, ne, si rationem non invenias, mox legem sine ratione esse clames.*** It is a fault which ought to be avoided, that if you cannot discover the reason you presently exclaim that the law is without reason. ***Ratio potest allegari deficiente lege; sed vera et legalis et non apparens.*** Where the law is deficient, the reason can be alleged, but it must be true and lawful and not merely apparent.

REASON *(Sound judgment),* ***noun*** ability to know, acumen, apperception, awareness, clearheadedness, cognition, cognizance, common sense, comprehension, *consilium,*

discernment, discretion, discrimination, good sense, insight, intellect, intelligence, judiciousness, knowledge, logic, logicalness, lucidity, *mens,* mental capacity, mind, perception, percipiency, rationality, recognition, sagacity, sanity, sense, sensibility, sensibleness, sobriety, thinking, thought, understanding, wisdom
ASSOCIATED CONCEPTS: business reason, rule of reason
FOREIGN PHRASES: ***Quaere de dubiis, quia per rationes pervenitur ad legitimam rationem.*** Inquire into doubtful matters, because by reasoning we arrive at legal reason. ***Lex est dictamen rationis.*** Law is the dictate of reason. ***Lex est ratio summa, quae jubet quae sunt utilia et necessaria, et contraria prohibet.*** That which is law is the consummation of reason, which commands those things useful and necessary, while prohibiting the contrary. ***Nihil quod est contra rationem est licitum.*** Nothing is lawful which is contrary to reason. ***Lex plus laudatur quando ratione probatur.*** The law is most praiseworthy when it is consistent with reason. ***Ratio non clauditur loco.*** Reason is not confined to any place. ***Ratio et auctoritas duo clarissima mundi lumina.*** Reason and authority are the two brightest lights in the world. ***Ratio legis est anima legis.*** The reason of the law is the spirit of the law. ***Ratio in jure aequitas integra.*** Reason in law is impartial equity. ***Ratio est formalis causa consuetudinis.*** Reason is the source and cause of custom. ***Lex semper intendit quod convenit rationi.*** The law always intends what is agreeable to reason. ***Quod naturalis ratio inter omnes homines constituit, vocatur jus gentium.*** The rule which natural reason has established among all men is called the law of nations. ***Ratio est legis anima; mutata legis ratione mutatur et lex.*** Reason is the soul of law; the reason of law being changed, the law is also changed.

REASON *(Conclude),* ***verb*** analyze, cerebrate, cogitate, conclude, consider, contemplate, deduce, deliberate, derive, draw inferences, examine, excogitate, figure out, gather, hypothesize, infer, intellectualize, judge, make deductions, philosophize, ponder, *ratiocinari,* ratiocinate, rationalize, reflect, resolve, study, suppose, theorize, think, think through, try conclusions, turn over in the mind, weigh

REASON *(Persuade),* ***verb*** advise, argue, bring to reason, coax, contend, convince, debate, demonstrate, discuss, dissuade, establish, explain, expostulate, expound, join issue, justify, move, persuade, plead, point out, prevail upon, prove, remonstrate, set forth, speak logically, talk over, urge, ventilate a question, win over

REASONABLE *(Fair),* ***adjective*** *aequus,* conscionable, equitable, fit, fitting, judicious, just, *modicus,* not excessive, not extreme, proper, *rationi consentaneus,* restrained, suitable, temperate, tempered, tolerable, unextravagant, unextreme
ASSOCIATED CONCEPTS: reasonable agreement, reasonable allowance, reasonable attorney's fees, reasonable market value, reasonable notice, reasonable opportunity to cure, reasonable restraint, reasonable return, reasonable time, reasonable value
FOREIGN PHRASES: ***Quam rationabilis debet esse finis, non definitur, sed omnibus circumstantiis inspectis pendet ex justiciariorum discretione.*** What a reasonable fine ought to be is not defined, but is left to the discretion of the judges, all the circumstances being considered. ***Quam longum debet esse rationabile tempus non definitur in lege, sed pendet ex discretione justiciariorum.*** How long a reasonable time ought to be is not defined by law, but is left to the discretion of the judges.

REASONABLE *(Rational),* ***adjective*** amenable to reason, broad-minded, capable of reason, clearheaded, cognitive, credible, discerning, fit, intelligent, judicious, justifiable, logical, lucid, perceiving, percipient, persuable, plausible, probable, proper, *prudens,* ratiocinative, rational, *rationis particeps,* realistic, right, sagacious, sapient, sensible, sound, tenable, understandable, unjaundiced, unprejudiced, valid, warrantable, well-advised, well-founded, wise
ASSOCIATED CONCEPTS: reasonable care, reasonable cause, reasonable certainty, reasonable degree of care, reasonable diligence, reasonable doubt, reasonable excuse, reasonable ground, reasonable inference, reasonable injury, reasonable interpretation, reasonable judgment, reasonable notice, reasonable person, reasonable probability, reasonable use

REASONING, ***noun*** analysis, argumentation, cogency, coherence, convincingness, deduction, intellectualization, logic, persuasiveness, rationale, rationality, sense, syllogism, synthesis, thinking, thought process

REASSESS, ***verb*** reappraise, reappreciate, reapprise, recalculate, recharge, reclass, reestimate, reevaluate, regauge, rejudge, relevy, remeasure, rerank, retax, revalue
ASSOCIATED CONCEPTS: reassessed tax

REASSIGN, ***verb*** assign again, change, commit again, consign again, deal again, portion out again, reallocate, reallot, reappoint, reappropriate, recommission, redistribute, redivide, reengage, reinstall, rezone, transfer
ASSOCIATED CONCEPTS: reassign a case

REASSURE, ***verb*** affirm, approve, assure again, bolster up, buoy up, certify, cheer, comfort, confirm, *confirmare,* convince, dismiss doubt, ease, embolden, encourage, enhearten, give confidence, give hope, guarantee, hearten, help, hold out hope, infuse courage, inspire, inspirit, nerve, rally, *recreare,* refresh, remove doubt, remove fear, restore courage to, restore to assurance, restore to confidence, sanction, satisfy, solace, strengthen, support, sustain, uphold, uplift, warrant

REBATE, ***noun*** allowance, cut, decrease, deduction, diminution, discount, lessening of price, markdown, reduction, refund, reimbursement, repayment

REBATE, ***verb*** allow, allow as a discount, cut, deduct, diminish, discount, give back, lessen, make allowance, mark down, offer a discount, pare, pay back, reduce, refund, reimburse, render, repay, replace, restore, return, slash, strike off, subtract, take off

REBEL, ***verb*** arise, be disloyal, be insubordinate, be treasonable, betray, break with, *concitare,* defy, denounce, dethrone, disobey, insurrect, mutiny, oppose, overthrow, recalcitrate, refuse to conform, refuse to support, renounce, resist, resist lawful authority, revolt, revolutionize, riot, rise, rise in arms, *seditionem,* strike, take up arms, tergiversate, turn against, undermine

REBELLION, ***noun*** breach of orders, contumacy, defiance, disobedience, indiscipline, insubordination, insurgence, insurgency, insurrection, lack of discipline, lese majesty, *motus,* mutiny, opposition, outbreak, overthrow, overturn, resistance, resistance movement, revolt, revolution, riot, rising, *seditio,* sedition, strike, subversion, treason, upheaval, uprising, upset, violation

REBUFF, *noun* admonition, censure, check, chiding, cold shoulder, condemnation, counteraction, criticism, defeat, defiance, disapproval, discouragement, discourtesy, disregard, flat refusal, insult, opposition, peremptory refusal, rebuke, recoil, refusal, rejection, renouncement, renunciation, reprimand, reproach, reproof, repudiation, *repulsa,* repulse, resistance, rudeness, scolding, slight, snub, spurn

REBUFF, *verb* affront, brush aside, cast aside, check, chide, decline, despise, disallow, discard, disdain, dismiss, disown, disregard, drive back, ignore, insult, jilt, keep at a distance, neglect, rebuke, refuse, *reicere,* reject, renounce, repel, *repellere,* reprobate, reprove, repudiate, repulse, resist, scorn, send away, set aside, slight, snub, spurn, turn away

REBUKE, *verb* accuse, admonish, animadvert on, berate, blame, bring to book, call down, call to account, call to task, castigate, censure, charge, chastise, chide, correct, criminate, criticize, disapprove, exprobrate, find fault with, judge, lecture, objurgate, rate, remonstrate with, reprehend, *reprehendere,* reprimand, reproach, reprove, revile, scold, slate, take to task, tax, upbraid, vituperate

REBUT, *verb* answer, argue, argue against, conflict, confute, contradict, contravene, controvert, countercharge, counterclaim, deny, disagree, disprove, dispute, explode, join issue, negate, negative, oppose, parry, prove false, rebuff, *redarguere,* refute, rejoin, *repellere,* reply, repudiate, respond, retaliate, retort, surrebut, surrejoin, take a stand against
ASSOCIATED CONCEPTS: rebut a presumption, rebut an argument

REBUTTAL, *noun* answer, arguments against the opposition, arguments in opposition, countercharges, defense, denials, pleading, refutation, reply, repudiation, reputation, response, retort, statement made in response
ASSOCIATED CONCEPTS: rebuttal evidence, rebuttal witness, rebutter, surrebuttal

REBUTTABLE PRESUMPTION, *noun* assumption that may be disproven, evidentiary assumption that may be overcome, fact that is assumed to be true by the court, presumption drawn from prima facie evidence, presumption that may be overcome by evidence

RECALCITRANT, *adjective* balky, callous, contrary, contumacious, defiant, disobedient, fractious, hardened, headstrong, immovable, insubordinate, intractable, mulish, mutinous, noncooperative, obstinate, obstreperous, opposing, oppugnant, pervicacious, rebellious, recusant, refractory, relentless, renitent, resistant, resistive, restive, stubborn, uncompliant, uncomplying, uncontrollable, uncooperative, ungovernable, unmanageable, unrelenting, unsubmissive, unwilling, unyielding, willful
ASSOCIATED CONCEPTS: recalcitrant witness

RECALL *(Call back),* ***verb*** abolish, abrogate, annul, cancel, disannul, dismiss, disqualify, invalidate, nullify, reanimate, reassemble, reconvene, repudiate, rescind, resuscitate, revive, revivify, *revocare,* revoke, summon back, take back, unsay, void, withdraw

RECALL *(Remember),* ***verb*** be reminded of, call up, commemorate, conjure up, dwell upon, evoke, fix in the mind, have memories of, keep in mind, know again, know by heart, look back upon, memorialize, memorize, place, recognize, recollect, *recordari,* recover knowledge of, refresh one's memory, relive, reminisce, retain, retrace, retrospect, review, revive, see in retrospect, summon up, think back to

RECANT, *verb* abjure, abrogate, annul, cancel, contradict, countermand, disaffirm, disannul, disavow, disclaim, disenact, disown, negate, nullify, recall, *recantare,* renounce, repudiate, rescind, retract, *retractare,* reverse, revoke, take back, tergiversate, unsay, vacate, void, withdraw
ASSOCIATED CONCEPTS: recant a confession, recant prior testimony

RECAPITULATE, *verb* *commemorare,* enumerate, give a summary of, go over, ingeminate, paraphrase, recite, recount, *referre,* reiterate, relate, repeat, rephrase, restate, retell, retrospect, reutter, review, reword, run over, say again, sum up, summarize, tell again

RECEIPT *(Act of receiving),* ***noun*** acceptance, *acceptio,* accession, acquirement, acquisition, admittance, assumption, attainment, gain, income, intake, obtainment, possession, reception, recipience
ASSOCIATED CONCEPTS: receipt of dividend, receipt of letters
FOREIGN PHRASES: ***Quicquid recipitur, recipitur secundum modum recipientis.*** Whatever is received is received in accordance with the intention of the recipient.

RECEIPT *(Proof of receiving),* ***noun*** acknowledgment of payment, acquittance, *apocha,* certificate of deposit, discharge, proof of delivery, proof of payment, quittance, release, signed notice, slip, stub, voucher
ASSOCIATED CONCEPTS: receipt in full, receipt of goods, receipt of letters, receipt of message, receipt of payment, rent receipt, warehouse receipt

RECEIPT *(Voucher),* ***noun*** assumption, bill, payment, reimbursement

RECEIVABLE, *adjective* due, due to be paid, in arrears, mature, outstanding, owed, owing, payable, redeemable, unpaid

RECEIVE *(Acquire),* ***verb*** accept, *accipere,* assume, be given, *capere,* catch, collect, come by, derive, draw, earn, gain, gather, get, inherit, make, obtain, pick up, pocket, procure, realize, reap, secure, seize, take, take in, take possession, win
ASSOCIATED CONCEPTS: contructively received, receive process, receive stolen property

RECEIVE *(Permit to enter),* ***verb*** absorb, accept, admit, adopt, allow, allow entrance, approve, embrace, entertain, give entrance, grant asylum, include, induct, initiate, install, let in, let through, permit, shelter, show in, take in, tolerate, usher in
ASSOCIATED CONCEPTS: receive into evidence, receive into the record

RECEIVER, *noun* accepter, assignee, benefactor, beneficiary, collector, consignee, depositary, fence, grantee, holder, receptacle, *receptor,* recipient, trustee
ASSOCIATED CONCEPTS: ancillary receiver, appointment of a receiver, equitable receiver, general receiver, joint receivers, legal receiver, principal receiver, provisional receiver, receiver in bankruptcy, receiver of stolen property, receivership, statutory receiver, temporary receiver

RECENT, *adjective* fresh, lately, new, newly arrived, not long past, novel, of recent occurrence, up-to-date
ASSOCIATED CONCEPTS: in recent memory, recent possession, recently

RECEPTION *(Ceremony),* ***noun*** celebration, custom, event, form, formality, function, observance, practice, protocol, ritual, service, solemnity, tradition

RECEPTION *(Welcome),* ***noun*** civilities, greeting, hail, hospitality, pleasantries, receipt, regards, respects, salute, wishes

RECEPTIVE, ***adjective*** accessible, admissive, admitting, affectible, alert, amenable, aware, broad-minded, cognitive, compassionate, comprehending, conscious, cordial, disposed, favorable, flexible, friendly, gracious, hospitable, impartial, impressible, impressionable, inclined, influenceable, interested, keen, movable, observant, open, open-minded, open to suggestion, perceptive, persuadable, reasonable, receiving, recipient, responsive, sensitive, susceptible, sympathetic, tolerant, tractable, unbiased, understanding, unjaundiced, unprejudiced, unswayed, welcoming, willing

RECESS, ***noun*** break, cessation, halt, hiatus, interim, interlude, intermission, interruption, interval, intervening period, lull, pause, repose, respite, rest, spell, stop, stoppage, time out, vacation, withdrawal

RECESS, ***verb*** adjourn, break, break up, dissolve, halt, hesitate, intermit, interrupt, lay off, pause, postpone, prorogue, relax, rest, retire, stop, suspend, take a recess, take a rest, take time out, vacation, withdraw
ASSOCIATED CONCEPTS: recess the court

RECESSION, ***noun*** downbeat, downdraft, downswing, downtrend, economic bust, economic crash, economic downturn, economic slump, failure, pullback, pullout, retirement, slowdown, stagnation, withdrawal

RECIDIVATE, ***verb*** backslide, degenerate, deteriorate, relapse, regress, retrograde, slip back

RECIDIVISM, ***noun*** backsliding, degeneration, deterioration, habitual relapse into crime, recreancy, regression, relapse, repeated relapse into crime, retrogradation, retrogression, reversion

RECIDIVIST, ***noun*** convict, criminal, delinquent, guilty person, habitual criminal, hardened offender, lawbreaker, malefactor, malfeasant, malfeasor, offender, outlaw, repeat offender, reprobate, transgressor, wrongdoer

RECIPIENT, ***noun*** accepter, assignee, beneficiary, consignee, devisee, donee, grantee, heir, holder, inheritor, legatee, liquidator, object, payee, receiver, repository, transferee

RECIPROCAL, ***adjective*** alternating, bilateral, common, commutual, complemental, complementary, contingent, correlative, corresponding, give and take, interchangeable, interconnected, interdependent, interrelated, mutual, *mutuus,* parallel, reciprocative, requited, responded to, retaliative, retaliatory, retributive, returned, two-sided
ASSOCIATED CONCEPTS: reciprocal agreements, reciprocal promises, reciprocal wills

RECIPROCATE, ***verb*** act interchangeably, alternate, cooperate, exchange, follow successively, give and take, give in return, *inter se dare,* interchange, pay back, perform by turns, perform responsively, recompense, refund, reimburse, repay, requite, respond, retaliate, return, share, switch, take a turn, trade

RECIPROCITY, ***noun*** concord, cooperation, correspondence, exchange, give and take, interchange, interplay, mutuality, reciprocality, reciprocalness, reciprocation, return, *vicissitudo*
ASSOCIATED CONCEPTS: reciprocity of enforcement of laws between states

RECITAL, ***noun*** account, depiction, description, detailed statement, discourse, dissertation, *enumeratio,* explanation, exposition, graphic account, iteration, lecture, *narratio,* narration, narrative, oration, reaffirmation, reassertation, recapitulation, recitation, recountal, recounting, reiteration, relation, rendition, report, representation, restatement, retelling, review, statement, story, summary, summing up, telling
ASSOCIATED CONCEPTS: recital in a deed, recital of consideration

RECITE, ***verb*** address, articulate, chant, communicate, declaim, delineate, deliver, detail, *dicere,* discourse, divulge, dramatize, enact, *enumerare,* enumerate, *exponere,* express, give a verbal account, give expression, hold forth, interpret, lecture, list, make a speech, mouth, narrate, orate, parrot, perform, portray, preach, prelect, present, pronounce, quote, recapitulate, recount, reel off, rehearse, reiterate, relate, render, repeat, repeat by rote, repeat from memory, report, retell, say by heart, set forth, soliloquize, speak, spout, state, talk, tell, utter, voice

RECKLESS, ***adjective*** careless, disregardful, foolhardy, foolish, hasty, heedless, impetuous, improvident, imprudent, impulsive, inattentive, incautious, *incautus,* inconsiderate, *inconsideratus,* indifferent, indiscreet, *injudicious,* insensible, irrational, irresponsible, mindless, neglectful, *neglegens,* negligent, overconfident, overhasty, precipitate, temerous, thoughtless, unaware, uncircumspect, unconcerned, unheeding, unmindful, unobservant, unthinking, unwary, unwatchful, unwise, wanton, wild, without caution, without prudence
ASSOCIATED CONCEPTS: reckless abandon, reckless conduct, reckless disregard, reckless driving, reckless endangerment, reckless indifference

RECLAIM, ***verb*** appropriate, develop, get back, reacquire, rebuild, recall, recover, redeem, reestablish, regain, regenerate, reinstate, reoccupy, replevin, replevy, repossess, retake, retrieve
ASSOCIATED CONCEPTS: reclaim land

RECLAMATION, ***noun*** exchange, recapture, reclaiming to its original state, recoupment, recovery, recycling, redemption, reform, rehabilitation, replenishment, rescue, restoration, retrieval

RECLASSIFICATION, ***noun*** change, changed ordering of priorities, changed priorities, reallocation, reallotment, reanalysis, reapportionment, rearrangement, reassignment, reassorting, reassortment, reconstitution, redistributing, redistribution, reestablishment, regradation, regrouping, reordering, reorganization, retabulating
ASSOCIATED CONCEPTS: reclassification of job titles

RECOGNITION, ***noun*** acceptance, acknowledgment, admission, apperception, appreciation, approval, attention, audition, avowal, award, awareness, citation, cognition, cognizance, commemoration, comprehension, consciousness, consideration, detection, diagnosis, discovery, distinguishment, divination, espial, finding, floor, gratitude, identification, insight, insite, knowledge, memory,

nod, notice, perception, prize, realization, recall, recollection, regard, remembrance, reward, thanks, tribute
ASSOCIATED CONCEPTS: identification of a defendent

RECOGNIZANCE, *noun* acknowledgment, assurance, avowal, bond, commitment, guaranty, obligation, promise, security, *sponsio,* surety, warranty

RECOGNIZE *(Acknowledge),* ***verb*** accept, admit, allow, appreciate, avow, cite, commemorate, concede, confess, consent, defer to, dignify, exalt, give the floor to, give the nod to, grant, greet, honor, *noscere,* own, permit, realize, salute, suffer, tolerate, yield to

RECOGNIZE *(Perceive),* ***verb*** *agnoscere,* apprehend, ascertain, be aware of, be familiar with, call to mind, catch sight of, *cognoscere,* comprehend, conceive, descry, diagnose, discern, discover, distinguish, espy, identify, know, make out, mark, *noscitare,* notice, place, recall, recollect, recover knowledge, reidentify, remember, retain the impression of, see, sight, spy, understand, verify, view

RECOLLECT, *verb* be reminded of, bring to mind, call to mind, *commeminisse,* conjure up, go back, know again, look back upon, place, recall, *recognize, recordari,* relive, remember, reminisce, *reminisci,* renew, retrospect, review, revive, summon up, think of

RECOLLECTION, *noun* afterthought, consciousness, contemplation of the past, memoir, *memoria,* memory, mental image, mental picture, mindfulness, recall, recognition, *recordatio,* remembrance, reminiscence, retrospection
ASSOCIATED CONCEPTS: past recollection recorded, present recollection revived

RECOMMEND, *verb* acclaim, advance, advise, advocate, applaud, approbate, approve, back, be satisfied with, celebrate, commend, *commendare,* compliment, counsel, countenance, direct, endorse, esteem, exalt, exhort, extol, favor, give credit, glorify, guarantee, guide, instruct, laud, lend approval, lend support, make desirable, make preferable, move, persuade, praise, prescribe, present as worthy, prize, *probare,* promote, prompt, propose, ratify, sanction, second, speak highly of, speak well of, stand by, suggest, support, think highly of, uphold, urge, value, vouch for

RECOMMENDATION, *noun* admonition, advice, advocacy, advocation, approbation, approval, boost, celebration, certificate, *commendatio,* commendation, counsel, credential, encouragement, endorsement, esteem, exhortation, good opinion, guidance, injunction, instruction, judgment, *laudatio,* laudation, motion, opinion, praise, precept, prescription, proposal, proposition, reference, sanction, suggestion, support, testimonial, tip, tribute
FOREIGN PHRASES: ***Simplex commendatio non obligat.*** A mere recommendation is not binding. ***Liberum est cuique apud se explorare an expediat sibi consilium.*** Everyone is free to determine for himself whether a recommendation is advantageous to his interests.

RECOMMIT, *verb* call back, commit again, commit anew, give back, order back, refer back, remand, remit, return, send back

RECOMPENSE, *noun* amends, compensation, consideration, damages, defrayment, deserts, earnings, emolument, fee, gratuity, guerdon, income, indemnification, indemnity, meed, *merces,* payment, *praemium,* price, quittance, recoupment, recovery, redress, reimbursement, *remuneratio,* remuneration, reparation, repayment, requital, requitement, restitution, return, reward, salary, satisfaction, settlement, solatium, substitution, wage

RECONCILE, *verb* accustom, adapt, adjust, appease, arbitrate, bring into harmony, bring to acquiescence, bring to terms, bring together, conciliate, dictate peace, harmonize, heal the breach, intercede, make compatible, make consistent, make contented, make peace, make up, mediate, mend, mollify, negotiate, pacify, placate, propitiate, render concordant, resign, restore harmony, restore to friendship, reunite, settle, unite, win over

RECONCILIATION, *noun* accord, adjustment, agreement, amnesty, appeasement, arbitration, conciliation, concord, concordance, forgiveness, harmony, improved relations, mediation, mollification, mutual forgiveness, pacification, peace, peacemaking, propitiation, rapprochement, reconcilement, restoration of harmony, reunion, settlement, understanding, union
ASSOCIATED CONCEPTS: reconciliation of contradictory clauses

RECONDITE, *adjective* abstract, abstruse, arcane, cabalistic, complex, complicated, concealed, convoluted, covert, crabbed, cryptic, cryptical, dark, deep, difficult, elusive, enigmatic, esoteric, *exquisitus,* hidden, impenetrable, imperspicuous, intricate, involved, knotty, little-known, mysterious, mystic, mystical, nebulous, obscure, occult, orphic, perdu, perplexing, profound, puzzling, *reconditus,* secret, subtle, tangled, transcendental, unfamiliar, unintelligible

RECONFIRM, *verb* make certain, make sure again, reacknowledge, reaffirm, reapprove, reauthenticate, recertify, recheck, reendorse, reenforce, reestablish, resanction, resubstantiate, revalidate, verify again

RECONSIDER, *verb* amend, consider again, consult again, *denuo,* go over, have second thoughts, redeliberate, reevaluate, reexamine, reflect again, rehear, rejudge, reponder, *reputare,* rethink, retry, review, revise one's thoughts, reweigh, rework, think better of, think over
ASSOCIATED CONCEPTS: reconsider a judicial decision

RECONSTITUTE, *verb* bring back, make over, put back, reactivate, rebuild, recondition, reconstruct, reconvert, redo, reestablish, reform, regenerate, reintegrate, remake, remodel, remold, renew, renovate, reorganize, replace, restore

RECONSTRUCT, *verb* duplicate, make over, modernize, rearrange, rebuild, recast, reclaim, recompose, recondition, reconstitute, re-create, redo, reestablish, refashion, *reficere,* reform, refresh, refurbish, regenerate, rehabilitate, remake, remodel, remold, renew, renovate, reorganize, *restituere,* restore, revamp, rework
ASSOCIATED CONCEPTS: reconstruct the scene of a crime

RECONVERSION, *noun* change, change over, demilitarization, disarmament, palingenesis, passage, readjustment, rebirth, redintegration, reestablishment, regenerateness, regeneration, regenesis, rehabilitation, renaissance, reorganization, restoration, retrogression, retroversion, return, reversal, reversion, shift, transformation, transit, transition

RECORD, *noun* account, affidavit, annal, archive, attestation, catalog, certificate, chronicle, contract, *diurna,* docket, documentation, dossier, entry, evidence, file, history, journal, list, log, memorandum, minute, note,

proceedings, recording, register, roll, roster, transcript, transcription, *urbana,* written material
ASSOCIATED CONCEPTS: courts of record, judicial record, liens of record, matter of record, public record, record of convictions, record of encumbrances, recording acts

RECORD, *verb* book, calendar, catalog, chronicle, copy, docket, document, enroll, enter, file, formalize, historify, historize, *in tabulas referre,* index, inscribe, insert, jot down, journalize, keep accounts, list, log, make a memorandum, make a note, make an entry, mark, note, *perscribere,* post, preserve, put in writing, put on paper, put on record, register, report, set down, tabulate, take down, take minutes, tally, write, write down
ASSOCIATED CONCEPTS: record a deed, record a lien, record a mortgage

RECORDATION, *noun* documentation instrument, filing, filing with copyright office
ASSOCIATED CONCEPTS: registration

RECORD-BREAKING, *adjective* astronomical, capper, climactic, exceptional, extreme, incredible, landmark, milepost, milestone, miraculous, outstanding, success, the best, the finest, transformative, turnaround, unbelievable, watershed, wonderful

RECOUNT, *verb* articulate, *commemorare,* communicate, convey, delineate, depict, describe, detail, divulge, *enarrare,* give an account, give the facts, give the particulars, hold forth, impart, iterate, narrate, particularize, picture, portray, recapitulate, recite, *referre,* reiterate, relate, render, repeat, report, retail, retell, reword, set forth, state, summarize, talk, tell, tell in detail, unfold

RECOUP *(Regain),* ***verb*** gain anew, get back, reacquire, reassume, recapture, reclaim, recover, redeem, reobtain, replace, replevin, replevy, repossess, retake, retrieve, take back, win back

RECOUP *(Reimburse),* ***verb*** compensate, give back, indemnify, make amends, make good, make reparations, make restitution, make up for, pay, pay back, quit, recompense, refund, remunerate, repay, replace, requite, restitute, restore, return, satisfy, settle

RECOURSE, *noun* avail, benefit, *confugere,* corrective device, corrective measure, device, disposal, legal redress, means, redress, remedy, resource, *se applicare, se conferre*
FOREIGN PHRASES: ***Electa una via, non datur recursus ad alteram.*** He who has chosen one course cannot have recourse to another.

RECOVER, *verb* achieve, acquire, attain, carry back, confer again, devolve again, *emergere,* gain anew, gain possession, get back, get by judgment, grant again, obtain, obtain by course of law, pass on again, procure, reacquire, realize, reassign, recapture, rechannel, reclaim, recoup, redeem, regain, reobtain, *reparare,* replevy, repossess, resell, retake, retransmit, retrieve, salvage, secure, transfer again, transfer back, transport back, win back

RECOVERY *(Award),* ***noun*** compensation, damages, defrayal, discharge, financial remuneration, indemnification, indemnity, reckoning, reclamation, recompense, recoupment, redress, remittal, remuneration, reparation, repayment, restitution, satisfaction
ASSOCIATED CONCEPTS: primary recovery, recovery from an adversary
FOREIGN PHRASES: ***Frustra agit qui judicium prosequi nequit cum effectu.*** He sues vainly who cannot prosecute his judgment with effect. ***Qui melius probat melius habet.*** He who proves most recovers most.

RECOVERY *(Repossession),* ***noun*** acquisition, *evictio,* obtainment, procuration, procurement, recapture, reclamation, recouping, redemption, regaining, regainment, replevin, replevy, rescue, restoration, retrieval, return, reversion, revindication, salvage, trover
ASSOCIATED CONCEPTS: recovery of chattels

RECREANT, *adjective* afraid, apostate, apostatic, apostatical, base, betraying, caitiff, conniving, corrupt, cowardly, cowering, craven, dastardly, deceitful, derelict, designing, disaffected, disgraceful, dishonest, dishonorable, disloyal, dissembling, double-dealing, fainthearted, faithless, false, falsehearted, fearful, frightened, guileful, hesitant, inglorious, insidious, knavish, lilylivered, perfidious, pigeonhearted, poltroon, pusillanimous, renegade, reprobate, scheming, sham, skulking, sneaking, spiritless, timid, timorous, traitorous, treacherous, treasonable, two-faced, unconscienced, uncourageous, undependable, unfaithful, unmanly, unreliable, unscrupulous, untrue, untrustworthy, villainous, without honor, yellow

RE-CREATE, *verb* create anew, duplicate, fascimile, heal, invigorate, make over, mend, reanimate, rebuild, recast, reconstruct, redo, reestablish, refashion, refocillate, reform, refresh, regenerate, rehabilitate, rejuvenate, remake, remodel, renew, *renovare,* renovate, reorganize, reproduce, restore, revamp, revive

RECRIMINATE, *verb* accuse, bring a countercharge, come back at, countercharge, get even with, give in kind, have revenge, hit back, lash back, match, pay back, requite, retaliate, retort, retort a charge, return an accusation, return the charge, shift the blame, strike back, turn on, turn the tables on

RECRUDESCENCE, *noun* backsliding, eruption, fresh outbreak, lapse, new outbreak, reactivation, reanimation, reappearance, recidivation, recrudescency, recurrence, regression, reinfection, relapse, renewal, resumption, resurgence, return, reversal, reverse, reversion, revival, revivification, reviviscence, reviviscency

RECRUIT, *verb* add, augment, call up, collect, *conscribere,* conscript, draft, employ, enlarge, enlist, enroll, find manpower, gain, gather, increase, induct, muster, obtain, provide, raise, raise troops, reinvigorate, replenish, select, sign up, strengthen, supply, swell the ranks, take in

RECTIFY, *verb* adjust, alter, ameliorate, amend, better, correct, *corrigere,* cure, emend, *emendare,* emendate, improve, make corrections, make right, meliorate, mend, perfect, put to rights, redress, reform, rehabilitate, remedy, renovate, repair, restore, revise, right, set right, set to rights, straighten, untangle

RECTITUDE, *noun* character, conscientiousness, correctness, equity, fairness, faithfulness, faultlessness, fidelity, goodness, honesty, honor, honorableness, impartiality, impeccability, *integritas,* integrity, justice, justness, loyalty, merit, morality, principle, *probitas,* probity, propriety, purity, reputability, responsibility, right, righteousness, scrupulousness, straight course, straightforwardness, straightness, trustworthiness, uncorruptibility, uprightness, upstandingness, veracity, virtue, worthiness

RECUR, ***verb*** be persistent, come again, come back, continue, crop up again, happen again, haunt, intermit, keep on, occur again, persevere, persist, reappear, recrudesce, renew, reoccur, repeat, resume, return, revert

RECURRENCE, ***noun*** analogue, carbon copy, copy, frequency, habit, habituation, intermittence, reappearance, regularity, reoccurrence, repeated happening, repetition, repetitiveness, return
ASSOCIATED CONCEPTS: recidivism

RECURRING, ***adjective*** chronic, constant, continuous, cyclical, expected, frequent, habitual, periodic, periodical, recurrent, regular, repeated, repetitious, rhythmic, round-the-clock, seasonal, serial, steady, 24/7, usual

RECUSANT, ***adjective*** abjuratory, antagonistic, apostate, contrary, contumacious, differing, disagreeing, discordant, disobedient, dissentient, dissenting, dissident, heretic, heterodox, hostile, iconoclastic, impenitent, inflexible, inimical, insubordinate, negative, nonconformist, nonjuring, nonobservant, obdurate, obstinate, oppugnant, protestant, rebellious, recalcitrant, resistant, restive, schismatic, uncompliant, unconformable, unconforming, unconsenting, unfriendly, unrepentant, unresigned, unsubmissive, unwilling

RECUSE, ***verb*** absent, avoid, brush aside, decline, disenable, disqualify, disregard, exclude, excuse, forgive, ignore, pardon, pass over, preclude

RED TAPE, ***noun*** barriers, blockades, bureaucracy, constraints, deterrents, drawbacks, embargos, encumbrances, hindrances, obstacles, obstructions, restraints, snags, stoppages, stops, stumbling blocks, trammels

REDACT, ***verb*** blot out, censor, cut out, delete, edit, edit out, erase, excise, expunge, extirpate, make deletions, redraft, revamp, rework, rewrite, strike out, work over
ASSOCIATED CONCEPTS: censorship, redact testimony

REDEEM *(Repurchase),* ***verb*** buy back, deliver, emancipate, get back, liberate, obtain, ransom, recall, recapture, reclaim, recoup, recover, regain, release, replevin, replevy, repossess, rescue, retrieve
ASSOCIATED CONCEPTS: right to redeem

REDEEM *(Satisfy debts),* ***verb*** absolve, atone, compensate, do penance, expiate, give satisfaction, make amends, make up for, offset bad debts, propitiate, reform, satisfy, set straight, shrive, turn from sin

REDEMPTION, ***noun*** deliverance, indemnification, reclamation, recovery, release, reparation, replevin, repossession, repurchase, rescue, restoration, retrieval, return, salvation
ASSOCIATED CONCEPTS: right of redemption

REDIRECT, ***verb*** change course, change direction, direct again, forward, mail again, post on, readdress, remail, reship, send forward, send on, transmit

REDISTRIBUTE, ***verb*** allot again, deal out again, dole out again, give out again, hand out again, parcel out again, readminister, reallot, reapportion, rearrange, reassign, reassort, reclass, reclassify, redivide, regroup, reissue, repartition, replace

REDOUND, ***verb*** accrue, arise, cause, conduce, contribute, effect, ensue, flow from, follow, germinate from, influence, lead, proceed, *redundare,* result, spring, sprout from, yield

REDRESS, ***verb*** adjust, aid, allay, alleviate, appease, atone, change, *compensare,* compensate, correct, cure, ease, expiate, fix, heal, help, improve, make amends, make good, make reparation, make up for, mend, pacify, palliate, propitiate, put right, readjust, rectify, relieve, remedy, repair, *restituere,* restore, right, satisfy, set right
ASSOCIATED CONCEPTS: legal redress

REDUCE, ***verb*** abate, abbreviate, abridge, attenuate, bring low, compact, compress, condense, contract, curtail, cut down, decimate, decrease, demean, diminish, disgrace, downgrade, humble, *imminuere,* lessen, lower, make less, make smaller, minimize, narrow, shorten, shrink, thin
ASSOCIATED CONCEPTS: reduce a sentence, reduce damages

REDUCED, ***adjective*** attenuated, brief, contracted, cut, decreased, deficient, depressed, diluted, diminished, inferior, less, lesser, lowered, minimal, minor, nominal, shorter, slashed, smaller, thinned
ASSOCIATED CONCEPTS: reduced charge, reduced sentence

REDUNDANCY, ***noun*** duplication, excess, excessiveness, immoderation, inordinacy, inordinate amount, needlessness, nimiety, overplus, oversupply, pleonasm, recurrence, redundance, *redundantia,* reiteration, repetition, restatement, retelling, superabundance, superfluity, surplus, tautology

REDUNDANT, ***adjective*** excessive, inordinate, needless, otiose, overmuch, periphrastic, pleonastic, repetitive, repetitious, superabundant, superfluous, supernumerary, *supervacaneus,* surplus, tautologic, tautological, uncalled-for, undue, unnecessary, unrequired, useless, verbose, wordy

REEXAMINE, ***verb*** check upon again, cross-examine, cross-question, go back over, reanalyze, recheck, reconsider, reinquire, reinvestigate, reprobe, requestion, rescrutinize, restudy, retrace, review

REFER *(Direct attention),* ***verb*** adduce, allude, appertain, apply, assign, bear upon, cite, concern, connect, connote, denote, hint at, indicate, mention, pertain, point, quote, relate, signify, suggest, touch on

REFER *(Send for action),* ***verb*** ask help of, assign, call in, call on, consign, consult, deliver, entrust, recommend, *referre,* seek advice, send, submit, transfer

REFEREE, ***noun*** adjudicator, arbiter, arbitrator, compromiser, conciliator, interceder, intercessor, intermediary, intermediate, intermediator, internuncio, intervener, judge, judicator, mediator, moderator, peacemaker, propitiator, reconciler, settler, umpire
ASSOCIATED CONCEPTS: appointment of referee, referee in bankruptcy, referee's findings, special referee, trial before referee

REFERENCE *(Allusion),* ***noun*** attribution, clue, connotation, cue, hint, implication, implied indication, imputation, incidental mention, indication, indirect implication, inference, inkling, innuendo, insinuation, intimation, mention, ratio, referment, subtle communication, suggestion

REFERENCE *(Citation),* ***noun*** ascription, assignation, assignment, authority, citing, connecting, credit, data,

derivation from, designation, documentation, enumeration, indicating, mention, mentioning, pointing out, quotation, quoted passage, quoting, recitation, referment, referral, relating, source, source material, substantiation
ASSOCIATED CONCEPTS: incorporation by reference
FOREIGN PHRASES: ***Verba relata hoc maxime operantur per referentiam, ut in eis inesse videntur.*** Words incorporated by reference have as great an effect through reference, as they are deemed to be inserted.

REFERENCE *(Recommendation),* ***noun*** affirmation, assurance, attestation, attesting declaration, authenticated confirmation, averment, avouchment, avowal, avowance, certificate of character, certification, commendation, confirmation, declaration, endorsement, laudation, letter in support, letter of introduction, letter of recommendation, substantiation, testification, testimony, validification, verification, voucher, vouching, witnessing

REFERENDUM, ***noun*** ballot, decision, determination, discretion, election, expression of choice, mandate, plebiscite, poll, popular choice, popular decision, popular vote, preference, say, selection, voice, vote

REFERRAL, ***noun*** allusion, implication, inference, innuendo, insinuation, making reference, mention, reference, referment

REFINANCE, ***verb*** back again, contribute to again, finance again, fund again, invest in again, lend to again, loan to again, provide capital again, provide funds for again, reinvest, sponsor again, subsidize again, support again, underwrite again

REFINE, ***verb*** advance, amend, better, clarify, cleanse, clear, correct, cultivate, develop, edit, elaborate, elevate, emend, enhance, filter, filtrate, improve, improve upon, make improvements, meliorate, modify, perfect, polish, purify, rectify, sanitize, sensitize, sharpen, soften, strain, temper, uplift

REFINEMENT, ***noun*** advancement, breakthrough, clarification, development, edification, elaboration, enhancement, evolution, growth, heightening, improvement, innovation, maturation, melioration, progression, strengthening, upgrade

REFLECT *(Mirror),* ***verb*** bounce back, cast back, copy, ditto, emulate, give back, give forth, imitate, *ostendere,* rebound, repeat, reproduce, send back, show an image, simulate, throw back

REFLECT *(Ponder),* ***verb*** analyze, brood over, cerebrate, *cogitare,* cogitate, commune with oneself, conceive, concentrate, consider, *considerare,* contemplate, deduce, deliberate, dream, dwell upon, excogitate, give thought to, meditate, mull over, muse, pore over, puzzle over, reason, revolve in the mind, ruminate, speculate, study, theorize, think, turn over, weigh, wonder

REFLECTION *(Image),* ***noun*** counterpart, double, duplicate, echo, *imago,* impression, likeness, semblance, specter

REFLECTION *(Thought),* ***noun*** absorption, analysis, cerebration, *cogitatio,* cogitation, concentration, *consideratio,* consideration, contemplation, deliberation, excogitation, exercise of the intellect, intellection, meditation, mentation, musing, pondering, *ratio,* reasoning, reverie, rumination, self-communing, self-counsel, speculation, study, thinking, weighing

FOREIGN PHRASES: ***Nemo cogitationis poenam patitur.*** No one suffers punishment on account of his thoughts.

REFLECTIVE, ***adjective*** abstruse, astute, complicated, deep, erudite, esoteric, intellectual, intellectually profound, penetrating, perceptive, philosophical, profound, recondite, sagacious, sage, scholarly, thoughtful, wise
ASSOCIATED CONCEPTS: deep constituted interpretation

REFORM, ***noun*** advancement, alteration, amelioration, amendment, betterment, change, *correctio,* correction, development, elevation, *emendatio,* enhancement, enrichment, improvement, innovation, melioration, progress, progression, progressivism, recast, reclamation, reconstitution, reconstruction, recovery, recreation, rectification, refinement, reformation, regeneration, remaking, renewal, renovation, repair, revision

REFORM, ***verb*** ameliorate, amend, better, change, convert, correct, *corrigere,* cure, emend, enhance, fix, form anew, improve, make better, make over, meliorate, mend, modify, rearrange, recast, reclaim, reconstitute, reconstruct, rectify, redeem, redo, redress, reestablish, refashion, refine, regenerate, rehabilitate, remake, remedy, remodel, renew, renovate, reorganize, repair, repent, reshape, restore, revise, revolutionize, rework, set straight, uplift
ASSOCIATED CONCEPTS: reform a contract, reform a deed, reform a lease, reform a will, reform an instrument

REFORMATORY, ***noun*** bridewell, correction facility, house of correction, house of detention, jail, penal institution, penitentiary, prison, reform school

REFRAIN, ***verb*** abstain, avoid, be temperate, break off, cease, check, contain oneself, curb oneself, decline, desist, discontinue, dispense with, do without, eschew, evade, exercise self-control, forbear, forestall, forgo, forsake, halt, have nothing to do with, hold back, keep from, leave off, refuse, renounce, *se abstinere, se continere,* shun, stop, swear off, take no part in, waive, withdraw, withhold

REFUGE, ***noun*** ark, asylum, citadel, covert, coverture, harbor, haven, hiding place, lee, *perfugium,* place of protection, place of safety, protection, *receptaculum, refugium,* resort, retreat, safe place, safety, sanctuary, security, shelter, stronghold
ASSOCIATED CONCEPTS: flight
FOREIGN PHRASES: ***Domus sua cuique est tutissimum refugium.*** Everyone's home is his safest refuge. ***Debet sua cuique domus esse perfugium tut issimum.*** Every man's home should be a perfectly safe refuge.

REFUND, ***noun*** compensation, cut, discount, indemnification, money back, payment for expenses, rebate, recompense, recoupment, reduction, refundment, reimbursement, repayment, replacement, restitution, return, satisfaction, settlement

REFUND, ***verb*** adjust, compensate, *dissolvere,* give back, honor a claim, indemnify, make amends, make compensation, make good, make restitution, pay back, rebate, recompense, *reddere,* redeem, reimburse, repay, replace, requite, restore, return, satisfy, settle, square

REFUSAL, ***noun*** abjuration, abnegation, ban, debarment, declination, declinature, defiance, denial, disallowance, disapprobation, disapproval, disavowal, disclaimer, discountenance, enjoinment, exclusion, incompliance, interdiction,

negation, negative answer, nonacceptance, noncompliance, nonconsent, prohibition, proscription, rebuff, *recusatio,* regrets, rejection, renouncement, renunciation, repudiation, repulse, resistance, unwillingness, veto
ASSOCIATED CONCEPTS: refusal to answer, refusal to bargain, refusal to proceed, refusal to testify, right of first refusal
FOREIGN PHRASES: ***Reprobata pecunia liberat solventem.*** Money refused releases the debtor.

REFUSE, *verb* abjure, abnegate, abstain, balk, bar, be obstinate, be unwilling, beg to be excused, cast aside, debar, decline, demur, deny, disaccord with, disallow, disapprove, disavow, disclaim, discountenance, discredit, dismiss, disown, dispense with, dissent, exclude, forswear, grudge, hesitate, hold back, negative, object to, oppose, pass up, prohibit, protest, rebuff, recoil, regret, reject, renege, renounce, repel, repudiate, resist, revoke, scruple, send regrets, shirk, shun, shy at, spurn, stick at, stickle, traverse, turn down, turn from, veto, withdraw, withhold consent

REFUTE, *verb* abnegate, belie, cancel, confute, contend, contradict, contravene, controvert, crush, debate, defeat, demolish, deny, destroy, disaffirm, disclaim, discredit, dispose of, disprove, explode, falsify, gainsay, impugn, invalidate, negate, oppose, oppugn, overthrow, parry, prove false, quash, rebut, *redarguere, refellere,* repel, repudiate, retort, squelch, tear down, traverse

REGARD *(Attention),* ***noun*** advertence, advertency, alertness, application, attentiveness, care, concentration, concern, consideration, examination, heed, heedfulness, intentness, interest, mindfulness, notice, observation, scrutiny, vigilance, watch, watchfulness

REGARD *(Esteem),* ***noun*** admiration, affection, appreciation, approbation, approval, attachment, awe, celebrity, consideration, credit, deference, devotion, distinction, eminence, estimation, fame, famousness, favor, fondness, good name, honor, interest, judgment, liking, loyalty, note, opinion, reputability, reputation, repute, respect, *respectus,* reverence, *studium,* valuation, value, veneration

REGARD *(Hold in esteem),* ***verb*** admire, adore, appreciate, approve, be fond of, be impressed, be in awe, care for, cherish, defer to, esteem, exalt, extol, glorify, have a liking for, have regard for, hold a high opinion of, hold dear, hold in affection, hold in regard, honor, idolize, look up to, pay homage to, pay tribute, praise, prize, respect, revere, reverence, think highly of, think well of, treasure, value, venerate, worship

REGARD *(Pay attention),* ***verb*** advert to, attend, be attentive, be aware of, be conscious of, be mindful, bear in mind, behold, consider, contemplate, deem, *ducere,* gaze, give heed to, heed, keep in sight, look, look at, look upon, mark, mind, note, notice, observe, perceive, peruse, scan, scrutinize, see, survey, take cognizance of, take notice, think about, view, watch, witness
ASSOCIATED CONCEPTS: due regard

REGARDLESS, *adverb* albeit, all the same, although, anyhow, anyway, anywise, at any rate, by any means, despite, even though, however, in any case, in any event, in spite of, *incuriosus,* irrespective of, *neglegens,* nevertheless, nonetheless, notwithstanding, still, though, without regard to, without respect to

REGIME, *noun* administration, authority, command, directorship, dominion, governance, government, incumbency, management, political system, power, primacy, regency, regimen, reign, rule, sovereignty, supervision, supremacy

REGIMENT, *verb* administrate, allocate, allot, arrange, categorize, classify, codify, command, control, coordinate, direct, discipline, incorporate, manage, organize, oversee, regulate, rehearse, sort

REGION, *noun* area, circle, circuit, clime, compass, confines, country, county, demesne, diocese, district, division, domain, environs, field, land, latitude, limited area, locale, locality, location, *locus,* neighborhood, part, place, portion, precinct, province, purlieus, quarter, range, realm, *regio,* scene, scope, section, sector, situation, space, sphere, spot, terrain, territory, *tractus,* vicinage, vicinity, ward, zone

REGIONAL, *adjective* circumscribed, district, divisional, geographical, insular, local, localized, native, neighborhood, parochial, provincial, restricted, sectional, specific, subdivisional, territorial, vernacular, zonal

REGISTER, *noun* agenda, *album,* almanac, archive, arrangement, balance sheet, calendar, catalog, chronicle, chronology, day book, diary, docket, ephemeris, file, invoice, journal, ledger, *liber,* list, log, log book, memorandum, minutes, notes, proceedings, record, registration book, roll, roster, schedule, *tabulae,* written record
ASSOCIATED CONCEPTS: register a complaint, register to vote

REGISTER, *verb* book, calendar, catalog, check in, chronicle, engage, enlist, enroll, enter, file, *in album,* index, inscribe, join, matriculate, note down, order, *perscribere,* post, program, record, reserve, schedule, sign in, sign up, subscribe, *tabulas referre,* tabulate
ASSOCIATED CONCEPTS: register to vote

REGISTRATION, *noun* booking, bookkeeping, cataloging, certification, chronicling, enlistment, enrolling, enrollment, filing, inscribing, installing, listing, matriculation, noting down, record keeping, recording, registry, reservation, signing up, tabulation

REGRESS, *verb* backslide, fall again into, fall back, fall behind, go back, move backward, pass back, recede, relapse, retrocede, retrograde, retrogress, return, reverse, revert, turn back

REGRESSIVE, *adjective* atavistic, backsliding, backward, decadent, degenerate, ill-advised, lapsing, on the decline, receding, recessive, recidivistic, recidivous, refluent, relapsing, retrocedent, retrograde, retrogressive, reverse, reversed, reversional, reversionary, tergiversating, withering
ASSOCIATED CONCEPTS: regressive tax

REGRET, *verb* apologize, be disturbed over, be penitent, be remorseful, be sorry for, bemoan, bewail, blame oneself, cry over, deplore, disapprove of, feel conscience stricken, feel uneasy about, fret, grieve at, have a bad conscience, have qualms about, lament, mourn for, repent, repine, reproach oneself, rue, sorrow for, weep over

REGRETTABLE, *adjective* adverse, calamitous, catastrophic, deplorable, dire, disadvantageous, disastrous, dreadful, grievous, ill-boding, ill-fated, ill-omened, inauspicious, inopportune, lamentable, *paenitendus,* regretted, ruinous, sad, scandalous, terrible, unfavorable, unfortunate, unhappy, unlucky, unpropitious, unsuccessful, untimely, untoward, woeful

REGULAR *(Conventional), **adjective*** according to rule, accustomed, average, classic, common, commonplace, conformable, consuetudinal, consuetudinary, conventional, customary, everyday, expected, familiar, general, habitual, *iustus,* natural, normal, *ordinarius,* ordinary, popular, predictable, prevailing, prevalent, routine, run of the mill, standard, stock, traditional, typical, unchanged, undeviating, unexceptional, usual, wonted, workaday
ASSOCIATED CONCEPTS: regular employment, regular interest

REGULAR *(Orderly), **adjective*** balanced, *certus, constans,* controlled, cyclic, established, even, fixed, invariable, measured, methodical, patterned, periodic, periodical, recurring, regulated, rhythmic, seasonal, stable, steady, successive, symmetrical, systematic, uniform, unvarying, well-regulated
ASSOCIATED CONCEPTS: presumption of regularity, regular course of business, regular election

REGULARITY, *noun* balance, clockwork precision, conformity, congruity, consistency, *constantia,* even tenor, evenness, exactness, harmony, homogeneity, invariability, levelness, method, methodicalness, order, orderliness, *ordo,* periodicity, precision, proportion, punctuality, recurrence, regular recurrence, regular return, regularness, rhythm, sameness, steadiness, symmetry, uniformity
ASSOCIATED CONCEPTS: presumption of regularity

REGULATE *(Adjust), **verb*** allocate, arrange, balance, coordinate, correct, dispose, level, make right, make uniform, methodize, moderate, modulate, normalize, order, organize, put in order, rectify, reduce to method, regularize, remedy, render accordant, restore equilibrium, set right, square, standardize, straighten out, systematize, temper

REGULATE *(Manage), **verb*** administer, conduct, control, determine, direct, discipline, govern, guide, handle, have authority over, have charge of, head, lead, order, oversee, police, preside over, rule, steer, superintend, supervise
ASSOCIATED CONCEPTS: regulate commerce, regulated by law

REGULATION *(Management), **noun*** adjustment, *administratio,* administration, arrangement, conduct, coordination, disposal, disposition, economy, government, guidance, handling, lawmaking, moderation, organization, regimentation, steerage, superintendence, supervision, systematization

REGULATION *(Rule), **noun*** act, bylaw, canon, code, command, commandment, decree, dictate, direction, directive, discipline, edict, enactment, injunction, instruction, *iussum,* law, legislation, mandate, measure, order, ordinance, *praeceptum,* precept, prescript, prescription, regimen, statute
ASSOCIATED CONCEPTS: municipal regulation, reasonable regulation, zoning regulation

REGULATIONS, *noun* code, codification, dictates, directives, instructions, ordinances, provisions of the regulations, rules, section of the regulations
ASSOCIATED CONCEPTS: promulgation of administrative rules, promulgation of regulations

REHABILITATE, *verb* ameliorate, amend, bring back, fix, furbish, improve, make over, meliorate, mend, readjust, rebuild, reclaim, recondition, reconstitute, reconstruct, reconvert, rectify, redeem, redintegrate, reestablish, refashion, refit, refurbish, reintegrate, reinvigorate, remake, renew, renovate, repair, reproduce, *restituere,* restore, revamp, revive, revivify, salvage
ASSOCIATED CONCEPTS: rehabilitate an offender, rehabilitate an insurance company

REHABILITATION, *noun* adjustment, alteration, amelioration, development, improvement, instauration, melioration, readjustment, rebuilding, reclamation, reconstitution, reconstruction, re-creation, recuperation, redemption, redintegration, reeducation, reestablishment, reformation, regeneration, reindoctrination, reinstatement, reinvigoration, remaking, remodeling, renewal, renovation, reorganization, repair, reparation, restitution, restoration, resurrection, resuscitation, return, revival, revivement, revivification, salvation
ASSOCIATED CONCEPTS: company rehabilitation

REHEARING, *noun* new hearing, reassessment, reexamination, reinquiry, retrial

REIGN, *noun* administration, authority, command, control, dominance, domination, dominion, government, hold, influence, jurisdiction, mastery, might, power, predominance, prerogative, privilege, regency, right, rule, sovereignty, supreme power, suzerainty, sway

REIGN, *verb* administer, command, dominate, exercise authority, govern, influence, master, predominate, preside, prevail, regulate, rule

REIMBURSE, *verb* compensate, indemnify, make good, make reparation, make restitution, pay back, rebate, recompense, *reddere,* redress, refund, remit, remunerate, repay, replace, requite, restore, satisfy, settle

REIMBURSEMENT, *noun* compensation, damages, defrayal, disbursement, giving back, indemnification, indemnity, paying back, payment, rebate, recompense, recoupment, redress, refund, remuneration, reparation, repayment, replacement, restitution, restoration
FOREIGN PHRASES: ***Frustra petis quod statim alteri reddere cogeris.*** You ask in vain that which you will immediately be compelled to restore to another.

REIN IN, *verb* arrest, bridle, check, choke, constrain, contain, control, curb, govern, hamper, handcuff, hinder, hold, impede, inhibit, keep, measure, muzzle, obstruct, pull in, regulate, repress, restrain, rule, shackle, smother, stifle, strangle, suppress, tame

REINFORCE, *verb* affirm, augment, avouch, back, bolster, boost, brace, buttress, confirm, confirmare, corroborate, energize, establish, fortify, intensify, prove, reconfirm, reconstitute, redouble, reestablish, refurbish, reinvigorate, reorganize, replenish, shore up, strengthen, substantiate, supplement, support, validate, verify

REINFORCEMENT, *noun* addition, additional strength, aid, assistance, augmentation, auxiliary, backing, boost, buttress, fresh supply, furtherance, help, helping hand, increase, prop, protection, relief, replenishment, strengthener, supplement, *supplementum,* support

REINSTATE, *verb* bring back, place in a former state, put back, put back into service, reappoint, reconstitute, reestablish, rehabilitate, rehire, reinaugurate, reinstall, reinvest, remit, replace, reseat, *restituere,* restore, restore to office, restore to power, return, revest, revive
ASSOCIATED CONCEPTS: reinstate to a job

REITERATE, ***verb*** duplicate, echo, go over, harp upon, ingeminate, *iterare,* iterate, reaffirm, reassert, recapitulate, redouble, repeat, rephrase, reproduce, restate, retell, re-utter, review, reword, say again, say repeatedly, state again

REITERATION, ***noun*** battology, duplication, echo, encore, iteration, reassertion, recapitulation, recital, recount, recounting, recurrence, redundancy, reechoing, rehash, repetition, repetitiveness, reproduction, restatement, retelling, review, summary, tautology

REJECT, ***verb*** abandon, abhor, abjure, abnegate, banish, blackball, boycott, brush aside, cashier, cast aside, cast away, cast off, challenge, contravene, controvert, decline, demur, deny, despise, detest, disaffirm, disallow, disapprove, disavow, disbelieve, discard, disclaim, discount, discredit, disdain, disinherit, dismiss, disown, dispute, disregard, dissent, dodge, eject, eliminate, eradicate, excise, exclude, expel, extirpate, extract, forbid, forswear, gainsay, get rid of, hold in contempt, ignore, impugn, jeer, jettison, jilt, keep out, lay aside, leave out, neglect, object, oppose, ostracize, oust, overrule, pass by, pass over, preclude, prohibit, proscribe, protest, rebuff, refuse, refuse to accept, refuse to consider, remove, renounce, repel, reprobate, *repudiare,* repudiate, repulse, revolt, scoff at, scout, scrap, screen out, set aside, shun, slight, snub, spurn, take exception to, throw aside, throw out, traverse, uproot, veto, vote against, waive, weed out

REJECTION, ***noun*** abandonment, abhorrence, abjuration, abnegation, averseness, ban, banishment, cashiering, contempt, contravention, debarment, declension, declination, declinature, defeat, denial, deportation, deposal, disaffirmation, disagreement, disallowance, disapprobation, disapproval, disbelief, discardure, discharge, discrediting, disdain, disfavor, disinheritance, dislike, dislodgment, dismissal, disownment, dissent, distrust, dubiety, dubiousness, elimination, eradication, erasure, eviction, excision, exclusion, excommunication, exile, exilement, expatriation, expulsion, extirpation, firing, gainsaying, hatred, intolerance, intoleration, mistrust, negation, neglect, nonacceptance, noninclusion, objection, omission, opposition, ostracism, ouster, overruling, prohibition, proscription, rebuff, recantation, refusal, *reiectio,* relegation, removal, renunciation, reprobation, *repudiatio,* repudiation, repulse, revilement, revolt, riddance, scorn, slight, snub, spurning, uprooting, veto, waiver
ASSOCIATED CONCEPTS: rejection of claim

REJOIN *(Congregate),* ***verb*** assemble, associate, cluster, collect, concentrate, convocate, forgather, meet with, muster, reassemble, reconcentrate, regroup, rendezvous with, reunite

REJOIN *(Retort),* ***verb*** acknowledge, answer, confute, counter, countercharge, rebut, refute, reply, respond, return and answer, riposte
ASSOCIATED CONCEPTS: pleadings, rejoinder

REJOINDER, ***noun*** answer, counteraccusation, counterargument, countercharge, counterstatement, defense, plea in rebuttal, reply, response, retort

REJUVENATE, ***verb*** freshen, make over, modernize, overhaul, recharge, recondition, re-create, redesign, reengineer, refresh, refurbish, rehabilitate, remodel, renovate, repair, replenish, restore, resupply, resurrect, resuscitate, revitalize, revive, revivify, transform, update

RELAPSE, ***noun*** backsliding, declension, declination, decline, degeneration, deterioration, escheat, fall, lapse, *recidere,* recidivation, recidivism, recrudescence, recrudescency, recurrence, regress, regression, reoccurrence, repetition, retrocession, retrogradation, retrogression, retroversion, return, reversal, reverse, reversion, setback, sinking, weakening

RELAPSE, ***verb*** backslide, decline, degenerate, deteriorate, fall, fall back, *recidere,* recidivate, recrudesce, regress, *relabi,* renew, retrocede, retrograde, retrogress, retrovert, return, reverse, revert, sink back, slide back, slip back, start again, start fresh, suffer a relapse, wane, weaken

RELATE *(Establish a connection),* ***verb*** affect, affiliate, ally, appertain to, apply, associate, bear upon, bracket, concern, connect, consociate, correlate, draw a parallel, filiate, group, have a bearing on, identify, integrate, interconnect, interrelate, link, parallel, pertain, *pertinere,* tie, unite

RELATE *(Tell),* ***verb*** acquaint, advise, air, announce, apprise, broadcast, communicate, convey, declare, describe, detail, disclose, divulge, elucidate, *enarrare,* express, give a report, give an account, impart, inform, make known, mention, narrate, notify, observe, particularize, phrase, portray, put into words, recite, recount, repeat, report, represent in words, retell, reveal, say, set forth, speak, state, utter, vent, ventilate, verbalize

RELATED, ***adjective*** affiliated, affined, affinitive, agnate, akin, allied, analogous, applicable, apposite, appropriate, appurtenant, associated, cognate, *cognatus,* collateral, commutual, complementary, congeneric, congenerical, congenerous, connate, connatural, connected, consanguine, consanguineous, consociate, contingent, correlated, correlative, correspondent, dependent, enmeshed, germane, implicated, interconnected, interdependent, interrelated, intertwined, interwoven, kindred, knit, like, linked, mutual, pertinent, *propinquus, proximus,* reciprocal, relative, relevant, tied

RELATION *(Connection),* ***noun*** affiliation, affinity, alliance, analogy, applicability, appositeness, apposition, association, bearing, bond, closeness, cognation, comparableness, connation, connaturalness, *connexion,* correlation, correspondence, homology, indentification, interconnection, interrelationship, liaison, likeness, link, mutuality, nearness, nexus, pertinence, propinquity, reference, relationship, relative position, relevance, resemblance, similarity, similitude, tie, tie-in

RELATION *(Kinship),* ***noun*** blood relative, blood tie, *cognatus,* common ancestry, common descent, common lineage, common stock, consanguinity, family connection, family tie, kin, kindred, kinsman, *propinquus,* relationship, relative

RELATIONSHIP *(Connection),* ***noun*** alignment, amalgamation, analogy, appositeness, association, bearing, bond, coaction, coalition, *cognatio,* cognation, combination, confederacy, *coniunctio,* connecting link, consociation, correlation, interconnection, interdependence, interrelation, interrelationship, involvement, likeness, link, linkage, mutuality, nearness, pertinence, rapport, reciprocity, relation, relevance, relevancy, tie, unification, union, unity
ASSOCIATED CONCEPTS: privity

RELATIONSHIP *(Family tie),* ***noun*** affinity, blood relation, blood ties, consanguinity, extraction, family connection, filiation, kindredship, kinship, lineage, *propinquitas,* relation
ASSOCIATED CONCEPTS: blood relationship, intestate succession, paternity proceeding
FOREIGN PHRASES: ***Affinis mei affinis non est mihi affinis.*** One who is a relative of my relative by marriage is not my relative.

RELATIVE *(Comparative),* ***adjective*** analogous, commensurable, commensurate, *comparare,* compared, contrastive, correlative, correspondent, corresponding, proportional, proportionate
ASSOCIATED CONCEPTS: dependent relative revocation, relative fault

RELATIVE *(Relevant),* ***adjective*** affinitive, allied, applicable, apposite, appositional, appropriate, appurtenant, apropos, apt, associated, bearing on, cognate, collateral, compatible, concerning, connected, connective, correlated, fit, fitting, germane, interconnected, kindred, material, pertaining, pertinent, referring, related, relating, relational, respecting, suitable

RELATIVE, ***noun*** blood relation, clansman, cognate, *cognatus,* connection, family, kin, kindred, kinsman, kith, member of the family, *propinquus,* relation, sib

RELAX, ***verb*** abate, allay, assuage, be lenient, bend, diminish, ease, give, lenify, lessen, milden, mitigate, moderate, modify, modulate, reduce, relent, remit, show clemency, show pity, slacken, soften, temper, weaken, yield
ASSOCIATED CONCEPTS: relax a restriction

RELAXATION OF LAW, ***noun*** absolution, acquittal, assuagement, discharge, dismissal, dispensation, exculpation, exemption, exoneration, grace, grant, immunity, indulgence, license, mollification, pardon, privilege, reduction, release from liability, release from obligation, relief, reprieve, special privilege, tolerance, toleration, vindication

RELAY, ***verb*** broadcast, conduct, convey, deliver, diffuse, disseminate, give, hand over, impart, send, spread, surrender, transfer, transfuse, transmit, turn over

RELEASE, ***noun*** abandonment, absolution, acquittal, acquittance, amnesty, casting away, cession, clearance, compurgation, deliverance, disbanding, discarding, discharge, disculpation, disengagement, disentanglement, disenthrallment, dismissal, dispensation, disposal, emancipation, exculpation, excusal, excuse, exemption, exoneration, extrication, forgiveness, freeing, immunity, laying aside, *liberatio,* liberation, manumission, *missio,* pardon, pardonment, quietus, relinquishment, salvation, setting free, sparing, unchaining, unfettering, unharnessing, untying, waiver, yielding
ASSOCIATED CONCEPTS: binding release
FOREIGN PHRASES: ***Eodem modo quo oritur, eodem modo dissolvitur.*** It is discharged in the same manner in which it was created. ***Quodque dissolvitur eodem modo quo ligatur.*** A thing is unbound in the same manner that it is made binding.

RELEASE, ***verb*** clear, deliver, discharge, disengage, disenthrall, dismiss, emancipate, enfranchise, exculpate, excuse, exempt, exonerate, *exsolvere,* extricate, forgive, free, give clearance, give up, *laxare,* let go, let out, *liberare,* liberate, manumit, relieve, relinquish, remit, reprieve, save, set at large, set at liberty, set free, set loose, spare, unburden, unfetter, yield
ASSOCIATED CONCEPTS: release a claim, release a lien

RELEASE FROM PRISON, ***verb*** deliver, demobilize, discharge, dismiss, free, let go, let go free, let loose, let off, let out, let out on bail, pardon, parole, release from custody, unbridle, unchain, unfetter, unharness, unlatch, unleash, unlock, unshackle
ASSOCIATED CONCEPTS: appeal, habeas corpus

RELEGATE, ***verb*** allocate, assign, ban, banish, bar, cast out, consign, convey, delegate, deport, depute, discard, dislodge, dismiss, dispatch, displace, elide, eliminate, entrust, eradicate, exclude, excommunicate, exile, expatriate, expel, isolate, omit, ostracize, oust, outlaw, proscribe, push aside, refer, reject, remand, remove, segregate, send away, separate, set apart, shut out, throw out, transfer, transport, turn over to

RELENT, ***verb*** abate severity, accede, acquiesce, be assuaged, be compassionate, be compliant, be forgiving, be merciful, be mollified, be placated, be pliant, be submissive, be tolerant, bend, defer to, feel compassion, feel for, forgive, give, give in, give quarter, give way, grow lenient, grow less severe, have mercy, have sympathy, *iram remittere, molliri,* pity, relax, remit, resign, show mercy, soften, spare, succumb, sympathize, unbend, yield

RELENTLESS, ***adjective*** assiduous, bowelless, brutish, cold, cold-blooded, cold-hearted, continuous, cruel, determined, dictatorial, endless, hard, hard of heart, hard-hearted, harsh, heedless, *immisericors,* impenitent, imperious, implacable, inclement, indefatigable, *inexorabilis,* inexorable, inflexible, insensitive, insistent, intolerant, intransigent, iron, merciless, obdurate, obstinate, perseverant, persevering, persistent, pertinacious, pitiless, pressing, rancorous, remorseless, resolute, rigid, ruthless, sedulous, severe, steadfast, stern, stony-hearted, stringent, stubborn, tenacious, truculent, tyrannical, unappeasable, unbending, uncompassionate, uncompromising, undaunted, undeviating, unfaltering, unfeeling, unflinching, unforgiving, unintermitting, unmerciful, unmitigable, unmoved by pity, unpitying, unrelenting, unremitting, unshrinking, unsparing, unswerving, unsympathetic, unyielding, vindictive, without regrets

RELEVANCE, ***noun*** affinity, applicability, application, appositeness, appropriateness, aptness, association, bearing, compatibility, concern, congruence, congruency, congruity, connection, correlation, correspondence, importance, materiality, pertinence, reference, relation, relationship, significance, suitability, suitableness, tie-in
ASSOCIATED CONCEPTS: objection as to relevance

RELEVANCY, ***noun*** accord, affinity, applicability, application, appositeness, appropriateness, aptness, association, bearing, comparability, compatibility, congruence, congruency, congruity, connection, correlation, correspondence, fitness, harmoniousness, importance, materiality, pertinence, propriety, reference, relation, relationship, scope, significance, suitability, suitableness, tie-in
ASSOCIATED CONCEPTS: legal relevancy, logical relevancy, relevancy of evidence

RELEVANT, ***adjective*** *ad rem spectare,* admissible, affinitive, allied, applicable, apposite, appropriate, appurtenant, apropos, apt, associated, cognate, compatible, concerning, conformant, conforming, congruent, congruous, connected, consentaneous, consistent, consonant, correlated, correspondent, felicitous, fit, fitting, germane, important, material, pertaining to, pertinent, proper, referring to,

related, relative, seasonable, suitable, tied in with, to the point, to the purpose
ASSOCIATED CONCEPTS: relevant evidence, relevant question

RELEVANT CONDUCT, *noun* conduct at issue, conduct in question, pertinent conduct, scope of behavior at issue, scope of behavior to be considered

RELIABILITY *(Authoritativeness)*, ***noun*** candor, certainty, certification, credibility, honor, loyalty, trustworthiness

RELIABILITY *(Predictability)*, ***noun*** constancy, dependability, firmness, punctuality, responsibility, secureness, solidity, soundness, stability, substantiality

RELIABLE, *adjective* accurate, assured, authentic, believable, certain, competent, conclusive, conscientious, constant, credible, definite, dependable, devoted, evidential, exact, faithful, genuine, guaranteed, honest, honorable, incontestable, incontrovertible, indisputable, indubitable, inerrable, inerrant, infallible, irrefutable, legitimate, loyal, proved, real, reputable, respectable, responsible, safe, scrupulous, secure, sincere, sound, stable, stanch, steadfast, steady, strong, sure, tried, true, trustworthy, trusty, truthful, undeniable, unequivocal, unerring, unfailing, unhazardous, unperilous, unquestionable, upright, veracious, veridical, worthy of trust
ASSOCIATED CONCEPTS: reliable evidence, reliable testimony, reliable witness

RELIANCE, *noun* acceptance, affiance, assurance, assuredness, belief, certainty, certitude, confidence, conviction, credence, credulity, dependability, dependence, expectation, faith, *fides, fiducia,* security, support, sureness, troth, trust

RELIEF *(Aid)*, ***noun*** accommodation, assistance, attention, *auxilium,* avail, backing, care, cooperation, encouragement, help, ministration, ministry, promotion, reinforcement, rescue, respite, salvation, *subsidium,* succor, support, sustenance, treatment

RELIEF *(Legal redress)*, ***noun*** award, compensation, correction, decision, indemnification, judgment, payment, recompense, rectification, remedy, reparation, restitution, restoration, retribution, satisfaction
ASSOCIATED CONCEPTS: affirmative relief, bill of discovery and relief, complete relief, declaratory relief, further relief, primary relief, supplemental relief
FOREIGN PHRASES: ***Judex non reddit plus quam quod petens ipse requirit.*** A judge should not render judgments for a larger sum than the plaintiff demands.

RELIEF *(Release)*, ***noun*** abatement, alleviation, amelioration, assuagement, deliverance, diminishment, diminution, discharge, disencumberance, easement, liberation, mitigation, palliation, reduction, *remedium,* remission, reprieve, respite, rest, *sublevatio*

RELIEVE *(Free from burden)*, ***verb*** abate, allay, assuage, deliver, disburden, disencumber, disengage, emancipate, exempt, extricate, free, liberate, lighten, manumit, mitigate, moderate, relax, release, rid, set free, unburden, unload

RELIEVE *(Give aid)*, ***verb*** aid, alleviate, ameliorate, assist, better, calm, comfort, cure, ease, give help, give relief, heal, help, improve, medicate, meliorate, minister to, palliate, reenforce, remedy, render assistance, salve, soothe, succor, treat

RELINQUISH, *verb* abandon, abdicate, abjure, cast off, cease, cede, deliver, demit, desert, disclaim, discontinue, dismiss, do without, drop, eliminate, forgo, forsake, forswear, give over, give up, give up claim to, go without, hand over, jettison, lay aside, leave, let go, part with, pull out, quit, reject, release, *relinquere,* renounce, resign, rid, sacrifice, secede from, sign away, spare, surrender, throw away, turn one's back on, vacate, waive, withdraw, yield
ASSOCIATED CONCEPTS: relinquish a claim

RELINQUISHMENT, *noun* abandonment, abdication, abjuration, cessation, demission, discontinuance, dismissal, elimination, forswearance, rejection, release, renouncement, renunciation, resignation, succession, surrender, vacation, waiver, withdrawal
ASSOCIATED CONCEPTS: custody relinquishment, relinquishment of rights

RELISH, *verb* appreciate, bask in, be fond of, be pleased with, delight in, derive pleasure from, enjoy, fancy, feel gratification, feel joy, feel pleasure, gloat over, like, luxuriate in, prefer, rejoice in, revel in, savor, take pleasure in

RELOCATE, *verb* reassign, reestablish, replace, reposition, rereside, resettle, resite, restation

RELUCTANCE, *noun* antipathy, averseness, aversion, coactus, deprecation, diffidence, disaffection, disapproval, disfavor, disinclination, dislike, dissent, distaste, doubt, hesitance, hesitancy, hesitation, indisposedness, indisposition, indocility, *invitus,* misgiving, nolition, objection, obstinacy, qualms, recoiling, renitence, renitency, repugnance, reservations, resistance, scruples, shyness, skepticism, squeamishness, uncertainty, unwillingness

RELUCTANT, *adjective* adverse, averse, avoiding, begrudging, diffident, discontented, disinclined, dissenting, dissentious, evasive, grudging, hesitant, hesitating, hesitative, inacquiescent, indisposed, involuntary, irreconcilable, not disposed, not inclined, opposed, protestant, querulous, recalcitrant, refusing, rejective, renitent, shrinking, shunning, squeamish, uncertain, uncomplaisant, uncomplying, unconsenting, uncooperated, uninclined, unwilling
ASSOCIATED CONCEPTS: reluctant witness

RELY, *verb* bank on, be confident, be dependent on, believe in, confide, *confidere,* count upon, depend, entrust, feel sure, have confidence in, have faith in, lean on, look to, place trust in, put confidence in, put faith in, rely on, trust

REMAIN *(Continue)*, ***verb*** adhere, be constant, be permanent, be steadfast, be tenacious, carry on, continue, endure, exist, extend, go on, hang on, hold out, keep, keep going, keep on, last, linger, maintain, outlast, outlive, perdure, perpetuate, persevere, persist, prevail, proceed, progress, prolong, pursue, stand fast, stand firm, stay, subsist, survive, sustain

REMAIN *(Occupy)*, ***verb*** be present, dwell, enjoy, have, have possession, hold, hold possession, inhabit, live in, lodge, maintain, own, possess, reside, retain

REMAIN *(Stay)*, ***verb*** adhere, await, be anchored, be dormant, be immobile, be immovable, be inert, be motionless, be sedentary, be stationary, be transfixed, come to stay, delay, *durare,* hold, last, linger, lodge, pause, *remanere,* repose, rest, set in, stand, stand fast, wait

ASSOCIATED CONCEPTS: remain in possession after the expiration of a lease, remain on premises

REMAINDER *(Estate in property),* ***noun*** estate, excess, expectancy, interest, property, residual estate, reversionary estate, surplus
ASSOCIATED CONCEPTS: contingent remainder, vested remainder

REMAINDER *(Remaining part),* ***noun*** balance, carryover, excess, leftover, overplus, *quod restat, reliquum,* remaining portion, remains, residuals, residue, *residuum,* rest, reversion, superfluity, surplus

REMAND, ***verb*** command back, commit, commit to an institution, consign, delegate, entrust, imprison again, order back, reassign, recommit, reincarcerate, reinstitutionalize, relegate, remit, *remittere,* replace, restore, return, return to prison, send, send back, transfer
ASSOCIATED CONCEPTS: general remand, reversed and remanded

REMARK, ***noun*** animadversion, assertion, averment, comment, commentary, declaration, *dictum,* exclamation, expression, interjection, mention, note, observation, point, pronouncement, recitation, reflection, saying, speech, statement, thought, utterance, word

REMARK, ***verb*** affirm, animadvert, articulate, assert, asseverate, aver, come out with, comment, communicate, convey, dare say, declare, deliver, *dicere,* discuss, emit, expound, express, give utterance, let fall, make mention, make note of, mention, note, observe, present, recite, relate, respond, say, speak, state, suggest, talk about, tell, utter, verbalize, vocalize, voice

REMARKABLE, ***adjective*** amazing, astonishing, astounding, celebrated, consequential, conspicuous, *conspicuus,* curious, distinct, distinctive, distinguished, egregious, exceptional, extraordinary, eye-catching, fabulous, flagrant, great, important, imposing, impressive, incredible, lofty, marked, marvelous, memorable, miraculous, momentous, monumental, notable, noteworthy, outstanding, overwhelming, peculiar, predominent, prominent, rare, salient, signal, significant, singular, *singularis,* special, strange, striking, stupendous, surprising, unbelievable, uncommon, unforgettable, unique, unparalleled, unspeakable, unusual, visible, wonderful, wondrous, worthy of note

REMEDIAL, ***adjective*** alleviating, alleviative, alterative, amendatory, analeptic, anodyne, antidotal, assuasive, balmy, beneficial, benign, bracing, calmative, cleansing, compensatory, corrective, counteracting, curative, curing, easing, emollient, healing, health-giving, healthful, invigorating, lenitive, medical, medicative, medicinal, palliative, prophylactic, purifying, recuperative, reformative, reparative, reparatory, restitutive, restorative, revivifying, roborant, salubrious, *salutaris,* salutary, salutiferous, sanative, sanatory, sanitary, soothing, stimulating, strengthening, therapeutic, tonic, wholesome
ASSOCIATED CONCEPTS: remedial act, remedial laws

REMEDIAL STATUTE, ***noun*** correction, corrective measure, cure, legislative cure, legislative redress, rectification, relief, remedial measure, remedy
ASSOCIATED CONCEPTS: remedial act, remedial action, remedial cases, remedial legislation, remedial right, remedial statute, remedial writ

REMEDY *(Legal means of redress),* ***noun*** aid, alleviation, amelioration, assistance, compensation, corrective measure, counteraction, effective help, help, recompense, rectification, rehabilitation, relief, remedial measure, reparation, reparative measure, restitution, solution
ASSOCIATED CONCEPTS: adequate remedy at law, ancillary relief, appropriate relief, equitable remedy, exclusive remedy, exhaustion of administrative remedies, extraordinary remedy, inadequate remedy, legal remedy, mutuality of remedy, provisional remedy, statutory remedy

REMEDY *(That which corrects),* ***noun*** aid, antidote, assistance, correction, corrective measure, cure, help, palliative, relief, remedial measure, remedium, restorative

REMEDY, ***verb*** adjust, aid, alleviate, ameliorate, amend, assist, assuage, attend, calm, change, correct, cure, ease, fix, heal, help, improve, indemnify, make amends, make better, make sound, *medicamentum,* medicate, *medicina,* meliorate, mend, minister to, mitigate, mollify, neutralize, overhaul, palliate, put into condition, put into shape, readjust, rectify, redress, reinvigorate, relieve, *remedium,* renew, repair, restore, resuscitate, retrieve, revise, revive, revivify, right, satisfy, save, set straight, solve, soothe, succor, treat, work a cure

REMEMBER, ***verb*** be reminded of, bear in memory, bear in mind, bring to mind, call to mind, call up, commemorate, conjure up, fix in the mind, keep in mind, know again, know by heart, look back, master, memorialize, memorize, not forget, place, preserve a memory, recall, recognize, recollect, *recordari,* recover knowledge of, reidentify, relive, remind oneself, reminisce, *reminisci,* retain, review, summon up, think back

REMEMBRANCE *(Commemoration),* ***noun*** acclaim, aggrandizement, celebration, ceremony, commendation, consecration, dignification, elevation, enshrinement, exaltation, glorification, holiday, homage, honoring, immortalization, keepsake, memento, memorial, memorialization, monument, observance, perpetuation, praise, ritual, salutation, solemnization, souvenir, testimonial, token, tribute

REMEMBRANCE *(Recollection),* ***noun*** *memoria,* memory, mental image, recall, recognition, recognizance, reconstruction, reidentification, reminiscence, retention, retrospect, retrospection, revival in the mind

REMIND, ***verb*** *admonere,* advise, awaken memories, bring back, bring to recollection, bring up, cause to recollect, cause to remember, *commonere,* cue, drop a hint, give notice, haunt, hint, jog the memory, make an allusion to, note, point out, prod, prompt, refresh the memory, renew memories, state, stress, suggest, tell, warn

REMINDER, ***noun*** allusion, commemoration, cue, hint, jog, keepsake, memento, memo, memorandum, memorial, mnemonic, mnemonic device, notation, note, phylactery, prod, prompt, reference, relic, remembrance, shrine, souvenir, suggestion, testimonial

REMISE, ***verb*** cede, give back, give up, grant, quit, quitclaim, release, relinquish, remit, resign, surrender

REMISS, ***adjective*** careless, delinquent, derelict, dilatory, disregardant, disregardful, dutiless, forgetful, heedless, idle, improvident, imprudent, inattentive, inconsiderate, indifferent, indolent, injudicious, lackadaisical, late, lax, lazy, loafing, neglectful, *neglegens,* negligent, omissive, procrastinative, reckless, shiftless, slack, slothful, tardy, temerarious, thoughtless, uncircumspect, unconcerned, unheeding, unmindful, unsolicitous, unthinking, unwatchful, unwilling

REMISSION, *noun* abatement, absolution, acquittal, acquittance, allayment, alleviation, amnesty, assuagement, break, cancellation, cessation, check, clearance, condonation, decrease, diminution, discharge, discontinuance, exculpation, exemption, exoneration, forbearance, forgiveness, grace, halt, indulgence, intermission, interruption, interval, lapse, lessening, letup, liberation, lull, mitigation, moderation, modulation, pardon, pause, quietus, quittance, recess, reduction, relaxation, release, relief, relinquishment, *remissio,* reprieve, respite, rest, standstill, stay, stop, stoppage, subsidence, suspense, suspension, tranquilization, *venia*

REMIT *(Relax),* ***verb*** abate, alleviate, assuage, attemper, brake, calm, check, *condonare,* decrease, diminish, ease, give up, halt, hold up, lenify, lessen, let slacken, let up, loosen, make less violent, minimize, mitigate, moderate, palliate, quell, quiet, reduce, relinquish, *remittere,* soften, soothe, stall, stop, suspend, tranquilize, weaken

REMIT *(Release from penalty),* ***verb*** absolve, acquit, amnesty, assoil, cancel, clear, condone, discharge, dismiss, disregard, drop charges, exculpate, excuse, exempt, exonerate, forgive, free, give amnesty, let go, let out, liberate, overlook, pardon, pass over, reinstate, release, reprieve, respite, show clemency, show mercy, spare, vindicate, waive

REMIT *(Send payment),* ***verb*** compensate, defray, disburse, discharge, forward payment, make payment, *mittere,* pay, recompense, remunerate, render, repay, requite, satisfy, send money, send payment, settle, tender, transmit payment

REMIT *(Submit for consideration),* ***verb*** advance, commit, consign, forward, offer, present, proffer, propose, refer, relegate, remand, send, tender, transmit

REMITTANCE, *noun* acquittal, defrayal, defrayment, disbursement, expenditure, money sent, payment, *pecunia,* quittance, recompense, reimbursement, remuneration, reparation, transmittal

REMONSTRANCE, *noun* admonishment, *admonitio,* admonition, animadversion, argument, castigation, censure, challenge, chastisement, correction, criticism, dehortation, demur, determent, discouragement, dissuasion, exception, exhortation, expostulation, exprobration, gainsaying, objection, objurgation, opposition, protest, protestation, rebuke, *reclamatio,* reprimand, reproach, reprobation, reproof, reproval, warning

REMONSTRATE, *verb* admonish, advise, advise against, altercate, animadvert, argue against, berate, castigate, censure, challenge, chastise, correct, counsel, counsel against, criticize, cry out against, decry, demur, deprecate, deter, disapprove, discourage, disparage, dispute, dissuade, exhort, expostulate, express disapproval, exprobate, find fault, find flaws, frown upon, make objections, object, objurgate, oppose, protest, raise objections, rebuke, reprehend, reproach, reprove, scold, stickle, take exception, upbraid, urge against, warn

REMONSTRATIVE, *adjective* admonitive, admonitory, argumentative, censorious, contentious, corrective, critical, dehortative, dehortatory, demurring, deprecative, deprecatory, discouraging, disputatious, dissuasive, enjoining, expostulatory, exprobrative, exprobratory, objecting, objurgatory, protesting, rebuking, remonstrant, reprimanding, reproachful, reprobative, reprobatory, reproving, warning

REMORSE, *noun* anguish, chagrin, compunction, concern, conscience, *conscientia mala,* contriteness, contrition, disquiet, feelings of guilt, grief, pangs of conscience, penitence, regret, regretfulness, remorsefulness, repentance, rue, self-accusation, self-condemnation, self-conviction, self-criticism, self-reproach, self-reproof, sorriness, sorrow

REMORSEFUL, *adjective* apologetic, compunctious, conscience-smitten, conscience-stricken, contrite, full of regret, lamenting, penitent, penitential, regretful, repentant, repenting, rueful, sad, self-accusatory, self-condemnatory, self-reproaching, sorrowful, sorry

REMORSELESS, *adjective* cruel, dispiteous, hardened, heartless, *immisericors,* impenitent, implacable, indurate, indurated, insensitive, intolerant, lacking remorse, merciless, obdurate, pitiless, relentless, ruthless, shameless, unappeasable, uncompassionate, unforgiving, unmerciful, unpitying, unregenerate, unrelenting, unremorseful, unrepentant

REMOTE *(Not proximate),* ***adjective*** at a great distance, distant, far, far-off, far removed, indirect, not immediate, *remotus,* removed
ASSOCIATED CONCEPTS: remote cause, remote damages
FOREIGN PHRASES: ***Id quod est magis remotum, non trahit ad se quod est magis junctum, sed e contrario in omni casu.*** That which is more remote does not draw to itself that which is more proximate, but the contrary in every case.

REMOTE *(Secluded),* ***adjective*** alone, apart, curtained, detached, disassociated, distant, far, far-off, faraway, hidden, inaccessible, insular, isolated, not close, not near, not nearby, out of the way, private, remote, removed, seclusive, segregated, separated, sequestered, shut away, solitary, unapproachable, unassociated, unconnected, unfrequented

REMOTE *(Small),* ***adjective*** diminutive, faint, in small amount, inappreciable, inconsequential, inconsiderable, insignificant, insubstantial, little, minimal, minute, scant, slight, slim, small, superficial, tiny, trivial, unessential, unimportant

REMOTE CAUSE, *noun* auxiliary cause, distant basis, distant cause, distant reason, far cause, far-off cause, far-removed cause, immaterial cause, indirect cause, insufficient legal basis, insufficient legal cause, insufficient legal factor, insufficient legal genesis, insufficient legal inducement, insufficient legal source, no imediate legal cause, nonimmediate legal basis, not immediate cause, not immediate legal genesis, removed cause
ASSOCIATED CONCEPTS: intervening cause, liability, negligence, proximate cause

REMOVAL, *noun* abatement, abolition, *amotio,* amotion, banishment, cashiering, change of place, conveyance, debarment, deduction, demission, demotion, departure, deportation, deposal, deposition, deprivation of office, detachment, discard, discharge, disemployment, dislocation, dislodgment, dismissal, displacement, divestment, ejection, elimination, eradication, erasure, evacuation, evulsion, exception, excision, exclusion, exile, expulsion,

extermination, extirpation, extraction, extrication, isolation, layoff, noninclusion, obliteration, omission, ousting, purge, reallocation, rejection, relegation, remotion, retirement, retreat, riddance, segregation, separation, sequestration, shift, sublation, subtraction, suppression, taking away, transfer, transference, transhipment, translocation, transplacement, transplantation, transportation, unseating, withdrawal
ASSOCIATED CONCEPTS: removal from office, removal of cloud from title, removal to federal court

REMOVE *(Dismiss from office),* ***verb*** cashier, depose, disassociate, disbar, discharge, dismiss, displace, dissociate, divest, eject, expel, fire, get rid of, impeach, oust, put out, relieve, replace, suspend, turn out
ASSOCIATED CONCEPTS: removal proceeding, remove from office

REMOVE *(Eliminate),* ***verb*** abolish, annihilate, bar, cancel, clear, confiscate, debar, deduct, delete, delocalize, detach, deterge, detruncate, disassociate, disconnect, disjoin, dislocate, dislodge, displace, disroot, dissociate, disturb, divest, drain, eliminate, eradicate, except, exclude, exhume, export, expunge, exterminate, extirpate, extract, extricate, isolate, kill, liquidate, obliterate, obviate, omit, part, purge, reject, segregate, separate, sequester, sequestrate, set apart, strip, subtract, take away, take out, truncate, unattach, unbind, unfasten, unload, untie, uproot, withdraw
ASSOCIATED CONCEPTS: remove a cloud on title, remove disabilities, remove obstructions

REMOVE *(Transfer),* ***verb*** *amovere,* change address, change place, change venue, convey to, deliver to, forward, move, relocate, *removere,* send, send forth, shift, switch, transmit
ASSOCIATED CONCEPTS: removal from the state, remove a case to federal court, remove a cause of action

REMUNERATE, ***verb*** acquit, award, compensate, defray, disburse, discharge, give payment, indemnify, make payment, make up for, pay, recompense, reimburse, remit, *remunerari,* repay, requite, reward, satisfy, settle
ASSOCIATED CONCEPTS: legal fees

REMUNERATION, ***noun*** award, compensation, defrayal, defrayment, indemnification, indemnity, money, pay, payment, *praemium,* quittance, recompense, reimbursement, *remuneratio,* requital, restitution, return, reward, satisfaction, settlement

REMUNERATIVE, ***adjective*** advantageous, beneficial, compensative, compensatory, gainful, fruitful, lucrative, maintaining, productive, profitable, reimbursing, rewardful, rewarding, salutary, satisfying, supporting, valuable, well-paying, worthwhile

RENASCENT, ***adjective*** awakened, overhauled, reanimated, reappearing, reborn, reclaimed, reconditioned, reconstituted, reconstructed, re-created, redintegrated, redivivus, reestablished, refashioned, reformed, refreshed, regenerated, rehabilitated, rejuvenated, remade, renewed, renovated, repaired, reproduced, restored, resurgent, resurrected, resuscitated, revived, revivified, salvaged

REND, ***verb*** break, burst, cleave, crack, cut, dilacerate, discerp, *disscindere,* dissect, dissever, disunite, divide, fracture, lacerate, lancinate, rip, rive, rupture, sever, shatter, shiver, slash, slice, snap, splinter, split, sunder, tear, tear asunder

RENDER *(Administer),* ***verb*** accomplish, accord, administrate, bring about, conduct, contribute, dispense, execute, furnish, give, mete out, perform, preside over, provide, provide with, put into effect

RENDER *(Deliver),* ***verb*** communicate, confer, convey, execute, give, give back, hand down, hand over, impart, pass down, present, *reddere, referre,* set down, submit, surrender, *tribuere*
ASSOCIATED CONCEPTS: render a judgment, render a verdict, render an accounting

RENDER *(Depict),* ***verb*** characterize, construe, define, delineate, describe, detail, elucidate, illustrate, interpret, outline, picture, portray, record, represent, reproduce, set forth, show, sketch, translate

RENDER A JUDGMENT, ***verb*** adjudge, adjudicate, authorize, award, constitute, decide, decree, deliver judgment, enact, establish by law, hand down a judgment, impose, institute, legalize, pass, pass judgment, pass upon, sanction
ASSOCIATED CONCEPTS: render a verdict

RENDER IMPOSSIBLE, ***verb*** ban, block, check, debar, disallow, enjoin, exclude, forbid, foreclose, halt, hinder, impede, interdict, obstruct, oppose, preclude, prevent, prohibit, proscribe, refuse permission, restrain, restrict, stop, thwart, veto

RENDER NULL AND VOID, ***verb*** abolish, abrogate, annul, cancel, countermand, deprive of legal force, disown, dissolve, frustrate, invalidate, make useless, make valueless, negate, neutralize, nullify, obliterate, offset, override, overrule, overturn, renege, renounce, repeal, rescind, reverse, revoke, suspend, vacate, vitiate, void

RENDEZVOUS, ***noun*** appointment, assembly, assignation, concourse, confluence, congregation, congress, date, encounter, engagement, gathering, gathering place, get-together, ingathering, meeting, meeting place, muster, place of assignation, place of meeting, tryst

RENDEZVOUS, ***verb*** assemble, be closeted with, become acquainted, come together, congregate, convene, encounter, forgather, gather, keep a date, keep an appointment, meet, muster

RENDITION *(Explication),* ***noun*** account, construction, definition, delineation, explanation, interpretation, reading, rendering, report, representation, rewording, statement, translation

RENDITION *(Restoration),* ***noun*** compensation, indemnification, recommitment, rehabilitation, reparation, restitution, return, submission, surrender

RENEGE, ***verb*** abandon, abolish, abrogate, annul, back out, bolt, break a promise, call back, contradict, counterorder, countermand, desert, disannul, dissolve, go back on a commitment, go back on a promise, invalidate, nullify, pull out, quit, recall, refuse to honor a commitment, refuse to honor a promise, repeal, rescind, retract, retreat, reverse, revoke, secede, vacate, withdraw

RENEW *(Begin again),* ***verb*** continue, launch again, progress, put back, readmit, recommence, *redintegrare,* reembark, reenter, regenerate, reinstall, reinstate, reinstitute, reintroduce, reopen, reorganize, repeat, *repetere,*

resume, return to, revive, set going again, start again, stimulate, transform
ASSOCIATED CONCEPTS: leave to renew, renew a motion, renew an objection

RENEW *(Refurbish),* ***verb*** ameliorate, amend, bring up to date, cure, enhance, fix, freshen, give new life to, improve, invigorate, make over, make perfect, make sound, make well, make whole, meliorate, mend, modernize, overhaul, patch up, perfect, put into shape, reanimate, reawaken, rebuild, reclaim, *reconcinnare,* recondition, reconstitute, reconstruct, reconvert, recover, re-create, rectify, redesign, redintegrate, redo, redress, refashion, *reficere,* refinish, refit, refresh, refurbish, regenerate, rehabilitate, reintegrate, reinvigorate, rejuvenate, rekindle, remake, remodel, *renovare,* renovate, repair, replace, replenish, reproduce, restore, resurge, resurrect, resuscitate, retouch, revamp, revise, revitalize, revive, rework, salvage, save

RENEWABLE ENERGY, ***noun*** alternative energy, energy efficiency, geothermal power, hydropower, replenishable energy, solar power, tidal power, wind power

RENEWAL, ***noun*** amelioration, comeback, continuance, enhancement, fixing, improvement, instauration, making over, melioration, mending, modernization, new start, readjustment, reanimation, rearrangement, rebirth, recharging, reclamation, recommencement, reconstitution, reconstruction, recrudescence, recrudescency, recurrence, redoubling, reestablishment, refitting, reformation, refreshment, regeneration, rehabilitation, reinstatement, reinvigoration, reissue, rejuvenation, relapse, renaissance, renascence, *renovatio,* renovation, reopening, repair, repetition, replenishment, reproduction, restoration, resumption, resurrection, resuscitation, return, revamping, revision, revival, revivification, salvage
ASSOCIATED CONCEPTS: motion to renew, renewal of a claim, renewal of a license, renewal of a motion

RENITENT, ***adjective*** adverse, antagonistic, antipathetic, antipathetical, conflicting, counteracting, counteractive, demurring, disapproving, disgusted, disinclined, dissenting, firm, indisposed, indocile, insurrectional, intractable, intransigent, loath, mutinous, opposed, opposing, reactionary, recalcitrant, reluctant, resistant, resisting, rigid, stiff, unsubmissive, unwilling

RENOUNCE, ***verb*** abandon, abdicate, abhor, abjure, abnegate, banish, break with, cast aside, cast off, cease, decline, demit, deny, deprive oneself, desert, desist from, despise, detest, disagree, disapprove, disavow, discard, disclaim, discountenance, disdain, dismiss, disown, dissent, divorce oneself from, drop, eliminate, exclude, forbear, forbid, forgo, forsake, forswear, give away, give up, give up claim to, go without, interdict, lay aside, leave, let go, oppose, ostracize, part with, proscribe, protest, quit, rebuff, recant, refuse, reject, relinquish, renege, repel, repudiate, repulse, resign, rid oneself of, scorn, spurn, surrender, swear off, take exception to, turn from, waive
ASSOCIATED CONCEPTS: renounce a will
FOREIGN PHRASES: ***Cuilibet licet juri pro se introducto renunciare.*** Anyone may renounce the benefit of a legal right that exists only for his protection.

RENOVATE, ***verb*** ameliorate, amend, convert, fix, improve, make better, make new, make over, make sound, make whole, meliorate, mend, modernize, perfect, readjust, reanimate, rebuild, recondition, reconstitute, reconstruct, reconvert, re-create, redeem, redintegrate, reestablish, refashion, *reficere,* refit, refresh, refurbish, regenerate, rehabilitate, reinvigorate, rejuvenate, remake, remodel, renew, renovize, reorganize, repair, replace, restore, resurrect, revamp, revive, revivify, salvage

RENOWNED, ***adjective*** acclaimed, applauded, celebrated, *clarus,* consequential, conspicuous, distinguished, eminent, exalted, extraordinary, famed, famous, far-famed, foremost, great, honored, illustrious, important, *inlustris,* known, leading, matchless, much touted, notable, noted, noteworthy, notorious, outstanding, popular, preeminent, prominent, recognized, remarkable, reputable, singular, talked about, top-flight, unexampled, unique, unparalled, unprecedented, well-known

RENT, ***noun*** assessment, compensation, cost, fee, income, income from real estate, land revenue, *merces,* payment, proceeds, *reditus,* remuneration, rental, return, revenue
ASSOCIATED CONCEPTS: action for rent, assignment of rent, ejectment, fair rent, fair rental value, holdover, month-to-month rental, prepayment of rent, reasonable rent, rent strike, rents and proceeds, security, suit for rent, tenancy by will, unaccrued rent

RENT, ***verb*** allow residency, allow the use of, charter, *conducere,* contract, demise, enjoy the use of premises, engage, give occupation, grant a lease, hire out, lease, lend, let, let out, *locare,* make available, sublease, sublet, subrent, take a lease, underlease, underlet, use premises
ASSOCIATED CONCEPTS: option to rent

RENUNCIATION, ***noun*** abandonment, abdication, abjuration, abnegation, cancellation, cession, declination, demission, denial, disaffirmation, disallowance, disapprobation, disapproval, disavowal, disavowment, discard, disclaimer, discontinuance, disinheritance, dismissal, disownment, elimination, exclusion, forswearing, giving up, negation, omission, proscription, rebuff, recantation, refusal, *reiectio,* rejection, relinquishment, renouncement, reprobation, *repudiatio,* repudiation, repulsion, resignation, retraction, sacrifice, shutting out, spurning, swearing off, veto, waiver, withdrawal, yielding
ASSOCIATED CONCEPTS: renunciation of a contract, renunciation of a will

REOPEN, ***verb*** *aperire,* begin again, carry on, come back to, commence again, continue, *iterum,* open again, proceed, recommence, reembark, reestablish, reinstitute, renew, repeat, resume, return to, revive, start over
ASSOCIATED CONCEPTS: motion to reopen, reopen a case, reopen a hearing, reopen an investigation

REORGANIZATION, ***noun*** alteration, amelioration, betterment, change, conversion, improvement, melioration, overhauling, readjustment, rearrangement, rebuilding, recasting, reconstitution, reconstruction, rectification, reestablishment, reformation, rehabilitation, remaking, remodeling, restoration, restructuring, revising, revision, transformation
ASSOCIATED CONCEPTS: bankruptcy, corporate reorganization

REPAIR, ***noun*** adjustment, alteration, amelioration, betterment, correction, cure, fixing, improvement, melioration, mending, overhaul, patching, reanimation, reassembling, reconditioning, reconstruction, recovery, rectification, redintegration, refitting, reform, reformation, rehabilitation, remedy, remodeling, renewal, renovation, reorganization, reparation, restoration, resurrection, retouching, revival

ASSOCIATED CONCEPTS: duty to repair, failure to keep in repair, opportunity to make repairs

REPAIR, *verb* adjust, ameliorate, amend, brush up, condition, correct, cure, darn, fix, improve, make better, make good, make improvements, meliorate, mend, overhaul, patch, piece, put in order, put into shape, put right, readjust, rebuild, recondition, reconstruct, rectify, redress, *reficere,* refit, reform, refresh, refurbish, rehabilitate, rejuvenate, remedy, render better, renew, *reparare,* reshape, restore, resurrect, retouch, retread, revamp, revive, right, salvage, service, tinker, touch up, vamp
ASSOCIATED CONCEPTS: duty to repair

REPARATION *(Act of keeping in repair),* ***noun*** correction, instauration, overhaul, readjustment, rebuilding, reconditioning, reconstruction, rectification, refurbishment, rehabilitation, rejuvenation, remedy, renewal, renovation, repair, replacement, restoral, restoration, revamping, salvage, service

REPARATION *(Indemnification),* ***noun*** adjustment, amends, atonement, compensation, conscience money, correction, damages, expiation, financial remuneration, indemnity, payment, peace offering, penalty, quittance, recompense, redress, reimbursement, relief, remedy, repayment, restitution, restoration, return, *satisfactio,* satisfaction, settlement, wergild

REPAY, *verb* avenge, compensate, get even, give back, give in exchange, indemnify, make amends, make payment, make reparation, make requital, make restitution, pay back, pay in kind, punish, rebate, reciprocate, recompense, *reddere,* refund, reimburse, remunerate, replace, *reponere,* requite, restore, retaliate, return, revenge, reward, satisfy, square accounts

REPEAL, *verb* abolish, *abrogare,* abrogate, annul, avoid, cancel, countermand, declare null and void, delete, eliminate, formally withdraw, invalidate, make void, negate, nullify, obliterate, officially withdraw, override, overrule, quash, recall, render invalid, rescind, *rescindere,* retract, reverse, revoke, set aside, vacate, void, withdraw
ASSOCIATED CONCEPTS: repeal a bylaw, repeal a law, repeal a statute, repeal by implication
FOREIGN PHRASES: ***Leges posteriores priores contrarias abrogant.*** Subsequent laws repeal prior laws that are repugnant to them. ***Jura eodem modo destituuntur quo constituuntur.*** Laws are abrogated by the same means by which they are enacted.

REPEAT *(Do again),* ***verb*** backslide, copy, do over, duplicate, give an encore, imitate, ingeminate, *iterare,* persist, reconstruct, re-create, recur, redo, reduplicate, reenact, regenerate, reinstitute, relapse, remake, renew, replicate, reproduce, resume, retrace, return, revert

REPEAT *(State again),* ***verb*** chant, drum, dwell on, echo, emphasize, harp on, insist upon, iterate, paraphrase, parrot, quote, read back, reaffirm, reassert, recapitulate, recite, recount, rehash, reiterate, relate, rephrase, report, restate, retell, review, reword, run over, say again, say over, sum up, summarize, tell again, tell over, utter again

REPEATED, *adjective* common, commonplace, consuetudinal, consuetudinary, copied, customary, done again, done over, duplicated, echoed, everyday, frequent, habitual, imitated, incessant, monotonous, multiple, paraphrased, periodic, persistent, recited, recurrent, recurring, redone, redoubled, redundant, reduplicated, reduplicative, regular, rehearsed, reiterated, renewed, repetitional, repetitionary, repetitious, repetitive, reproduced, restated, retold, reuttered, reworded, said again, standard, stock, successive, twice-told, uniform
ASSOCIATED CONCEPTS: repeated wrongdoing

REPEL *(Disgust),* ***verb*** alienate, appall, be unpalatable, cause aversion, cause dislike, displease, excite dislike, fill with loathing, frighten, give offense, grate, horrify, incense, irritate, make one shudder, make one sick, make unwelcome, nauseate, offend, repulse, revolt, scandalize, shock, sicken, vex

REPEL *(Drive back),* ***verb*** avert, beat back, cast aside, challenge, chase away, check, checkmate, confound, confront, deflect, dispel, disperse, divert, drive away, drive back, fend off, fight off, foil, forbid, force back, forestall, frustrate, *fugare,* keep at bay, make a stand against, oppose, parry, prevent, prohibit, push back, put to flight, rebuff, renounce, *repellere,* repercuss, repudiate, repulse, resist, retrude, rout, scatter, spurn, stave off, strive against, throw off, thrust back, traverse, ward off, withstand

REPENT, *verb* apologize, atone for, be conscience striken, be penitent, be sorry for, beg pardon, bemoan, bewail, cry over, deplore, do penance, expiate, feel contrition, feel regret, feel remorse, grieve, have a guilty conscience, have qualms, humble oneself, lament, make amends, make up for, mourn, pay the penalty, plead guilty, recant, redress, reform, regret, remember with sorrow, rue, show regret for, think better of, weep over

REPENTANT, *adjective* apologetic, atoning, compunctious, confessing, conscience-smitten, conscience-stricken, contrite, full of regrets, humble, lamenting, *paenitens,* penitent, penitential, reclaimed, reformative, reformatory, reformed, regretful, regretting, remorseful, rueful, self-abasing, self-accusatory, self-condemnatory, self-convicted, self-denouncing, self-reproachful, self-reproving, sorrowful, sorry, weeping

REPERCUSSION, *noun* backfire, backlash, blast, counteraction, echo, explosion, force, impact, reaction, rebound, reciprocal action, recoil, reflection, reflex, report, response, retroaction, reverberation, ricochet, shock

REPETITION, *noun* consistency, copy, duplication, iteration, over and over, recitation, redo, reduplication, rehearsal, reiteration, renewal, repeating, replay, reprise, reproduction, rerun, with frequency

REPETITIOUS, *adjective* duplicative, echoic, echoing, harping, incessant, invariable, monotonous, pleonastic, pleonastical, recapitulatory, recurrent, recurring, redundant, reduplicative, reechoed, reiterant, reiterative, repeated, repeating, repetitional, repetitionary, repetitive, stale, tedious

REPLACE, *verb* act for, alternate, change, commute, compensate, cover for, depute, deputize, duplicate, exchange, fill in for, interchange, make amends, pay back, put back, refund, reimburse, reinstall, reinstate, repay, *reponere,* represent, restitute, stand for, subrogate, *substituere,* substitute, succeed, supersede, supplant, supply an equivalent, surrogate, swap, switch, symbolize, understudy, vary

REPLACEMENT, *noun* alternate, alternative, change, commutation, compensation, counterfeit, delegate, deputy,

dislocation, displacement, envoy, equivalent, exchange, fill in, interchange, makeshift, proxy, reclamation, reconstitution, reconstruction, recovery, refund, reinstatement, relief, removal, renewal, renovation, reorganization, reparation, representative, reproduction, restitution, restoration, second, secondary, shift, stand in, subrogation, substitute, substitution, successor, supersedure, supersession, supplantation, supplanter, surrogate, surrogation, swap, switch, temporary expedient, transfer, transposition, understudy
ASSOCIATED CONCEPTS: replacement cost

REPLENISH, ***verb*** build up, complete, contribute, deposit, enrich, fill, fill in, fill up, furnish, give, make complete, make full, make up, make up a lack, make whole, present, provender, provide, provision, purvey, recharge, refill, refresh, refuel, reload, renew, replace, *replere,* restock, resupply, saturate, stock, store, supplement, *supplere,* supply, supply deficiencies

REPLETE, ***adjective*** abounding, abundant, affluent, ample, bounteous, bountiful, brimfull, brimming, chockfull, closely packed, cloyed, complete, completely full, copious, crammed, crammed solid, filled, filled to repletion, flush, fraught, full, fully supplied, gorged, jampacked, jammed, laden, lavish, loaded, luxurious, overflowing, packed, plenitudinous, plenteous, plentiful, plethoric, pregnant, profuse, refilled, replenished, rife, satiated, satisfied, saturated, stocked, stuffed, surfeited, teeming, well-provided, well-stocked

REPLEVIN, ***noun*** acquisition, action to recover personal chattels, action to recover personal property, action to regain possessions, action to regain property, action to revert ownership, articles of commerce, assets, backslide, belongings, chattels, delivery back, reclamation, recoupment, recovery, recovery of property, redelivery, redemption, repossession, retaking, retrieval, salvage, writ of replevin
ASSOCIATED CONCEPTS: bailment, conversion, detinue, *ex delicto, in specie,* personal replevin, replenish bond, replevin bond, trover

REPLICATE, ***verb*** clone, copy, copycat, counterfeit, duplicate, fake, forge, imitate, mimic, reconstruct, re-create, redo, reduplicate, reiterate, remake, render, renew, repeat, reprise, reproduce, simulate

REPLY, ***noun*** answer, counterstatement, reaction, rebuttal, reciprocation, rejoinder, remonstrance, replication, response, *responsio, responsum,* retort, return, surrebuttal
ASSOCIATED CONCEPTS: reply brief, sham reply, surreply
FOREIGN PHRASES: ***Ambigua responsio contra proferentem est accipienda.*** An ambiguous answer is to be taken against him who offers it.

REPLY, ***verb*** acknowledge, answer, come back at, confute, counter, make rejoinder, parry, react, rebut, refute, rejoin, respond, *respondere,* retort, return, riposte, surrebut, surrejoin
ASSOCIATED CONCEPTS: reply to a counterclaim, reply to new matter contained in an answer, surreply

REPORT *(Detailed account),* ***noun*** account, address, article, brief, broadcast, bulletin, chronicle, communication, criticism, description, digest, disclosure, dissemination, exposition, history, information, intelligence, manifesto, message, minute, narration, news, news story, note, notice, notification, proclamation, propagation, recapitulation, recital, recitation, record, recounting, *relatio,* relation, release, *renuntiatio,* revelation, review, saga, specification, statement, summary, talk, tidings, ventilation
ASSOCIATED CONCEPTS: accident report, grand jury report

REPORT *(Rumor),* ***noun*** bruit, *fama,* gossip, grapevine, hearsay, hint, intimation, scuttlebutt, talk, tattle, unconfirmed report, unverified news, whisper

REPORT *(Disclose),* ***verb*** acquaint, *adferre,* advise, air, announce, annunciate, apprise, broadcast, bruit, circulate publicly, communicate, declare, deliver information, describe, detail, disseminate, divulgate, divulge, enlighten, expose, expound, express, give an account of, give the facts, herald, impart, inform, make an announcement, make known, mention, notify, outline, proclaim, promulgate, publish, recite, recount, *referre, renuntiare,* report, reveal, set forth, speak about, specify, state, tell, testify to, unmask, voice, write up

REPORT *(Present oneself),* ***verb*** announce one's presence, answer, answer a summons, appear, appear for duty, arrive, attend, be at hand, be in attendance, check in, come, *comparere,* fulfill an engagement, meet, put in an appearance, reveal oneself, show oneself

REPOSE *(Place),* ***verb*** deposit, establish, fix, invest, lodge, plant, put, reposit, set, settle, store, vest in

REPOSE *(Rest),* ***verb*** be calm, be serene, be tranquil, compose oneself, lie down, recline, relax, rest, settle, sleep, slumber

REPOSITORY, ***noun*** arsenal, bank, bursary, cache, chest, coffer, conservatory, container, depository, depot, garner, promptuary, receptacle, *receptaculum,* reservatory, reservoir, safe, storehouse, storeroom, treasurehouse, treasury, warehouse

REPOSSESS, ***verb*** capture, foreclose, obtain again, reacquire, recall, recapture, reclaim, recoup, recover, redeem, regain, replevy, retrieve, secure, seize, take back, take possession of
ASSOCIATED CONCEPTS: attachment, security interest

REPREHEND, ***verb*** accuse, admonish, animadvert, berate, betongue, blame, bring to book, call down, call to account, cast blame upon, castigate, censure, charge, chastise, chide, condemn, correct, criticize, decry, denounce, disapprove, dress down, expostulate, exprobate, find fault with, impeach, impugn, increpate, lash, lay blame upon, lecture, object, objurgate, protest, punish, rate, rebuke, recriminate, *reprehendere,* reprimand, reproach, reprobate, reprove, run down, scold, slate, take exception, take to task, trounce, upbraid, voice disapproval

REPREHENSIBLE, ***adjective*** accusable, bad, base, blamable, blameful, blameworthy, censurable, chargeable, condemnable, convictable, criminal, *culpa dignus,* culpable, delinquent, deserving censure, deserving reproof, discreditable, disgraceful, disgusting, dishonorable, disreputable, evil, exceptionable, flagitious, flagrant, foul, guilty, hateful, heinous, horrendous, ignoble, illaudable, immoral, impeachable, incorrigible, indefensible, inexcusable, inexpiable, infamous, iniquitous, monstrous, naughty, nefarious, objectionable, obnoxious, odious, offensive, open to criticism, opprobrious, peccable, peccant, rebukable, recreant, *reprehendendus,* reproachable, reprobate, reprovable, shameful, shocking, sinful, uncommendable, unjustifiable, unpardonable, unprincipled, unrighteous, unworthy, vicious, villainous, wicked, wrong

REPRESENT *(Portray),* ***verb*** adumbrate, characterize, connote, delineate, denote, depict, designate, evoke, exemplify, *exprimere,* illustrate, image, indicate, mean, outline, picture, show, signify, stand for, symbolize, typify

REPRESENT *(Substitute),* ***verb*** act, act as broker, act as delegate, act for, act in place of, act on behalf of, act vicariously, appear for, be ambassador for, be an agent for, be attorney for, be deputy for, be proxy for, be spokesman for, factor, replace, speak for, stand in the place of, take the part of
ASSOCIATED CONCEPTS: agency, represent a client's interests, represent a defendant, represent a principal

REPRESENTATION *(Action of acting for others),* ***noun*** acting as attorney for, advocacy, agency, agentship, body of delegates, body of deputies, deputation, rendering legal advice, rendering legal assistance, speaking for another, substitution, supplying another's place

REPRESENTATION *(Statement),* ***noun*** account, assertion of facts, asseveration, declaration, depiction, description, *effigies,* explanation, illustration, *imago,* indication, narration, narrative, portraiture, portrayal, presentation, relation, report, setting forth
ASSOCIATED CONCEPTS: false representation, material representation, misrepresentation, public representation

REPRESENTATIVE, ***adjective*** acting, adumbrative, agential, characteristic, connotative, delegated, denotative, depictive, deputative, deputed, distinctive, emblematic, exemplary, faithful, figurative, graphic, graphical, illustrational, illustrative, indicative, indicatory, representational, sample, standard, symbolic, symbolical, typical, typifying
ASSOCIATED CONCEPTS: representative action, representative capacity, representative suit

REPRESENTATIVE *(Example),* ***noun*** exemplar, model, paragon, sample, specimen, symbol, typical example, typical instance

REPRESENTATIVE *(Proxy),* ***noun*** agent, barrister, broker, counsel, delegate, deputy, emissary, envoy, go-between, lawyer, messenger, middle man, solicitor, spokesman, substitute, substitution, trustee, *vicarius*
ASSOCIATED CONCEPTS: lawful representative, legal representative

REPRESS, ***verb*** allay, bottle up, bridle, censor, check, choke, *comprimere,* control, cork, crush, curb, damp, dampen, deaden, domineer, dull, enchain, gag, hinder, hobble, hold back, hold in, hush, inhibit, keep down, keep in, keep in check, keep under control, kill, leash, limit, master, muffle, mute, muzzle, *opprimere,* overbear, overcome, overmaster, overpower, pen up, press back, prohibit, put down, quell, quench, quiet, reduce to subjection, rein in, restrain, restrict, seal up, shackle, silence, smother, squash, stay, stifle, still, strangle, subdue, subjugate, suffocate, suppress, trammel, vanquish, withhold

REPRIEVE, ***noun*** day of grace, deferment, delay, delay in execution, delay in punishment, dispensation, interval of ease, moratorium, pause, postponement, postponement of penalty, quittance, respite, respite from impending punishment, stay, stay of execution, stop, suspension of execution, suspension of punishment, temporary escape, temporary relief, temporary suspension of the execution of a sentence, withdrawal of a sentence
ASSOCIATED CONCEPTS: executive reprieve, judicial reprieve, pardon

REPRIMAND, ***noun*** admonishment, admonition, animadversion, blame, castigation, censure, chiding, condemnation, correction, criticism, denunciation, derogation, disapprobation, disapproval, displeasure, dispraise, dressing down, exception, exprobration, improbation, increpation, jobation, lecture, objection, objurgation, rating, rebuke, remonstrance, *reprehensio,* reprehension, reproach, reprobation, reproof, reproval, revilement, scolding, sermon, sharp censure, sharp words, stricture, trimming, upbraiding, *vituperatio,* warning
ASSOCIATED CONCEPTS: reprimand issued by the grievance committee of the bar association

REPRIMAND, ***verb*** accuse, admonish, animadvert on, asperse, berate, blame, call to account, call to task, castigate, censure formally, chastise, chide, condemn, correct, criminate, decry, denounce, deprecate, disapprove, discommend, disparage, dispraise, dress down, execrate, exprobrate, find fault, flay, fulminate against, impeach, impugn, inveigh against, lash, lecture, objurgate, rail at, rant, rebuke, recriminate, remonstrate, reprehend, *reprehendere,* reproach, reprobate, reprove, revile, run down, scold, thunder against, trounce, upbraid, vilify, vilipend, *vituperare,* vituperate, warn
ASSOCIATED CONCEPTS: reprimand by the grievance committee

REPRISAL, ***noun*** avengement, counterattack, counterblast, counterplot, counterstroke, desert, disciplinary action, discipline, due, due punishment, getting even, measure for measure, nemesis, penalty, punishment, punition, punitive action, reaction, reciprocation, repayment, requital, retaliation, retribution, retributive justice, return, revenge, revengefulness, talion, vendetta, vengeance, vengefulness, vindictiveness

REPROACH, ***noun*** accusation, animadversion, blame, castigation, censure, chastisement, chiding, complaint, condemnation, contempt, *contumelia,* contumely, correction, degradation, denouncement, denunciation, derogation, disapprobation, disapproval, discredit, disgrace, dishonor, disparagement, disrepute, dressing down, exprobration, *exprobratio,* impeachment, increpation, incrimination, inculpation, indignity, jobation, objection, objurgation, obloquy, opprobrium, *probrum,* rating, rebuke, reprehension, reprimand, reprobation, reproof, revilement, scolding, shame, sharp criticism, slur, stigma, taint, tarnish, upbraiding, vilification

REPROACH, ***verb*** abuse, accuse, admonish, animadvert, asperse, berate, blame, brand, call to account, castigate, censure, chide, complain, condemn, criminate, criticize, decry, defame, denounce, denunciate, deprecate, disapprove, discredit, disgrace, dishonor, disparage, excoriate, express displeasure, exprobrate, find fault with, flay, frown upon, increpate, *increpitare,* incriminate, inculpate, *incusare,* inveigh against, lecture, malign, objurgate, protest against, put to shame, rail at, rant at, rebuke, reprehend, reprimand, reprobate, reprove, revile, scold, slate, speak ill of, take to task, tax, tongue lash, traduce, upbraid, vilify, vilipend, vituperate

REPROBATE, ***adjective*** accusable, bad, base, blameworthy, corrupt, criminal, culpable, degenerate, depraved, disgusting, disreputable, dissolute, evil-minded, facinorous, felonious, flagitious, flagrant, hardened, heinous, immoral, incorrigible, infamous, iniquitous, irreclaimable, irredeemable, irreverent, knavish, lost, morally abandoned, naughty, nefarious, obdurate, peccant, *perditus,* profligate, *profligatus,* rascally, recidivous, recreant, roguish, shameless, sinful, unconscionable, unprincipled, unregenerate, unrighteous, vicious, vile, vitiated, wicked, worthless

REPRODUCE, *verb* beget, breed, bring forth, conceive, copy, create, do again, double, duplicate, engender, father, fecundate, fructify, generate, give birth to, imitate, make again, manifold, mirror, multiply, parallel, portray, procreate, progenerate, proliferate, propagate, rebuild, reconstitute, reconstruct, re-create, redo, reduplicate, refashion, reform, *regignere,* remake, renew, repeat, replicate, sire, spawn
ASSOCIATED CONCEPTS: copyright, reproduce a record on appeal

REPROOF, *noun* admonishment, admonition, animadversion, aspersion, berating, blame, castigation, censure, charge, condemnation, contempt, criticism, denunciation, depreciation, derogation, diatribe, disapprobation, discipline, disparagement, execration, expostulation, exprobration, impeachment, objection, objurgation, obloquy, rebuff, rebuke, reprehension, reprimand, reproach, reprobation, reproval, revilement, scolding, upbraiding

REPUDIATE, *verb* abandon, abdicate, abjure, abnegate, abolish, abrogate, cancel, change sides, contradict, contravene, countermand, declare null and void, decline, default, demur, deny, disallow, disannul, disavow, disbar, discard, disclaim, dishonor, dissent, dissolve, exclude, forswear, negate, neglect, nullify, override, overrule, proscribe, protest, recant, refuse to accept, refuse to acknowledge, *reicere,* reject, renounce, repeal, *repudiare,* retract, reverse, revoke, set aside, spurn, withdraw
ASSOCIATED CONCEPTS: repudiate a cause of action, repudiate a contract

REPUDIATION, *noun* abjuration, abolition, abrogation, annulment, breach, cancellation, confutation, contradiction, counterorder, countermand, declination, defeasance, defection, denial, deposition, disaffirmation, disagreement, disallowance, disapproval, disavowal, disclaimer, disclamation, disproof, disproval, dissent, dissociation, exclusion, forswearing, negation, nonobservance, nullification, recantation, refusal, refutation, rejection, renouncement, renunciation, repeal, repellence, rescission, retractation, retraction, reversal, revocation, setting aside, veto, voidance, withdrawal
ASSOCIATED CONCEPTS: repudiation of a contract

REPUGNANCE, *noun* abhorrence, abomination, allergy, antipathy, aversion, disapproval, disfavor, disinclination, dislike, displeasure, distaste, execration, hate, hatred, horror, loathing, loss of appetite, nausea, repulsion, revulsion

REPUGNANT *(Exciting aversion),* ***adjective*** abhorrent, abominable, detestable, disagreeable, disgustful, disgusting, disliked, displeasing, distasteful, *diversus,* forbidding, fulsome, hateful, inedible, insufferable, loathsome, nauseating, noisome, objectionable, obnoxious, odious, offending, offensive, out of favor, painful, repellent, repelling, *repugnans,* repulsive, revolting, unacceptable, unappetizing, undesirable, unpalatable, unpleasant, unpopular, unsavory

REPUGNANT *(Incompatible),* ***adjective*** adverse, alien, antagonistic, at odds, at variance, clashing, conflicting, contradictory, contrary, different, disagreeing, discordant, hostile, inaccordant, incongruous, inconsistent, inharmonious, inimical, irreconcilable, jarring, opposed, opposing, unconformable
ASSOCIATED CONCEPTS: repugnant to the Constitution

REPULSE, *verb* beat back, beat off, chase, check, counteract, countervail, defeat, dispel, drive away, drive back, eschew, fend off, frustrate, gainsay, grapple with, hinder, impede, keep at bay, make a stand, obstruct, oppose, oppugn, overthrow, *propulsare,* push back, put to flight, rebuff, reject, repel, *repellere,* repercuss, repudiate, resist, retrude, rout, scorn, send away, shun, snub, spurn, stem, throw back, thwart, turn away, ward off, withstand

REPULSIVE, *adjective* abhorrent, abominable, appalling, arousing aversion, beastly, contemptible, despicable, detestable, dirty, disagreeable, disgusting, disliked, displeasing, distasteful, dreadful, execrable, fearful, feculent, filthy, *foedus,* forbidding, foul, frightful, ghastly, grim, grisly, gross, hateful, hideous, horrible, horrid, horrifying, insufferable, loathsome, misshapen, monstrous, nasty, nauseating, nauseous, noisome, noxious, objectionable, obnoxious, obscene, *odiosus,* odious, offensive, rank, repellent, repelling, repugnant, revolting, rotten, shocking, sickening, sloppy, squalid, ugly, unbearable, unclean, uninviting, unpalatable, unpleasant, unprepossessing, unsavory, unsightly, vile

REPUTABLE, *adjective* acclaimed, celebrated, conscientious, creditable, dependable, dignified, distinguished, eminent, esteemed, estimable, ethical, faithful, famed, held in esteem, held in good repute, high-principled, honest, hon*estus,* honorable, honored, illustrious, incorruptible, known, meritorious, moral, noble, notable, principled, prominent, reliable, renowned, respectable, respected, revered, reverenced, righteous, scrupulous, trustworthy, uncorrupt, unimpeachable, upright, venerated, virtuous, well-known, well thought of, worthy

REPUTATION, *noun* acclaim, celebration, celebrity, consequence, credit, distinction, eminence, esteem, estimation, *fama,* fame, famousness, glory, good name, illustriousness, importance, luster, mark, name, notability, note, notoriety, *opinio,* popular favor, position, position in society, precedence, preeminence, prestige, prominence, rank, regard, renown, report, repute, respect, respectability, standing, station, status
ASSOCIATED CONCEPTS: character witness, reputation evidence

REPUTED, *adjective* accepted by general opinion, accepted by public opinion, asserted, assumed, concluded, considered, declared, deduced, deemed, held out as, imagined to be, implied, inferred, insinuated, judged to be, known to be, maintained as, perceived as, presumed as, presupposed to be, proposed to be, propounded to be, purported, putative, regarded as, supposed, understood to be
ASSOCIATED CONCEPTS: reputed owner

REPUTEDLY, *adverb* according to general belief, according to reputation, allegedly, assumedly, assumptively, presumably, reportedly, rumored, seemingly, supposedly

REQUEST, *noun* appeal, application, asking, begging, behest, beseechment, bid, call, claim, demand, desideratum, entreaty, exaction, expressed desire, impetration, imploration, importunity, insistence, invitation, invocation, motion, obsecration, order, petition, plea, *postulatio,* postulation, prayer, *preces,* proposal, requirement, requisition, *rogatio,* solicitation, suggestion, supplication, wish

REQUEST, *verb* adjure, appeal, apply for, ask for, beckon, beg for, beseech, bid, cadge, call for, canvass, claim, clamor for, command, cry for, demand, desire, dun, enjoin, entreat, exact, impetrate, *implorare,* implore, importune, invite, make application, mendicate, nag, *obsecrare,* obtest, order, petition, petition for, plead for, pray, put in for, require, requisition, *rogare,* seek, send for, solicit, sue for, summon, supplicate, urge, want

REQUIRE *(Compel),* ***verb*** assess, call for, cause, coerce, command, constrain, decree, demand, dictate, direct, draft, drive, enact, enforce, enjoin, entail, exact, *exigere,* force, impose, insist on, issue a command, levy, make, necessitate, obligate, oblige, ordain, order, *poscere,* postulate, prescribe, requisition, subject, summon, tax
ASSOCIATED CONCEPTS: required by law

REQUIRE *(Need),* ***verb*** crave, demand, *desiderare,* desire, *egere,* fall short, feel the necessity for, have an insufficiency, lack, miss, necessitate, request, *requirere,* stand in need of, want

REQUIREMENT, *noun* adjuration, behest, bidding, call, claim, command, commandment, compulsion, conscription, constraint, decree, decretal, demand, dictate, direction, directive, edict, enforcement, enjoinment, essential, essential desideratum, exaction, exigency, extremity, fiat, imperative, imposition, indispensable item, injunction, mandate, matter of necessity, must, necessitation, necessity, need, obligation, obsession, onus, order, precondition, prerequisite, prescript, prescription, pressing concern, pressure, proviso, regulation, request, requisite, requisition, rescript, responsibility, ruling, specification, ukase, ultimatum, urgency, vital part, want, warrant
ASSOCIATED CONCEPTS: requirement contract

REQUISITE, *adjective* basic, binding, called for, compulsory, crying, demanded, entailed, essential, exigent, expedient, imperative, important, in demand, incumbent on, indispensable, ineluctable, inevasible, instant, mandatory, must, *necessarius,* necessary, necessitated, needed, needful, obligatory, postulated, prerequisite, pressing, required, requisitory, urgent, vital, wanted

REQUISITION, *noun* application, behest, bidding, call, claim, compulsory acquisition, demand, direction, exaction, forcible demand, formal request, indent, injunction, levy, mandate, necessitation, necessity, need, order, petition, *postulatio,* request, requirement, requisite, want

REQUITAL, *noun* acknowledgment, *compensare,* compensation, consideration, desert, emolument, guerdon, indemnification, indemnity, meed, pay, payment, quittance, recompense, redress, remuneration, reparation, repayment, reprisal, requitement, restitution, retaliation, return, reward, satisfaction

REQUITEMENT, *noun* compensation, consideration, indemnification, indemnity, payment, quittance, recompense, redress, remuneration, reparation, repayment, requital, restitution, restoration, satisfaction

RES IPSA LOQUITUR, *noun* automatic lack of due diligence, automatic negligence, automatic responsibility, breach of duty, certain dereliction, definite carelessness, doctrine of *res ipsa loquitur,* imprudence, irresponsibility, lack of attention, liability imposed for obvious responsibility, liability for sole and exclusive control, obvious and certain negligence, the thing speaks for itself
ASSOCIATED CONCEPTS: negligence

RES JUDICATA, *noun* accommodated, adjudication, adjusted, agreed, arranged, brought to termination, came to determination, concluded, decided, decision, decree, determination, judgment, negotiated, resolved

RESCIND, *verb* abolish, *abrogare,* abrogate, annul, call back, cancel, countermand, counterorder, cut off, cut short, declare null and void, disannul, discard, disestablish, dismiss, dissolve, do away with, end, erase, invalidate, negate, nullify, obliterate, override, overrule, quash, recall, recant, remove, render invalid, renege, renounce, repeal, repudiate, *rescindere,* retract, reverse, revoke, set aside, sweep aside, take back, vacate, void, wipe out, withdraw
ASSOCIATED CONCEPTS: rescind a contract, rescind an offer

RESCISION, *noun* abandonment, abjuration, abnegation, abolishment, abolition, abrogation, annulment, cancellation, change of mind, countermand, counterorder, defeasance, deletion, destruction, disannulment, disavowal, disclaimer, dissolution, eradication, invalidation, negation, nullification, overruling, overthrow, quashing, recall, recantation, renunciation, repeal, repudiation, rescindment, retraction, reversal, revocation, revokement, suspension, termination, vitiation, voidance, withdrawal
ASSOCIATED CONCEPTS: rescision and restriction

RESCUE, *verb* aid, deliver, disenthrall, disimprison, emancipate, *exsolvere,* extricate, free, free from confinement, free from danger, let escape, let out, *liberare,* liberate, manumit, preserve, ransom, recapture, reclaim, recover, redeem, release, retake, retrieve, safeguard, salvage, save, set free, set loose, take to safety, unbind, unchain, unfetter, unloose, unshackle, untrammel
ASSOCIATED CONCEPTS: Good Samaritan laws, rescue doctrine

RESEARCH, *noun* analysis, careful search, close inquiry, *eruditio,* examination, experimentation, exploration, fact-finding, indagation, inquest, inquiry, inquisition, inspection, investigation, observation, probe, pursuit, quest, questioning, reconnaissance, scrutiny, search, study, survey, testing program

RESEARCH, *verb* analyze, burrow, chase after, check on, delve into, dissect, examine, experiment, explore, go in quest of, hunt, indagate, inquire, inspect, investigate, look into, probe into, pry, pursue, pursue an inquiry, quest, read up on, scan, scrutinize, search, seek, sleuth, study, test, trace, track, unearth

RESEMBLANCE, *noun* affinity, agreement, alikeness, analogy, approximation, closeness, conformance, conformity, correspondence, counterpart, ditto, double, duplication, effigy, equality, fascimile, fellow, homogeneity, identicalness, identity, image, imitation, kinship, likeness, match, mate, mold, parallel, parity, reflection, replica, representation, reproduction, sameness, selfsameness, semblance, similarity, similitude, *similitudo,* type, uniformity

RESEMBLE, *verb* appear like, approximate, bear resemblance to, conform, copy, correspond, depict, double, duplicate, embolize, epitomize, equal, exemplify, imitate, impersonate, intend, match, mean, parallel, reflect, replicate, represent, reproduce, stand for, symbolize, typify

RESENT, ***verb*** be angry, be indignant, be insulted, be offended, be piqued, be provoked, be revengeful, be vengeful, be vexed, bear malice, bridle, bristle, chafe, dislike, express annoyance, express ill will, feel annoyance, feel displeasure, feel hurt, feel ill will, feel resentment, find intolerable, harbor a grudge, hate, *moleste ferre,* show indignation, take amiss, take exception to, take offense, take poorly, take umbrage, view with dissatisfaction

RESENTFUL, ***adjective*** acrimonious, angry, bitter, bristling, choleric, churlish, discontented, displeased, distrustful, embittered, envious, furious, galled, grouchy, grudging, grumpy, huffy, hurt, ill-disposed, implacable, in a huff, in high dudgeon, indignant, infuriated, *iracundus,* jealous, malevolent, malicious, malignant, miffed, mistrustful, moody, offended, outraged, pained, peevish, piqued, querulous, resentive, revengeful, sore, spiteful, splenetic, sulky, sullen, surly, suspicious, touchy, umbrageous, unforgiving, up in arms, vengeful, venomous, vindictive, waspish

RESENTMENT, ***noun*** acrimony, affront, anger, animosity, animus, antagonism, bile, bitterness, choler, dander, disaffection, discontent, displeasure, dissatisfaction, dudgeon, enmity, envy, fury, gall, grudge, hatred, huff, ill will, indignation, *ira,* ire, jealousy, malice, malignity, offense, pique, rankling, resentfulness, soreness, spite, spleen, stomachus, umbrage, vengefulness, venom, vindictiveness, wounded pride, wrath

RESERVATION *(Condition),* ***noun*** *exceptio,* exception, exemption, limitation, provision, proviso, qualification, requisite, restriction, *salvo,* saving clause, specification, stipulation
ASSOCIATED CONCEPTS: conditional contracts, reservation contained in acceptance, reservation contained in grant, reservation in deed, reservation in insurance policy

RESERVATION *(Engagement),* ***noun*** booking, preengagement, promise to set aside, registration, retaining, retainment, retention, saving, withholding
ASSOCIATED CONCEPTS: reservation of interest, reservation of life estate, reservation of rights, reservation of title
FOREIGN PHRASES: ***Quod sub certa forma concessum vel reservatum est non trahitur ad valorem vel compensationem.*** That which is granted or reserved under a certain form cannot be twisted into a valuation or compensation.

RESERVE, ***noun*** assets, cache, conservation, *copia,* depository, fund, means, provision, resource, resources, savings, stock, store, storehouse, supply
ASSOCIATED CONCEPTS: accumulated reserve, held in reserve, insurance reserve, legal reserve, minimum reserves, premium reserve, reserve funds, reserve valve, reserved powers

RESERVE, ***verb*** accumulate, amass, bank, bespeak, cache, create a fund, deposit, earmark, except, garner, hide, hoard, hold, hold back, keep, keep back, keep in reserve, keep on hand, lay away, maintain, preselect, preserve, put aside, *reponere,* retain, save, set apart, set aside, shelve, stock pile, store, store away, store up, withhold
ASSOCIATED CONCEPTS: reserve an interest, reserve one's rights

RESERVES, ***noun*** currency deposits, deposits in a bank, funds to meet the reserve requirements set, holdings of currency, means to ensure solvency requirement, monetary assets, money in the vault, protection against losses, savings of currency, vault cash
ASSOCIATED CONCEPTS: bank failures, posting of reserves, settling of reserves, solvency

RESERVOIR, ***noun*** cache, depository, fund, hoard, inventory, pool, resource, source, stock, stockpile, store

RESIDE, ***verb*** abide, be located, be quartered, be situated, become a citizen, bide, domicile, domiciliate, dwell, establish oneself, *habitare,* have an address, *incolere,* indwell, inhabit, *inhabitare,* live, live at, lodge, occupy, remain, settle, sojourn, squat, stay, take up abode, take up residence, tarry, tenant

RESIDENCE, ***noun*** abode, accommodations, address, billet, commorance, commorancy, domicile, domiciliation, *domicilium, domus,* dwelling, habitancy, habitat, habitation, home, housing, inhabitancy, inhabitation, living place, living quarters, lodgings, lodgment, place, place of residence, quarters, residency, sedes
ASSOCIATED CONCEPTS: domicile, legal residence, residency requirement

RESIDENT, ***noun*** addressee, boarder, burgess, denizen, dweller, habitant, *habitator,* indweller, inhabitant, inhabiter, inmate, lodger, native, occupant, occupier, oppidan, residentiary, resider, settler, sojourner, tenant, townsman, villager

RESIDENTIAL, ***adjective*** domestic, domiciliary, fit for habitation, home, household, inhabited, living, not commercial, not public, occupied, private
ASSOCIATED CONCEPTS: residential area, residential property, residential purposes, residential use

RESIDUAL, ***noun*** balance, excess, leftover, remainder, remains, residuary, residue, residuum, surplus

RESIDUARY, ***adjective*** excess, excessive, left over, outstanding, remaining, residual, resultant, spare, surplus, unspent
ASSOCIATED CONCEPTS: residuary bequest, residuary clause, residuary devise, residuary estate, residuary fund, residuary interest, residuary legacy, residuary legatee

RESIGN, ***verb*** abandon, abdicate, *abire,* abjure, capitulate, cease work, cede, *cedere,* demit, depart, *deponere,* desist from, disclaim, divest oneself of, drop out, forgo, forsake, give notice, give up, leave, quit, reject, relinquish, renounce, repudiate, retreat, stand aside, step down, surrender, tender one's resignation, vacate, withdraw, yield

RESIGNATION *(Passive acceptance),* ***noun*** acquiescence, *animus submissus,* capitulation, deference, docility, endurance, fatalism, forbearance, fortitude, lack of complaint, lack of resistance, longanimity, meekness, nonresistance, obedience, passiveness, passivity, patience, stoicism, submission, submissiveness, sufferance, surrender, tolerance, toleration, yeilding

RESIGNATION *(Relinquishment),* ***noun*** abandonment, *abdicatio,* abdication, abjuration, abjurement, cession, demission, departure, evacuation, forsaking, giving up, leaving, quitting, renouncement, renunciation, retirement, secession, surrender, termination, vacation, withdrawal, yielding
FOREIGN PHRASES: ***Resignatio est juris proprii spontanea refutatio.*** Resignation is a spontaneous relinquishment of one's own right.

RESIGNED, ***adjective*** adapted, adjusted, agreeable, biddable, defeatist, easily managed, enduring, forbearant, forbearing, long-suffering, manageable, meek, nonresistant, passive, patient, reconciled, resistless, stoic, stoical, submissive, surrendered, tame, tolerant, tractable, unassertive, uncomplaining, unrepining, unresisting, willing, yielding

RESILIENT, ***adjective*** able to endure, adaptable, adaptive, adjustable, bendable, bouncing, buoyant, durable, elastic, flexible, flexile, jaunty, malleable, *mollis,* pliable, pliant, recoiling, responsive, responsive to change, rubbery, sequacious, spongy, sprightly, springy, strong, tractable, wiry, yielding

RESIST *(Oppose),* ***verb*** assail, assault, bar, beat back, block, breast, check, combat, confront, contradict, contravene, counter, counteract, cross, defy, dissent, fight, hinder, impugn, make a stand against, obstruct, offer resistance, oppugn, parry, prevent, protest, rebel, rebuff, recalcitrate, refuse to yield, reluctate, repel, repulse, retaliate, rival, stem, stop, strike, strike back, strive against, thwart
FOREIGN PHRASES: ***Error qui non resistitur approbatur.*** An error which is not resisted or opposed is waived.

RESIST *(Withstand),* ***verb*** be immune, be strong, be unsusceptible, bear, bear up, challenge, continue, cope with, disregard, endure, fend off, hold off, hold out, hold up, last, maintain, persevere, persist, prevail against, refuse to submit, remain, stand, stand fast, stand firm, stand up to, stay, tolerate, weather
ASSOCIATED CONCEPTS: resisting arrest

RESISTANCE, ***noun*** antagonism, assault, attack, battle, blocking, check, combat, confrontation, contention, contrariety, contrariness, contravention, contumacy, counteraction, defiance, disobedience, fight, hindrance, immunity, imperviousness, insubordination, insurgence, insurrection, interference, mutiny, noncompliance, nonconformance, obstinacy, obstruction, oppugnance, oppugnation, protest, rebellion, rebuff, recalcitrance, recusancy, refusal, reluctance, renitence, repugnance, repulsion, revolt, revolution, sedition, stand, strife, strike, struggle, unalterableness, unsusceptibility, unwillingness, unyieldingness, uprising, withstanding

RESOLUTE, ***adjective*** adamant, bent, *constans,* constant, decided, determined, diligent, dogged, earnest, faithful, firm, *firmus,* fixed, *fortis,* immutable, indefatigable, indomitable, industrious, inexorable, inflexible, intent upon, intransigent, obdurate, obstinate, persevering, persistent, pertinacious, purposeful, relentless, resolved, sedulous, serious, set, settled, stanch, steadfast, steady, strong-willed, stubborn, tenacious, unalterable, unbending, unchanging, uncompromising, undaunted, undeviating, unfaltering, unflinching, unrelenting, unshaken, unswerving, untiring, unwavering, unyielding, vigorous, zealous

RESOLUTION *(Decision),* ***noun*** application, constancy, decretum, determination, earnestness, firmness, indefatigability, intention, obduracy, obstinacy, perseverance, persistence, purpose, resoluteness, resolve, *scitum, sententia,* spunk, staying power, steadfastness, steadiness, tenacity, will, will power, zealotry

RESOLUTION *(Formal statement),* ***noun*** declaration, deliverance, formal expression, plan, presentation, pronouncement, proposal, proposition, statement, written announcement

RESOLVE *(Decide),* ***verb*** arrive at a conclusion, arrive at a decision, ascertain, be firm, be settled in opinion, come to a determination, *constituere, decernere,* determine, devote oneself to, fix in purpose, make a choice, make a decision, make up one's mind, plan, propose, purpose, settle on by deliberate will, settle upon, take a stand, will

RESOLVE *(Solve),* ***verb*** clarify, clear up, decipher, disentangle, dispel misunderstanding, elucidate, enucleate, figure out, find a solution, find the answer, hit upon a solution, illuminate, interpret, make clear, make plain, provide the answer, remove misunderstanding, reveal, reveal the answer, shed light upon, throw light upon, understand, unravel, unscramble, untangle

RESOLVED, ***adjective*** absolutely set, bent, bound, certain, concluded, decided, decisive, determined, earnest, firm, inflexible, intent, intransigent, persistent, pertinacious, positive, purposeful, resolute, serious, set, single-minded, stead, stubborn, unfaltering, unrelenting, vehement, willful

RESORT, ***verb*** administer, adopt, apply, avail oneself of, bring into play, call forth, employ, enlist, exercise, fall back upon, have recourse, look to, make use of, practice, press into service, put to use, try, turn to for help, turn to for support, use, utilize

RESOUNDING, ***adjective*** absolute, booming, certain, clear, decided, definite, echoing, emphatic, explicit, forceful, incontestable, incontrovertible, intensive, loud, marked, overwhelming, pealing, positive, rebounding, repercussive, reverberant, reverberating, reverberatory, rich, ringing, sonorous, sounding, strong, thunderous, undisputed, vigorous

RESOURCE, ***noun*** accumulation, asset, available means, capital, contrivance, dependence, device, essential, estate, expedient, *facultates,* fund, income, instrument, material, means, property, provision, reserve, reserve fund, resort, revenue, source, stock, stock in trade, store, supply, support, tool, wealth, wherewithal

RESOURCEFUL, ***adjective*** able, able to meet situations, accomplished, adroit, apt, artful, bright, *callidus,* capable, clever, competent, conversant, crafty, creative, cunning, deft, dexterous, efficient, endowed, enterprising, experienced, facile, felicitous, fertile, gifted, habile, handy, imaginative, *ingeniosus,* ingenious, inventive, original, practiced, prepared, proficient, sagacious, sharp, shrewd, skillful, smart, *sollers,* talented, trained, venturesome, versatile

RESOURCES, ***noun*** capabilities, expedients, fortune, instruments, means, measures, method, mode, recourse, stock, stockpile, store, stratagem, substance, supplies, support, system, tools, wealth, worth

RESPECT, ***noun*** admiration, adoration, appreciation, approbation, approval, attention, awe, civility, commendation, consideration, courtesy, courtliness, credit, deference, devoirs, dignity, esteem, estimation, etiquette, favor, good manners, good will, homage, honor, humbleness, humility, idolization, laudation, note, obeisance, *observantia,* ovation, polite regard, politeness, praise, prestige, recognition, regard, repute, reverence, testimonial, tribute, veneration, worship, worth

RESPECTFULLY, ***adverb*** compliantly, courteously, decorously, deferentially, dutifully, humbly, obediently, politely,

regardfully, *reverenter,* reverently, submissively, *summisse,* unassumingly, *verecunde,* with all respect, with compliance, with deference, with due deference, with due respect, with the highest respect
ASSOCIATED CONCEPTS: respectfully submitted to the court

RESPECTIVELY, *adverb* apiece, each, each in turn, in turn, independently, individually, one at a time, one by one, separately, severally, singly

RESPITE *(Interval of rest),* ***noun*** abeyance, break, breathing spell, breathing time, cessation, halt, interim, interlude, intermediate time, intermission, interruption, lapse, letup, lull, pause, recess, relaxation, rest, spell, stay, stop, suspension, temporary stoppage, wait

RESPITE *(Reprieve),* ***noun*** acquittal, amnesty, clearance, deliverance, discharge, exemption, grace, immunity, pardon, release, stay of execution

RESPOND, *verb* acknowledge, answer, counterclaim, debate, discuss, exchange opinions, explain, give an answer, join issue, make a rejoinder, parry, plead, provide an answer, react, rebut, rejoin, reply, retort, return an answer

RESPONDEAT SUPERIOR, *noun* employer responsibility, employer responsibility for the acts of another, employer/employee responsibility, imposition of vicarious liability, master-servant rule, responsibility of a principal for the acts of an employee
ASSOCIATED CONCEPTS: agency relationship, best interests of employer, course of employment, general authority, master-servant rule, principal and agent, within the scope of employment

RESPONDENT, *noun* answerer, appellant, corespondent, defendant, party answering a summons or bill, replier, responder

RESPONSE, *noun* acknowledgment, answer, antiphon, countercharge, counterstatement, explanation, plea, reaction, rebuttal, rejoinder, replication, reply, respondence, responsal, retort, return, riposte, surrebutter, surrejoinder

RESPONSIBILITY *(Accountability),* ***noun*** accountableness, amenability, answerability, bounden duty, boundness, burden, chargeability, commitment, compulsion, culpability, duty, encumbrance, engagement, imperative duty, liability, obligation, obligatoriness, pledge, promise, *rationem rei,* subjection to, that which is owing
ASSOCIATED CONCEPTS: diminished responsibility

RESPONSIBILITY *(Conscience),* ***noun*** claims of conscience, compunction, conscientiousness, dependability, ethical judgment, faithfulness, feeling of obligation, incorruptibility, inviolability, inward monitor, moral consciousness, moral faculty, moral obligation, moral sense, morality, scruples, scrupulousness, sense of duty, sense of obligation, sense of right and wrong, stability, trustworthiness, unperfidiousness, untreacherousness, uprightness

RESPONSIBLE *(Dependable),* ***adjective*** accountable, answerable, assailable, at fault, blamable, blameworthy, chargeable, culpable, guilty, indebted, negligent, obligated, obliged, reckless
ASSOCIATED CONCEPTS: duty, responsible cause, responsible party

RESPONSIBLE *(Liable),* ***adjective*** accountable, answerable, dependable, dutiful, legally accountable, legally obligated, legitimate, liable, obligated, trustworthy

RESPONSIVE, *adjective* accessible, active, acute, admissive, alert, alive, answering, communicative, discerning, keen, perceptive, prudent, reacting, reactive, receptive, reciprocative, rejoining, replying, respondent, sensible, sensitive, sentient, sharp, susceptible
ASSOCIATED CONCEPTS: responsive answers, responsive pleading

REST *(Be supported by),* ***verb*** couch, lay, lean, lie, lounge, perch, prop, recline, squat

REST *(Cease from action),* ***verb*** abstain, be at ease, be peaceful, be quiet, be still, be tranquil, calm down, cease, come to a standstill, desist, discontinue, end, halt, idle, keep quiet, lounge, pause, recess, relax, repose, retire, settle, stand still, stay, stop, stop work, take a break, take time out, terminate

REST *(End a legal case),* ***verb*** cease to litigate, complete prosecution, conclude proceeding, end the introduction of evidence, end the presentation of evidence, finish litigation, submit the case, terminate a trial
ASSOCIATED CONCEPTS: rest a case

RESTATE, *verb* construe, copy, duplicate, echo, elucidate, explain, go over, go over the same ground, iterate, paraphrase, parrot, plagiarize, reaffirm, reassert, recapitulate, recite, recount, rehash, reiterate, repeat, rephrase, restate, retell, review, reword, run over, say over again, summarize, sum up, tautologize

RESTATEMENT, *noun* abridgment, abstract, brief, compendium, condensation, *conlectio,* conspectus, digest, *enumeratio,* epitome, explanation, going over, iteration, paraphrase, reaffirmation, reassertion, recapitulation, recital, recountal, recounting, rehash, reiteration, repetition, rephrasing, replay, retelling, review, rewording, summary, synopsis, translation

RESTITUTE, *verb* adjust, compensate, give back, honor a claim, indemnify, make amends, recompense, recoup, recuperate, redeem, redress, refund, reimburse, relinquish, remit, remunerate, repay, replace, restore, reward, settle

RESTITUTION, *noun* adjustment, amends, atonement, compensation, damages, emolument, expiation, giving back, indemnification, paying back, payment, quittance, rebate, reclamation, recompense, recoupment, recovery, reddition, redemption, redress, refund, reimbursement, reinstatement, remitter, remuneration, reparation, repayment, replacement, requital, requitement, restoration, retrieval, return, reversion, satisfaction, settlement
ASSOCIATED CONCEPTS: order of restitution, partial restitution, *quantum meruit,* writ of restitution
FOREIGN PHRASES: ***In restitutionibus benignissima interpretatio facienda est.*** The most favorable construction is to be adopted in restitutions.

RESTIVE, *adjective* averse, balking, balky, cantankerous, contumacious, crossgrained, crotchety, deaf to reason, demurring, difficult, discontented, disinclined, disobedient, exceptious, excitable, excited, fidgety, fractious, fretful, grumpy, headstrong, humorsome, ill at ease, impatient, incorrigible, inflexible, insubordinate, insurgent, intractable, intransigent, irreconcilable, lawless, loath, moody, mulish, mutinous, obdurate, obstinate, on edge, out of sorts, peevish, perverse, pervicacious, rebellious, recalcitrant, recusant, refractory, reluctant, renitent, resentful, resisting control, restiff, restless, revolutionary, seditious, skittish, splenetic, stickling, stubborn, sulky, sullen, unaccommodating, uncomplaisant, uncompliant, uncomplying, unconsenting, uncontrollable, uneasy, ungovernable, unmanageable, unquiet, unrestful, unruly, unsettled, unsubmissive, unwilling, unyielding, wayward, willful

RESTORE *(Renew),* ***verb*** ameliorate, amend, correct, cure, doctor up, energize, fix, heal, improve, make better, make whole, meliorate, mend, patch, patch up, put in order, put in repair, put right, reanimate, rearrange, rebuild, recondition, reconstitute, reconstruct, re-create, rectify, redintegrate, redo, refashion, refit, reform, refresh, regenerate, rehabilitate, reinvigorate, rejuvenate, remake, remedy, remodel, renovate, reorganize, repair, restitute, resuscitate, retouch, revive, revivify

RESTORE *(Return),* ***verb*** atone, bring back, give back, hand back, indemnify, make amends, make good, make reparation, make restitution, put back, recompense, recoup, *reddere,* redeem, redress, reestablish, *referre,* refund, reimburse, reinstall, reinstate, reinvest with, remit, render up, repay, replace, revest, satisfy, send back
ASSOCIATED CONCEPTS: restore to one's former position, restored to possession
FOREIGN PHRASES: ***Reddere, nil aliud est quam acceptum restituere seu reddere est quasi retro dare, et redditur dicitur a redeundo quia retro it.*** To render is nothing more than to restore that which has been received or to render is as it were to give back, and it is called "rendering" from "returning," because it goes back again.

RESTRAIN, ***verb*** arrest, bar, bind, blockade, bridle, call a halt, check, confine, constrain, contain, control, cramp, curb, curtail, debar, delimit, deprive of liberty, detain, deter, disallow, discountenance, enchain, enclose, enjoin, fasten, fetter, forbid, govern, hamper, handcuff, handicap, harness, hinder, hold, hold back, hold in check, hold in custody, immure, impound, imprison, incarcerate, inhibit, interdict, jail, keep, keep under control, keep within bounds, limit, lock up, manacle, moderate, obstruct, oppose, prevent, prohibit, proscribe, quell, repress, *reprimere,* restrict, *retinere,* shackle, stifle, stop, subdue, subjugate, suppress, take into custody, take prisoner, *tenere,* tie, trammel, vanquish, wall in, withhold
ASSOCIATED CONCEPTS: restraining order, restraining statute
FOREIGN PHRASES: ***Exempla illustrant non restrigunt legem.*** Examples illustrate but do not restrain the law.

RESTRAINT, ***noun*** arrest, ban, bar, barricade, blockade, bondage, brake, bridle, captivity, caution, censure, check, circumscription, confinement, constraint, containment, control, curb, custody, damper, deprivation of liberty, detention, determent, deterrence, deterrent, disallowance, discipline, dissuasion, durance, embargo, forbearance, forbiddance, guardianship, hamper, hindrance, holdback, impediment, *impedimentum,* imprisonment, incarceration, inhibition, injunction, interception, interference, limitation, *moderatio,* moderation, obstacle, obstruction, opposition, prevention, prohibition, proscription, repression, reserve, restriction, retardation, self-control, self-denial, servitude, shackle, slavery, stay, stop, stoppage, suppression, taboo, temperance, veto
ASSOCIATED CONCEPTS: combination in restraint of trade, conspiracy in restraint of trade, prior restraint, restraint on alienation

RESTRICT, ***verb*** astrict, bar, bind, bound, bridle, cage, censor, chain, check, circumscribe, *circumscribere,* cloister, *coercere,* confine, constrain, control, coop, cramp, curb, debar, define, delimit, delimitate, demarcate, diminish, disallow, enchain, encumber, entrammel, exclude, fetter, forbid, frustrate, hamper, handcuff, handicap, hedge in, hem in, hobble, hold back, immure, inhibit, interdict, keep within limits, limit, localize, manacle, modify, muzzle, narrow, obstruct, pen, pin down, pinion, preclude, prevent, prohibit, proscribe, put under restraint, qualify, reduce, repress, restrain, restringe, secure, shackle, shut out, specialize, stifle, stop, suppress, taboo, tether, tie up, trammel, veto, wall in
ASSOCIATED CONCEPTS: restricted allotment, restricted assets

RESTRICTED *(Confidential),* ***adjective*** close, confined, exclusive, intimate, inviolate, irrevealable, personal, private, privy, reserved, secret

RESTRICTED *(Limited),* ***adjective*** burdensome, conditional, confining, contingent, cumbrous, defining, definite, definitive, dependent, exact, exceptional, exclusive, hindering, impeditive, inhibitive, interdictive, limitative, local, narrow, onerous, partial, precise, prohibitive, prohibitory, proscriptive, provisional, qualified, qualifying, regional, repressive, restrictive, restringent, specific, suppressive
ASSOCIATED CONCEPTS: restricted covenant, restricted endorsement, restrictive condition

RESTRICTION, ***noun*** *angustiae,* bonds, boundary, bounds, check, circumscription, condition, confinement, constraint, constriction, containment, curb, demarcation, distinction, *finis,* impediment, interdiction, limitation, *modus,* obligation, prohibition, qualification, regulation, reservation, restraint
ASSOCIATED CONCEPTS: restriction on alienation

RESTRICTIVE, ***adjective*** circumscriptive, clannish, cliquish, conditional, contingent, defining, deterrent, exclusive, hindering, impeditive, inflexible, interdictive, interdictory, limitary, limitative, limiting, modificatory, modifying, narrow, preclusive, preventative, preventive, prohibitionary, prohibitive, prohibitory, proscriptive, provisional, provisory, qualifying, repressive, restraining, select, selective, stiff, straitlaced, suppressive
ASSOCIATED CONCEPTS: restrictive covenant, restrictive endorsement, restrictive interpretation, restrictive provisions, restrictive title

RESULT, ***noun*** aftermath, conclusion, consequence, *consequentia,* decision, denouement, determination, development, effect, end, eventuality, *exitus,* finding, *fructus,* fruit, fruition, harvest, judgment, outcome, outgrowth, output, product, resolution, resultant, termination, turnout, upshot, verdict, yield

RESULT, ***verb*** accrue, arise, be due to, be the effect, be the outcome, come forth, come from, conclude, *consequi,* derive from, develop, emanate, emerge, end, ensue, *evenire,* eventuate, *fieri,* flow, follow, issue, originate, proceed, proceed from, redound, rise, spring, terminate, turn out
ASSOCIATED CONCEPTS: causation, direct result, necessary result, probable result, proximate result, result in damages suffered

RESUME, ***verb*** advance, begin again, carry on, continue, follow, forge ahead, get a fresh start, go on, move ahead, proceed, progress, pursue, *recolere,* recommence, renew, *repetere,* return to, start afresh, start again, start forward again, take up again

RESUMPTION, *noun* continuance, fresh start, new beginning, recommencement, recrudescence, reentry, reinstatement, renewal, reopening, reprise, resurgence, resurrection, return to normal, revival

RESURGENCE, *noun* come back, fresh spurt, new energy, reanimation, reappearance, rebirth, recovery, recuperation, recurrence, reestablishment, regeneration, regenesis, rejuvenation, renaissance, renascence, renewal, restoration, resumption, resurgence, resurrection, resuscitation, reversion, revival, revivification

RESURRECT, *verb* bring back, bring to, call back, reanimate, rebuild, recall to life, recondition, regenerate, reincarnate, rejuvenate, rekindle, renew, reorganize, restore, resuscitate, revitalize, revive, revivify

RESUSCITATE, *verb* breath fresh life into, bring back to life, cure, improve, reanimate, re-create, recuperate, reestablish, refresh, regenerate, rehabilitate, reinvigorate, rekindle, remedy, renew, restore, restore to life, resurrect, revivify, renovate, revitalize, revive

RETAIL, *adjective* by the piece, commercial, engaged in commerce, marketing, mercantile, singly

RETAIN *(Employ),* ***verb*** book, commission, contract for, engage, enlist, give a job, hire, keep, keep in pay, maintain, put to work, recruit, reserve, secure

RETAIN *(Keep in possession),* ***verb*** bear in mind, call up, cause to be remembered, cling to, clutch, *conservare,* continue to hold, detain, grasp, have, hold, hold fast, hold in possession, impress upon the memory, keep, keep hold of, keep in mind, maintain, possess, preserve, put away, recall, recollect, remember, reserve, save, secure, sustain, *tenere,* withhold

RETAINER, *noun* *arrhabo,* compensation, employment fee, engaging fee, fee contingent on future legal services, fee paid to secure legal services, income, payment, professional fee, recompense, remuneration, retaining fee
ASSOCIATED CONCEPTS: attorney's retainer

RETALIATE, *verb* answer back, avenge, counter, exchange blows, get back, get even, give measure for measure, match, pay back, rebut, reciprocate, repay, repay in kind, requite, return, revenge, strike back, take retribution, take revenge, take vengeance, *ulcisci*

RETALIATION, *noun* amends, compensation, counterattack, counteroffensive, payback, punishment, reprisal, requital, retribution, settlement, vengeance, wrath

RETARD *(Delay),* ***verb*** check, countercheck, defer, detain, ease off, hamper, hinder, hold up, impede, inhibit, interfere, procrastinate, stall, stem

RETARD *(Obstruct),* ***verb*** arrest, bar, block, check, clog, condemn, constrict, control, cramp, curb, debar, diminish, disadvantage, discontinue, encumber, entrammel, hamper, hinder, hold up, impede, inhibit, intercept, interfere, interpose, interrupt, occlude, preclude, prevent, thwart, trammel, withstand

RETARD *(Slow up),* ***verb*** brake, check, crawl, dawdle, decelerate, hamper, hinder, inhibit, interfere, linger, move slowly, slow down

RETENTION, *noun* *conservatio,* constraint, control, custodianship, grasp, hold, holding action, holding power, keeping, memory, *possessio,* reservation, restraint, retainment, *retentio,* tenacity
ASSOCIATED CONCEPTS: retention of benefits

RETICENT, *adjective* cautious, concise, confidential, constrained, detached, distant, evasive, guarded, laconic, mute, noncommittal, recondite, remote, reserved, restrained, retiring, secretive, sparing of words, standoffish, succinct, taciturn, uncommunicative, unobtrusive, unresponsive, withdrawn

RETIRE *(Conclude a career),* ***verb*** abdicate, demit, drop out, give notice, give up office, give up work, leave, quit, relinquish, resign, stand aside, take leave, tender one's resignation, vacate

RETIRE *(Retreat),* ***verb*** abandon, *abire, concedere,* decamp, depart, discharge, fall back, go back, leave, part, recede, *recedere,* remove, retrocede, seclude oneself, separate oneself, shelve, take leave, turn in, vacate, withdraw

RETORT, *verb* answer, answer back, come back, counter, countercharge, counterclaim, make a rebuttal, parry, rebut, rejoin, replicate, reply, requite, respond, *respondere,* return, riposte, say in reply, snap back, surrebut, surrejoin

RETRACE, *verb* copy, go over again, recall, reexamine, regress, reminisce, repeat, return, revert, review, think back upon, trace back, turn back

RETRACT, *verb* abandon, abnegate, bolt, deny, disaffirm, disavow, disclaim, disown, forsake, forswear, gainsay, negate, relinquish, remove, renounce, repeal, repudiate, revoke, spurn, take back, withdraw

RETRACTION, *noun* abjuration, abolishment, annulment, cancellation, contradiction, countermand, counterorder, disannulment, disavowal, gainsaying, negation, nullification, palinode, recall, recantation, recision, renunciation, repeal, repudiation, rescindment, retractation, reversal, revocation, taking back, unsaying, voidance, withdrawal
ASSOCIATED CONCEPTS: retraction of erroneous or defamatory statements

RETREAT, *verb* abandon, back away, back out, backtrack, bolt, decamp, depart, desert, disengage, draw back, ebb, escape, evacuate, fall back, fall to the rear, flee, *fugere,* give way, go away, go back, leave, lose ground, make oneself scarce, move back, *pedem referre,* pull back, quit, recede, recoil, regrade, remove oneself, retire, retrocede, reverse, run away, rusticate, *se recipere,* seclude oneself, shrink, slip away, take flight, turn tail, vacate, withdraw

RETRENCH, *verb* abridge, be economical, be frugal, *circumcidere,* clip, confine, *contrahere,* curtail, cut, cut down, cut short, decrease, deduct, delete, diminish, economize, lessen, limit, lop, pare, pinch, practice economy, prune, reduce, reduce expenses, remove, shorten, subduct, subtract, *sumptus minuere*

RETRIBUTION, *noun* amends, atonement, avengement, compensation, counterstroke, desert, due, indemnification, justice, measure for measure, nemesis, payment, penalty, *poena,* punishment, punitive action, reciprocation, reparation, repayment, reprisal, requital, requitement, retaliation, retributive justice, return, revenge, reward, satisfaction, vengeance, vengefulness, vindictiveness

RETRIEVE, *verb* get back, reacquire, recapture, reclaim, recollect, recoup, recover, recruit, redeem, regain, repossess, repurchase, rescue, retake

RETROACTIVE, *adjective* affecting the past, beginning before, commencing before, effective before, having prior application, having prior effect, operational before, starting before, taking effect before
ASSOCIATED CONCEPTS: ex post facto, retroactive effect

RETROACTIVE APPLICATION, *noun* imposition of a statute retroactively, posthoc application of a law, retroactivity *in mitius,* statutory application after the fact

RETROCEDE *(Abate),* ***verb*** close, decline, decrease, diminish, drop, dwindle, ebb, fall back, recede, relent, retire, retreat, slacken, subside, taper, wane, weaken, withdraw, yield

RETROCEDE *(Cede back),* ***verb*** cast, cast off, cede off, depart with, give back, give off, regress, retrograde, retrogress, shed

RETROSPECT, *noun* afterthought, contemplation of the past, hindsight, looking back, memory, recall, recapitulation, recollection, reconsideration, reexamination, remembrance, rememoration, reminiscence, *respectus,* retentive memory, review, survey, thoughts of the past
ASSOCIATED CONCEPTS: ex post facto

RETRY, *verb* another trial, do once again, do over from the outset, mistrial, new trial, redo, repeat, replicate, represent, revise, start over, try once again

RETURN *(Go back),* ***verb*** backslide, come again, come back, double back, reappear, rebound, recidivate, *redire,* reenter, reestablish, relapse, resume, retrace one's steps, retreat, retrograde, reverse direction, revert, *reverti,* revisit

RETURN *(Refund),* ***verb*** compensate, give back, indemnify, make compensation, make good, make reparation, make restitution, pay back, *reddere,* reimburse, repay, restore, satisfy, settle

RETURN *(Respond),* ***verb*** acknowledge, answer, answer back, counter, countercharge, exchange, field questions, give an answer, interchange, make a rebuttal, make a rejoinder, make acknowledgment, react, rebut, reciprocate, recriminate, rejoin, reply, *respondere,* retaliate, retort, riposte, say in reply, surrebut, surrejoin

REVAMP, *verb* alter, change, fix, improve, make over, metapmorphose, modify, recast, redo, refashion, reform, regenerate, remake, remodel, repair, revamp, revise, revolutionize, rework, touch up, transfigure, transform, transmute, update, vary

REVEAL, *verb* acknowledge, admit, advise, affirm, announce, apprise, bare, blazon, blurt out, break the news, bring to light, bruit, circulate, communicate, concede, confess, confide, confirm, debunk, declare, describe, disabuse, disclose, display, disseminate, divulgate, divulge, enlighten, evince, *evulgare,* evulgate, explain, expose, give inside information, give out, grant, impart, indicate, inform, make known, make public, make publicly known, manifest, mention, notify, open, *patefacere,* promulgate, publish, set right, tell, uncloak, uncover, uncurtain, undeceive, unearth, unfold, unmask, unseal, unshroud, unveil, utter, vent, verify, voice
ASSOCIATED CONCEPTS: disclosure of grand jury secrets, disclosure of secret, scientific information

REVENGE, *noun* avengement, counterblast, counterstroke, desert, feud, implacability, nemesis, punishment, punitive action, quittance, reciprocation, repayment, reprisal, requital, retaliation, retaliatory punishment, retribution, retributive punishment, revengefulness, satisfaction, *ultio,* vendetta, vengeance, vengefulness, *vindicta,* vindictiveness

REVENUE, *noun* compensation, dividends, earnings, emolument, gain, hire, income, intake, interest, livelihood, pay, payment, perquisites, proceeds, profit, receipts, recompense, *reditus,* remuneration, return, reward, salary, *vectigal,* wages, yield
ASSOCIATED CONCEPTS: appropriation law, internal revenue, revenue bills, revenue law, revenue-producing income, revenue tax

REVERE, *verb* admire, adore, adulate, apotheosize, canonize, deify, delight in, dignify, done on, esteem, exalt, extol, glorify, honor, idealize, idolize, laud, lionize, love, magnify, praise, regard, respect, venerate, worship

REVERSAL, *noun* abolishment, abolition, about-face, abrogation, annulment, backslide, cancellation, change, change of mind, check, countermandment, counterorder, disavowal, invalidation, inversion, nonapproval, nullification, overriding, overruling, overthrowing, rebuff, rebuke, recantation, rejection, renouncement, renunciation, repeal, repudiation, rescission, retraction, reversion, revocation, revokement, tergiversation, turnabout, undoing, voidance, voiding
ASSOCIATED CONCEPTS: reversal of a lower court's decision

REVERSE, *verb* abrogate, alter, annul, backtrack, cancel, change, contradict, counteract, counterman, disapprove, do a 180 degree turnaround, do an about-face, interchange, invalidate, invert, negate, overturn, rebuke, recant, repeal, rescind, retract, revert, revoke, strike, strike down, switch, tergiversate, turn around, turn over, undo, upset, void

REVERSION *(Act of returning),* ***noun*** about-face, backslide, recidivism, regress, regression, relapse, retroaction, retrocession, retrogradation, retrogression, retroversion, return, reversal, reverse, reverting, throwback, turnabout, turnaround

REVERSION *(Remainder of an estate),* ***noun*** future interest, future possession, *hereditas,* remainder over, residue, right of future enjoyment, right of future possession, right of succession
ASSOCIATED CONCEPTS: equitable reversion, life estate, partial reversion, reversionary interest, right of reversion

REVERSION RIGHTS, *noun* automatic reversionary rights, retroaction, retroversion, reversal of rights, reversionary interest, reverting

REVERT, *verb* backslide, change back, lapse, recede, recoil, regress, retreat, retrograde, retrogress, retrovert, return, reverse, turn back

REVIEW *(Critical evaluation),* ***noun*** account, analysis, appraisal, comment, commentary, critical article, critical discussion, criticism, critique, editorial, essay, exposition, report
ASSOCIATED CONCEPTS: law review

REVIEW *(Official reexamination),* ***noun*** investigation, judicial reconsideration, recapitulation, reconsideration, reinquiry, scrutiny, second examination, study, survey
ASSOCIATED CONCEPTS: administrative review, judicial review, scope of review

REVIEW, ***verb*** abstract, analyze, brood over, check thoroughly, comment upon, *contemplari,* criticize, critique, deliberate, describe, digest, epitomize, examine, explain, go over, inspect, *inspicere,* interpret, investigate, look over, make corrections, make improvements, mull over, notice critically, overlook, recapitulate, recheck, reconsider, reexamine, rehearse, reiterate, remember, restate briefly, retell, retrace, revise, reword, run over, scrutinize, skim, study, sum up, summarize, survey, view retrospectively, weigh

REVILE, ***verb*** abuse, admonish, assail, berate, beset, blame, castigate, censure, chide, condemn, criticize, defame, demean, denigrate, denounce, disparage, impugn, lambaste, lecture, malign, reproach, scold

REVILEMENT, ***noun*** abuse, affront, animadversion, aspersion, berating, billingsgate, bitter words, castigation, censure, condemnation, contumely, criticism, cursing, denunciation, depreciation, detraction, diatribe, discommendation, disparagement, execration, exprobration, increpation, insult, invective, *maledictio,* malediction, objurgation, obloquy, opprobrium, philippic, reprehension, reproach, reprobation, reproof, stricture, tirade, traducement, upbraiding, verbal abuse, vilification, vituperation

REVISE, ***verb*** alter, amend, bring up to date, change, correct, develop, doctor, edit, examine, exchange, improve, modify, overhaul, polish, recast, reconsider, reconstruct, rectify, redact, reexamine, remold, *retractare,* revamp, review, rework, rewrite, touch up, work over
ASSOCIATED CONCEPTS: revise a statute

REVISION *(Corrected version),* ***noun*** corrected edition, current edition, *emendatio,* improved version, improvement, new edition, rescript, revised edition, rewrite, updated version

REVISION *(Process of correcting),* ***noun*** alteration, change, correcting, editing, elaboration, overhauling, rectification, refining, reform, removal of errors, restyling, review, revisal, rewriting
ASSOCIATED CONCEPTS: law revision commission, revision of a statute

REVITALIZE, ***verb*** freshen, make over, overhaul, recharge, recondition, re-create, redesign, redevelop, refresh, refurbish, regenerate, rejuvenate, renew, replenish, restore, resurrect, resuscitate, revise, revivify

REVIVAL, ***noun*** awakening, comeback, convalescence, freshening, improvement, invigoration, new version, palingenesis, phoenix, quickening, reanimation, reappearance, reawakening, rebirth, reclamation, recovery, recreation, recuperation, recurrence, redintegration, reestablishment, refreshment, regeneracy, regeneration, regenesis, reincarnation, rejuvenation, rejuvenescence, renaissance, renascence, renewal, reproduction, restoration, resumption, resurgence, resurrection, resuscitation, return, revivification, reviviscence, vivification
ASSOCIATED CONCEPTS: abatement and revival, revival of a cause of action

REVIVE, ***verb*** freshen, reanimate, reawaken, recharge, re-create, refresh, regenerate, rejuvenate, rekindle, renew, repair, restore, resurrect, resuscitate, revitalize, revivify, rewake
ASSOCIATED CONCEPTS: revive an action

REVOCABLE, ***adjective*** cancellable, changeable, erratic, inconstant, refundable, transformable, transitional, uncertain, unreliable, unsettled, unstable, varying, wavering

REVOCATION, ***noun*** abolishment, abolition, *abrogatio,* abrogation, annulment, cancellation, canceling, countermand, counterorder, defeasance, disavowal, disownment, invalidation, negation, nullification, recall, recantation, recission, renouncement, repeal, repudiation, rescindment, retractation, retraction, reversal, *revocatio,* revokement, revoking, vacatur, withdrawal
ASSOCIATED CONCEPTS: dependent relative revocation, express revocation, implied revocation, power of revocation, presumption of revocation, revocation of a contract, revocation of a license, revocation of a will
FOREIGN PHRASES: ***Non refert verbis an factis fit revocatio.*** It matters not whether a revocation is made by words or by acts. ***Quod inconsulto fecimus, consultius revocemus.*** That which we have done without due consideration, we should revoke upon further consideration.

REVOKE, ***verb*** abjure, abolish, *abrogare,* abrogate, annul, cancel, countermand, counterorder, declare null and void, disannul, discard, disclaim, dismiss, dissolve, expunge, invalidate, make void, negate, nullify, override, prohibit, quash, recall, recant, remove, renege, renounce, *renuntiare,* repeal, repudiate, rescind, *rescindere,* retract, reverse, revert, suppress, suspend, vacate, vitiate, void, wipe out, withdraw
ASSOCIATED CONCEPTS: dependent relative revocation, revoke a license, revoke a will

REVOLT, ***noun*** agitation, apostasy, change of sides, contrariety, counteraction, defection, *defectio,* defiance, desertion, disobedience, dissension, faithlessness, inconstancy, insubordination, insurgency, insurrection, *motus,* mutiny, noncompliance, opposition, outbreak, overthrow, overturn, political upheaval, rebellion, recalcitrance, resistance, revolution, rising, secession, *seditio,* sedition, strife, strike, subversion, tergiversation, *tumultus,* uprising

REVOLUTION, ***noun*** anarchy, *débâcle,* general uprising, insurrection, lawlessness, outbreak, overthrow, overthrow of authority, overturn of authority, overturn of government, political upheaval, public uprising, rebellion, resistance to government, revolt, sweeping change, tumult, turbulence, upheaval, uprising, violent change

REVULSION, ***noun*** abhorrence, abomination, allergy, antipathy, averseness, aversion, contempt, disapproval, dislike, displeasure, distaste, execration, hate, hatred, horror, loathing, nausea, odium, repugnance, repulsion

REWARD, ***noun*** acknowledgment, award, benefit, bonus, booty, bounty, compensation, consideration, donation, emolument, fee, gift, grant, gratuity, guerdon, honorarium, incentive, indemnification, indemnity, meed, pay, payment, perquisite, *praemium proponere,* premium, presentation, prize, purse, quittance, recognition, recompense, remembrance, remuneration, requital, requitement, return, solatium, tip, tribute

REWRITE, *verb* amend, bring up to date, change, copy, correct, edit, emend, improve, improve upon, make corrections, make improvements, modify, overhaul, recast, re-create, rectify, redraft, refine, reform, remold, revamp, revise, rework

RHETORIC *(Insincere language),* ***noun*** affectation, artificial eloquence, bombastic speech, declamation, euphuism, grandiloquence, grandiosity, inflated language, loftiness, magniloquence, pomposity, pompous speech, pompousness, pretension, pretentiousness

RHETORIC *(Skilled speech),* ***noun*** address, allocution, appeal, *ars dicendi,* art of composition, art of discourse, art of prose, command of words, compositional skill, delivery, diction, discourse, elocution, eloquence, exhortation, expression, flowery language, forensic oratory, language, oratory, parlance, phraseology, phrasing, public speaking, recitation, *rhetorica,* science of oratory, speech-making, wording

RICH *(Affluent),* ***adjective*** comfortable, moneyed, opulent, pecunious, prosperous, successful, wealthy, well-off, well provided for, well-to-do

RICH *(Plentiful),* ***adjective*** abundant, ample, bounteous, bountiful, copious, elaborate, eloquent, fecund, fertile, fruitful, full, generous, lavish, lush, luxuriant, magnificent, plenteous, prodigal, productive, profuse, prolific, replete, resounding, savory, strong, well-provided

RID, *verb* banish, clean, clear, clear out, deliver, disallow, disburden, discharge, disencumber, divest, eject, eliminate, emancipate, enfranchise, exit, expel, exterminate, extirpate, free, get rid of, leave, liberate, loose, loosen, manumit, release, relieve, relinquish, rescue, scour, snuff out, spring, terminate, unbind, unburden, uncage, unchain, unfetter

RIDER, *noun* accompaniment, addendum, additament, addition, additional clause, adjunct, affix, amendment, appendage, appendant, appendix, appurtenance, attachment, augmentation, complement, continuation, endorsement, extension, insertion, postscript, subjunction, subscript, supplement
ASSOCIATED CONCEPTS: codicil, rider to a contract

RIDICULE, *noun* buffoonery, burlesque, caricature, chaff, contempt, derision, derisiveness, disdain, disparagement, disrespect, game, gibe, jeer, lampoonery, ludicrous representation, mimicry, mockery, pasquinade, raillery, *ridiculum,* sarcasm, satire, scorn, scornful imitation, sneer, sniggering, sport, squib, taunt, travesty

RIFE, *adjective* abundant, accustomed, bristling, catholic, common, considerable, crowded, current, customary, dense, dominant, endless, epidemic, extensive, far-reaching, galore, general, manifold, many, multitudinous, numerous, pandemic, plenteous, plentiful, popular, populous, predominant, prevailing, prevalent, profuse, rampant, regnant, reigning, replete, swarming, teeming, thick, unending, universal, usual, well-supplied, widespread, worldwide

RIFT *(Disagreement),* ***noun*** argument, break, clash, contention, controversy, difference, disceptation, dispute, estrangement, fight, misunderstanding, parting, split, variance

RIFT *(Gap),* ***noun*** aperture, breach, break, chasm, chink, cleft, crack, cranny, crevice, disjunction, fault, fissure, fracture, gash, hiatus, interstice, opening, parting, rent, rima, rupture, scissure, separation, split

RIGHT *(Correct),* ***adjective*** aboveboard, accurate, equitable, ethical, fair, honest, honorable, in accordance with duty, in accordance with justice, in accordance with morality, in accordance with truth, legitimate, reasonable, righteous, rightful, scrupulous, truthful, unswerving, upright, upstanding, valid, veracious, virtuous

RIGHT *(Direct),* ***adjective*** absolute, exact, immediate, straight, straightaway, straightforward, undeviating, unswerving

RIGHT *(Suitable),* ***adjective*** accepted, admissible, allowable, appropriate, apt, conventional, customary, fit, fitting, orderly, perfect, proper, reasonable, recognized, satisfactory, seemly, suitable, valid, virtuous, well-done, well-performed, well-regulated

RIGHT *(Entitlement),* ***noun*** authority, authorization, due, fair claim, heritage, inalienable interest, *ius, iusta,* just claim, justification, legal claim, legal power, legal title, ownership, power, prerogative, privilege, sanction, stake, title, vested interest, warrant
ASSOCIATED CONCEPTS: absolute right, accrued rights, Bill of Rights, claim of right, color of right, constitutional right, contingent right, established right, exclusive right, future right, inchoate right, incorporeal right, inherent right, marital rights, material rights, mineral rights, natural rights, permissive right, preemptive right, preferential right, prescriptive right, prima facie right, proprietary right, prospective right, reciprocal rights, right of action, right of entry, right of privacy, right of redemption, right of way, right to bear arms, right to counsel, right to jury trial, right to vote, right-to-work laws, riparian rights, substantive right, vested rights
FOREIGN PHRASES: ***Assignatus utitur jure auctoris.*** An assignee is clothed with the right of his principal. ***Nul charter, nul vente, ne nul done vault perpetualment, si le donor n'est seise al temps de contracts de deux droits, sc. del droit de possession et del droit de propertie.*** No grant, no sale, no gift, is valid forever, unless the donor at the time of contract has two rights, namely, the right of possession and the right of property. ***Non videtur vim facere qui jure suo utitur et ordinaria actione experitur.*** He is not considered to use force who exercises his own right and proceeds by ordinary action. ***Nemo plus juris ad alienum transferre potest quam ipse habet.*** No one can transfer to another any greater right than he himself has. ***Cui jus est donandi, eidem et vendendi et concedendi jus est.*** He who has the right to give has also the right to sell and to grant. ***L'ou le ley done chose, la ceo done remedie a vener a ceo.*** Where the law gives a right, it gives a remedy to recover. ***Ubi jus, ibi remedium.*** Where there is a right, there is a remedy. ***Non debeo melioris conditionis esse, quam auctor meus a quo jus in me transit.*** I ought not to be in better condition than he to whose rights I succeed. ***Nemo potest plus juris ad alium transferre quam ipse habet.*** No one can transfer a greater right to another than he himself has. ***Jus publicum privatorum pactis mutari non potest.*** A public right cannot be changed by agreement of private persons. ***Nullus jus***

alienum forisfacere potest. No man can forfeit the right of another. ***Neminem laedit qui jure suo utitur.*** He who stands on his own rights injures no one. ***Cujus est instituere, ejus est abrogare.*** Whose right it is to institute anything, may also abrogate it. ***Qui jure suo utitur, nemini facit injuriam.*** One who exercises his legal rights, injures no one. ***Ignorantia juris sui non praejudicat juri.*** Ignorance of one's right does not prejudice the right. ***Jus triplex est,-propietatis, possessionis, et possibilitatis.*** Right is threefold—of property, of possession, and of possibility. ***Nullus videtur dolo facere qui suo jure utitur.*** No one is considered to have committed a wrong who exercises his legal rights. ***Cuilibet licet juri pro se introducto renunciare.*** Any one may wave the benefit of a legal right that exists only for his protection. ***Qui prior est tempore potior est jure.*** He who is first in time is first in right.

RIGHT *(Righteousness),* ***noun*** correctness, due, duty, equitableness, equity, evenhanded justice, excellence, fair treatment, fairness, good actions, good behavior, goodness, honor, integrity, justice, justness, merit, morality, morals, nobleness, principle, probity, propriety, rectitude, *rectus,* straight course, truth, uprightness, *verus,* virtue, worthiness
FOREIGN PHRASES: ***Fiat justitia, ruat coelum.*** Let right be done, though the heavens fall. ***Ipsae leges cupiunt ut jure regantur.*** The laws themselves are desirous of being governed by what is right. ***Jus et fraus nunquam cohabitant.*** Right and fraud never dwell together. ***Jus naturale est quod apud homines eandem habet potentiam.*** Natural right is that which has the same force among all mankind. ***Pacta privata juri publico derogare non possunt.*** Private compacts cannot derogate from public right. ***Jus est norma recti; et quicquid estcontra normam recti est injuria.*** Law is the rule of right; and whatever is contrary to the rule of right is an injury. ***Lex est norma recti.*** Law is the rule of right. ***Quid sit jus, et in quo consistit injuria, legis est definire.*** What constitutes right, and what injury, it is the business of the law to define. ***Jus ex injuria non oritur.*** A right does not arise from a wrong.

RIGHT OF RECOVERY, ***noun*** ability to recover, actionable claim, charge, ground to recovery, legitimate cause of action, means to compensate a party, means to compensate an aggrieved party, mechanism to compensate an injured party, right to recover

RIGHT TO CONTROL, ***noun*** authority, control, discretion, final determination, final say, force, power, prerogative, right to determine, right to determine one's course, right to settle issues

RIGHT TO COUNSEL, ***noun*** assistance of counsel, guaranty to be represented, right of representation, right to consult an attorney, right to legal assistance, Sixth Amendment

RIGHT TO DIE, ***noun*** choosing time of one's death, choosing to die, denial of life support, refusal of extraordinary means to prolong life, right to reject medical treatment to prolong life
Generally: choice to die, prerogative to die
ASSOCIATED CONCEPTS: living will

RIGHT TO LIFE, ***noun*** advocate, against abortion, antiabortion, diametrically opposed to abortion, in favor of life, in opposition to abortion, pro-life advocate
ASSOCIATED CONCEPTS: abortion, capital punishment, euthanasia, partial birth abortion

RIGHT TO PRIVACY, ***noun*** constitutional right to privacy, inalienable right to secretiveness, prerogative in favor of privacy, privilege in favor of privacy, right to privacy, right to solitude
ASSOCIATED CONCEPTS: civil liberties, genetic privacy, Internet privacy, medical privacy, political privacy, privacy from governmental interference

RIGHT TO REMAIN SILENT, ***noun*** Fifth Amendment, privilege against self-incrimination, protection against self-incrimination, right to refrain from testifying against oneself
ASSOCIATED CONCEPTS: Miranda warnings

RIGHTEOUS, ***adjective*** commendable, correct, creditable, decent, decorous, distinguished, esteemed, ethical, fair, guiltless, high-minded, honest, honorable, impartial, inoffensive, just, legitimate, noble, principled, proper, pure, respectable, right, right-minded, seemly, true, truthful, upright, virtuous

RIGHTFUL, ***adjective*** according to law, allowable, allowed, appropriate, authentic, authorized, becoming, befitting, chartered, constitutional, correct, deserved, due, enfranchised, equitable, fair, fitting, genuine, honest, inalienable, *iustus,* just, justifiable, lawful, legal, legalized, legitimate, licit, meet, merited, ordained, permitted, prescriptive, privileged, proper, real, reasonable, right, sanctioned, seemly, square, statutory, suitable, true, valid, warranted, within the law

RIGHT-MINDED, ***adjective*** angelic, correct, decent, decorous, ethical, fair, high-minded, honest, honorable, immaculate, impartial, incorrupt, incorruptible, just, law-abiding, legitimate, lily-white, meritorious, moral, proper, pure, respectable, right, righteous, scrupulous, seemly, straight, true, upright, virtuous

RIGID, ***adjective*** austere, dour, *durus,* exact, exacting, firm, firmly set, fixed, flinty, formal, hard, harsh, hidebound, indurate, indurated, indurative, inelastic, inexorable, inflexible, intractable, motionless, obdurate, obstinate, orthodox, precise, punctilious, puritanical, relentless, renitent, resistant, *rigidus,* rigorous, set, severe, *severus,* starched, starchy, static, steely, stern, stiff, stony, straitlaced, strict, stringent, stubborn, taut, tense, tough, unadaptable, unalterable, unbending, uncompromising, unconformable, undeviating, unmalleable, unmitigated, unmoving, unpliant, unrelaxed, unrelenting, unyielding, wooden

RIGOR, ***noun*** accuracy, asperity, austerity, care, carefulness, conscientiousness, discipline, *duritia,* exactitude, exactness, firmness, force, freedom from deviation, intensity, keenness, meticulousness, preciseness, precision, relentlessness, rigidity, rigidness, rigorousness, scrupulousness, *severitas,* sharpness, sternness, strictness, stringency, tenacity, uncompromisingness, unyieldingness

RIGOROUS, ***adjective*** arduous, backbreaking, burdensome, demanding, difficult, exacting, formidable, hard, heavy, inflexible, intense, intransigent, laborious, merciless, obdurate, onerous, rough, severe, strict, taxing, time-consuming, tough, trying, uncompromising

RIOT, ***noun*** affray, bedlam, brawl, breach of the peace, broil, commotion, confusion, disorder, disorderliness, disturbance, ferment, fracas, fray, furor, hubbub, insurgence, insurrection, lawlessness, melee, outbreak, outburst, pandemonium, rebellion, revolt, row, rumpus, shindy, tumult,

tumultus, turba, turmoil, unruliness, uprising, uproar, wild confusion
ASSOCIATED CONCEPTS: disturbing the peace, inciting a riot

RIPARIAN RIGHT, *noun* nonexclusive right to use water, reasonable use of water right, right to divert water, right to take water, right to use water, water right
ASSOCIATED CONCEPTS: common property right, usufructuary right

RIPE, *adjective* adult, advanced, brought to perfection, complete, consummate, filled out, finished, fit, full, full-blown, full-grown, fully developed, fully grown, grown, ideal, mature, *maturus,* mellow, perfect, prepared, prime, primed, ready, seasoned, *tempestivus,* usable, well-developed
ASSOCIATED CONCEPTS: ripe for adjudication

RIPOSTE, *noun* banter, comeback, counter, counterattack, defense, insult, put-down, reaction, rebuttal, refutation, rejoinder, repartee, replication, reply, response, retort, return, witticism

RISE *(Appreciation),* ***noun*** accession, acclivity, accretion, accrual, accumulation, addition, advance, advancement, amplification, appearance, appreciation, ascension, ascent, augmentation, boom, climb, derivation, elevation, enhancement, enlargement, expansion, extension, gain, grade, gradient, growth, inception, increment, inflation, hill, increase, lift, progress, progression, promotion, propagation, reaction, slope, uprising

RISE *(Origin),* ***noun*** beginning, cause, commencement, debut, derivation, development, fountainhead, genesis, germ, growth, inception, incipience, introduction, nascency, onset, origin, origination, outset, overture, preamble, preface, prelude, prologue, source, spring, start, starting point, uprising, upswing

RISE *(Originate),* ***verb*** arise, begin, come into existence, come to be, emanate, emerge, happen, inaugurate, increase, initiate, issue, occur, spring up

RISE *(Prosper),* ***verb*** appreciate, arise, bear fruit, benefit, be successful, blossom, build, excel, flourish, improve, incept from, originate from, progress, spring from, strive, succeed

RISE *(Soar),* ***verb*** arise, ascend, bear fruit, blossom, build, climb, elevate, emerge, erect, escalate, extend directly upward, flourish, go further, go higher, grow, heighten, hover, improve, inaugurate, inflate, initiate, levitate, mount, pullulate, raise, rear, rebel, rise up, scale, surmount, tower, transcend, uprise, wax

RISK, *noun* *alea,* bet, chance, danger, *discrimen,* endangerment, exposure, exposure to harm, gamble, gaming, hazard, imperilment, insecurity, instability, jeopardy, *periculum,* peril, plunge, possibility, possibility of injury, possibility of loss, precariousness, speculation, stake, uncertainty, venture, vulnerability, wager
ASSOCIATED CONCEPTS: acceptance of risk, assumption of risk, extraordinary risk, forseeable risk, incurred risk, insurance risk, limitation of risk, mutuality of risk, risk of loss, shifting of risk, unreasonable risk
FOREIGN PHRASES: ***Periculum rei venditae, nondum traditae, est emptoris.*** The risk of a thing sold, but not yet delivered, is the purchaser's. ***Ubi periculum ibi et lucrum collocatur.*** He who risks a thing should receive the profits arising from it. ***Cujus est dominium ejus est periculum.*** He who has the ownership should bear the risk.

RISK/REWARD ANALYSIS, *noun* answer, assay, assessment, breakdown, categorization, deconstruction, determination, diagnosis, dissection, evaluation, examination, inspection, investigation, scrutiny

RITUAL BEHAVIOR, *noun* characteristic, convention, custom, disposition, drill, fashion, form, formality, habit, inclination, manner, mode, pattern, practice, proclivity, regime, regimen, rote, routine, set, style, tendency, tradition, way

RIVAL, *noun* adversary, *aemulus,* antagonist, aspirant, bidder, candidate, challenger, combatant, competition, competitor, contender, contestant, corrival, disputant, enemy, entrant, foe, litigant, opponent, opposition

RIVALRY, *noun* battle, clash, collision, combat, competition, conflict, confrontation, contention, contest, controversy, dispute, dissention, dogfight, duel, face-off, match, quarrel, row, showdown, strife, struggle, war, warfare

ROAD, *noun* access, approach, arterial, artery, avenue, boulevard, carriageway, drag, drive, expressway, highway, means, method, pass, path, roadway, route, row, street, thoroughfare, thruway, way

ROB, *verb* appropriate illegally, burglarize, commit robbery, *despoliare, exspoliare,* hold up, loot, misappropriate, peculate, pilfer, pillage, plunder, purloin, seize, steal, take by force, take unlawful possession

ROBBERY, *noun* depredation, felonious taking, felonious taking of the property of another, holdup, larceny by force, *latrocinium,* piracy, plundering, *rapina, spoliatio,* stealing, theft, thievery

RODOMONTADE, *noun* bluster, boastfulness, boasting, brag, braggadocio, braggartism, bragging, bunkum, embroidery, empty talk, exaggeration, extravagance, fanfaronade, gasconade, hyperbole, inflation, jactitation, ostentation, pretense, pretension, pretentious talk, puffery, rant, swagger, swashbuckling, tall talk, turgescence, vainglorious boasting, vainglory, vaporing

ROLE, *noun* act, assignment, billet, capacity, character, characterization, department, false show, function, guise, impersonation, job, mission, part, *partes,* performance, place, pose, position, post, posture, presentation, pretense, province, representation, sham, task, undertaking, work

ROLL, *noun* account, *album,* catalog, census, chronicle, directory, docket, document, enumeration, index, inventory, ledger, list, membership, muster, record, register, registry, roster, schedule, *tabula*

ROLL-OVER CLAUSE, *noun* automatic renewal, automatic renewal terms, automatic restoration, automatic resumption
Generally: continuance, means to obtain the status quo

ROOM *(Area),* ***noun*** accommodation, apartment, berth, booth, cabin, chamber, compartment, cubicle, location, niche, place, space

ROOM *(Latitude),* ***noun*** capacity, compass, elbow room, freedom, latitude, leeway, means, method, opportunity, play, range, scope, way

ROOT, ***noun*** basis, bedrock, bottom, cornerstone, footing, foundation, ground, groundwork, keystone, origin, origination, reason, root, seedbed, spring, underpinning, warp, wellspring

ROUGH, ***adjective*** bitter, brutal, burdensome, complicated, cruel, difficult, excruciating, grievous, grim, hard, hardhanded, onerous, oppressive, rugged, severe, tough, trying

ROUSE, ***verb*** arise, arouse, awaken, get up, reawaken, revive, rewake, rise, roll out, stir, turn out, uprise, wake

ROUTE, ***noun*** access, approach, avenue, boulevard, course, means, method, path, road, row, thoroughfare, thruway, turnpike, way

ROUTINE, ***adjective*** accustomed, automatic, common, commonplace, conventional, customary, established, everyday, expected, familiar, fixed, frequent, general, habitual, ingrained, mechanical, normal, popular, prevalent, recurrent, recurring, regular, repeated, ritual, set, standard, stereotyped, stock, uniform, usual, *usus,* well-trodden

RUBRIC *(Authoritative rule),* ***noun*** act, bylaw, canon, code, convention, dictate, enactment, institution, law, legislation, measure, ordinance, precept, prescription, regulation, rule, ruling, statute

RUBRIC *(Title),* ***noun*** caption, classification, denomination, designation, division, genus, grouping, head, heading, headline, label, superscription

RUDE, ***adjective*** amateur, artless, backward, base, clumsy, contemptuous, crude, disdainful, immoral, impertinent, inexpert, insolent, jerry-built, jerry-rigged, jury-rigged, low, primeval, primitive, primordial, rough, rough-and-ready, rough-and-tumble, rough-hewn, unrefined

RUDIMENTARY, ***adjective*** abecedarian, basal, basic, beginning, crude, elemental, elementary, embryonic, essential, formative, fundamental, germinal, germinative, immature, inceptive, inchoate, *incohatus,* incomplete, initial, initiative, initiatory, original, originative, primal, primary, primitive, primordial, protomorphic, rudimental, simple, starting, uncompleted, underlying, undeveloped, unfinished

RUIN, ***verb*** annihilate, bankrupt, break, bust, crush, damage, decimate, demolish, desolate, despoil, destroy, devastate, eradicate, impair, impoverish, loot, maraud, obliterate, pauperize, pillage, plunder, rape, raze, reduce, scourge, strip, take under, wipe out

RULE *(Guide),* ***noun*** code, course, criterion, custom, direction, formula, habit, matter of course, method, model, norm, *norma,* order, pattern, policy, practice, procedure, protocol, prototype, *regula,* routine, standard, standing order, system

RULE *(Legal dictate),* ***noun*** act, bylaw, canon, charge, code, command, commandment, decree, dictate, direction, doctrine, dogma, edict, enactment, formula, formulary, formulation, law, legislation, maxim, order, ordinance, *praeceptum, praescriptum,* precept, prescription, principle, regulation, standing order, statute, tenet
ASSOCIATED CONCEPTS: administrative rule, court rule, cy pres rule, discriminatory rule, home rule, parol evidence rule, rule against perpetuities, Rule in Shelley's Case, rules of construction, rules of evidence, rules of procedure
FOREIGN PHRASES: ***Ubi non est condendi auctoritas, ibi non est parendi necessitas.*** Where there is no authority for establishing a rule, there is no need of obeying it. ***Exceptio probat regulam de rebus non exceptis.*** The exception proves the rule in matters not excepted. ***Exceptio firmat regulam in contrarium.*** An exception affirms the rule to be the contrary. ***Non est certandum de regulis juris.*** There is no disputing about rules of the law. ***Regula est, juris quidem ignorantiam cuique nocere, facti vero ignorantiam non nocere.*** The rule is that a person's ignorance of the law may prejudice him, but that his ignorance of fact will not. ***Non jus ex regula, sed regula ex jure.*** The law does not arise from the rule, but the rule comes from the law. ***Omnis regula suas patitur exceptiones.*** Every rule is subject to its own exceptions. ***Exceptio firmat regulam in casibus non exceptis.*** An exception confirms the rule in cases not excepted.

RULE *(Decide),* ***verb*** adjudge, adjudicate, ascertain, come to a conclusion, come to a determination, conclude, decide by judicial sentence, declare, declare authoritatively, decree, deliver judgment, determine, draw a conclusion, establish, exercise judgment, find, fix conclusively, give an opinion, give judgment, hold, make a decision, make a resolution, pass judgment, pass sentence, pass upon, pronounce, pronounce judgment, reach an official decision, resolve, settle, settle by decree, umpire
ASSOCIATED CONCEPTS: rule from the bench

RULE *(Govern),* ***verb*** administer, be in power, command, compel, conduct, control, decree, dictate, direct, dispose, domineer, enact, enforce obedience, exercise authority, exert authority, give orders, guide, have authority, have control, have jurisdiction over, have predominating influence, have responsibility, hold authority, hold dominion, hold office, keep in order, manage, manipulate, master, officiate, order, oversee, police, possess authority, predominate, prescribe, preside over, *regnare,* regulate, reign, restrain, run, serve the people, superintend, supervise

RULE OF LAW, ***noun*** consistent principles of the law, guardians of the law, means to rule society, procedural attributes, rule according to law, servants of the law, state of order

RULE OF REASON, ***noun*** antitrust standard involving relevant factors, consideration of relevant factors in evaluating possible monopolization, utilization of factors to determine monopolization
ASSOCIATED CONCEPTS: Sherman Antitrust Act (Sherman Act) (federal)

RULING, ***noun*** adjudication, award, command, conclusion, court's finding, decision, decree, determination, edict, finding, findings of fact and conclusions of law, holding, judgment, judicial determination, judicial proclamation, judicial pronouncement, opinion of the court, order, order of the court, pronouncement, resolution, rule, sentence, verdict
ASSOCIATED CONCEPTS: judicial ruling, ruling from the bench

RUMINATION, *noun* analyzing, close study, cogitation, concentrating, consideration, contemplation, deliberation, dialectic, excogitation, hindsight, meditation, musing, pondering, reflection, retrospection, speculation, thinking

RUN *(Contend),* ***verb*** announce a candidacy, aspire to political office, be a candidate, be designated a candidate, become an office seeker, campaign, campaign for office, campaign for public office, canvass, challenge an incumbent, compete, run for office, seek election, seek reelection, seek to become a public official, solicit votes, stand for election, strive, vie

RUN *(Flee),* ***verb*** abscond, break away, dash, decamp, depart, disengage, escape, fly, hasten, hurry, leave, move swiftly, quit, race, retreat, rush, scamper, take flight

RUN *(Flow),* ***verb*** advance, continue, drain out, elapse, extend, flood, go on, pass, proceed, pour, team, surge, trickle
ASSOCIATED CONCEPTS: conditions and deeds running with the land, covenants running with the land, running at large, running of the statute of limitations

RUN *(Manage),* ***verb*** carry on, conduct, direct, drive, function, govern, guide, handle, influence, maintain, operate, oversee, perform, regulate, steer, superintend, supervise, work

RUSE, *noun* art, artifice, bait, blind, camouflage, cheat, chicane, chicanery, chouse, circumvention, craft, crafty device, deceit, deception, decoy, delusion, design, disguise, dodge, *dolus,* duplicity, evasion, feint, fetch, finesse, flimflam, fraud, guile, hoax, humbug, imposture, jugglery, machination, maneuver, mask, masquerade, plot, pretext, scheme, sham, sharp practice, shift, snare, stratagem, strategy, subterfuge, trick, trickery, wile

RUSH, *noun* acceleration, bustle, celerity, crush, dash, deluge, expeditiousness, flood, flurry, haste, hurried activity, hurry, no time to lose, onrush, precipitance, press of work, promptitude, rampage, run, scamper, scramble, scurry, sprint, spurt, stampede, torrent, urgency, velocity, whirlwind
ASSOCIATED CONCEPTS: date certain, time of the essence

RUSH, *verb* accelerate, bustle, charge, expedite, hasten, hustle, lose no time, make haste, precipitate, quicken, rush to and fro, scramble, scurry, speed, spout, spur, spurt, surge, work under pressure

RUTHLESS, *adjective* atrocious, barbarous, bloodthirsty, brutal, brutish, callous, cold, cold-blooded, coldhearted, cruel, deadly, demoniac, devilish, diabolical, dispiteous, fell, feral, ferine, ferocious, fiendish, grim, hard, hardhearted, harsh, heartless, *immisericors,* implacable, inclement, *inexorabilis,* inexorable, inflexible, inhuman, inhumane, *inhumanus,* insensitive, lethal, maleficent, malevolent, malign, malignant, marble-hearted, merciless, murderous, obdurate, pitiless, poisonous, rancorous, relentless, remorseless, retaliative, revengeful, sadistic, sanguinary, savage, stony-hearted, treacherous, truculent, uncompassionate, unfeeling, unforgiving, unkind, unmerciful, unpitying, unrelenting, unsparing, unsympathetic, vengeful, venomous, vicious, vindictive, virulent, without pity

SABOTAGE, *verb* annihilate, annul, break down, damage, decimate, demolish, destroy, dismantle, disrupt, eradicate, extirpate, impair, injure, main, mar, maraud, obliterate, overthrow, spoil, subvert, take down, treason, undermine, vandalize, wreck

SABOTEURS, *noun* cell, enemy combatants, enemy group, extremist group, extremists, incendiaries, insurgents, rebel organization, revolutionaries, subversives, underground extremists
ASSOCIATED CONCEPTS: justice courts, military tribunals, Patriot Act, prison cells, sleeper cells, terrorism, terrorist cells

SACRED *(Holy),* ***adjective*** all-powerful, blessed, divine, godlike, godly, hallowed, heavenly, immortal, inviolate, supernatural, supreme

SACRED *(Protected),* ***adjective*** exempt, forbidden, immaculate, immune, not for discussion, not on the table, privileged, protected, reserved, shielded, unassailable, untouchable

SACRIFICE *(Forfeiture),* ***noun*** abandonment, capitulation, cessation, cost, deprivation, destruction, dispensation, expense, giving up, loss, oblation, release, relinquishment, renunciation, resignation, yielding

SACRIFICE *(Victim),* ***noun*** dupe, immolation, martyr, oblation, offering, peace offering, prey

SACRIFICE, *verb* cede, dispose of, drop, forbear, forfeit, forgo, forswear, give up, incur loss, let go, part with, release, relinquish, sell at a loss, spare, suffer loss, surrender, undercharge, underrate, waive, yield

SACROSANCT, ***adjective*** anointed, awesome, blessed, ceremonial, consecrated, dedicated, devotional, divine, elevated, enshrined, godly, hallowed, heavenly, holy, ineffable, inviolable, inviolate, mystical, purified, religious, revered, reverend, sacramental, sacred, sainted, sanctified, set apart, solemn, spiritual, theistic, theologic, theological, transcedent, venerable, venerated, worshiped

SAD, ***adjective*** bad, blue, brokenhearted, cast down, crestfallen, dejected, depressed, despondent, disconsolate, doleful, down, down in the mouth, downcast, downhearted, forlorn, gloomy, glum, heartbroken, heartsick, heartsore, heavyhearted, inconsolable, joyless, lamentable, low, low-spirited, melancholic, melancholy, miserable, mournful, pessimistic, saddened, sorrowful, sorry, unhappy, woeful, wretched

SAFE, ***adjective*** armed, armored, benign, cared for, certain, covered, defended, dependable, ensconced, entrenched, *fidus,* foolproof, free from danger, free from harm, free from hurt, free from injury, free from risk, guaranteed, guarded, harmless, impervious, impregnable, insured, intact, invulnerable, looked after, maintained, on guard, out of danger, panoplied, preserved, proof, protected, prudent, regulated, reliable, safeguarded, salubrious, scatheless, screened, screened from danger, secure, *securus,* sheltered, shielded, sound, sure, sustained, tested, trustworthy, *tutus,* unadventurous, unassailable, unattackable, unbroken, undamaged, undaring, under cover, unendangered, unexposed, unharmed, unhazarded, unhurt, unimpaired, uninjured, unmolested, unscathed, unshakable, unthreatened, whole, without risk

SAFE HAVEN, ***noun*** area free from danger, area free from harm, area of protection, area out of danger, area screened from danger, asylum, confined area, guaranteed safe area, harbor, place of safety, port, protected area, refuge, retreat, safe area, safe harbor, safeguarded area, sanctuary, secure area, shelter, sheltered area, shielded area, untreatened area
ASSOCIATED CONCEPTS: safe haven in contracts, safe haven in statutes

SAFE WORKPLACE, ***noun*** harmonious workplace, protected workplace, safe-guarded place, secure place of work, unhazardous workplace
ASSOCIATED CONCEPTS: labor law, OSHA standards, recalcitrant worker doctrine, safe standards, sanctity of the workplace

SAFEGUARD, ***noun*** armor, assurance, buffer, bulwark, cover, defense, fortification, insurance, *munimentum,* palladium, precaution, preventive measure, protection, provision, screen, security, shield, surety

SAFEKEEPING, ***noun*** aegis, auspices, care, charge, conservation, custody, defense, guard, guardianship, keeping, lee, patronage, preservation, protection, protective custody, salvation, security, shelter, superintendence, supervision, support, tutelage, upkeep, wardship, watch
ASSOCIATED CONCEPTS: bailment

SAFETY, ***noun*** asylum, cover, custody, immunity, inviolability, preservation, protection, refuge, safeguard, safekeeping, safeness, sanctuary, security, shelter
ASSOCIATED CONCEPTS: safety devices

SAFETY VALVE, ***noun*** alternative, aperture, boundary condition, choice, circumstance, clause condition, contingency, contrivance, definition, device, escalator clause, esca clause, escape valve, escape way, evasion, exception, excuse, exit strategy, expedient, frame of reference, given, grounds, hole to creep out of, limitation, limiting condition, loophole, means of escape, mechanism for evasion, obligation, opening, out, outlet, parameter, prerequisite, pretext, provision, proviso, requisite, saving clause, specification, stipulation, technicality, terms, ultimatum, uncommunicativeness, vehicle of escape, way of escape, way out, whereas
ASSOCIATED CONCEPTS: safety valve consideration, safety valve function, stop valve

SAFETY VALVE PROVISIONS, ***noun*** certain solution in statutes, escape hatch in statutes, impregnable solution in statutes, insured solution in statutes, invulnerable solution in statutes, means of resolution in statutes, method of preservation in statutes, safeguards in statutes, secure methodology in statutes, solution in statutes, sound solution in statutes, sure solution in statutes, unassailable solution in statutes

SAGA, ***noun*** account, adventure, chronicle, epic, epos, heroic story, history, legend, myth, mythology, report, story, tale, yarn

SAGACIOUS, ***adjective*** astute, circumspect, clever, cognizant, diplomatic, discerning, discreet, discriminating, enlightened, far-sighted, intelligent, judicial, judicious, keen-sighted, knowing, learned, lucid, omniscient, penetrating, perceptive, perspicacious, politic, prescient, profound, prudent, quick, rational, reasonable, resourceful, sage, sapient, sensible, sharp, shrewd, smart, solid, subtle, understanding, wise

SAGACITY, ***noun*** acuity, acumen, acuteness, apperception, arguteness, astuteness, awareness, brilliance, clear thinking, clear thought, cleverness, comprehension, discernment, discrimination, excellent judgment, farsightedness, foresight, genius, good judgment, incisiveness, insight, intelligence, intuition, judgment, keenness, keensightedness, levelheadedness, mentality, penetration, perception, percipience, perspicaciousness, *perspicacitas,* perspicacity, profundity, prudence, *prudentia,* quickness, rationality, reason, reasoning power, sagaciousness, *sagacitas,* sapience, sapiency, sense, sharpness, shrewdness, smartness, sobriety, understanding, vision, wisdom

SAGE, ***adjective*** acute, astute, brainy, bright, brilliant, cerebral, clever, discerning, discriminating, erudite, experienced, expert, insightful, keen, knowledgeable, learned, literate, master, mastermind, perceptive, percipient, perspicacious, prudent, sagacious, sapient, scholarly, smart, specialist

SAID, ***adjective*** above-mentioned, aforgoing, aforenamed, aforesaid, already indicated, before mentioned, earlier, exact, forgoing, forementioned, named, preceding, prevenient, previous, previously mentioned, previously named, previously referred to, prior, specific

SALACIOUS, ***adjective*** bawdy, carnal, coarse, *concupiscent,* corrupt, debauched, depraved, dirty, dissolute, erotic, Fescennine, filthy, foul, free, goatish, gross, immoral, impure, incontinent, indecent, lascivious, lecherous, lewd, libertine, libidinous, licentious, lickerish, lickerous, loose, lurid, lustful, obscene, offensive, Paphian, polluted, pornographic, profligate, provocative, prurient, ribald, risque, ruttish, satyric, satyrical, scabrous, scarlet, scrofulous, scurrile, scurrilous, sensual, sexy, shameful, shameless, sinful, smutty, spicy, suggestive, titillating, unblushing, unbowdlerized, unchaste, unclean, unexpurgated, unprintable, unvirtuous, virtueless, wanton

SALE, ***noun*** disposal, exchange, trade, transaction, transfer, vendition
ASSOCIATED CONCEPTS: sales and exchange, sale and return, sale at auction, sale by commercial broker, sale by sample, sale confirmed, sale for payment, sale of debt, sale of office, sale on credit, sale on return, sale on trial

SALIENT, ***adjective*** bold, capital, cardinal, chief, clear, commanding, conspicuous, distinct, distinguished, dominant, dominating, eminent, evident, exalted, explicit, extraordinary, flagrant, foremost, glaring, illustrious, important, imposing, indubitable, leading, main, marked, memorable, notable, noticeable, obvious, outstanding, overt, paramount, plain, *praecipuus,* predominant, primary, prime, principal, prominent, pronounced, protrudent, protruding, protrusive, protuberant, recognized, remarkable, showing, significant, standing out, striking, towering, unconcealed, unmistakable, visible, well-known, worthy of notice, worthy of remark

SALIENT POINT, ***noun*** basis, cardinal point, central point, core, cornerstone, elixir, essence, essential part, feature, focal point, gist, gravamen, highlight, implication, import, important point, kernel, keystone, main issue, main point, marrow, material point, nucleus, pith, prominent part, quintessence, significance, significant fundamental, substance, sum and substance

SALUBRIOUS, ***adjective*** advantageous, analeptic, beneficial, corrective, corroborant, curative, favorable to health, healing, health-promoting, healthful, healthy, invigorating, life-giving, medicinal, nourishing, nutritious, nutritive, recuperative, remedial, reparative, restorative, reviviscent, roborant, salutary, salutiferous, sanatory, stimulating, sustentative, therapeutic, therapeutical, tonic, wholesome

SALUTARY, ***adjective*** advantageous, aidant, analeptic, beneficial, benign, bracing, constitutional, corrective, corroborant, curative, edifying, favorable, good, harmless, healing, health-giving, health-preserving, healthful, healthy, helpful, hurtless, hygienic, innocuous, innoxious, invigorating, medicinal, nourishing, nutritious, nutritive, palliative, preventive, profitable, promoting health, prophylactic, protective, remedial, reparative, reparatory, restorative, roborant, safe, salubrious, *salutaris,* salutiferous, sanative, sanatory, sanitary, sustaining, sustentative, therapeutic, tonic, uninjurious, useful, *utilis,* wholesome

SALUTIFEROUS, ***adjective*** advantageous, advisable, ameliorative, auspicious, beneficial, benignant, bettering, constructive, desirable, favorable, friendly, gainful, good, gratifying, healthful, healthy, helpful, lucrative, medicinal, profitable, promising, propitious, remunerative, rewarding, salubrious, salutary, salutiferous, satisfying, supportive, wholesome

SALVAGE, ***noun*** conservation, deliverance, extrication, property saved, recapture, reclaimed materials, reclamation, recoupment, recovery, redemption, remains, reoccupation, repossession, rescue, retrieval, return, salvation, scrap
ASSOCIATED CONCEPTS: equitable salvage, net salvage, salvage charges, salvage loss, salvage service

SALVO, ***noun*** condition, defense, escape clause, evasion, exception, exemption, explosion, fusillade, general discharge, proviso, qualification, quibbling excuse, reservation, restriction, salute, saving clause, simultaneous discharge of shots, volley

SAMARITAN, ***noun*** aid, aider, altruist, assister, befriender, benefactor, champion, defender, friend, good neighbor, help, helper, helping hand, kind person, ministering angel, ministrant, patron, philanthropist, protector, savior, succorer, sympathizer, well-wisher
ASSOCIATED CONCEPTS: Good Samaritan laws, rescue doctrine

SAME, ***adjective*** alike, cognate, duplicate, equal, equivalent, exactly like, identical, one and the same, parallel, similar, synonymous, twin, uniform, without difference
ASSOCIATED CONCEPTS: same act or transaction, same as, same cause, same cause of action, same character of work, same class of subject, same compensation, same condition(s), same descriptive properties, same direction, same extent, same fees, same fund, same general business, same grade of employment, same grantor, same manner, same offense, same parties, same punishment, same rate of interest, same right

SAME, ***noun*** consistency, counterpart, double, equal, equivalent, idem, identical, match, mate, reciprocal, resemblance, similarity, synonym

SAME-SEX MARRIAGE, ***noun*** civil union (opponents), equality for gay marriage, gay marriage, laws governing gay marriage, marriage equality (proponents)
ASSOCIATED CONCEPTS: civil marriage, Federal Defense of Marriage Act (DOMA), gay rights

SAMPLE, ***noun*** archetype, case in point, cross section, *documentum,* ensample, example, exemplar, exemplification, *exemplum,* guide, illustration, instance, model, original, paradigm, prototype, representation, representative, representative selection, showpiece, specimen, standard of comparison, swatch, typical example

SANCTIFY, ***verb*** absolve, acquit, amend, authorize, baptize, canonize, chasten, cleanse, clear, consecrate, devote, elevate, ennoble, exonerate, hallow, heal, improve, purge, purify, refine, regenerate, restore, spiritualize, vindicate

SANCTIMONIOUS, ***adjective*** arrogant, authorized, canonized, chastened, condescending, deceiving, deceptive, devoted, elevated, ennobled, haughty, high and mighty, holier than thou, insincere, pharisaical, pietistic, pious, self-righteous, spiritualized, unctuous

SANCTION *(Permission),* ***noun*** acceptance, acquiescence, affirmance, affirmation, agreement, allowance, approbation, approval, assent, *auctoritas,* authorization, charter, *confirmatio,* consent, cooperation, countenance, empowerment, encouragement, endorsement, favor, grant, homologation, immunity, indulgence, legality, license, permission, permit, ratification, seal, stamp of approval, subscription, sufferance, support, tolerance, toleration, validation, vouchsafement, willingness
FOREIGN PHRASES: ***Multa conceduntur per obliquum quae non conceduntur de directo.*** Many things are allowed indirectly which are not allowed directly.

SANCTION *(Punishment),* ***noun*** condemnation, denunciation, deprivation, disciplinary action, discipline, imposition, infliction, penal retribution, penalty, retributive action, suffering

SANCTION, ***verb*** accede, accept, acquiesce, agree to, allow, approbate, approve, assent to, authenticate, authorize, charter, confer a privilege, confer a right, *confirmare,* consent to, countenance, empower, enable, endorse, entitle, foster, give approval, give permission, go along with, grant, gratify, homologate, indulge, legitimate, legitimatize, legitimize, license, permit, privilege, promote, ratify, *ratum facere, sancire,* stand behind, subscribe to, suffer, support, tolerate, uphold, validate, vouchsafe
ASSOCIATED CONCEPTS: civil sanctions, criminal sanctions, penal sanctions

SANCTUARY, ***noun*** asylum, harbor, harborage, haven, holy place, oasis, protection, refuge, sacred place, sanctorium, sanctum, shelter, shrine

SANE, ***adjective*** *animi,* balanced, clearheaded, competent, coolheaded, judicious, legitimate, levelheaded, logical, lucid, mentally sound, *mentis compos,* normal, rational, realistic, reasonable, responsible, *sanus,* sensible, sober, sober-minded, sound, understanding, undisturbed

SANGUINE, ***adjective*** anticipative, assured, bright, buoyant, cheerful, confident, encouraged, enthusiastic, expectant, full of hope, hopeful, in good spirits, inspirited, optimistic, reassured, sanguineous, trustful, trusting, undespairing, undoubting

SANITY, ***noun*** balance, clear thinking, clearmindedness, comprehension, health of mind, healthy mind, levelheadedness, lucidity, mental balance, mental equilibrium, mental health, normalcy, normality, rationality, reason, reasonableness, saneness, sense, sensibleness, sound understanding, soundmindedness, soundness, understanding
ASSOCIATED CONCEPTS: competency hearing, presumption of sanity

SAPID, ***adjective*** acceptable, affecting, agreeable, alluring, ambrosial, amusing, appealing, appetizing, arresting, attractive, bewitching, captivating, challenging, charming, delectable, delicious, delightful, dulcet, enchanting, engaging, entertaining, enthralling, enticing, entrancing, exciting, fascinating, fine, flavorful, flavorous, flavorsome, flavory, full-bodied, full-flavored, good, good-tasting, gratifying, gustable, gustful, impressive, inspiring, interesting, intriguing, inviting, likable, lovely, luscious, nectareous, palatable, piquant, pleasant, pleasing, pleasurable, popular, prepossessing, provocative, provoking, refreshing, relishable, saporous, satisfying, savory, scrumptious, seasoned, stirring, succulent, sweet, tantalizing, tasty, tempting, thought-provoking, titallative, titillating, welcome, winning, winsome

SAPIENCE, ***adjective*** acuity, astuteness, brilliance, cleverness, discernment, discrimination, insight, intellect, intelligence, judgment, keenness, perception, perceptiveness, percipience, sagaciousness, sagacity, sageness, sense, understanding, wit

SAPIENT, ***adjective*** acute, astute, bright, clear-headed, clever, deep, discerning, discriminating, farsighted, intellectual, intelligent, judicious, keen, knowing, learned, perceptive, perspicacious, profound, quick of apprehension, quick-witted, rational, sagacious, sage, *sapiens,* sensible, sharp, shrewd, thinking, wise

SARCASTIC, ***adjective*** acidulous, acrid, barbed, biting, bitter, caustic, corrosive, cutting, mordant, offensive, pungent, sardonic, satirical, scalding, scathing, sharp, sharp-tongued, tart

SATIATE, ***verb*** alleviate, assuage, fulfill, gratify, indulge, pacify, quench, relieve, satisfy, saturate, surfeit

SATISFACTION *(Discharge of debt),* ***noun*** acquitment, acquittal, acquittance, amortizement, clearance, compensation, damages, defrayal, defrayment, discharge, guerdon, indemnification, indemnity, payment, quittance, receipted payment, recompense, recoupment, redress, reimbursement, release from debt, remuneration, reparation, repayment, requital, requitement, restitution, return, settlement, solatium
ASSOCIATED CONCEPTS: accord and satisfaction, ademption, reasonable satisfaction, satisfaction of lien, satisfaction piece

SATISFACTION *(Fulfillment),* ***noun*** accomplishment, achievement, appeasement, attainment, consummation, content, contentedness, contentment, enjoyment, fruition, gratification, pleasure, realization, reparation, success, sufficiency
ASSOCIATED CONCEPTS: satisfaction of judgment

SATISFACTORY, ***adjective*** acceptable, adequate, agreeable, all right, ample, appropriate, average, bearable, copacetic, decent, endurable, fair, fine, good, palatable, passable, respectable, serviceable, standard, sufferable, tolerable, unexceptional

SATISFY *(Discharge),* ***verb*** arrange a settlement, carry into execution, carry out, clear, compensate, fulfill an obligation, make compensation, make good, make payment, meet an obligation, pay, pay in full, pay off, pay up, recompense, reimburse, remit, remunerate, render, repay, requite, settle, settle accounts, tender
ASSOCIATED CONCEPTS: satisfy a debt, satisfy a judgment

SATISFY *(Fulfill),* ***verb*** answer the purpose, appease, avail, be agreeable, be sufficient, carry out, comply with, conform to, content, fill, fit, gratify, meet requirements, please, prove acceptable, qualify, quench, sate, satiate, serve the purpose, set at ease, slake, suffice, suit, surfeit
ASSOCIATED CONCEPTS: satisfy to a moral certainty

SATURATION, ***noun*** abundance, cornucopia, feast, overdose, overflow, overkill, oversupply, plenitude, plethora, sufficiency, superabundance, surfeit, wealth

SAVAGE, ***adjective*** barbarian, barbaric, brutal, brute, coarse, crude, heathen, malevolent, malicious, primitive, rough, rude, uncivilized, uncouth, uncultivated, uncultured, unpolished, wanton, wild

SAVE, ***conjunction*** bar, barring, besides, but for, deducting, excepting, lacking, leaving out, not including, short of, without

SAVE, ***preposition*** but, except, exclusive of, less, minus, omitting

SAVE *(Conserve),* ***verb*** hold, keep safe, preserve, redeem, salvage

SAVE *(Hold back),* ***verb*** economize, hoard, keep, reserve, retain

SAVE *(Rescue),* ***verb*** avert, defend, fend off, give salvation, help, liberate, protect, safeguard, shield

SAVINGS CLAUSE, ***noun*** limitation on the scope of repeal, means to ensure a statute will not be struck down entirely, protection to ensure the validity of a contract, severability, the means to ensure enforceability if part of a contract is overturned

SAVORY, ***adjective*** agreeable, ambrosiac, ambrosial, ambrosian, appetizing, *conditus,* delectable, delicious, delightful, flavor, flavored, flavorous, flavorsome, full-bodied, full-flavored, good, good-tasting, gustable, gustative, likable, luscious, nectarean, nectareous, palatable, piquant, pleasant, pleasing, rich, sapid, sweet, tasty, tempting

SAY, ***verb*** air, allege, articulate, broadcast, claim, comment, declare, discuss, elaborate on, enunciate, express, formulate, post, proclaim, put, recite, reel off, remark, share, speak, state, talk, tell, utter, vent, verbalize, vocalize

SAY-SO, ***noun*** acceptance, accord, affirmance, affirmation, agreement, approval, assent, authorization, compliance, confirmation, consent, endorsement, go-ahead, green light, imprimatur, leave, liberty, license, nod, okay, permission, ratification, sanction, sign-off, special permission, validation, willingness

SCABROUS, ***adjective*** blotchy, boorish, coarse, difficult, immodest, improper, indiscreet, knotty, rough, rugged, scabby, scaly, scandalous, surly, treacherous, unconventional, unsmooth

SCALE *(Measurement),* ***noun*** analysis of measurement, balance, calibration, computation, graduated system of measurement, guide, index, meter, page, proportion, range of measurements, rule, scheme, scope

SCALE *(Order),* ***noun*** analytical assessment, arrangement, array, comparison, distribution, gamut, pecking order, progression, range, ranking, rate, reach, relative magnitude, rubric, scope, sequence, series, spectrum

SCANDAL, ***noun*** aspersion, attaint, bad name, bad reputation, bad repute, baseness, brand, censure, damaging report, dedecoration, defamation, degradation, disapprobation, disapproval, discredit, disesteem, disgrace, dishonor, disrepute, humiliation, ignominy, ill repute, imputation, infamy, ingloriousness, loss of honor, loss of reputation, malicious gossip, notoriety, obloquy, odium, opprobrium, reproach, shame, slur, stain, stigma, taint, talk, tarnish, tarnished honor, vilification
ASSOCIATED CONCEPTS: defamatory reports, deformatory rumors

SCANDALOUS, ***adjective*** arrant, atrocious, base, black, condemnatory, corrupt, damnatory, dastardly, defamatory, denunciatory, deplorable, despicable, discreditable, disgraceful, dishonorable, disreputable, disrespectable, execrable, facinorous, flagitious, flagrant, fulsome, heinous, horrifying, ignoble, ignominious, illaudable, immodest, immoral, indecent, infamous, inglorious, iniquitous, lewd, licentious, low, mean, nefarious, notorious, objurgatory, odious, offensive, opprobrious, outrageous, *probrosus,* profligate, reprehensible, scurrilous, shameful, shocking, thersitical, *turpis,* ugly, uncommendable, unworthy, wicked
ASSOCIATED CONCEPTS: motion to strike scandalous matter, scandalous allegations, scandalous pleading

SCANT, ***adjective*** bare, bare-bones, deficient, inadequate, insufficient, lacking, light, marginal, mere, minimal, poor, scanty, scarce, short, skimpy, slender, slim, spare, sparing, sparse, stingy, wanting

SCARCE, ***adjective*** at a premium, dear, deficient, few, inadequate, incomplete, inconsiderable, insufficient, limited, little, low, meager, minute, not abundant, not plentiful, out-of-the-way, paltry, rare, *rarus,* scant, seldom met with, short, skimpy, sparing, sparse, thinly scattered, unavailable, uncommon, unique, unobtainable, unplentiful, unusual, wanting

SCARE, ***verb*** intimidate, bowl over, chill, discomfort, discompose, disconcert, dismay, disquiet, distract, distress, disturb, floor, jolt, perturb, shake, shake up, unnerve, unsettle, unstring, upset, worry

SCATHING, ***adjective*** *acerbus,* acrimonious, *aculeatus,* biting, brutal, burning, cruel, cutting, damaging, envenomed, excoriating, harmful, harsh, hurtful, insulting, maleficent, malevolent, malicious, malignant, mordacious, *mordax,* rancorous, scatheful, searing, severe, sharp, spiteful, stinging, trenchant, unbenevolent, uncharitable, uncompromising, ungentle, unkind, venemous, virulent, vitriolic, withering

SCENARIO, ***noun*** abstract, analysis, brief, capsule, compression, condensation, contents, digest, essence, narrative, outline, plot, recap, recapitulation, report, review, script, sketch, story, sum and substance, summary, synopsis, text

SCENE, ***noun*** act, arena, background, display, episode, eyereach, eyeshot, field, landscape, locale, locality, location, locus, panorama, place, range, *scaena,* scope, setting, sight, site, spectacle, sphere, stage, stage setting, surroundings, theater, view, vista, whereabouts
ASSOCIATED CONCEPTS: scene of an accident

SCHEDULE, ***noun*** agenda, calendar, check list, docket, enumeration, index, inventory, *libellus,* list, outline, plan, program, roll, *tabula,* timetable
ASSOCIATED CONCEPTS: payment schedule, schedule of assets

SCHEME, ***noun*** arrangement, cabal, *consilium,* contrivance, course of action, delineation, design, device, enterprise, machination, maneuver, method, operation, order, organization, plan, plot, policy, procedure, program of action, project, *ratio,* schedule, stratagem, strategy, subterfuge, system, tactics
ASSOCIATED CONCEPTS: conspiracy

SCHEME, ***verb*** arrange, be cunning, cabal, calculate, chart, collude, complot, compose, concoct, connive, conspire, contrive, design, devise, diagram, engineer, excogitate, fabricate, fashion, frame, hatch, have designs, improvise, intrigue, invent, lay a plan, machinate, make arrangements, maneuver, manipulate, map, map out, organize, outline, plan, plot, predesign, predetermine, premeditate, prepare, project, *ratio,* think ahead, think out, weave a plot, work out, work up
ASSOCIATED CONCEPTS: collude, conspire

SCHISM, ***noun*** breach, break, cabal, desertion, difference, disassociation, disconnection, discord, dissension, dissent, disunion, division, faction, falling out, nonconformity, partition, recusancy, rent, rift, rupture, *schisma,* secession, sectarianism, sectarism, separation, severance, split, withdrawal

SCIENCE *(Study),* ***noun*** body of fact, branch of knowledge, data, discipline, facts, information, knowledge, learning, organized knowledge, *scientia,* system of knowledge

SCIENCE *(Technique),* ***noun*** ability, adroitness, aptitude, aptness, capacity, competence, competency, dexterity, expertness, facility, finesse, genius, highly developed skill, know-how, mastery, method, proficiency, skill, skillfulness

SCIENTER, ***noun*** appreciation, apprehension, awareness, cognition, cognizance, comprehension, consciousness, discernment, familiarity, intent, intention, knowledge, perception, recognition, understanding

SCIENTIAL, ***adjective*** able, accomplished, adapted, adept, adequate, capable, competent, deft, educated, efficacious, fitted, gifted, intelligent, knowing, knowledgeable, learned, proficient, qualified, schooled, skillful, suitable, suited, trained, up to, well-suited

SCINTILLA, ***noun*** bit, corpuscle, grain, insignificant amount, iota, minim, modicum, particle, small amount, small quantity, spark, tittle, trace, trifle, whit
ASSOCIATED CONCEPTS: scintilla of evidence

SCOFFLAW, ***noun*** a contemptuous violator of the law, habitual failure to answer allegations, habitual failure to answer charges, habitual failure to answer summons, habitual failure to pay debts, violator who fails to answer summonses

SCOLD, ***verb*** berate, castigate, chastise, flay, hammer, lambaste, lecture, rail against, rant, rebuke, reprimand, reproach, score, tongue-lash, upbraid

SCOPE, ***noun*** ambit, amplitude, area, boundary, bounds, circle, circuit, compass, confines, demesne, expanse, extent, field, latitude, limit, *locus,* margin, orbit, purview, range, reach, realm, region, room, space, span, sphere, spread, stretch, sweep, territory, zone
ASSOCIATED CONCEPTS: scope of a patent, scope of authority, scope of employment, scope of jurisdiction, scope of review

SCOPE OF REVIEW, ***noun*** issues that reviewing court will consider, limitation of issues available to the appellant, limitation on issues preserved by appellant, restriction on issues that an appellate court will consider, right to raise issues for review on appeal

SCORCHED EARTH POLICY, ***noun*** annihilation, decimation, demolishment, demolition, desolation, despoilment, destruction, devastation, dismantlement, effacement, eradication, extermination, extinction, obliteration, ruin, ruination, wreckage

SCORN, ***verb*** abhorrence, abomination, aversion, cattiness, contempt, contemptuousness, despisement, detestation, disdain, disgust, disrespect, distaste, execration, hate, hatefulness, hatred, horror, invidiousness, loathing, malevolence, malice, maliciousness, malignancy, malignity, meanness, misprision, odium, ridicule, spite, spitefulness

SCRAMBLE, ***noun*** chaos, commotion, confound, confuse, discord, jumble, mishmash, perplex, turbid, upheaval

SCREEN *(Guard),* ***verb*** camouflage, cloak, conceal, cover, defend, disguise, fence, harbor, haven, hide, mask, protect, safeguard, shade, shelter, shield, shroud, veil

SCREEN *(Select),* ***verb*** choose, class, classify, discard, discriminate, eliminate, evaluate, exclude, filter, grade, group, keep out, pick, *prefer,* segregate, separate, sieve, sift, single out, sort, strain, weed, winnow
ASSOCIATED CONCEPTS: screen prospective jurors

SCRIPT, ***noun*** book, calligraphy, characters, cursive hand, dialogue, handwriting, jottings, libretto, lines, longhand, manuscript, penmanship, penscript, playbook, printing, scrawl, scription, text, writing, written characters, written matter

SCRUPLE, ***noun*** anxiety, apprehension, apprehensiveness, compunction, concern, *cunctatio,* doubt, doubtfulness, drawback, dubiety, dubiousness, *dubitatio,* fear, fearfulness, *haesitatio,* hesitancy, hesitation, misgiving, objection, qualm, question, reluctance, uncertainty, unease, uneasiness, unwillingness

SCRUPULOUS, ***adjective*** aboveboard, *accuratus,* admirable, careful, choosy, *diligens,* discriminating, discriminative, equitable, ethical, fair, forthright, honest, honorable, laudable, legitimate, moral, noble, principled, reliable, reputable, sincere, sound, thorough, trustworthy, truthful, upright, worthy

SCRUTABLE, ***adjective*** apprehensible, beholdable, cognizable, comprehensible, conspicuous, discoverable, easily observed, easily seen, easily understood, evident, explicable, explicit, fathomable, intelligible, knowable, manifest, noticeable, observable, obvious, open, overt, penetrable, perceptible, plain, seeable, unconcealed, understandable, unhidden, unmasked, unveiled

SCRUTINIZE, ***verb*** analyze, anatomize, audit, canvass, check, contemplate, delve into, dissect, examine, explore, eye, give close attention, inquire into, inspect, *inspicere, investigare,* investigate, keep under surveillance, look at closely, look into, look over, observe, overhaul, peer into, *perscrutari,* peruse, probe, pry into, question, regard carefully, research, review, scan, search, search into, sift, stare, study, survey, view, watch

SCRUTINY, ***noun*** analysis, attention, careful examination, close investigation, close look, close search, consideration, critical examination, examination, exploration, indagation, inquest, inquiry, inquisition, inspection, investigation, minute attention, observance, observation, *perscrutatio,* perusal, probe, research, review, scrutation, search, study, surveillance, survey

SCURRILOUS, ***adjective*** abusive, coarse, *contumeliosus,* disgusting, disrespectful, foul, gross, indecent, indelicate, insulting, lascivious, lewd, libidinous, licentious, low, mean, obscene, offensive, opprobrious, *probrosus,* ribald, risque, salacious, scabrous, scurrile, *scurrilis,* shameless, vile, vulgar

SEAL *(Close),* ***verb*** bar, block off, bolt, close up, cover, keep from public view, keep in confidence, keep in secrecy, lock, occlude, secret, secure
ASSOCIATED CONCEPTS: sealed case, sealed grand jury report, sealed indictment, sealed instrument, sealed verdict

SEAL *(Solemnize),* ***verb*** accept, accredit, approve, attest, authenticate, authorize, bear witness, certify, confirm, endorse, enstamp, impress with mark, imprint, inscribe, legalize, license, ratify, sanction, sign, stamp, substantiate, support, undersign, validate, verify, vouch

SEALED RECORD, ***noun*** classified record, concealed record, confidential record, private record, record which cannot be disclosed, record which cannot be revealed, restricted record, secret record
ASSOCIATED CONCEPTS: open records policy, sealed instrument, sealed verdict

SEARCH, ***verb*** chase after, closely examine, comb, delve, examine, examine by inspection, explore, ferret, follow the trail of, go through, hunt, indagate, inquire into, inspect, investigate, look into, look over, look through, probe, pry into, pursue, scan, scour, scout, scrutinize, seek, trace, track, track down, trail
ASSOCIATED CONCEPTS: illegal search by law enforcement officers, searching premises, unlawful search, unreasonable search and seizure

SEARCH WARRANT, ***noun*** authority to search, bench warrant, court order, judicial order to search, judicial process, legal document to search, legal order, legal process, order authorizing a search, process, writ
ASSOCIATED CONCEPTS: illegal search warrant, probable cause to issue search warrant

SEASON, ***noun*** cycle, era, part of the year, period, semester, span, spell, stretch, term, time, time of year

SEASONABLE, ***adjective*** acceptable, apposite, appropriate, auspicious, befitting, convenient, due, expedient, favorable, fit, opportune, *opportunus,* proper, properly timed, propitious, seemly, suitable, *tempestivus,* timeful, timely, towardly, well-timed

SEAT, ***noun*** base, berth, capital, center, *domicilium,* headquarters, home, locale, locality, location, perch, place, position, post, region, residence, *sedes,* site, spot, station, vital center
ASSOCIATED CONCEPTS: county seat

SECEDE, ***verb*** abandon, *abire,* apostatize, break away, depart, desert, disaffiliate, dissent, evacuate, insurrect, leave, mutiny, pull out, quit, rebel, refuse to support, relinquish, remove oneself, repudiate, resign, retire, retract, revolt, separate, sever one's connections, tergiversate, vacate, walk out, withdraw

SECERN, ***verb*** differentiate, discern, discriminate, distinguish, note the distinctions, perceive differences

SECLUDE, ***verb*** banish, blockade, bury, conceal, confine, cover, cut off, deport, disassociate, dissociate, embargo, exclude, excommunicate, exile, expatriate, hide, imprison, insulate, isolate, keep apart, keep in detention, keep in private, keep out, maroon, ostracize, outlaw, quarantine, relegate, remove, *removere,* retire, retire from sight, retreat, rope off, screen out, *secludere, segregare,* segregate, separate, sequester, set apart, set aside, shut out, withdraw

SECOND *(Backer),* ***noun*** advocate, aide, angel, backer, champion, co signer, endorser, patron, promoter, supporter

SECOND *(Moment),* ***noun*** before you know it, brief period of time, flash, flash of an eyelid, instant

SECOND, ***verb*** approve, assist, authorize, back, back up, confirm, endorse, favor, pass, ratify, receipt, recommend, sanction, stand behind, subscribe, support, undersign, validate, vote for, warrant
ASSOCIATED CONCEPTS: second lien

SECONDARY, ***adjective*** accessory, alternative, ancillary, auxiliary, collateral, contingency, derived, following, indirect, inferior, junior, less important, lesser, minor, *secundarius,* subaltern, subordinate, subsequent, subsidiary, substitute, unessential, unimportant, vicarious
ASSOCIATED CONCEPTS: secondary boycott, secondary evidence, secondary liability

SECONDARY RIGHTS, ***noun*** ancillary rights, contingent rights, indirect rights, subordinated rights, subsequent rights

SECRECY, ***noun*** circumspection, closeness, concealment, confidentiality, covertness, discreteness, discretion, furtiveness, privacy, prudence, reserve, reticence, secretiveness, shiftiness, silence, stealth, subterfuge, taciturnity, underhandedness, wariness

SECRET, ***adjective*** abstruse, acroamatic, acroamatical, arcane, *arcanus,* clandestine, close, concealed, confidential, covert, cryptic, dark, esoteric, furtive, hidden, latent, mysterious, not public, obscure, occult, *occultus,* private, privy, recondite, secluded, secretus, shrouded, sly, surreptitious, undisclosed, undivulged, unknown, unpublished, unrevealed, unseen, untold, veiled
ASSOCIATED CONCEPTS: secret lien, undisclosed principal

SECRET, ***noun*** abstruse knowledge, *arcana,* cabal, classified information, concealed knowledge, confidence, confidential communication, confidential matter, enigma, hidden knowledge, inside information, intimacy, intrigue, mystery, obscure information, personal matter, private affair, private communication, private matter, privileged communication, privileged information, puzzle, recondite knowledge, *res arcana, res occulta,* unknown information, veiled information

SECTION *(Division),* ***noun*** category, class, compartment, component, department, detachment, fraction, fragment, group, grouping, part, segment, separate part, separation, subdivision, subgroup

SECTION *(Vicinity),* ***noun*** area, block, clime, demesne, environs, field, locale, locality, location, *locus,* milieu, neighborhood, parcel of land, part, plot, plot of ground, plot of land, province, purlieus, *regio,* region, surroundings, territory, tract, vicinage, *vicinitas*
ASSOCIATED CONCEPTS: block, plot, and section

SECTOR, ***noun*** area, arena, category, department, district, division, domain, part, precinct, province, quarter, realm, region, scene, section, segment, sphere, stratum, subdivision, territory, theater, zone

SECURE *(Confident),* ***adjective*** assured, carefree, certain, convinced, not nervous, not scared, positive, reassured, sure, unafraid, unanxious, unconcerned, undisturbed, unfrightened, unhesitating, unshaken, unsuspecting

SECURE *(Free from danger),* ***adjective*** armored, defended, dependable, guaranteed, guarded, impregnable, in safety, insured, inviolable, invulnerable, protected, safe, sheltered, stable, unassailable, unattackable, unharmable, unimperiled, unthreatened
ASSOCIATED CONCEPTS: secured transactions

SECURE *(Sound)*, ***adjective*** dependable, fast, fastened, firm, fixed, immovable, infallible, reliable, solid, sound, stable, strong, substantial, trustworthy, trusty, unerring, unfailing, unimpeachable

SECURITIES, *noun* assets, bonds, capital, evidences of debts, evidences of obligations, holdings, invested property, investment, negotiables, property, shares, stocks
ASSOCIATED CONCEPTS: corporate securities, investment securities, sale of securities

SECURITY *(Pledge)*, ***noun*** bail, bond, collateral, debenture, deposit, earnest, gage, guarantee, indemnity, insurance, lien, pawn, pignoration, promise, promissory note, stipulation, surety, token, vadium, voucher, warranty
ASSOCIATED CONCEPTS: collateral security, investment securities, issuing securities, public securities, real security, sale of securities, security agreement, security deposit, security interest, treasury securities, valuable securities

SECURITY *(Safety)*, ***noun*** anchor, assurance, asylum, bastion, bulwark, certainty, defense, dependability, faith, freedom from danger, freedom from harm, guard, immovability, immunity, impregnability, *incolumitas,* invulnerability, maintenance, palladium, preservation, protection, rampart, reliance, safe conduct, safeguard, safeness, *salus,* salvation, sanctuary, secureness, shelter, stability, support, trust, unassailability, unattackability
ASSOCIATED CONCEPTS: national security

SECURITY *(Stock)*, ***noun*** assets, bill of exchange, capital, certificate of debt, certificate of indebtedness, coupon, funds, indenture, invested property, investment, money invested, negotiable instrument, negotiable paper, obligation, *pignus,* secured debenture

SEDITION, *noun* apostasy, defection, defiance, desertion, disloyalty, disobedience, dissidence, infidelity, infraction, insubordination, insurgence, insurrection, *motus,* mutiny, noncompliance, overthrow, rebellion, recreance, recreancy, recusancy, resistance to authority, revolt, revolution, riot, rising, *seditio,* seditiousness, subversion, tergiversation, treachery, treason, underground activity, uprising, violation
ASSOCIATED CONCEPTS: alien and sedition acts, seditious libel

SEDITIOUS, *adjective* disloyal, incendiary, instigative, insubordinate, insurgent, insurrectionary, mutinous, provocative, rebellious, refractory, restive, revolutionary, treacherous, treasonous, turbulent, ungovernable, unruly

SEDUCTION, *noun* allure, allurement, attraction, bait, bewitchment, blandishment, cajolery, captivation, coaxing, *corruptela,* corruption, defilement, enchantment, enticement, fascination, inducement, inveiglement, invitation, lure, persuasion, seducement, solicitation, *stuprum,* tantalization, temptation

SEDULOUS, *adjective* active, *adsiduus,* alert, ardent, assiduous, attentive, avid, brisk, busily engaged, busy, conscientious, constant, diligent, dogged, eager, energetic, firm, hardworking, indefatigable, industrious, keen, laborious, painstaking, patient, perseverant, persevering, persistent, pertinacious, relentless, resolute, resolved, *sedulus,* stalwart, steadfast, tenacious, uncompromising, undeviating, unfaltering, unflagging, unrelenting, unremitting, unswerving, untiring, unwearying, unyielding, zealous

SEE *(Comprehend)*, ***verb*** ascertain, catch on to, comprehend, know, understand

SEE *(Feel)*, ***verb*** agree, consent, find out, have, learn, perceive, realize, sense, suffer, sustain

SEE *(Recall)*, ***verb*** call to mind, call up, conceive, conjure up, conjure up an image, contemplate in the imagination, envisage, envision, have a picture of, perceive, realize, view, visualize

SEE *(Observe)*, ***verb*** behold, catch, discern, espy, eye, look at, note, notice, perceive, regard, sight, spot, spy, view, witness

SEGMENT, *noun* bit, branch, cantle, cantlet, chapter, chunk, component, constituent, detached part, detail, division, element, fraction, fractional part, fragment, *fragmentum,* ingredient, installment, measure, moiety, *pars,* part, piece, portion, section, sector, *segmentum,* share, slice, small part, subdivision

SEGMENTATION, *noun* apportionment, bisection, breaking, breaking down, breaking up, carving, compartmentalizing, cutting up, demarcation, departmentalization, disconnection, dissolution, distribution, division, separation, split

SEGREGATE, *verb* confine, cut off, detach, detain, disengage, hold, immure, incarcerate, insulate, isolate, jail, keep, lock up, quarantine, remove, restrain, restrict, seclude, separate, sequester

SEGREGATION *(Isolation by races)*, ***noun*** apartheid, discrimination, division by races, ostracism, prejudice, racial prejudice, racialism, racism, separation by races
ASSOCIATED CONCEPTS: equal protection clause

SEGREGATION *(Separation)*, ***noun*** classification, detachment, differentiation, disassociation, disconnection, disengagement, dissociation, distinguishment, disunion, division, grouping, isolation, partition, *seiunctio,* setting apart
ASSOCIATED CONCEPTS: segregation of trust funds

SEISIN, *noun* control, hold, mastery, occupancy, occupation, ownership, possession, possessorship, tenancy, tenure, title
ASSOCIATED CONCEPTS: actual seisin, constructive seisin, covenant of seisin, equitable seisin, seisin in deed, seisin in fact, seisin in law

SEIZE *(Apprehend)*, ***verb*** *apprehendere,* arrest, arrest with authority, capture, catch, *comprehendere,* detain by criminal process, imprison, incarcerate, jail, put in duress, take, take in, take into custody, take prisoner

SEIZE *(Confiscate)*, ***verb*** annex, appropriate, arrogate, assume, capture, cause to be forfeited, commandeer, deprive of, dispossess, disseise, distrain, expropriate, grasp, impound, impress, mulct, pillage, pirate, pounce upon, put in possession, sequester, sequestrate, take, take possession of, usurp, wrest
ASSOCIATED CONCEPTS: attachment, execution on property, garnishment, seize property

SELECT, *adjective* accepted, adopted, appointed, best, capital, choice, chosen, culled, designated, elected, *electus,* elite, embraced, excellent, exceptional, exclusive, ex*quisitus,* first-rate, good, handpicked, matchless, named, picked, popular, preferable, preferred, prime, quality, rare, selected, superior, top-notch, unequaled, unexcelled
ASSOCIATED CONCEPTS: select committee

SELECT, ***verb*** abstract, adopt, appoint, assign, be jaundiced, be prejudiced, champion, choose, collect, cull, decide, designate, determine, differentiate, discriminate, distinguish between, draft, elect, *eligere,* eliminate, excerpt, exclude, extract, fix upon, glean, have a bias, isolate, lay aside, lean, *legere,* make a choice, make a distinction, make a selection, mark, name, nominate, pick, point out, prefer, prize, put aside, reject, segregate, seperate, set apart, shut out, sift, single out, sort out, specialize, specify, stipulate, take out, weed out, winnow
ASSOCIATED CONCEPTS: select a jury

SELECTION *(Choice),* ***noun*** adoption, appointment, appropriation, assignment, compilation, cooptation, decision, *delectus,* denomination, designation, determination, *electio,* election, extraction, indication, naming, nomination, ordainment, ordination, preference, reservation, segregation, separation, specification, stipulation
ASSOCIATED CONCEPTS: jury selection

SELECTION *(Collection),* ***noun*** accumulation, aggregation, anthology, arrangement, array, assemblage, assembly, assortment, batch, bunch, cluster, collectanea, combination, compilation, conglomeration, cumulation, examples, gathering, group, hoard, mass, pile, quantity, samples, treasury, variety

SELFISH, ***adjective*** egoistic, egomaniacal, egotistic, narcissistic, self-absorbed, self-centered, self-concerned, self-infatuated, self-interested, self-involved, selfish, self-loving, self-obsessed, self-oriented, self-preoccupied, self-regarding, self-seeking, self-serving, uncharitable

SELFLESS, ***adjective*** altruistic, benevolent, caring, charitable, chivalrous, devoted, generous, giving, helpful, humanitarian, incorruptible, indulgent, liberal, loving, magnanimous, noble, open-handed, philanthropic, self-denying, self-effacing, self-forgetting, self-sacrificing, supportive, unselfish

SELFSAMENESS, ***noun*** analogousness, close resemblance, cognate, comparability, complement, correspondence, corresponding, counterpart, equality, equivalence, exactness, general resemblance, identicalness, indistinguishability, likeness, oneness, parallelism, resemblance, sameness, semblance, similarity, similitude, synonymity, synonymy, the like

SELL, ***verb*** auction, barter, bring to market, deal in, dispense, dispose of for profit, *divendere,* drive a trade, effect a sale, exchange, furnish, give title to, handle, hawk, huckster, make a sale, market, merchandise, offer for sale, peddle, provide, put on sale, put up for sale, trade in, traffic in, transfer for a consideration, vend

SEMBLANCE, ***noun*** air, appearance, aspect, bearing, closeness, copy, counterpart, effect, example, exterior, guise, identity, illusion, image, *imago,* likeness, look, mien, outward form, replica, representation, resemblance, sameness, show, similarity, similitude, simulacrum, *species,* uniformity, visage

SEMI, ***adjective*** fractional, fragmentary, half, half-finished, not whole, partial, unfinished
ASSOCIATED CONCEPTS: semiannually

SEND, ***verb*** *ablegare,* advance, broadcast, cast, circulate, convey, direct, discharge, dismiss, dispatch, displace, drive, ejaculate, eject, emit, *emittere,* export, fling, forward, freight, give, give forth, hurl, impel, issue, jaculate, launch, mail, *mittere,* post, project, propel, relay, route, send forth, send out, ship, shoot, throw, toss, transfer, transmit

SENIOR *(Higher in priority),* ***noun*** chief, first, foremost, key major, most important, most significant, paramount, takes precedence, uppermost
ASSOCIATED CONCEPTS: bankruptcy, seniority

SENIOR *(Older),* ***noun*** adult, advanced in years, ancestor, ancient, antiquated, antique, archaic, early, elderly, matured, older, older man, older woman, one of the older generation, original, senior citizen, superannuated, veteran, vintage
ASSOCIATED CONCEPTS: elder law

SENIORITY, ***noun*** advantage, antiquity, ascendancy, command, control, eldership, leadership, pecking order, precedence, predominance, preference, priority, privilege, rank, ranking, standing, station, superiority

SENSATION *(Impression),* ***noun*** abstraction, cogitation, concept, conception, feeling, hint, image, intellection, notion, perception, reaction, response, sense, suggestion, thought

SENSATION *(Notoriety),* ***noun*** a star performer, a stellar function, esteemed event, excellence, outstanding event, popular, sought-after event, sought-after performance, success, talk of the town

SENSE *(Feeling),* ***noun*** apperception, apprehension, awareness, consciousness, discernment, idea, impression, instinct, mental image, mindfulness, notion, opinion, perception, realization, sensation, *sensus,* speculation, understanding

SENSE *(Intelligence),* ***noun*** acumen, astuteness, awareness, brightness, brilliance, cleverness, cognition, cognitive faculties, cognitive powers, comprehension, depth, enlightenment, foresight, genius, good judgment, grasp, insight, intellect, intellectual ability, intellectuality, *iudicium,* judgment, judiciousness, mentality, observation, perception, perspicacity, prudence, *prudentia,* rational faculty, rationality, reason, recognition, sagaciousness, sagacity, sapience, shrewdness, smartness, talent, understanding, wisdom, wiseness

SENSE OF RIGHT AND WRONG, ***noun*** accountableness, allegiance, conscience, decency, deference, devoir, faithfulness, good faith, honesty, inner voice, integrity, moral obligations, moral sense, morality, morals, principles, qualms, responsibility, scruples, sense of duty
ASSOCIATED CONCEPTS: intent, malice aforethought, mens rea

SENSELESS, ***adjective*** absurd, asinine, empty, fatuous, foolish, frivolous, ill-advised, inane, inconsequential, insignificant, little, minor, misadvised, negligible, pointless, ridiculous, slight, trifling, trivial, unimportant, useless, wasteful

SENSIBILITY, ***noun*** acuteness, affectibility, alertness, appreciation, attentiveness, awareness, comprehension, consciousness, delicacy, delicacy of feeling, discernment, discrimination, emotion, feeling, fineness, impressibility, judgment, keenness, mindfulness, perception, perceptivity, response, responsiveness, sensation, sensitiveness,

sensitivity, sharpness, susceptibility, sympathy, taste
ASSOCIATED CONCEPTS: peculiar sensibilities

SENSIBLE, *adjective* advisable, apprised, astute, conscious, cool-headed, discerning, discreet, discriminating, enlightened, farsighted, informed, intelligent, judicious, justifiable, knowing, knowledgeable, levelheaded, logical, observant, palpable, perceptive, politic, *prudens,* prudent, ratiocinative, rational, reasonable, sagacious, sage, sane, sapient, sapiential, shrewd, sober, sound, thinking, thoughtful, understanding, well-advised, wise

SENSITIVE *(Discerning),* ***adjective*** aesthetic, alert, alive to, apperceptive, appercipient, astute, attentive, awake to, aware, cognizant, conscious, critical, discriminating, discriminative, fastidious, heedful, keen, mindful, observant, penetrating, perceptive, percipient, perspicacious, quick of apprehension, responsive, *sensilis,* sentient, understanding

SENSITIVE *(Easily affected),* ***adjective*** easily excited, easily offended, emotive, feeling, high-strung, hypercritical, impassionable, impressible, impressionable, irritable, merciful, *mollis,* moving, overemotional, peevish, perceptive, quick-tempered, reactive, sentimental, softhearted, susceptible, susceptive, sympathetic, temperamental, tenderhearted, touchy, uncontrolled

SENTENCE, *noun* adjudication, award of punishment, censure, conviction, decision, declaration of penalty, decree of punishment, *decretum,* determination, determined punishment, doom, edict, formally pronounced judgment, *iudicium,* order of penalty, order of the court, penalty, prescribed punishment, pronouncement, punishment, ruling, verdict
ASSOCIATED CONCEPTS: concurrent sentences, consecutive sentences, cumulative sentences, excessive sentence, indeterminative sentence, life sentence, presentence hearing, suspended sentence

SENTENCE, *verb* adjudge, bring in a verdict, commit, condemn, *condemnare,* convict, *damnare,* decide, declare guilty of an offense, decree, determine, find, find guilty, hold, immure, impose penalty, imprison, inflict penalty, *multare,* order, pass judgment upon, prescribe punishment, pronounce guilty, pronounce judgment, proscribe, reprobate
ASSOCIATED CONCEPTS: presentence report

SENTENTIOUS, *adjective* abridged, aphoristic, apothegmatic, blunt, commatic, compact, compressed, concise, condensed, direct, economical of words, epigrammatic, epigrammatical, expressive, full of meaning, gnomic, laconic, meaningful, meaty, packed with meaning, pithy, pointed, precise, *sententiosus,* sparing of words, succinct, summarized, telegraphic, terse, to the point

SENTIMENT, *noun* angle, attitude, belief, chord, conviction, emotion, feeling, impression, mind, notion, opinion, outlook, passion, perception, perspective, receptivity, response, sensation, sense, standpoint, thoughts, view, viewpoint

SEPARABLE, *adjective* breakable, cleavable, detachable, divisible, partible, severable
ASSOCIATED CONCEPTS: joint and separable liability, separability of arbitration, separable controversy, separable interest, separate provision

SEPARATE, *adjective* alone, apart, asunder, departing, detached, different, disassociated, disconnected, *disiunctus,* disjoined, disjointed, disjunct, disparate, disrelated, dissimilar, dissociated, distinct, disunited, divergent, diverse, divided, divorced, independent, individual, insular, isolated, lone, loose, parted, removed, secluded, *secretus,* segregated, separated, *separatus,* set apart, severed, solitary, split, sundered, unaccompanied, unaffiliated, unallied, unassociated, unattached, unattended, unconnected
ASSOCIATED CONCEPTS: separate action, separate cause of action, separate maintenance

SEPARATE, *verb* alienate, break, break off, break up, cleave, come apart, come between, cut adrift, cut off, detach, disassociate, disband, disconnect, disengage, *disiungere,* disjoin, dismember, dispart, disperse, dissever, dissociate, dissolve, disunite, divide, exclude, fractionize, hold apart, intersect, keep apart, part, part company, part ways, rend, rive, rupture, section, sectionalize, segment, segregate, *separare,* set apart, sever, splinter, split, split up, sunder, tear, unbind, uncouple, unloose, unmarry, unravel, untie, unyoke, winnow
ASSOCIATED CONCEPTS: annul, divorce

SEPARATION, *noun* alienation, breach, break, cleavage, detachment, disassociation, *disiunctio,* disseverance, dissociation, dissolution, dissolution of marriage, disunion, division, divorce, divorcement, estrangement, legal dissolution of marriage, parting, rending, rupture, *separatio,* severance, split, sundering, tearing, termination of marital cohabitation, uncoupling
ASSOCIATED CONCEPTS: judgment of separation, judicial separation, just cause for separation, legal separation, separation agreement, separation by consent, separation decree, separation of powers, separation order, voluntary separation

SEQUACIOUS, *adjective* accommodating, acquiescent, adaptable, amenable, bendable, bending, compliant, deferential, dependent, docile, ductile, easily influenced, easily led, easily taught, easygoing, elastic, facile, fictile, flexible, flexile, giving, governable, impressible, impressionable, lacking individuality, malleable, manageable, meek, moldable, obedient, obeisant, obliging, obsequious, passive, plastic, pliable, pliant, reverential, servile, slavish, submissive, subordinate, sycophantic, teachable, toadying, tractable, unassertive, undeviating, unimaginative, without originality, yielding

SEQUENCE, *noun* alternation, arrangement, array, catenation, chain, classification, concatenation, consecution, continuum, cycle, flow, gradation, group, list, logical order, nexus, order, *ordo,* procession, progression, rotation, serialization, string, succession

SEQUESTER *(Seclude),* ***verb*** cloister, closet, conceal, confine, exclude, isolate, quarantine, remove, retire, secret, segregate, separate, withdraw
ASSOCIATED CONCEPTS: sequester a jury, sequester a witness

SEQUESTER *(Seize property),* ***verb*** annex, appropriate, arrogate, attach, confiscate, dispossess, distrain, impound, impress, levy, preempt, replevy, separate, sequestrate, set apart, set aside, take, take hold of, wrest
ASSOCIATED CONCEPTS: sequester assets

SEQUESTRATION *(Financial funds withheld),* ***noun*** across-the-board cuts imposed, automatic budget cuts, balancing the budget, cut in government spending, fiscal constraints which are automatically imposed, increased savings, process to cut the deficit, reduced spending, reduction in spending, separation
ASSOCIATED CONCEPTS: sequestration of budget cuts to curtail the deficit

SEQUESTRATION *(Isolation of a jury),* ***noun*** insulation of a jury, isolation of jury deliberations, means to ensure privacy for a jury, private deliberations of a jury, segregation of a jury, separation of a jury

SERIAL, ***noun*** consecution, fascicle, issue, periodical, procession, progression, series, successive portion

SERIOUS *(Devoted),* ***adjective*** ardent, assiduous, decided, dedicated, determined, devout, dogged, dutiful, eager, earnest, faithful, fervent, firm, fixed, intent, loyal, passionate, purposeful, relentless, resolute, resolved, settled, sincere, steadfast, steady, tenacious, true, uncompromising, unfaltering, unswerving, unyielding, zealous
ASSOCIATED CONCEPTS: serious crime, serious wrongdoing

SERIOUS *(Grave),* ***adjective*** *austerus,* consequential, critical, crucial, dangerous, dire, dreadful, fatal, *gravis,* great, grim, highly serious, important, intense, momentous, pensive, pressing, *serius,* severe, *severus,* sober, solemn, stern, weighty
ASSOCIATED CONCEPTS: serious and willful misconduct, serious bodily injury, serious crime, serious harm, serious wrongdoing

SERVE *(Assist),* ***verb*** accommodate, administer to, advance, afford aid, aid, assist, attend, be of use, care for, come to the aid of, *commodare,* comply, confer a benefit, contribute to, cooperate, *deservire,* discharge one's duty, do a service, do one's bidding, fill an office, forward, furnish aid, furnish assistance, give help, help, lend aid, minister to, promote, render help, *servire,* submit, succor, supply aid, take care of, tend, wait on, work for

SERVE *(Deliver a legal instrument),* ***verb*** afford notice, deliver, deliver a summons and complaint, deliver over, forward, give notice to, hand over, issue, make delivery of legal process, present, subpoena, summon, turn over
ASSOCIATED CONCEPTS: serve with process

SERVICE *(Assistance),* ***noun*** abetment, accommodation, advice, aid, attendance, backing, benefit, care, cooperation, favor, guidance, help, helping hand, *ministerium,* ministration, *opera,* relief, succor, support, useful office, usefulness
ASSOCIATED CONCEPTS: essential service, professional service, public service, service contract, service mark

SERVICE *(Delivery of legal process),* ***noun*** commencement of an action, delivery of a writ, delivery of process, handing over legal papers, institution of proceedings, notification of legal action
ASSOCIATED CONCEPTS: actual service of process, constructive service of process, personal service, service by mail, service by publication, service of notice, service of subpoena, service of summons, service rendered, special service, substituted service of process

SERVILE, ***adjective*** abiectus, abject, compliant, deferential, downtrodden, fawning, groveling, harnessed, humble, *humilis,* ingratiating, low, mean, meek, menial, obedient, obeisant, obsequious, passive, prostrate, respectful, *servilis,* slavish, subject, submissive, subordinate, supple, sycophantic, tractable, truckling, unassertive, unresisting, vernile

SERVITUDE, ***noun*** bonds, burden, captivity, charge, compulsion, enslavement, enthrallment, fetters, helotism, helotry, indenture, obedience, oppression, restraint, service, *servitium, servitus,* slavery, subjection, subjugation, submission, subordination, subservience, suppression, thrall, thralldom
ASSOCIATED CONCEPTS: involuntary servitude, penal servitude, real servitude

SESQUIPEDALIAN, ***adjective*** grandiloquent, lengthy, long, magniloquent, multisyllabic, pedantic, sonorous

SESSION, ***noun*** assembly, audience, caucus, conclave, conference, congregation, congress, consultation, convention, *conventus,* convocation, council, diet, forgathering, forum, gathering, hearing, meeting, parley, plenum, rendezvous, roundtable, sitting, synod, term, union
ASSOCIATED CONCEPTS: general sessions, joint session, regular session, session laws, special sessions

SET APART, ***adjective*** cloistered, covert, demarcated, distinct, distinguished, hidden, isolated, remote, secluded, secret, separate, separated, sheltered

SET ASIDE *(Annul),* ***verb*** abandon, abjure, abnegate, abrogate, accumulate, amass, cast off, discard, dispense with, dispose of, disuse, drop, omit, reject, relegate, relinquish, renounce, repudiate, shunt, spurn
ASSOCIATED CONCEPTS: set aside a verdict

SET ASIDE *(Reserve),* ***verb*** keep in reserve, lay aside, pigeonhole, pile up, put aside, put away, save up, set apart, shelve, store up

SET DOWN, ***verb*** book, calender, chronicle, commit to writing, docket, enter, jot down, line up, list, note, place, plan, post, program, put on record, record, register, schedule, slate
ASSOCIATED CONCEPTS: set down for trial

SET FORTH, ***verb*** allege, argue, articulate, assert, characterize, cite, commence, communicate, contend, convey, declare, delineate, demonstrate, depict, describe, detail, develop, disclose, display, divulge, enunciate, evince, expound, express, illustrate, issue, manifest, plead, portray, posit, present, proclaim, profess, proffer, promulgate, propose, propound, reason, recite, recount, relate, render, report, represent, show, signify, state, trace, unfold
ASSOCIATED CONCEPTS: set forth the allegations of a crime

SETBACK, ***noun*** breakdown, comedown, decline, descent, disappointment, downfall, failure, frustration, impediment, knock, lapse, letdown, loss, obstacle, recession, regression, relapse, retrogression, reversal, reversion, setback, snag, turnabout, turnaround

SETOFF, ***noun*** allowance, balance, compensation, counter, counter demand, counterbalance, credit, equalization, equivalent, offset, opposite, outstanding indebtedness, satisfaction
ASSOCIATED CONCEPTS: affirmative defense, counterclaim

SETTLE, ***verb*** settle order on notice, accommodate, adjust, agree, agree upon, approve, arrange, arrange matters,

arrange matters in dispute, ascertain, bring to terms, bring together, clear up, come to a determination, come to an agreement, come to an understanding, come to terms, compromise, conclude, *conficere, constituere,* decide, determine, determine once for all, dispose of, end, even the score, harmonize, make a compact, mend, negotiate, put in order, reach a compromise, reconcile, rectify, resolve, restore harmony, set at rest, set in place, settle, solve, stabilize, straighten out, strike a bargain, work out
ASSOCIATED CONCEPTS: settle a bill of exceptions, settle a claim, settle a judgment, settle an account, settle an estate, settle an order, settle issues, settle property, settled account

SETTLED METHOD, ***noun*** accordance, common practice, compliance, conformity, conventionalism, conventionality, custom, established mode, formality, mere form, observance of form, prescription, propriety, protocol, rigidity, rule of procedure, usual custom

SETTLEMENT, ***noun*** accommodation, adjustment, agreement, arrangement, arrangement of difficulties, bargain, *compositio,* composure of differences, composure of doubts, compromise, conciliation, concordat, *constitutio,* contract, determination by agreement, discharge, disposition, final terms, negotiation, pact, *pactum,* payment, reconciliation, release, satisfaction, set of terms, terms, understanding
ASSOCIATED CONCEPTS: deed of settlement, final settlement, settlement of a case, voluntary settlement

SEVER, ***verb*** break apart, break off, cleave, cut, cut adrift, detach, *dirimere,* disband, disconnect, disengage, disjoin, dismember, dispair, dispart, dissever, dissociate, dissolve, disunite, divide, *dividere,* divorce, fissure, isolate, keep apart, lacerate, lop off, part, partition, rend, rend asunder, rive, rupture, segment, segregate, *separare,* separate, set apart, slit, splinter, split, subdivide, sunder, tear, unbind, uncouple, unfasten, untie, wrench
ASSOCIATED CONCEPTS: sever a claim, sever a party, sever an action, severable cause of action, severable contract

SEVERABLE, ***adjective*** apportionable, cleavable, detachable, dissoluable, dividual, *dividuus,* divisible, fissile, fissionable, fractional, partible, scissile, *separabilis,* separable
ASSOCIATED CONCEPTS: severable contract, severable statute

SEVERAL *(Plural),* ***adjective*** assorted, certain, diverse, few, more than one, some, sundry

SEVERAL *(Separate),* ***adjective*** appropriate, certain, chosen, definite, different, distinctive, distinguishable, exclusive, fixed, independent, marked, peculiar, personal, private, proper, representative, singular, unique
ASSOCIATED CONCEPTS: several defendants, several liability, several ownership, several tracts, several trusts, several transactions, severally

SEVERANCE, ***noun*** bifurcation, cleavage, demarcation, detachment, differentiation, disassociation, discrimination, distinction, distinguishment, division, divorce, fission, isolation, scission, segregation, separation, sunderance, withdrawal
ASSOCIATED CONCEPTS: severance damage, severance of statute, severance pay, severance tax

SEVERE, ***adjective*** acrimonious, afflictive, agonizing, astringent, austere, *austerus,* bearish, brutal, censorious, churlish, coercive, cold, condemnatory, critical, cruel, despotic, difficult, domineering, dour, drastic, *durus,* exacting, excruciating, exigent, faultfinding, fierce, firm, forbidding, furious, grievous, grim, gruff, hard, hard to endure, harsh, hypercritical, ill-natured, ill-tempered, immovable, implacable, inclement, inexorable, inflexible, insufferable, intense, intractable, ironclad, ironhanded, mordant, nasty, obdurate, oppressive, overbearing, overpowering, painful, peremptory, pitiless, punitive, puritanic, puritanical, raging, relentless, rigid, rigorous, rough, rugged, ruthless, savage, *severus,* sharp, sour, stark, stern, stiff, stinging, stony, stony-hearted, stormy, straitlaced, strict, stringent, stubborn, tempestuous, tough, trying, tyrannical, unbending, uncompromising, unfeeling, ungentle, ungracious, unjust, unkind, unmerciful, unmitigated, unrelenting, unsparing, unyielding, vicious, vindictive, violent
ASSOCIATED CONCEPTS: severe penalties

SEVERE WEATHER, ***idiom*** astringent weather conditions, austere climate conditions, bitter weather conditions, cruel weather, extreme weather, harsh weather, onerous weather conditions, pitiless, unrelenting weather, unsparing weather
ASSOCIATED CONCEPTS: environmental conservation

SEVERITY, ***noun*** *acerbitas,* acerbity, acrimony, asperity, austerity, causticity, cruel treatment, cruelty, ferity, ferociousness, ferocity, fierceness, force, fury, *gravitas,* gravity, grimness, harshness, inclemency, inexorability, inflexibility, inhumanity, intensity, might, relentlessness, rigor, rigorousness, ruthlessness, savagery, seriousness, *severitas,* sharpness, sternness, strictness, stringency, turbulence, tyranny, unkindness, venom, violence, virulence

SEXUAL ABUSE, ***noun*** molestation, rape, sex offender, sexual assault, sexual harassment
ASSOCIATED CONCEPTS: Megan's Law

SEXUAL ASSAULT, ***noun*** crime, criminal action, criminal activity, criminal offense, felony, illegal action, illegality, offense against the state, serious offense against law, sexual abuse, sexual attack, sexual force, sexual injury

SEXUAL HARASSMENT, ***noun*** actionable annoyance at place of employment, actionable conduct, gender harassment in the workplace, offensive verbal abuse in the workplace, plan of physical harassment by superiors, policy of verbal harassment by superiors, unsolicited physical behavior in the workplace, unsolicited verbal abuse in the workplace, unwarranted advances, unwelcome sexual advances, verbal abuse at work
ASSOCIATED CONCEPTS: hostile workplace

SHALL, ***verb*** as required will, by compulsion will, by imperative will, mandatorily will, obligatorily will
ASSOCIATED CONCEPTS: shall be lawful, shall be legal, shall become, shall give, shall have, shall not, shall perform, shall work

SHAM, ***noun*** chicanery, counterfeit, deception, delusion, *dolus,* fabrication, fake, *fallacia,* false show, feint, forgery, *fraud,* fraus, guise, imitation, impersonation, impostor, imposture, masquerade, misrepresentation, mock, pretense, reproduction, simulacrum, simulation, trick, trickery
ASSOCIATED CONCEPTS: sham defense, sham pleading

SHAMBLES, ***noun*** cataclysm, chaos, confusion, destruction, disorder, disorganization, disruption, havoc, holocaust, jumble, *laniena,* madhouse, maelstrom, mayhem, mess, pandemonium, scene of destruction, scene of disorder, state of violence, turmoil, upheaval, uproar, welter

SHAME, ***noun*** abasement, abjectness, abuse, aspersion, attaint, bad name, baseness, blot, contempt, debasement, defamation, defilement, degradation, discredit, disesteem, disfavor, disgrace, dishonor, disrepute, disrespect, humiliation, *ignominia,* ignominy, ill repute, *infamia,* infamy, loss of honor, loss of reputation, obloquy, odium, opprobrium, reproach, scandal, scorn, smirch, stain, stigma, taint, tarnish, tarnished honor, turpitude, vileness

SHAPE, ***noun*** appearance, build, cast, color, complexion, condition, configuration, contour, criterion, cut, delineation, fashion, feature, features, figure, form, frame, guise, image, impression, likeness, look, manner, mien, mode, mold, motif, organization, outline, pattern, physique, posture, presence, profile, seeming, semblance, state, structure, style, turn

SHAPE, ***verb*** adapt, carve, compose, conform, create, delineate, design, devise, fashion, figure, form, formalize, formulate, frame, influence, make, manufacture, model, mold, pattern, produce, sculpture, style, tailor
ASSOCIATED CONCEPTS: shaping of a claim, shaping of a defense

SHARE *(Interest),* ***noun*** allocation, allotment, apportioned lot, commission, dole, measure, *pars,* part, percent, percentage, portion, proportion, quotum, ratio, ration, right, section, segment, slice
ASSOCIATED CONCEPTS: distributive share, equal share, share and share alike, share of capital, similiar share

SHARE *(Stock),* ***noun*** asset, capital, corporate interest, holding, invested property, investment, property, security, stockholding
ASSOCIATED CONCEPTS: bank shares, corporate shares, share of corporate stock, shareholder, treasury shares

SHAREHOLDER, ***noun*** investor, owner, property owner, stockholder, stockholder of record, stockowner
ASSOCIATED CONCEPTS: shareholder action, shareholder's derivative suit

SHED LIGHT ON, ***verb*** account for, clarify, clear the air, clear up, decipher, demonstrate, demystify, elucidate, enlighten, explain, explain away, explain oneself, explain the meaning of, expound on, get to the bottom of, get to the heart of, illuminate, illustrate, interpret, make sense of, provide insight, provide reason for, provide the meaning of, show, solve, spell out, unfold, unlock, unravel

SHELTER *(Protection),* ***noun*** aid, *asylum,* care, cover, covering, coverture, defense, habitation, harbor, haven, home, house, lodging, place of refuge, preservation, refuge, retreat, roof, safety, sanctuary, screen, security, shield, stronghold, support

SHELTER *(Tax benefit),* ***noun*** advantage, gain, hedge, refuge, security, tax haven, tax sanctuary
ASSOCIATED CONCEPTS: tax shelter

SHIELD, ***noun*** aegis, buckler, buffer, bulwark, *clipeus,* cover, covert, coverture, defense, guard, protection, protector, rampart, refuge, safeguard, sanctuary, screen, *scutum,* security, shelter

SHIFTING, ***adjective*** alternating, changeable, changing, deviating, digressive, discursive, drifting, fluctuating, inconstant, interim, roaming, roving, straying, transient, transitory, uncertain, vacillating, varying, wandering, wavering
ASSOCIATED CONCEPTS: shifting risk, shifting the burden of proof, shifting trust, shifting use

SHIP, ***verb*** bestow, contribute, convey, deliver, export, forward, import, pass, present, resend, return, send, transport
ASSOCIATED CONCEPTS: Interstate Commerce Clause

SHIRK, ***verb*** abstain, avoid, cheat, *detrectare,* dodge, duck, elude, escape from, evade, funk, ignore, keep away from, leave undone, malinger, neglect, quit, refuse, run from, shrink, shun, slink away, stay away, steer clear

SHOCK, ***verb*** amaze, astound, awe, daunt, discomfort, discompose, disconcert, displease, disquiet, distress, disturb, offend, outrage, overpower, overwhelm, perturb, repel, revolt, shake, startle, surprise, terrify, terrorize, unnerve, unsettle, unstring, upset

SHOOTING, ***noun*** accident, battle, gun down, killing, massacre, murder, raid, tragedy, war
ASSOCIATED CONCEPTS: manslaughter, murder

SHORT *(Brief),* ***adjective*** abbreviated, abridged, compact, compressed, concise, condensed, crisp, cursory, curtailed, deficient, delinquent, devoid, fleet, fleeting, fugacious, hasty, laconic, meager, minimal, momentary, perfunctory, petulant, poor, quick, scarce, short-lived, shy, skimpy, sparse, succinct, temporary, terse, transient, unelevated
ASSOCIATED CONCEPTS: short clause, short form decision of the court, short notice

SHORT *(Caustic),* ***adjective*** abrupt, acetous, acrimonious, blunt, brusque, curt, discourteous, froward, grouchy, gruff, impolite, irascible, peevish, sharp, sour, sullen, surly, terse, touchy, testy, trenchant, ungraceful, volatile

SHORT *(Imperfect),* ***adjective*** defective, inadequate, incommensurate, incomplete, insufficient, lacking, low, meager, needing, sparse, unenduring, wanting

SHORTAGE, ***noun*** absence, crunch, dearth, deficiency, deficit, delinquency, drought, failure, famine, inadequacy, inadequateness, insufficiency, lack, lacuna, need, paucity, pinch, poverty, scantiness, scarceness, scarcity, shortage, undersupply, want

SHORTCOMING, ***noun*** Achilles' heel, blemish, deficiency, demerit, dereliction, difficulty to overcome, disadvantage, failing, fall, flaw, foible, frailty, handicap, imperfection, inability, lack, nemesis, sin, soft spot, vice, want, weakness

SHORTEN, ***verb*** abbreviate, abridge, compress, constrict, contract, curtail, cut back, decrease, diminish, elide, encapsulate, epitomize, minimize, modify, pare, prune, reduce, shrink, slash, subtract, sum up, summarize, syncopate, taper, trim, truncate

SHORTSIGHTED, ***adjective*** careless, extravagant, heedless, imprudent, incautious, indulgent, injudicious, mindless, myopic, prodigal, profligate, reckless, spendthrift, thriftless, unguarded, unsafe, unwary, unwise, wasteful

SHOW *(Display)*, ***noun*** affectation, amusement, appearance, array, ceremony, chance, color, deceptive appearance, delusion, demonstration, distortion, exhibit, exhibition, expression, facade, flashiness, flourish, frills, front, illusion, impression, manifestation, materialization, occasion, outward show, parade, phenomenon, pomp, pomposity, pompousness, pose, presence, pretense, pretext, revelation, scene, semblance, show, showiness, sight, simulation, specious appearance, splash, trick, veneer, window dressing
ASSOCIATED CONCEPTS: show cause

SHOW *(Production)*, ***noun*** entertainment, exhibition, exposition, performance, presentation, spectacle

SHOW *(Come into view)*, ***verb*** be seen, be visible, bring under notice, make one see, materialize, present oneself

SHOW *(Detail)*, ***verb*** adduce, attest, bare, be visible, bear, cite, clarify, demean, demonstrate, denote, depict, designate, detail, disclose, display, document, edify, educate, establish, evidence, evince, exemplify, exhibit, explain, expose, express, furnish evidence, illustrate, indicate, inform, instruct, lay bare, make known, manifest, point out, point the way, portray, present, present oneself, produce, prove, render, represent, reveal, set forth, set straight, signify, specify, tell, testify, unveil, unfold, unmask

SHOW CAUSE, ***verb*** present a case, present argument, present cause, present reason, show grounds for
ASSOCIATED CONCEPTS: order to show cause

SHOWING, ***noun*** appearance, authentication, broadcast, communication, declaration, demonstration, display, dispute, documentation, evidence, explanation, exposé, manifestation, parade, placard, projection, proof, substantiation, support
ASSOCIATED CONCEPTS: showing of evidence, showing of proof

SHRINK, ***verb*** abbreviate, abridge, compress, constrict, contract, curtail, cut back, decrease, diminish, dock, elide, encapsulate, epitomize, minimize, modify, pare, prune, reduce, shrink, slash, subtract, sum up, syncopate, taper, trim, truncate

SHROUD, ***verb*** adumbrate, becloud, befog, blanket, bury, cloak, closet, conceal, cover, curtain, darken, eclipse, encase, ensconce, envelop, enwrap, hide, mask, muffle, obscure, overshadow, protect, render invisible, screen, seclude, sheathe, shelter, suppress, *tegere,* veil, *velare,* wrap

SHUN, ***verb*** abhor, abstain, avoid, back away, boycott, bypass, circumvent, cold-shoulder, *defugere,* deliberately avoid, disregard, dodge, draw back, elude, escape, eschew, evade, give a wide berth to, have no part of, have nothing to do with, hide from, ignore, keep away from, keep clear of, keep one's distance, leave, let alone, malinger, neglect, rebuff, recoil from, refrain, shirk, shrink from, shy away from, snub, spurn, stay away from, steer clear of, turn aside, turn away from, *vitare,* ward off

SHUT, ***verb*** bar, barricade, block, block off, block up, blockade, bound, bung, button, cease, choke off, clasp, *claudere,* cloister, close, close down, cork, corral, cover, dam, discontinue, encase, enclose, end, envelop, enwrap, fasten, fence in, finish, halt, hem in, *includere,* intern, latch, lock, obstruct, occlude, plug, prevent passage, retard flow, seal, secure, shut down, stop, stop up, stopper, terminate, throttle, turn off

SIDE, ***noun*** affiliation, angle, aspect, body of partisans, cause, coalition, conception, direction, facet, faction, outlook, *pars,* party, point of view, position, sect, slant, standpoint, surface, verge, view, viewpoint

SIDE, ***verb*** advocate, aid, assist, back up, befriend, bolster, brace, buttress, champion, defend, encourage, endorse, favor, further, help, plead for, promote, protect, rally around, reinforce, second, stand behind, stand by, stick up for, strengthen, support, sustain, take the part of, unite with, uphold, vote for, vouch for

SIEGE, ***noun*** assault, battle, confinement, containment, counterblockade, encampment, encirclement, encompassment, incarceration, insulation, internment, invasion, isolation, quarantine, raid, seclusion, segregation

SIGHT *(Appearance)*, ***noun*** apparency, curiosity, display, effect, exposure, figure, front, glance, guise, impression, inspection, ken, mien, object, panorama, perception, perspective, phenomenon, prospect, regard, respect, scene, scrutiny, show, spectacle, view, vision, vista

SIGHT *(Condition)*, ***noun*** complexion, eyesore, fright, look, mess

SIGHT *(Eyesight)*, ***noun*** eyeshot, field of view, line of sight, range or scope of vision, visualization

SIGHT, ***verb*** behold, contemplate, descry, detect, discern, distinguish, espy, gape, gaze, glimpse, look, look on or upon, notice, observe, peek, peer, perceive, recognize, regard, scan, scrutinize, see, set one's sights, set or lay eyes on, spot, spy, study, survey, view, take in, witness

SIGN, ***verb*** accept, accredit, acknowledge, affix a signature, affix one's name, affix one's signature to, agree to, approve, authenticate, authorize, autograph, certify, confirm, *consignare,* covenant, enter into a contract, execute, indorse, initial, inscribe one's name, inscribe one's signature, license, paraph, ratify, sanction, seal, set one's name to, subscribe, *subscribere,* undersign, underwrite, validate
ASSOCIATED CONCEPTS: countersign

SIGN OVER, ***verb*** assign, bequeath, bestow, commit, confer, consign, contribute, deliver, donate, entrust, grant, hand down, hand over, lease, leave, lend, let, move, pass, pass down, present, release, relinquish, surrender, transfer, transmit, trust, turn in, turn over, vest, will, yield
ASSOCIATED CONCEPTS: assignment of a contract, assignment of a lease

SIGNAL, ***noun*** flag, gesticulation, gesture, indication, indicator, knell, lights, manifestation, means of communication, motion, posture, red light, sign, sign language, signification, tocsin

SIGNIFICANCE, ***noun*** bearing, concern, concernment, consequence, distinction, eminence, essentiality, excellence, force, gist, gravity, greatness, import, importance, interest, mark, materiality, materialness, matter, meaning, merit, moment, momentousness, notability, note, paramountcy, pith, portent, precedence, preeminence, primacy, priority, prominence, relevance, salience, salient point, seriousness, *significatio,* signification, substance, substantiality, supremacy, value, *vis,* weight, weightiness, worth

SIGNIFICATION, ***noun*** acceptation, aim, connotation, designation, drift, effect, essence, explanation, force, gist, impact, implication, import, importance, indication, inference, intent, intention, interpretation, meaning, meat, moral, object, pith, point, purport, purpose, sense, significance, *significatio,* substance, tenor, value, vis, worth

SIGNIFY *(Denote),* ***verb*** betoken, connotate, connote, delineate, demonstrate, depict, evidence, evince, exemplify, hint, illustrate, imply, indicate, insinuates, intimate, manifest, mark, mean, point out, portray, purport, represent, reveal, show, stand for, suggest, symbolize, tell of, typify

SIGNIFY *(Inform),* ***verb*** acquaint, advance, advise, air, announce, apprise, assert, bruit, caution, communicate, convey, convey knowledge, declare, demonstrate, designate, direct the attention to, disclose, disseminate, divulge, enlighten, enumerate, express, give notice, give sign, impart, instruct, issue, make known, make obvious, make plain, make public, mention, notify, proclaim, promulgate, publish, report, reveal, set forth, specify, state, stipulate, tell, vent, voice

SILENCE, ***noun*** absolute quiet, hush, lack of sound, noiselessness, quiescence, quiescency, quiet, quietness, quietude, *silentium,* soundlessness, speechlessness, stillness, suppression of sound, *taciturnitas,* wordlessness
ASSOCIATED CONCEPTS: estopped by silence, silence as an admission
FOREIGN PHRASES: ***Qui tacet, consentire videtur.*** He who is silent is deemed to consent. ***Qui tacet consentire videtur, ubi tractatur de ejus commodo.*** He who is silent is deemed to consent, when his interest is at stake.

SIMILAR, ***adjective*** agreeing, allied, analogous, approximate, close, cognate, collateral, companion, comparable, conformable, congeneric, congenerical, congruent, connatural, consimilar, consubstantial, correspondent, corresponding, equivalent, homogeneous, identical, indistinguishable, kindred, like, matching, par, parallel, related, resembling, same, similis, synonymous, twin, uniform
FOREIGN PHRASES: ***Ubi eadem ratio, ibi idem jus; et de similibus, idem est judicium.*** Where there is the same reason, there is the same law; and where there are similar situations, the judgment is the same.

SIMILARITY, ***noun*** affinity, alikeness, analogousness, analogy, community, comparability, correlation, correspondence, equation, equivalence, identicalness, likeness, parallelism, parity, relation, resemblance, sameness, semblance, similitude

SIMPLE, ***adjective*** artless, bare, basal, basic, clear, crude, downright, elemental, elementary, frank, free of duplicity, fundamental, guileless, homespun, homogeneous, inartificial, incomplex, *inconditus,* ingenuous, inornate, intelligible, irreducible, mere, natural, open, plain, primary, pure, rudimentary, rustic, simple-minded, *simplex,* simplified, sincere, *sincerus,* single, straightforward, unadorned, unadulterated, unaffected, unalloyed, unblended, uncombined, uncomplicated, uncompounded, unconstrained, undecorated, understandable, undesigning, unembellished, uninvolved, unmingled, unmixed, unpretentious, unsophisticated, unstudied, unvarnished, without confusion
ASSOCIATED CONCEPTS: simple assault, simple battery, simple contract, simple larceny, simple will

SIMPLIFY *(Clarify),* ***verb*** clear up, elucidate, explain, make clear, make plain, unfold, untwist

SIMPLIFY *(Make easier),* ***verb*** disentangle, make plain, streamline, uncomplicate, unravel

SIMULATE, ***verb*** act, copy, counterfeit, fabricate, feign, imitate, make believe, mock, play-act, pretend, represent
ASSOCIATED CONCEPTS: simulated conveyance, simulated sale, simulation

SIMULTANEOUS, ***adjective*** accompanying, at the same time, coetaneous, coeval, coexistent, coexisting, coincident, coinstantaneous, concomitant, concurrent, contemporaneous, contemporary, cotemporary, *eodem tempore,* in concert, *simul,* synchronal, synchronic, synchronical, synchronistic, synchronistical, synchronous
ASSOCIATED CONCEPTS: simultaneous death

SIN, ***noun*** breach, crime, debt, error, lawbreaking, malefaction, misdeed, misdoing, offensive act, offensive action, transgression, trespass, violation, wrongdoing

SINCERE, ***adjective*** aboveboard, bona fide, candid, deceitless, direct, earnest, faithful, fervent, forthright, frank, genuine, guileless, honest, open, pure, real, reliable, scrupulous, serious, straight, straightforward, true, trustworthy, truthful, undeceitful, veracious, wholehearted

SINE DIE, ***adverb*** at no period, at no time, never, never again, on no occasion, without date

SINE QUA NON, ***noun*** absolute condition, absolute prerequisite, antecedent, condition, contingency, essential clause, essential condition, essential matter, essential part, essential qualification, indispensable condition, indispensable item, necessity, precondition, prerequisite, prime constituent, prime ingredient, qualification, requirement, vital concern

SINECURE, ***noun*** easily managed job, easy chore, easy employment, easy job, easy labor, effortless assignment, effortless employment, effortless undertaking, effortless work, light labor, light work, simple job, soft job, undemanding chore, undemanding job, undemanding task

SINEW, ***noun*** brawn, brawniness, effectiveness, endurance, energy, force, forcefulness, grit, lustiness, might, muscle, *nervus,* potence, potency, power, powerfulness, robustness, stamina, staying power, strength, thews, vigor, vigorousness

SINGLE *(Singular),* ***adjective*** exclusive, individual, lone, one of a kind, only, particular, unattached

SINGLE *(Unmarried),* ***adjective*** detached, disconnected, discrete, free, freestanding, uncommon, unconnected, unshared, unwed

SINGULAR, ***adjective*** different, distinct, eccentric, *egregius,* eminent, especial, exceptional, exclusive, extraordinary, individual, isolated, lone, matchless, nonpareil, odd, out of the ordinary, particular, peculiar, peerless, queer, rare, remarkable, separate, single, *singularis,* sole, special, unaccompanied, uncommon, uncustomary, unequaled, unexampled, *unicus,* unique, unparalleled, unprecedented, unusual

SINISTER, ***adjective*** alarming, baleful, baneful, blameworthy, censurable, cold-blooded, comminatory, conscienceless, contemptible, corrupt, creepy, cruel, culpable, dangerous, demoniac, demoniacal, deserving of condemnation, designing, despiteful, destructive, detrimental, diabolic, diabolical, dishonest, disingenuous, dismaying, disquieting, disreputable, disturbing, dreadful, eerie, envenomed, evil, exceptionable, facinorous, fear-inspiring, fearsome, fiendish, flagitious, flawed, frightening, ghoulish, harmful, heartless, heinous, horrible, horrid, hurtful, ignoble, ill-disposed, illaudable, immeritorious, immoral, impious, inauspicious, infamous, injurious, inquitous, insidious, intimidating, lawless, malefic, maleficent, maleficial, malevolent, malicious, malign, malignant, menacing, minatory, mischievous, miscreant, murderous, nefarious, nocuous, noisome, noxious, obliquitous, peccable, peccant, pernicious, perverse, portending evil, *pravus,* presageful, rascally, remorseless, reprehensible, satanic, scatheful, scheming, scoundrelly, sinful, spiteful, tainted, terrible, threatening, treacherous, truculent, unbenevolent, uncommendable, unfair, unfavorable, unjustifiable, unprincipled, unpromising, unpropitious, unrighteous, untrustworthy, unwholesome, venomous, villainous, virulent, wicked, worthy of blame, wrong

SINUOUS, ***adjective*** ambagious, ambagitory, anfractuous, circuitous, coiled, complex, complicated, convolute, convoluted, convolutional, crooked, curved, curvilinear, deviating, deviative, devious, entangled, flexuous, indirect, intricate, involute, involuted, involutional, involutionary, involved, labyrinthian, labyrinthine, mazy, meandering, meandrous, oblique, plexiform, rambling, reticular, roundabout, serpentine, sinuate, *sinuosus,* snaky, spiral, tangled, tortile, tortuous, turning, twisted, twisting, volute, winding, zigzag

SITE, ***noun*** address, base, environs, habitat, locale, locality, location, neighborhood, place, position, setting, situation, situs, stead, territory, vicinity

SITE, ***verb*** arrange, assign, base, center, localize, locate, place, position, situate

SITUATED, ***adjective*** anchored, bestead, *conlocatus,* embedded, ensconced, established, fixed, found, housed, implanted, installed, laid, located, lodged, occupying, placed, planted, posited, positioned, positus, posted, proximate to, put, quartered, rooted, seated, set, settled, *situs,* stationed
ASSOCIATED CONCEPTS: similarly situated

SITUATION, ***noun*** arrangement, case, circumstance, circumstances, condition, crisis, environment, exigency, happening, incidence, instance, juncture, lot, mishap, occurrence, plight, position, post, posture, predicament, *situs,* standing, state, station, status

SITUS, ***noun*** locale, locality, location, locus, place, placement, point, position, site, situation
ASSOCIATED CONCEPTS: situs of a crime

SIZE *(Frequency),* ***noun*** area, bigness, body, cubic content, expanse, extent, girth, intensity, quantity, scope, tonnage, volume

SIZE *(Physical magnitude),* ***noun*** amplitude, bulk, caliber, capacity, dimensions, extent, frequency, greatness, largeness, magnitude, mass, measurement, proportions
ASSOCIATED CONCEPTS: size of a market share, size of jury pool

SKEPTICAL, ***adjective*** agnostic, cynical, disbelieving, distrustful, distrusting, doubting, dubious, faithless, freethinking, heretical, heterodox, iconoclastic, incredulous, questioning, quizzical, scoffing, suspecting, suspicious, unbelieving, uncertain, unorthodox, unsure, untrusting, wary

SKILL, ***noun*** ability, adeptness, adroitness, aptitude, aptness, art, artistry, cleverness, command, competence, craft, cunning, deftness, dexterity, ease, endowment, excellence, experience, expertness, facility, felicity, finesse, fluency, gift, handiness, ingeniousness, ingenuity, knack, knowledge, mastery, *peritia,* proficiency, prowess, quickness, *scientia,* sollertia, talent

SLANDER, ***noun*** abusive language, accusation, aspersion, *calumnia,* calumniation, calumny, censure, character assassination, *criminatio,* damaging report, defamation, defamatory words, denigration, denunciation, disparagement, execration, false report, imprecation, insinuation, invective, libel, *maledictio,* malicious report, obloquy, opprobrium, reproach, revilement, scandal, scurrility, slur, smear, stricture, traducement, vilification
ASSOCIATED CONCEPTS: malice, publication, slander of title, slander per quod, slander per se

SLANT, ***verb*** angle, bias, color, distort, doctor, embroider, exaggerate, falsify, incline, interpret falsely, misapply, miscolor, misconstrue, misdirect, misinterpret, misquote, misrender, misrepresent, misstate, overstate, pervert, predispose, prejudice, prepossess, stretch, turn, twist, varnish, veer, warp, wrest

SLAPP SUIT, ***noun*** action against public, action to deter protests, harassment through legal means, infliction of punishment for protesting, judicial process as a means to discourage protests, lawsuit to deter opposition, litigation to deter opposition, participation suit, retaliation for protests, retribution for protesting, retributive justice, scare tactics, strategic lawsuit, vengeance
ASSOCIATED CONCEPTS: antislapp suit

SLAY, ***verb*** annihilate, assassinate, deprive of life, destroy, dispatch, dispose of, execute, exterminate, *interficere, interimere,* kill, liquidate, massacre, murder, *occidere,* put to death, slaughter, take a life, terminate, victimize
ASSOCIATED CONCEPTS: homicide

SLIGHT, ***adjective*** ancillary, auxiliary, diminutive, exiguous, *exiguus,* immaterial, inappreciable, inconsequential, inconsiderable, inferior, insignificant, *levis,* light, limited, little, meager, mean, minor, minute, modest, negligible, niggardly, nonessential, nugatory, of small account, of small importance, paltry, petty, scant, secondary, slender, slim, small, stinted, subaltern, subordinate, subsidiary, *tenuis,* tenuous, thin, trifling, trivial, unessential, unimportant, unsubstantial
ASSOCIATED CONCEPTS: slight care, slight evidence, slight fault, slight negligence

SLIP AND FALL CASE, ***noun*** accident, action, calamity, casualty claim, cause of action, claim, general liability claim, injurious occurrence, injury, liability claim, litigation, misfortune, mishap, negligence case, personal injury case, trip and fall
ASSOCIATED CONCEPTS: insurance, mitigating slip and fall liability, trial lawyers

SLIPSHOD, ***adjective*** careless, disordered, disorderly, disorganized, haphazard, heedless, imprecise, improper, inaccurate, indifferent, inexact, lackadaisical, lax, negligent, offhand, orderless, poor, remiss, shabby, sloppy, slovenly, thoughtless, uncareful, uncaring, uncoordinated, unmeticulous, unneat, unorganized, unseemly, untidy

SLOTH, *noun* acedia, apathy, *desidia,* disinclination to action, disinclination to labor, dullness, faineance, idleness, *ignavia,* inaction, inactivity, indifference, indolence, inertia, inertness, inexertion, languidness, laxness, laziness, leadenness, lethargy, listlessness, lumpishness, neglectfulness, otiosity, passivity, phlegm, *segnitia,* shiftlessness, slackness, sluggishness, stupor, supineness, torpescence, torpidity, torpor, unconcern

SLOWLY, *adverb* crawling, creeping, dallying, dawdling, deliberate, dilatory, dragging, laggard, lagging, languid, leisurely, restrained, sluggish, snail-like, snail-paced, tardy, unhurried

SLUR, *verb* brush off, bypass, denounce, disdain, disgrace, dishonor, disparage, disregard, forget, ignore, miss, overlook, pass over, reject, scant, scorn, skimp, slight, slough

SLY, *adjective* arch, artful, astute, *astutus,* calculating, clandestine, conniving, covert, covinous, crafty, crooked, cunning, deceitful, deceiving, deceptious, deceptive, delusive, designing, devious, dishonest, dishonorable, disingeuous, double-dealing, evasive, feline, foxy, furtive, guileful, hidden, insidious, intriguing, keen, obreptitious, plotting, scheming, secret, secretive, sharp, shifty, shrewd, skulking, slippery, sneaking, sneaky, stealthy, *subdolus,* subtle, surreptitious, treacherous, tricky, uncandid, undercover, underhand, underhanded, unscrupulous, vafer, vulpine, wily

SMALL, *adjective* bantam, diminutive, inconsiderable, infinitesimal, insignificant, meager, micro, microscopic, mini, miniature, miniscule, minor, nominal, slight, smallish, toylike, undersized

SMART, *adjective* able, able-minded, astute, brainy, bright, brilliant, canny, clever, creative, cunning, deft, educated, erudite, esoteric, highbrow, intelligent, keen, knowing, knowledgeable, learned, perspicacious, sharp, skilled, witty

SMEAR, *verb* asperse, attack, attaint, belittle, besmear, besmirch, besmut, blacken, blemish, brand, calumniate, cast a slur, contaminate, decry, defame, defile, degrade, denigrate, denounce, depreciate, derogate, destroy one's reputation, detract, discredit, dishonor, disparage, disrate, expose to infamy, hold up to shame, humiliate, *inlinere,* libel, make scandal, malign, mar, mark, *oblinere,* pillory, pollute, render unclean, ridicule, slander, slur, smirch, soil, speak evil of, stain, stigmatize, sully, taint, tarnish, traduce, undermine, vilify, vilipend
ASSOCIATED CONCEPTS: defamation

SMOOTH, *adjective* appealing, assured, calm, cavalier, civilized, couth, cultivated, cultured, debonair, deft, genteel, glib, graceful, placid, practiced, refined, serene, slick, smart, sophisticated, svelte, tranquil, undisturbed, unperturbed, urbane

SNARL, *noun* complexus, complication, confusion, disarray, disorder, entanglement, *gannitus,* imbroglio, involute, kink, knot, labyrinth, mat, maze, mess, ravel, snag, tangle, twist

SNEAK AND PEEK WARRANT, *noun* clandestine search, covert entry warrant, enhanced surveillance mechanism, no seizure warrant, nontraditional warrant, surreptitious entry search warrant

SOBRIQUET, *noun* byname, cognomen, fanciful name, fictitious, nickname, nom de plume, pseudonym

SOCIAL SECURITY, *noun* insurance coverage for aged Americans, retirement benefits, retirement coverage, retirement insurance, retirement protection
Generally: economic assistance, social insurance, support for the disabled, support of the retired

SOCIETY, *noun* alliance, aristocracy, association, bloc, body, brethren, brotherhood, circle, citizenry, civilization, class, clique, club, coalition, colleagueship, combine, commonwealth, community, companionship, comradeship, confederacy, confederation, confraternity, consociation, culture, denomination, faction, federation, fellowship, fold, folk, fraternal order, fraternity, fraternization, gentility, group, guild, higher class, *homines,* institute, league, order, organization, organized group, patriciate, peerage, polity, population, privileged class, religious order, sect, set, sodality, tribe, union, upper class

SODALITY, *noun* alignment, alliance, amity, association, bond, brotherhood, brotherliness, camaraderie, clique, club, colleagueship, combination, communion, community, community of interest, companionship, compatibility, comradeship, concord, confederacy, confederation, confraternity, consolidation, copartnership, faction, federation, fellowship, fraternity, fraternization, friendliness, friendly relations, friendship, group, guild, intercourse, league, order, organization, partnership, social group, society, sorosis, unification, union

SODOMY, *noun* buggery, degeneration, depravity, deviation, indecency, pederasty, perversion, sexual deviation, unlawful sexual intercourse, unnatural carnal intercourse, unnatural sexual intercourse, vice

SOFT, *adjective* bendable, compressible, cottony, downy, elastic, flexible, kneadable, malleable, mushy, pliable, pliant, satin, satiny, silken, silklike, silky, spongy, supple, velvetlike, velvety, willowy, workable, yielding

SOLACE, *noun* abatement, allayment, alleviation, amelioration, cheer, comfort, commiseration, condolence, *consolatio,* consolation, ease, easement, encouragement, help, kindliness, melioration, mitigation, palliation, reassurance, refreshment, relief, *solatium,* sympathy, tranquility

SOLE, *adjective* individual, insular, isolated, lone, one, only, separate, single, singular, solitary, solus, unaccompanied, unattended, *unicus,* unique, *unus*
ASSOCIATED CONCEPTS: sole actor, sole and exclusive cause, sole and unconditional owner, sole proprietor, sole surviving heir

SOLELY *(Purely),* ***adverb*** barely, merely, plainly, purely, simply

SOLELY *(Singly),* ***adverb*** alone, entirely, exclusively, only, wholly

SOLEMN, *adjective* august, awe-inspiring, awesome, ceremonial, ceremonious, devotional, devout, earnest, formal, funereal, gloomy, grave, *gravis,* grim, hallowed, holy, imposing, impressive, majestic, meditative, mirthless, mournful, pensive, quiet, reflective, religious, reverential, ritual, sacramental, sacred, sanctified, sedate, serious, *severus,* sober, somber, spiritual, staid, stately, stern, stirring, subdued, *tristis,* venerable, worshipful

SOLEMNITY, *noun* awesomeness, ceremoniousness, ceremony, dignity, graveness, *gravitas,* gravity, impressiveness, pomp, seriousness, *severitas,* soberness, sobriety, solemn feeling, stateliness, tradition, *tristitia*

SOLICIT, *verb* appeal for, appeal to, apply, ask, ask earnestly, beseech, call for, canvass, *captare,* clamor for, coax, demand, entreat, *flagitare,* implore, importune, induce, make a request, obsecrate, obtest, *petere,* petition, plead, press, request, supplicate, urge

SOLICITATION, *noun* appeal for, appeal to, application, asking, asking earnestly, beseechment, calling for, canvassing, clamor for, coaxing, entreatment, imploration, importuning, importunity, inducement, inquiry, making a request, obtestation, petition, pleading, press, request, supplication, urging, writing for contributions
ASSOCIATED CONCEPTS: criminal solicitation, peddlers and solicitors

SOLICITOR, *noun* arguer, attorney, attorney-at-law, lawyer, member of the bar, member of the legal profession, petitioner, professional, representative

SOLICITOUS, *adjective* ambitious, anxious, *anxius,* apprehensive, aspiring, bent on, beseeching, caring, concerned, craving, desirous, eager, hopeful, inclined, intent on, keen, optative, petitionary, *sollicitus,* supplicatory, wanting, willing, yearning

SOLID *(Compact),* ***adjective*** bunched, close, coagulated, compressed, concentrated, condensed, congealed, consolidated, dense, firm, grumose, hard, hardened, impenetrable, impermeable, incompressible, indiscerptible, indivisible, inflexible, insecable, inseparable, massed, massive, monolithical, nonporous, ossified, packed, packed together, pressed together, rigid, serried, solidified, stiff, thick, tight, undissolved, united, unyielding

SOLID *(Sound),* ***adjective*** able to pay, assured, considered, convincing, dependable, durable, enduring, established, faithworthy, fast, firm, *firmus,* guaranteed, incontestable, incontrovertible, irrefutable, judicious, just, lasting, logical, politic, precautional, precautionary, precautious, prudent, prudential, rational, reasonable, reliable, responsible, rugged, safe, sagacious, sage, sapient, secure, sensible, *solidus,* solvent, *stabilis,* stable, stanch, steadfast, steady, strong, sturdy, substantial, substantive, true, trustworthy, trusty, unconfutable, unerring, unfailing, unimpeachable, unquestionable, unrefutable, valid, weighty, well-built, well-constructed, well-established, well-founded, well-grounded, well-made, wise

SOLIDIFY, *verb* calcify, callus, cement, coagulate, congeal, crystallize, encrust, firm up, freeze, indurate, ossify, set, solidify, stiffen, strengthen, thicken

SOLITARY, *adjective* abandoned, aloof, anchoretic, anchoretical, avoiding the society of others, celibate, cloistered, companionless, deserted, desolate, detached, disjoined, disjunct, enisled, eremetical, eremitic, eremitish, estranged, fellowless, forsaken, friendless, hermitic, hermitical, homeless, insular, isolated, kithless, lone, lonely, lonesome, orphaned, private, reclusive, remote, removed, rootless, secluded, separate, separated, single, sole, solo, *solus,* unabetted, unaccompanied, unaided, unassisted, unattended, unconnected, unescorted, uninhabited, unmatched, unoccupied, unpaired, unseconded, unshared, unsupported, unvisited, without companions, without company
ASSOCIATED CONCEPTS: solitary confinement

SOLUTION *(Answer),* ***noun*** clarification, decipherment, determination, eludication, explanation, *explicatio,* explication, exposition, finding, illumination, interpretation, key, reason, resolution, right answer, *solutio*
ASSOCIATED CONCEPTS: equitable solution

SOLUTION *(Substance),* ***noun*** admixture, amalgam, blend, combination, commixture, composite, composition, compound, *dilutum,* emulsion, intermixture, mix, mixture, solvent, suspension

SOLVABLE, *adjective* ascertainable, cognizable, decipherable, decodable, determinable, discoverable, exegetical, explainable, explicative, explicatory, expository, fathomable, intelligible, recognizable, resolvable, scrutable, soluble, workable

SOLVE, *verb* account for, answer, arrive at the truth, ascertain, bring out, clear up, crack, decipher, decode, deduce, discover, disentangle, disinter, *dissolvere,* educe, elucidate, *enodare,* enucleate, *expedire,* explain, fathom, ferret out, figure out, find out, find the cause, find the key, find the solution, guess correctly, guess right, interpret, learn the answer, make out, make plain, penetrate, piece together, puzzle out, realize, reason out, render intelligible, resolve, root out, shed light upon, think out, throw light upon, trace, understand, unearth, unfold, unlock, unravel, unriddle, unscramble, untangle, work out
ASSOCIATED CONCEPTS: solve a crime

SOLVENT, *adjective* able to pay, clear of encumbrance, creditworthy, financially sound, in good financial condition, moneyed, not owing, out of debt, owing nothing, pecunious, unindebted, with funds, with good credit
ASSOCIATED CONCEPTS: solvent debt
FOREIGN PHRASES: ***Id solum nostrum quod debitis deductis nostrum est.*** That only is ours which remains to us after deduction of our debts.

SOMBER, *adjective* black, bleak, caliginous, darkened, darkish, darkling, darksome, despondent, dim, dimmed, disconsolate, dusk, dusky, gloomy, lightless, murky, obscure, obscured, pitch-black, pitch-dark, pitchy, rayless, tenebrific, tenebrous, unlit

SOOTHE, *verb* allay, alleviate, ameliorate, appease, assuage, attemper, balm, becalm, blunt, calm, comfort, compose, deaden, dulcify, dull, ease, free from anxiety, free from pain, give relief, humor, hush, lenify, *lenire,* lessen, lull, mitigate, moderate, mollify, *mulcere,* obtund, pacificate, pacify, palliate, *placare,* placate, propitiate, quell, quench, quiet, relax, relieve, relieve pressure, render less painful, salve, slake, smooth, soften, still, succor, tame, temper, tranquilize

SOPHISTIC, *adjective* *captiosus,* captious, casuistic, casuistical, contrary to reason, erroneous, fallacious, false, faulty in logic, groundless, ill-reasoned, illogical, inconsequent, inconsistent, incorrect, invalid, irrational, misleading, paralogical, sophistical, specious, tricky, unfounded, ungrounded, unreasonable, unsound, untenable, unwarranted, wrong

SOPHISTICATED, *adjective* advanced, avant-garde, complex, contemporary, forward looking, innovative, knowledgeable, modern, new, progressive, ultramodern, up-to-date, up-to-the minute, urbane

SOPHISTRY, *noun* casuistry, cavil, chicanery, deception, distortion, equivocation, evasion, evasive reasoning, fallacious reasoning, false logic, misrepresentation, specious reasoning

SORDID, *adjective* *abiectus,* abject, abominable, base, corrupt, debased, decayed, defiled, degraded, deteriorated, dilapidated, disgusting, foul, fouled, fulsome, fusty, grimy, gruesome, *inliberalis,* mucky, odious, repellent, slatternly, slovenly, *sordidus,* squalid, undesirable

SORROW, *noun* affliction, anguish, desolation, despair, despondence, despondency, disconsolateness, dispiritedness, distress, doldrums, dolefulness, dolor, downheartedness, dreariness, forlornness, gloom, gloominess, glumness, grief, heartache, heartbreak, heartsickness, joylessness, loss, melancholy, miserableness, misery, oppression, remorse, tragedy, woe

SORT, *verb* allocate, allot, apportion, arrange, array, assign places to, assort, catalog, categorize, class, classify, collocate, deal, *digerere,* disentangle, distribute, divide, file, grade, graduate, group, methodize, order, organize, parcel out, place in order, put in order, range, rank, reduce to order, screen, segregate, separate, sieve, sift, size, split, subdivide, systematize, tabulate

SOUND, *adjective* accurate, acknowledged, admitted, cogent, compelling, convincing, correct, credible, effective, effectual, efficacious, factual, forceful, incontrovertible, irrefutable, justified, legitimate, persuasive, potent, powerful, proven, right, rightful, scientific, solid, strong, substantial, true, truthful, unanswerable, unchallengeable, unconfutable, undisputable, undistorted, unexaggerated, unimagined, unimpeachable, veracious, veritable, weighty, well-founded, well-grounded
ASSOCIATED CONCEPTS: sound discretion, sound value

SOUND BITE, *idiom* banner, catchphrase, catchword, catchy expression, cliché, expression, idiom, maxim, motto, pithy saying, shibboleth, tagline, watchword

SOUND REASONING, *noun* accurate assessment, cogent reasoning, compelling reasoning, convincing logic, correct assessment, effective analysis, forceful reasoning, incontrovertible logic, irrefutable conclusions, judicious analysis, justified analysis, legitimate analysis, methodical analysis, persuasive reasoning, plausible reasoning, potent logic, powerful conclusions, proven reasoning, reasonable analysis, solid reasoning, sound rationale, strong reasoning, unchallengeable reasoning, undisputable reasoning, unimpeachable reasoning, well-founded logic, well-grounded logic, well-reasoned opinion
ASSOCIATED CONCEPTS: judicial opinions

SOURCE, *noun* ancestry, authority, basis, beginning, *caput,* cause, cradle, derivation, *fons,* font, foundation, fount, fountain, fountainhead, generator, genesis, germ, headspring, incunabula, informant, inspiration, lineage, motive, origin, original, origination, *origo,* parent, parentage, place, provenance, provenience, root, spring, springhead, stem, well, wellhead, wellspring
ASSOCIATED CONCEPTS: source of income, source of information

SOVEREIGN *(Absolute),* ***adjective*** authoritative, chief, commanding, controlling, dominant, governing, hegemonic, hegemonical, imperial, influential, leading, master, most powerful, paramount, potent, powerful, predominant, prepollent, prepotent, regent, regnant, reigning, royal, ruling, supreme

SOVEREIGN *(Independent),* ***adjective*** at liberty, autonomous, enjoying liberty, enjoying political independence, exempt from external authority, free, liberated, politically independent, removed from bondage, self-determined, self-directing, self-governed, self-ruling, *sui iuris,* unattached, unbound, unconquered, uncontrolled, unenslaved, unrestricted, unsubjected, unvanquished
ASSOCIATED CONCEPTS: sovereign right, sovereign states

SOVEREIGN IMMUNITY, *noun* immunity for state from a civil suit, immunity for state from criminal prosecution, judicial doctrine precluding suit against the government without consent, requirement that federal government must waive its immunity or consent to suit, state sovereign immunity

SPACE, *noun* accommodation, acreage, area, capaciousness, capacity, compass, distance, expanse, extent, field, footage, gap, interstice, interval, latitude, *locus,* margin, mileage, range, room, scope, size, spaciousness, span, *spatium,* stretch, sweep, territory, vastness, yardage

SPACE HATCH, *noun* avenue to explore, channel to pursue, door, egress, excuse, exit, harbor, loophole, means, opening, out, port, pretext, safety valve, shelter, vehicle, vent, way out

SPARSE, *adjective* a few, barren, contained, deficient, exiguous, insufficient, less than generous, light, limited, niggardly, parsimonious, poor, scant, scanty, scarce, skimp, skimpy, slender, slim, small, spare, sparing, thin

SPARTAN, *adjective* aggressive, *audax,* bellicose, bold, brave, courageous, daring, dauntless, determined, disciplined, doughty, fearless, fierce, firm, formidable, *fortis,* hardy, hero-like, heroic, highly disciplined, indomitable, intrepid, iron-hearted, lionhearted, manly, martial, mighty, militant, plucky, pugnacious, resisting, resolute, resolved, self-reliant, severe, soldierlike, soldierly, stalwart, stoic, stoical, stout, stout-hearted, *strenuus,* strong, unafraid, unapprehensive, unblenching, unconquerable, undaunted, unflinching, unshrinking, valiant, valorous, virile, warlike, well-disciplined

SPATE, *noun* abundance, cataract, deluge, flood, outburst, profusion, rush, torrent

SPEAK, *verb* address, air, announce, annunciate, apprise, articulate, aver, badinage, bandy words, bear witness, break silence, carry on a conversation, colloque, communicate with, converse, declaim, declare, deliver, deliver an address, denote, *dicere,* disclose, discourse, divulge, engage in a conversation, engage in a dialogue, enunciate, exchange opinions, explain, expound, express, give a talk, give expression, give indication of, give voice, give words to, have a dialogue, hold a conversation, hold a discussion, indicate, inform, issue a statement, join in a

conversation, make a speech, make a statement, make mention, make oral communication, make oral mention, make solemn affirmation, make solemn declaration, murmur, mutter, palaver, parley, phrase, pour forth, proclaim, pronounce, publish, put into words, recite, remark, render an account of, repeat, report, reveal, say, sermonize, state, state emphatically, state one's case, state with conviction, talk, tell, utter, utter forth, utter with conviction, utter words
FOREIGN PHRASES: ***Idem est nihil dicere et insufficienter dicere.*** It is the same thing to say nothing and to say a thing insufficiently.

SPEAKER *(Guest of honor),* ***noun*** celebrity, chairperson, elocutionist, featured reader, honored guest, keynote speaker, lector, lecturer, moderator, performer, president

SPEAKER *(Spokesperson),* ***noun*** ambassador, communicator, delegate, emissary, envoy, front, moderator, mouth, mouthpiece, point person, promoter, prophet, representative, sayer, talker, tongue

SPECIAL, ***adjective*** amazing, astonishing, astounding, atypical, awe-inspiring, awesome, certain, conspicuous, different, distinctive, distinguished, *egregius,* endemic, esoteric, especial, exceptional, *eximius,* extraordinary, fabulous, fantastic, gala, important, imposing, incredible, individualistic, infrequent, marked, marvelous, memorable, miraculous, notable, noteworthy, outstanding, particular, *praecipuus,* prodigious, rare, remarkable, significant, singular, specific, striking, stupendous, superior, unaccustomed, uncommon, uncustomary, unexampled, unfamiliar, unforgettable, unimitative, unique, unparalleled, unprecedented, unusual, wonderful
ASSOCIATED CONCEPTS: special act, special appearance, special assessment, special benefits, special case, special circumstances, special damages, special election, special interest, special law, special legislation, special proceeding, special remedy, special tax, special verdict
FOREIGN PHRASES: ***Statutum generaliter est intelligendum quando verba statuti sunt specialia, ratio autem generalis.*** When the words of a statute are special but the reason general, the statute is to be understood generally. ***Generalia praecedunt, specialia sequuntur.*** General matters precede, special matters follow.

SPECIAL INTEREST, ***noun*** advocate, appealer, aspirant, influencer, instigator, lobby, lobbyist, mover, petitioner, pressure group, prompter, seeker, solicitor, suggester, suitor, suppliant

SPECIALIST, ***noun*** authority, connoisseur, consultant, degreeholder, devotee, experienced person, expert, knowing person, learned person, master, practiced hand, practitioner, professional, professor, proficient, proficient person, qualified person, savant, scholar, skilled hand, skilled person, skilled practitioner, skilled worker, specializer, technician, trained person, veteran, virtuoso

SPECIALITY, ***noun*** badge, character, distinction, distinctive characteristic, distinctive mark, distinctive quality, distinctiveness, feature, identification, individual characteristic, individual trait, individuality, mark, oddity, particularity, peculiarity, quality, quirk, singularity, specialness, stamp

SPECIALIZATION, ***noun*** craft, department, employment, field, forte, gift, interest, job, mastery, occupation, profession, pursuit, savvy, skill, trade, vocation

SPECIALIZE, ***verb*** address oneself to, apply oneself, bound, concentrate on, concern oneself with, dedicate oneself to, devote oneself to, focus attention on, give attention to, limit, narrow, practice exclusively, pursue, qualify, restrict, select, take up, train

SPECIALTY *(Contract),* ***noun*** agreement, arrangement, bargain under seal, bond, commitment, compact, concordat, contractual obligation, contractual statement, covenant, covenant of indemnity, debenture, engagement, guaranty, hypothecation, indenture, legal agreement, obligation, pact, pledge, pledged word, promise under seal, recognizance, security, stipulation, understanding, undertaking, warranty
ASSOCIATED CONCEPTS: specialty debts, suit upon a specialty

SPECIALTY *(Distinctive mark),* ***noun*** attribute, badge, brand, character, characteristic, definiteness, disconformity, dissimilarity, distinction, distinctive feature, distinctiveness, distinctness, dominant characteristic, earmark, eccentricity, feature, idiosyncrasy, impress, inconsistency, individualism, mannerism, mark, oddity, particular characteristic, particular item, particular matter, particular point, particularity, peculiar idiom, peculiar temperament, peculiarity, personal characteristic, point of difference, property, quality, quirk, rarity, singularity, special characteristic, special item, special matter, special point, specific quality, specificness, stamp, token, trait, uniqueness, unlikeness

SPECIALTY *(Special aptitude),* ***noun*** ability, accomplishment, adeptness, aptness, artistry, calling, capability, career, competence, craft, dexterity, endowment, expertise, expertness, faculty, forte, function, genius, handicraft, inborn aptitude, ingenuity, innate ability, knowledge, main interest, mastership, mastery, natural ability, object of study, occupation, particular object of pursuit, professionalism, proficiency, pursuit, qualification, skill, skillfulness, special line of work, special project, special skill, special study, specialization, strong point, talent, task, technique, virtuosity, vocation

SPECIFIC, ***adjective*** appropriate, categorical, certain, characteristic, definite, denominational, determinate, determined, different, *disertus,* distinctive, divisional, endemic, endemical, esoteric, especial, exact, exceptional, exclusive, explicit, express, idiomatic, idiosyncratic, idiosyncratical, indigenous, individual, individualistic, limited, marked, narrow, out of the ordinary, particular, peculiar, *peculiaris,* precise, precisely formulated, *proprius,* respective, restricted, sectarian, select, special, uncommon, unique, unusual
ASSOCIATED CONCEPTS: specific bequest, specific denial, specific devise, specific legacy, specific performance

SPECIFICATION, ***noun*** assignment, condition, definition, delimitation, description, designation, detail, detailed statement, determination, distinction, enumeration, item, itemization, minute account, nicety, particular, particularization, proviso, recital, special point, statement of particulars, stipulation, written requirement

SPECIFY, ***verb*** advert to, circumscribe, cite, clearly define, demarcate, *denotare,* designate, detail, differentiate, disclose, *enumerare,* enumerate, explain, express, give full particulars, go into detail, indicate, instance, itemize, list, mark out, mention, name, particularize, point out, refer to, represent, select, show, state in detail, state precisely, stipulate

SPECIMEN, ***noun*** case in point, *documentum,* ensample, example, *exemplum,* exponent, guide, illustration, instance, model, paradigm, pattern, representative, representative selection, sample

SPECIOUS, ***adjective*** affected, apparent, appearing, artificial, assumed, believable, bogus, casuistic, casuistical, colorable, colored, convincing, counterfeit, credible, deceiving, deceptive, deluding, delusive, delusory, erroneous, exterior, external, fake, fallacious, false, hypocritical, illusional, illusive, illusory, misleading, ostensible, outward, persuasive, phony, plausible, posed, pretend, pretended, professed, purported, put on, resembling truth, seeming, simulated, so-called, sophistic, sophistical, *speciosus,* spurious, unfounded, would-be
ASSOCIATED CONCEPTS: specious argument, specious defense

SPECTACLE, ***noun*** attraction, big attraction, demonstration, display, drama, elaborate function, event, exhibition, exposition, main event, pageant, performance, phenomenon, play, production, representation, scene, show, sight, wonder

SPECTER, ***noun*** apparition, appearance, eidolon, form, illusion, presence, revenant, shadow, shape, spirit, sprite

SPECULATE *(Chance),* ***verb*** assume a risk, bet, chance, dare, deal in futures, gamble, hazard, invest, lay money on, play the market, plunge, risk, stake, take a chance, try one's luck, venture, wager

SPECULATE *(Conjecture),* ***verb*** assume, *cogitare,* consider, dare say, debate, deliberate, guess, have a theory, hypothesize, judge, muse, philosophize, ponder, puzzle over, *quaerere,* reckon, ruminate, suppose, surmise, theorize, think, turn over in the mind, venture, weigh, wonder about
ASSOCIATED CONCEPTS: speculative damages

SPECULATION *(Conjecture),* ***noun*** assumption, *coniectura,* contemplation, deliberation, guesswork, hypothesis, inference, presumption, reasoning, rumination, supposition, surmise, suspicion, theorization, theory
ASSOCIATED CONCEPTS: speculative damages, speculative testimony

SPECULATION *(Risk),* ***noun*** bet, calculated risk, chance, fortuity, fortune, gamble, gambling, gaming, hazard, uncertainty, venture, wager

SPECULATIVE, ***adjective*** abstract, academic, aleatory, assumptive, chancy, cogitative, *coniecturalis,* conjectural, contemplative, contestable, controvertible, debatable, deliberative, doubtful, dubious, experimental, hazardous, hypothetical, imaginary, impractical, indefinite, indistinct, insecure, irresolute, meditative, presumptive, projected, provisional, questionable, risky, speculatory, suppositional, tentative, theoretical, uncertain, unconfirmed, undemonstrated, undetermined, unproven, unsafe, unsettled
ASSOCIATED CONCEPTS: speculative testimony

SPECULATOR, ***noun*** adventurer, backer, bettor, entrepreneur, experimenter, gambler, hazarder, prospector, risk taker, trader, venturer, wagerer

SPEECH, ***noun*** address, allocution, articulation, audible expression, colloquy, confabulation, conversation, declamation, declaration, delivery, dialect, diction, discourse, enunciation, expression, idiom, interlocution, language, lecture, lingo, locution, oral communication, oral expression, *oratio,* oration, oratory, palaver, parlance, phonation, phraseology, prattle, pronouncement, pronunciation, recital, recitation, rhetoric, say, sermon, spoken language, spoken word, statement, talk, tongue, utterance, verbal expression, verbal intercourse, vocalization, words
ASSOCIATED CONCEPTS: First Amendment, freedom of speech
FOREIGN PHRASES: ***Lubricum linguae non facile trahendum est in poenam.*** A slip of the tongue ought not readily be subjected to punishment.

SPEECHLESS, ***adjective*** agape, aghast, amazed, aphonic, astonished, awe-struck, bewildered, dumb, dumbstruck, *elinguis,* gagged, inarticulate, incapable of utterance, indisposed to words, mum, mute, *mutus,* noiseless, open-mouthed, quiet, silent, soundless, stunned, stupefied, thunderstruck, tongue-tied, unable to speak, unvocal, voiceless, wordless

SPEEDY TRIAL, ***noun*** criminal trial held diligently, criminal trial held promptly, criminal trial held punctually, criminal trial held within allowed time, criminal trial held within designated periods of time, criminal trial held within imposed time frames, criminal trial held within prescribed deadlines, criminal trial held within required time frame, protection against delay between the time of an indictment and a trial, protection against delay of criminal trial, speedy trial period, sufficiently prompt trial, the right to have a trial proceed expeditiously, the right to have a trial proceed promptly, time limits for completing various stages of criminal prosecution
ASSOCIATED CONCEPTS: Sixth Amendment, Speedy Trial Act of 1974 (federal), Sixth Amendment, the right to a speedy and public trial, waiver

SPEND, ***verb*** apply, bestow, consume, *consumere,* contribute, deplete, devote, disburse, dispense, dispose of, donate, drain, employ, empty, exhaust, expend, give, go through, impoverish, incur expense, *insumere,* invest, lay out money, make expenditure, outlay, part with, pay, run through, splurge, use, use up, wear away, wear out
ASSOCIATED CONCEPTS: spendthrift

SPHERE, ***noun*** ambit, arena, ball, bounds, capacity, circle, circuit, demesne, department, domain, field, field of activity, field of operation, function, globe, globoid, globular mass, influence, office, orb, orbit, pale, province, *provincia,* range, realm, region, round body, scope, *sphaera,* spheroid

SPIN, ***noun*** angle, cover-up, delicate answer, evasion, illusion, mask, nicety, polished presentation, political approach, political response, propaganda, public relations, self-serving statement, smooth packaging, twist
ASSOCIATED CONCEPTS: political spin

SPIRIT, ***noun*** angel, *anima,* animation, apparition, ardor, boldness, bravery, character, characteristic quality, cheer, cheerfulness, complexion, courage, daring, dash, disposition, earnestness, energy, enterprise, enthusiasm, essence, essential part, fire, firmness, force, fortitude, frame of mind, gist, humor, hypostasis, immaterial substance, immortal part, *ingenium,* intent, life, liveliness, meaning, mettle, mood, nature, passion, psyche, purport, quintessence, resoluteness, resolution, sense, sentiment, significance, soul, sparkle, specter, spice, substance, supernatural

being, temper, temperament, tenor, turn of mind, verve, vigor, vim, vital essence, vitality, vivacity, zeal
ASSOCIATED CONCEPTS: spirit of the law

SPIRIT, *verb* actuate, animate, arouse, encourage, enliven, *excitare,* excite, exhilarate, exhort, impassion, impel, *incitare,* incite, inspire, inspirit, instigate, kindle, motivate, move, press, prod, prompt, propel, provoke, push, rouse, spur, *stimulare,* stimulate, stir up, urge on

SPIRITED, *adjective* active, adventurous, alive, animated, avid, bold, brisk, buoyant, dashing, dynamic, eager, ebullient, effervescent, energetic, enthusiastic, exuberant, fervent, fiery, full of life, full of pep, hearty, intense, intrepid, irrepressible, keen, lively, mettlesome, passionate, peppy, sparkling, sprightly, spry, stalwart, undaunted, unrestrained, vehement, venturesome, vibrant, vigorous, vivacious, zealous, zestful

SPITE, *noun* acrimoniousness, acrimony, animosity, animus, antagonism, bitterness, cattiness, contempt, defiance, despite, enmity, gall, grudge, harsh feeling, hate, hatred, hostility, ill feeling, ill nature, ill will, inimicality, intolerance, *livor,* malevolence, *malevolentia,* malice, maliciousness, malignance, malignancy, malignitas, malignity, rancor, resentment, revengefulness, spitefulness, vengeance, venom, viciousness, vindictiveness, virulence, virulency

SPITEFUL, *adjective* acrimonious, antagonistic, antipathetic, belligerent, caustic, contrary, despiteful, envenomed, evil-minded, froward, harsh, hateful, hostile, ill-disposed, ill-intentioned, ill-natured, inimical, invidious, *lividus,* malevolent, *malevolus,* malicious, malign, malignant, *malignus,* mean, rancorous, resentful, revengeful, testy, venemous, vicious, vindictive, viperous, virulent

SPLENDID, *adjective* cosmic, epic, glorious, grand, great, imperial, imposing, impressive, magnific, magnificent, majestic, massive, monumental, noble, prepossessing, princely, proud, regal, royal, stately, sublime, terrific, wonderful

SPLIT, *noun* aperture, bifurcation, bisection, breach, break, chasm, chink, cleavage, cleft, crack, crater, crevice, cut, detachment, dichotomy, difference, dilaceration, dimidiation, diremption, disagreement, disassociation, discerption, disconnection, disengagement, disjunction, dismemberment, disruption, dissection, dissension, disseverance, disunion, divarication, divergence, division, divorce, divulsion, faction, *fissura,* fissure, fork, fracture, furrow, gap, gash, gulf, hiatus, incision, interruption, lacuna, partage, partition, perforation, quarrel, rent, rift, *rima,* rip, scission, *scissura,* scissure, sect, segmentation, segregation, separation, severance, slit, slot, subdivision, sunderance, variance
ASSOCIATED CONCEPTS: split among the circuit courts, split in authority, split sentence, splitting a cause of action

SPLIT, *verb* abscind, allocate, allot, apportion, assign, bisect, break, break with, carve, chop, cleave, crack, cut, deal, detach, dichotomize, *diffindere,* disconnect, disjoin, dispense, dissect, dissever, distribute, disunite, divide, dole, fissure, fracture, give way, hack, halve, hew, incise, intersect, isolate, lance, mete, open, parcel out, part, part company, partition, rend, rift, rip, rive, rupture, *scindere,* section, segment, segregate, separate, sever, share, shiver, slash, slice, slit, snap, splinter, subdivide, sunder, tear, unbind, untie
ASSOCIATED CONCEPTS: split a cause of action

SPOIL *(Impair),* *verb* addle, blemish, blight, botch, break, bungle, butcher, *corrumpere,* corrupt, damage, damage irreparably, debase, decay, decompose, deface, defile, deform, demolish, destroy, deteriorate, dilapidate, disable, disfigure, go bad, harm, hurt, impair, injure, lay waste, mangle, mar, mess up, mutilate, *perdere,* putrefy, rot, ruin, ruinate, sabotage, smash, sour, turn, vitiate, wreck

SPOIL *(Pillage),* *verb* despoil, forage, foray, loot, maraud, pirate, plunder, raid, ransack, ravage, rob, *spoliare,* spoliate, steal, waste

SPOILAGE, *noun* blight, corrosion, corruption, decay, decomposition, decrement, deterioration, dilapidation, disintegration, dissolution, erosion, putrefaction, putrescence, rot, wastage, waste

SPOILS, *noun* booty, gains, grab, graft, haul, ill-gotten gains, loot, pelf, pickings, pillage, plunder, plunderage, prize, ravin, *spolia,* stolen goods, swag, take, takings, winnings

SPOKESMAN, *noun* advocate, agent, ambassador, attorney, *auctor,* broker, delegate, deputy, emissary, envoy, go-between, interlocutor, mediary, mediator, messenger, mouthpiece, negotiator, *patronus,* plenipotentiary, prolocutor, representative, speaker, speechmaker, *suasor,* vicar, voice

SPOLIATION, *noun* attack, brigandage, buccaneering, depredation, deprivation, desolation, despoliation, destruction, devastation, *direptio,* direption, *expilatio,* foray, looting, marauding, pilfering, pillage, pillaging, piracy, plunder, plunderage, plundering, raid, ransack, rapine, robbery, sack, theft, thievery

SPONSOR, *noun* advocate, *auctor,* backer, benefactor, champion, favorer, guarantor, guardian, insurer, patron, promoter, protector, succorer, surety, sympathizer
ASSOCIATED CONCEPTS: sponsor of legislation

SPONSOR, *verb* accept responsibility for, act as surety for, answer for, assure, back, be responsible for, befriend, certify, champion, defend, endorse, ensure, favor, finance, financier, guarantee, insure, patronize, pay for, promote, protect, provide for, put up the money, secure, stand behind, subscribe to, support, sustain, sympathize, take responsibility for, underwrite, uphold, vouch for, warrant
ASSOCIATED CONCEPTS: sponsor a bill

SPONTANEOUS, *adjective* discretional, discretionary, elective, extemporal, extemporaneous, extemporary, extempore, free, free-willed, impetuous, impromptu, improvisatorial, improvised, impulsive, indeliberate, independent, natural, optional, rash, self-acting, self-determined, snap, *spontaneus,* sudden, unbidden, uncompelled, unconstrained, uncontrived, uncontrolled, unforced, unintentional, unplanned, unpremeditated, unprepared, unprompted, unrehearsed, unstudied, untaught, unthinking, volitient, volitional, volitive, *voluntarius,* voluntary, willful
ASSOCIATED CONCEPTS: res gestae, spontaneous declaration

SPORADIC, *adjective* appearing at intervals, casual, changeable, desultory, disconnected, discontinuous, disjunct, dispersed, erratic, fitful, fluctuating, immethodical, inconstant, indefinite, infrequent, intermittent, intermitting, *inusitatus,* irregular, isolated, nonuniform, now and then, occasional, periodic, periodical, rare, *rarus,* recurrent, recurring, remittent, scattered, scrappy, separate, shifting, single, sparse, spasmodic, sporadical, spotty, stray, uncertain, uneven, unsteady, unsuccessive, unsystematic, variable, wavering

SPOUSAL SUPPORT, ***noun*** alimony, allotment, allowance, dispensation, maintenance, provision, support
Generally: emolument, subsidization, subsidy, subsistence, sustenance, upkeep

SPOUSE, ***noun*** *coniunx,* consort, espouse, helpmate, helpmeet, husband, marital partner, marriage partner, mate, wife

SPREAD, ***verb*** advertise, bestrew, bloat, branch, broadcast, broaden, bruit, circulate, cover, deploy, diffuse, dilate, disperse, disseminate, distribute, divaricate, *divulgare,* divulge, emanate, expand, *explicare,* extend, fan, fill out, flow, fork, inflate, irradiate, lengthen, make known, make public, mantle, open, outspread, overrun, overspread, penetrate, permeate, pervade, promulgate, propagate, publicize, publish, radiate, ramify, roll out, rumor, scatter, smear, sow, *spargere,* splay, sprawl, sprinkle, straggle, stretch, stretch out, strew, suffuse, swell, uncoil, unfold, unfurl, unravel, unroll, unwind, vent, widen

SPURIOUS, ***adjective*** apocryphal, artificial, bogus, counterfeit, deceitful, deceptive, delusive, ersatz, fabricated, fake, faked, false, feigned, fictitious, forged, fraudulent, illegitimate, imitation, misrepresented, mock, pinchbeck, pretend, pseudo, quasi, sham, simulated, synthetic, unauthentic, ungenuine, unreal, untrue
ASSOCIATED CONCEPTS: spurious claim

SPURN, ***verb*** *aspernari,* belittle, boot, brush aside, cast aside, cast out, censure, contemn, decline, depreciate, despise, disapprove, discard, disdain, disparage, disregard, drive away, drive back, elude, evade, *fastidire,* flout, frown upon, have nothing to do with, hold in contempt, ignore, jilt, kick, laugh at, look down upon, neglect, ostracize, rebuff, refuse, refuse to accept, reject, renounce, repel, reprobate, repudiate, repulse, scorn, scout, set at nought, shun, slight, slur, sneer, snub, trample, tread on, treat with disdain, turn down

SPY, ***noun*** agent, detective, *emissarius, explorator,* informant, informer, intelligence agent, intelligencer, investigator, lookout, observer, reconnoiterer, reporter, scout, secret agent, sleuth, snoop, snooper, source, *speculator,* undercover agent, undercover man, watcher
ASSOCIATED CONCEPTS: espionage

SPY, ***verb*** behold, catch sight of, descry, detect, discern, discover, discover by artifice, distinguish, eavesdrop, espy, examine secretely, *explorare,* follow, glimpse, inspect secretely, look at, look for, make a reconnaissance, make out, make secret observations, observe, peep, peer, perceive, pry, recognize, reconnoiter, scrutinize, search out, see, shadow, sight, snoop, *speculari,* spy upon, take note, trail, view, watch, watch secretely

STABILITY, ***noun*** certainty, cohesion, consistency, dependability, durability, enduringness, firmness, fixedness, immutability, invariability, lastingness, normalcy, permanence, regularity, reliability, sameness, security, solidity, solidness, soundness, stableness, status quo, steadiness, strength, sturdiness, substance, uniformity

STABILIZE, ***verb*** balance, clinch, counterbalance, establish, firm up, round, secure, set, settle, steady

STABLE, ***adjective*** abiding, anchored, chronic, constans, constant, continuing, deep-rooted, diligent, durable, endless, enduring, established, everlasting, faithful, fast, fastened, firm, *firmus,* fixed, grounded, immovable, immutable, indissoluble, indomitable, industrious, inert, inexorable, intact, invariable, inveterate, irremovable, irreversible, irrevocable, lasting, long-lasting, long-lived, longstanding, moored, motionless, perdurable, permanent, perpetual, persistent, plodding, relentless, reliable, riveted, rooted, secure, sedulous, settled, solid, sound, stabile, *stabilis,* stalwart, stanch, stationary, steadfast, steady, strong, sturdy, substantial, sure, tenacious, unalterable, unchangeable, unchanging, uncompromising, undeviating, unfailing, unfaltering, unflagging, unflinching, unhesitating, unremitting, unshakeable, unshaken, unswerving, untiring, unwavering, unyielding, well-built, well-grounded

STAFF, ***noun*** *adiutores,* aides, assistants, associates, body of employees, cadre, clerical staff, complement, corps, council, crew, deputies, employees, faculty, force, help, *legatio,* management, personnel, professional force, professional staff, servants, staff members, workers

STAGNANT, ***adjective*** apathetic, dormant, dull, hebetudinous, idle, immobile, inactive, indolent, inert, lacking activity, lazy, *lentus,* lethargic, lifeless, listless, lumpish, motionless, otiose, passive, phlegmatic, phlegmatical, *piger,* quiescent, sluggish, *stagnans,* stagnating, standing, static, stationary, still, supine, torpid, torporific, unflowing, unmoving, unstirring, without current, without motion

STAIN, ***verb*** attaint, bedaub, befoul, besmear, besmirch, blacken, blemish, blot, blotch, bring reproach upon, color, contaminate, corrupt, damage, daub, debase, defame, defile, detract from, dirty, discolor, discredit, disgrace, dishonor, dye, grime, impair, *inquinare, maculare,* maculate, malign, mar, mark, *polluere,* pollute, ruin, smear, smirch, smudge, soil, spatter, splotch, spoil, spot, stigmatize, sully, taint, tarnish, tinge, tint

STAKE *(Award),* ***noun*** ante, bet, pot, prize, purse, spoils, wager, winnings

STAKE *(Interest),* ***noun*** claim, equity, holding, ownership, right, share, title
ASSOCIATED CONCEPTS: interpleader stake deposited in court

STALE, ***adjective*** banal, boring, common, commonplace, decayed, declining, dull, effete, faded, fetid, flat, flavorless, fusty, hackneyed, humdrum, insipid, jejune, mildewed, moldy, monotonous, musty, *obsoletus,* off, old, pedestrian, prosaic, prosy, rancid, rotten, savorless, shopworn, sour, soured, spoiled, tasteless, timeworn, trite, unimaginative, uninteresting, unvaried, vapid, *vetus,* vitiated, wasted, wilted, withered, without novelty, worn out
ASSOCIATED CONCEPTS: stale cause of action, stale check

STALEMATE, ***noun*** bind, bottleneck, corner, dead end, dead heat, deadlock, difficulty, dilemma, draw, fix, gridlock, halt, hole, impasse, jam, loggerheads, logjam, morass, pinch, plight, predicament, problem, quagmire, quandary, spot, standoff, standstill
ASSOCIATED CONCEPTS: arbitration, litigation, mediation

STALL, ***verb*** arrest, avert, bar, block, bog, break down, bring to a standstill, check, dally, dawdle, defer, delay, detain, dillydally, disable, filibuster, halt, hamper, hinder, hold up, impede, incapacitate, inhibit, interrupt, keep back, lag,

linger, obstruct, paralyze, postpone, procrastinate, put off, render powerless, retard, *stabulare,* stalemate, still, stop, take time, temporize, ward off
ASSOCIATED CONCEPTS: dilatory motions

STAMP, *noun* attestation, authentication, brand, cast, certification, die, endorsement, engraving, form, hallmark, identification, impress, impression, imprint, intaglio, mark, *nota,* pattern, print, ratification, seal, sigil, signit, *signum,* validation
ASSOCIATED CONCEPTS: tax stamps

STANCE, *noun* approach, aspect, attack, attention, attitude, behavior, concept, conduct, course, demeanor, line, matter, mien, opinion, plan, plan of attack, poise, position, presence, procedure, station, studied approach, tack, technique

STAND *(Position),* ***noun*** attitude, belief, bent, bias, inclination, leaning, opinion, outlook, point of view, position, slant, standpoint, vantage point, view, viewpoint

STAND *(Witness' place in court),* ***noun*** booth, box, corner, place, platform, position, post, stall, station, witness box, witness stand

STANDARD, *noun* archetype, basis of comparison, canon, comparison, criterion, example, exemplar, frame of reference, gauge, grade of excellence, guide, ideal, level of excellence, measure, model, norm, *norma,* paradigm, paragon, pattern, precedent, prototype, *regula,* touchstone
ASSOCIATED CONCEPTS: standard established by law, standard of care, standard of conduct, standard of proof

STANDARD OF CARE, *noun* bar, barometer, baseline, benchmark, criterion, established grade, established mark, measure of conduct, method, metric, par, procedure, requirement, standard, touchstone, yardstick
ASSOCIATED CONCEPTS: medical malpractice, negligence

STANDARD OF REVIEW, *noun* degree of deference to a lower court, level of review by appellate court, level of review by reviewing court, threshold for appellate court to find error on appeal
ASSOCIATED CONCEPTS: arbitrary and capricious standard of review, clearly erroneous standard of review, de novo standard of review, plain error standard of review

STANDARD PROCEDURE, *noun* approach, avenue, behavior, common practice, conduct, consuetude, course of conduct, custom, customary course, fashion, line of conduct, manner, manner of operating, matter of course, means, method, mode, mode of operation, mode of procedure, *modus operandi,* pattern, practice, prescribed form, procedure, process, routine, tactics, technique, way of doing things

STANDARDIZE, *verb* average, conciliate, conform, coordinate, equalize, even, formalize, govern, harmonize, homogenize, integrate, normalize, order, organize, reconcile, regularize, regulate, rule, square, synthesize, systematize, systemize

STANDING, *adjective* constant, continued, continuing, conventional, enduring, established, fixed, lasting, permanent, perpetual, perpetuated, settled, stationary, still, traditional, unceasing, unchanging
ASSOCIATED CONCEPTS: standing committee

STANDPOINT, *noun* angle, aspect, attitude, belief, bent, conviction, direction, disposition, inclination, judgment, leaning, location, observation post, opinion, orientation, outlook, perspective, persuasion, point, point of view, position, post, predilection, proclivity, propensity, seat, *sententia,* situation, spot, station, tendency, vantage point, view, viewpoint, vision

STAR, *verb* be a headline performer, be a headlining actor, be featured, entertain, feature, give a command performance, headline, perform, play, receive an ovation

STARE DECISIS, *noun* authoritative example, basis, foundation, precedent, principle of law, rule, standard
ASSOCIATED CONCEPTS: *stare decisis et non quieta movere, stare in judicio*

STARK, *adjective* absolute, bald, bare, complete, conspicuous, decided, downright, entire, glaring, gross, obvious, outright, plain, positive, pure, *rigidus,* sheer, simple, staring, total, unmitigated, unqualified, utter, very

START, *noun* beginning, birth, commencement, dawn, derivation, embarkation, emergence, evolution, exordium, first step, foundation, genesis, inauguration, inception, inchoation, incipience, incipiency, infancy, initiation, *initium,* onset, opening, origin, origination, outbreak, outset, *profectio,* rise, scare, source, threshold

START, *verb* begin, commence, create, embark on, emerge, evolve, file, give birth to, inaugurate, incept, initiate, insinuate, install, introduce, invent, open, originate, set off, take the first step, take the initiative
ASSOCIATED CONCEPTS: commence an action, start proceedings

STATE *(Condition),* ***noun*** appearance, aspect, circumstance, class, complexion, disposition, grade, mien, mood, plight, position, posture, predicament, shape, situation, standing, station, *status,* way
ASSOCIATED CONCEPTS: state of mind

STATE *(Political unit),* ***noun*** body politic, civil community, *civitas,* commonwealth, governmental unit, mandated territory, nation, political division, polity, sovereign unit
ASSOCIATED CONCEPTS: state's evidence, state's rights
FOREIGN PHRASES: ***Privilegium non valet contra rempublicam.*** A privilege is of no avail against the state.

STATED, *adjective* aforementioned, aforesaid, arranged, ascertained, decided, defined, detailed, determined, established, expressed, fixed, prearranged, predetermined, prescribed, reported, said, set forth, settled, specified, stipulated, told, uttered, voiced
ASSOCIATED CONCEPTS: stated capital, stated term

STATEMENT, *noun* account, affidavit, affirmation, announcement, assertion, asseveration, averment, avowal, claim, comment, declaration, deposition, detailed account, dictum, enumeration, exclamation, explanation, exposition, manifesto, narrative, observation, prepared announcement, prepared text, pronouncement, recapitulation, recital, recitation, remark, report, story, summary, testimony, utterance
ASSOCIATED CONCEPTS: statement of claim, statement of defense, statement of particulars

STATEMENT OF FACTS, *noun* affirmation, allegation of facts, allegations, assertion, asseveration, attestation,

averment, avouchment, declaration, description, enumeration, one's position, one's stand, review, summary
ASSOCIATED CONCEPTS: brief, memorandum of law

STATIC, ***adjective*** changeless, dormant, fixed, immobile, *immobilis, immotus,* inactive, inert, motionless, passive, permanent, quiescent, quiet, resting, rigid, stable, stagnant, standing, statical, stationary, still, suspended, torpid, unmoving, unprogressive

STATIONARY, ***adjective*** fast, fixed, frozen, immobile, immotile, immovable, irremovable, motionless, moveless, nonmotile, nonmoving, permanent, rooted, stagnant, standing, static, steadfast, still, stuck, unbudging, unmovable, wedged

STATURE, ***noun*** account, altitude, appreciation, elevation, esteem, favor, highness, honor, inches, loftiness, prestige, prize, regard, respect, rise, tallness

STATUS, ***noun*** caliber, caste, circumstances, class, condition, degree, dignity, echelon, elevation, eminence, esteem, footing, grade, importance, level, notability, place, position, posture, prestige, prominence, quality, rank, ranking, rating, reach, reputation, rung, situation, standing, state, station, stratum, superiority

STATUS QUO, ***noun*** absence of change, conservation of the same situation, equilibrium, existing conditions, existing state, maintenance of regularity, preservation of the same conditions, same conditions, stable state, static condition, things as they are

STATUTE, ***noun*** act, canon, code, codified law, commandment, decree, dictate, edict, enactment, *ius,* law, legislation, legislative enactment, *lex,* mandate, measure, order, ordinance, provision of the law, regulation, rubric, rule, written law
ASSOCIATED CONCEPTS: affirmative statute, criminal statute, declaratory statute, enabling statute, penal statute, private statute, remedial statute, statute of frauds, statute of limitations
FOREIGN PHRASES: ***Quae communi lege derogant stricte interpretantur.*** Statutes which derogate from the common law are to be strictly construed. ***Optima statuti interpretatrix est ipsum statutum.*** The best interpreter of a statute is the statute itself. ***Ex malis moribus bonae leges natae sunt.*** Good laws arise from evil morals. ***Casus omissus et oblivioni datus dispositioni communis juris relinquitur.*** A case omitted and forgotten is left to the disposal of the common law. ***Statutum generaliter est intelligendum quando verba statuti sunt specialia ratio autem generalis.*** When the words of a statute are special but the reason general, the statute is to be understood generally. ***Constructio legis non facit injuriam.*** The interpretation of the law works no injury. ***Ad ea quae frequentius accidunt jura adaptantur.*** Laws are adapted to those cases which occur. ***Jus constitui oportet in his quae ut plurimum accidunt non quae ex inopinato.*** Laws ought to be made with a view to those cases which occur most frequently and not to those which are of rare or accidental occurrence. ***Nova constitutio futuris formam imponere debet non praeteritis.*** A new law ought to affect the future, not what is past. ***A verbis legis non est recendendum.*** From the words of a statute there must be no departure. ***Lex posterior derogat priori.*** A later law takes away the effect of a prior one. ***Leges posteriores priores contrarias abrogant.*** Subsequent laws repeal prior laws that are repugnant to them. ***Non est novum ut priores leges ad posteriores trahantur.*** It is not novel that prior statutes should give way to later ones. ***In rebus quae sunt favorabilia animae, quamvis sunt damnosa rebus, fiat aliquando extensio statuti.*** In matters that are favorable to the spirit, though injurious to things, an extension of a statute should sometimes be made. ***Est ipsorum legislatorum tanquam viva vox; rebus et non verbis legem imponimus.*** The voice of the lawmakers is like the living voice; we impose law upon things and not upon words. ***Statutum speciale statuto speciali non derogat.*** One special statute does not derogate from another special statute. ***Statutum affirmativum non derogat communi legi.*** An affirmative statute does not derogate from the common law.

STATUTE OF FRAUDS, ***noun*** evidentiary rule, signed writing of agreements requirement, signed writing of contracts requirement, signed writing requirement, unenforceability of oral contracts

STATUTORY, ***adjective*** according to law, authorized, established, fixed, lawful, legal, legalized, legislative, legislatorial, licit, sanctioned, within the law
ASSOCIATED CONCEPTS: statutory crime

STAUNCH, ***adjective*** *certus,* constant, dependable, devoted, faithful, fast, *fidus,* firm, *firmus,* inflexible, iron, loyal, reliable, resolute, solid, sound, stable, stalwart, steadfast, steady, strong, substantial, sure, tried, true, trustworthy, trusty, unfailing, unfaltering, unshakeable, unwavering, unyielding

STAVE, ***verb*** avert, avoid, beat off, block, check, deflect, drive away, fend off, *fugare,* hamper, hinder, hold off, impede, inhibit, intercept, keep at bay, keep off, obstruct, prevent, *propulsare,* push away, put off, repel, *repellere,* shun, turn aside, ward off

STAY, ***noun*** abeyance, abeyancy, bar, cessation, check, curb, delay, desistance, discontinuance, halt, hindrance, interruption, *mansio,* obstacle, obstruction, prevention, reprieve, respite, restraint, stop, stoppage, suspension, wait
ASSOCIATED CONCEPTS: judicial stay, stay of enforcement, stay of execution, stay of proceedings, stay pending appeal

STAY *(Continue),* ***verb*** endure, extend, keep on, last, persevere, persist, prolong, remain, subsist
ASSOCIATED CONCEPTS: stay in occupancy

STAY *(Halt),* ***verb*** arrest, bar, block, check, *cohibere,* constrain, curb, delay, *demorari,* desist, detain, deter, *detinere,* discontinue, forbid, foreclose, forestall, frustrate, hamper, hinder, hold, impede, intercept, interrupt, obstruct, obviate, preclude, prevent, prohibit, put an end to, quell, reprieve, respite, restrain, stem, stop, stymie, suppress, thwart
ASSOCIATED CONCEPTS: permanent injunction, stay enforcement, stay of execution, stay order, stay proceedings, temporary injunction, temporary restraining order

STAY *(Rest),* ***verb*** await, be anchored, be dormant, be fixed, be immobile, be inert, be inmovable, be motionless, be riveted, be sedentary, be stationary, be transfixed, halt, lodge, park, pause, remain, repose, stand, stop, wait

STAY OF EXECUTION, ***noun*** halt to execution, order delaying imposition of the death penalty, order precluding execution, respite for the ultimate penalty for murder, stay

of death sentence, stay of punishment for a person condemned to death, stay of the death warrant, stay of warrant of execution, suspension from capital punishment, suspension from execution, temporary reprieve
ASSOCIATED CONCEPTS: application for stay of execution, clemency request, pardon, vacate execution

STEADFAST, *adjective* abiding, anchored, assiduous, constans, constant, decided, dedicated, dependable, determined, devoted, diligent, enduring, established, faithful, fast, firm, firmly established, *firmus,* fixed, gritty, indissoluble, indomitable, industrious, inexorable, inflexible, intransigent, lasting, long-lasting, loyal, obstinate, patient, perseverant, persevering, persistent, pertinacious, plodding, relentless, reliable, resolute, resolved, riveted, rooted, secure, sedulous, serious, settled, single-minded, *stabilis,* stable, stationary, staunch, steady, strong, strong-willed, tenacious, tried, true, trustworthy, unalterable, unchanging, uncompromising, undaunted, undeviating, undistracted, unfailing, unfaltering, unflagging, unflinching, unhesitating, unmoved, unshaken, unswerving, untiring, unvarying, unwavering, unyielding, zealous

STEADFASTNESS, *noun* adherence, adhesion, allegiance, attachment, commitment, constancy, dedication, devotedness, devotion, faith, faithfulness, fastness, fealty, fidelity, firmness, loyalty, reliability, resolution, steadiness, trustworthiness

STEAL, *verb* abscond with, abstract, burglarize, depredate, despoil, embezzle, filch, fleece, *furari,* hold up, lift, mulct, nim, peculate, pilfer, pillage, pirate, plagiarize, plunder, poach, pocket, prig, purloin, rifle, rob, shoplift, snatch, *subducere, surripere,* take unlawfully, thieve, usurp

STEALTHY, *adjective* arcane, artful, catlike, clandestine, *clandestinus,* cloaked, concealed, covert, crafty, elusive, evasive, feline, furtive, furtivus, hidden, masked, obreptitious, obscure, *occultus,* privy, prowling, secret, secretive, shrouded, silent, skulking, sly, sneaking, sneaky, stealthful, surreptitious, thievish, undercover, underhand, undisclosed, unrevealed, unseen, veiled

STEER CLEAR, *idiom* avert, avoid, bypass, circumvent, deflect, deter, dodge, duck, elude, escape, eschew, evade, exclude, finesse, foil, get around, miss, outfox, preclude, rule out, scrape, shake, shirk, shun, thwart

STELLAR, *adjective* astral, capital, celebrated, celestial, chief, crowning, distinguished, dominant, eminent, eventful, extraordinary, famous, first, foremost, grand, heavenly, impressive, leading, main, marked, memorable, momentous, noteworthy, outstanding, paramount, predominant, primary, principal, prominent, sidereal, starlike, starry, uranic

STEM *(Check),* ***verb*** arrest, balk, bear up against, block, bung, checkmate, choke, clog, *cohibere,* cork, counteract, curb, dam up, deadlock, deter, foil, frustrate, halt, hamper, hinder, hold back, impede, intercept, interrupt, keep at bay, keep in, obstruct, oppose, plug, prevent, quell, rein in, repel, repulse, resist, restrain, retard, scotch, stall, stanch, stay, stop, suppress, thwart, veto

STEM *(Originate),* ***verb*** arise, begin, branch off, come, commence, derive, descend, emanate, ensue, flow, follow, germinate, grow, issue, originate, proceed, result, rise, spring, sprout, start, trail

STEP, *noun* achievement, act, action, advance, advancement, deed, degree, expedient, footpace, footstep, gait, gradation, grade, maneuver, milestone, move, pace, procedure, proceeding, process, progression, rundle, rung, stride, tramp, tread

STEP-BY-STEP, *adjective* by degrees, continuous, creeping, gradational, gradual, graduated, in steps, leisurely, measured, methodical, orderly, paced, part of a process, progressive, regular, slow, slow-paced, snail-like, systematic, unhurried

STERLING, *adjective* authentic, bona fide, *bonus,* consummate, costly, creditable, excellent, exceptional, exemplary, extraordinary, genuine, good, high-grade, high-quality, honest, honorable, matchless, meritorious, noble, peerless, precious, prime, pure, quality, real, splendid, superb, superior, superlative, true, unadulterated, unalloyed, unmingled, unsynthetic, upright, valuable, *verus,* virtuous, worthy

STERN, *adjective* austere, authoritarian, bleak, cold, dour, fierce, flinty, forbidding, gruff, hard, harsh, heavy-handed, hostile, inimical, ramrod, rigid, rigorous, rough, rugged, serious, solemn, strict, tough

STIFLE, *verb* annihilate, arrest, balk, bar, block, check, choke, conceal, constrain, contain, control, crush, damp, deaden, destroy, drown, dull, extinguish, frustrate, gag, hush, inhibit, kill, mask, muffle, mute, muzzle, obstruct, *opprimere,* prevent, put down, quell, quench, repress, reprimere, restrain, silence, smother, snuff out, squash, squelch, still, stop, strangle, strangulate, stymie, subdue, suffocate, suppress, throttle, withhold

STIGMA, *noun* badge of infamy, blemish, blot, brand, defect, disgrace, dishonor, disrepute, flaw, imputation, infamousness, infamy, mark of disgrace, mark of shame, nota, notoriety, notoriousness, reproach, *scandalum magnatum,* scar, shame, slur, smear, smirch, spot, stain, taint, tarnish

STILL, *adjective* Arcadian, calm, halcyon, hushed, motionless, not moving, peaceful, placid, quiet, restful, serene, silent, stationary, stopped, tranquil, unmoving, untroubled

STIMULATE, *verb* activate, actuate, animate, arouse, awaken, brace, drive, egg on, encourage, energize, enkindle, enliven, excite, fan, fillip, fire, foment, goad, impel, *incitare,* incite, inflame, initiate, *inritare,* inspire, inspirit, instigate, invigorate, jog, kindle, motivate, move, move to action, pique, prod, prompt, propel, provoke, rally, rouse, spur, stir up, vitalize, vivify, whet, work up

STIMULUS, *noun* activator, animator, arouser, calcar, catalyst, catalytic agent, cause, drive, encouragement, excitant, fillip, goad, impetus, impulse, incentive, *incitamentum,* incitement, inducement, influence, infrastructure funds, *inritamentum,* means to reinvigorate the economy, means to spark the economy, means to trigger a healthier economy, motivating force, motive, needle, prod, provocation, push, reason, shock, spur, stimulant, stimulation, stimulative, stimulator, sting, urge, whet

STIMULUS PROGRAM, *noun* economic reform, economic stimulation, encouragement, financial boost, financial stimulation, fiscal stimulation, incentive, infrastructure,

injection of funds, investment, motivation, stimulant, stimulus package
ASSOCIATED CONCEPTS: federal government economic programs to address a weak economy

STINT, *noun* assignment, chore, cycle, duration, duty, job, limitation, limited assignment, period, rein, role, shift, span, spell, standing, stretch, task, tenure, term, time, tour

STIPULATE, *verb* adjust, agree, arrange, assent, bargain, become bound, clarify, condition, contract, covenant, decide, denominate, designate, determine, engage, guarantee, include in an agreement, insist upon, lay down, make a condition, make a point of, make clear, make definition, mention, name, negotiate, pledge, postulate, predicate, promise, provide, set, settle, settle terms, signify, specify, state, *stipulari*
ASSOCIATED CONCEPTS: stipulated damages, stipulated fact, stipulation of a bill of particulars, stipulation of an adjournment, stipulation of appeal, stipulation of guilt, stipulation of judgment, stipulation of matters of law, stipulation of proof, stipulation of the record

STIPULATION, *noun* agreement, arrangement, article of agreement, bargain, bond, compact, concordat, condition, contract, convention, covenant, deal, engagement, pact, *pactum,* promise, provise, specification, *stipulatio,* treaty, understanding
ASSOCIATED CONCEPTS: stipulated facts, stipulation of settlement

STOCK *(Shares),* ***noun*** assets, capital, fund, holdings, invested property, investment, negotiables, property, security
ASSOCIATED CONCEPTS: bank stock, bonus stock, capital stock, common stock, debenture stock, ordinary stock, original stock, outstanding stock, preferred stock, prepaid stock, sale of stock, shares of stock, special stock, stock certificate, subscription to stock, treasury stock, value of stock, watered stock

STOCK *(Store),* ***noun*** accumulation, *copia,* effects, hoard, inventory, provision, reserve, reservoir, supply, *vis*

STOCK IN TRADE, *noun* articles of commerce, available assets, contents, equipment, goods, line, merchandise, products, provisions, resources, staple, stock, store, supply, supply on hand, vendibles, wares

STOCKHOLDER, *noun* backer, co-owner, corporate shareholder, investor, owner, shareholder
ASSOCIATED CONCEPTS: corporate law practice, directors and officers lawsuits

STOICAL, *adjective* apathetic, ascetic, controlled, dispassionate, impassive, imperturbable, indifferent, long-suffering, passionless, passive, patient, philosophic, placid, repressing emotion, resigned, self-controlled, self-disciplined, spartan, tolerant, undemonstrative, undisturbed, unimpassioned, unimpressible, unmoved, unresisting, unruffled

STOP, *verb* abandon, abolish, arrest, bar, barricade, block, block up, blockade, brake, break off, bring to a close, bring to a standstill, bring to naught, catch, cease, check, checkmate, choke, clog, close, come to a standstill, conclude, counteract, countermand, crush, cut off, cut short, cut out, dam up, delay, desist, desist from, detain, deter, die away, disallow, discontinue, disrupt, drop, end, expire, finish, foil, forbear, forbid, forestall, freeze, give over, halt, hamper, hinder, hold, hold back, hold up, impede, inhibere, intercept, interrupt, knock off, lapse, lay an embargo on, lay off, leave off, obstruct, occlude, pack up, pause, plug, preclude, prevent, prohibere, prohibit, put an end to, quell, quit, refrain, render impassable, repress, rest, restrain, silence, shut off, snag, sojourn, stall, stanch, staunch, stay, stem, stifle, still, stopper, stopple, stunt, stymie, suppress, suspend, tarry, terminate, thwart, ward off, wipe out, withdraw from
ASSOCIATED CONCEPTS: cease and desist, temporary injunction, permanent injunction, stop and frisk

STOP & FRISK, *noun* a frisk with reasonable fear of danger, a frisk with reasonable suspicion of criminal activity, a warrantless frisk, limited outer search, pat down

STOPGAP, *noun* alternate, alternative, auxiliary, expedient, impermanent fixture, makeshift, means, measure, provisional measure, replacement, reserve, resort, substitute, substitution, temporary arrangement, temporary expedient, temporary substitute

STORE *(Business),* ***noun*** booth, business house, concern, emporium, establishment, exchange, market, market place, mart, outlet, shop, stall

STORE *(Depository),* ***noun*** abundance, *abundantia,* accumulation, amassment, assets, backlog, cache, collection, conservatory, *copia,* deposit, depository, fund, great quantity, hoard, inventory, nest egg, plenty, profusion, provisions, reserve, reservoir, savings, stack, stock, stockpile, storehouse, sufficiency, supplies, supply, treasure, treasury, wealth

STORE, *verb* accumulate, acquire, amass, assemble, bank, cache, collect, conserve, *copia,* cumulate, deposit, garner, gather, hoard, hold, husband, keep, lay away, maintain, mass, pile up, put by, reposit, reserve, retain, save, stock, stockpile, stow away, treasure, warehouse

STORM *(Barrage),* ***noun*** assault, attack, battle, besiegement, blast, blitz, blitzkrieg, blizzard, bombardment, clash, combat, commotion, conflict, confusion, disquiet, disruption, embroilment, eruption, excitement, explosion, fight, flare-up, imbroglio, melee, mutiny, outbreak, outburst, rebellion, revolt, revolution, skirmish, stir, struggle, tempest, tumult, turbulence, turmoil, unrest, upheaval, uprising
ASSOCIATED CONCEPTS: damage, flood damage, hurricanes

STORM *(Rain),* ***noun*** blizzard, cloudburst, cyclone, deluge, downpour, endless rain, gale, hailstorm, heavy showers, heavy winds, hurricane, moisture, precipitation, rainstorm, sheets of rain, snowstorm, storming, stormy winds, tempest, thundershower, thunderstorm, tornado, torrent, tropical rains, tropical storm, turbulence, twister, typhoon, whirlwind
ASSOCIATED CONCEPTS: cyberstorm, storm models, storm predicting, storm victims, storm water

STORY *(Falsehood),* ***noun*** canard, concoction, deceit, deception, deliberate falsification, dissemblance, dissimulation, distortion, duplicity, evasion, fabrication, faithlessness, false statement, falsification, falsity, fantasy, fib, fiction, figment, inaccuracy, incorrectness, insincerity, intentional misstatement, intentional untruth, invention, inveracity, lie, *mendacium,* misrepresentation, misstatement, myth, perversion of truth, pretense, prevarication, suppression of truth, untrue statement, untruth, want of fidelity

STORY *(Narrative)*, ***noun*** account, adventures, article, chronicle, conte, description, dispatch, epic, *fabula,* historiette, history, legend, memoir, *narratio,* narration, news, news article, news item, newspaper report, particulars, piece, portrayal, press notice, publicity, recapitulation, recital, recitation, record, recountal, relation, report, saga, sketch, summary of facts, tale, tidings

STRAIGHT, ***adjective*** direct, ethical, honest, honorable, just, legitimate, linear, moral, moralistic, normal, proper, right, righteous, right-minded, seemly, steadfast, straightforward, true, unbend, unbending, uninterrupted, untwisted, upright, virtuous

STRAIGHTFORWARD, ***adjective*** aboveboard, *apertus,* artless, candid, direct, forthright, frank, guileless, honest, honorable, ingenuous, legitimate, open, outspoken, plain-spoken, scrupulous, *simplex,* sincere, straight, truth-speaking, truthful, unaffected, uncontrived, uncorrupt, undesigning, undeviating, undissembling, undistorted, unfeigned, unperjured, unswerving, unturned, unwavering, upright, veracious, veridical

STRAIGHT-OUT, ***adjective*** aboveboard, blunt, candid, clear, clear-cut, crystal clear, decent, direct, distinct, evident, explicit, express, forthright, frank, honest, ingenuous, manifest, obvious, on the up and up, open, open and aboveboard, open and genuine, open and sincere, sincere, straight, straightforward, unequivocal, unreserved, upfront
ASSOCIATED CONCEPTS: franking privilege

STRANGE, ***adjective*** abnormal, atypical, bizarre, crazy, curious, different, eccentric, freakish, idiosyncratic, irregular, mysterious, odd, off, offbeat, outrageous, peculiar, quaint, queer, quirky, rare, remarkable, shocking, singular, uncommon, unique, unusual, weird

STRANGER, ***noun*** *advena,* alien, foreign person, foreigner, *hospes,* newcomer, outsider, strange person, tramontane, unknown person

STRANGLE, ***verb*** arrest, block, check, choke off, crush, extinguish, hush, inhibit, keep back, keep down, mask, muzzle, put a stop to, quell, quiet, repress, reserve, restrain, silence, smother, snuff out, squelch, still, stop, *strangulare,* subdue, suppress, withhold

STRATAGEM, ***noun*** *ars,* artful contrivance, artifice, blind, cheat, chicane, contrivance, crafty device, cunning, deceit, deception, device, dodge, *dolus,* evasion, excuse, expedient, feint, finesse, gimmick, intrigue, machination, maneuver, manipulation, plan, plot, ploy, pretext, ruse, scheme, shift, strategy, subterfuge, tactic, trap, trick, wile

STRATEGIC, ***adjective*** calculated, clever, consequential, contrived, critical, crucial, decisive, designed, diplomatic, diplomatical, important, key, momentous, planned, politic, pregnant, significant, strategical, tactical, telling, tricky, turning, vital, well thought out

STRATEGIST, ***noun*** brains of the operation, conceiver, contriver, creator, expert, leader, mastermind, organizer, originator, planner, professional, schemer, strategist, tactician, technician

STRATEGY, ***noun*** approach, arrangement, art of war, artifice, battle maneuver, campaign, careful methods, careful plans, *consilium,* contrivance, course, course of action, cunning, design, devices, engineering, forethought, intrigue, intriguery, invention, machination, management, maneuvering, maneuvers, manipulation, method, military evolutions, military science, mode of operation, plan, plan of action, plan of attack, planned campaign, platform, policy, procedure, proceedings, program, proposal, proposed action, proposition, *propositum,* rules of war, scheme, schemery, set of maneuvers, skillful management, soldiership, system, tactics, technique
ASSOCIATED CONCEPTS: trial strategy

STRAW MAN, ***idiom*** argument, avenue, construct, device, example, figurehead, front, front man, imaginary position, mechanism, method, nominal head, ploy, refutation, sham argument, weak argument, weak position

STRENGTH, ***noun*** brawn, cogency, concentration, durability, efficacy, emphasis, endurance, energy, fervor, firmness, force, hardiness, health, impregnability, intensity, main, mainstay, might, mightiness, muscle, potency, power, proof, puissance, *robur,* robustness, solidity, soundness, stalwartness, stamina, stoutness, sturdiness, substantiality, substantialness, superiority, tenaciousness, tenacity, toughness, validity, vigor, *vires,* virility, vitality, vividness, willpower

STRENGTHEN, ***verb*** accentuate, amplify, beef up, bolder, boost, deepen, develop, enforce, enhance, firm up, fortify, galvanize, harden, heighten, indurate, insure, invigorate, magnify, redouble, reinforce, season, step up, support, tone up, toughen, vitalize

STRENUOUS, ***adjective*** active, arduous, burdensome, demanding, difficult, exacting, exhausting, grueling, hard, Herculean, intense, intensive, laborious, onerous, operose, oppressive, painstaking, rigorous, strenuous, toilsome, vigorous, wearisome
ASSOCIATED CONCEPTS: strenuous law enforcement

STRESS *(Accent)*, ***noun*** accentuation, attention, beat, distinction, emphasis, force, import, importance, inflection, insistence, intonation, paramountcy, primacy, prominence, pronunciation, significance, superiority, tone, urgency, weight

STRESS *(Strain)*, ***noun*** adversity, affliction, agony, alarm, anxiety, apprehension, apprehensiveness, burden, coercion, compulsion, cross, demand, disquiet, disquietude, distention, dread, duress, exertion, exigency, extension, fear, fearfulness, ferment, fluster, force, fright, load, misgiving, *momentum,* need, nervousness, overexertion, pinch, pondus, pressure, pull, stretch, tautness, tenseness, tension, tensity, tightness, traction, trepidation, trial, urgency

STRETCH *(Distance)*, ***noun*** amplitude, expansion, extension, extent, field, immensity, latitude, length, magnitude, reach, space, span, spell, spread

STRETCH *(Exaggeration)*, ***noun*** breadth, contrived reason, excuse, extension, fabrication, far-fetched, far-fetched explanation, far-fetched reason, improbable, inflation, lie, magnification

STRICT, ***adjective*** absolute, accurate, austere, authoritarian, authoritative, autocratic, careful, close, conscientious,

despotic, dictatorial, *diligens,* disciplined, exact, exacting, extreme, faithful, fastidious, formal, hard, harsh, high-principled, imperious, inexorable, inflexible, limited, literal, meticulous, obdurate, obligatory, orthodox, particular, positive, precise, principled, punctilious, puritanical, rigid, *rigidus,* rigorous, scrupulous, severe, *severus,* stern, stiff, straitlaced, stringent, tyrannical, unbending, uncompromising, unconditional, unerring, unyielding, veracious
ASSOCIATED CONCEPTS: strict construction, strict interpretation, strict necessity

STRICT CONSTRUCTION, *noun* absolutely by the snidest interpretation, according to the letter, by chapter and verse, by the rules, conservative interpretation, exactly as written, in a conservative interpretation, in an orthodox interpretation, literally as written, plainly within the language, precisely as written, specific interpretation, strictly read, with a strict interpretation, with fastidious rigidity, with hard-and-fast interpretation, with inflexible interpretation, with literal interpretation, with meticulous rigidity, with narrow interpretation, with punctilious rigidity, with rigid interpretation, with unyielding interpretation
ASSOCIATED CONCEPTS: constitutional interpretation, literal construction, loose construction

STRICT MEANING, *noun* accurate meaning, correct meaning, defined meaning, definition, distinct meaning, exact meaning, explanation, explicit meaning, express meaning, faithful meaning, inflexible meaning, literal meaning, methodical meaning, meticulous meaning, narrow meaning, not subject to interpretation, ordinary meaning, plain meaning, precise meaning, prescribed meaning, rigid meaning, rigorous meaning, sharply defined meaning, significance, specific meaning, unbending meaning, uncompromising meaning, unequivocal meaning
ASSOCIATED CONCEPTS: construction, literal contract, literal proof, plain meaning rule, rules of statutory, soft plain meaning rule, textualism

STRICT SCRUTINY, *noun* most heightened scrutiny, requirement that a law be narrowly tailored, requirement that a law be tailored with the least restrictive means, requirement that a law represent a compelling state interest, standard for considering when a fundamental constitutional right is infringed, standard for reviewing laws applying to suspect classifications

STRICTURE, *noun* accusation, adverse comment, adverse criticism, *animadversio,* animadversion, aspersion, blame, castigation, censure, critical remark, criticism, denunciation, deprecation, depreciation, diatribe, disapprobation, disapproval, exception, faultfinding, objection, objurgation, obloquy, philippic, rebuke, reprehension, reproach, reprobation, reproof, tirade, unfavorable remark, vituperation

STRIFE, *noun* agitation, altercation, animosity, battle, belligerency, broil, *certamen, certatio,* clash, combat, competition, conflict, contention, contest, contestation, contrariety, controversy, counteraction, disaccord, disaggreement, discord, disputation, dispute, disquiet, dissension, dissent, dissidence, encounter, engagement, eruption, faction, factionalism, fight, fighting, fray, friction, imbroglio, incompatibility, match, opposition, outbreak, outburst, polemics, quarrel, race, rift, rivalry, row, squabble, struggle, trouble, unrest, upheaval, variance, violence, war, warfare, wrangle

STRIKE, *noun* boycott, collective refusal to work, concerted refusal to work, group refusal to work, job action, labor dispute, organized refusal to work, shutdown, stoppage, suspension of work, walkout, work stoppage
ASSOCIATED CONCEPTS: lockout, mass strike, picketing, secondary strike

STRIKE *(Assault),* ***verb*** afflict, aggress, assail, attack, bat, batter, beat, besiege, damage, deal a blow, fall upon, harm, hit, hurt, inflict harm, inflict injury, lunge at, pound, slap, smash, smite, storm

STRIKE *(Collide),* ***verb*** butt, come in contact, come into collision, come together, *conlidere,* crash, encounter, hit, hit against, jar, jolt, knock into, meet, smash

STRIKE *(Refuse to work),* ***verb*** blockade, boycott, cease work, discontinue work, halt work, interrupt work, leave the job, obstruct work, quit work, rebel, refrain from working, revolt, stop work, suspend work, terminate work, walk out
ASSOCIATED CONCEPTS: economic strike, general strike, wildcat strike

STRIKE A BALANCE, *idiom* centrist, equality, equity, evenhandedness, fair-mindedness, fairness, impartiality, justice, moderation, neutralism, neutrality, nonpartisanship, objectivity, tolerance

STRINGENT, *adjective* authoritative, binding, compelling, compulsory, despotic, dictatorial, draconian, exact, exacting, exigent, forceful, hard, harsh, inescapable, inflexible, ironhanded, precise, puritanical, rigid, rigorous, rough, stern, stiff, straitlaced, strict, tyrannical, uncompromising, unyielding

STRIVE, *verb* aim, aspire, attempt, bestir oneself, bid for, carry into execution, compete, *conari,* contend, contest, do all one can, do one's best, do one's utmost, drive at, drudge, employ one's time, employ oneself, endeavor, endeavor to accomplish, endeavor to effect, *eniti,* exert one's energies, exert oneself, fight, go after, labor for, make a bid, make an attempt, make an effort, point at, pursue, put forth an effort, seek, strain, struggle, tackle, take action, take pains, take steps, take trouble, tax one's energies, toil, travail, trouble oneself, try, try for, try one's best, undertake, venture, vie, work, work hard

STRONG, *adjective* able, brawny, burly, clear, compelling, concentrated, crushing, determined, durable, effective, enduring, energetic, firm, forceful, forcible, formidable, *fortis,* hard, hardy, harsh, healthy, Herculean, husky, inflexible, intense, lasting, lusty, manly, mighty, omnipotent, overpowering, overwhelming, perseverant, persevering, persistent, persuasive, potent, powerful, puissant, reinforced, reliable, resolute, rich, robust, *robustus,* rugged, secure, solid, sound, stable, stalwart, staunch, steadfast, steady, stiff, stout, strapping, strengthful, sturdy, tenacious, titanic, tough, unflimsy, unmixed, unpliant, unremitting, unyielding, *valens,* vibrant, vigorous, violent, virile, vivid, well-built, well-made, wiry
ASSOCIATED CONCEPTS: strong case, strong evidence, strong probability

STRUCTURE *(Composition),* ***noun*** arrangement, configuration, constitution, design, disposition, essence, fabric, form, formation, layout, make up, organization, pattern, plan, set up, shape, style, substance

STRUCTURE *(Edifice),* ***noun*** building, establishment, erection, location, premises
ASSOCIATED CONCEPTS: corporate structure

STRUGGLE, *noun* affray, agitation, attempt, battle, broil, *certamen,* clash, combat, competition, conflict, confrontation, contention, contestation, controversy, disagreement, dissension, effort, encounter, endeavor, engagement, essay, exertion, feud, fight, force, fracas, grind, haul, labor, *luctatio,* opposition, pains, pursuit, push, quarrel, rencounter, resistance, scrimmage, scuffle, strain, striving, tussle, work

STUDIOUS, *adjective* academic, assiduous, bookish, bookworm, busy, careful, conscientious, contemplative, devoted, diligent, disciplined, eager, earnest, hard-working, industrious, intellectual, learned, lettered, meditative, reflective, sedulous, serious, thoughtful, well-informed, well-read

STUDY, *verb* acquire knowledge, analyze, apply the mind, attend, audit, cerebrate, consider, contemplate, devote oneself to, dissect, do research, educate oneself, examine, excogitate, explore, eye, *incumbere,* inquire into, inspect, intellectualize, investigate, learn, meditate, mull over, muse, note, observe, peruse, ponder, pore over, probe, pursue, read, reconnoiter, reflect upon, research, review, revolve in the mind, ruminate, scan, school oneself, scrutinize, search into, sift, specialize, *studere,* survey, think about, train in, view, weigh

STYLE, *noun* appearance, artistry, aspect, cast, character, class, custom, denomination, description, expression, fashion, form, genre, *genus,* guise, habit, individual method, kind, make, manner, manner of presentation, method, mode, model, *modus,* pattern, presentation, rage, *ratio,* school, shape, taste, technique, tone, trend, type, vogue, way

STYMIE, *verb* block, circumscribe, counteract, curb, deadlock, debar, delay, disadvantage, encumber, estop, forestall, frustrate, hamper, handicap, hinder, impede, inconvenience, inhibit, obstruct, parry, preclude, prevent, put an end to, stall, stand in the way, stay, stifle, stop, thwart, stump, suppress

SUA SPONTE, *noun* elective, offered, on one's own accord, on the court's own initiative, on the court's own volition, on the court's own will, optional and freely initiated, self-initiated, self-willed, uncompelled, volitional, voluntary, willful

SUASIBLE, *adjective* accessible, amenable, convincible, docile, easily convinced, easily persuaded, easygoing, facile, flexible, inducible, influenceable, movable, open, open-minded, persuadable, persuasible, pervious, pliable, pliant, receptive, responsive, swayable, tractable

SUASIVE, *adjective* apposite, apt, cogent, compelling, conclusive, consequential, convictive, convincing, fitting, forceful, influential, irresistible, justified, meaningful, momentous, persuasive, pertinent, potent, powerful, significant, strong

SUBALTERN, *adjective* baser, humble, inferior, junior, less, lesser, low, lower, lower in rank, lowly, minor, of lower rank, secondary, servile, subalternate, *subcenturio,* subordinate, subsidiary, under

SUBDIVIDE, *verb* apportion, bisect, break down, categorize, classify, cleave, cut, dissect, dissever, distribute, divide, divide into parcels, divide up, graduate, group, parcel, partition, portion, redistribute, redivide, separate, sever, share, split, sunder

SUBDIVISION, *noun* bisection, categorization, category, class, classification, compartment, component, division, fraction, fragment, group, grouping, *pars,* part, partition, section, sector, segment, separation, subcategory, subclass, subgroup, subheading
ASSOCIATED CONCEPTS: political subdivision, subdivision of a statute

SUBDUE, *verb* abate, allay, beat, beat down, bend, best, break, bring under rule, calm, captivate, capture, choke, conquer, control, crush, curb, deaden, defeat, discipline, discomfit, *domare,* dominate, dull, enthrall, foil, get the better of, harness, humble, inhibit, lessen, lower, make docile, make submissive, make tractable, master, moderate, mollify, muffle, mute, obtund, oppress, overbear, overcome, overpower, overwhelm, put down, quell, quiet, reduce, rein, repress, restrain, silence, slacken, smash, smother, soften, *subiungere,* subject, subjugate, suppress, tame, temper, tone down, tranquilize, triumph over, vanquish, worst
ASSOCIATED CONCEPTS: subdue an assailant

SUBHEADING, *noun* article, categorization, chapter, classification, clause, division, heading, paragraph, section, segment, subdivision, subgroup, subsection, title

SUBJECT *(Conditional),* ***adjective*** contingent, dependent, dependent on circumstances, depending upon, incident to, incidental, provisional, relying upon, *subiectus,* subordinate, uncertain
ASSOCIATED CONCEPTS: subject to approval, subject to defeasance, subject to review

SUBJECT *(Exposed),* ***adjective*** accountable, answerable, at the mercy of, chargeable, liable, open, prone, susceptible, unexempt from, vulnerable

SUBJECT *(Object),* ***noun*** case, experimentee, liegeman, recipient, testee, victim
ASSOCIATED CONCEPTS: subject of an investigation

SUBJECT *(Topic),* ***noun*** affair, *argumentum,* content, course, gist, issue, material, matter, motif, pith, point, point at issue, *quaestio,* study, text, theme, thesis
ASSOCIATED CONCEPTS: interest in subject matter, subject of agreement, subject of bailment, subject of commerce, subject of statute, subject of tax

SUBJECT, *verb* bring under domination, bring under rule, cause to undergo, conquer, control, crush, defeat, disfranchise, dominate, enslave, enthrall, expose, get the better of, govern, hold down, hold in bondage, hold in subjection, humble, keep down, make liable, make submissive, make subordinate, make subservient, master, *obnoxium reddere,* oppress, overcome, overmaster, overthrow, quell, repress, rule, subdue, *subicere,* subjugate, subordinate, suppress, tame, triumph over, vanquish, worst

SUBJECT MATTER, *noun* content, contents, context, framework, import, material, matter, scope, study, substance, sum and substance, text, writing
ASSOCIATED CONCEPTS: subject matter jurisdiction

SUBJECTION, *noun* bondage, captivity, conquest, control, disenfranchisement, disfranchisement, duress, enslavement, enthrallment, force, helotry, inferior rank, involuntary servitude, loss of freedom, *officium,* servitude, *servitus,* slavery, subdual, subjugation, submission, subordination, subserviency, thrall, yielding, yoke

SUBJECTIVE, ***adjective*** biased, colored by bias, emotional, individual, individualized, internal, introspective, nonobjective, personal, personalized, prejudiced, unrealistic

SUBJUGATE, ***verb*** beat, bring to terms, command, conquer, control, crush, defeat, dominate, enslave, enthrall, govern, hold captive, hold in bondage, hold sway over, humble, master, overbear, overcome, overpower, overrule, overthrow, overwhelm, put down, quash, quell, reduce, restrain, rob of freedom, rout, rule over, sell into slavery, subdue, subject, suppress, tame, trample, triumph over, vanquish

SUBLEASE, ***verb*** allow the use of, demise, grant a demise, grant a lease, hire, let out, make available for rent, rent, rent out, sublet, subrent, underlet

SUBLET, ***verb*** allow the use of, contract to lease, lease, let out, relet, rent, rent out, sublease, subrent, underlet
ASSOCIATED CONCEPTS: assignment, covenant against subletting, restriction against subletting

SUBMIT *(Give),* ***verb*** advance, commit, extend, hold out, introduce, make a motion, make a suggestion, present, propose, propound, put, put forth, put forward, refer, referre, suggest, tender
ASSOCIATED CONCEPTS: submit to arbitration, submit to the court, submit to the jury

SUBMIT *(Yield),* ***verb*** accede, accept, acknowledge defeat, acquiesce, admit defeat, bear with, bend, bow to, capitulate, cease resistance, comply, endure, give in, give up, give way to, heed, listen to, make the best of, mind, obey, put up with, reconcile oneself to, relent, resign, succumb, surrender, tolerate
ASSOCIATED CONCEPTS: submit to the jurisdiction of the court

SUBORDINATE, ***adjective*** subordinate position, accessory, ancillary, auxiliary, collateral, humble, inferior, junior, less important, less significant, lesser, low-level, lower, lower in rank, lowly, minor, secondary, subaltern, subject, subjected, submissive, subservient, subsidiary
ASSOCIATED CONCEPTS: subordinate interest, subordinate lien

SUBORN, ***verb*** bribe, bribe to take a false oath, buy off, corrupt, fraudulently induce, induce, induce another to commit perjury, induce by illegal gratuity, instigate, offer an inducement, procure another to commit perjury, procure indirectly, seduce, *subornare,* tamper with
ASSOCIATED CONCEPTS: suborn perjury

SUBPOENA, ***noun*** call, citation, command, command to appear, demand, denuntiatio *testimonii,* directive, imperative, instruction, invocation, judicial imperative, legal mandate, legal process, mandate, notification, order, order to appear, order to appear in court, process, request, requirement to attend, summons, writ
ASSOCIATED CONCEPTS: information subpoena, judicial subpoena, subpoena ad testificandum, subpoena duces tecum

SUBPOENA, ***verb*** beckon, call for the presence of, call forth, call out, call to witness, call with authority, command to appear, compel attendence, demand, *denuntiatio testimonii,* direct, direct the attendance of, issue a command, issue a court directive, issue a writ, issue process, notify to appear, order, order to appear, require compliance, require to attend, send for, summon, summon to court
ASSOCIATED CONCEPTS: subpoena a witness, subpoena before a jury, subpoena records, subpoena to a grand jury

SUBPOENA DUCES TECUM, ***noun*** judicial command, judicial demand for an accounting, judicial demand for archive, judicial demand for documentation, judicial demand for documents, judicial demand for files, judicial directive to produce documents, judicial mandate to produce documents, judicial order to produce documents
ASSOCIATED CONCEPTS: subpoena ad testificandum

SUBREPTION, ***noun*** deception, deliberate misrepresentation, fabrication, false swearing, falsehood, falsification, guile, invention, lying, mendacity, misrepresentation, perjury, prevarication, untruth

SUBROGATION, ***noun*** change, commutation, displacement, exchange, interchange, replacement, replacing, substitution, succession, supersedure, supersession, supplantation, supplanting, surrogation, switch, transfer, transference
ASSOCIATED CONCEPTS: conventional subrogation, legal subrogation, rights of subrogation

SUBSCRIBE *(Promise),* ***verb*** advocate, agree, assent, consent, donate to, enroll, guarantee, patronize, pledge, promise to contribute, register, support, warrant

SUBSCRIBE *(Sign),* ***verb*** acknowledge, affix one's signature, approve, attest, certify, confirm, endorse, inscribe, mark, ratify, seal, set a name to, sign a name to, undersign, underwrite, witness, write

SUBSCRIPTION, ***noun*** acceptance, affirmation, agreement, approval, assent, authentication, certification, confirmation, consent, endorsement, enrollment, ratification, registration, sanction, signature, validation

SUBSEQUENT, ***adjective*** coming, ensuing, eventual, following, future, *insequens,* later, latter, next, *posterior,* sequent, sequential, succeeding, trailing
ASSOCIATED CONCEPTS: subsequent condition, subsequent creditor

SUBSERVIENT, ***adjective*** abject, accessory, adjuvant, aidful, aiding, ancillary, auxiliary, base, contributory, cringing, deferential, dependent, enslaved, fawning, helpful, inferior, ingratiating, junior, lesser, lower, menial, ministrant, obedient, obeisant, *obsequens,* obsequious, prostrate, secondary, serviceable, servile, slavish, subaltern, subject, submissive, subordinate, subsidiary, sycophantic, toadying, tractable, truckling, unassertive, unctious, useful, utilitarian, valuable

SUBSIDE, ***verb*** abate, become less active, calm, *considere,* decline, decrease, descend, die away, diminish, dip, drop, dwindle, ebb, fall, fall away, fall off, grow less, lapse, lessen, let up, lull, melt away, mitigate, moderate, peter out, quiet, recede, relax, remit, *residere,* settle, shrink, sink, slack off, slacken, taper off, wane

SUBSIDIARY, ***noun*** adjuvant, aiding, assistant, auxiliary, cooperating, helping, secondary, subordinate, subservient, supplemental, supplementary
ASSOCIATED CONCEPTS: subsidiary corporation

SUBSIDIZE, ***verb*** abet, *adiuvare,* advance, afford aid, afford support, aid, assist, back, befriend, bestow, bolster, contribute, endow, finance, foster, furnish aid, furnish support, further, give, give a grant to, give aid, give support to, help, help with money, keep, lend one's aid, lend support, maintain, patronize, pay, pay for, pay toward, promote, provide capital for, provide financing, provide for, provide funds for, provide money for, render assistance, stand behind, stand by, subscribe, subserve, subventionize, supply aid, supply support, support, sustain, underwrite, uphold

SUBSIDY, ***noun*** allotment, allowance, backing, bounty, contribution, gift, grant, grant-in-aid, stipend, subsistence, subvention
ASSOCIATED CONCEPTS: government subsidy

SUBSIST, ***verb*** abide, be, be nurtured, be supported, be sustained, *constare,* continue, endure, exist, go on, hold on, last, live, maintain, outlast, outlive, perdure, persist, prevail, remain, remain alive, stand fast, stay, stay alive, survive

SUBSTANCE *(Essential nature),* ***noun*** actuality, backbone, basis, body, content, core, drift, essence, essential part, force, gist, heart, hypostasis, idea, import, marrow, material, meaning, pith, principle, purport, reality, sense, significance, signification, soul, sum, tenor, vital part

SUBSTANCE *(Material possessions),* ***noun*** assets, capital, command of money, *corpus,* estate, fortune, income, means, money, ownership, property, resources, revenue, riches, treasure, wealth, wherewithal

SUBSTANTIAL, ***adjective*** abundant, ample, concrete, consequential, considerable, established, existent, existing, *firmus,* flush, genuine, *gravis,* great, important, large, plentiful, real, significant, sizable, strong, substantive, valid
ASSOCIATED CONCEPTS: substantial breach, substantial claim, substantial compliance, substantial controversy, substantial damages, substantial error, substantial evidence, substantial factor, substantial impairment, substantial injury, substantial interest, substantial issue, substantial justice, substantial performance, substantial question, substantial right, substantial use

SUBSTANTIAL CAUSE SHOWN, ***noun*** good cause shown, legitimate basis proven, proper cause demonstrated, reasonable basis shown, substantial factors proven, sufficient foundation, sufficient grounds
ASSOCIATED CONCEPTS: temporary restraining orders

SUBSTANTIATE, ***verb*** actualize, affirm, attest, authenticate, bear out, bear witness, certify, circumstantiate, confirm, corroborate, demonstrate, embody, establish by proof, evidence, make good, materialize, objectify, prove, ratify, realize, reify, substantialize, support, uphold, validate, verify, vindicate
ASSOCIATED CONCEPTS: substantiate a claim, substantiate charges

SUBSTANTIATION, ***noun*** authenticating evidence, confirmation, confirming evidence, corroborating evidence, evidence which bears out the truth, evidence which proves a supposition, evidence which ratifies a position, evidence which validates a supposition, supporting evidence, verification
ASSOCIATED CONCEPTS: substantiation of charges

SUBSTANTIVE, ***adjective*** actual, appreciable, basic, concrete, considerable, constituent, elemental, essential, existent, existing, fundamental, important, independent, main, material, not subordinate, objective, palpable, positive, primary, principal, real, requisite, separate, solid, substantial, tangible, underlying, vital
ASSOCIATED CONCEPTS: substantive law, substantive right, substantive statute of limitations

SUBSTANTIVE DUE PROCESS, ***noun*** fundamental rights, limitation on government's power to restrict liberty, nonprocedural due process, protection of fundamental constitutional liberties, rights that must be preserved
ASSOCIATED CONCEPTS: Fifth and Fourteenth Amendments

SUBSTANTIVE ISSUE, ***noun*** benchmark, bookmark, critical point, crucial point, crux, essence, essential matter, fundamental part, gist, gravamen, heart, key point, linchpin, main point, material point, milestone, pivotal point, prime issue, salient point, substance, substantive point, turning point

SUBSTITUTE, ***noun*** agent, alternate, alternative, auxiliary, delegate, deputy, double, emissary, envoy, factor, lieutenant, pinch hitter, plenipotentiary, proxy, regent, relief, replacement, representation, representative, stand-in, steward, stopgap, substitution, supplanter, surrogate, symbol, temporary expedient, trustee, understudy

SUBSTITUTION OF COUNSEL, ***noun*** appointment of new counsel, change of counsel, hiring a new attorney, replacement of the current attorney, replacing the current counsel, retaining a new attorney-at-law, retaining a new barrister, retention of new counsel, substituting for the current lawyer
ASSOCIATED CONCEPTS: ineffective assistance of counsel, right to counsel

SUBSTITUTION OF COUNSEL, ***verb*** appointment of new counsel, change of counsel, change of legal representative, new representation, replacement of counsel, replacement of the current attorney, replacing the current counsel, retention of a new attorney-at-law, retention of new counsel, substitution for the current lawyer, substitution of attorney
ASSOCIATED CONCEPTS: attorney withdrawal, disqualification of counsel, ineffective assistance of counsel, right to counsel

SUBSUME, ***verb*** assimilate, carry, compose, comprehend, comprise, consist of, constitute, contain, embody, embrace, encompass, entail, form, have within, hold, include, incorporate, integrate into, involve, make, number, own, possess, receive, take in

SUBTERFUGE, ***noun*** artifice, camouflage, chicane, chicanery, concealment, counterfeit, deception, *deverticulum,* device, dodge, duplicity, elusion, evasion, excuse, fabrication, falsehood, fib, fiction, finesse, forgery, guise, imposture, jugglery, *latebra,* lie, loophole, machination, maneuver, mask, plan, pretense, pretext, prevarication, ruse, sham, shift, smoke screen, sophistry, strategem, subtlety, trick, untruth

SUBTLE *(Insidious),* ***adjective*** canny, contriving, crafty, cunning, deceitful, deceptive, designing, feline, guileful, illusive, implied, indistinct, inferred, insinuated, intriguing, serpentine, shifty, shrewd, sly, sophistical, stealthy, tricky, underhand, vulpine, wily

SUBTLE *(Refined),* ***adjective*** accomplished, airy, apt, artful, artistic, astute, clever, deft, delicate, diplomatic, discerning, discreet, discriminating, exact, expert, keen, light, masterly, meticulous, perceptive, politic, precise, sagacious, sharp, skillful, slender, sophisticated, strategic, subtile, superfine, tactful

SUBTRACT, ***verb*** abate, abbreviate, abridge, crop, curtail, cut, cut back, cut down, decrease, deduct, diminish, discount, downsize, dwindle, lessen, lower, minimize, pare down, prune, reduce, retrench, shorten, slash, take off, trim, truncate, whittle

SUBTRACTION, ***noun*** abstraction, ademption, curtailment, decrease, decrement, deduction, diminution, discount, exception, lessening, reduction, removal, retrenchment, shortening, shrinkage, subduction, withdrawal

SUBVERSION, ***noun*** abolition, annihilation, breakup, debacle, defeat, demolition, destruction, devastation, disestablishment, disruption, *eversio,* extinction, extirpation, incendiarism, inversion, overset, overthrow, overturn, perdition, rebellion, revolt, revolution, ruin, ruination, sabotage, sedition, subversive activities, upheaval, uprising, upset

SUBVERSIVES, ***noun*** cell, enemy combatant, enemy group, extremist group, extremists, incendiaries, insurgents, rebel organization, revolutionaries, saboteurs, underground extremists
ASSOCIATED CONCEPTS: justice courts, military tribunals, Patriot Act, prison cells, sleeper cell, terrorism, terrorist cell

SUBVERT, ***verb*** annihilate, confound, corrupt, defeat, demolish, demoralize, despoil, destroy, devastate, disestablish, dismantle, disrupt, *evertere,* extinguish, extirpate, impair, injure, lay waste, level, overset, overthrow, overturn, pervert, pull down, put an end to, ruin, spy against, *subvertere,* throw down, topple, tumble, turn over, undermine, undo, upset, vitiate
ASSOCIATED CONCEPTS: subvert the laws

SUCCEDANEUM, ***noun*** change, ersatz, exchange, replacement, secondary, substitute, substitution

SUCCEED *(Attain),* ***verb*** accomplish, achieve, acquire, advance, be victorious, bear fruit, bloom, capture, come through, conquer, do well, earn, fare well, flourish, fulfill, gain, gain a victory, make a hit, manage, master, meet with success, obtain, prevail, profit, progress, prosper, reach, realize, reap, *rem bene,* score a success, secure, surmount obstacles, thrive, triumph, vanquish, win, wrest

SUCCEED *(Follow),* ***verb*** arise, be subsequent, come after, come subsequently, derive, develop, displace, ensue, *excipere,* follow after, follow in order, give place to, go after, go next, outmode, postdate, relieve, remove, replace, serve as a substitute, set aside, subrogate, substitute for, *succedere,* supersede, supervene, supplant, take over, take the place of

SUCCESS, ***noun*** achievement, advantage, astronomical hit, attainment, blockbuster, blue chip, coup, extraordinary hit, gem, hit, jewel, marvel, phenomenon, prizewinner, progress, prosperity, record-breaker, sensation, smash, spectacular hit, treasure, triumph, victory, welfare, winner, wonder

SUCCESSFUL, ***adjective*** affluent, auspicious, blooming, blossoming, booming, champion, comfortable, effective, efficacious, felicitous, *felix,* flourishing, fortunate, *fortunatus,* fruitful, gainful, prevailing, profitable, prospering, prosperous, rich, satisfied, thriving, triumphant, unbeaten, undefeated, unvanquished, victorious, wealthy, well-off, well-situated, well-to-do, winning

SUCCESSION, ***noun*** chain, concatenation, consecution, consecutive order, *continuatio,* cycle, descent, devolution, family, issue, lineage, offspring, order, posterity, procession, progeny, progression, sequence, series, successorship, train
ASSOCIATED CONCEPTS: hereditary succession, intestate succession, legal succession, line of succession, natural succession, successor employer, successor interest, testamentary succession
FOREIGN PHRASES: ***Haereditas est successio in universum jus quod defunctus habuerit.*** Inheritance is the succession to every right which the deceased had possessed. ***Haereditas nihil aliud est, quam successio in universum jus, quod defunctus habuerit.*** An inheritance is nothing other than the succession to all the rights which the deceased had. ***Qui in jus dominiumve alterius succedit jure ejus uti debet.*** One who succeeds to the ownership rights of another should enjoy the rights of the other. ***Non debeo melioris conditionis esse, quam auctor meus a quo jus in me transit.*** I ought not to be in better condition than he to whose rights I succeed.

SUCCESSIVE, ***adjective*** after, consecutive, ensuing, following, later, subsequent, succeeding, sequent, sequential
ASSOCIATED CONCEPTS: successive application, successive continuance, successive proceeding, successive term of imprisonment, successive writ

SUCCESSOR, ***noun*** beneficiary, descendant, follower, grantee, newcomer, next in line, replacement, scion
ASSOCIATED CONCEPTS: successor in estate, successor in interest, successor in office, successor in trust

SUCCINCT, ***adjective*** abbreviated, *brevis,* brief, compact, compendious, concise, condensed, curt, epigrammatic, expressed in few words, irreducible, laconic, pauciloquent, pithy, sententious, short, summary, synoptic, terse, to the point, trenchant

SUCCUMB, ***verb*** accede, acquiesce, be defeated, bend, bow, break down, capitulate, cave in, cease, collapse, come to naught, come to terms, comply, concede, die, droop, drop, end, expire, fail, fall, flag, give in, give way, go down, go under, knuckle under, lose, perish, relent, resign, stoop, submit, *succumbere,* surrender, tire, yield

SUDDEN, ***adjective*** abrupt, fast, immediate, impromptu, improbable, improvised, instinctive, involuntary, knee-jerk, off-the-cuff, precipitant, precipitate, quick, reactive, reflex, spontaneous, spur-of-the-moment, unanticipated, unpremeditated, unrehearsed, unexpected, unforeseen, unintended, unlikely, unplanned, unpredictable, unpredicted
ASSOCIATED CONCEPTS: sudden and accidental pollution

SUE, ***verb*** appeal to the law, apply for, ask for relief, beseech, bring a legal action, bring an action, bring to justice, bring to the bar, claim, commence a suit, contest, entreat, file a legal claim, file suit, implore, initiate a civil action, institute a legal proceeding, institute process, legally pursue, litigate against, make appeal to, *orare,* petition,

plead, prefer a claim, press a claim, pursue a claim, put on trial, *rogare,* seek by request, supplicate, take to court
ASSOCIATED CONCEPTS: power to sue, right to sue, standing to sue
FOREIGN PHRASES: ***Nemo alieno nomine lege agere potest.*** No one can sue in the name of another.

SUFFER *(Permit),* ***verb*** abide, accede, accept, acquiesce, allow, assent, authorize, be reconciled, be resigned, bear with, brook, comply, concede, consent, empower, give consent, give leave, give permission, grant, grant permission, indulge, let, license, oblige, *pati, permittere,* put up with, *sinere,* tolerate

SUFFER *(Sustain loss),* ***verb*** agonize, ail, anguish, be afflicted, be impaired, be injured, be racked, be stricken, be subjected to, be wounded, bear, endure, experience loss, feel pain, hurt, incur loss, languish, lose, *minui,* sacrifice, sustain damage
ASSOCIATED CONCEPTS: suffer harm, suffer loss

SUFFERANCE, ***noun*** allowance, authorization, calmness, capacity to endure, composure, concession, control, countenance, forbearance, fortitude, imperturbation, indulgence, leave, license, longanimity, patience, patient endurance, *patientia,* permission, resignation, sanction, self-control, self-possession, self-restraint, stoicism, submission, suffering, tolerance, *toleratio,* toleration

SUFFERING *(Forbearance),* ***noun*** adversity, anguish, depression, despair, desperation, despondence, despondency, hurt, miserable condition, pain
ASSOCIATED CONCEPTS: damages, pain and suffering

SUFFERING *(Hardship),* ***noun*** acquiescence, amenability, compliance, conformism, docility, ennui, melancholy, obedience, passiveness, passivity, resignation, sadness, submission, subordination, tractability

SUFFICIENCY, ***noun*** abundance, accumulation, adequacy, adequate resources, affluence, ample stock, ampleness, amplitude, cache, capacity, competence, competency, copiousness, cornucopia, enough, fill, full measure, fullness, fund, glut, hoard, large amount, plenitude, plenty, plethora, profuseness, profusion, *quod satis est,* redundance, repletion, reservoir, satiety, satisfactoriness, saturation, shower, store, sufficientness, superabundance, supply, surfeit, treasure, wealth, wherewithal
ASSOCIATED CONCEPTS: legal sufficiency, sufficiency of the evidence

SUFFICIENT, ***adjective*** adequate, ample, capable, comfortable, commensurate, commensurate with, competent, enough, equal to, fair, in fair condition, in good condition, just, meritorious, operative, plentiful, plenty, qualified, replete, satisfactory, satisfying, suitable
ASSOCIATED CONCEPTS: sufficient cause, sufficient evidence, sufficient facts

SUFFICIENT FOUNDATION, ***noun*** good cause shown, legitimate basis proven, proper cause demonstrated, reasonable basis shown, substantial cause shown, substantial factors proven, sufficient grounds
ASSOCIATED CONCEPTS: temporary restraining orders

SUFFICIENT PROOF, ***noun*** adequate evidence, adequate proof legally presented at trial, burden of going forward, burden of proof, legal responsibility, obligation of going forward, sufficient corroboration, sufficient evidence in a case, sufficient evidence to establish a case, sufficient proof of facts, validation of proof of a case, verification of proof of a case
ASSOCIATED CONCEPTS: cause of action of claim, evidence, evidential burden, failure to sustain, preponderance of the evidence, *prima facie* case, rebuttal, weight of evidence
FOREIGN PHRASES: ***Onus probandi.*** Burden of proof.

SUFFRAGE, ***noun*** affranchisement, autonomy, choice, emancipation, enfranchisement, exemption from control, exemption from restraint, franchise, freedom, freedom of choice, liberation, liberty, license, manumission, option, popular decision, prerogative, right to vote, say, self-determination, self-government, *suffragium,* voice, vote
ASSOCIATED CONCEPTS: election law, voters' rights

SUGGEST, ***verb*** advise, advocate, allude, argue, charge, coax, connote, convey, counsel, denote, evidence, exhort, hint, implicate, imply, indicate, insinuate, instruct, mention, nominate, offer, persuade, pose, postulate, prescribe, present, proffer, promise, prompt, propose, propound, purport, put forth, put forward, recommend, refer, remark, remind, signify, submit, urge
ASSOCIATED CONCEPTS: suggestive terms, suggestive interrogatories

SUGGESTION, ***noun*** *admonitio,* advancement, advice, allusion, breath, clue, *consilium,* counsel, cue, exhortation, glimmer, hint, idea, implication, indication, inference, inkling, innuendo, insinuation, intimation, lead, motion, outline, overtone, pointer, possibility, prompting, prompture, proposal, proposition, recommendation, reminder, representation, resolution, scheme, slight trace, statement, suggested plan, suspicion, symbol, tentative statement, thought, tip, touch, trace, whisper
ASSOCIATED CONCEPTS: suggestion of error, suggestive interrogation

SUGGESTIVE *(Evocative),* ***adjective*** allusive, commemorative, commemoratory, connotative, demonstrative, expressive, graphic, graphical, implicative, indicant, indicative, indicatory, inferential, insinuative, insinuatory, intriguing, lifelike, meaningful, ominous, pictorial, provocative, recollective, redolent, referential, remindful, reminiscent, reminiscential, symbolic, thought-provoking, vivid
ASSOCIATED CONCEPTS: suggestive lineup

SUGGESTIVE *(Risqué),* ***adjective*** bawdy, carnal, coarse, erotic, improper, indecent, indelicate, lascivious, lecherous, lewd, libidinous, lickerish, loose, lurid, lustful, obscene, off-color, pornographic, provocative, racy, ribald, salacious, seductive, sexy, shameless, smutty, spicy, titillating, wanton

SUI GENERIS, ***noun*** in its own category, in its own group, of its own character, of its own class, of its own classification, of its own denomination, of its own designation, of its own genre, of its own kind, of its own nature, of its own type, of its own variety, peculiar, special, the only one of its kind, unique

SUIT, ***noun*** action, action at law, action to serve justice, case, *causa,* cause, cause in court, judicial contest, lawsuit, legal action, legal proceeding, legal remedy, *lis,* litigation, petition, proceeding, suit in law, trial
ASSOCIATED CONCEPTS: class suits, nonsuit, suit against state
FOREIGN PHRASES: ***Secta est pugna civilis; sicut actores armantur actionibus, et, quasi, accinguntur gladiis,***

ita rei muniuntur exceptionibus, et defenduntur, quasi, clypeis. A suit is a civil battle; for as the plaintiffs are armed with actions, and, as it were, girded with swords, so the defendants are fortified with pleas, and are defended, as it were, with shields. ***Frustra agit qui judicium prosequi nequit cum effectu.*** He sues vainly who cannot prosecute his judgment with effect. ***Nemo alieno nomine lege agere potest.*** No one can sue in the name of another.

SUITABILITY, *noun* accepted standard, adequacy, applicability, appropriateness, aptness, compatibility, correct standard, expediency, felicity, fitness, fittingness, happiness, justifiability, properness, propriety, relevance, right standard, rightness, serviceableness, suitableness, usefulness, utility
ASSOCIATED CONCEPTS: appropriate investment strategies

SUITABLE, *adjective* acceptable, accommodating, accordant, adapted, adequate, admissible, advantageous, advisable, applicable, apposite, appropriate, apropos, apt, *aptus,* becoming, befitting, commensurate, commodious, compatible, condign, conformable, congenial, congruent, congruous, *consentaneous,* consentaneus, consistent, consonant, convenient, correct, correspondent, decent, decorous, deserved, desirable, due, eligible, expedient, favorable, feasible, felicitous, fit, fitting, germane, harmonious, idoneous, *idoneus,* just, likely, meet, merited, opportune, pat, pertinent, practicable, proper, proportionate, qualified, reasonable, reconcilable, relevant, right, rightful, satisfactory, seasonable, seemly, sufficient, suited, timely, valid, worthy
ASSOCIATED CONCEPTS: suitable for a particular purpose

SUITOR, *noun* appellant, applicant, claimant, litigant, litigator, party to a suit, petitioner, plaintiff, pleader, seeker, solicitor, suppliant, supplicant

SULLY, *verb* asperse, attaint, bedim, begrime, belittle, bemire, besmear, blacken, blemish, blot, blur, brand, contaminate, corrupt, daub, debase, decry, deface, defame, defile, degrade, denigrate, denounce, deprecate, depreciate, dirty, discredit, disgrace, dishonor, disparage, dispraise, drabble, dull, foul, gibbet, impeach, impugn, injure, *inquinare,* knock, *maculare,* make unclean, malign, mar, pollute, put to shame, run down, shame, slur, smear, smirch, smudge, soil, spatter, speak ill of, splash, spoil, spot, stain, stigmatize, taint, tarnish, traduce, vilify, vilipend, vitiate

SUM *(Tally),* ***noun*** compendium, essence, figure, gist, idea conveyed, meaning, score, substance, summary

SUM *(Total),* ***noun*** aggregate amount, all, entirety, everything, gross amount, sum total, the whole, totality, wholeness
ASSOCIATED CONCEPTS: sum paid, sum and substance, sum in controversy, sum certain, sum demanded, sum in question

SUM, *verb* add, compute, count up, figure up, reckon up, summate, total

SUMMARIZATION, *noun* abbreviation, abridgment, analysis, brief, compendium, compilation, conclusion, condensation, core, digest, overview, recap, recapitulation, report, restatement, review, skeleton, summary, syllabus, synopsis
ASSOCIATED CONCEPTS: summarization presented to the jury

SUMMARIZE, *verb* abridge, abstract, boil down, brief, concentrate, condense, consolidate, cut, digest, encapsulate, epitomize, essentialize, extract, outline, recap, recapitulate, reprise, shorten, shrink, simplify, streamline, sum up, synopsize

SUMMARY, *adjective* *brevis,* concise, direct, done without delay, expeditious, hasty, hurried, immediate, instantaneous, prompt, quick, quickly executed, quickly performed, rapid, speedy, sudden, swift
ASSOCIATED CONCEPTS: summary action, summary contempt, summary conviction, summary hearing, summary judgment, summary proceeding, summary process, summary punishment

SUMMARY, *noun* abbreviation, abridgment, abstract, analysis, brief, compend, compendium, compilation, compressed statement, conspectus, core, digest, *epitoma,* epitome, minute, note, outline, pandect, recap, recapitulation, report, restatement, review, short version, skeleton, *summarium,* syllabus, synopsis

SUMMATION *(Presentation),* ***noun*** analysis, completion, conclusion, examination, oral argument, reasons
ASSOCIATED CONCEPTS: summation of a case

SUMMATION *(Sum),* ***noun*** addition, aggregate, aggregation, cumulative sum, result, total, totality

SUMMON, *verb* *advocare, appellare,* beckon, bid, call for, call for the presence of, call forth, call into action, call to witness, call with authority, charge, cite, command, command to appear, compel attendance, demand, give orders, issue a command, issue a court directive, issue process, notify to appear, order, order to appear, require compliance, require to attend, send for, subpoena
ASSOCIATED CONCEPTS: summon to appear in court

SUMMONS, *noun* authoritative citation to appear before a court, authoritative command, bid, calling to court, citation, command to appear, commandment, direction, invocation, legal process, mandate, notification to appear, official call, official court order, official notice, official order, order to appear, request to appear, writ, written notification to appear in court

SUNSET LAW, *noun* a law which will be discontinued, a law which will be eliminated, a statute which automatically ends, a statute which automatically terminates, a statute which expires, a statute which will cease, ending law, expiring law, statute with a fixed lifespan, terminating law

SUNSHINE LAWS, *noun* availability of government documents, availability of government information, availability of governmental records, freedom of information laws, freely available government information, open access to government information laws, open government laws
ASSOCIATED CONCEPTS: Freedom of Information Act

SUPER PAC, *noun* political committee capable of accepting boundless contributions, political committee capable of accepting limitless corporate contributions, political committee capable of accepting unbounded donations, political committee capable of accepting unlimited contributions, political committee capable of accepting unrestrained contributions
ASSOCIATED CONCEPTS: Federal Election Law

SUPERANNUATE, *verb* antiquate, cancel, dismiss, make extinct, make obsolete, make outdated, remove, replace, retire, shelve, withdraw

SUPERB, ***adjective*** astronomical, awesome, bang-up, banner, beautiful, best, blue-chip, capital, choice, classic, dynamite, fabulous, famous, five-star, grand, great, impressive, incredible, noble, outstanding, perfect, preeminent, premium, prime, quality, sensational, splendid, stellar, sterling, superior, superlative, terrific, top-notch

SUPERCILIOUS, ***adjective*** arrogant, assumptive, bumptious, cavalier, condescending, contemptuous, contumelious, derisive, dictatorial, disdainful, disrespectful, domineering, egotistic, *fastidiosus,* haughty, imperious, inso-lent, intolerant, irreverent, lofty, lordly, magisterial, overbearing, overweening, patronizing, peremptory, pompous, presumptuous, prideful, proud, puffed up, scornful, *superbus,* swollen, toplofty, uppish, uppity, vainglorious, withering

SUPERFICIAL, ***adjective*** careless, cursory, depthless, desultory, empty, exterior, external, frivolous, hasty, hurried, inane, insubstantial, *lax, levis,* outward, perfunctory, sciolistic, shallow, shoal, silly, skin-deep, slapdash, slight, surface, trifling, trivial, unthinking

SUPERFLUOUS, ***adjective*** additional, adscititious, dispensable, duplicate, excess, excrescent, expendable, extra, extravagant, inessential, inordinate, lavish, luxuriant, luxurious, more than enough, more than sufficient, needless, overflowing, overmuch, prodigal, profuse, redundant, remaining, remanent, residual, residuary, spare, superabundant, supererogative, supererogatory, supernumerary, supervacaneous, *supervacaneus, supervacuus,* supplemental, surplus, uncalled-for, unessential, unnecessary, useless, wasteful
ASSOCIATED CONCEPTS: superfluous lands

SUPERFUND, ***noun*** environmental cleanup, federal program to restore environmentally unsound sites, fund to reclaim the environment, mechanism to fund the environment, reserve for environment contingencies
Generally: fund for repairs, reserves for removing wastes

SUPERINTEND, ***verb*** administer, *administrare,* administrate, boss, caretake, command, control, direct, exercise charge over, exercise supervision over, govern, guide, handle, have charge of, head, instruct, keep in order, lead, look after, manage, overlook, oversee, pilot, praeesse, *procurare,* regulate, rule, see to, steer, supervise, watch

SUPERINTENDENT, ***noun*** administrator, agent, captain, caretaker, chief, controller, curator, custodian, director, foreman, governor, guardian, intendant, leader, manager, master, monitor, overseer, *praefectus,* proctor, steward, supervisor, taskmaster, warden

SUPERIOR *(Excellent),* ***adjective*** above average, above par, better, choice, deluxe, distinguished, exceptional, finer, first-rate, foremost, greater, high-class, high-grade, high-quality, illustrious, incomparable, matchless, *melior,* noble, nonpareil, peerless, *praestantior,* preferable, preferred, second to none, superexcellent, superlative, supreme, topping, transcendent, unequaled, unexcelled, unparalleled, unrivalled, unsurpassed

SUPERIOR *(Higher),* ***adjective*** chief, greater, more elevated, of greater influence, of higher rank, paramount, senior
ASSOCIATED CONCEPTS: respondeat superior, superior court, superior force

SUPERLATIVE, ***adjective*** best, champion, chief, consummate, crowning, excellent, excessive, *eximius,* extreme, first-rate, foremost, greatest, highest, immoderate, incomparable, inflated, inimitable, matchless, most eminent, nonpareil, *optimus,* paramount, peerless, prime, principal, second to none, sovereign, super, superexcellent, superfine, superior, supreme, surpassing, tiptop, transcendent, unequaled, unexcelled, unmatched, unparalleled, unrivaled, unsurpassed, utmost, without parallel

SUPERSEDE, ***verb*** abolish, annul, discard, displace, make obsolete, make void, nullify, obviate, oust, override, overrule, preclude, put in the place of, remove, repeal, replace, set aside, stand in stead of, subrogate, substitute, *succedere,* succeed, supplant, take the place of, void
ASSOCIATED CONCEPTS: superseding cause

SUPERSEDING CAUSE, ***noun*** annulment, break, displacement, immediate legal basis, immediate legal cause, immediate legal genesis, interceding break, nullification, obviation, ousting, overriding cause, overruling cause, preclusion, put in the place of, removal, replacement, substitution, succession, sufficient legal basis, sufficient legal cause, sufficient legal factor, sufficient legal genesis, sufficient legel inducements, sufficient legal source, supplanting legal cause, voidance
ASSOCIATED CONCEPTS: intervening clause

SUPERVENE, ***verb*** arise, be subsequent, bechance, befall, come to pass, *crop* up, ensue, eventuate, follow, happen, issue, occur, result, spring up, succeed, *supervenire,* take place

SUPERVISE, ***verb*** administer, care, caretake, check, command, conduct, control, direct, discipline, govern, guide, handle, have charge of, lead, look after, manage, moderate, officiate, operate, oversee, pilot, preside, preside over, regulate, rule, steer, watch over
ASSOCIATED CONCEPTS: employer/employee, principal and agent

SUPERVISION, ***noun*** administration, care, charge, command, control, direction, government, gubernation, guidance, inspection, jurisdiction, management, oversight, *procuratio,* proctorage, regulation, steerage, stewardship, superintendence, surveillance
ASSOCIATED CONCEPTS: direct supervision, general supervision, person in need of supervision, personal supervision, right of supervision, supervision and control, supervisory powers

SUPERVISOR, ***noun*** administrator, boss, chairperson, chief, director, executive, head, leader, manager, man in charge, official, organizer, overseer, superintendent

SUPPLANT, ***verb*** abolish, act for, bring low, cashier, cause the downfall of, depose, deracinate, dethrone, discharge, dismiss, displace, drive away, drive out, eject, eradicate, expel, extirpate, fire, force out, oust, overthrow, overpower, remove, replace, retire, subrogate, substitute, subvert, succeed, supersede, take over, take the place of, transfer, turn out, undermine, unseat, uproot, upset, usurp

SUPPLEMENT, ***verb*** add, add to, amend, amplify, augment, bolster, broaden, buttress, complement, contribute to, enhance, enlarge, enrich, expand, fortify, improve, increase, lengthen, magnify, reinforce, strengthen, subsidize, superadd, widen

SUPPLEMENTAL, ***adjective*** accompanying, additional, additive, adjunct, adventitious, ancillary, appurtenant, attendant, augmentative, auxiliary, collateral, concomitant, contributory, extra, extrinsic, incidental, nonessential, pendent, spare, submitted at a later time, subordinate, subsidiary, superfluous, supernumerary, supervenient, supplementary, unessential, unnecessary
ASSOCIATED CONCEPTS: supplemental affidavit, supplemental answer, supplemental claim, supplemental complaint, supplemental condition, supplemental findings, supplemental insurance, supplemental policy, supplemental procedure, supplemental questions

SUPPLEMENTARY, ***adjective*** accessory, additional, additive, adjunct, adscititious, ancillary, attendant, augmentative, auxiliary, collateral, concomitant, extra, incidental, nonessential, secondary, spare, subordinate, subsidiary, supervenient, supplemental, suppletive, suppletory, unessential
ASSOCIATED CONCEPTS: supplementary proceedings

SUPPLIER, ***noun*** caterer, chandler, commissary, contractor, furnisher, giver, merchant, provider, provisioner, purveyor, seller, steward, trader, victualer

SUPPLY, ***verb*** accommodate with, accouter, administer, afford, bestow, cater, contribute, deal out, deliver, distribute, endow, endue, equip, feed, fill up, fit out, furnish, give, grant, invest, lavish, maintain, minister, *ministrare,* oblige, outfit, present, provide, provision, purvey, recruit, refill, render, replenish, satisfy, serve, stock, *suppeditare,* suppeditate, sustain, victual, yield

SUPPORT *(Assistance),* ***noun*** accommodation, *adiumentum,* aid, assist, assistance, *auxilium,* backing, comfort, contribution, cooperation, defense, encouragement, endowment, help, helping hand, lift, livelihood, mainstay, maintenance, patronage, preservation, promotion, protection, relief, subsistence, succor, *subsidium,* sustenance, upkeep
ASSOCIATED CONCEPTS: alimony, child support, failure to provide support, inadequate support, maintenance

SUPPORT *(Corroboration),* ***noun*** affirmation, approval, attestation, authentication, backing, certification, circumstantiation, confirmation, documentation, endorsement, fortification, justification, ratification, strengthening, substantiation, validation, verification, vindication

SUPPORT *(Assist),* ***verb*** accommodate, *adesse,* aid, back, bolster, champion, come to the defense of, come to the help of, contribute, cooperate with, defend, endorse, facilitate, feed, finance, furnish funds, further, help, lend money to, maintain, minister to, nourish, patronize, promote, protect, provide for, reinforce, second, subsidize, *suffragari,* supply the necessities of, sustain, take care of, take the part of, uphold
FOREIGN PHRASES: ***Parentum est liberos alere atiam nothos.*** It is the duty of parents to support their children even when illegitimate.

SUPPORT *(Corroborate),* ***verb*** accredit, affirm, attest, authenticate, back up, bear out, buttress, certify, circumstantiate, confirm, establish, make absolute, make good, make more certain, prove, ratify, reinforce, strengthen, substantiate, sustain, uphold in evidence, validate, verify, vindicate, vouch for

SUPPORT *(Justify),* ***verb*** account for, approve, defend, defend successfully, explain, give grounds for, make defense for, make legitimate, provide justification, say in defense, stand up for, vindicate

SUPPORTER, ***noun*** adherent, advocate, apostle, applauder, backer, believer, booster, champion, cohort, contributor, encourager, espouser, expounder, financer, follower, friend, loyalist, paladin, partisan, promoter, proponent, stalwart, white knight

SUPPORTING EVIDENCE, ***noun*** authenticating evidence, certification, confirmation, confirming documentation, confirming documents, confirming evidence, confirming means of proof, corroboration, evidence which bears out the truth, evidence which buttresses a case, evidence which strengthens a case, reinforcing evidence, substantiating proof, substantiation, validation, verification
ASSOCIATED CONCEPTS: circumstantial evidence

SUPPOSE, ***verb*** allude to, anticipate, assume, believe, be of the opinion, calculate, conceive, conclude, conjecture, consider, deduce, deduct, deem, estimate, expect, feel, gather, gauge, generalize, guess, hint, hypothesize, imagine, imply, infer, insinuate, intimate, judge, opine, posit, predicate, presume, presuppose, propose, propound, reason, regard, speculate, surmise, suspect, take for granted, theorize, understand, view

SUPPOSITION, ***noun*** assumption, belief, conception, *coniectura,* conjecture, guess, hypothesis, likelihood, likeliness, *opinio,* opinion, position, postulate, premise, presumption, probability, speculation, supposal, surmise, suspicion, theorem, theory, thesis
FOREIGN PHRASES: ***In claris non est locus conjecturis.*** In matters which are obvious there is no room for conjecture.

SUPPRESS, ***verb*** arrest, ban, burke, bury, cancel, censor, check, choke, choke back, cloak, conceal, cover up, crush, delete, end, *exstinguere,* extinguish, gag, hush up, inhibit, keep back, keep down, keep out of sight, keep secret, mask, muffle, obstruct, overcome, overpower, overthrow, overwhelm, prevent, prohibit, quash, quell, quench, repress, *reprimere,* restrain, screen, shroud, silence, smother, stifle, still, stop, strangle, subdue, *supprimere,* vanquish, veil
ASSOCIATED CONCEPTS: motion to suppress evidence

SUPPRESSION OF EVIDENCE, ***verb*** extinguishment, judicial ban of evidence, prevention of the introduction of evidence, prohibition of the use of evidence, quashing evidence, repressing evidence, restraining the use of evidence, substantiation, that which furnishes proof, that which tends to prove, validation, vanquish veil, verification
ASSOCIATED CONCEPTS: exclusionary rule, Fifth Amendment, Fourteenth Amendment, illegal search and seizure

SUPREMACY, ***noun*** ascendancy, authority, championship, chieftaincy, command, control, direction, *dominatio,* domination, dominion, governance, headship, highest position, importance, influence, leadership, lordship, management, masterdom, mastership, mastery, omnipotence, paramountcy, power, precedence, predominance, predominancy, predomination, preeminence, primacy, *principatus,* regulation, rule, scepter, sovereignty, superintendence, superiority, supervision, supreme authority, supremeness, sway, transcendence, transcendency, triumph, upperhand, victory
ASSOCIATED CONCEPTS: Supremacy Clause

SUPREME, ***adjective*** absolute, best, chief, commanding, controlling, directing, first, foremost, greatest, highest, high-level, ideal, lead, main, major, officiating, overseeing, paramount, predominant, preeminent, premier, presiding, primary, prime, principal, regnant, reigning, ruling, senior, supereminent, supervisory, top, ultimate

SURCHARGE, ***noun*** added charge, additional charge, excessive burden, excessive charge, extra charge, extra fee, overassessment, overburden, overcharge, overload, penalty
ASSOCIATED CONCEPTS: identifiable surcharge, surcharge for services

SURE, ***adjective*** assured, axiomatic, certain, clear, confident, doubtless, positive, resolute, sanguine, self-assured, self-conceited, self-confident, unfaltering, unhesitating, unquestioning, unwavering

SURETY *(Certainty),* ***noun*** absolute confidence, absoluteness, affirmance, affirmation, aplomb, ascertainment, asseveration, assurance, assuredness, averment, avowal, avowance, certain knowledge, certification, certitude, complete conviction, confirmation, contract, conviction, convincement, declaration, definiteness, determination, earnest averment, earnest avowal, earnest declaration, firmness, guaranty, hardihood, persuasion, positiveness, pronouncement, reassurance, reliance on, self-assurance, self-conviction, solemn averment, solemn avowal, solemn declaration, sureness, unequivocalness, unmistakableness, unquestionableness, vow, warrant

SURETY *(Guarantor),* ***noun*** attester, backer, certifier, confirmer, consignee, endorser, financer, indemnitor, insurer, promisor, ratifier, signatory, signer, sponsor, subscriber, supporter, underwriter, voucher, warrantor
ASSOCIATED CONCEPTS: surety bond, surety company, surety insurance, surety of the peace
FOREIGN PHRASES: ***In veram quantitatem fidejussor teneatur, nisi pro certa quantitate accessit.*** A surety should be held for the true quantity, unless he agreed for a certain quantity. ***Natura fide jussionis sit strictissimi juris et non durat vel extendatur de re ad rem, de persona ad personam, de tempore ad tempus.*** The nature of a suretyship is one of strictest law and cannot endure or be extended from one thing to another, from one person to another, or from one time to another.

SURFEIT, ***noun*** avalanche, deluge, excess, excessive amount, fullness, glut, inundation, nimiety, overabundance, overdose, overflow, overfullness, overload, oversupply, plenty, profuseness, profusion, redundance, repletion, satiation, *satietas,* satiety, satisfaction, saturation, superabundance, superfluity, supersaturation, surplus, surplusage

SURGE, ***noun*** augmentation, billow, breaker, comber, curl, deluge, flood, flow, forward movement, gain, groundswell, growth, increase, intensification, inundation, mass, rise, roller, swell, upsurge, wave

SURMISE, ***verb*** apprehend, assume, *augurari,* be of the opinion, believe, conceive, conclude, conjecture, count, deduce, deem, divine, esteem, fancy, feel, gather, guess, have an idea, hazard a guess, hypothesize, imagine, infer, judge, opine, posit, predicate, presume, presuppose, regard, speculate, suppose, suspect, *suspicari,* theorize, think, trow, understand, view, ween

SURMOUNT, ***verb*** beat, clear, climb, command, conquer, crest, crown, defeat, dominate, exceed, excel, get the better of, go beyond, master, outdo, outmaneuver, outrival, overcome, overpass, overpower, overthrow, overturn, pass, prevail over, rise above, rout, scale, subdue, subjugate, surpass, top, transcend, triumph over, upset, vanquish, vault

SURPASS, ***verb*** *antecellere,* be greater, be superior, beat, better, break the record, cap, come first, distance, eclipse, exceed, excel, *excellere,* get ahead, go beyond, go one better, have the upper hand, improve upon, leave behind, outmaneuver, outclass, outdo, outmatch, outnumber, outplay, outrank, outrival, outrun, outshine, outstrip, outvie, outweigh, overshadow, pass, predominate, prevail, rank first, reach a new high, rise above, rival, supererogate, take precedence, top, tower over, transcend, triumph over

SURPLUS, ***noun*** balance, bonus, excess, expletive, glut, leavings, margin, nimiety, overabundance, overage, overflow, overmeasure, overplus, overrun, oversupply, redundance, redundancy, remainder, residue, *residuum,* spare, superabundance, superfluity, superplus, supersaturation, surfeit, surplusage
ASSOCIATED CONCEPTS: accumulated surplus, distribution of surplus, surplus after sale, surplus goods, surplus income, surplus of proceeds, transfer to surplus

SURPLUSAGE, ***noun*** balance, continuing, extra, left, leftover, over, spare, staying
ASSOCIATED CONCEPTS: no child left behind, remainder

SURPRISE, ***noun*** *admiratio,* amazement, astonishment, astoundment, bafflement, bewilderment, consternation, lack of warning, *miratio,* shock, unexpected event, unexpected occurrence, unforeseen contingency, unforeseen event, unforeseen occurrence, unsuspected event, unusual occurrence, wonder, wonderment
ASSOCIATED CONCEPTS: take an opposing party by surprise

SURRENDER *(Give back),* ***verb*** abdicate, abjure, abnegate, cede, disclaim, disown, forfeit, forgo, forsake, forswear, hand over, let go, part with, reinstate, relinquish, render up, renounce, resign, restore, return, waive

SURRENDER *(Yield),* ***verb*** acquiesce, agree to, back down, be submissive, capitulate, concede, *dedere,* give in, obey, relent, submit, succumb, *tradere*

SURREPTITIOUS, ***adjective*** artful, clandestine, *clandestinus,* concealed, conniving, covert, crafty, cunning, deceitful, deceptive, delitescent, disguised, done by stealth, evasive, faked, fraudulently introduced, furtive, *furtivus,* guileful, hidden, indirect, insidious, lurking, mysterious, obreptitious, private, secret, secretive, sneaky, stealthy, subdolous, subtle, tricky, uncommunicative, undercover, underground, underhand, undisclosed, unknown, unseen, unspied, unsuspected, veiled, vulpine, wily

SURROGATE, ***adjective*** acting, alternate, delegated, deputy, foster, imitation, makeshift, provisional, proxy, pseudo, representative, simulated, stand-in, substitute, substitutional, vicarial, vicarious, *vicarius*

SURROUND, ***verb*** band, circle, compass, embrace, encircle, enclose, encompass, envelop

SURVEILLANCE, ***noun*** care, charge, circumspection, examination, guard, heed, inspection, lookout, observation, oversight, protection, scrutiny, stewardship, superintendence, supervision, vigil, vigilance, watch, watchfulness

SURVEY *(Examine),* ***verb*** analyze, appraise, consider, *considerare, contemplari,* evaluate, inspect, keep an eye upon, keep watch, look at, observe, overlook, oversee, peruse, reconnoiter, review, scan, scrutinize, search, *spectare,* study, view, watch, weigh

SURVEY *(Poll),* ***verb*** canvass, compute, count, count ballots, count votes, enroll, enumerate, estimate, list, register, review, tabulate, take stock, test, total

SURVIVAL, ***noun*** being, continuance, continuation, continuation of life, durability, duration, endurance, existence, extension, life, maintenance, permanence, prolongation

SURVIVE, ***verb*** abide, be left, be spared, continue, endure, exist, last, live longer, live on, make a comeback, outlast, outlive, persevere, persist, remain, result, subsist, sustain, weather the storm
ASSOCIATED CONCEPTS: survival of a debt, survival of an action, survive a contract, surviving party, survivor statutes, survivorship

SUSCEPTIBILITY, ***noun*** affectability, aptitude, bent, capability of being affected, capacity for emotion, capacity for receiving impressions, empathy, impressibility, impressionability, inclination, leaning, penchant, proclivity, propensity, sensibility, sensitive feelings, sensitiveness, sensitivity, tendency, tendency to be emotionally affected

SUSCEPTIBLE *(Responsive),* ***adjective*** compassionate, easily affected, flexible, impressible, impressionable, influenceable, *mollis,* movable, persuadable, pliant, reactive, readily impressed, receptive, sensitive, susceptive, swayable, sympathetic

SUSCEPTIBLE *(Unresistent),* ***adjective*** exposed, helpless, in danger, liable, nonresistant, open, predisposed, resistless, sensitive, undefended, unprotected, unsafe, vulnerable, yielding

SUSPECT, ***noun*** accused, accused person, alleged malfeasor, alleged offender, alleged transgressor, alleged wrongdoer, individual under suspicion, one suspected of a crime, person accused of crime, presumed wrongdoer, suspected criminal
ASSOCIATED CONCEPTS: defendant

SUSPECT *(Distrust),* ***verb*** be doubtful, be dubious, be skeptical, be suspicious, disbelieve, doubt, feel distrust, harbor suspicious, have no confidence in, lack confidence in, misdoubt, misgive, mistrust, question, without reliance in
ASSOCIATED CONCEPTS: suspect of wrongdoing

SUSPECT *(Think),* ***verb*** assume, be of the opinion, believe, conclude, conjecture, consider, deduce, deem, divine, fancy, gather, guess, have the idea, hold, hypothesize, imagine, infer, judge, opine, posit, presume, presuppose, reckon, speculate, suppose, surmise, *suspicari, suspicionem habere,* take for granted, theorize, understand, view

SUSPEND, ***verb*** arrest, break off, bring to a standstill, bring to a stop, cease, check, defer, delay, desist, *differre,* discharge, discontinue, halt, hinder, hold in abeyance, interfere with, intermit, *intermittere,* interrupt, lay aside, lay off, leave off, postpone, put off, remit, remove, shelve, stall, stay, stop, table, temporize
ASSOCIATED CONCEPTS: suspend a license, suspend a sentence, suspend an employee, suspend payment, suspend the power of alienation, suspend the writ of habeas corpus

SUSPENSE, ***noun*** anticipation, apprehension, doldrums, dormancy, dread, expectancy, expectation, foreboding, hypnosis, impasse, inaction, indecision, inertness, latency, misgiving, moratorium, motionlessness, pendency, prospect, quiescence, standstill, suspended admiration, waiting

SUSPENSION, ***noun*** deep freeze, discontinuance, dormancy, downtime, holding pattern, idleness, impasse, inaction, inertia, inertness, latency, layoff, moratorium, motionlessness, pause, quiescence, recess, recession, remission, repose, rest, sleep, standstill, stop, stoppage, suspended animation, suspense, torpor
ASSOCIATED CONCEPTS: suspension pending discharge

SUSPICION *(Mistrust),* ***noun*** apprehension, cynicism, disbelief, distrust, doubt, doubtfulness, dubiety, dubiousness, fear, fearfulness, incredulity, lack of faith, lack of trust, misdoubt, misgiving, qualm, skepticism, suspiciousness, trepidation, unbelief
ASSOCIATED CONCEPTS: suspicious circumstances, suspicious origin
FOREIGN PHRASES: ***Dona clandestina sunt semper suspiciosa.*** Clandestine gifts are always open to suspicion.

SUSPICION *(Uncertainty),* ***noun*** chance, conjecture, doubtfulness, guess, hint, impression, incertitude, inconclusiveness, inference, inkling, insecurity, intimation, notion, postulate, postulation, question, speculation, suggestion, supposition, surmise, trace, unsureness

SUSPICIOUS *(Distrustful),* ***adjective*** apprehensive, cautious, concerned, disposed to doubt, doubting, dubious, fearful, hard to convince, hesitant, inconvincible, jealous, leery, mistrustful, nervous, quizzical, skeptical, suspecting, *suspiciosus,* untrustful, untrusting, untrustworthy, wary, watchful

SUSPICIOUS *(Questionable),* ***adjective*** abnormal, cryptic, doubtful, dubious, enigmatic, equivocal, farfetched, hard to believe, irregular, open to doubt, open to question, peculiar, strange, suspect, unbelievable, uncertain, unconvincing, unplausible, unworthy of belief
ASSOCIATED CONCEPTS: suspicious circumstances, suspicious origin

SUSTAIN *(Confirm),* ***verb*** affirm, approve, assent to, attest, authenticate, bear out, buttress, certify, circumstantiate, consent to, corroborate, defend, document, endorse, establish, evidence, justify, make firm, prove, ratify, reinforce, sanction, settle, strenghten, substantiate, support, uphold, uphold in evidence, validate, verify, vindicate
ASSOCIATED CONCEPTS: sustain a lower court's decision

SUSTAIN *(Prolong),* ***verb*** attentuate, bolster, conserve, continue, contribute to, elongate, extend, fortify, guard, keep going, keep up, lengthen, maintain, nourish, perpetuate, preserve, promote, protect, protract, reinforce, save, spare, strengthen, stretch, *sustentare, sustinere,* uphold

SUSTENANCE, ***noun*** aliment, alimentation, *alimentum,* food, keep, living, maintenance, means of sustaining life, necessities, nourishment, nutriment, nutrition, provisions, subsistence, supplies, support, sustentation, upkeep, victuals, victus

SWAY, *noun* authority, command, control, domain, dominance, domination, dominion, force, governance, influence, jurisdiction, leadership, power, predominance, prestige, primacy, reign, rule, supremacy

SWAY *(Persuade),* ***verb*** actuate, coax, control, convert, convince, dominate, encourage, force, goad, govern, incline, induce, influence, inspire, inveigle, manage, motivate, move, predispose, predominate, prejudice, preside, pressure, prevail, prevail upon, prod, prompt, spur, stimulate, urge

SWAY *(Vacillate),* ***verb*** falter, flounder, fluctuate, hesitate, lean, oscillate, pulsate, seesaw, shift, shuffle, swing, undulate, veer, waffle, waver

SWEAR, *verb* adjure, affirm, allege under oath, assert as true, assure, authenticate, aver, avow, bear witness, bind oneself by oath, certify, confirm, declare, declare solemnly, declare true, give a promise, give evidence, give one's word, guarantee, *iurare, iureiurando adfirmare,* maintain under oath, promise, put one's trust in, state, state under oath, utter an oath, vouch, vow
ASSOCIATED CONCEPTS: false swearing, public swearing
FOREIGN PHRASES: ***In judicio non creditur nisi juratis.*** In a court of justice no one is given credence who is not sworn.

SWEARING-IN, *noun* documentation, enlistment, inauguration, induction, initiation, installation of an officer, installment, investiture of official responsibilities, oath, official ceremonies
ASSOCIATED CONCEPTS: inauguration, public officer, public service

SWINDLE, *verb* beguile, bilk, cheat, con, cozen, deceive, defraud, dupe, house, misappropriate, scam, swindle, trick, victimize

SWITCH, *verb* about-face, abrogate, alternate, change, displace, hand over, interchange, oscillate, overturn, repeal, replace, rescind, revert, revoke, rock, shift, strike, substitute, surrender, swap, sway, swing, trade, waver, yield
ASSOCIATED CONCEPTS: bait and switch

SWORN, *verb* adjured, affirmed, alleged under oath, asserted as true under oath, assured under oath, authenticated under oath, averred, avowed, certified under oath, confirmed under oath, declared solemnly, declared true under oath, declared under oath, given evidence under oath, maintained under oath, stated under oath, vowed, witnessed
ASSOCIATED CONCEPTS: sworn enemy, sworn statements

SWORN DECLARANT, *noun* affiant, author, compiler, composer, declarant, drafter, party, scriptor, undersigned, writer
ASSOCIATED CONCEPTS: accommodation endorser, accommodation maker, dying declaration

SYCOPHANT, *noun* acolyte, adherent, admirer, camp follower, company man, convert, devotee, disciple, enthusiast, fan, fawner, follower, groveler, idolator, partisan, pawn, pupil, student, votary, worshipper, zealot

SYMBOL, *noun* abbreviation, badge, clue, connotation, cue, delineation, depiction, emblem, enactment, ensign, exponent, gesture, image, index, indication, manifestation, mark, model, notation, note, picture, portrayal, representation, seal, sign, signal, signification, *signum, symbolum,* symptom, token, trademark, visible sign
ASSOCIATED CONCEPTS: trademark

SYMBOLIC, *adjective* allegorical, characteristic, emblematic, example, explanatory, figural, figurative, indicative, metaphoric, representational, representative, suggestive, symbolical, typical

SYMPATHETIC, *adjective* affectionate, benevolent, benignant, bighearted, caring, charitable, clement, commiserative, compassionate, congenial, cordial, empathetic, empathic, friendly, genial, good-natured, good-tempered, gracious, humane, kind, kindhearted, kindly, largehearted, lenient, loving, magnanimous, merciful, pitying, responsive, ruthful, sensitive, softhearted, tender, tenderhearted, tolerant, understanding, warm, warmhearted, well-disposed

SYMPATHIZE, *verb* be compassionate, be moved, be sorry for, be touched, be understanding, comfort, commiserate, condole, *congruere,* console, *eadem sentire,* empathize, express sympathy, feel for, grieve with, have pity, identify with, lament with, *misereri,* mourn with, pity, share grief, share sorrow, show mercy, show tenderness, solace, soothe, understand

SYMPATHY, *noun* affinity, altruism, benevolence, benignity, charity, commiseration, compassion, condolence, feeling, generosity, goodwill, humaneness, humanitarianism, humanity, kindheartedness, kindness, largesse, magnanimity, mercy, philanthropy, pity, regard, regret, softheartedness, tolerance

SYMPTOM, *noun* alarm, augury, characteristic, clue, danger signal, diagnostic, evidence, evincement, feature, forewarning, guide, index, indicant, indication, indicator, indice, *indicium,* intimation, manifestation, mark, means of recognition, monition, monitor, notice, preindication, premonitor, premonitory sign, prognostic, sign, signal, token, trait, warning, warning sign

SYNCHRONISM, *noun* accompaniment, accord, *aequalitas temporum,* agreement, attunement, coexistence, coincidence, compatibility, concord, concurrence, conformity, consistency, harmony, simultaneity, simultaneousness, unison

SYNDICATE, *noun* alliance, association, cartel, coalition, combine, company, consortium, council, federation, guild, league, machine, merger, organization, partnership, pool, ring, union

SYNERGETIC, *adjective* coacting, coactive, collaborative, concurrent, concurring, co-operant, cooperative, coworking, in agreement, in concord

SYNERGY, *noun* coaction, coincidence, collaboration, combined action, combined effect, combined operation, concert, concurrence, cooperation, cooperative action, joint effect, synergism, united action

SYNONYMOUS, *noun* alike, analogous, carbon-copy, coincident, compatible, convertible, correlative, correspondent, corresponding, duplicate, equal, equal with, equivalent, identical, interchangeable, like, same, similar, substitute, synonymic, tantamount

SYNOPSIS, *noun* abridgment, abstract, brief, compend, compendium, condensation, conspectus, digest, *epitome,* minute, outline, recapitulation, review, *summarium,* summary, summation

SYNTHETIC, *adjective* artificial, counterfeit, ersatz, factitious, illegitimate, man-made, manufactured, mock, not genuine, not natural, pretended, pseudo, quasi, spurious, unnatural

SYSTEM, *noun* arrangement, *artificium,* classification, design, *formula,* logical process, manner, means, method, mode of management, operation, order, orderliness, orderly combination, organization, pattern, plan, policy, practice, procedure, process, program, recipe, regime, regimen, regularity, routine, scheme, settled procedure, state of order, strategy, technique, way
ASSOCIATED CONCEPTS: commercial system, governmental system, judicial system, legal system, retirement system

SYSTEMATIC, *adjective* according to rule, *accuratus,* arranged, businesslike, classified, disciplined, exact, habitual, in order, methodical, ordered, orderly, organized, precise, regular, regulated, routine, standardized, systematical, thorough, thoroughgoing, under control, uniform, well-ordered, well-organized, well-regulated

TABULATE, *noun* alphabetize, allocate, arrange, assign places to, catalog, chart, chronicle, codify, coordinate, docket, enumerate, file, grade, graduate, group, index, inventory, itemize, list, marshal, methodize, organize, rank, register, sort, systematize

TACIT, *adjective* allusive, assumed, connoted, implicit, implied, indicated, inferential, inferred, not openly expressed, silent, suggested, symbolized, *tacitus,* taken for granted, undeclared, understood, unexpressed, unmentioned, unpronounced, unsaid, unspoken, unstated, untold, unvoiced, wordless
ASSOCIATED CONCEPTS: tacit approval, tacit consent

TACITURN, *adjective* brusque, close, closemouthed, curt, dumb, guarded, habitually silent, inarticulate, laconic, mum, mute, pauciloquent, quiet, reserved, restrained, reticent, secretive, silent, sparing of words, speechless, *taciturnus,* uncommunicative, ungarrulous, unloquacious, unsociable, untalkative, unvocal, withdrawn

TACTIC, *noun* arrangement, blueprint, contrivance, design, device, expedient, formula, gambit, game plan, ground plan, maneuver, means, method, plot, ploy, project, ruse, scheme, stratagem, strategy, system

TACTICAL, *adjective* aimed, artful, *astutus,* blueprinted, calculated, *cautus,* considered, contrived, crafty, cunning, deliberate, designed, devised, diplomatic, diplomatical, engineered, intended, intriguing, knowing, maneuvering, organized, planned, plotted, politic, prepared, *prudens,* purposed, purposeful, skillful, strategic, strategical, studied, systematized, weighed, well-planned, well-thought-out

TACTICS, *noun* artifice, contrivance, course of action, devices, direction, evolution, expedients, intrigue, machination, maneuvering, manipulation, manner, mode of procedure, *modus operandi,* policy, politics, practice, procedure, process, scheme, stratagem, strategy, temporizing

TAINT *(Contaminate),* ***verb*** adulterate, alloy, befoul, besmirch, blemish, blight, *contaminare,* decay, defile, degrade, dirty, disease, envenom, foul, *imbuere,* infect, make noxious, make putrid, poison, pollute, putrefy, render impure, rot, soil, spoil, sully
ASSOCIATED CONCEPTS: tainted evidence

TAINT *(Corrupt),* ***verb*** cause to be dishonest, debase, debauch, defile, degenerate, demoralize, deprave, despoil, destroy the integrity of, lower morally, misuse, pervert, suborn, tarnish, violate, vitiate

TAINTED *(Contaminated),* ***adjective*** adulterated, befouled, blighted, defiled, dirtied, dirty, diseased, envenomed, foul, impaired, impure, infected, noxious, poisoned, polluted, putrefied, putrid, rancid, rotten, smirched, soiled, spoiled, stained, sullied, unclean
ASSOCIATED CONCEPTS: fruit of the poisonous tree doctrine, tainted evidence

TAINTED *(Corrupted),* ***adjective*** abandoned, criminal, debased, debauched, degenerate, degraded, demoralized, depraved, dishonest, dissolute, evil, immoral, low, perverted, profligate, reprobate, rotten, shameless, vicious, vitiated, warped, wicked

TAKE *(Acquire),* ***verb*** adopt, attach, carry, derive, endure, excise, gain, get, impound, impress, obtain, preempt, procure, profit, reap, secure, sequester
ASSOCIATED CONCEPTS: take effect, take over

TAKE *(Deceive),* ***verb*** betray, cheat, cozen, defraud, dupe, fool, gull, lead astray, mislead, victimize

TAKE *(Seize),* ***verb*** apprehend, appropriate, arrogate, capture, confiscate, embezzle, extort, grab, hijack, impound, loot, pilfer, plunder, purloin, usurp
ASSOCIATED CONCEPTS: burglary, grand larceny, grand theft, larceny, take a case from the jury, trespassing

TAKE *(Understand),* ***verb*** adopt, catch on, estimate, get the meaning of, grasp the meaning, hold as, set down as account as, take for, view as

TAKE ISSUE WITH, ***verb*** be against, be antagonistic to, be antipathetic to, be at odds with, be contra to, be contrary to, be different to, be hostile to, be inimical to, be opposed to, be repugnant to, challenge, clash, conflict with, contradict, oppose, render inopportune
ASSOCIATED CONCEPTS: take issue with the opportunity

TAKE POSSESSION OF, ***verb*** accumulate, achieve, acquire, appropriate, attain, capture, collect, earn, elicit, gain, gain possession of, gather, get, harvest, obtain, possess, procure, realize, receive, recover, secure, seize, take, take over
ASSOCIATED CONCEPTS: devices and bequests under a will, laws of intestacy

TAKE PRECENDENCE, ***verb*** abrograte, control, lead over, outrun, override, overstep, quash, replace, squash, supersede, surpass, top, tower over, transcend, vanquish
ASSOCIATED CONCEPTS: appellate review

TAKE THE NECESSARY MEASURE, ***verb*** accomplish, achieve, act, attain, be instrumental, bring to fruition, conclude, decide, determine, discharge, effectuate, enforce, execute, find a method, find the means, find the way, follow through, fulfill, gain, gain results, get, obtain, perform, produce, realize
ASSOCIATED CONCEPTS: attach, contempt, execution, filing a judgment, filing an appeal, order of the court

TAKE OVER, ***verb*** arrogate, assume, command, seize, take command, take charge, take possession, usurp

TAKEOVER, ***noun*** acquirement of a corporation, acquisition, acquisition of a company, appropriation, assumption of control over management, assumption of ownership, impropriation, obtainment, procurement, procurement of a business, purchase, transference
Generally: acquirement, assumption, attainment, obtainment, possession, procuration, securement
ASSOCIATED CONCEPTS: corporate raider, corporate takeover, friendly takeover, hostile takeover, tender offer, white knight

TAKING, ***noun*** abduction, *acceptio,* acquisition, ademption, appropriation, capture, confiscation, deprivation, dispossession, distraint, divestment, expropriation, foreclosure, impoundage, impoundment, *occupatio,* preemption, seizure, sequestration
ASSOCIATED CONCEPTS: attachment, eminent domain

TAKINGS CLAUSE, ***noun*** eminent domain, private property taken by the government, requirement of just compensation with government taking, taking of private land for public use
ASSOCIATED CONCEPTS: Fifth Amendment

TALENT, ***noun*** ability, adequacy, caliber, capability, capacity, competence, competency, creative thought, creativity, efficacy, efficiency, endowment, facility, faculty, fitness, flair, forte, genius, gift, high caliber, inspiration, long suit, proficiency, qualification, strength, strong point, strong suit, sufficiency, susceptibility

TALK, ***verb*** advise, answer, articulate, carry on a conversation, comment on, communicate with, confer with, consult with, debate, discuss, dissertate, exchange ideas, exchange views, express, have dialogue, have verbal intercourse with, impart thoughts, inform, interview, make a speech, make a statement, parley, recite, recount, relate, relate ideas, relay ideas, say, speak with, state, utter
ASSOCIATED CONCEPTS: freedom of speech, wiretaps

TALLY, ***noun*** account, accumulation, amount, analysis, bottom line, calculation, census, count, evaluation, examination, gross, impact, number, reckon, recount, score, sum, summation, total, upshot, whole

TAMPER, ***verb*** alter, change, convert, corrupt, debase, hinder, interfere, intermeddle, intervene, manipulate, meddle
ASSOCIATED CONCEPTS: tamper with a jury, tamper with evidence

TANGENTIAL, ***adjective*** akin, associated, attendant, connected, correlated, dependent on, digressive, excursive, extraneous, germane, incidental, interrelated, nonessential, pertinent, related, subordinate, tangent, touching

TANGIBLE, ***adjective*** actual, certain, clear-cut, concrete, corporal, corporeal, definite, discernible by touch, embodied, evident, manifest, material, not elusive, not vague, obvious, palpable, perceivable, perceptible, physical, plain, positive, real, solid, somatic, substantial, substantive, tactile, tactual, touchable, *tractabilis,* verifiable, visible, well-defined
ASSOCIATED CONCEPTS: tangible object, tangible property, tangible value

TANTAMOUNT, ***adjective*** analogous, comparable, corresponding to, ditto, equal, equivalent, identical, parallel, similar, synonymous

TARGET, ***noun*** aim, ambition, aspiration, butt, center, contemplation, design, desired object, destination, end, goal, hope, intention, mark, motive, object, objective, plan, point

TARIFF *(Bill),* ***noun*** account, itemized account, list, list of items, money's worth, quoted price, price list, scale of prices, table of charges

TARIFF *(Duties),* ***noun*** assessment, duty, excise, impost, levy, schedule of duties, tax

TARNISH, ***verb*** asperse, befoul, blacken, blemish, blot, brand, cloud, contaminate, corrode, darken, deface, defame, degrade, denigrate, desecrate, dim, dirty, discolor, discredit, disgrace, dishonor, dull, fade, foul, *inquinare,* lose luster, maculate, pollute, shame, slander, slur, smear, smirch, smudge, soil, spot, stain, stigmatize, sully, taint, vilify
ASSOCIATED CONCEPTS: defamation

TARTUFFISH, ***adjective*** affected, dissembling, false, feigned, hypocritical, insincere, pious, pretended, puritanical, sanctimonious, two-faced

TASK, *noun* act, activity, assigned work, assignment, burden, charge, chore, concern, duty, employment, endeavor, engagement, enterprise, function, job, labor, mission, obligation, operation, practice, project, pursuit, role, specialty, trade, undertaking, venture, work

TASTE, *noun* appetite, bias, choice, desire, discretion, fancy, favor, favoritism, fondness, like, option, palate, partiality, preference, relish, selection, sensibility, style, use

TAUNT, *verb* aggravate, bait, bully, deride, disparage, disturb, exasperate, gibe, grate, gripe, harass, hassle, haze, heckle, insult, mock, needle, nettle, peeve, perturb, pester, ride, ridicule, rile, ruffle, spite, trouble, vex
ASSOCIATED CONCEPTS: crime of bullying, cyberbullying

TAUTOLOGY, *noun* battology, duplication, loquacity, pleonasm, profuseness, redundancy, repetition, superfluousness, surfeit, verbiage, verbosity

TAWDRY, *adjective* baroque, bedizened, blatant, brummagem, catchpenny, cheap, common, crass, crude, flashy, garish, gaudy, glaring, glittering, inelegant, loud, meretricious, ostentatious, pretentious, shoddy, showy, sleazy, tasteless, tinsel, vulgar

TAX, *noun* assessment, capitation, charge, dues, duty, exaction, exactment, excise, imposition, impost, levy, pollage, *portorium,* scot, tariff, taxation, tithe, toll, tribute, *vectigal*
ASSOCIATED CONCEPTS: action for taxes, *ad valorem tax,* apportionment of taxes, back taxes, collection of taxes, current tax, delinquent tax, direct tax, discriminatory tax, double taxation, estate tax, evasion of taxation, excess profits tax, excessive tax, excise tax, federal estate tax, federal taxes, franchise tax, general tax, graduated tax, income tax, indirect tax, inheritance tax, land tax, levy a tax, personal tax, power of taxation, power to tax, progressive tax, property tax, proportional tax, regulatory tax, retroactive tax, sales tax, tax anticipation note, tax assessor, tax deed, tax district, tax lien, tax roll, tax sale, tax title, tax warrants, taxpayer, transfer tax, withholding taxes

TAX *(Levy),* ***verb*** assess, collect, exact, lay a duty, require

TAX *(Overwork),* ***verb*** burden, cumber, debilitate, deplete, deprive of strength, disable, drain, encumber, enervate, exact, fatigue, load, make excessive demands, oppress, overexercise, overexert, overfatigue, overload, overstrain, overtire, overuse, push too far, require, saddle with, strain, task, tire out, tyrannize, use hard, weaken, wear down, wear out, weary, weigh down

TEACH, *verb* advise, apprise, brief, catechize, communicate, convey, counsel, demonstrate, direct, disabuse, disseminate, edify, educate, elucidate, enlarge the mind, enlighten, explain, expound, give lessons to, guide, imbue, impart, impart knowledge, implant, inculcate, indoctrinate, inform, instill, instruct, lecture, moralize, nurture, persuade, preach, school, sermonize, show, tell, train, tutor

TEASE, *verb* aggravate, bait, belittle, bully, deride, disturb, exasperate, grate, gripe, harass, hassle, haze, heckle, mock, needle, peeve, perturb, pester, pick at, ridicule, rile, ruffle, spite, torment, trouble, vex

TECHNICAL, *adjective* abstruse, difficult to understand, highly specialized, highly specific, industrial, mechanical, occupational, professional, scientific, special, specialized, specific, trained, vocational

TECHNICALITY, *noun* aspect, detail, distinctive feature, fact, feature, fine point, inessentiality, item, method, minor point, minutiae, nuance, particular, particularity, peculiarity, petty detail, point, precept, rule, singularity, special point, speciality, specific, specification, subtlety, technical term, term, trifle, triviality

TECHNIQUE *(Method),* ***noun*** aptitude, art, deftness, dexterity, endowment, execution, felicity, finesse, flair, form, forte, genius for, gift, ingenuity, knack, know-how, mastery, proficiency, science, skillfulness, touch

TECHNIQUE *(Technical skill),* ***noun*** artistry, avenue, bravura, discretion, expedient, facility, skill, technology, virtuosity

TECHNOLOGY, *noun* best technical knowledge, know-how, latest scientific knowledge, scientific advancement, state of the art, state of the industry, updated scientific knowledge
Generally: application, development, latest products, modern science, science

TEDIOUS, *adjective* boring, colorless, drab, dreary, drudging, dull, jading, jejune, monotonous, numbing, pedestrian, ponderous, prosaic, repetitious, slow, stale, tiresome, tiring, uninteresting, wearisome, weary, wearying

TELECOMMUNICATIONS, *noun* information exchange, media, mode, phones, route, systems, telephone, technology, telephones
ASSOCIATED CONCEPTS: broadcasting laws, telecommunication laws

TELL, *verb* acquaint, advise, annunciate, apprise, betray, blurt out, come out with, communicate, confess, constrain, convey, declare, depict, detail, direct, disclose, distinguish, divulge, enumerate, enunciate, express, give an account of, give vent to, have a strong effect, impart, influence, inform, instruct, let on, make known, mention, narrate, notify, order, proclaim, profess, pronounce, publish, recite, record, recount, register, relate, remark, report, reveal, signify, speak, talk, tell a story
ASSOCIATED CONCEPTS: Fifth Amendment Rights, informant

TEMERARIOUS, *adjective* adventuresome, audacious, bold, careless, courageous, dare, daring, dashing, dauntless, fearless, foolhardy, foolish, gutsy, hasty, headlong, heedless, hot-blooded, intrepid, lionhearted, madcap, overbold, overconfident, precipitate, rash, reckless, undaunted, venturesome, venturous

TEMERITY, *noun* audacity, boldness, carelessness, daring, effrontery, foolhardiness, foolishness, gall, hastiness, heedlessness, impetuosity, improvidence, imprudence, impudence, incautiousness, inconsiderateness, indiscretion, injudiciousness, nerve, overconfidence, presumptuousness, procacity, rashness, recklessness, rudeness, shamelessness, *temeritas,* thoughtlessness, unthoughtfulness, venturesomeness, want of caution

TEMPERAMENT, *noun* aptitude, attitude, carriage, character, composition, constitution, demeanor, disposition, ethos, makeup, mentality, nature, patience, personality, qualities, structure, style, tendency, tenor, way

TEMPERANCE, ***noun*** abnegation, abstemiousness, abstention, abstinence, calmness, control, forbearance, frugality, indulgence, moderateness, *moderatio,* moderation, patience, prohibition, prudence, restraint, self-control, self-denial, self-restraint, soberness, sobriety, sparing use, teetotalism, *temperantia,* temperateness, tolerance, toleration, unexcessiveness

TEMPERATE, ***adjective*** controlled, disciplined, fair, gentle, inhibited, judicious, level-headed, mild, moderate, modest, normal, ordinary, rational, reasonable, regular, restrained, routine, self-controlled, sensible, typical, usual

TEMPERED, ***adjective*** adapted, adjusted, altered, changed, corrected, indurate, indurated, moderated, modified, recast, reconstructed, remolded, reshaped, revised, transformed, treated

TEMPESTUOUS, ***adjective*** angry, disgusted, enraged, frantic, frenzied, fuming, furious, hostile, inflamed, infuriated, ireful, livid, offended, offensive, outraged, raging, storming, tumultuous, turbulent

TEMPORARY, ***adjective*** acting, *ad tempus,* brief, changeable, deciduous, elusive, ephemeral, evanescent, fleeting, fugacious, fugitive, impermanent, interim, limited, makeshift, momentary, monohemerous, nondurable, passing, perishable, provisional, shifting, short-lived, stopgap, temporal, transient, transitional, transitive, transitory, unenduring, unstable, volatile
ASSOCIATED CONCEPTS: temporary restraining order

TEMPT, ***verb*** allure, bait, beguile, betray, bewitch, captivate, catch, charm, decoy, draw in, enchant, enmesh, ensnare, entice, entrap, fascinate, interest, lead on, magnetize, persuade, prompt, rope in, seduce, snow, solicit, wile

TENABLE, ***adjective*** acceptable, befitting, believable, capable of being maintained, defendable, defensible, dependable, deserving, fitting, immune, imperdible, impregnable, inviolable, invulnerable, justifiable, legitimate, logical, maintainable, plausible, proper, rational, reasonable, reliable, strong, supportable, trustworthy, unassailable, unattackable, unchallengeable, unquestionable, vindicable, warrantable, well-founded, well-grounded

TENACIOUS, ***adjective*** adamant, assured, certain, dedicated, determined, dogged, dogmatic, firm, indurate, industrious, insistent, intent, patient, persevering, pertinacious, positive, relentless, resolute, resolved, single-minded, steadfast, sure

TENACITY, ***noun*** ability to pursue, adhesiveness, backbone, cohesiveness, constancy, courage, determination, diligence, doggedness, endurance, firmness, grip, grit, immovability, indefatigability, intransigence, iron will, obduracy, obstinacy, perseverance, persistence, persistency, *pertinacia,* pertinaciousness, pertinacity, recalcitrance, res*oluteness,* resolution, stamina, steadfastness, strength, stubbornness, tenaciousness, *tenacitas,* toughness, unyieldingness, will

TENANCY, ***noun*** holding, holding by title, leasing, occupancy, occupation, ownership, possession, possessorship, proprietorship, renting, residency, temporary possession, tenure
ASSOCIATED CONCEPTS: joint tenancy, month-to-month tenancy, tenancy at sufferance, tenancy at will, tenancy by the entirety, tenancy for years, tenancy in common

TENANT, ***noun*** border, *conductor,* dweller, holder, householder, *incola,* inhabitant, *inquilinus,* landholder, landowner, leaseholder, lessee, lodger, occupant, occupier, one holding land of another, one occupying another's land, one occupying real property, one using real property, owner, paying guest, possessor, proprietor, rent payer, renter, resident
ASSOCIATED CONCEPTS: disorderly tenant, eviction, holdover tenant, joint tenant, life tenant, objectionable tenant, subtenant, tenant at sufferance, tenant at will, tenant by the entirety, tenant for a fixed term, tenant from month to month, tenant in common, tenant pur autre vie

TENDENCY, ***noun*** aptitude, aptness, bearing, bent, bias, character, direction, disposition, facility, gift, gravitation, idiosyncrasy, *inclinatio,* inclination, instinct, leaning, natural disposition, nature, partiality, penchant, predisposition, prejudice, *proclivitas,* proclivity, proneness, propensity, slant, susceptibility, temperament, trend, turn, twist, warp

TENDER, ***verb*** advance, *deferre,* deliver, extend, furnish, give, grant, hold out, issue, lay before, offer, pay, present, present for payment, proffer, propose, put forward, render, submit, urge upon, volunteer
ASSOCIATED CONCEPTS: tender payment, tender performance
FOREIGN PHRASES: ***Reprobata pecunia liberat solventem.*** Money refused releases the debtor.

TENDER OFFER, ***noun*** broad offer, broad request to purchase, broad solicitation, collective offer, offer to purchase a large number of shares, offer to purchase a large number of stock shares, offer to purchase a significant number of securities in a corporation, public offer, public offer to buy stock, takeover bid

TENOR, ***noun*** cast, character, content, course, cut, direction, drift, *exemplum,* feeling, form, gist, idea, import, manner, meaning, mode, mood, nature, purport, sense, *sententia,* significance, signification, spirit, stamp, subject matter, tendency, tone, trend, vein

TENSION, ***noun*** aggravation, anger, angst, annoyance, anxiety, apprehension, brooding, concern, conflict, distress, exasperation, fears, irritation, load, misfortune, strain, stress, uneasiness, weight, worry

TENTATIVE, ***adjective*** cautious, conditional, contingent, dependent, experimental, exploratory, groping, interim, probationary, probative, proposed, provisional, provisory, questionable, speculative, temporary, trial, undecided, unsettled
ASSOCIATED CONCEPTS: tentative agreement

TENUOUS, ***adjective*** airy, attenuated, delicate, diminutive, fine, flimsy, illusory, inconsequential, infinitesimal, insignificant, little, miniature, minute, narrow, paltry, petty, scant, slender, slight, small, thin, tiny, trifling, trivial, unimportant, unsubstantial

TENURE, ***noun*** duration, holding, occupancy, occupation, period, *possessio, possidere,* regime, term
ASSOCIATED CONCEPTS: tenure in office
FOREIGN PHRASES: ***Tenura est pactio contra communem feudi naturam ac rationem, in contractu interposita.*** Tenure is a compact contrary to the common nature and reason of the fee, put into a contract.

TERGIVERSATE, ***verb*** apostatize, avoid, be uncertain, be unsure, change one's mind, change sides, desert, dodge, equivocate, evade, hedge, quibble, recant, renege, renounce, shift, straddle, turn renegade, use evasions, use subterfuge, vacillate

TERM *(Duration),* ***noun*** age, course, era, incumbency, interval, lifetime, period, reign, season, session, span, *spatium temporis,* spell, stage, tenancy, tenure, time
ASSOCIATED CONCEPTS: term for years, term insurance, term of a lease, term of confinement, term of court, term of office
FOREIGN PHRASES: ***Terminus annorum certus debet esse et determinatus.*** A term of years ought to be certain and determinate.

TERM *(Expression),* ***noun*** appellation, appellative, cognomen, denomination, designation, epithet, heading, idiom, locution, name, phrase, title, verbalism, *verbum,* vocable, *vocabulum,* word
ASSOCIATED CONCEPTS: definition of terms

TERM *(Provision),* ***noun*** agreement, arrangement, article of agreement, bargain, clause, *condicio,* condition, covenant, item, *lex,* limitation, particular, point, proviso, qualification, specification, stipulation, understanding
ASSOCIATED CONCEPTS: terms and conditions of a contract, terms of a policy, terms of payment, terms of sale

TERMINABLE, ***adjective*** capable of being bounded, capable of being completed, capable of being concluded, capable of being conditioned, capable of being ended, capable of being fixed, capable of being limited, capable of being made definite, conditional, defeasible, finite, limitable
ASSOCIATED CONCEPTS: terminable at will, terminable fee, terminable interest, terminable trust, terminable upon a condition subsequent

TERMINALLY ILL, ***adjective*** incurable, *in extremis,* in final stages, *in terminus,* near an end, seriously ill, terminally diseased

TERMINATE, ***verb*** abolish, annul, bring to an end, bring to completion, cancel, cease, close, come to an end, complete, conclude, culminate, die, discontinue, drop, eliminate, end, expire, finish, fire from employment, halt, let go, put an end to, release, run out, stop, wind up
ASSOCIATED CONCEPTS: notice to terminate, terminate a contract, terminate a lease, terminate an action, terminate an agreement, terminate employment

TERMINATION, ***noun*** abatement, adjournment, cancellation, climax, close, completion, conclusion, confine, consequence, consummation, culmination, denouement, destination, discharge, discontinuance, effect, end, ending, end of the matter, end result, epilogue, expiration, extremity, finale, finality, finish, lapse, limit, outcome, pay-off, result, sequel, stoppage, terminal, upshot, windup
ASSOCIATED CONCEPTS: termination of a contract, termination of employment, termination of parental rights

TERMS *(Provisions),* ***noun*** conditions, contingencies, limitations, necessities, preconditions, prerequisites, provisions, provisos, qualifications, requirements, reservations, restrictions, specifics, stipulations, terms
ASSOCIATED CONCEPTS: terms in a contract between parties

TERMS *(Settlement),* ***noun*** acceptances, accords, agreements, alliances, approvals, arrangements, bargains, compacts, contracts, covenants, deals, final arrangements, pacts, pledges, promises, settlement, understanding
ASSOCIATED CONCEPTS: terms of a contract, terms of a settlement

TERRIBLE, ***adjective*** abhorrent, abominable, appalling, atrocious, contemptible, deplorable, despicable, detestable, dreadful, foul, frightening, frightful, ghastly, grisly, gruesome, heinous, hideous, horrendous, horrid, horrifying, macabre, monstrous, obnoxious, odious, offensive, outrageous, pathetic, pitiful, regrettable, repellent, reprehensible, repulsive, revolting, serious, severe, shameful, shocking, terrifying, vile

TERRIFIC, ***adjective*** celebrated, colossal, commanding, distinguished, enormous, esteemed, exalted, excellent, exceptional, expert, extraordinary, far-reaching, first-rate, gigantic, glorious, grand, great, high-minded, illustrious, immense, incredible, incredible performances, incredible results, leading, lofty, major, marvelous, massive, momentous, monstrous, notable, noted, outrageous, outstanding, paramount, perfect, potent, powerful, preeminent, prime, profound, remarkable, renowned, skillful, solid, splendid, strong, superior, supreme, vast, widely remarkable results, wonderful

TERROR *(Panic),* ***noun*** agitation, apprehension, concern, consternation, cowardice, creeps, discomposure, dismay, disquiet, faintheartedness, funk, hysteria, jitters, nervousness, pang, perturbation, phobia, qualm, timidity, timorousness, worry

TERROR *(Terrorism),* ***noun*** agitation by terrorists, concentrated efforts to achieve anarchy, concentrated efforts to subvert a society, concerted efforts to disrupt a government, homeland security crimes, incendiary efforts, radicalism, revolution through fear and intimidation, subversion, violence to obtain ideological goals

TERRORISM, ***noun*** acts by subversives, acts of annihilation, criminal act, demolition, destruction, extermination, fanaticism, revolution, terrorist act, tyranny

TERRORIST, ***noun*** abductor, active combatant in the foreign theater of conflict, anarchist, assailant, assassin, attacker, combatant, demoniac force, destroyer, enemy alien, enemy combatant, enemy force, enemy operation, faction at war, fanatic, foreign assailant, foreign force, hostile force, insurgent, killer, mercenary, militant, murderer, opponent, radical, rebel, revolutionary, revolutionist, revolutionizer, savage, subversive force
ASSOCIATED CONCEPTS: Department of Homeland Security, enemy combatant, military tribunals, terrorist attacks, terrorist demands, terrorist groups, terrorist incidents, terrorist networks, terrorist organizations

TERRORIST ACTIVITY, ***verb*** anarchist's act, assassin's plot, criminal act, destroyer's action, enemy deed, enemy pursuits, enemy undertakings, fanatical act, fanatical action, foreign combatant's efforts, insurgent's acts, insurgent's plans, operations of combatants, radical efforts, rebel cell's plot, revolutionary plot, subversive plans
ASSOCIATED CONCEPTS: enemy combatants, military tribunals, terrorist cells, U.S. Patriot Act, weapons of mass destruction

TERRORIST CELL, ***noun*** mutiny, outbreak, radical hideaway, radical holding cell, radical insurrection, radical revolt, radical uprising, revolution, terrorist rising, terrorist underground insurgency

TERRITORY, ***noun*** *ager,* area, beat, circuit, clime, demesne, district, division, domain, dominion, environs, expanse, field, land, latitude, locale, place, precinct, property, province, quarter, realm, *regio,* region, scene, section, terrain, tract, zone

TEST, ***noun*** analysis, audit, check, checkup, effort, endeavor, examination, experience, experiment, exploration, inquest, inquiry, inquisition, inspection, interrogation, investigation, observation, questioning, quiz, research, review, scrutiny, search, study, survey, trial, try, tryout
ASSOCIATED CONCEPTS: blood test, clear and present danger test, compelling state interest test, prudent man test, right from wrong test, substantial evidence test

TESTAMENT, ***noun*** agreement, binding agreement, contract, covenant, engagement, expression of conviction, formal declaration, legal will, promise, solemn agreement, solemn promise, testamentary declaration, testamentary decree, *testamentum,* will, writing
ASSOCIATED CONCEPTS: codicil, last will and testament, testamentary capacity, testamentary devise, testamentary trust
FOREIGN PHRASES: ***Omne testamentum morte consummatum est.*** Every will or testament is consummated by death.

TESTAMENTARY, ***adjective*** by way of a will, bequeathed by will, contained in a will, devised by will, distributed by will, given by testament, hereditary, patrimonial, set forth in a will, transferred by a legacy, transferred by bequest, transferred by devise
ASSOCIATED CONCEPTS: letters testamentary, testamentary assets, testamentary capacity, testamentary condition, testamentary devise, testamentary disposition, testamentary gifts, testamentary guardian, testamentary guardianship, testamentary instrument, testamentary intent, testamentary inventory, testamentary power, testamentary succession, testamentary trust, testamentary trustee

TESTATE, ***adjective*** having left a will, having written a testament, relating to a will, with a valid will, with an executed will
ASSOCIATED CONCEPTS: intestate succession

TESTIFY, ***verb*** acknowledge openly, affirm, affirm under oath, allege, assert, asseverate, attest, aver, avow, be sworn, bear witness, declare, depone, depose, establish, express, give evidence, give one's word, indicate, make solemn declaration, profess, prove, show, state, state a fact, state a truth, swear, take one's oath, take the stand, *testari, testificari,* verify
ASSOCIATED CONCEPTS: compulsion to testify, privilege against self-incrimination, testify in one's own defense, testify under oath

TESTILYING, ***noun*** dishonesty by the police, fabrication of evidence, fabrication of evidence by the police, false testimony, in-court deception by a police officer, law enforcer's perjury, police perjury, trumping up testimony by the police, untruthful testimony

TESTIMONY, ***noun*** affidavit, affirmation, assertion, asseveration, attestation, averment, avowal, declaration, declaration of facts, deposition, disclosure, evidence, evidence by a competent witness, evidence in support of, expression, profession, proof, proof by a witness, revelation, statement, statement of facts, *testimonium*
ASSOCIATED CONCEPTS: circumstantial testimony, compelled testimony, corroborative testimony, cross-examination, deposition, direct examination, expert testimony, impeachment of testimony, incompetent testimony, involuntary testimony, oral testimony, perjured testimony, preservation of testimony, testimony under oath

TEXTUALISM, ***noun*** a formalist statutory interpretation, adherence to text, construction, faithfulness to text, interpretation based solely on the text, literalism, ordinary meaning, original meaning, plain meaning, theory of the study of language
ASSOCIATED CONCEPTS: intentionalism, strict construction

THEFT, ***noun*** burglary, embezzlement, felonious taking, filchery, fraudulent taking, *furtum,* larceny, looting, misappropriation, peculation, pilferage, pilfering, purloining, purloinment, robbery, stealing, swindling, thievery, wrongful taking
ASSOCIATED CONCEPTS: theft of services
FOREIGN PHRASES: ***Contrectatio rei alienae animo furando, est furtum.*** The touching or removing of another's property, with an intention of stealing, is theft.

THEN *(Additionally),* ***adverb*** again, also, besides, either, further, furthermore, in addition, likewise, moreover, then, then too, too, yet

THEN *(At that time),* ***adverb*** at that juncture, at that moment, at that point, at which point, before, formerly, previously

THEORETICAL, ***adjective*** abstract, academic, assumed, conjectural, *doctrina,* doctrinaire, hypothetical, ideational, ideative, ideological, impractical, open to proof, philosophical, postulated, postulatory, presumed, presumptive, pure, *ratio,* speculative, speculatory, stated as a premise, supposable, suppositional, suppositive, unapplied, unproved, unproven, unsubstantiated, visionary

THEORY, ***noun*** assumption, belief, conjecture, *doctrina,* doctrine, dogma, guesswork, hypothesis, ideology, opinion, philosophy, postulate, presupposition, proposition, *ratio,* speculation, supposition, surmise, thesis, thought, untested opinion, view
ASSOCIATED CONCEPTS: conflicts of law theory, contract theory, inconsistent theories, rescue theory, theory of the case

THERE, ***adverb*** at a distance, at that established place, at that location, at that place, at that point, beyond, exactly at that place, exactly at that spot, in that place, in that respect, in that spot, in the distance, into that place, just there, not here, over there, precisely at that place, precisely at that point, precisely at that spot, to or toward that point

THEREBY, ***adverb*** by means of, by use of, by virtue of, in consequence of, per, through, through the medium of, whereby, with the aid of

THEREAFTER, ***adverb*** after, afterwards, at a later period, from that time, later, next, since, subsequently

THERETOFORE, ***adverb*** before, earlier, formerly, heretofore, previous to, prior to

THESIS, ***noun*** affirmation, argument, belief, claim, conjecture, debatable issue, debatable point, doctrine, dogma, hypothesis, issue, moot point, position, postulate, postulation, premise, principle, problem, proposition, question, speculation, stand, subject, supposition, tenet, theme, theory, topic, tract

THIEF, ***noun*** bandit, contrabandist, criminal, defalcator, defaulter, defrauder, depredator, embezzler, lawbreaker, lifter, marauder, outlaw, peculator, pilferer, pillager, pirate, purloiner, robber, stealer, swindler
ASSOCIATED CONCEPTS: burglary, larceny, robbery

THINK, ***verb*** anticipate, apprehend, believe, be of the opinion, cerebrate, cogitate, compass, conceive, conclude, consider, contemplate, contrive, deduce, deduct, deem, deliberate, determine, digest, dwell intently upon, envisage, envision, exercise the mind, expect, form ideas, guess, have the idea, hypothesize, ideate, imagine, intellectualize, judge, mean, meditate, mentalize, mull over, opine, philosophize, picture, plan, plot, ponder, presume, presuppose, propose, rationalize, reason, recall, reckon, recollect, reflect, reminisce, ruminate, speculate, surmise, theorize

THINKING, ***noun*** axioms, belief, conviction, credo, doctrine, dogma, gospel, ideology, manifesto, opinion, philosophy, rationale, tenets, theory

THOROUGH, ***adjective*** absolute, accurate, all-inclusive, assiduous, careful, complete, comprehensive, consummate, definitive, detailed, diligent, downright, entire, exhaustive, extensive, full, fully executed, inclusive, intensive, meticulous, painstaking, perfect, plenary, sheer, sound, sweeping, systematic, thoroughgoing, total, trustworthy, unabridged, uncompromising, unmitigated, unqualified, utter, zealous

THOUGHT *(Concept),* ***noun*** belief, conception, credo, creed, hint, idea, insight, notion, opinion, perspective, point, proposal, rationale, suggestion, tenet, view

THOUGHT *(Concern),* ***noun*** attentiveness, care, impression, philosophy, reaction, regard, sentiment, solicitousness, thoughtfulness

THOUGHT *(Thinking),* ***noun*** absorption, abstraction, application, apprehension, association of ideas, belief, brainwork, cerebration, cogitation, concept, conception, consciousness, consideration, contemplation, deliberation, fancy, introversion, meditation, mental process, perception, perspective, ratiocination, reason, recollection, reflection, remark, retrospection, reverie, rumination, self-communing, speculation, study, suggestion, theory, view

THOUGHTLESS, ***adjective*** absent-minded, abstracted, blank, blockish, careless, casual, dazed, disregardful, distracted, distrait, dull, flighty, foolhardy, giddy, harebrained, headlong, heedless, ill-advised, improvident, *imprudens,* imprudent, impulsive, inadvertent, inane, inattentive, incogitant, inconsiderate, *inconsultus,* indelicate, indifferent, indiscreet, insensate, irrational, irresponsible, neglectful, *neglegens,* negligent, precipitate, rash, reckless, regardless, remiss, scatterbrained, selfish, stupid, tactless, unaccommodating, unconcerned, unmindful, unobliging, unobservant, unreasoning, unreflecting, unreflective, unthinking, unthoughtful, unwatchful, vacant, vacuous, without consideration

THRALL, ***noun*** bondage, captivity, confinement, custody, durance, enslavement, enthrallment, helotry, oppression, servitude, *servitus,* slavery, subjection, subjugation, submission, thralldom, tyranny, vassalage, yoke

THREAT, ***noun*** alarm, augury, auspice, commination, danger, *denuntiatio,* foreboding, fulmination, hazard, imminence, impendence, impendency, insecurity, intimidation, jeopardy, menace, *minae,* omen, peril, portent, presage, risk, sign, warning
ASSOCIATED CONCEPTS: coercion
FOREIGN PHRASES: ***Non videtur consensum retinuisse si quis ex praescripto minantis aliquid immutavit.*** He does not appear to have retained consent who has changed anything at the command of a threatening party.

THREATEN, ***verb*** admonish, augur, be near at hand, blackmail, bode, browbeat, coerce, *comminari,* comminate, forebode, foreshadow, forewarn, frighten, fulminate, hector, intimidate, menace, portend, presage, terrorize, use threats

THRESHOLD *(Commencement),* ***noun*** beginning, foreword, inception, onset, outbreak, overture, preamble, prelude, prologue, start

THRESHOLD *(Entrance),* ***noun*** door, entrance way, entry, gateway, sill

THRESHOLD *(Verge),* ***noun*** brink, edge
ASSOCIATED CONCEPTS: monetary threshold

THRILL, ***noun*** arousal, charge, contentment, ecstasy, enchantment, excitement, exciting feeling, exhilaration, feeling of excitement, frisson, intoxication, jolt, joy, magical feeling, palpitation, passion, pleasure, shock, surprise, titillation

THROUGH, ***adjective*** completed, concluded, decided, done, done with, ended, finished, set at rest, settled, terminated

THROUGH *(By means of),* ***adverb*** by means of, by the hand of, by way of, using, using the help of

THROUGH *(From beginning to end),* ***adverb*** all along, all the way, by way of, via

THROUGH *(Until now),* ***adverb*** to this day

THROUGHOUT *(All over),* ***adverb*** all over, every bit, extensively, from beginning to end, from first to last, from the ground up, from the word go, inside and out, over all, to the end

THROUGHOUT *(During),* ***adverb*** for the duration, for the period of, in the course of, until the conclusion of

THRUST, ***noun*** accent, accentuation, centered theme, concentration, emphasis, focus, jist, stress, underscoring, weight
ASSOCIATED CONCEPTS: thrust of a memorandum of law, thrust of an argument

THUS, ***adverb*** accordingly, all together, coincidentally, concomitantly, conjointly, consequently, contemporaneously, in conclusion, moreover, then too

THWART, ***verb*** avert, baffle, balk, bar, blight, bring to naught, check, contravene, counteract, countermine, counterwork, cripple, cross, damp, debar, defeat, foil, forestall, frustrate, hamper, hinder, impede, inhibit, intercept, interfere, interrupt, nip, obstruct, oppose, outmaneuver, override, preclude, prevent, restrain, retard, ruin, spoil, stave off, stifle, stop, stultify, stymie, traverse, turn aside, undermine, ward off

TIDE TURNING, ***verb*** about-face, adoption, afterthoughts, backsliding, change like a chameleon, change of heart, change of mind, conversion, defection, divergence, diversion, dramatically opposed stance, flip-flop, 180-degree about-face, qualification, realignment, regression, restructuring, reversal, reversion, temporizer, tergiversation, turnabout
ASSOCIATED CONCEPTS: flip-flop on a political stance

TIES, ***noun*** adherences, adhesions, attachments, bands, bonds, chains, commitments, connections, engagements, interconnections, knots, liaisons, links, pledges, unions, vincula

TIME, ***noun*** age, chronology, duration, end of the matter, era, extent, interlude, interim, interval, period, tenancy, tenure, term
ASSOCIATED CONCEPTS: time being of the essence, time certificate, time deposit, time fixed by agreement, time of absence, time of adjudication, time of bankruptcy, time of injury, time of memory, time option, time policy, time studies, timetables

TIMELINESS, ***noun*** appropriateness, aptness, auspiciousness, climacteric, compliance, convenient time, felicitousness, fitness, matureness, opportuneness, proper time, seasonableness, suitability, suitable time, time, within appropriate time provided
ASSOCIATED CONCEPTS: laches, notice, statute of limitations

TIP *(Clue),* ***noun*** advice, aviso, communication, confidential information, cue, enlightenment, forewarning, guidance, head, hint, indication, inside information, insinuation, instruction, intimation, key, lead, mention, point, pointer, prenotification, recommendation, report, suggestion, warning, whisper

TIP *(Gratuity),* ***noun*** award, benefaction, bestowment, bonus, compensation, consideration, contribution, donation, donative, gift, guerdon, meed, offering, payment, perquisite, reward
ASSOCIATED CONCEPTS: unreported income

TITLE *(Designation),* ***noun*** appellation, caption, denomination, heading, inscription, label, name, rubric, sign, signification, superscription, tag
ASSOCIATED CONCEPTS: title of statute

TITLE *(Division),* ***noun*** article, branch, chapter, clause, item, paragraph, part, portion, provision, section, statement, term

TITLE *(Position),* ***noun*** employment, office, post, rank, situation, station, status

TITLE *(Right),* ***noun*** authority, authorization, claim, deed, domain, droit, entitlement, equity, interest, legal title, ownership, permission, possession, power, prerogative, prescription, proprietorship, right, sanction, stake, tenure, vested interest
ASSOCIATED CONCEPTS: absolute title, abstract of title, acquisition of title, apparent title, chain of title, claim of title, clear title, cloud on title, color of title, defeasible title, disparagement of title, documents of title, equitable title, failure of title, good title, imperfect title, marketable title, merchantable title, nominal title, paramount title, perfection of title, prima facie title, quieting title, reservation of title, superior title, title by adverse possession, title by deeds, title by prescription, title insurance, title search, title to property, unmarketable title, warranty of title, worthier title
FOREIGN PHRASES: ***Praescriptio est titulus ex usu et tempore substantiam capiens ab auctoritate legis.*** Prescription is a title by authority of law, deriving its force from use and time. ***A piratis et latronibus capta dominum non mutant.*** Things captured by pirates and robbers do not change title.

TOGETHER, ***adverb*** along with, altogether, coincidentally, coincidently, collectively, concertedly, concomitantly, concurrently, conjoined, conjointly, contemporaneously, inclusively, jointly, overall, simultaneously

TOKEN, ***noun*** augury, auspice, chip, device, emblem, evidence, expression, favor, figurehead, indicant, indicator, keepsake, manifestation, memento, omen, portent, proof, relic, remembrance, sign, souvenir, symbol

TOLERANCE, ***noun*** abiding, ability to bear, ability to endure, ability to tolerate, ability to withstand, allowance, bravery, broad-mindedness, capacity to endure, capacity to stand suffering, capacity to take pain, charter, compassion, constancy, courage, durability, endurance, fortitude, franchise, freedom, freedom from bigotry, freedom from prejudice, good will, humanity, immunity, immunization, impunity, indulgence, *indulgentia,* lack of bias, liberality, license, patience, perseverance, persistence, resignation, stamina, stoicism, strength, submission, sufferance, sustainment, sympathy, *tolerantia,* toleration, understanding

TOLERATE, ***verb*** abide, accept, acquiesce, allow, be lenient, bear, bear with, brook, carry on, consent, endure, forbear, indulge, make the best of, oblige, permit, put up with, receive, sanction, stand, stomach, submit to, suffer, swallow, take patiently, *tolerare,* undergo

TOLL *(Effect),* ***noun*** casualties, consequence, cost, damage, distress, effect, exaction, forfeit, grievous price, loss, payment, result, ruinous price, setback, suffering

TOLL *(Tax),* ***noun*** assessment, charge, exaction, excise, fare, fee, impost, levy, payment, *portorium,* tithe, vectigal
ASSOCIATED CONCEPTS: collection of tolls, toll bridges, toll roads

TOLL *(Exact payment),* ***verb*** collect payment, exact tribute, extort, levy, raise taxes, tax

TOLL *(Stop),* ***verb*** arrest, block, check, cut off, embar, estop, frustrate, halt, hinder, hold back, impede, inhibit, interrupt, limit, obstruct, put a stop to, restrain, restrict, stay, suspend, thwart
ASSOCIATED CONCEPTS: toll a statute of limitations

TONE DEAF, ***idiom*** absentminded, clueless, deaf, heedless, inattentive, incognizant, inconscient, insensible, oblivious, stubborn, unaware, undiscerning, uninformed, unknowing, unmindful, untrained, unwitting

TOOL, ***noun*** agent, apparatus, channel, contrivance, device, implement, instrument, machine, means, mechanism, medium, recourse, resource, utensil, vehicle

TOP-NOTCH, ***adjective*** apical, best, capital, chief, critical, crowning, crucial, crying, deep, desperate, earnest, essential, far-reaching, forcible, gravest, head, heavy, highest, intense, intensified, maximal, maximum, momentous,

most, of great force, of great number, overmost, paramount, potent, preeminent, pressing, principal, serious, sharp, strong, superlative, supreme, telling, tiptop, top, topmost, urgent, vigorous, violent, vital, weighty, zenithal
ASSOCIATED CONCEPTS: highest degree of care, highest proved value

TORMENT, *noun* abomination, acute distress, affliction, agony, angst, anguish, annoyance, bane, constant anxiety, convulsion, despair, distress, extreme pain, harassment, infliction, misery, oppression, pain, pique, scourge, torture, vexation

TORMENT, *verb* abuse, anguish, annoy, badger, bait, beset, besiege, chafe, crucify, discompose, distress, endanger, excruciate, harass, harrow, harry, haze, hector, ill-use, inflict, irritate, lacerate, maltreat, mistreat, molest, needle, nettle, obsess, persecute, pester, plague, press, provoke, rile, taunt, tease, treat maliciously, trouble, vex

TORPID, *adjective* apathetic, benumbed, comatose, dead, disinterested, dormant, drowsy, dull, heavy, idle, impervious, inactive, inanimate, indifferent, indolent, *iners,* inert, inexcitable, insensate, insensible, languid, languorous, lazy, leaden, *lentus,* lethargic, lifeless, listless, motionless, numb, otiose, passive, phlegmatic, sedentary, sleepy, slow, sluggish, somnolent, spiritless, stagnant, static, stupefied, stuperous, stupid, supine, torpescent, torporific, unconcerned, unconscious, unfeeling

TORT, *noun* breach of legal duty, civil wrong, dereliction of duty, error, fault, invasion of a legal right, legal wrong, malfeasance, misdeed, misdoing, misfeasance, negligent act, personal wrong, private wrong, transgression, violation of a legal duty, wrong, wrongdoing, wrongful act
ASSOCIATED CONCEPTS: action founded in tort, comparative negligence, continuing tort, contributory negligence, foreseeable consequences, intentional tort, prima facie tort, proximate cause, standard of care, strict liability in tort, successive torts, tort feasor, tortious act, tortious conduct

TORTIOUS ACT, *noun* actionable act, criminal act, felonious act, illegitimate act, improper act, incorrect act, nefarious act, punishable act, triable act, unlawful act, wrongful act

TORTIOUS INTERFERENCE, *noun* encouraging a breach, infringing on another's agreement, interceding, interfering with contract, interfering with contractual commitments, interfering with contractual obligation, interfering with contractual rights, intermeddling, intermeddling with business activities, obstruction, work against anothers contractual relationship, wrongful interference with business relationships, wrongful interference with contractual relationships
ASSOCIATED CONCEPTS: employment law

TORTUOUS *(Bending),* ***adjective*** anfractuous, circuitous, complicated, conniving, contorted, convoluted, curved, curvilinear, indirect, involved, irregular, labyrinthine, mazy, meandering, roundabout, serpentine, sinuate, sinuated, sinuous, snakelike, torsional, tortile, turning, twisted, twisting, undulatory, vermicular, vermiculate, vermiculated, winding, wreathed, zigzag

TORTUOUS *(Corrupt),* ***adjective*** crafty, crooked, deceitful, devious, dishonest, dishonorable, disingenuous, fraudulent, immoral, knavish, perfidious, treacherous, unscrupulous

TOTAL, *adjective* absolute, aggregate, all, complete, downright, entire, full, global, gross, inclusive, integral, *omnis,* outright, radical, thorough, thoroughgoing, *totus,* undivided, universal, *universus,* unqualified, utter, whole, with no exception, without omission

TOTALITY, *noun* aggregate, aggregation, allness, collectivity, completeness, comprehensiveness, entireness, entirety, entity, everything, gross, integration, lump, mass, sum, totalness, unity, whole
ASSOCIATED CONCEPTS: totality of the circumstances

TOUGH *(Difficult),* ***adjective*** arduous, bothersome, burdensome, complex, complicated, convoluted, difficult, enigmatic, entangled, grueling, hard, hard to deal with, hard to manage, hard to understand, impenetrable, incomprehensible, insoluble, insurmountable, intractable, involved, involving obstacles, labored, laborious, mettlesome, painstaking, perplexing, problematic, puzzling, troublesome, unachievable, unapproachable

TOUGH *(Durable),* ***adjective*** built to last, enduring, fortified, lasting, long-lasting, reinforced, rugged, solid, sound, stable, steady, strong, sturdy, well-built, well-constructed, well-established, well-made

TOUGH *(Strong),* ***adjective*** firm, hard, hard to deal with, hard to manage, impenetrable, intractable, intransigent, obdurate, obstinate, perplexing, resolute, rugged, strenuous, tenacious, too hard, troublesome
ASSOCIATED CONCEPTS: tough laws

TOXIC, *adjective* damaging, deadly, deleterious, fatal, festering, harmful, injurious, insalubrious, lethal, malign, noxious, pestilent, pernicious, poisonous, purulent, risky, unsafe, venomous, virulent
ASSOCIATED CONCEPTS: toxic chemicals, toxic dementia, toxic ingredients, toxic psychosis, toxic torts

TOXIC TORT, *noun*
Generally: lethal wrongdoing, noxious injury, poison
Specifically: asbestos poisoning, environmental poisoning
ASSOCIATED CONCEPTS: asbestos, electromagnetic fields, lead paint, lead poisoning, radon

TRACE *(Delineate),* ***verb*** copy, define, describe, *designare,* detail, draw, duplicate, explain, go over, mark out, reproduce, set forth, sketch

TRACE *(Follow),* ***verb*** chase, detect, ensue, ferret out, hound, hunt out, inquire, *investigare,* investigate, *odorari,* probe, pursue, scent, search, seek, shadow, track, track down, trail, unearth

TRACTABLE, *adjective* acquiescent, adaptable, amenable, bendable, compliant, conformable, controllable, docile, *docilis,* ductile, easily lead, easily managed, easily taught, easygoing, elastic, facile, *facilis,* flexible, flexile, formable, governable, guidable, impressionable, leadable, malleable, manageable, obedient, plastic, pliable, pliant, readily wrought, submissive, teachable, *tractabilis,* tractile, willing, yielding

TRADE *(Commerce),* ***noun*** barter, business, business affairs, business intercourse, buying and selling, commercial enterprise, deal, exchange, exchange of commodities, interchange, marketing, mercantile business, mercantile relations, *mercatus,* merchandising, merchantry, negotiation,

nundination, open market, patronage, purchase, sale, sales, swap, traffic, transaction, truck
ASSOCIATED CONCEPTS: combination in restraint of trade, hazardous trade, in the ordinary course of trade or business, restraint of trade, stock in trade, unfair trade

TRADE *(Occupation),* ***noun*** *ars,* assignment, avocation, berth, business, calling, concern, craft, duty, employment, engagement, function, handicraft, job, line, line of work, livelihood, living, metier, office, position, post, practice, profession, pursuit, situation, specialty, task, vocation

TRADE, ***verb*** bargain, barter, buy, buy and sell, carry on commerce, chaffer, *commercari,* deal, do business, drive a bargain, exchange, huckster, interchange, *mercaturam,* merchandise, negotiate, purchase, scorse, sell, shop, traffic, transact
ASSOCIATED CONCEPTS: combination in restraint of trade, trade acceptance, trade in interstate commerce

TRADE SECRET, ***noun*** knowledge which provides superiority, protected design used by a business, protected formula used by a business, protected information used by a business, protected instrument used by a business, protected knowledge which provides an edge, protected pattern used by a business, protected practice used by a business, protected special knowledge, protected unique knowledge
ASSOCIATED CONCEPTS: database rights, fair use, mask work, plant breeders' rights

TRADEMARK, ***noun*** badge, brand, countermark, countersign, hallmark, identification, imprint, label, mark, signet, symbol, ticket, trade sign

TRADITIONAL, ***adjective*** accepted, acknowledged, ancestral, classic, classical, common, confirmed, conformable, consuetudinal, consuetudinary, conventional, customary, established, fixed, habitual, handed down, historic, historical, ingrained, inherited, inveterate, long established, long-standing, old, orthodox, prescribed, prescriptive, regular, rooted, sanctioned, time-honored, traditionary, traditive
ASSOCIATED CONCEPTS: custom and usage, past practices, prior conduct between the parties

TRAGEDY, ***noun*** accident, adversity, affliction, bale, blow, calamity, casualty, cataclysm, catastrophe, disaster, doom, dreadful event, fatal affair, hardship, misadventure, misfortune, mishap, reverse, sorrow, *tragoedia,* woe

TRAIT, ***noun*** attribute, characteristic, detail, differentia, distinguished quality, feature, habit, idiosyncrasy, individualism, item, lineament, manner, mannerism, mark, nature, oddity, particularity, peculiarity, property, proprietas, quality, singularity, specialty, temperament

TRAMMEL, ***verb*** bind, bridle, check, clog, confine, constrain, control, cramp, cumber, curb, debar, discommode, enchain, encumber, entangle, entrammel, fasten, fetter, frustrate, hamper, handicap, hinder, hobble, hold back, impede, incommode, inconvenience, keep within bounds, manacle, obstruct, oppose, pinion, put in irons, repress, restrain, restrict, retard, shackle, suppress, tether, thwart, tie, tie up

TRANSACT, ***verb*** accomplish, achieve, carry on, carry on business, carry out, conduct, consummate, deal, deal with, discharge, do business, execute, fulfill, *gerere,* make terms, manage, negotiate, operate, perform, proceed with, put into practice, render, *transigere*
ASSOCIATED CONCEPTS: transact business

TRANSACTION, ***noun*** accomplishment, achievement, act, action, activity, administration, adventure, affair, business, commission, completion, consummation, deal, dealing, deed, direction, effectuation, enactment, enterprise, execution, exercise, exploit, management, measure, negotiation, *negotium,* operation, performance, proceeding, process, purchase, sale, undertaking
ASSOCIATED CONCEPTS: arm's-length transaction, transacting business, transactional immunity
FOREIGN PHRASES: ***Res inter alios judicatae nullum aliis praejudicium faciunt.*** Transactions between strangers ought not to injure those who are not parties to them.

TRANSCEND, ***verb*** be better, be superior, best, better, eclipse, exceed, excel, *excellere, exsuperare,* go beyond, outdistance, outdo, outrank, outrival, outshine, outstrip, outvie, outweigh, overpass, overshadow, overstep, overtop, pass, predominate, prevail, rise above, rival, surmount, surpass, take precedence, top, tower above

TRANSCRIPT, ***noun*** apograph, copy, *exemplar, exemplum,* facsimile, minutes, record, recording, reprint, reproduction, rescript, stenographic copy, transcription, written copy
ASSOCIATED CONCEPTS: stenographic transcript, transcript of proceedings, transcript on appeal, trial transcript

TRANSFER, ***verb*** assign, bequeath, bestow, carry, confer, consign, deed, deliver, deliver over, demise, devolve, forward, grant, hand on, pass, pass on, remove, send, shift, *traducere, transferre,* transmit, *transmittere,* transport
ASSOCIATED CONCEPTS: transfer an interest

TRANSFEREE, ***noun*** acceptor, allottee, assignee, beneficiary, consignee, devisee, donee, grantee, heir, inheritor, legatee, licensee, payee, recipient, successor, trustee

TRANSFEROR, ***noun*** allotter, assignor, consignor, devisor, donor, grantor, lessor, licensor, payor

TRANSFORM, ***verb*** adjust, alter, change, commute, convert, denature, do over, make over, metamorphose, modify, mutate, recast, recondition, reconstruct, reconvert, redo, reform, regenerate, remake, remodel, remold, render different, renovate, reorganize, restyle, revamp, revise, revolutionize, shift, substitute, switch, tailor, transfigure, translate, transmogrify, transmute, transshape, transubstantiate, turn, vary

TRANSGRESSION, ***noun*** abuse, breach, contravention, crime, *delictum,* delinquency, dereliction, disobedience, encroachment, error, fault, guilty act, illegal action, illegality, infraction, infringement, iniquity, misbehavior, misconduct, misdeed, misdoing, misfeasance, noncompliance, nonobservance, offense, *peccatum,* sin, slip, transcursion, trespass, violation, wrong, wrongdoing
FOREIGN PHRASES: ***Frustra legis auxilium quaerit qui in legem committit.*** He vainly seeks the aid of the law who transgresses the law.

TRANSGRESSOR, ***noun*** criminal, degenerate, delinquent, lawbreaker, malefactor, malfeasant, miscreant, offender, profligate, recreant, reprobate, violator, wrongdoer
ASSOCIATED CONCEPTS: target of an investigation

TRANSIENT, *adjective* *brevis,* brief, caducous, deciduous, elusive, ephemeral, ephemerous, evanescent, fading, fleeting, *fluxus,* fugacious, *fugax,* fugitive, hasty, impermanent, inconstant, interim, meteoric, migratory, momentary, passing, perishable, provisional, provisory, roaming, roving, short, short-lived, temporal, temporary, transitory, unenduring, unstable, vanishing, volatile

TRANSITION, *noun* alteration, break, change, changeover, conversion, development, flux, graduation, growth, jump, leap, metastasis, modification, motion, movement, passage, passing, phase, progress, realignment, shift, transference, transformation, transit, *transitio,* transmigration, transmutation, turn

TRANSITORY, *adjective* brief, cursory, ephemeral, evanescent, fleeting, flitting, fugacious, impermanent, momentary, not permanent, passing away, provisional, short lived, temporal, temporary, transient, unenduring, unstable, volatile
ASSOCIATED CONCEPTS: transitory actions, transitory causes of action, transitory possession of property, transitory seizen, transitory trade name, transitory use and occupation, transitory work

TRANSMIT, *verb* bear, carry, cede, communicate, conduct, consign, convey, deliver, dispatch, forward, give, hand on, hand over, impart, issue, pass, pass on, provide, radiate, remit, send, send a message, send on, ship, transfer, *transmittere,* transport

TRANSMITTAL, *noun* circulation, communication, conveyance, deliverance, delivery, direction, dispatch, forwarding, impartation, letter, movement, note, passage, propagation, remittance, sending, transfer, transference, translocation, transmission, transmittance, transplantation, transportation

TRANSPARENT, *adjective* apparent, candid, clear, clear as crystal, clear-cut, direct, distinct, evident, explicit, frank, honest, innocent, intelligible, lucent, lucid, manifest, obvious, open, palpable, patent, pellucid, perceivable, perceptible, perspicuous, pervious, plain, plain-speaking, porous, revealing, self-evident, simple, translucent, translucid, unambiguous, undisguised, unequivocal, unmistakable, visible

TRANSPORT, *verb* banish, bear, bring, carry, cart, conduct, consign, convey, deliver, deport, dispatch, drive out, exile, expel, extradite, fetch, imprison, move, ostracize, remove, send, ship, take, tote, transfer, transmit, *transmittere,* transplant, *transportare*
ASSOCIATED CONCEPTS: transport across state lines, transport contraband, transport illegal goods, transport in interstate commerce

TRAP, *noun* ambush, artifice, bait, catch, catch-all, lure, maneuver, net, pitfall, snare, stratagem

TRAP, *verb* bait, catch, ensnare, entangle, entrap, hook, inveigle, snare, snatch

TRAVEL, *noun* flying, get to, go, go abroad, go by air, go by airplane, go by car, go by jet, go by plane, go by sea, go to, ride to a spot, sail to a place, see the sights, see the world, sojourn, take a trip, take a vacation, tour on vacation, touring, traverse, visit during a vacation
ASSOCIATED CONCEPTS: emigration, immigration, travel law, travel rights

TRAVERSE, *verb* course, crisscross, cross, cross in opposition, cross in traveling, cut across, ford, go across, intersect, march, over pass, pass, pass from point to point, pass through, patrol, probe, survey carefully, tramp, travel over, trek

TRAVESTY, *noun* burlesque, burlesque translation, caricature, crude presentation, distortion, exaggeration, farce, imitation, lampoon, low comedy, ludicrous presentation, mimicry, mockery, parody, perversion, ridicule, take-off

TREASON, *noun* betrayal, betrayal of a trust, breach of allegiance, breach of faith, disloyalty, infidelity, insurgence, insurrection, *maiestas,* mutiny, *perfidia,* perfidy, rebellion, rebellion against the government, revolt, revolution, sedition, subversion, treachery, violation of allegiance
FOREIGN PHRASES: ***Felonia implicatur in qualibet proditione.*** Felony is implied in every treason. ***Reus laesae majestatis punitur ut pereat unus ne pereant omnes.*** A traitor is punished that one may die lest all perish. ***Crimen laesae majestatis omnia alia crimina excedit quoad poenam.*** The crime of high treason exceeds all other crimes in its punishment. ***In alta proditione nullus potest esse accessorius sed principalis solummodo.*** In high treason each one is a principal. ***Qui molitur insidias in patriam id facit quod insanus nauta perforans navem in qua vehitur.*** He who betrays his country is like the insane sailor who bores a hole in the ship which carries him.

TREASURY, *noun* accumulation, *aerarium,* bank, bursary, cache, capital, central money office, coffer, conservatory, deposit, depository, depot, exchequer, *fiscus,* fund, place of deposit, purse, receptacle, repertory, repository, reservatory, reserve, reserve fund, safe, store, storehouse, strongbox, thesaurus, till, treasure house, vault

TREAT, *noun* amusement, delight, diversion, festival, pleasure, refreshment, repast, revelry

TREAT *(Process),* ***verb*** act on, analyze, attend, bargain with, behave toward, comment upon, confer, correct, deal with, debate, deliberate, discuss, edit, entertain, examine, handle, heal, investigate, modify, negotiate, parley, reason, reason about, revise, use, work on, write about

TREAT *(Remedy),* ***verb*** ameliorate, better, cure, improve

TREATMENT, *noun* adjustment, analysis, arrangement, consideration, cure, design, examination, execution, handling, investigation, management, modification, process, processing, study, technique, therapy, transaction, way
ASSOCIATED CONCEPTS: inhuman treatment, medical treatment

TREATY, *noun* accord, agreement, agreement between nations, alliance, armistice, arrangement, bargain, bond, cartel, charter, compact, concordance, concordat, contract, *conventio,* convention, covenant, deal, entente, formal contract, international compact, negotiation, pact, *pactio,* protocol, settlement, truce, understanding
ASSOCIATED CONCEPTS: insurance treaty

TRENCHANT, *adjective* acrimonious, acute, biting, brisk, caustic, clear-cut, cutting, distinct, dynamic, energetic, explicit, forceful, incisive, intense, keen, mordant, penetrating, penetrative, piercing, pointed, powerful, pungent, sarcastic, scathing, severe, sharp, spirited, stinging, telling, thoroughgoing, unsparing, vigorous

TREPIDATION, ***noun*** affright, agitation, alarm, apprehension, awe, consternation, disconcertion, dismay, disquiet, disquietude, dread, fear, flutter, fret, fright, funk, horror, jitteriness, jumpiness, nervousness, oscillation, panic, perturbation, quaking, quivering, restlessness, scare, shaking, terror, trembling, tremor, tremulousness, *trepidatio,* trepidity, uneasiness, unrest

TRESPASS, ***verb*** advance upon, breach, break in, break the law, contravene, deviate from rectitude, disobey, disobey the law, disregard, encroach, enter unlawfully, exceed, go astray, ignore limits, *in alienum fundum ingredi,* infringe, intrude, invade, offend, overrun, overstep, sin, transgress, usurp, violate
ASSOCIATED CONCEPTS: action of trespass, constructive trespass, continuing trespass, forcible trespass, innocent trespass, malicious trespass, technical trespass, willful and deliberate trespass
FOREIGN PHRASES: ***Aedificare in tuo proprio solo non licet quod alteri noceat.*** It is not lawful to build upon one's own land what may injure another. ***Prohibetur ne quis faciat in suo quod nocere possit alieno.*** It is forbidden for anyone to do on his own property what may injure another's.

TRIABLE, ***adjective*** actionable, cognizable, justiciable, legally enforceable

TRIAL *(Experiment),* ***noun*** analysis, attempt, check, endeavor, evaluation, examination, experimental method, *experimentum,* exploration, in-depth analysis, inquiry, inspection, probe, review, scrutiny, study, test, testing
ASSOCIATED CONCEPTS: trial period

TRIAL *(Legal proceeding),* ***noun*** action, action at law, case, cause, contest, court action, examination, formal examination by a court of law, formal examination of facts by a court, hearing, *iudicium,* inquest, inquiry, inquisition, judicial contest, lawsuit, legal dispute, litigation, proceeding, *quaestio,* suit, suit at law
ASSOCIATED CONCEPTS: appeal from a trial, close of a trial, examination before trial, fair trial, former trial, impartial trial, joint trial, jury trial, mistrial, new trial, order of trial, post-trial evidence, pretrial evidence, proceed to trial, public trial, retrial, separate trial, speedy trial, trial by jury, trial by the court, trial court, trial de novo, trial judge
FOREIGN PHRASES: ***Triatio ibi semper debet fieri, ubi juratores meliorem possunt habere notitiam.*** Trial ought always to be had where the jurors can have the best information.

TRIAL BALLOON, ***noun*** attempt, dry run, effort, endeavor, experiment, experimental method, exploration, first attempt, inquiry, inspection, investigation, probe, rehearsal, research, search, stab, straw man, test, trial, trial run, try, undertaking, venture

TRIBUNAL, ***noun*** bench, chancery, court, court of justice, court of law, forum, *iudicium,* judges, judgment seat, judiciary, law court, panel of judges
ASSOCIATED CONCEPTS: administrative tribunal, appellate tribunal, fair tribunal, inferior tribunal, tribunal of limited jurisdiction

TRICK, ***noun*** antic, artifice, bunko, canard, caper, caprice, contrivance, deception, decoy, delusion, device, dodge, escapade, evasion, expedient, fake, false pretense, feint, fraud, gimmick, hoax, illusion, imposture, instinct, intrigue, knavery, legerdemain, machination, maneuver, peculiarity, plot, ploy, prank, prestidigitation, pretense, pretext, quirk, racket, ruse, scheme, sham, sleight, sophistry, stratagem, subterfuge, wile
ASSOCIATED CONCEPTS: false pretenses

TRICK, ***verb*** bait, bamboozle, beguile, betray, cheat, circumvent, cozen, deceive, decoy, defraud, delude, dupe, ensnare, evade, hoax, hoodwink, illude, inveigle, mislead, misrepresent, pettifog, swindle, take in, trap, victimize

TRIP AND FALL CASE, ***noun*** accident case, action, action for an injury, calamity, casualty claim, cause of action, claim of negligence, general liability claim, injurious occurrence, liability claim, litigation, misfortune, mishap, negligence case, personal injury, slip and fall
ASSOCIATED CONCEPTS: liability insurance, plaintiff law firms, trials bar

TRITE, ***adjective*** banal, boring, bromidic, common, commonplace, conventional, dull, familiar, hackneyed, known, much used, oft repeated, old, ordinary, overused, *pervulgatus,* platitudinous, prosaic, proverbial, routine, run-of-the-mill, shopworn, stale, stereotyped, stock, tedious, threadbare, too familiar, *tritus,* uncreative, unexciting, unimaginative, unoriginal, used, wearisome, well-known, widely known, worn, worn out

TRIVIAL, ***adjective*** cursory, empty, foolish, frivolous, inane, inappreciable, inconsiderable, indifferent, idle, immaterial, inconsequential, inferior, insignificant, *levis,* light, little, meager, meaningless, mediocre, minute, negligible, nominal, nonessential, nugatory, of little consequence, petty, picayune, scanty, shallow, slight, slim, small, superficial, trashy, trifling, unimportant, useless, worthless
ASSOCIATED CONCEPTS: trivial defect rule, trivial matter

TROUBLE, ***noun*** ado, adversity, affliction, ailment, annoyance, bane, blow, bother, burden, calamity, catastrophe, cause of distress, commotion, difficulty, discomfort, discontent, discord, dissatisfaction, distress, disturbance, fuss, grievance, hardship, hindrance, ill, inconvenience, misfortune, obstruction, ordeal, pitfall, plague, problem, reverse, row, setback, snag, *sollicitudo,* suffering, torment, trial, tribulation

TROVER, ***noun*** atonement, award, compensation, damages, fine, forfeiture, indemnification, indemnity, mulct, payment, penalty, quittance, recompense, recoupment, recovery, redress, reparation, requital, requitement, restitution, retrieval, retrievement, return, satisfaction, solatium

TRUANT, ***adjective*** absent, apathetic, dilatory, errant, flown, fugitive, idle, inattentive, indifferent, indolent, laggard, lazy, loitering, missing, neglectful, nonattendant, remiss, shiftless, shirking, slack, slothful, straying, unconcerned, unemployed, unpersevering, wandering

TRUCKLE, ***verb*** crawl, cringe, fawn, grovel, toady, yield to the wishes of others

TRUE *(Authentic),* ***adjective*** according to the facts, accurate, actual, as represented, authenticated, certain, correct, creditable, dependable, exact, factual, *fidelis, fidus,* founded on fact, genuine, honest, legitimate, literal, not false, not faulty, not fictitious, original, precise, pure, real, realistic, reliable, right, rightful, sound, trustworthy, truthful, unadulterated, unaffected, uncolored, undisguised, undisputed, undistorted, unexaggerated, unfabricated, unfallacious, unfeigned, unfictitious, unimagined, unimpeachable,

unmistaken, unperjured, unpretended, unquestionable, unspurious, unvarnished, valid, veracious, veridical, verifiable, veritable, *verus,* well-based, well-founded, well-grounded
ASSOCIATED CONCEPTS: true bill, true copy, true value, true verdict

TRUE *(Loyal),* ***adjective*** ardent, assiduous, compliant, complying, conscientious, constant, dedicated, dependable, devoted, duteous, dutiful, earnest, faithful, fervent, firm in adherence, firm in allegiance, incorruptible, obedient, reliable, resolute, responsible, sincere, stanch, steadfast, steady, sure, tried, truehearted, trustworthy, trusty, unbetraying, unfailing, unfalse, unperfidious, unswerving, untreacherous, unwavering, zealous

TRUST *(Combination of businesses),* ***noun*** association, cartel, combination of companies, combine, consortium, corporation, merger, monopolistic organization, monopoly, pool, syndicate
ASSOCIATED CONCEPTS: antitrust laws, combination in restraint of trade

TRUST *(Confidence),* ***noun*** assurance, belief, certainty, confident expectation, conviction, credence, credulity, dependence, faith, *fides, fiducia,* reassurance, reliance, sureness, trustworthiness
ASSOCIATED CONCEPTS: breach of trust, office of trust, public trust

TRUST *(Custody),* ***noun*** care, charge, control, duty, guardianship, holding, keeping, management, obligation, possession and control, power over, protection, responsibility, safety
ASSOCIATED CONCEPTS: beneficiary of trust, business trust, *cestui que trust,* charitable trust, constructive trust, continuing trust, corpus of trust, de facto trust, declaration of trust, discretionary trust, dormant trust, dry trust, execution of trust, executory trust, express trust, implied trust, parol trust, presumptive trust, principal of a trust, private trust, residuary trust, resultant trust, revocable trust, shifting trust, special trust, spendthrift trust, totten trust, trust agreement, trust certificate, trust company, trust deed, trust estate, trust funds, trust mortgage, trust receipts
FOREIGN PHRASES: ***Fides est obligatio conscientiae alicujus ad intentionem alterius.*** A trust is an obligation of conscience of one to the wishes of another.

TRUST, ***verb*** accept, accredit, assume, be confident, confide, *confidere,* count upon, *credere,* credit, depend upon, expect, feel sure, give credence to, give credit to, have faith in, have no doubt, have no reservations, hope, lean on, *mandare,* place reliance in, presume, put confidence in, rely on, swear by, take, take for granted

TRUSTEE, ***noun*** administrator, agent, appointee, caretaker, curator, custodian, *custos,* depositary, fiduciary, financier, functionary, guardian, holder of the legal estate, one to whom something is entrusted, person appointed to administer affairs, recipient
ASSOCIATED CONCEPTS: acting trustee, appointment of trustee, bare trustee, change of trustee, corporate trustee, cotrustees, de facto trustee, designation of trustee, disinterested trustee, duty of trustee, fiduciary responsibility, interested trustee, involuntary trustee, liability of trustee, nominal trustee, public trustee, qualification of trustees, quasi trustee, removal of trustee, successor trustee, testamentary trustee, trustee by deed, trustee of an estate, trustee ex maleficio, trustee in bankruptcy

TRUSTWORTHINESS, ***noun*** dependability, faithfulness, honesty, integrity, loyalty, probity, rectitude, reliability, uprightness

TRUTH, ***noun*** accuracy, actuality, authenticity, candor, conformity to fact, correctness, exactness, fact, genuineness, honesty, integrity, precision, probity, realism, reality, right, sincerity, veracity, *veritas,* verity
ASSOCIATED CONCEPTS: credibility of a witness, reputation for truth, truth in lending laws
FOREIGN PHRASES: ***Error fucatus nuda veritate in multis, est probabilior; et saepenumero rationibus vincit veritatem error.*** Error artfully disguised is, in many instances, more probable than naked truth; and frequently error overwhelms truth by argumentation. ***Veritas nimium altercando amittitur.*** Truth is lost by too much altercation. ***Sacramentum habet in se tres comites:veritatem, justitiam, et judicium–veritus habenda est in jurato; justitia et justicium in judice.*** An oath has in it three components:truth, justice, and judgment—truth in the party swearing; justice and judgment in the judge administering the oath. ***Fictio cedit veritati. Fictio juris non est ubi veritas.*** Fiction yields to truth. Where truth is, fiction of law does not exist. ***Qui non libere veritatem pronunciat proditor est veritatis.*** He who does not freely speak the truth is a betrayer of the truth. ***Veritas, quae minime defensatur opprimitur; et qui non improbat, approbat.*** Truth which is not sufficiently defended is overpowered; and he who does not disapprove, approves. ***Veritas nihil veretur nisi abscondi.*** Truth fears nothing but concealment.

TRUTHFUL, ***adjective*** aboveboard, accurate, actual, believable, credible, exact, fact, factual, faithful, honest, honorable, legitimate, right-minded, truth-loving, truth-speaking, truth-telling, upright, veracious
ASSOCIATED CONCEPTS: impeachment, the veracity of a witness, truthful testimony

TRY *(Attempt),* ***verb*** aim, aspire, *conari,* endeavor, exert oneself, make an effort, put forth effort, seek, strain, strive, tackle, take a chance, *temptare,* test, undertake, venture

TRY *(Conduct a trial),* ***verb*** adjudge, adjudicate, consider, decide, deliberate, examine, examine judicially, hear a case, hear a cause, *iudicare,* judge, legally determine, pronounce, rule, sit in judgment
ASSOCIATED CONCEPTS: try a case before a judge, try a case before a jury

TUMULTUOUS, ***adjective*** angry, disgusted, enraged, frantic, frenzied, fuming, furious, hostile, inflamed, infuriated, ireful, livid, offended, offensive, outraged, raging, storming, tempestuous, turbulent

TURGID, ***adjective*** bombastic, circumlocutory, declamatory, diffuse, digressive, euphuistic, flowery, fustian, grandiloquent, high-flown, inflated, long-winded, magniloquent, orotund, periphrastic, pleonastic, plethoric, pompous, prolix, puffed up, redundant, rhetorical, sesquipedalian, stilted, swelled, swollen, tumid, turgent, wordy

TURMOIL, ***noun*** activity, ado, agitation, bedlam, bustle, chaos, commotion, confusion, convulsion, discord, disorder, disquiet, distraction, disturbance, excitement, ferment, fracas, fuss, havoc, huddle, imbroglio, jumble, melee, muddle, pandemonium, perturbation, pother, row, rumpus, stir, storm, tempest, trouble, tumult, *turba,* turbulence, turbulency, unrest, upheaval, uproar, welter

TURN *(Change)*, ***noun*** bend, change of direction, curve, detour, deviation, diversion, particular interpretation, twist, vicissitude
ASSOCIATED CONCEPTS: turnover order

TURN *(Rotation)*, ***noun*** circuit, cycle, gyration, perambulation, revolution, shift, span stretch, stint

TURN *(Change)*, ***verb*** alter, avert, bend, change, change opinion, coil, contort, convert, curdle, curl, deviate, digress, ferment, form, induce, influence, metamorphose, mold, persuade, prevail upon, recast, reconstruct, reorganize, shift, sinuate, slue, sway, swerve, transform, transmute, transpose, veer, wind, win over

TURN *(Deflect)*, ***verb*** alter belief, argue, avert, change course, convince, gainsay, maneuver, outmaneuver, revolutionize, transform, vary
ASSOCIATED CONCEPTS: turn state's evidence

TURN *(Rotate)*, ***verb*** change, gyrate, jibe, move, move clockwise, move counterclockwise, pivot, pull, push, revolve, spin, swivel, whirl

TURNS ON, ***verb*** arises from, centers on, emanates from, ensues from, exists because of, hinges on, is decided on, issues from, springs from, the conclusion originates from, the critical point is, the crowning point is, the crucial moment is, the crux of the matter is, the culmination is, the determination is, the juncture is, the outcome is derived from, the pivotal moment is, the result is, the watershed event is

TURPITUDE, ***noun*** bad character, bad name, baseness, character, corruption, decadence, degeneracy, degradation, depravity, disrepute, ill repute, immorality, infamy, obscenity, perfidy, shady reputation, vileness, wickedness, wrongdoing

TWEAKING, ***noun*** accommodation, adjustment, advance, advancement, alteration, amelioration, amendment, bettering, betterment, breakthrough, change, change for the better, changeover, constructive change, deviation, difference, divergence, enhancement, enrichment, improvement, increase, lift, melioration, modification, progress, progression, progressive change, redesign, reform, reformation, reshaping, restoration, restructuring, transition, upgrade
ASSOCIATED CONCEPTS: punitive damages

TWO-PART TRIAL, ***noun*** bifurcated trial, bisection of a case, segmentation in a case, segregation in a case, separate liability and damage phases, separate quilt and insanity defense phases, separation in a case, severance in a case, split in a case, split trial, two or more hearings held
ASSOCIATED CONCEPTS: financial betterment, improvement in real estate value
FOREIGN PHRASES: ***Nul ne doit s'enrichir aux despens des autres.*** No man should enrich himself at the expense of others.

TYPICAL, ***adjective*** according to custom, according to routine, accustomed, average, characteristic, common, commonplace, conformable, conformable to rule, consistent, conventional, current, customary, everyday, exemplifying a class, familiar, habitual, illustrative, in character, indicative, indicatory, model, normal, of everyday occurrence, of frequent occurrence, oft-repeated, ordinary, orthodox, popular, prevailing, prevalent, *proprius,* prosaic, recurrent, regular, representative, *solitus,* standard, standardized, stereotyped, stock, traditional, true to type, *typicus,* unexceptional, usual

TYRANNOUS, ***adjective*** arbitrary, brutal, despotic, domineering, grinding, hard, harsh, high-handed, imperious, lordly, masterful, oppressive, overbearing, peremptory, severe, strict, tyrannical, uncompromising, unjustly severe

UBIQUITOUS, ***adjective*** ever-present, omnipresent, permeative, pervading, pervasive, ubiquitary, universal, worldwide

UGSOME, ***adjective*** aberrant, abhorrent, contemptible, despicable, dreadful, frightful, fulsome, ghastly, gross, hateful, horrific, loathsome, monstrous, nasty, odious, rancid, repellent, reprehensible, repugnant, repulsive, revolting, scandalous, shocking, unpleasant

ULTERIOR, ***adjective*** concealed, hidden, not manifest, obscure, secret, unadvertised, unavowed, undisclosed, undivulged, unevident, unexpressed, unknown, unmentioned, unobvious, unperceived, unrevealed, unseen
ASSOCIATED CONCEPTS: ulterior motive

ULTIMATE, ***adjective*** basic, conclusive, conclusory, crowning, elemental, elementary, end, ending, essential, eventual, extreme, extremus, farthest, final, fundamental,

furthermost, furthest, greatest possible, last, maximum, most distant, most remote, primary, rudimental, rudimentary, supreme, terminal, terminative, *ultimus*
ASSOCIATED CONCEPTS: ultimate facts

ULTIMATUM, *noun* condition, demand, exaction, *extrema condicio,* final condition, final offer, final proposal, final proposition, last offer, notice, proposition, provision, proviso, requirement, requisite, specification, stipulation, threat, warning

ULTRA VIRES, *adjective* illegitimate, unallowed, unauthorized, unchartered, unlicensed, unsanctioned, unwarranted
ASSOCIATED CONCEPTS: *ultra vires* act, *ultra vires* doctrine

UMBRAGE, *noun* acrimony, alienation, anger, animosity, annoyance, bad blood, bile, bitterness, choler, disaffection, discord, dislike, displeasure, dissatisfaction, dudgeon, enmity, estrangement, grudge, hatred, hostility, ill humor, ill will, indignation, irritation, offense, pique, rancor, resentment, soreness, spleen, wrath

UMPIRE, *noun* adjudicator, arbiter, arbitrator, compromiser, *disceptator,* go-between, interagent, intercessor, intermediary, intermediator, intermedium, intervenor, judge, mediator, moderator, peacemaker, reconciler, referee

UNABASHED, *adjective* aweless, barefaced, bold, brazen, forward, hardened, immodest, *impudens,* not ashamed, not disconcerted, shameless, unafraid, unapprehensive, unashamed, unawed, unblushing, unconcerned, uncringing, undaunted, undismayed, unembarrassed, unfearing, unflinching, unshaken, unshrinking, without shame

UNABLE, *adjective* defenseless, disabled, feckless, forceless, helpless, impotent, inadequate, incapable, incompetent, ineffective, inefficient, inept, inoperative, insufficient, lame, not able, powerless, unfit, unqualified, useless, worthless

UNACCEPTABLE, *adjective* displeasing, distasteful, exceptionable, impossible, inadmissable, inappropriate, *ingratus, iniucundus,* intolerable, not fitting, objectionable, offensive, repugnant, unappealing, unattractive, undesirable, undesired, uninviting, unpleasant, unpleasing, unpopular, unsatisfactory, unsuitable, unwanted, unwelcome

UNACCOUNTABLE, *adjective* anything goes, defiant, devolving on, disobedient, insubordinate, irresponsible, licentious, not accountable, mutinous, not properly accounted for, not responsible, not traceable, rebellious, riotous, seditious, unchecked, uncontrolled, uncurbed, undisciplined, ungoverned, unrestrained

UNACCUSTOMED, *adjective* a stranger to, aberrant, abnormal, amazing, anomalous, astonishing, bizarre, curious, different, disaccustomed, eccentric, exceptional, exotic, extraordinary, first time experiencing, first time for, foreign, freakish, green, ignorant, inexperienced, *insolitus, insuetus,* inusitate, irregular, naive, new, new to, not accustomed to, not common, not conversant with, not familiar with, not in the habit of, not usual, not used to, novel, odd, out of the habit of, out of the ordinary, outlandish, peculiar, queer, rare, raw, remarkable, rusty, shaky, singular, strange, surprising, unacquainted, unacquainted with, unaware of, uncommon, unconventional, unconversant, uncustomary, unfamiliar, unfamiliar with, unhabituated, uninitiated, uninured, unique, unnatural, unordinary, unpracticed, unseasoned, unskilled, untrained, untried, unusual, unversed

UNACQUAINTED, *adjective* *ignarus,* ignorant, inexperienced, *inscius,* new, strange, unaccustomed, unapprized, unaware, unconversant, unenlightened, unfamiliar, uninformed, unknowing, unversed

UNADULTERATED, *adjective* genuine, *integer, merus,* neat, pure, simple, *sincerus,* straight, true, unalloyed, uncombined, uncompounded, uncontaminated, uncorrupted, undebased, undefiled, undiluted, undistorted, unmingled, unmixed, unsophisticated, untouched, unvarnished, virgin

UNAFFECTED *(Sincere),* ***adjective*** aboveboard, artless, candid, *candidus,* childlike, direct, downright, forthright, frank, free from affectation, guileless, honest, inartificial, ingenuous, innocent, modest, naive, natural, open, outspoken, plain, plainspoken, simple, *simplex,* spontaneous, straightforward, truthful, unassuming, uncounterfeited, undeceptive, undesigning, unfeigning, unpretending, unpretentious, unreserved, unsimulated, unsophisticated, unsynthetic, upright, wholesome

UNAFFECTED *(Uninfluenced),* ***adjective*** aweless, callous, calm, *constans,* disdainful, frigid, hard-hearted, heartless, icy, *immotus,* impassive, impervious, implacable, indifferent, inflexible, insensitive, insentient, inured, obdurate, obtuse, pitiless, remorseless, steely, stoic, stoical, stony, unaltered, uncaring, unchanged, uncompassionate, unconcerned, unexcited, unfeeling, unimpressed, uninspired, unmoved, unresponsive, unstirred, unstruck, unswayed, unsympathetic, untouched, unyielding

UNALIENABLE, *adjective* absolute, actual, certain, conclusive, definite, fixed, imprescriptible, inalienable, incapable of being surrendered, indefeasible, inviolable, lawful, prescriptive, privileged, rightful, unalterable, unchallengeable, unimpeachable, untransferable
ASSOCIATED CONCEPTS: unalienable rights

UNALTERABLE, *adjective* adamant, changeless, constant, definite, determined, fated, firm, fixed, *immutabilis,* immutable, inalterable, incommutable, inevitable, inflexible, invariable, irreversible, obdurate, permanent, relentless, resolute, rigid, settled, stable, unbending, unchangeable, undeviating, unmodifiable, unpliant, unwavering, unyielding

UNAMBIGUOUS, *adjective* *apertus,* articulate, certain, *clarus,* clear, clear-cut, clearly defined, comprehensible, defined, definite, *definitus,* distinct, distinguishable, evident, exact, explicit, express, intelligible, lucid, not vague, obvious, perspicuous, plain, precise, recognizable, sure, transparent, unconfused, understandable, unequivocal, univocal, unmistakable, well-defined
ASSOCIATED CONCEPTS: plain language

UNANTICIPATED, *adjective* abrupt, *improvisus, inexspectatus, insperatus,* startling, sudden, surprising, uncontemplated, unexpected, unforeseen, unlooked for, unthought of

UNAPPROACHABLE, *adjective* aloof, austere, beyond reach, distant, far-off, faraway, forbidding, formidable, impregnable, inaccessible, inaffable, incomparable, inimitable, matchless, nongregarious, out of reach, out-of-the-way, peerless, *rari aditus,* remote, removed, reserved, secluded, separated, standoffish, stern, superior, superlative, supreme, unattainable, unequaled, unexcelled, unique, unobtainable, unparalleled, unreachable, unsociable, unsurpassed, withdrawn

UNASSAILABLE, ***adjective*** as strong as a fortress, completely defensible, impenetrable, impossible to disprove, impossible to dispute, impregnable, not attackable, not capable of being, not subject to attack, not vulnerable, strong, undeniable

UNATTAINABLE, ***adjective*** impossible, impracticable, impractical, inaccessible, infeasible, insuperable, insurmountable, out of reach, out of the question, unachievable, unacquirable, unapproachable, unavailable, unfeasible, ungettable, unobtainable, unperformable, unprocurable, unreachable, unsecurable

UNATTENDED, ***adjective*** abandoned, all by one's lonesome, alone, disregarded, forgotten, helpless, ignored, insular, isolated, left alone, lone, lonesome, neglected, not associated with, not cared for, on one's own, removed, separate, separated, unaccompanied, unaided, unassisted, unescorted, unguarded, unheeded, unprotected, unsheltered, unshielded, unsupported, unsuspecting, untended, unwarned, unwatched, withdrawn
ASSOCIATED CONCEPTS: attractive nuisance, negligence

UNAUTHORIZED, ***adjective*** disallowed, forbidden, inappropriate, incorrect, illegal, illegitimate, improper, prohibited, proscribed, unaccredited, unaffirmed, unapproved, uncertified, unchartered, uncommanded, uncommissioned, unconstitutional, undue, unempowered, unendorsed, unentitled, unjustified, unlawful, unlicensed, unpermitted, unratified, unsanctioned, unsuitable, unsupported, unwarranted, wrongful
ASSOCIATED CONCEPTS: unauthorized conduct, unauthorized use

UNAVAILABILITY, ***noun*** inaccessibility, unacquirability, unapproachability, unattainability, unobtainability

UNAVAILING, ***adjective*** abortive, barren, bootless, empty, fruitless, futile, *futilis,* idle, impotent, inadequate, incompetent, ineffective, ineffectual, inefficacious, inefficient, inoperative, *inritus,* inutile, invalid, nugatory, of no avail, pointless, profitless, purposeless, successless, to no end, to no purpose, uneventful, unproductive, unprofitable, unserviceable, unsuccessful, useless, vain, valueless, *vanus,* wasted, wasteful, worthless

UNAVOIDABLE *(Inevitable),* ***adjective*** avoidless, certain, coercive, compelling, compulsory, fated, fixed, impending, imperative, inavertible, ineluctable, ineludible, inescapable, inevasible, *inevitabilis,* inexorable, involuntary, irresistible, irrevocable, mandatory, *necessarius,* necessary, obligatory, resistless, sure, uncontrollable, unpreventable
ASSOCIATED CONCEPTS: unavoidable accident, unavoidable casualty, unavoidable cause, unavoidable consequences, unavoidable dangers

UNAVOIDABLE *(Not voidable),* ***adjective*** binding, fixed, indefeasible, *inrevocabilis,* irrebuttable, irrefutable, irrevocable, mandatory, settled, unable to be annulled, unchangeable

UNAWARE, ***adjective*** blinded, heedless, *ignarus,* ignorant, inattentive, incognizant, inexpectant, *inscius,* insensible, mindless, nescient, *nescius,* oblivious, off guard, surprised, unacquainted, unadvised, unapprised, unconscious, undiscerning, unenlightened, unfamiliar with, unforewarned, unguarded, unheeding, uninformed, unknowing, unmindful, unobservant, unprepared, unrealizing, unsuspecting, unversed, unwarned, unwary, without notice

UNBEARABLE, ***adjective*** enough to drive one mad, indefensible, inequitable, inexcusable, insufferable, insupportable, intolerable, not capable of being endured, too much, unconscionable, unendurable, unjustifiable, unwarranted
ASSOCIATED CONCEPTS: unbearable loss, unbearable suffering

UNBEATABLE, ***adjective*** beyond comparison, championship, first, in a class all by itself, incomparable, inimitable, matchless, never-to-be-equaled, peerless, top, unapproachable, unequaled, unexampled, unexcelled, unique, unmatchable, unmatched, unparalleled, unrivaled, unsurpassable, unsurpassed, without equal

UNBECOMING, ***adjective*** awkward, degrading, dishonorable, disreputable, graceless, improper, in bad taste, inapposite, inappropriate, incongruous, incorrect, indecent, indecorous, *indecorus,* indelicate, *indignus,* infelicitous, offensive, out of keeping, out of place, unapt, unbefitting, unbeseeming, uncomely, undignified, unfit, unfitted, ungenteel, unhandsome, unladylike, unmeet, unpraiseworthy, unseemly, unsuitable, unsuited, untasteful, vulgar

UNBELIEVABLE, ***adjective*** absurd, difficult to accept, difficult to believe, disbelieved, distrusted, doubtful, dubious, farfetched, hard to believe, implausible, improbable, inconceivable, incredible, open to doubt, open to suspicion, palpably false, questionable, staggering, suspect, suspicious, unconvincing, unimaginable, unlikely, untenable, unthinkable

UNBENDING, ***adjective*** adamant, *durus,* firm, fixed, hard, immobile, immovable, implacable, inflexible, intractable, intransigent, narrow-minded, obdurate, obstinate, relentless, renitent, resistant, resolute, rigid, *rigidus,* stern, stiff, straight, straitlaced, strict, strong-minded, stubborn, unchangeable, uncompromising, unpliant, unrelenting, unyielding, willful

UNBIASED, ***adjective*** broad-minded, detached, disinterested, dispassionate, equitable, fair, fair-minded, impartial, impersonal, independent, indifferent, just, liberal, neutral, nonpartisan, objective, open, open-minded, tolerant, unbigoted, uncolored, uninfluenced, unjaundiced, unprejudiced, unslanted, unswayed, unwarped

UNBLEMISHED *(Clean),* ***adjective*** above suspicion, acquitted, blameless, bright, clean-handed, clear, decent, faultless, free from criminal record, free from guilt, guiltless, honest, honorable, immaculate, impeccable, in the clear, incorrupt, incorruptible, innocent, irreproachable, law-abiding, lawful, pure, righteous, right-minded, scrupulous, soil-free, spotless, squeaky clean, stainless, strictly honest, unimpeachable, unobjectionable, unoffending, unsoiled, unstained, untainted, untarnished, veracious, virtuous, without a stain, without reproach
ASSOCIATED CONCEPTS: a clean criminal record

UNBLEMISHED *(Honest),* ***adjective*** above suspicion, absolute, acquitted, angelic, beyond all praise, beyond reproach, blameless, bloodless, chaste, clean, clean-handed, clean-minded, creditable, decent, defectless, entirely defensible, estimable, ethical, fair, faultless, flawless, free from

impurities, full of integrity, good, guileless, high-minded, high-principled, highly respectable, honorable, ideal, immaculate, impeccable, incorrupt, incorruptible, indefectible, indefective, infallible, innocent, inviolable, inviolate, irreprehensible, irreproachable, irreprovable, just, just right, law-abiding, lawful, law-loving, law-revering, matchless, moral, noble, not guilty, not responsible, not to be improved, number-one, peedess, perfect, principled, pure, pure in heart, reputable, respectable, right, righteous, right-minded, scrupulous, sinless, spotless, squeaky-clean, stainless, sterling, straight, strictly honest, taintless, true-dealing, true-devoted, true-disposing, truehearted, true-souled, true-spirited, unadulterated, unblamable, unbribed, uncontaminated, uncorrupt, uncorrupted, unculpable, unerring, unexceptionable, unfaultable, unflawed, unguilty, unimpeachable, uninvolved, unmixed, unmuddied, unobjectionable, unoffending, unstained, unsullied, untainted, untarnished, unviolated, uprighteous, upstanding, veracious, virtuous, without reproach, world-class, worthy
ASSOCIATED CONCEPTS: unblemished record

UNBOUND, ***adjective*** disunited, exempt, free, liberated, limitless, manumitted, paroled, released, set free, uncaught, unchained, unchecked, unconfined, unconstrained, uncontrolled, unencumbered, unfastened, unfettered, unfixed, unhindered, unlimited, unobstructed, unprevented, unrestrained, unrestricted, untied, untrammeled

UNBRIDLED AUTHORITY, ***noun*** absolute discretion, authority, blank check, carte blanche, complete liberty, discretion, every option, free hand, freedom, full authority, full delegated authority, full power, full range, latitude, leeway, maneuvering space, total discretion, unbridled discretion, unhampered authority

UNCANNY, ***adjective*** astonishing, exceptional, inconceivable, incredible, intuitional, magical, mysterious, mystifying, noteworthy, odd, peculiar, preternatural, rare, remarkable, secret, singular, strange, supernatural, unaccountable, unbelievable, uncommon, unearthly, unfamiliar, unheard of, unnatural, weird

UNCERTAIN *(Ambiguous),* ***adjective*** amphibolic, cryptic, enigmatical, inconclusive, indeterminate, indistinct, mistakable, mysterious, mystifying, nebulous, not certain, not clear, not plain, obscure, occult, open to various interpretations, perplexing, puzzling, unclear, unintelligible, vague
FOREIGN PHRASES: ***Ubi jus incertum, ibi jus nullum.*** Where the law is uncertain, there is no law. ***Res est misera ubi jus est vagum et incertum.*** It is a sorry state of affairs when law is vague and mutable. ***Incerta pro nullis habentur.*** Uncertain things are regarded as nothing.

UNCERTAIN *(Questionable),* ***adjective*** arguable, conjectural, contestable, contingent, controvertible, debatable, disputable, doubtful, dubious, equivocal, insecure, liable to question, not sure, open to discussion, open to question, precarious, problematic, problematical, provisional, suspect, suspicious, tentative, unconfirmed, undecided, undetermined, unreliable, unsettled, unsure, untrustworthy

UNCERTAINTY, ***noun*** ambiguity, ambivalence, chance, confusion, contingency, darkness, desultoriness, dilemma, dimness, doubt, doubtfulness, dubiousness, equivocation, faintness, feebleness, gamble, hazard, hesitancy, hesitation, improbability, incertitude, inconstancy, incredulity, indecision, indefiniteness, indetermination, insecurity, instability, irresolution, jeopardy, misgiving, obscurity, peril, perplexity, possibility, precariousness, qualm, quandary, reluctance, risk, shadowiness, speculation, suspense, undependability, unevenness, unpredictability, unreliability, unsteadiness, unsureness, vacillation, vagueness, wavering, weakness

UNCHECKED, ***adjective*** allowed, allowed freely, easy, lax, out of control, out of hand, permitted, rampant, riotous, tolerated, unbridled, unconditional, unconstrained, uncontrolled, uncurbed, ungoverned, unhampered, uninhibited, unregulated, unrepressed, unreserved, unrestrained, unruly
ASSOCIATED CONCEPTS: unchecked presidential power

UNCLAIMED, ***adjective*** forgotten, unallocated, unapplied, unappropriated, unasked for, uncalled-for, undemanded, unexacted, unpossessed, unrequisitioned, unsought, untaken
ASSOCIATED CONCEPTS: last property, unclaimed property

UNCLEAN HANDS, ***noun*** a blemished record, a record of proven fault, equitable defense, improper history, personal deficiencies, personal problems, problems in the past, tainted past

UNCLEAR, ***adjective*** ambiguous, blurred, blurry, clouded, cloudy, confused, difficult to comprehend, difficult to understand, dim, equivocal, faint, foggy, fuzzy, hazy, ill-defined, illegible, imperspicuous, incomprehensible, inconspicuous, indistinct, indistinguishable, misty, muddy, murky, obscure, out of focus, poorly defined, poorly seen, shadowy, sketchy, turbid, uncertain, undefined, unevident, unexplicit, unintelligible, unobvious, unplain, unreadable, unrecognizable, vague

UNCOMMON, ***adjective*** aberrant, abnormal, anomalous, bizarre, curious, different, distinctive, eccentric, exceptional, exotic, extraordinary, infrequent, *insolitus,* inusitate, *inusitatus,* marked, noteworthy, novel, occasional, odd, out-of-the-way, outstanding, peculiar, rare, *rarus,* remarkable, scarce, seldom met with, singular, special, startling, strange, surprising, unaccustomed, unconventional, uncustomary, unexampled, unfamiliar, unheard of, unimitated, unique, unorthodox, unparalleled, unprecedented, unusual

UNCOMPROMISING, ***adjective*** adamant, austere, conservative, determined, difficult, exacting, exigent, fanatic, fanatical, firm, hard, immovable, implacable, incorruptible, inexorable, inflexible, intransigent, irreconcilable, narrow, obdurate, obstinate, orthodox, puritanic, puritanical, relentless, resolute, resolved, rigid, ruthless, severe, steadfast, strict, stringent, unbending, unchangeable, unrelenting, unremitting, unyielding

UNCONCERNED, ***adjective*** aloof, apathetic, careless, casual, cold, cold-blooded, contemptuous, cool, cruel, derelict, disinterested, dispassionate, distant, free from anxiety, frigid, hard-hearted, heartless, heedless, icy, impartial, inaccessible, incurious, indifferent, insensitive, insouciant, lax, listless, negligent, neutral, nonchalant, obdurate, passionless, perfunctory, phlegmatic, remiss, serene, sluggish, stoical, stolid, stony, supercilious, thick-skinned, thoughtless, torpid, truant, unabashed, unaffected, unalarmed, unapprehensive, uncaring, unconcerned, undaunted, undismayed, unemotional, unfeeling, uninquisitive, uninterested, uninvolved, unmindful, unmoved, unperturbed, unresponsive, unshrinking, unsolicitous, unsusceptible, unsympathetic, untroubled
ASSOCIATED CONCEPTS: failure to cooperate, recalcitrant witness

UNCONDITIONAL, ***adjective*** absolute, categorical, complete, not limited by conditions, *purus, simplex,* unbounded, unchecked, unconfined, unqualified, unrestricted, utter, without conditions, without reservations
ASSOCIATED CONCEPTS: unconditional claim, unconditional guaranty, unconditional pardon, unconditional payment, unconditional promise, unconditional refusal

UNCONDITIONAL AUTHORITY, ***noun*** alternatives, artistic license, authority, blanket permission, carte blanche, civil liberty, decontrols, deregulation, discretion, emancipation, franchise, free choice, free will, freedom of choice, lack of censorship, laissez-faire, latitude, liberation, liberty, license, noninterference, nonintervention, openness, permission, prerogative, privilege, right of selection, self-determination, self-direction, unbridled discretion, unconstraint, unrestraint, unrestricted use

UNCONFIRMED, ***adjective*** inconclusive, indecisive, unascertained, unattested, unauthenticated, uncertain, uncertified, unchecked, uncorroborated, undemonstrated, unestablished, unproved, unproven, unratified, unsettled, unshown, unsubstantiated, unsupported, untried, unvalidated, unverified, unwitnessed

UNCONFORMABLE, ***adjective*** discordant, discrepant, disparate, disproportionate, dissident, dissimilar, eccentric, inadjustable, inapplicable, inappropriate, incommensurate, incompatible, incongruent, incongruous, inconsistent, inconsonant, irreconcilable, irreducible, irregular, lawless, nonconforming, original, peculiar, repugnant, rigid, unique, unorthodox, unrelated

UNCONNECTED, ***adjective*** absonant, alien, apart, broken, collateral, desultory, detached, disconnected, discontinued, discontinuous, disengaged, disjoined, disjunctive, disparate, distinct, disunited, divided, foreign, gratuitous, inapposite, incongruous, inconsequential, inconsistent, independent, individual, insular, irrelative, irrelevant, isolated, loose, obscure, parted, remote, removed, segregate, separate, separated, solitary, sundered, unaffiliated, unallied, unassociated, unattached, unrelated, without context
ASSOCIATED CONCEPTS: unconnected subjects in a bill

UNCONSCIONABLE, ***adjective*** atrocious, blackguard, completely unreasonable, conniving, conscienceless, corrupt, criminal, designing, dishonest, dishonorable, disingenuous, excessive, exorbitant, extreme, grievous, grossly unjust, immoderate, impermissible, incomprehensible, indefensible, inequitable, inexcusable, inexpiable, inordinate, intemperate, intriguing, knavish, monstrous, outrageous, preposterous, rascally, reprehensible, scheming, tricky, unbalanced, unconscienced, undue, unequal, unethical, unfair, unforgivable, unjust, unjustifiable, unpardonable, unprincipled, unreasonable, unscrupulous, unwarrantable, wrong
ASSOCIATED CONCEPTS: unconscionable bargain, unconscionable conduct, unconscionable contract

UNCONSCIONABILITY, ***noun*** amoral action, evil action, immoral action, inconceivableness, indefensibleness, inexcusableness, inexpiableness, shameless action, unethical actoin, unfair action, unfounded action, unprincipled action, unreasonable action, unreasonableness, unscrupulous action, unwarranted action, wicked action
ASSOCIATED CONCEPTS: contract of adhesion, enforcement of contracts, integration clause, unconscionable bargain, unconscionable conduct

UNCONTESTED, ***adjective*** accepted, admitted, axiomatic, believed, incontestable, incontrovertible, indubitable, irrefragable, irrefutable, not argued over, not challenged, not disputed, *sine certamine,* unchallengeable, unchallenged, uncontradicted, uncontroversial, uncontroverted, undeniable, undisputed, undoubted, unquestionable, unquestioned
ASSOCIATED CONCEPTS: uncontested action, uncontested divorce, uncontested election

UNCONTROLLABLE, ***adjective*** bullheaded, carried away, disobedient, disorderly, fractious, frenzied, headstrong, hysterical, impetuous, *impotens,* incorrigible, indocile, indomitable, insuppressible, insurgent, intractable, irrepressible, irresistable, lawless, mulish, obdurate, obstinate, obstreperous, opinionated, out of control, rampageous, rampant, recalcitrant, refractory, restive, riotous, rowdy, stubborn, troublesome, unappeasable, ungovernable, unmalleable, unmanageable, unrestrainable, unruly, unsubmissive, untoward, violent, wild, willful
ASSOCIATED CONCEPTS: uncontrollable impulse

UNCONTROVERTED, ***adjective*** beyond doubt, doubtless, indubious, past dispute, unchallenged, uncontested, uncontradicted, undisputed, undoubted, unquestioned
ASSOCIATED CONCEPTS: uncontroverted fact, uncontroverted truth

UNCORROBORATED, ***adjective*** unattested, unauthenticated, unauthorative, unconfirmed, undemonstrated, unofficial, unproven, unratified, unsubstantiated, unsupported, unvalidated, unverified
ASSOCIATED CONCEPTS: uncorroborated evidence, uncorroborated fact

UNCOUTH, ***adjective*** *agrestis,* awkward, barbaric, barbarous, boorish, brutish, callow, churlish, clownish, clumsy, coarse, crass, crude, discourteous, doltish, gawky, graceless, gross, heavy-handed, ill-bred, ill-mannered, impolite, *incultus,* indelicate, inelegant, loutish, plebeian, rough, rude, *rudis,* rustic, strange, uncivil, uncourteous, uncourtly, uncultivated, uncultured, ungainly, ungentlemanly, unmannerly, unpolished, unrefined, unseemly, vulgar

UNCURBED, ***adjective*** abandoned, *effrenatus, effusus,* incontinent, *infrenatus,* irresponsible, lawless, lax, licentious, out of control, out of hand, reinless, unaccountable, unanswerable, unbound, unbridled, unchained, unchecked, unconfined, unconstrained, uncontrolled, undisciplined, ungoverned, unhindered, unimpeded, uninhibited, unmuzzled, unobstructed, unprevented, unreined, unrepressed, unrestrained, unruly, unshackled, unsuppressed

UNDAUNTED, ***adjective*** bold, brave, courageous, daring, dauntless, doughty, dreadless, fearless, firm, gallant, gritty, heroic, *impavidus,* indefatigable, indomitable, *interritus,* intrepid, *intrepidus,* mettlesome, perseverant, persevering, persistent, persisting, resolute, stalwart, steady, stouthearted, tireless, unafraid, unalarmed, unapprehensive, unblenched, unconcerned, undiscouraged, undismayed, unfaltering, unfearing, unflinching, unfrightened, unrelenting, unshaken, unshrinking, unsubdued, unterrified, untimid, valiant, valorous

UNDECIDED, ***adjective*** ambiguous, *ambiguus,* changeful, contestable, debatable, disputable, doubtful, doubting, drawn, dubious, *dubius,* hesitant, *incertus,* indecisive, indefinite, irresolute, moot, open, pending, problematical, questionable, speculative, tentative, unascertained, uncertain, unconvinced, undetermined, unfixed, unresolved, unsettled, unsure, vacillating, vacillatory, vague, wavering

UNDEFINABLE, ***adjective*** esoteric, indefinable, indescribable, indeterminate, indistinct, ineffable, inexplicable, inexpressible, unexplainable, untranslatable, vague

UNDENIABLE, ***adjective*** axiomatic, axiomatical, beyond a doubt, beyond all question, beyond dispute, certain, clear, compelling, conclusive, convincing, demonstrable, established, *evidens,* evident, firm, *haud dubius,* inappealable, incontestable, incontrovertible, indisputable, indubitable, inescapable, infallible, irrefragable, irrefutable, obvious, past dispute, proven, sound, unanswerable, unavoidable, unimpeachable, unquestionable

UNDEPENDABLE, ***adjective*** capricious, careless, changeable, deceitful, dishonest, double-dealing, erratic, fickle, fluctuating, frivolous, inconstant, irresponsible, mercurial, open to error, perfidious, shifty, slippery, tergiversating, timeserving, treacherous, two-faced, uncertain, unpredictable, unreliable, unstable, unsteadfast, unsteady, unsure, untrustworthy, vacillating, variable, wavering

UNDER ARREST, ***noun*** captured, caught, collared, committed, confined, constrained, detained, held, held in custody, immurred, imprisoned, incarcerated, interned, jailed, kept in custody, legally restrained, made captive, made prisoner, remanded, remanded into custody, restrained, seized, sent to prison, taken, taken by force by the authorities, taken into custody

UNDER OATH, ***adjective*** adjure, affirm, allege under oath, assert as true, assure under oath, authenticate under oath, aver, avow, bear witness under oath, bind by oath, certify under oath, confirm under oath, declare under oath, declare solemnly, declare as true under oath, maintain under oath, promise under oath, provide evidence under oath, put one's trust in state, state under oath, vouch, vow under oath

UNDERESTIMATE, ***verb*** belittle, deprecate, depreciate, detract from, discredit, disesteem, disparage, do scant justice to, make light of, minimize, *minoris aestimare, minoris facere,* misjudge, misprize, rate below the true value, rate too low, run down, set at naught, set little store by, slight, think too little of, underprice, underprize, underrate, underreckon, undervalue

UNDERHANDED, ***adjective*** against the rules, backroom, bad, below-the-belt, calculating, clandestine, cloak-and dagger, corrupt, covert, criminal, crooked, cunning, deceitful, designing, dishonest, dishonorable, double-dealing, felonious, furtive, guileful, illegal, illicit, immoral, insidious, malfeasant, perfidious, plotting, scheming, secret, shady, slippery, sly, sneaking, stealthy, surreptitious, treacherous, unauthorized, unconscionable, undercover, underground, underhand, under-the-counter, under-the-table, unfair, unlawful, unobtrusive, unscrupulous, wily, wrong, wrongful

UNDERLYING, ***adjective*** based on, basic, built on, deep-rooted, elemental, elementary, essential, fundamental, latent, not evident, obscure, original, primal, primary, rudimentary, supporting, undermost, unseen
ASSOCIATED CONCEPTS: underlying contract, underlying fact, underlying obligation

UNDERMINE, ***verb*** deaden, debilitate, devitalize, dull, enervate, enfeeble, eviscerate, extenuate, harm, impair, incapacitate, injure, mitigate, negate, rattle, reduce, ruin, sabotage, sap the foundation out of, sap the strength out of, subvert, unnerve, unstrengthen, weaken
ASSOCIATED CONCEPTS: undermine credibility

UNDERSIGNED, ***noun*** attestant, attester, author, covenanter, endorser, petitioner, ratifier, signatory, signer, subscriber, supporter

UNDERSTAND, ***verb*** absorb, apperceive, appreciate, apprehend, assimilate, be apprised, be informed, cognize, comprehend, conceive, conclude, conjecture, deduce, digest, discern, fathom, gather, glean, grasp, infer, *intellegere,* internalize, know, learn, master, perceive, retain, take to mean
ASSOCIATED CONCEPTS: express understanding, want of understanding

UNDERSTANDABLE, ***adjective*** comprehensible, knowable

UNDERSTANDING *(Agreement),* ***noun*** accord, accordance, alliance, arrangement, common view, compact, compliance, concord, concordance, congruence, consentaneity, contract, cooperation, covenant, harmony, likemindedness, meeting of minds, mutual pledge, pact, rapport, unanimity
ASSOCIATED CONCEPTS: express understanding, understanding of the parties
FOREIGN PHRASES: ***Conventio facit legem.*** An agreement creates the law; i.e., the parties to a binding contract will be held to their promises.

UNDERSTANDING *(Comprehension),* ***noun*** apperception, apprehension, assimilation, awareness, conception, discernment, grasp, *ingenium,* insight, intelligence, knowledge, *mens,* mental ability, perception, power to understand, prehension, realization, reason, recognition, sense, wisdom
ASSOCIATED CONCEPTS: intent, want of understanding
FOREIGN PHRASES: ***Sermones semper accipiendi sunt secundum subjectam materiam et conditionem personarum.*** Language is always to be understood according to its subject matter and the condition of the person. ***Probationes debent esse evidentes, id est, perspicuae et faciles intelligi.*** Proofs ought to be evident, that is, clear and easily understood. ***Quod tacite intelligitur deesse non videtur.*** What is tacitly understood does not appear to be wanting.

UNDERSTANDING *(Tolerance),* ***noun*** acceptance, altruism, benevolence, charitableness, compassion, condonation, consideration, empathy, good will, humanity, indulgence, kindliness, lack of prejudice, mercy, patience, sensitivity, sufferance, sympathy, toleration

UNDERSTATEMENT, ***noun*** conservative estimate, grossly inadequate representation, minimization, misrepresentation, underestimation, undervaluation

UNDERTAKE, ***verb*** accept, address oneself to, agree, answer for, apply oneself to, assume, attempt, be answerable for, begin, carry on, carry out, commence, commit, commit oneself to, contract, covenant, devote oneself to, embark upon, endeavor, engage in, enter into, enter upon, execute, go in for, guarantee, *in se recipere,* incur a duty, indent, indenture, initiate, launch, make an effort, obligate oneself, pledge, pledge one's word, promise, pursue, set

about, set in motion, start, strive, *suscipere,* tackle, take in hand, take up, take upon oneself, try, venture, vow
ASSOCIATED CONCEPTS: overt act

UNDERTAKING *(Attempt),* ***noun*** design, effort, plan, purpose, quest, search, task undertaken, trial

UNDERTAKING *(Bond),* ***noun*** pledge, security

UNDERTAKING *(Business),* ***noun*** engagement, enterprise, project, pursuit, task, transaction, venture

UNDERTAKING *(Commitment),* ***noun*** agreement, contract, obligation, pledge

UNDERTAKING *(Enterprise),* ***noun*** adventure, affair, attempt, business, *coeptum,* concern, effort, emprise, endeavor, engagement, essay, exercise, *inceptum,* job, move, occupation, operation, plan, program, project, pursuit, quest, search, task, trial, venture
ASSOCIATED CONCEPTS: joint undertaking

UNDERTAKING *(Pledge),* ***noun*** agreement, assurance, avowal, commitment, compact, contract, covenant, engagement, guarantee, insurance, oath, obligation, parole, pledged word, promise, security, stipulation, troth, vow, warrant, word
ASSOCIATED CONCEPTS: bail undertaking, insufficiency of undertaking, statutory undertaking, undertaking

UNDERWRITE, ***verb*** agree to support, assume a risk, ensure, back, consent to support, countersign, endorse, finance, fund, guarantee, guaranty, insure, pledge, promise, secure, shoulder, sponsor, support, take responsibility, undertake, uphold, vouch for

UNDESIRABLE, ***adjective*** abominable, annoying, bothersome, defective, disadvantageous, disagreeable, disliked, displeasing, distasteful, dreaded, exceptionable, improper, inadvisable, inappropriate, incommodious, inconvenient, ineligible, inexpedient, insufferable, intolerable, loathed, loathsome, objectionable, obnoxious, out of character, out of keeping, outcast, rejected, repellent, repulsive, scorned, shunned, thankless, troublesome, unacceptable, unalluring, unappealing, unapprovable, unattractive, unbecoming, unbefitting, unfit, uninviting, unlikable, unmeet, unpalatable, unpleasant, unpleasing, unpopular, unsatisfactory, unseemly, unsought, unsuitable, unwanted, unwelcome, unwished, unworthy

UNDIMINISHED, ***adjective*** in full force, *indelibatus, inlibatus,* intact, *integer,* not decreased, not lessened, unabated, unallayed, unceasing, uncut, undamaged, undivided, unfaded, unimpaired, unincreased, unlessened, unreduced, unretarded, unsevered, unweakened, unworn, whole, without loss

UNDISCLOSED, ***adjective*** concealed, covert, hidden, invisible, latent, mysterious, occult, sealed, secret, suppressed, tacit, ulterior, unaired, unannounced, unapparent, unbreathed, uncommunicated, unconveyed, undeclared, undetected, undivulged, unexplained, unexposed, unexpressed, unheralded, unimparted, unknown, unmentioned, unproclaimed, unpronounced, unpublicized, unpublished, unrevealed, unsaid, unseen, untalked of, untold, unvoiced
ASSOCIATED CONCEPTS: undisclosed interest, undisclosed principal

UNDISPUTED, ***adjective*** absolute, accepted, acknowledged, assured, axiomatic, believed, beyond doubt, beyond question, certain, *certus,* conclusive, doubtless, *haud dubius,* incontestable, incontrovertible, indisputable, indubitable, irrefragable, irrefutable, past dispute, positive, questionless, trusted, unanswerable, unchallengeable, unchallenged, uncontroversial, undebatable, undeniable, undoubted, unquestioned, without doubt, without question
ASSOCIATED CONCEPTS: undisputed fact

UNDISTORTED, ***adjective*** authentic, direct, exact, faithful, genuine, natural, original, right, scrupulous, straight, true, true to nature, truthful, unbiased, undeviating, undisguised, unembroidered, unexaggerated, unfaked, unfictitious, unjaundiced, unperverted, unprejudiced, unswerving, unwarped, veracious

UNDO, ***verb*** abolish, abrogate, annul, answer, cancel, counteract, counterbalance, countermand, debug, decode, decrypt, defeat, destroy, disestablish, declare null and void, dispense with, eliminate, impeach, invalidate, neutralize, nullify, obviate, offset, put an end to, quash, ravel, remove, repeal, rescind, resolve, retract, reverse, revoke, ruin, terminate, thwart, unravel, untangle, untwist, unweave, vacate, vitiate, worst
ASSOCIATED CONCEPTS: undo charges, undo the law

UNDUE *(Excessive),* ***adjective*** disproportionate, exceeding propriety, excessive, exorbitant, extravagant, extreme, ill-advised, immoderate, *immodicus,* improper, inappropriate, indecorous, inordinate, needless, *nimius,* objectionable, out of bounds, outrageous, overmuch, profuse, superfluous, unbecoming, unbefitting, uncalled-for, undeserved, unfit, unjustified, unmerited, unnecessary, unneeded, unreasonable, unseemly, unsuitable, unwarranted
ASSOCIATED CONCEPTS: undue influence

UNDUE *(Not owing),* ***adjective*** not mature, not yet due, not yet payable, premature, unowed, unseasonable, untimely

UNDUE DELAY, ***noun*** culpability, default, delay, dereliction, dilatoriness, disregard, dutilessness, impropriety, inattention, indifference, laches, laxity, neglect, neglectfulness, negligence, noncompliance, non observance, nonperformance, peccadillo, procrastination, tardiness
ASSOCIATED CONCEPTS: undue delay as cause for a dismissal

UNDUE INFLUENCE, ***noun*** absolutism, arbitrary power, coercion, compulsion, conscription, constraint, despotism, dominance, domination, duress, enforcement, high-pressure methods, impelling, impressment, inducement, insistence, necessitation, predominance, pressure, repression, subjugation
ASSOCIATED CONCEPTS: exertion of undue influence, invalidation of a will

UNDULY, ***adverb*** excessively, exorbitantly, extremely, immoderately, inordinately, intemperately, overly
ASSOCIATED CONCEPTS: unduly harsh criminal sanctions

UNDYING, ***adjective*** abiding, ceaseless, constant, continuing, continuous, deathless, endless, eternal, fadeless, immortal, imperishable, impregnable, incessant, indefatigable, indelible, indestructible, indivisible, ineffaceable, ineradicable, inerasable, inexpugnable, inextinguishable, invulnerable, lasting, never-dying, never-ending, never-fading, nonperishable, permanent, perpetual, persistent, protracted, sustained, unceasing, undiminished, undying, unending, unfading, unremitting, untiring, unwavering

UNEMOTIONAL, ***adjective*** aloof, anesthetized, apathetic, arctic, callous, calm, catatonic, chilly, cold, coldblooded, coldhearted, composed, cool, demure, dispassionate, distant, emotionless, formal, frigid, frosted, frosty, frozen, hardened, heartless, impassive, imperturbable, impervious, indifferent, languid, neutral, nonchalant, obdurate, passionless, reserved, restrained, reticent, sedate, self-absorbed, self-centered, self-controlled, sober, soulless, spiritless, staid, stiff, stoical, thick-skinned, unaffectionate, unexcitable, unfeeling, unimpassioned, unimpressionable, unmoved, unperturbed, unresponsive, unruffled, unstirred, unsusceptible, unsympathetic

UNEMPLOYED, ***adjective*** disengaged, disused, doing nothing, idle, inactive, jobless, leisured, not employed, not working, *otiosus,* out of employment, out of work, unengaged, unoccupied, unused, *vacuus,* without employment, workless
ASSOCIATED CONCEPTS: unemployment insurance

UNEMPLOYMENT INSURANCE, ***noun*** coverage for the unemployed, insurance coverage for the unemployed, promise to pay benefits for the unemployed, unemployment benefits, unemployment compensation

UNENCUMBERED, ***adjective*** clear, disembarrassed, free, no encumbrances, no liens, unburdened, unhampered, unhindered, unimpeded, unobstructed
ASSOCIATED CONCEPTS: title

UNENDURABLE, ***adjective*** displeasing, excessive, extreme, impalatable, impossible, insufferable, intolerable, objectionable, obnoxious, offensive, past bearing, past enduring, unacceptable, unbearable, undesirable, unpalatable, unpleasant, unsavory

UNEQUAL *(Unequivalent),* ***adjective*** different, differing, *dispar,* disparate, disproportionate, dissimilar, *impar, inaequalis,* irregular, unbalanced, uneven, unlike, unmatched
ASSOCIATED CONCEPTS: unequal bargaining powers

UNEQUAL *(Unjust),* ***adjective*** biased, inequitable, influenced, jaundiced, one-sided, partial, prejudiced, prepossessed, unfair, unjustifiable

UNEQUIVOCAL, ***adjective*** absolute, categorical, certain, clear, clear-cut, decided, defined, definite, downright, evident, explicit, forthright, inappealable, incontestable, incontrovertible, indisputable, indubitable, irrefragable, irrefutable, outright, peremptory, plain, positive, straightforward, sure, unambiguous, unanswerable, unchallenged, undeniable, undisputed, unmistakable, unqualified, unquestionable, utter

UNERRING, ***adjective*** accurate, actual, authentic, certain, correct, errorless, exact, factual, faultless, flawless, inerrable, inerrant, not liable to err, on target, on the beam, perfect, positive, precise, real, right, sound, sure, true, unfailing, valid, veracious

UNESSENTIAL, ***adjective*** *adventicius,* dispensable, extraneous, extrinsic, immaterial, inapposite, incidental, inconsequential, inconsiderable, insignificant, irrelevant, meaningless, minor, needless, negligible, nonessential, of no account, of no consequence, secondary, superfluous, trifling, trivial, uncalled-for, unimportant, unnecessary, unneeded
ASSOCIATED CONCEPTS: *minimis*

UNETHICAL, ***adjective*** corrupt, corruptible, dishonest, dishonorable, disreputable, ignoble, immoral, inglorious, questionable, shady, uncommendable, unconscionable, underhanded, unfair, unprincipled, unprofessional, unscrupulous, unworthy, wrong

UNEXPECTED, ***adjective*** abrupt, accidental, astonishing, chance, extemperaneous, extempore, fortuitous, impetuous, impromptu, impulsive, *inexpectatus, insperatus,* instantaneous, precipitate, shocking, startling, subitaneous, sudden, surprising, unannounced, unanticipated, unawaited, uncontemplated, undesigned, unforeseen, unheralded, unintended, unintentional, unlooked for, unpredicted, unpremeditated, unprepared for, unthought of, untimely, unusual

UNEXPIRED TERM, ***noun*** remaining period, remaining time, residual time, surplus time, unelapsed period

UNFAIR, ***adjective*** biased, fraudulent, inequitable, iniquitous, jaundiced, not equitable, one-sided, prejudiced, unequal, uneven, unjust, unprincipled, unreasonable, unsporting, weighted
ASSOCIATED CONCEPTS: unfair advantage, unfair claim practices, unfair competition, unfair labor practices, unfair proceedings, unfair trade

UNFAIR PREJUDICE, ***noun*** evidence that may lead to an unfair decision, excessive prejudice, intolerable prejudice, reversible prejudice, undue prejudice

UNFAVORABLE, ***adjective*** adverse, adversus, antagonistic, bad, calamitous, contrary, damaging, derogatory, deterrent, disadvantageous, disapprobatory, discouraging, disparaging, foul, hopeless, hostile, ill-boding, ill-disposed, ill-omened, impedimental, impedimentary, impedimentive, inadvisable, inappropriate, inauspicious, inclement, inconvenient, indisposed, inexpedient, infelicitous, inhibitive, inimical, *iniquus,* inopportune, malapropos, malign, misfortunate, noxious, ominous, opposed, poor, prejudicial, repugnant, sinister, unfortunate, unfriendly, unlucky, unpromising, unpropitious, unsatisfactory, unsuited, untimely, untoward

UNFIT, ***adjective*** badly qualified, foolish, ill-adapted, ill-advised, impertinent, improper, inadequate, inadvisable, inapplicable, inapposite, inappropriate, inapt, incapable, *incommodus,* incompetent, incongruous, inconvenient, *indignus,* ineligible, inept, inexpedient, inexpert, injudicious, inopportune, inutile, *inutilis,* irrelevant, maladjusted, malapropros, objectionable, out of keeping, out of place, unable, unadapted, unbecoming, unbefitting, undesirable, undue, unequipped, unfitting, unlikely, unprepared, unpromising, unqualified, unseemly, unsuitable, unsuited, unusable, unwise, unworthy, useless, valueless, wrong
ASSOCIATED CONCEPTS: unfit for consumption, unfit for occupancy, unfit parent

UNFLAGGING, ***adjective*** ardent, assiduous, continuing, decided, determined, diligent, earnest, enduring, energetic, faithful, fervent, firm, fixed, gritty, hard, hardworking, immutable, inalterable, indefatigable, indomitable, insistent, intent, invincible, laborious, lasting, loyal, never idle, never-tiring, perseverant, persevering, persistent, persisting, pertinacious, plugging, purposeful, relentless, resolute, resolved, sedulous, single-minded, staunch, steadfast, steady, strenuous, stubborn, tenacious, tireless, undaunted, undeviating, undiscouraged, unfailing, unfaltering, unflinching, unhesitating, uninterrupted, unrelenting, unremitting, unsleeping, unswerving, untiring, unwavering, unwearied, unyielding, vehement, zealous

UNFORESEEABLE, ***adjective*** contrary to expectations, improbable, startling, subitaneous, sudden, surprise, unaccountable, unanticipated, uncertain, unexpected, unintended, unlooked for, unplanned, unprecedented, unpredictable, unpredicted, unprepared for, unthought of, unusual, unwonted
ASSOCIATED CONCEPTS: unforseeable consequences, unforseeable events

UNFORESEEN, ***adjective*** accidental, sudden, surprise, unanticipated, undesigned, unexpected, unheralded, unintended, unpredicted, unthought of
ASSOCIATED CONCEPTS: unforeseen cause, unforeseen difficulties, unforeseen event, unforeseen peril

UNFORESEEN CIRCUMSTANCES, ***adjective*** atypical, different, exceptional, extraordinary, first, first ever, improbable, incomparable, matchless, never before encountered, new, not to be expected, novel, of its own kind, off the beaten track, offbeat, original, out of the ordinary, out of the pale, out-of-the-way, rare, remarkable, sensational, singular, strange, surprising, tremendous, unaccustomed, uncommon, uncustomary, unequaled, unexampled, unexpected, unfamiliar, unheard of, unique, unmatched, unparalleled, unprecedented, unthought-of, unusual

UNFORTUNATE, ***adjective*** bad, bad timing, counterproductive, dire, discommodious, down on one's luck, failed, failing, fatal, fortuneless, fruitless, futile, hapless, hopeless, ill-considered, ill-timed, impolitic, impracticable, impractical, inadvisable, inappropriate, inapt, inauspicious, inconvenient, ineffectual, inefficacious, inexpedient, infelicitous, inopportune, intrusive, jinxed, luckless, malfunctioning, miscarried, miscarrying, mistimed, off-base, ominous, out of luck, pathetic, pitiable, poor, sad, too late, unbefitting, under adverse circumstances, underprivileged, undesirable, unfavorable, unlucky, unprofitable, unpropitious, unseasonable, unseemly, unsuccessful, unsuitable, untimely, unworkable, useless
ASSOCIATED CONCEPTS: Medicaid, welfare

UNFOUNDED, ***adjective*** baseless, empty, erroneous, fabricated, fallacious, false, fictitious, *fictus,* fraudulent, groundless, idle, illogical, insubstantial, invented, spurious, suppositional, supposititious, trumped-up, unattested, unauthenticated, unestablished, ungrounded, unproven, unsubstantial, unsupportable, unsupported, untenable, untrue, unwarranted, *vanus,* without basis, without foundation, without reality, without substance

UNGUARDED *(Direct),* ***adjective*** aboveboard, brash, candid, frank, genuine, honest, indiscreet, open, open and aboveboard, open and sincere, straightforward, up front

UNGUARDED *(Without protection),* ***adjective*** careless, defenseless, derelict, foolish, heedless, helpless, ill-advised, ill-considered, imprudent, inadvertent, inattentive, incautious, inconsiderate, indiscreet, injudicious, insecure, irresponsible, lax, mindless, neglectful, neglecting, negligent, nonobservant, nonrestrictive, permissive, pregnable, relaxed, remiss, slack, unattended, undefended, unfortified, unheeding, unmindful, unobservant, unprotected, unscreened, unsheltered, unshielded, unsuspecting, unthinking, unvigilant, unwarned, unwary, unwatched, unwatchful, unwise, vulnerable, weaponless
ASSOCIATED CONCEPTS: abandonment

UNHEARD OF, ***adjective*** atypical, different, exceptional, exemplary, extraordinary, first, first ever, improbable, incomparable, matchless, never before encountered, new, not to be expected, novel, of its own kind, original, out of the ordinary, out of the pale, out-of-the-way, rare, remarkable, sensational, singular, strange, surprising, tremendous, unaccustomed, uncommon, uncustomary, unequaled, unexampled, unexpected, unfamiliar, unheard of, unique, unknown, unmatched, unparalleled, unprecedented, unthought of, unusual

UNIFORM, ***adjective*** *aequabilis,* alike, compatible, conformable, consistent, consonant, *constans,* constant, conventional, correspondent, equable, equal, even, harmonious, homogeneous, identical, invariable, matched, orderly, orthodox, regular, same, similar, standard, steady, systematic, unaltered, unchanging, undeviating, undiversified, universal, unswerving, unvaried, unvarying, well-matched
ASSOCIATED CONCEPTS: uniform accounting system, Uniform Act, Uniform Commercial Code, Uniform Fiduciaries Act, uniform laws, uniformity of laws, uniform operation of laws, uniform rate of taxation, uniform rates, uniform rule of taxation, uniform sales, uniform taxation

UNIFORMITY, ***noun*** absence of diversity, absence of variation, conformity, consistency, constancy, continuity, equability, evenness, homogeneity, levelness, order, persistence, regularity, singleness, smoothness, stability, standardization, symmetry, unity

UNILATERAL, ***adjective*** independent, lone, not reciprocal, one-sided, single, singular, unaided
ASSOCIATED CONCEPTS: unilateral action, unilateral contract, unilateral mistake

UNIMPEACHABLE, ***adjective*** above reproach, approved, believable, beyond reproach, blameless, commendable, credible, creditable, excellent, faultless, guiltless, ideal, impeccable, incontestable, incontrovertible, inculpable, indefeasable, innocent, irrefragable, irrefutable, irreprehensible, irreproachable, laudable, *locuples,* meritorious, noncontroversial, perfect, questionless, reputable, *sanctus,* sinless, spotless, stainless, unable to be discredited, unassailable, unblamable, unblameworthy, unblemished, uncensurable, unchallengeable, unconfutable, undeniable, undisputed, undoubted, unexceptionable, unmarred, unobjectionable, unquestionable, unrefutable, untainted, upright, worthy

UNINTENTIONAL, ***adjective*** accidental, adventitious, casual, chance, fortuitous, inadvertent, *insciens,* involuntary, purposeless, spontaneous, uncalculated, unconscious, undeliberate, undesigned, unexpected, unforeseen, unintended, unknowing, unmeant, unpremeditated, unpurposeful, unthinking, unwitting
ASSOCIATED CONCEPTS: unintentional act

UNION *(Labor organization),* ***noun*** affiliation, alliance of workers, amalgamation, association, brotherhood, confederacy, consociation, council, federation, fellowship, fraternity, guild, league, organization, organized labor, sodality, trade association
ASSOCIATED CONCEPTS: anti-union animus, craft union, international union, labor union, local union, trade union, union membership, union shop

UNION *(Unity),* ***noun*** accord, accordance, agreement, coalition, coherence, combination, concert, concord, concurrence, *congregatio,* connection, consensus, *consociatio,* consolidation, cooperation, coupling, fusion, harmony, homogeneity, joining, junction, oneness, unification, uniformity, unison

UNIQUE, ***adjective*** anomalous, atypical, beyond comparison, bizarre, curious, different, dissimilar, exceptional, extraordinary, incomparable, individual, matchless, nonpareil, nonuniform, novel, odd, original, peculiar, peerless, rare, single, singular, *singularis,* sole, special, uncommon, unconformable, unequaled, unexampled, *unicus,* unimitated, unmatched, unparalleled, unprecedented, unrepeated, unrivaled, unusual

UNIT *(Department),* ***noun*** branch, division, group, staff

UNIT *(Item),* ***noun*** ace, component, constituent, element, formation, integral, measure, monad, one, part, piece, quantity

UNITE, ***verb*** act in concert, add, affiliate, agglomerate, agree, ally, amalgamate, amass, assemble, assimilate, associate, be one, become one, blend, bring together, cement, centralize, cluster, coact, coalesce, collect, combine, come together, commingle, concur, confederate, conglomerate, congregate, *coniungere,* conjoin, connect, consolidate, consubstantiate, converge, cooperate, coordinate, *copulare,* couple, cowork, entwine, fall in with, form a league, form a single unit, form an alliance, fuse, gather together, group, grow together, harmonize, incorporate, interfuse, join, join forces, league, link, marry, mass, meet, meld, merge, mingle, *miscere,* mix, pool, pull together, reconcile, side with, solidify, syncretize, unify, wed
ASSOCIATED CONCEPTS: join in an action, united in interest

UNITED, ***adjective*** affiliated, allied, amalgamated, associated, attached, banded together, blended, bonded, cemented, coadunate, coexistent, coherent, cohesive, collective, combined, compatible, composite, compound, concerted, concordant, concurrent, conglomerate, conjoint, conjunctive, connected, consolidated, coupled, fused, harmonious, incorporated, indivisible, infrangible, inseparable, interrelated, joined, joint, linked, merged, mutual, one, solid, undivided
ASSOCIATED CONCEPTS: unitary trial, unity of interest, unity of possession, unity of title

UNITY, ***noun*** accordance, affinity, agreement, assent, closeness, coherence, cohesion, community of interests, comradeship, concert, concord, concurrence, congeniality, congruence, congruity, congruousness, consensus, consentaneity, consentaneousness, equivalence, feeling of identity, fellowship, fraternity, friendship, fusion, good feeling, good vibrations, good will, harmony, identity, inseparability, integrality, integration, integrity, kinship, likeness, mutual supportiveness, mutuality, one voice, oneness, rapport, reciprocity, resemblance, sameness, selfsameness, sharing, similarity, similitude, simplicity, singleness, singularity, solidarity, solidification, solidity, team spirit, togetherness, unanimity, understanding, unification, uniformity, union, unison, uniting
ASSOCIATED CONCEPTS: unity of interest, unity of possession, unity of title

UNIVERSAL, ***adjective*** absolute, across-the-board, all-comprehensive, all-embracing, all-encompassing, all-including, all-inclusive, all-pervading, blanket, boundless, broad-based, complete, comprehensive, downright, encyclopedic, endless, every aspect, every facet, exhaustive, general, global, infinite, intensive, international, measureless, omnibus, outright, overall, panoramic, sweeping, the entire gamut, the entire universe, thorough, total, unlimited, unqualified, unrestricted, whole, wholesale, widespread, without exception
ASSOCIATED CONCEPTS: *ius cogens,* universal agar, universal causation, universal representation

UNJUST, ***adjective*** biased, crooked, dishonorable, heinous, immoral, improper, inequitable, influenced, iniquitous, *iniquus, iniurius, iniustus,* interested, jaundiced, partial, prejudiced, prepossessed, undeserved, unequal, unfair, unjustifiable, unmerited, unprincipled, unreasonable, unwarranted, venal, warped, wicked, wrong, wrongful
ASSOCIATED CONCEPTS: unjust decision, unjust enrichment, unjust penalty, unjust sentence

UNJUST ENRICHMENT, ***noun*** improper benefit, improper gain, inequitable benefit, inequitable gain, undeserved gain, unfair betterment, unfair gain, unfair profit, unjustifiable gain, unmerited benefit, wrongful benefit

UNJUSTIFIABLE, ***adjective*** accusable, blameworthy, censurable, chargeable, culpable, discreditable, dishonorable, groundless, impeachable, indefensible, inexcusable, *iniquus, iniurius, iniustus,* irremissible, objectionable, reprehensible, unallowable, unforgivable, unjust, unjustified, unpardonable, unreasonable, vicious, wicked, without excuse, wrong
ASSOCIATED CONCEPTS: unjustifiable cause, unjustifiable claim, unjustifiable deviation

UNKNOWINGLY, ***adverb*** adventitiously, fortuitously, ignorantly, inadvertently, innocently, insensibly, unawares, unconsciously, unintentionally, unmindfully, unsuspectingly, unwittingly, witlessly

UNKNOWN, ***adjective*** alien, anonymous, concealed, cryptic, esoteric, foreign, hidden, incognito, indeterminate, inscrutable, insoluble, insolvable, mysterious, nameless, never experienced before, new, no credit to, novel, obscure, secret, strange, to be announced, unaccounted for, unascertained, undesignated, undetermined, undiscovered, undistinguished, unfamiliar, unfixed, unheard-of, unidentified, uninvestigated, unlabeled, unmeasured, unnamed, unnoted, unnoticed, unpopular, unrenowned, unrevealed, unseen, unset, unsettled, unspecified, unstudied, untold, untraced, untracked, withheld, without a name

UNLAWFUL, ***adjective*** actionable, against the law, contraband, criminal, forbidden, illegal, illegitimate, illicit, *inlicitus,* lawless, *non legitimus,* not allowed by law, outlawed, prohibited, transgressive, unallowed, unauthorized, unconstitutional, unlicensed, unsanctioned, unwarranted, vetitus, wrongful, wrongous
ASSOCIATED CONCEPTS: unlawful accumulation, unlawful act, unlawful assembly, unlawful combination, unlawful contract, unlawful detainer, unlawful detention, unlawful enrichment, unlawful entrapment, unlawful entry, unlawful flight, unlawful force, unlawful picketing
FOREIGN PHRASES: ***Ex pacto illicito non oritur actio.*** From an unlawful agreement, no action will lie.

UNLESS, ***preposition*** except, excepting, however, precluding, save, without

UNLIKE, ***adjective*** alien, contrary, deviative, different, differing, discordant, discrepant, disparate, dissimilar, distinct, distinctive, divergent, diverse, heterogeneous, ill-matched, incongruous, irreconcilable, irrelative, not comparable, opposite, peculiar, unalike, unequal, unidentical, unrelated, unresembling, unsimilar, variant, varied

UNLIMITED, ***adjective*** boundless, endless, free, immeasurable, *immensus,* incalculable, indefinite, inexhaustible, infinite, *infinitus,* interminable, limitless, measureless, perpetual, termless, unbounded, unchecked, unconditional, unconfined, uncontrolled, unending, unfathomable, universal, unrestrained, unrestricted, untold, vast, without number
ASSOCIATED CONCEPTS: unlimited liability

UNMANAGEABLE *(Cumbersome),* ***adjective*** awkward, beyond control, bulky, difficult, impractical, incommodious, inconvenient, not disciplined, out of hand, uncomfortable, ungainly, unhandy, unruly

UNMANAGEABLE *(Defiant),* ***adjective*** incorrigible, indocile, indomitable, insuppressible, irascible, irrepressible, obstreperous, out of hand, rebellious, recalcitrant, refractory, resistant, resisting, uncontrollable, uncooperative, ungovernable, unreconstructed, untamable, unyielding

UNMARKETABLE, ***adjective*** not readily salable, nonsalable, unsalable, unvendible
ASSOCIATED CONCEPTS: unmarketable title

UNMISTAKABLE, ***adjective*** apparent, autoptic, autoptical, bald, certain, clear, conclusive, conspicuous, decided, defined, distinct, distinguishable, evident, explicit, express, glaring, identifiable, indubitable, intelligible, known, lucid, manifest, notorious, obvious, open, overt, palpable, patent, perspicuous, plain, positive, pronounced, recognizable, sure, unambiguous, unconcealed, unconfusing, uncontestable, undeniable, undisguised, undoubted, unequivocal, unquestionable, visible, well-defined

UNMITIGATED, ***adjective*** absolute, complete, consummate, downright, exhaustive, full, intensive, plenary, rank, rigid, severe, sheer, stark, thorough, unbounded, unconditional, unqualified, unsoftened, unsuppressed, untamed, untempered, unyielding, utter

UNNECESSARY, ***adjective*** auxiliary, avoidable, dispensable, excess, excessive, expendable, expletive, extra, extraneous, extrinsic, gratuitous, inessential, irrelevant, needless, *non necessarius,* noncompulsory, optional, overmuch, redundant, spare, supererogative, supererogatory, superfluous, *supervacaneus, supervacuus,* supplemental, supplementary, surplus, uncalled-for, uncritical, unessential, unimportant, unneeded, unrequired
ASSOCIATED CONCEPTS: unnecessary force

UNOBJECTIONABLE, ***adjective*** acceptable, adequate, admissible, allowable, condonable, defensible, harmless, inoffensive, irreprehensible, irreproachable, irreprovable, passable, satisfactory, tolerable, unblameworthy, uncensurable, unexceptionable, unimpeachable, vindicable

UNOBTRUSIVE, ***adjective*** clandestine, covert, humble, meek, modest, natural, passive, quiet, reserved, restrained, reticent, retiring, self-effacing, shrinking, simple, subdued, surreptitious, unassuming, unconspicuous, undercover, underground, unimposing, unostentatious, unseen

UNOFFICIAL, ***adjective*** casual, informal, not to be quoted, off the record, personal, unauthoritative, unauthorized, unendorsed, without authority, without ceremony
ASSOCIATED CONCEPTS: unofficial ruling

UNORTHODOX, ***adjective*** *a ceteris dissentire,* aberrant, anomalous, deviative, different, divergent, eccentric, heretical, heterodox, irregular, lawless, out of step, unaccepted, unapproved, uncanonical, uncommon, unconformable, unconventional, unfashionable, unobservant, unusual

UNPAID, ***adjective*** due, free, given, gratis, gratuitous, in arrears, outstanding, owing, payable, uncollected, uncompensated, undischarged, unrecompensed, unremunerated, unrequited, unrewarded, unsalaried, unsettled, volunteer

UNPALATABLE, ***adjective*** abrasive, bitter, disagreeable, dislikable, displeasing, distasteful, foul-tasting, hostile, ill-flavored, inedible, noisome, objectionable, obnoxious, offensive, rancid, repellent, repelling, repugnant, repulsive, revolting, savorless, sour, unappealing, unappetizing, undesirable, unfriendly, uninviting, unlikable, unpleasant, unpleasing, unsavory, unwelcome

UNPARALLELED, ***adjective*** best, beyond compare, beyond comparison, cardinal, exceptional, extraordinary, incomparable, inestimable, inimitable, invaluable, isolated, leading, major, marvelous, matchless, nonconforming, nonpareil, outstanding, paramount, peerless, phenomenal, premium, prime, prodigious, rare, remarkable, singular, special, stupendous, superior, superlative, unapproachable, uncommon, unequaled, unexampled, unexcelled, unheard of, unique, unmatched, unparagoned, unprecedented, unrivaled, unsurpassed, unusual, without parallel, wonderful

UNPOLITIC, ***adjective*** careless, clumsy, foolish, harebrained, hasty, heedless, ill-advised, ill-judged, impolitic, improvident, imprudent, incautious, inconsiderate, indiscreet, inexpedient, injudicious, rash, reckless, senseless, stupid, tactless, temerarious, undiplomatic, unsagacious, unshrewd, untactful, unwary, unwise

UNPRECEDENTED, ***adjective*** anomalous, exceptional, extraordinary, first, *inauditus,* incomparable, initial, miraculous, modern, new, newfangled, novel, *novus,* original, rare, singular, uncustomary, unequaled, unexampled, unexpected, unfamiliar, unheard of, unique, unknown, unmatched, unparalleled, unrivaled, untraditional, unusual

UNPREDICTABLE, ***adjective*** aberrant, arbitrary, capricious, causeless, changeable, changeful, deviative, eccentric, erratic, fanciful, fickle, fitful, incalculable, inconstant, irregular, mercurial, mutable, random, spasmodic, speculative, unaccountable, uncertain, undependable, uneven, unexpected, unforeseeable, unmethodical, unreliable, unstable, unsteadfast, unsteady, unsure, unsystematic, variable, vicissitudinous, wavering

UNPREJUDICED, ***adjective*** broadminded, detached, disinterested, dispassionate, equitable, even-handed, fair, fairminded, impartial, independent, *integer,* judicial, just, neutral, nonpartisan, objective, open, openminded, proper, reasonable, tolerant, unbiased, unbigoted, uncolored, uninfluenced, unjaundiced, unprepossessed, unslanted, unswayed, unwarped
ASSOCIATED CONCEPTS: right to fair trial

UNPREMEDITATED, ***adjective*** extemporaneous, extempore, hasty, impromptu, improvisate, improvised, impulsive, indeliberate, not intended, offhand, rash, snap, spontaneous, thoughtless, uncalculated, unconsidered, undesigned, unintended, unintentional, unmeant, unplanned, unprepared, unpurposeful, unrehearsed, unstudied, unthinking
ASSOCIATED CONCEPTS: manslaughter, unpremeditated murder

UNPRETENTIOUS, ***adjective*** artless, humble, *inadfectatus,* informal, matter of fact, meek, modest, *modicus,* natural, plain, quiet, retiring, simple, *simplex,* unaffected, unassuming, undistinguished, unelaborate, unobtrusive, unostentatious, without airs

UNPRODUCTIVE, ***adjective*** abortive, arid, barren, doomed, dry, effete, exhausted, fallow, fruitless, futile, impotent, ineffectual, inefficacious, inefficient, infecund, *infecundus,* infertile, inoperative, issueless, jejune, nugatory, otiose, profitless, sterile, *sterilis,* unavailing, unfruitful, unprofitable, unprolific, unremunerative, unrewarding, unsuccessful, unyielding, useless, wasteful, without results, worthless

UNPROFESSIONAL, ***adjective*** amateurish, contrary to professional ethics, improper, imprudent, inappropriate, indiscreet, injudicious, nonexpert, not of high standards, unbefitting, unbusinesslike, undignified, unethical, unfitting, unscholarly, unseemly, unsuitable
ASSOCIATED CONCEPTS: Code of Professional Responsibility, disbarment, grievance committee, unprofessional conduct

UNPROPITIOUS, ***adjective*** adverse, hopeless, ill-disposed, ill-omened, ill-timed, inauspicious, minatory, ominous, sinister, threatening, unfavorable, unfortunate, unpromising, untoward

UNQUALIFIED *(Not competent),* ***adjective*** deficient, disqualified, ill-qualified, inadequate, incapable, incompetent, ineffective, inefficient, ineligible, inept, inexperienced, inexpert, unable, unadapted, uneffective, unequipped, unfit, unprepared, unready, unsuited
ASSOCIATED CONCEPTS: unqualified opinion

UNQUALIFIED *(Unlimited),* ***adjective*** absolute, all-encompassing, boundless, complete, consummate, downright, full, illimitable, immoderate, limitless, measureless, not modified, outright, plenary, *summus,* sweeping, total, unbound, unchecked, unconditional, unconstrained, uncontrolled, unmitigated, unmodified, unreserved, unrestrained, unrestricted, unsparing, unstinted, utter
ASSOCIATED CONCEPTS: unqualified acceptance, unqualified ownership

UNQUESTIONABLE, ***adjective*** above criticism, above reproach, absolute, authoritative, believable, beyond all question, certain, clear, conclusive, decided, definite, definitive, doubtless, evident, ideal, incontrovertible, indisputable, indubitable, irrefutable, irreprehensible, irreproachable, irresponsible to question, manifest, obvious, patent, plausible, real, realistic, reliable, self-evident, sure, unassailable, unchallenged, uncontestable, undeniable, undisputed, undoubted, unimpeachable, unmistakable
ASSOCIATED CONCEPTS: that cannot be impeached, unquestionable integrity

UNREASONABLE, ***adjective*** absurd, asinine, capricious, contorted, contrary, exaggerated, excessive, exorbitant, extravagant, extreme, foolish, groundless, ill-advised, ill-judged, illogical, immoderate, *iniquus,* indefensible, injudicious, inordinate, intemperate, irrational, ludicrous, nonsensical, pervicacious, pointless, preposterous, recalcitrant, ridiculous, senseless, twisted, undue, unfair, unjust, unjustifiable, unsensible, unsound, untenable, unwarranted, unwise
ASSOCIATED CONCEPTS: arbitrary and capricious action, unreasonable delay, unreasonable force, unreasonable rate of interest, unreasonable restraint, unreasonable restraint on alienation, unreasonable search, unreasonable use

UNREFUTABLE, ***adjective*** accurate, certain, demonstrated, doubtless, factual, inappealable, incontestable, incontrovertible, indisputable, indubitable, irrefragable, irrefutable, positive, proved, proven, sure, true, unanswerable, unconfutable, uncontroversial, undeniable, unequivocal, unimpeachable, unquestionable, valid, veracious, veritable

UNRELATED, ***adjective*** alien, different, differing, discrepant, disparate, dissimilar, diverse, extraneous, foreign, heterogeneous, incomparable, incompatible, incongruous, independent, irrelative, irrelevant, mismatched, separate, strange, unaffiliated, unallied, unassociated, unattached, unconformable, unconnected, ungermane, unlike, unmatched
ASSOCIATED CONCEPTS: unrelated claims

UNRELENTING, ***adjective*** adamant, austere, ceaseless, constant, continual, continuous, cruel, determined, diligent, endless, enduring, hard, *immitis,* implacable, incessant, inclement, indefatigable, *inexorabilis,* inexorable, inflexible, merciless, obdurate, perseverant, persevering, persistent, pertinacious, pitiless, relentless, remorseless, resolved, rigid, rigorous, ruthless, sedulous, severe, steadfast, stern, stubborn, tenacious, unappeasable, unbending, uncompassionate, uncompromising, undeviating, unforgiving, unmerciful, unpitying, unsoftening, unsparing, unsympathetic, unwavering, unyielding

UNRELIABLE, ***adjective*** capricious, changeful, deceitful, faithless, fallible, false, fickle, inconstant, insecure, irresponsible, perfidious, precarious, shifty, tergiversating, treacherous, two-faced, undependable, unpredictable, unsound, unstable, unsteady, untrue, untrustworthy, vacillating, wavering
ASSOCIATED CONCEPTS: unreliable evidence, unreliable testimony, unreliable witness

UNREMITTING, ***adjective*** *adsiduus,* assiduous, ceaseless, constant, continual, continuous, *continuus,* diligent, durable, enduring, incessant, indefatigable, perennial, perpetual, perseverant, persevering, persistent, pertinacious, sedulous, tenacious, unabated, unbroken, unceasing, unchanging, unfailing, unintermittent, uninterrupted, unshifting, unswerving, untiring, unvarying, unwearied

UNREQUITED, ***adjective*** thankless, unacknowledged, unanswered, uncompensated, unrecompensed, unremunerated, unrepaid, unreturned, unrewarded

UNRESPONSIVE, ***adjective*** aloof, cold, cool, dispassionate, elusive, emotionless, evasive, impassive, inattentive, indifferent, insensitive, irresponsive, laconic, mum, mute, pitiless, reserved, reticent, secretive, taciturn, unanswering, uncommunicative, uncompassionate, unconcerned, unconversable, uncooperative, unemotional, unfeeling, unimpressible, unimpressionable, uninfluenceable, uninterested, unmoved, unreacting, unreplying, unresponding, unsociable, unsympathetic

ASSOCIATED CONCEPTS: evasive contempt, unresponsive answer, unresponsive testimony

UNRESTRAINED *(Not in custody),* ***adjective*** free, independent, unbounded, unbridled, unchecked, unconfined, unconstrained, uncurbed, unencumbered, unfettered, unhampered, unhindered, unimpeded, unlimited, unobstructed, unprevented, unshackled, unsuppressed, untrammeled

UNRESTRAINED *(Not repressed),* ***adjective*** dissolute, effusive, excessive, extravagant, immoderate, incontinent, intemperate, lawless, lewd, libertine, licentious, loose, prodigal, rampant, spirited, unbridled, unchecked, unconstrained, uncontrolled, uncurbed, undisciplined, unfettered, ungoverned, unhampered, unhindered, unlimited, unreined, unrepressed, unreserved, unsuppressed, wanton, wild

UNRESTRICTED, ***adjective*** boundless, *effrenatus,* free, immoderate, independent, limitless, open, permitted, unbound, unbounded, unbridled, unchecked, unconditional, unconfined, unconstrained, uncontained, uncontrolled, unfettered, unforbidden, unlimited, unobstructed, unqualified, unrestrained, unshackled, untrammeled, without strings
ASSOCIATED CONCEPTS: unrestricted use

UNRULY, ***adjective*** chaotic, contrary, contumacious, disobedient, disorderly, *effrenatus, ferox,* fractious, froward, hard to control, headstrong, incorrigible, indocile, insubordinate, intractable, irrepressible, lawless, mutinous, obstinate, obstreperous, out of control, perverse, rampant, rebellious, recalcitrant, refractory, resistive, restive, riotous, rowdy, stormy, stubborn, troublesome, turbulent, unbridled, uncompliant, uncomplying, uncontrollable, uncurbed, ungovernable, unmanageable, unrestrained, unsubmissive, untoward, unyielding, wanton, wayward, wild, willful

UNSATISFACTORY, ***adjective*** deficient, disagreeable, disappointing, disapproved, displeasing, disquieting, distressing, disturbing, faulty, feeble, imperfect, inadequate, inappropriate, inapt, inept, inexpedient, inferior, insufficient, intolerable, lame, *non idoneus,* not up to par, objectionable, offensive, poor, rejected, unacceptable, unapt, unbefitting, undesirable, unfavorable, unfit, ungratifying, unpleasant, unsatisfying, unseemly, unsuitable, untoward, unwelcome, unworthy, upsetting, useless, vexing, wanting, weak
ASSOCIATED CONCEPTS: unsatisfactory testimony

UNSATISFIED *(Delinquent),* ***adjective*** due, due and owing, in arrears, outstanding, payable, uncollected, unfilled, unpaid
ASSOCIATED CONCEPTS: unsatisfied judgment funds, unsatisfied judgments

UNSATISFIED *(Disappointed),* ***adjective*** despondent, discontented, disgruntled, displeased, dissatisfied, frustrated, greedy, insatiable, insatiate, malcontented, quenchless, thwarted, ungratified, unhappy, unquenchable, unslaked

UNSAVORY, ***adjective*** disagreeable, disgusting, disliked, distasteful, intolerable, loathsome, mawkish, nasty, nauseating, nauseous, objectionable, obnoxious, offensive, repelling, repugnant, revolting, sickening, unalluring, unappetizing, unattractive, undelectable, undesirable, uninviting, unpalatable, unpleasant, unpleasing

UNSCRUPULOUS, ***adjective*** base, conscienceless, corrupt, crooked, deceitful, dishonest, dishonorable, disingenuous, faithless, false, fraudulent, immoral, inequitable, iniquitous, lawless, perfidious, profligate, questionable, roguish, ruthless, shifty, sly, treacherous, two-faced, underhand, unethical, unfair, unjust, unlawful, unprincipled, unrestrained, vicious, villainous, wanton, wicked, without integrity, without scruples, wrongful

UNSEEMLY, ***adjective*** base, boorish, coarse, crude, discreditable, disreputable, distasteful, gross, ignoble, improper, in bad taste, inappropriate, incongruous, incorrect, indecent, indecorous, *indecorus,* indelicate, inelegant, offensive, out of character, out of place, preposterous, reprehensible, rude, shameful, unapt, unbecoming, unbefitting, undignified, undue, unfit, unfitting, ungenteel, unhandsome, unmanly, unmeet, unpraiseworthy, unpresentable, unrefined, unsightly, unsuitable, untasteful, vulgar, wrong

UNSETTLED, ***adjective*** adrift, afloat, agitated, capricious, changeable, changing, conjectural, deranged, desolate, disarranged, disputable, disturbed, doubtful, dubious, due, fickle, *incertus, inconstans,* inconstant, migratory, mutable, nervous, new, open, outstanding, owing, pending, perturbed, restless, speculative, tentative, transient, troubled, unadjusted, unattached, unbalanced, uncertain, unchartered, uncollected, undecided, undetermined, uneasy, unessayed, unexplored, unfixed, uninhabited, unnerved, unoccupied, unpaid, unresolved, unrooted, unstable, unstaid, unsteady, untried, untrodden, unventured, upset, vacillating, *varius,* wandering, wavering

UNSOLICITED, ***adjective*** complimentary, free, gratuitous, offered, proffered, unasked, unbidden, uncalled-for, undesired, uninvited, unrequested, unsought, unwanted, unwelcome, unwished, voluntary, volunteered
ASSOCIATED CONCEPTS: unsolicited response, unsolicited sale

UNSOUND *(Fallacious),* ***adjective*** absurd, defective, disputable, erroneous, false, faulty, groundless, ill-founded, illogical, improbable, incongruous, incorrect, insubstantial, invalid, irrational, mistaken, questionable, senseless, sophistical, speculative, unauthentic, ungrounded, unreal, unreasonable, unreasoned, unsubstantial, untenable, untrue, unwarranted, worthless, wrong

UNSOUND *(Not strong),* ***adjective*** below par, broken, decayed, decrepit, defective, deficient, deranged, deteriorated, diseased, disturbed, exhausted, faulty, feeble, ill, impaired, imperfect, infirm, insecure, insolvent, precarious, sickly, tainted, unbacked, unhealthy, unreliable, unsafe, unsettled, unstable, unsteady, unsubstantial, untrustworthy, unwell, warped, wasted, weak, worn

UNSPECIFIED, ***adjective*** anonymous, general, generic, indefinable, indefinite, indeterminate, indistinct, nonspecific, obscure, unacknowledged, unclear, undefined, undesignated, unfixed, unnamed, unsettled, vague

UNSUFRUCTARY RIGHT, ***noun*** a right to enjoy the property of another, right of nonowner to use an asset of another, right to use property of another, right to use property without ownership
ASSOCIATED CONCEPTS: riparian right

UNSUITABLE, ***adjective*** absurd, *alienus,* amiss, awkward, conflicting, contrary, discordant, discrepant, disparate, dissonant, disturbing, divergent, ill-adapted, impertinent,

improper, imprudent, in bad taste, inadequate, inadmissible, inadvisable, inapplicable, inapposite, inappropriate, inapt, incommodious, *incommodus,* incompatible, incongruous, inconvenient, indecorous, inexpedient, infelicitous, inharmonious, inopportune, intolerable, irrelevant, malapropos, mismatched, objectionable, out of character, out of keeping, out of place, poorly adapted, unacceptable, unapt, unbecoming, unbeseeming, uncongenial, undesirable, unfavorable, unfit, unfitting, unfortunate, unsatisfactory, unsatisfying, unseasonable, unseemly, unsuited, untimely, untoward
ASSOCIATED CONCEPTS: unsuitable for consumption

UNSUPPORTED, *adjective* based on conjecture, baseless, groundless, not authenticated, not established, not substantiated, suppositional, supposititious, unabetted, unaided, unassisted, unattested, unauthenticated, unbacked, uncertified, uncollaborated, unconfirmed, uncorroborated, undemonstrated, unfounded, unproved, unproven, unseconded, unsubstantiated, unsustained, untenable, unvalidated, unverified, without basis, without foundation
ASSOCIATED CONCEPTS: unsupported by a preponderance of the evidence

UNSURE, *adjective* ambiguous, ambivalent, between, betwixt, chancy, changeable, constrained, dicey, doubtful, doubting, dubious, equivocal, fickle, hesitant, hesitating, holding back, indecisive, indemonstrable, irresolute, not certain, not decided, not definitive, not resolved, not sure, of two minds, on the fence, precarious, provisional, shaky, skeptical, suspicious, tentative, unaccountable, uncountable, undecided, unpredictable, unsteady, unsubstantial, up in the air, wavering
ASSOCIATED CONCEPTS: unsure of guilt

UNSURPASSED, *adjective* absolute, best, beyond comparison, beyond praise, cardinal, consummate, dazzling, dominant, excellent, exceptional, incomparable, infallible, inimitable, leading, matchless, *ne plus ultra,* paramount, peerless, premium, primary, prime, second to none, superior, superlative, supreme, the acme, transcendent, unapproachable, unequaled, unexampled, unexcelled, unique, unmatched, unparagoned, unparalleled, unrivaled, without equal, without parallel

UNSUSPECTING, *adjective* believing, credulous, easily deceived, gullible, *incautus,* innocent, naive, off guard, simple, trustful, trusting, unaware, unconscious, undoubting, unexpectant, unguarded, unquestioning, unsuspecting, unsuspicious, unwarned, without suspicion

UNSUSTAINABLE, *adjective* baseless, controvertible, doubtful, erroneous, false, groundless, incorrect, insupportable, questionable, unauthentic, unconfirmable, undemonstrable, unmaintainable, unprovable, untenable, untrue, untrustworthy, unverifiable, wrong

UNTENABLE, *adjective* accessible, baseless, controvertible, defenseless, erroneous, exposed, fallacious, false, faulty, groundless, hollow, illogical, implausible, incapable of being defended, incapable of being held, incapable of being maintained, incorrect, indefensible, insupportable, invalid, irrational, powerless, pregnable, questionable, refutable, ridiculous, specious, undefended, undemonstrable, unfortified, unguarded, unjustifiable, unmaintainable, unprotected, unreasonable, unsound, unsustainable, unwarrantable, vincible, vulnerable, weak, wrong

UNTIL, *adverb* as far as, by the time that, down to, pending, til, to, to the time when, up to, up to the time of

UNTIMELY, *adjective* anachronic, anachronistic, anachronous, badly timed, erroneous in date, ill-advised, ill-considered, ill-timed, *immaturus,* improper, imprudent, inapposite, inappropriate, inappropriately timed, inauspicious, inconvenient, infelicitous, inopportune, *intempestivus,* malapropos, misjudged, mistimed, out of keeping, out of place, poorly timed, unfavorable, unpromising, unpropitious, unpunctual, unseasonable, unsuitably timed

UNTROUBLED, *adjective* balanced, calm, collected, composed, controlled, cool, dispassionate, easygoing, even-tempered, impassive, imperturbable, in control, laid-back, level-headed, mellow, peaceful, placid, poised, rational, reasonable, relaxed, self-controlled, sensible, steady, unbothered, undisturbed, unemotional, unexcited, unflappable, unflustered, unimpassioned, unmoved, unperturbed, unruffled, unstirred

UNTRUE, *adjective* all wrong, amiss, apocryphal, awry, bogus, contradictory, contrary to fact, counterfeit, deceitful, deceiving, deceptive, defective, delusive, devoid of truth, dishonest, disingenuous, disloyal, disobedient, duplicitous, errant, erring, erroneous, faithless, fake, faked, fallacious, false, false-principled, *falsus,* faulty, fictitious, flawed, forged, fraudulent, groundless, guileful, hypocritical, in error, inaccurate, inconstant, incorrect, incredulous, insidious, insincere, invalid, invented, lying, mendacious, miscalculated, misleading, misrepresentative, mistaken, mock, not true, off base, perfidious, perverse, perverted, prevaricating, recreant, scheming, sham, shifty, spurious, traitorous, treacherous, treasonable, trumped up, truthless, two-faced, uncandid, underhanded, undutiful, unfaithful, unfounded, ungrounded, unorthodox, unproved, unreal, unsound, unsubstantial, untrustworthy, unveracious, wrong
ASSOCIATED CONCEPTS: liable, slander

UNTRUSTWORTHY, *adjective* capricious, changeable, conniving, deceitful, deceptive, dishonest, dishonorable, disloyal, double-dealing, faithless, fallible, false, fickle, fly-by-night, fraudulent, frivolous, illusive, inconstant, insecure, insidious, irresponsible, mercurial, perfidious, precarious, questionable, shifty, slippery, tergiversating, treacherous, two-faced, unauthenticated, uncertain, undependable, unfaithful, unreliable, unsafe, unsound, unstable, unsteadfast, untrue, unworthy of confidence, unworthy of trust, variable, wavering

UNUSUAL, *adjective* aberrant, abnormal, alien, amazing, anomalous, astonishing, astounding, atypical, bizarre, choice, conspicuous, curious, different, distinctive, distinguished, exceptional, extraordinary, extreme, fantastic, fresh, important, incomparable, inconceivable, inconsistent, incredible, indescribable, individual, infrequent, inusitate, irregular, little-known, marked, marvelous, matchless, memorable, modern, new, newfangled, nonpareil, notable, noteworthy, novel, occasional, odd, offbeat, original, out of the ordinary, outlandish, outstanding, particular, peculiar, peerless, phenomenal, portentous, prodigious, prominent, radical, rare, refreshing, remarkable, scarce, significant, singular, special, startling, strange, striking, supernormal, surprising, unaccustomed, unclassifiable, uncommon, unconventional, uncustomary, unequaled, unexpected, unfamiliar, unhabitual, unheard of, unique, unmatched, unnatural, unorthodox, unparalleled, unprecedented, unprevalent, unrivaled, unroutine, untraditional, untypical, unwonted
ASSOCIATED CONCEPTS: cruel and unusual punishment

UNVEIL, *verb* *aperire,* bare, begin, bring to light, demonstrate, denude, *detegere,* disclose, display, divest, divulge, exhibit, expose, extract, lay open, make known, make plain, make visible, manifest, open up, originate, present, reveal, show, start, strip, uncase, uncloak, unconceal, uncover, uncurtain, undrape, undress, unfold, unmask, unrobe, unseal, unwrap

UNVERSED, *adjective* ignorant, illiterate, *imperitus,* inexperienced, inexpert, raw, *rudis,* unacquainted, unclever, unconversant, undisciplined, undrilled, uneducated, unexercised, unfamiliar, unindoctrinated, uninformed, uninitiated, unknowing, unknowledgeable, unlearned, unlettered, unpracticed, unprepared, unproficient, unqualified, unread, unschooled, unskilled, unstudied, untaught

UNWARRANTED, *adjective* arbitrary, baseless, excessive, fulsome, groundless, immoderate, improper, indefensible, inexcusable, inordinate, needless, objectionable, outrageous, overmuch, superabundant, superfluous, supernumerary, unauthorized, uncalled-for, unconscionable, undue, unentitled, unfair, unfounded, unjust, unjustifiable, unjustified, unlawful, unnecessary, unreasonable, unsanctioned, unwarrantable, wrongful

UNWILLING, *adjective* adverse, against, diametrically opposed, disagreeing, disinclined, disobedient, dissenting, forced, independent of one's will, indisposed, involuntary, loathe, not opposed, reluctant, renitent, resistant, unconscious, unintentional, unthinking, unwilled, unwitting, willingly
ASSOCIATED CONCEPTS: contumacious witness, hostile witness, unwilling witness

UNWILLINGLY, *adverb* adversely, demurringly, indisposedly, involuntarily, recalcitrantly, reluctantly, unconsentingly, without assent, without consent
ASSOCIATED CONCEPTS: unknowingly

UNWISE, *adjective* detrimental, disadvantageous, fatuous, foolish, ill-advised, ill-considered, ill-contrived, ill-devised, ill-judged, ill-managed, illogical, impolitic, imprudent, inadvisable, inane, inappropriate, inapt, incongruous, inept, inexpedient, injudicious, insensate, irrational, misadvised, reckless, senseless, short-sighted, stupid, thoughtless, unfit, unintelligent, unpolite, unreasonable, unreasoning, unsound, unthinking

UNWITTING, *adjective* accidental, adventitious, aimless, blind, chance, fortuitous, ignorant, inadvertent, *insciens, inscius,* involuntary, purposeless, thoughtless, unapprized, unaware, unconscious, undesigned, unexpected, uninformed, unintended, unintentional, unknowing, unmeant, unmindful, unpremeditated, unpurposed, unsuspecting, unthinking

UNWORKABLE, *adjective* effort-wasting, impossible, impracticable, impractical, inadequate, incapable of being done, inconceivable, ineffective, ineffectual, inefficacious, infeasible, inoperable, insurmountable, otiose, out of the question, useless, unachievable, unattainable, undoable, unfeasible, unnegotiable, unobtainable, unperformable, unrealizable, unviable

UNWORTHY, *adjective* base, contemptible, inferior, lacking worth, meager, meritless, not fit, undeserving, unfit, unqualified, worthless

UNYIELDING, *adjective* adamant, adamantine, constant, decided, dedicated, determined, devoted, enduring, faithful, firm, fixed, hard, headstrong, immobile, immovable, impliant, indomitable, inductile, inexorable, inflexible, intractable, intransigent, invariable, obdurate, obstinate, opinionated, perseverant, persevering, persistent, pertinacious, perverse, pervicacious, recalcitrant, refractory, relentless, renitent, resisting, resolute, resolved, rigid, sedulous, set, settled, solid, stable, stanch, steadfast, steady, stern, stiff, strong, stubborn, tenacious, tough, true, unbending, unchangeable, uncompromising, uncontrollable, undeviating, ungovernable, unimpressible, uninfluenceable, unmanageable, unpliable, unwavering, wayward, willful, zealous

UPBRAID, *verb* admonish, berate, blame, blast, call on the carpet, call to account, castigate, censure, chastise, chew out, chide, condemn, correct, criticize, curse, decry, denounce, denunciate, fulminate against, give a piece of one's mind, give a tongue-lashing, have harsh words with, indict, inveigh against, lash, lay out in lavender, lecture, objurgate, rail against, rake over the coals, rap on the knuckles, read the riot act, rebuke, remonstrate, reprehend, reprimand, reproach, reprobate, reprove, revile, scold, set straight, straighten out, take a hard line with, take to task, tell off, vilify, vilipend

UPHEAVAL, *noun* blowup, break, chaos, collapse, convulsion, disorder, disquiet, disruption, eruption, explosion, furor, hurricane, insurrection, irruption, quake, rebellion, revolt, revolution, sudden change, tempest, tornado, tumult, unrest
ASSOCIATED CONCEPTS: terrorism

UPHOLD, *verb* accept, acknowledge, advocate, affirm, agree with, aid, approve, assert, assist, authenticate, back, back up, bear up, bolster, brace, buttress, carry, champion, confirm, corroborate, countenance, decide in favor of, defend, elevate, encourage, endorse, espouse, favor, guard, help, hold up, justify, keep, maintain, perpetuate, preserve, prop, protect, raise, sanction, second, speak for, stand by, stand up for, stay, *substantiate,* support, sustain, *sustentare,* upraise, vindicate, warrant
ASSOCIATED CONCEPTS: uphold a decision, uphold the law

UPKEEP, *noun* aid, backing, care, caregiving, caring, economic support, endowment, fosterage, life support, maintenance, nourishment, nurturance, operating costs, preservation, provision, relief, safekeeping, subsidization, subsidy, subsistence, support, support services, sustenance, sustentation, total support, welfare
ASSOCIATED CONCEPTS: maintenance

UPRIGHT, *adjective* aboveboard, candid, circumspect, conscientious, erect, estimable, ethical, fair, forthright, good, guileless, highly principled, honest, *honestus,* honorable, incorruptible, *integer,* just, laudable, legitimate, moral, *probus,* pure, reasonable, reputable, respectable, righteous, scrupulous, square, straightforward, trustworthy, truthful, uncorrupt, unimpeachable, upstanding, veracious, virtuous, worthy

UPRISING, *noun* anarchy, chaos, civil disorder, coup d'etat, fighting in the streets, general uprising, insurgence, insurgency, insurrection, mass confusion, mutiny, outbreak, overthrow, rebellion, resistance, revolt, revolution, riot, rise, upheaval

UPROAR, *noun* ado, affray, agitation, bedlam, blowup, bluster, boiling, brawl, brouhaha, chaos, clamor, commotion, conflict, disorder, disruption, disturbance, embroilment, fracas, furor, hullabaloo, pandemonium, ruckus, scuffle, struggle, tumult, turbulence, turmoil

UPSET, *verb* agitate, beat, bother, capsize, confuse, conquer, crush, defeat, demolish, derange, destroy, disarrange, discomfit, discompose, disconcert, disorganize, displace, disquiet, distress, disturb, embarrass, enrage, *evertere,* fluster, invert, overpower, overthrow, overturn, overwhelm, perturb, put out of order, quash, reverse, ruin, shock, startle, subvert, *subvertere,* supersede, tip over, topple, tumble, turn upside down, undo, unnerve, unsettle, upend, vanquish, worst
ASSOCIATED CONCEPTS: upset a lower court's ruling

URGE, *verb* activate, adjure, advance, advise, advocate, appeal to, beg, beseech, coax, drive, encourage, entreat, evoke, exhort, expostulate, goad, hurry, impel, *impellere,* implore, importune, *incitare,* incite, insist, instigate, invite, motivate, move, persuade, prescribe, press, prevail upon, prod, promote, prompt, propel, provoke, push, recommend, request, rouse, solicit, spur, stimulate, *urgere*

URGENCY, *noun* crisis, critical situation, crucial situation, dire necessity, emergency, exigency, expeditious need, hurried need, immediate need, importance, instant need, matter of life and death, necessity, pressing need, urgent need
ASSOCIATED CONCEPTS: good samaritan laws, *in extremis,* stay of execution, statute of limitations, temporary restraining order

URGENT, *adjective* clamant, compelling, compulsory, critical, crucial, crying, demanding, earnest, essential, exigent, grave, *gravis,* impelling, imperative, important, importunate, indispensable, insistent, instant, *necessarius,* necessary, necessitous, pressing, required, serious, vital, weighty

USABLE, *adjective* appliable, applicable, appropriateness, compliant, effective, effectual, employable, exploitable, fitting, operable, practical, recyclable, reusable, serviceable, utilizable
ASSOCIATED CONCEPTS: fit for the intended purpose

USAGE, *noun* application, conduct, consuetude, *consuetudo,* convention, custom, customary use, disposition, employment, established custom, established practice, fashion, fixed procedure, form, formula, habit, habitual use, habitude, management, manner, method, mode, *mos,* operation, practice, prescription, prevalence, routine, service, style, system, tradition, treatment, use, utilization, vogue, wear, wont
ASSOCIATED CONCEPTS: common usage, custom and usage, general usage
FOREIGN PHRASES: ***Consuetudo ex certa causa rationabili usitata privat communem legem.*** A custom based on a certain and reasonable cause supersedes the common law. ***Optimus interpres rerum usus.*** Usage is the best interpreter of things. ***In contractibus, tacite insunt quae sunt moris et consuetudinis.*** In contracts, matters of custom and usage are tacitly implied. ***Non ex opinionibus singulorum, sed ex communi usu, nomina exaudiri debent.*** The names of things ought to be understood, not according to individual opinions, but according to common usage. ***Obtemperandum est consuetudini rationabili tanquam legi.*** A reasonable custom is to be obeyed like law. ***Quae praeter consuetudinem et morem majorum fiunt neque placent neque recta videntur.*** Things which are done contrary to the custom and manner of our ancestors neither please nor appear right.

USE, *noun* adhibition, adoption, application, avail, benefit, convenience, disposal, disposition, employment, enjoyment, exercitation, exploitation, function, means, practice, purpose, service, serviceability, suitability, usage, usefulness, *usus, utilitas,* utility, utilization
ASSOCIATED CONCEPTS: actual use, apparent use, beneficial use, best and highest use, business use, charitable use, common use, contingent use, convenient use, corporate use, customary use, declared use, domestic use, dominent use, exclusive use, existing use, forseeable use, hostile use, lawful use, mutual use, nonconforming use, nonpublic use, normal use, offensive use, official use, ordinary use, permissive use, personal use, primary use, principal use, private use, reasonable use, resulting use, secondary use, shifting use, Statute of Uses, suitable use, unfit for use, use and derivate use

USEFUL, *adjective* advantageous, advisable, applicable, appropriate, availing, befitting, beneficial, commodious, conducive, congruous, constructive, contributing, contributory, convenient, decent, desirable, doable, effective, effectual, efficacious, employable, expedient, favorable, feasible, fit, fitting, functional, good, handy, instrumental, of use, operative, opportune, positive, practical, pragmatic, productive, profitable, proper, remedial, rewarding, right, salutary, seemly, suitable, usable, valuable, wise, worthwhile
ASSOCIATED CONCEPTS: usefulness

USELESS, *adjective* aimless, barren, counterproductive, effete, empty, failed fatuitous, fatuous, feckless, for naught, frivolous, fruitless, functionless, futile, idle, impotent, impracticable, inadequate, inane, incapable, incompetent, inconsequential, ineffective, ineffectual, inefficacious, inefficient, inept, inessential, inoperative, inutile, invalid, meaningless, needless, no go, no good, not serving any purpose, nugatory, null and void, of no avail, of no force, of no purpose, of no use, otiose, pointless, powerless, profitless, purposeless, redundant, superfluous, to no avail, to no purpose, trivial, unavailing, unfit, unhelpful, unimportant, unnecessary, unproductive, unprofitable, unsatisfactory, unserviceable, unsuccessful, unusable, vain, valueless, void, worthless

USUAL, *adjective* abundant, accepted, accustomed, acknowledged, average, banal, casual, characteristic, characterless, colorless, common, commonplace, conformable, conforming, consistent, consuetudinal, consuetudinary, conventional, current, customary, daily, established, everyday, expected, familiar, frequent, general, habitual, humdrum, inconspicuous, indifferent, insignificant, known, mediocre, middling, moderate, monotonous, natural, nondescript, normal, ordinary, orthodox, pat, pedestrian, plain, plentiful, popular, prevailing, prevalent, prosaic, prosy, recurrent, regular, repeated, representative, rife, routine, set, stale, standard, stereotyped, stock, tedious, traditional, trivial, typical, undistinctive, undistinguished, unexceptional, unimaginitive, unimpressive, uninteresting, universal, unmarked, unmemorable, unoriginal, unremarkable, unsophisticated, unsurprising, unvaried, vernacular, well-known, well-trodden, wonted, workaday
ASSOCIATED CONCEPTS: usual conduct, usual course of conduct, usual place of abode, usual terms

USURIOUS, *adjective* criminal interest, excessive, exorbitant, extortionate, illegal, immoderate, improper rate of interest, inordinate, unconscionable, undue, unreasonable

USURP, *verb* accroach, appropriate unlawfully, arrogate, assume, assume command, assume without authority, commandeer, encroach, help oneself to, hold by force, lay hold of, seize, seize power, *sibi adsumere,* squat, steal, take, take charge, take possession, wrest

USURY, *noun* criminal rate of interest, excessive interest, excessive rate, exorbitant interest, exploitation, *faeneratio,* high interest, illegal interest, overcharge, unconscionable rate of interest

UTILITY *(Public service),* ***noun*** public business, public company, public corporation, public industry

UTILITY *(Usefulness),* ***noun*** adequacy, advantage, advantageousness, applicability, avail, benefit, convenience, efficacy, employability, fruitfulness, function, helpfulness, practicality, productiveness, productivity, profit, profitability, service, serviceability, suitability, usability, use, value
FOREIGN PHRASES: ***Omne magnum exemplum habet aliquid ex iniquo, quod publica utilitate compensatur.*** Every great example has some unfairness, which is compensated by the public utility.

UTILIZATION, *noun* applicability, employability, practicality, serviceability, usability, usefulness

UTILIZE, *verb* adopt, apply, avail, benefit, employ, enjoy, exploit, incorporate, practice, purpose, service, use

UTMOST, *adjective* extreme, furthest, greatest, highest, maximal, maximum, most, superlative, supreme
ASSOCIATED CONCEPTS: utmost care

UTMOST, *noun* best, degree, extreme limit, extremity, farthest reach, furthest point, greatest amount, greatest degree, highest, maximum, optimum, the most possible

UTTER, *verb* air, announce, articulate, assert, asseverate, aver, breathe, broach, circulate, come out with, communicate, declaim, declare, deliver, *dicere,* disclose, divulge, emit, enunciate, express, give expression to, give forth, impart, issue, make known, mouth, proclaim, pronounce, propound, publicize, publish, recite, reveal, sound, speak, spread, state, talk, tell, vent, voice

UTTERANCE, *noun* account, affirmation, announcement, assertion, asseveration, averment, avowal, comment, declaration, deposition, detailed account, enumeration, exclamation, explanation, exposition, observation, pronouncement, recapitulation, recital, recitation, remark, report, statement, story, summary, testimony

VACANT, *adjective* bare, blank, clear, depleted, deserted, devoid, disengaged, empty, exhausted, free, hollow, idle, not in use, not occupied, open, unemployed, unfilled, uninhabited, unoccupied, unpossessed, untenanted, unused, unutilized, vacuous, *vacuus,* void

VACATE *(Leave),* ***verb*** abandon, cease, depart, depart from, desert, empty, evacuate, exit, forgo, go away, move, move out, quit, relinquish, remove, retreat, surrender, *vacuefacere,* withdraw
ASSOCIATED CONCEPTS: vacate premises

VACATE *(Void),* ***verb*** abandon, abdicate, abolish, abrogate, annul, cancel, countermand, deprive of force, disannul, do away with, eliminate, evacuate, invalidate, make void, negate, nullify, overrule, quash, recant, relinquish, render inoperative, repeal, rescind, retract, reverse, revoke, set aside
ASSOCIATED CONCEPTS: vacate a default, vacate a judgment, vacate an award, vacate an order, vacate occupancy, vacate office

VACATION, *noun* absence, break, breather, cruise, day off, escape, excursion, holiday, interval, jaunt, leave, leave of absence, paid vacation, respite, rest, rest and recuperation, sabbatical, time off, tour, trip, voyage, week off

VACATUR, *noun* abolishment, abrogation, annulment, canceling, cancellation, cessation, defeasance, deprivation, dissolution, invalidation, neutralization, nullification, rescission, revocation, undoing, vacation, vitiation
ASSOCIATED CONCEPTS: vacating a judgment

VACILLATE, *verb* alternate, be capricious, be inconstant, be irresolute, be uncertain, be unsettled, be unsteady, be unsure, change, debate, demur, equivocate, falter, feel uncertain, fluctuate, hesitate, hover, librate, move to and fro, oscillate, rock, seesaw, shift, show indecision, stagger, sway, swing, totter, undulate, *vacillare,* vibrate, waver

VACUOUS, *adjective* absent, barren, blank, depleted, devoid, drained, dull, empty, empty-headed, exhausted, expressionless, fatuous, foolish, hollow, idle, inadequate, inane, incogitative, insufficient, lacking content, missing, null, purposeless, senseless, silly, stupid, thoughtless, unfilled, unintelligent, unoccupied, unreasoning, unthinking, vacant, void, wanting

VAGRANCY, ***noun*** evagation, hoboism, indolence, itinerancy, pererration, roaming, roving, shiftlessness, vagabondage, vagabondism, wandering, wayfaring
ASSOCIATED CONCEPTS: common-law vagrancy, loitering

VAGUE, ***adjective*** ambiguous, *ambiguus,* amorphous, blurred, blurry, broad, cloudy, confused, cryptic, dim, doubtful, dubious, *dubius,* enigmatic, equivocal, evasive, faint, general, ill-defined, impalpable, imprecise, *incertus,* incomprehensible, indecisive, indefinite, indeterminate, indistinct, indistinguishable, inexplicit, intangible, misunderstood, mysterious, nebulous, obscure, perplexing, poorly defined, problematical, questionable, shadowy, uncertain, unclear, undefined, undetermined, unsettled, unspecified, unsure
ASSOCIATED CONCEPTS: void for vagueness
FOREIGN PHRASES: ***Res est misera ubi jus est vagum et incertum.*** It is a sorry state of affairs when law is vague and mutable.

VAIN ATTEMPT, ***noun*** aborted mission, all talk and no action, barren, efforts to no avail, efforts to no purpose, empty effort, fruitless effort, futile effort, hallow efforts, idle efforts, impotent efforts, inadequate efforts, inane efforts, ineffective efforts, ineffectual efforts, inefficacious efforts, interrupted mission, meaningless attempt, unavailing efforts, unsuccessful efforts, useless attempt, worthless effort

VALIANT, ***adjective*** adventurous, bold, bold-spirited, brave, chivalric, chivalrous, courageous, daring, dashing, dauntless, fearless, gallant, gutsy, herolike, heroic, intrepid, knightly, lionhearted, nervy, reckless, self-assured, self-reliant, soldierly, stalwartlike, stout, stouthearted, unafraid, unalarmed, undaunted, valorous, virile

VALID, ***adjective*** accurate, attested, authentic, authoritative, authorized, binding, bona fide, canonic, canonical, conclusive, confirmed, constitutional, correct, credible, effective, effectual, enforceable, executed with proper formalities, factual, *firmus,* forcible, good, *gravis,* having legal force, having legal strength, *iustus,* lawful, legal, legalized, legally binding, legitimate, licit, logical, official, potent, powerful, proved, sanctioned, scientific, solid, sound, statutory, strong, substantial, supportable by law, sustainable in law, true, truthful, veritable, warranted, well-grounded
ASSOCIATED CONCEPTS: valid argument, valid case, valid claim, valid commitment, valid consideration, valid contract, valid delivery, valid existing marriage, valid gift, valid judgment, valid obligation, valid reasoning, valid reasons, valid statute

VALIDATE, ***verb*** accept, affirm, approve, attest, authorize, certify, circumstantiate, confirm, corroborate, declare legal, declare valid, endorse, give legal force, legalize, legitimatize, legitimize, make binding, make legal, make valid, prove, qualify, ratify, sanction, seal, stamp, substantiate, verify, warrant
ASSOCIATED CONCEPTS: validate a sale, validate records

VALIDATION, ***noun*** affirmation, approval, authentication, authorization, backing, certification, confirmation, documentation, endorsement, fortification, justification, ratification, strengthening, substantiation, verification, vindication

VALIDITY, ***noun*** authenticity, authority, correctness, force, forcefulness, genuineness, *gravitas,* lawfulness, legal force, legality, legitimacy, legitimateness, meritoriousness, *pondus,* potency, power, puissance, reality, realness, significance, soundness, strength, trueness, truth, veracity, verity
ASSOCIATED CONCEPTS: validity of a statute
FOREIGN PHRASES: ***Quod in minori valet valebit in majori; et quod in majori non valet nec valebit in minori.*** That which is valid in the greater shall be valid in the less; and that which is not valid in the greater shall neither be valid in the less. ***Nul charter, nul vente, ne nul done vault perpetualment, si le donor n'est seise al temps de contracts de deux droits, sc. del droit de possession et del droit de propertie.*** No grant, no sale, no gift, is valid forever, unless the donor, at the time of the contract, has two rights, namely, the right of possession and the right of property. ***Quae ab initio non valent, ex post facto convalescere non possunt.*** Things invalid from the beginning cannot be made valid by a subsequent act. ***Semper praesumitur pro matrimonio.*** The presumption is always in favor of the validity of a marriage. ***Quod initio vitiosum est non potest tractu temporis convalescere.*** That which is void from the beginning cannot become valid by lapse of time. ***Pacta conventa quae neque contra leges neque dolo malo inita sunt omni modo observanda sunt.*** Agreements which are not contrary to the laws nor entered into with a fraudulent design must be observed in all respects. ***Quod initio non valet, tractu temporis non valet.*** That which is void at the beginning does not become valid by lapse of time.

VALOROUS, ***adjective*** adventurous, audacious, bold, bold as a lion, bold-spirited, brave, chivalric, chivalrous, courageous, daring, dauntless, fearless, foolhardy, gallant, heroic, herolike, high-spirited, intrepid, knightly, lionhearted, rash, reckless, soldierly, stalwart, stout, stouthearted, unafraid, unalarmed, undaunted, valiant, virile

VALUABLE, ***adjective*** above par, advantageous, beneficial, choice, commanding a good price, costly, dear, desirable, edifying, effective, effectual, efficacious, esteemed, estimable, excellent, expensive, favorable, fine, gainful, good, helpful, important, in demand, inestimable, invaluable, marketable, operative, precious, *pretiosus,* prizable, profitable, rare, relevant, remunerative, rewarding, salable, select, serviceable, significant, suitable, superior, treasured, useful, utilitarian, worthy
ASSOCIATED CONCEPTS: valuable consideration

VALUATION, ***noun*** assessment, calculation, computation, determination, estimate, estimated value, estimation, evaluation, examination, fixing a price, measurement, quantification, reckoning, setting a price, setting the value, summary, survey
ASSOCIATED CONCEPTS: property

VALUE, ***noun*** advantage, *aestimatio,* amount, appraisal, assessment, benefit, caliber, consequence, cost, desirability, effect, equivalent, esteem, estimate, estimation, excellence, expense, force, impact, importance, merit, price, purport, quality, quotation, significance, substance, superiority, use, usefulness, utility, valuation, worth, worthiness
ASSOCIATED CONCEPTS: acquisition value, actual cash value, actual market value, appraised value, assessed value, book value, cash market value, cash surrender value, current market value, face value, fair and reasonable value, fair market value, fair value, full cash value, good faith purchaser for value, gross value, highest market value, holder for value, instrument of value, insurable value, intrinsic value, market value, negotiable instrument, nominal value,

nuisance value, par value, pecuniary value, present value, probative value, prospective value, purchaser for value, real value, reasonable value, relative value, rental value, reserve value, residual value, retention value, substantial value, sufficient value, surrender value, tangible value, taxable value, transfer for value, true value, value received
FOREIGN PHRASES: ***Libertas non recipit aestimationem.*** Freedom does not admit a valuation. ***Tantum bona valent, quantum vendipossunt.*** Goods are worth as much as they are sold for. ***Res per pecuniam aestimatur, et non pecunia per rem.*** The value of a thing is estimated according to its worth in money, but the value of money is not estimated by reference to property. ***Sapientia legis nummario pretio non est aestimanda.*** The wisdom of the law cannot be computed in money value.

VANDAL, ***noun*** criminal, defacer, demolisher, destroyer, evildoer, lawbreaker, pillager, plunderer, raider, ravager, reprobate, robber, ruiner, spoiler, transgressor, wrecker

VANQUISH, ***adjective*** baffle, bar, beat, best, block, break, bring down, check, checkmate, circumvent, confound, conquer, crush, defeat, destroy, discomfit, dispel, dissipate, end, floor, foil, get the better of, humble, master, outmaneuver, outwit, overcome, overpower, override, overrun, overthrow, overwhelm, prevail over, prevent, put a stop to, put an end to, quash, quell, rout, smash, stop, subdue, suppress, surmount, surpass, terminate, thwart, trample, triumph over, trounce

VANWARD, ***adverb*** forward, frontward, headward, in advance, in front, in the lead, onward

VARIABLE, ***adjective*** aberrant, alterable, capricious, changeable, changeful, erratic, faithless, fanciful, fast and loose, fickle, fitful, fluctuating, inconstant, irregular, irresponsible, mercurial, modifiable, oscillating, protean, shifting, spasmodic, uneven, unreliable, unsettled, unstable, unsteadfast, unsteady, vagrant, variant, volatile, wavering, wayward

VARIANCE *(Disagreement),* ***noun*** alienation, altercation, breach, contention, contrariety, controversy, difference, disaccord, discongruity, discord, *discordia,* discrepancy, disharmony, disparity, dispute, *dissensio,* dissension, dissent, dissidence, disunity, divergence, diversity, division, incompatibility, nonagreement, odds, opposition, quarrel, rupture, split, strife, unconformity

VARIANCE *(Exemption),* ***noun*** anomaly, deviation, divergence, exception, leave, special dispensation

VARIATION, ***noun*** adaptation, adjustment, adverseness, alteration, antipathy, antithesis, array, change, choice, contrast, departure, deviation, difference, differentiation, disaccord, disagreement, discontinuity, discord, discordance, discrepancy, disharmony, disjunction, disparity, dissemblance, dissension, dissimilarity, dissimilitude, dissonance, distinctness, distortion, divergence, divergency, diverseness, exchange, fluctuation, incongruence, incongruity, incongruousness, inconsistency, inconsonance, inconstancy, inharmoniousness, metamorphosis, modification, modulation, mutual exclusiveness, nonconformity, oppositeness, opposition, reformation, reforming, remake, revision, revolutionize, separateness, substitution, switch, transfiguration, transformation, uniqueness, unlikeness, variance, variety

VARIED, ***adjective*** assorted, complex, composite, compound, conglomerate, different, differing, disparate, dissimilar, distinct, diverse, diversified, indiscriminate, intricate, jumbled, medley, mixed, multifarious, multifold, multiform, multiple, scrambled, separate, thrown together, variant, variegated, varying

VARY, ***verb*** alter, alternate, assort, be inconstant, be unlike, change, contrast, depart, deviate, differ, diverge, diversify, exchange, fluctuate, give variety, innovate, interchange, make a change, make different, modify, *mutare,* mutate, reorganize, rotate, shift, show variety, transfigure, transform, transmute, turn into, vacillate, *variare,* variegate, veer, waver
ASSOCIATED CONCEPTS: vary the terms of an agreement

VARYING, ***verb*** altering, bearing no resemblance, being at variance, being contrary, being dissimilar, being distinctly different, being distinguished from, being inharmonious, being opposite, unique, being unlike, contrasting, departing from, differing, digressing, disagreeing, diverging from, having a dissimilar opinion, lacking resembalance, not comparing with, not conforming, showing contrasting, showing variety

VEHEMENT, ***adjective*** agitated, angry, ardent, boisterous, burning, clamorous, demonstrative, eager, earnest, emphatic, enthusiastic, excited, explosive, fanatical, *fervens,* fervent, fervid, fierce, fiery, forceful, forcible, frenzied, furious, glowing, headstrong, heated, hot, impassioned, impetuous, impulsive, *incitatus,* inflamed, insistent, intense, lusty, mighty, passionate, perfervid, powerful, rabid, rampant, strong, tempestuous, turbulent, unequivocal, urgent, violent, volcanic, wild, zealous

VEHICLE *(Car),* ***noun*** automobile, carriage, means of carriage, means of transportation, means to an end, medium of transportation, method of transportation, motor vehicle, transportation

VEHICLE *(Means),* ***noun*** access, agency, agent, channel, conduit, contrivance, conveyor, course, device, expediter, facilitator, intermediate, means to an end, mechanism, medium, method, path

VEIL, ***noun*** camouflage, cloak, cloud, concealment, cover, covering, curtain, guise, *involucrum, integumentum,* mantle, mask, pall, protection, screen, shade, shelter, shield, shroud, visor, vizard
ASSOCIATED CONCEPTS: pierce the corporate veil

VENAL, ***adjective*** avaricious, bribable, corrupt, corruptible, dishonorable, extortionate, grasping, greedy, mercenary, *nummarius,* purchasable, self-seeking, *venalis*

VEND, ***verb*** auction, deal in, dispense, make a sale, market, offer for sale, peddle, put up for sale, retail, sell, trade, unload
ASSOCIATED CONCEPTS: vendee, vendor, vendor's lien

VENDOR, ***noun*** businessman, chapman, dealer, hawker, huckster, merchant, monger, peddler, retailer, salesman, seller, trader, tradesman
ASSOCIATED CONCEPTS: good faith vendor, vendor's liability, vendor's lien, vendor's title

VENERABLE, ***adjective*** advanced in life, ageless, at an advanced age, august, creditable, dateless, eminent, esteemed, estimable, hallowed, held in esteem, highly regarded, highly reputed, highly respectable, honorable, honored, illustrious, immemorial, in favor, in high favor, noble, of repute, patriarchal, prestigious, reputable, respectable, respected, revered, time-honored, timeless, venerated, well-thought-of, worthy

VENGEANCE, *noun* avengement, enmity, implacability, malevolence, nemesis, punishment, rancor, repayment, reprisal, retaliation, retribution, retributive punishment, revengefulness, *ultio,* vendetta, vengefulness, *vindicta,* vindictiveness

VENGEFULNESS, *noun* acrimony, anger, avengement, danger, dangerousness, feud, getting even, hostility, implacableness, inexorableness, intractableness, punitiveness, recrimination, reprisal, retaliation, retribution, revenge, spitefulness, unappeasableness, unforgivingness, vendetta, vengeance, vindictiveness, wrath, wrathfulness

VENIRE, *noun* authoritative citation to appear before a court, command to appear, notification to appear, required to attend, subpoena, summons

VENTURE, *noun* adventure, alea, attempt, business, campaign, chance, crusade, danger, dangerous undertaking, endeavor, enterprise, essay, experiment, *facinus,* gamble, hazard, investment, jeopardy, move, *periculum,* peril, plunge, project, quest, risk, risky undertaking, speculation, step, task, test, trial, uncertainty, wager
ASSOCIATED CONCEPTS: business venture, joint venture, private venture

VENUE, *noun* county, jurisdiction, locale, locality, location, neighborhood, place of jurisdiction, political subdivision, position, seat, site, station, territory
ASSOCIATED CONCEPTS: *forum non conveniens*
FOREIGN PHRASES: ***Triatio ibi semper debet fieri, ubi juratores meliorem possunt habere notitiam.*** Trial ought always to be had where the jurors can have the best information.

VERACIOUS, *adjective* aboveboard, accurate, believable, candid, credible, ethical, factual, frank, honest, honorable, ingenuous, legitimate, noble, precise, principled, sincere, straightforward, straight-talking, truthful, truth-telling, upstanding, with certitude, with verity
ASSOCIATED CONCEPTS: veracious witness

VERACITY, *noun* accuracy, actuality, artlessness, authenticity, candidness, candor, conformity to fact, correctness, credibility, exactitude, exactness, factualness, faithfulness, frankness, genuiness, guilelessness, honesty, ingenuousness, integrity, precision, principle, probity, rectitude, sincerity, trustworthiness, truth, truthfulness, veraciousness, veridicality, *veritas,* verity, virtue
ASSOCIATED CONCEPTS: reputation for veracity, veracity of a witness

VERBAL, *adjective* audible, expressed, nuncupative, oral, parole, pronounced, recited, spoken, stated, unwritten, uttered, *verbum,* voiced, *vox*
ASSOCIATED CONCEPTS: statute of frauds, verbal acts, verbal agreements, verbal contracts, verbal gift, verbal no fault threshold

VERBATIM, *adjective* exact, following the letter, literal, precise, true to the letter, word-for-word

VERBATIM, *adverb* chapter and verse, in the same words, literally, literatim, strictly to the letter, to the letter, word for word

VERBOSE, *adjective* conversational, expressive, inconcise, superfluous, talkative, verbal, wordy

VERDICT, *noun* adjudication, answer, assessment, award, conclusion, decision, decision of a jury, declaration of a jury, decree of a jury, definitive answer, determination, finding, *iudicium,* judgment, opinion of the jury, pronouncement of a jury, resolution by a jury, ruling, sentence, *sententia*
ASSOCIATED CONCEPTS: adverse verdict, arbitrary verdict, compromise verdict, directed verdict, estoppel by verdict, excessive verdict, final verdict, general verdict, incongruous verdict, informal verdict, judgment notwithstanding verdict, open verdict, partial verdict, quotient verdict, recorded verdict, rendering of a verdict, special verdict, unanimous verdict, void verdict
FOREIGN PHRASES: ***Veredictum, quasi dictum veritatis; ut judicium, quasi juris dictum.*** A verdict is, as it were, the expression of the truth; as a judgment is, as it were, the expression of the law. ***Non obstante veredicto.*** Notwithstanding the verdict.

VERIDICAL, *adjective* authentic, bona fide, genuine, honest, inartificial, legitimate, natural, real, sincere, true, truth-telling, truthful, uncounterfeited, unfaked, unfictitious, unperjured, unpretending, unsynthetic, veracious, verifiable

VERIFICATION, *verb* acceptance, accord, acknowledgment, affidavit, affirmance, affirmation, approval, assent, assurance, attestation, authentication, authorization, averment, avouchment, certification, check, confirmation of authority, confirmation of truth, declaration, formal assertion, legal pledge, oath, solemn averment, solemn avowal, solemn declaration, substantiation, swearing, validation, warrant

VERIFY *(Prove),* ***verb*** accredit, acknowledge, agree to, agree with, approve, assent, assure, attest, authenticate, authorize, avow, bear out, certify, charter, check, circumstantiate, commend, concur, confirm, *confirmare,* consent, corroborate, document, endorse, establish, establish the truth of fortify, give evidence, guarantee, license, make certain, make sure, pass, permit, *probare,* produce evidence, prove, prove the accuracy, prove the truth, review and approve, sanction, seal, second, substantiate, support, sustain, uphold, validate

VERIFY *(Swear),* ***verb*** affirm, asseverate, attest, avouch, avow, declare, evidence, guarantee, state, testify, vouch for, vow, warrant, witness
ASSOCIATED CONCEPTS: verify pleadings

VERSATILE, *adjective* able, adaptable, all-around, all-purpose, capable, changeable, gifted, handy, inconstant, many-sided, multifaceted, multipurpose, resourceful, talented

VEST, *verb* authorize, bestow upon, clothe, confer, consign, empower, enable, endow, entrust, establish, furnish, give authority, give control, invest, place authority, place control, put in possession, sanction
ASSOCIATED CONCEPTS: contingently vested, estate vested subject to being divested, indefeasibly vested, vested estate, vested future estate, vested gift, vested in possession, vested interest, vested legacy, vested property right, vested remainder, vested remainder subject to open, vested right, vesting of title

VEST IN, ***verb*** authorize, become effective, confer, consign, empower, enable, endow, entrust, establish, furnish, give, give authority, give control, grant a right in, invest, place authority, place control, sanction, start effectively

VESTED, ***adjective*** bestowed, earned, empowered, endowed, established, owned, vouchsafed
ASSOCIATED CONCEPTS: pension rights

VETERAN, ***adjective*** adept, adroit, apt, capable, deft, dexterous, disciplined, experienced, expert, facile, finished, knowing, practiced, proficient, qualified, seasoned, skilled, sophisticated, talented, trained, tried, world-wise

VETERAN, ***noun*** dean, expert, knowing person, old campaigner, old soldier, person of experience, practiced hand, senior statesman, sophisticate

VETO, ***noun*** ban, bar, denial, disallowance, embargo, forbiddance, inhibition, injunction, *intercessio,* interdict, interdiction, interference, negative, prevention, prohibition, proscription, refusal of approval, refusal to sanction, rejection, restraint, restriction, taboo

VEX, ***verb*** acerbate, aggravate, anger, annoy, badger, bedevil, beleaguer, beset, bother, chafe, chivy, concern, distress, disturb, envenom, gall, harass, harry, incense, infuriate, irk, irritate, miff, offend, pester, provoke, rankle, roil

VEXATIOUS, ***adjective*** aggravating, annoying, bothersome, disturbing, exasperating, galling, harassing, irksome, irritating, maddening, pestering, provocative, provoking, syncophantic, tiresome, troublesome, trying, wearisome

VEXATIOUS LITIGATION, ***noun*** bad faith litigation, harassment through the courts, nuisance action, pursuit of a meritless action, sanctionable litigation
ASSOCIATED CONCEPTS: frivolous lawsuit, meritless motions

VIABLE, ***adjective*** acceptable, actable, alive, appropriate, apt, capable of development, capable of growth, conceivable, doable, effective, effectual, efficacious, encouraging, expedient, favorable, feasible, functional, imaginable, legitimate, likely, living, logical, operative, performable, plausible, possible, potential, practicable, practical, promising, propitious, reasonable, sensible, sound, suitable, thinkable, usable, useful, valid, vital, workable

VIATICAL AGREEMENT, ***noun*** buying a life insurance policy for a lump sum, financial assistance, investment in a policyholder's life insurance policy, policy purchase

VIATICAL SETTLEMENT, ***noun*** life insurance agreement, life insurance payment, life insurance settlement, reformation of a life insurance policy, revision of a life insurance agreement

VICARIOUS *(Delegated),* ***adjective*** acting, acting as a substitute, commissioned, deputed, empathic, intermediary, mental, perceptive, procuratory, sympathetic, sympathizing, taking the place of another, understanding

VICARIOUS *(Substitutional),* ***adjective*** alternate, alternative, equivalent, ersatz, makeshift, provisional, representational, temporary, tentative
ASSOCIATED CONCEPTS: vicarious liability

VICE, ***noun*** atrocity, bad habit, blemish, corruption, debauchery, defect, deficiency, degeneracy, delinquency, depravation, depravity, dereliction, dissipation, dissoluteness, evil, excess, failing, failure, fault, flaw, foible, fraility, immoral habit, immorality, imperfection, impurity, inadequacy, incontinence, indecency, indulgence, infamy, infirmity, iniquity, lack, lewdness, libertinism, licentiousness, looseness, mar, maleficence, malignance, misconduct, misdeed, obliquity, outrage, perversion, profligacy, shortcoming, sin, sinfulness, transgression, turpitude, unchastity, vileness, wantonness, weak point, weakness, wickedness, wrong, wrongdoing

VICINITY, ***noun*** area, confines, environs, neighborhood, outskirts, precincts, propinquity, proximity, purlieu, region, scene, setting, suburbs, surroundings, territory, zone

VICIOUS, ***adjective*** abandoned, acrimonious, atrocious, barbarous, beastly, blameworthy, brutal, censurable, contrary, corrupt, criminal, cruel, dangerous, debased, degenerate, demoralized, depraved, devilish, diabolical, disgraceful, evil, evil-minded, ferocious, fierce, flawed, foul, frightful, given to vice, guilty, hateful, heinous, horrid, ill-disposed, ill-natured, immoral, imperfect, improper, impure, incorrigible, inhuman, inimical, iniquitous, malevolent, malicious, malign, malignant, mean, merciless, mischievous, nasty, offensive, pernicious, perverse, profligate, recalcitrant, refractory, reprehensible, reprobate, savage, scandalous, shameless, spiteful, steeped in vice, treacherous, *turpis,* uncivilized, unfriendly, unprincipled, unrighteous, unruly, untamed, venomous, vile, villainous, virulent, vitiosus, wicked, wrong
ASSOCIATED CONCEPTS: vicious propensity

VICISSITUDES, ***noun*** alteration, alternating conditions, alternation, changes, fluctuations, interchanges, modifications, successions, successive phases, transformations, ups and downs, variations

VICTIM, ***noun*** casualty, complainant, complaining witness, *hostia,* injured, prey, quarry, sufferer, target, unfortunate person, unlucky person, *victima*

VICTIMIZE, ***verb*** beguile, betray, cheat, con, damage, deceive, defraud, delude, do out of, dupe, exploit, fast-talk, finagle, fleece, flimflam, fool, hoodwink, injure, mislead, obtain under false pretenses, prey on, snooker, subject to a swindle, subject to fraud, swindle, take advantage of, to subject to fraud, trick, use

VIEW *(Opinion),* ***noun*** advice, apprehension, aspect, assumption, attitude, belief, concept, conception, conclusion, conviction, credence, creed, discernment, doctrine, estimate, estimation, idea, impression, intent, judgment, notion, perception, perspective, platform, position, posture, regard, representation, respect, sentiment, slant, stand, standpoint, supposition, theory, thought

VIEW *(Sight),* ***noun*** appearance, aspect, complexion, conspectus, contemplation, coverage, design, gaze, glimpse, ken, lookout, object, observation, outlook, panorama, posture, preview, prospect, purpose, purview, reaction, scene, scenery, scrutiny, show, side, spectacle, vision, vista
ASSOCIATED CONCEPTS: demand of a view, inspection of the scene of an accident, view of an inquest

VIEW, ***verb*** apprehend, attend, behold, consider, contemplate, detect, discern, envisage, examine, explore, glance at, have in sight, inspect, look at, look on, notice, observe, opine, perceive, pierce, recognize, reconnoiter,

reflect upon, regard, scan, scrutinize, see, study, surmise, survey, take stock of, think about, watch, witness
ASSOCIATED CONCEPTS: view the crime scene

VIEWPOINT, *noun* angle, attitude, basis, conception, feeling, frame of reference, framework, impression, inclination, mental view, opinion, orientation, outlook, perspective, point of observation, point of vantage, point of view, position, posture, reference, respect, sentiment, slant, stance, stand, standpoint, vantage point, view

VIGILANT, *adjective* alert, apprehensive, attentive, canny, careful, cautious, circumspect, guarded, heedful, *intentus,* judicious, keenly aware, observant, on guard, precautious, prescient, provident, *providus,* prudent, regardful, scrupulous, searching, sharp, suspicious, unsleeping, unslumbering, *vigilans,* wakeful, wary, watchful, wide awake

VIGOROUS, *adjective* active, acute, aggressive, all-out, animated, brisk, dynamic, energetic, enthusiastic, feisty, forceful, forcible, full of life, go-getting, go-go, hardy, healthy, intense, keen, lively, lusty, proactive, robust, spirited, strenuous, strong, strong and healthy, vibrant, vivacious, vivid, wholehearted, zestful, zesty

VILE, *adjective* bawdy, debauched, foul, immoral, impure, indecent, indelicate, lewd, lurid, offensive, offensive to decency, offensive to modesty, offensive to morality, patently offensive, profane, profligate, ribald, salacious, shameful, shameless, vulgar, wanton

VILIFICATION, *noun* abuse, abusive language, blackening, calumniation, calumny, contemptuous language, contumely, defamation, denigration, denunciation, detraction, impugnment, invective, malediction, opprobrium, revilement, scorn, slander, smear, traducement, verbal attack, vituperation

VILLAINOUS, *adjective* abhorrent, abominable, accursed, arrant, atrocious, baleful, baneful, base, criminal, cursed, damnable, deceiving, delinquent, depraved, despicable, detestable, devilish, diabolic, disgraceful, dishonorable, dissipated, dissolute, evil, evildoing, evil-minded, execrable, facinorous, faithless, fell, felon, felonious, flagitious, foul, hateful, heinous, horrible, ignoble, ill-intentioned, immoral, incorrigible, infamous, iniquitous, knavish, lawless, loathsome, malefic, maleficent, malevolent, malicious, malignant, mean, menacing, misfeasant, monstrous, nefarious, nefast, notorious, obnoxious, odious, offensive, opprobrious, perfidious, pernicious, profligate, rancorous, rascally, repellent, reprehensible, reprobate, repugnant, repulsive, revolting, roguish, ruffianly, satanic, shameful, unregenerate, unrepentant, unscrupulous, venomous, vile, virulent, wicked

VINDICATE, *verb* absolve, account for, acquit, clear, declare innocent, discharge, dismiss, exculpate, excuse, exonerate, give good reasons for, justify, pardon, *probare,* pronounce not guilty, *purgare,* release, relieve of burden, reprieve, set free

VINDICTIVE, *adjective* angry, avenging, grudgeful, implacable, inclined to vengeance, malevolent, malicious, malignant, punitive, punitory, rancorous, resentful, retaliative, retaliatory, retributive, revengeful, spiteful, *ulciscendi cupidus,* unforgiving, unrelenting, vengeful, vindicatory

VIOLATE, *verb* act illegally, break, constuprate, contravene, defy, desecrate, dishonor, disobey, disregard, disrespect, do violence to, encroach upon, fail to keep, fail to observe, infringe, injure, invade, offend against the law, *rumpere,* trample on, transgress, treat improperly, treat without reverence, trespass, *violare*
ASSOCIATED CONCEPTS: violate the law

VIOLATION, *noun* abuse, breach, *contra leges,* dereliction, desecration, disturbance, encroachment, illegality, impiety, infraction, infringement, interruption, invasion, irreverence, lawbreaking, misbehavior, mistreatment, misuse, nonobservance, offense, recusancy, transgression, trespass, wrong
ASSOCIATED CONCEPTS: crime, felony, misdemeanor
FOREIGN PHRASES: ***Mulcta damnum famae non irrogat.*** A fine does not impose a loss of reputation.

VIOLENCE, *noun* assault, attack, brutality, clash, convulsion, disorder, eruption, explosion, ferocity, force, fracas, furiousness, fury, inclemency, *manus,* onslaught, outburst, rage, rampage, ruthlessness, savagery, severity, unlawful force, vehemence, *violentia,* wildness
FOREIGN PHRASES: ***Insanus est qui, abjecta ratione, omnia cum impetu et furore facit.*** A person is insane who, deprived of reason, does everything with violence and rage. ***Paci sunt maxime contraria vis et injuria.*** Violence and injury are especially hostile to peace. ***Est autem vis legem simulans.*** Violence may also be masquerading as the law.

VIOLENT, *adjective* acrimonious, afire, aflame, astir, astringent, blown-up, brutal, brutish, caustic, clamorous, crazed, cruel, damaging, destructive, disorderly, excited, explosive, ferocious, feverish, forceful, frantic, frenetic, frenzied, furious, in a furious rage, in a furor, in rage, inflamed, raging, raised to a fever pitch, ruthless, seething, severe, sharp, uncontrollable, ungovernable, vicious

VIRTUAL, *adjective* basic, capable, constructive, deep down, deep-rooted, deep-seated, equivalent, essential, fundamental, implicit, indirect, inherent, intrinsic, material, potent, potential, powerful, practical, substantive, tantamount to, underlying, viable
ASSOCIATED CONCEPTS: virtual adoption, virtual representation

VIRULENT, *adjective* *acerbus,* acrid, acrimonious, antagonistic, baleful, baneful, bitter, deadly, deleterious, despiteful, destructive, envenomed, *gravis,* harmful, hateful, hostile, hurtful, injurious, lethal, malevolent, malicious, malign, malignant, mordacious, noxious, pernicious, poison, poisonous, rancorous, spiteful, toxic, treacherous, unfriendly, venomous, violent

VISIBLE *(In full view),* ***adjective*** clear, distinct, in focus, in full view, in plain sight, in sight, in view, manifest, perceptible, plain, seeable, showing, viewable, well defined

VISIBLE *(Noticeable),* ***adjective*** apparent, conspicuous, detectable, discernible, observable, perceivable, recognizable
ASSOCIATED CONCEPTS: visible easements, visible mark, visible means of support, visible possession, visible property, visible risk, visible sign of injury

VISION *(Dream),* ***noun*** abstraction, apparition, appearance, concept, conception, discernment, fantasy, form, glance, glimpse, illusion, image, look, perception, perspective, phenomenon, picture, presence, revelation, shape, spectacle, specter

VISION *(Sight),* ***noun*** field of view, vista

VITAL, *adjective* basic, cardinal, chief, critical, essential, extremely important, fundamental, important, indispensable, irreplaceable, life-supporting, main, necessary to life, needed, paramount, pressing, primary, principal, radical, required, requisite, urgent, vitalic, *vitalis*

VITIATE, *verb* abolish, abrogate, annul, blight, cancel, counteract, damage, *depravare,* destroy, disannul, impair, injure, invalidate, make faulty, make imperfect, make impure, make ineffective, make void, mar, negate, negative, neutralize, nullify, overturn, pervert, poison, pollute, quash, render defective, render inefficacious, rescind, reverse, spoil, sully, tamper with, undo, *vitiare,* weaken
FOREIGN PHRASES: ***Crimen omnia ex se nata vitiat.*** Crime vitiates all that is born of it.

VIVID, *adjective* bright, clear, colorful, demonstrative, direct, distinct, emphatic, evident, exact, explicit, express, expressive, graphic, identifiable, in bold relief, in evidence, in strong relief, manifest, observable, outspoken, overt, patent, pellucid, perceivable, perceptible, perspicuous, plain, prominent, pronounced, salient, self-evident, showing, shown, straightforward, striking, transparent, unblurred, unclouded, uncovered, unequivocal, unmistakable, visible, well-defined, well-marked, well-seen

VOICE, *verb* announce authoritatively, announce officially, assert, avow, break silence, clarify, communicate, declare, deliver, emphasize, enounce, enunciate, express, form, frame, observe, phrase, present, proclaim, pronounce, recite, recount, remark, say, sound, speak, state, stress, tell, utter, verbalize, vocalize

VOID *(Empty),* ***adjective*** abandoned, bare, barren, blank, deserted, desolate, destitute, devoid, forsaken, free, hollow, *inanis,* lacking, unfilled, unfurnished, uninhabited, unoccupied, unsupplied, untenanted, vacant, vacuous, vacuus, wanting, without contents

VOID *(Invalid),* ***adjective*** canceled, ineffective, ineffectual, inoperative, *irritus,* insubstantial, meaningless, not binding, not in force, nugatory, null, null and void, unenforceable, useless, *vanus,* without legal force
ASSOCIATED CONCEPTS: void act, void contract, void in part, void in toto, void judgment, void marriage, void on its face, void process, voidable
FOREIGN PHRASES: ***Quae ab initio non valent, ex post facto convalescere non possunt.*** Things invalid from the beginning cannot be made valid by a subsequent act. ***Judicium a non suo judice datum nullius est momenti.*** A judgment rendered by one who is not the proper judge is of no force. ***Quod initio non valet, tractu temporis non valet.*** That which is void at the beginning does not become valid by lapse of time. ***Quod initio vitiosum est non potest tractu temporis convalescere.*** That which is void from the beginning cannot become valid by lapse of time.

VOIDABLE, *adjective* capable of being adjudged invalid, capable of being adjudged void, capable of being annulled, capable of being declared ineffectual, capable of being declared void, defeasible, liable to be annulled, nullifiable, revocable, subject to being revoked, subject to cancellation
ASSOCIATED CONCEPTS: voidable contract, voidable judgment, voidable marriage, voidable preference

VOIR DIRE, *noun* examination for qualification for jury service, hearing before the court, hearing without jury's presence, inquiry, judicial examination

VOLATILE, *adjective* active, animated, brief, brisk, buoyant, capricious, changeable, cometary, deciduous, desultory, effervescent, elastic, elusive, ephemeral, erratic, evanescent, evaporable, excitable, explosive, fickle, fleeting, flighty, full of spirit, giddy, humorsome, inconstant, instable, irresolute, *levis,* lively, mercurial, *mobilis,* momentary, passing, precarious, quick, shallow, short-lived, spirited, sprightly, transient, transitory, unstable, unsteady, vacillating, vaporable, vaporizable, vaporous, *volaticus,* wavering

VOLITION, *noun* accord, choice, decision, desire, determination, discretion, election, elective preference, exercise of will, free agency, free will, intent, option, pick, power of choice, preference, purpose, resolution, selection, *voluntas,* will, willingness, wish

VOLUBLE, *adjective* copious, declamatory, discursive, eloquent, effusive, expansive, fluent, garrulous, glib, long-winded, loquacious, multiloquent, profuse, rambling, ready-tongued, rhetorical, talkative, verbose, wordy

VOLUNTARY, *adjective* conative, deliberate, designed, discretionary, effected by choice, elective, facultative, free, intended, intentional, offered, optional, purposeful, self-willed, unaccidental, unbidden, uncoerced, uncompelled, unconstrained, unforced, unprompted, unrestrained, volens, volitient, volitional, volitionary, *voluntarius,* willful, without compulsion, without constraint
ASSOCIATED CONCEPTS: voluntary abandonment, voluntary acceptance, voluntary act, voluntary agreement, voluntary appearance, voluntary assignment, voluntary confession, voluntary conveyance, voluntary discontinuance, voluntary dismissal, voluntary exposure, voluntary gift, voluntary grant, voluntary homocide, voluntary manslaughter, voluntary partition, voluntary payment, voluntary petition in bankruptcy, voluntary retirement, voluntary separation, voluntary statement, voluntary suspension, voluntary testimony, voluntary trust, voluntary waste

VOLUNTEER, *noun* amateur, enlisted man, enlisted person, enlistee, freewill worker, gratuitous worker, nonprofessional, recruit, taker, unpaid worker, voluntary worker
ASSOCIATED CONCEPTS: Good Samaritan

VOTE, *noun* ballot, chirotony, choice, choosing, decision, determination, election, formal expression of choice, judgment, option, pick, poll, predilection, preference, *punctum,* selection, *sententia, suffragium*

VOTE, *verb* approve, ballot, be counted, cast a ballot, cast a vote, choose, elect, exercise the right of suffrage, judge, poll, *suffragium ferre*

VOTER ID LAW, *noun* election law preconditions to voting, identification requirements to vote, photo requirements to vote, proof of identity, voter identification law, voter integrity, voter requirements, voter restrictions, voter suppression
ASSOCIATED CONCEPTS: disenfranchisement, Help America Vote Act (HAVA) (federal), integrity of the election process

VOUCH, *verb* acknowledge, *adseverare,* affirm, asserverate, assure, attest, authenticate, aver, avouch, back, bear witness, certify, confirm, corroborate, declare, depone, depose, endorse, give assurance, give evidence, give one's word, guarantee, maintain by affirmation, pledge, promise, *rem praestare,* secure, support, sustain, swear to, testify, underwrite, uphold, warrant, witness

VOUCHSAFE, ***verb*** accord, acquiesce, admit, allow, assent, bear with, bestow, comply with, concede, *concedere,* condescend, condescend to grant, consent, deign to give, deign to grant, favor with, give in, grant, grant by favor, gratify, humor, indulge, let, permit, satisfy, show favor, stoop, suffer, tolerate, yield

VOW, ***noun*** affirmation, asseveration, assurance, aver, avow, covenant, *devotio,* endorsement, *fides,* formal guaranty, oath, pledge, promise, *promissum,* solemn assertion, solemn declaration, solemn promise, subscription, undertaking, vouch, warrant, word, word of honor, written assurance

VULGAR, ***adjective*** bawdy, broad, debauched, disgusting, foul, immodest, immoral, impure, indecent, indelicate, lascivious, lecherous, lewd, licentious, lubricous, lurid, lustful, obscene, offensive, offensive to decency, offensive to modesty, offensive to the senses, patently offensive, pornographic, profane, profligate, prurient, ribald, salacious, scabrous, sensual, sexy, shameful, shameless, vile, wanton

VULNERABLE, ***adjective*** accessible, approachable, assailable, attainable, beatable, capable of receiving injuries, defenseless, exposed, fallible, guardless, indefensible, insecure, liable to attack, obtainable, open, penetrable, precarious, pregnable, *qui vulnerari potest,* reachable, risky, susceptible, unguarded, unprepared, unprotected, unsafe, unshielded, untenable, vincible, weak, woundable

WAGE, ***noun*** allowance, compensation, earnings, emolument, fee, hire, income, meed, *merces,* pay, payment, quittance, rate of pay, recompense, remuneration, revenue, reward for service, salary, stipend
ASSOCIATED CONCEPTS: minimum wage, wage rate

WAIT, ***verb*** abide, await, be patient, bear with composure, bide, continue, defer, delay, discontinue, extend, forbear, halt, hesitate, linger, loiter, mark time, pause, postpone, procrastinate, prorogate, protract, put off, remain, remand, reserve, retard, shelve, stall, stay, suspend, table, tarry, waive

WAIT, ***noun*** adjournment, cessation, deferment, delay, dilatoriness, halt, hindrance, moratorium, obstacle, pause, postponement, procrastination, prorogation, remand, reprieve, respite, retardation, stay, stop, suspension

WAIVE, ***verb*** cast off, cease, *de re decedere,* desist from, disclaim, dismiss, disown, dispense with, forgo, give up, give up claim to, not retain, not use, put aside, refrain from, refuse, reject, relinquish, *rem concedere,* renounce, repudiate, sacrifice, set aside, surrender, yield
ASSOCIATED CONCEPTS: election of remedy, waive a jury trial, waive jurisdictional requirements, waive objections, waive rights, waive rights to payment under a contract

WAIVER, ***noun*** abandonment, abandonment of a known right, abdication, abrogation, absolution, acquittal, act of relinquishing a right, clearance, deed of release, discharge, excusal, forgoing, giving up, intentional relinquishment, loss of right, release, relinquishment, renunciation, surrender, voluntary relinquishment
ASSOCIATED CONCEPTS: express waiver, implied waiver, waiver of immunity
FOREIGN PHRASES: ***Omnis consensus tollit errorem.*** Every consent removes error. ***Potest quis renunciare pro se et suis juri quod pro se introductum est.*** One may relinquish for himself and his successors a right which was introduced for his own benefit. ***Cuilibet licet juri pro se introducto renunciare.*** Anyone may waive a legal right which is for his protection. ***Ab assuetis non fit injuria.*** No legal injury is done by things long acquiesced in. ***Omnes licentiam habere his quae pro se indulta sunt, renunciare.*** All are free to renounce those privileges which have been allowed for their benefit.

WALL, ***noun*** blockage, divider, dividing wall, division, impediment, impenetrable obstacle, insurmountable task, isolated part, lone part, obstacle, obstruction, occlusion, overwhelming obstacle, separation
ASSOCIATED CONCEPTS: Chinese wall, common wall, party wall

WANT, ***noun*** absence, *conatus,* dearth, default, defect, deficiency, deficit, desideratum, desire, destitution, distress, exigency, impoverishment, insufficiency, lack, meagerness, necessitude, necessity, need, needfulness, neediness, paucity, pauperism, pennilessness, privation, request, requirement, requisition, scarcity, shortness, shortage
ASSOCIATED CONCEPTS: want of capacity, want of consideration, want of jurisdiction, want of knowledge

WANT, ***verb*** be deficient in, be desirous, be destitute of, be found wanting, be without, covet, crave, desiderate, desire, fancy, feel the lack of, have occasion for, hope for, lack, like, long for, miss, need, request, require, stand in need of, will, wish

WANT OF CAPACITY *(Mental deficiency),* ***noun*** amentia, defectiveness, dementedness, dementia, feeblemindedness, imbecility, moronity, retardment
ASSOCIATED CONCEPTS: insanity defense

WANT OF CAPACITY *(Underage),* ***noun*** callowness, defectiveness, immaturity, inexperience, juvenile, lack of development, minor, undevelopment, unfledged

WANT OF JURISDICTION, ***adverb*** beyond the jurisdiction of the court, improper jurisdiction, not legitimate, want of authority, without judicial authority

WANT OF KNOWLEDGE, ***noun*** denseness, ignorance, illiteracy, incomprehension, inerudition, inexperience, lack of education, lack of knowledge, lack of learning, unenlightenment, unfamiliarity, unintellectuality, unintelligence, unknowingness, unlearnedness, untaught state
ASSOCIATED CONCEPTS: ignorance of the law

WANTON, ***adjective*** careless, dissolute, froward, groundless, heedless, immoral, *impudicus,* intemperate, *lascivus,* lewd, libidinous, licentious, lustful, luxuriant, reckless, unjustifiable, unmanageable, unprovoked
ASSOCIATED CONCEPTS: wanton act, wanton disregard, wanton indifference, wanton injury, wanton misconduct, wanton negligence

WARD, ***noun*** care, charge, custody, defense, guard, guardianship, keeping, preservation, protection, safeguard, safekeeping, security, trusteeship, tutelage, vigilance, watch, watchfulness
ASSOCIATED CONCEPTS: ward of the state

WARDEN, ***noun*** chaperon, claviger, custodian, *custos,* gatekeeper, guard, guardian, jailer, overseer, patrolman, protector, sentry, superintendent, supervisor, supervisory official, turnkey, warder, watchman

WARN, ***verb*** admonish, advise, alert, apprise, caution, caution against danger, communicate to, counsel, deter, discourage, dissuade, exhort, expostulate, forebode, forewarn, give warning, herald, inform, make aware, notice, notify, portend, predict, premonish, presage, put on one's guard, remind, remonstrate, reprimand, signal, sound the alarm, urge to take heed
ASSOCIATED CONCEPTS: warning order, warning regarding product liability, warn of a danger, warn of known and obvious defects

WARNING, ***noun*** *admonitio,* admonition, alarm, alert, augury, caution, caveat, commination, contraindication, foreboding, foreshadow, monition, *monitus,* notice of danger, omen, portent, presage, prognostic, symptom, threat, ultimatum
ASSOCIATED CONCEPTS: adequate warning, ample warning, duty to warn, failure to warn, proper warning, sufficient warning, timely warning, warning attached to a products label

WARRANT *(Authorization),* ***noun*** *auctoritas,* authority, brevet, charter, commission, credentials, license, *mandatum,* permission, permit, *potestas,* power, sanction, voucher
ASSOCIATED CONCEPTS: warrant of attorney

WARRANT *(Guaranty),* ***noun*** agreement, assurance, authentication, covenant, pledge, promise, security, surety, warranty

WARRANT *(Judicial writ),* ***noun*** certificate, decree, edict, judicial authorization, judicial order, legal process, mandate of a court, order, process, subpoena, summons
ASSOCIATED CONCEPTS: arrest warrant, bench warrant, dispossess warrant, fugitive warrant, search warrant, tax warrant, warrant of attachment, warrant of commitment

WARRANTLESS SEARCH, ***noun*** a search conducted without proper procedures, a search resulting in suppressible evidence, improper search, inadmissible search, objectionable search, prohibited search
ASSOCIATED CONCEPTS: emergency aid exception

WARRANTY, ***noun*** assurance, certificate, contractual assurance, contractual promise, contractual representation, covenant, guarantee, guaranty, pledge, promise, *satisdatio,* voucher
ASSOCIATED CONCEPTS: affirmative warranty, breach of warranty, disclaimer of warranty, express warranty, implied warranty, limited warranty, material warranty, prospective warranty, warranty deed, warranty of fitness, warranty of merchantability, warranty of title
FOREIGN PHRASES: ***Ea quae, commendandi causa, in venditionibus dicuntur, si palam appareant, venditorem non obligant.*** Those things which are said as praise of the things sold, if they are openly apparent, do not bind the seller.

WASTE, ***noun*** careless loss, consumption, depletion, diminution, *dispendium,* dispersion, dissipation, *effusio,* excessive use, exhaustion, expenditure, extravagance, ill usage, improvidence, intemperance, lavishness, misapplication, misemployment, misusage, misuse, prodigality, profusion, ruination, squandering, *sumptus,* unnecessary loss, unthriftiness, useless consumption, wanton destruction, wastage, wastefulness, wasting
ASSOCIATED CONCEPTS: economic waste, permissive waste, voluntary waste, waste of public property, wasting assets

WATCH, ***noun*** advertency, alertness, attention, charge, concern, custody, guard, heed, inspection, lookout, observance, observation, oversight, precaution, regard, safeguard, safekeeping, sentinel, sentry, shift, spell of work, superintendence, supervision, surveillance, view, vigil, vigilance, ward, watchfulness

WATCH, ***verb*** attend, be a spectator, be careful, be cautious of, be closely observant, be on guard, be on the alert, be on the lookout, behold, contemplate, espy, eye, gaze at, guard, heed, inspect, keep under observation, look after, look at, mark, mind, monitor, not lose sight of, note, notice, observe, oversee, pay attention to, peer, perceive, police, preserve, regard, safeguard, scan, scrutinize, stare at, superintend, survey, take care, take care of, tend, view, witness

WAVERING, ***adjective*** between changing, debating, delaying, deliberating, demurring, dubitating, equivocating, faltering, feeling unsure, fluctuating, having difficulty deciding, having qualms, having reservations, hesitating, holding off, in a quandary, in between, irresolute, judgmental, pausing, pondering, pushing aside, putting off a decision, puzzled, puzzling over, scrupling, stopping to consider, tabling, thinking it over, uncertain, undecided, undermined, vacillating, withholding

WAY *(Channel),* ***noun*** alley, artery, avenue, custom, direction, lane, mode, path, pathway, plan, road, roadway, route, throughway

WAY *(Manner),* ***noun*** behavior, fashion, habit, means, progression, ritual
ASSOCIATED CONCEPTS: way appurtenant, way by dedication, way of necessity, way reserved, wayfarer, waylay

WEAK *(Decrepit),* ***adjective*** ailing, atonic, brittle, debilitated, delicate, dilapidated, dim, enervated, enfeebled, faint, feeble, flaccid, fragile, impotent, infirm, passive, spent, timorous, unfortified, unhealthy, vulnerable, wasted

WEAK *(Deficient),* ***adjective*** confused, defective, fallible, flimsy, helpless, illogical, imperfect, inadequate, incapable, ineffective, ineffectual, insubstantial, insufficient, invalid, jejune, languid, marginal, not thought out, obscure, poor, powerless, tenuous, thin, uncertain, unsound, unsteady, untenable, vague

WEAKENED, ***adjective*** debilitating, defective, deficient, fallible, flimsy, helpless, imperfect, improper, inadequate, incapable, ineffective, ineffectual, inferior, insubstantial, insufficient, invalid, languid, marginal, poor, unsound, untenable, weak

WEALTH, ***noun*** abundance, achievement, affluence, assessed valuation, assets, assets and liabilities, blessings, bottom line, circumstances, comfort, condition, current assets, dividends, earnings, ease, fixed assets, fortune, funds, gain, gains, good fortune, good luck, good times, gross profit, handsome fortune, high income, intangible assets, intangibles, interest, liquid assets, material assets, material wealth, means, money, money to burn, net assets, net worth, opulence, possessions, proceeds, profit, profits, property, prosperity, prosperousness, resources, riches, richness, spoils, success, successfulness, tangible assets, tangibles, thriving condition, total assets, total resources, treasure, wealthiness, well-being, what one is worth, winnings, worth

WEALTHY, ***adjective*** abundantly affluent, affluent, established and affluent, extraordinarily affluent, fabulously rich, incredibly affluent, loaded (slang), made of money (slang), moneyed, of extreme means, of great achievement, of great means, of substantial means, old money, rich, rich and powerful, well-endowed, well-established, well-heeled, well-off, well-to-do, worth substantial funds
ASSOCIATED CONCEPTS: fat cats, maximum campaign contributions, millionaire

WEAPONS, ***noun*** armaments, *armorum,* arms, deadly devices, deadly weapons, instruments of combat, lethal instruments, lethal weapons, munitions
ASSOCIATED CONCEPTS: concealed weapons, deadly weapons, possession of a weapon
FOREIGN PHRASES: ***Arma in armatos sumere jura sinunt.*** The laws permit the use of arms against those who are armed.

WEAR AND TEAR, ***noun*** corrosion, damage, decay, depletion, depreciation, deterioration, dissolution, dilapidation, diminution, erosion, exhaustion, impairment, ravage, ruination, wastage
ASSOCIATED CONCEPTS: award with wear and tear excepted

WEIGH, ***verb*** balance, bear heavily, burden, cogitate, consider, *considerare,* contemplate, cumber, deliberate, determine the heaviness of, encumber, estimate, evaluate, examine, find the weight of, gauge, load down, measure according to weight, meditate upon, mull over, ponder, press, put on the scale, reflect upon, *reputare,* ruminate, study
ASSOCIATED CONCEPTS: weigh the evidence

WEIGHT *(Burden),* ***noun*** care, cumbrance, duty, encumbrance, incubus, liability, load, mass, obligation, onus, oppression, ponderousness, pressure, responsibility

WEIGHT *(Credibility),* ***noun*** belief, certainty, confidence, credence, credibleness, credit, faith, impressiveness, likelihood, positiveness, reliance, trustworthiness, validity

WEIGHT *(Importance),* ***noun*** authority, consequence, degree of importance, effect, efficacy, eminence, emphasis, enormity, force, import, impressiveness, influence, interest, magnitude, merit, moment, potency, power, prominence, quality, seriousness, significance, value
ASSOCIATED CONCEPTS: weight of the evidence
FOREIGN PHRASES: ***Ponderantur testes, non numerantur.*** Witnesses are weighed, not counted. ***Testimonia ponderanda sunt, non numeranda.*** Evidence is to be weighed, not counted.

WEIGHT OF EVIDENCE, ***noun*** adequate evidence, adequate proof legally presented at trial, burden of going forward, legal responsibility, obligation of going forward, sufficient corroboration, sufficient evidence in a case, sufficient evidence to establish a case, sufficient proof, sufficient proof of facts, validation of proof of a case, verification of proof of a case
ASSOCIATED CONCEPTS: cause of action or claim, evidence, evidential burden, failure to sustain, preponderance of the evidence, prima facie case, rebuttal
FOREIGN PHRASES: ***Onus probani.*** Burden of proof.

WELFARE, ***noun*** advantage, affluence, assistance, benefit, *commodis consulere,* fortune, good, haleness, happiness, health, *hominis,* interest, luck, prosperity, prosperousness, soundness, success, weal, well-being
ASSOCIATED CONCEPTS: public welfare

WELL-BEING, ***noun*** abounding in riches, affluent, blooming, booming, comfortable, established, flourishing, fortunate, lucky, moneyed, profiting, providential, rich, safety, security, successful, thriving, wealthy, well-off, well-situated well-to-do

WELL-FOUNDED, ***adjective*** according to law, age-old, allowed, appropriate, authorized, correct, enacted, established, genuine, in accord with the law, in accord with legal provisions, in accord with statutory law, justification, law-abiding, lawful, legal, legalized, legislated, licensed, mandated, official, permitted, proper, recognized by law, real, sanctioned, sanctioned by law, sanctioned by legal authority, sound, statutory, suitable, valid, well-grounded, within the law

WELL-GROUNDED, ***adjective*** firm, legitimate, positive, solid, sound, steady, strong, well-based, well-founded

WELL-KNOWN, ***adjective*** acclaimed, celebrated, established, esteemed, famed, famous, glorified, illustrious,

important, notable, noted, notorious, popular, preeminent, prominent, respected, universally known, well-established, well-positioned, widely known, with a distinct name, with a luster, with celebrity status, with distinction, with eminence, with prestige, with regard, with renown, with standing, with star quality, with station, with status
ASSOCIATED CONCEPTS: judicial notice

WELL-OFF, ***adjective*** booming, doing quite well, flourishing, fortuitous, fortunate, halcyon, happy, moneyed, of adequate means, on top of the world, prosperous, successful, thriving, triumphant, wealthy, well-heard

WHARTON RULE, ***noun*** concert-of-action rule, prohibition of conspiracy due to the nature of crime, prohibition on conspiracy charges when the crime requires a plurality of offenders, prohibition on conspiracy charges when the crime requires concerted criminal activity
ASSOCIATED CONCEPTS: judicial presumption, merger, nature of act, plurality of offenders

WHATEVER, ***adverb*** at all, of any description, of any kind or sort, whatsoever, whichever

WHATSOEVER, ***adjective*** all without specification, any, anything, every, everything, some, whatever
ASSOCIATED CONCEPTS: plain language

WHATSOEVER, ***adverb*** any kind, any sort, at all, of any description, whatever

WHENEVER, ***adverb*** at whatever time, at which time, no matter when, once, when

WHEREABOUTS, ***noun*** abode, address, area, coordinates, direction, district, emplacement, environment, habitat, latitude and longitude, locale, locality, location, neighborhood, pinpointed location, place, placement, point of location, position, region, setting, site, situation, spot, venue, the very point of location, the very spot of location, vicinage, vicinity
ASSOCIATED CONCEPTS: plain language

WHEREBY, ***conjunction*** as a result of which, by which, in accordance with which, through which
ASSOCIATED CONCEPTS: plain language

WHEREIN, ***adverb*** concerning, during which, herein, in regard to which, in the course of which, in what, in which, inwardly, of which, regarding, respecting, therein touching, whereon, whereupon, within
ASSOCIATED CONCEPTS: plain language

WHILE, ***conjunction*** although, at the same time that, concurrently with, contemporaneously, currently, during, during the time that, even though, in the time that, simultaneously with, though, throughout the time that

WHISTLE-BLOWER, ***noun*** disclosure of illegality, disclosure of mismanagement, exposure of corruption, informant as the source of evidence of a crime, informant turning in evidence of a crime, public disclosure of wrongdoing
ASSOCIATED CONCEPTS: retaliation, reprisal

WHOEVER, ***noun*** any individual, any person, anybody, anyone, no matter who, whomever, whomsoever, whosoever

WHOLE *(Undamaged),* ***adjective*** aggregate, all, complete, entire, gross, intact, solid, total, undiminished, unhurt, unimpaired, unreduced, without loss
ASSOCIATED CONCEPTS: whole capital, whole estate, whole quantity, whole truth

WHOLE *(Unified),* ***adjective*** holistic, indivisible, one, single, total, undivisible, universal

WHOLE, ***noun*** aggregate, all, allness, assemblage, collectiveness, collectivity, completeness, entirety, everything, gross amount, indivisibility, intactness, integer, integrity, sum total, totality, undividedness, universality, wholeness

WHOLLY, ***adverb*** altogether, as a whole, collectively, completely, entirely, fully, in all respects, in the aggregate, in the main, in the mass, in toto, outright, roundly, throughout, totally, utterly
ASSOCIATED CONCEPTS: wholly dependant, wholly liable

WHOLLY INADEQUATE, ***adjective*** abhorrent, abominable, atrocious, awful, beneath contempt, contemptible, deplorable, despicable, detestable, dreadful, drive, foul, frightening, frightful, ghastly, ghoulish, gruesome, harrowing, hateful, heinous, horrendous, horrid, horrifying, indefensible, loathsome, macabre, obnoxious, odious, offensive, outrageous, pathetic, pitiful, repellent, reprehensible, repulsive, revolting, shameful, shocking, terrible, terrifying, unspeakable, vile, villainous
ASSOCIATED CONCEPTS: deplorable conditions

WICKED, ***adjective*** abhorrent, abominable, arrant, atrocious, bad, baleful, baneful, base, criminal, crude, damnable, dastardly, debased, despicable, detestable, dishonorable, dissolute, dreadful, evil, evildoing, evil-minded, hateful, heinous, hideous, horrible, horrid, ignoble, ignominious, incorrigible, infamous, iniquitous, invidious, knavish, loathsome, malefic, maleficent, malevolent, malicious, malignant, monstrous, noxious, obnoxious, opprobrious, pernicious, perverse, perverted, reprehensible, repulsive, revolting, satanic, scurrilous, unseemly, unspeakable, untoward, vicious, vile, villainous, vulgar, wanton
ASSOCIATED CONCEPTS: moral turpitude

WIDESPREAD, ***adjective*** ample, broad, capacious, collective, common, comprehensive, current, diffuse, epidemic, extensive, familiar, far-flung, far-reaching, general, global, indiscriminate, large-scale, omnibus, ordinary, predominant, prevailing, prevalent, rampant, rife, spacious, sparse, sporadic, spreading, substantial, sweeping, wide-open, wide-ranging

WIDE-SWEEPING, ***adjective*** boundless, broad, capacious, commodious, comprehensive, deep, endless, expansive, extended, far-flung, far-reaching, general, global, inclusive, infinite, limitless, massive, rangy, roomy, spacious, sweeping, wide, widespread
ASSOCIATED CONCEPTS: wide-sweeping changes to a draft of a contract

WIELD, ***verb*** avail oneself of, brandish, carry, command, control, direct, employ, exercise, exert, govern, handle, make use of, manage, manipulate, operate, ply, rule, sway, swing, *tractare,* use, utilize, work

WILL *(Desire),* ***noun*** *animus,* aspiration, backbone, choice, command, decision, desideration, determination, disposition, grit, hankering, hope, inclination, intent, longing, mind, pleasure, power of choosing, power of determination, preference, purpose, resoluteness, resolution, self-control, self-discipline, velleity, volition, *voluntas,* want, wish, yearning

FOREIGN PHRASES: ***Voluntas donatoris in charta doni sui manifeste expressa observetur.*** The will of the donor which is clearly expressed in his deed of gift should be observed. ***Furiosi nulla voluntas est.*** A madman has no will.

WILL *(Testamentary instrument),* ***noun*** bequeathal, bestowal, document, dispensation, disposition, instrument, legacy, testament, *testamentum*

ASSOCIATED CONCEPTS: absolute will, alienation, alteration, ambulatory will, appointment of an administrator, attempt to defeat will, bequest, cancellation, challenge to a will, codicil, commercial will, conditional will, conjoint will, contested will, contractual wills, counter wills, devise, election, execute a will, executor named in a will, existence of a will, forgery of a will, gift inter vivos, holographic will, incorporation by reference, instructions, joint wills, mutual wills, nuncupative will, precatory words, probate, property which passes by will, pursuant to terms of will, reciprocal wills, revocation of a will, suit for construction of a will, suit to annul or suspend a will, unconditional will, validity of a will, voidable will, witness to a will, written instrument

FOREIGN PHRASES: ***Da tua dum tua sunt, post mortem tunc tua non sunt.*** Give that which is yours while it is yours; after death it is not yours. ***Haereditas est successio in universum jus quod defunctus habuerit.*** Inheritance is the succession to every right which the deceased had possessed. ***Sola ac per se senectus donationem testamentum aut transactionem non vitiat.*** Old age does not alone and of itself vitiate a will, gift, or transaction. ***Haereditas nihil aliud est, quam successio in universum jus, quod defunctus habuerit.*** An inheritance is nothing other than the succession to all the rights which the deceased had. ***In testamentis plenius testatoris intentionem scrutamur.*** In wills, the intentions of the testators should be fully regarded. ***In testamentis ratio tacita non debet considerari, sed verba solum spectari debent; adeo per divinationem mentis a verbis recedere durum est.*** In wills, an unexpressed intention ought not to be considered, but the words alone ought to be regarded; for it is difficult to recede from the words by guessing at their intention. ***In dubiis, non praesumitur pro testamento.*** In doubtful cases, there is no presumption in favor of the will. ***Interest reipublicae suprema hominum testamenta rata haberi.*** It concerns the state that men's last wills be held valid. ***Quae in testamento ita sunt scripta ut intelligi non possint, perinde sunt ac si scripta non essent.*** Things which are so written in a will that they cannot be understood, are the same as if they had not been written at all. ***Testatoris ultima voluntas est perimplenda secundum veram intentionem suam.*** The last will of a testator is to be thoroughly fulfilled according to his true intention. ***Non aliter a significatione verborum recedi oportet quam cum manifestum est, aliud sensisse testatorem.*** The ordinary meaning of the words ought not to be departed from unless it is evident that the testator intended otherwise. ***Ubi pugnantia inter se in testamento juberentur, neutrum ratum est.*** When two directions conflicting with each other are given in a will, neither is held valid. ***Cum in testamento ambigue aut etiam perperam scriptum est benigne interpretari et secundum id quod credibile est cogitatum credendum est.*** When an ambiguous or even an incorrectly written expression is found in a will, it should be interpreted liberally and according to what is the probable intention of the testator. ***Omne testamentum morte consummatum est.*** Every will or testament is consummated by death. ***Nemo plus commodi haeredi suo relinquit quam ipse habuit.*** No one leaves a greater advantage for his heir than he himself had. ***Ambulatoria est voluntas defunctiusque ad vitae supremum exitum.*** The will of a deceased person is revocable until the last moment of life. ***Relatio semper fiat ut valeat dispositio.*** Reference should always be made that a testamentary disposition may be effective. ***Cum duo inter se pugnantia reperiuntur in testamento, ultimum ratum est.*** When two repugnant matters are found in a will, the last one will be confirmed. ***Voluntas facit quod in testamento scriptum valeat.*** The will of the testator gives validity to what is written in the will. ***Opinio quae favet testamento est tenenda.*** An opinion which favors a will is to be followed.

WILLFUL, ***adjective*** conscious, contemplated, contumax, deliberate, designed, inflexible, intended, intentional, intractable, intransigent, obdurate, obstinate, *obstinatus, pertinax,* planned, premeditated, purposed, purposeful, restive, retractory, studied, tenacious, uncompromising, unconstrained, unyielding, volitional, volitive, voluntary

ASSOCIATED CONCEPTS: willful acts

WILLING *(Desirous),* ***adjective*** assenting, disposed, eager, earnest, enthusiastic, partial to, ready, volitional, zealous

WILLING *(Not averse),* ***adjective*** acquiescent, agreeable, amenable, compliant, content, consenting, fain, favorably inclined, favorable, genial, receptive, responsive, susceptible, tractable, unreluctant, voluntary, yielding

WILLING *(Uncompelled),* ***adjective*** gratuitous, unbidden, unforced

WILLINGNESS, ***noun*** acceptableness, accommodation, accordance, acquiescence, amiability, appropriateness, complaisance, compliance, concordance, conformableness, congeniality, congruousness, consent, cordiality, courteousness, delightfulness, enjoyableness, flexibleness, friendliness, geniality, pliancy, suitability

WISDOM, ***noun*** acumen, astuteness, caliber, clear thinking, cognition, common sense, comprehension, discernment, discretion, edification, enlightenment, erudition, experience, good judgment, information, insight, intellectuality, intelligence, knowledge, learning, lore, perspicuity, prescience, profound thought, profundity, rationality, reason, sagacity, sapience, savvy, scholarship, sense, shrewdness, sound understanding, understanding, wiseness, worldly wisdom

ASSOCIATED CONCEPTS: expert witness, in the wisdom of the court

WITHDRAW, ***verb*** abandon, abdicate, abjure, abolish, abscond, absent oneself, abstract, back out, backtrack, cease, deduct, depart, desert, disappear, disassociate, disavow, disengage, disestablish, dissociate, draw out, evacuate, extract, invalidate, keep apart, leave, nullify, overrule, pull back, quash, quit, recall, recant, recede, relinquish, remove, renege, repeal, rescind, resign, retire, retract, retreat, reverse, revoke, secede, separate, sequester, sequestrate, subduce, subduct, subtract, surrender, take away, take back, unsheathe, vacate, wean

WITHDRAWAL, ***noun*** abandonment, abdication, abjuration, abolition, abrogation, absence, annulment, cancellation,

clearance, cloture, defeasance, denial, departure, desertion, disavowal, discontinuance, disengagement, dissociation, eradication, evacuation, evulsion, exit, exodus, extraction, hegira, invalidation, leave-taking, nullification, parting, recall, recantation, recess, relinquishment, removal, renunciation, repudiation, rescindment, rescission, resignation, retirement, retraction, retreat, revocation, riddance, secession
ASSOCIATED CONCEPTS: error cured by withdrawal, withdrawal from the commission of a crime, withdrawal of a case, withdrawal of a default, withdrawal of a judgment, withdrawal of a partner from a partnership, withdrawal of an action, withdrawal of charges, withdrawal of pleadings

WITHHOLD, *verb* abstain, begrudge, block, censor, check, *comprimere,* conceal, constrain, curb, debar, deny, disallow, forbear, forbid, hide, hinder, hold, hold back, hold in, hold out, hush up, inhibit, keep, keep back, keep in, keep secret, muzzle, prohibit, refrain, refuse, refuse to disclose, rein in, repress, reserve, restrain, restrict, *retinere,* smother, stifle, suppress, *supprimere*

WITHOUT A SHRED OF EVIDENCE, *noun* absence of confirmation, basis for belief, corroboration, documentation, grounds to believe, indicia of evidence, modicum of evidence, modicum of proof, some evidence, some grounds, some means of proof, some persuasive evidence, some proof, some proof of facts, substantiation, validation, verification
ASSOCIATED CONCEPTS: circumstantial evidence, direct evidence, relevant evidence

WITHOUT JUDICIAL AUTHORITY, *idiom* beyond authority of the court, beyond judicial power, beyond the bounds of the court, lack of legal authority, want of legal authority, without jurisdiction, without legal authority

WITHOUT RECOURSE, *adverb* conditional endorsement, qualified endorsement, restricted, subject to terms
ASSOCIATED CONCEPTS: endorsement without recourse

WITHOUT RESTRAINT, *adjective* all-encompassing, all-inclusive, all-out, broad, complete, comprehensive, entire, every possible combination, extensive, full-fledged, liberal, maximum, thorough, total, unabridged, unbridled, unrestrained, vast, voluminous, whole, without abridgment, without limitation, without reduction

WITHSTAND, *verb* block, breast, challenge, check, confront, contravene, cope with, counteract, countercheck, countervail, defy, endure, face, face danger, face up to, fight, foil, hamper, hinder, hold out, impede, inhibit, interrupt, last, *obsistere, obstare,* obstruct, offer resistance, oppose, preclude, prevail against, prevent, refuse to submit, repel, repulse, resist, *resistere,* retard, stand fast, stand firm, stand up to, stave off, stay, stem, stop, thwart, weather
ASSOCIATED CONCEPTS: withstand a challenge on appeal

WITNESS, *noun* attestant, attestor, beholder, bystander, compurgator, corroborator, deponent, informant, informer, looker, looker-on, observer, one who gives testimony, onlooker, person affording evidence, reporter, swearer, testifier, *testis*
ASSOCIATED CONCEPTS: adverse witness, attestation, attesting witness, available witness, call as a witness, compel the attendance of witnesses, competent disinterested witness, competent witness, confronting a witness, credible witness, cross-examination, discredited witness, disinterested witness, expert witness, eyewitness, hostile witness, impeachment of a witness, material witness, nonexpert witness, prosecution witness, res gestae witness, skilled witness, specially qualified witness, state witness, subscribing witness, tampering with a witness, voluntary witness
FOREIGN PHRASES: ***Habemus optimum testem, confitentem reum.*** We have the best witness, a confessing defendant. ***Nemo allegans suam turpitudinem audien dus est.*** No one should be permitted to testify as a witness to his own baseness or wickedness. ***Nullus idoneus testis in re sua intelligitur.*** No person is deemed to be a competent witness in his own behalf. ***Judex non potest esse testis in propria causa.*** A judge cannot be a witness in his own case. ***Jurato creditur in judicio.*** He who makes an oath is to be believed in a judicial proceeding. ***Quod constat curiae opere testium non indiget.*** That which is clear to the court needs not the help of witnesses. ***Nemo tenetur edere instrumenta contra se.*** No one is bound to produce writings against himself. ***Nemo tenetur jurare in suam turpitudinem.*** No one is bound to testify to his own turpitude. ***Nemo tenetur prodere seipsum.*** No one is bound to betray himself. ***Testis nemo in sua causa esse potest.*** No one can be a witness in his own cause. ***Testis de visu praeponderat aliis.*** An eyewitness is preferred to others. ***Nemo in propria causa testis esse debet.*** No one ought to be a witness in his own cause.

WITNESS *(Attest to),* ***verb*** acknowledge, affirm, authenticate, bear out, bear witness, certify, confirm, corroborate, cosign, countersign, endorse, give evidence, give testimony, say under oath, sign, substantiate, sustain, swear, take one's oath, testari, *testificari,* testify to, *testimonium dicere,* undersign, uphold, validate, verify, vouch for, warrant
ASSOCIATED CONCEPTS: witness a crime, witness a document, witness a will

WITNESS *(Have direct knowledge of),* ***verb*** be a spectator, be present and note, behold, mark, note, notice, observe, recognize, see, sight, *spectare,* spot, take cognizance of, *videre,* view, watch

WORD *(News),* ***noun*** account, advice, bulletin, communication, dispatch, information, intelligence, mention, message, report, statement

WORD *(Promise),* ***noun*** affirmation, agreement, assurance, averment, avouchment, avowal, declaration, pledge, profession, solemn declaration, statement, undertaking, vow, warrant

WORD *(Term),* ***noun*** adage, antonym, argument, articulation, coined word, colloquy, command, contention, conversation, dialogue, discourse, expression, homonym, maxim, mot, motto, observation, palaver, parlay, part of speech, phrase, proverb, remark, saying, statement, synonym, utterance, verbalism
ASSOCIATED CONCEPTS: actionable words, words of art, words of limitation

WORK *(Effort),* ***noun*** application, attempt, campaign, chore, diligence, drudgery, endeavor, enterprise, essay, exercise, exertion, grind, industry, labor, opus, strain, stress, strife, struggle, toil, undertaking

WORK *(Employment),* ***noun*** assignment, avocation, business, calling, charge, craft, duty, engagement, function, incumbency, industry, job, line, metier, occupation, office, position, post, profession, pursuit, specialty, task, trade, vocation

WORK FOR HIRE, *noun* appointed subauthor, delegated author, subauthor, underauthor

WORLDWIDE, *adjective* all-embracing, all-inclusive, complete, comprehensive, extensive, far-reaching, global, international, nonsectarian, omnipresent, overall, pandemic, prevailing, prevalent, total, universal, widespread

WORRY, *noun* affliction, annoyance, anxiety, apprehension, apprehensiveness, care, concern, consternation, difficulty, discomfort, discomposure, dismay, disquiet, distress, distress one's self, dread, fear, fearfulness, grief, malaise, mental agitation, misgiving, nuisance, pain, perplexity, perturbation, premonition, qualm, restiveness, solicitude, torment, trepidation, trouble, troubles, unease, uneasiness, vexation

WORRY, *verb* agitate, agonize, annoy, badger, be anxious, be apprehensive, be troubled, bedevil, beset, bother, brood over, despair, discommode, discompose, displease, disquiet, distress, disturb, dread, embarrass, feel uneasy, fret, grieve over, harass, harry, hector, hound, incommode, irritate, mistreat, oppress, pain, perplex, persecute, perturb, pique, plague, press, trouble, upset, vex

WORTH, *noun* account, advantage, *aestimatio,* appraisal, appraisement, avail, benefit, caliber, charge, cost, credit, desert, esteem, estimation, excellence, expense, importance, merit, par, *pretium,* price, profit, profitableness, quality, quotation, rate, regard, respect, service, serviceableness, use, utility, valuation, value, *virtus,* worthiness
FOREIGN PHRASES: ***Tantum bona valent, quantum vendi possunt.*** Goods are worth as much as they are sold for.

WRIT, *noun* bid, bidding, command, commandment, decree, decretal, dictate, direction, directive, fiat, mandate, order, ordinance, precept, regulation, requirement
ASSOCIATED CONCEPTS: concurrent writ, judicial writ, original writ, preemptory writ, prerogative writ, writ of attachment, writ of certiorari, writ of covenant, writ of detinue, writ of error, writ of error coram nobis, writ of execution, writ of habeas corpus, writ of inquiry, writ of mandemus, writ of prohibition, writ of protection, writ of quo warranto, writ of replevin, writ of right

WRITE OFF, *verb* abandon, abdicate, abjure, abstain, avoid, cease, cede, deny oneself, desist from, dispense with, disposed of, do without, drop, eschew, fast, forbear, forfeit, forgo, forswear, give up, give up on, go without, hold back, hold off, lay down, leave off, let alone, make do without, not use, pass up, refrain, release, relinquish, renounce, reserve, resign, sacrifice, shun, surrender, waive, withhold, yield, yield up
ASSOCIATED CONCEPTS: forgo interest owed, forgo opportunity

WRONG, *noun* abomination, abuse, atrocity, crime, delinquency, dereliction, evil, grievance, harm, illegality, immorality, improbity, infraction, iniquity, *iniuria,* injury, injustice, lawlessness, malfeasance, malpractice, miscreancy, misdeed, misdoing, mistake, mistreatment, obliquity, offense, outrage, sin, transgression, trespass, turpitude, unfairness, unrighteousness, vice, villainy, violation, violation of right, wickedness
FOREIGN PHRASES: ***Scienti et volenti non fit injuria.*** A wrong is not done to a person who understands and consents. ***Peccatum peccato addit qui culpae quam facit patrocinium defensionis adjungit.*** He adds one offense to another who connects a wrong which he has committed with his defense. ***Nemo ex suo delicto meliorem suam conditionem facere potest.*** No one can improve his condition by his own misdeed. ***Nemo ex proprio dolo consequitur actionem.*** No one acquires a right of action from his own fraud. ***Un ne doit prise advantage de son tort demesne.*** One ought not to take advantage of his own wrong. ***Nemo damnum facit, nisi qui id fecit quod facere jus non habet.*** No one is considered as doing damage, except he who does that which he has no right to do. ***Jus ex injuria non oritur.*** A right does not arise from a wrong. ***Injuria non excusat injuriam.*** One wrong does not excuse another. ***Ubi et dantis et accipientis turpitudo versatur, non posse repeti dicimus; quotiens autem accipientis turpitudo versatur, repeti posse.*** Where there is turpitude by both giver and receiver, we say it cannot be recovered back; but whenever the turpitude is in the receiver only, it can be recovered. ***Ubicunque est injuria, ibi damnum sequitur.*** Wherever there is a wrong, there damage follows. ***Nullum iniquum est praesumendum in jure.*** Nothing iniquitous is to be presumed in law. ***Nullus videtur dolo facere qui suo jure utitur.*** No one is considered to have committed a wrong who exercises his legal rights. ***Aliquid conceditur ne injuria remaneat impunita, quod alias non concederetur.*** Something is conceded lest a wrong remain unredressed, which otherwise would not be conceded.

WRONGDOER, *noun* criminal, debauchee, delinquent, evildoer, homo *maleficus,* lawbreaker, malefactor, malfeasant, miscreant, misdemeanant, misdoer, offender, outlaw, profligate, reprobate, scoundrel, sinner, transgressor, villain
FOREIGN PHRASES: ***In pari delicto potior est conditio possidentis, defendentis.*** Where the parties are equally guilty of wrongdoing, the defendant holds the stronger position. ***Nullus videtur dolo facere qui suo jure utitur.*** No one is considered to have committed a wrong who exercises his legal rights.

WRONGFUL, *adjective* against the law, bad, criminal, felonious, illegal, illegitimate, illicit, improper, incorrect, iniquitous, *iniuriosus, iniustus,* lawless, malicious, mischievous, unauthorized, undue, unfair, unjust, unlawful, unseemly, unsuitable, wrong
ASSOCIATED CONCEPTS: wrongful act, wrongful conversion, wrongful death, wrongful detention, wrongful discharge, wrongful interference
FOREIGN PHRASES: ***Fictio legis inique operatur alieni damnum vel injuriam.*** Fiction of law is wrongful if it works loss or harm to anyone.

WRONGFUL ACT, *noun* breach, breach of legal duty, civil wrong, contravention, delinquency, dereliction, dereliction of duty, guilty act, illegality, impropriety, injustice, malefaction, malpractice, misbehavior, misconduct, misdeed, misdoing, misfeasance, offense, offense against the law, tort, transgression, trespass, violation, willful wrongdoing, wrong, wrongful conduct
ASSOCIATED CONCEPTS: criminal act, illegality, perjury, tortuous act, wrongful attachment, wrongful conviction, wrongful death, wrongful execution, wrongful foreclosure, wrongful injunction, wrongful institution of an action, wrongful levy, wrongful testimony

WRONGFUL CONDUCT, *noun* bad conduct, breach, contravention, corruption, crime, delinquency, dereliction, deviation from rectitude, ill conduct, illegal action, illegality, impropriety, infringement, injurious action, injustice, malfeasance, malpractice, misbehavior, misdeed, misdoing, transgression, violation, wrongful action

WRONGFUL USE, ***noun*** abuse, corrupt use, deformation, distortion, errancy, incorrect usage, malapropism, misapplication, misappropriation, misconstruction, misdirection, misemployment, mishandling, mismanagement, misusage, misuse, wrong application, wrong use
ASSOCIATED CONCEPTS: product liability, warnings

YARDSTICK, ***noun*** aspect, benchmark, borderline indication, boundary, confinement, dictate, dimension, direction, formula, gauge, general guideline, guide, guideline, idea, instruction, key, limitation, margin, marker, measure, outer limits, parameter, perimeter, restraint, restriction, rule, specific, standard

YET, ***adverb*** additionally, again, also, besides, further, furthermore, likewise, moreover, on the other hand, then, then too, too

YIELD *(Produce a return),* ***verb*** accord, accrue, afford, bear, bestow, bring, bring about, bring forth, bring in, fetch, furnish, generate, give, provide, render, return, supply

YIELD *(Submit),* ***verb*** abandon, abdicate, accede, accept, acquiesce, admit, agree to, allow, assent, back down, be submissive, bend, bow, capitulate, cede, comply, concede, *concedere,* consent, *dedere,* forgo, give in, give up, give way, grant, leave, let go, make way, obey, pay homage to, permit, quit, relent, relinquish, renounce, resign, sacrifice, succumb, suffer defeat, surrender, waive

YIELDING, ***adjective*** accommodating, acquiescent, alterable, amenable, complaisant, compliant, docile, easy, easygoing, elastic, facile, *facilis,* flexible, impressible, impressionable, malleable, manageable, obedient, obliging, *obsequens,* obsequious, passive, pliable, pliant, soft, submissive, supple, tractable, unresistant, unresisting
ASSOCIATED CONCEPTS: confessions

YOUR HONOR, ***noun*** adjudicator, administrator of justice, her honor, his honor, honorable justice, interpreter, judge, jurist, justice, magistrate, member of the judiciary, one who dispenses justice, the court

ZEALOUS, ***adjective*** active, ardent, assiduous, attentive, bent upon, dedicated, desirous, devoted, devout, eager, earnest, enthusiastic, fanatical, fervent, fervid, fiery, hearty, impassioned, impetuous, industrious, infatuated, keen, loving, passionate, perfervid, perseverant, persistent, pious, rabid, raving, ready, sedulous, solicitous, *studiosus,* willing
ASSOCIATED CONCEPTS: overly zealous representation of a client

ZONE, *noun* accommodation, address, area, arena, bailiwick, band, belt, circumference, compartment, confines, corridor, department, district, division, domain, environs, hemisphere, land, latitude, locale, locality, location, neighborhood, orb, orbit, permieter, periphery, place, precinct, premises, province, region, section, sector, sphere, terrain, territory, turf, vicinage, vicinity
ASSOCIATED CONCEPTS: economic zone, free trade zone, zone of employment, zoning ordinances

ZONING, *noun* governmental planning requirements, laws governing various categorized zones, municipal planning restrictions, zoning codes, zoning laws, zoning ordinances, zoning statutes
ASSOCIATED CONCEPTS: commercial zones, industrial zones, residential zones

ZONING LAWS, *noun* building laws, building restrictions, construction laws, limitations on commercial buildings, by area, limitations on private residences by area, restrictions by area, restrictions set by zones, statutory provisions of the zoning law, zoning ordinances
ASSOCIATED CONCEPTS: variances permitted under the law

COMPREHENSIVE INDEX

A

a ceteris dissentire unorthodox
a commanding portion bulk
a fortiori discursive *(analytical)*. SEE MAIN ENTRY
a good deal of considerable
a posteriori discursive *(analytical)*
a priori axiomatic. SEE MAIN ENTRY
a priori discursive *(analytical)*
à propos admissible, applicable
a savoir SEE MAIN ENTRY
a.k.a. alias
ab initio SEE MAIN ENTRY
ab origine ab initio
ab ovo ab initio
ab re desistere abandon *(withdraw)*
ab re discrepare contradict
abalienare alienate *(estrange)*, alienate *(transfer title)*, estrange
abalienate alienate *(transfer title)*, assign *(transfer ownership)*, cede, consign, convey *(transfer)*. SEE MAIN ENTRY
abalienatio alienation *(transfer of title)*, pass *(advance)*
abalienation alienation *(transfer of title)*, assignment *(transfer of ownership)*, cession, demise *(conveyance)*, estrangement. SEE MAIN ENTRY
abandon betray *(lead astray)*, cede, disclaim, disinherit, disown *(refuse to acknowledge)*, fail *(neglect)*, flee, forfeit, forgo, forswear, leave *(depart)*, pretermit, quit *(discontinue)*, quit *(evacuate)*, reject, relinquish, renege, renounce, repudiate, resign, retire *(retreat)*, retreat, secede, set aside *(annul)*, stop, vacate *(leave)*, vacate *(void)*, withdraw, yield *(submit)*. SEE MAIN ENTRY
abandon allegiance defect
abandon nationality expatriate
abandoned dissolute, helpless *(defenseless)*, licentious, obsolete, solitary, tainted *(corrupted)*, uncurbed, vicious, void *(empty)*. SEE MAIN ENTRY
abandoned child orphan
abandoned infant orphan
abandoned to vice profligate *(corrupt)*
abandoning cancellation
abandonment abdication, abjuration, absence *(nonattendance)*, cancellation, capitulation, cessation *(termination)*, cloture, dereliction, desertion, desuetude, disclaimer, disuse, estrangement, expense *(sacrifice)*, halt, neglect, negligence, rejection, release, renunciation, rescision, resignation *(relinquishment)*, waiver. SEE MAIN ENTRY
abandonment of a known right waiver
abandonment of a trademark SEE MAIN ENTRY
abandonment of allegiance desertion, infidelity
abase adulterate, betray *(lead astray)*, damage, debase, demean *(make lower)*, demote, denigrate, depress, derogate, disgrace, dishonor *(deprive of honor)*, humiliate. SEE MAIN ENTRY
abasement attaint, bad repute, degradation, deterioration, disgrace, dishonor *(shame)*, disrepute, ignominy, infamy, obloquy, opprobrium, perversion, prostration, shame
abash browbeat, confound, confuse *(bewilder)*, disconcert, disgrace, disorient, dissuade, embarrass, humiliate, intimidate, perturb
abashed diffident
abashment embarrassment
abasing contemptuous
abate abolish, allay, alleviate, assuage, cease, check *(restrain)*, commute, curtail, decrease, deduct *(reduce)*, diminish, discount *(minimize)*, discount *(reduce)*, ease, enjoin, give *(yield)*, lapse *(cease)*, lessen, mitigate, moderate *(temper)*, modify *(moderate)*, mollify, obtund, quash, reduce, relax, relieve *(free from burden)*, remit *(relax)*, subdue, subside. SEE MAIN ENTRY
abate in intensity mitigate
abate severity relent
abatement abridgment *(disentitlement)*, curtailment, decline, decrease, decrement, deduction *(diminution)*, diminution, discount, lull, mitigation, mollification, outflow, relief *(release)*, remission, removal, solace. SEE MAIN ENTRY
abatement of differences adjustment, arrangement *(understanding)*, collective bargaining, compromise, conciliation
abating mitigating
abbreviate abridge *(shorten)*, abstract *(summarize)*, commute, condense, constrict *(compress)*, curtail, decrease, digest *(summarize)*, dilute, diminish, discount *(minimize)*, lessen, minimize, reduce
abbreviated brief, compact *(pithy)*, concise, laconic, minimal, succinct
abbreviation abridgment *(condensation)*, abstract, capsule, compendium, curtailment, decrease, digest, diminution, outline *(synopsis)*, summary, symbol
abbreviatory compact *(pithy)*
abbreviature abridgment *(condensation)*, abstract, curtailment
abdere hide
abdicate abandon *(withdraw)*, cede, defect, demit, forfeit, leave *(depart)*, quit *(discontinue)*, relinquish, renounce, repudiate, resign, retire *(conclude a career)*, surrender *(give back)*, vacate *(void)*, withdraw, yield *(submit)*. SEE MAIN ENTRY
abdicatio abdication, renunciation, resignation *(relinquishment)*
abdication abandonment *(discontinuance)*, renunciation, resignation *(relinquishment)*, waiver. SEE MAIN ENTRY
abditus latent
abduce carry away
abduct carry away, hijack, kidnap. SEE MAIN ENTRY
abduction taking. SEE MAIN ENTRY
abecedarian elementary, neophyte, rudimentary
aberemurder SEE MAIN ENTRY
aberrance deviation, error, indirection *(indirect action)*, irregularity, perversion. SEE MAIN ENTRY
aberrancy deviation, digression, error, indirection *(indirect action)*, irregularity, perversion. SEE MAIN ENTRY
aberrant anomalous, astray, atypical, deviant, devious, disordered, disorderly, disparate, dissimilar, divergent, eccentric, errant, erroneous, faulty, irregular *(not usual)*, licentious, nonconforming, peccant *(culpable)*, peculiar *(curious)*, unaccustomed, uncommon, unorthodox, unpredictable, unusual, variable. SEE MAIN ENTRY
aberrare detour, deviate, digress
aberration deviation, digression, discrepancy, error, fault *(mistake)*, insanity, irregularity, nonconformity, perversion, quirk *(idiosyncrasy)*. SEE MAIN ENTRY
aberration of mind insanity
abet aid, assist, bear *(support)*, conduce, conspire, contribute *(assist)*, countenance, enable, espouse, foment, foster, help, maintain *(sustain)*, promote *(organize)*, subsidize. SEE MAIN ENTRY
abetment aid *(help)*, auspices, collusion, conspiracy, contribution *(participation)*, favor *(sanction)*, help, service *(assistance)*. SEE MAIN ENTRY
abetting ancillary *(auxiliary)*, concerted, concurrent *(united)*, promotion *(encouragement)*. SEE MAIN ENTRY
abettor accessory, accomplice, advocate *(espouser)*, assistant, backer, benefactor, catalyst, coactor, coadjutant, coconspirator, cohort, colleague, confederate, consociate, conspirator, conspirer, contributor *(contributor)*, copartner *(coconspirator)*, participant, partner, proponent. SEE MAIN ENTRY
abeyance cessation *(interlude)*, check *(bar)*, cloture, desuetude, discontinuance *(act of discontinuing)*, extension *(postponement)*, halt, hiatus, inaction, interruption, interval, moratorium, nonuse, pause, pendency, respite *(interval of rest)*, stay. SEE MAIN ENTRY
abeyancy stay
abeyant dormant, inactive, prospective
abhor blame, condemn *(ban)*, contemn, disdain, forswear, reject, renounce, shun. SEE MAIN ENTRY
abhorrence alienation *(estrangement)*, contempt *(disdain)*, disapprobation, disapproval, disdain, hatred, odium, phobia, rejection
abhorrent antipathetic *(distasteful)*, bad *(offensive)*, contemptible, heinous, loathsome, objectionable, obnoxious, offensive *(offending)*, repugnant *(exciting aversion)*, repulsive. SEE MAIN ENTRY
abide adhere *(persist)*, allow *(endure)*, bear *(tolerate)*, continue *(persevere)*, dwell *(reside)*, endure *(last)*, inhabit, lodge *(reside)*, occupy *(take possession)*, persist, reside, subsist, suffer *(permit)*, tolerate. SEE MAIN ENTRY
abide by accede *(concede)*, adhere *(maintain loyalty)*, comply, concede, conform, defer *(yield in judgment)*, fulfill, keep *(fulfill)*, obey, observe *(obey)*, perform *(adhere to)*
abide together cohabit
abider habitant, inhabitant
abiding constant, continuance, durable, habitation *(act of inhabiting)*, indestructible, lasting, live *(existing)*, noncancellable, permanent, persistent, stable, steadfast, tolerance. SEE MAIN ENTRY
abiding place building *(structure)*, domicile, habitation *(dwelling place)*
abiding together cohabitation *(living together)*
abiectus contemptible, servile, sordid
ability aptitude, caliber *(mental capacity)*, capacity *(aptitude)*, efficiency, facility *(easiness)*, force *(strength)*, gift *(flair)*, performance *(workmanship)*, potential, proclivity, propensity, qualification *(fitness)*, quality *(excellence)*, quality *(grade)*, science *(technique)*, skill, specialty *(special aptitude)*. SEE MAIN ENTRY
ability to bear tolerance
ability to distinguish judgment *(discernment)*
ability to endure tolerance
ability to get along with others discretion *(quality of being discreet)*

ability to know comprehension, reason *(sound judgment)*
ability to make distinctions perception
ability to perceive intellect
ability to pursue tenacity
ability to reason intellect
ability to tolerate tolerance
ability to understand insight, intellect
ability to withstand tolerance
abire disappear, resign, retire *(retreat)*, secede
abject base *(inferior)*, blameful, blameworthy, caitiff, contemptible, contemptuous, ignoble, loathsome, odious, servile, sordid, subservient. SEE MAIN ENTRY
abject fear phobia
abject slavery bondage
abjection bad faith, bad repute, degradation, dishonor *(shame)*, ignominy. SEE MAIN ENTRY
abjectness bad faith, bad repute, disgrace, dishonor *(shame)*, disrepute, ignominy, shame. SEE MAIN ENTRY
abjudge hold *(decide)*. SEE MAIN ENTRY
abjudicate hold *(decide)*
abjuration abdication, denial, desertion, disclaimer, disdain, negation, refusal, rejection, renunciation, repudiation, rescision, resignation *(relinquishment)*, retraction. SEE MAIN ENTRY
abjuratory contradictory, recusant
abjure abandon *(relinquish)*, abrogate *(annul)*, cede, controvert, disaffirm, disallow, disown *(deny the validity)*, disown *(refuse to acknowledge)*, forfeit, forgo, forswear, leave *(depart)*, quit *(discontinue)*, recant, refuse, reject, relinquish, renounce, repudiate, resign, revoke, set aside *(annul)*, surrender *(give back)*, withdraw. SEE MAIN ENTRY
abjurement confutation, disclaimer, resignation *(relinquishment)*
able adequate, artful, capable, competent, deft, effective *(efficient)*, efficient, expert, fit, omnipotent, potent, powerful, practiced, professional *(trained)*, proficient, qualified *(competent)*, ready *(prepared)*, resourceful, sciential, strong. SEE MAIN ENTRY
able to be altered ambulatory
able to be confirmed deductible *(provable)*
able to be felt palpable
able to be handled palpable
able to be pierced penetrable
able to be seen apparent *(perceptible)*, ostensible
able to be shown deductible *(provable)*
able to be subducted deductible *(capable of being deducted from taxes)*
able to be subtracted for tax purposes deductible *(capable of being deducted from taxes)*
able to be touched palpable
able to contain a great deal capacious
able to endure resilient
able to improve corrigible
able to meet situations resourceful
able to pay solid *(sound)*, solvent
able to recognize conscious *(awake)*
able to withstand insusceptible *(resistant)*
able-bodied powerful
ablegare send
ableness ability, caliber *(mental capacity)*, capacity *(aptitude)*, dint, efficiency, faculty *(ability)*, force *(strength)*, quality *(excellence)*, quality *(grade)*. SEE MAIN ENTRY
ablude conflict, disaccord
abnegate abrogate *(annul)*, adeem, annul, condemn *(ban)*, controvert, countercharge, decline *(reject)*, deny *(refuse to grant)*, disaffirm, disallow, disapprove *(reject)*, disavow, disclaim, disown *(deny the validity)*, forgo, forswear, negate, refuse, refute, reject, renounce, repudiate, set aside *(annul)*, surrender *(give back)*. SEE MAIN ENTRY
abnegation abandonment *(repudiation)*, ademption, declination, denial, disdain, negation, refusal, rejection, renunciation, rescision, temperance. SEE MAIN ENTRY
abnegative contrary
abnormal anomalous, atypical, deviant, disordered, irregular *(not usual)*, non compos mentis, peculiar *(curious)*, prodigious *(amazing)*, suspicious *(questionable)*, unaccustomed, uncommon, unusual. SEE MAIN ENTRY
abnormality deviation, incongruity, insanity, irregularity, nonconformity, perversion, quirk *(idiosyncrasy)*. SEE MAIN ENTRY
abnormity irregularity, nonconformity, quirk *(idiosyncrasy)*. SEE MAIN ENTRY
abnormous peculiar *(curious)*
abode address, base *(place)*, building *(structure)*, domicile, dwelling, habitation *(dwelling place)*, home *(domicile)*, house, inhabitation *(place of dwelling)*, lodging, residence. SEE MAIN ENTRY
abolere abolish, annul, obliterate
abolish abate *(extinguish)*, abrogate *(annul)*, abrogate *(rescind)*, adeem, annul, cancel, destroy *(void)*, disaffirm, discharge *(release from obligation)*, discontinue *(abandon)*, eliminate *(eradicate)*, eradicate, extinguish, extirpate, invalidate, kill *(defeat)*, negate, nullify, obliterate, overthrow, overturn, quash, recall *(call back)*, remove *(eliminate)*, renege, repeal, repudiate, rescind, revoke, stop, supersede, supplant, terminate, vacate *(void)*, vitiate, withdraw. SEE MAIN ENTRY
abolish the organization of disorganize
abolished inactive, null *(invalid)*, null and void
abolishing cancellation
abolishment abolition, ademption, annulment, cancellation, countermand, defeasance, discharge *(annulment)*, discontinuance *(act of discontinuing)*, dissolution *(termination)*, disuse, negation, rescision, retraction, reversal, revocation. SEE MAIN ENTRY
abolition abatement *(extinguishment)*, ademption, annulment, cancellation, censorship, countermand, defeasance, destruction, discharge *(annulment)*, discharge *(release from obligation)*, discontinuance *(act of discontinuing)*, dissolution *(termination)*, disuse, negation, obviation, removal, repudiation, rescision, reversal, revocation, subversion. SEE MAIN ENTRY
abominable bad *(offensive)*, contemptible, contemptuous, depraved, disgraceful, disreputable, heinous, invidious, loathsome, nefarious, objectionable, obnoxious, odious, offensive *(offending)*, outrageous, repugnant *(exciting aversion)*, repulsive, sordid, undesirable. SEE MAIN ENTRY
abominableness disrepute
abominari deprecate
abominate contemn
abomination alienation *(estrangement)*, atrocity, bad repute, contaminate, contempt *(disdain)*, defilement, disgrace, hatred, misdeed, perversion, wrong
aboriginal incipient, native *(domestic)*, prime *(original)*, primordial
abort cancel, conclude *(complete)*, destroy *(efface)*, discontinue *(abandon)*, dissolve *(terminate)*, extinguish, frustrate, invalidate, negate, quit *(discontinue)*. SEE MAIN ENTRY
aborted attempt failure *(lack of success)*
aborticide abortion *(feticide)*
abortio abortion *(feticide)*
abortion miscarriage. SEE MAIN ENTRY
abortive futile, imperfect, ineffective, ineffectual, otiose, unavailing, unproductive
abortive attempt frustration, miscarriage
abortive effort miscarriage
abound increase, proliferate. SEE MAIN ENTRY
abounding ample, copious, full, profuse, replete
abounding in error fallacious, false *(inaccurate)*
abounding in riches opulent, prosperous
about to be imminent, prospective
about to happen forthcoming, immediate *(imminent)*, imminent, inevitable, pending *(imminent)*, proximate
about-face reversal, reversion *(act of returning)*
aboutir abut
above before mentioned, last *(preceding)*. SEE MAIN ENTRY
above all a fortiori, particularly
above all price inestimable
above all value inestimable
above appraisal inestimable
above average extraordinary, superior *(excellent)*
above meanness magnanimous
above par meritorious, notable, noteworthy, preferable, superior *(excellent)*, valuable
above pettiness magnanimous
above reproach blameless, unimpeachable
above suspicion blameless, clean, incorruptible, inculpable, irreprehensible, not guilty. SEE MAIN ENTRY
above the average best
above the law SEE MAIN ENTRY
above-cited before mentioned, last *(preceding)*, previous
above-mentioned aforesaid, before mentioned, last *(preceding)*, previous, said. SEE MAIN ENTRY
above-named before mentioned, last *(preceding)*, previous. SEE MAIN ENTRY
above-stated before mentioned, last *(preceding)*
aboveboard bona fide, candid, direct *(forthright)*, ethical, honest, ingenuous, irreprehensible, moral, right *(correct)*, scrupulous, straightforward, unaffected *(sincere)*, upright
abrade diminish, erode, expunge
abrasion deterioration, erosion
abrasive caustic
abreaction catharsis
abreast equal, informed *(having information)*
abrégé capsule
abri cache *(hiding place)*
abridge abstract *(summarize)*, commute, condense, constrict *(compress)*, curtail, decrease, digest *(summarize)*, diminish, discount *(minimize)*, expurgate, extract, lessen, minimize, reduce, retrench. SEE MAIN ENTRY

abridged brief, compact *(pithy)*, concise, laconic, minimal, partial *(relating to a part)*, sententious. SEE MAIN ENTRY
abridgment abstract, brief, capsule, censorship, compendium, curtailment, decrease, decrement, deduction *(diminution)*, denial, deterrence, digest, mitigation, outline *(synopsis)*, paraphrase, restatement, summary, synopsis. SEE MAIN ENTRY
abrogare abrogate *(annul)*, annul, discredit, repeal, rescind, revoke
abrogate abate *(extinguish)*, abolish, adeem, annul, ban, bear false witness, cancel, cease, condemn *(ban)*, contradict, controvert, countervail, debar, disallow, discharge *(release from obligation)*, disclaim, discontinue *(abandon)*, disinherit, dissolve *(terminate)*, invalidate, kill *(defeat)*, negate, nullify, overrule, proscribe *(prohibit)*, recall *(call back)*, recant, renege, repeal, repudiate, rescind, revoke, set aside *(annul)*, vacate *(void)*, vitiate. SEE MAIN ENTRY
abrogated defunct, inactive, invalid, lifeless *(dead)*, null *(invalid)*, null and void, powerless. SEE MAIN ENTRY
abrogatio revocation
abrogation abandonment *(desertion)*, abandonment *(discontinuance)*, abatement *(extinguishment)*, abolition, ademption, annulment, avoidance *(cancellation)*, cancellation, condemnation *(seizure)*, countermand, default, defeasance, desuetude, discharge *(annulment)*, discharge *(release from obligation)*, dissolution *(termination)*, inaction, mistrial, negation, nollo prosequi, obviation, repudiation, rescision, reversal, revocation, waiver. SEE MAIN ENTRY
abrupt caustic, impulsive *(rash)*, instantaneous, precipitate, unanticipated, unexpected. SEE MAIN ENTRY
abruption impasse
abruptness disrespect
abscind break *(violate)*, excise *(cut away)*, split. SEE MAIN ENTRY
abscission cancellation
abscond abandon *(physically leave)*, defect, depart, disappear, elude, escape, evacuate, flee, leave *(depart)*, move *(alter position)*, quit *(evacuate)*, withdraw. SEE MAIN ENTRY
abscond with hold up *(rob)*, jostle *(pickpocket)*, loot, pilfer, steal
abscondence bad faith
absconder fugitive
abscondere hide
absconding flight
absconditus hidden, latent
absence blank *(emptiness)*, dearth, deficiency, deficit, desuetude, furlough, insufficiency, need *(deprivation)*, nonresidence, nonuse, paucity, poverty, privation. SEE MAIN ENTRY
absence of authority anarchy
absence of ceremony informality
absence of change status quo
absence of diversity uniformity
absence of doubt certainty
absence of fear prowess *(bravery)*
absence of feeling insentience
absence of foreign rule liberty
absence of guilt innocence
absence of meaning incoherence, platitude
absence of restraint latitude, liberty
absence of sensation insentience
absence of servitude liberty
absence of variation uniformity
absence without leave desertion, nonappearance
absent lost *(taken away)*, oblivious, truant, vacuous. SEE MAIN ENTRY
absent oneself abandon *(physically leave)*, abscond, depart, evacuate, flee, withdraw
absent-minded perfunctory, thoughtless
absentation leave *(absence)*, nonappearance
absenteeism nonappearance
absentia absence *(nonattendance)*
absentminded lax, oblivious
absentmindedness neglect
absinthal bitter *(acrid tasting)*
absinthian bitter *(acrid tasting)*
absolute actual, affirmative, arbitrary and capricious, axiomatic, cardinal *(outstanding)*, categorical, certain *(fixed)*, certain *(positive)*, clear *(certain)*, compelling, complete *(all-embracing)*, conclusive *(determinative)*, convincing, decisive, definite, definitive, demonstrable, dogmatic, explicit, gross *(flagrant)*, implicit, inappealable, incontrovertible, indubious, outright, plenary, positive *(incontestable)*, pure, radical *(extreme)*, resounding, right *(direct)*, stark, strict, thorough, total, unalienable, unconditional, undisputed, unequivocal, unmitigated, unqualified *(unlimited)*. SEE MAIN ENTRY
absolute assertion affirmance *(legal affirmation)*, affirmation
absolute certainty certification *(certainness)*, certitude, fact
absolute condition sine qua non
absolute confidence certainty, certification *(certainness)*, surety *(certainty)*
absolute difference antipode, antithesis
absolute inheritance fee *(estate)*
absolute interest in realty fee *(estate)*
absolute leader dictator
absolute prerequisite sine qua non
absolute quiet silence
absolute reality fact
absolute requisite necessity
absolute right birthright
absolute ruler dictator
absolutely de facto, fairly *(clearly)*, faithfully, in toto, ipso facto, purely *(positively)*
absolutely clear incontestable
absoluteness belief *(state of mind)*, certainty, certitude, surety *(certainty)*
absolutio acquittal
absolution acquittal, amnesty, clemency, compurgation, condonation, discharge *(liberation)*, discharge *(release from obligation)*, dispensation *(exception)*, exoneration, grace, immunity, impunity, liberation, pardon, release, remission, waiver. SEE MAIN ENTRY
absolution of a charge exoneration
absolutistic dictatorial
absolutus absolute *(complete)*
absolve acquit, clear, condone, discharge *(liberate)*, discharge *(release from obligation)*, exculpate, excuse, exonerate, extenuate, forgive, free, justify, palliate *(excuse)*, purge *(wipe out by atonement)*, quit *(free of)*, redeem *(satisfy debts)*, remit *(release from penalty)*, vindicate. SEE MAIN ENTRY
absolve of a charge exonerate
absolve of fault exculpate
absolve of wrongdoing exculpate
absolved blameless, clear *(free from criminal charges)*, exempt, free *(relieved from a burden)*, immune. SEE MAIN ENTRY
absolvere absolve, acquit, dispatch *(dispose of)*, perfect
absonant contradictory, opposite
absorb comprehend *(understand)*, conceive *(comprehend)*, concern *(involve)*, digest *(comprehend)*, engage *(involve)*, immerse *(engross)*, impress *(affect deeply)*, include, incorporate *(include)*, interest, merge, monopolize, occupy *(engage)*, penetrate, realize *(understand)*, receive *(permit to enter)*, understand. SEE MAIN ENTRY
absorb the attention occupy *(engage)*
absorb the mind occupy *(engage)*
absorb the thoughts occupy *(engage)*
absorbed internal, oblivious, pensive
absorbed interest preoccupation
absorbent penetrable
absorbing moving *(evoking emotion)*
absorption centralization, contemplation, interest *(concern)*, merger, notice *(heed)*, obsession, osmosis, preoccupation, reflection *(thought)*
absorption of mind diligence *(care)*
abstain abandon *(relinquish)*, decline *(reject)*, defer *(yield in judgment)*, desist, discontinue *(abandon)*, eschew, forbear, refrain, refuse, rest *(cease from action)*, shirk, shun, withhold. SEE MAIN ENTRY
abstain from avoid *(evade)*, cease, forgo
abstain from inserting omit
abstain from recognizing ignore
abstainment abstention, continence
abstemious frugal. SEE MAIN ENTRY
abstemiousness abstention, austerity, moderation, temperance
abstention absence *(nonattendance)*, continence, desuetude, temperance. SEE MAIN ENTRY
abstention from buying boycott
abstention from using boycott
absterge decontaminate
absterrere deter
abstinence abstention, continence, disuse, moderation, nonuse, temperance
abstinence from action abstention, inaction, laissez faire
abstract abridgment *(condensation)*, capsule, compendium, condense, delineation, digest, digest *(summarize)*, extract, hold up *(rob)*, intangible, lessen, moot, note *(brief comment)*, outline *(synopsis)*, recondite, restatement, review, scenario, select, speculative, steal, summary, synopsis, theoretical, withdraw. SEE MAIN ENTRY
abstract idea concept
abstract on the law hornbook
abstracted compact *(pithy)*, concise, disconnected, oblivious, pensive, perfunctory, thoughtless
abstraction concept, generality *(vague statement)*, idea, impalpability, larceny, notion, preoccupation, vision *(dream)*
abstruse ambiguous, complex, elusive, esoteric, hidden, inapprehensible, incomprehensible, indefinable, inexplicable, mysterious, nebulous, private *(confidential)*, profound *(esoteric)*, recondite, secret, technical. SEE MAIN ENTRY
abstruse knowledge secret
abstruseness ambiguity, mystery
absumere consume, exhaust *(deplete)*
absurd egregious, fatuous, impossible, incredible, inept *(inappropriate)*, infeasible, irrational, ludicrous, lunatic, outrageous, unbelievable, unreasonable, unsound *(fallacious)*, unsuitable. SEE MAIN ENTRY
absurd story myth. SEE MAIN ENTRY
absurdity incongruity
absurdly foolish fatuous

absurdness incongruity
absurdus illogical, irrational
abundance boom *(prosperity)*, bulk, plethora, prosperity, quantity, quorum, spate, store *(depository)*, sufficiency
abundant ample, considerable, copious, full, liberal *(generous)*, multiple, predominant, prevailing *(current)*, prevalent, profuse, prolific, replete, rife, substantial, usual. SEE MAIN ENTRY
abundantia store *(depository)*
abuse aspersion, atrocity, attack, badger, beat *(strike)*, contumely, criticism, damage, debauch, defamation, diatribe, dissipate *(expend foolishly)*, endanger, exploit *(take advantage of)*, harm, ill use, imprecation, infliction, injury, injustice, malign, maltreat, misapplication, misappropriation, misemploy, mishandle *(maltreat)*, mishandle *(mismanage)*, mistreat, misusage, misuse, molest *(subject to indecent advances)*, molestation, obloquy, offend *(insult)*, oppression, persecute, perversion, pervert, provocation, rape, reproach, revilement, shame, transgression, vilification, violation, wrong. SEE MAIN ENTRY
abuse a privilege infringe
abuse of privilege infringement
abuse of public trust corruption
abuse one's rights infringe
abused aggrieved *(harmed)*. SEE MAIN ENTRY
abusive calumnious, contemptuous, hostile, impertinent *(insolent)*, insolent, libelous, offensive *(offending)*, outrageous, pejorative, scurrilous. SEE MAIN ENTRY
abusive harangue diatribe
abusive language diatribe, obloquy, philippic, slander, vilification
abusive speech harangue, malediction
abusiveness oppression
abut contact *(touch)*, juxtapose. SEE MAIN ENTRY
abut on adjoin
abut upon border *(approach)*, border *(bound)*
abuti abuse *(misuse)*, ill use, misemploy
abutment bulwark, contact *(touching)*. SEE MAIN ENTRY
abuttal connection *(abutment)*, contact *(touching)*
abutting adjacent, coalescence, contiguous, immediate *(not distant)*, proximate
abysmal profound *(intense)*
abyss pitfall. SEE MAIN ENTRY
academic didactic, disciplinary *(educational)*, moot, speculative, theoretical. SEE MAIN ENTRY
academic honor degree *(academic title)*
academician pedagogue
academy institute
accede acknowledge *(respond)*, admit *(concede)*, agree *(comply)*, allow *(endure)*, assent, cede, coincide *(concur)*, concede, confirm, conform, consent, defer *(yield in judgment)*, grant *(concede)*, obey, relent, sanction, submit *(yield)*, succumb, suffer *(permit)*, yield *(submit)*. SEE MAIN ENTRY
accede to accept *(admit as sufficient)*, accept *(assent)*, approve, bear *(tolerate)*, certify *(approve)*, comply, concur *(agree)*, countenance, inherit, pass *(approve)*
accedence acceptance, acquiescence, compliance, consent
accedere approach
accedere ad approximate
accelerare hasten, precipitate *(hasten)*
accelerate expedite, facilitate, hasten, precipitate *(hasten)*, race. SEE MAIN ENTRY
accelerated expeditious, rapid
accelerated decision accelerated judgment
accelerated judgment SEE MAIN ENTRY
accelerating cumulative *(intensifying)*
acceleration boom *(increase)*, haste. SEE MAIN ENTRY
acceleration lane causeway
accendere incense
accent consequence *(significance)*, dwell *(linger over)*, emphasis, enunciate, inflection, insist, pronounce *(speak)*, reaffirm
accentuate dwell *(linger over)*, insist, pronounce *(speak)*, reaffirm. SEE MAIN ENTRY
accentuation emphasis, inflection, intonation, stress *(accent)*
accept abide, accede *(concede)*, accommodate, accredit, acquire *(receive)*, admit *(concede)*, adopt, agree *(comply)*, allow *(endure)*, approve, assent, assume *(undertake)*, bear *(tolerate)*, certify *(approve)*, coincide *(concur)*, collect *(recover money)*, comply, concede, conceive *(comprehend)*, concur *(agree)*, condone, conform, consent, defer *(yield in judgment)*, espouse, gain, grant *(concede)*, obey, partake, pass *(approve)*, receive *(acquire)*, receive *(permit to enter)*, recognize *(acknowledge)*, sanction, seal *(solemnize)*, sign, submit *(yield)*, suffer *(permit)*, tolerate, trust, undertake, uphold, validate, yield *(submit)*. SEE MAIN ENTRY
accept a liability promise *(vow)*
accept advice hear *(give attention to)*
accept an obligation assume *(undertake)*, promise *(vow)*
accept an offer close *(agree)*, contract
accept as a citizen naturalize *(make a citizen)*
accept as a member enroll
accept responsibility promise *(vow)*
accept responsibility for sponsor
accept the loan of borrow
acceptability admissibility, expedience, mediocrity, qualification *(fitness)*
acceptable adequate, admissible, allowable, allowed, applicable, commensurate, convenient, conventional, desirable *(qualified)*, eligible, fair *(satisfactory)*, fit, justifiable, mediocre, meritorious, palatable, passable, proper, qualified *(competent)*, sapid, seasonable, suitable, tenable, unobjectionable, viable. SEE MAIN ENTRY
acceptable evidence admissible evidence
acceptably fairly *(moderately)*
acceptance acquiescence, acquisition, affirmance *(judicial sanction)*, approval, assent, assumption *(adoption)*, charter *(sanction)*, compliance, concession *(compromise)*, confirmation, consent, credence, faith, indorsement, lenience, ratification, receipt *(act of receiving)*, recognition, reliance, sanction *(permission)*, subscription, understanding *(tolerance)*. SEE MAIN ENTRY
acceptance bill draft
acceptance of penalty nollo contendere
acceptation acquisition, meaning, signification
accepted allowable, allowed, assumed *(inferred)*, boiler plate, common *(customary)*, conventional, customary, familiar *(customary)*, formal, general, ordinary, plausible, popular, prescriptive, prevailing *(current)*, prevalent, right *(suitable)*, select, traditional, uncontested, undisputed, usual
accepted belief principle *(axiom)*
accepted fact common knowledge
accepted language plain language
accepted meaning content *(meaning)*
acceptedly admittedly
accepter disciple, receiver, recipient
accepting orthodox
acceptio acceptance, receipt *(act of receiving)*, taking
acceptor bearer, customer, devisee, donee, feoffee, grantee, heir, payee, transferee
access admission *(entry)*, admittance *(means of approach)*, entrance, entry *(entrance)*, ingress, outlet, portal. SEE MAIN ENTRY
access road causeway
accesses approaches
accessibility access *(opening)*
accessible amenable, available, convenient, destructible, indefensible, obvious, open-minded, passable, penetrable, potential, present *(attendant)*, public *(open)*, ready *(prepared)*, receptive, responsive, suasible, untenable, vulnerable. SEE MAIN ENTRY
accessible to all competitive *(open)*
accessible to bribery mercenary
accessibleness amenability
accessio accession *(annexation)*, addition, appendix *(supplement)*, augmentation
accession acceptance, acknowledgment *(acceptance)*, acquiescence, addition, appurtenance, arrogation, collection *(accumulation)*, cumulation, receipt *(act of receiving)*. SEE MAIN ENTRY
accessories paraphernalia *(apparatus)*, paraphernalia *(personal belongings)*, property *(possessions)*
accessory abettor, accomplice, addition, additional, adjunct, ancillary *(auxiliary)*, appendix *(accession)*, appliance, appurtenance, appurtenant, assistant, attachment *(thing affixed)*, augmentation, circumstantial, clerical, coactor, coadjutant, coconspirator, codicil, cohort, collateral *(accompanying)*, colleague, confederate, consociate, conspirer, contributor *(contributor)*, contributory, copartner *(coconspirator)*, expendable, extrinsic, incident, incidental, inferior *(lower in position)*, minor, nonessential, participant, partner, secondary, subordinate, subservient, supplementary. SEE MAIN ENTRY
accessory after the fact accomplice, coactor, coconspirator, conspirer, copartner *(coconspirator)*
accessory before the fact accomplice, coactor, coconspirator, conspirer, copartner *(coconspirator)*
accessus access *(right of way)*
accident act of god, casualty, catastrophe, contingency, emergency, happenstance, misfortune, tragedy. SEE MAIN ENTRY
accidental coincidental, fortuitous, haphazard, inadvertent, incidental, random, unexpected, unforeseen, unintentional, unwitting. SEE MAIN ENTRY
accidental death fatality
accidental homocide manslaughter
accidental occurrence happenstance, quirk *(accident)*
accipere accept *(take)*, construe *(comprehend)*, enfranchise, hear *(give attention to)*, receive *(acquire)*
accipient assignee
acclaim honor *(outward respect)*, honor, mention *(tribute)*, recommend, remembrance *(commemoration)*, reputation

acclaimed famous, illustrious, notable, renowned, reputable
acclamation consensus, mention *(tribute)*
acclamatory favorable *(expressing approval)*
acclimate inure *(accustom)*
acclimated accustomed *(familiarized)*
acclimation compatibility, habituation
acclimatization habituation
acclimatize adapt, attune, conform, inure *(accustom)*
acclimatized accustomed *(familiarized)*
accolade prize
accommodare accommodate, adjust *(regulate)*
accommodate adjust *(regulate)*, agree *(comply)*, assist, attune, comply, compromise *(settle by mutual agreement)*, conform, contribute *(assist)*, fund, furnish, help, loan, naturalize *(acclimate)*, negotiate, obey, pacify, propitiate, provide *(supply)*, serve *(assist)*, settle, support *(assist)*. SEE MAIN ENTRY
accommodate oneself adapt, condescend *(deign)*
accommodate with lend, supply
accommodated fit, res judicata
accommodating benevolent, charitable *(lenient)*, civil *(polite)*, consenting, malleable, philanthropic, pliable, pliant, propitious, sequacious, suitable, yielding. SEE MAIN ENTRY
accommodatio adjustment
accommodation accord, accordance *(compact)*, accordance *(understanding)*, adjustment, advance *(allowance)*, advancement *(loan)*, advantage, aid *(help)*, amenity, arrangement *(understanding)*, assistance, benefit *(betterment)*, comity, compatibility, compliance, conciliation, condonation, conformity *(agreement)*, consideration *(recompense)*, consideration *(sympathetic regard)*, consortium *(marriage companionship)*, coverage *(scope)*, dispensation *(act of dispensing)*, favor *(act of kindness)*, help, latitude, loan, lodging, provision *(act of supplying)*, relief *(aid)*, service *(assistance)*, settlement, space, support *(assistance)*. SEE MAIN ENTRY
accommodations domicile, habitation *(dwelling place)*, house, residence
accommodative concordant, nonmilitant
accommodativeness amenability
accommodatus adequate, appropriate, convenient, qualified *(conditioned)*
accompanied composite
accompanier colleague, consort, copartner *(coconspirator)*
accompaniment appurtenance, attendance, codicil, rider, synchronism
accompaniments paraphernalia *(apparatus)*
accompany coincide *(correspond)*, concur *(coexist)*. SEE MAIN ENTRY
accompanying coincidental, concomitant, concurrent *(at the same time)*, incidental, simultaneous. SEE MAIN ENTRY
accompanying events circumstances
accomplice abettor, accessory, assistant, coactor, coadjutant, coconspirator, cohort, colleague, confederate, consociate, conspirer, contributor *(contributor)*, copartner *(coconspirator)*, participant, partner. SEE MAIN ENTRY
accomplice in crime abettor, accessory, coactor, conspirer, copartner *(coconspirator)*
accomplish attain, avail *(bring about)*, carry *(succeed)*, commit *(perpetrate)*, complete, compose, consummate, culminate, discharge *(perform)*, dispatch *(dispose of)*, effectuate, evoke, finish, fulfill, gain, implement, make, operate, pass *(satisfy requirements)*, perfect, perform *(execute)*, perpetrate, procure, produce *(manufacture)*, reach, realize *(make real)*, render *(administer)*, succeed *(attain)*, transact
accomplish promptly expedite
accomplished capable, cognizant, competent, complete *(ended)*, deft, expert, facile, familiar *(informed)*, informed *(educated)*, learned, literate, practiced, proficient, qualified *(competent)*, resourceful, sciential, subtle *(refined)*
accomplished efficiently expeditious
accomplished fact fait accompli, performance *(execution)*
accomplished practitioner professional
accomplishment act *(undertaking)*, action *(performance)*, boom *(prosperity)*, commission *(act)*, development *(outgrowth)*, discharge *(performance)*, effect, end *(termination)*, fait accompli, finality, fruition, output, performance *(execution)*, performance *(workmanship)*, product, progress, realization, satisfaction *(fulfilment)*, specialty *(special aptitude)*, transaction. SEE MAIN ENTRY
accomplishments civilization, education
accord accede *(concede)*, accordance *(compact)*, adjust *(resolve)*, adjustment, administer *(tender)*, agree *(comply)*, agreement *(concurrence)*, allow *(endure)*, approval, arbitrate *(conciliate)*, arrangement *(understanding)*, ascribe, assent *(noun)*, assent *(verb)*, attune, authorize, bargain, bestow, cartel, certify *(approve)*, cohere *(be logically consistent)*, coincide *(concur)*, comity, compatibility, compliance, concert, concession *(compromise)*, conciliation, concordance, concur *(agree)*, condescend *(deign)*, confer *(give)*, confirm, confirmation, conform, conformity *(agreement)*, consensus, consent *(noun)*, consent *(verb)*, contact *(association)*, contract, contribute *(supply)*, correspondence *(similarity)*, defer *(yield in judgment)*, delegate, endue, give *(grant)*, grant *(concede)*, impart, indorsement, league, leave *(give)*, mutual understanding, peace, present *(make a gift)*, propinquity *(similarity)*, provide *(supply)*, rapport, rapprochement, reconciliation, render *(administer)*, synchronism, treaty, understanding *(agreement)*, union *(unity)*, volition, vouchsafe, yield *(produce a return)*. SEE MAIN ENTRY
accord one's approval certify *(approve)*, notarize, permit
accord recognition to accept *(recognize)*
accord superiority to defer *(yield in judgment)*
accord with comport *(agree with)*
accordance acceptance, accommodation *(adjustment)*, accord, acquiescence, adjustment, arrangement *(understanding)*, assent, bargain, capacity *(authority)*, cartel, coalescence, compatibility, compliance, concert, conciliation, concordance, confirmation, conformity *(agreement)*, contract, indulgence, leave *(permission)*, license, propriety *(appropriateness)*, rapport, rapprochement, understanding *(agreement)*, union *(unity)*. SEE MAIN ENTRY
accordance with law legality
accordant agreed *(harmonized)*, apposite, appropriate, commensurate, concerted, concordant, concurrent *(united)*, congruous, consensual, consenting, consistent, consonant, contractual, correlative, felicitous, germane, harmonious, suitable
accordant with the facts authentic
according to pursuant to
according to contract as agreed upon
according to custom orthodox, typical
according to desires arbitrary
according to edict licit
according to established form formal
according to fiat lawful
according to general belief reputedly
according to habit habitual
according to law choate lien, de jure, due *(regular)*, jural, juridical, just, law-abiding, lawful, legitimate *(rightful)*, licit, permissible, rightful, statutory. SEE MAIN ENTRY
according to plan purposely
according to regulation orthodox
according to reputation reputedly
according to routine typical
according to rule normal *(regular)*, orthodox, regular *(conventional)*, systematic
according to the agreement as agreed upon
according to the bargain as agreed upon
according to the book orthodox
according to the contract as agreed upon
according to the facts authentic, true *(authentic)*
according to the law legal
according to usage customary
according to value ad valorem
accordingly a fortiori, a priori, consequently. SEE MAIN ENTRY
accost approach, assail, assault, confront *(encounter)*. SEE MAIN ENTRY
accost bellicosely assault
accoster assailant
account amount *(sum)*, behalf, bill *(invoice)*, brief, calculate, census, computation, deem, delineation, description, distinction *(reputation)*, entry *(record)*, intelligence *(news)*, invoice *(bill)*, narration, rationale, reason *(basis)*, recital, record, rendition *(explication)*, report *(detailed account)*, representation *(statement)*, review *(critical evaluation)*, roll, statement, story *(narrative)*, tariff *(bill)*, worth. SEE MAIN ENTRY
account book ledger
account debtor debtor
account for enlighten, explain, exposit, justify, rationalize, solve, support *(justify)*, vindicate
account of goods shipped invoice *(itemized list)*
account of merchandise invoice *(itemized list)*
account of transactions ledger
account outstanding debt
account owing debt
account rendered invoice *(bill)*
accountability blame *(responsibility)*, burden, charge *(lien)*, charge *(responsibility)*, commitment *(responsibility)*, duty *(obligation)*, fault *(responsibility)*, liability, obligation *(liability)*. SEE MAIN ENTRY
accountable actionable, bound, cognizable, determinable *(ascertainable)*, liable, subject *(exposed)*. SEE MAIN ENTRY
accountableness charge *(responsibility)*, commitment *(responsibility)*, liability, responsibility *(accountability)*
accountancy budget, computation

accountant comptroller. SEE MAIN ENTRY
accounted detailed
accounted for present *(attendant)*
accounting attribution, computation. SEE MAIN ENTRY
accounts budget, finance, ledger
accounts collectable due
accounts outstanding due
accounts payable bill *(invoice)*
accouple cement, join *(bring together)*
accouplement marriage *(intimate relationship)*
accouter clothe, furnish, supply
accouterment equipment
accouterments paraphernalia *(apparatus)*
accredit allow *(authorize)*, ascribe, authorize, bestow, certify *(approve)*, concur *(agree)*, confirm, cosign, countenance, delegate, empower, honor, indorse, notarize, qualify *(meet standards)*, seal *(solemnize)*, sign, support *(corroborate)*, trust, verify *(confirm)*. SEE MAIN ENTRY
accredit with attribute
accreditation jurat
accredited authentic, documentary, official, popular
accreted coherent *(joined)*
accretion accession *(enlargement)*, boom *(increase)*, collection *(accumulation)*, compilation, cumulation, development *(progression)*, increment. SEE MAIN ENTRY
accretive coherent *(joined)*
accroach annex *(arrogate)*, assume *(seize)*, condemn *(seize)*, impropriate, obtrude, overreach, overstep, usurp. SEE MAIN ENTRY
accroachment appropriation *(taking)*
accrual accession *(enlargement)*, additive, appreciation *(increased value)*, augmentation, boom *(increase)*, interest *(profit)*
accruance profit
accrue accumulate *(enlarge)*, arise *(originate)*, bear *(yield)*, compound, develop, hoard, increase, mature, redound, result, yield *(produce a return)*. SEE MAIN ENTRY
accrued SEE MAIN ENTRY
accruement appreciation *(increased value)*, augmentation, boom *(increase)*, cumulation
accruing cumulative *(increasing)*
accumulare accumulate *(amass)*
accumulate accrue *(increase)*, aggregate, codify, collect *(gather)*, compile, concentrate *(consolidate)*, congregate, conjoin, consolidate *(unite)*, convene, crystallize, cull, expand, fund, garner, glean, hoard, increase, inure *(benefit)*, join *(bring together)*, keep *(shelter)*, obtain, procure, raise *(collect)*, reserve, set aside *(annul)*, store. SEE MAIN ENTRY
accumulated accrued, collective, conglomerate
accumulation accession *(enlargement)*, agglomeration, appreciation *(increased value)*, arsenal, assemblage, augmentation, boom *(increase)*, boom *(prosperity)*, bulk, compilation, conglomeration, cumulation, deposit, development *(progression)*, entirety, fund, growth *(increase)*, hoard, plethora, profit, resource, selection *(collection)*, stock *(store)*, store *(depository)*, sufficiency, treasury. SEE MAIN ENTRY
accumulative collective, cumulative *(increasing)*, lucrative
accuracy honesty, rigor, truth, veracity
accurate absolute *(conclusive)*, actual, appropriate, authentic, bona fide, definite, definitive, detailed, documentary, exact, explicit, factual, faithful *(true to fact)*, genuine, honest, literal, particular *(exacting)*, precise, proper, punctilious, punctual, real, reliable, right *(correct)*, sound, strict, thorough, true *(authentic)*, unrefutable, valid. SEE MAIN ENTRY
accurately duly, faithfully
accuratus careful, circumstantial, scrupulous, systematic
accursed arrant *(onerous)*, diabolic, iniquitous, loathsome, odious, peccant *(culpable)*
accusable bad *(offensive)*, blameful, blameworthy, culpable, delinquent *(guilty of a misdeed)*, illicit, peccant *(culpable)*, reprehensible, reprobate, unjustifiable
accusal accusation, blame *(culpability)*, complaint, denunciation, impeachment, incrimination, indictment, information *(charge)*
accusant accuser, claimant, complainant
accusare accuse, arraign, charge *(accuse)*, complain *(charge)*, fault, impeach, indict, prosecute *(charge)*
accusatio accusation, charge *(accusation)*, denunciation, impeachment, indictment
accusation arraignment, blame *(culpability)*, claim *(legal demand)*, complaint, condemnation *(blame)*, count, criticism, denunciation, diatribe, disparagement, impeachment, incrimination, inculpation, indictment, information *(charge)*, innuendo, libel, objurgation, obloquy, onus *(blame)*, outcry, pleading, presentment, reproach, slander, stricture. SEE MAIN ENTRY
accusation in court arraignment
accusative inculpatory
accusator prosecutor
accusatory contemptuous, incriminatory, inculpatory. SEE MAIN ENTRY
accusatory instrument SEE MAIN ENTRY
accusatrix accuser
accuse arraign, blame, book, complain *(charge)*, complain *(criticize)*, condemn *(blame)*, contemn, defame, denigrate, denounce *(inform against)*, fault, impeach, implicate, incriminate, indict, inform *(betray)*, involve *(implicate)*, lodge *(bring a complaint)*, pillory, present *(prefer charges)*, proscribe *(denounce)*, rebuke, recriminate, reprehend, reprimand, reproach. SEE MAIN ENTRY
accuse falsely defame, frame *(charge falsely)*, libel
accuse in writing libel
accuse of maladministration impeach
accuse of misconduct impeach
accuse of wrong arraign
accuse unfairly frame *(charge falsely)*
accuse unjustly frame *(charge falsely)*
accused convict, suspect. SEE MAIN ENTRY
accused litigant defendant
accused party defendant
accused person convict, suspect
accuser claimant, complainant, district attorney, informant, informer *(one providing criminal information)*, plaintiff. SEE MAIN ENTRY
accusing critical *(faultfinding)*, incriminatory, inculpatory
accustom discipline *(train)*, inure *(accustom)*, naturalize *(acclimate)*, reconcile
accustom oneself to endure *(suffer)*
accustomary habitual, mundane, ordinary, prevailing *(current)*, prevalent
accustomed addicted, conventional, customary, daily, familiar *(customary)*, frequent, habitual, household *(familiar)*, inveterate, ordinary, orthodox, prevailing *(current)*, prevalent, regular *(conventional)*, rife, routine, typical, usual. SEE MAIN ENTRY
accustoming habituation
ace unit *(item)*
acedia sloth
acer acute, intense
acerb harsh
acerbate aggravate *(annoy)*, annoy, bitter *(acrid tasting)*
acerbic bitter *(acrid tasting)*, harsh, mordacious
acerbitas intolerance, severity
acerbity ill will, rancor, severity
acerbus bitter *(acrid tasting)*, caustic, scathing, virulent
acervation assemblage, collection *(accumulation)*, cumulation
acervus collection *(accumulation)*, hoard
ache pain
achievability feasibility, possibility
achievable passable, possible, potential, practicable
achieve accomplish, acquire *(receive)*, attain, build *(construct)*, carry *(succeed)*, commit *(perpetrate)*, complete, compose, consummate, discharge *(perform)*, dispatch *(dispose of)*, earn, effectuate, evoke, execute *(accomplish)*, finish, fulfill, function, gain, implement, make, obtain, operate, pass *(satisfy requirements)*, perform *(adhere to)*, perform *(execute)*, perpetrate, procure, produce *(manufacture)*, reach, realize *(make real)*, realize *(obtain as a profit)*, reap, recover, succeed *(attain)*, transact. SEE MAIN ENTRY
achieve by continued effort earn
achieve liberty escape
achieved complete *(ended)*
achievement act *(undertaking)*, action *(performance)*, boom *(prosperity)*, commission *(act)*, development *(outgrowth)*, discharge *(performance)*, effect, end *(termination)*, endeavor, fait accompli, finality, fruition, monument, objective, outcome, output, performance *(execution)*, performance *(workmanship)*, progress, prosperity, realization, satisfaction *(fulfilment)*, step, transaction
achievement of liberty liberation
aching painful
acid astringent, bitter *(acrid tasting)*, harsh, mordacious
acidulous bitter *(acrid tasting)*
acidus bitter *(acrid tasting)*
acknowledge abide, accede *(concede)*, accept *(recognize)*, admit *(concede)*, agree *(comply)*, allow *(authorize)*, answer *(reply)*, appreciate *(comprehend)*, assent, avouch *(avow)*, avow, bear *(adduce)*, betray *(disclose)*, certify *(approve)*, certify *(attest)*, comply, concede, concur *(agree)*, confess, confirm, correspond *(communicate)*, corroborate, defer *(yield in judgment)*, disclose, grant *(concede)*, hear *(give attention to)*, keep *(fulfill)*, note *(notice)*, notice *(observe)*, posit, prescriptive, profess *(avow)*, reply, respond, return *(respond)*, reveal, sign, subscribe *(sign)*, uphold, vouch, witness *(attest to)*. SEE MAIN ENTRY
acknowledge defeat quit *(discontinue)*, submit *(yield)*
acknowledge one's guilt confess
acknowledge openly bear *(adduce)*, testify
acknowledge through possession prescriptive

acknowledge through use prescriptive
acknowledged alleged, allowed, customary, familiar *(customary)*, nunc pro tunc, orthodox, proverbial, public *(known)*, putative, sound, traditional, undisputed, usual. SEE MAIN ENTRY
acknowledged elsewhere as alias
acknowledged judgment cognovit
acknowledgment acceptance, acquiescence, admission *(disclosure)*, adoption *(acceptance)*, affirmance *(authentication)*, affirmation, answer *(reply)*, approval, assent, asseveration, attribution, avouchment, avowal, charter *(sanction)*, common knowledge, concession *(compromise)*, confession, confirmation, consensus, consent, corroboration, disclosure *(something disclosed)*, expiation, grant, honorarium, ratification, recognition, recognizance, requital, response, reward. SEE MAIN ENTRY
acknowledgment of guilt confession
acknowledgment of payment receipt *(proof of receiving)*
acme ceiling, culmination, pinnacle
acme of perfection paragon
acolyte coactor
acquaint apprise, communicate, convey *(communicate)*, disabuse, disclose, divulge, enlighten, impart, inform *(notify)*, instruct *(teach)*, inure *(accustom)*, mention, notify, relate *(tell)*, report *(disclose)*, signify *(inform)*
acquaintance cognition, experience (background), knowledge *(awareness)*. SEE MAIN ENTRY
acquaintanceship contact *(association)*
acquainted accustomed *(familiarized)*, cognizant, expert, familiar *(informed)*, informed *(having information)*, knowing. SEE MAIN ENTRY
acquainted with conscious *(aware)*, learned, privy
acquainting informatory
acquest demesne
acquiesce abide, accede *(concede)*, accept *(admit as sufficient)*, accept *(assent)*, admit *(concede)*, agree *(comply)*, allow *(endure)*, assent, bear *(tolerate)*, coincide *(concur)*, concede, concur *(agree)*, confirm, consent, defer *(yield in judgment)*, grant *(concede)*, obey, observe *(obey)*, pass *(approve)*, relent, sanction, submit *(yield)*, succumb, suffer *(permit)*, surrender *(yield)*, tolerate, vouchsafe, yield *(submit)*. SEE MAIN ENTRY
acquiesce in approve, authorize, comply, countenance, indorse
acquiesced in consensual
acquiescence acceptance, acknowledgment *(acceptance)*, affirmance *(judicial sanction)*, affirmation, amenability, approval, assent, capitulation, charter *(sanction)*, compliance, concession *(compromise)*, confession, confirmation, conformity *(agreement)*, consent, deference, discipline *(obedience)*, dispensation *(exception)*, indorsement, indulgence, leave *(permission)*, permission, resignation *(passive acceptance)*, sanction *(permission)*. SEE MAIN ENTRY
acquiescent amenable, charitable *(lenient)*, concurrent *(united)*, congruous, consensual, consenting, favorable *(expressing approval)*, harmonious, inclined, law-abiding, malleable, obedient, open *(persuasible)*, passive, patient, permissive, pliable, pliant, ready *(willing)*, sequacious, tractable, willing *(not averse)*, yielding
acquiescently faithfully
acquiescing consenting
acquire accept *(take)*, accrue *(arise)*, accrue *(increase)*, aggregate, appropriate, attain, collect *(gather)*, collect *(recover* money), condemn *(seize)*, derive *(receive)*, gain, garner, hoard, impress *(procure by force)*, incur, inherit, obtain, occupy *(take possession)*, possess, procure, profit, purchase, realize *(obtain as a profit)*, reap, recover, store, succeed *(attain)*. SEE MAIN ENTRY
acquire beforehand preempt
acquire by purchase buy
acquire by service earn
acquire currency circulate
acquire from ancestors inherit
acquire information ascertain
acquire information about find *(discover)*
acquire intelligence about ascertain
acquire knowledge study
acquire ownership of buy, purchase
acquire the habit practice *(train by repetition)*
acquired facts information *(knowledge)*, intelligence *(news)*
acquired knowledge civilization, information *(knowledge)*
acquired mode of behavior habit
acquired right option *(contractual provision)*
acquirement acquisition, distress *(seizure)*, edification, realization, receipt *(act of receiving)*
acquirements education
acquisition accession *(enlargement)*, adverse possession, appropriation *(taking)*, assumption *(adoption)*, boom *(prosperity)*, collection *(accumulation)*, cumulation, distress *(seizure)*, profit, realization, receipt *(act of receiving)*, recovery *(repossession)*, replevin, takeover, taking. SEE MAIN ENTRY
acquisition by right of eminent domain condemnation *(seizure)*
acquisition of knowledge discovery, education
acquisitive confiscatory, insatiable, mercenary, parsimonious
acquisitiveness greed
acquit absolve, clear, comport *(behave)*, demean *(deport oneself)*, deport *(conduct oneself)*, discharge *(liberate)*, exculpate, excuse, exonerate, extenuate, forgive, free, liberate, palliate *(excuse)*, pardon, pay, purge *(wipe out by atonement)*, quit *(free of)*, remit *(release from penalty)*, remunerate, vindicate. SEE MAIN ENTRY
acquitment acquittal, discharge *(payment)*, satisfaction *(discharge of debt)*
acquittal absolution, compurgation, condonation, discharge *(liberation)*, discharge *(payment)*, discharge *(release from obligation)*, emancipation, exoneration, immunity, impunity, liberation, pardon, payment *(act of paying)*, release, remission, remittance, respite *(reprieve)*, satisfaction *(discharge of debt)*, waiver. SEE MAIN ENTRY
acquittance acquittal, amnesty, collection *(payment)*, compurgation, discharge *(payment)*, exoneration, liberation, payment *(act of paying)*, quitclaim, receipt *(proof of receiving)*, release, remission, satisfaction *(discharge of debt)*
acquitted blameless, clean, clear *(free from criminal charges)*, free *(relieved from a burden)*. SEE MAIN ENTRY
acreage homestead, parcel, plot *(land)*, property *(land)*, real estate, space
acres estate *(property)*, freehold, homestead, property *(land)*, realty
acrid astringent, bitter *(acrid tasting)*, caustic, harsh, mordacious, virulent
acrimonious astringent, bitter *(penetrating)*, bitter *(reproachful)*, caustic, cruel, cynical, harsh, hostile, libelous, malevolent, malicious, mordacious, negative, outrageous, pejorative, petulant, resentful, scathing, severe, spiteful, trenchant, vicious, virulent. SEE MAIN ENTRY
acrimoniousness spite
acrimony alienation *(estrangement)*, malice, philippic, rancor, resentment, severity, spite, umbrage
acroamatic esoteric, inapprehensible, incomprehensible, inexplicable, profound *(esoteric)*, secret
acroamatical esoteric, inapprehensible, incomprehensible, inexplicable, profound *(esoteric)*, secret
acroatic esoteric, inapprehensible, incomprehensible, inexplicable, learned, profound *(esoteric)*
act amendment *(legislation)*, canon, codification, commit *(perpetrate)*, comport *(behave)*, constitution, course, demean *(deport oneself)*, deport *(conduct oneself)*, dictate, enactment, execute *(accomplish)*, exercise *(discharge a function)*, fake, false pretense, function, law, measure, mock *(imitate)*, officiate, operate, operation, palter, performance *(execution)*, portray, prescription *(directive)*, pretend, procedure, proceed *(go forward)*, regulation *(rule)*, represent *(substitute)*, role, rubric *(authoritative rule)*, rule *(legal dictate)*, scene, simulate, statute, step, transaction. SEE MAIN ENTRY
act a part impersonate
act against counter, gainsay
act against with equal force compensate *(counterbalance)*, countervail
act as assume *(simulate)*, pose *(impersonate)*
act as agent intercede. SEE MAIN ENTRY
act as assistant to assist
act as broker represent *(substitute)*
act as chairman moderate *(preside over)*, preside
act as delegate represent *(substitute)*
act as go-between intercede
act as mediator intercede
act as moderator moderate *(preside over)*
act as one combine *(act in concert)*
act as president moderate *(preside over)*, preside
act as surety for sponsor
act committed in violation of law misdemeanor
act contrary disoblige
act demanded by social custom decorum
act despite override
act dishonestly cheat
act effectively function
act falsely fake
act foolishly mismanage
act for displace *(replace)*, replace, represent *(substitute)*, supplant
act illegally disobey, violate. SEE MAIN ENTRY
act improperly mismanage
act in accordance with orders obey
act in advance forestall
act in collusion plot
act in combination conspire
act in concert concur *(agree)*, connive, conspire, cooperate, federalize *(associate)*,

federate, involve *(participate)*, join *(associate oneself with)*, participate, unite. SEE MAIN ENTRY
act in harmony conspire
act in opposition fight *(battle)*
act in opposition to antagonize, confront *(oppose)*, counter, counteract, cross *(disagree with)*, fight *(counteract)*, oppose
act in place of represent *(substitute)*
act in response to answer *(reply)*
act in support adhere *(maintain loyalty)*
act insincerely palter
act interchangeably alternate *(take turns)*, reciprocate
act jointly combine *(act in concert)*, cooperate
act of bearing witness attestation
act of believing credence
act of berating diatribe, disparagement
act of bribing corruption
act of bringing in introduction
act of coming together chain *(nexus)*
act of compassing coverage *(scope)*
act of comprehending coverage *(scope)*
act of containing coverage *(scope)*
act of copying counterfeit
act of coupling chain *(nexus)*
act of crumbling decline
act of despising disdain
act of discrediting disdain, impeachment
act of dissembling color *(deceptive appearance)*
act of driving out eviction
act of dwelling together cohabitation *(living together)*
act of dwindling decline
act of embracing coverage *(scope)*
act of encircling coverage *(scope)*
act of encompassing coverage *(scope)*
act of engrossing coverage *(scope)*
act of facing confrontation *(act of setting face to face)*
act of falling away decline
act of ferocity atrocity
act of forestalling constraint *(restriction)*
act of forsaking desertion
act of generosity favor *(act of kindness)*
act of giving one's word pledge *(binding promise)*
act of God calamity. SEE MAIN ENTRY
act of grace amnesty, favor (act of kindness)
act of hampering constraint *(restriction)*
act of hardening congealment
act of holding harmless indemnity
act of hostility assault
act of indemnity exoneration
act of inhumanity brutality
act of joining chain *(nexus)*
act of judgment adjudication, award, choice *(decision)*, holding *(ruling of a court)*
act of keeping in constraint *(imprisonment)*
act of killing dispatch *(act of putting to death)*, murder
act of lawbreaking misdemeanor
act of lessening decline
act of living together as husband and wife cohabitation *(married state)*
act of loathing disdain
act of looking backward hindsight
act of losing ground decline
act of maneuvering connivance
act of mercy amnesty
act of oath-breaking perjury
act of pairing cohabitation *(married state)*
act of profiteering corruption
act of promise-making coverage *(insurance)*
act of protecting custody *(supervision)*
act of pursuing course
act of quelling constraint *(restriction)*
act of relinquishing a right waiver
act of reverting escheatment
act of running down disparagement
act of scheming connivance
act of scorning disdain
act of setting forth delineation
act of shrinking decline
act of shunning disdain
act of slaying dispatch *(act of putting to death)*, murder
act of slipping back decline
act of spanning coverage *(scope)*
act of spurning disdain
act of stifling constraint *(restriction)*
act of strangling constraint *(restriction)*
act of subsuming coverage *(scope)*
act of surrounding coverage *(scope)*
act of taking life murder
act of taunting disdain
act of throwing out eviction
act of thwarting constraint *(restriction)*
act of uniting chain *(nexus)*
act of wasting away decline
act of weakening decline
act of working together collusion
act of worsening decline
act on affect, award, commit *(perpetrate)*, discharge *(perform)*, militate, obey, treat *(process)*
act on *(complete)*. SEE MAIN ENTRY
act on *(rule)*. SEE MAIN ENTRY
act on behalf of represent *(substitute)*
act on one's own authority choose
act out impersonate
act prohibited by law crime
act the part of displace *(replace)*, exemplify, impersonate, pose *(impersonate)*
act together cooperate, participate
act upon execute *(accomplish)*, operate
act vicariously represent *(substitute)*
acta diurna journal
actable viable
acte act *(enactment)*
acting histrionics, operative, representative, surrogate, temporary, vicarious *(delegated)*. SEE MAIN ENTRY
acting as a substitute vicarious *(delegated)*
acting as attorney for representation *(acting for others)*
acting in conjunction concurrent *(united)*
acting out catharsis
acting with force drastic
acting without due consideration ill-judged
actio action *(proceeding)*, delivery, proceeding, suit
action act *(undertaking)*, award, campaign, case *(lawsuit)*, cause *(lawsuit)*, cause of action, contest *(dispute)*, controversy (lawsuit), course, day in court, fight *(battle)*, happening, hearing, holding *(ruling of a court)*, lawsuit, matter *(case)*, operation, overt act, performance *(execution)*, performance (workmanship), ploy, procedure, proceeding, process *(course)*, prosecution *(criminal trial)*, step, suit, transaction, trial *(legal proceeding)*. SEE MAIN ENTRY
action at law action *(proceeding)*, cause of action, lawsuit, proceeding, suit, trial *(legal proceeding)*
action in court cause *(lawsuit)*
action to defeat plaintiff's demand counterclaim
action to serve justice suit
actionable illegal, illicit, impermissible, justiciable, litigable, litigious, moot, triable, unlawful. SEE MAIN ENTRY
actionable act tortious act
actions behavior, conduct, dealings, deportment, manner *(behavior)*. SEE MAIN ENTRY
activate empower, launch *(initiate)*, maintain *(commence)*, motivate, originate, prompt, stimulate, urge. SEE MAIN ENTRY
activating impulsive *(impelling)*
activator catalyst, stimulus
active alert *(vigilant)*, conscious *(awake)*, effective *(operative)*, expeditious, fervent, industrious, moving *(in motion)*, operative, potent, rapid, responsive, sedulous, volatile, zealous. SEE MAIN ENTRY
active application diligence *(care)*
active attention diligence *(care)*
active discouragement deterrence
active element catalyst
active espousal advocacy
active giving charity
active ill will malice
active partisan catalyst
active partisans lobby
active reformer catalyst
active reformers lobby
active study diligence *(care)*, examination *(study)*
active supporters lobby
active thought diligence *(care)*
actively opposed hostile, malevolent
actively represent lobby
activeness life *(vitality)*
activism campaign
activists lobby
activities affairs, dealings. SEE MAIN ENTRY
activity agency *(legal relationship)*, business *(affair)*, business *(occupation)*, calling, campaign, career, course, employment, enterprise *(undertaking)*, life *(vitality)*, occupation *(vocation)*, project, pursuit *(occupation)*, transaction, turmoil. SEE MAIN ENTRY
actor actor. SEE MAIN ENTRY
acts conduct, dealings, legislation *(enactments)*, manner *(behavior)*. SEE MAIN ENTRY
actual absolute *(conclusive)*, accurate, authentic, bona fide, certain *(positive)*, clear *(certain)*, corporeal, de facto, definite, documentary, factual, genuine, honest, material *(physical)*, objective, peremptory *(absolute)*, physical, real, realistic, substantive, tangible, true *(authentic)*, unalienable. SEE MAIN ENTRY
actual existence reality
actual occurrence fact
actual possession occupancy
actual reality fact
actuality entity, fact, fait accompli, reality, substance *(essential nature)*, truth, veracity
actualization commission *(act)*, embodiment, fait accompli, realization
actualize compose, consummate, embody, exemplify, forge *(produce)*, implement, make, realize *(make real)*, substantiate
actually de facto
actuary SEE MAIN ENTRY
actuate agitate *(activate)*, bait *(lure)*, constrain *(compel)*, impel, induce, influence, inspire, lobby, motivate, persuade, prevail *(persuade)*, prompt, provoke, spirit, stimulate

actuating impulsive *(impelling),* persuasive
actuation commission *(act),* impetus, impulse, incentive, instigation, persuasion, provocation, reason *(basis)*
actuator abettor, catalyst
actus reus SEE MAIN ENTRY
acuity insight, perception, sagacity
aculeatus scathing
acumen caliber *(mental capacity),* common sense, discrimination *(good judgment),* insight, intelligence *(intellect),* judgment *(discernment),* perception, reason *(sound judgment),* sagacity, sense *(intelligence).* SEE MAIN ENTRY
acuminate acute
acute artful, caustic, conscious *(awake),* critical *(crucial),* crucial, exigent, important *(urgent),* incisive, insufferable, intense, intensive, knowing, mordacious, perceptive, politic, profound *(intense),* responsive, sapient, trenchant. SEE MAIN ENTRY
acute alcoholism dipsomania
acute dissatisfaction ill will
acuteness caliber *(mental capacity),* discretion *(quality of being discreet),* discrimination *(good judgment),* insight, judgment *(discernment),* perception, sagacity, sensibility
acutus acute, perspicacious
ad administrationem pertimens clerical
ad aerarium pertinens financial
ad captandum colorable *(plausible)*
ad damnum clause SEE MAIN ENTRY
ad hoc SEE MAIN ENTRY
ad hominem confugere apply *(request)*
ad infinitum SEE MAIN ENTRY
ad inritum redigere frustrate, nullify
ad interim SEE MAIN ENTRY
ad persuadendum accommodatus convincing
ad pugnam provocare challenge
ad rem apposite
ad rem spectare relevant
ad sententiam adopt
ad tempus temporary
ad tempus advenire punctual
ad vadimonium non venire default *(noun),* default *(verb)*
ad valorem SEE MAIN ENTRY
ad vanum frustrate
adage catchword, maxim, phrase, principle *(axiom)*
adamant callous, immutable, implacable, inexorable, inflexible, intractable, irreconcilable, persistent, pertinacious, resolute, unalterable, unbending, uncompromising, unrelenting, unyielding. SEE MAIN ENTRY
adamantine callous, unyielding
adapertus open *(unclosed)*
adapt accommodate, adjust *(regulate),* agree *(comply),* alter, apply *(put in practice),* arrange *(methodize),* attune, change, conform, modify *(alter),* naturalize *(acclimate),* orchestrate, reconcile. SEE MAIN ENTRY
adapt to correspond *(be equivalent)*
adaptability ability, amenability, compliance, conciliation
adaptable applicable, corrigible, disposable, flexible, malleable, pliable, pliant, practical, resilient, sequacious, tractable. SEE MAIN ENTRY
adaptable to change liberal *(broad-minded)*
adaptation accommodation *(adjustment),* adjustment, compromise, habituation, innovation, modification, propriety *(appropriateness)*
adapted accustomed *(familiarized),* agreed *(harmonized),* apposite, congruous, consonant, correlative, effective *(efficient),* felicitous, fit, fitting, harmonious, pertinent, proper, qualified *(competent),* resigned, sciential, suitable, tempered. SEE MAIN ENTRY
adapted to applicable, appropriate
adapted to argumentation forensic
adapted to teach didactic
adapted to the understanding coherent *(clear)*
adaption arrangement *(ordering)*
adaptive pliable, resilient
add affix, append, attach *(join),* conjoin, contribute *(supply),* extend *(enlarge),* heighten *(augment),* interject, recruit, sum, supplement, unite. SEE MAIN ENTRY
add as a third party implead
add as an accessory attach *(join)*
add details embellish
add on accrue *(increase),* increase
add strength to confirm
add to accumulate *(enlarge),* aggravate *(exacerbate),* amend, amplify, build *(augment),* collect *(gather),* compound, conjoin, consolidate *(strengthen),* elaborate, enhance, enlarge, expand, increase, intensify, magnify, supplement
add to the payroll employ *(engage services),* hire
add together aggregate
add up to consist
add water dilute
add weight to aggravate *(exacerbate)*
added additional, ancillary *(auxiliary),* attached *(annexed),* expendable, extrinsic, incidental, nonessential
added charge surcharge
added monetary worth appreciation *(increased value)*
added protection buffer zone
added time extension *(postponement)*
added to accrued
added together cumulative *(increasing)*
addend addition
addendum addition, additive, adjunct, allonge
addendum appendix *(supplement)*
addendum appurtenance, attachment *(thing affixed),* codicil, insertion, rider. SEE MAIN ENTRY
addere append, appendix *(supplement)*
addicere adjudge, allot, award
addict SEE MAIN ENTRY
addicted accustomed *(familiarized),* inveterate. SEE MAIN ENTRY
addicted to lewdness lecherous
addictedness dipsomania
addiction dipsomania
adding augmentation, computation
additament addendum, addition, adjunct, allonge, appendix *(accession),* appurtenance, boom *(increase),* codicil, insertion, rider
addition accession *(annexation),* accession *(enlargement),* accretion, addendum, additive, adjunct, allonge, appendix *(supplement),* appreciation *(increased value),* appurtenance, boom *(increase),* codicil, collection *(accumulation),* continuation *(prolongation),* corollary, cumulation, exaggeration, expletive, extension *(expansion),* growth *(increase),* increment, insertion, offshoot, reinforcement, rider. SEE MAIN ENTRY
addition to adjoiner
addition to a will codicil
addition to realty fixture
additional ancillary *(auxiliary),* circumstantial, collateral *(accompanying),* contributory, cumulative *(increasing),* expendable, extraneous, extrinsic, gratuitous *(unwarranted),* incidental, nonessential, pendent, superfluous, supplementary. SEE MAIN ENTRY
additional charge surcharge
additional clause rider
additional strength reinforcement
additional time extension *(postponement)*
additionally also, further. SEE MAIN ENTRY
additive addition, additional, bonus, codicil, cumulative *(increasing),* factor *(ingredient),* supplementary. SEE MAIN ENTRY
additory boom *(increase),* cumulative *(increasing)*
additum attachment *(thing affixed),* codicil
additur SEE MAIN ENTRY
additus additional
addle confuse *(bewilder),* decay, discompose, muddle, obfuscate, spoil *(impair)*
addlebrained opaque
addled fatuous
addleheaded opaque
addlepated opaque
address abode, accost, bestow, building *(structure),* call *(appeal),* conduct, converse, declaim, declamation, deportment, discourse *(noun),* discourse *(verb),* dispatch *(send off),* domicile, habitation *(dwelling place),* locality, lodging, manner *(behavior),* parlance, peroration, recite, report *(detailed account),* residence, rhetoric *(skilled speech),* site, speak, speech. SEE MAIN ENTRY
address a petition call *(appeal to)*
address a request call *(appeal to),* plead *(implore),* pray
address a warning to admonish *(warn),* notice *(give formal warning)*
address oneself to call *(appeal to),* endeavor, occupy *(engage),* specialize, undertake
address to dedicate
address to the jury charge *(statement to the jury)*
addressee inhabitant, lodger, occupant, resident
addriri assault
adduce allege, depose *(testify),* mention, proffer, quote, rationalize, refer *(direct attention).* SEE MAIN ENTRY
adduce evidence corroborate
adduced alleged. SEE MAIN ENTRY
adducere adduce, induce
adeem assume *(seize),* attach *(seize),* confiscate. SEE MAIN ENTRY
adeemed attached *(seized)*
ademption taking. SEE MAIN ENTRY
adept artful, capable, competent, deft, diplomatic, expert, practiced, professional *(trained),* proficient, qualified *(competent),* sciential, veteran. SEE MAIN ENTRY
adept practitioner professional
adeptness ability, efficiency, facility *(easiness),* gift *(flair),* prowess *(ability),* skill, specialty *(special aptitude)*
adequacy ability, caliber *(mental capacity),* competence *(ability),* quorum, sufficiency, utility *(usefulness).* SEE MAIN ENTRY
adequate ample, capable, commensurate, competent, effective *(efficient),* fair *(satisfactory),* fit, functional, habitable, mediocre, operative, prima facie *(legally*

sufficient), proficient, qualified *(competent),* sciential, suitable, unobjectionable. SEE MAIN ENTRY
adequate notice SEE MAIN ENTRY
adequate proof SEE MAIN ENTRY
adequate resources sufficiency
adequately fairly *(moderately)*
adequately perceive appreciate *(value)*
adequateness admissibility, mediocrity, quorum
adesse appear *(attend court proceedings),* support *(assist)*
adeundi copiam admit *(give access)*
adferre entail, quote, report *(disclose)*
adficere affect
adfigere affix, attach *(join)*
adfinis germane
adfirmare affirm *(uphold),* assert, contend *(maintain),* maintain *(carry on)*
adfirmatio affirmation, allegation, assertion, indorsement, possess
adfligere overthrow
adgredi assail, assault, attack
adherance concrescence
adhere abide, affix, attach *(join),* cement, confirm, join *(bring together),* maintain (sustain), persevere, remain *(continue),* remain *(stay).* SEE MAIN ENTRY
adhere to bear *(tolerate),* comply, conform, fulfill, keep *(fulfill),* obey, observe *(obey),* pursue *(carry on).* SEE MAIN ENTRY
adherence accession *(annexation),* adhesion *(affixing),* adhesion *(loyalty),* allegiance, coalescence, coherence, compliance, conformity *(obedience),* continuation *(prolongation),* loyalty. SEE MAIN ENTRY
adherence to duty adhesion *(loyalty),* allegiance
adherences ties
adherency loyalty
adherent addict, advocate *(espouser),* backer, coadunate, coherent *(joined),* cohesive *(sticking),* consociate, disciple, partisan, protégé. SEE MAIN ENTRY
adhering coadunate, coherent *(joined),* cohesive *(sticking),* inextricable
adhering to a purpose pertinacious
adhering to an original faithful *(true to fact)*
adhesion accession *(annexation),* coalescence, coherence, contact *(touching).* SEE MAIN ENTRY
adhesions ties
adhesive coadunate, coherent *(joined),* cohesive *(sticking)*
adhesiveness adhesion *(affixing),* coherence, tenacity. SEE MAIN ENTRY
adhibition use
adhortari exhort
adiacere adjoin, border *(bound)*
adiectio addition
adiectus additional
adipisci acquire *(receive),* obtain
adit access *(right of way),* entrance, entry *(entrance)*
aditus access *(right of way),* entrance
adiudicare adjudge, award
adiumentum assistance, support *(assistance)*
adiungere append, appendix *(accession)*
adiutor assistant, promoter
adiutores staff
adiutrix assistant
adiuvare abet, contribute *(assist),* cooperate, subsidize
adjacency conjunction, contact *(touching),* propinquity *(proximity)*
adjacent close *(near),* contiguous, immediate *(not distant),* local, present *(attendant),* proximate. SEE MAIN ENTRY
adjective procedural
adjective law procedure. SEE MAIN ENTRY
adjoin abut, affix, attach *(join),* border *(approach),* border *(bound),* contact *(touch),* juxtapose, overlap. SEE MAIN ENTRY
adjoiner SEE MAIN ENTRY
adjoining accession *(annexation),* adjacent, close *(near),* contiguous, immediate *(not distant),* local, proximate
adjourn cease, conclude *(complete),* defer *(put off),* delay, discontinue *(break continuity),* halt, hold up *(delay),* postpone, procrastinate, recess. SEE MAIN ENTRY
adjournal adjournment, cloture
adjourned arrested *(checked)*
adjournment cessation *(interlude),* close *(conclusion),* cloture, deferment, discontinuance *(act of discontinuing),* end *(termination),* extension *(postponement),* hiatus, pendency. SEE MAIN ENTRY
adjournment of a cause continuance
adjournment of a proceeding continuance
adjudge adjudicate, ascertain, award, condemn *(punish),* confer *(give),* criticize *(evaluate),* decide, decree, deem, determine, find *(determine),* gauge, judge, opine, pronounce *(pass judgment),* rule *(decide),* sentence, try *(conduct a trial).* SEE MAIN ENTRY
adjudge innocent absolve, palliate *(excuse)*
adjudge the validity of a will probate
adjudge to be due award
adjudged juridical
adjudger judge, juror
adjudgment adjudication, arbitration, award, conviction *(finding of guilt),* decree, determination, judgment *(formal court decree)*
adjudgment body jury
adjudicate adjudge, arbitrate *(adjudge),* award, decide, decree, determine, find *(determine),* hear *(give a legal hearing),* judge, pronounce *(pass judgment),* rule *(decide),* try *(conduct a trial).* SEE MAIN ENTRY
adjudicate the validity of a will probate
adjudication award, cognovit, conclusion *(determination),* conviction *(finding of guilt),* decree, determination, direction *(order),* holding *(ruling of a court),* judgment *(formal court decree),* opinion *(judicial decision),* res judicata, ruling, sentence, verdict. SEE MAIN ENTRY
adjudicator arbiter, arbitrator, judge, juror, referee, umpire
adjudicators jury
adjunct addendum, addition, additive, allonge, ancillary *(auxiliary),* appendix *(supplement),* appliance, appurtenance, appurtenant, associate, attachment *(thing affixed),* backer, coactor, codicil, colleague, confederate, consociate, copartner *(coconspirator),* corollary, pendent, rider, supplementary. SEE MAIN ENTRY
adjunct in crime coconspirator
adjunction addition, attachment *(act of affixing)*
adjuration affirmance *(legal affirmation),* asseveration, assurance, attestation, averment, avouchment, call *(appeal),* charge *(statement to the jury),* claim *(legal demand),* entreaty, oath, petition, requirement. SEE MAIN ENTRY
adjure attest, bear *(adduce),* call *(appeal to),* command, direct *(order),* exhort, importune, motivate, order, petition, pray, press *(beseech),* pressure, promise *(vow),* request, swear, urge. SEE MAIN ENTRY
adjurement affirmation, averment, avowal
adjust accommodate, adapt, alter, amend, apply *(put in practice),* arrange *(methodize),* attune, change, check *(restrain),* compromise *(settle by mutual agreement),* conform, coordinate, decide, defray, discharge *(pay a debt),* discharge *(perform),* emend, fix *(arrange),* fix *(repair),* inure *(accustom),* liquidate *(determine liability),* mediate, mitigate, modify *(alter),* naturalize *(acclimate),* orchestrate, organize *(arrange),* pay, reconcile, rectify, redress, refund, remedy, repair, settle, stipulate, transform. SEE MAIN ENTRY
adjust differences agree *(comply),* agree *(contract),* arbitrate *(conciliate),* dicker
adjust difficulties mediate
adjust oneself to countenance
adjustable flexible, malleable, pliable, resilient
adjusted accustomed *(familiarized),* fit, harmonious, res judicata, resigned, tempered
adjuster SEE MAIN ENTRY
adjustment accord, accordance *(compact),* accordance *(understanding),* amendment *(correction),* arbitration, arrangement *(understanding),* collection *(payment),* collective bargaining, compatibility, compromise, conciliation, conformity *(agreement),* correction *(change),* disposition *(determination),* disposition *(final arrangement),* expiation, habituation, justification, mediation, mitigation, modification, order *(arrangement),* reconciliation, regulation *(management),* rehabilitation, repair, reparation *(indemnification),* restitution, settlement, treatment. SEE MAIN ENTRY
adjustment by agreement arrangement *(understanding)*
adjustment of differences peace
adjustment of difficulties mediation
adjutant abettor, acting, assistant, backer, coactor, coadjutant, colleague, confederate, consociate, conspirer, copartner *(coconspirator),* partner
adjutant in crime coconspirator
adjutor partner
adjuvancy assistance
adjuvant ancillary *(auxiliary),* assistant, backer, coactor, coadjutant, colleague, confederate, copartner *(business associate),* copartner *(coconspirator),* participant, partner, subservient, subsidiary. SEE MAIN ENTRY
adjuvant in crime coconspirator
adlevare alleviate
adlicere lure
adligare affix, attach *(join),* connect *(join together)*
admeasure distribute, divide *(distribute),* dole, measure, mete. SEE MAIN ENTRY
admeasurement estimate *(approximate cost),* estimation *(calculation),* measurement
administer allocate, allot, apportion, bestow, commit *(perpetrate),* conduct, confer *(give),* contribute *(supply),* control *(regulate),* direct *(supervise),* disburse *(distribute),* discharge *(perform),* discipline *(control),* dispense, disperse *(disseminate),* distribute,

divide *(distribute)*, dominate, drug, exercise *(discharge a function)*, govern, handle *(manage)*, manage, mete, moderate *(preside over)*, officiate, operate, overlook *(superintend)*, oversee, parcel, predominate *(command)*, prescribe, preside, provide *(supply)*, regulate *(manage)*, resort, rule *(govern)*, superintend, supply. SEE MAIN ENTRY
administer a penalty inflict
administer a rebuke admonish *(warn)*, blame, censure
administer badly misgovern
administer correction condemn *(punish)*, discipline *(punish)*
administer improperly misgovern, mishandle *(mismanage)*, mismanage
administer inefficiently mismanage
administer poorly misgovern, mismanage
administer punishment inflict
administer to accommodate, assist, bequeath, care *(regard)*, concern *(care)*, serve *(assist)*
administrare conduct, direct *(supervise)*, manage, regulate *(adjust)*, superintend. SEE MAIN ENTRY
administrate administer *(conduct)*, conduct, control *(regulate)*, direct *(supervise)*, govern, manage, operate, preside, render *(administer)*, superintend
administrating clerical
administratio administration, government *(administration)*, management *(supervision)*, regulation *(management)*
administration act *(enactment)*, action *(performance)*, agency *(commission)*, apportionment, authorities, bureau, bureaucracy, charge *(custody)*, control *(supervision)*, custody *(supervision)*, direction *(guidance)*, dispensation *(act of dispensing)*, disposition *(final arrangement)*, economy *(economic system)*, enforcement, generalship, government *(political administration)*, management (directorate), management *(supervision)*, regime, regulation *(management)*, supervision, transaction. SEE MAIN ENTRY
administration of economics economy *(economic system)*
administration of justice judicature, judiciary. SEE MAIN ENTRY
administration of resources economy *(economic system)*
administrative clerical, executive, ministerial, political. SEE MAIN ENTRY
administrative head administrator, official
administrative unit bureau
administrator caretaker *(one fulfilling the function of office)*, director, employer, executive, executor, functionary, liaison, official, procurator, superintendent, trustee. SEE MAIN ENTRY
administrator of a will executor
administrator of justice judge
administrator of the decedent's estate executor
administrators hierarchy *(persons in authority)*, management *(directorate)*, management *(supervision)*
administratorship generalship
administratrix executor
adminster enforce, give *(grant)*
admirable high-minded, laudable, meritorious, professional *(stellar)*, scrupulous
admiratio surprise
admiration affection, estimation *(esteem)*, honor *(outward respect)*, interest *(concern)*, regard *(esteem)*, respect. SEE MAIN ENTRY
admire regard *(hold in esteem)*
admired popular
admirer disciple
admiring favorable *(expressing approval)*
admiscere implicate
admissibility propriety *(appropriateness)*, qualification *(fitness)*. SEE MAIN ENTRY
admissible allowable, allowed, appropriate, justifiable, licit, pardonable, passable, permissible, relevant, right *(suitable)*, suitable, unobjectionable. SEE MAIN ENTRY
admissible evidence SEE MAIN ENTRY
admission access *(right of way)*, acknowledgment *(avowal)*, admittance *(acceptance)*, admittance *(means of approach)*, adoption *(acceptance)*, charter *(sanction)*, concession *(compromise)*, confession, confirmation, consent, declaration, disclosure *(act of disclosing)*, disclosure *(something disclosed)*, entrance, entry *(entrance)*, ingress, installation, recognition. SEE MAIN ENTRY
admission of fault confession
admission of foreigners immigration
admission of guilt confession. SEE MAIN ENTRY
admission of postponement continuance
admission of the facts nollo contendere
admissive receptive, responsive
admit accede *(concede)*, acknowledge *(declare)*, acknowledge *(verify)*, adopt, authorize, avow, bare, bear *(adduce)*, betray *(disclose)*, certify *(approve)*, confess, disclose, grant *(concede)*, induct, initiate, instate, profess *(avow)*, receive *(permit to enter)*, recognize *(acknowledge)*, reveal, vouchsafe, yield *(submit)*. SEE MAIN ENTRY
admit a right acknowledge *(verify)*
admit as satisfactory accept *(admit as sufficient)*
admit citizenship naturalize *(make a citizen)*
admit defeat quit *(discontinue)*, submit *(yield)*
admit frankly avow
admit guilt confess
admit the charge acknowledge *(verify)*
admit to citizenship enfranchise
admittance access *(right of way)*, acknowledgment *(acceptance)*, admission *(entry)*, ingress, introduction, receipt *(act of receiving)*. SEE MAIN ENTRY
admitted allowed, prescriptive, sound, uncontested. SEE MAIN ENTRY
admitted judgment cognovit
admitted maxim principle *(axiom)*
admitted testimony evidence
admittedly SEE MAIN ENTRY
admittere admit *(give access)*
admitting concession *(compromise)*, receptive
admitting of decision determinable *(ascertainable)*
admitting of doubt debatable, disputable
admitting of no deviation exact
admix amalgamate, combine *(join together)*, commingle, desegregate
admixed composite, miscellaneous
admixture coalescence, integration *(amalgamation)*, melange, solution *(substance)*. SEE MAIN ENTRY
admonere admonish *(advise)*, remind
admonish blame, castigate, caution, censure, charge *(instruct on the law)*, complain *(criticize)*, decry, disabuse, disapprove *(condemn)*, exhort, expostulate, fault, impeach, lash *(attack verbally)*, rebuke, remonstrate, reprehend, reprimand, reproach, threaten. SEE MAIN ENTRY
admonish beforehand forewarn
admonishment admonition, caveat, deterrent, disapprobation, disparagement, monition *(warning)*, notice *(warning)*, objurgation, remonstrance, reprimand
admonitio remonstrance, suggestion, warning
admonition caution *(warning)*, caveat, charge *(statement to the jury)*, criticism, deterrence, deterrent, diatribe, direction *(guidance)*, guidance, impeachment, monition *(warning)*, notice *(warning)*, objurgation, rebuff, recommendation, remonstrance, reprimand, warning. SEE MAIN ENTRY
admonitive remonstrative
admonitor monitor
admonitory hortative, informatory, remonstrative
admovere apply *(put in practice)*
adnectere affix
adnotare note *(record)*
adnotatio note *(brief comment)*
adnuere assent
ado furor, noise, trouble, turmoil
adolescence nonage. SEE MAIN ENTRY
adolescent child, jejune *(lacking maturity)*, juvenile, minor. SEE MAIN ENTRY
adolescere develop
adopt accept *(embrace)*, acquire *(receive)*, agree *(comply)*, apply *(put in practice)*, appropriate, approve, assume *(seize)*, choose, copy, embrace *(accept)*, espouse, gain, impropriate, naturalize *(make a citizen)*, pass *(approve)*, prefer, receive *(permit to enter)*, resort, select. SEE MAIN ENTRY
adopt a measure enact
adopt an opinion deem
adopt and pass off as one's own pirate *(reproduce without authorization)*
adopt as a citizen naturalize *(make a citizen)*
adopt as one's own plagiarize
adopt into a nation naturalize *(make a citizen)*
adoptare adopt
adopted assumed *(feigned)*, preferred *(favored)*, select
adoptio adoption *(affiliation)*
adoption acceptance, appropriation *(taking)*, approval, arrogation, consent, distress *(seizure)*, selection *(choice)*, use. SEE MAIN ENTRY
adoptive SEE MAIN ENTRY
adoptivus adoptive
adorable attractive
adoration affection, respect
adore regard *(hold in esteem)*
adoriri accost, assail, attack
adorn embellish, meliorate
adorned pretentious *(ostentatious)*
adornment motif
adquirere acquire *(secure)*
adrift astray, derelict *(abandoned)*, disconnected, insecure, lost *(disoriented)*, unsettled
adrogans impervious, presumptuous
adrogantia intolerance
adroit artful, capable, competent, deft, efficient, expert, practiced, proficient, resourceful, veteran. SEE MAIN ENTRY

adroit practitioner professional
adroitness competence *(ability)*, efficiency, experience *(background)*, facility *(easiness)*, faculty *(ability)*, gift *(flair)*, prowess *(ability)*, science *(technique)*, skill
adsciscere enfranchise
adscititious circumstantial, nonessential, pendent, superfluous, supplementary
adscribere encompass *(include)*, enroll, include
adsecula parasite
adsensio assent
adsensus acquiescence, assent
adsentari assent
adsentire consent
adsequi attain
adseverare vouch
adsiduitas continuance, continuation *(prolongation)*, diligence *(care)*, industry *(activity)*
adsiduus continual *(perpetual)*, incessant, industrious, perpetual, sedulous, unremitting
adsignare allot, apportion, ascribe, attribute, impute
adsignatio allotment
adstrictorius astringent
adstrictus laconic
adstringere bind *(obligate)*
adsuefacere inure *(accustom)*
adsuetus accustomed *(customary)*
adsumere assume *(seize)*
adulate overestimate. SEE MAIN ENTRY
adulation doxology, honor *(outward respect)*, mention *(tribute)*. SEE MAIN ENTRY
adulescentia adolescence
adult ripe. SEE MAIN ENTRY
adulterare adulterate
adulterate contaminate, corrupt, debase, denature, deteriorate, fake, falsify, harm, impair, infect, lessen, pollute, taint *(contaminate)*. SEE MAIN ENTRY
adulterated inferior *(lower in quality)*, tainted *(contaminated)*. SEE MAIN ENTRY
adulteration contaminate, defilement, detriment, dissolution *(disintegration)*. SEE MAIN ENTRY
adultered bad *(inferior)*
adulterine artificial, bastard, illegitimate *(born out of wedlock)*
adulterium adultery
adultery SEE MAIN ENTRY
adulthood maturity
adultus adult
adumbrare delineate
adumbrate blind *(obscure)*, camouflage, hint, obfuscate, obnubilate, obscure, portend, portray, predict, presage, represent *(portray)*, shroud
adumbratio delineation, outline (synopsis)
adumbration hint, obscuration. SEE MAIN ENTRY
adumbrative representative. SEE MAIN ENTRY
advance abet, accession *(enlargement)*, accretion, accrue *(increase)*, adduce, advancement *(loan)*, aid *(help)*, aid, allege, ameliorate, appreciate *(increase)*, approach, argue, assert, augmentation, bid, boom *(increase)*, boom *(prosperity)*, capitalize *(provide capital)*, certify *(attest)*, cite *(state)*, compound, conduce, contend *(maintain)*, contribute *(assist)*, course, credit *(delayed payment)*, cultivate, declare, develop, development *(progression)*, elevate, evolve, expand, expedite, extend *(offer)*, facilitate, favor, finance, foster, further, gain, hasten, headway, heighten *(augment)*, help, honor, installment, inure *(benefit)*, invest *(fund)*, invitation, lend, loan *(noun)*, loan *(verb)*, lobby, meliorate, nurture, offer (tender), onset *(assault)*, overture, plead (allege in a legal action), pose *(propound)*, posit, postulate, precipitate *(hasten)*, precursory, preface, prefer, proceed *(go forward)*, proffer, profit, progress *(noun)*, progress *(verb)*, promotion *(advancement)*, propose, propound, prosecute *(carry forward)*, recommend, remit *(submit for consideration)*, resume, send, serve *(assist)*, signify *(inform)*, step, submit *(give)*, subsidize, succeed *(attain)*, tender, urge. SEE MAIN ENTRY
advance against assail
advance beyond proper limits overstep
advance guard precursor
advance in rank promote *(advance)*
advance in successive gradation develop
advance in value enhance
advance in worth appreciation *(increased value)*
advance near to approximate
advance notice admonition, caveat
advance planning forethought, premeditation
advance stealthily infringe
advance toward perfection mature
advance upon assail, attack, impinge, trespass
advanced alleged, liberal *(broad minded)*, proficient, progressive *(advocating change)*, ripe, sophisticated. SEE MAIN ENTRY
advanced in years elderly, old
advancement advocacy, application, augmentation, boom *(increase)*, boom *(prosperity)*, civilization, development *(progression)*, edification, elevation, favor *(sanction)*, growth *(evolution)*, growth *(increase)*, incursion, loan, longevity, preference *(priority)*, profit, progress, reform, step, suggestion. SEE MAIN ENTRY
advancement of knowledge civilization
advancing cumulative *(increasing)*, forthcoming, future, progressive *(going forward)*
advantage behalf, benefit *(betterment)*, chance *(fortuity)*, dividend, edification, help, interest *(profit)*, inure *(benefit)*, leverage, patronage *(power to appoint jobs)*, precedence, preference *(priority)*, prerogative, priority, privilege, prize, profit, shelter *(tax benefit)*, utility *(usefulness)*, value, welfare, worth. SEE MAIN ENTRY
advantage in land easement
advantage in votes cast plurality
advantageous ancillary *(auxiliary)*, beneficial, constructive *(creative)*, convenient, disposable, effective *(efficient)*, fit, functional, gainful, instrumental, lucrative, operative, opportune, practical, preferential, productive, profitable, propitious, purposeful, salubrious, salutary, suitable, valuable. SEE MAIN ENTRY
advantageous position edge *(advantage)*
advantageousness expedience, feasibility, utility *(usefulness)*
advena alien, stranger
advent occasion
adventare approach
adventicius foreign, unessential
adventitious fortuitous, haphazard, unintentional, unwitting. SEE MAIN ENTRY
adventitiously unknowingly
adventitiousness accident *(chance occurrence)*
adventure bet, enterprise *(undertaking)*, event, experience *(encounter)*, transaction, undertaking *(enterprise)*, venture. SEE MAIN ENTRY
adventurer pioneer, speculator
adventures story *(narrative)*
adventurous aleatory *(perilous)*, imprudent, impulsive *(rash)*
adventus appearance *(emergence)*, immigration
adversarius adversary, foe, opponent, opposite
adversary contender, contestant, disputant, foe, litigant, opponent, party *(litigant)*, plaintiff, rival. SEE MAIN ENTRY
adversative contradictory, contrary
adverse antipathetic *(oppositional)*, averse, competitive *(antagonistic)*, contradictory, contrary, deleterious, detrimental, disadvantageous, discordant, disinclined, hostile, inadvisable, inauspicious, inimical, malevolent, noxious, ominous, opposite, pernicious, regrettable, reluctant, renitent, repugnant *(incompatible)*, unfavorable, unpropitious. SEE MAIN ENTRY
adverse argument objection
adverse charge objection
adverse circumstance disadvantage, plight. SEE MAIN ENTRY
adverse circumstances adversity, predicament
adverse comment criticism, diatribe, disapprobation, disapproval, impugnation, objection, stricture
adverse criticism disparagement, exception *(objection)*, impugnation, stricture
adverse event misfortune. SEE MAIN ENTRY
adverse fortune adversity, calamity, misfortune
adverse lot misfortune
adverse luck misfortune
adverse party adversary, contender, contestant, disputant, foe, litigant, opponent
adverse possession SEE MAIN ENTRY
adverse reason objection
adverse to contra *(adverb)*, contra *(preposition)*, deviant. SEE MAIN ENTRY
adversely unwillingly
adversely affected aggrieved *(victimized)*. SEE MAIN ENTRY
adverseness antipode, antithesis, conflict, contradiction, difference, ill will
adversity accident *(misfortune)*, burden, calamity, casualty, catastrophe, damage, debacle, detriment, disadvantage, disaster, hardship, injury, misfortune, pain, plight, predicament, stress *(strain)*, tragedy, trouble. SEE MAIN ENTRY
adversus adverse *(opposite)*, antipode, contrary, unfavorable
advert allude, hear *(give attention to)*, hint, imply. SEE MAIN ENTRY
advert to consider, indicate, mention, note *(notice)*, regard *(pay attention)*, specify
advertence diligence *(care)*, notice *(heed)*, observation, regard *(attention)*. SEE MAIN ENTRY
advertency consideration *(contemplation)*, diligence *(care)*, notice *(heed)*, observation, regard *(attention)*

advertent prudent
advertise communicate, divulge, expose, herald, inform *(notify)*, notify, post, proclaim, proffer, promote *(organize)*, propagate *(spread)*, publish, spread. SEE MAIN ENTRY
advertisement publication *(disclosure)*, publicity
advertising promotion *(encouragement)*, publicity
advice admonition, advocacy, charge *(statement to the jury)*, direction *(guidance)*, guidance, help, instruction *(direction)*, monition *(warning)*, recommendation, service *(assistance)*, suggestion, tip *(clue)*. SEE MAIN ENTRY
advice of counsel SEE MAIN ENTRY
advisability propriety *(appropriateness)*
advisable favorable *(advantageous)*, fit, profitable, sensible, suitable. SEE MAIN ENTRY
advise advocate, alert, annunciate, apprise, charge *(instruct on the law)*, communicate, confer *(consult)*, contribute *(assist)*, converse, convey *(communicate)*, counsel, disabuse, disclose, exhort, forewarn, help, impart, incite, inform *(notify)*, instruct *(direct)*, motivate, notice *(give formal warning)*, notify, persuade, predict, presage, prognosticate, prompt, propose, reason *(persuade)*, recommend, relate *(tell)*, remind, remonstrate, report *(disclose)*, reveal, signify *(inform)*, urge. SEE MAIN ENTRY
advise against admonish *(warn)*, caution, discourage, dissuade, expostulate, forewarn, remonstrate
advise beforehand forewarn
advise together deliberate
advise with consult *(ask advice of)*, deliberate
advised acquainted, deliberate, express, familiar *(informed)*, informed *(having information)*
advisedly knowingly
advisement advice, caveat, consideration *(contemplation)*, deliberation, disclosure *(act of disclosing)*, guidance
advising hortative, informatory, juridical
advisor accessory, accomplice, advocate (counselor), arbiter, counsel, counselor, esquire, informant, informer (a person who provides information), pedagogue, procurator. SEE MAIN ENTRY
advisors management (directorate)
advisory hortative, informative, informatory, juridical, precatory. SEE MAIN ENTRY
advisory board council *(assembly)*
advisory body congress, panel *(discussion group)*
advisory group commission *(agency)*, committee
advisory limitation guideline
advocacy advice, aid *(help)*, assistance, behalf, direction *(guidance)*, favor *(sanction)*, guidance, persuasion, recommendation, representation *(acting for others)*. SEE MAIN ENTRY
advocare call *(summon)*, summon
advocate abet, abettor, adhere *(maintain loyalty)*, admonish *(advise)*, advise, amicus curiae, apologist, approve, assistant, attorney, authorize, backer, barrister, benefactor, certify *(attest)*, claim *(maintain)*, coactor, colleague, conduit *(intermediary)*, corroborate, council *(consultant)*, counsel *(noun)*, counsel *(verb)*, counselor, countenance, defend, disciple, embrace *(accept)*, espouse, esquire, exhort, favor, foster, incite, indorse, instruct *(direct)*, jurist, lawyer, maintain *(sustain)*, partisan, pass *(approve)*, patron *(influential supporter)*, petition, plead *(argue a case)*, plenipotentiary, posit, prescribe, pressure, proctor, profess *(avow)*, promote *(advance)*, promote *(organize)*, promoter, proponent, propose, propound, recommend, side, special interest, spokesman, sponsor, subscribe *(promise)*, uphold, urge. SEE MAIN ENTRY
advocated alleged
advocates bar *(body of lawyers)*, lobby
advocating change radical *(favoring drastic change)*
advocation labor *(work)*, recommendation
adynamic languid, nonsubstantial *(not sturdy)*, powerless
adynamy incapacity
aedes house
aedificatio building *(business of assembling)*
aedificium building *(structure)*, premises *(buildings)*
aeger patient
aegis auspices, custody *(supervision)*, favor *(sanction)*, protection, safekeeping, shield. SEE MAIN ENTRY
aegrotus patient
aemulus contestant, rival
aenigma enigma
aeonian constant, durable
aequabilis impartial, uniform
aequalis coequal, equal, par *(equality)*
aequalitas temporum synchronism
aeque fairly *(impartially)*
aequiperare compare
aequitas equity *(justice)*, fairness, justice, objectivity
aequo animo nonchalant
aequum equity *(justice)*
aequus admissible, equal, equitable, fair *(just)*, impartial, just, par *(equality)*, reasonable *(fair)*
aequus animus composure
aerarium finance, treasury
aerial intangible
aes money
aes alienum debt
aes alienum contrahere overdraw
Aesculapian medicinal
aesthetic elegant, sensitive *(discerning)*. SEE MAIN ENTRY
aesthetic judgment discretion *(quality of being discreet)*
aestimare appreciate *(value)*, assess *(appraise)*, estimate, rate
aestimatio assessment *(estimation)*, estimate *(approximate cost)*, value, worth
aetas age, lifetime
aetate provectus elderly
aevum lifetime
affability comity, courtesy, informality
affable amicable, benevolent, civil *(polite)*, obeisant
affair event, happening, incident, occasion, occurrence, subject *(topic)*, transaction, undertaking *(enterprise)*. SEE MAIN ENTRY
affairs case *(set of circumstances)*, dealings. SEE MAIN ENTRY
affect appertain, apply *(pertain)*, concern *(involve)*, dispose *(incline)*, emotion, fake, feign, interest, militate, modify *(alter)*, motivate, prejudice *(influence)*, pretend, prevail upon, profess *(pretend)*, relate *(establish a connection)*. SEE MAIN ENTRY
affect detrimentally prejudice *(injure)*
affect dishonorably disgrace
affect entirely pervade
affect injuriously impair
affectation bombast, color *(deceptive appearance)*, false pretense, fustian, histrionics, pretense *(ostentation)*, pretext, pride, rhetoric *(insincere language)*
affected bogus, formal, grandiose, histrionic, inclined, interested, orgulous, orotund, pretentious *(pompous)*, proud *(conceited)*, specious, tartuffish
affected manner pride
affectedness false pretense, histrionics, pretense *(ostentation)*, pride
affecter pedant
affectibility sensibility
affectible receptive
affecting moving *(evoking emotion)*, potent, sapid. SEE MAIN ENTRY
affecting a previous act ex post facto
affecting the nation as a whole national
affecting the past retroactive
affection affinity *(regard)*, benevolence *(disposition to do good)*, predilection, predisposition, regard *(esteem)*. SEE MAIN ENTRY
affiance confidence *(faith)*, reliance
affiant declarant, deponent. SEE MAIN ENTRY
affidavit certificate, confirmation, record, statement, testimony. SEE MAIN ENTRY
affiliate adopt, ascribe, chapter *(branch)*, connect *(relate)*, consolidate *(unite)*, corporate *(associate)*, corporation, correlate, correlative, embrace *(accept)*, federalize *(associate)*, federate, incorporate *(form a corporation)*, join *(associate oneself with)*, member *(individual in a group)*, organ, organize *(unionize)*, relate *(establish a connection)*, unite. SEE MAIN ENTRY
affiliate with combine *(act in concert)*, participate, pool
affiliated akin *(germane)*, akin *(related by blood)*, allied, apposite, associated, cognate, collateral *(accompanying)*, conjoint, consanguineous, correlative, incident, interested, interrelated, related. SEE MAIN ENTRY
affiliates constituency
affiliation affinity *(family ties)*, ancestry, association *(alliance)*, bloodline, cartel, chain *(nexus)*, coalescence, coalition, combination, compatibility, confederacy *(compact)*, connection *(relation)*, consolidation, consortium *(marriage companionship)*, contact *(association)*, corporation, degree *(kinship)*, federation, filiation, integration *(amalgamation)*, kinship, league, merger, nexus, organization *(association)*, privity, propinquity *(kinship)*, relation *(connection)*, side, union *(labor organization)*. SEE MAIN ENTRY
affined cognate, correlative, related
affinitive allied, apposite, correlative, germane, interrelated, pendent, pertinent, related, relative *(relevant)*, relevant
affinity analogy, blood, chain *(nexus)*, conformity *(agreement)*, consortium *(marriage companionship)*, inclination, instinct, kinship, partiality, penchant, predilection, propensity, propinquity *(kinship)*, propinquity *(similarity)*, rapport, relation *(connection)*, relationship *(family tie)*, relevance, resemblance. SEE MAIN ENTRY
affinity of nature propinquity *(similarity)*
affirm accept *(assent)*, accredit, acknowledge *(declare)*, admit *(concede)*, allege, annunciate, approve, argue, assert, assure *(insure)*, attest, authorize, avouch *(avow)*,

avow, bear *(adduce),* certify *(attest),* claim *(maintain),* concede, concur *(agree),* consent, contend *(maintain),* convey *(communicate),* corroborate, countenance, declare, depose *(testify),* enunciate, express, indorse, mention, notarize, pass *(approve),* plead *(allege in a legal action),* posit, profess *(avow),* promise *(vow),* reassure, remark, reveal, substantiate, support *(corroborate),* sustain *(confirm),* swear, testify, uphold, validate, verify *(swear),* vouch, witness *(attest to).* SEE MAIN ENTRY
affirm explicitly certify *(attest),* plead *(allege in a legal action)*
affirm in an official capacity certify *(attest)*
affirm positively promise *(vow)*
affirm the contrary bear false witness, contradict, disown *(deny the validity)*
affirm under oath depose *(testify),* testify
affirm with confidence avouch *(avow)*
affirmance affirmation, approval, assent, asseveration, averment, avouchment, avowal, certification *(certification of proficiency),* confirmation, consensus, consent, indorsement, sanction *(permission),* surety *(certainty).* SEE MAIN ENTRY
affirmant declarant. SEE MAIN ENTRY
affirmation acknowledgment *(avowal),* adjuration, approval, assent, assertion, asseveration, assurance, attestation, attribution, averment, avouchment, avowal, certification *(attested copy),* claim *(assertion),* confirmation, consensus, consent, corroboration, declaration, declaratory judgment, disclosure *(something disclosed),* jurat, legalization, oath, parole, permit, profession *(declaration),* promise, pronouncement, reference *(recommendation),* sanction *(permission),* statement, subscription, support *(corroboration),* surety *(certainty),* testimony, thesis, vow. SEE MAIN ENTRY
affirmation of truth oath
affirmation of truth of a statement oath
affirmation under oath affidavit. SEE MAIN ENTRY
affirmations premises *(hypotheses)*
affirmative SEE MAIN ENTRY
affirmative action SEE MAIN ENTRY
affirmatory affirmative
affirmed agreed *(promised),* alleged, alleged
affirmer affirmant
affix addendum, allonge, annex *(add),* append, attach *(join),* cement, cohere *(adhere),* combine *(join together),* levy, rider. SEE MAIN ENTRY
affix a date to date
affix a legal signature notarize
affix a signature sign
affix an earlier date antedate
affix an impost assess *(tax)*
affix one's name sign
affix one's signature subscribe *(sign)*
affix one's signature to notarize, sign
affixation accession *(annexation),* attachment *(act of affixing),* codicil
affixed attached *(annexed),* conjoint
affixed property immovable
affixed to realty fixture
affixture attachment *(thing affixed),* codicil
afflicting pernicious
afflict affront, badger, bait *(harass),* beat *(strike),* discommode, discompose, distress, harass, harm, ill use, mistreat, persecute, plague, strike *(assault).* SEE MAIN ENTRY
afflicted aggrieved *(harmed),* deplorable, disconsolate
afflicting detrimental, harmful, peccant *(unhealthy)*
affliction accident *(misfortune),* adversity, burden, calamity, casualty, catastrophe, damage, detriment, disability *(physical inability),* disaster, disease, disorder *(abnormal condition),* grievance, handicap, hardship, misfortune, nuisance, onus *(burden),* pain, stress *(strain),* tragedy, trouble. SEE MAIN ENTRY
afflictive adverse *(negative),* bitter *(penetrating),* oppressive, painful, severe
affluence boom *(prosperity),* money, prosperity, sufficiency, welfare
affluent full, opulent, profuse, prosperous, replete, successful
afford administer *(tender),* allow *(endure),* bear *(yield),* bequeath, bestow, contribute *(supply),* fund, furnish, give *(grant),* lend, provide *(supply),* supply, yield *(produce a return).* SEE MAIN ENTRY
afford advantages favor
afford aid abet, assist, capitalize *(provide capital),* contribute *(assist),* serve *(assist),* subsidize
afford notice serve *(deliver a legal instrument)*
afford proof of bear *(adduce)*
afford sanctuary harbor, lodge *(house)*
afford support capitalize *(provide capital),* subsidize
affordable care act SEE MAIN ENTRY
affording no undue advantage fair *(just),* just
affording proof demonstrative *(illustrative)*
affranchise enfranchise, free, let *(permit),* liberate
affranchisement freedom, liberation, liberty, privilege, suffrage
affray altercation, belligerency, collision *(dispute),* commotion, conflict, confrontation *(altercation),* disaccord, disturbance, embroilment, fight *(battle),* fracas, fray, outbreak, outburst, pandemonium, riot, struggle. SEE MAIN ENTRY
affreightment carriage
affright consternation, discourage, fear, fright, frighten, intimidate, menace, panic, trepidation
affront accost, annoy, aspersion, bait *(harass),* challenge, contumely, defiance, defy, discommode, disoblige, disparage, disregard *(lack of respect),* disrespect, flout, humiliate, irritate, offend *(insult),* pique, provocation, provoke, rebuff, resentment, revilement. SEE MAIN ENTRY
affront hostilely assault
affronting outrageous
afield astray
afloat unsettled
aforecited aforesaid
aforedescribed aforesaid. SEE MAIN ENTRY
aforegiven aforesaid
aforegoing aforesaid, last *(preceding),* said. SEE MAIN ENTRY
aforehand before mentioned. SEE MAIN ENTRY
aforementioned aforesaid, last *(preceding),* preliminary, previous, stated. SEE MAIN ENTRY
aforenamed aforesaid, before mentioned, said
aforesaid before mentioned, last *(preceding),* previous, said, stated
aforestated aforesaid, before mentioned. SEE MAIN ENTRY
aforethought express, premeditated, premeditation. SEE MAIN ENTRY
afraid caitiff, leery, recreant. SEE MAIN ENTRY
afresh anew, de novo
after ensuing, ex post facto, successive, thereafter
after death posthumous
after the act is committed ex post facto
after the fact ex post facto
after the same pattern boiler plate
after time dilatory, late *(tardy)*
after-comer heir
after-generations heir
aftereffect consequence *(conclusion),* outcome, outgrowth
aftergrowth consequence *(conclusion),* development *(outgrowth)*
aftermath consequence *(conclusion),* development *(outgrowth),* effect, outcome, outgrowth, result. SEE MAIN ENTRY
aftermost last *(final)*
afterthought hindsight, recollection, retrospect
afterward ex post facto
afterwards hereafter *(henceforth),* thereafter
agacerie catalyst
again anew, de novo. SEE MAIN ENTRY
against contiguous, contra *(adverb),* contra *(preposition),* disinclined. SEE MAIN ENTRY
against fair trade antitrust act
against free commerce antitrust act
against free mercantilism antitrust act
against free trade antitrust act
against one's will compulsory, involuntary. SEE MAIN ENTRY
against open business antitrust act
against open markets antitrust act
against reason ill-judged
against the admonition of law felonious
against the law felonious, illegal, illegitimate *(illegal),* illicit, impermissible, lawless, unlawful, wrongful
against the rules deviant, felonious, irregular *(improper)*
agape open *(unclosed),* penetrable, speechless
age annum, cycle, duration, lifetime, longevity, mature, period, phase *(period),* term *(duration),* time. SEE MAIN ENTRY
age of discretion majority *(adulthood).* SEE MAIN ENTRY
age of majority majority *(adulthood)*
age of responsibility majority *(adulthood)*
aged elderly
ageless durable, immutable, permanent
agellus plot *(land)*
agency bureau, bureaucracy, committee, conduit *(channel),* delegation *(assignment),* department, expedient, facility *(institution),* facility *(instrumentality),* forum *(medium),* instrument *(tool),* medium, organ, proxy, representation *(acting for others).* SEE MAIN ENTRY
agency of the state government *(political administration)*
agenda calendar *(list of cases),* calendar *(record of yearly periods),* docket, outline *(synopsis),* plan, program, register, schedule. SEE MAIN ENTRY

agent assistant, broker, cause *(reason)*, conduit *(intermediary)*, dealer, deputy, detective, determinant, employee, factor *(commission merchant)*, factor *(ingredient)*, fiduciary, forum *(medium)*, go-between, instrument *(tool)*, interagent, intermediary, liaison, medium, plenipotentiary, proctor, procurator, protagonist, proxy, representative *(proxy)*, spokesman, spy, substitute, superintendent, tool, trustee. SEE MAIN ENTRY
agent provocateur catalyst
agent provocateur conspirer
agential ministerial, representative
agents deputation *(delegation)*
agentship delegation *(assignment)*, representation *(acting for others)*
ager district, estate *(property)*, territory
agger causeway
agglomerate accumulate *(amass)*, agglomeration, aggregate *(noun)*, aggregate *(verb)*, cement, coadunate, cohere *(adhere)*, compile, composite, concentrate *(consolidate)*, conglomerate, corporation, cumulation, desegregate, hoard, unite
agglomeration adhesion *(affixing)*, arsenal, assemblage, coalescence, collection *(accumulation)*, compilation, conglomeration, cumulation. SEE MAIN ENTRY
agglutinate adhere *(fasten)*, affix, attach *(join)*, cement, cohere *(adhere)*, coherent *(joined)*, cohesive *(sticking)*, combine *(join together)*
agglutinated attached *(annexed)*
agglutination adhesion *(affixing)*, agglomeration, coalescence
agglutinative coherent *(joined)*, cohesive *(sticking)*
aggrandize accrue *(increase)*, accumulate *(enlarge)*, bear *(yield)*, build *(augment)*, compound, elevate, empower, enhance, enlarge, expand, extend *(enlarge)*, honor, increase, inflate, magnify, overestimate, promote *(advance)*, raise *(advance)*
aggrandized extreme *(exaggerated)*, inflated *(overestimated)*
aggrandizement accession *(enlargement)*, advancement *(improvement)*, augmentation, boom *(prosperity)*, elevation, eminence, exaggeration, extension *(expansion)*, growth *(increase)*, honor *(outward respect)*, hyperbole, inflation *(increase)*, overstatement, remembrance *(commemoration)*. SEE MAIN ENTRY
aggravate alienate *(estrange)*, annoy, badger, bait *(harass)*, compound, deteriorate, discommode, discompose, distress, exacerbate, expand, harm, heighten *(augment)*, incense, intensify, irritate, plague, press *(goad)*, provoke. SEE MAIN ENTRY
aggravated gross *(flagrant)*
aggravating provocative, vexatious
aggravating factor SEE MAIN ENTRY
aggravation complication, damage, detriment, harm, molestation, nuisance, pain. SEE MAIN ENTRY
aggravative cumulative *(intensifying)*
aggregate accumulate *(amass)*, agglomeration, amount *(quantity)*, coadunate, collect *(gather)*, collection *(accumulation)*, collective, combination, compile, complex *(development)*, composite, compound, comprise, concentrate *(consolidate)*, conglomerate, conglomeration, congregate, congregation, corpus, cumulation, entirety, garner, glean, gross *(total)*, hoard, in solido, join *(bring together)*, mass *(body of persons)*, multiple, quantity, total, totality, whole *(undamaged)*, whole. SEE MAIN ENTRY
aggregate amount sum *(total)*
aggregated coadunate, collective, composite, compound, miscellaneous
aggregation adhesion *(affixing)*, affiliation *(amalgamation)*, agglomeration, aggregate, assemblage, assembly, body *(collection)*, centralization, chamber *(body)*, collection *(accumulation)*, collection *(assembly)*, combination, company *(assemblage)*, compilation, complex *(development)*, conglomeration, congregation, consolidation, corpus, cumulation, hoard, incorporation *(blend)*, organization *(association)*, selection *(collection)*, totality. SEE MAIN ENTRY
aggress antagonize, assail, assault, attack, impinge, infringe, invade, oppugn, strike *(assault)*
aggression assault, belligerency, foray, incursion, infringement, intrusion, invasion, offense, onset *(assault)*, outbreak, provocation. SEE MAIN ENTRY
aggressive contentious, disorderly, forcible, hostile, hot-blooded, industrious, litigious, malevolent, obtrusive, offensive *(taking the initiative)*, pugnacious, spartan
aggressive action assault
aggressive argument dispute
aggressiveness belligerency, main force
aggressor assailant, offender. SEE MAIN ENTRY
aggrieve affront, aggravate *(annoy)*, badger, bait *(harass)*, distress, harrow, harry *(harass)*, mistreat, persecute, plague
aggrieved despondent. SEE MAIN ENTRY
aggrieved party actor, appellant, complainant
aggroup aggregate, congregate, convene, hoard, join *(bring together)*
aghast speechless
agile deft
agilis movable
agio brokerage
agitare discuss
agitari oscillate
agitate bait *(harass)*, bicker, debate, discommode, discompose, disconcert, dislocate, disorganize, disrupt, distress, disturb, foment, harass, harrow, impel, incense, incite, inflict, irritate, militate, obsess, oscillate, perturb, pique, provoke, upset. SEE MAIN ENTRY
agitate against counter, counteract, countervail
agitated disordered, disorderly, unsettled, vehement
agitating moving *(evoking emotion)*
agitatio commotion
agitation affray, aggravation *(exacerbation)*, apprehension *(fear)*, commotion, consternation, distress *(anguish)*, disturbance, embroilment, emotion, entanglement *(confusion)*, fright, furor, instigation, outbreak, outburst, pandemonium, panic, passion, provocation, revolt, strife, struggle, trepidation, turmoil
agitational offensive *(taking the initiative)*
agitative incendiary
agitator catalyst, demagogue, hoodlum, insurgent, malcontent
agitators lobby
agnate associated, cognate, consanguineous, correlate, correlative, interrelated, related
agnation affiliation *(bloodline)*, blood, propinquity *(kinship)*
agnomen call *(title)*
agnoscere recognize *(perceive)*
agnostic skeptical
agonize bait *(harass)*, brood, distress, harass, inflict, persecute, press *(goad)*, suffer *(sustain loss)*. SEE MAIN ENTRY
agonizing cruel, insufferable, painful, severe
agony distress *(anguish)*, pain, plaint, stress *(strain)*
agora market *(business)*, market place
agree abide, accommodate, acknowledge *(respond)*, admit *(concede)*, allow *(endure)*, assent, bond *(secure a debt)*, certify *(approve)*, cohere *(be logically consistent)*, coincide *(concur)*, compromise *(settle by mutual agreement)*, concede, conform, consent, conspire, contract, correspond *(be equivalent)*, decide, defer *(yield in judgment)*, fix *(settle)*, grant *(concede)*, obey, promise *(vow)*, settle, stipulate, subscribe *(promise)*, undertake, unite. SEE MAIN ENTRY
agree beforehand predetermine
agree in principle concede
agree to accede *(concede)*, accept *(admit as sufficient)*, accept *(assent)*, approve, authorize, certify *(approve)*, confirm, countenance, embrace *(accept)*, pass *(approve)*, permit, sanction, sign, surrender *(yield)*, yield *(submit)*. SEE MAIN ENTRY
agree to beforehand prearrange
agree to indemnify for loss assure *(insure)*
agree to support underwrite
agree upon settle
agree with comply, confirm, uphold
agreeability compliance
agreeable amenable, attractive, benevolent, concordant, congruous, consensual, consenting, convenient, favorable *(expressing approval)*, harmonious, inclined, malleable, nonmilitant, palatable, patient, peaceable, pliant, prone, ready *(willing)*, resigned, sapid, savory, willing *(not averse)*. SEE MAIN ENTRY
agreeable manner amenity
agreeable to pursuant to
agreeable to reason rational
agreeable way amenity
agreeableness amenability, amenity, benevolence *(disposition to do good)*, comity, propriety *(appropriateness)*
agreed concerted, congruous, conjoint, contractual, res judicata. SEE MAIN ENTRY
agreed to contractual
agreed upon consensual
agreeing coequal, coextensive, commensurate, concerted, concordant, concurrent *(united)*, consenting, consistent, consonant, correlative, felicitous, harmonious, proportionate, similar
agreeing to pursuant to
agreement acceptance, accommodation *(adjustment)*, accord, accordance *(compact)*, accordance *(understanding)*, acknowledgment *(acceptance)*, acquiescence, adjustment, analogy, approval, arrangement *(understanding)*, assent, attornment, bargain, cartel, coherence, collusion, commitment *(responsibility)*, compact, compatibility, compliance, composition *(agreement in bankruptcy)*, compromise, concert, concession *(compromise)*, conciliation, concordance, conformity *(agreement)*, conjunction, consensus, consent, contract, correspondence *(similarity)*, covenant, deal, identity *(similarity)*, indenture, indorsement,

integration *(assimilation)*, league, lease, leave *(permission)*, mutual understanding, obligation *(duty)*, option *(contractual provision)*, pact, peace, pledge *(binding promise)*, policy *(contract)*, promise, quid pro quo, rapport, rapprochement, reconciliation, resemblance, sanction *(permission)*, settlement, specialty *(contract)*, stipulation, subscription, synchronism, term *(provision)*, testament, treaty, undertaking *(commitment)*, undertaking *(pledge)*, union *(unity)*, warrant *(guaranty)*. SEE MAIN ENTRY
agreement as to time and place of meeting appointment *(meeting)*
agreement before marriage antenuptial agreement
agreement between nations treaty
agreement between parties compact. SEE MAIN ENTRY
agreement for fraud collusion
agreement to accomplish an unlawful end conspiracy
agreement to commit a crime conspiracy
agreement to pay insurance
agreement to work indenture
agressive eager
agrestis uncouth
agrorum possessor landlord, landowner
ahead of time premature
aid abet, accommodate, accomplice, advantage, advocacy, assist, assistance, associate, avail *(be of use)*, bear *(support)*, behalf, benefactor, benefit *(conferment)*, bolster, capitalize *(provide capital)*, charity, coactor, coadjutant, conduce, confederate, conspire, conspirer, contribute *(assist)*, contribution *(participation)*, copartner *(coconspirator)*, countenance, enable, endow, endowment, espouse, expedite, facilitate, factor *(ingredient)*, favor *(sanction)*, favor, finance, foment, foster, harbor, help *(noun)*, help *(verb)*, instrument *(tool)*, inure *(benefit)*, largess *(generosity)*, lend, loan, maintain *(sustain)*, maintenance *(support of spouse)*, nurture, participant, participate, partner, patronage *(support)*, promotion *(encouragement)*, redress, reinforcement, relieve *(give aid)*, remedy *(legal means of redress)*, remedy *(that which corrects)*, remedy, rescue, samaritan, serve *(assist)*, service *(assistance)*, shelter *(protection)*, side, subsidize, support *(assistance)*, support *(assist)*, uphold
aid a judge clerk
aid in organizing promote *(organize)*
aid with a subsidy capitalize *(provide capital)*
aidance aid *(help)*, behalf
aidant salutary
aide abettor, assistant, coadjutant, consociate, contributor *(contributor)*, good samaritan. SEE MAIN ENTRY
aide in crime coconspirator
aide in wrongdoing coconspirator
aide-de-camp assistant
aide-de-camp associate, coactor, copartner *(coconspirator)*
aide-mémoire memorandum
aider abettor, accessory, accomplice, assistant, backer, benefactor, coactor, coadjutant, confederate, conspirer, donor, good samaritan, partner, promoter, samaritan
aider and abettor accomplice, coactor, cohort, colleague, conspirer, copartner *(coconspirator)*
aider in wrongdoing coconspirator
aides staff
aidful ancillary *(auxiliary)*, beneficial, subservient
aiding ancillary *(auxiliary)*, beneficial, concurrent *(united)*, contributory, donative, instrumental, practical, profitable, subservient, subsidiary
aiding and abetting concerted
aidless helpless *(defenseless)*
ail languish, suffer *(sustain loss)*
ailment disability *(physical inability)*, disease, disorder *(abnormal condition)*, pain, trouble. SEE MAIN ENTRY
aim cause *(reason)*, contemplation, content *(meaning)*, desideratum, design *(intent)*, destination, direction *(course)*, end *(intent)*, endeavor *(noun)*, endeavor *(verb)*, forethought, goal, idea, intend, intent, intention, mission, motive, object, objective, plan, point *(purpose)*, predetermination, project, purpose, pursue *(strive to gain)*, pursuit *(goal)*, reason *(basis)*, signification, strive, target, try *(attempt)*. SEE MAIN ENTRY
aim at attempt
aimed deliberate, direct *(straight)*, tactical
aiming for effect flagrant, histrionic
aiming to destroy deadly
aiming to kill deadly
aimless casual, discursive *(digressive)*, disjointed, random, unwitting
air appearance *(look)*, atmosphere, bare, behavior, betray *(disclose)*, conduct, deportment, disabuse, disclose, discuss, divulge, expose, express, flaunt, herald, issue *(publish)*, manifest, manner *(behavior)*, posture *(attitude)*, presence *(poise)*, proclaim, produce *(offer to view)*, promulgate, propagate *(spread)*, publish, relate *(tell)*, report *(disclose)*, semblance, signify *(inform)*, speak, utter. SEE MAIN ENTRY
air pollution SEE MAIN ENTRY
aired public *(known)*
airfreight carriage
airing publicity
airs disdain, histrionics, pretense *(ostentation)*, pride
airspace atmosphere
airtight impervious
airy insubstantial, intangible, subtle *(refined)*, tenuous
airy spirit phantom
ajar open *(unclosed)*, penetrable
akin allied, analogous, associated, cognate, comparable *(capable of comparison)*, congruous, consanguineous, correlative, interrelated, related, tangential. SEE MAIN ENTRY
alacritas life *(vitality)*
alacritious expeditious
alacritous eager, ready *(willing)*
alacrity dispatch *(promptness)*, haste, industry *(activity)*. SEE MAIN ENTRY
alarm admonition, agitate *(perturb)*, alert, apprehension *(fear)*, caution *(warning)*, consternation, disconcert, disturb, fear, forewarn, fright, frighten, harrow, intimidate, menace, monition *(warning)*, panic, perturb, phobia, stress *(strain)*, symptom, threat, trepidation, warning. SEE MAIN ENTRY
alarming dangerous, formidable, imminent, ominous, portentous *(ominous)*, precarious, prophetic, sinister
albeit regardless
album register, roll
alcohol SEE MAIN ENTRY
alcoholic addiction dipsomania
alcoholic beverage alcohol
alcoholism dipsomania, inebriation
alcove chamber *(compartment)*
alderman lawmaker
alderwoman lawmaker
alea risk, venture
alea ludere gamble
aleatory speculative
alere develop, foster
alert acute, admonish *(advise)*, advise, apprise, careful, caution *(warning)*, caveat, circumspect, cognizant, conscious *(awake)*, forewarn, guarded, meticulous, monition *(warning)*, notify, perspicacious, preventive, prompt, provident *(showing foresight)*, ready *(willing)*, receptive, responsive, sedulous, sensitive *(discerning)*, vigilant, warning. SEE MAIN ENTRY
alert to danger forewarn
alertness comprehension, diligence *(care)*, life *(vitality)*, notice *(heed)*, precaution, regard *(attention)*, sensibility
alexipharmic medicinal
alford plea SEE MAIN ENTRY
alias call *(title)*. SEE MAIN ENTRY
alias dictus alias
alibi compurgation, excuse, pretext. SEE MAIN ENTRY
alien antipathetic *(oppositional)*, apart, different, extraneous, extrinsic, foreign, impertinent *(irrelevant)*, inapplicable, inapposite, inappropriate, incongruous, irrelative, irrelevant, nonconforming, novel, obscure *(remote)*, peculiar *(curious)*, repugnant *(incompatible)*, stranger, unrelated, unusual. SEE MAIN ENTRY
alienable heritable, negotiable
alienate antagonize, assign *(transfer ownership)*, cede, convey *(transfer)*, disaffect, disown *(refuse to acknowledge)*, estrange, repel *(disgust)*, separate. SEE MAIN ENTRY
alienate by breach of condition forfeit
alienated antipathetic *(oppositional)*, hostile, inimical, irreconcilable
alienatio alienation *(estrangement)*, estrangement
alienation assignment *(transfer of ownership)*, conveyance, demise *(conveyance)*, disposition *(transfer of property)*, estrangement, feud, ill will, insanity, odium, separation, umbrage, variance *(disagreement)*. SEE MAIN ENTRY
alienation of affection estrangement
alienation of mind insanity
alienation of property conveyance
alienigena alien
alienus averse, extraneous, incongruous, irrelevant, unsuitable
alight SEE MAIN ENTRY
align conform, convert *(persuade)*, file *(arrange)*, fix *(arrange)*, join *(associate oneself with)*, juxtapose, organize *(arrange)*, persuade. SEE MAIN ENTRY
align convergently border *(approach)*
aligned coextensive, concerted, concomitant, concordant
alignment affiliation *(connectedness)*, confederacy *(compact)*, league, persuasion, relationship *(connection)*, sodality
alike akin *(germane)*, analogous, approximate, cognate, comparable *(capable of comparison)*, consistent, consonant, equal, equivalent, identical, same, uniform. SEE MAIN ENTRY
alikeness comparison, identity *(similarity)*, parity, propinquity *(similarity)*, resemblance
aliment sustenance

alimentation sustenance
alimentum sustenance
alimony maintenance *(support of spouse).* SEE MAIN ENTRY
alius different, diverse
alive alert *(agile),* alert *(vigilant),* conscious *(awake),* extant, responsive, viable
alive to sensitive *(discerning)*
all complete *(all-embracing),* entirety, sum *(total),* total, whole *(undamaged),* whole. SEE MAIN ENTRY
all along through *(from beginning to end)*
all gone defunct
all in all in toto
all over throughout *(all over)*
all over with defunct
all right mediocre
all the more a fortiori
all the same notwithstanding, regardless
all the time always *(forever)*
all the way through *(from beginning to end)*
all the while always *(forever)*
all together en banc, en masse
all-comprehending complete *(all-embracing)*
all-comprehensive complete *(all-embracing),* nonsectarian
all-covering complete *(all-embracing),* comprehensive
all-destroying disastrous
all-embracing composite, comprehensive, inclusive, nonsectarian, omnibus, prevailing *(current),* prevalent
all-encompassing unqualified *(unlimited).* SEE MAIN ENTRY
all-important necessary *(required)*
all-including nonsectarian
all-inclusive complete *(all-embracing),* comprehensive, detailed, gross *(total),* nonsectarian, omnibus, thorough
all-knowing expert, omniscient
all-out outright
all-pervading complete *(all-embracing),* comprehensive
all-powerful cardinal *(outstanding),* invincible, omnipotent, predominant
all-purpose practical
all-searching interrogative
all-seeing omniscient
all-sufficing complete *(all-embracing)*
all-wise omniscient
allay alleviate, ameliorate, assuage, commute, decrease, discount *(minimize),* lessen, lull, mitigate, moderate *(temper),* modify *(moderate),* mollify, obtund, palliate *(abate),* placate, redress, relax, relieve *(free from burden),* repress, soothe, subdue. SEE MAIN ENTRY
allay fears disarm *(set at ease)*
allay mistrust disarm *(set at ease)*
allaying palliative *(abating)*
allayment mollification, remission, solace
allegation accusation, assertion, attestation, bad repute, charge *(accusation),* claim *(assertion),* color *(deceptive appearance),* complaint, contention *(argument),* count, indictment, information *(charge),* mention *(reference),* plea, pleading. SEE MAIN ENTRY
allegation of criminal wrongdoing arraignment
allegation of facts bill *(formal declaration),* pleading
allege adduce, argue, avouch *(avow),* bear *(adduce),* certify *(attest),* cite *(accuse),* claim *(maintain),* comment, express, plead *(allege in a legal action),* posit, propound, purport, testify. SEE MAIN ENTRY
allege as a fact avouch *(avow),* avow
allege in support advocate, assert, defend, justify
allege in vindication justify
allege to be guilty implicate
allege to belong ascribe
allege under oath swear. SEE MAIN ENTRY
alleged colorable *(plausible),* purported, putative. SEE MAIN ENTRY
alleged malfeasor suspect
alleged motive color *(deceptive appearance)*
alleged offender suspect
alleged purpose pretext
alleged reason cover *(pretext),* gist *(ground for a suit),* pretext
alleged transgressor suspect
alleged wrongdoer suspect
allegedly reputedly
allegiance adherence *(devotion),* adhesion *(loyalty),* charge *(responsibility),* commitment *(responsibility),* duty *(obligation),* faith, fealty, fidelity, homage, loyalty, nationality. SEE MAIN ENTRY
allegiant loyal
allegorical demonstrative *(illustrative)*
alleviate abate *(lessen),* allay, assuage, commute, diminish, disencumber, ease, help, lessen, lull, mitigate, moderate *(temper),* mollify, obtund, pacify, palliate *(abate),* redress, relieve *(give aid),* remedy, remit *(relax),* soothe. SEE MAIN ENTRY
alleviating mitigating, palliative *(abating),* remedial
alleviating circumstances extenuating circumstances
alleviation abatement *(reduction),* decrease, mitigation, moderation, mollification, relief *(release),* remedy *(legal means of redress),* remission, solace
alleviative corrigible, medicinal, narcotic, palliative *(abating),* remedial
alleviator narcotic
alley way *(channel)*
alliance adhesion *(loyalty),* affiliation *(amalgamation),* agreement *(contract),* band, cartel, centralization, chain *(nexus),* coaction, coalescence, coalition, cohabitation *(living together),* collusion, committee, concert, confederacy *(compact),* conformity *(agreement),* conjunction, connection *(relation),* connivance, consortium *(marriage companionship),* contact *(association),* contribution *(participation),* cooperative, corporation, federation, integration *(amalgamation),* integration *(assimilation),* league, marriage *(intimate relationship),* matrimony, merger, mutual understanding, nexus, organization *(association),* pact, partnership, peace, pool, propinquity *(kinship),* rapport, rapprochement, relation *(connection),* society, sodality, syndicate, treaty, understanding *(agreement).* SEE MAIN ENTRY
alliance of workers union *(labor organization)*
allied affiliated, akin *(germane),* analogous, apposite, associated, close *(intimate),* coadunate, cognate, coherent *(joined),* concomitant, concordant, concurrent *(united),* conjoint, consanguineous, corporate *(associate),* correlative, federal, germane, harmonious, incident, incidental, interrelated, intimate, joint, nuptial, related, relative *(relevant),* relevant, similar. SEE MAIN ENTRY
allied to pendent
allness totality, whole
allocate allot, apportion, arrange *(methodize),* assign *(allot),* classify, delegate, demarcate, detail *(assign),* disburse *(distribute),* dispense, disperse *(disseminate),* distribute, divide *(distribute),* dole, expend *(disburse),* marshal, mete, parcel, partition, pigeonhole, prorate, regulate *(adjust),* relegate, sort, split, tabulate. SEE MAIN ENTRY
allocated per capita
allocation allotment, appointment *(act of designating),* apportionment, appropriation *(allotment),* assignment *(allotment),* budget, circulation, classification, consignment, coupon, dispensation *(act of dispensing),* distribution *(apportionment),* division *(act of dividing),* order *(arrangement),* part *(portion),* quota, share *(interest).* SEE MAIN ENTRY
allocute converse
allocution declamation, discourse, parlance, rhetoric *(skilled speech),* speech
allot allocate, apportion, attorn, bear *(yield),* bestow, classify, commit *(entrust),* contribute *(supply),* delegate, delimit, demarcate, devise *(give),* devote, disburse *(distribute),* dispense, distribute, divide *(distribute),* dole, endow, endue, expend *(disburse),* fund, give *(grant),* leave *(give),* marshal, mete, parcel, partition, pigeonhole, present *(make a gift),* prorate, sort, split. SEE MAIN ENTRY
allot again reapportion, redistribute
allot the parts orchestrate
alloted pro rata
alloting disbursement *(act of disbursing)*
allotment alimony, annuity, appointment *(act of designating),* apportionment, budget, circulation, classification, commission *(fee),* consignment, disbursement *(act of disbursing),* dispensation *(act of dispensing),* distribution *(apportionment),* dividend, division *(act of dividing),* dower, endowment, equity *(share of ownership),* grant, installment, loan, moiety, order *(arrangement),* payment *(remittance),* pension, proportion, quantity, quota, ration, share *(interest),* subsidy. SEE MAIN ENTRY
allotment by chance lottery
allottee assignee, heir, transferee
allotter transferor
allow accept *(admit as sufficient),* accept *(assent),* accept *(recognize),* agree *(comply),* approve, assent, authorize, bear *(tolerate),* bequeath, bestow, certify *(approve),* concede, concur *(agree),* condone, consent, countenance, deign, dole, empower, enable, endow, endue, enfranchise, grant *(concede),* indorse, let *(permit),* loan, pass *(approve),* permit, provide *(supply),* qualify *(meet standards),* rebate, receive *(permit to enter),* recognize *(acknowledge),* sanction, suffer *(permit),* tolerate, vouchsafe, yield *(submit).* SEE MAIN ENTRY
allow a margin discount *(reduce)*
allow as a discount rebate
allow credit lend
allow entrance admit *(give access),* receive *(permit to enter)*
allow for compensate *(counterbalance),* compensate *(remunerate),* excuse, extenuate, palliate *(excuse)*
allow residency rent
allow the use of lease, let *(lease),* rent, sublease, sublet

allow with condescension deign
allowable admissible, allowed, deductible *(capable of being deducted from taxes),* due *(regular),* justifiable, lawful, legal, licit, open *(accessible),* pardonable, passable, permissible, potential, right *(suitable),* rightful, unobjectionable. SEE MAIN ENTRY
allowableness admissibility, legality
allowance acceptance, acquiescence, advancement *(loan),* alimony, annuity, apportionment, appropriation *(allotment),* approval, assignment *(allotment),* budget, capacity *(authority),* cession, charter *(sanction),* commission *(fee),* concession *(authorization),* concession *(compromise),* condonation, consent, disbursement *(funds paid out),* discount, dispensation *(exception),* dower, endowment, excuse, exemption, franchise *(license),* gift *(present),* grant, indulgence, justification, leave *(permission),* license, maintenance *(support of spouse),* offset, option *(contractual provision),* part *(portion),* pay, payment *(remittance),* payroll, pension, permission, perquisite, privilege, quota, ration, rebate, sanction *(permission),* subsidy, sufferance, tolerance, wage
allowed admissible, choate lien, definite, entitled, lawful, legal, legitimate *(rightful),* licit, open *(accessible),* permissible, potential, privileged, rightful. SEE MAIN ENTRY
allowedly admittedly
allowing consenting, lenient, permissive
allowing no departure from the standard exact
alloy commingle, incorporate *(include),* join *(bring together),* pollute, taint *(contaminate)*
alloyed composite, promiscuous
allude adduce, hint, purport, refer *(direct attention).* SEE MAIN ENTRY
allude to appertain, bear *(adduce),* connote, disclose, imply, indicate, mention
alluded to implied
allure amenity, bait *(lure),* cajole, coax, convince, decoy, ensnare, entice, entrap, incentive, inveigle, lure, motivate, seduction
allurement bribery, cause *(reason),* decoy, incentive, inducement, invitation, seduction
alluring attractive, provocative, sapid
allusion attribution, connotation, hint, implication *(inference),* indication, inference, innuendo, insinuation, intimation, mention *(reference),* referral, reminder, suggestion
allusive implicit, implied, indirect, suggestive *(evocative),* tacit. SEE MAIN ENTRY
allusory allusive
alluvion cataclysm. SEE MAIN ENTRY
ally affiliate, backer, bear *(support),* benefactor, coactor, coadjutant, cohort, colleague, combine *(act in concert),* confederate, confirm, conjoin, connect *(relate),* consociate, consolidate *(unite),* contributor *(contributor),* cooperate, correlate, disciple, espouse, federalize *(associate),* federate, involve *(implicate),* join *(associate oneself with),* merge, participant, partisan, partner, pool, proponent, relate *(establish a connection),* unite. SEE MAIN ENTRY
ally in crime coconspirator
ally in wrongdoing coconspirator
almanac calendar *(record of yearly periods),* register
almightiness predominance
almighty omnipotent, predominant
almoner contributor *(giver)*
almost approximate, quasi. SEE MAIN ENTRY
almost as quasi
almost certainly high probability
alms contribution *(donation),* donation, largess *(gift)*
almsgiver contributor *(giver),* donor
almsgiving charitable *(benevolent),* charity, largess *(generosity),* liberal *(generous),* philanthropic, philanthropy
alodium domain *(land owned)*
alone apart, insular, only, remote *(secluded),* separate, solely *(singly).* SEE MAIN ENTRY
along SEE MAIN ENTRY
along in years elderly
along the river banks fluvial
along the way en route
alonge SEE MAIN ENTRY
alongside adjacent
aloof cold-blooded, controlled *(restrained),* disdainful, dispassionate, insusceptible *(uncaring),* orgulous, phlegmatic, proud *(conceited),* solitary, unapproachable, unresponsive
aloofness disinterest *(lack of interest),* disregard *(lack of respect),* indifference, neutrality
alphabetize tabulate
already indicated previous, said
already mentioned aforesaid
already said aforesaid
also alias. SEE MAIN ENTRY
also acknowledged as alias
also acknowledging the name of alias
also answering to alias
also called alias
also known as alias. SEE MAIN ENTRY
also known by alias
also known under the name of alias
also recognized as alias
alter adapt, amend, change, commute, convert *(change use),* countervail, denature, edit, emend, falsify, fix *(repair),* fluctuate, qualify *(condition),* rectify, revise, tamper, transform, vary. SEE MAIN ENTRY
alter course deviate, digress
alter ego counterpart *(complement).* SEE MAIN ENTRY
alter fraudulently falsify
alter one's course detour
alter the appearance of camouflage, disguise
alter the position move *(alter position)*
alter with intent to deceive fake
alterable aleatory *(uncertain),* conditional, indefinite, mutable, pliable, protean, provisional, variable, yielding
alterant drug
alteration conversion *(change),* correction *(change),* deviation, digression, diversification, innovation, modification, reform, rehabilitation, reorganization, repair, revision *(process of correcting),* transition, vicissitudes. SEE MAIN ENTRY
alterative ambulatory, corrigible, remedial
altercari dispute *(contest)*
altercate bicker, brawl, collide *(clash),* contend *(dispute),* contest, debate, discacord, dispute *(contest),* fight *(battle),* litigate, remonstrate
altercatio altercation, controversy *(argument),* dispute
altercation affray, argument *(contention),* belligerency, brawl, collision *(dispute),* commotion, conflict, contest *(dispute),* controversy *(argument),* disagreement, dispute, feud, fight *(argument),* fracas, strife, variance *(disagreement).* SEE MAIN ENTRY
altered different, tempered
altered for the worse dilapidated
alternare alternate *(take turns)*
alternate agent, alter ego, attorney in fact, beat *(pulsate),* cover *(substitute),* deputy, disjunctive *(alternative),* fluctuate, intermittent, oscillate, reciprocate, replace, replacement, stopgap, substitute, surrogate, vacillate, vary, vicarious *(substitutional).* SEE MAIN ENTRY
alternate choice alternative *(option),* option *(choice)*
alternate route detour
alternating reciprocal, shifting
alternating conditions vicissitudes
alternation cycle, interchange, sequence, vicissitudes
alternative call *(option),* cover *(substitute),* elective *(selective),* expedient, loophole, option *(choice),* plan, replacement, secondary, stopgap, substitute, vicarious *(substitutional).* SEE MAIN ENTRY
alternative dispute resolution SEE MAIN ENTRY
alterner alternate *(take turns)*
although notwithstanding, regardless
altiloquence fustian
altiloquent inflated *(bombastic)*
altior heighten *(elevate)*
altisonant inflated *(bombastic)*
altitude ceiling, elevation
altogether in toto, outright, radical *(extreme),* wholly
altruism benevolence *(disposition to do good),* charity, goodwill, humanity *(humaneness),* largess *(generosity),* philanthropy, understanding *(tolerance)*
altruist benefactor, contributor *(giver),* donor, good samaritan, samaritan
altruistic benevolent, charitable *(benevolent),* humane, liberal *(generous),* magnanimous, nonprofit, philanthropic
always invariably. SEE MAIN ENTRY
amalgam melange, solution *(substance)*
amalgamate cement, collect *(gather),* combine *(join together),* commingle, connect *(join together),* consolidate *(unite),* cooperate, crystallize, desegregate, federalize *(associate),* federate, hoard, join *(bring together),* merge, organize *(unionize),* pool, unite. SEE MAIN ENTRY
amalgamated collective, composite, compound, concerted, concurrent *(united),* conglomerate, conjoint, correlative, joint, miscellaneous, promiscuous
amalgamating concrescence
amalgamation association *(alliance),* building *(business of assembling),* cartel, centralization, coalescence, coalition, combination, consolidation, federation, incorporation *(blend),* merger, pool, relationship *(connection),* union *(labor organization)*
amalgamative coadunate, coherent *(joined)*
amanuensis SEE MAIN ENTRY
amaranthine durable, perpetual
amass accrue *(increase),* aggregate, collect *(gather),* compile, concentrate *(consolidate),* congregate, conjoin, consolidate *(strengthen),* consolidate *(unite),* convene, cull, fund, garner, glean, hoard, join *(bring together),* keep *(shelter),* meet, reserve, set aside *(annul),* store, unite. SEE MAIN ENTRY
amassed collective, composite, conglomerate. SEE MAIN ENTRY

amassing centralization
amassment agglomeration, assemblage, collection *(accumulation)*, conglomeration, congregation, corpus, cumulation, hoard, store *(depository)*
amateur inexperienced, layman, neophyte, novice, volunteer. SEE MAIN ENTRY
amateurish incompetent, unprofessional
amaze impress *(affect deeply)*. SEE MAIN ENTRY
amazed speechless
amazement incredulity, phenomenon *(unusual occurrence)*, surprise
amazing extraordinary, ineffable, noteworthy, portentous *(eliciting amazement)*, remarkable, special, unaccustomed, unusual
amazing thing phenomenon *(unusual occurrence)*
ambages enigma, evasion
ambagious circuitous, devious, indirect, labyrinthine, sinuous
ambagitory labyrinthine, sinuous
ambassador deputy, plenipotentiary, spokesman
ambassadorial function embassy
ambassadorial office embassy
ambassadorial residence embassy
ambience atmosphere
ambigere dispute *(debate)*
ambiguitas ambiguity
ambiguity doubt *(indecision)*, incertitude. SEE MAIN ENTRY
ambiguous aleatory *(uncertain)*, allusive, debatable, disputable, dubious, enigmatic, equivocal, inapprehensible, incomprehensible, indefinite, indeterminate, indistinct, inexact, inscrutable, nebulous, opaque, problematic, unclear, undecided, vague. SEE MAIN ENTRY
ambiguous saying enigma
ambiguus ambiguous, equivocal, evasive, indefinite, undecided, vague
ambire canvass
ambit border, capacity *(sphere)*, circuit, contour *(outline)*, coverage *(scope)*, frontier, limit, outline *(boundary)*, periphery, purview, range, scope, sphere. SEE MAIN ENTRY
ambition desideratum, design *(intent)*, desire, end *(intent)*, goal, intention, objective, plan, project, prospect *(outlook)*, purpose, pursuit *(goal)*, target
ambitious eager, solicitous
ambivalence SEE MAIN ENTRY
ambivalent ambiguous, equivocal, evasive, oblique *(evasive)*
amble perambulate
ambrosiac savory
ambrosial palatable, sapid, savory
ambrosian palatable, savory
ambulant itinerant, moving *(in motion)*
ambulative moving *(in motion)*
ambulator pedestrian
ambulatory itinerant, moving *(in motion)*. SEE MAIN ENTRY
ambuscade cache *(hiding place)*, ensnare, lurk
ambush accost, decoy, ensnare, trap. SEE MAIN ENTRY
ambushed hidden
ameliorable corrigible
ameliorate amend, commute, cure, ease, emend, fix *(repair)*, help, meliorate, mitigate, modify *(alter)*, mollify, progress, rectify, reform, rehabilitate, relieve *(give aid)*, remedy, renew *(refurbish)*, renovate, repair, restore *(renew)*, soothe, treat *(remedy)*. SEE MAIN ENTRY
amelioration amendment *(correction)*, boom *(prosperity)*, correction *(change)*, development *(progression)*, improvement, mollification, progress, promotion *(advancement)*, reform, rehabilitation, relief *(release)*, remedy *(legal means of redress)*, renewal, reorganization, repair, solace
ameliorative mitigating
amenability decorum, liability, responsibility *(accountability)*. SEE MAIN ENTRY
amenable actionable, corrigible, facile, inclined, liable, malleable, obedient, open *(persuasible)*, open-minded, palatable, passive, pliable, receptive, sequacious, suasible, tractable, willing *(not averse)*, yielding. SEE MAIN ENTRY
amenable to law justiciable, permissible
amenable to measurement determinable *(ascertainable)*
amenable to reason reasonable *(rational)*
amenableness decorum, liability
amend adjust *(resolve)*, alter, convert *(change use)*, edit, emend, fix *(repair)*, meliorate, modify *(alter)*, reconsider, rectify, reform, rehabilitate, remedy, renew *(refurbish)*, renovate, repair, restore *(renew)*, revise, supplement. SEE MAIN ENTRY
amend by removing expurgate
amendable ambulatory, corrigible
amendatory ambulatory, remedial
amending correction *(change)*
amendment correction *(change)*, reform, rider. SEE MAIN ENTRY
amends collection *(payment)*, compensation, damages, expiation, indemnification, indemnity, recompense, reparation *(indemnification)*, restitution, retribution
amenities decorum. SEE MAIN ENTRY
amenity comity, courtesy. SEE MAIN ENTRY
amentia insanity
amerce fine, mulct *(fine)*, penalize, punish
amercement correction *(punishment)*, cost *(penalty)*, discipline *(punishment)*, fine, forfeiture *(thing forfeited)*, penalty, punishment. SEE MAIN ENTRY
amercing disciplinary *(punitory)*
amiability benevolence *(disposition to do good)*, comity, courtesy, rapprochement
amiable amenable, amicable, benevolent, civil *(polite)*, malleable, obeisant, peaceable
amicability rapprochement
amicable benevolent, harmonious, nonmilitant, peaceable. SEE MAIN ENTRY
amicableness benevolence *(disposition to do good)*
amicire clothe
amicus curiae SEE MAIN ENTRY
amid among
amidst among
amiss astray, defective, disordered, errant, erroneous, faulty, improper, inaccurate, inappropriate, incorrect, unsuitable
amittere lose *(be deprived of)*
amity accordance *(understanding)*, agreement *(concurrence)*, comity, compatibility, concordance, goodwill, mutual understanding, peace, rapprochement, sodality
ammassment arsenal
ammount accrued cumulation
ammunition bomb. SEE MAIN ENTRY
amnesty absolution, acquittal, clear, clemency, condonation, dispensation *(exception)*, exoneration, impunity, pardon, reconciliation, release, remission, remit *(release from penalty)*, respite *(reprieve)*. SEE MAIN ENTRY
amoenitas amenity
among SEE MAIN ENTRY
amoral bad *(offensive)*, diabolic, immoral, peccant *(culpable)*
amoralism bad repute
amoralistic diabolic
amorality bad repute, laxity
amorous hot-blooded
amorousness affection
amorphic indefinite
amorphous indefinite, intangible, vague
amortization discharge *(payment)*, payment *(act of paying)*. SEE MAIN ENTRY
amortize discharge *(pay a debt)*
amortizement discharge *(payment)*, payment *(act of paying)*, satisfaction *(discharge of debt)*
amotio removal
amotion removal
amount aggregate, bulk, caliber *(measurement)*, compound, degree *(magnitude)*, entirety, expenditure, expense *(cost)*, extent, measurement, par *(face amount)*, part *(portion)*, payment *(remittance)*, price, quantity, rate, value. SEE MAIN ENTRY
amount accrued collection *(accumulation)*
amount assessed as payable assessment *(levy)*
amount computed computation
amount deducted discount
amount due bill *(invoice)*, debit, debt, obligation *(liability)*
amount expended outlay
amount for which anything is insured coverage *(insurance)*
amount of surface area *(surface)*
amount over par premium *(excess value)*
amount owing debt
amount paid periodically premium *(insurance payment)*
amount payable debit
amount produced output
amount reserved margin *(spare amount)*
amount to aggregate, comprise, consist, reach
amovere avert, remove *(transfer)*
amphibolic uncertain *(ambiguous)*
amphibological equivocal
amphibolous equivocal
amphigory parody
ample adequate, broad, capacious, considerable, copious, extensive, liberal *(generous)*, multiple, operative, profuse, replete, substantial. SEE MAIN ENTRY
ample notice adequate notice
ample stock sufficiency
ampleness capacity *(maximum)*, maximum *(amplitude)*, quorum, sufficiency
ampliare adjourn, compound
ampliation development *(progression)*, discontinuance *(interruption of a legal action)*
amplificare compound, enhance, enlarge, heighten *(augment)*, increase, intensify, magnify
amplificatio augmentation, promotion *(encouragement)*
amplification accession *(enlargement)*, advance *(increase)*, advancement *(improvement)*, aggravation *(exacerbation)*, augmentation, boom *(increase)*, clarification,

development *(progression),* explanation, extension *(expansion),* growth *(increase),* hyperbole, inflation *(increase),* overstatement. SEE MAIN ENTRY
amplified extreme *(exaggerated),* inflated *(enlarged),* inflated *(overestimated)*
amplify accrue *(increase),* accumulate *(enlarge),* aggravate *(exacerbate),* build *(augment),* detail *(particularize),* develop, elaborate, enhance, enlarge, expand, extend *(enlarge),* heighten *(augment),* increase, inflate, magnify, supplement. SEE MAIN ENTRY
amplifying cumulative *(intensifying)*
amplissimus gradus eminence
amplitude boom *(increase),* boom *(prosperity),* caliber *(measurement),* capacity *(maximum),* degree *(magnitude),* latitude, magnitude, mass *(weight),* plethora, quantity, scope, sufficiency
amplitudinous broad
amplitudo bulk, magnitude
amplus broad, extensive, illustrious
amputate mutilate
amuse occupy *(engage)*
amusement enjoyment *(pleasure),* treat
amusing jocular, ludicrous, sapid
an equal percentage per capita
anabasis development *(progression)*
anachronic untimely
anachronistic obsolete, outdated, outmoded, untimely. SEE MAIN ENTRY
anachronize antedate
anachronous obsolete, outdated, outmoded, untimely
anacoluthon non sequitur. SEE MAIN ENTRY
analagous coextensive, commensurable, commensurate, comparable *(capable of comparison).* SEE MAIN ENTRY
analagous to comparative
analagousness balance *(equality)*
analect abstract
analeptic curative, medicinal, remedial, salubrious, salutary
analgesic drug
analogical analogous, cognate, commensurable, comparable *(capable of comparison),* congruous
analogical procedure collation, comparison
analogize compare
analogous akin *(germane),* coequal, cognate, congruous, correlative, interrelated, proportionate, related, relative *(comparative),* similar, tantamount. SEE MAIN ENTRY
analogue correlate, counterpart *(complement)*
analogy collation, comparison, connection *(relation),* correspondence *(similarity),* parity, relation *(connection),* relationship *(connection),* resemblance. SEE MAIN ENTRY
analysis capsule, choice *(decision),* classification, criticism, deliberation, diagnosis, digest, discretion *(power of choice),* discrimination *(differentiation),* examination *(study),* hornbook, indagation, judgment *(discernment),* measurement, pandect *(treatise),* probe, proposal *(report),* prospectus, rating, ratiocination, reflection *(thought),* research, review *(critical evaluation),* scenario, scrutiny, summary, test, treatment, trial *(experiment).* SEE MAIN ENTRY
analytic deductive, discursive *(analytical),* logical
analytical clinical, deductive, demonstrative *(illustrative),* empirical, logical, rational. SEE MAIN ENTRY
analyzation hornbook, inquiry *(systematic investigation)*
analyze canvass, classify, consider, construe *(comprehend),* construe *(translate),* deliberate, detail *(particularize),* diagnose, digest *(comprehend),* discuss, examine *(study),* identify, investigate, peruse, ponder, rationalize, reason *(conclude),* reflect *(ponder),* research, review, scrutinize, study, survey *(examine),* treat *(process).* SEE MAIN ENTRY
anamorphosis distortion
anarchic disorderly, lawless
anarchical disordered, disorderly, lawless
anarchism disorder *(lack of order),* misrule
anarchist insurgent, malcontent
anarchistic contumacious, disorderly, incendiary
anarchy confusion *(turmoil),* disorder *(lack of order),* havoc, insurrection, lynch law, misrule, pandemonium, revolution. SEE MAIN ENTRY
anathema denunciation, expletive, imprecation, malediction
anathematize blame, condemn *(blame),* defame, denounce *(condemn),* malign, proscribe *(denounce)*
anatomical organic
anatomize analyze, examine *(study),* scrutinize
anatomy body *(person),* configuration *(form),* content *(structure)*
anceps critical *(crucial),* dubious, equivocal, indeterminate
ancestor ascendant, derivation, forerunner, kindred, parents, precursor, predecessor, primogenitor, progenitor. SEE MAIN ENTRY
ancestorial hereditary
ancestors lineage
ancestral consanguineous, hereditary, paternal, traditional
ancestral descent origin *(ancestry)*
ancestral relation kindred, primogenitor
ancestral relative primogenitor
ancestry affiliation *(bloodline),* affinity *(family ties),* birth *(lineage),* birthright, blood, bloodline, derivation, descent *(lineage),* family *(common ancestry),* heritage, lineage, origination, parentage, paternity, race, source. SEE MAIN ENTRY
anchor adhere *(fasten),* mainstay, security *(safety)*
anchorage haven
anchored firm, fixed *(securely placed),* situated, stable, steadfast
anchoretic solitary
anchoretical solitary
ancient antique, hereditary, obsolete, old, outdated, outmoded
ancillary appurtenant, collateral *(accompanying),* dependent, pendent, secondary, slight, subordinate, subservient, supplementary. SEE MAIN ENTRY
ancillary relief SEE MAIN ENTRY
and all et al.
and everyone et al.
and more of the same et al.
and other parties et al.
and other things et al.
and others et al.
and the rest et al.
anecdotal narrative
anemic languid
anent correlative
anesthetic drug, narcotic *(adjective),* narcotic *(noun)*
anesthetic agent drug
anesthetize drug, obtund
anew de novo. SEE MAIN ENTRY
anfractuous circuitous, sinuous, tortuous *(bending)*
angel spirit
angelic clean
anger bait *(harass),* harass, incense, irritate, molest *(annoy),* offend *(insult),* passion, pique, provoke, resentment, umbrage. SEE MAIN ENTRY
angering provocation
angle outlook, phase *(aspect),* side, slant, standpoint
angle of vision perspective
angle off deviate
angled oblique *(slanted)*
angry resentful, vehement, vindictive
angry disagreement dissension
angry dispute altercation
anguilliform circuitous
anguine circuitous
anguish pain, plaint, remorse, suffer *(sustain loss).* SEE MAIN ENTRY
anguished aggrieved *(harmed),* disconsolate
anguishing painful
angustiae predicament, restriction
angustus limited
anility incapacity
anima life *(period of existence),* spirit
animadversio correction *(punishment),* notice *(heed),* stricture
animadversion admonition, bad repute, comment, condemnation *(blame),* correction *(punishment),* criticism, diatribe, disapprobation, disapproval, discredit, impeachment, impugnation, obloquy, remark, remonstrance, reprimand, reproach, revilement, stricture. SEE MAIN ENTRY
animadvert blame, comment, complain *(criticize),* condemn *(blame),* criticize *(find fault with),* denounce *(condemn),* disapprove *(condemn),* fault, impeach, remark, remonstrate, reprehend, reproach
animadvert on rebuke, reprimand
animadvert upon censure, expostulate, lash *(attack verbally)*
animadvertere notice *(observe),* observe *(watch)*
animal SEE MAIN ENTRY
animalism bestiality
animam edere expire
animans animal
animate conscious *(awake),* exhort, generate, incite, inspire, live *(conscious),* motivate, prompt, provoke, spirit, stimulate
animated alert *(agile),* born *(alive),* fervent, live *(conscious),* ready *(willing),* volatile
animating impulsive *(impelling),* moving *(evoking emotion)*
animation birth *(beginning),* instigation, life *(vitality),* spirit
animator catalyst, stimulus
animi sane
animi motus emotion, impression
animosity alienation *(estrangement),* belligerency, conflict, contempt *(disdain),* discord, discord, feud, hatred, ill will, incompatibility *(difference),* malice, odium, rancor, resentment, spite, strife, umbrage. SEE MAIN ENTRY
animum attendere concentrate *(pay attention)*

animum frangere discourage
animus character *(personal quality)*
animus design *(intent)*, feud
animus frame *(mood)*
animus hatred, ill will, malice, odium, resentment, spite
animus will *(desire)*. SEE MAIN ENTRY
animus ingratus ingratitude
animus submissus resignation *(passive acceptance)*
annal record
annals calendar *(record of yearly periods)*, documentation
annex accrue *(increase)*, acquire *(secure)*, addendum, addition, adopt, affix, append, appropriate, appurtenance, assume *(seize)*, attach *(join)*, attach *(seize)*, attachment *(thing affixed)*, cement, codicil, combine *(join together)*, compound, confiscate, conjoin, connect *(join together)*, contact *(touch)*, distrain, enlarge, impropriate, increase, join *(bring together)*, juxtapose, occupy *(take possession)*, offshoot, organ, preempt, seize *(confiscate)*, sequester *(seize property)*. SEE MAIN ENTRY
annex for public use eminent domain
annexation accretion, addendum, addition, appendix *(accession)*, appropriation *(taking)*, appurtenance, assumption *(seizure)*, attachment *(act of affixing)*, attachment *(seizure)*, boom *(increase)*, coalescence, codicil, distraint, distress *(seizure)*, garnishment, sequestration
annexe addendum, appurtenance
annexed accrued, appurtenant, attached *(seized)*, provincial
annexing accession *(annexation)*, coalescence
annexion attachment *(act of affixing)*
annihilate abolish, annul, cancel, consume, destroy *(efface)*, eliminate *(eradicate)*, eradicate, extinguish, extirpate, negate, obliterate, overturn, remove *(eliminate)*, slay, stifle, subvert. SEE MAIN ENTRY
annihilated lifeless *(dead)*, lost *(taken away)*
annihilating deadly, destructive
annihilation abolition, assassination, demise *(death)*, destruction, dissolution *(termination)*, homicide, killing, subversion
annihilative dire, disastrous, fatal, lethal
annotate comment, describe, edit, elucidate, explain, interpret, note *(record)*
annotated detailed
annotated text hornbook
annotation caption, comment, explanation, memorandum, notation, note *(brief comment)*, observation
annotative demonstrative *(illustrative)*, interpretive
announce allege, annunciate, apprise, assert, bare, circulate, communicate, convey *(communicate)*, declare, disabuse, disclose, disseminate, enunciate, herald, inform *(betray)*, inform *(notify)*, issue *(publish)*, mention, notify, observe *(remark)*, pass *(determine)*, portend, posit, proclaim, profess *(avow)*, promulgate, pronounce *(speak)*, protest, publish, relate *(tell)*, report *(disclose)*, reveal, signify *(inform)*, speak, utter. SEE MAIN ENTRY
announce a conclusion find *(determine)*
announce authoritatively pronounce *(pass judgment)*, pronounce *(speak)*
announce in advance anticipate *(prognosticate)*, predict, presage
announce officially pronounce *(speak)*
announce one's presence report *(present oneself)*
announce publicly post
announced alleged, oral, public *(known)*
announcement assertion, averment, caveat, charter *(declaration of rights)*, common knowledge, communication *(statement)*, declaration, declaratory judgment, dictum, disclosure *(act of disclosing)*, disclosure *(something disclosed)*, issuance, judgment *(formal court decree)*, notification, proclamation, profession *(declaration)*, pronouncement, prospectus, publication *(disclosure)*, publicity, statement. SEE MAIN ENTRY
announcer harbinger, informant, informer *(a person who provides information)*, precursor
annoy aggravate *(annoy)*, badger, bait *(harass)*, discommode, discompose, disconcert, disrupt, distress, disturb, embarrass, harass, harrow, harry *(harass)*, hinder, inconvenience, irritate, mistreat, obsess, offend *(insult)*, persecute, perturb, pique, plague, press *(goad)*, provoke. SEE MAIN ENTRY
annoy excessively badger
annoyance dissatisfaction, disturbance, grievance, hindrance, mischief, molestation, nuisance, provocation, trouble, umbrage
annoyed petulant
annoying irksome, loathsome, objectionable, obnoxious, odious, offensive *(offending)*, provocative, undesirable, vexatious
annua pension
annua pecunia annuity
annual allowance annuity, pension
annual commitment premium *(insurance payment)*
annual encumbrance premium *(insurance payment)*
annual fee premium *(insurance payment)*
annual installment premium *(insurance payment)*
annual liability premium *(insurance payment)*
annual obligation premium *(insurance payment)*
annual payment premium *(insurance payment)*
annual rate of insurance premium *(insurance payment)*
annual remittance premium *(insurance payment)*
annually per annum
annuciative declaratory
annuity allotment, pension, perquisite. SEE MAIN ENTRY
annul abate *(extinguish)*, abolish, abrogate *(rescind)*, adeem, avoid *(cancel)*, cancel, cease, contradict, counteract, destroy *(void)*, disable, discharge *(release from obligation)*, disclaim, discontinue *(abandon)*, disinherit, disown *(deny the validity)*, divorce, eradicate, expunge, extinguish, extirpate, frustrate, impede, invalidate, kill *(defeat)*, negate, neutralize, nullify, obliterate, overreach, override, overrule, quash, recall *(call back)*, recant, renege, repeal, rescind, revoke, supersede, terminate, vacate *(void)*, vitiate. SEE MAIN ENTRY
annul a marriage divorce
annulled defunct, lifeless *(dead)*, null *(invalid)*, null and void
annulling avoidance *(cancellation)*, cancellation
annulment abatement *(extinguishment)*, abolition, ademption, avoidance *(cancellation)*, cancellation, countermand, defeasance, disclaimer, dismissal *(termination of a proceeding)*, dissolution *(termination)*, invalidity, mistrial, negation, repudiation, rescision, retraction, reversal, revocation. SEE MAIN ENTRY
annulment of debt discharge *(payment)*
annulment of marriage divorce
annum SEE MAIN ENTRY
annunciate allege, assert, convey *(communicate)*, disseminate, enunciate, inform *(notify)*, mention, notify, proclaim, promulgate, report *(disclose)*, speak. SEE MAIN ENTRY
annunciation common knowledge, communication *(statement)*, declaration, notification, proclamation, pronouncement
annunciator harbinger, informant, informer *(a person who provides information)*
annunciatory declaratory
annus annum
anodyne beneficial, drug, medicinal, narcotic *(adjective)*, narcotic *(noun)*, remedial
anodynous narcotic
anoint drug
anointed sacrosanct
anomalistic anomalous, irregular *(not usual)*, peculiar *(curious)*
anomalistical peculiar *(curious)*
anomalous atypical, disordered, eccentric, irregular *(not usual)*, noteworthy, novel, peculiar *(curious)*, prodigious *(amazing)*, unaccustomed, uncommon, unique, unorthodox, unprecedented, unusual. SEE MAIN ENTRY
anomalousness deviation, nonconformity
anomaly deviation, discrepancy, irregularity, nonconformity, quirk *(idiosyncrasy)*, variance *(exemption)*. SEE MAIN ENTRY
anon instantly
anonymous unspecified. SEE MAIN ENTRY
another additional
another addressee cotenant
another denizen cotenant
another dweller cotenant
another inhabitant cotenant
another inhabiter cotenant
another leaseholder cotenant
another lessee cotenant
another lodger cotenant
another occupant cotenant
another occupier cotenant
another paying guest cotenant
another possessor cotenant
another renter cotenant
another resident cotenant
another residentiary cotenant
another time anew, de novo
answer acknowledge *(respond)*, acknowledgment *(acceptance)*, appear *(attend court proceedings)*, appearance *(coming into court)*, controvert, converse, counterargument, countercharge, disclosure *(something disclosed)*, find *(discover)*, fulfill, key *(solution)*, outcome, panacea, plea, pleading, reaction *(response)*, rebut, rejoinder, reply *(noun)*, reply *(verb)*, report *(present oneself)*, respond, response, retort, return *(respond)*, solve, verdict. SEE MAIN ENTRY
answer a purpose function
answer a summons report *(present oneself)*
answer back contradict, countercharge, retaliate, retort, return *(respond)*

answer conclusively controvert
answer for assure *(insure)*, cosign, displace *(replace)*, guarantee, indemnify, justify, sponsor, undertake. SEE MAIN ENTRY
answer the purpose correspond *(be equivalent)*, satisfy *(fulfill)*
answer to obey
answerability duty *(obligation)*, fault *(responsibility)*, liability, responsibility *(accountability)*
answerable accountable *(responsible)*, actionable, ascertainable, blameworthy, bound, consonant, liable, subject *(exposed)*
answerer respondent
answering contrary, responsive
antagonism alienation *(estrangement)*, argument *(contention)*, bad repute, belligerency, collision *(dispute)*, conflict, contention *(opposition)*, contest *(dispute)*, contradistinction, contraposition, contravention, controversy *(argument)*, disaccord, discord, feud, hatred, ill will, impugnation, incompatibility *(difference)*, malice, rancor, resentment, resistance, spite. SEE MAIN ENTRY
antagonist adversary, aggressor, assailant, contender, contestant, disputant, foe, rival
antagonistic adverse *(hostile)*, antipathetic *(oppositional)*, averse, contradictory, different, discordant, disinclined, dissident, hostile, inimical, litigious, malevolent, malicious, negative, offensive *(taking the initiative)*, opposite, pugnacious, recusant, renitent, repugnant *(incompatible)*, spiteful, unfavorable, virulent
antagonistic to contrary
antagonistical adverse *(hostile)*
antagonize affront, alienate *(estrange)*, collide *(clash)*, counter, counteract, disaffect, disoblige, incense, provoke. SEE MAIN ENTRY
antagonized irreconcilable
antagonizing obnoxious
ante bet, parlay *(bet)*, stake *(award)*
ante nuptial agreement SEE MAIN ENTRY
ante up bet
antecede precede. SEE MAIN ENTRY
antecedence precedence, priority
antecedens antecedent, last *(preceding)*
antecedent aforesaid, ascendant, before mentioned, derivation, forerunner, former, last *(preceding)*, original *(initial)*, precur-sor, precursory, predecessor, preexist-ing, preliminary, previous, primogenitor, prior, progenitor, sine qua non. SEE MAIN ENTRY
antecedents family *(common ancestry)*, lineage, parentage
antecedere precede
antecellere surpass
antecessor forerunner, predecessor, progenitor
antechamber chamber *(compartment)*
antecursor harbinger
antedate antecede, precede. SEE MAIN ENTRY
antedeluvian antique
antediluvian obsolete, outdated, outmoded
antegredi precede
anteire precede
anteponere prefer
anterior aforesaid, antecedent, before mentioned, last *(preceding)*, preexisting, preliminary, previous, prior
anteroom chamber*(compartment)*, entrance
antetype model, pattern
antevertere anticipate *(expect)*, forestall
anthologize compile
anthology compilation, digest, selection *(collection)*
antibiotic drug
anticipatable foreseeable
anticipate forestall, precede, preconceive, predict, presage, presume. SEE MAIN ENTRY
anticipate danger fear
anticipate injury fear
anticipate needs provide *(arrange for)*
anticipated foreseeable, forseen, forthcoming, future, immediate *(imminent)*, pending *(imminent)*, possible, potential, presumptive, prospective
anticipated loan advance *(allowance)*
anticipating provident *(showing foresight)*
anticipation advancement *(loan)*, expectation, forethought, likelihood, possibility, precaution, preconception, preparation, presumption, probability, prospect *(outlook)*. SEE MAIN ENTRY
anticipation of adversity apprehension *(fear)*
anticipative sanguine
anticipatory premature, preparatory
antidotal medicinal, preventive, remedial
antidote cure, remedy *(that which corrects)*
antifebrile medicinal
antilogy contrary, inconsistency, paradox
antimony antipode
antinomy inconsistency, opposition, paradox
antipathetic averse, bitter *(reproachful)*, contrary, disinclined, hostile, inimical, malevolent, negative, objectionable, obnoxious, offensive *(offending)*, renitent, spiteful. SEE MAIN ENTRY
antipathetical discordant, disinclined, inimical, malevolent, negative, renitent
antipathy alienation *(estrangement)*, antipode, conflict, contradiction, deviation, difference, hatred, ill will, incompatibility *(difference)*, malice, odium, phobia, rancor, reluctance. SEE MAIN ENTRY
antiphon response
antipodal adverse *(opposite)*, hostile, inverse, opposite
antipode antithesis, contra, contrary. SEE MAIN ENTRY
antipodean adverse *(opposite)*, antipathetic *(oppositional)*, inverse, opposite
antipodes antipode
antipoison cure
antipole antipode
antipollution project ecology
antiquate superannuate
antiquated obsolete, old, outdated, outmoded. SEE MAIN ENTRY
antique obsolete, old, outdated, outmoded. SEE MAIN ENTRY
antiseptic preventive
antisepticize decontaminate
antithesis antipode, contra, contradiction, contradistinction, contraposition, contrary, deviation, difference, distinction *(difference)*, incompatibility *(inconsistency)*. SEE MAIN ENTRY
antithetic antipathetic *(oppositional)*, contrary, different, hostile, opposite
antithetical adverse *(opposite)*, antipathetic *(oppositional)*, contradictory, contrary, discordant, hostile, inverse, opposite. SEE MAIN ENTRY
antitheticalness difference
antitoxin cure
antitrust act SEE MAIN ENTRY
antonomasia call *(title)*
antonym contra
antonymous adverse *(opposite)*, discordant, hostile
anxietude disturbance, misgiving
anxiety apprehension *(fear)*, burden, concern *(interest)*, consternation, distress *(anguish)*, disturbance, doubt *(indecision)*, fear, fright, interest *(concern)*, misgiving, nuisance, panic, phobia, pressure, problem, qualm, scruple, stress *(strain)*. SEE MAIN ENTRY
anxious eager, ready *(willing)*, solicitous. SEE MAIN ENTRY
anxious concern consternation, misgiving
anxiousness consternation, distress *(anguish)*, disturbance, misgiving, pressure
anxius solicitous
any individual whoever
any person whoever
anybody whoever
anyhow regardless
anyone whoever
anyway regardless
anywise regardless
apart alone *(solitary)*, bipartite, disconnected, discrete, extrinsic, insular, irrelative, only, partial *(part)*, private *(secluded)*, remote *(secluded)*, separate. SEE MAIN ENTRY
apartheid exclusion, segregation *(isolation by races)*
apartment chamber *(compartment)*, home *(domicile)*, lodging. SEE MAIN ENTRY
apartness exception *(exclusion)*
apathetic casual, cursory, inactive, indolent, inexpressive, insensible, insusceptible *(uncaring)*, languid, lax, lifeless *(dull)*, nonchalant, otiose, passive, perfunctory, phlegmatic, stagnant, stoical, torpid, truant. SEE MAIN ENTRY
apathetical languid
apathy disinterest *(lack of interest)*, indifference, inertia, languor, laxity, sloth
ape copy, impersonate, mock *(imitate)*, pose *(impersonate)*
aperçu abridgment *(condensation)*
aperire betray *(disclose)*, disclose, manifest, reopen, unveil
aperte fairly *(clearly)*
aperture loophole, outlet, portal, rift *(gap)*, split
apertus evident, explicit, ingenuous, manifest, obvious, open *(in sight)*, open *(persuasible)*, overt, patent, straightforward, unambiguous
apertus sincerus candid
apery caricature, parody
apex ceiling, culmination, pinnacle
aphonic speechless
aphorism maxim, phrase
aphoristic axiomatic, brief, compact *(pithy)*, proverbial, sententious
aphoristic expression maxim
aphoristical compact *(pithy)*
apical cardinal *(basic)*
apiece respectively
aplomb composure, confidence *(faith)*
aplomb indestructibility
aplomb surety *(certainty)*. SEE MAIN ENTRY
apocha receipt *(proof of receiving)*
apocryphal assumed *(feigned)*, disputable, fictitious, ill-founded, spurious, untrue

apodictic axiomatic, categorical, incontrovertible
apodosis denouement
apogee ceiling, culmination, pinnacle
apograph transcript
apologetic contrite, palliative *(excusing)*, penitent, remorseful, repentant
apologist advocate *(counselor)*, advocate *(espouser)*, proponent. SEE MAIN ENTRY
apologize regret, repent
apology expiation. SEE MAIN ENTRY
apostasize abandon *(relinquish)*, defect, discontinue *(abandon)*
apostasy abandonment *(desertion)*, bad faith, blasphemy, desertion, disloyalty, dissent *(difference of opinion)*, infidelity, nonconformity, revolt, sedition
apostate heretic, recreant, recusant
apostatic recreant
apostatical recreant
apostatize bear false witness, quit *(discontinue)*, secede, tergiversate
apostatizing disobedient, faithless, false *(disloyal)*
apostil clarification
apostle disciple, partisan
apotheca depository
apothegm phrase
apothegmatic compact *(pithy)*, sententious
apothegmatical compact *(pithy)*
apotheosis exemplar
appall discompose, disconcert, harrow, repel *(disgust)*
appalling deplorable, dire, disastrous, egregious, formidable, loathsome, lurid, repulsive
appalling SEE MAIN ENTRY
appanage addendum, adjunct, appurtenance, codicil, dower, grant, inheritance
apparatus appliance, device *(mechanism)*, equipment, expedient, facility *(instrumentality)*, instrument *(tool)*, paraphernalia *(apparatus)*, tool
apparatus belli ammunition
apparent axiomatic, blatant *(conspicuous)*, candid, circumstantial, coherent *(clear)*, colorable *(plausible)*, conclusive *(determinative)*, conspicuous, constructive *(inferential)*, demonstrable, discernible, distinct *(clear)*, elementary, evident, flagrant, lucid, manifest, naked *(perceptible)*, obvious, open *(in sight)*, ostensible, overt, palpable, patent, pellucid, perceivable, perceptible, plausible, presumptive, probable, prominent, public *(known)*, specious, unmistakable, visible *(noticeable)*. SEE MAIN ENTRY
apparent character color *(complexion)*, complexion
apparent right color *(deceptive appearance)*
apparent state complexion
apparentation affiliation *(bloodline)*
apparently prima facie *(self-evident)*, quasi
apparently right colorable *(plausible)*
apparere appear *(materialize)*
apparition phantom, phenomenon *(manifestation)*, specter, spirit, vision *(dream)*
appeal address *(petition)*, amenity, call *(appeal to)*, challenge, coax, entreaty, habeas corpus, importune, incentive, invitation, motivate, press *(beseech)*, request *(noun)*, request *(verb)*, rhetoric *(skilled speech)*. SEE MAIN ENTRY
appeal against expostulate
appeal for petition, solicit
appeal on the merits SEE MAIN ENTRY
appeal to bait *(lure)*, pray, propitiate, solicit, urge
appeal to a higher court certiorari
appeal to arms fight *(battle)*, fight *(battle)*
appeal to the law litigate, sue
appealable litigable
appealer appellant, special interest
appealing attractive, precatory, sapid
appealing conclusively cogent
appealing forcibly cogent
appealing to reason disputable
appear bare, comport *(behave)*, demean *(deport oneself)*, emerge, report *(present oneself)*. SEE MAIN ENTRY
appear for represent *(substitute)*
appear for duty report *(present oneself)*
appearance aspect, color *(deceptive appearance)*, complexion, condition *(state)*, configuration *(form)*, demeanor, deportment, expression *(manifestation)*, face value *(first blush)*, first appearance, manifestation, manner *(behavior)*, phantom, phenomenon *(manifestation)*, presence *(poise)*, pretense *(pretext)*, semblance, specter, state *(condition)*, style, vision *(dream)*. SEE MAIN ENTRY
appearance of truth credibility, probability
appearing apparent *(presumptive)*, colorable *(specious)*, evident, ostensible, perceivable, specious
appearing at intervals sporadic
appeasable nonmilitant, placable
appease allay, assuage, disarm *(set at ease)*, mitigate, moderate *(temper)*, mollify, pacify, palliate *(abate)*, placate, propitiate, reconcile, redress, satisfy *(fulfill)*, soothe. SEE MAIN ENTRY
appeased agreed *(harmonized)*
appeasement conciliation, mollification, reconciliation, satisfaction *(fulfilment)*. SEE MAIN ENTRY
appeaser go-between
appelare appeal
appelation cognomen
appellant claimant, contender, contestant, litigant, party *(litigant)*, respondent, suitor. SEE MAIN ENTRY
appellare summon
appellate court SEE MAIN ENTRY
appellate review appeal
appellatio appeal
appellation call *(title)*, denomination, designation *(naming)*, identification, term *(expression)*, title *(designation)*. SEE MAIN ENTRY
appellative call *(title)*, cognomen, term *(expression)*
appellator appellant
appellee litigant, party *(litigant)*
append affix, annex *(add)*, attach *(join)*, combine *(join together)*, compound, connect *(join together)*, join *(bring together)*. SEE MAIN ENTRY
appendage accession *(annexation)*, addendum, adjoiner, adjunct, allonge, appendix *(accession)*, appendix *(supplement)*, appurtenance, attachment *(thing affixed)*, codicil, organ, rider
appendant appurtenance, attached *(annexed)*, rider
appended additional, appurtenant, attached *(annexed)*
appendix addendum, allonge, appurtenance, attachment *(thing affixed)*, codicil, insertion, rider. SEE MAIN ENTRY
apperceive note *(notice)*, perceive, understand
apperception appreciation *(perception)*, cognition, insight, judgment *(discernment)*, knowledge *(awareness)*, perception, realization, reason *(sound judgment)*, recognition, sagacity, sense *(feeling)*, understanding *(comprehension)*. SEE MAIN ENTRY
apperceptive cognizant, conscious *(aware)*, judicious, knowing, omniscient, perceptive, perspicacious, sensitive *(discerning)*
appercipient sensitive *(discerning)*
appertain correspond *(be equivalent)*, pertain, refer *(direct attention)*. SEE MAIN ENTRY
appertain to concern *(involve)*, connect *(relate)*, relate *(establish a connection)*
appertaining akin *(germane)*, applicable, appurtenant, cognate, collateral *(accompanying)*, pertinent
appertaining to incident
appetence predilection, predisposition, proclivity
appetency desire, greed, predilection, predisposition, proclivity
appetent eager
appetere assault
appetite desire, penchant, predilection, predisposition
appetitio desire
appetitus instinct
appetizing palatable, sapid, savory
applaud honor, recommend
applauded famous, illustrious, renowned
applause mention *(tribute)*
appliable applicable
appliance device *(mechanism)*, expedient, facility *(instrumentality)*, instrument *(tool)*. SEE MAIN ENTRY
appliances paraphernalia *(apparatus)*
applicability admissibility, aptitude, connection *(relation)*, propriety *(appropriateness)*, qualification *(fitness)*, relation *(connection)*, relevance, utility *(usefulness)*, utilization. SEE MAIN ENTRY
applicable admissible, akin *(germane)*, apposite, appropriate, congruous, constructive *(creative)*, convenient, correlative, felicitous, fit, functional, germane, operative, pertinent, practical, related, relative *(relevant)*, relevant, suitable. SEE MAIN ENTRY
applicable to a class generic
applicant candidate, claimant, contender, petitioner, prospect *(prospective patron)*, suitor. SEE MAIN ENTRY
application arrogation, assignation, call *(appeal)*, call *(title)*, connection *(relation)*, connotation, diligence *(care)*, diligence *(perseverance)*, endeavor, industry *(activity)*, infliction, interest *(concern)*, means *(opportunity)*, motion, obsession, petition, prayer, purpose, regard *(attention)*, relevance, request, requisition, resolution *(decision)*, usage, use, work *(effort)*. SEE MAIN ENTRY
application for a ruling motion
application for an order motion
application for discharge habeas corpus
application for liberty habeas corpus
application for proposed relief motion
application for relief prayer
application for retrial appeal, certiorari

application for review by a higher tribunal appeal
application of force compulsion *(coercion)*
applied functional
applied energy effort
applied from without extrinsic
applied logic dialectic
apply ascribe, concern *(involve)*, devote, employ *(make use of)*, exercise *(use)*, exert, expend *(consume)*, exploit *(make use of)*, impute, inflict, manipulate *(utilize skillfully)*, move *(judicially request)*, refer *(direct attention)*, relate *(establish a connection)*, resort, solicit, spend. SEE MAIN ENTRY
apply a closure complete
apply a remedy cure, drug, help
apply dishonestly convert *(misappropriate)*
apply for desire, petition, request, sue
apply for a loan borrow
apply for a reexamination of a case appeal
apply for a retrial appeal
apply for a review of a case to a higher tribunal appeal
apply one's self to practice *(train by repetition)*
apply oneself labor, persevere, specialize
apply oneself to address *(direct attention to)*, commit *(perpetrate)*, endeavor, occupy *(engage)*, undertake
apply pressure coerce, constrain *(compel)*, foist, force *(coerce)*
apply reason deduce, deduct *(conclude by reasoning)*
apply the attention to occupy *(engage)*
apply the closure close *(terminate)*
apply the mind concentrate *(pay attention)*, ponder, study
apply the mind to occupy *(engage)*
apply to appertain, call *(appeal to)*, importune, petition, pray
apply to one's own uses impropriate, plagiarize
applying to apposite, germane
appoint allocate, allot, assign *(designate)*, authorize, bestow, charge *(empower)*, choose, clothe, delegate, designate, detail *(assign)*, dispense, employ *(engage services)*, empower, engage *(hire)*, entrust, furnish, hire, induct, instate, invest *(vest)*, nominate, parcel, provide *(arrange for)*, select. SEE MAIN ENTRY
appoint as agent delegate
appoint as representative delegate
appoint beforehand preordain
appoint by act enact
appoint by vote elect *(select by a vote)*
appoint in advance preordain
appoint the time of date
appointed select
appointed counsel SEE MAIN ENTRY
appointed group commission *(agency)*, committee
appointee agent, deputy, licensee, nominee *(delegate)*, proctor, procurator, trustee
appointer licensor
appointing deputation *(selection of delegates)*
appointive adoptive, elective *(voluntary)*
appointment agency *(legal relationship)*, allotment, assignment *(designation)*, charge *(responsibility)*, delegation *(assignment)*, deputation *(selection of delegates)*, designation *(naming)*, dispensation *(act of dispensing)*, election *(choice)*, employment, equipment, mission, nomination, office, position *(business status)*, post, province, pursuit *(occupation)*, rendezvous, selection *(choice)*. SEE MAIN ENTRY
appointment by vote election *(selection by vote)*
appointments paraphernalia *(personal belongings)*, property *(possessions)*
apportion allocate, allot, arrange *(methodize)*, assign *(allot)*, bestow, classify, demarcate, devote, dichotomize, disburse *(distribute)*, dispense, disperse *(disseminate)*, divide *(distribute)*, dole, endue, expend *(disburse)*, fund, furnish, leave *(give)*, marshal, mete, parcel, partition, prorate, sort, split, subdivide. SEE MAIN ENTRY
apportion anew reapportion
apportion by measure mete
apportion pro rata prorate
apportionable divisible, severable
apportioned pro rata. SEE MAIN ENTRY
apportioned lot share *(interest)*
apportioning disbursement *(act of disbursing)*
apportionment allotment, appropriation *(allotment)*, arbitration, assignment *(allotment)*, classification, decentralization, disbursement *(act of disbursing)*, dispensation *(act of dispensing)*, division *(act of dividing)*, equity *(share of ownership)*, order *(arrangement)*, proportion, quantity, quota, ration. SEE MAIN ENTRY
appose adjoin, border *(bound)*, contrast, juxtapose
apposite appropriate, congruous, correlative, felicitous, fit, germane, harmonious, pertinent, proper, related, relative *(relevant)*, relevant, seasonable, suitable. SEE MAIN ENTRY
appositeness admissibility, affiliation *(connectedness)*, collation, qualification *(fitness)*, relation *(connection)*, relationship *(connection)*, relevance
apposition affiliation *(connectedness)*, propinquity *(proximity)*, relation *(connection)*. SEE MAIN ENTRY
appositional relative *(relevant)*
appraisable appreciable, determinable *(ascertainable)*
appraisal account *(evaluation)*, appreciation *(perception)*, arbitration, assessment *(estimation)*, choice *(decision)*, computation, concept, cost *(price)*, determination, discretion *(power of choice)*, discrimination *(differentiation)*, estimate *(approximate cost)*, estimation *(calculation)*, expense *(cost)*, generalization, idea, inspection, judgment *(discernment)*, measurement, par *(face amount)*, perception, price, proposal *(report)*, rating, review *(critical evaluation)*, value, worth. SEE MAIN ENTRY
appraise calculate, charge *(assess)*, consider, criticize *(evaluate)*, diagnose, estimate, evaluate, excise *(levy a tax)*, gauge, judge, measure, opine, ponder, rate, survey *(examine)*. SEE MAIN ENTRY
appraised ad valorem
appraisement ad valorem, appraisal, assessment *(estimation)*, determination, estimate *(approximate cost)*, estimation *(calculation)*, expense *(cost)*, measurement, par *(face amount)*, price, worth
appraiser juror
appraising discriminating *(judicious)*
appraisment appreciation *(perception)*
appreciable corporeal, determinable *(ascertainable)*, perceivable, ponderable, substantive. SEE MAIN ENTRY
appreciate accrue *(increase)*, apprehend *(perceive)*, comprehend *(understand)*, conceive *(comprehend)*, digest *(comprehend)*, discern *(detect with the senses)*, enhance, gauge, increase, note *(notice)*, notice *(observe)*, perceive, pierce *(discern)*, realize *(understand)*, recognize *(acknowledge)*, regard *(hold in esteem)*, relish, understand. SEE MAIN ENTRY
appreciation accession *(enlargement)*, augmentation, boom *(increase)*, cognition, comprehension, computation, concept, determination, discretion *(quality of being discreet)*, discrimination *(differentiation)*, estimation *(esteem)*, honor *(outward respect)*, knowledge *(awareness)*, mention *(tribute)*, perception, realization, recognition, regard *(esteem)*, respect, scienter, sensibility. SEE MAIN ENTRY
appreciation of differences diagnosis
appreciative conscious *(aware)*
appreciativeness discretion *(quality of being discreet)*, knowledge *(awareness)*
apprehend appreciate *(comprehend)*, capture, comprehend *(understand)*, conceive *(comprehend)*, construe *(comprehend)*, detain *(hold in custody)*, discern *(detect with the senses)*, ensnare, expect *(consider probable)*, fear, find *(discover)*, jail, mistrust, perceive, pierce *(discern)*, presume, read, realize *(understand)*, recognize *(perceive)*, surmise, understand. SEE MAIN ENTRY
apprehend clearly discern *(detect with the senses)*
apprehend danger fear
apprehend harm fear
apprehend punishment fear
apprehendere seize *(apprehend)*
apprehending attachment *(seizure)*, conscious *(aware)*, knowing
apprehensibility coherence
apprehensible cognizable, coherent *(clear)*, comprehensible, perceivable, perceptible, scrutable. SEE MAIN ENTRY
apprehension appropriation *(taking)*, arrest, cloud *(suspicion)*, cognition, comprehension, concept, consternation, constraint *(imprisonment)*, detection, dialectic, doubt *(indecision)*, doubt *(suspicion)*, fear, fright, idea, impression, misgiving, notion, perception, phobia, position *(point of view)*, qualm, realization, scienter, scruple, sense *(feeling)*, stress *(strain)*, suspicion *(mistrust)*, trepidation, understanding *(comprehension)*. SEE MAIN ENTRY
apprehension and transfer extradition
apprehension of danger fear
apprehension of harm fear
apprehension of injury fear
apprehension of punishment fear
apprehensive cognizant, leery, perceptive, solicitous, suspicious *(distrustful)*, vigilant. SEE MAIN ENTRY
apprehensiveness apprehension *(fear)*, cloud *(suspicion)*, consternation, doubt *(indecision)*, fear, misgiving, qualm, scruple, stress *(strain)*
apprentice amateur, assistant, coadjutant, disciple, employee, neophyte, novice, probationer *(one being tested)*, protégé. SEE MAIN ENTRY
apprenticed indentured
apprenticeship experience *(background)*, preparation

apprenticeship agreement indenture
apprisal disclosure *(act of disclosing)*
apprise advise, annunciate, caution, communicate, convey *(communicate)*, disabuse, disclose, disseminate, divulge, enlighten, enunciate, herald, impart, inform *(notify)*, mention, notice *(give formal warning)*, notify, relate *(tell)*, report *(disclose)*, reveal, signify *(inform)*, speak. SEE MAIN ENTRY
apprised acquainted, cognizant, conscious *(aware)*, familiar *(informed)*, knowing, literate, sensible
apprised of learned
apprisement determination
appriser informant
apprize assess *(appraise)*, rate
apprized informed *(having information)*
apprizement determination
apprizer affirmant, bystander, deponent
approach access *(right of way)*, accost, address *(direct attention to)*, admittance *(means of approach)*, approximate, avenue *(means of attainment)*, avenue *(route)*, bid, confrontation *(act of setting face to face)*, converge, correspond *(be equivalent)*, course, design *(intent)*, direction *(course)*, entrance, gravitate, impend, inflow, ingress, invitation, maneuver *(tactic)*, manner *(behavior)*, modus operandi, overture, policy *(plan of action)*, portal, practice *(procedure)*, progress, proposition, reach, strategy. SEE MAIN ENTRY
approach closely approximate
approach in amount approximate
approach of danger peril
approach one another converge
approach road causeway
approachability access *(opening)*
approachable available, open *(accessible)*, passable, public *(open)*, vulnerable
approaches SEE MAIN ENTRY
approaching approximate, close *(near)*, forthcoming, future, immediate *(imminent)*, imminent, inevitable, instant, pending *(imminent)*, prospective, proximate
approaching an end determinable *(liable to be terminated)*
approaching death in extremis
approaching the finish determinable *(liable to be terminated)*
approbare approve, countenance, pass *(satisfy requirements)*
approbate approve, concur *(agree)*, countenance, pass *(approve)*, recommend, sanction. SEE MAIN ENTRY
approbatio approval
approbation acceptance, adoption *(acceptance)*, advocacy, approval, assent, consent, estimation *(esteem)*, favor *(sanction)*, honor *(outward respect)*, indorsement, leave *(permission)*, license, mention *(tribute)*, permit, ratification, recommendation, regard *(esteem)*, respect, sanction *(permission)*. SEE MAIN ENTRY
approbative favorable *(expressing approval)*
appropinquare approach
appropriate accroach, acquire *(secure)*, admissible, adopt, allocate, annex *(arrogate)*, applicable, apposite, ascribe, assign *(allot)*, assume *(seize)*, attach *(seize)*, certain *(specific)*, collect *(recover money)*, commensurate, condemn *(seize)*, condign, confiscate, congruous, consonant, convenient, correlative, devote, dispense, distrain, distribute, divide *(distribute)*, dole, due *(regular)*, eligible, fair *(just)*, favorable *(advantageous)*, felicitous, fit, fitting, garnish, germane, hijack, hold up *(rob)*, impound, impress *(procure by force)*, impropriate, loot, mete, monopolize, obtain, occupy *(take possession)*, opportune, parcel, pertinent, pirate *(reproduce without authorization)*, plagiarize, poach, preempt, procure, proper, reclaim, related, relative *(relevant)*, relevant, right *(suitable)*, rightful, seasonable, seize *(confiscate)*, sequester *(seize property)*, several *(separate)*, specific, suitable, viable. SEE MAIN ENTRY
appropriate activity function
appropriate behavior decorum
appropriate criminally peculate
appropriate dishonestly peculate, purloin
appropriate for federal use nationalize
appropriate for government use nationalize
appropriate for residence habitable
appropriate for use preempt
appropriate fraudulently bilk, embezzle, purloin
appropriate illegally peculate, pilfer, rob
appropriate to one's own use defalcate, embezzle
appropriate to public use confiscate
appropriate unlawfully usurp
appropriate wrongfully convert *(misappropriate)*, peculate
appropriated attached *(seized)*
appropriately pro rata
appropriateness admissibility, decorum, expedience, fairness, qualification *(fitness)*, relevance, timeliness
appropriating confiscatory
appropriation acquisition, adverse possession, allotment, arrogation, assignment *(allotment)*, assumption *(seizure)*, budget, condemnation *(seizure)*, consignment, conversion *(misappropriation)*, distraint, distress *(seizure)*, distribution *(apportionment)*, embezzlement, endowment, garnishment, housebreaking, larceny, pillage, plagiarism, preemption, quota, ration, selection *(choice)*, sequestration, taking. SEE MAIN ENTRY
appropriation for a dishonest use misappropriation
appropriation for a wrongful use misappropriation
appropriation of a literary composition plagiarism
approvable admissible, allowable, allowed, laudable, meritorious, permissible
approval acceptance, adoption *(acceptance)*, advantage, advocacy, affirmation, assent, charter *(sanction)*, confirmation, consent, designation *(naming)*, dispensation *(exception)*, estimation *(esteem)*, favor *(partiality)*, favor *(sanction)*, honor *(outward respect)*, indorsement, indulgence, leave *(permission)*, legalization, license, mention *(tribute)*, option *(contractual provision)*, permission, permit, ratification, recognition, recommendation, regard *(esteem)*, respect, sanction *(permission)*, subscription, support *(corroboration)*. SEE MAIN ENTRY
approve accede *(concede)*, accredit, advocate, affirm *(uphold)*, agree *(comply)*, allow *(authorize)*, allow *(endure)*, appoint, assent, authorize, bear *(tolerate)*, coincide *(concur)*, concur *(agree)*, confirm, conform, consent, cosign, countenance, enable, endorse, favor, grant *(concede)*, legalize, legitimate, let *(permit)*, notarize, permit, prefer, reassure, receive *(permit to enter)*, recommend, regard *(hold in esteem)*, sanction, seal *(solemnize)*, settle, sign, subscribe *(sign)*, support *(justify)*, sustain *(confirm)*, uphold, validate, vote. SEE MAIN ENTRY
approve of countenance, permit
approved agreed *(promised)*, allowable, allowed, conventional, eligible, formal, legal, meritorious, official, orthodox, permissible, preferred *(favored)*, unimpeachable. SEE MAIN ENTRY
approving consensual, consenting, ecstatic, favorable *(expressing approval)*, propitious
approximate border *(approach)*, close *(near)*, comparable *(capable of comparison)*, copy, correspond *(be equivalent)*, inaccurate, inexact, similar. SEE MAIN ENTRY
approximate calculation estimate *(approximate cost)*, estimation *(calculation)*
approximate judgment of value estimate *(approximate cost)*, estimation *(calculation)*
approximate value estimate *(approximate cost)*
approximately almost, on or about
approximation estimate *(approximate cost)*, estimation *(calculation)*, parity, resemblance. SEE MAIN ENTRY
approximative inexact
appulsion meeting *(encounter)*
appurtenance additive, appliance, attachment *(thing affixed)*, augmentation, boom *(increase)*, corollary, droit, rider. SEE MAIN ENTRY
appurtenances goods
appurtenant apposite, cognate, germane, pendent, pertinent, related, relative *(relevant)*, relevant. SEE MAIN ENTRY
apriorism prolepsis
apropos akin *(germane)*, apposite, appropriate, felicitous, fit, germane, incident, pertinent, relative *(relevant)*, relevant, suitable. SEE MAIN ENTRY
apt acute, applicable, apposite, appropriate, artful, consonant, deft, expert, felicitous, fit, germane, harmonious, inclined, opportune, pertinent, possible, practiced, probable, prone, proper, qualified *(competent)*, relative *(relevant)*, relevant, resourceful, right *(suitable)*, subtle *(refined)*, suitable, veteran, viable. SEE MAIN ENTRY
apt to change suddenly capricious
apt to distrust cynical
apt to flee elusive
apt to quarrel fractious
aptare adapt, adjust *(regulate)*
aptitude ability, caliber *(mental capacity)*, chance *(possibility)*, competence *(ability)*, disposition *(inclination)*, faculty *(ability)*, gift *(flair)*, inclination, instinct, intelligence *(intellect)*, performance *(workmanship)*, potential, predisposition, proclivity, propensity, propriety *(appropriateness)*, qualification *(fitness)*, science *(technique)*, skill, temperament, tendency. SEE MAIN ENTRY
aptness ability, admissibility, capacity *(aptitude)*, expedience, inclination, instinct, liability, performance *(workmanship)*, predisposition, proclivity, propensity, propriety *(appropriateness)*, qualification *(fitness)*, quality *(excellence)*, quality *(grade)*,

relevance, science *(technique)*, skill, specialty *(special aptitude)*, tendency, timeliness
aptum qualify *(meet standards)*
aptus adequate, appropriate, attached *(annexed)*, capable, fit, proper, suitable
aqua et igni interdicere outlaw
arable fertile
arbiter arbitrator, eyewitness, go-between, intermediary, judge, juror, referee, umpire. SEE MAIN ENTRY
arbiters jury
arbitrage adjudication, arbitration, collective bargaining, intercession
arbitrament adjudication, collective bargaining, conclusion *(determination)*, judgment *(formal court decree)*, negotiation
arbitrari opine
arbitrarily invented fictitious
arbitrary contemptuous, dictatorial, disobedient, haphazard, irresponsible, tyrannous, unpredictable, unwarranted. SEE MAIN ENTRY
arbitrary and capricious SEE MAIN ENTRY
arbitrary power force *(compulsion)*
arbitrate adjudge, adjudicate, decide, intercede, judge, mediate, negotiate, reconcile. SEE MAIN ENTRY
arbitrate terms dicker
arbitrated agreed *(harmonized)*
arbitrater adjuster
arbitration adjudication, collective bargaining, intercession, mediation, negotiation, reconciliation. SEE MAIN ENTRY
arbitrator arbiter, go-between, intermediary, judge, magistrate, referee, umpire. SEE MAIN ENTRY
arbitrators jury
arbitrium arbitration, determination, freedom
arca coffer
arcana secret
arcane clandestine, confidential, esoteric, hidden, latent, mysterious, private *(confidential)*, privy, recondite, secret, stealthy. SEE MAIN ENTRY
arcanum enigma, mystery
arcanus confidential, mysterious, private *(confidential)*, secret
arch jocular, machiavellian, master, paramount, project *(extend beyond)*, sly
archaic antique, obsolete, old, outdated, outmoded. SEE MAIN ENTRY
archaism desuetude, disuse
archaistic obsolete
archetypal primordial
archetype example, exemplar, model, paradigm, pattern, precedent, prototype, sample, standard
architect author *(originator)*, contractor. SEE MAIN ENTRY
architectural monument edifice
architecture building *(business of assembling)*
architectus architect
archive dossier, file, record, register
archives depository
archivist caretaker *(one caring for property)*, clerk
ardency ardor, passion
ardens fervent, intense
ardent eager, fanatical, fervent, industrious, intense, intensive, ready *(willing)*, sedulous, serious *(devoted)*, true *(loyal)*, vehement, zealous. SEE MAIN ENTRY
ardent admirer addict
ardent champion of change malcontent
ardent impulse desire
ardor adhesion *(loyalty)*, affection
ardor ardor
ardor compulsion *(obsession)*, desire, diligence *(perseverance)*, emotion, industry *(activity)*, life *(vitality)*, passion, penchant, predisposition, spirit. SEE MAIN ENTRY
arduous difficult, formidable, onerous, operose, oppressive, painful. SEE MAIN ENTRY
arduousness effort
area area *(province)*
area bailiwick, caliber *(measurement)*, capacity *(sphere)*, circuit, department, dimension, district, division *(administra-tive unit)*, extent, locality, location, parcel, part *(place)*, province, purview, range, realm, region, scope, section *(vicinity)*, space, territory, vicinity, zone. SEE MAIN ENTRY
area of disagreement contention *(argument)*
area of education discipline *(field of study)*
area of learning discipline *(field of study)*
arena area *(province)*, bailiwick, capacity *(sphere)*, enclosure, focus, purview, range, scene, sphere
argot jargon *(technical language)*, phraseology
arguable controversial, debatable, disputable, doubtful, dubious, forensic, justiciable, litigable, moot, plausible, uncertain *(questionable)*. SEE MAIN ENTRY
argue bear *(adduce)*, bespeak, bicker, challenge, collide *(clash)*, conflict, contend *(dispute)*, contend *(maintain)*, contest, contradict, controvert, cross *(disagree with)*, debate, differ *(vary)*, disaccord, disagree, dispute *(debate)*, dissent *(differ in opinion)*, expostulate, haggle, insist, posit, propound, reason *(persuade)*, rebut. SEE MAIN ENTRY
argue a case dispute *(debate)*
argue a point dispute *(debate)*
argue against confront *(oppose)*, discourage, dispute *(contest)*, dissuade, oppose, rebut, remonstrate
argue at the bar plead *(argue a case)*
argue for adhere *(maintain loyalty)*, advocate, assert, defend, espouse, justify
argue for and against discuss
argue in opposition dispute *(debate)*
argue into convince, prevail *(persuade)*
argue price dicker
argue pros and cons debate
argue the case controvert, discuss
argue the point controvert, discuss, plead *(argue a case)*
argue to no purpose bicker
argue vehemently dispute *(contest)*
argued alleged
arguendo SEE MAIN ENTRY
arguer contender
arguer in defense apologist
arguere accuse, charge *(accuse)*
argufy dispute *(debate)*
arguing disputable, dissenting, hostile, litigious
argument altercation, brief, conflict, confrontation *(altercation)*, contest *(dispute)*, contravention, disaccord, disagreement, discourse, disparity, dispute, dissent *(difference of opinion)*, dissidence, persuasion, pleading, point *(item)*, reason *(basis)*, remonstrance, rift *(disagreement)*, thesis. SEE MAIN ENTRY
argument at the bar argument *(pleading)*
argumental litigious, polemic
argumentari argue
argumentation conflict, contention *(argument)*, controversy *(argument)*, dialectic, disaccord, disagreement, discord, discourse, dissension, ratiocination. SEE MAIN ENTRY
argumentative contentious, discursive *(analytical)*, disputable, dissenting, forensic, hostile, insistent, litigable, litigious, negative, petulant, polemic, pugnacious, remonstrative. SEE MAIN ENTRY
argumentative person disputant
arguments at the bar plea
argumentum context, proof, subject *(topic)*
argus guardian
argute perspicacious
arguteness caliber *(mental capacity)*, sagacity
arid barren, lifeless *(dull)*, otiose, pedestrian, unproductive
arise appear *(materialize)*, commence, disobey, emerge, ensue, occur *(happen)*, proceed *(go forward)*, rebel, redound, result, stem *(originate)*, succeed *(follow)*, supervene. SEE MAIN ENTRY
arise from develop, emanate, evolve
aristocracy elite, society
ark refuge
arm affiliate, clothe, cudgel, empower, enable, endue, furnish, organ, protect
arm of the law judiciary, marshal, peace officer, police, posse
arma homini adimere disarm *(divest of arms)*
armament ammunition, bomb, gun
armaments weapons
armature ammunition, panoply
armatus armed
armed defensible, ready *(prepared)*, safe. SEE MAIN ENTRY
armed action fight *(battle)*
armed attack foray
armed band posse
armed enemy foe
armiger esquire
armipotent powerful
armistice cessation *(interlude)*, halt, interruption, lull, pause, peace, treaty. SEE MAIN ENTRY
armor panoply, protect, protection, safeguard
armored immune, protective, safe, secure *(free from danger)*
armored protection panoply
armorum weapons
arms ammunition, gun, weapons
army band
arouse abet, agitate *(activate)*, alert, bait *(harass)*, discommode, disturb, elicit, evoke, exacerbate, exhort, foment, harass, impel, impress *(affect deeply)*, incense, incite, influence, inspire, interest, lobby, molest *(annoy)*, originate, perturb, prompt, provoke, spirit, stimulate
arouse desire motivate
arouse ire incense
arouse notice interest
arouse one's enthusiasm interest
arouse resentment incense, pique
arouse to action incite
arouser cannabis, stimulus
arousing moving *(evoking emotion)*, persuasive, provocative
arousing aversion repulsive
arraign blame, charge *(accuse)*, complain *(charge)*, denounce *(inform against)*, prosecute *(charge)*. SEE MAIN ENTRY

arraigned accused *(charged)*
arraignment charge *(accusation)*, impeachment, presentment. SEE MAIN ENTRY
arrange accommodate, adapt, adjust *(resolve)*, allocate, arbitrate *(adjudge)*, arbitrate *(conciliate)*, classify, codify, compile, compose, contrive, coordinate, devise *(invent)*, disentangle, dispose *(incline)*, distribute, edit, fix *(settle)*, form, formulate, frame *(formulate)*, frame *(prearrange)*, maneuver, marshal, orchestrate, pigeonhole, plan, plot, program, regulate *(adjust)*, scheme, settle, site, sort, stipulate, tabulate. SEE MAIN ENTRY
arrange a settlement satisfy *(discharge)*
arrange beforehand prearrange
arrange by mutual concession compromise *(settle by mutual agreement)*
arrange differences mediate
arrange for negotiate
arrange for the services of engage *(hire)*
arrange for the use of engage *(hire)*
arrange in advance prearrange
arrange in succession continue *(prolong)*
arrange itself crystallize
arrange materials for publication compile
arrange matters settle
arrange matters in dispute settle
arrange methodically file *(arrange)*
arrange side by side juxtapose
arrange terms dicker
arranged agreed *(harmonized)*, agreed *(promised)*, consonant, contractual, fixed *(settled)*, harmonious, prospective, ready *(prepared)*, res judicata, stated, systematic. SEE MAIN ENTRY
arranged within a small space compact *(dense)*
arrangement accommodation *(adjustment)*, accord, accordance *(compact)*, adjustment, agreement *(concurrence)*, agreement *(contract)*, allotment, array *(order)*, attornment, bargain, building *(business of assembling)*, case *(set of circumstances)*, classification, combination, compact, compilation, composition *(agreement in bankruptcy)*, composition *(makeup)*, conciliation, configuration *(form)*, contract, covenant, creation, deal, digest, disposition *(final arrangement)*, expedient, formation, hierarchy *(arrangement in a series)*, honorarium, indenture, lineup, method, motif, organization *(structure)*, pact, plan, policy *(contract)*, practice *(procedure)*, preparation, program, proposition, protocol *(agreement)*, provision *(act of supplying)*, register, regulation *(management)*, scheme, selection *(collection)*, sequence, settlement, situation, specialty *(contract)*, stipulation, strategy, structure *(composition)*, system, term *(provision)*, treatment, treaty, understanding *(agreement)*. SEE MAIN ENTRY
arrangement for disposal disposition *(transfer of property)*
arrangement of difficulties settlement
arrangement of laws codification
arrangement of parts content *(structure)*
arrangement of rules codification
arrangement of statutes code, codification
arrangements dealings
arrangment course
arrant bad *(offensive)*, blameworthy, disreputable, egregious, flagrant, heinous, immoral, lawless, nefarious, notorious, outrageous, scandalous. SEE MAIN ENTRY
array assemblage, band, chain *(series)*, clothe, composition *(makeup)*, conglomeration, disposition *(final arrangement)*, distribute, embellish, file *(arrange)*, fix *(arrange)*, form *(arrangement)*, formation, jury, marshal, order *(arrangement)*, selection *(collection)*, sequence, sort. SEE MAIN ENTRY
arraying arrangement *(ordering)*
arrear default
arrearage arrears, debt, delinquency *(shortage)*
arrears debit, debt, deficit, delinquency *(shortage)*, due. SEE MAIN ENTRY
arrest abeyance, apprehension *(act of arresting)*, avert, block, bondage, book, capture, cease, cessation *(interlude)*, check *(bar)*, check *(restrain)*, clog, cloture, commit *(institutionalize)*, confine, constrain *(imprison)*, constraint *(imprisonment)*, constrict *(inhibit)*, contain *(restrain)*, control *(restrain)*, curb, custody *(incarceration)*, debar, defer *(put off)*, delay, desist, desuetude, detain *(hold in custody)*, detain *(restrain)*, detention, discontinue *(abandon)*, discontinue *(break continuity)*, durance, forestall, halt *(noun)*, halt *(verb)*, hamper, hinder, hindrance, hold up *(delay)*, impede, incarceration, inhibit, interdict, interfere, interrupt, interruption, keep *(restrain)*, kill *(defeat)*, lock, obstacle, occlude, palliate *(abate)*, prevent, quit *(discontinue)*, restrain, restraint, seize *(apprehend)*, stall, stay *(halt)*, stem *(check)*, stifle, stop, strangle, suppress, suspend, toll *(stop)*. SEE MAIN ENTRY
arrest temporarily continue *(adjourn)*, delay, hold up *(delay)*, postpone
arrest the attention occupy *(engage)*
arrest with authority seize *(apprehend)*
arrested SEE MAIN ENTRY
arresting moving *(evoking emotion)*, obviation, preventive, sapid
arrestment custody *(incarceration)*
arrêt arrest *(apprehend)*
arrhabo retainer
arrière pensée propaganda
arrival birth *(beginning)*, birth *(emergence of young)*, inflow
arrival into view appearance *(emergence)*
arrive emerge, enter *(go in)*, reach, report *(present oneself)*. SEE MAIN ENTRY
arrive at attain, obtain
arrive at a conclusion arbitrate *(adjudge)*, ascertain, deduce, deduct *(conclude by reasoning)*, determine, find *(determine)*, fix *(settle)*, gauge, resolve *(decide)*
arrive at a decision resolve *(decide)*
arrive at a judgment decide
arrive at a price dicker
arrive at a settlement agree *(contract)*
arrive at a verdict find *(determine)*
arrive at an agreement close *(agree)*, coincide *(concur)*, concede, fix *(settle)*
arrive at an understanding coincide *(concur)*
arrive at terms coincide *(concur)*, conform
arrive at the end of finish
arrive at the truth solve
arriving future
arrogance contempt *(disdain)*, contumely, disdain, disrespect
arrogant brazen, contemptuous, cynical, dictatorial, disdainful, dogmatic, impertinent *(insolent)*, inflated *(vain)*, insolent, orgulous, presumptuous, pretentious *(pompous)*, proud *(conceited)*, supercilious. SEE MAIN ENTRY
arrogate accroach, adopt, appropriate, assume *(seize)*, attach *(seize)*, collect *(recover money)*, condemn *(seize)*, demand, deprive, harass, hijack, impress *(procure by force)*, impropriate, infringe, invade, seize *(confiscate)*, sequester *(seize property)*, takeover, usurp. SEE MAIN ENTRY
arrogate to oneself preempt
arrogated attached *(seized)*
arrogation assignation, assumption *(seizure)*, condemnation *(seizure)*, disseisin, distress *(seizure)*, infringement, misappropriation. SEE MAIN ENTRY
arrondissement circuit
ars performance *(workmanship)*, stratagem, trade *(occupation)*
ars dicendi rhetoric *(skilled speech)*
ars ludicra histrionics
arsenal repository. SEE MAIN ENTRY
arson SEE MAIN ENTRY
arsonist lawbreaker
art performance *(workmanship)*, propensity, ruse, skill
art of composition rhetoric *(skilled speech)*
art of discourse rhetoric *(skilled speech)*
art of monetary relations finance
art of negotiating discretion *(quality of being discreet)*
art of prose rhetoric *(skilled speech)*
art of speaking declamation
art of war strategy
arterial causeway
arterial highway causeway
artery causeway, conduit *(channel)*, way *(channel)*
artful collusive, colorable *(specious)*, competent, delusive, devious, diplomatic, disingenuous, evasive, expert, insidious, machiavellian, mendacious, original *(creative)*, perspicacious, politic, practiced, resourceful, sly, stealthy, subtle *(refined)*, surreptitious, tactical. SEE MAIN ENTRY
artful contrivance artifice, stratagem
artful dodge evasion, machination, maneuver *(trick)*
artful management discretion *(quality of being discreet)*
artfully contrived politic
artfulness artifice, discretion *(quality of being discreet)*, fraud, hypocrisy, improbity, knavery, performance *(workmanship)*, pettifoggery
article chapter *(division)*, clause, condition *(contingent provision)*, instrument *(tool)*, item, law, member *(constituent part)*, pandect *(treatise)*, particular, product, report *(detailed account)*, story *(narrative)*, subheading, title *(division)*. SEE MAIN ENTRY
article of agreement provision *(clause)*, stipulation, term *(provision)*
article of belief principle *(axiom)*
article of commerce freight
article of faith dogma, principle *(axiom)*
article of merchandise product
article of trade product
articled indentured
articles commodities, merchandise, paraphernalia *(apparatus)*
articles of agreement contract
articles of commerce commodities, goods, merchandise, stock in trade
articles of merchandise commodities

articles of trade commodities
articulate avow, clarify, coherent *(clear)*, communicate, comprehensible, converse, convey *(communicate)*, eloquent, enunciate, express, lucid, observe *(remark)*, phrase, pronounce *(speak)*, recite, recount, remark, speak, unambiguous, utter. SEE MAIN ENTRY
articulated nuncupative, oral
articulation conversation, expression *(comment)*, speech
artifex artisan
artifice bad faith, contrivance, deception, device *(contrivance)*, disguise, duplicity, evasion, expedient, false pretense, fraud, hoax, knavery, machination, maneuver *(trick)*, pettifoggery, ploy, ruse, stratagem, strategy, subterfuge, trap. SEE MAIN ENTRY
artificer architect, artisan, contractor, materialman, practitioner
artificial bogus, deceptive, disingenuous, false *(not genuine)*, fictitious, histrionic, imitation, inflated *(bombastic)*, meretricious, orotund, pretentious *(ostentatious)*, specious, spurious, synthetic. SEE MAIN ENTRY
artificial behavior for effect histrionics
artificial eloquence rhetoric *(insincere language)*
artificial entity corporation
artificial person corporation
artificiality artifice, false pretense, pretense *(ostentation)*
artificiosus artificial
artificium maneuver *(trick)*, performance *(workmanship)*, pursuit *(occupation)*, system
artillery fire barrage
artisan practitioner. SEE MAIN ENTRY
artist practitioner
artistic aesthetic, artful, subtle *(refined)*
artistic effort creation
artistic judgment discretion *(quality of being discreet)*
artistry skill, specialty *(special aptitude)*, style
artless honest, inadept, inexperienced, ingenuous, natural, simple, straightforward, unaffected *(sincere)*, unpretentious
artless person philistine
artlessness honesty, veracity
as a body en masse
as a consequence a priori, consequently. SEE MAIN ENTRY
as a favor gratis
as a group en masse
as a matter of course as a rule, consequently
as a matter of fact de facto
as a matter of form pro forma
as a matter of right SEE MAIN ENTRY
as a result consequently
as a result of a priori
as a rule generally, invariably. SEE MAIN ENTRY
as a start ab initio
as a substitute for in lieu of
as a substitute for a parent loco parentis
as a unit en banc
as a whole en banc, en masse, in toto, wholly
as agreed upon SEE MAIN ENTRY
as an alternative in lieu of
as an alternative for a parent loco parentis
as arranged by the agreement as agreed upon
as contained as so defined
as contained in the statutes as provided by law
as contracted for as agreed upon
as delineated as so defined
as explained as so defined
as far as until
as good as equivalent
as great as another coequal
as if quasi
as is a priori. SEE MAIN ENTRY
as it is as is
as it stands as is
as matters stand consequently
as near as may be cy pres
as near as possible cy pres
as near as practicable cy pres
as negotiated for as agreed upon
as offered as is
as one en masse
as pledged as agreed upon
as presented as is
as promised as agreed upon
as provided by law SEE MAIN ENTRY
as proxy for in lieu of
as represented actual, as is, authentic, bona fide, honest, true *(authentic)*
as required duly
as required will shall
as seen as is
as set forth as so defined. SEE MAIN ENTRY
as set forth by law as provided by law
as settled upon as agreed upon
as shown as is
as so defined SEE MAIN ENTRY
as soon as can be reasonably expected forthwith
as soon as feasible SEE MAIN ENTRY
as soon as possible as soon as feasible
as soon as reasonably possible as soon as feasible
as specified as so defined
as specified in the law as provided by law
as the case may be consequently
as things are as is
as though quasi
as though it were quasi
as well also
ascend expand, progress
ascendance dominance, hegemony, influence, prestige. SEE MAIN ENTRY
ascendancy advantage, dominance, dominion *(supreme authority)*, force *(strength)*, hegemony, influence, occupation *(possession)*, primacy, supremacy
ascendant ancestor, dominant, predominant, prevailing *(having superior force)*, prevalent, primogenitor, prosperous. SEE MAIN ENTRY
ascendants ancestry
ascendency predominance, prestige
ascent headway
ascertain assess *(appraise)*, bear *(adduce)*, decide, deduce, deduct *(conclude by reasoning)*, determine, discern *(detect with the senses)*, discover, distinguish, elucidate, ensure, establish *(show)*, find *(determine)*, find *(discover)*, fix *(settle)*, gauge, hold *(decide)*, judge, notice *(observe)*, prove, recognize *(perceive)*, resolve *(decide)*, rule *(decide)*, settle, solve. SEE MAIN ENTRY
ascertain a position locate
ascertain after reasoning arbitrate *(adjudge)*
ascertain and declare find *(determine)*
ascertain as truth prove
ascertain by judicial inquiry find *(determine)*
ascertain dimensions measure
ascertain liability liquidate *(determine liability)*
ascertain mathematically calculate
ascertain size measure
ascertain the amount of evaluate
ascertain the amount of indebtedness liquidate *(determine liability)*
ascertain the balance due liquidate *(determine liability)*
ascertain the meaning of construe *(comprehend)*
ascertain the time of date
ascertainable appreciable, cognizable, comprehensible, deductible *(provable)*, perceptible, ponderable, provable, solvable. SEE MAIN ENTRY
ascertained actual, axiomatic, certain *(positive)*, certain *(specific)*, clear *(certain)*, cognizable, common *(customary)*, conclusive *(determinative)*, conclusive *(settled)*, definite, definitive, factual, genuine, incontrovertible, indubious, positive *(incontestable)*, real, stated. SEE MAIN ENTRY
ascertained fact certification *(certainness)*, certitude
ascertained principle conviction *(persuasion)*
ascertainment analysis, certification *(certainness)*, collation, conclusion *(determination)*, detection, determination, discovery, finding, holding *(ruling of a court)*, identification, inspection, observation, opinion *(judicial decision)*, perception, surety *(certainty)*
ascetic dispassionate, harsh, stoical
asceticism continence
ascribable derivative
ascribe acknowledge *(declare)*, assign *(designate)*, attribute, impute. SEE MAIN ENTRY
ascribe blame incriminate
ascribe personal qualities to personify
ascribe to blame
ascribere ascribe, impute, inscribe
ascription accusation, arrogation, assignation, attribution, blame *(responsibility)*, citation *(attribution)*, condemnation *(blame)*, reference *(citation)*. SEE MAIN ENTRY
aseptic preventive
aside innuendo
aside from the point extraneous, inapposite, irrelevant
asinine fatuous, ludicrous, obtuse, opaque, puerile, unreasonable
asininity opacity
ask apply *(request)*, call *(appeal to)*, canvass, consult *(ask advice of)*, demand, desire, inquire, investigate, pose *(propound)*, solicit. SEE MAIN ENTRY
ask advice consult *(ask advice of)*
ask an opinion consult *(ask advice of)*
ask earnestly canvass, pray, press *(beseech)*, solicit
ask for call *(appeal to)*, claim *(demand)*, delve, desire, exact, move *(judicially request)*, petition, request
ask for credit borrow
ask for recommendations consult *(ask advice of)*
ask for relief sue
ask for suggestions consult (ask ad-vice of)
ask for with authority call *(demand)*, demand

ask help of refer *(send for action)*
ask questions cross-examine
ask solemnly for invoke
ask to come call *(summon)*
ask urgently importune
asked for popular
asker petitioner
askew disordered, oblique *(slanted)*
asking inquiry *(systematic investigation)*, precatory, question *(inquiry)*, request
asking for what is due demand
asking price cost *(price)*
asking questions cross-examination
aslant oblique *(slanted)*
asleep dormant
asomatous incorporeal, intangible
aspect appearance *(look)*, characteristic, complexion, component, condition *(state)*, conduct, demeanor, deportment, detail, factor *(ingredient)*, feature *(appearance)*, feature *(characteristic)*, ingredient, manner *(behavior)*, outlook, particular, posture *(attitude)*, presence *(poise)*, property *(distinctive attribute)*, semblance, side, standpoint, state *(condition)*, style, technicality. SEE MAIN ENTRY
aspects character *(personal quality)*, color *(complexion)*. SEE MAIN ENTRY
aspectus appearance *(look)*, aspect
asper bitter *(acrid tasting)*
asperity rigor, severity
aspernari disdain, spurn
asperse brand *(stigmatize)*, complain *(criticize)*, condemn *(blame)*, contemn, defame, denigrate, denounce *(condemn)*, deprecate, derogate, discommend, discredit, dishonor *(deprive of honor)*, disparage, libel, malign, pillory, reprimand, reproach, smear, sully, tarnish
aspersion bad repute, contempt *(disdain)*, contumely, conviction *(finding of guilt)*, criticism, defamation, denunciation, disapprobation, discredit, dishonor *(shame)*, disparagement, imprecation, infamy, innuendo, insinuation, libel, obloquy, phillipic, revilement, scandal, shame, slander, stricture. SEE MAIN ENTRY
aspersive libelous
aspirant amateur, applicant *(candidate)*, candidate, contender, novice, rival, special interest
aspiration desideratum, design *(intent)*, desire, destination, end *(intent)*, goal, objective, purpose, target, will *(desire)*
aspire desire, endeavor, strive, try *(attempt)*
aspire to intend, pursue *(strive to gain)*
aspirer candidate
aspiring eager, solicitous
assail accost, ambush, assault, attack, badger, censure, complain *(criticize)*, confront *(oppose)*, defame, denounce *(condemn)*, despoil, engage *(involve)*, fight *(battle)*, harass, harrow, harry *(plunder)*, impugn, invade, lash *(attack verbally)*, maltreat, mishandle *(maltreat)*, mistreat, persecute, resist *(oppose)*, strike *(assault)*. SEE MAIN ENTRY
assail by argument impugn
assail with censure condemn *(blame)*, denounce *(condemn)*
assailability danger
assailable dangerous, destructible, inadequate, indefensible, penetrable, vulnerable. SEE MAIN ENTRY
assailant aggressor, disputant, foe, offender, offensive *(taking the initiative)*. SEE MAIN ENTRY
assailer aggressor, assailant
assailing offensive *(taking the initiative)*
assailment assault, onset *(assault)*
assassinate dispatch *(put to death)*, extinguish, kill *(murder)*, slay
assassination aberemurder, dispatch *(act of putting to death)*, homicide, killing, murder. SEE MAIN ENTRY
assault accost, ambush, assail, attack, barrage, battery, belligerency, denounce *(condemn)*, fight *(battle)*, fight *(battle)*, incursion, invade, invasion, mishandle *(maltreat)*, mistreat, molest *(subject to indecent advances)*, offense, oppugn, outbreak, rape, resist *(oppose)*, resistance, violence. SEE MAIN ENTRY
assault belligerently accost, assail, assault
assaulter aggressor, assailant
assaulting hostile
assay analysis, attempt, diagnosis, endeavor, experiment, inquiry *(systematic investigation)*. SEE MAIN ENTRY
assemblage agglomeration, aggregate
assemblage assemblage. SEE MAIN ENTRY
assemblage assembly, body *(collection)*, caucus, coalescence, collection *(assembly)*, combination, compilation, congregation, congress, consolidation, corpus, cumulation, distribution *(arrangement)*, entirety, joinder, manufacture, mass *(body of persons)*, selection *(collection)*, whole
assemble accumulate *(amass)*, aggregate, attach *(join)*, build *(construct)*, call *(summon)*, codify, collect *(gather)*, commingle, compile, concentrate *(consolidate)*, congregate, conjoin, connect *(join together)*, convene, converge, federate, form, garner, glean, join *(bring together)*, make, manufacture, meet, orchestrate, produce *(manufacture)*, raise *(collect)*, rendezvous, store, unite
assemble and apportion assets liquidate *(determine liability)*
assemble by summons call *(summon)*
assemble parts fabricate *(construct)*
assemble the facts document
assembled coadunate, collective, composite, conglomerate
assembled body company *(assemblage)*
assemblée caucus, chamber *(body)*, company *(assemblage)*
assembling building *(business of assembling)*, centralization
assembly aggregate, assemblage, caucus, chamber *(body)*, company *(assemblage)*, conference, conglomeration, congregation, congress, cumulation, legislature, manufacture, meeting *(conference)*, parley, rendezvous, selection *(collection)*, session. SEE MAIN ENTRY
assembly of persons congregation
assemblyman lawmaker
assemblywoman lawmaker
assent abide, accede *(concede)*, acceptance, accordance *(understanding)*, acknowledgment *(acceptance)*, acquiescence, admit *(concede)*, affirmance *(judicial sanction)*, agree *(comply)*, agreement *(concurrence)*, allow *(endure)*, approval, bear *(adduce)*, capitulation, certify *(approve)*, charter *(sanction)*, coincide *(concur)*, compliance, concede, concession *(compromise)*, concordance, confirm, confirmation, conformity *(agreement)*, consent *(noun)*, consent *(verb)*, corroborate, defer *(yield in judgment)*, deference, franchise *(license)*, grant *(concede)*, indorsement, leave *(permission)*, let *(permit)*, obey, pass *(approve)*, permission, permit, ratification, sanction *(permission)*, stipulate, subscribe *(promise)*, subscription, suffer *(permit)*, vouchsafe, yield *(submit)*. SEE MAIN ENTRY
assent to approve, authorize, certify *(approve)*, comply, concur *(agree)*, countenance, indorse, sanction, sustain *(confirm)*
assented consensual
assentient consenting
assenting concerted, concordant, concurrent *(united)*, congruous, consenting, favorable *(expressing approval)*, harmonious, inclined, pliable, ready *(willing)*, willing *(desirous)*
assentive concordant, consenting
assererate vouch
assert acknowledge *(declare)*, adduce, advocate, affirm *(claim)*, allege, annunciate, argue, attest, avouch *(avow)*, avow, bear *(adduce)*, cast *(register)*, certify *(attest)*, claim *(maintain)*, comment, communicate, contend *(maintain)*, convey *(communicate)*, declare, enunciate, express, mention, observe *(remark)*, plead *(allege in a legal action)*, pose *(propound)*, posit, proclaim, profess *(avow)*, promise *(vow)*, pronounce *(speak)*, remark, signify *(inform)*, testify, uphold, utter. SEE MAIN ENTRY
assert a right to call *(demand)*, demand
assert absolutely bear *(adduce)*
assert an oath promise *(vow)*
assert as one's own claim *(demand)*
assert as one's right claim *(demand)*
assert as true swear
assert formally certify *(attest)*, issue *(publish)*, plead *(allege in a legal action)*
assert in court litigate
assert incorrectly misrepresent
assert on oath avow
assert one's rights demand
assert oneself certify *(attest)*, constrain *(compel)*
assert peremptorily avouch *(avow)*, avow
assert positively avouch *(avow)*, certify *(attest)*, plead *(allege in a legal action)*, promise *(vow)*
assert solemnly pledge *(promise the performance of)*, promise *(vow)*
assert the contrary contradict
assert the opposite contradict
assert under oath avouch *(avow)*, avow, certify *(attest)*, promise *(vow)*
assertative declaratory
asserted alleged
asserted formally alleged
asserter claimant
asserting the contrary contradictory
asserting the opposite contradictory
assertion accusation, acknowledgment *(avowal)*, admission *(disclosure)*, affirmance *(authentication)*, affirmation, allegation, asseveration, attestation, averment, avouchment, avowal, comment, confession, confirmation, count, declaration, dictum, disclosure *(act of disclosing)*, disclosure *(something disclosed)*, expression *(comment)*, hypothesis, mention *(reference)*, observation, plea, postulate, principle *(axiom)*, profession *(declaration)*, pronouncement, proposition, remark, statement, testimony. SEE MAIN ENTRY
assertion against the plaintiff counterclaim
assertion of facts representation *(statement)*
assertion of legal right demand

assertion of the contrary contradiction
assertion of the opposite contradiction
assertions premises *(hypotheses)*
assertive certain *(positive)*, compelling, declaratory, dogmatic, insistent, peremptory *(imperative)*. SEE MAIN ENTRY
assertment averment
assertory dogmatic
assertory oath affidavit, affirmance *(legal affirmation)*, affirmation, averment
assess arbitrate *(adjudge)*, calculate, consider, criticize *(evaluate)*, encumber *(financially obligate)*, evaluate, exact, excise *(levy a tax)*, gauge, judge, levy, measure, mete, notice *(observe)*, rate, require *(compel)*, tax *(levy)*. SEE MAIN ENTRY
assess a tax upon charge *(assess)*
assess pro rata charge *(assess)*, prorate
assess proportionally prorate
assessable ad valorem, appreciable, determinable *(ascertainable)*
assessment account *(evaluation)*, ad valorem, appraisal, appreciation *(perception)*, arbitration, charge *(cost)*, choice *(decision)*, computation, concept, conclusion *(determination)*, cost *(price)*, determination, discretion *(power of choice)*, discrimination *(differentiation)*, duty *(tax)*, estimate *(approximate cost)*, estimation *(calculation)*, excise, expense *(cost)*, idea, inspection, judgment *(discernment)*, judgment *(formal court decree)*, levy, measurement, opinion *(judicial decision)*, perception, rate, rating, rent, tariff *(duties)*, tax, toll *(tax)*, value, verdict. SEE MAIN ENTRY
assessment of damages additur
assessor judge, juror, magistrate. SEE MAIN ENTRY
assessor of liability and damages juror
assessors jury
asset advantage, chattel, holding *(property owned)*, item, possession *(property)*, resource, share *(stock)*
assets capital, commodities, effects, estate *(property)*, fund, goods, interest *(ownership)*, means *(funds)*, merchandise, money, paraphernalia *(personal belongings)*, personalty, possessions, principal *(capital sum)*, property *(possessions)*, reserve, securities, security *(stock)*, stock *(shares)*, store *(depository)*, substance *(material possessions)*. SEE MAIN ENTRY
assets and liabilities estate *(property)*
assets in hand principal *(capital sum)*
assever assert
asseverate acknowledge *(declare)*, affirm *(claim)*, affirm *(declare solemnly)*, allege, assert, assure *(insure)*, avouch *(avow)*, avow, bear *(adduce)*, certify *(attest)*, claim *(maintain)*, contend *(maintain)*, declare, depose *(testify)*, enunciate, express, posit, proclaim, profess *(avow)*, promise *(vow)*, remark, testify, utter, verify *(swear)*
asseverated alleged
asseveration acknowledgment *(avowal)*, affirmance *(legal affirmation)*, affirmation, assertion, attestation, averment, avouchment, avowal, claim *(assertion)*, expression *(comment)*, jurat, oath, promise, pronouncement, representation *(statement)*, statement, surety *(certainty)*, testimony, vow. SEE MAIN ENTRY
assidous pertinacious. SEE MAIN ENTRY
assiduity diligence *(perseverance)*, effort, endeavor, industry *(activity)*, interest *(concern)*
assiduous active, circumspect, close *(rigorous)*, conscientious, diligent, eager, earnest, faithful *(diligent)*, industrious, meticulous, painstaking, patient, persistent, relentless, sedulous, serious *(devoted)*, steadfast, thorough, true *(loyal)*, unremitting, zealous
assiduousness diligence *(perseverance)*, effort, industry *(activity)*
assign abalienate, adduce, alienate *(transfer title)*, allocate, allot, appoint, apportion, ascribe, attorn, attribute, authorize, bear *(yield)*, cede, charge *(assess)*, charge *(empower)*, commit *(entrust)*, contribute *(supply)*, convey *(transfer)*, delegate, demarcate, designate, devise *(give)*, devote, direct *(supervise)*, disburse *(distribute)*, dispense, disperse *(disseminate)*, distribute, divide *(distribute)*, dole, employ *(engage services)*, empower, endue, entrust, expend *(disburse)*, give *(grant)*, grant *(transfer formally)*, impute, induct, leave *(give)*, marshal, mete, nominate, parcel, refer *(direct attention)*, refer *(send for action)*, relegate, select, site, split, transfer. SEE MAIN ENTRY
assign a duty delegate
assign a meaning to construe *(translate)*, explain
assign a time to date
assign again reassign
assign dower bequeath
assign one's share to charge *(assess)*
assign places to distribute, file *(arrange)*, fix *(arrange)*, sort, tabulate
assign power of attorney to delegate
assign the care of entrust
assign the parts orchestrate
assign to blame, consign
assign to a place locate
assign to a position delegate, hire
assign to an earlier date antedate
assign to battle stations deploy
assign to lodgings lodge *(house)*
assign to positions deploy
assignable heritable, negotiable. SEE MAIN ENTRY
assignable rights of action intangible
assignation alienation *(transfer of title)*, arrogation, assignment *(allotment)*, assignment *(transfer of ownership)*, attribution, blame *(responsibility)*, consignment, conveyance, incrimination, reference *(citation)*, rendezvous. SEE MAIN ENTRY
assignation of title feoffment
assigned certain *(specific)*, positive *(prescribed)*
assigned task office, province
assigned time date
assignee deputy, feoffee, licensee, payee, receiver, recipient, transferee. SEE MAIN ENTRY
assignee in fact licensee
assigning designation *(naming)*
assigning by lot disbursement *(act of disbursing)*
assignment activity, agency *(legal relationship)*, alienation *(transfer of title)*, allotment, appointment *(act of designating)*, apportionment, arrogation, assignation, attribution, blame *(responsibility)*, burden, capacity *(job)*, cession, charge *(responsibility)*, citation *(attribution)*, classification, commitment *(responsibility)*, consignment, conveyance, deed, department, deputation *(selection of delegates)*, designation *(naming)*, devolution, dispensation *(act of dispensing)*, disposition *(transfer of property)*, distribution *(apportionment)*, duty *(obligation)*, employment, function, job, labor *(work)*, mission, nomination, position *(business status)*, project, province, quota, ration, reference *(citation)*, role, selection *(choice)*, specification, trade *(occupation)*, work *(employment)*. SEE MAIN ENTRY
assignment by share allotment
assignment in proportion apportionment
assignment of cause hypothesis
assignment of paternity filiation
assignor contributor *(giver)*, donor, feoffor, grantor, licensor, transferor
assimilate adopt, comprehend *(understand)*, conceive *(comprehend)*, conform, construe *(comprehend)*, coordinate, desegregate, digest *(comprehend)*, naturalize *(acclimate)*, naturalize *(make a citizen)*, realize *(understand)*, understand, unite. SEE MAIN ENTRY
assimilated compound, conjoint
assimilation adoption *(acceptance)*, conformity *(obedience)*, incorporation *(blend)*, merger, osmosis, understanding *(comprehension)*
assist abet, accommodate, aid, avail *(be of use)*, bear *(support)*, conduce, contribute *(assist)*, countenance, enable, espouse, expedite, facilitate, favor, finance, foster, help *(noun)*, help *(verb)*, indorse, inure *(benefit)*, lend, maintain *(sustain)*, nurture, pander, profit, promote *(organize)*, relieve *(give aid)*, remedy, serve *(assist)*, side, subsidize, support *(assistance)*, uphold. SEE MAIN ENTRY
assist a judge clerk
assist in accomplishing a purpose avail *(be of use)*
assist substantially contribute *(assist)*
assist the progress facilitate
assistance accommodation *(backing)*, advantage, advocacy, aid *(help)*, auspices, behalf, benefit *(betterment)*, benevolence *(act of kindness)*, charity, consortium *(marriage companionship)*, contribution *(donation)*, contribution *(participation)*, endowment, favor *(sanction)*, help, largess *(generosity)*, largess *(gift)*, loan, maintenance *(support of spouse)*, panacea, patronage *(power to appoint jobs)*, patronage *(support)*, promotion *(encouragement)*, reinforcement, relief *(aid)*, remedy *(legal means of redress)*, remedy *(that which corrects)*, support *(assistance)*. SEE MAIN ENTRY
assistant abettor, accessory, accomplice, affiliate, agent, ancillary *(auxiliary)*, associate, clerical, coactor, coadjutant, coconspirator, cohort, colleague, confederate, consociate, conspirer, contributor *(contributor)*, copartner *(coconspirator)*, employee, good samaritan, participant, partner, plenipotentiary, procurator, subsidiary. SEE MAIN ENTRY
assistants personnel, staff
assister backer, benefactor, good samaritan, samaritan
assisting clerical, contributory, instrumental, practical, profitable
assize bar *(court)*, forum *(court)*
associate abettor, accomplice, affiliate *(noun)*, affiliate *(verb)*, appertain, assistant, chapter *(branch)*, coactor, coadjutant, cohort, colleague, combine *(act in concert)*, commingle, confederate, connect *(relate)*, consociate, consort, conspire, conspirer, constituent *(member)*, contributor *(contributor)*, cooperate, copartner *(business associ-*

ate), copartner *(coconspirator),* corporation, correlate, desegregate, engage *(involve),* federalize *(associate),* federate, implicate, involve *(implicate),* involve *(participate),* join *(associate oneself with),* meet, member *(individual in a group),* merge, organ, organize *(unionize),* participant, participate, partner, peer, pool, relate *(establish a connection),* unite. SEE MAIN ENTRY
associate in crime accomplice, coconspirator
associate in guilt accomplice, coconspirator
associate with accompany, espouse
associated affiliated, akin *(germane),* allied, analogous, apposite, coadunate, cognate, collateral *(accompanying),* collective, comparable *(capable of comparison),* compound, concomitant, concurrent *(at the same time),* conjoint, corporate *(joint),* correlative, federal, germane, incident, incidental, interested, interrelated, joint, pertinent, related, relative *(relevant),* relevant, tangential. SEE MAIN ENTRY
associated concepts SEE MAIN ENTRY
associated with intimate
associates constituency, staff
associating concurrent *(united)*
association adhesion *(loyalty),* affiliation *(amalgamation),* affiliation *(connectedness),* assemblage, attribution, band, cartel, centralization, chain *(nexus),* coaction, coalescence, coalition, collection *(assembly),* collusion, committee, company *(enterprise),* comparison, complex *(development),* confederacy *(compact),* conformity *(obedience),* congregation, conjunction, connection *(relation),* connivance, consolidation, consortium *(business cartel),* consortium *(marriage companionship),* contribution *(participation),* cooperative, corporation, denomination, federation, firm, foundation *(organization),* incorporation *(formation of a business entity),* institute, integration *(amalgamation),* integration *(assimilation),* kinship, league, merger, nexus, partnership, party *(political organization),* profession *(vocation),* propinquity *(kinship),* relation *(connection),* relationship *(connection),* relevance, society, sodality, syndicate, trust *(combination of businesses),* union *(labor organization).* SEE MAIN ENTRY
associative apposite, correlative, pertinent
assoil condone, palliate *(excuse),* remit *(release from penalty)*
assonance accordance *(understanding),* consensus
assonant concurrent *(united)*
assort allocate, apportion, classify, codify, distribute, fix *(arrange),* organize *(arrange),* pigeonhole, sort, vary
assorted composite, diverse, heterogeneous, manifold, miscellaneous, multiple, several *(plural)*
assortment class, classification, conglomeration, diversification, diversity, melange, selection *(collection)*
assuage allay, alleviate, diminish, disarm *(set at ease),* lessen, lull, meliorate, mitigate, moderate *(temper),* modify *(moderate),* mollify, obtund, pacify, palliate *(abate),* placate, relax, relieve *(free from burden),* remedy, remit *(relax),* soothe. SEE MAIN ENTRY
assuagement mitigation, moderation, mollification, relief *(release),* remission
assuager cure
assuaging mitigating, narcotic, palliative *(abating)*
assuasive medicinal, narcotic, palliative *(abating),* remedial
assuasive drug narcotic
assumable constructive *(inferential),* ostensible
assume accede *(succeed),* accroach, acquire *(secure),* adopt, annex *(arrogate),* anticipate *(expect),* appropriate, collect *(recover money),* condemn *(seize),* confiscate, copy, deduce, deduct *(conclude by reasoning),* deem, embrace *(accept),* endeavor, expect *(consider probable),* forejudge, gain, generalize, guess, impropriate, incur, occupy *(take possession),* opine, posit, postulate, preconceive, preempt, presume, presuppose, pretend, receive *(acquire),* seize *(confiscate),* speculate *(conjecture),* surmise, suspect *(think),* takeover, trust, undertake, usurp. SEE MAIN ENTRY
assume a character impersonate
assume a fighting attitude defy
assume a lofty bearing patronize *(condescend toward)*
assume a mask camouflage
assume a patronizing air condescend *(patronize)*
assume a pattern crystallize
assume a risk speculate *(chance),* underwrite
assume authority federalize *(place under federal control),* hold *(possess)*
assume command govern, hijack, hold *(possess),* preside, usurp
assume definite characteristics crystallize
assume for public use eminent domain
assume ownership acquire *(secure),* annex *(arrogate),* appropriate, condemn *(seize),* distrain, impropriate, occupy *(take possession),* possess, purchase
assume responsibility conduct, guarantee, operate
assume responsibility for avouch *(guarantee)*
assume the appearance of mock *(imitate)*
assume the character of pose *(impersonate)*
assume the offensive attack, fight *(battle)*
assume the role of pose *(impersonate)*
assume unlawful rights of ownership convert *(misappropriate)*
assume without authority usurp
assumed artificial, false *(not genuine),* hypothetical, implied, ostensible, presumptive, purported, putative, specious, tacit, theoretical. SEE MAIN ENTRY
assumed position platform
assumed positions premises *(hypotheses)*
assumed truth postulate
assumedly reputedly
assuming brazen, impertinent *(insolent),* insolent, obtrusive, orgulous, presumptuous, proud *(conceited)*
assuming different forms protean
assuming ownership disseisin
assuming that provided
assumption acquisition, adoption *(acceptance),* adverse possession, appropriation *(taking),* arrogation, basis, concept, condemnation *(seizure),* conjecture, conviction *(persuasion),* deduction *(conclusion),* distress *(seizure),* estimate *(idea),* estimation *(calculation),* generalization, ground, hypothesis, inference, opinion *(belief),* postulate, preconception, presumption, prolepsis, proposition, receipt *(act of receiving),* receipt *(voucher),* speculation *(conjecture),* supposition, theory. SEE MAIN ENTRY
assumptive apparent *(presumptive),* presumptive, speculative, supercilious
assumptively reputedly
assurance acceptance, accommodation *(backing),* affirmance *(authentication),* approval, avouchment, bail, belief *(state of mind),* binder, bond, certainty, certification *(attested copy),* certification *(certainness),* certitude, commitment *(responsibility),* confidence *(faith),* confirmation, consent, contract, conviction *(persuasion),* corroboration, coverage *(insurance),* credence, expectation, faith, guaranty, license, mainstay, pact, pledge *(binding promise),* principle *(axiom),* profession *(declaration),* promise, proof, prospect *(outlook),* recognizance, reference *(recommendation),* reliance, safeguard, security *(safety),* surety *(certainty),* trust *(confidence),* undertaking *(pledge),* vow, warrant *(guaranty),* warranty. SEE MAIN ENTRY
assurance against loss indemnity, insurance
assurance of secrecy confidence *(relation of trust)*
assure avouch *(guarantee),* bear *(adduce),* bond *(secure a debt),* certify *(attest),* contend *(maintain),* convince, corroborate, cosign, declare, disarm *(set at ease),* ensure, guarantee, pledge *(promise the performance of),* profess *(avow),* promise *(vow),* sponsor, swear, underwrite, verify *(confirm),* vouch. SEE MAIN ENTRY
assure again reassure
assure oneself ascertain
assured agreed *(promised),* alleged, axiomatic, categorical, certain *(fixed),* certain *(positive),* conclusive *(determinative),* convincing, credible, decisive, definite, demonstrable, dependable, dogmatic, incontrovertible, indubious, inevitable, infallible, official, positive *(confident),* reliable, sanguine, secure *(confident),* solid *(sound),* undisputed
assured belief conviction *(persuasion)*
assured expectation faith
assuredly admittedly
assuredness assurance, belief *(state of mind),* certainty, certification *(certainness),* certitude, reliance, surety *(certainty)*
assurer insurer
assuring convincing
assymetrical disproportionate
asthenic languid, nonsubstantial *(not sturdy),* powerless
astir conscious *(awake)*
astonish confound, confuse *(bewilder),* overcome *(overwhelm),* overwhelm. SEE MAIN ENTRY
astonished speechless
astonishing moving *(evoking emotion),* notable, noteworthy, peculiar *(curious),* portentous *(eliciting amazement),* prodigious *(amazing),* remarkable, special, unaccustomed, uncanny, unexpected, unusual
astonishing thing phenomenon *(unusual occurrence)*
astonishment bombshell, phenomenon *(unusual occurrence),* surprise

astound confound, discommode, discompose, disconcert, impress *(affect deeply)*
astounding ineffable, noteworthy, prodigious *(amazing)*, remarkable, special, unusual
astoundment surprise
astral stellar
astray errant, lost *(disoriented)*, peccant *(culpable)*. SEE MAIN ENTRY
astrict clog, constrict *(inhibit)*, debar, disadvantage, restrict
astriction constraint *(restriction)*
astringe constrict *(compress)*
astringent bitter *(penetrating)*, caustic, harsh, particular *(exacting)*, severe. SEE MAIN ENTRY
astronomical prodigious *(enormous)*
astucious SEE MAIN ENTRY
astute acute, artful, circumspect, cognizant, discreet, discriminating *(judicious)*, judicious, knowing, perceptive, perspicacious, politic, profound *(esoteric)*, sapient, sensible, sensitive *(discerning)*, sly, subtle *(refined)*. SEE MAIN ENTRY
astuteness common sense, insight, intelligence *(intellect)*, judgment *(discernment)*, perception, sagacity, sense *(intelligence)*
astutus artful, politic, sly, tactical
asunder apart, disconnected, discrete, disperse *(scatter)*, separate
asylum bulwark, haven, lodging, protection, refuge, security *(safety)*. SEE MAIN ENTRY
asylum shelter *(protection)*
asymmetric irregular *(not usual)*
asymmetrical dissimilar, irregular *(not usual)*
asymmetry difference, discrepancy, disparity, inequality, irregularity
at a fixed interval per annum
at a fixed time hereafter *(eventually)*
at a great distance remote *(not proximate)*
at a later period ex post facto, thereafter
at a later time ex post facto
at a premium scarce
at a subsequent period ex post facto
at a succeeding time ex post facto
at all whatever
at all times always *(forever)*
at an end complete *(ended)*
at any rate regardless
at close quarters contiguous, present *(attendant)*
at cross purposes contra, contrary, discordant
at cross-purposes antipathetic *(oppositional)*, dissenting
at ease complacent
at fault blameful, blameworthy, culpable, delinquent *(guilty of a misdeed)*, errant, guilty. SEE MAIN ENTRY
at first ab initio
at first glance prima facie *(self-evident)*
at first sight prima facie *(self-evident)*
at first view prima facie *(self-evident)*
at hand available, close *(near)*, forthcoming, immediate *(imminent)*, immediate *(not distant)*, imminent, inevitable, pending *(imminent)*, present *(attendant)*, present *(current)*, proximate, ready *(prepared)*
at home household *(domestic)*
at issue arguable, competitive *(antagonistic)*, contestable, contrary, controversial, debatable, disputable, dissenting, doubtful. SEE MAIN ENTRY
at large free *(not restricted)*
at least only
at liberty autonomous *(self governing)*, clear *(free from criminal charges)*, exempt, free *(not restricted)*, sovereign *(independent)*
at loggerheads dissenting
at no period sine die
at no time sine die
at odds contradictory, controversial, disproportionate, dissenting, hostile, incongruous, repugnant *(incompatible)*
at odds with dissident, negative, nonconforming
at once forthwith, instant, instantly
at one concordant, consonant
at one with consensual
at one's disposal available
at one's end in extremis
at one's own risk caveat emptor
at other times known as alias
at peace placid
at peril at risk
at rest dead, dormant, lifeless *(dead)*
at risk SEE MAIN ENTRY
at sight prima facie *(self-evident)*
at the beginning ab initio
at the conclusion of life in extremis
at the edge extreme *(last)*
at the first opportunity as soon as feasible
at the first possible moment as soon as feasible
at the last stage in extremis
at the mercy of subject *(exposed)*
at the point of death in extremis
at the present time instant
at the same instant concurrent *(at the same time)*
at the same time ad interim, coincidental, en masse, simultaneous
at the start ab initio
at the termination of life in extremis
at the utmost point extreme *(last)*
at the very least only
at the wrong time inopportune
at this moment instant, present *(current)*
at this time present *(current)*
at variance adverse *(opposite)*, competitive *(antagonistic)*, contradictory, contrary, controversial, discordant, disproportionate, dissenting, hostile, inapplicable, inapposite, inapt, incommensurate, incongruous, inconsistent, inept *(inappropriate)*, inimical, irreconcilable, litigious, repugnant *(incompatible)*
at variance with dissident, nonconforming
at variance with the facts ludicrous
at war with inimical
at whatever time whenever
at which time whenever
at will employment SEE MAIN ENTRY
at work active, effective *(operative)*, operative
atavistic genetic, regressive
athirst eager, hot-blooded
athwart contra
atmosphere climate, environment. SEE MAIN ENTRY
atomization dissolution *(disintegration)*
atomize dissolve *(disperse)*
atone compensate *(counterbalance)*, redeem *(satisfy debts)*, redress, restore *(return)*
atone for repent
atonement compensation, expiation, reparation *(indemnification)*, restitution, retribution, trover
atoning compensatory, penitent, repentant
atrabilious deplorable, disconsolate
atrocious arrant *(onerous)*, bad *(offensive)*, brutal, contemptible, cruel, deplorable, disgraceful, gross *(flagrant)*, heinous, inexcusable, iniquitous, loathsome, malignant, outrageous, ruthless, scandalous, vicious. SEE MAIN ENTRY
atrocious crime atrocity
atrocitas atrocity
atrocity abuse *(physical misuse)*, cruelty, delinquency *(misconduct)*, misdeed, vice, wrong. SEE MAIN ENTRY
atrophy decay, decline, degenerate, depreciate, deteriorate, deterioration, detriment, dissolution *(disintegration)*
attach abridge *(divest)*, abut, adhere *(fasten)*, affiliate, affix, annex *(add)*, append, ascribe, bond *(hold together)*, border *(bound)*, cement, cohere *(adhere)*, combine *(join together)*, condemn *(seize)*, confiscate, conjoin, connect *(join together)*, contact *(touch)*, deprive, distrain, divest, fix *(make firm)*, garnish, impound, impress *(procure by force)*, impute, join *(bring together)*, levy, lock, sequester *(seize property)*. SEE MAIN ENTRY
attach a legal signature notarize
attach little importance to minimize
attach oneself to adopt
attach too much importance to overestimate
attache employee
attached addicted, appurtenant, cohesive *(sticking)*, conjoint, inextricable, inseparable, proximate. SEE MAIN ENTRY
attached to another jurisdiction foreign
attaching attachment *(act of affixing)*, confiscatory
attachment accession *(annexation)*, addendum, addition, additive, adherence *(adhesion)*, adherence *(devotion)*, adhesion *(affixing)*, adhesion *(loyalty)*, adjoiner, affection, affinity *(regard)*, allegiance, allonge, appendix *(accession)*, appendix *(supplement)*, appliance, appurtenance, arrogation, boom *(increase)*, chain *(nexus)*, coalescence, codicil, coherence, connection *(fastening)*, consortium *(marriage companionship)*, disseisin, distraint, distress *(seizure)*, expropriation *(divestiture)*, favor *(partiality)*, favoritism, levy, loyalty, nexus, partiality, penchant, predilection, predisposition, privation, privity, regard *(esteem)*, rider, sequestration. SEE MAIN ENTRY
attachment to adoption *(acceptance)*
attachment to realty fixture
attachments paraphernalia *(apparatus)*, ties
attack accost, accuse, ambush, assail, assault *(noun)*, assault *(verb)*, bait *(harass)*, barrage, battery, beat *(strike)*, belligerency, cavil, censure, charge *(accusation)*, charge *(accuse)*, condemn *(blame)*, condemnation *(blame)*, controvert, course, denigrate, denounce *(condemn)*, despoil, discommend, disease, engage *(involve)*, fault, fight *(battle)*, fight *(battle)*, foray, grapple, harm, harry *(plunder)*, impeach, impeachment, impinge, impugn, impugnation, incursion, intrusion, invade, invasion, inveigh, malign, mistreat, molest *(subject to indecent advances)*, object, offense, onset *(assault)*, oppugn, outbreak, outburst, persecute, protest, resistance, smear, spoliation, strike *(assault)*, violence. SEE MAIN ENTRY

attack by words impugn
attack from a concealed position ambush
attack on rights invasion
attack physically assault
attack the reputation of malign
attackable penetrable
attacked accused *(attacked)*
attacker aggressor, assailant, foe
attacking negative, offensive *(taking the initiative)*
attain accede *(succeed)*, accomplish, acquire *(secure)*, carry *(succeed)*, consummate, discharge *(perform)*, dispatch *(dispose of)*, earn, effectuate, execute *(accomplish)*, gain, make, obtain, operate, pass *(satisfy requirements)*, procure, reach, realize *(obtain as a profit)*, reap, recover. SEE MAIN ENTRY
attain by effort find *(discover)*
attain majority mature
attain maturity mature
attain the goal consummate
attainability chance *(possibility)*, feasibility, possibility
attainable available, facile, open *(accessible)*, possible, potential, practicable, public *(open)*, vulnerable
attainment accession *(enlargement)*, acquisition, adverse possession, boom *(prosperity)*, caliber *(mental capacity)*, commission *(act)*, development *(outgrowth)*, discharge *(performance)*, edification, end *(termination)*, fait accompli, fruition, outcome, performance *(execution)*, performance *(workmanship)*, realization, receipt *(act of receiving)*, satisfaction *(fulfilment)*
attaint bad repute, brand *(stigmatize)*, convict, denigrate, discredit, disgrace *(noun)*, disgrace *(verb)*, dishonor *(shame)*, dishonor *(deprive of honor)*, ignominy, impeach, notoriety, opprobrium, pillory, scandal, shame, smear, stain, sully. SEE MAIN ENTRY
attemper adjust *(regulate)*, assuage, attune, check *(restrain)*, denature, extenuate, moderate *(temper)*, mollify, palliate *(abate)*, qualify *(condition)*, remit *(relax)*, soothe
attempt assume *(undertake)*, conatus, effort, endeavor *(noun)*, endeavor *(verb)*, enterprise *(undertaking)*, experiment, project, pursue *(strive to gain)*, pursuit *(effort to secure)*, strive, struggle, trial *(experiment)*, undertake, undertaking *(enterprise)*, venture, work *(effort)*. SEE MAIN ENTRY
attempt strenuously endeavor
attempt to disprove debate
attempt to divert dissuade, expostulate
attempt to equal competition
attempt to obstruct legislation filibuster
attempt to prevent dissuade
attempt violence to assault
attempted monopolization SEE MAIN ENTRY
attend care *(regard)*, concentrate *(pay attention)*, concern *(care)*, devote, focus, immerse *(engross)*, maintain *(sustain)*, monitor, note *(notice)*, observe *(obey)*, observe *(watch)*, overhear, pander, patrol, protect, regard *(pay attention)*, remedy, report *(present oneself)*, serve *(assist)*, study, treat *(process)*. SEE MAIN ENTRY
attend *(To be present at)* SEE MAIN ENTRY
attend as consequence ensue
attend minutely concentrate *(pay attention)*, focus
attend to assume *(undertake)*, care *(regard)*, concern *(care)*, hear *(give attention to)*, heed, notice *(observe)*, obey, oversee, preserve
attend to business labor
attend to instructions conform
attend to orders comply, obey
attendance service *(assistance)*. SEE MAIN ENTRY
attendant ancillary *(auxiliary)*, caretaker *(one caring for property)*, clerical, coactor, coadjutant, cohort, collateral *(accompanying)*, colleague, concomitant, concurrent *(at the same time)*, consociate, copartner *(coconspirator)*, guardian, incidental, ministerial, participant, party *(participant)*, present *(current)*, supplementary, tangential
attendant conditions circumstances
attended by obstacles difficult
attended with death deadly
attended with risk dangerous
attending circumspect, clerical, concomitant, concurrent *(at the same time)*, ministerial
attention adhesion *(loyalty)*, caution *(vigilance)*, concern *(interest)*, consideration *(contemplation)*, contemplation, diligence *(care)*, discretion *(quality of being discreet)*, emphasis, homage, industry *(activity)*, interest *(concern)*, notice *(heed)*, observation, perception, precaution, prudence, recognition, relief *(aid)*, respect, scrutiny, stress *(accent)*. SEE MAIN ENTRY
attention to detail diligence *(care)*, interest *(concern)*
attentive alert *(vigilant)*, careful, circumspect, close *(rigorous)*, conscientious, conscious *(aware)*, deliberate, diligent, faithful *(diligent)*, guarded, meticulous, obedient, painstaking, particular *(exacting)*, pensive, punctilious, punctual, sedulous, sensitive *(discerning)*, vigilant, zealous
attentive to detail particular *(exacting)*
attentiveness caution *(vigilance)*, comprehension, consideration *(contemplation)*, consideration *(sympathetic regard)*, notice *(heed)*, observation, preoccupation, regard *(attention)*, sensibility
attentuate deduct *(reduce)*, sustain *(prolong)*
attentus careful, economical, intent
attenuare attenuate
attenuate alleviate, decrease, depreciate, dilute, disarm *(divest of arms)*, discount *(minimize)*, extenuate, lessen, minimize, reduce. SEE MAIN ENTRY
attenuated deficient, impalpable, narrow, nonsubstantial *(not sturdy)*, tenuous
attenuation decrease, deduction *(diminution)*, mitigation
attest affirm *(declare solemnly)*, affirmation, allege, assert, assure *(insure)*, attestation, averment, avouch *(avow)*, avouchment, avow, bear *(adduce)*, bespeak, certify *(attest)*, cite *(state)*, claim *(maintain)*, confirm, contend *(maintain)*, corroborate, depose *(testify)*, endorse, establish *(show)*, evidence, manifest, posit, profess *(avow)*, promise *(vow)*, seal *(solemnize)*, subscribe *(sign)*, substantiate, support *(corroborate)*, sustain *(confirm)*, testify, validate, verify *(confirm)*, verify *(swear)*, vouch. SEE MAIN ENTRY
attest to acknowledge *(declare)*, converse, notarize, plead *(allege in a legal action)*
attestable convincing
attestant affiant, affirmant, bystander, deponent, eyewitness, indicator, undersigned, witness
attestation adjuration, admission *(disclosure)*, affirmance *(authentication)*, affirmance *(legal affirmation)*, affirmation, assertion, asseveration, assurance, averment, avouchment, avowal, certificate, certification *(attested copy)*, certitude, confirmation, corroboration, declaration, jurat, oath, pledge *(binding promise)*, profession *(declaration)*, proof, record, reference *(recommendation)*, stamp, support *(corroboration)*, testimony. SEE MAIN ENTRY
attestator affirmant, deponent
attested agreed *(promised)*, authentic, certain *(fixed)*, certain *(positive)*, definite, documentary, factual, indubious, official, valid
attested statement affidavit
attester affiant, affirmant, bystander, deponent, eyewitness, indicator, surety *(guarantor)*, undersigned
attesting declaration attestation, certification *(attested copy)*, reference *(recommendation)*
attesting statement jurat
attestor deponent, witness
attestor of documents notary public
attinere concern *(involve)*
attingere adjoin, allude, border *(bound)*
attire oneself clothe
attitude conduct, conviction *(persuasion)*, demeanor, deportment, frame *(mood)*, generalization, habit, manner *(behavior)*, opinion *(belief)*, outlook, perspective, platform, position *(point of view)*, property *(distinctive attribute)*, reaction *(response)*, stand *(position)*, standpoint, temperament. SEE MAIN ENTRY
attollere elevate
attonement consensus
attorn SEE MAIN ENTRY
attorney advocate *(counselor)*, barrister, counsel, counselor, esquire, jurist, lawyer, practitioner, spokesman. SEE MAIN ENTRY
attorney for the people district attorney
attorney general prosecutor
attorney in fact SEE MAIN ENTRY
attorney representing the state's interest district attorney
attorney-at-law advocate *(counselor)*, attorney, barrister, counsel, counselor, esquire, jurist, lawyer
attorney-client-privilege SEE MAIN ENTRY
attorneys bar *(body of lawyers)*
attorneys-at-law bar *(body of lawyers)*
attorney's fees SEE MAIN ENTRY
attornment SEE MAIN ENTRY
attract bait *(lure)*, coax, interest, inveigle, lure, motivate. SEE MAIN ENTRY
attract notice interest
attract the attention occupy *(engage)*
attract the mind occupy *(engage)*
attract the thoughts occupy *(engage)*
attracting attractive
attraction affinity *(regard)*, chain *(nexus)*, decoy, desire, favor *(partiality)*, incentive, inducement, invitation, obsession, partiality, penchant, predisposition, propensity, seduction
attractive popular, provocative, sapid. SEE MAIN ENTRY
attractive feature amenity
attractive nuisance SEE MAIN ENTRY
attractive quality amenity
attractiveness amenity, draw *(attraction)*

attrahent attractive
attribuere ascribe, assign *(allot),* bestow, impute
attributable derivative
attribute ascribe, assign *(designate),* caliber *(quality),* character *(personal quality),* characteristic, color *(complexion),* differential, feature *(characteristic),* impute, property *(distinctive attribute),* specialty *(distinctive mark),* trait. SEE MAIN ENTRY
attribute to blame
attribute vicariously impute
attributed putative
attributed to contingent
attributes personality
attribution accusation, arrogation, assignation, blame *(responsibility),* incrimination, reference *(allusion).* SEE MAIN ENTRY
attrition erosion. SEE MAIN ENTRY
attroupement caucus, company *(assemblage),* cumulation
attune accommodate, comport *(agree with),* conform. SEE MAIN ENTRY
attuned consonant
attuned to acquainted, consensual
attunement adjustment, compatibility, synchronism
atypical anomalous, deviant, different, disordered, disparate, dissimilar, infrequent, irregular *(not usual),* notable, noteworthy, peculiar *(distinctive),* special, unique, unusual. SEE MAIN ENTRY
atypicality difference
auctio auction
auction handle *(trade),* sell, vend. SEE MAIN ENTRY
auctione vendere auction
auctor advocate *(espouser),* author *(originator),* informant, informer *(one providing criminal information),* promoter, spokesman, sponsor
auctor esse authorize
auctor generis ancestor
auctor gentis ancestor
auctorem esse advise
auctoritas authority *(power),* consequence *(significance),* credibility, patronage *(power to appoint jobs),* sanction *(permission),* warrant *(authorization)*
auctus development *(progression),* growth *(increase)*
audacia audacity
audacious brazen, bumptious, disdainful, flagrant, impertinent *(insolent),* insolent, presumptuous. SEE MAIN ENTRY
audaciousness audacity
audacity contempt *(disobedience to the court),* disrespect, temerity. SEE MAIN ENTRY
audax lawless, spartan
audi alteram partem counterargument
audible coherent *(clear),* oral, verbal
audible expression speech
audience assemblage, bystander, collection *(assembly),* confrontation *(act of setting face to face),* congregation, interview, session. SEE MAIN ENTRY
audiendi inquisitive
audio rights SEE MAIN ENTRY
audit analysis, analyze, bill *(invoice),* canvass, check *(inspect),* computation, examination *(study),* examine *(study),* indagation, monitor, scrutinize, study, test. SEE MAIN ENTRY
auditing accounting
auditio hearsay
audition hear *(give attention to),* interview, recognition
auditor comptroller
auditor disciple
augere compound, enhance, enlarge, extend *(enlarge),* heighten *(augment),* increase, intensify, magnify
augeri develop
augment accrue *(increase),* accumulate *(enlarge),* aggravate *(exacerbate),* aid, amplify, append, bear *(yield),* boom *(increase),* conduce, develop, elaborate, enhance, enlarge, exacerbate, expand, extend *(enlarge),* hoard, increase, intensify, magnify, raise *(advance),* recruit, reinforce, supplement
augmentation accession *(enlargement),* accretion, addition, additive, adjunct, advance *(increase),* aggravation *(exacerbation),* boom *(increase),* boom *(prosperity),* codicil, continuation *(prolongation),* cumulation, exaggeration, extension *(expansion),* growth *(increase),* increment, profit, progress, reinforcement, rider. SEE MAIN ENTRY
augmentative cumulative *(intensifying),* supplementary
augmented inflated *(enlarged)*
augur anticipate *(prognosticate),* forewarn, harbinger, herald, indicate, portend, predict, presage, prognosticate, threaten. SEE MAIN ENTRY
augur well promise *(raise expectations)*
augural portentous *(ominous),* presageful, prophetic
augurari guess, presage, surmise
augurate portend, presage, prognosticate
augurial ominous, presageful
augurous portentous *(ominous)*
augury caution *(warning),* caveat, harbinger, indicant, indication, indicator, precursor, premonition, symptom, threat, token, warning
august meritorious, outstanding *(prominent),* solemn
aura atmosphere, climate, environment, prestige
aura popularis distinction *(reputation)*
auribus hear *(perceive by ear)*
auricular confidential, privy
aurora onset *(commencement)*
ausculate hear *(give attention to)*
auspicate anticipate *(prognosticate),* commence, embark, portend, predict, presage, prognosticate
auspice forerunner, harbinger, indicant, indication, indicator, premonition, threat, token
auspices advocacy, aid *(help),* behalf, charge *(custody),* control *(supervision),* custody *(supervision),* direction *(guidance),* favor *(sanction),* power, safekeeping. SEE MAIN ENTRY
auspicial ominous, presageful
auspicious favorable *(advantageous),* fitting, opportune, propitious, seasonable, successful. SEE MAIN ENTRY
auspiciousness boom *(prosperity),* opportunity, timeliness
auspicium auspices
austere astringent, bitter *(penetrating),* bleak *(severely simple),* caustic, draconian, harsh, rigid, severe, strict, unapproachable, uncompromising, unrelenting
austeritas austerity
austerity cruelty, rigor, severity. SEE MAIN ENTRY
austerus serious *(grave),* severe
autarch dictator
autarchic autonomous *(self-governing)*
autarkic independent
authentic accurate, actual, convincing, de facto, definitive, documentary, factual, genuine, honest, literal, natural, original *(initial),* positive *(incontestable),* prime *(original),* real, realistic, reliable, rightful, sterling, undistorted, valid, veridical. SEE MAIN ENTRY
authentically admittedly
authenticate accredit, affirm *(uphold),* approve, attest, avouch *(guarantee),* avow, bear *(adduce),* certify *(attest),* cite *(state),* confirm, corroborate, demonstrate *(establish),* document, endorse, establish *(show),* evidence, indorse, notarize, prove, sanction, seal *(solemnize),* sign, substantiate, support *(corroborate),* sustain *(confirm),* swear, uphold, vouch, witness *(attest to).* SEE MAIN ENTRY
authenticate a will probate
authenticated actual, definitive, fully executed *(signed),* genuine, official, true *(authentic)*
authenticated confirmation certification *(attested copy),* reference *(recommendation)*
authenticated incident fact
authentication acknowledgment *(avowal),* affirmation, approval, attestation, avowal, certificate, confirmation, consent, corroboration, deed, documentation, jurat, stamp, subscription, support *(corroboration),* warrant *(guaranty)*
authentication of a will probate
authentication proceeding probate
authenticity honesty, reality, truth, validity, veracity
authentification certification *(attested copy)*
author architect, compose, derivation, elicit, engender, generate, invent *(produce for the first time),* make, maker, originate, undersigned. SEE MAIN ENTRY
authoritarian dictatorial, dogmatic, ex officio, strict
authoritative arbitrary and capricious, assertive, authentic, categorical, certain *(positive),* clear *(certain),* cogent, compelling, compulsory, consequential *(substantial),* decisive, definite, definitive, determinative, dictatorial, documentary, dogmatic, dominant, factual, forcible, incontrovertible, influential, juridical, master, official, peremptory *(imperative),* persuasive, powerful, predominant, prevailing *(having superior force),* sovereign *(absolute),* strict, stringent, valid. SEE MAIN ENTRY
authoritative assertion dictum
authoritative attestation certification *(attested copy)*
authoritative citation to appear monition *(legal summons)*
authoritative citation to appear before a court process *(summons),* summons, venire
authoritative command edict, mandate, monition *(legal summons),* order *(judicial directive),* process *(summons),* summons
authoritative decision adjudication, award, decree
authoritative estimate determination
authoritative example authority *(documentation),* precedent, stare decisis
authoritative law codification
authoritative opinion conclusion *(determination),* determination
authoritative order fiat, mandate

authoritative power clout
authoritative request demand
authoritative rule ordinance, precedent
authoritative rule for future similar cases authority *(documentation)*
authoritative statement instruction *(direction)*, opinion *(judicial decision)*, pronouncement
authoritative stoppage of trade embargo
authoritative suggestion dictate
authoritatively admittedly
authoritativeness authority *(power)*, certainty, certification *(certainness)*, force *(strength)*, puissance
authorities bureaucracy, hierarchy *(persons in authority)*. SEE MAIN ENTRY
authority advantage, agency *(commission)*, agency *(legal relationship)*, auspices, bailiwick, basis, bureau, certification *(certification of proficiency)*, charter *(license)*, charter *(sanction)*, clout, concession *(authorization)*, consent, control *(supervision)*, copyright, derivation, determinant, dint, documentation, dominance, dominion *(supreme authority)*, droit, eminence, expert, force *(compulsion)*, generalship, government *(political administration)*, hegemony, influence, judicature, jurisdiction, license, management *(directorate)*, management *(supervision)*, mastermind, occupation *(possession)*, patronage *(power to appoint jobs)*, permission, permit, possession *(ownership)*, power, precedence, precedent, predominance, prerogative, prescription *(claim of title)*, prescription *(directive)*, prestige, primacy, privilege, professional, realm, reference *(citation)*, regime, right *(entitlement)*, source, specialist, supremacy, title *(right)*, validity, warrant *(authorization)*, weight *(importance)*. SEE MAIN ENTRY
authority *(Legal expert)*. SEE MAIN ENTRY
authority to act for another proxy
authority to hear and decide a case jurisdiction
authority to search search warrant
authorization appointment *(act of designating)*, approval, assent, assignment *(designation)*, brevet, capacity *(authority)*, certificate, certification *(certification of proficiency)*, charter *(sanction)*, concession *(authorization)*, confirmation, consent, copyright, credentials, delegation *(assignment)*, deputation *(selection of delegates)*, designation *(naming)*, dispensation *(exception)*, droit, fiat, franchise *(license)*, government *(administration)*, indorsement, leave *(permission)*, legality, legalization, legitimacy, license, mittimus, nomination, option *(contractual provision)*, permission, permit, prerogative, privilege, right *(entitlement)*, sanction *(permission)*, sufferance, title *(right)*. SEE MAIN ENTRY
authorize accept *(assent)*, accredit, appoint, approve, assent, assign *(designate)*, bestow, certify *(approve)*, charge *(empower)*, command, commit *(entrust)*, confirm, consent, consign, cosign, delegate, designate, detail *(assign)*, employ *(engage services)*, empower, enable, enfranchise, entrust, grant *(concede)*, hire, indorse, invest *(vest)*, legalize, legislate, legitimate, let *(permit)*, notarize, pass *(approve)*, permit, qualify *(meet standards)*, sanction, seal *(solemnize)*, sign, suffer *(permit)*, validate, vest. SEE MAIN ENTRY
authorize formally charge *(empower)*, delegate
authorize to represent delegate
authorized admissible, allowable, allowed, de jure, due *(regular)*, entitled, fully executed *(signed)*, juridical, legal, legitimate *(rightful)*, licit, permissible, privileged, rightful, statutory, valid
authorized by law de jure, lawful, legal
authorized might force *(legal efficacy)*
authorizing deputation *(selection of delegates)*
authorless anonymous
authors press
authorship creation
authortative decision precedent
authortative principle of law precedent
autochthonal native *(domestic)*
autochthonic native *(domestic)*
autochthonous native *(domestic)*
autocrat dictator
autocratic dictatorial, powerful, strict
autocratic master dictator
autocratical powerful
autograph brand *(mark)*, inscription, sign
autography handwriting
automated industrial
automatic habitual, routine. SEE MAIN ENTRY
automatic lack of due diligence res ipsa loquitur
automatic negligence res ipsa loquitur
automatic reaction instinct
autonomic autonomous *(self-governing)*, free *(enjoying civil liberty)*
autonomical free *(enjoying civil liberty)*
autonomous free *(enjoying civil liberty)*, independent, nonpartisan, sovereign *(independent)*. SEE MAIN ENTRY
autonomous being individual, person
autonomy freedom, home rule, latitude, liberty, suffrage
autoptic unmistakable
autoptical unmistakable
auxiliari assist
auxiliary abettor, additional, adjunct, affiliate, appurtenance, appurtenant, associate, backer, clerical, coactor, coadjutant, cohort, collateral *(accompanying)*, colleague, confederate, consociate, contributor *(contributor)*, contributory, copartner *(business associate)*, expedient, expendable, inferior *(lower in position)*, instrumental, ministerial, nonessential, participant, pendent, reinforcement, secondary, slight, stopgap, subordinate, subservient, subsidiary, substitute, supplementary, unnecessary. SEE MAIN ENTRY
auxiliary in crime coconspirator
auxilium assistance, help, relief *(aid)*, support *(assistance)*
avail advantage, aid, behalf, benefit *(betterment)*, edification, enjoyment *(use)*, function, gain, help *(noun)*, help *(verb)*, inure *(benefit)*, output, profit, promote *(organize)*, purpose, recourse, relief *(aid)*, satisfy *(fulfill)*, use, utility *(usefulness)*, worth. SEE MAIN ENTRY
avail against countervail
avail oneself of adopt, capitalize *(seize the chance)*, employ *(make use of)*, exercise *(use)*, expend *(consume)*, exploit *(make use of)*, impropriate, plagiarize, resort, wield
availability access *(opening)*, possibility
available amenable, convenient, disposable, open *(accessible)*, present *(attendant)*, present *(current)*, public *(open)*, ready *(prepared)*, ready *(willing)*. SEE MAIN ENTRY
available assets stock in trade
available facts information *(knowledge)*
available means assets, capital, cash, personalty, property *(possessions)*, resource
availing adequate, beneficial
avails boom *(prosperity)*, proceeds, profit
avalanche cataclysm, overage, surfeit
avant garde sophisticated
avant-courier precursor
avarice greed
avaricious illiberal, insatiable, mercenary, parsimonious, rapacious, venal
avariciousness greed
avaritia greed
avarus illiberal
avenge penalize, repay, retaliate
avengement conviction *(finding of guilt)*, punishment, reprisal, retribution, revenge, vengeance
avenging punitive, vindictive
avenue admission *(entry)*, admittance *(means of approach)*, causeway, conduit *(channel)*, outlet, way *(channel)*. SEE MAIN ENTRY
avenues approaches
aver adduce, affirm *(claim)*, affirm *(declare solemnly)*, allege, annunciate, assert, assure *(insure)*, attest, avouch *(avow)*, avow, bear *(adduce)*, certify *(attest)*, claim *(maintain)*, contend *(maintain)*, convey *(communicate)*, corroborate, declare, depose *(testify)*, enunciate, express, observe *(remark)*, posit, profess *(avow)*, promise *(vow)*, propound, remark, speak, swear, testify, utter, vouch, vow. SEE MAIN ENTRY
average cross section, customary, general, imperfect, intermediate, marginal, mediocre, mediocrity, mundane, nondescript, norm, normal *(regular)*, ordinary, regular *(conventional)*, typical, usual. SEE MAIN ENTRY
average out calculate
averageness mediocrity
averment adjuration, affidavit, affirmance *(legal affirmation)*, affirmation, allegation, assertion, asseveration, assurance, attestation, avouchment, avowal, claim *(assertion)*, comment, confirmation, corroboration, count, disclosure *(something disclosed)*, profession *(declaration)*, pronouncement, proof, reference *(recommendation)*, remark, statement, surety *(certainty)*, testimony. SEE MAIN ENTRY
averred alleged
averse antipathetic *(oppositional)*, contrary, disinclined, disobedient, hesitant, involuntary, negative, reluctant, restive. SEE MAIN ENTRY
averseness disincentive, rejection, reluctance
aversion alienation *(estrangement)*, consternation, contempt *(disdain)*, hatred, ill will, intolerance, malice, odium, phobia, rancor, reluctance
aversus averse, disinclined
avert arrest *(stop)*, avoid *(evade)*, balk, bar *(hinder)*, block, counter, deter, discourage, estop, forestall, parry, prevent, repel *(drive back)*, save *(rescue)*, stall, stave, thwart. SEE MAIN ENTRY
avertere alienate *(estrange)*, avert, divert, embezzle, purloin
averting preventive
aveu avowal
avid eager, fervent, hot-blooded, ready *(willing)*, sedulous
aviditas greed
avidity desire, greed, passion

avidus eager, rapacious
aviso dispatch *(message)*, intelligence *(news)*, notification, tip *(clue)*
avocare disengage
avocat lawyer
avocation business *(occupation)*, career, employment, job, occupation *(vocation)*, position *(business status)*, practice *(professional business)*, profession *(vocation)*, pursuit *(occupation)*, trade *(occupation)*, work *(employment)*
avoid abscond, adeem, annul, avert, cancel, default, deter, detour, discriminate *(treat differently)*, disdain, disfavor, elude, escape, eschew, estrange, evade *(deceive)*, evade *(elude)*, exclude, fail *(neglect)*, forestall, forgo, forswear, parry, picket, pretermit, prevent, refrain, repeal, shirk, shun, stave, tergiversate. SEE MAIN ENTRY
avoid a straight answer equivocate
avoid arrest escape
avoid capture escape
avoid doing circumvent
avoid peril escape
avoid using conserve
avoidable needless, nonessential, unnecessary
avoidance absence *(nonattendance)*, abstention, boycott, default, evasion, exclusion, flight, nonperformance, odium, ostracism. SEE MAIN ENTRY
avoidance of extremes moderation
avoidance of waste economy *(frugality)*
avoided derelict *(abandoned)*
avoider fugitive
avoiding evasive, reluctant
avoiding extravagance economical
avoiding the society of others solitary
avoidless certain *(positive)*, necessary *(inescapable)*, unavoidable *(inevitable)*
avoison SEE MAIN ENTRY
avouch affirm *(declare solemnly)*, allege, assert, assure *(insure)*, avow, bear *(adduce)*, certify *(attest)*, claim *(maintain)*, corroborate, depose *(testify)*, evidence, posit, profess *(avow)*, promise *(vow)*, verify *(swear)*, vouch. SEE MAIN ENTRY
avouched alleged
avouchment adjuration, affidavit, affirmance *(legal affirmation)*, affirmation, assertion, asseveration, attestation, averment, avowal, certification *(attested copy)*, claim *(assertion)*, confirmation, contract, corroboration, jurat, oath, reference *(recommendation)*. SEE MAIN ENTRY
avow acknowledge *(declare)*, affirm *(declare solemnly)*, agree *(comply)*, assert, assurance, assure *(insure)*, bear *(adduce)*, betray *(disclose)*, certify *(attest)*, claim *(maintain)*, confirm, contend *(maintain)*, convey *(communicate)*, declare, depose *(testify)*, pledge *(promise the performance of)*, posit, promise *(vow)*, recognize *(acknowledge)*, swear, testify, verify *(swear)*, vow. SEE MAIN ENTRY
avowal adjuration, admission *(disclosure)*, affidavit, affirmance *(legal affirmation)*, affirmation, assertion, asseveration, assurance, attestation, averment, avouchment, claim *(assertion)*, contract, conviction *(persuasion)*, covenant, disclosure *(something disclosed)*, jurat, oath, pledge *(binding promise)*, profession *(declaration)*, promise, recognition, recognizance, reference *(recommendation)*, statement, surety *(certainty)*, testimony, undertaking *(pledge)*. SEE MAIN ENTRY
avowal of guilt confession
avowance acknowledgment *(avowal)*, adjuration, affidavit, assurance, avouchment, avowal, common knowledge, oath, pledge *(binding promise)*, reference *(recommendation)*, surety *(certainty)*
avowed agreed *(promised)*, alleged, manifest, ostensible, putative
avowedly admittedly, purported
avulsion evulsion. SEE MAIN ENTRY
await expect *(anticipate)*, forestall, remain *(stay)*, stay *(rest)*
awaited forseen, forthcoming, prospective
awaiting expectation
awake guarded
awake a suspicion doubt *(distrust)*
awake to discern *(detect with the senses)*, discover, sensitive *(discerning)*
awaken disabuse, elicit, foment, incite, inspire, originate, perceive, provoke, stimulate
awaken memories remind
awakened acquainted, penitent, renascent
awakening moving *(evoking emotion)*, revival
award adjudge, adjudicate, adjudication, apportion, benefit *(conferment)*, bestow, bounty, cession, confer *(give)*, contribute *(supply)*, contribution *(donation)*, convey *(transfer)*, decide, decree *(noun)*, decree *(verb)*, dedicate, degree *(academic title)*, delegate, demise, determination, determine, dole, dower, endow, endowment, endue, finding, gift *(present)*, give *(grant)*, grant, grant *(transfer formally)*, gratuity *(present)*, largess *(gift)*, leave *(give)*, parcel, pass *(advance)*, pay *(noun)*, pay *(verb)*, present *(make a gift)*, prize, provide *(supply)*, recognition, relief *(legal redress)*, remunerate, remuneration, reward, ruling, tip *(gratuity)*, trover, verdict. SEE MAIN ENTRY
award assent permit
award judgment adjudicate
award of punishment sentence
awarding donative
aware acute, artful, cognizant, guarded, knowing, learned, literate, perceptive, receptive, sensitive *(discerning)*. SEE MAIN ENTRY
aware of acquainted, familiar *(informed)*
awareness appreciation *(perception)*, cognition, comprehension, insight, judgment *(discernment)*, perception, realization, reason *(sound judgment)*, recognition, sagacity, scienter, sense *(feeling)*, sense *(intelligence)*, sensibility, understanding *(comprehension)*
awareness of comprehension
away SEE MAIN ENTRY
awe fear, impress *(affect deeply)*, interest *(concern)*, panic, phobia, regard *(esteem)*, respect, trepidation. SEE MAIN ENTRY
awe-inspiring formidable, ineffable, notable, solemn, special
awe-strike overcome *(overwhelm)*
awe-struck speechless
aweless brazen, unabashed, unaffected *(uninfluenced)*
awesome formidable, ineffable, notable, sacrosanct, solemn, special
awesomeness solemnity
awestricken diffident
awestruck diffident
awful dire, heinous, lamentable. SEE MAIN ENTRY
awkward difficult, improper, inadept, incompetent, inelegant, inept *(incompetent)*, ponderous, unbecoming, uncouth, unsuitable. SEE MAIN ENTRY
awkward predicament dilemma
awkward situation dilemma, embarrassment, plight
awkwardness embarrassment
AWOL desertion
awry anomalous, astray, defective, disordered, errant, faulty, incorrect, oblique *(slanted)*
axiom dogma, maxim, postulate, precept, prescription *(directive)*
axiomatic absolute *(conclusive)*, certain *(positive)*, definite, evident, irrefutable, obvious, peremptory *(absolute)*, positive *(incontestable)*, proverbial, uncontested, undeniable, undisputed. SEE MAIN ENTRY
axiomatical evident, irrefutable, obvious, positive *(incontestable)*, undeniable
axioms premises *(hypotheses)*
axis center *(central position)*, league
ayslum inhabitation *(place of dwelling)*

B

babble jargon *(unintelligible language)*, prattle
babbling loquacious
babel imbroglio
babies children
baby infant, minor. SEE MAIN ENTRY
babyish jejune *(lacking maturity)*
babyishness puerility
bacchanalia debauchery
bacchanalianism inebriation
back abet, adhere *(maintain loyalty)*, advocate, assist, avouch *(guarantee)*, bear *(support)*, bolster, capitalize *(provide capital)*, cosign, countenance, delinquent *(overdue)*, document, encourage, endorse, espouse, favor, finance, guarantee, help, invest *(fund)*, justify, nurture, parlay *(bet)*, promote *(organize)*, recommend, sponsor, subsidize, support *(assist)*, underwrite, uphold, vouch. SEE MAIN ENTRY
back again refinance
back away retreat, shun
back away from eschew
back down abandon *(withdraw)*, accede *(concede)*, disavow, surrender *(yield)*, yield *(submit)*
back off abandon *(withdraw)*
back out abandon *(physically leave)*, abandon *(withdraw)*, defect, disavow, quit *(discontinue)*, renege, retreat, withdraw
back payments arrears
back up bear *(support)*, capitalize *(provide capital)*, encourage, side, support *(corroborate)*, uphold
back-up data
backbiting denunciation, diatribe
backbone cornerstone, gist *(substance)*, ground, main point, mainstay, prowess *(bravery)*, substance *(essential nature)*, tenacity, will *(desire)*. SEE MAIN ENTRY
backbreaking onerous, operose
backed-up fully secured
backer abettor, advocate *(espouser)*, assistant, benefactor, colleague, creditor, disciple, donor, mainstay, partisan, patron *(influential supporter)*, promoter, proponent, speculator, sponsor, surety *(guarantor)*. SEE MAIN ENTRY
backfire reaction *(opposition)*, repercussion
background atmosphere, basis, case *(set of circumstances)*, context, determinant, preparation, scene. SEE MAIN ENTRY

backhanded indirect, oblique *(evasive)*
backing advocacy, aid *(help)*, auspices, charity, coverage *(insurance)*, favor *(sanction)*, guaranty, guidance, help, indorsement, investment, loan, patronage *(power to appoint jobs)*, patronage *(support)*, promotion *(encouragement)*, reinforcement, relief *(aid)*, service *(assistance)*, subsidy, support *(assistance)*, support *(corroboration)*. SEE MAIN ENTRY
backlash reaction *(opposition)*, repercussion
backlog store *(depository)*
backroom cache *(hiding place)*
backset casualty, damper *(depressant)*, misfortune
backslide recidivate, regress, relapse, repeat *(do again)*, return *(go back)*, reversal, reversion *(act of returning)*, revert
backsliding recidivism, recrudescence, regressive, relapse. SEE MAIN ENTRY
backstair furtive
backtrack retreat, withdraw
backward back *(in reverse)*, regressive. SEE MAIN ENTRY
backward step decline
backwood provincial
baculum cudgel
bad deleterious, delinquent *(guilty of a misdeed)*, deplorable, depraved, detrimental, disastrous, disreputable, harmful, heinous, immoral, imperfect, iniquitous, nefarious, noxious, peccable, peccant *(culpable)*, perverse, poor *(inferior in quality)*, profane, reprehensible, reprobate, unfavorable, wrongful. SEE MAIN ENTRY
bad behavior miscarriage, misdeed
bad blood umbrage
bad character bad repute, disgrace, dishonor *(shame)*, disrepute, turpitude. SEE MAIN ENTRY
bad check SEE MAIN ENTRY
bad conduct malfeasance, misconduct
bad debt nonpayment. SEE MAIN ENTRY
bad example convict
bad faith dishonesty, infidelity. SEE MAIN ENTRY
bad favor dishonor *(shame)*
bad feeling odium
bad fortune calamity, casualty, misfortune, privation
bad habit vice
bad idea miscue
bad influence bad repute
bad intent ill will, malice
bad intention malice
bad job maladministration
bad judgment misestimation, misjudgment. SEE MAIN ENTRY
bad language expletive
bad light opprobrium
bad logic non sequitur
bad luck misfortune, privation
bad management misconduct
bad manners disregard *(lack of respect)*
bad match misjoinder
bad name attaint, bad character, bad repute, disgrace, dishonor *(shame)*, ignominy, ill repute, infamy, opprobrium, scandal, shame, turpitude
bad report disgrace, notoriety
bad reporting misstatement
bad reputation attaint, bad character, disgrace, dishonor *(shame)*, disrepute, ignominy, infamy, notoriety, scandal
bad repute attaint, bad character, disgrace, dishonor *(shame)*, disrepute, ignominy, ill repute, notoriety, scandal. SEE MAIN ENTRY
bad review disparagement
bad taste impropriety
bad treatment abuse *(physical misuse)*, misusage
bad turn disservice
bad wishes imprecation
bad-hearted diabolic
bad-natured perverse
bad-tempered fractious, perverse, petulant
badge brand, designation *(symbol)*, indicant, indication, indicator, manifestation, onus *(stigma)*, speciality, specialty *(distinctive mark)*, symbol, trademark
badge of infamy disgrace, dishonor *(shame)*, ignominy, stigma
badge of office device *(distinguishing mark)*
badger annoy, bait *(harass)*, browbeat, discommode, discompose, disturb, harass, harrow, harry *(harass)*, hector, importune, intimidate, irritate, mistreat, molest *(annoy)*, persecute, perturb, plague, press *(goad)*, provoke. SEE MAIN ENTRY
badinage speak
badly advised misadvised
badly calculated inopportune
badly made inferior *(lower in quality)*, poor *(inferior in quality)*
badly needed exigent
badly qualified unfit
badly timed inopportune, untimely
badness delinquency *(misconduct)*, misdoing
baffle balk, confound, confuse *(bewilder)*, dilemma, disadvantage, disorient, elude, embarrass, foil, frustrate, muddle, obfuscate, perplex, perturb, prevent, thwart. SEE MAIN ENTRY
baffled lost *(disoriented)*
bafflement ambiguity, complication, confusion *(ambiguity)*, dilemma, embarrassment, problem, quandary, surprise
baffling debatable, elusive, enigmatic, inexplicable, inscrutable, labyrinthine, mysterious
bag gain, procure
baggage cargo
baggy full
bail security *(pledge)*. SEE MAIN ENTRY
bail out discharge *(liberate)*, disenthrall, liberate
bailiff marshal
bailiwick domain *(sphere of influence)*, realm. SEE MAIN ENTRY
bailment SEE MAIN ENTRY
bailout SEE MAIN ENTRY
bait badger, bilk, cajole, coax, decoy, ensnare, entice, entrap, harry *(harass)*, hector, incentive, inveigle, lure, mislead, pique, plague, provoke, ruse, seduction, trap *(noun)*, trap *(verb)*. SEE MAIN ENTRY
bait a trap ambush
baiting bribery
balance adjust *(regulate)*, collation, comparison, compatibility, compensate *(counterbalance)*, composure, coordinate, countervail, earnings, equipoise, fairness, moderation, neutralize, offset, overage, par *(equality)*, parity, proceeds, regularity, regulate *(adjust)*, remainder *(remaining part)*, residual, sanity, stabilize, surplus, weigh. SEE MAIN ENTRY
balance accounts check *(inspect)*, quit *(repay)*
balance against compare
balance due arrears, bill *(invoice)*, nonpayment
balance owed debt
balance sheet budget, ledger, register
balance statement budget
balance to pay debt, deficit, due
balanced agreed *(harmonized)*, coextensive, consonant, equal, fair *(just)*, firm, proportionate, rational, regular *(orderly)*, sane. SEE MAIN ENTRY
balanced contrast antithesis
balanced judgment common sense
balances capital
balancing compensatory, equivalent
bald evident, honest, manifest, obvious, stark, unmistakable. SEE MAIN ENTRY
baldness honesty
bale adversity, assemblage, disaster, misfortune, tragedy
baleful bad *(offensive)*, dangerous, deadly, deleterious, destructive, dire, disadvantageous, harmful, heinous, insalubrious, lethal, malevolent, malignant, noxious, ominous, pernicious, pestilent, portentous *(ominous)*, sinister, virulent. SEE MAIN ENTRY
balefulness harm
balk bar *(obstruction)*, contravene, disadvantage, discontinue *(break continuity)*, disoblige, foil, frustrate, halt, hamper, hesitate, hold out *(resist)*, interrupt, obstacle, obstruction, oppose, prevent, refuse, stem *(check)*, stifle, thwart. SEE MAIN ENTRY
balk at avoid *(evade)*
balking disinclined, hesitant, restive
balky hesitant, intractable, recalcitrant, restive
ball sphere
ballistics ammunition
balloon expand, inflate, magnify
ballooned inflated *(enlarged)*
ballot cast *(register)*, franchise *(right to vote)*, plebiscite, poll *(casting of votes)*, poll, primary, referendum, vote. SEE MAIN ENTRY
balloter constituent *(part)*
balloting election *(selection by vote)*
balm cure, panacea, soothe
balmy medicinal, placid, remedial
bamboozle bait *(lure)*, betray *(lead astray)*, bilk, ensnare, inveigle
bamboozlement bunko, pettifoggery
ban bar *(obstruction)*, bar *(exclude)*, block, boycott, censor, constrain *(restrain)*, countermand, debar, deter, disapprobation, eliminate *(exclude)*, embargo, enjoin, estop, estoppel, exclude, exclusion, expulsion, forbid, inhibit, injunction, obstruction, ostracism, preclude, prohibit, prohibition, proscribe *(prohibit)*, proscription, refusal, rejection, relegate, restraint, suppress, veto. SEE MAIN ENTRY
banal insipid, lifeless *(dull)*, mediocre, mundane, ordinary, pedestrian, stale, trite, usual. SEE MAIN ENTRY
banality platitude
band assemblage, cabal, commingle, connect *(join together)*, consolidate *(unite)*, denomination, desegregate, federate, join *(bring together)*, league, lock, posse, zone. SEE MAIN ENTRY
band in a federation federalize *(associate)*
band of armed men posse
band of employees personnel
band of men armed with legal authority posse
band of union affiliation *(connectedness)*

band together adhere *(fasten)*, combine *(act in concert)*, concur *(agree)*, connect *(join together)*, federalize *(associate)*, join *(associate oneself with)*, meet, merge, organize *(unionize)*, pool
banded corporate *(associate)*, federal
banded together concordant, concurrent *(united)*, conjoint
bandit burglar, criminal, hoodlum, malefactor, outlaw, thief
bands ties
bandy circulate, debate
bandy with fight *(battle)*
bandy words bicker, communicate, discuss, dispute *(debate)*, speak
bane detriment, disaster, injury, trouble
baneful bad *(offensive)*, dangerous, deleterious, disadvantageous, disastrous, harmful, heinous, hostile, insalubrious, lethal, malevolent, malignant, noxious, pernicious, pestilent, sinister, virulent. SEE MAIN ENTRY
bang impinge
bang into jostle *(bump into)*
banish ban, condemn *(ban)*, dislodge, dispel, displace *(remove)*, eliminate *(exclude)*, exclude, expatriate, expel, isolate, oust, outlaw, prohibit, proscribe *(denounce)*, reject, relegate, renounce, seclude, transport. SEE MAIN ENTRY
banishment deportation, disqualification *(rejection)*, expulsion, layoff, ostracism, prohibition, proscription, rejection, removal. SEE MAIN ENTRY
bank coffer, deposit *(submit to a bank)*, edge *(border)*, fund, garner, hoard, keep *(shelter)*, margin *(outside limit)*, pool, repository, reserve, store, treasury. SEE MAIN ENTRY
bank annuities capital
bank check draft
bank note draft, money
bank notes currency
bank on rely
bank paper check *(instrument)*, draft
bank robber burglar
bankbook ledger
banker comptroller
banknote check *(instrument)*
bankroll money
bankrupt destitute, impecunious, insolvent, poor *(underprivileged)*. SEE MAIN ENTRY
bankruptcy default, privation. SEE MAIN ENTRY
banned barred, illegal, illegitimate *(illegal)*, illicit, impermissible, inadmissible
banned goods contraband
banner caption, heading
banner head caption
banner line caption
banning boycott
banshee phantom
bantling bastard
baptism call *(title)*
bar abrogate *(rescind)*, balk, ban, barrier, bench, block, blockade *(barrier)*, censor, censorship, clog, condemn *(ban)*, constrain *(restrain)*, constraint *(restriction)*, court, cudgel, damper *(stopper)*, debar, deport *(banish)*, deter, disable, disapprobation, disqualify, eliminate *(exclude)*, embargo, enjoin, estop, estoppel, exclude, exclusion, forbid, halt, hamper, impasse, impediment, inhibit, interdict, interfere, interruption, judiciary, keep *(restrain)*, key *(passport)*, lock, obstruct, obstruction, obviation, occlude, outlaw, preclude, prevent, prohibit, prohibition, proscribe *(prohibit)*, refuse, relegate, remove *(eliminate)*, resist *(oppose)*, restrain, restraint, restrict, save, seal *(close)*, shut, stall, stay, stay *(halt)*, stifle, stop, thwart, veto. SEE MAIN ENTRY
bar from access preclude
bar of justice bench, court, judicatory
bad sinister SEE MAIN ENTRY
bar someone's way halt
bar to an allegation estoppel
barbaric disorderly, uncouth
barbarity atrocity, bestiality, brutality, cruelty
barbarize brutalize
barbarous brutal, cold-blooded, cruel, disorderly, hot-blooded, malevolent, malignant, ruthless, uncouth, vicious
barbarousness bestiality, cruelty
barbiturate narcotic
bare barren, betray *(disclose)*, bleak *(exposed and barren)*, brief, clarify, confess, convey *(communicate)*, denude, devoid, disclose, disinter, divulge, expose, find *(discover)*, manifest *(adjective)*, manifest *(verb)*, marginal, mere, naked *(lacking embellishment)*, only *(no more than)*, open *(in sight)*, reveal, simple, stark, unveil, vacant, void *(empty)*. SEE MAIN ENTRY
bare possibility chance *(possibility)*, improbability
bare subsistence austerity, indigence, paucity, poverty
barefaced brazen, outrageous, unabashed
barely purely *(simply)*, solely *(purely)*
barely acceptable marginal
barely adequate marginal
barely passable poor *(inferior in quality)*
barely possible ludicrous
barely seen impalpable, inconspicuous, indefinite
bargain adjustment, agree *(contract)*, agreement *(contract)*, barter, close *(agree)*, compact, compromise, compromise *(settle by mutual agreement)*, contract, deal *(noun)*, deal *(verb)*, dicker, discount, exchange, haggle, negotiate, pact, settlement, stipulate, stipulation, term *(provision)*, trade, treaty. SEE MAIN ENTRY
bargain for buy, expect *(anticipate)*, incur. SEE MAIN ENTRY
bargain under seal specialty *(contract)*
bargain with treat *(process)*
bargainer customer
bargaining collective bargaining, commerce, negotiation
bargaining agent broker
barge in impinge, interrupt
barnacle parasite
barometer criterion. SEE MAIN ENTRY
baroque elaborate, tawdry
barrage onset *(assault)*. SEE MAIN ENTRY
barratry disloyalty
barred blind *(impassable)*, inadmissible. SEE MAIN ENTRY
barren bleak *(exposed and barren)*, deficient, devoid, futile, ineffective, ineffectual, lifeless *(dull)*, otiose, pedestrian, unavailing, unproductive, vacuous, void *(empty)*. SEE MAIN ENTRY
barrenness blank *(emptiness)*
barricade bar *(obstruction)*, bar *(hinder)*, barrier, block, blockade *(barrier)*, bulwark, check *(bar)*, clog, confine, constrict *(inhibit)*, contain *(restrain)*, damper *(stopper)*, debar, deter, enjoin, estop, halt, hamper, hinder, impede, lock, obstacle, obstruct, obstruction, occlude, protect, protection, restraint, shut, stop. SEE MAIN ENTRY
barricaded blind *(impassable)*
barrier bar *(obstruction)*, bulwark, check *(bar)*, complication, damper *(stopper)*, deterrence, deterrent, enclosure, estoppel, handicap, hindrance, impediment, limitation, mete, obstacle, obstruction, panoply, predicament, prohibition. SEE MAIN ENTRY
barring deterrent, estoppel, save
barring out lockout
barrister advocate *(counselor)*, attorney, counsel, counselor, esquire, jurist, lawyer, representative *(proxy)*. SEE MAIN ENTRY
barrister-at-law advocate *(counselor)*, counsel, counselor, lawyer
barristerial forensic
barristers bar *(body of lawyers)*
barter alienate *(transfer title)*, business *(commerce)*, commerce, deal, dealings, dicker, exchange, handle *(trade)*, interchange, sell, trade *(commerce)*, trade. SEE MAIN ENTRY
bartering commerce
basal cardinal *(basic)*, central *(essential)*, elementary, essential *(inherent)*, fundamental, naked *(lacking embellishment)*, organic, original *(initial)*, primary, prime *(original)*, primordial, rudimentary, simple
base arrant *(onerous)*, bad *(inferior)*, bad *(offensive)*, basis, caitiff, cause *(reason)*, center *(essence)*, consequence *(significance)*, contemptible, contemptuous, cornerstone, depraved, derivation, determinant, disgraceful, disreputable, felonious, foundation *(basis)*, gist *(ground for a suit)*, ground, headquarters, heinous, ignoble, immoral, inelegant, inexpiable, inferior *(lower in quality)*, iniquitous, loathsome, machiavellian, nefarious, objectionable, obnoxious, odious, outrageous, peccant *(culpable)*, perfidious, perverse, plant *(place firmly)*, poor *(inferior in quality)*, profligate *(corrupt)*, recreant, reprehensible, reprobate, scandalous, seat, site *(noun)*, site *(verb)*, sordid, subservient, unscrupulous, unseemly, unworthy. SEE MAIN ENTRY
base camp headquarters
base conduct bad faith
base of authority headquarters
base of operations headquarters
base-minded depraved, dissolute
baseborn caitiff, ignoble, illegitimate *(born out of wedlock)*
based on underlying. SEE MAIN ENTRY
based on conjecture unsupported
based on evidence deductible *(provable)*
based on evidence of the senses empirical
based on observation empirical
based on proof deductible *(provable)*
baseless arbitrary and capricious, gratuitous *(unwarranted)*, ill-founded, immaterial, insubstantial, invalid, unfounded, unsupported, unsustainable, untenable, unwarranted. SEE MAIN ENTRY
baseless charge frame up
baseness abuse *(corrupt practice)*, bad character, corruption, degradation, delinquency *(misconduct)*, discredit, disgrace, dishonor *(shame)*, disrepute, ill repute, infamy, mediocrity, perversion, scandal, shame, turpitude
baser subaltern
bases circumstances, premises *(hypotheses)*
bashful diffident
basic central *(essential)*, elementary, essential *(inherent)*, essential *(required)*,

fundamental, implicit, indispensable, initial, innate, integral, material *(important)*, naked *(lacking embellishment)*, native *(inborn)*, necessary *(required)*, organic, original *(initial)*, primary, prime *(original)*, primordial, requisite, rudimentary, simple, substantive, ultimate, underlying, virtual, vital. SEE MAIN ENTRY
basic doctrine principle *(axiom)*
basic facts SEE MAIN ENTRY
basic ingredient necessity
basic law principle *(axiom)*
basic part essence
basic rule principle *(axiom)*
basic substance component
basic truth principle *(axiom)*
basilar essential *(inherent)*, fundamental, original *(initial)*
basilary essential *(inherent)*, fundamental
basilica court
basis assumption *(supposition)*, base *(foundation)*, cause *(reason)*, center *(essence)*, consequence *(significance)*, content *(meaning)*, criterion, derivation, determinant, documentation, gist *(ground for a suit)*, gist *(substance)*, ground, main point, pattern, precedent, preparation, purpose, rationale, source, stare decisis, substance *(essential nature)*. SEE MAIN ENTRY
basis for development embryo
basis for relief cause of action
basis of argument gist *(ground for a suit)*
basis of comparison standard
basis of litigation gist *(ground for a suit)*
bask in relish
bastard illegitimate *(born out of wedlock)*. SEE MAIN ENTRY
bastardism bar sinister
bastardization bar sinister
bastardize debase
bastardy bar sinister
baste beat *(strike)*
bastille prison
bastinado beat *(strike)*, cudgel, lash *(strike)*
bastion bulwark, mainstay, security *(safety)*. SEE MAIN ENTRY
bat cudgel, strike *(assault)*
batch assemblage, body *(collection)*, bulk, congregation, quantity, selection *(collection)*
batch together glean, hoard
bate abridge *(shorten)*, attenuate, check *(restrain)*, commute, decrease, deduct *(reduce)*, dilute, diminish, ease, lessen, palliate *(abate)*
bathe imbue, immerse *(plunge into)*, permeate, pervade
baton bar sinister
batter beat *(strike)*, force *(break)*, lash *(strike)*, mishandle *(maltreat)*, mutilate, strike *(assault)*
battering ram cudgel
battery SEE MAIN ENTRY
battle affray, bicker, collision *(dispute)*, compete, conflict, confrontation *(altercation)*, contend *(dispute)*, contest *(dispute)*, contest, defy, disagree, engage *(involve)*, fracas, fray, grapple, oppose, resistance, strife, struggle. SEE MAIN ENTRY
battle maneuver strategy
battle verbally debate
battlement bulwark
battler contestant
battling belligerency, hostile, offensive *(taking the initiative)*
battology tautology
batture alluvion
bawdiness obscenity, pornography
bawdy lascivious, lecherous, lewd, licentious, obscene, prurient, salacious, suggestive *(risqué)*
bazaar exchange, market *(business)*
be exist, subsist
be a benefactor fund
be a candidate compete
be a coward fear
be a customer of patronize *(trade with)*
be a drag on impede
be a drunkard carouse
be a factor concern *(involve)*
be a feature constitute *(compose)*
be a good investment pay
be a name for denote
be a part of involve *(participate)*
be a participator in commit *(perpetrate)*
be a party to commit *(perpetrate)*, connive, contribute *(assist)*, cooperate, involve *(participate)*, partake, participate
be a reproach to disgrace
be a sign of denote, indicate
be a sound argument cohere *(be logically consistent)*
be a spectator observe *(watch)*, witness *(have direct knowledge of)*
be a suppliant call *(appeal to)*
be a token of indicate
be a winner prevail *(triumph)*
be a witness observe *(watch)*
be absorbed in devote
be abstracted muse
be accepted pass *(satisfy requirements)*
be accordant agree *(comply)*, cohere *(be logically consistent)*, coincide *(concur)*, comport *(agree with)*, correspond *(be equivalent)*
be accorded hold *(possess)*
be accountable answer *(be responsible)*
be acquainted comprehend *(understand)*
be acquainted with apprehend *(perceive)*, perceive, pierce *(discern)*
be active with occupy *(engage)*
be adjacent to abut, adjoin, border *(bound)*
be afflicted suffer *(sustain loss)*
be afraid fear
be after desire
be against confront *(oppose)*, disapprove *(reject)*
be agreeable satisfy *(fulfill)*
be ahead of precede
be akin appertain, correspond *(be equivalent)*
be alarmed fear
be alive exist
be all over cease
be allowable lie *(be sustainable)*
be ambassador for represent *(substitute)*
be ambiguous equivocate
be an accomplice commit *(perpetrate)*
be an agent for represent *(substitute)*
be an impediment constrict *(inhibit)*, hinder
be an indication of denote
be an obstacle constrict *(inhibit)*, hinder, interfere
be an obstacle to impede, interpose
be an omen portend
be anchored remain *(stay)*, stay *(rest)*
be angry resent
be annihilated perish
be answerable allow *(endure)*, answer *(be responsible)*
be answerable for avouch *(guarantee)*, justify, pledge *(promise the performance of)*, promise *(vow)*, undertake
be antagonistic collide *(clash)*
be anxious fear, mistrust
be apologist for justify
be applicable appertain, apply *(pertain)*, comport *(agree with)*
be applicable to concern *(involve)*
be apposite comport *(agree with)*
be apprehensive doubt *(distrust)*, fear, misdoubt, mistrust
be apprised understand
be apprized comprehend *(understand)*
be apprized of apprehend *(perceive)*, perceive, pierce *(discern)*
be appropriate comport *(agree with)*, lie *(be sustainable)*, pertain
be apt comport *(agree with)*
be armed forestall
be associated with attend *(accompany)*, pertain
be assuaged relent
be at an end cease
be at cross purposes conflict, counter, counteract, differ *(vary)*, dispute *(contest)*, oppose
be at cross-purposes collide *(clash)*, confront *(oppose)*, fight *(counteract)*
be at ease rest *(cease from action)*
be at fault lapse *(fall into error)*
be at hand impend, report *(present oneself)*
be at loggerheads bicker
be at one with agree *(comply)*, coincide *(concur)*, conform
be at the head of moderate *(preside over)*, preside
be at the helm overlook *(superintend)*, oversee
be at variance bicker, collide *(clash)*, conflict, demurrer, deviate, differ *(vary)*, disaccord, disagree, dispute *(contest)*, dissent *(differ in opinion)*, except *(object)*, object
be at work attempt
be at work on occupy *(engage)*
be attendant on attend *(take care of)*
be attentive consider, devote, hear *(give attention to)*, heed, immerse *(engross)*, note *(notice)*, notice *(observe)*, observe *(watch)*, regard *(pay attention)*
be attentive to attend *(heed)*, perceive
be attorney for represent *(substitute)*
be attracted gravitate
be augmented compound, expand
be auxiliary to aid
be available lie *(be sustainable)*
be averse object
be aware comprehend *(understand)*, heed, observe *(watch)*
be aware of appreciate *(comprehend)*, apprehend *(perceive)*, construe *(comprehend)*, perceive, pierce *(discern)*, recognize *(perceive)*, regard *(pay attention)*
be banded together conspire
be beholden owe
be benevolent help
be bent upon desire, pursue *(strive to gain)*
be bereft of lack
be better transcend
be better for gain, profit
be bewildered misjudge
be biased favor, preconceive, predetermine, presuppose
be blind to ignore

be born arise *(originate)*
be bound answer *(be responsible)*, avow, owe
be calm repose *(rest)*
be capable of holding accommodate
be capricious vacillate
be careful beware, hedge, heed
be careless neglect
be careless with endanger
be caused by ensue
be cautious beware, care *(be cautious)*, hedge, heed, mistrust
be censorious denounce *(condemn)*
be certain expect *(anticipate)*
be changeful fluctuate
be characteristic of appertain
be chargeable answer *(be responsible)*
be chary beware
be circumjacent encompass *(surround)*
be circumjacent to border *(bound)*
be circumspect beware
be clear cohere *(be logically consistent)*
be closeted with rendezvous
be cognizant comprehend *(understand)*
be cognizant of appreciate *(comprehend)*, apprehend *(perceive)*, perceive
be coherent cohere *(be logically consistent)*
be compassionate relent, sympathize
be compelled answer *(be responsible)*
be complemental correspond *(be equivalent)*
be compliant relent
be composed of comprehend *(include)*, comprise, consist, contain *(comprise)*, include
be compounded of contain *(comprise)*
be comprised of comprehend *(include)*, consist
be concealed camouflage, elude
be concerned care *(be cautious)*, care *(regard)*, fear
be concerned for care *(regard)*
be concerned with appertain, apply *(pertain)*, occupy *(engage)*, pertain
be concomitant coincide *(correspond)*
be concomittant concur *(coexist)*
be confident expect *(anticipate)*, rely, trust
be confounded lose *(undergo defeat)*
be confused misconstrue, misunderstand
be congruent appertain, coincide *(correspond)*, correspond *(be equivalent)*
be congruous cohere *(be logically consistent)*
be connected to pertain
be connected with appertain, apply *(pertain)*, attend *(accompany)*
be conscience striken repent
be conscious comprehend *(understand)*, observe *(watch)*
be conscious of appreciate *(comprehend)*, apprehend *(perceive)*, detect, heed, notice *(observe)*, perceive, pierce *(discern)*, regard *(pay attention)*
be consistent comport *(agree with)*
be consonant comport *(agree with)*
be conspicuous flaunt
be constant adhere *(persist)*, endure *(last)*, keep *(continue)*, persevere, remain *(continue)*
be constituted of contain *(comprise)*
be consumed decrease
be contained in consist
be contemporaneous coincide *(correspond)*, concur *(coexist)*
be contemporary concur *(coexist)*
be contemptuous condescend *(patronize)*
be contemptuous of contemn, disdain, flout, misprize
be conterminous border *(bound)*
be contiguous abut, border *(bound)*, contact *(touch)*
be continguous to adjoin
be contrary collide *(clash)*, conflict, counter, counteract, countervail, differ *(vary)*, disagree, disapprove *(reject)*, dispute *(debate)*, dissent *(differ in opinion)*, fight *(counteract)*, gainsay, oppugn
be contrary to contravene, oppose
be conversant with comprehend *(understand)*
be converted change
be convinced opine
be convivial carouse
be counted vote
be courteous condescend *(deign)*
be cowardly fear
be critical complain *(criticize)*
be cunning cheat, circumvent, delude, illude, scheme
be daunted fear
be debited with overdraw
be deceitful bear false witness, fake, palter, pretend
be deceived err, misapprehend, misconceive, misread, mistake
be deceptive misstate, palter
be defeated fail *(lose)*, lose *(undergo defeat)*, succumb
be deficient default, lack
be dejected brood
be delinquent default
be demoted fail *(lose)*
be dense cohere *(adhere)*
be dependent on rely
be dependent upon appertain
be deprived of forfeit, lack, lose *(be deprived of)*
be deputy for represent *(substitute)*
be derelict break *(violate)*, default, disobey
be derived accrue *(arise)*, arise *(originate)*
be derogatory derogate
be deserving earn
be desirous lack
be destitute lack
be destroyed degenerate, lose *(undergo defeat)*, perish
be determined persevere, persist
be determined to intend
be determined to get pursue *(strive to gain)*
be devoid of truth bear false witness
be devoted adhere *(maintain loyalty)*, adhere *(persist)*
be devoted to obey
be different conflict, deviate
be diffuse digress
be dilatory defer *(put off)*, delay, hesitate, hold up *(delay)*, procrastinate
be diligent labor
be disappointed lose *(undergo defeat)*
be disclosed bare
be discordant bicker, collide *(clash)*, conflict, contend *(dispute)*, differ *(disagree)*, disagree
be discourteous offend *(insult)*
be dishonest bear false witness, betray *(lead astray)*, cheat, hoodwink, lie *(falsify)*, mislead, palter, prevaricate
be disjoined estrange
be disloyal defect, disobey, rebel
be disposed to choose
be disrespectful flout
be dissatisfied complain *(criticize)*
be dissimilar differ *(vary)*
be distended expand
be distinct differ *(vary)*
be distinguished from deviate, differ *(vary)*
be distracted muse
be disturbed over regret
be disunited disagree
be dormant remain *(stay)*, stay *(rest)*
be doubtful disbelieve, doubt *(distrust)*, misdoubt, mistrust, oscillate, suspect *(distrust)*
be drunk carouse
be dubious doubt *(distrust)*, hesitate, mistrust, pause, suspect *(distrust)*
be due owe
be due to ensue, result
be durable continue *(persevere)*, endure *(last)*
be eager desire
be economical retrench
be effaced disappear
be effective function, prevail *(triumph)*
be efficacious prevail *(triumph)*
be effusive outpour
be employed labor, occupy *(engage)*, practice *(engage in)*
be engaged in commit *(perpetrate)*
be engrossed in commit *(perpetrate)*, concentrate *(pay attention)*, devote
be entitled to as a matter of right, earn
be equivalent compensate *(counterbalance)*
be eradicated perish
be erased disappear
be erroneous bear false witness, err, miscalculate, misread, misstate, mistake
be established lie *(be sustainable)*
be established in inhabit
be evasive evade *(deceive)*, palter, prevaricate
be even with quit *(repay)*
be evidence of manifest
be evident lie *(be sustainable)*
be extinguished perish
be extravagant dissipate *(expend foolishly)*
be faithful adhere *(maintain loyalty)*
be faithful to comply, fulfill, keep *(fulfill)*, obey, observe *(obey)*, perform *(adhere to)*
be faithless bear false witness, default
be fallacious bear false witness
be false bear false witness, equivocate, misrepresent, palter, perjure
be false to betray *(lead astray)*
be familiar with recognize *(perceive)*
be favorable to authorize, bestow, favor
be fearful fear
be firm endure *(last)*, maintain *(sustain)*, resolve *(decide)*
be firmly fixed maintain *(sustain)*
be fitting lie *(be sustainable)*
be fixed stay *(rest)*
be foiled lose *(undergo defeat)*
be fond of prefer, regard *(hold in esteem)*, relish
be forewarned beware, forestall
be forfeited back escheat
be forgiving relent
be formed of comprise, consist, contain *(comprise)*, include
be forsworn bear false witness

be forthcoming impend
be fraudulent bear false witness, palter
be frightened fear
be frugal retrench
be fruitful proliferate, propagate *(increase)*, pullulate
be frustrated lose *(undergo defeat)*
be given acquire *(receive)*, collect *(recover money)*, receive *(acquire)*
be given to understand construe *(comprehend)*
be gluttonous overindulge
be gone abandon *(physically leave)*, depart, part *(leave)*
be good to avail *(be of use)*
be governed by obey
be gracious condescend *(deign)*
be graduated pass *(satisfy requirements)*
be granted a legacy inherit
be greater surpass
be greater in value outbalance
be greater in weight outbalance
be greedy overindulge
be guarded beware
be guided by hear *(give attention to)*, heed, obey, observe *(obey)*
be guilty of perpetrate
be guilty of infraction break *(violate)*
be handed down to devolve
be handed over devolve
be harbinger portend
be harmonious attune
be hateful alienate *(estrange)*
be heir to hold *(possess)*
be helpful contribute *(assist)*
be horrified fear
be humbled lose *(undergo defeat)*
be hurtful ill use, mistreat
be hypocritical palter, pretend
be identical coincide *(correspond)*
be idle loiter, procrastinate
be ignorant misunderstand
be imminent impend
be immobile remain *(stay)*, stay *(rest)*
be immoderate carouse, dissipate *(expend foolishly)*
be immovable remain *(stay)*
be immune resist *(withstand)*
be impaired suffer *(sustain loss)*
be impolite offend *(insult)*
be impoverished lose *(be deprived of)*
be impressed regard *(hold in esteem)*
be improved by gain, profit
be in a quandary doubt *(hesitate)*
be in a reverie muse
be in accordance with comport *(agree with)*
be in action attempt
be in antagonism collide *(clash)*
be in arrears default
be in attendance appear *(attend court proceedings)*, report *(present oneself)*
be in authority moderate *(preside over)*, preside
be in awe fear, regard *(hold in esteem)*
be in charge preside
be in collusion maneuver, plot
be in collusion with connive
be in conflict with contravene
be in conjunction with border *(bound)*
be in contact with border *(bound)*
be in control prevail *(triumph)*
be in debt default, overdraw, owe
be in effect exist
be in error misapprehend, miscalculate, misconstrue
be in favor of approve, authorize, consent, countenance, embrace *(accept)*, pass *(approve)*, permit
be in general use prevail *(be in force)*, prevail *(triumph)*
be in harmony conform
be in harmony with agree *(comply)*
be in keeping comport *(agree with)*, conform
be in league with involve *(participate)*, participate
be in need lack
be in operation function
be in opposition disagree
be in possession of hold *(possess)*, own, possess
be in possession of the facts comprehend *(understand)*
be in power govern, manage, rule *(govern)*
be in present force exist
be in proximity approach
be in receipt of obtain, own, possess
be in sight appear *(materialize)*
be in sight of approach
be in store impend
be in the ascendant prevail *(triumph)*
be in the chair preside
be in the majority predominate *(outnumber)*
be in the neighborhood of approach
be in the running compete
be in the vicinity of approach, approximate, border *(approach)*
be in the way impede
be in the wrong err, mistake, misunderstand
be in tune with comport *(agree with)*
be in unison agree *(comply)*
be in want lack
be inadequate lack
be inattentive ignore, muse, neglect
be inattentive to overlook *(superintend)*
be incident to appertain
be inclined to think assume *(suppose)*, deem, presuppose
be incompatible collide *(clash)*
be incongruent differ *(disagree)*
be inconsistent conflict
be inconstant change, palter, vacillate, vary
be incredulous disbelieve, doubt *(distrust)*
be incurious disregard
be indebted owe
be indecisive oscillate
be indifferent disregard
be indifferent to discount *(disbelieve)*
be indignant resent
be indiscreet impart
be indulgent of allow *(endure)*, permit
be indulgent toward favor
be industrious labor
be inert procrastinate, remain *(stay)*, stay *(rest)*
be inferior lack
be influenced predetermine
be influential prevail upon
be informed comprehend *(understand)*, pierce *(discern)*, understand
be informed of perceive
be inharmonious conflict, differ *(disagree)*, differ *(vary)*
be inherent constitute *(compose)*
be inimical collide *(clash)*, counter
be injured suffer *(sustain loss)*
be inmovable stay *(rest)*
be insensitive disregard
be insincere bear false witness, palter
be insolent disparage
be instrumental pander
be insubordinate disobey, rebel
be insufficient lack
be insulted resent
be intelligible cohere *(be logically consistent)*
be intemperate carouse, debauch, dissipate *(expend foolishly)*, overindulge
be intent upon pursue *(strive to gain)*
be interdependent with concern *(involve)*
be intermittent fluctuate
be intimate cohabit
be intimidated fear
be intolerant persecute
be intrinsic appertain
be involved concern *(involve)*, participate
be irresolute change, doubt *(hesitate)*, hesitate, misdoubt, oscillate, pause, vacillate
be jaundiced preconceive, predetermine, presuppose, select
be joined conjoin
be joined to adjoin
be juxtaposed border *(bound)*
be lax neglect
be left behind lose *(undergo defeat)*
be lenient bear *(tolerate)*, condone, palliate *(excuse)*, relax, tolerate
be liable answer *(be responsible)*, owe
be loath disfavor, mistrust
be located dwell *(reside)*, reside
be logical cohere *(be logically consistent)*
be long-lived last
be lost to view disappear
be loyal adhere *(maintain loyalty)*
be loyal to obey
be lucid cohere *(be logically consistent)*
be made of comprise, consist
be made up of comprehend *(include)*, consist, include
be malevolent bait *(harass)*, endanger, harass, harm, ill use, mistreat, persecute
be malicious persecute
be manifest appear *(attend court proceedings)*, appear *(materialize)*
be master direct *(supervise)*
be master of handle *(manage)*, hold *(possess)*, own
be mendacious bear false witness, palter
be merciful condone, relent
be mindful concern *(care)*, regard *(pay attention)*
be misguided err, miscalculate, misconceive, mistake, misunderstand
be misinformed misconceive
be misled err, misapprehend, miscalculate, misconceive, misconstrue, misinterpret, mistake, misunderstand
be mistaken err, misapprehend, miscalculate, misconceive, misread, mistake, misunderstand
be mixed desegregate
be mollified relent
be more specific elaborate
be motionless remain *(stay)*, stay *(rest)*
be moved sympathize
be mutinous disobey
be mutually opposed collide *(clash)*
be near approach, approximate, border *(approach)*, impend
be near at hand impend, threaten
be needy lack
be neglectful default, procrastinate

be negligent default, disobey
be nervous doubt *(distrust)*, fear, misdoubt, mistrust
be no more die
be noisy brawl
be null and void perish
be numerous compound, proliferate
be nurtured subsist
be obedient obey
be obligated answer *(be responsible)*, owe
be obliged answer *(be responsible)*
be oblique deviate
be obstinate adhere *(persist)*, insist, persevere, persist, refuse
be obstructive balk, clog, counter, fight *(counteract)*, foil, frustrate, inconvenience
be occupied in concentration muse
be occupied in study muse
be occupied with address *(direct attention to)*
be of contrary sentiment dissent *(differ in opinion)*
be of different opinions disagree
be of greater significance outweigh
be of help assist
be of service aid, avail *(be of use)*, contribute *(assist)*, pander
be of the opinion assume *(suppose)*, deem, guess, surmise, suspect *(think)*
be of the same mind coincide *(concur)*
be of use assist, help, inure *(benefit)*, profit, serve *(assist)*
be of value avail *(be of use)*
be off abandon *(physically leave)*, leave *(depart)*
be offended resent
be offensive affront, bait *(harass)*, harry *(harass)*, mistreat, persecute
be offered hold *(possess)*
be on one's guard beware
be on the alert beware, patrol
be on the lookout beware, patrol
be on the watch beware, patrol
be one unite
be one of concern *(involve)*
be one with coincide *(concur)*, merge
be opposed conflict, disagree
be opposed to conflict, cross *(disagree with)*, disapprove *(reject)*
be opposite confront *(oppose)*, differ *(vary)*
be ostentatious flaunt
be outdistanced lose *(undergo defeat)*
be outvoted lose *(undergo defeat)*
be overawed fear
be overbearing condescend *(patronize)*
be overthrown lose *(undergo defeat)*
be paid collect *(recover money)*
be parallel concur *(coexist)*
be part of appertain, constitute *(compose)*
be partial discriminate *(treat differently)*
be partial to favor, prefer
be partisan adhere *(maintain loyalty)*
be patent appear *(seem to be)*
be patient bear *(tolerate)*, forbear
be peaceful rest *(cease from action)*
be penitent regret, repent
be peremptory insist
be perfidious bear false witness, disobey, palter
be periodic alternate *(fluctuate)*, fluctuate
be perjured bear false witness
be permanent continue *(persevere)*, endure *(last)*, remain *(continue)*
be permissible lie *(be sustainable)*
be permitted lie *(be sustainable)*
be perplexed misjudge
be persistent recur
be persuaded concede, grant *(concede)*, opine
be pertinent appertain, apply *(pertain)*
be pertinent to concern *(involve)*
be petrified fear
be piqued resent
be pitiless brutalize, mistreat
be placated relent
be pleased with relish
be plentiful proliferate
be pliant relent
be poor lack
be possessed of hold *(possess)*, occupy *(take possession)*, own
be possible lie *(be sustainable)*
be precise detail *(particularize)*
be predisposed discriminate *(treat differently)*
be prejudiced favor, forejudge, preconceive, predetermine, presuppose, select
be prepared beware, expect *(anticipate)*
be prepossessed predetermine
be present appear *(attend court proceedings)*, dwell *(reside)*, remain *(occupy)*
be present and note witness *(have direct knowledge of)*
be present to answer appear *(attend court proceedings)*
be preserved endure *(last)*
be prevalent prevail *(triumph)*
be prewarned beware
be prodigal bestow, dissipate *(expend foolishly)*, overdraw
be productive pullulate
be proffered hold *(possess)*
be profitable avail *(be of use)*, inure *(benefit)*, pay
be prolix outpour
be prolonged endure *(last)*
be promoted pass *(satisfy requirements)*
be prone to gravitate
be proper lie *(be sustainable)*
be proper to apply *(pertain)*
be protracted endure *(last)*
be provoked resent
be proxy for represent *(substitute)*
be prudent beware
be public bare, circulate
be published circulate
be puzzled doubt *(hesitate)*
be quartered reside
be quiescent desist
be quiet rest *(cease from action)*
be racked suffer *(sustain loss)*
be rash forejudge
be rationally connected cohere *(be logically consistent)*
be ready for anticipate *(expect)*
be reasonable cohere *(be logically consistent)*
be recalcitrant disobey
be reconciled condone, suffer *(permit)*
be recusant disobey
be reduced in worth decay, degenerate
be regulated by conform, obey, observe *(obey)*
be related correspond *(be equivalent)*
be related to concern *(involve)*
be relevant apply *(pertain)*, concern *(involve)*
be reminded of recall *(remember)*, recollect, remember
be remiss default
be remorseful regret
be resident in inhabit
be resigned suffer *(permit)*
be resolute choose, endeavor, insist, persevere, persist
be resolute in prosecute *(carry forward)*
be respondent countercharge
be responsible cause, compose, create, induce
be responsible for guarantee, sponsor
be responsive acknowledge *(respond)*, answer *(reply)*, countercharge
be revengeful resent
be rewarded reap
be rife pervade, predominate *(outnumber)*
be riveted stay *(rest)*
be rude affront, disparage, harry *(harass)*, ignore, mistreat
be ruined lose *(undergo defeat)*, perish
be ruled by obey
be ruthless persecute
be satisfied opine
be satisfied with approve, recommend
be scared fear
be scornful flout
be sedentary remain *(stay)*, stay *(rest)*
be seized of possess
be selfish overindulge
be sensitive to perceive
be serene repose *(rest)*
be servile pander
be settled dwell *(reside)*
be settled in opinion resolve *(decide)*
be severe castigate
be severed part *(separate)*
be showy flaunt
be silent cease
be simultaneous coincide *(correspond)*
be situated dwell *(reside)*, reside
be skeptical disbelieve, doubt *(distrust)*, impugn, misdoubt, mistrust, suspect *(distrust)*
be sly circumvent
be so good as to deign
be so minded choose
be solid crystallize
be sorry for deplore, regret, repent, sympathize
be sovereign predominate *(command)*
be specific describe, designate, enumerate, itemize, pinpoint
be spokesman for represent *(substitute)*
be spurious bear false witness
be stable last
be startled fear
be stationary remain *(stay)*, stay *(rest)*
be stationed dwell *(reside)*
be steadfast adhere *(maintain loyalty)*, adhere *(persist)*, keep *(continue)*, persevere, persist, prolong, prosecute *(carry forward)*, remain *(continue)*
be steady adhere *(persist)*, persevere, persist
be stealthy conspire, lurk, prowl
be still rest *(cease from action)*
be stricken suffer *(sustain loss)*
be strong resist *(withstand)*
be stubborn persevere
be subject answer *(be responsible)*, obey
be subjected to bear *(tolerate)*, endure *(suffer)*, suffer *(sustain loss)*
be submissive relent, surrender *(yield)*, yield *(submit)*
be submissive to observe *(obey)*
be subsequent ensue, succeed *(follow)*, supervene
be subservient pander

be successful attain, earn, pass *(satisfy requirements),* prevail *(triumph)*
be sufficient fulfill, satisfy *(fulfill)*
be suitable comport *(agree with),* lie *(be sustainable),* pertain
be suited lie *(be sustainable)*
be sundered part *(separate)*
be superior beat *(defeat),* outbalance, surpass, transcend
be superior in number predominate *(outnumber)*
be supportable lie *(be sustainable)*
be supported subsist
be supreme beat *(defeat),* predominate *(command)*
be surety answer *(be responsible)*
be surety for avouch *(guarantee),* cosign
be suspicious doubt *(distrust),* suspect *(distrust)*
be sustained subsist
be swallowed up merge
be swayed predetermine
be sworn certify *(attest),* testify
be tacked together cohere *(adhere)*
be taken for exemplify
be temperate forbear, refrain
be tenacious persevere, persist, remain *(continue)*
be tentative hesitate
be terrified fear
be the agent compose, create
be the author create
be the author of cause
be the cause generate
be the cause of compose, create, engender, evoke
be the chairman preside
be the effect result
be the effect of ensue
be the embodiment personify
be the equivalent of exemplify
be the guiding force oversee
be the heir of inherit
be the outcome result
be the reason compose, create
be the victor prevail *(triumph)*
be thorough follow-up
be thwarted lose *(undergo defeat)*
be timeless endure *(last),* last
be timid fear
be tolerant condone, forbear, relent
be touched sympathize
be tranquil repose *(rest),* rest *(cease from action)*
be transferred devolve
be transfixed remain *(stay),* stay *(rest)*
be treasonable rebel
be treasonous disobey
be triumphant prevail *(triumph)*
be true adhere *(maintain loyalty)*
be true to keep *(fulfill)*
be unable to respect decry, disgrace
be unaccommodating disoblige
be uncandid palter
be uncertain confound, doubt *(distrust),* doubt *(hesitate),* hesitate, misdoubt, mistrust, oscillate, pause, tergiversate, vacillate
be unclear equivocate
be unconsumed last
be unconvinced disbelieve
be uncooperative inconvenience
be undecided doubt *(hesitate),* oscillate
be under legal obligation answer *(be responsible)*
be under obligation owe
be under the impression apprehend *(perceive),* deem
be understandable cohere *(be logically consistent)*
be understanding sympathize
be undetermined doubt *(hesitate),* misdoubt, oscillate
be undisciplined disobey
be unexhausted last
be unfaithful default
be unfriendly alienate *(estrange)*
be unique differ *(vary)*
be united join *(associate oneself with)*
be unlike differ *(vary),* vary
be unpalatable repel *(disgust)*
be unresolved oscillate
be unruly disobey
be unseen lurk
be unsettled alternate *(fluctuate),* vacillate
be unsteady fluctuate, oscillate, vacillate
be unsuccessful fail *(lose),* lose *(undergo defeat)*
be unsure oscillate, tergiversate, vacillate
be unsusceptible resist *(withstand)*
be untruthful bear false witness, equivocate, fabricate *(make up),* lie *(falsify),* palter, perjure, prevaricate
be unwilling conflict, disoblige, dissent *(withhold assent),* hold out *(resist),* refuse
be unyielding adhere *(persist),* persevere, persist
be uppermost in the mind occur *(come to mind)*
be useful avail *(be of use),* function, pander
be vagrant loiter
be vague equivocate
be vengeful resent
be vexed resent
be vicious to brutalize
be victorious carry *(succeed),* pass *(satisfy requirements),* prevail *(triumph),* succeed *(attain)*
be victorious over beat *(defeat),* overthrow
be vigilant caution, concern *(care),* observe *(watch)*
be violent fight *(battle),* mistreat
be voracious overindulge
be vouchsafed hold *(possess)*
be wanting lack
be warned beware
be warranted lie *(be sustainable)*
be wary beware
be watchful concern *(care)*
be wicked to brutalize
be willing agree *(comply),* comply, consent
be willing to bear assume *(undertake)*
be without lack, lose *(be deprived of)*
be worse degenerate
be worthy earn
be wounded suffer *(sustain loss)*
be wrong miscalculate, misconstrue
beach littoral
beachfront littoral
beacon indicant, indicator
beam emit, radiate
bear allow *(endure),* carry *(transport),* demean *(deport oneself),* endure *(suffer),* engender, produce *(manufacture),* propagate *(increase),* resist *(withstand),* suffer *(sustain loss),* tolerate, transmit, transport, yield *(produce a return).* SEE MAIN ENTRY
bear a grudge against discriminate *(treat differently)*
bear a part contribute *(assist)*
bear away distrain, hijack, impropriate
bear down coerce, pressure
bear down against compel
bear down on press *(constrain)*
bear down upon attack
bear false witness frame *(charge falsely),* lie *(falsify),* misrepresent, palter, perjure, prevaricate. SEE MAIN ENTRY
bear fruit avail *(bring about),* succeed *(attain)*
bear hard upon compel
bear heavily weigh
bear in memory remember
bear in mind care *(be cautious),* regard *(pay attention),* remember, retain *(keep in possession)*
bear malice alienate *(estrange),* discriminate *(treat differently),* mistreat, resent
bear no malice forgive
bear no resemblance deviate, differ *(vary)*
bear off deviate, kidnap
bear on appertain
bear oneself deport *(conduct oneself)*
bear out attest, certify *(attest),* corroborate, document, evidence, justify, substantiate, support *(corroborate),* sustain *(confirm),* verify *(confirm),* witness *(attest to)*
bear pain endure *(suffer)*
bear resemblance correspond *(be equivalent)*
bear the cost bear the expense, defray, pay
bear the cost of disburse *(pay out),* expend *(disburse)*
bear the expense defray. SEE MAIN ENTRY
bear the expense of disburse *(pay out),* expend *(disburse)*
bear the responsibility of hold *(possess)*
bear up resist *(withstand),* uphold
bear up against maintain *(sustain),* stem *(check)*
bear up under endure *(suffer)*
bear upon affect, apply *(pertain),* based on, pertain, prejudice *(influence),* refer *(direct attention),* relate *(establish a connection).* SEE MAIN ENTRY
bear with condone, excuse, forbear, submit *(yield),* suffer *(permit),* tolerate, vouchsafe
bear without resistance endure *(suffer)*
bear witness acknowledge *(declare),* avouch *(avow),* avow, certify *(attest),* corroborate, notarize, promise *(vow),* seal *(solemnize),* speak, substantiate, swear, testify, vouch, witness *(attest to).* SEE MAIN ENTRY
bear witness against betray *(disclose),* denounce *(inform against),* inform *(betray)*
bear witness to attest, certify *(attest),* depose *(testify),* evidence
bearable fair *(satisfactory),* passable
beard defy
beardless inexperienced
bearer SEE MAIN ENTRY
bearing behavior, color *(complexion),* conduct, connection *(relation),* connotation, content *(meaning),* demeanor, deportment, direction *(course),* magnitude, manner *(behavior),* position *(point of view),* posture *(attitude),* presence *(poise),* relation *(connection),* relationship *(connection),* relevance, semblance, significance, tendency
bearing good will benevolent
bearing no name anonymous
bearing offspring freely fertile
bearing on relative *(relevant)*
bearing on the question pertinent
bearing out corroboration

bearing revenue lucrative
bearing the cost collection *(payment)*
bearing upon apposite, cognate, germane, incident
bearings locality
bearish brutal, fractious, petulant, severe
beast animal
beast of burden animal
beast of the field animal
beastliness bestiality, disrepute
beastly brutal, disreputable, heinous, obnoxious, odious, repulsive, vicious
beat attack, defeat, kill *(defeat)*, lash *(strike)*, oscillate, outweigh, overcome *(surmount)*, overwhelm, stress *(accent)*, strike *(assault)*, subdue, subjugate, surmount, surpass, territory, upset. SEE MAIN ENTRY
beat a retreat quit *(evacuate)*
beat back repel *(drive back)*, repulse, resist *(oppose)*
beat down browbeat, haggle, subdue
beat off parry, repulse, stave
beatable vulnerable
beaten despondent, passable
beatific ecstatic
beatify elevate
beating battery, defeat, failure *(lack of success)*
beauteous attractive
beautification motif
beautified elaborate
beautiful attractive, elegant
beautify embellish, meliorate
becalm pacify, soothe
becalmed dormant
because consequently. SEE MAIN ENTRY
because of this a priori
bechance supervene
beckon call *(summon)*, entrap, request, subpoena, summon
beckoning attractive
becloud blind *(obscure)*, camouflage, confound, cover *(conceal)*, disguise, muddle, obfuscate, obnubilate, obscure, shroud
become arise *(originate)*, comport *(agree with)*, convert *(change use)*, develop, evolve, germinate. SEE MAIN ENTRY
become a citizen reside
become a component incorporate *(include)*
become a fact occur *(happen)*
become a member join *(associate oneself with)*
become a participator espouse
become a partisan espouse
become a party to an action intervene
become a reality crystallize
become acquainted rendezvous
become acquainted with ascertain, discern *(detect with the senses)*, find *(discover)*
become added accrue *(increase)*
become an ingredient incorporate *(include)*
become apparent develop, emerge
become apprised of find *(discover)*
become apprized discern *(detect with the senses)*
become aware note *(notice)*, occur *(come to mind)*, realize *(understand)*
become aware of apprehend *(perceive)*, detect, discern *(detect with the senses)*, hear *(perceive by ear)*, notice *(observe)*, overhear, perceive
become bankrupt fail *(lose)*, overdraw
become better progress
become bound promise *(vow)*, stipulate
become bound to pledge *(promise the performance of)*
become broad expand
become connected with join *(associate oneself with)*
become conscious note *(notice)*, realize *(understand)*
become conscious of hear *(perceive by ear)*, notice *(observe)*, perceive
become definite crystallize
become delineated crystallize
become depraved degenerate
become detached disengage
become deteriorated degenerate, depreciate
become disheartened languish
become due accrue *(arise)*, mature
become enfeebled decay, degenerate
become enforceable accrue *(arise)*
become extinct disappear, perish
become familiar with practice *(train by repetition)*
become firm crystallize
become flexible give *(yield)*
become forfeit lapse *(cease)*
become free escape
become fully developed mature
become greater accrue *(increase)*, appreciate *(increase)*, compound, expand, increase
become habituated naturalize *(acclimate)*
become heir to accede *(succeed)*
become ill languish
become impaired degenerate
become imperceptible disappear
become inactive quit *(discontinue)*
become informed discern *(detect with the senses)*, discover, find *(discover)*
become insolvent fail *(lose)*, overdraw
become involved care *(regard)*, engage *(involve)*
become involved with participate
become known convey *(communicate)*, occur *(happen)*
become larger accrue *(increase)*, compound, expand, increase
become less active subside
become less rigid give *(yield)*
become liable guarantee
become liable for incur
become like conform
become lower in quality decay, degenerate
become manifest arise *(appear)*, emerge
become more numerous appreciate *(increase)*
become notably worse degenerate
become noticeable arise *(appear)*
become of greater value appreciate *(increase)*
become of less worth depreciate
become one consolidate *(unite)*, unite
become operative arise *(occur)*
become payable mature
become perfected mature
become perverted degenerate
become plain emerge
become pliant give *(yield)*
become poorer by lose *(be deprived of)*
become present accrue *(arise)*
become prime mature
become public circulate
become putrescent decay
become responsible for assume *(undertake)*, incur
become ripe mature
become settled crystallize
become similar conform
become smaller decrease, diminish
become solid cohere *(adhere)*, crystallize
become surety for guarantee
become tainted degenerate
become unable to meet obligations default
become visible appear *(materialize)*, arise *(appear)*, crystallize, emerge, occur *(come to mind)*
become void cease, expire, lapse *(cease)*
become weak languish
become worse degenerate, deteriorate
becoming attractive, consonant, favorable *(advantageous)*, felicitous, fit, fitting, harmonious, palatable, proper, rightful, suitable
becoming greater cumulative *(increasing)*
becoming larger cumulative *(increasing)*
becoming more intense cumulative *(intensifying)*
becomingness propriety *(appropriateness)*
becripple disable
becurtain blind *(obscure)*, camouflage
bed lodge *(house)*, plant *(place firmly)*
bedaub stain
bedazzle discompose, disconcert
bedeck clothe, embellish
bedecked elaborate
bedevil annoy, discompose, disconcert, disorganize, distress, disturb, embarrass, harass, harrow, obsess, perplex, persecute, pique, plague
bedevilment detriment, harm, nuisance
bedim blind *(obscure)*, camouflage, obfuscate, obnubilate, obscure, sully
bedizen embellish
bedizened meretricious, tawdry
bedlam imbroglio, pandemonium, riot, turmoil
bedraggled disordered
bedrape clothe
bedridden disabled *(made incapable)*
bedrock center *(essence)*, foundation *(basis)*. SEE MAIN ENTRY
bedwarf minimize
befall supervene
befalling accident *(chance occurrence)*, chance *(fortuity)*, contingency, experience *(encounter)*
befit applicable, comport *(agree with)*, pertain
befitting applicable, apposite, appropriate, condign, convenient, due *(regular)*, eligible, favorable *(advantageous)*, felicitous, fit, just, opportune, proper, rightful, seasonable, suitable, tenable
befog blind *(obscure)*, camouflage, confuse *(bewilder)*, cover *(conceal)*, disorganize, muddle, obscure, shroud
befogged lost *(disoriented)*
befool bait *(lure)*, betray *(lead astray)*, bilk, cheat, deceive, defraud, delude, dupe, entrap, hoodwink, humiliate, illude, inveigle, misguide, mislead
before theretofore. SEE MAIN ENTRY
before further examination prima facie *(self-evident)*
before mentioned last *(preceding)*, said
before now heretofore
before one's eyes perceivable
before time premature
before-mentioned aforesaid. SEE MAIN ENTRY

beforehand aforethought. SEE MAIN ENTRY
beforesaid aforesaid
befoul contaminate, corrupt, debase, infect, pillory, pollute, stain, taint *(contaminate),* tarnish
befouled tainted *(contaminated)*
befoulment contaminate
befriend favor, foster, promote *(organize),* side, sponsor, subsidize
befriender good samaritan, samaritan
befuddle confuse *(bewilder),* discompose, disorganize, disorient, disturb, muddle, obfuscate
befuddled lost *(disoriented)*
befuddlement confusion *(ambiguity)*
beg exhort, importune, press *(beseech),* pressure, urge
beg a favor call *(appeal to),* desire
beg for invoke, request
beg leave call *(appeal to)*
beg pardon repent
beg the question prevaricate
beg to be excused refuse
beg to differ demur
beget create, elicit, engender, generate, make, originate, produce *(manufacture),* propagate *(increase),* reproduce
begetter architect, author *(originator),* derivation, parents
begettor progenitor
beggar deplete, parasite
beggared impecunious, poor *(underprivileged)*
beggarliness poverty
beggarly destitute, ignoble, impecunious, petty, poor *(inferior in quality)*
beggary poverty, privation
begging request
begin arise *(originate),* assume *(undertake),* commence, conceive *(invent),* embark, establish *(launch),* generate, initiate, launch *(initiate),* maintain *(commence),* originate, preface, provoke, stem *(originate),* undertake, unveil. SEE MAIN ENTRY
begin a corporation incorporate *(form a corporation)*
begin again continue *(resume),* proceed *(continue),* reopen, resume
begin from develop
begin hostilities against attack
begin over continue *(resume)*
begin where one left off proceed *(continue)*
beginner amateur, apprentice, neophyte, novice, probationer *(one being tested)*
beginning causative, creation, derivation, elementary, embryo, foundation *(basis),* genesis, inception, inchoate, incipient, initial, nascency, onset *(commencement),* origin *(source),* original *(initial),* origination, outset, overture, preamble, precursory, preface, preliminary, prelude, preparatory, prime *(original),* primordial, rudimentary, source, start, threshold *(commencement).* SEE MAIN ENTRY
beginning before retroactive
beginnings overt act
begird circumscribe *(surround by boundary),* embrace *(encircle),* encompass *(surround),* include
begloom obfuscate, obscure
begotten born *(alive)*
begrime deface, pollute, sully
begrudge withhold
begrudging jealous, reluctant
beguile bait *(lure),* betray *(lead astray),* bilk, cheat, circumvent, cloak, deceive, defraud, delude, disarm *(set at ease),* dupe, ensnare, entrap, evade *(deceive),* fabricate *(make up),* fake, feign, foist, hoodwink, illude, interest, inveigle, lure, misguide, mislead, misrepresent, palter, pettifog, pretend, propitiate
beguilement artifice, deceit, deception, falsification, fraud, hoax, knavery, pretense *(pretext)*
beguiling attractive, collusive, deceptive, delusive, dishonest, evasive, fallacious, false *(not genuine),* fraudulent, insidious
begun but not completed inchoate
behalf SEE MAIN ENTRY
behave demean *(deport oneself),* deport *(conduct oneself),* obey
behave towards treat *(process)*
behaved obedient
behavior conduct, demeanor, deportment, modus operandi, practice *(custom),* presence *(poise),* procedure, protocol *(etiquette),* way *(manner).* SEE MAIN ENTRY
behavior pattern conduct, manner *(behavior)*
behaviorism casuistry
behest canon, demand, dictate, directive, mandate, order *(judicial directive),* process *(summons),* request, requirement, requisition
behind back *(in arrears),* delinquent *(overdue)*
behind bars in custody
behind the age outdated, outmoded
behind the scenes clandestine, latent
behind the times outdated, outmoded
behind time back *(in arrears),* dilatory, late *(tardy),* overdue
behindhand delinquent *(overdue)*
behold detect, discern *(detect with the senses),* discover, notice *(observe),* observe *(watch),* pierce *(discern),* regard (pay attention), spy, witness (have direct knowledge of). SEE MAIN ENTRY
beholdable discernible, manifest, open *(in sight),* perceivable, perceptible, scrutable
beholden accountable *(responsible),* bound, indebted, loyal
beholder bystander, witness
behoof advantage, behalf, benefit *(betterment)*
behoove pertain
being character *(an individual),* entity, identity *(individuality),* individual, person, personality, presence *(attendance),* reality, survival. SEE MAIN ENTRY
being analyzed at issue
being done current
being in ill repute disreputable
being in two corresponding parts bipartite
being of no importance collateral *(immaterial)*
bejewel embellish
belated back *(in arrears),* dilatory, late *(tardy),* overdue
belaud honor. SEE MAIN ENTRY
belay handcuff
beleaguer attack, contain *(enclose),* envelop, harry *(harass)*
belie bear false witness, cloak, deceive, disguise, disprove, fake, falsify, feign, lie *(falsify),* misrepresent, prevaricate, refute
belief assumption *(supposition),* concept, conjecture, credence, credulity, doctrine, dogma, estimate *(idea),* faith, idea, impression, notion, presumption, principle *(axiom),* reliance, stand *(position),* standpoint, supposition, theory, thesis, trust *(confidence),* weight *(credibility).* SEE MAIN ENTRY
beliefs behavior
believability credibility, probability
believable convincing, credible, defensible, ostensible, plausible, possible, presumptive, probable, reliable, specious, tenable, unimpeachable. SEE MAIN ENTRY
believableness credibility
believe deem, expect *(consider probable),* guess, opine, presume, presuppose, surmise, suspect *(think).* SEE MAIN ENTRY
believe in confide *(trust),* rely
believe on consideration deem
believed convincing, putative, uncontested, undisputed
believer addict, disciple, partisan
believing convincing, credulous, naive, orthodox, positive *(confident),* unsuspecting
belittle cavil, condescend *(patronize),* contemn, decry, defame, demean *(make lower),* demote, denigrate, denounce *(condemn),* deprecate, depreciate, derogate, dilute, diminish, disapprove *(condemn),* discommend, discount *(disbelieve),* disdain, disparage, lessen, minimize, misprize, pillory, smear, spurn, sully, underestimate. SEE MAIN ENTRY
belittlement disparagement, disregard *(lack of respect)*
belittling derogatory, disparagement, pejorative
bellicose contentious, disorderly, impertinent *(insolent),* inimical, insolent, litigious, malevolent, offensive *(taking the initiative),* perverse, provocative, pugnacious, spartan
bellicosity belligerency
belligerance belligerency
belligerant inimical
belligerency argument *(contention),* conflict, ill will, strife. SEE MAIN ENTRY
belligerent aggressor, argumentative, contentious, contestant, disputant, foe, litigious, malevolent, negative, perverse, pugnacious, spiteful
bellowing blatant *(obtrusive)*
belong comport *(agree with),* constitute *(compose),* correspond *(be equivalent),* pertain
belong as a part appertain
belong as an attribute appertain
belong intrinsically constitute *(compose)*
belong to affiliate, apply *(pertain),* join *(associate oneself with)*
belonger member *(individual in a group)*
belonging applicable, appurtenant, chattel, cognate, collateral *(accompanying),* correlative, holding *(property owned),* incident, pertinent, possession *(property)*
belonging equally to common *(shared)*
belonging to apposite, germane
belonging to all common *(shared)*
belonging to another country foreign
belonging to courts of justice forensic
belonging to debate forensic
belonging to many common *(shared)*
belonging to the house domestic *(household)*
belonging to the time current
belongings assets, capital, effects, estate *(property),* goods, interest *(ownership),* merchandise, personalty, possessions, property *(possessions)*
beloved popular
below a savoir. SEE MAIN ENTRY

below contempt loathsome
below par defective, deficient, faulty, ignoble, imperfect, inferior *(lower in quality)*, marginal, nonsubstantial *(not sturdy)*, paltry, peccable, perfunctory, poor *(inferior in quality)*, unsound *(not strong)*
below standard poor *(inferior in quality)*
below standards defective
below the mark minimal
below the surface latent
belt circumscribe *(surround by boundary)*, contain *(enclose)*, embrace *(encircle)*, encompass *(surround)*
bemask blind *(obscure)*, camouflage, disguise, pretend
bemingle denature
bemire pollute, sully
bemist obfuscate
bemoan deplore, regret, repent
bemock disparage, jape
bemuddle confuse *(bewilder)*
bemuddled disordered, lost *(disoriented)*
bemuse perplex
ben trovato colorable *(plausible)*
bench bar *(court)*, chamber *(body)*, court, judicatory, judicature, judiciary, tribunal. SEE MAIN ENTRY
bench of judges chamber *(body)*
bench warrant search warrant
bencher jurist
benchmark SEE MAIN ENTRY
bend conform, contort, dispose *(incline)*, distort, relax, relent, subdue, submit *(yield)*, succumb, yield *(submit)*
bend out of shape contort
bend to obey
bend to one's will persuade, prejudice *(influence)*
bendable flexible, malleable, pliable, pliant, resilient, sequacious, tractable
bending flexible, malleable, sequacious
bene moratus law-abiding, moral
beneath consideration inappreciable
beneath contempt blameworthy, loathsome, offensive *(offending)*, paltry. SEE MAIN ENTRY
beneath notice inappreciable, inconsiderable, negligible, null *(insignificant)*, paltry
beneath one's dignity disgraceful
beneath standards defective
benediction laudation
benefaction aid *(subsistence)*, appropriation *(donation)*, behalf, benefit *(betterment)*, benefit *(conferment)*, benevolence *(act of kindness)*, boom *(prosperity)*, bounty, charity, clemency, contribution *(donation)*, donation, endowment, favor *(act of kindness)*, favor *(sanction)*, gift *(present)*, goodwill, grant, gratuity *(present)*, help, inheritance, largess *(generosity)*, largess *(gift)*, perquisite, profit, tip *(gratuity)*
benefactor backer, contributor *(giver)*, donor, good samaritan, patron *(influential supporter)*, promoter, proponent, receiver, samaritan, sponsor. SEE MAIN ENTRY
benefactress donor
beneficence benevolence *(act of kindness)*, benevolence *(disposition to do good)*, clemency, consideration *(sympathetic regard)*, goodwill, humanity *(humaneness)*, largess *(generosity)*, philanthropy
beneficent beneficial, charitable *(benevolent)*, charitable *(lenient)*, donative, humane, liberal *(generous)*, magnanimous, nonprofit, philanthropic
beneficent friend benefactor
beneficentia charity
bénéficiaire heir
beneficial ancillary *(auxiliary)*, contributory, convenient, corrigible, favorable *(advantageous)*, gainful, instrumental, lucrative, medicinal, operative, palliative *(abating)*, practical, profitable, propitious, purposeful, remedial, salubrious, salutary, valuable. SEE MAIN ENTRY
beneficial interest claim *(right)*
bénéfficiare beneficiary
beneficiary devisee, donee, grantee, heir, legatee, receiver, recipient, successor, transferee. SEE MAIN ENTRY
beneficience benefit *(conferment)*
beneficient benevolent
beneficium favor *(act of kindness)*, privilege
beneficus charitable *(benevolent)*
benefit accommodate, advantage, aid *(help)*, aid *(subsistence)*, aid, assistance, avail *(be of use)*, behalf, bonus, capitalize *(seize the chance)*, contribution *(donation)*, dividend, edge *(advantage)*, edification, endowment, favor *(act of kindness)*, favor, function, gain, grant, help *(noun)*, help *(verb)*, largess *(gift)*, output, preference *(priority)*, prerogative, privilege, proceeds, profit *(noun)*, profit *(verb)*, promote *(organize)*, promotion *(encouragement)*, realize *(obtain as a profit)*, reap, recourse, reward, service *(assistance)*, use, utility *(usefulness)*, value, welfare, worth. SEE MAIN ENTRY
benefit of doubt compurgation
benefiter benefactor
benefits consideration *(recompense)*
benevolence assistance, behalf, benefit *(conferment)*, bounty, charity, clemency, comity, consideration *(sympathetic regard)*, favor *(act of kindness)*, goodwill, help, humanity *(humaneness)*, indulgence, lenience, philanthropy, understanding *(tolerance)*. SEE MAIN ENTRY
benevolent charitable *(lenient)*, donative, humane, lenient, liberal *(generous)*, meritorious, nonprofit, paternal, philanthropic, placable, propitious. SEE MAIN ENTRY
benevolentia benevolence *(act of kindness)*, philanthropy
benevolently fairly *(impartially)*
benevolentness charity
benevolus benevolent
benight blind *(obscure)*, obscure
benighted blind *(not discerning)*, incognizant, opaque
benightedness ignorance
benign beneficial, benevolent, charitable *(lenient)*, favorable *(expressing approval)*, harmless, humane, nontoxic, paternal, philanthropic, propitious, remedial, safe, salutary. SEE MAIN ENTRY
benign favor auspices
benignancy benevolence *(disposition to do good)*, humanity *(humaneness)*, largess *(generosity)*, philanthropy
benignant beneficial, charitable *(lenient)*, philanthropic, propitious
benignitas indulgence
benignity clemency, consideration *(sympathetic regard)*, favor *(act of kindness)*, humanity *(humaneness)*, largess *(generosity)*, philanthropy
benignus charitable *(benevolent)*
bent animus, aptitude, character *(personal quality)*, design *(intent)*, desire, direction *(course)*, disposition *(inclination)*, favor *(partiality)*, frame *(mood)*, inclination, inclined, instinct, partiality, penchant, pertinacious, position *(point of view)*, posture *(attitude)*, preconception, predilection, predisposition, prejudice *(preconception)*, proclivity, prone, propensity, resolute, stand *(position)*, standpoint, tendency
bent on solicitous
bent upon eager, earnest, insistent, zealous
benumb drug, obtund
benumbed insensible, torpid
benumbing chilling effect, lifeless *(dull)*
bepraise honor
bequeath abalienate, bestow, cede, contribute *(supply)*, convey *(transfer)*, demise, descend, devise *(give)*, devolve, endow, give *(grant)*, grant *(transfer formally)*, leave *(give)*, pass *(advance)*, present *(make a gift)*, transfer. SEE MAIN ENTRY
bequeathable heritable
bequeathal bequest, demise *(conveyance)*, devolution, endowment, grant, legacy, will *(testamentary instrument)*
bequeathed by will testamentary
bequeather donor, feoffor, grantor
bequest benefit *(conferment)*, contribute *(supply)*, contribution *(donation)*, devolution, donation, dower, endowment, estate *(hereditament)*, grant, hereditament, heritage, inheritance, legacy. SEE MAIN ENTRY
berate blame, castigate, censure, complain *(criticize)*, condemn *(blame)*, criticize *(find fault with)*, decry, defame, denounce *(condemn)*, deprecate, disapprove *(condemn)*, fault, lash *(attack verbally)*, mistreat, pillory, rebuke, remonstrate, reprehend, reprimand, reproach. SEE MAIN ENTRY
berating contumely, objurgation, obloquy, revilement
bereave deprive, despoil
bereaved disconsolate
bereaved child orphan
bereavement cost *(penalty)*, privation
bereft bankrupt, destitute
bereft of devoid, insufficient
bereft of funds poor *(underprivileged)*
bereft of life dead, deceased, lifeless *(dead)*
bereft of reason deranged, lunatic, non compos mentis
beribbon embellish
berserk frenetic
berth employment, lodge *(house)*, lodging, office, post, seat, trade *(occupation)*
beseech call *(appeal to)*, exhort, importune, petition, plead *(implore)*, pray, pressure, prevail upon, request, solicit, sue, urge. SEE MAIN ENTRY
beseeching precatory, solicitous
beseechment call *(appeal)*, entreaty, prayer, request
beseige dun, envelop
beset accost, assail, attack, badger, bait *(harass)*, discommode, dun, embarrass, envelop, harass, harrow, harry *(harass)*, hector, importune, inflict, obsess, perplex, persecute, pique, plague, press *(goad)*, provoke
beset with danger dangerous
beset with difficulties painful
beset with difficulty difficult
beset with perils aleatory *(perilous)*
besetting hostile

besetting idea compulsion (*obsession*)
beside adjacent, contiguous
beside oneself ecstatic
beside the mark impertinent (*irrelevant*), inapposite, irrelevant
beside the point immaterial, impertinent (*irrelevant*), inapposite, irrelevant, needless, nonessential, peripheral
beside the question immaterial, impertinent (*irrelevant*), irrelevant, nonessential
besides also, further, save
besiege assault, attack, bait (*harass*), harass, harrow, importune, obsess, overwhelm, strike (*assault*)
besiegement assault
besieger aggressor
besmear brand (*stigmatize*), defame, denigrate, denounce (*condemn*), disgrace, dishonor (*deprive of honor*), disparage, pillory, smear, stain, sully
besmirch brand (*stigmatize*), contemn, defame, denigrate, denounce (*condemn*), derogate, discredit, dishonor (*deprive of honor*), infect, libel, malign, pillory, pollute, smear, stain, taint (*contaminate*). SEE MAIN ENTRY
besmirched blemished
besmirching defilement
besmut smear
bespangle embellish
bespangled pretentious (*ostentatious*)
bespatter brand (*stigmatize*), defame, denigrate, derogate, disparage, humiliate, pillory, pollute
bespeak call (*appeal to*), denote, evince, indicate, manifest, reserve. SEE MAIN ENTRY
bespread diffuse
besprinkle diffuse
best absolute (*ideal*), cardinal (*outstanding*), premium, prime (*most valuable*), select, subdue, superlative, transcend, utmost. SEE MAIN ENTRY
best behavior decorum
best evidence rule SEE MAIN ENTRY
best of taste decorum
best part elite
best people elite
bestead avail (*be of use*), promote (*organize*), situated
bestial brutal
bestiality brutality. SEE MAIN ENTRY
bestir oneself endeavor, strive
bestow bear (*yield*), confer (*give*), contribute (*supply*), dedicate, delegate, descend, devise (*give*), dispel, dispense, dole, endow, endue, fund, furnish, give (*grant*), grant (*transfer formally*), impart, leave (*give*), mete, parcel, post, present (*make a gift*), provide (*supply*), spend, subsidize, supply, transfer, vouchsafe, yield (*produce a return*). SEE MAIN ENTRY
bestow by judicial decree award
bestow by will demise
bestow in shares disperse (*disseminate*)
bestow on administer (*tender*)
bestow thought upon muse
bestow upon bequeath, dispense, vest
bestow voluntarily grant (*transfer formally*)
bestowable heritable
bestowal appropriation (*donation*), benefit (*conferment*), cession, charity, concession (*authorization*), contribution (*donation*), conveyance, dedication, dispensation (*act of dispensing*), dower, endowment, grant, legacy, will (*testamentary instrument*)
bestowed gratuitous (*given without recompense*)
bestowed by ballot elective (*selective*)
bestower contributor (*giver*), donor, feoffor, grantor, obligee
bestowing donative
bestowment conveyance, dispensation (*act of dispensing*), donation, dower, endowment, gift (*present*), largess (*gift*), tip (*gratuity*)
bestowment of a share contribution (*donation*)
bestrew cast (*throw*), diffuse, dispel, disperse (*disseminate*), dissipate (*spread out*), spread
bet gamble, lottery, risk, speculate (*chance*), speculation (*risk*), stake (*award*). SEE MAIN ENTRY
bet on parlay (*bet*)
betoken anticipate (*prognosticate*), denote, evince, exemplify, herald, indicate, label, manifest, portend, predict, presage, prognosticate, promise (*raise expectations*), signify (*denote*)
betokening success auspicious
betongue lash (*attack verbally*), reprehend
betray bear false witness, bilk, cheat, defect, disobey, misrepresent, palter, rebel. SEE MAIN ENTRY
betray the secret inform (*betray*)
betrayal bad faith, bad repute, disloyalty, infidelity, treason
betrayal of a trust treason
betrayal of oath infidelity
betrayal of trust disloyalty, infidelity
betraying perfidious, recreant
betrayment bad faith
betrothed conjugal, nuptial
better ameliorate, amend, bettor, embellish, emend, enhance, help, meliorate, meritorious, outbalance, outweigh, preferable, preferential, promote (*advance*), rectify, reform, relieve (*give aid*), superior (*excellent*), surpass, transcend, treat (*remedy*). SEE MAIN ENTRY
better part generality (*bulk*), majority (*greater part*)
betterment advancement (*improvement*), amendment (*correction*), behalf, correction (*change*), development (*progression*), edification, headway, improvement, progress, promotion (*advancement*), reform, reorganization, repair
betterment SEE MAIN ENTRY
bettor betterment speculator. SEE MAIN ENTRY
between among, intermediate
bevy assemblage, band
bewail deplore, regret, repent
bewailing querulous
beware care (*be cautious*). SEE MAIN ENTRY
bewilder confound, discompose, disorganize, disorient, disturb, embarrass, misguide, muddle, obfuscate, overcome (*overwhelm*), overwhelm, perplex, perturb
bewildered insensible, lost (*disoriented*), speechless
bewildering complex, enigmatic, equivocal, labyrinthine, opaque
bewilderment ambiguity, bombshell, confusion (*ambiguity*), enigma, ignorance, incertitude, quandary, surprise
bewitch lure, obsess
bewitching attractive, sapid
bewitchment seduction
beyond further
beyond a doubt definitive, undeniable
beyond a question demonstrable
beyond a reasonable doubt SEE MAIN ENTRY
beyond a shadow of a doubt clear (*certain*), incontrovertible
beyond a shadow of doubt categorical, certain (*positive*)
beyond all dispute certain (*positive*), clear (*certain*), decisive, definite, definitive, inappealable
beyond all doubt demonstrable
beyond all praise prime (*most valuable*)
beyond all question axiomatic, categorical, certain (*positive*), decisive, definite, inappealable, incontestable, positive (*incontestable*), undeniable
beyond belief implausible, incredible, ludicrous
beyond compare absolute (*ideal*), best, leading (*ranking first*), paramount, prime (*most valuable*)
beyond comparison paramount, unique
beyond comprehension inapprehensible, incomprehensible
beyond contradiction incontrovertible
beyond control impracticable, insuperable, intractable
beyond correction irremediable
beyond cure irremediable
beyond dispute axiomatic, conclusive (*settled*), undeniable
beyond doubt absolute (*conclusive*), explicit, irrefutable, positive (*incontestable*), uncontroverted, undisputed
beyond expression indefinable, ineffable
beyond help incorrigible
beyond hope irremediable
beyond one's power insurmountable
beyond one's reach difficult, insurmountable
beyond price inestimable, invaluable, priceless
beyond question inappealable, undisputed
beyond reach inaccessible, unapproachable
beyond recall irrecoverable, irremediable, irrevocable
beyond redress irremediable
beyond reform incorrigible
beyond remedy irredeemable, irremediable, irreversible
beyond reproach unimpeachable
beyond the bounds of possibility insurmountable
beyond the jurisdiction of the court want of jurisdiction
beyond the limit extreme (*exaggerated*)
beyond the ordinary extraordinary
beyond understanding inapprehensible
bhang cannabis
bi-facial bilateral
bias bait (*lure*), discrimination (*bigotry*), dispose (*incline*), disposition (*inclination*), favor (*partiality*), favoritism, inclination, inequality, inequity, injustice, intolerance, nepotism, partiality, penchant, position (*point of view*), preconception, predetermination, predilection, predisposition, preference (*choice*), prejudice (*preconception*), prejudice (*influence*), proclivity, propensity, slant, stand (*position*), tendency. SEE MAIN ENTRY
biased disadvantageous, ex parte, exclusive (*limited*), illiberal, interested, one-sided, parochial, partisan, preferential, prejudicial,

prone, subjective, unequal *(unjust)*, unfair, unjust
biased judgment inequity, partiality
bibacity dipsomania
bibliophilic learned
bibulosity inebriation
bibulousness inebriation
bicameral bipartite. SEE MAIN ENTRY
bicker brawl, contend *(dispute)*, dicker, differ *(disagree)*, disaccord, disagree, dispute *(debate)*, dissent *(differ in opinion)*. SEE MAIN ENTRY
bickering altercation, argument *(contention)*, contest *(dispute)*, discord, dispute, dissension, dissidence, fight *(argument)*, fracas, fractious, negative, pugnacious
bid appeal *(noun)*, appeal *(verb)*, application, call *(appeal)*, command, detail *(assign)*, dictate, direct *(order)*, endeavor *(noun)*, endeavor *(verb)*, enjoin, impose *(enforce)*, insist, instruct *(direct)*, invitation, invoke, mandate, offer *(propose)*, overture, petition *(noun)*, petition *(verb)*, pray, prescribe, proffer, proposition, request *(noun)*, request *(verb)*, summon, summons, writ. SEE MAIN ENTRY
bid against counter, counteract
bid come call *(summon)*
bid defiance to challenge
bid fair promise *(raise expectations)*
bid farewell leave *(depart)*
bid for attempt, dicker, haggle, negotiate, pursue *(strive to gain)*, strive
bid-rigging SEE MAIN ENTRY
biddable loyal, obedient, pliable, resigned
bid-rigging SEE MAIN ENTRY
bidder applicant *(candidate)*, customer, rival
bidding demand, directive, guidance, injunction, instruction *(direction)*, invitation, monition *(legal summons)*, process *(summons)*, requirement, requisition, writ
bide continue *(persevere)*, defer *(put off)*, endure *(suffer)*, last, persist, reside
bide time pause
bienséance decorum
bifurcate dichotomize, divergent, part *(separate)*. SEE MAIN ENTRY
bifurcated bicameral, bipartite, divergent
bifurcated trial SEE MAIN ENTRY
bifurcation dichotomy, severance, split
bifurcous bipartite
big capacious, extensive, gross *(flagrant)*, important *(significant)*, major, momentous, ponderous, prodigious *(enormous)*. SEE MAIN ENTRY
big-hearted benevolent
biggest part generality *(bulk)*
biggest share majority *(greater part)*
bighearted philanthropic
bigness mass *(weight)*
bigot SEE MAIN ENTRY
bigoted exclusive *(limited)*, illiberal, narrow, partial *(biased)*
bigotry bias, inequity, intolerance
bilateral mutual *(reciprocal)*, reciprocal. SEE MAIN ENTRY
bilateral contract mutual understanding
bile resentment, umbrage
bileful bilious
bilious bitter *(penetrating)*, dyseptic, malevolent. SEE MAIN ENTRY
bilk defraud, dupe, ensnare, peculate, pilfer. SEE MAIN ENTRY
bilked aggrieved *(harmed)*
bill act *(enactment)*, amendment *(legislation)*, cash, charge *(assess)*, check *(instrument)*, codification, debt, draft, enactment, instrument *(document)*, measure, receipt *(voucher)*. SEE MAIN ENTRY
bill drafter lawmaker
bill of accounts dun
bill of attainder SEE MAIN ENTRY
bill of complaint allegation, claim *(legal demand)*
bill of costs dun
bill of exchange check *(instrument)*, draft, security *(stock)*
bill of indemnity exoneration
bill of indictment accusation, complaint
bill of lading invoice *(itemized list)*
bill of particulars SEE MAIN ENTRY
billet domicile, dwell *(reside)*, employment, job, lodging, note *(brief comment)*, office, post, residence, role
billing publicity
billingsgate profanity, revilement
bills currency, debit, legislation *(enactments)*
billy cudgel
bind affix, amalgamate, annex *(add)*, attach *(join)*, cement, combine *(join together)*, confine, connect *(join together)*, consolidate *(strengthen)*, constrain *(imprison)*, constrict *(compress)*, contain *(enclose)*, contain *(restrain)*, detain *(restrain)*, engage *(hire)*, estop, fetter, hamper, handcuff, impose *(enforce)*, join *(bring together)*, limit, pledge *(promise the performance of)*, press *(constrain)*, promise *(vow)*, restrain, restrict, trammel. SEE MAIN ENTRY
bind by a pledge promise *(vow)*
bind oneself pledge *(promise the performance of)*, promise *(vow)*
bind oneself by oath promise *(vow)*, swear
bind together commingle
binder connection *(fastening)*. SEE MAIN ENTRY
binding accession *(annexation)*, attachment *(act of affixing)*, choate lien, coalescence, coalition, compelling, compulsory, concurrent *(united)*, contractual, decretal, essential *(required)*, forcible, fully executed *(signed)*, indefeasible, irrevocable, mandatory, necessary *(required)*, obligatory, positive *(prescribed)*, prescriptive, requisite, stringent, unavoidable *(not voidable)*, valid. SEE MAIN ENTRY
binding agreement adjustment, contract, covenant, testament
binding promise agreement *(contract)*
bioecology ecology
bioethic SEE MAIN ENTRY
bioethics SEE MAIN ENTRY
biographical record journal
bionomics ecology
bipartisanship conciliation, consensus
bipartite bicameral. SEE MAIN ENTRY
bipartition dichotomy
birch lash *(strike)*
birdbrained opaque
birth bloodline, creation, derivation, descent *(lineage)*, family *(common ancestry)*, genesis, inception, nascency, nationality, onset *(commencement)*, origin *(ancestry)*, origin *(source)*, origination, outset, parentage, race, start. SEE MAIN ENTRY
birth out of wedlock bar sinister
birthplace derivation, home *(place of origin)*, origin *(source)*
birthright bequest, descent *(lineage)*, droit, estate *(hereditament)*, heritage. SEE MAIN ENTRY
bisect bifurcate, cross *(intersect)*, dichotomize, divide *(separate)*, split, subdivide
bisectable divisible
bisected bicameral, bipartite, divisive
bisection dichotomy, split, subdivision
bit iota, minimum, part *(portion)*, scintilla, segment
biting bitter *(acrid tasting)*, bitter *(penetrating)*, bitter *(reproachful)*, caustic, harsh, incisive, mordacious, offensive *(offending)*, scathing, trenchant
bitter antipathetic *(distasteful)*, astringent, dyseptic, harsh, hostile, malevolent, malignant, mordacious, resentful, virulent. SEE MAIN ENTRY
bitter animosity malice
bitter enemy foe
bitter feelings ill will, rancor
bitter harangue diatribe
bitter language philippic
bitter words diatribe, phillipic, revilement
bitterness alienation *(estrangement)*, feud, ill will, rancor, resentment, spite, umbrage
bivium intersection
bizarre eccentric, egregious, inept *(inappropriate)*, irrational, ludicrous, noteworthy, novel, peculiar *(curious)*, prodigious *(amazing)*, unaccustomed, uncommon, unique, unusual. SEE MAIN ENTRY
bizarreness nonconformity, quirk *(idiosyncrasy)*
blabber jargon *(unintelligible language)*
blabbing loquacious
black deplorable, heinous, iniquitous, outrageous, portentous *(ominous)*, scandalous
black marketeer bootlegger
black out eradicate, expunge
black-listing boycott
black-market impermissible
blackball condemn *(ban)*, denounce *(condemn)*, exclusion, humiliate, ostracism, picket, reject
blackballing boycott
blacken brand *(stigmatize)*, deface, defame, denigrate, denounce *(condemn)*, derogate, disgrace, disparage, humiliate, obfuscate, obnubilate, obscure, pillory, smear, stain, sully, tarnish
blacken one's good name denigrate
blackening calumnious, defilement, pejorative, vilification
blackguard criminal, hoodlum, lash *(attack verbally)*, unconscionable
blackhearted malignant
blackjack cudgel
blacklist bar *(exclude)*, denounce *(condemn)*, isolate, ostracism
blackmail coercion, compel, extort, extortion, graft, hush money, threaten. SEE MAIN ENTRY
blackmailer extortionist
blackout censorship, insentience, obscuration
blamable blameful, blameworthy, culpable, delinquent *(guilty of a misdeed)*, guilty, peccable, reprehensible
blame accuse, arraign, assignation, censure, charge *(accusation)*, charge *(accuse)*, cite *(accuse)*, complain *(charge)*, complain *(criticize)*, conviction *(finding of guilt)*, criticism, criticize *(find fault with)*, culpability, denounce *(inform against)*, denunciation, diatribe, disparagement, fault *(responsibility)*, fault, guilt, impeach, impeachability, impeachment, impute, incriminate, incrimination, inculpation,

indict, involve *(implicate)*, obloquy, odium, ostracism, outcry, present *(prefer charges)*, proscribe *(denounce)*, rebuke, reprehend, reprimand *(noun)*, reprimand *(verb)*, reproach *(noun)*, reproach *(verb)*, stricture. SEE MAIN ENTRY
blame falsely frame *(charge falsely)*
blame oneself regret
blame unfairly frame *(charge falsely)*
blame unjustly frame *(charge falsely)*
blameful blameworthy, delinquent *(guilty of a misdeed)*, peccant *(culpable)*, reprehensible. SEE MAIN ENTRY
blameless clean, incorruptible, inculpable, innocent, irreprehensible, not guilty, pardonable, unimpeachable. SEE MAIN ENTRY
blamelessness innocence
blameworthiness blame *(culpability)*, culpability, guilt, impeachability, onus *(blame)*
blameworthy blameful, contemptible, culpable, delinquent *(guilty of a misdeed)*, disgraceful, guilty, inexcusable, inexpiable, loathsome, notorious, obnoxious, odious, peccable, peccant *(culpable)*, reprehensible, reprobate, sinister, unjustifiable, vicious. SEE MAIN ENTRY
blameworthy conduct criminality
blaming critical *(faultfinding)*, incriminatory, inculpatory
blandish coax, inveigle, persuade, pressure
blandishment bribery, inducement, mention *(tribute)*, persuasion, seduction
blank bleak *(exposed and barren)*, devoid, form *(document)*, inexpressive, inscrutable, nonentity, oblivious, thoughtless, vacant, vacuous, void *(empty)*. SEE MAIN ENTRY
blanked blind *(impassable)*
blanket absolute *(complete)*, blind *(obscure)*, broad, camouflage, complete *(all-embracing)*, cover *(protection)*, ensconce, enshroud, envelop, generic, indiscriminate, omnibus, shroud
blankness indifference, insentience, nullity
blare barrage, noise, proclaim
blase casual
blasé dispassionate
blase nonchalant
blaspheme malign
blaspheming expletive
blasphemous offensive *(offending)*, profane
blasphemy imprecation, profanity. SEE MAIN ENTRY
blast barrage, destroy *(efface)*, discharge *(shot)*, discharge *(shoot)*, extirpate, inveigh, outburst, repercussion
blasting blasphemy, discharge *(shot)*
blatancy noise, pretense *(ostentation)*
blatant brazen, flagrant, manifest, open *(in sight)*, tawdry. SEE MAIN ENTRY
blatant violation of law lynch law
blather jargon *(unintelligible language)*, prattle *(noun)*, prattle *(verb)*
blaze brand *(mark)*, burn, conflagration, deflagrate, outburst, promulgate, propagate *(spread)*
blaze abroad proclaim
blazon disclose, embellish, herald, inform *(notify)*, promulgate, propagate *(spread)*, publish, reveal
bleak devoid, jejune *(dull)*. SEE MAIN ENTRY
bleakness damper *(depressant)*
blear blind *(obscure)*
bleared nebulous
bleed deplete, exude
blemish damage, deface, defacement, defame, defect, denigrate, detriment, disgrace, dishonor *(shame)*, flaw, foible, frailty, handicap, mutilate, onus *(stigma)*, smear, spoil *(impair)*, stain, stigma, sully, taint *(contaminate)*, tarnish, vice. SEE MAIN ENTRY
blemished defective, deficient, faulty, imperfect, inferior *(lower in quality)*, marred. SEE MAIN ENTRY
blend amalgamate, attune, bond *(hold together)*, combine *(join together)*, commingle, conjoin, connect *(join together)*, consolidate *(strengthen)*, converge, denature, desegregate, integration *(amalgamation)*, join *(bring together)*, melange, merge, pool, solution *(substance)*, unite
blended composite, compound, concerted, concurrent *(united)*, conglomerate, conjoint, harmonious, inseparable, miscellaneous, promiscuous
blending coherence, concordant, concrescence, integration *(amalgamation)*
blessed sacrosanct
blessing laudation, permission
blessings prosperity
blight calamity, casualty, damage, decay, destroy *(efface)*, disaster, distress *(anguish)*, impair, infect, pain, spoil *(impair)*, spoilage, taint *(contaminate)*, thwart, vitiate. SEE MAIN ENTRY
blight one's optical powers blind *(deprive of sight)*
blighted marred, tainted *(contaminated)*
blighted hope pessimism
blighting disastrous
blind camouflage, cloak, deceive, deception, decoy, heedless, hidden, hoodwink, ill-judged, inadvertent, incognizant, injudicious, insensible, insusceptible *(uncaring)*, obfuscate, obnubilate, obscure, opaque, random, ruse, stratagem, unwitting. SEE MAIN ENTRY
blind chance accident *(chance occurrence)*
blind faith credulity
blind to impervious
blind zeal discrimination *(bigotry)*
blinded unaware
blindfold hoodwink
blindness ignorance, nescience
bliss enjoyment *(pleasure)*
blissful ecstatic
blister burn
blistered blemished
blitz barrage
blitzkrieg onset *(assault)*
bloat inflate, spread
bloated inflated *(enlarged)*
bloatedness inflation *(increase)*
bloc cartel, league, organization *(association)*, society
block arrest *(stop)*, balk, ban, bar *(obstruction)*, bar *(hinder)*, bind *(restrain)*, blockade *(barrier)*, bulk, censorship, check *(bar)*, check *(restrain)*, clog, condemn *(ban)*, constrain *(restrain)*, constrict *(inhibit)*, contain *(restrain)*, damper *(stopper)*, deadlock, debar, defeat, delay, deter, deterrence, deterrent, disadvantage, disqualify, encumber *(hinder)*, enjoin, exclude, forbid, halt *(noun)*, halt *(verb)*, hamper, hinder, hold up *(delay)*, impasse, impede, impediment, interdict, interfere, interpose, interruption, keep *(restrain)*, kill *(defeat)*, limitation, lock, obstacle, obstruct, obstruction, obturate, occlude, oppose, parcel, parry, plot *(land)*, preclude, prevent, procrastinate, prohibit, prohibition, real estate, resist *(oppose)*, section *(vicinity)*, shut, stall, stave, stay *(halt)*, stem *(check)*, stifle, stop, strangle, toll *(stop)*, withhold, withstand. SEE MAIN ENTRY
block off seal *(close)*, shut
block out delineate, frame *(construct)*, plan, program
block the way estop
block up clog, encumber *(hinder)*, estop, shut, stop
blockade bar *(hinder)*, block, contain *(enclose)*, control *(restriction)*, deterrence, disadvantage, eliminate *(exclude)*, enclose, enclosure, enjoin, estop, exclude, halt, hindrance, impasse, impede, impediment, lock, obstruction, occlude, ostracism, picket, restrain, restraint, seclude, shut, stop, strike *(refuse to work)*. SEE MAIN ENTRY
blockaded blind *(impassable)*
blockage bar *(obstruction)*, blockade *(barrier)*, censorship, check *(bar)*, damper *(stopper)*, deadlock, disadvantage, estoppel, filibuster, impasse, impediment, obstruction, obviation
blockbuster bomb
blocked arrested *(checked)*, blind *(impassable)*, impervious
blocking preventive, resistance
blockish obtuse, opaque, thoughtless
blockishness opacity
blood ancestry, bloodline, descent *(lineage)*. SEE MAIN ENTRY
blood connection family *(common ancestry)*
blood kindred next of kin
blood money hush money
blood related consanguineous
blood relation affiliation *(bloodline)*, degree *(kinship)*, next of kin, relationship *(family tie)*, relative
blood relations kindred
blood relationship affiliation *(bloodline)*, ancestry, degree *(kinship)*, filiation
blood relative affinity *(family ties)*, next of kin, relation *(kinship)*
blood relatives kindred, lineage
blood tie ancestry, relation *(kinship)*
blood ties relationship *(family tie)*
blood-thirsty cruel
bloodless clean, insipid, peaceable, phlegmatic
bloodline ancestry, birth *(lineage)*, descent *(lineage)*, lineage, origin *(ancestry)*, parentage, posterity, progeny. SEE MAIN ENTRY
bloodshed dispatch *(act of putting to death)*, fight *(battle)*, outbreak
bloodsucker parasite
bloodthirstiness bestiality, cruelty
bloodthirsty malevolent, malignant, predatory, ruthless
bloody brutal
bloody murder killing
bloom pullulate, succeed *(attain)*
blooming prosperous, successful
blossom proliferate, pullulate
blossoming successful
blot brand *(stigmatize)*, deface, defacement, defect, derogate, disgrace *(noun)*, disgrace *(verb)*, dishonor *(shame)*, dishonor *(deprive of honor)*, disparage, flaw, ignominy, infamy, onus *(stigma)*, opprobrium, pillory, shame, stain, stigma, sully, tarnish
blot out censor, condone, deface, delete, destroy *(efface)*, eliminate *(eradicate)*,

eradicate, expunge, extinguish, extirpate, obliterate, redact
blotch deface, defacement, onus *(stigma)*, stain
blotting out defacement
blow bombshell, debacle, detriment, infliction, misfortune, tragedy, trouble
blow up expand, inflate, outbreak
blowing up inflation *(increase)*
blown up inflated *(enlarged)*
blowout outburst
blows fracas
blowup outburst
bludgeon coerce, cudgel, harass
bludgeon man assailant
blue ribbon prize
blue sky law SEE MAIN ENTRY
blue-pencil expurgate
blue-penciling censorship
blueprint agenda, arrange *(plan)*, delineate, delineation, design *(construction plan)*, direction *(course)*, method, program, prospectus. SEE MAIN ENTRY
blueprinted tactical
bluff betray *(lead astray)*, bilk, brazen, cloak, deception, delude, ensnare, fake, palter, pettifog, pretend, pretense *(pretext)*
bluffer pedant
bluffing lying
blunder abortion *(fiasco)*, disaster, err, fault *(mistake)*, indiscretion, maladministration, misapprehend, miscalculate, misconceive, misconstrue, miscue, misdeed, misdoing, misinterpret, misjudge, mismanage, misread, misstatement, mistake, misunderstand, oversight *(carelessness)*. SEE MAIN ENTRY
blundering erroneous, inaccurate, inept *(incompetent)*
blunt allay, alleviate, assuage, candid, clear *(apparent)*, decrease, deter, direct *(forthright)*, harmless, honest, impair, ingenuous, moderate *(temper)*, modify *(moderate)*, mollify, obtund, obtuse, sententious, soothe. SEE MAIN ENTRY
blunt-witted obtuse
bluntness candor *(straightforwardness)*, disrespect, honesty
blur blind *(obscure)*, deface, indistinctness, obfuscate, obnubilate, obscuration, obscure, sully. SEE MAIN ENTRY
blur the outline blind *(obscure)*
blurred inconspicuous, indefinite, indistinct, nebulous, obscure *(faint)*, unclear, vague
blurriness indistinctness
blurry indefinite, indistinct, nebulous, obscure *(faint)*, unclear, vague
blurt interject
blurt out divulge, reveal
blushful diffident
blushing diffident
bluster hector, outburst, rodomontade. SEE MAIN ENTRY
blustering disorderly, orgulous, orotund
blustery disorderly
board bench, bureau, chamber *(body)*, commission *(agency)*, committee, council *(assembly)*, enter *(go in)*, inhabit, lodge *(reside)*, management *(directorate)*. SEE MAIN ENTRY
board of directors management *(directorate)*, management *(supervision)*
board of inquiry commission *(agency)*
boarder habitant, inhabitant, lessee, lodger, resident
boardinghouse building *(structure)*
boast bluster *(speech)*, exaggeration, flaunt, include, jactation
boastful grandiose, inflated *(vain)*, orgulous, pretentious *(pompous)*, proud *(conceited)*
boastfulness bombast, jactation, pride, rodomontade
boasting bombast, orgulous, overstatement, pretentious *(pompous)*, rodomontade
boatload cargo
bode portend, predict, presage, prognosticate, threaten
bodeful ominous, portentous *(ominous)*, prophetic
bodement caveat
bodiless immaterial, incorporeal, insubstantial, intangible
bodilessness impalpability
bodiliness materiality *(physical existence)*
bodily concrete, corporal, corporeal, in person, material *(physical)*, mundane, physical. SEE MAIN ENTRY
bodily deviation from health disease
bodily existence materiality *(physical existence)*
bodily presentation embodiment
bodily representation embodiment
boding consternation, inauspicious, portentous *(ominous)*, premonition
body aggregate, assemblage, assembly, band, character *(an individual)*, committee, community, confederacy *(compact)*, configuration *(form)*, content *(structure)*, cornerstone, corporation, corpse, corpus, entity, generality *(bulk)*, individual, majority *(greater part)*, mass *(body of persons)*, mass *(weight)*, materiality *(physical existence)*, party *(political organization)*, society, substance *(essential nature)*. SEE MAIN ENTRY
body corporate cartel, company *(enterprise)*, corporation
body of commissioners commission *(agency)*
body of consultants committee
body of delegates commission *(agency)*, delegation *(envoy)*, deputation *(delegation)*, representation *(acting for others)*
body of deputies commission *(agency)*, representation *(acting for others)*
body of employees personnel, staff
body of fact science *(study)*
body of facts on which belief is based evidence
body of judges chamber *(body)*, judiciary
body of jurors array *(jury)*, jury, panel *(jurors)*
body of knowledge education
body of law constitution, pandect *(code of laws)*
body of laws code, jurisprudence
body of laws enacted legislation *(enactments)*
body of members constituency
body of men armed with legal process posse
body of men summoned by a sheriff posse
body of office holders government *(political administration)*
body of partisans caucus, side
body of persons summoned as jurors panel *(jurors)*
body of persons sworn to render a verdict panel *(jurors)*
body of persons who formulate laws legislature
body of principles platform
body of professors faculty *(teaching staff)*
body of representatives delegation *(envoy)*, deputation *(delegation)*
body of rules law
body of rules of government constitution
body politic community, nationality, polity, populace, population, public, state *(political unit)*
bodyguard guardian
boeotian opaque
bog stall
boggle mismanage
bogus assumed *(feigned)*, counterfeit, deceptive, delusive, dishonest, false *(not genuine)*, fraudulent, imitation, specious, spurious. SEE MAIN ENTRY
Bohemian nonconforming
Bohemianism nonconformity
boil down abridge *(shorten)*, distill, lessen
boiler plate SEE MAIN ENTRY
boisterous blatant *(obtrusive)*, disorderly, vehement
boisterousness bluster *(commotion)*
bold brazen, flagrant, heroic, hot-blooded, impertinent *(insolent)*, impulsive *(rash)*, indomitable, insolent, obtrusive, palpable, perceivable, presumptuous, prominent, salient, spartan, unabashed, undaunted. SEE MAIN ENTRY
bold front audacity
boldfaced brazen
boldness audacity, confidence *(faith)*, prowess *(bravery)*, spirit, temerity
bolster bear *(support)*, favor, inure *(benefit)*, justify, maintain *(sustain)*, nurture, preserve, promote *(organize)*, reinforce, side, subsidize, supplement, support *(assist)*, sustain *(prolong)*, uphold. SEE MAIN ENTRY
bolster up corroborate, reassure
bolt abscond, assemblage, bar *(hinder)*, escape, impede, lock, race, renege, retreat, seal *(close)*
bomb SEE MAIN ENTRY
bombard attack
bombardment barrage, discharge *(shot)*, onset *(assault)*
bombast fustian, harangue, peroration. SEE MAIN ENTRY
bombastic flatulent, fustian, grandiose, orotund, pretentious *(pompous)*, prolix, turgid. SEE MAIN ENTRY
bombastic language fustian
bombastic speech rhetoric *(insincere language)*
bombastical flatulent
bombastry fustian
bombings barrage
bombshell bomb. SEE MAIN ENTRY
bona assets, effects, possession *(property)*, property *(possessions)*
bona fide accurate
bona fide actual, adherence *(devotion)*, adhesion *(loyalty)*
bona fide authentic, convincing. SEE MAIN ENTRY
bona fide corporeal, de facto
bona fide genuine, good faith, in good faith, sterling, valid, veridical
bonafide real
bonanza bounty

bond adherence *(adhesion)*, adherence *(devotion)*, adhesion *(loyalty)*, affiliation *(connectedness)*, agreement *(contract)*, association *(connection)*, attachment *(act of affixing)*, bail, chain *(nexus)*, charge *(lien)*, coalescence, coalition, connection *(fastening)*, contact *(association)*, contract, coverage *(insurance)*, debenture, fetter, guaranty, handcuff, hostage, kinship, liaison, loyalty, marriage *(intimate relationship)*, nexus, note *(written promise to pay)*, pact, pawn, pledge *(deposit)*, promise, propinquity *(kinship)*, recognizance, relation *(connection)*, relationship *(connection)*, security *(pledge)*, sodality, specialty *(contract)*, stipulation, treaty. SEE MAIN ENTRY
bond against risk insurance
bond of matrimony cohabitation *(married state)*, marriage *(wedlock)*
bond of slavery bondage
bond of union chain *(nexus)*
bondage captivity, coercion, constraint *(imprisonment)*, custody *(incarceration)*, durance, duress, incarceration, restraint, subjection, thrall. SEE MAIN ENTRY
bonded allied, concerted, concordant, concurrent *(united)*, fully secured, harmonious
bondman captive
bonds bondage, constraint *(imprisonment)*, durance, restriction, securities, servitude, ties
bondsman captive
bone of contention problem, question *(issue)*
bonfire conflagration
boni bonus
bonorum possessions
bonus benefit *(conferment)*, bounty, commission *(fee)*, contribution *(donation)*, gratuity *(present)*, largess *(gift)*, perquisite, premium *(excess value)*, prize, reward
bonus sterling
bonus surplus, tip *(gratuity)*. SEE MAIN ENTRY
bony ossified
book document, engage *(hire)*, enroll, file *(place among official records)*, program, publication *(printed matter)*, record, register, retain *(employ)*, script, set down. SEE MAIN ENTRY
book learning information *(knowledge)*
book of accounts ledger
book of records ledger
booking registration, reservation *(engagement)*
bookish learned
bookkeeper accountant, comptroller
bookkeeping accounting, computation, registration. SEE MAIN ENTRY
bookkeeping expert comptroller
books ledger
boom barrage, prosperity. SEE MAIN ENTRY
booming prosperous, resounding, successful
booming economy boom *(prosperity)*, prosperity
boon behalf, benefit *(conferment)*, benevolence *(act of kindness)*, bonus, bounty, contribution *(donation)*, endowment, favor *(act of kindness)*, grant, help, largess *(gift)*
boorish ignoble, inelegant, perverse, provincial, uncouth, unseemly
boost boom *(increase)*, elevate, encourage, enhance, favor, help, impetus, increase, increment, intensify, magnify, parlay *(exploit successfully)*, raise *(advance)*, recommendation, reinforce, reinforcement
boost in prices inflation *(decrease in value of currency)*
boosting cumulative *(intensifying)*, promotion *(encouragement)*
boot spurn
booth stand *(witness' place in court)*, store *(business)*
bootlegged commerce contraband
bootlegged goods contraband
bootlegged trade contraband
bootlegged traffic contraband
bootlegger SEE MAIN ENTRY
bootless futile, otiose, unavailing
booty pillage, plunder, prize, reward, spoils
border ambit, boundary, circumscribe *(define)*, circumscribe *(surround by boundary)*, connection *(abutment)*, contact *(touch)*, contain *(enclose)*, demarcate, enclosure, encompass *(surround)*, end *(termination)*, extremity *(furthest point)*, frontier, hedge, juxtapose, limit, margin *(outside limit)*, mete, outline *(boundary)*, periphery, tenant. SEE MAIN ENTRY
border on abut, adjoin, approximate, contact *(touch)*, correspond *(be equivalent)*
bordering adjacent, close *(near)*, contiguous, immediate *(not distant)*, proximate
bordering upon proximate
borderland border, frontier, mete, periphery
borderline boundary, end *(termination)*, extremity *(furthest point)*, insecure, marginal, mete, purview
borders configuration *(confines)*, confines, extent
bore enter *(penetrate)*, penetrate, pierce *(lance)*
boredom disinterest *(lack of interest)*
boresome irksome, jejune *(dull)*, pedestrian, prolix, prosaic
boring insipid, irksome, jejune *(dull)*, lifeless *(dull)*, nondescript, ordinary, pedestrian, ponderous, prolix, prosaic, stale, trite
born native *(inborn)*. SEE MAIN ENTRY
born in wedlock legitimate *(lawfully conceived)*. SEE MAIN ENTRY
born of parents legally married legitimate *(lawfully conceived)*
borough community
borrow adopt, appropriate, copy. SEE MAIN ENTRY
borrow dishonestly pirate *(reproduce without authorization)*, plagiarize
borrower debtor, obligor, parasite
borrowing limit SEE MAIN ENTRY
bosom close *(intimate)*
boss chief, direct *(supervise)*, director, employer, manage, principal *(director)*, superintend
botch fail *(lose)*, failure *(lack of success)*, miscue, mismanage, muddle, spoil *(impair)*
botchery maladministration
bother aggravate *(annoy)*, annoy, badger, bait *(harass)*, burden, care *(regard)*, discommode, disorganize, distress, disturb, embarrass, harass, harrow, harry *(harass)*, hector, hinder, hindrance, impede, importune, inconvenience, irritate, mistreat, molest *(annoy)*, molestation, nuisance, perplex, persecute, perturb, pique, plague, press *(goad)*, provoke, trouble, upset
botheration burden
bothering enigmatic
bothersome difficult, irksome, operose, undesirable, vexatious
bottle up repress
bottleneck blockade *(barrier)*
bottomless baseless, profound *(intense)*
boulevard avenue *(route)*
bounce oscillate
bounce back reflect *(mirror)*
bouncing resilient
bound abut, accountable *(responsible)*, actionable, attached *(annexed)*, barrier, boundary, circumscribe *(surround by boundary)*, confine, definite, delimit, demarcate, detain *(restrain)*, diminish, en route, enclose, encompass *(surround)*, end *(termination)*, frontier, hedge, include, indebted, inextricable, limit, loyal, mete, palliate *(abate)*, periphery, purposeful, qualify *(condition)*, restrict, shut, specialize. SEE MAIN ENTRY
bound by agreement indentured
bound by contract indentured
bound by convention orthodox
bound by duty moral
bound in equity liable
bound in law liable
bound to liable
bound to respond liable
bound together conjoint
boundaries capacity *(sphere)*, confines, dimension, range
boundary ambit, barrier, border, configuration *(confines)*, edge *(border)*, enclosure, end *(termination)*, extremity *(furthest point)*, frontier, guideline, limit, margin *(outside limit)*, mete, purview, restriction, scope. SEE MAIN ENTRY
boundary line ambit, frontier, limit, mete, periphery
boundary lines confines
boundary mark mete
boundary marker landmark *(conspicuous object)*
bounded certain *(specific)*, limited
bounded with precision definite
bounden indebted, loyal, mandatory, necessary *(required)*
bounden duty allegiance, burden, liability, responsibility *(accountability)*
bounding contiguous, immediate *(not distant)*
boundless continual *(perpetual)*, far reaching, indefinite, indeterminate, infinite, innumerable, myriad, open-ended, profuse, unlimited, unqualified *(unlimited)*, unrestricted
boundlessly ad infinitum
boundlessness perpetuity
boundness responsibility *(accountability)*
bounds ambit, area *(province)*, border, capacity *(sphere)*, circuit, configuration *(confines)*, confines, constraint *(imprisonment)*, contour *(outline)*, coverage *(scope)*, custody *(incarceration)*, edge *(border)*, extent, margin *(outside limit)*, mete, outline *(boundary)*, premises *(buildings)*, purview, range, restriction, scope, sphere. SEE MAIN ENTRY
bounteous benevolent, charitable *(benevolent)*, humane, liberal *(generous)*, philanthropic, profuse, replete
bounteousness charity, largess *(generosity)*, philanthropy
bountiful ample, benevolent, copious, donative, liberal *(generous)*, philanthropic, profuse, replete
bountifulness benevolence *(disposition to do good)*, boom *(prosperity)*, charity, largess *(generosity)*, philanthropy

bounty bonus, consideration *(recompense),* contribution *(donation),* donation, endowment, favor *(act of kindness),* grant, largess *(generosity),* largess *(gift),* philanthropy, premium *(excess value),* prize, reward, subsidy. SEE MAIN ENTRY
bourgeois ordinary, prevailing *(current)*
bourn destination, end *(intent),* outline *(boundary)*
bourse exchange, market *(business)*
bout competition, confrontation *(altercation),* contest *(competition),* fight *(battle),* period
bout of sickness disease
bovine phlegmatic
bow prostration, succumb, yield *(submit)*
bow to obey, observe *(obey),* submit *(yield)*
bowdlerization censorship
bowdlerize censor, expurgate. SEE MAIN ENTRY
bowelless relentless
bowing compliance
bowl over overcome *(overwhelm)*
box chamber *(compartment),* envelop, stand *(witness' place in court)*
box number address
boy child
boycott condemn *(ban),* disapprove *(reject),* eschew, exclude, exclusion, ignore, picket, proscription, reject, shun, strike, strike *(refuse to work).* SEE MAIN ENTRY
boyishness puerility
brabble affray, bicker, disaccord, fray
brace bear *(support),* mainstay, reinforce, side, stimulate, uphold
bracing remedial, salutary
bracket class, connect *(relate),* enclose, enclosure, include, pigeonhole, relate *(establish a connection)*
brag exaggeration, jactation, rodomontade
braggadocio jactation, pride, rodomontade
braggardism jactation
braggardly pretentious *(pompous)*
braggart inflated *(vain),* pretentious *(pompous),* proud *(conceited)*
braggartism pride, rodomontade
braggery bombast
bragging bluster *(speech),* orgulous, rodomontade
braid cross *(intersect),* intertwine
brain intellect
brain child invention
brain damage insanity
brainless fatuous, irrational, opaque
brains intelligence *(intellect)*
braintwister enigma
brainwash convert *(persuade),* influence
brainwashing propaganda
brainwork dialectic
brake control *(restriction),* curb, hamper, hold up *(delay),* impede, impediment, obstruct, remit *(relax),* restraint, stop
branch adjunct, affiliate, bifurcate, bureau, class, denomination, department, dichotomize, division *(administrative unit),* member *(constituent part),* offshoot, organ, segment, spread, title *(division),* unit *(department)*
branch member chapter *(branch)*
branch of instruction discipline *(field of study)*
branch of knowledge discipline *(field of study),* science *(study)*
branch off bifurcate, stem *(originate)*
branch office chapter *(branch),* organ
branch organization affiliate
branch out accrue *(increase),* bifurcate, compound, deploy, deviate, digress, expand, increase, radiate
branching divergent, extensive
branching off deviation
branching out circulation, decentralization
brand arraign, attaint, burn, class, classify, defame, denigrate, denounce *(condemn),* derogate, disapprove *(condemn),* discredit, disgrace *(noun),* disgrace *(verb),* dishonor *(shame),* dishonor *(deprive of honor),* disparagement, disrepute, earmark, humiliate, ignominy, implicate, indicant, indication, infamy, involve *(implicate),* label *(noun),* label *(verb),* manner *(kind),* onus *(stigma),* opprobrium, pillory, reproach, scandal, smear, specialty *(distinctive mark),* stamp, stigma, sully, tarnish, trademark. SEE MAIN ENTRY
brand incorrectly mislabel
brand with reproach arraign
brandish display, flaunt, wield. SEE MAIN ENTRY
brangle bicker, brawl *(noun),* brawl *(verb),* disaccord
brash brazen, caustic, impertinent *(insolent),* improvident, imprudent, obtrusive, presumptuous
brashness disrespect
brassy pretentious *(ostentatious)*
bravado audacity, pretense *(ostentation)*
brave bear *(tolerate),* confront *(encounter),* defy, endure *(suffer),* heroic, indomitable, spartan, undaunted. SEE MAIN ENTRY
brave SEE MAIN ENTRY
brave face audacity
braveness prowess *(bravery)*
bravery spirit, tolerance
bravura audacity
brawl affray, bicker, bluster *(commotion),* commotion, confrontation *(altercation),* contend *(dispute),* contest *(dispute),* controversy *(argument),* disaccord, embroilment, fight *(battle),* fracas, fray, outbreak, outcry, riot. SEE MAIN ENTRY
brawler malcontent
brawn force *(strength),* puissance, sinew, strength
brawniness sinew
brawny powerful, strong
braying blatant *(obtrusive)*
braze cement
brazen contemptuous, flagrant, impertinent *(insolent),* insolent, obtrusive, outrageous, presumptuous, unabashed. SEE MAIN ENTRY
brazenness disrespect
breach alienation *(estrangement),* argument *(contention),* break *(violate),* conflict, default, delinquency *(failure of duty),* dereliction, difference, disassociation, disloyalty, embroilment, encroach, encroachment, estrangement, feud, flaw, force *(break),* incursion, infraction, infringe, infringement, invasion, irregularity, neglect, offense, omission, outbreak, repudiation, rift *(gap),* schism, separation, split, transgression, trespass, variance *(disagreement),* violation. SEE MAIN ENTRY
breach of a promise delinquency *(failure of duty)*
breach of allegiance treason
breach of duty negligence, res ipsa loquitur
breach of faith bad faith, bribery, corruption, dishonor *(nonpayment),* disloyalty, infidelity, infraction, treason
breach of law crime, guilt, infraction, misdemeanor, misfeasance
breach of legal duty tort
breach of orders default, disregard *(omission),* infraction, rebellion
breach of peace disorder *(lack of order)*
breach of practice deviation, exception *(exclusion),* malpractice
breach of privilege infraction
breach of profession malpractice
breach of promise dishonor *(nonpayment),* disloyalty, infidelity, infraction, nonperformance
breach of the law delinquency *(misconduct),* offense
breach of the peace brawl, fracas, infraction, outbreak, outburst, riot
breach of trust abuse *(corrupt practice),* corruption, disloyalty, embezzlement, improbity, infidelity, infraction, misappropriation
breach the agreement default
breadth caliber *(measurement),* capacity *(maximum),* extent, gamut, purview, range
break adjournment, alienation *(estrangement),* breach, cessation *(interlude),* cloture, controversy *(argument),* damage, digression, disable, disassociation, discontinue *(abandon),* discontinue *(break continuity),* estrangement, extension *(postponement),* halt *(noun),* halt *(verb),* hiatus, infringe, interrupt, interruption, interval, leave *(absence),* lull, luxate, moratorium, part *(separate),* pause *(noun),* pause *(verb),* pendency, recess *(noun),* recess *(verb),* remission, rend, respite *(interval of rest),* rift *(disagreement),* rift *(gap),* schism, separate, separation, split *(noun),* split *(verb),* spoil *(impair),* subdue, transition, violate. SEE MAIN ENTRY
break a law disobey, offend *(violate the law)*
break a promise renege
break a rule disobey
break apart disband, disjoint, disrupt, dissolve *(separate),* sever
break away defect, elude, leave *(depart),* part *(leave),* secede
break bounds accroach, deviate, impinge, infringe
break camp evacuate, move *(alter position)*
break down classify, codify, damage, decay, erode, overcome *(overwhelm),* pigeonhole, stall, subdivide, succumb
break faith bear false witness, cheat, inform *(betray),* misrepresent, palter
break faith with betray *(lead astray)*
break fealty defect
break forth issue *(send forth)*
break from prison escape
break ground initiate, originate
break in discipline *(train),* interfere, interrupt, intervene, invade, obtrude, trespass
break in on impinge
break in upon infringe, overstep
break into infringe, interpose, loot, penetrate
break loose elude, escape
break news divulge
break off alienate *(estrange),* close *(terminate),* conclude *(complete),* detach, discontinue *(abandon),* discontinue *(break continuity),* forbear, forswear, halt, quit *(discontinue),* refrain, separate, sever, stop, suspend
break one's oath perjure

break one's promise betray *(lead astray)*, fail *(neglect)*
break one's promise to disappoint
break one's trust default
break one's word fail *(neglect)*, perjure
break out escape
break silence pronounce *(speak)*, speak
break the association of disband
break the connection with disengage
break the contract default
break the law disobey, offend *(violate the law)*, trespass. SEE MAIN ENTRY
break the news notify, reveal
break the pattern deviate
break the peace brawl, fight *(battle)*
break the record surpass
break through emerge, lancinate
break to pieces destroy *(efface)*
break trust inform *(betray)*
break up decay, degenerate, destroy *(void)*, diffuse, disband, disintegrate, disjoint, dispel, dissipate *(spread out)*, dissociate, dissolve *(separate)*, dissolve *(terminate)*, overthrow, partition, recess, separate
break up into opposing factions polarize
break with defect, disaccord, disagree, estrange, rebel, renounce, split
breakability frailty
breakable destructible, divisible, nonsubstantial *(not sturdy)*, separable
breakage injury
breakdown debacle, decentralization, defeat, diagnosis, disassociation, disaster, disease, erosion, failure *(lack of success)*, miscarriage, prostration. SEE MAIN ENTRY
breakdown of administration anarchy, lynch law, misrule
breaking division *(act of dividing)*, infraction
breaking an obligation contravention
breaking and entering burglary, housebreaking
breaking down decadent, destruction
breaking of precedent innovation
breaking of the law offense
breaking off discontinuance *(act of discontinuing)*
breaking up dissolution *(disintegration)*, dissolution *(termination)*
breaking with tradition anomalous, peculiar *(curious)*
breakneck dangerous, impulsive *(rash)*, precipitate
breakup defeasance, division *(act of dividing)*, subversion
breast confront *(encounter)*, defy, resist *(oppose)*, withstand
breath suggestion
breathe communicate, divulge, exist, express, pause, utter
breathe one's last die
breather lull, pause
breathing born *(alive)*, conscious *(awake)*, live *(conscious)*
breathing spell halt, lull, pause, respite *(interval of rest)*
breathing time lull, respite *(interval of rest)*
breathless dead, lifeless *(dead)*
breathtaking moving *(evoking emotion)*, noteworthy, portentous *(eliciting amazement)*
breed bear *(yield)*, blood, cause, class, descent *(lineage)*, engender, foster, generate, kind, occasion, originate, produce *(manufacture)*, proliferate, propagate *(increase)*, pullulate, race, reproduce
breeding conduct, deportment
breedy prolific
breeziness life *(vitality)*
brethren affinity *(family ties)*, blood, kindred, society
brevet warrant *(authorization)*. SEE MAIN ENTRY
breviary compendium
brevis ephemeral, laconic, limited, succinct, summary, transient
brew maneuver
brewing imminent, inevitable
bribable mercenary, venal
bribe coax, corrupt, hush money, lure, suborn. SEE MAIN ENTRY
bribe to take a false oath suborn
bribery corruption, graft. SEE MAIN ENTRY
bribing bribery
bridal conjugal, nuptial
bridewell reformatory
bridge chain *(nexus)*, connect *(join together)*, connect *(relate)*, connection *(fastening)*, contact *(touch)*, join *(bring together)*, nexus
bridle bar *(hinder)*, block, clog, constrain *(imprison)*, constrain *(restrain)*, contain *(restrain)*, damper *(stopper)*, disadvantage, discipline *(control)*, fetter, hamper, handcuff *(noun)*, handcuff *(verb)*, handicap, inhibit, limit, obstacle, obstruct, obstruction, repress, resent, restrain, restraint, restrict, trammel
bridled arrested *(checked)*
brief abridgment *(condensation)*, abstract, account *(report)*, apprise, capsule, compact *(pithy)*, compendium, concise, cursory, digest, disabuse, dossier, edify, educate, ephemeral, impart, indicate, inform *(notify)*, instruct *(direct)*, laconic, memorandum, minimal, note *(brief comment)*, notify, outline *(synopsis)*, paraphrase, pithy, report *(detailed account)*, restatement, scenario, succinct, summary, synopsis, temporary, transient, transitory, volatile. SEE MAIN ENTRY
brief silence lull
briefed acquainted, familiar *(informed)*, informed *(having information)*
briefing guidance
briefly pro tempore
brigand hoodlum, malefactor, outlaw
brigandage foray, larceny, pillage, spoliation
brigandine panoply
brigandish larcenous
bright illustrious, obvious, perspicacious, resourceful, sanguine, sapient. SEE MAIN ENTRY
brighten enhance
brightness sense *(intelligence)*
brilliance distinction *(reputation)*, intellect, intelligence *(intellect)*, sagacity, sense *(intelligence)*. SEE MAIN ENTRY
brilliant illustrious, politic, prominent
brim border, edge *(border)*, margin *(outside limit)*
brimful full, replete
brimming replete
brimming over full
bring carry *(transport)*, cause, commence, procure, transport, yield *(produce a return)*
bring a case lodge *(bring a complaint)*
bring a charge accuse, cite *(accuse)*, impeach
bring a countercharge recriminate
bring a formal accusation against indict
bring a legal action sue
bring a person to his senses persuade
bring a suit complain *(charge)*, lodge *(bring a complaint)*
bring about accomplish, attain, bear *(yield)*, cause, commit *(perpetrate)*, compose, conduce, constitute *(establish)*, create, discharge *(perform)*, dispatch *(dispose of)*, elicit, engender, establish *(launch)*, evoke, execute *(accomplish)*, fulfill, generate, implement, incite, induce, inflict, inspire, make, occasion, operate, originate, perpetrate, produce *(manufacture)*, prosecute *(carry forward)*, provoke, realize *(make real)*, render *(administer)*, yield *(produce a return)*
bring about by force constrain *(compel)*
bring about by legislation constitute *(establish)*
bring about change militate
bring accusation accuse, arraign, charge *(accuse)*, denounce *(inform against)*, incriminate, involve *(implicate)*, lodge *(bring a complaint)*
bring action against litigate, prosecute *(charge)*
bring aid capitalize *(provide capital)*, contribute *(assist)*
bring an action cite *(accuse)*, complain *(charge)*, litigate, sue
bring an action against lodge *(bring a complaint)*
bring around convert *(persuade)*, disarm *(set at ease)*, persuade, prevail *(persuade)*
bring back reconstitute, rehabilitate, reinstate, remind, restore *(return)*, resurrect
bring before a court arraign, prosecute *(charge)*
bring before the public circulate, publish
bring charges complain *(charge)*, denounce *(inform against)*, impeach, involve *(implicate)*
bring charges against incriminate, lodge *(bring a complaint)*
bring discredit on decry
bring disgrace upon discredit
bring disrepute upon defame
bring down cause, demean *(make lower)*, demote, depress, derogate, disgrace, dispatch *(put to death)*, overthrow
bring forth avail *(bring about)*, bear *(yield)*, develop, educe, elicit, engender, evoke, extract, generate, make, manifest, produce *(manufacture)*, reproduce, yield *(produce a return)*
bring forward bear *(adduce)*, certify *(attest)*, cite *(state)*, elicit, exhibit, manifest, offer *(propose)*, plead *(allege in a legal action)*, posit, prefer, produce *(offer to view)*, proffer
bring from obscurity into view disinter
bring in induct, introduce, yield *(produce a return)*
bring in a supply bear *(yield)*
bring in a true bill accuse
bring in a verdict award, determine, sentence
bring in as a third party implead
bring in contact join *(bring together)*
bring in contact with commingle, connect *(join together)*
bring in question canvass, dispute *(contest)*
bring into a small compass concentrate *(consolidate)*
bring into accord attune
bring into agreement arbitrate *(conciliate)*, attune
bring into being compose, conceive *(invent)*, create, develop, engender, establish

(launch), fabricate *(construct),* forge *(produce),* generate, invent *(produce for the first time),* make, produce *(manufacture),* propagate *(increase)*
bring into close connection affiliate
bring into close relation affiliate
bring into comparison compare, contrast, measure
bring into concord agree *(contract)*
bring into conflict engage *(involve)*
bring into conformity with law legalize
bring into connection with implicate
bring into consistency accommodate
bring into court plead *(argue a case)*
bring into custody imprison
bring into danger compromise *(endanger)*
bring into discredit brand *(stigmatize),* censure, condemn *(blame),* denounce *(condemn),* derogate, discommend, disgrace, dishonor *(deprive of honor),* fault, impeach, malign
bring into disfavor discredit
bring into disorder confound, discompose, perturb
bring into disrepute decry, demean *(make lower)*
bring into effect compose
bring into existence cause, compose, conceive *(invent),* engender, establish *(launch),* fabricate *(construct),* forge *(produce),* generate, make, originate, produce *(manufacture)*
bring into focus converge, focus
bring into harmony arbitrate *(conciliate),* intercede, reconcile
bring into meaningful relation with compare
bring into operation exert, perform *(execute)*
bring into order arrange *(methodize),* codify, file *(arrange),* fix *(arrange),* orchestrate
bring into peril endanger
bring into play exercise *(use),* exert, exploit *(make use of),* resort
bring into question audit
bring into relation compare
bring into relation with correspond *(be equivalent)*
bring into the open betray *(disclose),* disclose, find *(discover),* issue *(publish),* manifest, promulgate
bring into use initiate
bring into view bare, disclose, evince, produce *(offer to view)*
bring low demean *(make lower),* demote, depress, derogate, reduce, supplant
bring near converge, juxtapose
bring new evidence appeal
bring off dispatch *(dispose of),* implement
bring off successfully attain
bring on cause, conduce, create, incite, incur, induce, originate, precipitate *(hasten)*
bring out circulate, comment, create, disclose, disinter, educe, elicit, evoke, manifest, produce *(offer to view),* publish, solve
bring out in evidence bare
bring out more clearly elucidate
bring over disarm *(set at ease),* persuade, prevail upon
bring pressure to bear coerce, influence, lobby, prejudice *(influence),* press *(constrain)*
bring pressure to bear upon compel, constrain *(compel)*
bring proceedings against complain *(charge),* incriminate, lodge *(bring a complaint)*
bring reproach upon discredit, disgrace, disparage, stain
bring shame upon derogate, disgrace, dishonor *(deprive of honor),* humiliate, pillory
bring suit litigate, prosecute *(charge)*
bring the mind to bear upon focus
bring to resurrect
bring to a close complete, conclude *(complete),* consummate, discontinue *(abandon),* finish, stop
bring to a common center collect *(gather)*
bring to a complete condition develop
bring to a conclusion dispatch *(dispose of),* perfect
bring to a more advanced state develop
bring to a point of union collect *(gather)*
bring to a standstill arrest *(stop),* check *(restrain),* delay, discontinue *(break continuity),* enjoin, forestall, halt, hold up *(delay),* impede, obstruct, palliate *(abate),* stall, stop, suspend
bring to a state of obedience discipline *(control)*
bring to a stop arrest *(stop),* estop, suspend
bring to account condemn *(punish),* denounce *(condemn),* impeach, penalize
bring to acquiescence reconcile
bring to agreement adjust *(resolve)*
bring to an end cease, close *(terminate),* complete, conclude *(complete),* determine, discontinue *(abandon),* dispatch *(dispose of),* dissolve *(terminate),* extinguish, finish, perfect, quit *(discontinue),* terminate
bring to an understanding intercede, mediate
bring to attention address *(direct attention to)*
bring to bear avail *(be of use),* exercise *(use),* exert
bring to book rebuke, reprehend
bring to completion finish, fulfill, perfect, terminate
bring to conclusion complete, dissolve *(terminate)*
bring to effect consummate, create, make
bring to full development mature
bring to fullness perfect
bring to its peak mature
bring to justice convict, determine, impeach, lodge *(bring a complaint),* prosecute *(charge),* sue
bring to light bare, bear *(adduce),* betray *(disclose),* clarify, denude, detect, disclose, discover, display, divulge, educe, evidence, exhibit, expose, ferret, locate, manifest, produce *(offer to view),* reveal, unveil. SEE MAIN ENTRY
bring to light by degrees develop
bring to market handle *(trade),* sell
bring to maturity complete, effectuate, mature, nurture
bring to mind allude, recollect, remember
bring to naught destroy *(void),* foil, stop, thwart
bring to nothing obliterate
bring to notice address *(direct attention to),* exhibit, manifest
bring to nought frustrate
bring to order marshal
bring to pass attain, carry *(succeed),* cause, commit *(perpetrate),* create, discharge *(perform),* dispatch *(dispose of),* effectuate, enforce, evoke, execute *(accomplish),* fulfill, implement, induce, make, originate, perform *(execute),* perpetrate, produce *(manufacture),* prosecute *(carry forward),* realize *(make real)*
bring to perfection complete, mature
bring to reason convince, persuade, prevail upon, reason *(persuade)*
bring to recollection remind
bring to rest conclude *(complete)*
bring to retribution discipline *(punish),* punish
bring to ruin destroy *(efface),* extirpate, pillage
bring to terms accommodate, arbitrate *(conciliate),* arrange *(methodize),* beat *(defeat),* intercede, mediate, negotiate, pacify, placate, reconcile, settle, subjugate
bring to the bar litigate, lodge *(bring a complaint),* sue
bring to the fore adduce, produce *(offer to view)*
bring to the front manifest, produce *(offer to view)*
bring to trial arraign, litigate, lodge *(bring a complaint)*
bring to view evidence, exhibit, manifest
bring together accumulate *(amass),* aggregate, annex *(add),* arbitrate *(conciliate),* collect *(gather),* compile, congregate, conjoin, consolidate *(strengthen),* consolidate *(unite),* convene, converge, crystallize, focus, garner, glean, hoard, incorporate *(include),* intercede, juxtapose, mediate, orchestrate, raise *(collect),* reconcile, settle, unite
bring together in a crowd congregate
bring toward a central point concentrate *(consolidate)*
bring unawares into danger entrap
bring unawares into evil entrap
bring under domination subject
bring under rule impose *(subject),* subdue, subject
bring under subjection discipline *(control)*
bring up bear *(adduce),* discipline *(train),* educate, foster, nurture, raise *(advance),* remind
bring up for investigation arraign, impeach
bring up on charges arraign, complain *(charge),* incriminate, lodge *(bring a complaint)*
bring up to date renew *(refurbish),* revise
bring upon inflict
bring upon oneself incur
bring word communicate, mention, notify
bringing forth creation
bringing to trial prosecution *(criminal trial)*
bringing together centralization, combination, cumulation, joinder
brink border, edge *(border),* extremity *(furthest point),* margin *(outside limit),* outline *(boundary),* penumbra, threshold *(verge).* SEE MAIN ENTRY
brisk brief, expeditious, incisive, sedulous, trenchant, volatile
briskness dispatch *(promptness),* haste, life *(vitality)*
bristle resent
bristling hostile, resentful, rife
bristling with arms armed
brittle nonsubstantial *(not sturdy)*
brittleness frailty

broach assume *(undertake)*, commence, initiate, mention, pose *(propound)*, proclaim, utter
broad capacious, collective, comprehensive, extensive, general, generic, inaccurate, inclusive, indefinite, indiscriminate, inexact, liberal *(not literal)*, nonsectarian, obscene, omnibus, passable, vague. SEE MAIN ENTRY
broad enough ample
broad guage caliber *(measurement)*
broad meaning connotation, gist *(substance)*, implication *(inference)*
broad statement generality *(vague statement)*, generalization
broad-based complete *(all-embracing)*, extensive, nonsectarian
broad-minded impartial, nonpartisan, objective, open-minded, permissive, reasonable *(rational)*, receptive, unbiased, unprejudiced
broad-mindedness disinterest *(lack of prejudice)*, objectivity, tolerance
broadcast circulate, communicate, convey *(communicate)*, diffuse, dispel, disseminate, divulge, issuance, issue *(publish)*, proclaim, promulgate, propagate *(spread)*, public *(known)*, publication *(disclosure)*, publicity, publish, relate *(tell)*, report *(detailed account)*, report *(disclose)*, send, spread. SEE MAIN ENTRY
broaden accrue *(increase)*, accumulate *(enlarge)*, deploy, develop, enlarge, expand, extend *(enlarge)*, increase, inflate, magnify, parlay *(exploit successfully)*, spread, supplement. SEE MAIN ENTRY
broadening accession *(enlargement)*, augmentation, boom *(increase)*, cumulative *(increasing)*, extension *(expansion)*
broadness caliber *(measurement)*
broadside barrage
broil altercation, brawl *(noun)*, brawl *(verb)*, controversy *(argument)*, disaccord, embroilment, fight *(argument)*, fracas, fray, furor, imbroglio, riot, strife, struggle
broke bankrupt, impecunious, insolvent
broken bankrupt, defective, desultory, disconnected, disjunctive *(tending to disjoin)*, imperfect, intermittent, unsound *(not strong)*. SEE MAIN ENTRY
broken faith bad faith, infidelity
broken in spirit contrite
broken marriage divorce
broken off disconnected
broken promise bad faith, disloyalty
broken silence outcry
broken thread anacoluthon
broken word infidelity
brokenhearted disconsolate
broker dealer, deputy, factor *(commission merchant)*, interagent, medium, plenipotentiary, proctor, procurator, proxy, representative *(proxy)*, spokesman. SEE MAIN ENTRY
brokerage SEE MAIN ENTRY
bromidic ordinary, trite
brood blood, children, deliberate, family *(household)*, muse, offspring, progeny. SEE MAIN ENTRY
brood over deplore, dwell *(linger over)*, ponder, reflect *(ponder)*, review
brooding contemplation, deliberation
brook allow *(endure)*, endure *(suffer)*, suffer *(permit)*, tolerate
brook no denial insist
brother colleague, counterpart *(complement)*
brotherhood denomination, goodwill, kinship, peace, philanthropy, society, sodality, union *(labor organization)*
brotherliness benevolence *(disposition to do good)*, philanthropy, sodality
brotherly close *(intimate)*, humane, intimate, philanthropic
brotherly love philanthropy
brought about by force forcible
brought charges accused *(charged)*
brought to a conclusion complete *(ended)*
brought to fruition choate lien
brought to light naked *(perceptible)*
brought to perfection best, ripe
brought to termination res judicata
brought together collective, conglomerate
brouillerie dissension
browbeat bait *(harass)*, discompose, frighten, harass, harrow, harry *(harass)*, hector, intimidate, persecute, plague, press *(goad)*, threaten. SEE MAIN ENTRY
browse peruse
bruise beat *(strike)*, damage, harm, ill use, lash *(strike)*, mistreat, mutilate
bruised blemished, defective, marred
bruit declare, disseminate, notoriety, outcry, proclaim, promulgate, report *(rumor)*, report *(disclose)*, reveal, signify *(inform)*, spread
bruit abroad circulate
bruited about public *(known)*
brummagem meretricious, tawdry
brunt burden, pressure
brush affray, confrontation *(altercation)*
brush aside discount *(disbelieve)*, disdain, dismiss *(put out of consideration)*, ignore, rebuff, reject, spurn
brush off parry
brush up repair
brusque harsh, laconic, taciturn
brusqueness disrespect
brutal bitter *(penetrating)*, callous, cold-blooded, cruel, diabolic, disorderly, harsh, hot-blooded, inexcusable, malevolent, malicious, malignant, noxious, pernicious, ruthless, scathing, severe, tyrannous, vicious. SEE MAIN ENTRY
brutality bestiality, cruelty, oppression, violence. SEE MAIN ENTRY
brutalize SEE MAIN ENTRY
brutalized diabolic
brutalness brutality, cruelty
brute animal
brute creation animal
brute force coercion, main force, oppression, pressure
brute-like brutal
brutify brutalize
brutilization brutality
brutish brutal, caitiff, cold-blooded, malignant, relentless, ruthless, uncouth
brutishness bestiality, brutality, cruelty
brutum fulmen disaster
buccaneer criminal, plunder
buccaneering spoliation
buck defy, oppose, oppugn
buckler protection, shield
bucolic provincial
bud embryo, germinate, proliferate, pullulate
budding inchoate, incipient
budget appropriation *(allotment)*, estimate, finance, overhead, program. SEE MAIN ENTRY
budgetary financial, fiscal, pecuniary
budgeted items expense *(cost)*, outlay
budgeting appropriation *(allotment)*
buffer bulwark, intermediary, panoply, safeguard, shield
buffer zone SEE MAIN ENTRY
buffered impervious
buffet beat *(strike)*, ill use, jostle *(bump into)*
buffoonery parody, ridicule
buggery sodomy
build accrue *(increase)*, compose, create, enlarge, establish *(launch)*, fabricate *(construct)*, forge *(produce)*, form, frame *(structure)*, frame *(construct)*, increase, invent *(produce for the first time)*, make, manufacture, organization *(structure)*, produce *(manufacture)*. SEE MAIN ENTRY
build up accrue *(increase)*, accumulate *(enlarge)*, aggregate, compound, consolidate *(strengthen)*, cumulation, develop, elevate, enlarge, expand, extend *(enlarge)*, heighten *(augment)*, heighten *(elevate)*, hoard, magnify, parlay *(exploit successfully)*, promote *(organize)*, replenish. SEE MAIN ENTRY
build-up augmentation
builder architect, contractor, developer, materialman
building creation, edifice, frame *(structure)*, preparation, structure *(edifice)*. SEE MAIN ENTRY
building entrepeneur developer
building of imposing appearance edifice
built on based on, underlying
bulge project *(extend beyond)*
bulk amount *(quantity)*, assemblage, cargo, corpus, cumulation, majority *(greater part)*, mass *(weight)*, measurement, plurality, quantity. SEE MAIN ENTRY
bulk transfer SEE MAIN ENTRY
bulkhead buffer zone, bulwark
bulky ponderous
bulletin declaration, dispatch *(message)*, entry *(record)*, issuance, notice *(announcement)*, notification, prospectus, publicity, report *(detailed account)*. SEE MAIN ENTRY
bullheaded pertinacious, uncontrollable
bully badger, browbeat, brutalize, endanger, frighten, harrow, harry *(harass)*, hector, intimidate, irritate, mistreat, persecute, pique
bullyrag frighten, pique, plague
bulwark barrier, bear *(support)*, buffer zone, mainstay, protect, protection, safeguard, security *(safety)*, shield. SEE MAIN ENTRY
bump collide *(crash against)*, impinge, jostle *(bump into)*
bump against jostle *(bump into)*
bump into collide *(crash against)*
bumper crop SEE MAIN ENTRY
bumptious contemptuous, disdainful, inflated *(vain)*, insolent, perverse, supercilious. SEE MAIN ENTRY
bunch assemblage, compile, congregate, hoard, quantity, selection *(collection)*
bunch together compile
bunched compact *(dense)*, solid *(compact)*
bundle assemblage
bung shut, stem *(check)*
bungle fail *(lose)*, miscue, misdoing, mismanage, mistake, muddle, spoil *(impair)*
bungling fault *(mistake)*, incompetent, inept *(incompetent)*, maladministration, neglect, negligent
bunk dwell *(reside)*
bunker depository
bunko SEE MAIN ENTRY
bunkum rodomontade
buoy up assure *(give confidence to)*, bear *(support)*, bolster, reassure

buoyant resilient, sanguine, volatile
burden bind *(obligate)*, charge *(lien)*, charge *(responsibility)*, clog, cloud *(incumbrance)*, commitment *(responsibility)*, compel, constrain *(compel)*, disadvantage *(noun)*, disadvantage *(verb)*, duty *(obligation)*, duty *(tax)*, embarrass, encumber *(financially obligate)*, encumber *(hinder)*, encumbrance, grievance, hamper, handicap, harass, impede, impediment, impose *(enforce)*, inflict, interfere, liability, load, mistreat, nuisance, obligation *(duty)*, overcome *(overwhelm)*, overload, parasite, part *(role)*, pressure, responsibility *(accountability)*, servitude, stress *(strain)*, tax *(overwork)*, trouble, weigh. SEE MAIN ENTRY
burden of going forward SEE MAIN ENTRY
burden of proof SEE MAIN ENTRY
burdened disadvantaged, disconsolate
burdensome difficult, onerous, operose, oppressive, ponderous
burdensome requirement onus *(burden)*
bureau agency *(commission)*, board, chapter *(branch)*, commission *(agency)*, committee, department, facility *(institution)*, firm, management *(directorate)*, office, organ. SEE MAIN ENTRY
bureaucracy hierarchy *(persons in authority)*, management *(directorate)*. SEE MAIN ENTRY
bureaucrat functionary, incumbent, official
bureaucratic ministerial, political
burgeon compound, expand, germinate, increase, proliferate, pullulate
burgeoning accession *(enlargement)*, boom *(increase)*, boom *(prosperity)*
burgess resident
burgher denizen
burglar criminal, hoodlum. SEE MAIN ENTRY
burglarious larcenous
burglarize loot, pillage, purloin, rob, steal
burglarizing housebreaking
burglary housebreaking, theft. SEE MAIN ENTRY
buried blind *(concealed)*, dead, hidden, personal *(private)*, privy
burke suppress
burlesque imitation, jape, mock *(imitate)*, parody, ridicule, travesty
burlesque translation travesty
burly strong
burn deflagrate, destroy *(efface)*, expend *(consume)*. SEE MAIN ENTRY
burn fiercely deflagrate
burn to a cinder burn
burn up consume, deflagrate, dissipate *(expend foolishly)*
burning bitter *(penetrating)*, caustic, fanatical, harsh, hot-blooded, perfervid, scathing, vehement
burrow delve, hunt, research
bursal financial, fiscal
bursar comptroller
bursary bank, repository, treasury
burst barrage, break *(fracture)*, discharge *(shot)*, discharge *(shoot)*, outbreak, outburst, rend
burst forth emerge, issue *(send forth)*, pullulate
burst in obtrude
burst in upon penetrate
burst into flame burn, deflagrate
burst of sound outcry
bury camouflage, cloak, cover *(conceal)*, embed, hide, immerse *(engross)*, inundate, overwhelm, plant *(covertly place)*, seclude, shroud, suppress. SEE MAIN ENTRY
busily employed active
busily engaged active, industrious, sedulous
busily intent diligent
business agenda, assignment *(task)*, calling, career, commerce, commercial, company *(enterprise)*, concern *(business establishment)*, corporation, dealings, employment, enterprise *(economic organization)*, firm, function, job, livelihood, mercantile, mission, occupation *(vocation)*, office, position *(business status)*, post, practice *(professional business)*, profession *(vocation)*, province, pursuit *(occupation)*, trade *(commerce)*, trade *(occupation)*, transaction, undertaking *(enterprise)*, venture, work *(employment)*. SEE MAIN ENTRY
business affairs agenda, commerce, trade *(commerce)*
business agreement consortium *(business cartel)*
business association corporation
business combine consortium *(business cartel)*
business contact client, customer, patron *(regular customer)*
business deals commerce
business entente consortium *(business cartel)*
business establishment company *(enterprise)*, corporation, enterprise *(economic organization)*, firm, house
business expense cost *(expenses)*
business expenses overhead
business firm house
business house firm, store *(business)*
business intercourse commerce, dealings, exchange, trade *(commerce)*
business judgment rule SEE MAIN ENTRY
business manager comptroller
business on hand agenda, matter *(subject)*
business owner lessor
business profits income
business representative procurator
business science finance
business transaction deal, dealings
business transactions commerce
businesslike commercial, diligent, formal, professional *(stellar)*, prompt, systematic
businessman dealer, vendor
businessperson dealer, merchant
bustle dispatch *(promptness)*, industry *(activity)*, turmoil
bustling rapid
busy active, diligent, engage *(involve)*, industrious, sedulous. SEE MAIN ENTRY
busy oneself with occupy *(engage)*, ply
busyness industry *(activity)*
but only, save
but for save
but for the fact that only
butcher extinguish, mutilate, spoil *(impair)*
butchery homicide
butt abut, border *(bound)*, jostle *(bump into)*, object, strike *(collide)*, target
butt against collide *(crash against)*, contact *(touch)*, impinge
butt in interrupt, obtrude
button shut
buttress bear *(support)*, bulwark, corroborate, document, mainstay, maintain *(sustain)*, reaffirm, reinforce, reinforcement, side, supplement, support *(corroborate)*, sustain *(confirm)*, uphold. SEE MAIN ENTRY
buy procure, purchase, trade. SEE MAIN ENTRY
buy and sell barter, deal, trade
buy back redeem *(repurchase)*
buy from patronize *(trade with)*
buy into invest *(fund)*
buy off suborn
buy stock invest *(fund)*
buy up purchase
buyer consumer, customer, patron *(regular customer)*. SEE MAIN ENTRY
buyer of labor client, consumer, customer
buyer of stolen goods fence
buyer of stolen property fence
buying and selling business *(commerce)*, commerce, dealings, exchange, trade *(commerce)*
buying power money
buying price expense *(cost)*
by a stronger reason a fortiori
by all appearances prima facie *(self-evident)*
by and large as a rule
by and large each and every time always *(without exception)*
by any means regardless
by choice purposely
by circumstance coincidental
by compulsion will shall
by course of conduct pro forma
by custom pro forma
by degrees piecemeal
by design intentional, purposely
by divine right ex officio
by habit pro forma
by imperative will shall
by inference a fortiori, circumstantial
by law de jure, ex officio. SEE MAIN ENTRY
by means of hereby, thereby, through *(by means of)*
by one party ex parte
by order de jure
by past practice pro forma
by proxy in lieu of
by reason of a priori, consequently
by right as a matter of right, ex officio
by right of law de jure
by statute de jure
by the act itself ipso facto
by the aid of hereby
by the fact itself ipso facto
by the hand of through *(by means of)*
by the mere fact ipso facto
by the piece retail
by the same sign consequently
by the same token consequently
by the time that until
by the very fact ipso facto
by trade and usage pro forma
by usage pro forma
by use of thereby
by virtue of hereby, thereby
by vote elective *(selective)*
by way of through *(by means of)*, through *(from beginning to end)*
by way of a will testamentary
by way of gift gratuitous *(given without recompense)*
by will purposely
by word of mouth oral
by-passage causeway, detour
by-product development *(outgrowth)*, follow-up
bygone antique, former, obsolete, outdated, outmoded
bylaw code, regulation *(rule)*, rubric *(authoritative rule)*, rule *(legal dictate)*
bylaws codification
byname cognomen, sobriquet

bypass avoidance *(evasion)*, circumvent, detour, eschew, forgo, ignore, omit, pretermit, shun. SEE MAIN ENTRY
byproduct offshoot
bystander eyewitness, witness. SEE MAIN ENTRY
byword call *(title)*, catchword, cognomen, maxim, phrase

C

cabal band, collusion, confederacy *(conspiracy)*, conspire, cooperate, faction, frame up, machination, maneuver, plan *(noun)*, plan *(verb)*, plot *(secret plan)*, plot, scheme *(noun)*, scheme *(verb)*, schism, secret. SEE MAIN ENTRY
cabala mystery
cabalism mystery
cabalistic esoteric, mysterious, recondite
cabalistical esoteric
cabinet bench, board, chamber *(body)*, commission *(agency)*, committee
cache depository, fund, garner, harbor, hide, hoard *(noun)*, hoard *(verb)*, keep *(shelter)*, plant *(covertly place)*, provision *(something provided)*, repository, reserve *(noun)*, reserve *(verb)*, store *(depository)*, store, sufficiency, treasury. SEE MAIN ENTRY
cachet earmark, label
cacoethes dipsomania
cacophonous discordant
cacophony noise
cadaver body *(person)*. SEE MAIN ENTRY
cadaver corpse
cadaveric lifeless *(dead)*
cadaverous dead, lifeless *(dead)*
cadeau bounty
cadence inflection, intonation
cadenced periodic
cadent periodic
cadere abate *(extinguish)*, fail *(lose)*, miscarriage
cadet offspring
cadge request
cadger parasite
cadre division *(administrative unit)*, staff
caducity deterioration, impuissance, incapacity. SEE MAIN ENTRY
caducous ephemeral, transient
caducus ephemeral
caecus blind *(sightless)*
caedere beat *(strike)*
caedes assassination, homicide, murder
caelum climate
caerimonia ceremony
cage cell, confine, contain *(restrain)*, envelop, keep *(restrain)*, lock, restrict
cagey machiavellian
cairn landmark *(conspicuous object)*, monument
caitiff recreant. SEE MAIN ENTRY
cajole coax, entice, importune, influence, inveigle, lure, persuade, pressure, prevail *(persuade)*. SEE MAIN ENTRY
cajolement bribery, persuasion
cajolery bribery, instigation, persuasion, seduction
cajoling persuasion
calamitas adversity, calamity, catastrophe, disaster, misfortune
calamitosus disastrous
calamitous adverse *(negative)*, deadly, deplorable, dire, disastrous, fatal, harmful, hostile, insalubrious, pernicious, regrettable, unfavorable
calamity accident *(misfortune)*, adversity, casualty, catastrophe, debacle, disaster, fatality, loss, misfortune, pain, tragedy, trouble. SEE MAIN ENTRY
calcar stimulus
calcified ossified
calculable appreciable, foreseeable
calculate arrange *(plan)*, assess *(appraise)*, conspire, deduce, deduct *(conclude by reasoning)*, devise *(invent)*, evaluate, find *(determine)*, gauge, intend, measure, plan, rate, scheme. SEE MAIN ENTRY
calculate approximately estimate
calculate on anticipate *(expect)*
calculate upon expect *(anticipate)*
calculate wrongly miscalculate
calculated aforethought, cold-blooded, deliberate, express, intentional, premeditated, purposeful, strategic, tactical
calculated risk speculation *(risk)*
calculated to give a false impression deceptive
calculated to provoke resentment invidious
calculated to stir eloquent
calculatedly purposely
calculating artful, cold-blooded, collusive, discreet, judicious, machiavellian, pensive, politic, provident *(showing foresight)*, prudent, sly
calculation appraisal, assessment *(estimation)*, census, computation, contemplation, deduction *(conclusion)*, deliberation, estimate *(approximate cost)*, expectation, forethought, idea, ledger, measurement, prospect *(outlook)*, prudence. SEE MAIN ENTRY
calculator accountant
calculator of insurance risks actuary
calendar agenda, date, docket, empanel, file *(place among official records)*, note *(record)*, program *(noun)*, program *(verb)*, record, register *(noun)*, register *(verb)*, schedule. SEE MAIN ENTRY
calender set down
caliber degree *(magnitude)*, materiality *(consequence)*, performance *(workmanship)*, quality *(excellence)*, status, value, worth. SEE MAIN ENTRY
calibrate adjust *(regulate)*, assess *(appraise)*, gauge, measure
caliginosus lurid
call bespeak, charge *(command)*, contact *(communicate)*, convene, deem, demand, denominate, detail *(assign)*, entreaty, identify, impetus, invitation, label, market *(demand)*, monition *(legal summons)*, nominate, phrase, prayer, request, requirement, requisition, subpoena. SEE MAIN ENTRY
call a halt check *(restrain)*, close *(terminate)*, condemn *(ban)*, halt, hold up *(delay)*, quit *(discontinue)*, restrain
call attention to address *(direct attention to)*, admonish *(advise)*, indicate, notice *(observe)*, notify
call back annul, disavow, recommit, renege, rescind, resurrect
call before a court arraign
call by a distinctive title label
call by name denominate
call down rebuke, reprehend
call for command, demand, desire, entail, exact, market *(demand)*, necessitate, request, require *(compel)*, solicit, summon
call for aid call *(appeal to)*, petition
call for help call *(appeal to)*
call for the presence of subpoena, summon
call forth educe, elicit, engender, evoke, foment, incite, induce, order, provoke, resort, subpoena, summon
call in consult *(ask advice of)*, refer *(send for action)*
call in question disown *(deny the validity)*, dispute *(contest)*, except *(object)*, impeach, impugn, object, oppugn
call into action summon
call into being compose, engender, fabricate *(construct)*, generate, make
call into existence compose, generate, make
call names defame, denigrate
call of duty allegiance, burden, commitment *(responsibility)*
call off desist, discontinue *(abandon)*, dissolve *(terminate)*, hold up *(delay)*
call on refer *(send for action)*
call on for a blessing invoke
call on for help invoke
call out challenge, proclaim, subpoena
call public attention to issue *(publish)*, post, publish
call the roll poll
call to account arraign, blame, castigate, cite *(accuse)*, condemn *(blame)*, convict, denounce *(condemn)*, disapprove *(condemn)*, discipline *(punish)*, impeach, indict, lodge *(bring a complaint)*, penalize, punish, rebuke, reprehend, reprimand, reproach
call to answer challenge, contest
call to mind bear *(adduce)*, conjure, recognize *(perceive)*, recollect, remember
call to notice address *(direct attention to)*
call to task rebuke, reprimand
call to witness corroborate, subpoena, summon
call together convene
call up convene, evoke, induct, invoke, recall *(remember)*, recruit, remember, retain *(keep in possession)*
call upon address *(petition)*, call *(appeal to)*, command, delegate, direct *(order)*, importune, instruct *(direct)*, order, petition, plead *(implore)*, pray, press *(beseech)*
call with authority subpoena, summon
called by duty bound
called for essential *(required)*, important *(urgent)*, indispensable, mandatory, requisite
callidus artful, expert, resourceful
calligraphy handwriting, script
calling business *(occupation)*, career, designation *(naming)*, employment, job, labor *(work)*, livelihood, mission, occupation *(vocation)*, position *(business status)*, practice *(professional business)*, profession *(vocation)*, pursuit *(occupation)*, specialty *(special aptitude)*, trade *(occupation)*, work *(employment)*. SEE MAIN ENTRY
calling to account incrimination
calling to court summons
callosus callous
callous cold-blooded, diabolic, impervious, insensible, insusceptible *(uncaring)*, obdurate, obtuse, phlegmatic, recalcitrant, ruthless, unaffected *(uninfluenced)*. SEE MAIN ENTRY
calloused ossified
callousness disinterest *(lack of interest)*, disregard *(lack of respect)*
callow inexperienced, jejune *(lacking maturity)*, juvenile, naive, puerile, uncouth
calm allay, alleviate, composure, controlled *(restrained)*, dispassionate, ease, lull *(noun)*, lull *(verb)*, moderate *(temper)*, mollify, nonchalant, obtund, pacify, passive,

patient, peace, peaceable, phlegmatic, placate, placid, propitiate, relieve *(give aid)*, remedy, remit *(relax)*, soothe, subdue, subside, unaffected *(uninfluenced)*. SEE MAIN ENTRY
calm before a storm crossroad *(turning point)*
calm down rest *(cease from action)*
calmant narcotic
calmative mitigating, narcotic *(adjective)*, narcotic *(noun)*, palliative *(abating)*, placid, remedial
calme dispassionate
calmness common sense, composure, lull, moderation, mollification, peace, sufferance, temperance
calumnia aspersion, slander
calumniari cavil, defame, misrepresent
calumniate contemn, defame, denigrate, denounce *(condemn)*, derogate, disparage, lessen, libel, malign, pillory, smear
calumniating contemptuous
calumniation aspersion, bad repute, defamation, slander, vilification
calumniatory calumnious, contemptuous, derogatory
calumnious contemptuous, derogatory, libelous, pejorative. SEE MAIN ENTRY
calumny aspersion, bad repute, defamation, denunciation, dishonor *(shame)*, libel, lie, slander, vilification
camarade copartner *(coconspirator)*
camaraderie comity, contact *(association)*, sodality
camarilla cabal, faction
came to determination res judicata
camera chamber *(compartment)*
camouflage blind *(obscure)*, cloak, conceal, concealment, cover *(pretext)*, cover *(conceal)*, deceit, deception, decoy, disguise *(noun)*, disguise *(verb)*, distort, distortion, ensconce, enshroud, evasion, falsify, hide, misrepresent, plant *(covertly place)*, pretense *(pretext)*, pretext, ruse, screen *(guard)*, subterfuge, veil. SEE MAIN ENTRY
camouflaged blind *(concealed)*, clandestine, deceptive, hidden, indiscernible, latent
camp dwelling, lodge *(reside)*
campaign activity, course, endeavor, enterprise *(undertaking)*, expedient, fight *(battle)*, operation, plan, program, promotion *(encouragement)*, pursuit *(effort to secure)*, strategy, venture, work *(effort)*. SEE MAIN ENTRY
campaign promises platform
campaigner contender, politician
campaigning politics
canaille populace
canard falsehood, fiction, figment, hoax, story *(falsehood)*. SEE MAIN ENTRY
canation license
cancel abate *(extinguish)*, abolish, abrogate *(annul)*, abrogate *(rescind)*, adeem, annul, cease, censor, condemn *(ban)*, countervail, debar, delete, disable, discharge *(release from obligation)*, disclaim, discontinue *(abandon)*, dissolve *(terminate)*, eliminate *(eradicate)*, expunge, expurgate, extinguish, extirpate, forestall, forgive, frustrate, invalidate, kill *(defeat)*, negate, neutralize, nullify, obliterate, override, overrule, quash, recall *(call back)*, recant, refute, remit *(release from penalty)*, remove *(eliminate)*, repeal, repudiate, rescind, revoke, superannuate, suppress, terminate, vacate *(void)*, vitiate. SEE MAIN ENTRY
cancel a punishment pardon
cancel an offense pardon
cancel debts liquidate *(determine liability)*
cancel out annul, counteract, countervail, neutralize
canceled inactive, invalid, lifeless *(dead)*, null *(invalid)*, null and void, powerless
canceling defeasance, discharge *(annulment)*
cancellation abandonment *(repudiation)*, abatement *(extinguishment)*, abolition, ademption, annulment, censorship, condonation, countermand, defeasance, desuetude, discharge *(annulment)*, discharge *(release from obligation)*, discontinuance *(act of discontinuing)*, dismissal *(termination of a proceeding)*, dissolution *(termination)*, invalidity, mistrial, negation, nollo prosequi, obviation, remission, renunciation, repudiation, rescision, retraction, reversal, revocation. SEE MAIN ENTRY
cancellation of a legacy ademption
cancelled defunct, void *(invalid)*
cancelling avoidance *(cancellation)*, discontinuance *(act of discontinuing)*, dissolution *(termination)*, revocation
cancerous malignant
candid bona fide, direct *(forthright)*, honest, ingenuous, objective, straightforward, unaffected *(sincere)*, upright. SEE MAIN ENTRY
candidate contender, contestant, politician, probationer *(one being tested)*, prospect *(prospective patron)*, rival. SEE MAIN ENTRY
candidate under consideration applicant *(candidate)*
candidatus candidate
candidness candor *(straightforwardness)*, honesty, probity, veracity
candidus candid, open *(persuasible)*, unaffected *(sincere)*
candied nectarious
candor disinterest *(lack of prejudice)*, honesty, probity, truth, veracity. SEE MAIN ENTRY
cane cudgel
canker decay, degenerate, infect, pervert
cankered decadent, marred
cannabis SEE MAIN ENTRY
cannabis sativa cannabis
cannonade barrage
canny artful, deft, machiavellian, perspicacious, politic, practiced, prudent, subtle *(insidious)*, vigilant
canon article *(precept)*, belief *(something believed)*, bylaw, code, codification, constitution, direction *(order)*, doctrine, dogma, edict, law, legislation *(enactments)*, mandate, maxim, ordinance, pandect *(code of laws)*, precept, prescription *(directive)*, principle *(axiom)*, regulation *(rule)*, rubric *(authoritative rule)*, rule *(legal dictate)*, standard, statute. SEE MAIN ENTRY
canon of laws pandect *(code of laws)*
canonic valid
canonical dogmatic, orthodox, valid
canonization elevation
canonize elevate, honor
canons legislation *(enactments)*
canons of ethics SEE MAIN ENTRY
canons regarding securities blue sky law
canorus harmonious
cant jargon *(technical language)*, palter, phraseology
cantankerous contentious, fractious, froward, hostile, inflexible, negative, perverse, petulant, restive. SEE MAIN ENTRY
canting querulous
cantle element, segment
cantlet segment
canton division *(administrative unit)*, province
canvass analyze, check *(inspect)*, debate, examine *(study)*, poll, request, scrutinize, solicit, survey *(poll)*. SEE MAIN ENTRY
canvassing analysis, inquiry *(systematic investigation)*
cap culminate, culmination, finish, pinnacle, surpass. SEE MAIN ENTRY
cap and trade SEE MAIN ENTRY
capability ability, caliber *(mental capacity)*, caliber *(quality)*, capacity *(aptitude)*, competence *(ability)*, competence *(sanity)*, comprehension, efficiency, facility *(easiness)*, faculty *(ability)*, force *(strength)*, gift *(flair)*, performance *(workmanship)*, potential, qualification *(fitness)*, specialty *(special aptitude)*
capable adequate, artful, competent, deft, effective *(efficient)*, efficient, eligible, expert, familiar *(informed)*, fit, omnipotent, operative, possible, potent, practiced, proficient, qualified *(competent)*, resourceful, sciential, veteran, virtual. SEE MAIN ENTRY
capable of being adjudged invalid voidable
capable of being adjudged void voidable
capable of being annulled voidable
capable of being appeased placable
capable of being bounded terminable
capable of being completed terminable
capable of being concluded terminable
capable of being conditioned terminable
capable of being conquered indefensible
capable of being debated debatable, forensic, litigable
capable of being decided by a court justiciable
capable of being declared ineffectual voidable
capable of being declared void voidable
capable of being deducted deductible *(capable of being deducted from taxes)*
capable of being demonstrated provable
capable of being divided divisible
capable of being done practicable
capable of being ended terminable
capable of being examined cognizable
capable of being exchanged convertible
capable of being figured out deductible *(provable)*
capable of being fixed terminable
capable of being inhabited habitable
capable of being limited terminable
capable of being made definite terminable
capable of being maintained tenable
capable of being overcome indefensible
capable of being pacified placable
capable of being perceived appreciable
capable of being proved deductible *(provable)*
capable of being proven provable
capable of being rebated deductible *(capable of being deducted from taxes)*
capable of being shown provable
capable of being transferred negotiable

capable of being tried in the court cognizable
capable of conforming to new situations flexible
capable of decision determinable *(ascertainable)*
capable of development viable
capable of growth viable
capable of holding much capacious
capable of loss at risk
capable of passing passable
capable of positive proof provable
capable of proof certain *(positive)*, incontrovertible, provable
capable of reason reasonable *(rational)*
capable of receiving injuries vulnerable
capable of resisting insusceptible *(resistant)*, insusceptible *(uncaring)*
capable of responding to changing situations flexible
capable of withstanding insusceptible *(uncaring)*
capableness caliber *(mental capacity)*, capacity *(aptitude)*, efficiency
capacious ample, complete *(all-embracing)*, comprehensive, extensive. SEE MAIN ENTRY
capaciousness measurement, space
capacitate empower, enable
capacity ability, appointment *(position)*, caliber *(mental capacity)*, cargo, competence *(ability)*, coverage *(scope)*, employment, faculty *(ability)*, gift *(flair)*, maximum *(amplitude)*, means *(opportunity)*, measurement, occupation *(vocation)*, office, penchant, performance *(workmanship)*, post, potential, propensity, province, pursuit *(occupation)*, qualification *(fitness)*, role, science *(technique)*, space, sphere, sufficiency. SEE MAIN ENTRY
capacity to decide the matter in issue jurisdiction
capacity to endure sufferance, tolerance
capacity to hear the controversy jurisdiction
capacity to stand suffering tolerance
capacity to take pain tolerance
capacity to understand comprehension
capere capture, contain *(comprise)*, ensnare, entrap, gain, occupy *(take possession)*, receive *(acquire)*
capital assets, cardinal *(basic)*, cash, central *(essential)*, deadly, fund, important *(significant)*, leading *(ranking first)*, master, material *(important)*, monetary, money, possessions, premium, prime *(most valuable)*, principal *(capital sum)*, resource, salient, seat, securities, security *(stock)*, select, share *(stock)*, stellar, stock *(shares)*, substance *(material possessions)*, treasury. SEE MAIN ENTRY
capital crime felony, homicide
capital gains boom *(prosperity)*
capital goods merchandise
capital invested investment
capital murder homicide
capital outlay investment
capital punishment SEE MAIN ENTRY
capitalize finance. SEE MAIN ENTRY
capitalize on exploit *(make use of)*
capitalize upon employ *(make use of)*
capitation assessment *(levy)*, duty *(tax)*, excise, poll *(canvass)*, tax
capitulary code, codification
capitulate accede *(concede)*, defer *(yield in judgment)*, forfeit, quit *(discontinue)*, resign, submit *(yield)*, succumb, surrender *(yield)*, yield *(submit)*
capitulation capsule, concession *(compromise)*, hornbook, resignation *(passive acceptance)*. SEE MAIN ENTRY
caprice notion
capricious aleatory *(uncertain)*, arbitrary, disordered, haphazard, inconsistent, irresolute, irresponsible, lawless, mutable, undependable, unpredictable, unreasonable, unreliable, unsettled, untrustworthy, variable, volatile. SEE MAIN ENTRY
capriciousness inconsistency
capsize upset
capsule abridgment *(condensation)*, abstract, brief, compendium, concise, digest, hornbook, scenario. SEE MAIN ENTRY
capsulize abridge *(shorten)*, abstract *(summarize)*, condense, constrict *(compress)*, digest *(summarize)*
capsulized concise
captain chief, superintendent
captainship generalship
captare solicit
captio fallacy
caption apprehension *(act of arresting)*, call *(title)*, denomination, heading, inscription, phrase, rubric *(title)*, title *(designation)*. SEE MAIN ENTRY
captiosus sophistic
captious contentious, contrary, critical *(faultfinding)*, fractious, froward, perverse, petulant, querulous, sophistic. SEE MAIN ENTRY
captivate coax, lure, motivate, occupy *(engage)*, subdue
captivating attractive, moving *(evoking emotion)*, provocative, sapid
captivation seduction
captive convict, hostage, in custody, inmate, prisoner. SEE MAIN ENTRY
captivitas captivity
captivity bondage, constraint *(imprisonment)*, custody *(incarceration)*, detention, durance, duress, incarceration, restraint, servitude, subjection, thrall. SEE MAIN ENTRY
captivus captive
capture apprehend *(arrest)*, apprehension *(act of arresting)*, appropriate, appropriation *(taking)*, arrest, arrest *(apprehend)*, carry away, confine, deprive, detain *(hold in custody)*, disseisin, distraint, distress *(seizure)*, enclose, ensnare, gain, hijack, jail, kidnap, obtain, occupy *(take possession)*, preempt, prize, procure, repossess, seize *(apprehend)*, seize *(confiscate)*, subdue, succeed *(attain)*, taking. SEE MAIN ENTRY
capture and deportation extradition
captured arrested *(apprehended)*
captured goods contraband
captured person captive
capturing confiscatory
captus captive, inmate
caput article *(precept)*, capital, chapter *(division)*, chief, clause, main point, person, point *(item)*, principal *(capital sum)*, source
carbine gun
carbon counterpart *(parallel)*, duplicate
carbon copy counterpart *(parallel)*, duplicate
carcass body *(person)*, cadaver, corpse
carcer custody *(supervision)*, incarceration, jail, prison
card coupon, form *(document)*
card index file
cardholder member *(individual in a group)*
cardinal central *(essential)*, considerable, dominant, fundamental, indispensable, integral, leading *(ranking first)*, material *(important)*, paramount, prime *(most valuable)*, principal, salient, vital. SEE MAIN ENTRY
cardinal feature main point
cardinal point center *(essence)*, content *(meaning)*, cornerstone, gist *(ground for a suit)*, gravamen, landmark *(significant change)*, main point
care administration, agency *(legal relationship)*, alimony, apprehension *(fear)*, auspices, burden, caution *(vigilance)*, charge *(custody)*, concern *(interest)*, consideration *(sympathetic regard)*, constraint *(imprisonment)*, control *(supervision)*, custody *(supervision)*, direction *(guidance)*, discretion *(quality of being discreet)*, generalship, help, interest *(concern)*, maintenance *(upkeep)*, management *(supervision)*, notice *(heed)*, particularity, patronage *(support)*, precaution, preservation, problem, prudence, regard *(attention)*, relief *(aid)*, rigor, safekeeping, service *(assistance)*, shelter *(protection)*, supervision, surveillance, trust *(custody)*, ward, weight *(burden)*. SEE MAIN ENTRY
care for attend *(take care of)*, cover *(guard)*, foster, harbor, hold *(possess)*, keep *(shelter)*, maintain *(sustain)*, manage, nurture, police, preserve, protect, provide *(arrange for)*, regard *(hold in esteem)*, serve *(assist)*
care nothing for condescend *(patronize)*, disdain, flout
cared for safe
career business *(occupation)*, calling, employment, livelihood, occupation *(vocation)*, position *(business status)*, post, practice *(professional business)*, profession *(vocation)*, professional *(trained)*, pursuit *(occupation)*, specialty *(special aptitude)*. SEE MAIN ENTRY
carefree complacent, convenient, nonchalant, secure *(confident)*
careful accurate, circumspect, close *(rigorous)*, conscientious, deliberate, discreet, economical, exact, faithful *(diligent)*, frugal, guarded, judicious, leery, literal, meticulous, noncommittal, painstaking, particular *(exacting)*, politic, precise, preventive, provident *(frugal)*, provident *(showing foresight)*, prudent, punctilious, scrupulous, strict, thorough, vigilant. SEE MAIN ENTRY
careful appreciation diagnosis
careful attention notice *(heed)*
careful budgeting prudence
careful consideration deliberation
careful examination scrutiny
careful management economy *(frugality)*
careful methods strategy
careful noting of details examination *(study)*
careful plans strategy
careful scrutiny inspection
careful search indagation, investigation, probe, research
careful study indagation, investigation
carefully considered deliberate
carefully weighed deliberate
carefulness caution *(vigilance)*, deliberation, diligence *(care)*, discretion *(quality of being discreet)*, economy *(frugality)*, notice *(heed)*, particularity, precaution, prudence, rigor
carefulness in outlay economy *(frugality)*
careless blind *(not discerning)*, cursory, derelict *(negligent)*, disorderly, heedless,

hot-blooded, ill-judged, impolitic, improvident, imprudent, impulsive *(rash)*, inaccurate, inadvertent, inexact, lax, negligent, oblivious, perfunctory, prodigal, reckless, remiss, slipshod, superficial, thoughtless, undependable, unpolitic, wanton. SEE MAIN ENTRY
careless abandon neglect
careless loss waste
careless mistake oversight *(carelessness)*
careless omission oversight *(carelessness)*
carelessness delinquency *(failure of duty)*, dereliction, disinterest *(lack of interest)*, disregard *(unconcern)*, inconsideration, indiscretion, laxity, malpractice, neglect, negligence, omission, temerity
caretake operate, superintend
caretaker custodian *(warden)*, fiduciary, guardian, proctor, procurator, superintendent, trustee. SEE MAIN ENTRY
caretakers management *(directorate)*
careworn disconsolate
carfare fare
cargo freight, merchandise. SEE MAIN ENTRY
caricature copy, disguise, distort, distortion, exaggeration, jape, mock *(imitate)*, parody, ridicule, travesty. SEE MAIN ENTRY
caring solicitous
caritas dearth
carload cargo, freight
carmen famosum libel
carnage aberemurder, havoc, homicide
carnal bodily, dissolute, lascivious, lewd, mundane, physical, promiscuous, prurient, salacious, suggestive *(risqué)*
carnivorous predatory
carouse SEE MAIN ENTRY
carp blame, cavil, complain *(criticize)*
carp at discompose, persecute, press *(goad)*
carpenter build *(construct)*, frame *(construct)*
carpere cavil, cull
carping critical *(faultfinding)*, criticism, denunciation, diatribe, fractious, petulant, querulous
carriage behavior, complexion, conduct, demeanor, deportment, manner *(behavior)*, presence *(poise)*, temperament. SEE MAIN ENTRY
carried consensual
carried away ecstatic, uncontrollable
carried through complete *(ended)*
carrier bearer. SEE MAIN ENTRY
carrion body *(person)*, corpse
carry bear *(support)*, convey *(transfer)*, deliver, demean *(deport oneself)*, handle *(trade)*, move *(alter position)*, pass *(approve)*, transfer, transmit, transport, uphold, wield. SEE MAIN ENTRY
carry a report disseminate
carry a suggestion connote, imply
carry authority dominate, prevail *(triumph)*
carry away abduct, capture, displace *(remove)*, distrain, hijack, hold up *(rob)*, impropriate. SEE MAIN ENTRY
carry back recover
carry beyond the limit extend *(enlarge)*
carry conviction convince
carry forward keep *(continue)*, perpetuate
carry further extend *(enlarge)*
carry into effect comply, consummate, discharge *(perform)*, effectuate, enforce, execute *(accomplish)*, fulfill, implement, make, realize *(make real)*
carry into execution abide, commit *(perpetrate)*, comply, compose, discharge *(perform)*, effectuate, enforce, execute *(accomplish)*, exercise *(discharge a function)*, implement, make, operate, perform *(adhere to)*, perform *(execute)*, perpetrate, satisfy *(discharge)*, strive
carry off carry away, dislodge, distrain, hijack, hold up *(rob)*, kidnap, loot, perpetrate, plunder, poach
carry on adhere *(persist)*, attempt, bear *(tolerate)*, commit *(perpetrate)*, conduct, continue *(resume)*, endure *(last)*, exercise *(discharge a function)*, function, keep *(continue)*, last, manage, militate, operate, oversee, perpetrate, perpetuate, persevere, persist, ply, proceed *(continue)*, promote *(organize)*, prosecute *(carry forward)*, remain *(continue)*, reopen, resume, tolerate, transact, undertake. SEE MAIN ENTRY
carry on a conversation converse, discuss, speak
carry on a lawsuit litigate
carry on a trade handle *(trade)*
carry on an argument contend *(dispute)*, dispute *(debate)*
carry on an inquiry canvass
carry on business handle *(trade)*, practice *(engage in)*, transact
carry on commerce handle *(trade)*, trade
carry on hostilities engage *(involve)*
carry on intensive research delve
carry on negotiations deal, handle *(trade)*
carry on under allow *(endure)*
carry on war fight *(battle)*
carry oneself deport *(conduct oneself)*
carry out administer *(conduct)*, apply *(put in practice)*, commit *(perpetrate)*, complete, comply, conduct, consummate, discharge *(perform)*, dispatch *(dispose of)*, enforce, execute *(accomplish)*, exercise *(discharge a function)*, finish, function, implement, keep *(fulfill)*, obey, observe *(obey)*, officiate, operate, perfect, perform *(adhere to)*, perpetrate, prosecute *(carry forward)*, realize *(make real)*, satisfy *(discharge)*, satisfy *(fulfill)*, transact, undertake. SEE MAIN ENTRY
carry out a sentence condemn *(punish)*, discipline *(punish)*, penalize
carry over continue *(resume)*, holdover
carry tales inform *(notify)*
carry through attain, commit *(perpetrate)*, complete, consummate, discharge *(perform)*, dispatch *(dispose of)*, effectuate, enforce, finish, follow-up, implement, perpetrate, realize *(make real)*
carry to completion complete, conclude *(complete)*, consummate, dispatch *(dispose of)*, exhaust *(try all possibilities)*
carry to excess carouse, overindulge
carry too far overindulge
carry weight influence, motivate, predominate *(command)*, prejudice *(influence)*
carry weight with prevail *(persuade)*, prevail upon
carry-over balance *(amount in excess)*, remainder *(remaining part)*
carrying carriage
carrying charge cost *(price)*, maintenance *(upkeep)*
carrying into effect enforcement, performance *(execution)*
carrying on continuation *(resumption)*
carrying out action *(performance)*, commission *(act)*, enforcement
carrying through discharge *(performance)*, fait accompli, performance *(execution)*
cart carry *(transport)*, deliver, transport
cart away dislodge, displace *(remove)*
cartage carriage
carte blanche dispensation *(exception)*
carte blanche latitude
carte blanche permit
cartel business *(commercial enterprise)*, coalition, compact, confederacy *(compact)*, consortium *(business cartel)*, league, pool, syndicate, treaty, trust *(combination of businesses)*. SEE MAIN ENTRY
cartload cargo
cartoon caricature, copy, parody
cartridges ammunition
carve create, disjoint, divide *(distribute)*, parcel, part *(separate)*, partition, split
carve up apportion
cascade outpour
case action *(proceeding)*, cause *(lawsuit)*, check *(inspect)*, complaint, controversy *(lawsuit)*, day in court, enshroud, example, incident, instance, lawsuit, matter *(subject)*, particular, patient, plight, predicament, proceeding, question *(issue)*, situation, subject *(object)*, suit, trial *(legal proceeding)*. SEE MAIN ENTRY
case at law controversy *(lawsuit)*, hearing
case for decision lawsuit
case for the prosecution complaint, count
case history dossier. SEE MAIN ENTRY
case in point example, illustration, instance, sample, specimen. SEE MAIN ENTRY
case in question matter *(subject)*
case of conscience allegiance
cases ready for argument calendar *(list of cases)*
cash currency, money. SEE MAIN ENTRY
cash box bank
cash in liquidate *(convert into cash)*
cash in on gain, profit
cash paid expenditure
cash payment advance *(allowance)*, collection *(payment)*
cash supplies capital
cashbook journal, ledger
casher bearer
cashier comptroller, demote, discharge *(dismiss)*, dislodge, dismiss *(discharge)*, eliminate *(exclude)*, reject, remove *(dismiss from office)*, supplant
cashier's check draft
cashiering dismissal *(discharge)*, layoff, rejection, removal
cassation cancellation, defeasance, negation
cast allocate, build *(construct)*, characteristic, configuration *(form)*, copy, discharge *(dismiss)*, disposition *(inclination)*, fabricate *(construct)*, frame *(formulate)*, inclination, launch *(project)*, make, nuance, personnel, posture *(attitude)*, predisposition, project *(impel forward)*, send, stamp, style, tenor. SEE MAIN ENTRY
cast a ballot vote
cast a reproach censure
cast a shadow obnubilate, obscure
cast a slur smear
cast a slur on blame, dishonor *(deprive of honor)*, involve *(implicate)*
cast a slur upon brand *(stigmatize)*, censure, denounce *(condemn)*, derogate, disgrace, fault, humiliate, malign, pillory
cast a vote vote

cast accounts calculate
cast adrift dispel
cast an imputation upon impeach
cast anchor pause
cast aside abandon *(relinquish),* condemn *(ban),* derelict *(abandoned),* forgo, forswear, nullify, omit, pretermit, rebuff, refuse, reject, renounce, repel *(drive back),* spurn
cast aspersions complain *(criticize),* contemn, denigrate, denounce *(condemn),* deprecate, derogate, dishonor *(deprive of honor),* malign. SEE MAIN ENTRY
cast aspersions at brand *(stigmatize)*
cast aspersions on defame, disapprove *(condemn),* discredit, pillory
cast away abandon *(relinquish),* depose *(remove),* disown *(refuse to acknowledge),* forswear, reject
cast back reflect *(mirror)*
cast blame upon censure, condemn *(blame),* convict, disapprove *(condemn),* fault, impeach, incriminate, lodge *(bring a complaint),* reprehend
cast dishonor upon disgrace
cast doubt impugn
cast doubt upon debunk
cast down disconsolate, discourage, humiliate, overthrow
cast eyes on discern *(detect with the senses)*
cast forth diffuse, disperse *(disseminate),* dissipate *(spread out),* eject *(expel),* outpour
cast into prison arrest *(apprehend),* immure, imprison, jail
cast light upon elucidate. SEE MAIN ENTRY
cast loose discharge *(dismiss),* free *(not restricted),* parole
cast lots bet
cast off abandon *(physically leave),* abandon *(relinquish),* defect, derelict *(abandoned),* disencumber, disown *(refuse to acknowledge),* dispel, disperse *(disseminate),* forgo, forswear, reject, relinquish, renounce, set aside *(annul),* waive
cast out condemn *(ban),* deport *(banish),* depose *(remove),* disinherit, dislocate, dislodge, dismiss *(discharge),* dispel, displace *(remove),* eject *(evict),* eject *(expel),* eliminate *(exclude),* emit, exclude, expatriate, expose, ineligible, oust, relegate, spurn
cast overboard jettison
cast reflection upon censure, denounce *(condemn),* impugn
cast reproach upon denounce *(condemn),* disgrace, dishonor *(deprive of honor),* expostulate, lash *(attack verbally)*
cast shame upon discredit
cast the majority of ballots for elect *(select by a vote)*
castaway derelict *(abandoned),* discard, orphan, pariah
caste bloodline, class, status
castigare castigate, punish
castigate blame, censure, complain *(criticize),* condemn *(blame),* criticize *(find fault with),* denounce *(condemn),* disapprove *(condemn),* discipline *(punish),* expostulate, fault, ill use, impeach, lash *(attack verbally),* penalize, proscribe *(denounce),* punish, rebuke, remonstrate, reprehend, reprimand, reproach. SEE MAIN ENTRY
castigating critical *(faultfinding)*
castigatio correction *(punishment),* punishment
castigation bad repute, blame *(culpability),* charge *(accusation),* condemnation *(blame),* contumely, correction *(punishment),* denunciation, diatribe, discipline *(punishment),* discredit, disparagement, impeachment, indictment, infliction, objurgation, obloquy, outcry, penalty, phillipic, punishment, remonstrance, reprimand, reproach, revilement, stricture
castigatory calumnious, disciplinary *(punitory),* pejorative, penal, punitive
casting away release
casting of ballots poll *(casting of votes)*
casting out deportation
castoff discard
casual careless, coincidental, cursory, fortuitous, haphazard, informal, lax, nonchalant, perfunctory, promiscuous, random, sporadic, thoughtless, unintentional, unofficial, usual. SEE MAIN ENTRY
casualness informality
casualties toll *(effect)*
casualty accident *(misfortune),* corpse, damage, disaster, expense *(sacrifice),* fatality, happenstance, misfortune, quirk *(accident),* tragedy, victim. SEE MAIN ENTRY
casuistic artificial, illusory, sophistic, specious
casuistical illusory, sophistic, specious
casuistry duplicity, ethics, sophistry. SEE MAIN ENTRY
casus accident *(chance occurrence),* chance *(fortuity),* contingency, emergency, fatality, happening, hazard, incident, occurrence
casus foederis counteroffer
catachresis SEE MAIN ENTRY
cataclysm calamity, catastrophe, debacle, disaster, fatality, havoc, misfortune, outbreak, prostration, shambles, tragedy. SEE MAIN ENTRY
cataclysmal disastrous
cataclysmic deadly, dire, disastrous, harmful
catalog codify, docket, enumerate, impanel, index *(relate),* itemize
catalogue classify, detail *(particularize),* digest *(summarize),* directory, enroll, enter *(record),* file, file *(arrange),* fix *(arrange),* identify, inventory, note *(record),* order *(arrangement),* organize *(arrange),* pigeonhole, program, prospectus, record *(noun),* record *(verb),* register *(noun),* register *(verb),* roll, sort, tabulate. SEE MAIN ENTRY
catalogue of persons poll *(canvass)*
cataloguing classification, registration
catalyst stimulus. SEE MAIN ENTRY
catalytic agent catalyst, stimulus
catapult cast *(throw),* impel, launch *(project),* precipitate *(throw down violently)*
cataract spate
catastrophe adversity, calamity, casualty, debacle, disaster, fatality, loss, misfortune, tragedy, trouble. SEE MAIN ENTRY
catastrophic adverse *(negative),* deplorable, dire, disastrous, fatal, harmful, pernicious, regrettable. SEE MAIN ENTRY
catastrophical dire
catch apprehend *(arrest),* apprehension *(act of arresting),* arrest *(apprehend),* capture, connection *(fastening),* ensnare, entrap, lock, obstacle, obstruction, overhear, pitfall, preempt, prize, receive *(acquire),* seize *(apprehend),* trap *(noun),* trap *(verb).* SEE MAIN ENTRY
catch a glimpse of find *(discover)*
catch again rearrest
catch by artifice entrap
catch by perfidy ambush
catch fire burn
catch phrase catchword
catch sight of discern *(detect with the senses),* recognize *(perceive),* spy
catch the attention occupy *(engage)*
catch the eye interest
catch unprepared ensnare
catch up reach
catch-all trap
catchall depository. SEE MAIN ENTRY
catching attractive, contagious
catchpenny tawdry
catchword SEE MAIN ENTRY
catchy attractive
catechization interrogation
catechize cross-examine, examine *(interrogate),* inquire
catechumen neophyte, novice
categorical absolute *(conclusive),* actual, affirmative, axiomatic, certain *(specific),* clear (certain), *compelling, conclusive* (determinative), *convincing, decisive, definite, dogmatic, explicit, express, positive* (incontestable), *specific, unconditional, unequivocal.* SEE MAIN ENTRY
categorical imperative conscience, instruction *(direction)*
categorically true actual, candid
categorization classification, denomination, department, designation *(naming),* diagnosis, distribution *(arrangement),* hierarchy *(arrangement in a series),* manner *(kind),* order *(arrangement),* subdivision, subheading
categorization of laws codification
categorize classify, codify, file *(arrange),* index *(docket),* organize *(arrange),* pigeonhole, sort, subdivide
category class, classification, denomination, department, diagnosis, division *(administrative unit),* kind, manner *(kind),* member *(constituent part),* section *(division),* subdivision. SEE MAIN ENTRY
catena chain *(series),* fetter
catenas fetter
catenation chain *(series),* connection *(fastening),* sequence
cater bestow, pander, supply
cater to excessively overindulge
caterer supplier
catering provision *(act of supplying)*
catharsis SEE MAIN ENTRY
catholic general, omnibus, prevailing *(current),* prevalent, rife
catholicity disinterest *(lack of prejudice)*
catholicon cure, panacea
catlike furtive, stealthy
cattiness spite
caucas company *(assemblage)*
caucus assemblage, assembly, chamber *(body),* meeting *(conference),* panel *(discussion group),* party *(political organization),* session. SEE MAIN ENTRY
caught arrested *(apprehended)*
causa cause *(reason),* cause, ground, inducement, issue *(matter in dispute),* matter *(case),* motive, reason *(basis),* suit
causal causative. SEE MAIN ENTRY
causality derivation, incentive
causam hear *(give a legal hearing)*
causam agere plead *(argue a case)*
causation building *(business of assembling),* cause *(reason),* creation, derivation, incentive, instigation, motive, origination, provocation, reason *(basis)*
causative causal, constructive *(creative),* productive. SEE MAIN ENTRY
cause action *(proceeding),* activity, answer *(solution),* avail *(bring about),* base

(foundation), basis, bear *(yield)*, campaign, case *(lawsuit)*, catalyst, cause of action, compel, compose, conduce, contention *(argument)*, contrive, controversy *(lawsuit)*, create, derivation, effectuate, elicit, endeavor, engender, enterprise *(undertaking)*, evoke, factor *(ingredient)*, forge *(produce)*, generate, gist *(ground for a suit)*, ground, impel, incentive, incite, induce, inducement, inflict, inspire, issue *(matter in dispute)*, make, matter *(case)*, motivate, occasion, operate, origin *(source)*, originate, origination, proceeding, procure, prompt, provocation, provoke, rationale, reason *(basis)*, redound, require *(compel)*, side, source, stimulus, suit, trial *(legal proceeding)*. SEE MAIN ENTRY
cause a discontinuance discontinue *(abandon)*
cause a fuss perturb
cause a mistake misguide
cause a rift disaffect
cause a scandal pillory
cause a stoppage check *(restrain)*, close *(terminate)*, hold up *(delay)*, quit *(discontinue)*
cause against an opposing party counterclaim
cause agitation perturb
cause alarm menace, perturb
cause aversion repel *(disgust)*
cause chaos disrupt
cause confusion disrupt, embarrass, perturb
cause damage to prejudice *(injure)*
cause detriment damage, prejudice *(injure)*
cause discomfort embarrass
cause discontent disappoint, disconcert, discourage
cause dislike affront, alienate *(estrange)*, antagonize, disaffect, discourage, incense, repel *(disgust)*
cause disorder perturb
cause displeasure disoblige
cause doubt discourage, dissuade
cause error delude, err, misguide, mislead
cause evil ill use, mistreat
cause for alarm hazard
cause for blame fault *(responsibility)*
cause for complaint ground
cause for concern problem
cause for protest ground
cause growth magnify
cause hostility disaffect
cause illness infect
cause in court action *(proceeding)*, lawsuit, matter *(case)*, suit
cause-in-fact SEE MAIN ENTRY
cause injury damage
cause loathing alienate *(estrange)*, incense
cause mischief damage
cause of action claim *(legal demand)*, gist *(ground for a suit)*, incentive. SEE MAIN ENTRY
cause of action in favor of defendants counterclaim. SEE MAIN ENTRY
cause of distress nuisance, trouble
cause of reproach disgrace
cause of shame disgrace
cause of sorrow grievance
cause offense affront, antagonize
cause pain aggravate *(annoy)*, harm, mistreat, prejudice *(injure)*
cause problems disadvantage
cause resentment bait *(harass)*, incense, pique
cause scission disrupt
cause suffering distress
cause the downfall of supplant
cause to constrain *(compel)*
cause to alter affect
cause to arrive late hold up *(delay)*
cause to be compose, fabricate *(construct)*, generate
cause to be continued perpetuate
cause to be dishonest corrupt, taint *(corrupt)*
cause to be forfeited confiscate, seize *(confiscate)*
cause to be nugatory foil
cause to be remembered retain *(keep in possession)*
cause to be smaller diminish
cause to be still allay
cause to be understood explain
cause to bend divert
cause to bulge inflate
cause to cease eradicate, interrupt
cause to contract constrict *(compress)*
cause to curve divert
cause to delay impede, interrupt
cause to descend demote
cause to deviate divert
cause to diminish decrease
cause to disappear expunge
cause to endure establish *(entrench)*, keep *(shelter)*, perpetuate
cause to exist compose, create, engender, fabricate *(construct)*, make
cause to expand develop
cause to feel certain assure *(give confidence to)*
cause to feel ill at ease embarrass
cause to forfeit dispossess
cause to grow develop, extend *(enlarge)*
cause to halt cease, enjoin, quit *(discontinue)*
cause to happen carry *(succeed)*, effectuate, evoke
cause to last keep *(shelter)*, perpetuate
cause to move with undue slowness hold up *(delay)*
cause to pass to another devolve
cause to put off to a later time hold up *(delay)*
cause to recollect remind
cause to relax lull
cause to remember remind
cause to rise elevate
cause to sink demote, depress
cause to subside allay
cause to suffer inflict
cause to taper diminish
cause to turn from divert
cause to undergo subject
cause to vary affect
cause to yield force *(coerce)*
cause umbrage antagonize
cause upset perturb
caused causative, derivative
causeless casual, gratuitous *(unwarranted)*, needless, unpredictable
causer author *(originator)*
causerie conversation
causeway SEE MAIN ENTRY
causey causeway
causidical actionable
causing danger dangerous, noxious
causing death fatal
causing destruction fatal
causing disagreement divisive
causing disassociation divisive
causing disjunction divisive
causing pleasure palatable
causing separation divisive
caustic astringent, bitter *(acrid tasting)*, bitter *(reproachful)*, calumnious, critical *(faultfinding)*, cynical, harsh, incisive, malignant, mordacious, spiteful, trenchant. SEE MAIN ENTRY
causticity severity
cautel notice *(heed)*
cauterize burn
cautio caution *(vigilance)*, prudence, security *(stock)*
caution admonish *(warn)*, admonition, advise, alert, castigate, caveat, charge *(instruct on the law)*, counsel, deliberation, deter, deterrent, diligence *(care)*, discourage, discretion *(quality of being discreet)*, dissuade, exhort, expostulate, forewarn, hesitation, indicant, monition *(warning)*, notice *(heed)*, notice *(warning)*, notification, notify, portend, precaution, premonition, prudence, restraint, signify *(inform)*, warning. SEE MAIN ENTRY
caution against danger forewarn
caution beforehand forewarn
caution in advance forewarn
caution money bail, binder
cautionary advisory, portentous *(ominous)*
cautious careful, circumspect, deliberate, diffident, discreet, frugal, guarded, hesitant, judicious, leery, noncommittal, politic, preventive, provident *(showing foresight)*, prudent, suspicious *(distrustful)*, tentative, vigilant. SEE MAIN ENTRY
cautious in dealing diplomatic
cautiousness deliberation, discretion *(quality of being discreet)*, notice *(heed)*
cautus circumspect, discreet, guarded, prudent, tactical
cavalier cynical, disdainful, impertinent *(insolent)*, presumptuous, supercilious
cavalierness disrespect
cave in break *(fracture)*, succumb
caveat admonition
caveat caution *(warning)*, deterrence, deterrent, instruction *(direction)*, measure, monition *(warning)*, notice *(warning)*, warning. SEE MAIN ENTRY
caveat emptor SEE MAIN ENTRY
cavil bicker, blame, complain *(criticize)*, denounce *(condemn)*, differ *(disagree)*, disagree, disapprove *(condemn)*, disparage, pettifog, sophistry. SEE MAIN ENTRY
caviler disputant, malcontent
caviling contentious, critical *(faultfinding)*, criticism, disaccord, disapprobation, dissension, dissent *(difference of opinion)*, dissenting, fractious
cavillari flout, jeer
cavilling petulant
cease abandon *(relinquish)*, close *(terminate)*, cloture, conclude *(complete)*, desist, discontinue *(abandon)*, dissipate *(spread out)*, dissolve *(terminate)*, expire, finish, forbear, forgo, halt, interrupt, leave *(allow to remain)*, palliate *(abate)*, pause, perish, quit *(discontinue)*, refrain, relinquish, renounce, rest *(cease from action)*, shut, stop, succumb, suspend, terminate, vacate *(leave)*, waive, withdraw. SEE MAIN ENTRY
cease existing decease
cease living decease, die, perish
cease progress quit *(discontinue)*
cease resistance comply, submit *(yield)*

cease to be decease, dissipate *(spread out)*, expire, perish
cease to exist decease, die, perish
cease to litigate rest *(end a legal case)*
cease to live decease, perish
cease to use quit *(discontinue)*
cease using discontinue *(abandon)*
cease work quit *(discontinue)*, resign, strike *(refuse to work)*
ceaseless chronic, continual *(perpetual)*, continuous, durable, incessant, infinite, open-ended, permanent, perpetual, unrelenting, unremitting
ceaselessness indestructibility, perpetuity
ceasing cessation *(interlude)*
cede abandon *(relinquish)*, attorn, bequeath, bestow, confer *(give)*, contribute *(supply)*, convey *(transfer)*, defer *(yield in judgment)*, devolve, disown *(refuse to acknowledge)*, forfeit, give *(grant)*, grant *(concede)*, grant *(transfer formally)*, offer *(tender)*, pass *(advance)*, relinquish, remise, resign, surrender *(give back)*, transmit, yield *(submit)*. SEE MAIN ENTRY
cede back escheat
cedere resign
ceiling cap, pinnacle. SEE MAIN ENTRY
celare hide
celeber famous, populous
celebrare honor
celebrate carouse, honor, keep *(fulfill)*, recommend. SEE MAIN ENTRY
celebrated blatant *(conspicuous)*, famous, household *(familiar)*, illustrious, notable, noteworthy, notorious, outstanding *(prominent)*, popular, prominent, remarkable, renowned, reputable, stellar
celebrated in public famous
celebration ceremony, dedication, holiday, memory *(commemoration)*, mention *(tribute)*, recommendation, remembrance *(commemoration)*, reputation
celebrity character *(reputation)*, distinction *(reputation)*, eminence, notoriety, prestige, regard *(esteem)*, reputation. SEE MAIN ENTRY
celer expeditious
celerity dispatch *(promptness)*, haste
celestial stellar
celibate solitary
cell chamber *(compartment)*, jail, penitentiary, prison. SEE MAIN ENTRY
cella cell
cement adhere *(fasten)*, bond *(hold together)*, cohere *(adhere)*, conjoin, connect *(join together)*, crystallize, lock, merge, unite. SEE MAIN ENTRY
cement a union affiliate, organize *(unionize)*
cementation accession *(annexation)*, adherence *(adhesion)*, adhesion *(affixing)*
cemented concordant, concurrent *(united)*, conjoint, inseparable
cementitious cohesive *(sticking)*
cenotaph monument
censeo comment
censere comment, estimate, judge
censor assessor
censor ban, bowdlerize. SEE MAIN ENTRY
censor censor
censor condemn *(ban)*, constrain *(restrain)*, delete, eliminate *(exclude)*, exclude, expunge, expurgate, forestall, redact, repress, restrict, suppress, withhold
censored illicit
censorious blameful, calumnious, critical *(faultfinding)*, cynical, derogatory, dictatorial, pejorative, petulant, querulous, remonstrative, severe
censorious writing libel
censoriousness bad repute
censorship SEE MAIN ENTRY
censurability blame *(culpability)*, guilt, impeachability
censurable blameful, blameworthy, contemptible, culpable, delinquent *(guilty of a misdeed)*, disgraceful, guilty, inexpiable, obnoxious, peccable, peccant *(culpable)*, reprehensible, sinister, unjustifiable, vicious
censurableness blame *(culpability)*, culpability
censure admonish *(warn)*, admonition, aspersion, bad repute, blame *(culpability)*, blame, charge *(accusation)*, charge *(accuse)*, cite *(accuse)*, complain *(charge)*, complain *(criticize)*, condemnation *(blame)*, contemn, convict, conviction *(finding of guilt)*, correction *(punishment)*, criticism, criticize *(find fault with)*, decry, defame, denounce *(condemn)*, denunciation, depreciate, diatribe, disapprobation, disapproval, disapprove *(condemn)*, discommend, discredit, disparage, fault, impeach, impeachment, impugnation, incrimination, judgment *(formal court decree)*, lessen, libel, notoriety, obloquy, odium, onus *(stigma)*, ostracism, outcry, phillipic, proscribe *(denounce)*, proscription, punishment, rebuff, rebuke, remonstrance, remonstrate, reprehend, reprimand, reproach *(noun)*, reproach *(verb)*, restraint, revilement, scandal, sentence, slander, spurn, stricture. SEE MAIN ENTRY
censure as faulty decry
censure bitterly castigate
censure formally reprimand
censure frivolously cavil
censured blameful
censurer malcontent
censuring critical *(faultfinding)*
census assessment *(levy)*, census
census poll *(canvass)*, roll. SEE MAIN ENTRY
census report poll *(canvass)*
census return poll *(canvass)*
center average *(midmost)*, base *(place)*, central *(situated near center)*, concentrate *(consolidate)*, focus *(noun)*, focus *(verb)*, gravamen, headquarters, interior, seat, site, target. SEE MAIN ENTRY
center around meet
center of activity focus
center of attention focus. SEE MAIN ENTRY
center of attraction focus
center of authority headquarters
center of consciousness focus
center of focus SEE MAIN ENTRY
center of gravity center *(central position)*
center of interest focus
center of operations headquarters
center upon converge
centering centralization
centermost average *(midmost)*, central *(situated near center)*
cento melange
central cardinal *(basic)*, cardinal *(outstanding)*, federal, fundamental, indispensable, integral, intermediate, leading *(ranking first)*, master, material *(important)*, primary. SEE MAIN ENTRY
central element necessity
central headquarters base *(place)*
central idea main point
central money office treasury
central nature center *(essence)*
central office management *(directorate)*
central point center *(central position)*, focus, gravamen, highlight
central station headquarters
centralism centralization
centrality focus
centralization affiliation *(amalgamation)*, coalescence, consolidation, federation, incorporation *(blend)*, merger. SEE MAIN ENTRY
centralize amalgamate, concentrate *(consolidate)*, consolidate *(unite)*, converge, federalize *(associate)*, focus, incorporate *(include)*, organize *(unionize)*, unite
centralized coadunate, concurrent *(united)*
centric central *(situated near center)*
centrical central *(situated near center)*
centrist SEE MAIN ENTRY
cerebral rational
cerebrate consider, deliberate, muse, ponder, reason *(conclude)*, reflect *(ponder)*, study
cerebration contemplation, deliberation, dialectic, intellect, ratiocination, reflection *(thought)*
ceremonial formal, sacrosanct, solemn
ceremonial rite formality
ceremonious formal, official, punctilious, solemn
ceremoniously pro forma
ceremoniousness formality, solemnity
ceremony custom, form *(arrangement)*, formality, protocol *(etiquette)*, remembrance *(commemoration)*, solemnity. SEE MAIN ENTRY
ceremony of induction into an office installation
certain absolute *(conclusive)*, actual, affirmative, axiomatic, conclusive *(determinative)*, concrete, constant, convincing, corporeal, de facto, decisive, definite, dependable, dogmatic, explicit, express, incontrovertible, indubious, inevitable, irrefutable, lucid, necessary *(inescapable)*, official, palpable, peremptory *(absolute)*, pertinacious, positive *(confident)*, positive *(incontestable)*, reliable, resounding, safe, secure *(confident)*, several *(plural)*, several *(separate)*, special, specific, tangible, true *(authentic)*, unalienable, unambiguous, unavoidable *(inevitable)*, undeniable, undisputed, unequivocal, unmistakable, unrefutable. SEE MAIN ENTRY
certain dereliction res ipsa loquitur
certain knowledge certification *(certainness)*, surety *(certainty)*
certainly a fortiori, admittedly, fairly *(clearly)*
certainness certitude
certainty belief *(state of mind)*, certification *(certainness)*, certitude, confidence *(faith)*, constant, conviction *(persuasion)*, credence, fact, fait accompli, faith, proof, prospect *(outlook)*, reliance, security *(safety)*, trust *(confidence)*, weight *(credibility)*. SEE MAIN ENTRY
certainty of meaning certitude
certamen contest *(competition)*, fight *(argument)*, strife, struggle
certare compete
certatio contest *(competition)*, strife
certifiable ascertainable, determinable *(ascertainable)*
certificate charter *(license)*, check *(instrument)*, coupon, deed, degree *(academic title)*, document, instrument *(document)*,

permit, recommendation, record, warrant *(judicial writ)*, warranty. SEE MAIN ENTRY
certificate of character reference *(recommendation)*
certificate of debt bond, security *(stock)*
certificate of deposit receipt *(proof of receiving)*
certificate of exemption dispensation *(exception)*
certificate of indebtedness bond, security *(stock)*
certificate of invention copyright, patent
certificate of permission charter *(license)*
certificates credentials
certification acknowledgment *(avowal)*, affirmance *(authentication)*, affirmation, appointment *(act of designating)*, asseveration, attestation, capacity *(authority)*, certainty, certificate, confirmation, consent, copyright, corroboration, credentials, documentation, droit, guaranty, indorsement, jurat, leave *(permission)*, license, proof, ratification, reference *(recommendation)*, registration, stamp, subscription, support *(corroboration)*, surety *(certainty)*. SEE MAIN ENTRY
certified alleged, allowed, certain *(fixed)*, certain *(positive)*, definite, documentary, familiar *(informed)*, fully secured, official
certified public accountant accountant
certifier comaker, surety *(guarantor)*
certify accredit, acknowledge *(declare)*, affirm *(uphold)*, allow *(authorize)*, approve, ascertain, assert, assure *(insure)*, attest, audit, authorize, avouch *(avow)*, avouch *(guarantee)*, avow, bear *(adduce)*, bond *(secure a debt)*, cite *(state)*, claim *(maintain)*, corroborate, cosign, countersign, depose *(testify)*, endorse, ensure, establish *(show)*, evidence, guarantee, indorse, legitimate, let *(permit)*, manifest, notarize, posit, promise *(vow)*, qualify *(meet standards)*, reassure, seal *(solemnize)*, sign, sponsor, subscribe *(sign)*, substantiate, support *(corroborate)*, sustain *(confirm)*, swear, validate, verify *(confirm)*, vouch, witness *(attest to)*. SEE MAIN ENTRY
certify a will probate
certiorari SEE MAIN ENTRY
certitude belief *(state of mind)*, certainty, certification *(certainness)*, confidence *(faith)*, conviction *(persuasion)*, faith, reliance, surety *(certainty)*. SEE MAIN ENTRY
certus authentic, certain *(particular)*, certain *(positive)*, certainty, conclusive *(settled)*, definite, fixed *(securely placed)*, infallible, irrefutable, positive *(confident)*, regular *(orderly)*, staunch, undisputed
cess assessment *(levy)*
cessare loiter
cessatio delay, inaction
cessation abandonment *(discontinuance)*, abeyance, avoidance *(cancellation)*, check *(bar)*, close *(conclusion)*, cloture, conclusion *(outcome)*, defeasance, desuetude, discharge *(annulment)*, discontinuance *(act of discontinuing)*, discontinuance *(interruption of a legal action)*, dissolution *(termination)*, end *(termination)*, expiration, finality, halt, hiatus, impasse, inaction, interruption, layoff, lull, moratorium, pause, pendency, recess, remission, respite *(interval of rest)*, stay. SEE MAIN ENTRY
cessation of activity lull
cessation of being extremity *(death)*
cessation of employment lockout
cessation of existence extremity *(death)*
cessation of life death, demise *(death)*, extremity *(death)*
cessation of sound lull
cessation of the furnishing of work lockout
cessation of use disuse
cession abandonment *(desertion)*, alienation *(transfer of title)*, assignment *(transfer of ownership)*, consignment, demise *(conveyance)*, expense *(sacrifice)*, release, renunciation, resignation *(relinquishment)*. SEE MAIN ENTRY
cession of a fee feoffment
chafe affront, aggravate *(annoy)*, annoy, badger, bait *(harass)*, discommode, discompose, harrow, incense, irritate, resent
chaff jape, mock *(deride)*, ridicule
chaffer haggle, handle *(trade)*, trade
chaffering commerce
chagrin disconcert, dissatisfaction, distress, embarrass, embarrassment, harrow, ignominy, ill will, offend *(insult)*, remorse. SEE MAIN ENTRY
chain constrain *(imprison)*, constrain *(restrain)*, contain *(restrain)*, detain *(restrain)*, fetter *(noun)*, fetter *(verb)*, handcuff *(noun)*, handcuff *(verb)*, hierarchy *(arrangement in a series)*, restrict, sequence, succession. SEE MAIN ENTRY
chain of custody SEE MAIN ENTRY
chain of evidence SEE MAIN ENTRY
chain of reasoning dialectic
chains bondage, ties
chair chairman, management *(directorate)*, moderate *(preside over)*, preside
chairman chief. SEE MAIN ENTRY
chairmen management *(directorate)*
chairperson chief
chalk out compose
challenge argue, charge *(accuse)*, cite *(accuse)*, claim *(legal demand)*, compete, competition, complain *(charge)*, conflict, confront *(oppose)*, confutation, contend *(dispute)*, contention *(opposition)*, contest *(competition)*, contest *(dispute)*, contest, contradict, counter, counterargument, cross-examination, cross-examine, defiance, defy, demonstrate *(protest)*, demur, demurrer, denial, denounce *(condemn)*, disaccord, disaffirm, disagree, disagreement, disbelieve, disown *(deny the validity)*, dispute, dispute *(contest)*, dissent *(difference of opinion)*, dissent *(withhold assent)*, doubt *(distrust)*, examine *(interrogate)*, except *(object)*, exception *(objection)*, fight *(battle)*, impeach, impeachment, impugnation, indagation, invitation, misdoubt, motivate, object, objection, oppose, opposition, oppugn, protest *(noun)*, protest *(verb)*, provoke, reaction *(opposition)*, reject, remonstrance, remonstrate, repel *(drive back)*, resist *(withstand)*, withstand. SEE MAIN ENTRY
challenge as false impugn
challenge the credibility of impeach
challenge to the sufficiency of the pleading demurrer
challenger accuser, candidate, complainant, contender, contestant, opponent, party *(litigant)*, rival
challenging competitive *(antagonistic)*, contemptuous, dissident, hostile, provocative, sapid
chamber bench, cell. SEE MAIN ENTRY
chambers lodging
chambre chamber *(compartment)*
champain bar sinister
champion absolute *(ideal)*, adhere *(maintain loyalty)*, advocate *(counselor)*, advocate *(espouser)*, advocate, amicus curiae, apologist, assistant, backer, bear *(support)*, benefactor, colleague, custodian *(protector)*, defend, espouse, favor, guardian, justify, mainstay, maintain *(sustain)*, paragon, paramount, partisan, patron *(influential supporter)*, preserve, prime *(most valuable)*, promote *(organize)*, proponent, protagonist, protect, samaritan, select, side, sponsor *(noun)*, sponsor *(verb)*, successful, superlative, support *(assist)*, uphold. SEE MAIN ENTRY
championing accommodation *(backing)*
championship advocacy, assistance, favor *(sanction)*, indorsement, supremacy
chance access *(opening)*, bet, coincidental, contingency, fortuitous, gamble, haphazard, happenstance, hazard, likelihood, lottery, occasion, opportunity, possibility, potential, privilege, probability, prospect *(outlook)*, quirk *(accident)*, random, risk, speculate *(chance)*, speculation *(risk)*, suspicion *(uncertainty)*, unexpected, unintentional, unwitting, venture. SEE MAIN ENTRY
chance event happening
chance happening happenstance. SEE MAIN ENTRY
chance occurrence act of god
chance the odds bet
chance to borrow money on time credit *(delayed payment)*
chance upon discover, find *(discover)*
chancellor judge, plenipotentiary
chancery equity *(justice)*, tribunal
chancy dubious, precarious, speculative
chandler dealer, merchant, supplier
change adapt, adjust *(resolve)*, affect, alter, alternative *(substitute)*, amend, amendment *(correction)*, commute, conflict, convert *(change use)*, denature, development *(progression)*, difference, digression, diversification, emend, exchange, fluctuate, innovation, interchange, modification, modify *(alter)*, money, nonconformity, pass *(advance)*, progress, reassign, reclassification, reconversion, redress, reform *(noun)*, reform *(verb)*, remedy, reorganization, replace, replacement, reversal, revise, revision *(process of correcting)*, subrogation, succedaneum, tamper, transform, transition, vacillate, vary. SEE MAIN ENTRY
change address remove *(transfer)*
change an abode move *(alter position)*
change back revert
change by alternation alternate *(take turns)*
change continuously fluctuate
change course redirect
change direction detour, deviate, digress, redirect
change for displace *(replace)*
change for the better ameliorate, improvement
change for the worse adulterate
change from higher to lower descent *(declination)*
change from one to another devolve
change hands bequeath, circulate
change in method innovation
change into convert *(change use)*, develop, evolve
change into cash liquidate *(convert into cash)*

change into money liquidate *(convert into cash)*
change national allegiance expatriate
change of direction deviation
change of hands devolution
change of mind rescision, reversal
change of national location immigration
change of place extradition, removal
change of position deviation
change of sides revolt
change one's mind tergiversate
change out of recognition distort
change over convert *(change use)*, reconversion
change ownership devolve, grant *(transfer formally)*, pass *(advance)*
change penalties commute
change place move *(alter position)*, remove *(transfer)*
change places circulate
change residence move *(alter position)*
change sides defect, repudiate, tergiversate
change the appearance of disguise
change the bearing detour
change the course of avert, divert
change the face of camouflage, disguise, distort
change the guise of disguise
change the place of displace *(remove)*
change venue remove *(transfer)*
change-over devolution, transition
changeable aleatory *(uncertain)*, ambulatory, capricious, conditional, convertible, debatable, disordered, faithless, inconsistent, indefinite, insecure, irresolute, irresponsible, mutable, noncommittal, pliable, precarious, protean, shifting, sporadic, temporary, undependable, unpredictable, unsettled, untrustworthy, variable, volatile
changeableness incertitude, inconsistency, indecision, irregularity
changed different, tempered
changed ordering of priorities reclassification
changed priorities reclassification
changeful aleatory *(uncertain)*, capricious, disordered, insecure, irresolute, mutable, protean, undecided, unpredictable, unreliable, variable
changeless certain *(fixed)*, certain *(positive)*, constant, durable, fixed *(settled)*, indelible, inflexible, irrevocable, permanent, static, unalterable
changelessly invariably
changelessness indestructibility
changer dealer
changes circumstances, vicissitudes
changing capricious, moving *(in motion)*, open-ended, shifting, unsettled
channel avenue *(route)*, facility *(instrumentality)*, forum *(medium)*, instrument *(tool)*, instrumentality, medium, outlet, tool. SEE MAIN ENTRY
channels approaches
chant recite, repeat *(state again)*
chaos anarchy, confusion *(turmoil)*, disorder *(lack of order)*, embroilment, entanglement *(confusion)*, havoc, imbroglio, incoherence, misrule, pandemonium, shambles, turmoil. SEE MAIN ENTRY
chaotic complex, disordered, haphazard, labyrinthine, promiscuous, unruly. SEE MAIN ENTRY
chaotic state havoc
chap person
chaperon guardian, warden
chaperonage charge *(custody)*
chaperone protect
chapman vendor
chapter affiliate, article *(distinct section of a writing)*, constituency, department, division *(administrative unit)*, organ, segment, subheading, title *(division)*. SEE MAIN ENTRY
chapter and verse verbatim
char burn
character animus, behavior, caliber *(quality)*, color *(complexion)*, complexion, condition *(state)*, configuration *(form)*, disposition *(inclination)*, entity, frame *(mood)*, honor *(good reputation)*, individual, integrity, kind, merit, part *(role)*, person, personality, predisposition, principle *(virtue)*, property *(distinctive attribute)*, quality *(excellence)*, quality *(grade)*, rectitude, role, speciality, specialty *(distinctive mark)*, spirit, style, temperament, tendency, tenor, turpitude. SEE MAIN ENTRY
character assassination slander
characteristic certain *(specific)*, customary, demonstrative *(illustrative)*, differential, disposition *(inclination)*, distinct *(distinguished from others)*, distinctive, general, identity *(individuality)*, indicant, natural, nondescript, ordinary, particular *(individual)*, particular *(specific)*, particularity, peculiar *(distinctive)*, personal *(individual)*, prevailing *(current)*, prevalent, property *(distinctive attribute)*, quality *(attribute)*, representative, specialty *(distinctive mark)*, specific, symptom, trait, typical, usual. SEE MAIN ENTRY
characteristic behavior habit
characteristic difference distinction *(difference)*
characteristic feature necessity
characteristic marks indicia
characteristic mood character *(personal quality)*, disposition *(inclination)*
characteristic part epitome
characteristic quality particularity, spirit
characteristic way custom
characteristically repeated action habit
characteristics color *(complexion)*, indicia, personality
characterization caption, caricature, cross section, denomination, description, role
characterize call *(title)*, construe *(translate)*, define, depict, describe, designate, differentiate, discriminate *(distinguish)*, distinguish, interpret, label, personify, portray, render *(depict)*, represent *(portray)*. SEE MAIN ENTRY
characterize precisely construe *(translate)*, define
characterized by argument argumentative
characterized by art artful
characterized by decision decisive
characterized by excess excessive
characterized by reflection deliberate
characterizing descriptive
characterless arrant *(onerous)*, disreputable, inexpressive, lifeless *(dull)*, pedestrian, usual
characters script
charade pretext
charge accusation, ad valorem, admonish *(advise)*, agency *(commission)*, agency *(legal relationship)*, allegation, allege, ammunition, appoint, arraign, assessment *(levy)*, assign *(designate)*, assignation, assignment *(task)*, attack, auspices, authorize, bad repute, bind *(obligate)*, blame *(responsibility)*, blame, bomb, brevet, brokerage, burden, cargo, cite *(accuse)*, claim *(maintain)*, cloud *(incumbrance)*, command, commit *(entrust)*, commitment *(responsibility)*, complaint, condemn *(blame)*, condemnation *(blame)*, consign, constrain *(compel)*, constraint *(imprisonment)*, control *(supervision)*, conviction *(finding of guilt)*, cost *(expenses)*, cost *(price)*, count, criticism, custody *(supervision)*, decree, defame, delegate, delegation *(assignment)*, denigrate, denounce *(inform against)*, denunciation, dependent, deprecate, detail *(assign)*, dictate *(noun)*, dictate *(verb)*, direct *(order)*, direction *(guidance)*, direction *(order)*, directive, due, duty *(obligation)*, duty *(tax)*, encumber *(financially obligate)*, encumber *(hinder)*, encumbrance, enjoin, estimate *(approximate cost)*, exact, exception *(objection)*, excise, excise *(levy a tax)*, exhort, expenditure, expense *(cost)*, fare, fault, generalship, grievance, impeach, impeachment, implicate, impose *(enforce)*, imposition *(tax)*, incriminate, incrimination, indict, indictment, inform *(betray)*, information *(charge)*, innuendo, instruct *(direct)*, instruction *(direction)*, invest *(vest)*, involve *(implicate)*, levy, lien, management *(supervision)*, mandamus, mandate, mechanics lien, mission, mortgage, motivate, obligation *(duty)*, obligation *(liability)*, occupation *(possession)*, office, onset *(assault)*, onus *(blame)*, onus *(burden)*, outcry, outlay, part *(role)*, payment *(remittance)*, plead *(implore)*, post, precept, prescribe, prescription *(directive)*, present *(prefer charges)*, presentment, price, proscribe *(denounce)*, protégé, province, rate, rebuke, reprehend, rule *(legal dictate)*, safekeeping, servitude, summon, supervision, surveillance, tax, toll *(tax)*, trust *(custody)*, ward, work *(employment)*, worth. SEE MAIN ENTRY
charge beyond normal premium *(excess value)*
charge duty excise *(levy a tax)*
charge falsely frame *(prearrange)*
charge for carriage of passengers fare
charge for conveyance of a person fare
charge for services fee *(charge)*
charge imposed on specific property lien, mechanics lien
charge levied assessment *(levy)*
charge to impeach, impute
charge to excess premium *(excess value)*
charge unfairly frame *(charge falsely)*
charge unjustly frame *(charge falsely)*
charge upon impute
charge with accuse, ascribe, attribute, commit *(entrust)*, complain *(charge)*, impeach, lodge *(bring a complaint)*
charge with a duty entrust
charge with a trust entrust
charge with an errand delegate
charge with an offense incriminate
charge with offense indict
charge with one's share assess *(tax)*
charge with the commission of a crime indict
chargeability blame *(culpability)*, impeachability, responsibility *(accountability)*
chargeable accountable *(responsible)*,

actionable, ad valorem, blameful, blameworthy, bound, culpable, delinquent *(overdue)*, due *(owed)*, guilty, liable, peccant *(culpable)*, reprehensible, subject *(exposed)*, unjustifiable
chargeableness culpability
charged accused *(charged)*, ad valorem, full
charged party defendant
chargeless gratuitous *(given without recompense)*
charger assessor, complainant, contender, party *(litigant)*
charges bill *(invoice)*, brokerage, overhead
chargeship appointment *(position)*
charging with fault inculpation
charging with guilt incriminatory, inculpation, inculpatory
chariness austerity, discretion *(quality of being discreet)*, doubt *(suspicion)*, economy *(frugality)*
charismatic leader demagogue
charitable benevolent, donative, gratuitous *(given without recompense)*, humane, lenient, liberal *(generous)*, magnanimous, meritorious, nonprofit, philanthropic, placable. SEE MAIN ENTRY
charitable effort benevolence *(act of kindness)*
charitable institution foundation *(organization)*
charitableness benevolence *(disposition to do good)*, humanity *(humaneness)*, largess *(generosity)*, philanthropy, understanding *(tolerance)*
charity aid *(subsistence)*, benefit *(conferment)*, benevolence *(act of kindness)*, benevolence *(disposition to do good)*, clemency, condonation, contribution *(donation)*, donation, favor *(act of kindness)*, foundation *(organization)*, goodwill, gratuity *(present)*, help, largess *(generosity)*, largess *(gift)*, lenience, philanthropy. SEE MAIN ENTRY
charivari noise
charlatan fake
charlatanism fraud, hypocrisy
charlatanry artifice, deception, fraud, hypocrisy
charm lure
charming attractive, moving *(evoking emotion)*, sapid
chart delineation, design *(construction plan)*, scheme, tabulate
charter allow *(authorize)*, appoint, appointment *(act of designating)*, authorize, bestow, brevet, bylaw, capacity *(authority)*, certificate, certify *(approve)*, code, confirm, constitute *(establish)*, constitution, contract, countenance, deed, delegate, enactment, engage *(hire)*, establish *(launch)*, franchise *(license)*, immunity, incorporate *(form a corporation)*, instrument *(document)*, invest *(vest)*, law, lease, let *(lease)*, license, ordinance, pact, pandect *(code of laws)*, permit, prerogative, privilege, protocol *(agreement)*, rent, sanction *(permission)*, sanction, tolerance, treaty, warrant *(authorization)*. SEE MAIN ENTRY
chartered allowed, licit, privileged, rightful
chartered accountant accountant, comptroller
chartering incorporation *(formation of a business entity)*
chary circumspect, discreet, frugal, guarded, leery, parsimonious, penurious, provident *(showing foresight)*, prudent
chary of expense economical
chase embellish, hunt, pursuit *(chase)*, quest, race, repulse, trace *(follow)*. SEE MAIN ENTRY
chase after hunt, research, search
chase away parry, repel *(drive back)*
chase off parry
chase out oust
chasm hiatus, pitfall, rift *(gap)*, split
chassis frame *(structure)*
chaste pure
chasten assuage, castigate, discipline *(punish)*, moderate *(temper)*, punish
chastened contrite, penitent
chastening condemnation *(blame)*, correction *(punishment)*, disciplinary *(punitory)*, discipline *(punishment)*, punishment
chastise blame, castigate, censure, complain *(criticize)*, denounce *(condemn)*, disapprove *(condemn)*, discipline *(punish)*, expostulate, fault, lash *(attack verbally)*, penalize, punish, rebuke, remonstrate, reprehend, reprimand
chastisement condemnation *(blame)*, correction *(punishment)*, discipline *(punishment)*, obloquy, phillipic, punishment, remonstrance, reproach
chastity continence
chat conversation
chattel holding *(property owned)*, merchandise, possession *(property)*. SEE MAIN ENTRY
chattel property effects
chattels assets, commodities, effects, estate *(property)*, goods, paraphernalia *(personal belongings)*, personalty, possessions, property *(possessions)*
chattels personal movable
chattels real demesne, estate *(property)*, real estate
chatter bombast, prattle
chattering loquacious
chatty informatory, loquacious
chauvinism intolerance
cheap base *(inferior)*, disreputable, economical, frugal, inferior *(lower in quality)*, meretricious, nominal, paltry, parsimonious, penurious, poor *(inferior in quality)*, tawdry. SEE MAIN ENTRY
cheapen damage, debase, deduct *(reduce)*, demean *(make lower)*, denature, depreciate, depress, dilute, diminish, disparage, minimize
cheapening decline
cheapness of operation economy *(frugality)*
cheat betray *(lead astray)*, bilk, copy, deceive, deception, defalcate, defraud, delude, dupe, ensnare, fake, feign, hoax, hoodwink, illude, imposture, inveigle, knavery, maneuver, mislead, mulct *(defraud)*, overreach, palter, peculate, pretend, pretense *(pretext)*, purloin, ruse, shirk, stratagem. SEE MAIN ENTRY
cheat out of money defraud
cheated aggrieved *(victimized)*
cheater embezzler
cheating artifice, bunko, deceit, deceptive, dishonest, dishonesty, embezzlement, fraud, fraudulent, insidious, knavery, machiavellian, perfidious, pettifoggery
check abeyance, allay, alleviate, arrest *(stop)*, assuage, audit, avert, balk, ban, barrier, bill *(invoice)*, bind *(restrain)*, block, cease, cloture, collation, concern *(care)*, condemn *(ban)*, constrain *(restrain)*, constrict *(inhibit)*, contain *(restrain)*, control *(restriction)*, control *(regulate)*, countervail, coupon, cross-examine, curb, damper *(stopper)*, deadlock, debar, desist, detain *(restrain)*, deter, deterrence, disadvantage *(noun)*, disadvantage *(verb)*, discipline *(control)*, discontinue *(abandon)*, discontinue *(break continuity)*, disincentive, disqualify, draft, ensure, examination *(study)*, examine *(study)*, fetter *(noun)*, fetter *(verb)*, foil, forbid, forestall, frisk, frustrate, halt *(noun)*, halt *(verb)*, hamper, heed, hinder, hindrance, hold up *(delay)*, impasse, impede, impediment, indagation, inhibit, interdict, interfere, interrupt, interruption, keep *(restrain)*, kill *(defeat)*, lessen, limit, lock, mitigate, moderate *(temper)*, modify *(moderate)*, mollification, mollify, monitor, note *(written promise to pay)*, observation, obstacle, obstruct, obstruction, obviation, occlude, palliate *(abate)*, peruse, police, preclude, prevent, prohibit, prohibition, quit *(discontinue)*, quota, rebuff *(noun)*, rebuff *(verb)*, refrain, remission, remit *(relax)*, repel *(drive back)*, repress, repulse, resist *(oppose)*, resistance, restrain, restraint, restrict, restriction, reversal, scrutinize, stall, stave, stay, stay *(halt)*, stifle, stop, strangle, suppress, suspend, test, thwart, toll *(stop)*, trammel, trial *(experiment)*, verify *(confirm)*, withhold, withstand. SEE MAIN ENTRY
check a reference consult *(seek information from)*
check a source consult *(seek information from)*
check holder bearer
check in enter *(record)*, register, report *(present oneself)*
check list invoice *(itemized list)*, schedule
check on audit, research
check over probe
check thoroughly review
check up check *(inspect)*
check upon again reexamine
check-up diligence *(care)*
checked broken *(interrupted)*, limited, qualified *(conditioned)*
checking collation, cross-examination, discovery, limiting, preventive
checklist inventory
checkmate beat *(defeat)*, check *(bar)*, clog, deadlock, defeat, frustrate, prevent, repel *(drive back)*, stem *(check)*, stop
checkup test
cheer assure *(give confidence to)*, honor, promise *(raise expectations)*, reassure, solace, spirit
cheerful ready *(willing)*, sanguine
cheerful consent goodwill
cheerful giver donor
cheerful willingness goodwill
cheerfulness spirit
cheering propitious
cheerless bleak *(severely simple)*, disconsolate, grave *(solemn)*, lugubrious, pessimistic
cheerlessness damper *(depressant)*, pessimism
chemical substance drug
cheque coupon
cherish foster, keep *(shelter)*, nurture, preserve, protect, regard *(hold in esteem)*
cherish a belief opine
cherish doubts misdoubt, mistrust
cherishing preservation
chest repository
chevy persecute
chic elegant

chicane deceive, deception, dishonesty, evasion, false pretense, fraud, imposture, pettifoggery, plot *(secret plan)*, ruse, stratagem, subterfuge
chicanery artifice, bunko, collusion, connivance, deception, dishonesty, duplicity, evasion, false pretense, fraud, hoax, knavery, maneuver *(trick)*, pettifoggery, ruse, sham, sophistry, subterfuge. SEE MAIN ENTRY
chide blame, browbeat, castigate, censure, complain *(criticize)*, condemn *(blame)*, criticize *(find fault with)*, denounce *(condemn)*, disapprove *(condemn)*, expostulate, fault, lash *(attack verbally)*, rebuff, rebuke, reprehend, reprimand, reproach
chiding condemnation *(blame)*, critical *(faultfinding)*, criticism, denunciation, diatribe, disapprobation, objurgation, obloquy, outcry, rebuff, reprimand, reproach
chief best, cardinal *(basic)*, cardinal *(outstanding)*, central *(essential)*, critical *(crucial)*, director, dominant, employer, essential *(required)*, grave *(important)*, important *(significant)*, leading *(ranking first)*, major, master, necessary *(required)*, outstanding *(prominent)*, paramount, prevailing *(having superior force)*, prevalent, primary, prime *(most valuable)*, principal, principal *(director)*, salient, sovereign *(absolute)*, stellar, superintendent, superior *(higher)*, superlative, vital. SEE MAIN ENTRY
chief accounting officer comptroller
chief actor principal *(director)*
chief authority principal *(director)*
chief constituent content *(meaning)*
chief controller chief
chief executive administrator, principal *(director)*
chief feature main point
chief issue main point
chief office headquarters
chief part bulk, center *(essence)*, content *(meaning)*, corpus, main point
chief party principal *(director)*
chief point main point
chief reliance mainstay
chiefly a fortiori, ab initio, as a rule, generally, particularly
chieftain chief, principal *(director)*
chieftaincy supremacy
child dependent, descendant, infant, issue *(progeny)*, juvenile, minor, offspring. SEE MAIN ENTRY
child born before marriage bastard
child born out of wedlock bastard
child without parents orphan
child-stealing abduction
childbirth birth *(emergence of young)*
childhood minority *(infancy)*, nonage
childish frivolous, jejune *(lacking maturity)*, juvenile, naive, puerile
childishly foolish puerile
childishness puerility
childless barren
childlike ingenuous, juvenile, naive, puerility, unaffected *(sincere)*
children blood, issue *(progeny)*, offspring, posterity, progeny. SEE MAIN ENTRY
chill damper *(depressant)*, deter
chilling effect SEE MAIN ENTRY
chime in interrupt
chime in with comport *(agree with)*
chimera figment, phantom
chimerical delusive, fictitious, illusory, immaterial, insubstantial, nonexistent, quixotic
chinese wall SEE MAIN ENTRY
chink rift *(gap)*, split
chip part *(portion)*, token
chipped blemished
chirographum bond, handwriting
chirography handwriting
chirotony vote
chisel bilk, create
chivalric civil *(polite)*, meritorious
chivalrous civil *(polite)*, magnanimous, meritorious
chivalry consideration *(sympathetic regard)*, courtesy. SEE MAIN ENTRY
choate lien SEE MAIN ENTRY
chock-full full, replete
choice adoption *(acceptance)*, advantage, alternative *(option)*, appointment *(act of designating)*, best, call *(option)*, certain *(specific)*, conatus, decision *(judgment)*, discretion *(power of choice)*, exclusive *(limited)*, franchise *(right to vote)*, inestimable, intent, latitude, liberty, meritorious, nomination, noteworthy, option *(choice)*, patronage *(power to appoint jobs)*, plebiscite, poll *(casting of votes)*, predilection, preferable, preferential, preferred *(favored)*, premium, primary, prime *(most valuable)*, professional *(stellar)*, rare, select, suffrage, superior *(excellent)*, unusual, valuable, volition, vote, will *(desire)*. SEE MAIN ENTRY
choice between alternatives election *(choice)*
choice group elite
choice of language phraseology
choice of words parlance, phraseology
choiceless necessary *(inescapable)*
choke bar *(hinder)*, block, clog, constrict *(inhibit)*, extinguish, hamper, inhibit, obstruct, overload, preclude, repress, stem *(check)*, stifle, stop, subdue, suppress
choke back suppress
choke off bar *(hinder)*, occlude, shut, strangle
choler resentment, umbrage
choleric bilious, bitter *(penetrating)*, critical *(faultfinding)*, dyseptic, fractious, petulant, resentful
choose adopt, appoint, conclude *(decide)*, cull, decide, delegate, designate, determine, edit, espouse, extract, nominate, prefer, screen *(select)*, select, vote. SEE MAIN ENTRY
choose a course of action decide
choose an alternative decide
choose an option decide
choose for office elect *(select by a vote)*
choosing adoptive, decision *(election)*, designation *(naming)*, elective *(selective)*, nomination, vote
choosing by vote election *(selection by vote)*
choosy particular *(exacting)*, scrupulous
chop split
chore assignment *(task)*, burden, duty *(obligation)*, function, job, part *(role)*, work *(effort)*
chorus outcry
chose in action estate *(property)*, intangible
chosen particular *(specific)*, preferable, preferred *(favored)*, select, several *(separate)*
chosen career practice *(professional business)*
chosen few elite
chosen field practice *(professional business)*
chosen profession practice *(professional business)*
chosen representative nominee *(candidate)*
chosen work calling, career, occupation *(vocation)*, profession *(vocation)*, pursuit *(occupation)*
chouse bait *(lure)*, illude, inveigle, ruse
christen call *(title)*, denominate
chronic constant, durable, habitual, incorrigible, inveterate, permanent, perpetual, persistent, stable. SEE MAIN ENTRY
chronic alcoholism dipsomania
chronic disability disease
chronical inveterate
chronicle book, calendar *(record of yearly periods)*, detail *(particularize)*, enter *(record)*, entry *(record)*, file *(place among official records)*, journal, memorandum, narration, notation, note *(record)*, record *(noun)*, record *(verb)*, register *(noun)*, register *(verb)*, report *(detailed account)*, roll, set down, story *(narrative)*, tabulate. SEE MAIN ENTRY
chronicled documentary
chronicler clerk
chronicling registration
chronological consecutive
chronologize date
chronology calendar *(record of yearly periods)*, journal, order *(arrangement)*, register, time. SEE MAIN ENTRY
chuck precipitate *(throw down violently)*
chunk part *(portion)*, segment
churlish brutal, caitiff, disorderly, fractious, illiberal, impertinent *(insolent)*, inelegant, malevolent, penurious, perverse, petulant, provincial, resentful, severe, uncouth
churn disturb, perturb. SEE MAIN ENTRY
chute outlet
cibarious palatable
cinch lock
cincture border *(bound)*, embrace *(encircle)*, enclosure, encompass *(surround)*
cingere enclose, encompass *(surround)*
cipher blank *(emptiness)*, calculate, designation *(symbol)*, indicant, nonentity
ciphering census
circle bailiwick, contour *(outline)*, cycle, enclosure, encompass *(surround)*, hedge, perambulate, region, scope, society, sphere
circonvenir circumvent
circuit bench, circulate, circumscribe *(surround by boundary)*, contour *(outline)*, cycle, detour, district, encompass *(surround)*, extent, gamut, outline *(boundary)*, periphery, province, region, scope, sphere, territory. SEE MAIN ENTRY
circuitous astray, complex, devious, discursive *(digressive)*, indirect, labyrinthine, oblique *(evasive)*, sinuous, tortuous *(bending)*. SEE MAIN ENTRY
circuitous action indirection *(indirect action)*
circuitous route detour, indirection *(indirect action)*
circuitousness indirection *(indirect action)*
circuitus circuit
circuity digression, indirection *(indirect action)*
circular dispatch *(message)*, notice *(announcement)*
circular reasoning non sequitur
circularize circulate
circulate diffuse, disburse *(distribute)*, disclose, disperse *(disseminate)*, disseminate, herald, issue *(publish)*, post, proclaim,

promulgate, propagate *(spread)*, publish, reveal, send, spread, utter. SEE MAIN ENTRY
circulate publicly report *(disclose)*
circulated public *(known)*
circulating capital principal *(capital sum)*
circulating medium currency
circulation coverage *(scope)*, publication *(disclosure)*, transmittal. SEE MAIN ENTRY
circulus circuit, cycle
circumagere circulate, circulation
circumambience atmosphere
circumambiency climate, periphery
circumambulate detour, perambulate
circumambulating circuitous, indirect
circumcidere abridge *(shorten)*, retrench
circumcludere encompass *(surround)*
circumduction cancellation
circumference ambit, border, contour *(outline)*, margin *(outside limit)*, outline *(boundary)*, periphery, zone
circumferential peripheral
circumflexion indirection *(indirect action)*
circumfluent circuitous
circumfluous circuitous
circumfundere envelop
circumfuse diffuse
circumire patrol
circumjacence blockade *(enclosure)*, border, enclosure
circumjacencies frontier
circumlocution indirection *(indirect action)*
circumlocutory circuitous, indirect, oblique *(evasive)*, prolix, turgid
circumplecti encompass *(surround)*
circumpose border *(bound)*
circumscribe bar *(exclude)*, comprehend *(include)*, confine, constrain *(imprison)*, delimit, delineate, demarcate, detain *(restrain)*, deter, disadvantage, embrace *(encircle)*, enclose, encompass *(surround)*, envelop, hedge, impede, imprison, include, limit, obstruct, palliate *(abate)*, prohibit, proscribe *(prohibit)*, restrict, specify. SEE MAIN ENTRY
circumscribed arrested *(checked)*, certain *(specific)*, limited, narrow, qualified *(conditioned)*, regional
circumscribere circumscribe *(define)*, circumvent, define, defraud, limit, overreach, qualify *(condition)*, restrict
circumscribing limiting
circumscriptio fraud, limit, limitation
circumscription bar *(obstruction)*, blockade *(enclosure)*, boundary, configuration *(confines)*, constraint *(restriction)*, contour *(outline)*, coverage *(scope)*, custody *(incarceration)*, delineation, detention, enclosure, limit, limitation, mete, outline *(boundary)*, periphery, prohibition, purview, quota, restraint, restriction
circumscriptive limited, restrictive
circumspect careful, discreet, guarded, irreprehensible, leery, meticulous, politic, provident *(showing foresight)*, prudent, upright, vigilant. SEE MAIN ENTRY
circumspectio prudence
circumspection caution *(vigilance)*, deliberation, diligence *(care)*, discretion *(quality of being discreet)*, discrimination *(good judgment)*, forethought, judgment *(discernment)*, notice *(heed)*, precaution, prudence, surveillance
circumspective circumspect
circumspectness discretion *(quality of being discreet)*
circumspectus guarded, prudent
circumstance accident *(chance occurrence)*, case *(set of circumstances)*, chance *(fortuity)*, condition *(state)*, context, contingency, detail, experience *(encounter)*, happenstance, occurrence, particular, plight, posture *(situation)*, predicament, quirk *(accident)*, situation, state *(condition)*, status
circumstanced qualified *(conditioned)*
circumstances environment, position *(situation)*, situation. SEE MAIN ENTRY
circumstances in a case evidence
circumstantial coincidental, descriptive, fortuitous, incident, presumptive. SEE MAIN ENTRY
circumstantial event contingency
circumstantial evidence SEE MAIN ENTRY
circumstantiality detail, particularity
circumstantiate bear *(adduce)*, cite *(state)*, corroborate, demonstrate *(establish)*, detail *(particularize)*, document, establish *(show)*, evidence, itemize, quote, substantiate, support *(corroborate)*, sustain *(confirm)*, validate, verify *(confirm)*
circumstantiation corroboration, documentation, support *(corroboration)*
circumvalate border *(bound)*
circumvallate circumscribe *(surround by boundary)*, enclose
circumvallation blockade *(enclosure)*, enclosure
circumvenire circumvent, overreach
circumvent betray *(lead astray)*, bilk, border *(bound)*, deceive, dupe, escape, evade *(deceive)*, illude, overreach, pettifog, prevent, shun. SEE MAIN ENTRY
circumvention artifice, deception, device *(contrivance)*, evasion, false pretense, hoax, knavery, maneuver *(trick)*, pettifoggery, ruse
circumvention of truth false pretense
cista coffer
citadel bulwark, haven, protection, refuge
citare accuse, arraign
citation accusation, canon, certification *(certification of proficiency)*, charge *(accusation)*, complaint, count, direction *(order)*, excerpt, mention *(tribute)*, monition *(legal summons)*, paraphrase, presentment, process *(summons)*, recognition, subpoena, summons. SEE MAIN ENTRY
cite accuse, allege, allude, arraign, bear *(adduce)*, blame, charge *(accuse)*, complain *(charge)*, denounce *(condemn)*, exemplify, extract, honor, illustrate, mention, order, posit, present *(prefer charges)*, quote, recognize *(acknowledge)*, refer *(direct attention)*, specify, summon. SEE MAIN ENTRY
cite a holding of a case quote
cite evidence establish *(show)*
cited alleged
citing reference *(citation)*
citizen denizen, domiciliary, inhabitant. SEE MAIN ENTRY
citizenize naturalize *(make a citizen)*
citizenry community, nationality, populace, population, public, society
citizens population
city community. SEE MAIN ENTRY
civic civil (public), local, political, public *(affecting people)*. SEE MAIN ENTRY
civic-minded philanthropic
civicus civic
civil civic, obeisant, public *(affecting people)*. SEE MAIN ENTRY
civil code code
civil community state *(political unit)*
civil constitution polity
civil law constitution. SEE MAIN ENTRY
civil liberty freedom
civil liberties SEE MAIN ENTRY
civil officer peace officer
civil wrong misfeasance, tort
civilian civil *(public)*, layman
civilian police posse
civilis civic, political
civilis ratio politics
civility amenity, comity, consideration *(sympathetic regard)*, courtesy, decorum, respect
civilization community, society. SEE MAIN ENTRY
civilize educate
civilized civil *(polite)*
civilized behavior decorum
civilized life civilization
civilized society civilization
civis citizen
civitas community, state *(political unit)*
civitatis constitution
civium population
clades calamity, disaster
claim adduce, allegation, allege, appeal, appropriate, argue, assert, bear *(adduce)*, bill *(formal declaration)*, call *(demand)*, case *(lawsuit)*, cause of action, certify *(attest)*, cloud *(incumbrance)*, contend *(maintain)*, count, cover *(pretext)*, declare, demand *(noun)*, demand *(verb)*, dominion *(absolute ownership)*, droit, due, dun, encumbrance, equity *(share of ownership)*, exact, excise *(levy a tax)*, impropriate, interest *(ownership)*, lawsuit, lien, matter *(case)*, matter *(subject)*, motion, need, occupy *(take possession)*, own, ownership, plea, pleading, posit, prayer, prerogative, prescription *(claim of title)*, pretense *(pretext)*, pretext, profess *(pretend)*, profession *(declaration)*, purport, request *(noun)*, request *(verb)*, requirement, requisition, stake *(interest)*, statement, sue, thesis, title *(right)*. SEE MAIN ENTRY
claim a victory beat *(defeat)*
claim advanced by defendant counterclaim
claim as a right call *(demand)*
claim as one's due demand
claim falsely fake, pretend
claim for damages ad damnum clause
claim for relief cause of action
claim for relief by defendant counterclaim
claim on property charge *(lien)*, cloud *(incumbrance)*, lien, mechanics lien
claim one's thoughts occupy *(engage)*
claim presented by defendant counterclaim
claim to know contend *(maintain)*
claim unduly impropriate
claimable due *(owed)*
claimant applicant *(petitioner)*, complainant, contender, contestant, litigant, party *(litigant)*, plaintiff, suitor. SEE MAIN ENTRY
claimed alleged, ostensible, purported, putative
claimer claimant
claims of conscience responsibility *(conscience)*
clairvoyance precognition
clairvoyant prophetic
clamant exigent, important *(urgent)*, urgent
clamare call *(appeal to)*
clamor barrage, brawl, commotion, confusion *(turmoil)*, demonstrate *(protest)*, exception *(objection)*, furor, noise, outburst, outcry, pandemonium, protest. SEE MAIN ENTRY

clamor against decry, discommend
clamor for call *(demand)*, desire, exact, importune, necessitate, need, petition, plead *(implore)*, pray, request, solicit
clamor for payment dun
clamorous blatant *(obtrusive)*, important *(urgent)*, insistent, querulous, vehement
clamorousness noise, outcry
clamp adhere *(fasten)*
clan affinity *(family ties)*, blood, descent *(lineage)*, family *(common ancestry)*, house, kindred, lineage
clandestine allusive, collusive, covert, evasive, furtive, hidden, mysterious, personal *(private)*, private *(confidential)*, privy, secret, sly, stealthy, surreptitious, unobtrusive. SEE MAIN ENTRY
clandestinus clandestine, stealthy, surreptitious
clangor noise
clannish exclusive *(limited)*, partisan, restrictive
clansman relative
clansmen kindred
clap together conjoin
claque assemblage
clare fairly *(clearly)*
clarification clarification, comment, construction, definition, explanation, illustration, instance, solution *(answer)*. SEE MAIN ENTRY
clarified clear *(apparent)*
clarify adjust *(resolve)*, comment, construe *(translate)*, define, demonstrate *(establish)*, describe, detail *(particularize)*, distill, elucidate, enlighten, explain, explicate, exposit, expound, illustrate, interpret, purge *(purify)*, resolve *(solve)*, stipulate. SEE MAIN ENTRY
clarifying demonstrative *(illustrative)*, informatory, interpretive
clarifying statement justification
clarus conspicuous, distinct *(clear)*, open *(in sight)*, patent, renowned, unambiguous
clash affray, bicker, collision *(dispute)*, commotion, compete, conflict *(noun)*, conflict *(verb)*, confrontation *(altercation)*, contend *(dispute)*, contest *(competition)*, contest *(dispute)*, contradict, contravene, contravention, counter, counteract, deviate, differ *(disagree)*, disaccord, disagree, discrepancy, dispute *(contest)*, dissent *(difference of opinion)*, dissent *(differ in opinion)*, embroilment, feud, fight *(argument)*, fracas, fray, incompatibility *(difference)*, incompatibility *(inconsistency)*, meeting *(encounter)*, oppugn, reaction *(opposition)*, rift *(disagreement)*, strife, struggle, violence. SEE MAIN ENTRY
clash of arms conflict, fight *(battle)*
clash of opinions dispute
clash of temperament difference
clash with deviate
clashing argument *(contention)*, belligerency, competitive *(antagonistic)*, contention *(opposition)*, contradictory, contradistinction, controversy *(argument)*, deviant, difference, different, disaccord, discord, discordant, disparate, dissension, dissenting, dissidence, dissident, dissimilar, hostile, inapplicable, inapposite, inappropriate, inapt, incongruous, inept *(inappropriate)*, negative, opposite, repugnant *(incompatible)*
clasp adhere *(fasten)*, cohere *(adhere)*, grapple, lock, shut
clasp together conjoin
class allocate, classification, classify, denomination, department, distribute, division *(administrative unit)*, evaluate, file *(arrange)*, fix *(arrange)*, form *(arrangement)*, gauge, index *(relate)*, kind, manner *(kind)*, organize *(arrange)*, pigeonhole, quality *(excellence)*, race, rate, screen *(select)*, section *(division)*, society, sort, state *(condition)*, status, style, subdivision. SEE MAIN ENTRY
class action law suit SEE MAIN ENTRY
class prejudice discrimination *(bigotry)*
classic regular *(conventional)*, traditional
classical conventional, traditional
classification array *(order)*, chain *(series)*, class, compilation, degree *(station)*, denomination, department, diagnosis, distribution *(arrangement)*, division *(administrative unit)*, form *(arrangement)*, hierarchy *(arrangement in a series)*, identification, kind, label, manner *(kind)*, method, order *(arrangement)*, organization *(structure)*, rating, rubric *(title)*, segregation *(separation)*, sequence, subdivision, subheading, system. SEE MAIN ENTRY
classificatory descriptive
classificatory description diagnosis
classified confidential, systematic
classified communication confidence *(relation of trust)*
classified index file
classified information secret
classify allocate, apportion, call *(title)*, characterize, codify, denominate, diagnose, differentiate, digest *(summarize)*, discriminate *(distinguish)*, distinguish, distribute, file *(arrange)*, fix *(arrange)*, identify, include, index *(relate)*, label, organize *(arrange)*, rate, screen *(select)*, sort, subdivide. SEE MAIN ENTRY
classify as classify, constitute *(compose)*
classify incorrectly mislabel
classis class
classmaster pedagogue
clatter noise
claudere close *(terminate)*, shut
clause amendment *(legislation)*, article *(distinct section of a writing)*, caption, chapter *(division)*, condition *(contingent provision)*, limitation, phrase, subheading, term *(provision)*, title *(division)*. SEE MAIN ENTRY
claviger warden
clean blameless, decontaminate, honest, meticulous, pure, purge *(purify)*. SEE MAIN ENTRY
clean up expurgate
clean-cut precise
clean-handed clean, not guilty
cleaned out impecunious
cleanminded clean
cleanse decontaminate, expurgate, purge *(purify)*
cleansing medicinal, remedial
clear absolute *(conclusive)*, absolve, acquit, apparent *(perceptible)*, arrant *(definite)*, blameless, blatant *(conspicuous)*, certain *(positive)*, clean, cognizable, comment, comprehensible, conclusive *(settled)*, condone, conspicuous, decisive, definite, demonstrable, descriptive, direct *(forthright)*, discharge *(liberate)*, discharge *(pay a debt)*, disencumber, disentangle, earn, evident, exculpate, excuse, exonerate, explicit, express, extenuate, extricate, facilitate, flagrant, forgive, free *(relieved from a burden)*, free, gain, immune, inappealable, incontestable, lucid, manifest, naked *(perceptible)*, net, obvious, open *(in sight)*, orotund, ostensible, overt, palliate *(excuse)*, palpable, passable, patent, pay, pellucid, perceivable, perceptible, positive *(incontestable)*, profit, propitious, pure, purge *(purify)*, purge *(wipe out by atonement)*, quit *(free of)*, realize *(obtain as a profit)*, reap, release, remit *(release from penalty)*, remove *(eliminate)*, resounding, salient, satisfy *(discharge)*, simple, strong, surmount, unambiguous, unblemished, undeniable, unequivocal, unmistakable, vacant, vindicate, visible *(in full view)*. SEE MAIN ENTRY
clear a debt quit *(repay)*
clear accounts quit *(repay)*
clear away disencumber, displace *(remove)*
clear cut exact
clear demonstration proof
clear from free *(not restricted)*
clear from a charge exculpate
clear from alleged guilt exculpate
clear from imputation of fault exculpate
clear from obscurity ascertain
clear indication proof
clear language plain language
clear of an imputation of guilt exonerate
clear of doubt ascertain
clear of encumbrance solvent
clear of obscurity ascertain, elucidate, explain, expound
clear out eliminate *(eradicate)*, evacuate, flee
clear perception appreciation *(perception)*
clear sight perception
clear the mind disabuse
clear the way expedite, facilitate
clear thinking common sense, sagacity, sanity
clear thought sagacity
clear to the mind distinct *(clear)*
clear to the senses distinct *(clear)*
clear up clarify, construe *(translate)*, elucidate, explain, exposit, expound, interpret, resolve *(solve)*, settle, simplify *(clarify)*, solve. SEE MAIN ENTRY
clear-cut accurate, categorical, certain *(positive)*, certain *(specific)*, clear *(apparent)*, coherent *(clear)*, comprehensible, conspicuous, definite, demonstrable, distinct *(clear)*, incontrovertible, lucid, manifest, palpable, pellucid, precise, tangible, trenchant, unambiguous, unequivocal
clear-headed sapient
clear-minded lucid
clear-sighted acute, cognizant, discriminating *(judicious)*, perspicacious
clear-thinking lucid, pragmatic
clear-witted lucid
clearance absolution, acquittal, amortization, collection *(payment)*, composition *(agreement in bankruptcy)*, compurgation, concession *(authorization)*, condonation, discharge *(liberation)*, discharge *(payment)*, dispensation *(exception)*, exoneration, indulgence, justification, liberty, license, margin *(spare amount)*, pardon, payment *(act of paying)*, profit, release, remission, respite *(reprieve)*, satisfaction *(discharge of debt)*, waiver
cleared acquitted, clear *(free from criminal charges)*, exempt, free *(relieved from a burden)*. SEE MAIN ENTRY
clearheaded lucid, perspicacious, rational, reasonable *(rational)*, sane
clearheadedness reason *(sound judgment)*

clearing exoneration
clearly define specify
clearly defined absolute *(conclusive)*, certain *(specific)*, decisive, distinct *(clear)*, explicit, perceptible, unambiguous. SEE MAIN ENTRY
clearly expressed explicit
clearly formulated explicit
clearly indicated express
clearly known certain *(positive)*
clearly marked perceptible
clearly stated certain *(specific)*, explicit, express
clearmindedness competence *(sanity)*, sanity
cleavable divisible, divisive, separable, severable
cleavage coherence, disaccord, division *(act of dividing)*, estrangement, separation, severance, split
cleave bifurcate, break *(separate)*, cohere *(adhere)*, detach, disjoint, divide *(separate)*, lancinate, rend, separate, sever, split, subdivide
cleave in two dichotomize
cleaving coherent *(joined)*, cohesive *(sticking)*
cleaving together coherent *(joined)*
cleft rift *(gap)*, split
clemency benevolence *(disposition to do good)*, charity, condonation, consideration *(sympathetic regard)*, grace, humanity *(humaneness)*, indulgence, lenience, pardon. SEE MAIN ENTRY
clemens humane, lenient
clement charitable *(lenient)*, humane, lenient, placable, propitious
clementia clemency, humanity *(humaneness)*
clementness clemency
clench constrict *(compress)*
clerical SEE MAIN ENTRY
clerical error SEE MAIN ENTRY
clerical staff personnel, staff
clerk accountant, amanuensis, assistant. SEE MAIN ENTRY
clerk of the court notary public
clever artful, deft, expert, machiavellian, original *(creative)*, perspicacious, politic, practiced, proficient, resourceful, sapient, strategic, subtle *(refined)*. SEE MAIN ENTRY
clever in deception mendacious
cleverness artifice, discretion *(quality of being discreet)*, faculty *(ability)*, gift *(flair)*, insight, intelligence *(intellect)*, perception, prowess *(ability)*, sagacity, sense *(intelligence)*, skill
clew catchword
cliché catchword
cliche expression *(comment)*, platitude
cliched familiar *(customary)*
click comport *(agree with)*
cliens client
client consumer, customer, patron *(regular customer)*. SEE MAIN ENTRY
clientele consumer
climacteric critical *(crucial)*, crossroad *(turning point)*, crucial, emergency, timeliness
climactic critical *(crucial)*, last *(final)*
climactical last *(final)*
climate atmosphere. SEE MAIN ENTRY
climate change SEE MAIN ENTRY
climatic condition atmosphere
climax ceiling, cessation *(termination)*, conclude *(complete)*, consequence *(conclusion)*, crossroad *(turning point)*, culminate, culmination, denouement, pinnacle
climb headway, progress, surmount
climb down alight
clime climate, region, section *(vicinity)*, territory
clinch complete, ensure, grapple, stabilize
clinch an argument convince
cling cohere *(adhere)*, persevere
cling tenaciously adhere *(persist)*, persevere
cling to adhere *(fasten)*, hold *(possess)*, keep *(shelter)*, observe *(obey)*, perform *(adhere to)*, persist, prefer, pursue *(carry on)*, retain *(keep in possession)*
clinging adhesion *(affixing)*, coadunate, coherent *(joined)*, cohesive *(sticking)*
clinical SEE MAIN ENTRY
clip curtail, excise *(cut away)*, minimize, retrench
clipeus shield
clipping excerpt
clique cabal, denomination, faction, society, sodality
cliquish exclusive *(limited)*, partisan, restrictive
cloak blind *(obscure)*, camouflage, circumvent, clothe, color *(deceptive appearance)*, conceal, cover *(conceal)*, disguise *(noun)*, disguise *(verb)*, ensconce, enshroud, envelop, harbor, hide, obfuscate, obnubilate, obscure, plant *(covertly place)*, pretense *(pretext)*, screen *(guard)*, shroud, suppress, veil. SEE MAIN ENTRY
cloaked clandestine, covert, furtive, hidden, mysterious, oblique *(evasive)*, stealthy
clockwork precision regularity
cloddish inelegant, opaque
clog block, damper *(stopper)*, hamper, hinder, impediment, interfere, interrupt, interruption, obstruction, obturate, stem *(check)*, stop, trammel. SEE MAIN ENTRY
cloister circumscribe *(surround by boundary)*, envelop, restrict, sequester *(seclude)*, shut
cloistered private *(secluded)*, solitary
clone SEE MAIN ENTRY
cloning SEE MAIN ENTRY
close approximate, block, brief, cease, cessation *(termination)*, clog, cognate, coherent *(joined)*, cohesive *(compact)*, compact *(dense)*, comparable *(capable of comparison)*, complete, conclude *(complete)*, conclusion *(outcome)*, constrict *(inhibit)*, contestable, contiguous, culminate, defeasance, denouement, discontinue *(abandon)*, dispatch *(dispose of)*, dissolution *(termination)*, end *(termination)*, exact, expiration, expire, extremity *(death)*, faithful *(true to fact)*, finality, finish, future, grapple, halt, hidden, illiberal, immediate *(imminent)*, immediate *(not distant)*, inarticulate, indivisible, inseparable, instant, intense, intimate, literal, local, lock, moratorium, noncommittal, obturate, occlude, outcome, parsimonious, pendent, pending *(imminent)*, penurious, populous, precise, present *(attendant)*, proximate, secret, shut, similar, solid *(compact)*, stop, strict, taciturn, terminate. SEE MAIN ENTRY
close application diligence *(care)*
close around circumscribe *(surround by boundary)*
close association propinquity *(kinship)*
close at hand close *(near)*, forthcoming, future, immediate *(imminent)*, immediate *(not distant)*, instant, pending *(imminent)*, present *(attendant)*, prospective, proximate
close attention deliberation, diligence *(care)*, interest *(concern)*
close by close *(near)*, present *(attendant)*, proximate
close contact adhesion *(affixing)*
close correspondence parity
close down shut
close fast lock
close identification adhesion *(loyalty)*
close in border *(bound)*, circumscribe *(surround by boundary)*, contain *(enclose)*, enclose, envelop, include
close in upon converge
close inquiry analysis, cross-questioning, examination *(study)*, hearing, indagation, investigation, research
close investigation scrutiny
close look scrutiny
close observance conformity *(obedience)*
close observation examination *(study)*, judgment *(discernment)*
close off clog
close on border *(approach)*
close relation analogy
close relationship marriage *(intimate relationship)*
close relative next of kin
close resemblance analogy
close search scrutiny
close study deliberation, diligence *(care)*
close the curtain camouflage
close thought diligence *(care)*
close to almost
close together compact *(dense)*
close union contact *(association)*
close up seal *(close)*
close watch prudence
close with fight *(battle)*, grapple
close-fisted penurious
close-fitting limiting
close-handed penurious
close-knit compact *(dense)*
close-lipped mute
close-minded SEE MAIN ENTRY
close-out lockout
close-set compact *(dense)*
closed blind *(impassable)*, complete *(ended)*, fixed *(settled)*, impervious, personal *(private)*, private *(not public)*
closed purse austerity
closed-minded provincial
closed-minded person pedant
closed-mindedness predetermination
closefisted illiberal, parsimonious
closely faithfully
closely acquainted familiar *(informed)*, intimate
closely allied affiliated, associated, cognate, consanguineous
closely associated intimate
closely connected pendent
closely examine search
closely packed populous, replete
closely related affiliated, akin *(germane)*, associated, cognate, collateral *(accompanying)*, consanguineous
closely resemble approximate
closely united compact *(dense)*
closemouthed laconic, mute, taciturn
closeness affection, affinity *(regard)*, coalescence, consortium *(marriage companionship)*, density, identity *(similarity)*, kinship, marriage *(intimate relationship)*, propinquity *(proximity)*, rapport, relation *(connection)*, resemblance, semblance
closest proximate

closet chamber *(compartment)*, hide, private *(confidential)*, sequester *(seclude)*, shroud
closing cessation *(termination)*, close *(conclusion)*, cloture, conclusive *(settled)*, definitive, denouement, dissolution *(termination)*, expiration, final, halt, last *(final)* closing arguments SEE MAIN ENTRY
closing in imminent
closing piece end *(termination)*
closure cessation *(termination)*, close *(conclusion)*, cloture, conclusion *(outcome)*, denouement, end *(termination)*, expiration, finality, obstruction, payoff *(result)*
clot cohere *(adhere)*
clothe vest. SEE MAIN ENTRY
clothe in words phrase
cloture cessation *(interlude)*. SEE MAIN ENTRY
cloud blind *(obscure)*, camouflage, cloak, damper *(depressant)*, ensconce, enshroud, hide, muddle, obfuscate, obnubilate, obscuration, obscure, tarnish, veil. SEE MAIN ENTRY
cloud over obnubilate
clouded hidden, nebulous, opaque, unclear
cloudless propitious
cloudy equivocal, indefinite, inscrutable, nebulous, opaque, unclear, vague
clout SEE MAIN ENTRY
clownish uncouth
cloyed full, replete
cloying nectarious
club beat *(strike)*, cudgel, league, organization *(association)*, party *(political organization)*, society, sodality
clue catchword, hint *(noun)*, hint *(verb)*, indicant, indication, indicator, insinuation, reference *(allusion)*, suggestion, symbol, symptom. SEE MAIN ENTRY
clueless incognizant, insensible
clump aggregate, assemblage, bulk
clumsiness abortion *(fiasco)*
clumsy incompetent, inept *(incompetent)*, ponderous, uncouth, unpolitic
clumsy performance miscue
cluster agglomeration, aggregate, assemblage, bulk, compile, concentrate *(consolidate)*, congregate, hoard, mass *(body of persons)*, meet, selection *(collection)*, unite
clustered compact *(dense)*, composite
clutch grapple, retain *(keep in possession)*
clutter complex *(entanglement)*, confuse *(create disorder)*, confusion *(turmoil)*, disorganize
co-existent contemporary
co-obligor comaker
co-operant synergetic
co-opt adopt, choose
co-optation adoption *(acceptance)*
co-respondent respondent
coacervare accumulate *(amass)*, hoard
coach advise, counsel, direct *(supervise)*, discipline *(train)*, edify, educate, foster, instruct *(direct)*, nurture, oversee. SEE MAIN ENTRY
coaching direction *(guidance)*, discipline *(training)*, education, guidance
coact combine *(act in concert)*, consolidate *(unite)*, conspire, cooperate, join *(bring together)*, unite
coacting concerted, concurrent *(at the same time)*, concurrent *(united)*, synergetic
coaction affiliation *(connectedness)*, concert, concordance, contribution *(participation)*, duress, enforcement, force *(compulsion)*, relationship *(connection)*, synergy. SEE MAIN ENTRY
coactive associated, compulsory, concerted, concurrent *(at the same time)*, concurrent *(united)*, insistent, obligatory, synergetic
coactor accomplice, confederate, conspirer. SEE MAIN ENTRY
coactor in crime coconspirator
coactus involuntary, reluctance
coaddressee cotenant
coadjument concert
coadjutant associate, backer, coactor, colleague, concerted, confederate, conspirer, copartner *(business associate)*, copartner *(coconspirator)*, mutual *(collective)*, partner. SEE MAIN ENTRY
coadjutive mutual *(collective)*
coadjutor abettor, assistant, associate, backer, coactor, coadjutant, coconspirator, cohort, colleague, confederate, consociate, conspirer, contributor *(contributor)*, copartner *(coconspirator)*, participant, partner
coadjutorship combination
coadjutress colleague, copartner *(coconspirator)*
coadjutrix colleague
coadjuvancy affiliation *(connectedness)*, aid *(help)*, association *(connection)*, cartel, collusion, concert
coadjuvant ancillary *(auxiliary)*, associate, backer, colleague, concerted, mutual *(collective)*
coadjuvate consolidate *(unite)*
coadunate amalgamate, associated, coherent *(joined)*, joint, mutual *(collective)*. SEE MAIN ENTRY
coadunation adhesion *(affixing)*, coalescence, consolidation, integration *(amalgamation)*
coagency collusion, concert, connivance
coagent plenipotentiary
coagulate bond *(hold together)*, cement, cohere *(adhere)*, coherent *(joined)*, crystallize
coagulated coadunate, coherent *(joined)*, solid *(compact)*
coagulation adhesion *(affixing)*, agglomeration, coalescence, congealment
coagulative coadunate
coaid assistant, colleague, copartner *(coconspirator)*
coaider in crime coconspirator
coalesce adhere *(fasten)*, amalgamate, bond *(hold together)*, cement, cohere *(adhere)*, combine *(join together)*, commingle, concentrate *(consolidate)*, conjoin, connect *(join together)*, consolidate *(strengthen)*, consolidate *(unite)*, converge, desegregate, incorporate *(include)*, unite
coalesced coadunate
coalescence centralization, combination, concrescence, conspiracy, incorporation *(blend)*, joinder, merger. SEE MAIN ENTRY
coalescent coadunate, coherent *(joined)*, concerted, conjoint
coalescing centralization
coalition affiliation *(amalgamation)*, affiliation *(connectedness)*, association *(alliance)*, association *(connection)*, band, cabal, cartel, centralization, coaction, coalescence, combination, company *(assemblage)*, concert, confederacy *(compact)*, connection *(relation)*, consortium *(business cartel)*, conspiracy, contact *(association)*, contribution *(participation)*, corporation, federation, incorporation *(formation of a business entity)*, institute, integration *(amalgamation)*, integration *(assimilation)*, league, merger, organization *(association)*, pact, partnership, party *(political organization)*, pool, relationship *(connection)*, side, society, syndicate, union *(unity)*. SEE MAIN ENTRY
coalitional concurrent *(united)*, conjoint, joint, mutual *(collective)*
coapplicant comaker
coaptation adjustment
coarct constrict *(compress)*
coarctate decrease
coarctation bondage
coarguere expose
coarse blatant *(obtrusive)*, brutal, disreputable, impertinent *(insolent)*, inelegant, lascivious, lurid, odious, offensive *(offending)*, poor *(inferior in quality)*, profane, prurient, salacious, scurrilous, suggestive *(risqué)*, uncouth, unseemly. SEE MAIN ENTRY
coarsen debase
coarseness obscenity
coartare curtail
coastal littoral
coastland littoral
coating cover *(protection)*
coax agitate *(activate)*, cajole, entice, exhort, importune, inveigle, lure, persuade, pressure, prevail *(persuade)*, prevail upon, reason *(persuade)*, solicit, urge. SEE MAIN ENTRY
coaxing instigation, persuasion, persuasive, seduction
coborrower comaker
cockiness pride
cocksureness confidence *(faith)*
coconspirator accessory, accomplice. SEE MAIN ENTRY
coddle excessively overindulge
code act *(enactment)*, bylaw, canon, conduct, criterion, digest, ethics, jargon *(technical language)*, law, ordinance, pandect *(code of laws)*, precept, protocol *(etiquette)*, regulation *(rule)*, rubric *(authoritative rule)*, rule *(guide)*, rule *(legal dictate)*, statute. SEE MAIN ENTRY
code of behavior protocol *(etiquette)*
code of duty conscience
code of honor conscience
code of laws constitution
code of morals ethics
code of right and wrong ethics
code of what is fitting decorum
coded mysterious
codefendant accomplice
codenizen cotenant
codes legislation *(enactments)*
codex accepti et expensi ledger
codicil addendum, appendix *(supplement)*. SEE MAIN ENTRY
codicilli note *(brief comment)*
codification classification, code, compilation, constitution, enactment, legalization, pandect *(code of laws)*. SEE MAIN ENTRY
codification of laws legislation *(lawmaking)*
codified law code, constitution, pandect *(code of laws)*, statute
codify classify, constitute *(establish)*, digest *(summarize)*, enact, file *(arrange)*, fix *(arrange)*, index *(docket)*, legislate, tabulate. SEE MAIN ENTRY
codirector accessory, accomplice, colleague
codweller cotenant
coefficiency concert
coemptor consumer
coeptum undertaking *(enterprise)*
coequal analogous, coextensive, commensurable, commensurate, comparable

(equivalent), counterpart *(complement)*, equal, equivalent, identical, peer. SEE MAIN ENTRY
coequality identity *(similarity)*, mutuality, parity
coerce compel, constrain *(compel)*, enforce, exact, extort, foist, harass, impose *(enforce)*, impose *(subject)*, inflict, intimidate, necessitate, press *(constrain)*, pressure, require *(compel)*, threaten. SEE MAIN ENTRY
coercere coerce, confine, control *(regulate)*, govern, restrict, shut, stem *(check)*
coercion constraint *(restriction)*, duress, extortion, force *(compulsion)*, oppression, pressure, stress *(strain)*. SEE MAIN ENTRY
coercitio coercion
coercive binding, compelling, compulsory, forcible, insistent, involuntary, mandatory, necessary *(required)*, obligatory, severe, unavoidable *(inevitable)*. SEE MAIN ENTRY
coercive refusal to furnish work lockout
coetaneous concurrent *(at the same time)*, simultaneous
coetus company *(enterprise)*, congregation
coeval concerted, concurrent *(at the same time)*, contemporaneous, simultaneous
coexist accompany, coincide *(correspond)*
coexistence compatibility, integration *(amalgamation)*, integration *(assimilation)*, peace, synchronism. SEE MAIN ENTRY
coexistent coincidental, concerted, concordant, concurrent *(at the same time)*, congruous, contemporaneous, harmonious, simultaneous
coexisting coincidental, concerted, concordant, concurrent *(at the same time)*, congruous, contemporaneous, harmonious, simultaneous
coextending coextensive
coextensive coequal, commensurable, commensurate, equal. SEE MAIN ENTRY
coffer bank, depository, repository, treasury. SEE MAIN ENTRY
cofunction cooperate
cog deceive
cogency force *(strength)*, strength
cogent clear *(certain)*, coherent *(clear)*, convincing, important *(urgent)*, influential, irresistible, logical, persuasive, potent, powerful, predominant, sound. SEE MAIN ENTRY
cogere compel, constrain *(compel)*, necessitate
cogitable plausible, possible
cogitare intend, reflect *(ponder)*, speculate *(conjecture)*
cogitate brood, consider, deliberate, muse, ponder, rationalize, reason *(conclude)*, reflect *(ponder)*, weigh
cogitatio idea, reflection *(thought)*
cogitation consideration *(contemplation)*, contemplation, deliberation, dialectic, ratiocination, reflection *(thought)*
cogitative deliberate, speculative. SEE MAIN ENTRY
cogitatus deliberate, intentional
cognate analogous, apposite, comparable *(capable of comparison)*, consanguineous, correlate, correlative, germane, interrelated, pendent, related, relative *(relevant)*, relative, relevant, same, similar. SEE MAIN ENTRY
cognati kindred
cognatio affinity *(family ties)*, relationship *(connection)*
cognation affinity *(family ties)*, ancestry, blood, degree *(kinship)*, filiation, kinship, propinquity *(kinship)*, relation *(connection)*, relationship *(connection)*
cognatus related, relation *(kinship)*, relative
cognitio cognition, hearing, inquiry *(systematic investigation)*, insight, knowledge *(learning)*
cognition appreciation *(perception)*, apprehension *(perception)*, comprehension, insight, intellect, intelligence *(intellect)*, knowledge *(awareness)*, observation, perception, realization, reason *(sound judgment)*, recognition, scienter, sense *(intelligence)*. SEE MAIN ENTRY
cognitive cognizant, familiar *(informed)*, knowing, perceptive, rational, reasonable *(rational)*, receptive
cognitive faculties judgment *(discernment)*, sense *(intelligence)*
cognitive faculty intellect, intelligence *(intellect)*
cognitive powers judgment *(discernment)*, sense *(intelligence)*
cognitive process cognition
cognitus acquainted
cognizable appreciable, ascertainable, coherent *(clear)*, comprehensible, concrete, determinable *(ascertainable)*, discernible, justiciable, naked *(perceptible)*, perceivable, perceptible, ponderable, scrutable, solvable, triable. SEE MAIN ENTRY
cognizable in courts of law legal
cognizance appreciation *(perception)*, apprehension *(perception)*, cognition, comprehension, experience *(background)*, identification, insight, knowledge *(awareness)*, notice *(heed)*, observation, perception, realization, reason *(sound judgment)*, recognition, scienter
cognizant certain *(positive)*, circumspect, conscious *(aware)*, expert, familiar *(informed)*, knowing, learned, perceptive, sensitive *(discerning)*. SEE MAIN ENTRY
cognizant of acquainted, privy
cognize apprehend *(perceive)*, comprehend *(understand)*, construe *(comprehend)*, digest *(comprehend)*, discern *(detect with the senses)*, note *(notice)*, notice *(observe)*, perceive, pierce *(discern)*, realize *(understand)*, understand
cognized household *(familiar)*
cognomen call *(title)*, sobriquet, term *(expression)*. SEE MAIN ENTRY
cognomination call *(title)*
cognoscere ascertain, discover, find *(discover)*, hear *(give a legal hearing)*, hear *(give attention to)*, investigate, perceive, recognize *(perceive)*, try *(conduct a trial)*
cognoscible comprehensible
cognovit SEE MAIN ENTRY
cohabit SEE MAIN ENTRY
cohabitant inhabitant
cohabitation marriage *(intimate relationship)*, marriage *(wedlock)*, matrimony. SEE MAIN ENTRY
cohaerens coherent *(clear)*, coherent *(joined)*
cohaerere cohere *(adhere)*, cohere *(be logically consistent)*
cohelper associate, coactor, cohort, colleague, consociate, conspirer, contributor *(contributor)*, copartner *(business associate)*, copartner *(coconspirator)*, partner
cohere adhere *(fasten)*, adjoin, affix, attach *(join)*, bond *(hold together)*, cement, combine *(join together)*, comport *(agree with)*, conjoin, connect *(join together)*, connect *(relate)*, consolidate *(strengthen)*, conspire, contact *(touch)*, correspond *(be equivalent)*, crystallize. SEE MAIN ENTRY
coherence adherence *(adhesion)*, adhesion *(affixing)*, coalescence, competence *(sanity)*, connection *(relation)*, contact *(touching)*, continuity, union *(unity)*. SEE MAIN ENTRY
coherency coherence, connection *(relation)*
coherent agreed *(harmonized)*, cohesive *(sticking)*, commensurable, consensual, consistent, consonant, convincing, logical. SEE MAIN ENTRY
cohering coadunate, coherent *(joined)*, cohesive *(sticking)*, consistent
cohesion accession *(annexation)*, adherence *(adhesion)*, adhesion *(affixing)*, attachment *(act of affixing)*, coaction, coalescence, coherence, congealment, connection *(fastening)*
cohesive coadunate, coherent *(joined)*, compact *(dense)*, concerted, concurrent *(united)*, conjoint, inextricable, infrangible. SEE MAIN ENTRY
cohesiveness adherence *(adhesion)*, adhesion *(affixing)*, coalescence, coherence, tenacity
cohibere confine, keep *(restrain)*, stay *(halt)*, stem *(check)*
cohibit block
cohors cohort
cohort associate, consociate, copartner *(coconspirator)*. SEE MAIN ENTRY
cohouseholder cotenant
coiled sinuous
coin cash, conceive *(invent)*, currency, denominate, frame *(construct)*, invent *(produce for the first time)*, make, money, originate, produce *(manufacture)*
coin of the realm cash
coinage cash, formation, invention, money, origination
coincide agree *(comply)*, certify *(approve)*, comport *(agree with)*, concur *(coexist)*, correspond *(be equivalent)*. SEE MAIN ENTRY
coincidence concordance, conformity *(agreement)*, connivance, contingency, happenstance, synchronism, synergy
coincident coequal, coincidental, concerted, concomitant, concurrent *(at the same time)*, congruous, consonant, contemporaneous, corporate *(joint)*, simultaneous
coincident with consensual
coincidental contingent, fortuitous. SEE MAIN ENTRY
coinciding coincidental, concerted, concordant, congruous, contemporaneous, correlative
coined words jargon *(technical language)*
coinhabitant cotenant
coinhabiter cotenant
coinstantaneous coincidental, concurrent *(at the same time)*, contemporaneous, simultaneous
coire converge
cojugate conjugal
cold bleak *(exposed and barren)*, bleak *(severely simple)*, callous, cold-blooded, cruel, disdainful, dispassionate, inexpressive, insusceptible *(uncaring)*, malevolent, obdurate, pedestrian, phlegmatic, relentless, ruthless, severe, unresponsive. SEE MAIN ENTRY
cold of heart callous

cold shoulder rebuff
cold-blooded callous, cruel, dispassionate, malevolent, malignant, phlegmatic, relentless, ruthless, sinister. SEE MAIN ENTRY
cold-hearted cold-blooded, cruel, dispassionate, relentless
cold-shoulder shun
coldhearted callous, malignant, ruthless
coldness indifference
coleaseholder cotenant
colere cultivate, honor
colessee cotenant
collaborate aid, combine *(act in concert),* cooperate, federalize *(associate),* federate, involve *(participate),* organize *(unionize),* participate, pool. SEE MAIN ENTRY
collaborated mutual *(collective)*
collaborating concerted, consensual
collaboration bad faith, coaction, collusion, concert, conformity *(agreement),* connivance, contribution *(participation),* league, pool, synergy
collaborationist coactor, conspirer
collaborative concurrent *(united),* joint, mutual *(collective),* synergetic
collaborator abettor, accessory, accomplice, assistant, associate, coactor, coadjutant, coconspirator, cohort, colleague, confederate, consociate, conspirer, contributor *(contributor),* copartner *(business associate),* copartner *(coconspirator),* participant, partner. SEE MAIN ENTRY
collapse catastrophe, debacle, decline, defeat, destruction, deteriorate, detriment, disaster, disease, disrepair, fail *(lose),* failure *(lack of success),* give *(yield),* languish, miscarriage, mistrial, prostration, succumb. SEE MAIN ENTRY
collar handcuff
collared arrested *(apprehended)*
collateral additional, akin *(germane),* ancillary *(auxiliary),* bail, binder, circumstantial, coextensive, concurrent *(at the same time),* consanguineous, correlative, deposit, downpayment, extrinsic, hostage, hypothecation, incident, pendent, peripheral, pledge *(security),* related, relative *(relevant),* secondary, security *(pledge),* similar, subordinate, supplementary. SEE MAIN ENTRY
collateral relative next of kin
collateral review of detention habeas corpus
collateral security binder, deposit, mortgage
collaterial review habeas corpus
collation SEE MAIN ENTRY
colleague affiliate, assistant, associate, coactor, coadjutant, cohort, confederate, consociate, consort, conspirer, contributor *(contributor),* copartner *(business associate),* participant. SEE MAIN ENTRY
colleague in crime coconspirator
colleagueship affiliation *(connectedness),* association *(connection),* cartel, coaction, society, sodality
collect accrue *(increase),* accumulate *(amass),* aggregate, codify, compile, concentrate *(consolidate),* congregate, conjoin, convene, cull, excise *(levy a tax),* extract, fund, gain, garner, glean, hoard, hold *(possess),* join *(bring together),* levy, meet, obtain, purchase, read, reap, receive *(acquire),* recruit, select, store, tax *(levy),* unite. SEE MAIN ENTRY
collect evidence document
collect facts investigate
collect into a focus congregate
collect into a mass accumulate *(amass),* aggregate
collect knowledge discover
collect payment collect *(recover money),* toll *(exact payment)*
collect the vote poll
collect together accumulate *(amass)*
collectable due *(owed),* payable
collectanea selection *(collection)*
collected composite, conglomerate, dispassionate, miscellaneous, nonchalant, placid
collected writings information *(knowledge)*
collection agglomeration, aggregate, assemblage, assembly, band, code, combination, compilation, conglomeration, congregation, corpus, cumulation, depository, digest, hoard, levy, store *(depository).* SEE MAIN ENTRY
collection of facts investigation
collection of laws code, constitution, pandect *(code of laws)*
collection of statutes code, codification
collective broad, common *(shared),* composite, conjoint, cooperative, generic, joint, nonsectarian, omnibus, pool, public *(affecting people).* SEE MAIN ENTRY
collective action coaction
collective agreement bargain, contract, covenant
collective assets estate *(property)*
collective bargaining SEE MAIN ENTRY
collective members constituency
collective refusal to work strike
collectively en banc, en masse, in toto, wholly. SEE MAIN ENTRY
collectively agreed contractual
collectiveness entirety, whole
collectivism pool
collectivity complex *(development),* corpus, entirety, totality, whole
collectivized conglomerate
collector assessor, caretaker *(one fulfilling the function of office),* receiver
college institute
collegiate distinction degree *(academic title)*
collide conflict, counter, counteract, cross *(disagree with),* disagree, dispute *(contest),* dissent *(differ in opinion),* impinge, jostle *(bump into),* meet, oppose. SEE MAIN ENTRY
collide with contact *(touch)*
colliding competitive *(antagonistic),* discordant
colligate accumulate *(amass),* aggregate, **combine** *(join together), join (bring together)*
colligation assemblage, body *(collection),* collection *(assembly),* compilation, corpus
collision antipode, conflict, confrontation *(altercation),* meeting *(encounter).* SEE MAIN ENTRY
collocate allocate, arrange *(methodize),* classify, file *(arrange),* fix *(arrange),* join *(bring together),* marshal, pigeonhole, sort
collocation arrangement *(ordering),* array *(order),* building *(business of assembling),* chamber *(body),* collection *(assembly),* compilation, distribution *(arrangement),* hierarchy *(arrangement in a series)*
collocution communication *(discourse),* conversation, parley
collop part *(portion)*
colloque speak
colloquial ordinary, prevailing *(current),* prevalent
colloquial discourse conversation
colloquialism catchword
colloquy communication *(discourse),* conference, confrontation *(act of setting face to face),* conversation, interview, meeting *(conference),* parley, speech
collude combine *(act in concert),* connive, conspire, contrive, cooperate, involve *(participate),* maneuver, plan, plot, scheme. SEE MAIN ENTRY
colluder coactor, coconspirator, confederate, conspirator, conspirer, copartner *(coconspirator),* partner
colluding concerted
collusion bad faith, bribery, cabal, coaction, confederacy *(conspiracy),* connivance, conspiracy, contribution *(participation),* contrivance, deceit, fraud, machination, plot *(secret plan).* SEE MAIN ENTRY
collusive clandestine, deceptive, machiavellian, mendacious. SEE MAIN ENTRY
collusory machiavellian
colonial provincial
colonies possessions
colonist migrant, pioneer
colonization immigration
colonize inhabit, occupy *(take possession)*
colonizer pioneer
colony province
colophon brand
color camouflage
color complexion
color falsify, misrepresent, prejudice *(influence),* pretense *(pretext),* slant, stain. SEE MAIN ENTRY
colorable ostensible, plausible, specious. SEE MAIN ENTRY
colored one-sided, prejudicial, specious
colored by bias subjective
coloring connotation, context, implication *(inference),* overstatement
colorless insipid, jejune *(dull),* lifeless *(dull),* mediocre, pedestrian, prosaic, usual
colossal capacious, gross *(flagrant),* prodigious *(enormous)*
colporteur dealer
column chapter *(division)*
columnists press
comaker SEE MAIN ENTRY
comate accomplice, associate, cohort, colleague, confederate, consociate, consort, copartner *(business associate),* copartner *(coconspirator),* participant, partner
comatose inactive, insensible, phlegmatic, torpid
comb search
combat affray, attack, belligerency, collision *(dispute),* compete, competition, conflict *(noun),* conflict *(verb),* confrontation *(altercation),* contend *(dispute),* contention *(opposition),* contest *(dispute),* contest, dispute *(contest),* embroilment, engage *(involve),* fight *(battle),* fight *(battle),* fray, grapple, oppose, oppugn, resist *(oppose),* resistance, strife, struggle. SEE MAIN ENTRY
combat an opinion challenge
combatant aggressor, competitive *(antagonistic),* contender, contestant, disputant, foe, opponent, rival
combative argumentative, competitive *(antagonistic),* contentious, hostile, litigious, offensive *(taking the initiative),* pugnacious
combativeness belligerency

combatting competitive *(antagonistic)*
combination accession *(annexation)*, affiliation *(amalgamation)*, affiliation *(connectedness)*, assemblage, association *(alliance)*, association *(connection)*, band, cabal, cartel, centralization, coalescence, coalition, company *(enterprise)*, compilation, composition *(makeup)*, concert, confederacy *(compact)*, connection *(fastening)*, consolidation, consortium *(business cartel)*, conspiracy, contact *(association)*, content *(structure)*, contribution *(participation)*, corporation, federation, incorporation *(blend)*, integration *(amalgamation)*, integration *(assimilation)*, joinder, league, melange, merger, organization *(association)*, partnership, pool, relationship *(connection)*, selection *(collection)*, sodality, solution *(substance)*, union *(unity)*. SEE MAIN ENTRY
combination for fraud collusion
combination of companies trust *(combination of businesses)*
combination of financial institutions consortium *(business cartel)*
combination of funds pool
combinative concordant, concurrent *(united)*
combine accumulate *(amass)*, affix, amalgamate, annex *(add)*, association *(alliance)*, attach *(join)*, bond *(hold together)*, business *(commercial enterprise)*, cartel, cement, coalition, cohere *(adhere)*, commingle, compile, concentrate *(consolidate)*, confederacy *(compact)*, conjoin, connect *(join together)*, connive, consolidate *(strengthen)*, consolidate *(unite)*, conspire, cooperate, coordinate, corporation, crystallize, federalize *(associate)*, federate, federation, include, incorporate *(include)*, join *(associate oneself with)*, join *(bring together)*, league, merge, organize *(arrange)*, organize *(unionize)*, party *(political organization)*, pool *(noun)*, pool *(verb)*, society, syndicate, trust *(combination of businesses)*, unite. SEE MAIN ENTRY
combine for some evil design conspire
combine forces cooperate
combine operations conspire
combine racially desegregate
combine with desegregate
combine with water dilute
combined associated, coadunate, coherent *(joined)*, collective, composite, compound, concerted, concurrent *(united)*, conglomerate, conjoint, federal, harmonious, inextricable, inseparable, joint, miscellaneous, mutual *(collective)*
combined action concert, synergy
combined effect synergy
combined effort coaction, concert
combined operation collusion, conformity *(agreement)*, connivance, conspiracy, synergy
combining accession *(annexation)*, concerted, concrescence, congruous
come accrue *(arise)*, report *(present oneself)*, stem *(originate)*
come about arise *(occur)*, occur *(happen)*
come across confront *(encounter)*
come after accede *(succeed)*, ensue, succeed *(follow)*
come afterward ensue
come again recur, return *(go back)*
come and go beat *(pulsate)*
come apart separate
come at call obey
come away move *(alter position)*
come back recur, resurgence, retort, return *(go back)*
come back at recriminate, reply
come back to reopen
come before precede
come between alienate *(estrange)*, disaffect, interpose, interrupt, intervene, separate
come by attain, gain, procure, realize *(obtain as a profit)*, receive *(acquire)*
come clean betray *(disclose)*
come close border *(approach)*
come close in estimation approximate
come close to approximate
come closer converge
come down decline *(fall)*, degenerate
come down by transmission descend
come down lineally descend
come face to face meet
come face to face with confront *(encounter)*
come first outweigh, precede, surpass
come formally before a tribunal appear *(attend court proceedings)*
come forth arise *(appear)*, confess, emanate, emerge, pullulate, result
come forward approach, emerge, issue *(send forth)*
come from arise *(originate)*, emanate, evolve, result
come gradually into existence develop
come in enter *(go in)*
come in conflict with confront *(oppose)*, contradict, counter, counteract, disap-prove *(reject)*, except *(object)*, grapple, oppose
come in contact collide *(crash against)*, confront *(encounter)*, congregate, strike *(collide)*
come in last lose *(undergo defeat)*
come in sight arise *(appear)*
come in view arise *(appear)*
come into gain
come into action arise *(originate)*
come into being arise *(originate)*, occur *(happen)*
come into collision collide *(crash against)*, conflict, impinge, strike *(collide)*
come into court appear *(attend court proceedings)*
come into existence arise *(originate)*, commence, exist, occur *(happen)*
come into notice emerge
come into possession derive *(receive)*, obtain
come into possession as an heir inherit
come into possession of acquire *(receive)*, possess
come into sight appear *(materialize)*
come into the world commence
come into view appear *(materialize)*, emerge, occur *(come to mind)*
come near approach, approximate
come near in position approximate
come next accede *(succeed)*, ensue
come of age mature
come onto the horizon issue *(send forth)*
come out circulate, declare, emerge, issue *(send forth)*
come out in the open issue *(send forth)*
come out of hiding emerge
come out with phrase, remark, utter
come round conform
come short fail *(lose)*
come subsequently succeed *(follow)*
come through succeed *(attain)*
come to attain, reach
come to a close cease, expire, finish
come to a conclusion ascertain, decide, deduce, deduct *(conclude by reasoning)*, determine, find *(determine)*, hold *(decide)*, rule *(decide)*
come to a decision determine
come to a determination conclude *(decide)*, determine, fix *(settle)*, resolve *(decide)*, rule *(decide)*, settle
come to a focus converge
come to a hasty conclusion presume
come to a point border *(approach)*, converge, focus
come to a resolution fix *(settle)*
come to a standstill cease, pause, quit *(discontinue)*, rest *(cease from action)*, stop
come to a stop close *(terminate)*, halt
come to an agreement agree *(contract)*, arrange *(methodize)*, coincide *(concur)*, compromise *(settle by mutual agreement)*, concur *(agree)*, decide, fix *(settle)*, settle
come to an arrangement close *(agree)*
come to an end cease, close *(terminate)*, decease, expire, finish, lapse *(cease)*, perish, terminate
come to an understanding agree *(comply)*, agree *(contract)*, close *(agree)*, coincide *(concur)*, compromise *(settle by mutual agreement)*, concur *(agree)*, settle
come to be arise *(originate)*, develop, evolve
come to blows fight *(battle)*
come to know apprehend *(perceive)*, ascertain, discover, perceive
come to light appear *(materialize)*, arise *(appear)*, emerge
come to maturity develop
come to naught fail *(lose)*, perish, succumb
come to nothing fail *(lose)*
come to notice arise *(appear)*
come to pass arise *(occur)*, occur *(happen)*, supervene
come to pieces disorganize
come to ruin perish
come to stay remain *(stay)*
come to terms agree *(comply)*, agree *(contract)*, arrange *(methodize)*, close *(agree)*, coincide *(concur)*, compromise *(settle by mutual agreement)*, concede, concur *(agree)*, consent, decide, dicker, negotiate, settle, succumb
come to the aid of assist, help, promote *(organize)*, serve *(assist)*
come to the defense of maintain *(sustain)*, support *(assist)*
come to the help of support *(assist)*
come to the rescue free
come to understand comprehend *(understand)*
come together cohere *(adhere)*, collide *(crash against)*, concur *(agree)*, congregate, contact *(touch)*, converge, crystallize, meet, rendezvous, strike *(collide)*, unite
come uninvited intrude
come up to the standard pass *(satisfy requirements)*
come upon discover, find *(discover)*, invent *(produce for the first time)*, locate
comeback renewal, revival
comedown descent *(declination)*, disgrace, misfortune
comely attractive
comes consort, count
comestible palatable

cometary brief, volatile
comfort accommodate, assuage, assure *(give confidence to)*, benefit *(betterment)*, consortium *(marriage companionship)*, ease, prosperity, reassure, relieve *(give aid)*, solace, soothe, support *(assistance)*, sympathize. SEE MAIN ENTRY
comfortable habitable, opulent, prosperous, successful. SEE MAIN ENTRY
comfortable circumstances prosperity
comforting mitigation
comfortless bleak *(severely simple)*, disconsolate, lamentable
comic jocular
comical ludicrous
comical representation parody
coming appearance *(emergence)*, close *(near)*, forthcoming, future, immediate *(imminent)*, imminent, onset *(commencement)*, pending *(imminent)*, prospective, subsequent
coming after consecutive
coming before preliminary
coming between mesne
coming down descent *(declination)*
coming events prospect *(outlook)*
coming from derivative
coming from another land alien *(foreign)*
coming from without extraneous
coming in inflow
coming soon forthcoming
coming to an end determinable *(liable to be terminated)*
coming together coalition, confrontation *(act of setting face to face)*
comissari carouse
comitas courtesy
comity compatibility, courtesy. SEE MAIN ENTRY
command agency *(commission)*, agency *(legal relationship)*, call *(demand)*, canon, claim *(legal demand)*, coerce, coercion, compel, conduct, constrain *(compel)*, control *(supervision)*, control *(regulate)*, decree *(noun)*, decree *(verb)*, demand *(noun)*, demand *(verb)*, detail *(assign)*, dictate *(noun)*, dictate *(verb)*, direct *(order)*, direct *(supervise)*, direction *(order)*, directive, discipline *(control)*, dominate, dominion *(supreme authority)*, edict, efficiency, enact, enjoin, exhort, fiat, force *(compulsion)*, force *(strength)*, force *(coerce)*, generalship, govern, government *(administration)*, handle *(manage)*, hegemony, hold *(possess)*, impose *(enforce)*, influence, injunction, insist, instruct *(direct)*, instruction *(direction)*, jurisdiction, knowledge *(learning)*, law, manage, management *(directorate)*, management *(supervision)*, mandamus, mandate, manipulate *(utilize skillfully)*, mittimus, moderate *(preside over)*, monition *(legal summons)*, motivate, occupation *(possession)*, occupy *(take possession)*, officiate, operate, order *(judicial directive)*, order, ordinance, overcome *(surmount)*, overlook *(superintend)*, oversee, own, possess, power, precept, predominance, predominate *(command)*, prescribe, prescription *(directive)*, preside, press *(constrain)*, pressure, prevail *(triumph)*, primacy, process *(summons)*, regime, regulation *(rule)*, request, require *(compel)*, requirement, rule *(legal dictate)*, rule *(govern)*, ruling, skill, subjugate, subpoena, summon, superintend, supervision, supremacy, surmount, takeover, wield, will *(desire)*, writ. SEE MAIN ENTRY
command a view observe *(watch)*
command a view of discern *(detect with the senses)*, overlook *(superintend)*
command back remand
command by the court mandate
command influence constrain *(compel)*
command not to do forbid
command of idiom parlance, phraseology
command of language parlance, phraseology
command of money substance *(material possessions)*
command of one's faculties composure
command of temper composure
command of thought comprehension
command of words parlance, rhetoric *(skilled speech)*
command to appear call *(summon)*, citation *(charge)*, subpoena *(noun)*, subpoena *(verb)*, summon, summons, venire
command to incarcerate mittimus
command to undo wrong injunction
commandant chief, principal *(director)*
commanded compulsory, decretal, mandatory, obligatory, positive *(prescribed)*
commanded by long use prescriptive
commandeer assume *(seize)*, carry away, deprive, garnish, hijack, procure, seize *(confiscate)*, usurp
commandeering condemnation *(seizure)*, confiscatory, disseisin
commander chief, principal *(director)*
commanders authorities, hierarchy *(persons in authority)*
commanding cardinal *(outstanding)*, cogent, compelling, considerable, convincing, critical *(crucial)*, decisive, decretal, dictatorial, dominant, forcible, important *(significant)*, influential, insistent, mandatory, master, noteworthy, peremptory *(imperative)*, potent, powerful, predominant, prescriptive, prevailing *(having superior force)*, salient, sovereign *(absolute)*
commanding a good price valuable
commanding a high price priceless
commanding belief credible, fiduciary, plausible
commanding confidence credible, fiduciary
commanding position priority
commandment canon, charge *(command)*, codification, decree, dictate, direction *(order)*, directive, instruction *(direction)*, mandate, monition *(legal summons)*, order *(judicial directive)*, precept, regulation *(rule)*, requirement, rule *(legal dictate)*, statute, summons, writ
commatic sententious
commeasurable commensurate, proportionate
commeatus furlough, leave *(absence)*
commeminisse recollect
commemorare recapitulate, recount
commemorate honor, keep *(fulfill)*, recall *(remember)*, recognize *(acknowledge)*, remember. SEE MAIN ENTRY
commemoratio mention *(reference)*
commemoration ceremony, recognition, reminder
commemorative honorary, suggestive *(evocative)*
commemoratory suggestive *(evocative)*
commence embark, initiate, originate, preface, stem *(originate)*, undertake. SEE MAIN ENTRY
commence a suit sue
commence again reopen
commence proceedings against a third party implead
commencement birth *(beginning)*, derivation, embryo, genesis, inception, nascency, origin *(source)*, origination, outset, overt act, preface, prelude, start
commencement of an action service (delivery of legal process)
commencing incipient, initial, original *(initial)*
commencing before retroactive
commend advocate, confirm, counsel, countenance, endorse, honor, indorse, recommend. SEE MAIN ENTRY
commendable congruous, laudable, meritorious, moral, professional *(stellar)*, unimpeachable
commendableness expedience
commendare recommend
commendatio recommendation
commendation consent, credit *(recognition)*, estimation *(esteem)*, honor *(outward respect)*, mention *(tribute)*, patronage *(support)*, recommendation, reference *(recommendation)*, remembrance *(commemoration)*, respect
commendatory honorary, meritorious
commending favorable *(expressing approval)*
commensurability balance *(equality)*
commensurable commensurate, comparable *(capable of comparison)*, correlative, relative *(comparative)*. SEE MAIN ENTRY
commensurate adequate, coequal, cognate, commensurable, comparable *(equivalent)*, congruous, consonant, correlative, proportionate, relative *(comparative)*, suitable. SEE MAIN ENTRY
commensurate notice adequate notice
commensurate with pursuant to
commensuration proportion
comment construction, convey *(communicate)*, discourse, discuss, express, interject, mention *(reference)*, muse, notation, note *(brief comment)*, notice *(observe)*, observation, observe *(remark)*, phrase, pronouncement, remark *(noun)*, remark *(verb)*, review *(critical evaluation)*, statement. SEE MAIN ENTRY
comment on converse, edit
comment upon clarify, discuss, elucidate, expound, instruct *(teach)*, mention, review, treat *(process)*
commentary clarification, comment, construction, criticism, discourse, explanation, hornbook, marginalia, notation, note *(brief comment)*, observation, pandect *(treatise)*, proposal *(report)*, remark, review *(critical evaluation)*. SEE MAIN ENTRY
commentate elucidate, expound
commentators press
commenticius fictitious
commentum falsehood, fiction
commercari trade
commerce contact *(association)*, deal, dealings, exchange. SEE MAIN ENTRY
commerce with communicate
commercial industrial, marketable, mercantile, retail. SEE MAIN ENTRY
commercial activity SEE MAIN ENTRY
commercial advantage goodwill
commercial agent factor *(commission merchant)*
commercial backing patronage *(support)*

commercial building development *(building)*
commercial enterprise company *(enterprise)*, corporation, dealings, firm, trade *(commerce)*
commercial establishment enterprise *(economic organization)*, house
commercial failure failure *(bankruptcy)*
commercial house firm
commercial instrument check *(instrument)*
commercial intercourse business *(commerce)*, commerce, dealings
commercial paper check *(instrument)*, draft
commercial profits income
commercial rights SEE MAIN ENTRY
commercial speech SEE MAIN ENTRY
commercial theory finance
commercial transaction deal
commercialize deal
commercium commerce, commercial
comminari threaten
comminate denounce *(condemn)*, menace, threaten
commination denunciation, disapprobation, imprecation, menace, notice *(warning)*, phillipic, threat, warning
comminatory calumnious, critical *(faultfinding)*, sinister
commingle accompany, amalgamate, combine *(join together)*, desegregate, diffuse, join *(bring together)*, unite. SEE MAIN ENTRY
commingled miscellaneous, promiscuous
comminisci invent *(falsify)*
comminuque SEE MAIN ENTRY
comminute break *(fracture)*
commiscere commingle
commiserate sympathize
commiseration pity, solace
commissaries deputation *(delegation)*
commissary deputy, functionary, supplier
commission act *(undertaking)*, agency *(legal relationship)*, allow *(authorize)*, appoint, assign *(designate)*, assignment *(designation)*, assignment *(task)*, authorize, bestow, board, brokerage, bureau, charge *(command)*, charge *(empower)*, commit *(entrust)*, committee, constitute *(establish)*, delegate, delegation *(assignment)*, delegation *(envoy)*, deputation *(delegation)*, deputation *(selection of delegates)*, designate, detail *(assign)*, dictate, discharge *(performance)*, duty *(obligation)*, earnings, embassy, employ *(engage services)*, employment, empower, engage *(hire)*, hire, induct, infliction, instruction *(direction)*, invest *(vest)*, let *(permit)*, mission, nominate, performance *(execution)*, post, retain *(employ)*, share *(interest)*, transaction, warrant *(authorization)*. SEE MAIN ENTRY
commission agent broker, dealer
commission man dealer
commission merchant broker
commissioned allowed, vicarious *(delegated)*
commissioner caretaker *(one fulfilling the function of office)*, deputy, functionary, incumbent
commissioner of oaths notary public
commissioning delegation *(assignment)*, designation *(naming)*
commit apprehend *(arrest)*, arrest *(apprehend)*, confide *(trust)*, confine, consign, constrain *(imprison)*, contribute *(supply)*, delegate, deliver, deposit *(submit to a bank)*, detain *(hold in custody)*, entrust, execute *(accomplish)*, give *(grant)*, inflict, perpetrate, remand, remit *(submit for consideration)*, sentence, submit *(give)*, undertake. SEE MAIN ENTRY
commit a breach infringe
commit a breach of the law offend *(violate the law)*
commit a crime disobey, offend *(violate the law)*
commit a debauch carouse
commit a fault offend *(violate the law)*
commit again reassign, recommit
commit an error err, lapse *(fall into error)*, miscalculate, mistake, misunderstand
commit an infraction encroach, offend *(violate the law)*
commit anew recommit
commit breach of trust cheat, defraud
commit forgery forge *(counterfeit)*
commit hostilities attack, fight *(battle)*
commit larceny embezzle, pilfer, purloin
commit murder dispatch *(put to death)*
commit offense offend *(violate the law)*
commit oneself assume *(undertake)*, avow, cast *(register)*, decide, guarantee, pledge *(promise the performance of)*, promise *(vow)*
commit oneself to undertake
commit oneself to a course choose
commit perjury lie *(falsify)*
commit piracy pirate *(take by violence)*
commit powers to another assign *(designate)*, delegate
commit robbery hold up *(rob)*, pirate *(take by violence)*, rob
commit sin offend *(violate the law)*
commit to an institution arrest *(apprehend)*, constrain *(imprison)*, immure, imprison, jail, remand
commit to another's trust assign *(transfer ownership)*, consign
commit to prison arrest *(apprehend)*, confine, constrain *(imprison)*, contain *(restrain)*, immure, imprison, jail
commit to the hands of delegate
commit to writing inscribe, note *(record)*, set down. SEE MAIN ENTRY
commit violence prey
commitment adhesion *(loyalty)*, agreement *(contract)*, allegiance, assurance, attornment, captivity, charge *(lien)*, charge *(responsibility)*, cloud *(incumbrance)*, compact, constraint *(imprisonment)*, contract, covenant, custody *(incarceration)*, debit, detention, durance, duty *(obligation)*, guaranty, incarceration, incumbrance *(lien)*, indenture, infliction, obligation *(duty)*, pledge *(binding promise)*, promise, recognizance, responsibility *(accountability)*, specialty *(contract)*, undertaking *(pledge)*. SEE MAIN ENTRY
commitments ties
committal captivity, commitment *(confinement)*, detention
committed agreed *(promised)*, arrested *(apprehended)*, bound, contractual, loyal
committed to payment promissory
committee agency *(commission)*, assemblage, bureau, caucus, chamber *(body)*, council *(assembly)*, delegation *(envoy)*, deputation *(delegation)*, management *(directorate)*. SEE MAIN ENTRY
committeeperson member *(individual in a group)*
committere consign, delegate, entrust, perpetrate
commix amalgamate, combine *(join together)*, commingle, desegregate
commixed composite, compound, concerted, miscellaneous
commixtion incorporation *(blend)*
commixture coalescence, melange, solution *(substance)*
commodare lend, loan, serve *(assist)*
commodious ample, capacious, convenient, extensive, practical, suitable
commodis consulere welfare
commodities cargo, goods, merchandise. SEE MAIN ENTRY
commodity appliance, chattel, item, object, product
commodus favorable *(advantageous)*, fit, opportune
common accustomed *(customary)*, average *(standard)*, base *(inferior)*, blatant *(obtrusive)*, boiler plate, civic, cognate, competitive *(open)*, concurrent *(united)*, conjoint, conventional, customary, daily, familiar *(customary)*, frequent, general, generic, habitual, household *(familiar)*, ignoble, inelegant, informal, jejune *(dull)*, joint, mediocre, mundane, mutual *(collective)*, national, nondescript, normal *(regular)*, orthodox, poor *(inferior in quality)*, predominant, prevailing *(current)*, prevalent, pro forma, profane, prosaic, proverbial, public *(affecting people)*, reciprocal, regular *(conventional)*, repeated, rife, routine, stale, tawdry, traditional, trite, typical, usual. SEE MAIN ENTRY
common agreement mutual understanding
common ancestry affinity *(family ties)*, blood, propinquity *(kinship)*, relation *(kinship)*
common assent agreement *(concurrence)*, concordance
common consent agreement *(concurrence)*, cartel, consensus
common course practice *(custom)*
common denominator connection *(relation)*
common derivation affiliation *(bloodline)*
common descent relation *(kinship)*
common effort coaction
common extraction family *(common ancestry)*
common feature analogy
common folk populace
common forebears family *(common ancestry)*
common fund pool
common knowledge publicity. SEE MAIN ENTRY
common lineage family *(common ancestry)*, relation *(kinship)*
common lot mediocrity
common occurrence frequency
common ownership pool
common parentage family *(common ancestry)*
common people populace
common practice habit, matter of course, procedure
common reference connection *(relation)*
common run generality *(bulk)*, matter of course
common saying catchword
common sense prudence, reason *(sound judgment)*. SEE MAIN ENTRY

common state of affairs matter of course
common stock relation *(kinship)*
common to many general
common understanding mutual understanding
common usage custom
common view accordance *(understanding)*, agreement *(concurrence)*, compatibility, understanding *(agreement)*
commonage populace
commonality mutuality
commonalty community, populace, population, public
commonere admonish *(warn)*, remind
commoners populace
commonition admonition
commonly as a rule, generally, invariably
commonly considered putative
commonly known household *(familiar)*, proverbial, public *(known)*
commonly observed customary
commonly practiced customary
commonness frequency, mediocrity
commonplace accustomed *(customary)*, average *(standard)*, boiler plate, common *(customary)*, customary, familiar *(customary)*, habitual, household *(familiar)*, jejune *(dull)*, lifeless *(dull)*, mediocre, mundane, nondescript, normal *(regular)*, ordinary, orthodox, pedestrian, prevailing *(current)*, prevalent, prosaic, proverbial, regular *(conventional)*, repeated, routine, stale, trite, typical, usual
commonplace expression platitude
commonplace idea platitude
commonplace phrase platitude
commonplaceness mediocrity
commonwealth community, nationality, polity, public, society, state *(political unit)*
commorance residence
commorancy residence
commotion affray, altercation, brawl, confusion *(turmoil)*, disorder *(lack of order)*, disturbance, embroilment, entanglement *(confusion)*, fracas, fray, furor, imbroglio, outbreak, outburst, pandemonium, riot, trouble, turmoil. SEE MAIN ENTRY
commovere affect, disturb, move *(alter position)*
communal civic, civil *(public)*, common *(shared)*, concurrent *(united)*, joint, mutual *(collective)*, public *(affecting people)*
communal business establishment cooperative
communal society cooperative
communalistic mutual *(collective)*
commune communicate, community, cooperative
commune with converse, discourse
commune with oneself muse, ponder, reflect *(ponder)*
communicable contagious
communicant deponent, informant, informer *(a person who provides information)*
communicare communicate, impart
communicate advise, annunciate, apprise, bestow, circulate, connote, declare, deliver, depict, disabuse, disclose, disseminate, divulge, express, herald, impart, inform *(betray)*, inform *(notify)*, issue *(publish)*, mention, notice *(give formal warning)*, notify, observe *(remark)*, pass *(advance)*, phrase, post, proclaim, promulgate, pronounce *(speak)*, publish, recite, recount, relate *(tell)*, remark, render *(deliver)*, report *(disclose)*, reveal, signify *(inform)*, transmit, utter. SEE MAIN ENTRY
communicate effectively SEE MAIN ENTRY
communicate orally discourse
communicate to caution
communicate with converse, reach, speak
communicated oral
communicatio communication *(discourse)*
communication admission *(disclosure)*, caveat, contact *(association)*, conversation, correspondence *(communication by letters)*, disclosure *(act of disclosing)*, disclosure *(something disclosed)*, dispatch *(message)*, expression *(comment)*, information *(knowledge)*, intelligence *(news)*, issuance, language, mention *(reference)*, note *(brief comment)*, notice *(announcement)*, notice *(warning)*, notification, parley, publication *(disclosure)*, report *(detailed account)*, tip *(clue)*, transmittal. SEE MAIN ENTRY
communication of knowledge advice, declaration
communicative declaratory, demonstrative *(expressive of emotion)*, eloquent, informative, informatory, loquacious, narrative, responsive
communicator deponent, informant, informer *(a person who provides information)*
communicatory advisory, informative
communion accordance *(understanding)*, concordance, mutual understanding, sodality
communiqué communication *(discourse)*, declaration, dispatch *(message)*
communique information *(facts)*, information *(knowledge)*, intelligence *(news)*, issuance, notice *(announcement)*, notification
communis common *(shared)*, general, joint, ordinary
community body *(collection)*, civic, coalition, constituency, contact *(association)*, denomination, joint, organization *(association)*, populace, population, public *(open)*, public, society, sodality. SEE MAIN ENTRY
community of interest cartel, sodality
community of interests agreement *(concurrence)*, peace
community of possession pool
commutability mutuality
commutable convertible, mutable
commutare alter, modify *(alter)*
commutation clemency, compensation, compromise, exchange, immunity, mutuality, replacement, subrogation
commutative convertible, mutual *(reciprocal)*
commute alter, convert *(change use)*, replace, transform. SEE MAIN ENTRY
commutual common *(shared)*, concurrent *(united)*, conjoint, correlative, mutual *(collective)*, reciprocal, related
compact abstract *(summarize)*, adjustment, agreement *(contract)*, arrangement *(understanding)*, attornment, bargain, brief, cartel, coadunate, composition *(agreement in bankruptcy)*, concentrate *(consolidate)*, conciliation, concise, concordance, conjoint, consensus, consolidate *(strengthen)*, consolidation, consortium *(marriage companionship)*, conspiracy, constrict *(compress)*, contract, corporate *(joint)*, covenant, crystallize, decrease, indenture, league, mutual understanding, pact, pithy, pledge *(binding promise)*, populous, promise, protocol *(agreement)*, reduce, sententious, specialty *(contract)*, stipulation, succinct, treaty, understanding *(agreement)*, undertaking *(pledge)*. SEE MAIN ENTRY
compact to govern constitution
compacted compact *(dense)*, concise
compacting centralization
compactness congealment, density
compages complex *(development)*, corpus
compages frame *(structure)*
companion associate, cohort, colleague, complement, confederate, consociate, consort, copartner *(business associate)*, copartner *(coconspirator)*, correlate, participant, partner, peer, similar. SEE MAIN ENTRY
companion in crime coconspirator
companionless solitary
companionship compatibility, consortium *(marriage companionship)*, contact *(association)*, society, sodality
company assemblage, assembly, association *(alliance)*, body *(collection)*, business *(commercial enterprise)*, collection *(assembly)*, concern *(business establishment)*, corporation, enterprise *(economic organization)*, firm, house, organization *(association)*, personnel, syndicate. SEE MAIN ENTRY
comparabilis comparable *(capable of comparison)*
comparability analogy, balance *(equality)*, collation, correspondence *(similarity)*, identity *(similarity)*, parity
comparable analogous, apposite, approximate, coequal, coextensive, cognate, commensurable, commensurate, comparative, correlative, equivalent, identical, proportionate, similar, tantamount. SEE MAIN ENTRY
comparableness balance *(equality)*, relation *(connection)*
comparare compare, contrast, procure, relative *(comparative)*
comparatio comparison
comparative cognate, correlative, proportionate. SEE MAIN ENTRY
comparative estimate collation, comparison
comparative size proportion
comparativeness balance *(equality)*
comparativus comparative
compare correspond *(be equivalent)*, discriminate *(distinguish)*, measure. SEE MAIN ENTRY
compare by observing differences contrast
compare critically diagnose
compare opinions confer *(consult)*
compare to contrast
compare with approximate, contrast
compared cognate, relative *(comparative)*
comparere appear *(attend court proceedings)*, report *(present oneself)*
comparison analogy, collation, correlate, identification, parity, propinquity *(similarity)*, proportion, standard. SEE MAIN ENTRY
compartment cell, section *(division)*, subdivision, zone
compartmentalize insulate, part *(separate)*, partition
compass blockade *(enclosure)*, boundary, caliber *(measurement)*, capacity *(maximum)*, circumscribe *(surround by boundary)*, comprehend *(include)*, demarcate, embrace *(encircle)*, enclose, encompass *(surround)*, envelop, extent, frontier, gamut, hedge, include, outline *(boundary)*, periphery, province, purview, range, region, scope, space
compassion benevolence *(disposition to do good)*, clemency, condonation,

consideration *(sympathetic regard)*, humanity *(humaneness)*, indulgence, lenience, pity, tolerance, understanding *(tolerance)*
compassionate lenient, placable, receptive, susceptible *(responsive)*
compatibility accordance *(understanding)*, concert, conformity *(agreement)*, consensus, propinquity *(similarity)*, propriety *(appropriateness)*, qualification *(fitness)*, rapport, relevance, sodality, synchronism. SEE MAIN ENTRY
compatible apposite, concordant, concurrent *(united)*, congruous, conjoint, consensual, consistent, consonant, correlative, fit, harmonious, proportionate, relative *(relevant)*, relevant, suitable, uniform
compatible to pursuant to
compeer associate, colleague, consort, contributor *(contributor)*, copartner *(business associate)*, partner, peer
compel bait *(harass)*, bait *(lure)*, bind *(obligate)*, bind *(restrain)*, cause, coerce, command, constrain *(compel)*, convince, detail *(assign)*, dictate, dominate, enforce, exact, extort, foist, force *(coerce)*, impose *(enforce)*, impose *(subject)*, instruct *(direct)*, make, motivate, necessitate, obsess, order, persuade, press *(constrain)*, pressure, rule *(govern)*. SEE MAIN ENTRY
compel attendance summon
compel attendence subpoena
compel belief convince
compel by intimidation extort
compel by threat extort
compel obedience enforce
compel payment excise *(levy a tax)*
compel to accept foist
compellare accost
compellation call *(title)*
compelled bound
compeller extortionist
compellere compel, constrain *(compel)*
compelling binding, causal, cogent, compulsory, considerable, convincing, decisive, dictatorial, eloquent, exigent, forcible, important *(urgent)*, impulsive *(impelling)*, insistent, irresistible, material *(important)*, necessary *(inescapable)*, necessary *(required)*, obligatory, persuasive, potent, powerful, sound, stringent, strong, unavoidable *(inevitable)*, undeniable, urgent. SEE MAIN ENTRY
compelling government interest SEE MAIN ENTRY
compelling quality necessity
compend capsule, compendium, outline *(synopsis)*, summary, synopsis
compendious brief, compact *(pithy)*, comprehensive, concise, laconic, omnibus, pithy, succinct
compendium abridgment *(condensation)*, abstract, brief, capsule, codification, digest, hornbook, outline *(synopsis)*, pandect *(treatise)*, restatement, sum *(tally)*, summary, synopsis. SEE MAIN ENTRY
compensare compensate *(counterbalance)*, redress, requital
compensate bear the expense, contribute *(indemnify)*, defray, disburse *(pay out)*, indemnify, outbalance, pay, quit *(repay)*, recoup *(reimburse)*, redeem *(satisfy debts)*, redress, refund, reimburse, remit *(send payment)*, remunerate, repay, replace, return *(refund)*, satisfy *(discharge)*. SEE MAIN ENTRY
compensate for cover *(provide for)*
compensate for injury indemnify
compensate for loss indemnify
compensate for loss sustained indemnify
compensating compensatory, disbursement *(act of disbursing)*, lucrative
compensatio collection *(payment)*, compensation
compensation advance *(allowance)*, aid *(subsistence)*, benefit *(conferment)*, brokerage, collection *(payment)*, commission *(fee)*, consideration *(recompense)*, contribution *(indemnification)*, damages, disbursement *(funds paid out)*, discharge *(payment)*, earnings, expiation, fee *(charge)*, honorarium, income, indemnification, indemnity, offset, out of pocket, pay, payment *(act of paying)*, payment *(remittance)*, payroll, pension, perquisite, price, profit, recompense, recovery *(award)*, refund, reimbursement, relief *(legal redress)*, remedy *(legal means of redress)*, remuneration, rendition *(restoration)*, rent, reparation *(indemnification)*, replacement, requital, restitution, retainer, retribution, revenue, reward, satisfaction *(discharge of debt)*, tip *(gratuity)*, trover, wage. SEE MAIN ENTRY
compensation for delay demurrage
compensation for injury insurance
compensation for labor fee *(charge)*
compensation for loss insurance
compensation for professional service fee *(charge)*
compensation owed due
compensative compensatory
compensator insurer
compensatory equivalent, lucrative, remedial. SEE MAIN ENTRY
comperire ascertain, discover
compes fetter
compete contend *(dispute)*, dispute *(contest)*, engage *(involve)*, participate, race, strive. SEE MAIN ENTRY
compete for endeavor
compete with antagonize, counter, fight *(battle)*, grapple
competence ability, caliber *(mental capacity)*, capacity *(aptitude)*, discretion *(quality of being discreet)*, efficiency, experience *(background)*, facility *(easiness)*, faculty *(ability)*, force *(strength)*, gift *(flair)*, penchant, performance *(workmanship)*, potential, power, prowess *(ability)*, science *(technique)*, skill, specialty *(special aptitude)*, sufficiency. SEE MAIN ENTRY
competency ability, capacity *(aptitude)*, efficiency, experience *(background)*, faculty *(ability)*, performance *(workmanship)*, prowess *(ability)*, qualification *(fitness)*, quality *(excellence)*, science *(technique)*, sufficiency. SEE MAIN ENTRY
competent adequate, capable, deft, effective *(efficient)*, efficient, expert, familiar *(informed)*, fit, operative, practiced, professional *(trained)*, proficient, reliable, resourceful, sane, sciential. SEE MAIN ENTRY
competent practitioner professional
competere competent
competing competitive *(antagonistic)*, contestable
competition conflict, contention *(opposition)*, rival, strife, struggle. SEE MAIN ENTRY
competitive contentious, hostile, jealous. SEE MAIN ENTRY
competitiveness contention *(opposition)*
competitor adversary, candidate, contender, foe, peer, rival
competitory competitive *(antagonistic)*
compilare hold up *(rob)*, plunder
compilation abstract, assemblage, body *(collection)*, building *(business of assembling)*, centralization, code, codification, collection *(accumulation)*, composition *(makeup)*, conglomeration, corpus, cumulation, digest, selection *(choice)*, selection *(collection)*, summary. SEE MAIN ENTRY
compilation of law code, constitution
compilation of laws code
compilations information *(knowledge)*
compile accumulate *(amass)*, aggregate, build *(construct)*, codify, collect *(gather)*, compose, congregate, garner. SEE MAIN ENTRY
compiled collective
compiler author *(writer)*
compiler of tables of mortality actuary
complacence composure
complacent benevolent. SEE MAIN ENTRY
complain cite *(accuse)*, criticize *(find fault with)*, deplore, object, protest, reproach. SEE MAIN ENTRY
complain against accuse, arraign, blame, charge *(accuse)*, denounce *(inform against)*, impeach, incriminate
complain frivolously cavil
complain publicly demonstrate *(protest)*
complainant accuser, actor, claimant, contender, contestant, declarant, informer *(one providing criminal information)*, litigant, malcontent, party *(litigant)*, plaintiff, victim. SEE MAIN ENTRY
complained of accused *(charged)*
complainer malcontent
complaining criticism, diatribe, disapproval, fractious, querulous
complaining party complainant
complaining witness victim
complaint allegation, charge *(accusation)*, claim *(legal demand)*, condemnation *(blame)*, criticism, denunciation, disapprobation, disapproval, disorder *(abnormal condition)*, disparagement, dissatisfaction, exception *(objection)*, grievance, ground, impeachment, incrimination, indictment, outcry, plaint, pleading, protest, reproach. SEE MAIN ENTRY
complaint to a higher court habeas corpus
complaint to a superior court appeal
complaisance consideration *(sympathetic regard)*, courtesy, deference
complaisant complacent, obedient, obeisant, permissive, yielding. SEE MAIN ENTRY
complecti embrace *(encircle)*, encompass *(include)*, include
complement addendum, addition, adjunct, allonge, appendix *(accession)*, boom *(increase)*, codicil, component, content *(structure)*, corollary, correlate, correspond *(be equivalent)*, rider, staff, supplement. SEE MAIN ENTRY
complemental concomitant, correlative, mutual *(reciprocal)*, reciprocal
complemental term correlate
complementary cognate, concordant, concurrent *(united)*, convertible, correlative, mutual *(reciprocal)*, pendent, reciprocal, related
complementing ancillary *(subsidiary)*
complementum complement
complete accomplish, adjust *(resolve)*, arrant *(definite)*, attain, cap, carry *(succeed)*, categorical, close *(terminate)*, commit *(perpetrate)*, comply, comprehensive, conclusive *(settled)*, consummate, culminate,

definitive, detailed, discharge *(perform)*, discontinue *(abandon)*, dispatch *(dispose of)*, effectuate, execute *(accomplish)*, exhaust *(try all possibilities)*, fabricate *(construct)*, finish, follow-up, fulfill, full, gross *(total)*, implement, intact, inviolate, keep *(fulfill)*, lapse *(cease)*, make, omnibus, outright, peremptory *(absolute)*, perfect, perform *(adhere to)*, perform *(execute)*, plenary, pure, radical *(extreme)*, realize *(make real)*, replenish, replete, ripe, stark, terminate, thorough, total, unconditional, unmitigated, unqualified *(unlimited)*, whole *(undamaged)*. SEE MAIN ENTRY
complete a purchase buy
complete body of laws pandect *(code of laws)*
complete conviction certainty, certification *(certainness)*, surety *(certainty)*
complete digest pandect *(treatise)*
complete lawsuit day in court
complete prosecution rest *(end a legal case)*
complete report accounting
complete sequence gamut
complete series gamut
complete standstill impasse
complete substitution novation
complete trust credence
completed complete *(ended)*, conclusive *(settled)*, definitive, fully executed *(consummated)*, fully executed *(signed)*, through
completely fairly *(clearly)*, in toto, wholly
completely end destroy *(void)*
completely full replete
completeness conclusion *(outcome)*, entirety, fait accompli, finality, quorum, totality, whole
completing ancillary *(auxiliary)*, conclusive *(settled)*, final
completion cessation *(termination)*, close *(conclusion)*, commission *(act)*, complement, conclusion *(outcome)*, consequence *(conclusion)*, course, denouement, discharge *(performance)*, dissolution *(termination)*, end *(termination)*, entirety, expiration, extremity *(death)*, fait accompli, finality, follow-up, maturity, outcome, performance *(execution)*, realization, transaction. SEE MAIN ENTRY
completive complete *(ended)*, comprehensive, conclusive *(settled)*, last *(final)*
completory last *(final)*
complex composite, compound, conglomerate, difficult, elaborate, inextricable, intricate, labyrinthine, obscure *(abstruse)*, problematic, recondite, sinuous, sophisticated. SEE MAIN ENTRY
complexion appearance *(look)*, condition *(state)*, spirit, state *(condition)*. SEE MAIN ENTRY
complexity complication, confusion *(turmoil)*, enigma, entanglement *(confusion)*, imbroglio, impasse, involution, problem
complexness complication
complexus complex *(entanglement)*
complexus complication
complexus corpus, snarl
compliable complacent, consenting, consistent, facile, obedient, obsequious, passive, pliant
compliance acceptance, accordance *(understanding)*, acknowledgment *(acceptance)*, acquiescence, adherence *(devotion)*, amenability, assent, capitulation, comity, compatibility, conciliation, conduct, conformity *(obedience)*, conjunction, consent, consortium *(marriage companionship)*, conspiracy, deference, discipline *(obedience)*, fealty, homage, indorsement, loyalty, timeliness, understanding *(agreement)*. SEE MAIN ENTRY
compliancy amenability, compliance
compliant amenable, charitable *(lenient)*, complacent, concordant, consensual, consenting, facile, favorable *(expressing approval)*, loyal, malleable, obedient, obeisant, obsequious, orthodox, passive, patient, pliable, pliant, prone, ready *(willing)*, sequacious, servile, tractable, true *(loyal)*, willing *(not averse)*, yielding. SEE MAIN ENTRY
compliantly faithfully, respectfully
complicate aggravate *(exacerbate)*, confound, dislocate, disorganize, muddle, obfuscate, perplex, perturb. SEE MAIN ENTRY
complicated circuitous, complex, compound, difficult, elaborate, inextricable, intricate, labyrinthine, problematic, profound *(esoteric)*, recondite, sinuous, tortuous *(bending)*
complicated misunderstanding imbroglio
complicated state complication
complication aggravation *(annoyance)*, complex *(entanglement)*, confusion *(ambiguity)*, embroilment, entanglement *(confusion)*, hindrance, imbroglio, involution, predicament, problem, quagmire, snarl. SEE MAIN ENTRY
complicity bad faith, bribery, cabal, coaction, collusion, concert, confederacy *(conspiracy)*, connivance, conspiracy, contribution *(participation)*, contrivance, corruption, implication *(incriminating involvement)*, league, plot *(secret plan)*. SEE MAIN ENTRY
compliment belaud, doxology, honor, mention *(tribute)*, recommend
complimentary free *(at no charge)*, gratis, gratuitous *(given without recompense)*, unsolicited
complot cabal, collusion, confederacy *(conspiracy)*, connivance, connive, maneuver, plan *(noun)*, plan *(verb)*, plot *(secret plan)*, scheme
complotter conspirator
comply abide, accede *(concede)*, accept *(admit as sufficient)*, accept *(assent)*, adhere *(maintain loyalty)*, assent, concur *(agree)*, conform, consent, defer *(yield in judgment)*, discharge *(perform)*, hear *(give attention to)*, heed, obey, serve *(assist)*, submit *(yield)*, succumb, suffer *(permit)*, yield *(submit)*. SEE MAIN ENTRY
comply with adapt, agree *(comply)*, concede, correspond *(be equivalent)*, fulfill, keep *(fulfill)*, observe *(obey)*, perform *(adhere to)*, satisfy *(fulfill)*, vouchsafe
complying law-abiding, obedient, passive, true *(loyal)*
component adjunct, affiliate, chapter *(branch)*, chapter *(division)*, color *(complexion)*, constituent *(part)*, detail, element, factor *(ingredient)*, feature *(characteristic)*, ingredient, integral, item, member *(constituent part)*, organ, part *(portion)*, section *(division)*, segment, subdivision, unit *(item)*. SEE MAIN ENTRY
component part component, constituent *(part)*, detail, element, ingredient
components contents
componere agree *(comply)*, arrange *(methodize)*, compare, compile, compose, constitute *(compose)*, frame *(formulate)*, organize *(arrange)*, pacify
comport demean *(deport oneself)*. SEE MAIN ENTRY
comport oneself deport *(conduct oneself)*
comport with cohere *(be logically consistent)*, correspond *(be equivalent)*
comportment behavior, conduct, demeanor, deportment, manner *(behavior)*, presence *(poise)*
compose accommodate, allay, alleviate, assuage, build *(construct)*, compile, conceive *(invent)*, contrive, create, devise *(invent)*, fabricate *(construct)*, forge *(produce)*, form, formulate, frame *(construct)*, invent *(produce for the first time)*, lull, make, manufacture, marshal, mollify, orchestrate, originate, produce *(manufacture)*, scheme, soothe. SEE MAIN ENTRY
compose differences intercede
compose oneself repose *(rest)*
composed complacent, dispassionate, nonchalant, patient, peaceable, placid
composed of several elements multiple
composer architect, author *(originator)*
composer of a literary work author *(writer)*
composite coherent *(joined)*, collective, complex *(development)*, compound, concerted, conglomerate, conjoint, content *(structure)*, miscellaneous, omnibus, promiscuous, solution *(substance)*. SEE MAIN ENTRY
composite representation cross section
compositio accommodation *(adjustment)*, arrangement *(ordering)*, composition *(makeup)*, settlement
composition adjustment, arrangement *(ordering)*, array *(order)*, building *(business of assembling)*, combination, compromise, configuration *(form)*, conspiracy, content *(structure)*, coverage *(scope)*, creation, formation, invention, language, manufacture, melange, motif, order *(arrangement)*, organization *(structure)*, origination, performance *(workmanship)*, phraseology, solution *(substance)*, temperament. SEE MAIN ENTRY
composition of differences accommodation *(adjustment)*
compositional skill rhetoric *(skilled speech)*
compositus composite, compound
composure common sense, longanimity, moderation, sufferance. SEE MAIN ENTRY
composure of differences settlement
composure of doubts settlement
compound adhere *(fasten)*, close *(enclosed area)*, coalescence, collective, combination, combine *(join together)*, commingle, complex *(development)*, composite, confines, conglomerate, conjoin, consolidate *(strengthen)*, consolidate *(unite)*, desegregate, incorporate *(include)*, incorporation *(blend)*, join *(bring together)*, make, melange, merge, solution *(substance)*. SEE MAIN ENTRY
compounded composite, conglomerate, inextricable. SEE MAIN ENTRY
compounding building *(business of assembling)*, composition *(makeup)*
comprehend apprehend *(perceive)*, discern *(detect with the senses)*, include, perceive, pierce *(discern)*, realize *(understand)*, recognize *(perceive)*, understand. SEE MAIN ENTRY
comprehendable comprehensible

comprehended from accompanying words noscitur a sociis
comprehendere apprehend *(arrest)*, apprehend *(perceive)*, arrest *(apprehend)*, capture, comprehend *(understand)*, contain *(comprise)*, embrace *(encircle)*, include, realize *(understand)*, seize *(apprehend)*
comprehending cognizant, conscious *(aware)*, knowing, lucid, omniscient, perceptive, receptive
comprehensibility coherence
comprehensible cognizable, coherent *(clear)*, explicit, lucid, obvious, pellucid, perceptible, ponderable, scrutable, unambiguous. SEE MAIN ENTRY
comprehensio comprehension
comprehension appreciation *(perception)*, apprehension *(perception)*, caliber *(mental capacity)*, cognition, connotation, coverage *(scope)*, discrimination *(differentiation)*, information *(knowledge)*, insight, intellect, intelligence *(intellect)*, judgment *(discernment)*, knowledge *(awareness)*, perception, realization, reason *(sound judgment)*, recognition, sagacity, sanity, scienter, sense *(intelligence)*, sensibility. SEE MAIN ENTRY
comprehensive absolute *(complete)*, ample, broad, capacious, collective, competitive *(open)*, complete *(all-embracing)*, detailed, extensive, far reaching, full, generic, gross *(total)*, inclusive, indiscriminate, major, nonsectarian, omnibus, outright, plenary, prevailing *(current)*, radical *(extreme)*, thorough. SEE MAIN ENTRY
comprehensive digest pandect *(treatise)*
comprehensively in toto
comprehensiveness capacity *(maximum)*, corpus, coverage *(scope)*, entirety, extent, totality. SEE MAIN ENTRY
compress abridge *(shorten)*, abstract *(summarize)*, cohere *(adhere)*, concentrate *(consolidate)*, condense, consolidate *(strengthen)*, consolidate *(unite)*, crystallize, decrease, diminish, impact, lessen, reduce
compressed brief, coherent *(joined)*, cohesive *(compact)*, compact *(dense)*, concise, laconic, narrow, pithy, sententious, solid *(compact)*
compressed statement summary
compression abridgment *(condensation)*, abstract, blockade *(limitation)*, capsule, centralization, curtailment, outline *(synopsis)*, scenario
comprimere repress, withhold
comprisal composition *(makeup)*, coverage *(scope)*
comprise comprehend *(include)*, consist, constitute *(compose)*, encompass *(include)*. SEE MAIN ENTRY
comprising comprehensive, inclusive
comprobare approve, confirm, corroborate
comprobatio acceptance, approval, indorsement
compromisable convertible
compromise accommodation *(adjustment)*, accord, adjustment, agree *(contract)*, arrangement *(understanding)*, bargain, collective bargaining, compact, conciliation, contract, deal, denigrate, endanger, find *(determine)*, give *(yield)*, mediate, negotiation, pact, settle, settlement. SEE MAIN ENTRY
compromise agreement composition *(agreement in bankruptcy)*
compromised agreed *(harmonized)*
compromiser referee, umpire
compromising calumnious, contemptuous, disgraceful, intermediate
compromittere compromise *(settle by mutual agreement)*
compte rendu account *(evaluation)*
comptroller SEE MAIN ENTRY
compulsatory obligatory
compulsion coercion, constraint *(restriction)*, deterrence, dipsomania, duress, enforcement, extortion, force *(compulsion)*, main force, motive, need *(requirement)*, obligation *(duty)*, obsession, oppression, pressure, requirement, responsibility *(accountability)*, servitude, stress *(strain)*. SEE MAIN ENTRY
compulsive compelling, obligatory
compulsorily acquire condemn *(seize)*, confiscate, distrain
compulsory binding, choate lien, compelling, essential *(required)*, exigent, forcible, imperative, indispensable, involuntary, mandatory, necessary *(required)*, obligatory, peremptory *(imperative)*, positive *(prescribed)*, prescriptive, requisite, stringent, unavoidable *(inevitable)*, urgent. SEE MAIN ENTRY
compulsory acquisition condemnation *(seizure)*, disseisin, requisition
compulsory detail necessity, need *(requirement)*
compulsory execution enforcement
compulsory payment fine, penalty, punishment
compulsory purchase expropriation *(right of eminent domain)*
compulsory service bondage
compunction conscience, qualm, remorse, responsibility *(conscience)*, scruple
compunctious blameful, contrite, penitent, remorseful, repentant
compurgate acquit, confess
compurgation acquittal, deposition, justification, pardon, release. SEE MAIN ENTRY
compurgator deponent, eyewitness, witness
computable appreciable, determinable *(ascertainable)*
computare calculate
computation accounting, appraisal, census, estimate *(approximate cost)*, estimation *(calculation)*, ledger, measurement. SEE MAIN ENTRY
compute assess *(appraise)*, calculate, charge *(assess)*, gauge, measure, poll, rate, sum, survey *(poll)*
comrade cohort, colleague, confederate, consociate, consort, contributor *(contributor)*, copartner *(coconspirator)*, member *(individual in a group)*, participant, partisan, peer
comrade in crime coconspirator
comrade in wrongdoing coconspirator
comradeship consortium *(marriage companionship)*, contribution *(participation)*, society, sodality
con contra, deception, peruse, read
con game bunko
conari attempt, endeavor, strive, try *(attempt)*
conation conatus
conative discretionary, voluntary
conative will conatus
conatus effort, endeavor. SEE MAIN ENTRY
concatenate combine *(join together)*, consolidate *(strengthen)*, join *(bring together)*
concatenation chain *(series)*, conjunction, connection *(fastening)*, joinder, sequence, succession
conceal blind *(obscure)*, camouflage, circumvent, cloak, clothe, disguise, distort, ensconce, enshroud, envelop, expurgate, harbor, hedge, hide, misguide, misinform, obfuscate, obliterate, obnubilate, obscure, screen *(guard)*, seclude, sequester *(seclude)*, shroud, stifle, suppress, withhold. SEE MAIN ENTRY
conceal from knowledge hide
conceal from sight blind *(obscure)*, hide
conceal oneself lurk
conceal the truth cloak, prevaricate
concealed clandestine, confidential, covert, esoteric, evasive, furtive, hidden, impalpable, incomprehensible, inconspicuous, indiscernible, inexplicable, inscrutable, latent, mysterious, oblique *(evasive)*, obscure *(faint)*, opaque, personal *(private)*, potential, private *(confidential)*, privy, recondite, secret, stealthy, surreptitious, ulterior, undisclosed. SEE MAIN ENTRY
concealed knowledge secret
concealment artifice, color *(deceptive appearance)*, confidence *(relation of trust)*, disguise, evasion, mystery, nonappearance, obscuration, privacy, subterfuge, veil. SEE MAIN ENTRY
concealment of truth indirection *(deceitfulness)*
concede abandon *(relinquish)*, acknowledge *(verify)*, agree *(comply)*, allow *(endure)*, assent, authorize, bear *(tolerate)*, bestow, cede, compromise *(settle by mutual agreement)*, confess, confirm, conform, forfeit, give *(grant)*, give *(yield)*, let *(permit)*, recognize *(acknowledge)*, reveal, succumb, suffer *(permit)*, surrender *(yield)*, vouchsafe, yield *(submit)*. SEE MAIN ENTRY
conceded agreed *(harmonized)*, allowed, consensual
conceded judgment cognovit
concededly admittedly
concedere admit *(concede)*, cede, comply, concede, grant *(concede)*, grant *(transfer formally)*, let *(permit)*, retire *(retreat)*, vouchsafe, yield *(submit)*
conceit idea, jactation
conceited inflated *(vain)*, orgulous, presumptuous, pretentious *(pompous)*
conceivability chance *(possibility)*, likelihood, possibility, probability
conceivable believable, colorable *(plausible)*, comprehensible, constructive *(inferential)*, plausible, possible, potential, presumptive, probable, prospective, viable. SEE MAIN ENTRY
conceivableness chance *(possibility)*, likelihood, possibility
conceive appreciate *(comprehend)*, compose, comprehend *(understand)*, conjure, contrive, create, deem, devise *(invent)*, frame *(formulate)*, initiate, invent *(produce for the first time)*, originate, presume, produce *(manufacture)*, recognize *(perceive)*, reflect *(ponder)*, reproduce, surmise, understand. SEE MAIN ENTRY
conceive of apprehend *(perceive)*, construe *(comprehend)*
conceived of parents legally married legitimate *(lawfully conceived)*
concent consensus
concenter concentrate *(consolidate)*, converge, focus
concentralization centralization
concentralize converge
concentrate accumulate *(amass)*, border *(approach)*, collect *(gather)*,

congregate, consolidate *(strengthen)*, consolidate *(unite)*, constrict *(compress)*, converge, decrease, devote, distill, draw *(extract)*, intensify, muse, reflect *(ponder)*. SEE MAIN ENTRY
concentrate on focus, occupy *(engage)*, specialize
concentrate the mind focus
concentrate the thoughts focus
concentrate upon ponder
concentrated cohesive *(compact)*, collective, compact *(dense)*, intense, intensive, solid *(compact)*, strong
concentrating cumulative *(intensifying)*, earnest, pensive
concentration assemblage, barrage, centralization, collection *(accumulation)*, contemplation, corpus, cumulation, density, emphasis, interest *(concern)*, observation, preoccupation, reflection *(thought)*, regard *(attention)*, strength. SEE MAIN ENTRY
concentric coextensive
concentus consensus
concept conviction *(persuasion)*, idea, impression, notion, vision *(dream)*. SEE MAIN ENTRY
conception apprehension *(perception)*, arrangement *(plan)*, cognition, comprehension, concept, conviction *(persuasion)*, design *(construction plan)*, idea, impression, notion, perspective, presumption, side, supposition, understanding *(comprehension)*, vision *(dream)*
conceptualize conceive *(comprehend)*, conjure
concern affinity *(regard)*, agitate *(perturb)*, appertain, apply *(pertain)*, apprehension *(fear)*, business *(affair)*, business *(commercial enterprise)*, calling, caution *(vigilance)*, charge *(custody)*, company *(enterprise)*, consideration *(sympathetic regard)*, corporation, devote, diligence *(care)*, discretion *(quality of being discreet)*, enterprise *(economic organization)*, fear, firm, house, importance, institute, interest, magnitude, market *(business)*, matter *(subject)*, misgiving, mission, object, part *(role)*, pertain, position *(business status)*, profession *(vocation)*, prudence, pursuit *(occupation)*, purview, qualm, refer *(direct attention)*, regard *(attention)*, relate *(establish a connection)*, relevance, remorse, scruple, significance, store *(business)*, trade *(occupation)*, undertaking *(enterprise)*. SEE MAIN ENTRY
concern oneself with address *(direct attention to)*, discharge *(perform)*, occupy *(engage)*, specialize
concerned careful, interested, solicitous, suspicious *(distrustful)*
concerning correlative, germane, pertinent, relative *(relevant)*, relevant, wherein
concerning the law forensic, juridical
concernment concern *(interest)*, importance, significance
concerns affairs
concert affiliation *(connectedness)*, cartel, coherence, collusion, combine *(act in concert)*, conciliation, concordance, conformity *(agreement)*, conjunction, connivance, connive, consensus, consolidate *(unite)*, conspiracy, conspire, contribution *(participation)*, cooperate, federate, federation, orchestrate, propinquity *(similarity)*, synergy, union *(unity)*. SEE MAIN ENTRY
concert of action coaction
concertare dispute *(contest)*
concerted associated, coadunate, collective, concurrent *(at the same time)*, concurrent *(united)*, conjoint, consonant, joint. SEE MAIN ENTRY
concerted refusal to work strike
concessio admission *(disclosure)*, concession *(authorization)*
concession accord, acknowledgment *(acceptance)*, acquiescence, admission *(disclosure)*, advancement *(loan)*, appropriation *(allotment)*, cession, compliance, compromise, conciliation, consent, consignment, copyright, disclosure *(act of disclosing)*, disclosure *(something disclosed)*, expense *(sacrifice)*, franchise *(license)*, grace, grace period, grant, sufferance. SEE MAIN ENTRY
concessive obsequious, passive, pliant
concidere fail *(lose)*
concierge caretaker *(one caring for property)*
conciliable nonmilitant
conciliate arbitrate *(adjudge)*, compromise *(settle by mutual agreement)*, disarm *(set at ease)*, intercede, mediate, mollify, pacify, placate, propitiate, reconcile
conciliated agreed *(harmonized)*
conciliatio conciliation
conciliation accordance *(compact)*, amnesty, arbitration, collective bargaining, condonation, intercession, mediation, mollification, peace, reconciliation, settlement. SEE MAIN ENTRY
conciliative nonmilitant
conciliator go-between, intermediary
conciliator referee
conciliatory nonmilitant, obeisant, penitent, placable. SEE MAIN ENTRY
concinere agree *(comply)*
concinnity accordance *(understanding)*, conformity *(agreement)*, consensus, proportion
concinnous felicitous, harmonious
concipere conceive *(invent)*, frame *(formulate)*
concise brief, coherent *(clear)*, cohesive *(compact)*, compact *(pithy)*, laconic, pithy, sententious, succinct, summary. SEE MAIN ENTRY
concise treatment compendium
concitare rebel
conclave assemblage, assembly, caucus, company *(assemblage)*, conference, congregation, council *(assembly)*, meeting *(conference)*, parley, session
conclude adjudge, adjudicate, adjust *(resolve)*, ascertain, assume *(suppose)*, award, cap, cease, close *(terminate)*, complete, construe *(comprehend)*, consummate, culminate, decide, deduce, deduct *(conclude by reasoning)*, deem, derive *(deduce)*, determine, discharge *(perform)*, discontinue *(abandon)*, dispatch *(dispose of)*, dissolve *(terminate)*, expect *(consider probable)*, expire, find *(determine)*, finish, fix *(settle)*, generalize, hold *(decide)*, infer, judge, lapse *(cease)*, liquidate *(convert into cash)*, opine, perfect, perform *(adhere to)*, presume, pronounce *(pass judgment)*, read, reason *(conclude)*, result, rule *(decide)*, settle, stop, surmise, suspect *(think)*, terminate, understand. SEE MAIN ENTRY
conclude from evidence construe *(comprehend)*, infer
conclude proceeding rest *(end a legal case)*
concluded complete *(ended)*, res judicata, through. SEE MAIN ENTRY
concludere conclude *(decide)*, infer, lock
concluding dialectic, extreme *(last)*, final, last *(final)*
concluding part end *(termination)*
conclusible deductible *(provable)*
conclusio close *(conclusion)*, conclusion *(determination)*, conclusion *(outcome)*, inference
conclusion adjudication, alternative *(option)*, amount *(result)*, belief *(something believed)*, belief *(state of mind)*, cessation *(termination)*, choice *(decision)*, concept, consequence *(conclusion)*, conviction *(persuasion)*, defeasance, denouement, destination, determination, development *(outgrowth)*, diagnosis, discharge *(performance)*, disposition *(determination)*, dissolution *(termination)*, divorce, end *(termination)*, expiration, extremity *(death)*, finality, finding, generalization, holding *(ruling of a court)*, inference, judgment *(discernment)*, judgment *(formal court decree)*, observation, opinion *(belief)*, opinion *(judicial decision)*, payoff *(result)*, position *(point of view)*, result, ruling, verdict. SEE MAIN ENTRY
conclusion beforehand predetermination
conclusion drawn from accepted truths hypothesis
conclusion in advance predetermination
conclusion of a proceeding dismissal *(termination of a proceeding)*
conclusion of an action dismissal *(termination of a proceeding)*
conclusion of the matter holding *(ruling of a court)*, opinion *(judicial decision)*
conclusive categorical, certain *(fixed)*, certain *(positive)*, clear *(certain)*, cogent, complete *(ended)*, convincing, crucial, decisive, definite, definitive, demonstrable, determinative, extreme *(last)*, final, inappealable, incontestable, incontrovertible, last *(final)*, official, positive *(incontestable)*, reliable, ultimate, unalienable, undeniable, undisputed, unmistakable, valid. SEE MAIN ENTRY
conclusive evidence corroboration
conclusive proof certification *(certainness)*, corroboration
conclusiveness certainty, certification *(certainness)*, certitude, proof. SEE MAIN ENTRY
conclusory conclusive *(settled)*, decisive, definitive, final, last *(final)*, ultimate
concoct conceive *(invent)*, contrive, create, feign, forge *(produce)*, frame *(construct)*, frame *(formulate)*, invent *(produce for the first time)*, lie *(falsify)*, make, maneuver, originate, palter, plan, prearrange, prevaricate, produce *(manufacture)*, profess *(pretend)*, scheme
concoct a plot conspire
concocted artificial, false *(inaccurate)*, fictitious, mendacious
concoction arrangement *(plan)*, composition *(makeup)*, creation, fiction, figment, formation, invention, myth, story *(falsehood)*
concomitance conjunction
concomitant addendum, appurtenance, coincidental, collateral *(accompanying)*, concurrent *(at the same time)*, conjoint, consensual, contemporaneous, simultaneous, supplementary. SEE MAIN ENTRY
concord accord, accordance *(compact)*, affirmance *(judicial sanction)*, agree

(comply), agreement *(concurrence)*, arrangement *(understanding)*, assent, bargain, cartel, collusion, comity, compact, compatibility, compliance, concert, conciliation, concordance, condonation, conformity *(agreement)*, conjunction, connivance, consensus, consent, cooperate, league, pact, partnership, peace, propinquity *(similarity)*, protocol *(agreement)*, rapport, rapprochement, reciprocity, reconciliation, sodality, synchronism, understanding *(agreement)*, union *(unity)*
concord before marriage antenuptial agreement
concordance acceptance, accord, accordance *(compact)*, acquiescence, affirmance *(judicial sanction)*, agreement *(concurrence)*, approval, assent, bargain, cartel, compatibility, concert, consensus, consent, consortium *(marriage companionship)*, mutual understanding, pact, peace, rapport, rapprochement, reconciliation, treaty, understanding *(agreement)*. SEE MAIN ENTRY
concordancy peace
concordant agreed *(harmonized)*, appropriate, commensurable, commensurate, concerted, concurrent *(united)*, congruous, consensual, consenting, consistent, consonant, correlative, felicitous, fit, harmonious, joint, nonmilitant. SEE MAIN ENTRY
concordat agreement *(contract)*, bargain, cartel, compact, contract, covenant, league, pact, protocol *(agreement)*, settlement, specialty *(contract)*, stipulation, treaty
concordia agreement *(contract)*, peace
concors concordant, harmonious
concours meeting *(encounter)*
concourse assemblage, assembly, caucus, causeway, coaction, intersection, rendezvous
concredere entrust
concrescence coalescence. SEE MAIN ENTRY
concrete actual, appreciable, cement, certain *(positive)*, certain *(specific)*, cohesive *(compact)*, corporeal, distinct *(clear)*, material *(physical)*, objective, physical, substantial, substantive, tangible. SEE MAIN ENTRY
concrete expression embodiment
concrete results action *(performance)*
concreteness congealment, materiality *(physical existence)*
concretion adherence *(adhesion)*, adhesion *(affixing)*, congealment, corpus, density
concupiscence desire
concupiscent dissolute, lascivious, lecherous, lewd, licentious, prurient, salacious
concur abide, accede *(concede)*, acknowledge *(respond)*, admit *(concede)*, agree *(comply)*, assent, certify *(approve)*, comply, comport *(agree with)*, confirm, conform, consent, conspire, cooperate, correspond *(be equivalent)*, grant *(concede)*, meet, unite. SEE MAIN ENTRY
concur in approve, certify *(approve)*, countenance, embrace *(accept)*, indorse
concurred in consensual
concurrence accordance *(compact)*, accordance *(understanding)*, acknowledgment *(acceptance)*, acquiescence, adjustment, approval, assent, cartel, charter *(sanction)*, coaction, coalescence, coalition, collusion, compatibility, compliance, concert, concession *(compromise)*, conciliation, concordance, confederacy *(compact)*, conformity *(agreement)*, conjunction, connivance, consensus, consent, indorsement, league, leave *(permission)*, mutual understanding, permission, rapport, synchronism, synergy, union *(unity)*
concurrence in opinions concordance
concurrency concert
concurrent coextensive, cognate, coincidental, collateral *(accompanying)*, collective, commensurable, concerted, concomitant, concordant, congruous, conjoint, consensual, consonant, contemporaneous, corporate *(joint)*, correlative, current, joint, mutual *(reciprocal)*, simultaneous, synergetic. SEE MAIN ENTRY
concurrent cause SEE MAIN ENTRY
concurrent effort cooperative
concurrent opinion conformity *(agreement)*, conjunction, connivance
concurrent power SEE MAIN ENTRY
concurrere coincide *(correspond)*, meet
concurring concerted, concordant, concurrent *(united)*, contemporaneous, synergetic
concursio collision *(dispute)*
concursus collision *(dispute)*, meeting *(conference)*
concuss beat *(strike)*, necessitate
concussion collision *(accident)*
condemn blame, cavil, censure, charge *(accuse)*, complain *(criticize)*, confiscate, convict, criticize *(find fault with)*, decry, defame, denigrate, discommend, disparage, execute *(sentence to death)*, fault, impeach, incriminate, judge, libel, proscribe *(denounce)*, punish, reprehend, reprimand, reproach, sentence. SEE MAIN ENTRY
condemn after judicial investigation convict
condemn as worthless decry
condemn beforehand prejudge
condemn openly denounce *(condemn)*
condemn to death execute *(sentence to death)*
condemn to public use confiscate
condemnable blameful, blameworthy, contemptible, culpable, delinquent *(guilty of a misdeed)*, felonious, guilty, inexcusable, inexpiable, irregular *(improper)*, reprehensible
condemnare condemn *(blame)*, disapprove *(reject)*, sentence
condemnatio condemnation *(blame)*
condemnation aspersion, bad repute, blame *(culpability)*, charge *(accusation)*, confutation, contempt *(disdain)*, conviction *(finding of guilt)*, correction *(punishment)*, count, criticism, denunciation, diatribe, disapprobation, disapproval, discredit, disparagement, expropriation *(right of eminent domain)*, ignominy, impeachment, impugnation, inculpation, judgment *(formal court decree)*, onus *(stigma)*, ostracism, outcry, proscription, rebuff, reprimand, reproach, revilement, sanction *(punishment)*. SEE MAIN ENTRY
condemnation for public use expropriation *(right of eminent domain)*
condemnatory blameworthy, calumnious, contemptible, critical *(faultfinding)*, cynical, derogatory, incriminatory, inculpatory, libelous, scandalous, severe
condemned blameful, blameworthy, dilapidated
condemned person convict
condemned prisoner convict
condemning critical *(faultfinding)*, incriminatory, inculpatory
condensation abstract, adhesion *(affixing)*, brief, capsule, centralization, compendium, congealment, curtailment, digest, hornbook, outline *(synopsis)*, paraphrase, restatement, scenario, synopsis
condense abridge *(shorten)*, abstract *(summarize)*, concentrate *(consolidate)*, consolidate *(strengthen)*, constrict *(compress)*, crystallize, decrease, digest *(summarize)*, discount *(minimize)*, distill, draw *(extract)*, lessen, reduce. SEE MAIN ENTRY
condensed brief, compact *(dense)*, compact *(pithy)*, concise, laconic, pithy, sententious, solid *(compact)*, succinct
condere garner, keep *(shelter)*
condescend deign, vouchsafe. SEE MAIN ENTRY
condescend to grant vouchsafe
condescending disdainful, inflated *(vain)*, orgulous, proud *(conceited)*, supercilious
condescension disrespect, pride
condicio article *(precept)*, condition *(contingent provision)*, condition *(state)*, contract, overture, posture *(situation)*, proposition, provision *(clause)*, qualification *(condition)*, stipulation, term *(provision)*
condicio mortalis mortality
condign appropriate, due *(owed)*, just, proper, suitable. SEE MAIN ENTRY
condire preserve
condisciple disciple
condition aspect, attornment, case *(set of circumstances)*, clause, climate, discipline *(train)*, disease, disorder *(abnormal condition)*, frame *(mood)*, health, inure *(accustom)*, limitation, modify *(moderate)*, plight, position *(situation)*, posture *(situation)*, practice *(train by repetition)*, predicament, prerequisite, provision *(clause)*, quality *(grade)*, repair, reservation *(condition)*, restriction, salvo, sine qua non, situation, specification, status, stipulation, term *(provision)*, ultimatum. SEE MAIN ENTRY
condition of a married woman coverture
condition of infamy disgrace
condition of insufficiency emergency
conditional circumstantial, dependent, doubtful, dubious, provisional, qualified *(conditioned)*, restrictive, tentative, terminable. SEE MAIN ENTRY
conditional conveyance of land mortgage
conditional deed held in trust escrow
conditional deliverance parole
conditional discharge parole. SEE MAIN ENTRY
conditional disenthrallment parole
conditional disimprisonment parole
conditional emancipation parole
conditional endorsement without recourse
conditional event contingency
conditional freedom parole
conditional freedom from confinement parole
conditional independence parole
conditional instrument escrow
conditional intent SEE MAIN ENTRY
conditional liberation parole
conditional liberty parole
conditional property transfer mortgage
conditional release parole
conditional reprieve parole
conditional suspension of sentence probation

conditionally release parole
conditionally release from imprisonment parole
conditioned accustomed *(familiarized)*,
conditional, contingent, controlled (restrained), *dependent*
conditioning discipline *(training)*, habituation, propaganda
conditions circumstances
conditiosine qua non clause
conditus savory
condole sympathize
condolement pity
condolence pity, solace
condolent benevolent
condonable blameless, defensible, justifiable, palliative *(excusing)*, pardonable, unobjectionable
condonare forgive, overlook *(superintend)*, remit *(relax)*
condonation amnesty, impunity, lenience, remission, understanding *(tolerance)*. SEE MAIN ENTRY
condone bear *(tolerate)*, concur *(agree)*, excuse, extenuate, forgive, justify, overlook *(excuse)*, palliate *(excuse)*, pardon, remit *(release from penalty)*. SEE MAIN ENTRY
condoned clear *(free from criminal charges)*
condoning charitable *(lenient)*, lenient, palliative *(excusing)*
conduce affect, avail *(bring about)*, contribute *(assist)*, generate, induce, redound. SEE MAIN ENTRY
conduce to cause
conducere conduce, engage *(hire)*, hire, rent
conducive ancillary *(auxiliary)*, beneficial, contributory, convenient, favorable *(advantageous)*, instrumental, practical, propitious. SEE MAIN ENTRY
conduct administration, agency *(legal relationship)*, behavior, comport *(behave)*, control *(regulate)*, course, decorum, demean *(deport oneself)*, demeanor, deportment, direct *(show)*, direct *(supervise)*, direction *(guidance)*, discipline *(training)*, ethics, exercise *(discharge a function)*, govern, handle *(manage)*, manage, management *(judicious use)*, manipulate *(utilize skillfully)*, manner *(behavior)*, modus operandi, officiate, operate, orchestrate, overlook *(superintend)*, oversee, practice *(procedure)*, prescribe, presence *(poise)*, procedure, process *(course)*, prosecute *(carry forward)*, protect, pursue *(carry on)*, regulate *(manage)*, regulation *(management)*, render *(administer)*, rule *(govern)*, transact, transmit, transport, usage. SEE MAIN ENTRY
conduct a search frisk, hunt
conduct a trial hear *(give a legal hearing)*
conduct an inquiry analyze, audit, canvass, delve, investigate, monitor, probe
conduct business handle *(trade)*
conduct dishonestly mishandle *(mismanage)*
conduct involving graft corruption
conduct of a lawsuit proceeding
conduct of affairs agency *(legal relationship)*
conduct research inquire
conduct research on examine *(study)*, peruse, poll, probe
conduct without efficiency mishandle *(mismanage)*
conduct without honesty mishandle *(mismanage)*
conductio contract, lease
conductive causal
conductor chairman, guardian
conductor lessee
conductor procurator
conductor tenant
conductus mercenary
conduit dealer, outlet. SEE MAIN ENTRY
conectere join *(bring together)*
confabulate communicate, converse, discourse, discuss. SEE MAIN ENTRY
confabulation conference, conversation, speech
confectio consumption
confederacy affiliation *(amalgamation)*, association *(alliance)*, cabal, chamber *(body)*, coaction, coalescence, collusion, committee, company *(enterprise)*, connivance, consortium *(business cartel)*, conspiracy, corporation, federation, league, partnership, pool, relationship *(connection)*, society, sodality, union *(labor organization)*. SEE MAIN ENTRY
confederate abettor, accessory, accomplice, affiliate, allied, assistant, associate, coactor, coadjutant, coconspirator, cohort, colleague, collective, combine *(act in concert)*, conjoint, consociate, consolidate *(unite)*, conspirator, conspire, conspirer, contributor *(contributor)*, cooperate, copartner *(coconspirator)*, desegregate, federal, federalize *(associate)*, federate, involve *(participate)*, join *(associate oneself with)*, joint, member *(individual in a group)*, organize *(unionize)*, participant, participate, partisan, partner, pool, unite. SEE MAIN ENTRY
confederate for an unlawful purpose conspire
confederated affiliated, associated, concurrent *(united)*, conjoint, mutual *(collective)*
confederation affiliation *(amalgamation)*, association *(alliance)*, band, cartel, chamber *(body)*, coalescence, committee, concert, confederacy *(compact)*, consolidation, contribution *(participation)*, federation, integration *(amalgamation)*, integration *(assimilation)*, league, merger, partnership, party *(political organization)*, pool, society, sodality
confer administer *(tender)*, attorn, bear *(yield)*, bestow, cede, consider, consult *(ask advice of)*, contribute *(supply)*, counsel, dedicate, devise *(give)*, discourse, discuss, dispense, enable, endue, give *(grant)*, grant *(transfer formally)*, impart, leave *(give)*, present *(make a gift)*, provide *(supply)*, render *(deliver)*, transfer, treat *(process)*, vest. SEE MAIN ENTRY
confer a benefit serve *(assist)*
confer a benefit on avail *(be of use)*, profit
confer a corporate franchise upon incorporate *(form a corporation)*
confer a privilege authorize, bestow, grant *(concede)*, permit, sanction
confer a right authorize, qualify *(meet standards)*, sanction
confer a trust commit *(entrust)*
confer again recover
confer an honor elevate
confer by will demise
confer corporate status upon incorporate *(form a corporation)*
confer distinction bestow
confer distinction on honor
confer formally deliberate, grant *(transfer formally)*
confer honor on dedicate
confer on price dicker
confer ownership attorn, devolve, grant *(transfer formally)*, pass *(advance)*
confer ownership on oneself impropriate
confer power invest *(vest)*
confer power on charge *(empower)*, delegate, empower
confer privileges of a native citizen naturalize *(make a citizen)*
confer rights of citizenship naturalize *(make a citizen)*
confer with advise, converse, debate, discuss
conference assembly, caucus, collective bargaining, communication *(discourse)*, company *(assemblage)*, confrontation *(act of setting face to face)*, congregation, council *(assembly)*, discourse, inquiry *(systematic investigation)*, interview, negotiation, panel *(discussion group)*, parlance, parley, session. SEE MAIN ENTRY
conferment alienation *(transfer of title)*, assignment *(transfer of ownership)*, bounty, concession *(authorization)*, contribution *(donation)*, conveyance, demise *(conveyance)*, deputation *(selection of delegates)*, dispensation *(act of dispensing)*, legacy
conferment between the living inter vivos
conferral alienation *(transfer of title)*, assignment *(transfer of ownership)*, concession *(authorization)*, demise *(conveyance)*, dispensation *(act of dispensing)*
conferral of a fee feoffment
conferre bestow, collect *(gather)*, compare, confer *(give)*, contribution *(donation)*, converse
conferrer donor, grantor
conferring donative
conferrment of title feoffment
confess acknowledge *(verify)*, admit *(concede)*, avow, bare, betray *(disclose)*, certify *(attest)*, disclose, inform *(betray)*, recognize *(acknowledge)*, reveal. SEE MAIN ENTRY
confessed judgment cognovit
confessedly admittedly
confessing repentant
confessio acknowledgment *(avowal)*, avowal
confession acknowledgment *(avowal)*, admission *(disclosure)*, avowal, disclosure *(act of disclosing)*, disclosure *(something disclosed)*, profession *(declaration)*. SEE MAIN ENTRY
confessor penitent
conficere conclude *(complete)*, consummate, dispatch *(dispose of)*, exhaust *(deplete)*, finish, kill *(defeat)*, kill *(murder)*, settle
confidant confederate, consociate
confidante associate
confide commit *(entrust)*, convey *(communicate)*, delegate, divulge, impart, inform *(notify)*, notify, rely, reveal, trust. SEE MAIN ENTRY
confide for care delegate
confide for use delegate
confide in confer *(consult)*
confide to mention
confidence assurance, belief *(state of mind)*, certification *(certainness)*, certitude, credence, credit *(delayed payment)*, faith, prospect *(outlook)*, reliance, secret, weight *(credibility)*. SEE MAIN ENTRY

confidence in one's powers audacity
confidence trick bunko
confident assertive, categorical, certain *(fixed)*, certain *(positive)*, definite, dogmatic, indubious, sanguine
confident expectation likelihood, trust *(confidence)*
confidential clandestine, close *(intimate)*, collusive, esoteric, fiduciary, intimate, personal *(private)*, privy, secret. SEE MAIN ENTRY
confidential communication confidence *(relation of trust)*, secret. SEE MAIN ENTRY
confidential information tip *(clue)*
confidential matter confidence *(relation of trust)*, secret
confidentiality privacy. SEE MAIN ENTRY
confidentialness privacy
confidentness assurance, certainty, certitude, confidence *(faith)*
confidere rely, trust
confiding intimate
configuration boundary, construction, content *(structure)*, contour *(outline)*, contour *(shape)*, delineation, formation, organization *(structure)*, structure *(composition)*. SEE MAIN ENTRY
configurattion dimension
confine apprehend *(arrest)*, arrest *(apprehend)*, bind *(restrain)*, border, border *(bound)*, boundary, capture, circumscribe *(surround by boundary)*, close *(enclosed area)*, commit *(institutionalize)*, conceal, constrain *(imprison)*, contain *(enclose)*, contain *(restrain)*, control *(restrain)*, debar, delimit, demarcate, detain *(hold in custody)*, detain *(restrain)*, enclose, enclosure, envelop, fetter, hamper, immure, impede, imprison, isolate, jail, keep *(restrain)*, limit, lock, mete, outline *(boundary)*, periphery, purview, qualify *(condition)*, restrain, restrict, retrench, seclude, sequester *(seclude)*, trammel. SEE MAIN ENTRY
confine forcibly constrain *(imprison)*
confined arrested *(apprehended)*, in custody, insular, limited, narrow, partial *(part)*, private *(not public)*
confined individual prisoner
confined room cell
confined to a select circle esoteric
confinement apprehension *(act of arresting)*, arrest, blockade *(limitation)*, bondage, boundary, cache *(hiding place)*, captivity, cell, concealment, constraint *(imprisonment)*, custody *(incarceration)*, detention, durance, duress, enclosure, fetter, incarceration, quarantine, restraint, restriction, thrall. SEE MAIN ENTRY
confinement by public authority incarceration
confinement in a jail incarceration
confinement in a penitentiary incarceration
confinement under legal process incarceration
confinements confines
confines area *(province)*, barrier, circuit, edge *(border)*, region, scope, vicinity. SEE MAIN ENTRY
confining binding, commitment *(confinement)*, limited, limiting, oppressive
confinis contiguous
confinium frontier
confirm accept *(admit as sufficient)*, accept *(assent)*, accredit, acknowledge *(verify)*, admit *(concede)*, affirm *(uphold)*, agree *(comply)*, appoint, approve, ascertain, assent, assure *(insure)*, attest, authorize, avouch *(avow)*, avow, bind *(obligate)*, bond *(secure a debt)*, certify *(approve)*, certify *(attest)*, corroborate, cosign, countenance, countersign, demonstrate *(establish)*, determine, document, endorse, ensure, establish *(show)*, evidence, fix *(make firm)*, indorse, legalize, notarize, pass *(approve)*, prove, reaffirm, reassure, reveal, seal *(solemnize)*, sign, subscribe *(sign)*, substantiate, support *(corroborate)*, swear, uphold, validate, vouch, witness *(attest to)*. SEE MAIN ENTRY
confirm as correct certify *(attest)*
confirm by law legalize
confirm by oath avouch *(avow)*
confirm in conviction assure *(give confidence to)*
confirm officially authorize, certify *(approve)*, indorse, notarize
confirm the validity of a will probate
confirmable ascertainable, convincing, provable
confirmare affirm *(uphold)*, assert, certify *(attest)*, contend *(maintain)*, enforce, establish *(entrench)*, instate, maintain *(carry on)*, reassure, reinforce, sanction, verify *(confirm)*
confirmatio assurance, indorsement, sanction *(permission)*
confirmation acknowledgment *(avowal)*, admittance *(acceptance)*, affirmance *(authentication)*, affirmation, approval, assent, asseveration, averment, avowal, certification *(attested copy)*, certification *(certification of proficiency)*, charter *(sanction)*, collation, confession, consent, contract, corroboration, disclosure *(something disclosed)*, document, documentation, evidence, indorsement, jurat, legalization, license, permit, proof, ratification, reference *(recommendation)*, subscription, support *(corroboration)*, surety *(certainty)*. SEE MAIN ENTRY
confirmation under oath affidavit
confirmative affirmative, definitive, demonstrative *(illustrative)*
confirmatory affirmative, convincing, demonstrative *(illustrative)*
confirmed accustomed *(customary)*, agreed *(promised)*, arrant *(definite)*, certain *(fixed)*, chronic, customary, firm, formal, habitual, immutable, indefeasible, ingrained, inveterate, permanent, traditional, valid
confirmed habit habituation, practice *(custom)*
confirmed judgment cognovit
confirmed opposition dissent *(difference of opinion)*
confirmed way habit
confirmer surety *(guarantor)*
confirming conclusive *(settled)*, consensual, convincing, demonstrative *(illustrative)*
confirmist affirmant
confiscate annex *(arrogate)*, assume *(seize)*, attach *(seize)*, condemn *(seize)*, deprive, distrain, divest, garnish, impound, levy, penalize, remove *(eliminate)*, sequester *(seize property)*. SEE MAIN ENTRY
confiscated attached *(seized)*, lost *(taken away)*
confiscated goods contraband
confiscated property contraband
confiscation appropriation *(taking)*, attachment *(seizure)*, condemnation *(seizure)*, disseisin, distraint, distress *(seizure)*, escheatment, expropriation *(divestiture)*, foreclosure, forfeiture *(act of forfeiting)*, garnishment, levy, privation, sequestration, taking
confiscatory SEE MAIN ENTRY
confiteri avow, confess
confixation attachment *(act of affixing)*
conflagrate burn, deflagrate
conflagration SEE MAIN ENTRY
conflate amalgamate. SEE MAIN ENTRY
conflation merger. SEE MAIN ENTRY
conflict affray, altercation, antipode, antithesis, argument *(contention)*, belligerency, bicker, collision *(dispute)*, commotion, competition, confrontation *(altercation)*, contend *(dispute)*, contention *(argument)*, contention *(opposition)*, contest, contradict, contradiction, contrary, contravention, controversy *(argument)*, disaccord *(noun)*, disaccord *(verb)*, disagree, disagreement, discord, discrepancy, dispute, dispute *(contest)*, dissension, dissent *(difference of opinion)*, dissent *(differ in opinion)*, dissidence, embroilment, estrangement, feud, fight *(argument)*, fracas, ill will, impugnation, incompatibility *(difference)*, incompatibility *(inconsistency)*, opposition, oppugn, outbreak, reaction *(opposition)*, rebut, strife, struggle. SEE MAIN ENTRY
conflict of interest disagreement
conflict of opinion conflict, controversy *(argument)*, difference, disaccord, disagreement, disparity, dispute, dissension, dissent *(difference of opinion)*. SEE MAIN ENTRY
conflict with antagonize, collide *(clash)*, contravene, counter, counteract, countervail, cross *(disagree with)*, defy, deviate, differ *(disagree)*, disaffirm, gainsay
conflicting adverse *(opposite)*, antipathetic *(oppositional)*, competitive *(antagonistic)*, contradictory, contrary, discordant, disparate, disproportionate, dissenting, hostile, incongruous, inconsistent, litigious, negative, opposite, polemic, renitent, repugnant *(incompatible)*, unsuitable
conflicting evidence contradiction
conflictive adverse *(opposite)*, dissenting
conflictory discordant, dissenting
confligere collide *(crash against)*
confluence assemblage, coalescence, coalition, company *(assemblage)*, corpus, crossroad *(intersection)*, rendezvous. SEE MAIN ENTRY
confluent coadunate
confluere meet
conflux assemblage, chamber *(body)*, collection *(assembly)*, company *(assemblage)*
confodere pierce *(lance)*
conform abide, accede *(concede)*, adapt, adhere *(maintain loyalty)*, adjust *(resolve)*, cohere *(be logically consistent)*, comport *(agree with)*, copy, correspond *(be equivalent)*, obey, observe *(obey)*. SEE MAIN ENTRY
conform to adopt, assent, coincide *(concur)*, coincide *(correspond)*, comply, defer *(yield in judgment)*, keep *(fulfill)*, pass *(satisfy requirements)*, satisfy *(fulfill)*
conform with concur *(agree)*
conformability amenability, compliance, conciliation, identity *(similarity)*
conformable appropriate, commensurable, concerted, concordant, congruous, consistent, consonant, conventional, correlative, faithful *(true to fact)*, felicitous, fit, malleable, obedient, orthodox, passive, pliable, pliant, prevailing *(current)*, prevalent, regular *(conventional)*, similar, suitable, tractable, traditional, typical, uniform, usual
conformable to fact real
conformable to law lawful

conformable to rule typical
conformable with the law juridical, lawful
conformance accordance *(understanding)*, adjustment, agreement *(concurrence)*, compliance, concordance, conduct, conformity *(agreement)*, conformity *(obedience)*, consensus, resemblance
conformant relevant
conformare form
conformatio formation
conformation adjustment, arrangement *(ordering)*, building *(business of assembling)*, composition *(makeup)*, configuration *(form)*, conformity *(agreement)*, conformity *(obedience)*, consensus, construction, content *(structure)*, contour *(shape)*, dimension, formation, organization *(structure)*
conforming agreed *(harmonized)*, concerted, concordant, concurrent *(united)*, congruous, consonant, conventional, harmonious, law-abiding, malleable, normal *(regular)*, obedient, orthodox, pliable, pliant, relevant, usual
conforming to consensual, pursuant to
conforming to accepted standards conventional
conforming to moral standards ethical
conforming to professional conduct ethical
conformist philistine
conformity accordance *(understanding)*, adjustment, compatibility, compliance, conciliation, concordance, conjunction, consensus, constant, correspondence *(similarity)*, decorum, propriety *(appropriateness)*, regularity, resemblance, synchronism, uniformity. SEE MAIN ENTRY
conformity to fact truth, veracity
conformity to law legality, legitimacy
conformity with the law legality
confound confuse *(bewilder)*, defeat, discompose, disconcert, dislocate, disorganize, disorient, disturb, fight *(counteract)*, foil, frustrate, harass, misdirect, mismanage, muddle, negate, obfuscate, overcome *(overwhelm)*, overwhelm, perplex, perturb, repel *(drive back)*, subvert. SEE MAIN ENTRY
confounded heinous, nefarious, odious
confounded meaning ambiguity
confounding enigmatic, labyrinthine
confoundment confusion *(ambiguity)*, dilemma, quandary
confraternity confederacy *(compact)*, society, sodality
confrère accessory, accomplice, assistant
confrere associate
confrère colleague
confrere confederate, consociate
confrère consort
confrere contributor *(contributor)*
confrère copartner *(business associate)*, copartner *(coconspirator)*
confront accost, approach, challenge, collide *(clash)*, contrast, cross *(disagree with)*, defy, fight *(battle)*, grapple, oppose, oppugn, repel *(drive back)*, resist *(oppose)*, withstand. SEE MAIN ENTRY
confrontation contraposition, contravention, disaccord, experience *(encounter)*, fight *(argument)*, impugnation, meeting *(encounter)*, resistance, struggle. SEE MAIN ENTRY
confrontment confrontation *(altercation)*, contraposition
confugere recourse
confundere confound, confuse *(bewilder)*, disorganize, muddle
confuse circumvent, confound, discompose, disconcert, dislocate, disorganize, disrupt, disturb, embarrass, misapprehend, misconstrue, misdirect, misinterpret, misread, mistake, misunderstand, muddle, obfuscate, overwhelm, perplex, perturb, upset. SEE MAIN ENTRY
confused ambiguous, complex, deranged, disjointed, disordered, disorderly, haphazard, inextricable, lost *(disoriented)*, nebulous, opaque, promiscuous, unclear, vague
confused language jargon *(unintelligible language)*
confused mass melange
confused meaning ambiguity
confused talk jargon *(unintelligible language)*
confusedness confusion *(ambiguity)*, entanglement *(confusion)*, pandemonium, panic, quandary
confusing dubious, enigmatic, equivocal, indefinable, labyrinthine, opaque
confusing situation imbroglio
confusing statement enigma
confusio confusion *(turmoil)*
confusion ambiguity, anarchy, commotion, complex *(entanglement)*, complication, dilemma, disorder *(lack of order)*, disturbance, doubt *(indecision)*, embarrassment, embroilment, enigma, havoc, imbroglio, involution, irregularity, jargon *(unintelligible language)*, misrule, opacity, pandemonium, panic, quandary, riot, shambles, snarl, turmoil. SEE MAIN ENTRY
confutable contestable, controversial, debatable, defeasible, disputable, dubious, litigable
confutation answer *(judicial response)*, bad repute, contradiction, counterargument, defeat, defense, demurrer, denial, disparagement, negation, opposition, repudiation. SEE MAIN ENTRY
confutative contradictory, contrary, negative
confute answer *(reply)*, argue, challenge, contradict, controvert, counter, counteract, countercharge, countervail, cross *(disagree with)*, debate, disagree, disapprove *(reject)*, disown *(deny the validity)*, disprove, dispute *(contest)*, dispute *(debate)*, dissent *(differ in opinion)*, fight *(counteract)*, impeach, impugn, invalidate, negate, oppose, parry, rebut, refute, reply. SEE MAIN ENTRY
confuting contradictory, contrary
congé dispensation *(exception)*
congeal cement, cohere *(adhere)*, consolidate *(strengthen)*, consolidate *(unite)*
congealed coherent *(joined)*, ossified, solid *(compact)*
congealment SEE MAIN ENTRY
congelation adhesion *(affixing)*, congealment
congener complement, correlate, counterpart *(complement)*
congeneric apposite, cognate, comparable *(capable of comparison)*, correlative, identical, pendent, related, similar
congenerical pendent, related, similar
congenerous apposite, cognate, consanguineous, correlative, identical, pendent, related
congenial apposite, cognate, consonant, harmonious, informal, palatable, suitable
congeniality compatibility, concordance, conformity *(agreement)*, propinquity *(similarity)*
congenital born *(innate)*, genetic, hereditary, innate, native *(inborn)*
congerere collect *(gather)*
congeries agglomeration, assemblage, body *(collection)*, entirety
congest concentrate *(consolidate)*, obstruct, overload
congestion confusion *(turmoil)*, obstruction, plethora
congestus collection *(accumulation)*
congiarium largess *(generosity)*
conglomerate agglomeration, aggregate, assemblage, coadunate, coalition, coherent *(joined)*, collect *(gather)*, collection *(accumulation)*, combine *(join together)*, commingle, compile, complex *(development)*, composite, compound, concentrate *(consolidate)*, congregate, consolidate *(unite)*, corporation, corpus, crystallize, cumulation, desegregate, join *(bring together)*, merge, unite. SEE MAIN ENTRY
conglomeratic coadunate, coherent *(joined)*
conglomeration adhesion *(affixing)*, agglomeration, aggregate, arsenal, assemblage, body *(collection)*, centralization, coalescence, collection *(accumulation)*, compilation, complex *(development)*, cumulation, melange, selection *(collection)*. SEE MAIN ENTRY
conglutemate bond *(hold together)*. SEE MAIN ENTRY
conglutinare cement
conglutinate cement, combine *(join together)*, join *(bring together)*
conglutination adherence *(adhesion)*, adhesion *(affixing)*, coalescence
conglutinative cohesive *(sticking)*
congratulate honor
congregari congregate
congregate collective, concentrate *(consolidate)*, conglomerate, convene, converge, meet, rendezvous, unite. SEE MAIN ENTRY
congregated coadunate, compound, conglomerate
congregated body congregation
congregatio union *(unity)*
congregation assemblage, assembly, band, centralization, collection *(assembly)*, combination, committee, company *(assemblage)*, cumulation, mass *(body of persons)*, rendezvous, session. SEE MAIN ENTRY
congregational collective
congregative collective
congress assemblage, chamber *(body)*, coalition, company *(assemblage)*, government *(political administration)*, legislature, parley, rendezvous, session. SEE MAIN ENTRY
congressio interview, meeting *(conference)*
congressional legislative
congressman lawmaker, legislator
congresswoman lawmaker
congruence adjustment, agreement *(concurrence)*, coherence, concordance, conformity *(agreement)*, consensus, correspondence *(similarity)*, relevance, understanding *(agreement)*. SEE MAIN ENTRY
congruency agreement *(concurrence)*, concordance, conformity *(agreement)*, relevance
congruens appropriate, coherent *(clear)*, coherent *(joined)*, consonant, harmonious
congruent coequal, coextensive, commensurate, concerted, concordant, congruous, conjoint, consensual, consonant,

correlative, germane, harmonious, relevant, similar, suitable
congruent with consistent
congruentia correspondence *(similarity)*
congruere agree *(comply)*, coincide *(correspond)*, correspond *(be equivalent)*, sympathize
congruity adjustment, agreement *(concurrence)*, analogy, coherence, compatibility, conformity *(agreement)*, consortium *(marriage companionship)*, correspondence *(similarity)*, propriety *(appropriateness)*, rapport, regularity, relevance
congruous appropriate, commensurable, commensurate, concerted, concordant, consistent, consonant, correlative, felicitous, fit, germane, harmonious, relevant, suitable. SEE MAIN ENTRY
congruousness compatibility, consortium *(marriage companionship)*
conicere cast *(throw)*, interpret
coniectio discharge *(shot)*
coniectura hypothesis, inference, presumption, speculation *(conjecture)*, supposition
coniecturalis speculative
coniectus discharge *(shot)*
coniugalis conjugal
coniugium marriage *(wedlock)*
coniunctio affinity *(family ties)*, combination, incorporation *(formation of a business entity)*, relationship *(connection)*
coniunctus intimate
coniungere combine *(join together)*, join *(bring together)*, unite
coniunx spouse
coniurare conspire, plot
coniuratio confederacy *(conspiracy)*, conspiracy, plot *(secret plan)*
coniuratus conspirator
conjacent cohesive *(compact)*
conjecturable colorable *(plausible)*, debatable, ostensible, plausible, presumptive, probable
conjectural apparent *(presumptive)*, circumstantial, debatable, disputable, doubtful, enigmatic, hypothetical, presumptive, speculative, theoretical, uncertain *(questionable)*, unsettled. SEE MAIN ENTRY
conjecture anticipate *(prognosticate)*, assume *(suppose)*, assumption *(supposition)*, concept, deduce, deduct *(conclude by reasoning)*, estimate *(idea)*, estimate, estimation *(calculation)*, expect *(consider probable)*, guess, hypothesis, idea, infer, inference, opine, opinion *(belief)*, postulate *(noun)*, postulate *(verb)*, presume, presumption, presuppose, prognosis, prognosticate, proposition, supposition, surmise, suspect *(think)*, suspicion *(uncertainty)*, theory, thesis, understand. SEE MAIN ENTRY
conjectured assumed *(inferred)*, presumptive, putative
conjoin abut, adjoin, affix, annex *(add)*, append, attach *(join)*, border *(bound)*, cement, cohere *(adhere)*, combine *(join together)*, commingle, concentrate *(consolidate)*, connect *(join together)*, consolidate *(strengthen)*, consolidate *(unite)*, conspire, contact *(touch)*, cooperate, correspond *(be equivalent)*, desegregate, federate, join *(bring together)*, merge, pool, unite. SEE MAIN ENTRY
conjoined attached *(annexed)*, coadunate, coherent *(joined)*, collateral *(accompanying)*, concerted, concordant, concurrent *(united)*, promiscuous
conjoiner adjoiner
conjoining accession *(annexation)*, coalition, conjunction, contiguous, immediate *(not distant)*
conjoint associated, coadunate, common *(shared)*, composite, compound, concerted, concomitant, consolidate *(strengthen)*, corporate *(joint)*, correlative, joint, mutual *(collective)*. SEE MAIN ENTRY
conjugal nuptial. SEE MAIN ENTRY
conjugal bliss cohabitation *(married state)*
conjugal partner consort
conjugal union marriage *(wedlock)*
conjugality cohabitation *(married state)*, coverture, marriage *(wedlock)*, matrimony
conjugate coadunate, cohabit, compound, interrelated, joint
conjugation coalescence, combination, joinder
conjunct associated, coadunate, coherent *(joined)*, cohesive *(compact)*, composite, compound, concerted, conjoint, consensual, contiguous, corporate *(joint)*, correlative, inextricable, joint. SEE MAIN ENTRY
conjunctio coalition
conjunction adhesion *(affixing)*, affiliation *(connectedness)*, association *(connection)*, attachment *(act of affixing)*, building *(business of assembling)*, cartel, chain *(nexus)*, coalescence, coalition, coherence, collusion, combination, concert, concordance, conformity *(agreement)*, connection *(fastening)*, connivance, consolidation, contact *(association)*, intersection, joinder, league, partnership. SEE MAIN ENTRY
conjunctional coincidental, concomitant, concordant
conjunctive composite, concomitant, concurrent *(at the same time)*, conjoint, correlative
conjuncture case *(set of circumstances)*, coalition, consolidation, crossroad *(intersection)*, crossroad *(turning point)*, occasion, point *(period of time)*, posture *(situation)*, predicament
conjure invoke. SEE MAIN ENTRY
conjure up conceive *(comprehend)*, occur *(come to mind)*, recall *(remember)*, recollect, remember. SEE MAIN ENTRY
conjuring illusory, prestidigitation
conlatio collation, comparison
conlectio restatement
conlega colleague
conlegium association *(alliance)*, association *(connection)*, board, corporation, facility *(institution)*, foundation *(organization)*, institute
conlidere strike *(collide)*
conligere argue, concentrate *(consolidate)*, conclude *(decide)*, hoard, infer, raise *(collect)*
conlocatio arrangement *(ordering)*, disposition *(final arrangement)*
conlocatus situated
conlocutio discourse
conloqui discourse, parley
conloquium conversation, discourse, interview, negotiation
conlusio collusion
connatal hereditary
connate akin *(related by blood)*, associated, born *(innate)*, correlative, hereditary, inherent, native *(inborn)*, natural, related
connation degree *(kinship)*, relation *(connection)*
connatural apposite, born *(innate)*, consanguineous, correlative, interrelated, native *(inborn)*, pendent, related, similar
connaturalness relation *(connection)*
connect abut, adjoin, affiliate, affix, annex *(add)*, append, attach *(join)*, bond *(hold together)*, border *(bound)*, cement, combine *(join together)*, commingle, conjoin, consolidate *(strengthen)*, consolidate *(unite)*, contact *(touch)*, desegregate, engage *(involve)*, implicate, involve *(implicate)*, involve *(participate)*, join *(bring together)*, juxtapose, lock, pool, refer *(direct attention)*, relate *(establish a connection)*, unite. SEE MAIN ENTRY
connect with ascribe, attribute
connect with a crime incriminate
connected affiliated, akin *(germane)*, allied, apposite, appurtenant, associated, attached *(annexed)*, coadunate, cognate, coherent *(joined)*, cohesive *(sticking)*, collateral *(accompanying)*, composite, compound, concurrent *(united)*, conjoint, consecutive, contiguous, correlative, direct *(uninterrupted)*, germane, incident, inextricable, interested, interrelated, pertinent, proximate, related, relative *(relevant)*, relevant, tangential. SEE MAIN ENTRY
connected series chain *(series)*
connected with comparative
connectedness adherence *(adhesion)*, association *(connection)*, chain *(nexus)*, coherence, continuity
connectere connect *(join together)*
connecting proximate, reference *(citation)*
connecting link chain *(nexus)*, go-between, intermediary, nexus, relation-ship *(connection)*
connecting medium chain *(nexus)*, privity
connection adhesion *(affixing)*, adjoiner, affiliation *(connectedness)*, affinity *(family ties)*, ancestry, attachment *(act of affixing)*, attribution, chain *(nexus)*, coalescence, coalition, coherence, conjunction, contact *(association)*, contact *(touching)*, context, continuity, degree *(kinship)*, go-between, implication *(incriminating involvement)*, intermediary, intersection, joinder, kinship, liaison, nexus, partnership, privity, propinquity *(kinship)*, relative, relevance, union *(unity)*. SEE MAIN ENTRY
connections ties
connective concerted, contact *(touching)*, correlative, interlocking, nexus, relative *(relevant)*
connexion relation *(connection)*
connivance artifice, bad faith, bribery, cabal, collusion, confederacy *(conspiracy)*, conspiracy, contrivance. SEE MAIN ENTRY
connivant collusive
connive conspire, contrive, cooperate, maneuver, pettifog, plan, plot, scheme. SEE MAIN ENTRY
conniver conspirator
conniving collusive, concerted, dishonest, fraudulent, insidious, machiavellian, perfidious, recreant, sly, surreptitious, tortuous *(bending)*, unconscionable, untrustworthy
connoisseur expert, specialist
connotate signify *(denote)*
connotation context, gist *(substance)*, hint, implication *(inference)*, import, indication, innuendo, meaning, reference *(allusion)*, signification, symbol. SEE MAIN ENTRY
connotative allusive, demonstrative *(illustrative)*, representative, suggestive *(evocative)*
connote allude, bespeak, construe *(translate)*, depict, exemplify, hint, imply,

indicate, purport, refer *(direct attention)*, represent *(portray)*, signify *(denote)*. SEE MAIN ENTRY
connoted assumed *(inferred)*, constructive *(inferential)*, implied, tacit
connubial conjugal, nuptial
connubiality cohabitation *(married state)*, marriage *(wedlock)*, matrimony
conprehensible ascertainable
conquer beat *(defeat)*, defeat, demean *(make lower)*, occupy *(take possession)*, overcome *(surmount)*, overthrow, overturn, overwhelm, pass *(satisfy requirements)*, prevail *(triumph)*, subdue, subject, subjugate, succeed *(attain)*, surmount, upset. SEE MAIN ENTRY
conquerable facile, helpless *(defenseless)*, indefensible, penetrable
conqueri de rem complain *(criticize)*
conquering confiscatory, prevailing *(having superior force)*
conquest subjection
conquirere hoard
consanguine akin *(related by blood)*, cognate, consanguineous, related
consanguineal relations next of kin
consanguinean akin *(related by blood)*
consanguinei kindred
consanguineous akin *(related by blood)*, cognate, interrelated, related. SEE MAIN ENTRY
consanguineus akin *(related by blood)*
consanguinitas affinity *(family ties)*
consanguinity affiliation *(bloodline)*, affinity *(family ties)*, ancestry, blood, connection *(relation)*, contact *(association)*, degree *(kinship)*, family *(common ancestry)*, kinship, propinquity *(kinship)*, relation *(kinship)*, relationship *(family tie)*
conscendere embark
conscience commitment *(responsibility)*, probity, remorse. SEE MAIN ENTRY
conscience money reparation *(indemnification)*
conscience-smitten contrite, penitent, remorseful, repentant
conscience-smitten person penitent
conscience-stricken contrite, penitent, remorseful, repentant
conscience-stricken person penitent
conscienceless brazen, delinquent *(guilty of a misdeed)*, diabolic, dishonest, disingenuous, disreputable, immoral, machiavellian, sinister, unconscionable, unscrupulous
conscientia conscience
conscientia mala remorse
conscientious accurate, circumspect, close *(rigorous)*, dependable, diligent, earnest, faithful *(diligent)*, high-minded, honest, loyal, meritorious, meticulous, moral, painstaking, particular *(exacting)*, punctilious, punctual, reliable, reputable, sedulous, strict, true *(loyal)*, upright. SEE MAIN ENTRY
conscientiously faithfully
conscientiousness adhesion *(loyalty)*, caution *(vigilance)*, conscience, fidelity, honesty, interest *(concern)*, particularity, rectitude, responsibility *(conscience)*, rigor
conscionable reasonable *(fair)*
conscious circumspect, cognizant, deliberate, express, familiar *(informed)*, intentional, knowing, perceptive, premeditated, receptive, sensible, sensitive *(discerning)*, willful. SEE MAIN ENTRY
conscious of acquainted
conscious purpose deliberation
conscious violation of law malice
consciously purposely
consciousness appreciation *(perception)*, cognition, comprehension, impression, insight, knowledge *(awareness)*, perception, realization, recognition, recollection, scienter, sense *(feeling)*, sensibility
conscius accessory, accomplice, cognizant, conscious *(aware)*
conscribere recruit
conscript bind *(obligate)*, coerce, impose *(enforce)*, induct, levy, recruit
conscription requirement
consecrare dedicate, devote
consecrate dedicate, devote, elevate, honor
consecrated inviolate, sacrosanct
consecration adhesion *(loyalty)*, dedication, elevation, remembrance *(commemoration)*
consectari hunt, pursue *(chase)*, pursue *(strive to gain)*
consectatio pursuit *(chase)*, pursuit *(effort to secure)*
consecutio consequence *(conclusion)*, effect
consecution chain *(series)*, continuity, cycle, sequence, serial, succession
consecutive continuous, direct *(uninterrupted)*, progressive *(going forward)*, successive. SEE MAIN ENTRY
consecutive order succession
consecutiveness continuity
consensual concerted, concordant, congruous, contractual. SEE MAIN ENTRY
consensus accordance *(understanding)*, concordance, conformity *(agreement)*. SEE MAIN ENTRY
consensus consent
consensus poll *(casting of votes)*, union *(unity)*
consensus omnium compatibility
consent accede *(concede)*, acceptance, acquiescence, advocate, agree *(comply)*, agree *(contract)*, agreement *(concurrence)*, allow *(endure)*, approval, assent *(noun)*, assent *(verb)*, bestow, capacity *(authority)*, capitulation, certify *(approve)*, charter *(sanction)*, close *(agree)*, coincide *(concur)*, compatibility, compliance, concede, concordance, concur *(agree)*, confirm, conformity *(agreement)*, conformity *(obedience)*, contribution *(participation)*, defer *(yield in judgment)*, dispensation *(exception)*, enable, franchise *(license)*, grant *(concede)*, indorsement, leave *(permission)*, let *(permit)*, license, obey, option *(contractual provision)*, pass *(approve)*, permission, permit, promise, promise *(vow)*, ratification, recognize *(acknowledge)*, sanction *(permission)*, subscribe *(promise)*, subscription, suffer *(permit)*, tolerate, vouchsafe, yield *(submit)*. SEE MAIN ENTRY
consent decree SEE MAIN ETNRY
consent order SEE MAIN ENTRY
consent to approve, authorize, comply, countenance, embrace *(accept)*, indorse, sanction, sustain *(confirm)*
consent to support underwrite
consentaneity agreement *(concurrence)*, assent, compatibility, concert, concordance, consensus, pact, peace, understanding *(agreement)*
consentaneous concerted, concordant, concurrent *(united)*, congruous, consensual, consenting, consonant, correlative, harmonious, relevant, suitable
consentaneousness agreement *(concurrence)*, concordance, consensus, peace
consentaneus consonant, rational, suitable
consented allowed
consentience accordance *(understanding)*, agreement *(concurrence)*, consensus
consentient concerted, congruous, consensual, consenting, consonant, contractual, harmonious
consenting concerted, concordant, inclined, ready *(willing)*, willing *(not averse)*. SEE MAIN ENTRY
consentire agree *(contract)*, consent, plot
consenus cartel
consequence amount *(result)*, clout, concern *(interest)*, conclusion *(outcome)*, degree *(magnitude)*, development *(outgrowth)*, effect, eminence, emphasis, follow-up, force *(strength)*, import, importance, influence, interest *(concern)*, magnitude, outcome, prestige, primacy, reputation, result, significance, toll *(effect)*, value, weight *(importance)*. SEE MAIN ENTRY
consequent conclusion *(outcome)*, consecutive, consonant, derivative, development *(outgrowth)*
consequentia result
consequential considerable, contingent, crucial, decisive, derivative, grave *(important)*, important *(significant)*, influential, major, material *(important)*, momentous, outstanding *(prominent)*, powerful, prominent, remarkable, renowned, serious *(grave)*, strategic, substantial. SEE MAIN ENTRY
consequentialism SEE MAIN ENTRY
consequently a fortiori, a priori. SEE MAIN ENTRY
consequi attain, gain, obtain, result
conservare conserve, observe *(obey)*, preserve, retain *(keep in possession)*
conservatio maintenance *(upkeep)*, preservation, retention
conservation ecology, maintenance *(upkeep)*, preservation, protection, prudence, reserve, safekeeping, salvage. SEE MAIN ENTRY
conservation of the same situation status quo
conservational protective
conservatism continence, moderation, prudence
conservative frugal, guarded, illiberal, orthodox, protective, uncompromising
conservative estimate understatement
conservative reading SEE MAIN ETNRY
conservator guardian
conservatory protective, repository, store *(depository)*, treasury
conserve fund, hold *(possess)*, keep *(shelter)*, maintain *(sustain)*, preserve, protect, store, sustain *(prolong)*. SEE MAIN ENTRY
consider analyze, assess *(appraise)*, assume *(suppose)*, brood, calculate, care *(be cautious)*, concern *(care)*, contrive, criticize *(evaluate)*, debate, deem, deliberate, digest *(comprehend)*, discuss, gauge, heed, investigate, judge, muse, opine, pause, peruse, ponder, postulate, reason *(conclude)*, reflect *(ponder)*, regard *(pay attention)*, speculate *(conjecture)*, study, survey *(examine)*, suspect *(think)*, try *(conduct a trial)*, weigh. SEE MAIN ENTRY
consider again reconsider
consider again with a view to a change or action appeal
consider as belonging to attribute
consider as true accept *(embrace)*, presume
consider attentively deliberate, probe

consider beforehand prearrange
consider beneath notice condescend *(patronize)*, disdain
consider beneath oneself disdain
consider carefully deliberate
consider closely concentrate *(pay attention)*
consider implausible disbelieve
consider in advance anticipate *(expect)*
consider likely expect *(consider probable)*
consider not to be true disbelieve
consider pro and con deliberate
consider probable deduce, deduct *(conclude by reasoning)*, infer, presume, read
consider unproven disbelieve
consider untrue disbelieve
consider unworthy of regard disdain
considerable appreciable, consequential *(substantial)*, copious, critical *(crucial)*, extensive, far reaching, gross *(flagrant)*, important *(significant)*, major, manifold, material *(important)*, multiple, noteworthy, ponderable, rife, substantial, substantive. SEE MAIN ENTRY
considerare consider, deliberate, ponder, reflect *(ponder)*, survey *(examine)*, weigh
considerate benevolent, charitable *(lenient)*, circumspect, humane, judicial, judicious, lenient, philanthropic, politic, prudent
considerateness charity, comity, consideration *(sympathetic regard)*, discretion *(quality of being discreet)*, philanthropy, prudence
consideratio consideration *(contemplation)*, reflection *(thought)*
consideration advancement *(loan)*, analysis, benevolence *(disposition to do good)*, cause *(reason)*, caution *(vigilance)*, charity, clemency, comity, commission *(fee)*, compensation, concept, concern *(interest)*, conclusion *(determination)*, contemplation, conviction *(persuasion)*, cost *(price)*, courtesy, credit *(recognition)*, decorum, deference, deliberation, determinant, determination, dialectic, diligence *(care)*, discretion *(power of choice)*, discretion *(quality of being discreet)*, discrimination *(differentiation)*, emphasis, estimate *(idea)*, examination *(study)*, expense *(cost)*, extenuating circumstances, fee *(charge)*, forethought, hindsight, homage, honor *(outward respect)*, honorarium, impression, incentive, inducement, interest *(concern)*, judgment *(discernment)*, judgment *(formal court decree)*, lenience, magnitude, motive, notice *(heed)*, observation, opinion *(belief)*, opinion *(judicial decision)*, pay, payment *(remittance)*, perquisite, phase *(aspect)*, philanthropy, point *(item)*, prudence, reason *(basis)*, recognition, recompense, reflection *(thought)*, regard *(attention)*, regard *(esteem)*, requital, respect, reward, scrutiny, tip *(gratuity)*, treatment, understanding *(tolerance)*. SEE MAIN ENTRY
consideration in advance forethought
consideratus deliberate, discreet, intentional
considere subside
considered deliberate, intentional, judicious, meticulous, premeditated, prospective, solid *(sound)*, tactical
considered decision choice *(decision)*
considered guess estimate *(approximate cost)*, estimation *(calculation)*
considered opinion determination, holding *(ruling of a court)*
considered together collective
considered true assumed *(inferred)*
consign alienate *(transfer title)*, allocate, assign *(transfer ownership)*, attorn, authorize, cede, commit *(entrust)*, commit *(institutionalize)*, confide *(trust)*, contribute *(supply)*, convey *(transfer)*, delegate, detail *(assign)*, disperse *(disseminate)*, divide *(distribute)*, entrust, give *(grant)*, grant *(transfer formally)*, leave *(give)*, mete, refer *(send for action)*, relegate, remand, remit *(submit for consideration)*, transfer, transmit, transport, vest. SEE MAIN ENTRY
consign again reassign
consignable assignable, heritable, negotiable
consignare indorse, inscribe, sign
consignation alienation *(transfer of title)*, assignment *(transfer of ownership)*, consignment, conveyance
consignee heir, licensee, nominee *(delegate)*, payee, receiver, recipient, surety *(guarantor)*, transferee
consigner dealer, merchant
consignify construe *(comprehend)*
consigning delegation *(assignment)*
consignment alienation *(transfer of title)*, apportionment, assignment *(transfer of ownership)*, cargo, delegation *(assignment)*, freight. SEE MAIN ENTRY
consignor donor, licensor, transferor
consiliari advise
consilium advice, assembly, committee, counsel, design *(intent)*, determination, direction *(guidance)*, end *(intent)*, expedient, facility *(instrumentality)*, guidance, intention, judgment *(discernment)*, object, panel *(discussion group)*, policy *(plan of action)*, project, reason *(sound judgment)*, scheme, strategy, suggestion
consilium dare advise
consimilar identical, similar
consimilarity identity *(similarity)*
consimilitude identity *(similarity)*
consimility identity *(similarity)*
consist SEE MAIN ENTRY
consist of comprehend *(include)*, comprise, constitute *(compose)*, contain *(comprise)*, encompass *(include)*, include
consistence congealment
consistency adjustment, coherence, compatibility, concordance, conformity *(obedience)*, consensus, constant, continuity, method, regularity, same, synchronism, uniformity. SEE MAIN ENTRY
consistent apposite, appropriate, certain *(positive)*, cohesive *(sticking)*, commensurable, commensurate, concordant, consonant, constant, fit, harmonious, logical, natural, proportionate, relevant, suitable, typical, uniform, usual. SEE MAIN ENTRY
consistent with concerted, congruous, consensual, pursuant to
consistent with the agreement as agreed upon
consistently faithfully
consistere consist, halt, stand *(position)*
consisting of inclusive
consisting of a guarantee promissory
consisting of a pledge promissory
consistory board, meeting *(conference)*
consociare combine *(join together)*
consociate accessory, accomplice, affiliate, coactor, coadjutant, cohort, colleague, confederate, connect *(relate)*, conspirer, contact *(communicate)*, copartner *(business associate)*, copartner *(coconspirator)*, correlative, federalize *(associate)*, federate, interrelated, involve *(implicate)*, join *(associate oneself with)*, partner, relate *(establish a connection)*, related. SEE MAIN ENTRY
consociate in crime coconspirator
consociated intimate
consociatio union *(unity)*
consociation affiliation *(connectedness)*, association *(connection)*, cartel, coalescence, coalition, company *(enterprise)*, connection *(relation)*, consortium *(marriage companionship)*, contact *(association)*, corporation, integration *(assimilation)*, partnership, relationship *(connection)*, society, union *(labor organization)*
consolatio solace
consolation pity, solace
consolatory palliative *(abating)*
console alleviate, assure *(give confidence to)*, ease, sympathize
consolidate amalgamate, annex *(add)*, attach *(join)*, bond *(hold together)*, cement, cohere *(adhere)*, collect *(gather)*, combine *(join together)*, commingle, condense, conjoin, connect *(join together)*, constrict *(compress)*, convene, converge, crystallize, desegregate, federalize *(associate)*, fix *(make firm)*, include, incorporate *(include)*, join *(bring together)*, merge, organize *(unionize)*, pool, unite. SEE MAIN ENTRY
consolidated coadunate, coherent *(joined)*, cohesive *(compact)*, collective, compact *(dense)*, concerted, concurrent *(united)*, conjoint, inseparable, joint, solid *(compact)*
consolidation abridgment *(condensation)*, abstract, accession *(annexation)*, adhesion *(affixing)*, agglomeration, centralization, coalescence, coalition, coherence, combination, compilation, concrescence, confederacy *(compact)*, congealment, conglomeration, connection *(fastening)*, consortium *(business cartel)*, corporation, digest, incorporation *(blend)*, integration *(amalgamation)*, merger, pool, sodality, union *(unity)*. SEE MAIN ENTRY
consonance accordance *(compact)*, accordance *(understanding)*, agreement *(concurrence)*, assent, coherence, compatibility, compliance, concert, conciliation, concordance, conformity *(agreement)*, consensus, propriety *(appropriateness)*, rapport. SEE MAIN ENTRY
consonancy accordance *(understanding)*, cartel, compliance
consonant apposite, appropriate, boiler plate, commensurable, concerted, concordant, concurrent *(united)*, congruous, consistent, correlative, felicitous, fit, harmonious, relevant, suitable, uniform. SEE MAIN ENTRY
consonant with pursuant to
consort accompany, cartel, coactor, colleague, consociate, contributor *(contributor)*, copartner *(business associate)*, join *(associate oneself with)*, spouse. SEE MAIN ENTRY
consort with commingle
consortem participate
consortio partnership
consortium affiliation *(amalgamation)*, cartel, coalition, consolidation, contact *(association)*, matrimony, pact, partnership, pool, syndicate, trust *(combination of businesses)*. SEE MAIN ENTRY
consortship consortium *(marriage companionship)*
conspecific correlative
conspectus abridgment *(condensation)*, abstract, brief, capsule, compendium, digest, outline *(synopsis)*, pandect *(treatise)*, restatement, summary, synopsis

conspici appear *(materialize)*
conspicuous apparent *(perceptible)*, appreciable, arrant *(definite)*, conclusive *(determinative)*, distinct *(clear)*, distinctive, evident, famous, flagrant, illustrious, manifest, naked *(perceptible)*, notable, noteworthy, notorious, obvious, open *(in sight)*, outrageous, outstanding *(prominent)*, palpable, patent, pretentious *(ostentatious)*, prominent, remarkable, renowned, salient, scrutable, special, stark, unmistakable, unusual, visible *(noticeable)*. SEE MAIN ENTRY
conspicuously fairly *(clearly)*
conspicuousness notoriety
conspicuus conspicuous, remarkable
conspiracy cabal, collusion, connivance, faction, frame up, machination, plan, plot *(secret plan)*, racket. SEE MAIN ENTRY
conspirare conspire, plot
conspiratio coalition, plot *(secret plan)*
conspirational collusive
conspirative collusive
conspirator abettor, coactor, confederate, conspirer. SEE MAIN ENTRY
conspiratorial collusive, malevolent
conspire combine *(act in concert)*, connive, contrive, cooperate, maneuver, plan, plot, scheme. SEE MAIN ENTRY
conspire against frame *(charge falsely)*, frame *(prearrange)*
conspirer coactor, confederate, copartner *(coconspirator)*. SEE MAIN ENTRY
conspiring clandestine, collusive
constable peace officer
constabulary police
constancy adherence *(devotion)*, adhesion *(loyalty)*, allegiance, constant, continuity, diligence *(perseverance)*, discipline *(obedience)*, faith, fealty, fidelity, homage, indestructibility, industry *(activity)*, loyalty, perpetuity, prowess *(bravery)*, purpose, resolution *(decision)*, tenacity, tolerance, uniformity. SEE MAIN ENTRY
constans consistent, constant *(adjective)*, constant *(noun)*, immutable, regular *(orderly)*, resolute, stable, steadfast, unaffected *(uninfluenced)*, uniform
constant chronic, continual *(connected)*, continuous, dependable, diligent, durable, faithful *(diligent)*, faithful *(loyal)*, habitual, immutable, incessant, loyal, patient, permanent, perpetual, reliable, resolute, sedulous, stable, standing, staunch, steadfast, true *(loyal)*, unalterable, uniform, unrelenting, unremitting, unyielding. SEE MAIN ENTRY
constant flow chain *(series)*
constant progression perpetuity
constantia fidelity, regularity
constantly faithfully, in good faith, invariably
constantly recurring continual *(connected)*
constantly together inseparable
constare persevere, subsist
consternation apprehension *(fear)*, bombshell, cloud *(suspicion)*, confusion *(ambiguity)*, doubt *(suspicion)*, fear, fright, panic, surprise, trepidation. SEE MAIN ENTRY
constituency chamber *(body)*, constituent *(member)*, district. SEE MAIN ENTRY
constituent component, element, factor *(ingredient)*, feature *(characteristic)*, ingredient, integral, item, member *(individual in a group)*, part *(portion)*, segment, substantive, unit *(item)*. SEE MAIN ENTRY
constituent part component, ingredient
constituents constituency, contents
constituere adopt, agree *(contract)*, appoint, arrange *(methodize)*, constitute *(establish)*, decide, determine, establish *(launch)*, fix *(arrange)*, fix *(settle)*, instate, legislate, resolve *(decide)*, settle
constitute comprehend *(include)*, comprise, consist, create, embody, establish *(launch)*, frame *(construct)*, make, nominate. SEE MAIN ENTRY
constituting creation
constituting a difference differential
constitutio settlement
constitution building *(business of assembling)*, character *(personal quality)*, characteristic, charter *(declaration of rights)*, code, color *(complexion)*, composition *(makeup)*, configuration *(form)*, construction, content *(structure)*, disposition *(inclination)*, frame *(mood)*, organization *(structure)*, polity, structure *(composition)*, temperament. SEE MAIN ENTRY
constitutional fundamental, hereditary, innate, lawful, legal, legitimate *(rightful)*, licit, organic, permissible, rightful, salutary, valid
constitutionality legality
constitutionally opposed antipathetic *(oppositional)*
constitutive causal, causative, primary
constitutive element determinant, factor *(ingredient)*
constitutive principle center *(essence)*
constitutus definite
constrain allay, apprehend *(arrest)*, arrest *(apprehend)*, bind *(obligate)*, bind *(restrain)*, check *(restrain)*, coerce, command, commit *(institutionalize)*, compel, confine, constrict *(inhibit)*, contain *(restrain)*, control *(restrain)*, debar, detain *(restrain)*, disadvantage, enjoin, exact, foist, force *(coerce)*, hinder, immure, impose *(enforce)*, impose *(subject)*, imprison, inhibit, jail, keep *(restrain)*, limit, make, moderate *(temper)*, pressure, require *(compel)*, restrain, restrict, stay *(halt)*, stifle, trammel, withhold. SEE MAIN ENTRY
constrain again rearrest
constrain by force extort
constrained arrested *(apprehended)*, bound, controlled *(restrained)*, obligatory
constraining binding, compelling, compulsory, necessary *(inescapable)*
constraining force pressure
constraining power force *(compulsion)*
constraint bar *(obstruction)*, bondage, captivity, coercion, commitment *(confinement)*, composure, compulsion *(coercion)*, control *(restriction)*, custody *(incarceration)*, detention, deterrence, deterrent, discipline *(obedience)*, disincentive, duress, embarrassment, enforcement, fetter, force *(compulsion)*, incarceration, limitation, moderation, obstacle, obstruction, pressure, prohibition, quota, requirement, restraint, restriction, retention. SEE MAIN ENTRY
constraint by force bondage, coercion
constraint to obedience compulsion *(coercion)*
constrict attenuate, block, clog, concentrate *(consolidate)*, decrease, deter, limit. SEE MAIN ENTRY
constricted compact *(dense)*, limited
constricting limiting
constriction compulsion *(coercion)*, constraint *(restriction)*, curtailment, decrease, deterrence, deterrent, force *(compulsion)*, hindrance, obstruction, restriction
constringe attenuate, constrict *(compress)*, decrease
constringed compact *(dense)*
constringent bitter *(penetrating)*
construability construction
construable accountable *(explainable)*, circumstantial, determinable *(ascertainable)*
construal construction
construct build *(construct)*, compose, create, devise *(invent)*, establish *(launch)*, forge *(produce)*, form, generate, invent *(produce for the first time)*, make, manufacture, orchestrate, produce *(manufacture)*
construct a figure delineate
construction building *(business of assembling)*, building *(structure)*, composition *(makeup)*, configuration *(form)*, connotation, content *(structure)*, creation, development *(building)*, edifice, formation, frame *(structure)*, manufacture, motif, organization *(structure)*, performance *(workmanship)*, rendition *(explication)*. SEE MAIN ENTRY
constructional constructive *(inferential)*
constructive beneficial, causative, interpretive, productive, virtual. SEE MAIN ENTRY
constructive criticism advocacy
constructive notice SEE MAIN ENTRY
constructor architect, contractor, materialman
construe characterize, clarify, deduce, deduct *(conclude by reasoning)*, define, derive *(deduce)*, elucidate, expound, infer, interpret, rationalize, render *(depict)*. SEE MAIN ENTRY
construe falsely cloak
construe wrongly misconstrue
constuprate violate
constupration rape
consubstantial congruous, identical, similar
consubstantiate unite
consuescere cohabit
consuetude behavior, custom, habit, manner *(behavior)*, practice *(custom)*, usage
consuetudinal accustomed *(customary)*, frequent, regular *(conventional)*, repeated, traditional, usual
consuetudinary accustomed *(customary)*, customary, familiar *(customary)*, frequent, habitual, ordinary, regular *(conventional)*, repeated, traditional, usual
consuetudo habit, practice *(procedure)*, usage
consul plenipotentiary
consulate deputation *(delegation)*, embassy
consulere provide *(arrange for)*
consult consider, counsel, deliberate, discuss, refer *(send for action)*. SEE MAIN ENTRY
consult again reconsider
consult with advise, confer *(consult)*, converse, debate
consultant specialist
consultants commission *(agency)*
consultare confer *(consult)*, consult *(ask advice of)*, deliberate
consultatio deliberation
consultation caucus, conference, confrontation *(act of setting face to face)*, conversation, guidance, interview, meeting *(conference)*, negotiation, parley, session
consultation meeting conference
consultative hortative
consultative body board

consulting advisory
consultive body congress
consulto design *(intent)*
consultor client, patron *(regular customer)*
consultum edict
consumable disposable
consume burn, decay, deflagrate, degenerate, deplete, despoil, destroy *(efface)*, diminish, dissipate *(expend foolishly)*, eliminate *(eradicate)*, erode, exhaust *(deplete)*, exploit *(make use of)*, extirpate, obliterate, prey, spend. SEE MAIN ENTRY
consume completely exhaust *(deplete)*
consume one's substance dissipate *(expend foolishly)*
consumed irredeemable
consumer client, customer, patron *(regular customer)*. SEE MAIN ENTRY
consumer demand market *(demand)*
consumer durables goods, merchandise
consumer goods merchandise
consumere consume, exhaust *(deplete)*, spend
consuming deadly, deleterious, harmful, malignant
consummare consummate, finish
consummate absolute *(ideal)*, accomplish, arrant *(definite)*, attain, cease, close *(terminate)*, commit *(perpetrate)*, complete *(all-embracing)*, complete, comprehensive, conclude *(complete)*, culminate, definitive, discharge *(perform)*, discontinue *(abandon)*, dispatch *(dispose of)*, finish, fulfill, implement, mature, outright, perfect, perform *(adhere to)*, realize *(make real)*, ripe, sterling, superlative, thorough, transact, unmitigated, unqualified *(unlimited)*. SEE MAIN ENTRY
consummated choate lien, complete *(ended)*
consummation action *(performance)*, cessation *(termination)*, close *(conclusion)*, commission *(act)*, conclusion *(outcome)*, consequence *(conclusion)*, denouement, destination, discharge *(performance)*, end *(termination)*, expiration, fait accompli, finality, fruition, maturity, outcome, payoff *(result)*, performance *(execution)*, pinnacle, realization, satisfaction *(fulfilment)*, transaction
consumptio consumption
consumption decline, destruction, deterioration, erosion, expense *(sacrifice)*, prostration, waste. SEE MAIN ENTRY
consumptive fatal, harmful
contact coalescence, collision *(accident)*, connection *(abutment)*, convey *(communicate)*, correspond *(communicate)*, impinge, liaison, meeting *(encounter)*, notify, reach. SEE MAIN ENTRY
contactual proximate
contactus contact *(touching)*, contact *(communicate)*
contagion contaminate, disease
contagious pestilent. SEE MAIN ENTRY
contain accommodate, border *(bound)*, circumscribe *(surround by boundary)*, comprehend *(include)*, comprise, confine, consist, constitute *(compose)*, detain *(hold in custody)*, detain *(restrain)*, embrace *(encircle)*, enclose, encompass *(include)*, hold up *(delay)*, include, incorporate *(include)*, keep *(restrain)*, limit, own, restrain, stifle. SEE MAIN ENTRY
contain oneself refrain
contained arrested *(checked)*
contained in a will testamentary
container catchall, coffer, depository, enclosure, repository
containing comprehensive, inclusive, limiting
containing a penalty penal
containing a pledge promissory
containing an assurance promissory
containing error erroneous
containing power capacity *(maximum)*
containing stipulations conditional
containment blockade *(enclosure)*, constraint *(imprisonment)*, enclosure, quota, restraint, restriction
contaminare infect, taint *(contaminate)*
contaminate adulterate, corrupt, damage, debase, impair, infect, pervert, pollute, smear, stain, sully, tarnish. SEE MAIN ENTRY
contaminated marred, noxious, peccant *(unhealthy)*
contaminating contagious
contamination air pollution, defilement, detriment, perversion
contankerous contumacious
conte story *(narrative)*
contemn condescend *(patronize)*, decry, denounce *(condemn)*, depreciate, discommend, disdain, dishonor *(deprive of honor)*, disparage, flout, humiliate, misprize, spurn. SEE MAIN ENTRY
contemned blameworthy, contemptible
contemnendus contemptible
contemplari review, survey *(examine)*
contemplate anticipate *(expect)*, brood, concentrate *(pay attention)*, conjure, consider, deliberate, devote, digest *(comprehend)*, examine *(study)*, muse, peruse, ponder, presume, reason *(conclude)*, reflect *(ponder)*, regard *(pay attention)*, scrutinize, study, weigh. SEE MAIN ENTRY
contemplated apparent *(presumptive)*, deliberate, foreseeable, intentional, willful
contemplatio contemplation
contemplation deliberation, design *(intent)*, dialectic, diligence *(care)*, discretion *(power of choice)*, discrimination *(differentiation)*, expectation, forethought, hindsight, intent, introspection, judgment *(discernment)*, prospect *(outlook)*, purview, reflection *(thought)*, speculation *(conjecture)*, target. SEE MAIN ENTRY
contemplation of past events hindsight
contemplation of the past hindsight, recollection, retrospect
contemplative circumspect, cogitative, deliberate, pensive, politic, speculative
contemplativeness deliberation
contemporaneous coincidental, concomitant, concurrent *(at the same time)*, current, present *(current)*, simultaneous. SEE MAIN ENTRY
contemporary concomitant, concurrent *(at the same time)*, contemporaneous, current, peer, present *(current)*, prevailing *(current)*, simultaneous, sophisticated. SEE MAIN ENTRY
contemporary account journal
contempt contumely, disdain, disgrace, dishonor *(shame)*, disparagement, disregard *(lack of respect)*, disrespect, ignominy, impertinent *(insolent)*, infamy, malice, misprision, obloquy, odium, opprobrium, rejection, reproach, ridicule, shame, spite. SEE MAIN ENTRY
contempt of danger prowess *(bravery)*
contemptibility bad repute, disrepute, ignominy, ill repute
contemptible bad *(offensive)*, base *(bad)*, blameful, blameworthy, contemptuous, depraved, disgraceful, disreputable, heinous, ignoble, inferior *(lower in quality)*, loathsome, nefarious, notorious, obnoxious, odious, offensive *(offending)*, outrageous, paltry, perverse, petty, poor *(inferior in quality)*, repulsive, sinister, unworthy. SEE MAIN ENTRY
contemptibleness ignominy, ill repute
contemptio disdain
contemptousness disregard *(lack of respect)*
contemptuous blameful, blameworthy, calumnious, contumacious, cynical, disdainful, impertinent *(insolent)*, inflated *(vain)*, insolent, libelous, orgulous, proud *(conceited)*, supercilious. SEE MAIN ENTRY
contemptuous language vilification
contemptuous resistance contempt *(disobedience to the court)*
contemptuous treatment contumely
contemptuousness contempt *(disdain)*, contumely, disdain, disrespect
contemptus contempt *(disdain)*, contemptible
contend allege, answer *(reply)*, argue, assert, avouch *(avow)*, avow, bear *(adduce)*, bicker, claim *(maintain)*, collide *(clash)*, compete, conflict, contest, counter, counteract, cross *(disagree with)*, debate, declare, dicker, differ *(disagree)*, disaccord, dispute *(contest)*, engage *(involve)*, fight *(battle)*, insist, litigate, oppose, oppugn, plead *(allege in a legal action)*, posit, postulate, profess *(avow)*, propose, propound, reason *(persuade)*, refute, strive. SEE MAIN ENTRY
contend against antagonize, confront *(oppose)*
contend against in discussion controvert
contend for advocate, dispute *(contest)*, justify, plead *(argue a case)*
contend in argument argue, dispute *(debate)*
contend in words discuss
contend with confront *(oppose)*
contended alleged
contender adversary, aggressor, appellant, candidate, contestant, disputant, foe, litigant, opponent, party *(litigant)*, peer, rival. SEE MAIN ENTRY
contendere contend *(dispute)*, contend *(maintain)*, contest, endeavor, exert, hasten, labor, maintain *(carry on)*, strive
contending competitive *(antagonistic)*
content complacent, component, composure, disarm *(set at ease)*, element, factor *(ingredient)*, inclined, ingredient, meaning, propitiate, proud *(self-respecting)*, satisfaction *(fulfilment)*, satisfy *(fulfill)*, subject *(topic)*, substance *(essential nature)*, tenor, willing *(not averse)*. SEE MAIN ENTRY
contented complacent, peaceable, proud *(self-respecting)*
contentedness satisfaction *(fulfilment)*
contentio antithesis, competition, effort, endeavor
contention avowal, case *(lawsuit)*, collision *(dispute)*, conflict, confrontation *(altercation)*, contest *(dispute)*, contravention, controversy *(argument)*, disaccord, disagreement, discord, dispute, dissension, embroilment, feud, fracas, fray, lawsuit, opposition, resistance, rift *(disagreement)*, strife, struggle, variance *(disagreement)*. SEE MAIN ENTRY

contentious argumentative, competitive *(antagonistic)*, debatable, dissenting, forensic, fractious, hostile, litigious, moot, negative, offensive *(taking the initiative)*, petulant, polemic, pugnacious, querulous, remonstrative. SEE MAIN ENTRY
contentious group faction
contentiousness argument *(contention)*, belligerency, conflict, contention *(opposition)*
contentment composure, satisfaction *(fulfilment)*
contents capsule, cargo, composition *(makeup)*, effects, inventory, merchandise, outline *(synopsis)*, scenario, stock in trade. SEE MAIN ENTRY
conterminal proximate
conterminous adjacent, contiguous, immediate *(not distant)*, proximate
contest answer *(reply)*, answer *(respond legally)*, appeal, argue, bicker, compete, competition, conflict *(noun)*, conflict *(verb)*, contend *(dispute)*, contention *(argument)*, contention *(opposition)*, contravene, contravention, controversy *(argument)*, controversy *(lawsuit)*, controvert, cross *(disagree with)*, debate, disagree, discuss, disown *(deny the validity)*, embroilment, engage *(involve)*, fight *(argument)*, fight *(battle)*, fight *(battle)*, fray, gainsay, grapple, hearing, impugn, lawsuit, oppose, prevent, primary, strife, strive, sue, trial *(legal proceeding)*. SEE MAIN ENTRY
contest a case by asking for review appeal
contest in court litigate
contest in law litigate
contestability cloud *(suspicion)*
contestable arguable, controversial, debatable, disputable, doubtful, dubious, dubitative, forensic, litigable, moot, polemic, problematic, speculative, uncertain *(questionable)*, undecided. SEE MAIN ENTRY
contestant adversary, candidate, contender, disputant, foe, litigant, party *(litigant)*, rival. SEE MAIN ENTRY
contestation affray, altercation, belligerency, confrontation *(altercation)*, contention *(opposition)*, controversy *(argument)*, primary, strife, struggle
contested litigious, moot
contester adversary, contender, contestant
contesting hostile, negative
context case *(set of circumstances)*, connotation, environment, posture *(situation)*. SEE MAIN ENTRY
contextual incident
contexture content *(structure)*
contextus coherence, coherent *(joined)*
contiguity border, contact *(touching)*, propinquity *(proximity)*
contiguous adjacent, close *(near)*, immediate *(not distant)*, proximate. SEE MAIN ENTRY
contiguousness connection *(abutment)*, contact *(touching)*
contiguus adjacent
continence moderation. SEE MAIN ENTRY
continens consecutive, contiguous
continentia continence, moderation
continere contain *(enclose)*, control *(restrain)*, encompass *(include)*, involve *(implicate)*
contingence contact *(touching)*, contingency
contingency chance *(possibility)*, incident, occurrence, secondary, sine qua non. SEE MAIN ENTRY
contingent circumstantial, contingency, correlative, dependent, dubious, executory, extrinsic, incident, provisional, quota, reciprocal, related, restrictive, subject *(conditional)*, tentative, uncertain *(questionable)*. SEE MAIN ENTRY
contingent deed held in trust escrow
contingent event contingency
contingent-fee agreement SEE MAIN ENTRY
contingent interest claim *(right)*
contingent on conditional
contingent upon based on, qualified *(conditioned)*
continual chronic, consecutive, constant, continuous, direct *(uninterrupted)*, durable, habitual, immutable, incessant, periodic, unrelenting, unremitting. SEE MAIN ENTRY
continually increasing cumulative *(increasing)*
continually recurring constant
continualness continuity, perpetuity
continuance continuation *(prolongation)*, continuation *(resumption)*, continuity, diligence *(perseverance)*, duration, extension *(postponement)*, habitation *(act of inhabiting)*, indestructibility, life *(period of existence)*, longevity, pendency, period, perpetuity, phase *(period)*, renewal, survival. SEE MAIN ENTRY
continuance in time duration
continuatio continuance, continuation *(prolongation)*, continuity, succession
continuation adjournment, appendix *(supplement)*, continuance, continuity, extension *(postponement)*, longevity, perpetuity, rider, survival. SEE MAIN ENTRY
continuation in time duration
continuation of life survival
continue adhere *(persist)*, adjourn, bear *(tolerate)*, dwell *(linger over)*, endure *(last)*, exist, extend *(enlarge)*, last, maintain *(carry on)*, pass *(advance)*, persevere, persist, preserve, prolong, propagate *(increase)*, prosecute *(carry forward)*, protract *(stall)*, pursue *(carry on)*, recur, remain *(continue)*, renew *(begin again)*, reopen, resist *(withstand)*, resume, subsist, sustain *(prolong)*. SEE MAIN ENTRY
continue onward progress
continue to be endure *(last)*, exist
continue to exist endure *(last)*
continue to hold retain *(keep in possession)*
continue to live exist
continue under pain endure *(suffer)*
continued continual *(connected)*, live *(existing)*, open-ended, permanent, persistent, standing
continued existence perpetuity
continued movement process *(course)*
continuing chronic, consecutive, constant, continual *(connected)*, continuous, durable, infallible, lasting, live *(existing)*, open-ended, patient, permanent, persistent, pertinacious, protracted, stable, standing
continuing after death posthumous
continuing development process *(course)*
continuing for a short time ephemeral
continuing offer option *(contractual provision)*
continuing offer to buy option *(contractual provision)*
continuity chain *(series)*, coherence, frequency, indestructibility, uniformity. SEE MAIN ENTRY
continuous adjacent, chronic, consecutive, constant, continual *(perpetual)*, direct *(uninterrupted)*, immutable, incessant, perpetual, persistent, progressive *(going forward)*, relentless, unrelenting, unremitting. SEE MAIN ENTRY
continuous time perpetuity
continuousness continuity, perpetuity
continuum continuity, sequence
continuum of days annum
continuus continual *(connected)*, incessant, unremitting
contio assembly, harangue
contorquere launch *(project)*
contort distort, misrepresent. SEE MAIN ENTRY
contorted circuitous, tortuous *(bending)*, unreasonable
contortion distortion
contour ambit, boundary, circumscribe *(surround by boundary)*, complexion, configuration *(confines)*, configuration *(form)*, delineate, delineation, outline *(boundary)*, periphery. SEE MAIN ENTRY
contra SEE MAIN ENTRY
contra dicere recusare object
contra leges violation
contra rem facere militate
contraband impermissible, unlawful. SEE MAIN ENTRY
contrabandist bootlegger, racketeer, thief
contract abridge *(shorten)*, abstract *(summarize)*, accordance *(compact)*, adjustment, arrangement *(understanding)*, assume *(undertake)*, attenuate, bargain, bond *(secure a debt)*, buy, cartel, clause, commitment *(responsibility)*, compact, composition *(agreement in bankruptcy)*, condense, consolidate *(strengthen)*, constrict *(compress)*, covenant, deal, decrease, diminish, employ *(engage services)*, incur, indenture, lease, lessen, let *(lease)*, mutual understanding, obligation *(duty)*, pact, pledge *(binding promise)*, promise, promise *(vow)*, protocol *(agreement)*, provide *(arrange for)*, record, reduce, rent, settlement, stipulate, stipulation, surety *(certainty)*, testament, treaty, understanding *(agreement)*, undertake, undertaking *(commitment)*, undertaking *(pledge)*. SEE MAIN ENTRY
contract a debt owe
contract against future loss insurance
contract against unknown contingencies insurance
contract an obligation pledge *(promise the performance of)*, promise *(vow)*
contract before marriage antenuptial agreement
contract for assume *(undertake)*, engage *(hire)*, hire, retain *(employ)*
contract for exclusive possession lease
contract for exclusive possession of lands lease
contract for possession and profits lease
contract for possession of land lease
contract for use and occupation lease
contract obligation liability. SEE MAIN ENTRY
contract of mortgage hypothecation
contract of pledge hypothecation
contract payment installment, premium *(insurance payment)*
contract talks negotiation
contract to lease sublet
contract to work indenture

contracted agreed *(promised),* brief, compact *(dense),* compact *(pithy),* concise, indentured, laconic, narrow
contracting party privy
contraction abridgment *(condensation),* abstract, blockade *(limitation),* compendium, curtailment, decline, decrease, decrement, digest, diminution, outline *(synopsis)*
contractor materialman, supplier. SEE MAIN ENTRY
contracts dealings
contractual SEE MAIN ENTRY
contractual assurance warranty. SEE MAIN ENTRY
contractual bond privity
contractual clause article *(distinct section of a writing)*
contractual obligation bill *(formal declaration),* compact, covenant, indenture, mortgage, policy *(contract),* specialty *(contract)*
contractual promise warranty
contractual representation warranty
contractual statement agreement *(contract),* compact, covenant, indenture, policy *(contract),* specialty *(contract)*
contractual terms condition *(contingent provision),* counteroffer
contractus narrow
contradicere contradict
contradict abrogate *(annul),* annul, answer *(reply),* bear false witness, challenge, collide *(clash),* conflict, confront *(oppose),* contend *(dispute),* contest, contravene, controvert, counter, counteract, countercharge, countervail, cross *(disagree with),* demur, differ *(disagree),* disaccord, disagree, disallow, disapprove *(reject),* disown *(deny the validity),* dispute *(contest),* dispute *(debate),* dissent *(differ in opinion),* except *(object),* fight *(counteract),* gainsay, impugn, negate, oppose, oppugn, protest, rebut, recant, refute, renege, repudiate, resist *(oppose).* SEE MAIN ENTRY
contradict absolutely controvert
contradicting contradictory, contrary, dissenting
contradictio objection
contradiction antipode, antithesis, collision *(dispute),* conflict, confutation, contradistinction, contraposition, contrary, contravention, counterargument, denial, difference, disaccord, disagreement, disapproval, discrepancy, disparity, dissidence, exception *(objection),* impugnation, incongruity, inconsistency, negation, paradox, reaction *(opposition),* repudiation, retraction. SEE MAIN ENTRY
contradiction of terms non sequitur
contradictive opposite
contradictoriness contradistinction, incompatibility *(difference),* incongruity, inconsistency
contradictory adverse *(opposite),* antipathetic *(oppositional),* contrary, different, discordant, disparate, hostile, illogical, incongruous, inconsistent, negative, opposite, polemic, repugnant *(incompatible).* SEE MAIN ENTRY
contradictory evidence answer *(judicial response)*
contradistinct adverse *(opposite),* antipathetic *(oppositional),* contradictory, contrary, different, discordant, discriminating *(distinguishing)*
contradistinction antipode, antithesis, contradiction, contraposition, contrary, difference, disparity. SEE MAIN ENTRY
contradistinctive different
contradistinguish demarcate, distinguish
contrahere abridge *(shorten),* concentrate *(consolidate),* contract, retrench
contraindicate discourage
contraindicating contradictory, contrary
contraindication admonition, antipode, contradiction, deterrence, deterrent, warning
contrapose confront *(oppose),* polarize
contraposition antipode, antithesis, conflict, contradiction, difference, disagreement, disparity, dissent *(difference of opinion).* SEE MAIN ENTRY
contrapositive adverse *(opposite),* antipathetic *(oppositional),* contradictory, contrary
contraption invention
contraremonstrance counterargument, counterclaim
contrariae irreconcilable
contrariant adverse *(opposite),* hostile
contraries contradiction
contrariety admonition, antipode, antithesis, collision *(dispute),* conflict, confutation, contention *(opposition),* contradiction, contradistinction, contraposition, difference, disaccord, disagreement, dissent *(nonconcurrence),* dissidence, distinction *(difference),* exception *(exclusion),* ill will, impugnation, incompatibility *(difference),* incongruity, inconsistency, opposition, paradox, reaction *(opposition),* resistance, revolt, strife, variance *(disagreement)*
contrarily contra
contrariness antipode, conflict, contradiction, difference, disaccord, disagreement, impugnation, incongruity, resistance
contrarious adverse *(opposite),* contradictory, discordant, hostile, lawless
contrarium antithesis
contrarius adverse *(opposite),* contradictory, contrary, inconsistent, opposite
contrariwise contra *(adverb),* contra *(preposition)*
contrary adverse *(opposite),* antipathetic *(oppositional),* antipode, antithesis, competitive *(antagonistic),* contentious, contra, contradictory, deviant, different, discordant, disinclined, disobedient, dissident, dissimilar, eccentric, fractious, froward, hostile, incongruous, inconsistent, inimical, intractable, inverse, litigious, negative, nonconforming, opposite, perverse, recalcitrant, recusant, repugnant *(incompatible),* spiteful, unfavorable, unreasonable, unruly, unsuitable, vicious. SEE MAIN ENTRY
contrary action opposition
contrary advice admonition
contrary assertion confutation, contradiction, denial
contrary to common sense ludicrous
contrary to decency improper
contrary to expectations unforeseeable
contrary to experience implausible
contrary to fact dishonest, fallacious, false *(inaccurate),* fraudulent, untrue. SEE MAIN ENTRY
contrary to good business antitrust act
contrary to good taste improper
contrary to law felonious, illegal, illegally, illegitimate *(illegal),* illicit, impermissible. SEE MAIN ENTRY
contrary to professional ethics unprofessional
contrary to reason arbitrary, contradictory, disproportionate, illogical, impossible, irrational, ludicrous, sophistic
contrary to the rules of logic illogical
contrast antipode, antithesis, collation, compare, comparison, conflict *(noun),* conflict *(verb),* contradict, contradiction, contradistinction, contraposition, contrary, deviate, deviation, differ *(vary),* difference, differentiate, discrepancy, discriminate *(distinguish),* disparity, distinction *(difference),* diversification, incompatibility *(difference),* incompatibility *(inconsistency),* inequality, nonconformity, offset, polarize, vary. SEE MAIN ENTRY
contrast with collide *(clash),* confront *(oppose)*
contrastable adverse *(opposite)*
contrasted antipathetic *(oppositional),* contradictory, contrary, dissimilar, distinct *(distinguished from others),* negative, opposite, peculiar *(distinctive)*
contrasting contrary, different, discriminating *(distinguishing),* discrimination *(differentiation),* disparate, dissimilar, distinct *(distinguished from others),* distinctive, negative, opposite, peculiar *(distinctive)*
contrasting quality differential
contrastive comparative, different, diverse, peculiar *(distinctive),* relative *(comparative)*
contravene abrogate *(annul),* annul, answer *(reply),* circumvent, collide *(clash),* complain *(criticize),* confront *(oppose),* contest, contradict, controvert, counter, countervail, cross *(disagree with),* defeat, demonstrate *(protest),* demur, deny *(contradict),* disaccord, disaffirm, disagree, disallow, disapprove *(reject),* discommode, disobey, disown *(deny the validity),* disprove, dispute *(contest),* except *(object),* gainsay, negate, object, offend *(violate the law),* oppose, oppugn, protest, rebut, refute, reject, repudiate, resist *(oppose),* thwart, trespass, violate, withstand. SEE MAIN ENTRY
contravened broken *(unfulfilled)*
contravening contradictory, negative
contravention ademption, annulment, breach, conflict, confutation, contention *(opposition),* contradiction, counterargument, crime, criticism, denial, disagreement, disapproval, exception *(objection),* impugnation, infraction, infringement, negation, opposition, rejection, resistance, transgression. SEE MAIN ENTRY
contraway contrary
contrawise contra
contretemps accident *(misfortune),* adversity
contretemps casualty, catastrophe, debacle
contretemps deterrence, disaster
contribuere contribution *(donation)*
contribute abet, bear *(yield),* bequeath, bestow, capitalize *(provide capital),* convey *(transfer),* cooperate, create, defray, dole, endow, fund, furnish, give *(grant),* help, inure *(benefit),* involve *(participate),* participate, pay, present *(make a gift),* profit, provide *(supply),* redound, render *(administer),* replenish, spend, subsidize, supply, support *(assist).* SEE MAIN ENTRY
contribute to bear *(support),* cause, compound, espouse, further, promote *(organize),* serve *(assist),* supplement, sustain *(prolong)*
contribute to again refinance
contribute toward conduce, conspire
contributing concerted, concurrent *(united),* contributory, donative

contributing force determinant, expedient, factor *(ingredient)*, instrument *(tool)*
contribution appropriation *(donation)*, behalf, benefit *(conferment)*, charity, collection *(payment)*, donation, endowment, gift *(present)*, gratuity *(present)*, help, largess *(gift)*, subsidy, support *(assistance)*, tip *(gratuity)*. SEE MAIN ENTRY
contributive beneficial, constructive *(creative)*, lucrative
contributor benefactor, determinant, donor, grantor. SEE MAIN ENTRY
contributors press
contributory ancillary *(auxiliary)*, beneficial, donative, gratuitous *(given without recompense)*, instrumental, purposeful, subservient. SEE MAIN ENTRY
contrite penitent, remorseful, repentant. SEE MAIN ENTRY
contrite person penitent
contriteness remorse
contrition remorse
contrivance appliance, arrangement *(plan)*, artifice, collusion, conduit *(channel)*, connivance, conspiracy, expedient, facility *(instrumentality)*, instrument *(tool)*, invention, loophole, machination, ploy, project, resource, scheme, stratagem, strategy, tool. SEE MAIN ENTRY
contrivances paraphernalia *(apparatus)*
contrive arrange *(plan)*, build *(construct)*, cause, circumvent, compose, conceive *(invent)*, conspire, create, devise *(invent)*, forge *(produce)*, form, frame *(construct)*, frame *(formulate)*, frame *(prearrange)*, generate, invent *(produce for the first time)*, make, maneuver, manufacture, militate, originate, plan, produce *(manufacture)*, scheme. SEE MAIN ENTRY
contrive a result frame *(prearrange)*, predetermine
contrive to gain pursue *(strive to gain)*
contrived aforethought, assumed *(feigned)*, controlled *(automatic)*, strategic, tactical
contrived in advance aforethought
contriver accomplice, architect, author *(originator)*, coactor, conspirer
contriving artful, building *(business of assembling)*, collusion, creation, machiavellian, subtle *(insidious)*
control administer *(conduct)*, administration, agency *(commission)*, agency *(legal relationship)*, allay, authority *(power)*, capacity *(authority)*, censor, censorship, charge *(custody)*, check *(bar)*, check *(restrain)*, coercion, compel, composure, conduct, confine, constrain *(restrain)*, constraint *(imprisonment)*, constrict *(inhibit)*, contain *(restrain)*, curb, custody *(supervision)*, damper *(stopper)*, detain *(hold in custody)*, detain *(restrain)*, detention, deterrence, dint, direct *(supervise)*, discipline *(obedience)*, disposition *(final arrangement)*, dominance, dominate, dominion *(absolute ownership)*, dominion *(supreme authority)*, duress, fetter, force *(compulsion)*, force *(strength)*, force *(coerce)*, govern, government *(administration)*, handle *(manage)*, hegemony, hold *(possess)*, hold up *(delay)*, impose *(subject)*, influence, inhibit, jurisdiction, keep *(restrain)*, longanimity, manage, management *(supervision)*, manipulate *(utilize skillfully)*, militate, mitigate, moderate *(preside over)*, moderation, monitor, monopolize, monopoly, obsess, occupancy, occupation *(possession)*, occupy *(take possession)*, operate, overlook *(superintend)*, oversee, own, ownership, patronage *(power to appoint jobs)*, police, possess, power, preclude, predominance, prescribe, preside, prestige, prevail *(be in force)*, prevail *(triumph)*, primacy, prohibit, qualify *(condition)*, quota, regulate *(manage)*, repress, restrain, restraint, restrict, retention, rule *(govern)*, seisin, stifle, subdue, subject, subjection, subjugate, sufferance, superintend, supervision, supremacy, temperance, trammel, trust *(custody)*, wield. SEE MAIN ENTRY
control market supply monopolize
control of the market monopoly
control of trade embargo, monopoly
control prices monopolize
control the flow of news censor
control trade monopolize
controllable corrigible, malleable, obedient, pliable, tractable
controlled arrested *(checked)*, deliberate, dispassionate, limited, patient, qualified *(conditioned)*, regular *(orderly)*, stoical. SEE MAIN ENTRY
controlled by dependent
controller caretaker *(one fulfilling the function of office)*, employer, principal *(director)*, superintendent
controllers hierarchy *(persons in authority)*, management *(directorate)*, management *(supervision)*
controlling cardinal *(basic)*, cardinal *(outstanding)*, dictatorial, dominant, forcible, influential, leading *(guiding)*, master, powerful, predominant, prevailing *(having superior force)*, principal, sovereign *(absolute)*. SEE MAIN ENTRY
controlling factors circumstances
controlling force main force
controlling influence predominance
controlling power clout, main force, patronage *(power to appoint jobs)*, pressure
controlment power
controversia controversy *(argument)*, dispute, lawsuit
controversial arguable, contestable, debatable, disputable, dubious, dubitative, equivocal, forensic, litigable, litigious, moot, polemic, problematic. SEE MAIN ENTRY
controversialist contender, disputant, litigant, party *(litigant)*
controversion contest *(dispute)*, contradiction, contravention, counterargument
controversus controversial
controversy altercation, argument *(contention)*, belligerency, case *(lawsuit)*, conflict, contention *(argument)*, contention *(opposition)*, contest *(dispute)*, contradiction, difference, disaccord, disagreement, discord, disparity, dispute, dissension, dissidence, feud, fight *(argument)*, incompatibility *(difference)*, lawsuit, rift *(disagreement)*, strife, struggle, variance *(disagreement)*. SEE MAIN ENTRY
controversy before a court lawsuit
controvert answer *(reply)*, answer *(respond legally)*, argue, bicker, challenge, collide *(clash)*, conflict, confront *(oppose)*, contest, contradict, cross *(disagree with)*, debate, demonstrate *(protest)*, demur, deny *(contradict)*, disaccord, disaffirm, disagree, disallow, disapprove *(reject)*, disown *(deny the validity)*, disprove, dispute *(contest)*, dispute *(debate)*, gainsay, impugn, negate, object, oppose, oppugn, rebut, refute, reject. SEE MAIN ENTRY
controvertibility cloud *(suspicion)*
controvertible actionable, arguable, contestable, controversial, debatable, disputable, doubtful, dubious, dubitative, forensic, indefinite, litigable, litigious, moot, problematic, speculative, uncertain *(questionable)*, unsustainable, untenable
controverting dissenting
controvertist disputant
contumacious contentious, disobedient, disorderly, froward, impertinent *(insolent)*, inflexible, insolent, insubordinate, intractable, lawless, perverse, recalcitrant, recusant, restive, unruly. SEE MAIN ENTRY
contumaciousness contempt *(disobedience to the court)*, dissidence
contumacy contempt *(disobedience to the court)*, defiance, disloyalty, disrespect, rebellion, resistance
contumax contumacious, froward, insolent, willful
contumelia contumely, reproach
contumeliosus outrageous, scurrilous
contumelious blameworthy, bumptious, calumnious, contemptible, contemptuous, cynical, derogatory, disdainful, impertinent *(insolent)*, insolent, offensive *(offending)*, outrageous, perverse, presumptuous, supercilious
contumeliousness disdain
contumely aspersion, bad repute, contempt *(disdain)*, contempt *(disobedience to the court)*, denunciation, disapprobation, discredit, dishonor *(shame)*, disregard *(lack of respect)*, disrespect, phillipic, reproach, revilement, vilification. SEE MAIN ENTRY
contund beat *(strike)*
conturbare disturb, embarrass
contuse beat *(strike)*
convalesce progress
convalescence revival
convalescent patient
convalescent case patient
convenance decorum
convenant certify *(attest)*
convene call *(summon)*, collect *(gather)*, congregate, converge, join *(bring together)*, meet, rendezvous. SEE MAIN ENTRY
convenience accommodate, advantage, appliance, benefit *(betterment)*, easement, expedience, expedient, opportunity, use, utility *(usefulness)*. SEE MAIN ENTRY
conveniences paraphernalia *(apparatus)*
conveniens consistent, consonant
convenient available, beneficial, constructive *(creative)*, effective *(efficient)*, favorable *(advantageous)*, fitting, functional, opportune, practical, present *(attendant)*, seasonable, suitable. SEE MAIN ENTRY
convenient time timeliness
convenientia coherence, conformity *(agreement)*
convenire coincide *(correspond)*
conventicle collection *(assembly)*
conventio contract, covenant, treaty
convention agreement *(contract)*, assemblage, assembly, bargain, caucus, collection *(assembly)*, compact, company *(assemblage)*, conference, conformity *(agreement)*, congregation, constant, covenant, custom, decorum, formality, habit, meeting *(conference)*, mode, pact, parley, prescription *(custom)*, propriety *(correctness)*, rubric *(authoritative rule)*, session, stipulation, treaty, usage. SEE MAIN ENTRY
conventional accustomed *(customary)*, average *(standard)*, boiler plate, common

(customary), customary, familiar *(customary)*, formal, household *(familiar)*, mundane, nondescript, normal *(regular)*, ordinary, orthodox, popular, prevailing *(current)*, prevalent, proper, regular *(conventional)*, right *(suitable)*, routine, standing, traditional, trite, typical, uniform, usual. SEE MAIN ENTRY
conventional conduct propriety *(correctness)*
conventional language plain language
conventional practice protocol *(etiquette)*
conventional usage prescription *(custom)*
conventionalism custom
conventionalist philistine
conventionalities propriety *(correctness)*, protocol *(etiquette)*
conventionality ceremony, conformity *(obedience)*, custom, decorum, formality, habit, practice *(custom)*
conventionalize conform, formalize
conventionally invariably
conventions decorum
conventions of society decorum
conventus assembly, collection *(assembly)*, compact, congregation, meeting *(conference)*, session
converge adjoin, border *(approach)*, collide *(crash against)*, concentrate *(consolidate)*, congregate, contact *(touch)*, convene, meet, unite. SEE MAIN ENTRY
converge upon approach
convergence adjoiner, caucus, center *(central position)*, centralization, coalescence, coalition, collection *(accumulation)*, collision *(accident)*, company *(assemblage)*, congregation, contact *(touching)*, focus, meeting *(encounter)*
convergency meeting *(encounter)*
convergent adjacent, concurrent *(at the same time)*, contiguous
converging centralization, coalescence, concerted, concurrent *(at the same time)*
converging point center *(central position)*, focus
conversance competence *(ability)*
conversant cognizant, competent, expert, familiar *(informed)*, learned, literate, practiced, proficient, resourceful
conversant with acquainted, informed *(educated)*
conversation communication *(discourse)*, discourse, interview, parlance, parley, speech. SEE MAIN ENTRY
conversational nuncupative
conversations conference
converse adverse *(opposite)*, antipathetic *(oppositional)*, antipode, antithesis, communicate, contra, contradictory, contraposition, contrary *(adjective)*, contrary *(noun)*, discourse, discuss, inverse, negative, opposite, speak. SEE MAIN ENTRY
conversely contra
conversing conversation
conversion appropriation *(taking)*, exchange, misappropriation, persuasion, propaganda, reorganization, transition. SEE MAIN ENTRY
conversion to the government escheatment
conversus inverse
convert adapt, alter, annex *(arrogate)*, change, convince, denature, deprive, impropriate, modify *(alter)*, persuade, pilfer, prevail *(persuade)*, reform, renovate, tamper, transform. SEE MAIN ENTRY
convert to use apply *(put in practice)*, capitalize *(seize the chance)*. SEE MAIN ENTRY
convertere convert *(change use)*
convertere in change
convertible SEE MAIN ENTRY
convertible terms call *(title)*
convey abalienate, advise, alienate *(transfer title)*, allude, annunciate, assign *(transfer ownership)*, attorn, bear *(yield)*, bespeak, bestow, carry *(transport)*, cede, circulate, commit *(entrust)*, communicate, confer *(give)*, connote, consign, construe *(translate)*, contribute *(supply)*, dedicate, delegate, deliver, demise, depict, devise *(give)*, devolve, disabuse, disperse *(disseminate)*, displace *(remove)*, disseminate, express, grant *(transfer formally)*, impart, indicate, let *(lease)*, move *(alter position)*, notify, pass *(advance)*, phrase, post, present *(make a gift)*, purport, recount, relate *(tell)*, relegate, remark, render *(deliver)*, send, signify *(inform)*, transmit, transport. SEE MAIN ENTRY
convey a meaning denote
convey a verbal image portray
convey an impression exemplify, portray
convey an impression of delineate
convey away abduct, carry away, hijack, jostle *(pickpocket)*, kidnap
convey by deed grant *(transfer formally)*
convey for a designated period lease
convey information instruct *(teach)*, mention
convey knowledge apprise, mention, signify *(inform)*
convey knowledge to notice *(give formal warning)*
convey real property for a specified period lease
convey the impression appear *(seem to be)*, demean *(deport oneself)*
convey the meaning of interpret
convey to remove *(transfer)*
conveyable assignable, contagious, heritable, moving *(in motion)*, negotiable
conveyance alienation *(transfer of title)*, assignment *(transfer of ownership)*, cargo, carriage, cession, consignment, deed, delivery, devolution, disposition *(transfer of property)*, removal, transmittal. SEE MAIN ENTRY
conveyance between the living inter vivos
conveyance in consideration of recompense lease
conveyance of interest in real property lease
conveyance of land for a designated period lease
conveyance of realty feoffment
conveyancing alienation *(transfer of title)*, assignment *(transfer of ownership)*, consignment, delivery, demise *(conveyance)*, disposition *(transfer of property)*, feoffment
conveyed orally nuncupative
conveying donative
conveying title feoffment
conveyor carrier
convicium outcry
convict captive, condemn *(punish)*, criminal, felon, hoodlum, inmate, lawbreaker, malefactor, outlaw, prisoner, recidivist, sentence. SEE MAIN ENTRY
convictable culpable, reprehensible
convicted blameworthy, guilty
convicting incriminatory, inculpatory
conviction belief *(something believed)*, belief *(state of mind)*, certainty, certification *(certainness)*, certitude, condemnation *(punishment)*, confidence *(faith)*, credence, determination, dogma, faith, idea, notion, opinion *(belief)*, principle *(axiom)*, principle *(virtue)*, reliance, sentence, standpoint, surety *(certainty)*, trust *(confidence)*. SEE MAIN ENTRY
convictive convincing, persuasive. SEE MAIN ENTRY
convince assure *(give confidence to)*, coax, convert *(persuade)*, inculcate, induce, influence, inspire, motivate, persuade, prejudice *(influence)*, prevail *(persuade)*, prevail upon, reason *(persuade)*, reassure. SEE MAIN ENTRY
convince to the contrary discourage, dissuade, expostulate
convinced affirmative, categorical, certain *(positive)*, definite, indubious, inexorable, positive *(confident)*, secure *(confident)*
convincement surety *(certainty)*
convincible suasible
convincing believable, categorical, cogent, colorable *(plausible)*, credible, determinative, eloquent, forcible, influential, persuasive, plausible, potent, solid *(sound)*, sound, specious, undeniable. SEE MAIN ENTRY
convocare call *(summon)*, collect *(gather)*, convene
convocate call *(summon)*, congregate, converge
convocation assemblage, assembly, caucus, chamber *(body)*, commission *(agency)*, company *(assemblage)*, conference, congregation, meeting *(conference)*, session
convoke call *(summon)*, convene, meet
convolute sinuous
convoluted circuitous, complex, compound, difficult, inextricable, recondite, sinuous, tortuous *(bending)*. SEE MAIN ENTRY
convolution complex *(entanglement)*, digression, distortion, involution
convolutional circuitous, sinuous
convoy accompany, caretaker *(one caring for property)*, carry *(transport)*, protect
convulse agitate *(shake up)*, beat *(pulsate)*, churn, discompose, harass
convulsion cataclysm, commotion, outbreak, outburst, pandemonium, turmoil, violence
cooccupant cotenant
cooccupier cotenant
cool controlled *(restrained)*, inimical, insusceptible *(uncaring)*, moderate *(temper)*, mollify, nonchalant, phlegmatic, placid, unresponsive
cool-headed dispassionate, sensible, sane
coolness disinterest *(lack of interest)*, ill will, indifference, moderation
coop restrict
cooperancy coaction
cooperant associated, mutual *(collective)*
cooperate abide, agree *(comply)*, agree *(contract)*, combine *(act in concert)*, concur *(agree)*, conduce, connive, consolidate *(unite)*, conspire, contribute *(assist)*, espouse, federalize *(associate)*, help, involve *(participate)*, join *(associate oneself with)*, observe *(obey)*, participate, promote *(organize)*, reciprocate, serve *(assist)*, unite. SEE MAIN ENTRY

cooperate with abet, aid, assist, comply, support *(assist)*
cooperate with secretly connive
cooperating concerted, consonant, subsidiary
cooperation accommodation *(backing)*, agreement *(concurrence)*, aid *(help)*, assistance, cartel, coaction, coalition, collusion, compatibility, compliance, concert, conciliation, concordance, conformity *(agreement)*, conjunction, connivance, consensus, contact *(association)*, contact *(association)*, contribution *(participation)*, favor *(sanction)*, federation, help, integration *(assimilation)*, league, pact, partnership, peace, pool, reciprocity, relief *(aid)*, sanction *(permission)*, service *(assistance)*, support *(assistance)*, synergy, understanding *(agreement)*, union *(unity)*. SEE MAIN ENTRY
cooperation for fraud collusion
cooperative ancillary *(auxiliary)*, associated, beneficial, benevolent, coadunate, common *(shared)*, concerted, concurrent *(united)*, consensual, constructive *(creative)*, favorable *(expressing approval)*, harmonious, joint, mutual *(collective)*, synergetic. SEE MAIN ENTRY
cooperative action synergy
cooperative society partnership
cooperativeness coaction
cooperator abettor, accessory, accomplice, assistant, associate, coactor, coadjutant, cohort, colleague, confederate, consociate, conspirer, contributor *(contributor)*, copartner *(business associate)*, copartner *(coconspirator)*, member *(individual in a group)*, participant, partner, party *(participant)*
cooperator in crime coconspirator
cooptatio incorporation *(formation of a business entity)*
cooptation election *(choice)*, selection *(choice)*
cooptive elective *(selective)*
coordinate adjust *(regulate)*, arrange *(methodize)*, centralization, classify, codify, coequal, coextensive, cognate, combine *(act in concert)*, commensurable, complement, concordant, conform, correlate, correlative, correspond *(be equivalent)*, counterpart *(complement)*, equal, file *(arrange)*, fix *(arrange)*, juxtapose, marshal, orchestrate, pool, regulate *(adjust)*, tabulate, unite. SEE MAIN ENTRY
coordinated harmonious, joint
coordination adjustment, compatibility, contribution *(participation)*, regulation *(management)*
coowner partner
copartner accessory, assistant, associate, coactor, consociate, consort, contributor *(contributor)*, member *(individual in a group)*, participant, partisan, partner. SEE MAIN ENTRY
copartner in crime coconspirator, copartner *(coconspirator)*
copartnership affiliation *(connectedness)*, association *(connection)*, company *(enterprise)*, league, partnership, pool, sodality
cope with manage, resist *(withstand)*, withstand
copia fund, hoard, license, opportunity, permission, reserve, stock *(store)*, store *(depository)*, store
copied false *(not genuine)*, imitation, repeated
copiosus copious
copious ample, comprehensive, liberal *(generous)*, profuse, prolific, prolix, replete, voluble. SEE MAIN ENTRY
copious in speech loquacious
copiousness boom *(prosperity)*, sufficiency
copossessor cotenant
copula connection *(fastening)*
copulare join *(bring together)*, unite
copulate cohabit
copy certification *(certification of proficiency)*, correspond *(be equivalent)*, counterfeit, counterpart *(parallel)*, duplicate, facsimile, fake, forgery, form *(document)*, impersonate, mock *(imitate)*, model, personify, pirate *(reproduce without authorization)*, pose *(impersonate)*, record, reflect *(mirror)*, repeat *(do again)*, reproduce, semblance, simulate, trace *(delineate)*, transcript. SEE MAIN ENTRY
copy fraudulently forge *(counterfeit)*
copy from plagiarize
copy in miniature model
copycat killing SEE MAIN ENTRY
copying plagiarism
copyist clerk
copyright SEE MAIN ENTRY
copyright infringement plagiarism
copyright label brand
coquere mature
coratifier comaker
cordial amicable, benevolent, civil *(polite)*, receptive. SEE MAIN ENTRY
cordial assistance patronage *(support)*
cordial relations rapprochement
cordiality benevolence *(disposition to do good)*, comity, consideration *(sympathetic regard)*, courtesy, goodwill, rapprochement
cordon blockade *(barrier)*, chain *(series)*, prize
core body *(main part)*, center *(central position)*, center *(essence)*, consequence *(significance)*, content *(structure)*, cornerstone, corpus, epitome, essence, gist *(substance)*, gravamen, interior, main point, outline *(synopsis)*, point *(purpose)*, substance *(essential nature)*, summary. SEE MAIN ENTRY
core holding SEE MAIN ENTRY
core political speech SEE MAIN ENTRY
corenter cotenant
coresident cotenant
coresidentiary cotenant
corival adversary
cork damper *(stopper)*, obstruction, obturate, occlude, repress, shut, stem *(check)*
cormorant rapacious
corner edge *(border)*, monopolize, perplex, plight, predicament, stand *(witness' place in court)*
corner the market monopolize
cornerstone corpus, foundation *(basis)*, gravamen, mainstay. SEE MAIN ENTRY
cornucopia boom *(prosperity)*, sufficiency
corollary adjunct. SEE MAIN ENTRY
coronation elevation
corporal bodily, corporeal, physical, tangible. SEE MAIN ENTRY
corporal hereditament fee *(estate)*
corporal punishment SEE MAIN ENTRY
corporality body *(person)*, corpus, materiality *(physical existence)*
corporalness body *(person)*
corporate collective, conjoint, joint. SEE MAIN ENTRY
corporate body company *(enterprise)*, corporation, enterprise *(economic organization)*
corporate interest share *(stock)*
corporate governance SEE MAIN ENTRY
corporation affiliation *(amalgamation)*, association *(alliance)*, business *(commercial enterprise)*, company *(enterprise)*, concern *(business establishment)*, enterprise *(economic organization)*, league, trust *(combination of businesses)*. SEE MAIN ENTRY
corporeal bodily, corporal, material *(physical)*, mundane, objective, physical, tangible. SEE MAIN ENTRY
corporeal body object
corporeality body *(person)*
corporealize embody
corporeity corpus, embodiment, materiality *(physical existence)*
corporeous bodily, physical
corporeus bodily, material *(physical)*
corps assemblage, band, organization *(association)*, staff
corps of employees personnel
corpse body *(person)*, cadaver, dead. SEE MAIN ENTRY
corpulent ponderous
corpus body *(main part)*, body *(person)*. SEE MAIN ENTRY
corpus bulk, cornerstone, corpse, entity
corpus substance *(material possessions)*
corpus delecti cadaver
corpus juris code
corpus juris jurisprudence
corpuscle scintilla
corral border *(bound)*, encompass *(surround)*, envelop, shut
correal corporate *(joint)*, joint
correct accurate, actual, adjust *(resolve)*, admonish *(advise)*, ameliorate, amend, appropriate, certain *(positive)*, cure, definite, disabuse, discipline *(punish)*, documentary, due *(regular)*, edit, emend, exact, expostulate, factual, faithful *(true to fact)*, fitting, fix *(repair)*, help, honest, literal, meliorate, meticulous, modify *(alter)*, moral, official, orthodox, penalize, perfect, precise, proper, punctilious, punish, qualify *(condition)*, real, rebuke, rectify, redress, reform, regulate *(adjust)*, remedy, remonstrate, repair, reprehend, reprimand, restore *(renew)*, revise, rightful, sound, suitable, treat *(process)*, true *(authentic)*, valid. SEE MAIN ENTRY
correct behavior protocol *(etiquette)*
correct English plain language
correct valuation appreciation *(perception)*
correctable corrigible
corrected tempered
corrected edition revision *(corrected version)*
correcting revision *(process of correcting)*
correctio amendment *(correction)*, correction *(change)*, reform
correction adjustment, discipline *(punishment)*, modification, panacea, punishment, reform, relief *(legal redress)*, remedial statute, remedy *(that which corrects)*, remonstrance, repair, reparation *(indemnification)*, reparation *(keeping in repair)*, reprimand, reproach. SEE MAIN ENTRY
correction facility reformatory
correctitude propriety *(correctness)*, protocol *(etiquette)*
corrective curative, cure, disciplinary *(punitory)*, medicinal, palliative *(abating)*,

panacea, penal, progressive *(advocating change)*, remedial, remonstrative, salubrious, salutary. SEE MAIN ENTRY
corrective device recourse
corrective measure correction *(punishment)*, recourse, remedial statute, remedy *(legal means of redress)*, remedy *(that which corrects)*
correctly as a matter of right, duly
correctness conduct, decorum, formality, propriety *(correctness)*, protocol *(etiquette)*, qualification *(fitness)*, rectitude, right *(righteousness)*, truth, validity, veracity
correlate adapt, classify, compare, complement, conform, connect *(relate)*, correspond *(be equivalent)*, counterpart *(complement)*, measure, organize *(arrange)*, relate *(establish a connection)*. SEE MAIN ENTRY
correlated apposite, cognate, collateral *(accompanying)*, concordant, germane, interrelated, related, relative *(relevant)*, relevant, tangential
correlation analogy, chain *(nexus)*, collation, comparison, connection *(relation)*, corollary, correspondence *(similarity)*, counterpart *(complement)*, mutuality, parity, proportion, relation *(connection)*, relationship *(connection)*, relevance. SEE MAIN ENTRY
correlative agreed *(harmonized)*, akin *(germane)*, analogous, apposite, coequal, coextensive, cognate, comparable *(capable of comparison)*, comparative, concomitant, concordant, congruous, convertible, counterpart *(complement)*, harmonious, incident, interlocking, interrelated, mutual *(reciprocal)*, proportionate, reciprocal, related, relative *(comparative)*. SEE MAIN ENTRY
correlative agreement mutual understanding
correlativeness mutuality
correlativity mutuality
correspond agree *(comply)*, cohere *(be logically consistent)*, coincide *(concur)*, communicate, compensate *(counterbalance)*, comport *(agree with)*, conform, contact *(communicate)*. SEE MAIN ENTRY
correspondence analogy, balance *(equality)*, coherence, communication *(discourse)*, concordance, conformity *(agreement)*, consensus, consortium *(marriage companionship)*, corollary, dispatch *(message)*, mutuality, parity, propinquity *(similarity)*, propriety *(appropriateness)*, reciprocity, relation *(connection)*, relevance, resemblance. SEE MAIN ENTRY
correspondency coherence
correspondent agreed *(harmonized)*, akin *(germane)*, analogous, apposite, appropriate, coequal, coextensive, cognate, collateral *(accompanying)*, commensurable, complement, concomitant, concordant, congruous, consistent, consonant, contemporaneous, correlate, correlative, counterpart *(complement)*, fit, germane, harmonious, litigant, mutual *(reciprocal)*, pendent, related, relative *(comparative)*, relevant, similar, suitable, uniform. SEE MAIN ENTRY
correspondents press
corresponding akin *(germane)*, analogous, apposite, coequal, coextensive, cognate, coincidental, collateral *(accompanying)*, commensurate, concerted, concomitant, concordant, congruous, consonant, contemporaneous, correlative, faithful *(true to fact)*, harmonious, mutual *(reciprocal)*, pendent, proportionate, reciprocal, relative *(comparative)*, similar. SEE MAIN ENTRY
corresponding part complement, counterpart *(parallel)*
corresponding to comparative, tantamount
corresponding to the contract as agreed upon
corridor avenue *(route)*, portal
corrigendum error, miscue
corrigere ameliorate, amend, emend, rectify, reform
corrigible SEE MAIN ENTRY
corrival contender, contestant, opponent, peer, rival
corrivalry competition, conflict, contest *(competition)*
corroborant salubrious, salutary
corroborate attest, bear *(adduce)*, certify *(attest)*, confirm, countenance, countersign, demonstrate *(establish)*, document, ensure, establish *(show)*, prove, quote, substantiate, sustain *(confirm)*, uphold, validate, verify *(confirm)*, vouch, witness *(attest to)*. SEE MAIN ENTRY
corroborating convincing, demonstrative *(illustrative)*
corroboration avowal, certainty, certification *(attested copy)*, confirmation, consent, documentation, evidence, ratification. SEE MAIN ENTRY
corroborative convincing, deductible *(provable)*. SEE MAIN ENTRY
corroborative excuse alibi
corroborative statement confirmation
corroborator bystander, eyewitness, witness
corrode corrupt, decay, depreciate, destroy *(efface)*, deteriorate, harm, tarnish
corroding caustic, deleterious, peccant *(unhealthy)*
corrosion decline, deterioration, detriment, disrepair, dissolution *(disintegration)*, spoilage, wear and tear
corrosive adverse *(negative)*, bitter *(penetrating)*, caustic, decadent, deleterious, disadvantageous, harmful, harsh, malignant, mordacious, peccant *(unhealthy)*, pernicious. SEE MAIN ENTRY
corrumpere adulterate, corrupt, debase, debauch, deteriorate, falsification, falsify, pervert, spoil *(impair)*
corrupt adulterate, bad *(offensive)*, betray *(lead astray)*, blameful, blameworthy, brand *(stigmatize)*, brutalize, contaminate, contemptible, damage, debase, debauch, decadent, decay, degenerate, delinquent *(guilty of a misdeed)*, denature, depraved, deteriorate, disgrace, dishonest, disreputable, dissolute, distort, faithless, false *(disloyal)*, fraudulent, harm, ignoble, immoral, imperfect, infect, iniquitous, lascivious, lawless, lecherous, lewd, machiavellian, mercenary, misemploy, misguide, mislead, nefarious, odious, outrageous, perfidious, perverse, pervert, pollute, recreant, reprobate, salacious, scandalous, sinister, sordid, spoil *(impair)*, stain, suborn, subvert, sully, tamper, unconscionable, unethical, unscrupulous, venal, vicious. SEE MAIN ENTRY
corrupt agreement connivance, conspiracy
corrupt collusion connivance
corrupt consent connivance
corrupt consenting connivance
corrupt cooperation connivance
corrupt demander extortionist
corrupt demanding extortion
corrupt inducement bribery, corruption
corrupt money bribe, hush money
corrupt offering bribe
corrupt payment bribery
corrupt person degenerate
corrupt use misapplication
corrupted dissolute, marred, perverse, profligate *(corrupt)*
corruptela corruption, seduction
corruptibility bribery, corruption, nepotism
corruptible dishonest, faithless, mercenary, unethical, venal
corrupting detrimental, noxious
corrupting gift gratuity *(bribe)*
corruptio corruption, perversion
corruption bad repute, bribery, crime, decline, defilement, delict, delinquency *(misconduct)*, deterioration, detriment, dishonesty, dissolution *(disintegration)*, graft, gratuity *(bribe)*, guilt, improbity, knavery, malfeasance, misusage, nepotism, perversion, pettifoggery, racket, seduction, spoilage, turpitude, vice. SEE MAIN ENTRY
corruption of purity defilement
corruptness criminality, dishonesty, illegality
coruscate radiate
cosh cudgel
cosharer member *(individual in a group)*
cosharing pool
cosign indorse, witness *(attest to)*. SEE MAIN ENTRY
cosignatory comaker
cosigner comaker
cosmopolitanism experience *(background)*
cost bill *(invoice)*, detriment, expenditure, fee *(charge)*, forfeiture *(thing forfeited)*, loss, maintenance *(upkeep)*, outlay, overhead, penalty, price, rate, rent, toll *(effect)*, value, worth. SEE MAIN ENTRY
cost effective economic
cost incurred expenditure, expense *(cost)*, overhead
cost of commutation fare
cost of conveyance fare
cost of living overhead
cost of reclamation ransom
cost of recovery ransom
cost of transportation fare
cost reducing economic
cost-reducing economical
costing nothing free *(at no charge)*
costless free *(at no charge)*, gratis, gratuitous *(given without recompense)*
costliness expense *(cost)*, expense *(sacrifice)*
costly harmful, inestimable, invaluable, priceless, sterling, valuable
costs damages, disbursement *(funds paid out)*, out of pocket. SEE MAIN ENTRY
costume clothe
cotemporary simultaneous
cotenant SEE MAIN ENTRY
coterie association *(alliance)*, band, confederacy *(compact)*, denomination, organization *(association)*
cottage home *(domicile)*
couch camouflage, cloak, phrase, rest *(be supported by)*
couch in terms express, observe *(remark)*
council bench, board, cabal, caucus, chamber *(body)*, commission *(agency)*, committee, congress, panel *(discussion group)*, parley, session, staff, syndicate, union *(labor organization)*. SEE MAIN ENTRY

council meeting caucus
councilman lawmaker
councilwoman lawmaker
counsel admonish *(advise),* admonition, advice, advise, advocate, apprise, attorney, bar *(body of lawyers),* barrister, caution, charge *(instruct on the law),* confer *(consult),* counselor, deliberation, direction *(guidance),* esquire, exhort, forewarn, guidance, incite, instruct *(direct),* jurist, lawyer, notice *(warning),* notify, persuade, prognosticate, propose, recommend, recommendation, remonstrate, representative *(proxy),* suggestion. SEE MAIN ENTRY
counsel against admonish *(warn),* remonstrate
counsel learned in the law advocate *(counselor)*
counseled familiar *(informed)*
counselling advisory
counselor attorney, barrister, council *(consultant),* counsel, esquire, jurist, lawyer, practitioner. SEE MAIN ENTRY
counselor-at-law advocate *(counselor),* attorney, barrister, counsel, counselor, esquire, jurist, lawyer
counselors bar *(body of lawyers)*
counselors-at-law bar *(body of lawyers)*
count amount *(quantity),* amount *(sum),* assess *(appraise),* calculate, canvass, census, charge *(accusation),* complaint, computation, enumerate, item, itemize, poll *(canvass),* poll, surmise, survey *(poll).* SEE MAIN ENTRY
count against confront *(oppose)*
count ballots survey *(poll)*
count for displace *(replace)*
count on anticipate *(expect),* expect *(anticipate)*
count out eliminate *(exclude),* except *(exclude),* exclude, omit
count up sum
count upon presume, presuppose, rely, trust
count votes survey *(poll)*
countable appreciable, determinable *(ascertainable)*
counted upon foreseeable
countenance advocacy, aid *(help),* allow *(endure),* approval, approve, auspices, authorize, behalf, certify *(approve),* charter *(sanction),* concur *(agree),* condone, consent, demeanor, embrace *(accept),* endure *(suffer),* favor *(sanction),* favor, feature *(appearance),* foster, goodwill, indorse, justify, leave *(permission),* maintain *(sustain),* patronage *(support),* permission, recommend, sanction *(permission),* sanction, sufferance, uphold. SEE MAIN ENTRY
countenancer advocate *(espouser)*
counter adverse *(opposite),* answer *(reply),* antipathetic *(oppositional),* balk, collide *(clash),* condemn *(ban),* contest, contra *(adverb),* contra *(noun),* contra *(preposition),* contradict, contradictory, contrary, controvert, counteract, countercharge, countervail, demonstrate *(protest),* discordant, disinclined, fight *(counteract),* foil, frustrate, gainsay, negate, offset, oppose, opposite, oppugn, parry, prevent, reply, resist *(oppose),* retaliate, retort, return *(respond),* setoff. SEE MAIN ENTRY
counter order nollo prosequi
counter to deviant
counteraccusation contradiction, counterargument, rejoinder
counteract antagonize, avert, balk, circumvent, collide *(clash),* compensate *(counterbalance),* conflict, confront *(oppose),* contradict, contravene, counter, countervail, demonstrate *(protest),* discommode, disprove, disqualify, foil, forestall, frustrate, halt, hamper, interfere, kill *(defeat),* negate, nullify, oppose, outbalance, override, prevent, prohibit, repulse, resist *(oppose),* stem *(check),* stop, thwart, vitiate, withstand. SEE MAIN ENTRY
counteractant contradictory, cure, disadvantageous, offset, preventive
counteracting contrary, hostile, preventive, remedial, renitent
counteraction antipode, collision *(dispute),* conflict, contention *(opposition),* contradiction, contravention, counterattack, counterclaim, deterrent, impediment, impugnation, opposition, protest, rebuff, remedy *(legal means of redress),* repercussion, resistance, revolt, strife
counteractive adverse *(opposite),* competitive *(antagonistic),* hostile, negative, renitent
counteragent offset
counterapplication counterclaim
counterargument contradiction, defense, objection, rejoinder. SEE MAIN ENTRY
counterassault counterattack
counterattack confront *(oppose),* oppose, opposition, reprisal. SEE MAIN ENTRY
counterbalance counteract, cover *(provide for),* equipoise, neutralize, offset, oppose, outbalance, quid pro quo, setoff, stabilize. SEE MAIN ENTRY
counterbalanced agreed *(harmonized)*
counterbid counteroffer
counterblast answer *(respond legally),* counterattack, offset, reprisal, revenge
counterblow counterattack
counterchangeable convertible
countercharge answer *(judicial response),* answer *(respond legally),* charge *(accusation),* confutation, contradiction, count, counterargument, counterclaim, diatribe, impeachment, objection, rebut, recriminate, rejoinder, response, retort, return *(respond).* SEE MAIN ENTRY
countercheck arrest *(stop),* balk, check *(restrain),* counter, prevent, withstand
counterclaim answer *(judicial response),* answer *(reply),* answer *(respond legally),* claim *(legal demand),* counterargument, rebut, respond, retort. SEE MAIN ENTRY
counterclause counteroffer
counterconditions counteroffer
counterdebt setoff
counterdeclaration counterclaim
counterdemand counterclaim, setoff
counterevidence answer *(judicial response),* confutation, contradiction
counterexception counteroffer
counterfeit assume *(simulate),* assumed *(feigned),* bogus, copy, deception, deceptive, disguise *(noun),* disguise *(verb),* dishonest, disingenuous, dupe, erroneous, fabricate *(make up),* fake, false *(not genuine),* falsification, feign, fictitious, forgery, hoax, illusory, imitation, imposture, invent *(falsify),* lie *(falsify),* mendacious, meretricious, mislead, mock *(imitate),* palter, pirate *(reproduce without authorization),* plagiarize, pose *(impersonate),* pretend, prevaricate, profess *(pretend),* replacement, sham, simulate, specious, spurious, subterfuge, synthetic, untrue. SEE MAIN ENTRY
counterfeit copy fake
counterfeit evidence frame up
counterfeited artificial, fraudulent
counterfeiting forgery
countering negative
counterintelligence SEE MAIN ENTRY
counterlimitation counteroffer
countermand abrogate *(rescind),* annul, cancel, cancellation, counter, counteract, debar, disown *(deny the validity),* negate, nollo prosequi, nullify, override, overrule, proscription, quash, recant, renege, repeal, repudiate, repudiation, rescind, rescision, retraction, revocation, revoke, stop, vacate *(void).* SEE MAIN ENTRY
countermandment reversal
countermark trademark
countermeaning antipode
countermeasure counterattack, counter offer
countermine connive, conspiracy, conspire, counteract, fight *(counteract),* foil, maneuver, oppose, thwart
countermotion counterclaim
countermovement counterattack
counteroath contradiction
counteroffensive counterattack
counteroffer SEE MAIN ENTRY
counterorder annul, cancel, cancellation, countermand, prohibition, renege, repudiation, rescind, rescision, retraction, reversal, revocation, revoke
counterpart alter ego, antipode, antithesis, complement, conspirer, contraposition, copy, correlate, reflection *(image),* resemblance, same, semblance. SEE MAIN ENTRY
counterpetition counterclaim
counterplan counteroffer
counterplot collusion, connive, conspiracy, conspire, contrive, counterattack, maneuver, opposition, plan, plot *(secret plan),* reprisal
counterpoint contradistinction, difference
counterpoise cancel, compensate *(counterbalance),* counteract, countervail, equipoise, negate, neutralize, offset, oppose, outbalance, quid pro quo, setoff. SEE MAIN ENTRY
counterpole antipode, antithesis
counterpose fight *(counteract)*
counterpostulation counterclaim
counterpresentation counteroffer
counterpressure deterrent
counterproposal counterclaim, counter offer
counterproposition counteroffer
counterprotest counterargument
counterprovision counteroffer
counterpush counterattack
counterqualification counteroffer
counterreclamation counterclaim
counterrecommendation counteroffer
counterreply answer *(judicial response),* counterargument
counterrequest counterclaim, counteroffer
counterreservation counteroffer
countersign certify *(attest),* confirm, corroborate, cosign, indorse, trademark, underwrite, witness *(attest to).* SEE MAIN ENTRY
countersignature affirmance *(authentication),* affirmance *(judicial sanction)*
counterstatement answer *(judicial response),* argument *(pleading),* confutation, contradiction, counterargument, plea, pleading, rejoinder, reply, response
counterstipulation counteroffer
counterstrike counterattack

counterstroke counterattack, reprisal, retribution, revenge
countersuggestion counteroffer
countersuit counterclaim
countertendency reaction *(opposition)*
counteterrorism SEE MAIN ENTRY
counterthrust counterattack
countervail collide *(clash)*, compensate *(counterbalance)*, contradict, contravention, counter, counteract, disprove, interfere, neutralize, obstruct, oppose, oppugn, outbalance, repulse, withstand. SEE MAIN ENTRY
countervailing contradictory, contrary
counterweigh compensate *(counterbalance)*, oppose, outbalance
counterweight equipoise, offset, setoff
counterwork circumvent, collide *(clash)*, confront *(oppose)*, contradict, counteract, fight *(counteract)*, impugnation, oppose, oppugn, thwart
counterworking contradictory, opposition
counting census, computation
countless copious, infinite, innumerable, myriad, profuse. SEE MAIN ENTRY
country home *(place of origin)*, nationality, polity, realm, region
country house homestead
country of origin home *(place of origin)*
country-wide national, public *(affecting people)*
county province, region, venue
county officer marshal
coup de bec denunciation, diatribe
coup de grâce dispatch *(put to death)*
couple affix, attach *(join)*, bond *(hold together)*, cement, cohabit, combine *(join together)*, commingle, connect *(join together)*, connection *(fastening)*, consolidate *(unite)*, incorporate *(include)*, join *(bring together)*, lock, unite
coupled affiliated, associated, coherent *(joined)*, composite, concomitant, concurrent *(at the same time)*, concurrent *(united)*, conjoint, conjugal, contiguous, nuptial
coupled with along, collateral *(accompanying)*
couplement marriage *(intimate relationship)*
coupling accession *(annexation)*, coalescence, joinder, marriage *(intimate relationship)*, nexus, union *(unity)*
coupon security *(stock)*. SEE MAIN ENTRY
courage confidence *(faith)*, prowess *(bravery)*, spirit, tenacity, tolerance. SEE MAIN ENTRY
courageous heroic, indomitable, spartan, undaunted. SEE MAIN ENTRY
courageous deeds prowess *(bravery)*
courageousness prowess *(bravery)*
courier harbinger, informer *(a person who provides information)*
course access *(right of way)*, act *(undertaking)*, admission *(entry)*, admittance *(means of approach)*, array *(order)*, avenue *(means of attainment)*, avenue *(route)*, behavior, conduit *(channel)*, cycle, discipline *(field of study)*, duration, expedient, method, mode, modus operandi, perambulate, period, platform, policy *(plan of action)*, polity, practice *(procedure)*, procedure, program, rule *(guide)*, strategy, subject *(topic)*, tenor, term *(duration)*, traverse. SEE MAIN ENTRY
course of action arrangement *(plan)*, avenue *(means of attainment)*, campaign, design *(intent)*, direction *(course)*, manner *(behavior)*, method, operation, plan, platform, policy *(plan of action)*, practice *(custom)*, practice *(procedure)*, procedure, proposition, scheme, strategy. SEE MAIN ENTRY
course of an action at law proceeding
course of behavior conduct
course of business custom
course of conduct action *(performance)*, behavior, campaign, habit, maneuver *(tactic)*, manner *(behavior)*, modus operandi, policy *(plan of action)*, practice *(custom)*, practice *(procedure)*. SEE MAIN ENTRY
course of events case *(set of circumstances)*, circumstances, happening
course of law certiorari
course of life behavior
course of proceeding campaign
course of reasoning argument *(pleading)*
coursing fluvial
court bench, board, chamber *(body)*, chamber *(compartment)*, close *(enclosed area)*, courtroom, curtilage, homage, judicatory, judicature, lure, pursue *(strive to gain)*, tribunal. SEE MAIN ENTRY
court action case *(lawsuit)*, lawsuit, matter *(case)*, trial *(legal proceeding)*
court commandment order *(judicial directive)*
court decision determination
court employee clerk
court favor pander
court instruction order *(judicial directive)*
court of appellate jurisdiction appellate court
court of justice bar *(court)*, bench, forum *(court)*, judicatory, tribunal
court of law bar *(court)*, bench, forum *(court)*, judicatory, judicature, tribunal
court of review appellate court
court officer marshal
court official clerk
court order search warrant
court order of imprisonment mittimus
court proceeding action *(proceeding)*
court rule authority *(documentation)*
court scribe clerk
court's finding ruling
court's jurisdiction judicature
court's log calendar *(list of cases)*
courteous civil *(polite)*, obeisant
courteous conduct courtesy
courteously respectfully
courteousness consideration *(sympathetic regard)*, courtesy, propriety *(correctness)*
courtesy benefit *(conferment)*, benevolence *(disposition to do good)*, comity, consideration *(sympathetic regard)*, decorum, deference, favor *(act of kindness)*, honor *(outward respect)*, propriety *(correctness)*, protocol *(etiquette)*, respect. SEE MAIN ENTRY
courtliness consideration *(sympathetic regard)*, courtesy, respect
courtly civil *(polite)*
courtly politeness comity
courtroom forum *(court)*. SEE MAIN ENTRY
courts judiciary
courts of justice judiciary
courtyard close *(enclosed area)*, curtilage
cove haven
coven assemblage
covenant adjustment, agree *(contract)*, agreement *(contract)*, assurance, bargain, bond *(secure a debt)*, cartel, certificate, clause, commitment *(responsibility)*, compact, contract *(noun)*, contract *(verb)*, coverage *(insurance)*, deed, indenture, league, obligation *(duty)*, pact, pledge *(binding promise)*, pledge *(promise the performance of)*, promise, promise *(vow)*, protocol *(agreement)*, sign, specialty *(contract)*, stipulate, stipulation, term *(provision)*, testament, treaty, understanding *(agreement)*, undertake, undertaking *(pledge)*, vow, warrant *(guaranty)*, warranty. SEE MAIN ENTRY
covenant of indemnity specialty *(contract)*
covenanted agreed *(promised)*
covenanter undersigned
coventry ostracism
cover artifice, blind *(obscure)*, camouflage, circumvent, cloak, clothe, comprehend *(include)*, conceal, concealment, consist, disguise *(noun)*, disguise *(verb)*, embrace *(encircle)*, encompass *(include)*, ensconce, enshroud, envelop, harbor, hedge, hide, include, incorporate *(include)*, maintain *(sustain)*, obfuscate, obliterate, obnubilate, obscure, occlude, outbalance, overlap, patrol, penumbra, perambulate, pretense *(pretext)*, pretext, protect, publish, safeguard, screen *(guard)*, seal *(close)*, seclude, shelter *(protection)*, shield, shroud, shut, spread, veil. SEE MAIN ENTRY
cover a beat patrol
cover against loss insure
cover for replace
cover up blind *(obscure)*, camouflage, cloak, clothe, conceal, deface, ensconce, fake, hide, obliterate, obnubilate, obscure, plant *(covertly place)*, suppress. SEE MAIN ENTRY
cover with water immerse *(plunge into)*
coverage extent. SEE MAIN ENTRY
covered blind *(concealed)*, covert, fully secured, hidden, impalpable, ironclad, latent, safe
covering cover *(protection)*, disguise, panoply, protection, protective, shelter *(protection)*, veil
covering a wide area extensive
covering all cases broad
covering fire barrage
covering up evasion
coverless open *(unclosed)*
covert allusive, asylum *(hiding place)*, blind *(concealed)*, clandestine, esoteric, evasive, furtive, hidden, impalpable, inconspicuous, indirect, latent, mysterious, personal *(private)*, potential, private *(confidential)*, privy, protection, recondite, refuge, secret, shield, sly, stealthy, surreptitious, undisclosed, unobtrusive. SEE MAIN ENTRY
covert allusion hint
coverture cohabitation *(married state)*, cover *(protection)*, protection, refuge, shelter *(protection)*, shield. SEE MAIN ENTRY
covet desire, pursue *(strive to gain)*
coveted popular
covetous eager, illiberal, insatiable, jealous, mercenary
covetousness desire, greed
covey band
covin collusion, fraud, machination
covinous collusive, deceptive, evasive, insidious, lying, machiavellian, mendacious, sly
cow browbeat, deter, frighten, hector, humiliate, intimidate
cowardice fear, fright, panic
cowardliness fear
cowardly base *(bad)*, ignoble, recreant
cower fear

cowering recreant
cowork consolidate *(unite)*, conspire, cooperate, unite
coworker accessory, accomplice, assistant, associate, coactor, coadjutant, cohort, colleague, confederate, consociate, contributor *(contributor)*, copartner *(business associate)*, participant, partisan, partner
coworker in crime coconspirator
coworkers personnel
coworking affiliation *(connectedness)*, associated, association *(connection)*, coaction, concerted, concurrent *(united)*, conjoint, synergetic
coxcombry pride
cozen bait *(lure)*, betray *(lead astray)*, bilk, cheat, deceive, defraud, delude, dupe, ensnare, fake, hoodwink, illude, inveigle, mislead, palter, peculate, pretend
cozenage artifice, bad faith, deceit, deception, dishonesty, false pretense, fraud, hoax, indirection *(deceitfulness)*, knavery, maneuver *(trick)*, pettifoggery
crabbed perverse, petulant, recondite
crabby fractious, petulant
crack break *(separate)*, deface, defacement, flaw, force *(break)*, rend, rift *(gap)*, solve, split *(noun)*, split *(verb)*
cradle bear *(support)*, genesis, lull, origin *(source)*, origination, source
craft business *(occupation)*, calling, career, contrivance, deception, device *(contrivance)*, discretion *(quality of being discreet)*, employment, imposture, indirection *(deceitfulness)*, knavery, labor *(work)*, livelihood, occupation *(vocation)*, performance *(workmanship)*, pettifoggery, profession *(vocation)*, prowess *(ability)*, pursuit *(occupation)*, ruse, skill, specialty *(special aptitude)*, trade *(occupation)*, work *(employment)*
craftiness artifice, deceit, deception, evasion, fraud, improbity, indirection *(deceitfulness)*, knavery, pettifoggery
craftsman artisan, practitioner
craftsmanship building *(business of assembling)*, performance *(workmanship)*
craftworker artisan
crafty artful, colorable *(specious)*, deceptive, delusive, devious, disingenuous, evasive, fraudulent, furtive, insidious, machiavellian, perspicacious, politic, practiced, resourceful, sly, stealthy, subtle *(insidious)*, surreptitious, tactical, tortuous *(corrupt)*
crafty design machination
crafty device artifice, machination, maneuver *(trick)*, ruse, stratagem
crafty plan machination
cram constrict *(compress)*, impact, load, overload
crammed compact *(dense)*, full, inordinate, populous, replete
crammed solid replete
cramp block, constrict *(compress)*, deter, disadvantage, encumber *(hinder)*, hamper, hinder, impede, interfere, obstruct, preclude, restrain, restrict, trammel
cramped limited, narrow
cranky fractious, perverse, petulant
cranny rift *(gap)*
crapulence dipsomania, greed
crapulent gluttonous
crapulous gluttonous
crash cataclysm, collision *(accident)*, debacle, discharge *(shot)*, fail *(lose)*, intrude, strike *(collide)*
crash into collide *(crash against)*, jostle *(bump into)*
crash together collide *(crash against)*
crasis condition *(state)*
crass blatant *(obtrusive)*, disreputable, inelegant, tawdry, uncouth
crater split
crave desire, lack, need, require *(need)*
craven caitiff, ignoble, recreant
cravenness fear
craving desire, eager, insatiable, solicitous
craving for drink dipsomania
crawl truckle
crawling obsequious
crawling with people populous
craze compulsion *(obsession)*, furor, mode, obsess, obsession, passion
crazed frenetic, lunatic, non compos mentis
craziness insanity, lunacy
crazy frenetic, irrational, ludicrous, lunatic, non compos mentis
cream main point
cream of society elite
creare appoint, create, elect *(choose)*, make
create appoint, bear *(yield)*, build *(construct)*, cause, conceive *(invent)*, conjure, constitute *(compose)*, constitute *(establish)*, devise *(invent)*, engender, establish *(launch)*, fabricate *(construct)*, find *(discover)*, forge *(produce)*, form, frame *(construct)*, frame *(formulate)*, generate, induce, invent *(produce for the first time)*, make, manufacture, occasion, organize *(unionize)*, originate, produce *(manufacture)*, propagate *(increase)*, reproduce. SEE MAIN ENTRY
create a corporation incorporate *(form a corporation)*
create a disturbance brawl, disrupt
create a false appearance feign
create a false impression delude, dupe, misdirect, misguide, misinform, mislead, profess *(pretend)*
create a fund reserve
create a need necessitate
create a riot brawl
create a stoppage estop
create an opening admit *(give access)*, capitalize *(seize the chance)*
create anew recreate
create by law constitute *(establish)*, legislate
create disorder disrupt
create havoc harry *(plunder)*, mistreat
create strife disagree
create the impression appear *(seem to be)*, demean *(deport oneself)*
created being animal
creating building *(business of assembling)*
creating dissension divisive
creating disunity divisive
creating hostility divisive
creation birth *(beginning)*, composition *(makeup)*, formation, genesis, invention, manufacture, nascency, origin *(source)*, origination, outcome, output, performance *(workmanship)*, product. SEE MAIN ENTRY
creation of a lien hypothecation
creation of housing project development *(building)*
creation of the imagination phantom
creation of the mind figment, phantom
creational productive
creative causal, causative, fertile, primordial, productive, prolific, resourceful
creative effort invention
creative fabrication invention
creative genius mastermind
creative worker practitioner
creator architect, author *(originator)*, derivation, developer, mastermind, parents
creature animal, entity
creature of habit addict
creber frequent
crebritas frequency
credal convincing
credence belief *(state of mind)*, confidence *(faith)*, conviction *(persuasion)*, faith, reliance, trust *(confidence)*, weight *(credibility)*. SEE MAIN ENTRY
credendum doctrine, dogma
credential believable, certification *(certification of proficiency)*, recommendation
credentials certificate, certification *(certification of proficiency)*, degree *(academic title)*, warrant *(authorization)*. SEE MAIN ENTRY
credere delegate, presume, trust
credibilis credible
credibility probability, veracity. SEE MAIN ENTRY
credible authentic, believable, colorable *(plausible)*, competent, convincing, defensible, ostensible, persuasive, plausible, possible, presumptive, probable, reasonable *(rational)*, reliable, sound, specious, unimpeachable, valid. SEE MAIN ENTRY
credible evidence SEE MAIN ENTRY
credibleness credibility, probability, weight *(credibility)*
credit advance *(allowance)*, authorize, character *(reputation)*, citation *(attribution)*, coupon, credence, degree *(academic title)*, distinction *(reputation)*, estimation *(esteem)*, honor *(outward respect)*, impute, loan, mention *(tribute)*, merit, prestige, reference *(citation)*, regard *(esteem)*, reputation, respect, trust, weight *(credibility)*, worth. SEE MAIN ENTRY
credit account letter of credit
credit check coupon
credit note letter of credit
credit with ascribe
credit-worthy meritorious
creditable believable, convincing, honest, laudable, meritorious, moral, reputable, sterling, true *(authentic)*, unimpeachable. SEE MAIN ENTRY
creditable evidence admissible evidence
credited prominent
creditor SEE MAIN ENTRY
credits capital
creditworthy candid, credible, solvent
credo belief *(something believed)*, doctrine, dogma, principle *(axiom)*
credulitas credulity
credulity belief *(state of mind)*, confidence *(faith)*, reliance, trust *(confidence)*. SEE MAIN ENTRY
credulous certain *(positive)*, naive, unsuspecting. SEE MAIN ENTRY
credulousness credulity
credulus credulous
creed belief *(something believed)*, conviction *(persuasion)*, doctrine, dogma
creedal dogmatic
creep prowl
creepy sinister
cremate burn, deflagrate
crescere develop, increase
crest culmination, pinnacle, surmount
crestfallen disappointed, disconsolate, lugubrious
crevice rift *(gap)*, split

crew band, personnel, staff
crib pirate *(reproduce without authorization)*
crier harbinger, informer *(a person who provides information)*
crime bribery, burglary, corruption, delict, delinquency *(misconduct)*, guilt, homicide, infraction, misconduct, misdeed, misdoing, offense, transgression, wrong. SEE MAIN ENTRY
crime committed misdemeanor
crime graver than a misdemeanor felony
crime of violence SEE MAIN ENTRY
crimen accusation, charge *(accusation)*, indictment
criminal aggressor, assailant, blameful, blameworthy, burglar, convict, culpable, delinquent *(guilty of a misdeed)*, delinquent, embezzler, felon, felonious, guilty, hoodlum, illegal, illegitimate *(illegal)*, illicit, immoral, impermissible, iniquitous, irregular *(improper)*, larcenous, lawbreaker, lawless, malefactor, nefarious, offender, outlaw, peccant *(culpable)*, prisoner, racketeer, recidivist, reprehensible, reprobate, tainted *(corrupted)*, thief, unconscionable, unlawful, vandal, vicious, wrongdoer, wrongful. SEE MAIN ENTRY
criminal ablation asportation
criminal accusal information *(charge)*
criminal act misdemeanor, offense, overt act, tortious act
criminal activity crime, felony, guilt, misdemeanor, racket
criminal agreement confederacy *(conspiracy)*
criminal attitude criminality
criminal conduct criminality
criminal deed guilt, offense
criminal design mens rea
criminal guilt mens rea
criminal imitation counterfeit
criminal information supplier informer *(one providing criminal information)*
criminal intent mens rea
criminal interest usurious
criminal offense crime, felony, guilt, misdemeanor
criminal proceeding impeachment
criminal purpose mens rea
criminal rate of interest usury
criminal released at large probationer *(released offender)*
criminal remotion asportation
criminal removement asportation
criminal setting of fires arson
criminal transmission asportation
criminal trial lawyer for the people prosecutor
criminal unchastity adultery
criminal under suspension of sentence probationer *(released offender)*
criminality bad repute, bribery, conviction *(finding of guilt)*, corruption, culpability, delinquency *(misconduct)*, guilt, illegality, knavery, mens rea, mischief, offense, racket. SEE MAIN ENTRY
criminally illegally
criminate accuse, arraign, blame, charge *(accuse)*, complain *(charge)*, denounce *(condemn)*, implicate, incriminate, involve *(implicate)*, present *(prefer charges)*, rebuke, reprimand, reproach
criminate falsely frame *(charge falsely)*
criminate unfairly frame *(charge falsely)*
criminate unjustly frame *(charge falsely)*
criminatio accusation, slander
crimination accusation, allegation, bad repute, blame *(culpability)*, charge *(accusation)*, complaint, count, impeachment, implication *(incriminating involvement)*, incrimination, inculpation
crimination through law enforcement arraignment
criminative critical *(faultfinding)*, incriminatory, inculpatory
criminatory calumnious, critical *(faultfinding)*, incriminatory, inculpatory
criminologist detective
criminosus calumnious
criminous blameful, blameworthy, culpable, felonious, guilty, irregular *(improper)*, peccant *(culpable)*. SEE MAIN ENTRY
criminousness guilt
cringe truckle
cringing obsequious, subservient
cripple damage, debilitate, disable, disarm *(divest of arms)*, foil, frustrate, harm, hinder, impair, interfere, maim, mutilate, obstruct, preclude, thwart
crippled defective, disabled *(made incapable)*, helpless *(powerless)*, imperfect, incapable, marred, powerless
crippling detriment, detrimental, disabling, harmful, pernicious
crisis crossroad *(turning point)*, danger, emergency, exigency, jeopardy, peril, plight, predicament, pressure, problem, quagmire, situation. SEE MAIN ENTRY
crisp compact *(pithy)*
crisscross cross *(intersect)*, intertwine, traverse
criterion canon, pattern, precedent, rule *(guide)*, standard. SEE MAIN ENTRY
critic malcontent
critical acute, crucial, cynical, decisive, discriminating *(judicious)*, essential *(required)*, exigent, grave *(important)*, imperative, important *(urgent)*, indispensable, key, material *(important)*, momentous, necessary *(required)*, nonconsenting, particular *(exacting)*, pejorative, precarious, precise, remonstrative, sensitive *(discerning)*, serious *(grave)*, severe, strategic, urgent, vital. SEE MAIN ENTRY
critical analysis proposal *(report)*
critical appraisal diagnosis
critical article review *(critical evaluation)*
critical attitude doubt *(suspicion)*, misgiving
critical discussion review *(critical evaluation)*
critical examination analysis, criticism, inspection, probe, scrutiny
critical faculty judgment *(discernment)*
critical feature main point
critical happening landmark *(significant change)*
critical juncture landmark *(significant change)*. SEE MAIN ENTRY
critical moment crossroad *(turning point)*
critical occasion landmark *(significant change)*
critical period crossroad *(turning point)*
critical point cornerstone, crossroad *(turning point)*, emergency, main point. SEE MAIN ENTRY
critical remark stricture
critical remarks criticism
critical scrutiny diagnosis
critical situation exigency, plight, predicament, quagmire
critical spirit judgment *(discernment)*
critical viewing inspection
criticalness judgment *(discernment)*, particularity
criticism bad repute, blame *(culpability)*, complaint, condemnation *(blame)*, denunciation, diatribe, disapprobation, disapproval, discredit, disparagement, exception *(objection)*, grievance, ground, guidance, impeachment, impugnation, objection, obloquy, odium, ostracism, outcry, protest, rebuff, remonstrance, report *(detailed account)*, reprimand, review *(critical evaluation)*, revilement, stricture. SEE MAIN ENTRY
criticize blame, comment, condemn *(blame)*, contemn, decry, defame, denigrate, denounce *(condemn)*, disapprove *(condemn)*, discommend, disparage, evaluate, fault, impeach, impugn, judge, minimize, object, proscribe *(denounce)*, rebuke, remonstrate, reprehend, reproach, review. SEE MAIN ENTRY
criticize adversely oppugn
criticize frivolously cavil
criticize severely castigate, denounce *(condemn)*
criticize severly lash *(attack verbally)*
criticized blameful, blameworthy
criticizing severely critical *(faultfinding)*
critique analysis, criticism, diagnosis, inspection, judgment *(discernment)*, review *(critical evaluation)*, review. SEE MAIN ENTRY
cromlech monument
crook convict, embezzler
crooked circuitous, devious, fraudulent, indirect, labyrinthine, machiavellian, sinuous, sly, tortuous *(corrupt)*, unjust, unscrupulous
crookedness criminality, fraud, improbity, indirection *(indirect action)*, irregularity
crop output, product
crop up emerge, occur *(come to mind)*, supervene
crop up again recur
cross annoy, antagonize, bitter *(reproachful)*, conflict, confront *(oppose)*, contentious, contravene, counter, counteract, countervail, discompose, disobey, fight *(counteract)*, fractious, froward, harrow, inimical, interfere, intertwine, oppugn, pass *(advance)*, perambulate, perverse, petulant, plague, querulous, resist *(oppose)*, stress *(strain)*, thwart, traverse. SEE MAIN ENTRY
cross dimension caliber *(measurement)*
cross fire barrage, counterattack
cross in opposition traverse
cross in traveling traverse
cross interrogate cross-examine
cross interrogation cross-examination
cross measurement caliber *(measurement)*
cross off delete, expunge
cross one's mind occur *(come to mind)*
cross out deface, delete, edit, expunge, expurgate
cross purposes contention *(opposition)*
cross question cross-examine
cross section sample
cross the threshold enter *(go in)*
cross with commingle
cross-action counterclaim
cross-bill counterclaim
cross-check collation
cross-examination cross-questioning, interrogation. SEE MAIN ENTRY
cross-examine inquire, reexamine. SEE MAIN ENTRY
cross-grained fractious

cross-interrogation cross-questioning
cross-purposes argument *(contention)*, disaccord. SEE MAIN ENTRY
cross-questioning SEE MAIN ENTRY
cross-tempered petulant
cross-way crossroad *(intersection)*
crossable passable
crossbred promiscuous
crosscut cross *(intersect)*
crossed promiscuous
crossgrained restive
crossing crossroad *(intersection)*, intersection
crossing point intersection
crosspoint intersection
crossroad causeway, intersection. SEE MAIN ENTRY
crosswalk intersection
crossways crossroad *(intersection)*, crossroad *(turning point)*
crotchet obsession
crotchety restive
crouch lurk
crouching obsequious
crowd assembly, collection *(assembly)*, company *(assemblage)*, congregation, constrict *(compress)*, impact, jostle *(bump into)*, mass *(body of persons)*, overload, populace, quantity
crowd together concentrate *(consolidate)*, congregate
crowded compact *(dense)*, populous, profuse, rife
crown culminate, culmination, honor, maximum *(pinnacle)*, pinnacle, surmount
crowning absolute *(ideal)*, best, cardinal *(outstanding)*, definitive, final, last *(final)*, master, paramount, prime *(most valuable)*, stellar, superlative, ultimate. SEE MAIN ENTRY
crowning point crossroad *(turning point)*, pinnacle
crowning touch culmination
crucial acute, central *(essential)*, decisive, essential *(required)*, exigent, imperative, important *(significant)*, important *(urgent)*, indispensable, key, major, mandatory, material *(important)*, momentous, necessary *(required)*, peremptory *(imperative)*, serious *(grave)*, strategic, urgent. SEE MAIN ENTRY
crucial feature main point
crucial moment crossroad *(turning point)*
crucial part necessity, need *(requirement)*
crucial period emergency
crucial point cornerstone, landmark *(significant change)*, main point. SEE MAIN ENTRY
cruciare harry *(harass)*
cruciation intersection
crucify persecute
crude blatant *(obtrusive)*, elementary, harsh, imperfect, inelegant, inexact, inferior *(lower in quality)*, natural, poor *(inferior in quality)*, rudimentary, simple, tawdry, uncouth, unseemly. SEE MAIN ENTRY
crude presentation travesty
crudelis cruel
crudelitas cruelty
cruel bad *(offensive)*, brutal, caustic, cold-blooded, diabolic, harmful, harsh, inexcusable, malevolent, malicious, malignant, oppressive, outrageous, pernicious, relentless, remorseless, ruthless, scathing, severe, sinister, unrelenting, vicious. SEE MAIN ENTRY
cruel act cruelty, misdeed, misdoing
cruel conduct cruelty
cruel hearted cold-blooded
cruel treatment severity
cruelness brutality
cruelty bestiality, brutality, inconsideration, mischief, oppression, severity. SEE MAIN ENTRY
cruise prowl
crumb iota
crumble decay, degenerate, disintegrate, ebb, give *(yield)*, impair, perish
crumbled broken *(fractured)*
crumbling decadent, dissolution *(disintegration)*, erosion, old, precarious
crusade activity, campaign, operation, quest, venture
crusader malcontent
crush beat *(defeat)*, constrict *(compress)*, damage, defeat, demean *(make lower)*, disable, extinguish, foil, humiliate, kill *(defeat)*, overcome *(overwhelm)*, override, overturn, refute, repress, stifle, stop, strangle, subdue, subject, subjugate, suppress, upset
crushed disconsolate, pessimistic
crushed spirits damper *(depressant)*
crushing disastrous, harmful, insufferable, onerous, operose, oppressive, strong
crushing reverse disaster
crusty fractious, froward, perverse, petulant
crutch mainstay
crux cornerstone, gravamen, main point
cry call *(appeal)*, call *(appeal to)*, entreaty, herald, noise, outcry, plaint, proclaim. SEE MAIN ENTRY
cry down decry, denounce *(condemn)*
cry for call *(demand)*, exact, need, request
cry for help pray
cry out against challenge, decry, demonstrate *(protest)*, denounce *(condemn)*, except *(object)*, inveigh, protest, remonstrate
cry out for desire
cry over deplore, regret, repent
cry to call *(appeal to)*, importune
crying blatant *(obtrusive)*, exigent, important *(urgent)*, insistent, manifest, requisite, urgent
cryptic covert, debatable, disputable, enigmatic, esoteric, hidden, indefinable, indefinite, indeterminate, indistinct, mysterious, obscure *(abstruse)*, opaque, oracular, personal *(private)*, private *(confidential)*, privy, problematic, recondite, secret, suspicious *(questionable)*, uncertain *(ambiguous)*, vague. SEE MAIN ENTRY
cryptical covert, obscure *(abstruse)*, private *(confidential)*, privy, problematic, recondite
crystal clear distinct *(clear)*, manifest, palpable
crystal-clear explicit
crystalline lucid, pellucid
crystallization congealment
crystallize cement, consolidate *(strengthen)*. SEE MAIN ENTRY
crystallized ossified
cubicle cell, chamber *(compartment)*
cubiculum cell, chamber *(compartment)*
cuckoldry adultery, infidelity
cudgel beat *(strike)*, lash *(strike)*. SEE MAIN ENTRY
cue frame *(mood)*, guidance, hint *(noun)*, hint *(verb)*, indicant, indication, indicator, reference *(allusion)*, remind, reminder, suggestion, symbol, tip *(clue)*
cue word catchword
cuff beat *(strike)*
cuirass panoply
cul-de-sac impasse
cull choose, compile, extract, glean, reap, select. SEE MAIN ENTRY
culled select
cully bilk, delude, dupe, mislead
culminate carry *(succeed)*, cease, conclude *(complete)*, discharge *(perform)*, mature, perfect, terminate. SEE MAIN ENTRY
culminated complete *(ended)*
culminating conclusive *(settled)*, decisive
culmination ceiling, conclusion *(outcome)*, consequence *(conclusion)*, crossroad *(turning point)*, discharge *(performance)*, end *(termination)*, issuance, maturity, maximum *(pinnacle)*, outcome, performance *(execution)*, pinnacle. SEE MAIN ENTRY
culpa blame *(culpability)*
culpa dereliction
culpa fault *(responsibility)*, guilt
culpa negligence
culpa dignus reprehensible
culpa vacuus innocent
culpability conviction *(finding of guilt)*, criminality, delinquency *(misconduct)*, fault *(responsibility)*, guilt, ignominy, impeachability, implication *(incriminating involvement)*, mens rea, misdoing, onus *(blame)*, opprobrium, responsibility *(accountability)*. SEE MAIN ENTRY
culpable at fault, blameful, blameworthy, contemptible, delinquent *(guilty of a misdeed)*, disobedient, felonious, guilty, iniquitous, peccable, reprehensible, reprobate, sinister, unjustifiable. SEE MAIN ENTRY
culpable conduct criminality
culpable omission misdeed
culpable professional neglect malpractice
culpable recklessness malice
culpableness blame *(culpability)*, ignominy
culpae socius accessory, accomplice
culpandus culpable
culpare blame, condemn *(blame)*, criticize *(find fault with)*, fault
culprit convict, delinquent, embezzler, felon, malefactor. SEE MAIN ENTRY
cultivate ameliorate, cause, develop, discipline *(train)*, educate, enhance, foster, meliorate, nurture, promote *(organize)*, pursue *(carry on)*. SEE MAIN ENTRY
cultivate a habit naturalize *(acclimate)*, practice *(train by repetition)*
cultivated civil *(polite)*, literate
cultivated taste decorum
cultivation civilization, development *(progression)*, discipline *(training)*, education, promotion *(encouragement)*
cultural disciplinary *(educational)*
cultural group race
culture civilization, education, race, society
cultured aesthetic, informed *(educated)*, literate
cultus homage
cum homine contendere compete
cumber clog, deter, disadvantage, encumber *(hinder)*, hold up *(delay)*, impede, load, overload, tax *(overwork)*, trammel, weigh
cumbersome onerous, oppressive, ponderous
cumbrance burden, weight *(burden)*
cumbrous oppressive, ponderous
cumulare perfect
cumulate accumulate *(amass)*, aggregate, compile, glean, hoard, store
cumulated conglomerate
cumulation agglomeration, assemblage, collection *(accumulation)*, conglomeration, corpus, hoard, provision *(something provided)*, selection *(collection)*. SEE MAIN ENTRY

cumulative collective, consecutive. SEE MAIN ENTRY
cumulative effect augmentation
cumulativeness augmentation
cunctari hesitate
cunctatio delay, hesitation, scruple
cunctation deferment, delay, filibuster
cunctative indolent
cunning artful, artifice, clandestine, collusive, color *(deceptive appearance),* deceit, deception, deceptive, deft, delusive, devious, diplomatic, dishonest, disingenuous, faculty *(ability),* fraud, fraudulent, furtive, gift *(flair),* imposture, indirection *(deceitfulness),* insidious, knavery, lying, machiavellian, mendacious, perspicacious, pettifoggery, politic, proficient, prudence, resourceful, skill, sly, stratagem, strategy, subtle *(insidious),* surreptitious, tactical. SEE MAIN ENTRY
cunning contrivance maneuver *(trick)*
cunning practice management *(judicious use)*
cunningness artifice, evasion, knavery
cup prize
cupere desire
cupiditas desire, greed
cupidity desire, greed
cupidus inquisitive, partial *(biased)*
cura caution *(vigilance),* management *(supervision)*
curable corrigible
curare care *(be cautious),* care *(regard),* charge *(custody),* concern *(care),* heed
curative correction *(change),* medicinal, palliative *(abating),* panacea, remedial, salubrious, salutary. SEE MAIN ENTRY
curative preparation drug
curator administrator, caretaker *(one caring for property),* custodian *(protector),* director, guardian
curator procurator
curator superintendent, trustee
curb adjust *(resolve),* allay, arrest *(stop),* assuage, balk, bar *(obstruction),* bar *(hinder),* block, blockade *(barrier),* censorship, check *(bar),* check *(restrain),* constrain *(restrain),* constraint *(restriction),* constrict *(inhibit),* contain *(restrain),* control *(restriction),* damper *(stopper),* debar, delay, detain *(restrain),* deterrence, deterrent, diminish, disadvantage *(noun),* disadvantage *(verb),* discipline *(obedience),* discipline *(control),* disincentive, encumbrance, enjoin, fetter *(noun),* fetter *(verb),* halt, hamper, hinder, hold up *(delay),* impede, inhibit, interfere, keep *(restrain),* lessen, limit, limitation, lock, margin *(outside limit),* mitigate, moderate *(temper),* modify *(moderate),* mollification, mollify, obstacle, obstruct, obstruction, palliate *(abate),* preclude, prohibit, prohibition, quota, repress, restrain, restraint, restrict, restriction, stay, stay *(halt),* stem *(check),* subdue, trammel, withhold. SEE MAIN ENTRY
curb oneself refrain
curbed arrested *(checked),* limited, qualified *(conditioned)*
curbing limiting
curbs confines
cure correction *(change),* drug, help *(noun),* help *(verb),* meliorate, panacea, preserve, rectify, redress, reform, relieve *(give aid),* remedial statute, remedy *(that which corrects),* remedy, renew *(refurbish),* repair *(noun),* repair *(verb),* restore *(renew),* treat *(remedy),* treatment. SEE MAIN ENTRY
cure for all ills panacea
cure-all panacea
cureless incorrigible, inoperable *(incurable),* irredeemable, irremediable, irreversible
curia bar *(court),* board
curing preservation, remedial
curiosa pornography
curiosity interest *(concern),* phenomenon *(unusual occurrence).* SEE MAIN ENTRY
curiosus inquisitive
curious eccentric, extraordinary, inquisitive, noteworthy, prodigious *(amazing),* rare, remarkable, unaccustomed, uncommon, unique, unusual
curiousness interest *(concern)*
curmudgeonly parsimonious, petulant
currency cash, money, publication *(disclosure).* SEE MAIN ENTRY
currency devaluation inflation *(decrease in value of currency)*
current common *(customary),* extant, familiar *(customary),* instant, outflow, popular, present *(current),* prevailing *(current),* prevalent, rife, typical, usual. SEE MAIN ENTRY
current edition revision *(corrected version)*
current expenses overhead
currently existing extant
currently perceived common *(customary)*
curricular didactic
curriculum career
curriculum discipline *(field of study),* plan, program. SEE MAIN ENTRY
currish caitiff
curse expletive, imprecation, malediction, malign, proscribe *(denounce).* SEE MAIN ENTRY
cursed diabolic, odious
cursing blasphemy, profanity, revilement
cursive holographic
cursive hand script
cursive writing handwriting
cursory brief, careless, casual, informal, minor, perfunctory, random, superficial, transitory, trivial. SEE MAIN ENTRY
cursus career, direction *(course)*
curt caustic, compact *(pithy),* laconic, succinct, taciturn
curtail abate *(lessen),* abridge *(shorten),* allay, arrest *(stop),* attenuate, bowdlerize, commute, condense, decrease, diminish, discount *(minimize),* lessen, minimize, palliate *(abate),* reduce, restrain, retrench. SEE MAIN ENTRY
curtailed brief, concise
curtailment abatement *(reduction),* abridgment *(condensation),* abridgment *(disentitlement),* decrease, decrement. SEE MAIN ENTRY
curtain blind *(obscure),* camouflage, cessation *(termination),* cloak, conceal, cover *(conceal),* disguise, end *(termination),* ensconce, enshroud, envelop, hide, obfuscate, obnubilate, obscure, shroud, veil
curtained remote *(secluded)*
curtate concise
curtilage SEE MAIN ENTRY
curtilages confines
curtness disrespect
curved circuitous, sinuous, tortuous *(bending)*
curvilinear sinuous, tortuous *(bending)*
cushion bear *(support),* ease, mitigate, modify *(moderate),* protect
custodia charge *(custody),* custody *(supervision),* detention, incarceration
custodial protective. SEE MAIN ENTRY
custodial detention arrest
custodian administrator, caretaker *(one caring for property),* executor, fiduciary, guardian, superintendent, trustee, warden. SEE MAIN ENTRY
custodian of the law peace officer
custodians management *(directorate)*
custodians of the law police, posse
custodianship bondage, constraint *(imprisonment),* custody *(supervision),* detention, incarceration, retention. SEE MAIN ENTRY
custodire protect
custody adoption *(affiliation),* auspices, bondage, captivity, constraint *(imprisonment),* control *(supervision),* detention, durance, enclosure, incarceration, possession *(ownership),* preservation, protection, quarantine, restraint, safekeeping, thrall, ward. SEE MAIN ENTRY
custom criterion, decorum, excise, form *(arrangement),* formality, habit, manner *(behavior),* method, mode, procedure, rule *(guide),* style, usage, way *(channel).* SEE MAIN ENTRY
customarily as a rule, generally, invariably
customariness habituation
customary boiler plate, conventional, current, formal, frequent, general, habitual, household *(familiar),* inveterate, mundane, normal *(regular),* ordinary, orthodox, popular, prescriptive, prevailing *(current),* prevalent, pro forma, regular *(conventional),* repeated, rife, right *(suitable),* routine, traditional, typical, usual. SEE MAIN ENTRY
customary action habit
customary conduct habit
customary course practice *(custom)*
customary manner of procedure course
customary procedure manner *(behavior),* matter of course
customary use usage. SEE MAIN ENTRY
customary way avenue *(means of attainment)*
customer client, consumer, patron *(regular customer).* SEE MAIN ENTRY
customer approval goodwill
customer encouragement goodwill
customers' man broker
customs protocol *(etiquette)*
customs documents bill *(formal declaration)*
custos guardian, trustee, warden
cut bowdlerize, break *(fracture),* censor, commute, curtail, decrease *(noun),* decrease *(verb),* decrement, deduct *(reduce),* deduction *(diminution),* delete, depreciate, discontinue *(break continuity),* discount *(reduce),* divide *(separate),* division *(act of dividing),* edit, excise *(cut away),* expurgate, ignore, interrupt, lancinate, lessen, minimal, mutilate, reap, rebate *(noun),* rebate *(verb),* refund, rend, retrench, sever, split *(noun),* split *(verb),* subdivide, tenor. SEE MAIN ENTRY
cut across cross *(intersect),* traverse
cut adrift dissociate, separate, sever
cut apart disconnected
cut back decrease, diminish
cut down abridge *(shorten),* curtail, decrease, deduct *(reduce),* digest *(summarize),* diminish, dispatch *(put to death),* extirpate, lessen, minimize, reduce, retrench

cut down to size minimize
cut in halves dichotomize
cut in two bifurcate, dichotomize, disconnected, part *(separate)*
cut into enter *(penetrate)*, lancinate
cut loose disengage, extricate
cut off border *(bound)*, check *(restrain)*, decrease, disband, discrete, disengage, disinherit, disown *(refuse to acknowledge)*, dissociate, estop, estrange, insulate, isolate, lock, preclude, prevent, rescind, seclude, separate, toll *(stop)*. SEE MAIN ENTRY
cut off from inheritance disinherit
cut out bowdlerize, delete, eliminate *(eradicate)*, eviscerate, excise *(cut away)*, expel, expurgate, extinguish, omit, quit *(discontinue)*, redact. SEE MAIN ENTRY
cut out of one's will disinherit, disown *(refuse to acknowledge)*
cut short brief, condense, curtail, decrease, discontinue *(break continuity)*, halt, minimize, rescind, retrench, stop
cut through enter *(penetrate)*, penetrate, pierce *(lance)*
cut up disjoint, partition
cut-back curtailment
cut-rate nominal
cutback decrease
cutting acute, bitter *(acrid tasting)*, bitter *(penetrating)*, caustic, division *(act of dividing)*, incisive, mordacious, part *(portion)*, scathing, trenchant
cutting down curtailment
cutting off curtailment
cutting words diatribe
cy press SEE MAIN ENTRY
cyber crime SEE MAIN ENTRY
cyberbullying SEE MAIN ENTRY
cyberterrorism SEE MAIN ENTRY
cycle annum, frequency, life *(period of existence)*, sequence, succession. SEE MAIN ENTRY
cyclic intermittent, periodic, regular *(orderly)*
cyclical chronic, intermittent, periodic
cyclopean prodigious *(enormous)*
cynical critical *(faultfinding)*, disdainful, inconvincible, ironic, pejorative, pessimistic, skeptical. SEE MAIN ENTRY
cynicism irony, pessimism, suspicion *(mistrust)*. SEE MAIN ENTRY
cynosure highlight, landmark *(conspicuous object)*
cyprian prurient

D

dab iota
daedal elaborate
daft lunatic
daftness insanity
daily habitual, ordinary, usual. SEE MAIN ENTRY
daily paper journal
daily register journal
dalliance deferment, delay
dally hesitate, pause, procrastinate, stall
dallying hesitant, otiose
dam block, clog, constrict *(inhibit)*, halt, lock, obstacle, obstruction, shut
dam up discontinue *(break continuity)*, impede, occlude, stem *(check)*, stop
damage abuse *(physical misuse)*, cost *(penalty)*, countervail, decrement, deface, defacement, defect, detriment, disable, disadvantage *(noun)*, disadvantage *(verb)*, disrepair, disservice, drawback, endanger, eviscerate, expense *(sacrifice)*, harm *(noun)*, harm *(verb)*, ill use, impair, injury, maim, mischief, mutilate, persecute, pillage, prejudice *(injury)*, prejudice *(injure)*, spoil *(impair)*, stain, strike *(assault)*, toll *(effect)*, vitiate, wear and tear. SEE MAIN ENTRY
damage a reputation pillory
damage irreparably spoil *(impair)*
damage one's reputation defame
damaged aggrieved *(victimized)*, blemished, broken *(fractured)*, defective, dilapidated, faulty, imperfect, inferior *(lower in quality)*, marred
damages amercement, compensation, cost *(penalty)*, expiation, out of pocket, punishment, recompense, recovery *(award)*, reimbursement, reparation *(indemnification)*, restitution, satisfaction *(discharge of debt)*, trover. SEE MAIN ENTRY
damaging calumnious, chilling effect, contemptuous, deleterious, destructive, detrimental, disabling, disadvantageous, disastrous, disgraceful, harmful, incriminatory, inculpatory, insalubrious, libelous, malevolent, malignant, noxious, pejorative, pernicious, pestilent, prejudicial, scathing, toxic, unfavorable. SEE MAIN ENTRY
damaging report scandal, slander
damn proscribe *(denounce)*
damnable contemptible, heinous, odious
damnare condemn *(punish)*, sentence
damnatio conviction *(finding of guilt)*
damnation blame *(culpability)*, conviction *(finding of guilt)*, denunciation, disapprobation, disparagement, imprecation, malediction
damnatory blameful, blameworthy, calumnious, critical *(faultfinding)*, incriminatory, inculpatory, libelous, profane, scandalous
damnified aggrieved *(harmed)*
damning incriminatory, inculpatory
damnosus prejudicial
damnum detriment, harm, injury, loss, mischief
damnum restituere indemnify
damnum sarcire indemnify
damp repress, stifle, thwart
damp down diminish
dampen alleviate, decrease, depress, deter, diminish, discourage, moderate *(temper)*, repress. SEE MAIN ENTRY
damper check *(bar)*, deterrent, disincentive, impediment, restraint. SEE MAIN ENTRY
dander resentment
dandify embellish
dandyism pride
danger hazard, jeopardy, menace, mischief, peril, pitfall, predicament, risk, threat, venture. SEE MAIN ENTRY
danger signal symptom
danger-loving hot-blooded
dangerous aleatory *(perilous)*, deadly, formidable, harmful, insalubrious, insecure, lethal, malignant, noxious, ominous, peccant *(unhealthy)*, pestilent, precarious, serious *(grave)*, sinister, vicious. SEE MAIN ENTRY
dangerous condition predicament
dangerous course hazard
dangerous person delinquent
dangerous situation hazard, jeopardy, menace, peril
dangerous spot pitfall
dangerous to life deadly
dangerous undertaking venture
dangerousness jeopardy
dangle before the eyes brandish
dare defiance, defy, endanger
dare grant *(concede)*
dare speculate *(chance)*
dare not fear
dare say opine, presume, remark, speculate *(conjecture)*
daredevil hot-blooded
daring audacity, brazen, defiance, flagrant, heroic, hot-blooded, impulsive *(rash)*, original *(creative)*, presumptuous, prowess *(bravery)*, spartan, spirit, temerity, undaunted. SEE MAIN ENTRY
dark bleak *(not favorable)*, covert, hidden, incomprehensible, lugubrious, mysterious, ominous, opaque, portentous *(ominous)*, private *(confidential)*, privy, recondite, secret
dark *(devoid of light)*. SEE MAIN ENTRY
dark *(dismal)*. SEE MAIN ENTRY
dark *(evil)*. SEE MAIN ENTRY
darken depress, obfuscate, obnubilate, obscure, shroud, tarnish
darkening obscuration
darkle obscure
darkness ignorance, nescience, obscuration, opacity
darn repair
dart race
dash beat *(defeat)*, dispatch *(promptness)*, foil, haste, hasten, iota, minimum, race, spirit
dash against impinge
dash one's expectation disappoint
dash one's hopes foil
dashed disappointed
dashed hopes pessimism
dastardly caitiff, recreant, scandalous
data clue, documentation, dossier, ground, information *(facts)*, intelligence *(news)*, proof, reference *(citation)*, science *(study)*. SEE MAIN ENTRY
data paper pandect *(treatise)*
data sheet blank *(form)*, form *(document)*
database SEE MAIN ENTRY
date age, appointment *(meeting)*, rendezvous. SEE MAIN ENTRY
date back antedate
date before the true date antedate
date before the true time antedate
date earlier than the fact antedate
date rape. SEE MAIN ENTRY
dated obsolete, outdated, outmoded
dated *(antiquated)*. SEE MAIN ENTRY
dated *(date-stamped)*. SEE MAIN ENTRY
dateless permanent
daub stain, sully
daughter child
daunt browbeat, discourage, dissuade, frighten, intimidate
dauntless heroic, indomitable, spartan, undaunted
dauntlessness prowess *(bravery)*
dawdle pause, procrastinate, stall
dawn emerge, genesis, inception, onset *(commencement)*, origin *(source)*, origination, outset, start
dawning prime *(original)*
day date
day *(24 hours)*. SEE MAIN ENTRY
day *(morning)*. SEE MAIN ENTRY
day book register
day in court SEE MAIN ENTRY
day of festivities holiday
day of grace reprieve
day of the week date

day off holiday
daybook calendar *(record of yearly periods)*, journal, ledger
daydream muse
daydreaming preoccupation
daze confuse *(bewilder)*, discompose, disorganize, muddle, obfuscate, overcome *(overwhelm)*, overwhelm
dazed insensible, thoughtless
dazzle delude, discompose, prestige
dazzling meritorious
de facto actual
de facto bodily. SEE MAIN ENTRY
de facto material *(physical)*
de jure ex officio. SEE MAIN ENTRY
de jure jural
de minimus SEE MAIN ENTRY
de novo SEE MAIN ENTRY
de re decedere waive
de re disserere argue
de rigueur binding
déabacle disaster
deactivate counteract, disable, disarm *(divest of arms)*, disband, disorganize, neutralize, palliate *(abate)*. SEE MAIN ENTRY
deactivated dormant, lifeless *(dull)*
deactivation deterrent
dead deceased, defunct, late *(defunct)*, null *(invalid)*, obsolete, pedestrian, torpid. SEE MAIN ENTRY
dead body cadaver, corpse
dead certainty certitude
dead end deadlock, impasse, quagmire
dead heat deadlock, draw *(tie)*
dead man decedent
dead person corpse, decedent
dead set SEE MAIN ENTRY
dead stop impasse
dead-end blind *(impassable)*
deaden allay, drug, extinguish, mollify, neutralize, obtund, repress, soothe, stifle, subdue
deadened lifeless *(dull)*
deadening abatement *(extinguishment)*, mollification, narcotic
deadliness fatality, harm
deadlock abeyance, check *(bar)*, clog, draw *(tie)*, halt *(noun)*, halt *(verb)*, impasse, impede, interruption, quagmire, stem *(check)*. SEE MAIN ENTRY
deadly dangerous, deleterious, diabolic, dire, disastrous, fatal, irremediable, lethal, malevolent, malignant, peccant *(unhealthy)*, pedestrian, pernicious, pestilent, ruthless, toxic, virulent. SEE MAIN ENTRY
deadly accident fatality
deadly device cudgel
deadly devices weapons
deadly weapon cudgel
deadly weapons weapons
deadpan inexpressive, inscrutable
deadstop check *(bar)*
deadweight incumbrance *(burden)*
deaf heedless, incognizant, insensible, insusceptible *(uncaring)*
deaf to impervious
deaf to reason restive
deafening powerful
deafening row brawl
deal agreement *(contract)*, allocate, allot, attornment, barter, bestow, compact, compromise, contract, dicker, dispense, disperse *(disseminate)*, distribute, dole, exchange, give *(grant)*, haggle, inflict, league, pact, project, sort, split, stipulation, trade *(commerce)*, trade, transact, transaction, treaty. SEE MAIN ENTRY
deal a blow assault, oppugn, strike *(assault)*
deal a blow to lash *(strike)*
deal a death blow dispatch *(put to death)*
deal a stroke lash *(strike)*
deal again reassign
deal crookedly palter
deal destruction destroy *(efface)*, eradicate, extinguish, extirpate
deal hard measure to ill use
deal in handle *(trade)*, sell, vend
deal in futures invest *(fund)*, speculate *(chance)*
deal in generalities generalize
deal out administer *(tender)*, allocate, apportion, assign *(allot)*, diffuse, disburse *(distribute)*, dispel, disperse *(disseminate)*, dispose *(apportion)*, disseminate, marshal, mete, parcel, supply
deal out again redistribute
deal out anew reapportion
deal retributive justice castigate, condemn *(punish)*, discipline *(punish)*
deal secretly plot
deal to dispense
deal with appertain, apply *(pertain)*, communicate, concern *(involve)*, conduct, correspond *(be equivalent)*, handle *(manage)*, militate, operate, patronize *(trade with)*, transact, treat *(process)*
deal with definitely dispatch *(dispose of)*
deal with gently favor
dealer broker, go-between, merchant, vendor. SEE MAIN ENTRY
dealer in illicit goods racketeer
dealing act *(undertaking)*, commerce, management *(judicious use)*, transaction
dealing death aberemurder, capital punishment
dealing out disbursement *(act of disbursing)*, distribution *(apportionment)*
dealings business *(commerce)*, conduct, contact *(association)*, overt act. SEE MAIN ENTRY
deals dealings
dean veteran
dear close *(intimate)*, exorbitant, priceless, scarce, valuable
dearth deficiency, deficit, delinquency *(shortage)*, indigence, insufficiency, need *(deprivation)*, paucity, poverty, privation. SEE MAIN ENTRY
dearth of ideas platitude
death capital punishment, dissolution *(termination)*, end *(termination)*, expiration, fatality, mortality. SEE MAIN ENTRY
death by accident fatality
death by violence dispatch *(act of putting to death)*
death sentence capital punishment
death-bringing deadly, lethal, malignant, pernicious
death-dealing deadly, fatal, lethal, malignant, pernicious, pestilent
death penalty SEE MAIN ENTRY
death sentence SEE MAIN ENTRY
deathblow dispatch *(act of putting to death)*
deathful deadly, pernicious
deathless perpetual
deathly deadly, fatal, lethal, malignant, pernicious, pestilent
débâcle casualty
debacle cataclysm
débâcle catastrophe
debacle failure *(lack of success)*
débâcle revolution
debacle subversion. SEE MAIN ENTRY
debar bar *(exclude)*, block, condemn *(ban)*, constrain *(restrain)*, disable, disqualify, eliminate *(exclude)*, exclude, fight *(counteract)*, forbid, halt, hamper, inhibit, interdict, obstruct, occlude, preclude, prevent, prohibit, refuse, remove *(eliminate)*, restrain, restrict, thwart, trammel, withhold. SEE MAIN ENTRY
debarkation point destination
debarment embargo, exclusion, expulsion, prohibition, refusal, rejection, removal
debarred barred
debarring blockade *(limitation)*, boycott
debase adulterate, brand *(stigmatize)*, contaminate, contemn, corrupt, damage, debauch, degenerate, demean *(make lower)*, demote, depreciate, derogate, deteriorate, disapprove *(condemn)*, discredit, disgrace, dishonor *(deprive of honor)*, disoblige, disparage, harm, humiliate, infect, libel, mistreat, pillory, pollute, spoil *(impair)*, stain, sully, taint *(corrupt)*, tamper. SEE MAIN ENTRY
debase in quality degenerate
debased depraved, dissolute, ignoble, sordid, tainted *(corrupted)*, vicious
debased person degenerate
debasement abuse *(physical misuse)*, attaint, bad faith, bad repute, contempt *(disdain)*, corruption, defilement, degradation, depression, deterioration, discredit, disgrace, dishonor *(shame)*, disrepute, ignominy, misusage, obloquy, odium, opprobrium, perversion, shame
debatable arguable, contestable, controversial, disputable, doubtful, dubious, equivocal, indefinite, litigious, moot, polemic, problematic, speculative, uncertain *(questionable)*, undecided. SEE MAIN ENTRY
debatable issue thesis
debatable point issue *(matter in dispute)*, matter *(subject)*, thesis
debate answer *(reply)*, argue, argument *(contention)*, challenge, conflict *(noun)*, conflict *(verb)*, consider, contention *(argument)*, contention *(opposition)*, contest *(dispute)*, contest, contravention, controversy *(argument)*, controvert, converse, cross *(disagree with)*, deliberate, deliberation, discord *(noun)*, disaccord *(verb)*, disagree, disagreement, discourse, discuss, dispute, doubt *(hesitate)*, fight *(argument)*, muse, oppose, oscillate, parley, ponder, reason *(persuade)*, refute, respond, speculate *(conjecture)*, treat *(process)*, vacillate. SEE MAIN ENTRY
debater contender
debating dissenting, hesitant
debauch abuse *(violate)*, betray *(lead astray)*, carouse, contemn, corrupt, debase, degenerate, deteriorate, dishonor *(deprive of honor)*, pervert, pollute, taint *(corrupt)*. SEE MAIN ENTRY
débauche delineation
debauched bad *(offensive)*, decadent, depraved, dissolute, gluttonous, immoral, lascivious, lecherous, licentious, obscene, peccant *(culpable)*, perverse, profligate *(corrupt)*, promiscuous, prurient, salacious, tainted *(corrupted)*
debauchee degenerate, wrongdoer
debauchery perversion, vice. SEE MAIN ENTRY

debauchment debauchery, defilement. SEE MAIN ENTRY
debenture bond, charge *(lien)*, check *(instrument)*, draft, note *(written promise to pay)*, security *(pledge)*, specialty *(contract)*. SEE MAIN ENTRY
debere owe
deberi due
debilitare disable, impair
debilitate adulterate, attenuate, depreciate, deteriorate, disable, disarm *(divest of arms)*, eviscerate, exhaust *(deplete)*, extenuate, impair, mutilate, tax *(overwork)*. SEE MAIN ENTRY
debilitated disabled *(made incapable)*, helpless *(powerless)*, lifeless *(dull)*, powerless
debilitating disabling
debilitation disability *(physical inability)*, impotence
debility disability *(physical inability)*, fault *(weakness)*, frailty, impotence, impuissance, languor, prostration
debit arrears, charge *(cost)*, debt, due, expense *(cost)*, liability, obligation *(liability)*. SEE MAIN ENTRY
debitus condign, due *(owed)*, overdue
debouch emanate
debouchment issuance
debrief SEE MAIN ENTRY
debris discard
debt arrears, cloud *(incumbrance)*, debit, delinquency *(shortage)*, due, duty *(obligation)*, liability, lien, obligation *(duty)*, obligation *(liability)*. SEE MAIN ENTRY
debt limit SEE MAIN ENTRY
debt owed setoff
debt service SEE MAIN ENTRY
debt unpaid though due arrears
debtee creditor
debtor obligor. SEE MAIN ENTRY
debunk disabuse, disapprove *(reject)*, disgrace, reveal. SEE MAIN ENTRY
debut birth *(beginning)*, first appearance, inception, nascency. SEE MAIN ENTRY
debutant neophyte
decadence caducity, degradation, delinquency *(misconduct)*, deterioration, detriment, disrepair, turpitude. SEE MAIN ENTRY
decadency decline, degradation, disrepair
decadent dissolute, old, regressive. SEE MAIN ENTRY
decadent person degenerate
decamp abandon *(physically leave)*, abduct, abscond, depart, disappear, escape, evacuate, flee, leave *(depart)*, quit *(evacuate)*, retire *(retreat)*, retreat. SEE MAIN ENTRY
decampment abandonment *(desertion)*, flight
decant outpour
decay caducity, consumption, corrupt, decline, decline *(fall)*, degenerate, depreciate, deteriorate, deterioration, detriment, disintegrate, disrepair, dissolution *(disintegration)*, disuse, ebb, erode, erosion, languish, prostration, spoil *(impair)*, spoilage, taint *(contaminate)*, wear and tear. SEE MAIN ENTRY
decayed old, sordid, stale, unsound *(not strong)*
decaying bad *(inferior)*, decadent
decease death, demise *(death)*, die, end *(termination)*, expire. SEE MAIN ENTRY
deceased corpse, dead, decedent, defunct, late *(defunct)*, lifeless *(dead)*. SEE MAIN ENTRY
deceased person decedent
decedent dead. SEE MAIN ENTRY
decedere secede
deceit artifice, bad faith, canard, collusion, color *(deceptive appearance)*, deception, dishonesty, evasion, false pretense, falsification, fraud, hoax, hypocrisy, imposture, improbity, indirection *(deceitfulness)*, knavery, lie, misstatement, pettifoggery, pretense *(pretext)*, ruse, story *(falsehood)*, stratagem. SEE MAIN ENTRY
deceitful collusive, colorable *(specious)*, deceptive, delusive, devious, dishonest, disingenuous, evasive, faithless, fallacious, false *(disloyal)*, false *(not genuine)*, fraudulent, furtive, insidious, lying, machiavellian, mendacious, meretricious, perfidious, politic, recreant, sly, spurious, subtle *(insidious)*, surreptitious, tortuous *(corrupt)*, undependable, unreliable, unscrupulous, untrue, untrustworthy. SEE MAIN ENTRY
deceitful agreement collusion
deceitful compact collusion
deceitful practice fraud
deceitfulness bad faith, collusion, concealment, deceit, dishonesty, duplicity, evasion, false pretense, falsification, fraud, hypocrisy, improbity, infidelity, knavery, misrepresentation
deceivability credulity
deceivable credulous, naive
deceive bait *(lure)*, betray *(lead astray)*, bilk, camouflage, cheat, circumvent, cloak, defraud, delude, disguise, dupe, ensnare, entrap, equivocate, fabricate *(make up)*, fake, feign, foist, hide, hoodwink, illude, inveigle, lie *(falsify)*, misguide, misinform, mislabel, mislead, misrepresent, misstate, mulct *(defraud)*, overreach, palter, peculate, pettifog, pretend, prevaricate. SEE MAIN ENTRY
deceive by treachery betray *(lead astray)*
deceive oneself miscalculate, misconceive
deceiver conspirator
deceiving colorable *(specious)*, deceptive, delusive, dishonest, disingenuous, evasive, fallacious, false *(inaccurate)*, fictitious, fraudulent, illusory, insidious, machiavellian, mendacious, ostensible, perfidious, sly, specious
decelerate decrease, diminish, hold up *(delay)*, impede, moderate *(temper)*, palliate *(abate)*
deceleration decrease, delay
decencies decorum
decency clemency, decorum, propriety *(correctness)*
decent benevolent, clean, ethical, fair *(satisfactory)*, honest, humane, mediocre, meritorious, moral, suitable
decently fairly *(moderately)*
decentralization SEE MAIN ENTRY
decentralize diffuse, disperse *(scatter)*, dissolve *(separate)*, distribute
deception artifice, bad faith, canard, collusion, color *(deceptive appearance)*, contrivance, corruption, counterfeit, deceit, decoy, disguise, dishonesty, distortion, duplicity, evasion, fallacy, falsehood, falsification, figment, forgery, fraud, hoax, hypocrisy, imposture, indirection *(deceitfulness)*, knavery, lie, maneuver *(trick)*, misrepresentation, misstatement, pettifoggery, plot *(secret plan)*, pretense *(pretext)*, pretext, ruse, sham, sophistry, story *(falsehood)*, stratagem, subreption, subterfuge. SEE MAIN ENTRY
deceptious sly
deceptive artificial, assumed *(feigned)*, collusive, colorable *(specious)*, delusive, dishonest, disingenuous, equivocal, evasive, fallacious, false *(inaccurate)*, false *(not genuine)*, fraudulent, illusory, imitation, insidious, lying, machiavellian, meretricious, ostensible, sly, specious, spurious, subtle *(insidious)*, surreptitious, untrue, untrustworthy. SEE MAIN ENTRY
deceptive belief fallacy
deceptive check bad check
deceptive covering color *(deceptive appearance)*, disguise
deceptive representation of fact false pretense
deceptive statement misrepresentation
deceptiveness deceit, fraud, misrepresentation
decernere contend *(dispute)*, decide, determine, resolve *(decide)*
decerpere cull
decessio discount, discount *(disbelieve)*
decide adjudge, adjudicate, arbitrate *(adjudge)*, ascertain, award, choose, deem, determine, dispose *(incline)*, elect *(choose)*, find *(determine)*, fix *(settle)*, gauge, hear *(give a legal hearing)*, judge, pass *(determine)*, prescribe, pronounce *(pass judgment)*, select, sentence, settle, stipulate, try *(conduct a trial)*. SEE MAIN ENTRY
decide a question of fact find *(determine)*
decide against overrule
decide beforehand predetermine, presuppose
decide between opposing parties arbitrate *(adjudge)*
decide by judicial sentence rule *(decide)*
decide in advance forejudge, predetermine, preordain, presuppose
decide in favor of uphold
decide legally hold *(decide)*
decide upon conclude *(decide)*, determine, find *(determine)*
decided absolute *(conclusive)*, actual, affirmative, axiomatic, categorical, certain *(fixed)*, certain *(positive)*, complete *(ended)*, conclusive *(settled)*, definite, definitive, demonstrable, dogmatic, explicit, express, fixed *(settled)*, inappealable, inevitable, inexorable, inflexible, intentional, necessary *(inescapable)*, obdurate, official, patient, peremptory *(absolute)*, pertinacious, positive *(confident)*, positive *(incontestable)*, purposeful, res judicata, resolute, resounding, serious *(devoted)*, stark, stated, steadfast, through, unequivocal, unmistakable, unyielding. SEE MAIN ENTRY
decided by competition vying competitive *(antagonistic)*
decided upon preferred *(favored)*
decidedly fairly *(clearly)*, purely *(positively)*
decidedly different distinct *(distinguished from others)*
deciding critical *(crucial)*, crucial, determinative
deciduous ephemeral, temporary, transient, volatile
decimate destroy *(efface)*, diminish, disarm *(divest of arms)*, eliminate *(eradicate)*, lessen, minimize, reduce
decimation aberemurder, catastrophe, destruction, killing
decipere mislead
decipher ascertain, clarify, construe *(comprehend)*, construe *(translate)*, detect, elucidate,

explain, find *(discover)*, interpret, read, resolve *(solve)*, solve
decipherable ascertainable, cognizable, coherent *(clear)*, comprehensible, determinable *(ascertainable)*, solvable
deciphering clarification, explanation
decipherment definition, solution *(answer)*
decision adjudication, alternative *(option)*, animus, arbitration, authority *(documentation)*, award, call *(option)*, cognovit, conclusion *(determination)*, consequence *(conclusion)*, conviction *(finding of guilt)*, decree, determination, dilemma, discretion *(power of choice)*, disposition *(determination)*, election *(choice)*, finding, holding *(ruling of a court)*, judgment *(discernment)*, judgment *(formal court decree)*, opinion *(judicial decision)*, outcome, poll *(casting of votes)*, pronouncement, referendum, relief *(legal redress)*, res judicata, result, ruling, selection *(choice)*, sentence, verdict, volition, vote, will *(desire)*. SEE MAIN ENTRY
decision beforehand predetermination
decision in advance predetermination
decision making government *(administration)*
decision of a jury verdict
decision-making body management *(directorate)*
decision-making power over the case jurisdiction
decisive absolute *(conclusive)*, axiomatic, categorical, certain *(fixed)*, certain *(positive)*, compelling, conclusive *(settled)*, convincing, critical *(crucial)*, crucial, definite, definitive, determinative, final, inappealable, key, last *(final)*, major, material *(important)*, peremptory *(absolute)*, peremptory *(imperative)*, positive *(confident)*, strategic. SEE MAIN ENTRY
decisive factor determinant
decisive moment crossroad *(turning point)*
decisive turn landmark *(significant change)*
decisively fairly *(clearly)*
decivilize brutalize
deck embellish
declaim enunciate, recite, speak, utter. SEE MAIN ENTRY
declaim against censure, complain *(charge)*, condemn *(blame)*, decry, denounce *(condemn)*, disapprove *(condemn)*, expostulate, fault, impeach
declaimer demagogue
declamatio bluster *(speech)*, declamation
declamation bombast, charge *(statement to the jury)*, discourse, fustian, harangue, peroration, rhetoric *(insincere language)*, speech. SEE MAIN ENTRY
declamatory flatulent, fustian, inflated *(bombastic)*, orotund, turgid, voluble
declamatory speech harangue
declarant SEE MAIN ENTRY
declarare declare, express, manifest, proclaim, prove
declaratio declaration, manifestation
declaration acknowledgment *(avowal)*, adjudication, adjuration, admission *(disclosure)*, affirmance *(authentication)*, affirmation, alibi, allegation, assertion, asseveration, assurance, attestation, averment, avouchment, avowal, brevet, certificate, certification *(attested copy)*, certification *(certification of proficiency)*, claim *(assertion)*, claim *(legal demand)*, cognovit, common knowledge, communication *(statement)*, conclusion *(determination)*, confession, confirmation, count, declaratory judgment, decree, determination, dictum, directive, disclosure *(act of disclosing)*, disclosure *(something disclosed)*, discovery, edict, expression *(comment)*, judgment *(formal court decree)*, measure, notice *(announcement)*, notification, observation, opinion *(judicial decision)*, order *(judicial directive)*, parole, platform, proclamation, promise, pronouncement, proposition, reference *(recommendation)*, remark, representation *(statement)*, resolution *(formal statement)*, speech, statement, surety *(certainty)*, testimony. SEE MAIN ENTRY
declaration of a jury verdict
declaration of disapproval protest
declaration of dissent protest
declaration of facts testimony
declaration of faith conviction *(persuasion)*, dogma, principle *(axiom)*, profession *(declaration)*
declaration of opposition protest
declaration of penalty sentence
declaration of policy platform
declaration of war outbreak
declaration under oath affidavit, deposition. SEE MAIN ENTRY
declarative declaratory, demonstrative *(illustrative)*, narrative
declaratory narrative. SEE MAIN ENTRY
declaratory judgment SEE MAIN ENTRY
declare adduce, admit *(concede)*, allege, annunciate, assert, attest, avouch *(avow)*, avow, bare, bear *(adduce)*, betray *(disclose)*, claim *(maintain)*, comment, communicate, conclude *(decide)*, confess, contend *(maintain)*, convey *(communicate)*, designate, determine, disclose, enact, enunciate, express, inform *(betray)*, issue *(publish)*, manifest, notify, observe *(remark)*, pass *(determine)*, phrase, pose *(propound)*, posit, proclaim, profess *(avow)*, promise *(vow)*, promulgate, pronounce *(speak)*, propose, publish, purport, relate *(tell)*, remark, report *(disclose)*, reveal, rule *(decide)*, signify *(inform)*, speak, swear, testify, utter, verify *(swear)*, vouch. SEE MAIN ENTRY
declare a verdict find *(determine)*
declare authoritatively rule *(decide)*
declare blameless exonerate
declare forfeit dispossess
declare guiltless exculpate, justify, palliate *(excuse)*
declare guilty of an offense convict, sentence
declare illegal ban, forbid, interdict, outlaw
declare incidentally mention
declare innocent acquit, exonerate, vindicate
declare invalid cancel, negate
declare lawful authorize, constitute *(establish)*, legitimate, pass *(approve)*
declare legal validate
declare not guilty exculpate, exonerate
declare not to be true disavow
declare null and void abolish, abrogate *(annul)*, abrogate *(rescind)*, adeem, cancel, discharge *(release from obligation)*, disclaim, negate, nullify, quash, repeal, repudiate, rescind, revoke
declare one's right claim *(demand)*
declare openly avouch *(avow)*, avow
declare opposition demonstrate *(protest)*
declare positively avow
declare solemnly affirm *(declare solemnly)*, swear
declare the truth of attest, avow, certify *(attest)*
declare to be pronounce *(pass judgment)*
declare to be fact affirm *(claim)*, bear *(adduce)*
declare to be false deny *(contradict)*
declare to be forfeited condemn *(seize)*
declare to be genuine evidence
declare to be true certify *(attest)*, evidence
declare to be untrue deny *(contradict)*
declare true swear
declare under oath depose *(testify)*
declare unlawful outlaw
declare valid validate
declare war fight *(battle)*
declare with positiveness avouch *(avow)*, purport
declared agreed *(promised)*, alleged, nuncupative, ostensible
declared insane non compos mentis
declared intention proposition
declarer SEE MAIN ENTRY
déclassé discard
declension curtailment, decrease, decrement, degradation, deterioration, rejection, relapse
declinare deviate
declinatio deviation
declination abandonment *(repudiation)*, abatement *(reduction)*, damage, decrease, degradation, deterioration, disdain, dishonor *(nonpayment)*, negation, refusal, rejection, relapse, renunciation, repudiation. SEE MAIN ENTRY
declinatory nonconsenting
declinature negation, refusal, rejection
decline abate *(lessen)*, abatement *(reduction)*, avoid *(evade)*, caducity, curtailment, damage, decay, decrease *(noun)*, decrease *(verb)*, deduction *(diminution)*, degenerate, degradation, depreciate, depress, depression, deteriorate, disavow, disdain, dismiss *(put out of consideration)*, disoblige, dissent *(withhold assent)*, ebb, end *(termination)*, expense *(sacrifice)*, fail *(lose)*, forbear, forgo, forswear, languish, lapse *(expiration)*, lessen, loss, rebuff, refrain, refuse, reject, relapse *(noun)*, relapse *(verb)*, renounce, repudiate, spurn, subside. SEE MAIN ENTRY
decline and fall decrease
decline to agree dissent *(withhold assent)*
decline to pay dishonor *(refuse to pay)*
decline to redeem dishonor *(refuse to pay)*
decline to sanction disapprove *(reject)*
declining decadent, old, stale
declining to agree dissenting
decoct distill
decoctor bankrupt
decodable solvable
decode construe *(comprehend)*, construe *(translate)*, elucidate, find *(discover)*, interpret, solve
decoding definition
decommission SEE MAIN ENTRY
decompose decay, degenerate, deteriorate, disintegrate, disorganize, dissolve *(disperse)*, spoil *(impair)*
decomposed dilapidated
decomposing decadent
decomposition consumption, destruction, deterioration, dissolution *(disintegration)*, spoilage

decompound decay
decontaminate SEE MAIN ENTRY
decontrol disengage, freedom
decorare embellish, garnish, honor
decorate embellish, honor
decorated elaborate, pretentious *(ostentatious)*
decoration mention *(tribute),* motif, prize
decorous formal, obeisant, proper, suitable
decorously respectfully
decorousness decorum, propriety *(correctness)*
decorum behavior, conduct. SEE MAIN ENTRY
decorum decorum
decorum deportment, formality, manner *(behavior),* presence *(poise),* propriety *(correctness),* protocol *(etiquette)*
decoy bait *(lure),* betray *(lead astray),* cloak, deceive, deception, delude, ensnare, entice, entrap, fake, illude, inveigle, lure, maneuver *(trick),* mislead, ruse. SEE MAIN ENTRY
decrease abate *(lessen),* abatement *(reduction),* abridge *(shorten),* allay, attenuate, attrition, curtail, curtailment, decline, decrement, deduct *(reduce),* deduction *(diminution),* deplete, depreciate, depress, deteriorate, diminish, diminution, discount, discount *(reduce),* ebb, erode, erosion, lessen, minimize, mitigate, mitigation, moderate *(temper),* modify *(moderate),* mollification, mollify, palliate *(abate),* rebate, reduce, remission, remit *(relax),* retrench, subside. SEE MAIN ENTRY
decrease a punishment commute
decrease in excellence impair
decrease in importance demote
decrease in purchasing power inflation *(decrease in value of currency)*
decreased qualified *(conditioned)*
decree adjudge, adjudicate, adjudication, appointment *(act of designating),* arbitrate *(adjudge),* arbitration, award *(noun),* award *(verb),* brevet, canon, charter *(declaration of rights),* citation *(charge),* codification, cognovit, command, compel, conclude *(decide),* conclusion *(determination),* constitute *(establish),* constrain *(compel),* conviction *(finding of guilt),* decide, decision *(judgment),* declaration, detail *(assign),* determination, determine, dictate *(noun),* dictate *(verb),* direct *(order),* direction *(order),* directive, edict, enact, enactment, enjoin, fiat, finding, hold *(decide),* holding *(ruling of a court),* impose *(enforce),* instruct *(direct),* instruction *(direction),* issuance, judge, judgment *(formal court decree),* law, legislate, mandamus, mandate, measure, mittimus, monition *(legal summons),* necessitate, notice *(announcement),* opinion *(judicial decision),* order *(judicial directive),* order, ordinance, pass *(approve),* pass *(determine),* precept, prescribe, prescription *(directive),* press *(constrain),* proclamation, pronounce *(pass judgment),* pronouncement, regulation *(rule),* require *(compel),* requirement, res judicata, rule *(legal dictate),* rule *(decide),* rule *(govern),* ruling, sentence, statute, warrant *(judicial writ),* writ. SEE MAIN ENTRY
decree absolute law
decree authoritatively arbitrate *(adjudge)*
decree beforehand preordain
decree by deliberate judgment award
decree by judicial authority conclude *(decide),* determine
decree by law legalize
decree having the force of law fiat
decree of a jury verdict
decree of nullity annulment, divorce
decree of punishment sentence
decree to be merited award
decreed decretal, legal, mandatory, necessary *(inescapable),* positive *(prescribed)*
decreeing legislative
decreement declaration, opinion *(judicial decision)*
decrement abatement *(reduction),* consumption, damage, decline, decrease, deduction *(diminution),* discount, erosion, loss, spoilage. SEE MAIN ENTRY
decremental drawback
decrepit decadent, dilapidated, disabled *(made incapable),* imperfect, old, powerless, unsound *(not strong)*
decrepitude decline, deterioration, disrepair, impuissance, prostration
decreptitude caducity
decrescence curtailment, decrease, decrement, deduction *(diminution)*
decrescere abate *(lessen)*
decretal declaratory, determinative, directive, mandate, mittimus, prescriptive, proclamation, requirement, writ. SEE MAIN ENTRY
decretive compulsory, declaratory, decretal
decretory declaratory, decretal
decretum decree, edict, holding *(ruling of a court),* ordinance, principle *(axiom),* resolution *(decision),* sentence
decrial bad repute, blame *(culpability),* conviction *(finding of guilt),* denunciation, disapprobation, dishonor *(shame),* disparagement, impugnation, incrimination, ostracism
decried blameful
decry brand *(stigmatize),* cavil, censure, complain *(criticize),* condemn *(blame),* contemn, criticize *(find fault with),* debunk, defame, denigrate, denounce *(condemn),* deprecate, depreciate, derogate, disapprove *(condemn),* discommend, discredit, disdain, disparage, except *(object),* fault, impeach, lash *(attack verbally),* lessen, libel, malign, minimize, remonstrate, reprehend, reprimand, reproach, smear, sully. SEE MAIN ENTRY
decrying calumnious, contemptuous, cynical, pejorative
decurrence decline
decursio maneuver *(tactic)*
decursus maneuver *(tactic)*
decussatio intersection
decussation intersection
dedecorare disgrace, dishonor *(deprive of honor)*
dedecorate demote
dedecoration ignominy, notoriety, scandal
dedecori esse disgrace
dedecus degradation, discredit, opprobrium
dedere deliver, devote, surrender *(yield),* yield *(submit)*
dedicare dedicate
dedicate devote. SEE MAIN ENTRY
dedicate oneself to specialize
dedicated industrious, loyal, obedient, purposeful, sacrosanct, serious *(devoted),* steadfast, true *(loyal),* unyielding, zealous
dedication adherence *(devotion),* inscription, loyalty. SEE MAIN ENTRY
dedicatory honorary
deditum esse adhere *(maintain loyalty)*
deduce ascertain, assume *(suppose),* conclude *(decide),* construe *(comprehend),* deduct *(conclude by reasoning),* detect, determine, discover, educe, extract, find *(determine),* gauge, infer, interpret, judge, presume, presuppose, read, reason *(conclude),* reflect *(ponder),* solve, surmise, suspect *(think),* understand. SEE MAIN ENTRY
deduce by interpretation construe *(comprehend)*
deduce the meaning of construe *(comprehend)*
deduced circumstantial
deducere derive *(deduce),* divert
deducible accountable *(explainable),* convincing, deductible *(provable),* deductive, determinable *(ascertainable),* provable
deducibly a priori
deducing dialectic
deduct construe *(comprehend),* decrease, deduce, depreciate, diminish, except *(exclude),* excise *(cut away),* lessen, minimize, rebate, remove *(eliminate),* retrench, withdraw. SEE MAIN ENTRY
deduct from discount *(reduce)*
deductible SEE MAIN ENTRY
deducting save
deductio deduction *(diminution),* discount, discount *(disbelieve)*
deduction computation, concept, conclusion *(determination),* consequence *(conclusion),* construction, corollary, decrease, decrement, dialectic, diminution, discount, estimate *(idea),* estimation *(calculation),* holding *(ruling of a court),* hypothesis, inference, perception, presumption, ratiocination, rebate, removal. SEE MAIN ENTRY
deductive discursive *(analytical),* logical. SEE MAIN ENTRY
deductively a priori
deed act *(enactment),* act *(undertaking),* alienate *(transfer title),* cede, contribute *(supply),* convey *(transfer),* descend, dominion *(absolute ownership),* endeavor, give *(grant),* grant *(transfer formally),* instrument *(document),* overt act, performance *(execution),* present *(make a gift),* step, title *(right),* transaction, transfer. SEE MAIN ENTRY
deed done fait accompli
deed exculpating the transferor quitclaim
deed of agreement indenture
deed of release quitclaim, waiver
deed of savagery atrocity
deeding alienation *(transfer of title),* demise *(conveyance)*
deeds conduct, dealings
deem adjudge, adjudicate, conclude *(decide),* deduce, deduct *(conclude by reasoning),* guess, judge, opine, presume, presuppose, regard *(pay attention),* surmise, suspect *(think).* SEE MAIN ENTRY
deem true assume *(suppose)*
deem unbecoming disdain
deem unsuitable disdain
deemed putative
deemphasize SEE MAIN ENTRY
deep broad, capacious, esoteric, extensive, incomprehensible, ingrained, intense, obscure *(abstruse),* profound *(intense),* recondite, sapient. SEE MAIN ENTRY
deep application diligence *(care)*
deep attention diligence *(care)*

deep down virtual
deep pockets SEE MAIN ENTRY
deep rooted virtual. SEE MAIN ENTRY
deep-rooted chronic, inherent, inveterate, organic, stable, underlying
deep-rooted belief faith
deep seated intrinsic *(deep down),* virtual. SEE MAIN ENTRY
deep-seated chronic, ingrained, permanent
deep study diligence *(care),* preoccupation, probe
deep thought diligence *(care)*
deepen aggravate *(exacerbate),* enhance, expand, extend *(enlarge),* intensify, magnify
deepening aggravation *(exacerbation),* boom *(increase),* cumulative *(intensifying)*
deeply felt profound *(intense)*
deescalate disarm *(divest of arms)*
deface damage, destroy *(efface),* harm, maim, mutilate, spoil *(impair),* sully, tarnish. SEE MAIN ENTRY
defaced blemished, marred
defacement flaw. SEE MAIN ENTRY
defacer vandal
defalcate cheat, embezzle, loot, purloin. SEE MAIN ENTRY
defalcation bad faith, embezzlement, misappropriation
defalcator embezzler, thief
defamation aspersion, denunciation, dishonor *(shame),* hatred, infamy, libel, malediction, obloquy, opprobrium, phillipic, scandal, shame, slander, vilification. SEE MAIN ENTRY
defamatory calumnious, contemptuous, critical *(faultfinding),* cynical, derogatory, incriminatory, libelous, pejorative, scandalous
defamatory words slander
defamatory writing libel
defame brand *(stigmatize),* denigrate, denounce *(condemn),* depreciate, derogate, disgrace, dishonor *(deprive of honor),* disparage, expose, humiliate, lessen, libel, malign, pillory, reproach, smear, stain, sully, tarnish. SEE MAIN ENTRY
defame by a published writing libel
defamed accused *(attacked)*
default arrears, breach, defeat, defect, deficit, delinquency *(failure of duty),* delinquency *(shortage),* dereliction, dishonor *(nonpayment),* disregard *(omission),* failure *(bankruptcy),* forfeit, infraction, lapse *(expiration),* maladministration, miscarriage, neglect, nonappearance, nonpayment, nonperformance, omission, repudiate. SEE MAIN ENTRY
default in performance omission
defaultant delinquent *(overdue)*
defaulter convict, fugitive, thief
defaulting bankrupt, bankruptcy, delinquent *(overdue),* insolvent
defeasance abolition, countermand, discharge *(annulment),* discharge *(release from obligation),* discontinuance *(act of discontinuing),* dissolution *(termination),* repudiation, rescision, revocation. SEE MAIN ENTRY
defeasible terminable, voidable. SEE MAIN ENTRY
defeat abate *(extinguish),* abatement *(extinguishment),* answer *(reply),* avoid *(cancel),* balk, circumvent, contravene, controvert, counteract, debacle, failure *(lack of success),* foil, frustrate, frustration, halt, miscarriage, negate, nonsuit, obliterate, overcome *(surmount),* override, overthrow, overturn, overwhelm, preclude, prevent, prostration, rebuff, refute, rejection, repulse, subdue, subject, subjugate, subversion, subvert, surmount, thwart, upset. SEE MAIN ENTRY
defeat of the prosecution compurgation
defeat one's own purpose overreach
defeat oneself by overdoing matters overreach
defeated despondent, disappointed, null *(invalid),* null and void. SEE MAIN ENTRY
defeating prevailing *(having superior force)*
defeatism pessimism
defeatist cynical, despondent, pessimistic, resigned
defect abandon *(physically leave),* defacement, deficiency, disadvantage, disease, disqualification *(factor that disqualifies),* drawback, fault *(weakness),* flaw, foible, frailty, handicap, leave *(depart),* part *(leave),* quit *(evacuate),* stigma, vice. SEE MAIN ENTRY
defect-free accurate
defectio failure *(falling short),* revolt
defection abandonment *(desertion),* abjuration, absence *(nonattendance),* bad faith, dereliction, desertion, disloyalty, infidelity, repudiation, revolt, sedition
defective bad *(inferior),* blemished, broken *(fractured),* deficient, faulty, imperfect, inferior *(lower in quality),* insufficient, marred, non compos mentis, nonsubstantial *(not sturdy),* peccable, poor *(inferior in quality),* undesirable, unsound *(fallacious),* unsound *(not strong).* SEE MAIN ENTRY
defective check bad check
defectiveness failure *(falling short),* frailty
defectless absolute *(ideal),* infallible
defend adhere *(maintain loyalty),* advocate, answer *(reply),* answer *(respond legally),* corroborate, countercharge, cover *(guard),* espouse, harbor, justify, lobby, maintain *(sustain),* palliate *(excuse),* preserve, protect, save *(rescue),* screen *(guard),* side, sponsor, support *(assist),* support *(justify),* sustain *(confirm),* uphold. SEE MAIN ENTRY
defend a case plead *(argue a case)*
defend as conformable to law justify
defend as conformable to right justify
defend successfully support *(justify)*
defendable defensible, justifiable, tenable
defendant convict, litigant, party *(litigant),* respondent. SEE MAIN ENTRY
defendant's answer to charges plea, pleading
defended guarded, insusceptible *(resistant),* ironclad, safe, secure *(free from danger)*
defender advocate *(counselor),* advocate *(espouser),* apologist, backer, benefactor, custodian *(protector),* guardian, partisan, patron *(influential supporter),* proponent, samaritan
defendere parry, protect
defense advocacy, alibi, ammunition, answer *(judicial response),* argument *(pleading),* behalf, bulwark, compurgation, counterargument, excuse, explanation, justification, panoply, plea, pleading, preservation, pretext, protection, reason *(basis),* rejoinder, safeguard, safekeeping, salvo, security *(safety),* shelter *(protection),* shield, support *(assistance),* ward. SEE MAIN ENTRY
defenseless disabled *(made incapable),* indefensible, insecure, open *(accessible),* powerless, precarious, unable, untenable, vulnerable
defenselessness danger, impotence
defensible inexpugnable, justifiable, pardonable, plausible, tenable, unobjectionable. SEE MAIN ENTRY
defensio assertion
defensive preventive, protective
defensive arms panoply
defensive clothing panoply
defensive equipment panoply
defensive evidence alibi
defensive plea alibi
defensor apologist, guardian
defer accommodate, adjourn, continue *(adjourn),* delay, discontinue *(break continuity),* hold up *(delay),* postpone, procrastinate, stall, suspend. SEE MAIN ENTRY
defer to acknowledge *(verify),* comply, concur *(agree),* hear *(give attention to),* honor, obey, recognize *(acknowledge),* regard *(hold in esteem),* relent
deference allegiance, character *(reputation),* comity, consideration *(sympathetic regard),* courtesy, discipline *(obedience),* estimation *(esteem),* fealty, homage, honor *(outward respect),* regard *(esteem),* resignation *(passive acceptance),* respect. SEE MAIN ENTRY
deferential civil *(polite),* malleable, obedient, obeisant, obsequious, pliant, sequacious, servile, subservient
deferentially respectfully
deferment adjournment, delay, extension *(postponement),* pause, reprieve. SEE MAIN ENTRY
deferral deferment, extension *(postponement),* moratorium
deferre devolve, invest *(vest),* tender
deferred arrested *(checked),* back *(in arrears),* late *(tardy)*
deferred payment arrears, bill *(invoice),* debit, debt, nonpayment
deferring dilatory, obeisant
defiance conflict, contradiction, disrespect, impugnation, infraction, insurrection, mutiny, negation, noncompliance *(nonobservance),* nonconformity, protest, provocation, rebellion, rebuff, refusal, resistance, revolt, sedition, spite. SEE MAIN ENTRY
defiance of custom deviation, exception *(exclusion),* quirk *(idiosyncrasy)*
defiance of danger audacity, prowess *(bravery)*
defiance of orders contempt *(disobedience to the court),* infraction
defiance of precedent creation
defiant brazen, contemptuous, contumacious, disobedient, disorderly, impertinent *(insolent),* indomitable, insolent, insubordinate, intractable, nonconforming, nonconsenting, proud *(conceited),* provocative, pugnacious, recalcitrant
deficere fail *(lose)*
deficiency absence *(omission),* dearth, defect, deficit, delinquency *(shortage),* disadvantage, failure *(falling short),* fault *(weakness),* flaw, foible, frailty, handicap, insufficiency, mediocrity, need *(deprivation),* paucity, poverty, vice. SEE MAIN ENTRY
deficient defective, delinquent *(overdue),* devoid, fallible, faulty, imperfect, inadequate, incompetent, inferior *(lower in quality),* insufficient, minimal, nonsubstantial *(not sturdy),* nonsubstantial *(not sufficient),* paltry, partial *(relating to a part),* perfunctory,

poor *(inferior in quality)*, scarce, unqualified *(not competent)*, unsatisfactory, unsound *(not strong)*. SEE MAIN ENTRY

deficient in reason fatuous

deficient work noncompliance *(improper completion)*

deficit arrears, debt, decrement, deficiency, delinquency *(shortage)*, due, insufficiency, need *(deprivation)*, poverty. SEE MAIN ENTRY

defile abuse *(violate)*, adulterate, betray *(lead astray)*, brand *(stigmatize)*, contaminate, contemn, damage, debase, deteriorate, disgrace, dishonor *(deprive of honor)*, infect, malign, misemploy, mishandle *(maltreat)*, molest *(subject to indecent advances)*, pillory, pollute, smear, spoil *(impair)*, stain, sully, taint *(contaminate)*, taint *(corrupt)*. SEE MAIN ENTRY

defiled sordid, tainted *(contaminated)*

defilement abuse *(physical misuse)*, air pollution, attaint, bad repute, contaminate, contempt *(disdain)*, debauchment, disgrace, dishonor *(shame)*, misusage, perversion, rape, seduction, shame. SEE MAIN ENTRY

definability construction

definable accountable *(explainable)*, ascertainable, determinable *(ascertainable)*

define border *(bound)*, call *(title)*, clarify, comment, construe *(translate)*, delimit, delineate, demarcate, describe, designate, distinguish, elucidate, explain, explicate, expound, illustrate, interpret, label, render *(depict)*, restrict, trace *(delineate)*. SEE MAIN ENTRY

define limits locate

define location locate

defined actual, coherent *(clear)*, comprehensible, exact, express, manifest, narrow, perceptible, precise, qualified *(conditioned)*, stated, unambiguous, unequivocal, unmistakable. SEE MAIN ENTRY

defined meaning SEE MAIN ENTRY

defining restrictive

definire circumscribe *(define)*, define, fix *(settle)*

definite absolute *(conclusive)*, actual, apparent *(perceptible)*, axiomatic, categorical, certain *(fixed)*, certain *(positive)*, certain *(specific)*, clear *(certain)*, cogent, cognizable, coherent *(clear)*, conclusive *(determinative)*, concrete, conspicuous, corporeal, decisive, definitive, demonstrable, distinct *(clear)*, dogmatic, explicit, express, factual, fixed *(settled)*, inappealable, incontrovertible, indubious, inevitable, irrevocable, limited, official, overt, palpable, particular *(individual)*, peremptory *(absolute)*, positive *(confident)*, positive *(incontestable)*, precise, reliable, resounding, several *(separate)*, specific, tangible, unalienable, unalterable, unambiguous, unequivocal. SEE MAIN ENTRY

definite carelessness res ipsa loquitur

definite form embodiment

definite procedure avenue *(means of attainment)*, modus operandi

definitely fairly *(clearly)*

definiteness belief *(state of mind)*, certainty, certitude, specialty *(distinctive mark)*, surety *(certainty)*

definition clarification, construction, description, explanation, identification, meaning, rendition *(explication)*, specification. SEE MAIN ENTRY

definitional descriptive

definitions on the law charge *(statement to the jury)*

definitive absolute *(conclusive)*, categorical, clear *(certain)*, cogent, complete *(ended)*, conclusive *(settled)*, crucial, decisive, descriptive, determinative, dogmatic, extreme *(last)*, factual, final, inappealable, interpretive, last *(final)*, thorough. SEE MAIN ENTRY

definitive answer verdict

definitiveness finality

definitus categorical, definite, explicit, unambiguous

deflagrate burn. SEE MAIN ENTRY

deflagration conflagration

deflate attenuate, browbeat, debunk, decrease, deduct *(reduce)*, demean *(make lower)*, demote, denounce *(condemn)*, depreciate, depress, diminish, disable, discount *(minimize)*, disgrace, disparage, exhaust *(deplete)*, humiliate, lessen, minimize. SEE MAIN ENTRY

deflated disgraceful

deflation decline, decrease, depression, diminution, disgrace

deflect avert, counter, deter, detour, deviate, discourage, divert, parry, prevent, repel *(drive back)*, stave. SEE MAIN ENTRY

deflection alienation *(estrangement)*, detour

deflere deplore

defloration debauchment, rape

deflower dishonor *(deprive of honor)*

deflowering debauchment, defilement

defluxion outflow

defoliate denude

deform camouflage, contort, damage, deface, denature, disorganize, distort, mutilate, spoil *(impair)*

deform one's character brutalize

deformare deface

deformation defacement, detriment, distortion

deformed blemished, defective, marred

deformity defacement, defect, distortion, flaw

defraud betray *(lead astray)*, bilk, cheat, circumvent, corrupt, deceive, defalcate, delude, dupe, embezzle, ensnare, evade *(deceive)*, fake, hoodwink, illude, inveigle, mislabel, mislead, misrepresent, overreach, palter, peculate, prevaricate, purloin. SEE MAIN ENTRY

defraudare defraud

defraudation bunko, conversion *(misappropriation)*, deception, hoax, knavery, misappropriation

defrauded aggrieved *(victimized)*

defrauder criminal, embezzler, lawbreaker, thief

defrauding collusive

defraudment deception

defray bear the expense, compensate *(remunerate)*, disburse *(pay out)*, pay, remit *(send payment)*, remunerate. SEE MAIN ENTRY

defray expenses bear the expense

defray in advance prepay

defray the cost bear the expense, disburse *(pay out)*

defrayal amortization, collection *(payment)*, compensation, disbursement *(funds paid out)*, discharge *(payment)*, expenditure, expense *(cost)*, pay, payment *(act of paying)*, recovery *(award)*, reimbursement, remittance, remuneration, satisfaction *(discharge of debt)*. SEE MAIN ENTRY

defrayment advance *(allowance)*, amortization, collection *(payment)*, commission *(fee)*, compensation, consideration *(recompense)*, disbursement *(funds paid out)*, discharge *(payment)*, expenditure, expense *(cost)*, pay, payment *(act of paying)*, recompense, remittance, remuneration, satisfaction *(discharge of debt)*

defrock disgrace

deft artful, capable, competent, diplomatic, efficient, expert, facile, familiar *(informed)*, practiced, proficient, qualified *(competent)*, resourceful, sciential, subtle *(refined)*, veteran. SEE MAIN ENTRY

deftness discretion *(quality of being discreet)*, efficiency, facility *(easiness)*, faculty *(ability)*, gift *(flair)*, propensity, prowess *(ability)*, skill

defugere shun

defunct dead, deceased, lifeless *(dead)*, null *(invalid)*, null and void, outdated. SEE MAIN ENTRY

defy break *(violate)*, challenge, complain *(criticize)*, conflict, confront *(oppose)*, contest, contravene, counter, counteract, cross *(disagree with)*, disaffirm, disagree, disobey, dissent *(withhold assent)*, fight *(counteract)*, flout, oppose, oppugn, provoke, rebel, resist *(oppose)*, violate, withstand. SEE MAIN ENTRY

defying contemptuous

defying lawful authority contumacious

degeneracy bad repute, caducity, decline, delinquency *(misconduct)*, turpitude, vice

degenerare degenerate

degenerate bad *(offensive)*, contaminate, corrupt, debauch, decadent, decay, decline *(fall)*, depraved, depreciate, deteriorate, dissolute, ebb, ignoble, immoral, lawless, lessen, nefarious, perverse, pervert, profligate *(corrupt)*, recidivate, regressive, relapse, reprobate, taint *(corrupt)*, tainted *(corrupted)*, vicious. SEE MAIN ENTRY

degenerateness decline

degeneratess degradation

degenerating decadent

degeneration decline, degradation, detriment, disrepair, recidivism, relapse, sodomy

degenerative bad *(inferior)*

degradation attaint, bad repute, defilement, deterioration, discredit, disgrace, dishonor *(shame)*, disrepute, ignominy, ill repute, infamy, libel, misusage, misuse, notoriety, obloquy, odium, onus *(stigma)*, opprobrium, perversion, reproach, scandal, shame, turpitude. SEE MAIN ENTRY

degrade abuse *(violate)*, adulterate, contaminate, damage, debase, debauch, decry, defame, degenerate, demean *(make lower)*, demote, denigrate, denounce *(condemn)*, depreciate, deteriorate, discredit, disgrace, dishonor *(deprive of honor)*, disoblige, disparage, humiliate, libel, minimize, pillory, pollute, smear, sully, taint *(contaminate)*, tarnish

degraded bad *(inferior)*, bad *(offensive)*, depraved, disreputable, dissolute, ignoble, notorious, sordid, tainted *(corrupted)*

degraded person degenerate

degrading disgraceful, unbecoming

degredi deviate

degree caliber *(measurement)*, extent, magnitude, nuance, prestige, step, utmost. SEE MAIN ENTRY

degree of importance weight *(importance)*

degreeholder specialist

dehiscent open *(unclosed)*, penetrable

dehonestare disgrace, dishonor *(deprive of honor)*
dehort admonish *(warn)*, discourage, expostulate, protest
dehortari dissuade
dehortation admonition, monition *(warning)*, notice *(warning)*, remonstrance
dehortative remonstrative
dehortatory remonstrative
dehumanize brutalize, debase
dehumanized diabolic
deicere disappoint, dislodge, eject *(evict)*, overthrow, precipitate *(throw down violently)*
deific omniscient
deifical omniscient
deification elevation
deify elevate
deign accede *(concede)*, bestow, patronize *(condescend toward)*. SEE MAIN ENTRY
deign to give vouchsafe
deign to grant vouchsafe
deject depress, discourage
dejected despondent, disappointed, disconsolate, lugubrious, pessimistic. SEE MAIN ENTRY
dejectedness pessimism
dejection depression, dissatisfaction, pessimism, prostration
delate complain *(charge)*, denigrate, implicate, involve *(implicate)*
delatio denunciation
delation accusation, blame *(culpability)*, charge *(accusation)*, count, denunciation, indictment
delation by criminal charges arraignment
delator accuser, appellant, complainant, informant
delator informer *(a person who provides information)*
delay abeyance, adjourn, arrest *(stop)*, balk, block, cessation *(interlude)*, check *(bar)*, check *(restrain)*, constrict *(inhibit)*, continue *(adjourn)*, curb, damper *(stopper)*, defer *(put off)*, deferment, detain *(restrain)*, discontinue *(break continuity)*, doubt *(hesitate)*, extension *(postponement)*, filibuster, halt, hamper, hesitate, hesitation, hiatus, impede, inhibit, interrupt, interruption, keep *(restrain)*, laches, moratorium, obstacle, obstruct, pause *(noun)*, pause *(verb)*, postpone, prevent, procrastinate, protract *(prolong)*, remain *(stay)*, reprieve, stall, stay, stay *(halt)*, stop, suspend. SEE MAIN ENTRY
delay attended by change of position laches
delay enforcing rights forbear
delay in execution reprieve
delay in legislation filibuster
delay in punishment reprieve
delay that results in disadvantage laches
delayed arrested *(checked)*, back *(in arrears)*, dilatory, late *(tardy)*, overdue. SEE MAIN ENTRY
delaying dilatory
dele delete, edit
delectable nectarious, palatable, sapid, savory
delectare interest
delectation enjoyment *(pleasure)*
delectus choice *(alternatives offered)*, choice *(decision)*, selection *(choice)*
delegare delegate
delegate agent, appoint, assign *(designate)*, charge *(empower)*, commit *(entrust)*, conduit *(intermediary)*, deliver, deputy, detail *(assign)*, employ *(engage services)*, empower, entrust, executor, factor *(commission merchant)*, functionary, hire, induct, intermediary, invest *(vest)*, liaison, medium, plenipotentiary, proctor, procurator, proxy, relegate, remand, replacement, representative *(proxy)*, spokesman, substitute. SEE MAIN ENTRY
delegate authority to charge *(empower)*
delegate to authorize
delegate upon another devolve
delegated representative, surrogate
delegated authority bureaucracy
delegates delegation *(envoy)*, deputation *(delegation)*, government *(political administration)*
delegating delegation *(assignment)*, designation *(naming)*
delegation agency *(commission)*, agency *(legal relationship)*, appointment *(act of designating)*, assignment *(designation)*, charter *(sanction)*, commission *(agency)*, committee, constituency, decentralization, deputation *(delegation)*, deputation *(selection of delegates)*, designation *(naming)*, devolution, embassy, mission, nomination. SEE MAIN ENTRY
delegation of duties devolution
delere abolish, cancel, expunge, obliterate
delete abolish, bowdlerize, censor, deface, diminish, edit, eliminate *(eradicate)*, eradicate, except *(exclude)*, excise *(cut away)*, expunge, expurgate, obliterate, omit, redact, remove *(eliminate)*, repeal, retrench, suppress. SEE MAIN ENTRY
deleted null *(invalid)*
deleterious adverse *(negative)*, bad *(inferior)*, detrimental, disadvantageous, disastrous, fatal, harmful, inadvisable, insalubrious, malevolent, malignant, noxious, peccant *(unhealthy)*, pernicious, pestilent, prejudicial, toxic, virulent. SEE MAIN ENTRY
deletion annulment, cancellation, rescission
deliberare deliberate. SEE MAIN ENTRY
deliberate aforethought, circumspect, cogitative, cold-blooded, confer *(consult)*, consider, consult *(ask advice of)*, debate, discreet, doubt *(hesitate)*, express, hesitant, intentional, judicious, knowing, muse, oscillate, pause, ponder, premeditated, purposeful, reason *(conclude)*, reflect *(ponder)*, review, speculate *(conjecture)*, tactical, treat *(process)*, try *(conduct a trial)*, voluntary, weigh, willful. SEE MAIN ENTRY
deliberate application diligence *(care)*
deliberate attention diligence *(care)*
deliberate burning of property arson
deliberate choice election *(choice)*
deliberate determination adjudication
deliberate falsification story *(falsehood)*
deliberate intent premeditation
deliberate intention forethought, premeditation
deliberate malice cruelty, ill will
deliberate misrepresentation subreption
deliberate omission dispensation *(exception)*. SEE MAIN ENTRY
deliberate over brood
deliberate study diligence *(care)*
deliberate thought diligence *(care)*
deliberate upon discuss, investigate
deliberately knowingly, purposely
deliberately avoid shun
deliberately intended premeditated
deliberately slow dilatory
deliberateness animus, contemplation, moderation
deliberatio deliberation
deliberation conference, contemplation, conversation, council *(consultant)*, dialectic, discretion *(quality of being discreet)*, examination *(study)*, forethought, hindsight, negotiation, parley, prudence, purpose, reflection *(thought)*, speculation *(conjecture)*. SEE MAIN ENTRY
deliberative circumspect, cogitative, deliberate, pensive, speculative
deliberative body panel *(discussion group)*
deliberative group commission *(agency)*
delicacy consideration *(sympathetic regard)*, decorum, discretion *(quality of being discreet)*, fault *(weakness)*, frailty, nuance, propriety *(correctness)*, sensibility
delicacy of feeling sensibility
delicate destructible, impalpable, intricate, nonsubstantial *(not sturdy)*, palatable, precarious, subtle *(refined)*, tenuous. SEE MAIN ENTRY
delicate distinction differential
delicatus particular *(exacting)*
delicious nectarious, palatable, sapid, savory
delict crime, guilt, misdeed, offense. SEE MAIN ENTRY
delictum crime, delict, delinquency *(misconduct)*, fault *(responsibility)*, misconduct, misdeed, misdemeanor, offense, transgression
deligere choose, elect *(choose)*
delight enjoyment *(pleasure)*, treat
delight in relish
delighted ecstatic, inclined, proud *(self-respecting)*, ready *(willing)*
delightful attractive, palatable, sapid, savory
delightfulness amenity
delimit allot, apportion, border *(bound)*, circumscribe *(define)*, demarcate, determine, hedge, restrain, restrict. SEE MAIN ENTRY
delimitate border *(bound)*, demarcate, hedge, restrict
delimitation boundary, definition, periphery, purview, specification
delimited qualified *(conditioned)*
delineate amplify, analyze, border *(bound)*, characterize, circumscribe *(define)*, circumscribe *(surround by boundary)*, clarify, construe *(translate)*, define, depict, describe, detail *(particularize)*, draw *(depict)*, exemplify, expound, hedge, identify, interpret, locate, portray, recite, recount, render *(depict)*, represent *(portray)*, signify *(denote)*. SEE MAIN ENTRY
delineated detailed
delineation analysis, boundary, clarification, configuration *(confines)*, construction, contour *(outline)*, definition, description, design *(construction plan)*, explanation, identification, narration, rendition *(explication)*, scheme, symbol. SEE MAIN ENTRY
delineation lines ambit
delineative descriptive
delineatory demonstrative *(illustrative)*
delinquence default
delinquency arrears, bad repute, blame *(culpability)*, breach, crime, culpability, default, dereliction, dishonor *(nonpayment)*,

disregard *(omission)*, failure *(falling short)*, fault *(responsibility)*, guilt, lapse *(expiration)*, misconduct, misdeed, misdoing, misprision, neglect, negligence, nonfeasance, nonpayment, nonperformance, offense, omission, transgression, vice, wrong. SEE MAIN ENTRY
delinquent blameful, blameworthy, broken *(unfulfilled)*, convict, culpable, derelict *(negligent)*, disobedient, due *(owed)*, felon, guilty, lawbreaker, malefactor, negligent, offender, outlaw, outstanding *(unpaid)*, overdue, recidivist, remiss, reprehensible, wrongdoer. SEE MAIN ENTRY
deliquare clarify
deliquesce lessen
delirious *(incoherent)*. SEE MAIN ENTRY
delirious *(wildly happy)*. SEE MAIN ENTRY
delirious with joy ecstatic
delirium insanity
delitescence indistinctness, privacy
delitescency indistinctness
delitescent covert, hidden, indiscernible, indistinct, latent, surreptitious
delitescere abscond, lurk
deliver assign *(transfer ownership)*, attorn, bear *(yield)*, bestow, cede, clear, confer *(give)*, consign, contribute *(supply)*, convey *(transfer)*, delegate, devolve, discharge *(liberate)*, disengage, disenthrall, dole, extricate, free, give *(grant)*, grant *(transfer formally)*, impart, liberate, pardon, parole, pass *(determine)*, phrase, post, present *(make a gift)*, pronounce *(speak)*, provide *(supply)*, publish, quit *(free of)*, recite, redeem *(repurchase)*, refer *(send for action)*, release, relieve *(free from burden)*, relinquish, remark, rescue, serve *(deliver a legal instrument)*, speak, supply, tender, transfer, transmit, transport, utter. SEE MAIN ENTRY
deliver a charge discharge *(shoot)*
deliver a judgment pass *(determine)*
deliver a speech discourse
deliver a summons and complaint serve *(deliver a legal instrument)*
deliver a talk address *(talk to)*, discourse
deliver an address discourse, pronounce *(speak)*, speak
deliver an instrument file *(place among official records)*
deliver as one's act and deed certify *(attest)*
deliver formally consign, pronounce *(speak)*
deliver from a hindrance disencumber
deliver from bondage disenthrall, free
deliver from uncertainty assure *(give confidence to)*
deliver in trust delegate
deliver information report *(disclose)*
deliver into custody commit *(institutionalize)*
deliver judgment adjudge, adjudicate, award, conclude *(decide)*, decree, determine, find *(determine)*, pronounce *(pass judgment)*, rule *(decide)*
deliver oratorically declaim
deliver over alienate *(transfer title)*, consign, convey *(transfer)*, delegate, demise, pass *(advance)*, serve *(deliver a legal instrument)*, transfer
deliver over to a successor devolve
deliver to bequeath, remove *(transfer)*
deliver to the care of confide *(trust)*
deliver up betray *(lead astray)*, forfeit
deliverable assignable
deliverance absolution, alienation *(transfer of title)*, catharsis, delivery, demise *(conveyance)*, devolution, discharge *(liberation)*, discharge *(release from obligation)*, disposition *(transfer of property)*, emancipation, freedom, help, holding *(ruling of a court)*, liberation, liberty, mainstay, parole, pronouncement, ransom, redemption, release, relief *(release)*, resolution *(formal statement)*, respite *(reprieve)*, salvage, transmittal
deliverance from bondage emancipation
delivered clear *(free from criminal charges)*, free *(relieved from a burden)*
deliverer donor, good samaritan
delivering to consignment
delivery alienation *(transfer of title)*, assignment *(transfer of ownership)*, birth *(emergence of young)*, cession, conveyance, course, demise *(conveyance)*, devolution, discharge *(release from obligation)*, disposition *(transfer of property)*, intonation, issuance, liberation, parlance, rhetoric *(skilled speech)*, speech, transmittal. SEE MAIN ENTRY
delivery back replevin
delivery of a writ service *(delivery of legal process)*
delivery of process service *(delivery of legal process)*
delivery of title feoffment
delocalization asportation
delocalize dislodge, displace *(remove)*, remove *(eliminate)*
deludable naive
delude bait *(lure)*, betray *(lead astray)*, bilk, circumvent, deceive, defraud, dupe, ensnare, evade *(deceive)*, fabricate *(make up)*, fake, feign, hoodwink, illude, inveigle, lie *(falsify)*, misguide, misinform, mislead, misrepresent, misstate, palter, pretend, prevaricate. SEE MAIN ENTRY
delude oneself err, misconceive, misunderstand
deluded blind *(not discerning)*
deludere delude
deluding delusive, illusory, ostensible, prestidigitation, specious
deluge cataclysm, immerse *(plunge into)*, inundate, overage, overcome *(overwhelm)*, overload, overwhelm, plethora, spate, surfeit
delusion artifice, bad faith, deception, error, fallacy, false pretense, figment, hoax, insanity, lunacy, phantom, ruse, sham
delusional ostensible
delusional insanity paranoia
delusions paranoia
delusive assumed *(feigned)*, colorable *(specious)*, deceptive, dishonest, disingenuous, evasive, fallacious, false *(inaccurate)*, fictitious, fraudulent, illusory, lying, machiavellian, meretricious, ostensible, sly, specious, spurious, untrue. SEE MAIN ENTRY
delusiveness bad faith, deceit, fraud
delusory colorable *(specious)*, deceptive, delusive, dishonest, disingenuous, fallacious, false *(not genuine)*, fraudulent, lying, ostensible, specious
deluxe elaborate, elegant, superior *(excellent)*
delve search. SEE MAIN ENTRY
delve for hunt
delve into analyze, canvass, examine *(study)*, inquire, investigate, peruse, probe, research, scrutinize
delving into evidence inquiry *(systematic investigation)*
demagnetize neutralize
demagogue insurgent. SEE MAIN ENTRY
demand call *(demand)*, canon, cause of action, coerce, command, compel, compulsion *(coercion)*, constrain *(compel)*, detail *(assign)*, dictate *(noun)*, dictate *(verb)*, direct *(order)*, direction *(order)*, directive, dun *(noun)*, dun *(verb)*, entail, exact, excise, excise *(levy a tax)*, force *(compulsion)*, force *(coerce)*, importune, impose *(enforce)*, insist, instruct *(direct)*, levy, motion, necessitate, need *(deprivation)*, need *(requirement)*, need, order, outlet, petition, prerequisite, prescribe, press *(constrain)*, request *(noun)*, request *(verb)*, require *(compel)*, require *(need)*, requirement, requisition, solicit, stress *(strain)*, subpoena *(noun)*, subpoena *(verb)*, summon, ultimatum. SEE MAIN ENTRY
demand a payment assess *(tax)*
demand and obtain payment collect *(recover money)*
demand for payment bill *(invoice)*
demand made on a stock holder call *(option)*
demand payment charge *(assess)*, dun, exact, excise *(levy a tax)*
demand toll assess *(tax)*, exact, excise *(levy a tax)*
demand with threats dun
demanded compulsory, decretal, essential *(required)*, mandatory, necessary *(req-uired)*, popular, positive *(prescribed)*, requisite
demanded damages ad damnum clause
demander extortionist
demanding exigent, imperative, insistent, operose, particular *(exacting)*, peremptory *(imperative)*, urgent
demanding attention important *(urgent)*
demanding belief plausible
demands interrogatories
demarcate allot, apportion, border *(bound)*, circumscribe *(define)*, delimit, differentiate, distinguish, divide *(separate)*, hedge, label, locate, restrict, specify. SEE MAIN ENTRY
demarcation definition, discrimination *(differentiation)*, limitation, outline *(boundary)*, periphery, restriction, severance
demarcation line edge *(border)*, frontier
demark circumscribe *(define)*, demarcate
dematerialize disappear, dissipate *(spread out)*
demean comport *(behave)*, demote, deprecate, derogate, disgrace, humiliate, reduce. SEE MAIN ENTRY
demeaning disgraceful
demeanor appearance *(look)*, behavior, complexion, conduct, decorum, deportment, manner *(behavior)*, posture *(attitude)*, presence *(poise)*, temperament. SEE MAIN ENTRY
démêlé dispute
demens deranged
demensum ration
dement discompose, disorient, obsess
dementate lunatic
demented deranged, lunatic, non compos mentis
dementedness insanity
dementia insanity
dementia lunacy
demergere overwhelm
demerit defect, flaw, foible, frailty
demesne area *(province)*, domain *(land owned)*, dominion *(absolute ownership)*, locality, location, possession *(ownership)*, property *(land)*, province, realm, region, scope, section *(vicinity)*, sphere, territory. SEE MAIN ENTRY

demetere reap
demetiri measure
demilitarization reconversion
demilitarize disarm *(divest of arms)*
deminuere decrease, diminish, lessen
deminutio abatement *(reduction),* decline, decrease, deduction *(diminution)*
demise abalienate, alienate *(transfer title),* alienation *(transfer of title),* assignment *(transfer of ownership),* attorn, bequeath, bequest, contribute *(supply),* convey *(transfer),* conveyance, death, decease, descend, devolution, die, dissolution *(termination),* end *(termination),* extremity *(death),* grant *(transfer formally),* lease, leave *(give),* let *(lease),* rent, sublease, transfer. SEE MAIN ENTRY
demised dead, deceased, decedent, defunct, late *(defunct),* lifeless *(dead)*
demission abandonment *(desertion),* abdication, deterioration, removal, renunciation, resignation *(relinquishment)*
demit abandon *(relinquish),* defect, discontinue *(abandon),* forfeit, relinquish, renounce, resign, retire *(conclude a career).* SEE MAIN ENTRY
demiurgic original *(creative),* productive
demiurgical original *(creative),* productive
demobilize disarm *(divest of arms),* disband, dismiss *(discharge),* disorganize, dissociate, dissolve *(separate).* SEE MAIN ENTRY
democratic equal, free *(enjoying civil liberty)*
demode outdated
demoded outmoded
demography census
demolish consume, damage, defeat, destroy *(efface),* devastate, eliminate *(eradicate),* eradicate, extinguish, extirpate, harm, impair, obliterate, overturn, prejudice *(injure),* refute, spoil *(impair),* subvert, upset
demolisher vandal
demolishing dire, disastrous, fatal
demolishment debacle, destruction, detriment
demolition debacle, destruction, dissolution *(disintegration),* prostration, subversion
demoniac cold-blooded, diabolic, malevolent, malicious, ruthless, sinister
demoniacal cruel, malevolent, malicious, malignant, sinister
demonial malevolent
demonic diabolic
demonstrability corroboration
demonstrable actual, ascertainable, certain *(positive),* cogent, concrete, convincing, corporeal, de facto, deductible *(provable),* definite, genuine, incontrovertible, indubious, irrefutable, provable, undeniable. SEE MAIN ENTRY
demonstrate bear *(adduce),* clarify, communicate, construe *(translate),* disagree, display, document, elucidate, establish *(show),* evidence, evince, exemplify, exhibit, explain, illustrate, manifest, picket, present *(introduce),* produce *(offer to view),* prove, reason *(persuade),* signify *(denote),* signify *(inform),* substantiate, unveil. SEE MAIN ENTRY
demonstrate against picket
demonstrate protest picket
demonstrated actual, authentic, certain *(positive),* conclusive *(determinative),* indubious, unrefutable
demonstrating cogent
demonstratio manifestation
demonstration argument *(pleading),* case *(example),* clarification, corroboration, example, explanation, expression *(manifestation),* instance, manifestation, pretense *(ostentation),* proof, protest
demonstrative clear *(apparent),* declaratory, probative, suggestive *(evocative),* vehement. SEE MAIN ENTRY
demonstrator malcontent
demoralization bad repute, confusion *(turmoil),* defilement, perversion
demoralize brutalize, debase, deteriorate, discompose, discourage, disgrace, pervert, subvert, taint *(corrupt)*
demoralized bad *(offensive),* tainted *(corrupted),* vicious
demoralizing deplorable, disgraceful, disreputable
demorari stay *(halt)*
demortuus late *(defunct)*
demote depose *(remove),* derogate, dislodge, humiliate, minimize. SEE MAIN ENTRY
demotion degradation, ignominy, removal
demulcent medicinal
demur demonstrate *(protest),* disaffirm, disagree, disapprove *(reject),* disoblige, disown *(deny the validity),* dissent *(difference of opinion),* dissent *(withhold assent),* doubt *(hesitate),* except *(object),* hesitate, negate, object, oppose, pause *(noun),* pause *(verb),* protest, refuse, reject, remonstrance, remonstrate, repudiate, vacillate. SEE MAIN ENTRY
demure diffident. SEE MAIN ENTRY
demureness propriety *(correctness)*
demurrage SEE MAIN ENTRY
demurral delay, disagreement, pause
demurrer disapproval, exception *(objection).* SEE MAIN ENTRY
demurring disapproval, disinclined, dissenting, hesitant, negative, remonstrative, renitent, restive
demurringly unwillingly
den chamber *(compartment)*
denaturalize contaminate, denature, pollute
denature adulterate, convert *(change use),* debilitate, deteriorate, transform. SEE MAIN ENTRY
deniability cloud *(suspicion)*
deniable contestable, debatable, disputable, dubitative
denial abandonment *(repudiation),* abjuration, answer *(judicial response),* answer *(reply),* contravention, counterargument, declination, disapproval, disclaimer, disdain, embargo, exclusion, incredulity, injunction, negation, opposition, pleading, prohibition, proscription, refusal, rejection, renunciation, repudiation, veto. SEE MAIN ENTRY
denial of entry exclusion
denial of justice injustice
denial of the allegations demurrer
denial of the pleading demurrer
denial of the statements demurrer
denigrate cavil, censure, condemn *(blame),* contemn, decry, defame, denounce *(condemn),* deprecate, depreciate, derogate, discommend, discredit, dishonor *(deprive of honor),* disoblige, disparage, fault, impeach, libel, malign, pillory, smear, sully, tarnish. SEE MAIN ENTRY
denigrating pejorative
denigration aspersion, bad repute, condemnation *(blame),* contempt *(disdain),* defamation, defilement, denunciation, disparagement, impeachment, libel, slander, vilification
denigratory calumnious, contemptuous
dénigrement disparagement
denizen citizen, domiciliary, dwell *(reside),* habitant, inhabitant, lodger, occupant, occupy *(take possession),* resident. SEE MAIN ENTRY
denizenize adopt, naturalize *(make a citizen)*
denominare denominate
denominate call *(title),* define, denote, designate, identify, label, mention, nominate, phrase. SEE MAIN ENTRY
denomination class, classification, cognomen, color *(complexion),* designation *(naming),* identification, kind, manner *(kind),* nomination, rubric *(title),* selection *(choice),* society, style, term *(expression),* title *(designation).* SEE MAIN ENTRY
denominational partisan, specific
denotare specify
denotate denote
denotation connotation, content *(meaning),* designation *(naming),* meaning
denotative representative
denote bear *(adduce),* bespeak, connote, construe *(translate),* denominate, designate, evidence, evince, exemplify, express, identify, imply, label, manifest, purport, refer *(direct attention),* represent *(portray),* speak. SEE MAIN ENTRY
dénouement cessation *(termination)*
denouement conclusion *(outcome),* consequence *(conclusion).* SEE MAIN ENTRY
dénouement denouement
denouement end *(termination),* finality, outcome, result
denounce accuse, arraign, blame, cavil, censure, challenge, charge *(accuse),* cite *(accuse),* complain *(charge),* complain *(criticize),* condemn *(blame),* contemn, convict, decry, defame, demonstrate *(protest),* denigrate, deprecate, depreciate, disapprove *(condemn),* discommend, dishonor *(deprive of honor),* disoblige, except *(object),* expose, fault, impeach, implicate, impugn, incriminate, inform *(betray),* inveigh, involve *(implicate),* libel, malign, oppugn, pillory, protest, rebel, reprehend, reprimand, reproach, smear, sully. SEE MAIN ENTRY
denounce falsely frame *(charge falsely)*
denounce unfairly frame *(charge falsely)*
denounce unjustly frame *(charge falsely)*
denouncement blame *(culpability),* charge *(accusation),* complaint, conviction *(finding of guilt),* denunciation, disapprobation, disapproval, disparagement, impeachment, incrimination, reproach
denouncer accuser, complainant, contender
denouncing inculpatory
dense cohesive *(compact),* impervious, obtuse, opaque, ossified, ponderous, populous, rife, solid *(compact)*
denseness ignorance, opacity
densified compact *(dense)*
densify concentrate *(consolidate),* consolidate *(strengthen)*
density mass *(weight),* opacity. SEE MAIN ENTRY
dented blemished
denudate denude
denude abduct, bare, deprive, despoil, expose, unveil. SEE MAIN ENTRY

denuded of devoid, insufficient
denunciate arraign, censure, charge *(accuse)*, complain *(charge)*, convict, denounce *(condemn)*, disapprove *(condemn)*, impeach, proscribe *(denounce)*, reproach. SEE MAIN ENTRY
denunciation allegation, aspersion, bad repute, blame *(culpability)*, charge *(accusation)*, complaint, condemnation *(blame)*, contempt *(disdain)*, contradiction, conviction *(finding of guilt)*, count, criticism, diatribe, disapprobation, disapproval, discredit, disparagement, expletive, ignominy, impeachment, imprecation, inculpation, indictment, libel, malediction, notoriety, objection, objurgation, obloquy, onus *(stigma)*, outcry, phillipic, profanity, proscription, reprimand, reproach, revilement, sanction *(punishment)*, slander, stricture, vilification. SEE MAIN ENTRY
denunciatory calumnious, contemptuous, critical *(faultfinding)*, cynical, derogatory, incriminatory, inculpatory, libelous, pejorative, scandalous
denuntiatio innuendo, intimation, notice *(announcement)*, notice *(warning)*, notice *(give formal warning)*, notification, threat
denuntiatio testimonii subpoena *(noun)*, subpoena *(verb)*
denuo reconsider
deny adeem, annul, answer *(reply)*, ban, bar *(exclude)*, bear false witness, cancel, condemn *(ban)*, confront *(oppose)*, constrain *(restrain)*, contradict, contravene, controvert, demur, disaccord, disaffirm, disagree, disallow, disapprove *(reject)*, disavow, disclaim, dismiss *(put out of consideration)*, disown *(deny the validity)*, disprove, dispute *(contest)*, disqualify, forbid, forswear, gainsay, interdict, negate, oppose, prohibit, protest, rebut, refuse, refute, reject, renounce, repudiate, withhold. SEE MAIN ENTRY
deny absolutely disavow, disown *(deny the validity)*, dispute *(contest)*
deny access deter
deny any knowledge of disclaim
deny connection with disavow
deny emphatically disavow, dispute *(contest)*
deny entirely disavow, dispute *(contest)*
deny entry exclude
deny flatly dispute *(contest)*
deny oneself eschew, forbear
deny oneself nothing dissipate *(expend foolishly)*
deny peremptorily disavow, disown *(deny the validity)*, dispute *(contest)*
deny permission forbid
deny respect decry, disfavor, disgrace
deny responsibility for disavow
deny the genuineness of dispute *(contest)*
deny the possibility disown *(deny the validity)*
deny wholly disavow, disown *(deny the validity)*
denying contradictory, contrary, dissenting, negative
deobstruct extricate, facilitate
deontology casuistry. SEE MAIN ENTRY
depart abscond, alight, decease, defect, die, digress, disagree, disperse *(scatter)*, evacuate, expire, move *(alter position)*, part *(leave)*, perish, resign, retire *(retreat)*, retreat, secede, vacate *(leave)*, vary, withdraw. SEE MAIN ENTRY
depart custody escape
depart from abandon *(physically leave)*, avoid *(evade)*, conflict, detour, deviate, differ *(vary)*, quit *(evacuate)*, vacate *(leave)*
depart from life decease
depart from one's course detour, deviate
depart unlawfully escape
departed corpse, dead, deceased, decedent, defunct, late *(defunct)*, lifeless *(dead)*
departed this life dead
departing divergent, flight, separate
departing from deviant, disparate, distinct *(distinguished from others)*
departing from the usual course eccentric
department agency *(commission)*, bailiwick, board, bureau, chapter *(branch)*, district, division *(administrative unit)*, domain *(sphere of influence)*, member *(constituent part)*, organ, post, province, pursuit *(occupation)*, purview, realm, role, section *(division)*, sphere. SEE MAIN ENTRY
department of justice judiciary
department store market *(business)*
departmentalization bureaucracy, division *(act of dividing)*
departure abandonment *(desertion)*, abdication, demise *(death)*, desertion, detour, deviation, difference, digression, discrepancy, egress, end *(termination)*, extremity *(death)*, flight, indirection *(indirect action)*, innovation, leave *(absence)*, nonconformity, quirk *(idiosyncrasy)*, removal, resignation *(relinquishment)*. SEE MAIN ENTRY
departure from contradistinction, difference
departure from life death
departure from usage deviation
departure from usual exception *(exclusion)*
dépêche dispatch *(promptness)*
depellere dislodge, evict
depend rely
depend upon appertain, trust
dependability adhesion *(loyalty)*, certification *(certainness)*, loyalty, probity, reliance, responsibility *(conscience)*, security *(safety)*, trustworthiness. SEE MAIN ENTRY
dependable accurate, authentic, believable, certain *(positive)*, constant, credible, demonstrable, diligent, factual, faithful *(loyal)*, incorruptible, infallible, loyal, official, punctual, real, reliable, reputable, safe, secure *(free from danger)*, secure *(sound)*, solid *(sound)*, staunch, steadfast, tenable, true *(authentic)*, true *(loyal)*. SEE MAIN ENTRY
dependence faith, mainstay, mutuality, reliance, resource, trust *(confidence)*
dependence on credence
dependency appurtenance
dependent ancillary *(subsidiary)*, contingent, correlative, dubious, helpless *(powerless)*, insecure, minor, protégé, qualified *(conditioned)*, related, sequacious, subject *(conditional)*, subservient, tentative. SEE MAIN ENTRY
dependent event contingency
dependent on appurtenant, based on, conditional, contingent, incident, tangential
dependent on circumstances contingent, provisional, subject *(conditional)*
depending aleatory *(uncertain)*, contingent
depending on conditional
depending on a future event conditional
depending upon subject *(conditional)*
depict characterize, construe *(translate)*, copy, delineate, denote, describe, detail *(particularize)*, exemplify, interpret, portray, recount, represent *(portray)*, signify *(denote)*. SEE MAIN ENTRY
depict the essential qualities of define
depiction brief, caricature, delineation, description, design *(construction plan)*, illustration, narration, recital, representation *(statement)*, symbol. SEE MAIN ENTRY
depiction of essential features delineation
depictive demonstrative *(illustrative)*, realistic, representative
depictment illustration, narration
depicture denote, portray
depingere delineate, depict, describe, portray
depletable destructible
deplete deduct *(reduce)*, dissipate *(expend foolishly)*, expend *(consume)*, impair, lessen, overdraw, spend, tax *(overwork)*. SEE MAIN ENTRY
depleted deficient, destitute, inadequate, lost *(taken away)*, nonsubstantial *(not sufficient)*, poor *(underprivileged)*, vacant, vacuous
depletion consumption, decrement, delinquency *(shortage)*, insufficiency, poverty, waste, wear and tear
deplorable arrant *(onerous)*, bad *(inferior)*, bad *(offensive)*, blameful, blameworthy, contemptible, disgraceful, disreputable, gross *(flagrant)*, heinous, lamentable, loathsome, nefarious, notorious, objectionable, obnoxious, outrageous, regrettable, scandalous. SEE MAIN ENTRY
deplorare deplore
deplore blame, deprecate, except *(object)*, regret, repent. SEE MAIN ENTRY
deplored blameful
deploy maneuver, spread. SEE MAIN ENTRY
deplume despoil, plunder
depone acknowledge *(declare)*, affirm *(declare solemnly)*, attest, bear *(adduce)*, certify *(attest)*, depose *(testify)*, testify, vouch
deponent affiant, affirmant, witness. SEE MAIN ENTRY
deponere deposit *(place)*, give *(yield)*, resign
depopulate devastate, diminish, pillage
deport comport *(behave)*, dislodge, displace *(remove)*, eliminate *(exclude)*, exclude, expatriate, expel, relegate, seclude, transport. SEE MAIN ENTRY
deportation banishment, exclusion, expulsion, extradition, ostracism, rejection, removal. SEE MAIN ENTRY
deportee pariah
deportment behavior, conduct, demeanor, manner *(behavior)*, presence *(poise)*. SEE MAIN ENTRY
deposal abolition, disqualification *(rejection)*, rejection, removal
deposcere call *(demand)*
depose acknowledge *(declare)*, affirm *(declare solemnly)*, assert, attest, avouch *(avow)*, avow, bear *(adduce)*, certify *(attest)*, demote, discharge *(dismiss)*, dislodge, dismiss *(discharge)*, dispossess, divest, oust, remove *(dismiss from office)*, supplant, testify, vouch. SEE MAIN ENTRY
deposed powerless
deposit alluvion, binder, downpayment, embed, fund, garner, handsel, hoard,

installment, keep *(shelter)*, leave *(allow to remain)*, locate, pawn, pay, plant *(place firmly)*, pledge *(security)*, replenish, repose *(place)*, reserve, security *(pledge)*, store *(depository)*, store, treasury. SEE MAIN ENTRY
deposit among records of the court file *(place among official records)*
deposit as collateral pawn
deposit as security pawn
deposit formally cast *(register)*
deposit with consign, delegate
depositary comptroller, receiver, trustee
deposition abdication, affirmation, alluvion, confirmation, disclosure *(something disclosed)*, dismissal *(discharge)*, entry *(record)*, removal, repudiation, statement, testimony. SEE MAIN ENTRY
depository arsenal, bank, cache *(storage place)*, catchall, coffer, repository, reserve, store *(depository)*, treasury. SEE MAIN ENTRY
depositum deposit
depot depository, repository, treasury
depravare contort, corrupt, debauch, deteriorate, misrepresent, pervert, vitiate
depravatio corruption, perversion
depravation damage, defilement, perversion, vice
deprave corrupt, debase, debauch, degenerate, pervert, pollute, taint *(corrupt)*
depraved bad *(offensive)*, blameworthy, contemptible, decadent, dissolute, ignoble, immoral, iniquitous, lascivious, lecherous, lewd, nefarious, perverse, profligate *(corrupt)*, reprobate, salacious, tainted *(corrupted)*, vicious. SEE MAIN ENTRY
depraved person degenerate
depravity bad repute, delinquency *(misconduct)*, dishonor *(shame)*, perversion, sodomy, turpitude, vice
deprecari intercede
deprecate admonish *(warn)*, blame, cavil, censure, complain *(criticize)*, condemn *(blame)*, criticize *(find fault with)*, decry, denounce *(condemn)*, disapprove *(condemn)*, disapprove *(reject)*, discommend, discourage, discredit, disoblige, fault, jeer, malign, misprize, remonstrate, reprimand, reproach, sully, underestimate. SEE MAIN ENTRY
deprecating diffident, disdainful
deprecatio intercession
deprecation admonition, bad repute, condemnation *(blame)*, contempt *(disdain)*, contempt *(disobedience to the court)*, criticism, denunciation, diatribe, disapprobation, disapproval, disparagement, reluctance, stricture
deprecative diffident, remonstrative
deprecator intermediary
deprecatory adverse *(hostile)*, calumnious, derogatory, remonstrative
depreciate adulterate, blame, censure, contemn, criticize *(find fault with)*, debase, decay, decrease, decry, deduct *(reduce)*, defame, demean *(make lower)*, demote, denigrate, denounce *(condemn)*, depress, derogate, deteriorate, dilute, diminish, discommend, discount *(disbelieve)*, discount *(reduce)*, discredit, disparage, fault, humiliate, jeer, lessen, minimize, misprize, smear, spurn, sully, underestimate. SEE MAIN ENTRY
depreciate publicly decry
depreciating contemptuous
depreciation contempt *(disdain)*, criticism, damage, decline, decrease, denunciation, depression, deterioration, diatribe, disapprobation, disparagement, disregard *(lack of respect)*, disrespect, revilement, stricture, wear and tear
depreciative calumnious, contemptuous, derogatory, pejorative
depreciatory calumnious, derogatory, pejorative
depredate despoil, devastate, hold up *(rob)*, loot, pillage, plunder, prey, steal
depredation foray, havoc, pillage, plunder, rape, robbery, spoliation. SEE MAIN ENTRY
depredator thief
depredatory predatory, rapacious
deprehendere arrest *(apprehend)*
depress debase, decrease, depreciate, derogate, diminish, discourage, disgrace. SEE MAIN ENTRY
depressant narcotic *(adjective)*, narcotic *(noun)*
depressed despondent, disconsolate, pessimistic
depressing bleak *(not favorable)*, bleak *(severely simple)*, deplorable, lamentable, lugubrious, ominous, oppressive
depressing influence damper *(depressant)*
depression curtailment, decrease, distress *(anguish)*, pessimism, prostration. SEE MAIN ENTRY
depressive deplorable, lamentable
deprival expense *(sacrifice)*
deprival of honor degradation
deprivation abridgment *(disentitlement)*, absence *(omission)*, attachment *(seizure)*, censorship, condemnation *(seizure)*, constraint *(restriction)*, conversion *(misappropriation)*, curtailment, defeasance, deficiency, detriment, discipline *(punishment)*, disqualification *(rejection)*, disseisin, distress *(seizure)*, escheatment, expense *(sacrifice)*, expropriation *(divestiture)*, expulsion, foreclosure, forfeiture *(act of forfeiting)*, injury, loss, ouster, paucity, penalty, pillage, privation, punishment, sanction *(punishment)*, sequestration, spoliation, taking. SEE MAIN ENTRY
deprivation of a right forfeiture *(act of forfeiting)*
deprivation of liberty restraint
deprivation of office removal
deprivation of possession disseisin, eviction
deprivation of rights SEE MAIN ENTRY
deprivative confiscatory
deprive abduct, condemn *(ban)*, confiscate, demote, derogate, despoil, diminish, disfranchise, disinherit, dispossess, divest, exclude, forbid, impress *(procure by force)*, keep *(restrain)*, mulct *(fine)*. SEE MAIN ENTRY
deprive dishonestly defraud
deprive illegally pilfer
deprive of abridge *(divest)*, adeem, confiscate, distrain, impound, seize *(confiscate)*
deprive of advantage disadvantage
deprive of an important part mutilate
deprive of arms disarm *(divest of arms)*
deprive of corporal possession condemn *(seize)*
deprive of courage discourage
deprive of credit discredit
deprive of dishonestly cheat
deprive of efficacy nullify
deprive of essential parts eviscerate
deprive of force abolish, cancel, dismiss *(discharge)*, eviscerate, negate, vacate *(void)*
deprive of form deface
deprive of freedom of movement imprison
deprive of hereditary succession disinherit, disown *(refuse to acknowledge)*
deprive of legal effect invalidate
deprive of legal force nullify
deprive of liberty arrest *(apprehend)*, imprison, restrain
deprive of life dispatch *(put to death)*, execute *(sentence to death)*, kill *(murder)*, slay
deprive of means of defense disarm *(divest of arms)*
deprive of occupancy dispossess
deprive of office discharge *(dismiss)*, oust
deprive of organization disorganize
deprive of ownership condemn *(seize)*
deprive of possession evict
deprive of power abrogate *(rescind)*, disable, disarm *(divest of arms)*, disqualify, impair
deprive of protection expose
deprive of rank depose *(remove)*
deprive of strength debilitate, disable, disarm *(divest of arms)*, exhaust *(deplete)*, extenuate, tax *(overwork)*
deprive of the right to inherit disown *(refuse to acknowledge)*
deprive of vital parts eviscerate
deprive of weapons disarm *(divest of arms)*
deprive oneself renounce
deprived destitute, disadvantaged, nonsubstantial *(not sufficient)*, poor *(underprivileged)*
deprived of devoid
deprived of legal rights aggrieved *(harmed)*
deprived of life dead, deceased
deprived of one's wits non compos mentis
deprived of sensation insensible
deprived of sight blind *(sightless)*
deprived of strength disabled *(made incapable)*
deprivement abridgment *(disentitlement)*, attachment *(seizure)*, denial, distress *(seizure)*, privation
depriving confiscatory
depth caliber *(mental capacity)*, sense *(intelligence)*
depth of thought preoccupation
depthless superficial
depurate decontaminate, expurgate, purge *(purify)*
depurative medicinal
deputation agency *(legal relationship)*, appointment *(act of designating)*, assignment *(designation)*, delegation *(assignment)*, designation *(naming)*, embassy, representation *(acting for others)*. SEE MAIN ENTRY
deputative acting, representative
depute appoint, assign *(designate)*, authorize, delegate, detail *(assign)*, empower, entrust, hire, invest *(vest)*, relegate, replace
deputed representative, vicarious *(delegated)*
deputies delegation *(envoy)*, staff
deputization delegation *(assignment)*, deputation *(selection of delegates)*, nomination
deputize charge *(empower)*, empower, entrust, replace
deputy acting, assistant, broker, coadjutant, conduit *(intermediary)*, factor

(commission merchant), liaison, medium, plenipotentiary, proctor, procurator, proxy, replacement, representative *(proxy),* spokesman, substitute, surrogate. SEE MAIN ENTRY
dequantitate lessen
deracinate disinter, dislodge, eliminate *(eradicate),* eradicate, extinguish, extirpate, obliterate, supplant
deracination evulsion
derail dislocate
derange confuse *(create disorder),* degenerate, discompose, dislocate, disorganize, disorient, disrupt, disturb, mismanage, muddle, obsess, perturb, upset
deranged anomalous, broken *(interrupted),* disjointed, disorderly, frenetic, lunatic, non compos mentis, unsettled, unsound *(not strong).* SEE MAIN ENTRY
deranged intellect insanity
derangement complex *(entanglement),* disorder *(lack of order),* embroilment, entanglement *(confusion),* havoc, insanity, lunacy, pandemonium
derelict broken *(unfulfilled),* degenerate, delinquent *(guilty of a misdeed),* discard, disobedient, faithless, lax, negligent, pariah, recreant, remiss. SEE MAIN ENTRY
derelictio abandonment *(discontinuance),* desertion
dereliction abandonment *(desertion),* abortion *(fiasco),* bad faith, blame *(culpability),* breach, contempt *(disobedience to the court),* crime, culpability, default, delinquency *(misconduct),* failure *(falling short),* fault *(responsibility),* laches, lapse *(expiration),* laxity, malfeasance, misconduct, misdeed, misdemeanor, misfeasance, neglect, negligence, nonfeasance, omission, transgression, vice, violation, wrong. SEE MAIN ENTRY
dereliction of allegiance disloyalty
dereliction of duty bad faith, default, delict, delinquency *(failure of duty),* disregard *(omission),* laches, maladministration, malpractice, nonperformance, tort
deride bait *(harass),* brand *(stigmatize),* cavil, contemn, decry, denigrate, depreciate, discommend, disdain, disgrace, dishonor *(deprive of honor),* disparage, flout, harry *(harass),* humiliate, illude, jeer, lessen
deridere jeer, mock *(deride)*
derisible ludicrous
derision aspersion, bad repute, contempt *(disdain),* contumely, disdain, disrespect, ignominy, infamy, obloquy, odium, ridicule
derisive calumnious, caustic, contemptuous, cynical, disdainful, impertinent *(insolent),* insolent, pejorative, supercilious. SEE MAIN ENTRY
derisive language profanity
derisiveness disrespect, ridicule
derisory caustic, contemptuous
derivable deductible *(provable)*
derivare divert
derivate derivative
derivation ancestry, birth *(lineage),* blood, bloodline, cause *(reason),* citation *(attribution),* connotation, consequence *(conclusion),* corollary, descent *(lineage),* development *(outgrowth),* genesis, inception, origin *(ancestry),* origin *(source),* origination, parentage, paternity, reason *(basis),* source, start. SEE MAIN ENTRY
derivation from reference *(citation)*
derivational ancillary *(subsidiary),* derivative
derivative ancillary *(subsidiary),* consequence *(conclusion),* consequential *(deducible),* dependent, offshoot. SEE MAIN ENTRY
derivative authority agency *(legal relationship)*
derivative interest privity
derivative work SEE MAIN ENTRY
derivatively a priori
derive acquire *(receive),* ascertain, deduce, deduct *(conclude by reasoning),* draw *(extract),* educe, ensue, extract, gain, infer, judge, presume, read, reap, reason *(conclude),* receive *(acquire),* stem *(originate),* succeed *(follow).* SEE MAIN ENTRY
derive by reasoning construe *(comprehend),* infer
derive from ascribe, develop, emanate, evolve, inherit, result
derive pleasure from relish
derived derivative, secondary
derived from dependent
derived from experience empirical
derived from within innate, organic
derived from without extraneous, extrinsic
derived principle conclusion *(determination),* corollary
deriving derivative, dialectic
derogare derogate, discredit
derogate brand *(stigmatize),* condemn *(blame),* contemn, debunk, decry, demean *(make lower),* denounce *(condemn),* deprecate, diminish, discommend, disgrace, disparage, humiliate, lessen, libel, malign, minimize, smear. SEE MAIN ENTRY
derogate from depreciate, discredit
derogation attaint, bad repute, condemnation *(blame),* contempt *(disdain),* criticism, defamation, denunciation, disapprobation, discredit, disgrace, dishonor *(shame),* disparagement, ignominy, obloquy, opprobrium, reprimand, reproach
derogation of religion blasphemy
derogative contemptuous, cynical, pejorative
derogatory bad *(offensive),* calumnious, contemptuous, critical *(faultfinding),* cynical, disgraceful, libelous, pejorative, unfavorable. SEE MAIN ENTRY
derogatory criticism aspersion
derring-do audacity
derringdo prowess *(bravery)*
descant censure, comment, converse, declaim
descend alight, condescend *(deign),* deign, demean *(make lower),* stem *(originate),* subside. SEE MAIN ENTRY
descend by inheritance devolve
descend from develop, emanate, evolve
descend on attack
descend to particulars characterize
descend upon devolve, oppugn
descendant derivative, heir, kindred, offshoot, successor. SEE MAIN ENTRY
descendants children, issue *(progeny),* offspring, posterity, progeny
descended derivative
descendere alight, condescend *(deign),* descend
descension decline
descent affiliation *(bloodline),* ancestry, birth *(lineage),* blood, bloodline, decline, derivation, family *(common ancestry),* heritage, lineage, origin *(ancestry),* parentage, paternity, posterity, race, succession. SEE MAIN ENTRY
descent by forfeiture escheatment
descrial discovery
describable accountable *(explainable)*
describe apprise, characterize, construe *(translate),* convey *(communicate),* define, delineate, depict, detail *(particularize),* disclose, draw *(depict),* elucidate, explain, explicate, express, identify, inform *(notify),* interpret, label, phrase, portray, recount, relate *(tell),* render *(depict),* report *(disclose),* reveal, review, trace *(delineate).* SEE MAIN ENTRY
describe incorrectly mislabel
describe the properties of define
described detailed, documentary
describere delineate, depict, describe
descriptio delineation, description, design *(construction plan),* organization *(structure)*
description account *(report),* brief, call *(title),* caption, character *(personal quality),* clarification, color *(complexion),* construction, definition, delineation, denomination, designation *(naming),* explanation, label, manner *(kind),* narration, paraphrase, prospectus, recital, report *(detailed account),* representation *(statement),* specification, story *(narrative),* style. SEE MAIN ENTRY
descriptive demonstrative *(illustrative),* detailed, informatory, narrative. SEE MAIN ENTRY
descriptive account narration
descriptivism SEE MAIN ENTRY
descry ascertain, comprehend *(understand),* detect, discern *(detect with the senses),* discover, expose, identify, observe *(watch),* pierce *(discern),* recognize *(perceive),* spy
desecrate contaminate, contemn, debase, dishonor *(deprive of honor),* impair, misemploy, mistreat, pollute, tarnish, violate
desecration blasphemy, defilement, misusage, profanity, violation
desegrate SEE MAIN ENTRY
desensitize drug, obtund
deserere neglect
desert abandon *(physically leave),* abandon *(relinquish),* abscond, default, defect, depart, disclaim, escape, fail *(neglect),* flee, forswear, leave *(depart),* merit, quit *(evacuate),* relinquish, renege, renounce, reprisal, requital, retreat, retribution, revenge, secede, tergiversate, vacate *(leave),* withdraw, worth
deserted bleak *(exposed and barren),* derelict *(abandoned),* devoid, helpless *(defenseless),* solitary, vacant, void *(empty)*
deserter fugitive
desertion absence *(nonattendance),* dereliction, disloyalty, flight, infidelity, revolt, schism, sedition. SEE MAIN ENTRY
deserts recompense
deserve earn
deserved condign, due *(owed),* entitled, equitable, fair *(just),* just, rightful, suitable
deservedly duly
deservedness merit
deserving entitled, laudable, meritorious, moral, tenable
deserving belief credible, fiduciary, plausible
deserving blame culpable
deserving censure culpable, reprehensible
deserving of blame guilty
deserving of commendation meritorious

deserving of compliment meritorious
deserving of condemnation sinister
deserving of confidence credible
deserving of praise meritorious
deserving of preference preferable
deserving of punishment guilty
deserving of reward meritorious
deserving reproach disgraceful
deserving reproof guilty, reprehensible
deservingness probity
deservire serve *(assist)*
deses indolent
desiderare desire, require *(need)*
desiderate desire, lack
desideration desideratum, end *(intent)*, need *(requirement)*, will *(desire)*
desideratum condition *(contingent provision)*, end *(intent)*, need *(requirement)*, request. SEE MAIN ENTRY
desiderium desire
desidia sloth
design animus, arrange *(plan)*, array *(order)*, artifice, blueprint, building *(business of assembling)*, cabal, calculate, campaign, cause *(reason)*, composition *(makeup)*, conceive *(invent)*, configuration *(form)*, conspire, contemplation, content *(meaning)*, content *(structure)*, contrivance, contrive, course, criterion, delineation, device *(contrivance)*, device *(distinguishing mark)*, devise *(invent)*, direction *(course)*, direction *(guidance)*, end *(intent)*, expedient, forethought, form *(arrangement)*, form, frame *(construct)*, frame *(formulate)*, function, goal, intend, intent, intention, invent *(produce for the first time)*, machination, maneuver *(trick)*, maneuver, mission, mode, model, motif, motive, object, objective, order *(arrangement)*, organization *(structure)*, pattern, plan *(noun)*, plan *(verb)*, plot *(secret plan)*, point *(purpose)*, premeditation, program *(noun)*, program *(verb)*, project, proposal *(suggestion)*, proposition, purpose, purview, reason *(basis)*, ruse, scheme *(noun)*, scheme *(verb)*, strategy, structure *(composition)*, system, target, treatment, undertaking *(attempt)*. SEE MAIN ENTRY
designare allude, characterize, constitute *(establish)*, denote, designate, nominate, trace *(delineate)*
designate allocate, allot, appoint, call *(title)*, connote, define, delegate, denominate, denote, detail *(assign)*, direct *(show)*, discriminate *(distinguish)*, enumerate, future, identify, instate, itemize, label, manifest, nominate, phrase, prescribe, represent *(portray)*, select, signify *(inform)*, specify, stipulate. SEE MAIN ENTRY
designate a place locate
designate for appointment nominate
designate for election nominate
designate for office by vote elect *(select by a vote)*
designate incorrectly mislabel
designate to a post delegate, hire
designated certain *(specific)*, necessary *(inescapable)*, select
designated ground point *(item)*
designated public forum SEE MAIN ENTRY
designating descriptive
designatio designation *(naming)*, nomination
designation admittance *(acceptance)*, allotment, call *(title)*, caption, choice *(decision)*, citation *(attribution)*, class, classification, cognomen, color *(complexion)*, delegation *(assignment)*, denomination, department, deputation *(selection of delegates)*, device *(distinguishing mark)*, diagnosis, discretion *(power of choice)*, earmark, election *(choice)*, identification, kind, manner *(kind)*, nomination, reference *(citation)*, rubric *(title)*, selection *(choice)*, signification, specification, term *(expression)*. SEE MAIN ENTRY
designation of use appropriation *(allotment)*
designation to office appointment *(act of designating)*
designed aforethought, deliberate, intentional, knowing, purposeful, strategic, tactical, voluntary, willful
designed for the initiated esoteric
designed misrepresentation false pretense
designed to deceive false *(not genuine)*
designedly knowingly, purposely
designee candidate
designer architect, contractor, developer, materialman
designing collusive, creation, deceptive, devious, dishonest, disingenuous, fraudulent, insidious, machiavellian, perfidious, recreant, sinister, sly, subtle *(insidious)*, unconscionable
designing power contrivance
designless casual, fortuitous, haphazard, indiscriminate, random
desinere cease, desist
desirability qualification *(fitness)*, value
desirable attractive, constructive *(creative)*, convenient, eligible, entitled, favorable *(advantageous)*, felicitous, fitting, meritorious, popular, premium, profitable, provocative, suitable, valuable. SEE MAIN ENTRY
desirable feature amenity
desire choose, conatus, desideratum, design *(intent)*, end *(intent)*, intend, intention, lack, market *(demand)*, need, notion, objective, passion, predilection, predisposition, purpose, pursue *(strive to gain)*, request, require *(need)*, volition. SEE MAIN ENTRY
desire the presence of call *(summon)*
desire to buy market *(demand)*
desire to hoard wealth greed
desire to know interest *(concern)*
desire to obtain market *(demand)*
desired objective, popular, preferential
desired object objective, target
desired result end *(intent)*, purpose
desirer candidate
desiring jealous
desirous eager, hot-blooded, inclined, jealous, lecherous, solicitous, zealous
desirous of forgiveness contrite
desist abandon *(relinquish)*, cease, discontinue *(abandon)*, dissolve *(terminate)*, halt, interrupt, leave *(allow to remain)*, palliate *(abate)*, pause, refrain, rest *(cease from action)*, stay *(halt)*, stop, suspend. SEE MAIN ENTRY
desist from discontinue *(abandon)*, forbear, forgo, quit *(discontinue)*, renounce, resign, waive
desistance abandonment *(discontinuance)*, abeyance, cessation *(interlude)*, cloture, desuetude, discontinuance *(act of discontinuing)*, discontinuance *(interruption of a legal action)*, halt, impasse, layoff, lull, moratorium, stay
desistere cease, desist
desk book hornbook
desolate barren, bleak *(exposed and barren)*, derelict *(abandoned)*, despoil, despondent, destroy *(efface)*, devastate, devoid, disconsolate, eliminate *(eradicate)*, extirpate, obliterate, pillage, plunder, solitary, unsettled, void *(empty)*
desolating disastrous
desolation catastrophe, consumption, distress *(anguish)*, havoc, prostration, spoliation
despair brood, consternation, distress *(anguish)*, languish, panic, pessimism, prostration
despairing despondent, disconsolate, pessimistic
despatch delegate
desperado convict, malefactor
desperate drastic, hot-blooded, pessimistic
desperate criminal convict
desperate situation peril
desperation pessimism
despicability bad repute, disrepute
despicable bad *(offensive)*, base *(bad)*, blameful, blameworthy, caitiff, contemptible, deplorable, disgraceful, disreputable, heinous, ignoble, loathsome, nefarious, objectionable, obnoxious, odious, outrageous, paltry, repulsive, scandalous. SEE MAIN ENTRY
despicableness bad repute, disrepute
despicere disdain
despise contemn, decry, disdain, disfavor, dishonor *(deprive of honor)*, flout, misprize, rebuff, reject, renounce, spurn. SEE MAIN ENTRY
despised base *(bad)*, contemptible, disreputable, notorious
despisedness ignominy
despising cynical, disdainful
despite contumely, irrespective, notwithstanding, odium, regardless, spite
despiteful bitter *(reproachful)*, harsh, malevolent, malignant, outrageous, sinister, spiteful, virulent
despiteful treatment contumely
despoil debauch, deface, deprive, devastate, divest, harry *(plunder)*, hold up *(rob)*, loot, pillage, pirate *(take by violence)*, plunder, prey, spoil *(pillage)*, steal, subvert, taint *(corrupt)*. SEE MAIN ENTRY
despoiled marred
despoiler burglar
despoilment defilement, pillage
despoliare rob
despoliation pillage, rape, spoliation
despond brood, languish
despondence depression, pessimism
despondency depression, distress *(anguish)*, pessimism, prostration
despondent disappointed, disconsolate, lugubrious, pessimistic. SEE MAIN ENTRY
despot dictator. SEE MAIN ENTRY
despotic brutal, dictatorial, peremptory *(imperative)*, severe, strict, stringent, tyrannous
despotic commander dictator
despotic master dictator
despotism oppression
destillare distill
destinare appoint
destinate predetermine
destination design *(intent)*, end *(intent)*, end *(termination)*, goal, intention, object, objective, purpose, pursuit *(goal)*, target. SEE MAIN ENTRY
destine allocate, predetermine, preordain
destined bound, forthcoming, future, imminent, inevitable, necessary *(inescapable)*, prospective

destined lot predetermination
destiny destination, end *(termination)*, predetermination, prospect *(outlook)*
destituere abandon *(physically leave)*
destitute bankrupt, impecunious, insolvent, poor *(underprivileged)*, void *(empty)*. SEE MAIN ENTRY
destitute of devoid, insufficient
destitute of good faith dishonest, fraudulent
destitute of integrity dishonest, fraudulent
destitute of life dead, deceased, lifeless *(dead)*
destitute of reason fatuous
destituteness bankruptcy
destitution bankruptcy, dearth, deficiency, indigence, paucity, poverty, privation
destroy abate *(extinguish)*, abolish, abrogate *(rescind)*, annul, break *(fracture)*, consume, countervail, damage, deface, denounce *(condemn)*, devastate, discontinue *(abandon)*, dispatch *(put to death)*, dissolve *(terminate)*, eliminate *(eradicate)*, eradicate, expunge, extinguish, extirpate, kill *(defeat)*, kill *(murder)*, mistreat, negate, obliterate, overcome *(surmount)*, overturn, overwhelm, pillage, pollute, prejudice *(injure)*, prey, quash, refute, slay, spoil *(impair)*, stifle, subvert, upset, vitiate. SEE MAIN ENTRY
destroy a reputation pillory
destroy confidence discourage
destroy form deface
destroy good will antagonize
destroy goodwill alienate *(estrange)*
destroy one's perception blind *(deprive of sight)*
destroy one's reputation defame, smear
destroy the affection of disaffect
destroy the effect of counteract, neutralize
destroy the efficacy of avoid *(cancel)*
destroy the form of disorganize
destroy the integrity of taint *(corrupt)*
destroy thoroughly eradicate
destroyable destructible
destroyed broken *(fractured)*, inactive, lost *(taken away)*
destroyer vandal
destroying deadly, destructive, dire, disastrous, fatal
destruct destroy *(efface)*
destructibility frailty
destructible nonsubstantial *(not sturdy)*. SEE MAIN ENTRY
destruction abatement *(extinguishment)*, abolition, assassination, calamity, catastrophe, consumption, damage, debacle, defacement, defeat, deterioration, detriment, dispatch *(act of putting to death)*, dissolution *(termination)*, fatality, havoc, killing, misfortune, mortality, murder, pillage, prostration, rescision, shambles, spoliation, subversion. SEE MAIN ENTRY
destruction of a right forfeiture *(act of forfeiting)*
destruction of human life murder
destruction of life aberemurder, homicide, murder
destruction of property by fire arson
destructive adverse *(negative)*, bad *(offensive)*, dangerous, deadly, detrimental, dire, disadvantageous, disastrous, disorderly, fatal, harmful, hostile, insalubrious, lethal, malicious, malignant, noxious, pernicious, pestilent, prejudicial, sinister, virulent. SEE MAIN ENTRY
destructive agency parasite
destructive criticism disparagement
destructive fire conflagration
destructiveness murder
destruere destroy *(efface)*
desuete outmoded
desuetude abolition, disuse, nonuse. SEE MAIN ENTRY
desuetudo desuetude
desultoriness irregularity
desultory broken *(interrupted)*, casual, cursory, deviant, discursive *(digressive)*, disjointed, disjunctive *(tending to disjoin)*, haphazard, indirect, intermittent, random, sporadic, superficial, volatile. SEE MAIN ENTRY
detach abstract *(separate)*, alienate *(estrange)*, break *(separate)*, dichotomize, disband, disengage, disentangle, disjoint, displace *(remove)*, dissociate, dissolve *(separate)*, divide *(separate)*, divorce, extricate, insulate, isolate, luxate, part *(separate)*, remove *(eliminate)*, separate, sever, split. SEE MAIN ENTRY
detachable divisible, moving *(in motion)*, separable, severable
detachable part of a certificate coupon
detachable portion coupon
detached alien *(unrelated)*, alone *(solitary)*, apart, autonomous *(independent)*, bipartite, clinical, controlled *(restrained)*, disconnected, discrete, disjunctive *(tending to disjoin)*, dispassionate, equitable, evenhanded, fair *(just)*, foreign, impartial, impervious, independent, individual, insular, insusceptible *(uncaring)*, irrelative, just, nonpartisan, objective, open-minded, phlegmatic, remote *(secluded)*, separate, solitary, unbiased, unprejudiced
detached part segment
detachment candor *(impartiality)*, disassociation, disinterest *(lack of interest)*, disinterest *(lack of prejudice)*, division *(act of dividing)*, estrangement, exception *(exclusion)*, fairness, indifference, neutrality, objectivity, part *(portion)*, quarantine, removal, section *(division)*, segregation *(separation)*, separation, severance, split
detachment of police posse
detail allocate, assign *(designate)*, band, characterize, convey *(communicate)*, delegate, delineate, depict, describe, designate, develop, dispatch *(send off)*, dispense, elaborate, element, elucidate, enumerate, explicate, feature *(characteristic)*, inform *(notify)*, item, itemize, motif, part *(portion)*, particular, particularity, point *(item)*, portray, posse, quote, recite, recount, relate *(tell)*, render *(depict)*, report *(disclose)*, segment, specification, specify, technicality, trace *(delineate)*, trait. SEE MAIN ENTRY
detail the law charge *(instruct on the law)*
detailed descriptive, elaborate, exact, full, narrative, precise, stated, thorough. SEE MAIN ENTRY
detailed account statement
detailed examination investigation
detailed plan blueprint
detailed statement instruction *(teaching)*, recital, specification
details circumstances, contents, description, intelligence *(news)*. SEE MAIN ENTRY
details now to be provided a savoir
details on the law charge *(statement to the jury)*
detain apprehend *(arrest)*, arrest *(apprehend)*, arrest *(stop)*, balk, check *(restrain)*, clog, confine, constrain *(imprison)*, constrict *(inhibit)*, contain *(restrain)*, curb, debar, defer *(put off)*, delay, hinder, hold up *(delay)*, immure, impede, imprison, jail, keep *(restrain)*, preclude, prevent, restrain, retain *(keep in possession)*, stall, stay *(halt)*, stop. SEE MAIN ENTRY
detain by criminal process arrest *(apprehend)*, seize *(apprehend)*
detain by legal process apprehend *(arrest)*
detain in custody imprison
detained arrested *(apprehended)*, back *(in arrears)*, in custody, late *(tardy)*
detainee prisoner
detainer SEE MAIN ENTRY
detainment check *(bar)*, constraint *(imprisonment)*, constraint *(restriction)*, delay, detainer, detention, deterrence, disadvantage, obstacle
detect apprehend *(perceive)*, comprehend *(understand)*, discern *(detect with the senses)*, discover, disinter, expose, find *(discover)*, hear *(perceive by ear)*, identify, locate, notice *(observe)*, overhear, perceive, pierce *(discern)*, spy, trace *(follow)*. SEE MAIN ENTRY
detect differences discern *(discriminate)*
detectable apparent *(perceptible)*, appreciable, discernible, palpable, perceivable, perceptible, visible *(noticeable)*
detectible determinable *(ascertainable)*
detection discovery, observation, perception, recognition. SEE MAIN ENTRY
detective peace officer, spy. SEE MAIN ENTRY
detective force police
detegere betray *(disclose)*, disclose, expose, unveil
detention apprehension *(act of arresting)*, bondage, captivity, check *(bar)*, commitment *(confinement)*, constraint *(imprisonment)*, custody *(incarceration)*, delay, durance, fetter, halt, hindrance, incarceration, restraint. SEE MAIN ENTRY
detention camp penitentiary
detention cell jail
detention center jail, penitentiary
detention of ships embargo
detention station jail
deter arrest *(stop)*, avert, check *(restrain)*, constrict *(inhibit)*, debar, discourage, divert, expostulate, forbid, forestall, forewarn, frighten, halt, hamper, hold up *(delay)*, impede, interdict, interfere, keep *(restrain)*, limit, occlude, preclude, prevent, remonstrate, restrain, stay *(halt)*, stem *(check)*, stop. SEE MAIN ENTRY
deter from one's purpose dissuade
deterge decontaminate, purge *(purify)*, remove *(eliminate)*
deterimental inadvisable
deterior inferior *(lower in position)*
deterior condicio deterioration
deteriorate adulterate, aggravate *(exacerbate)*, debase, decay, decline *(fall)*, degenerate, depreciate, depress, disorganize, ebb, erode, exacerbate, fail *(lose)*, languish, lessen, recidivate, relapse, spoil *(impair)*. SEE MAIN ENTRY
deteriorated bad *(inferior)*, blemished, decadent, depraved, imperfect, old, sordid, unsound *(not strong)*
deteriorating decadent
deterioration caducity, damage, decline, decrease, degradation, detriment, disability *(physical inability)*, disease, disrepair,

dissolution *(disintegration)*, erosion, expense *(sacrifice)*, recidivism, relapse, spoilage, wear and tear. SEE MAIN ENTRY
determent constraint *(restriction)*, damper *(stopper)*, deterrent, disadvantage, disincentive, prohibition, remonstrance, restraint
determinable accountable *(explainable)*, appreciable, ascertainable, provable, solvable. SEE MAIN ENTRY
determinant causal, causative, decisive, derivation, factor *(ingredient)*. SEE MAIN ENTRY
determinate absolute *(conclusive)*, actual, axiomatic, certain *(fixed)*, certain *(specific)*, concrete, de facto, definite, definitive, demonstrable, explicit, express, peremptory *(absolute)*, positive *(incontestable)*, precise, specific
determinatio limitation
determination adjudication, alternative *(option)*, animus, appraisal, assessment *(estimation)*, award, cessation *(termination)*, choice *(decision)*, cognovit, collation, conatus, consequence *(conclusion)*, contemplation, conviction *(finding of guilt)*, decision *(judgment)*, denouement, design *(intent)*, diligence *(perseverance)*, discretion *(power of choice)*, election *(choice)*, end *(termination)*, estimate *(idea)*, finality, finding, goal, holding *(ruling of a court)*, industry *(activity)*, intent, intention, judgment *(formal court decree)*, motive, opinion *(belief)*, opinion *(judicial decision)*, payoff *(result)*, perception, poll *(casting of votes)*, project, purpose, rating, referendum, res judicata, resolution *(decision)*, result, ruling, selection *(choice)*, sentence, solution *(answer)*, specification, surety *(certainty)*, tenacity, verdict, volition, vote, will *(desire)*. SEE MAIN ENTRY
determination by agreement settlement
determination of a child's paternity filiation
determination of damages inquest. SEE MAIN ENTRY
determination of issues adjudication
determination prepense deliberation
determinative causal, cause *(reason)*, cogent, decisive, definitive, extreme *(last)*, final, influential, last *(final)*. SEE MAIN ENTRY
determine adjudge, adjudicate, arbitrate *(adjudge)*, arrange *(methodize)*, ascertain, assess *(appraise)*, award, calculate, call *(title)*, choose, circumscribe *(define)*, complete, conclude *(decide)*, constitute *(establish)*, construe *(comprehend)*, decide, deduce, deduct *(conclude by reasoning)*, deem, delimit, delineate, demarcate, designate, detect, discover, dispose *(incline)*, elucidate, fix *(settle)*, gauge, hold *(decide)*, identify, judge, opine, pass *(determine)*, postulate, predominate *(command)*, program, pronounce *(pass judgment)*, rate, regulate *(manage)*, resolve *(decide)*, rule *(decide)*, select, sentence, settle. SEE MAIN ENTRY
determine a controversy arbitrate *(adjudge)*, find *(determine)*
determine a point at issue arbitrate *(adjudge)*
determine after judicial inquiry find *(determine)*
determine an issue find *(determine)*
determine beforehand predetermine, preordain, presuppose
determine boundaries circumscribe *(surround by boundary)*, demarcate
determine exactly construe *(comprehend)*
determine finally adjudicate
determine in advance forejudge, predetermine, presuppose
determine in favor of elect *(choose)*
determine once for all settle
determine size measure
determine the amount of indebtedness liquidate *(determine liability)*
determine the essential qualities of define
determine the essentials discriminate *(distinguish)*
determine the heaviness of weigh
determine the worth of evaluate
determine upon choose, intend, plan
determine value measure
determine with precision define
determined certain *(fixed)*, definite, deliberate, earnest, fixed *(settled)*, indomitable, industrious, inevitable, inexorable, inflexible, intentional, obdurate, patient, peremptory *(absolute)*, persistent, pertinacious, positive *(confident)*, prescriptive, purposeful, relentless, resolute, serious *(devoted)*, spartan, specific, stated, steadfast, strong, unalterable, uncompromising, unrelenting, unyielding. SEE MAIN ENTRY
determined by conditional
determined by chance haphazard
determined by no principle arbitrary
determined punishment sentence
determiner arbiter, arbitrator
determiners jury
determining conclusive *(settled)*, contributory, critical *(crucial)*, crucial, decisive, definitive, prevailing *(having superior force)*, primary. SEE MAIN ENTRY
determining circumstance determinant
determining element determinant
determining influence determinant
determining of a controversy arbitration
deterred arrested *(checked)*
deterrence control *(restriction)*, deterrent, disadvantage, disincentive, fetter, impasse, prohibition, restraint. SEE MAIN ENTRY
deterrent ammunition, control *(restriction)*, cudgel, damper *(stopper)*, deterrence, disadvantage, disincentive, fetter, halt, hindrance, impediment, obviation, panoply, preventive, prohibition, prohibitive *(restrictive)*, restraint, restrictive, unfavorable. SEE MAIN ENTRY
deterrere deter, discourage, dissuade, intimidate
deterring chilling effect, formidable, preventive
detersion catharsis
detest contemn, disdain, reject, renounce. SEE MAIN ENTRY
detestabilis heinous
detestable contemptible, contemptuous, disgraceful, disreputable, heinous, loathsome, nefarious, objectionable, obnoxious, odious, offensive *(offending)*, repugnant *(exciting aversion)*, repulsive
detestableness infamy
detestation contempt *(disdain)*, disdain, disgrace, hatred, ill will, malice, odium, phobia
dethrone demote, depose *(remove)*, dislodge, overthrow, rebel, supplant
dethronement abdication, disqualification *(rejection)*
detinere delay, hold up *(delay)*, stay *(halt)*
detineri employ *(engage services)*
detonate discharge *(shoot)*
detonation discharge *(shot)*, noise, outburst
detonator bomb
detorquere contort
detour avoidance *(evasion)*, deter, deviation, digress, digression. SEE MAIN ENTRY
detract bait *(harass)*, blame, debunk, decry, denounce *(condemn)*, deprecate, derogate, diminish, discommend, discount *(minimize)*, discount *(reduce)*, disparage, lessen, minimize, smear. SEE MAIN ENTRY
detract from decrease, decry, demean *(make lower)*, depreciate, dilute, diminish, stain, underestimate
detracting abusive, contemptuous, derogatory, harmful, libelous, pejorative
detraction aspersion, bad repute, contempt *(disdain)*, criticism, defamation, denunciation, detriment, disapprobation, disapproval, disdain, dishonor *(shame)*, disparagement, disrespect, phillipic, revilement, vilification
detractive libelous
detractor foe, malcontent
detractory calumnious, derogatory
detrahere derogate
detrectare depreciate, disparage, shirk
detriment damage, disadvantage, disservice, expense *(sacrifice)*, handicap, harm, hindrance, impairment *(damage)*, impairment *(drawback)*, injury, mischief, prejudice *(injury)*. SEE MAIN ENTRY
detrimental adverse *(negative)*, bad *(inferior)*, bad *(offensive)*, destructive, disadvantageous, disastrous, harmful, insalubrious, malignant, noxious, oppressive, peccant *(unhealthy)*, pernicious, prejudicial, sinister. SEE MAIN ENTRY
detrimentum detriment, disservice, harm, injury, loss, prejudice *(injury)*
detrition erosion
detritus discard
detrude dislodge, eject *(expel)*, outpour
detrudere evict
detruncate condense, excise *(cut away)*, remove *(eliminate)*
detrusion expulsion
deturbare dispossess, evict
deuterogamy digamy
devaluate deduct *(reduce)*, depreciate, depress, lessen
devaluation decline, decrease
devalue adulterate, corrupt, damage, denature, depreciate, depress, deteriorate, disable, impair. SEE MAIN ENTRY
devastate damage, despoil, destroy *(efface)*, extinguish, extirpate, harm, obliterate, pillage, prejudice *(injure)*, subvert. SEE MAIN ENTRY
devastating dire, disastrous, fatal
devastation catastrophe, conflagration, consumption, debacle, defilement, destruction, disaster, havoc, plunder, spoliation, subversion. SEE MAIN ENTRY
develop accrue *(arise)*, ameliorate, amplify, bear *(yield)*, build *(augment)*, cause, compose, compound, conceive *(invent)*, constitute *(establish)*, convert *(change use)*, create, crystallize, cultivate, elaborate, engender, enhance, enlarge, ensue, establish *(launch)*, evolve, expand, explicate, expound, extend *(enlarge)*, forge *(produce)*, generate, germinate, increase, make, mature, nurture, occur *(happen)*, parlay *(exploit successfully)*, progress, promote

(organize), pullulate, reclaim, result, revise, succeed *(follow).* SEE MAIN ENTRY
develop a course contrive
develop in greater detail expand
develop too fast overextend
develop too much overextend
developed complete *(all-embracing)*
developed minutely elaborate
developer SEE MAIN ENTRY
development accession *(enlargement),* advancement *(improvement),* augmentation, boom *(increase),* boom *(prosperity),* building *(business of assembling),* complication, consequence *(conclusion),* creation, denouement, discipline *(training),* effect, event, growth *(evolution),* happening, headway, manufacture, nascency, offshoot, outcome, outgrowth, preparation, progress, reform, rehabilitation, result, transition. SEE MAIN ENTRY
development of industrial sites development *(building)*
developmental constructive *(creative),* corrigible
deversari lodge *(reside)*
deversor lodger
deversorium lodging
devertere lodge *(reside)*
deverticulum lodging, subterfuge
devestation pillage
deviant eccentric, errant. SEE MAIN ENTRY
deviate alter, change, conflict, depart, detour, digress, disaccord, disagree, disobey, divert, miscalculate, palter, prevaricate, vary. SEE MAIN ENTRY
deviate from differ *(vary)*
deviate from a direct course detour
deviate from rectitude trespass
deviate from the proper path lapse *(fall into error)*
deviate from the truth bear false witness, lie *(falsify),* perjure, prevaricate. SEE MAIN ENTRY
deviate from virtue lapse *(fall into error)*
deviating astray, circuitous, desultory, deviant, devious, different, discursive *(digressive),* disordered, disparate, dissimilar, divergent, eccentric, errant, indirect, individual, irrelevant, labyrinthine, nonconforming, peculiar *(distinctive),* perverse, shifting, sinuous. SEE MAIN ENTRY
deviating from the common rule anomalous
deviating from the general rule irregular *(not usual)*
deviating from the norm irregular *(not usual).* SEE MAIN ENTRY
deviating from the standard irregular *(not usual)*
deviation avoidance *(evasion),* defect, detour, difference, digression, discrepancy, disparity, diversification, error, exception *(exclusion),* incongruity, inconsistency, indirection *(indirect action),* inequality, irregularity, miscue, nonconformity, quirk *(idiosyncrasy),* sodomy, variance *(exemption).* SEE MAIN ENTRY
deviation from a direct course detour
deviation from probity dishonesty
deviation from rectitude abuse *(corrupt practice),* attaint, bad faith, bad repute, blame *(culpability),* corruption, crime, disgrace, dishonor *(shame),* guilt, malfeasance, misconduct, misdoing, misfeasance, misprision. SEE MAIN ENTRY
deviation from truth fallacy, misstatement
deviation from virtue bad repute
deviative anomalous, devious, discursive *(digressive),* divergent, diverse, eccentric, irregular *(not usual),* sinuous, unorthodox, unpredictable
deviatory circuitous, divergent, errant, indirect
device appliance, artifice, color *(deceptive appearance),* conduit *(channel),* contrivance, deception, evasion, expedient, facility *(instrumentality),* false pretense, hoax, instrument *(tool),* instrumentality, loophole, maneuver *(tactic),* maneuver *(trick),* ploy, project, recourse, resource, scheme, stratagem, subterfuge, token, tool. SEE MAIN ENTRY
devices means *(opportunity),* strategy
devil plague
devil-like diabolic
devilish cold-blooded, cruel, diabolic, heinous, malevolent, malignant, nefarious, ruthless, vicious
devilishness delinquency *(misconduct)*
devilment mischief, nuisance
deviltry cruelty, mischief
devious artful, blameworthy, circuitous, discursive *(digressive),* disingenuous, disreputable, indirect, insidious, machiavellian, oblique *(evasive),* sinuous, sly, tortuous *(corrupt).* SEE MAIN ENTRY
deviousness bad faith, bad repute, corruption, improbity, indirection *(deceitfulness),* indirection *(indirect action),* knavery
devisable assignable, heritable
devisal bequest
devise arrange *(methodize),* arrange *(plan),* attorn, benefit *(conferment),* bequeath, bequest, build *(construct),* calculate, circumvent, compose, conceive *(invent),* conjure, conspire, constitute *(establish),* contrive, conveyance, create, demise, devolution, estate *(hereditament),* fabricate *(construct),* forge *(produce),* form, formulate, frame *(construct),* frame *(formulate),* give *(grant),* grant, grant *(transfer formally),* hereditament, inheritance, invent *(produce for the first time),* leave *(give),* make, maneuver, manufacture, originate, plan, plot, produce *(manufacture),* program, scheme. SEE MAIN ENTRY
devise falsely fabricate *(make up)*
devise treachery conspire
devised controlled *(automatic),* tactical
devised by will testamentary
devisee donee, feoffee, grantee, heir, legatee, payee, recipient, transferee. SEE MAIN ENTRY
deviser architect, author *(originator),* coactor, contractor, materialman
devising building *(business of assembling),* creation
devisor donor, feoffor, grantor, maker, transferor
devitalization fault *(weakness)*
devitalize adulterate, attenuate, debilitate, disable, disarm *(divest of arms),* eviscerate, exhaust *(deplete),* kill *(defeat)*
devitalized disabled *(made incapable)*
devius devious, indirect
devoid deficient, vacant, vacuous, void *(empty).* SEE MAIN ENTRY
devoid of insufficient
devoid of consideration naked *(lacking embellishment)*
devoid of dissimulation ingenuous
devoid of expression inexpressive
devoid of feeling insusceptible *(uncaring)*
devoid of life dead, deceased, defunct, lifeless *(dead)*
devoid of truth dishonest, erroneous, fallacious, false *(inaccurate),* fraudulent, lying, mendacious. SEE MAIN ENTRY
devoir burden
devoir commitment *(responsibility)*
devoirs respect
devolution conveyance, delegation *(assignment),* deputation *(selection of delegates),* succession. SEE MAIN ENTRY
devolve alienate *(transfer title),* cede, convey *(transfer),* detail *(assign),* entrust, pass *(advance),* transfer. SEE MAIN ENTRY
devolve again recover
devolve on delegate
devolve upon assign *(transfer ownership),* attorn, bequeath, demise, grant *(transfer formally),* hold *(possess),* possess
devolvement assignment *(transfer of ownership)*
devolving on accountable *(responsible)*
devote contribute *(supply),* dedicate, give *(grant),* occupy *(engage),* spend. SEE MAIN ENTRY
devote attention to consider, observe *(watch)*
devote oneself adhere *(maintain loyalty)*
devote oneself to address *(direct attention to),* concern *(care),* discharge *(perform),* labor, peruse, ply, practice *(engage in),* resolve *(decide),* specialize, study, undertake
devote thought to ponder
devoted close *(intimate),* dependable, earnest, faithful *(loyal),* fanatical, fervent, indebted, industrious, inseparable, loyal, obedient, partisan, purposeful, reliable, staunch, steadfast, true *(loyal),* unyielding, zealous. SEE MAIN ENTRY
devoted to convention orthodox
devoted to others philanthropic
devotedly faithfully, in good faith
devotedness adherence *(devotion),* adhesion *(loyalty),* allegiance, diligence *(perseverance),* fidelity, homage, industry *(activity),* loyalty
devotee addict, disciple, partisan, specialist
devotio vow
devotion adhesion *(loyalty),* affection, affinity *(regard),* allegiance, dedication, diligence *(perseverance),* discipline *(obedience),* fealty, fidelity, homage, honor *(outward respect),* industry *(activity),* loyalty, preoccupation, regard *(esteem).* SEE MAIN ENTRY
devotion to others philanthropy
devotional sacrosanct, solemn
devour consume, despoil, destroy *(efface),* eliminate *(eradicate),* expend *(consume),* extirpate, obliterate, prey
devouring harmful, oppressive, pernicious, predatory, rapacious
devouring element conflagration
devout faithful *(loyal),* serious *(devoted),* solemn, zealous
devoutness adhesion *(loyalty)*
devovere devote
dexterity competence *(ability),* efficiency, facility *(easiness),* faculty *(ability),* gift *(flair),* performance *(workmanship),* propensity, prowess *(ability),* science *(technique),* skill, specialty *(special aptitude)*
dexterous artful, competent, deft, diplomatic, efficient, expert, facile, familiar *(informed),* proficient, resourceful, veteran

dexterousness efficiency
dextrous practiced
dextrousness gift *(flair)*
diabolic bad *(offensive)*, cold-blooded, heinous, malevolent, malicious, odious, pernicious, sinister. SEE MAIN ENTRY
diabolical cruel, malevolent, malicious, malignant, nefarious, ruthless, sinister, vicious. SEE MAIN ENTRY
diacritical discriminating *(distinguishing)*, distinctive
diagnose decide, detect, discover, interpret, opine, recognize *(perceive)*. SEE MAIN ENTRY
diagnosis construction, determination, judgment *(discernment)*, recognition. SEE MAIN ENTRY
diagnostic empirical, indicant, interrogative, symptom
diagnosticate detect
diagonal oblique *(slanted)*
diagram blueprint, characterize, contour *(outline)*, delineate, delineation, depict, design *(construction plan)*, scheme
dialect language, phraseology, speech. SEE MAIN ENTRY
dialectic controversial, discursive *(analytical)*, logical, polemic
dialectical argumentative, logical, polemic
dialectics ratiocination
dialogize discuss
dialogue communication *(discourse)*, conference, confrontation *(act of setting face to face)*, conversation, discourse, interview, parley, script. SEE MAIN ENTRY
diameter caliber *(measurement)*
diameter of a cylindrical body caliber *(measurement)*
diametric different
diametrically opposed opposite
diametrically opposite adverse *(opposite)*, antipathetic *(oppositional)*, contradictory, contrary, inverse
diaphanous lucid, pellucid
diary calendar *(record of yearly periods)*, journal, ledger, register
diatribe bombast, denunciation, disapprobation, harangue, obloquy, outcry, phillipic, revilement, stricture. SEE MAIN ENTRY
dicendi genus phraseology
dicere appoint, assert, call *(title)*, nominate, pronounce *(speak)*, recite, remark, speak, utter
dichotomize bifurcate, split. SEE MAIN ENTRY
dichotomous bipartite
dichotomy disassociation, split. SEE MAIN ENTRY
dicio dominion *(supreme authority)*
dicker barter, haggle, negotiate. SEE MAIN ENTRY
dickering negotiation
dictate act *(enactment)*, canon, charge *(command)*, citation *(charge)*, coerce, compel, constitution, decree *(noun)*, decree *(verb)*, detail *(assign)*, direct *(order)*, direction *(order)*, directive, dominate, edict, enact, enactment, enforce, enjoin, fiat, govern, holding *(ruling of a court)*, impose *(enforce)*, insist, instruct *(direct)*, legislate, manage, mandamus, mandate, measure, monition *(legal summons)*, necessitate, order *(judicial directive)*, order, oversee, pass *(approve)*, precept, prescribe, prescription *(directive)*, prevail *(be in force)*, regulation *(rule)*, require *(compel)*, requirement, rubric *(authoritative rule)*, rule *(legal dictate)*, rule *(govern)*, statute, writ. SEE MAIN ENTRY
dictate of conscience duty *(obligation)*
dictate peace reconcile
dictated boiler plate, indispensable, necessary *(required)*, nuncupative, obligatory, positive *(prescribed)*, prescriptive
dictated term article *(precept)*
dictates legislation *(enactments)*, protocol *(etiquette)*
dictates of society custom, decorum
dictating master
dictation canon, coercion, compulsion *(coercion)*, enforcement, force *(compulsion)*, mandate
dictator SEE MAIN ENTRY
dictatorial arbitrary and capricious, dogmatic, peremptory *(imperative)*, presumptuous, relentless, strict, stringent, supercilious. SEE MAIN ENTRY
dictatorial mogul dictator
dictatorius dictatorial
dictators hierarchy *(persons in authority)*
dictatorship oppression
dictio delivery
diction parlance, phraseology, rhetoric *(skilled speech)*, speech
dicto audiens obedient
dicto oboediens amenable
dictum canon, comment
dictum declaration
dictum dogma, law
dictum observation
dictum phrase, pronouncement. SEE MAIN ENTRY
dictum remark
dictum statement
didactic disciplinary *(educational)*, hortative, informative. SEE MAIN ENTRY
didactical disciplinary *(educational)*
die decease, expire, pattern, perish, stamp, succumb, terminate. SEE MAIN ENTRY
die away expire, lessen, perish, stop, subside
die down decrease
die out expire, perish
die-hard bigot
diehard malcontent
dies date
dies festus holiday
diet session
differ bicker, challenge, collide *(clash)*, complain *(criticize)*, conflict, contend *(dispute)*, contradict, contrast, demur, depart, deviate, disaccord, disaffirm, disagree, dispute *(contest)*, dispute *(debate)*, dissent *(differ in opinion)*, except *(object)*, vary. SEE MAIN ENTRY
differ in opinion collide *(clash)*, conflict, disaccord, disagree
differ in sentiment dissent *(differ in opinion)*
differ violently collide *(clash)*
difference conflict, contention *(opposition)*, contradistinction, deviation, disaccord, disagreement, disapproval, discord, discrepancy, disparity, dispute, dissidence, diversification, estrangement, feud, fight *(argument)*, identity *(individuality)*, impugnation, incongruity, inconsistency, inequality, nonconformity, nuance, objection, rift *(disagreement)*, schism, split, variance *(disagreement)*. SEE MAIN ENTRY
difference of degree differential
difference of opinion argument *(contention)*, contest *(dispute)*, contradiction, controversy *(argument)*, disagreement, disapproval, dispute, dissension, embroilment
differences dissension, reaction *(opposition)*
different alien *(unrelated)*, contrary, discrete, disparate, dissimilar, distinct *(distinguished from others)*, distinctive, divergent, diverse, eccentric, extraordinary, foreign, heterogeneous, inconsistent, individual, multifarious, multiple, nonconforming, noteworthy, novel, original *(creative)*, peculiar *(distinctive)*, rare, repugnant *(incompatible)*, separate, several *(separate)*, singular, special, specific, unaccustomed, uncommon, unequal *(unequivalent)*, unique, unorthodox, unrelated, unusual. SEE MAIN ENTRY
differentia characteristic, distinction *(difference)*, trait
differential characteristic, discrepancy, distinction *(difference)*, particular *(specific)*. SEE MAIN ENTRY
differentiate call *(title)*, characterize, compare, contrast, define, demarcate, discern *(discriminate)*, discriminate *(distinguish)*, distinguish, enumerate, except *(exclude)*, label, secern, select, specify. SEE MAIN ENTRY
differentiated disparate, individual, particular *(specific)*, peculiar *(distinctive)*
differentiating discriminating *(distinguishing)*, distinctive, personal *(individual)*
differentiating trait differential
differentiation collation, denomination, diagnosis, difference, discrepancy, distinction *(difference)*, diversification, nuance, segregation *(separation)*, severance. SEE MAIN ENTRY
differentiative discriminating *(distinguishing)*, distinctive
differing discordant, discriminating *(distinguishing)*, disparate, dissenting, dissident, dissimilar, distinct *(distinguished from others)*, distinctive, divergent, diverse, eccentric, nonconforming, peculiar *(distinctive)*, recusant, unequal *(unequivalent)*, unrelated. SEE MAIN ENTRY
differre defer *(put off)*, postpone, procrastinate, suspend
difficile difficult
difficilis difficult, fractious, froward, intractable
difficult complex, elusive, formidable, fractious, froward, impracticable, insuperable, intricate, labyrinthine, lawless, obscure *(abstruse)*, onerous, opaque, operose, oppressive, painful, perverse, petulant, problematic, querulous, recondite, restive, severe, uncompromising. SEE MAIN ENTRY
difficult choice dilemma
difficult situation imbroglio, nuisance
difficult to accept unbelievable
difficult to alter ironclad
difficult to appraise intangible
difficult to bear oppressive
difficult to believe unbelievable
difficult to break ironclad
difficult to catch elusive
difficult to change ironclad
difficult to classify nondescript
difficult to comprehend ambiguous, elusive, esoteric, incomprehensible, opaque, unclear
difficult to describe nondescript
difficult to endure painful
difficult to explain indefinable
difficult to feel impalpable
difficult to perceive impalpable

difficult to please particular *(exacting)*, querulous
difficult to see impalpable
difficult to translate indefinable
difficult to understand elusive, indefinable, obscure *(abstruse)*, opaque, technical, unclear
difficultas predicament
difficulty adversity, aggravation *(annoyance)*, bar *(obstruction)*, burden, complex *(entanglement)*, complication, confusion *(ambiguity)*, confusion *(turmoil)*, damper *(stopper)*, dilemma, disadvantage, distress *(anguish)*, emergency, encumbrance, enigma, exigency, handicap, hindrance, imbroglio, impasse, impediment, impossibility, nuisance, obstacle, obstruction, plight, poverty, predicament, problem, quagmire, quandary, trouble. SEE MAIN ENTRY
diffidence fear, hesitation, qualm, reluctance
diffidens diffident
diffident hesitant, reluctant. SEE MAIN ENTRY
diffindere split
diffiteri disavow
diffluent fluvial
diffundere diffuse
diffundi diffuse
diffuse broad, circulate, deploy, desultory, disburse *(distribute)*, disintegrate, dispel, disperse *(scatter)*, disseminate, dissipate *(spread out)*, dissolve *(disperse)*, extensive, intersperse, pedestrian, permeate, pervade, prevailing *(current)*, profuse, prolix, propagate *(spread)*, publish, radiate, spread, turgid. SEE MAIN ENTRY
diffusion circulation, decentralization, osmosis
diffusive extensive
dig down into delve
dig into canvass, delve, investigate, probe
dig out disinter, eviscerate, extract, ferret
dig up disinter, expose, procure
dig up out of the earth disinter
digerere arrange *(methodize)*, codify, sort
digest abridgment *(condensation)*, abstract, brief, capsule, code, compendium, conceive *(comprehend)*, condense, consider, muse, outline *(synopsis)*, pandect *(code of laws)*, pandect *(treatise)*, ponder, read, realize *(understand)*, report *(detailed account)*, restatement, review, scenario, summary, synopsis, understand. SEE MAIN ENTRY
digest of law pandect *(code of laws)*
digest of the law hornbook
digested compact *(pithy)*
digestion osmosis
dignification degree *(academic title)*, elevation, remembrance *(commemoration)*
dignified civil *(polite)*, elegant, important *(significant)*, meritorious, prominent, proud *(self-respecting)*, reputable
dignify bestow, elevate, prefer, promote *(advance)*, raise *(advance)*, recognize *(acknowledge)*
dignitary functionary, incumbent
dignitas distinction *(reputation)*, honor *(good reputation)*, merit
dignity decorum, deportment, distinction *(reputation)*, eminence, prestige, propriety *(correctness)*, respect, solemnity, status
dignus eligible
digredi detour, digress
digress depart, detour, deviate, differ *(vary)*. SEE MAIN ENTRY
digressing indirect
digressio deviation, digression
digression detour, indirection *(indirect action)*, innovation. SEE MAIN ENTRY
digressive alien *(unrelated)*, circuitous, desultory, disparate, indirect, labyrinthine, shifting, tangential, turgid
diiudicare decide, discriminate *(distinguish)*
dijudicare arbitrate *(adjudge)*
dilacerate rend
dilaceration damage, split
dilapidate decay, degenerate, deteriorate, impair, spoil *(impair)*
dilapidated base *(inferior)*, decadent, old, sordid. SEE MAIN ENTRY
dilapidation decline, deterioration, detriment, disrepair, dissolution *(disintegration)*, spoilage, wear and tear
dilatare compound, deploy, enlarge, expand, increase
dilatation extension *(expansion)*
dilate compound, declaim, discourse, enlarge, expand, extend *(enlarge)*, increase, inflate, spread
dilate upon comment
dilated inflated *(enlarged)*
dilatio adjournment
dilation extension *(expansion)*, inflation *(increase)*
dilatoriness deferment, delay
dilatory indolent, otiose, remiss, truant. SEE MAIN ENTRY
dilatory obstruction filibuster
dilemma complication, confusion *(ambiguity)*, deadlock, emergency, entanglement *(involvement)*, imbroglio, impasse, incertitude, indecision, plight, predicament, problem, quagmire, quandary. SEE MAIN ENTRY
diligence caution *(vigilance)*
diligence dispatch *(promptness)*
diligence industry *(activity)*, tenacity, work *(effort)*. SEE MAIN ENTRY
diligens careful, diligent, economical, exact, meticulous, precise, punctilious, scrupulous, strict
diligent circumspect, close *(rigorous)*, conscientious, eager, earnest, industrious, intense, meticulous, painstaking, patient, persistent, pertinacious, punctual, resolute, sedulous, stable, steadfast, thorough, unrelenting, unremitting. SEE MAIN ENTRY
diligent application diligence *(care)*
diligent attention diligence *(care)*, examination *(study)*, interest *(concern)*
diligent exercise discipline *(training)*
diligent practice discipline *(training)*
diligent study diligence *(care)*
diligent thought diligence *(care)*
diligentia diligence *(care)*, industry *(activity)*
diligently faithfully
dilly dally procrastinate
dillydally stall
diluere dilute
dilute commute, deduct *(reduce)*, denature, depreciate, diminish, disarm *(divest of arms)*, extenuate, lessen. SEE MAIN ENTRY
diluted insipid
dilutum solution *(substance)*
dim blind *(concealed)*, blind *(obscure)*, equivocal, incomprehensible, inconspicuous, indefinite, indistinct, inexpressive, intangible, nebulous, obfuscate, obnubilate, obscure *(faint)*, obscure, opaque, tarnish, unclear, vague
dim-sighted blind *(sightless)*
dim-witted non compos mentis
dimension degree *(magnitude)*, magnitude, mass *(weight)*. SEE MAIN ENTRY
dimensions area *(surface)*, caliber *(measurement)*, configuration *(confines)*, extent, measurement
dimidiate bifurcate
dimidiation split
diminish abate *(lessen)*, abridge *(shorten)*, allay, alleviate, assuage, attenuate, check *(restrain)*, commute, curtail, damage, decrease, deduct *(reduce)*, demean *(make lower)*, demote, depress, derogate, discount *(minimize)*, disgrace, erode, excise *(cut away)*, extenuate, impair, lessen, minimize, mitigate, moderate *(temper)*, mollify, palliate *(abate)*, rebate, reduce, relax, remit *(relax)*, restrict, retrench, subside. SEE MAIN ENTRY
diminish in effect attenuate
diminish in quality impair
diminish the price of depreciate
diminish the value of depreciate
diminished minimal, qualified *(conditioned)*
diminishing abatement *(reduction)*, decline, mitigating
diminishment consumption, curtailment, decrease, decrement, diminution, erosion, mitigation, mollification, relief *(release)*
diminution abatement *(reduction)*, consumption, curtailment, damage, decrease, decrement, discount, erosion, mitigation, moderation, mollification, rebate, relief *(release)*, remission, waste, wear and tear. SEE MAIN ENTRY
diminutive immaterial, minimal, paltry, petty, remote *(small)*, slight, tenuous
dimissio discharge *(dismissal)*, dismissal *(discharge)*
dimittere disband, discharge *(dismiss)*, dispense, forgo
dimming obscuration
dimness indistinctness, obscuration, opacity
dimwitted opaque
din brawl, noise, outcry, pandemonium
dint puissance. SEE MAIN ENTRY
diocese region
dioristic perspicacious
dip immerse *(plunge into)*, subside
diploma degree *(academic title)*, document
diplomacy consideration *(sympathetic regard)*, discretion *(quality of being discreet)*, intercession, negotiation, parley
diplomat go-between, intermediary, plenipotentiary
diplomatic civil *(polite)*, discreet, judicious, politic, strategic, subtle *(refined)*, tactical. SEE MAIN ENTRY
diplomatic agent plenipotentiary
diplomatic agreement protocol *(agreement)*
diplomatic code protocol *(etiquette)*
diplomatic corps embassy
diplomatical strategic, tactical
diplomatis patent
dipsomania inebriation. SEE MAIN ENTRY
dirae malediction
dire adverse *(negative)*, bad *(offensive)*, deplorable, disastrous, drastic, fatal, gross *(flagrant)*, harmful, heinous, ominous, outrageous, pernicious, portentous *(ominous)*, regrettable, serious *(grave)*. SEE MAIN ENTRY
direct accurate, administer *(conduct)*, advise, appoint, arrange *(methodize)*, candid,

cause, charge *(instruct on the law)*, clear *(apparent)*, coherent *(clear)*, command, compact *(pithy)*, conduct, control *(regulate)*, counsel, decree, demand, determine, dictate, discipline *(control)*, discipline *(train)*, dispatch *(send off)*, edify, educate, enjoin, explicit, express, govern, handle *(manage)*, hold *(possess)*, impose *(enforce)*, inculcate, indicate, influence, initiate, instill, manage, mandamus, manipulate *(utilize skillfully)*, militate, moderate *(preside over)*, motivate, nurture, officiate, operate, order, overlook *(superintend)*, oversee, predominate *(command)*, prescribe, preside, prevail *(be in force)*, program, provide *(arrange for)*, recommend, regulate *(manage)*, require *(compel)*, rule *(govern)*, send, sententious, straightforward, subpoena, summary, superintend, unaffected *(sincere)*, undistorted, wield. SEE MAIN ENTRY
direct a threat against menace
direct affairs conduct
direct again redirect
direct approach access *(right of way)*
direct attention devote
direct attention to indicate, note *(notice)*, notice *(give formal warning)*
direct cause SEE MAIN ENTRY
direct imperatively command
direct one's attention instruct *(teach)*
direct one's thoughts to focus
direct opposite antipode, antithesis, contradiction
direct the attendance of subpoena
direct the attention to concern *(care)*, convey *(communicate)*, disabuse, mention, occupy *(engage)*, signify *(inform)*
direct the eyes to observe *(watch)*
direct the mind to occupy *(engage)*
direct the mind upon concentrate *(pay attention)*
direct to address *(direct attention to)*
direct toward one object focus
directed against prejudicial
directed verdict nonsuit
directing advisory, determinative, executive, leading *(guiding)*, prevailing *(having superior force)*
directing agency patronage *(power to appoint jobs)*
directing head chief, principal *(director)*
directing power clout
direction administration, advice, agency *(legal relationship)*, canon, caveat, charge *(command)*, charge *(statement to the jury)*, conatus, control *(supervision)*, course, custody *(supervision)*, decree, design *(intent)*, dictate, directive, disposition *(final arrangement)*, edification, education, fiat, forethought, generalship, government *(administration)*, guidance, inclination, intention, management *(supervision)*, mandate, monition *(legal summons)*, occupation *(possession)*, order *(judicial directive)*, ordinance, penchant, precept, prescription *(directive)*, process *(summons)*, purpose, regulation *(rule)*, requirement, requisition, rule *(guide)*, rule *(legal dictate)*, side, standpoint, summons, supervision, supremacy, tendency, tenor, transaction, transmittal, way *(channel)*, writ. SEE MAIN ENTRY
direction post landmark *(conspicuous object)*
direction to imprison mittimus
directive causative, decretal, direction *(order)*, fiat, guidance, mandate, order *(judicial directive)*, procedural, regulation *(rule)*, requirement, subpoena, writ. SEE MAIN ENTRY
directly instantly
directly affected by the outcome of a controversy interested
directly after ex post facto
directness candor *(straightforwardness)*
director administrator, caretaker *(one fulfilling the function of office)*, chairman, chief, employer, principal *(director)*, procurator, superintendent. SEE MAIN ENTRY
directorate board, generalship, management *(supervision)*
directorial administrative
directors authorities, hierarchy *(persons in authority)*, management *(directorate)*, management *(supervision)*. SEE MAIN ENTRY
directorship board, direction *(guidance)*, generalship, hegemony, management *(directorate)*, management *(supervision)*, regime
directory roll. SEE MAIN ENTRY
direful dire, ominous, portentous *(ominous)*
diremption split
direptio pillage, spoliation
direption spoliation
dirge plaint
dirigere direct *(supervise)*
dirimere sever
dirtied tainted *(contaminated)*
dirtiness defilement, obscenity
dirty base *(inferior)*, brand *(stigmatize)*, infect, machiavellian, odious, pollute, profane, prurient, repulsive, salacious, stain, sully, taint *(contaminate)*, tainted *(contaminated)*, tarnish
diruere destroy *(efface)*, overthrow
disability detriment, disadvantage, disease, disorder *(abnormal condition)*, disqualification *(factor that disqualifies)*, handicap, impediment, impuissance, inability, incapacity, inefficacy, pain. SEE MAIN ENTRY
disable damage, disarm *(divest of arms)*, disqualify, foil, impede, maim, mutilate, neutralize, obstruct, spoil *(impair)*, stall, tax *(overwork)*. SEE MAIN ENTRY
disabled helpless *(powerless)*, inactive, inadequate, incapable, ineffective, marred, powerless, unable. SEE MAIN ENTRY
disablement abortion *(fiasco)*, detriment, disability *(legal disqualification)*, disability *(physical inability)*, disadvantage, disqualification *(factor that disqualifies)*, harm, impuissance, inability, incapacity, inefficacy
disabling SEE MAIN ENTRY
disabuse debunk, inform *(notify)*, reveal. SEE MAIN ENTRY
disaccommodate disadvantage, discommode, disoblige
disaccord altercation, argument *(contention)*, bicker, collide *(clash)*, conflict *(noun)*, conflict *(verb)*, contend *(dispute)*, contention *(opposition)*, contest *(dispute)*, contradiction, controversy *(argument)*, deviation, differ *(vary)*, difference, disagreement, discord, discrepancy, disparity, dispute, dissension, dissent *(difference of opinion)*, dissidence, distinction *(difference)*, division *(act of dividing)*, faction, feud, incompatibility *(difference)*, inconsistency, inequality, strife, variance *(disagreement)*. SEE MAIN ENTRY
disaccord with differ *(vary)*, disapprove *(reject)*, refuse
disaccordance deviation, discord
disaccordant discordant, disproportionate, dissenting, incongruous, negative
disaccustom forswear
disadvantage damper *(stopper)*, detriment, discommode, drawback, encumber *(hinder)*, encumbrance, expense *(sacrifice)*, fetter, handicap, harm, hindrance, impairment *(drawback)*, inconvenience, incumbrance *(burden)*, inexpedience, liability, misfortune, penalty, prejudice *(injury)*, prejudice *(injure)*. SEE MAIN ENTRY
disadvantaged SEE MAIN ENTRY
disadvantageous adverse *(negative)*, deleterious, detrimental, harmful, ill-advised, inadvisable, inauspicious, injudicious, insalubrious, noxious, peccant *(unhealthy)*, pernicious, prejudicial, regrettable, undesirable, unfavorable. SEE MAIN ENTRY
disadvantageousness inexpedience
disaffect alienate *(estrange)*, antagonize, discourage, disfavor, estrange. SEE MAIN ENTRY
disaffected faithless, false *(disloyal)*, hostile, inimical, malevolent, recreant
disaffection abandonment *(desertion)*, alienation *(estrangement)*, bad faith, contempt *(disobedience to the court)*, desertion, disaccord, dissatisfaction, dissension, estrangement, ill will, infidelity, malice, odium, reluctance, resentment, umbrage. SEE MAIN ENTRY
disaffiliate disaffirm, disown *(refuse to acknowledge)*, secede
disaffirm contest, controvert, deny *(contradict)*, disaccord, disallow, disavow, disclaim, disinherit, disown *(deny the validity)*, gainsay, negate, oppose, protest, recant, refute, reject. SEE MAIN ENTRY
disaffirmation abjuration, denial, disclaimer, negation, rejection, renunciation, repudiation. SEE MAIN ENTRY
disaffirming contrary
disaggreement strife
disagree argue, bicker, challenge, collide *(clash)*, complain *(criticize)*, conflict, contend *(dispute)*, contest, contradict, contravene, debate, demur, deny *(contradict)*, deviate, differ *(vary)*, disaccord, disaffirm, disallow, disown *(deny the validity)*, dispute *(debate)*, dissent *(differ in opinion)*, gainsay, object, oppose, oppugn, protest, rebut, renounce. SEE MAIN ENTRY
disagree in opinion dissent *(differ in opinion)*
disagree with confront *(oppose)*, controvert, disapprove *(reject)*, dispute *(contest)*
disagreeable adverse *(hostile)*, antipathetic *(distasteful)*, bitter *(acrid tasting)*, deplorable, disorderly, invidious, loathsome, objectionable, obnoxious, odious, offensive *(offending)*, petulant, repugnant *(exciting aversion)*, repulsive, undesirable, unsatisfactory, unsavory. SEE MAIN ENTRY
disagreeing contradictory, contrary, discordant, disparate, dissenting, dissident, dissimilar, diverse, hostile, inapplicable, inapposite, inappropriate, incongruous, inconsistent, litigious, nonconforming, opposite, peculiar *(distinctive)*, recusant, repugnant *(incompatible)*
disagreeing party faction
disagreement antipode, antithesis, argument *(contention)*, belligerency, collision *(dispute)*, conflict, confrontation *(altercation)*, contention *(opposition)*, contest *(dispute)*, contradiction, contraposition,

contravention, controversy *(argument)*, deviation, difference, disaccord, disapprobation, disapproval, discord, discrepancy, disparity, dispute, dissatisfaction, dissension, dissent *(difference of opinion)*, dissent *(nonconcurrence)*, dissidence, distinction *(difference)*, division *(act of dividing)*, estrangement, feud, fight *(argument)*, fracas, fray, imbroglio, impugnation, incompatibility *(difference)*, incompatibility *(inconsistency)*, incongruity, inconsistency, inequality, negation, nonconformity, objection, opposition, paradox, reaction *(opposition)*, rejection, repudiation, split, struggle. SEE MAIN ENTRY

disallow ban, bar *(exclude)*, censor, condemn *(ban)*, constrain *(restrain)*, controvert, debar, deny *(contradict)*, disaffirm, disapprove *(reject)*, dismiss *(put out of consideration)*, disown *(deny the validity)*, disown *(refuse to acknowledge)*, dissent *(withhold assent)*, eliminate *(exclude)*, enjoin, exclude, forbid, forestall, gainsay, halt, inhibit, interdict, interfere, negate, prohibit, proscribe *(prohibit)*, rebuff, refuse, reject, repudiate, restrain, restrict, stop, withhold. SEE MAIN ENTRY

disallow payment dishonor *(refuse to pay)*

disallowance abjuration, constraint *(restriction)*, control *(restriction)*, countermand, defeasance, denial, disapproval, disclaimer, estoppel, limitation, obstacle, obstruction, prohibition, proscription, refusal, rejection, renunciation, repudiation, restraint, veto. SEE MAIN ENTRY

disallowance of trade embargo

disallowed barred, impermissible, inadmissible, ineligible, unauthorized

disallowing prohibitive *(restrictive)*

disannul abolish, abrogate *(annul)*, abrogate *(rescind)*, disclaim, disown *(deny the validity)*, invalidate, nullify, quash, recall *(call back)*, recant, renege, repudiate, rescind, revoke, vacate *(void)*, vitiate. SEE MAIN ENTRY

disannulled null *(invalid)*, null and void

disannulment mistrial, rescision, retraction

disappear abandon *(physically leave)*, abscond, consume, depart, dissipate *(spread out)*, escape, evacuate, expire, flee, leave *(depart)*, perish, quit *(evacuate)*, withdraw. SEE MAIN ENTRY

disappearance absence *(omission)*, concealment, erosion, flight, obscuration. SEE MAIN ENTRY

disappearing ephemeral

disappoint fail *(lose)*, foil, frustrate. SEE MAIN ENTRY

disappointed SEE MAIN ENTRY

disappointing deficient, inadequate, nonsubstantial *(not sufficient)*, unsatisfactory

disappointment defeat, dissatisfaction, failure *(lack of success)*, miscarriage, misfortune

disapprobation abandonment *(repudiation)*, attaint, bad repute, charge *(accusation)*, condemnation *(blame)*, conflict, constraint *(restriction)*, contempt *(disdain)*, denunciation, disapproval, discredit, disdain, disgrace, dishonor *(shame)*, disparagement, disqualification *(rejection)*, dissatisfaction, exception *(objection)*, ignominy, impugnation, infamy, negation, notoriety, objection, obloquy, opposition, opprobrium, outcry, reaction *(opposition)*, refusal, rejection, renunciation, reprimand, reproach, scandal, stricture. SEE MAIN ENTRY

disapprobatory derogatory, unfavorable

disapproval abandonment *(repudiation)*, blame *(culpability)*, condemnation *(blame)*, contempt *(disdain)*, criticism, denunciation, disapprobation, discredit, disdain, disgrace, disparagement, dissatisfaction, dissent *(nonconcurrence)*, exception *(objection)*, ignominy, ill repute, impeachment, impugnation, infamy, negation, objection, odium, opposition, outcry, protest, rebuff, refusal, rejection, reluctance, renunciation, reprimand, reproach, repudiation, scandal, stricture. SEE MAIN ENTRY

disapprove abrogate *(annul)*, blame, cavil, censor, censure, challenge, complain *(criticize)*, condemn *(ban)*, condemn *(blame)*, conflict, confront *(oppose)*, contemn, counter, criticize *(find fault with)*, decry, demur, denounce *(condemn)*, deprecate, disaccord, disagree, disallow, discommend, disfavor, dissent *(withhold assent)*, enjoin, except *(object)*, expostulate, fault, fight *(counteract)*, forbid, impeach, object, oppose, protest, rebuke, refuse, reject, remonstrate, renounce, reprehend, reprimand, reproach, spurn. SEE MAIN ENTRY

disapprove of decry, discriminate *(treat differently)*, regret

disapproved blameful, disadvantageous, impermissible, inadmissible, inadvisable, ineligible, nonconforming, outmoded, unsatisfactory

disapproving calumnious, contemptuous, critical *(faultfinding)*, cynical, derogatory, disdainful, dissenting, nonconsenting, pejorative, renitent

disarm disable, disqualify, placate, propitiate. SEE MAIN ENTRY

disarmament reconversion

disarmed disabled *(made incapable)*

disarrange agitate *(shake up)*, confuse *(create disorder)*, discompose, dislocate, disorganize, disorient, disrupt, disturb, mismanage, muddle, perturb, upset. SEE MAIN ENTRY

disarranged anomalous, broken *(interrupted)*, deranged, desultory, disjointed, disordered, disorderly, unsettled

disarrangement complex *(entanglement)*, confusion *(turmoil)*, disorder *(lack of order)*, disturbance, embroilment, entanglement *(confusion)*, irregularity, pandemonium

disarray complex *(entanglement)*, confuse *(create disorder)*, confusion *(turmoil)*, disorder *(lack of order)*, pandemonium, snarl

disarry entanglement *(confusion)*

disarticulate disjoint

disarticulated disjunctive *(tending to disjoin)*

disassemble disable, disjoint

disassembly dissolution *(disintegration)*

disassociate depart, disjoint, dissociate, part *(separate)*, remove *(dismiss from office)*, remove *(eliminate)*, seclude, separate, withdraw. SEE MAIN ENTRY

disassociated disconnected, discrete, disjointed, distinct *(distinguished from others)*, remote *(secluded)*, separate. SEE MAIN ENTRY

disassociation division *(act of dividing)*, estrangement, inconsequence, privacy, schism, segregation *(separation)*, separation, severance, split. SEE MAIN ENTRY

disaster abortion *(fiasco)*, accident *(misfortune)*, adversity, calamity, casualty, cataclysm, catastrophe, debacle, fatality, loss, misfortune, tragedy. SEE MAIN ENTRY

disastrous adverse *(negative)*, bad *(offensive)*, dangerous, deadly, deplorable, detrimental, dire, fatal, harmful, hostile, insalubrious, ominous, pernicious, pestilent, regrettable. SEE MAIN ENTRY

disavow controvert, defect, demur, deny *(contradict)*, disaccord, disaffirm, disallow, disapprove *(reject)*, disclaim, disdain, dismiss *(put out of consideration)*, disown *(deny the validity)*, gainsay, negate, recant, refuse, reject, renounce, repudiate, withdraw. SEE MAIN ENTRY

disavowal abandonment *(desertion)*, abandonment *(repudiation)*, abjuration, bad faith, confutation, declination, denial, disclaimer, disdain, dissent *(nonconcurrence)*, negation, refusal, renunciation, repudiation, rescision, retraction, reversal, revocation

disavowing contrary, negative

disavowment renunciation

disband break *(separate)*, degenerate, diffuse, disintegrate, disjoint, disorganize, disperse *(scatter)*, dissociate, dissolve *(separate)*, dissolve *(terminate)*, estrange, separate, sever. SEE MAIN ENTRY

disbanding dissolution *(disintegration)*, release

disbandment decentralization, division *(act of dividing)*

disbar discharge *(dismiss)*, disgrace, dislodge, eliminate *(exclude)*, exclude, remove *(dismiss from office)*, repudiate. SEE MAIN ENTRY

disbarment disqualification *(rejection)*, exclusion, expulsion, ostracism

disbelief cloud *(suspicion)*, discredit, doubt *(suspicion)*, incredulity, rejection, suspicion *(mistrust)*

disbelieve disavow, disclaim, disown *(deny the validity)*, doubt *(distrust)*, impugn, misdoubt, reject, suspect *(distrust)*. SEE MAIN ENTRY

disbelieved unbelievable

disbelieving doubtful, inconvincible, skeptical

disbench disbar

disburden alleviate, clear, disencumber, disentangle, ease, extricate, facilitate, free, relieve *(free from burden)*

disburden one's conscience confess

disburdened clear *(free from criminal charges)*, clear *(unencumbered)*, free *(relieved from a burden)*

disburse administer *(tender)*, defray, manage, pay, remit *(send payment)*, remunerate, spend. SEE MAIN ENTRY

disbursement advance *(allowance)*, amortization, appropriation *(donation)*, charge *(cost)*, collection *(payment)*, commission *(fee)*, consideration *(recompense)*, cost *(expenses)*, expenditure, fee *(charge)*, installment, maintenance *(upkeep)*, outlay, overhead, payment *(act of paying)*, price, reimbursement, remittance. SEE MAIN ENTRY

disbursement of salary payroll

discard abandon *(relinquish)*, cancel, delete, depose *(remove)*, disavow, discharge *(dismiss)*, disclaim, discontinue *(abandon)*, disdain, disinherit, displace *(remove)*, eject *(expel)*, eliminate *(exclude)*, exclusion,

expel, forgo, forswear, ignore, jettison, leave *(allow to remain)*, omit, override, quash, rebuff, reject, relegate, removal, renounce, renunciation, repudiate, rescind, revoke, screen *(select)*, set aside *(annul)*, spurn, supersede. SEE MAIN ENTRY
discarded derelict *(abandoned)*, obsolete, outdated, outmoded
discarding desuetude, layoff, release
discardure rejection
discarnate intangible
discedere depart, leave *(depart)*
discept contend *(dispute)*, debate, differ *(vary)*, disaccord, dispute *(debate)*
disceptare arbitrate *(conciliate)*, discuss, dispute *(debate)*, parley
disceptatio controversy *(argument)*, dispute
disceptation contest *(dispute)*, controversy *(argument)*, rift *(disagreement)*
disceptator arbiter, arbitrator, umpire
discern appreciate *(comprehend)*, apprehend *(perceive)*, comprehend *(understand)*, conceive *(comprehend)*, construe *(comprehend)*, detect, diagnose, discover, distinguish, find *(discover)*, judge, locate, note *(notice)*, notice *(observe)*, perceive, read, realize *(understand)*, recognize *(perceive)*, secern, spy, understand. SEE MAIN ENTRY
discern between differentiate
discern something audible hear *(perceive by ear)*
discernere discriminate *(distinguish)*
discernible apparent *(perceptible)*, appreciable, ascertainable, blatant *(conspicuous)*, cognizable, coherent *(clear)*, conspicuous, determinable *(ascertainable)*, evident, manifest, naked *(perceptible)*, obvious, open *(in sight)*, ostensible, palpable, perceivable, perceptible, ponderable, prominent, visible *(noticeable)*. SEE MAIN ENTRY
discernible by touch tangible
discernibly fairly *(clearly)*
discerning acute, circumspect, cognizant, conscious *(aware)*, discreet, discriminating *(judicious)*, incisive, judicious, juridical, lucid, omniscient, perceptive, perspicacious, provident *(showing foresight)*, rational, reasonable *(rational)*, responsive, sapient, sensible, subtle *(refined)*. SEE MAIN ENTRY
discernment alternative *(option)*, appreciation *(perception)*, apprehension *(perception)*, caliber *(mental capacity)*, cognition, comprehension, conclusion *(determination)*, diagnosis, discovery, discretion *(quality of being discreet)*, discrimination *(good judgment)*, insight, knowledge *(awareness)*, notice *(heed)*, perception, realization, reason *(sound judgment)*, sagacity, scienter, sense *(feeling)*, sensibility, understanding *(comprehension)*, vision *(dream)*. SEE MAIN ENTRY
discerp lancinate, rend
discerpted disjointed
discerption disassociation, split
discharge absolution, absolve, accomplish, acquit, acquittal, action *(performance)*, amnesty, amortization, banishment, bear the expense, clear, collection *(payment)*, commission *(act)*, commit *(perpetrate)*, complete, composition *(agreement in bankruptcy)*, conclude *(complete)*, condonation, conduct, defeasance, defray, depose *(remove)*, disband, disburse *(distribute)*, disclaim, disenthrall, dislodge, dispel, displace *(remove)*, disqualification *(rejection)*, divest, egress, eject *(expel)*, emancipation, emit, excuse, execute *(accomplish)*, exemption, exonerate, exoneration, expel, expenditure, expulsion, extricate, exude, free, freedom, fulfill, immunity, implement, issuance, keep *(fulfill)*, layoff, liberate, liberation, liquidate *(determine liability)*, observe *(obey)*, operate, outburst, outflow, outpour, output, palliate *(excuse)*, pardon *(noun)*, pardon *(verb)*, parole *(noun)*, parole *(verb)*, payoff *(payment in full)*, perform *(execute)*, precipitate *(throw down violently)*, project *(impel forward)*, purge *(purify)*, quit *(free of)*, receipt *(proof of receiving)*, recovery *(award)*, rejection, release *(noun)*, release *(verb)*, relief *(release)*, remission, remit *(release from penalty)*, remit *(send payment)*, removal, remove *(dismiss from office)*, remunerate, respite *(reprieve)*, retire *(retreat)*, satisfaction *(discharge of debt)*, send, settlement, supplant, suspend, transact, vindicate, waiver. SEE MAIN ENTRY
discharge a debt compensate *(remunerate)*, pay, quit *(repay)*
discharge a duty perform *(execute)*
discharge a function officiate
discharge a liability liquidate *(determine liability)*
discharge debts liquidate *(determine liability)*
discharge from accusation acquit
discharge from employment dismissal *(discharge)*
discharge from office depose *(remove)*
discharge in advance prepay
discharge of a debt expense *(cost)*, payment *(act of paying)*
discharge of emotions catharsis
discharge of responsibility exonerate
discharge one's duty serve *(assist)*
discharge the duties of commit *(perpetrate)*
discharged clear *(free from criminal charges)*, exempt, free *(relieved from a burden)*, fully executed *(consummated)*
discidium divorce, estrangement
disciple addict, amateur, novice, partisan, protégé. SEE MAIN ENTRY
disciplina discipline *(obedience)*
disciplinarian dictator
disciplinary penal, punitive. SEE MAIN ENTRY
disciplinary action condemnation *(punishment)*, correction *(punishment)*, penalty, punishment, reprisal, sanction *(punishment)*
discipline castigate, comport *(behave)*, condemn *(punish)*, control *(supervision)*, correction *(punishment)*, criterion, edify, educate, force *(compulsion)*, inculcate, labor *(exertion)*, method, moderate *(preside over)*, penalize, practice *(train by repetition)*, punish, punishment, regulate *(manage)*, regulation *(rule)*, reprisal, restraint, rigor, sanction *(punishment)*, science *(study)*, subdue. SEE MAIN ENTRY
disciplined controlled *(restrained)*, literate, spartan, strict, systematic, veteran
discipulus disciple
disclaim answer *(reply)*, cancel, contradict, controvert, deny *(contradict)*, deprecate, disaccord, disaffirm, disallow, disapprove *(reject)*, disavow, disdain, disinherit, disown *(deny the validity)*, disown *(refuse to acknowledge)*, forswear, gainsay, ignore, negate, protest, recant, refuse, refute, reject, relinquish, renounce, repudiate, resign, revoke, surrender *(give back)*, waive. SEE MAIN ENTRY
disclaim the responsibility for disown *(refuse to acknowledge)*
disclaimer abjuration, declination, denial, dissent *(nonconcurrence)*, negation, refusal, renunciation, repudiation, rescision. SEE MAIN ENTRY
disclaiming contradictory
disclamation abjuration, ademption, denial, disclaimer, disdain, repudiation
disclose acknowledge *(declare)*, adduce, admit *(concede)*, apprise, bare, communicate, confess, confide *(divulge)*, construe *(translate)*, convey *(communicate)*, declare, denude, disabuse, display, divulge, enlighten, evidence, exhibit, expose, express, find *(discover)*, impart, inform *(betray)*, inform *(notify)*, issue *(publish)*, manifest, mention, notice *(give formal warning)*, notify, present *(introduce)*, produce *(offer to view)*, profess *(avow)*, promulgate, publish, relate *(tell)*, reveal, signify *(inform)*, speak, specify, unveil, utter. SEE MAIN ENTRY
disclose intentionally inform *(betray)*
disclose secrets inform *(betray)*
disclose something secret confide *(divulge)*
disclosed comprehensible, evident, manifest, naked *(perceptible)*, overt, palpable, patent, pellucid, perceivable, perceptible, public *(known)*
disclosed judgment cognovit
disclosing disclosure *(act of disclosing)*, informative, informatory
disclosure assertion, common knowledge, communication *(statement)*, confession, denouement, deposition, detection, discovery, divulgation, exhibit, expression *(manifestation)*, identification, manifestation, notice *(announcement)*, notification, profession *(declaration)*, publicity, report *(detailed account)*, testimony. SEE MAIN ENTRY
disclosure of fault confession
disclosure proceedings discovery
discolor stain, tarnish
discoloration defacement
discolored blemished, marred
discomfit beat *(defeat)*, discompose, disconcert, disturb, embarrass, overcome *(overwhelm)*, overwhelm, perturb, subdue, upset
discomfiture confusion *(ambiguity)*, disturbance, embarrassment
discomfort agitate *(perturb)*, badger, discompose, disconcert, disease, dissatisfaction, distress *(anguish)*, embarrass, embarrassment, nuisance, pain, trouble
discomforting painful
discommend blame, denounce *(condemn)*, deprecate, disapprove *(condemn)*, fault, lessen, reprimand. SEE MAIN ENTRY
discommendable blameful
discommendation bad repute, criticism, defamation, denunciation, diatribe, disapprobation, disapproval, exception *(objection)*, ignominy, impeachment, revilement
discommode annoy, badger, bait *(harass)*, condemn *(ban)*, deter, disadvantage, discompose, disoblige, encumber *(hinder)*, hinder, inconvenience, molest *(annoy)*, plague, trammel. SEE MAIN ENTRY
discommodious detrimental
discommodity disadvantage, handicap
discompose annoy, badger, confuse *(bewilder)*, disconcert, disorganize, disorient,

disrupt, distress, disturb, embarrass, harass, harrow, harry *(harass)*, incense, irritate, muddle, obsess, perplex, perturb, pique, plague, provoke, upset. SEE MAIN ENTRY
discomposed disordered, disorderly
discomposure disorder *(lack of order)*, distress *(anguish)*, disturbance, embarrassment, pandemonium, panic
disconcert affront, agitate *(perturb)*, badger, confuse *(bewilder)*, counteract, discommode, discompose, disorganize, disorient, disturb, embarrass, frustrate, harrow, harry *(harass)*, menace, muddle, obfuscate, obsess, perplex, perturb, upset. SEE MAIN ENTRY
disconcerted deranged
disconcerting enigmatic
disconcertion ambiguity, confusion *(ambiguity)*, disturbance, quandary, trepidation
disconformity exception *(exclusion)*, incompatibility *(inconsistency)*, nonconformity, specialty *(distinctive mark)*
discongruity controversy *(argument)*, deviation, difference, disaccord, discord, discrepancy, dissidence, distinction *(difference)*, diversity, incompatibility *(inconsistency)*, variance *(disagreement)*
disconnect break *(separate)*, detach, dichotomize, disband, discontinue *(abandon)*, discontinue *(break continuity)*, disengage, disentangle, disjoint, dislocate, dissociate, dissolve *(separate)*, divide *(separate)*, estrange, interrupt, isolate, luxate, part *(separate)*, remove *(eliminate)*, separate, sever, split
disconnectable divisible
disconnected alien *(unrelated)*, apart, bipartite, broken *(interrupted)*, desultory, discrete, discursive *(digressive)*, disjunctive *(tending to disjoin)*, foreign, impertinent *(irrelevant)*, independent, separate, sporadic. SEE MAIN ENTRY
disconnectedness anacoluthon, non sequitur
disconnection difference, disassociation, division *(act of dividing)*, estrangement, hiatus, incoherence, inconsequence, interruption, pause, schism, segregation *(separation)*, split
disconsolate despondent, lugubrious, pessimistic. SEE MAIN ENTRY
disconsolation pessimism
discontent disapprobation, disparagement, dissatisfaction, dissent *(nonconcurrence)*, exception *(objection)*, grievance, ill will, outcry, plaint, resentment, trouble
discontented disappointed, dissident, insatiable, jealous, nonconsenting, querulous, reluctant, resentful, restive
discontentedness dissatisfaction
discontenting deficient
discontentment dissatisfaction
discontinu discrete
discontinuance abatement *(extinguishment)*, abeyance, abolition, ademption, annulment, cancellation, cessation *(interlude)*, close *(conclusion)*, cloture, defeasance, desuetude, discharge *(annulment)*, dismissal *(termination of a proceeding)*, dissolution *(termination)*, disuse, expiration, extremity *(death)*, halt, impasse, interruption, layoff, lull, moratorium, remission, renunciation, stay. SEE MAIN ENTRY
discontinuance of activity impasse
discontinuance of business failure *(bankruptcy)*
discontinuation abandonment *(discontinuance)*, abeyance, adjournment, avoidance *(cancellation)*, cessation *(interlude)*, close *(conclusion)*, cloture, disassociation, discontinuance *(act of discontinuing)*, discontinuance *(interruption of a legal action)*, disuse, expiration, extremity *(death)*, halt, impasse, layoff, lull
discontinue abandon *(relinquish)*, abate *(extinguish)*, abolish, annul, cancel, cease, close *(terminate)*, conclude *(complete)*, continue *(adjourn)*, defer *(put off)*, desist, discharge *(release from obligation)*, disrupt, dissolve *(terminate)*, expire, finish, forgo, forswear, halt, interrupt, lapse *(cease)*, negate, palliate *(abate)*, pause, refrain, relinquish, rest *(cease from action)*, shut, stay *(halt)*, stop, suspend, terminate. SEE MAIN ENTRY
discontinue work strike *(refuse to work)*
discontinued obsolete, old
discontinuity anacoluthon, deviation, difference, disturbance, hiatus, incoherence, irregularity, non sequitur, pendency
discontinuous broken *(interrupted)*, desultory, disconnected, discrete, disordered, disorderly, infrequent, intermittent, sporadic
discord anarchy, argument *(contention)*, belligerency, collision *(dispute)*, conflict, confrontation *(altercation)*, confusion *(turmoil)*, contend *(dispute)*, contention *(argument)*, contention *(opposition)*, contest *(dispute)*, contradiction, contravention, controversy *(argument)*, deviation, difference, disaccord, disagree, disagreement, discrepancy, disparity, dispute, dissension, dissent *(difference of opinion)*, dissidence, division *(act of dividing)*, estrangement, faction, feud, fight *(argument)*, fracas, impugnation, incompatibility *(difference)*, incompatibility *(inconsistency)*, inconsistency, noise, schism, strife, trouble, turmoil, umbrage, variance *(disagreement)*. SEE MAIN ENTRY
discordance conflict, controversy *(argument)*, difference, disaccord, disagreement, disapproval, discord, discrepancy, disparity, dissension, dissent *(difference of opinion)*, dissidence, incompatibility *(difference)*, incompatibility *(inconsistency)*, incongruity, inconsistency
discordancy disaccord, disagreement, dissidence, incompatibility *(inconsistency)*, incongruity, inconsistency
discordant adverse *(hostile)*, argumentative, competitive *(antagonistic)*, contentious, contradictory, contrary, deviant, different, disjointed, disparate, disproportionate, dissenting, dissident, dissimilar, divisive, harsh, hostile, improper, inapplicable, inapposite, inappropriate, inapt, incommensurate, incongruous, inconsistent, inept *(inappropriate)*, litigious, negative, nonconforming, opposite, peculiar *(distinctive)*, polemic, recusant, repugnant *(incompatible)*, unsuitable. SEE MAIN ENTRY
discordia discord, dissension, variance *(disagreement)*
discors discordant
discount brokerage, deduct *(reduce)*, deduction *(diminution)*, depreciate, discredit, disparage, drawback, except *(exclude)*, exclude, lessen, minimize, rebate *(noun)*, rebate *(verb)*, refund, reject. SEE MAIN ENTRY
discountable deductible *(capable of being deducted from taxes)*
discountenance bad repute, blame, censor, condemn *(ban)*, condemn *(blame)*, condemnation *(blame)*, denounce *(condemn)*, denunciation, deter, disapprobation, disapproval, disapprove *(condemn)*, disclaim, disconcert, discount *(disbelieve)*, discourage, disfavor, dismiss *(put out of consideration)*, enjoin, except *(object)*, fault, forbid, forswear, protest, reaction *(opposition)*, refusal, refuse, renounce, restrain
discountenancing disdain
discounting mitigating
discourage browbeat, check *(restrain)*, debar, depress, deter, disappoint, dissuade, expostulate, forbid, forewarn, frustrate, hinder, preclude, prevent, remonstrate. SEE MAIN ENTRY
discouraged arrested *(checked)*, disappointed, disconsolate, lugubrious, pessimistic
discouragement damper *(depressant)*, damper *(stopper)*, deterrence, deterrent, disadvantage, disincentive, dissatisfaction, hindrance, impediment, pessimism, prohibition, rebuff, remonstrance. SEE MAIN ENTRY
discouraging chilling effect, remonstrative, unfavorable
discourse address *(talk to)*, charge *(statement to the jury)*, conversation, converse, declaim, declamation, discuss, instruction *(teaching)*, narration, pandect *(treatise)*, parlance, peroration, recital, recite, rhetoric *(skilled speech)*, speak, speech. SEE MAIN ENTRY
discourse about deliberate, discuss
discourse at length outpour
discourse designed to convince argument *(pleading)*
discourse on the law hornbook
discourse upon comment
discourse with communicate
discourteous contemptuous, disdainful, disorderly, impertinent *(insolent)*, insolent, offensive *(offending)*, pejorative, perverse, presumptuous, uncouth
discourteousness disrespect
discourtesy contumely, disparagement, disregard *(lack of respect)*, disrespect, rebuff
discover ascertain, detect, discern *(detect with the senses)*, disinter, educe, expose, ferret, initiate, invent *(produce for the first time)*, locate, manifest, note *(notice)*, notice *(observe)*, perceive, pierce *(discern)*, recognize *(perceive)*, solve, spy. SEE MAIN ENTRY
discover by artifice spy
discover by observation apprehend *(perceive)*
discover by search locate
discover by survey locate
discover the location of locate
discover the place of locate
discoverable appreciable, ascertainable, cognizable, conspicuous, determinable *(ascertainable)*, naked *(perceptible)*, obvious, open *(in sight)*, palpable, patent, perceivable, perceptible, ponderable, provable, scrutable, solvable. SEE MAIN ENTRY
discoverer author *(originator)*, pioneer
discovery detection, disclosure *(something disclosed)*, invention, manifestation, observation, origination, perception, realization, recognition. SEE MAIN ENTRY
discredit attaint, bad character, bad repute, brand *(stigmatize)*, cavil, cite *(accuse)*, condemnation *(blame)*, contemn, debase,

decry, defame, degradation, demean *(make lower)*, denounce *(condemn)*, deprecate, depreciate, derogate, disaccord, disallow, disapprove *(condemn)*, disavow, disbelieve, discommend, discount *(disbelieve)*, disfavor, disgrace *(noun)*, disgrace *(verb)*, dishonor *(shame)*, dishonor *(deprive of honor)*, disparage, disprove, doubt *(suspicion)*, doubt *(distrust)*, humiliate, ignominy, impeach, impeachability, impugn, incredulity, infamy, lessen, libel, negate, notoriety, obloquy, onus *(stigma)*, opprobrium, pillory, refuse, refute, reject, reproach *(noun)*, reproach *(verb)*, scandal, shame, smear, stain, sully, tarnish, underestimate. SEE MAIN ENTRY
discredit in writing libel
discreditable arrant *(onerous)*, blameful, blameworthy, calumnious, contemptible, culpable, disgraceful, dishonest, disreputable, fraudulent, ignoble, libelous, nefarious, notorious, reprehensible, scandalous, unjustifiable, unseemly
discreditableness bad character, disrepute, ignominy
discredited blameful, blameworthy, blemished, disreputable
discrediting derogatory, libelous, rejection
discreet careful, circumspect, diplomatic, guarded, judicious, noncommittal, politic, provident *(showing foresight)*, prudent, sensible, subtle *(refined)*. SEE MAIN ENTRY
discreetness discretion *(quality of being discreet)*, discrimination *(good judgment)*
discrepance inequality
discrepancy conflict, deviation, difference, disaccord, disagreement, discord, disparity, distinction *(difference)*, incompatibility *(inconsistency)*, incongruity, inconsistency, inequality, paradox, variance *(disagreement)*. SEE MAIN ENTRY
discrepans different, discordant
discrepant contradictory, deviant, different, discordant, disparate, disproportionate, dissenting, dissident, dissimilar, distinct *(distinguished from others)*, divergent, diverse, divisive, improper, inapplicable, inapposite, inappropriate, inapt, incommensurate, incongruous, inconsistent, inept *(inappropriate)*, peculiar *(distinctive)*, polemic, unrelated, unsuitable. SEE MAIN ENTRY
discrepantia contradiction, difference, disagreement, diversity
discrepare conflict, contrast, differ *(vary)*, disagree
discrete disconnected, disjunctive *(tending to disjoin)*, distinct *(distinguished from others)*, individual, insular. SEE MAIN ENTRY
discretion alternative *(option)*, call *(option)*, choice *(alternatives offered)*, diagnosis, discrimination *(good judgment)*, franchise *(right to vote)*, latitude, option *(choice)*, preference *(choice)*, prudence, reason *(sound judgment)*, referendum, volition. SEE MAIN ENTRY
discretional adoptive, discreet, discretionary, disjunctive *(alternative)*, permissive, spontaneous
discretionary circumspect, discreet, disjunctive *(alternative)*, elective *(voluntary)*, judicious, juridical, spontaneous, voluntary. SEE MAIN ENTRY
discretionary order call *(option)*
discretive discrete
discrimen danger, discrimination *(differentiation)*, distinction *(difference)*, emergency, risk

discriminate call *(title)*, choose, contrast, demarcate, designate, differentiate, discreet, discriminating *(distinguishing)*, distinct *(distinguished from others)*, distinguish, except *(exclude)*, identify, perceive, screen *(select)*, secern, select. SEE MAIN ENTRY
discriminate between choose, compare
discriminating circumspect, cognizant, discreet, distinctive, judicious, juridical, lucid, particular *(exacting)*, perceptive, perspicacious, preferential, prudent, rational, sapient, scrupulous, sensible, sensitive *(discerning)*, subtle *(refined)*. SEE MAIN ENTRY
discriminating judgment diagnosis, perception
discriminating taste discretion *(quality of being discreet)*
discriminatingness particularity
discrimination alternative *(option)*, caliber *(mental capacity)*, choice *(alternatives offered)*, decorum, diagnosis, difference, discretion *(power of choice)*, discretion *(quality of being discreet)*, distinction *(difference)*, expedience, favoritism, ine-quity, insight, intolerance, judgment *(discernment)*, nu-ance, partiality, particularity, perception, prejudice *(preconception)*, propriety *(correctness)*, prudence, reason *(sound judgment)*, sagacity, segregation *(isolation by races)*, sensibility, severance. SEE MAIN ENTRY
discriminative aesthetic, circumspect, discreet, discretionary, juridical, particular *(exacting)*, perceptive, personal *(individual)*, perspicacious, preferential, scrupulous, sensitive *(discerning)*
discriminatory inequitable, one-sided, partial *(biased)*. SEE MAIN ENTRY
discriminatory powers discretion *(quality of being discreet)*
discrown demote
disculpate palliate *(excuse)*
disculpated clear *(free from criminal charges)*
disculpation amnesty, release
discursive circuitous, comprehensive, desultory, forensic, profuse, prolix, shifting, voluble. SEE MAIN ENTRY
discursive faculties judgment *(discernment)*
discursive reasoning dialectic
discuss address *(talk to)*, canvass, comment, confer *(consult)*, consult *(ask advice of)*, controvert, converse, counsel, debate, deliberate, discourse, investigate, mention, reason *(persuade)*, remark, respond, treat *(process)*. SEE MAIN ENTRY
discuss in the abstract generalize
discuss private affairs confide *(divulge)*
discussant disputant
discussion caucus, conference, confrontation *(act of setting face to face)*, conversation, deliberation, discourse, interview, meeting *(conference)*, negotiation, pandect *(treatise)*, parley. SEE MAIN ENTRY
discutere breach, dispel
disdain affront, condemn *(blame)*, condemnation *(blame)*, condescend *(patronize)*, contemn, contumely, criticism, debunk, decry, deprecate, disapprobation, disapproval, disavow, discount *(disbelieve)*, disfavor, disinterest *(lack of interest)*, disoblige, disown *(refuse to acknowledge)*, disregard *(lack of respect)*, disrespect, eliminate *(exclude)*, exclude, flout, forswear, ignore, misprize, neglect, rebuff, reject, rejection, renounce, ridicule, spurn. SEE MAIN ENTRY

disdainful blameworthy, contemptuous, cynical, derogatory, hostile, impertinent *(insolent)*, inflated *(vain)*, insolent, offensive *(offending)*, orgulous, pejorative, presumptuous, proud *(conceited)*, supercilious, unaffected *(uninfluenced)*. SEE MAIN ENTRY
disdainfulness contempt *(disdain)*, contumely
disease contaminate, disorder *(abnormal condition)*, pain, taint *(contaminate)*. SEE MAIN ENTRY
disease-ridden pestilent
diseased peccant *(unhealthy)*, pestilent, tainted *(contaminated)*, unsound *(not strong)*
diseased in mind non compos mentis
diseased mind insanity, paranoia
disembark alight
disembarrass extricate
disembarrassed free *(relieved from a burden)*
disembodied disconnected, intangible
disembodied spirit phantom
disembody disband
disembogue exude, outpour
disemboguement outflow
disembowel eviscerate
disembroil clear, disencumber, disengage, disentangle, extricate, free, liberate, quit *(free of)*
disembroiling liberation
disemploy depose *(remove)*, discharge *(dismiss)*, dislodge, dismiss *(discharge)*
disemployment dismissal *(discharge)*, layoff, removal
disenable disable, disarm *(divest of arms)*, disqualify, neutralize
disenabled disabled *(deprived of legal right)*, disabled *(made incapable)*
disenablement incapacity
disenact recant
disenchant debunk, deter, disaffect, disappoint, discourage, dissuade
disenchanted disappointed
disencourage deter
disencumber clear, disengage, disentangle, dissociate, ease, extricate, facilitate, free, quit *(free of)*, relieve *(free from burden)*. SEE MAIN ENTRY
disencumberance relief *(release)*
disencumbered clear *(unencumbered)*, free *(relieved from a burden)*
disendow deprive, disinherit, disown *(refuse to acknowledge)*, dispossess, divest. SEE MAIN ENTRY
disendowment defeasance, disseisin
disenfranchise disable
disenfranchisement forfeiture *(act of forfeiting)*, subjection
disengage abstract *(separate)*, break *(separate)*, depart, detach, disband, discontinue *(break continuity)*, disencumber, disentangle, disenthrall, disjoint, dissociate, dissolve *(separate)*, divide *(separate)*, extricate, free, isolate, liberate, luxate, part *(separate)*, quit *(free of)*, release, relieve *(free from burden)*, retreat, separate, sever, withdraw. SEE MAIN ENTRY
disengaged apart, bipartite, controlled *(restrained)*, discrete, dispassionate, free *(not restricted)*, free *(relieved from a burden)*, idle, neutral, nonpartisan, otiose, unemployed, vacant
disengagement disassociation, division *(act of dividing)*, estrangement, evulsion, exemption, freedom, liberation, release, segregation *(separation)*, split

disengaging divisive
disentail disencumber
disentangle ascertain, break *(separate)*, clarify, clear, construe *(comprehend)*, detach, disencumber, disengage, elucidate, explain, extricate, facilitate, find *(discover)*, free, part *(separate)*, quit *(free of)*, resolve *(solve)*, simplify *(make easier)*, solve, sort. SEE MAIN ENTRY
disentangled free *(relieved from a burden)*
disentanglement denouement, release
disenthrall disengage, enfranchise, extricate, free, liberate, release, rescue. SEE MAIN ENTRY
disenthrallment discharge *(liberation)*, freedom, liberation, release
disenthrone dislodge
disentitle condemn *(seize)*, confiscate, depose *(remove)*, deprive, disinherit, dispossess, disqualify, divest, impress *(procure by force)*
disentitled ineligible
disentitlement denial, disqualification *(rejection)*, foreclosure, forfeiture *(act of forfeiting)*
disentomb disinter
disequalization discrimination *(differentiation)*
disequilibrium difference, disparity
disertus eloquent, specific
disestablish abolish, annul, cancel, depose *(remove)*, dislodge, quash, rescind, subvert, withdraw
disestablished null *(invalid)*, null and void
disestablishment annulment, defeasance, subversion
disesteem attaint, bad character, bad repute, contemn, contempt *(disdain)*, decry, depreciate, disapprobation, disapproval, discount *(disbelieve)*, discredit, disdain *(noun)*, disdain *(verb)*, disgrace, dishonor *(shame)*, disparage, disparagement, disregard *(lack of respect)*, disrepute, disrespect, dissatisfaction, ignominy, ill repute, infamy, malign, misprize, notoriety, obloquy, odium, opprobrium, scandal, shame, underestimate
disfavor alienation *(estrangement)*, bad character, bad repute, condemn *(ban)*, condemnation *(blame)*, contempt *(disdain)*, deprecate, disaffect, disapprobation, disapproval, disapprove *(condemn)*, discommend, discredit, discriminate *(treat differently)*, disdain, disgrace, dishonor *(shame)*, disparage, disparagement, disqualification *(rejection)*, disregard *(lack of respect)*, dissatisfaction, estrangement, ignominy, ill repute, impugnation, infamy, notoriety, obloquy, odium, proscription, rejection, reluctance, shame. SEE MAIN ENTRY
disfiguration defacement
disfigure damage, deface, harm, mutilate, spoil *(impair)*
disfigured blemished, imperfect, marred
disfigurement defacement, flaw
disfranchise disable, disqualify, subject. SEE MAIN ENTRY
disfranchisement disqualification *(rejection)*, infringement, subjection
disfurnish denude
disgorge eject *(expel)*, forfeit, outpour
disgorgement expulsion, outburst
disgrace attaint, bad character, bad repute, brand, brand *(stigmatize)*, corruption, debase, defame, defilement, degradation, demean *(make lower)*, depreciate, derogate, discredit *(noun)*, discredit *(verb)*, dishonor *(shame)*, dishonor *(deprive of honor)*, disparage, humiliate, ignominy, ill repute, infamy, notoriety, obloquy, odium, onus *(stigma)*, opprobrium, pillory, reduce, reproach *(noun)*, reproach *(verb)*, scandal, shame, stain, stigma, sully, tarnish. SEE MAIN ENTRY
disgraced bad *(offensive)*, blemished, disreputable
disgraceful arrant *(onerous)*, contemptible, disorderly, disreputable, heinous, ignoble, inexcusable, inexpiable, nefarious, notorious, odious, outrageous, profligate *(corrupt)*, recreant, reprehensible, scandalous, vicious. SEE MAIN ENTRY
disgracefulness bad repute, disrepute
disgracing libelous
disgruntle disappoint, discourage
disgruntled disappointed
disgruntlement dissatisfaction
disguise artifice, camouflage, cloak, clothe, conceal, concealment, cover *(pretext)*, cover *(conceal)*, deception, decoy, denature, distort, distortion, ensconce, enshroud, equivocate, fake, false pretense, falsification, feign, hide, misrepresent, obnubilate, obscure, palter, plant *(covertly place)*, pretend, pretense *(pretext)*, pretext, profess *(pretend)*, ruse, screen *(guard)*. SEE MAIN ENTRY
disguised assumed *(feigned)*, blind *(concealed)*, clandestine, covert, deceptive, hidden, indiscernible, mysterious, surreptitious
disguisement concealment
disgust contempt *(disdain)*, dissatisfaction, distress, odium, pique
disgusted renitent
disgustful repugnant *(exciting aversion)*
disgusting antipathetic *(distasteful)*, bad *(offensive)*, contemptible, gross *(flagrant)*, heinous, loathsome, lurid, objectionable, obnoxious, odious, offensive *(offending)*, reprehensible, reprobate, repugnant *(exciting aversion)*, repulsive, scurrilous, sordid, unsavory. SEE MAIN ENTRY
disharmonious dissenting, divergent, incongruous
disharmonize disaccord
disharmony conflict, contention *(opposition)*, contest *(dispute)*, controversy *(argument)*, deviation, difference, disaccord, disagreement, discord, discrepancy, disorder *(lack of order)*, disparity, dissension, dissent *(difference of opinion)*, dissidence, distinction *(difference)*, division *(act of dividing)*, estrangement, incompatibility *(inconsistency)*, incongruity, pandemonium, variance *(disagreement)*. SEE MAIN ENTRY
dishearten deter, disappoint, discommode, discourage, dissuade
disheartened disconsolate, lugubrious, pessimistic
disheartener damper *(depressant)*
disheartening bleak *(not favorable)*, deplorable, disastrous, lamentable
disheartenment depression, pessimism
disherit deprive, disinherit
dishevel agitate *(shake up)*, discompose, disorganize, disrupt, disturb
disheveled disordered, disorderly
dishevelment disorder *(lack of order)*, disturbance
dishonest culpable, deceptive, delinquent *(guilty of a misdeed)*, disgraceful, disingenuous, disreputable, faithless, false *(disloyal)*, felonious, fraudulent, ignoble, immoral, iniquitous, insidious, irregular *(improper)*, larcenous, lying, machiavellian, mendacious, peccant *(culpable)*, perfidious, recreant, sinister, sly, tainted *(corrupted)*, tortuous *(corrupt)*, unconscionable, undependable, unethical, unscrupulous, untrue, untrustworthy. SEE MAIN ENTRY
dishonest application misapplication
dishonest management misconduct
dishonest use misapplication
dishonesty abuse *(corrupt practice)*, bad faith, corruption, deception, false pretense, fraud, guilt, hypocrisy, improbity, indirection *(deceitfulness)*, knavery, misdoing, pettifoggery, racket. SEE MAIN ENTRY
dishonor abuse *(physical misuse)*, abuse *(violate)*, aspersion, attaint, bad character, bad faith, bad repute, brand *(stigmatize)*, browbeat, contemn, contumely, corruption, debase, defame, default, defilement, degradation, demean *(make lower)*, denigrate, denounce *(condemn)*, derogate, discredit *(noun)*, discredit *(verb)*, disfavor, disgrace *(noun)*, disgrace *(verb)*, dishonesty, disoblige, disparage, disparagement, disregard *(lack of respect)*, disrepute, disrespect, fail *(lose)*, humiliate, ignominy, ill repute, impeachability, infamy, infidelity, malign, nonpayment, notoriety, obloquy, odium, onus *(stigma)*, opprobrium, pillory, pollute, reproach *(noun)*, reproach *(verb)*, repudiate, scandal, shame, smear, stain, stigma, sully, tarnish, violate. SEE MAIN ENTRY
dishonor by false reports malign
dishonorable bad *(offensive)*, blameful, blameworthy, contemptible, contemptuous, disgraceful, dishonest, disreputable, faithless, false *(disloyal)*, fraudulent, ignoble, immoral, libelous, machiavellian, nefarious, notorious, outrageous, perfidious, recreant, reprehensible, scandalous, sly, tortuous *(corrupt)*, unbecoming, unconscionable, unethical, unjust, unjustifiable, unscrupulous, untrustworthy, venal. SEE MAIN ENTRY
dishonorableness bad character, bad repute, disrepute, ignominy
dishonored blemished
dishonored bill bad debt, nonpayment
dishonoring abuse *(physical misuse)*, contemptuous, default, derogatory, libelous
disillusion debunk, disabuse, disaffect, disappoint, discourage, dissuade
disillusioned cynical, disappointed
disillusionize disappoint
disillusionment disparagement
disimprison liberate, parole, rescue
disimprisonment freedom, liberation
disincentive deterrence, deterrent. SEE MAIN ENTRY
disinclination bias, disincentive, reluctance
disinclination to action sloth
disinclination to labor sloth
disincline deter, discourage, expostulate
disinclined adverse *(hostile)*, averse, dissident, reluctant, renitent, restive. SEE MAIN ENTRY
disinfect decontaminate
disinfectant preventive
disinfected pure
disingenuity improbity, indirection *(deceitfulness)*
disingenuous deceptive, dishonest, fraudulent, lying, machiavellian, oblique *(evasive)*, sinister, tortuous *(corrupt)*, unconscionable, unscrupulous, untrue. SEE MAIN ENTRY

disingenuousness bad faith, color *(deceptive appearance)*, dishonesty, evasion, improbity, indirection *(deceitfulness)*
disingeuous sly
disinherit adeem, confiscate, deprive, disown *(refuse to acknowledge)*, reject. SEE MAIN ENTRY
disinheritance rejection, renunciation
disinhume disinter
disintegrate break *(separate)*, decay, degenerate, destroy *(efface)*, diffuse, disorganize, dispel, disperse *(scatter)*, dissipate *(spread out)*, dissolve *(disperse)*, erode, obliterate. SEE MAIN ENTRY
disintegrated broken *(fractured)*, old
disintegrating decadent
disintegration attrition, decentralization, deterioration, detriment, erosion, spoilage
disinter detect, ferret, find *(discover)*, solve. SEE MAIN ENTRY
disinterest discourage, disregard *(unconcern)*, neutrality, objectivity. SEE MAIN ENTRY
disinterested dispassionate, equitable, evenhanded, factual, impartial, judicial, just, neutral, objective, open-minded, perfunctory, phlegmatic, torpid, unbiased, unprejudiced
disinterestedly fairly *(impartially)*
disinterestedness candor *(impartiality)*, disinterest *(lack of interest)*, disregard *(unconcern)*, fairness, indifference, neutrality, objectivity
disinterestness candor *(impartiality)*
disinvigorate disarm *(divest of arms)*
disinvolve disentangle. SEE MAIN ENTRY
disiunctio separation
disiunctus separate
disiungere detach, divide *(separate)*, separate
disjoin abstract *(separate)*, break *(separate)*, depart, detach, dichotomize, disband, discontinue *(abandon)*, discontinue *(break continuity)*, disencumber, disengage, disentangle, disjoint, dislocate, disorganize, disperse *(scatter)*, disrupt, dissociate, dissolve *(separate)*, divide *(separate)*, divorce, excise *(cut away)*, extricate, interrupt, isolate, luxate, part *(separate)*, remove *(eliminate)*, separate, sever, split. SEE MAIN ENTRY
disjoined alien *(unrelated)*, apart, bipartite, desultory, disconnected, discrete, disjunctive *(tending to disjoin)*, divisive, individual, separate, solitary
disjoining decentralization
disjoint apart, disband, discrete, disjunctive *(tending to disjoin)*, dislocate, force *(break)*, luxate. SEE MAIN ENTRY
disjointed apart, bipartite, deranged, disconnected, disjunctive *(tending to disjoin)*, disorderly, separate. SEE MAIN ENTRY
disjointure disassociation
disjunct anomalous, apart, bipartite, broken *(interrupted)*, desultory, disconnected, discrete, disordered, individual, separate, solitary, sporadic
disjunction abandonment *(discontinuance)*, decentralization, difference, disassociation, division *(act of dividing)*, estrangement, hiatus, incoherence, inconsequence, interruption, rift *(gap)*, split
disjunctive disconnected, disjointed, divisive, elective *(selective)*. SEE MAIN ENTRY
disjuncture division *(act of dividing)*
dislikable contemptuous, objectionable
dislike conflict *(noun)*, conflict *(verb)*, contempt *(disdain)*, deprecate, disapprobation, disapproval, disapprove *(condemn)*, disdain, disfavor, disparagement, dissatisfaction, exception *(objection)*, hatred, ignominy, ill repute, ill will, incompatibility *(difference)*, intolerance, malice, odium, outcry, phobia, rejection, reluctance, resent, umbrage. SEE MAIN ENTRY
disliked disreputable, invidious, loathsome, repugnant *(exciting aversion)*, repulsive, undesirable, unsavory
disliking averse
dislocate break *(separate)*, contort, disband, discompose, disjoint, dislodge, disorient, displace *(remove)*, disturb, isolate, luxate, remove *(eliminate)*. SEE MAIN ENTRY
dislocated anomalous, deranged, disordered
dislocation deportation, disturbance, removal, replacement. SEE MAIN ENTRY
dislodge deport *(banish)*, depose *(remove)*, disengage, dislocate, disorient, displace *(remove)*, dispossess, disturb, divest, eject *(evict)*, evict, expel, extricate, liberate, oust, relegate, remove *(eliminate)*. SEE MAIN ENTRY
dislodgment dismissal *(discharge)*, disqualification *(rejection)*, eviction, exclusion, expropriation *(divestiture)*, expulsion, foreclosure, liberation, ostracism, ouster, rejection, removal
disloyal broken *(unfulfilled)*, disobedient, faithless, hostile, insidious, insubordinate, irresponsible, perfidious, recreant, untrue, untrustworthy. SEE MAIN ENTRY
disloyalty bad faith, corruption, desertion, estrangement, infidelity, mutiny, noncompliance *(nonobservance)*, sedition, treason. SEE MAIN ENTRY
dismal bleak *(not favorable)*, bleak *(severely simple)*, deplorable, despondent, dire, disconsolate, lamentable, lifeless *(dull)*, lugubrious. SEE MAIN ENTRY
dismantle break *(separate)*, destroy *(void)*, disable, disjoint, disorganize, dissolve *(separate)*, eviscerate, extinguish, mutilate, subvert. SEE MAIN ENTRY
dismantlement dissolution *(disintegration)*
dismask disclose
dismay aggravate *(annoy)*, agitate *(perturb)*, consternation, deter, discompose, disconcert, discourage, disturb, doubt *(suspicion)*, fear, fright, harrow, intimidate, perturb, pique, trepidation. SEE MAIN ENTRY
dismayed pessimistic
dismaying ominous, sinister
dismember disband, disjoint, divide *(separate)*, mutilate, part *(separate)*, separate, sever
dismembered broken *(fractured)*, disjunctive *(tending to disjoin)*
dismemberment disassociation, division *(act of dividing)*, split
dismiss cancel, cede, clear, condone, controvert, decry, deport *(banish)*, depose *(remove)*, disband, discharge *(release from obligation)*, discontinue *(abandon)*, dislodge, dispel, displace *(remove)*, disregard, eject *(expel)*, eliminate *(exclude)*, except *(exclude)*, exclude, exculpate, expel, forgo, free, liberate, oust, override, quash, rebuff, recall *(call back)*, refuse, reject, release, relegate, relinquish, remit *(release from penalty)*, remove *(dismiss from office)*, renounce, rescind, revoke, send, superannuate, supplant, vindicate, waive. SEE MAIN ENTRY
dismiss all doubt assure *(give confidence to)*
dismiss charges palliate *(excuse)*. SEE MAIN ENTRY
dismiss doubt ensure, reassure
dismiss from favor demote, disgrace
dismiss from service disband
dismiss from the bar disbar
dismiss from the legal profession disbar
dismissal abandonment *(repudiation)*, absolution, acquittal, avoidance *(cancellation)*, banishment, cancellation, compurgation, condonation, deportation, discharge *(release from obligation)*, discontinuance *(act of discontinuing)*, discontinuance *(interruption of a legal action)*, disqualification *(rejection)*, dissolution *(termination)*, exclusion, expulsion, layoff, liberation, ostracism, pardon, rejection, release, removal, renunciation. SEE MAIN ENTRY
dismissal from office degradation
dismissal of an accusation absolution
dismissal of charges exoneration
dismissed clear *(free from criminal charges)*, free *(relieved from a burden)*, obsolete. SEE MAIN ENTRY
dismissible defeasible
dismount alight
disobedience anarchy, bad faith, breach, contempt *(disobedience to the court)*, defiance, disloyalty, disregard *(lack of respect)*, disrespect, infraction, infringement, insurrection, invasion, mutiny, nonconformity, offense, rebellion, resistance, revolt, sedition, transgression
disobedient adverse *(hostile)*, broken *(unfulfilled)*, contumacious, disorderly, dissident, froward, insolent, insubordinate, intractable, irresponsible, lawless, nonconforming, nonconsenting, perfidious, perverse, recalcitrant, recusant, restive, uncontrollable, unruly, untrue. SEE MAIN ENTRY
disobey break *(violate)*, defect, defy, rebel, trespass, violate. SEE MAIN ENTRY
disobey the law offend *(violate the law)*, trespass
disobeyed lawless
disobeying lawless
disoblige affront, disaffect, discommode, mistreat. SEE MAIN ENTRY
disobliging insolent, invidious, malevolent, negative, outrageous
disorder agitate *(shake up)*, anarchy, commotion, complex *(entanglement)*, confuse *(create disorder)*, confusion *(turmoil)*, degenerate, detriment, disability *(physical inability)*, discompose, disease, dislocate, disorganize, disorient, disrupt, disturb, disturbance, embroilment, entanglement *(confusion)*, havoc, imbroglio, incoherence, insurrection, irregularity, misrule, muddle, pandemonium, panic, perturb, riot, shambles, snarl, turmoil, violence. SEE MAIN ENTRY
disordered anomalous, broken *(interrupted)*, deranged, disjointed, haphazard, lunatic, slipshod. SEE MAIN ENTRY
disordered intellect insanity
disordered mind insanity, lunacy
disordered reason insanity, paranoia
disorderliness anarchy, commotion, confusion *(turmoil)*, irregularity, lynch law, riot
disorderly culpable, disjointed, disobedient, haphazard, lawless, licentious, perverse, slipshod, uncontrollable, unruly. SEE MAIN ENTRY

disorderly conduct disorder *(lack of order),* misconduct, misdoing
disorganization anarchy, commotion, complex *(entanglement),* confusion *(turmoil),* disorder *(lack of order),* dissolution *(disintegration),* disturbance, entanglement *(confusion),* havoc, misrule, pandemonium, shambles
disorganize confuse *(create disorder),* disband, discompose, dislocate, disorient, disrupt, disturb, muddle, upset. SEE MAIN ENTRY
disorganized anomalous, deranged, disjointed, disordered, disorderly, lax, slipshod
disorient dislocate, perplex. SEE MAIN ENTRY
disorientate disorganize, disturb
disorientation insanity
disoriented non compos mentis
disown condemn *(ban),* defect, deny *(contradict),* deprive, disaffirm, disallow, disavow, disclaim, disdain, disinherit, exclude, expel, rebuff, recant, refuse, reject, renounce, surrender *(give back),* waive. SEE MAIN ENTRY
disowned blameful, derelict *(abandoned)*
disownment abandonment *(repudiation),* abjuration, ademption, attachment *(seizure),* disclaimer, disdain, exclusion, rejection, renunciation, revocation
dispair sever
dispar dissimilar, diverse, unequal *(unequivalent)*
disparage blame, brand *(stigmatize),* censure, complain *(criticize),* condemn *(blame),* condescend *(patronize),* contemn, criticize *(find fault with),* damage, debunk, decry, defame, demean *(make lower),* denounce *(condemn),* deprecate, depreciate, derogate, disapprove *(condemn),* discommend, discount *(disbelieve),* discredit, disdain, dishonor *(deprive of honor),* disoblige, fault, humiliate, impeach, jeer, lessen, libel, malign, minimize, misprize, mock *(deride),* pillory, remonstrate, reprimand, reproach, smear, spurn, sully, underestimate. SEE MAIN ENTRY
disparage frivolously cavil
disparagement aspersion, bad repute, blame *(culpability),* condemnation *(blame),* contempt *(disdain),* criticism, defamation, denunciation, diatribe, disapprobation, disapproval, discredit, disgrace, dishonor *(shame),* disrepute, disrespect, exception *(objection),* ignominy, libel, notoriety, obloquy, phillipic, profanity, reproach, revilement, ridicule, slander. SEE MAIN ENTRY
disparaging calumnious, contemptuous, cynical, derogatory, incriminatory, inculpatory, libelous, nonconsenting, pejorative, unfavorable. SEE MAIN ENTRY
disparate different, disconnected, disproportionate, dissimilar, divergent, diverse, heterogeneous, miscellaneous, multifarious, peculiar *(distinctive),* separate, unequal *(unequivalent),* unrelated, unsuitable. SEE MAIN ENTRY
disparity contradistinction, contraposition, deviation, difference, disaccord, discord, discrepancy, dissent *(difference of opinion),* distinction *(difference),* distortion, incompatibility *(inconsistency),* incongruity, inconsistency, inequality, nonconformity, variance *(disagreement).* SEE MAIN ENTRY
dispart break *(separate),* detach, disengage, disjoint, disperse *(scatter),* dissociate, dissolve *(separate),* divide *(separate),* estrange, luxate, separate, sever
dispassion disinterest *(lack of prejudice),* objectivity
dispassionate clinical, cold-blooded, deliberate, discriminating *(judicious),* equitable, evenhanded, fair *(just),* impartial, just, neutral, nonchalant, objective, openminded, perfunctory, phlegmatic, stoical, unbiased, unprejudiced, unresponsive. SEE MAIN ENTRY
dispassionately fairly *(impartially)*
dispassionateness candor *(impartiality),* disinterest *(lack of prejudice),* fairness, moderation, neutrality, objectivity
dispatch acceleration, accomplish, close *(terminate),* commission *(act),* complete, conduct, delegate, discharge *(performance),* discharge *(perform),* dismiss *(discharge),* displace *(remove),* eliminate *(eradicate),* execute *(sentence to death),* expedite, haste, hasten, intelligence *(news),* issuance, kill *(defeat),* kill *(murder),* note *(brief comment),* notice *(announcement),* notification, relegate, send, slay, story *(narrative),* transmit, transmittal, transport. SEE MAIN ENTRY
dispatch news annunciate, disseminate
dispatcher carrier, informant
dispatches correspondence *(communication by letters)*
dispatching assassination
dispatchment consignment
dispel disband, disorganize, disperse *(scatter),* disprove, dissolve *(disperse),* extinguish, obliterate, quash, repel *(drive back),* repulse. SEE MAIN ENTRY
dispel misunderstanding resolve *(solve)*
dispellere dispel, disperse *(scatter)*
dispendium expense *(cost),* waste
dispensable disposable, expendable, extraneous, gratuitous *(unwarranted),* inconsequential, minor, needless, negligible, nonessential, null *(insignificant),* otiose, petty, superfluous, unessential, unnecessary. SEE MAIN ENTRY
dispensation administration, alimony, allotment, appointment *(act of designating),* appropriation *(allotment),* assignment *(allotment),* benefit *(conferment),* capacity *(authority),* charter *(license),* circulation, contribution *(donation),* discharge *(release from obligation),* disposition *(final arrangement),* disposition *(transfer of property),* distribution *(apportionment),* donation, excuse, exoneration, franchise *(license),* gift *(present),* grant, gratuity *(present),* impunity, inheritance, leave *(permission),* legacy, pardon, privilege, quota, ration, release, reprieve, will *(testamentary instrument).* SEE MAIN ENTRY
dispense adjudge, administer *(tender),* allocate, allot, apportion, assign *(allot),* bear *(yield),* bequeath, bestow, confer *(give),* contribute *(supply),* convey *(transfer),* disburse *(distribute),* dispense, disperse *(disseminate),* disseminate, distribute, divide *(distribute),* dole, endue, fund, give *(grant),* impart, issue *(publish),* mete, parcel, present *(make a gift),* reapportion, render *(administer),* sell, spend, split, vend. SEE MAIN ENTRY
dispense judgment adjudge
dispense with abandon *(relinquish),* abolish, censor, disavow, disclaim, dismiss *(discharge),* disown *(refuse to acknowledge),* extinguish, forbear, forgo, forswear, jettison, refrain, refuse, set aside *(annul),* waive. SEE MAIN ENTRY
dispensed with derelict *(abandoned)*
dispensing circulation, donative
dispergere circulate, circulation, disperse *(scatter),* disseminate
dispersal circulation, decentralization, disbursement *(act of disbursing),* dispensation *(act of dispensing),* dissolution *(disintegration),* division *(act of dividing)*
disperse administer *(tender),* allocate, allot, break *(separate),* circulate, diffuse, disband, disintegrate, disorganize, dispel, dispense, displace *(remove),* disseminate, dissipate *(spread out),* dissociate, divide *(distribute),* issue *(publish),* move *(alter position),* radiate, repel *(drive back),* separate, spread. SEE MAIN ENTRY
disperse completely dispel
dispersed desultory, sporadic
dispersion circulation, decentralization, dispensation *(act of dispensing),* division *(act of dividing),* havoc, waste. SEE MAIN ENTRY
dispertire apportion, distribute
dispirit depress, discourage, dissuade, harass, intimidate
dispirited despondent, disconsolate, lugubrious, pessimistic
dispiritedness depression, pessimism
dispiriting ominous
dispiteous remorseless, ruthless
displace accede *(succeed),* change, confuse *(create disorder),* deport *(banish),* depose *(remove),* discharge *(dismiss),* discompose, disjoint, dislocate, dislodge, dismiss *(discharge),* dispossess, dissociate, disturb, divest, eject *(evict),* eradicate, evict, exclude, inconvenience, luxate, oust, relegate, remove *(dismiss from office),* remove *(eliminate),* send, succeed *(follow),* supersede, supplant, upset. SEE MAIN ENTRY
displaced deranged
displaced person derelict
displacement banishment, deportation, discharge *(dismissal),* dismissal *(discharge),* disqualification *(rejection),* disturbance, evulsion, exclusion, expulsion, layoff, ostracism, preemption, removal, replacement, sequestration, subrogation
displacement of rightful owner disseisin
displacency bad repute
displant disengage, dislodge, disturb
display bare, bear *(adduce),* brandish, color *(deceptive appearance),* complexion, demonstrate *(establish),* disinter, evidence, evince, exemplify, exhibit *(noun),* exhibit *(verb),* expose, expression *(manifestation),* flaunt, histrionics, illustrate, illustration, manifest, manifestation, phenomenon *(manifestation),* present *(introduce),* pretense *(ostentation),* produce *(offer to view),* reveal, scene, unveil. SEE MAIN ENTRY
display line caption
display oneself boldly flaunt
display with effrontery flaunt
displease agitate *(perturb),* annoy, antagonize, bait *(harass),* disappoint, discommode, disturb, harrow, harry *(harass),* irritate, offend *(insult),* pique, plague, provoke, repel *(disgust).* SEE MAIN ENTRY
displeased disappointed, resentful
displeasing antipathetic *(distasteful),* deplorable, inadequate, inferior *(lower in quality),* objectionable, obnoxious, odious,

offensive *(offending)*, repugnant *(exciting aversion)*, repulsive, unacceptable, undesirable, unendurable, unsatisfactory
displeasure disapprobation, disapproval, disparagement, dissatisfaction, exception *(objection)*, nuisance, odium, pain, plaint, reprimand, resentment, umbrage. SEE MAIN ENTRY
displume plunder
disponere marshal
disposable assignable, expendable. SEE MAIN ENTRY
disposal administration, allotment, cession, conveyance, disbursement *(act of disbursing)*, dismissal *(termination of a proceeding)*, dispatch *(act of putting to death)*, dispensation *(act of dispensing)*, disposition *(determination)*, disposition *(final arrangement)*, disposition *(transfer of property)*, distribution *(apportionment)*, enjoyment *(use)*, expense *(sacrifice)*, management *(judicious use)*, order *(arrangement)*, recourse, regulation *(management)*, release, sale, use
dispose abolish, allocate, allot, bait *(lure)*, classify, convince, disperse *(disseminate)*, divide *(distribute)*, prompt, regulate *(adjust)*, rule *(govern)*. SEE MAIN ENTRY
dispose of abandon *(relinquish)*, administer *(conduct)*, assign *(transfer ownership)*, attorn, bequeath, bestow, close *(terminate)*, complete, conclude *(complete)*, contribute *(supply)*, debar, decide, discharge *(perform)*, dispatch *(put to death)*, dispense, dissolve *(terminate)*, eliminate *(eradicate)*, eradicate, expel, expunge, forgo, give *(grant)*, jettison, liquidate *(determine liability)*, parcel, post, refute, set aside *(annul)*, settle, slay, spend
dispose of for profit sell
disposed eager, inclined, prone, ready *(willing)*, receptive, willing *(desirous)*
disposed of complete *(ended)*
disposed to believe credulous
disposed to bestow favors propitious
disposed to cavil fractious
disposed to cheat dishonest
disposed to controversy litigious
disposed to doubt cynical, inconvincible, incredulous, suspicious *(distrustful)*
disposed to envy jealous
disposed to fight pugnacious
disposed to good benevolent
disposed to insist insistent
disposed to mercy placable
disposed to peace peaceable
disposed to question debatable, doubtful
disposed to talk freely loquacious
disposed to yield flexible
disposer of stolen goods fence
dispositio disposition *(final arrangement)*
disposition adjudication, adjustment, administration, allotment, animus, apportionment, array *(order)*, assignment *(transfer of ownership)*, bias, cession, character *(personal quality)*, choice *(decision)*, classification, complexion, conatus, dispensation *(act of dispensing)*, distribution *(arrangement)*, favor *(partiality)*, frame *(mood)*, habit, legacy, penchant, personality, posture *(attitude)*, predilection, predisposition, preference *(choice)*, proclivity, propensity, property *(distinctive attribute)*, regulation *(management)*, settlement, spirit, standpoint, state *(condition)*, structure *(composition)*, temperament, tendency, usage, use, will *(desire)*, will *(testamentary instrument)*. SEE MAIN ENTRY
disposition of mind posture *(attitude)*
disposition of personalty legacy
disposition to believe credulity
disposition to deceive dishonesty
disposition to defraud dishonesty
disposition to inquire interest *(concern)*
disposition to lie dishonesty
disposition to mercy clemency, lenience
disposition to pardon clemency, condonation
disposition to please comity
disposition to resist contempt *(disobedience to the court)*
dispositioned inclined
dispossess assume *(seize)*, condemn *(seize)*, confiscate, demote, depose *(remove)*, deprive, despoil, dislodge, dismiss *(discharge)*, disown *(refuse to acknowledge)*, displace *(remove)*, divest, eject *(evict)*, evict, expel, hijack, oust, seize *(confiscate)*, sequester *(seize property)*. SEE MAIN ENTRY
dispossess of abridge *(divest)*
dispossess of hereditary right disinherit, disown *(refuse to acknowledge)*
dispossess of right disqualify
dispossess oneself of abandon *(relinquish)*
dispossessed poor *(underprivileged)*
dispossession abridgment *(disentitlement)*, appropriation *(taking)*, assumption *(seizure)*, attachment *(seizure)*, condemnation *(seizure)*, disqualification *(rejection)*, disseisin, distraint, distress *(seizure)*, eviction, expropriation *(divestiture)*, expulsion, foreclosure, forfeiture *(act of forfeiting)*, garnishment, infringement, ouster, privation, taking. SEE MAIN ENTRY
disposure array *(order)*, distribution *(arrangement)*
dispraise blame *(culpability)*, blame, censure, condemn *(blame)*, condemnation *(blame)*, contempt *(disdain)*, criticism, criticize *(find fault with)*, decry, defame, denounce *(condemn)*, denunciation, deprecate, depreciate, derogate, diatribe, disapprobation, disapprove *(condemn)*, discommend, discredit, exception *(objection)*, fault, ignominy, inveigh, lessen, malediction, malign, onus *(stigma)*, reprimand *(noun)*, reprimand *(verb)*, sully. SEE MAIN ENTRY
dispraised blameful
dispread diffuse
disprison extricate
disprize contemn, decry, derogate, minimize, misprize
disproof confutation, contradiction, counterargument, negation, repudiation
disproportion difference, distort, distortion, exaggeration, inequality, inequity
disproportionate disparate, excessive, inapposite, inappropriate, inapt, incommensurate, incongruous, inept *(inappropriate)*, undue *(excessive)*, unequal *(unequivalent)*. SEE MAIN ENTRY
disproportionateness inequality
disprovable defeasible
disproval repudiation
disprove answer *(reply)*, contradict, controvert, disown *(deny the validity)*, impugn, invalidate, negate, rebut, refute. SEE MAIN ENTRY
disputability cloud *(suspicion)*
disputable actionable, arguable, contestable, controversial, debatable, doubtful, dubious, dubitative, equivocal, forensic, justiciable, litigable, litigious, moot, problematic, uncertain *(questionable)*, undecided, unsettled, unsound *(fallacious)*. SEE MAIN ENTRY
disputant adversary, apologist, contender, contestant, foe, litigant, opponent, party *(litigant)*, rival. SEE MAIN ENTRY
disputare discuss, dispute *(debate)*
disputatio argument *(contention)*, contention *(argument)*
disputation altercation, argument *(contention)*, argument *(pleading)*, belligerency, collision *(dispute)*, contention *(argument)*, contention *(opposition)*, contest *(dispute)*, controversy *(argument)*, disaccord, disagreement, fight *(argument)*, impugnation, strife
disputatious argumentative, competitive *(antagonistic)*, contentious, debatable, disputable, dissenting, fractious, hostile, litigious, moot, petulant, polemic, pugnacious, querulous, remonstrative. SEE MAIN ENTRY
disputative dissenting, forensic, litigious
dispute altercation, answer *(reply)*, argue, argument *(contention)*, bicker, brawl, challenge, collide *(clash)*, conflict *(noun)*, conflict *(verb)*, confront *(oppose)*, confrontation *(altercation)*, contention *(argument)*, contention *(opposition)*, contest *(dispute)*, contest, contradict, contradiction, contravene, controversy *(argument)*, controvert, cross *(disagree with)*, debate, deny *(contradict)*, differ *(disagree)*, disaccord *(noun)*, disaccord *(verb)*, disaffirm, disagree, disallow, disapprove *(reject)*, disbelieve, discord, dissension, dissent *(differ in opinion)*, doubt *(distrust)*, except *(object)*, exception *(objection)*, feud, fight *(argument)*, fight *(battle)*, fracas, fray, gainsay, haggle, impeach, impugn, impugnation, incompatibility *(difference)*, lawsuit, matter *(case)*, matter *(subject)*, negate, nonconformity, object, oppose, oppugn, proceeding, protest, rebut, reject, remonstrate, rift *(disagreement)*, strife, variance *(disagreement)*. SEE MAIN ENTRY
dispute angrily brawl
dispute resolution SEE MAIN ENTRY
disputed moot
disputed point conflict, contention *(argument)*, controversy *(argument)*, discrepancy
disputed point of law issue *(matter in dispute)*. SEE MAIN ENTRY
disputed question controversy *(argument)*, issue *(matter in dispute)*
disputer malcontent
disputing dissenting, negative
disqualification disability *(physical inability)*, expulsion, inability, incapacity, invalidity, prohibition. SEE MAIN ENTRY
disqualified disabled *(deprived of legal right)*, incompetent, ineligible, inept *(incompetent)*, powerless, unqualified *(not competent)*
disqualify ban, censor, condemn *(ban)*, disable, eliminate *(exclude)*, exclude, invalidate, prohibit, recall *(call back)*. SEE MAIN ENTRY
disqualify as an attorney disbar
disqualifying prohibitive *(restrictive)*
disquiet affront, agitate *(perturb)*, annoy, badger, commotion, confusion *(turmoil)*, consternation, discommode, discompose, disconcert, disrupt, dissatisfaction, distress

(anguish), distress, disturb, disturbance, embarrass, embroilment, frighten, harass, harrow, ill will, incense, inflict, intimidate, menace, misgiving, molest *(annoy)*, outburst, perplex, perturb, pique, plague, press *(goad)*, provoke, qualm, remorse, stress *(strain)*, strife, trepidation, turmoil, upset. SEE MAIN ENTRY

disquieting ominous, sinister, unsatisfactory

disquietude commotion, concern *(interest)*, confusion *(turmoil)*, consternation, distress *(anguish)*, disturbance, fear, fright, outburst, pandemonium, panic, stress *(strain)*, trepidation

disquisition charge *(statement to the jury)*, discourse, harangue, inquiry *(systematic investigation)*, narration, pandect *(treatise)*

disquisitional discursive *(analytical)*, narrative

disrank humiliate

disrate contemn, demote, derogate, humiliate, smear

disregard anarchy, breach, break *(violate)*, condonation, condone, contemn, contempt *(disdain)*, contravene, default, defiance, defy, dereliction, disaffirm, discount *(disbelieve)*, disdain *(noun)*, disdain *(verb)*, disfavor, dishonor *(nonpayment)*, dishonor *(refuse to pay)*, disinterest *(lack of interest)*, dismiss *(put out of consideration)*, disobey, disoblige, disown *(deny the validity)*, disparage, disrespect, disuse, eliminate *(exclude)*, except *(exclude)*, exclude, flout, ignore, inconsideration, indifference, jeer, laxity, misprize, muse, negate, neglect *(noun)*, neglect *(verb)*, negligence, nonfeasance, nonperformance, omission, overlook *(excuse)*, override, pretermit, rebuff *(noun)*, rebuff *(verb)*, reject, remit *(release from penalty)*, resist *(withstand)*, shun, spurn, trespass, violate. SEE MAIN ENTRY

disregard of duty nonfeasance

disregard of orders contempt *(disobedience to the court)*, defiance, noncompliance *(nonobservance)*

disregard one's duty default

disregard one's obligations default

disregard prestige condescend *(deign)*

disregard the law offend *(violate the law)*

disregardant negligent, remiss

disregarded broken *(unfulfilled)*, inappreciable, null *(insignificant)*

disregardful broken *(unfulfilled)*, careless, contemptuous, derelict *(negligent)*, heedless, inadvertent, insolent, negligent, perfunctory, reckless, remiss, thoughtless

disregardfulness disregard *(lack of respect)*, disregard *(omission)*, disregard *(unconcern)*

disregarding disobedient, lax

disrelated alien *(unrelated)*, apart, separate

disrepair damage, deterioration, impairment *(damage)*. SEE MAIN ENTRY

disreputability attaint, bad character, bad repute, discredit, disgrace, dishonor *(shame)*, disrepute, ignominy, ill repute, notoriety

disreputable arrant *(onerous)*, bad *(offensive)*, base *(bad)*, blameful, blameworthy, contemptible, delinquent *(guilty of a misdeed)*, depraved, disgraceful, dishonest, fraudulent, ignoble, immoral, iniquitous, lawless, notorious, profligate *(corrupt)*, reprehensible, reprobate, scandalous, sinister, unbecoming, unethical, unseemly. SEE MAIN ENTRY

disreputable person degenerate

disreputableness bad repute, disrepute, ignominy, notoriety

disreputation ignominy, ill repute

disrepute attaint, bad character, bad faith, bad repute, contempt *(disdain)*, corruption, defamation, degradation, discredit, disgrace, dishonor *(shame)*, disparagement, ignominy, impeachability, infamy, notoriety, obloquy, odium, opprobrium, reproach, scandal, shame, stigma, turpitude. SEE MAIN ENTRY

disreputed blameful

disrespect attaint, blasphemy, condescend *(patronize)*, contemn, contempt *(disobedience to the court)*, contumely, decry, disapprobation, disdain, disfavor, disgrace *(noun)*, disgrace *(verb)*, dishonor *(shame)*, disparage, disparagement, disregard *(lack of respect)*, disrepute, inconsideration, infamy, jeer, notoriety, obloquy, opprobrium, profanity, ridicule, shame, violate. SEE MAIN ENTRY

disrespectability bad repute, ill repute

disrespectable blameworthy, disreputable, notorious, scandalous

disrespectful brazen, calumnious, contemptuous, disdainful, disobedient, harsh, impertinent *(insolent)*, insolent, offensive *(offending)*, outrageous, pejorative, presumptuous, profane, scurrilous, supercilious

disrespectfulness bad repute, contempt *(disobedience to the court)*, disparagement, disrespect, inconsideration

disrobe denude, divest

disroot remove *(eliminate)*

disrupt circumvent, counteract, damage, disconcert, discontinue *(break continuity)*, disorganize, foil, overthrow, subvert. SEE MAIN ENTRY

disrupter insurgent

disruption abandonment *(discontinuance)*, alienation *(estrangement)*, check *(bar)*, debacle, disaccord, disassociation, discontinuance *(act of discontinuing)*, dissolution *(disintegration)*, estrangement, exception *(exclusion)*, furor, havoc, outbreak, outburst, pandemonium, shambles, split, subversion

disruptive offensive *(taking the initiative)*

dissatisfaction disapprobation, disapproval, dissent *(nonconcurrence)*, distress *(anguish)*, exception *(objection)*, ill will, objection, outcry, plaint, resentment, trouble, umbrage. SEE MAIN ENTRY

dissatisfactory loathsome

dissatisfied disappointed, dissident, jealous, querulous

dissatisfiedness dissatisfaction

dissatisfy disaffect, disappoint

disscindere rend

dissect analyze, canvass, dichotomize, disjoint, examine *(study)*, investigate, partition, probe, rend, research, scrutinize, split, study, subdivide. SEE MAIN ENTRY

dissectible divisible

dissection analysis, dichotomy, hornbook, indagation, split

disseise abridge *(divest)*, adeem, annex *(arrogate)*, attach *(seize)*, condemn *(seize)*, confiscate, dispossess, impress *(procure by force)*, impropriate, levy, seize *(confiscate)*

disseised attached *(seized)*

disseisin appropriation *(taking)*, distress *(seizure)*, expropriation *(divestiture)*. SEE MAIN ENTRY

disseize deprive, dispossess, divest

disseizing confiscatory

dissemblance color *(deceptive appearance)*, difference, distortion, false pretense, story *(falsehood)*

dissemble assume *(simulate)*, camouflage, cheat, cloak, deceive, delude, disguise, distort, equivocate, evade *(deceive)*, fabricate *(make up)*, fake, falsify, feign, hide, misguide, mislead, misrepresent, misstate, palter, pretend, prevaricate, profess *(pretend)*

dissembling deceit, fraud, hypocrisy, lying, perfidious, recreant, tartuffish

disseminare disseminate

disseminate annunciate, apportion, cast *(throw)*, circulate, convey *(communicate)*, correspond *(communicate)*, diffuse, disburse *(distribute)*, disclose, dispel, dispense, dissipate *(spread out)*, distribute, herald, intersperse, issue *(publish)*, notify, proclaim, promulgate, propagate *(spread)*, publish, report *(disclose)*, reveal, signify *(inform)*, spread. SEE MAIN ENTRY

disseminated pervade, public *(known)*

disseminating disbursement *(act of disbursing)*

dissemination circulation, common knowledge, communication *(statement)*, disbursement *(act of disbursing)*, disclosure *(act of disclosing)*, dispensation *(act of dispensing)*, distribution *(apportionment)*, division *(act of dividing)*, divulgation, notification, publication *(disclosure)*, publicity, report *(detailed account)*

dissensio conflict, disagreement, discord, dissent *(difference of opinion)*, variance *(disagreement)*

dissension argument *(contention)*, belligerency, breach, case *(lawsuit)*, conflict, contempt *(disobedience to the court)*, contention *(opposition)*, contest *(dispute)*, contradiction, controversy *(argument)*, difference, disaccord, disagreement, discord, dispute, dissent *(difference of opinion)*, dissent *(nonconcurrence)*, dissidence, distinction *(difference)*, division *(act of dividing)*, embroilment, faction, feud, fight *(argument)*, fracas, fray, incompatibility *(difference)*, opposition, revolt, schism, split, strife, struggle, variance *(disagreement)*. SEE MAIN ENTRY

dissent argument *(contention)*, bicker, challenge, collide *(clash)*, conflict *(noun)*, conflict *(verb)*, contend *(dispute)*, contention *(opposition)*, contest *(dispute)*, contradict, contradiction, contravention, demonstrate *(protest)*, demur, denial, deny *(contradict)*, differ *(vary)*, disaccord *(noun)*, disaccord *(verb)*, disaffirm, disagree, disagreement, disallow, disapprobation, disapproval, disavow, discord, disown *(deny the validity)*, dispute *(debate)*, dissatisfaction, dissension, dissidence, except *(object)*, exception *(objection)*, faction, gainsay, impugnation, incompatibility *(difference)*, negation, nonconformity, object, objection, oppugn, outcry, protest *(noun)*, protest *(verb)*, refuse, reject, rejection, reluctance, renounce, repudiate, repudiation, resist *(oppose)*, schism, secede, strife, variance *(disagreement)*. SEE MAIN ENTRY

dissent from dispute *(contest)*

dissenter disputant, heretic, malcontent. SEE MAIN ENTRY

dissentience breach, disapproval, discord, dispute, dissension, dissent *(difference of opinion)*, embroilment

dissentient adversary, argumentative, contradictory, discordant, dissenting, dissident, divisive, heretic, hostile, malcontent, negative, nonconforming, nonconsenting, polemic, recusant
dissentient voice dissent *(nonconcurrence)*
dissenting contradictory, discordant, disinclined, dissident, hostile, nonconforming, nonconsenting, recusant, reluctant, renitent. SEE MAIN ENTRY
dissentious contentious, dissenting, dissident, hostile, litigious, pugnacious, reluctant
dissentire conflict, differ *(vary)*, disagree, dissent *(differ in opinion)*
disserere discuss
dissertate converse, declaim, discourse, discuss
dissertation communication *(discourse)*, conversation, discourse, pandect *(treatise)*, recital
dissertation on the law hornbook
disserve damage, harm
disservice grievance, harm, injury, mischief, prejudice *(injure)*. SEE MAIN ENTRY
disserviceable adverse *(negative)*, deleterious, disadvantageous, harmful, peccant *(unhealthy)*, pernicious, prejudicial
dissever detach, dichotomize, disband, discontinue *(abandon)*, discontinue *(break continuity)*, disengage, disjoint, dissociate, dissolve *(separate)*, divide *(separate)*, estrange, excise *(cut away)*, interrupt, isolate, luxate, part *(separate)*, rend, separate, sever, split, subdivide
disseverable divisible
disseverance division *(act of dividing)*, separation, split
disseverence disassociation
dissevering estrangement
dissidence argument *(contention)*, conflict, contention *(opposition)*, contravention, controversy *(argument)*, deviation, disaccord, disagreement, disapprobation, disapproval, discord, dispute, dissension, dissent *(difference of opinion)*, incompatibility *(difference)*, nonconformity, protest, sedition, strife, variance *(disagreement)*. SEE MAIN ENTRY
dissident competitive *(antagonistic)*, deviant, discordant, dissenting, divisive, heretic, hostile, insubordinate, malcontent, negative, nonconforming, nonconsenting, recusant. SEE MAIN ENTRY
dissidere differ *(vary)*, disagree, dissent *(differ in opinion)*
dissidium disagreement, discord
dissimilar atypical, different, discordant, disparate, distinct *(distinguished from others)*, divergent, diverse, heterogeneous, multifarious, nonconforming, peculiar *(distinctive)*, separate, unequal *(unequivalent)*, unique, unrelated. SEE MAIN ENTRY
dissimilarity contradistinction, contraposition, deviation, difference, discord, discrepancy, distortion, diversity, identity *(individuality)*, incompatibility *(inconsistency)*, incongruity, inconsistency, inequality, nonconformity, specialty *(distinctive mark)*
dissimilis dissimilar, heterogeneous
dissimilitude difference, disagreement, discrepancy, disparity, distortion, diversity, incompatibility *(inconsistency)*, incongruity, inconsistency, inequality
dissimilitudo disparity, inequality
dissimulare cloak, pretend
dissimulate assume *(simulate)*, cloak, deceive, disguise, equivocate, fabricate *(make up)*, fake, feign, lie *(falsify)*, misrepresent, palter, pretend, prevaricate, profess *(pretend)*
dissimulatio hypocrisy, irony
dissimulation color *(deceptive appearance)*, deceit, deception, disguise, duplicity, false pretense, falsehood, falsification, fraud, indirection *(deceitfulness)*, story *(falsehood)*
dissipare dispel, disperse *(scatter)*, dissipate *(spread out)*
dissipate carouse, debauch, deplete, diffuse, disappear, disorganize, dispel, disperse *(scatter)*, dissolve *(disperse)*, exhaust *(deplete)*, expend *(consume)*, impair, misemploy, obliterate, overdraw. SEE MAIN ENTRY
dissipated depraved, dissolute, immoral, improvident, irredeemable, irretrievable, lascivious, lecherous, licentious, lost *(taken away)*, prodigal, profligate *(corrupt)*, prurient
dissipation consumption, debauchery, decentralization, decrease, decrement, dissolution *(disintegration)*, division *(act of dividing)*, expense *(sacrifice)*, privation, vice, waste
dissipative prodigal, profligate *(corrupt)*
dissociability ostracism
dissociate abstract *(separate)*, break *(separate)*, depart, detach, disband, disengage, disjoint, disrupt, dissolve *(separate)*, divide *(separate)*, divorce, estrange, isolate, luxate, part *(separate)*, remove *(dismiss from office)*, remove *(eliminate)*, seclude, separate, sever, withdraw. SEE MAIN ENTRY
dissociate oneself disagree, disavow, disown *(refuse to acknowledge)*
dissociated alien *(unrelated)*, apart, discrete, foreign, independent, separate
dissociation disassociation, disclaimer, division *(act of dividing)*, estrangement, inconsequence, privacy, repudiation, segregation *(separation)*, separation
dissoluable severable
dissoluble defeasible
dissolute culpable, depraved, disorderly, disreputable, felonious, immoral, iniquitous, lascivious, lecherous, lewd, licentious, nefarious, profligate *(corrupt)*, promiscuous, prurient, reprobate, salacious, tainted *(corrupted)*, unrestrained *(not repressed)*, wanton. SEE MAIN ENTRY
dissoluteness debauchery, delinquency *(misconduct)*, vice
dissolutio abolition, dissolution *(termination)*
dissolution abatement *(extinguishment)*, abolition, ademption, annulment, cancellation, cessation *(termination)*, debacle, decentralization, decline, defeasance, denouement, destruction, disassociation, discharge *(annulment)*, end *(termination)*, erosion, expense *(sacrifice)*, expiration, extremity *(death)*, interruption, rescision, separation, spoilage, wear and tear. SEE MAIN ENTRY
dissolution of marriage divorce, separation
dissolution of the marriage bond divorce
dissolutus dissolute, lax, licentious
dissolvable destructible
dissolve abate *(extinguish)*, abolish, abrogate *(annul)*, cancel, degenerate, destroy *(efface)*, disappear, discharge *(release from obligation)*, discontinue *(abandon)*, discontinue *(break continuity)*, disintegrate, disorganize, dispel, disperse *(scatter)*, dissipate *(spread out)*, eliminate *(eradicate)*, eradicate, erode, extirpate, interrupt, nullify, obliterate, part *(separate)*, quash, recess, renege, repudiate, rescind, revoke, separate, sever. SEE MAIN ENTRY
dissolve by dismissal disband
dissolve of the bonds of matrimony divorce
dissolve the marriage of divorce
dissolved irretrievable
dissolvere disburse *(pay out)*, dissolve *(disperse)*, refund, solve
dissolving cancellation
dissonance conflict, contention *(opposition)*, contest *(dispute)*, controversy *(argument)*, deviation, difference, disaccord, disagreement, discord, discrepancy, disparity, dissension, dissent *(difference of opinion)*, dissidence, distinction *(difference)*, division *(act of dividing)*, estrangement, incompatibility *(inconsistency)*, incongruity, inconsistency, inequality, paradox. SEE MAIN ENTRY
dissonant deranged, deviant, different, discordant, dissenting, divisive, inapposite, inappropriate, inapt, incongruous, inconsistent, inept *(inappropriate)*, peculiar *(distinctive)*, polemic, unsuitable. SEE MAIN ENTRY
dissonus discordant
dissuade caution, check *(restrain)*, counsel, debar, deter, discourage, expostulate, forewarn, reason *(persuade)*, remonstrate. SEE MAIN ENTRY
dissuade from entering picket
dissuadere dissuade
dissuasion admonition, deterrence, deterrent, disincentive, persuasion, remonstrance, restraint
dissuasive adverse *(hostile)*, remonstrative
distance extent, ostracism, perspective, range, space, surpass. SEE MAIN ENTRY
distant controlled *(restrained)*, disdainful, distinct *(distinguished from others)*, foreign, inaccessible, insusceptible *(uncaring)*, obscure *(remote)*, phlegmatic, remote *(not proximate)*, remote *(secluded)*, unapproachable
distant *(detached)* SEE MAIN ENTRY
distant *(far)* SEE MAIN ENTRY
distantly related consanguineous
distare apart
distaste dissatisfaction, odium, phobia, reluctance
distasteful bitter *(acrid tasting)*, deplorable, heinous, loathsome, objectionable, offensive *(offending)*, repugnant *(exciting aversion)*, repulsive, unacceptable, undesirable, unsavory, unseemly. SEE MAIN ENTRY
distemper discompose, disease, disorder *(abnormal condition)*, disturb, pique
distend compound, enlarge, expand, extend *(enlarge)*, inflate, overextend
distended inflated *(enlarged)*
distension boom *(increase)*, inflation *(increase)*
distention extension *(expansion)*, growth *(increase)*, stress *(strain)*
distill extract. SEE MAIN ENTRY
distillation corpus
distinct apparent *(perceptible)*, categorical, certain *(particular)*, certain *(positive)*, certain *(specific)*, clear *(apparent)*, cognizable, coherent *(clear)*, concrete,

conspicuous, definite, different, discrete, disjunctive *(tending to disjoin)*, disparate, distinctive, diverse, evident, exclusive *(singular)*, explicit, express, individual, insular, lucid, manifest, naked *(perceptible)*, nonconforming, obvious, open *(in sight)*, overt, palpable, particular *(individual)*, particular *(specific)*, peculiar *(distinctive)*, perceivable, perceptible, personal *(individual)*, precise, prominent, remarkable, salient, separate, singular, trenchant, unambiguous, unmistakable, visible *(in full view)*. SEE MAIN ENTRY
distinct indivisible entity individual
distinct intention deliberation
distinct meaning SEE MAIN ENTRY
distinct purpose forethought, premeditation
distinct statement count
distincte fairly *(clearly)*
distinctio discrimination *(differentiation)*, distinction *(difference)*
distinction alternative *(option)*, character *(reputation)*, characteristic, color *(complexion)*, consequence *(significance)*, contradistinction, credit *(recognition)*, degree *(academic title)*, denomination, difference, differential, discretion *(power of choice)*, discretion *(quality of being discreet)*, discrimination *(differentiation)*, eminence, emphasis, feature *(characteristic)*, honor *(outward respect)*, identity *(individuality)*, importance, inequality, materiality *(consequence)*, merit, notoriety, nuance, personality, prestige, prize, property *(distinctive attribute)*, quality *(grade)*, regard *(esteem)*, reputation, restriction, severance, significance, speciality, specialty *(distinctive mark)*, specification, stress *(accent)*. SEE MAIN ENTRY
distinctive different, discriminating *(distinguishing)*, distinct *(distinguished from others)*, individual, meritorious, noteworthy, novel, outstanding *(prominent)*, particular *(individual)*, particular *(specific)*, prominent, remarkable, representative, several *(separate)*, special, specific, uncommon, unusual. SEE MAIN ENTRY
distinctive characteristic speciality
distinctive feature characteristic, differential, highlight, identity *(individuality)*, particularity, specialty *(distinctive mark)*, technicality
distinctive mark speciality
distinctive quality speciality
distinctive social attitude manner *(behavior)*
distinctive trait feature *(characteristic)*
distinctively fairly *(clearly)*
distinctiveness caliber *(quality)*, identity *(individuality)*, personality, speciality, specialty *(distinctive mark)*
distinctly fairly *(clearly)*, particularly
distinctly expressed explicit
distinctly indicated express
distinctly stated explicit, express
distinctness contradistinction, deviation, difference, emphasis, identity *(individuality)*, nonconformity, specialty *(distinctive mark)*
distinctus distinct *(clear)*, distinct *(distinguished from others)*
distinguere discriminate *(distinguish)*, distinguish
distinguish call *(title)*, characterize, circumscribe *(define)*, classify, contrast, demarcate, detect, diagnose, differentiate, discern *(discriminate)*, elevate, honor, identify, notice *(observe)*, perceive, pierce *(discern)*, recognize *(perceive)*, secern, spy. SEE MAIN ENTRY
distinguish between compare, contrast, select
distinguish by a mark label
distinguish by mark brand *(mark)*
distinguish by name denominate
distinguish by special selection elect *(choose)*
distinguishable appreciable, ascertainable, cognizable, conspicuous, determinable *(ascertainable)*, distinct *(clear)*, diverse, individual, naked *(perceptible)*, obvious, particular *(specific)*, peculiar *(distinctive)*, perceivable, perceptible, ponderable, several *(separate)*, unambiguous, unmistakable SEE MAIN ENTRY
distinguishably fairly *(clearly)*
distinguished best, certain *(specific)*, conspicuous, discrete, disparate, elegant, famous, illustrious, important *(significant)*, influential, major, meritorious, nonconforming, notable, noteworthy, outstanding *(prominent)*, paramount, particular *(individual)*, particular *(specific)*, peculiar *(distinctive)*, preferential, prominent, remarkable, renowned, reputable, salient, special, stellar, superior *(excellent)*, unusual. SEE MAIN ENTRY.
distinguished by nature distinct *(distinguished from others)*
distinguished by station distinct *(distinguished from others)*
distinguished quality trait
distinguishing discovery, discreet, distinctive, personal *(individual)*
distinguishing characteristic distinction *(difference)*, identity *(individuality)*
distinguishing feature differential
distinguishing mark designation *(symbol)*, earmark
distinguishing quality distinction *(difference)*, identity *(individuality)*, property *(distinctive attribute)*
distinguishing trait characteristic, property *(distinctive attribute)*
distinguishment discrimination *(differentiation)*, recognition, segregation *(separation)*, severance
distorquere contort, distort
distort bear false witness, camouflage, cloak, contort, corrupt, deface, denature, disguise, fabricate *(make up)*, fake, falsify, invent *(falsify)*, misapprehend, misconstrue, misemploy, misguide, misinform, misinterpret, mislead, misread, misrepresent, misstate, misunderstand, mutilate, palter, prejudice *(influence)*, prevaricate, slant. SEE MAIN ENTRY
distort intentionally misrepresent
distort the meaning misconceive. SEE MAIN ENTRY
distort the truth feign
distorted defective, fallacious, false *(inaccurate)*, faulty, mendacious
distorted conception error
distorted idea misestimation
distorted impression misestimation
distortio distortion
distortion abuse *(corrupt practice)*, artifice, catachresis, color *(deceptive appearance)*, defacement, difference, error, evasion, exaggeration, fallacy, falsehood, falsification, irregularity, lie, misapplication, misrepresentation, misstatement, misusage, overstatement, parody, propaganda, sophistry, story *(falsehood)*, travesty. SEE MAIN ENTRY
distortion of the truth perjury. SEE MAIN ENTRY
distortion of truth falsehood
distract bait *(harass)*, confuse *(bewilder)*, disorganize, disorient, disrupt, disturb, divert, interrupt, perturb
distracted oblivious, thoughtless
distraction confusion *(ambiguity)*, confusion *(turmoil)*, preoccupation, turmoil. SEE MAIN ENTRY
distrahere perplex
distrain annex *(arrogate)*, assume *(seize)*, attach *(seize)*, compel, condemn *(seize)*, confiscate, deprive, divest, garnish, impound, levy, mulct *(fine)*, seize *(confiscate)*, sequester *(seize property)*. SEE MAIN ENTRY
distrained attached *(seized)*
distrainer attachment *(seizure)*
distraining confiscatory
distraint attachment *(seizure)*, condemnation *(seizure)*, disseisin, distress *(seizure)*, expropriation *(divestiture)*, foreclosure, garnishment, sequestration, taking. SEE MAIN ENTRY
distrait thoughtless
distraught deranged, non compos mentis
distress adversity, affront, aggravation *(annoyance)*, annoy, attach *(seize)*, attachment *(seizure)*, badger, bait *(harass)*, condemnation *(seizure)*, discommode, disseisin, distraint, disturb, embarrass, expropriation *(divestiture)*, foreclosure, garnishment, harass, harry *(harass)*, hector, inflict, mistreat, obsess, offend *(insult)*, pain, persecute, perturb, plague, plaint, poverty, privation, prostration, provoke, quagmire, sequestration, toll *(effect)*, trouble, upset. SEE MAIN ENTRY
distressed aggrieved *(harmed)*, destitute, disappointed, disconsolate, impecunious, poor *(underprivileged)*
distressful lamentable, painful
distressing bleak *(not favorable)*, cruel, deplorable, detrimental, disastrous, insufferable, irksome, lamentable, loathsome, oppressive, painful, pernicious, unsatisfactory
distribuere allot, apportion, dispense, distribute, divide *(distribute)*, parcel
distribute administer *(tender)*, allocate, allot, apportion, assign *(allot)*, bequeath, bestow, cast *(throw)*, circulate, classify, deploy, detail *(assign)*, diffuse, dispense, disperse *(disseminate)*, dispose *(apportion)*, disseminate, dole, expend *(disburse)*, file *(arrange)*, fix *(arrange)*, give *(grant)*, intersperse, issue *(publish)*, marshal, mete, parcel, partition, post, prorate, publish, sort, split, spread, subdivide, supply. SEE MAIN ENTRY
distribute again reapportion
distribute anew reapportion
distribute assets liquidate *(convert into cash)*
distribute proportionally prorate
distribute proportionately apportion
distributed pro rata
distributed by will testamentary
distributee legatee
distributer merchant
distributing center headquarters
distributing justice equitable
distribution administration, allotment, appointment *(act of designating)*, apportionment, appropriation *(allotment)*, assignment *(allotment)*, assignment *(transfer of ownership)*, budget, circulation, classification,

consignment, decentralization, dispensation *(act of dispensing)*, disposition *(final arrangement)*, disposition *(transfer of property)*, division *(act of dividing)*, form *(arrangement)*, hierarchy *(arrangement in a series)*, order *(arrangement)*, proportion, ration. SEE MAIN ENTRY
distribution by lot allotment
distribution of earnings dividend
distribution of profits dividend
distributional proportionate
distributor merchant
distributor of largess donor
district bailiwick, circuit, constituency, department, division *(administrative unit)*, local, locality, location, parcel, province, region, regional, territory. SEE MAIN ENTRY
district attorney prosecutor. SEE MAIN ENTRY
district officer caretaker *(one fulfilling the function of office)*
distrust apprehension *(fear)*, cloud *(suspicion)*, disbelieve, discount *(disbelieve)*, discredit, doubt *(suspicion)*, incredulity, misdoubt, misgiving, mistrust, qualm, rejection, suspicion *(mistrust)*. SEE MAIN ENTRY
distrusted unbelievable
distrustful cynical, doubtful, inconvincible, incredulous, jealous, leery, pessimistic, resentful, skeptical
distrustfulness cloud *(suspicion)*, doubt *(suspicion)*, incredulity
distrusting skeptical
distrusting the motives of others cynical
disturb affront, aggravate *(annoy)*, agitate *(perturb)*, annoy, badger, bait *(harass)*, confuse *(create disorder)*, discommode, discompose, disconcert, discontinue *(break continuity)*, dislocate, dislodge, disorganize, disorient, displace *(remove)*, disrupt, distress, embarrass, evict, harass, harrow, harry *(harass)*, hector, impair, inconvenience, interfere, interrupt, irritate, menace, mistreat, molest *(annoy)*, muddle, obfuscate, offend *(insult)*, perplex, persecute, perturb, pique, plague, remove *(eliminate)*, upset. SEE MAIN ENTRY
disturb keenly badger
disturb the composure of discompose
disturbance affray, altercation, belligerency, bluster *(commotion)*, brawl, cataclysm, commotion, confusion *(turmoil)*, consternation, detriment, disorder *(lack of order)*, dispute, embarrassment, embroilment, fracas, fray, furor, imbroglio, insurrection, molestation, nuisance, outbreak, outburst, outcry, pandemonium, panic, phobia, riot, trouble, turmoil, violation. SEE MAIN ENTRY
disturbed disorderly, unsettled, unsound *(not strong)*
disturbing detrimental, formidable, ominous, painful, sinister, unsatisfactory, unsuitable, vexatious
disunion anarchy, argument *(contention)*, conflict, contravention, controversy *(argument)*, disaccord, disagreement, disassociation, discord, dissension, dissidence, division *(act of dividing)*, divorce, estrangement, hiatus, incompatibility *(difference)*, interruption, schism, segregation *(separation)*, separation, split
disunite abstract *(separate)*, alienate *(estrange)*, bicker, break *(separate)*, demarcate, detach, dichotomize, disaccord, disaffect, disband, discontinue *(abandon)*, discontinue *(break continuity)*, disengage, disintegrate, disjoint, dislocate, disperse *(scatter)*, dissociate, dissolve *(separate)*, divide *(separate)*, divorce, estrange, interrupt, isolate, luxate, part *(separate)*, rend, separate, sever, split
disunited apart, bipartite, disconnected, discrete, disjunctive *(tending to disjoin)*, dissenting, separate, unbound
disuniting division *(act of dividing)*
disunity argument *(contention)*, conflict, contravention, controversy *(argument)*, disaccord, disagreement, discord, disparity, dispute, dissension, dissent *(nonconcurrence)*, dissidence, division *(act of dividing)*, estrangement, incompatibility *(difference)*, variance *(disagreement)*
disusage abolition, desuetude, disuse, nonuse
disuse abandon *(relinquish)*, abolition, cancellation, desuetude, discontinuance *(act of discontinuing)*, dissolution *(termination)*, leave *(allow to remain)*, nonuse, set aside *(annul)*. SEE MAIN ENTRY
disused barren, obsolete, otiose, outdated, outmoded, unemployed
disvaluation contempt *(disdain)*, criticism, ignominy
disvalue denounce *(condemn)*, deprecate, discommend, lessen
dithyrambic ecstatic
ditto copy, duplicate, reflect *(mirror)*, resemblance, tantamount
diurna record
diurnal daily
diuturnity period
divagate digress
divagation deviation, digression, indirection *(indirect action)*
divaricate bifurcate, bipartite, break *(separate)*, conflict, deviate, dichotomize, digress, disaccord, disagree, disjoint, spread
divaricate from differ *(vary)*
divaricating disparate, divergent
divarication dichotomy, digression, disassociation, split
divendere sell
diverge bifurcate, change, depart, deploy, detour, deviate, dichotomize, digress, disaccord, disagree, dissipate *(spread out)*, vary. SEE MAIN ENTRY
diverge from conflict, differ *(vary)*
divergence antithesis, circulation, conflict, contention *(opposition)*, contradiction, contradistinction, controversy *(argument)*, deviation, difference, digression, disaccord, disassociation, discrepancy, disparity, dispute, dissension, dissent *(difference of opinion)*, dissidence, incompatibility *(difference)*, incompatibility *(inconsistency)*, inconsistency, inequality, innovation, irregularity, nonconformity, quirk *(idiosyncrasy)*, split, variance *(disagreement)*, variance *(exemption)*
divergent anomalous, deviant, different, disconnected, discordant, disordered, disparate, disproportionate, dissenting, dissident, dissimilar, distinct *(distinguished from others)*, diverse, eccentric, inapplicable, inappropriate, incongruous, inconsistent, irregular *(not usual)*, multiple, peculiar *(distinctive)*, separate, unorthodox, unsuitable. SEE MAIN ENTRY
divergent opinion contradiction
divergent opinions conflict, controversy *(argument)*, disagreement, discord, dispute, dissension
diverging divergent, divisive
divers dissimilar, diverse, manifold
diverse atypical, different, discordant, disordered, dissimilar, distinct *(distinguished from others)*, divergent, heterogeneous, manifold, miscellaneous, multifarious, multiple, promiscuous, separate, several *(plural)*, unrelated. SEE MAIN ENTRY
diverseness deviation, difference, distinction *(difference)*, diversity, nonconformity
diversification innovation. SEE MAIN ENTRY
diversified composite, dissimilar, divergent, diverse, heterogeneous, manifold, miscellaneous, multifarious, multifold, multiple, nonconforming
diversiform different, diverse, heterogeneous, miscellaneous, multifold
diversify convert *(change use)*, differ *(vary)*, differentiate, vary. SEE MAIN ENTRY
diversion decoy, detour, deviation, digression, enjoyment *(pleasure)*, misappropriation, misusage, treat. SEE MAIN ENTRY
diversitas difference, diversity
diversity difference, discord, disparity, inconsistency, inequality, nonconformity, variance *(disagreement)*. SEE MAIN ENTRY
diversity of opinion disaccord, disagreement, dissension, dissent *(difference of opinion)*
diversus apart, contradictory, different, diverse, heterogeneous, miscellaneous, repugnant *(exciting aversion)*
divert alleviate, avert, cloak, deter, detour, digress, discourage, entice, hold up *(rob)*, misemploy, peculate, pervert, repel *(drive back)*. SEE MAIN ENTRY
divert by appeal dissuade, expostulate
divert by persuasion expostulate
divert from deter, dissuade
divert from its course detour, deviate
divert from original use estrange
divert from the original possessor estrange
divert funds defalcate
divert one's attention interest
divert to one's own use embezzle
diverting jocular
divest adeem, confiscate, demote, denude, depose *(remove)*, deprive, despoil, diminish, disinherit, disown *(refuse to acknowledge)*, dispossess, distrain, eject *(evict)*, excise *(cut away)*, expose, levy, plunder, remove *(dismiss from office)*, remove *(eliminate)*, unveil. SEE MAIN ENTRY
divest of abridge *(divest)*
divest of legal office disbar
divest of office dislodge, oust
divest of property condemn *(seize)*
divest of right disqualify
divest of suspicion disarm *(set at ease)*
divest oneself forswear
divest oneself of abandon *(relinquish)*, disclaim, resign
divesting confiscatory
divestiture abridgment *(disentitlement)*, garnishment
divestiture of property forfeiture *(act of forfeiting)*
divestment appropriation *(taking)*, attachment *(seizure)*, condemnation *(seizure)*, curtailment, denial, disseisin, distraint, distress *(seizure)*, eviction, expropriation *(divestiture)*, foreclosure, forfeiture *(act of forfeiting)*, privation, removal, sequestration, taking
dividable divisible

divide alienate *(estrange)*, allocate, allot, apportion, classify, codify, cross *(intersect)*, demarcate, detach, dichotomize, disaccord, disaffect, disagree, disburse *(distribute)*, discontinue *(break continuity)*, discriminate *(distinguish)*, disjoint, disperse *(disseminate)*, disperse *(scatter)*, dissociate, dissolve *(separate)*, distinguish, distribute, dole, estrange, fix *(arrange)*, hedge, interrupt, lancinate, mete, parcel, part *(separate)*, partition, pigeonhole, prorate, rend, separate, sever, sort, split, subdivide. SEE MAIN ENTRY
divide according to rule apportion
divide and bestow in shares allocate
divide in portions assign *(allot)*, dispense
divide into distinct portions partition
divide into parcels subdivide
divide into portions partition
divide into shares apportion, parcel, partition
divide into two bifurcate
divide on differ *(disagree)*, dispute *(debate)*
divide proportionally prorate
divide proportionately apportion, partition
divide up apportion, partition, subdivide
divided bicameral, bipartite, broken *(fractured)*, broken *(interrupted)*, discrete, disjunctive *(tending to disjoin)*, dissident, hostile, partial *(part)*, partial *(relating to a part)*, polemic, separate
divided on dissenting
dividend bonus, commission *(fee)*, coupon, installment, interest *(profit)*, profit. SEE MAIN ENTRY
dividends revenue
dividere distribute, divide *(distribute)*, divide *(separate)*, parcel, part *(separate)*, sever
dividing disbursement *(act of disbursing)*, divisive
dividing line edge *(border)*
dividing point crossroad *(turning point)*
dividual divisible, severable
dividuus severable
divinare guess
divination deduction *(conclusion)*, premonition, recognition
divinatory ominous, oracular, portentous *(ominous)*, prophetic
divine anticipate *(prognosticate)*, assume *(suppose)*, construe *(comprehend)*, deduce, deduct *(conclude by reasoning)*, detect, discover, expect *(consider probable)*, find *(discover)*, guess, portend, predict, presage, presume, presuppose, prognosticate, sacrosanct, surmise, suspect *(think)*
divinus prophetic
divisible divisive, partial *(part)*, partial *(relating to a part)*, separable, severable. SEE MAIN ENTRY
divisio division *(act of dividing)*
division affiliate, alienation *(estrangement)*, apportionment, argument *(contention)*, article *(distinct section of a writing)*, assignment *(allotment)*, bureau, capacity *(sphere)*, chamber *(compartment)*, chapter *(branch)*, class, classification, component, conflict, constituency, constituent *(part)*, decentralization, denomination, de-partment, detail, dichotomy, disaccord, disassociation, discord, discrimination *(differentiation)*, dispensation *(act of dispensing)*, dissension, distribution *(apportionment)*, equity *(share of ownership)*, estrangement, faction, incompatibility *(difference)*, installment, kind, manner *(kind)*, member *(constituent part)*, moiety, offshoot, organ, part *(place)*, part *(portion)*, plot *(land)*, province, ration, region, rubric *(title)*, schism, segment, segregation *(separation)*, separation, severance, split, subdivision, subheading, territory, unit *(department)*, variance *(disagreement)*. SEE MAIN ENTRY
division by races segregation *(isolation by races)*
division in proportion apportionment
division line boundary, mete
division lines confines
divisional local, provincial, regional, specific
divisive SEE MAIN ENTRY
divisiveness argument *(contention)*, contravention, discord
divorce depart, detach, disassociation, disband, disengage, disjoint, disown *(refuse to acknowledge)*, dissociate, dissolve *(separate)*, divide *(separate)*, division *(act of dividing)*, estrangement, separation, sever, severance, split. SEE MAIN ENTRY
divorce oneself from renounce
divorced disconnected, disjunctive *(tending to disjoin)*, distinct *(distinguished from others)*, separate
divorcement disassociation, estrangement, separation
divortium divorce
divulgare circulate, circulation, publish, spread
divulgate bare, circulate, confide *(divulge)*, convey *(communicate)*, divulge, report *(disclose)*, reveal
divulgation disclosure *(act of disclosing)*, notification, publicity. SEE MAIN ENTRY
divulge adduce, admit *(concede)*, apprise, bare, bear *(adduce)*, betray *(disclose)*, circulate, communicate, confess, convey *(communicate)*, declare, denounce *(inform against)*, disabuse, disclose, display, enlighten, expose, find *(discover)*, inform *(betray)*, inform *(notify)*, issue *(publish)*, manifest, mention, notice *(give formal warning)*, notify, proclaim, produce *(offer to view)*, profess *(avow)*, promulgate, publish, recite, recount, relate *(tell)*, report *(disclose)*, reveal, signify *(inform)*, speak, spread, unveil, utter. SEE MAIN ENTRY
divulged alleged, public *(known)*
divulgement communication *(statement)*, confession, disclosure *(act of disclosing)*, divulgation, publicity
divulgence admission *(disclosure)*, confession, disclosure *(act of disclosing)*, disclosure *(something disclosed)*, discovery, divulgation, manifestation, publicity
divulger informant, informer *(a person who provides information)*
divulsion avulsion, split
dizen embellish
DNA SEE MAIN ENTRY
DNA sampling SEE MAIN ENTRY
do conduct, discharge *(perform)*, execute *(accomplish)*, fulfill, generate, implement, operate, perform *(execute)*, perpetrate, realize *(make real)*. SEE MAIN ENTRY
do a favor for accommodate
do a job labor
do a service assist, help, serve *(assist)*
do a service for accommodate
do again reproduce
do all one can endeavor, strive
do an injustice to exploit *(take advantage of)*, ill use, mistreat, persecute
do away with delete, destroy *(efface)*, dispatch *(put to death)*, dispel, dispense, eliminate *(eradicate)*, eliminate *(exclude)*, eradicate, expunge, extinguish, extirpate, override, rescind, vacate *(void)*
do away with completely eradicate
do battle with grapple
do business deal, handle *(trade)*, trade, transact
do business with deal, patronize *(trade with)*
do disservice to damage
do duty exercise *(discharge a function)*, officiate
do evil harm, ill use
do harm persecute
do harm to ill use
do honor dedicate
do honor to defer *(yield in judgment)*
do like copy
do likewise mock *(imitate)*
do mischief harm, persecute
do nothing procrastinate
do of one's own accord choose
do one's best attempt, endeavor, strive
do one's bidding serve *(assist)*
do one's utmost endeavor, strive
do over emend, repeat *(do again)*, transform
do penance redeem *(satisfy debts)*, repent
do repairs fix *(repair)*
do repeatedly practice *(train by repetition)*
do research study
do scant justice to underestimate
do service avail *(be of use)*, pander
do subtraction diminish
do the deed dispatch *(dispose of)*
do the needful attempt
do the will of obey, observe *(obey)*
do thoroughly consummate
do violence harm, ill use, persecute
do violence to damage, mistreat, violate
do well pass *(satisfy requirements)*, succeed *(attain)*
do without dispense, eschew, forbear, forgo, forswear, refrain, relinquish
do work labor
do work with ply
do wrong ill use, lapse *(fall into error)*, mistreat
do wrong to persecute
doable potential, practicable, viable
docere edify, inform *(notify)*, instruct *(teach)*
docile facile, malleable, obedient, obsequious, passive, patient, pliable, pliant, sequacious, suasible, tractable, yielding
docilis tractable
docility amenability, capitulation, resignation *(passive acceptance)*
dock diminish, lessen
docket agenda, book, calendar *(list of cases)*, calendar *(record of yearly periods)*, empanel, enroll, file, file *(place among official records)*, label *(noun)*, label *(verb)*, note *(record)*, pigeonhole, program *(noun)*, program *(verb)*, record *(noun)*, record *(verb)*, register, roll, schedule, set down, tabulate. SEE MAIN ENTRY
docket incorrectly mislabel
doctor cure, denature, falsify, meliorate, palter, revise, slant
doctor assisted suicide SEE MAIN ENTRY

doctor up restore *(renew)*
doctrina instruction *(teaching)*, knowledge *(learning)*, theoretical, theory
doctrinaire bigot, dogmatic, theoretical
doctrinaire opinion dogma
doctrinal disciplinary *(educational)*, dogmatic, informatory, orthodox
doctrinal statement belief *(something believed)*
doctrine belief *(something believed)*, codification, concept, conviction *(persuasion)*, discipline *(field of study)*, dogma, idea, platform, policy *(plan of action)*, precept, prescription *(directive)*, principle *(axiom)*, rule *(legal dictate)*, theory, thesis. SEE MAIN ENTRY
doctrines of lawmaking jurisprudence
doctus learned
document bear *(adduce)*, blank *(form)*, certify *(attest)*, cite *(state)*, confirm, corroborate, deed, dossier, establish *(show)*, evidence, file *(place among official records)*, index *(relate)*, itemize, note *(record)*, quote, record, roll, sustain *(confirm)*, verify *(confirm)*, will *(testamentary instrument)*. SEE MAIN ENTRY
document granting permission permit
document produced as evidence exhibit
document which passes a present interest deed
documentable deductible *(provable)*
documental documentary
documentary convincing, informatory. SEE MAIN ENTRY
documentary evidence certification *(attested copy)*
documentation certification *(attested copy)*, certification *(certification of proficiency)*, confirmation, corroboration, deposition, dossier, evidence, jurat, proof, record, reference *(citation)*, support *(corroboration)*. SEE MAIN ENTRY
documented authentic, convincing, documentary
documented event fact
documents credentials, data, evidence. SEE MAIN ENTRY
documentum example, sample, specimen
dodge abscond, avoid *(evade)*, avoidance *(evasion)*, contrivance, deception, default, elude, equivocate, evade *(deceive)*, evade *(elude)*, evasion, hedge, ignore, imposture, machination, maneuver *(trick)*, omit, palter, parry, pettifog, prevaricate, reject, ruse, shirk, shun, stratagem, subterfuge, tergiversate
dodgery artifice, pettifoggery
dodging disingenuous
doff denude
dogged diligent, faithful *(diligent)*, inexorable, inflexible, intractable, obdurate, patient, persistent, pertinacious, purposeful, resolute, sedulous, serious *(devoted)*
doggedness diligence *(perseverance)*, prowess *(bravery)*, purpose, tenacity
dogma article *(precept)*, belief *(something believed)*, conviction *(persuasion)*, doctrine. SEE MAIN ENTRY
dogma dogma
dogma idea, precept, principle *(axiom)*, rule *(legal dictate)*, theory, thesis
dogmatic arbitrary and capricious, assertive, categorical, dictatorial, fanatical, illiberal, insistent, narrow, obdurate, parochial, provincial. SEE MAIN ENTRY
dogmatic theorist bigot
dogmatical obdurate
dogmatist bigot, pedant
dogmatizer bigot
doing act *(undertaking)*, action *(performance)*, commission *(act)*
doing away with dispatch *(act of putting to death)*
doing good benevolent
doing nothing unemployed
doings dealings, overt act
dole allot, allotment, bestow, disperse *(disseminate)*, distribute, distribution *(apportionment)*, divide *(distribute)*, fund, gratuity *(present)*, largess *(gift)*, loan, prorate, ration, share *(interest)*, split. SEE MAIN ENTRY
dole out administer *(tender)*, allocate, apportion, assign *(allot)*, contribute *(supply)*, disburse *(distribute)*, dispense, disperse *(disseminate)*, dispose *(apportion)*, divide *(distribute)*, mete, parcel, partition, present *(make a gift)*, reapportion
dole out again redistribute
doleful deplorable, disconsolate, lamentable, lugubrious
dolefulness depression, pessimism
doling out apportionment
dollar currency cash
dolmen monument
dolor pain
dolorous deplorable, despondent, disconsolate, grave *(solemn)*, lugubrious
dolosus fraudulent, insidious
doltish obtuse, opaque, uncouth
doltishness opacity
dolus deceit, machination, maneuver *(trick)*, ruse, sham, stratagem
domain ambit, area *(province)*, bailiwick, capacity *(sphere)*, circuit, coverage *(scope)*, demesne, department, district, dominion *(absolute ownership)*, freehold, holding *(property owned)*, jurisdiction, locality, possessions, property *(land)*, province, real estate, realm, region, sphere, territory, title *(right)*. SEE MAIN ENTRY
domare subdue
domestic internal, local, national, native *(domestic)*, residential. SEE MAIN ENTRY
domestic circle family *(household)*, household
domestic domicile household
domestic establishment family *(household)*, household
domesticate inure *(accustom)*
domestication cohabitation *(married state)*
domesticus household *(domestic)*, internal
domicile abode, address, building *(structure)*, dwell *(reside)*, dwelling, habitation *(dwelling place)*, house, inhabit, inhabitation *(place of dwelling)*, lodge *(house)*, lodge *(reside)*, lodging, reside, residence. SEE MAIN ENTRY
domiciled household *(domestic)*
domiciles premises *(buildings)*
domiciliary domestic *(household)*, habitant, household *(domestic)*, residential. SEE MAIN ENTRY
domiciliate dwell *(reside)*, reside
domiciliated household *(domestic)*
domiciliation residence
domicilium domicile, dwell *(reside)*, dwelling, habitation *(dwelling place)*, home *(domicile)*, house, inhabitation *(place of dwelling)*, residence, seat
dominance advantage, authority *(power)*, control *(supervision)*, dominion *(supreme authority)*, duress, hegemony, influence, patronage *(power to appoint jobs)*, power, predominance, preponderance, puissance. SEE MAIN ENTRY
dominancy clout, dominance, dominion *(supreme authority)*
dominant cardinal *(outstanding)*, causative, central *(essential)*, compelling, considerable, forcible, influential, leading *(ranking first)*, master, omnipotent, potent, powerful, predominant, prevailing *(current)*, prevailing *(having superior force)*, prevalent, primary, prime *(most valuable)*, principal, rampant, rife, salient, sovereign *(absolute)*, stellar. SEE MAIN ENTRY
dominant characteristic specialty *(distinctive mark)*
dominant quality character *(personal quality)*
dominant strength main force
dominant theme motif
dominate coerce, constrain *(compel)*, control *(regulate)*, direct *(supervise)*, discipline *(control)*, govern, handle *(manage)*, hold *(possess)*, manage, manipulate *(control unfairly)*, monopolize, obsess, occupy *(take possession)*, outbalance, outweigh, overcome *(surmount)*, override, oversee, own, predominate *(command)*, prevail *(be in force)*, prevail *(triumph)*, subdue, subject, subjugate, surmount. SEE MAIN ENTRY
dominating leading *(ranking first)*, omnipotent, powerful, predominant, prevailing *(having superior force)*, salient
dominating action obsession
dominatio supremacy
domination authority *(power)*, compulsion *(coercion)*, control *(supervision)*, dominance, dominion *(supreme authority)*, force *(strength)*, hegemony, influence, jurisdiction, monopoly, occupation *(possession)*, oppression, patronage *(power to appoint jobs)*, possession *(ownership)*, power, predominance, preponderance, primacy, supremacy. SEE MAIN ENTRY
domineer browbeat, dominate, impose *(subject)*, prevail *(be in force)*, repress, rule *(govern)*
domineering brutal, dictatorial, dogmatic, influential, peremptory *(imperative)*, presumptuous, severe, supercilious, tyrannous
dominion agency *(legal relationship)*, ambit, bailiwick, circuit, clout, control *(supervision)*, coverage *(scope)*, demesne, domain *(sphere of influence)*, dominance, force *(strength)*, government *(administration)*, hegemony, influence, interest *(ownership)*, jurisdiction, occupancy, occupation *(possession)*, ownership, possession *(ownership)*, power, predominance, primacy, province, realm, regime, supremacy, territory. SEE MAIN ENTRY
dominions possessions, property *(land)*
dominium ownership
dominus proprietor
domus abode, building *(structure)*, domicile, dwelling, habitation *(dwelling place)*, home *(domicile)*, house, household, premises *(buildings)*, residence
don assume *(simulate)*, pedagogue
donare impart, present *(make a gift)*
donate bequeath, bestow, cede, contribute *(supply)*, convey *(transfer)*, dedicate, dispense, endow, endue, fund, give *(grant)*, leave *(give)*, present *(make a gift)*, proffer, provide *(supply)*, spend. SEE MAIN ENTRY

donate to subscribe *(promise)*
donated gratuitous *(given without recompense)*
donation benefit *(conferment)*, bonus, cession, charity, endowment, gift *(present)*, grant, largess *(gift)*, perquisite, provision *(act of supplying)*, reward, tip *(gratuity)*. SEE MAIN ENTRY
donative gift *(present)*, gratuity *(present)*, largess *(gift)*, tip *(gratuity)*. SEE MAIN ENTRY
donator contributor *(giver)*, donor, grantor
done complete *(ended)*, through
done again repeated
done at pleasure arbitrary
done by force forcible
done by one person ex parte
done by stealth surreptitious
done for effect flagrant
done on purpose deliberate
done over repeated
done quickly expeditious
done reciprocally mutual *(reciprocal)*
done with through
done with expedition expeditious
done with intent to commit crime felonious
done with skill artful
done with thoroughness elaborate
done without delay summary
done without reason random
donee assignee, beneficiary, devisee, feoffee, grantee, heir, legatee, licensee, payee, recipient, transferee. SEE MAIN ENTRY
donee of a corporeal hereditament feoffee
donor benefactor, contributor *(giver)*, feoffor, good samaritan, maker, transferor. SEE MAIN ENTRY
donum donation, gift *(present)*, grant
doom condemn *(punish)*, convict, predetermine, sentence, tragedy
doomed unproductive
doomful portentous *(ominous)*
door entrance, outlet, portal, threshold *(entrance)*
doorway egress, portal
dope narcotic
doppelganger counterpart *(complement)*
dormancy abeyance, cessation *(interlude)*, desuetude, inaction, inertia
dormant dead, inactive, insensible, lifeless *(dull)*, otiose, passive, potential, stagnant, static, torpid. SEE MAIN ENTRY
dormant energy potential
dormitory dwelling, home *(domicile)*, lodging
dos dower
dose drug
dossier blank *(form)*, file, record. SEE MAIN ENTRY
dotage caducity, incapacity
dotation charity, donation, dower, largess *(gift)*, legacy
doted on popular
double alter ego, copy, correlate, counterpart *(parallel)*, duplicate, reflection *(image)*, reproduce, resemblance, same, substitute. SEE MAIN ENTRY
double back return *(go back)*
double dealing deceptive. SEE MAIN ENTRY
double for displace *(replace)*, impersonate, pose *(impersonate)*
double jeopardy SEE MAIN ENTRY
double prosecution double jeopardy
double punishment double jeopardy
double talk jargon *(unintelligible language)*
double-cross betray *(disclose)*, mislead
double-crossing machiavellian, perfidious
double-dealing bad faith, bunko, collusion, deceit, deception, dishonest, duplicity, faithless, false *(disloyal)*, fraud, fraudulent, hypocrisy, infidelity, knavery, lying, machiavellian, perfidious, recreant, sly, undependable, untrustworthy
double-edged bitter *(penetrating)*
double-tongued false *(disloyal)*, machiavellian
doubling boom *(increase)*
doubt cloud *(suspicion)*, confusion *(ambiguity)*, disbelieve, discount *(disbelieve)*, dispute *(contest)*, hesitate, hesitation, improbability, incertitude, incredulity, indecision, misdoubt, misgiving, mistrust, qualm, quandary, reluctance, scruple, suspect *(distrust)*, suspicion *(mistrust)*. SEE MAIN ENTRY
doubt the truth of impugn
doubtable debatable, disputable, doubtful, dubitative, impalpable, implausible, ludicrous
doubtful ambiguous, controversial, cynical, debatable, disputable, dubious, dubitative, equivocal, hesitant, implausible, inconclusive, inconvincible, incredible, incredulous, indefinite, irresolute, leery, moot, precarious, problematic, speculative, suspicious *(questionable)*, unbelievable, uncertain *(questionable)*, undecided, unsettled, unsustainable, vague. SEE MAIN ENTRY
doubtful event contingency
doubtful meaning ambiguity
doubtful narrative myth
doubtfulness ambiguity, confusion *(ambiguity)*, doubt *(suspicion)*, improbability, incertitude, incredulity, indecision, misgiving, qualm, quandary, scruple, suspicion *(mistrust)*, suspicion *(uncertainty)*
doubting cynical, disputable, doubtful, hesitant, inconvincible, incredulous, irresolute, jealous, leery, skeptical, suspicious *(distrustful)*, undecided. SEE MAIN ENTRY
doubtless axiomatic, categorical, certain *(positive)*, clear *(certain)*, definite, demonstrable, indubious, uncontroverted, undisputed, unrefutable
doubtlessly a priori, admittedly, fairly *(clearly)*
douceur grant
doughtiness prowess *(bravery)*
doughty heroic, indomitable, spartan, undaunted
dour astringent, bleak *(severely simple)*, rigid, severe
douse immerse *(plunge into)*
dovetail correspond *(be equivalent)*
dower SEE MAIN ENTRY
down *(dejected)* SEE MAIN ENTRY
down *(lowest point)* SEE MAIN ENTRY
down payment deposit, handsel, installment. SEE MAIN ENTRY
down to until
downcast despondent, disconsolate, lugubrious, pessimistic
downcastness pessimism
downfall catastrophe, debacle, decline, defeat, disaster, failure *(lack of success)*, fatality, miscarriage, prostration. SEE MAIN ENTRY
downgrade debase, decline, deduct *(reduce)*, demote, deteriorate, discredit, disgrace, disparage, humiliate, reduce. SEE MAIN ENTRY
downhearted disconsolate, pessimistic
downheartedness damper *(depressant)*, pessimism
downhill decline
downright absolute *(complete)*, clear *(apparent)*, honest, ingenuous, outright, purely *(positively)*, simple, stark, thorough, total, unaffected *(sincere)*, unequivocal, unmitigated, unqualified *(unlimited)*
downrush descent *(declination)*
downthrow prostration
downtrend decline, decrease
downtrodden servile
downturn decline, decrease
downward inclination decline
downward incline decline
downward trend decline, decrease
dowry endowment
doxology laudation. SEE MAIN ENTRY
doxy dogma
drab ordinary, pedestrian
drabble sully
draconian harsh, stringent. SEE MAIN ENTRY
draft bill *(proposed act)*, blueprint, check *(instrument)*, coerce, compose, conceive *(invent)*, contrive, delineate, design *(construction plan)*, direction *(course)*, enroll, formulate, frame *(construct)*, frame *(formulate)*, instrument *(document)*, invent *(produce for the first time)*, make, nominate, note *(written promise to pay)*, originate, pattern, plan, program *(noun)*, program *(verb)*, proposal *(suggestion)*, recruit, require *(compel)*, select. SEE MAIN ENTRY
draft a brief SEE MAIN ENTRY
rdraft a document SEE MAIN ENTRY
draft a will SEE MAIN ENTRY
draft holder bearer
drafter author *(writer)*
draftsman architect
drag impede
drag away carry away
drag on persist
drag out continue *(prolong)*, prolong, protract *(prolong)*
dragged out protracted
dragonnade onset *(assault)*
dragoon bait *(harass)*, coerce, persecute
drain consume, decrease, decrement, deplete, diminish, dissipate *(expend foolishly)*, exhaust *(deplete)*, expense *(sacrifice)*, exude, outflow, outpour, remove *(eliminate)*, spend, tax *(overwork)*
drain of resources deplete
drain on resources expense *(cost)*, expense *(sacrifice)*, maintenance *(upkeep)*, overhead
drainage outflow
drained insufficient, nonsubstantial *(not sufficient)*, poor *(underprivileged)*, vacuous
dramatic histrionic, moving *(evoking emotion)*, potent
dramatic art histrionics
dramatic representation histrionics
dramatic rights SEE MAIN ENTRY
dramatically opposed SEE MAIN ENTRY
dramatize produce *(offer to view)*, recite
dramaturgy histrionics
drape clothe
drastic extreme *(exaggerated)*, forcible, harsh, outrageous, severe. SEE MAIN ENTRY
draw bait *(lure)*, bet, characterize, choose, copy, deadlock, delineate, depict, detail *(particularize)*, educe, exhaust *(deplete)*, extract, gain, inveigle, lottery, motivate, portray, reap, receive *(acquire)*, trace *(delineate)*. SEE MAIN ENTRY
draw a comparison contrast
draw a conclusion ascertain, deduce, deduct *(conclude by reasoning)*, derive

(deduce), determine, find *(determine)*, infer, judge, read, rule *(decide)*
draw a distinction distinguish
draw a parallel compare, connect *(relate)*, correspond *(be equivalent)*, relate *(establish a connection)*
draw a picture delineate
draw an inference construe *(comprehend)*, derive *(deduce)*, gauge, infer, presuppose
draw apart estrange
draw as an implication construe *(comprehend)*
draw as by a lure entrap
draw aside divert
draw away divert
draw back retreat, shun. SEE MAIN ENTRY
draw by artful inducements entrap
draw forth disinter, distill, educe, elicit, evoke, extract
draw from derive *(receive)*, exact
draw gradually together converge
draw in converge, engage *(involve)*, entrap, implicate, incriminate, involve *(implicate)*
draw inferences generalize, reason *(conclude)*
draw lots bet
draw near accost, approach, approximate, border *(approach)*, gravitate, impend
draw off disengage
draw on exercise *(use)*, lure
draw one's sword brandish
draw out compose, continue *(prolong)*, disinter, distill, educe, elicit, evoke, exhaust *(deplete)*, extend *(enlarge)*, extract, prolong, withdraw
draw out by compulsion extort
draw out by force extort
draw out the essence distill
draw profit from profit
draw rein check *(restrain)*
draw the inference assume *(suppose)*
draw the line delimit, differentiate, discriminate *(distinguish)*. SEE MAIN ENTRY
draw the veil camouflage
draw to a close cease, complete, dissolve *(terminate)*, expire
draw together collect *(gather)*, compile, consolidate *(unite)*, constrict *(compress)*, convene, glean, hoard
draw toward gravitate
draw up compile, compose, devise *(invent)*, formulate, frame *(construct)*, frame *(formulate)*, make, produce *(manufacture)*
drawback burden, check *(bar)*, defect, disadvantage, encumbrance, fault *(weakness)*, handicap, hindrance, impediment, liability, obstacle, onus *(burden)*, scruple
drawee debtor, obligor
drawer payee
drawing attractive, design *(construction plan)*, lottery
drawing conclusions dialectic
drawing near forthcoming, immediate *(imminent)*, imminent
drawing out evulsion
drawing to a close determinable *(liable to be terminated)*
drawn undecided
drawn battle deadlock
drawn game deadlock
drawn out chronic, protracted
drayage carriage
dread consternation, fear *(noun)*, fear *(verb)*, fright, mistrust, panic, phobia, portentous *(ominous)*, stress *(strain)*, trepidation
dreaded dire, undesirable
dreadful adverse *(negative)*, bad *(inferior)*, deplorable, detrimental, dire, disastrous, disreputable, formidable, gross *(flagrant)*, heinous, hostile, insufferable, lamentable, loathsome, nefarious, portentous *(ominous)*, regrettable, repulsive, serious *(grave)*, sinister
dreadful event tragedy
dreadless undaunted
dream end *(intent)*, objective, phantom, reflect *(ponder)*
dream up conceive *(invent)*, conjure, invent *(produce for the first time)*
dreaminess preoccupation
dreaming pensive
dreamy delusive, oblivious, pensive, quixotic
drear bleak *(severely simple)*
drearisome jejune *(dull)*, lifeless *(dull)*, pedestrian, ponderous, prolix
dreary bleak *(severely simple)*, deplorable, despondent, insipid, jejune *(dull)*, lifeless *(dull)*, lugubrious, pedestrian, ponderous, portentous *(ominous)*
drench imbue, immerse *(plunge into)*, inundate, overload, permeate, pervade
dress clothe
dress as impersonate
dress down browbeat, denounce *(condemn)*, disapprove *(condemn)*, fault, reprehend, reprimand
dress to conceal disguise
dress up camouflage, cloak, disguise, embellish
dressing down diatribe, obloquy, reprimand, reproach
dried up otiose
drift conatus, connotation, content *(meaning)*, contents, detour, deviate, digress, digression, direction *(course)*, gist *(substance)*, import, main point, meaning, prowl, signification, substance *(essential nature)*, tenor
drifter derelict, itinerant
drifting discursive *(digressive)*, moving *(in motion)*, shifting
drill discipline *(training)*, educate, enter *(penetrate)*, practice *(train by repetition)*
drilling discipline *(training)*
drink carouse
drink to excess carouse
drinkable palatable
drip exude
drive activity, ardor, bind *(obligate)*, browbeat, campaign, causeway, coerce, compel, compulsion *(obsession)*, constrain *(compel)*, enforce, foray, force *(compulsion)*, impact, impetus, impose *(enforce)*, impulse, incite, inducement, industry *(activity)*, life *(vitality)*, manipulate *(utilize skillfully)*, obsess, operate, press *(constrain)*, press *(goad)*, pressure *(noun)*, pressure *(verb)*, project *(impel forward)*, provoke, purpose, require *(compel)*, send, stimulate, stimulus, urge. SEE MAIN ENTRY
drive a bargain dicker, haggle, handle *(trade)*, trade
drive a trade deal, sell
drive against collide *(crash against)*
drive apart estrange
drive at attempt, intend, strive
drive away deport *(banish)*, dispel, parry, repel *(drive back)*, repulse, spurn, stave, supplant
drive away by scattering dispel
drive back parry, rebuff, repel *(drive back)*, repulse, spurn
drive firmly in impact
drive forward hasten, impel
drive from one's native land expatriate
drive in inject
drive into collide *(crash against)*, pierce *(lance)*
drive off in various directions dispel
drive on expedite
drive onward impel
drive out deport *(banish)*, depose *(remove)*, divest, expel, oust, supplant, transport
driveway causeway
driving compelling, important *(urgent)*, impulsive *(impelling)*, insistent
driving force determinant, incentive, motive
driving out deportation, expulsion
droit birthright, capacity *(authority)*, due, franchise *(license)*, interest *(ownership)*, prerogative, title *(right)*. SEE MAIN ENTRY
droning ponderous
dronish lifeless *(dull)*, obtuse
droop descent *(declination)*, languish, succumb
drooping languid, powerless
droopy powerless
drop abandon *(relinquish)*, cancel, cease, decline, decline *(fall)*, decrease *(noun)*, decrease *(verb)*, delete, demote, depose *(remove)*, depreciate, depress, descent *(declination)*, discharge *(dismiss)*, discontinue *(abandon)*, distill, ebb, exude, forswear, iota, languish, leave *(allow to remain)*, minimum, omit, precipitate *(throw down violently)*, quit *(discontinue)*, relinquish, renounce, set aside *(annul)*, stop, subside, succumb, terminate. SEE MAIN ENTRY
drop a case SEE MAIN ENTRY
drop a hint imply, remind
drop by drop piecemeal
drop charges remit *(release from penalty)*
drop in strength decline *(fall)*
drop off diminish, ebb, lessen
drop out leave *(depart)*, resign, retire *(conclude a career)*
drought paucity
drove assemblage, mass *(body of persons)*
drown immerse *(plunge into)*, overcome *(overwhelm)*, stifle
drown out extinguish
drowsiness languor
drowsy torpid
drub defeat, lash *(strike)*, overcome *(surmount)*
drubbing failure *(lack of success)*
drudge labor, palliative *(abating)*, strive
drudgery work *(effort)*
drug cannabis, narcotic. SEE MAIN ENTRY
drugged insensible
drum repeat *(state again)*
drum out of the legal profession disbar
drunk SEE MAIN ENTRY
drunkenness dipsomania, inebriation
dry jejune *(dull)*, languid, lifeless *(dull)*, pedestrian, prosaic, unproductive
dry run experiment
dry up deplete
dual bilateral
dual chambered bicameral
duality duplicity
dub denominate, phrase
dubiety ambiguity, ambivalence, confusion *(ambiguity)*, doubt *(suspicion)*,

hesitation, incertitude, incredulity, indecision, misgiving, qualm, quandary, rejection, scruple, suspicion *(mistrust)*
dubiosity incertitude, quandary
dubious aleatory *(uncertain)*, ambiguous, controversial, cynical, debatable, disputable, doubtful, dubitative, equivocal, inconvincible, incredulous, indefinite, leery, moot, poor *(inferior in quality)*, precarious, problematic, skeptical, speculative, suspicious *(distrustful)*, suspicious *(questionable)*, unbelievable, uncertain *(questionable)*, undecided, unsettled, vague. SEE MAIN ENTRY
dubiousness ambiguity, confusion *(ambiguity)*, doubt *(suspicion)*, incertitude, incredulity, indecision, qualm, quandary, rejection, scruple, suspicion *(mistrust)*
dubitable controversial, debatable, disputable, doubtful, dubitative, impalpable, implausible, ludicrous
dubitancy ambivalence, incertitude, indecision
dubitare hesitate
dubitate doubt *(hesitate)*
dubitatio doubt *(indecision)*, hesitation, indecision, scruple
dubitation confusion *(ambiguity)*, doubt *(suspicion)*, hesitation, incertitude, indecision, quandary
dubitative debatable, disputable, dubious. SEE MAIN ENTRY
dubito doubt *(indecision)*
dubius critical *(crucial)*, doubtful, dubious, equivocal, indefinite, indeterminate, irresolute, precarious, problematic, undecided, vague
ducere regard *(pay attention)*
duck immerse *(plunge into)*, shirk
ductile flexible, malleable, obedient, pliable, pliant, sequacious, tractable
ductilis malleable
ductility amenability
ductus generalship, guidance
dudgeon estrangement, odium, resentment, umbrage
due birthright, charge *(cost)*, claim *(right)*, condign, delinquent *(overdue)*, droit, entitled, expense *(cost)*, forthcoming, just, liability, opportune, outstanding *(unpaid)*, overdue, payable, prerogative, price, receivable, reprisal, retribution, right *(entitlement)*, right *(righteousness)*, rightful, seasonable, suitable, unpaid, unsettled. SEE MAIN ENTRY
due date maturity. SEE MAIN ENTRY
due order array *(order)*
due process SEE MAIN ENTRY
due punishment reprisal
due to contingent, dependent
due to be paid receivable
duel compete, fight *(battle)*
dueness droit, propriety *(appropriateness)*
dues charge *(cost)*, fee *(charge)*, tax
dulce domum building *(structure)*
dulcet nectarious, palatable, sapid
dulcification mollification
dulcify alleviate, lull, mollify, pacify, placate, soothe
dulcis palatable
dull allay, alleviate, bleak *(severely simple)*, diminish, drug, impair, inexpressive, insensible, insipid, languid, lessen, moderate *(temper)*, mollify, nondescript, obfuscate, obnubilate, obscure, obtund, obtuse, opaque, pedestrian, phlegmatic, ponderous, prosaic, repress, soothe, stagnant, stale, stifle, subdue, sully, tarnish, thoughtless, torpid, trite, vacuous. SEE MAIN ENTRY
dull comment platitude
dull-witted non compos mentis, obtuse, opaque
dull-wittedness opacity
dulling narcotic
dullness indistinctness, inertia, languor, opacity, sloth
duly as a matter of right, ex officio. SEE MAIN ENTRY
dumb fatuous, mute, speechless, taciturn
dumb-struck speechless
dumbfound confound
dumbfounding prodigious *(amazing)*
dummy imitation, proxy
dump deposit *(place)*
dun charge *(assess)*, claim *(demand)*, exact, importune, request. SEE MAIN ENTRY
duncelike opaque
duncical opaque
dunk immerse *(plunge into)*
dupable naive
dupe bait *(lure)*, betray *(lead astray)*, bilk, cheat, cloak, deceive, defraud, delude, ensnare, entrap, fake, hoodwink, illude, mislead, misrepresent, overreach, palter, pettifog, pretend, prevaricate. SEE MAIN ENTRY
dupery bunko, deception, false pretense, falsification, fraud, hoax, knavery
duplexity duplicity
duplexity in meaning ambiguity
duplicate copy *(noun)*, copy *(verb)*, correlate, counterpart *(parallel)*, expendable, facsimile, identical, mock *(imitate)*, plagiarize, quote, reconstruct, recreate, reflection *(image)*, reiterate, repeat *(do again)*, replace, reproduce, same, superfluous, trace *(delineate)*. SEE MAIN ENTRY
duplicated repeated
duplication boom *(increase)*, copy, counterpart *(parallel)*, identity *(similarity)*, plagiarism, redundancy, resemblance, tautology. SEE MAIN ENTRY
duplicative iterative, repetitious
duplicitous agreement conspiracy
duplicity artifice, bad faith, collusion, concealment, deceit, deception, dishonesty, false pretense, falsification, fraud, hoax, hypocrisy, imposture, improbity, indirection *(deceitfulness)*, knavery, misstatement, pettifoggery, pretense *(pretext)*, ruse, story *(falsehood)*, subterfuge. SEE MAIN ENTRY
durability indestructibility, longevity, strength, survival, tolerance
durable constant, firm, immutable, indelible, indestructible, infrangible, noncancellable, permanent, persistent, resilient, solid *(sound)*, stable, strong, unremitting. SEE MAIN ENTRY
durableness indestructibility, longevity
durables goods
durance bondage, captivity, commitment *(confinement)*, custody *(incarceration)*, restraint, thrall. SEE MAIN ENTRY
durance vile detention
durare continue *(prolong)*, endure *(last)*, last, remain *(stay)*
duration life *(period of existence)*, longevity, period, phase *(period)*, survival, tenure, time. SEE MAIN ENTRY
duration of existence age
duration of life lifetime
duress captivity, coercion, compulsion *(coercion)*, constraint *(restriction)*, force *(compulsion)*, intimidate, main force, pressure, stress *(strain)*, subjection. SEE MAIN ENTRY
during the interval ad interim. SEE MAIN ENTRY
during the journey en route
during the last moments of life in extremis
during travel en route
duritia rigor
durus callous, rigid, severe, unbending
dusk obscure
dusky indistinct, nebulous
duteous conscientious, faithful *(loyal)*, loyal, meritorious, moral, obedient, obeisant, passive, true *(loyal)*
duteously faithfully
duteousness allegiance, fealty
dutiable ad valorem
dutiful conscientious, faithful *(loyal)*, law-abiding, loyal, meritorious, moral, obedient, obeisant, passive, patient, punctilious, serious *(devoted)*, true *(loyal)*
dutiful adherence fidelity
dutifully faithfully, respectfully
dutifulness adhesion *(loyalty)*, allegiance, compliance, conformity *(obedience)*, discipline *(obedience)*, fidelity
dutiless broken *(unfulfilled)*, derelict *(negligent)*, irresponsible, remiss
dutilessness dereliction, infidelity, misdeed, misdoing, nonperformance
duty ad valorem, agency *(legal relationship)*, assignment *(task)*, burden, business *(affair)*, business *(occupation)*, charge *(lien)*, commitment *(responsibility)*, compulsion *(coercion)*, employment, excise, fealty, function, imposition *(tax)*, job, labor *(work)*, levy, liability, loyalty, mission, office, position *(business status)*, province, responsibility *(accountability)*, right *(righteousness)*, tariff *(duties)*, tax, trade *(occupation)*, trust *(custody)*, weight *(burden)*, work *(employment)*. SEE MAIN ENTRY
duty owed obligation *(duty)*
duty to pay liability
duty to pay money obligation *(liability)*
duty unfulfilled delict
dux chief, marshal
dwarf lessen, minimize. SEE MAIN ENTRY
dwell lodge *(reside)*, occupy *(take possession)*, pause, remain *(occupy)*, reside. SEE MAIN ENTRY
dwell in inhabit, occupy *(take possession)*
dwell on repeat *(state again)*
dwell permanently inhabit
dwell together cohabit
dwell upon brood, recall *(remember)*, reflect *(ponder)*
dweller citizen, denizen, domiciliary, habitant, inhabitant, inmate, lodger, occupant, resident, tenant
dwellers population
dwelling abode, address, building *(structure)*, domicile, habitation *(act of inhabiting)*, habitation *(dwelling place)*, home *(domicile)*, house, inhabitation *(act of dwelling in)*, inhabitation *(place of dwelling)*, lodging, residence. SEE MAIN ENTRY
dwelling place abode, address, building *(structure)*, home *(domicile)*, house, inhabitation *(place of dwelling)*, lodging
dwellings premises *(buildings)*
dwindle consume, decrease, deduct *(reduce)*, depreciate, diminish, ebb, lessen, subside
dwindling attrition, decrease, deduction *(diminution)*
dye stain
dying death, expiration, in extremis

dynamic impulsive *(impelling)*, intense, potent, powerful, progressive *(going forward)*, trenchant. SEE MAIN ENTRY
dynamic quality life *(vitality)*
dynamical impulsive *(impelling)*
dynamism industry *(activity)*, life *(vitality)*
dynamite bomb
dynamite charge SEE MAIN ENTRY
dynasty bloodline, descent *(lineage)*, family *(common ancestry)*, origin *(ancestry)*. SEE MAIN ENTRY
dyspeptic bilious, bitter *(penetrating)*. SEE MAIN ENTRY

E

e-signature SEE MAIN ENTRY
each respectively. SEE MAIN ENTRY
each and every collective, in solido
each in turn respectively
each to each per capita, pro rata
eadem sentire sympathize
eager earnest, fervent, hot-blooded, inclined, industrious, prompt, prone, ready *(willing)*, sedulous, serious *(devoted)*, solicitous, vehement, willing *(desirous)*, zealous. SEE MAIN ENTRY
eager for knowledge inquisitive
eager to please obeisant
eagerly readily
eagerness ardor, desire, emotion, greed, industry *(activity)*, interest *(concern)*, life *(vitality)*, passion, penchant, purpose
eagerness to act quickly haste
earlier antecedent, back *(in arrears)*, before mentioned, former, heretofore, last *(preceding)*, precursory, preexisting, previous, prior, said, theretofore. SEE MAIN ENTRY
earliest original *(initial)*, primary, prime *(original)*
earliest stage embryo
early initial, instant, obsolete, old, preliminary, preparatory, previous, prime *(original)*, prompt, punctual. SEE MAIN ENTRY
early stage nonage
earmark allocate, allot, brand, brand *(mark)*, designate, designation *(symbol)*, device *(distinguishing mark)*, distinction *(difference)*, index *(catalog)*, label, property *(distinctive attribute)*, quality *(grade)*, reserve, specialty *(distinctive mark)*. SEE MAIN ENTRY
earmarked prospective
earn attain, bear *(yield)*, gain, obtain, pass *(satisfy requirements)*, procure, realize *(obtain as a profit)*, reap, receive *(acquire)*, succeed *(attain)*. see main entry
earn out SEE MAIN ENTRY
earned condign, due *(owed)*, entitled
earned income earnings
earnest bail, binder, close *(rigorous)*, eager, fervent, honest, industrious, intense, painstaking, pertinacious, pledge *(security)*, purposeful, resolute, security *(pledge)*, serious *(devoted)*, solemn, true *(loyal)*, urgent, vehement, willing *(desirous)*, zealous. SEE MAIN ENTRY
earnest averment surety *(certainty)*
earnest avowal surety *(certainty)*
earnest declaration assurance, surety *(certainty)*
earnest entreaty prayer
earnest money handsel. SEE MAIN ENTRY
earnest payment pledge *(security)*
earnest pledge deposit
earnest request call *(appeal)*, entreaty, petition, prayer
earnest seeking market *(demand)*
earnestly faithfully
earnestness adhesion *(loyalty)*, compulsion *(obsession)*, diligence *(care)*, diligence *(perseverance)*, goodwill, industry *(activity)*, intention, resolution *(decision)*, spirit
earnings annuity, boom *(prosperity)*, commission *(fee)*, compensation, honorarium, income, interest *(profit)*, output, pay, payment *(remittance)*, possessions, proceeds, profit, recompense, revenue, wage. SEE MAIN ENTRY
earshot range
earthly material *(physical)*, mundane, physical
earthly possessions estate *(property)*
earthquake cataclysm
earthshaking momentous
earthy inelegant
earwitness bystander
ease alleviate, ameliorate, assuage, commute, disencumber, disentangle, expedite, facilitate, facility *(easiness)*, favor, give *(yield)*, help, informality, lessen, lull, mitigate, moderate *(temper)*, modify *(moderate)*, mollify, obtund, pacify, palliate *(abate)*, prosperity, reassure, redress, relax, relieve *(give aid)*, remedy, remit *(relax)*, skill, solace, soothe. SEE MAIN ENTRY
ease of movement latitude
ease the burden alleviate, disencumber, ease
easeful palliative *(abating)*, placid
easement advantage, droit, instigation, mollification, relief *(release)*, solace. SEE MAIN ENTRY
easily readily
easily *(by far)*. SEE MAIN ENTRY
easily *(without trouble)*. SEE MAIN ENTRY
easily accessible convenient
easily affected perceptive, susceptible *(responsive)*
easily bent flexible, malleable, pliable, pliant
easily convinced credulous, suasible
easily deceived credulous, unsuspecting
easily done convenient, facile
easily duped credulous
easily excited sensitive *(easily affected)*
easily influenced facile, malleable, pliable, sequacious
easily lead tractable
easily led sequacious
easily managed flexible, resigned, tractable
easily managed job sinecure
easily observed scrutable
easily offended sensitive *(easily affected)*
easily perceived distinct *(clear)*, palpable
easily persuaded facile, malleable, pliable, pliant, prone, suasible
easily seen apparent *(perceptible)*, evident, gross *(flagrant)*, overt, palpable, scrutable
easily taken in credulous
easily taught sequacious, tractable
easily understood coherent *(clear)*, comprehensible, distinct *(clear)*, scrutable
easiness informality
easiness of belief credulity
easing mitigating, mitigation, mollification, remedial
easy convenient, elementary, facile, lenient, malleable, passable, promiscuous, yielding
easy *(effortless)*. SEE MAIN ENTRY
easy *(lenient)*. SEE MAIN ENTRY
easy *(obvious)*. SEE MAIN ENTRY
easy chore sinecure
easy employment sinecure
easy job sinecure
easy labor sinecure
easy to be seen patent, perceptible
easy to believe presumptive
easy to grasp coherent *(clear)*
easy to perceive evident
easy to see evident, manifest, naked *(perceptible)*, perceivable
easy to understand coherent *(clear)*, comprehensible, elementary, explicit, pellucid
easy-mannered civil *(polite)*
easygoing facile, lenient, malleable, nonchalant, patient, peaceable, placid, pliable, sequacious, suasible, tractable, yielding
easygoingness informality
eat consume, prey
eat away diminish
eat excessively overindulge
eatable palatable
eavesdrop monitor, overhear, spy. SEE MAIN ENTRY
ebb decline, decline *(fall)*, decrease *(noun)*, decrease *(verb)*, degenerate, depreciate, depress, deteriorate, diminish, languish, lessen, outflow, retreat, subside. SEE MAIN ENTRY
ebb and flow beat *(pulsate)*
ebb of life death
eblandiri elicit
ebrietas inebriation
ebriosity dipsomania
ebrius drunk
ebullient SEE MAIN ENTRY
ebullition bluster *(speech)*, commotion, emotion, outbreak, outburst
eccentric anomalous, deviant, divergent, irregular *(not usual)*, ludicrous, nonconforming, novel, original *(creative)*, particular *(specific)*, peculiar *(curious)*, singular, unaccustomed, uncommon, unorthodox, unpredictable. SEE MAIN ENTRY
eccentricity irregularity, nonconformity, quirk *(idiosyncrasy)*, specialty *(distinctive mark)*
echelon class, degree *(station)*, position *(business status)*
echo concur *(agree)*, copy, mock *(imitate)*, reflection *(image)*, reiterate, repeat *(state again)*, repercussion. SEE MAIN ENTRY
echoed repeated
echoic repetitious
echoing iterative, repetitious, resounding
eclat notoriety
éclat prestige
eclat prestige
eclectic miscellaneous
eclipse blind *(obscure)*, cloak, conceal, ensconce, enshroud, obfuscate, obnubilate, obscure, outbalance, outweigh, overcome *(surmount)*, predominate *(outnumber)*, shroud, surpass, transcend. SEE MAIN ENTRY
eclipsed allusive, hidden
ecology SEE MAIN ENTRY
economic commercial, fiscal, mercantile, pecuniary. SEE MAIN ENTRY
economic decline depression
economic downfall failure *(bankruptcy)*
economic liberties SEE MAIN ENTRY

economic prosperity boom *(prosperity)*
economic resources capital, principal *(capital sum)*
economic science economy *(economic system)*
economic use management *(judicious use)*
economical economic, frugal, parsimonious, pecuniary, provident *(frugal)*, prudent. SEE MAIN ENTRY
economical of space compact *(dense)*
economical of words laconic, sententious
economically imprudent profligate *(extravagant)*
economicalness austerity, economy *(frugality)*
economics finance
economize diminish, preserve, retrench, save *(hold back)*
economizing economical
economy austerity, conservation, moderation, prudence, regulation *(management)*. SEE MAIN ENTRY
economy-minded frugal
ecphonesis expletive
ecstasy enjoyment *(pleasure)*, passion
ecstatic SEE MAIN ENTRY
ectype copy, duplicate
ecumenical general, nonsectarian
edacious gluttonous
edacity greed
eddying fluvial
edere issue *(publish)*
edge advantage, border, border *(bound)*, boundary, circumscribe *(surround by boundary)*, delimit, enclosure, encompass *(surround)*, end *(termination)*, envelop, extremity *(furthest point)*, frontier, hedge, margin *(outside limit)*, outline *(boundary)*, penumbra, periphery, threshold *(verge)*. SEE MAIN ENTRY
edge close to approach
edges configuration *(confines)*, confines
edging border, contiguous, edge *(border)*, outline *(boundary)*, proximate
edible palatable
edicere enunciate, order
edico direction *(order)*
edict act *(enactment)*, adjudication, award, brevet, canon, constitution, declaration, decree, dictate, direction *(order)*, directive, enactment, fiat, mandate, measure, mittimus, monition *(legal summons)*, order *(judicial directive)*, ordinance, precept, prescription *(directive)*, proclamation, pronouncement, regulation *(rule)*, requirement, rule *(legal dictate)*, ruling, sentence, statute, warrant *(judicial writ)*. SEE MAIN ENTRY
edictum declaration, decree, edict, order *(judicial directive)*, ordinance, proclamation
edification education, guidance, instruction *(direction)*, instruction *(teaching)*. SEE MAIN ENTRY
edifice building *(structure)*, dwelling, inhabitation *(place of dwelling)*. SEE MAIN ENTRY
edifices premises *(buildings)*
edify disabuse, educate, enlighten, instruct *(teach)*, profit. SEE MAIN ENTRY
edifying beneficial, didactic, informative, meritorious, profitable, salutary, valuable
edit amend, digest *(summarize)*, redact, revise, treat *(process)*. SEE MAIN ENTRY
edit out bowdlerize, delete, expunge, redact
editing revision *(process of correcting)*
editio libri publication *(printed matter)*
edition publication *(printed matter)*
editorial review *(critical evaluation)*. SEE MAIN ENTRY
editorialize SEE MAIN ENTRY
editors press
educare develop, educate
educate convey *(communicate)*, direct *(supervise)*, disabuse, discipline *(train)*, edify, enlighten, impart, inculcate, inform *(notify)*, instill, instruct *(teach)*, nurture. SEE MAIN ENTRY
educate oneself study
educated cognizant, familiar *(informed)*, knowing, learned, literate, sciential
educated guess estimate *(approximate cost)*, estimation *(calculation)*
educating didactic
education direction *(guidance)*, discipline *(field of study)*, edification, experience *(background)*, guidance, information *(knowledge)*, instruction *(teaching)*, knowledge *(learning)*, preparation. SEE MAIN ENTRY
educational didactic, informative, informatory
educational clarification edification
educational institution institute
educational knowledge edification
educative didactic, disciplinary *(educational)*, informative
educator pedagogue
educe deduce, deduct *(conclude by reasoning)*, detect, disinter, elicit, evoke, extract, solve. SEE MAIN ENTRY
edulcorate purge *(purify)*
eel-shaped circuitous
eellike circuitous
eerie sinister
efface annul, deface, delete, dissolve *(terminate)*, eliminate *(eradicate)*, eradicate, expunge, expurgate, extinguish, extirpate, obliterate. SEE MAIN ENTRY
effaced lost *(taken away)*
effacement annulment, defacement, dissolution *(termination)*
effect accomplish, administer *(conduct)*, amount *(result)*, article *(commodity)*, attain, avail *(bring about)*, carry *(succeed)*, cast *(register)*, cause, chattel, chilling effect, commit *(perpetrate)*, compose, conclusion *(outcome)*, conduce, consequence *(conclusion)*, consequence *(significance)*, constitute *(establish)*, consummate, contrive, create, culminate, development *(outgrowth)*, discharge *(perform)*, dispatch *(dispose of)*, effectuate, elicit, enforce, engender, evoke, execute *(accomplish)*, fulfill, generate, holding *(property owned)*, implement, impose *(subject)*, impression, induce, influence, inspire, item, legislate, lobby, magnitude, make, occasion, operate, originate, outcome, outgrowth, perform *(execute)*, perpetrate, possession *(property)*, proceeds, procure, produce *(manufacture)*, product, provoke, reaction *(response)*, realize *(make real)*, redound, result, semblance, signification, toll *(effect)*, value, weight *(importance)*. SEE MAIN ENTRY
effect a change modify *(alter)*
effect a cure cure
effect a dissolution dissolve *(terminate)*
effect a sale handle *(trade)*, sell
effect an agreement mediate
effect an entrance enter *(go in)*
effect by legislation constitute *(establish)*
effected complete *(ended)*
effected by choice voluntary
effecter author *(originator)*
effectible practicable
effecting commission *(act)*
effectio operation
effective active, capable, causal, cogent, competent, constructive *(creative)*, efficient, eloquent, expert, felicitous, functional, incisive, influential, material *(important)*, omnipotent, operative, persuasive, politic, potent, powerful, practical, predominant, prevailing *(having superior force)*, proficient, sound, strong, successful, valid, valuable, viable. SEE MAIN ENTRY
effective before retroactive
effective help remedy *(legal means of redress)*
effective rejoinder confutation
effectiveness competence *(ability)*, dint, efficiency, force *(strength)*, influence, sinew
effectless null *(invalid)*, null and void
effects assets, dower, estate *(property)*, goods, merchandise, movable, paraphernalia *(personal belongings)*, personalty, possessions, property *(possessions)*, stock *(store)*. SEE MAIN ENTRY
effectual active, adequate, capable, causal, cogent, competent, constructive *(creative)*, decisive, effective *(efficient)*, effective *(operative)*, efficient, functional, influential, ministerial, omnipotent, operative, potent, powerful, practical, prevailing *(having superior force)*, sound, valid, valuable, viable. SEE MAIN ENTRY
effectuality capacity *(aptitude)*, competence *(ability)*, dint, force *(strength)*, influence
effectuate administer *(conduct)*, attain, avail *(bring about)*, bear *(yield)*, carry *(succeed)*, cause, constitute *(establish)*, consummate, discharge *(perform)*, dispatch *(dispose of)*, elicit, enforce, engender, evoke, execute *(accomplish)*, fulfill, function, generate, implement, induce, inspire, make, operate, perfect, perform *(execute)*, perpetrate, produce *(manufacture)*, realize *(make real)*. SEE MAIN ENTRY
effectuated complete *(ended)*
effectuation act *(undertaking)*, action *(performance)*, building *(business of assembling)*, commission *(act)*, conclusion *(outcome)*, course, development *(progression)*, discharge *(performance)*, effect, enforcement, fait accompli, fruition, output, realization, transaction. SEE MAIN ENTRY
effectus effect, realization
effervescence life *(vitality)*
effervescent volatile
effete decadent, ineffective, ineffectual, otiose, powerless, stale, unproductive
efficacious active, beneficial, cogent, competent, effective *(efficient)*, functional, influential, politic, potent, powerful, practical, predominant, prevailing *(having superior force)*, proficient, qualified *(competent)*, sciential, sound, successful, valuable, viable. SEE MAIN ENTRY
efficacy caliber *(mental capacity)*, competence *(ability)*, dint, efficiency, force *(strength)*, strength, utility *(usefulness)*, weight *(importance)*
efficax effective *(efficient)*, operative
efficere compose, constitute *(compose)*, execute *(accomplish)*, exercise *(discharge a function)*, fulfill, realize *(make real)*
efficiency caliber *(mental capacity)*, qualification *(fitness)*. SEE MAIN ENTRY

efficient active, competent, constructive *(creative)*, deft, economical, expeditious, expert, functional, operative, potent, practical, practiced, productive, proficient, prompt, resourceful. SEE MAIN ENTRY
efficientia efficiency
effigies counterpart *(parallel)*, embodiment, imitation, representation *(statement)*
effigy counterpart *(parallel)*, resemblance
effingere depict
efflagitare insist
effluence issuance, outflow
effluency issuance
efflux outflow
effodere disinter
efform compose, forge *(produce)*, formulate, make
efformation building *(business of assembling)*, composition *(makeup)*, form *(arrangement)*, formation
effort campaign, course, endeavor, enterprise *(undertaking)*, industry *(activity)*, labor *(exertion)*, main force, performance *(workmanship)*, pursuit *(effort to secure)*, struggle, test, undertaking *(attempt)*, undertaking *(enterprise)*. SEE MAIN ENTRY
effort to secure pursuit *(chase)*
effortful operose
effortless convenient, facile, practiced
effortless *(accomplished)*. SEE MAIN ENTRY
effortless *(easy)* SEE MAIN ENTRY
effortless assignment sinecure
effortless employment sinecure
effortless undertaking sinecure
effortless work sinecure
effortlessly readily
effortlessness facility *(easiness)*
effractura burglary
effrenatus lawless, uncurbed, unrestricted, unruly
effrontery contumely, disrespect, temerity
effugere flee
effugium flight
effulgent lucid
effundi emanate
effuse diffuse, emanate, exude, outpour. SEE MAIN ENTRY
effusio waste
effusion expulsion, harangue, issuance, outflow, prolixity
effusive demonstrative *(expressive of emotion)*, loquacious, unrestrained *(not repressed)*, voluble. SEE MAIN ENTRY
effusiveness ardor
effusus profuse, uncurbed
egens poor *(underprivileged)*
egere require *(need)*
egestas indigence, necessity, privation
egg on provoke, stimulate
ego SEE MAIN ENTRY
egocentric inflated *(vain)*, orgulous
egohood personality
egoism pride
egoistic inflated *(vain)*, orgulous, presumptuous, proud *(conceited)*
egoistical inflated *(vain)*, orgulous, proud *(conceited)*
egotism pride
egotistic inflated *(vain)*, orgulous, presumptuous, supercilious
egotistical inflated *(vain)*, orgulous, presumptuous
egredi issue *(send forth)*
egregious contemptible, gross *(flagrant)*, heinous, noteworthy, notorious, outrageous, remarkable. SEE MAIN ENTRY
egregius singular, special
egress alight, avenue *(route)*, issuance, issue *(send forth)*, outlet, quit *(evacuate)*. SEE MAIN ENTRY
egression egress, issuance, outflow
egressus egress, outlet
eicere eject *(expel)*, expel
eidetic distinct *(clear)*
eidolon phantom, specter
either SEE MAIN ENTRY
eiuratio abdication
ejaculate precipitate *(throw down violently)*, send
ejaculation outburst
eject cast *(throw)*, censor, deport *(banish)*, depose *(remove)*, discharge *(dismiss)*, dislocate, dislodge, dismiss *(discharge)*, dispel, displace *(remove)*, eliminate *(exclude)*, emanate, emit, eradicate, evict, exclude, expatriate, expel, jettison, launch *(project)*, luxate, oust, outpour, project *(impel forward)*, reject, remove *(dismiss from office)*, send, supplant. SEE MAIN ENTRY
eject from possession dispossess
ejection banishment, deportation, discharge *(dismissal)*, dismissal *(discharge)*, disqualification *(rejection)*, eviction, evulsion, exclusion, expropriation *(divestiture)*, expulsion, layoff, ostracism, ouster, removal
ejectment deportation, eviction, expulsion, layoff
elabi escape
elaborare elaborate
elaborate amplify, compound *(adjective)*, compound *(verb)*, develop, embellish, enhance, enlarge, expand, intricate, meliorate, painstaking. SEE MAIN ENTRY
elaborated complex, detailed
elaboration accession *(enlargement)*, advance *(increase)*, advancement *(improvement)*, amendment *(correction)*, development *(progression)*, overstatement, revision *(process of correcting)*. SEE MAIN ENTRY
elaboratus elaborate
élan ardor
elapse expire. SEE MAIN ENTRY
elapsed back *(in arrears)*
elastic flexible, malleable, pliable, pliant, resilient, sequacious, tractable, volatile, yielding
elated ecstatic. SEE MAIN ENTRY
elatio elevation
elbow jostle *(bump into)*
elbowroom margin *(spare amount)*
elder adult, predecessor, primogenitor. SEE MAIN ENTRY
elderliness longevity
elderly old. SEE MAIN ENTRY
elect adopt, choose, decide, entrust, intend, prefer, premium, select, vote. SEE MAIN ENTRY
elected preferred *(favored)*, select
elected representative officer
electio election *(choice)*, selection *(choice)*
election adoption *(acceptance)*, alternative *(option)*, choice *(alternatives offered)*, choice *(decision)*, discretion *(power of choice)*, nomination, option *(choice)*, plebiscite, poll *(casting of votes)*, preference *(choice)*, primary, referendum, selection *(choice)*, volition, vote. SEE MAIN ENTRY
election contest primary
electioneering politics
elective adoptive, discretionary, disjunctive *(alternative)*, spontaneous, voluntary. SEE MAIN ENTRY
elective preference volition
elective privilege poll *(casting of votes)*
electorate constituency. SEE MAIN ENTRY
electors constituency
electric incisive, provocative
electrify agitate *(activate)*, impress *(affect deeply)*
electrifying moving *(evoking emotion)*, provocative
electronic monitoring SEE MAIN ENTRY
electronic rights SEE MAIN ENTRY
electus select
electrocution SEE MAIN ENTRY
eleemosynary benevolent, charitable *(benevolent)*, donative, nonprofit, philanthropic
eleemosynary corporation foundation *(organization)*
elegance propriety *(correctness)*
elegance of manners courtesy
elegans critical *(faultfinding)*, elegant, particular *(exacting)*, precise
elegant attractive. SEE MAIN ENTRY
elegiac disconsolate, lugubrious
element aspect, atmosphere, component, constituent *(part)*, detail, determinant, factor *(ingredient)*, feature *(characteristic)*, ingredient, item, member *(constituent part)*, segment, unit *(item)*. SEE MAIN ENTRY
elemental cardinal *(basic)*, central *(essential)*, elementary, essential *(inherent)*, fundamental, inchoate, incipient, integral, organic, original *(initial)*, primary, prime *(original)*, primordial, rudimentary, simple, substantive, ultimate, underlying. SEE MAIN ENTRY
elementary cardinal *(basic)*, fundamental, inchoate, incipient, initial, naked *(lacking embellishment)*, original *(initial)*, primary, prime *(original)*, primordial, rudimentary, simple, ultimate, underlying. SEE MAIN ENTRY
elementary detail necessity
elementary unit component, factor *(ingredient)*
elementum constituent *(part)*, element
elephantine ponderous, prodigious *(eno-rmous)*
elevare disparage
elevate ameliorate, build *(augment)*, build *(construct)*, cultivate, enhance, expand, honor, meliorate, parlay *(exploit successfully)*, prefer, promote *(advance)*, raise *(advance)*, uphold. SEE MAIN ENTRY
elevated ecstatic, famous, magnanimous, meritorious, outstanding *(prominent)*, prominent, sacrosanct
elevated place elevation
elevated rank eminence
elevation advance *(progression)*, adv-ancement *(improvement)*, building *(structure)*, eminence, inflation *(increase)*, precedence, promotion *(advancement)*, reform, remembrance *(commemoration)*, status. SEE MAIN ENTRY
elevation in rank promotion *(advancement)*
élève disciple
eleventh hour crossroad *(turning point)*, dilatory
elicere elicit, evoke
elicit cause, compel, discover, disinter, educe, evoke, exact, extract, ferret, find *(discover)*, generate, inspire, originate, provoke. SEE MAIN ENTRY
elicit by threat coerce, extort
elicitation evulsion

elide delete, eliminate *(exclude)*, relegate. SEE MAIN ENTRY
eligere elect *(choose)*, select
eligibility admissibility, competence *(ability)*, droit, qualification *(fitness)*
eligible admissible, allowed, convenient, desirable *(qualified)*, entitled, fit, qualified *(competent)*, suitable. SEE MAIN ENTRY
eliminate abate *(extinguish)*, abolish, abrogate *(annul)*, abrogate *(rescind)*, censor, close *(terminate)*, debar, delete, deplete, destroy *(efface)*, dislodge, eject *(expel)*, eradicate, except *(exclude)*, exclude, expel, expurgate, extirpate, exude, forgo, jettison, obliterate, palliate *(abate)*, purge *(purify)*, reject, relegate, relinquish, remove *(eliminate)*, renounce, repeal, screen *(select)*, select, terminate, vacate *(void)*. SEE MAIN ENTRY
eliminate racial segregation desegregate
eliminate the alternatives choose, elect *(choose)*
eliminated ineligible, lost *(taken away)*
elimination abatement *(extinguishment)*, aberemurder, abolition, cancellation, censorship, curtailment, deduction *(diminution)*, deportation, discharge *(dismissal)*, dismissal *(discharge)*, disqualification *(rejection)*, dissolution *(termination)*, end *(termination)*, evulsion, expulsion, homicide, killing, layoff, murder, obviation, ostracism, ouster, prohibition, proscription, rejection, removal, renunciation. SEE MAIN ENTRY
elimination of ambiguousness clarification
elimination of complexity clarification
elimination of complication clarification
elinguis speechless
elite preferential, select. SEE MAIN ENTRY
elixir cure, main point
elliptical brief
elocutio delivery
elocution declamation, parlance, rhetoric *(skilled speech)*
elocutionary orotund
elongate extend *(enlarge)*, protract *(stall)*, sustain *(prolong)*
elongated protracted
elongation SEE MAN ENTRY
eloquence parlance, rhetoric *(skilled speech)*
eloquens eloquent
eloquent descriptive, persuasive, voluble. SEE MAIN ENTRY
else further
elsewhere SEE MAIN ENTRY
elsewhere known as alias
elucidate argue, bear *(adduce)*, characterize, clarify, comment, construe *(translate)*, convey *(communicate)*, define, demonstrate *(establish)*, describe, detail *(particularize)*, enlighten, exemplify, explain, explicate, exposit, expound, illustrate, instruct *(teach)*, notice *(observe)*, relate *(tell)*, render *(depict)*, resolve *(solve)*, simplify *(clarify)*, solve. SEE MAIN ENTRY
elucidating declaratory
elucidation answer *(solution)*, clarification, comment, definition, discourse, education, explanation, illustration, instance, paraphrase, rationale. SEE MAIN ENTRY
elucidative demonstrative *(illustrative)*, interpretive
elucidatory informatory
elude abscond, avoid *(evade)*, bilk, circumvent, default, equivocate, escape, eschew, ignore, parry, prevaricate, shirk, shun, spurn. SEE MAIN ENTRY
eludere balk, elude, foil
eludication solution *(answer)*
eluding evasive
eluding clear perception elusive
elusion abstention, avoidance *(evasion)*, flight, subterfuge
elusive delusive, ephemeral, evasive, inaccessible, oblique *(evasive)*, recondite, stealthy, temporary, transient, unresponsive, volatile. SEE MAIN ENTRY
elusiveness evasion
elusory elusive, evasive, oblique *(evasive)*. SEE MAIN ENTRY
elutriate purge *(purify)*
emaciate decrease
emaciation deterioration
emanare emanate
emanate accrue *(arise)*, arise *(originate)*, develop, emerge, issue *(send forth)*, proceed *(go forward)*, result, spread, stem *(originate)*. SEE MAIN ENTRY
emanate in rays radiate
emanation circulation, consequence *(conclusion)*, development *(outgrowth)*, discharge *(shot)*, face value *(first blush)*, issuance, outflow, output, product
emancipate discharge *(liberate)*, disencumber, disengage, disenthrall, enable, enfranchise, free, liberate, pardon, parole, quit *(free of)*, redeem *(repurchase)*, release, relieve *(free from burden)*, rescue
emancipated free *(enjoying civil liberty)*, liberal *(broad minded)*
emancipation discharge *(liberation)*, discharge *(release from obligation)*, freedom, liberation, liberty, parole, release, suffrage. SEE MAIN ENTRY
emasculate bowdlerize, debilitate, disable, inadequate
emasculated ineffective, ineffectual, powerless
emasculating operose
emasculation fault *(weakness)*, languor. SEE MAIN ENTRY
embankment bulwark
embar bar *(hinder)*, obstruct, toll *(stop)*
embargo attachment *(seizure)*
embargo ban, bar *(obstruction)*, boycott, check *(bar)*, condemn *(ban)*, debar, enjoin, hindrance, interdict, obstacle, obstruction, prohibit, prohibition, proscribe *(prohibit)*, proscription, restraint, seclude, veto. SEE MAIN ENTRY
embargoed goods contraband
embark launch *(initiate)*, leave *(depart)*. SEE MAIN ENTRY
embark on commence
embark upon assume *(undertake)*, maintain *(commence)*, undertake
embarkation birth *(beginning)*, inception, onset *(commencement)*, outset, start
embarrass confuse *(bewilder)*, disgrace, humiliate, impede, offend *(insult)*, perplex, perturb, upset. SEE MAIN ENTRY
embarrassed diffident, impecunious, poor *(underprivileged)*
embarrassed circumstances poverty
embarrassing position plight, predicament
embarrassing situation imbroglio, plight
embarrassment confusion *(ambiguity)*, disadvantage, disgrace, ignominy, indigence, obstruction, predicament. SEE MAIN ENTRY
embassage embassy
embassy commission *(agency)*, delegation *(envoy)*, mission. SEE MAIN ENTRY
embed fix *(make firm)*, inseminate, plant *(place firmly)*. SEE MAIN ENTRY
embedded ingrained, situated
embellish camouflage, cloak, falsify, meliorate. SEE MAIN ENTRY
embellished elaborate, inflated *(overestimated)*, pretentious *(ostentatious)*
embellishment bombast, exaggeration, expletive, motif
embezzle bilk, cheat, convert *(misappropriate)*, defalcate, defraud, impropriate, loot, mulct *(defraud)*, peculate, pilfer, purloin, steal. SEE MAIN ENTRY
embezzlement conversion *(misappropriation)*, larceny, misappropriation, theft. SEE MAIN ENTRY
embezzler hoodlum, thief. SEE MAIN ENTRY
embitter affront, alienate *(estrange)*, antagonize, bait *(harass)*, discompose, incense
embittered bitter *(reproachful)*, dyseptic, hostile, malevolent, resentful
embittering operose
emblaze brand *(mark)*
emblazon embellish
emblem brand, designation *(symbol)*, device *(distinguishing mark)*, earmark, indicant, indication, indicator, label, manifestation, symbol, token. SEE MAIN ENTRY
emblematic representative. SEE MAIN ENTRY
embodied bodily, compound, concrete, corporeal, physical, tangible
embodied terms contract
embodiment affiliation *(amalgamation)*, appearance *(look)*, body *(person)*, composition *(makeup)*, corpus, coverage *(scope)*, cross section, entity, epitome, essence, instance, materiality *(physical existence)*. SEE MAIN ENTRY
embody attach *(join)*, commingle, comprehend *(include)*, comprise, concern *(involve)*, consist, constitute *(compose)*, contain *(comprise)*, depict, exemplify, form, include, incorporate *(include)*, personify, substantiate. SEE MAIN ENTRY
embodying inclusive
embolden abet, assure *(give confidence to)*, encourage, promise *(raise expectations)*, reassure. SEE MAIN ENTRY
embolium cessation *(interlude)*
emboss brand *(mark)*, embellish
embowel eviscerate
embox contain *(enclose)*, envelop
embrace accept *(embrace)*, adopt, affiliate, attach *(join)*, border *(bound)*, choose, circumscribe *(surround by boundary)*, collect *(gather)*, comprehend *(include)*, comprise, concern *(involve)*, constitute *(compose)*, contact *(touch)*, contain *(comprise)*, contain *(enclose)*, coverage *(scope)*, enclose, enclosure, encompass *(include)*, envelop, espouse, include, incorporate *(include)*, keep *(shelter)*, personify, prefer, receive *(permit to enter)*. SEE MAIN ENTRY
embrace an offer assent
embrace an opinion deem
embraced select
embracement adoption *(acceptance)*, alt-ernative *(option)*
embracing inclusive
embracing a large area extensive
embrangle confound, disorganize, muddle
embrangled inextricable
embranglement brawl, disaccord, dispute, embroilment, imbroglio
embroider camouflage, cloak, clothe, embellish, falsify, invent *(falsify)*, misrepresent, slant

embroidered histrionic, mendacious
embroidery distortion, exaggeration, overstatement, rodomontade
embroil bicker, collide *(clash)*, confound, confuse *(create disorder)*, disrupt, implicate, incense
embroilment affray, belligerency, bluster *(commotion)*, brawl, collision *(dispute)*, commotion, conflict, contest *(dispute)*, controversy *(argument)*, disaccord, dispute, disturbance, entanglement *(confusion)*, fight *(argument)*, imbroglio, involution, pandemonium. SEE MAIN ENTRY
embryo SEE MAIN ENTRY
embryonic inchoate, incipient, initial, original *(initial)*, premature, prime *(original)*, rudimentary. SEE MAIN ENTRY
emend amend, convert *(change use)*, edit, fix *(repair)*, meliorate, modify *(alter)*, rectify, reform. SEE MAIN ENTRY
emendable ambulatory, corrigible
emendare amend, emend, rectify
emendate adjust *(resolve)*, amend, edit, emend, modify *(alter)*, rectify
emendatio amendment *(correction)*, correction *(change)*, reform, revision *(corrected version)*
emendation advancement *(improvement)*, amendment *(correction)*, correction *(change)*, progress
emendatory ambulatory, curative, progressive *(advocating change)*
emerge appear *(materialize)*, arise *(appear)*, develop, emanate, evolve, germinate, issue *(send forth)*, occur *(come to mind)*, occur *(happen)*, result. SEE MAIN ENTRY
emergence egress, expression *(manifestation)*, issuance, manifestation, nascency, origination, outflow, start. SEE MAIN ENTRY
emergency casualty, catastrophe, debacle, disaster, peril, plight, predicament, quagmire. SEE MAIN ENTRY
emergency aid SEE MAIN ENTRY
emergere emerge, recover
emersion egress, outflow
emigrant alien
emigrate abandon *(physically leave)*, abscond, depart, leave *(depart)*, move *(alter position)*, quit *(evacuate)*
emigration egress, outflow
eminence advantage, caliber *(quality)*, character *(reputation)*, clout, distinction *(reputation)*, dominance, elevation, emphasis, importance, influence, magnitude, materiality *(consequence)*, notoriety, power, prestige, primacy, regard *(esteem)*, reputation, significance, status, weight *(importance)*. SEE MAIN ENTRY
eminency elevation
eminent consequential *(substantial)*, dominant, famous, illustrious, influential, master, meritorious, notable, noteworthy, outstanding *(prominent)*, prime *(most valuable)*, prominent, renowned, reputable, salient, singular, stellar
eminent domain dominion *(supreme authority)*. SEE MAIN ENTRY
eminent person paragon
eminently particularly
emissaries deputation *(delegation)*
emissarium outlet
emissarius spy
emissary agent, conduit *(intermediary)*, deputy, intermediary, liaison, medium, plenipotentiary, procurator, proxy, representative *(proxy)*, spokesman, substitute
emissio discharge *(shot)*
emission issuance, outburst
emit bear *(yield)*, cast *(throw)*, discharge *(shoot)*, emanate, enunciate, expel, exude, outpour, project *(impel forward)*, promulgate, pronounce *(speak)*, publish, remark, send, utter. SEE MAIN ENTRY
emit heat radiate
emit rays radiate
emittere emit, send
emmission discharge *(shot)*
emollient cure, medicinal, remedial
emolument advance *(allowance)*, alimony, bounty, brokerage, commission *(fee)*, compensation, consideration *(recompense)*, disbursement *(funds paid out)*, earnings, fee *(charge)*, honorarium, pay, payment *(remittance)*, pension, perquisite, profit, recompense, requital, restitution, revenue, reward, wage. SEE MAIN ENTRY
emolumental profitable
emotion ardor, passion, reaction *(response)*, sensibility. SEE MAIN ENTRY
emotional demonstrative *(expressive of emotion)*, ecstatic, impulsive *(rash)*, intense, subjective
emotional display for effect histrionics
emotional release catharsis
emotional tone outlook
emotionless insensible, unresponsive
emotive demonstrative *(expressive of emotion)*, sensitive *(easily affected)*
empanel SEE MAIN ENTRY
empathetic benevolent, charitable *(lenient)*
empathic vicarious *(delegated)*. SEE MAIN ENTRY
empathize sympathize. SEE MAIN ENTRY
empathy rapport, understanding *(tolerance)*. SEE MAIN ENTRY
emper charge *(empower)*
empery dominion *(supreme authority)*
emphasis content *(meaning)*
emphasis emphasis
emphasis importance, inflection, strength, stress *(accent)*, weight *(importance)*. SEE MAIN ENTRY
emphasize argue, assert, bear *(adduce)*, contend *(maintain)*, dwell *(linger over)*, enhance, insist, intensify, magnify, plead *(allege in a legal action)*, pronounce *(speak)*, reaffirm, repeat *(state again)*. SEE MAIN ENTRY
emphatic categorical, clear *(apparent)*, compelling, dogmatic, express, forcible, insistent, resounding, vehement. SEE MAIN ENTRY
emphatic assertion asseveration
emphatic inquiry demand
empierce enter *(penetrate)*, lancinate, penetrate, pierce *(lance)*
empire demesne, realm
empiric probative
empirical probative. SEE MAIN ENTRY
empiricism casuistry, experience *(background)*
employ agency *(legal relationship)*, apply *(put in practice)*, appoint, capitalize *(seize the chance)*, commit *(entrust)*, delegate, employment, engage *(hire)*, exercise *(use)*, exert, expend *(consume)*, exploit *(make use of)*, exploitation, hire, impropriate, induct, labor *(work)*, manipulate *(utilize skillfully)*, ply, practice *(engage in)*, recruit, resort, spend, wield. SEE MAIN ENTRY
employ capital invest *(fund)*
employ force compel, enforce
employ improperly misemploy
employ one's professional skill practice *(engage in)*
employ one's time strive
employ oneself attempt, commit *(perpetrate)*, perform *(execute)*, strive
employ oneself in practice *(engage in)*
employ stratagem compete
employability utility *(usefulness)*, utilization
employable disposable, eligible, functional, practical
employed operative
employee assistant. SEE MAIN ENTRY
employee-numerosity agreement SEE MAIN ENTRY
employees personnel, staff
employees' earnings payroll
employees' salaries payroll
employer chief, executive, principal *(director)*. SEE MAIN ENTRY
employer of legal advice client
employer work stoppage lockout
employment agency *(legal relationship)*, appointment *(position)*, business *(occupation)*, calling, career, course, enjoyment *(use)*, function, industry *(activity)*, job, labor *(work)*, livelihood, management *(judicious use)*, means *(opportunity)*, occupation *(vocation)*, office, position *(business status)*, post, practice *(professional business)*, profession *(vocation)*, project, pursuit *(occupation)*, title *(position)*, trade *(occupation)*, usage, use. SEE MAIN ENTRY
employment discrimination SEE MAIN ENTRY
employment fee retainer
employment of capital investment
employment of force compulsion *(coercion)*
empoison infect
emporium market *(business)*, market place, store *(business)*
empower allow *(authorize)*, appoint, assign *(designate)*, authorize, bestow, certify *(approve)*, clothe, commit *(entrust)*, constitute *(establish)*, countenance, delegate, detail *(assign)*, employ *(engage services)*, enable, endue, enfranchise, entrust, grant *(concede)*, invest *(vest)*, let *(permit)*, permit, qualify *(meet standards)*, sanction, suffer *(permit)*, vest. SEE MAIN ENTRY
empower to act for another delegate
empowered allowed, entitled, ex officio, influential, permissible, powerful, privileged
empowering consent, deputation *(selection of delegates)*
empowerment charter *(sanction)*, droit, force *(strength)*, freedom, license, sanction *(permission)*
emprise campaign, endeavor, undertaking *(enterprise)*
emptiness insufficiency
emptor consumer
emptor customer, patron *(regular customer)*
empty barren, baseless, consume, deficient, deplete, devoid, diminish, dissipate *(expend foolishly)*, evacuate, exhaust *(deplete)*, ill-founded, inexpressive, languid, lifeless *(dull)*, null *(insignificant)*, outpour, purge *(purify)*, spend, superficial, trivial, unavailing, unfounded, vacant, vacate *(leave)*, vacuous. SEE MAIN ENTRY
empty *(noting left)*. SEE MAIN ENTRY
empty *(without substance)*. SEE MAIN ENTRY
empty of devoid
empty out deplete

empty show pretense *(ostentation)*
empty talk bombast, fustian, jargon *(unintelligible language)*, rodomontade
empty words pretense *(pretext)*
empty-handed poor *(underprivileged)*
empty-headed vacuous
emulate copy, mock *(imitate)*, pose *(impersonate)*, reflect *(mirror)*. SEE MAIN ENTRY
emulation contest *(competition)*, fake
emulative competitive *(antagonistic)*
emulous SEE MAIN ENTRY
emulsion solution *(substance)*
en attendant ad interim
en banc SEE MAIN ENTRY
en bloc en banc, en masse
en masse en banc. SEE MAIN ENTRY
en rapport concurrent *(united)*, conjoint
en route SEE MAIN ENTRY
enable allow *(authorize)*, authorize, charge *(empower)*, clothe, delegate, empower, endue, facilitate, furnish, grant *(concede)*, invest *(vest)*, let *(permit)*, permit, qualify *(meet standards)*, sanction, vest. SEE MAIN ENTRY
enable to comprehend enlighten
enable to see enlighten
enablement ability, capacity *(authority)*, competence *(ability)*, faculty *(ability)*, force *(strength)*
enabling legislation SEE MAIN ENTRY
enact accomplish, command, conduct, constitute *(establish)*, effectuate, execute *(accomplish)*, govern, impersonate, implement, impose *(enforce)*, instruct *(direct)*, legislate, make, pass *(approve)*, perform *(adhere to)*, perform *(execute)*, pursue *(carry on)*, recite, require *(compel)*, rule *(govern)*. SEE MAIN ENTRY
enact beforehand preordain
enact by law legalize
enact laws legislate
enacted legitimate *(rightful)*, positive *(prescribed)*
enacting legislative
enacting laws legislation *(lawmaking)*
enacting punishment penal
enactment code, codification, commission *(act)*, constitution, dictate, direction *(order)*, edict, fiat, law, mandate, measure, ordinance, pandect *(code of laws)*, performance *(execution)*, prescription *(directive)*, regulation *(rule)*, rubric *(authoritative rule)*, rule *(legal dictate)*, statute, symbol, transaction. SEE MAIN ENTRY
enactment of rules code
enarrare recount, relate *(tell)*
enarratio description
encage immure
encamp lodge *(reside)*
encapsulate comprise, contain *(enclose)*, envelop
encase border *(bound)*, clothe, contain *(enclose)*, enclose, encompass *(surround)*, ensconce, enshroud, envelop, shroud, shut
encasement enclosure
enchain confine, contain *(restrain)*, fetter, handcuff, repress, restrain, restrict, trammel
enchanted ecstatic
enchanting attractive, moving *(evoking emotion)*, provocative, sapid. SEE MAIN ENTRY
enchantment affection, compulsion *(obsession)*, seduction
enchase border *(bound)*
enchorial native *(domestic)*
enchoric native *(domestic)*
encincture blockade *(enclosure)*, constraint *(imprisonment)*, contain *(enclose)*, embrace *(encircle)*, enclose, encompass *(surround)*
encircle border *(bound)*, circumscribe *(surround by boundary)*, comprehend *(include)*, contain *(enclose)*, delimit, detour, enclose, encompass *(surround)*, envelop, hedge, include, incorporate *(include)*, lock
encirclement blockade *(enclosure)*, enclosure
encircling comprehensive, inclusive
enclasp concern *(involve)*, contain *(encl ose)*
enclave bailiwick, parcel
enclose affix, border *(bound)*, circumscribe *(surround by boundary)*, confine, constrain *(imprison)*, delimit, demarcate, embrace *(encircle)*, encompass *(surround)*, ensconce, enshroud, envelop, fetter, hedge, immure, imprison, keep *(restrain)*, limit, lock, restrain, shut. SEE MAIN ENTRY
enclose on all sides encompass *(surround)*
enclose within bounds border *(bound)*
enclose within walls immure
enclosed internal, limited
enclosed cage cell
enclosed space enclosure
enclosing blockade *(enclosure)*, inclusive
enclosure barrier, boundary, chamber *(compartment)*, close *(enclosed area)*, constraint *(imprisonment)*, coverage *(scope)*, curtilage, parcel. SEE MAIN ENTRY
enclosures confines
encloud obscure
encomiastic favorable *(expressing appr oval)*
encomium laudation
encompass border *(bound)*, circumscribe *(surround by boundary)*, comprehend *(include)*, comprise, consist, constitute *(compose)*, contain *(enclose)*, delimit, demarcate, embrace *(encircle)*, enclose, envelop, hedge, include, incorporate *(include)*. SEE MAIN ENTRY
encompass with gloom obnubilate
encompassed with difficulties difficult
encompassing a wide area extensive
encompassment blockade *(enclosure)*, coverage *(scope)*, enclosure
encore de novo
encounter affray, affront, assail, assault, belligerency, collide *(clash)*, collision *(accident)*, collision *(dispute)*, commotion, compete, competition, conflict, confrontation *(act of setting face to face)*, contact *(touch)*, contend *(dispute)*, contest *(competition)*, contest *(dispute)*, discover, embroilment, endure *(suffer)*, engage *(involve)*, fight *(battle)*, find *(discover)*, grapple, meet, meeting *(conference)*, onset *(assault)*, oppose, rendezvous *(noun)*, rendezvous *(verb)*, strife, strike *(collide)*, struggle. SEE MAIN ENTRY
encounter the risk bet
encounter with a shock collide *(crash against)*
encourage abet, assure *(give confidence to)*, coax, conduce, contribute *(assist)*, counsel, exhort, expedite, facilitate, favor, foment, foster, help, impel, incite, indorse, inspire, lobby, motivate, nurture, prevail upon, promise *(raise expectations)*, promote *(advance)*, promote *(organize)*, prompt, reassure, side, spirit, stimulate, uphold, urge. SEE MAIN ENTRY
encourage repose lull
encouraged sanguine
encouragement advocacy, approval, auspices, catalyst, contribution *(participation)*, favor *(sanction)*, guidance, help, impetus, impulse, incentive, indorsement, inducement, influence, instigation, invitation, motive, patronage *(support)*, persuasion, recommendation, relief *(aid)*, sanction *(permission)*, solace, stimulus, support *(assistance)*
encourager abettor, accessory, accomplice, advocate *(espouser)*, catalyst, partisan, promoter
encouraging auspicious, favorable *(advantageous)*, favorable *(expressing approval)*, moving *(evoking emotion)*, propitious, viable
encroach accroach, border *(approach)*, impinge, impose *(intrude)*, interfere, intervene, intrude, invade, obtrude, overlap, overreach, overstep, trespass, usurp. SEE MAIN ENTRY
encroach upon violate
encroached upon broken *(unfulfilled)*
encroaching culpable, obtrusive
encroachment assumption *(seizure)*, bre ach, contempt *(disobedience to the court)*, crime, imposition *(excessive burden)*, incursion, infraction, injustice, intrusion, invasion, offense, transgression, violation. SEE MAIN ENTRY
encrust embellish
encumber bind *(obligate)*, bind *(restrain)*, block, check *(restrain)*, contain *(restrain)*, detain *(restrain)*, disadvantage, embarrass, estop, hamper, hinder, hold up *(delay)*, impede, impose *(enforce)*, inconvenience, interfere, obstruct, overcome *(overwhelm)*, overload, perplex, preclude, restrict, tax *(overwork)*, trammel, weigh. SEE MAIN ENTRY
encumbered arrested *(checked)*, disconsolate, indebted
encumbrance barrier, burden, charge *(lien)*, constraint *(restriction)*, damper *(stopper)*, debt, disadvantage, fetter, handicap, hindrance, impediment, imposition *(excessive burden)*, liability, mortgage, onus *(burden)*, pressure, responsibility *(accountability)*, weight *(burden)*. SEE MAIN ENTRY
encyclic public *(known)*
encyclical public *(known)*
encyclopedia hornbook
encyclopedic broad, collective, complete *(all-embracing)*, comprehensive, expert, omnibus, omniscient
encyclopedical omnibus
end annul, arrest *(stop)*, border, cancel, cap, cause *(reason)*, cease, cessation *(termination)*, close *(conclusion)*, close *(terminate)*, complete, conclude *(complete)*, conclusion *(outcome)*, consummate, culminate, decide, defeasance, denouement, design *(intent)*, desist, destination, discontinue *(abandon)*, dispatch *(put to death)*, dissolution *(termination)*, dissolve *(terminate)*, eliminate *(eradicate)*, expiration, expire, extinguish, extirpate, extremity *(death)*, extremity *(furthest point)*, final, finality, finish, goal, halt *(noun)*, halt *(verb)*, impasse, intent, lapse *(cease)*, last *(final)*, mete, moratorium, motive, object, objective, outcome, output, payoff *(result)*, perform *(adhere to)*, periphery, point *(purpose)*, project, purpose, pursuit *(goal)*, quash, reason *(basis)*, rescind, rest *(cease from action)*, result *(noun)*, result *(verb)*, settle, shut, stop, succumb, suppress, target, terminate, ultimate. SEE MAIN ENTRY

end at abut
end by a decision arbitrate *(adjudge)*, conclude *(decide)*, determine
end in view design *(intent)*, intention
end intended intention
end life dispatch *(put to death)*, execute *(sentence to death)*
end of hostilities peace
end of life death, demise *(death)*, extremity *(death)*
end of the matter defeasance, time
end one's life decease, die
end product conclusion *(outcome)*, effect, outcome, output
end result amount *(result)*, conclusion *(outcome)*, destination, effect, outgrowth, proceeds, product
end the introduction of evidence rest *(end a legal case)*
end the presentation of evidence rest *(end a legal case)*
end to end contiguous
endamage disable, harm, persecute
endanger expose, jeopardize. SEE MAIN ENTRY
endangered aleatory *(perilous)*, insecure
endangerment hazard, jeopardy, peril, risk
endearment affection
endeavor activity, attempt, business *(occupation)*, calling, campaign, conatus, course, creation, effort, enterprise *(undertaking)*, experiment, industry *(activity)*, intend, labor *(exertion)*, labor, profession *(vocation)*, project, pursuit *(effort to secure)*, pursuit *(occupation)*, strive, struggle, test, trial *(experiment)*, try *(attempt)*, undertake, undertaking *(enterprise)*, venture, work *(effort)*. SEE MAIN ENTRY
endeavor to accomplish strive
endeavor to effect strive
endeavor to gain pursue *(strive to gain)*
endeavor to overtake chase
ended dead, defunct, lifeless *(dead)*, through
endemic domestic *(indigenous)*, native *(domestic)*, special, specific. SEE MAIN ENTRY
endemical native *(domestic)*, specific
endenizen adopt
ending cessation *(termination)*, close *(conclusion)*, conclusion *(outcome)*, defeasance, denouement, destination, development *(outgrowth)*, dissolution *(termination)*, end *(termination)*, expiration, extreme *(last)*, final, finality, halt, last *(final)*, moratorium, outcome, ultimate
ending of a proceeding dismissal *(termination of a proceeding)*
ending of an action dismissal *(termination of a proceeding)*
endless chronic, constant, continual *(perpetual)*, continuous, durable, far reaching, incessant, indestructible, indeterminate, infinite, innumerable, myriad, permanent, perpetual, profuse, progressive *(going forward)*, relentless, rife, stable, unlimited, unrelenting. SEE MAIN ENTRY
endless duration perpetuity
endless time perpetuity
endlessly ad infinitum
endlessness indestructibility, perpetuity
endmost extreme *(last)*, last *(final)*
endorse abet, accept *(assent)*, accredit, acknowledge *(declare)*, advocate, affirm *(uphold)*, allow *(authorize)*, approve, assent, assist, assure *(insure)*, attest, authorize, avouch *(guarantee)*, bear *(adduce)*, bond *(secure a debt)*, brand *(mark)*, certify *(approve)*, certify *(attest)*, close *(agree)*, coincide *(concur)*, concede, concur *(agree)*, confirm, consent, constitute *(establish)*, corroborate, cosign, countenance, countersign, embrace *(accept)*, encourage, ensure, espouse, favor, justify, let *(permit)*, pass *(approve)*, qualify *(meet standards)*, recommend, sanction, seal *(solemnize)*, side, sponsor, subscribe *(sign)*, support *(assist)*, sustain *(confirm)*, underwrite, uphold, validate, vouch, witness *(attest to)*. SEE MAIN ENTRY
endorse over assign *(transfer ownership)*
endorsed agreed *(promised)*, allowed, consensual, official, preferred *(favored)*
endorsee holder, payee
endorsement acceptance, accommodation *(backing)*, acknowledgment *(acceptance)*, advocacy, affirmance *(authentication)*, affirmance *(judicial sanction)*, affirmation, aid *(help)*, approval, assent, attestation, avowal, certificate, certification *(attested copy)*, charter *(sanction)*, confirmation, consent, corroboration, favor *(sanction)*, guaranty, jurat, leave *(permission)*, license, ratification, recommendation, reference *(recommendation)*, rider, sanction *(permission)*, stamp, subscription, support *(corroboration)*, vow. SEE MAIN ENTRY
endorsement *(signature)*. SEE MAIN ENTRY
endorser backer, comaker, patron *(influential supporter)*, proponent, surety *(guarantor)*, undersigned
endow authorize, bear *(yield)*, bestow, charge *(empower)*, clothe, confer *(give)*, contribute *(supply)*, convey *(transfer)*, dedicate, demise, descend, devise *(give)*, divide *(distribute)*, empower, enable, endue, fund, furnish, give *(grant)*, impart, instate, leave *(give)*, pass *(advance)*, present *(make a gift)*, provide *(supply)*, subsidize, supply, vest. SEE MAIN ENTRY
endow the power charge *(empower)*
endow with bequeath
endow with authority invest *(vest)*
endow with political privilege enfranchise
endow with power authorize
endow with rights of citizenship naturalize *(make a citizen)*
endowed resourceful
endowed institution foundation *(organization)*
endowed with consciousness cognizant
endowed with life conscious *(awake)*, live *(conscious)*
endowed with reason cognizant, rational
endowing donative
endowment aid *(subsistence)*, appropriation *(donation)*, aptitude, behalf, benefit *(conferment)*, bequest, caliber *(mental capacity)*, charity, color *(complexion)*, competence *(ability)*, concession *(authorization)*, contribution *(donation)*, dedication, donation, dower, faculty *(ability)*, foundation *(organization)*, fund, gift *(flair)*, gift *(present)*, grant, inheritance, investment, largess *(gift)*, legacy, pension, performance *(workmanship)*, perquisite, potential, provision *(act of supplying)*, qualification *(fitness)*, quality *(attribute)*, quality *(grade)*, skill, specialty *(special aptitude)*, support *(assistance)*. SEE MAIN ENTRY
ends confines
endue clothe, endow, fund, furnish, supply. SEE MAIN ENTRY
endurance continuance, diligence *(perseverance)*, force *(strength)*, indestructibility, industry *(activity)*, lenience, life *(period of existence)*, longanimity, longevity, resignation *(passive acceptance)*, sinew, strength, survival, tenacity, tolerance
endure abide, adhere *(persist)*, bear *(tolerate)*, concede, exist, forbear, keep *(continue)*, last, persevere, persist, remain *(continue)*, resist *(withstand)*, stay *(continue)*, submit *(yield)*, subsist, suffer *(sustain loss)*, tolerate, withstand. SEE MAIN ENTRY
endure the cost of disburse *(pay out)*
enduring chronic, constant, diligent, durable, indelible, indestructible, infallible, infinite, lasting, lenient, live *(existing)*, passive, patient, permanent, perpetual, persistent, pertinacious, resigned, solid *(sound)*, stable, standing, steadfast, strong, unrelenting, unremitting, unyielding
enduring only a very short time ephemeral
enemy adversary, foe, rival. SEE MAIN ENTRY
enemy alien SEE MAIN ENTRY
enemy combatant SEE MAIN ENTRY
energetic active, forcible, indomitable, industrious, intense, painstaking, potent, sedulous, strong, trenchant. SEE MAIN ENTRY
energize agitate *(activate)*, empower, incite, reinforce, restore *(renew)*, stimulate. SEE MAIN ENTRY
energizing impulsive *(impelling)*
energumen bigot
energy ardor, force *(strength)*, impetus, industry *(activity)*, labor *(exertion)*, life *(vitality)*, main force, puissance, sinew, spirit, strength. SEE MAIN ENTRY
enervare disable
enervate debilitate, depreciate, disable, disarm *(divest of arms)*, eviscerate, exhaust *(deplete)*, extenuate, impair, tax *(overwork)*. SEE MAIN ENTRY
enervate oneself carouse
enervated helpless *(powerless)*, nonsubstantial *(not sturdy)*
enervating operose
enervation frailty, languor, prostration
enfeeble debilitate, depreciate, disable, disarm *(divest of arms)*, eviscerate, exhaust *(deplete)*, extenuate, impair
enfeebled disabled *(made incapable)*, old
enfeeblement decline
enfeebling disabling
enfeoff alienate *(transfer title)*, bequeath, convey *(transfer)*
enfeoffment alienation *(transfer of title)*
enflame bait *(harass)*
enfold clothe, consist, contain *(comprise)*, embrace *(encircle)*, enclose, envelop
enfoldment enclosure
enforce administer *(conduct)*, compel, constrain *(compel)*, discharge *(perform)*, effectuate, exact, force *(coerce)*, implement, inflict, insist, make, operate, perform *(adhere to)*, press *(constrain)*, require *(compel)*. SEE MAIN ENTRY
enforce censorship censor, expurgate
enforce obedience constrain *(compel)*, force *(coerce)*, rule *(govern)*
enforce payment excise *(levy a tax)*
enforceable choate lien, valid
enforceable claim cause of action
enforceable in a court of law legal

enforced compulsory, forcible, obligatory
enforced abstention prohibition
enforced withdrawal expulsion
enforcement action *(performance)*, commission *(act)*, compulsion *(coercion)*, discharge *(performance)*, duress, force *(compulsion)*, requirement. SEE MAIN ENTRY
enforcement of judgment collection *(payment)*
enforcement of mortgage foreclosure
enforcing compelling
enframe frame *(construct)*
enframement border
enfranchise allow *(authorize)*, authorize, bestow, disenthrall, free, let *(permit)*, liberate, release. SEE MAIN ENTRY
enfranchised allowed, autonomous *(self governing)*, free *(enjoying civil liberty)*, rightful
enfranchisement charter *(sanction)*, copyright, emancipation, franchise *(right to vote)*, freedom, home rule, liberation, liberty, license, privilege, suffrage
engage agree *(contract)*, appoint, assume *(undertake)*, book, charge *(empower)*, coax, commit *(entrust)*, contend *(dispute)*, contract, delegate, employ *(engage services)*, fight *(battle)*, hire, immerse *(engross)*, implicate, induct, lease, monopolize, nominate, participate, promise *(vow)*, provide *(arrange for)*, pursue *(carry on)*, register, rent, retain *(employ)*, stipulate. SEE MAIN ENTRY
engage in commence, endeavor, exercise *(discharge a function)*, labor, operate, participate, ply, practice *(engage in)*, undertake. SEE MAIN ENTRY
engage in a contest compete
engage in a contest of speed race
engage in a conversation communicate, discuss, speak
engage in a dialogue speak
engage in an enterprise embark
engage in conflict with confront *(oppose)*
engage in conversation discuss
engage in hostilities attack
engage in oral controversy debate, discuss
engage in solemn manner promise *(vow)*
engage premises for a designated period lease
engage solemnly pledge *(promise the performance of)*
engage the attention interest, occupy *(engage)*
engage the mind interest, occupy *(engage)*
engage the thoughts interest, occupy *(engage)*
engage to give pledge *(promise the performance of)*
engage with grapple
engaged bound, indentured
engaged in business industrial
engaged in commerce commercial, retail
engaged in traffic industrial
engagement agreement *(contract)*, appointment *(meeting)*, assurance, burden, charge *(responsibility)*, commitment *(responsibility)*, competition, conflict, confrontation *(act of setting face to face)*, confrontation *(altercation)*, contest *(competition)*, contract, covenant, duty *(obligation)*, embroilment, employment, enterprise *(undertaking)*, fight *(battle)*, meeting *(encounter)*, mortgage, profession *(vocation)*, project, promise, pursuit *(occupation)*, rendezvous, responsibility *(accountability)*, specialty *(contract)*, stipulation, strife, struggle, testament, trade *(occupation)*, undertaking *(business)*, undertaking *(enterprise)*, undertaking *(pledge)*, work *(employment)*. SEE MAIN ENTRY
engagements ties
engager of services principal *(director)*
engaging attractive, sapid
engaging fee retainer
engaging in bigamy polygamous
engaging in unlawful marriage polygamous
engender avail *(bring about)*, bear *(yield)*, cause, constitute *(establish)*, create, foment, generate, make, originate, produce *(manufacture)*, propagate *(increase)*, reproduce. SEE MAIN ENTRY
engenderment creation
engine SEE MAIN ENTRY
engineer administer *(conduct)*, arrange *(plan)*, build *(construct)*, cause, compose, connive, contractor, control *(regulate)*, create, devise *(invent)*, direct *(supervise)*, manage, maneuver, manipulate *(utilize skillfully)*, manufacture, materialman, militate, operate, originate, oversee, plan, plot, program, realize *(make real)*, scheme. SEE MAIN ENTRY
engineered tactical
engineering building *(business of assembling)*, contrivance, strategy
engird circumscribe *(surround by boundary)*, contain *(enclose)*, embrace *(encircle)*, encompass *(surround)*, include
engorgement plethora
engraft embed, plant *(place firmly)*
engrafted ingrained, permanent
engrave brand *(mark)*, delineate, inscribe
engraving inscription, stamp
engross engage *(involve)*, interest, monopolize, occupy *(engage)*. SEE MAIN ENTRY
engross the mind interest, occupy *(engage)*
engross the thoughts interest, occupy *(engage)*
engrossed pensive
engrossment compulsion *(obsession)*, contemplation, notice *(heed)*, obsession, preoccupation
engulf immerse *(plunge into)*, inundate, overcome *(overwhelm)*. SEE MAIN ENTRY
engulfing oppressive
engulfment osmosis
enhance ameliorate, amend, build *(augment)*, compound, embellish, enlarge, expand, heighten *(augment)*, intensify, inure *(benefit)*, magnify, meliorate, progress, raise *(advance)*, reform, renew *(refurbish)*, supplement. SEE MAIN ENTRY
enhance the degree of appreciate *(increase)*
enhanced sentencing SEE MAIN ENTRY
enhancement accession *(enlargement)*, additive, advance *(increase)*, amendment *(correction)*, augmentation, boom *(increase)*, development *(progression)*, hyperbole, progress, reform, renewal. SEE MAIN ENTRY
enhancing cumulative *(intensifying)*
enhearten assure *(give confidence to)*, promise *(raise expectations)*, reassure
enigma confusion *(ambiguity)*, mystery, paradox, problem, question *(issue)*, secret. SEE MAIN ENTRY
enigmatic complex, debatable, difficult, disputable, elusive, equivocal, esoteric, inapprehensible, incomprehensible, indefinable, indefinite, indistinct, inexplicable, inexpressive, inscrutable, mysterious, obscure *(abstruse)*, opaque, oracular, problematic, recondite, suspicious *(questionable)*, vague. SEE MAIN ENTRY
enigmatical equivocal, esoteric, hidden, inapprehensible, incomprehensible, indefinable, indefinite, indistinct, inexplicable, inexpressive, mysterious, obscure *(abstruse)*, problematic, uncertain *(ambiguous)*
enisle isolate
enisled insular, solitary
eniti endeavor, strive
enixus earnest
enjoin admonish *(advise)*, arrest *(stop)*, ban, bar *(hinder)*, coerce, condemn *(ban)*, debar, demand, detail *(assign)*, dictate, direct *(order)*, enact, exact, exhort, expostulate, forbid, force *(coerce)*, forestall, impose *(enforce)*, inhibit, insist, interdict, necessitate, prescribe, press *(beseech)*, prohibit, proscribe *(prohibit)*, request, require *(compel)*, restrain. SEE MAIN ENTRY
enjoin from contain *(restrain)*
enjoinder injunction
enjoined positive *(prescribed)*
enjoining bar *(obstruction)*, obstacle, obstruction, prohibition, remonstrative
enjoinment directive, refusal, requirement
enjoy own, possess, realize *(obtain as a profit)*, relish, remain *(occupy)*. SEE MAIN ENTRY
enjoy the use of premises rent
enjoyable desirable *(pleasing)*, palatable, preferable
enjoyed popular
enjoying liberty free *(enjoying civil liberty)*, sovereign *(independent)*
enjoying political independence sovereign *(independent)*
enjoyment benefit *(betterment)*, occupancy, satisfaction *(fulfilment)*, use. SEE MAIN ENTRY
enkindle burn, foment, incense, inspire, provoke, stimulate
enlace intertwine
enlarge accrue *(increase)*, amplify, bear *(yield)*, build *(augment)*, compound, develop, enhance, expand, extricate, heighten *(augment)*, increase, inflate, magnify, overestimate, raise *(advance)*, recruit, supplement. SEE MAIN ENTRY
enlarge in size accumulate *(enlarge)*
enlarge on expand
enlarge the mind disabuse, edify
enlarge the scope of extend *(enlarge)*
enlarge upon develop, elaborate, outpour
enlarged extreme *(exaggerated)*, inflated *(overestimated)*, liberal *(not literal)*
enlarged by swelling inflated *(enlarged)*
enlargement accretion, addition, advance *(increase)*, advancement *(improvement)*, aggravation *(exacerbation)*, augmentation, bombast, boom *(increase)*, distortion, exaggeration, extension *(expansion)*, growth *(increase)*, hyperbole, increment, inflation *(increase)*, overstatement. SEE MAIN ENTRY
enlarging augmentation, cumulative *(increasing)*
enlighten admit *(concede)*, advise, apprise, clarify, comment, communicate, construe *(translate)*, convey *(communicate)*, disabuse, discipline *(train)*, disclose, divulge, edify, educate, elucidate, explain,

explicate, exposit, herald, illustrate, impart, inform *(notify)*, initiate, instruct *(teach)*, mention, notify, report *(disclose)*, reveal, signify *(inform)*. SEE MAIN ENTRY
enlightened acquainted, cognizant, familiar *(informed)*, informed *(educated)*, informed *(having information)*, judicious, juridical, learned, literate, politic, rational, sensible
enlightener bystander, deponent, informant
enlightening advisory, demonstrative *(illustrative)*, didactic, informative, informatory, interpretive
enlightenment admission *(disclosure)*, civilization, clarification, cognition, comprehension, direction *(guidance)*, disclosure *(act of disclosing)*, dispatch *(message)*, edification, education, experience *(background)*, guidance, information *(knowledge)*, insight, intelligence *(news)*, knowledge *(awareness)*, knowledge *(learning)*, mention *(reference)*, monition *(warning)*, notice *(announcement)*, notification, publication *(disclosure)*, sense *(intelligence)*, tip *(clue)*. SEE MAIN ENTRY
enlist appoint, bait *(lure)*, coax, convert *(persuade)*, convince, employ *(engage services)*, engage *(hire)*, enroll, hire, instate, join *(associate oneself with)*, levy, lobby, persuade, prevail *(persuade)*, prevail upon, procure, recruit, register, resort, retain *(employ)*
enlist employees in a labor union organize *(unionize)*
enlist in a labor union organize *(unionize)*
enlist in one's service engage *(hire)*
enlist jurors empanel
enlist with combine *(act in concert)*
enlisted man volunteer
enlisted person volunteer
enlistee member *(individual in a group)*, volunteer
enlistment persuasion, registration
enliven inspire, spirit, stimulate
enlivened born *(alive)*, conscious *(awake)*
enmesh bait *(lure)*, betray *(lead astray)*, engage *(involve)*, ensnare, entrap, implicate, incriminate, intertwine. SEE MAIN ENTRY
enmeshed interrelated, related
enmeshment complex *(entanglement)*, entanglement *(confusion)*, implication *(incriminating involvement)*
enmity alienation *(estrangement)*, belligerency, breach, conflict, contention *(opposition)*, cruelty, disaccord, discord, estrangement, feud, hatred, ill will, malice, odium, opposition, rancor, resentment, spite, umbrage, vengeance. SEE MAIN ENTRY
ennoble honor, raise *(advance)*. SEE MAIN ENTRY
enodare explicate, solve
enormity degree *(magnitude)*, magnitude, weight *(importance)*. SEE MAIN ENTRY
enormous exorbitant, far reaching, flagrant, grandiose, gross *(flagrant)*, major, outrageous, ponderous. SEE MAIN ENTRY
enough adequate, quorum, sufficiency. SEE MAIN ENTRY
enounce declare, enunciate, proclaim, promulgate, pronounce *(speak)*
enquiry cross-examination
enrage aggravate *(annoy)*, alienate *(estrange)*, annoy, bait *(harass)*, discompose, disturb, exacerbate, harass, incense, irritate, offend *(insult)*, persecute, pique, provoke, upset. SEE MAIN ENTRY
enraptured ecstatic
enregister note *(record)*
enrich amend, bestow, compound, contribute *(supply)*, cultivate, elaborate, embellish, endow, endue, enhance, impart, inure *(benefit)*, meliorate, nurture, progress, replenish, supplement
enriched literate
enriching didactic, informative
enrichment advance *(increase)*, development *(progression)*, endowment, progress, reform. SEE MAIN ENTRY
enring encompass *(surround)*
enrobe clothe
enroll empanel, employ *(engage services)*, enter *(record)*, enumerate, file *(place among official records)*, inscribe, instate, join *(associate oneself with)*, record, recruit, register, subscribe *(promise)*, survey *(poll)*. SEE MAIN ENTRY
enrolled person member *(individual in a group)*
enrolling registration
enrollment constituency, registration, subscription
ensample instance, sample, specimen
ensconce blind *(obscure)*, camouflage, cloak, enshroud, harbor, hide, instate, plant *(place firmly)*, preserve, shroud. SEE MAIN ENTRY
ensconce oneself lurk
ensconced clandestine, safe, situated. SEE MAIN ENTRY
enscroll inscribe
ensemble assemblage, corpus, en masse, entirety
enshield ensconce
enshrine dedicate
enshrined sacrosanct
enshrinement dedication, remembrance *(commemoration)*
enshrining honorary
enshroud blind *(obscure)*, camouflage, cloak, conceal, cover *(conceal)*, ensconce, envelop, obnubilate, obscure. SEE MAIN ENTRY
enshrouded hidden
ensign device *(distinguishing mark)*, indicant, indicator, symbol
enslave force *(coerce)*, impose *(subject)*, subject, subjugate
enslaved indentured, obsequious, subservient
enslavement bondage, captivity, oppression, servitude, subjection, thrall
enslaving dictatorial
ensnare abduct, ambush, bait *(lure)*, betray *(lead astray)*, bilk, coax, deceive, dupe, entrap, hunt, illude, inveigle, kidnap, mislead, pettifog, trap. SEE MAIN ENTRY
ensnarement bunko
ensnaring insidious
ensphere border *(bound)*, circumscribe *(surround by boundary)*, contain *(enclose)*, encompass *(surround)*, envelop, hedge
enstamp seal *(solemnize)*
ensual consequence *(conclusion)*, development *(outgrowth)*
ensue accrue *(arise)*, arise *(originate)*, proceed *(go forward)*, redound, result, stem *(originate)*, succeed *(follow)*, supervene, trace *(follow)*. SEE MAIN ENTRY
ensue from emanate
ensuing ancillary *(subsidiary)*, consecutive, derivative, forthcoming, future, subsequent, successive. SEE MAIN ENTRY
ensure avouch *(guarantee)*, bond *(secure a debt)*, certify *(attest)*, cover *(guard)*, guarantee, preserve, protect, sponsor. SEE MAIN ENTRY
ensure a result frame *(prearrange)*, prearrange
ensured certain *(positive)*, definite
ensurer backer
entail bequest, concern *(involve)*, consist, require *(compel)*. SEE MAIN ENTRY
entailed proprietary, requisite
entangle bait *(lure)*, bicker, bilk, collide *(clash)*, confound, confuse *(create disorder)*, disorganize, encumber *(hinder)*, engage *(involve)*, ensnare, entrap, implicate, incriminate, interest, intertwine, inveigle, involve *(implicate)*, muddle, perplex, perturb, trammel, trap
entangled complex, compound, disordered, inextricable, labyrinthine, sinuous
entangled by difficulties difficult
entanglement commotion, complication, confusion *(turmoil)*, embroilment, imbroglio, implication *(incriminating involvement)*, involution, pandemonium, predicament, quagmire, snarl. SEE MAIN ENTRY
entente arrangement *(understanding)*, bargain, compact
entente compatibility
entente conciliation
entente contract
entente mutual understanding, pact, treaty
entente cordiale accordance *(compact)*, compact
enter book, compete, embark, enroll, file *(place among official records)*, impanel, inscribe, introduce, join *(associate oneself with)*, note *(record)*, penetrate, pervade, record, register, set down. SEE MAIN ENTRY
enter a competition race
enter a demurrer demur, object
enter a plea address *(petition)*
enter a protest challenge, object
enter a suit for address *(petition)*
enter an appearance appear *(attend court proceedings)*. SEE MAIN ENTRY
enter by stealth encroach
enter competition compete
enter hostilely invade
enter into contract, contribute *(assist)*, engage *(involve)*, espouse, incur, involve *(participate)*, participate, undertake
enter into a contract sign
enter into a contractual obligation close *(agree)*
enter into a league organize *(unionize)*
enter into an account deposit *(submit to a bank)*
enter into collision collide *(crash against)*
enter into conflict with engage *(involve)*
enter into detail designate, develop, expand, itemize
enter into partnership with combine *(act in concert)*, pool
enter into possession obtain, possess
enter on a list enroll
enter on a record enroll
enter on a register enroll
enter the mind occur *(come to mind)*
enter the picture emerge, occur *(come to mind)*
enter those names designated as jurors empanel
enter uninvited intrude

enter unlawfully impose *(intrude)*, intrude, trespass
enter upon assume *(undertake)*, commence, embark, initiate, undertake
enter upon the domain of another encroach
enter wrongfully encroach
enterprise act *(undertaking)*, activity, calling, campaign, corporation, employment, endeavor, firm, industry *(activity)*, industry *(business)*, labor *(exertion)*, livelihood, occupation *(vocation)*, operation, project, pursuit *(occupation)*, scheme, spirit, transaction, undertaking *(business)*, venture, work *(effort)*. SEE MAIN ENTRY
enterpriser architect, developer, promoter
enterprising active, competent, progressive *(advocating change)*, resourceful
entertain engage *(involve)*, interest, occupy *(engage)*, receive *(permit to enter)*, treat *(process)*. SEE MAIN ENTRY
entertain doubts doubt *(distrust)*, misdoubt, mistrust
entertain suspicions doubt *(distrust)*, misdoubt, mistrust
entertaining sapid
entertaining suspicion leery
entertainment enjoyment *(pleasure)*. SEE MAIN ENTRY
entêté contumacious
enthrall coerce, commit *(institutionalize)*, confine, constrain *(imprison)*, detain *(hold in custody)*, force *(coerce)*, immerse *(engross)*, interest, lock, monopolize, obsess, occupy *(engage)*, subdue, subject, subjugate. SEE MAIN ENTRY
enthralling attractive, sapid
enthrallment constraint *(imprisonment)*, constraint *(restriction)*, custody *(incarceration)*, preoccupation, servitude, subjection, thrall
enthuse incite
enthusiasm ardor, compulsion *(obsession)*, emotion, industry *(activity)*, interest *(concern)*, life *(vitality)*, penchant, spirit. SEE MAIN ENTRY
enthusiast addict, partisan, proponent. SEE MAIN ENTRY
enthusiastic eager, earnest, ecstatic, fanatical, fervent, industrious, ready *(willing)*, sanguine, vehement, willing *(desirous)*, zealous. SEE MAIN ENTRY
enthusiastically readily
entice bait *(lure)*, betray *(lead astray)*, cajole, coax, ensnare, entrap, interest, inveigle, lure, prevail upon. SEE MAIN ENTRY
enticement bribery, cause *(reason)*, decoy, draw *(attraction)*, hush money, incentive, inducement, invitation, persuasion, seduction. SEE MAIN ENTRY
enticing attractive, sapid
entire absolute *(complete)*, collective, complete *(all-embracing)*, full, gross *(total)*, intact, outright, plenary, pure, radical *(extreme)*, stark, thorough, total, whole *(undamaged)*. SEE MAIN ENTRY
entire amount entirety
entire number aggregate
entire quantity aggregate
entirely en banc, in toto, purely *(positively)*, solely *(singly)*, wholly
entirely defensible blameless, clean, inculpable
entirely occupied full
entireness entirety, finality, totality
entirety aggregate, finality, sum *(total)*, totality, whole. SEE MAIN ENTRY
entitle allow *(authorize)*, authorize, bestow, call *(title)*, certify *(approve)*, delegate, denominate, designate, label, let *(permit)*, nominate, permit, phrase, qualify *(meet standards)*, sanction
entitled desirable *(qualified)*, meritorious, privileged, qualified *(competent)*. SEE MAIN ENTRY
entitled to acceptance and belief auth-entic
entitlement birthright, certification *(certification of proficiency)*, charter *(sanction)*, consent, droit, due, freedom, license, privilege, qualification *(fitness)*, title *(right)*
entitlement for a term of years copyright
entitlements SEE MAIN ENTRY
entity body *(collection)*, body *(person)*, item, materiality *(physical existence)*, totality. SEE MAIN ENTRY
entomb conceal, constrain *(imprison)*, immure, imprison
entombment bondage, captivity
entrammel arrest *(apprehend)*, encumber *(hinder)*, fetter, handcuff, interfere, restrict, trammel
entrance access *(right of way)*, admission *(entry)*, admittance *(acceptance)*, admittance *(means of approach)*, avenue *(route)*, entry *(entrance)*, incursion, inflow, ingress, nascency, occupy *(engage)*, onset *(commencement)*, outset, portal. SEE MAIN ENTRY
entrance by stealth encroachment
entrance in a case appearance *(coming into court)*
entrance into a lawsuit intervention *(imposition into a lawsuit)*
entrance of a third party intervention *(imposition into a lawsuit)*
entrance upon domain of another infringement
entrance upon the domain of another encroachment
entrance way access *(right of way)*, threshold *(entrance)*
entranced ecstatic
entrances approaches
entranceway portal
entranceways approaches
entrancing attractive, provocative, sapid
entrant amateur, applicant *(candidate)*, candidate, contender, neophyte, novice, probationer *(one being tested)*, rival
entrap ambush, bait *(lure)*, betray *(lead astray)*, deceive, dupe, ensnare, inveigle, mislead, trap. SEE MAIN ENTRY
entrapment entanglement *(involvement)*
entreat bait *(lure)*, call *(appeal to)*, desire, exhort, invoke, petition, plead *(implore)*, pray, press *(beseech)*, pressure, prevail upon, request, solicit, sue, urge
entreat against except *(object)*
entreat earnestly petition
entreat persistently importune, pray
entreating precatory
entreaty bait *(lure)*, call *(appeal)*, dun, petition, prayer, request. SEE MAIN ENTRY
entree admittance *(acceptance)*
entrench embed, fix *(make firm)*, impose *(intrude)*, overstep. SEE MAIN ENTRY
entrench on impinge
entrenched chronic, constant, fixed *(settled)*, indefeasible, ingrained, inveterate, irreversible, permanent, safe
entrepreneur merchant, speculator. SEE MAIN ENTRY
entries ledger
entrust appoint, assign *(designate)*, assign *(transfer ownership)*, authorize, charge *(empower)*, confide *(trust)*, consign, delegate, deliver, deposit *(submit to a bank)*, descend, detail *(assign)*, empower, endue, give *(grant)*, instate, invest *(vest)*, leave *(give)*, lend, let *(permit)*, refer *(send for action)*, relegate, rely, remand, vest. SEE MAIN ENTRY
entrust to the care of another delegate
entrust with a task employ *(engage services)*
entrust with information notice *(give formal warning)*
entrust with management employ *(engage services)*
entrust with private information confide *(divulge)*
entrusted cause charge *(custody)*
entrusted object charge *(custody)*
entrusting delegation *(assignment)*
entrustment delegation *(assignment)*, deputation *(selection of delegates)*, escrow, loan
entry access *(right of way)*, admittance *(acceptance)*, admittance *(means of approach)*, avenue *(route)*, entrance, file, inflow, ingress, inscription, insertion, item, marginalia, nascency, notation, note *(brief comment)*, portal, record, threshold *(entrance)*. SEE MAIN ENTRY
entry book docket
entry of aliens immigration
entry under paramount title eviction
entryway admission *(entry)*, admittance *(means of approach)*, entrance
entryways approaches
entwine combine *(join together)*, commingle, conjoin, connect *(join together)*, intertwine, join *(bring together)*, lock, merge, unite
entwined cognate, collateral *(accompanying)*
enucleate comment, elucidate, enlighten, exemplify, explain, explicate, exposit, expound, resolve *(solve)*, solve
enucleation comment, explanation, illustration, paraphrase
enumerare enumerate, recite, specify
enumerate book, calculate, define, detail *(particularize)*, express, impanel, index *(relate)*, itemize, mention, pinpoint, poll, recapitulate, recite, signify *(inform)*, specify, survey *(poll)*, tabulate. SEE MAIN ENTRY
enumerated detailed
enumeratio recital, restatement
enumeration account *(evaluation)*, census, computation, disclosure *(act of disclosing)*, docket, index *(catalog)*, inventory, invoice *(itemized list)*, poll *(canvass)*, reference *(citation)*, roll, schedule, specification, statement. SEE MAIN ENTRY
enumeration of causes arranged for trial calendar *(list of cases)*
enumeration of the essential qualities delineation
enunciate affirm *(claim)*, allege, annunciate, argue, assert, avow, cite *(state)*, communicate, construe *(translate)*, declare, depict, express, herald, issue *(publish)*, notify, pass *(determine)*, phrase, plead *(allege in a legal action)*, posit, pronounce *(speak)*, propagate *(spread)*, speak, utter. SEE MAIN ENTRY
enunciated alleged, nuncupative, oral
enunciation assertion, declaratory

judgment, disclosure *(something disclosed)*, notice *(announcement)*, notification, profession *(declaration)*, pronouncement, publicity, speech. SEE MAIN ENTRY
enunciative declaratory
enunciatory declaratory
enuntiare pronounce *(speak)*
envelop blind *(obscure)*, border *(bound)*, camouflage, circumscribe *(surround by boundary)*, cloak, clothe, comprehend *(include)*, conceal, consist, contain *(comprise)*, contain *(enclose)*, embrace *(encircle)*, enclose, encompass *(surround)*, ensconce, enshroud, hide, include, shroud, shut. SEE MAIN ENTRY
envelopment blockade *(enclosure)*, coverage *(scope)*, enclosure, panoply. SEE MAIN ENTRY
envenom aggravate *(annoy)*, alienate *(estrange)*, antagonize, bait *(harass)*, disaffect, discompose, incense, infect, provoke, taint *(contaminate)*
envenomed bitter *(reproachful)*, caustic, deadly, deleterious, malevolent, malignant, peccant *(unhealthy)*, pernicious, scathing, sinister, spiteful, tainted *(contaminated)*, virulent
envenomed tongue aspersion
enviable meritorious. SEE MAIN ENTRY
envious jealous, resentful
environ border *(bound)*, enclose, envelop
environing influence atmosphere
environment atmosphere, climate, locality, location, situation. SEE MAIN ENTRY
environmental conditions climate
environmental conservation SEE MAIN ENTRY
environmental science ecology
environmental studies ecology
environs confines, environment, locality, region, section *(vicinity)*, site, territory, vicinity
envisage compose, conceive *(comprehend)*, conjure, invent *(produce for the first time)*
envisagement contemplation
envision conceive *(comprehend)*, expect *(consider probable)*, predict, presage. SEE MAIN ENTRY
envisioning original *(creative)*
envisionment contemplation
envoy agent, conduit *(intermediary)*, deputy, factor *(commission merchant)*, informant, informer *(a person who provides information)*, liaison, medium, plenipotentiary, procurator, proxy, replacement, representative *(proxy)*, spokesman, substitute
envoys deputation *(delegation)*
envy resentment
enwrap clothe, contain *(enclose)*, encompass *(surround)*, ensconce, enshroud, envelop, shroud, shut
eodem tempore simultaneous
eon age, cycle, period
epagogic discursive *(analytical)*
epexegesis clarification
ephemeral brief, insubstantial, nonsubstantial *(not sturdy)*, temporary, transient, transitory, volatile. SEE MAIN ENTRY
ephemerally SEE MAIN ENTRY
ephemeris journal
ephemeris register
ephemerous ephemeral, transient
epic narrative, story *(narrative)*. SEE MAIN ENTRY
epicenter center *(central position)*
epicurean palatable, particular *(exacting)*
epidemic contagious, disease, far reaching, general, pestilent, predominant, prevailing *(current)*, prevalent, rife. SEE MAIN ENTRY
epigrammatic brief, compact *(pithy)*, concise, laconic, pithy, proverbial, sententious, succinct
epigrammatical sententious
epilogue codicil, denouement
epilogus peroration
epiphany SEE MAIN ENTRY
episode event, experience *(encounter)*, happening, incident, occasion, occurrence, scene. SEE MAIN ENTRY
epistle dispatch *(message)*
epistolize correspond *(communicate)*
epistula dispatch *(message)*, note *(brief comment)*
epistulae correspondence *(communication by letters)*
epithet blasphemy, call *(title)*, term *(expression)*
epitoma abstract, compendium, summary
epitome abridgment *(condensation)*, abstract, capsule, compendium, cross section, digest, outline *(synopsis)*, restatement, summary. SEE MAIN ENTRY
epitome synopsis
epitomization abridgment *(condensation)*
epitomize abridge *(shorten)*, abstract *(summarize)*, condense, extract, review. SEE MAIN ENTRY
epitomized brief, compact *(pithy)*, concise
epoch age, cycle, duration, lifetime, period, phase *(period)*
eponym call *(title)*
equability composure, parity, uniformity
equable agreed *(harmonized)*, coextensive, comparable *(equivalent)*, consistent, consonant, equal, harmonious, just, peaceable, placid, uniform
equably fairly *(impartially)*
equal agreed *(harmonized)*, coequal, coextensive, cognate, commensurable, competitive *(open)*, congruous, consistent, consonant, correlate, correspond *(be equivalent)*, counterpart *(parallel)*, equitable, equivalent, evenhanded, fair *(just)*, identical, peer, reach, same *(adjective)*, same *(noun)*, tantamount, uniform. SEE MAIN ENTRY
equal distribution of weight equipoise
equal footing par *(equality)*
equal in effect equivalent
equal in extent commensurate
equal in force equivalent
equal in measure commensurate
equal in power equivalent
equal in scope coextensive
equal in significance equivalent
equal in space coextensive
equal in time coextensive
equal in value comparable *(equivalent)*, equivalent
equal part moiety
equal share moiety
equal to capable, commensurate, effective *(efficient)*, proficient, qualified *(competent)*
equal to the need adequate
equal value par *(equality)*
equal worth par *(equality)*
equality fairness, identity *(similarity)*, par *(equality)*, parity, resemblance. SEE MAIN ENTRY
equality of force equipoise
equality of weight equipoise
equalization balance *(equality)*, offset
equalize compensate *(counterbalance)*, conform, coordinate, counteract, neutralize, outbalance. SEE MAIN ENTRY
equalized agreed *(harmonized)*, coextensive, equal, equivalent
equally fairly *(impartially)*
equally divided equal
equalness par *(equality)*
equanimity compatibility, composure, moderation
equate compare, compensate *(counterbalance)*. SEE MAIN ENTRY
equation balance *(equality)*, comparison, parity
equibalanced coequal
equidistance center *(central position)*
equidistant central *(situated near center)*, coextensive, equal, intermediate
equilateral coextensive, equal
equilibrate compensate *(counterbalance)*
equilibration balance *(equality)*, equipoise
equilibrium balance *(equality)*, composure, equipoise, parity, status quo
equip bear *(yield)*, bestow, clothe, contribute *(supply)*, fund, furnish, give *(grant)*, provide *(supply)*, supply
equipage paraphernalia *(apparatus)*
equipment appliance, chattel, competence *(ability)*, device *(mechanism)*, expedient, faculty *(ability)*, instrument *(tool)*, instrumentality, paraphernalia *(apparatus)*, preparation, stock in trade. SEE MAIN ENTRY
equipoise balance *(equality)*, parity, quid pro quo. SEE MAIN ENTRY
equipollence balance *(equality)*, identity *(similarity)*, par *(equality)*
equipollency identity *(similarity)*
equipollent analogous, coequal, coextensive, comparable *(equivalent)*, equal, equivalent
equiponderance balance *(equality)*, equi poise
equiponderant coequal, coextensive
equiponderate counteract, countervail, outbalance
equipondious coextensive
equipped practiced, provident *(showing foresight)*, qualified *(competent)*, ready *(prepared)*. SEE MAIN ENTRY
equipped with arms armed
equitable equal, evenhanded, fair *(just)*, honest, impartial, judicial, juridical, just, neutral, nonpartisan, objective, open-minded, reasonable *(fair)*, right *(correct)*, rightful, scrupulous, unbiased, unprejudiced. SEE MAIN ENTRY
equitable estoppel SEE MAIN ENTRY
equitable interest claim *(right)*
equitable treatment fairness
equitableness candor *(impartiality)*, disinterest *(lack of prejudice)*, fairness, justice, objectivity, probity, right *(righteousness)*
equitably fairly *(impartially)*
equity candor *(impartiality)*, disinterest *(lack of prejudice)*, estate *(property)*, fairness, justice, objectivity, possessions, probity, propriety *(appropriateness)*, rectitude, right *(righteousness)*, stake *(interest)*, title *(right)*. SEE MAIN ENTRY
equivalence analogy, balance *(equality)*, correspondence *(similarity)*, identity *(similarity)*, par *(equality)*, parity, propinquity *(similarity)*. SEE MAIN ENTRY
equivalency parity

equivalent agreed *(harmonized),* analogous, coequal, coextensive, cognate, commensurable, commensurate, compensatory, congruous, correlate, correlative, counterpart *(parallel),* disjunctive *(alternative),* faithful *(true to fact),* identical, mutual *(reciprocal),* offset, peer, pendent, proportionate, replacement, same *(adjective),* same *(noun),* similar, tantamount, value, vicarious *(substitutional),* virtual. SEE MAIN ENTRY
equivalent claim setoff
equivalent given for injury compensation
equivalent given for loss sustained compensation
equivalent item cover *(substitute)*
equivalent meaning definition, paraphrase
equivalently pro rata
equivocal aleatory *(uncertain),* ambiguous, conditional, disputable, doubtful, dubious, elusive, hesitant, impalpable, indefinite, indeterminate, oblique *(evasive),* precarious, problematic, provisional, suspicious *(questionable),* uncertain *(questionable),* unclear, vague. SEE MAIN ENTRY
equivocalness ambiguity, ambivalence, color *(deceptive appearance),* indecision, qualm
equivocate bicker, doubt *(hesitate),* evade *(deceive),* lie *(falsify),* misrepresent, palter, prevaricate, tergiversate, vacillate. SEE MAIN ENTRY
equivocating equivocal, evasive, lying, oblique *(evasive)*
equivocation ambiguity, color *(deceptive appearance),* deceit, deception, duplicity, evasion, falsehood, hesitation, pettifoggery, sophistry
equivocatory equivocal
era age, cycle, duration, lifetime, period, phase *(period),* term *(duration),* time
eradere eradicate
eradicable destructible
eradicare extirpate
eradicate abolish, cancel, censor, consume, delete, destroy *(efface),* excise *(cut away),* exclude, expunge, extinguish, extirpate, overthrow, purge *(purify),* quash, reject, relegate, remove *(eliminate),* supplant. SEE MAIN ENTRY
eradicated lost *(taken away)*
eradication abolition, cancellation, catastrophe, destruction, dissolution *(termination),* evulsion, prohibition, rejection, removal, rescision
eradicative dire, disastrous, fatal
erase censor, deface, delete, destroy *(efface),* dissolve *(terminate),* edit, eliminate *(eradicate),* eradicate, expunge, expurgate, extinguish, extirpate, invalidate, obliterate, redact, rescind. SEE MAIN ENTRY
erasure cancellation, defacement, dissolution *(termination),* rejection, removal
erasure of ambiguity clarification
eratic disjunctive *(tending to disjoin)*
erect build *(construct),* create, devise *(invent),* elevate, fabricate *(construct),* frame *(construct),* honest, make, produce *(manufacture),* upright
erect a barrier bar *(hinder),* impede
erection building *(structure),* development *(building),* elevation, structure *(edifice)*
erectus intent
eremetical solitary
eremitic solitary
eremitish solitary
ergo a fortiori, a priori, consequently
eripere disabuse, hold up *(rob)*
eristic argumentative, controversial, debatable, disputable, litigious, polemic
eristical argumentative, litigious, polemic
ernest decisive
erode degenerate, depreciate, diminish, impair, lessen. SEE MAIN ENTRY
erogare expend *(disburse)*
erosion attrition, decline, decrement, deterioration, detriment, dissolution *(disintegration),* expense *(sacrifice),* spoilage, wear and tear. SEE MAIN ENTRY
erosive caustic
erotic lascivious, lecherous, prurient, salacious, suggestive *(risqué)*
erotica pornography
erotical lecherous
err deviate, fail *(lose),* lapse *(fall into error),* misapprehend, miscalculate, misconceive, misinterpret, misjudge, misread, mistake, misunderstand, offend *(violate the law).* SEE MAIN ENTRY
err in judgment misjudge
errable fallible
errancy misapplication
errand burden, mission
errant astray, blameful, blameworthy, deviant, devious, discursive *(digressive),* fallible, faulty, truant. SEE MAIN ENTRY
errare err, lapse *(fall into error),* miscalculate
erratic anomalous, astray, broken *(interrupted),* capricious, desultory, disjointed, eccentric, inconsistent, infrequent, irregular *(not usual),* irresolute, periodic, sporadic, undependable, unpredictable, variable, volatile. SEE MAIN ENTRY
erratum error
erratum fault *(mistake),* miscue, misstatement
erratum oversight *(carelessness)*
erring at fault, blameworthy, delinquent *(guilty of a misdeed),* errant, erroneous, fallible, guilty, inaccurate, incorrect, peccable
erroneous baseless, errant, fallacious, false *(inaccurate),* faulty, fictitious, ill-founded, improper, inaccurate, incorrect, inexact, peccant *(culpable),* sophistic, specious, unfounded, unsound *(fallacious),* unsustainable, untenable, untrue. SEE MAIN ENTRY
erroneous in date untimely
erroneous reasoning fallacy
erroneous statement error
erroneous trial mistrial
erroneous use abuse *(corrupt practice),* misuse
erroneousness fallacy, invalidity, misestimation
error delinquency *(failure of duty)*
error error
error failure *(lack of success),* fallacy, fault *(mistake),* flaw, indiscretion
error lapse *(expiration)*
error lapse *(expiration),* misapplication, misconduct, miscue, misdoing, misestimation, misjudgment, misstatement, onus *(blame),* oversight *(carelessness),* tort, transgression. SEE MAIN ENTRY
error in naming misnomer
error of judgment fault *(mistake)*
error of the court injustice
errori obnoxius fallible
errorless accurate, factual, infallible
ersatz artificial, counterfeit, imitation, spurious, succedaneum, synthetic, vicarious *(substitutional)*
erstwhile former, late *(defunct),* previous
eruct eject *(expel),* outpour
eructate eject *(expel),* emit, outpour
erudire educate, instruct *(teach)*
erudite cognizant, didactic, familiar *(informed),* informed *(educated),* learned, literate, profound *(esoteric).* SEE MAIN ENTRY
eruditio instruction *(teaching),* research
erudition comprehension, education, information *(knowledge),* knowledge *(learning)*
eruditus learned
eruere disinter
erumpere issue *(send forth)*
erupt emit, penetrate
eruption bluster *(commotion),* cataclysm, commotion, disturbance, expulsion, furor, outbreak, outburst, outflow, passion, recrudescence, strife, violence
escalate accrue *(increase),* enhance, enlarge, expand, increase, inflate, intensify, parlay *(exploit successfully)*
escalating cumulative *(intensifying)*
escalation boom *(increase),* boom *(prosperity),* growth *(increase),* inflation *(increase).* SEE MAIN ENTRY
escapade experience *(encounter)*
escape abscond, avoid *(evade),* circumvent, disappear, egress, elude, evacuate, evade *(elude),* exude, flee, impunity, issuance, leave *(depart),* outflow, parry, part *(leave),* quit *(evacuate),* retreat, shun. SEE MAIN ENTRY
escape by artifice elude
escape by cleverness evasion
escape by trickery evasion
escape clause loophole, salvo. SEE MAIN ENTRY
escape detection elude, lurk
escape from shirk
escape hatch loophole. SEE MAIN ENTRY
escape notice elude, evade *(elude),* lurk
escape observation lurk
escape recognition lurk
escape valve loophole
escape-clause dispensation *(exception)*
escaped prisoner fugitive
escapee convict, fugitive
escaper fugitive
escaping elusive, flight
escheat forfeit, relapse. SEE MAIN ENTRY
escheatment SEE MAIN ENTRY
eschew abscond, avoid *(evade),* decline *(reject),* forgo, forswear, refrain, repulse, shun. SEE MAIN ENTRY
eschewal abstention, continence
eschewment avoidance *(evasion)*
escort consort, guardian, protect
escrow binder. SEE MAIN ENTRY
esculent palatable
esoteric certain *(specific),* enigmatic, exclusive *(limited),* hidden, incomprehensible, inexplicable, mysterious, obs-cure *(abstruse),* private *(confidential),* profound *(esoteric),* recondite, secret, special, specific, undefinable. SEE MAIN ENTRY
esoterical esoteric, private *(confidential)*
especial certain *(particular),* certain *(specific),* exclusive *(singular),* extraordinary, noteworthy, outstanding *(prominent),* particular *(individual),* particular *(specific),* singular, special, specific
especially a fortiori, particularly
especially liked preferred *(favored)*
especially prepared express
espial discovery, espionage, observation, perception, recognition

espieglerie artifice
espier detective
espionage observation. SEE MAIN ENTRY
espousal adoption *(acceptance),* aid *(help),* alternative *(option),* defense, favor *(sanction),* marriage *(wedlock),* matrimony
espouse adhere *(maintain loyalty),* adopt, advocate, assert, assure *(insure),* defend, embrace *(accept),* justify, lobby, prefer, spouse, uphold. SEE MAIN ENTRY
espouse the cause of justify, maintain *(sustain)*
espoused conjugal, nuptial
espousement marriage *(wedlock),* matrimony
espouser proponent
espy detect, discern *(detect with the senses),* identify, observe *(watch),* perceive, recognize *(perceive),* spy
esquire SEE MAIN ENTRY
essay attempt, effort, endeavor *(noun),* endeavor *(verb),* experiment, pandect *(treatise),* project, question *(inquiry),* review *(critical evaluation),* struggle, undertaking *(enterprise),* venture, work *(effort)*
essayist author *(writer)*
esse exist, subsist
esse participem participate
essence basis, capsule, character *(personal quality),* characteristic, compendium, connotation, consequence *(significance),* content *(meaning),* contents, cornerstone, corpus, digest, epitome, gist *(substance),* gravamen, import, interior, main point, necessary, outline *(synopsis),* point *(purpose),* scenario, signification, spirit, structure *(composition),* substance *(essential nature),* sum *(tally).* SEE MAIN ENTRY
essence of a grievance gravamen
essential actual, cardinal *(basic),* critical *(crucial),* crucial, exigent, fundamental, grave *(important),* imperative, important *(urgent),* indispensable, ingrained, inherent, innate, integral, major, mandatory, material *(important),* native *(inborn),* necessary *(required),* necessary, necessity, obligatory, peremptory *(imperative),* primary, principal, requirement, requisite, resource, rudimentary, substantive, ultimate, underlying, urgent, virtual, vital. SEE MAIN ENTRY
essential clause sine qua non
essential condition sine qua non
essential desideratum prerequisite, requirement
essential element necessity, need *(requir
ement)*
essential ground gist *(ground for a suit)*
essential matter content *(meaning),* cornerstone, gist *(ground for a suit),* main point, sine qua non
essential meaning connotation, content *(meaning),* gist *(substance)*
essential nature materiality *(physical existence)*
essential object of desire desideratum
essential part body *(main part),* center *(essence),* character *(personal quality),* characteristic, content *(meaning),* element, essence, gist *(ground for a suit),* gist *(substance),* gravamen, ingredient, main point, sine qua non, spirit, substance *(essential nature)*
essential point gravamen, main point
essential provision condition *(contingent provision)*
essential qualification sine qua non
essential quality consequence *(significance)*
essential quality of one's nature character *(personal quality)*
essential status priority
essential to completeness integral
essentiality importance, magnitude, market *(demand),* necessary, need *(requirement),* significance
essentially ipso facto, purely *(positively),* purely *(simply)*
essentially different disparate
essentialness character *(personal quality),* main point, need *(requirement)*
essentials basic facts
establish affirm *(claim),* affirm *(uphold),* appoint, argue, ascertain, authorize, award, bear *(adduce),* build *(construct),* cast *(register),* certify *(approve),* circumscribe *(define),* cite *(state),* confirm, create, decide, decree, define, document, enact, evidence, fabricate *(construct),* fix *(arrange),* fix *(make firm),* fix *(settle),* form, instate, launch *(initiate),* legislate, locate, make, organize *(unionize),* originate, pass *(approve),* plant *(place firmly),* prove, quote, reason *(persuade),* repose *(place),* rule *(decide),* stabilize, support *(corroborate),* sustain *(confirm),* testify, verify *(confirm),* vest. SEE MAIN ENTRY
establish a corporation incorporate *(form a corporation)*
establish as facts find *(determine)*
establish as truth prove
establish beforehand preordain
establish boundaries demarcate
establish by agreement close *(agree)*
establish by law enact, legislate, pass *(approve)*
establish by proof substantiate
establish connection contact *(communicate),* contact *(touch)*
establish equilibrium adjust *(regulate)*
establish guide lines organize *(arrange)*
establish guidelines for plan
establish in an office instate
establish oneself lodge *(reside),* reside
establish parameters organize *(arrange)*
establish the authenticity of a will probate
establish the genuineness of prove
establish the genuineness of a will probate
establish the truth of verify *(confirm)*
establish the validity of prove
establish the validity of a will probate
establish with certainty ascertain
establishable convincing, provable
established accustomed *(customary),* certain *(positive),* chronic, common *(customary),* conventional, convincing, customary, daily, definite, demonstrable, durable, familiar *(customary),* firm, fixed *(settled),* habitual, inappealable, incontrovertible, indefeasible, ingrained, inveterate, lawful, normal *(regular),* official, ordinary, orthodox, permanent, positive *(prescribed),* prescriptive, prevailing *(current),* prevalent, professional *(trained),* prosperous, regular *(orderly),* routine, situated, solid *(sound),* stable, standing, stated, statutory, steadfast, substantial, traditional, undeniable, usual. SEE MAIN ENTRY
established by custom customary
established by general consent conventional
established by law legal
established by the federal government national
established custom usage
established division of time calendar *(record of yearly periods)*
established law code
established matter fact
established method procedure
established mode formality
established order code, method, policy *(plan of action),* practice *(custom),* practice *(procedure)*
established patronage goodwill
established phenomenon fact
established popularity goodwill
established practice conduct, form *(arran-gement),* usage
established principle canon, maxim
established reputation goodwill
established rule law, principle *(axiom)*
established way of doing things custom
establisher developer, pioneer
establishing guilt incriminatory, inculpatory
establishment affirmance *(authentication),* affirmation, birth *(beginning),* building *(business of assembling),* building *(structure),* business *(commercial enterprise),* company *(enterprise),* composition *(makeup),* concern *(business establishment),* corporation, corroboration, creation, enactment, facility *(institution),* firm, formation, foundation *(organization),* household, industry *(business),* inhabitation *(place of dwelling),* installation, institute, market *(business),* onset *(commencement),* organization *(association),* preparation, proof, store *(business),* structure *(edifice)*
establishment of a firm incorporation *(formation of a business entity)*
establishment of an ambassador embassy
establishment of foreign residence immigration
establishment of proof corroboration
estate assets, demesne, domain *(land owned),* dower, effects, freehold, holding *(property owned),* homestead, paraphernalia *(personal belongings),* parcel, possessions, property *(land),* property *(possessions),* rating, real estate, realty, remainder *(estate in property),* resource, substance *(material possessions).* SEE MAIN ENTRY
estate for a fixed term leasehold
estate for a fixed term of years leasehold
estate for life freehold
estate in fee freehold
estate in realty leasehold
estate owner landholder, landowner
estate planning SEE MAIN ENTRY
esteem appreciate *(value),* character *(reputation),* consideration *(sympathetic regard),* credit *(recognition),* deem, defer *(yield in judgment),* deference, eminence, homage, honor *(outward respect),* honor, indorsement, interest *(concern),* mention *(tribute),* opine, prestige, rate, recommend, recommendation, regard *(hold in esteem),* reputation, respect, status, surmise, value, worth. SEE MAIN ENTRY
esteem of no account disdain
esteem of small account disdain
esteem slightly flout
esteemed famous, important *(significant),* influential, outstanding *(prominent),* popular, reputable, valuable

estimable appreciable, considerable, determinable *(ascertainable),* high-minded, honest, laudable, meritorious, moral, popular, premium, reputable, upright, valuable
estimableness honesty, integrity
estimate appraisal, assess *(appraise),* assessment *(estimation),* bid, calculate, charge *(assess),* computation, concept, determine, diagnose, estimation *(calculation),* evaluate, gauge, generalization, guess, idea, judge, judgment *(discernment),* measure, measurement, opine, opinion *(belief),* perception, presume, presuppose, price, prognosis, rate, survey *(poll),* value, weigh. SEE MAIN ENTRY
estimate incorrectly miscalculate, misconceive, misjudge
estimate relatively compare
estimate too highly overestimate
estimated approximate, inexact
estimated by comparison comparative
estimated expenditures budget
estimated value appraisal
estimation appraisal, appreciation *(perception),* character *(reputation),* computation, conclusion *(determination),* consideration *(sympathetic regard),* diagnosis, discrimination *(differentiation),* estimate *(approximate cost),* generalization, homage, honor *(outward respect),* idea, judgment *(discernment),* measurement, notion, observation, opinion *(belief),* prestige, price, rating, regard *(esteem),* reputation, respect, value, worth
estimator juror
estop balk, ban, bar *(hinder),* block, check *(restrain),* constrict *(inhibit),* debar, forestall, halt, hamper, impede, inhibit, obstruct, preclude, prevent, toll *(stop).* SEE MAIN ENTRY
estoppage end *(termination),* halt
estoppel bar *(obstruction),* check *(bar),* halt, impediment, obstacle, prohibition. SEE MAIN ENTRY
estrange antagonize, disaffect. SEE MAIN ENTRY
estranged hostile, inimical, irreconcilable, solitary
estrangement feud, fight *(argument),* rift *(disagreement),* separation, umbrage. SEE MAIN ENTRY
et al SEE MAIN ENTRY
etch delineate
eternal constant, continual *(perpetual),* durable, immutable, incessant, infinite, permanent, perpetual
eternally ad infinitum
eternalness indestructibility, perpetuity
eternity perpetuity. SEE MAIN ENTRY
eternization preservation
eternize perpetuate
ethereal immaterial, incorporeal, intangible
ethical high-minded, honest, incorruptible, just, law-abiding, meritorious, moral, proper, reputable, right *(correct),* scrupulous, upright. SEE MAIN ENTRY
ethical judgment conscience, responsibility *(conscience)*
ethical philosophy casuistry, conscience
ethical self conscience
ethicality propriety *(correctness)*
ethics conduct, conscience, principle *(virtue).* SEE MAIN ENTRY
ethnic group blood, family *(common ancestry),* race
ethnic stock race
ethnicity family *(common ancestry)*
ethology casuistry
ethos character *(personal quality),* temperament
etiquette conduct, courtesy, custom, decorum, formality, manner *(behavior),* propriety *(correctness),* respect
étranger alien
etymology origination
eulogistic favorable *(expressing approval)*
eulogistic speech mention *(tribute)*
eulogistical favorable *(expressing approval)*
eulogize belaud, honor
eulogy laudation, mention *(tribute)*
euphemism bombast
euphuism fustian, rhetoric *(insincere language)*
euphuistic turgid
eurhythmy proportion
euthauasis SEE MAIN ENTRY
evacuate abandon *(physically leave),* alight, depart, deplete, dislocate, dislodge, eliminate *(eradicate),* eliminate *(exclude),* flee, leave *(depart),* outpour, part *(leave),* purge *(purify),* retreat, secede, vacate *(leave),* vacate *(void),* withdraw. SEE MAIN ENTRY
evacuation abandonment *(desertion),* egress, flight, outflow, removal, resignation *(relinquishment).* SEE MAIN ENTRY
évacué discard
evade abscond, bilk, circumvent, default, dishonor *(refuse to pay),* elude, equivocate, escape, eschew, fail *(neglect),* flee, hedge, ignore, palter, parry, pettifog, prevaricate, refrain, shirk, shun, spurn, tergiversate. SEE MAIN ENTRY
evade the truth palter, prevaricate
evader fugitive
evadere escape
evagari maneuver
evagation vagrancy
evaluate assess *(appraise),* calculate, consider, estimate, gauge, measure, ponder, rate, screen *(select),* survey *(examine),* weigh. SEE MAIN ENTRY
evaluated ad valorem
evaluation appraisal, census, computation, concept, conclusion *(determination),* determination, discretion *(power of choice),* discrimination *(differentiation),* estimate *(approximate cost),* estimation *(calculation),* idea, inspection, judgment *(discernment),* judgment *(formal court decree),* opinion *(belief),* par *(face amount),* perception, poll *(canvass),* rating, trial *(experiment).* SEE MAIN ENTRY
evaluator juror
evanesce disappear, dissipate *(spread out),* dissolve *(disperse),* perish
evanescence mortality
evanescent elusive, ephemeral, indiscernible, temporary, transient, transitory, volatile
evanescere disappear
evaporable volatile
evaporate consume, disappear, lessen, perish. SEE MAIN ENTRY
evasion abstention, artifice, avoidance *(evasion),* color *(deceptive appearance),* concealment, dereliction, duplicity, falsehood, flight, loophole, nonpayment, nonperformance, pettifoggery, pretext, privacy, ruse, salvo, sophistry, story *(falsehood),* stratagem, subterfuge. SEE MAIN ENTRY
evasion of duty default, infidelity, infraction, maladministration, nonperformance
evasion of truth false pretense
evasive allusive, clandestine, disingenuous, elusive, furtive, indefinite, machiavellian, noncommittal, reluctant, sly, stealthy, surreptitious, unresponsive, vague. SEE MAIN ENTRY
evasive action avoidance *(evasion)*
evasive reasoning sophistry
evasiveness privacy
evellere eradicate, extract
even adjust *(regulate),* coequal, coextensive, commensurable, comparable *(equivalent),* compensate *(counterbalance),* equal, equivalent, impartial, notwithstanding, placid, precise, proportionate, regular *(orderly),* uniform. SEE MAIN ENTRY
even balance equipoise
even more a fortiori
even tenor regularity
even the score settle
even though regardless
even-handed dispassionate, unprejudiced. SEE MAIN ENTRY
even-handedness candor *(impartiality)*
even-sided coextensive
even-tempered dispassionate
evenhanded equal, equitable, fair *(just),* honest, impartial, just, law-abiding, nonpartisan, open-minded
evenhanded justice fairness, right *(righteousness)*
evenhandedly fairly *(impartially)*
evenhandedness disinterest *(lack of prejudice),* equity *(justice),* fairness
evenire result
evenly fairly *(impartially)*
evenly balanced impartial
evenness candor *(impartiality),* composure, equipoise, par *(equality),* regularity, uniformity
event chance *(fortuity),* development *(outgrowth),* experience *(encounter),* fact, happening, incident, landmark *(significant change),* occasion, occurrence, particular. SEE MAIN ENTRY
eventful cardinal *(outstanding),* critical *(crucial),* stellar
events circumstances
eventual forthcoming, future, pending *(imminent),* prospective, subsequent, ultimate
eventuality conclusion *(outcome),* consequence *(conclusion),* development *(outgrowth),* occurrence, outcome, outgrowth, result
eventually in due course. SEE MAIN ENTRY
eventuate accrue *(arise),* arise *(occur),* arise *(originate),* crystallize, ensue, result, supervene
eventuation denouement, development *(outgrowth),* effect, outcome, outgrowth
eventus effect, event
ever-abiding perpetual
ever-present chronic, ubiquitous
ever-victorious invincible
ever-widening cumulative *(increasing)*
everchanging capricious, protean
everlasting chronic, continual *(perpetual),* durable, incessant, indestructible, infallible, infinite, infrangible, permanent, perpetual, perpetuity, persistent, stable
everlastingness indestructibility
evermore now and forever
eversio subversion
evertere overturn, subvert, upset
every collective

every bit throughout *(all over)*
everyday common *(customary)*, conventional, customary, familiar *(customary)*, household *(familiar)*, mediocre, mundane, nondescript, normal *(regular)*, prevailing *(current)*, prevalent, prosaic, regular *(conventional)*, repeated, routine, typical, usual. SEE MAIN ENTRY
everything entirety, sum *(total)*, totality, whole. SEE MAIN ENTRY
everywhere rampant
evict deport *(banish)*, depose *(remove)*, dislocate, dislodge, displace *(remove)*, dispossess, divest, eliminate *(exclude)*, expel. SEE MAIN ENTRY
evictio eviction, recovery *(repossession)*
eviction banishment, deportation, discharge *(dismissal)*, disqualification *(rejection)*, expropriation *(divestiture)*, expulsion, foreclosure, forfeiture *(act of forfeiting)*, ostracism, ouster, proscription, rejection. SEE MAIN ENTRY
evidence adduce, bear *(adduce)*, certification *(attested copy)*, certify *(attest)*, cite *(state)*, clue, connote, corroboration, data, disclose, display, document *(noun)*, document *(verb)*, documentation, evince, exemplify, exhibit *(noun)*, exhibit *(verb)*, expression *(manifestation)*, ground, indicate, indication, indicia, manifest, manifestation, notarize, produce *(offer to view)*, proof, record, signify *(denote)*, substantiate, sustain *(confirm)*, symptom, testimony, token, verify *(swear)*. SEE MAIN ENTRY
evidence against confutation
evidence by a competent witness testimony
evidence from impersonal knowledge hearsay
evidence in support of testimony
evidence of a debt bond
evidence on oath affidavit, affirmance *(legal affirmation)*
evidence on the other side confutation
evidence-seeking cross-examination
evidenced solely by speech parol
evidences of debts securities
evidences of obligations securities
evidens evident, manifest, palpable, undeniable
evident apparent *(perceptible)*, appreciable, certain *(positive)*. SEE MAIN ENTRY
évident clear *(apparent)*
evident clear *(apparent)*, coherent *(clear)*, comprehensible, conclusive *(determinative)*, conspicuous, convincing, definite, demonstrable, discernible, distinct *(clear)*, explicit, gross *(flagrant)*, lucid, manifest, naked *(perceptible)*, obvious, open *(in sight)*, ostensible, overt, palpable, patent, perceivable, perceptible, positive *(incontestable)*, prominent, public *(known)*, salient, scrutable, tangible, unambiguous, undeniable, unequivocal, unmistakable
evident demonstration proof
evidential apparent *(presumptive)*, categorical, certain *(positive)*, cogent, conclusive *(settled)*, deductive, definite, documentary, presumptive, probative, reliable
evidential record documentation
evidential writing instrument *(document)*
evidentiary probative. SEE MAIN ENTRY
evidentiary privilege SEE MAIN ENTRY
evidentiary record document, documentation
evidently fairly *(clearly)*
evil arrant *(onerous)*, bad *(offensive)*, contemptible, delinquency *(misconduct)*, delinquent *(guilty of a misdeed)*, depraved, detriment, diabolic, harm, harmful, heinous, immoral, inexpiable, iniquitous, lethal, malevolent, malicious, malignant, mischief, nefarious, objectionable, odious, peccant *(culpable)*, pernicious, perverse, pestilent, profane, profligate *(corrupt)*, reprehensible, sinister, tainted *(corrupted)*, vice, vicious, wrong. SEE MAIN ENTRY
evil adumbration premonition
evil behavior delinquency *(misconduct)*, offense, perversion
evil conduct mischief
evil deed misdeed, offense
evil disposition malice
evil fame infamy
evil fortune calamity, misfortune
evil intent malice
evil lot calamity
evil luck calamity
evil-doing delinquent *(guilty of a misdeed)*, diabolic
evil-minded cruel, delinquent *(guilty of a misdeed)*, diabolic, dissolute, malevolent, malicious, malignant, perverse, profligate *(corrupt)*, reprobate, spiteful, vicious
evil-speaking calumnious, malediction
evildoer convict, criminal, delinquent, embezzler, felon, hoodlum, malefactor, offender, outlaw, vandal, wrongdoer
evildoing felonious, misdoing
evince adduce, allude, attest, bare, bear *(adduce)*, certify *(attest)*, cite *(state)*, convey *(communicate)*, demonstrate *(establish)*, depict, disclose, disinter, display, divulge, evidence, exemplify, exhibit, expose, indicate, manifest, produce *(offer to view)*, prove, reveal, signify *(denote)*. SEE MAIN ENTRY
evincement appearance *(emergence)*, expression *(manifestation)*, indication, manifestation, symptom
evincible ascertainable, convincing
evincive explicit
eviscerate bowdlerize, debilitate, extract. SEE MAIN ENTRY
evitare elude
evocare elicit, evoke
evocative moving *(evoking emotion)*
evoke bait *(lure)*, cause, coax, depict, disinter, educe, elicit, extract, generate, inspire, originate, provoke, recall *(remember)*, represent *(portray)*, urge. SEE MAIN ENTRY
evolution civilization, course, development *(progression)*, maturity, nascency, preparation, start
evolve arise *(originate)*, avail *(bring about)*, bear *(yield)*, build *(construct)*, change, convert *(change use)*, develop, devise *(invent)*, educe, forge *(produce)*, germinate, make, manufacture, mature. SEE MAIN ENTRY
evolved derivative
evolved from dependent
evolvement development *(progression)*, growth *(evolution)*, nascency
evolvere evolve
evulgare reveal
evulgate bare, propagate *(spread)*, reveal
evulgation divulgation, notification, publicity
evulse disinter
evulsion avulsion, removal. SEE MAIN ENTRY
ex concesso a priori
ex officio clerical. SEE MAIN ENTRY
ex parte determinative. SEE MAIN ENTRY
ex post facto SEE MAIN ENTRY
exacerbare exacerbate
exacerbate compound, distress, expand, harm, heighten *(augment)*, incense, intensify, irritate, prejudice *(injure)*, provoke. SEE MAIN ENTRY
exacerbation damage
exact absolute *(conclusive)*, accurate, acquire *(secure)*, actual, appropriate, attach *(seize)*, bind *(obligate)*, brief, call *(demand)*, certain *(particular)*, certain *(specific)*, charge *(assess)*, clear *(apparent)*, close *(rigorous)*, coerce, coherent *(clear)*, command, compel, constrain *(compel)*, decree, definite, definitive, demand, detailed, diligent, dun, enforce, enjoin, excise *(levy a tax)*, explicit, express, extort, factual, faithful *(true to fact)*, genuine, honest, identical, impose *(enforce)*, insist, instruct *(direct)*, laconic, levy, literal, meticulous, narrow, necessitate, need, precise, prescribe, press *(constrain)*, punctilious, punctual, realistic, reliable, request, require *(compel)*, right *(direct)*, rigid, said, specific, strict, stringent, subtle *(refined)*, systematic, tax *(levy)*, tax *(overwork)*, true *(authentic)*, unambiguous, undistorted, verbatim. SEE MAIN ENTRY
exact a charge assess *(tax)*
exact a fine mulct *(fine)*
exact a penalty condemn *(punish)*, discipline *(punish)*, fine, penalize
exact a toll assess *(tax)*
exact amount face amount
exact as due claim *(demand)*
exact by force extort
exact copy facsimile
exact data information *(facts)*
exact meaning definition
exact moment point *(period of time)*
exact payment collect *(recover money)*
exact retribution condemn *(punish)*, discipline *(punish)*, fine, penalize, punish
exact statement definition
exact tribute toll *(exact payment)*
exacted positive *(prescribed)*
exacter extortionist
exacting circumspect, confiscatory, conscientious, critical *(faultfinding)*, dictatorial, draconian, faithful *(diligent)*, ironclad, mercenary, meticulous, onerous, operose, oppressive, painstaking, punctilious, punctual, rigid, severe, strict, stringent, uncompromising
exactingness particularity
exactio expulsion
exaction assessment *(levy)*, assumption *(seizure)*, blackmail, charge *(cost)*, claim *(legal demand)*, coercion, dun, duress, duty *(tax)*, enforcement, excise, expense *(cost)*, extortion, force *(compulsion)*, forfeiture *(act of forfeiting)*, levy, price, request, requirement, requisition, tax, toll *(effect)*, toll *(tax)*, ultimatum
exaction by oppression extortion
exaction of penalty condemnation *(punishment)*, conviction *(finding of guilt)*
exactitude caution *(vigilance)*, diligence *(care)*, honesty, particularity, rigor, veracity
exactly faithfully
exactly alike identical
exactly like same
exactly the same identical
exactment assessment *(levy)*, charge *(cost)*, duty *(tax)*, excise, expense *(cost)*, fee *(charge)*, levy, tax

exactness caution *(vigilance)*, diligence *(care)*, particularity, regularity, rigor, truth, veracity
exactus exact
exaggerare accumulate *(enlarge)*, heighten *(augment)*, magnify
exaggerate cloak, compound, distort, enhance, enlarge, expand, falsify, inflate, intensify, invent *(falsify)*, magnify, misinform, misrepresent, overestimate, slant. SEE MAIN ENTRY
exaggerated excessive, histrionic, inflated *(overestimated)*, inordinate, lurid, outrageous, unreasonable
exaggerated likeness caricature
exaggerated statement overstatement
exaggerating cumulative *(intensifying)*
exaggeration bombast, caricature, catachresis, color *(deceptive appearance)*, distortion, falsification, histrionics, hyperbole, inflation *(increase)*, misrepresentation, overstatement, parody, rodomontade, travesty. SEE MAIN ENTRY
exaggerative inflated *(overestimated)*
exagitare harass, plague
exalt belaud, compound, elevate, honor, magnify, overestimate, parlay *(exploit successfully)*, promote *(advance)*, raise *(advance)*, recognize *(acknowledge)*, recommend, regard *(hold in esteem)*
exaltation distinction *(reputation)*, elevation, eminence, homage, honor *(outward respect)*, laudation, mention *(tribute)*, precedence, prestige, promotion *(advancement)*, remembrance *(commemoration)*
exalted famous, irreprehensible, magnanimous, outstanding *(prominent)*, prominent, renowned, salient. SEE MAIN ENTRY
examinant detective
examination analysis, appraisal, collation, consideration *(contemplation)*, contemplation, cross-examination, deliberation, discretion *(power of choice)*, discrimination *(differentiation)*, experiment, habeas corpus, hearing, indagation, inquest, inquiry *(request for information)*, inquiry *(systematic investigation)*, inspection, interrogation, investigation, judgment *(discernment)*, observation, probe, proposal *(report)*, question *(inquiry)*, regard *(attention)*, research, scrutiny, surveillance, test, treatment, trial *(experiment)*, trial *(legal proceeding)*. SEE MAIN ENTRY
examination for qualification for jury service voir dire
examination for the purpose of ascertaining facts discovery
examination into facts or principles inquiry *(request for information)*
examine analyze, audit, canvass, check *(inspect)*, consider, criticize *(evaluate)*, cross-examine, deliberate, delve, discern *(detect with the senses)*, frisk, inquire, investigate, judge, monitor, muse, observe *(watch)*, overlook *(superintend)*, oversee, peruse, ponder, probe, reason *(conclude)*, research, review, revise, scrutinize, search, study, treat *(process)*, try *(conduct a trial)*, weigh. SEE MAIN ENTRY
examine a question debate
examine a source consult *(seek information from)*
examine by argument debate
examine by inspection search
examine carefully deliberate
examine closely concentrate *(pay attention)*, focus, frisk, notice *(observe)*
examine critically analyze, diagnose
examine financial accounts audit
examine in detail investigate
examine intently concern *(care)*, frisk, notice *(observe)*
examine judicially hear *(give a legal hearing)*, try *(conduct a trial)*
examine searchingly canvass
examine secretely spy
examine the accounts officially audit
examine the particulars investigate
examine the witnesses hear *(give a legal hearing)*
examine with care and accuracy investigate
examinee contender
examiner detective, juror
examiner of business accounts comptroller
example comment, criterion, cross section, exemplar, illustration, indicant, instance, model, paradigm, paragon, pattern, precedent, prototype, sample, semblance, specimen, standard. SEE MAIN ENTRY
examples selection *(collection)*
exanimate dead, deceased, defunct, insensible, languid, lifeless *(dead)*
exanimis dead
exanimus dead, lifeless *(dead)*
exasperate aggravate *(annoy)*, annoy, badger, bait *(harass)*, discommode, discompose, disturb, incense, irritate, perturb, pique, plague, provoke. SEE MAIN ENTRY
exasperating provocative, vexatious
exasperation provocation
exauctorare disband
exaudire overhear
excavate disinter, extract
excavation evulsion
excedere leave *(depart)*
exceed carouse, outbalance, outweigh, overestimate, overlap, overreach, overstep, predominate *(outnumber)*, prevail *(triumph)*, surmount, surpass, transcend, trespass. SEE MAIN ENTRY
exceed in importance outweigh
exceed in value outweigh
exceeding drastic, excessive, extreme *(exaggerated)*, inordinate, intemperate
exceeding propriety undue *(excessive)*
exceeding the bounds of moderation extreme *(exaggerated)*
exceeding the law illegal, illicit
exceeding the usual extraordinary
exceeding what is usual excessive
exceedingly ardent perfervid
excel beat *(defeat)*, outweigh, prevail *(triumph)*, surmount, surpass, transcend. SEE MAIN ENTRY
excellence caliber *(quality)*, efficiency, merit, prowess *(ability)*, right *(righteousness)*, significance, skill, value, worth. SEE MAIN ENTRY
excellence of behavior courtesy
excellency primacy
excellent cardinal *(outstanding)*, competent, exemplary, felicitous, illustrious, laudable, meritorious, noteworthy, outstanding *(prominent)*, preferable, premium, professional *(stellar)*, proficient, rare, select, sterling, superlative, unimpeachable, valuable. SEE MAIN ENTRY
excellent judgment sagacity. SEE MAIN ENTRY
excellent prospect likelihood
exceller paragon
excellere surpass, transcend
excelling absolute *(ideal)*, outstanding *(prominent)*, preferable, prime *(most valuable)*
except bar *(exclude)*, eliminate *(exclude)*, exclude, object, remove *(eliminate)*, reserve, save, unless. SEE MAIN ENTRY
excepted barred, inadmissible, privileged
excepting palliative *(excusing)*, save, unless
excepting that only
exceptio exception *(exclusion)*, plea, qualification *(condition)*, reservation *(condition)*
exception clause, condition *(contingent provision)*, criticism, demurrer, disagreement, disapproval, discharge *(release from obligation)*, disparagement, dispensation *(exception)*, exemption, extenuating circumstances, immunity, irregularity, license, loophole, modification, nonconformity, objection, phenomenon *(unusual occurrence)*, qualification *(condition)*, quirk *(idiosyncrasy)*, remonstrance, removal, reprimand, reservation *(condition)*, salvo, stricture, variance *(exemption)*. SEE MAIN ENTRY
exception in favor of dispensation *(exception)*
exception to a pleading demurrer
exceptionable blameful, objectionable, peccable, reprehensible, sinister, unacceptable, undesirable
exceptional atypical, best, extraordinary, individual, infrequent, irregular *(not usual)*, notable, noteworthy, novel, original *(creative)*, outstanding *(prominent)*, particular *(specific)*, peculiar *(distinctive)*, portentous *(eliciting amazement)*, preferential, prime *(most valuable)*, prodigious *(amazing)*, rare, remarkable, select, singular, special, specific, sterling, superior *(excellent)*, unaccustomed, uncanny, uncommon, unique, unprecedented, unusual
exceptionality nonconformity
exceptionem facere demur
exceptious fractious, litigious, querulous, restive
excerpere extract
excerpt choose, digest *(summarize)*, extract, part *(portion)*, quote, select. SEE MAIN ENTRY
excerption excerpt
excess balance *(amount in excess)*, boom *(prosperity)*, debauchery, exaggeration, expendable, greed, needless, nonessential, overage, plethora, redundancy, remainder *(estate in property)*, remainder *(remaining part)*, residual, residuary, superfluous, surfeit, surplus, unnecessary, vice. SEE MAIN ENTRY
excessive brutal, disproportionate, drastic, egregious, excess, exorbitant, expendable, extreme *(exaggerated)*, fanatical, gluttonous, gratuitous *(unwarranted)*, harsh, hot-blooded, inflated *(overestimated)*, inordinate, intemperate, needless, onerous, outrageous, prodigal, profuse, rampant, redundant, residuary, superlative, unconscionable, undue *(excessive)*, unendurable, unnecessary, unreasonable, unrestrained *(not repressed)*, unwarranted, usurious. SEE MAIN ENTRY
excessive amount surfeit
excessive burden surcharge
excessive charge premium *(excess value)*, surcharge
excessive demand imposition *(excessive burden)*

excessive drinking dipsomania
excessive interest usury
excessive rate usury
excessive use abuse *(corrupt practice)*, waste
excessively unduly
excessively bold presumptuous
excessively confident presumptuous
excessively critical particular *(exacting)*
excessively frugal parsimonious
excessiveness debauchery, dipsomania, exaggeration, redundancy
exchange barter, business *(commerce)*, change, commerce, communication *(discourse)*, commute, conference, contact *(association)*, conversation, convert *(change use)*, cover *(substitute)*, deal *(noun)*, deal *(verb)*, dealings, displace *(replace)*, finance, handle *(trade)*, interchange, market *(business)*, market place, mercantile, mutuality, novation, quid pro quo, reciprocate, reciprocity, replace, replacement, return *(respond)*, revise, sale, sell, store *(business)*, subrogation, succedaneum, trade *(commerce)*, trade, vary. SEE MAIN ENTRY
exchange blows fight *(battle)*, retaliate
exchange fisticuffs fight *(battle)*
exchange for money liquidate *(convert into cash)*
exchange ideas converse
exchange in commerce handle *(trade)*
exchange letters correspond *(communicate)*
exchange observations confer *(consult)*, consult *(ask advice of)*, counsel, discourse, discuss
exchange of blows fight *(battle)*
exchange of commodities trade *(commerce)*
exchange of letters correspondence *(communication by letters)*
exchange of obligations innovation
exchange of views conversation, discourse, interview, meeting *(conference)*, negotiation, panel *(discussion group)*, parley
exchange opinions discuss, respond, speak
exchange penalties commute
exchange value price
exchange views converse
exchangeable assignable, convertible, correlative, heritable, marketable, negotiable
exchequer treasury
excidere eradicate, extirpate
excipere disqualify, except *(exclude)*, overhear, succeed *(follow)*
excisable ad valorem
excise assess *(tax)*, bowdlerize, cancel, delete, diminish, duty *(tax)*, expunge, imposition *(tax)*, levy, redact, reject, tariff *(duties)*, tax, toll *(tax)*. SEE MAIN ENTRY
exciseman assessor
excision cancellation, expulsion, rejection, removal
excitability passion
excitable demonstrative *(expressive of emotion)*, fractious, hot-blooded, restive, volatile
excitant catalyst, stimulus
excitare evoke, inspire, spirit, stimulate
excitation aggravation *(exacerbation)*, dispatch *(promptness)*, instigation, provocation
excitation of feeling affection
excitation of feelings ardor
excite aggravate *(annoy)*, agitate *(activate)*, bait *(harass)*, bait *(lure)*, discompose, engender, evoke, exacerbate, foment, harass, incense, incite, interest, perturb, prompt, provoke, spirit, stimulate. SEE MAIN ENTRY
excite anger irritate
excite disapprobation brand *(stigmatize)*, denounce *(condemn)*
excite dislike repel *(disgust)*
excite expectation promise *(raise expectations)*
excite hate antagonize
excite hatred incense
excite impatience irritate
excite indignation bait *(harass)*, incense
excite the attention occupy *(engage)*
excited eager, ecstatic, fervent, frenetic, restive, vehement
excitement ardor, commotion, furor, interest *(concern)*, passion, provocation, turmoil. SEE MAIN ENTRY
exciter catalyst, demagogue
exciting moving *(evoking emotion)*, offensive *(taking the initiative)*, provocative, sapid
exciting fear formidable
excitive moving *(evoking emotion)*
exclaim interject, observe *(remark)*, proclaim
exclaim against censure, denounce *(condemn)*, disapprove *(condemn)*, expostulate, inveigh, protest
exclamation confession, proclamation, remark, statement. SEE MAIN ENTRY
exclude abrogate *(rescind)*, ban, block, censor, clog, condemn *(ban)*, debar, deport *(banish)*, discharge *(dismiss)*, dislodge, displace *(remove)*, disqualify, eject *(expel)*, eliminate *(exclude)*, estrange, expatriate, expel, forbid, isolate, omit, outlaw, preclude, preempt, prohibit, proscribe *(prohibit)*, refuse, reject, relegate, remove *(eliminate)*, renounce, repudiate, restrict, screen *(select)*, seclude, select, separate, sequester *(seclude)*. SEE MAIN ENTRY
exclude from inheritance disinherit
exclude from the profession of law disbar
excluded barred, derelict *(abandoned)*, exempt, inadmissible, ineligible, privileged
excludere debar, exclude
excluding omission
exclusio exclusion
exclusion bar *(obstruction)*, blockade *(limitation)*, boycott, control *(restriction)*, deportation, disapprobation, dismissal *(discharge)*, dispensation *(exception)*, disqualification *(rejection)*, disregard *(unconcern)*, expulsion, omission, ostracism, ouster, preemption, prohibition, proscription, refusal, rejection, removal, renunciation, repudiation. SEE MAIN ENTRY
exclusion from commerce embargo
exclusion from favor disgrace
exclusion of entitled owner disseisin
exclusion of workers lockout
exclusionary exclusive *(limited)*
exclusionary rule SEE MAIN ENTRY
exclusive certain *(particular)*, certain *(specific)*, distinctive, only *(sole)*, particular *(individual)*, preferential, private *(not public)*, privy, prohibitive *(restrictive)*, proprietary, restrictive, select, several *(separate)*, singular, specific. SEE MAIN ENTRY
exclusive application diligence *(care)*
exclusive area circuit
exclusive attention diligence *(care)*, obsession
exclusive competition primary
exclusive contest primary
exclusive control monopoly. SEE MAIN ENTRY
exclusive election primary
exclusive license patent
exclusive of save
exclusive political competition primary
exclusive political contest primary
exclusive possession holding *(property owned)*, monopoly
exclusive privilege patent, prerogative
exclusive privilege of publication copyright
exclusive privilege of publication and sale copyright
exclusive privilege to carry on a traffic monopoly
exclusive right monopoly, patent, possession *(ownership)*, prerogative
exclusive right of production copyright
exclusive study diligence *(care)*
exclusive thought diligence *(care)*
exclusive title patent
exclusively only, solely *(singly)*
exclusory exclusive *(limited)*, prohibitive *(restrictive)*
excogitare conjure, contrive, devise *(invent)*, invent *(produce for the first time)*, program
excogitate conceive *(invent)*, conjure, deliberate, frame *(formulate)*, invent *(produce for the first time)*, ponder, rationalize, reason *(conclude)*, reflect *(ponder)*, scheme, study
excogitatio contrivance
excogitation contemplation, deliberation, idea, reflection *(thought)*
excogitative deliberate
excolere develop
excommunicate condemn *(ban)*, debar, eliminate *(exclude)*, exclude, expel, isolate, relegate, seclude
excommunication banishment, expulsion, ostracism, rejection
excorciating caustic
excoriate castigate, censure, denounce *(condemn)*, deprecate, disapprove *(condemn)*, lash *(attack verbally)*, reproach
excoriating scathing
excoriation bad repute, blame *(culpability)*, denunciation, disapprobation
excrescence outgrowth
excrescent superfluous
excrete exude, purge *(purify)*
excruciare harrow
excruciate badger, harass
excruciating caustic, insufferable, painful, severe
exculpable blameless, inculpable, not guilty, palliative *(excusing)*. SEE MAIN ENTRY
exculpate absolve, acquit, clear, discharge *(liberate)*, excuse, exonerate, extenuate, forgive, free, justify, liberate, palliate *(excuse)*, purge *(wipe out by atonement)*, release, remit *(release from penalty)*, vindicate. SEE MAIN ENTRY
exculpated acquitted, blameless, clear *(free from criminal charges)*
exculpating palliative *(excusing)*
exculpation absolution, acquittal, amnesty, compurgation, discharge *(liberation)*, discharge *(release from obligation)*, dispensation *(exception)*, excuse, exoneration, immunity, innocence, justification, liberation, release, remission

exculpatory defensible, mitigating. SEE MAIN ENTRY
exculpatory clause SEE MAIN ENTRY
exculpatory excuse alibi
excurse detour
excursion detour
excursive circuitous, devious, indirect, labyrinthine, tangential
excursus appendix *(supplement)*, digression, discourse, hornbook, pandect *(treatise)*
excusabilis pardonable
excusable allowable, defensible, justifiable, pardonable
excusal condonation, release, waiver
excusare exculpate, excuse, justify
excusatio excuse, justification, plea
excusatory palliative *(excusing)*
excuse absolve, acquit, alibi, clear, clemency, compurgation, condone, cover *(pretext)*, discharge *(release from obligation)*, discharge *(liberate)*, discharge *(release from obligation)*, dispensation *(exception)*, exclude, exculpate, exonerate, exoneration, extenuate, forgive, free, grace, justification, justify, loophole, overlook *(excuse)*, pardon, pretense *(pretext)*, pretext, purge *(wipe out by atonement)*, rationalize, reason *(basis)*, release *(noun)*, release *(verb)*, remit *(release from penalty)*, stratagem, subterfuge, vindicate. SEE MAIN ENTRY
excuse oneself decline *(reject)*
excused clear *(free from criminal charges)*, exempt, free *(relieved from a burden)*, immune, privileged
excuser apologist
excusing mitigating
execrable arrant *(onerous)*, bad *(offensive)*, blameful, blameworthy, contemptible, contemptuous, depraved, diabolic, heinous, loathsome, malignant, nefarious, objectionable, obnoxious, odious, offensive *(offending)*, outrageous, peccant *(culpable)*, repulsive, scandalous
execrableness disrepute
execrate blame, castigate, censure, condemn *(blame)*, contemn, denounce *(condemn)*, proscribe *(denounce)*, reprimand
execration alienation *(estrangement)*, aspersion, blasphemy, condemnation *(blame)*, condemnation *(punishment)*, denunciation, disapprobation, expletive, imprecation, malediction, obloquy, odium, outcry, phillipic, profanity, revilement, slander
execrative profane
execute abide, accomplish, apply *(put in practice)*, certify *(attest)*, close *(agree)*, collect *(recover money)*, commit *(perpetrate)*, compose, conclude *(complete)*, conduct, consummate, countersign, culminate, discharge *(perform)*, dispatch *(dispose of)*, dispatch *(put to death)*, effectuate, enforce, engender, exercise *(discharge a function)*, fabricate *(construct)*, fulfill, function, garnish, generate, handle *(manage)*, implement, impose *(enforce)*, kill *(murder)*, levy, make, manage, obey, observe *(obey)*, officiate, operate, oversee, perfect, perform *(adhere to)*, perpetrate, produce *(manufacture)*, pursue *(carry on)*, render *(administer)*, render *(deliver)*, sign, slay, transact, undertake. SEE MAIN ENTRY
execute a sentence condemn *(punish)*, discipline *(punish)*, penalize
execute judgment discipline *(punish)*, penalize
execute justice condemn *(punish)*, discipline *(punish)*
executed complete *(ended)*, fully executed *(signed)*
executed and delivered writing instrument *(document)*
executed with care accurate
executed with exactness elaborate
executed with proper formalities valid
execution act *(undertaking)*, action *(performance)*, administration, assassination, attachment *(seizure)*, capital punishment, commission *(act)*, consequence *(conclusion)*, course, discharge *(performance)*, dispatch *(act of putting to death)*, distraint, enforcement, fait accompli, finality, fruition, garnishment, infliction, killing, manufacture, operation, realization, sequestration, transaction, treatment. SEE MAIN ENTRY
execution of sentence conviction *(finding of guilt)*
executions dealings
executive administrator, director, employer, official, principal *(director)*. SEE MAIN ENTRY
executive arm management *(supervision)*
executive charge administration
executive committee commission *(agency)*, management *(directorate)*
executive office management *(directorate)*
executive officer official, principal *(director)*
executive privilege SEE MAIN ENTRY
executives authorities, management *(directorate)*, management *(supervision)*
executor director, fiduciary, procurator. SEE MAIN ENTRY
executory SEE MAIN ENTRY
exegesis comment, construction, content *(meaning)*, explanation, note *(brief comment)*
exegetic demonstrative *(illustrative)*, narrative
exegetical demonstrative *(illustrative)*, narrative, solvable
exemplar representative *(example)*, sample, standard. SEE MAIN ENTRY
exemplary absolute *(ideal)*, best, laudable, meritorious, moral, prime *(most valuable)*, professional *(stellar)*, representative, sterling. SEE MAIN ENTRY
exempli gratia cross section
exemplification case *(example)*, clarification, comment, construction, corroboration, cross section, epitome, example, explanation, illustration, instance, sample
exemplify bear *(adduce)*, characterize, cite *(state)*, clarify, comment, define, demonstrate *(establish)*, depict, elucidate, evidence, explain, illustrate, personify, represent *(portray)*, signify *(denote)*. SEE MAIN ENTRY
exemplifying a class typical
exemplum cross section, duplicate, example, exemplar, illustration, instance, model, pattern, precedent, prototype, sample, specimen, tenor, transcript
exempt acquit, clear *(unencumbered)*, clear, condone, discharge *(release from obligation)*, eliminate *(exclude)*, except *(exclude)*, exclude, excuse, forgive, free, immune, palliate *(excuse)*, privileged, purge *(wipe out by atonement)*, release, relieve *(free from burden)*, remit *(release from penalty)*, unbound. SEE MAIN ENTRY
exempt from external authority free *(enjoying civil liberty)*, sovereign *(independent)*
exempted clear *(free from criminal charges)*, exempt, free *(relieved from a burden)*, privileged
exemptible justifiable
exempting palliative *(excusing)*
exemption clause, clemency, condonation, discharge *(liberation)*, discharge *(release from obligation)*, dispensation *(exception)*, exception *(exclusion)*, exclusion, excuse, franchise *(license)*, freedom, grace period, immunity, impunity, leave *(permission)*, privilege, probation, qualification *(condition)*, release, remission, reservation *(condition)*, respite *(reprieve)*, salvo. SEE MAIN ENTRY
exemption from control latitude, liberty, suffrage
exemption from external control freedom, liberty
exemption from judgment impunity
exemption from law dispensation *(exception)*
exemption from penalty impunity
exemption from punishment immunity, impunity, pardon
exemption from restraint freedom, liberty, suffrage
exenterate eviscerate
exercere discipline *(control)*, exercise *(discharge a function)*, plague, ply, practice *(engage in)*
exercise apply *(put in practice)*, campaign, commission *(act)*, discipline *(training)*, employ *(make use of)*, endeavor, exert, exploit *(make use of)*, labor, officiate, operate, ply, practice *(train by repetition)*, problem, resort, transaction, undertaking *(enterprise)*, wield, work *(effort)*. SEE MAIN ENTRY
exercise an option elect *(choose)*
exercise authority command, dictate, direct *(supervise)*, govern, handle *(manage)*, manage, police, prescribe, rule *(govern)*
exercise charge over superintend
exercise critical judgment compare
exercise direction over discipline *(control)*, handle *(manage)*, hold *(possess)*
exercise discretion discern *(discriminate)*, distinguish, elect *(choose)*
exercise discrimination differentiate, distinguish
exercise exclusive rights monopolize
exercise federal authority over federalize *(place under federal control)*
exercise influence lobby, persuade
exercise influence over induce, prejudice *(influence)*, prevail upon
exercise influence upon prejudice *(influence)*, prevail upon
exercise influence with prevail upon
exercise judgment adjudge, gauge, rule *(decide)*
exercise judicial authority adjudicate
exercise of the intellect reflection *(thought)*
exercise of will volition
exercise one's choice cast *(register)*, choose
exercise one's discretion choose
exercise one's option adopt, choose
exercise one's options cast *(register)*
exercise one's preference choose
exercise power over force *(coerce)*, govern, handle *(manage)*, operate
exercise self-control refrain
exercise supervision direct *(supervise)*, preside

exercise supervision over superintend
exercise the function of legislation legislate
exercise the judgment determine
exercise the right of suffrage vote
exercise the will choose
exercising commission *(act)*
exercising reason rational
exercitatio practice *(procedure)*
exercitation course, use
exert apply *(put in practice)*, expend *(consume)*, operate, wield. SEE MAIN ENTRY
exert authority federalize *(place under federal control)*, govern, handle *(manage)*, police, rule *(govern)*
exert effort endeavor
exert energy labor
exert federal control federalize *(place under federal control)*
exert influence affect, constrain *(compel)*, convince, incite, inspire, lobby, motivate, persuade, prejudice *(influence)*
exert one's energies strive
exert oneself attempt, endeavor, labor, persevere, strive, try *(attempt)*
exert oneself for pursue *(strive to gain)*
exert pressure bait *(lure)*, coax, incite, insist, lobby
exert pressure on browbeat
exertion campaign, effort, endeavor, industry *(activity)*, pressure, pursuit *(effort to secure)*, stress *(strain)*, struggle, work *(effort)*
exhale emit
exhaurire exhaust *(try all possibilities)*
exhaust conclude *(complete)*, consume, debilitate, deplete, disable, dissipate *(expend foolishly)*, emit, expend *(consume)*, outlet, outpour, overdraw, spend. SEE MAIN ENTRY
exhausted inadequate, languid, lost *(taken away)*, otiose, powerless, unproductive, unsound *(not strong)*, vacant, vacuous
exhaustible destructible
exhausting operose, oppressive
exhaustion consumption, decrement, impuissance, insufficiency, privation, prostration, waste, wear and tear
exhaustive absolute *(complete)*, complete *(all-embracing)*, comprehensive, definitive, detailed, full, gross *(total)*, inclusive, intensive, omnibus, outright, plenary, radical *(extreme)*, thorough, unmitigated. SEE MAIN ENTRY
exhaustive inquiry analysis, examination *(study)*, hearing, indagation, judgment *(discernment)*
exhaustive study indagation, investigation, probe
exhaustive tract pandect *(treatise)*
exhaustiveness entirety
exhaustless infallible, infinite, innumerable
exheredare disinherit
exhibere exhibit
exhibit bare, bear *(adduce)*, brandish, cite *(state)*, demonstrate *(establish)*, denude, depict, disclose, disinter, display, document, documentation, evidence, evince, exemplify, expose, expression *(manifestation)*, flaunt, illustrate, manifest, manifestation, present *(introduce)*, produce *(offer to view)*, propound, unveil. SEE MAIN ENTRY
exhibit boastfully flaunt
exhibit hostile intentions menace
exhibit in visible form embody
exhibit the differences between contrast
exhibited palpable
exhibiting equity equitable
exhibiting lust lewd
exhibiting pros and cons controversial
exhibiting purpose pertinacious
exhibition exhibit, expression *(manifestation)*, manifestation, performance *(workmanship)*
exhibitionistic histrionic
exhibits evidence
exhibits submitted to jury evidence
exhilarate spirit
exhilaration ardor, enjoyment *(pleasure)*
exhort admonish *(advise)*, admonish *(warn)*, advocate, agitate *(activate)*, bait *(harass)*, bait *(lure)*, caution, charge *(instruct on the law)*, coax, coerce, confer *(consult)*, enjoin, forewarn, incite, insist, motivate, notify, persuade, press *(beseech)*, pressure, prevail upon, prompt, recommend, remonstrate, spirit, urge. SEE MAIN ENTRY
exhort against dissuade, expostulate, protest
exhort to take heed caution
exhortation admonition, caution *(warning)*, charge *(statement to the jury)*, direction *(guidance)*, discourse, guidance, harangue, inducement, instigation, monition *(warning)*, persuasion, pressure, proposal *(suggestion)*, recommendation, remonstrance, rhetoric *(skilled speech)*, suggestion
exhortative hortative
exhortatory hortative
exhume disinter, remove *(eliminate)*
exigence exigency
exigency coercion, cornerstone, demand, desideratum, emergency, necessity, need *(deprivation)*, paucity, poverty, predicament, prerequisite, pressure, priority, quagmire, requirement, situation, stress *(strain)*. SEE MAIN ENTRY
exigent astringent, compulsory, critical *(crucial)*, crucial, essential *(required)*, grave *(important)*, imperative, important *(urgent)*, indispensable, insistent, mandatory, necessary *(required)*, obligatory, particular *(exacting)*, peremptory *(imperative)*, requisite, severe, stringent, uncompromising, urgent. SEE MAIN ENTRY
exigere expel, require *(compel)*
exiguitas insignificance
exiguity dearth, insufficiency, paucity
exiguous minimal, slight
exiguousness dearth, insufficiency
exiguus inconsiderable, slight
exile asylum *(hiding place)*, banishment, bar *(exclude)*, deport *(banish)*, deportation, depose *(remove)*, derelict, dislodge, displace *(remove)*, eliminate *(exclude)*, exclude, exclusion, expatriate, expel, expulsion, isolate, ostracism, pariah, rejection, relegate, removal, seclude, transport. SEE MAIN ENTRY
exilement banishment, deportation, ostracism, rejection
eximere except *(exclude)*, exclude, free
eximious illustrious, outstanding *(prominent)*
eximius special, superlative
exire issue *(send forth)*
exist continue *(persevere)*, endure *(last)*, last, lie *(be sustainable)*, remain *(continue)*, subsist. SEE MAIN ENTRY
exist together coincide *(correspond)*, concur *(coexist)*
exist uninterruptedly endure *(last)*
exist widely prevail *(be in force)*
exist without break endure *(last)*
existence entity, life *(period of existence)*, materiality *(physical existence)*, reality, survival. SEE MAIN ENTRY
existenceless nonentity
existent actual, bodily, concrete, conscious *(awake)*, corporeal, current, de facto, extant, instant, live *(conscious)*, live *(existing)*, present *(current)*, substantial, substantive
existent thing fact
existimatio character *(reputation)*, honor *(good reputation)*
existing actual, bodily, certain *(positive)*, concrete, conscious *(awake)*, current, de facto, definite, extant, live *(conscious)*, present *(current)*, substantial, substantive
existing as an independent entity autonomous *(independent)*
existing conditions status quo
existing for a short time ephemeral
existing from birth innate
existing in equity equitable
existing in fact de facto
existing state case *(set of circumstances)*, posture *(situation)*, status quo
exit alight, depart, disappear, egress, emerge, evacuate, issuance, issue *(send forth)*, leave *(depart)*, move *(alter position)*, outlet, quit *(evacuate)*, vacate *(leave)*. SEE MAIN ENTRY
exitialis deadly, fatal, lethal
exitiosus pernicious
exitus egress, end *(termination)*, event, outlet, result
exodus egress, flight, outflow
exomologesis confession
exonerate absolve, acquit, clear, condone, discharge *(liberate)*, discharge *(release from obligation)*, disencumber, exculpate, excuse, extenuate, extricate, forgive, free, justify, liberate, palliate *(excuse)*, pardon, quit *(free of)*, release, remit *(release from penalty)*, vindicate. SEE MAIN ENTRY
exonerated acquitted, blameless, clear *(free from criminal charges)*, free *(relieved from a burden)*
exonerating circumstance justification
exonerating fact justification
exoneration absolution, acquittal, amnesty, compurgation, condonation, discharge *(liberation)*, discharge *(release from obligation)*, dispensation *(exception)*, excuse, innocence, justification, liberation, pardon, release, remission. SEE MAIN ENTRY
exorabilis placable
exorable charitable *(lenient)*, lenient, placable
exorare prevail upon
exorbitance boom *(prosperity)*, exaggeration, plethora
exorbitancy boom *(prosperity)*, exaggeration, plethora
exorbitant excess, excessive, extreme *(exaggerated)*, grandiose, inordinate, intemperate, needless, outrageous, profuse, prohibitive *(costly)*, unconscionable, undue *(excessive)*, unreasonable, usurious. SEE MAIN ENTRY
exorbitant interest usury
exorbitantly unduly
exordial preliminary
exordium birth *(beginning)*

exordium genesis, inception, onset *(commencement)*, origination, outset, overture
exordium preamble
exordium preface, prelude, start
exornare embellish, garnish
exoteric coherent *(clear)*, comprehensible, obvious, pellucid, perceivable, public *(known)*
exoterical coherent *(clear)*, obvious
exotic nonconforming, unaccustomed, uncommon
expand accrue *(increase)*, accumulate *(enlarge)*, amplify, build *(augment)*, compound, declaim, deploy, develop, elaborate, enhance, extend *(enlarge)*, heighten *(augment)*, increase, inflate, magnify, overestimate, parlay *(exploit successfully)*, progress, spread, supplement. SEE MAIN ENTRY
expand on comment
expand upon develop
expanded capacious, extensive, inflated *(enlarged)*
expanding cumulative *(increasing)*
expange deface
expanse area *(province)*, area *(surface)*, caliber *(measurement)*, coverage *(scope)*, degree *(magnitude)*, extent, latitude, scope, space, territory
expansion accession *(enlargement)*, advance *(increase)*, advancement *(improvement)*, area *(surface)*, augmentation, bombast, boom *(increase)*, boom *(prosperity)*, development *(progression)*, distortion, exaggeration, growth *(evolution)*, growth *(increase)*, increment, inflation *(increase)*, latitude, overstatement, prosperity. SEE MAIN ENTRY
expansive ample, broad, capacious, complete *(all-embracing)*, comprehensive, ext-ensive, omnibus, open-ended, voluble
exparte one-sided
expatiate declaim, digress, discourse, enlarge
expatiate on expand
expatiation harangue
expatriate alien, deport *(banish)*, dislodge, displace *(remove)*, eliminate *(exclude)*, exclude, expel, pariah, relegate, seclude. SEE MAIN ENTRY
expatriate oneself abscond, depart
expatriation banishment, deportation, exclusion, expulsion, immigration, ostracism, rejection
expect intend, plan, presume, presuppose, trust. SEE MAIN ENTRY
expectable deductible *(provable)*
expectance contemplation, expectation, likelihood, possibility, prospect *(outlook)*
expectancy claim *(right)*, expectation, likelihood, possibility, prospect *(outlook)*, remainder *(estate in property)*
expectant pending *(imminent)*, preparatory, prospective, ready *(prepared)*, sanguine. SEE MAIN ENTRY
expectare expect *(anticipate)*
expectation belief *(something believed)*, belief *(state of mind)*, contemplation, design *(intent)*, end *(intent)*, likelihood, objective, possibility, probability, prospect *(outlook)*, purpose, reliance. SEE MAIN ENTRY
expectations heritage
expected apparent *(presumptive)*, customary, foreseeable, forseen, forthcoming, future, habitual, immediate *(imminent)*, imminent, necessary *(inescapable)*, ordinary, potential, prospective, proximate, regular *(conventional)*, routine, usual
expedience advantage, behalf, feasibility, pragmatism, propriety *(appropriateness)*, qualification *(fitness)*. SEE MAIN ENTRY
expediency artifice, benefit *(betterment)*, boom *(prosperity)*, expedience, feasibility, pragmatism, propriety *(appropriateness)*
expedient appropriate, convenient, due *(regular)*, effective *(efficient)*, efficient, favorable *(advantageous)*, fitting, functional, help, instrumentality, loophole, medium, necessary *(required)*, opportune, plan, politic, practical, pragmatic, profitable, propitious, requisite, resource, seasonable, step, stopgap, stratagem, suitable, viable. SEE MAIN ENTRY
expediential practical
expediousness dispatch *(promptness)*
expedire disengage, disentangle, expedite, explain, extricate, facilitate, solve
expedite conduce, dispatch *(send off)*, ease, facilitate, hasten, help, precipitate *(hasten)*. SEE MAIN ENTRY
expedited determination accelerated judgment
expedited judgment accelerated judgment
expedition acceleration, advance *(progression)*, campaign
expédition dispatch *(promptness)*
expedition haste, quest
expeditious alert *(agile)*, efficient, instantaneous, prompt, punctual, rapid, ready *(willing)*, summary. SEE MAIN ENTRY
expeditious performance acceleration, dispatch *(promptness)*
expeditiously as soon as feasible, instantly
expeditiousness haste
expel condemn *(ban)*, delete, deport *(banish)*, depose *(remove)*, discharge *(dismiss)*, discharge *(shoot)*, dislocate, dislodge, dismiss *(discharge)*, dispel, displace *(remove)*, dispossess, distill, divest, eject *(evict)*, eliminate *(exclude)*, emit, evict, exclude, expatriate, jettison, luxate, oust, outlaw, outpour, precipitate *(throw down violently)*, project *(impel forward)*, purge *(purify)*, reject, relegate, remove *(dismiss from office)*, supplant, transport. SEE MAIN ENTRY
expel from the bar disbar
expel from the legal profession disbar
expelled ineligible
expellere dislodge, eject *(expel)*, expel
expelling expulsion
expend bear the expense, consume, defray, deplete, disburse *(pay out)*, dissipate *(expend foolishly)*, emit, exert, exhaust *(deplete)*, pay, spend. SEE MAIN ENTRY
expend gradually conserve
expend slowly conserve
expendable disposable, minor, needless, negligible, nonessential, null *(insignificant)*, otiose, petty, superfluous, unnecessary. SEE MAIN ENTRY
expended irredeemable
expendere consider, expend *(disburse)*
expenditure advance *(allowance)*, charge *(cost)*, collection *(payment)*, consumption, cost *(expenses)*, decrement, disbursement *(funds paid out)*, expense *(cost)*, fee *(charge)*, finance, maintenance *(upkeep)*, outflow, outlay, payment *(act of paying)*, payment *(remittance)*, price, remittance, waste. SEE MAIN ENTRY
expenditure of energy effort
expenditures bill *(invoice)*, overhead
expense charge *(cost)*, disbursement *(funds paid out)*, expenditure, fare, fee *(charge)*, maintenance *(upkeep)*, outflow, outlay, overhead, payment *(remittance)*, price, rate, value, worth. SEE MAIN ENTRY
expense of transportation fare
expense outlay binder
expenseless free *(at no charge)*, gratis, gratuitous *(given without recompense)*
expenses bill *(invoice)*, damages, expenditure, out of pocket
expensive exorbitant, invaluable, priceless, prohibitive *(costly)*, valuable. SEE MAIN ENTRY
expensiveness cost *(price)*
expensum debit
experience bear *(tolerate)*, common knowledge, common sense, competence *(ability)*, discern *(detect with the senses)*, endure *(suffer)*, event, fact, happening, incident, information *(knowledge)*, occasion, occurrence, partake, particular, perceive, phenomenon *(unusual occurrence)*, skill, test. SEE MAIN ENTRY
experience a loss lose *(be deprived of)*
experience loss suffer *(sustain loss)*
experience unpleasantly endure *(suffer)*
experienced artful, competent, expert, familiar *(informed)*, learned, practiced, professional *(trained)*, proficient, qualified *(competent)*, resourceful, veteran
experienced hand expert
experienced person expert, professional, specialist
experienced personnel expert
experienced view common sense
experientia experience *(background)*
experiment check *(inspect)*, endeavor *(noun)*, endeavor *(verb)*, research, test, venture. SEE MAIN ENTRY
experimental probative, speculative, tentative
experimental method trial *(experiment)*
experimentation research
experimentee subject *(object)*
experimenter speculator
experimentum experiment, trial *(experiment)*
expers corporis immaterial
expert capable, cognizant, competent, deft, efficient, familiar *(informed)*, informed *(educated)*, learned, mastermind, practiced, professional *(trained)*, professional, proficient, qualified *(competent)*, specialist, subtle *(refined)*, veteran *(adjective)*, veteran *(noun)*. SEE MAIN ENTRY
expertise comprehension, experience *(background)*, facility *(easiness)*, faculty *(ability)*, gift *(flair)*, knowledge *(learning)*, prowess *(ability)*, specialty *(special aptitude)*. SEE MAIN ENTRY
expertness discretion *(quality of being discreet)*, efficiency, experience *(background)*, facility *(easiness)*, faculty *(ability)*, gift *(flair)*, performance *(workmanship)*, prowess *(ability)*, science *(technique)*, skill, specialty *(special aptitude)*
expetere desire
expiable justifiable, pardonable
expiate redeem *(satisfy debts)*, redress, repent
expiating compensatory, palliative *(excusing)*
expiatio expiation

expiation condonation, damages, reparation *(indemnification)*, restitution. SEE MAIN ENTRY
expiatory compensatory, penitent
expilare hold up *(rob)*, plunder
expilatio pillage, spoliation
expiration cessation *(termination)*, close *(conclusion)*, death, defeasance, demise *(death)*, dissolution *(termination)*, end *(termination)*, extremity *(death)*, finality. SEE MAIN ENTRY
expire cease, close *(terminate)*, decease, die, discontinue *(abandon)*, dissolve *(terminate)*, lapse *(cease)*, perish, stop, succumb, terminate. SEE MAIN ENTRY
expired back *(in arrears)*, dead, defunct, lifeless *(dead)*, obsolete, outdated, outmoded
expiring in extremis
expiry end *(termination)*, expiration, finality, lapse *(expiration)*
explain annunciate, argue, clarify, comment, construe *(comprehend)*, construe *(translate)*, convey *(communicate)*, define, depict, describe, detail *(particularize)*, discourse, discuss, educate, elucidate, enlighten, enunciate, explicate, exposit, expound, illustrate, inform *(notify)*, instruct *(teach)*, interject, interpret, justify, manifest, rationalize, reason *(persuade)*, respond, reveal, review, simplify *(clarify)*, solve, speak, specify, support *(justify)*, trace *(delineate)*. SEE MAIN ENTRY
explain away negate, rationalize
explain incorrectly misinterpret
explain the meaning interpret
explain the nature of define
explain wrongly misrepresent
explainable ascertainable, determinable *(ascertainable)*, solvable
explained coherent *(clear)*
explanare elucidate, explain, interpret
explanatio explanation
explanation alibi, answer *(solution)*, clarification, comment, construction, content *(meaning)*, definition, description, disclosure *(something disclosed)*, education, illustration, instruction *(teaching)*, justification, meaning, pandect *(treatise)*, paraphrase, rationale, reason *(basis)*, recital, rendition *(explication)*, representation *(statement)*, response, restatement, signification, solution *(answer)*, statement. SEE MAIN ENTRY
explanation for some delinquency excuse
explanatory coherent *(clear)*, declaratory, demonstrative *(illustrative)*, descriptive, explicit, informative, informatory, interpretive, narrative. SEE MAIN ENTRY
explanatory comment note *(brief comment)*
explanatory note comment
explanatory remark note *(brief comment)*
explere fulfill
expletio satisfaction *(fulfilment)*
expletive blasphemy, expendable, imprecation, needless, surplus, unnecessary. SEE MAIN ENTRY
explicability construction
explicable accountable *(explainable)*, cognizable, coherent *(clear)*, comprehensible, determinable *(ascertainable)*, scrutable. SEE MAIN ENTRY
explicare clear, deploy, describe, disentangle, evolve, explicate, spread
explicate clarify, comment, construe *(translate)*, depict, elucidate, enlighten, exemplify, explain, exposit, expound, interpret. SEE MAIN ENTRY
explicatio analysis, development *(progression)*, explanation, solution *(answer)*
explication clarification, comment, construction, content *(meaning)*, definition, explanation, illustration, paraphrase, rationale, solution *(answer)*
explicative demonstrative *(illustrative)*, informative, informatory, interpretive, narrative, solvable
explicators of the law judiciary
explicatory coherent *(clear)*, demonstrative *(illustrative)*, descriptive, informative, informatory, narrative, solvable. SEE MAIN ENTRY
explicit absolute *(conclusive)*, accurate, apparent *(perceptible)*, candid, certain *(specific)*, clear *(apparent)*, cognizable, coherent *(clear)*, comprehensible, concrete, demonstrative *(illustrative)*, detailed, direct *(forthright)*, distinct *(clear)*, evident, exact, express, informative, lucid, manifest, naked *(perceptible)*, obvious, ostensible, overt, palpable, pellucid, perceivable, perceptible, positive *(incontestable)*, precise, resounding, salient, scrutable, specific, trenchant, unambiguous, unequivocal, unmistakable. SEE MAIN ENTRY
explicit utterance declaration
explicitly fairly *(clearly)*
explode discharge *(shoot)*, rebut, refute
exploit bilk, capitalize *(seize the chance)*, employ *(make use of)*, endeavor, manipulate *(control unfairly)*, operation, ply, transaction. SEE MAIN ENTRY
exploitable disposable, naive
exploitation abuse *(corrupt practice)*, function, graft, misusage, use, usury. SEE MAIN ENTRY
exploitative immoral, mercenary
explorare ascertain, spy
exploration analysis, cross-examination, cross-questioning, discovery, examination *(study)*, indagation, inquiry *(request for information)*, inquiry *(systematic investigation)*, inspection, interrogation, investigation, probe, quest, question *(inquiry)*, research, scrutiny, test, trial *(experiment)*
explorator spy
exploratory interrogative, precursory, probative, tentative
exploratory examination indagation, probe
explore analyze, canvass, check *(inspect)*, delve, examine *(study)*, find *(discover)*, frisk, hunt, inquire, investigate, peruse, probe, research, scrutinize, search, study. SEE MAIN ENTRY
explorer pioneer
explosion discharge *(shot)*, outbreak, outburst, outcry, passion, repercussion, salvo, violence. SEE MAIN ENTRY
explosions barrage
explosive ammunition, bomb, dangerous, disorderly, vehement, volatile. SEE MAIN ENTRY
explosive device bomb
exponent abettor, advocate *(espouser)*, amicus curiae, apologist, backer, example, exemplar, illustration, indicant, indication, proponent, specimen, symbol. SEE MAIN ENTRY
exponere elucidate, exhibit, explain, expose, recite
export displace *(remove)*, outflow, remove *(eliminate)*, send
export and import deal
exportation outflow
exporter dealer
exposcere dun, insist
expose accuse, admit *(concede)*, bare, bear *(adduce)*, betray *(disclose)*, clarify
exposé common knowledge
expose confess, contemn, convey *(communicate)*, debunk, denigrate, denude
exposé denunciation
expose detect, disabuse, disclose. SEE MAIN ENTRY
exposé disclosure *(something disclosed)*
expose discover, dishonor *(deprive of honor)*, disinter, divulge, emerge, endanger, evidence, exhibit, find *(discover)*, impeach, implicate, incriminate, inform *(betray)*, issue *(publish)*, locate, manifest, manifestation, pillory, produce *(offer to view)*, publish, report *(disclose)*, reveal, subject, unveil. SEE MAIN ENTRY
expose onself to incur
expose to danger compromise *(endanger)*, endanger, jeopardize
expose to infamy humiliate, pillory, smear
expose to injury endanger
expose to loss endanger
expose to public contempt libel
expose to view bare, disinter, manifest, present *(introduce)*
exposed aleatory *(perilous)*, apparent *(perceptible)*, blatant *(conspicuous)*, bleak *(exposed and barren)*, conspicuous, evident, helpless *(defenseless)*, indefensible, insecure, manifest, naked *(perceptible)*, obvious, open *(in sight)*, overt, patent, perceivable, perceptible, precarious, susceptible *(unresistent)*, untenable, vulnerable
exposed to liable
exposed to penalty liable
exposed to risk aleatory *(perilous)*, dangerous, insecure
exposed to view conspicuous, distinct *(clear)*, open *(in sight)*, patent, perceivable, perceptible
exposit clarify, construe *(translate)*, elucidate, expound. SEE MAIN ENTRY
exposit on comment
expositer apologist
expositio description, narration, publication *(disclosure)*
exposition body *(main part)*, clarification, comment, construction, content *(meaning)*, declaration, disclosure *(act of disclosing)*, disclosure *(something disclosed)*, discourse, discovery, exhibit, explanation, expression *(manifestation)*, hornbook, illustration, instruction *(teaching)*, justification, manifestation, market place, narration, pandect *(treatise)*, rationale, recital, report *(detailed account)*, review *(critical evaluation)*, solution *(answer)*, statement
expositive descriptive, informative, informatory, narrative
expository declaratory, demonstrative *(illustrative)*, descriptive, didactic, informative, informatory, narrative, solvable. SEE MAIN ENTRY
expostulate admonish *(warn)*, argue, blame, castigate, censure, charge *(accuse)*, counsel, demonstrate *(protest)*, discourage, forewarn, reason *(persuade)*, remonstrate, reprehend, urge. SEE MAIN ENTRY
expostulation admonition, blame *(culpability)*, complaint, condemnation *(blame)*,

criticism, disapprobation, dissent *(difference of opinion)*, guidance, objection, objurgation, remonstrance. SEE MAIN ENTRY
expostulative hortative
expostulatory hortative, remonstrative
exposure admission *(disclosure)*, bad repute, detection, disclosure *(act of disclosing)*, discovery, expression *(manifestation)*, impeachment, manifestation, publicity, risk. SEE MAIN ENTRY
exposure to danger peril, pitfall
exposure to destruction peril
exposure to harm danger, peril, pitfall, risk
exposure to injury peril
exposure to loss peril
expound clarify, comment, construe *(translate)*, declaim, define, describe, discourse, elucidate, enlighten, explain, explicate, exposit, illustrate, instruct *(teach)*, interpret, reason *(persuade)*, remark, report *(disclose)*, speak. SEE MAIN ENTRY
expounder advocate *(espouser)*, apologist, pedagogue
expounding comment, construction, explanation
express absolute *(conclusive)*, acknowledge *(declare)*, advise, affirm *(claim)*, allege, annunciate, apparent *(perceptible)*, argue, assert, avow, bear *(adduce)*, bespeak, candid, causeway, certain *(specific)*, cite *(state)*, clear *(apparent)*, coherent *(clear)*, comment, communicate, compose, comprehensible, connote, construe *(translate)*, contend *(maintain)*, convey *(communicate)*, declaratory, definite, denote, depict, designate, display, distinct *(clear)*, enunciate, evident, exact, exemplify, exhibit, expeditious, explicit, frame *(formulate)*, interject, lucid, manifest *(adjective)*, manifest *(verb)*, mention, naked *(perceptible)*, observe *(remark)*, ostensible, overt, particular *(specific)*, pellucid, perceivable, perceptible, peremptory *(absolute)*, phrase, portray, posit, precise, pronounce *(speak)*, publish, purport, rapid, recite, relate *(tell)*, remark, report *(disclose)*, signify *(inform)*, speak, specific, specify, testify, unambiguous, unmistakable, utter. SEE MAIN ENTRY
express a wish to obtain desire
express agreement quid pro quo
express an objection object
express an opinion evaluate, opine
express annoyance resent
express briefly indicate
express concurrence assent, grant *(concede)*
express deep grief for deplore
express disagreement demonstrate *(pro-test)*
express disapproval demonstrate *(protest)*, except *(object)*, object, remonstrate
express displeasure reproach
express dissatisfaction criticize *(find fault with)*, demonstrate *(protest)*
express generally indicate
express highway causeway
express ill will resent
express in a formula formulate
express in a systematic way formulate
express in concrete form embody
express in fuller form expand
express in precise form formulate
express opposition protest
express permission charter *(license)*
express precisely characterize
express shipper carrier
express sympathy sympathize
expressage consignment
expressed certain *(specific)*, oral, parol, stated, verbal
expressed command law
expressed concisely compact *(pithy)*
expressed desire request
expressed in few words succinct
expressed in words nuncupative, oral
expressed in writing in writing
expressed indirectly implied
expressed meaning definition
expressed opinion expression *(comment)*
expressed outright explicit
expressed solely by speech parol
expressing disdain contemptuous
expressing entreaty precatory
expression admission *(disclosure)*, assertion, call *(title)*, comment, connotation, creation, declaration, demeanor, disclosure *(something disclosed)*, inflection, language, manifestation, maxim, mention *(reference)*, parlance, phraseology, pronouncement, remark, rhetoric *(skilled speech)*, speech, style, testimony, token. SEE MAIN ENTRY
expression of choice referendum
expression of contrary opinions fight *(argument)*
expression of conviction testament
expression of disapproval reaction *(opposition)*
expression of discontent plaint
expression of grief plaint
expression of ideas phraseology
expression of merit mention *(tribute)*
expression of opinion observation
expression of opinion for or against argument *(pleading)*
expression of pain plaint
expression of satisfaction approval
expression of views discourse
expression of will poll *(casting of votes)*
expressionless inexpressive, inscrutable, vacuous
expressions indicia
expressive clear *(apparent)*, coherent *(clear)*, declaratory, demonstrative *(expressive of emotion)*, demonstrative *(illustrative)*, eloquent, informative, moving *(evoking emotion)*, sententious, suggestive *(evocative)*. SEE MAIN ENTRY
expressive of opinion advisory
expressly faithfully, particularly, purposely
expressway causeway
exprimere express, extort, force *(coerce)*, represent *(portray)*
exprobate contemn, deprecate, remonstrate, reprehend
exprobation blame *(culpability)*
exprobrate lash *(attack verbally)*, rebuke, reprimand, reproach
exprobratio reproach
exprobration obloquy, remonstrance, reprimand, reproach, revilement
exprobrative remonstrative
exprobratory remonstrative
expropriate abridge *(divest)*, annex *(arrogate)*, assume *(seize)*, attach *(seize)*, carry away, condemn *(seize)*, confiscate, convert *(misappropriate)*, deprive, dislodge, displace *(remove)*, dispossess, divest, hijack, impress *(procure by force)*, occupy *(take possession)*, plagiarize, seize *(confiscate)*. SEE MAIN ENTRY
expropriated attached *(seized)*
expropriation appropriation *(taking)*, assumption *(seizure)*, attachment *(seizure)*, condemnation *(seizure)*, disseisin, distraint, distress *(seizure)*, foreclosure, forfeiture *(act of forfeiting)*, garnishment, taking. SEE MAIN ENTRY
expropriatory confiscatory
expugnable helpless *(defenseless)*
expulsio expulsion
expulsion banishment, deportation, discharge *(dismissal)*, dismissal *(discharge)*, disqualification *(rejection)*, eviction, exception *(exclusion)*, exclusion, expropriation *(divestiture)*, foreclosure, layoff, ostracism, outburst, outflow, rejection, removal. SEE MAIN ENTRY
expulsion of a fetus abortion *(feticide)*
expunction cancellation, dissolution *(termination)*
expunge annul, bowdlerize, cancel, censor, delete, destroy *(efface)*, edit, eliminate *(eradicate)*, eradicate, excise *(cut away)*, expurgate, extinguish, obliterate, redact, remove *(eliminate)*, revoke. SEE MAIN ENTRY
expunge the record of pardon
expurgare excuse, expurgate
expurgate bowdlerize, censor, censure, diminish, eliminate *(eradicate)*, eradicate, excise *(cut away)*, purge *(purify)*. SEE MAIN ENTRY
expurgated pure. SEE MAIN ENTRY
expurgation censorship
exquisite attractive, elegant, prime *(most valuable)*, rare. SEE MAIN ENTRY
exquisitus recondite, select
exsanguis lifeless *(dull)*
exsecratio imprecation, malediction
exsect eviscerate
exsection evulsion
exsequi enforce
exsistere appear *(materialize)*, exist
exsolvere disburse *(pay out)*, disentangle, extricate, pay, release, rescue
exspectatio expectation
exspirare expire
exspiratio expiration
exspoliare rob
exstare exist, extant
exstinguere abolish, suppress
exstirpare eradicate, extirpate
exsuperare surmount, transcend
extant conscious *(awake)*, live *(existing)*, present *(current)*. SEE MAIN ENTRY
extemperaneous unexpected
extemplo instantly
extemporal spontaneous
extemporaneous ad hoc, impulsive *(rash)*, informal, spontaneous, unpremeditated. SEE MAIN ENTRY
extemporaneousness informality
extemporary impulsive *(rash)*, spontaneous
extempore informal, spontaneous, unexpected, unpremeditated
extend accrue *(increase)*, accumulate *(enlarge)*, administer *(tender)*, amplify, append, bestow, build *(augment)*, compound, continue *(prolong)*, defer *(put off)*, deploy, develop, dwell *(linger over)*, endure *(last)*, enhance, enlarge, expand, increase, inflate, keep *(continue)*, lie *(be sustainable)*, magnify, offer *(tender)*, postpone, present *(make a gift)*, proceed *(go forward)*, proffer, prolong, protract *(stall)*, remain *(continue)*, spread, stay *(continue)*, submit *(give)*, sustain *(prolong)*, tender. SEE MAIN ENTRY

extend beyond overlap, overreach
extend citizenship to an alien naturalize *(make a citizen)*
extend credit capitalize *(provide capital)*, lend, loan
extend in duration continue *(prolong)*
extend over overreach
extend through pervade
extend to abut, border *(bound)*, reach
extended broad, capacious, chronic, comprehensive, continuous, extensive, far reaching, inflated *(enlarged)*, liberal *(not literal)*, prolix, prominent, protracted
extended meaning context
extendere expand, extend *(enlarge)*, prolong
extending broad, cumulative *(intensifying)*, extensive
extension accession *(enlargement)*, accretion, addition, additive, adjournment, adjunct, advance *(increase)*, appendix *(accession)*, appurtenance, augmentation, boom *(increase)*, continuance, continuation *(prolongation)*, deferment, development *(progression)*, growth *(increase)*, increment, inflation *(increase)*, insertion, latitude, magnitude, offshoot, organ, rider, stress *(strain)*, survival. SEE MAIN ENTRY
extension in time duration
extension of credit loan
extension of time deferment
extensive ample, broad, capacious, complete *(all-embracing)*, comprehensive, far reaching, general, inclusive, major, material *(important)*, omnibus, predominant, prevailing *(current)*, prevalent, rife, thorough. SEE MAIN ENTRY
extensive flood cataclysm
extensively generally, throughout *(all over)*
extent amount *(quantity)*, caliber *(measurement)*, capacity *(maximum)*, capacity *(sphere)*, circuit, configuration *(confines)*, degree *(magnitude)*, duration, gamut, magnitude, mass *(weight)*, measurement, purview, quota, range, scope, space, time. SEE MAIN ENTRY
extent of authority jurisdiction
extent of surface area *(surface)*
extent of the court's authority judicature
extent of view coverage *(scope)*
extents confines
extenuare attenuate, decrease, disparage, qualify *(condition)*
extenuate alleviate, attenuate, dilute, diminish, ease, excuse, lessen, modify *(moderate)*, palliate *(excuse)*. SEE MAIN ENTRY
extenuating mitigating, palliative *(excusing)*
extenuating circumstances SEE MAIN ENTRY
extenuation clemency, condonation, exc-use, extenuating circumstances, justification, reason *(basis)*
extenuative palliative *(excusing)*
exterior extrinsic, peripheral, periphery, semblance, specious, superficial
exterminate abate *(extinguish)*, abolish, annul, cancel, destroy *(efface)*, dispatch *(put to death)*, eliminate *(eradicate)*, eradicate, extinguish, extirpate, kill *(murder)*, obliterate, overthrow, remove *(eliminate)*, slay
exterminated lost *(taken away)*
extermination abatement *(extinguishment)*, aberemurder, abolition, dispatch *(act of putting to death)*, homicide, killing, removal
exterminative dire, disastrous, fatal
exterminatory disastrous
external alien *(foreign)*, extrinsic, peripheral, physical, specious, superficial. SEE MAIN ENTRY
external appearance color *(deceptive appearance)*, complexion, feature *(appearance)*
external aspect appearance *(look)*
external form configuration *(form)*, outline *(boundary)*
externalize perceive
externus foreign
exterrere frighten
extinct dead, defunct, lifeless *(dead)*, null *(invalid)*, null and void, obsolete, outdated, outmoded. SEE MAIN ENTRY
extinction aberemurder, abolition, ademption, cancellation, catastrophe, death, demise *(death)*, destruction, dissolution *(termination)*, end *(termination)*, extremity *(death)*, mortality, prostration, subversion
extinction of a debt amortization
extinguere extinguish
extinguish abolish, annul, cancel, cease, destroy *(efface)*, destroy *(void)*, disappear, eradicate, expunge, extirpate, inhibit, kill *(defeat)*, obliterate, quash, stifle, strangle, subvert, suppress. SEE MAIN ENTRY
extinguish indebtedness liquidate *(determine liability)*
extinguish visual discernment blind *(deprive of sight)*
extinguishable destructible
extinguished dead, lost *(taken away)*, null *(invalid)*, null and void
extinguishment abolition, death, demise *(death)*, deterrence, dissolution *(termination)*, end *(termination)*, extremity *(death)*
extinguishment of claim amortization
extirpate abolish, bowdlerize, delete, destroy *(efface)*, eliminate *(eradicate)*, eradicate, expunge, extinguish, obliterate, overthrow, quash, redact, reject, remove *(eliminate)*, subvert, supplant. SEE MAIN ENTRY
extirpated lost *(taken away)*
extirpation abolition, destruction, dissolution *(termination)*, evulsion, rejection, removal, subversion
extirpative detrimental, dire, disastrous, fatal, pernicious
extirpatory dire
extol belaud, honor, overestimate, recommend, regard *(hold in esteem)*
extorquere extort, force *(coerce)*
extort acquire *(secure)*, coerce, deprive, exact, force *(coerce)*, impose *(enforce)*, press *(constrain)*, prey, toll *(exact payment)*. SEE MAIN ENTRY
extort belief convince
extorter racketeer
extortion blackmail, coercion. SEE MAIN ENTRY
extortionary confiscatory
extortionate exorbitant, inordinate, prohibitive *(costly)*, usurious, venal
extortionist criminal. SEE MAIN ENTRY
extra additional, also, ancillary *(auxiliary)*, balance *(amount in excess)*, bonus, excess, excessive, expendable, extraneous, extrinsic, further, gratuity *(present)*, needless, nonessential, overage, premium *(excess value)*, superfluous, supplementary, unnecessary. SEE MAIN ENTRY
extra amount for contingencies margin *(spare amount)*
extra amount for emergencies margin *(spare amount)*
extra charge surcharge
extra compensation commission *(fee)*
extra fee surcharge
extra time extension *(postponement)*
extract abridgment *(condensation)*, abstract, acquire *(secure)*, brief, compendium, deduce, deduct *(conclude by reasoning)*, derive *(deduce)*, derive *(receive)*, detect, digest, disencumber, disinter, dislodge, distill, educe, elicit, eradicate, eviscerate, evoke, except *(exclude)*, excerpt, excise *(cut away)*, gain, glean, infer, liberate, quote, reject, remove *(eliminate)*, select, unveil, withdraw. SEE MAIN ENTRY
extract from other works compile
extracted individual
extraction birth *(lineage)*, blood, bloodline, degree *(kinship)*, derivation, descent *(lineage)*, evulsion, family *(common ancestry)*, lineage, origin *(ancestry)*, parentage, race, relationship *(family tie)*, removal, selection *(choice)*
extradite deport *(banish)*, transport
extradition banishment, deportation, expulsion. SEE MAIN ENTRY
extrahere extract
extrajudicial opinion dictum
extralegal felonious
extramarital promiscuity adultery
extramarital relations adultery
extraneous circumstantial, collateral *(im-material)*, expendable, extrinsic, foreign, gratuitous *(unwarranted)*, immaterial, impertinent *(irrelevant)*, inapposite, irrelevant, needless, nonessential, peripheral, tangential, unessential, unnecessary, unrelated. SEE MAIN ENTRY
extraneus extraneous
extraordinally particularly
extraordinarily burdensome requirement imposition *(excessive burden)*
extraordinarius extraordinary
extraordinary best, eccentric, individual, infrequent, inordinate, irregular *(not usual)*, major, meritorious, notable, noteworthy, novel, outstanding *(prominent)*, paramount, particular *(specific)*, peculiar *(distinctive)*, portentous *(eliciting amazement)*, preferential, priceless, prodigious *(amazing)*, rare, remarkable, renowned, salient, singular, special, stellar, sterling, unaccustomed, uncommon, unique, unprecedented, unusual. SEE MAIN ENTRY
extraordinary remedy habeas corpus
extraordinary writ habeas corpus
extravagance exaggeration, hyperbole, misapplication, overstatement, rodomontade, waste
extravagancy overstatement
extravagant copious, egregious, excess, excessive, exorbitant, improvident, inordinate, intemperate, pretentious *(pompous)*, prodigal, profuse, prohibitive *(costly)*, rampant, superfluous, undue *(excessive)*, unreasonable, unrestrained *(not repressed)*
extravagant statement exaggeration
extravasate outpour
extravasation outflow
extrema condicio ultimatum
extrema lineamenta outline *(boundary)*
extreme brutal, ceiling, conclusive *(settled)*, contra, dire, draconian, drastic, end *(termination)*, excess, excessive, exorbitant, fanatical, final, gross *(flagrant)*, harsh, hot-blooded, inordinate, insufferable, intemperate, intense, last *(final)*, lurid,

noteworthy, outrageous, strict, superlative, ultimate, unconscionable, undue *(excessive)*, unendurable, unreasonable, unusual, utmost. SEE MAIN ENTRY
extreme boundary limit
extreme edge periphery
extreme fear fright
extreme limit extremity *(furthest point)*, utmost
extreme penalty capital punishment
extreme point end *(termination)*
extremely unduly
extremely important vital
extremes exaggeration
extremist bigot, malcontent
extremitas extremity *(furthest point)*
extremities confines
extremity border, boundary, ceiling, disaster, edge *(border)*, emergency, end *(termination)*, finality, need *(deprivation)*, outline *(boundary)*, pinnacle, prostration, requirement, utmost. SEE MAIN ENTRY
extremus extreme *(last)*, final, ultimate
extricable corrigible
extricate clear, discharge *(liberate)*, disencumber, disengage, disentangle, disenthrall, disinter, educe, free, quit *(free of)*, release, relieve *(free from burden)*, remove *(eliminate)*, rescue. SEE MAIN ENTRY
extrication condonation, discharge *(liberation)*, discharge *(release from obligation)*, emancipation, evulsion, freedom, ransom, release, removal, salvage
extrinsic alien *(foreign)*, extraneous, foreign, incidental, nonessential, unessential, unnecessary. SEE MAIN ENTRY
extrinsical extraneous, extrinsic, nonessential
extrude expel
extrudere eject *(expel)*
extrusion deportation, eviction, expulsion, ostracism, outflow
exuberance life *(vitality)*
exuberant copious, loquacious, profuse, rampant
exudation outflow
exude emanate, emit, issue *(send forth)*, radiate. SEE MAIN ENTRY
exultant ecstatic
eye center *(central position)*, observe *(watch)*, scrutinize, study
eye opener bombshell
eye-catching manifest, open *(in sight)*, remarkable
eyeless blind *(sightless)*
eyereach perspective, scene
eyeshot scene
eyewitness bystander. SEE MAIN ENTRY

F

faber artisan
fable fiction, lie *(falsify)*, myth
fabled famous, fictitious
fabric building *(structure)*, frame *(structure)*, structure *(composition)*
fabrica manufacture
fabricari fabricate *(construct)*, form, make, manufacture
fabricate build *(construct)*, conceive *(invent)*, conjure, contrive, create, devise *(invent)*, fake, falsify, feign, forge *(produce)*, form, formulate, frame *(construct)*, generate, invent *(falsify)*, invent *(produce for the first time)*, lie *(falsify)*, make, manufacture, misrepresent, originate, palter, plagiarize, prevaricate, produce *(manufacture)*, profess *(pretend)*, scheme, simulate. SEE MAIN ENTRY
fabricate evidence frame *(charge falsely)*
fabricated assumed *(feigned)*, fictitious, illusory, mendacious, spurious, unfounded
fabricating lying
fabrication artifice, building *(business of assembling)*, canard, composition *(makeup)*, counterfeit, creation, deceit, deception, evasion, fake, false pretense, falsehood, falsification, fiction, figment, formation, fraud, hoax, invention, lie, manufacture, misrepresentation, myth, origination, pretense *(pretext)*, pretext, sham, story *(falsehood)*, subreption, subterfuge. SEE MAIN ENTRY
fabricative constructive *(creative)*
fabricator author *(originator)*
fabula fiction, myth, story *(narrative)*
fabulous exorbitant, remarkable, special
facade disguise, false pretense
face appearance *(look)*, confront *(encounter)*, endure *(suffer)*, withstand. SEE MAIN ENTRY
face amount SEE MAIN ENTRY
face danger fight *(battle)*, withstand
face to face direct *(forthright)*
face up to withstand
face value cost *(price)*, par *(face amount)*. SEE MAIN ENTRY
facere appoint, exercise *(discharge a function)*, glean, make, practice *(engage in)*, realize *(make real)*
facet aspect, complexion, phase *(aspect)*, side
facetious jocular
facies form *(arrangement)*
facile artful, capable, deft, expert, pliable, practiced, proficient, resourceful, sequacious, suasible, tractable, veteran, yielding. SEE MAIN ENTRY
facillity instrument *(tool)*
facilis facile, flexible, tractable, yielding
facilitas facility *(easiness)*
facilitate abet, aid, bestow, ease, enable, expedite, favor, further, hasten, help, permit, promote *(organize)*, support *(assist)*. SEE MAIN ENTRY
facilitated decision accelerated judgment
facilitation advance *(progression)*, aid *(help)*, help. SEE MAIN ENTRY
facility appliance, competence *(ability)*, device *(mechanism)*, discretion *(quality of being discreet)*, gift *(flair)*, power, prison, proclivity, propensity, prowess *(ability)*, science *(technique)*, skill, tendency. SEE MAIN ENTRY
facing opposite
facinorous heinous, inexpiable, iniquitous, reprobate, scandalous, sinister
facinus crime, venture
facsimile copy, delineation, duplicate, fake, model. SEE MAIN ENTRY
fact fait accompli, ground, particular, technicality, truth. SEE MAIN ENTRY
fact of comprehending coverage *(scope)*
fact put in controversy by the pleadings issue *(matter in dispute)*. SEE MAIN ENTRY
fact-finding interrogative. SEE MAIN ENTRY
factfinding research
factio cabal, faction
faction cabal, conflict, constituency, contention *(opposition)*, denomination, discord, disagreement, discord, dissidence, disturbance, division *(act of dividing)*, feud, incompatibility *(difference)*, organization *(association)*, party *(political organization)*, schism, side, society, sodality, split, strife. SEE MAIN ENTRY
factional divergent, partial *(part)*,partisan
factional part proportion
factionalism strife
factionary demagogue, partisan
factioneer demagogue
factious argumentative, contentious, controversial, contumacious, dissenting, dissident, divergent, divisive, hostile, negative, polemic, pugnacious. SEE MAIN ENTRY
factious leader demagogue
factiousness contention *(opposition)*
factitare practice *(engage in)*
factitious assumed *(feigned)*, colorable *(specious)*, false *(not genuine)*, imitation, synthetic. SEE MAIN ENTRY
factor aspect, broker, cause *(reason)*, component, constituent *(part)*, dealer, deputy, determinant, element, feature *(characteristic)*, ingredient, member *(constituent part)*, part *(portion)*, plenipotentiary, procurator, represent *(substitute)*, substitute. SEE MAIN ENTRY
factorage brokerage
factors case *(set of circumstances)*, circumstances, deputation *(delegation)*
factory-made industrial
factotum employee
factotums personnel
facts circumstances, data, dossier, evidence, proof, science *(study)*
facts admitted at trial evidence
facts judicially noted evidence
facts which bear on the point in question evidence
facts which establish the point in issue evidence
factual accurate, actual, authentic, certain *(positive)*, de facto, documentary, genuine, honest, incontrovertible, indubious, literal, objective, real, sound, true *(authentic)*, unrefutable, valid. SEE MAIN ENTRY
factual basis documentation
factual matter evidence
factual statement affirmation
factualness honesty, reality, veracity
factum action *(performance)*, event, fact
facultas ability, facility *(instrumentality)*, permission, possibility
facultate bestow
facultatem facere enable
facultates resource
facultative voluntary
faculty ability, aptitude, caliber *(mental capacity)*, capacity *(aptitude)*, color *(complexion)*, competence *(ability)*, droit, gift *(flair)*, performance *(workmanship)*, specialty *(special aptitude)*, staff. SEE MAIN ENTRY
faculty member pedagogue
faculty of speech language
fad mode
fade decay, depart, disappear, dissipate *(spread out)*, languish, perish, tarnish. SEE MAIN ENTRY
fade away diminish, disappear, dissipate *(spread out)*, ebb, expire, perish
fade out perish
faded blemished, indistinct, stale
faded reputation ignominy
fadeless indelible, indestructible
fading attrition, brief, transient
faeneratio usury
faenus interest *(profit)*
fagging operose
fall decay, default, disappoint, ebb, languish, lapse *(fall into error)*, lose *(undergo*

defeat), mismanage, neglect, perish, succumb. SEE MAIN ENTRY
fail in duty default
fail in health languish
fail to accommodate disoblige
fail to act default
fail to answer default
fail to appear default
fail to appreciate decry, overlook *(disregard)*
fail to comply disobey
fail to comply with disoblige
fail to do omit
fail to exact a penalty pardon
fail to find lose *(be deprived of)*
fail to include omit
fail to insert omit
fail to keep forfeit, lose *(be deprived of),* violate
fail to meet financial engagements default
fail to mention omit
fail to notice disregard
fail to observe disregard, overlook *(disregard),* violate
fail to pay default
fail to perform default
fail to recognize misjudge
fail to retain forfeit
fail to see overlook *(disregard)*
fail to understand misapprehend, misconceive, misconstrue, misinterpret, misunderstand
fail to win lose *(undergo defeat)*
failed bankrupt, insolvent
failing decadent, decline, defect, deficiency, disadvantage, fault *(mistake),* fault *(weakness),* flaw, foible, frailty, imperfect, insufficient, misconduct, perfunctory, vice. SEE MAIN ENTRY
failing in duty delinquent *(overdue),* derelict *(negligent)*
failure abortion *(fiasco),* bankruptcy, breach, debacle, defeat, delinquency *(failure of duty),* disaster, dishonor *(nonpayment),* disqualification *(factor that disqualifies),* flaw, foible, frailty, frustration, impossibility, impotence, impuissance, inability, incapacity, inefficacy, infraction, lapse *(expiration),* loss, miscarriage, misconduct, mistrial, neglect, negligence, nonfeasance, nonpayment, offense, omission, oversight *(carelessness),* vice. SEE MAIN ENTRY
failure in duty culpability, dereliction
failure of credit default
failure of duty default, infraction, laches, maladministration
failure of obligation delinquency *(failure of duty)*
failure of strength frailty
failure of vital functions death
failure to act delinquency *(failure of duty),* inaction
failure to agree conflict, contest *(dispute),* controversy *(argument),* difference, disaccord, disagreement, discord, disparity, dispute, dissent *(difference of opinion)*
failure to answer default
failure to appear default, nonappearance
failure to carry out disregard *(omission)*
failure to comply deficiency. SEE MAIN ENTRY
failure to correspond discrepancy
failure to establish a cause of action nonsuit
failure to litigate within reasonable period laches
failure to maintain solvency failure *(bankruptcy)*
failure to make a case nonsuit
failure to meet one's obligations default
failure to meet the burden of proof nonsuit
failure to notice oversight *(carelessness)*
failure to pay default, nonpayment
failure to perform nonperformance, omission
failure to present sufficient evidence nonsuit
failure to use desuetude, disuse
fain willing *(not averse)*
fainaigue deceive
faineance sloth
faineant otiose
faint inconspicuous, indefinite, indistinct, insufficient, languid, nebulous, powerless, prostration, remote *(small),* unclear, vague
faint hope pessimism
faint outline hint
faint suggestion hint
faint-hearted caitiff
fainthearted diffident, recreant
faintheartedness fear
faintish powerless
faintness indistinctness, obscuration
fair adequate, attractive, average *(standard),* clean, dispassionate, equal, equitable, evenhanded, high-minded, honest, impartial, imperfect, judicial, juridical, just, marginal, market *(business),* mediocre, neutral, nonpartisan, objective, open-minded, passable, right *(correct),* rightful, scrupulous, unbiased, unprejudiced, upright. SEE MAIN ENTRY
fair chance likelihood, opportunity, probability, prospect *(outlook)*
fair claim right *(entitlement)*
fair expectation probability
fair notice adequate notice
fair play disinterest *(lack of prejudice),* fairness, justice, objectivity, probity
fair prospect likelihood
fair sample cross section
fair sharing dispensation *(act of dispensing)*
fair trade agreement SEE MAIN ENTRY
fair treatment candor *(impartiality),* disinterest *(lack of prejudice),* equity *(justice),* fairness, justice, right *(righteousness)*
fair use SEE MAIN ENTRY
fair value expense *(cost)*
fair-dealing honest
fair-haired popular
fair-minded equal, equitable, evenhanded, fair *(just),* impartial, just, liberal *(broad minded),* neutral, nonpartisan, objective, open-minded, unbiased
fair-mindedness equity *(justice),* fairness, justice, objectivity
fairish mediocre
fairly duly, in good faith. SEE MAIN ENTRY
fairminded unprejudiced
fairness candor *(impartiality),* disinterest *(lack of prejudice),* equity *(justice),* honesty, integrity, justice, mediocrity, moderation, objectivity, probity, rectitude, right *(righteousness).* SEE MAIN ENTRY
fait accompli denouement. SEE MAIN ENTRY
faith allegiance, conviction *(persuasion),* credence, fealty, fidelity, probity, prospect *(outlook),* reliance, security *(safety),* trust *(confidence),* weight *(credibility).* SEE MAIN ENTRY
faithful accurate, actual, authentic, bona fide, close *(intimate),* conscientious, constant, credible, dependable, diligent, exact, factual, identical, infallible, intimate, literal, loyal, meticulous, obedient, persistent, pertinacious, precise, punctilious, realistic, reliable, representative, reputable, resolute, serious *(devoted),* stable, staunch, steadfast, strict, true *(loyal),* undistorted, unyielding. SEE MAIN ENTRY
faithful companion cohort
faithfully in good faith, invariably. SEE MAIN ENTRY
faithfulness adherence *(devotion),* adhesion *(loyalty),* allegiance, commitment *(responsibility),* conformity *(obedience),* credibility, discipline *(obedience),* fealty, fidelity, homage, integrity, loyalty, rectitude, responsibility *(conscience),* trustworthiness, veracity. SEE MAIN ENTRY
faithless derelict *(negligent),* dishonest, false *(disloyal),* lying, machiavellian, malevolent, perfidious, profane, recreant, skeptical, unreliable, unscrupulous, untrue, untrustworthy, variable. SEE MAIN ENTRY
faithlessness dereliction, dishonesty, disloyalty, doubt *(suspicion),* incredulity, infidelity, revolt, story *(falsehood)*
faithworthy credible, solid *(sound)*
fake assumed *(feigned),* camouflage, cloak, copy, counterfeit, deceive, deception, disguise, dishonest, fabricate *(make up),* false *(not genuine),* false pretense, falsification, falsify, fictitious, forge *(counterfeit),* forgery, frame *(prearrange),* fraudulent, hoax, imposture, invent *(falsify),* meretricious, misrepresent, mock *(imitate),* palter, pretend, sham, specious, spurious, untrue. SEE MAIN ENTRY
fake charges against frame *(charge falsely)*
fake the evidence frame *(prearrange)*
faked artificial, dishonest, fictitious, fraudulent, imitation, lying, spurious, surreptitious
faked charge frame up
fakery false pretense
faking disguise
fall debacle, decline, decline *(fall),* decrease *(noun),* decrease *(verb),* depreciate, ebb, failure *(lack of success),* prostration, relapse *(noun),* relapse *(verb),* subside, succumb. SEE MAIN ENTRY
fall again into regress
fall against impinge
fall apart decay, degenerate
fall away degenerate, diminish, ebb, subside
fall back regress, relapse, retire *(retreat),* retreat
fall back on exploit *(make use of)*
fall back upon resort
fall behind decrease, regress
fall below decrease
fall by inheritance devolve
fall by succession devolve
fall due accrue *(arise),* mature
fall exactly together coincide *(correspond)*
fall foul of bicker
fall from grace lapse *(fall into error)*
fall from repute degradation
fall heir to inherit
fall ill languish
fall in conform
fall in with comply, comport *(agree with),* defer *(yield in judgment),* obey, unite

fall into incur
fall into decay degenerate
fall into error deviate, err, miscalculate, misconceive, misread, mistake, misunderstand
fall into line conform, crystallize
fall off decrease, degenerate, ebb, subside
fall out alienate *(estrange)*, bicker, disaccord, emanate, estrange. SEE MAIN ENTRY
fall short fail *(lose)*, lack, require *(need)*
fall sick languish
fall to pieces decay, degenerate, disintegrate
fall to the rear retreat
fall upon accost, assail, attack, oppugn, strike *(assault)*
fallabity frailty
fallacia deceit, fraud, imposture, sham
fallacious deceptive, delusive, dishonest, errant, erroneous, false *(inaccurate)*, faulty, fraudulent, ill-founded, illogical, illusory, inaccurate, incorrect, invalid, ludicrous, nonsubstantial *(not sturdy)*, sophistic, specious, unfounded, untenable, untrue. SEE MAIN ENTRY
fallacious argument fallacy, non sequitur
fallacious reasoning non sequitur, sophistry
fallaciousness bad faith, deceit, fraud, invalidity, misestimation. SEE MAIN ENTRY
fallacy invalidity, misjudgment, non sequitur. SEE MAIN ENTRY
fallax delusive, fallacious, insidious
fallen peccable, profligate *(corrupt)*
fallen into desuetude obsolete, outdated, outmoded
fallen into disuse obsolete, outdated, outmoded
fallen into ruin dilapidated
fallere hoodwink, mislead
falli err, miscalculate
fallible disputable, dubious, peccable, unreliable, untrustworthy, vulnerable. SEE MAIN ENTRY
falling decadent, descent *(declination)*
falling away decline
falling due maturity
falling into ruin decadent
falling off attrition
falling out disaccord, schism
falling short defective, deficiency, deficient, insufficiency
falling-off decline, decrease
fallow barren, idle, otiose, unproductive
falsa docere misinform
false artificial, assumed *(feigned)*, baseless, bogus, colorable *(specious)*, deceptive, delusive, dishonest, disingenuous, erroneous, faithless, fallacious, faulty, fictitious, fraudulent, ill-founded, illusory, imitation, immoral, improper, inaccurate, incorrect, insidious, lying, mendacious, meretricious, perfidious, recreant, sophistic, specious, spurious, tartuffish, unfounded, unreliable, unscrupulous, unsound *(fallacious)*, unsustainable, untenable, untrue, untrustworthy. SEE MAIN ENTRY
false accusation defamation, libel
false alarm hoax
false and injurious libelous
false appearance color *(deceptive appearance)*, deception, disguise, fallacy, pretense *(ostentation)*, pretense *(pretext)*, pretext
false assertion falsehood
false charge frame up
false claim artifice
false coloring catachresis, distortion
false colors disguise
false conception error
false conduct duplicity, fraud, imposture
false construction catachresis, distortion, misapplication
false copy counterfeit, disguise, distortion
false duplication counterfeit
false evidence frame up
false fabrication forgery
false front deception, disguise
false ground pretext
false hearted disingenuous, false *(disloyal)*
false idea misestimation
false impression error, misestimation
false information frame up
false logic sophistry
false motive pretext
false plea pretense *(pretext)*
false pretense pretext. SEE MAIN ENTRY
false pretenses bad faith
false pretension bad faith
false pretensions artifice
false profession hypocrisy
false publication defamation, libel
false reading catachresis, distortion
false reason pretext
false reasoning non sequitur
false report canard, defamation, hoax, slander
false representation counterfeit, fake, fraud, misrepresentation
false representation of fact false pretense
false reproduction counterfeit
false rumor canard
false show histrionics, pretense *(ostentation)*, pretense *(pretext)*, pretext, role, sham
false statement canard, falsehood, fiction, libel, lie, misrepresentation, misstatement, perjury, story *(falsehood)*. SEE MAIN ENTRY
false step fault *(mistake)*
false story myth
false swearing bad faith, dishonesty, perjury, subreption
false teaching propaganda
false-hearted dishonest
falsehearted faithless, insidious, machiavellian, perfidious, recreant
falseheartedness bad faith, deceit, dishonesty, duplicity, infidelity
falsehood canard, counterfeit, deceit, deception, dishonesty, fake, false pretense, fiction, figment, improbity, indirection *(deceitfulness)*, libel, lie, misrepresentation, misstatement, myth, perjury, pretense *(pretext)*, subreption, subterfuge. SEE MAIN ENTRY
falsely call to account frame *(charge falsely)*
falsely characterize mislabel
falsely testify bear false witness
falseness bad faith, color *(deceptive appearance)*, counterfeit, deceit, deception, dishonesty, disloyalty, duplicity, fallacy, false pretense, fraud, improbity, indirection *(deceitfulness)*, invalidity, libel, perjury, pretense *(pretext)*
falsification artifice, canard, color *(deceptive appearance)*, counterfeit, deceit, deception, dishonesty, distortion, fake, false pretense, falsehood, fiction, figment, forgery, fraud, hoax, hypocrisy, libel, lie, misrepresentation, misstatement, overstatement, perjury, pretense *(pretext)*, pretext, story *(falsehood)*, subreption. SEE MAIN ENTRY
falsified dishonest, fraudulent, mendacious
falsify bear false witness, cloak, copy, deceive, defame, delude, disguise, distort, evade *(deceive)*, fabricate *(make up)*, fake, feign, forge *(counterfeit)*, invent *(falsify)*, lie *(falsify)*, malign, misguide, misinform, mislead, misrepresent, misstate, negate, palter, perjure, pervert, plagiarize, pretend, prevaricate, refute, slant. SEE MAIN ENTRY
falsify accounts defalcate
falsify testimony perjure
falsity counterfeit, deceit, dishonesty, disloyalty, fallacy, false pretense, falsehood, fraud, improbity, infidelity, invalidity, lie, misrepresentation, story *(falsehood)*
falsum falsehood, lie
falsus counterfeit, delusive, erroneous, false pretense, illusory, inaccurate, incorrect, putative, untrue
falter beat *(pulsate)*, doubt *(hesitate)*, hesitate, oscillate, vacillate
faltering diffident, disinclined, doubt *(indecision)*, hesitant, hesitation, irresolute, noncommittal
fama character *(reputation)*, honor *(good reputation)*, notoriety, prestige, report *(rumor)*, reputation
fame character *(reputation)*, credit *(recognition)*, distinction *(reputation)*, eminence, importance, notoriety, prestige, publicity, regard *(esteem)*, reputation. SEE MAIN ENTRY
famed famous, illustrious, notable, notorious, outstanding *(prominent)*, renowned, reputable
familia family *(household)*, household
familiar accustomed *(familiarized)*, brazen, close *(intimate)*, cognizable, cognizant, common *(customary)*, conventional, customary, frequent, habitual, informal, informed *(having information)*, intimate, learned, mundane, nondescript, ordinary, presumptuous, prevailing *(current)*, prevalent, proverbial, public *(known)*, regular *(conventional)*, routine, trite, typical, usual. SEE MAIN ENTRY
familiar discourse conversation
familiar object landmark *(conspicuous object)*
familiar through use accustomed *(familiarized)*
familiar way custom
familiaris familiar *(customary)*, intimate
familiarity cognition, common knowledge, comprehension, consortium *(marriage companionship)*, experience *(background)*, informality, information *(knowledge)*, knowledge *(awareness)*, knowledge *(learning)*, scienter
familiarization habituation, knowledge *(learning)*
familiarize advise, apprise, communicate, educate, inform *(notify)*, initiate, instruct *(teach)*, inure *(accustom)*, naturalize *(acclimate)*
familiarize oneself perceive
familiarize with instill, practice *(train by repetition)*
familiarized informed *(having information)*
family affiliation *(bloodline)*, affinity *(family ties)*, ancestry, bloodline, derivation, descendant, domestic *(household)*, house,

household *(domestic)*, household, issue *(progeny)*, kindred, kinship, lineage, next of kin, offspring, origin *(ancestry)*, parentage, paternal, posterity, progeny, race, relative, succession. SEE MAIN ENTRY
family abode household
family circle household
family connection affiliation *(bloodline)*, affinity *(family ties)*, ancestry, blood, degree *(kinship)*, filiation, kinship, next of kin, parentage, propinquity *(kinship)*, relation *(kinship)*, relationship *(family tie)*
family dwelling place household
family patronage nepotism
family related consanguineous
family relationship blood, degree *(kinship)*
family tie affiliation *(bloodline)*, blood, degree *(kinship)*, next of kin, relation *(kinship)*
family tree ancestry, blood, bloodline, descent *(lineage)*, parentage
family unit family *(household)*
famine paucity, poverty, privation
famous blatant *(conspicuous)*, household *(familiar)*, illustrious, important *(significant)*, notable, noteworthy, notorious, outstanding *(prominent)*, popular, prominent, renowned, stellar. SEE MAIN ENTRY
famousness notoriety, prestige, publicity, regard *(esteem)*, reputation
fan addict, spread, stimulate
fan out deploy, expand
fanatic addict, addicted, bigot, demagogue, dictatorial, drastic, eager, fanatical, malcontent, outrageous, partisan, uncompromising
fanatical demonstrative *(expressive of emotion)*, dogmatic, draconian, drastic, eager, excessive, extreme *(exaggerated)*, illiberal, inordinate, narrow, outrageous, parochial, provincial, radical *(favoring drastic change)*, uncompromising, vehement, zealous. SEE MAIN ENTRY
fanaticism ardor, compulsion *(obsession)*, obsession, passion
fanaticus fanatical
fancied delusive, fictitious, illusory, nonexistent, preferred *(favored)*
fancier addict
fanciful arbitrary, arbitrary and capricious, capricious, delusive, fictitious, ill-founded, illusory, insubstantial, original *(creative)*, quixotic, unpredictable, variable
fanciful name sobriquet
fancy affection, compulsion *(obsession)*, conatus, concept, conjure, desire, elaborate, expect *(consider probable)*, favor, fiction, figment, idea, notion, obsession, opine, opinion *(belief)*, penchant, predilection, predisposition, prefer, preference *(choice)*, propensity, quirk *(idiosyncrasy)*, relish, surmise, suspect *(think)*
fanfare noise
fanfaronade histrionics, jactation, pretense *(ostentation)*, rodomontade
fanfaronading orgulous
fantasied capricious
fantastic delusive, ludicrous, nonexistent, noteworthy, prodigious *(amazing)*, special, unusual. SEE MAIN ENTRY
fantastical capricious, delusive, ludicrous, nonexistent
fantasy fiction, figment, myth, story *(falsehood)*, vision *(dream)*
far inaccessible, obscure *(remote)*, remote *(not proximate)*, remote *(secluded)*. SEE MAIN ENTRY
far away inaccessible
far from the point irrelevant
far off inaccessible
far removed remote *(not proximate)*
far-famed outstanding *(prominent)*, renowned
far-fetched inapposite. SEE MAIN ENTRY
far-flung broad, extensive, far reaching
far-gone dilapidated
far-off remote *(not proximate)*, remote *(secluded)*, unapproachable
far-ranging extensive, far reaching
far-reaching broad, comprehensive, critical *(crucial)*, extensive, important *(significant)*, major, material *(important)*, momentous, rife. SEE MAIN ENTRY
far-spread broad
faraway oblivious, remote *(secluded)*, unapproachable
farce caricature, parody, travesty. SEE MAIN ENTRY
farcical ludicrous
fare fee *(charge)*, price, rate, toll *(tax)*. SEE MAIN ENTRY
fare well succeed *(attain)*
farfetched suspicious *(questionable)*, unbelievable
farm cultivate, homestead
farm land homestead
farmplace homestead
farmstead homestead
farrago confusion *(turmoil)*, melange
farseeing omniscient, perspicacious, prophetic, provident *(showing foresight)*
farsighted perspicacious, politic, prophetic, prudent, sapient, sensible
farsightedness sagacity
farthest extreme *(last)*, last *(final)*, peripheral, ultimate
farthest end extremity *(furthest point)*
farthest point ceiling, extremity *(furthest point)*
farthest reach extremity *(furthest point)*, utmost
farthest removed extreme *(last)*
fascicle serial
fascimile recreate, resemblance, transcript
fascinate immerse *(engross)*, interest, occupy *(engage)*. SEE MAIN ENTRY
fascinating attractive, sapid
fascination compulsion *(obsession)*, obsession, preoccupation, seduction. SEE MAIN ENTRY
fascist dictatorial
fashion adapt, build *(construct)*, complexion, compose, conduct, contrive, create, crystallize, custom, devise *(invent)*, fabricate *(construct)*, forge *(produce)*, form *(arrangement)*, form, formulate, frame *(construct)*, frame *(formulate)*, habit, invent *(produce for the first time)*, make, manner *(behavior)*, manner *(kind)*, manufacture, means *(opportunity)*, mode, parlance, prescription *(custom)*, produce *(manufacture)*, scheme, style, usage, way *(manner)*. SEE MAIN ENTRY
fashionable customary, elegant, popular
fashionable society elite
fashionableness custom
fashioning building *(business of assembling)*, creation, manufacture, onset *(commencement)*
fast close *(intimate)*, expeditious, firm, fixed *(securely placed)*, indelible, inextricable, inseparable, instantly, loyal, permanent, rapid, secure *(sound)*, solid *(sound)*, stable, staunch, steadfast. SEE MAIN ENTRY
fast and loose variable
fast rate dispatch *(promptness)*
fasten affix, annex *(add)*, append, attach *(join)*, bar *(hinder)*, cement, cohere *(adhere)*, combine *(join together)*, commingle, handcuff, lock, occlude, restrain, shut, trammel
fasten in position securely fix *(make firm)*
fasten oneself upon hunt
fasten securely fix *(make firm)*
fasten together attach *(join)*, connect *(join together)*
fasten upon grapple
fastened attached *(annexed)*, firm, fixed *(securely placed)*, secure *(sound)*, stable
fastened together conjoint
fastener connection *(fastening)*, handcuff
fastening accession *(annexation)*, attachment *(act of affixing)*
fastidiosus disdainful, supercilious
fastidious conscientious, diligent, discriminating *(judicious)*, meticulous, particular *(exacting)*, precise, punctilious, sensitive *(discerning)*, strict. SEE MAIN ENTRY
fastidiousness decorum, diligence *(care)*, particularity
fastidire disdain, spurn
fastidium contempt *(disdain)*, disdain
fastigium eminence
fastness dispatch *(promptness)*
fat cat SEE MAIN ENTRY
fatal deadly, deleterious, dire, lethal, malignant, noxious, pernicious, pestilent, serious *(grave)*, toxic. SEE MAIN ENTRY
fatal accident fatality
fatal affair tragedy
fatal casualty dead, fatality
fatal mishap fatality
fatalism resignation *(passive acceptance)*
fatality dead, death, mortality. SEE MAIN ENTRY
fate end *(termination)*, happenstance, predetermination, predetermine, prospect *(outlook)*, quirk *(accident)*. SEE MAIN ENTRY
fated forthcoming, future, inevitable, necessary *(inescapable)*, unalterable, unavoidable *(inevitable)*. SEE MAIN ENTRY
fateful critical *(crucial)*, fatal, key, major, momentous, necessary *(inescapable)*, portentous *(ominous)*, prophetic
fateri admit *(concede)*, avow, confess
father generate, originate, parents, primogenitor, propagate *(increase)*, reproduce
fatherhood filiation, paternity
fatherland home *(place of origin)*, nationality
fatherlike paternal
fatherly paternal
fathership filiation, paternity
fathom apprehend *(perceive)*, ascertain, comprehend *(understand)*, conceive *(comprehend)*, construe *(comprehend)*, delve, digest *(comprehend)*, discern *(detect with the senses)*, find *(discover)*, gauge, measure, pierce *(discern)*, realize *(understand)*, solve, understand
fathomable appreciable, cognizable, coherent *(clear)*, comprehensible, determinable *(ascertainable)*, scrutable, solvable
fathomless incomprehensible, profound *(intense)*
fatidic ominous, oracular, prophetic
fatidical ominous, oracular, prophetic
fatidicus prophetic
fatigare importune

fatigue exhaust *(deplete)*, languor, prostration, tax *(overwork)*
fatigued languid
fatiguing difficult, onerous, operose, oppressive
fatiloquent portentous *(ominous)*, prophetic
fatten enlarge, expand, inflate
fatten upon prey
fatuitous fatuous, illusory, opaque
fatuity opacity
fatuous ludicrous, misadvised, nugatory, opaque, puerile, vacuous. SEE MAIN ENTRY
fatuus fatuous
faubourg frontier
fault blame *(culpability)*, blame, culpability, decry, defacement, defect, deficiency, delinquency *(misconduct)*, deprecate, depreciate, disadvantage, discommend, drawback, error, flaw, foible, frailty, guilt, impeach, mischief, misconduct, misdeed, misdoing, onus *(blame)*, rift *(gap)*, tort, transgression, vice. SEE MAIN ENTRY
fault finding cynical
fault of the court injustice
fault-finding criticism, dissatisfaction
faultfind cavil, complain *(criticize)*
faultfinder malcontent
faultfinding denunciation, derogatory, diatribe, disapproval, disparagement, fractious, impugnation, inculpation, nonconsenting, obloquy, particular *(exacting)*, pejorative, querulous, severe, stricture
faultful defective, errant, fallacious, peccant *(culpable)*
faultiness defect, deficiency, fallacy, handicap
faultless absolute *(ideal)*, accurate, best, blameless, clean, faithful *(true to fact)*, incorruptible, inculpable, infallible, innocent, intact, irreprehensible, literal, not guilty, pardonable, precise, pure, unblemished, unimpeachable. SEE MAIN ENTRY
faultlessness rectitude
faulty bad *(inferior)*, blameful, blemished, defective, deficient, derelict *(negligent)*, errant, erroneous, fallacious, fallible, false *(inaccurate)*, illogical, imperfect, inaccurate, incorrect, inexact, inferior *(lower in quality)*, invalid, marred, obnoxious, peccable, poor *(inferior in quality)*, unsatisfactory, unsound *(fallacious)*, unsound *(not strong)*, untenable. SEE MAIN ENTRY
faulty in logic fallacious, sophistic
faulty reasoning fallacy
faulty work noncompliance *(improper completion)*
fautor backer
fautor partisan, promoter
favere favor, patronize *(trade with)*
favor accommodate, advantage, advocate, approval, approve, assent, auspices, behalf, benefit *(conferment)*, benevolence *(act of kindness)*, bounty, capitalize *(provide capital)*, complexion, concur *(agree)*, conduce, countenance, deign, discriminate *(treat differently)*, embrace *(accept)*, espouse, estimation *(esteem)*, foster, franchise *(license)*, further, gift *(present)*, goodwill, grace, grant, grant *(concede)*, gratuity *(present)*, help, honor *(outward respect)*, indorsement, indulgence, inequity, largess *(gift)*, leave *(permission)*, lenience, let *(permit)*, nepotism, option *(contractual provision)*, partiality, pass *(approve)*. SEE MAIN ENTRY
favor patronage *(power to appoint jobs)*
favor patronage *(support)*, patronize *(condescend toward)*, predilection, predisposition, prefer, preserve, prestige, privilege, promote *(advance)*, propensity, recommend, regard *(esteem)*, respect, sanction *(permission)*, service *(assistance)*, side, sponsor, token, uphold
favor excessively overindulge
favor owed due
favor with bestow, impart, vouchsafe
favor with one's patronage patronize *(trade with)*
favorable auspicious, beneficial, constructive *(creative)*, fitting, inclined, profitable, prone, propitious, receptive, salutary, seasonable, suitable, valuable, viable, willing *(not averse)*. SEE MAIN ENTRY
favorable chance likelihood, opportunity, probability
favorable decision SEE MAIN ENTRY
favorable disposition goodwill
favorable opinion credit *(recognition)*, estimation *(esteem)*
favorable opportunity advantage, possibility
favorable position edge *(advantage)*. SEE MAIN ENTRY
favorable prospect chance *(possibility)*, high probability, likelihood, possibility
favorable reception adoption *(acceptance)*
favorable recognition estimation *(esteem)*
favorable regard goodwill
favorable repute estimation *(esteem)*
favorable time chance *(fortuity)*, opportunity
favorable to health salubrious
favorable trade balance boom *(prosperity)*
favorable verdict acquittal
favorable verdict to the defendant compurgation
favorableness expedience
favorably disposed partial *(biased)*
favorably inclined consenting, propitious, willing *(not averse)*
favorably minded ready *(willing)*
favorably prejudiced favorable *(expressing approval)*
favored exempt, popular, preferential, privileged
favored by fortune auspicious
favored treatment preference *(priority)*
favorer abettor, advocate *(espouser)*, apologist, benefactor, disciple, partisan, patron *(influential supporter)*, sponsor
favoring auspicious, favorable *(expressing approval)*, inequitable, lenient
favoring circumstance advantage
favoring influence auspices
favorite best, popular, preferable, preference *(choice)*, preferred *(favored)*. SEE MAIN ENTRY
favoritism bias, discrimination *(bigotry)*, favor *(partiality)*, inequity, injustice, nepotism, partiality, predisposition, prejudice *(preconception)*. SEE MAIN ENTRY
fawn truckle
fawning obsequious, servile, subservient
fealty adherence *(devotion)*, adhesion *(loyalty)*, allegiance, fidelity, loyalty. SEE MAIN ENTRY
fear cloud *(suspicion)*, consternation, fright, misgiving, mistrust, panic, phobia, scruple, stress *(strain)*, suspicion *(mistrust)*, trepidation. SEE MAIN ENTRY
fear of danger fright
fear-inspiring formidable, ominous, sinister
fear-stricken caitiff
fearful dire, formidable, ineffable, ominous, pending *(imminent)*, portentous *(ominous)*, recreant, repulsive, suspicious *(distrustful)*
fearfulness consternation, fear, misgiving, panic, scruple, stress *(strain)*, suspicion *(mistrust)*. SEE MAIN ENTRY
fearless heroic, indomitable, spartan, undaunted. SEE MAIN ENTRY
fearlessness confidence *(faith)*, prowess *(bravery)*
fearsome dangerous, sinister
feasibility expedience, possibility, potential. SEE MAIN ENTRY
feasible colorable *(plausible)*, plausible, possible, potential, practicable, pragmatic, presumptive, probable, suitable, viable. SEE MAIN ENTRY
feasibleness feasibility
feast carouse
feast upon prey
feat act *(undertaking)*, endeavor
featherbrained opaque
feature aspect, characteristic, complexion, component, constituent *(part)*, contour *(shape)*, detail, differential, element, exhibit, expose, factor *(ingredient)*, ingredient, item, member *(constituent part)*, particular, particularity, phase *(aspect)*, phenomenon *(manifestation)*, point *(item)*, property *(distinctive attribute)*, quality *(attribute)*, quality *(grade)*, speciality, specialty *(distinctive mark)*, symptom, technicality, trait. SEE MAIN ENTRY
featured attraction feature *(special attraction)*
featureless indeterminate
features character *(personal quality)*, circumstances, color *(complexion)*, configuration *(form)*, indicia
febrifugal medicinal
febrile hot-blooded
feckless futile, inadept, inadequate, ineffective, ineffectual, lax, otiose, unable. SEE MAIN ENTRY
feculent repulsive
fecund fertile, original *(creative)*, productive, prolific
fecundate proliferate, propagate *(increase)*, reproduce
fecundify proliferate
fecundus fertile
federal mutual *(collective)*, national, public *(affecting people)*. SEE MAIN ENTRY
federal officer marshal
federal union federation
federalization integration *(amalgamation)*
federalize affiliate, join *(bring together)*. SEE MAIN ENTRY
federate affiliate, allied, associated, combine *(act in concert)*, consolidate *(unite)*, cooperate, federal, federalize *(associate)*, intimate, join *(bring together)*, mutual *(collective)*, organize *(unionize)*, pool. SEE MAIN ENTRY
federated affiliated, associated, conjoint, mutual *(collective)*
federation affiliation *(amalgamation)*, association *(alliance)*, cartel, chamber *(body)*, coaction, coalescence, coalition, committee, company *(enterprise)*, confederacy *(compact)*, consolidation, contact

(association), contribution (participation), cooperative, corporation, integration (assimilation), league, merger, organization (association), partnership, pool, society, sodality, syndicate, union (labor organization). SEE MAIN ENTRY
federative collective, conjoint, corporate (associate), federal, mutual (collective)
fee advance (allowance), brokerage, charge (cost), compensation, due, excise, expense (cost), fare, honorarium, pay, payment (remittance), pension, perquisite, price, rate, real estate, recompense, rent, reward, toll (tax), wage. SEE MAIN ENTRY
fee contingent on future legal services retainer
fee-for-service SEE MAIN ENTRY
fee paid to secure legal services retainer
fee simple freehold. SEE MAIN ENTRY
feeble decadent, helpless (powerless), imperfect, inadept, inadequate, incapable, inconspicuous, ineffective, ineffectual, insipid, insubstantial, insufficient, languid, lifeless (dull), nonsubstantial (not sturdy), passive, powerless, unsatisfactory, unsound (not strong). SEE MAIN ENTRY
feeble-eyed blind (sightless)
feeble-minded non compos mentis
feebleness caducity, disability (physical inability), fault (weakness), frailty, impotence, impuissance, incapacity, inefficacy, languor, prostration
feed maintain (sustain), nurture, provide (supply), supply, support (assist)
feed upon prey
feedback SEE MAIN ENTRY
feel deem, detect, endure (suffer), opine, perceive, surmise. SEE MAIN ENTRY
feel a dearth lack
feel annoyance resent
feel compassion relent
feel conscience stricken regret
feel contempt for contemn, disdain, flout, misprize
feel contrition repent
feel disapproval except (object)
feel displeasure resent
feel distrust doubt (distrust), suspect (distrust)
feel for relent, sympathize
feel gratification relish
feel hurt resent
feel ill will resent
feel joy relish
feel no concern disregard
feel out peruse
feel pain suffer (sustain loss)
feel pleasure relish
feel regret repent
feel remorse repent
feel resentment resent
feel sure rely, trust
feel sure of confide (trust)
feel terror fear
feel the necessity for need, require (need)
feel the want of need
feel uncertain vacillate
feel uneasy about regret
feel unsure doubt (hesitate)
feel utter contempt for decry, disdain
feeling affection, climate, concept, fervent, humanity (humaneness), impression, notion, opinion (belief), passion, perceptive, perspective, pity, position (point of view), posture (attitude), premonition, reaction (response), sensibility, sensitive (easily affected), tenor. SEE MAIN ENTRY
feeling of dejection damper (depressant)
feeling of depression damper (depressant)
feeling of obligation responsibility (conscience)
feeling of uncertainty doubt (indecision), qualm
feelingless cold-blooded
feelings of guilt remorse
fees consideration (recompense), disbursement (funds paid out)
feign assume (simulate), cloak, disguise, fabricate (make up), fake, falsify, forge (counterfeit), invent (falsify), misrepresent, mock (imitate), palter, perjure, pretend, prevaricate, profess (pretend), simulate. SEE MAIN ENTRY
feigned artificial, colorable (specious), deceptive, delusive, dishonest, disingenuous, evasive, false (not genuine), fictitious, fraudulent, illusory, imitation, lying, mendacious, spurious, tartuffish. SEE MAIN ENTRY
feigned copy fake
feigned story fiction, figment
feint artifice, color (deceptive appearance), deception, false pretense, maneuver (trick), pretense (pretext), pretext, ruse, sham, stratagem. SEE MAIN ENTRY
felicitous auspicious, ecstatic, favorable (advantageous), propitious, relevant, resourceful, successful, suitable. SEE MAIN ENTRY
felicitousness expedience, timeliness
felicity gift (flair), propensity, propriety (appropriateness), prosperity, skill
feline furtive, machiavellian, politic, sly, stealthy, subtle (insidious)
felix auspicious, successful
fell brutal, dire, disastrous, fatal, harmful, lethal, malignant, overthrow, pernicious, precipitate (throw down violently), ruthless
fell stroke disaster
fellow cohort, colleague, confederate, consort, contributor (contributor), copartner (business associate), correlate, correlative, member (individual in a group), participant, peer, person, resemblance. SEE MAIN ENTRY
fellow companion colleague, consociate, consort
fellow conspirator accessory, accomplice, coactor, coconspirator, cohort, colleague, consociate, conspirer
fellow feeling comity, philanthropy, pity, rapprochement
fellow machinator coconspirator
fellow plotter coconspirator
fellow schemer coconspirator
fellow strategist coconspirator
fellow suffering pity
fellow traiter coconspirator
fellow worker associate, coadjutant, colleague, consociate, copartner (business associate), participant, partisan, partner
fellow workers personnel
fellowless solitary
fellowship coaction, coalition, committee, confederacy (compact), contact (association), contribution (participation), informality, integration (assimilation), league, merger, partnership, peace, rapprochement, society, sodality, union (labor organization)
fellowship in sorrow pity
felon assailant, captive, convict, criminal, hoodlum, lawbreaker, malefactor, offender, outlaw, prisoner. SEE MAIN ENTRY
felonious culpable, illegal, illicit, impermissible, iniquitous, larcenous, lawless, nefarious, reprobate, wrongful. SEE MAIN ENTRY
felonious abreption asportation
felonious act tortious act
felonious conduct criminality, guilt
felonious removal asportation
felonious stealing larceny
felonious taking robbery, theft
felonious taking of the property of another robbery
felonious transference asportation
felonious translocation asportation
feloniously illegally
feloniousness corruption, criminality
felony burglary, crime, delict, homicide, housebreaking, misdeed, offense. SEE MAIN ENTRY
felony murder homicide
female SEE MAIN ENTRY
fence bar (hinder), barrier, bicker, enclosure, equivocate, hedge, obstacle, obstruction, palter, parry, pettifog, prevaricate, receiver, screen (guard). SEE MAIN ENTRY
fence in circumscribe (surround by boundary), confine, contain (enclose), enclose, encompass (surround), envelop, shut
fence off demarcate
fenced curtilage, guarded
fenced in area enclosure
fend counter, deter
fend off avert, block, deter, estop, parry, prevent, repel (drive back), repulse, resist (withstand), save (rescue), stave
fender panoply
feod fee (estate)
feoffee legatee. SEE MAIN ENTRY
feoffment SEE MAIN ENTRY
feoffor SEE MAIN ENTRY
feracious fertile, prolific. SEE MAIN ENTRY
feral deadly, destructive, fatal, harsh, lethal, malicious, malignant, pestilent, ruthless
ferax fertile, productive
fergiversate prevaricate
feriae holiday
ferine harsh, ruthless
ferire beat (strike)
ferity atrocity, cruelty, severity
ferment agitate (activate), catalyst, commotion, confusion (turmoil), decompose, discompose, disturb, disturbance, embroilment, emotion, entanglement (confusion), foment, furor, pandemonium, passion, perturb, riot, stress (strain), turmoil. SEE MAIN ENTRY
fermentation commotion
ferocious brutal, cruel, harsh, malevolent, malicious, malignant, outrageous, ruthless, vicious
ferociousness bestiality, cruelty, severity
ferocity atrocity, bestiality, cruelty, furor, outbreak, severity, violence. SEE MAIN ENTRY
ferox rampant, unruly
ferre bear (support), legalize
ferret hunt, search. SEE MAIN ENTRY
ferret out ascertain, cross-examine, delve, detect, discover, disinter, educe, find (discover), locate, pursue (chase), solve, trace (follow). SEE MAIN ENTRY
ferrier carrier
fertile beneficial, gainful, lucrative, original (creative), productive, prolific, resourceful. SEE MAIN ENTRY
fertilis fertile

fertility maternity
ferule cudgel
ferus brutal
fervency affection, ardor, compulsion *(obsession),* furor, passion
fervens fervent, vehement
fervent demonstrative *(expressive of emotion),* eager, earnest, fanatical, hot-blooded, intense, intensive, ready *(willing),* serious *(devoted),* true *(loyal),* vehement, zealous. SEE MAIN ENTRY
fervid fervent, hot-blooded, vehement, zealous. SEE MAIN ENTRY
fervidness ardor
fervidus eager, fervent
fervor affection. SEE MAIN ENTRY
fervor ardor
fervor emotion, passion, strength
Fescennine salacious
fester annoy
festering toxic
festinatio dispatch *(promptness),* haste
festival holiday, treat
festive occasion ceremony
festivity ceremony
festooned elaborate
fetch procure, ruse, transport, yield *(produce a return)*
fetching attractive
fete holiday
fetid stale
fetish compulsion *(obsession),* obsession
fetter apprehend *(arrest),* bind *(restrain),* constraint *(imprisonment),* constraint *(restriction),* constrict *(inhibit),* contain *(restrain),* custody *(incarceration),* detain *(restrain),* detention, deter, hamper, handcuff *(noun),* handcuff *(verb),* hinder, impede, impediment, interfere, restrain, restrict, trammel. SEE MAIN ENTRY
fetters bondage, servitude
fettle color *(complexion)*
fetus embryo
feud altercation, argument *(contention),* belligerency, brawl, collide *(clash),* contention *(opposition),* contest *(dispute),* controversy *(argument),* disaccord, disagreement, dispute, fee *(estate),* freehold, revenge, struggle. SEE MAIN ENTRY
feuder contender
feuding malevolent
fever furor SEE MAIN ENTRY
fever pitch SEE MAIN ENTRY
feverish demonstrative *(expressive of emotion),* frenetic, hot-blooded, rapid
feverish haste dispatch *(promptness)*
feverishness ardor
few deficient, infrequent, scarce, several *(plural).* SEE MAIN ENTRY
few and far between SEE MAIN ENTRY
fewness insufficiency, paucity
fiasco debacle, disaster, failure *(lack of success),* miscarriage
fiat brevet, canon, declaration, decree, dictate, direction *(order),* directive, edict, enactment, law, license, mandate, monition *(legal summons),* order *(judicial directive),* ordinance, permit, precept, proclamation, pronouncement, requirement, writ. SEE MAIN ENTRY
fib invent *(falsify),* lie *(falsify),* mislead, prevaricate, story *(falsehood),* subterfuge
fibbing falsification
fiber character *(personal quality),* frame *(mood),* prowess *(bravery)*
fickle capricious, faithless, false *(disloyal),* inconsistent, irresolute, mutable, undependable, unpredictable, unreliable, unsettled, untrustworthy, variable, volatile
fickleness disloyalty, indecision, infidelity
fictile pliable, sequacious
fiction canard, falsehood, figment, lie, misstatement, myth, phantom, story *(falsehood),* subterfuge. SEE MAIN ENTRY
fiction of the mind figment
fictional fictitious
fictionalize fabricate *(make up),* invent *(falsify)*
fictitious artificial, assumed *(feigned),* erroneous, evasive, false *(inaccurate),* illusory, lying, mendacious, sobriquet, spurious, unfounded, untrue. SEE MAIN ENTRY
fictitious story myth
fictive evasive, fictitious, original *(creative)*
fictive creation phantom
fictus apparent *(perceptible),* false *(not genuine),* false pretense, fictitious, ostensible, unfounded
fidelis faithful *(diligent),* loyal, true *(authentic)*
fidelitas fidelity, loyalty
fideliter faithfully
fidelity adherence *(devotion),* adhesion *(loyalty),* allegiance, conformity *(obedience),* discipline *(obedience),* faith, fealty, homage, honesty, integrity, loyalty, rectitude. SEE MAIN ENTRY
fides allegiance, confidence *(faith),* credibility, duty *(obligation),* faith, fidelity, guarantee, honesty, loyalty, promise, reliance, trust *(confidence),* vow
fidgety restive
fiducia assurance, confidence *(faith),* reliance, trust *(confidence)*
fiducial fiduciary, pecuniary
fiduciary executor, pecuniary, trustee. SEE MAIN ENTRY
fiduciary currency check *(instrument)*
fidus confidential, faithful *(diligent),* loyal, safe, staunch, true *(authentic)*
fief fee *(estate),* freehold
field area *(province),* bailiwick, calling, capacity *(sphere),* career, circuit, coverage *(scope),* department, employment, latitude, occupation *(vocation),* parcel, plot *(land),* post, profession *(vocation),* province, pursuit *(occupation),* range, realm, region, scene, scope, section *(vicinity),* space, sphere, territory. SEE MAIN ENTRY
field of activity department, sphere
field of inquiry issue *(matter in dispute),* matter *(subject)*
field of interest discipline *(field of study)*
field of learning discipline *(field of study)*
field of operation sphere
field of view outlook, perspective, vision *(sight)*
field of vision perception, perspective
field questions return *(respond)*
fiend *(addiet)* SEE MAIN ENTRY
fiend *(enthusiast)* SEE MAIN ENTRY
fiendish cold-blooded, cruel, diabolic, harmful, malevolent, malignant, peccant *(culpable),* pernicious, ruthless, sinister
fiendishness atrocity, bestiality
fiendlike diabolic, malignant
fierce brutal, cruel, demonstrative *(expressive of emotion),* fervent, formidable, intense, severe, spartan, vehement, vicious. SEE MAIN ENTRY
fierceness bestiality, cruelty, passion, severity
fieri occur *(happen),* result
fieriness life *(vitality)*
fiery demonstrative *(expressive of emotion),* fervent, hot-blooded, intense, vehement, zealous
Fifth Amendment SEE MAIN ENTRY
fifty percent moiety
fifty-two weeks annum
fight affray, altercation, beat *(strike),* bicker, brawl *(noun),* brawl *(verb),* collision *(dispute),* commotion, conflict, confrontation *(altercation),* contend *(dispute),* contention *(opposition),* contest *(dispute),* contest, disagree, fracas, fray, grapple, incompatibility *(difference),* oppose, oppugn, resist *(oppose),* resistance, rift *(disagreement),* strife, strive, struggle, withstand. SEE MAIN ENTRY
fight against counter, counteract
fight for protect
fight off counter, parry, repel *(drive back)*
fight offensively attack
fight with engage *(involve)*
fighter aggressor, contender, foe, malcontent
fighting belligerency, conflict, litigious, offensive *(taking the initiative),* pugnacious, strife
figment fiction, myth, phantom, story *(falsehood).* SEE MAIN ENTRY
figment of the imagination phantom
figmental fictitious
figura contour *(shape),* form *(arrangement)*
figurare form
figuration configuration *(form),* contour *(outline),* contour *(shape),* formation, motif, organization *(structure)*
figurative representative. SEE MAIN ENTRY
figure bill *(invoice),* body *(main part),* build *(construct),* calculate, character *(an individual),* color *(complexion),* complexion, configuration *(form),* contour *(outline),* contour *(shape),* delineate, estimate, indicant, motif, organization *(structure),* phenomenon *(manifestation),* plan, price, rate, sum *(tally).* SEE MAIN ENTRY
figure costs estimate, evaluate
figure of speech phrase
figure out ascertain, calculate, conceive *(comprehend),* construe *(comprehend),* find *(discover),* interpret, reason *(conclude),* resolve *(solve),* solve. SEE MAIN ENTRY
figure up sum
figure work computation
figure-work census
figurehead ineffective, ineffectual, nonentity, powerless, token
figures census, information *(facts)*
figuring census, computation
filch embezzle, pilfer, poach, purloin, steal
filcher burglar, criminal
filchery theft
filching burglary, housebreaking
file book, classify, defer *(put off),* distribute, dossier, enroll, enter *(record),* entry *(record),* erode, fix *(arrange),* index *(docket),* ledger, lineup, organize *(arrange),* pigeonhole, record *(noun),* record *(verb),* register *(noun),* register *(verb),* sort, tabulate. SEE MAIN ENTRY
file a charge complain *(charge),* prosecute *(charge)*
file a claim charge *(accuse),* complain *(charge),* impeach, lodge *(bring a complaint),* prosecute *(charge)*
file a legal claim sue
file a suit complain *(charge),* lodge *(bring a complaint)*

file for petition
file suit sue
filed charges accused *(charged)*
filed notice lis pendens
filia child
filial loyal
filiality affiliation *(bloodline)*
filiate ascribe, relate *(establish a connection)*
filiation affiliation *(bloodline)*, affinity *(family ties)*, ancestry, blood, degree *(kinship)*, descent *(lineage)*, family *(common ancestry)*, origin *(ancestry)*, parentage, propinquity *(kinship)*, relationship *(family tie)*. SEE MAIN ENTRY
filibuster detain *(restrain)*, forestall, hold up *(delay)*, procrastinate, protract *(prolong)*, stall. SEE MAIN ENTRY
filing registration
filing of charges accusation
filius child
filius familias minor
fill fulfill, imbue, impact, load, penetrate, permeate, pervade, replenish, satisfy *(fulfill)*, sufficiency. SEE MAIN ENTRY
fill a position employ *(engage services)*, engage *(hire)*, hire
fill a post hold *(possess)*
fill a vacancy employ *(engage services)*, hire
fill an office officiate, serve *(assist)*
fill an opening employ *(engage services)*
fill another's position displace *(replace)*
fill identical times coincide *(correspond)*
fill in compound, develop, replacement, replenish
fill in for displace *(replace)*, replace
fill one's time engage *(involve)*
fill out compound, develop, enlarge, expand, inflate, spread
fill to capacity impact
fill to superfluity inundate
fill up load, replenish, supply
fill with air inflate
fill with doubt perplex
fill with enthusiasm inspire
fill with information disabuse, instruct *(teach)*
fill with loathing repel *(disgust)*
fill with longing motivate
fill with shame humiliate
filled copious, full, inflated *(enlarged)*, replete
filled out ripe
filled to repletion replete
filled to utmost capacity full
filled with pride disdainful
fillip inducement, stimulate, stimulus
filminess indistinctness
filmy indistinct
filter distill, purge *(purify)*, screen *(select)*. SEE MAIN ENTRY
filter in penetrate
filter through pervade
filth pornography
filthify pollute
filthiness defilement
filthy objectionable, repulsive, salacious
filtrate distill
fimbriae edge *(border)*
finagling fraudulent
final absolute *(complete)*, absolute *(conclusive)*, binding, categorical, certain *(positive)*, complete *(ended)*, conclusive *(determinative)*, conclusive *(settled)*, crucial, decisive, definitive, determinative, extreme *(last)*, inappealable, irrevocable, last *(final)*, peremptory *(absolute)*, positive *(incontestable)*, ultimate. SEE MAIN ENTRY
final appeal SEE MAIN ENTRY
final assessment determination
final authority arbiter
final cause object, purpose
final condemnation conviction *(finding of guilt)*
final condition ultimatum
final demand dun
final determination adjudication
final event end *(termination)*
final happening denouement
final judgment adjudication, conclusion *(determination)*, decree, holding *(ruling of a court)*, opinion *(judicial decision)*
final notice dun
final offer ultimatum
final outcome product
final point extremity *(furthest point)*, limit, objective
final proposal ultimatum
final proposition ultimatum
final result conclusion *(outcome)*, consequence *(conclusion)*, effect, issuance
final settlement of a matter disposition *(determination)*
final state end *(termination)*
final statement denouement
final terms condition *(contingent provision)*, settlement
final touch denouement
finale cessation *(termination)*, close *(conclusion)*, conclusion *(outcome)*, consequence *(conclusion)*. SEE MAIN ENTRY
finale denouement
finale end *(termination)*, payoff *(result)*
finality divorce, end *(termination)*. SEE MAIN ENTRY
finality of judgment SEE MAIN ENTRY
finalization denouement
finalize close *(agree)*, complete, conclude *(complete)*, consummate, decide, finish. SEE MAIN ENTRY
finalize an agreement close *(agree)*
finally consequently. SEE MAIN ENTRY
finally settled inappealable
finalty conclusion *(outcome)*
finance bear *(support)*, bestow, capitalize *(provide capital)*, fund, invest *(fund)*, lend, maintain *(sustain)*, pay, sponsor, subsidize, support *(assist)*, underwrite. SEE MAIN ENTRY
finance again refinance
financer patron *(influential supporter)*, surety *(guarantor)*
finances capital, cash, means *(funds)*, money
financial commercial, fiscal, mercantile, monetary, pecuniary. SEE MAIN ENTRY
financial affairs finance
financial assistance consideration *(recompense)*
financial backer promoter
financial backing investment, maintenance *(support of spouse)*
financial center market *(business)*, market place
financial disaster bankruptcy, default, failure *(bankruptcy)*
financial failure bankruptcy
financial loss failure *(bankruptcy)*
financial officer comptroller
financial provision capital
financial remuneration compensation, honorarium, income, pension, perquisite, recovery *(award)*, reparation *(indemnification)*
financial resources capital, finance, income, property *(possessions)*
financial reward perquisite, profit
financial ruin bankruptcy, failure *(bankruptcy)*
financial shortage deficit
financial statement account *(evaluation)*
financial straits privation
financially prudent economical
financially sound solvent
financier obligee, promoter, sponsor, trustee
financing investment, loan, maintenance *(support of spouse)*
find acquisition, adjudge, adjudicate, ascertain, award, conclude *(decide)*, decide, decree, detect, determine, disinter, ferret, hold *(decide)*, invent *(produce for the first time)*, judge, locate, prize, procure, pronounce *(pass judgment)*, rule *(decide)*, sentence. SEE MAIN ENTRY
find a clue elucidate
find a middle ground compromise *(settle by mutual agreement)*
find a place for lodge *(house)*
find a remedy counteract
find a solution resolve *(solve)*
find a way devise *(invent)*
find against convict
find an indictment against impeach
find cause to blame criticize *(find fault with)*
find fault blame, complain *(criticize)*, decry, deprecate, discommend, except *(object)*, object, remonstrate, reprimand
find fault with cavil, censure, complain *(criticize)*, denounce *(condemn)*, depreciate, disapprove *(condemn)*, disparage, expostulate, impugn, incriminate, rebuke, reprehend, reproach
find flaws remonstrate
find freedom escape
find guilty condemn *(blame)*, convict, sentence
find hard to believe doubt *(distrust)*
find help employ *(engage services)*
find indispensable need
find intolerable resent
find liable convict
find manpower recruit
find necessary need
find not guilty absolve, acquit, clear
find nothing to praise decry
find one's advantage in capitalize *(seize the chance)*
find out ascertain, detect, discover, disinter, overhear, solve
find out exactly ascertain
find out the meaning of construe *(comprehend)*
find outlet exude
find passage exude
find probable assume *(suppose)*
find room for lodge *(house)*
find the answer ascertain, resolve *(solve)*
find the cause solve
find the key solve
find the solution ascertain, solve
find the value of evaluate
find the weight of weigh
find unfounded disprove
find useful exploit *(make use of)*
find vent exude

find words for express
find words to express communicate, phrase
finding adjudication, answer *(solution)*, arbitration, award, choice *(decision)*, clue, cognovit, comment, conclusion *(determination)*, consequence *(conclusion)*, conviction *(finding of guilt)*, decree, detection, determination, dictum, disposition *(determination)*, holding *(ruling of a court)*, invention, judgment *(formal court decree)*, observation, opinion *(judicial decision)*, outcome, perception, recognition, result, ruling, solution *(answer)*, verdict. SEE MAIN ENTRY
finding a middle course mediation
finding another mate digamy
finding another spouse digamy
finding of guilt condemnation *(punishment)*. SEE MAIN ENTRY
finding out discovery
findings of fact and conclusions of law ruling
fine acute, amercement, appropriate, cost *(penalty)*, damages, forfeiture *(thing forfeited)*, impalpable, meritorious, narrow, penalize, penalty, premium, rare, sapid, tenuous, trover, valuable. SEE MAIN ENTRY
fine-mannered civil *(polite)*
fine point technicality
fine print SEE MAIN ENTRY
fineness quality *(excellence)*, sensibility
finer superior *(excellent)*
finesse artifice, discretion *(quality of being discreet)*, management *(judicious use)*, performance *(workmanship)*, prowess *(ability)*, ruse, science *(technique)*, skill, stratagem, subterfuge. SEE MAIN ENTRY
finest cardinal *(outstanding)*, leading *(ranking first)*, premium, prime *(most valuable)*
fingere conjure, create, feign, pretend
fingerprints SEE MAIN ENTRY
finical meticulous, particular *(exacting)*, precise, punctilious
finicality particularity
finicalness particularity
finicking meticulous, punctilious
finicky meticulous, particular *(exacting)*, precise, punctilious
finire conclude *(complete)*, limit
finis boundary, cessation *(termination)*, close *(conclusion)*, conclusion *(outcome)*
finis denouement, dissolution *(termination)*
finis end *(termination)*, frontier, limit, object, restriction
finish accomplish, attain, cap, cease, cessation *(termination)*, close *(conclusion)*, close *(terminate)*, commit *(perpetrate)*, complete, conclude *(complete)*, conclusion *(outcome)*, consequence *(conclusion)*, consummate, culminate, defeasance, denouement, deplete, desist, destination, discontinue *(abandon)*, dispatch *(dispose of)*, dissolution *(termination)*, dissolve *(terminate)*, end *(termination)*, exhaust *(try all possibilities)*, expend *(consume)*, expiration, expire, extremity *(death)*, finality, fulfill, liquidate *(convert into cash)*, mature, outcome, pass *(satisfy requirements)*, payoff *(result)*, perfect, perform *(adhere to)*, quit *(discontinue)*, shut, stop, terminate. SEE MAIN ENTRY
finish litigation rest *(end a legal case)*
finish off cap, extinguish
finish up close *(terminate)*
finished absolute *(complete)*, choate lien, complete *(ended)*, conclusive *(settled)*, defunct, expert, irredeemable, ripe, through, veteran. SEE MAIN ENTRY
finished product fait accompli, performance *(execution)*
finishing conclusive *(settled)*, extreme *(last)*, final, last *(final)*
finishing stroke denouement
finite terminable
finite quantity paucity
finitimus adjacent
fire ardor, barrage, burn, conflagration, deflagrate, depose *(remove)*, discharge *(dismiss)*, discharge *(shoot)*, dismiss *(discharge)*, foment, life *(vitality)*, passion, provoke, remove *(dismiss from office)*, spirit, stimulate, supplant. SEE MAIN ENTRY
fire at discharge *(shoot)*
fire from employment terminate
fire up motivate
fire-raising arson
firearm gun
firearms ammunition
fireball bomb
firebrand demagogue, hoodlum
fireside home *(domicile)*
firing arson, discharge *(dismissal)*, discharge *(shot)*, dismissal *(discharge)*, layoff, rejection
firing a charge discharge *(shot)*
firm business *(commercial enterprise)*, certain *(fixed)*, cohesive *(compact)*, compact *(dense)*, company *(enterprise)*, concern *(business establishment)*, concrete, constant, corporation, corporeal, definite, durable, earnest, enterprise *(economic organization)*, faithful *(loyal)*, fixed *(securely placed)*, house, immutable, indomitable, inexorable, inflexible, infrangible, inseparable, institute, intractable, ironclad, irreconcilable, irrevocable, loyal, obdurate, ossified, partnership, patient, peremptory *(imperative)*, pertinacious, purposeful, renitent, resolute, rigid, secure *(sound)*, sedulous, serious *(devoted)*, severe, solid *(compact)*, solid *(sound)*, spartan, stable, staunch, steadfast, strong, unalterable, unbending, uncompromising, undaunted, undeniable, unyielding, well-grounded. SEE MAIN ENTRY
firm advice instruction *(direction)*
firm attachment affection
firm belief confidence *(faith)*, conviction *(persuasion)*, credence, faith
firm hold coherence
firm in adherence true *(loyal)*
firm in allegiance true *(loyal)*
firm in principle high-minded
firm opposition conflict
firm principle code, law
firm up stabilize
firmly faithfully
firmly established fixed *(securely placed)*, ingrained, inveterate, steadfast
firmly fixed ingrained
firmly implanted fixed *(securely placed)*
firmly seated fixed *(securely placed)*
firmly set fixed *(securely placed)*, rigid
firmly united compact *(dense)*
firmness adherence *(adhesion)*, adhesion *(loyalty)*, certainty, constant, force *(strength)*, inertia, prowess *(bravery)*, purpose, resolution *(decision)*, rigor, spirit, strength, surety *(certainty)*, tenacity. SEE MAIN ENTRY
firmness of belief certainty
firmness of purpose diligence *(perseverance)*
firmus constant *(adjective)*, constant *(noun)*, durable, firm, irrefutable, resolute, solid *(sound)*, stable, staunch, steadfast, substantial, valid
first ab initio, cardinal *(basic)*, central *(essential)*, dominant, important *(significant)*, initial, leading *(ranking first)*, original *(initial)*, paramount, precursory, preferred *(given priority)*, previous, primary, prime *(original)*, primordial, principal, prior, prototype, stellar, unprecedented. SEE MAIN ENTRY
First Amendment SEE MAIN ENTRY
first and foremost ab initio
first and last only *(sole)*
first appearance nascency, onset *(commencement)*. SEE MAIN ENTRY
first attempt experiment
first cause derivation
first charge first offense
first competition primary
first contest primary
first crime first offense
first criminal violation first offense
first election primary
first impression SEE MAIN ENTRY
first in quality prime *(most valuable)*
first installment handsel
first move onset *(commencement)*, outset
first occasion derivation
first of all ab initio
first offender convict
first offense SEE MAIN ENTRY
first payment handsel
first place primacy, priority, prize
first pleading complaint
first political competition primary
first political contest primary
first position SEE MAIN ENTRY
first receipts handsel
first sale doctrine SEE MAIN ENTRY
first sight discovery
first stage embryo, nascency
first step nascency, onset *(commencement)*, outset, start. SEE MAIN ENTRY
first violation first offense
first-class best, premium, prime *(most valuable)*
firsthand SEE MAIN ENTRY
first-rate best, meritorious, preferential, premium, prime *(most valuable)*, select, superior *(excellent)*, superlative
firstly ab initio
fiscal commercial, financial, mercantile, monetary, pecuniary. SEE MAIN ENTRY
fiscal cliff SEE MAIN ENTRY
fiscal exchange commerce
fiscalis fiscal
fiscus finance, treasury
fish out ferret
fishing expedition SEE MAIN ENTRY
fissile divisible, severable
fission severance
fissionable divisible, severable
fissura split
fissure break *(fracture)*, force *(break)*, part *(separate)*, rift *(gap)*, sever, split *(noun)*, split *(verb)*
fisticuffs affray, brawl
fit accommodate, adapt, adequate, agree *(comply)*, applicable, apposite, appropriate, available, capable, competent, comply, comport *(agree with)*, condign, conform, congruous, consonant, due *(regular)*, effective *(efficient)*, eligible, entitled, familiar *(informed)*, favorable *(advantageous)*, felicitous, just, normal *(sane)*, opportune, outbreak, outburst, pertinent, qualified

(competent), ready (prepared), reasonable (fair), reasonable (rational), relative (relevant), relevant, right (suitable), ripe, satisfy (fulfill), seasonable, suitable. SEE MAIN ENTRY
fit exactly coincide (correspond)
fit for a purpose attune
fit for appointment eligible
fit for dwelling habitable
fit for election eligible
fit for habitation habitable, residential
fit for sale marketable
fit for selection eligible
fit for travel open (accessible), passable
fit for use disposable, effective (operative), functional
fit in comport (agree with), conform
fit out clothe, furnish, supply
fit the pattern naturalize (acclimate)
fit time opportunity
fit to be chosen eligible
fit to be occupied habitable
fit to live in habitable
fit together comport (agree with), frame (construct), join (bring together)
fitful broken (interrupted), disjunctive (tending to disjoin), disorderly, haphazard, inconsistent, intermittent, sporadic, unpredictable, variable
fitfulness inconsistency, irregularity
fitness ability, admissibility, aptitude, competence (ability), expedience, faculty (ability), health, instinct, propriety (appropriateness), timeliness. SEE MAIN ENTRY
fitted capable, commensurate, convenient, familiar (informed), fit, sciential
fitted for legal argumentation forensic
fitted for public argumentation forensic
fitted to teach didactic
fittedness ability
fitting applicable, apposite, appropriate, as a matter of right, condign, congruous, consonant, convenient, conventional, correlative, eligible, fair (just), favorable (advantageous), felicitous, fit, germane, just, opportune, permissible, pertinent, practical, proper, reasonable (fair), relative (relevant), relevant, right (suitable), rightful, suitable, tenable. SEE MAIN ENTRY
fitting occasion opportunity
fitting time opportunity
fittingness decorum, expedience, qualification (fitness)
fix adjust (resolve), affix, allocate, annex (add), arrange (methodize), award, bind (restrain), bond (hold together), cement, decide, define, delimit, designate, dispose (apportion), embed, emend, entanglement (involvement), help, hold (decide), marshal, plant (place firmly), predicament, redress, reform, rehabilitate, remedy, renew (refurbish), renovate, repair, repose (place), restore (renew). SEE MAIN ENTRY
fix a charge charge (assess)
fix a valuation assess (tax)
fix attention on note (notice)
fix beforehand preordain
fix blame accuse
fix bounds circumscribe (surround by boundary)
fix by agreement close (agree)
fix conclusively arbitrate (adjudge), rule (decide)
fix deeply establish (entrench)
fix firmly embed
fix in pinpoint
fix in purpose resolve (decide)
fix in the mind recall (remember), remember
fix limits circumscribe (surround by boundary), demarcate
fix on focus
fix one's attention concentrate (pay attention)
fix permanently establish (entrench)
fix the blame for lodge (bring a complaint)
fix the burden of impute
fix the date date
fix the meaning define
fix the mind upon intend
fix the order arrange (methodize), file (arrange)
fix the position locate
fix the price at charge (assess)
fix the price of rate
fix the responsibility present (prefer charges)
fix the responsibility for impute
fix the thoughts upon focus
fix the time date
fix the value assess (appraise)
fix together cement
fix up embellish
fix upon determine, impute, prefer, select
fix with precision define
fixable ascertainable, corrigible, determinable (ascertainable)
fixation compulsion (obsession), constant, location, obsession, preoccupation. SEE MAIN ENTRY
fixed absolute (conclusive), accustomed (customary), attached (annexed), certain (specific), constant, conventional, customary, definite, definitive, deliberate, durable, express, firm, formal, habitual, immutable, inappealable, indelible, inevitable, inextricable, inflexible, ingrained, inherent, inveterate, irrevocable, limited, necessary (inescapable), ordinary, permanent, perpetual, positive (prescribed), prescriptive, regular (orderly), resolute, rigid, routine, secure (sound), serious (devoted), several (separate), situated, stable, standing, stated, static, statutory, steadfast, traditional, unalienable, unalterable, unavoidable (inevitable), unavoidable (not voidable), unbending, unyielding. SEE MAIN ENTRY
fixed amount of damages ad damnum clause
fixed assets immovable
fixed belief credence
fixed capital principal (capital sum)
fixed charge fee (charge)
fixed chattel immovable
fixed conviction compulsion (obsession)
fixed direction intention
fixed future predetermination
fixed idea compulsion (obsession), obsession, preconception, preoccupation
fixed intention project
fixed opinion conviction (persuasion)
fixed order array (order), method
fixed procedure usage
fixed property immovable
fixed purpose animus, design (intent), forethought, goal, intention, objective
fixed residence abode, home (domicile)
fixed ways practice (custom)
fixedly invariably
fixedness adherence (adhesion)
fixing attachment (act of affixing), designation (naming), renewal, repair
fixing a bid SEE MAIN ENTRY
fixing a price appraisal
fixity of purpose diligence (perseverance)
fixture attachment (thing affixed), device (mechanism), immovable. SEE MAIN ENTRY
flaccid powerless
flag indicant, indicator, languish, succumb
flag bearer nominee (candidate)
flagellare lash (strike)
flagellate beat (strike), ill use, lash (strike)
flagging languid
flagitare call (demand), dun, solicit
flagitiosus disgraceful
flagitious bad (offensive), blameworthy, depraved, disgraceful, flagrant, heinous, immoral, inexcusable, inexpiable, iniquitous, nefarious, outrageous, profligate (corrupt), reprehensible, reprobate, scandalous, sinister. SEE MAIN ENTRY
flagitious villainy atrocity
flagitiousness atrocity, bad repute, crime
flagitous blameful
flagrancy atrocity, bad repute, notoriety, pretense (ostentation)
flagrant arrant (onerous), bad (offensive), blameworthy, brazen, conspicuous, delinquent (guilty of a misdeed), disgraceful, egregious, extreme (exaggerated), heinous, manifest, nefarious, notorious, outrageous, outright, prominent, remarkable, reprehensible, reprobate, salient, scandalous. SEE MAIN ENTRY
flagrant abuse of the law lynch law
flagrante delicto blameworthy, delinquency (misconduct)
flagrantly bad arrant (onerous)
flail beat (strike)
flair aptitude, competence (ability), faculty (ability). SEE MAIN ENTRY
flam falsehood
flamboyant elaborate, grandiose, pretentious (ostentatious). SEE MAIN ENTRY
flame deflagrate
flame up burn, deflagrate
flaming hot-blooded, intense
flaming into notice flagrant
flange border
flank border (bound), hedge, protect
flap brandish, oscillate
flare burn, deflagrate, discharge (shot)
flare up deflagrate, outburst
flare-up bluster (commotion), furor, outbreak
flaring blatant (obtrusive)
flash deflagrate, discharge (shot), flaunt, immediate (at once)
flashiness pretense (ostentation)
flashy elaborate, flagrant, grandiose, pretentious (ostentatious), tawdry
flat impecunious, insipid, jejune (dull), lifeless (dull), pedestrian, prosaic, stale
flat broke impecunious
flat refusal rebuff
flat saying platitude
flatten depress
flatter overestimate
flattering obsequious
flattery mention (tribute)
flatulence bombast
flatulent fustian, inflated (bombastic), loquacious, orotund. SEE MAIN ENTRY
flaunt brandish, display. SEE MAIN ENTRY
flaunting blatant (obtrusive), brazen, flagrant, grandiose, orgulous, proud (conceited)

flavor color *(complexion)*, savory. SEE MAIN ENTRY
flavored savory
flavorful palatable, sapid
flavorless insipid, jejune *(dull)*, stale
flavorous palatable, sapid, savory
flavorsome palatable, sapid, savory
flavory sapid
flaw deface, defacement, defect, deficiency, drawback, error, fault *(mistake)*, fault *(weakness)*, foible, frailty, miscue, onus *(blame)*, stigma, vice. SEE MAIN ENTRY
flaw in reasoning fallacy
flaw in the argument non sequitur
flawed blemished, defective, deficient, fallible, faulty, imperfect, incorrect, inexact, marred, peccable, sinister, vicious. SEE MAIN ENTRY
flawless absolute *(ideal)*, best, infallible, intact, precise, pure, unblemished. SEE MAIN ENTRY
flay denude, lash *(attack verbally)*, lash *(strike)*, plunder, reprimand, reproach
flebilis deplorable, lamentable, lugubrious
fledging amateur
fledgling juvenile, neophyte, novice
flee abscond, depart, disappear, elude, escape, evacuate, evade *(elude)*, leave *(depart)*, move *(alter position)*, quit *(evacuate)*, retreat. SEE MAIN ENTRY
flee from avoid *(evade)*, eschew
fleece betray *(lead astray)*, defraud, deprive, dupe, prey, steal
fleeced aggrieved *(victimized)*
fleeing flight
fleer flout, fugitive, mock *(deride)*
fleet expeditious, rapid
fleeting brief, elusive, ephemeral, temporary, transient, transitory, volatile
fleeting expletives SEE MAIN ENTRY
flesh and blood physical
fleshly corporeal, lascivious, lecherous, mundane, physical, prurient
fleshy corporal
flexibilis flexible, pliable
flexibility amenability, facility *(easiness)*, informality, lenience
flexible amenable, deft, facile, liberal *(broad minded)*, malleable, open *(persuasible)*, passive, pliable, pliant, receptive, resilient, sequacious, suasible, susceptible *(responsive)*, tractable, yielding. SEE MAIN ENTRY
flexibleness amenability
flexile flexible, malleable, pliable, resilient, sequacious, tractable
flexuous circuitous, complex, laby-rinthine, sinuous
flicker beat *(pulsate)*
flickering intermittent
flier notice *(announcement)*
flight abandonment *(desertion)*, desertion, evasion. SEE MAIN ENTRY
flight of fancy figment
flightiness inconsistency
flighty capricious, frivolous, inconsistent, irresponsible, thoughtless, volatile
flimflam bunko, falsification, ruse. SEE MAIN ENTRY
flimsiness frailty, impalpability
flimsy frivolous, inconclusive, inconsequential, inferior *(lower in quality)*, insubstantial, nonsubstantial *(not sturdy)*, poor *(inferior in quality)*, tenuous
fling cast *(throw)*, dispatch *(send off)*, impel, launch *(project)*, precipitate *(throw down violently)*, project *(impel forward)*, send
fling dishonor upon disgrace
fling downward precipitate *(throw down violently)*
fling off dispel
flint-hearted brutal, malignant
flinty rigid
flip a coin bet
flipflop SEE MAIN ENTRY
flippancy disrespect
flippant brazen, frivolous, impertinent *(insolent)*, insolent, presumptuous
flitter beat *(pulsate)*
flitting transitory
float finance. SEE MAIN ENTRY
flock assemblage, mass *(body of persons)*, meet
flog beat *(strike)*, lash *(strike)*, punish
flood assemblage, cataclysm, immerse *(plunge into)*, inundate, load, outflow, overcome *(overwhelm)*, overload, plethora, spate. SEE MAIN ENTRY
floodgate crossroad *(turning point)*, outlet. SEE MAIN ENTRY
floor recognition. SEE MAIN ENTRY
florens prosperous
floridness bombast
flounder mismanage
floundering incompetent
flourish brandish, display, flaunt, gain, germinate, increase, pretense *(ostentation)*, proliferate, pullulate, succeed *(attain)*
flourishing cumulative *(increasing)*, opulent, prosperous, rampant, successful
flourishing condition boom *(prosperity)*
flout contemn, defy, disdain, disrespect, jape, mock *(deride)*, override, spurn. SEE MAIN ENTRY
flouting contemptuous, disdainful
flow accrue *(arise)*, arise *(originate)*, circulate, circulation, cycle, ensue, issue *(send forth)*, pass *(advance)*, proceed *(go forward)*, progress, result, sequence, spread, stem *(originate)*. SEE MAIN ENTRY
flow forth emanate
flow from redound
flow in penetrate
flow into pervade
flow of language parlance
flow of words parlance
flow out exude, issue *(send forth)*
flow over inundate
flower proliferate, pullulate
flowering fertile, fruition, growth *(evolution)*
flowery turgid
flowery language rhetoric *(skilled speech)*
flowing circulation, copious, eloquent, facile, fluvial, full
flown truant
fluctuant indeterminate
fluctuare fluctuate
fluctuate beat *(pulsate)*, change, doubt *(hesitate)*, oscillate, vacillate, vary. SEE MAIN ENTRY
fluctuating capricious, disorderly, faithless, hesitant, intermittent, irresolute, irresponsible, mutable, periodic, shifting, sporadic, undependable, variable
fluctuation hesitation, indecision
fluctuations vicissitudes
fluency facility *(easiness)*, parlance, skill
fluent eloquent, facile, fluvial, loquacious, voluble
fluere emanate
fluff SEE MAIN ENTRY
fluid fluvial, indeterminate, protean. SEE MAIN ENTRY
fluidic fluvial
fluke SEE MAIN ENTRY
flunk fail *(lose)*
flurry confuse *(bewilder)*, dispatch *(promptness)*, haste, outburst, perturb
flush full, opulent, profuse, prosperous, replete, substantial
fluster agitate *(perturb)*, confuse *(bewilder)*, confusion *(ambiguity)*, discompose, disconcert, disorient, disrupt, disturb, embarrass, embarrassment, harry *(harass)*, muddle, obfuscate, perturb, stress *(strain)*, upset
flutter beat *(pulsate)*, oscillate, panic, trepidation
fluvial SEE MAIN ENTRY
fluviatic fluvial
fluviatile fluvial
fluvicoline fluvial
flux circulation, outflow, transition
fluxus transient
fly flee, leave *(depart)*, race
fly at attack
fly in the face of override
fly off at a tangent deviate, digress
fly-by-night untrustworthy
fob off on foist
focal central *(situated near center)*
focal point center *(central position)*, focus, gravamen, highlight. SEE MAIN ENTRY
focal point of the complaint gist *(ground for a suit)*
focalization centralization
focalize concentrate *(consolidate)*, converge
focus center *(central position)*, concentrate *(consolidate)*, concentrate *(pay attention)*, converge, devote, gravamen, pinpoint. SEE MAIN ENTRY
focus attention on concentrate *(pay attention)*, specialize
focus of attention center *(central position)*
fodere delve
fodicare jostle *(bump into)*
foe adversary, aggressor, contender, contestant, rival. SEE MAIN ENTRY
foedare deface
foederatus federal
foedere sociatus federal
foedus confederacy *(compact)*, league, loathsome, pact, repulsive
foeman foe
fog confuse *(bewilder)*, discompose, ignorance, incertitude, indistinctness, muddle, obfuscate, obnubilate, obscure, perplex
fogginess indistinctness, obscuration
foggy indistinct, nebulous, opaque, unclear
foible defect, deficiency, fault *(weakness)*, flaw, frailty, vice. SEE MAIN ENTRY
foil arrest *(stop)*, balk, check *(bar)*, circumvent, constrict *(inhibit)*, contravene, counter, counteract, defeat, deter, disadvantage, discontinue *(break continuity)*, enjoin, fight *(counteract)*, frustrate, frustration, halt, hamper, interfere, interrupt, keep *(restrain)*, oppugn, overturn, parry, preclude, prevent, repel *(drive back)*, stem *(check)*, stop, subdue, thwart, withstand. SEE MAIN ENTRY
foiled disappointed
foist coerce. SEE MAIN ENTRY
foist off fake
foist oneself intrude
foist upon bilk
fold fail *(lose)*, society
folder file

folio publication *(printed matter)*
folk family *(common ancestry)*, kindred, lineage, populace, population, public, race, society
folk speech language
folklore myth
folks populace
folktale myth
follow abide, accrue *(arise)*, adhere *(maintain loyalty)*, adopt, arise *(originate)*, chase, conform, copy, ensue, evolve, fulfill, heed, hunt, keep *(fulfill)*, mock *(imitate)*, obey, observe *(obey)*, observe *(watch)*, proceed *(go forward)*, pursue *(carry on)*, pursue *(chase)*, redound, result, resume, spy, stem *(originate)*, supervene. SEE MAIN ENTRY
follow a calling practice *(engage in)*
follow a course proceed *(go forward)*
follow a profession practice *(engage in)*
follow a trail pursue *(chase)*
follow after succeed *(follow)*
follow as a consequence ensue
follow as a model plagiarize
follow as an occupation practice *(engage in)*
follow close upon hunt
follow from emanate
follow in a train of events ensue
follow in order accede *(succeed)*, succeed *(follow)*
follow one another interchangeably alternate *(take turns)*
follow one another reciprocally alternate *(take turns)*
follow one's vocation labor
follow orders obey
follow precedent conform
follow routine conform
follow successively reciprocate
follow suit copy, mock *(imitate)*
follow the example of copy, mock *(imitate)*
follow the trail delve, hunt
follow the trail of search
follow through complete, consummate, exhaust *(try all possibilities)*, follow-up, perpetrate. SEE MAIN ENTRY
follow to a conclusion perfect
follow up maintain *(carry on)*, persevere, probe, prosecute *(carry forward)*. SEE MAIN ENTRY
follow up an inquiry canvass
follower addict, coadjutant, cohort, consociate, disciple, member *(individual in a group)*, parasite, partisan, protégé, successor
following ancillary *(subsidiary)*, business *(occupation)*, consequential *(deducible)*, continuous, deductible *(provable)*, deductive, derivative, ensuing, forthcoming, future, immediate *(imminent)*, imminent, inevitable, malleable, proximate, secondary, subsequent, successive. SEE MAIN ENTRY
following death posthumous
following established custom formal
following established form formal
following established rules formal
following in a series consecutive
following in time ex post facto
following the letter verbatim
following upon incident
folly abortion *(fiasco)*, inexpedience, lunacy. SEE MAIN ENTRY
foment abet, agitate *(activate)*, cause, conduce, incite, outbreak, outburst, stimulate. SEE MAIN ENTRY
fomentation aggravation *(exacerbation)*, commotion, disturbance, instigation, origination, outbreak, outburst, provocation
fomenter demagogue
fomentor abettor, determinant
fond of home household *(domestic)*
fond of investigation inquisitive
fondness affection, affinity *(regard)*, desire, estimation *(esteem)*, favor *(partiality)*, favoritism, inclination, partiality, penchant, predilection, predisposition, propensity, regard *(esteem)*. SEE MAIN ENTRY
fons origin *(source)*, source
font origin *(source)*, origination, source
food sustenance. SEE MAIN ENTRY
fool bilk, deceive, defraud, delude, dupe, ensnare, entrap, evade *(deceive)*, illude, inveigle, jape, lie *(falsify)*, misguide, mislead, misrepresent, overreach, palter, pretend. SEE MAIN ENTRY
foolable naive
foolhardiness inconsideration, temerity
foolhardy hot-blooded, imprudent, impulsive *(rash)*, precipitate, presumptuous, reckless, thoughtless
foolish fatuous, ill-advised, impolitic, imprudent, inept *(incompetent)*, irrational, ludicrous, lunatic, puerile, reckless, trivial, unfit, unpolitic, unreasonable, vacuous. SEE MAIN ENTRY
foolishness credulity, ignorance, inexpedience, jargon *(unintelligible language)*, lunacy, temerity
foolproof indubious, infallible, safe
foot pay
foot passenger pedestrian
foot the bill defray
foot traveler pedestrian
footage space
footing ground, plight, position *(situation)*, posture *(situation)*, status
footnote comment, marginalia, notation, note *(brief comment)*. SEE MAIN ENTRY
footpace step
footstep step
foppishness pride
for in furtherance, in lieu of. SEE MAIN ENTRY
for a beginning ab initio
for a certainty a fortiori
for a select few esoteric
for a still stronger reason a fortiori
for a time ad interim, pro tempore, provisional
for all history always *(forever)*
for all to see distinct *(clear)*
for cause SEE MAIN ENTRY
for each and every day per diem
for each day per diem
for ever and ever now and forever
for every day per diem
for just reason for cause
for legitimate reason for cause
for mere discussion only arguendo
for nothing free *(at no charge)*, gratis, gratuitous *(given without recompense)*
for one party ex parte
for one's good beneficial
for one's interest beneficial
for reasons given consequently
for that cause consequently
for that reason a priori, consequently
for the duration throughout *(during)*
for the moment pro tempore
for the most part as a rule, generally
for the period of throughout *(during)*
for the present occasion pro tempore
for the sake of ad hoc, in furtherance
for the sake of appearances pro forma
for the sake of argument arguendo
for the sake of form pro forma
for the time being ad interim, pro tempore
for the use of all common *(shared)*
for this case alone ad hoc
for this reason a priori, consequently
for which reason a priori, consequently
forage despoil, harry *(plunder)*, hunt, loot, prey, spoil *(pillage)*
foramen loophole
foraminated penetrable
foraminous penetrable
foray depredation, despoil, harry *(plunder)*, impinge, incursion, invasion, onset *(assault)*, pillage, plunder, prey, spoil *(pillage)*, spoliation. SEE MAIN ENTRY
forbear abandon *(relinquish)*, allow *(endure)*, avoid *(evade)*, bear *(tolerate)*, cease, condone, defer *(put off)*, desist, endure *(suffer)*, eschew, forgo, leave *(allow to remain)*, palliate *(excuse)*, pause, refrain, renounce, stop, tolerate, withhold. SEE MAIN ENTRY
forbearance abstention, benevolence *(disposition to do good)*, clemency, composure, continence, grace, lenience, longanimity, moderation, remission, resignation *(passive acceptance)*, restraint, sufferance, temperance. SEE MAIN ENTRY
forbearant passive, placable, resigned
forbearing charitable *(lenient)*, lenient, patient, placable, resigned
forbid ban, bar *(exclude)*, bar *(hinder)*, block, censor, clog, condemn *(ban)*, constrain *(restrain)*, debar, deny *(refuse to grant)*, deter, enjoin, estop, forestall, forewarn, gainsay, halt, inhibit, interdict, interfere, obstruct, preclude, prevent, prohibit, proscribe *(prohibit)*, reject, renounce, repel *(drive back)*, restrain, restrict, stay *(halt)*, stop, withhold. SEE MAIN ENTRY
forbid by law enjoin, outlaw
forbiddance bar *(obstruction)*, constraint *(restriction)*, embargo, estoppel, obstacle, obstruction, prohibition, proscription, restraint, veto
forbidden illegal, illegitimate *(illegal)*, illicit, impermissible, improper, unauthorized, unlawful
forbidden by law illicit
forbidding bleak *(not favorable)*, censorship, loathsome, lugubrious, odious, ominous, portentous *(ominous)*, repugnant *(exciting aversion)*, repulsive, severe, unapproachable
forbodement misgiving
forboding ominous
force ardor, attack, authority *(power)*, band, bind *(obligate)*, cast *(throw)*, catalyst, clout, coerce, coercion, command, compel, compulsion *(coercion)*, connotation, consequence *(significance)*, constrain *(compel)*, constraint *(restriction)*, content *(meaning)*, context, dint, dominance, draw *(attraction)*, duress, emphasis, enforce, enforcement, entail, exact, extort, foist, hijack, impact, impetus, impose *(subject)*, inflict, infliction, infringement, leverage, levy, main point, make, mistreat, misusage, necessitate, obtrude, oppression, overload, potential, power, press *(constrain)*, pressure *(noun)*, pressure *(verb)*, prestige, puissance, purpose, repercussion, require *(compel)*, rigor, severity, significance, signification, sinew, spirit, staff, strength, stress *(accent)*, stress *(strain)*, struggle, subjection, substance *(essential nature)*, validity, value, violence, weight *(importance)*. SEE MAIN ENTRY

force a passage penetrate, pervade
force an entrance impose *(intrude)*
force apart break *(separate)*
force armed with legal authority posse
force away expel
force back parry, repel *(drive back)*
force from acquire *(secure)*, preempt, procure
force in inject, interject, interpose
force of argument dialectic
force of circumstances predetermination
force of expression emphasis
force of voice emphasis
force oneself intrude
force oneself in impinge, impose *(intrude)*
force open break *(separate)*
force out deport *(banish)*, dislodge, eject *(expel)*, exclude, expel, oust, supplant
force payment exact, excise *(levy a tax)*
force together impact
force upon foist, impose *(enforce)*, inflict, insist
forced bound, compulsory, inappropriate, involuntary, obligatory, ponderous
forced confinement bondage, durance
forced departure deportation
forced entrance intrusion, onset *(assault)*
forced entry incursion
forced into smaller space compact *(dense)*
forced labor bondage
forced leave taking deportation
forced sale condemnation *(seizure)*
forceful categorical, cogent, convincing, decisive, dogmatic, drastic, eloquent, forcible, indomitable, insistent, intensive, irresistible, orotund, persuasive, potent, powerful, predominant, prevailing *(having superior force)*, resounding, sound, stringent, strong, trenchant, vehement. SEE MAIN ENTRY
forceful persuasion advocacy
forcefulness ardor, dint, force *(strength)*, influence, main force, sinew, validity
forceless null *(invalid)*, null and void, powerless, unable
forcelessness impotence, inefficacy
forces of law and order police
forces of nature climate
forcible cogent, compelling, compulsory, indomitable, irresistible, obligatory, potent, powerful, strong, valid, vehement. SEE MAIN ENTRY
forcible demand dun, requisition
forcible detention durance
forcible entry burglary, housebreaking
forcible expulsion from property eviction
forcible extraction avulsion
forcible inducement compulsion *(coercion)*
forcible restraint of liberty bondage
forcible seizure condemnation *(seizure)*, disseisin, distraint, expropriation *(divestiture)*, forfeiture *(act of forfeiting)*
forcible urging compulsion *(coercion)*, enforcement
forcible violation rape
forcing coercion, compulsion *(coercion)*
ford traverse
fordable passable
fore antecedent, back *(in arrears)*, last *(preceding)*, previous
forearm anticipate *(expect)*, caution, prearrange
forearmed prudent
forearming precaution
forebear ancestor, ascendant, forerunner, parents, primogenitor, progenitor
forebearance nonuse
forebearer precursor, predecessor
forebears ancestry, lineage, parentage
forebode admonish *(warn)*, anticipate *(prognosticate)*, forewarn, portend, predict, presage, prognosticate, promise *(raise expectations)*, threaten. SEE MAIN ENTRY
foreboding admonition, apprehension *(fear)*, caution *(warning)*, expectation, fear, misgiving, pessimistic, portentous *(ominous)*, precognition, premonition, presageful, prognosis, prophetic, qualm, threat, warning. SEE MAIN ENTRY
forecast anticipate *(prognosticate)*, contrive, expect *(consider probable)*, forsee, forewarn, herald, portend, predetermine, predict, presage, prognosis, prognosticate, promise *(raise expectations)*, prospect *(outlook)*. SEE MAIN ENTRY
forecasted foreseeable, imminent
forecasting prophetic, provident *(showing foresight)*
foreclose arrest *(stop)*, ban, bar *(hinder)*, block, clog, condemn *(seize)*, confiscate, deprive, deter, dispossess, impede, preclude, prevent, prohibit, repossess, stay *(halt)*. SEE MAIN ENTRY
foreclosed attached *(seized)*
foreclosing confiscatory
foreclosure attachment *(seizure)*, bar *(obstruction)*, condemnation *(seizure)*, disseisin, expropriation *(divestiture)*, forfeiture *(act of forfeiting)*, taking. SEE MAIN ENTRY
foredate antedate
foredoom predetermination, preordain
forefather ancestor, ascendant, precursor, predecessor, primogenitor, progenitor
forefathers ancestry, lineage, parentage
forefeeling expectation, premonition
forefeiture penalty
forefend balk
foregathering caucus
forego abandon *(relinquish)*, disclaim, forswear, resign, surrender *(give back)*. SEE MAIN ENTRY
foregoer ancestor, precursor, predecessor, progenitor
foregoing aforesaid, antecedent, before mentioned, former, last *(preceding)*, precursory, preliminary, previous, prior, said. SEE MAIN ENTRY
foregone previous
foregone conclusion bias, inequity, preconception, predetermination, predisposition. SEE MAIN ENTRY
forehanded economical, provident *(showing foresight)*
forehandedness economy *(frugality)*
foreign apart, different, extraneous, extrinsic, inapplicable, inapposite, irrelevant, novel, obscure *(remote)*, peculiar *(curious)*, unaccustomed, unrelated. SEE MAIN ENTRY
foreign influx immigration
foreign language rights SEE MAIN ENTRY
foreign person stranger
foreign-born alien *(foreign)*
foreigner alien, stranger
forejudge guess, preconceive, predetermine, prejudge, preordain, presume, presuppose. SEE MAIN ENTRY
forejudgment foregone conclusion, preconception, predetermination, prejudice *(preconception)*
foreknow anticipate *(prognosticate)*, predict, presage
foreknowable foreseeable
foreknowing oracular, prophetic
foreknowledge expectation, precognition, prognosis
forelay bait *(lure)*
foreman chief, director, superintendent. SEE MAIN ENTRY
forementioned before mentioned, previous, said
foremost best, cardinal *(basic)*, cardinal *(outstanding)*, central *(essential)*, critical *(crucial)*, dominant, famous, important *(significant)*, influential, leading *(ranking first)*, master, notable, noteworthy, outstanding *(prominent)*, paramount, predominant, prime *(most valuable)*, principal, professional *(stellar)*, prominent, renowned, salient, stellar, superior *(excellent)*, superlative. SEE MAIN ENTRY
forenamed aforesaid, before mentioned
forensic juridical. SEE MAIN ENTRY
forensic oratory rhetoric *(skilled speech)*
forensis forensic, judicial
foreordain prearrange, predetermine
foreordained inevitable, necessary *(inescapable)*, premeditated
foreordainment predetermination
foreordinate predetermine
foreordination foregone conclusion
foreparent predecessor
foreparents parentage
foreperson chief, principal *(director)*
forerun antecede, herald, precede
forerunner ancestor, ascendant, harbinger, pioneer, precursor, predecessor, primogenitor, progenitor. SEE MAIN ENTRY
forerunning antecedent, precursory, previous
foresee expect *(consider probable)*, preconceive, predict, presage, prognosticate. SEE MAIN ENTRY
foresee the future prognosticate
foreseeable forthcoming, future, probable. SEE MAIN ENTRY
foreseeing acute, omniscient, prophetic, provident *(showing foresight)*, prudent
foreseen foreseeable, immediate *(imminent)*, pending *(imminent)*, prospective. SEE MAIN ENTRY
foreshadow forewarn, portend, predict, preordain, presage, prognosticate, promise *(raise expectations)*, threaten, warning. SEE MAIN ENTRY
foreshadowing hint, indicator, pending *(imminent)*, precursory, premonition
foreshorten abridge *(shorten)*, condense
foreshow anticipate *(prognosticate)*, caution, forewarn, herald, portend, predict, presage, prognosticate, promise *(raise expectations)*
foresight diligence *(care)*, expectation, precaution, precognition, preparation, prognosis, prudence, sagacity, sense *(intelligence)*. SEE MAIN ENTRY
foresighted careful, perspicacious, prophetic, prudent
forespeak anticipate *(prognosticate)*, predict
forestall arrest *(stop)*, avert, balk, clog, condemn *(ban)*, debar, defer *(put off)*, detain *(restrain)*, deter, discourage, enjoin, estop, frustrate, prevent, refrain, repel *(drive back)*, stay *(halt)*, stop, thwart. SEE MAIN ENTRY
forestalling bar *(obstruction)*, deterrence, deterrent, obviation, preventive
foretell herald, portend, predict, presage, prognosticate, promise *(raise expectations)*

foretellable foreseeable
foretelling caution *(warning)*, oracular, portentous *(ominous)*, prognosis, prophetic
forethought caution *(vigilance)*, consideration *(contemplation)*, contemplation, deliberation, design *(intent)*, plan, precaution, precognition, predetermination, premeditation, preparation, prudence, strategy. SEE MAIN ENTRY
forethoughtful discreet, perspicacious
foretoken caveat, harbinger, herald, indicant, indicate, indication, portend, predict, premonition, presage, prognosticate
foretold forseen
forever chronic, now and forever, perpetuity
forevermore now and forever
forewarn admonish *(warn)*, advise, caution, counsel, notice *(give formal warning)*, notify, portend, predict, presage, promise *(raise expectations)*, threaten. SEE MAIN ENTRY
forewarned informed *(having information)*
forewarning admonition, caution *(warning)*, caveat, harbinger, monition *(warning)*, notice *(warning)*, portentous *(ominous)*, precursory, premonition, prophetic, symptom, tip *(clue)*
foreword overture, preamble, preface, prelude, threshold *(commencement)*
forfeit amercement, confiscate, deposit, detriment, discontinue *(abandon)*, disfranchise, disinherit, divest, expense *(sacrifice)*, fine, lose *(be deprived of)*, lose *(undergo defeat)*, loss, penalize, penalty, surrender *(give back)*, toll *(effect)*. SEE MAIN ENTRY
forfeited attached *(seized)*, irretrievable, lost *(taken away)*
forfeiting confiscatory
forfeiture amercement, cost *(penalty)*, detriment, disqualification *(rejection)*, escheatment, expense *(sacrifice)*, fine, foreclosure, loss, punishment, trover. SEE MAIN ENTRY
forfeiture by wrongdoing SEE MAIN ENTRY
forfend ban, contain *(restrain)*, deter, forbid, forestall, prevent, prohibit
forgather meet, rendezvous
forgathering collection *(assembly)*, conglomeration, congregation, session
forge copy, create, fake, form, formulate, frame *(construct)*, frame *(formulate)*, invent *(produce for the first time)*, make, manufacture, originate, plagiarize. SEE MAIN ENTRY
forge ahead continue *(persevere)*, endure *(last)*, keep *(continue)*, progress, resume
forged artificial, false *(not genuine)*, fictitious, spurious, untrue
forged check bad check
forged copy counterfeit
forged duplicate fake
forgery artifice, copy, counterfeit, deceit, deception, fake, false pretense, falsification, imposture, plagiarism, pretense *(pretext)*, sham, subterfuge. SEE MAIN ENTRY
forget condone, forgive, leave *(allow to remain)*, lose *(be deprived of)*, neglect, overlook *(disregard)*, pretermit. SEE MAIN ENTRY
forgetful careless, lax, oblivious, remiss
forgetfulness inconsideration
forging manufacture, onset *(commencement)*
forgivable justifiable, pardonable
forgive absolve, clear, condone, discharge *(liberate)*, discharge *(release from obligation)*, excuse, exonerate, extenuate, free, justify, overlook *(excuse)*, palliate *(excuse)*, pardon, purge *(wipe out by atonement)*, release, relent, remit *(release from penalty)*. SEE MAIN ENTRY
forgiven clear *(free from criminal charges)*
forgiveness absolution, amnesty, clemency, condonation, dispensation *(exception)*, exoneration, grace, indulgence, lenience, longanimity, pardon, reconciliation, release, remission
forgiveness of sins absolution
forgiving charitable *(lenient)*, lenient, magnanimous, nonmilitant, palliative *(excusing)*, patient, peaceable, placable
forgivingness clemency, lenience, longanimity
forgo forbear, forfeit, quit *(discontinue)*, refrain, relinquish, renounce, vacate *(leave)*, waive, yield *(submit)*. SEE MAIN ENTRY
forgoing waiver
forgotten back *(in arrears)*, derelict *(abandoned)*, outdated, outmoded, unclaimed
fork bifurcate, split, spread
forking divergent
forlorn derelict *(abandoned)*, disappointed, disconsolate, lugubrious, pessimistic
forlorn hope pessimism
form appearance *(look)*, body *(main part)*, build *(construct)*, color *(complexion)*, complexion, compose, consist, constant, constitute *(compose)*, construction, content *(structure)*, contour *(outline)*, contour *(shape)*, contrive, create, criterion, crystallize, decorum, delineation, devise *(invent)*, discipline *(train)*, embodiment, embody, establish *(launch)*, fabricate *(construct)*, feature *(appearance)*, fix *(arrange)*, forge *(produce)*, formalize, formulate, frame *(construct)*, frame *(formulate)*, generate, influence, invent *(produce for the first time)*, kind, make, manner *(kind)*, manufacture, means *(opportunity)*, mode, motif, order *(arrangement)*, organization *(structure)*, organize *(unionize)*, originate, pattern, phenomenon *(manifestation)*, practice *(procedure)*, principle *(axiom)*, produce *(manufacture)*, pronounce *(speak)*, protocol *(etiquette)*, specter, stamp, structure *(composition)*, style, tenor, usage, vision *(dream)*. SEE MAIN ENTRY
form a cartel federalize *(associate)*
form a circle round circumscribe *(surround by boundary)*, encompass *(surround)*
form a coalition conspire
form a company incorporate *(form a corporation)*
form a conception conceive *(comprehend)*
form a connection affiliate
form a core crystallize
form a fork bifurcate
form a judgment conclude *(decide)*, deem, determine
form a labor union organize *(unionize)*
form a league unite
form a network intertwine
form a plan plot, program
form a plot maneuver
form a resolution conclude *(decide)*, decide, determine
form a single unit unite
form a union combine *(act in concert)*, combine *(join together)*, federalize *(associate)*
form an alliance unite
form an estimate calculate, gauge, measure
form an estimation guess
form an image conjure
form an opinion conclude *(decide)*, construe *(comprehend)*, decide, deem, estimate, evaluate, gauge, measure, presume. SEE MAIN ENTRY
form anew reform
form into a body organize *(unionize)*
form into classes classify, organize *(arrange)*, partition, pigeonhole
form into ranks marshal
form of expression language
form of government polity
form plots conspire
forma aspect, contour *(shape)*, design *(construction plan)*, form *(arrangement)*, formation, kind
formable flexible, malleable, pliable, pliant, tractable
formal official, orthodox, perfunctory, proper, punctilious, rigid, solemn, strict. SEE MAIN ENTRY
formal accusal arraignment
formal accusation indictment, information *(charge)*
formal allegation complaint
formal assertion declaration, pleading
formal averment allegation, information *(charge)*, pleading
formal charge accusation, information *(charge)*
formal complaint charge *(accusation)*
formal consent permission
formal contract treaty
formal criminal charge information *(charge)*
formal criminal complaint information *(charge)*
formal criticism protest
formal declaration acknowledgment *(avowal)*, affirmation, protest, testament
formal declaration of dissent protest
formal discourse pandect *(treatise)*
formal discussion discourse
formal essay pandect *(treatise)*
formal examination by a court of law trial *(legal proceeding)*
formal examination of facts by a court trial *(legal proceeding)*
formal expression resolution *(formal statement)*
formal expression of choice poll *(casting of votes)*, vote
formal guaranty vow
formal notice declaration
formal occasion ceremony
formal permission license
formal petition bill *(formal declaration)*
formal presentation introduction
formal proceeding hearing
formal prosecution action *(proceeding)*
formal questioning hearing, interrogation
formal request requisition
formal scrutiny investigation
formal speech peroration
formal statement opinion *(judicial decision)*, pronouncement
formal writing instrument *(document)*
formal writing embodying a request petition
formal written plea petition
formal written request petition
formalis formal
formalistic draconian, formal

formalities decorum, protocol *(etiquette)*
formality ceremony, custom, decorum, form *(arrangement)*. SEE MAIN ENTRY
formalization of laws codification
formalize authorize, characterize, codify, define, frame *(formulate)*, record. SEE MAIN ENTRY
formally pro forma
formally accuse arraign
formally advise notice *(give formal warning)*
formally charge arraign, indict
formally charge with a crime indict
formally criminate arraign
formally incriminate arraign
formally pronounced judgment sentence
formally sanction authorize
formally urge petition
formally withdraw repeal
formalness formality
format configuration *(form)*, content *(structure)*, form *(arrangement)*, formation, motif. SEE MAIN ENTRY
formation arrangement *(ordering)*, building *(business of assembling)*, composition *(makeup)*, configuration *(form)*, content *(structure)*, contour *(shape)*, coverage *(scope)*, creation, distribution *(arrangement)*, embodiment, form *(arrangement)*, genesis, invention, lineup, manufacture, nascency, order *(arrangement)*, organization *(structure)*, performance *(workmanship)*, structure *(composition)*, unit *(item)*. SEE MAIN ENTRY
formation of a company incorporation *(formation of a business entity)*
formation of a corporation incorporation *(formation of a business entity)*
formation of an organization incorporation *(formation of a business entity)*
formative causal, causative, constructive *(creative)*, original *(initial)*, pliable, primary, prime *(original)*, productive, rudimentary
formative notion concept
former aforesaid, antecedent, back *(in arrears)*, before mentioned, deceased, last *(preceding)*, late *(defunct)*, outdated, outmoded, preliminary, previous, prior. SEE MAIN ENTRY
former generations ancestry, parentage
former incumbent predecessor
former officeholder predecessor
formerly heretofore, theretofore
formidable important *(significant)*, indomitable, inexpugnable, insuperable, insurmountable, irresistible, onerous, operose, oppressive, potent, spartan, strong, unapproachable. SEE MAIN ENTRY
formidolosus formidable
forming creation, manufacture, onset *(commencement)*
formless indefinite, indeterminate
formula avenue *(means of attainment)*, criterion, expedient, expression *(comment)*, form *(arrangement)*, method, mode, phrase, prescription *(directive)*, principle *(axiom)*, rule *(guide)*, rule *(legal dictate)*. SEE MAIN ENTRY
formula system
formula usage
formularize formulate
formulary boiler plate, code, form *(arrangement)*, prescription *(directive)*, rule *(legal dictate)*
formulate arrange *(plan)*, avow, bear *(adduce)*, codify, compose, conceive *(invent)*, conjure, constitute *(establish)*, create, crystallize, define, designate, devise *(invent)*, express, forge *(produce)*, form, frame *(construct)*, generate, legislate, make, manufacture, organize *(unionize)*, originate, phrase, produce *(manufacture)*. SEE MAIN ENTRY
formulate by law constitute *(establish)*
formulated belief doctrine, principle *(axiom)*
formulated intention objective, proposition
formulating questions cross-examination
formulating rules for the future legislation *(lawmaking)*
formulation averment, avouchment, building *(business of assembling)*, code, composition *(makeup)*, construction, creation, definition, description, expression *(comment)*, language, parlance, phraseology, rule *(legal dictate)*. SEE MAIN ENTRY
formulation of a mental image creation
formulation of a principle creation
formulation of an idea creation
formulation of laws codification
formulator of laws lawmaker
formulize formulate
fors hazard
forsake abandon *(physically leave)*, abandon *(relinquish)*, abandon *(withdraw)*, avoid *(evade)*, default, defect, depart, disclaim, discontinue *(abandon)*, disinherit, disown *(refuse to acknowledge)*, fail *(neglect)*, forgo, forswear, leave *(depart)*, quit *(discontinue)*, quit *(evacuate)*, refrain, relinquish, renounce, resign, surrender *(give back)*. SEE MAIN ENTRY
forsaken derelict *(abandoned)*, helpless *(defenseless)*, solitary, void *(empty)*
forsaking desertion, resignation *(relinquishment)*
forswear abandon *(relinquish)*, answer *(reply)*, bear false witness, betray *(lead astray)*, cloak, deceive, deny *(contradict)*, disaffirm, disavow, disclaim, disown *(deny the validity)*, eschew, exclude, fabricate *(make up)*, forfeit, forgo, lie *(falsify)*, palter, perjure, prevaricate, quit *(discontinue)*, refuse, reject, relinquish, renounce, repudiate, surrender *(give back)*. SEE MAIN ENTRY
forswearing abjuration, bad faith, desertion, falsification, negation, renunciation, repudiation
forsworn fraudulent, lying
fort bulwark
forte competence *(ability)*, gift *(flair)*, performance *(workmanship)*, propensity, specialty *(special aptitude)*
forte oblatus fortuitous, incidental
forthcoming close *(near)*, future, immediate *(imminent)*, imminent, inevitable, instant, pending *(imminent)*, portentous *(ominous)*, prospective, proximate. SEE MAIN ENTRY
forthright bona fide, candid, coherent *(clear)*, direct *(forthright)*, explicit, genuine, honest, ingenuous, scrupulous, straightforward, unaffected *(sincere)*, unequivocal, upright. SEE MAIN ENTRY
forthrightness candor *(straightforwardness)*
forthwith as soon as feasible, instant, instantly. SEE MAIN ENTRY
fortification barrier, bulwark, corroboration, panoply, protection, safeguard, support *(corroboration)*
fortified armed, insusceptible *(resistant)*, protective
fortify bear *(support)*, certify *(attest)*, compound, confirm, consolidate *(strengthen)*, corroborate, document, endue, help, nurture, protect, reaffirm, reinforce, supplement, sustain *(prolong)*. SEE MAIN ENTRY
fortis heroic, resolute, spartan, strong
fortis et invictus heroic
fortitude composure, longanimity, resignation *(passive acceptance)*, spirit, sufferance, tolerance
fortress bear *(support)*, bulwark
fortuitous casual, coincidental, random, unexpected, unintentional, unwitting. SEE MAIN ENTRY
fortuitous event accident *(chance occurrence)*, quirk *(accident)*
fortuitously unknowingly
fortuitousness act of god, chance *(fortuity)*, happenstance
fortuitus coincidental, fortuitous
fortuity accident *(chance occurrence)*, act of god, happenstance, occurrence, opportunity, quirk *(accident)*, speculation *(risk)*. SEE MAIN ENTRY
fortuna adversa misfortune
fortunate auspicious, favorable *(advantageous)*, felicitous, propitious, prosperous, successful. SEE MAIN ENTRY
fortunate condition prosperity
fortunatus successful
fortune chattel, contingency, money, possessions, predetermination, prospect *(outlook)*, speculation *(risk)*, substance *(material possessions)*, welfare. SEE MAIN ENTRY
fortuneless poor *(underprivileged)*
forum bar *(court)*
forum bench, chamber *(body)*, conference, council *(assembly)*. SEE MAIN ENTRY
forum forum *(court)*
forum judicatory, judicature
forum market place
forum meeting *(conference)*, panel *(discussion group)*, session, tribunal
forum for adjusting disputes court
forum non conveniens SEE MAIN ENTRY
forum of justice bench, court, judiciary
forum shopping SEE MAIN ENTRY
forward along, ameliorate, brazen, bumptious, contemptuous, countenance, cultivate, deliver, dispatch *(send off)*, eager, expedite, facilitate, foster, further, hasten, help, impertinent *(insolent)*, inure *(benefit)*, meliorate, nurture, obtrusive, precipitate *(hasten)*, presumptuous, progressive *(going forward)*, promote *(advance)*, redirect, remit *(submit for consideration)*, remove *(transfer)*, send, serve *(assist)*, serve *(deliver a legal instrument)*, transfer, transmit, unabashed, vanward. SEE MAIN ENTRY
forward looking progressive *(advocating change)*, sophisticated
forward motion advance *(progression)*, headway
forward movement advance *(progression)*
forward moving progressive *(going forward)*
forward payment remit *(send payment)*
forwarding advance *(progression)*, promotion *(advancement)*, transmittal
fossil prime *(original)*
fossilized ossified

foster abet, adopt, assist, bear *(support)*, bestow, care *(regard)*, concern *(care)*, conduce, cultivate, discipline *(train)*, expedite, facilitate, foment, further, keep *(shelter)*, nurture, preserve, promote *(organize)*, protect, sanction, subsidize, surrogate. SEE MAIN ENTRY
foster child child
foster hope promise *(raise expectations)*
fosterage adoption *(affiliation)*, auspices, favor *(sanction)*, guidance, help
fostering conservation, promotion *(encouragement)*
foul arrant *(onerous)*, bad *(inferior)*, contemptible, debase, deface, deleterious, depraved, disgraceful, disreputable, harmful, heinous, infect, iniquitous, irregular *(improper)*, loathsome, malignant, nefarious, objectionable, obnoxious, obscene, odious, offensive *(offending)*, outrageous, peccant *(culpable)*, pestilent, pollute, profligate *(corrupt)*, prurient, reprehensible, repulsive, salacious, scurrilous, sordid, sully, taint *(contaminate)*, tainted *(contaminated)*, tarnish, unfavorable, vicious
foul invective expletive
foul language expletive, imprecation, malediction, profanity. SEE MAIN ENTRY
foul play collusion, frame up, grievance, inequity, knavery, machination, mischief, misdoing, pettifoggery. SEE MAIN ENTRY
foul talk profanity
foul-spoken profane
fouled marred, sordid
foulmouthed profane
foulness defilement, delinquency *(misconduct)*, perversion
found build *(construct)*, create, establish *(launch)*, generate, initiate, instate, launch *(initiate)*, originate, situated. SEE MAIN ENTRY
found guilty blameful, blameworthy
found wanting blameful, devoid, faulty
foundation assumption *(supposition)*, basis, building *(business of assembling)*, cause *(reason)*, cornerstone, corporation, creation, criterion, derivation, facility *(institution)*, formation, fund, genesis, ground, institute, mainstay, nascency, onset *(commencement)*, organization *(association)*, origin *(source)*, origination, outset, postulate, preamble, precedent, preparation, principle *(axiom)*, reason *(basis)*, source, stare decisis, start. SEE MAIN ENTRY
foundation of a suit gist *(ground for a suit)*
foundational central *(essential)*, elementary, incipient, original *(initial)*, precursory, preparatory
foundationless baseless
foundations premises *(hypotheses)*
founded in confidence fiduciary
founded in law jural
founded on based on
founded on circumstances circumstantial
founded on fact authentic, documentary, true *(authentic)*
founded on fiction fictitious
founder architect, author *(originator)*, pioneer, predecessor, promoter
founder of the family parents, primogenitor
founding nascency
founding father pioneer
foundling discard, orphan
fount derivation, fund, source
fountain origination, source
fountainhead derivation, origin *(source)*, origination, source
four corners crossroad *(intersection)*
Fourteenth Amendment SEE MAIN ENTRY
fovea pitfall
fovere foment
foxy devious, insidious, machiavellian, politic, sly
foyer entrance
fracas affray, altercation, belligerency, bluster *(commotion)*, brawl, collision *(dispute)*, commotion, confrontation *(altercation)*, contest *(dispute)*, disaccord, disorder *(lack of order)*, disturbance, embroilment, fight *(battle)*, fray, furor, imbroglio, noise, outbreak, outcry, pandemonium, riot, struggle, turmoil, violence. SEE MAIN ENTRY
fracking SEE MAIN ENTRY
fraction constituent *(part)*, element, installment, member *(constituent part)*, modicum, moiety, part *(portion)*, paucity, proportion, section *(division)*, segment, subdivision
fractional broken *(fractured)*, partial *(relating to a part)*, semi, severable
fractional part detail, segment
fractionalize lancinate
fractionize divide *(separate)*, separate
fractious adverse *(hostile)*, contumacious, disobedient, froward, insubordinate, negative, perverse, petulant, pugnacious, querulous, recalcitrant, restive, uncontrollable, unruly. SEE MAIN ENTRY
fractiousness contempt *(disobedience to the court)*
fracture hiatus, rend, rift *(gap)*, split *(noun)*, split *(verb)*
fradulent copy counterfeit
fragile insecure, insubstantial, nonsubstantial *(not sturdy)*, powerless
fragilitas frailty
fragility frailty
fragment break *(fracture)*, chapter *(division)*, component, constituent *(part)*, detail, dichotomize, disintegrate, divide *(separate)*, element, ingredient, iota, lancinate, minimum, modicum, moiety, part *(portion)*, section *(division)*, segment, subdivision. SEE MAIN ENTRY
fragmentable divisive
fragmentary broken *(fractured)*, imperfect, inchoate, minimal, partial *(part)*, partial *(relating to a part)*, semi
fragmentation decentralization
fragmentum segment
frail imperfect, insecure, insubstantial, nonsubstantial *(not sturdy)*, powerless
fraility vice
frailty defect, disability *(physical inability)*, disadvantage, fault *(weakness)*, flaw, foible, impuissance. SEE MAIN ENTRY
frailty of character foible
frame arrange *(plan)*, border, border *(bound)*, build *(construct)*, building *(structure)*, circumscribe *(surround by boundary)*, compose, conceive *(invent)*, configuration *(form)*, conjure, conspire, construction, contain *(enclose)*, contour *(outline)*, contour *(shape)*, contrive, create, delineate, devise *(invent)*, edge *(border)*, envelop, forge *(produce)*, form, formulate, foundation *(basis)*, frame up, generate, make, maneuver, margin *(outside limit)*, originate, outline *(boundary)*, plan, plot, program, pronounce *(speak)*, scheme. SEE MAIN ENTRY
frame of mind character *(personal quality)*, disposition *(inclination)*, outlook, position *(point of view)*, spirit
frame of reference cornerstone, criterion, exemplar, instance, outlook, precedent, standard
frame up SEE MAIN ENTRY
framer architect
framework building *(structure)*, configuration *(confines)*, configuration *(form)*, construction, content *(structure)*, contour *(outline)*, delineation, foundation *(basis)*, frame *(structure)*, organization *(structure)*, perspective. SEE MAIN ENTRY
framing blockade *(enclosure)*, building *(business of assembling)*, creation
franchise charter *(sanction)*, droit, empower, enfranchise, free, freedom, home rule, immunity, let *(permit)*, liberate, liberty, license, prerogative, privilege, suffrage, tolerance. SEE MAIN ENTRY
franchised free *(enjoying civil liberty)*, permissible, privileged
franchisement freedom, liberation
frangere impair, infringe
frangible nonsubstantial *(not sturdy)*
frank candid, clear *(apparent)*, credible, direct *(forthright)*, genuine, honest, ingenuous, simple, straightforward, unaffected *(sincere)*. SEE MAIN ENTRY
frankhearted candid
frankness candor *(straightforwardness)*, honesty, probity, veracity
frantic frenetic, hot-blooded
fraternal akin *(related by blood)*, close *(intimate)*, consanguineous, harmonious, humane, interrelated, intimate
fraternal order society
fraternalism peace
fraternity coaction, concordance, society, sodality, union *(labor organization)*
fraternization rapprochement, society, sodality
fraternize cooperate, join *(associate oneself with)*
fraud bad faith, bad repute, betray *(lead astray)*, bilk, canard, collusion, conversion *(misappropriation)*, deceit, deception, duplicity, embezzlement, fake, false pretense, falsehood, falsification, forgery, hoax, hypocrisy, imposture, improbity, indirection *(deceitfulness)*, knavery, lie, maneuver *(trick)*, misappropriation, misrepresentation, pettifoggery, pretense *(pretext)*, pretext, racket, ruse, sham. SEE MAIN ENTRY
fraudare cheat
fraudulence artifice, bad repute, collusion, corruption, criminality, deceit, deception, dishonesty, false pretense, falsehood, forgery, fraud, hoax, hypocrisy, imposture, improbity, knavery, pettifoggery, pretense *(pretext)*, racket
fraudulency abuse *(corrupt practice)*, bad faith, corruption, deception, dishonesty, false pretense, hoax, improbity, indirection *(deceitfulness)*, pettifoggery
fraudulent assumed *(feigned)*, collusive, colorable *(specious)*, deceptive, delusive, dishonest, disingenuous, fallacious, false *(not genuine)*, felonious, insidious, larcenous, lying, machiavellian, mendacious, meretricious, perfidious, spurious, tortuous *(corrupt)*, unfair, unfounded, unscrupulous, untrue, untrustworthy. SEE MAIN ENTRY
fraudulent application misapplication
fraudulent appropriation embezzlement
fraudulent appropriation of money embezzlement
fraudulent check bad check
fraudulent conversion embezzlement, misappropriation

fraudulent document forgery
fraudulent expedient maneuver *(trick)*
fraudulent imitation counterfeit
fraudulent income graft
fraudulent practice pettifoggery
fraudulent replica fake
fraudulent taking larceny, theft
fraudulently induce suborn
fraudulently introduced surreptitious
fraudulentus dishonest, fraudulent
fraught full, replete
fraught with danger aleatory *(perilous)*, dangerous, insalubrious, insecure, noxious, precarious
fraught with evil pernicious
fraught with harm disastrous, pernicious
fraught with peril dangerous
fraus deceit, dishonesty, fraud, hypocrisy, imposture, knavery, sham
fray affray, brawl, collision *(dispute)*, commotion, confrontation *(altercation)*, contest *(dispute)*, embroilment, fight *(battle)*, fracas, furor, outbreak, outburst, riot, strife. SEE MAIN ENTRY
frayed dilapidated
freak quirk *(accident)*
freak occurrence phenomenon *(unusual occurrence)*
freakish irregular *(not usual)*, prodigious *(amazing)*, unaccustomed
free absolve, alleviate, autonomous *(independent)*, autonomous *(self governing)*, clear *(unencumbered)*, clear, competitive *(open)*, condone, discharge *(liberate)*, disencumber, disengage, disentangle, disenthrall, dissociate, enfranchise, exculpate, excuse, exempt, extricate, gratis, gratuitous *(given without recompense)*, immune, independent, liberal *(generous)*, liberate, licentious, parole, passable, philanthropic, promiscuous, release, relieve *(free from burden)*, remit *(release from penalty)*, rescue, salacious, sovereign *(independent)*, spontaneous, unbound, unlimited, unpaid, unrestrained *(not in custody)*, unrestricted, unsolicited, vacant, void *(empty)*, voluntary. SEE MAIN ENTRY
free agency volition
free course latitude
free decision discretion *(power of choice)*, latitude, option *(choice)*
free enterprise SEE MAIN ENTRY
free fight affray
free for use disposable
free from a mistaken belief disabuse
free from accusation exonerate
free from affectation natural, unaffected *(sincere)*
free from ambiguity clarify
free from anxiety ease, soothe
free from bias impartial
free from blame exculpate, exonerate
free from bondage disenthrall
free from burden clear *(unencumbered)*
free from confinement rescue
free from confusion clarify
free from danger rescue, safe
free from desecration inviolate
free from difficulty facilitate
free from doubt assure *(give confidence to)*, clear *(certain)*
free from encumbrance clear *(unencumbered)*, disencumber
free from engagement disengage
free from error disabuse
free from extraneous matter distill
free from fault inculpable, irreprehensible
free from fraud honest
free from guilt blameless, clean, inculpable, innocent, not guilty
free from harm safe
free from hindrance clear *(unencumbered)*, facilitate
free from hurt safe
free from ignorance enlighten
free from impairment inviolate
free from impediment clear *(unencumbered)*, facilitate
free from imperfection infallible, intact, unblemished
free from impurities clean
free from impurity purge *(purify)*
free from injury safe
free from limitation clear *(unencumbered)*
free from mistake infallible
free from narrowness liberal *(not literal)*
free from objectionable content expurgate
free from obstruction clear *(unencumbered)*, facilitate
free from pain soothe
free from pledge disengage
free from political disabilities enfranchise
free from prejudice enlighten, fairly *(impartially)*
free from reserve ingenuous
free from risk safe
free from sin clean
free from superstition enlighten
free from thralldom disenthrall
free from uncertainty assure *(give confidence to)*
free from vindictiveness charitable *(lenient)*, lenient
free from vow disengage
free from war peaceable
free from waste economical
free from wrong blameless
free giver benefactor, donor
free giving largess *(generosity)*, philanthropy
free hand latitude. SEE MAIN ENTRY
free in expression demonstrative *(expressive of emotion)*
free of privileged
free of access open *(accessible)*
free of binding obligation exempt
free of charge gratis
free of cost gratis, gratuitous *(given without recompense)*
free of duplicity simple
free of error accurate, proper
free of expense gratis, gratuitous *(given without recompense)*
free of guilt irreprehensible
free of pettiness magnanimous
free play latitude
free selection alternative *(option)*, option *(choice)*
free thought latitude
free to all competitive *(open)*, open *(accessible)*, patent, public *(open)*
free to choose autonomous *(independent)*, impartial
free trade SEE MAIN ENTRY
free translation paraphrase
free will discretion *(power of choice)*, latitude, liberty, option *(choice)*, volition
free wording paraphrase
free-handedness philanthropy
free-living dissolute
free-willed spontaneous
freed clear *(free from criminal charges)*, free *(enjoying civil liberty)*
freed from exempt
freed of wrongdoing acquitted
freedom dispensation *(exception)*, emancipation, exemption, exoneration, immunity, impunity, informality, latitude, liberation, liberty, license, option *(choice)*, parole, prerogative, privilege, probation, suffrage, tolerance. SEE MAIN ENTRY
freedom from accusation exoneration
freedom from affectation informality
freedom from ailment health
freedom from bias disinterest *(lack of prejudice)*, justice
freedom from bigotry tolerance
freedom from blame innocence
freedom from captivity liberty
freedom from danger asylum *(protection)*, preservation, protection, security *(safety)*
freedom from deviation rigor
freedom from difficulty facility *(easiness)*
freedom from disease health
freedom from domination home rule
freedom from doubt faith
freedom from duty exemption, leave *(absence)*
freedom from error certification *(certainness)*, certitude
freedom from exemption immunity
freedom from extravagance economy *(frugality)*
freedom from guilt exoneration, innocence
freedom from harm security *(safety)*
freedom from illegality innocence
freedom from interference home rule
freedom from judgment impunity
freedom from liability exemption
freedom from obligation exemption, immunity
freedom from penalty impunity
freedom from prejudice disinterest *(lack of prejudice)*, tolerance
freedom from prosecution immunity
freedom from punishment impunity
freedom from requirements exemption
freedom from self-interest disinterest *(lack of prejudice)*
freedom from service exemption
freedom from vindictiveness lenience
freedom from war peace
freedom of action home rule, latitude, liberty
freedom of association SEE MAIN ENTRY
freedom of choice call *(option)*, discretion *(power of choice)*, franchise *(right to vote)*, home rule, liberty, option *(choice)*, suffrage. SEE MAIN ENTRY
freedom of information request SEE MAIN ENTRY
freedom of press SEE MAIN ENTRY
freedom to discharge SEE MAIN ENTRY
freehanded benevolent, charitable *(bene-volent)*, donative, philanthropic
freehandedness largess *(generosity)*
freehold demesne, domain *(land owned)*, dominion *(absolute ownership)*, estate *(property)*, fee *(estate)*, leasehold, property *(land)*, real estate. SEE MAIN ENTRY
freeholder landholder, landowner, occupant
freeing liberation, release

freeing from blame exoneration
freeing from prison parole
freelance independent
freely readily
freely giving liberal *(generous)*
freeness largess *(generosity)*
freethinking liberal *(broad minded)*, licentious, radical *(favoring drastic change)*, skeptical
freeway causeway
freewill worker volunteer
freeze check *(restrain)*, desist, embargo, stop
freight cargo, load, merchandise, send. SEE MAIN ENTRY
freightage cargo, freight
frenetic deranged, lunatic. SEE MAIN ENTRY
frenzied deranged, frenetic, lunatic, uncontrollable, vehement
frenzy bluster *(commotion)*, confusion *(turmoil)*, furor, haste, insanity, lunacy, outburst, pandemonium, panic, passion
frequence draw *(attendance)*, frequency
frequency SEE MAIN ENTRY
frequens frequent, populous
frequent attend *(be present at)*, chronic, common *(customary)*, customary, familiar *(customary)*, habitual, incessant, innumerable, inveterate, mundane, ordinary, patronize *(trade with)*, periodic, prevailing *(current)*, prevalent, repeated, routine, usual. SEE MAIN ENTRY
frequent as a customer patronize *(trade with)*
frequent repetition practice *(custom)*
frequenter addict, patron *(regular customer)*
frequentia frequency
frequently invariably
frequently met prevalent
frequently repeated act habit
fresh impertinent *(insolent)*, insolent, novel, original *(creative)*, recent, unusual
fresh outbreak recrudescence
fresh spurt resurgence
fresh start continuation *(resumption)*
fresh supply reinforcement
freshen fix *(repair)*, renew *(refurbish)*
freshen up fix *(repair)*
freshening revival
freshest last *(preceding)*
freshly de novo
freshman amateur, neophyte, novice
fret agitate *(perturb)*, annoy, badger, brood, discompose, fear, harrow, harry *(harass)*, hector, irritate, languish, oscillate, perturb, pique, plague, provoke, regret, trepidation
fret over deplore
fretful fractious, petulant, querulous, restive
fretter malcontent
friable dilapidated
fribble petty
friction collision *(dispute)*, conflict, contention *(opposition)*, contravention, controversy *(argument)*, disaccord, discord, dissension, dissent *(difference of opinion)*, strife. SEE MAIN ENTRY
frictional hostile
frictionless harmonious
friend associate, benefactor, cohort, confederate, partisan, patron *(influential supporter)*, proponent, samaritan. SEE MAIN ENTRY
friend at court advocate *(counselor)*
friend in court advocate *(counselor)*, amicus curiae
friendless derelict *(abandoned)*, helpless *(defenseless)*, solitary
friendliness affinity *(regard)*, benevolence *(disposition to do good)*, comity, consideration *(sympathetic regard)*, courtesy, informality, peace, rapprochement, sodality
friendly amicable, benevolent, close *(intimate)*, harmonious, intimate, peaceable, propitious, receptive. SEE MAIN ENTRY
friendly agreement accommodation *(adjustment)*
friendly association affiliation *(connectedness)*
friendly disposition goodwill
friendly interest patronage *(support)*
friendly relations sodality
friendly turn favor *(act of kindness)*
friendship affinity *(regard)*, benevolence *(disposition to do good)*, concordance, consortium *(marriage companionship)*, patronage *(support)*, peace, rapprochement, sodality
fright consternation, fear, frighten, panic, phobia, stress *(strain)*, trepidation. SEE MAIN ENTRY
frighten browbeat, intimidate, menace, repel *(disgust)*, threaten. SEE MAIN ENTRY
frighten away discourage, dissuade
frightened leery, recreant
frightening dire, formidable, odious, portentous *(ominous)*, sinister
frightful deplorable, disastrous, formidable, insufferable, loathsome, ominous, portentous *(ominous)*, repulsive, vicious. SEE MAIN ENTRY
frigid cold-blooded, insensible, insusceptible *(uncaring)*, phlegmatic, unaffected *(uninfluenced)*
frigidus insipid, lifeless *(dull)*, prosaic
frill embellish
fringe border, edge *(border)*, extremity *(furthest point)*, frontier, limit, margin *(outside limit)*, penumbra, peripheral, periphery. SEE MAIN ENTRY
fringement crime
fringes confines, outline *(boundary)*
fringing contiguous, proximate
frisk SEE MAIN ENTRY
frisky jocular
frivolous capricious, inconsequential, irresolute, irresponsible, jocular, nonessential, nugatory, petty, superficial, trivial, undependable, untrustworthy. SEE MAIN ENTRY
frock clothe
frolic carouse. SEE MAIN ENTRY
frolicsome jocular
frolicsomeness mischief
from a general law to a particular instance a priori
from abroad alien *(foreign)*
from beginning to end throughout *(all over)*
from cause to effect a priori
from competent sources authentic
from first to last throughout *(all over)*
from here on hereafter *(henceforth)*
from its birth ab initio
from now on hereafter *(henceforth)*
from nowhere alien *(unrelated)*
from that cause a priori, consequently
from that time thereafter
from the beginning ab initio, de novo
from the ground up throughout *(all over)*
from the original data authentic
from the river fluvial
from the start heretofore
from the word go throughout *(all over)*
from this cause a priori
from this time on hereafter *(henceforth)*
fronder censure
front defy, hypocrisy, prime *(most valuable)*. SEE MAIN ENTRY
front office management *(directorate)*
front position preference *(priority)*
frontage SEE MAIN ENTRY
frontier border, edge *(border)*, extremity *(furthest point)*, limit, outline *(boundary)*, periphery. SEE MAIN ENTRY
frontiers configuration *(confines)*
frontiersman pioneer
frontward vanward
frothy nugatory
froward disobedient, disorderly, insolent, insubordinate, intractable, perverse, petulant, spiteful, unruly, wanton. SEE MAIN ENTRY
frown on disfavor
frown upon denounce *(condemn)*, disparage, remonstrate, reproach, spurn
frowning grave *(solemn)*
fructiferous fertile, productive
fructify ameliorate, bear *(yield)*, reproduce. SEE MAIN ENTRY
fructuosus profitable
fructuous fertile, productive
fructus enjoyment *(pleasure)*, fruition, profit, result
frugal economical, parsimonious, penurious, prudent. SEE MAIN ENTRY
frugality austerity, management *(judicious use)*, moderation, prudence, temperance. SEE MAIN ENTRY
frugalness austerity, economy *(frugality)*
frugi economical, frugal
frugifer profitable
fruit effect, issuance, outcome, outgrowth, output, product, progeny, result
fruit of labor earnings
fruitbearing prolific
fruitful fertile, gainful, lucrative, operative, productive, profitable, prolific, successful
fruitfulness utility *(usefulness)*
fruition commission *(act)*, consequence *(conclusion)*, creation, denouement, discharge *(performance)*, effect, fait accompli, growth *(evolution)*, outcome, realization, result, satisfaction *(fulfilment)*. SEE MAIN ENTRY
fruitless barren, futile, idle, ineffective, ineffectual, needless, otiose, unavailing, unproductive
fruitless effort failure *(lack of success)*
fruitless trial mistrial
fruits profit
frustrari balk, disappoint
frustrari frustrate
frustrate arrest *(stop)*, balk, bar *(hinder)*, block, check *(restrain)*, clog, condemn *(ban)*, constrict *(inhibit)*, contravene, counteract, defeat, deter, disadvantage, discontinue *(break continuity)*, encumber *(hinder)*, enjoin, fight *(counteract)*, foil, forestall, halt, hamper, impede, inhibit, interrupt, keep *(restrain)*, obstruct, perturb, preclude, prevent, repel *(drive back)*, repulse, restrict, stay *(halt)*, stem *(check)*, stifle, thwart, toll *(stop)*, trammel. SEE MAIN ENTRY
frustrate by contrary action counter, counteract
frustrated disappointed

frustration abortion *(fiasco)*, aggravation *(annoyance)*, check *(bar)*, deadlock, deterrence, failure *(lack of success)*, impediment, miscarriage. SEE MAIN ENTRY
fuddle confusion *(ambiguity)*, muddle
fudge mulct *(defraud)*
fuga flight, lapse *(break)*
fugacious ephemeral, temporary, transient, transitory
fugaciousness mortality
fugacity mortality
fugam petere flee
fugare repel *(drive back)*, stave
fugax transient
fugere escape, retreat
fugitive convict, criminal, derelict, elusive, ephemeral, moving *(in motion)*, outlaw, pariah, temporary, transient, truant. SEE MAIN ENTRY
fugitive from the law outlaw
fugitivus fugitive
fulcrum basis, center *(central position)*
fulfill accomplish, close *(terminate)*, commit *(perpetrate)*, complete, comply, conclude *(complete)*, consummate, discharge *(perform)*, dispatch *(dispose of)*, effectuate, execute *(accomplish)*, implement, obey, observe *(obey)*, operate, pass *(satisfy requirements)*, perform *(adhere to)*, perpetrate, succeed *(attain)*, transact. SEE MAIN ENTRY
fulfill an engagement report *(present oneself)*
fulfill an obligation satisfy *(discharge)*
fulfill the commands of obey
fulfilled complacent, fully executed *(consummated)*
fulfillment cessation *(termination)*, conclusion *(outcome)*, discharge *(performance)*, end *(termination)*, fait accompli, finality, fruition, maturity, outcome
fulfilment collection *(payment)*, commission *(act)*, performance *(execution)*, realization
fulgent pretentious *(ostentatious)*
fulgere radiate
fulgid lucid, pretentious *(ostentatious)*
fulguration discharge *(shot)*
full absolute *(complete)*, broad, complete *(all-embracing)*, comprehensive, copious, gross *(total)*, inclusive, intact, orotund, outright, plenary, populous, profuse, replete, ripe, thorough, total, unmitigated, unqualified *(unlimited)*. SEE MAIN ENTRY
full age majority *(adulthood)*, maturity
full appraisal appreciation *(perception)*
full array panoply
full assurance credence
full authority permission
full belief credence
full chance day in court
full complement capacity *(maximum)*
full development maturity
full effect amount *(result)*
full extent capacity *(maximum)*
full force main force
full growth maturity
full legal age majority *(adulthood)*
full measure plethora, quorum, sufficiency
full observance conformity *(obedience)*
full of affectation pretentious *(pompous)*
full of contempt disdainful
full of curves labyrinthine
full of details detailed
full of enterprise eager
full of enthusiasm eager
full of exhortation hortative
full of faults faulty
full of feeling ecstatic, eloquent
full of fun jocular
full of good will benevolent
full of hate hostile, malevolent
full of hope sanguine
full of initiative eager
full of life live *(conscious)*
full of malice hostile, malevolent
full of meaning eloquent, pithy, sententious
full of mischief peccant *(culpable)*
full of power forcible
full of promise favorable *(advantageous)*, probable, propitious
full of regret remorseful
full of regrets contrite, penitent, repentant
full of remorse contrite
full of revenge malevolent
full of risk aleatory *(perilous)*, dangerous, precarious
full of sin diabolic
full of spirit volatile
full of spite malevolent
full of strength forcible
full of substance eloquent
full of thought deliberate, pensive
full of turns labyrinthine
full of urgency hortative
full of verbiage prolix
full pardon condonation
full particulars circumstances
full play latitude
full purse prosperity
full report accounting
full round of the seasons annum
full satisfaction collection *(payment)*, discharge *(payment)*, expiation, indemnity
full size caliber *(measurement)*
full stop check *(bar)*
full throttle SEE MAIN ENTRY
full volume capacity *(maximum)*
full-blown plenary, ripe
full-bodied sapid, savory
full-charged plenary
full-flavored sapid, savory
full-fledged outright. SEE MAIN ENTRY
full-grown ripe
fullness capacity *(maximum)*, corpus, entirety, finality, mass *(weight)*, maximum *(amplitude)*, plethora, quantity, sufficiency, surfeit
fullness of heart affection
fully fairly *(clearly)*, in toto, wholly
fully constituted plenary
fully convinced certain *(positive)*, definite, positive *(confident)*
fully detailed analysis accounting
fully developed ripe
fully developed person adult
fully executed thorough. SEE MAIN ENTRY
fully furnished plenary
fully grown ripe
fully grown person adult
fully realized comprehensive
fully secured SEE MAIN ENTRY
fully sufficient adequate
fully supplied replete
fulminate defame, discharge *(shoot)*, inveigh, threaten. SEE MAIN ENTRY
fulminate against censure, condemn *(blame)*, denounce *(condemn)*, disapprove *(condemn)*, lash *(attack verbally)*, malign, reprimand
fulmination denunciation, discharge *(shot)*, imprecation, malediction, threat
fulsome arrant *(onerous)*, bad *(inferior)*, bad *(offensive)*, contemptible, detrimental, excessive, gross *(flagrant)*, heinous, loathsome, lurid, objectionable, obnoxious, odious, outrageous, repugnant *(exciting aversion)*, scandalous, sordid, unwarranted
fumble miscue, mismanage
fumigate decontaminate
fun SEE MAIN ENTRY
function activity, agency *(legal relationship)*, appointment *(position)*, assignment *(task)*, business *(occupation)*, calling, capacity *(job)*, charge *(responsibility)*, demean *(deport oneself)*, duty *(obligation)*, employment, job, office, officiate, operate, operation, part *(role)*, perform *(execute)*, position *(business status)*, post, province, purpose, pursuit *(occupation)*, role, specialty *(special aptitude)*, sphere, trade *(occupation)*, use, utility *(usefulness)*, work *(employment)*. SEE MAIN ENTRY
functional beneficial, corrigible, effective *(efficient)*, efficient, ministerial, operative, practical, procedural, viable. SEE MAIN ENTRY
functionary agent, conduit *(intermediary)*, incumbent, notary public, officer, official, proctor, trustee. SEE MAIN ENTRY
functioning acting, active, in full force, operative
functionless barren, expendable
functus officio defeasible
fund bear *(yield)*, bestow, capitalize *(provide capital)*, endow, endowment, finance, garner, hoard, principal *(capital sum)*, provide *(supply)*, provision *(something provided)*, reserve, resource, stock *(shares)*, store *(depository)*, sufficiency, treasury, underwrite. SEE MAIN ENTRY
fund again refinance
fund invested for a charitable purpose foundation *(organization)*
fundamenta foundation *(basis)*
fundamental born *(innate)*, cardinal *(basic)*, central *(essential)*, cornerstone, elementary, essential *(inherent)*, essential *(required)*, gravamen, inchoate, incipient, indispensable, initial, innate, integral, material *(important)*, naked *(lacking embellishment)*, native *(inborn)*, natural, necessary *(required)*, necessity, need *(requirement)*, organic, original *(initial)*, prerequisite, primary, prime *(original)*, primordial, rudimentary, simple, substantive, ultimate, underlying, virtual, vital. SEE MAIN ENTRY
fundamental doctrine principle *(axiom)*
fundamental feature main point
fundamental law constitution, principle *(axiom)*
fundamental part component, essence, ingredient, main point
fundamental point main point
fundamental principle canon, foundation *(basis)*, necessity
fundamental principles policy *(plan of action)*
fundamental principles of government polity
fundamental reason rationale
fundamental research inquiry *(systematic investigation)*
fundamental rule principle *(axiom)*
fundamental unit necessity
fundamentally purely *(positively)*
fundamentals basis, gist *(substance)*
fundemental part element
funding appropriation *(donation)*, endowment, loan. SEE MAIN ENTRY

funds assets, capital, cash, finance, money, personalty, possessions, principal *(capital sum)*, property *(possessions)*, security *(stock)*. SEE MAIN ENTRY
funds for investment capital
funds in hand capital
funds paid out expenditure
fundus basis
funereal disconsolate, lugubrious, solemn
funestus disastrous, fatal, lethal
funk shirk, trepidation
funny jocular, ludicrous. SEE MAIN ENTRY
furari pilfer, purloin, steal
furbish rehabilitate
furcate bifurcate, bipartite, dichotomize, divergent
furcated divergent
furcular bipartite
furens frenetic
furibund frenetic
furious demonstrative *(expressive of emotion)*, resentful, severe, vehement. SEE MAIN ENTRY
furiousness violence
furlough holiday, leave *(absence)*. SEE MAIN ENTRY
furnish accommodate, adduce, bear *(yield)*, bequeath, bestow, clothe, contribute *(supply)*, dole, endow, endue, engender, fund, give *(grant)*, lend, pander, present *(make a gift)*, produce *(manufacture)*, provide *(supply)*, render *(administer)*, replenish, sell, supply, tender, vest, yield *(produce a return)*. SEE MAIN ENTRY
furnish aid abet, assist, capitalize *(provide capital)*, contribute *(assist)*, inure *(benefit)*, serve *(assist)*, subsidize
furnish an equivalent compensate *(counterbalance)*
furnish an estimate calculate
furnish an example illustrate
furnish assistance bear *(support)*, help, serve *(assist)*
furnish credit lend
furnish evidence bear *(adduce)*, evince
furnish foundations capitalize *(provide capital)*
furnish funds loan, support *(assist)*
furnish occupation for employ *(engage services)*, hire
furnish room for lodge *(house)*
furnish support bear *(support)*, capitalize *(provide capital)*, subsidize
furnish sustenance bear *(support)*
furnish with a date date
furnish with quarters lodge *(house)*
furnish with rank invest *(vest)*
furnished with weapons armed
furnisher supplier
furnishing donative, provision *(act of supplying)*
furnishings cargo
furor ardor, commotion, emotion, outburst, outcry, passion, riot. SEE MAIN ENTRY
furrow split
further accrue *(increase)*, additional, aggravate *(exacerbate)*, aid, assist, compound, countenance, cultivate, develop, expand, expedite, facilitate, favor, foster, help, inure *(benefit)*, nurture, parlay *(exploit successfully)*, precipitate *(hasten)*, prefer, promote *(advance)*, promote *(organize)*, raise *(advance)*, side, subsidize, support *(assist)*. SEE MAIN ENTRY
further time extension *(postponement)*
furtherance advancement *(improvement)*, advocacy, aid *(help)*, assistance, behalf, course, development *(progression)*, favor *(sanction)*, headway, help, longevity, progress, promotion *(encouragement)*, reinforcement. SEE MAIN ENTRY
furthermore also, further. SEE MAIN ENTRY
furthermost ultimate
furthermost part end *(termination)*
furthest extreme *(last)*, last *(final)*, ultimate, utmost
furthest extent ambit
furthest point ambit, limit, utmost
furtim feras intercipere poach
furtive clandestine, collusive, covert, evasive, fraudulent, insidious, mysterious, oblique *(evasive)*, privy, secret, sly, stealthy, surreptitious. SEE MAIN ENTRY
furtive removal asportation
furtiveness bad faith, concealment, deceit, dishonesty, fraud, improbity
furtivus clandestine, furtive, stealthy, surreptitious
furtum burglary, larceny, theft
fury furor, outbreak, outburst, passion, resentment, severity, violence
fuscus dun
fuse adhere *(fasten)*, amalgamate, bond *(hold together)*, cement, combine *(join together)*, commingle, conjoin, connect *(join together)*, consolidate *(strengthen)*, consolidate *(unite)*, desegregate, incorporate *(include)*, join *(bring together)*, lock, merge, unite. SEE MAIN ENTRY
fused coadunate, coherent *(joined)*, composite, compound, concerted, concurrent *(united)*, conjoint, inseparable, promiscuous
fusillade discharge *(shot)*, onset *(assault)*, salvo
fusing coalescence, coalition, concordant
fusion accession *(annexation)*, adhesion *(affixing)*, affiliation *(amalgamation)*, cartel, centralization, coaction, coalescence, coalition, coherence, combination, concrescence, confederacy *(compact)*, consolidation, incorporation *(blend)*, integration *(amalgamation)*, league, meeting *(encounter)*, merger, union *(unity)*
fusion of interests coalition, concert
fuss disturbance, fracas, furor, outburst, pretense *(ostentation)*, trouble, turmoil
fussiness particularity
fussy meticulous, particular *(exacting)*, precise, punctilious, punctual
fustian bombast, flatulent, grandiose, inflated *(bombastic)*, orotund, turgid. SEE MAIN ENTRY
fustigate beat *(strike)*, lash *(strike)*
fustis cudgel
fusty sordid, stale
futile expendable, idle, ineffective, ineffectual, invalid, minor, needless, nugatory, otiose, powerless, unavailing, unproductive. SEE MAIN ENTRY
futile effort frustration, miscarriage
futilis futile, unavailing
futility impossibility. SEE MAIN ENTRY
future forthcoming, imminent, potential, prospective, subsequent. SEE MAIN ENTRY
future generation descendant
future interest reversion *(remainder of an estate)*
future payment credit *(delayed payment)*
future possession heritage, reversion *(remainder of an estate)*
future relatives posterity
futures portfolio
futurity prospect *(outlook)*
futurus future, prospective
fuzziness indistinctness, obscuration
fuzzy unclear

G

gab prattle
gabble prattle
gabby loquacious
gad prowl
gadget device *(mechanism)*, item
gag inhibit, repress, stifle, suppress
gag rule SEE MAIN ENTRY
gage bail, binder, defiance, deposit, guaranty, security *(pledge)*
gagged speechless
gaiety enjoyment *(pleasure)*
gain accession *(enlargement)*, accretion, accrue *(increase)*, accumulate *(enlarge)*, acquire *(receive)*, acquire *(secure)*, acquisition, advancement *(improvement)*, advantage, appreciation *(increased value)*, attain, augmentation, bear *(yield)*, benefit *(betterment)*, boom *(increase)*, boom *(prosperity)*, carry *(succeed)*, collect *(gather)*, collect *(recover money)*, development *(progression)*, dividend, earn, edification, expand, headway, increase, increment, inherit, interest *(profit)*, inure *(benefit)*, obtain, output, perquisite, possess, prize, proceeds, procure, profit *(noun)*, profit *(verb)*, progress *(noun)*, progress *(verb)*, purchase, reach, realize *(obtain as a profit)*, reap, receipt *(act of receiving)*, receive *(acquire)*, recruit, revenue, shelter *(tax benefit)*, succeed *(attain)*. SEE MAIN ENTRY
gain a victory prevail *(triumph)*, succeed *(attain)*
gain admittance enter *(go in)*
gain advantage profit
gain anew recoup *(regain)*, recover
gain by labor earn
gain by service earn
gain by wrongful methods extort
gain control over defeat
gain derived from capital income
gain derived from labor income
gain entry enter *(go in)*
gain for oneself possess
gain ground compound, increase, proceed *(go forward)*, progress
gain in worth appreciate *(increase)*, appreciation *(increased value)*
gain indemnity against loss insure
gain insight comprehend *(understand)*
gain insight into perceive
gain knowledge detect
gain liberty escape
gain more time postpone
gain one's end attain
gain over disarm *(set at ease)*, prejudice *(influence)*
gain possession obtain, preempt, recover
gain strength compound, expand
gain the advantage prevail *(triumph)*
gain the ascendancy outbalance
gain the confidence of convince, disarm *(set at ease)*, persuade, prevail *(persuade)*
gain the favor of propitiate
gain the upper hand predominate *(command)*, prevail *(triumph)*
gain time defer *(put off)*, hold up *(delay)*, procrastinate, protract *(prolong)*
gain wrongfully extort
gainful beneficial, functional, lucrative, productive, profitable, successful, valuable. SEE MAIN ENTRY

gaingiving misgiving
gainless disadvantageous, futile, ineffective, ineffectual
gains earnings, income, spoils
gainsay contend *(dispute)*, contest, contravene, cross *(disagree with)*, debar, deny *(contradict)*, disaccord, disaffirm, disagree, disapprove *(reject)*, dispute *(contest)*, except *(object)*, expostulate, negation, oppugn, prohibit, refute, reject, repulse. SEE MAIN ENTRY
gainsaying contravention, counterargument, denial, diatribe, disagreement, disapprobation, negation, negative, rejection, remonstrance, retraction
gait step
gala holiday, special
galbe configuration *(form)*
gall affront, annoy, irritate, offend *(insult)*, perturb, pique, plague, provoke, resentment, spite, temerity
gallant heroic, magnanimous, undaunted
gallant acts prowess *(bravery)*
gallantness prowess *(bravery)*
gallantry consideration *(sympathetic regard)*, courtesy, prowess *(bravery)*
galled resentful
gallimaufry melange
galling malevolent, oppressive, outrageous, provocative, vexatious
gallop race
galloping rapid
galore rife
galvanic incisive, provocative
galvanical provocative
galvanize foment, impress *(affect deeply)*. SEE MAIN ENTRY
gambit first appearance
gamble bet, hazard, invest *(fund)*, lottery, parlay *(bet)*, possibility, risk, speculate *(chance)*, speculation *(risk)*, venture. SEE MAIN ENTRY
gambler bettor, speculator
gambling speculation *(risk)*
game bet, contest *(competition)*, ridicule
game change SEE MAIN ENTRY
game of chance lottery
gamesome jocular
gamester bettor
gaming risk, speculation *(risk)*
gammon bait *(lure)*, betray *(lead astray)*, palter
gamut range. SEE MAIN ENTRY
gang assemblage, band, cabal, league
gangleader racketeer
gangster burglar, criminal, malefactor, racketeer
gangway entrance
gannitus snarl
gap flaw, hiatus, interruption, interval, pause, space, split
gaping open *(unclosed)*, penetrable
garb clothe
garble cloak, falsify, misconstrue, misinterpret, misread. SEE MAIN ENTRY
garbled imperfect, inaccurate, marred
garbling catachresis
garden cultivate, curtilage
gargantuan prodigious *(enormous)*
garish meretricious, pretentious *(ostentatious)*, tawdry. SEE MAIN ENTRY
garishness pretense *(ostentation)*
garner accumulate *(amass)*, collect *(gather)*, compile, fund, glean, hoard, repository, reserve, store. SEE MAIN ENTRY
garner up hoard
garnering arsenal
garnish attach *(seize)*, distrain, embellish, impress *(procure by force)*, levy. SEE MAIN ENTRY
garnished elaborate
garnisheed attached *(seized)*
garnishing bombast, confiscatory
garnishment attachment *(seizure)*, distraint, motif, sequestration. SEE MAIN ENTRY
garrison bear *(support)*, lodge *(house)*, protect
garrulous flatulent, loquacious, profuse, voluble. SEE MAIN ENTRY
garrulus loquacious
gasconade exaggeration, jactation, rodomontade
gasconading orgulous
gash lancinate, mutilate, rift *(gap)*, split
gate egress, entrance, immure, outlet, portal
gatekeeper guardian, warden
gates approaches
gateway easement, egress, entrance, outlet, portal, threshold *(entrance)*
gather accrue *(increase)*, accumulate *(amass)*, aggregate, assume *(suppose)*, call *(summon)*, compile, concentrate *(consolidate)*, congregate, conjoin, connect *(join together)*, construe *(comprehend)*, convene, converge, cull, deduce, deduct *(conclude by reasoning)*, expect *(consider probable)*, extract, gain, garner, glean, guess, hold *(possess)*, infer, join *(bring together)*, levy, obtain, presume, presuppose, procure, read, reap, reason *(conclude)*, receive *(acquire)*, recruit, rendezvous, store, surmise, suspect *(think)*, understand. SEE MAIN ENTRY
gather for oneself hoard
gather in hoard
gather into a mass accumulate *(amass)*
gather knowledge find *(discover)*
gather together accumulate *(amass)*, aggregate, collect *(gather)*, compile, consolidate *(unite)*, convene, meet, raise *(collect)*, unite
gather up accumulate *(amass)*, hoard
gathered collective, composite
gathered into a round mass conglomerate
gathered into a whole composite
gathering assemblage, assembly, body *(collection)*, caucus, chamber *(body)*, collection *(assembly)*, company *(assemblage)*, compilation, conference, congregation, levy, mass *(body of persons)*, meeting *(conference)*, rendezvous, selection *(collection)*, session. SEE MAIN ENTRY
gathering place focus, rendezvous
gathering together centralization
gauche incompetent, provincial
gaudiness pretense *(ostentation)*
gaudium enjoyment *(pleasure)*
gaudy blatant *(obtrusive)*, meretricious, pretentious *(ostentatious)*, tawdry
gauge assess *(appraise)*, calculate, consider, criterion, criticize *(evaluate)*, estimate *(approximate cost)*, estimate, estimation *(calculation)*, evaluate, extent, magnitude, mass *(weight)*, measure, measurement, model, rate, standard, weigh. SEE MAIN ENTRY
gaugeable appreciable, determinable *(ascertainable)*
gausape fustian *(adjective)*, fustian *(noun)*
gavel SEE MAIN ENTRY
gawky incompetent, provincial, uncouth
gay jocular. SEE MAIN ENTRY
gay marriage SEE MAIN ENTRY
gaze regard *(pay attention)*
gaze at observe *(watch)*
gazette herald, journal, proclaim
gear clothe, device *(mechanism)*, furnish, paraphernalia *(apparatus)*
gear with engage *(involve)*
geared to fitting
gelatinization congealment
gelling congealment
gemination duplicate
gemmate germinate
gender SEE MAIN ENTRY
gender bias SEE MAIN ENTRY
gender discrimination SEE MAIN ENTRY
gene patent SEE MAIN ENTRY
genealogical hereditary
genealogical tree blood, origin *(ancestry)*, parentage
genealogy ancestry, blood, bloodline, descent *(lineage)*, family *(common ancestry)*, lineage, origin *(ancestry)*, parentage, race
genera class
general broad, chief, collective, competitive *(open)*, conventional, customary, familiar *(customary)*, generic, habitual, inaccurate, inclusive, inexact, liberal *(not literal)*, mutual *(collective)*, national, nonsectarian, omnibus, ordinary, predominant, prevailing *(current)*, prevalent, proverbial, public *(affecting people)*, regular *(conventional)*, rife, routine, unspecified, usual, vague. SEE MAIN ENTRY
general agreement consensus. SEE MAIN ENTRY
general course practice *(custom)*
general denial demurrer
general discharge salvo
general expenses overhead
general fire conflagration
general guidelines policy *(plan of action)*, practice *(procedure)*
general information common knowledge, education
general law generality *(vague statement)*
general meaning connotation, content *(meaning)*, gist *(substance)*. SEE MAIN ENTRY
general notion impression
general pardon amnesty
general performance norm
general principle generality *(vague statement)*
general principles policy *(plan of action)*. SEE MAIN ENTRY
general public populace, population, public
general reciprocity comity
general release SEE MAIN ENTRY
general rule canon, generality *(vague statement)*
general run matter of course
general statement generality *(vague statement)*, generalization
general store market *(business)*
general uprising revolution
generalis general
generality generalization, majority *(greater part)*, norm. SEE MAIN ENTRY
generalization generality *(vague statement)*. SEE MAIN ENTRY
generalize SEE MAIN ENTRY
generalized broad, inaccurate
generally as a rule, invariably. SEE MAIN ENTRY
generally accepted prevailing *(current)*, prevalent
generally known common *(customary)*, notorious
generally practiced ordinary
generally seen familiar *(customary)*

generally speaking as a rule
generals management *(directorate)*
generalship management *(supervision).* SEE MAIN ENTRY
generare engender, generate
generate avail *(bring about),* bear *(yield),* cause, compose, conceive *(invent),* create, elicit, engender, evoke, fabricate *(construct),* germinate, induce, inspire, launch *(initiate),* make, manufacture, occasion, originate, produce *(manufacture),* propagate *(increase),* provoke, pullulate, reproduce, yield *(produce a return).* SEE MAIN ENTRY
generatim generalize
generating causal
generation formation, lifetime
generations of man humanity *(mankind)*
generative causal, causative, constructive *(creative),* potent, prime *(original),* prolific
generator architect, author *(originator),* cause *(reason),* derivation, determinant, source
generic broad, omnibus, unspecified. SEE MAIN ENTRY
generic class kind
generical omnibus
generis kind
generosity benevolence *(disposition to do good),* charity, clemency, consideration *(sympathetic regard),* contribution *(donation),* indulgence, largess *(generosity),* philanthropy
generous ample, benevolent, capacious, charitable *(benevolent),* copious, donative, favorable *(expressing approval),* humane, lenient, liberal *(generous),* magnanimous, meritorious, multiple, philanthropic, placable, profuse, propitious. SEE MAIN ENTRY
generous giver donor
generous giving charity
generousness clemency, indulgence, largess *(generosity),* lenience
genesis ancestry, birth *(beginning),* cause *(reason),* derivation, determinant, embryo, formation, inception, nascency, onset *(commencement),* origin *(source),* origination, outset, parentage, reason *(basis),* source, start. SEE MAIN ENTRY
genetic born *(innate),* hereditary, native *(inborn).* SEE MAIN ENTRY
genetic engineering SEE MAIN ENTRY
genial amicable, benevolent, civil *(polite),* willing *(not averse)*
genialis nuptial
geniality consideration *(sympathetic regard),* courtesy, goodwill
genitor ancestor, ascendant, parents, progenitor
genius caliber *(mental capacity),* expert, gift *(flair),* intellect, intelligence *(intellect),* mastermind, propensity, sagacity, science *(technique),* sense *(intelligence),* specialty *(special aptitude).* SEE MAIN ENTRY
genocide murder. SEE MAIN ENTRY
genre class, denomination, kind, style. SEE MAIN ENTRY
gens lineage
gens humana humanity *(mankind)*
genteel civil *(polite)*
gentility blood, comity, courtesy, decorum, presence *(poise),* society
gentle harmless, lenient, nonmilitant, peaceable, placid
gentleman of fortune bettor
gentlemanlike civil *(polite)*
gentlemanliness decorum
gentlemanly civil *(polite)*
gentleness clemency, consideration *(sympathetic regard),* humanity *(humaneness),* lenience, moderation
gentry elite
genuflection prostration
genuine accurate, actual, authentic, bona fide, convincing, de facto, direct *(forthright),* documentary, factual, faithful *(true to fact),* honest, ingenuous, legitimate *(rightful),* natural, prime *(original),* real, realistic, reliable, rightful, sterling, substantial, true *(authentic),* unadulterated, undistorted, veridical. SEE MAIN ENTRY
genuine in origin authentic
genuinely admittedly
genuineness candor *(straightforwardness),* honesty, legitimacy, reality, truth, validity
genuiness veracity
genus ancestry, blood, class
genus kind
genus lineage, parentage
genus race
genus range
genus rubric *(title)*
genus style
geographical regional
gerere conduct, transact
germ consequence *(significance),* embryo, source
germane applicable, apposite, appropriate, cognate, congruous, correlative, felicitous, interrelated, pertinent, related, relative *(relevant),* relevant, suitable, tangential. SEE MAIN ENTRY
germanus genuine, real
germicidal preventive
germinal original *(initial),* prime *(original),* rudimentary
germinare germinate
germinate develop, pullulate, stem *(originate).* SEE MAIN ENTRY
germinate from redound
germination development *(progression),* growth *(evolution)*
germinative rudimentary
gerrymander illude. SEE MAIN ENTRY
gestare bear *(support)*
gesture brandish, symbol. SEE MAIN ENTRY
get acquire *(secure),* attain, derive *(receive),* gain, incur, obtain, possess, procure, raise *(collect),* reach, realize *(obtain as a profit),* reap, receive *(acquire).* SEE MAIN ENTRY
get a fresh start resume
get a glimpse of discover
get a profit earn
get abroad circulate
get across annunciate, convey *(communicate).* SEE MAIN ENTRY
get ahead compound, proceed *(go forward),* progress, surpass
get ahead of outbalance, outweigh
get as one's own possess
get at reach
get away elude
get away from evade *(elude),* part *(leave)*
get away with *(let off)* SEE MAIN ENTRY
get away with *(put over on).* SEE MAIN ENTRY
get back collect *(recover money),* reclaim, recoup *(regain),* recover, redeem *(repurchase),* retaliate
get back to work proceed *(continue)*
get by pass *(satisfy requirements)*
get by effort attain, earn
get by judgment recover
get control hold *(possess)*
get done attain, cap
get down alight
get even repay, retaliate
get even with discipline *(punish),* recriminate. SEE MAIN ENTRY
get free break *(separate)*
get going originate
get hold of grapple, obtain
get in exchange buy
get in formation organize *(arrange)*
get in the act participate
get in the way disrupt, hinder, interrupt
get in the way of foil
get in touch convey *(communicate)*
get in touch with reach
get loose break *(separate)*
get money collect *(recover money)*
get near approach
get off alight
get off the subject deviate
get on proceed *(continue),* proceed *(go forward)*
get on credit borrow
get on the nerves of annoy
get out quit *(evacuate)*
get possession of attain, collect *(recover money),* gain, hold *(possess),* obtain
get ready provide *(arrange for)*
get rid of delete, discharge *(dismiss),* disown *(refuse to acknowledge),* dispel, eject *(evict),* eliminate *(eradicate),* expel, extirpate, jettison, purge *(purify),* reject, remove *(dismiss from office)*
get temporary use of borrow
get the best of beat *(defeat)*
get the better of beat *(defeat),* overcome *(surmount),* overreach, subdue, subject, surmount
get the start on anticipate *(expect)*
get the upper hand overcome *(overwhelm),* overcome *(surmount),* prevail *(triumph)*
get through annunciate, cease, pass *(satisfy requirements)*
get through to contact *(communicate),* reach
get through with cap
get to contact *(communicate)*
get to safety escape
get to the bottom of find *(discover)*
get together congregate, hoard, meet
get under way arise *(occur),* dispatch *(send off),* embark
get up originate
get used to inure *(accustom),* naturalize *(acclimate)*
get worse degenerate, depreciate
get wrong misconstrue, mistake
get-together rendezvous
getting even reprisal
getting less decrease
getting together congregation
ghastly deplorable, heinous, loathsome, lurid, repulsive
ghost phantom. SEE MAIN ENTRY
ghostly nonsubstantial *(not sturdy)*
ghostly form phantom
ghoulish sinister
giant prodigious *(enormous)*
gibberish jargon *(unintelligible language)*
gibbet defame, denigrate, denounce *(condemn),* pillory, sully
gibe disdain, disparage, flout, hector, jeer, mock *(deride),* plague, ridicule
gibe at jape
giddy capricious, frivolous, thoughtless, volatile

gift appropriation *(donation)*, aptitude, behalf, benefit *(conferment)*, bequest, bonus, bounty, caliber *(mental capacity)*, cession, charity, competence *(ability)*, contribution *(donation)*, donation, endowment, faculty *(ability)*, grant, gratuity *(present)*, inheritance, perquisite, proclivity, propensity, reward, skill, subsidy, tendency, tip *(gratuity)*. SEE MAIN ENTRY
gift by succession estate *(hereditament)*
gift by will legacy
gift of a freehold interest feoffment
gift of property by will legacy
gifted artful, capable, deft, original *(creative)*, practiced, resourceful, sciential
giftedness capacity *(aptitude)*
gigantic capacious, copious, gross *(flagrant)*, prodigious *(enormous)*
gignere engender, generate, propagate *(increase)*
gild camouflage, embellish
gimcrack poor *(inferior in quality)*
gimmick device *(contrivance)*, stratagem. SEE MAIN ENTRY
gingerly meticulous
gird border *(bound)*, circumscribe *(surround by boundary)*, embrace *(encircle)*, enclose, encompass *(surround)*
girdle circumscribe *(surround by boundary)*, embrace *(encircle)*, enclose, enclosure, encompass *(surround)*, hedge, include
girdling blockade *(enclosure)*
girl child
girlishness puerility
girth caliber *(measurement)*, measurement
gist center *(essence)*, connotation, content *(meaning)*, contents, context, essence, gravamen, import, main point, significance, signification, spirit, subject *(topic)*, substance *(essential nature)*, sum *(tally)*, tenor. SEE MAIN ENTRY
gist of a charge gravamen
gite abode
givable heritable
give adduce, administer *(tender)*, allow *(authorize)*, ascribe, attorn, bear *(yield)*, bequeath, bestow, cede, confer *(give)*, contribute *(supply)*, convey *(transfer)*, dedicate, delegate, descend, devise *(give)*, devolve, disburse *(distribute)*, dole, endow, endue, extend *(offer)*, fund, furnish, grant *(concede)*, grant *(transfer formally)*, lend, loan, mete, pander, present *(make a gift)*, proffer, provide *(supply)*, relax, relent, render *(administer)*, render *(deliver)*, replenish, send, spend, subsidize, supply, tender, transmit, yield *(produce a return)*. SEE MAIN ENTRY
give a bad name defame, denigrate, pillory
give a beating lash *(strike)*
give a blow beat *(strike)*
give a color to camouflage
give a detailed explanation explicate
give a directive direct *(order)*, instruct *(direct)*, prescribe
give a false appearance camouflage, pretend
give a false coloring camouflage, cloak, disguise, misrepresent
give a false idea delude, distort, mislead
give a false impression delude, distort, misdirect, misinform, mislead, misstate, profess *(pretend)*
give a false representation misrepresent
give a favorable verdict acquit
give a final notice charge *(assess)*
give a formal hearing to hear *(give a legal hearing)*
give a formal speech declaim
give a grant to subsidize
give a guarantee certify *(attest)*, pledge *(promise the performance of)*
give a guilty verdict convict
give a hand assist
give a hint imply, mention
give a job retain *(employ)*
give a job to employ *(engage services)*, engage *(hire)*, hire
give a judicial hearing to hear *(give a legal hearing)*
give a lesson exposit
give a mandate appoint, delegate, entrust, instruct *(direct)*, invest *(vest)*, prescribe
give a name call *(title)*
give a name to denominate, identify
give a new form to modify *(alter)*
give a performance produce *(offer to view)*
give a permit qualify *(meet standards)*
give a position to employ *(engage services)*
give a post to employ *(engage services)*
give a present bestow
give a prize dedicate
give a promise swear
give a recommendation counsel
give a report inform *(notify)*, relate *(tell)*
give a reprieve clear, condone, free
give a responsibility to delegate, entrust
give a right authorize
give a ruling conclude *(decide)*, determine, pronounce *(pass judgment)*
give a sense to comment
give a signal indicate
give a situation to engage *(hire)*
give a solemn declaration depose *(testify)*
give a speech address *(talk to)*, discourse
give a start expedite
give a strained meaning distort
give a summary of recapitulate
give a talk discourse, speak
give a thrashing beat *(strike)*, lash *(strike)*
give a turn distort
give a verbal account recite
give a vote cast *(register)*
give a warrant qualify *(meet standards)*
give a wide berth eschew
give a wide berth to shun
give a wrong idea misstate
give ability empower, enable
give absolution clear, condone, exonerate, forgive, free, pardon
give absolution to exculpate, excuse
give additional information elaborate
give admittance to instate
give advice admonish *(advise)*, advise, advocate, caution, charge *(instruct on the law)*, confer *(consult)*, counsel, incite
give advice against expostulate
give aid aid, assist, capitalize *(provide capital)*, contribute *(assist)*, nurture, subsidize
give allegiance to obey
give amnesty condone, palliate *(excuse)*, remit *(release from penalty)*
give an account communicate, convey *(communicate)*, depict, describe, detail *(particularize)*, inform *(notify)*, recount, relate *(tell)*
give an account of characterize, depose *(testify)*, report *(disclose)*
give an address discourse
give an answer respond, return *(respond)*
give an appellation to identify
give an approximate value estimate
give an encore copy, repeat *(do again)*
give an estimate evaluate
give an example exemplify
give an explanation elucidate
give an impetus impel, inspire
give an inclination prejudice *(influence)*
give an inkling hint
give an instance exemplify, illustrate
give an interpretation elucidate
give an introduction present *(introduce)*
give an official hearing to hear *(give a legal hearing)*
give an opinion adjudge, advise, conclude *(decide)*, determine, evaluate, find *(determine)*, pass *(determine)*, pronounce *(pass judgment)*, rule *(decide)*
give an order direct *(order)*, instruct *(direct)*, prescribe
give and bequeath devise *(give)*
give and take barter, interchange, quid pro quo, reciprocal, reciprocate, reciprocity. SEE MAIN ENTRY
give approval bestow, consent, pass *(approve)*, sanction
give as a gift present *(make a gift)*
give as a guarantee pledge *(deposit)*
give as an excuse justify
give as example cite *(state)*
give as security pawn
give as security for a debt pledge *(deposit)*
give as security for an obligation pledge *(deposit)*
give as surety pledge *(deposit)*
give assent accede *(concede)*, agree *(comply)*, bestow, certify *(approve)*, coincide *(concur)*, defer *(yield in judgment)*
give assurance agree *(contract)*, avouch *(guarantee)*, close *(agree)*, cosign, guarantee, pledge *(promise the performance of)*, promise *(vow)*, vouch
give attention concern *(care)*, devote, focus
give attention to concentrate *(pay attention)*, note *(notice)*, observe *(watch)*, perceive, specialize
give audience hear *(give attention to)*
give authoritative instructions to instruct *(direct)*
give authority allow *(authorize)*, authorize, empower, enable, grant *(concede)*, invest *(vest)*, vest
give authority to charge *(empower)*, delegate
give away abandon *(relinquish)*, bestow, betray *(disclose)*, cede, contribute *(supply)*, devise *(give)*, disburse *(distribute)*, disperse *(disseminate)*, dole, expose, forfeit, grant *(transfer formally)*, parcel, post, renounce
give away at death bequeath
give back bestow, contribute *(indemnify)*, indemnify, rebate, recommit, recoup *(reimburse)*, reflect *(mirror)*, refund, remise, render *(deliver)*, repay, restore *(return)*, return *(refund)*
give base bear *(support)*
give being to develop
give birth propagate *(increase)*
give birth to conceive *(invent)*, create, make, originate, produce *(manufacture)*, reproduce
give by way of information instruct *(teach)*

give by will bequeath, demise, descend, devise *(give)*, leave *(give)*
give cause for occasion
give cause for alarm disconcert, frighten, perturb
give chase hunt
give clearance bestow, certify *(approve)*, facilitate, grant *(concede)*, permit, release
give close attention scrutinize
give color to disguise
give compensation for defray
give compensation for in advance prepay
give concrete form to embody, exemplify
give confidence reassure
give consent agree *(comply)*, assent, bestow, certify *(approve)*, consent, defer *(yield in judgment)*, grant *(concede)*, permit, suffer *(permit)*
give consent to comply
give control vest
give counsel admonish *(advise)*, advise
give credence to trust
give credit concur *(agree)*, lend, recommend
give credit to trust
give currency promulgate
give currency to circulate
give definite form to embody
give denial to contradict, controvert, dispute *(contest)*
give details detail *(particularize)*
give directions command, direct *(order)*, discipline *(train)*, prescribe
give dispensation bestow, excuse, palliate *(excuse)*
give earnestly dedicate
give employment delegate, employ *(engage services)*
give employment to engage *(hire)*, hire
give entrance receive *(permit to enter)*
give entrance to induct, initiate, instate, penetrate
give equal value compensate *(remunerate)*
give evidence bear *(adduce)*, confess, depose *(testify)*, swear, testify, verify *(confirm)*, vouch, witness *(attest to)*
give expectation promise *(raise expectations)*
give explanation to construe *(translate)*
give expression communicate, enunciate, recite, speak
give expression to depict, express, observe *(remark)*, phrase, utter
give fair warning caution, forewarn, notice *(give formal warning)*
give final notice dun
give force to implement
give form to formalize, formulate
give formal approval to formalize
give formal status to formalize
give forth circulate, develop, emit, post, reflect *(mirror)*, send, utter
give foundation bear *(support)*
give freedom liberate
give freely bestow
give full particulars specify
give good reasons for vindicate
give ground bear *(support)*
give grounds for support *(justify)*
give heed concentrate *(pay attention)*
give heed to attend *(heed)*, care *(be cautious)*, notice *(observe)*, observe *(watch)*, regard *(pay attention)*
give help relieve *(give aid)*, serve *(assist)*
give honor dedicate
give hope assure *(give confidence to)*, promise *(raise expectations)*, reassure
give impetus incite
give impulse to originate
give in accede *(concede)*, concede, defer *(yield in judgment)*, relent, submit *(yield)*, succumb, surrender *(yield)*, vouchsafe, yield *(submit)*. SEE MAIN ENTRY
give in charge delegate
give in custody arrest *(apprehend)*
give in earnest pawn
give in exchange barter, change, repay
give in kind recriminate
give in return reciprocate
give in trust confide *(trust)*, consign, delegate
give increase bear *(yield)*
give indication of evidence, speak
give indirect information connote, imply
give information advise, apprise, bear *(adduce)*, notice *(give formal warning)*
give inside information reveal
give instructions direct *(order)*, discipline *(train)*
give intimation of impending evil caution, forewarn
give into another's keeping deliver
give judgment adjudicate, arbitrate *(adjudge)*, conclude *(decide)*, decree, determine, find *(determine)*, pronounce *(pass judgment)*, rule *(decide)*
give leave allow *(authorize)*, authorize, bestow, grant *(concede)*, let *(permit)*, permit, suffer *(permit)*
give legal force validate
give legal form to constitute *(establish)*
give legislative sanction enact
give legislative sanction to pass *(approve)*
give lessons educate
give lessons in discipline *(train)*, instruct *(teach)*
give liberty to disenthrall, enfranchise, liberate
give life to generate
give means enable
give measure for measure retaliate
give money bear the expense, disburse *(pay out)*, expend *(disburse)*, fund
give money over lend
give new life to renew *(refurbish)*
give no credence to disbelieve, doubt *(distrust)*, misdoubt
give no credit to disbelieve, misdoubt, mistrust
give no heed disregard
give notice admonish *(advise)*, advise, alert, annunciate, apprise, caution, communicate, convey *(communicate)*, demand, discharge *(dismiss)*, forewarn, inform *(notify)*, mention, notify, predict, remind, resign, retire *(conclude a career)*, signify *(inform)*. SEE MAIN ENTRY
give notice of proclaim, promulgate
give notice to serve *(deliver a legal instrument)*
give notification communicate
give occasion for cause
give occupation rent
give off emit, exude
give offense irritate, pique, provoke, repel *(disgust)*
give offense to affront, bait *(harass)*, disoblige, humiliate
give one a talking to browbeat
give one an idea of interpret
give one an impression of interpret
give one his deserts discipline *(punish)*
give one pause discourage
give one to understand advise, communicate
give one's attention concern *(care)*
give one's blessing countenance
give one's hand to bestow
give one's honor promise *(vow)*
give one's signature cosign, pledge *(deposit)*
give one's word bear *(adduce)*, certify *(attest)*, guarantee, pledge *(promise the performance of)*, promise *(vow)*, swear, testify, vouch
give one's word for confirm
give one's word of honor promise *(vow)*
give opportunity for permit
give oral evidence affirm *(declare solemnly)*
give orders command, decree, dictate, direct *(order)*, enjoin, govern, rule *(govern)*, summon
give origin provoke
give origin to avail *(bring about)*, cause, create, make, originate
give out allocate, assign *(allot)*, bestow, circulate, deliver, disburse *(distribute)*, dispense, distribute, divide *(distribute)*, dole, emit, issue *(publish)*, mete, parcel, post, proclaim, publish, reveal
give out again redistribute
give out among a number disperse *(disseminate)*
give out in payment disburse *(pay out)*
give out in shares bestow
give out information inform *(notify)*
give over abandon *(relinquish)*, cease, present *(make a gift)*, relinquish
give over to grant *(transfer formally)*
give over to the foe betray *(lead astray)*, inform *(betray)*
give pain aggravate *(annoy)*, harrow, inflict, mistreat
give payment pay, remunerate
give permission allow *(authorize)*, authorize, bestow, certify *(approve)*, consent, empower, enable, grant *(concede)*, let *(permit)*, permit, sanction, suffer *(permit)*
give place to succeed *(follow)*
give play to the imagination conjure
give political privileges to enfranchise
give power authorize, bestow, delegate, empower, enable, invest *(vest)*, permit
give power of attorney delegate
give power to charge *(empower)*
give precise meaning to characterize
give previous notice to forewarn
give previous warning to forewarn
give proof depose *(testify)*
give proof by a witness depose *(testify)*
give public notice of issue *(publish)*, post, publish
give publicity to promulgate
give quarter relent
give reason for enlighten, explain, exposit
give references document
give refuge harbor
give relief mitigate, mollify, relieve *(give aid)*, soothe
give repose ease
give rest ease
give right empower
give right of entry to admit *(give access)*

give rise provoke
give rise to avail *(bring about)*, cause, compose, create, develop, engender, establish *(launch)*, evoke, generate, make, originate, produce *(manufacture)*
give salvation save *(rescue)*
give satisfaction indemnify, redeem *(satisfy debts)*
give satisfaction for damage compensate *(remunerate)*
give satisfaction for injury compensate *(remunerate)*
give security assure *(insure)*, bond *(secure a debt)*, confirm, ensure, pledge *(deposit)*, promise *(vow)*
give sense to construe *(translate)*
give shape to form
give sign signify *(inform)*
give strength to compound
give suggestions advise
give suggestions to charge *(instruct on the law)*, counsel
give support adhere *(maintain loyalty)*, aid, assist, bear *(support)*, capitalize *(provide capital)*, preserve
give support to subsidize
give surety ensure
give sworn evidence affirm *(declare solemnly)*
give sworn testimony depose *(testify)*
give tangible form to embody
give terms dicker
give testimony witness *(attest to)*
give the cold shoulder ignore
give the death blow dispatch *(put to death)*
give the details of characterize, delineate
give the effect appear *(seem to be)*
give the facts communicate, inform *(notify)*, notify, recount, report *(disclose)*
give the floor to recognize *(acknowledge)*
give the impression appear *(seem to be)*
give the meaning define
give the mind to focus
give the nod to recognize *(acknowledge)*
give the particulars recount
give the right to vote enfranchise
give the signal instruct *(direct)*
give the sum and substance abridge *(shorten)*
give the word instruct *(direct)*
give the word of command instruct *(direct)*
give thought to ponder, reflect *(ponder)*
give tidings herald, inform *(notify)*
give title to denominate, sell
give to delegate
give to the world circulate
give to understand disabuse, instruct *(teach)*, notify
give token portend
give tongue communicate
give tongue to observe *(remark)*, phrase
give trouble balk, inconvenience
give twist distort
give umbrage pique
give umbrage to bait *(harass)*
give up abandon *(relinquish)*, bestow, cede, demit, disclaim, discontinue *(abandon)*, disown *(refuse to acknowledge)*, forfeit, forgo, forswear, leave *(allow to remain)*, quit *(discontinue)*, release, relinquish, remise, remit *(relax)*, renounce, resign, submit *(yield)*, waive, yield *(submit)*
give up claim to abandon *(relinquish)*, cede, forfeit, forgo, relinquish, renounce, waive
give up office retire *(conclude a career)*
give up the argument forfeit
give up the point forfeit
give up the right to forgo
give up treacherously betray *(lead astray)*
give up work retire *(conclude a career)*
give utterance communicate, enunciate, mention, phrase, remark
give utterance to betray *(disclose)*, disclose, observe *(remark)*
give validity to implement
give variety vary
give vent to express
give verbal evidence affirm *(declare solemnly)*
give voice communicate, speak
give voice to express, observe *(remark)*, phrase
give warning admonish *(warn)*, advise, caution, notice *(give formal warning)*, notify
give warning of possible harm caution, forewarn
give way defer *(yield in judgment)*, hear *(give attention to)*, obey, relent, retreat, split, succumb, yield *(submit)*
give way to submit *(yield)*
give witness bear *(adduce)*
give word for word quote
give words to phrase, portray, speak
give work to employ *(engage services)*, hire
given assumed *(inferred)*, free *(at no charge)*, gratuitous *(given without recompense)*, prone, ready *(willing)*, unpaid. SEE MAIN ENTRY
given away donative, free *(at no charge)*, gratuitous *(given without recompense)*
given by testament testamentary
given due consideration deliberate
given name call *(title)*
given over addicted
given preference preferred *(given priority)*
given to accustomed *(familiarized)*
given to controversy argumentative
given to deceit false *(not genuine)*
given to disputation litigious
given to fighting pugnacious
given to joking jocular
given to lying mendacious
given to research inquisitive
given to suspicion inconvincible
given to thought pensive
given to vice vicious
given up derelict *(abandoned)*, irretrievable
giver benefactor, donor, feoffor, good samaritan, grantor, supplier
giver of evidence eyewitness
giving charitable *(benevolent)*, concession *(authorization)*, dedication, disposition *(transfer of property)*, donative, philanthropic, sequacious
giving back reimbursement, restitution
giving beforehand advance *(allowance)*
giving each his due equitable
giving in concession *(compromise)*
giving over delegation *(assignment)*
giving up bailment, cession, renunciation, resignation *(relinquishment)*, waiver
giving up claim to cession
giving way capitulation
glad ecstatic, inclined, ready *(willing)*
gladly readily
glamor prestige
glamorize embellish
glamorous attractive
glance vision *(dream)*. SEE MAIN ENTRY
glance at notice *(observe)*
glance off deviate
glance over peruse
glare pretense *(ostentation)*
glaring blatant *(obtrusive)*, clear *(apparent)*, distinct *(clear)*, egregious, evident, flagrant, gross *(flagrant)*, manifest, notorious, obvious, open *(in sight)*, outrageous, overt, palpable, patent, perceivable, perceptible, prominent, salient, stark, tawdry, unmistakable. SEE MAIN ENTRY
glaringly bad arrant *(onerous)*
glaringly vivid lurid
glean acquire *(receive)*, compile, construe *(comprehend)*, cull, derive *(receive)*, extract, gain, infer, procure, read, reap, select, understand. SEE MAIN ENTRY
glean information peruse
glean knowledge of overhear
gleaning acquisition
gleeful jocular
gleesome jocular
glib loquacious, voluble
glimmer suggestion
glimpse find *(discover)*, pierce *(discern)*, spy, vision *(dream)*. SEE MAIN ENTRY
gliscere increase
glitter pretense *(ostentation)*
glittering tawdry
gloat over relish
global complete *(all-embracing)*, nonsectarian, prevailing *(current)*, prevalent, total. SEE MAIN ENTRY
global warming SEE MAIN ENTRY
globe sphere
globoid sphere
globular mass sphere
glomerate composite, conglomerate
glomeration agglomeration, conglomeration, cumulation
gloom damper *(depressant)*, depression, indistinctness, obscuration, pessimism. SEE MAIN ENTRY
gloominess obscuration, pessimism
gloomy bleak *(not favorable)*, bleak *(severely simple)*, despondent, disconsolate, lugubrious, ominous, pessimistic, portentous *(ominous)*, solemn. SEE MAIN ENTRY
gloomy outlook pessimism
gloria prestige
glorification doxology, homage, honor *(outward respect)*, laudation, mention *(tribute)*, remembrance *(commemoration)*
glorified famous
glorify belaud, compound, elevate, honor, magnify, overestimate, raise *(advance)*, recommend, regard *(hold in esteem)*. SEE MAIN ENTRY
gloriosus pretentious *(pompous)*
glorious famous, illustrious, meritorious. SEE MAIN ENTRY
glory eminence, honor *(outward respect)*, prestige, reputation. SEE MAIN ENTRY
gloss color *(deceptive appearance)*, comment *(noun)*, comment *(verb)*, distortion, note *(brief comment)*
gloss over cloak, discount *(disbelieve)*, neglect, pretermit, prevaricate
glow passion
glowing moving *(evoking emotion)*, vehement
glue adhere *(fasten)*, bond *(hold together)*, cement, combine *(join together)*, join *(bring together)*, lock
glued inseparable

glum disconsolate, lugubrious, pessimistic
glumness damper *(depressant)*, pessimism
glut inundate, overage, overcome *(overwhelm)*, overload, plethora, sufficiency, surfeit, surplus
glutinosity adhesion *(affixing)*
glutinous cohesive *(sticking)*
glutted full
gluttonous inordinate, insatiable, lecherous. SEE MAIN ENTRY
gluttonous appetite greed
gluttony greed
gnarus familiar *(informed)*
gnaw obsess, pique
gnomic compact *(pithy)*, pithy, sententious
gnomic saying maxim
gnomical compact *(pithy)*
gnostic profound *(esoteric)*
go expire, leave *(depart)*, move *(alter position)*, part *(leave)*, pass *(advance)*, perish, proceed *(go forward)*, quit *(evacuate)*. SEE MAIN ENTRY
go about discharge *(perform)*, occupy *(engage)*
go about stealthily prowl
go across cross *(intersect)*, traverse
go adrift deviate
go after attempt, chase, hunt, prosecute *(carry forward)*, pursue *(chase)*, strive, succeed *(follow)*
go against antagonize, confront *(oppose)*, contradict, contravene, counter, counteract, disapprove *(reject)*, oppose, oppugn
go ahead proceed *(go forward)*, progress. SEE MAIN ENTRY
go ahead of precede
go all out for attempt
go along with attend *(accompany)*, authorize, coincide *(concur)*, comply, concur *(agree)*, conform, cooperate, countenance, defer *(yield in judgment)*, participate, sanction. SEE MAIN ENTRY
go amiss deviate, err, miscalculate, mistake
go apart disband
go around detour, envelop, perambulate
go astray deviate, digress, err, lapse *(fall into error)*, miscalculate, mistake, trespass
go away leave *(depart)*, move *(alter position)*, part *(leave)*, quit *(evacuate)*, retreat, vacate *(leave)*
go awry deviate, lapse *(fall into error)*, miscalculate
go back escheat, recollect, regress, retire *(retreat)*, retreat
go back on abandon *(relinquish)*
go back on a commitment renege
go back on a promise renege
go back on one's word bear false witness
go back over reexamine
go back to continue *(resume)*
go bad degenerate, spoil *(impair)*
go before antecede, precede
go between SEE MAIN ENTRY
go beyond outweigh, overlap, overstep, predominate *(outnumber)*, surmount, surpass, transcend
go by pass *(advance)*
go contrary to collide *(clash)*, conflict, contradict, counter, except *(object)*, oppose, protest
go counter to contradict, countervail, disobey
go deep into delve
go different ways disband, disperse *(scatter)*
go down succumb
go down in defeat lose *(undergo defeat)*
go downhill decrease
go for a walk perambulate
go forth circulate, leave *(depart)*, move *(alter position)*, part *(leave)*, proceed *(go forward)*, quit *(evacuate)*
go forward persevere, persist, progress
go from home move *(alter position)*
go in advance precede
go in different directions diffuse, disperse *(scatter)*
go in for pursue *(carry on)*, undertake
go in front of precede
go in many directions diffuse
go in opposition to collide *(clash)*, conflict, contradict, counter, counteract
go in pursuit of chase, delve, hunt, pursue *(chase)*
go in quest of chase, research
go in search of delve, hunt
go into deliberate, embark, enter *(go in)*, investigate
go into a decline languish
go into detail develop, elaborate, expand, quote, specify
go into litigation litigate
go into partnership cooperate, federalize *(associate)*
go into retirement demit, quit *(discontinue)*
go into the particulars detail *(particularize)*
go near approach
go next succeed *(follow)*
go off on a tangent deviate
go on continue *(persevere)*, endure *(last)*, exist, keep *(continue)*, maintain *(carry on)*, move *(alter position)*, pass *(advance)*, persevere, persist, progress, remain *(continue)*, resume, subsist
go on a spree carouse
go on an outing perambulate
go on foot perambulate
go one better surpass
go one's way move *(alter position)*
go out quit *(evacuate)*
go out of emanate
go out of business fail *(lose)*, quit *(discontinue)*
go out of one's way detour, deviate
go out of the path detour
go out of the way detour
go over check *(inspect)*, examine *(study)*, overstep, peruse, reaffirm, recapitulate, reconsider, reiterate, review, trace *(delineate)*
go past pass *(advance)*
go round about detour, deviate
go separate ways disband, disperse *(scatter)*
go the rounds patrol
go through bear *(tolerate)*, delve, endure *(suffer)*, penetrate, permeate, pervade, search, spend
go through phases change
go through the books audit
go through the motions fake
go through with commit *(perpetrate)*, discharge *(perform)*, follow-up
go to attend *(be present at)*
go to any lengths adhere *(persist)*
go to contract close *(agree)*. SEE MAIN ENTRY
go to pieces degenerate
go to press publish
go to the limit adhere *(persist)*
go to the polls cast *(register)*
go to war fight *(battle)*
go too far overextend, overstep
go under fail *(lose)*, succumb
go undercover cloak
go up against SEE MAIN ENTRY
go with coincide *(correspond)*
go without relinquish, renounce
go wrong deviate, err, mistake
go-between agent, broker, conduit *(intermediary)*, interagent, intermediary, liaison, medium, procurator, representative *(proxy)*, spokesman, umpire
goad abet, agitate *(activate)*, badger, bait *(harass)*, bait *(lure)*, browbeat, catalyst, constrain *(compel)*, discompose, exhort, foment, harass, hector, impetus, incentive, incite, inducement, motivate, pique, pressure, prompt, provocation, stimulate, stimulus, urge. SEE MAIN ENTRY
goading instigation
goal cause *(reason)*, contemplation, desideratum, design *(intent)*, destination, end *(intent)*, focus, intention, mission, motive, object, objective, point *(purpose)*, predetermination, project, purpose, reason *(basis)*, target. SEE MAIN ENTRY
goatish lascivious, lecherous, salacious
god-forsaken diabolic
godless profane
godlike omnipotent, omniscient
godly sacrosanct
going before in time antecedent
going contrary to dissenting
going down descent *(declination)*
going on open-ended, present *(current)*
going over restatement
going to the utmost lengths extreme *(exaggerated)*
going too far extreme *(exaggerated)*
golden propitious
gone defunct, irredeemable, irretrievable, lifeless *(dead)*, lost *(taken away)*, null *(invalid)*. SEE MAIN ENTRY
gone by outdated
gone out outdated, outmoded
gone out of existence defunct
gone to waste irredeemable, lost *(taken away)*
good advantage, appropriate, auspicious, behalf, benefit *(betterment)*, clean, competent, ethical, favorable *(advantageous)*, item, meritorious, moral, palatable, preferable, proficient, salutary, sapid, savory, select, sterling, upright, valid, valuable, welfare. SEE MAIN ENTRY
good actions merit, right *(righteousness)*
good and effectual in law legal
good at deft
good behavior courtesy, merit, propriety *(correctness)*, protocol *(etiquette)*, right *(righteousness)*. SEE MAIN ENTRY
good breeding courtesy, propriety *(correctness)*
good cause shown SEE MAIN ENTRY
good chance likelihood, opportunity, prospect *(outlook)*
good conduct ethics
good deed benevolence *(act of kindness)*, favor *(act of kindness)*
good disposition benevolence *(disposition to do good)*
good enough fair *(satisfactory)*, mediocre
good example exemplar, paragon
good excuse justification
good faith fidelity, integrity, loyalty, probity. SEE MAIN ENTRY

good faith reliance SEE MAIN ENTRY
good for nothing ineffective, ineffectual
good for one's advantage beneficial
good form decorum, protocol *(etiquette)*
good fortune boom *(prosperity)*, chance *(fortuity)*, opportunity, prosperity
good intention benevolence *(disposition to do good)*
good judgment caliber *(mental capacity)*, common sense, sagacity, sense *(intelligence)*
good luck prosperity
good management austerity, economy *(frugality)*
good manners consideration *(sympathetic regard)*, courtesy, decorum, propriety *(correctness)*, protocol *(etiquette)*, respect
good men and true array *(jury)*
good name credit *(recognition)*, goodwill, honor *(good reputation)*, regard *(esteem)*, reputation
good nature benevolence *(disposition to do good)*, goodwill, philanthropy
good neighbor samaritan
good notice adequate notice
good offices patronage *(power to appoint jobs)*
good opinion estimation *(esteem)*, favor *(sanction)*, honor *(good reputation)*, recommendation
good order array *(order)*
good prospect likelihood
good reputation estimation *(esteem)*, goodwill
good repute prestige
Good Samaritan benefactor, donor. SEE MAIN ENTRY
good sense common sense, discretion *(quality of being discreet)*, discrimination *(good judgment)*, reason *(sound judgment)*
good service favor *(act of kindness)*
good standing estimation *(esteem)*. SEE MAIN ENTRY
good taste decorum
good times prosperity
good to eat palatable
good treatment benevolence *(act of kindness)*
good turn benefit *(conferment)*, benevolence *(act of kindness)*, favor *(act of kindness)*, help
good understanding agreement *(concurrence)*
good will affinity *(regard)*, benevolence *(disposition to do good)*, charity, clemency, comity, humanity *(humaneness)*, peace, philanthropy, respect, tolerance, understanding *(tolerance)*. SEE MAIN ENTRY
good works philanthropy
good-fellowship comity
good-hearted philanthropic
good-heartedness philanthropy
good-humored benevolent, obeisant
good-natured benevolent, obeisant, philanthropic
good-quality meritorious
good-tasting palatable, sapid, savory
good-tempered peaceable
goodly major
goodness benevolence *(disposition to do good)*, decorum, ethics, good faith, honor *(good reputation)*, integrity, merit, principle *(virtue)*, probity, quality *(excellence)*, rectitude, right *(righteousness)*
goodness and mercy benevolence *(disposition to do good)*
goods assets, cargo, commodities, effects, estate *(property)*, freight, merchandise, movable, paraphernalia *(personal belongings)*, possession *(property)*, possessions, property *(possessions)*, stock in trade. SEE MAIN ENTRY
goods exported illegally contraband
goods for sale merchandise
goods imported illegally contraband
goods shipped consignment
goods subject to confiscation contraband
goods subject to seizure contraband
gore enter *(penetrate)*, lancinate, penetrate, pierce *(lance)*
gorge overload
gorged full, replete
gorgeous elegant
gospel doctrine, principle *(axiom)*
gossip hearsay, report *(rumor)*
gossipy informatory
govern administer *(conduct)*, command, control *(regulate)*, curb, direct *(order)*, direct *(supervise)*, discipline *(control)*, dominate, handle *(manage)*, inhibit, manage, manipulate *(utilize skillfully)*, moderate *(preside over)*, officiate, operate, overlook *(superintend)*, oversee, predominate *(command)*, preside, prevail *(be in force)*, qualify *(condition)*, regulate *(manage)*, restrain, subject, subjugate, superintend, wield. SEE MAIN ENTRY
govern badly misgovern
govern strictly discipline *(control)*
governable corrigible, malleable, obedient, pliable, sequacious, tractable
governance agency *(legal relationship)*, authority *(power)*, bureaucracy, dominance, government *(administration)*, hegemony, influence, management *(supervision)*, politics, regime, supremacy. SEE MAIN ENTRY
governed arrested *(checked)*
governed by inferior *(lower in position)*
governed by law legal
governing dominant, influential, master, predominant, prevailing *(having superior force)*, sovereign *(absolute)*. SEE MAIN ENTRY
governing body board, management *(directorate)*
governing course of action policy *(plan of action)*, practice *(procedure)*
governing factors circumstances
governing plan policy *(plan of action)*, practice *(procedure)*
governing principle policy *(plan of action)*. SEE MAIN ENTRY
government authorities, bureaucracy, civic, control *(supervision)*, dominion *(supreme authority)*, hierarchy *(persons in authority)*, management *(directorate)*, national, politics, public *(affecting people)*, regime, regulation *(management)*, supervision. SEE MAIN ENTRY
government appropriation of private land expropriation *(right of eminent domain)*
government attorney prosecutor
government by bureaus bureaucracy
government notes currency
government office bureaucracy
government officers police
government paper bond
government servant caretaker *(one fulfilling the function of office)*
government-owned national
governmental civic, civil *(public)*, federal, national, political, public *(affecting people)*
governmental body congress
governmental control censorship
governmental grant patent
governmental leader politician
governmental order of prohibition em-bargo
governmental procedure bureaucracy
governmental system for decision-making bureaucracy
governmental unit state *(political unit)*
governor caretaker *(one caring for property)*, director, pedagogue, principal *(director)*, superintendent. SEE MAIN ENTRY
governorship direction *(guidance)*
grab obtain, prey, spoils
grace absolution, amenity, amnesty, charity, clemency, condonation, consent, decorum, dispensation *(exception)*, embellish, facility *(easiness)*, favor *(act of kindness)*, franchise *(license)*, leave *(permission)*, lenience, permission, proportion, propriety *(correctness)*, remission, respite *(reprieve)*. SEE MAIN ENTRY
grace period SEE MAIN ENTRY
graceful diplomatic, elegant, eloquent
gracefulness facility *(easiness)*
graceless dissolute, immoral, inelegant, pedestrian, unbecoming, uncouth
gracious benevolent, charitable *(benevolent)*, charitable *(lenient)*, civil *(polite)*, favorable *(expressing approval)*, meritorious, obeisant, philanthropic, placable, propitious, receptive. SEE MAIN ENTRY
graciously readily
graciousness benevolence *(disposition to do good)*, comity, consideration *(sympathetic regard)*, courtesy, largess *(generosity)*, philanthropy
gradation array *(order)*, chain *(series)*, class, classification, degree *(station)*, differential, distribution *(arrangement)*, hierarchy *(arrangement in a series)*, order *(arrangement)*, sequence, step. SEE MAIN ENTRY
grade caliber *(measurement)*, caliber *(quality)*, class, classify, condition *(state)*, degree *(station)*, differential, file *(arrange)*, fix *(arrange)*, measure, organize *(arrange)*, pigeonhole, quality *(excellence)*, rate, rating, screen *(select)*, sort, state *(condition)*, status, step, tabulate. SEE MAIN ENTRY
grade A premium
grade of excellence standard
grading rating
gradual deliberate. SEE MAIN ENTRY
gradual crumbling decline
gradual decline deterioration
gradual eating away erosion
gradual evolution development *(progression)*
gradual impairment decline, deterioration
gradual wearing away erosion
gradually piecemeal
gradually eat away erode
graduate file *(arrange)*, fix *(arrange)*, measure, prefer, promote *(advance)*, sort, subdivide, tabulate
graduation differential, distribution *(arra-ngement)*, promotion *(advancement)*, transition
graduation certificate degree *(academic title)*
gradus degree *(station)*
gradus amplior advancement *(improvement)*
graft bribe, connect *(join together)*, corruption, crime, gratuity *(bribe)*, hush money, improbity, spoils. SEE MAIN ENTRY
grafter criminal

grain character *(personal quality)*, disposition *(inclination)*, frame *(mood)*, iota, modicum, scintilla
grand elegant, illustrious, important *(significant)*, momentous, orgulous, paramount, prodigious *(enormous)*, proud *(self-respecting)*, stellar. SEE MAIN ENTRY
grand jury's accusation indictment
grand larceny SEE MAIN ENTRY
grand total corpus
grand vizier caretaker *(one fulfilling the function of office)*
grandchild child
grandeur character *(reputation)*, distinction *(reputation)*, eminence, importance, prestige
grandiloquence bombast, declamation, peroration, rhetoric *(insincere language)*. SEE MAIN ENTRY
grandiloquent flatulent, fustian, gra-ndiose, inflated *(bombastic)*, orotund, pretentious *(pompous)*, sesquipedalian, turgid
grandiose elaborate, fustian, inflated *(vain)*, orgulous, orotund, pretentious *(pompous)*. SEE MAIN ENTRY
grandiosity bombast, pretense *(ostentation)*, rhetoric *(insincere language)*
grandsire ancestor, primogenitor
grant abalienate, accede *(concede)*, acquiescence, admit *(concede)*, alimony, allocate, allow *(authorize)*, appropriation *(donation)*, assign *(transfer ownership)*, assignment *(transfer of ownership)*, attorn, authorize, award, bear *(yield)*, bequeath, bestow, bounty, brevet, cede, cession, charge *(empower)*, charity, charter *(license)*, charter *(sanction)*, concede, concession *(authorization)*, concession *(compromise)*, condescend *(deign)*, confer *(give)*, consent *(noun)*, consent *(verb)*, contribute *(supply)*, contribution *(donation)*, convey *(transfer)*, copyright, deign, descend, devise *(give)*, devolve, dispensation *(exception)*, dispense, dole, donation, empower, enable, endow, endowment, endue, enfranchise, franchise *(license)*, fund, furnish, gift *(present)*, gratuity *(present)*, indulgence, largess *(gift)*, lease, leave *(permission)*, leave *(give)*, legacy, lend, let *(lease)*, let *(permit)*, liberty, license, loan, option *(contractual provision)*, parcel, patent, patronize *(condescend toward)*, pay, pension, permit, prerogative, present *(make a gift)*, privilege, provide *(supply)*, recognize *(acknowledge)*, remise, reveal, reward, sanction *(permission)*, sanction, subsidy, suffer *(permit)*, supply, tender, transfer, vouchsafe, yield *(submit)*. SEE MAIN ENTRY
grant a boon bestow
grant a demise sublease
grant a lease rent, sublease
grant a reprieve clear, exonerate, free
grant a request bestow
grant absolution palliate *(excuse)*, purge *(wipe out by atonement)*
grant again recover
grant amnesty clear, condone, exonerate, forgive, free, palliate *(excuse)*, pardon
grant amnesty to excuse, quit *(free of)*
grant asylum harbor, receive *(permit to enter)*
grant authority empower, invest *(vest)*
grant authority to commit *(entrust)*. SEE MAIN ENTRY
grant by favor vouchsafe
grant by will demise
grant claims authorize
grant clemency pardon
grant exclusive possession for a designated period lease
grant exemption palliate *(excuse)*
grant favors to favor, prefer
grant for support pension
grant forgiveness pardon
grant immunity condone, palliate *(excuse)*
grant in aid pension
grant monetary compensation indemnify
grant of a share contribution *(donation)*
grant of authority patent
grant of realty lease
grant of rights SEE MAIN ENTRY
grant of use and possession lease
grant pardon forgive, free
grant permission allow *(authorize)*, authorize, bestow, permit, suffer *(permit)*
grant power empower, invest *(vest)*
grant remission acquit, clear, pardon
grant the occupancy of let *(lease)*
grant use and possession lease
grant-in-aid subsidy
grantable assignable, plausible, possible
granted allowable, allowed, assumed *(inferred)*, consensual, definite, permissible
granted amnesty immune
granted on certain terms conditional, dependent
grantee assignee, bearer, beneficiary, devisee, donee, feoffee, legatee, payee, receiver, recipient, successor, transferee. SEE MAIN ENTRY
granter contributor *(giver)*
granting concession *(compromise)*, donative, permissive
granting freedom parole
grantor contributor *(giver)*, donor, feoffor, obligee, transferor. SEE MAIN ENTRY
grapevine report *(rumor)*
graph delineation, design *(construction plan)*, measure
graphic clear *(apparent)*, coherent *(clear)*, comprehensible, demonstrative *(illustrative)*, descriptive, detailed, distinct *(clear)*, holographic, lurid, narrative, realistic, representative, suggestive *(evocative)*. SEE MAIN ENTRY
graphic account recital
graphic treatment caricature
graphical comprehensible, representative, suggestive *(evocative)*
grapple lock. SEE MAIN ENTRY
grapple with contest, fight *(battle)*, repulse
grasp apprehension *(perception)*, cognition, cohere *(adhere)*, competence *(ability)*, comprehend *(understand)*, comprehension, conceive *(comprehend)*, coverage *(scope)*, digest *(comprehend)*, gain, grapple, hold *(possess)*, information *(knowledge)*, judgment *(discernment)*, jurisdiction, knowledge *(awareness)*, perception, pierce *(discern)*, read, realize *(understand)*, retain *(keep in possession)*, retention, seize *(confiscate)*, sense *(intelligence)*, understand, understanding *(comprehension)*. SEE MAIN ENTRY
grasp mentally construe *(comprehend)*
grasping illiberal, insatiable, mercenary, parsimonious, rapacious, venal
grass cannabis
grass-roots SEE MAIN ENTRY
grate annoy, badger, bait *(harass)*, irritate, plague, provoke, repel *(disgust)*
gratia patronage *(power to appoint jobs)*
gratification benefit *(betterment)*, bounty, enjoyment *(pleasure)*, fruition, indulgence, satisfaction *(fulfilment)*. SEE MAIN ENTRY
gratification of desire indulgence
gratified complacent, proud *(self-respecting)*
gratify accommodate, bestow, consent, favor, grant *(concede)*, pander, sanction, satisfy *(fulfill)*, vouchsafe. SEE MAIN ENTRY
gratify to excess overindulge
gratifying desirable *(pleasing)*, palatable, sapid
gratiis gratis
grating harsh, provocative
gratis free *(at no charge)*, gratuitous *(given without recompense)*, unpaid. SEE MAIN ENTRY
gratitude recognition SEE MAIN ENTRY
gratuito gratis
gratuitous baseless, donative, elective *(voluntary)*, expendable, free *(at no charge)*, impertinent *(irrelevant)*, inappropriate, irrelevant, needless, nonessential, unnecessary, unpaid, unsolicited, willing *(uncompelled)*. SEE MAIN ENTRY
gratuitous remark dictum
gratuitous worker volunteer
gratuitus free *(at no charge)*, gratuitous *(unwarranted)*
gratuity benefit *(conferment)*, bonus, bounty, consideration *(recompense)*, contribution *(donation)*, dedication, donation, gift *(present)*, grant, honorarium, hush money, largess *(gift)*, payment *(remittance)*, perquisite, recompense, reward. SEE MAIN ENTRY
gravamen center *(essence)*, content *(meaning)*, cornerstone, gist *(ground for a suit)*, impugnation, main point. SEE MAIN ENTRY
gravamen of a charge complaint, gist *(ground for a suit)*
gravamen of the complaint gist *(ground for a suit)*
grave bleak *(not favorable)*, critical *(crucial)*, crucial, deadly, dire, earnest, exigent, gross *(flagrant)*, important *(significant)*, lamentable, major, momentous, solemn, urgent. SEE MAIN ENTRY
grave consequence SEE MAIN ENTRY
grave culpability impeachability
grave injustice ground, misjudgment
graveness solemnity
gravis compelling, considerable, earnest, grave *(important)*, important *(significant)*, influential, insalubrious, irksome, offensive *(offending)*, onerous, peccant *(unhealthy)*, ponderous, serious *(grave)*, solemn, substantial, urgent, valid, virulent
gravitas severity, solemnity, validity
gravitate SEE MAIN ENTRY
gravitate toward border *(approach)*
gravitation penchant, proclivity, tendency
gravity draw *(attraction)*, import, importance, interest *(concern)*, magnitude, materiality *(consequence)*, severity, significance, solemnity. SEE MAIN ENTRY
gray area SEE MAIN ENTRY
grayness indistinctness
graze contact *(touch)*
graze against jostle *(bump into)*
great capacious, compelling, consequential *(substantial)*, considerable, copious, extensive, far reaching, gross *(flagrant)*, illustrious, ineffable, inordinate, magnanimous, major, master, meritorious, momentous, outstanding *(prominent)*,

paramount, portentous *(eliciting amazement)*, powerful, prodigious *(enormous)*, profound *(intense)*, remarkable, renowned, serious *(grave)*, substantial. SEE MAIN ENTRY
great fear panic
great feeling emotion
great misfortune catastrophe, disaster
great mishap disaster
great number plurality
great person paragon
great point gist *(ground for a suit)*
great quantity boom *(prosperity)*, plethora, store *(depository)*
great span of life longevity
great station eminence
greaten accrue *(increase)*, accumulate *(enlarge)*, compound, expand, heighten *(augment)*, increase
greater best, superior *(excellent)*, superior *(higher)*
greater number majority *(greater part)*
greater part body *(main part)*, generality *(bulk)*
greatest cardinal *(outstanding)*, leading *(ranking first)*, maximum *(amplitude)*, paramount, primary, prime *(most valuable)*, superlative, utmost
greatest amount cap, capacity *(maximum)*, utmost
greatest degree utmost
greatest extent capacity *(maximum)*
greatest number generality *(bulk)*
greatest part bulk
greatest possible cardinal *(outstanding)*, ultimate
greatest size capacity *(maximum)*
greathearted charitable *(benevolent)*, meritorious
greatness degree *(magnitude)*, dint, distinction *(reputation)*, eminence, importance, mass *(weight)*, materiality *(consequence)*, measurement, merit, prestige, primacy, significance
greed SEE MAIN ENTRY
greediness greed
greedy exorbitant, gluttonous, illiberal, insatiable, jealous, mercenary, penurious, predatory, rapacious, venal
green credulous, inexperienced, naive, premature, puerile, unaccustomed
greenback money
greenness ignorance, nescience
greet recognize *(acknowledge)*
greet with skepticism doubt *(distrust)*
grenade bomb
grew accrued
grex band, company *(enterprise)*
grief pain, plaint, remorse. SEE MAIN ENTRY
grief-stricken disconsolate
grievance aggravation *(annoyance)*, complaint, criticism, damage, dissatisfaction, exception *(objection)*, gravamen, impugnation, nuisance, objection, outcry, provocation, trouble, wrong. SEE MAIN ENTRY
grieve affront, annoy, brood, discommode, distress, harass, languish, perturb, repent. SEE MAIN ENTRY
grieve at regret
grieve for deplore
grieve with sympathize
grieved aggrieved *(harmed)*, disconsolate, pessimistic
grieving disconsolate, lugubrious, plaint
grievous arrant *(onerous)*, deplorable, detrimental, dire, disastrous, gross *(flagrant)*, lamentable, oppressive, painful, regrettable, severe. SEE MAIN ENTRY
grievous harm calamity
grievous price toll *(effect)*
grievous trouble pain
grill cross-examine
grilling cross-examination, interrogation
grim bleak *(not favorable)*, bleak *(severely simple)*, brutal, dire, disastrous, grave *(solemn)*, harsh, malevolent, ominous, portentous *(ominous)*, repulsive, ruthless, serious *(grave)*, severe, solemn
grime pollute, stain
grimness severity
grimy sordid
grind erode, ill use, struggle, work *(effort)*
grinding erosion, onerous, operose, oppressive, tyrannous
grip dominion *(supreme authority)*, grapple, immerse *(engross)*, interest, monopolize, tenacity
gripe discompose
griper malcontent
gripping moving *(evoking emotion)*
grisly repulsive
grit prowess *(bravery)*, sinew, tenacity, will *(desire)*
gritty steadfast, undaunted
groan deplore, plaint
groom discipline *(train)*
groomed ready *(prepared)*
grooming discipline *(training)*
grope for hunt
groping blind *(sightless)*, hesitant, tentative
gross aggregate, blatant *(obtrusive)*, brutal, depraved, entirety, excessive, exorbitant, extreme *(exaggerated)*, flagrant, heinous, improper, inelegant, iniquitous, lurid, manifest, nefarious, objectionable, obnoxious, outrageous, repulsive, salacious, scurrilous, stark, total, totality, uncouth, unseemly, whole *(undamaged)*. SEE MAIN ENTRY
gross amount aggregate, corpus, entirety, principal *(capital sum)*, sum *(total)*, whole
gross injustice misjudgment
gross offense atrocity, felony
gross offense against law crime
gross profit proceeds
gross return income
gross revenues SEE MAIN ENTRY
gross wrong ground
grossly inadequate representation understatement
grossly offensive outrageous
grossness bestiality, brutality, debauchery
grotesque odious, prodigious *(amazing)*
grotesque portrayal caricature
grotesque rendition caricature
grouchy fractious, petulant, querulous, resentful
ground assumption *(supposition)*, basis, cause *(reason)*, cause of action, contention *(argument)*, derivation, fix *(make firm)*, gist *(ground for a suit)*, instill, parcel, plant *(place firmly)*, plot *(land)*, point *(item)*, position *(situation)*, property *(land)*, rationale, real estate, reason *(basis)*. SEE MAIN ENTRY
ground for believing presumption
ground for excusing justification
ground gained headway
ground of argument discrepancy
ground of proof evidence
ground oneself alight
ground plan arrangement *(plan)*, blueprint
ground rules criterion
grounded stable
grounded on based on
groundless arbitrary and capricious, baseless, erroneous, fallacious, false *(inaccurate)*, gratuitous *(unwarranted)*, ill-founded, illogical, immaterial, inaccurate, insubstantial, needless, sophistic, unfounded, unjustifiable, unreasonable, unsound *(fallacious)*, unsupported, unsustainable, untenable, untrue, unwarranted, wanton. SEE MAIN ENTRY
groundless rumor hearsay
groundless story canard
grounds case *(set of circumstances)*, circumstances, close *(enclosed area)*, data, documentation, estate *(property)*, homestead, premises *(buildings)*, premises *(hypotheses)*, property *(land)*, realty. SEE MAIN ENTRY
grounds for belief documentation, evidence
grounds for complaint grievance
groundwork basis, cornerstone, foundation *(basis)*, frame *(structure)*, preparation, prerequisite
group aggregate, allocate, arrange *(methodize)*, assemblage, assembly, band, call *(summon)*, cartel, chamber *(body)*, class, classification, classify, coalition, codify, collect *(gather)*, collection *(accumulation)*, collection *(assembly)*, combine *(join together)*, community, company *(assemblage)*, compile, complex *(development)*, conglomeration, congregate, connect *(relate)*, constituency, convene, denomination, division *(administrative unit)*, file *(arrange)*, fix *(arrange)*, garner, hoard, index *(relate)*, join *(bring together)*, kind, league, marshal, meet, organization *(association)*, organize *(arrange)*, partition, party *(political organization)*, pigeonhole, race, relate *(establish a connection)*, screen *(select)*, section *(division)*, selection *(collection)*, sequence, society, sodality, sort, subdivide, subdivision, tabulate, unit *(department)*, unite. SEE MAIN ENTRY
group feeling loyalty
group of delegates committee
group of deputies posse
group of jurors panel *(jurors)*
group of persons organized with legal authorization posse
group refusal to work strike
group together compile
grouped collective
grouping building *(business of assembling)*, centralization, class, classification, corpus, denomination, disposition *(final arrangement)*, distribution *(arrangement)*, division *(administrative unit)*, form *(arrangement)*, hierarchy *(arrangement in a series)*, lineup, manner *(kind)*, order *(arrangement)*, organization *(structure)*, rating, rubric *(title)*, section *(division)*, segregation *(separation)*, subdivision
grovel truckle
groveling obsequious, servile
grow accrue *(increase)*, accumulate *(enlarge)*, build *(augment)*, develop, enlarge, expand, germinate, increase, inflate, progress, proliferate, stem *(originate)*. SEE MAIN ENTRY
grow aware comprehend *(understand)*, construe *(comprehend)*
grow better develop, progress
grow from develop, emanate, evolve
grow in number proliferate

grow in value appreciate *(increase)*
grow larger accumulate *(enlarge)*, compound, expand
grow lenient relent
grow less decrease, depreciate, diminish, subside
grow less severe relent
grow out of arise *(originate)*, emanate, ensue
grow together cohere *(adhere)*, unite
grow too fast overextend
grow too much overextend
grow up mature, progress
grow weak degenerate, languish
grow worse decay, degenerate, depreciate
growing cumulative *(increasing)*, live *(conscious)*, progressive *(going forward)*, rampant
growing by successive additions cumulative *(increasing)*
growling petulant
grown ripe
grown old outdated, outmoded
grown-up person adult
growth accession *(enlargement)*, accretion, advancement *(improvement)*, appreciation *(increased value)*, augmentation, boom *(increase)*, boom *(prosperity)*, development *(progression)*, extension *(expansion)*, headway, increment, inflation *(increase)*, profit, progress, transition. SEE MAIN ENTRY
growth by addition collection *(accumulation)*, cumulation
growth in value appreciation *(increased value)*
grudge dissatisfaction, feud, rancor, refuse, resentment, spite, umbrage
grudgeful malevolent, vindictive
grudging disinclined, illiberal, jealous, malevolent, parsimonious, penurious, reluctant, resentful
grueling difficult, harsh, onerous, operose, painful. SEE MAIN ENTRY
gruesome lurid, sordid
gruff brutal, harsh, severe
grumbler malcontent
grumbling criticism, petulant, querulous
grumbly petulant
grumose solid *(compact)*
grumpy petulant, resentful, restive
guage caliber *(measurement)*
guarantee accommodation *(backing)*, assure *(insure)*, bear *(adduce)*, bond, bond *(secure a debt)*, certificate, certify *(attest)*, charge *(lien)*, close *(agree)*, confirm, consent, contract, corroborate, cosign, covenant, coverage *(insurance)*, deposit, ensure, hostage, hypothecation, indemnify, indorse, insurer, oath, pact, pawn, pledge *(binding promise)*, pledge *(security)*, pledge *(deposit)*, pledge *(promise the performance of)*, precaution, promise, promise *(vow)*, protection, reassure, recommend, security *(pledge)*, sponsor, stipulate, subscribe *(promise)*, swear, undertake, undertaking *(pledge)*, underwrite, verify *(swear)*, vouch, warranty. SEE MAIN ENTRY
guarantee against loss insurance, insure
guaranteed agreed *(promised)*, certain *(fixed)*, certain *(positive)*, conclusive *(determinative)*, definite, dependable, fully secured, indubious, inevitable, official, promissory, reliable, safe, secure *(free from danger)*, solid *(sound)*. SEE MAIN ENTRY
guarantor backer, insurer, sponsor. SEE MAIN ENTRY
guaranty assurance, bail, binder, bond, certify *(attest)*, charge *(lien)*, coverage *(insurance)*, letter of credit, option *(contractual provision)*, recognizance, specialty *(contract)*, surety *(certainty)*, underwrite, warranty. SEE MAIN ENTRY
guard attend *(take care of)*, bulwark, care *(be cautious)*, caretaker *(one caring for property)*, conserve, control *(restrain)*, cover *(protection)*, defend, detain *(hold in custody)*, diligence *(care)*, ensconce, enshroud, guarantee, guaranty, guardian, harbor, hedge, keep *(shelter)*, maintain *(sustain)*, monitor, notice *(heed)*, panoply, patrol, peace officer, preserve, protect, protection, safekeeping, security *(safety)*, shield, surveillance, sustain *(prolong)*, uphold, ward, warden. SEE MAIN ENTRY
guard against anticipate *(expect)*. SEE MAIN ENTRY
guarded alert *(vigilant)*, careful, circumspect, controlled *(restrained)*, discreet, inarticulate, intimate, leery, noncommittal, politic, preventive, prudent, safe, secure *(free from danger)*, taciturn, vigilant. SEE MAIN ENTRY
guardedness caution *(vigilance)*, discretion *(quality of being discreet)*, precaution
guardian administrator, caretaker *(one caring for property)*, custodian *(protector)*, fiduciary, patron *(influential supporter)*, protective, sponsor, superintendent, trustee, warden. SEE MAIN ENTRY
guardian of the peace peace officer
guardianship administration, adoption *(affiliation)*, auspices, bondage, charge *(custody)*, control *(supervision)*, custody *(supervision)*, detention, patronage *(support)*, preservation, protection, restraint, safekeeping, trust *(custody)*, ward. SEE MAIN ENTRY
guarding bondage, conservation, preservation, preventive
guardless helpless *(defenseless)*, precarious, vulnerable
gubernare overrule
gubernatio direction *(guidance)*, government *(administration)*
gubernation supervision
guerdon appropriation *(donation)*, bounty, collection *(payment)*, compensation, consideration *(recompense)*, contribution *(indemnification)*, expiation, honorarium, payment *(remittance)*, prize, recompense, requital, reward, satisfaction *(discharge of debt)*, tip *(gratuity)*
guess concept, conjecture, deduce, deduct *(conclude by reasoning)*, estimate *(idea)*, estimate, estimation *(calculation)*, expect *(consider probable)*, hypothesis, idea, infer, inference, opine, opinion *(belief)*, postulate, presume, presuppose, prognosis, read, speculate *(conjecture)*, supposition, surmise, suspect *(think)*, suspicion *(uncertainty)*. SEE MAIN ENTRY
guess correctly solve
guess right solve
guess wrong misconceive
guessed inexact
guesswork conjecture, estimate *(idea)*, estimation *(calculation)*, inference, speculation *(conjecture)*, theory
guest SEE MAIN ENTRY
guidable tractable
guidance administration, advice, advocacy, aid *(help)*, auspices, charge *(custody)*, charge *(statement to the jury)*, control *(supervision)*, custody *(supervision)*, discipline *(training)*, edification, education, generalship, government *(administration)*, help, instruction *(direction)*, instruction *(teaching)*, management *(supervision)*, patronage *(support)*, recommendation, regulation *(management)*, service *(assistance)*, supervision, tip *(clue)*. SEE MAIN ENTRY
guide administer *(conduct)*, advise, charge *(instruct on the law)*, clue, code, conduct, control *(regulate)*, counsel, criterion, direct *(show)*, direct *(supervise)*, director, discipline *(train)*, edify, educate, example, exemplar, generalization, govern, guideline, handle *(manage)*, inculcate, index *(gauge)*, indicate, indication, influence, instill, instruct *(direct)*, instruct *(teach)*, manage, manipulate *(utilize skillfully)*, marshal, model, motivate, officiate, overlook *(superintend)*, oversee, paradigm, pattern, pedagogue, precedent, precept, precursor, predominate *(command)*, prescribe, preside, prevail *(be in force)*, prevail *(persuade)*, prototype, recommend, regulate *(manage)*, rule *(govern)*, sample, specimen, standard, superintend, symptom. SEE MAIN ENTRY
guide astray mislead
guide into error mislead
guide the studies of instruct *(teach)*
guide wrongly mislead
guidebook directory
guided direct *(straight)*
guided by experiment empirical
guideline code. SEE MAIN ENTRY
guidepost landmark *(conspicuous object)*
guiding administrative, advisory
guiding conception impression
guiding principle end *(intent)*, purpose
guild association *(alliance)*, company *(enterprise)*, confederacy *(compact)*, cooperative, institute, league, partnership, society, sodality, syndicate, union *(labor organization)*
guildsman member *(individual in a group)*
guile artifice, bad faith, collusion, color *(deceptive appearance)*, deception, duplicity, evasion, fraud, hoax, hypocrisy, imposture, improbity, indirection *(deceitfulness)*, knavery, pettifoggery, ruse, subreption
guileful collusive, delusive, dishonest, evasive, fallacious, fraudulent, insidious, machiavellian, perfidious, recreant, sly, subtle *(insidious)*, surreptitious
guileless clean, direct *(forthright)*, genuine, honest, ingenuous, pure, simple, straightforward, unaffected *(sincere)*, upright
guilelessness candor *(straightforwardness)*, honesty, probity, veracity
guilt blame *(culpability)*, criminality, culpability. SEE MAIN ENTRY
guilt-free blameless, not guilty
guiltiness blame *(culpability)*, culpability, impeachability, onus *(blame)*
guiltless blameless, clean, clear *(free from criminal charges)*, incorruptible, inculpable, innocent, irreprehensible, meritorious, not guilty, pardonable, pure, unblemished, unimpeachable
guiltlessness innocence
guilty arrant *(onerous)*, at fault, blameful, blameworthy, contrite, culpable, delinquent *(guilty of a misdeed)*, diabolic, illicit, peccable, peccant *(culpable)*, reprehensible, vicious. SEE MAIN ENTRY

guilty act crime, misconduct, misdeed, misdemeanor, misdoing, transgression. SEE MAIN ENTRY
guilty man convict, delinquent
guilty of transgression peccant *(culpable)*
guilty person convict, criminal, felon, lawbreaker, recidivist
guilty plea SEE MAIN ENTRY
guilty verdict condemnation *(punishment)*
guise appearance *(look)*, color *(deceptive appearance)*, complexion, conduct, cover *(pretext)*, demeanor, deportment, disguise, false pretense, manner *(behavior)*, means *(opportunity)*, mode, presence *(poise)*, pretense *(pretext)*, pretext, role, semblance, sham, style, subterfuge, veil. SEE MAIN ENTRY
gulf hiatus, split
gull deceive, delude, dupe, ensnare, foist, illude, inveigle
gullibility credulity
gullible credulous, naive, unsuspecting
gullibleness credulity
gulosity greed
gumminess adhesion *(affixing)*
gummosity adhesion *(affixing)*
gumshoe prowl
gun SEE MAIN ENTRY
gun control SEE MAIN ENTRY
gun for hunt
gunfire barrage
gunman criminal, hoodlum
gunnery ammunition
gunpowder ammunition, bomb
gunrunner bootlegger
gush emit, exude, issuance, outburst, outflow
gushy loquacious
gustable sapid, savory
gustative savory
gustful sapid
gusto enjoyment *(pleasure)*, passion
gut burn, destroy *(efface)*, devastate, eviscerate, extirpate, obliterate, prey
gyp bunko
gypsy migrant
gyve detain *(restrain)*, fetter *(noun)*, fetter *(verb)*, handcuff

H

habere dwell *(reside)*, hold *(possess)*, own, possess
habeus corpus SEE MAIN ENTRY
habile resourceful
habilis convenient, efficient
habilitated proficient
habit custom, manner *(behavior)*, method, mode, norm, practice *(custom)*, prescription *(custom)*, procedure, quirk *(idiosyncrasy)*, rule *(guide)*, style, trait, usage, way *(manner)*. SEE MAIN ENTRY
habit of a majority custom
habitabilis habitable
habitable SEE MAIN ENTRY
habitance domicile
habitancy abode, domicile, habitation *(act of inhabiting)*, inhabitation *(act of dwelling in)*, nationality, population, residence
habitant citizen, denizen, domiciliary, inhabitant, inmate, lodger, occupant, resident. SEE MAIN ENTRY
habitants populace, population
habitare dwell *(reside)*, inhabit, reside
habitat abode, building *(structure)*, domicile, habitation *(dwelling place)*, home *(domicile)*, locality, lodging, residence, site
habitation abode, address, building *(structure)*, domicile, dwelling, enjoyment *(use)*, home *(domicile)*, house, household, inhabitation *(act of dwelling in)*, lodging, occupancy, residence, shelter *(protection)*. SEE MAIN ENTRY
habitator habitant, inhabitant, resident
habits behavior, conduct
habitual accustomed *(customary)*, boiler plate, chronic, constant, conventional, customary, daily, familiar *(customary)*, frequent, general, household *(familiar)*, ingrained, inveterate, mundane, normal *(regular)*, ordinary, orthodox, periodic, prevailing *(current)*, prevalent, regular *(conventional)*, repeated, routine, systematic, traditional, typical, usual. SEE MAIN ENTRY
habitual activity custom
habitual course practice *(custom)*
habitual criminal outlaw, recidivist
habitual devotion diligence *(perseverance)*
habitual offender outlaw
habitual practice custom, manner *(behavior)*
habitual relapse into crime recidivism
habitual use usage
habitually generally, invariably
habitually silent taciturn
habituate discipline *(train)*, inure *(accustom)*, naturalize *(acclimate)*
habituated accustomed *(familiarized)*, addicted, inveterate, practiced
habituation behavior, custom, practice *(custom)*. SEE MAIN ENTRY
habitude behavior, condition *(state)*, custom, practice *(custom)*, usage
habitus deportment, habit
hack split
hacking SEE MAIN ENTRY
hacking into SEE MAIN ENTRY
hackneyed familiar *(customary)*, mundane, nondescript, ordinary, pedestrian, prosaic, stale, trite
hackneyed expression platitude
hackneyed idea platitude
hackneyed phrase platitude
hackneyed saying platitude
hactenus extent
haerere hesitate
haereticus heretic
haesitatio hesitation, indecision, scruple
haggle barter, cavil, dicker, negotiate. SEE MAIN ENTRY
haggling negotiation
hail honor
hairsplitting particular *(exacting)*
halcyon harmonious, nonmilitant, peaceable, placid
halcyonian peaceable, placid
haleness health, welfare
half moiety, semi
half believe doubt *(distrust)*
half distance center *(central position)*
half finished semi
half-begun inchoate
half-done inchoate
half-seen indistinct
halfhearted hesitant, insipid, lax, perfunctory, phlegmatic
halfway center *(central position)*, central *(situated near center)*, intermediate
hall chamber *(compartment)*
hallmark brand, designation *(symbol)*, device *(distinguishing mark)*, label, stamp, trademark. SEE MAIN ENTRY
hallow dedicate
hallowed infrangible, inviolate, laudable, sacrosanct, solemn. SEE MAIN ENTRY
hallowing honorary
hallucination figment, insanity, phantom
hallucinative delusive
hallucinatory delusive, insubstantial, nonexistent
halt abeyance, balk, block, cease, cessation *(interlude)*, check *(bar)*, check *(restrain)*, close *(terminate)*, cloture, conclude *(complete)*, condemn *(ban)*, constrict *(inhibit)*, curtail, debar, defeat, desist, desuetude, detain *(restrain)*, deterrence, discontinue *(abandon)*, dissolve *(terminate)*, embargo, end *(termination)*, estop, finality, finish, forestall, hiatus, hinder, hold up *(delay)*, impasse, interdict, interruption, interval, keep *(restrain)*, layoff, lull, moratorium, obstruct, pause *(noun)*, pause *(verb)*, pendency, prevent, prohibit, proscribe *(prohibit)*, quit *(discontinue)*, recess *(noun)*, recess *(verb)*, refrain, remission, remit *(relax)*, respite *(interval of rest)*, rest *(cease from action)*, shut, stall, stay, stay *(rest)*, stem *(check)*, stop, suspend, terminate, toll *(stop)*. SEE MAIN ENTRY
halt work strike *(refuse to work)*
halting broken *(interrupted)*
halve bifurcate, cross *(intersect)*, dichotomize, divide *(separate)*, part *(separate)*, split
halved bipartite
halving dichotomy
hammer in impact
hammer out forge *(produce)*, formulate, make
hammer together frame *(construct)*
hamper balk, bar *(hinder)*, bind *(restrain)*, block, clog, condemn *(ban)*, constrain *(restrain)*, constrict *(inhibit)*, control *(restrain)*, damper *(stopper)*, debar, delay, detain *(restrain)*, deter, disadvantage *(noun)*, disadvantage *(verb)*, encumber *(hinder)*, enjoin, estop, fetter *(noun)*, fetter *(verb)*, foil, halt, handcuff, hinder, hindrance, hold up *(delay)*, impede, impediment, inconvenience, interfere, keep *(restrain)*, limit, lock, obstacle, obstruct, obstruction, occlude, overcome *(overwhelm)*, prevent, prohibit, restrain, restraint, restrict, stall, stave, stay *(halt)*, stem *(check)*, stop, thwart, trammel, withstand. SEE MAIN ENTRY
hampered arrested *(checked)*, limited
hampering binding, deterrent, encumbrance, limiting
hamstring deter, hinder, obstruct
hamstrung marred
hand deliver, employee, handwriting, help, present *(make a gift)*
hand back restore *(return)*
hand down abalienate, bequeath, confer *(give)*, convey *(transfer)*, deliver, demise, descend, endow, leave *(give)*, render *(deliver)*
hand down an opinion SEE MAIN ENTRY
hand grenade bomb
hand in one's resignation demit
hand on bequeath, descend, transfer, transmit
hand out allocate, bestow, convey *(transfer)*, disburse *(distribute)*, dispense, dole, endow, endue, fund, mete
hand out again redistribute
hand over abalienate, bestow, consign, contribute *(supply)*, delegate, discharge *(pay a debt)*, dole, endow, pay, present

(make a gift), relinquish, render *(deliver)*, serve *(deliver a legal instrument)*, surrender *(give back)*, transmit. SEE MAIN ENTRY
hand over to bequeath
hand-to-hand fight affray
handbook directory, pandect *(treatise)*
handcuff fetter, restrain, restrict. SEE MAIN ENTRY
handed down traditional
handicap burden, clog, constrict *(inhibit)*, detriment, disability *(physical inability)*, disadvantage *(noun)*, disadvantage *(verb)*, disease, disorder *(abnormal condition)*, disqualification *(factor that disqualifies)*, estop, fetter *(noun)*, fetter *(verb)*, hamper, hinder, hindrance, impede, impediment, incumbrance *(burden)*, interfere, liability, nuisance, obstacle, obstruct, onus *(burden)*, penalty, preclude, prevent, restrain, restrict, trammel. SEE MAIN ENTRY
handicapped disabled *(made incapable)*, disadvantaged
handicraft business *(occupation)*, performance *(workmanship)*, specialty *(special aptitude)*, trade *(occupation)*
handicraftsman artisan
handiness efficiency, faculty *(ability)*, gift *(flair)*, means *(opportunity)*, performance *(workmanship)*, skill
handing out disbursement *(act of disbursing)*, distribution *(apportionment)*
handing over cession
handing over into custody commitment *(confinement)*
handing over legal papers service *(delivery of legal process)*
handiwork building *(business of assembling)*, invention, performance *(workmanship)*, product
handle administer *(conduct)*, conduct, control *(regulate)*, deal, manage, manipulate *(utilize skillfully)*, militate, operate, oversee, ply, regulate *(manage)*, sell, superintend, treat *(process)*, wield. SEE MAIN ENTRY
handle badly mishandle *(maltreat)*, mishandle *(mismanage)*
handler merchant
handling administration, agency *(legal relationship)*, course, management *(judicious use)*, operation, process *(course)*, regulation *(management)*, treatment. SEE MAIN ENTRY
handout donation, gratuity *(present)*, largess *(gift)*
handpicked preferred *(favored)*, select
hands-off policy laissez faire
handsel binder, bounty, grant, largess *(gift)*, launch *(initiate)*, originate. SEE MAIN ENTRY
handsome elegant, liberal *(generous)*, magnanimous
handwriting script. SEE MAIN ENTRY
handwritten holographic
handy available, close *(near)*, deft, effective *(efficient)*, expert, functional, immediate *(not distant)*, practical, practiced, present *(attendant)*, proficient, resourceful
hang SEE MAIN ENTRY
hang around loiter
hang back pause, procrastinate
hang on cohere *(adhere)*, endure *(last)*, grapple, last, persevere, remain *(continue)*
hang on to hoard
hang over project *(extend beyond)*
hang together cohere *(be logically consistent)*
hangdog furtive
hanger on partisan
hanger-on disciple
hankering desire, will *(desire)*
hap contingency, event, opportunity, quirk *(accident)*
haphazard casual, fortuitous, indiscriminate, random, slipshod. SEE MAIN ENTRY
hapless ominous
happen arise *(occur)*, supervene. SEE MAIN ENTRY
happen again recur
happen at the same time concur *(coexist)*
happen simultaneously concur *(coexist)*
happen together coincide *(correspond)*, concur *(coexist)*
happen upon find *(discover)*
happening accident *(chance occurrence)*, chance *(fortuity)*, contingency, event, experience *(encounter)*, incident, occasion, occurrence, situation. SEE MAIN ENTRY
happening by chance fortuitous
happenings circumstances
happenstance occurrence. SEE MAIN ENTRY
happiness welfare
happy ecstatic, felicitous, inclined, propitious, prosperous, proud *(self-respecting)*, ready *(willing)*. SEE MAIN ENTRY
happy medium compromise
happy-go-lucky improvident
harangue address *(talk to)*, bombast, declaim, declamation, diatribe, outpour, phillipic. SEE MAIN ENTRY
haranguer demagogue
harass annoy, badger, browbeat, discompose, distress, harrow, hector, importune, incense, inflict, intimidate, irritate, mistreat, molest *(annoy)*, persecute, perturb, pique, prey, provoke. SEE MAIN ENTRY
harassing vexatious
harassment aggravation *(annoyance)*, infliction, nuisance, oppression. SEE MAIN ENTRY
harbinger anticipate *(prognosticate)*, forerunner, herald, indicator, informant, informer *(a person who provides information)*, precede, precursor. SEE MAIN ENTRY
harbor conceal, cover *(guard)*, foster, haven, hide, lodge *(house)*, lodging, nurture, preserve, protect, refuge, screen *(guard)*, shelter *(protection)*
harbor a design intend, plan
harbor a grudge harass, resent
harbor doubts disbelieve, doubt *(distrust)*, mistrust
harbor suspicions disbelieve, discount *(disbelieve)*, doubt *(distrust)*, misdoubt, mistrust. SEE MAIN ENTRY
harbor suspicious suspect *(distrust)*
harboring conservation
harborless insecure
hard callous, close *(rigorous)*, cohesive *(compact)*, cold-blooded, compact *(dense)*, cruel, difficult, durable, impervious, inflexible, insusceptible *(uncaring)*, obdurate, onerous, operose, oppressive, ossified, powerful, relentless, rigid, ruthless, severe, solid *(compact)*, strict, stringent, strong, tyrannous, unbending, uncompromising, unrelenting, unyielding
hard bargaining counteroffer
hard blow disaster
hard cash currency, money
hard core SEE MAIN ENTRY
hard feelings argument *(contention)*, ill will, malice
hard money cash
hard of heart callous, malignant, relentless
hard task campaign
hard to believe debatable, disputable, implausible, incredible, ludicrous, suspicious *(questionable)*, unbelievable
hard to comprehend opaque
hard to control unruly
hard to convince impervious, inconvincible, incredulous, suspicious *(distrustful)*
hard to cope with operose
hard to deal with difficult, impracticable, perverse
hard to define elusive
hard to endure painful, severe
hard to explain indefinable
hard to express elusive
hard to get rid of pertinacious
hard to grasp elusive
hard to lift ponderous
hard to maintain elusive
hard to manage difficult, perverse
hard to overcome formidable
hard to please particular *(exacting)*, querulous
hard to see obscure *(faint)*
hard to translate indefinable
hard to understand difficult, elusive, enigmatic, equivocal, incomprehensible, indefinable, inexplicable, opaque
hard up impecunious, poor *(underprivileged)*
hard upon critical *(faultfinding)*
hard work effort, industry *(activity)*
hard working industrious, patient
hard-bitten obdurate
harden cement, cohere *(adhere)*, consolidate *(strengthen)*, fix *(make firm)*, inure *(accustom)*
harden the heart alienate *(estrange)*
hardened callous, cold-blooded, impervious, incorrigible, inexpressive, inflexible, insusceptible *(uncaring)*, inveterate, obdurate, ossified, recalcitrant, remorseless, reprobate, solid *(compact)*, unabashed. SEE MAIN ENTRY
hardened criminal malefactor, outlaw
hardened offender criminal, recidivist
hardheaded perspicacious
hardhearted brutal, callous, cold-blooded, cruel, malevolent, obdurate, relentless, ruthless, unaffected *(uninfluenced)*
hardheartedness malice
hardhitting critical *(faultfinding)*
hardihood audacity, prowess *(bravery)*, surety *(certainty)*
hardiness force *(strength)*, health, prowess *(bravery)*, strength
hardly SEE MAIN ENTRY
hardly begun inchoate
hardly credible incredible
hardly possible implausible, insurmountable
hardly worth mention nominal
hardness brutality, congealment
hardness of heart brutality
hardship adversity, burden, calamity, casualty, catastrophe, damage, detriment, grievance, misfortune, nuisance, plight, pressure, privation, tragedy, trouble. SEE MAIN ENTRY
hardworking diligent, painstaking, sedulous
hardy durable, indestructible, indomitable, inexpugnable, spartan, strong
harebrained impolitic, precipitate, th-oughtless, unpolitic

hark heed
harm abuse *(violate)*, annoy, assault, cost *(penalty)*, damage *(noun)*, damage *(verb)*, detriment, disable, disadvantage *(noun)*, disadvantage *(verb)*, disaster, disservice, drawback, endanger, eviscerate, expense *(sacrifice)*, harrow, ill use, impair, impairment *(damage)*, infect, inflict, injury, mischief, mistreat, molest *(annoy)*, penalize, prejudice *(injury)*, prejudice *(injure)*, spoil *(impair)*, strike *(assault)*, wrong. SEE MAIN ENTRY
harmed imperfect, marred
harmful adverse *(negative)*, dangerous, deleterious, destructive, detrimental, disadvantageous, disastrous, fatal, hostile, inadvisable, incendiary, inimical, insalubrious, invidious, lethal, malevolent, malicious, malignant, noxious, oppressive, outrageous, painful, peccant *(unhealthy)*, pernicious, pestilent, prejudicial, scathing, sinister, toxic, virulent. SEE MAIN ENTRY
harmful act injury
harmful action mischief
harmful desire malice
harmful physical contact battery
harming disabling, incriminatory
harmless innocuous, nontoxic, powerless, safe, salutary, unobjectionable. SEE MAIN ENTRY
harmonious amicable, appropriate, concerted, concordant, congruous, consensual, consistent, consonant, felicitous, fit, joint, proportionate, suitable, uniform. SEE MAIN ENTRY
harmonious relation rapport
harmoniousness peace
harmonization accommodation *(adjustment)*, accordance *(understanding)*, arrangement *(understanding)*
harmonize accommodate, arbitrate *(conciliate)*, attune, cohere *(be logically consistent)*, coincide *(concur)*, combine *(act in concert)*, commingle, comport *(agree with)*, compromise *(settle by mutual agreement)*, concur *(agree)*, coordinate, correspond *(be equivalent)*, merge, naturalize *(acclimate)*, orchestrate, reconcile, settle, unite
harmonize with comply
harmonized concerted, congruous, consensual
harmonizing concurrent *(united)*
harmony accordance *(understanding)*, adjustment, agreement *(concurrence)*, coherence, comity, compatibility, compliance, composure, concert, conciliation, concordance, conformity *(agreement)*, conjunction, consensus, consent, contribution *(participation)*, correspondence *(similarity)*, peace, propinquity *(similarity)*, proportion, propriety *(appropriateness)*, rapport, rapprochement, reconciliation, regularity, synchronism, understanding *(agreement)*, union *(unity)*
harness confine, constrain *(imprison)*, constrain *(restrain)*, curb, discipline *(control)*, handcuff, inhibit, join *(bring together)*, restrain, subdue. SEE MAIN ENTRY
harness together connect *(join together)*
harnessed servile
harp SEE MAIN ENTRY
harp on repeat *(state again)*
harp upon dwell *(linger over)*, reiterate
harping insistent, iterative, repetitious
harrassed aggrieved *(victimized)*
harried aggrieved *(victimized)*
harrow badger, distress, harass, hector, mistreat, prey. SEE MAIN ENTRY
harrowing disastrous, insufferable, onerous, painful
harry annoy, badger, bait *(harass)*, discommode, discompose, distress, harass, harrow, hector, loot, mistreat, molest *(annoy)*, perturb, pique, plague, press *(goad)*. SEE MAIN ENTRY
harsh astringent, bitter *(penetrating)*, blatant *(obtrusive)*, brutal, caustic, close *(rigorous)*, contemptuous, cruel, draconian, drastic, hostile, incisive, insufferable, lurid, malevolent, mordacious, obdurate, offensive *(offending)*, onerous, oppressive, pejorative, relentless, rigid, ruthless, scathing, severe, spiteful, strict, stringent, strong, tyrannous. SEE MAIN ENTRY
harsh feeling spite
harsh sound noise
harshness brutality, cruelty, oppression, rancor, severity
haruspical prophetic
harvest gain, glean, output, product, profit *(noun)*, profit *(verb)*, reap, result
has as a component consist
hash cannabis, melange
hashish cannabis
haste dispatch *(promptness)*. SEE MAIN ENTRY
hasten dispatch *(send off)*, evoke, expedite, facilitate, induce, race. SEE MAIN ENTRY
hasten away flee
hasten on dispatch *(send off)*
hasten one's end dispatch *(put to death)*
hastening acceleration
hastily instantly
hastiness dispatch *(promptness)*, inconsideration, temerity
hasty brief, careless, cursory, expeditious, heedless, hot-blooded, ill-advised, ill-judged, impolitic, improvident, imprudent, impulsive *(rash)*, injudicious, instantaneous, perfunctory, precipitate, premature, rapid, reckless, summary, superficial, transient, unpolitic, unpremeditated
hasty departure abandonment *(desertion)*, flight
hatch conceive *(invent)*, engender, frame *(formulate)*, make, outlet, produce *(manufacture)*, scheme
hatch a plot conspire
hatch a plot against frame *(charge falsely)*
hatched illusory
hate malice, odium, rancor, resent, spite. SEE MAIN ENTRY
hate crime SEE MAIN ENTRY
hateful antipathetic *(distasteful)*, contemptible, contemptuous, disreputable, heinous, invidious, loathsome, malevolent, malicious, malignant, nefarious, objectionable, obnoxious, odious, offensive *(offending)*, outrageous, reprehensible, repugnant *(exciting aversion)*, repulsive, spiteful, vicious, virulent
hatred conflict, incompatibility *(difference)*, intolerance, malice, odium, rancor, rejection, resentment, spite, umbrage. SEE MAIN ENTRY
haud accuratus inexact
haud dubius infallible, undeniable, undisputed
haud sufficiens insufficient
haughtiness contumely, disdain, pride
haughty cynical, disdainful, impertinent *(insolent)*, inflated *(vain)*, insolent, orgulous, presumptuous, pretentious *(pompous)*, proud *(conceited)*, supercilious
haughty contempt disdain
haughty indifference disdain
haul cargo, carry *(transport)*, deliver, plunder, spoils, struggle
haunt bailiwick, harass, obsess, plague, recur, remind
haunting ominous, portentous *(ominous)*
hauteur disdain
have accommodate, hold *(possess)*, keep *(shelter)*, own, possess, remain *(occupy)*, retain *(keep in possession)*
have a bad conscience regret
have a bearing on concern *(involve)*, relate *(establish a connection)*
have a bias forejudge, preconceive, presuppose, select
have a care beware
have a certain semblance appear *(seem to be)*
have a common origin evolve
have a comparison correspond *(be equivalent)*
have a conference on discuss
have a connection concern *(involve)*, correspond *(be equivalent)*
have a connection to apply *(pertain)*
have a deed for own, possess
have a dialogue speak
have a dissimilar opinion differ *(vary)*
have a fancy for prefer
have a feud with dispute *(contest)*
have a firm grip on hold *(possess)*
have a good influence meliorate
have a guilty conscience repent
have a habitation dwell *(reside)*
have a hand in involve *(participate)*, partake, participate
have a hunch expect *(consider probable)*, guess, opine
have a impulse desire
have a liking for regard *(hold in esteem)*
have a loan owe
have a part in participate
have a part of participate
have a policy plan
have a portion of partake
have a prejudice forejudge
have a prepossession forejudge
have a presentiment anticipate *(prognosticate)*, expect *(consider probable)*, presage
have a proclivity desire
have a proclivity for gravitate
have a propensity for gravitate
have a reference concern *(involve)*
have a relation concern *(involve)*, correspond *(be equivalent)*
have a right claim *(demand)*
have a right to earn
have a row brawl
have a share of partake, participate
have a strong effect impress *(affect deeply)*
have a theory speculate *(conjecture)*
have a title to hold *(possess)*, own, possess
have a verbal controversy over dispute *(debate)*
have a vision conjure
have a wrong impression misjudge
have a yearning desire
have absolute disposal of hold *(possess)*, possess
have all to oneself monopolize
have an address reside

have an affection for discriminate *(treat differently)*
have an altercation bicker, contend *(dispute),* dispute *(contest)*
have an appetite desire
have an effect upon affect
have an exchange contact *(communicate)*
have an idea conceive *(comprehend),* devise *(invent),* opine, surmise
have an idea that assume *(suppose)*
have an impression apprehend *(perceive)*
have an incorrect impression misconstrue
have an insufficiency require *(need)*
have an obligation owe
have an opinion deem, opine
have an understanding of apprehend *(perceive)*
have an urge for need
have anxiety mistrust
have as its foundation consist
have as property hold *(possess),* possess
have at one's command possess
have at one's disposal possess
have authority govern, handle *(manage),* police, rule *(govern)*
have authority over oversee, preside, prevail *(be in force),* regulate *(manage)*
have bearing on apply *(pertain)*
have being exist
have business relations deal
have by inheritance hold *(possess)*
have by tenure hold *(possess)*
have capacity for accommodate
have charge of control *(regulate),* handle *(manage),* moderate *(preside over),* operate, overlook *(superintend),* oversee, police, prevail *(be in force),* regulate *(manage),* superintend
have charges against accused *(charged)*
have claim upon hold *(possess),* own
have cognizance of apprehend *(perceive),* perceive
have commerce deal, handle *(trade)*
have confidence in confide *(trust),* rely
have control command, conduct, manage, preside, rule *(govern)*
have conveyed consign, dispatch *(send off)*
have currency circulate
have dealings dicker
have dealings with contact *(communicate),* deal, patronize *(trade with)*
have designs plot, scheme
have designs on desire
have dialogue converse
have differences conflict, disaccord, dispute *(contest)*
have dissension disagree
have dominion over prevail *(be in force)*
have done with discontinue *(abandon),* quit *(discontinue)*
have doubts disbelieve, doubt *(distrust),* mistrust
have doubts about misdoubt
have duration endure *(last)*
have effect function, prevail *(persuade)*
have effect on militate
have efficacy avail *(be of use)*
have every indication appear *(seem to be)*
have evidence bear *(adduce)*
have executed enforce
have executive charge of administer *(conduct),* govern
have existence exist
have faith opine
have faith in confide *(trust),* rely, trust
have fears doubt *(distrust),* misdoubt, mistrust
have for one's own possess
have for sale handle *(trade)*
have force avail *(bring about),* prevail *(be in force)*
have foreknowledge preconceive
have hold of own
have ill feelings toward discriminate *(treat differently)*
have implications for pertain
have in hand hold *(possess),* own, possess
have in mind intend
have in one's charge control *(regulate)*
have in one's possession hold *(possess)*
have in production make
have in prospect anticipate *(expect),* expect *(anticipate)*
have in sight discern *(detect with the senses),* observe *(watch),* pierce *(discern)*
have in store hoard
have in view intend
have influence affect, constrain *(compel),* predominate *(command)*
have influence on militate
have influence over prejudice *(influence),* prevail upon
have influence upon prejudice *(influence),* prevail upon
have influence with prevail upon
have inherited hold *(possess)*
have insight diagnose, discern *(discriminate)*
have intercourse communicate
have interrelationship with concern *(involve),* pertain
have it out bicker
have jurisdiction over govern, rule *(govern)*
have knowledge of apprehend *(perceive),* perceive, pierce *(discern)*
have life exist
have mastery prevail *(triumph)*
have memories of recall *(remember)*
have mercy relent
have misgivings doubt *(distrust),* mistrust
have need for need
have no concern with dissociate
have no confidence in misdoubt, suspect *(distrust)*
have no doubt opine, trust
have no end endure *(last)*
have no faith in misdoubt, mistrust
have no objection authorize, consent, grant *(concede),* let *(permit),* permit
have no part of shun
have no regard for decry, disfavor, jeer
have no reservations trust
have no respect for decry, disfavor, disgrace
have no trust in mistrust
have no use for decry, disdain, disfavor
have nothing to do with avoid *(evade),* disown *(refuse to acknowledge),* eschew, exclude, refrain, shun, spurn
have occasion for need
have offspring proliferate
have one's address at dwell *(reside)*
have one's heart set on desire
have one's plans backfire overreach
have origin arise *(originate)*
have pity sympathize
have possession remain *(occupy)*
have possession of occupy *(take possession)*
have power dominate
have precedence antecede
have predominating influence rule *(govern)*
have printed publish
have progeny proliferate
have qualms disbelieve, doubt *(hesitate),* fear, mistrust, repent
have qualms about regret
have quarters inhabit
have questions doubt *(distrust),* misdoubt
have recourse resort
have recourse to employ *(make use of)*
have reference appertain, apply *(pertain)*
have reference to pertain
have regard care *(be cautious)*
have regard for regard *(hold in esteem)*
have relation appertain, apply *(pertain)*
have relation to pertain
have relevance pertain
have reservations disbelieve, doubt *(hesitate),* hesitate, misdoubt, mistrust
have responsibility rule *(govern)*
have revenge recriminate
have rights to hold *(possess),* occupy *(take possession),* own, possess
have run its course close *(terminate)*
have second thoughts reconsider
have significance for pertain
have succession as an heir inherit
have superiority prevail *(triumph)*
have superiority over prevail *(be in force)*
have suspicions doubt *(distrust),* misdoubt, mistrust
have sway predominate *(command)*
have sympathy relent
have tenacity adhere *(persist)*
have the advantage beat *(defeat),* outbalance
have the care of handle *(manage),* hold *(possess)*
have the charge of hold *(possess)*
have the direction of control *(regulate),* handle *(manage),* hold *(possess),* oversee
have the edge on outbalance
have the idea suspect *(think)*
have the impression deem
have the mien demean *(deport oneself)*
have the qualifications qualify *(meet standards)*
have the requisites qualify *(meet standards)*
have the upper hand predominate *(command),* surpass
have the wrong impression misapprehend, miscalculate
have title to hold *(possess),* occupy *(take possession)*
have to do with deal
have to one's name own
have under command manage
have under control control *(regulate),* handle *(manage),* hold *(possess)*
have underwritten insure
have use of need
have verbal intercourse converse
have volition choose
have words bicker
have words with brawl, contend *(dispute),* disaccord, dispute *(contest),* fight *(battle)*

haven asylum *(hiding place),* bulwark, harbor, home *(domicile),* preserve, protect, protection, refuge, screen *(guard),* shelter *(protection).* SEE MAIN ENTRY
having a bad reputation disreputable
having a common measure commensurate
having a double meaning ambiguous
having a natural contrariety antipathetic *(oppositional)*
having a significant impact far reaching
having a strong effect forcible
having direct bearing pertinent
having fixed limits definite
having force forcible
having formal education literate
having great strength forcible
having home interests household *(domestic)*
having immunity insusceptible *(resistant)*
having independent qualities apart
having integrity incorruptible
having investments in interested
having left a will testate
having legal force effective *(operative),* valid
having legal strength valid
having multiple husbands polygamous
having multiple wives polygamous
having no acknowledged name anonymous
having no alternative bound
having no force invalid
having no foundation baseless. SEE MAIN ENTRY
having no limit comprehensive, perpetual
having plurality of wives or husbands polygamous
having prior application retroactive
having prior effect retroactive
having priority preferred *(given priority)*
having resistance insusceptible *(resistant)*
having seniority preferred *(given priority)*
having substance corporeal
having suffered invasion of legal rights aggrieved *(harmed)*
having the possibility of termination determinable *(liable to be terminated)*
having the privilege to choose disjunctive *(alternative)*
having the right entitled
having to do with pertinent
having unique features apart
having unique qualities apart
having violated the law culpable
having written a testament testate
havoc catastrophe, confusion *(turmoil),* debacle, depredation, disturb, pillage, shambles, turmoil. SEE MAIN ENTRY
hawk handle *(trade),* hunt, sell
hawk about proclaim, promulgate, propagate *(spread)*
hawker dealer, merchant, vendor
hayseed provincial
hazard accident *(chance occurrence),* bet, compromise *(endanger),* danger, endanger, expose, jeopardy, menace, parlay *(bet),* peril, pitfall, risk, speculate *(chance),* speculation *(risk),* threat, venture. SEE MAIN ENTRY
hazard a guess presume, surmise
hazard a supposition postulate
hazard an opinion deem
hazarder bettor, speculator
hazardous aleatory *(perilous),* dangerous, imprudent, insalubrious, insecure, noxious, precarious, speculative. SEE MAIN ENTRY
haze bait *(harass),* harry *(harass),* ignorance, incertitude, obnubilate, obscure
haziness confusion *(ambiguity),* indistinctness
hazy dubious, equivocal, indeterminate, indistinct, inexact, nebulous, opaque, unclear
he who has passed away decedent
head call *(title),* caption, chairman, chapter *(division),* chief, culmination, derivation, direct *(supervise),* employer, govern, heading, manage, master, moderate *(preside over),* officiate, oversee, paramount, pinnacle, preface, preside, prime *(most valuable),* principal *(director),* regulate *(manage),* rubric *(title),* superintend, tip *(clue).* SEE MAIN ENTRY
head of affairs administrator
head of government official
head of the household parents
head off avert, check *(restrain)*
head-on SEE MAIN ENTRY
head start advantage, edge *(advantage)*
head toward gravitate
heading caption, chapter *(division),* denomination, direction *(course),* prevailing *(having superior force),* rubric *(title),* subheading, term *(expression),* title *(designation).* SEE MAIN ENTRY
headline caption, heading, rubric *(title).* SEE MAIN ENTRY
headlong blind *(not discerning),* impolitic, improvident, precipitate, thoughtless
headman chairman, chief
headmaster pedagogue
headmen management *(directorate)*
headnote caption
headperson chief, principal *(director)*
headquarters address, base *(place),* building *(structure),* habitation *(dwelling place),* management *(directorate),* seat. SEE MAIN ENTRY
heads authorities, hierarchy *(persons in authority)*
headship direction *(guidance),* generalship, hegemony, primacy, supremacy
headspring source
headstrong contumacious, disobedient, froward, hot-blooded, ill-judged, inexorable, inflexible, intractable, obdurate, pertinacious, perverse, precipitate, recalcitrant, restive, uncontrollable, unruly, unyielding, vehement. SEE MAIN ENTRY
headward vanward
headway advance *(progression),* margin *(spare amount),* progress, promotion *(advancement).* SEE MAIN ENTRY
heady precipitate
heal cure, drug, fix *(repair),* help, recreate, redress, relieve *(give aid),* remedy, restore *(renew),* treat *(process).* SEE MAIN ENTRY
heal the breach placate, reconcile
healing curative, medicinal, remedial, salubrious, salutary
healing agent cure, panacea
health strength, welfare. SEE MAIN ENTRY
health care SEE MAIN ENTRY
health maintenance organization SEE MAIN ENTRY
health of mind sanity
health-giving medicinal, remedial, salutary
health-preserving salutary
health-promoting salubrious
healthful remedial, salubrious, salutary
healthy salubrious, salutary, strong
healthy mind sanity
healthy mindedness competence *(sanity)*
heap assemblage, bulk, collection *(accumulation),* hoard *(noun),* hoard *(verb),* plethora, quantity
heap upon bestow
hear adjudicate, heed, notice *(observe),* overhear. SEE MAIN ENTRY
hear a case try *(conduct a trial).* SEE MAIN ENTRY
hear a cause try *(conduct a trial)* * *
hear the case adjudicate
hearer juror
hearing action *(proceeding),* day in court, inquest, inquiry *(request for information),* inquiry *(systematic investigation),* interview, parley, proceeding, range, session, trial *(legal proceeding).* SEE MAIN ENTRY
hearing before the court voir dire
hearing of evidence inquiry *(systematic investigation)*
hearing officer SEE MAIN ENTRY
hearing on the merits action *(proceeding)*
hearing without jury's presence voir dire
hearken concentrate *(pay attention),* defer *(yield in judgment),* eavesdrop
hearken to heed, note *(notice)*
hearsay report *(rumor).* SEE MAIN ENTRY
heart center *(essence),* confidence *(faith),* consequence *(significance),* cornerstone, essence, focus, frame *(mood),* main point, substance *(essential nature).* SEE MAIN ENTRY
heart of stone brutality
heart-stirring profound *(intense)*
heartbreaking disastrous
heartbroken disconsolate
hearten assure *(give confidence to),* encourage, reassure
heartening propitious. SEE MAIN ENTRY
heartfelt ecstatic, profound *(intense)*
heartily readily
heartiness health
heartless callous, cold-blooded, cruel, dispassionate, insusceptible *(uncaring),* obdurate, remorseless, ruthless, sinister, unaffected *(uninfluenced).* SEE MAIN ENTRY
heartlessness brutality, cruelty
heartsick disconsolate
hearty fervent, powerful, zealous
heat passion
heated hot-blooded, vehement
heated debate altercation
heave impel, launch *(project),* precipitate *(throw down violently)*
heave up elevate
heaven SEE MAIN ENTRY
heaven sent propitious
heavenly sacrosanct, stellar
heaviness damper *(depressant),* languor, pressure
heaviness of heart pessimism
heaviness of spirit damper *(depressant),* pessimism
heavy grave *(solemn),* onerous, oppressive, pedestrian, ponderous, profound *(intense),* torpid. SEE MAIN ENTRY
heavy demand market *(demand)*
heavy-handed uncouth. SEE MAIN ENTRY
heavy-hearted lugubrious
heavy-laden disconsolate
heavyhearted pessimistic

hebes obtuse
hebetude languor, opacity
hebetudinous languid, lifeless *(dull)*, phlegmatic, stagnant
heckle annoy, badger, bait *(harass)*, discompose, harass, harry *(harass)*, hector, mistreat, mock *(deride)*, pique, plague, press *(goad)*, provoke
hector annoy, badger, bait *(harass)*, intimidate, irritate, plague, press *(goad)*, provoke, threaten. SEE MAIN ENTRY
hectoring insolent
hedge equivocate, evade *(deceive)*, offset, outbalance, parry, prevaricate, protection, shelter *(tax benefit)*, tergiversate. SEE MAIN ENTRY
hedge in circumscribe *(surround by boundary)*, envelop, occlude, restrict
hedging evasive, noncommittal
heed abide, care *(be cautious)*, caution *(vigilance)*, consider, consideration *(contemplation)*, deliberation, devote, diligence *(care)*, discretion *(quality of being discreet)*, fulfill, hear *(give attention to)*, interest *(concern)*, keep *(fulfill)*, note *(notice)*, notice *(observe)*, obey, observation, observe *(obey)*, observe *(watch)*, precaution, prudence, regard *(attention)*, regard *(pay attention)*, submit *(yield)*, surveillance. SEE MAIN ENTRY
heedful careful, circumspect, conscientious, conscious *(aware)*, diligent, guarded, judicious, knowing, leery, meticulous, noncommittal, painstaking, particular *(exacting)*, politic, protective, provident *(showing foresight)*, prudent, sensitive *(discerning)*, vigilant
heedfulness caution *(vigilance)*, deliberation, diligence *(care)*, discretion *(quality of being discreet)*, interest *(concern)*, notice *(heed)*, observation, precaution, prudence, regard *(attention)*
heedless blind *(not discerning)*, careless, cursory, derelict *(negligent)*, hot-blooded, ill-judged, impolitic, improvident, imprudent, impulsive *(rash)*, inadvertent, incognizant, injudicious, insensible, intractable, irrational, lawless, lax, negligent, oblivious, passive, perfunctory, prodigal, reckless, relentless, remiss, slipshod, thoughtless, unaware, unpolitic, wanton. SEE MAIN ENTRY
heedlessness dereliction, disinterest *(lack of interest)*, disregard *(lack of respect)*, disregard *(unconcern)*, inconsideration, ingratitude, laxity, neglect, negligence, oversight *(carelessness)*, temerity
heft elevate
hegemonic influential, master, paramount, powerful, prevailing *(having superior force)*, principal, sovereign *(absolute)*
hegemonical dominant, influential, master, paramount, powerful, prevailing *(having superior force)*, principal, sovereign *(absolute)*
hegemony clout, dominion *(supreme authority)*, influence, primacy. SEE MAIN ENTRY
hegira flight
height ceiling, culmination, elevation, eminence, pinnacle, primacy. SEE MAIN ENTRY
height of one's ambition objective
height of perfection paragon
heighten accrue *(increase)*, aggravate *(exacerbate)*, build *(augment)*, compound, elevate, enhance, exacerbate, expand, intensify, magnify, raise *(advance)*. SEE MAIN ENTRY
heightened inflated *(overestimated)*, intense
heightening aggravation *(exacerbation)*, boom *(increase)*, cumulative *(intensifying)*, growth *(increase)*
heinous arrant *(onerous)*, bad *(offensive)*, base *(bad)*, blameful, contemptible, depraved, diabolic, disgraceful, disorderly, disreputable, gross *(flagrant)*, immoral, inexcusable, inexpiable, iniquitous, loathsome, malevolent, malignant, nefarious, objectionable, obnoxious, odious, offensive *(offending)*, outrageous, peccant *(culpable)*, profligate *(corrupt)*, reprehensible, reprobate, scandalous, sinister, unjust, vicious. SEE MAIN ENTRY
heinous conduct criminality
heinous crime felony
heinous misconduct felony
heinousness atrocity, delinquency *(misconduct)*, disrepute
heir beneficiary, descendant, devisee, offspring, recipient, transferee. SEE MAIN ENTRY
heir apparent legatee
heir at law legatee
heirdom bequest
heiress beneficiary, legatee
heirloom bequest, hereditament
heirs children, issue *(progeny)*, posterity, progeny
held arrested *(apprehended)*, in custody
held back arrested *(checked)*
held in contempt blameful, disreputable, notorious
held in custody arrested *(apprehended)*
held in esteem reputable
held in good repute reputable
held in high esteem famous
held in pledge bailment, in trust
held in trust in trust
held responsible accused *(charged)*
held up late *(tardy)*
helical circuitous
helicoid circuitous
helicoidal circuitous
hellbent precipitate
hellish cruel, diabolic, heinous, loathsome, malevolent, malignant, obnoxious
helm SEE MAIN ENTRY
helot captive
helotism servitude
helotry bondage, servitude, subjection, thrall
help abet, accommodate, advantage, advocacy, aid *(help)*, aid, ameliorate, assist, assistance, avail *(be of use)*, behalf, benefactor, capitalize *(provide capital)*, charity, coadjutant, consortium *(marriage companionship)*, contribute *(assist)*, contribution *(participation)*, countenance, emend, employee, enable, endow, espouse, expedite, facilitate, favor *(sanction)*, favor, foster, guidance, inure *(benefit)*, largess *(generosity)*, largess *(gift)*, mainstay, nurture, pander, patronage *(support)*, personnel, profit, promote *(advance)*, promote *(organize)*, promotion *(encouragement)*, reassure, redress, reinforcement, relief *(aid)*, relieve *(give aid)*, remedy *(legal means of redress)*, remedy *(that which corrects)*, remedy, samaritan, save *(rescue)*, serve *(assist)*, service *(assistance)*, side, solace, staff, subsidize, support *(assistance)*, support *(assist)*, uphold. SEE MAIN ENTRY
help a judge clerk
help along assist, ease, hasten
help oneself to assume *(seize)*, hijack, impropriate, occupy *(take possession)*, pirate *(reproduce without authorization)*, procure, usurp
help to bestow
help with money subsidize
helper abettor, accessory, accomplice, assistant, backer, benefactor, coactor, coadjutant, cohort, colleague, confederate, consociate, conspirer, contributor *(contributor)*, copartner *(business associate)*, copartner *(coconspirator)*, donor, employee, good samaritan, participant, partner, patron *(influential supporter)*, samaritan
helpful ancillary *(auxiliary)*, beneficial, benevolent, charitable *(lenient)*, constructive *(creative)*, contributory, convenient, disposable, effective *(efficient)*, favorable *(advantageous)*, favorable *(expressing approval)*, functional, humane, instrumental, medicinal, ministerial, obeisant, operative, palliative *(abating)*, philanthropic, practical, profitable, propitious, purposeful, salutary, subservient, valuable
helpfulness aid *(help)*, assistance, benevolence *(act of kindness)*, benevolence *(disposition to do good)*, consideration *(sympathetic regard)*, efficiency, goodwill, help, instigation, largess *(generosity)*, philanthropy, utility *(usefulness)*
helping beneficial, clerical, contributory, ministerial, part *(portion)*, propitious, ration, subsidiary
helping hand good samaritan, reinforcement, samaritan, service *(assistance)*, support *(assistance)*
helpless dependent, derelict *(abandoned)*, disabled *(deprived of legal right)*, disabled *(made incapable)*, inadequate, indefensible, insecure, powerless, susceptible *(unresistent)*, unable. SEE MAIN ENTRY
helpless person dependent
helplessness danger, disability *(physical inability)*, impotence, impuissance, inability, incapacity, inefficacy, languor, peril, prostration
helpmate accessory, accomplice, assistant, confederate, consociate, consort, conspirer, contributor *(contributor)*, copartner *(coconspirator)*, spouse
helpmeet spouse
hem border, margin *(outside limit)*
hem in border *(bound)*, circumscribe *(surround by boundary)*, enclose, encompass *(surround)*, envelop, limit, occlude, restrict, shut
hemisphere circuit, zone
hemp cannabis
hence a savoir, consequently. SEE MAIN ENTRY
henceforth SEE MAIN ENTRY
henchman abettor, coactor, coadjutant. SEE MAIN ENTRY
her honor judge
herald anticipate *(prognosticate)*, declare, forerunner, harbinger, indicator, inform *(notify)*, informant, informer *(a person who provides information)*, notify, portend, precede, precursor, predict, preface, proclaim, prognosticate, promulgate, propagate *(spread)*, publish, report *(disclose)*. SEE MAIN ENTRY
heralding portentous *(ominous)*
Herculean omnipotent, onerous, operose, powerful, prodigious *(enormous)*, strong
herd together congregate
here present *(current)*. SEE MAIN ENTRY
hereabouts SEE MAIN ENTRY
hereafter SEE MAIN ENTRY

hereby SEE MAIN ENTRY
hereditable hereditary, heritable
hereditament bequest, demesne, domain *(land owned)*, estate *(property)*, fee *(estate)*, freehold, heritage, real estate. SEE MAIN ENTRY
hereditaments property *(possessions)*
hereditarius hereditary
hereditary born *(innate)*, consanguineous, derivative, genetic, heritable, native *(inborn)*, testamentary. SEE MAIN ENTRY
hereditary enmity feud
hereditas heritage, inheritance, reversion *(remainder of an estate)*
hereditas caduca escheat
heredity affiliation *(bloodline)*, ancestry, birth *(lineage)*, blood, bloodline, descent *(lineage)*
heredium heritage
herein wherein. SEE MAIN ENTRY
hereinafter SEE MAIN ENTRY
hereof SEE MAIN ENTRY
heresy blasphemy, nonconformity
heretic malcontent, pariah, recusant. SEE MAIN ENTRY
heretical deviant, nonconforming, skeptical, unorthodox
heretofore theretofore. SEE MAIN ENTRY
hereunder a savoir
hereupon a savoir
herewith SEE MAIN ENTRY
heriditary innate
heritable bequest, hereditament, hereditary. SEE MAIN ENTRY
heritage affinity *(family ties)*, bequest, birth *(lineage)*, birthright, blood, claim *(right)*, descent *(lineage)*, estate *(hereditament)*, hereditament, inheritance, origin *(ancestry)*, right *(entitlement)*. SEE MAIN ENTRY
heritance birthright, estate *(hereditament)*, hereditament, heritage, legacy
hermetic impervious
hermitic solitary
hermitical solitary
hero paragon, protagonist. SEE MAIN ENTRY
hero worship doxology
hero-like spartan
heroic illustrious, meritorious, spartan, undaunted. SEE MAIN ENTRY
heroic achievement prowess *(bravery)*
heroism prowess *(bravery)*
herolike heroic
hesitance pause, qualm, reluctance
hesitancy doubt *(indecision)*, hesitation, incertitude, indecision, pause, qualm, reluctance, scruple
hesitant disinclined, irresolute, leery, noncommittal, recreant, reluctant, suspicious *(distrustful)*, undecided. SEE MAIN ENTRY
hesitate defer *(put off)*, discontinue *(break continuity)*, misdoubt, mistrust, oscillate, pause, procrastinate, recess, refuse, vacillate. SEE MAIN ENTRY
hesitating diffident, disinclined, hesitant, irresolute, leery, noncommittal, reluctant
hesitation ambivalence, cloud *(suspicion)*, doubt *(suspicion)*, halt, incertitude, indecision, misgiving, pause, qualm, reluctance, scruple. SEE MAIN ENTRY
hesitative hesitant, reluctant
hest directive, fiat
heteroclite irregular *(not usual)*
heterodox recusant, skeptical, unorthodox
heterodoxy disaccord, nonconformity
heterogeneity difference, diversification, diversity, nonconformity
heterogeneous composite, different, disordered, dissimilar, diverse, miscellaneous, multifarious, promiscuous, unrelated. SEE MAIN ENTRY
hew break *(fracture)*, split
heyday prosperity
hiatus absence *(omission)*, blank *(emptiness)*, cessation *(interlude)*. SEE MAIN ENTRY
hiatus hiatus
hiatus interruption, interval, lapse *(break)*, pendency, recess, rift *(gap)*, split
hibernating dormant
hic current
hidden blind *(concealed)*, clandestine, confidential, covert, enigmatic, esoteric, furtive, impalpable, inapprehensible, incomprehensible, inconspicuous, indirect, indiscernible, inexplicable, inscrutable, lost *(taken away)*, mysterious, obscure *(abstruse)*, obscure *(faint)*, personal *(private)*, private *(confidential)*, private *(secluded)*, privy, recondite, remote *(secluded)*, secret, sly, stealthy, surreptitious, ulterior, undisclosed. SEE MAIN ENTRY
hidden from view latent
hidden knowledge secret
hidden meaning implication *(inference)*, mystery, nuance
hide abscond, blind *(obscure)*, camouflage, cloak, conceal, cover *(conceal)*, disguise, elude, ensconce, enshroud, envelop, flee, harbor, hedge, hoard, lurk, obfuscate, obnubilate, obscure, reserve, screen *(guard)*, seclude, shroud, withhold. SEE MAIN ENTRY
hide away blind *(obscure)*, camouflage, cloak, ensconce, hoard, plant *(covertly place)*
hide from evade *(elude)*, shun
hide from view ensconce
hide one's identity camouflage, disguise
hide securely ensconce
hide the identity of blind *(obscure)*
hide the truth perjure
hide under a mask pretend
hide underground blind *(obscure)*
hideaway cache *(hiding place)*
hidebound illiberal, parochial, rigid
hideous loathsome, odious, offensive *(offending)*, repulsive. SEE MAIN ENTRY
hideout haven
hiding concealment, disguise, nonappearance
hiding place refuge
hie race
hierarchy class
hieroglyphic hidden
higgle haggle
high disdainful, priceless
high character honesty, integrity
high coloring bombast
high degree of probability SEE MAIN ENTRY
high explosive bomb
high honor prestige
high ideals conscience
high interest usury
high land elevation
high level executive
high official caretaker *(one fulfilling the function of office)*
high opinion estimation *(esteem)*, mention *(tribute)*
high point landmark *(significant change)*
high position eminence, primacy
high powered in full force
high pressure duress
high pressure methods compulsion *(coercion)*
high prices inflation *(decrease in value of currency)*
high principles honesty, probity
high priority exigent
high probability SEE MAIN ENTRY
high rank eminence
high regard credit *(recognition)*, estimation *(esteem)*, homage, honor *(good reputation)*, honor *(outward respect)*
high repute prestige
high reward character *(reputation)*
high society elite
high spot highlight
high standards conscience
high station eminence
high structure edifice
high worth cost *(price)*
high-class superior *(excellent)*
high-flown flatulent, fustian, inflated *(bombastic)*, orotund, turgid
high-grade preferential, premium, sterling, superior *(excellent)*
high-handed tyrannous
high-level important *(significant)*, major
high-minded clean, law-abiding, magnanimous, meritorious, moral. SEE MAIN ENTRY
high-mindedness honesty, integrity
high-paying lucrative
high-potency powerful
high-powered SEE MAIN ENTRY
high-pressure intense
high-priced exorbitant, priceless, prohibitive *(costly)*
high-principled clean, high-minded, incorruptible, law-abiding, meritorious, moral, reputable, strict
high-priority important *(urgent)*, indispensable
high-quality premium, sterling, superior *(excellent)*
high-sounding fustian, grandiose, inflated *(bombastic)*
high-sounding words bombast, fustian
high-spirited hot-blooded
high-strung hot-blooded, sensitive *(easily affected)*
high-technology SEE MAIN ENTRY
higher class society
higher court appellate court
highest absolute *(ideal)*, best, cardinal *(outstanding)*, paramount, primary, prime *(most valuable)*, principal, superlative, utmost *(adjective)*, utmost *(noun)*. SEE MAIN ENTRY
highest degree ceiling, pinnacle
highest point ceiling, culmination, pinnacle
highest position supremacy
highest quality professional *(stellar)*
highest ranking person chief
highhanded dictatorial
highlight cornerstone, emphasis, feature *(special attraction)*, indicate. SEE MAIN ENTRY
highly SEE MAIN ENTRY
highly developed skill science *(technique)*
highly disciplined spartan
highly important central *(essential)*
highly important detail necessity, need *(requirement)*
highly principled upright
highly reputed famous
highly serious serious *(grave)*
highly specialized technical

highly specific technical
highly thought of popular
highly wrought elaborate
highness elevation
highroad causeway
highway causeway
highways approaches
hijack SEE MAIN ENTRY
hike boom *(increase)*, perambulate
hike in prices inflation *(decrease in value of currency)*
hilarious jocular
hinder arrest *(stop)*, balk, bind *(restrain)*, block, check *(restrain)*, clog, conflict, constrain *(restrain)*, constrict *(inhibit)*, contain *(restrain)*, control *(restrain)*, counter, counteract, countervail, curb, debar, defer *(put off)*, delay, detain *(restrain)*, deter, disable, disadvantage, disappoint, discommode, discontinue *(break continuity)*, discourage, disrupt, enjoin, estop, fetter, fight *(counteract)*, foil, forbid, forestall, frustrate, halt, hamper, hold up *(delay)*, impair, impede, inconvenience, inhibit, interdict, interfere, interpose, interrupt, keep *(restrain)*, limit, lock, obstruct, obturate, occlude, oppugn, preclude, prevent, prohibit, repress, repulse, resist *(oppose)*, restrain, stall, stave, stay *(halt)*, stem *(check)*, stop, suspend, tamper, thwart, toll *(stop)*, trammel, withhold, withstand. SEE MAIN ENTRY
hinder movement encumber *(hinder)*
hindered arrested *(checked)*, broken *(interrupted)*
hinderer deterrent
hindering binding, detrimental, disadvantageous, encumbrance, intrusive, limiting, preventive, prohibitive *(restrictive)*, restrictive
hindermost back *(in reverse)*, extreme *(last)*, last *(final)*
hindmost back *(in reverse)*, extreme *(last)*, last *(final)*
hindrance admonition, bar *(obstruction)*, barrier, burden, censorship, check *(bar)*, complication, constraint *(restriction)*, damper *(stopper)*, deterrence, deterrent, disadvantage, disincentive, disturbance, encumbrance, estoppel, fetter, filibuster, frustration, handicap, impediment, imposition *(excessive burden)*, interruption, liability, nuisance, obstacle, obstruction, onus *(burden)*, pressure, prohibition, resistance, restraint, stay, trouble. SEE MAIN ENTRY
hindsight retrospect. SEE MAIN ENTRY
hindward back *(in reverse)*
hinge crossroad *(turning point)*. SEE MAIN ENTRY
hint allude, clue, connotation, connote, guidance, implication *(inference)*, indicant, indicate, indication, indicator, infer, inference, innuendo, insinuation, intimation, mention *(reference)*, monition *(warning)*, prompt, reference *(allusion)*, remind, reminder, report *(rumor)*, signify *(denote)*, suggestion, suspicion *(uncertainty)*, tip *(clue)*. SEE MAIN ENTRY
hint at imply, mention, refer *(direct attention)*
hints indicia
hire delegate, employ *(engage services)*, fare, let *(lease)*, pay, procure, rate, retain *(employ)*, revenue, sublease, wage. SEE MAIN ENTRY
hire out let *(lease)*, rent
hired mercenary
hired hand employee
hireling employee, mercenary
hirer client
his honor judge
historic traditional
historical honest, traditional
historical record journal
historically speaking heretofore
historiette story *(narrative)*
historify record
historize record
history account *(report)*, ancestry, bloodline, calendar *(record of yearly periods)*, common knowledge, record, report *(detailed account)*, story *(narrative)*. SEE MAIN ENTRY
histrionic demonstrative *(expressive of emotion)*, orotund. SEE MAIN ENTRY
histrionics exaggeration, pretense *(ostentation)*. SEE MAIN ENTRY
hit attack, beat *(strike)*, collide *(crash against)*, contact *(touch)*, impinge, impress *(affect deeply)*, lash *(strike)*, strike *(assault)*, strike *(collide)*. SEE MAIN ENTRY
hit against jostle *(bump into)*, strike *(collide)*
hit and run SEE MAIN ENTRY
hit back recriminate
hit upon find *(discover)*
hit upon a solution resolve *(solve)*
hitch connection *(fastening)*, damper *(stopper)*, encumbrance, obstruction, period
hive hoard
hoard accumulate *(amass)*, collection *(accumulation)*, fund *(noun)*, fund *(verb)*, garner, preserve, provision *(something provided)*, reserve, save *(hold back)*, selection *(collection)*, stock *(store)*, store *(depository)*, store, sufficiency. SEE MAIN ENTRY
hoary elderly, old
hoax artifice, betray *(lead astray)*, bilk, bunko, canard, circumvent, collusion, deceive, deception, defraud, delude, dupe, ensnare, evade *(deceive)*, fake *(noun)*, fake *(verb)*, false pretense, falsification, frame up, hoodwink, illude, imposture, knavery, maneuver *(trick)*, misrepresent, palter, pretense *(pretext)*, ruse. SEE MAIN ENTRY
hobble block, maim, repress, restrict, trammel
hoboism vagrancy
hodgepodge melange
hoggish insatiable
hoist elevate. SEE MAIN ENTRY
hold accommodate, adjudge, advantage, apprehend *(arrest)*, arrest *(apprehend)*, arrest *(stop)*, chamber *(compartment)*, claim *(maintain)*, comprise, conclude *(decide)*, confine, consist, constrain *(imprison)*, contain *(comprise)*, contend *(maintain)*, decide, deem, delay, depository, desist, detain *(hold in custody)*, determine, dominance, dominion *(supreme authority)*, embrace *(encircle)*, encompass *(include)*, find *(determine)*, grapple, halt, handcuff, immerse *(engross)*, immure, include, influence, judge, keep *(restrain)*, keep *(shelter)*, lock, moratorium, obtain, occupy *(take possession)*, opine, own, possess, power, primacy, remain *(occupy)*, remain *(stay)*, reserve, restrain, retain *(keep in possession)*, retention, rule *(decide)*, save *(conserve)*, seisin, sentence, stay *(halt)*, stop, store, suspect *(think)*, withhold. SEE MAIN ENTRY
hold a brief for bear *(support)*
hold a conference confer *(consult)*, discourse
hold a consultation confer *(consult)*, deliberate
hold a conversation speak
hold a convocation meet
hold a discussion speak
hold a high opinion of regard *(hold in esteem)*
hold a meeting convene, meet
hold a position of authority preside
hold a session convene, meet
hold accountable denounce *(inform against)*, incriminate. SEE MAIN ENTRY
hold aloft elevate
hold an argument dispute *(debate)*
hold an inquiry analyze, audit, canvass, delve, investigate
hold an office officiate
hold an opinion deem
hold apart separate
hold as a hostage confine
hold as hostage constrain *(imprison)*
hold at bay counter, parry
hold at fault impeach
hold authority govern, handle *(manage)*, preside, rule *(govern)*
hold back arrest *(stop)*, avoid *(evade)*, balk, clog, confine, constrain *(restrain)*, constrict *(inhibit)*, contain *(restrain)*, control *(restrain)*, curb, debar, decline *(reject)*, defer *(put off)*, delay, detain *(restrain)*, deter, disadvantage, forbear, forestall, hamper, hesitate, hinder, hoard, impede, inhibit, keep *(restrain)*, limit, mistrust, parry, pause, prevent, procrastinate, refrain, refuse, repress, reserve, restrain, restrict, stem *(check)*, stop, toll *(stop)*, trammel, withhold
hold back action encumber *(hinder)*
hold back by force constrain *(imprison)*, constrain *(restrain)*
hold by force usurp
hold captive capture, confine, constrain *(imprison)*, detain *(hold in custody)*, immure, imprison, jail, obsess, subjugate
hold cheap decry, disdain, disfavor, misprize
hold conclave deliberate, discuss
hold conference converse, discuss
hold conversations discuss
hold court adjudicate, hear *(give a legal hearing)*
hold dear foster, regard *(hold in esteem)*
hold different views differ *(disagree)*
hold dominion predominate *(command)*, rule *(govern)*
hold down constrain *(restrain)*, dominate, extinguish, subject
hold fast adhere *(fasten)*, cohere *(adhere)*, grapple, hold *(possess)*, hold out *(resist)*, persevere, persist, retain *(keep in possession)*
hold firmly adhere *(fasten)*
hold for ransom kidnap
hold forth declaim, exposit, offer *(propose)*, recite, recount
hold in constrain *(restrain)*, inhibit, keep *(restrain)*, repress, withhold
hold in abeyance adjourn, defer *(put off)*, delay, discontinue *(break continuity)*, forbear, hold up *(delay)*, suspend. SEE MAIN ENTRY
hold in affection regard *(hold in esteem)*
hold in belief deem
hold in bondage subject, subjugate
hold in captivity capture, confine, immure, imprison, jail
hold in check balk, check *(restrain)*, clog, confine, constrain *(restrain)*, contain *(restrain)*, control *(restrain)*, curb, detain *(hold in custody)*, disadvantage, enjoin, immure, impede, moderate *(preside over)*, restrain

hold in constraint commit *(institutionalize)*
hold in contempt condescend *(patronize),* contemn, decry, disdain, flout, ignore, misprize, reject, spurn
hold in custody contain *(restrain),* jail, restrain
hold in derision flout, humiliate, jeer, mock *(deride)*
hold in despite contemn
hold in disrespect condescend *(patronize),* flout, humiliate
hold in esteem defer *(yield in judgment),* honor
hold in leash discipline *(control)*
hold in legal custody impound
hold in line discipline *(control)*
hold in one's grasp hold *(possess)*
hold in possession retain *(keep in possession)*
hold in preventive custody detain *(hold in custody)*
hold in regard regard *(hold in esteem)*
hold in restraint commit *(institutionalize),* constrain *(imprison),* imprison
hold in subjection subject
hold in thrall confine, detain *(hold in custody)*
hold in view anticipate *(expect),* observe *(watch)*
hold intercourse discuss
hold liable convict, encumber *(financially obligate)*
hold no brief for blame, disown *(deny the validity)*
hold not to be true disbelieve
hold off cease, counter, defer *(put off),* doubt *(hesitate),* forbear, parry, pause, postpone, resist *(withstand),* stave. SEE MAIN ENTRY
hold office govern, predominate *(command),* rule *(govern)*
hold on adhere *(persist),* cohere *(adhere),* last, persevere, persist, subsist
hold on property charge *(lien),* cloud *(incumbrance),* lien, mechanics lien
hold one's ground endure *(last)*
hold ones own hold out *(resist)*
hold opposite views collide *(clash),* conflict, disaccord, disagree
hold out endure *(last),* extend *(offer),* last, offer *(propose),* persevere, persist, profess *(avow),* proffer, remain *(continue),* resist *(withstand),* submit *(give),* tender, withhold, withstand. SEE MAIN ENTRY
hold out against counter, oppugn
hold out allurement bait *(lure),* entrap, lure
hold out hope reassure
hold out temptation entrap, lure
hold over adjourn, continue *(adjourn),* delay, prolong
hold possession remain *(occupy)*
hold prisoner confine
hold questionable misdoubt
hold responsible blame, charge *(accuse),* convict, delegate, denounce *(inform against),* implicate
hold responsible for confide *(trust).* SEE MAIN ENTRY
hold spellbound immerse *(engross),* monopolize
hold sway govern, preside
hold sway over moderate *(preside over),* subjugate
hold the advantage beat *(defeat)*
hold the attention interest
hold the chair moderate *(preside over),* preside
hold the interest of engage *(involve),* monopolize
hold the opinion assume *(suppose),* contend *(maintain)*
hold the reins overlook *(superintend)*
hold tight adhere *(persist)*
hold to blame fault
hold together annex *(add),* cement, cohere *(adhere),* cohere *(be logically consistent),* conjoin, conspire
hold under duress detain *(hold in custody)*
hold up bear *(support),* clog, cohere *(adhere),* curb, defer *(put off),* delay, detain *(restrain),* deter, elevate, encumber *(hinder),* heighten *(elevate),* impede, keep *(restrain),* last, maintain *(sustain),* manifest, procrastinate, promote *(organize),* protract *(prolong),* remit *(relax),* resist *(withstand),* rob, stall, steal, uphold. SEE MAIN ENTRY
hold up one's hand cast *(register)*
hold up to execration censure, disapprove *(condemn)*
hold up to public ridicule expose
hold up to reprobation blame, censure, disapprove *(condemn)*
hold up to ridicule mock *(deride),* pillory
hold up to scorn flout. SEE MAIN ENTRY
hold up to shame brand *(stigmatize),* discredit, disgrace, pillory, smear
hold up to view manifest, produce *(offer to view)*
hold upon the property of another lien
hold with concur *(agree),* countenance
hold within bounds immure
hold-over adjournment
holdback disadvantage, hindrance, impediment, restraint. SEE MAIN ENTRY
holder bearer, catchall, coffer, depository, receiver, recipient, tenant. SEE MAIN ENTRY
holder of an estate by virtue of a lease lessee
holder of an office incumbent
holder of legal title landholder, landowner
holder of the legal estate trustee
holdfast connection *(fastening)*
holding chattel, custody *(incarceration),* demesne, domain *(land owned),* dominion *(absolute ownership),* fee *(estate),* interest *(ownership),* occupancy, ownership, possession *(property),* property *(land),* ruling, share *(stock),* stake *(interest),* tenancy, tenure, trust *(custody).* SEE MAIN ENTRY
holding a low opinion of mankind cynical
holding ability capacity *(maximum)*
holding action retention
holding back hesitation
holding by title tenancy
holding company corporation, firm
holding in constraint commitment *(confinement)*
holding in custody apprehension *(act of arresting)*
holding in restraint commitment *(confinement)*
holding legal rights conferred by another acting
holding off abstention
holding power retention
holding property proprietary
holding public interest famous
holding to a purpose pertinacious
holding together adherence *(adhesion),* coherence, coherent *(joined),* cohesive *(sticking)*
holding up well durable
holdings assets, capital, commodities, effects, estate *(property),* paraphernalia *(personal belongings),* personalty, portfolio, possessions, principal *(capital sum),* property *(possessions),* realty, securities, stock *(shares)*
holdover SEE MAIN ENTRY
holdup robbery
holdup man burglar, hoodlum
hole outlet, predicament. SEE MAIN ENTRY
holiday furlough, leave *(absence),* remembrance *(commemoration).* SEE MAIN ENTRY
holistic whole *(unified)*
hollow chamber *(compartment),* deficient, jejune *(dull),* perfunctory, untenable, vacant, vacuous, void *(empty).* SEE MAIN ENTRY
hollow place chamber *(compartment)*
hollow pretense hypocrisy, imposture
hollowness blank *(emptiness)*
holocaust atrocity, cataclysm, catastrophe, disaster, havoc, shambles
holographic SEE MAIN ENTRY
holy infrangible, sacrosanct, solemn
homage adherence *(devotion),* adhesion *(loyalty),* allegiance, estimation *(esteem),* fealty, fidelity, honor *(outward respect),* mention *(tribute),* remembrance *(commemoration),* respect. SEE MAIN ENTRY
home abode, address, apartment, building *(structure),* domestic *(household),* domestic *(indigenous),* domicile, habitation *(dwelling place),* homestead, house, household *(domestic),* household, inhabitation *(place of dwelling),* lodging, residence, residential, seat, shelter *(protection).* SEE MAIN ENTRY
home base headquarters
home circle family *(household)*
home invasion SEE MAIN ENTRY
home office headquarters
home rule SEE MAIN ENTRY
home-grown native *(domestic)*
home-loving household *(domestic)*
home-owning household *(domestic)*
homeland home *(domicile),* home *(place of origin),* nationality
homeless derelict *(abandoned),* solitary
homeless child orphan
homely familiar *(customary),* inelegant, nondescript, ordinary
homemade domestic *(indigenous).* SEE MAIN ENTRY
homemaking domestic *(household),* ho-usehold *(domestic)*
homeostasis balance *(equality)*
homes premises *(buildings)*
homespun inelegant, mundane, ordinary, simple
homestead abode, building *(structure),* dwelling, habitation *(dwelling place),* home *(domicile),* house, household, property *(land).* SEE MAIN ENTRY
homicidal deadly
homicide aberemurder, assassination, dispatch *(act of putting to death),* killing, manslaughter, murder. SEE MAIN ENTRY
homicidium manslaughter
homiletic informative
homiletical informative
homily peroration
hominem endow
hominem adire apply *(request)*

hominem adloqui address *(talk to)*
hominem armis exuere disarm *(divest of arms)*
hominem deserere abandon *(physically leave)*
hominem imitari impersonate
hominem iubere facere command
hominem permulcere coax
homines public, society
homini blandiri coax
homini civitatem dare naturalize *(make a citizen)*
homini gratiam debere obligation *(duty)*
homini imperare command
homini obsistere cross *(disagree with)*
homini placere appeal
homini praecipere ut faciat command
homini rei empower, enable
homini suadere advise
homini viam monstrare direct *(show)*
hominis welfare
hominis bona vendere distrain
hominis caedes manslaughter
hominis nomen deferre inform *(betray)*
hominum generis humanity *(mankind)*
homo inhabitant, person
homo maleficus delinquent *(guilty of a misdeed)*, delinquent, malefactor, wrongdoer
homo peritus specialist
homo rerum novarum cupidus malcontent
homo sapiens humanity *(mankind)*
homo sceleratus malefactor
homo studiosus partisan
homo trium literarum burglar
homogeneity identity *(similarity)*, propinquity *(similarity)*, regularity, resemblance, uniformity, union *(unity)*
homogeneous boiler plate, cognate, comparable *(capable of comparison)*, identical, pure, similar, simple, uniform
homologate agree *(comply)*, assent, authorize, concur *(agree)*, confirm, correspond *(be equivalent)*, countenance, sanction
homologation sanction *(permission)*
homological correlative
homologize coordinate, correspond *(be equivalent)*
homologous analogous, coequal, coextensive, cognate, comparable *(capable of comparison)*, equal
homologue counterpart *(complement)*
homology analogy, relation *(connection)*
homosexual SEE MAIN ENTRY
honest actual, authentic, bona fide, candid, clean, conscientious, credible, direct *(forthright)*, equitable, ethical, factual, fair *(just)*, faithful *(true to fact)*, genuine, high-minded, impartial, incorruptible, ingenuous, irreprehensible, just, law-abiding, meritorious, moral, proper, reliable, reputable, right *(correct)*, rightful, scrupulous, sterling, straightforward, true *(authentic)*, unaffected *(sincere)*, upright, veridical. SEE MAIN ENTRY
honest effort good faith
honestly fairly *(impartially)*, faithfully, in good faith
honestus moral, reputable, upright
honesty candor *(straightforwardness)*, conscience, equity *(justice)*, ethics, fairness, integrity, principle *(virtue)*, probity, rectitude, trustworthiness, truth, veracity. SEE MAIN ENTRY
honeyed nectarious
honor accept *(recognize)*, character *(reputation)*, compensate *(remunerate)*, conscience, credit *(recognition)*, dedicate, defer *(yield in judgment)*, deference, discharge *(pay a debt)*, distinction *(reputation)*, elevate, eminence, estimation *(esteem)*, ethics, homage, integrity, keep *(fulfill)*, laudation, mention *(tribute)*, merit, observe *(obey)*, pay, prestige, principle *(virtue)*, privilege, prize, probity, raise *(advance)*, recognize *(acknowledge)*, rectitude, regard *(esteem)*, regard *(hold in esteem)*, respect, right *(righteousness)*. SEE MAIN ENTRY
honor a bill defray
honor a claim refund
honor with bestow
honorable bona fide, clean, conscientious, equitable, ethical, exemplary, fair *(just)*, high-minded, honest, impartial, incorruptible, ingenuous, just, law-abiding, loyal, magnanimous, meritorious, moral, obeisant, outstanding *(prominent)*, pure, reliable, reputable, right *(correct)*, scrupulous, sterling, straightforward, upright. SEE MAIN ENTRY
honorable justice judge
honorableness honesty, integrity, principle *(virtue)*, probity, rectitude
honorably fairly *(impartially)*, faithfully
honorarium bonus, bounty, contribution *(donation)*, payment *(remittance)*, reward. SEE MAIN ENTRY
honorary nominal. SEE MAIN ENTRY
honored famous, illustrious, influential, outstanding *(prominent)*, prominent, proud *(self-respecting)*, renowned, reputable. SEE MAIN ENTRY
honorific honorary
honorifical honorary
honoring dedication, obedient, remembrance *(commemoration)*
hood enshroud
hoodlum lawbreaker, malefactor. SEE MAIN ENTRY
hoodwink betray *(lead astray)*, bilk, deceive, delude, ensnare, fake, pretend, prevaricate. SEE MAIN ENTRY
hook connect *(join together)*, ensnare, trap
hooligan malefactor
hoot mock *(deride)*
hope chance *(possibility)*, design *(intent)*, end *(intent)*, expectation, faith, goal, objective, plan, possibility, prospect *(outlook)*, purpose, target, trust, will *(desire)*. SEE MAIN ENTRY
hope for desire
hoped for prospective
hopeful apparent *(presumptive)*, auspicious, candidate, novice, propitious, sanguine, solicitous
hopeless despondent, diabolic, disconsolate, futile, impossible, impracticable, incorrigible, inoperable *(incurable)*, irredeemable, irremediable, irreversible, ominous, pessimistic, unfavorable, unpropitious. SEE MAIN ENTRY
hopeless failure miscarriage
hopelessly lost irretrievable
hopelessness impasse, impossibility, peril, pessimism
horde assemblage, band, congregation
horizon SEE MAIN ENTRY
horizontality prostration
horn in intrude
hornbook SEE MAIN ENTRY
horrendous contemptible, depraved, disastrous, disreputable, heinous, reprehensible. SEE MAIN ENTRY
horrible contemptible, deplorable, diabolic, dire, disastrous, disgraceful, formidable, gross *(flagrant)*, heinous, lamentable, loathsome, lurid, nefarious, obnoxious, odious, offensive *(offending)*, repulsive, sinister. SEE MAIN ENTRY
horrid deplorable, dire, disastrous, disreputable, heinous, lamentable, loathsome, objectionable, obnoxious, odious, offensive *(offending)*, repulsive, sinister, vicious. SEE MAIN ENTRY
horrific deplorable
horrify frighten, offend *(insult)*, repel *(disgust)*. SEE MAIN ENTRY
horrifying deplorable, dire, formidable, lurid, outrageous, repulsive, scandalous
horror consternation, fear, fright, odium, panic, phobia, trepidation. SEE MAIN ENTRY
hors de combat disabled *(made incapable)*
hortans hortative
hortation instigation
hortative informative, informatory, persuasive. SEE MAIN ENTRY
hortatory hortative, informative, informatory, persuasive
hospes stranger
hospitable benevolent, humane, liberal *(generous)*, philanthropic, receptive
hospitableness largess *(generosity)*, philanthropy
hospital case patient
hospitality charity, largess *(generosity)*, philanthropy
hospitalized person patient
hospitio excipere lodge *(house)*
host body *(collection)*, mass *(body of persons)*, plurality, quantity. SEE MAIN ENTRY
hostage captive, prisoner. SEE MAIN ENTRY
hostel lodge *(house)*
hostia victim
hostile averse, bitter *(reproachful)*, discordant, disobedient, impertinent *(insolent)*, inimical, irreconcilable, litigious, malevolent, malicious, malignant, negative, nonconsenting, offensive *(taking the initiative)*, opposite, prejudicial, pugnacious, recusant, repugnant *(incompatible)*, spiteful, unfavorable, virulent. SEE MAIN ENTRY
hostile attack diatribe, impugnation
hostile contest confrontation *(altercation)*
hostile criticism diatribe, disparagement, impeachment
hostile demonstration protest
hostile eloquence diatribe
hostile encounter confrontation *(altercation)*, fight *(battle)*
hostile entrance incursion
hostile entry invasion
hostile invasion foray
hostile person foe
hostile verdict conviction *(finding of guilt)*, nonsuit
hostile witness SEE MAIN ENTRY
hostilities conflict
hostility alienation *(estrangement)*, argument *(contention)*, belligerency, collision *(dispute)*, conflict, contention *(opposition)*, discord, estrangement, feud, hatred, ill will, impugnation, incompatibility *(difference)*, malice, odium, ostracism, rancor, spite, umbrage. SEE MAIN ENTRY
hostis foe
hot vehement
hot-blooded SEE MAIN ENTRY
hot-headed hot-blooded, imprudent, outrageous, petulant, precipitate
hot-tempered fractious, hot-blooded, petulant

hotheaded impulsive *(rash)*
hound badger, bait *(harass)*, harry *(harass)*, hector, hunt, importune, molest *(annoy)*, obsess, press *(goad)*, prompt, provoke, trace *(follow)*
hour point *(period of time)*
hour of decision crossroad *(turning point)*
house abode, building *(structure)*, concern *(business establishment)*, domicile, dwelling, enterprise *(economic organization)*, family *(common ancestry)*, firm, habitation *(dwelling place)*, home *(domicile)*, homestead, inhabitation *(place of dwelling)*, institute, locate, market *(business)*, parentage, preserve, protect, shelter *(protection)*. SEE MAIN ENTRY
house arrest SEE MAIN ENTRY
house of correction jail, penitentiary, prison, reformatory
house of detention jail, penitentiary, prison, reformatory
house of reform prison
house of representatives legislature
house with the grounds belonging to it premises *(buildings)*
house-building program development *(building)*
housebreaker burglar
housebreaking burglary. SEE MAIN ENTRY
housed situated
household domestic *(household)*, familiar *(customary)*, home *(domicile)*, homestead, house, ordinary, prevalent, property *(land)*, residential. SEE MAIN ENTRY
householder inhabitant, occupant, proprietor, tenant
housekeeping domestic *(household)*, household *(domestic)*
housing development *(building)*, habitation *(dwelling place)*, lodging, residence
hover prowl, vacillate
however notwithstanding, regardless, unless
howl outcry
hub body *(main part)*, focus
hubbub bluster *(commotion)*, brawl, noise, riot
hubris pride
huckster dealer, merchant, sell, trade, vendor
huddle meet, turmoil
hue color *(complexion)*
huff resentment
huffy petulant, resentful
huge capacious, exorbitant, far reaching, formidable, grandiose, gross *(flagrant)*, prodigious *(enormous)*
hulking ponderous
hullabaloo noise, outcry
human bodily, character *(an individual)*, person, physical. SEE MAIN ENTRY
human being body *(person)*, character *(an individual)*, individual, person
human beings humanity *(mankind)*
human creature person
human environment ecology
human race mortality
human weakness foible, frailty
humane benevolent, charitable *(lenient)*, lenient, liberal *(generous)*, philanthropic. SEE MAIN ENTRY
humaneness benevolence *(disposition to do good)*, charity, clemency, philanthropy
humanism benevolence *(disposition to do good)*
humanitarian benefactor, benevolent, charitable *(lenient)*, donor, good samaritan, humane, liberal *(generous)*, nonprofit, philanthropic
humanitarianism aid *(subsistence)*, charity, help, philanthropy
humanitas civilization, humanity *(humaneness)*, philanthropy
humanity benevolence *(disposition to do good)*, charity, clemency, consideration *(sympathetic regard)*, goodwill, lenience, mortality, populace, population, tolerance, understanding *(tolerance)*. SEE MAIN ENTRY
humanize personify
humankind humanity *(mankind)*
humanness mortality
humanum genus humanity *(mankind)*
humanus humane, philanthropic
humble browbeat, contrite, debase, demean *(make lower)*, demote, derogate, diffident, familiar *(customary)*, humiliate, ignoble, marginal, obeisant, obsequious, paltry, penitent, reduce, repentant, servile, subaltern, subdue, subject, subjugate, subordinate, unobtrusive, unpretentious. SEE MAIN ENTRY
humble entreaty prayer
humble oneself condescend *(deign)*, repent
humble oneself to obey
humble service fealty
humbled contrite, diffident
humbled pride disgrace
humbleness poverty, respect
humbling disgrace
humbly respectfully
humbug bilk, deceive, invent *(falsify)*, pettifoggery, ruse
humbuggery deception, knavery
humdrum ordinary, prosaic, stale, usual
humiliate browbeat, debase, demean *(make lower)*, denigrate, disgrace, disparage, smear. SEE MAIN ENTRY
humiliating disgraceful, libelous
humiliating rudeness contumely
humiliation attaint, contumely, degradation, disgrace, dishonor *(shame)*, embarrassment, ignominy, infamy, obloquy, odium, opprobrium, scandal, shame. SEE MAIN ENTRY
humiliative disgraceful
humilis ignoble, servile
humility homage, respect
humor characteristic, disposition *(inclination)*, notion, pander, placate, propitiate, soothe, spirit, vouchsafe. SEE MAIN ENTRY
humor excessively overindulge
humoring indulgence, lenient
humorless grave *(solemn)*, pedestrian
humorous jocular, ludicrous
humorsome restive, volatile
hunch premonition
hunger desire, passion
hunger for lack, need
hunt chase, ferret, frisk, prey, pursue *(chase)*, pursuit *(chase)*, pursuit *(effort to secure)*, quest, research, search. SEE MAIN ENTRY
hunt down expose
hunt for delve
hunt out trace *(follow)*
hunt through delve, frisk
hunted person fugitive
hurdle bar *(obstruction)*, barrier, deterrence, deterrent, encumbrance, handicap, negotiate, obstacle, obstruction. SEE MAIN ENTRY
hurl cast *(throw)*, emit, impel, launch *(project)*, project *(impel forward)*, send
hurl defiance at challenge
hurl headlong precipitate *(throw down violently)*
hurricane SEE MAIN ENTRY
hurried brief, careless, cursory, ephemeral, impulsive *(rash)*, instantaneous, perfunctory, precipitate, rapid, summary, superficial
hurriedly instantly
hurriedness haste
hurry dispatch *(promptness)*, dispatch *(send off)*, expedite, haste, hasten, precipitate *(hasten)*, race, urge. SEE MAIN ENTRY
hurry along dispatch *(send off)*, hasten
hurry away quit *(evacuate)*
hurry off with distrain
hurry on dispatch *(send off)*
hurrying acceleration
hurt abuse *(physical misuse)*, aggravate *(annoy)*, aggrieved *(harmed)*, brutalize, damage *(noun)*, damage *(verb)*, deface, detriment, disable, disconsolate, distress, drawback, endanger, expense *(sacrifice)*, harm *(noun)*, harm *(verb)*, harrow, ill use, impair, impairment *(damage)*, imperfect, inflict, injury, maim, marred, mischief, mistreat, molest *(annoy)*, offend *(insult)*, pain, penalize, pique, prejudice *(injury)*, prejudice *(injure)*, resentful, spoil *(impair)*, strike *(assault)*, suffer *(sustain loss)*. SEE MAIN ENTRY
hurt the feelings affront, discompose
hurtful adverse *(negative)*, bitter *(reproachful)*, caustic, dangerous, detrimental, disadvantageous, disastrous, fatal, harmful, inadvisable, inimical, insalubrious, insufferable, invidious, lethal, malevolent, malignant, noxious, oppressive, painful, pernicious, pestilent, prejudicial, scathing, sinister, virulent
hurtfulness harm
hurting disabling, painful
hurtle against collide *(crash against)*
hurtless harmless, innocuous, nontoxic, salutary
husband consort, hoard, keep *(shelter)*, preserve, spouse, store
husband one's resources hoard
husbanding of resources economy *(frugality)*
husbandry austerity, prudence
hush allay, lull *(noun)*, lull *(verb)*, moderate *(temper)*, mollify, peace, placate, repress, silence, soothe, stifle, strangle
hush money blackmail, bribe, graft, gratuity *(bribe)*. SEE MAIN ENTRY
hush up hide, suppress, withhold
hushed mute
husky strong
hustle haste, hasten, jostle *(bump into)*, race
hyaline pellucid
hybridize commingle
hybridized compound
hygienic preventive, salutary
hygienize decontaminate
hyperbole bombast, caricature, distortion, exaggeration, overstatement, rodomontade. SEE MAIN ENTRY
hyperbolic extreme *(exaggerated)*, inflated *(overestimated)*. SEE MAIN ENTRY
hyperbolical outrageous
hyperbolism overstatement
hypercritical critical *(faultfinding)*, particular *(exacting)*, querulous, sensitive *(easily affected)*, severe
hypercriticism diatribe, disparagement

hypersensitive querulous
hyphenate connect *(join together)*
hypnotic narcotic *(adjective),* narcotic *(noun)*
hypocrisy bad faith, duplicity, indirection *(deceitfulness),* pretense *(pretext).* SEE MAIN ENTRY
hypocritical dishonest, disingenuous, evasive, faithless, false *(disloyal),* insidious, machiavellian, perfidious, specious, tartuffish, untrue
hypostasis center *(essence),* essence, spirit, substance *(essential nature)*
hypothecate bond *(secure a debt),* guarantee, pawn, pledge *(deposit),* promise *(vow)*
hypothecated fully secured
hypothecation charge *(lien),* cloud *(incumbrance),* guaranty, specialty *(contract).* SEE MAIN ENTRY
hypothesis assumption *(supposition),* basis, conjecture, deduction *(conclusion),* generalization, idea, inference, opinion *(belief),* postulate, presumption, prolepsis, proposition, speculation *(conjecture),* supposition, theory, thesis. SEE MAIN ENTRY
hypothesization assumption *(supposition)*
hypothesize generalize, guess, opine, posit, postulate, presume, presuppose, propound, reason *(conclude),* speculate *(conjecture),* surmise, suspect *(think)*
hypothesized assumed *(inferred),* presumptive
hypothetic hypothetical
hypothetical conditional, debatable, disputable, moot, nonexistent, speculative, theoretical. SEE MAIN ENTRY
hypothetically arguendo
hysteria furor, outburst, panic
hysterical frenetic, uncontrollable
hysterical state outburst
hystericalness panic
hysterics outburst

I

iacere dormant
iactans pretentious *(ostentatious),* pretentious *(pompous)*
iactare cast *(throw),* flaunt
iactura loss
iconoclasm blasphemy
iconoclast heretic
iconoclastic radical *(favoring drastic change),* recusant, skeptical
icy disdainful, unaffected *(uninfluenced)*
icy aloofness disdain
idea apprehension *(perception),* clue, concept, connotation, end *(intent),* hint, import, intimation, meaning, notion, objective, opinion *(belief),* perception, project, proposal *(suggestion),* proposition, purpose, sense *(feeling),* substance *(essential nature),* suggestion, tenor. SEE MAIN ENTRY
idea conveyed gist *(substance),* sum *(tally)*
ideal criterion, example, exemplar, exemplary, felicitous, model, nonexistent, paradigm, paragon, pattern, prototype, ripe, standard, unimpeachable. SEE MAIN ENTRY
ideal justice equity *(justice)*
idealism casuistry
idealistic ethical, meritorious, moral, quixotic
idealize magnify
ideals conscience, ethics
ideate conceive *(comprehend),* create
ideational theoretical
ideative cogitative, theoretical
idée fixe preoccupation
idem identical
idem same
identical comparable *(equivalent),* equivalent, same *(adjective),* same *(noun),* similar, tantamount, uniform. SEE MAIN ENTRY
identical in amount equal
identical in quantity equal
identical in size commensurable, equal, equivalent
identical in value coequal, equal, equivalent
identical value parity
identicalness identity *(similarity),* par *(equality),* parity, resemblance
identifiable apparent *(perceptible),* arrant *(definite),* clear *(apparent),* manifest, palpable, unmistakable
identification classification, connection *(relation),* credentials, definition, denomination, designation *(naming),* discovery, earmark, fingerprints, label, recognition, speciality, stamp, trademark. SEE MAIN ENTRY
identification mark brand, designation *(symbol),* device *(distinguishing mark)*
identification records fingerprints
identification tag brand, label
identified with congruous
identifier eyewitness
identify brand *(mark),* call *(title),* characterize, classify, define, describe, detect, diagnose, discover, find *(discover),* label, recognize *(perceive),* relate *(establish a connection).* SEE MAIN ENTRY
identify by name call *(title)*
identify incorrectly mislabel, mistake
identify with compare, sympathize. SEE MAIN ENTRY
identifying descriptive
identity par *(equality),* personality, resemblance, semblance. SEE MAIN ENTRY
identity classification identification
identity comparison identification
identity theft SEE MAIN ENTRY
identity verification identification
ideological theoretical. SEE MAIN ENTRY
ideology theory
idiocrasy characteristic, quality *(attribute),* quirk *(idiosyncrasy)*
idiom expression *(comment),* language, parlance, phrase, phraseology, speech, term *(expression)*
idiomatic distinctive, specific
idiosyncrasy characteristic, disposition *(inclination),* feature *(characteristic),* identity *(individuality),* irregularity, nonconformity, quality *(attribute),* specialty *(distinctive mark),* tendency, trait. SEE MAIN ENTRY
idiosyncratic different, distinct *(distinguished from others),* distinctive, eccentric, noteworthy, particular *(specific),* peculiar *(distinctive),* personal *(individual),* specific
idiosyncratical specific
idiotic fatuous, ludicrous, non compos mentis, obtuse
idle barren, baseless, inactive, indolent, ineffectual, lax, loiter, otiose, procrastinate, remiss, rest *(cease from action),* stagnant, torpid, trivial, truant, unavailing, unemployed, unfounded, vacant, vacuous. SEE MAIN ENTRY
idle expenditure misapplication
idle fancy figment
idle speech fustian
idle speeches bombast
idle threat SEE MAIN ENTRY
idleness desuetude, inaction, languor, lull, neglect, nonperformance, sloth
idling layoff
idolatory doxology
idolatry laudation
idolization respect
idolize honor, regard *(hold in esteem)*
idoneous suitable
idoneus adequate, capable, convenient, eligible, fit, opportune, proper, qualified *(conditioned),* suitable
ieiunus prosaic
if it were not that only
igitur consequently
ignarus inexperienced, unacquainted, unaware
ignavia sloth
ignavus idle, inactive, indolent
ignis conflagration
ignite burn, deflagrate, discharge *(shoot)*
igniting discharge *(shot)*
ignobility bad character, bad repute, dishonor *(shame),* disrepute, ignominy, infamy, odium, opprobrium
ignoble bad *(offensive),* caitiff, calumnious, disgraceful, disreputable, immoral, machiavellian, nefarious, notorious, odious, offensive *(offending),* outrageous, reprehensible, scandalous, sinister, unethical, unseemly. SEE MAIN ENTRY
ignominia degradation, discredit, disgrace, dishonor *(shame),* ignominy, infamy, shame
ignominious blameful, blameworthy, caitiff, calumnious, contemptible, contem-ptuous, disgraceful, disreputable, ignoble, libelous, notorious, odious, scandalous. SEE MAIN ENTRY
ignominiousness bad repute, disrepute, infamy, opprobrium
ignominy attaint, bad character, bad faith, bad repute, degradation, discredit, disgrace, dishonor *(shame),* disrepute, infamy, notoriety, obloquy, odium, opprobrium, scandal, shame. SEE MAIN ENTRY
ignomy ignominy, notoriety
ignorance nescience. SEE MAIN ENTRY
ignorance of law SEE MAIN ENTRY
ignorant incognizant, incompetent, inept *(incompetent),* inexperienced, insensible, obtuse, opaque, unacquainted, unaware, unversed, unwitting. SEE MAIN ENTRY
ignorantly unknowingly
ignorare mistake
ignoration nescience
ignore discount *(disbelieve),* disdain, dismiss *(put out of consideration),* disobey, disoblige, disregard, exclude, fail *(neglect),* neglect, overlook *(superintend),* override, pretermit, rebuff, reject, shirk, shun, spurn. SEE MAIN ENTRY
ignore distinctions generalize, muddle
ignore ethics cheat
ignore limits trespass
ignore one's obligations default
ignored derelict *(abandoned)*
ignorement disuse
ignoscere amnesty, forgive, overlook *(superintend)*
ii qui reipublicae praesunt government *(political administration)*
ilk class, kind, manner *(kind)*
ill pain, trouble, unsound *(not strong).* SEE MAIN ENTRY
ill at ease restive

ill conduct guilt, malfeasance
ill consequence mischief
ill disposition ill will
ill fame attaint, opprobrium
ill favor attaint, bad character, ignominy, obloquy
ill feeling argument *(contention),* discord, hatred, malice, rancor, spite
ill fortune calamity, casualty, expense *(sacrifice),* loss, misfortune
ill hap casualty
ill health disease
ill humor umbrage
ill individual patient
ill judgment indiscretion
ill luck loss, misfortune
ill management misconduct
ill nature spite
ill repute attaint, bad character, bad repute, ignominy, infamy, notoriety, obloquy, opprobrium, scandal, shame, turpitude
ill treat misemploy, mishandle *(maltreat),* mistreat, persecute
ill treatment abuse *(physical misuse),* injury, misusage, misuse, molestation, oppression
ill turn disservice
ill usage abuse *(corrupt practice),* abuse *(physical misuse),* misusage, misuse, molestation
ill use abuse *(corrupt practice),* abuse *(physical misuse),* misemploy, mishandle *(maltreat),* mistreat, misuse, persecute
ill will argument *(contention),* discord, estrangement, feud, hatred, malice, odium, rancor, resentment, spite, umbrage
ill wishes imprecation, malediction
ill-adapted disproportionate, improper, inapplicable, inapposite, inapt, inept *(inappropriate),* unfit, unsuitable
ill-advised detrimental, fatuous, ill-judged, impolitic, imprudent, inadvisable, inept *(inappropriate),* injudicious, irrational, misadvised, regressive, thoughtless, undue *(excessive),* unfit, unpolitic, unreasonable, untimely. SEE MAIN ENTRY
ill-behaved blatant *(obtrusive),* disobedient, perverse
ill-boding dire, ominous, portentous *(ominous),* regrettable, unfavorable
ill-bred blatant *(obtrusive),* inelegant, offensive *(offending),* presumptuous, uncouth
ill-chosen ill-judged, inopportune
ill-conceived SEE MAIN ENTRY
ill-consequence harm
ill-considered ill-advised, ill-judged, impolitic, imprudent, impulsive *(rash),* inadvisable, irrational, misadvised, negligent, premature, untimely. SEE MAIN ENTRY
ill-contrived detrimental, ill-judged. SEE MAIN ENTRY
ill-defined inconspicuous, indefinite, ind-eterminate, indistinct, nebulous, opaque, unclear, vague
ill-disciplined lawless
ill-disposed hostile, malevolent, malicious, resentful, sinister, spiteful, unfavorable, unpropitious, vicious. SEE MAIN ENTRY
ill-done perfunctory
ill-fame dishonor *(shame),* disrepute
ill-fated ominous, portentous *(ominous),* regrettable
ill-favor disgrace, dishonor *(shame),* disrepute
ill-feeling ill will
ill-founded baseless, improper, unsound *(fallacious).* SEE MAIN ENTRY
ill-furnished devoid
ill-gotten gains spoils
ill-gotten goods plunder
ill-humored petulant
ill-intent ill will
ill-intentioned cruel, harmful, malevolent, malignant, spiteful
ill-judged ill-advised, impolitic, imprudent, inadvisable, injudicious, irrational, misadvised, unpolitic, unreasonable. SEE MAIN ENTRY
ill-manage mismanage
ill-mannered blatant *(obtrusive),* disorderly, impertinent *(insolent),* inelegant, presumptuous, provincial, uncouth
ill-matched disparate, disproportionate, incongruous
ill-nature cruelty
ill-natured cruel, harsh, malevolent, malicious, perverse, severe, spiteful, vicious. SEE MAIN ENTRY
ill-omened dire, disastrous, ominous, regrettable, unfavorable, unpropitious
ill-proportioned disproportionate
ill-provided devoid
ill-provided for poor *(underprivileged)*
ill-qualified inept *(incompetent),* inexperienced, unqualified *(not competent)*
ill-reasoned sophistic
ill-repute disgrace, dishonor *(shame),* disrepute. SEE MAIN ENTRY
ill-seasoned inopportune
ill-sorted disproportionate
ill-starred ominous, portentous *(ominous)*
ill-stored devoid
ill-suited disproportionate, inapt, inept *(inappropriate)*
ill-tempered fractious, perverse, petulant, severe
ill-timed improper, inapposite, inapt, inauspicious, inept *(inappropriate),* inopportune, premature, unpropitious, untimely
ill-treat affront, exploit *(take advantage of),* harass, harm, harrow, ill use, maltreat
ill-treated aggrieved *(harmed)*
ill-treatment harm. SEE MAIN ENTRY
ill-usage cruelty, waste
ill-use abuse *(misuse),* abuse *(violate),* exploit *(take advantage of),* harass, harm, harrow, maltreat. SEE MAIN ENTRY
ill-used aggrieved *(victimized)*
ill-will cruelty. SEE MAIN ENTRY
ill-willed cruel, hostile, libelous, negative
ill-wishing malevolent
illapse entrance
illaqueate inveigle
illation consequence *(conclusion),* deduction *(conclusion),* generalization, inference
illative deductible *(provable)*
illaudable blameful, blameworthy, immoral, objectionable, peccable, reprehensible, scandalous, sinister
illegal felonious, illicit, immoral, impermissible, irregular *(improper),* lawless, peccant *(culpable),* unauthorized, unlawful, usurious, wrongful. SEE MAIN ENTRY
illegal act offense
illegal action malfeasance, transgression
illegal agreement confederacy *(conspiracy)*
illegal amotion asportation
illegal application misapplication
illegal carriage asportation
illegal compact confederacy *(conspiracy)*
illegal compulsion blackmail, coercion, extortion
illegal conduct offense
illegal custody detainer
illegal detention detainer
illegal donation bribe
illegal evasion breach
illegal exacter extortionist
illegal gain gratuity *(bribe)*
illegal incentive bribe
illegal incitation bribe, bribery
illegal inducement bribe, bribery
illegal infliction of punishment lynch law
illegal interest usury
illegal intrusion encroachment
illegal lure bribe
illegal offer bribe
illegal offering bribe
illegal pact collusion
illegal present bribe
illegal profit graft
illegal property contraband
illegal restraint detainer
illegal reward bribe
illegal subduction asportation
illegal taker extortionist
illegal traffic contraband
illegal transmittance asportation
illegal transplantation asportation
illegal transshipment asportation
illegal use of property misappropriation
illegal withholding detainer
illegality burglary, corruption, crime, criminality, felony, infringement, injustice, irregularity, misconduct, misdeed, misdemeanor, misdoing, offense, prohibition, transgression, violation, wrong. SEE MAIN ENTRY
illegalize disfranchise
illegally SEE MAIN ENTRY
illegally exported goods contraband
illegally imported goods contraband
illegibility incoherence
illegible indistinct, unclear
illegitimacy bar sinister, illegality, incompetence, prohibition
illegitimate felonious, illegal, illicit, impermissible, irregular *(improper),* spurious, synthetic, ultra vires, unauthorized, unlawful, wrongful. SEE MAIN ENTRY
illegitimate act tortious act
illegitimate child bastard
illegitimate undertaking racket
illegitimately illegally
illegitimateness bar sinister
illegitimation bar sinister
illiberal bigot, exclusive *(limited),* narrow, parochial, parsimonious, penurious, provincial. SEE MAIN ENTRY
illiberality discrimination *(bigotry),* intolerance
illicit illegal, illegitimate *(illegal),* immoral, impermissible, improper, irregular *(improper),* unlawful, wrongful. SEE MAIN ENTRY
illicit business racket
illicit dealer bootlegger, racketeer
illicit gains contraband, plunder
illicit intercourse adultery
illicit love adultery
illicit procreation bar sinister
illicit profit graft
illicit revenue graft
illicit scheme racket
illicit sexual intercourse adultery
illicitly illegally
illicitly covert collusive

illicitness breach, criminality
illimitable infinite, myriad, omnipotent, open-ended, profuse, unqualified *(unlimited)*
illimitably ad infinitum
illimited open-ended
illiteracy ignorance. SEE MAIN ENTRY
illiterate unversed
illiterateness ignorance
illness disability *(physical inability)*, disease, disorder *(abnormal condition)*, prostration. SEE MAIN ENTRY
illogical arbitrary, baseless, disordered, disproportionate, erroneous, fatuous, ill-judged, improper, inapposite, incongruous, inconsistent, inept *(inappropriate)*, irrational, misadvised, nonsubstantial *(not sturdy)*, sophistic, unfounded, unreasonable, unsound *(fallacious)*, untenable. SEE MAIN ENTRY
illogical conclusion non sequitur
illogical deduction non sequitur
illogical result non sequitur
illude delude. SEE MAIN ENTRY
illuminate clarify, comment, construe *(translate)*, delineate, demonstrate *(establish)*, depict, describe, detail *(particularize)*, elucidate, embellish, enlighten, exemplify, explain, explicate, exposit, illustrate, interpret, manifest, resolve *(solve)*. SEE MAIN ENTRY
illuminated coherent *(clear)*, lucid
illuminating demonstrative *(illustrative)*, descriptive, informative, informatory, interpretive, narrative
illumination civilization, clarification, cognition, comment, construction, definition, explanation, illustration, motif, realization, solution *(answer)*. SEE MAIN ENTRY
illuminative demonstrative *(illustrative)*, descriptive, narrative
illumine disabuse, enlighten, instruct *(teach)*
illumined lucid
illusion artifice, deception, distortion, fallacy, figment, phantom, prestidigitation, semblance, specter, vision *(dream)*. SEE MAIN ENTRY
illusional ostensible, specious
illusionary delusive, ostensible
illusive deceptive, delusive, fallacious, fictitious, illusory, insubstantial, ostensible, specious, subtle *(insidious)*, untrustworthy
illusory artificial, deceptive, delusive, fallacious, fictitious, insubstantial, nonexistent, ostensible, quixotic, specious, tenuous. SEE MAIN ENTRY
illustrate bear *(adduce)*, characterize, cite *(state)*, clarify, comment, construe *(translate)*, define, delineate, demonstrate *(establish)*, depict, describe, detail *(particularize)*, display, elucidate, embellish, enlighten, evidence, evince, exemplify, exhibit, explain, explicate, expound, interpret, manifest, portray, render *(depict)*, represent *(portray)*, signify *(denote)*. SEE MAIN ENTRY
illustration case *(example)*, clarification, comment, example, explanation, expression *(manifestation)*, instance, representation *(statement)*, sample, specimen. SEE MAIN ENTRY
illustrational representative
illustrative descriptive, exemplary, general, narrative, representative, typical. SEE MAIN ENTRY
illustrative statement dictum
illustrious famous, important *(significant)*, influential, magnanimous, notable, noteworthy, outstanding *(prominent)*, professional *(stellar)*, prominent, renowned, reputable, salient, superior *(excellent)*. SEE MAIN ENTRY
illustriousness distinction *(reputation)*, prestige, reputation
image apprehension *(perception)*, color *(complexion)*, complexion, conceive *(comprehend)*, concept, copy, counterpart *(parallel)*, impression, model, perception, phantom, phenomenon *(manifestation)*, presence *(poise)*, represent *(portray)*, resemblance, semblance, symbol, vision *(dream)*. SEE MAIN ENTRY
image in the mind impression
imaginability chance *(possibility)*
imaginable plausible, possible, potential, prospective, viable
imaginal original *(creative)*
imaginary artificial, delusive, fictitious, hypothetical, illusory, insubstantial, nonexistent, speculative. SEE MAIN ENTRY
imagination comprehension, creation. SEE MAIN ENTRY
imaginative artful, fertile, original *(creative)*, productive, resourceful. SEE MAIN ENTRY
imagine compose, conceive *(comprehend)*, conjure, contrive, deem, devise *(invent)*, expect *(consider probable)*, feign, gauge, guess, invent *(produce for the first time)*, opine, presuppose, pretend, profess *(pretend)*, surmise, suspect *(think)*. SEE MAIN ENTRY
imagined artificial, delusive, fictitious, illusory, insubstantial, nonexistent, presumptive
imagined thought figment
imago phantom, reflection *(image)*, representation *(statement)*, semblance
imbalance difference, disparity, distortion, inequality. SEE MAIN ENTRY
imbecilic fatuous, obtuse, opaque
imbecillitas impotence
imbed inject
imbibe carouse
imbricate overlap
imbroglio brawl, commotion, complex *(entanglement)*, complication, confusion *(turmoil)*, dilemma, disaccord, dispute, embroilment, entanglement *(confusion)*, fight *(argument)*, involution, pandemonium, plight, predicament, quagmire, snarl, strife, turmoil. SEE MAIN ENTRY
imbrue infuse, penetrate, pervade
imbruement infusion
imbue inculcate, infuse, inject, inspire, permeate, pervade. SEE MAIN ENTRY
imbued full
imbued with addicted
imbued with life conscious *(awake)*, live *(conscious)*
imbuement infusion
imbuere imbue, initiate, taint *(contaminate)*
imitari copy
imitate adopt, copy, fake, forge *(counterfeit)*, impersonate, plagiarize, pose *(impersonate)*, pretend, reflect *(mirror)*, repeat *(do again)*, reproduce, simulate. SEE MAIN ENTRY
imitate deceptively feign
imitate falsely forge *(counterfeit)*
imitate fraudulently forge *(counterfeit)*
imitate insultingly disparage, jape
imitated imitation, repeated
imitation artificial, caricature, copy, counterfeit, decoy, disguise, duplicate, fake, false *(not genuine)*, forgery, imposture, meretricious, model, parody, plagiarism, pretense *(pretext)*, quasi, resemblance, sham, spurious, surrogate, travesty. SEE MAIN ENTRY
imitation of an original plagiarism
imitative artificial, derivative, imitation
imitator disciple
immaculate absolute *(ideal)*, blameless, clean, pure, unblemished. SEE MAIN ENTRY
immanence characteristic
immanent born *(innate)*, essential *(inherent)*, inherent, innate. SEE MAIN ENTRY
immanis brutal, outrageous, prodigious *(enormous)*
immanitas brutality
immaterial frivolous, impertinent *(irrelevant)*, imponderable, inapposite, inconsequential, inconsiderable, incorporeal, insubstantial, intangible, irrelevant, minor, negligible, nugatory, null *(insignificant)*, slight, trivial, unessential. SEE MAIN ENTRY
immaterial substance spirit
immateriality impalpability, inconsequence, insignificance. SEE MAIN ENTRY
immaterialness impalpability
immateriate impalpable, imponderable, incorporeal
immature inchoate, incipient, inexperienced, jejune *(lacking maturity)*, juvenile, naive, puerile, rudimentary. SEE MAIN ENTRY
immature person juvenile
immature stage embryo
immaturity adolescence, minority *(infancy)*, nonage
immaturus premature, untimely
immeasurable far reaching, indeterminate, inestimable, infinite, innumerable, profuse, unlimited. SEE MAIN ENTRY
immeasurably ad infinitum
immediacy SEE MAIN ENTRY
immediate current, direct *(straight)*, expeditious, instantaneous, pending *(imminent)*, precipitate, present *(current)*, prompt, prospective, proximate, right *(direct)*, summary. SEE MAIN ENTRY
immediate forebear parents
immediately forthwith, instantly. SEE MAIN ENTRY
immediateness dispatch *(promptness)*
immedicable chronic, inoperable *(incurable)*, irremediable
immemor oblivious
immense broad, capacious, exorbitant, far reaching, grandiose, gross *(flagrant)*, innumerable, myriad, outrageous, prodigious *(enormous)*. SEE MAIN ENTRY
immensity magnitude, mass *(weight)*
immensurable inestimable
immensus unlimited
immeritorious arrant *(onerous)*, blameful, depraved, sinister
immerse concern *(involve)*, inundate, occupy *(engage)*, overcome *(overwhelm)*, overwhelm. SEE MAIN ENTRY
immersion obsession, preoccupation
immethodical cursory, disordered, disorderly, haphazard, indiscriminate, random, sporadic
immigrant alien *(foreign)*, alien. SEE MAIN ENTRY
immigration entry *(entrance)*, inflow. SEE MAIN ENTRY
imminence threat
imminent close *(near)*, forthcoming, future, inevitable, instant, necessary *(inescapable)*, prospective, proximate. SEE MAIN ENTRY
imminent danger menace, pitfall

imminere command, imminent, impend, overlap
imminuere decrease, impair, lessen, reduce
imminui abate *(lessen)*
imminutio decrease
immiscere intersperse
immisericors relentless, remorseless, ruthless
immitigable irredeemable, irremediable, irrevocable
immitis unrelenting
immittere launch *(project)*
immix combine *(join together)*, commingle
immixture coalescence
immobile firm, inflexible, stagnant, static, unbending, unyielding
immobilis immovable, static
immobility abeyance, inaction, inertia, insentience, languor
immobilization inertia
immobilize bind *(restrain)*, fetter, lock. SEE MAIN ENTRY
immoderacy exaggeration
immoderate disorderly, dissolute, drastic, egregious, excess, excessive, exorbitant, extreme *(exaggerated)*, fanatical, gluttonous, hot-blooded, incendiary, inordinate, intemperate, outrageous, prodigal, profligate *(extravagant)*, profuse, prohibitive *(costly)*, superlative, unconscionable, undue *(excessive)*, unqualified *(unlimited)*, unreasonable, unrestrained *(not repressed)*, unrestricted, unwarranted, usurious. SEE MAIN ENTRY
immoderately unduly
immoderateness exaggeration
immoderation debauchery, exaggeration, redundancy
immoderatus excessive, inordinate, outrageous
immodest brazen, flagrant, improper, inflated *(vain)*, lascivious, lewd, obscene, orgulous, pretentious *(pompous)*, promiscuous, prurient, scandalous, unabashed
immodesty obscenity, pride
immodicus excessive, exorbitant, inordinate, undue *(excessive)*
immoral bad *(offensive)*, base *(bad)*, brazen, decadent, delinquent *(guilty of a misdeed)*, depraved, diabolic, dishonest, disreputable, dissolute, felonious, illicit, improper, inexcusable, iniquitous, irregular *(improper)*, lascivious, lawless, lecherous, lewd, licentious, machiavellian, nefarious, obscene, peccant *(culpable)*, profligate *(corrupt)*, promiscuous, reprehensible, reprobate, salacious, scandalous, sinister, tainted *(corrupted)*, tortuous *(corrupt)*, unethical, unjust, unscrupulous, vicious, wanton. SEE MAIN ENTRY
immoral habit vice
immoral person degenerate
immorality bad repute, delinquency *(misconduct)*, guilt, misdoing, obscenity, perversion, turpitude, vice, wrong. SEE MAIN ENTRY
immortal constant, durable, permanent, perpetual. SEE MAIN ENTRY
immortal part spirit
immortality distinction *(reputation)*, indestructibility. SEE MAIN ENTRY
immortalization dedication, preservation, remembrance *(commemoration)*
immortalize dedicate, perpetuate
immotile firm
immotus immovable, static, unaffected *(uninfluenced)*
immovability inertia, objectivity, security *(safety)*, tenacity
immovable dispassionate, durable, firm, fixed *(securely placed)*, immutable, implacable, indelible, inexorable, inextricable, inflexible, irreconcilable, irrevocable, obdurate, pertinacious, recalcitrant, secure *(sound)*, severe, stable, unbending, uncompromising, unyielding. SEE MAIN ENTRY
immovables property *(possessions)*
immune clear *(free from criminal charges)*, exempt. SEE MAIN ENTRY
immune freehold
immune inexpugnable, insusceptible *(resistant)*, privileged, tenable
immune from restriction free *(not restricted)*
immunis exempt, free *(relieved from a burden)*, immune, privileged
immunitas exemption, immunity, privilege
immunitio infraction, infringement
immunity dispensation *(exception)*, exclusion, exemption, franchise *(license)*, impunity, privilege, protection, release, resistance, respite *(reprieve)*, sanction *(permission)*, security *(safety)*, tolerance. SEE MAIN ENTRY
immunity from assault inviolability
immunization tolerance
immunize protect. SEE MAIN ENTRY
immunized immune, insusceptible *(resistant)*, privileged
immuration bondage, captivity, constraint *(imprisonment)*, custody *(incarceration)*, detention
immure arrest *(apprehend)*, capture, commit *(institutionalize)*, confine, constrain *(imprison)*, contain *(enclose)*, detain *(hold in custody)*, enclose, encompass *(surround)*, imprison, jail, lock, restrain, restrict, sentence. SEE MAIN ENTRY
immurement bondage, captivity, constraint *(imprisonment)*, custody *(incarceration)*, detention, durance, enclosure, incarceration
immuring commitment *(confinement)*
immurred arrested *(apprehended)*
immutabilis immutable, unalterable
immutability constant, indestructibility
immutable conclusive *(determinative)*, constant, definite, durable, indefeasible, indelible, inexorable, inflexible, ironclad, irreconcilable, irreversible, irrevocable, obdurate, permanent, pertinacious, resolute, stable, unalterable. SEE MAIN ENTRY
immutably invariably
immutare alter, change
impact collision *(accident)*, connotation, contact *(touching)*, content *(meaning)*, effect, force *(strength)*, impression, reaction *(response)*, repercussion, signification, value. SEE MAIN ENTRY
impacted inextricable
impair abrogate *(annul)*, adulterate, aggravate *(exacerbate)*, check *(restrain)*, contaminate, damage, debase, debilitate, deface, denature, disable, disadvantage, disorient, endanger, eviscerate, harm, hinder, impede, infect, maim, mistreat, mutilate, pollute, prejudice *(injure)*, spoil *(impair)*, stain, subvert, vitiate. SEE MAIN ENTRY
impair in worth debase
impair one's reputation libel
impair the force of obtund
impair the legibility of deface
impair the looks of deface
impair the reputation of discredit
impaired defective, deficient, dilapidated, disabled *(made incapable)*, faulty, imperfect, inadequate, marred, tainted *(contaminated)*, unsound *(not strong)*
impaired condition disrepair. SEE MAIN ENTRY
impaired reputation bad repute, discredit
impairing disabling, noxious
impairment abuse *(physical misuse)*, cost *(penalty)*, damage, defacement, defect, deficiency, defilement, deterioration, detriment, disability *(legal disqualification)*, disability *(physical inability)*, disrepair, expense *(sacrifice)*, fault *(weakness)*, handicap, harm, injury, prejudice *(injury)*, wear and tear. SEE MAIN ENTRY
impairment of mental faculties lunacy
impairment of reputation libel
impalatable objectionable, obnoxious, unendurable
impale enter *(penetrate)*, lancinate, penetrate, pierce *(lance)*
impalpability SEE MAIN ENTRY
impalpable elusive, imponderable, inappreciable, incorporeal, indiscernible, insubstantial, intangible, minimal, obscure *(abstruse)*, obscure *(faint)*, vague. SEE MAIN ENTRY
impanel SEE MAIN ENTRY
impar disproportionate, inadequate, insufficient, one-sided, unequal *(unequivalent)*
imparity difference, inequality
impart administer *(tender)*, advise, annunciate, attorn, bear *(yield)*, bestow, betray *(disclose)*, cast *(throw)*, communicate, concede, confer *(give)*, contribute *(supply)*, convey *(communicate)*, convey *(transfer)*, deliver, disabuse, disclose, disseminate, divulge, enlighten, express, give *(grant)*, grant *(transfer formally)*, inform *(betray)*, inform *(notify)*, instill, instruct *(teach)*, leave *(give)*, manifest, mention, notify, observe *(remark)*, pass *(determine)*, phrase, post, present *(make a gift)*, produce *(offer to view)*, provide *(supply)*, publish, recount, relate *(tell)*, render *(deliver)*, report *(disclose)*, reveal, signify *(inform)*, transmit, utter. SEE MAIN ENTRY
impart gradually instill
impart knowledge apprise
impart knowledge of notice *(give formal warning)*
impart momentum impel, incite
impart motion dispatch *(send off)*, impel
impart motion to agitate *(shake up)*
impart power to empower
impart thoughts converse
impart to notice *(give formal warning)*
impartation dispensation *(act of dispensing)*, donation, transmittal
imparted alleged
imparted in secret confidential
impartial discriminating *(judicious)*, dispassionate, equal, equitable, evenhanded, fair *(just)*, honest, judicial, juridical, just, liberal *(broad minded)*, neutral, nonpartisan, objective, open-minded, receptive, unbiased, unprejudiced. SEE MAIN ENTRY
impartial justice equity *(justice)*
impartiality disinterest *(lack of prejudice)*, fairness, honesty, justice, neutrality, objectivity, probity, rectitude
impartialness disinterest *(lack of prejudice)*

impartible contagious, indivisible, inseparable
imparting donative
imparting of skill education
imparting of thoughts conversation
impartment concession *(authorization),* delivery, dispensation *(act of dispensing),* donation, legacy
impassable difficult, impervious, impossible, impracticable, insurmountable
impasse deadlock, dilemma, draw *(tie),* halt, imbroglio, predicament, quagmire. SEE MAIN ENTRY
impassible insuperable
impassion foment, incite, inspire, spirit. SEE MAIN ENTRY
impassionable sensitive *(easily affected)*
impassioned eager, earnest, eloquent, fanatical, fervent, intense, perfervid, vehement, zealous
impassionedness ardor, life *(vitality)*
impassive callous, controlled *(restrained),* dispassionate, impervious, inexpressive, inscrutable, insusceptible *(uncaring),* nonchalant, phlegmatic, stoical, unaffected *(uninfluenced),* unresponsive
impassiveness indifference
impatience SEE MAIN ENTRY
impatient eager, fractious, hot-blooded, ill-judged, petulant, restive
impavidus undaunted
impeach accuse, blame, cite *(accuse),* condemn *(blame),* defame, denounce *(inform against),* depose *(remove),* disapprove *(condemn),* discharge *(dismiss),* except *(object),* fault, impugn, inform *(betray),* remove *(dismiss from office),* reprehend, reprimand, sully. SEE MAIN ENTRY
impeach falsely frame *(charge falsely)*
impeach unfairly frame *(charge falsely)*
impeach unjustly frame *(charge falsely)*
impeachability guilt. SEE MAIN ENTRY
impeachable blameful, blameworthy, reprehensible, unjustifiable
impeached accused *(charged)*
impeacher accuser, complainant, informer *(one providing criminal information)*
impeachment charge *(accusation),* condemnation *(blame),* disparagement, incrimination, reproach. SEE MAIN ENTRY
impeachment of virtue libel
impeccability rectitude
impeccable absolute *(ideal),* best, blameless, clean, honest, incorruptible, inculpable, irreprehensible, meritorious, not guilty, unblemished, unimpeachable. SEE MAIN ENTRY
impecuniosity bankruptcy, indigence, poverty, privation
impecunious bankrupt, destitute, insolvent, poor *(underprivileged).* SEE MAIN ENTRY
impecuniousness poverty, privation
impedance deterrent, offset
impede arrest *(stop),* balk, bar *(hinder),* bind *(restrain),* block, check *(restrain),* clog, condemn *(ban),* constrain *(restrain),* constrict *(inhibit),* contain *(restrain),* control *(restrain),* counter, curb, debar, defer *(put off),* delay, detain *(restrain),* deter, disadvantage, discommode, disrupt, encumber *(hinder),* enjoin, estop, fetter, fight *(counteract),* foil, forbid, forestall, halt, hamper, hinder, hold up *(delay),* inconvenience, inhibit, interdict, interfere, interpose, keep *(restrain),* limit, lock, obstruct, occlude, preclude, prevent, prohibit, repulse, stall, stave, stay *(halt),* stem *(check),* stop, thwart, toll *(stop),* trammel, withstand. SEE MAIN ENTRY
impede the progress of delay, hold up *(delay)*
impeded arrested *(checked),* disadvantaged, limited
impeder deterrent
impediment bar *(obstruction),* barrier, blockade *(barrier),* burden, censorship, check *(bar),* complication, constraint *(restriction),* damper *(stopper),* delay, deterrence, disadvantage, drawback, encumbrance, estoppel, fetter, filibuster, frustration, halt, handicap, hindrance, impasse, imposition *(excessive burden),* incumbrance *(burden),* interruption, obstacle, obstruction, onus *(burden),* predicament, prohibition, restraint, restriction. SEE MAIN ENTRY
impedimenta cargo, paraphernalia *(apparatus)*
impedimental preventive, unfavorable
impedimentary unfavorable
impedimentive unfavorable
impedimentum check *(bar),* encumbrance, handicap, hindrance, impediment, obstacle, obstruction, restraint
impeding limiting, preventive, prohibitive *(restrictive)*
impedire clog, embarrass, encumber *(financially obligate),* fetter, hamper, hinder, impede, incriminate, prevent
impedite balk, check *(restrain),* clog, disadvantage, hamper, obstruct
impedition bar *(obstruction),* check *(bar),* damper *(stopper),* deterrence, obstruction
impeditive preventive, restrictive. SEE MAIN ENTRY
impeditus difficult, impervious, labyrinthine
impel agitate *(activate),* bait *(harass),* bait *(lure),* cast *(throw),* coax, coerce, compel, constrain *(compel),* convince, dispatch *(send off),* enforce, entail, exact, exhort, further, impose *(enforce),* influence, inspire, motivate, necessitate, operate, persuade, press *(constrain),* prevail *(persuade),* prevail upon, prompt, provoke, send, spirit, stimulate, urge. SEE MAIN ENTRY
impel forward launch *(project)*
impelled bound
impellent impetus, impulsive *(impelling)*
impeller abettor, catalyst
impellere induce, influence, urge
impelling causative, coercion, compelling, decisive, force *(compulsion),* forcible, important *(urgent),* insistent, moving *(evoking emotion),* persuasive, potent, powerful, urgent
impelling force impetus, impulse
impelling power motive
impend menace, presage. SEE MAIN ENTRY
impendence threat
impendency threat
impendent immediate *(imminent),* imminent, proximate
impendere expend *(disburse),* imminent, impend, overlap
impending close *(near),* forthcoming, future, immediate *(imminent),* imminent, inevitable, instant, necessary *(inescapable),* pending *(imminent),* prospective, proximate, unavoidable *(inevitable).* SEE MAIN ENTRY
impendium expense *(cost)*
impenetrabilis impervious
impenetrability congealment, inviolability, opacity
impenetrable callous, cohesive *(compact),* complex, difficult, impervious, inapprehensible, incomprehensible, indefinable, inexplicable, inexpressive, inexpugnable, inscrutable, insurmountable, mysterious, opaque, recondite, solid *(compact).* SEE MAIN ENTRY
impenitent callous, incorrigible, recusant, relentless, remorseless
impensa cost *(price),* expense *(cost),* outlay
imperare order
imperative binding, canon, charge *(command),* compelling, compulsory, critical *(crucial),* crucial, decisive, decree, dictate, dictatorial, direction *(order),* directive, exigent, grave *(important),* important *(urgent),* indispensable, injunction, insistent, mandate, mandatory, necessary *(required),* necessity, obligatory, order *(judicial directive),* ordinance, positive *(prescribed),* pronouncement, requirement, requisite, subpoena, unavoidable *(inevitable),* urgent. SEE MAIN ENTRY
imperative duty allegiance, charge *(responsibility),* responsibility *(accountability)*
imperative request demand
imperativeness exigency, pressure
imperceptibility impalpability, indistinctness, nonappearance, opacity
imperceptible blind *(concealed),* impalpable, inappreciable, inconspicuous, indiscernible, indistinct, intangible, latent, negligible, obscure *(faint).* SEE MAIN ENTRY
imperceptive insensible, obtuse, opaque
impercipient insensible, lifeless *(dead),* obtuse
imperdible inexpugnable, tenable
imperfect bad *(inferior),* blemished, defective, deficient, dilapidated, errant, fallible, faulty, inchoate, incorrect, inexact, inferior *(lower in quality),* insufficient, marred, partial *(relating to a part),* peccable, perfunctory, poor *(inferior in quality),* unsatisfactory, unsound *(not strong),* vicious. SEE MAIN ENTRY
imperfection defect, deficiency, disadvantage, fault *(weakness),* flaw, foible, frailty, handicap, irregularity, vice. SEE MAIN ENTRY
imperfectness disadvantage, flaw, frailty
imperfectus defective, executory, imperfect
imperforate impervious
imperial sovereign *(absolute).* SEE MAIN ENTRY
imperil compromise *(endanger),* endanger, expose, jeopardize. SEE MAIN ENTRY
imperiled aleatory *(perilous)*
imperilment danger, hazard, jeopardy, menace, peril, risk
imperiosus dictatorial, impervious
imperious dictatorial, disdainful, dogmatic, influential, insolent, oppressive, orgulous, peremptory *(absolute),* peremptory *(imperative),* powerful, presumptuous, proud *(conceited),* relentless, strict, supercilious, tyrannous. SEE MAIN ENTRY
imperious commandant dictator
imperious direction dictate
imperishability indestructibility
imperishable constant, durable, indefeasible, indelible, indestructible, infallible, infinite, permanent, perpetual
imperitus inexperienced, unversed
imperium direction *(order),* dominion *(supreme authority),* fiat, injunction
imperium predominance

impermanence mortality
impermanent acting, ephemeral, interim, precarious, temporary, transient, transitory
impermanent fixture stopgap
impermeability congealment
impermeable cohesive *(compact)*, impervious, solid *(compact)*. SEE MAIN ENTRY
impermissible illegal, illegitimate *(illegal)*, illicit. SEE MAIN ENTRY
impermissibly illegally
impero imperative
impersonal clinical, dispassionate, impartial, neutral, objective, unbiased. SEE MAIN ENTRY
impersonality disinterest *(lack of prejudice)*, objectivity
impersonally fairly *(impartially)*. SEE MAIN ENTRY
impersonate assume *(simulate)*, copy, feign, mock *(imitate)*, pretend. SEE MAIN ENTRY
impersonation artifice, part *(role)*, role, sham
imperspicuity incoherence
imperspicuous allusive, equivocal, indefinite, nebulous, opaque, problematic, recondite, unclear
impersuadable impervious
impersuadible inflexible
impersuasible impervious, inflexible
impertinence contempt *(disobedience to the court)*, disrespect, inconsequence
impertinency inconsequence
impertinent brazen, collateral *(immaterial)*, contemptuous, extraneous, immaterial, inapplicable, inapposite, inappropriate, inconsequential, insolent, irrelative, irrelevant, obtrusive, offensive *(offending)*, peripheral, presumptuous, unfit, unsuitable. SEE MAIN ENTRY
impertire bestow, impart
imperturable placid
imperturbability composure, indifference
imperturbable callous, clinical, cold-blooded, controlled *(restrained)*, dispassionate, impervious, inexpressive, nonchalant, patient, peaceable, phlegmatic, stoical. SEE MAIN ENTRY
imperturbation composure, longanimity, sufferance
imperviable impervious
impervious callous, cold-blooded. SEE MAIN ENTRY
impervious impervious
impervious inexpressive, insuperable, insusceptible *(uncaring)*, obdurate, opaque, safe, torpid, unaffected *(uninfluenced)*
impervious to change durable
imperviousness resistance
impetrate call *(appeal to)*, importune, pray, press *(beseech)*, request
impetration call *(appeal)*, dun, entreaty, request
impetuosity dispatch *(promptness)*, inconsideration, outburst, passion, temerity
impetuous arbitrary and capricious, careless, disordered, impulsive *(rash)*, precipitate, reckless, spontaneous, uncontrollable, unexpected, vehement, zealous. SEE MAIN ENTRY
impetus assault
impetus boom *(prosperity)*, catalyst, determinant. SEE MAIN ENTRY
impetus force *(strength)*, impulse
impetus incentive, instigation, reason *(basis)*, stimulus
impietas profanity
impiety blasphemy, violation. SEE MAIN ENTRY
impiger active
impignorate guarantee, pawn, pledge *(deposit)*
impinge border *(bound)*, collide *(crash against)*, contact *(touch)*, encroach, infringe, invade, overlap, overstep. SEE MAIN ENTRY
impingement collision *(accident)*, encroachment
impingi impinge
impious diabolic, nefarious, offensive *(offending)*, peccant *(culpable)*, profane, sinister. SEE MAIN ENTRY
impious utterance blasphemy
impiousness blasphemy
impishness mischief
impius profane
implacabilis implacable, irreconcilable
implacability alienation *(estrangement)*, revenge, vengeance
implacable callous, cruel, immutable, inexorable, irreconcilable, malevolent, pertinacious, relentless, remorseless, resentful, ruthless, severe, unaffected *(uninfluenced)*, unbending, uncompromising, unrelenting, vindictive. SEE MAIN ENTRY
implacably opposed irreconcilable
implant educate, embed, enter *(insert)*, fix *(make firm)*, imbue, inculcate, infuse, initiate, inject, inseminate, instill, instruct *(teach)*, interject, pervade, plant *(place firmly)*
implant firmly establish *(entrench)*
implantation infusion, propaganda
implanted ingrained, internal, organic, situated. SEE MAIN ENTRY
implausibility improbability
implausible doubtful, incredible, ludicrous, unbelievable, untenable. SEE MAIN ENTRY
implead SEE MAIN ENTRY
implement appliance, consummate, device *(mechanism)*, discharge *(perform)*, dispatch *(dispose of)*, empower, enable, enforce, expedient, exploit *(make use of)*, facility *(instrumentality)*, instrument *(tool)*, instrumentality, operate, perpetrate, realize *(make real)*, tool. SEE MAIN ENTRY
implemental effective *(efficient)*, ministerial, practical
implementation act *(undertaking)*, action *(performance)*, building *(business of assembling)*, campaign, commission *(act)*, course, discharge *(performance)*, enforcement, fait accompli, finality, fruition, performance *(execution)*, realization. SEE MAIN ENTRY
implements paraphernalia *(apparatus)*
implere fulfill
impletion plethora
impliant unyielding
implicare hamper, implicate, incriminate
implicate accuse, arraign, blame, cite *(accuse)*, complain *(charge)*, condemn *(blame)*, denigrate, denounce *(inform against)*, impeach, incriminate, indict, inform *(betray)*, present *(prefer charges)*. SEE MAIN ENTRY
implicate falsely frame *(charge falsely)*
implicate oneself acknowledge *(declare)*
implicate unfairly frame *(charge falsely)*
implicate unjustly frame *(charge falsely)*
implicated complex, incident, related
implicating incriminatory, inculpatory
implicatio complication, embarrassment, entanglement *(involvement)*, involution
implication affiliation *(connectedness)*, attribution, blame *(responsibility)*, caveat, condemnation *(blame)*, connotation, content *(meaning)*, context, deduction *(conclusion)*, entanglement *(involvement)*, gist *(substance)*, hint, incrimination, inculpation, indicant, indication, inference, innuendo, insinuation, intimation, main point, mention *(reference)*, nuance, reference *(allusion)*, referral, signification, suggestion. SEE MAIN ENTRY
implicational allusive, circumstantial, leading *(guiding)*
implicative allusive, circumstantial, constructive *(inferential)*, incriminatory, inculpatory, leading *(guiding)*, suggestive *(evocative)*. SEE MAIN ENTRY
implicatory circumstantial, constructive *(inferential)*, incriminatory, inculpatory, leading *(guiding)*
implicit assumed *(inferred)*, constructive *(inferential)*, essential *(inherent)*, implied, indirect, inherent, intrinsic *(belonging)*, peremptory *(absolute)*, tacit, virtual. SEE MAIN ENTRY
implicit belief credence, faith
implicit confidence faith
implied constructive *(inferential)*, implicit, subtle *(insidious)*, tacit. SEE MAIN ENTRY
implied assent connivance
implied consent acquiescence
implied in law constructive *(inferential)*
implied indication innuendo, reference *(allusion)*
implied rather than expressly stated implicit
implode SEE MAIN ENTRY
implorare invoke, petition, request
imploratio prayer
imploration call *(appeal)*, entreaty, prayer, request
imploratory precatory
implore call *(appeal to)*, exhort, importune, invoke, petition, pray, press *(beseech)*, pressure, request, solicit, sue, urge. SEE MAIN ENTRY
imploring precatory
imply allude, bear *(adduce)*, bespeak, connote, denote, evidence, hint, indicate, infer, purport, signify *(denote)*. SEE MAIN ENTRY
impolicy misrule
impolite disorderly, impertinent *(insolent)*, insolent, perverse, presumptuous, uncouth
impoliteness disregard *(lack of respect)*, disrespect
impolitic detrimental, disadvantageous, ill-advised, imprudent, inadvisable, inappropriate, inapt, inept *(inappropriate)*, injudicious, misadvised, unpolitic. SEE MAIN ENTRY
impolitical injudicious
impoliticness indiscretion
imponderable intangible. SEE MAIN ENTRY
imponderous imponderable
imponere impose *(enforce)*, inflict
imporous impervious
import allude, amount *(result)*, bespeak, connotation, consequence *(significance)*, content *(meaning)*, context, corpus, degree *(magnitude)*, gist *(substance)*, implication *(inference)*, importance, interest *(concern)*, magnitude, main point, materiality *(consequence)*, meaning, point *(purpose)*, prestige, significance, signification, stress

(accent), substance (essential nature), tenor, weight (importance). SEE MAIN ENTRY
importance authority (power), caliber (quality), clout, concern (interest), consequence (significance), corpus, degree (magnitude), distinction (reputation), dominance, eminence, emphasis, force (strength), hegemony, import, influence, interest (concern), magnitude, materiality (consequence), power, precedence, prestige, primacy, priority, relevance, reputation, significance, signification, status, stress (accent), supremacy, value, worth. SEE MAIN ENTRY
important consequential (substantial), considerable, constructive (creative), critical (crucial), crucial, decisive, determinative, essential (required), exigent, famous, germane, illustrious, indispensable, influential, key, major, momentous, necessary (required), notable, noteworthy, outstanding (prominent), peremptory (imperative), potent, powerful, predominant, primary, prime (most valuable), prominent, relevant, remarkable, renowned, requisite, salient, serious (grave), special, strategic, substantial, substantive, unusual, urgent, valuable, vital. SEE MAIN ENTRY
important event highlight
important feature main point
important part center (essence), main point
important point gist (ground for a suit), main point
important station eminence
importation inflow
imported alien (foreign)
importunate important (urgent), insistent, obligatory, precatory, urgent
importunateness pressure
importune annoy, badger, bait (harass), bait (lure), cajole, call (appeal to), dun, exhort, harry (harass), insist, inveigle, persuade, plead (implore), pray, press (beseech), prevail upon, request, solicit, urge. SEE MAIN ENTRY
importunitas intrusion
importunity call (appeal), dun, entreaty, prayer, request
impose bind (obligate), charge (assess), coerce, command, compel, constrain (compel), decree, demand, detail (assign), encumber (hinder), enforce, enjoin, exact, foist, force (coerce), impinge, impose (intrude), inflict, infringe, insist, intrude, levy, necessitate, obtrude, order, perpetrate, prescribe, press (constrain), require (compel). SEE MAIN ENTRY
impose a ban censor, enjoin, exclude. SEE MAIN ENTRY
impose a charge assess (tax), encumber (financially obligate)
impose a duty compel, constrain (compel), delegate, enjoin, exact, instruct (direct), order
impose a duty on excise (levy a tax)
impose a fine mulct (fine)
impose a forfeiture fine
impose a levy assess (tax)
impose a lien encumber (financially obligate)
impose a mulct fine
impose a penalty condemn (punish), demote, discipline (punish), fine, penalize. SEE MAIN ENTRY
impose a penalty on convict
impose a task enjoin, instruct (direct), order
impose a tax exact
impose an order dictate
impose by fraud foist
impose difficulties discourage
impose hardship inconvenience
impose payment for misconduct fine
impose pecuniary punishment fine
impose penalty condemn (punish), sentence
impose punishment inflict
impose restraint fetter
impose restrictions coerce, constrain (restrain)
impose upon accroach, discommode, mishandle (maltreat)
impose with authority enjoin
imposed indispensable, necessary (required), obligatory, positive (prescribed)
imposed upon aggrieved (victimized)
imposing critical (crucial), important (significant), major, moving (evoking emotion), outstanding (prominent), prominent, proud (self-respecting), remarkable, salient, solemn, special
imposing a condition conditional, dependent
imposing building edifice
imposition ad valorem, assessment (levy), burden, canon, charge (command), compulsion (coercion), conviction (finding of guilt), deception, demand, disadvantage, duty (tax), encroachment, encumbrance, enforcement, excise, fiat, force (compulsion), forgery, hoax, incumbrance (lien), infliction, injustice, intrusion, misjudgment, nuisance, requirement, sanction (punishment), tax. SEE MAIN ENTRY
imposition of veil of secrecy censorship
impossibility impasse, improbability. SEE MAIN ENTRY
impossible impracticable, incredible, infeasible, insufferable, insuperable, insurmountable, intolerable, ludicrous, prohibitive (restrictive), unacceptable, unattainable, unendurable. SEE MAIN ENTRY
impossible task impasse
impossible to alter ironclad
impossible to better irremediable
impossible to break ironclad
impossible to calculate imponderable
impossible to change ironclad, irreversible, irrevocable
impossible to defeat invincible
impossible to describe ineffable
impossible to explain indefinable
impossible to express ineffable
impossible to influence obdurate
impossible to measure imponderable
impossible to overcome irresistible
impossible to reach inaccessible
impossible to resist irresistible
impossible to reverse irreversible
impossible to stop perpetual
impossible to translate indefinable
impossible to understand inapprehensible, incomprehensible, indefinable, inscrutable
impossible to vanquish invincible
impossible to weigh imponderable
impossible to withstand irresistible
impossibleness impossibility
impost assessment (levy), duty (tax), excise, excise (levy a tax), levy, tariff (duties), tax, toll (tax)
imposter fake
impostor sham
impostrous deceptive
imposture artifice, deception, false pretense, falsification, forgery, hoax, hypocrisy, ruse, sham, subterfuge. SEE MAIN ENTRY
impotence desuetude, detriment, disability (physical inability), fault (weakness), frailty, impuissance, inability, inaction, incapacity, inefficacy, languor, prostration. SEE MAIN ENTRY
impotency defect, disability (physical inability), impotence
impotens powerless, uncontrollable
impotent barren, devoid, disabled (deprived of legal right), disabled (made incapable), expendable, harmless, helpless (powerless), inadept, inadequate, ineffective, ineffectual, inept (incompetent), insipid, languid, null (invalid), null and void, otiose, powerless, unable, unavailing, unproductive. SEE MAIN ENTRY
impound annex (arrogate), attach (seize), commit (institutionalize), condemn (seize), confine, confiscate, constrain (imprison), contain (restrain), deprive, detain (hold in custody), distrain, enclose, garnish, immure, impress (procure by force), jail, lock, restrain, seize (confiscate), sequester (seize property). SEE MAIN ENTRY
impoundage attachment (seizure), distraint, distress (seizure), sequestration, taking
impounded attached (seized)
impounding condemnation (seizure), confiscatory
impoundment appropriation (taking), attachment (seizure), bondage, captivity, commitment (confinement), constraint (imprisonment), custody (incarceration), detention, distraint, distress (seizure), enclosure, garnishment, incarceration, sequestration, taking
impoverish deplete, depreciate, deprive, despoil, plunder, spend
impoverished bankrupt, deficient, destitute, impecunious, insolvent, penurious, poor (underprivileged)
impoverishment dearth, indigence, poverty
impower delegate
impracticability impossibility
impracticable impossible, infeasible, insuperable, insurmountable, otiose, quixotic, unattainable. SEE MAIN ENTRY
impractical hot-blooded, impracticable, otiose, quixotic, speculative, theoretical, unattainable.
impracticality impossibility
imprecation contempt (disdain), expletive, malediction, slander. SEE MAIN ENTRY
imprecation of evil blasphemy
imprecative calumnious, profane
imprecatory calumnious, profane
imprecise approximate, equivocal, faulty, inaccurate, incorrect, indefinite, inexact, lax, liberal (not literal), slipshod, vague. SEE MAIN ENTRY
imprecise statement generalization
imprecision generality (vague statement), laxity, misstatement
impregnability incontestability, inviolability, security (safety), strength
impregnable defensible, immune, inappealable, incontestable, indomitable, inexpugnable, insuperable, insurmountable, powerful, safe, secure (free from danger), tenable, unapproachable. SEE MAIN ENTRY
impregnate infuse, inject, inseminate, penetrate, permeate, pervade, plant (place firmly)

impregnation infusion
imprescriptible indefeasible, unalienable
impress abduct, affect, attach *(seize),* brand, brand *(mark),* capture, coerce, confiscate, convince, copy, distrain, distress *(seizure),* dwell *(linger over),* embed, hijack, hold up *(rob),* inculcate, induct, influence, kidnap, overwhelm, persuade, reach, seize *(confiscate),* sequester *(seize property),* specialty *(distinctive mark),* stamp. SEE MAIN ENTRY
impress by repeated statement inculcate
impress on insist
impress upon the memory instruct *(teach),* retain *(keep in possession)*
impress upon the mind discipline *(train),* imbue, inculcate, instill, instruct *(teach)*
impress with mark seal *(solemnize)*
impressed with oneself inflated *(vain)*
impressibility credulity, sensibility
impressible open *(persuasible),* perceptive, pliant, receptive, sensitive *(easily affected),* sequacious, susceptible *(responsive),* yielding
impression apprehension *(perception),* assumption *(supposition),* color *(deceptive appearance),* complexion, concept, conviction *(persuasion),* copy, estimate *(idea),* fingerprints, idea, inference, notion, opinion *(belief),* pattern, perception, perspective, reaction *(response),* reflection *(image),* sense *(feeling),* stamp, suspicion *(uncertainty).* SEE MAIN ENTRY
impression of fingers fingerprints
impressionable amenable, facile, malleable, open *(persuasible),* perceptive, pliable, pliant, receptive, sensitive *(easily affected),* sequacious, susceptible *(responsive),* tractable, yielding
impressive considerable, eloquent, forcible, important *(significant),* influential, major, momentous, moving *(evoking emotion),* notable, noteworthy, outstanding *(prominent),* persuasive, potent, prodigious *(amazing),* profound *(intense),* proud *(self-respecting),* remarkable, sapid, solemn, stellar. SEE MAIN ENTRY
impressive effect pretense *(ostentation)*
impressiveness emphasis, solemnity, weight *(credibility),* weight *(importance)*
impressment abduction, attachment *(seizure),* compulsion *(coercion),* distress *(seizure),* duress, force *(compulsion),* levy, sequestration
imprest loan
imprimatur charter *(license),* leave *(permission),* license. SEE MAIN ENTRY
imprint brand, brand *(mark),* caption, copy, embed, fingerprints, impression, inculcate, inscribe, label, seal *(solemnize),* stamp, trademark
imprison arrest *(apprehend),* capture, commit *(institutionalize),* confine, contain *(restrain),* detain *(hold in custody),* enclose, immure, jail, lock, restrain, seclude, seize *(apprehend),* sentence, transport. SEE MAIN ENTRY
imprison again remand
imprisoned arrested *(apprehended),* in custody
imprisoned person captive
imprisonment apprehension *(act of arresting),* arrest, bondage, captivity, commitment *(confinement),* custody *(incarceration),* detention, enclosure, fetter, incarceration, restraint. SEE MAIN ENTRY
improbability doubt *(indecision),* doubt *(suspicion).* SEE MAIN ENTRY
improbable disputable, doubtful, implausible, impossible, incredible, unbelievable, unforeseeable, unsound *(fallacious).* SEE MAIN ENTRY
improbare impugn
improbatio disapproval
improbation bad repute, exception *(objection),* reprimand
improbitas dishonesty
improbity attaint, bad faith, bad repute, bribery, contempt *(disobedience to the court),* corruption, culpability, delinquency *(misconduct),* dishonesty, dishonor *(nonpayment),* dishonor *(shame),* disloyalty, fraud, guilt, hypocrisy, indirection *(deceitfulness),* injustice, misdemeanor, misdoing, racket, wrong. SEE MAIN ENTRY
improbus bad *(offensive),* dishonest, incorrect, iniquitous
improficient incompetent, libelous
impromptu impulsive *(rash),* spontaneous, unexpected, unpremeditated. SEE MAIN ENTRY
improper bad *(offensive),* blatant *(obtrusive),* culpable, delinquent *(guilty of a misdeed),* disgraceful, disorderly, disreputable, drastic, false *(inaccurate),* faulty, illegal, illegitimate *(illegal),* illicit, immoral, impertinent *(insolent),* inaccurate, inadmissible, inapplicable, inapposite, inappropriate, inapt, incongruous, incorrect, inelegant, ineligible, inept *(inappropriate),* iniquitous, lascivious, nefarious, objectionable, perverse, profane, slipshod, suggestive *(risqué),* unauthorized, unbecoming, undesirable, undue *(excessive),* unfit, unjust, unprofessional, unseemly, unsuitable, untimely, unwarranted, vicious, wrongful. SEE MAIN ENTRY
improper act tortious act
improper action impropriety, misfeasance
improper behavior impropriety, misdeed
improper conduct guilt, misconduct
improper jurisdiction want of jurisdiction
improper performance misfeasance
improper professional action malpractice
improper professional conduct malpractice
improper rate of interest usurious
improper usage abuse *(corrupt practice),* misusage, misuse
improper use abuse *(corrupt practice),* misapplication, misusage, misuse
improper venue SEE MAIN ENTRY
improperly illegally
improperly proportioned disproportionate
improperness ill repute, irregularity
impropriate condemn *(seize),* hold *(possess),* impress *(procure by force),* preempt. SEE MAIN ENTRY
impropriation appropriation *(taking),* arrogation, assignment *(transfer of ownership),* assumption *(seizure),* condemnation *(seizure),* disseisin, distress *(seizure)*
impropriety bad repute, breach, delinquency *(misconduct),* fault *(mistake),* ill repute, illegality, incongruity, indecency, misapplication, misconduct, miscue, misdeed, misdemeanor, misdoing, misusage, obscenity, offense. SEE MAIN ENTRY
improvable corrigible
improve accrue *(increase),* ameliorate, amend, appreciate *(increase),* cultivate, cure, develop, edify, edit, elevate, embellish, emend, enhance, fix *(repair),* gain, heighten *(augment),* help, inure *(benefit),* meliorate, modify *(alter),* mollify, nurture, profit, progress, rectify, redress, reform, rehabilitate, relieve *(give aid),* remedy, renew *(refurbish),* renovate, repair, restore *(renew),* revise, supplement, treat *(remedy).* SEE MAIN ENTRY
improve upon elaborate, fix *(repair),* modify *(alter),* surpass
improved relations rapprochement, reconciliation
improved version correction *(change),* revision *(corrected version)*
improvement advance *(increase),* advantage, amendment *(correction),* augmentation, behalf, benefit *(betterment),* boom *(increase),* boom *(prosperity),* correction *(change),* development *(progression),* edification, growth *(evolution),* headway, panacea, profit, progress, promotion *(advancement),* reform, rehabilitation, renewal, reorganization, repair, revision *(corrected version),* revival. SEE MAIN ENTRY
improvement of the mind education
improvement-minded progressive *(advocating change)*
improvidence disregard *(unconcern),* inconsideration, laches, laxity, neglect, negligence, temerity, waste
improvident careless, derelict *(negligent),* heedless, imprudent, injudicious, lax, negligent, prodigal, profligate *(extravagant),* profuse, reckless, remiss, thoughtless, unpolitic. SEE MAIN ENTRY
improvidus improvident
improving beneficial, constructive *(creative)*
improvisate unpremeditated
improvisation invention
improvisatorial spontaneous
improvise compose, conjure, contrive, create, devise *(invent),* invent *(produce for the first time),* make, originate, scheme. SEE MAIN ENTRY
improvised ad hoc, impulsive *(rash),* spontaneous, unpremeditated
improvisus unanticipated
imprudence disregard *(unconcern),* impropriety, inconsideration, indiscretion, inexpedience, neglect, negligence, res ipsa loquitur, temerity. SEE MAIN ENTRY
imprudens impolitic, improvident, inadvertent, thoughtless
imprudent careless, heedless, hot-blooded, ill-advised, ill-judged, impolitic, improvident, impulsive *(rash),* inadvisable, inept *(inappropriate),* injudicious, irrational, lax, misadvised, negligent, precipitate, prodigal, reckless, remiss, thoughtless, unpolitic, unprofessional, unsuitable, untimely. SEE MAIN ENTRY
imprudentia ignorance
impudence contempt *(disobedience to the court),* defiance, disregard *(lack of respect),* disrespect, temerity. SEE MAIN ENTRY
impudency defiance
impudens brazen, flagrant, insolent, unabashed
impudent brazen, contemptuous, impertinent *(insolent),* insolent, offensive *(offending),* perverse, presumptuous
impudentia indiscretion

impudicity debauchery
impudicus lewd, licentious, wanton
impugn answer *(reply)*, attack, bear false witness, blame, brand *(stigmatize)*, censure, condemn *(blame)*, contend *(dispute)*, contest, contradict, contravene, criticize *(find fault with)*, demonstrate *(protest)*, denounce *(condemn)*, deprecate, disaccord, disaffirm, disallow, disapprove *(condemn)*, disown *(deny the validity)*, dispute *(contest)*, doubt *(distrust)*, except *(object)*, fault, gainsay, impeach, inveigh, lash *(attack verbally)*, malign, negate, protest, refute, reject, reprehend, reprimand, resist *(oppose)*, sully. SEE MAIN ENTRY
impugn a witness SEE MAIN ENTRY
impugnare impugn
impugnation bad repute, belligerency, contest *(dispute)*, controversy *(argument)*, disparagement, dispute, exception *(objection)*, opposition. SEE MAIN ENTRY
impugning negative
impugnment belligerency, contest *(dispute)*, impugnation, opposition, vilification
impuissance fault *(weakness)*, impotence, inability, incapacity. SEE MAIN ENTRY
impuissant incapable, null *(insignificant)*, powerless
impulse catalyst, cause *(reason)*, desire, impetus, incentive, motive, passion, stimulus. SEE MAIN ENTRY
impulsio impulse
impulsion impetus, impulse, incentive, instigation, provocation
impulsive careless, heedless, improvident, imprudent, precipitate, reckless, spontaneous, thoughtless, unexpected, unpremeditated, vehement. SEE MAIN ENTRY
impulsiveness inconsideration
impulsus impulse
impunitas impunity
impunity condonation, tolerance. SEE MAIN ENTRY
impure bad *(inferior)*, blemished, disreputable, dissolute, immoral, lewd, licentious, marred, obscene, profane, prurient, salacious, tainted *(contaminated)*, vicious. SEE MAIN ENTRY
impure air air pollution
impurity vice
impurus lascivious, lewd
imputable blameful, guilty
imputation accusation, allegation, aspersion, assignation, attaint, attribution, blame *(responsibility)*, charge *(accusation)*, condemnation *(blame)*, conjecture, count, criticism, defamation, disapprobation, discredit, disgrace, dishonor *(shame)*, disparagement, ignominy, incrimination, inculpation, innuendo, notoriety, onus *(stigma)*, opprobrium, presentment, reference *(allusion)*, scandal, stigma. SEE MAIN ENTRY
imputation from criminal proceeding arraignment
imputation of blame accusation
imputation of dereliction impeachment
imputation of fault impeachment
imputation of wrongdoing incrimination
imputative calumnious, incriminatory, inculpatory
impute ascribe, attribute, charge *(accuse)*, cite *(accuse)*, complain *(charge)*, denounce *(inform against)*, fault, implicate, present *(prefer charges)*. SEE MAIN ENTRY
impute fault to impeach
impute guilt to incriminate
impute shame to discredit, disgrace, pillory
impute to blame
imputed accused *(attacked)*, alleged
imputing blame incriminatory, inculpatory
in herein
in a body en banc
in a certain sense quasi
in a different class peculiar *(distinctive)*
in a dilemma doubtful
in a fair manner fairly *(impartially)*
in a huff resentful
in a line consecutive
in a manner quasi
in a mass en banc
in a quandary doubtful
in a row consecutive
in a state of action active
in a state of uncertainty contingent, indeterminate, pending *(unresolved)*, provisional
in abeyance back *(in arrears)*, dormant, pending *(unresolved)*
in accord commensurate, concerted, concordant, concurrent *(united)*, congruous, consenting, consonant, contractual
in accord with pursuant to
in accord with ethics ethical
in accordance therefore consequently
in accordance with apposite, concerted, congruous, contractual, in strict conformity, pursuant to. SEE MAIN ENTRY
in accordance with conventional requirements formal
in accordance with duty right *(correct)*
in accordance with justice right *(correct)*
in accordance with law de jure, legitimate *(rightful)*
in accordance with legal provisions legitimate *(rightful)*
in accordance with morality right *(correct)*
in accordance with the contract as agreed upon
in accordance with the law juridical, lawful, licit
in accordance with the ordinance de jure
in accordance with the rules for right conduct ethical
in accordance with the standards of a profession ethical
in accordance with the statute de jure
in accordance with truth right *(correct)*
in action effective *(operative)*, functional, operative
in actual process active
in addition also, ancillary *(auxiliary)*, further. SEE MAIN ENTRY
in advance vanward
in agreement commensurate, concerted, concordant, concurrent *(united)*, consensual, consenting, consonant, synergetic. SEE MAIN ENTRY
in album register
in alienum fundum ingredi trespass
in all in toto
in all cases invariably
in all likelihood high probability. SEE MAIN ENTRY
in all respects in toto, purely *(positively)*, wholly. SEE MAIN ENTRY
in alliance concerted, conjoint, consensual
in any case notwithstanding, regardless
in any event notwithstanding, regardless
in arms armed
in arrears deficient, delinquent *(overdue)*, due *(owed)*, indebted, insolvent, outstanding *(unpaid)*, overdue, past due, receivable, unpaid. SEE MAIN ENTRY
in assembly en masse
in attendance present *(attendant)*
in authority ex officio
in bad taste inappropriate, inelegant, unbecoming, unseemly, unsuitable
in behalf of one party ex parte
in being extant
in between SEE MAIN ENTRY
in black and white holographic, in writing
in bold relief clear *(apparent)*, conspicuous, manifest, perceptible
in camera SEE MAIN ENTRY
in carcerem imprison, jail
in chaos disordered
in character typical
in charge ex officio
in check controlled *(restrained)*
in chief a fortiori
in close proximity close *(near)*, contiguous, proximate
in clover prosperous
in cogitatione defixus pensive
in common conjoint, mutual *(collective)*
in common boundaries with contiguous
in common with cognate
in company with along
in compensation compensatory
in competition competitive *(antagonistic)*
in concert concordant, simultaneous
in conclusion consequently. SEE MAIN ENTRY
in concord consonant, synergetic
in conflict dissenting
in conflict with contra *(adverb)*, contra *(preposition)*
in conformity contractual
in conformity to the law juridical, lawful
in conformity with law legal
in conjunction concordant, conjoint
in conjunction with along, apposite
in connection with comparative, incident
in consequence a priori
in consequence of thereby
in consideration of ad hoc
in consonance pari materia
in conspiracy with SEE MAIN ENTRY
in contact contiguous
in contemplation at issue
in contrast to contra
in control ex officio
in correspondence with the contract as agreed upon
in current use extant
in custodiam imprison, jail
in custodiam dare arrest *(apprehend)*
in custody guarded. SEE MAIN ENTRY
in danger helpless *(defenseless)*, liable, susceptible *(unresistent)*
in darkness blind *(sightless)*
in debt indebted, past due
in decadence decadent
in decline decadent
in default insufficient, past due
in default of devoid
in defiance of the law lawless
in demand important *(urgent)*, popular, requisite, valuable

in despair despondent, disconsolate
in disagreement different, discordant, dissenting
in disarray disjointed, disordered
in discrimen endanger
in disgrace disreputable
in disguise evasive
in disorder anomalous, deranged, disjointed
in dispute arguable, at issue, controversial, debatable, disputable, doubtful, dubious, litigable, moot
in distress penurious, poor *(underprivileged)*
in doubt disputable, doubtful, dubious, dubitative, indefinite, indeterminate, leery
in dubio esse abeyance
in due course SEE MAIN ENTRY
in due form pro forma
in easy circumstances prosperous
in effect constructive *(inferential)*, effective *(operative)*, operative. SEE MAIN ENTRY
in embarrassed circumstances poor *(underprivileged)*
in equal shares pro rata
in equilibrium coextensive
in error at fault, culpable, delinquent *(guilty of a misdeed)*, fallacioadmit *(give access)*, cause, commence, constitute *(establish)*, create, embark, establish *(launch)*, generate, induct, initiate, instate, invest *(vest)*, launch *(initiate)*, originate, preface
in every respect faithfully
in evidence clear *(apparent)*, coherent *(clear)*, conspicuous, evident, manifest, obvious, palpable, perceivable, perceptible
in exact agreement commensurate
in existence conscious *(awake)*, corporeal, de facto, extant
in extremis SEE MAIN ENTRY
in fact actual, de facto
in fashion current
in fault blameworthy, delinquent *(guilty of a misdeed)*
in favor popular
in favor of in furtherance
in focus manifest, visible *(in full view)*
in force effective *(operative)*, operative
in front vanward
in full in toto
in full effect in full force
in full force undiminished. SEE MAIN ENTRY
in full gear SEE MAIN ENTRY
in full view distinct *(clear)*, evident, manifest, open *(in sight)*, overt, patent, perceivable, perceptible, visible *(in full view)*
in furtherance SEE MAIN ENTRY
in genera describere classify
in general as a rule, generally. SEE MAIN ENTRY
in good faith bona fide, faithfully. SEE MAIN ENTRY
in good financial condition solvent
in good order intact
in good spirits sanguine
in good taste elegant
in good time in due course
in harmony concordant, consonant, pari material. SEE MAIN ENTRY
in harmony with congruous, consenting, pursuant to. SEE MAIN ENTRY
in harness operative, ready *(prepared)*
in heavy spirits disconsolate
in high dudgeon resentful
in high esteem popular
in high favor popular
in hysterics disordered
in installments in part, piecemeal
in issue debatable, disputable, moot
in its entirety in toto
in its infancy ab initio, inchoate
in its present condition as is
in its present form as is
in its present state as is
in iudicium venire appear *(attend court proceedings)*
in ius vocare implead
in keeping fit
in keeping with in strict conformity
in league conjoint
in lieu of SEE MAIN ENTRY
in light of SEE MAIN ENTRY
in line with in strict conformity
in loco apposite
in longhand holographic
in margine positus marginal
in margine scriptus marginal
in mass en masse
in memory of honorary
in most cases as a rule, generally
in most instances high probability
in name only nominal, purported, quasi
in narrow circumstances poor *(underprivileged)*
in nature is consist
in need impecunious, penurious, poor *(underprivileged)*
in obedience to the agreement as agreed upon
in obedience with in strict conformity
in office ex officio
in one piece intact
in one's last moments in extremis
in one's own person in person
in operation active, effective *(operative)*, functional, operative
in opposition hostile
in opposition to contra *(adverb)*, contra *(preposition)*, contrary
in order consecutive, functional, ready *(prepared)*, systematic
in part SEE MAIN ENTRY
in partnership common *(shared)*
in passage en route
in penury poor *(underprivileged)*
in perfect condition intact
in periculum endanger, jeopardize
in perpetuum ratus indefeasible
in person SEE MAIN ENTRY
in pinched circumstances poor *(underprivileged)*
in place felicitous, fit
in place of in lieu of
in place of a parent loco parentis
in plain sight conspicuous, overt, perceivable, perceptible, visible *(in full view)*
in plain view naked *(perceptible)*. SEE MAIN ENTRY
in play operative
in point congruous, exemplary
in point of fact de facto
in position ready *(prepared)*
in posse colorable *(plausible)*
in practice active, constructive *(inferential)*
in print holographic
in prison in custody
in process instant
in profusion copious
in progress en route
in proportion pro rata
in proportion to comparative
in prospect prospective
in question aleatory *(uncertain)*, arguable, at issue, controversial, debatable, disputable, doubtful, dubious, moot, pending *(unresolved)*
in rapport concordant, congruous, consonant
in re commorari dwell *(linger over)*
in re connivere connive
in re stare adhere *(persist)*
in re versari occupy *(engage)*
in readiness ready *(prepared)*
in reality de facto
in receivership bankrupt
in reduced circumstances poor *(underprivileged)*
in regard to which wherein
in regular order consecutive
in relation to comparative, incident
in relation with apposite, comparative
in residence household *(domestic)*
in respect to comparative
in safety secure *(free from danger)*
in se recipere undertake
in sequence consecutive
in set form pro forma
in sight apparent *(perceptible)*, discernible, evident, manifest, perceivable, perceptible, visible *(in full view)*
in small amount remote *(small)*
in small doses piecemeal
in small quantities piecemeal
in solido SEE MAIN ENTRY
in solitude alone *(solitary)*
in some measure in part
in spite of irrespective, notwithstanding, regardless
in store forthcoming, imminent, in-evitable, prospective
in straitened circumstances impecunious, poor *(underprivileged)*
in strict compliance with in strict conformity
in strict conformity SEE MAIN ENTRY
in strong relief clear *(apparent)*
in style current
in substance is consist
in sum en banc
in suspense dormant, doubtful, outstanding *(unresolved)*
in tabulas referre record
in tempus provisional
in terrorem SEE MAIN ENTRY
in that case consequently
in that event consequently
in the absence of devoid
in the aggregate en masse, in toto, wholly
in the area close *(near)*
in the background clandestine
in the beginning ab initio
in the blood born *(innate)*
in the clear clean
in the company of present *(attendant)*
in the course of ad interim, throughout *(during)*
in the eyes of the law de jure
in the fad current
in the field of public debate forensic
in the final moments of life in extremis
in the first place ab initio
in the foreground conspicuous, manifest
in the general time frame on or about
in the habit addicted
in the habit of accustomed *(familiarized)*
in the hands of receivers bankrupt
in the heat of SEE MAIN ENTRY
in the immediate vicinity of on or about
in the interest of one party ex parte

in the interim ad interim
in the intervening time ad interim
in the jaws of death in extremis
in the lead vanward
in the limelight famous
in the long run in due course
in the main a fortiori, as a rule, generally, wholly
in the market commercial
in the mass wholly
in the meantime ad interim
in the meanwhile ad interim
in the middle of among
in the name of in furtherance
in the neighborhood close *(near)*
in the neighborhood of on or about
in the offing immediate *(imminent)*, imminent, inevitable
in the opposite scale contradictory
in the past heretofore
in the power of inferior *(lower in position)*
in the presence of present *(attendant)*
in the public eye famous
in the red impecunious
in the same category cognate, comparative
in the same way as is
in the same words verbatim
in the service of in furtherance
in the spotlight famous
in the usual course of things as a rule, generally
in the vicinity close *(near)*, present *(attendant)*
in the vicinity of approximate
in the whole in toto
in the wind imminent
in the wrong blameful, blameworthy, culpable, delinquent *(guilty of a misdeed)*, guilty
in the wrong place anomalous
in time in due course
in toto en banc
in toto wholly. SEE MAIN ENTRY
in transit en route
in tribute honorary
in trust SEE MAIN ENTRY
in truth purely *(positively)*
in turn consecutive, respectively
in two bipartite
in unbroken sequence consecutive
in uninterrupted succession consecutive
in unison concerted, concordant, concurrent *(united)*, consonant
in unison with congruous
in unum vergere converge
in view apparent *(perceptible)*, conspicuous, evident, immediate *(imminent)*, imminent, manifest, obvious, patent, perceivable, perceptible, present *(attendant)*, present *(current)*, prospective, visible *(in full view)*
in violation of deviant
in violation of law felonious, illegally
in vogue current, popular, prevailing *(current)*
in want impecunious, penurious, poor *(underprivileged)*
in want of devoid
in which case consequently
in whole in solido
in working order ready *(prepared)*
in writing documentary, holographic. SEE MAIN ENTRY
in-depth analysis proposal *(report)*, trial *(experiment)*

inability abortion *(fiasco)*, disability *(physical inability)*, disqualification *(factor that disqualifies)*, failure *(falling short)*, impairment *(drawback)*, impotence, impuissance, incapacity, inefficacy. SEE MAIN ENTRY
inability of performance frustration
inability to accept incredulity
inability to act inertia, insentience
inability to be completed frustration
inability to believe incredulity
inability to decide doubt *(indecision)*, indecision
inability to doubt certainty
inability to maintain solvency failure *(bankruptcy)*
inability to meet financial obligations failure *(bankruptcy)*
inability to pay bankruptcy, delinquency *(shortage)*, dishonor *(nonpayment)*
inability to perceive insentience
inability to wait dispatch *(promptness)*, haste
inability to work disability *(physical inability)*
inabstinence indulgence
inabstinent gluttonous, inordinate, intemperate
inaccessibility impossibility, unavailability
inaccessible immune, impervious, impossible, infeasible, insuperable, insurmountable, private *(secluded)*, remote *(secluded)*, unapproachable, unattainable. SEE MAIN ENTRY
inaccessus inaccessible
inaccordance controversy *(argument)*, difference, discrepancy
inaccordant discordant, dissident, inapposite, inapt, incommensurate, incongruous, inept *(inappropriate)*, repugnant *(incompatible)*
inaccuracy error, exaggeration, fallacy, falsehood, fault *(mistake)*, figment, laxity, misestimation, misjudgment, misrepresentation, misstatement, story *(falsehood)*. SEE MAIN ENTRY
inaccurate erroneous, fallacious, faulty, ill-founded, improper, incorrect, inexact, lax, slipshod, untrue. SEE MAIN ENTRY
inaccurateness misestimation, misjudgment
inacquiescent dissident, hostile, nonconsenting, reluctant
inaction abeyance, abstention, cessation *(interlude)*, desuetude, inertia, insentience, languor, neglect, sloth. SEE MAIN ENTRY
inactivate disable
inactive barren, dead, defunct, dormant, idle, indolent, insipid, languid, lifeless *(dull)*, otiose, powerless, stagnant, static, torpid, unemployed. SEE MAIN ENTRY
inactivity abeyance, cessation *(interlude)*, desuetude, halt, inertia, insentience, languor, leave *(absence)*, lull, nonperformance, sloth
inadept inept *(incompetent)*. SEE MAIN ENTRY
inadequacy absence *(omission)*, dearth, defect, deficiency, deficit, delinquency *(shortage)*, detriment, disability *(physical inability)*, disadvantage, disqualification *(factor that disqualifies)*, fault *(weakness)*, frailty, impotence, inability, incapacity, incompetence, inefficacy, insufficiency, invalidity, need *(deprivation)*, paucity, vice
inadequate defective, deficient, faulty, imperfect, incapable, incompetent, ineffective, ineffectual, inept *(incompetent)*, inferior *(lower in quality)*, insubstantial, insufficient, invalid, nonsubstantial *(not sturdy)*, nonsubstantial *(not sufficient)*, nugatory, paltry, peccable, perfunctory, poor *(inferior in quality)*, powerless, puerile, scarce, unable, unavailing, unfit, unqualified *(not competent)*, unsatisfactory, unsuitable, vacuous. SEE MAIN ENTRY
inadequate final work noncompliance *(improper completion)*
inadequateness dearth, deficiency, insufficiency
inadfectatus unpretentious
inadmissable unacceptable. SEE MAIN ENTRY
inadmissibility disqualification *(rejection)*. SEE MAIN ENTRY
inadmissible impertinent *(irrelevant)*, improper, inapplicable, inapposite, inappropriate, inapt, ineligible, inept *(inappropriate)*, unsuitable
inadvertence contingency, inconsideration, laxity, miscue, neglect, negligence, omission, quirk *(accident)*
inadvertency inconsideration, laxity, miscue, negligence, oversight *(carelessness)*. SEE MAIN ENTRY
inadvertent blind *(not discerning)*, careless, lax, negligent, thoughtless, unintentional, unwitting. SEE MAIN ENTRY
inadvertently unknowingly
inadvisability detriment, inexpedience
inadvisable disadvantageous, ill-advised, impolitic, imprudent, inapt, inauspicious, inept *(inappropriate)*, inopportune, misadvised, objectionable, undesirable, unfavorable, unfit, unsuitable. SEE MAIN ENTRY
inaequabilis irregular *(not usual)*
inaequalis disproportionate, one-sided, unequal *(unequivalent)*
inaequalitas inequality
inaestimabilis inestimable, invaluable, priceless
inaffable offensive *(offending)*, perverse, unapproachable. SEE MAIN ENTRY
inalienable absolute *(conclusive)*, indefeasible, rightful, unalienable. SEE MAIN ENTRY
inalienable interest right *(entitlement)*
inalienable right prerogative, prescription *(claim of title)*
inalterable certain *(positive)*, constant, unalterable
inane barren, fatuous, ludicrous, nugatory, puerile, superficial, thoughtless, trivial, vacuous. SEE MAIN ENTRY
inanimate inactive, insensible, lifeless *(dead)*, torpid
inanimateness insentience
inanimation desuetude, insentience
inanis frivolous, futile, void *(empty)*
inanitas nullity
inanity bombast, jargon *(unintelligible language)*, platitude
inappealable certain *(positive)*, definite, incontestable, incontrovertible, irrefutable, positive *(incontestable)*, undeniable, unequivocal, unrefutable. SEE MAIN ENTRY
inappetance disinterest *(lack of interest)*
inappetancy disinterest *(lack of interest)*
inapplicability incongruity, inconsequence, inconsistency
inapplicable collateral *(immaterial)*, disproportionate, expendable, extraneous, immaterial, impertinent *(irrelevant)*, impracticable, improper, inadmissible, inapposite, inappropriate, inapt, incongruous,

inconsequential, inept *(inappropriate)*, irrelative, irrelevant, unfit, unsuitable. SEE MAIN ENTRY
inapposite disproportionate, extraneous, gratuitous *(unwarranted)*, impertinent *(irrelevant)*, improper, inadmissible, inapplicable, inappropriate, inapt, incongruous, inept *(inappropriate)*, irrelative, irrelevant, unbecoming, unessential, unfit, unsuitable, untimely. SEE MAIN ENTRY
inappositeness inconsequence
inappreciability impalpability
inappreciable immaterial, impalpable, inconsequential, inconsiderable, intangible, marginal, minimal, minor, negligible, null *(insignificant)*, petty, remote *(small)*, slight, trivial. SEE MAIN ENTRY
inappreciation disregard *(lack of respect)*, ingratitude
inapprehensibility incoherence, opacity
inapprehensible impalpable, incomprehensible, inexplicable, inscrutable. SEE MAIN ENTRY
inapproachable inaccessible
inappropos irrelevant
inappropriate alien *(unrelated)*, collateral *(immaterial)*, detrimental, disproportionate, gratuitous *(unwarranted)*, ill-advised, immaterial, impertinent *(irrelevant)*, improper, inadmissible, inadvisable, inapplicable, inapposite, inapt, incongruous, inconsequential, incorrect, ineligible, injudicious, inopportune, irrelevant, objectionable, unacceptable, unauthorized, unbecoming, undesirable, undue *(excessive)*, unfavorable, unfit, unprofessional, unsatisfactory, unseemly, unsuitable, untimely. SEE MAIN ENTRY
inappropriate behavior impropriety
inappropriately timed untimely
inappropriateness impropriety, incongruity, inconsistency, inexpedience
inapropos impertinent *(irrelevant)*
inapt improper, inapplicable, inapposite, inappropriate, ineligible, inept *(inappropriate)*, inept *(incompetent)*, inexperienced, irrelevant, nugatory, powerless, unfit, unsatisfactory, unsuitable. SEE MAIN ENTRY
inaptitude disadvantage, disqualification *(factor that disqualifies)*, impuissance, incapacity
inarticulate mute, speechless, taciturn. SEE MAIN ENTRY
inarticulated indeterminate
inartificial authentic, genuine, honest, ingenuous, real, simple, unaffected *(sincere)*, veridical
inartificiality honesty
inartistic poor *(inferior in quality)*
inattention dishonor *(nonpayment)*, disinterest *(lack of interest)*, disregard *(unconcern)*, disuse, inconsideration, indifference, laches, laxity, neglect, negligence, nonfeasance, oversight *(carelessness)*
inattention to consequences inconsideration
inattentive blind *(not discerning)*, careless, casual, cursory, derelict *(negligent)*, heedless, hot-blooded, inadvertent, lax, negligent, oblivious, perfunctory, reckless, remiss, thoughtless, truant, unaware, unresponsive. SEE MAIN ENTRY
inattentiveness disinterest *(lack of interest)*, disregard *(lack of respect)*, disregard *(unconcern)*, laxity, neglect, negligence
inaudibility indistinctness
inaudible inarticulate, indistinct. SEE MAIN ENTRY
inauditus unprecedented
inaugural initial, original *(initial)*, precursory, preliminary, preparatory, primary, prime *(original)*, prior. SEE MAIN ENTRY
inaugural competition primary
inaugural contest primary
inaugural election primary
inaugural political competition primary
inaugural political contest primary
inaugurare induct, instate
inaugurate admit *(give access)*, cause, commence, constitute *(establish)*, create, embark, establish *(launch)*, generate, induct, initiate, instate, invest *(vest)*, launch *(initiate)*, originate, preface
inauguration birth *(beginning)*, first appearance, inception, installation, na-scency, onset *(commencement)*, origination, outset, prelude, start
inaugurator author *(originator)*
inauguratory original *(initial)*, precursory
inauspicious adverse *(hostile)*, bleak *(not favorable)*, dire, inopportune, ominous, portentous *(ominous)*, regrettable, sinister, unfavorable, unpropitious, untimely. SEE MAIN ENTRY
inavertible unavoidable *(inevitable)*
inborn born *(innate)*, hereditary, ingrained, inherent, innate, natural, organic
inborn ability penchant
inborn aptitude gift *(flair)*, specialty *(special aptitude)*
inborn proclivity instinct
inbred born *(innate)*, hereditary, ingrained, inherent, innate, native *(inborn)*, natural, organic. SEE MAIN ENTRY
incalculable aleatory *(uncertain)*, imponderable, incomprehensible, indeterminate, inestimable, infinite, innumerable, invaluable, myriad, priceless, profuse, unlimited, unpredictable. SEE MAIN ENTRY
incalculably ad infinitum
incandesce burn, deflagrate
incapabable of being done impossible
incapability disability *(physical inability)*, disqualification *(factor that disqualifies)*, impotence, impuissance, inability, incapacity, incompetence, inefficacy
incapable helpless *(powerless)*, inadept, inadequate, incompetent, inept *(incompetent)*, insufficient, powerless, unable, unfit, unqualified *(not competent)*. SEE MAIN ENTRY
incapable of being accomplished impracticable
incapable of being affected impervious
incapable of being appraised invaluable
incapable of being bought back irredeemable
incapable of being conveyed inalienable
incapable of being counted innumerable
incapable of being defeated indefeasible
incapable of being defended untenable
incapable of being deleted indelible
incapable of being divided indivisible
incapable of being done insurmountable
incapable of being evaluated imponderable
incapable of being explained inexplicable
incapable of being held untenable
incapable of being impaired impervious
incapable of being influenced impervious
incapable of being injured impervious
incapable of being justified inexcusable
incapable of being maintained untenable
incapable of being overcome insuperable, insurmountable, invincible
incapable of being parted inseparable
incapable of being perceived impalpable
incapable of being reviewed inappealable
incapable of being revoked indefeasible
incapable of being satisfied insatiable
incapable of being separated indivisible
incapable of being sold inalienable
incapable of being subdued indomitable
incapable of being surmounted insuperable
incapable of being surrendered unalienable
incapable of being transferred inalienable
incapable of caring insusceptible *(uncaring)*
incapable of correction incorrigible
incapable of deceit honest
incapable of discharging liabilities bankrupt
incapable of error infallible
incapable of existing impossible
incapable of feeling insensible
incapable of happening impossible
incapable of knowing right from wrong SEE MAIN ENTRY
incapable of managing one's own affairs fatuous
incapable of perceiving insensible
incapable of revocation irrevocable
incapable of speech mute
incapable of success insurmountable
incapable of utterance speechless
incapacious narrow
incapacitate damage, debilitate, disable, disarm *(divest of arms)*, disqualify, harm, maim, mutilate, neutralize, stall
incapacitated disabled *(deprived of legal right)*, disabled *(made incapable)*, incompetent, powerless
incapacitating disabling
incapacitation disability *(physical inability)*, disqualification *(factor that disqualifies)*, impotence, inability, incapacity, inefficacy
incapacity abortion *(fiasco)*, disability *(physical inability)*, disqualification *(factor that disqualifies)*, fault *(weakness)*, frustration, ignorance, impotence, impuissance, inability, incompetence, inefficacy. SEE MAIN ENTRY
incapacity to endure intolerance
incarcerate arrest *(apprehend)*, capture, commit *(institutionalize)*, confine, constrain *(imprison)*, contain *(restrain)*, detain *(hold in custody)*, enclose, immure, imprison, jail, lock, restrain, seize *(apprehend)*. SEE MAIN ENTRY
incarcerated arrested *(apprehended)*, in custody
incarcerated person captive, prisoner
incarcerating commitment *(confinement)*

incarceration apprehension *(act of arresting),* arrest, bondage, captivity, cell, commitment *(confinement),* constraint *(imprisonment),* detention, durance, enclosure, fetter, restraint. SEE MAIN ENTRY
incarceration facility prison
incarnate bodily, born *(innate),* corporal, corporeal, embody, genetic, live *(conscious),* personify, physical
incarnation embodiment
incase contain *(enclose)*
incaution disregard *(unconcern),* inconsideration, indiscretion
incautious careless, cursory, heedless, hot-blooded, impolitic, improvident, imprudent, impulsive *(rash),* injudicious, lax, misadvised, negligent, perfunctory, reckless, unpolitic
incautiousness inconsideration, indiscretion, negligence, temerity
incautus heedless, improvident, reckless, unsuspecting
incendere incense, inspire
incendiarism arson, conflagration, subversion
incendiarize burn
incendiary disorderly. SEE MAIN ENTRY
incendium conflagration
incense aggravate *(annoy),* alienate *(estrange),* bait *(harass),* disaffect, discompose, exacerbate, harass, irritate, molest *(annoy),* offend *(insult),* pique, provoke, repel *(disgust).* SEE MAIN ENTRY
incensurable blameless
incentive bonus, catalyst, consideration *(recompense),* impetus, impulse, instigation, motive, premium *(excess value),* profit, provocation, reason *(basis),* reward, stimulus. SEE MAIN ENTRY
incentor demagogue
incept commence
inception birth *(beginning),* causal, derivation, genesis, nascency, onset *(commencement),* origin *(source),* origination, outset, prelude, start, threshold *(commencement).* SEE MAIN ENTRY
inceptive causative, elementary, inchoate, incipient, initial, preparatory, prime *(original),* rudimentary
inceptum enterprise *(undertaking),* inception, project, undertaking *(enterprise)*
incertitude ambiguity, ambivalence, confusion *(ambiguity),* doubt *(indecision),* hesitation, indecision, qualm, quandary, suspicion *(uncertainty).* SEE MAIN ENTRY
incertus dubious, indefinite, indeterminate, insecure, irresolute, precarious, problematic, undecided, unsettled, vague
incessancy continuity, perpetuity
incessant chronic, constant, continual *(perpetual),* continuous, durable, insistent, perpetual, repeated, repetitious, unrelenting, unremitting. SEE MAIN ENTRY
incessere inveigh
incest SEE MAIN ENTRY
incestuous SEE MAIN ENTRY
incestus lewd
inch by inch piecemeal
inchoate conceive *(invent),* establish *(launch),* incipient, initial, initiate, original *(initial),* premature, rudimentary. SEE MAIN ENTRY
inchoation embryo, genesis, inception, nascency, onset *(commencement),* origination, outset, start
inchoative fundamental, incipient, original *(initial)*
incidence situation. SEE MAIN ENTRY
incident accident *(chance occurrence),* appurtenant, casualty, contingency, event, experience *(encounter),* happening, occasion, occurrence, particular. SEE MAIN ENTRY
incident to contingent, dependent, subject *(conditional)*
incidental appurtenance, casual, circumstantial, collateral *(immaterial),* extraneous, extrinsic, impertinent *(irrelevant),* inapposite, nonessential, particular, random, subject *(conditional),* supplementary, tangential, unessential. SEE MAIN ENTRY
incidental mention reference *(allusion)*
incidental opinion dictum
incidental profits perquisite
incidentals circumstances
incidere impinge, occur *(happen)*
incinerate burn, deflagrate, destroy *(efface).* SEE MAIN ENTRY
incipere commence, engage *(involve),* initiate
incipience birth *(beginning),* embryo, genesis, inception, nascency, onset *(commencement),* origination, outset, start
incipiency birth *(beginning),* genesis, inception, nascency, origination, outset, start
incipient inchoate, initial, original *(initial),* preliminary, preparatory, prime *(original).* SEE MAIN ENTRY
incipient organism embryo
incircumspection inconsideration, indiscretion, negligence
incise break *(separate),* lancinate, split
incision split
incisive bitter *(penetrating),* compelling, eloquent, harsh, mordacious, pithy, trenchant. SEE MAIN ENTRY
incisiveness judgment *(discernment),* sagacity
incitamentum incentive, inducement, stimulus
incitare impel, incite, inspire, spirit, stimulate, urge
incitation catalyst, inducement, influence, instigation, persuasion, reason *(basis)*
incitatus vehement
incite abet, agitate *(activate),* bait *(harass),* bait *(lure),* cause, coax, engender, evoke, exacerbate, exhort, foment, hasten, impel, induce, influence, inspire, motivate, pique, press *(goad),* prevail *(persuade),* prompt, provoke, spirit, stimulate, urge. SEE MAIN ENTRY
incite to action impel
incitement catalyst, cause *(reason),* incentive, inducement, influence, instiga-tion, invitation, persuasion, provocation, stimulus
inciter demagogue
inciting incendiary, moving *(evoking emotion),* offensive *(taking the initiative),* provocative
incitive incendiary
incivility contempt *(disdain),* disregard *(lack of respect),* disrespect. SEE MAIN ENTRY
inclemency severity, violence
inclement callous, harsh, relentless, ruthless, severe, unfavorable, unrelenting. SEE MAIN ENTRY
inclinatio bias, inclination, penchant, predisposition, tendency
inclination affection, affinity *(regard),* amenability, animus, aptitude, bias, character *(personal quality),* characteristic, color *(complexion),* conatus, conviction *(persuasion),* design *(intent),* desire, direction *(course),* disposition *(inclination),* favor *(partiality),* habit, instinct, notion, partiality, penchant, perspective, position *(point of view),* posture *(attitude),* preconception, predilection, predisposition, preference *(choice),* prejudice *(preconception),* proclivity, propensity, stand *(position),* standpoint, tendency, will *(desire).* SEE MAIN ENTRY
inclination downward descent *(declination)*
inclination to ask questions interest *(concern)*
incline convince, desire, dispose *(incline),* gravitate, lobby, motivate, preconceive, prompt, slant
incline to conduce
incline toward discriminate *(treat differently)*
incline toward each other converge
inclined eager, oblique *(slanted),* partial *(biased),* pliable, prone, ready *(willing),* receptive, solicitous. SEE MAIN ENTRY
inclined to anger fractious
inclined to assent consenting
inclined to delay dilatory
inclined to judge with severity critical *(faultfinding)*
inclined to lewdness lecherous
inclined to suspect inconvincible
inclined to vengeance vindictive
inclining oblique *(slanted)*
inclose contain *(enclose)*
inclosure jail
include append, circumscribe *(surround by boundary),* comprise, consist, constitute *(compose),* contain *(comprise),* embrace *(encircle),* implicate, interject, receive *(permit to enter).* SEE MAIN ENTRY
include as a necessary consequence entail
include by implication imply
include in an agreement stipulate
included additional, constituent *(part)*
includere confine, embody, enclose, immure, imprison, shut
including also
inclusion accession *(annexation),* addendum, admittance *(acceptance),* affiliation *(connectedness),* appendix *(accession),* composition *(makeup),* coverage *(scope),* insertion. SEE MAIN ENTRY
inclusive broad, complete *(all-embracing),* comprehensive, detailed, extensive, general, gross *(total),* omnibus, thorough, total. SEE MAIN ENTRY
inclusiveness corpus, coverage *(scope),* entirety
inclusivity coverage *(scope)*
inclusory inclusive, omnibus
incogitant thoughtless
incogitative vacuous
incognito anonymous, concealment. SEE MAIN ENTRY
incognizable inapprehensible, inscrutable
incognizance ignorance, insentience, nescience
incognizant blind *(not discerning),* unaware. SEE MAIN ENTRY
incognoscible incomprehensible
incohatus inchoate, rudimentary
incoherence jargon *(unintelligible language).* SEE MAIN ENTRY
incoherent disconnected, disjointed, disordered, incomprehensible. SEE MAIN ENTRY
incoherent discourse jargon *(unintelligible language)*

incola denizen, habitant, inhabitant, tenant
incolarum numerus population
incolere inhabit, reside
incolumitas security *(safety)*
income alimony, annuity, capital, earnings, finance, honorarium, money, pay, proceeds, profit, receipt *(act of receiving)*, recompense, rent, resource, retainer, revenue, substance *(material possessions)*, wage. SEE MAIN ENTRY
income from real estate rent
incoming inflow, ingress. SEE MAIN ENTRY
incoming population immigration
incommensurability difference, disparity
incommensurable different, disparate, disproportionate, inapplicable, incommensurate. SEE MAIN ENTRY
incommensurate disproportionate, insufficient. SEE MAIN ENTRY
incommode annoy, badger, bait *(harass)*, deter, disadvantage, discommode, disoblige, disturb, embarrass, encumber *(hinder)*, harass, hinder, hold up *(delay)*, impede, inconvenience, molest *(annoy)*, pique, plague, trammel
incommoded aggrieved *(harmed)*
incommodious undesirable, unsuitable
incommodum detriment, disadvantage *(noun)*, disadvantage *(verb)*, disservice, infliction, injury, mischief, misfortune
incommodus disadvantageous, unfit, unsuitable
incommunicable ineffable. SEE MAIN ENTRY
incommunicative inarticulate, mute, noncommittal
incommutable certain *(positive)*, conclusive *(determinative)*, definite, irreversible, irrevocable, permanent, unalterable
incomparable absolute *(ideal)*, best, cardinal *(outstanding)*, different, diverse, master, outstanding *(prominent)*, paramount, premium, priceless, professional *(stellar)*, rare, superior *(excellent)*, superlative, unapproachable, unique, unprecedented, unrelated, unusual. SEE MAIN ENTRY
incompatability feud
incompatibility antithesis, conflict, contraposition, contrary, disaccord, disagreement, discord, discrepancy, disparity, estrangement, ill will, incongruity, inconsistency, inequality, paradox, strife, variance *(disagreement)*. SEE MAIN ENTRY
incompatible different, discordant, disproportionate, dissident, divergent, hostile, inapplicable, inapposite, inappropriate, inapt, incongruous, inconsistent, inept *(inappropriate)*, negative, opposite, unrelated, unsuitable. SEE MAIN ENTRY
incompetence abortion *(fiasco)*, disability *(physical inability)*, disqualification *(factor that disqualifies)*, impotence, impuissance, inability, incapacity, inefficacy, insufficiency, invalidity. SEE MAIN ENTRY
incompetency abortion *(fiasco)*, disability *(physical inability)*, disqualification *(factor that disqualifies)*, impotence, inability, incapacity, inefficacy, maladministration. SEE MAIN ENTRY
incompetent deficient, deranged, disabled *(made incapable)*, helpless *(powerless)*, inadept, inadequate, inadmissible, incapable, ineffective, ineffectual, inept *(incompetent)*, insufficient, nugatory, powerless, unable, unavailing, unfit, unqualified *(not competent)*. SEE MAIN ENTRY
incomplete broken *(interrupted)*, defective, deficient, devoid, imperfect, inadequate, inchoate, insufficient, nonsubstantial *(not sufficient)*, outstanding *(unresolved)*, paltry, partial *(part)*, partial *(relating to a part)*, perfunctory, rudimentary, scarce. SEE MAIN ENTRY
incompletely in part
incompleteness dearth, defect, deficiency, deficit, hiatus, insufficiency, need *(deprivation)*
incompletion defect, deficiency, delinquency *(failure of duty)*
incomplex simple
incompliance refusal
incompositus disjointed
incomprehensibility complication, incoherence, opacity
incomprehensible difficult, inapprehensible, inarticulate, indefinable, indistinct, inexplicable, inexpressive, innumerable, inscrutable, mysterious, obscure *(abstruse)*, opaque, unclear, vague. SEE MAIN ENTRY
incomprehensibly ad infinitum
incomprehensive SEE MAIN ENTRY
incomprehension ignorance, incapacity, insentience
incompressibility congealment
incompressible solid *(compact)*
incomputable imponderable, innumerable
inconceivability impossibility
inconceivable debatable, doubtful, implausible, impossible, impracticable, incomprehensible, incredible, ineffable, infeasible, portentous *(eliciting amazement)*, prodigious *(amazing)*, rare, unbelievable, uncanny, unusual. SEE MAIN ENTRY
inconclusive circumstantial, indeterminate, uncertain *(ambiguous)*, unconfirmed. SEE MAIN ENTRY
inconclusiveness suspicion *(uncertainty)*
incondite defective
inconditus simple
inconformable disproportionate, incongruous, peculiar *(distinctive)*
inconformity diversity
incongruence conflict, controversy *(argument)*, difference, disaccord, discord, discrepancy, disparity, dissidence
incongruency discrepancy
incongruens incongruous
incongruent discordant, disjointed, disparate, disproportionate, dissimilar, distinct *(distinguished from others)*, inapplicable, inapposite, inappropriate, inapt, incongruous, inept *(inappropriate)*, peculiar *(distinctive)*. SEE MAIN ENTRY
incongruity conflict, contradiction, deviation, difference, disaccord, discord, discrepancy, disparity, dissidence, incompatibility *(inconsistency)*, inconsistency, inequality, misjoinder, nonconformity, paradox. SEE MAIN ENTRY
incongruous different, discordant, disjointed, disparate, disproportionate, dissenting, distinct *(distinguished from others)*, heterogeneous, impertinent *(irrelevant)*, improper, inapplicable, inapposite, inappropriate, inapt, inconsistent, inept *(inappropriate)*, irrelevant, ludicrous, nonconforming, peculiar *(distinctive)*, repugnant *(incompatible)*, unbecoming, unfit, unrelated, unseemly, unsound *(fallacious)*, unsuitable. SEE MAIN ENTRY
incongruousness difference, impropriety, incongruity, inconsistency, inequality
inconsequence immateriality, insignificance, non sequitur. SEE MAIN ENTRY
inconsequent disproportionate, extraneous, impertinent *(irrelevant)*, inapposite, incongruous, inconsequential, irrelevant, sophistic
inconsequential collateral *(immaterial)*, de minimus, expendable, extraneous, immaterial, inapposite, inappreciable, inconsiderable, insubstantial, irrelevant, mediocre, minor, negligible, nonessential, nugatory, null *(insignificant)*, paltry, peripheral, petty, remote *(small)*, slight, tenuous, trivial, unessential. SEE MAIN ENTRY
inconsequentiality inconsequence, insignificance
inconsiderable inappreciable, inconsequential, insubstantial, insufficient, minimal, minor, negligible, nominal, null *(insignificant)*, paltry, petty, remote *(small)*, scarce, slight, trivial, unessential. SEE MAIN ENTRY
inconsiderableness inconsequence, mediocrity
inconsiderate blind *(not discerning)*, careless, derelict *(negligent)*, ill-advised, ill-judged, impolitic, imprudent, injudicious, oblivious, reckless, remiss, thoughtless, unpolitic. SEE MAIN ENTRY
inconsiderateness disregard *(lack of respect)*, inconsideration, ingratitude, temerity
inconsideration disinterest *(lack of interest)*, disregard *(lack of respect)*, disregard *(unconcern)*, indifference, ingratitude, negligence. SEE MAIN ENTRY
inconsideratus injudicious, reckless
inconsistence inconsequence
inconsistency antipode, conflict, contradiction, contrary, controversy *(argument)*, deviation, difference, disaccord, discrepancy, exception *(exclusion)*, incongruity, inconsequence, inequality, irregularity, nonconformity, paradox, specialty *(distinctive mark)*. SEE MAIN ENTRY
inconsistent anomalous, contradictory, deranged, desultory, disconnected, discordant, discriminating *(distinguishing)*, disjunctive *(tending to disjoin)*, disordered, disparate, disproportionate, dissenting, divergent, illogical, inapplicable, inapposite, inappropriate, inapt, incommensurate, incongruous, inept *(inappropriate)*, ludicrous, miscellaneous, opposite, repugnant *(incompatible)*, sophistic, unusual. SEE MAIN ENTRY
inconsistent with dissident, hostile
inconsolable despondent, disconsolate
inconsonance deviation, difference, disaccord, disagreement, incompatibility *(inconsistency)*, incongruity, inconsistency, inequality, paradox
inconsonant discordant, disparate, disproportionate, incongruous, inconsistent
inconspicuous blind *(concealed)*, impalpable, indiscernible, intangible, obscure *(faint)*, unclear, usual. SEE MAIN ENTRY
inconspicuousness concealment
inconstancy disloyalty, inconsistency, infidelity, lapse *(expiration)*, revolt
inconstans capricious, desultory, inconsistent, mutable, unsettled
inconstant broken *(interrupted)*, capricious, desultory, faithless, false *(disloyal)*, inconsistent, infrequent, insidious, irresponsible, mutable, noncommittal, perfidious, shifting, sporadic, transient, undependable, unpredictable, unreliable, unsettled, untrue, untrustworthy, variable, volatile

inconstantia inconsistency, indecision
inconsultus ill-advised, impolitic, imprudent, injudicious, precipitate, thoughtless
incontestability certainty, certification *(certainness)*, certitude. SEE MAIN ENTRY
incontestable axiomatic, believable, categorical, certain *(fixed)*, certain *(positive)*, clear *(certain)*, cogent, conclusive *(determinative)*, decisive, definite, definitive, demonstrable, factual, inappealable, incontrovertible, indefeasible, indubious, infallible, irrebuttable, irrefutable, positive *(incontestable)*, provable, real, reliable, resounding, solid *(sound)*, uncontested, undeniable, undisputed, unequivocal, unimpeachable, unrefutable. SEE MAIN ENTRY
incontestably admittedly. SEE MAIN ENTRY
incontinence debauchery, greed, vice
incontinent dissolute, gluttonous, promiscuous, salacious, uncurbed, unrestrained *(not repressed)*
incontrollable disordered
incontrovertibility certainty, certification *(certainness)*, certitude, incontestability
incontrovertible axiomatic, believable, categorical, certain *(fixed)*, certain *(positive)*, clear *(certain)*, cogent, conclusive *(determinative)*, definitive, factual, immutable, inappealable, incontestable, indefeasible, infallible, irrefutable, peremptory *(absolute)*, positive *(incontestable)*, reliable, resounding, solid *(sound)*, sound, uncontested, undeniable, undisputed, unequivocal, unimpeachable, unrefutable. SEE MAIN ENTRY
incontrovertible incident fact
incontrovertibly admittedly
inconvenience aggravation *(annoyance)*, annoy, bait *(harass)*, detriment, disadvantage *(noun)*, disadvantage *(verb)*, discommode, drawback, encumber *(hinder)*, encumbrance, handicap, hinder, hindrance, hold up *(delay)*, impede, impediment, molest *(annoy)*, molestation, nuisance, obstacle, trammel, trouble. SEE MAIN ENTRY
inconvenient ill-advised, inopportune, undesirable, unfavorable, unfit, unsuitable, untimely. SEE MAIN ENTRY
inconversable inarticulate
inconvertible certain *(positive)*, constant, irredeemable
inconvertible bill bad debt
inconvincability incredulity
inconvincible cynical, doubtful, suspicious *(distrustful)*. SEE MAIN ENTRY
incorporal incorporeal, intangible
incorporality impalpability
incorporate affix, annex *(add)*, attach *(join)*, cement, collect *(gather)*, commingle, comprehend *(include)*, comprise, conjoin, consist, consolidate *(unite)*, constitute *(compose)*, contain *(comprise)*, corporate *(associate)*, desegregate, digest *(comprehend)*, embody, embrace *(encircle)*, encompass *(include)*, federalize *(associate)*, include, intangible, interject, join *(bring together)*, merge, organize *(unionize)*, unite. SEE MAIN ENTRY
incorporated affiliated, associated, coadunate, coherent *(joined)*, composite, compound, conjoint
incorporation accession *(annexation)*, building *(business of assembling)*, centralization, coalescence, combination, compilation, consolidation, coverage *(scope)*, integration *(amalgamation)*, merger. SEE MAIN ENTRY
incorporeal immaterial, impalpable, insubstantial, intangible. SEE MAIN ENTRY
incorporeal being phantom
incorporeal entity intangible
incorporeal hereditament heritage
incorporealism impalpability
incorporeality immateriality, impalpability
incorporeity impalpability
incorrect defective, errant, erroneous, fallacious, false *(inaccurate)*, faulty, ill-founded, improper, inaccurate, inexact, mendacious, sophistic, unauthorized, unbecoming, unseemly, unsound *(fallacious)*, unsustainable, untenable, untrue, wrongful. SEE MAIN ENTRY
incorrect act tortious act
incorrect application misapplication
incorrect appraisal misestimation
incorrect assertion misrepresentation
incorrect belief error
incorrect evaluation misestimation
incorrect statement misstatement
incorrect usage catachresis, misapplication, misuse
incorrect use misapplication, misuse
incorrect valuation misestimation
incorrectness impropriety, misdoing, story *(falsehood)*
incorrigible delinquent *(guilty of a misdeed)*, disobedient, disorderly, dissolute, inexcusable, iniquitous, intractable, irrecoverable, irredeemable, lawless, obdurate, peccant *(culpable)*, perverse, reprehensible, reprobate, restive, uncontrollable, unruly, vicious. SEE MAIN ENTRY
incorrupt blameless, clean, dependable, equitable, high-minded, honest, impartial, law-abiding, loyal, meritorious, moral, not guilty, pure
incorruptibility adhesion *(loyalty)*, honesty, honor *(good reputation)*, integrity, inviolability, loyalty, principle *(virtue)*, probity, responsibility *(conscience)*
incorruptible clean, conscientious, credible, equitable, faithful *(loyal)*, high-minded, honest, irreprehensible, just, law-abiding, loyal, meritorious, moral, reputable, true *(loyal)*, uncompromising, upright. SEE MAIN ENTRY
incorruptibly faithfully
incorruption innocence
incorruptus impartial, incorruptible
incrassate ossified
incrassated ossified
increase accession *(enlargement)*, accumulate *(enlarge)*, addition, advance *(increase)*, advancement *(improvement)*, aggravate *(exacerbate)*, aggravation *(exacerbation)*, amplify, appreciation *(increased value)*, augmentation, build *(augment)*, compound, enlarge, exacerbate, expand, extend *(enlarge)*, extension *(expansion)*, heighten *(augment)*, increment, inflate, inflation *(increase)*, intensify, magnify, profit, progress *(noun)*, progress *(verb)*, prolong, promotion *(advancement)*, pullulate, raise *(advance)*, recruit, reinforcement, supplement. SEE MAIN ENTRY
increase clarity explain
increase dimensions inflate
increase in amount of wealth income
increase in bulk expand
increase in extent expand
increase in size development *(progression)*
increase of clarity clarification
increase of clearness clarification
increase of damages additur
increase of intelligibility clarification
increase of jury award additur
increase of size extension *(expansion)*
increase of speed acceleration
increase the capacity of expand
increase the chances conduce
increase the length of extend *(enlarge)*
increase the market price of appreciate *(increase)*
increase the number of proliferate
increase the numbers compound
increase the size of magnify
increase the strength of develop
increase the value of enhance
increased accrued
increased price appreciation *(increased value)*
increased value premium *(excess value)*
increasement boom *(increase)*
increasing augmentation, boom *(increase)*
incredibilis gross *(total)*, incredible, ineffable
incredibility doubt *(suspicion)*. SEE MAIN ENTRY
incredible debatable, disputable, doubtful, implausible, impossible, ludicrous, noteworthy, portentous *(eliciting amazement)*, prodigious *(amazing)*, remarkable, special, unbelievable, uncanny, unusual. SEE MAIN ENTRY
incredulity cloud *(suspicion)*, discredit, doubt *(suspicion)*, suspicion *(mistrust)*. SEE MAIN ENTRY
incredulous inconvincible, skeptical. SEE MAIN ENTRY
incredulousness cloud *(suspicion)*, doubt *(suspicion)*, incredulity
incredulus incredulous
increment accretion, addition, additive, advance *(increase)*, appreciation *(increased value)*, augmentation, behalf, boom *(increase)*, boom *(prosperity)*, commission *(fee)*, dividend, extension *(expansion)*, growth *(increase)*, interest *(profit)*, profit, progress. SEE MAIN ENTRY
incremental cumulative *(increasing)*
incrementum growth *(increase)*, increment
increpare inveigh
increpate lash *(attack verbally)*, reprehend, reproach
increpation admonition, bad repute, reprimand, reproach, revilement
increpitare reproach
incriminate accuse, arraign, blame, charge *(accuse)*, cite *(accuse)*, complain *(charge)*, condemn *(blame)*, denigrate, denounce *(inform against)*, implicate, indict, inform *(betray)*, involve *(implicate)*, libel, lodge *(bring a complaint)*, present *(prefer charges)*, proscribe *(denounce)*, reproach. SEE MAIN ENTRY
incriminate unjustly frame *(charge falsely)*, frame *(prearrange)*
incriminated guilty
incriminating inculpatory
incriminating statement confession
incrimination accusation, arraignment, attribution, blame *(culpability)*, charge *(accusation)*, complaint, condemnation *(blame)*, denunciation, entanglement *(involvement)*, inculpation, innuendo, reproach. SEE MAIN ENTRY
incriminator accuser, complainant
incriminatory inculpatory. SEE MAIN ENTRY
incubare brood

incubate SEE MAIN ENTRY
incubus weight *(burden)*
inculcare inculcate, obtrude
inculcate discipline *(train),* educate, imbue, infuse, instill, instruct *(teach).* SEE MAIN ENTRY
inculcation discipline *(training),* education, guidance, infusion, instruction *(teaching),* propaganda
inculcator pedagogue
inculculate initiate
inculpable blameless, incorruptible, irreprehensible, justifiable, not guilty, unimpeachable. SEE MAIN ENTRY
inculpate accuse, arraign, blame, charge *(accuse),* complain *(charge),* confess, denigrate, denounce *(condemn),* denounce *(inform against),* deprecate, impeach, implicate, incriminate, indict, inform *(betray),* involve *(implicate),* lodge *(bring a complaint),* reproach. SEE MAIN ENTRY
inculpate falsely frame *(charge falsely)*
inculpate unfairly frame *(charge falsely)*
inculpate unjustly frame *(charge falsely)*
inculpating inculpatory
inculpation accusation, allegation, bad repute, blame *(culpability),* charge *(accusation),* condemnation *(blame),* count, denunciation, diatribe, entanglement *(involvement),* implication *(incriminating involvement),* incrimination, reproach. SEE MAIN ENTRY
inculpation by prosecution arraignment
inculpatory incriminatory. SEE MAIN ENTRY
inculpatory statement confession
incultus uncouth
incumbency appointment *(position),* commitment *(responsibility),* employment, office, position *(business status),* post, regime, term *(duration),* work *(employment)*
incumbent binding, forcible, necessary *(required).* SEE MAIN ENTRY
incumbent on mandatory, obligatory, requisite
incumbent upon compulsory, essential *(required)*
incumbere study
incumbrance lien. SEE MAIN ENTRY
incunabula birth *(beginning),* genesis, nascency, onset *(commencement),* origination, source
incunabular incipient, original *(initial)*
incur SEE MAIN ENTRY
incur a debt charge *(assess),* overdraw, owe
incur a duty assume *(undertake),* promise *(vow),* undertake
incur a loss forfeit, lose *(be deprived of)*
incur an expense expend *(disburse)*
incur blame denounce *(inform against),* humiliate, impeach
incur costs bear the expense, disburse *(pay out),* expend *(disburse).* SEE MAIN ENTRY
incur disapproval disoblige
incur disgrace derogate
incur expense spend
incur expenses bear the expense, disburse *(pay out).* SEE MAIN ENTRY
incur loss suffer *(sustain loss)*
incur the hostility of antagonize
incur the risk bet
incurable deadly, incorrigible, irredeemable, irremediable, irreparable, irreversible. SEE MAIN ENTRY
incuria neglect, negligence, oversight *(carelessness)*
incuriosity disinterest *(lack of interest)*
incuriosus regardless
incuriousness disinterest *(lack of interest)*
incurrere incur, invade
incursio incursion, invasion
incursion assault, encroachment, foray, inflow, infringement, ingress, intrusion, invasion, onset *(assault).* SEE MAIN ENTRY
incursionem invade
incursive offensive *(taking the initiative)*
incursus assault
incusare reproach
incutere infuse, intimidate
indagate probe, research, search
indagatio investigation
indagation probe, research, scrutiny. SEE MAIN ENTRY
indagator detective
indebted insolvent, loyal. SEE MAIN ENTRY
indebtedness arrears, charge *(lien),* cloud *(incumbrance),* debit, debt, due, duty *(obligation),* liability, lien, mortgage, obligation *(liability).* SEE MAIN ENTRY
indebtment arrears, cloud *(incumbrance),* delinquency *(shortage),* lien
indecency impropriety, obscenity, pornography, sodomy, vice. SEE MAIN ENTRY
indecent bad *(offensive),* brazen, depraved, disgraceful, disreputable, dissolute, ignoble, immoral, improper, lascivious, lewd, licentious, nefarious, obscene, offensive *(offending),* profligate *(corrupt),* prurient, salacious, scandalous, scurrilous, suggestive *(risqué),* unbecoming, unseemly. SEE MAIN ENTRY
indecent assault abuse *(physical misuse)*
indeciduous constant, durable
indecipherable SEE MAIN ENTRY
indecision ambivalence, dilemma, hesitation, incertitude, inertia, quandary. SEE MAIN ENTRY
indecisive circumstantial, debatable, doubtful, equivocal, hesitant, inconclusive, indefinite, ineffective, ineffectual, irresolute, noncommittal, open-ended, pliant, unconfirmed, undecided, vague. SEE MAIN ENTRY
indecisiveness ambivalence, confusion *(ambiguity)*
indecorous blatant *(obtrusive),* brazen, disorderly, disreputable, improper, inappropriate, inelegant, inept *(inappropriate),* unbecoming, undue *(excessive),* unseemly, unsuitable
indecorousness impropriety, indecency
indecorum bad repute, disrespect, impropriety, obscenity
indecorus improper, unbecoming, unseemly
indeed SEE MAIN ENTRY
indefatigability diligence *(perseverance),* industry *(activity),* resolution *(decision),* tenacity
indefatigable diligent, faithful *(diligent),* incessant, indomitable, industrious, infallible, patient, permanent, persistent, pertinacious, potent, relentless, resolute, sedulous, undaunted, unrelenting, unremitting. SEE MAIN ENTRY
indefeasable unimpeachable
indefeasibility incontestability, indestructibility
indefeasible certain *(positive),* clear *(certain),* compulsory, conclusive *(determinative),* definite, incontestable, indelible, indestructible, irreversible, irrevocable, permanent, unalienable, unavoidable *(not voidable).* SEE MAIN ENTRY
indefeasible right birthright
indefectible infallible
indefective infallible
indefensible blameful, blameworthy, illogical, inadequate, inexcusable, inexpiable, powerless, reprehensible, unjustifiable, unreasonable, untenable, unwarranted, vulnerable. SEE MAIN ENTRY
indefinable ineffable, inexplicable, undefinable, unspecified. SEE MAIN ENTRY
indefinite aleatory *(uncertain),* ambiguous, broad, conditional, debatable, disputable, equivocal, impalpable, incomprehensible, inconspicuous, indeterminate, intangible, obscure *(faint),* open-ended, outstanding *(unresolved),* pending *(unresolved),* provisional, speculative, sporadic, undecided, unlimited, unspecified, vague. SEE MAIN ENTRY
indefinite meaning ambiguity
indefinite portion moiety
indefinite share moiety
indefinitely ad infinitum
indefiniteness ambiguity, confusion *(am-biguity),* doubt *(indecision),* indistinctness, perpetuity
indelibatus undiminished
indeliberate impulsive *(rash),* spontaneous, unpremeditated
indelibilis indelible
indelibility indestructibility
indelible constant, durable, indestructible, ingrained, irrevocable, noncancellable, permanent, perpetual, profound *(intense).* SEE MAIN ENTRY
indelicacy impropriety, indecency, obscenity
indelicate blatant *(obtrusive),* disreputable, gross *(flagrant),* improper, inelegant, lewd, licentious, lurid, obscene, profane, scurrilous, suggestive *(risqué),* thoughtless, unbecoming, uncouth, unseemly
indemnification collection *(payment),* compensation, consideration *(recompense),* damages, expiation, indemnity, insurance, payment *(remittance),* recompense, recovery *(award),* redemption, refund, reimbursement, relief *(legal redress),* remuneration, rendition *(restoration),* requital, restitution, retribution, reward, satisfaction *(discharge of debt),* trover. SEE MAIN ENTRY
indemnificatory compensatory
indemnifier insurer
indemnify bear the expense, compensate *(remunerate),* defray, outbalance, pay, quit *(repay),* recoup *(reimburse),* refund, reimburse, remedy, remunerate, repay, restore *(return),* return *(refund).* SEE MAIN ENTRY
indemnify against loss ensure
indemnitor insurer, surety *(guarantor)*
indemnity bail, binder, clemency, collection *(payment),* compensation, condonation, consideration *(recompense),* contribute *(indemnify),* contribution *(indemnification),* coverage *(insurance),* damages, expiation, guaranty, honorarium, indemnification, pay, payment *(remittance),* recompense, recovery *(award),* reimbursement, remuneration, reparation *(indemnification),* requital, reward, satisfaction *(discharge of debt),* security *(pledge),* trover. SEE MAIN ENTRY
indemnity against loss insurance
indemonstrable SEE MAIN ENTRY
indent bind *(obligate),* depress, requisition, undertake
indentification relation *(connection)*

indenture bind *(obligate)*, bond, bond *(secure a debt)*, compact, obligation *(liability)*, pact, security *(stock)*, servitude, specialty *(contract)*, undertake. SEE MAIN ENTRY
indentured SEE MAIN ENTRY
independence freedom, home rule, latitude, liberty, nonconformity. SEE MAIN ENTRY
independent alien *(unrelated)*, apart, disparate, eccentric, foreign, free *(enjoying civil liberty)*, free *(not restricted)*, impartial, impertinent *(irrelevant)*, individual, irrelative, neutral, nonconforming, nonpartisan, open-minded, peremptory *(absolute)*, separate, several *(separate)*, spontaneous, substantive, unbiased, unilateral, unprejudiced, unrelated, unrestrained *(not in custody)*, unrestricted. SEE MAIN ENTRY
independent of law arbitrary
independent of rule arbitrary
independent of volition involuntary
independently alone *(solitary)*, respectively
indescribable indefinable, ineffable, nondescript, portentous *(eliciting amazement)*, prodigious *(amazing)*, undefinable, unusual. SEE MAIN ENTRY
indestructibility inviolability. SEE MAIN ENTRY
indestructible certain *(positive)*, constant, immutable, indefeasible, indelible, infinite, infrangible, invincible, irrevocable, permanent, perpetual. SEE MAIN ENTRY
indeterminable conditional, open-ended
indeterminableness confusion *(ambiguity)*
indeterminacy ambiguity, ambivalence, chance *(possibility)*
indeterminate broad, casual, conditional, debatable, disputable, equivocal, generic, indefinite, nebulous, oblique *(evasive)*, pending *(unresolved)*, provisional, uncertain *(ambiguous)*, undefinable, unspecified, vague. SEE MAIN ENTRY
indeterminately ad infinitum
indeterminateness chance *(possibility)*, confusion *(ambiguity)*, doubt *(indecision)*
indetermination ambivalence, doubt *(in-decision)*, incertitude, indecision, quandary. SEE MAIN ENTRY
index book, classify, clue, codify, directory, enumerate, fix *(arrange)*. SEE MAIN ENTRY
index gist *(substance)*
index indicant, indicate, indication, indicator
index inscription, inventory
index itemize, ledger, marshal, pigeonhole, record, register, roll, schedule, symbol, symptom, tabulate
indicant device *(distinguishing mark)*, index *(catalog)*, indication, suggestive *(evocative)*, symptom, token. SEE MAIN ENTRY
indicare denote, disclose, enunciate, imply, indicate, purport
indicate adduce, allot, allude, bear *(adduce)*, bespeak, cite *(state)*, connote, construe *(translate)*, convey *(communicate)*, demonstrate *(establish)*, denote, depict, designate, direct *(show)*, disabuse, disclose, display, evidence, evince, exemplify, exhibit, express, hint, imply, infer, label, manifest, mention, notify, portend, predict, purport, refer *(direct attention)*, represent *(portray)*, reveal, signify *(denote)*, speak, specify, testify. SEE MAIN ENTRY
indicate beforehand portend, predict, presage, prognosticate
indicate in advance presage, prognosticate
indicate willingness consent
indicated assumed *(inferred)*, constructive *(inferential)*, implied, tacit
indicating reference *(citation)*
indicating difference distinctive
indication admonition, attribution, call *(title)*, caveat, clue, designation *(naming)*, earmark, expression *(comment)*, expression *(manifestation)*, guideline, hint, implication *(inference)*, indicant, innuendo, manifestation, mention *(reference)*, monition *(warning)*, reference *(allusion)*, representation *(statement)*, selection *(choice)*, signification, suggestion, symbol, symptom, tip *(clue)*. SEE MAIN ENTRY
indication of contents caption
indications indicia
indicative allusive, circumstantial, distinctive, portentous *(ominous)*, prophetic, representative, suggestive *(evocative)*, typical
indicator bystander, clue, deponent, designation *(symbol)*, index *(catalog)*, indicant, indication, symptom, token. SEE MAIN ENTRY
indicatory circumstantial, representative, suggestive *(evocative)*, typical
indice symptom
indicia SEE MAIN ENTRY
indicium designation *(symbol)*
indicium disclosure *(something disclosed)*, evidence *(noun)*, evidence *(verb)*, indication, manifestation, proof, symptom
indict accuse, blame, charge *(accuse)*, condemn *(blame)*, defame, denounce *(inform against)*, impeach, incriminate. SEE MAIN ENTRY
indict for maladministration impeach
indictable blameful, blameworthy, culpable, guilty
indictable offense crime, felony
indicted accused *(charged)*
indicter complainant, informer *(one providing criminal information)*
indictment accusation, bill *(formal declaration)*, charge *(accusation)*, complaint, count, criticism, denunciation, diatribe, disapprobation, impeachment, incrimination, presentment. SEE MAIN ENTRY
indictor accuser, complainant
indifference dereliction, disinterest *(lack of interest)*, disregard *(lack of respect)*, disregard *(unconcern)*, insentience, languor, laxity, neglect, negligence, neutrality, nonfeasance, sloth. SEE MAIN ENTRY
indifference to act delinquency *(failure of duty)*
indifferent blind *(not discerning)*, callous, careless, casual, cold-blooded, collateral *(immaterial)*, cursory, derelict *(negligent)*, disdainful, dispassionate, evenhanded, faithless, impartial, imperfect, impervious, inactive, indolent, inferior *(lower in quality)*, insusceptible *(uncaring)*, jejune *(dull)*, languid, lax, marginal, mediocre, negligent, neutral, nonchalant, obdurate, oblivious, open-minded, passive, perfunctory, phlegmatic, poor *(inferior in quality)*, reckless, remiss, slipshod, stoical, thoughtless, torpid, trivial, truant, unaffected *(uninfluenced)*, unbiased, unresponsive, usual. SEE MAIN ENTRY
indifferent to suffering cruel
indigen citizen
indigence bankruptcy, dearth, need *(deprivation)*, poverty, privation. SEE MAIN ENTRY
indigene citizen
indigenous born *(innate)*, hereditary, innate, native *(domestic)*, native *(inborn)*, natural, organic, specific
indigent bankrupt, destitute, impecunious, penurious, poor *(underprivileged)*
indignant bitter *(reproachful)*, contemptuous, disdainful, resentful
indignant aversion contempt *(disdain)*, disdain
indignation disparagement, resentment, umbrage. SEE MAIN ENTRY
indignity contumely, defilement, disgrace, dishonor *(shame)*, notoriety, opprobrium, reproach
indignus improper, unbecoming, unfit
indiligence neglect
indiligens inaccurate, negligent
indiligentia neglect, negligence
indirect allusive, astray, circuitous, circumstantial, collusive, constructive *(inferential)*, deceptive, devious, discursive *(digressive)*, furtive, insidious, labyrinthine, oblique *(evasive)*, remote *(not proximate)*, secondary, sinuous, surreptitious, tortuous *(bending)*, virtual. SEE MAIN ENTRY
indirect allusion innuendo, insinuation
indirect comment insinuation
indirect evidence hearsay
indirect hint mention *(reference)*
indirect implication insinuation, reference *(allusion)*
indirect influence impression
indirect path detour
indirect quotation paraphrase
indirect suggestion hint
indirection corruption, deceit, deception, falsification, improbity, pettifoggery. SEE MAIN ENTRY
indirectly meant constructive *(inferential)*
indirectly state imply
indirectness deception
indiscernable hidden
indiscernibility nonappearance, opacity
indiscernible blind *(concealed)*, inconspicuous, inscrutable, intangible, latent, obscure *(faint)*. SEE MAIN ENTRY
indiscerptibility entirety
indiscerptible indivisible, infrangible, inseparable, solid *(compact)*
indiscerptibleness entirety
indiscipline anarchy, contempt *(disobedience to the court)*, latitude, rebellion
indiscreet careless, culpable, impolitic, improvident, imprudent, misadvised, precipitate, reckless, thoughtless, unpolitic, unprofessional. SEE MAIN ENTRY
indiscrete injudicious
indiscretion bad faith, delinquency *(misconduct)*, impropriety, inconsideration, misconduct, misdemeanor, misdoing, temerity. SEE MAIN ENTRY
indiscriminate blind *(not discerning)*, broad, casual, conglomerate, disjointed, haphazard, miscellaneous, omnibus, promiscuous, random. SEE MAIN ENTRY
indiscriminating blind *(not discerning)*
indiscrimination disinterest *(lack of prejudice)*
indiscriminative promiscuous
indispensability market *(demand)*, need *(requirement)*
indispensable cardinal *(basic)*, central *(essential)*, compulsory, essential *(required)*, exigent, fundamental, grave *(important)*, imperative, important *(urgent)*, instrumental,

integral, mandatory, material *(important)*, necessary *(required)*, necessity, obligatory, requisite, urgent, vital. SEE MAIN ENTRY
indispensable condition sine qua non
indispensable item prerequisite, requirement, sine qua non
indispensable party SEE MAIN ENTRY
indispensable person key man
indispensable provision necessity, need *(requirement)*
indispensable thing necessary
indispose deter, disable, discourage
indisposed adverse *(hostile)*, averse, disabled *(made incapable)*, disinclined, disobedient, reluctant, renitent, unfavorable. SEE MAIN ENTRY
indisposed to action indolent
indisposed to believe cynical, inconvincible, incredulous
indisposed to mercy callous
indisposed to talk mute
indisposed to words speechless
indisposedly unwillingly
indisposedness reluctance
indisposition disability *(physical inability)*, disease, disincentive, disorder *(abnormal condition)*, reluctance
indisposition to admit incredulity
indisposition to believe incredulity
indisposition to move inertia
indisputability certainty, certification *(certainness)*, certitude, incontestability
indisputable absolute *(conclusive)*, believable, categorical, certain *(fixed)*, certain *(positive)*, clear *(certain)*, conclusive *(determinative)*, credible, definite, definitive, demonstrable, evident, explicit, inappealable, incontestable, incontrovertible, irrebuttable, irrefutable, lucid, manifest, obvious, official, palpable, positive *(incontestable)*, provable, real, reliable, undeniable, undisputed, unequivocal, unrefutable. SEE MAIN ENTRY
indisputable event fact
indisputably admittedly
indissolubility indestructibility
indissoluble constant, firm, indefeasible, indestructible, inextricable, infrangible, inseparable, irreversible, irrevocable, stable, steadfast
indissoluble entity aggregate
indissolvable infrangible, irreversible, irrevocable
indistinct ambiguous, impalpable, inapprehensible, inarticulate, inconspicuous, indefinite, indeterminate, nebulous, obscure *(faint)*, opaque, speculative, subtle *(insidious)*, uncertain *(ambiguous)*, unclear, undefinable, unspecified, vague. SEE MAIN ENTRY
indistinct in character or meaning doubtful
indistinctness confusion *(ambiguity)*, obscuration, opacity. SEE MAIN ENTRY
indistinguishability indistinctness, opacity
indistinguishable identical, inarticulate, indefinite, indiscernible, indistinct, promiscuous, similar, unclear, vague. SEE MAIN ENTRY
indisturbance composure
indite formulate
individual certain *(particular)*, certain *(specific)*, corpse, different, discrete, disjunctive *(tending to disjoin)*, distinct *(distinguished from others)*, eccentric, entity, noteworthy, only *(sole)*, original *(creative)*, particular *(specific)*, patent, peculiar *(distinctive)*, person, private *(not public)*, separate, singular, sole, specific, subjective, unique, unusual. SEE MAIN ENTRY
individual admitted to the bar counselor
individual characteristic speciality
individual held in custody prisoner
individual in possession holder
individual jailed prisoner
individual method style
individual part detail
individual rights SEE MAIN ENTRY
individual selected for jury service juror
individual trait speciality
individual under age minor
individual under guardianship dependent
individual under suspicion suspect
individual under the age of majority minor
individual who brings a lawsuit plaintiff
individual who stays on holdover
individual's nearest relative next of kin
individualism character *(personal quality)*, disposition *(inclination)*, home rule, identity *(individuality)*, personality, quality *(attribute)*, specialty *(distinctive mark)*, trait. SEE MAIN ENTRY
individualistic distinctive, noteworthy, special, specific
individuality character *(personal quality)*, characteristic, difference, distinction *(difference)*, feature *(characteristic)*, individual, nonconformity, particularity, personality, property *(distinctive attribute)*, quirk *(idiosyncrasy)*, speciality. SEE MAIN ENTRY
individualization discrimination *(differentiation)*
individualize call *(title)*, characterize, define, detail *(particularize)*, discriminate *(distinguish)*, distinguish
individualized individual, private *(not public)*, subjective
individualizing discriminating *(distinguishing)*, distinctive
individually in person, particularly, respectively
individuals populace
individuate characterize, define
individuus indivisible
indivisibility congealment, whole
indivisible coherent *(joined)*, cohesive *(compact)*, conjoint, inextricable, infrangible, inseparable, solid *(compact)*, whole *(unified)*. SEE MAIN ENTRY
indivisible entity aggregate
indocile contumacious, fractious, froward, indomitable, inflexible, insubordinate, intractable, petulant, renitent, uncontrollable, unruly
indocilis intractable
indocility contempt *(disobedience to the court)*, reluctance
indoctrinate convince, discipline *(train)*, educate, imbue, inculcate, initiate, instill, instruct *(teach)*, persuade, prevail *(persuade)*. SEE MAIN ENTRY
indoctrination discipline *(training)*, education, guidance, instruction *(teaching)*, propaganda
indolen truant
indolence inaction, inertia, languor, laxity, sloth, vagrancy
indolent dilatory, idle, inactive, lax, lifeless *(dull)*, otiose, passive, remiss, stagnant, torpid. SEE MAIN ENTRY
indoles disposition *(inclination)*
indomitable contumacious, formidable, inexorable, inexpugnable, infallible, inflexible, insuperable, insurmountable, intractable, invincible, irresistible, pertinacious, potent, powerful, resolute, spartan, stable, steadfast, uncontrollable, undaunted, unyielding. SEE MAIN ENTRY
indomitus indomitable
indorse certify *(approve)*, cosign, pledge *(deposit)*, sign. SEE MAIN ENTRY
indorsement certification *(certification of proficiency)*, leave *(permission)*. SEE MAIN ENTRY
indorser notary public
indubious axiomatic, decisive, definite, incontestable, incontrovertible, irrefutable, uncontroverted. SEE MAIN ENTRY
indubitability certainty, certification *(certainness)*, certitude
indubitable absolute *(conclusive)*, apparent *(perceptible)*, axiomatic, believable, categorical, certain *(fixed)*, certain *(positive)*, clear *(certain)*, cogent, conclusive *(determinative)*, credible, definite, definitive, demonstrable, distinct *(clear)*, evident, incontestable, incontrovertible, indefeasible, irrebuttable, irrefutable, manifest, ostensible, palpable, perceptible, positive *(incontestable)*, probable, reliable, salient, uncontested, undeniable, undisputed, unequivocal, unmistakable, unrefutable
indubitable fact certification *(certainness)*, certitude
indubitableness certainty, certitude, incontestability
indubitably admittedly, fairly *(clearly)*
induce affect, agitate *(activate)*, bait *(lure)*, cause, coax, coerce, constrain *(compel)*, contrive, convert *(persuade)*, convince, create, dispose *(incline)*, engender, entice, evoke, exhort, generate, impel, incite, influence, inspire, inveigle, launch *(initiate)*, lobby, lure, motivate, occasion, originate, persuade, pressure, prevail *(persuade)*, prevail upon, prompt, provoke, solicit, suborn. SEE MAIN ENTRY
induce another to commit perjury suborn
induce by illegal gratuity suborn
induce forgetfulness lull
induce pain mistreat
induced causative
inducement bribery, catalyst, cause *(reason)*, coercion, consideration *(recompense)*, decoy, determinant, force *(compulsion)*, hush money, incentive, instigation, invitation, motive, persuasion, prize, provocation, reason *(basis)*, seduction, stimulus. SEE MAIN ENTRY
inducer abettor
inducere cancel, expunge, induce, introduce
inducible open *(persuasible)*, suasible
inducing causal, causative
inducive advisory, cogent, compelling
induct admit *(give access)*, enroll, hire, initiate, instate, introduce, invest *(vest)*, receive *(permit to enter)*, recruit. SEE MAIN ENTRY
inductile unyielding
inductio introduction
induction admittance *(acceptance)*, consequence *(conclusion)*, dialectic, inflow, installation, introduction, nascency, outset, prelude
inductional logical
inductive causative, discursive *(analytical)*, logical, persuasive

induere sibi vestem clothe
indulge bestow, enable, foster, furnish, give *(grant)*, grant *(concede)*, let *(permit)*, pander, patronize *(condescend toward)*, sanction, suffer *(permit)*, tolerate, vouchsafe
indulge in argument discuss, dispute *(debate)*
indulge in dissipation carouse
indulge in extravagance dissipate *(expend foolishly)*
indulge one's fancy prefer
indulge oneself carouse, dissipate *(expend foolishly)*
indulgence benevolence *(disposition to do good)*, clemency, condonation, consent, dispensation *(exception)*, favor *(act of kindness)*, franchise *(license)*, grace, grant, greed, largess *(generosity)*, leave *(permission)*, lenience, longanimity, philanthropy, privilege, remission, sanction *(permission)*, sufferance, temperance, tolerance, understanding *(tolerance)*, vice. SEE MAIN ENTRY
indulgent addicted, benevolent, dissolute, gluttonous, intemperate, lenient, patient, permissive, philanthropic, placable, pliant, propitious
indulgentia connivance, indulgence, patronage *(power to appoint jobs)*, tolerance
indulging lenient
indurate callous, cold-blooded, impervious, insusceptible *(uncaring)*, obdurate, remorseless, rigid, tempered. SEE MAIN ENTRY
indurated callous, cold-blooded, impervious, insusceptible *(uncaring)*, obdurate, ossified, remorseless, rigid, tempered
indurative rigid
industria diligence *(care)*, industry *(activity)*
industrial commercial, mercantile, productive, technical. SEE MAIN ENTRY
industrial area development *(building)*
industrial building development *(building)*
industrialist executive
industrialized industrial
industrious active, diligent, eager, faithful *(diligent)*, meticulous, painstaking, pertinacious, resolute, sedulous, stable, steadfast, zealous. SEE MAIN ENTRY
industriousness diligence *(perseverance)*
industrius active, diligent, industrious
industry building *(business of assembling)*, business *(commerce)*, business *(commercial enterprise)*, calling, commerce, corporation, effort, employment, enterprise *(economic organization)*, firm, labor *(exertion)*, occupation *(vocation)*, work *(effort)*, work *(employment)*. SEE MAIN ENTRY
industry and trade commerce
indwell dwell *(reside)*, occupy *(take possession)*, reside
indweller citizen, denizen, domiciliary, habitant, inhabitant, lodger, resident
indwelling ingrained
inebriant alcohol
inebriated drunk
inebriation dipsomania. SEE MAIN ENTRY
inebriety dipsomania, inebriation
inedible repugnant *(exciting aversion)*
ineducation illiteracy
ineffable mysterious, sacrosanct, undefinable. SEE MAIN ENTRY
ineffaceable indelible, indestructible, ingrained, inherent, noncancellable
ineffective disabled *(made incapable)*, futile, inadept, inadequate, incapable, incompetent, inconclusive, ineffectual, inept *(incompetent)*, insipid, invalid, languid, nugatory, null *(invalid)*, null and void, otiose, powerless, unable, unavailing, unqualified *(not competent)*, void *(invalid)*. SEE MAIN ENTRY
ineffective assistance of counsel SEE MAIN ENTRY
ineffective counsel SEE MAIN ENTRY
ineffective trial mistrial
ineffectiveness disability *(physical inability)*, impotence, inefficacy, invalidity, miscarriage
ineffectual disabled *(deprived of legal right)*, expendable, futile, inadept, inadequate, incapable, incompetent, ineffective, inept *(incompetent)*, invalid, minor, nugatory, null *(invalid)*, null and void, otiose, powerless, unavailing, unproductive, void *(invalid)*. SEE MAIN ENTRY
ineffectual attempt miscarriage
ineffectuality abortion *(fiasco)*, disability *(physical inability)*, impotence, inefficacy
ineffectualness detriment, disability *(physical inability)*, failure *(lack of success)*, impotence, inability, inefficacy
inefficacious defunct, disabled *(made incapable)*, futile, inadept, inadequate, ineffective, ineffectual, inept *(incompetent)*, invalid, nugatory, null *(invalid)*, null and void, otiose, powerless, unavailing, unproductive. SEE MAIN ENTRY
inefficaciousness impotence, inefficacy
inefficacy abortion *(fiasco)*, disability *(physical inability)*, impotence, impuissance, inability, incapacity, nullity. SEE MAIN ENTRY
inefficiency detriment, disability *(physical inability)*, impotence, impuissance, inability, incapacity, incompetence, inefficacy, maladministration
inefficient inadept, incompetent, inept *(incompetent)*, otiose, unable, unavailing, unproductive, unqualified *(not competent)*. SEE MAIN ENTRY
inefficient management maladministration
inelastic inflexible, rigid
inelegance impropriety
inelegans inelegant
inelegant disreputable, imperfect, inferior *(lower in quality)*, pedestrian, tawdry, uncouth, unseemly. SEE MAIN ENTRY
ineligibility disqualification *(rejection)*
ineligible inadmissible, inappropriate, undesirable, unfit, unqualified *(not competent)*. SEE MAIN ENTRY
ineluctable inevitable, irrevocable, necessary *(inescapable)*, requisite, unavoidable *(inevitable)*
ineludible inevitable, necessary *(in-escapable)*, unavoidable *(inevitable)*
inept amateur, disabled *(made incapable)*, fatuous, ill-judged, improper, inadept, inadequate, inapposite, incapable, incompetent, ineffective, ineffectual, inexperienced, nugatory, powerless, unable, unfit, unqualified *(not competent)*, unsatisfactory. SEE MAIN ENTRY
ineptitude abortion *(fiasco)*, disqualification *(factor that disqualifies)*, ignorance, impotence, impuissance, inability, incapacity. SEE MAIN ENTRY
ineptness inability
ineptus fatuous, inept *(incompetent)*, insipid
inequality difference, discrepancy, disparity, favoritism, incompatibility *(inconsistency)*, inconsistency, injustice. SEE MAIN ENTRY
inequitable iniquitous, unequal *(unjust)*, unfair, unjust, unscrupulous. SEE MAIN ENTRY
inequitable action injustice
inequitableness inequity, misjudgment, nepotism
inequity favoritism, ground, injustice, misjudgment, nepotism. SEE MAIN ENTRY
ineradicable durable, indefeasible, indelible, invincible, irreversible, irrevocable, permanent, perpetual
ineradicableness indestructibility
inerasable durable, indelible, indestructible
inerasableness indestructibility
inermis helpless *(defenseless)*
inerrability certainty, certitude
inerrable infallible, reliable
inerrancy certainty, certification *(certainness)*, certitude
inerrant accurate, certain *(positive)*, infallible, reliable
iners inactive, indolent, torpid
inert dead, dormant, idle, inactive, languid, lifeless *(dull)*, otiose, phlegmatic, stable, stagnant, static, torpid
inertia desuetude. SEE MAIN ENTRY
inertia insentience
inertia sloth
inertion abeyance
inertness abeyance, inaction, inertia, insentience, languor, sloth
inerudition ignorance, illiteracy
inescapable certain *(fixed)*, certain *(positive)*, compulsory, definite, exigent, forthcoming, important *(urgent)*, inevitable, irrevocable, obligatory, positive *(incontestable)*, stringent, unavoidable *(inevitable)*, undeniable. SEE MAIN ENTRY
inescapable duty allegiance, charge *(responsibility)*, onus *(burden)*
inessential circumstantial, expendable, gratuitous *(unwarranted)*, immaterial, inapposite, inappropriate, inconsequential, irrelevant, minor, nonessential, null *(insignificant)*, peripheral, superfluous, unnecessary
inessentiality immateriality, insignificance, technicality
inestimable imponderable, invaluable, priceless, valuable. SEE MAIN ENTRY
inevasible definite, inevitable, irrevocable, requisite, unavoidable *(inevitable)*
inevitabilis inevitable, unavoidable *(inevitable)*
inevitability predetermination
inevitable categorical, certain *(fixed)*, certain *(positive)*, definite, forthcoming, future, irremediable, irrevocable, necessary *(in-escapable)*, necessity, unalterable. SEE MAIN ENTRY
inevitable occurrence accident *(chance occurrence)*
inevitable result foregone conclusion
inevitableness certification *(certainness)*, certitude, predetermination
inexact ambiguous, approximate, erroneous, generic, ill-judged, imperfect, improper, inaccurate, incorrect, indefinite, lax, liberal *(not literal)*, oblique *(evasive)*, open-ended, partial *(relating to a part)*, perfunctory, slipshod. SEE MAIN ENTRY
inexact statement generalization
inexactitude exaggeration, generality *(vague statement)*, informality, laxity, misestimation, misjudgment, misstatement

inexactness confusion *(ambiguity)*, error, exaggeration, generality *(vague statement)*, informality, laxity, misestimation, misjudgment, misstatement
inexcitability composure, inertia, languor, longanimity
inexcitable callous, dispassionate, insensible, lifeless *(dull)*, torpid
inexcusability misdoing
inexcusable blameful, indefensible, inexpiable, peccant *(culpable)*, reprehensible, unjustifiable, unwarranted. SEE MAIN ENTRY
inexcusable delay laches. SEE MAIN ENTRY
inexcusable delay in assertion of rights laches
inexcusable neglect SEE MAIN ENTRY
inexecution neglect, nonperformance
inexertion neglect, sloth
inexhaustible copious, durable, infallible, infinite, innumerable, myriad, perpetual, profuse, unlimited
inexistence blank *(emptiness)*, nonappearance, nonentity, nullity
inexistent nonexistent
inexorabilis implacable, inexorable, irreconcilable, relentless, ruthless, unrelenting
inexorability certainty, certitude, severity
inexorable brutal, callous, certain *(positive)*, definite, dictatorial, immutable, implacable, inflexible, ironclad, irreconcilable, necessary *(inescapable)*, obdurate, peremptory *(imperative)*, pertinacious, purposeful, relentless, resolute, rigid, ruthless, severe, stable, steadfast, strict, unavoidable *(inevitable)*, uncompromising, unrelenting, unyielding. SEE MAIN ENTRY
inexorable fate predetermination
inexpectant unaware
inexpectation bombshell, happenstance, improbability
inexpectatus unexpected
inexpedience detriment, disadvantage, hindrance, impropriety
inexpediency detriment, impropriety, inexpedience. SEE MAIN ENTRY
inexpedient harmful, ill-advised, ill-judged, impolitic, imprudent, inadvisable, inappropriate, inapt, inauspicious, inept *(inappropriate)*, injudicious, inopportune, misadvised, objectionable, undesirable, unfavorable, unfit, unpolitic, unsatisfactory, unsuitable. SEE MAIN ENTRY
inexpensive economical, nominal
inexperience ignorance, minority *(infancy)*, nescience
inexperienced incompetent, jejune *(lacking maturity)*, juvenile, naive, unaccustomed, unacquainted, unqualified *(not competent)*, unversed. SEE MAIN ENTRY
inexperienced person amateur, juvenile, novice
inexpert inadept, incompetent, inept *(incompetent)*, inexperienced, unfit, unqualified *(not competent)*, unversed
inexpertness abortion *(fiasco)*, disqualification *(factor that disqualifies)*, incompetence
inexpiable implacable, indefensible, inexcusable, irreconcilable, irremediable, peccant *(culpable)*, reprehensible. SEE MAIN ENTRY
inexplebilis insatiable
inexplicabilis inexpiable, inexplicable, inextricable
inexplicable enigmatic, inapprehensible, incomprehensible, indefinable, inexpressive, inscrutable, mysterious, peculiar *(curious)*, undefinable. SEE MAIN ENTRY
inexplicable statement enigma
inexplicableness mystery
inexplicit indefinite, vague
inexpressible inapprehensible, indefinable, ineffable, undefinable
inexpressive SEE MAIN ENTRY
inexpugnabilis inexpugnable
inexpugnability inviolability
inexpugnable immune, insurmountable, invincible. SEE MAIN ENTRY
inexpungeable durable
inexspectatus unanticipated
inexsuperabilis invincible
inextinguishable certain *(positive)*, constant, indefeasible, indelible, indestructible, indomitable, inexpugnable, invincible, irreversible, irrevocable, permanent
inextinguished chronic
inextricabilis inextricable, labyrinthine
inextricability complication, constant, impasse
inextricable complex, inseparable. SEE MAIN ENTRY
infallibilism certitude
infallibility certainty, certification *(certainness)*, certitude
infallible certain *(fixed)*, certain *(positive)*, conclusive *(determinative)*, factual, positive *(incontestable)*, reliable, secure *(sound)*, undeniable. SEE MAIN ENTRY
infallibleness certitude
infamia discredit, disgrace, dishonor *(shame)*, disrepute, ignominy, infamy, notoriety, shame
infamis disputable, disreputable
infamous arrant *(onerous)*, bad *(offensive)*, contemptible, contemptuous, disgraceful, disreputable, flagrant, heinous, ignoble, illicit, inexpiable, iniquitous, machiavellian, malevolent, nefarious, notorious, odious, outrageous, peccant *(culpable)*, profligate *(corrupt)*, reprehensible, reprobate, scandalous, sinister. SEE MAIN ENTRY
infamous conduct criminality, misconduct, misdeed, misdemeanor, misdoing
infamous misbehavior criminality
infamousness bad repute, disrepute, infamy, notoriety, opprobrium, stigma
infamy atrocity, attaint, bad character, bad repute, contempt *(disdain)*, defamation, discredit, disgrace, dishonor *(shame)*, disrepute, ignominy, ill repute, notoriety, obloquy, odium, onus *(stigma)*, opprobrium, scandal, shame, stigma, turpitude, vice. SEE MAIN ENTRY
infancy birth *(beginning)*, nascency, nonage, onset *(commencement)*, origination, outset, start
infandus ineffable
infans child, infant
infant child, inchoate, incipient, minor, original *(initial)*. SEE MAIN ENTRY
infant status minority *(infancy)*
infantile jejune *(lacking maturity)*, puerile
infantilism puerility
infantine jejune *(lacking maturity)*, juvenile, puerile
infants children
infarction bar *(obstruction)*
infatuate bigot, obsess
infatuated zealous
infatuation affection, compulsion *(obsession)*, obsession, passion, predilection
infeasibility impossibility
infeasible impossible, unattainable. SEE MAIN ENTRY
infect adulterate, contaminate, foment, harm, motivate, pervert, pollute, taint *(contaminate)*. SEE MAIN ENTRY
infected marred, tainted *(contaminated)*
infection contaminate, disease
infectious contagious, harmful, pestilent
infective contagious
infectus executory
infecund barren, unproductive
infecundus unproductive
infelicitous disconsolate, disproportionate, ill-advised, improper, inadvisable, inapplicable, inapposite, inappropriate, inapt, inept *(inappropriate)*, misadvised, unbecoming, unfavorable, unsuitable, untimely
infelicity distress *(anguish)*, inexpedience, misfortune
infelix inauspicious
infensus adverse *(hostile)*, hostile
infer allude, assume *(suppose)*, conclude *(decide)*, connote, construe *(comprehend)*, deduce, deduct *(conclude by reasoning)*, derive *(deduce)*, determine, educe, evidence, expect *(consider probable)*, guess, hint, implicate, imply, judge, opine, postulate, presume, presuppose, purport, read, reason *(conclude)*, surmise, suspect *(think)*, understand. SEE MAIN ENTRY
inferable constructive *(inferential)*, deductible *(provable)*, deductive, presumptive, provable
inferable harm SEE MAIN ENTRY
inference conclusion *(determination)*, conjecture, connotation, construction, generalization, hint, hypothesis, idea, innuendo, insinuation, intimation, mention *(reference)*, presumption, reference *(allusion)*, referral, signification, speculation *(conjecture)*, suggestion, suspicion *(uncertainty)*. SEE MAIN ENTRY
inferential accountable *(explainable)*, allusive, circumstantial, consequential *(deducible)*, deductible *(provable)*, deductive, discursive *(analytical)*, implied, leading *(guiding)*, suggestive *(evocative)*, tacit
inferentially a priori
inferior deficient, faulty, ignoble, imperfect, inadequate, mediocre, minor, null *(insignificant)*, pedestrian, poor *(inferior in quality)*, secondary, slight, subaltern, subordinate, subservient, trivial, unsatisfactory, unworthy. SEE MAIN ENTRY
inferior rank subjection
inferiority disadvantage, flaw, handicap, mediocrity
inferiorness mediocrity
infernal blameworthy, diabolic, heinous, malevolent, malignant, nefarious, odious
infernal machine bomb
inferre entail, inflict
inferred allusive, constructive *(inferential)*, implied, presumptive, subtle *(insidious)*, tacit
inferred in law constructive *(inferential)*. SEE MAIN ENTRY
inferring dialectic
infertile barren, otiose, unproductive
infest annoy, harass. SEE MAIN ENTRY
infestus hostile
inficere imbue
infidel heretic
infidelis faithless
infidelitas disloyalty, infidelity
infidelity adultery, bad faith, bad repute, breach, dishonesty, disloyalty, sedition, treason. SEE MAIN ENTRY

infiltrate encroach, enter *(penetrate),* interject, interpose, penetrate, permeate, pervade. SEE MAIN ENTRY
infiltration encroachment, entrance, incursion, inflow, infusion, intrusion, invasion, osmosis
infinite continual *(perpetual),* far reaching, incessant, indeterminate, inestimable, innumerable, myriad, open-ended, permanent, perpetual, profuse, unlimited. SEE MAIN ENTRY
infinite duration perpetuity
infinitely powerful omnipotent
infinitely wise omniscient
infiniteness perpetuity
infinitesimal impalpable, inappreciable, intangible, minimal, tenuous
infinitus arbitrary, infinite, unlimited
infinity perpetuity. SEE MAIN ENTRY
infirm defective, imperfect, insecure, insubstantial, nonsubstantial *(not sturdy),* powerless, precarious, unsound *(not strong).* SEE MAIN ENTRY
infirm of purpose irresolute, irresponsible, noncommittal
infirmare quash
infirmitas frailty, impotence, inability
infirmity defect, deficiency, disability *(physical inability),* disadvantage, disease, disorder *(abnormal condition),* fault *(weakness),* flaw, frailty, impuissance, inability, incapacity, vice
infirmity of old age caducity
infirmity of purpose doubt *(indecision),* indecision
infirmus invalid, powerless
infitiari disavow, disown *(deny the validity),* disown *(refuse to acknowledge)*
infitias ire deny *(contradict),* disavow
infitiatio negation
infix embed, fix *(make firm),* inculcate, inject, instill, plant *(place firmly)*
infixed ingrained, innate, internal
inflame aggravate *(annoy),* agitate *(activate),* bait *(harass),* burn, deflagrate, discompose, exacerbate, foment, incense, intensify, irritate, molest *(annoy),* motivate, offend *(insult),* perturb, pique, provoke, stimulate. SEE MAIN ENTRY
inflame with wrath incense
inflamed hot-blooded, painful, vehement
inflamer demagogue
inflaming moving *(evoking emotion),* provocative
inflammable fractious
inflammation aggravation *(exacerbation),* provocation
inflammatory disorderly, hot-blooded, incendiary, offensive *(taking the initiative),* provocative. SEE MAIN ENTRY
inflare inflate
inflate compound, distort, enlarge, expand, extend *(enlarge),* increase, magnify, overestimate, spread. SEE MAIN ENTRY
inflated flatulent, fustian, grandiose, orgulous, orotund, pretentious *(pompous),* superlative, turgid. SEE MAIN ENTRY
inflated language fustian, rhetoric *(insincere language)*
inflated speech fustian
inflated statement overstatement
inflated style fustian
inflatio inflation *(increase)*
inflation bombast, boom *(prosperity),* exaggeration, growth *(increase),* overstatement, pretense *(ostentation),* rodomontade. SEE MAIN ENTRY
inflatus inflated *(bombastic),* inflated *(enlarged),* pretentious *(pompous)*
inflection intonation, stress *(accent).* SEE MAIN ENTRY
inflexibility severity
inflexible callous, certain *(positive),* constant, decisive, definite, draconian, firm, formal, immutable, implacable, inexorable, insusceptible *(uncaring),* intractable, ironclad, irreconcilable, irrevocable, obdurate, orthodox, particular *(exacting),* peremptory *(imperative),* pertinacious, precise, provincial, recusant, relentless, resolute, restive, restrictive, rigid, ruthless, severe, solid *(compact),* staunch, steadfast, strict, stringent, strong, unaffected *(uninfluenced),* unalterable, unbending, uncompromising, unrelenting, unyielding, willful. SEE MAIN ENTRY
inflexible routine bureaucracy
inflict bait *(harass),* beat *(strike),* commit *(perpetrate),* compel, encumber *(hinder),* foist, levy, perpetrate. SEE MAIN ENTRY
inflict a penalty penalize
inflict a penalty on convict
inflict a penalty upon fine
inflict capital punishment execute *(sentence to death)*
inflict evil mistreat, persecute
inflict harm strike *(assault)*
inflict injury harm, prejudice *(injure),* strike *(assault)*
inflict pain harrow, mistreat
inflict pain on plague
inflict penalty condemn *(punish),* discipline *(punish),* punish, sentence
inflict penance upon discipline *(punish)*
inflict punishment condemn *(punish),* convict, penalize
inflicting commission *(act)*
infliction casualty, catastrophe, commission *(act),* condemnation *(punishment),* correction *(punishment),* damage, discipline *(punishment),* encumbrance, ground, imposition *(excessive burden),* mischief, nuisance, pain, penalty, punishment, sanction *(punishment).* SEE MAIN ENTRY
infliction of pain cruelty
inflictive disciplinary *(punitory),* penal
infligere inflict
inflow penetrate. SEE MAIN ENTRY
influence advantage, affect, agitate *(activate),* authority *(power),* bait *(lure),* cause *(reason),* cause, clout, coax, concern *(involve),* conduce, consequence *(significance),* convert *(persuade),* convince, dint, dispose *(incline),* dominance, dominate, draw *(attraction),* eminence, exhort, force *(strength),* hegemony, imbue, impetus, importance, impress *(affect deeply),* impression, incentive, incite, induce, inducement, inspire, instigation, inveigle, leverage, lobby, manipulate *(control unfairly),* militate, motivate, motive, occupation *(possession),* patronage *(power to appoint jobs),* patronage *(support),* persuade, persuasion, power, predominance, predominate *(command),* pressure *(noun),* pressure *(verb),* prestige, prevail *(persuade),* prevail upon, primacy, prompt, reach, redound, sphere, stimulus, supremacy, weight *(importance).* SEE MAIN ENTRY
influence against prejudice *(influence)*
influence by a gift gratuity *(bribe)*
influence of liquor inebriation
influenceability amenability
influenceable amenable, open *(persuasible),* pliant, receptive, suasible, susceptible *(responsive)*
influenced interested, one-sided, partial *(biased),* partisan, passive, unequal *(unjust),* unjust. SEE MAIN ENTRY
influencer special interest
influencers lobby
influences climate
influencing moving *(evoking emotion)*
influential assertive, causal, causative, cogent, compelling, consequential *(substantial),* considerable, contributory, convincing, crucial, decisive, dominant, forcible, important *(significant),* key, master, material *(important),* outstanding *(prominent),* persuasive, potent, powerful, predominant, prevailing *(having superior force),* prominent, provocative, sovereign *(absolute).* SEE MAIN ENTRY
influential persons lobby
influential sponsor patron *(influential supporter)*
influentiality clout, force *(strength),* patronage *(power to appoint jobs),* pressure, prestige
influx entrance, incursion, inflow
infold contain *(enclose)*
inform admonish *(advise),* advise, annunciate, apprise, bear *(adduce),* betray *(disclose),* caution, charge *(instruct on the law),* communicate, construe *(translate),* contact *(communicate),* converse, convey *(communicate),* declare, denounce *(inform against),* disabuse, disclose, disseminate, divulge, edify, educate, enlighten, enunciate, forewarn, herald, impart, initiate, instill, instruct *(teach),* issue *(publish),* mention, notice *(give formal warning),* notify, posit, proclaim, publish, relate *(tell),* report *(disclose),* reveal, speak. SEE MAIN ENTRY
inform against betray *(disclose),* cite *(accuse),* complain *(charge),* implicate, incriminate
inform on betray *(disclose),* denounce *(inform against),* expose
informal casual, unofficial, unpretentious. SEE MAIN ENTRY
informality SEE MAIN ENTRY
informalness informality
informant bystander, deponent, eyewitness, indicator, informer *(one providing criminal information),* source, spy, witness. SEE MAIN ENTRY
information accusation, advice, charge *(accusation),* clue, communication *(statement),* complaint, comprehension, connotation, data, direction *(guidance),* disclosure *(something disclosed),* dispatch *(message),* edification, file, guidance, intelligence *(news),* knowledge *(awareness),* knowledge *(learning),* monition *(warning),* notice *(announcement),* notification, presentment, publicity, report *(detailed account),* science *(study).* SEE MAIN ENTRY
information against complaint
information blank form *(document)*
information giver informant
information preserved in writing entry *(record)*
information supplier informer *(one providing criminal information)*
informational didactic, disciplinary *(educational),* informatory, narrative. SEE MAIN ENTRY
informative demonstrative *(illustrative),* didactic, disciplinary *(educational),* eloquent, informatory, loquacious, narrative. SEE MAIN ENTRY
informed acquainted, cognizant, conscious *(aware),* knowing, learned, literate,

omniscient, perspicacious, practiced, sensible. SEE MAIN ENTRY
informer accuser, bystander, deponent, eyewitness, harbinger, indicator, informant, spy, witness. SEE MAIN ENTRY
informing demonstrative *(illustrative)*, disclosure *(act of disclosing)*
informing against denunciation
infract infringe
infraction bad faith, breach, delinquency *(misconduct)*, disregard *(omission)*, encroachment, illegality, infringement, invasion, misdeed, offense, perversion, sedition, transgression, violation, wrong. SEE MAIN ENTRY
infraction of rule exception *(exclusion)*
infraction of the law delinquency *(misconduct)*
infrangible callous, inseparable. SEE MAIN ENTRY
infrenatus uncurbed
infrequency improbability, paucity
infrequent extraordinary, intermittent, noteworthy, rare, special, sporadic, uncommon, unusual. SEE MAIN ENTRY
infringe accroach, break *(violate)*, contravene, disobey, disrupt, encroach, impinge, impose *(intrude)*, interfere, interpose, intervene, intrude, invade, obtrude, offend *(violate the law)*, overlap, overstep, plagiarize, trespass, violate. SEE MAIN ENTRY
infringe a law deviate, offend *(violate the law)*
infringe copyright copy
infringe custom deviate
infringed broken *(unfulfilled)*
infringement assumption *(seizure)*, breach, conflict, contempt *(disobedience to the court)*, contravention, crime, delinquency *(misconduct)*, disregard *(omission)*, encroachment, illegality, imposition *(excessive burden)*, incursion, infraction, injustice, intrusion, invasion, irregularity, malfeasance, misdeed, misfeasance, nuisance, offense, plagiarism, transgression, violation. SEE MAIN ENTRY
infringement of custom quirk *(idiosyncrasy)*
infringing broken *(unfulfilled)*, intrusive
infundere infuse, inject
infuriate aggravate *(annoy)*, bait *(harass)*, discompose, exacerbate, harass, incense, irritate, offend *(insult)*, perturb, pique, provoke
infuriated resentful
infuriating outrageous
infuse denature, develop, discipline *(train)*, enter *(insert)*, imbue, inculcate, inject, instill, permeate, pervade. SEE MAIN ENTRY
infuse courage reassure
infuse funds invest *(fund)*
infuse life into foment
infused compound
infusio infusion
infusion incorporation *(blend)*. SEE MAIN ENTRY
ingather congregate
ingathering assemblage, caucus, chamber *(body)*, collection *(assembly)*, company *(assemblage)*, conglomeration, congregation, rendezvous
ingeminate recapitulate, reiterate, repeat *(do again)*
ingenerate hereditary, native *(inborn)*, natural
ingeniosus resourceful
ingenious artful, competent, deft, expert, fertile, original *(creative)*, politic, proficient, resourceful. SEE MAIN ENTRY
ingeniousness gift *(flair)*, skill
ingenit native *(inborn)*
ingenium ability, character *(personal quality)*, disposition *(inclination)*, personality, spirit, understanding *(comprehension)*
ingens prodigious *(enormous)*
ingenue child
ingenuity artifice, gift *(flair)*, performance *(workmanship)*, skill, specialty *(special aptitude)*
ingenuous bona fide, candid, credible, direct *(forthright)*, honest, simple, straightforward, unaffected *(sincere)*. SEE MAIN ENTRY
ingenuousness candor *(straightforwardness)*, honesty, informality, probity, veracity
ingerere obtrude
inglorious blameworthy, contemptible, disgraceful, disreputable, ignoble, mediocre, notorious, recreant, scandalous, unethical. SEE MAIN ENTRY
ingloriousness attaint, degradation, discredit, disgrace, dishonor *(shame)*, disrepute, ignominy, infamy, notoriety, obloquy, opprobrium, scandal
ingoing inflow, ingress
ingraft fix *(make firm)*
ingrain embed, establish *(entrench)*, fix *(make firm)*, infuse. SEE MAIN ENTRY
ingrained born *(innate)*, genetic, habitual, indelible, inherent, innate, internal, inveterate, native *(inborn)*, natural, organic, permanent, routine, traditional. SEE MAIN ENTRY
ingrained with accustomed *(familiarized)*
ingratiate propitiate
ingratiate oneself pander
ingratiating obsequious, servile, subservient
ingratitude SEE MAIN ENTRY
ingratus unacceptable
ingredient component, constituent *(part)*, detail, element, feature *(characteristic)*, inherent, item, member *(constituent part)*, part *(portion)*, segment. SEE MAIN ENTRY
ingress access *(right of way)*, admission *(entry)*, admittance *(means of approach)*, avenue *(route)*, entrance, entry *(entrance)*, immigration, incursion, inflow, osmosis, portal. SEE MAIN ENTRY
ingress wrongfully encroach
ingresses approaches
ingression entry *(entrance)*, incursion, inflow, ingress
ingressus ingress
ingrown ingrained, provincial
inhabilis incapable, incompetent
inhabit dwell *(reside)*, lodge *(reside)*, occupy *(take possession)*, remain *(occupy)*, reside. SEE MAIN ENTRY
inhabitable habitable
inhabitance domicile, habitation *(act of inhabiting)*, lodging
inhabitancy abode, address, domicile, habitation *(act of inhabiting)*, inhabitation *(act of dwelling in)*, lodging, nationality, occupancy, residence
inhabitant citizen, denizen, domiciliary, habitant, inmate, lodger, occupant, resident, tenant. SEE MAIN ENTRY
inhabitants community, populace, population
inhabitare reside
inhabitation abode, habitation *(act of inhabiting)*, nationality, occupation *(possession)*, residence. SEE MAIN ENTRY
inhabited populous, residential
inhabiter citizen, domiciliary, habitant, inhabitant, lodger, resident
inhabitual infrequent
inhaerere adhere *(fasten)*
inharmonious different, discordant, disproportionate, dissenting, divisive, harsh, improper, inapposite, inapt, incongruous, inept *(inappropriate)*, offensive *(offending)*, opposite, polemic, repugnant *(incompatible)*, unsuitable. SEE MAIN ENTRY
inharmoniousness conflict, controversy *(argument)*, deviation, difference, discaccord, disagreement, disparity, dissidence, incompatibility *(inconsistency)*, incongruity
inharmony contest *(dispute)*, controversy *(argument)*, difference, disaccord, incompatibility *(inconsistency)*, inconsistency
inhere appertain, exist
inhere in constitute *(compose)*
inherence characteristic
inherent implicit, ingrained, innate, interior, intrinsic *(belonging)*, native *(inborn)*, organic, virtual. SEE MAIN ENTRY
inherent ability proclivity
inherent in incident
inherit accede *(succeed)*, hold *(possess)*, receive *(acquire)*. SEE MAIN ENTRY
inheritable heritable
inheritable property hereditament
inheritance bequest, birth *(lineage)*, birthright, dower, estate *(hereditament)*, hereditament, heritage, legacy. SEE MAIN ENTRY
inherited born *(innate)*, genetic, hereditary, innate, native *(inborn)*, traditional
inherited characteristics character *(personal quality)*
inherited lot heritage
inherited portion heritage
inherited property inheritance
inherited rights birthright
inheritor beneficiary, devisee, heir, legatee, recipient, transferee
inheritrix heir
inhersion characteristic
inhibere stop
inhibit arrest *(stop)*, bar *(hinder)*, bind *(restrain)*, censor, check *(restrain)*, constrain *(restrain)*, contain *(restrain)*, control *(restrain)*, counter, counteract, countervail, curb, debar, detain *(restrain)*, deter, disadvantage, disqualify, encumber *(hinder)*, enjoin, estop, fight *(counteract)*, forbid, forestall, halt, hamper, hinder, hold up *(delay)*, impede, interdict, interfere, interrupt, keep *(restrain)*, lock, obstruct, occlude, prevent, prohibit, repress, restrain, restrict, stall, stave, stifle, strangle, subdue, suppress, thwart, toll *(stop)*, withhold, withstand. SEE MAIN ENTRY
inhibit motion fetter
inhibit movement fetter
inhibited arrested *(checked)*, controlled *(restrained)*. SEE MAIN ENTRY
inhibiting binding
inhibition censorship, constraint *(restriction)*, control *(restriction)*, damper *(stopper)*, deterrence, deterrent, disadvantage, estoppel, fetter, hindrance, impediment, obstacle, prohibition, proscription, quota, restraint, veto
inhibitive preventive, prohibitive *(restrictive)*, unfavorable
inhibitor deterrent
inhibitory preventive, prohibitive *(restrictive)*

inhonestus disgraceful, ignoble
inhospitable illiberal
inhospitality ostracism
inhuman brutal, cruel, diabolic, harsh, malignant, oppressive, ruthless, vicious
inhumane cold-blooded, cruel, harsh, ruthless
inhumanity atrocity, bestiality, brutality, cruelty, oppression, severity
inhumanus brutal, ruthless
inicere infuse, intimidate
inimical adverse *(hostile),* antipathetic *(oppositional),* averse, contentious, detrimental, discordant, hostile, irreconcilable, litigious, negative, opposite, pernicious, perverse, prejudicial, pugnacious, recusant, repugnant *(incompatible),* spiteful, unfavorable, vicious. SEE MAIN ENTRY
inimical descent foray
inimicality belligerency, conflict, contention *(opposition),* feud, ill will, incompatibility *(difference),* spite
inimicalness odium
inimicitia feud
inimicus foe, hostile, inimical
inimitable best, cardinal *(outstanding),* inestimable, original *(creative),* paramount, premium, superlative, unapproachable. SEE MAIN ENTRY
iniquitas disadvantage, partiality
iniquitous bad *(offensive),* blameful, blameworthy, delinquent *(guilty of a misdeed),* depraved, diabolic, disgraceful, dishonest, disreputable, dissolute, fraudulent, heinous, illicit, immoral, impermissible, malevolent, malignant, nefarious, outrageous, peccable, peccant *(culpable),* profligate *(corrupt),* reprehensible, reprobate, scandalous, unfair, unjust, unscrupulous, vicious, wrongful. SEE MAIN ENTRY
iniquity atrocity, delinquency *(misconduct),* grievance, ground, guilt, injustice, misdeed, transgression, vice, wrong
iniquus detrimental, iniquitous, one-sided, oppressive, partial *(biased),* unfavorable, unjust, unjustifiable, unreasonable
inire enter *(go in)*
initial designation *(symbol),* first appearance, inchoate, incipient, indorse, original *(initial),* preliminary, preparatory, previous, primary, prime *(original),* rudimentary, sign, unprecedented. SEE MAIN ENTRY
initially ab initio
initiare initiate, instate
initiate admit *(give access),* amateur, arise *(originate),* cause, commence, conceive *(invent),* create, educate, elicit, embark, enroll, establish *(launch),* evoke, form, generate, incite, induct, instate, invent *(produce for the first time),* maintain *(commence),* make, novice, originate, preface, probationer *(one being tested),* prompt, protégé, receive *(permit to enter),* stimulate, undertake. SEE MAIN ENTRY
initiate a civil action sue
initiate a corporation incorporate *(form a corporation)*
initiated practiced
initiation admittance *(acceptance),* discipline *(training),* genesis, inception, inflow, installation, instigation, nascency, onset *(commencement),* origin *(source),* origination, outset, prelude, preparation, propaganda, start
initiative initial, original *(initial),* overture, preparatory, rudimentary
initiative seizer aggressor
initiator author *(originator),* maker
initiatory elementary, incipient, initial, original *(initial),* precursory, preliminary, preparatory, previous, rudimentary
initium creation, inception, outset, start
iniucundus unacceptable
iniungere impose *(enforce)*
iniuria encroachment, grievance, injustice, oppression, wrong
iniuriosus wrongful
iniurius unjust, unjustifiable
iniustitia injustice
iniustus iniquitous, unjust, unjustifiable, wrongful
inject drug, enter *(insert),* imbue, impact, infuse, inseminate, instill, interject, interpose, introduce, penetrate, permeate, pervade, plant *(place firmly).* SEE MAIN ENTRY
injection expletive, infusion
injudicial illicit
injudicious arbitrary, careless, ill-advised, ill-judged, impolitic, improvident, imprudent, impulsive *(rash),* inadvisable, inept *(inappropriate),* irrational, misadvised, negligent, precipitate, puerile, reckless, remiss, unfit, unpolitic, unprofessional, unreasonable. SEE MAIN ENTRY
injudicious treatment malpractice
injudiciousness inconsideration, indiscretion, inexpedience, temerity
injunction bar *(obstruction),* charge *(command),* check *(bar),* dictate, direction *(guidance),* direction *(order),* fiat, obstacle, obstruction, precept, prescription *(directive),* prohibition, proscription, recommendation, regulation *(rule),* requirement, requisition, restraint, veto. SEE MAIN ENTRY
injunctive prohibitive *(restrictive)*
injure abuse *(misuse),* abuse *(victimize),* aggravate *(annoy),* brutalize, damage, debase, debilitate, deface, disable, disadvantage, endanger, eviscerate, harm, harrow, ill use, impair, inflict, maim, mishandle *(maltreat),* mistreat, molest *(annoy),* mutilate, offend *(insult),* persecute, spoil *(impair),* subvert, sully, violate, vitiate. SEE MAIN ENTRY
injure another's reputation libel
injure by a published writing libel
injure fatally kill *(murder)*
injure one's reputation libel
injure persistently harass
injure the credit of discredit
injure the good name of defame
injure the good reputation of defame
injured aggrieved *(harmed),* aggrieved *(victimized),* blemished, broken *(fractured),* defective, faulty, imperfect, marred, victim
injuring contemptuous, disabling, inculpatory
injurious adverse *(negative),* bad *(inferior),* bad *(offensive),* blameworthy, calumnious, contemptuous, dangerous, derogatory, destructive, detrimental, disadvantageous, disastrous, fatal, harmful, inadvisable, insalubrious, invidious, lethal, libelous, malevolent, malignant, noxious, outrageous, peccant *(unhealthy),* pejorative, pernicious, pestilent, prejudicial, sinister, toxic, virulent. SEE MAIN ENTRY
injurious act delict
injurious action malfeasance
injurious conduct mischief
injurious exercise of authority misfeasance
injurious exercise of lawful authority misfeasance
injurious force battery
injurious interference nuisance
injurious occurrence accident *(misfortune)*
injurious to health deleterious
injurious treatment by a professional malpractice
injuriousness adversity, detriment, mischief
injury abuse *(physical misuse),* adversity, assault, casualty, cost *(penalty),* damage, damages, defacement, delict, detriment, disadvantage, disservice, drawback, expense *(sacrifice),* flaw, grievance, ground, harm, impairment *(damage),* infliction, mischief, misdeed, offense, pain, wrong. SEE MAIN ENTRY
injury to character libel
injury to one's reputation libel
injury to outward appearance defacement
injustice corruption, disservice, error, grievance, ground, inequality, inequity, infringement, mischief, misdeed, misdoing, misjudgment, nepotism, oppression, partiality, prejudice *(injury),* wrong. SEE MAIN ENTRY
inkling clue, hint, inference, intimation, notion, perception, reference *(allusion),* suggestion, suspicion *(uncertainty)*
inland interior
inlay plant *(place firmly)*
inlecebra inducement
inlet access *(right of way),* admission *(entry),* admittance *(means of approach),* entrance, ingress, portal
inlets approaches
inlex decoy
inlibatus undiminished
inliberalis ignoble, illiberal, sordid
inlicere ensnare, entrap, lure
inlicitus felonious, illegal, illicit, inadmissible, unlawful
inligare implicate
inlinere smear
inludere hoodwink
inluminare enlighten
inlustrare enlighten, illustrate
inlustris famous, illustrious, renowned
inmate captive, citizen, convict, denizen, habitant, inhabitant, lodger, occupant, patient, prisoner, resident. SEE MAIN ENTRY
inmost central *(situated near center),* internal, intimate, privy
inmost nature center *(essence),* essence
inmost recesses cache *(hiding place)*
inmost substance center *(essence)*
innate genetic, hereditary, implicit, ingrained, inherent, interior, internal, native *(inborn),* natural, organic. SEE MAIN ENTRY
innate ability aptitude, gift *(flair),* penchant, specialty *(special aptitude)*
innate disposition proclivity
innate inclination instinct
innate proclivity instinct
innate quality gift *(flair)*
innate sense proclivity
innatus inherent, innate, natural
innavigable impossible, insuperable
innectere intertwine
inner central *(situated near center),* interior, internal, intrinsic *(deep down)*
inner being essence
inner drive motive
inner nature character *(personal quality)*
inner part interior
inner reality center *(essence)*
inner voice conscience

innermost interior, internal, intimate
innermost thoughts introspection
innocence compurgation, credulity, ignorance. SEE MAIN ENTRY
innocency innocence
innocens harmless, inculpable, innocent, irreprehensible
innocent blameless, clean, harmless, honest, inculpable, inexperienced, infant, ingenuous, innocuous, irreprehensible, moral, naive, nontoxic, not guilty, pardonable, pure, unaffected *(sincere),* unblemished, unimpeachable, unsuspecting. SEE MAIN ENTRY
innocent bystander SEE MAIN ENTRY
innocent owner SEE MAIN ENTRY
innocentia innocence, integrity
innocently unknowingly
innocents children
innocuous blameless, harmless, nontoxic, salutary. SEE MAIN ENTRY
innocuousness moderation
innocuus harmless, innocuous
innominate anonymous
innovate alter, change, conceive *(invent),* vary. SEE MAIN ENTRY
innovater author *(originator)*
innovation invention, reform. SEE MAIN ENTRY
innovative novel, sophisticated
innovator pioneer
innoxious harmless, innocuous, irreprehensible, nontoxic, salutary
innoxius harmless
innuendo connotation, implication *(inference),* indication, insinuation, intimation, reference *(allusion),* referral, suggestion. SEE MAIN ENTRY
innumerabilis innumerable
innumerable copious, infinite, manifold, multiple, myriad, profuse. SEE MAIN ENTRY
innumerably ad infinitum
innumerous myriad. SEE MAIN ENTRY
innumerus innumerable
inobservance breach, contempt *(disobedience to the court),* delinquency *(failure of duty),* dishonor *(nonpayment),* disregard *(unconcern),* informality, infraction, laches, laxity, negligence, offense
inobservant broken *(unfulfilled),* negligent
inoccupation inaction
inoculate inject, protect. SEE MAIN ENTRY
inoculation propaganda
inoffensive blameless, harmless, innocuous, irreprehensible, nontoxic, pardonable, peaceable, unobjectionable
inoperability impossibility
inoperable impracticable. SEE MAIN ENTRY
inoperative defective, defunct, disabled *(deprived of legal right),* dormant, expendable, inactive, inadequate, ineffective, ineffectual, invalid, nugatory, null *(invalid),* null and void, otiose, powerless, unable, unavailing, unproductive, void *(invalid).* SEE MAIN ENTRY
inopia dearth, inability, indigence, insufficiency, privation
inopportune detrimental, disadvantageous, ill-advised, improper, imprudent, inadvisable, inapposite, inappropriate, inapt, inauspicious, inept *(inappropriate),* injudicious, premature, regrettable, unfavorable, unfit, unsuitable, untimely. SEE MAIN ENTRY
inopportuneness impropriety, inexpedience
inopportunus ineligible, inopportune
inops deficient, destitute, helpless *(defenseless),* poor *(underprivileged)*
inordinacy exaggeration, redundancy
inordinate disproportionate, drastic, egregious, excess, excessive, exorbitant, extreme *(exaggerated),* fanatical, gluttonous, intemperate, needless, outrageous, profuse, prohibitive *(costly),* redundant, superfluous, unconscionable, undue *(excessive),* unreasonable, unwarranted, usurious. SEE MAIN ENTRY
inordinate amount redundancy
inordinate desire greed
inordinate desire to gain greed
inordinately particularly, unduly
inordinateness exaggeration
inornate simple
inosculate amalgamate, combine *(join together),* contact *(touch),* intertwine, join *(bring together)*
inosculated associated
inpermeable invincible
inpour inflow
inpouring inflow
input *(data)* SEE MAIN ENTRY
input *(thinking)* SEE MAIN ENTRY
inquest cross-examination, examination *(study),* hearing, indagation, inquiry *(systematic investigation),* inspection, interrogation, pursuit *(chase),* research, scrutiny, test, trial *(legal proceeding).* SEE MAIN ENTRY
inquietude commotion, consternation, dissatisfaction, distress *(anguish),* disturbance, misgiving, pandemonium, panic
inquilinus lodger, tenant
inquinare stain, sully, tarnish
inquinatus obscene
inquire canvass, examine *(interrogate),* research, trace *(follow).* SEE MAIN ENTRY
inquire for delve, hunt
inquire into analyze, canvass, check *(inspect),* delve, examine *(study),* hear *(give a legal hearing),* investigate, monitor, peruse, probe, scrutinize, search, study. SEE MAIN ENTRY
inquire into systematically investigate
inquire of consult *(seek information from),* cross-examine
inquire to ascertain facts investigation
inquirer applicant *(candidate),* detective
inquirere examine *(interrogate)*
inquiries interrogatories
inquiring inquisitive
inquiry analysis, conversation, cross-examination, cross-questioning, deliberation, discovery, hearing, indagation, inquest, inspection, interrogation, investigation, judgment *(discernment),* market *(demand),* matter *(case),* poll *(canvass),* probe, pursuit *(chase),* quest, research, scrutiny, test, trial *(experiment),* trial *(legal proceeding),* voir dire. SEE MAIN ENTRY
inquiry agent detective
inquisitio examination *(study),* inquiry *(systematic investigation),* investigation
inquisition cross-examination, examination *(study),* hearing, indagation, inquiry *(request for information),* inquiry *(systematic investigation),* interrogation, pursuit *(chase),* question *(inquiry),* research, scrutiny, test, trial *(legal proceeding).* SEE MAIN ENTRY
inquisitional interrogative
inquisitive interrogative. SEE MAIN ENTRY
inquisitive attention diligence *(care)*
inquisitor detective, dictator
inquisitorial dictatorial, interrogative
inquitous sinister
inreparabilis irretrievable
inretire ensnare, entrap
inrevocabilis irrevocable, unavoidable *(not voidable)*
inridere jeer, mock *(deride)*
inritamentum incentive, stimulus
inritare irritate, stimulate
inritum facere invalidate, quash
inritus invalid, null *(invalid),* unavailing, void *(invalid)*
inroad encroachment, entrance, foray, incursion, inflow, ingress, invasion. SEE MAIN ENTRY
inrumpere force *(break)*
inruptio invasion
inrush inflow
insagacious inept *(inappropriate)*
insalubrious adverse *(negative),* blameful, blameworthy, deleterious, detrimental, disadvantageous, harmful, inadvisable, malignant, noxious, peccant *(unhealthy),* pernicious, pestilent, toxic. SEE MAIN ENTRY
insalubriousness disadvantage
insalubris insalubrious, peccant *(unhealthy)*
insalubrity disease
insane deranged, lunatic, non compos mentis. SEE MAIN ENTRY
insanely deluded non compos mentis
insaneness lunacy
insania insanity
insanity lunacy, paranoia. SEE MAIN ENTRY
insanus deranged, frenetic
insatiabilis insatiable
insatiability greed
insatiable gluttonous, rapacious. SEE MAIN ENTRY
insatiableness greed
insatiate rapacious
insciens unintentional, unwitting
inscientia ignorance
inscitia ignorance, incapacity
inscitus incompetent
inscius unacquainted, unaware, unwitting
inscribe book, brand *(mark),* dedicate, enroll, enter *(record),* file *(place among official records),* record, register, seal *(solemnize),* subscribe *(sign).* SEE MAIN ENTRY
inscribe one's name sign
inscribe one's signature indorse, sign
inscribed holographic
inscribere inscribe
inscribing registration
inscriptio address, device *(distinguishing mark),* inscription
inscription caption, dedication, entry *(record),* marginalia, notation, phrase, title *(designation).* SEE MAIN ENTRY
inscriptional holographic
inscroll enter *(record)*
inscrutability complication, mystery, opacity
inscrutable complex, dispassionate, inapprehensible, incomprehensible, indefinable, inexplicable, inexpressive, mysterious, opaque. SEE MAIN ENTRY
inscrutable person enigma
inscrutableness mystery
insecable solid *(compact)*
insectari inveigh
insecure dubious, open *(accessible),* precarious, speculative, uncertain *(questionable),* unreliable, unsound *(not strong),* untrustworthy, vulnerable. SEE MAIN ENTRY

insecurity doubt *(indecision)*, hazard, incertitude, jeopardy, peril, risk, suspicion *(uncertainty)*, threat. SEE MAIN ENTRY
inseminate SEE MAIN ENTRY
insensate callous, deranged, impervious, insensible, insusceptible *(uncaring)*, irrational, lifeless *(dead)*, lunatic, thoughtless, torpid. SEE MAIN ENTRY
insensateness insentience
insensibility ignorance, ingratitude, insentience
insensible blind *(not discerning)*, callous, incognizant, insusceptible *(uncaring)*, intangible, lifeless *(dull)*, oblivious, phlegmatic, reckless, torpid, unaware. SEE MAIN ENTRY
insensibleness insentience
insensibly unknowingly
insensient lifeless *(dead)*
insensitive blind *(not discerning)*, callous, cold-blooded, cruel, draconian, impervious, insensible, insusceptible *(un-caring)*, obdurate, obtuse, relentless, remorseless, ruthless, unaffected *(uninfluenced)*, unresponsive. SEE MAIN ENTRY
insensitivity disinterest *(lack of interest)*, disregard *(lack of respect)*, insentience
insentience SEE MAIN ENTRY
insentient callous, inactive, insensible, unaffected *(uninfluenced)*
inseparability adhesion *(affixing)*
inseparable close *(intimate)*, coherent *(joined)*, cohesive *(compact)*, compound, conglomerate, conjoint, indivisible, inextricable, infrangible, joint, solid *(compact)*. SEE MAIN ENTRY
inseparable intermixture confusion *(turmoil)*
inseparableness adhesion *(affixing)*
insequens subsequent
inserere graft, incorporate *(form a corporation)*
insert affix, append, attach *(join)*, book, embed, immerse *(plunge into)*, impact, infuse, inject, inscribe, inseminate, interject, interpose, introduce, penetrate, pierce *(lance)*, plant *(place firmly)*, record. SEE MAIN ENTRY
insert in a wrapper enclose
insert in an envelope enclose
insert names on a register empanel
insert surreptitiously foist
inserted intermediate
insertion addendum, appendix *(accession)*, attachment *(act of affixing)*, codicil, enclosure, entrance, expletive, inflow, infusion, intervention *(imposition into a lawsuit)*, rider. SEE MAIN ENTRY
inset insertion, plant *(place firmly)*
inseverable indivisible, inextricable, inseparable. SEE MAIN ENTRY
inside herein, interior, internal. SEE MAIN ENTRY
inside and out throughout *(all over)*
inside information disclosure *(something disclosed)*, secret, tip *(clue)*. SEE MAIN ENTRY
insider bystander, member *(individual in a group)*
insider trading SEE MAIN ENTRY
insidiosus insidious
insidious bad *(offensive)*, collusive, contemptible, covert, deceptive, detrimental, devious, dishonest, disingenuous, fraudulent, furtive, harmful, illusory, lawless, machiavellian, perfidious, pernicious, recreant, sinister, sly, surreptitious, untrue, untrustworthy. SEE MAIN ENTRY
insidiousness artifice, bad faith, deceit, fraud, improbity
insight cognition, comprehension, discretion *(quality of being discreet)*, discrimination *(good judgment)*, intelligence *(intellect)*, judgment *(discernment)*, perception, reason *(sound judgment)*, recognition, sagacity, sense *(intelligence)*, understanding *(comprehension)*. SEE MAIN ENTRY
insignia brand, designation *(symbol)*, device *(distinguishing mark)*, label
insignificance immateriality, inconsequence, mediocrity, nonentity, nullity. SEE MAIN ENTRY
insignificancy nonentity
insignificant collateral *(immaterial)*, de minimus, expendable, frivolous, futile, ignoble, immaterial, inapposite, inappreciable, inconsequential, inconsiderable, inferior *(lower in position)*, insubstantial, irrelevant, mediocre, minor, negligible, nominal, nonessential, nonsubstantial *(not sufficient)*, nugatory, paltry, petty, remote *(small)*, slight, tenuous, trivial, unessential, usual. SEE MAIN ENTRY
insignificant amount modicum, scintilla
insignificant number minority *(outnumbered group)*
insincere deceptive, dishonest, disingenuous, disreputable, faithless, false *(disloyal)*, histrionic, machiavellian, mendacious, tartuffish, untrue. SEE MAIN ENTRY
insincerity bad faith, deceit, deception, dishonesty, disloyalty, duplicity, falsification, hypocrisy, improbity, indirection *(deceitfulness)*, knavery, misstatement, pretense *(ostentation)*, pretext, story *(falsehood)*
insinuate allude, connote, hint, imply, impose *(intrude)*, incriminate, indicate, infer, mention, purport. SEE MAIN ENTRY
insinuated assumed *(inferred)*, constructive *(inferential)*, implied, subtle *(insidious)*
insinuates signifies *(denotes)*
insinuating calumnious, contemptuous, leading *(guiding)*
insinuation attribution, charge *(accusation)*, clue, connotation, criticism, defamation, disparagement, hint, implication *(inference)*, indication, innuendo, intimation, mention *(reference)*, reference *(allusion)*, referral, slander, suggestion, tip *(clue)*. SEE MAIN ENTRY
insinuative leading *(guiding)*, suggestive *(evocative)*
insinuatory circumstantial, suggestive *(evocative)*
insipid inferior *(lower in quality)*, jejune *(dull)*, lifeless *(dull)*, nondescript, ordinary, pedestrian, stale. SEE MAIN ENTRY
insipid remark platitude
insist certify *(attest)*, claim *(maintain)*, coax, coerce, compel, constrain *(compel)*, contend *(maintain)*, demand, dun, dwell *(linger over)*, force *(coerce)*, importune, persist, posit, press *(constrain)*, pressure, reaffirm, urge. SEE MAIN ENTRY
insist on call *(demand)*, constrain *(compel)*, enforce, enjoin, order, require *(compel)*
insist upon assert, claim *(demand)*, enforce, exact, impose *(enforce)*, necessitate, repeat *(state again)*
insistance instigation
insisted alleged
insistence assertion, coercion, diligence *(perseverance)*, dun, enforcement, force *(compulsion)*, instigation, persuasion, pressure, request, stress *(accent)*
insistence on a claim assertion
insistence on a right assertion
insistence upon enforcement
insistent dogmatic, exigent, persistent, pertinacious, positive *(confident)*, relentless, urgent, vehement. SEE MAIN ENTRY
insistent demand call *(appeal)*, dun
insisting on notice insistent
insite recognition
insitus ingrained, inherent, innate
insobriety dipsomania, inebriation
insolence bad repute, contempt *(disdain)*, contempt *(disobedience to the court)*, contumely, defiance, disdain, disregard *(lack of respect)*, disrespect. SEE MAIN ENTRY
insolens impertinent *(insolent)*, insolent
insolent brazen, calumnious, contemptuous, contumacious, disdainful, disorderly, lawless, obtrusive, offensive *(offending)*, orgulous, outrageous, presumptuous, proud *(conceited)*, supercilious. SEE MAIN ENTRY
insolentia disrespect
insolently disobedient contumacious
insolicitous insusceptible *(uncaring)*
insolitus unaccustomed, uncommon
insoluble difficult, incomprehensible, inexplicable, inextricable, infrangible, inscrutable, inseparable, insurmountable, problematic. SEE MAIN ENTRY
insoluble difference deadlock, impasse
insolvable incomprehensible, inexplicable
insolvency bankruptcy, default, dishonor *(nonpayment)*, failure *(bankruptcy)*, indigence, poverty
insolvent bankrupt, destitute, impecunious, poor *(underprivileged)*, unsound *(not strong)*. SEE MAIN ENTRY
insolvent debtor delinquent
insons innocent
insouciance disinterest *(lack of interest)*, disregard *(unconcern)*, indifference
insouciant careless, casual, heedless, insusceptible *(uncaring)*, nonchalant
inspect audit, canvass, consider, discern *(detect with the senses)*, examine *(study)*, frisk, investigate, monitor, notice *(observe)*, observe *(watch)*, overlook *(superintend)*, patrol, peruse, probe, research, review, scrutinize, search, study, survey *(examine)*. SEE MAIN ENTRY
inspect accounts officially audit
inspect secretely spy
inspection contemplation, cross-questioning, deliberation, diligence *(care)*, discovery, examination *(study)*, indagation, interrogation, judgment *(discernment)*, observation, probe, research, scrutiny, supervision, surveillance, test, trial *(experiment)*. SEE MAIN ENTRY
inspector detective, director
inspector of accounts comptroller
insperatus unanticipated, unexpected
inspicere examine *(interrogate)*, review, scrutinize
inspiration catalyst, incentive, inducement, influence, instigation, motive, provocation, reason *(basis)*, source. SEE MAIN ENTRY
inspirational provocative
inspire agitate *(activate)*, assure *(give confidence to)*, cause, coax, convince, encourage, evoke, exhort, imbue, impress *(affect deeply)*, incite, inculcate, influence, infuse, interest, motivate, originate, prevail

(persuade), prompt, reassure, spirit, stimulate. SEE MAIN ENTRY
inspire fear discourage, menace
inspire hope assure *(give confidence to)*
inspired causative, felicitous, original *(creative)*
inspirer abettor, catalyst
inspiring persuasive, potent, sapid
inspirit agitate *(activate),* exhort, foment, incite, infuse, lobby, motivate, promise *(raise expectations),* reassure, spirit, stimulate
inspirited conscious *(awake),* sanguine
inspiriting auspicious, moving *(evoking emotion),* potent, propitious
instabilis insecure
instability doubt *(indecision),* fault *(weakness),* frailty, inconsistency, indecision, jeopardy, risk
instability of mental powers lunacy
instable volatile
install admit *(give access),* bestow, commence, constitute *(establish),* deposit *(place),* hire, induct, initiate, instate, invest *(vest),* locate, lodge *(house),* nominate, plant *(place firmly),* receive *(permit to enter).* SEE MAIN ENTRY
installation appointment *(act of designating),* building *(business of assembling),* deputation *(selection of delegates),* designation *(naming).* SEE MAIN ENTRY
installed situated
installing registration
installment advance *(allowance),* binder, collection *(payment),* component, constituent *(part),* deposit, downpayment, handsel, honorarium, installation, pledge *(security),* segment
installment buying credit *(delayed payment)*
instance call *(appeal),* case *(example),* detail, evidence, example, exemplify, expression *(manifestation),* illustrate, illustration, occasion, occurrence, particular, quote, sample, situation, specify, specimen. SEE MAIN ENTRY
instances circumstances
instant crucial, current, expeditious, immediate *(at once),* imminent, important *(urgent),* insistent, instantaneous, pending *(imminent),* point *(period of time),* present *(current),* prompt, rapid, requisite, urgent. SEE MAIN ENTRY
instantaneity dispatch *(promptness)*
instantaneous immediate *(at once),* prompt, summary, unexpected. SEE MAIN ENTRY
instantaneously forthwith, instantly
instantly forthwith. SEE MAIN ENTRY
instar omnium pendent
instare insist
instate delegate, induct, invest *(vest).* SEE MAIN ENTRY
instatement installation
instauration rehabilitation, renewal, reparation *(keeping in repair)*
instead of in lieu of
instead of a parent loco parentis
instigare incite, press *(goad)*
instigate abet, agitate *(activate),* bait *(harass),* evoke, exhort, foment, impel, incite, induce, inspire, lobby, motivate, pique, press *(goad),* prompt, provoke, spirit, stimulate, suborn, urge. SEE MAIN ENTRY
instigating moving *(evoking emotion),* offensive *(taking the initiative)*
instigation cause *(reason),* determinant, impetus, incentive, inducement, influence, origination, provocation, reason *(basis).* SEE MAIN ENTRY
instigative incendiary, offensive *(taking the initiative)*
instigator abettor, catalyst, demagogue, malcontent, special interest
instill communicate, discipline *(train),* imbue, inculcate, infuse, initiate, inject, instruct *(teach),* pervade, plant *(place firmly).* SEE MAIN ENTRY
instillare instill
instillation infusion
instinct caliber *(mental capacity),* gift *(flair),* proclivity, sense *(feeling),* tendency. SEE MAIN ENTRY
instinctive born *(innate),* hereditary, inherent, innate, native *(inborn),* natural, organic. SEE MAIN ENTRY
instinctive belief credence
instinctual born *(innate),* hereditary, native *(inborn),* natural
instituere discipline *(train),* educate, establish *(launch),* instate, instruct *(teach)*
institute admit *(give access),* building *(structure),* cause, chamber *(body),* commence, company *(enterprise),* constitute *(establish),* corporation, create, embark, establish *(launch),* facility *(institution),* foundation *(organization),* generate, initiate, invest *(vest),* launch *(initiate),* legislate, maintain *(commence),* make, organization *(association),* organize *(unionize),* originate, pass *(approve),* preface, produce *(manufacture),* society. SEE MAIN ENTRY
institute a comparison contrast
institute a lawsuit complain *(charge).* SEE MAIN ENTRY
institute a legal proceeding sue
institute an action against a third party implead
institute an inquiry analyze, canvass, delve, probe
institute by law enact, pass *(approve)*
institute commingling of races desegregate
institute legal proceedings litigate
institute process sue
instituted positive *(prescribed)*
institutio instruction *(teaching)*
institution building *(business of assembling),* concern *(business establishment),* corporation, custom, firm, formation, foundation *(organization),* installation, institute, organization *(association),* prescription *(custom),* rubric *(authoritative rule).* SEE MAIN ENTRY
institution of commercial sites development *(building)*
institution of learning institute
institution of proceedings service *(delivery of legal process)*
institution where justice is rendered judicatory
institutionalize confine, constrain *(imprison),* jail
institutive causal, causative, prime *(original)*
institutor author *(originator)*
institutum determination, intention, matter *(subject),* principle *(axiom),* purpose
instruct admonish *(advise),* apprise, charge *(instruct on the law),* command, communicate, control *(regulate),* convey *(communicate),* counsel, decree, demonstrate *(establish),* dictate, direct *(order),* direct *(show),* disabuse, discipline *(train),* edify, educate, enjoin, enlighten, exhort, impart, inculcate, inform *(notify),* initiate, instill, notice *(give formal warning),* notify, nurture, order, oversee, prescribe, recommend, signify *(inform),* superintend. SEE MAIN ENTRY
instruct badly misdirect
instructed acquainted, familiar *(informed),* informed *(educated),* knowing, learned
instructing advisory
instruction admonition, advice, canon, caveat, charge *(command),* dictate, direction *(guidance),* directive, discipline *(training),* dispatch *(message),* edification, education, experience *(background),* fiat, guidance, law, mandate, order *(judicial directive),* precept, preparation, prescription *(directive),* principle *(axiom),* recommendation, regulation *(rule),* subpoena, tip *(clue).* SEE MAIN ENTRY
instruction to appear process *(summons)*
instructional didactic, disciplinary *(educational),* informative, leading *(guiding)*
instructional corps faculty *(teaching staff)*
instructional personnel faculty *(teaching staff)*
instructions charge *(statement to the jury),* direction *(order)*
instructive decretal, didactic, disciplinary *(educational),* informative, informatory, leading *(guiding)*
instructor counselor, pedagogue
instructors faculty *(teaching staff)*
instruere endow, furnish, garnish, marshal
instrument appliance, blank *(form),* certificate, charter *(license),* conduit *(channel),* deed, device *(mechanism),* document, expedient, facility *(instrumentality),* form *(document),* forum *(medium),* indenture, instrumentality, interagent, lease, medium, organ, proctor, resource, tool, will *(testamentary instrument).* SEE MAIN ENTRY
instrument evidencing an agreement contract
instrument for use in combat cudgel
instrument granting possession of premises lease
instrument held until the performance of a condition escrow
instrument in proof affidavit, averment
instrument of proof certification *(attested copy),* evidence
instrument of war cudgel
instrument of warfare bomb
instrument which transfers title to realty deed
instrumental causal, clerical, constructive *(creative),* contributory, effective *(efficient),* functional, intermediate, ministerial, operative, practical. SEE MAIN ENTRY
instrumentality agency *(legal relationship),* intercession, medium, organ. SEE MAIN ENTRY
instruments paraphernalia *(apparatus)*
instruments of combat weapons
instrumentum appliance, document, instrument *(tool)*
insubmission contempt *(disobedience to the court),* defiance
insubmissive froward, insubordinate
insubordinate broken *(unfulfilled),* contumacious, disobedient, froward, impertinent *(insolent),* insurgent, intractable, lawless, malcontent, nonconsenting,

perverse, recalcitrant, recusant, restive, unruly. SEE MAIN ENTRY
insubordination anarchy, contempt *(disobedience to the court)*, defiance, disloyalty, disrespect, insurrection, mutiny, rebellion, resistance, revolt, sedition
insubstantial circumstantial, collateral *(immaterial)*, deficient, delusive, ill-founded, illusory, immaterial, inadequate, inappreciable, inconsiderable, insipid, intangible, minor, negligible, nonsubstantial *(not sufficient)*, nugatory, null *(insignificant)*, perfunctory, remote *(small)*, superficial, unfounded, unsound *(fallacious)*, void *(invalid)*. SEE MAIN ENTRY
insubstantiality artifice, blank *(emptiness)*, immateriality, impalpability, insignificance, nonentity
insuetus unaccustomed
insufferable contemptible, deplorable, intolerable, loathsome, objectionable, obnoxious, odious, painful, repugnant *(exciting aversion)*, repulsive, severe, undesirable, unendurable. SEE MAIN ENTRY
insufferable harm SEE MAIN ENTRY
insufficiency abortion *(fiasco)*, dearth, defect, deficiency, deficit, delinquency *(shortage)*, detriment, disability *(physical inability)*, disadvantage, disqualification *(factor that disqualifies)*, failure *(falling short)*, fault *(weakness)*, handicap, immateriality, impotence, inability, incompetence, indigence, inefficacy, market *(demand)*, need *(deprivation)*, paucity, privation. SEE MAIN ENTRY
insufficiency as a matter of law nonsuit
insufficiency of funds failure *(bankruptcy)*
insufficiency of service emergency
insufficient barren, defective, deficient, devoid, imperfect, inadept, inadequate, incapable, incompetent, ineffective, ineffectual, inferior *(lower in quality)*, minimal, null *(insignificant)*, partial *(relating to a part)*, scarce, unable, unsatisfactory, vacuous. SEE MAIN ENTRY
insufficient evidence nonsuit. SEE MAIN ENTRY
insufficient funds default
insufficient income indigence
insufficiently considered injudicious
insular alien *(unrelated)*, alone *(solitary)*, disjunctive *(tending to disjoin)*, limited, parochial, private *(secluded)*, provincial, regional, remote *(secluded)*, separate, sole, solitary. SEE MAIN ENTRY
insulate isolate, protect, seclude. SEE MAIN ENTRY
insulation buffer zone, bulwark
insulator bulwark
insulse lifeless *(dull)*
insulsus insipid
insult affront, aspersion, bait *(harass)*, contumely, defamation, defilement, denigrate, diatribe, disoblige, disparage, disregard *(lack of respect)*, disrespect, flout, hector, humiliate, jeer, mock *(deride)*, pique, provocation, provoke, rebuff *(noun)*, rebuff *(verb)*, revilement. SEE MAIN ENTRY
insulting abusive, calumnious, caustic, contemptuous, disdainful, impertinent *(insolent)*, insolent, libelous, offensive *(offending)*, outrageous, pejorative, perverse, presumptuous, scathing, scurrilous
insumere spend
insuperabilis irresistible
insuperability impasse, impossibility
insuperable impossible, impracticable, indomitable, inexpugnable, insurmountable, invincible, unattainable. SEE MAIN ENTRY
insuperable obstacle deterrent, impasse
insuperableness impossibility
insupportable indefensible, insufferable, intolerable, unsustainable, untenable
insuppressible hot-blooded, intractable, manifest, uncontrollable
insurable interest SEE MAIN ENTRY
insurance guaranty, safeguard, security *(pledge)*, undertaking *(pledge)*. SEE MAIN ENTRY
insurance adviser actuary
insurance company insurer
insurance contract policy *(contract)*
insure avouch *(guarantee)*, bond *(secure a debt)*, certify *(attest)*, cosign, cover *(guard)*, cover *(provide for)*, ensure, guarantee, harbor, indemnify, pledge *(deposit)*, preserve, promise *(vow)*, sponsor, underwrite. SEE MAIN ENTRY
insured agreed *(promised)*, definite, fully secured, official, safe, secure *(free from danger)*
insurer sponsor, surety *(guarantor)*. SEE MAIN ENTRY
insurgence anarchy, commotion, defiance, insurrection, mutiny, outbreak, outburst, rebellion, resistance, riot, sedition, treason
insurgency defiance, disloyalty, insurrection, mutiny, rebellion, revolt. SEE MAIN ENTRY
insurgent disobedient, insubordinate, malcontent, radical *(favoring drastic change)*, restive, uncontrollable. SEE MAIN ENTRY
insurmountability impossibility
insurmountable cardinal *(outstanding)*, difficult, impossible, impracticable, indomitable, inexpugnable, insuperable, invincible, unattainable. SEE MAIN ENTRY
insurrect disobey, rebel, secede
insurrection anarchy, commotion, defiance, disloyalty, mutiny, outbreak, outburst, rebellion, resistance, revolt, revolution, riot, sedition, treason. SEE MAIN ENTRY
insurrectional disobedient, renitent
insurrectionary disorderly, insubordinate, insurgent, radical *(favoring drastic change)*
insurrectionist insurgent, malcontent
insusceptibility to change indestructibility
insusceptible indestructible. SEE MAIN ENTRY
insusceptible of change indefeasible
insusceptible to change permanent
insusceptire insusceptible *(uncaring)*
intact gross *(total)*, inviolate, live *(existing)*, safe, stable, unblemished, undiminished, whole *(undamaged)*. SEE MAIN ENTRY
intactile intangible
intactilis intangible *(adjective)*, intangible *(noun)*
intactness entirety, whole
intactus intact, inviolate
intaglio stamp
intake receipt *(act of receiving)*, revenue
intakes approaches
intaking acquisition
intangibility immateriality, impalpability
intangible elusive, immaterial, impalpable, imponderable, inappreciable, incorporeal, nonsubstantial *(not sturdy)*, vague. SEE MAIN ENTRY
intangible assets estate *(property)*
integer full, impartial, incorruptible, inculpable
integer individual
integer intact, inviolate, pure, unadulterated, unblemished, undiminished, unprejudiced, upright
integer whole
integral essential *(inherent)*, indispensable, inherent, necessary *(required)*, total, unit *(item)*. SEE MAIN ENTRY
integral part component, constituent *(part)*, detail, element, factor *(ingredient)*, ingredient, member *(constituent part)*, necessity, need *(requirement)*
integrality corpus
integrant constituent *(part)*, detail, integral
integrant part constituent *(part)*
integrate aggregate, connect *(relate)*, coordinate, desegregate, embody, embrace *(encircle)*, relate *(establish a connection)*. SEE MAIN ENTRY
integrated coadunate, collective, composite, compound, conjoint, inseparable
integration affiliation *(amalgamation)*, coalition, consolidation, corpus, federation, merger, totality. SEE MAIN ENTRY
integrative collective
integritas innocence, integrity, principle *(virtue)*, rectitude
integrity adhesion *(loyalty)*, conscience, credibility, ethics, fairness, honesty, honor *(good reputation)*, principle *(virtue)*, probity, rectitude, right *(righteousness)*, trustworthiness, truth, veracity, whole. SEE MAIN ENTRY
integument cover *(protection)*
integumentum veil
intellect caliber *(mental capacity)*, character *(personal quality)*, comprehension, mastermind, reason *(sound judgment)*, sense *(intelligence)*. SEE MAIN ENTRY
intellection apprehension *(perception)*, cognition, deliberation, knowledge *(awareness)*, ratiocination, reflection *(thought)*
intellectional faculty intelligence *(intellect)*
intellectual literate, mastermind, profound *(esoteric)*, sapient
intellectual ability sense *(intelligence)*
intellectual faculties judgment *(discernment)*
intellectual gill-netting SEE MAIN ENTRY
intellectual power caliber *(mental capacity)*, comprehension, intelligence *(intellect)*
intellectual powers intellect, judgment *(discernment)*
intellectual prodigy mastermind
intellectual property rights SEE MAIN ENTRY
intellectualism comprehension
intellectuality comprehension, education, intellect, intelligence *(intellect)*, sense *(intelligence)*
intellectualization concept, contemplation, ratiocination
intellectualize muse, ponder, reason *(conclude)*, study
intellectually deep profound *(esoteric)*
intellegentia comprehension, discrimination *(good judgment)*, insight, intellect, intelligence *(intellect)*
intellegere realize *(understand)*, understand
intellegi non potest incomprehensible
intelligence aptitude, caliber *(mental capacity)*, common sense, competence

(*ability*), discrimination (*good judgment*), espionage, information (*knowledge*), intellect, knowledge (*awareness*), notification, reason (*sound judgment*), report (*detailed account*), sagacity, understanding (*comprehension*). SEE MAIN ENTRY
intelligence agent spy
intelligencer harbinger, informant, informer (*a person who provides information*), spy
intelligent discreet, perspicacious, rational, reasonable (*rational*), sapient, sciential, sensible. SEE MAIN ENTRY
intelligent grip information (*knowledge*)
intelligibility coherence
intelligible clear (*apparent*), cognizable, coherent (*clear*), comprehensible, distinct (*clear*), explicit, lucid, obvious, pellucid, scrutable, simple, solvable, unambiguous, unmistakable. SEE MAIN ENTRY
intelligibly fairly (*clearly*)
intemperance debauchery, dipsomania, exaggeration, greed, inebriation, waste
intemperate disorderly, dissolute, drastic, drunk, egregious, excessive, exorbitant, extreme (*exaggerated*), gluttonous, hot-blooded, incendiary, inordinate, insatiable, lawless, prodigal, profligate (*extravagant*), profuse, promiscuous, unconscionable, unreasonable, unrestrained (*not repressed*), wanton. SEE MAIN ENTRY
intemperately unduly
intemperateness exaggeration
intempestivus untimely
intend allocate, attempt, plan, predetermine, purport, pursue (*strive to gain*). SEE MAIN ENTRY
intendance generalship
intendancy generalship
intendant administrator, director, procurator, superintendent
intended aforethought, apparent (*presumptive*), bona fide, deliberate, express, intentional, knowing, premeditated, prospective, purposeful, tactical, voluntary, willful
intended for a specific purpose express
intended for instruction didactic
intended for teaching didactic
intended for youth juvenile
intended result end (*intent*), purpose
intended to bring about delay dilatory
intended to defer decision dilatory
intended to gain time dilatory
intendere exert, intend
intendment animus, end (*intent*), plan
intense acute, close (*rigorous*), drastic, eager, fervent, forcible, harsh, hot-blooded, intensive, major, potent, powerful, profound (*intense*), purposeful, serious (*grave*), severe, strong, trenchant, vehement. SEE MAIN ENTRY
intense application diligence (*care*)
intense desire ardor, greed
intense study diligence (*care*)
intense thought diligence (*care*)
intensification advance (*increase*), aggravation (*exacerbation*), augmentation, boom (*increase*), exaggeration, growth (*increase*)
intensified intense
intensify accrue (*increase*), aggravate (*exacerbate*), compound, consolidate (*strengthen*), develop, dwell (*linger over*), enhance, enlarge, exacerbate, expand, heighten (*augment*), magnify, reinforce. SEE MAIN ENTRY
intensity degree (*magnitude*), force (*strength*), life (*vitality*), main force, passion, pressure, rigor, severity, strength. SEE MAIN ENTRY
intensity of expression emphasis
intensive comprehensive, cumulative (*intensifying*), radical (*extreme*), resounding, thorough, unmitigated. SEE MAIN ENTRY
intent animus, cause (*reason*), circumspect, connotation, contemplation, content (*meaning*), destination, earnest, forethought, goal, hot-blooded, idea, industrious, intense, objective, pertinacious, plan, point (*purpose*), project, purpose, purposeful, reason (*basis*), scienter, serious (*devoted*), signification, spirit, volition, will (*desire*). SEE MAIN ENTRY
intent on solicitous
intent upon decisive, insistent, resolute
intention animus, cause (*reason*), conatus, connotation, contemplation, content (*meaning*), design (*intent*), destination, end (*intent*), expectation, forethought, goal, idea, objective, plan, point (*purpose*), predetermination, project, prospect (*outlook*), purpose, reason (*basis*), resolution (*decision*), scienter, signification, target. SEE MAIN ENTRY
intentional deliberate, express, knowing, premeditated, purposeful, voluntary, willful. SEE MAIN ENTRY
intentional act overt act
intentional deception fraud
intentional distortion lie
intentional exaggeration lie
intentional exclusion of lessee eviction
intentional killing murder
intentional misstatement falsehood, lie, misrepresentation, perjury, story (*falsehood*)
intentional relinquishment waiver
intentional untruth lie, story (*falsehood*)
intentional wrongdoing malice
intentionality animus, design (*intent*)
intentionally knowingly, purposely
intentionally disregard ignore
intentionally untrue false (*not genuine*)
intentiveness interest (*concern*)
intentivus intensive
intentness compulsion (*obsession*), diligence (*care*), diligence (*perseverance*), industry (*activity*), interest (*concern*), observation, preoccupation, regard (*attention*)
intentus earnest, intense, intent, vigilant
inter se congredi meet
inter se dare reciprocate
inter se repugnare contradict
inter vivos SEE MAIN ENTRY
interacting correlative, interlocking
interaction course
interactive concerted, mutual (*reciprocal*)
interaffiliated interrelated
interaffiliation mutuality
interagency medium
interagent adjuster, advocate (*counselor*), arbiter, arbitrator, factor (*commission merchant*), go-between, instrumentality, liaison, medium, umpire. SEE MAIN ENTRY
interallied associated, concurrent (*united*), interrelated
interassociated interrelated
interassociation mutuality
interblend combine (*join together*), consolidate (*unite*), desegregate, embody, incorporate (*include*)
interbreed commingle
intercalate enter (*insert*), interject, interpose
intercalation insertion, intervention (*interference*)
intercapedo interruption, pause
intercede arbitrate (*conciliate*), impose (*intrude*), interfere, interpose, intervene, mediate, negotiate, reconcile. SEE MAIN ENTRY
intercede for assist, contribute (*assist*), help
interceder adjuster, advocate (*counselor*), arbiter, arbitrator, go-between, intermediary, referee
intercedere intervene, protest
intercept avert, block, check (*restrain*), clog, discontinue (*break continuity*), disrupt, eavesdrop, foil, forestall, hamper, hijack, hinder, inhibit, interfere, interpose, interrupt, occlude, overhear, parry, prevent, stave, stay (*halt*), stem (*check*), stop, thwart. SEE MAIN ENTRY
interception interruption, intervention (*interference*), restraint
interceptor embezzler
intercessio veto
intercession advocacy, arbitration, assistance, collective bargaining, interven-tion (*interference*), mediation. SEE MAIN ENTRY
intercessor adjuster, advocate (*counselor*), amicus curiae, arbiter, arbitrator, counselor, intermediary, judge, jurist, liaison, referee, umpire
interchange alternate (*take turns*), barter, bequeath, change, commerce, communication (*discourse*), consignment, contact (*association*), contact (*communicate*), conversation, conversion (*change*), convert (*change use*), crossroad (*intersection*), devolution, devolve, displace (*replace*), exchange, handle (*trade*), mutuality, quid pro quo, reciprocate, reciprocity, replace, replacement, return (*respond*), subrogation, trade (*commerce*), trade, vary. SEE MAIN ENTRY
interchange ideas converse
interchange information converse
interchange of commodities commerce
interchange of goods commerce
interchange of information conversation
interchange of opinions conference, conversation
interchange of speech conversation
interchange of thoughts conversation
interchange of views discourse, meeting (*conference*)
interchange opinions converse
interchange regularly alternate (*take turns*)
interchange successively alternate (*take turns*)
interchange thoughts communicate, converse
interchange views confer (*consult*), consult (*ask advice of*), discuss
interchangeability identity (*similarity*), mutuality
interchangeable akin (*germane*), coequal, cognate, comparable (*equivalent*), convertible, disjunctive (*alternative*), equivalent, identical, negotiable, reciprocal
interchangeable commitment mutual understanding
interchangeableness par (*equality*)
interchanged mutual (*reciprocal*)
interchanges vicissitudes

intercipere embezzle
interclasped conjoint
interclude deter, occlude
intercommunicate communicate, contact *(communicate)*
intercommunication communication *(discourse),* contact *(association),* conversation, notification, parley
intercommunion consortium *(marriage companionship),* contact *(association)*
interconnect connect *(relate),* contact *(touch),* involve *(implicate),* juxtapose, relate *(establish a connection)*
interconnected interrelated, reciprocal, related, relative *(relevant)*
interconnection chain *(nexus),* coalescence, connection *(fastening),* intersection, mutuality, nexus, privity, relation *(connection),* relationship *(connection)*
interconnections ties
intercourse business *(commerce),* commerce, communication *(discourse),* contact *(association),* dealings, exchange, interchange, sodality
intercross cross *(intersect)*
intercrossing crossroad *(intersection),* intersection
intercurrent intermediate
interdenominational nonsectarian
interdependence mutuality, relationship *(connection)*
interdependent cognate, conjoint, correlative, inseparable, mutual *(collective),* reciprocal, related
interdicere forbid, inhibit, interdict
interdict ban, bar *(obstruction),* bar *(exclude),* block, coerce, condemn *(ban),* constraint *(restriction),* debar, enjoin, forbid, inhibit, prohibit, prohibition, proscription, renounce, restrain, restrict, veto. SEE MAIN ENTRY
interdicted illegitimate *(illegal),* illicit
interdictio aquae et ignis banishment
interdiction canon, constraint *(restriction),* decree, injunction, obviation, prohibition, proscription, refusal, restriction, veto
interdictive prohibitive *(restrictive),* restrictive
interdictory prohibitive *(restrictive),* restrictive
interdictum prohibition
interest activity, advocacy, appertain, behalf, benefit *(betterment),* birthright, boom *(increase),* business *(affair),* claim *(right),* commission *(fee),* concern *(involve),* contribution *(participation),* dividend, dominion *(absolute ownership),* engage *(involve),* equity *(share of ownership),* fee *(estate),* holding *(property owned),* immerse *(engross),* market *(demand),* motivate, nepotism, occupy *(engage),* part *(portion),* patronage *(support),* prescription *(claim of title),* profit, regard *(attention),* regard *(esteem),* remainder *(estate in property),* revenue, significance, title *(right),* weight *(importance),* welfare. SEE MAIN ENTRY
interest certificate coupon
interest group constituency
interest in land easement, estate *(property)*
interest in real estate leasehold
interest in real property freehold
interest of a lessee leasehold
interested eager, inquisitive, interrogative, one-sided, partial *(biased),* receptive, unjust
interested party privy, prospect *(prospective patron)*
interesting attractive, moving *(evoking emotion),* provocative, sapid
interests affairs, dealings
interfere arrest *(stop),* censor, clog, constrict *(inhibit),* counter, countervail, debar, defer *(put off),* delay, disqualify, disrupt, disturb, encroach, encumber *(hinder),* estop, fight *(counteract),* forestall, hamper, hinder, hold up *(delay),* impede, impose *(intrude),* infringe, intercede, interpose, interrupt, intervene, intrude, mediate, militate, obtrude, obturate, overstep, parry, prevent, prohibit, tamper, thwart. SEE MAIN ENTRY
interfere with bar *(hinder),* block, collide *(clash),* conflict, counteract, deter, disadvantage, discontinue *(break continuity),* molest *(annoy),* obstruct, oppugn, preclude, suspend
interfere with the law SEE MAIN ENTRY
interference bar *(obstruction),* barrier, check *(bar),* collision *(dispute),* conflict, damper *(stopper),* deterrence, deterrent, disadvantage, embargo, encroachment, encumbrance, fetter, filibuster, frustration, handicap, hiatus, hindrance, impediment, imposition *(excessive burden),* infringement, intercession, interruption, intervention *(imposition into a lawsuit),* intrusion, invasion, mediation, molestation, nuisance, obstruction, onus *(burden),* opposition, prohibition, resistance, restraint, veto. SEE MAIN ENTRY
interfering intrusive, mesne, obtrusive, preventive, prohibitive *(restrictive)*
interficere dispatch *(put to death),* kill *(defeat),* kill *(murder),* slay
interfuse combine *(join together),* consolidate *(unite),* converge, desegregate, embody, incorporate *(include),* intersperse, penetrate, pervade, unite
interfused conjoint
interfusion coalescence, incorporation *(blend)*
intericere interject, interpose
interim abeyance, cessation *(interlude),* hiatus, interlocutory, interruption, interval, moratorium, pause, pendency, provisional, recess, respite *(interval of rest),* shifting, temporary, tentative, time, transient. SEE MAIN ENTRY
interim agreement modus vivendi
interim dividend coupon
interimere dispatch *(put to death),* slay
interior internal. SEE MAIN ENTRY
interire perish
interjacence arbitration, intervention *(interference)*
interjacent intermediate, mesne
interjaculate inject, interject
interject comment, discontinue *(break continuity),* enter *(insert),* inject, interfere, interpose. SEE MAIN ENTRY
interjection expletive, insertion, intercession, intervention *(imposition into a lawsuit),* intervention *(interference),* remark
interjection into a lawsuit intervention *(imposition into a lawsuit)*
interknit intertwine
interlace commingle, conjoin, desegregate, implicate, incorporate *(include),* intertwine
interlaced complex, compound
interlacement incorporation *(blend)*
interlard commingle, desegregate, intersperse
interlarded promiscuous
interlink annex *(add),* combine *(join together),* connect *(join together),* intertwine, join *(bring together)*
interlinked coadunate, coherent *(joined),* correlative, interrelated
interlinking interlocking
interlock bond *(hold together),* conjoin, connect *(join together),* engage *(involve),* join *(bring together)*
interlocked coadunate, coherent *(joined)*
interlocking coalition. SEE MAIN ENTRY
interlocution communication *(discourse),* conference, conversation, discourse, parlance, parley, speech
interlocutor adjuster, advocate *(counselor),* spokesman
interlocutory SEE MAIN ENTRY
interlope accroach, balk, encroach, impinge, impose *(intrude),* infringe, intrude, obtrude
interloper alien
interloping encroachment, intervention *(interference),* intrusion, intrusive, invasion
interlude abeyance, hiatus, interruption, interval, lapse *(break),* leave *(absence),* lull, pause, pendency, recess, respite *(interval of rest),* time
intermeddle intercede, interfere, interpose, intervene, obtrude, tamper
intermeddling intercession, intervention *(interference)*
intermedial interlocutory, ministerial
intermediary adjuster, advocate *(counselor),* agent, arbiter, arbitrator, broker, clerical, deputy, factor *(commission merchant),* forum *(medium),* go-between, instrumentality, interagent, interlocutory, intermediate, liaison, medium, mesne, ministerial, procurator, referee, umpire, vicarious *(delegated).* SEE MAIN ENTRY
intermediate adjuster, advocate *(counselor),* agent, arbiter, arbitrator, average *(midmost),* go-between, instrumentality, interagent, intercede, interim, interpose, medium, mesne, ministerial, negotiate, procurator, referee. SEE MAIN ENTRY
intermediate agent advocate *(counselor),* go-between, interagent, medium
intermediate time cessation *(interlude),* pendency, respite *(interval of rest)*
intermediation agency *(legal relationship),* arbitration, collective bargaining, intercession, intervention *(interference)*
intermediator adjuster, advocate *(counselor),* arbiter, go-between, interagent, referee, umpire
intermedium adjuster, advocate *(counselor),* agent, broker, chain *(nexus),* conduit *(intermediary),* instrumentality, liaison, nexus, procurator, umpire
interminability indestructibility, perpetuity
interminable continual *(perpetual),* durable, incessant, indeterminate, infinite, innumerable, open-ended, permanent, perpetual, profuse, unlimited. SEE MAIN ENTRY
interminably ad infinitum
interminate incessant
intermingle commingle, confuse *(create disorder),* desegregate, interject, intersperse, merge
intermingled compound
intermissio cessation *(interlude),* cessation *(termination),* halt, interruption, pause
intermission abeyance, adjournment, cessation *(interlude),* delay, extension *(postponement),* halt, hiatus, interruption, interval, leave *(absence),* lull, pause, pendency, recess, remission, respite *(interval of rest).* SEE MAIN ENTRY

intermit adjourn, cease, delay, desist, discontinue *(break continuity)*, disrupt, fluctuate, interfere, interrupt, pause, quit *(discontinue)*, recess, recur, suspend
intermittence irregularity
intermittent broken *(interrupted)*, disjunctive *(tending to disjoin)*, infrequent, periodic, sporadic. SEE MAIN ENTRY
intermittere interrupt, neglect, pause, suspend
intermitti abeyance
intermitting disjunctive *(tending to disjoin)*, intermittent, sporadic
intermix combine *(join together)*, commingle, denature, desegregate, diffuse, embody, incorporate *(include)*, intertwine, merge
intermixed composite, conjoint, miscellaneous, promiscuous
intermixture incorporation *(blend)*, integration *(amalgamation)*, melange, solution *(substance)*
intermutation mutuality
intern arrest *(apprehend)*, commit *(institutionalize)*, confine, constrain *(imprison)*, detain *(hold in custody)*, imprison, lock, shut
internal domestic *(household)*, inherent, interior, intrinsic *(deep down)*, subjective. SEE MAIN ENTRY
internalize accept *(embrace)*, understand
international compact treaty
internecine deadly, destructive, detrimental, harmful, lethal, noxious
internecive lethal
interned arrested *(apprehended)*
internee captive, convict, hostage, prisoner
interning commitment *(confinement)*
internment apprehension *(act of arresting)*, arrest, bondage, captivity, commitment *(confinement)*, constraint *(imprisonment)*, detention, durance, incarceration. SEE MAIN ENTRY
internoscere discriminate *(distinguish)*, distinguish
internuncio advocate *(counselor)*, broker, plenipotentiary, referee
interpellare interfere, interrupt
interpellate cross-examine, examine *(interrogate)*
interpellation citation *(charge)*, cross-examination, question *(inquiry)*
interpenetrate break *(fracture)*, enter *(penetrate)*, intersperse, permeate, pervade
interpenetration osmosis
interplay mutuality, reciprocity
interpolare falsification, falsify
interpolate inject, interject, intersperse
interpolation expletive, insertion, intervention *(interference)*
interponere interject, interpose
interpose comment, discontinue *(break continuity)*, enter *(insert)*, impose *(intrude)*, inject, intercede, interfere, interject, interrupt, intersperse, intervene, introduce, obtrude. SEE MAIN ENTRY
interpose no obstacles authorize
interposed intermediate
interpositio insertion
interposition arbitration, collective bargaining, deterrent, hindrance, intercession, intervention *(imposition into a lawsuit)*, intervention *(interference)*, introduction. SEE MAIN ENTRY
interpres broker, go-between
interpret characterize, clarify, comment, construe *(comprehend)*, construe *(translate)*, define, determine, educate, elucidate, enlighten, explain, explicate, expound, illustrate, judge, read, recite, render *(depict)*, resolve *(solve)*, review, solve. SEE MAIN ENTRY
interpret falsely slant
interpret incorrectly misconceive, misread
interpretability construction
interpretable accountable *(explainable)*, determinable *(ascertainable)*
interpretari construe *(translate)*, elucidate, explicate, interpret
interpretatio construction, explanation, paraphrase
interpretation clarification, comment, connotation, construction, content *(meaning)*, definition, diagnosis, explanation, meaning, paraphrase, rendition *(explication)*, signification, solution *(answer)*. SEE MAIN ENTRY
interpretational interpretive
interpretative demonstrative *(illustrative)*, discursive *(analytical)*. SEE MAIN ENTRY
interpreted coherent *(clear)*
interpreter judge
interpreters of the law judiciary
interpretive demonstrative *(illustrative)*, descriptive
interregnum abeyance, anarchy, cessation *(interlude)*, duration, hiatus, interval, lull, pendency
interrelate connect *(relate)*, involve *(implicate)*, relate *(establish a connection)*
interrelated coadunate, cognate, coherent *(joined)*, collateral *(accompanying)*, correlative, mutual *(reciprocal)*, reciprocal, related, tangential. SEE MAIN ENTRY
interrelation building *(business of assembling)*, chain *(nexus)*, coherence, connection *(relation)*, contact *(association)*, content *(structure)*, mutuality, nexus, proportion, relationship *(connection)*. SEE MAIN ENTRY
interrelation of parts organization *(structure)*
interrelationship relation *(connection)*, relationship *(connection)*
interritus undaunted
interrogate cross-examine, inquire, investigate, pose *(propound)*, probe. SEE MAIN ENTRY
interrogatio inquiry *(request for information)*, interrogation
interrogation cross-examination, cross-questioning, examination *(test)*, hearing, indagation, inquest, inquiry *(request for information)*, inquiry *(systematic investigation)*, investigation, question *(inquiry)*, test. SEE MAIN ENTRY
interrogational interrogative
interrogative inquisitive. SEE MAIN ENTRY
interrogativus interrogative
interrogatories SEE MAIN ENTRY
interrogatory question *(inquiry)*
interrumpere break *(fracture)*
interrupt arrest *(stop)*, balk, cease, check *(restrain)*, close *(terminate)*, condemn *(ban)*, continue *(adjourn)*, cross *(intersect)*, defer *(put off)*, desist, discontinue *(break continuity)*, disorganize, disrupt, disturb, encumber *(hinder)*, estop, halt, hamper, hinder, hold up *(delay)*, impede, inhibit, interfere, interject, interpose, intervene, intrude, molest *(annoy)*, obstruct, obtrude, occlude, pause, preclude, prevent, recess, stall, stay *(halt)*, stem *(check)*, stop, suspend, thwart, toll *(stop)*, withstand. SEE MAIN ENTRY
interrupt work strike *(refuse to work)*
interrupted arrested *(checked)*, desultory, disconnected, disjointed, disjunctive *(tending to disjoin)*, intermittent
interrupting obtrusive
interruption abeyance, adjournment, cessation *(interlude)*, check *(bar)*, cloture, damper *(stopper)*, deferment, delay, disassociation, discontinuance *(act of discontinuing)*, disturbance, frustration, halt, hiatus, hindrance, impediment, interval, intervention *(interference)*, intrusion, lapse *(break)*, layoff, lull, molestation, obstruction, pause, pendency, recess, remission, respite *(interval of rest)*, split, stay, violation. SEE MAIN ENTRY
interruptive intrusive, obtrusive
intersect cross *(intersect)*, separate, split, traverse
intersecting road crossroad *(intersection)*
intersection crossroad *(intersection)*, meeting *(encounter)*. SEE MAIN ENTRY
intersperse diffuse, dissolve *(disperse)*. SEE MAIN ENTRY
interstate commerce commerce
interstice hiatus, interruption, interval, rift *(gap)*, space
interthread intertwine
intertwine combine *(join together)*, connect *(join together)*, consolidate *(unite)*, implicate, join *(bring together)*, merge. SEE MAIN ENTRY
intertwined inseparable, related
intertwist annex *(add)*, combine *(join together)*, conjoin, intertwine, join *(bring together)*
interval abeyance, cessation *(interlude)*, discontinuance *(act of discontinuing)*, duration, hiatus, moratorium, pause, pendency, period, point *(period of time)*, recess, remission, space, term *(duration)*, time. SEE MAIN ENTRY
interval of ease reprieve
interval of rest leave *(absence)*
interval of years age
intervallum interruption, interval, pause
intervene arbitrate *(conciliate)*, check *(restrain)*, defer *(put off)*, discontinue *(break continuity)*, disrupt, estop, forestall, hold up *(delay)*, impose *(intrude)*, intercede, interfere, interject, interpose, mediate, obstruct, obtrude, parry, tamper. SEE MAIN ENTRY
intervener actor, adjuster, advocate *(counselor)*, arbiter, interagent, medium, party *(litigant)*, referee
intervenient intermediate, mesne
intervening interlocutory, intermediate, mesne, ministerial
intervening agent interagent
intervening cause SEE MAIN ENTRY
intervening episode cessation *(interlude)*
intervening party amicus curiae
intervening period cessation *(interlude)*, hiatus, pause, pendency, recess
intervening space cessation *(interlude)*
intervening time cessation *(interlude)*, interval
intervenire interfere, intervene
intervenor amicus curiae, arbitrator, litigant, umpire
intervention agency *(legal relationship)*, arbitration, collective bargaining, intercession, invasion, mediation. SEE MAIN ENTRY

intervention to facilitate a compromise mediation
interventional interlocutory
interventionist advocate *(counselor),* arbitrator
interventor advocate *(counselor)*
interventus intervention *(interference)*
intervertere embezzle
interview appointment *(meeting),* confrontation *(act of setting face to face),* conversation, converse, examination *(test),* examine *(interrogate),* parley. SEE MAIN ENTRY
interviewers press
interweave combine *(join together),* conjoin, connect *(join together),* interject, intersperse, intertwine, join *(bring together)*
interwoven complex, compound, interrelated, promiscuous, related
intestate individual decedent
intestinus internal
intimacy confidence *(relation of trust),* consortium *(marriage companionship),* contact *(association),* marriage *(intimate relationship),* privacy, rapport, secret
intimate advise, connote, consociate, familiar *(informed),* hint, imply, indicate, infer, inseparable, mention, personal *(private),* private *(confidential),* purport, signify *(denote).* SEE MAIN ENTRY
intimate connection affiliation *(connectedness)*
intimated assumed *(inferred)*
intimately allied affiliated, cognate
intimately related affiliated, cognate, consanguineous
intimation cloud *(suspicion),* clue, hint, implication *(inference),* indication, insinuation, mention *(reference),* premonition, reference *(allusion),* report *(rumor),* suggestion, suspicion *(uncertainty),* symptom, tip *(clue).* SEE MAIN ENTRY
intimidate bait *(harass),* browbeat, coerce, deter, discourage, frighten, harass, hector, menace, pressure, threaten. SEE MAIN ENTRY
intimidating chilling effect, dictatorial, portentous *(ominous),* sinister
intimidating force menace
intimidation admonition, coercion, deterrence, deterrent, fear, fright, menace, pressure, threat
intimus intimate
intitle delegate
intolerabilis insufferable
intolerable deplorable, insufferable, loathsome, objectionable, obnoxious, odious, offensive *(offending),* onerous, oppressive, outrageous, painful, peccant *(culpable),* unacceptable, undesirable, unendurable, unsatisfactory, unsavory, unsuitable. SEE MAIN ENTRY
intolerance bias, cruelty, discrimination *(bigotry),* exclusion, feud, hatred, ill will, incompatibility *(difference),* inequity, ostracism, partiality, prejudice *(preconception),* proscription, rejection, spite. SEE MAIN ENTRY
intolerant SEE MAIN ENTRY
intolerandus insufferable
intolerant adverse *(hostile),* bigot, callous, disdainful, dogmatic, draconian, illiberal, insolent, narrow, orgulous, parochial, provincial, relentless, remorseless, supercilious
intoleration rejection
intonate enunciate
intonation inflection, stress *(accent).* SEE MAIN ENTRY
intone enunciate
intorted circuitous
intoxicant alcohol
intoxicated drunk
intoxicating provocative
intoxicating liquor alcohol
intoxication dipsomania, inebriation, passion. SEE MAIN ENTRY
intractable contumacious, difficult, disobedient, froward, immutable, incorrigible, indomitable, inexorable, inflexible, insubordinate, lawless, nonconsenting, obdurate, pertinacious, perverse, recalcitrant, renitent, restive, rigid, severe, unbending, uncontrollable, unruly, unyielding, willful. SEE MAIN ENTRY
intractableness contempt *(disobedience to the court)*
intransient permanent, perpetual
intransigence incompatibility *(difference),* tenacity
intransigency incompatibility *(difference)*
intransigent implacable, incorrigible, inflexible, irreconcilable, obdurate, purposeful, relentless, renitent, resolute, restive, steadfast, unbending, uncompromising, unyielding, willful. SEE MAIN ENTRY
intransmutable definite, durable, indefeasible, irrevocable, permanent
intransparency density
intrare enter *(go in)*
intrepid heroic, spartan, undaunted
intrepidity audacity, confidence *(faith),* diligence *(perseverance),* prowess *(bravery)*
intrepidus undaunted
intricacy complex *(entanglement),* complication, entanglement *(confusion),* involution, predicament
intricate complex, compound, elaborate, incomprehensible, inextricable, labyrinthine, obscure *(abstruse),* recondite, sinuous. SEE MAIN ENTRY
intricate involvement imbroglio
intricate plot imbroglio
intricately wrought elaborate
intrigant confederate, conspirator, conspirer
intrigant copartner *(coconspirator)*
intrigue artifice, cabal, coax, collusion, complication, confederacy *(conspiracy),* connivance, connive, conspiracy, conspire, contrivance, contrive, deceive, deception, frame up, fraud, impress *(affect deeply),* indirection *(deceitfulness),* machination, maneuver, pettifoggery, plan, plot *(secret plan),* plot, scheme, secret, stratagem, strategy. SEE MAIN ENTRY
intriguer conspirator, conspirer, copartner *(coconspirator)*
intriguery collusion, conspiracy, strategy
intriguing artful, attractive, collusive, insidious, machiavellian, perfidious, provocative, sapid, sly, subtle *(insidious),* suggestive *(evocative),* tactical, unconscionable
intrinsic born *(innate),* central *(essential),* essential *(inherent),* implicit, ingrained, inherent, innate, native *(inborn),* organic, virtual. SEE MAIN ENTRY
intrinsic nature gist *(substance)*
intrinsical central *(essential),* essential *(inherent),* organic
intrinsicality character *(personal quality)*
intrinsicalness character *(personal quality)*
introduce adduce, bear *(adduce),* commence, enter *(insert),* establish *(launch),* extend *(offer),* herald, induct, infuse, initiate, inject, inseminate, instate, interject, interpose, invent *(produce for the first time),* launch *(initiate),* maintain *(commence),* move *(judicially request),* originate, pose *(propound),* precede, preface, propose, propound, submit *(give).* SEE MAIN ENTRY
introduce a change affect
introduce a system classify, organize *(arrange)*
introduce as an example cite *(state)*
introduce changes denature, modify *(alter),* qualify *(condition)*
introduce into office induct, instate
introduce new conditions qualify *(condition)*
introduce order codify, marshal, organize *(arrange)*
introduce order into fix *(arrange)*
introduced alleged
introduced to acquainted
introducer architect, author *(originator)*
introducere introduce, present *(introduce)*
introductio introduction
introduction appearance *(emergence),* birth *(beginning),* genesis, inflow, infusion, insertion, installation, nascency, onset *(commencement),* origination, outset, overture, preamble, preface, prelude. SEE MAIN ENTRY
introductory aforesaid, antecedent, elementary, inchoate, incipient, initial, last *(preceding),* original *(initial),* precursory, preliminary, preparatory, previous, prime *(original),* prior
introductory part preamble, preface
introductory statement preamble
introgression entrance, incursion, inflow, osmosis
introire enter *(go in)*
introitus entrance
intromit enter *(insert),* inject, interject
introspect muse, ponder
introspection contemplation. SEE MAIN ENTRY
introspective circumspect, cogitative, pensive, subjective
introversion introspection
intrude accroach, discontinue *(break continuity),* disrupt, disturb, encroach, impinge, infringe, interfere, interpose, interrupt, intervene, invade, obtrude, overstep, pervade, trespass. SEE MAIN ENTRY
intrude illegally encroach
intrude upon harass
intruder alien
intruding obtrusive
intrusion assault, disturbance, encroachment, incursion, infringement, interruption, intervention *(imposition into a lawsuit),* intervention *(interference),* invasion, molestation, nuisance, onset *(assault).* SEE MAIN ENTRY
intrusive impertinent *(insolent),* obtrusive, presumptuous. SEE MAIN ENTRY
intrust delegate
intuit anticipate *(expect),* preconceive, presuppose
intuition belief *(state of mind),* common sense, comprehension, discretion *(quality of being discreet),* discrimination *(good judgment),* insight, instinct, judgment *(discernment),* sagacity. SEE MAIN ENTRY
intuitional uncanny
intuitive acute, innate
intuitive truth principle *(axiom)*

intuitiveness insight
intwine combine *(join together)*
inundate immerse *(plunge into)*, load, outpour, overcome *(overwhelm)*, overload, overwhelm. SEE MAIN ENTRY
inundation cataclysm, inflow, overage, plethora, surfeit
inurbane provincial
inurbanity disrespect
inurbanus inelegant
inure accrue *(arise)*, naturalize *(acclimate)*. SEE MAIN ENTRY
inured impervious, inveterate, nonchalant, unaffected *(uninfluenced)*
inurement habituation
inusitate novel, unaccustomed, uncommon, unusual
inusitation desuetude, disuse
inusitatus eccentric, extraordinary, irregular *(not usual)*, rare, sporadic, uncommon
inutile expendable, futile, ineffective, ineffectual, nugatory, unavailing, unfit
inutile check bad check
inutilis incompetent, ineffective, ineffectual, unfit
inutilitas inexpedience
inutility desuetude
invade accroach, assail, attack, break *(violate)*, despoil, encroach, enter *(penetrate)*, force *(break)*, harry *(plunder)*, impinge, impose *(intrude)*, infringe, interfere, intrude, obtrude, occupy *(take possession)*, overlap, overstep, pervade, preempt, trespass, violate. SEE MAIN ENTRY
invade unlawfully encroach
invader aggressor, assailant
invadere encroach, invade
invading intrusive, offensive *(taking the initiative)*
invalid disabled *(deprived of legal right)*, disabled *(made incapable)*, fallacious, false *(inaccurate)*, faulty, helpless *(powerless)*, illegal, inactive, inconsequential, ineffective, ineffectual, nugatory, null and void, otiose, patient, sophistic, unavailing, unsound *(fallacious)*, untenable. SEE MAIN ENTRY
invalid check bad check
invalid trial mistrial
invalidate abate *(extinguish)*, abolish, abrogate *(annul)*, abrogate *(rescind)*, annul, avoid *(cancel)*, cancel, denature, destroy *(void)*, disable, disarm *(divest of arms)*, disavow, discharge *(release from obligation)*, discontinue *(abandon)*, disown *(deny the validity)*, disprove, disqualify, frustrate, kill *(defeat)*, negate, neutralize, nullify, obliterate, override, overrule, quash, recall *(call back)*, refute, renege, repeal, rescind, revoke, vacate *(void)*, vitiate, withdraw. SEE MAIN ENTRY
invalidate an attorney's license disbar
invalidated disabled *(deprived of legal right)*
invalidating cancellation
invalidation abatement *(extinguishment)*, abolition, ademption, annulment, avoidance *(cancellation)*, cancellation, counterargument, countermand, defeasance, defeat, disability *(legal disqualification)*, discharge *(annulment)*, discharge *(release from obligation)*, discontinuance *(act of discontinuing)*, dismissal *(termination of a proceeding)*, disqualification *(factor that disqualifies)*, disqualification *(rejection)*, dissolution *(termination)*, negation, rescision, reversal, revocation
invalidism disease
invalidity disability *(legal disqualification)*, disqualification *(factor that disqualifies)*, impuissance, nullity. SEE MAIN ENTRY
invalidus ineffective, ineffectual, powerless
invaluable beneficial, constructive *(creative)*, functional, inestimable, lucrative, practical, priceless, profitable, valuable. SEE MAIN ENTRY
invariability constant, regularity
invariable certain *(positive)*, chronic, constant *(adjective)*, constant *(noun)*, definite, durable, immutable, indefeasible, inflexible, obdurate, regular *(orderly)*, repetitious, stable, unalterable, uniform, unyielding. SEE MAIN ENTRY
invariably always *(without exception)*. SEE MAIN ENTRY
invariant constant *(adjective)*, constant *(noun)*
invasion encroachment, entrance, foray, incursion, inflow, infringement, intrusion, onset *(assault)*, outbreak, violation. SEE MAIN ENTRY
invasion of a legal right injury, tort
invasion of a right infringement
invasive intrusive, obtrusive, offensive *(taking the initiative)*
invectio introduction
invective aspersion, condemnation *(blame)*, contumely, correction *(punishment)*, defamation, denunciation, diatribe, disparagement, harangue, libel, malediction, obloquy, outcry, phillipic, profanity, revilement, slander, vilification
invehere introduce
invehi in attack
inveigh demonstrate *(protest)*, denounce *(condemn)*, entice, lash *(attack verbally)*, protest. SEE MAIN ENTRY
inveigh against censure, condemn *(blame)*, contemn, decry, defame, impugn, reprimand, reproach
inveigle bait *(lure)*, betray *(lead astray)*, bilk, cheat, coax, convince, deceive, defraud, delude, dupe, entrap, hoodwink, illude, importune, influence, lure, palter, persuade, prevail *(persuade)*, trap. SEE MAIN ENTRY
inveiglement bribery, decoy, persuasion, seduction
invenire contrive, devise *(invent)*, discover, find *(discover)*, invent *(produce for the first time)*
invent compose, conjure, contrive, create, fabricate *(make up)*, find *(discover)*, forge *(produce)*, frame *(formulate)*, generate, initiate, lie *(falsify)*, make, manufacture, originate, palter, prevaricate, produce *(manufacture)*, scheme. SEE MAIN ENTRY
invented assumed *(feigned)*, fictitious, illusory, mendacious, unfounded, untrue
inventio contrivance
invention contrivance, creation, device *(mechanism)*, expedient, false pretense, falsehood, falsification, fiction, figment, formation, innovation, lie, myth, nascency, origination, pretense *(pretext)*, pretext, product, story *(falsehood)*, strategy, subreption. SEE MAIN ENTRY
invention of lies perjury
inventive fertile, original *(creative)*, productive, resourceful
inventiveness contrivance
inventor architect, author *(originator)*, pioneer
inventories assets
inventory check *(inspect)*, enumerate, index *(relate)*, inspection, invoice *(itemized list)*, itemize, roll, schedule, stock *(store)*, store *(depository)*, tabulate. SEE MAIN ENTRY
inventory expert comptroller
inventum invention
invenustus inelegant
inveracity bad faith, dishonesty, falsehood, improbity, story *(falsehood)*
inverse adverse *(opposite)*, antipode, antithesis, contra, contradictory, contrary, discordant, negative, opposite. SEE MAIN ENTRY
inversely contra
inversion antipode, reversal, subversion
inversus inverse
invert alter, disorganize, disorient, overthrow, overturn, upset
inverted disordered, inverse, opposite
invest admit *(give access)*, allow *(authorize)*, assign *(designate)*, bequeath, bestow, capitalize *(provide capital)*, clothe, commit *(entrust)*, confer *(give)*, constitute *(establish)*, contribute *(supply)*, delegate, deposit *(submit to a bank)*, embrace *(encircle)*, empower, enable, endue, enshroud, finance, induct, instate, lend, repose *(place)*, speculate *(chance)*, spend, supply, vest. SEE MAIN ENTRY
invest empower entrust
invest in purchase
invest in again refinance
invest money fund
invest the power charge *(empower)*
invest with devolve
invest with a body embody
invest with authoritative power charge *(empower)*, delegate
invest with matter embody
invest with power authorize, clothe, commit *(entrust)*
invested capital investment
invested money investment
invested property investment, securities, security *(stock)*, share *(stock)*, stock *(shares)*
invested sum principal *(capital sum)*
investigare examine *(interrogate)*, scrutinize, trace *(follow)*
investigate analyze, audit, canvass, check *(inspect)*, consider, deliberate, delve, discover, examine *(study)*, frisk, inquire, monitor, notice *(observe)*, peruse, probe, research, review, scrutinize, search, study, trace *(follow)*, treat *(process)*. SEE MAIN ENTRY
investigate judicially hear *(give a legal hearing)*
investigating committee commission *(agency)*
investigatio examination *(study)*, investigation
investigation analysis, cross-examination, cross-questioning, discovery, examination *(study)*, experiment, hearing, indagation, inquest, inquiry *(request for information)*, inquiry *(systematic investigation)*, interrogation, observation, probe, pursuit *(chase)*, pursuit *(effort to secure)*, question *(inquiry)*, research, review *(official reexamination)*, scrutiny, test, treatment. SEE MAIN ENTRY
investigation to uncover facts discovery
investigative inquisitive, interrogative
investigator detective, spy
investing with authority delegation *(assignment)*
investiture delegation *(assignment)*, deputation *(selection of delegates)*, installation

investiture of title feoffment
investment advance *(allowance),* advancement *(loan),* binder, deputation *(selection of delegates),* equity *(share of ownership),* expenditure, fund, securities, security *(stock),* share *(stock),* stock *(shares),* venture. SEE MAIN ENTRY
investment portfolio capital
investments capital, finance, personalty, portfolio, property *(possessions)*
investor backer, contributor *(giver),* creditor, customer, grantor, patron *(influential supporter),* shareholder
inveteracy behavior, constant, habituation
inveterate constant, durable, familiar *(customary),* habitual, incorrigible, ingrained, pertinacious, stable, traditional. SEE MAIN ENTRY
inveterate habit habituation, practice *(custom)*
inveterate hatred feud
inveterate practice habit
inveterate strife feud
inveterateness habituation
inveteratus habitual, ingrained, inveterate, old
invictus indomitable, insuperable, invincible, irresistible
invidia disfavor, malice, rancor
invidiosus invidious, odious
invidious caustic, heinous, loathsome, malevolent, malicious, malignant, objectionable, obnoxious, odious, offensive *(offending),* provocative, spiteful. SEE MAIN ENTRY
invidiousness malice
invidus jealous, malicious
invigilate police
invigorate develop, endue, fix *(repair),* meliorate, nurture, recreate, renew *(refurbish),* stimulate. SEE MAIN ENTRY
invigorating medicinal, remedial, salubrious, salutary. SEE MAIN ENTRY
invigoration instigation, revival
invincible defensible, forcible, in-domitable, inexpugnable, insuperable, insurmountable, irresistible, potent, powerful. SEE MAIN ENTRY
inviolability responsibility *(conscience).* SEE MAIN ENTRY
inviolable clean, immune, indefeasible, inexpugnable, infrangible, invincible, lawful, private *(confidential),* sacrosanct, secure *(free from danger),* tenable, unalienable. SEE MAIN ENTRY
inviolable refuge asylum *(hiding place)*
inviolableness inviolability
inviolate certain *(positive),* clean, definite, durable, gross *(total),* honest, intact, law-abiding, sacrosanct. SEE MAIN ENTRY
inviolatus inviolate
invious impervious
invisibility concealment, nonappearance
invisible covert, hidden, impalpable, inconspicuous, indiscernible, intangible, obscure *(faint),* undisclosed. SEE MAIN ENTRY
invisibleness nonappearance
invisus obnoxious, odious
invitatio invitation
invitation instigation, monition *(legal summons),* overture, provocation, request, seduction. SEE MAIN ENTRY
invitation to combat defiance
invite call *(appeal to),* call *(summon),* motivate, offer *(propose),* proffer, request, urge
invite competition challenge
invite the attention occupy *(engage)*
invite to contest challenge
inviting attractive, palatable, persuasive, provocative, sapid
invitingness amenity
invitus involuntary, reluctance
invocare invoke
invocate invoke
invocation call *(appeal),* entreaty, laudation, petition, prayer, request, subpoena, summons
invocation of evil imprecation
invocatory plea call *(appeal)*
invocatory prayer call *(appeal)*
invoice charge *(assess),* register. SEE MAIN ENTRY
invoke bear *(adduce),* call *(appeal to),* call *(summon).* SEE MAIN ENTRY
involucrum veil
involuntarily unwillingly
involuntariness happenstance, instinct
involuntary compelling, fortuitous, innate, mandatory, obligatory, reluctant, unavoidable *(inevitable),* unintentional, unwitting. SEE MAIN ENTRY
involuntary exile banishment
involuntary liquidation bankruptcy
involuntary loss of right forfeiture *(act of forfeiting)*
involuntary manslaughter SEE MAIN ENTRY
involuntary servitude bondage, subjection
involute elaborate, inextricable, la-by-rinthine, sinuous, snarl
involuted complex, inextricable, la-by-rinthine, sinuous
involution complex *(entanglement),* complication. SEE MAIN ENTRY
involutional complex, sinuous
involutionary sinuous
involve appertain, apply *(pertain),* bear *(adduce),* comprehend *(include),* comprise, confound, connote, consist, constitute *(compose),* denounce *(inform against),* embrace *(encircle),* entail, immerse *(engross),* implicate, imply, include, incorporate *(include),* incriminate, interest, monopolize, occupy *(engage),* perplex. SEE MAIN ENTRY
involve in criminal proceeding incriminate
involve in error misdirect
involve in guilt incriminate
involve in shame brand *(stigmatize),* discredit, disgrace
involve in suspicion impugn
involve together commingle, pool
involved at risk, complex, compound, constructive *(inferential),* difficult, disordered, elaborate, esoteric, inextricable, interested, intricate, labyrinthine, obscure *(abstruse),* problematic, recondite, sinuous, tortuous *(bending).* SEE MAIN ENTRY
involved situation imbroglio
involved state complication
involvement affiliation *(connectedness),* association *(connection),* complex *(entanglement),* complication, embroilment, involution, preoccupation, quagmire, relationship *(connection).* SEE MAIN ENTRY
involvere envelop
involving death fatal
involving in guilt incriminatory, inculpatory
involving risk dangerous
involving ruin fatal
invulnerability inviolability, protection, security *(safety)*
invulnerable certain *(positive),* defensible, immune, indestructible, inexpugnable, infrangible, insuperable, invincible, permanent, safe, secure *(free from danger),* tenable. SEE MAIN ENTRY
inward interior, intrinsic *(deep down)*
inward monitor conscience, responsibility *(conscience)*
inward perception impression
inwardly herein, wherein
inweave intertwine
inwrought born *(innate),* ingrained
iocosus jocular
iocularis jocular
iota minimum, modicum, scintilla. SEE MAIN ENTRY
ipse actual
ipse dixit allegation, assertion, bigot, declaration
ipso facto SEE MAIN ENTRY
ipsum se inspicere introspection
ira resentment
iracund petulant
iracundus resentful
iram remittere relent
irascibility outburst
irascible contentious, disobedient, fractious, froward, perverse, petulant. SEE MAIN ENTRY
irascibleness outburst
ire passion, resentment
irenic nonmilitant, placid
irenical nonmilitant, placid
irk aggravate *(annoy),* annoy, badger, bait *(harass),* discommode, discompose, distress, disturb, irritate, molest *(annoy),* offend *(insult),* perturb, pique, plague, provoke. SEE MAIN ENTRY
irksome invidious, operose, oppressive, painful, provocative, vexatious. SEE MAIN ENTRY
iron fetter, relentless, staunch
iron grip adhesion *(affixing)*
iron rule oppression
iron will tenacity
iron-handed peremptory *(imperative)*
iron-hearted obdurate, spartan
ironbound ironclad
ironclad severe. SEE MAIN ENTRY
ironclad agreement contract. SEE MAIN ENTRY
ironhanded dictatorial, severe, stringent
ironia irony
ironic SEE MAIN ENTRY
ironical ironic
irony SEE MAIN ENTRY
irradiate radiate, spread
irrational arbitrary, disconnected, disproportionate, fatuous, ill-judged, illogical, injudicious, ludicrous, lunatic, misadvised, reckless, sophistic, thoughtless, unreasonable, unsound *(fallacious),* untenable. SEE MAIN ENTRY
irrational conclusion non sequitur
irrational terror panic
irrebuttable unavoidable *(not voidable).* SEE MAIN ENTRY
irreclaimable incorrigible, iniquitous, irredeemable, irretrievable, irreversible, irrevocable, lost *(taken away),* obdurate, reprobate. SEE MAIN ENTRY
irreconcilability antithesis, conflict, contention *(opposition),* difference, discrepancy, disparity, incompatibility *(difference),* paradox. SEE MAIN ENTRY
irreconcilable adverse *(opposite),* contradictory, discordant, disparate, disproportionate,

dissenting, dissident, hostile, implacable, inapposite, inapt, incongruous, inconsistent, inept *(inappropriate)*, inimical, litigious, reluctant, repugnant *(incompatible)*, restive, uncompromising. SEE MAIN ENTRY

irreconcilable differences incompatibility *(difference)*. SEE MAIN ENTRY

irreconcilableness incompatibility *(difference)*

irrecoverable incorrigible, irredeemable, irremediable, irreparable, irretrievable, irreversible, lifeless *(dead)*, lost *(taken away)*. SEE MAIN ENTRY

irredeemable delinquent *(guilty of a misdeed)*, diabolic, incorrigible, irrecoverable, irremediable, irreparable, irretrievable, irreversible, irrevocable, lost *(taken away)*, reprobate. SEE MAIN ENTRY

irredeemable bill bad debt

irreducible certain *(positive)*, complex, inextricable, net, simple, succinct

irreformable incorrigible, irredeemable, irreversible

irrefragability certainty, certification *(certainness)*, certitude

irrefragable believable, categorical, certain *(fixed)*, certain *(positive)*, clear *(certain)*, cogent, conclusive *(determinative)*, convincing, definite, incontestable, incontrovertible, indefeasible, infallible, irrefutable, positive *(incontestable)*, uncontested, undeniable, undisputed, unequivocal, unimpeachable, unrefutable

irrefragably admittedly, fairly *(clearly)*

irrefragibility incontestability

irrefutability certainty, certification *(certainness)*, certitude, incontestability

irrefutable axiomatic, believable, categorical, certain *(fixed)*, certain *(positive)*, clear *(certain)*, cogent, conclusive *(determinative)*, convincing, credible, definite, definitive, factual, inappealable, incontestable, incontrovertible, indubious, irrebuttable, positive *(incontestable)*, provable, real, reliable, solid *(sound)*, sound, unavoidable *(not voidable)*, uncontested, undeniable, undisputed, unequivocal, unimpeachable, unrefutable. SEE MAIN ENTRY

irrefutably admittedly, fairly *(clearly)*

irregular anomalous, broken *(interrupted)*, casual, deviant, disjunctive *(tending to disjoin)*, disorderly, disparate, dissimilar, eccentric, extraordinary, haphazard, impermissible, incongruous, infrequent, intermittent, multifarious, nonconforming, novel, peculiar *(curious)*, random, sporadic, suspicious *(questionable)*, tortuous *(bending)*, unaccustomed, unequal *(unequivalent)*, unorthodox, unpredictable, unusual, variable. SEE MAIN ENTRY

irregularity deviation, disorder *(lack of order)*, diversity, entanglement *(confusion)*, exception *(exclusion)*, inequality, informality, misapplication, miscue, misdoing, nonconformity, quirk *(idiosyncrasy)*. SEE MAIN ENTRY

irrelated alien *(unrelated)*

irrelation difference, disparity, distinction *(difference)*, distortion

irrelative apart, disconnected, dissimilar, extraneous, gratuitous *(unwarranted)*, heterogeneous, impertinent *(irrelevant)*, inapposite, independent, irrelevant, unrelated. SEE MAIN ENTRY

irrelevance immateriality, inconsequence, insignificance

irrelevancy immateriality, inconsequence, insignificance, non sequitur

irrelevant collateral *(immaterial)*, expendable, extraneous, extrinsic, gratuitous *(unwarranted)*, immaterial, improper, inadmissible, inapplicable, inapposite, inappreciable, inappropriate, inconsequential, inconsiderable, irrelative, minor, needless, negligible, nugatory, null *(insignificant)*, paltry, peripheral, unessential, unfit, unnecessary, unrelated, unsuitable. SEE MAIN ENTRY

irreligious diabolic, mundane, profane

irremediable blameworthy, incorrigible, irrevocable. SEE MAIN ENTRY

irremedial irreversible

irremissible inexcusable, unjustifiable

irremovable durable, firm, fixed *(securely placed)*, immutable, indefeasible, indelible, inextricable, irreversible, irrevocable, permanent, stable

irrepair deterioration

irreparable incorrigible, irrecoverable, irredeemable, irremediable, irretrievable, irreversible, irrevocable. SEE MAIN ENTRY

irreparable harm SEE MAIN ENTRY

irrepealable conclusive *(determinative)*, irreversible, irrevocable, noncancellable

irreplaceability importance, need *(requirement)*

irreplaceable indispensable, inestimable, integral, priceless, vital

irreplaceable feature necessity, need *(requirement)*

irrepoachable honest

irrepproachable law-abiding

irreprehensible blameless, clean, inculpable, unimpeachable, unobjectionable. SEE MAIN ENTRY

irrepressible hot-blooded, indomitable, intractable, rampant, uncontrollable, unruly

irreproachable blameless, clean, incorruptible, inculpable, infallible, irreprehensible, meritorious, unimpeachable, unobjectionable

irreprovable blameless, clean, irreprehensible, unobjectionable

irresistable uncontrollable

irresistible certain *(positive)*, cogent, compelling, compulsory, definite, in-domitable, inexpugnable, invincible, necessary *(inescapable)*, omnipotent, powerful, provocative, unavoidable *(inevitable)*. SEE MAIN ENTRY

irresistible compulsion necessity

irresistible impulse compulsion *(obsession)*, obsession

irresistible urge passion

irresoluble certain *(positive)*

irresolute capricious, doubtful, hesitant, insipid, mutable, noncommittal, passive, pliant, speculative, undecided, volatile. SEE MAIN ENTRY

irresoluteness ambivalence, indecision

irresolution ambivalence, doubt *(indecision)*, hesitation, incertitude, indecision, inertia, quandary

irresolved noncommittal, outstanding *(unresolved)*

irrespective SEE MAIN ENTRY

irrespective of regardless

irresponsibility anarchy, inconsideration, negligence, res ipsa loquitur

irresponsible capricious, careless, disobedient, heedless, ill-advised, lawless, misadvised, negligent, reckless, thoughtless, uncurbed, undependable, unreliable, untrustworthy, variable. SEE MAIN ENTRY

irresponsive unresponsive

irretrievable irrecoverable, irredeemable, irremediable, irreversible, irrevocable, lost *(taken away)*. SEE MAIN ENTRY

irretrievable debt bad debt

irrevealable clandestine, confidential

irreverant profane

irreverence bad repute, blasphemy, contempt *(disobedience to the court)*, disparagement, disrespect, expletive, ignominy, violation

irreverent contemptuous, impertinent *(insolent)*, pejorative, presumptuous, reprobate, supercilious. SEE MAIN ENTRY

irreverent behavior blasphemy

irreversible certain *(positive)*, decisive, definite, indefeasible, indelible, ironclad, irrecoverable, irredeemable, irremediable, irreparable, irrevocable, noncancellable, permanent, stable, unalterable. SEE MAIN ENTRY

irreversible damage prejudice *(injury)*

irrevocability certitude

irrevocable certain *(positive)*, compulsory, conclusive *(determinative)*, decisive, definite, final, immutable, inappealable, indefeasible, indelible, indestructible, ironclad, irredeemable, irremediable, irreversible, lost *(taken away)*, necessary *(inescapable)*, permanent, stable, unavoidable *(inevitable)*, unavoidable *(not voidable)*. SEE MAIN ENTRY

irrevocable decision adjudication

irritable fractious, froward, petulant, querulous, sensitive *(easily affected)*

irritant aggravation *(annoyance)*

irritate affront, aggravate *(annoy)*, agitate *(activate)*, annoy, antagonize, badger, bait *(harass)*, disaffect, discommode, discompose, distress, exacerbate, harass, harrow, harry *(harass)*, hector, incense, inconvenience, molest *(annoy)*, offend *(insult)*, perturb, pique, plague, press *(goad)*, provoke, repel *(disgust)*. SEE MAIN ENTRY

irritating caustic, irksome, loathsome, offensive *(offending)*, painful, provocative, vexatious

irritation aggravation *(annoyance)*, dissatisfaction, instigation, molestation, nuisance, provocation, umbrage

irrupt encroach, intrude

irruption assault, encroachment, incursion, inflow, intrusion, outbreak, outburst

is composed of consist

is essentially consist

island isolate

isolate abstract *(separate)*, constrain *(imprison)*, detain *(hold in custody)*, dissociate, estrange, exclude, immure, insulate, jail, part *(separate)*, relegate, remove *(eliminate)*, seclude, select, sequester *(seclude)*, sever, split. SEE MAIN ENTRY

isolated alone *(solitary)*, apart, derelict *(abandoned)*, disconnected, discrete, disjunctive *(tending to disjoin)*, exclusive *(singular)*, inapposite, individual, insular, obscure *(remote)*, private *(secluded)*, remote *(secluded)*, separate, singular, sole, solitary, sporadic

isolation exclusion, expulsion, ostracism, privacy, removal, segregation *(separation)*, severance. SEE MAIN ENTRY

isolationist neutral

issuance apportionment, circulation, dispensation *(act of dispensing)*, distribution *(apportionment)*, output, publication *(disclosure)*, publicity. SEE MAIN ENTRY

issue accrue *(arise)*, administer *(tender)*, bestow, blood, cause of action, cessation *(termination)*, child, children, circulate, confer *(give)*, contention *(argument)*, denouement, derivation, descendant, dispense,

disperse *(disseminate)*, disseminate, divide *(distribute)*, dole, effect, emanate, emerge, emit, ensue, evolve, exude, family *(household)*, impart, issuance, matter *(subject)*, mete, offshoot, offspring, outcome, outflow, outgrowth, output, point *(item)*, post, posterity, proceed *(go forward)*, product, progeny, promulgate, propagate *(spread)*, publication *(printed matter)*, publish, result, send, serial, serve *(deliver a legal instrument)*, signify *(inform)*, stem *(originate)*, subject *(topic)*, succession, supervene, tender, thesis, transmit, utter. SEE MAIN ENTRY
issue a command command, constrain *(compel)*, dictate, direct *(order)*, enact, instruct *(direct)*, require *(compel)*, subpoena, summon
issue a court directive subpoena, summon
issue a decree command, direct *(order)*, instruct *(direct)*, order
issue a fiat decree
issue a proclamation decree, notify
issue a pronouncement notify
issue a statement certify *(attest)*, posit, post, publish, speak
issue a ukase decree
issue a writ charge *(accuse)*, subpoena
issue an edict decree
issue an invitation call *(summon)*
issue an order command, dictate, direct *(order)*, enjoin, instruct *(direct)*, prescribe
issue counterfeit money forge *(counterfeit)*
issue for distribution publish
issue for public sale publish
issue forth arise *(originate)*, depart
issue of fact SEE MAIN ENTRY
issue one's fiat order
issue process subpoena, summon
issue rays radiate
issue threats coerce
issued positive *(prescribed)*
issued weapons armed
issueless barren, otiose, unproductive
it follows that consequently
itaque consequently
itch passion
item article *(commodity)*, article *(distinct section of a writing)*, component, count, detail, element, entity, entry *(record)*, member *(constituent part)*, object, particular, particularity, possession *(property)*, product, specification, technicality, term *(provision)*, title *(division)*, trait. SEE MAIN ENTRY
item in the indictment count
item of evidence exhibit
item of information particular
item of personalty possession *(property)*
item on the agenda issue *(matter in dispute)*, matter *(subject)*
itemization inventory, specification
itemize delineate, describe, designate, detail *(particularize)*, enumerate, impanel, index *(relate)*, specify, tabulate. SEE MAIN ENTRY
itemized detailed
itemized account bill *(invoice)*, invoice *(itemized list)*, tariff *(bill)*
itemized list inventory
itemized specification bill *(formal declaration)*
items circumstances, commodities, contents, goods
items for sale merchandise
items of business agenda
items of personalty possessions
iter course
iterare reiterate, renew *(begin again)*, repeat *(do again)*
iterate copy, reaffirm, recount, reiterate, repeat *(state again)*
iteration narration, recital, restatement. SEE MAIN ENTRY
iterative incessant, insistent. SEE MAIN ENTRY
iterum reopen
itinerancy vagrancy
itinerant moving *(in motion)*. SEE MAIN ENTRY
itinerary plan
iubeo direction *(order)*
iubere order, pass *(approve)*
iucundus palatable
iudex judge, juror
iudicare criticize *(evaluate)*, judge, try *(conduct a trial)*
iudices jury
iudicialis forensic, judicial
iudicium court, criticism, determination, discretion *(quality of being discreet)*, discrimination *(good judgment)*, estimate *(idea)*, holding *(ruling of a court)*, insight, judgment *(discernment)*, judgment *(formal court decree)*, opinion *(belief)*, perception, sense *(intelligence)*, sentence, trial *(legal proceeding)*, tribunal, verdict
iudicium exercere judge
iungere connect *(join together)*
iurare swear
iureiurando adfirmare swear
iurgium altercation
iuridicialis forensic, juridical
iuris consultus jurist
iuris peritus jurist
iuris prudentia jurisprudence
iurisconsultus lawyer
iurisdictio judicature, jurisdiction
iurisperitus lawyer
ius law, right *(entitlement)*, statute
iusiurandum oath
iussum fiat, injunction, order *(judicial directive)*, regulation *(rule)*
iusta right *(entitlement)*
iuste fairly *(impartially)*
iustitia equity *(justice)*, fairness, justice
iustus equitable, just, justifiable, regular *(conventional)*, rightful, valid
iuvenilis juvenile *(adjective)*, juvenile *(noun)*

J

jab jostle *(bump into)*
jabber jargon *(unintelligible language)*, prattle
jabbering loquacious
jack up elevate
jackpot prize
jactation SEE MAIN ENTRY
jactitation jactation, rodomontade
jaculate impel, launch *(project)*, precipitate *(throw down violently)*, send
jaggedness irregularity
jail arrest *(apprehend)*, captivity, capture, cell, commit *(institutionalize)*, confine, constrain *(imprison)*, contain *(restrain)*, detain *(hold in custody)*, imprison, lock, penitentiary, prison, reformatory, restrain, seize *(apprehend)*. SEE MAIN ENTRY
jail inmate convict
jailbreak SEE MAIN ENTRY
jailed arrested *(apprehended)*, in custody
jailed person prisoner
jailer custodian *(warden)*, warden
jailhouse cell, penitentiary
jailing commitment *(confinement)*
jam block, imbroglio, impact
jam-packed replete
jammed inextricable, replete
jangle altercation, brawl *(noun)*, brawl *(verb)*, controversy *(argument)*, fracas, fray, noise
jangling altercation
jape SEE MAIN ENTRY
jar agitate *(perturb)*, bicker, collision *(accident)*, discompose, fracas, irritate, jostle *(bump into)*, perturb, strike *(collide)*
jargon language, phraseology. SEE MAIN ENTRY
jarring inapplicable, inapposite, inapt, incongruous, inconsistent, inept *(inappropriate)*, repugnant *(incompatible)*
jaundice bias, intolerance, predetermination, prejudice *(influence)*
jaundiced bilious, dyseptic, one-sided, parochial, partial *(biased)*, unequal *(unjust)*, unfair, unjust
jaunt perambulate
jaunty resilient
jealous resentful, suspicious *(distrustful)*. SEE MAIN ENTRY
jealousy resentment
jeer disdain, disparage, flout, hector, jape, mock *(deride)*, reject, ridicule. SEE MAIN ENTRY
jeering disdainful
jejune deficient, irksome, nugatory, otiose, pedestrian, prosaic, puerile, stale, unproductive. SEE MAIN ENTRY
jellification congealment
jeopardize compromise *(endanger)*, endanger, expose. SEE MAIN ENTRY
jeopardous noxious, precarious
jeopardy danger, hazard, peril, predicament, risk, threat, venture. SEE MAIN ENTRY
jest jape
jesting jocular
jet emit, outburst, outflow
jettison abandon *(relinquish)*, disown *(refuse to acknowledge)*, eject *(expel)*, evict, reject, relinquish. SEE MAIN ENTRY
jettisoned derelict *(abandoned)*
jibe comport *(agree with)*, concur *(agree)*
jilt rebuff, reject, spurn
jingoism intolerance
jitteriness trepidation
job appointment *(position)*, burden, business *(occupation)*, calling, career, employment, enterprise *(undertaking)*, labor *(work)*, livelihood, mission, occupation *(vocation)*, office, part *(role)*, position *(business status)*, post, profession *(vocation)*, project, province, pursuit *(occupation)*, role, trade *(occupation)*, undertaking *(enterprise)*, work *(employment)*. SEE MAIN ENTRY
job action strike
job holder incumbent
job seeker candidate
jobation reprimand, reproach
jobber dealer
jobbery abuse *(corrupt practice)*, artifice, bribery, corruption, crime, gratuity *(bribe)*, improbity, pettifoggery. SEE MAIN ENTRY
jobbing commercial
jobholder employee
jobless idle, otiose, unemployed
jockey maneuver
jocose jocular

jocular SEE MAIN ENTRY
jocularity life *(vitality)*
jocund jocular
jocundity life *(vitality)*
jog impetus, reminder, stimulate
jog the memory remind
join abut, accompany, adhere *(fasten)*, affiliate, affix, aggregate, amalgamate, annex *(add)*, append, bond *(hold together)*, border *(approach)*, border *(bound)*, cement, collect *(gather)*, commingle, congregate, connect *(join together)*, consolidate *(unite)*, conspire, contact *(touch)*, correspond *(be equivalent)*, enroll, espouse, federalize *(associate)*, federate, incorporate *(include)*, juxtapose, lock, meet, merge, organize *(unionize)*, participate, register, unite. SEE MAIN ENTRY
join as a third party implead
join battle with engage *(involve)*
join forces affiliate, combine *(act in concert)*, concur *(agree)*, connive, consolidate *(unite)*, conspire, cooperate, federalize *(associate)*, federate, involve *(participate)*, merge, participate, unite
join forces with consolidate *(unite)*
join in concur *(agree)*, contribute *(assist)*, cooperate, involve *(participate)*, participate
join in a compact confirm
join in a conversation discuss, speak
join in partnership with participate
join issue bicker, collide *(clash)*, disaccord, oppose, reason *(persuade)*, rebut, respond
join the majority conform
join together affiliate, concur *(agree)*, conjoin, converge, desegregate, organize *(unionize)*
join with combine *(act in concert)*, concur *(agree)*, connive, cooperate
joinder attachment *(act of affixing)*, merger. SEE MAIN ENTRY
joinder of a party SEE MAIN ENTRY
joined additional, associated, attached *(annexed)*, coadunate, collective, composite, concerted, concurrent *(united)*, conjoint, contiguous, correlative, inextricable, inseparable, interrelated, joint, promiscuous
joined in a union federal
joined together conjoint
joined with affiliated
joiner connection *(fastening)*
joining accession *(annexation)*, addition, attachment *(act of affixing)*, coalescence, combination, contact *(touching)*, joinder, marriage *(intimate relationship)*, matrimony, meeting *(encounter)*, union *(unity)*
joining place intersection
joining road crossroad *(intersection)*
joint common *(shared)*, concerted, concomitant, concordant, concurrent *(united)*, conjoint, connection *(fastening)*, consensual, federal, harmonious, intersection, mutual *(collective)*. SEE MAIN ENTRY
joint action concert, cooperative
joint agreement mutual understanding
joint and several *in solido*. SEE MAIN ENTRY
joint and several liability SEE MAIN ENTRY
joint concern cartel, coalition, company *(enterprise)*, corporation, firm, merger, organization *(association)*, pool
joint custody SEE MAIN ENTRY
joint discussion panel *(discussion group)*
joint effect synergy
joint effort coaction, collusion, conformity *(agreement)*, conjunction, connivance, conspiracy
joint endeavor coalition
joint enterprise affiliation *(connectedness)*, association *(connection)*
joint interest partnership
joint operation concert, cooperative
joint ownership pool
joint pact mutual understanding
joint participation coaction
joint planning collusion, conformity *(agreement)*, connivance, conspiracy
joint possession cooperative, pool
joint-operator coactor
jointure dower
joke jape
joke about mock *(deride)*
joking jocular
jolly jocular
jolt bombshell, collision *(accident)*, discompose, impetus, jostle *(bump into)*, perturb, strike *(collide)*
joshing jocular
jot iota, minimum
jot down enter *(record)*, note *(record)*, record, set down
jottings script
journal calendar *(record of yearly periods)*, dossier, record, register. SEE MAIN ENTRY
journalistic writers press
journalists press
journalize record
journey move *(alter position)*, perambulate, quest
journey's end destination
journeying itinerant, moving *(in motion)*
journeyman artisan, practitioner
joust compete, fight *(battle)*
jovial jocular
joviality life *(vitality)*
joyful ecstatic, felicitous, jocular
joyless bleak *(not favorable)*, bleak *(severely simple)*, despondent, disconsolate, grave *(solemn)*, lamentable, lugubrious, pessimistic
joylessness damper *(depressant)*, pessimism
joyous ecstatic, felicitous, jocular
jubilant ecstatic
jubilee holiday
judge adjudge, adjudicate, arbitrate *(adjudge)*, assess *(appraise)*, bench, censor, conclude *(decide)*, construe *(comprehend)*, criticize *(evaluate)*, decide, decree, deduce, deduct *(conclude by reasoning)*, deem, deliberate, determine, diagnose, discern *(discriminate)*, distinguish, estimate, evaluate, expect *(consider probable)*, find *(determine)*, gauge, guess, hear *(give a legal hearing)*, hold *(decide)*, intercede, jurist, magistrate, measure, opine, presume, presuppose, pronounce *(pass judgment)*, rate, reason *(conclude)*, rebuke, referee, speculate *(conjecture)*, surmise, suspect *(think)*, try *(conduct a trial)*, umpire, vote. SEE MAIN ENTRY
judge at random guess
judge before hearing prejudge
judge beforehand forejudge, preconceive, prejudge
judge erroneously misjudge
judge from premises infer
judge in advance forejudge, prejudge, presuppose
judge inaccurately misjudge
judge innocent palliate *(excuse)*
judge the future presage
judge with indulgence excuse
judge with uncertainty guess
judge wrongly misjudge
judged deliberate
judged by comparison comparative
judgelike judicial, juridical
judges tribunal
judge's chamber SEE MAIN ENTRY
judges of the facts jury
judgmatic determinative, discriminating *(judicious)*, judicial, judicious, juridical. SEE MAIN ENTRY
judgment adjudication, alternative *(option)*, apprehension *(perception)*, arbitration, authority *(documentation)*, belief *(state of mind)*, caliber *(mental capacity)*, choice *(decision)*, common sense, concept, conclusion *(determination)*, condemnation *(punishment)*, consideration *(contemplation)*, conviction *(finding of guilt)*, conviction *(persuasion)*, decision *(election)*, decree, deliberation, determination, diagnosis, dialectic, dictate, direction *(order)*, discipline *(punishment)*, edict, estimate *(idea)*, estimation *(calculation)*, experience *(background)*, fiat, finding, holding *(ruling of a court)*, idea, inference, notion, opinion *(belief)*, opinion *(judicial decision)*, outcome, perception, position *(point of view)*, pronouncement, prudence, recommendation, regard *(esteem)*, relief *(legal redress)*, res judicata, result, ruling, sagacity, sense *(intelligence)*, sensibility, standpoint, verdict, vote. SEE MAIN ENTRY
judgment dissolving a marriage divorce
judgment for the defendant as a matter of law nonsuit
judgment of the court declaratory judgment
judgment on facts adjudication, determination, holding *(ruling of a court)*, opinion *(judicial decision)*. SEE MAIN ENTRY
judgment seat bench, court, tribunal
judicable determinable *(ascertainable)*
judicate adjudge, arbitrate *(adjudge)*
judication award
judicative judicial, juridical
judicator arbitrator, referee
judicatorial juridical
judicatory bench, board, chamber *(body)*, forensic, forum *(court)*, judicature, judiciary, jural, juridical, licit. SEE MAIN ENTRY
judicature bar *(court)*, bench, council *(assembly)*, forum *(court)*, judgment *(formal court decree)*, judicatory, judiciary. SEE MAIN ENTRY
judicial forensic, jural, juridical, licit, objective, open-minded, politic, unprejudiced. SEE MAIN ENTRY
judicial administrator clerk
judicial antecedent precedent
judicial assembly bench, court
judicial assertion dictum, judgment *(formal court decree)*
judicial assistant clerk
judicial authorization warrant *(judicial writ)*
judicial branch chamber *(body)*, judiciary
judicial branch of government judiciary
judicial charge arraignment
judicial command mandate, order *(judicial directive)*
judicial comment dictum
judicial conclusion finding
judicial contest action *(proceeding)*, case *(lawsuit)*, controversy *(lawsuit)*, lawsuit, suit, trial *(legal proceeding)*. SEE MAIN ENTRY
judicial decision adjudication, award, decree, holding *(ruling of a court)*

juxtaposit adjoin, border *(approach)*, border *(bound)*
juxtaposition collation, connection *(abutment)*, contact *(touching)*, propinquity *(proximity)*. SEE MAIN ENTRY
juxtapositional immediate *(not distant)*

K

kaleidoscopic complex, protean
keen acute, bitter *(penetrating)*, close *(rigorous)*, cognizant, discriminating *(judicious)*, eager, fervent, incisive, intense, perceptive, perspicacious, ready *(willing)*, receptive, responsive, sapient, sedulous, sensitive *(discerning)*, sly, solicitous, subtle *(refined)*, trenchant, zealous. SEE MAIN ENTRY
keen sight perception
keen-eyed perspicacious
keen-sighted perspicacious
keen-witted perspicacious
keeness comprehension, perception
keenly aware vigilant
keenly sensitive acute
keenness insight, intelligence *(intellect)*, judgment *(discernment)*, predisposition, rigor, sagacity, sensibility
keensightedness sagacity
keep accompany, concern *(care)*, conserve, constrict *(inhibit)*, continue *(persevere)*, detain *(restrain)*, endure *(last)*, fulfill, fund, harbor, hoard, hold *(possess)*, jail, livelihood, obey, observe *(obey)*, occupy *(take possession)*, own, perform *(adhere to)*, possess, preserve, prolong, protect, remain *(continue)*, reserve, restrain, retain *(employ)*, retain *(keep in possession)*, save *(hold back)*, store, subsidize, sustenance, uphold, withhold. SEE MAIN ENTRY
keep a date rendezvous
keep a secret cloak
keep accounts note *(record)*, record
keep alive keep *(shelter)*, maintain *(carry on)*, perpetuate, preserve
keep aloof elude, estrange
keep aloof from forgo
keep an account deposit *(submit to a bank)*
keep an appointment rendezvous
keep an eye on observe *(watch)*, patrol
keep an eye upon survey *(examine)*
keep apart dichotomize, dissociate, estrange, insulate, isolate, part *(separate)*, seclude, separate, sever, withdraw
keep as captive constrain *(imprison)*, imprison
keep as one's own hold *(possess)*
keep at persist
keep at a distance eschew, estrange, rebuff
keep at a distance from avoid *(evade)*
keep at bay parry, repel *(drive back)*, repulse, stave, stem *(check)*
keep away eschew, parry
keep away from avoid *(evade)*, forgo, shirk, shun
keep back arrest *(stop)*, check *(restrain)*, constrain *(restrain)*, constrict *(inhibit)*, delay, detain *(restrain)*, deter, discourage, encumber *(hinder)*, forbear, hinder, hoard, impede, reserve, stall, strangle, suppress, withhold
keep behind bars enclose, imprison
keep busy occupy *(engage)*
keep clandestine blind *(obscure)*, conceal, enshroud, plant *(covertly place)*
keep clear of avoid *(evade)*, eschew, evade *(elude)*, parry, shun
keep company with accompany
keep count enumerate
keep count of poll
keep down extinguish, repress, strangle, subject, suppress
keep driving persevere
keep entirely to oneself monopolize
keep faith adhere *(maintain loyalty)*
keep for hold *(possess)*
keep for future action postpone
keep from conceal, deny *(refuse to grant)*, deter, discourage, forbear, forgo, prevent, refrain
keep from being successful foil
keep from contact with others isolate
keep from danger ensconce
keep from entering exclude
keep from happening enjoin, prevent
keep from harm ensure, preserve
keep from loss conserve
keep from notice enshroud
keep from proceeding delay
keep from public view seal *(close)*
keep from sight camouflage
keep from view camouflage, enshroud
keep going adhere *(persist)*, keep *(continue)*, maintain *(carry on)*, persevere, proceed *(go forward)*, progress, remain *(continue)*, sustain *(prolong)*. SEE MAIN ENTRY
keep guard patrol, police
keep guarded ensconce
keep hidden cloak, ensconce, enshroud, plant *(covertly place)*
keep hold of occupy *(take possession)*, retain *(keep in possession)*
keep house inhabit, occupy *(take possession)*
keep in circumscribe *(surround by boundary)*, contain *(enclose)*, enclose, encompass *(surround)*, immure, inhibit, repress, stem *(check)*, withhold
keep in bounds condemn *(ban)*, enjoin
keep in captivity contain *(restrain)*, immure, imprison
keep in check balk, constrain *(restrain)*, contain *(restrain)*, control *(restrain)*, fetter, immure, impede, repress
keep in confidence seal *(close)*
keep in countenance coax
keep in custody confine, constrain *(imprison)*, detain *(hold in custody)*, enclose, immure, imprison. SEE MAIN ENTRY
keep in detention constrain *(imprison)*, detain *(hold in custody)*, immure, imprison, seclude
keep in existence conserve, perpetuate
keep in hand hold *(possess)*
keep in ignorance cloak
keep in mind recall *(remember)*, remember, retain *(keep in possession)*
keep in order handle *(manage)*, manage, police, rule *(govern)*, superintend
keep in pay retain *(employ)*
keep in perspective discern *(discriminate)*. SEE MAIN ENTRY
keep in private seclude
keep in readiness hold *(possess)*
keep in reserve fund, garner, hoard, hold *(possess)*, reserve, set aside *(reserve)*
keep in safety cover *(guard)*
keep in secrecy seal *(close)*
keep in service employ *(engage services)*
keep in sight monitor, observe *(watch)*, regard *(pay attention)*
keep in solitude isolate
keep in the dark camouflage, obscure
keep in the shade camouflage
keep in view monitor, observe *(watch)*, patrol, police
keep intact preserve
keep moving proceed *(go forward)*, progress
keep off deter, parry, stave
keep on adhere *(persist)*, bear *(tolerate)*, hold *(possess)*, maintain *(carry on)*, persevere, persist, pursue *(carry on)*, recur, remain *(continue)*, stay *(continue)*
keep on hand reserve
keep one guessing obfuscate
keep one waiting delay, hold up *(delay)*, procrastinate
keep one's countenance bear *(tolerate)*
keep one's distance shun
keep one's word perform *(adhere to)*
keep order handle *(manage)*, police, preside
keep orderly police
keep out bar *(exclude)*, clog, condemn *(ban)*, eliminate *(exclude)*, exclude, reject, screen *(select)*, seclude
keep out of harm's way beware
keep out of sight blind *(obscure)*, conceal, cover *(conceal)*, elude, enshroud, harbor, hide, lurk, suppress
keep out of the way eschew
keep out of view camouflage, hide
keep pace with concur *(coexist)*, reach
keep pending adjourn, continue *(adjourn)*, defer *(put off)*, delay, hold up *(delay)*
keep posted annunciate, convey *(communicate)*, inform *(notify)*
keep prepared hold *(possess)*
keep prisoner constrain *(imprison)*, contain *(restrain)*, immure
keep quiet rest *(cease from action)*
keep safe conserve, ensconce, ensure, harbor, keep *(shelter)*, preserve, save *(conserve)*
keep safe from harm cover *(guard)*
keep score poll
keep secret camouflage, cloak, conceal, ensconce, harbor, hide, plant *(covertly place)*, suppress, withhold
keep sound preserve
keep subjugated dominate
keep the peace SEE MAIN ENTRY
keep to conform
keep to oneself conceal, hide
keep under arrest contain *(restrain)*, detain *(hold in custody)*, immure, imprison
keep under close watch cover *(guard)*
keep under control check *(restrain)*, confine, contain *(restrain)*, control *(restrain)*, detain *(hold in custody)*, detain *(restrain)*, handle *(manage)*, police, repress, restrain
keep under cover ensconce, enshroud, hide, preserve
keep under surveillance examine *(study)*, scrutinize
keep undercover cloak
keep underground conceal
keep unimpaired conserve
keep up last, maintain *(carry on)*, persevere, preserve, pursue *(carry on)*, sustain *(prolong)*
keep vigil patrol, police
keep watch check *(inspect)*, patrol, police, survey *(examine)*
keep watch over preserve
keep within bounds censor, condemn *(ban)*, confine, detain *(hold in custody)*, detain *(restrain)*, immure, moderate *(temper)*, restrain, trammel
keep within limits curb, qualify *(condition)*, restrict

keeper caretaker *(one caring for property),* custodian *(protector),* guardian, holder
keeping administration, charge *(custody),* compliance, conservation, constraint *(imprisonment),* control *(supervision),* custody *(supervision),* detention, retention, safekeeping, trust *(custody),* ward
keeping back detention
keeping in detention
keeping in custody detention
keepsake remembrance *(commemoration),* reminder, token
ken apprehend *(perceive),* cognition, comprehend *(understand),* construe *(comprehend),* digest *(comprehend),* experience *(background),* find *(discover),* insight, knowledge *(awareness),* knowledge *(learning),* perceive, realization. SEE MAIN ENTRY
kept in custody arrested *(apprehended)*
kept in prison in custody
kept in remembrance honorary
kept out ineligible
kernel main point
key cardinal *(basic),* cardinal *(outstanding),* catchword, central *(essential),* clue, cornerstone, critical *(crucial),* explanation, fundamental, gravamen, indispensable, main point, major, material *(important),* necessary *(required),* primary, solution *(answer),* strategic, tip *(clue).* SEE MAIN ENTRY
key man chairman, executive. SEE MAIN ENTRY
key person caretaker *(one fulfilling the function of office),* executive
key point landmark *(significant change)*
key woman executive
keynote cornerstone, corpus, highlight, main point. SEE MAIN ENTRY
keystone cornerstone, foundation *(basis),* gist *(ground for a suit),* gravamen, main point, mainstay
kick beat *(strike),* impetus, spurn
kick out evict, expel
kick the can down the road SEE MAIN ENTRY
kickback graft, gratuity *(bribe).* SEE MAIN ENTRY
kicker malcontent
kiddish puerile
kidnap abduct, carry away. SEE MAIN ENTRY
kidnapper criminal
kidnapping abduction
kill destroy *(efface),* dispatch *(put to death),* eliminate *(eradicate),* execute *(sentence to death),* extinguish, prey, remove *(eliminate),* repress, slay, stifle. SEE MAIN ENTRY
kill by suffocation extinguish
kill time procrastinate
killer criminal. SEE MAIN ENTRY
killing aberemurder, assassination, capital punishment, deadly, dispatch *(act of putting to death),* fatal, homicide, lethal, manslaughter, murder, pernicious, pestilent. SEE MAIN ENTRY
killing with malice aforethought aberemurder
kin descendant, descent *(lineage),* family *(common ancestry),* house, kindred, next of kin, relation *(kinship),* relative. SEE MAIN ENTRY
kind benevolent, blood, character *(personal quality),* charitable *(lenient),* class, color *(complexion),* denomination, favorable *(expressing approval),* form *(arrangement),* humane, lenient, magnanimous, manner *(kind),* philanthropic, propitious, race, style. SEE MAIN ENTRY
kind act favor *(act of kindness)*
kind office benevolence *(act of kindness)*
kind person benefactor, good samaritan, samaritan
kind regard favor *(partiality)*
kind treatment benevolence *(act of kindness)*
kindhearted benevolent, charitable *(lenient),* humane, lenient, philanthropic, propitious. SEE MAIN ENTRY
kindhearte benevolence *(disposition to do good),* consideration *(sympathetic regard),* humanity *(humaneness)*
kindle agitate *(activate),* burn, create, foment, generate, incite, induce, inspire, make, originate, provoke, spirit, stimulate. SEE MAIN ENTRY
kindle one's wrath incense
kindle wrath pique
kindliness benevolence *(disposition to do good),* consideration *(sympathetic regard),* largess *(generosity),* philanthropy, pity, solace, understanding *(tolerance)*
kindly benevolent, humane, paternal, peaceable, philanthropic, propitious
kindly disposed benevolent
kindness affection, benefit *(conferment),* benevolence *(disposition to do good),* charity, clemency, consideration *(sympathetic regard),* goodwill, help, humanity *(humaneness),* largess *(generosity),* lenience, philanthropy. SEE MAIN ENTRY
kindred affiliation *(bloodline),* affinity *(family ties),* akin *(related by blood),* allied, analogous, blood, comparable *(capable of comparison),* consanguineous, family *(common ancestry),* house, interrelated, next of kin, propinquity *(kinship),* related, relation *(kinship),* relative *(relevant),* relative, similar. SEE MAIN ENTRY
kindredship kinship, relationship *(family tie)*
kinetic impulsive *(impelling),* moving *(in motion)*
kinfolk affiliation *(bloodline)*
king SEE MAIN ENTRY
kingdom domain *(sphere of influence),* realm. SEE MAIN ENTRY
kink quirk *(idiosyncrasy),* snarl
kinsfolk blood, kindred
kinship affiliation *(bloodline),* affinity *(family ties),* ancestry, blood, chain *(nexus),* community, connection *(relation),* contact *(association),* family *(common ancestry),* filiation, nexus, relationship *(family tie),* resemblance. SEE MAIN ENTRY
kinsman blood, next of kin, relation *(kinship),* relative
kinsmen affiliation *(bloodline),* blood, family *(common ancestry),* kindred
kinspeople kindred, next of kin
kinswoman blood
kismet predetermination
kith relative
kith and kin origin *(ancestry)*
kithless solitary
kleptomaniac SEE MAIN ENTRY
knack faculty *(ability),* gift *(flair),* propensity, skill
knave criminal, hoodlum
knavery artifice, collusion, corruption, deception, dishonesty, evasion, hoax, imposture, improbity, mischief, misdoing, pettifoggery. SEE MAIN ENTRY
knavish artful, deceptive, disreputable, false *(disloyal),* immoral, iniquitous, lawless, machiavellian, perfidious, recreant, reprobate, tortuous *(corrupt),* unconscionable
knavishness dishonesty, knavery
kneel to obey
kneeling prostration
knife lancinate, pierce *(lance)*
knifelike mordacious
knit connect *(join together),* join *(bring together),* related
knock impinge, jostle *(bump into),* sully
knock about ill use
knock against collide *(crash against),* impinge, jostle *(bump into)*
knock-and-announce rule SEE MAIN ENTRY
knock down beat *(strike).* SEE MAIN ENTRY
knock into collide *(crash against),* strike *(collide)*
knock out of shape mutilate
knot connection *(fastening),* contort, intertwine, involution, snarl
knots ties
knotted complex, inextricable
knotty problematic, recondite
knotty point enigma
know appreciate *(comprehend),* comprehend *(understand),* conceive *(comprehend),* digest *(comprehend),* discern *(detect with the senses),* find *(discover),* identify, perceive, pierce *(discern),* read, realize *(understand),* recognize *(perceive),* understand. SEE MAIN ENTRY
know again recall *(remember),* recollect, remember
know by heart recall *(remember),* remember
know entirely apprehend *(perceive)*
know of apprehend *(perceive)*
know well apprehend *(perceive)*
know-all bigot
know-how experience *(background),* faculty *(ability),* knowledge *(awareness),* knowledge *(learning),* prowess *(ability),* science *(technique).* SEE MAIN ENTRY
know-it-all bigot
knowable appreciable, ascertainable, cognizable, coherent *(clear),* comprehensible, determinable *(ascertainable),* discernible, perceivable, perceptible, ponderable, scrutable
knowing certain *(positive),* cognizant, conscious *(aware),* discriminating *(judicious),* expert, familiar *(informed),* intentional, judicial, learned, literate, omniscient, oracular, perceptive, perspicacious, politic, practiced, proficient, profound *(esoteric),* qualified *(competent),* rational, sapient, sciential, sensible, tactical, veteran. SEE MAIN ENTRY
knowing person expert, specialist, veteran
knowingly purposely. SEE MAIN ENTRY
knowledge apprehension *(perception),* caliber *(mental capacity),* certainty, certification *(certainness),* cognition, comprehension, concept, disclosure *(something disclosed),* discrimination *(good judgment),* edification, education, experience *(background),* information *(knowledge),* intelligence *(news),* notification, realization, reason *(sound judgment),* recognition, science *(study),* scienter, skill, specialty *(special aptitude),* understanding *(comprehension).* SEE MAIN ENTRY
knowledge of facts information *(knowledge)*
knowledge of law jurisprudence
knowledgeable acquainted, acute, cognizant, expert, familiar *(informed),* informed

(*educated*), knowing, learned, literate, omniscient, sciential, sensible, sophisticated
known apparent (*perceptible*), cognizable, famous, illustrious, ordinary, outstanding (*prominent*), prominent, proverbial, renowned, reputable, trite, unmistakable, usual. SEE MAIN ENTRY
known elsewhere as alias
known elsewhere by alias
known elsewhere under the name alias
known facts information (*knowledge*), intelligence (*news*)
known in advance foreseeable
known name goodwill
known otherwise as alias
known previously as alias
known variously as alias
knuckle under succumb
kudos SEE MAIN ENTRY

L

"lettre de change" draft
labefactare invalidate
label brand, brand (*mark*), call (*title*), classify, define, denominate, denomination, denote, designation (*naming*), designation (*symbol*), device (*distinguishing mark*), discriminate (*distinguish*), earmark, heading, identification, identify, nominate, pigeonhole, rubric (*title*), title (*designation*), trademark. SEE MAIN ENTRY
label incorrectly mislabel
labeled entitled
labor employment, endeavor (*noun*), endeavor (*verb*), industry (*activity*), job, persevere, struggle, work (*effort*). SEE MAIN ENTRY
labor at one's vocation practice (*engage in*)
labor dispute strike
labor expense payroll
labor for attempt, pursue (*strive to gain*), strive
labor in vain failure (*lack of success*)
labor saving economic
labor supply personnel
labor under bear (*tolerate*)
labor under a misapprehension err, miscalculate, misconceive, mistake, misunderstand. SEE MAIN ENTRY
labor under an error miscalculate
labor-saving economical
labor-saving device appliance
laborare labor
labored difficult, elaborate, painstaking, ponderous
laborer artisan, employee
laborers personnel
laboring force personnel
laborious difficult, faithful (*diligent*), industrious, onerous, operose, oppressive, painful, painstaking, sedulous. SEE MAIN ENTRY
laborious application pursuit (*effort to secure*)
laboriousness effort, industry (*activity*)
labyrinth complex (*entanglement*), complication, confusion (*ambiguity*), imbroglio, involution, snarl
labyrinthian labyrinthine, sinuous
labyrinthic labyrinthine
labyrinthine circuitous, complex, devious, difficult, indirect, inextricable, sinuous, tortuous (*bending*). SEE MAIN ENTRY
lace connect (*join together*), intertwine
lacerate damage, harrow, lancinate, mutilate, rend, sever
lacerated broken (*fractured*)
laches neglect. SEE MAIN ENTRY
lachrymose disconsolate
lack absence (*omission*), dearth, defect, deficiency, deficit, delinquency (*shortage*), disadvantage, failure (*falling short*), foible, insufficiency, market (*demand*), need (*deprivation*), paucity, poverty, privation, require (*need*), vice. SEE MAIN ENTRY
lack ability SEE MAIN ENTRY
lack belief in mistrust
lack candor feign, palter
lack confidence misdoubt
lack confidence in doubt (*distrust*), mistrust, suspect (*distrust*)
lack conviction misdoubt
lack faith disbelieve, misdoubt
lack faith in mistrust
lack harmony disaccord, disagree
lack honesty cheat
lack information misunderstand
lack of ability inability
lack of accord discrepancy, inconsistency
lack of activity inertia
lack of agreement discrepancy, exception (*objection*), incompatibility (*difference*), incompatibility (*inconsistency*), nonconformity, paradox
lack of allurement disincentive
lack of appreciation ingratitude
lack of attention disinterest (*lack of interest*), negligence, res ipsa loquitur
lack of awareness insentience, nescience
lack of belief incredulity
lack of bias objectivity, tolerance
lack of candidness indirection (*deceitfulness*)
lack of capacity incapacity. SEE MAIN ENTRY
lack of care disregard (*unconcern*), inconsideration
lack of caution inconsideration
lack of certainty cloud (*suspicion*), indecision, misgiving, qualm. SEE MAIN ENTRY
lack of certitude doubt (*indecision*)
lack of charm disincentive
lack of circumspection indiscretion
lack of clarity incoherence
lack of clearness confusion (*ambiguity*)
lack of competence inability
lack of complaint resignation (*passive acceptance*)
lack of comprehension insentience
lack of concern disinterest (*lack of interest*)
lack of concert discrepancy
lack of concord argument (*contention*), contravention, controversy (*argument*), discord
lack of confidence cloud (*suspicion*), discredit, doubt (*indecision*), doubt (*suspicion*), misgiving, qualm. SEE MAIN ENTRY
lack of conformity discrepancy, exception (*objection*)
lack of congruence discrepancy
lack of congruity discrepancy
lack of connection difference
lack of conscience bad faith, corruption, dishonesty, dishonor (*shame*), improbity, indirection (*deceitfulness*)
lack of consideration disregard (*unconcern*), disrespect, inconsideration, indiscretion, ingratitude
lack of consonance discrepancy, incongruity
lack of control laxity. SEE MAIN ENTRY
lack of conviction doubt (*indecision*), qualm
lack of corruption fairness
lack of courteousness disrespect
lack of courtesy disrespect
lack of decision indecision
lack of depth immateriality
lack of desire disincentive
lack of dexterity disqualification (*factor that disqualifies*)
lack of diligence laches, negligence
lack of discipline rebellion
lack of doubt credulity
lack of dubiety credulity
lack of dubiousness credulity
lack of due process lynch law
lack of education ignorance
lack of enthusiasm pessimism
lack of enticement disincentive
lack of equality inequality
lack of esteem discredit
lack of excess moderation
lack of expectation pessimism
lack of faith cloud (*suspicion*), doubt (*indecision*), doubt (*suspicion*), incredulity, infidelity, suspicion (*mistrust*)
lack of feeling brutality
lack of fidelity bad faith, disloyalty
lack of fitness incapacity
lack of force impuissance
lack of funds failure (*bankruptcy*)
lack of good taste impropriety
lack of gratitude ingratitude
lack of harmony dissension, dissent (*difference of opinion*), impugnation, incompatibility (*inconsistency*), incongruity, paradox
lack of honesty dishonesty
lack of honor dishonor (*shame*)
lack of impetus disincentive
lack of incentive disincentive
lack of inducement disincentive
lack of integrity bad repute, dishonesty, improbity
lack of interest disregard (*unconcern*), laxity
lack of jaundice objectivity
lack of judgment indiscretion
lack of justice lynch law
lack of knowledge ignorance, insentience, nescience
lack of learning ignorance, nescience
lack of legal sanction lynch law
lack of loyalty disloyalty, infidelity
lack of luxury austerity
lack of maintenance disrepair
lack of might impuissance
lack of motion inertia
lack of motivation disincentive
lack of movement inertia
lack of observation disregard (*unconcern*)
lack of order irregularity, pandemonium
lack of perception insentience
lack of personal jurisdiction SEE MAIN ENTRY
lack of piety blasphemy
lack of politeness disrespect
lack of possibility impossibility
lack of potentiality impossibility
lack of power impotence, impuissance, inability, incapacity, inefficacy
lack of prejudice fairness, objectivity, understanding (*tolerance*)
lack of principle bad faith, corruption, dishonesty, dishonor (*shame*), improbity, knavery

lack of probity bad faith, corruption, dishonesty, dishonor *(shame)*, fraud, indirection *(deceitfulness)*, knavery
lack of proficiency disqualification *(factor that disqualifies)*
lack of propriety irregularity
lack of protection danger
lack of qualification disqualification *(factor that disqualifies)*
lack of regular order disorder *(lack of order)*
lack of relation disparity
lack of resemblance difference, discrepancy
lack of resistance resignation *(passive acceptance)*
lack of respect disrespect, ignominy, inconsideration
lack of reverence blasphemy, inconsideration
lack of safety danger
lack of skepticism credulity
lack of sophistication credulity
lack of sound silence
lack of spirit damper *(depressant)*
lack of stimulus disincentive
lack of strength fault *(weakness)*, impotence, impuissance, inefficacy, languor
lack of strictness lenience
lack of subject matter SEE MAIN ENTRY
lack of substance immateriality, impalpability
lack of suspicion credulity
lack of symmetry disparity, inequality, irregularity
lack of temptation disincentive
lack of thoroughness laxity
lack of toleration intolerance
lack of trust doubt *(suspicion)*, suspicion *(mistrust)*
lack of understanding opacity
lack of vigor impuissance
lack of warmth damper *(depressant)*
lack of warning surprise
lack resemblance differ *(vary)*
lack self-control carouse, overindulge
lack trust in mistrust
lackadaisical careless, dilatory, indolent, languid, lax, lifeless *(dull)*, otiose, phlegmatic, remiss, slipshod
lacking defective, deficient, delinquent *(overdue)*, devoid, essential *(required)*, faulty, imperfect, inadept, inadequate, insufficient, nonsubstantial *(not sufficient)*, paltry, peccable, perfunctory, save, void *(empty)*
lacking accord inconsistent
lacking activity stagnant
lacking agreement incongruous
lacking authority invalid
lacking caution imprudent
lacking clarity indistinct, nebulous, oblique *(evasive)*, opaque
lacking clearness ambiguous
lacking confidence hesitant
lacking content vacuous
lacking continuity desultory
lacking decency profligate *(corrupt)*
lacking dexterity inept *(incompetent)*
lacking dexterousness inept *(incompetent)*
lacking discretion ill-judged, injudicious
lacking elegance inelegant
lacking enthusiasm nonchalant
lacking experience inexperienced
lacking feeling insusceptible *(uncaring)*
lacking firmness insubstantial
lacking force invalid
lacking foresight improvident
lacking frankness disingenuous
lacking funds destitute, insolvent
lacking good taste inelegant
lacking grace inelegant
lacking harmony incongruous, inconsistent
lacking importance inapposite
lacking in quality poor *(inferior in quality)*
lacking individuality sequacious
lacking interest nonchalant
lacking judgment imprudent
lacking morals immoral
lacking nothing gross *(total)*
lacking order disjointed
lacking precision indistinct
lacking prejudice impartial
lacking principle profligate *(corrupt)*
lacking proficiency inexperienced
lacking proportion disproportionate
lacking prudence imprudent
lacking qualification incompetent
lacking refinement inelegant
lacking relevance inapposite
lacking remorse remorseless
lacking respect presumptuous
lacking self-confidence diffident
lacking shame profligate *(corrupt)*
lacking skill inept *(incompetent)*, inexperienced
lacking stability insecure
lacking strength invalid
lacking substance insubstantial
lacking truth mendacious
lacking vigor indolent
lacking warmth nonchalant
lacking worth unworthy
lackluster inexpressive, lifeless *(dull)*. SEE MAIN ENTRY
laconic brief, compact *(pithy)*, concise, inarticulate, noncommittal, pithy, sententious, succinct, taciturn, unresponsive. SEE MAIN ENTRY
lactare dupe
lacuna hiatus, split
lade encumber *(hinder)*, load
laden full, replete
lading cargo, freight
lading of a ship cargo
laedere harm, offend *(insult)*
lag delay, pause, procrastinate, stall. SEE MAIN ENTRY
laggard disinclined, indolent, lifeless *(dull)*, otiose, truant
laggardness laches
lagging late *(tardy)*, otiose
lagniappe contribution *(donation)*, grant
laic civil *(public)*, layman, profane
laical civil *(public)*, profane
laid situated
laid bare naked *(lacking embellishment)*
laid down positive *(prescribed)*
laissez faire SEE MAIN ENTRY
lakeside littoral
lambaste beat *(strike)*
lamblike passive, patient, peaceable, pliable
lame defective, disable, imperfect, inadept, ineffective, ineffectual, insubstantial, maim, nonsubstantial *(not sturdy)*, otiose, unable, unsatisfactory
lamed marred
lament deplore, languish, outcry, plaint, regret, repent. SEE MAIN ENTRY
lament with sympathize
lamenta plaint
lamentabilis lamentable
lamentable deplorable, gross *(flagrant)*, regrettable. SEE MAIN ENTRY
lamentation disapprobation, plaint
lamentative querulous
lamenting disconsolate, querulous, remorseful, repentant
laming detriment
lampoon caricature, disparage, jape, mock *(deride)*, parody, pillory, travesty
lampoonery ridicule
lance enter *(penetrate)*, lancinate, launch *(project)*, penetrate, split
lancinate harrow, rend. SEE MAIN ENTRY
land alight, circuit, curtilage, demesne, domain *(land owned)*, fee *(estate)*, freehold, holding *(property owned)*, immovable, parcel, premises *(buildings)*, property *(land)*, real estate, realm, realty, region, territory. SEE MAIN ENTRY
land a blow beat *(strike)*
land and buildings estate *(property)*
land developer developer
land held by lease leasehold
land leased leasehold
landlocked SEE MAIN ENTRY
land owned realty
land revenue rent
landed proprietary
landed estate demesne, fee *(estate)*, freehold, holding *(property owned)*, real estate
landed interests property *(land)*
landed property demesne, fee *(estate)*, freehold, property *(land)*
landed proprietor landowner
landholder landowner, tenant. SEE MAIN ENTRY
landing haven
landlord landholder, landowner, lessor, proprietor. SEE MAIN ENTRY
landmark cornerstone, crossroad *(turning point)*, indicant, indicator. SEE MAIN ENTRY
landowner landholder, proprietor, tenant. SEE MAIN ENTRY
lands estate *(property)*, fee *(estate)*
landscape scene
landslide (avalanche) SEE MAIN ENTRY
lane causeway, way *(channel)*
language discourse, phraseology, rhetoric *(skilled speech)*, speech. SEE MAIN ENTRY
language of a particular profession jargon *(technical language)*
languens languid
languere languish
languescere languish
languid inactive, indolent, insipid, lifeless *(dull)*, phlegmatic, powerless, torpid. SEE MAIN ENTRY
languidness disinterest *(lack of interest)*, sloth
languish decay, degenerate, suffer *(sustain loss)*. SEE MAIN ENTRY
languishing disconsolate, powerless
languor inaction, inertia. SEE MAIN ENTRY
languor disinterest *(lack of interest)*
languorous languid, otiose, passive, phlegmatic, torpid. SEE MAIN ENTRY
languourness lifeless *(dull)*
laniena shambles
lap embrace *(encircle)*
lap over overlap
lapidified ossified
lapis landmark *(conspicuous object)*
lapse abeyance, cease, cessation *(interlude)*, cloture, decline *(fall)*, default, degenerate,

descent *(declination)*, deteriorate, error, expire, halt, hiatus, interval, misdeed, nonpayment, oversight *(carelessness)*, pendency, recrudescence, relapse, remission, respite *(interval of rest)*, revert, stop, subside. SEE MAIN ENTRY
lapse in conduct delinquency *(failure of duty)*
lapse in judgment SEE MAIN ENTRY
lapse in time SEE MAIN ENTRY
lapsing regressive
lapsus lapse *(expiration)*
larcener burglar, hoodlum
larcenist hoodlum
larcenous SEE MAIN ENTRY
larceny burglary, conversion *(misappropriation)*, embezzlement, housebreaking, misappropriation, theft. SEE MAIN ENTRY
larceny by force robbery
lard meliorate
lares household *(domestic)*
large broad, capacious, considerable, copious, extensive, gross *(flagrant)*, major, ponderous, prodigious *(enormous)*, substantial. SEE MAIN ENTRY
large amount plurality, sufficiency
large asset transfer bulk transfer
large enough ample
large number plurality, quantity
large quantity plurality
large scale far reaching
large undertaking campaign
large-scale broad, extensive
largehearted magnanimous
largeness capacity *(maximum)*, degree *(magnitude)*, latitude, mass *(weight)*, measurement
larger number majority *(greater part)*
larger part majority *(greater part)*
largess benefit *(conferment)*, bounty, consideration *(recompense)*, donation, grant, philanthropy. SEE MAIN ENTRY
largesse contribution *(donation)*, grant
largest part generality *(bulk)*
largiri bestow
largitas bounty
largitio largess *(generosity)*
larrup lash *(strike)*
lascivious dissolute, lecherous, lewd, licentious, obscene, prurient, salacious, scurrilous, suggestive *(risqué)*. SEE MAIN ENTRY
lasciviousness debauchery
lascivire frisk
lascivus lascivious, wanton
lash beat *(strike)*, denounce *(condemn)*, handcuff, inveigh, punish, reprehend, reprimand. SEE MAIN ENTRY
lash back recriminate
lashing caustic, obloquy
lassitude inertia, languor, prostration
lassus languid
last continue *(persevere)*, definitive, exist, extreme *(last)*, final, keep *(continue)*, persevere, persist, remain *(continue)*, remain *(stay)*, resist *(withstand)*, stay *(continue)*, subsist, ultimate, withstand. SEE MAIN ENTRY
last act denouement
last minute dilatory
last minute need emergency
last of a series end *(termination)*
last offer ultimatum
last part close *(conclusion)*, end *(termination)*
last stage close *(conclusion)*, conclusion *(outcome)*
last stop destination
lasting chronic, constant, continuance, durable, indelible, indestructible, infallible, infinite, infrangible, irreversible, irrevocable, live *(existing)*, noncancellable, permanent, perpetual, persistent, solid *(sound)*, stable, standing, steadfast, strong. SEE MAIN ENTRY
lasting a very short time ephemeral
lasting period duration
lasting reminder monument
lastingness indestructibility, life *(period of existence)*, longevity
latch adhere *(fasten)*, shut
late back *(in arrears)*, deceased, dilatory, former, lifeless *(dead)*, overdue, prior, remiss. SEE MAIN ENTRY
late patens comprehensive
late payment delinquency *(shortage)*
latebra evasion, subterfuge
lately recent
latency cessation *(interlude)*, inaction. SEE MAIN ENTRY
lateness delay
latent blind *(concealed)*, covert, dormant, hidden, inactive, potential, secret, underlying, undisclosed. SEE MAIN ENTRY
latent power potential
later ensuing, ex post facto, future, hereafter *(eventually)*, subsequent, successive, thereafter. SEE MAIN ENTRY
later generations posterity
later in time ex post facto
later meditation hindsight
later thought hindsight
laterality contour *(outline)*
latere abscond, lurk
latest contemporary, current, present *(current)*, prevailing *(current)*. SEE MAIN ENTRY
latitare lurk
latitude coverage *(scope)*, freedom, informality, liberty, margin *(spare amount)*, purview, region, scope, space, territory, zone. SEE MAIN ENTRY
latitudinarian nonpartisan, open-minded
latitudinous broad
latitudo purview
latrocinium robbery
latter before mentioned, subsequent
latter day current
latus broad, extensive
laud belaud, honor *(outward respect)*, honor, mention *(tribute)*, recommend. SEE MAIN ENTRY
laudabilis laudable, meritorious
laudable exemplary, honest, meritorious, moral, professional *(stellar)*, scrupulous, unimpeachable, upright. SEE MAIN ENTRY
laudatio recommendation
laudation doxology, honor *(outward respect)*, mention *(tribute)*, recommendation, reference *(recommendation)*, respect. SEE MAIN ENTRY
laudatory favorable *(expressing approval)*, meritorious
laudatus laudable
laude dignus laudable, meritorious
laugh at disdain, disparage, flout, humiliate, jape, jeer, mock *(deride)*, pillory, spurn. SEE MAIN ENTRY
laugh-provoking ludicrous
laughable ludicrous
laughing jocular
launch cast *(throw)*, cause, commence, create, discharge *(shoot)*, embark, generate, impel, incite, initiate, inspire, instate, maintain *(commence)*, originate, precipitate *(throw down violently)*, preface, project *(impel forward)*, send, undertake. SEE MAIN ENTRY
launch again renew *(begin again)*
launch an inquiry SEE MAIN ENTRY
launching genesis, installation, nascency, onset *(commencement)*, outset
lavish bestow, copious, excess, furnish, inordinate, liberal *(generous)*, philanthropic, prodigal, profuse, replete, superfluous, supply. SEE MAIN ENTRY
lavishment largess *(generosity)*
lavishness largess *(generosity)*, philanthropy, waste
law act *(enactment)*, brevet, canon, constitution, criterion, dictate, edict, enactment, holding *(ruling of a court)*, measure, ordinance, precept, prescription *(directive)*, principle *(axiom)*, regulation *(rule)*, rubric *(authoritative rule)*, rule *(legal dictate)*, statute. SEE MAIN ENTRY
law and order peace
law court bench, judicatory, tribunal. SEE MAIN ENTRY
law courts judiciary
law enforcement agency police
law enforcement agent district attorney, marshal, peace officer
law enforcement agents police
law enforcement body police, posse
law firm SEE MAIN ENTRY
law of conduct principle *(axiom)*
law of the case holding *(ruling of a court)*. SEE MAIN ENTRY
law officer peace officer
law-abiding clean, ethical, honest, lawful, legitimate *(rightful)*, licit, moral, obedient. SEE MAIN ENTRY
law-breaker delinquent
law-breaking guilt
law-giving decretal
law-making body chamber *(body)*, legislature
law-making branch of government legislature
law-revering law-abiding
lawbreaker convict, criminal, embezzler, felon, hoodlum, inmate, malefactor, offender, outlaw, recidivist, thief, vandal, wrongdoer. SEE MAIN ENTRY
lawbreaker under suspension of sentence probationer *(released offender)*
lawbreaking bribery, culpable, delinquency *(misconduct)*, delinquent *(guilty of a misdeed)*, disobedient, disorderly, felonious, illegitimate *(illegal)*, larcenous, lawless, offense, racket, violation. SEE MAIN ENTRY
lawful allowable, allowed, choate lien, civic, clean, de jure, due *(regular)*, forensic, juridical, just, justifiable, legal, legitimate *(rightful)*, licit, permissible, rightful, statutory, unalienable, valid. SEE MAIN ENTRY
lawful authority hegemony. SEE MAIN ENTRY
lawful cause cause of action
lawful claim due
lawful possession dominion *(absolute ownership)*, interest *(ownership)*. SEE MAIN ENTRY
lawful power force *(legal efficacy)*. SEE MAIN ENTRY
lawful vigor force *(legal efficacy)*
lawfully de jure, fairly *(impartially)*. SEE MAIN ENTRY
lawfully sufficient prima facie *(legally sufficient)*
lawfulness legality, legitimacy, validity. SEE MAIN ENTRY
lawgiver lawmaker, legislator, politician
lawgivers government *(political administration)*, legislature

lawgiving legislative
lawless broken *(unfulfilled)*, culpable, dis-obedient, disordered, disorderly, felonious, illegal, illicit, iniquitous, insubordinate, irresponsible, nonconforming, profligate *(corrupt)*, restive, sinister, uncontrollable, uncurbed, unlawful, unorthodox, unrestrained *(not repressed)*, unruly, unscrupulous, wrongful. SEE MAIN ENTRY
lawless individual malefactor, outlaw
lawlessness anarchy, burglary, criminality, delinquency *(misconduct)*, disorder *(lack of order)*, illegality, irregularity, lynch law, misdeed, misdoing, misrule, offense, racket, revolution, riot, wrong
lawlike licit
lawmaker legislator, politician. SEE MAIN ENTRY
lawmakers chamber *(body)*, government *(political administration)*, legislature
lawmaking codification, legislative, regulation *(management)*
laws code, legislation *(enactments)*
laws of a profession ethics
lawsuit action *(proceeding)*, matter *(case)*, proceeding, suit, trial *(legal proceeding)*. SEE MAIN ENTRY
lawyer advocate *(counselor)*, attorney, barrister, counsel, counselor, esquire, jurist, practitioner, proctor, representative *(proxy)*. SEE MAIN ENTRY
lawyers bar *(body of lawyers)*
lax careless, cursory, derelict *(negligent)*, improvident, indolent, negligent, peccable, perfunctory, promiscuous, remiss, slipshod, superficial, uncurbed. SEE MAIN ENTRY
laxare release
laxity bad repute, dereliction, disinterest *(lack of interest)*, indifference, informality, laches, neglect, negligence, nonfeasance, nonperformance, omission, oversight *(carelessness)*. SEE MAIN ENTRY
laxness dereliction, laches, neglect, negligence, omission, oversight *(carelessness)*, sloth
lay deposit *(place)*, profane, rest *(be supported by)*
lay a duty tax *(levy)*
lay a duty on exact, excise *(levy a tax)*
lay a duty upon charge *(assess)*
lay a plan program, scheme
lay a plot frame *(charge falsely)*
lay a snare for entrap
lay a trap inveigle
lay a trap for ambush, ensnare, entrap
lay a wager bet, gamble, parlay *(bet)*
lay an embargo on condemn *(ban)*, stop
lay an impost assess *(tax)*
lay an information complain *(charge)*
lay aside abandon *(relinquish)*, continue *(adjourn)*, defer *(put off)*, dismiss *(put out of consideration)*, exclude, forgo, forswear, hold *(possess)*, hold up *(delay)*, keep *(shelter)*, neglect, postpone, pretermit, quit *(discontinue)*, reject, relinquish, renounce, select, set aside *(reserve)*, suspend. SEE MAIN ENTRY
lay away hold *(possess)*, keep *(shelter)*, reserve, store
lay bare bare, betray *(disclose)*, denude, disclose, divest, divulge, evidence, exhibit, expose, inform *(betray)*, manifest, produce *(offer to view)*, profess *(avow)*
lay before communicate, offer *(propose)*, pose *(propound)*, proffer, propose, propound, tender
lay before the public circulate, issue *(publish)*, publish
lay blame upon complain *(charge)*, denounce *(inform against)*, incriminate, reprehend
lay by deposit *(submit to a bank)*, hoard
lay charges against denounce *(inform against)*
lay claim to call *(demand)*, exact, excise *(levy a tax)*
lay down pose *(propound)*, posit, stipulate. SEE MAIN ENTRY
lay down a plan devise *(invent)*. prearrange
lay down guide lines organize *(arrange)*
lay down limits demarcate
lay down one's office demit
lay down the law instruct *(direct)*. SEE MAIN ENTRY
lay even money bet
lay eyes on discern *(detect with the senses)*, observe *(watch)*, pierce *(discern)*
lay hands on attack, procure
lay hands upon obtain
lay hold of distrain, hijack, impropriate, pirate *(take by violence)*, usurp
lay in ashes pillage
lay in ruins pillage, plunder
lay in store fund, glean, hoard
lay into attack
lay money down bet
lay money on gamble, parlay *(bet)*, speculate *(chance)*
lay odds bet
lay off dislodge, dismiss *(discharge)*, recess, suspend
lay on levy
lay oneself open to incur
lay open bare, clarify, confess, denude, disabuse, disinter, divest, divulge, educe, elucidate, exhibit, expose, inform *(betray)*, manifest, profess *(avow)*, unveil
lay open to harm expose
lay open to view expose
lay out demonstrate *(establish)*, devise *(invent)*, disburse *(pay out)*, invest *(fund)*, manifest, orchestrate, plan, prescribe, produce *(offer to view)*, program
lay out a boundary delimit
lay out money spend
lay over continue *(adjourn)*, delay
lay plans contrive, frame *(formulate)*, maneuver
lay responsibility on complain *(charge)*
lay responsibility upon charge *(accuse)*
lay stress on insist
lay the blame on complain *(charge)*, involve *(implicate)*
lay the foundation build *(construct)*, initiate, plan, plant *(place firmly)*
lay the foundation for originate
lay the foundation of generate
lay the foundations cause, commence, create, establish *(launch)*, instate, launch *(initiate)*
lay under embargo enjoin
lay under restraint arrest *(apprehend)*, check *(restrain)*, constrain *(restrain)*, detain *(restrain)*, hold up *(delay)*, immure
lay up fund, hoard
lay upon impose *(enforce)*
lay waste beat *(defeat)*, damage, denude, despoil, destroy *(efface)*, eliminate *(eradicate)*, eradicate, extirpate, harry *(plunder)*, loot, mistreat, pillage, plunder, spoil *(impair)*, subvert. SEE MAIN ENTRY
lay waste to extinguish
layer SEE MAIN ENTRY
layer of society class
laying aside release
laying out disbursement *(act of disbursing)*
layman amateur. SEE MAIN ENTRY
laymen public
layoff dismissal *(discharge)*, removal. SEE MAIN ENTRY
layout arrangement *(plan)*, array *(order)*, configuration *(form)*, design *(construction plan)*, formation, method, order *(arrangement)*, pattern, structure *(composition)*
lazare expand
lazaretto asylum *(hospital)*
laziness inertia, laches, languor, laxity, sloth
lazy idle, inactive, indolent, lax, lifeless *(dull)*, otiose, phlegmatic, remiss, stagnant, torpid, truant. SEE MAIN ENTRY
lead advantage, clue, coax, command, conduct, control *(regulate)*, direct *(show)*, direct *(supervise)*, dominate, edge *(advantage)*, generalship, govern, guidance, influence, initiate, manage, manipulate *(utilize skillfully)*, marshal, moderate *(preside over)*, motivate, officiate, operate, originate, oversee, persuade, pioneer, plurality, preamble, precede, predominance, predominate *(command)*, prescribe, preside, prevail *(triumph)*, prevail upon, primacy, prior, prompt, protagonist, redound, regulate *(manage)*, suggestion, superintend, tip *(clue)*. SEE MAIN ENTRY
lead astray bait *(lure)*, brutalize, corrupt, debauch, delude, ensnare, entrap, illude, inveigle, misdirect, misguide, mislabel, mislead, misstate, palter, pervert
lead by inducement entrap
lead counsel SEE MAIN ENTRY
lead in preface
lead into captivity immure
lead into danger by artifice entrap
lead into error delude, illude, misdirect, misguide, mislabel, mislead, misstate
lead into temptation bait *(lure)*, entrap
lead into trouble mistreat
lead item feature *(special attraction)*
lead on entrap, inveigle
lead on by artifice ensnare
lead one to induce
lead one to expect promise *(raise expectations)*
lead the way initiate, instate, precede, preface
lead to cause, conduce, engender
lead to a decision arbitrate *(adjudge)*
lead to believe assure *(give confidence to)*, convert *(persuade)*, convince, persuade
leadable tractable
leaden indolent, languid, lifeless *(dull)*, otiose, ponderous, torpid
leadenness sloth
leader administrator, chairman, chief, demagogue, director, employer, forerunner, mastermind, official, patron *(influential supporter)*, pioneer, protagonist, superintendent. SEE MAIN ENTRY
leader of affairs official
leaders management *(directorate)*
leadership direction *(guidance)*, generalship, guidance, hegemony, influence, management *(directorate)*, management *(supervision)*, predominance, primacy, supremacy. SEE MAIN ENTRY
leadership power hierarchy *(persons in authority)*
leading cardinal *(outstanding)*, dominant, famous, important *(significant)*, influential,

initial, major, master, material *(important)*, notable, noteworthy, paramount, precursory, prevailing *(having superior force)*, primary, prime *(most valuable)*, principal, prior, prominent, renowned, salient, sovereign *(absolute)*, stellar. SEE MAIN ENTRY
leading case SEE MAIN ENTRY
leading character protagonist
leading inquiry cross-examination
leading nowhere blind *(impassable)*
leaf through read
league affiliation *(amalgamation)*, association *(alliance)*, band, cabal, cartel, chamber *(body)*, coaction, coalescence, coalition, collusion, commingle, committee, company *(assemblage)*, conciliation, confederacy *(compact)*, conformity *(agreement)*, connect *(join together)*, connection *(relation)*, connivance, consolidate *(unite)*, consolidation, consortium *(business cartel)*, consortium *(marriage companionship)*, contribution *(participation)*, cooperate, federalize *(associate)*, federate, federation, organization *(association)*, pact, partnership, party *(political organization)*, pool *(noun)*, pool *(verb)*, society, sodality, syndicate, union *(labor organization)*, unite. SEE MAIN ENTRY
league together concur *(agree)*, conspire, join *(associate oneself with)*
league with combine *(act in concert)*, conspire
leagued affiliated, allied, associated, coadunate, collective, concurrent *(united)*, conjoint, corporate *(associate)*, federal, harmonious, joint, mutual *(collective)*, partisan
leak decrement, divulge, exude
leak into penetrate
leakage decrement, outflow
lean gravitate, insufficient, minimal, rest *(be supported by)*, select
lean against abut, border *(bound)*
lean on rely, trust
lean toward discriminate *(treat differently)*, prefer
leaning character *(personal quality)*, characteristic, conatus, conviction *(persuasion)*, disposition *(inclination)*, favor *(partiality)*, favoritism, habit, inclination, inclined, inequity, nepotism, oblique *(slanted)*, partiality, penchant, perspective, position *(point of view)*, posture *(attitude)*, preconception, predilection, predisposition, preference *(choice)*, prejudice *(preconception)*, proclivity, propensity, stand *(position)*, standpoint, tendency. SEE MAIN ENTRY
leanness dearth, poverty
leap transition
leap of faith SEE MAIN ENTRY
learn apprehend *(perceive)*, detect, discover, find *(discover)*, gain, perceive, realize *(understand)*, study, understand. SEE MAIN ENTRY
learn a habit naturalize *(acclimate)*, practice *(train by repetition)*
learn a lesson from profit
learn about ascertain
learn for a certainty discover
learn of discover
learn the answer solve
learnable ascertainable
learned cognizant, competent, didactic, expert, familiar *(informed)*, informed *(educated)*, literate, practiced, professional *(trained)*, profound *(esoteric)*, sapient, sciential. SEE MAIN ENTRY
learned counsel advocate *(counselor)*, attorney, barrister, jurist
learned in the law forensic
learned man pedagogue
learned person mastermind, specialist
learned profession calling, profession *(vocation)*
learnedly knowingly
learner apprentice, disciple, neophyte, novice, probationer *(one being tested)*, protégé
learning aptitude, common knowledge, comprehension, detection, discipline *(field of study)*, edification, education, experience *(background)*, information *(knowledge)*, science *(study)*. SEE MAIN ENTRY
lease convey *(transfer)*, engage *(hire)*, rent, sublet. SEE MAIN ENTRY
leased mercenary
leasehold property *(land)*. SEE MAIN ENTRY
leaseholder landholder, lessee, lodger, occupant, tenant
leaser consumer, customer
leash handcuff, inhibit, limit, repress
leasing tenancy
least minimal. SEE MAIN ENTRY
least amount minimum
least part minimum
least quantity minimum
least restrictive means SEE MAIN ENTRY
leave abscond, alight, bequeath, capacity *(authority)*, charter *(sanction)*, concession *(authorization)*, consent, defect, demise, demit, depart, devise *(give)*, disappear, discontinue *(abandon)*, dispensation *(exception)*, evacuate, fail *(neglect)*, favor *(sanction)*, forgo, forswear, franchise *(license)*, freedom, furlough, give *(grant)*, holiday, indulgence, liberty, license, move *(alter position)*, option *(choice)*, permission, permit, pretermit, quit *(evacuate)*, relinquish, renounce, resign, retire *(conclude a career)*, retire *(retreat)*, retreat, secede, shun, sufferance, variance *(exemption)*, withdraw, yield *(submit)*. SEE MAIN ENTRY
leave a legacy bequeath, demise, descend. SEE MAIN ENTRY
leave a place move *(alter position)*
leave a will SEE MAIN ENTRY
leave alone neglect
leave an inference allude, imply
leave behind abandon *(physically leave)*, surpass
leave by will bequeath, demise, devise *(give)*
leave defenseless endanger
leave destitute deprive, despoil
leave empty evacuate
leave in the lurch abandon *(physically leave)*
leave no choice necessitate
leave no option compel, constrain *(compel)*, impose *(enforce)*, necessitate
leave no trace disappear, expunge, perish
leave no trace of eradicate
leave no vestige of eradicate
leave nothing to be desired consummate
leave of absence furlough
leave off cease, desist, discontinue *(abandon)*, discontinue *(break continuity)*, forbear, interrupt, quit *(discontinue)*, refrain, stop, suspend
leave one's country expatriate
leave out bar *(exclude)*, block, censor, delete, disregard, eliminate *(exclude)*, estrange, except *(exclude)*, exclude, omit, overlook *(disregard)*, pretermit, reject. SEE MAIN ENTRY
leave out of consideration disregard
leave the impression demean *(deport oneself)*
leave the job strike *(refuse to work)*
leave to bequeath, devolve
leave to chance bet
leave undone omit, overlook *(disregard)*, pretermit, shirk
leave unfinished quit *(discontinue)*
leave unlawfully defect
leave unprotected endanger, jeopardize
leave unregarded exclude
leaven determinant, imbue, penetrate, permeate
leavetaking egress
leaving abdication, desertion, discard, flight, resignation *(relinquishment)*
leaving no choice obligatory
leaving off moratorium
leaving out disregard *(unconcern)*, omission, save
leavings surplus
lecherous depraved, immoral, lascivious, lewd, obscene, prurient, salacious, suggestive *(risqué)*. SEE MAIN ENTRY
lechery debauchery, obscenity
lecture address *(talk to)*, charge *(statement to the jury)*, criticism, declaim, declamation, discourse *(noun)*, discourse *(verb)*, harangue, inculcate, instruct *(teach)*, instruction *(teaching)*, objurgation, peroration, rebuke, recital, recite, reprehend, reprimand *(noun)*, reprimand *(verb)*, reproach, speech. SEE MAIN ENTRY
lecturer pedagogue
lecturers faculty *(teaching staff)*
led astray blind *(not discerning)*
ledge border, margin *(outside limit)*
ledger account *(evaluation)*, journal, register, roll. SEE MAIN ENTRY
lee refuge, safekeeping
leech parasite
leery suspicious *(distrustful)*. SEE MAIN ENTRY
leeway freedom, margin *(spare amount)*. SEE MAIN ENTRY
left derelict *(abandoned)*. SEE MAIN ENTRY
left in penury bankrupt
left over residuary. SEE MAIN ENTRY
left to discretion discretionary
left to individual judgment discretionary
leftover balance *(amount in excess)*, expendable, net, overage, remainder *(remaining part)*, residual
legacy benefit *(conferment)*, bequest, claim *(right)*, dower, estate *(hereditament)*, gift *(present)*, grant, heritage, inheritance, will *(testamentary instrument)*. SEE MAIN ENTRY
legal admissible, allowable, allowed, choate lien, civic, de jure, due *(regular)*, forensic, honest, jural, juridical, just, justifiable, lawful, legitimate *(rightful)*, licit, permissible, rightful, statutory, valid. SEE MAIN ENTRY
legal abstract brief
legal action action *(proceeding)*, cause *(lawsuit)*, controversy *(lawsuit)*, day in court, lawsuit, matter *(case)*, proceeding, prosecution *(criminal trial)*, suit. SEE MAIN ENTRY
legal administration bench
legal adversary litigant
legal adviser advocate *(counselor)*, attorney, barrister, counsel, counselor, esquire, jurist
legal advisor lawyer. SEE MAIN ENTRY
legal advocate lawyer

legal age majority *(adulthood)*
legal agreement lease, specialty *(contract)*. SEE MAIN ENTRY
legal appointee attorney in fact
legal approval affirmance *(judicial sanction)*
legal argument answer *(judicial response)*, case *(lawsuit)*, controversy *(lawsuit)*, lawsuit, plea. SEE MAIN ENTRY
legal arrangement before marriage antenuptial agreement
legal assertion cause of action
legal assistance maintenance *(support of spouse)*. SEE MAIN ENTRY
legal authority judicature, jurisdiction. SEE MAIN ENTRY
legal authorization affirmance *(judicial sanction)*
legal battle dispute
legal body corporation, corpus
legal call process *(summons)*
legal capacity capacity *(authority)*
legal cession grant
legal chicanery bunko
legal claim demand, right *(entitlement)*. SEE MAIN ENTRY
legal code code, constitution, jurisprudence, law, pandect *(code of laws)*
legal command ordinance
legal competence competence *(ability)*, majority *(adulthood)*
legal confinement commitment *(confinement)*
legal constraint commitment *(confinement)*
legal consultant lawyer
legal contest action *(proceeding)*, day in court, lawsuit
legal controversy lawsuit
legal costs damages
legal counsel advice
legal course to adhere to adjective law
legal decision cognovit, judgment *(formal court decree)*
legal defender counselor
legal defense compurgation, justification, plea
legal disclosure SEE MAIN ENTRY
legal dispute case *(lawsuit)*, contention *(argument)*, lawsuit, trial *(legal proceeding)*. SEE MAIN ENTRY
legal dissolution of marriage divorce, separation
legal document agreement *(contract)*, blank *(form)*, brief, contract, policy *(contract)*
legal document to search search warrant
legal documents SEE MAIN ENTRY
legal enforcement of a lien fore-closure
legal entity corporation, corpus, partnership
legal epitome brief
legal estate effects, fee *(estate)*, holding *(property owned)*
legal evidence admissible evidence, affirmance *(legal affirmation)*, affirmation, corroboration. SEE MAIN ENTRY
legal expense cost *(expenses)*
legal expert jurist. SEE MAIN ENTRY
legal fitness competence *(ability)*
legal force validity
legal forum judiciary
legal heir legatee
legal immaturity minority *(infancy)*, nonage
ligdally in force SEE MAIN ENTRY
legal incapacity disability *(legal disqualification)*, minority *(infancy)*
legal incompetence minority *(infancy)*
legal inquiry investigation
legal instructions charge *(statement to the jury)*
legal investigation inquest
legal issue case *(lawsuit)*, contention *(argument)*. SEE MAIN ENTRY
legal learning jurisprudence
legal liability damages, fine
legal mandate subpoena
legal maturity majority *(adulthood)*
legal memorandum brief
legal methods adjective law
legal minimum quorum
legal minority nonage
legal notice monition *(legal summons)*, notification
legal nullification of marriage divorce
legal obligation liability
legal opponent litigant
legal order mittimus, precept, search warrant
legal philosophy jurisprudence
legal pledge adjuration, affirmance *(legal affirmation)*, affirmation, asseveration, avowal, certification *(attested copy)*, confirmation
legal power authority *(right)*, droit, judicature, jurisdiction, prerogative, right *(entitlement)*
legal power to decide a case jurisdiction
legal practice jurisprudence
legal practitioner advocate *(counselor)*, attorney, barrister, counsel, counselor, esquire, jurist, lawyer. SEE MAIN ENTRY
legal precedent jurisprudence. SEE MAIN ENTRY
legal procedure certiorari, proceeding
legal proceeding action *(proceeding)*, controversy *(lawsuit)*, suit. SEE MAIN ENTRY
legal proceedings case *(lawsuit)*, cause *(lawsuit)*, hearing, lawsuit, matter *(case)*
legal process certiorari, citation *(charge)*, controversy *(lawsuit)*, prosecution *(criminal trial)*, search warrant, subpoena, summons, warrant *(judicial writ)*. SEE MAIN ENTRY
legal profession bar *(body of lawyers)*. SEE MAIN ENTRY
legal program agenda
legal ratification affirmance *(judicial sanction)*
legal recourse SEE MAIN ENTRY
legal redress recourse
legal relation of spouses to each other cohabitation *(married state)*
legal relationship privity
legal release from confinement discharge *(liberation)*
legal response SEE MAIN ENTRY
legal remedy suit
legal representative administrator, advocate *(counselor)*, attorney in fact, counselor, executor, jurist
legal representation SEE MAIN ENTRY
legal residence address
legal responsibility liability, obligation *(duty)*
legal restraint constraint *(imprisonment)*, detention, deterrence, deterrent, durance, embargo, estoppel, incarceration
legal right birthright, droit, freedom, jurisdiction, patent. SEE MAIN ENTRY
legal science jurisprudence
legal status of a married woman coverture
legal support maintenance *(support of spouse)*
legal tender cash, currency, money
legal termination of marriage divorce
legal title droit, right *(entitlement)*, title *(right)*
ligally in force SEE MAIN ENTRY
legal trial day in court, hearing, inquiry *(systematic investigation)*, prosecution *(criminal trial)*
legal union of a man and a woman cohabitation *(married state)*
legal vitality force *(legal efficacy)*
legal will testament
legal wrong tort
legalese jargon *(technical language)*
legalism legality. SEE MAIN ENTRY
legalist jurist
legalistic forensic, juridical. SEE MAIN ENTRY
legality admissibility, legitimacy, sanction *(permission)*, validity. SEE MAIN ENTRY
legalization consent, leave *(permission)*, permit. SEE MAIN ENTRY
legalize allow *(authorize)*, authorize, certify *(approve)*, confirm, constitute *(establish)*, formalize, legitimate, notarize, pass *(approve)*, seal *(solemnize)*, validate. SEE MAIN ENTRY
legalized allowable, allowed, choate lien, entitled, juridical, justifiable, lawful, legal, legitimate *(rightful)*, licit, prescriptive, rightful, statutory, valid
legally de jure, fairly *(impartially)*
legally adequate prima facie *(legally sufficient)*
legally binding valid. SEE MAIN ENTRY
legally bound liable
legally determine try *(conduct a trial)*
legally discard a spouse divorce
legally enforceable triable. SEE MAIN ENTRY
legally incapable disabled *(deprived of legal right)*
legally in force SEE MAIN ENTRY
legally obliged to repay indebted
legally pursue sue
legally qualified eligible
legally responsible liable
legally restrain apprehend *(arrest)*, arrest *(apprehend)*
legally restrain again rearrest
legally restrained arrested *(apprehended)*
legally sound permissible
legare leave *(give)*
legatary legatee
legate advocate *(counselor)*, plenipotentiary
legatee beneficiary, devisee, donee, feoffee, heir, recipient, transferee. SEE MAIN ENTRY
legateship embassy
legati deputation *(delegation)*
legatio deputation *(delegation)*, embassy, staff
legation delegation *(envoy)*, deputation *(delegation)*, embassy, mission
legatum bequest, legacy
legatus deputy, procurator
legend caption, fiction, inscription, myth, story *(narrative)*. SEE MAIN ENTRY
legendary famous, fictitious, nonexistent, proverbial. SEE MAIN ENTRY
legendary story myth
legerdemain deception, knavery, maneuver *(trick)*, prestidigitation
legere cull, select
leges facere legislate
legible coherent *(clear)*, comprehensible
legibly fairly *(clearly)*

legion assemblage, band, quantity
legionary innumerable
legis violator lawbreaker
legislate authorize, constitute *(establish),* enact, govern, legalize, mandamus, pass *(approve).* SEE MAIN ENTRY
legislated due *(regular),* legitimate *(rightful),* licit, positive *(prescribed)*
legislating legislative
legislation act *(enactment),* amendment *(legislation),* bill *(proposed act),* canon, code, codification, edict, enactment, measure, ordinance, regulation *(rule),* rubric *(authoritative rule),* rule *(legal dictate),* statute. SEE MAIN ENTRY
legislative executive, statutory. SEE MAIN ENTRY
legislative act amendment *(legislation)*
legislative bill amendment *(legislation)*
legislative body chamber *(body),* congress, legislature
legislative cure remedial statute
legislative declaration bill *(formal declaration)*
legislative decree act *(enactment),* ordinance. SEE MAIN ENTRY
legislative draftsman lawmaker
legislative edict ordinance
legislative enactment measure, statute. SEE MAIN ENTRY
legislative intent SEE MAIN ENTRY
legislative mandate measure. SEE MAIN ENTRY
legislative precedent authority *(documentation)*
legislative process legislation *(lawmaking)*
legislative proclamation measure
legislative redress remedial statute
legislative sanction legalization
legislator lawmaker, politician. SEE MAIN ENTRY
legislatorial statutory
legislators government *(political administration)*
legislature chamber *(body),* congress. SEE MAIN ENTRY
legist advocate *(counselor),* attorney, barrister, counsel, counselor, esquire, jurist, lawyer, magistrate
legists bar *(body of lawyers)*
legitimacy admissibility, authority *(right),* honesty, legality, reality, validity. SEE MAIN ENTRY
legitimate admissible, allowable, allowed, authentic, authorize, bona fide, choate lien, constitute *(establish),* de jure, due *(regular),* ethical, fit, formalize, genuine, honest, justifiable, justify, lawful, legal, legalize, licit, official, permissible, plausible, proper, rational, real, reliable, right *(correct),* rightful, sanction, sane, scrupulous, sound, straightforward, tenable, true *(authentic),* upright, valid, veridical, viable, well-grounded. SEE MAIN ENTRY
legitimate puissance force *(legal efficacy)*
legitimately de jure, duly, in good faith
legitimateness legality, legitimacy, validity
legitimation legitimacy
legitimatization legalization
legitimatize allow *(authorize),* authorize, constitute *(establish),* formalize, legalize, legitimate, sanction, validate. SEE MAIN ENTRY
legitimization legitimacy
legitimize authorize, constitute *(establish),* pass *(approve),* sanction, validate. SEE MAIN ENTRY
legitimized choate lien, fully executed *(signed)*
legitimus justifiable, lawful, legal, licit
leisure furlough, holiday, leave *(absence)*
leisured unemployed
leisurely deliberate
lend bestow, capitalize *(provide capital),* finance, invest *(fund),* let *(lease),* loan, rent. SEE MAIN ENTRY
lend a hand facilitate, help, promote *(organize)*
lend aid help, serve *(assist)*
lend approval recommend
lend assistance contribute *(assist)*
lend force to compound
lend money to support *(assist)*
lend on security invest *(fund),* lease
lend one's aid capitalize *(provide capital),* subsidize
lend one's name to indorse
lend one's support to cooperate
lend oneself to cooperate, espouse, involve *(participate),* partake
lend support bear *(support),* capitalize *(provide capital),* help, preserve, recommend, subsidize
lend to again refinance
lender backer, creditor, obligee
lending assistance contributory
length extent, gamut. SEE MAIN ENTRY
length of life longevity
length of time duration, period
lengthen compound, continue *(prolong),* enlarge, expand, extend *(enlarge),* increase, keep *(continue),* project *(extend beyond),* prolong, spread, supplement, sustain *(prolong).* SEE MAIN ENTRY
lengthen out protract *(stall)*
lengthened protracted
lengthening continuance, continuation *(prolongation),* cumulative *(increasing),* development *(progression)*
lengthwise along
lengthy prolix, protracted, sesquipedalian. SEE MAIN ENTRY
lenience clemency, condonation, humanity *(humaneness),* indulgence, longanimity, moderation, pity. SEE MAIN ENTRY
leniency clemency, grace period, humanity *(humaneness),* indulgence, lenience, longanimity, moderation, pardon, pity. SEE MAIN ENTRY
lenient palliative *(abating),* perfunctory, permissive, placable. SEE MAIN ENTRY
lenify palliate *(abate),* relax, remit *(relax),* soothe
lenire allay, mitigate, mollify, pacify, soothe
lenis lenient
lenitive medicinal, narcotic, remedial
lenity clemency, humanity *(humaneness),* indulgence, lenience, moderation, pity
lentus flexible, intentional, malleable, phlegmatic, pliable, pliant, stagnant, torpid
leonine powerful
lese majesty rebellion
less save, subaltern. SEE MAIN ENTRY
less important minor, secondary, subordinate
less powerful inferior *(lower in position)*
less significant subordinate
less than necessary deficient
less than perfect faulty, peccable
less valuable inferior *(lower in quality)*
lessee consumer, customer, lodger, occupant, tenant. SEE MAIN ENTRY
lessen abridge *(shorten),* adulterate, allay, alleviate, assuage, attenuate, commute, curtail, debilitate, decrease, deduct *(reduce),* deplete, depreciate, depress, derogate, diminish, discount *(minimize),* ease, erode, expend *(consume),* extenuate, minimize, mitigate, moderate *(temper),* modify *(moderate),* mollify, palliate *(abate),* rebate, reduce, relax, remit *(relax),* retrench, soothe, subdue, subside. SEE MAIN ENTRY
lessen importance of demote
lessen in force mitigate
lessen in power impair
lessen in value impair. SEE MAIN ENTRY
lessen in worth degenerate
lessen one's reputation defame
lessen the labor facilitate
lessen the price of depreciate
lessen the reputation of derogate
lessen the self-confidence of discourage
lessen the strength of dilute
lessening abatement *(reduction),* attrition, curtailment, decline, decrease, decrement, deduction *(diminution),* derogatory, diminution, erosion, mitigating, mitigation, mollification, remission
lessening of price rebate
lesser ancillary *(subsidiary),* inferior *(lower in position),* inferior *(lower in quality),* mediocre, minimal, minor, secondary, subaltern, subordinate, subservient. SEE MAIN ENTRY
lesser group minority *(outnumbered group)*
lesser included offense SEE MAIN ENTRY
lesser part minority *(outnumbered group)*
lesson caveat, correction *(punishment),* guidance. SEE MAIN ENTRY
lessor landlord, obligee, transferor. SEE MAIN ENTRY
let attorn, bestow, enable, engage *(hire),* grant *(concede),* lease, permit, rent, suffer *(permit),* vouchsafe. SEE MAIN ENTRY
let alone forswear, shun
let be leave *(allow to remain)*
let continue leave *(allow to remain)*
let down betray *(lead astray),* disappoint, disappointed, frustrate. SEE MAIN ENTRY
let drop divulge
let escape free, rescue
let fall outpour, precipitate *(throw down violently),* remark
let fly precipitate *(throw down violently),* project *(impel forward)*
let go acquitted, clear, disband, discharge *(dismiss),* discharge *(liberate),* disenthrall, disown *(refuse to acknowledge),* forfeit, free, leave *(allow to remain),* liberate, omit, palliate *(excuse),* release, relinquish, remit *(release from penalty),* renounce, surrender *(give back),* terminate, yield *(submit).* SEE MAIN ENTRY
let go free parole
let have present *(make a gift)*
let in receive *(permit to enter)*
let know apprise, communicate, confide *(divulge),* disabuse, inform *(notify),* mention, notify
let lapse discontinue *(abandon)*
let loose discharge *(dismiss),* discharge *(liberate),* disenthrall, extricate, free, liberate, pardon
let off absolve, acquit, acquitted, cast *(throw),* clear, excuse, palliate *(excuse).* SEE MAIN ENTRY
let one down fail *(neglect)*
let out communicate, disband, discharge *(liberate),* disengage, disenthrall, emit, free *(not restricted),* free, liberate, release, remit

(release from penalty), rent, rescue, sublease, sublet. SEE MAIN ENTRY
let out of jail parole
let out of prison discharge *(liberate)*, disenthrall, free, parole
let pass condone, forgo, omit, pretermit
let premises for a designated period lease
let ride overlook *(disregard)*
let slacken remit *(relax)*
let slide ignore, procrastinate
let slip betray *(disclose)*, divulge, forfeit, ignore, omit, procrastinate
let stand leave *(allow to remain)*. SEE MAIN ENTRY
let the matter stand procrastinate
let through receive *(permit to enter)*
let up diminution, ease, lessen, remit *(relax)*, subside
letdown damper *(depressant)*
lethal deadly, deleterious, dire, fatal, insalubrious, malevolent, malignant, noxious, peccant *(unhealthy)*, pernicious, pestilent, ruthless, toxic, virulent. SEE MAIN ENTRY
lethal instrument cudgel, gun
lethal instruments weapons
lethal weapon cudgel
lethal weapons weapons
lethality fatality
lethargic inactive, indolent, languid, lifeless *(dull)*, otiose, phlegmatic, stagnant, torpid
lethargical inactive, languid, lifeless *(dull)*, otiose, phlegmatic
lethargy inertia, languor, sloth. SEE MAIN ENTRY
lethiferous deadly, fatal, insalubrious, lethal, pestilent
letter dispatch *(message)*, inscribe, transmittal. SEE MAIN ENTRY
letter in support reference *(recommendation)*
letter of credit draft. SEE MAIN ENTRY
letter of introduction reference *(recommendation)*
letter of recognition certification *(certification of proficiency)*
letter of recommendation reference *(recommendation)*
letter of the law SEE MAIN ENTRY
letter writing correspondence *(communication by letters)*
lettered cognizant, familiar *(informed)*, informed *(educated)*, learned, literate
letters correspondence *(communication by letters)*, education
letting go layoff
letting off acquittal
lettre de cachet durance
letup cloture, pause, remission, respite *(interval of rest)*
levamentum mitigation
levant abscond, bilk, defraud, escape
levanter fugitive
levare assuage, elevate, extenuate
levatio mitigation
level balance *(equality)*, coequal, commensurable, destroy *(efface)*, extirpate, obliterate, pillage, regulate *(adjust)*, subvert. SEE MAIN ENTRY
level of attendance draw *(attendance)*
level of development degree *(station)*
level of education civilization
level of excellence standard
level off compensate *(counterbalance)*, decrease
level with inform *(notify)*
level-headedness common sense, deliberation
levelheaded patient, prudent, rational, sane, sensible
levelheadedness sagacity, sanity
levelness regularity, uniformity
lever devastate
leverage advantage, clout, influence, latitude. SEE MAIN ENTRY
leviable ad valorem
leviathan prodigious *(enormous)*
levied attached *(seized)*. SEE MAIN ENTRY
levis capricious, frivolous, inconsiderable, negligible, slight, superficial, trivial, volatile
levy ad valorem, assess *(tax)*, attach *(seize)*, charge *(assess)*, collect *(recover money)*, confiscate, distrain, distraint, distress *(seizure)*, dun, duty *(tax)*, exact, excise, excise *(levy a tax)*, garnishment, imposition *(tax)*, impress *(procure by force)*, raise *(collect)*, require *(compel)*, requisition, sequester *(seize property)*, sequestration, tariff *(duties)*, tax, toll *(tax)*, toll *(exact payment)*. SEE MAIN ENTRY
levy a distress distrain
levy an excise on excise *(levy a tax)*
levy upon garnish
lewd depraved, immoral, lascivious, lecherous, licentious, obscene, promiscuous, prurient, salacious, scandalous, scurrilous, suggestive *(risqué)*, unrestrained *(not repressed)*, wanton. SEE MAIN ENTRY
lewdness debauchery, obscenity, perversion, pornography, vice
lex act *(enactment)*, canon, code, enactment, law, statute, term *(provision)*
lex loci SEE MAIN ENTRY
lex oblivionis indemnity
liabilities overhead
liability arrears, attornment, blame *(responsibility)*, burden, chance *(possibility)*, characteristic, charge *(lien)*, cloud *(incumbrance)*, debit, debt, delinquency *(shortage)*, detriment, disadvantage, drawback, due, duty *(obligation)*, encumbrance, excise, fault *(responsibility)*, fine, impairment *(drawback)*, impeachability, incumbrance *(lien)*, lien, penalty, probability, responsibility *(accountability)*, weight *(burden)*. SEE MAIN ENTRY
liability to disaster fatality
liability to err frailty
liability to injury danger, hazard, peril
liable accountable *(responsible)*, at fault, blameful, blameworthy, bound, inclined, possible, probable, prone, subject *(exposed)*, susceptible *(unresistent)*. SEE MAIN ENTRY
liable to conditional
liable to attack vulnerable
liable to be annulled voidable
liable to be completed determinable *(liable to be terminated)*
liable to be discontinued determinable *(liable to be terminated)*
liable to be dropped determinable *(liable to be terminated)*
liable to be ended determinable *(liable to be terminated)*
liable to be erroneous fallible
liable to come to an end determinable *(liable to be terminated)*
liable to disappear elusive
liable to err peccable
liable to expire determinable *(liable to be terminated)*
liable to mistake fallible
liable to prosecution actionable, blameful, blameworthy, justiciable
liable to question uncertain *(questionable)*
liable to sin peccable
liableness probability
liaison chain *(nexus)*, collusion, connection *(fastening)*, connection *(relation)*, connivance, contact *(association)*, nexus, relation *(connection)*. SEE MAIN ENTRY
liaisons ties
libation grant
libel aspersion, defamation, defame, denigrate, malign, slander, smear. SEE MAIN ENTRY
libelant accuser, claimant, complainant, contender, contestant, party *(litigant)*
libellus indictment, invoice *(itemized list)*, petition, schedule
libellus famosus libel
libelous calumnious, contemptuous, derogatory. SEE MAIN ENTRY
liber candid, exempt, free *(not restricted)*, independent, ingenuous, liberty, register
liberal ample, benevolent, broad, charitable *(benevolent)*, charitable *(lenient)*, copious, extensive, lenient, magnanimous, open-minded, permissive, philanthropic, prodigal, profuse, progressive *(advocating change)*, unbiased. SEE MAIN ENTRY
liberalis charitable *(lenient)*, liberal *(broad minded)*
liberalism latitude
liberalistic broad
liberalitas bounty, charity
liberality benefit *(conferment)*, benevolence *(disposition to do good)*, candor *(impartiality)*, clemency, disinterest *(lack of prejudice)*, largess *(generosity)*, lenience, philanthropy, tolerance. SEE MAIN ENTRY
liberalness charity, largess *(generosity)*
liberare absolve, acquit, disengage, exonerate, extricate, free, liberate, release, rescue
liberate absolve, acquit, clear, disencumber, disengage, disentangle, disenthrall, dissociate, enable, enfranchise, exclude, exculpate, excuse, exonerate, extricate, free, let *(permit)*, palliate *(excuse)*, pardon, parole, quit *(free of)*, redeem *(repurchase)*, release, relieve *(free from burden)*, remit *(release from penalty)*, rescue, save *(rescue)*. SEE MAIN ENTRY
liberate from connection disengage
liberate from oppression disenthrall
liberated exempt, free *(enjoying civil liberty)*, free *(not restricted)*, free *(relieved from a burden)*, liberal *(broad minded)*, sovereign *(independent)*, unbound. SEE MAIN ENTRY
liberatio acquittal, emancipation, liberation, release
liberation absolution, acquittal, compurgation, emancipation, exemption, exoneration, freedom, immunity, impunity, parole, probation, release, relief *(release)*, remission, suffrage. SEE MAIN ENTRY
liberation from foreign restraint liberty
liberi issue *(progeny)*
libertas freedom, latitude, liberty
liberticide oppression
libertinage debauchery
libertine dissolute, lascivious, lecherous, lewd, licentious, salacious, unrestrained *(not repressed)*
libertinism debauchery, vice
liberty capacity *(authority)*, charter *(sanction)*, dispensation *(exception)*, emancipa-

tion, exemption, freedom, furlough, immunity, informality, latitude, leave *(absence),* leave *(permission),* license, opportunity, option *(choice),* parole, prerogative, privilege, suffrage. SEE MAIN ENTRY
liberty of action call *(option)*
liberty of approach admittance *(means of approach)*
liberty of choice franchise *(right to vote)*
liberty of choosing discretion *(power of choice)*
liberty of judgment discretion *(power of choice)*
liberty of use easement
liberty to enter ingress
liberty to vote franchise *(right to vote)*
libidinosus arbitrary, lascivious, licentious, prurient
libidinous dissolute, immoral, lascivious, lecherous, lewd, obscene, prurient, salacious, scurrilous, suggestive *(risqué),* wanton
librate oscillate, vacillate
libretto script
libro balance *(equality)*
librum edere edit
license allow *(authorize),* appoint, approval, authorize, bestow, brevet, capacity *(authority),* certificate, certification *(certification of proficiency),* certify *(approve),* charter *(sanction),* concession *(authorization),* confirm, consent *(noun),* consent *(verb),* constitute *(establish),* copyright, countenance, delegate, delegation *(assignment),* discretion *(power of choice),* dispensation *(exception),* droit, empower, enable, enfranchise, entrust, exemption, freedom, grant *(concede),* immunity, impunity, induct, indulgence, informality, invest *(vest),* latitude, leave *(permission),* let *(permit),* liberty, option *(contractual provision),* palliate *(excuse),* patent, permission, permit *(noun),* permit *(verb),* prerogative, prescription *(claim of title),* privilege, qualify *(meet standards),* sanction *(permission),* sanction, seal *(solemnize),* sign, suffer *(permit),* sufferance, suffrage, tolerance, warrant *(authorization).* SEE MAIN ENTRY
licensed admissible, allowed, entitled, lawless, legitimate *(rightful),* licit, official, permissible, privileged, qualified *(competent)*
licensee nominee *(delegate),* transferee. SEE MAIN ENTRY
licensing of rights SEE MAIN ENTRY
licensor transferor. SEE MAIN ENTRY
licentia anarchy, freedom, latitude, leave *(permission),* liberty
licentious depraved, disobedient, disorderly, disreputable, dissolute, immoral, lecherous, lewd, obscene, promiscuous, prurient, salacious, scandalous, scurrilous, uncurbed, unrestrained *(not repressed),* wanton. SEE MAIN ENTRY
licentiousness debauchery, vice
licet permissible
licit allowable, allowed, de jure, due *(regular),* honest, just, justifiable, law-abiding, lawful, legal, legitimate *(rightful),* permissible, rightful, statutory, valid. SEE MAIN ENTRY
licitatio bid
licitly de jure
licitness droit, legitimacy
licitus permissible
lickerish lascivious, lecherous, prurient, salacious, suggestive *(risqué)*
lickerous salacious
lid cap. SEE MAIN ENTRY
lidless open *(unclosed)*
lie bear false witness, canard, deceive, deception, equivocate, evade *(deceive),* fabricate *(make up),* fake, false pretense, falsehood, falsify, fiction, figment, hoax, invent *(falsify),* misguide, mislead, misrepresent, misrepresentation, misstate, misstatement, palter, perjure, posture *(attitude),* pretend, pretense *(pretext),* pretext, prevaricate, rest *(be supported by),* story *(falsehood),* subterfuge. SEE MAIN ENTRY
lie about feign
lie across cross *(intersect)*
lie adjacent to contact *(touch)*
lie against frame *(charge falsely),* frame *(prearrange)*
lie beside adjoin
lie concealed lurk
lie contiguous to border *(bound)*
lie down repose *(rest)*
lie hidden lurk
lie in ambush lurk, prowl
lie in wait lurk, prowl
lie in wait for ambush
lie low lurk
lie near border *(approach)*
lie near to adjoin
lie next to border *(bound)*
lie over overlap
lief readily
liegeman subject *(object)*
lien encumbrance, hypothecation, security *(pledge).* SEE MAIN ENTRY
lien on an estate encumbrance
lieutenant coadjutant, deputy, liaison, plenipotentiary, proctor, procurator, proxy, substitute
life entity, lifetime, practice *(professional business),* spirit, survival. SEE MAIN ENTRY
life estate freehold
life span lifetime
life support SEE MAIN ENTRY
life's duration lifetime
life's work practice *(professional business)*
life-giving productive, salubrious
life-supporting vital
lifeblood main point. SEE MAIN ENTRY
lifeless dead, deceased, defunct, languid, mediocre, otiose, pedestrian, phlegmatic, ponderous, stagnant, torpid. SEE MAIN ENTRY
lifeless body corpse
lifeless object article *(commodity)*
lifelessness inertia, insentience, languor
lifelike descriptive, natural, realistic, suggestive *(evocative)*
lifelong durable
lifetime life *(period of existence),* term *(duration).* SEE MAIN ENTRY
lifework calling, career, employment, profession *(vocation),* pursuit *(occupation)*
lift bolster, build *(augment),* elevate, elevation, enhance, jostle *(pickpocket),* promotion *(advancement),* raise *(advance),* steal, support *(assistance).* SEE MAIN ENTRY
lift a ban facilitate. SEE MAIN ENTRY
lift controls disengage, quit *(free of)*
lift up heighten *(elevate)*
lifter thief
ligament chain *(nexus)*
ligation attachment *(act of affixing)*
ligature chain *(nexus),* connection *(fastening)*
light deft, frivolous, jocular, minimal, negligible, slight, subtle *(refined),* trivial. SEE MAIN ENTRY
light labor sinecure
light up burn
light upon find *(discover)*
light work sinecure
light-footed rapid
light-minded frivolous
lighten abate *(lessen),* allay, alleviate, attenuate, commute, diminish, ease, extenuate, facilitate, lessen, mitigate, moderate *(temper),* modify *(moderate),* relieve *(free from burden).* SEE MAIN ENTRY
lighten the labor disencumber
lightening abatement *(reduction),* mitigation, mollification
lightness immateriality, informality
lightweight immaterial
likable palatable, preferable, sapid, savory
like akin *(germane),* analogous, approximate, cognate, comparable *(capable of comparison),* congruous, correlate, equal, equivalent, faithful *(true to fact),* identical, related, relish, similar. SEE MAIN ENTRY
like better prefer
like in degree coequal, equal
like in quantity coequal, equal
like-kind SEE MAIN ENTRY
like quality analogy
like to desire
like-minded consensual. SEE MAIN ENTRY
likeable attractive
liked popular, preferred *(favored)*
likelihood chance *(possibility),* feasibility, possibility, presumption, probability, prospect *(outlook),* supposition, weight *(credibility).* SEE MAIN ENTRY
likeliness likelihood, probability, prospect *(outlook),* supposition
likely apparent *(presumptive),* appropriate, believable, circumstantial, convincing, deductible *(provable),* fitting, future, ostensible, possible, potential, presumptive, probable, prone, prospective, suitable, viable. SEE MAIN ENTRY
likely client prospect *(prospective patron)*
likely customer prospect *(prospective patron)*
likely patron prospect *(prospective patron)*
likely person prospect *(prospective patron)*
likely to decrease taxes deductible *(capable of being deducted from taxes)*
likely to excite ill will invidious
likely to happen imminent
likely to harm dangerous
likeminded consenting
likemindedness concordance, understanding *(agreement)*
liken compare, conform, correspond *(be equivalent),* measure
likeness analogy, appearance *(look),* color *(complexion),* conformity *(agreement),* copy, correspondence *(similarity),* counterpart *(parallel),* duplicate, identity *(similarity),* par *(equality),* parity, peer, propinquity *(similarity),* reflection *(image),* relation *(connection),* relationship *(connection),* resemblance, semblance. SEE MAIN ENTRY
likewise also
liking affinity *(regard),* desire, disposition *(inclination),* favor *(partiality),* inclination, indorsement, partiality, penchant, predilection, predisposition, preference *(choice),* proclivity, propensity, regard *(esteem)*
Lilliputian minimal
lilylivered recreant

limare file *(arrange)*
limber flexible, malleable, pliable, pliant
limelight publicity
limit abate *(lessen)*, abridge *(divest)*, ambit, bar *(obstruction)*, bar *(exclude)*, barrier, bind *(restrain)*, block, border, border *(bound)*, boundary, cap, capacity *(maximum)*, ceiling, censor, check *(restrain)*, commute, compel, condemn *(ban)*, confine, constrain *(imprison)*, constrain *(restrain)*, constrict *(inhibit)*, control *(restrain)*, curb, debar, defeasance, define, demarcate, detain *(restrain)*, deter, determine, diminish, disadvantage, discipline *(control)*, disfranchise, duration, edge *(border)*, enclose, enclosure, encumber *(hinder)*, end *(termination)*, enjoin, expiration, extent, extremity *(furthest point)*, frontier, gamut, guideline, hamper, hedge, impede, margin *(outside limit)*, maximum *(pinnacle)*, measurement, mete, moderate *(temper)*, modify *(moderate)*, obstruct, palliate *(abate)*, periphery, prevent, prohibit, prohibition, purview, qualify *(condition)*, quota, range, repress, restrain, restrict, retrench, scope, specialize, toll *(stop)*. SEE MAIN ENTRY
limit of endurance capacity *(maximum)*
limitable terminable
limitary qualified *(conditioned)*, restrictive
limitation abatement *(reduction)*, abridgment *(disentitlement)*, alienation *(transfer of title)*, bar *(obstruction)*, boundary, capacity *(maximum)*, censorship, check *(bar)*, clause, compulsion *(coercion)*, condition *(contingent provision)*, constraint *(restriction)*, control *(restriction)*, custody *(incarceration)*, damper *(stopper)*, detention, deterrence, deterrent, disadvantage, discipline *(obedience)*, enclosure, end *(termination)*, extent, fetter, flaw, foible, guideline, handicap, impairment *(drawback)*, impediment, mete, moderation, modification, obstacle, obstruction, periphery, prohibition, provision *(clause)*, purview, qualification *(condition)*, quota, reservation *(condition)*, restraint, restriction, term *(provision)*. SEE MAIN ENTRY
limitations configuration *(confines)*, confines, frontier, outline *(boundary)*
limitative conditional, prohibitive *(restrictive)*, restrictive
limited arrested *(checked)*, brief, certain *(specific)*, conditional, dependent, imperfect, infrequent, local, minimal, narrow, parochial, partial *(part)*, partial *(relating to a part)*, petty, private *(not public)*, privy, provisional, qualified *(conditioned)*, scarce, slight, specific, strict, temporary. SEE MAIN ENTRY
limited amount paucity
limited area region
limited choice dilemma
limited time period
limiting binding, determinative, mitigating, prohibitive *(restrictive)*, restrictive. SEE MAIN ENTRY
limitive determinative
limitless far reaching, indeterminate, infinite, innumerable, myriad, omnibus, open-ended, plenary, profuse, unbound, unlimited, unqualified *(unlimited)*, unrestricted
limitlessly ad infinitum
limits area *(province)*, boundary, capacity *(sphere)*, configuration *(confines)*, confines, outline *(boundary)*, premises *(buildings)*, purview. SEE MAIN ENTRY
limn delineate, depict, portray
limp insipid, languid, nonsubstantial *(not sturdy)*
limpid clear *(apparent)*, lucid, pellucid
line ancestry, birth *(lineage)*, blood, bloodline, business *(occupation)*, calling, career, chain *(series)*, derivation, descent *(lineage)*, direction *(course)*, employment, family *(common ancestry)*, lineage, merchandise, occupation *(vocation)*, origin *(ancestry)*, parentage, policy *(plan of action)*, polity, post, posterity, progeny, pursuit *(occupation)*, race, range, stock in trade, trade *(occupation)*, work *(employment)*. SEE MAIN ENTRY
line drawn round delineation
line of achievement calling
line of action action *(performance)*, campaign, course, maneuver *(tactic)*, manner *(behavior)*, policy *(plan of action)*, practice *(custom)*, practice *(procedure)*, procedure, process *(course)*
line of ancestors bloodline, descent *(lineage)*, family *(common ancestry)*, origin *(ancestry)*, parentage
line of business calling, labor *(work)*, position *(business status)*, practice *(professional business)*
line of circumvallation boundary, mete
line of conduct behavior, campaign, course, manner *(behavior)*, modus operandi, platform, policy *(plan of action)*, practice *(procedure)*
line of credit capital
line of demarcation border, boundary, configuration *(confines)*, crossroad *(turning point)*, frontier, limit, mete, outline *(boundary)*, periphery
line of descent affiliation *(bloodline)*, birth *(lineage)*, degree *(kinship)*, family *(common ancestry)*, lineage, origin *(ancestry)*
line of duty burden
line of goods merchandise
line of proceeding campaign, practice *(custom)*
line of sight perspective
line of work calling, labor *(work)*, livelihood, position *(business status)*, practice *(professional business)*, profession *(vocation)*, trade *(occupation)*
line up allocate, file *(arrange)*, fix *(arrange)*, juxtapose, marshal, set down
lineage affiliation *(bloodline)*, affinity *(family ties)*, ancestry, blood, bloodline, children, derivation, descendant, family *(common ancestry)*, filiation, heritage, house, issue *(progeny)*, kindred, off-spring, origin *(ancestry)*, parentage, paternity, posterity, progeny, relationship *(family tie)*, source, succession. SEE MAIN ENTRY
lineal hereditary
lineal descendant child
lineal descendants issue *(progeny)*
lineament color *(complexion)*, feature *(appearance)*, particularity, trait
lineamenta contour *(outline)*, design *(construction plan)*
lineaments boundary, outline *(boundary)*
lineamentum feature *(appearance)*
linear direct *(straight)*
lined up coextensive
lines ambit, boundary, configuration *(form)*, contour *(outline)*, contour *(shape)*, feature *(appearance)*, script
lines of demarcation confines
lineup order *(arrangement)*. SEE MAIN ENTRY
linger continue *(persevere)*, defer *(put off)*, delay, last, loiter, pause, persist, procrastinate, prolong, remain *(continue)*, remain *(stay)*, stall
linger on endure *(last)*
lingering chronic, lasting, protracted
lingo phraseology, speech
lingua language
lingual parol
linguistics language
link affiliation *(connectedness)*, affix, appertain, association *(connection)*, attach *(join)*, broker, chain *(nexus)*, combine *(join together)*, commingle, connection *(fastening)*, connection *(relation)*, consolidate *(unite)*, contact *(association)*, contact *(touch)*, engage *(involve)*, go-between, implicate, implication *(incriminating involvement)*, intermediary, join *(bring together)*, kinship, liaison, lock, medium, member *(constituent part)*, nexus, privity, propinquity *(kinship)*, relate *(establish a connection)*, relation *(connection)*, relationship *(connection)*, unite. SEE MAIN ENTRY
link together connect *(join together)*, connect *(relate)*, involve *(implicate)*
linkage affiliation *(connectedness)*, affinity *(family ties)*, association *(connection)*, chain *(nexus)*, coalescence, connection *(fastening)*, connection *(relation)*, contact *(association)*, joinder, liaison, marriage *(intimate relationship)*, relationship *(connection)*. SEE MAIN ENTRY
linked affiliated, akin *(germane)*, associated, coadunate, cognate, concurrent *(united)*, conjoint, correlative, interrelated, intimate, related. SEE MAIN ENTRY
linking joinder, marriage *(intimate relationship)*
links chain *(series)*, ties
lion's share majority *(greater part)*
lionhearted heroic, spartan
lionize honor
lip edge *(border)*, margin *(outside limit)*
liquefacere dissolve *(disperse)*
liquid assets capital, estate *(property)*
liquidate defray, destroy *(efface)*, discharge *(pay a debt)*, disorganize, dispatch *(put to death)*, eliminate *(eradicate)*, eradicate, extinguish, extirpate, kill *(murder)*, obliterate, pay, remove *(eliminate)*, slay. SEE MAIN ENTRY
liquidation aberemurder, assassination, cancellation, composition *(agreement in bankruptcy)*, discharge *(payment)*, dispatch *(act of putting to death)*, dissolution *(termination)*, homicide, killing, murder, payment *(act of paying)*
liquidation of a debt amortization
liquidator recipient
liquor alcohol
lis action *(proceeding)*, lawsuit, process *(summons)*, suit
lis pendens SEE MAIN ENTRY
lissome flexible, malleable, pliable
list bill *(invoice)*, book, census, classify, codify, docket, enroll, enter *(record)*, enumerate, file, file *(place among official records)*, fix *(arrange)*, impanel, index *(catalog)*, index *(relate)*, inscribe, inventory, itemize, organize *(arrange)*, pigeonhole, poll, program *(noun)*, program *(verb)*, recite, record *(noun)*, record *(verb)*, register, roll, schedule, sequence, set down, specify, survey *(poll)*, tabulate, tariff *(bill)*. SEE MAIN ENTRY
list for jury duty empanel
list jurors empanel

list of appointments calendar *(record of yearly periods)*
list of cases docket
list of cases set down for hearing calendar *(list of cases)*
list of causes arranged for trial calendar *(list of cases)*
list of causes instituted in court calendar *(list of cases)*
list of causes ready for trial calendar *(list of cases)*
list of events calendar *(record of yearly periods)*
list of goods invoice *(itemized list)*
list of items invoice *(itemized list),* tariff *(bill)*
list of items shipped invoice *(itemized list)*
list of jurors panel *(jurors)*
list of mercantile goods invoice *(itemized list)*
list of paid employees payroll
list of properties inventory
list of receipts and payments account *(evaluation)*
list of salaried employees payroll
list of wages to be paid out payroll
listen attend *(heed),* concentrate *(pay attention),* eavesdrop, hear *(give attention to),* monitor, obey. SEE MAIN ENTRY
listen in on overhear
listen stealthily eavesdrop, overhear
listen to heed, submit *(yield)*
listener bystander
listing census, docket, index *(catalog),* registration
listing of contents index *(catalog)*
listless despondent, idle, inactive, indolent, inexpressive, languid, lifeless *(dull),* otiose, phlegmatic, powerless, stagnant, torpid. SEE MAIN ENTRY
listlessness disinterest *(lack of interest),* languor, sloth
literacy education. SEE MAIN ENTRY
literal accurate, actual, authentic, exact, factual, faithful *(true to fact),* honest, narrow, orthodox, parochial, precise, strict, true *(authentic),* verbatim. SEE MAIN ENTRY
literal interpretation connotation, content *(meaning)*
literal meaning connotation, content *(meaning).* SEE MAIN ENTRY
literal sense connotation, content *(meaning)*
literally SEE MAIN ENTRY
literality connotation, content *(meaning)*
literalize construe *(translate)*
literally faithfully, verbatim
literary literate
literary artistry phraseology
literary forgery plagiarism
literary magazine publication *(printed matter)*
literary person author *(writer)*
literary piracy plagiarism
literary publications press
literary style phraseology
literary theft plagiarism
literate familiar *(informed),* informed *(educated),* learned. SEE MAIN ENTRY
literati faculty *(teaching staff)*
literatim verbatim
literature publication *(printed matter).* SEE MAIN ENTRY
lithe flexible, malleable, pliable, pliant
lithesome malleable, pliable
litigable actionable, justiciable. SEE MAIN ENTRY
litigant accuser, actionable, actor, adversary, appellant, claimant, complainant, contender, contestant, disputant, petitioner, plaintiff, rival, suitor. SEE MAIN ENTRY
litigare litigate
litigate contend *(dispute).* SEE MAIN ENTRY
litigate against sue
litigate completely exhaust *(try all possibilities)*
litigating counsel SEE MAIN ENTRY
litigation action *(proceeding),* case *(lawsuit),* cause *(lawsuit),* complaint, contest *(dispute),* controversy *(lawsuit),* day in court, dispute, hearing, lawsuit, matter *(case),* proceeding, prosecution *(criminal trial),* suit, trial *(legal proceeding).* SEE MAIN ENTRY
litigation of the charges action *(proceeding)*
litigationist litigant
litigator contender, litigant, suitor. SEE MAIN ENTRY
litigatory litigious
litigiosus litigious
litigious actionable, argumentative, contentious, forensic. SEE MAIN ENTRY
litterae correspondence *(communication by letters),* dispatch *(message),* document
litteratus learned
little impalpable, inappreciable, minimal, minor, negligible, nominal, paltry, petty, remote *(small),* scarce, slight, tenuous, trivial. SEE MAIN ENTRY
little by little piecemeal
little chance improbability
little one infant
little-known peculiar *(curious),* recondite, unusual. SEE MAIN ENTRY
littleness dearth
littoral SEE MAIN ENTRY
livable habitable
live born *(alive),* conscious *(awake),* dwell *(reside),* exist, inhabit, lodge *(reside),* occupy *(take possession),* reside, subsist. SEE MAIN ENTRY
live at reside
live by obey
live dissolutely carouse
live idly dissipate *(expend foolishly)*
live in occupy *(take possession),* remain *(occupy)*
live in sexual intimacy cohabit
live in terror fear
live on endure *(last),* exist, keep *(continue),* last, persist
live through bear *(tolerate)*
live together cohabit
live under unfavorable conditions languish
live up to fulfill, keep *(fulfill)*
live with cohabit
livelihood business *(occupation),* calling, career, employment, occupation *(vocation),* revenue, support *(assistance),* trade *(occupation).* SEE MAIN ENTRY
liveliness ardor, dispatch *(promptness),* life *(vitality),* spirit
lively rapid, volatile
lively pace dispatch *(promptness)*
liverish petulant
livery of seisin feoffment
livid SEE MAIN ENTRY
lividus jealous, spiteful
living appointment *(position),* bodily, born *(alive),* business *(occupation),* calling, conscious *(awake),* durable, employment, extant, inhabitation *(act of dwelling in),* live *(conscious),* livelihood, present *(current),* pursuit *(occupation),* residential, sustenance, trade *(occupation),* viable. SEE MAIN ENTRY
living as man and wife coverture
living being person
living by prey predatory
living expenses overhead
living image alter ego
living on prey rapacious
living place abode, house, lodging, residence
living quarters building *(structure),* domicile, dwelling, habitation *(dwelling place),* home *(domicile),* house, inhabitation *(place of dwelling),* residence. SEE MAIN ENTRY
living soul person
living space inhabitation *(place of dwelling)*
living thing entity
living together in sexual intimacy cohabitation *(living together)*
living will SEE MAIN ENTRY
livor spite
load burden, cargo, encumbrance, freight, impact, impede, incumbrance *(burden),* onus *(burden),* plethora, pressure, stress *(strain),* tax *(overwork),* weight *(burden).* SEE MAIN ENTRY
load down weigh
load to excess overload
load up hoard
loaded full, ready *(prepared),* replete
loaf procrastinate
loafer parasite
loafing indolent, remiss
loan capitalize *(provide capital),* credit *(delayed payment),* finance, invest *(fund),* investment, lend, let *(lease).* SEE MAIN ENTRY
loan applicant obligor
loan at interest investment
loan to again refinance
loan transaction mortgage
loanee debtor, obligor
loath averse, disinclined, disobedient, dissident, hesitant, renitent, restive
loathe contemn, disdain. SEE MAIN ENTRY
loathe to contra
loathed undesirable
loathful loathsome, obnoxious
loathing alienation *(estrangement),* hatred, malice, odium, phobia
loathsome antipathetic *(distasteful),* bad *(offensive),* contemptible, disreputable, heinous, invidious, objectionable, obnoxious, odious, offensive *(offending),* repugnant *(exciting aversion),* repulsive, undesirable, unsavory. SEE MAIN ENTRY
loathsomeness disrepute
lobby bait *(lure),* constituency, entrance, party *(political organization),* special interest. SEE MAIN ENTRY
lobbyist special interest. SEE MAIN ENTRY
local chapter *(branch),* domestic *(indigenous),* native *(domestic),* organ, provincial, regional. SEE MAIN ENTRY
local law ordinance
local legislation ordinance
local office chapter *(branch)*
local representative dealer
local rule ordinance
locale district, locality, location, part *(place),* region, scene, seat, section *(vicinity),* site, situs, territory, venue. SEE MAIN ENTRY
locality community, district, environment, home *(domicile),* location, region,

scene, seat, section *(vicinity)*, site, situs, venue. SEE MAIN ENTRY

localize restrict, site

localized local, regional

locally born native *(domestic)*

locare contract, lease, rent

locate allocate, deposit *(place)*, detect, discover, find *(discover)*, lodge *(house)*, pinpoint, plant *(place firmly)*, site. SEE MAIN ENTRY

locate oneself lodge *(reside)*

located situated

location area *(province)*, locality, part *(place)*, region, scene, seat, section *(vicinity)*, site, situs, standpoint, structure *(edifice)*, venue. SEE MAIN ENTRY

lock connect *(join together)*, fetter, fix *(make firm)*, occlude, seal *(close)*, shut. SEE MAIN ENTRY

lock in immure, imprison, jail

lock out bar *(exclude)*, eliminate *(exclude)*. SEE MAIN ENTRY

lock up capture, commit *(institutionalize)*, confine, contain *(restrain)*, detain *(hold in custody)*, fetter, immure, imprison, jail, lock, restrain. SEE MAIN ENTRY

locked conjoint, impervious, inseparable

locker coffer

locking up commitment *(confinement)*

lockout ostracism

lockup penitentiary

loco movere depose *(remove)*

loco parentis SEE MAIN ENTRY

loco suo movere displace *(remove)*

locomotive moving *(in motion)*

locum vacuefacere evacuate

locuples unimpeachable

locus address, circuit, locality

locus location. SEE MAIN ENTRY

locus position *(situation)*, post, purview, region, scene, scope, section *(vicinity)*

locus situs

locus space

locus classicus cross section

locus qui petitur objective

locus standi character *(reputation)*

locutio phraseology

locution expression *(comment)*, parlance, phraseology, speech, term *(expression)*

lodge chapter *(branch)*, deposit *(place)*, dwell *(reside)*, embed, fix *(make firm)*, harbor, inhabit, locate, occupy *(take possession)*, organ, remain *(occupy)*, remain *(stay)*, repose *(place)*, reside, stay *(rest)*. SEE MAIN ENTRY

lodge a complaint accuse, blame, charge *(accuse)*, cite *(accuse)*, complain *(charge)*, denounce *(inform against)*, implicate, incriminate, indict, involve *(implicate)*, present *(prefer charges)*. SEE MAIN ENTRY

lodge together cohabit

lodged situated

lodger habitant, inhabitant, lessee, occupant, resident, tenant. SEE MAIN ENTRY

lodging address, building *(structure)*, chamber *(compartment)*, domicile, dw-elling, habitation *(dwelling place)*, home *(domicile)*, house, household, inhabitation *(act of dwelling in)*, inhabitation *(place of dwelling)*, shelter *(protection)*. SEE MAIN ENTRY

lodging house building *(structure)*

lodging place address, building *(structure)*, dwelling, home *(domicile)*, inhabitation *(place of dwelling)*, lodging

lodging together cohabitation *(living together)*

lodging together as husband and wife cohabitation *(living together)*

lodgings building *(structure)*, premises *(buildings)*, residence

lodgment address, building *(structure)*, domicile, dwelling, habitation *(act of inhabiting)*, habitation *(dwelling place)*, inhabitation *(act of dwelling in)*, inhabitation *(place of dwelling)*, lodging, residence

loftiness bombast, distinction *(reputation)*, elevation, eminence, pretense *(ostentation)*, rhetoric *(insincere language)*

lofty grandiose, magnanimous, meritorious, orgulous, presumptuous, prominent, proud *(self-respecting)*, remarkable, supercilious. SEE MAIN ENTRY

log book, calendar *(record of yearly periods)*, enter *(record)*, journal, ledger, note *(record)*, record *(noun)*, record *(verb)*, register

log book register

logbook calendar *(record of yearly periods)*, journal, ledger

logic common sense, data, dialectic, ratiocination, reason *(sound judgment)*. SEE MAIN ENTRY

logic of discursive argument dialectic

logical apparent *(presumptive)*, cogent, coherent *(clear)*, colorable *(plausible)*, consistent, convincing, deductive, discursive *(analytical)*, normal *(sane)*, persuasive, plausible, probable, rational, reasonable *(rational)*, sane, sensible, solid *(sound)*, tenable, valid, viable. SEE MAIN ENTRY

logical argumentation dialectic

logical discussion deliberation, dialectic

logical order array *(order)*, method, sequence

logical process deduction *(conclusion)*, dialectic, system

logical reasoning rationale

logical relation analogy

logical result consequence *(conclusion)*

logical sequence corollary, deduction *(conclusion)*, dialectic

logically appealing coherent *(clear)*

logically consistent coherent *(clear)*, consonant

logically then consequently

logically unsound illogical

logicalness reason *(sound judgment)*

logomachic argumentative

logomachical argumentative

logomachy fight *(argument)*

loiter delay, pause, procrastinate, prowl. SEE MAIN ENTRY

loitering truant

lone exclusive *(singular)*, only *(sole)*, separate, singular, sole, solitary, unilateral. SEE MAIN ENTRY

lonely derelict *(abandoned)*, solitary

lonesome derelict *(abandoned)*, solitary

long prolix, protracted, sesquipedalian. SEE MAIN ENTRY

long and short of it SEE MAIN ENTRY

long-drawn *(protracted)* SEE MAIN ENTRY

long for desire, lack, need

long gone dead

long life longevity

long odds improbability

long vehement speech diatribe

long windedness prolixity

long-arm jurisdiction SEE MAIN ENTRY

long-continued protracted

long-continuing chronic, durable

long-delayed back *(in arrears)*, overdue

long-drawn protracted

long-enduring durable

long-established conventional, customary, prescriptive, traditional

long-lasting durable, incessant, permanent, stable, steadfast. SEE MAIN ENTRY

long-lived chronic, durable, stable

long-spun prolix

long-standing chronic, durable, inveterate, stable, traditional. SEE MAIN ENTRY

long-suffering lenient, patient, resigned, stoical

long-winded flatulent, loquacious, profuse, prolix, turgid, voluble

longanimity lenience, resignation *(passive acceptance)*, sufferance. SEE MAIN ENTRY

longanimous lenient, patient, placable

longevity age. SEE MAIN ENTRY

longevous durable

longhand handwriting, holographic, script

longiloquent loquacious

longing desire, eager, jealous, predisposition, will *(desire)*

longlivedness longevity

longsighted perspicacious

longstanding chronic, prescriptive

longus prolix

look appear *(seem to be)*, aspect, complexion, condition *(state)*, configuration *(form)*, demean *(deport oneself)*, demeanor, deportment, feature *(appearance)*, manner *(behavior)*, notice *(observe)*, observation, observe *(watch)*, presence *(poise)*, regard *(pay attention)*, semblance, vision *(dream)*. SEE MAIN ENTRY

look about for canvass

look about one beware

look after concern *(care)*, conduct, control *(regulate)*, direct *(supervise)*, foster, handle *(manage)*, harbor, keep *(shelter)*, maintain *(sustain)*, manage, operate, overlook *(superintend)*, oversee, preserve, protect, provide *(arrange for)*, superintend

look ahead plan

look ahead to prognosticate

look around for delve

look as if appear *(seem to be)*

look askance at disfavor

look at discern *(detect with the senses)*, note *(notice)*, notice *(observe)*, observe *(watch)*, regard *(pay attention)*, spy, survey *(examine)*

look at closely scrutinize

look back remember

look back upon recall *(remember)*, recollect

look behind the scenes delve

look down on condescend *(patronize)*, disdain, disfavor, disparage, patronize *(condescend toward)*

look down upon discriminate *(treat differently)*, misprize, spurn

look for delve, expect *(anticipate)*, ferret, hunt, spy

look for flaws check *(inspect)*, examine *(study)*

look forward to anticipate *(prognosticate)*, expect *(anticipate)*, forestall, prognosticate

look into canvass, check *(inspect)*, delve, examine *(study)*, frisk, inquire, investigate, probe, research, scrutinize, search. SEE MAIN ENTRY

look on discern *(detect with the senses)*

look out beware, overlook *(superintend)*, patrol

look out for care *(be cautious)*

look over check *(inspect)*, examine *(study)*, frisk, overlook *(superintend)*, peruse, review, scrutinize, search. SEE MAIN ENTRY
look through delve, examine *(study)*, frisk, search
look to focus, heed, rely, resort
look up SEE MAIN ENTRY
look up information in consult *(seek information from)*
look up to honor, regard *(hold in esteem)*
look upon deem, discern *(detect with the senses)*, opine, regard *(pay attention)*
look with scorn on disdain
look with scorn upon condescend *(patronize)*
looked after safe
looked for foreseeable, forseen, immediate *(imminent)*, prospective
looked toward future
looker bystander, witness
looker-on bystander, eyewitness, witness
looking back hindsight, retrospect
looking within introspection
lookout caretaker *(one caring for property)*, spy, surveillance
loom emerge, impend
looming forthcoming, future, imminent, inevitable, instant, pending *(imminent)*, prospective. SEE MAIN ENTRY
loop detour
loophole flaw, subterfuge. SEE MAIN ENTRY
loose careless, discharge *(liberate)*, disconnected, disencumber, disengage, disjunctive *(tending to disjoin)*, dispel, free *(not restricted)*, inaccurate, inexact, lax, lecherous, liberal *(not literal)*, liberate, licentious, open-ended, promiscuous, salacious, separate, suggestive *(risqué)*, unrestrained *(not repressed)*. SEE MAIN ENTRY
loose rendering paraphrase
loose statement generality *(vague statement)*
loose thinking non sequitur
loose translation paraphrase
loosen disencumber, disentangle, disenthrall, dissociate, ease, extricate, give *(yield)*, remit *(relax)*. SEE MAIN ENTRY
looseness informality, laxity, vice
looseness of morals perversion
loosing discharge *(liberation)*, discharge *(release from obligation)*
loot despoil, jostle *(pickpocket)*, pilfer, pillage, pirate *(take by violence)*, plunder *(noun)*, plunder *(verb)*, prey, prize, rob, spoil *(pillage)*, spoils. SEE MAIN ENTRY
looting burglary, foray, housebreaking, spoliation, theft
lop break *(separate)*, curtail, retrench
lop off sever
loquacious profuse, voluble. SEE MAIN ENTRY
loquacity prolixity, tautology
loquax loquacious
loqui generalize
lordliness pride
lordly dictatorial, disdainful, inflated *(vain)*, orgulous, presumptuous, proud *(conceited)*, supercilious, tyrannous
lordship dominion *(supreme authority)*, hegemony, possession *(ownership)*, supremacy
lore discipline *(field of study)*, information *(knowledge)*
lose deplete, erode, fail *(lose)*, forfeit, succumb, suffer *(sustain loss)*. SEE MAIN ENTRY
lose an opportunity forfeit
lose by breach of condition forfeit
lose by default forfeit. SEE MAIN ENTRY
lose by failure to appear default, forfeit
lose control carouse
lose courage fear
lose ground retreat. SEE MAIN ENTRY
lose heart languish
lose identity merge
lose individuality merge
lose life decease, perish
lose luster tarnish
lose morale degenerate
lose no time hasten
lose one's life die
lose sight of neglect
lose spirit languish
lose strength languish
lose value depreciate
losel improvident
loss abridgment *(disentitlement)*, bad debt, bankruptcy, calamity, consumption, cost *(penalty)*, damage, damages, decline, decrease, decrement, defeat, deficiency, deficit, detriment, disadvantage, erosion, expense *(sacrifice)*, failure *(lack of success)*, forfeiture *(thing forfeited)*, impairment *(damage)*, injury, miscarriage, penalty, prejudice *(injury)*, privation, toll *(effect)*. SEE MAIN ENTRY
loss consequent to a default forfeiture *(thing forfeited)*
loss of affection estrangement. SEE MAIN ENTRY
loss of belief discredit
loss of credence discredit
loss of credit discredit
loss of fortune bankruptcy, poverty, privation
loss of freedom bondage, subjection
loss of health disease
loss of honor bad repute, disgrace, disrepute, ignominy, notoriety, opprobrium, scandal, shame
loss of identity merger
loss of life death, demise *(death)*
loss of opportunity SEE MAIN ENTRY
loss of power prostration
loss of reason insanity
loss of reputation attaint, bad repute, disgrace, dishonor *(shame)*, disrepute, ignominy, infamy, notoriety, opprobrium, scandal, shame. SEE MAIN ENTRY
loss of repute discredit
loss of respect ignominy
loss of right disqualification *(rejection)*, forfeiture *(act of forfeiting)*, waiver
loss of standing opprobrium
loss of strength failure *(falling short)*, fault *(weakness)*, frailty
loss of value decline, decrease. SEE MAIN ENTRY
lost astray, disconsolate, incorrigible, irredeemable, irretrievable, reprobate. SEE MAIN ENTRY
lost cause SEE MAIN ENTRY
lost connection anacoluthon, non sequitur
lost labor miscarriage
lost to principle profligate *(corrupt)*
lost to virtue profligate *(corrupt)*
lot assemblage, bulk, conglomeration, entirety, lottery, parcel, plight, plot *(land)*, posture *(situation)*, predetermination, property *(land)*, quantity, real estate, situation. SEE MAIN ENTRY
lottery SEE MAIN ENTRY
loud blatant *(obtrusive)*, disorderly, flagrant, powerful, resounding, tawdry. SEE MAIN ENTRY
loud noise outcry
loud protest outcry
loudness noise
lounge rest *(be supported by)*, rest *(cease from action)*
loutish opaque, provincial, uncouth
love affection, affinity *(regard)*, predilection. SEE MAIN ENTRY
love of mankind philanthropy
loved popular
lovely elegant, sapid
loving zealous
low caitiff, depraved, heinous, ignoble, inelegant, lamentable, minimal, nominal, nonsubstantial *(not sufficient)*, odious, offensive *(offending)*, outrageous, poor *(inferior in quality)*, scandalous, scarce, scurrilous, servile, subaltern, tainted *(corrupted)*. SEE MAIN ENTRY
low comedy travesty
low estimation dishonor *(shame)*, disparagement, disregard *(lack of respect)*
low grade mediocrity
low opinion disapproval, disparagement
low quality mediocrity
low regard bad repute
low spirited disconsolate
low spirits damper *(depressant)*, pessimism
low standard bad repute
low standing ignominy
low valuation disparagement
low-class mediocre
low-grade inferior *(lower in quality)*, mediocre, poor *(inferior in quality)*
low-level minor, subordinate
low-minded depraved, dissolute
low-priced nominal
low-quality marginal, mediocre
low-spirited lugubrious, pessimistic
low-spiritedness pessimism
lowborn caitiff, ignoble
lower debase, decrease, deduct *(reduce)*, defame, demean *(make lower)*, demote, denigrate, depreciate, depress, derogate, deteriorate, diminish, discount *(reduce)*, disgrace, humiliate, inferior *(lower in position)*, lessen, minimize, minor, modify *(moderate)*, pervert, pillory, reduce, subaltern, subdue, subordinate, subservient. SEE MAIN ENTRY
lower in authority inferior *(lower in position)*
lower in price depreciate
lower in rank demote, inferior *(lower in position)*, subaltern, subordinate
lower in reputation depreciate
lower in the scale inferior *(lower in position)*
lower in value debase, depreciate
lower morally taint *(corrupt)*
lower oneself condescend *(deign)*, patronize *(condescend toward)*
lower price discount
lower the courage of discourage
lower the estimation of disparage
lower the sale price discount *(reduce)*
lower the standard adulterate
lower the value of depreciate
lowering decline, decrease, deduction *(diminution)*, depression, diminution
lowest *(far below)* SEE MAIN ENTRY
lowest quantity minimum
lowliness prostration
lowly base *(inferior)*, ignoble, inferior *(lower in position)*, subaltern, subordinate

lowness bad character, depression
loyal constant, dependable, obedient, reliable, serious *(devoted),* staunch, steadfast. SEE MAIN ENTRY
loyalist disciple
loyally faithfully
loyalty adherence *(devotion),* allegiance, discipline *(obedience),* faith, fealty, fidelity, homage, rectitude, regard *(esteem),* trustworthiness. SEE MAIN ENTRY
lubric lascivious, lecherous
lubricious prurient
lubricity obscenity, pornography
lubricous lascivious, lecherous, lewd, licentious, obscene
lucent lucid
lucid cognizable, coherent *(clear),* comprehensible, distinct *(clear),* evident, explicit, manifest, normal *(sane),* obvious, palpable, pellucid, rational, reasonable *(rational),* sane, unambiguous, unmistakable. SEE MAIN ENTRY
lucidity competence *(sanity),* reason *(sound judgment),* sanity
lucidly fairly *(clearly)*
lucidus lucid
luck contingency, opportunity, prosperity, quirk *(accident),* welfare. SEE MAIN ENTRY
luckless ominous
lucky auspicious, fortuitous, propitious, prosperous
lucrari gain
lucrative gainful, profitable. SEE MAIN ENTRY
lucre boom *(prosperity)*
lucrosus gainful, lucrative
lucrum earnings, profit
luctatio struggle
lucubration pandect *(treatise)*
luculent comprehensible, lucid
ludibrio mock *(deride)*
ludicrous fatuous, inept *(inappropriate),* irrational, unreasonable. SEE MAIN ENTRY
ludicrous imitation parody
ludicrous presentation travesty
ludicrous representation ridicule
ludicrousness incongruity, inexpedience
ludificari flout, hoodwink
ludificatio hoax
luggage cargo
lugubrious despondent, lamentable. SEE MAIN ENTRY
lugubris lugubrious
lukewarm irresolute, languid, nonchalant, noncommittal, perfunctory
lukewarmness indifference
lull allay, alleviate, cessation *(interlude),* cloture, halt, hiatus, holiday, interruption, interval, lapse *(break),* mollification, mollify, moratorium, pause, peace, pendency, recess, remission, respite *(interval of rest),* soothe, subside. SEE MAIN ENTRY
lumbering ponderous
luminary mastermind
luminous cognizable, coherent *(clear),* notable, outstanding *(prominent)*
lump assemblage, entirety, part *(portion),* totality
lump sum payment SEE MAIN ENTRY
lump together commingle, compile, consolidate *(unite),* hoard
lumpiness irregularity
lumpish lifeless *(dull),* obtuse, opaque, ponderous, stagnant
lumpishness opacity, sloth
lunacy insanity, paranoia. SEE MAIN ENTRY
lunatic non compos mentis. SEE MAIN ENTRY
lunge at beat *(strike),* strike *(assault)*
lupine predatory, rapacious
lurch oscillate
lure amenity, betray *(lead astray),* cajole, coax, ensnare, entice, entrap, incentive, inveigle, persuade, prevail *(persuade),* seduction, trap. SEE MAIN ENTRY
lure into a compromising act entrap
lurid licentious, obscene, salacious, suggestive *(risqué).* SEE MAIN ENTRY
luridus lurid
luring attractive, bribery
lurk prowl. SEE MAIN ENTRY
lurking hidden, surreptitious
luscious nectarious, palatable, sapid, savory
lush fertile
lust debauchery, desire, passion
lust for need
lust for money greed
luster prestige, reputation
lusterless lifeless *(dull),* ponderous
lustful dissolute, hot-blooded, lascivious, lecherous, lewd, obscene, prurient, salacious, suggestive *(risqué),* wanton
lustiness life *(vitality),* prowess *(bravery),* puissance, sinew
lustless languid, powerless
lustrate decontaminate
lustrous outstanding *(prominent)*
lusty powerful, strong, vehement
luxate disjoint, dislocate. SEE MAIN ENTRY
luxuriant copious, fertile, productive, profuse, superfluous, wanton
luxuriate pullulate
luxuriate in relish
luxuriosus dissolute
luxurious replete, superfluous
luxury prosperity. SEE MAIN ENTRY
lyceum institute
lying deceit, deceptive, dishonest, dishonesty, disingenuous, falsification, improbity, insidious, mendacious, perfidious, subreption, untrue. SEE MAIN ENTRY
lymphatic languid, otiose, phlegmatic, ponderous
lynch law SEE MAIN ENTRY

M

macabre SEE MAIN ENTRY
macellum market *(business)*
macerate bait *(harass),* plague
Machiavellian artful. SEE MAIN ENTRY
Machiavellism artifice
machina device *(contrivance),* expedient, machination
machinari conjure, contrive
machinate connive, conspire, contrive, maneuver, plan, plot, scheme
machination artifice, cabal, connivance, contrivance, deception, device *(contrivance),* expedient, frame up, hoax, maneuver *(trick),* premeditation, ruse, scheme, stratagem, strategy, subterfuge. SEE MAIN ENTRY
machinator conspirator, copartner *(coconspirator)*
machine appliance, expedient, instrument *(tool),* make, syndicate, tool. SEE MAIN ENTRY
machine like controlled *(automatic)*
machine-made industrial
machiner artisan
machinery conduit *(channel),* facility *(instrumentality),* instrument *(tool),* instrumentality, medium SEE MAIN ENTRY
macroscopic perceivable, perceptible
macula defilement
maculare stain, sully
maculate pollute, stain, tarnish
maculation bad repute, flaw
mad deranged, lunatic, non compos mentis, outrageous, quixotic. SEE MAIN ENTRY
madcap hot-blooded, outrageous, precipitate
madden aggravate *(annoy),* incense, irritate, obsess, offend *(insult),* perturb, pique, provoke
maddened deranged, non compos mentis
maddening vexatious
made captive arrested *(apprehended)*
made fast fixed *(securely placed)*
made poorly insubstantial
made prisoner arrested *(apprehended)*
made public naked *(perceptible)*
made up mendacious
madhouse shambles
madness furor, insanity, lunacy, paranoia
maelstrom bluster *(commotion),* commotion, disturbance, furor, shambles. SEE MAIN ENTRY
maeror depression
maestus disconsolate
magazine depository, journal, publication *(printed matter)*
magic prestidigitation. SEE MAIN ENTRY
magical mysterious, uncanny
magister pedagogue, principal *(director)*
magisterial dogmatic, insolent, juridical, official, powerful, presumptuous, supercilious
magistracy bench, judiciary
magistrate bench, caretaker *(one fulfilling the function of office),* judge, jurist. SEE MAIN ENTRY
magistrates court
magistrature bench
magistratus authorities, magistrate
magnanimity charity, clemency, condonation, indulgence, largess *(generosity),* longanimity, philanthropy. SEE MAIN ENTRY
magnanimous benevolent, charitable *(benevolent),* lenient, liberal *(generous),* meritorious, philanthropic, placable. SEE MAIN ENTRY
magnanimousness clemency, largess *(generosity)*
magnanimus magnanimous
magnate SEE MAIN ENTRY
magnetic attractive SEE MAIN ENTRY
magnetism draw *(attraction)*
magni momenti momentous
magnification aggravation *(exacerbation),* augmentation, bombast, boom *(increase),* distortion, exaggeration, extension *(expansion),* hyperbole, laudation, overstatement SEE MAIN ENTRY
magnificent elegant, meritorious, proud *(self-respecting)* SEE MAIN ENTRY
magnified extreme *(exaggerated),* inflated *(overestimated)*
magnify aggravate *(exacerbate),* build *(augment),* compound, develop, elaborate, enhance, enlarge, expand, extend *(enlarge),* heighten *(augment),* inflate, intensify, overestimate, promote *(advance),* supplement. SEE MAIN ENTRY
magnifying cumulative *(intensifying)*
magniloquence ardor, bombast, fustian, overstatement, peroration, rhetoric *(insincere language)*

magniloquent grandiose, inflated *(bombastic),* orotund, sesquipedalian, turgid
magnitude amount *(quantity),* bulk, caliber *(measurement),* consequence *(significance),* extent, importance, mass *(weight),* materiality *(consequence),* measurement, purview, weight *(importance).* SEE MAIN ENTRY
magnitudo bulk, magnitude
magno rate
magnus considerable, extensive, gross *(total),* important *(significant)*
maiden incipient, initial, original *(initial)*
maiestas treason
mail correspondence *(communication by letters),* dispatch *(message),* send. SEE MAIN ENTRY
mail again redirect
maim damage, disable, harm, mutilate, prejudice *(injure)*
maimed disabled *(made incapable),* marred
maiming disabling
main cardinal *(basic),* central *(essential),* dominant, essential *(inherent),* important *(significant),* indispensable, leading *(ranking first),* master, material *(important),* noteworthy, paramount, primary, principal, prominent, salient, stellar, strength, substantive, vital. SEE MAIN ENTRY
main asset transfer bulk transfer
main attraction feature *(special attraction)*
main body cornerstone, corpus, generality *(bulk),* majority *(greater part),* principal *(capital sum)*
main business agenda
main character protagonist
main charge complaint, count, gist *(ground for a suit),* indictment
main element cornerstone
main feature motif
main features contour *(outline)*
main focus SEE MAIN ENTRY
main force SEE MAIN ENTRY
main idea main point
main ingredient necessity
main interest specialty *(special aptitude)*
main item feature *(special attraction)*
main meaning context
main office headquarters
main part body *(main part),* bulk, center *(essence),* corpus, generality *(bulk),* majority *(greater part),* plurality
main point center *(essence),* content *(meaning),* cornerstone, gist *(ground for a suit),* gravamen. SEE MAIN ENTRY
main thing cornerstone, main point
mainly a fortiori, ab initio, as a rule, generally, particularly. SEE MAIN ENTRY
mainspring cause *(reason),* derivation, reason *(basis)*
mainstay abettor, backer, cornerstone, partisan, strength, support *(assistance).* SEE MAIN ENTRY
maintain adhere *(persist),* allege, argue, assert, authorize, avouch *(avow),* avow, bear *(adduce),* bear *(support),* bestow, cite *(state),* conserve, continue *(persevere),* continue *(prolong),* control *(regulate),* corroborate, declare, defend, endure *(last),* fund, harbor, justify, keep *(continue),* keep *(shelter),* nurture, own, perpetuate, persevere, persist, plead *(allege in a legal action),* posit, possess, preserve, profess *(avow),* prolong, promote *(organize),* propound, prosecute *(carry forward),* protect, provide *(supply),* pursue *(carry on),* remain *(continue),* remain *(occupy),* reserve, resist *(withstand),* retain *(employ),* retain *(keep in possession),* store, subsidize, subsist, supply, support *(assist),* sustain *(prolong),* uphold. SEE MAIN ENTRY
maintain a course persevere
maintain a middle position compromise *(settle by mutual agreement)*
maintain as conformable to duty justify
maintain as conformable to justice justify
maintain by affirmation vouch
maintain by arguments plead *(argue a case)*
maintain continuity continue *(prolong)*
maintain under oath swear
maintainable defensible, justifiable, tenable
maintained alleged, chronic, durable, lasting, plausible, safe
maintained in prison in custody
maintainer abettor, advocate *(counselor),* advocate *(espouser),* backer, benefactor, mainstay, partisan
maintaining conservation, convincing
maintenance aid *(help),* aid *(subsistence),* alimony, conservation, continuation *(prolongation),* ecology, livelihood, longevity, preservation, promotion *(encouragement),* provision *(something provided),* security *(safety),* support *(assistance),* survival, sustenance. SEE MAIN ENTRY
maintenance allowance alimony
maintenance of regularity status quo
maior numerus majority *(greater part)*
maior pars majority *(greater part)*
majestic important *(significant),* outstanding *(prominent),* proud *(self-respecting),* solemn. SEE MAIN ENTRY
majesty eminence, prestige
major cardinal *(outstanding),* central *(essential),* critical *(crucial),* important *(significant),* indispensable, key, material *(important),* momentous. SEE MAIN ENTRY
major business asset transfer bulk transfer
major event cornerstone
major misfortune calamity
major part body *(main part),* bulk, cornerstone, corpus, main point, majority *(greater part)*
majority bulk, generality *(bulk),* maturity, plurality, preponderance. SEE MAIN ENTRY
make build *(construct),* cause, color *(complexion),* create, fabricate *(construct),* forge *(produce),* form, frame *(construct),* gain, generate, impose *(enforce),* manner *(kind),* manufacture, occasion, originate, press *(constrain),* produce *(manufacture),* realize *(obtain as a profit),* receive *(acquire),* require *(compel),* style. SEE MAIN ENTRY
make a bargain agree *(contract),* close *(agree),* contract, handle *(trade)*
make a beginning embark
make a benefaction bestow
make a bequest bequeath, demise, descend, devise *(give),* leave *(give)*
make a bet parlay *(bet)*
make a bid attempt, endeavor, offer *(propose),* proffer, strive
make a butt of mock *(deride)*
make a change affect, vary
make a choice cast *(register),* decide, discriminate *(distinguish),* elect *(choose),* resolve *(decide),* select
make a circuit detour
make a clean breast betray *(disclose)*
make a common cause with federalize *(associate)*
make a commotion brawl
make a compact settle
make a comparison contrast, measure
make a complaint cite *(accuse)*
make a compromise compromise *(settle by mutual agreement)*
make a computation calculate
make a condition stipulate
make a confession confess
make a deal compromise *(settle by mutual agreement)*
make a decision adjudge, adjudicate, arbitrate *(adjudge),* cast *(register),* choose, conclude *(decide),* decide, determine, find *(determine),* fix *(settle),* hold *(decide),* resolve *(decide),* rule *(decide)*
make a declaration declare
make a decree instruct *(direct)*
make a deduction derive *(deduce)*
make a demand call *(demand),* move *(judicially request)* SEE MAIN ENTRY
make a departure evacuate, quit *(evacuate)*
make a detour deviate
make a distinction differentiate, discriminate *(distinguish),* discriminate *(treat differently),* select
make a duplicate of copy
make a false show of feign
make a finding SEE MAIN ENTRY
make a fool of delude, dupe, hoodwink, humiliate, illude, mock *(deride)*
make a formal proclamation notice *(give formal warning)*
make a gaudy display flaunt
make a generalization generalize
make a getaway escape
make a gift give *(grant)*
make a good return pay
make a hit succeed *(attain)*
make a judgment diagnose
make a legacy demise, descend
make a likeness delineate
make a list enumerate
make a loan bestow
make a member enroll
make a memorandum note *(record),* record
make a mess of muddle
make a mistake err, miscalculate, misconceive, misconstrue, misinterpret, misjudge, misread, misunderstand
make a mixture combine *(join together)*
make a motion move *(judicially request),* pose *(propound),* proffer, propose, propound, submit *(give)* SEE MAIN ENTRY
make a new beginning continue *(resume)*
make a note record
make a party to implicate, incriminate, involve *(implicate)*
make a passage penetrate
make a path for facilitate
make a petition call *(appeal to),* move *(judicially request)*
make a place for locate, lodge *(house),* plant *(place firmly)*
make a plan devise *(invent),* maneuver, plot
make a positive statement affirm *(claim)*
make a prediction predict, presage, prognosticate, promise *(raise expectations)*

make a present grant *(transfer formally)*
make a present of bequeath, bestow
make a presentation give *(grant)*
make a pretext of pretend
make a proclamation proclaim
make a profit gain
make a prognosis predict
make a promise assure *(insure)*, pledge *(promise the performance of)*
make a proposition offer *(propose)*
make a public announcement issue *(publish)*
make a purchase buy, procure
make a racket brawl
make a reality implement
make a rebuttal converse, retort, return *(respond)* SEE MAIN ENTRY
make a reconnaissance check *(inspect)*, spy
make a record enroll
make a rejoinder answer *(reply)*, controvert, dispute *(debate)*, respond, return *(respond)*
make a remark observe *(remark)*
make a replica copy
make a request call *(appeal to)*, move *(judicially request)*, plead *(implore)*, pray, solicit
make a request for desire
make a requisition call *(appeal to)*, move *(judicially request)*, order, petition
make a resolute stand hold out *(resist)*
make a resolution conclude *(decide)*, determine, rule *(decide)*
make a sale handle *(trade)*, sell, vend
make a selection cast *(register)*, cull, decide, discriminate *(distinguish)*, elect *(choose)*, extract, select
make a shambles pillage
make a shift with displace *(replace)*
make a show pretend
make a show of fake, flaunt, profess *(pretend)*
make a showy appearance flaunt
make a solemn declaration affirm *(declare solemnly)*
make a solemn resolution promise *(vow)*
make a spectacle flaunt
make a speech converse, declaim, discourse, recite, speak
make a spurious copy of forge *(counterfeit)*
make a stand repulse
make a stand against counter, counteract, cross *(disagree with)*, fight *(counteract)*, repel *(drive back)*, resist *(oppose)*
make a start preface
make a statement avow, bear *(adduce)*, claim *(maintain)*, contend *(maintain)*, converse, declare, express, profess *(avow)*, speak. SEE MAIN ENTRY
make a suggestion propose, submit *(give)*
make a summary of digest *(summarize)*
make a survey canvass, poll
make a testamentary disposition leave *(give)*
make a transcript of copy
make a transition change
make a trial run check *(inspect)*
make a try attempt
make able charge *(empower)*, empower, enable
make absolute certify *(attest)*, support *(corroborate)*
make acceptable rationalize
make accordant attune
make accountable for encumber *(financially obligate)*
make acknowledgment return *(respond)*
make acquainted convey *(communicate)*, present *(introduce)*
make acquainted with forewarn, notice *(give formal warning)*
make active implement, launch *(initiate)*
make adjustments attune, modify *(alter)*
make again reproduce
make agree attune
make allowance condone, rebate
make allowance for discount *(reduce)*, extenuate, palliate *(excuse)*, provide *(arrange for)*
make allowances rationalize
make allowances for countenance, excuse
make allusion to mention
make amends propitiate, recoup *(reimburse)*, redeem *(satisfy debts)*, redress, refund, remedy, repay, repent, replace, restore *(return)*
make an accusation complain *(charge)*
make an adjustment compromise *(settle by mutual agreement)*
make an affidavit depose *(testify)*, plead *(allege in a legal action)*
make an agenda program
make an agreement agree *(contract)*, close *(agree)* SEE MAIN ENTRY
make an agreement with connive, conspire, cooperate, join *(associate oneself with)*
make an allusion hint
make an allusion to imply, remind
make an analysis analyze, examine *(study)*
make an announcement enunciate, notice *(give formal warning)*, notify, report *(disclose)*
make an antagonist of antagonize
make an appearance appear *(attend court proceedings)*, arise *(appear)*, emerge
make an arrest capture
make an assertion affirm *(claim)*, allege, argue, avouch *(avow)*, avow, bear *(adduce)*, claim *(maintain)*, contend *(maintain)*, express, plead *(allege in a legal action)*, profess *(avow)*
make an asseveration affirm *(declare solemnly)*
make an attempt endeavor, strive
make an attestation affirm *(declare solemnly)*
make an authoritative request call *(demand)*, exact
make an averment affirm *(declare solemnly)*
make an avowal promise *(vow)*
make an effort endeavor, strive, try *(attempt)*, undertake
make an effort at attempt
make an end of cease, close *(terminate)*, conclude *(complete)*, dispatch *(dispose of)*, quit *(discontinue)*
make an engagement promise *(vow)*
make an entrance enter *(go in)*, pervade
make an entry book, cast *(register)*, enter *(record)*, inscribe, note *(record)*, record
make an error misinterpret, misjudge
make an escape elude, flee
make an estimate calculate, measure
make an estimation gauge
make an examination probe
make an example of discipline *(punish)*
make an exception except *(exclude)*, exclude
make an exit depart, quit *(evacuate)*
make an expenditure expend *(disburse)*
make an impact upon impress *(affect deeply)*
make an impression on impress *(affect deeply)*
make an incision lancinate
make an incursion encroach
make an inquiry analyze
make an introduction present *(introduce)*
make an investment invest *(fund)*
make an issue contend *(dispute)*
make an oath promise *(vow)*
make an offer proffer
make an onset against attack
make an opening capitalize *(seize the chance)*
make an order instruct *(direct)*
make an overture offer *(propose)*, proffer
make an uproar brawl
make angry affront, offend *(insult)*
make apparent bare, characterize, delineate, elucidate
make appeal call *(appeal to)*
make appeal to sue
make application call *(appeal to)*, demand, move *(judicially request)*, petition, request. SEE MAIN ENTRY
make application for desire
make arrangements arrange *(plan)*, deal, devise *(invent)*, frame *(formulate)*, maneuver, plan, plot, program, scheme
make aseptic decontaminate
make ashamed demean *(make lower)*, derogate
make available disburse *(distribute)*, let *(lease)*, rent
make available for rent sublease
make averse alienate *(estrange)*
make aware apprise, caution, convey *(communicate)*, enlighten, forewarn
make away with dispatch *(put to death)*, distrain
make beautiful embellish
make believe assume *(simulate)*, fake, false *(not genuine)*, feign, invent *(falsify)*, pretend, prevaricate, profess *(pretend)*, simulate
make better ameliorate, cultivate, emend, enhance, expurgate, meliorate, mollify, reform, remedy, renovate, repair, restore *(renew)*
make binding validate
make blunt obtund
make bold to ask call *(appeal to)*, importune
make book parlay *(bet)*
make brief condense, constrict *(compress)*, decrease, digest *(summarize)*, minimize
make by mechanical industry manufacture
make calm lull
make capable empower, enable, qualify *(meet standards)*
make capital gain
make capital out of profit
make captive arrest *(apprehend)*, fetter, immure
make captive again rearrest
make certain ascertain, assure *(give confidence to)*, assure *(insure)*, certify *(attest)*,

document, ensure, find *(discover)*, reconfirm, verify *(confirm)* SEE MAIN ENTRY
make charges against denounce *(inform against)*
make claims upon call *(demand)*, charge *(assess)*, dun
make clear characterize, clarify, comment, define, delineate, demonstrate *(establish)*, describe, detail *(particularize)*, elucidate, enlighten, evince, exhibit, explain, explicate, exposit, expound, interpret, manifest, profess *(avow)*, resolve *(solve)*, simplify *(clarify)*, stipulate SEE MAIN ENTRY
make clear by examples exemplify
make cognizant apprise
make comfortable ease
make common cause affiliate
make common cause with combine *(act in concert)*, cooperate, involve *(participate)*
make compatible arbitrate *(conciliate)*, reconcile
make compensation bear the expense, contribute *(indemnify)*, cover *(provide for)*, outbalance, pay, quit *(repay)*, refund, return *(refund)*, satisfy *(discharge)*
make competent qualify *(meet standards)*
make complete conclude *(complete)*, replenish
make comprehensible clarify
make compulsory enforce
make concessions compromise *(settle by mutual agreement)*
make concise condense, digest *(summarize)*
make confident assure *(give confidence to)*, convince
make conformable adapt
make connection contact *(communicate)*
make consistent reconcile
make conspicuous manifest
make contact collide *(crash against)*, overlap
make contented pander, reconcile
make contiguous juxtapose
make conveyance of grant *(transfer formally)*
make corporeal embody
make corrections edit, emend, fix *(repair)*, modify *(alter)*, rectify, review
make corrupt pervert
make deductions construe *(comprehend)*, reason *(conclude)*
make defense for justify, support *(justify)*
make definite stipulate
make deletions redact
make delivery of legal process serve *(deliver a legal instrument)*
make demands exact, petition
make demands on claim *(demand)*, dun, order
make dense constrict *(compress)*
make denser condense
make deposition depose *(testify)*
make desirable recommend
make despondent depress
make different change, vary
make difficult perplex
make dim obscure
make discontented disaffect
make disease-free decontaminate
make disloyal disaffect
make dissatisfied disappoint
make distasteful discredit
make distinctions discern *(discriminate)*, distinguish
make distinctive differentiate
make distribution of disburse *(distribute)*
make docile subdue
make durable establish *(entrench)*
make earnest entreaty call *(appeal to)*
make earnest petition for pray
make easier favor
make easy ease, facilitate, help, naturalize *(acclimate)*
make effective enforce
make elaborate embellish
make equal compensate *(counterbalance)*
make essential entail
make eternal perpetuate
make even juxtapose
make everlasting perpetuate
make evident bare, bear *(adduce)*, cite *(state)*, demonstrate *(establish)*, document, evince, exemplify, explain, illustrate, manifest, profess *(avow)*
make excessive demands tax *(overwork)*
make excessive use of abuse *(misuse)*
make exchanges barter
make excuses rationalize
make excuses for extenuate, justify
make expenditure bear the expense, disburse *(pay out)*, spend
make explanation of justify
make explicit clarify, explain, explicate, express
make extinct superannuate
make eyeless blind *(deprive of sight)*
make false pretenses palter
make false statements falsify, frame *(charge falsely)*, palter
make fast fix *(make firm)*, handcuff, lock
make faulty vitiate
make favorably inclined propitiate
make feeble debilitate
make final disposition of dispatch *(dispose of)*
make firm affirm *(uphold)*, cement, concentrate *(consolidate)*, confirm, consolidate *(strengthen)*, establish *(entrench)*, sustain *(confirm)*
make forbidden forbid
make formal formalize
make formal accusation against denounce *(inform against)*, indict
make formal application move *(judicially request)*
make formal request apply *(request)*
make foul pollute
make free acquit, disengage, disenthrall, extricate, parole
make free with assume *(seize)*
make friendly disarm *(set at ease)*
make full replenish
make fun of disparage, jape, jeer, mock *(deride)*, pillory
make germ-free decontaminate
make good fulfill, indemnify, keep *(fulfill)*, pay, recoup *(reimburse)*, redress, refund, reimburse, repair, restore *(return)*, return *(refund)*, satisfy *(discharge)*, substantiate, support *(corroborate)*
make good against anticipated loss indemnify
make good use of profit
make great magnify
make greater accumulate *(enlarge)*, compound, enlarge, expand, increase, inflate
make haste hasten, precipitate *(hasten)*
make havoc confound, disorganize, disorient, muddle, perturb, pillage
make headway develop, persist, proceed *(go forward)*, progress
make healthful decontaminate
make heavy load, overload
make higher build *(augment)*, elevate, heighten *(augment)*, heighten *(elevate)*
make hostile disaffect
make hygienic decontaminate
make ill infect
make illegal annul, prohibit
make illegible deface
make illegitimate disfranchise
make impact collide *(crash against)*, impinge
make imperfect vitiate
make important honor
make impossible condemn *(ban)*, disqualify, preclude
make improper use of abuse *(misuse)*
make improvement profit
make improvements edit, embellish, emend, enhance, meliorate, modify *(alter)*, repair, review
make impure adulterate, denature, infect, vitiate
make inactive close *(terminate)*, delay, desist, disable, disarm *(divest of arms)*, halt
make incapable disable
make inconspicuous blind *(obscure)*, conceal
make incumbent entail
make indifferent alienate *(estrange)*
make indirect reference allude
make indirect suggestion connote
make indiscernible blind *(obscure)*, conceal
make indispensable necessitate
make indistinct obnubilate, obscure
make ineffective neutralize, vitiate
make ineffectual override
make inescapable entail
make inevitable necessitate
make inferior in value degenerate
make inimical alienate *(estrange)*, disaffect
make innovations alter
make innoxious decontaminate
make inoperative avoid *(cancel)*
make inquiries probe
make inquiry delve
make inroads encroach, impinge SEE MAIN ENTRY
make inroads on impair
make insecure endanger
make insensitive brutalize
make inseperable lock
make intelligible clarify, construe *(translate)*, elucidate
make into convert *(change use)*
make into a statute enact
make into law legislate, pass *(approve)*
make intricate perplex
make its appearance issue *(send forth)*
make known advise, annunciate, apprise, bare, betray *(disclose)*, circulate, communicate, confide *(divulge)*, convey *(communicate)*, declare, disabuse, disclose, disinter, divulge, enlighten, exhibit, express, herald, impart, inform *(betray)*, inform *(notify)*, instruct *(teach)*, issue *(publish)*, manifest, mention, notice *(give formal warning)*, notify, phrase, post, present *(introduce)*, proclaim, produce *(offer to view)*, profess *(avow)*, promulgate,

propagate *(spread)*, publish, relate *(tell)*, report *(disclose)*, reveal, signify *(inform)*, spread, unveil, utter SEE MAIN ENTRY
make known publicly annunciate
make languid debilitate
make larger build *(augment)*, compound, enlarge, expand, extend *(enlarge)*, heighten *(augment)*, increase, inflate, magnify
make last perpetuate
make lasting establish *(entrench)*
make lawful legalize, legitimate
make laws enact, legislate
make leeway outbalance
make legacies bequeath
make legal authorize, constitute *(establish)*, legalize, legislate, legitimate, pass *(approve)*, validate SEE MAIN ENTRY
make legitimate justify, legitimate, support *(justify)*
make less decrease, deduct *(reduce)*, diminish, minimize, moderate *(temper)*, reduce
make less concentrated dilute
make less confusing elucidate
make less extreme commute, modify *(moderate)*
make less friendly disaffect
make less harsh commute
make less important demote
make less intense commute, modify *(moderate)*
make less rigorous commute
make less rough commute
make less serious extenuate
make less severe commute, mitigate, modify *(moderate)*, palliate *(abate)*
make less violent obtund, remit *(relax)*
make level compensate *(counterbalance)*
make liable expose, subject
make liable to danger compromise *(endanger)*, endanger
make liable to injury endanger
make light of discount *(disbelieve)*, disparage, underestimate
make lighter commute
make little of decry, depreciate, derogate, minimize, misprize
make longer prolong
make lower in character degenerate
make lower in quality adulterate, denature
make lowly demean *(make lower)*, derogate, humiliate
make lucid clarify, elucidate, exposit
make manifest bare, elicit, evince, exemplify, explain
make manifold proliferate
make mention remark, speak
make mention of notice *(give formal warning)*, observe *(remark)*
make mild palliate *(abate)*
make milder commute
make mischief mistreat
make miserable distress
make money gain
make money by profit
make more attractive enhance
make more certain support *(corroborate)*
make more comprehensive expand, extend *(enlarge)*
make more fluid dilute
make more important magnify
make more liquid dilute
make more offensive aggravate *(exacerbate)*
make more serious aggravate *(exacerbate)*
make more severe aggravate *(exacerbate)*, exacerbate
make more valuable enhance
make much of belaud
make naked denude
make national nationalize
make national in character nationalize
make natural naturalize *(acclimate)*
make necessary constrain *(compel)*, entail, indicate, necessitate, press *(constrain)*
make needed indicate
make nervous browbeat
make new renovate
make no racial distinctions desegregate
make note of remark
make notes comment
make nothing of misprize
make noxious taint *(contaminate)*
make null destroy *(void)*, overrule
make null and void override SEE MAIN ENTRY
make objection except *(object)*
make objections remonstrate
make obligatory exact, force *(coerce)*, impose *(enforce)*
make observations comment
make obsolete superannuate, supersede
make obvious educe, evidence, exemplify, exhibit, manifest, signify *(inform)*
make of greater value appreciate *(increase)*
make of no effect avoid *(cancel)*
make off abscond, avoid *(evade)*, flee
make off with carry away, despoil, hijack, hold up *(rob)*, loot, pilfer, poach
make official formalize
make one attach *(join)*, conjoin, consolidate *(unite)*
make one a third party implead
make one feel small browbeat
make one lose one's temper incense
make one shudder repel *(disgust)*
make one sick repel *(disgust)*
make one's choice cast *(register)*, choose, determine
make one's debut commence
make one's exit abandon *(physically leave)*
make one's home dwell *(reside)*
make one's home at lodge *(reside)*, occupy *(take possession)*
make one's mark pass *(satisfy requirements)*
make one's oath certify *(attest)*
make one's own acquire *(secure)*, adopt, buy, embrace *(accept)*, impropriate
make one's point persuade
make one's selection cast *(register)*, choose
make one's submission move *(judicially request)*
make oneself acquainted with ascertain
make oneself answerable promise *(vow)*
make oneself answerable for guarantee
make oneself felt persuade
make oneself scarce retreat
make oneself useful pander
make open affirmation avouch *(avow)*
make oral communication speak
make oral mention speak
make orderly file *(arrange)*
make out detect, discern *(detect with the senses)*, hear *(perceive by ear)*, note *(notice)*, perceive, pierce *(discern)*, read, realize *(understand)*, recognize *(perceive)*, solve, spy
make outdated superannuate
make over change, convert *(change use)*, deliver, devolve, fix *(repair)*, grant *(transfer formally)*, present *(make a gift)*, reconstitute, reconstruct, recreate, reform, rehabilitate, renew *(refurbish)*, renovate, transform
make over to another assign *(transfer ownership)*
make overtures hold out *(deliberate on an offer)*
make participator involve *(implicate)*
make pay exact
make payment bear *(yield)*, bear the expense, compensate *(remunerate)*, defray, disburse *(pay out)*, expend *(disburse)*, pay, quit *(repay)*, remit *(send payment)*, remunerate, repay, satisfy *(discharge)*
make payment for purchase
make payment in advance prepay
make peace negotiate, pacify, placate, propitiate, reconcile
make peace between arbitrate *(conciliate)*, intercede
make pecuniary provision endow
make perfect renew *(refurbish)*
make permanent establish *(entrench)*, perpetuate
make perpetual perpetuate
make plain demonstrate *(establish)*, describe, elucidate, evidence, evince, exemplify, exhibit, explain, explicate, exposit, expound, express, illustrate, interpret, manifest, resolve *(solve)*, signify *(inform)*, simplify *(clarify)*, simplify *(make easier)*, solve, unveil
make possible enable, facilitate, let *(permit)*, permit, proffer
make possible the avoidance of avert
make potent empower
make practicable enable
make preferable recommend
make preparations anticipate *(expect)*, arrange *(plan)*, plan, plot, provide *(arrange for)*
make prisoner arrest *(apprehend)*, capture, fetter, hijack
make probable conduce
make proclamation annunciate
make progress ameliorate, develop, proceed *(go forward)*, progress SEE MAIN ENTRY
make provision bear *(yield)*, maintain *(sustain)*, provide *(arrange for)*
make provision for bestow, cover *(provide for)*, endue
make provisions forestall
make provisions for nurture
make public bare, betray *(disclose)*, circulate, convey *(communicate)*, denude, disclose, disseminate, divulge, notice *(give formal warning)*, notify, post, proclaim, propagate *(spread)*, publish, reveal, signify *(inform)*, spread
make publicly known reveal
make pure decontaminate
make putrid taint *(contaminate)*
make rapid strides proceed *(go forward)*
make ready plan, provide *(arrange for)*
make ready for publication edit
make realize convince
make reference quote
make reference to bear *(adduce)*, cite *(state)*
make rejoinder reply

make relevant connect *(relate)*
make remarks comment
make repairs emend
make reparation contribute *(indemnify)*, discharge *(pay a debt)*, indemnify, quit *(repay)*, redress, reimburse, repay, restore *(return)*, return *(refund)*
make reparations recoup *(reimburse)*
make repayment defray
make requisite entail
make requisition call *(demand)*, exact
make requital repay
make resplendent embellish
make responsible for commit *(entrust)*, encumber *(financially obligate)*
make restitution bear the expense, compensate *(remunerate)*, contribute *(indemnify)*, defray, discharge *(pay a debt)*, indemnify, liquidate *(determine liability)*, pay, quit *(repay)*, recoup *(reimburse)*, refund, reimburse, repay, restore *(return)*, return *(refund)* SEE MAIN ENTRY
make restoration fix *(repair)*
make right rectify, regulate *(adjust)*
make rigid fix *(make firm)*
make rounds perambulate
make routine inure *(accustom)*
make sad depress
make safe cover *(guard)*, maintain *(sustain)*
make salubrious decontaminate
make scandal smear
make secret arrangements conspire
make secret observations spy
make self-conscious embarrass
make sense cohere *(be logically consistent)*
make sense of elucidate, interpret
make sensible pierce *(discern)*
make sightless blind *(deprive of sight)*
make simple elucidate, exposit
make smaller constrict *(compress)*, curtail, decrease, deduct *(reduce)*, derogate, diminish, minimize, reduce
make solemn bear *(adduce)*
make solemn affirmation avouch *(avow)*, confess, speak
make solemn declaration speak, testify
make solid concentrate *(consolidate)*, consolidate *(strengthen)*
make someone a trustee of delegate
make someone guardian of delegate, entrust
make sorrowful distress
make sound fix *(repair)*, remedy, renew *(refurbish)*, renovate
make sport of disparage
make stable establish *(entrench)*
make steadfast establish *(entrench)*
make steady compensate *(counterbalance)*
make strong nurture
make submissive impose *(subject)*, subdue, subject
make subordinate subject
make subservient subject
make suitable adapt, qualify *(meet standards)*
make supplication pray
make sure ascertain, assure *(insure)*, certify *(attest)*, ensure, verify *(confirm)*
make sure again reconfirm
make swollen inflate
make terms agree *(contract)*, conclude *(decide)*, contract, determine, dicker, haggle, negotiate, transact
make terse condense
make testamentary disposition demise
make testamentary dispositions devise *(give)*
make the best of endure *(suffer)*, submit *(yield)*, tolerate
make the effort attempt
make the most of capitalize *(seize the chance)*, exploit *(make use of)*
make the round of circulate
make thin attenuate, dilute, diminish, erode, minimize
make toe the line discipline *(control)*
make too much of overestimate
make tractable subdue
make tumid inflate
make ugly deface
make unable to see blind *(deprive of sight)*
make unapparent blind *(obscure)*, conceal
make unavoidable entail, necessitate
make unclean disgrace, sully
make uncomfortable embarrass
make understandable elucidate, exposit
make understood clarify
make uneasy discommode, discompose, disturb, perturb
make unfaithful disaffect
make unfit disable
make unfriendly alienate *(estrange)*, antagonize
make unhappy distress
make uniform conform, juxtapose, regulate *(adjust)*
make unlawful enjoin, outlaw
make unlike distort
make unperceptible blind *(obscure)*, conceal
make unrecognizable camouflage, disguise
make unsafe endanger
make unsightly deface
make unsound damage
make unwelcome eschew, ignore, repel *(disgust)*
make up compile, conceive *(invent)*, conjure, consist, constitute *(compose)*, contrive, create, devise *(invent)*, feign, indemnify, invent *(falsify)*, manufacture, originate, produce *(manufacture)*, reconcile, replenish, structure *(composition)*
make up a lack replenish
make up for compensate *(counterbalance)*, outbalance, recoup *(reimburse)*, redeem *(satisfy debts)*, redress, remunerate, repent
make up one's mind conclude *(decide)*, decide, determine, resolve *(decide)*
make use of capitalize *(seize the chance)*, exercise *(use)*, exert, impropriate, manipulate *(utilize skillfully)*, ply, profit, resort, wield
make use of without permission pirate *(reproduce without authorization)*
make useless disable, disarm *(divest of arms)*, disqualify, maim, nullify
make valid approve, authorize, certify *(approve)*, confirm, countenance, formalize, implement, indorse, notarize, validate
make valueless nullify
make visible embody, expose, manifest, produce *(offer to view)*, unveil
make vivid characterize, delineate, describe, detail *(particularize)*, illustrate
make void abrogate *(annul)*, adeem, annul, avoid *(cancel)*, cancel, discharge *(release from obligation)*, invalidate, nullify, override, overrule, quash, repeal, revoke, supersede, vacate *(void)*, vitiate SEE MAIN ENTRY
make vulnerable compromise *(endanger)*, endanger
make war fight *(battle)*
make way yield *(submit)*
make way for demit, displace *(replace)*
make weak dilute
make well cure, renew *(refurbish)*
make whole cure, fix *(repair)*, renew *(refurbish)*, renovate, replenish, restore *(renew)*
make wholesome decontaminate
make wholly without effect avoid *(cancel)*
make wicked brutalize
make worse aggravate *(exacerbate)*, degenerate, exacerbate, impair
make wrathful bait *(harass)*, pique
make written application petition
make-believe delusive, fictitious, hypothetical, illusory, imitation, mendacious, pretext
maker architect, author *(originator)*, contractor. SEE MAIN ENTRY
makeshift expedient, interim, provisional, replacement, stopgap, surrogate, temporary, vicarious *(substitutional)*
makeup character *(personal quality)*, characteristic, configuration *(form)*, content *(structure)*, disposition *(inclination)*, frame *(mood)*, organization *(structure)*, personality, temperament
making building *(business of assembling)*, commission *(act)*, manufacture, onset *(commencement)*
making amends collection *(payment)*, penitent
making apparent clarification
making aware disclosure *(act of disclosing)*
making distinct clarification
making evident clarification
making intelligible definition
making less decrease, deduction *(diminution)*
making lucid clarification
making one concrescence
making over renewal
making perspicuous clarification
making precise clarification
making public disclosure *(act of disclosing)*, divulgation
making ready preparation
making reference referral
making sense coherent *(clear)*
making specific clarification
making trenchant clarification
making useless avoidance *(cancellation)*
mala fides bad faith
maladjusted inappropriate, unfit
maladjustment disaccord
maladminister misgovern, misguide, mishandle *(mismanage)*, mismanage
maladministration misconduct, misdoing, misrule, misusage, misuse. SEE MAIN ENTRY
maladroit incompetent, inept *(incompetent)*. SEE MAIN ENTRY
malady disability *(physical inability)*, disease, disorder *(abnormal condition)*, pain SEE MAIN ENTRY
malaise pain
malapert brazen, impertinent *(insolent)*, insolent, obtrusive, presumptuous

malapropism error, misapplication, misusage
malapropos impertinent *(irrelevant)*, inapplicable, inapposite, inappropriate, inapt, inept *(inappropriate)*, inopportune, irrelevant, unfavorable, unsuitable, untimely
malapropros unfit. SEE MAIN ENTRY
malcontent actor, dissident. SEE MAIN ENTRY
male administrare misgovern
male computare miscalculate
male interpretari misinterpret
male iudicare misjudge
male moratus immoral
male parentage paternity
male regere misgovern
maledicent contemptuous, querulous
maledictio revilement, slander
malediction aspersion, blasphemy, contempt *(disdain)*, denunciation, expletive, imprecation, phillipic, profanity, revilement, vilification. SEE MAIN ENTRY
maledictive profane
maledictory abusive, calumnious, profane
maledictum obloquy
malefaction delict, delinquency *(misconduct)*, disregard *(omission)*, fault *(responsibility)*, guilt, illegality, misdeed, misdoing, misprision, offense, perversion SEE MAIN ENTRY
malefactor convict, criminal, delinquent, embezzler, felon, hoodlum, lawbreaker, offender, outlaw, racketeer, recidivist. SEE MAIN ENTRY
malefactor wrongdoer
malefactor under suspension of sentence probationer *(released offender)*
malefic adverse *(negative)*, deleterious, detrimental, disadvantageous, disastrous, harmful, heinous, insalubrious, lethal, malevolent, malicious, malignant, noxious, peccant *(unhealthy)*, pernicious, pestilent, sinister. SEE MAIN ENTRY
maleficence vice
maleficent bad *(offensive)*, dangerous, deleterious, delinquent *(guilty of a misdeed)*, diabolic, disadvantageous, harmful, insalubrious, lethal, malevolent, malicious, malignant, peccant *(culpable)*, peccant *(unhealthy)*, pernicious, pestilent, ruthless, scathing, sinister SEE MAIN ENTRY
maleficial lethal, malicious, peccant *(culpable)*, pernicious, sinister
maleficient adverse *(negative)*
maleficium crime, mischief, misdeed
malevolence alienation *(estrangement)*, atrocity, bad repute, belligerency, feud, hatred, ill will, malediction, malice, odium, rancor, spite, vengeance SEE MAIN ENTRY
malevolent bad *(offensive)*, calumnious, caustic, cold-blooded, contemptuous, convict, cruel, delinquent *(guilty of a misdeed)*, diabolic, hoodlum, hostile, inimical, iniquitous, libelous, malicious, malignant, outrageous, pernicious, resentful, ruthless, scathing, sinister, spiteful, vicious, vindictive, virulent. SEE MAIN ENTRY
malevolentia ill will, malice, spite
malevolus malevolent, malicious, spiteful
malfeasance abuse *(corrupt practice)*, blame *(culpability)*, conversion *(misappropriation)*, crime, delict, delinquency *(misconduct)*, disloyalty, disservice, guilt, knavery, maladministration, misconduct, misdeed, misdemeanor, misprision, misrule, offense, tort, wrong. SEE MAIN ENTRY
malfeasant convict, criminal, delinquent *(guilty of a misdeed)*, felonious, hoodlum, illegitimate *(illegal)*, offender, recidivist, wrongdoer SEE MAIN ENTRY
malfeasor convict, delinquent, hoodlum, lawbreaker, recidivist. SEE MAIN ENTRY
malformation irregularity
malformed blemished, faulty, inferior *(lower in quality)*
malfunction disorder *(abnormal condition)*, irregularity. SEE MAIN ENTRY
malice alienation *(estrangement)*, cruelty, ill will, odium, rancor, resentment, spite. SEE MAIN ENTRY
malice aforethought cruelty
malice afterthought SEE MAIN ENTRY
malice prepense cruelty
malicious caustic, cold-blooded, contemptuous, cruel, felonious, harmful, invidious, libelous, malevolent, malignant, mordacious, noxious, outrageous, resentful, scathing, sinister, spiteful, vicious, vindictive, virulent, wrongful. SEE MAIN ENTRY
malicious action mischief
malicious burning of property arson
malicious defamation libel
malicious falsehood libel
malicious gossip scandal
malicious prosecution SEE MAIN ENTRY
malicious publication libel
malicious report slander
maliciously defame libel
maliciousness cruelty, ill will, malice, odium, spite
malific bad *(offensive)*
malign bait *(harass)*, brand *(stigmatize)*, cold-blooded, complain *(criticize)*, contemn, cruel, damage, decry, defame, denigrate, denounce *(condemn)*, depreciate, derogate, destructive, disapprove *(condemn)*, disastrous, discommend, discredit, dishonor *(deprive of honor)*, disoblige, disparage, harass, harmful, humiliate, ill use, lessen, lethal, libel, malevolent, malignant, misrepresent, mistreat, outrageous, pernicious, pestilent, pillory, reproach, ruthless, sinister, smear, spiteful, stain, sully, toxic, unfavorable, vicious, virulent. SEE MAIN ENTRY
malignance cruelty, fatality, harm, ill will, spite, vice
malignancy corruption, cruelty, fatality, harm, ill will, spite
malignant bad *(inferior)*, caustic, contemptuous, cruel, dangerous, deadly, deleterious, detrimental, diabolic, disadvantageous, fatal, lethal, libelous, malevolent, malicious, nefarious, noxious, offensive *(offending)*, outrageous, peccant *(unhealthy)*, pernicious, pestilent, resentful, ruthless, scathing, sinister, spiteful, vicious, vindictive, virulent. SEE MAIN ENTRY
maligned accused *(attacked)*
maligning contemptuous
malignitas malice, spite
malignity bad repute, cruelty, fatality, harm, malice, mischief, rancor, resentment, spite
malignus spiteful
malinger fake, pretend, shirk, shun
malison imprecation, malediction
malitia knavery
malleability amenability, discipline *(obedience)*
malleable facile, flexible, open *(persuasible)*, passive, pliable, pliant, resilient, sequacious, tractable, yielding. SEE MAIN ENTRY
mallet cudgel
malpractice delinquency *(failure of duty)*, disregard *(omission)*, guilt, misapplication, misconduct, misdeed, misdoing, misprision, misusage, misuse, offense, wrong. SEE MAIN ENTRY
maltreat abuse *(misuse)*, abuse *(victimize)*, bait *(harass)*, brutalize, damage, disoblige, endanger, exploit *(take advantage of)*, harass, harm, harrow, ill use, inflict, misemploy, mistreat, persecute. SEE MAIN ENTRY
maltreatment abuse *(physical misuse)*, atrocity, infliction, injustice, mischief, misuse, molestation, oppression
malum delinquency *(misconduct)*
malus bad *(inferior)*, bad *(offensive)*, dishonest
malversation abuse *(corrupt practice)*, bad faith, bad repute, crime, criminality, delict, delinquency *(misconduct)*, embezzlement, guilt, maladministration, misappropriation, misconduct, misdeed, misdemeanor, misdoing, misprision, misusage, offense. SEE MAIN ENTRY
mammoth prodigious *(enormous)* SEE MAIN ENTRY
man character *(an individual)*, humanity *(mankind)*, mortality
man of business dealer
man of erudition expert
man of law advocate *(counselor)*
man of learning expert
man of letters author *(writer)*, pedagogue
man of mark key man, paragon
man with a grievance actor
man-made artificial, synthetic
manacle constrain *(imprison)*, contain *(restrain)*, detain *(restrain)*, fetter *(noun)*, fetter *(verb)*, hamper, handcuff *(noun)*, handcuff *(verb)*, restrain, restrict, trammel
manacles bondage
manage administer *(conduct)*, arrange *(methodize)*, assume *(undertake)*, comport *(behave)*, conduct, control *(regulate)*, demean *(deport oneself)*, direct *(supervise)*, discipline *(control)*, dominate, effectuate, execute *(accomplish)*, function, govern, maneuver, manipulate *(control unfairly)*, marshal, militate, moderate *(preside over)*, officiate, operate, oversee, predominate *(command)*, preside, program, provide *(arrange for)*, rule *(govern)*, succeed *(attain)*, superintend, transact, wield. SEE MAIN ENTRY
manage badly misgovern, mishandle *(mismanage)*
manage poorly mismanage
manage unskillfully mismanage
manageability amenability
manageable corrigible, facile, flexible, malleable, obedient, pliable, pliant, resigned, sequacious, tractable, yielding SEE MAIN ENTRY
managed care SEE MAIN ENTRY
management administration, agency *(legal relationship)*, auspices, authorities, board, bureaucracy, conduct, control *(supervision)*, course, custody *(supervision)*, direction *(guidance)*, disposition *(final arrangement)*, distribution *(arrangement)*, dominion *(supreme authority)*, economy *(economic system)*, economy *(frugality)*, employer, generalship, government *(administration)*, guidance, hierarchy *(persons in authority)*, maneuver *(tactic)*, operation, oversight *(control)*, policy *(plan of action)*, regime, staff, strategy, supervision,

supremacy, transaction, treatment, trust *(custody)*, usage. SEE MAIN ENTRY
management of money finance
management of natural resources ecology
management of resources economy *(economic system)*
manager administrator, caretaker *(one fulfilling the function of office)*, chief, comptroller, custodian *(protector)*, director, employer, executive, factor *(commission merchant)*, principal *(director)*, proctor, procurator, proprietor, superintendent
manager's office headquarters
managerial administrative
managers hierarchy *(persons in authority)*, management *(supervision)*
managership control *(supervision)*, direction *(guidance)*, generalship, management *(supervision)*
managing administrative, executive, ministerial
manare exude
mancus deficient
mandamus fiat. SEE MAIN ENTRY
mandare delegate, devolve, entrust, instruct *(direct)*, invest *(vest)*, trust
mandate act *(enactment)*, agency *(legal relationship)*, article *(precept)*, assignment *(designation)*, brevet, burden, canon, charge *(command)*, citation *(charge)*, command, decree, delegation *(assignment)*, dictate, direction *(order)*, directive, edict, instruction *(direction)*, law, measure, mission, mittimus, monition *(legal summons)*, order *(judicial directive)*, ordinance, plebiscite, precept, prescribe, proclamation, referendum, regulation *(rule)*, requirement, requisition, statute, subpoena, summons, writ. SEE MAIN ENTRY
mandate of a court warrant *(judicial writ)*
mandated legitimate *(rightful)*, licit
mandated territory state *(political unit)*
mandatorily will shall
mandatory binding, compulsory, conclusive *(determinative)*, decretal, essential *(required)*, exigent, imperative, indispensable, involuntary, necessary *(required)*, obligatory, peremptory *(imperative)*, positive *(prescribed)*, requisite, unavoidable *(inevitable)*, unavoidable *(not voidable)*. SEE MAIN ENTRY
mandatory factor necessity, need *(requirement)*
mandatory minimum sentence SEE MAIN ENTRY
mandatum charge *(command)*, commission *(act)*, fiat, injunction, instruction *(direction)*, mandate, order *(judicial directive)*, warrant *(authorization)*
manere adhere *(persist)*
maneuver act *(undertaking)*, connive, conspire, contrivance, contrive, device *(contrivance)*, devise *(invent)*, evasion, expedient, inveigle, machination, manage, manipulate *(utilize skillfully)*, militate, operate, overt act, perpetrate, plot, ploy, ruse, scheme *(noun)*, scheme *(verb)*, step, stratagem, subterfuge, trap. SEE MAIN ENTRY
maneuverability latitude
maneuverable negotiable
maneuverer catalyst
maneuvering artifice, campaign, conspiracy, strategy, tactical
maneuvers campaign, strategy
manger liaison
mangle damage, deface, disable, mutilate, spoil *(impair)*
mangled broken *(fractured)*, marred
manhandle abuse *(misuse)*, abuse *(victimize)*, ill use, mishandle *(maltreat)*, mistreat, persecute
manhood majority *(adulthood)*
mania compulsion *(obsession)*, furor, lunacy, market *(demand)*, obsession, paranoia, passion
maniacal deranged, frenetic, lunatic, non compos mentis, outrageous
manic lunatic, non compos mentis. SEE MAIN ENTRY
manicae handcuff
manifest adduce, apparent *(perceptible)*, apparent *(presumptive)*, appreciable, axiomatic, bare, bear *(adduce)*, bear *(yield)*, bill *(invoice)*, blatant *(conspicuous)*, bodily, cite *(state)*, clear *(apparent)*, coherent *(clear)*, comprehensible, conspicuous, convey *(communicate)*, corroborate, demonstrate *(establish)*, denude, depict, disabuse, discernible, discover, disinter, distinct *(clear)*, divulge, document, elucidate, embody, emerge, establish *(show)*, evidence, evident, evince, exemplify, exhibit, explain, explicit, expose, flagrant, gross *(flagrant)*, illustrate, inventory, lucid, naked *(perceptible)*, obvious, open *(in sight)*, ostensible, overt, palpable, patent, pellucid, perceivable, perceptible, personify, produce *(offer to view)*, prominent, prove, public *(known)*, reveal, scrutable, signify *(denote)*, tangible, unmistakable, unveil, visible *(in full view)*. SEE MAIN ENTRY
manifest act overt act
manifest directly express
manifest itself appear *(materialize)*, arise *(appear)*, issue *(send forth)*, occur *(come to mind)*
manifestation appearance *(emergence)*, common knowledge, complexion, disclosure *(something disclosed)*, embodiment, face value *(first blush)*, illustration, indicant, proof, symbol, symptom, token. SEE MAIN ENTRY
manifestations indicia
manifesting contempt contemptuous
manifestly fairly *(clearly)*
manifesto brevet, canon, issuance, proclamation, pronouncement, report *(detailed account)*, statement
manifestus apparent *(perceptible)*, conspicuous, evident, flagrant, obvious, open *(in sight)*, overt, palpable, patent, perceptible
manifold compound, diverse, miscellaneous, multifarious, multifold, myriad, reproduce, rife. SEE MAIN ENTRY
manifoldness diversity
manipulable pliable
manipulate capitalize *(seize the chance)*, coax, control *(regulate)*, employ *(make use of)*, exercise *(use)*, exert, exploit *(make use of)*, exploit *(take advantage of)*, handle *(manage)*, ill use, manage, militate, operate, perpetrate, ply, rule *(govern)*, scheme, tamper, wield. SEE MAIN ENTRY
manipulate improperly misemploy
manipulation act *(undertaking)*, connivance, contrivance, machination, management *(judicious use)*, maneuver *(tactic)*, performance *(workmanship)*, plot *(secret plan)*, stratagem, strategy SEE MAIN ENTRY
mankind mortality
manliness prowess *(bravery)*
manly potent, spartan, strong
manner appearance *(look)*, avenue *(means of attainment)*, behavior, character *(personal quality)*, color *(complexion)*, complexion, conduct, conduit *(channel)*, course, custom, degree *(station)*, demeanor, deportment, facility *(instrumentality)*, form *(arrangement)*, instrumentality, means *(opportunity)*, method, mode, modus operandi, parlance, posture *(attitude)*, practice *(custom)*, presence *(poise)*, process *(course)*, style, system, tenor, trait, usage. SEE MAIN ENTRY
manner of conduct dealings
manner of construction organization *(structure)*
manner of disposal disposition *(transfer of property)*
manner of expression phraseology
manner of life behavior
manner of living modus vivendi
manner of operating modus operandi
manner of presentation style
manner of proceeding policy *(plan of action)*, practice *(procedure)*, procedure
manner of speaking parlance
manner of working avenue *(means of attainment)*, procedure
mannered formal, histrionic
mannerism characteristic, habit, identity *(individuality)*, quirk *(idiosyncrasy)*, specialty *(distinctive mark)*, trait. SEE MAIN ENTRY
mannerless disorderly
mannerliness decorum
mannerly civil *(polite)*
manners behavior, conduct, courtesy, decorum, propriety *(correctness)*, protocol *(etiquette)*. SEE MAIN ENTRY
manor demesne, domain *(land owned)*, dominion *(absolute ownership)*, homestead
manpower personnel
mansio stay
manslaughter homicide. SEE MAIN ENTRY
manslayer criminal
mansuetuda clemency
mansuetude amenability, comity
mantic portentous *(ominous)*, prophetic
mantle enshroud, plant *(covertly place)*, spread, veil
manual directory, hornbook, pandect *(treatise)* SEE MAIN ENTRY
manual of instruction hornbook
manufactural industrial
manufacture build *(construct)*, building *(business of assembling)*, business *(commercial enterprise)*, composition *(makeup)*, creation, devise *(invent)*, engender, fabricate *(construct)*, forge *(produce)*, form, formation, frame *(construct)*, generate, industry *(business)*, invent *(produce for the first time)*, make, originate, palter, performance *(workmanship)*. SEE MAIN ENTRY
manufactured assumed *(feigned)*, industrial, synthetic
manufactured for sale commercial, industrial
manufactured goods merchandise
manufactured product output
manufacturer author *(originator)*
manufacturing productive
manumissio emancipation, liberation
manumission emancipation, liberation, release, suffrage
manumit disengage, disenthrall, enfranchise, free, liberate, quit *(free of)*, release, relieve *(free from burden)*, rescue
manumitted clear *(free from criminal charges)*, free *(enjoying civil liberty)*, unbound
manumittere liberate
manus force *(strength)*, handwriting, profession *(vocation)*, violence

manuscript holographic, script
many ample, innumerable, manifold, miscellaneous, multifarious, multifold, multiple, myriad, rife. SEE MAIN ENTRY
many sidedness multiplicity
map blueprint, delineate, delineation, design *(construction plan)*, direction *(course)*, scheme
map out devise *(invent)*, frame *(construct)*, frame *(formulate)*, locate, plan, prearrange, predetermine, program, scheme
mar adulterate, contaminate, damage, deface, eviscerate, frustrate, harm, impair, impede, mutilate, prejudice *(injure)*, smear, spoil *(impair)*, stain, sully, vice, vitiate. SEE MAIN ENTRY
mar the appearance of deface
marathon SEE MAIN ENTRY
maraud despoil, foray, harry *(plunder)*, hold up *(rob)*, loot, onset *(assault)*, pillage *(noun)*, pillage *(verb)*, plunder *(noun)*, plunder *(verb)*, prey, spoil *(pillage)*
marauder burglar, criminal, thief
marauding burglary, depredation, rapacious, spoliation
marble-hearted malignant, ruthless
marcescence decline
march demonstrate *(protest)*, frontier, patrol, perambulate, periphery, progress, traverse
march off depart, part *(leave)*
march out evacuate
marcher pedestrian
marge border
margin balance *(amount in excess)*, border, edge *(border)*, extremity *(furthest point)*, latitude, mete, outline *(boundary)*, penumbra, periphery, plethora, scope, space, surplus. SEE MAIN ENTRY
marginal inappreciable, petty. SEE MAIN ENTRY
marginal annotation comment, note *(brief comment)*
marginalia notation. SEE MAIN ENTRY
margo edge *(border)*
marijuana cannabis
marital conjugal, nuptial
marital infidelity adultery
marital partner consort, spouse
maritus consort
mark attaint, attend *(heed)*, brand, characterize, clue, color *(complexion)*, consider, deface, degree *(station)*, demarcate, denote, designate, designation *(symbol)*, discriminate *(distinguish)*, earmark, eminence, expression *(manifestation)*, feature *(characteristic)*, goal, heed, importance, impression, index *(catalog)*, indicant, indication, indicator, inscribe, inscription, intention, interest *(concern)*, label *(noun)*, label *(verb)*, magnitude, manifest, manifestation, monument, note *(notice)*, note *(record)*, notice *(observe)*, objective, observe *(watch)*, particularity, perceive, prestige, property *(distinctive attribute)*, recognize *(perceive)*, record, regard *(pay attention)*, reputation, select, significance, signify *(denote)*, smear, speciality, specialty *(distinctive mark)*, stain, stamp, subscribe *(sign)*, symbol, symptom, target, trademark, trait, witness *(have direct knowledge of)*. SEE MAIN ENTRY
mark against confront *(oppose)*
mark down book, cast *(register)*, decrease, deduct *(reduce)*, discount *(reduce)*, enter *(record)*, note *(record)*, rebate
mark incorrectly mislabel
mark limits delimit, demarcate
mark of Cain onus *(stigma)*
mark of disgrace stigma
mark of honor mention *(tribute)*
mark of identification caption, earmark, label
mark of identity earmark
mark of shame stigma
mark off border *(bound)*, characterize, circumscribe *(surround by boundary)*, delimit, hedge, measure
mark off by differences differentiate
mark out circumscribe *(surround by boundary)*, delimit, demarcate, designate, differentiate, distinguish, indicate, prescribe, specify, trace *(delineate)*
mark out a course arrange *(plan)*, plan
mark out for choose
mark that designates device *(distinguishing mark)*
mark the difference between discriminate *(distinguish)*
mark the limits define
mark the time of date
mark time pause
mark up cost *(price)*
markdown discount, rebate
marked certain *(particular)*, certain *(specific)*, considerable, conspicuous, distinct *(distinguished from others)*, distinctive, important *(significant)*, manifest, marred, momentous, notable, noteworthy, open *(in sight)*, outstanding *(prominent)*, palpable, particular *(specific)*, peculiar *(distinctive)*, perceptible, preferential, prominent, remarkable, resounding, salient, several *(separate)*, special, specific, stellar, uncommon, unusual
marked by consent consenting
marked by excessive effort elaborate
marked feature characteristic, property *(distinctive attribute)*
marked occurrence event
marked off the calendar SEE MAIN ENTRY
marked price cost *(price)*
marked quality characteristic, property *(distinctive attribute)*
marked superiority distinction *(reputation)*
marked time date
marked traits character *(personal quality)*
markedly fairly *(clearly)*, particularly
marker indication, label, landmark *(conspicuous object)*
market barter, deal, exchange, handle *(trade)*, mercantile, outlet, sell, store *(business)*, vend. SEE MAIN ENTRY
market place store *(business)*. SEE MAIN ENTRY
market price estimate *(approximate cost)*, expense *(cost)*, par *(face amount)*
marketable negotiable, valuable. SEE MAIN ENTRY
marketing commerce, retail, trade *(commerce)*
marks fingerprints, indicia
marks left by a person's finger fingerprints
maroon isolate, seclude
marred blemished, defective, deficient, dilapidated, imperfect, poor *(inferior in quality)*. SEE MAIN ENTRY
marriage cohabitation *(married state)*, matrimony. SEE MAIN ENTRY
marriage accord consortium *(marriage companionship)*
marriage compatibility consortium *(marriage companionship)*
marriage concord consortium *(marriage companionship)*
marriage lines coverture
marriage partner consort, spouse
marriage tie marriage *(wedlock)*, matrimony
marriage to a second partner digamy
married conjugal, nuptial
married life marriage *(wedlock)*, matrimony
married state coverture, marriage *(wedlock)*, matrimony
married status cohabitation *(married state)*, marriage *(wedlock)*, matrimony
married tie coverture
marring defacement
marring feature flaw
marrow consequence *(significance)*, gist *(substance)*, main point, substance *(essential nature)*
marrowless powerless
marry combine *(act in concert)*, connect *(join together)*, join *(bring together)*, unite. SEE MAIN ENTRY
marshal allocate, arrange *(methodize)*, classify, file *(arrange)*, fix *(arrange)*, organize *(arrange)*, tabulate. SEE MAIN ENTRY
marshaling array *(order)*, disposition *(final arrangement)*, distribution *(arrangement)*
mart exchange, market *(business)*, store *(business)*
martial spartan
martial law force *(compulsion)*
martiality belligerency
martinet dictator
marvel phenomenon *(unusual occurrence)*
marvelous ineffable, meritorious, portentous *(eliciting amazement)*, prodigious *(amazing)*, remarkable, special, unusual. SEE MAIN ENTRY
mask camouflage, cloak, conceal, cover *(pretext)*, cover *(conceal)*, denature, disguise *(noun)*, disguise *(verb)*, ensconce, enshroud, envelop, false pretense, hide, obliterate, obnubilate, obscure, plant *(covertly place)*, pretend, pretense *(pretext)*, pretext, ruse, screen *(guard)*, shroud, stifle, strangle, subterfuge, suppress, veil
masked blind *(concealed)*, clandestine, furtive, hidden, mysterious, stealthy
masquerade camouflage, deception, disguise *(noun)*, disguise *(verb)*, evasion, false pretense, hoax, palter, pretend, ruse, sham
masquerade as impersonate, pose *(impersonate)*
mass accumulate *(amass)*, agglomeration, aggregate *(noun)*, aggregate *(verb)*, amount *(quantity)*, assemblage, assembly, body *(collection)*, bulk, caliber *(measurement)*, chamber *(body)*, cohere *(adhere)*, collect *(gather)*, collection *(accumulation)*, compile, concentrate *(consolidate)*, conglomerate, conglomeration, congregate, congregation, conjoin, consolidate *(st-rengthen)*, corpus, cumulation, desegregate, entirety, generality *(bulk)*, hoard, join *(bring together)*, load, majority *(greater part)*, materiality *(physical existence)*, measurement, meet, quantity, selection *(collection)*, store, totality, unite, weight *(burden)*. SEE MAIN ENTRY
mass meeting assemblage, caucus, congregation

mass produce manufacture
mass produced industrial
massacre aberemurder, dispatch *(act of putting to death),* dispatch *(put to death),* homicide, kill *(murder),* killing, murder, slay. SEE MAIN ENTRY
massed collective, compact *(dense),* populous, solid *(compact)*
masses populace, population
massing centralization
massive capacious, compact *(dense),* copious, gross *(flagrant),* major, ponderous, prodigious *(enormous),* solid *(compact).* SEE MAIN ENTRY
master apprehend *(perceive),* comprehend *(understand),* construe *(comprehend),* defeat, dominant, dominate, employer, expert, gain, impose *(subject),* manage, mastermind, moderate *(preside over),* overcome *(surmount),* oversee, overthrow, overwhelm, paramount, pass *(satisfy requirements),* pedagogue, predominate *(command),* prevail *(triumph),* principal *(director),* professional, proprietor, remember, repress, rule *(govern),* sovereign *(absolute),* specialist, subdue, subject, subjugate, succeed *(attain),* superintendent, surmount, understand. SEE MAIN ENTRY
master craftsman artisan
master hand expert
master of ceremonies chairman
master of jurisprudence jurist
master plan arrangement *(plan),* blueprint, direction *(course),* method
master worker practitioner
master workman artisan
masterdom supremacy
masterful competent, deft, dictatorial, expert, indomitable, potent, practiced, proficient, tyrannous SEE MAIN ENTRY
masterfulness influence, puissance
masterless independent
masterly artful, capable, competent, deft, expert, practiced, subtle *(refined)*
mastermind administer *(conduct),* direct *(supervise),* expert, manage, operate, oversee, predominate *(command).* SEE MAIN ENTRY
masters hierarchy *(persons in authority)*
mastership ability, clout, generalship, performance *(workmanship),* power, prowess *(ability),* specialty *(special aptitude),* supremacy
mastery ability, advantage, apprehension *(perception),* cognition, competence *(ability),* control *(supervision),* dominance, dominion *(supreme authority),* efficiency, experience *(background),* force *(strength),* gift *(flair),* hegemony, influence, knowledge *(learning),* occupation *(possession),* ownership, performance *(workmanship),* power, predominance, prowess *(ability),* science *(technique),* seisin, skill, specialty *(special aptitude),* supremacy SEE MAIN ENTRY
mastery of thought comprehension
mat snarl
match alter ego, coincide *(correspond),* compare, comport *(agree with),* conform, connect *(join together),* connect *(relate),* connection *(relation),* contest *(competition),* correlate, correspond *(be equivalent),* counterpart *(parallel),* countervail, duplicate, equipoise, identity *(similarity),* join *(bring together),* matrimony, measure, peer, recriminate, resemblance, retaliate, same, strife SEE MAIN ENTRY
match against confront *(oppose),* counteract
match strength with compete
match wits with compete
matched coextensive, comparable *(equivalent),* conjugal, correlative, equal, fit, uniform
matching agreed *(harmonized),* analogous, coequal, commensurable, commensurate, comparable *(equivalent),* comparative, congruous, harmonious, identical, pendent, similar
matchless absolute *(ideal),* best, inestimable, invaluable, laudable, major, paramount, premium, priceless, prime *(most valuable),* rare, renowned, select, singular, sterling, superior *(excellent),* superlative, unapproachable, unique, unusual
matchless effort main force
matchmaker broker
mate coadjutant, colleague, consociate, consort, contributor *(contributor),* copartner *(business associate),* correlate, counterpart *(complement),* participant, peer, resemblance, same, spouse
mated conjugal, nuptial
material appreciable, article *(commodity),* bodily, cardinal *(basic),* concrete, considerable, corporal, corporeal, critical *(crucial),* crucial, equipment, essential *(required),* expedient, important *(significant),* major, momentous, mundane, noteworthy, objective, paraphernalia *(apparatus),* pertinent, physical, relative *(relevant),* relevant, resource, subject *(topic),* substance *(essential nature),* substantive, tangible, virtual. SEE MAIN ENTRY
material assets estate *(property),* merchandise, principal *(capital sum),* property *(possessions)*
material existence body *(person),* materiality *(physical existence)*
material figuration embodiment
material object article *(commodity)*
material part component, gravamen
material point cornerstone, issue *(matter in dispute),* landmark *(significant change),* main point SEE MAIN ENTRY
material point deduced by the pleadings issue *(matter in dispute)*
material product object
material representation embodiment
material substance object
material things which are owned estate *(property)*
material wealth possessions
materialistic mercenary
materiality corpus, importance, magnitude, relevance, significance. SEE MAIN ENTRY
materialization corpus, embodiment, manifestation, phenomenon *(manifestation),* realization
materialize embody, emerge, form, occur *(happen),* realize *(make real),* substantiate
materialman SEE MAIN ENTRY
materialness consequence *(significance),* importance, magnitude, materiality *(consequence),* materiality *(physical existence),* significance
materials goods, merchandise
materials of combat ammunition
materiate bodily, physical
maternal consanguineous
maternity SEE MAIN ENTRY
mating matrimony
matriarch parents
matriculate register
matriculation registration
matrilinear consanguineous
matrimonial conjugal, nuptial
matrimonium marriage *(wedlock),* matrimony
matrimony cohabitation *(married state),* coverture, marriage *(wedlock).* SEE MAIN ENTRY
matrix pattern
matronage coverture
matronhood coverture
matronship coverture
matronymic call *(title)*
matted inextricable
matter article *(commodity),* business *(affair),* case *(lawsuit),* content *(meaning),* corpus, entity, gist *(substance),* happening, import, issue *(matter in dispute),* materiality *(consequence),* materiality *(physical existence),* object, particular, point *(item),* proceeding, significance, subject *(topic).* SEE MAIN ENTRY
matter for judgment case *(lawsuit),* controversy *(lawsuit),* lawsuit
matter in dispute problem SEE MAIN ENTRY
matter in hand issue *(matter in dispute)*
matter in question issue *(matter in dispute)* SEE MAIN ENTRY
matter legally submitted to the jury evidence
matter of cognition content *(meaning)*
matter of concern cornerstone
matter of contention issue *(matter in dispute)*
matter of course behavior, custom, practice *(custom),* procedure, rule *(guide).* SEE MAIN ENTRY
matter of disputation discrepancy
matter of dubitation doubt *(indecision),* doubt *(suspicion)*
matter of duty allegiance
matter of fact certification *(certainness),* fait accompli, prosaic, unpretentious
matter of factness pragmatism
matter of importance cornerstone
matter of necessity requirement
matter of no consequence nonentity
matter of no importance nonentity
matter of record certificate SEE MAIN ENTRY
matter-of-fact pragmatic
mattering much important *(significant)*
matters affairs, dealings
matters of fact evidence
matters of state politics
matters to be attended to agenda
maturare expedite, hasten, mature, precipitate *(hasten)*
maturate conclude *(complete),* mature, progress
maturation finality, growth *(evolution)*
mature accrue *(arise),* develop, full, payable, progress, ready *(prepared),* receivable, ripe. SEE MAIN ENTRY
mature consideration deliberation
mature person adult
mature reflection deliberation
mature responsibility discretion *(quality of being discreet)*
matured choate lien, elderly, old
maturely considered deliberate, premeditated
matureness majority *(adulthood),* maturity, timeliness
maturing payable
maturitas maturity
maturity age, discretion *(quality of being discreet),* experience *(background),* finality, majority *(adulthood).* SEE MAIN ENTRY

maturus expeditious, ripe
maudlin demonstrative *(expressive of emotion)*
maul beat *(strike)*, lash *(strike)*, mishandle *(maltreat)*, mistreat
maundering prolix
mawkish unsavory
maxim article *(precept)*, belief *(something believed)*, catchword, code, constant, constitution, doctrine, dogma, expression *(comment)*, holding *(ruling of a court)*, law, ordinance, precedent, prescription *(directive)*, principle *(axiom)*, rule *(legal dictate)*. SEE MAIN ENTRY
maxim effort main force
maximal cardinal *(outstanding)*, radical *(extreme)*, utmost
maxime particularly
maximize enhance, expand, increase, magnify, overestimate, parlay *(exploit successfully)*. SEE MAIN ENTRY
maximizing cumulative *(intensifying)*
maximum best, ceiling, full, ultimate, utmost *(adjective)*, utmost *(noun)*. SEE MAIN ENTRY
maximum amount cap
mayhem commotion, outbreak, outburst, shambles. SEE MAIN ENTRY
maze complex *(entanglement)*, entanglement *(confusion)*, ignorance, imbroglio, involution, snarl SEE MAIN ENTRY
mazy circuitous, inextricable, labyrinthine, sinuous, tortuous *(bending)*
meager de minimus, deficient, inappreciable, inconsiderable, insufficient, marginal, mediocre, minimal, negligible, nominal, nonsubstantial *(not sufficient)*, paltry, petty, poor *(inferior in quality)*, scarce, slight, trivial, unworthy SEE MAIN ENTRY
meagerness austerity, dearth, deficiency, deficit, immateriality, insufficiency, poverty
mean average *(midmost)*, base *(inferior)*, bespeak, brutal, connote, denote, heinous, ignoble, illiberal, inappreciable, inconsiderable, inimical, intend, intermediate, loathsome, machiavellian, malevolent, mediocre, mediocrity, mesne, moderation, odious, paltry, parsimonious, penurious, perverse, petty, petulant, poor *(inferior in quality)*, purport, represent *(portray)*, scandalous, scurrilous, servile, signify *(denote)*, slight, spiteful, vicious. SEE MAIN ENTRY
mean proportioned average *(midmost)*
mean-spirited caitiff
mean-tempered petulant
meander detour, deviate, digress, perambulate, prowl
meandering circuitous, discursive *(digressive)*, indirect, labyrinthine, moving *(in motion)*, protracted, sinuous, tortuous *(bending)*
meandrous circuitous, sinuous
meaning connotation, consequence *(significance)*, construction, contents, context, definition, design *(intent)*, essence, explanation, gist *(substance)*, import, intent, main point, paraphrase, purview, significance, signification, spirit, substance *(essential nature)*, sum *(tally)*, tenor. SEE MAIN ENTRY
meaningful cognizable, coherent *(clear)*, eloquent, pithy, sententious, suggestive *(evocative)*
meaningfulness content *(meaning)*, import
meaningless collateral *(immaterial)*, frivolous, immaterial, incomprehensible, inexpressive, minor, nominal, null *(insignificant)*, pedestrian, trivial, unessential, void *(invalid)* SEE MAIN ENTRY
meaningless saying platitude
meaninglessness incoherence
meanness inconsideration, mediocrity, mischief
means access *(opening)*, appliance, conduit *(channel)*, determinant, effects, expedient, facility *(instrumentality)*, forum *(medium)*, instrument *(tool)*, instrumentality, livelihood, medium, method, mode, modus operandi, money, organ, process *(course)*, recourse, reserve, resource, stopgap, substance *(material possessions)*, system, tool, use, way *(manner)*. SEE MAIN ENTRY
means of access access *(right of way)*, approaches, avenue *(means of attainment)*, entrance, ingress, portal
means of approach access *(right of way)*
means of attack ammunition
means of communication language
means of earning a living calling
means of entering entrance
means of entry ingress
means of escape loophole, outlet
means of exit egress
means of expression forum *(medium)*
means of identification fingerprints
means of livelihood employment, position *(business status)*, post, pursuit *(occupation)*
means of offense cudgel
means of proof evidence
means of protection panoply
means of proving a fact evidence
means of recognition indicia, symptom
means of restraint deterrence, deterrent, fetter
means of subsistence maintenance *(support of spouse)*
means of support business *(occupation)*, employment
means of sustaining life sustenance
means to an end contrivance, device *(contrivance)*, expedient
meant bona fide, express, implied, knowing, purposeful
meantime ad interim
meanwhile ad interim
measly paltry
measurable appreciable, determinable *(ascertainable)* SEE MAIN ENTRY
measure act *(undertaking)*, allot, amendment *(legislation)*, amount *(quantity)*, assess *(appraise)*, assessment *(estimation)*, bill *(proposed act)*, calculate, caliber *(measurement)*, capacity *(maximum)*, compare, coverage *(scope)*, criterion, criticize *(evaluate)*, degree *(magnitude)*, delimit, dimension, enactment, evaluate, expedient, extent, gauge, index *(gauge)*, magnitude, mass *(weight)*, measurement, mete *(noun)*, mete *(verb)*, moiety, parcel, part *(portion)*, prescription *(directive)*, procedure, proportion, proposal *(suggestion)*, quantity, quota, rate, ration, regulation *(rule)*, rubric *(authoritative rule)*, segment, share *(interest)*, standard, statute, stopgap, transaction, unit *(item)*. SEE MAIN ENTRY
measure according to weight weigh
measure for measure quid pro quo, reprisal, retribution
measure of value money
measure out administer *(tender)*, apportion, dole, mete
measure up qualify *(meet standards)*
measure up to conform
measured deliberate, periodic, regular *(orderly)*
measured size area *(surface)*, caliber *(measurement)*
measured time phase *(period)*
measureless indeterminate, inestimable, infinite, myriad, open-ended, profuse, unlimited, unqualified *(unlimited)*
measurelessly ad infinitum
measurement amount *(quantity)*, appraisal, appreciation *(perception)*, census, comparison, computation, degree *(magnitude)*, estimate *(approximate cost)*, estimation *(calculation)*, magnitude, mass *(weight)*, quantity, rating. SEE MAIN ENTRY
measurement across caliber *(measurement)*
measurements area *(surface)*
measures campaign, course, legislation *(enactments)*, means *(opportunity)*
measuring out apportionment
meat signification
meaty compact *(pithy)*, pithy, sententious
mechanic artisan
mechanical controlled *(automatic)*, industrial, perfunctory, routine, technical
mechanical aid device *(mechanism)*
mechanical construction instrument *(tool)*
mechanical drawing blueprint
mechanician artisan
mechanics lien SEE MAIN ENTRY
mechanism appliance, contrivance, expedient, facility *(instrumentality)*, forum *(medium)*, instrument *(tool)*, medium, ploy, tool. SEE MAIN ENTRY
mechanism for evasion loophole
mechanistic controlled *(automatic)*
mechanized industrial
medal prize
meddle disrupt, disturb, infringe, intercede, interfere, interrupt, intervene, militate, obtrude, overstep, tamper SEE MAIN ENTRY
meddlesome obtrusive
meddling interest *(concern)*, intrusion, molestation, obtrusive
mederi cure
media press
media pars center *(central position)*
medial average *(midmost)*, central *(situated near center)*, intermediate
median average *(midmost)*, central *(situated near center)*, intermediate, mesne, norm
mediary agent, conduit *(intermediary)*, go-between, intermediary, spokesman
mediate adjudicate, average *(midmost)*, compromise *(settle by mutual agreement)*, intercede, interpose, mollify, negotiate, pacify, reconcile. SEE MAIN ENTRY
mediated agreed *(harmonized)*
mediating agency interagent, liaison, medium
mediation collective bargaining, conciliation, intercession, mollification, negotiation, reconciliation. SEE MAIN ENTRY
mediator adjuster, advocate *(counselor)*, arbiter, broker, conduit *(intermediary)*, go-between, interagent, intermediary, liaison, medium, referee, spokesman, umpire
mediatorial intermediate
mediatorship collective bargaining
mediatory intermediate

Medicaid SEE MAIN ENTRY
medical medicinal, remedial
medical case patient
medical confidentiality SEE MAIN ENTRY
medical preparation drug
medical segregation quarantine
medical treatment cure
medicament cure, drug, panacea
medicamentum drug, remedy
Medicare SEE MAIN ENTRY
medicare drug
medicate cure, drug, relieve *(give aid)*, remedy
medication drug, narcotic
medicative medicinal, remedial
medicina remedy *(that which corrects)*, remedy
medicinal remedial, salubrious, salutary. SEE MAIN ENTRY
medicinal component drug
medicinal ingredient drug
medicine cure, narcotic, panacea
mediocre average *(standard)*, fair *(satisfactory)*, imperfect, inferior *(lower in quality)*, marginal, nondescript, nonsubstantial *(not sturdy)*, ordinary, paltry, passable, pedestrian, poor *(inferior in quality)*, prosaic, trivial, usual. SEE MAIN ENTRY
mediocris mediocre, poor *(inferior in quality)*
mediocritas mediocrity
mediocriter fairly *(moderately)*
mediocrity SEE MAIN ENTRY
meditari practice *(train by repetition)*
meditate concentrate *(pay attention)*, deliberate, muse, ponder, reflect *(ponder)*, study
meditate on brood, consider
meditate upon devote, focus, weigh
meditated deliberate, intentional
meditation consideration *(contemplation)*, deliberation, hindsight, introspection, reflection *(thought)*
meditative circumspect, cogitative, deliberate, pensive, solemn, speculative
medium advocate *(counselor)*, agent, atmosphere, average *(midmost)*, broker, buffer zone, conduit *(channel)*, conduit *(intermediary)*, determinant, expedient, facility *(instrumentality)*, factor *(commission merchant)*, fair *(satisfactory)*, instrument *(tool)*, instrumentality, interagent, intermediary, intermediate, mediocre, tool. SEE MAIN ENTRY
medium of exchange cash, currency, money
medium of proof documentation, evidence
medius center *(central position)*, intermediate, neutral
medley assemblage, composite, diversity, integration *(amalgamation)*, melange, miscellaneous
medullosus pithy
meed appropriation *(donation)*, compensation, honorarium, pay, prize, profit, recompense, requital, reward, tip *(gratuity)*, wage
meek malleable, nonmilitant, obedient, obeisant, patient, placid, pliable, pliant, resigned, sequacious, servile, unobtrusive, unpretentious
meekness resignation *(passive acceptance)*
meet abut, adjoin, appropriate, border *(approach)*, caucus, coincide *(concur)*, collection *(assembly)*, collide *(crash against)*, concur *(agree)*, confront *(encounter)*, congregate, connect *(join together)*, consolidate *(unite)*, contact *(touch)*, convene, converge, discharge *(pay a debt)*, endure *(suffer)*, engage *(involve)*, felicitous, fulfill, keep *(fulfill)*, pay, reach, rendezvous, report *(present oneself)*, rightful, strike *(collide)*, suitable, unite. SEE MAIN ENTRY
meet an obligation satisfy *(discharge)*
meet charges disburse *(pay out)*
meet death decease, perish
meet end to end border *(bound)*
meet halfway compromise *(settle by mutual agreement)*, negotiate
meet in a body congregate
meet in conflict confront *(oppose)*
meet one's death die
meet payments liquidate *(determine liability)*
meet requirements pass *(satisfy requirements)*, satisfy *(fulfill)*
meet the bill bear the expense, defray, disburse *(pay out)*
meet the bill ahead of time prepay
meet the demand avail *(bring about)*
meet the demands qualify *(meet standards)*
meet the expense of disburse *(pay out)*, expend *(disburse)*
meet the specifications qualify *(meet standards)*
meet the wants of accommodate
meet with bear *(tolerate)*, border *(bound)*, contact *(communicate)*, find *(discover)*, incur
meet with a loss forfeit, lose *(be deprived of)*
meet with success prevail *(triumph)*, succeed *(attain)*
meeting adjacent, assemblage, assembly, caucus, chamber *(body)*, coalition, collection *(assembly)*, collision *(accident)*, company *(assemblage)*, concurrent *(united)*, conference, confrontation *(act of setting face to face)*, congregation, contact *(touching)*, contiguous, interview, parley, rendezvous, session. SEE MAIN ENTRY
meeting hall chamber *(compartment)*
meeting of events crossroad *(turning point)*
meeting of minds accordance *(understanding)*, mutual understanding, understanding *(agreement)*. SEE MAIN ENTRY
meeting of political leaders caucus
meeting of the minds agreement *(concurrence)*
meeting place intersection, rendezvous
meeting point intersection
meeting standards palatable
meetness expedience
megalopolis city
melancholia pessimism
melancholic despondent, disconsolate, pessimistic
melancholy despondent, disconsolate, lamentable, lugubrious, pessimism, pessimistic
melange SEE MAIN ENTRY
meld amalgamate, combine *(join together)*, desegregate, incorporate *(include)*, join *(bring together)*, unite
melee affray
melee altercation, belligerency, bluster *(commotion)*
mèlée brawl
mèlée collision *(dispute)*, commotion, confrontation *(altercation)*
melee fracas, fray, imbroglio, pandemonium, riot, turmoil
melior preferable, superior *(excellent)*
meliorate ameliorate, commute, cure, develop, embellish, emend, fix *(repair)*, mitigate, modify *(alter)*, mollify, progress, rectify, reform, rehabilitate, relieve *(give aid)*, remedy, renew *(refurbish)*, renovate, repair, restore *(renew)*. SEE MAIN ENTRY
melioration amendment *(correction)*, correction *(change)*, development *(progression)*, improvement, mollification, progress, reform, rehabilitation, renewal, reorganization, repair, solace
meliorative mitigating
melliferous nectarious
mellifluous eloquent
mellow mollify, orotund, pacify, ripe
melodramatic histrionic
melodramatics histrionics
melt burn
melt away decrease, disappear, dissolve *(disperse)*, lessen, perish, subside
melt into one consolidate *(unite)*, merge
meltdown SEE MAIN ENTRY
member chapter *(branch)*, element, ingredient, offshoot, organ, party *(participant)*. SEE MAIN ENTRY
member of a governmental body legislator
member of a jury juror
member of a legislative body legislator
member of a legislature lawmaker
member of a partnership partner
member of Congress lawmaker
member of organized crime racketeer
member of parliament legislator
member of the Assembly lawmaker
member of the bar attorney, barrister, counsel, counselor, esquire, jurist
member of the family relative
member of the House lawmaker
member of the human race person
member of the legal profession advocate *(counselor)*, counsel, counselor, esquire, jurist, lawyer SEE MAIN ENTRY
member of the police force peace officer
member of the Senate lawmaker
members constituency, personnel
members of the bar chamber *(body)*
members of the media press
members of the press press
membership affiliation *(connectedness)*, constituency, roll
membrum clause, ingredient
memento remembrance *(commemoration)*, reminder, token
memo entry *(record)*, reminder
memoir account *(report)*, memorandum, recollection, story *(narrative)*
memorability importance, materiality *(consequence)*
memorable famous, illustrious, important *(significant)*, major, material *(important)*, momentous, notable, noteworthy, outstanding *(prominent)*, paramount, portentous *(eliciting amazement)*, prominent, remarkable, salient, special, stellar, unusual SEE MAIN ENTRY
memorable part highlight
memorableness importance
memoranda calendar *(record of yearly periods)*
memorandum brief, entry *(record)*, marginalia, notation, note *(brief comment)*, notice *(announcement)*, record, register, reminder. SEE MAIN ENTRY

memorandum of law brief SEE MAIN ENTRY
memoria account *(report)*, recollection, remembrance *(recollection)*
memorial honorary, monument, remembrance *(commemoration)*, reminder
memorialization ceremony, remembrance *(commemoration)*
memorialize honor, recall *(remember)*, remember
memorize recall *(remember)*, remember
memory hindsight, recognition, recollection, remembrance *(recollection)*, retention, retrospect. SEE MAIN ENTRY
men SEE MAIN ENTRY
menace bait *(harass)*, challenge, danger, endanger, frighten, hazard, hector, impend, intimidate, jeopardize, jeopardy, portend, threat, threaten. SEE MAIN ENTRY
menacing abusive, dangerous, formidable, imminent, insalubrious, noxious, ominous, pernicious, portentous *(ominous)*, precarious, prophetic, sinister
mend ameliorate, amend, cure, develop, emend, fix *(repair)*, meliorate, progress, reconcile, recreate, rectify, redress, reform, rehabilitate, remedy, renew *(refurbish)*, renovate, repair, restore *(renew)*, settle
mendable corrigible
mendacious deceptive, disingenuous, false *(inaccurate)*, fictitious, lying, untrue. SEE MAIN ENTRY
mendaciousness bad faith, dishonesty, improbity, indirection *(deceitfulness)*
mendacity artifice, bad faith, deceit, deception, dishonesty, false pretense, falsification, fraud, improbity, indirection *(deceitfulness)*, lie, misstatement, pretense *(pretext)*, subreption SEE MAIN ENTRY
mendacium falsehood, lie, misstatement, story *(falsehood)*
mendax mendacious
mendicancy poverty, privation
mendicant parasite
mendicate request
mendicitas indigence
mendicity poverty, privation
mendicus poor *(underprivileged)*
mending correction *(change)*, renewal, repair
mendosus faulty
mendum defect, flaw
menial base *(inferior)*, ignoble, inferior *(lower in position)*, servile, subservient. SEE MAIN ENTRY
menology calendar *(record of yearly periods)*
mens intellect, intelligence *(intellect)*, purpose, reason *(sound judgment)*, understanding *(comprehension)*
mens rea SEE MAIN ENTRY
mensio measurement
mensura measurement
mensurable appreciable, determinable *(ascertainable)*
mensural appreciable
mensurate assess *(appraise)*
mensuration assessment *(estimation)*, estimation *(calculation)*, measurement
mental non compos mentis, vicarious *(delegated)*
mental aberration lunacy, paranoia
mental ability intellect, intelligence *(intellect)*, understanding *(comprehension)*. SEE MAIN ENTRY
mental abnormality insanity, lunacy
mental acuteness intellect, intelligence *(intellect)*
mental agony distress *(anguish)*
mental alienation insanity
mental and spiritual makeup character *(personal quality)*
mental attitude impression
mental balance competence *(sanity)*, sanity
mental capacity apprehension *(perception)*, competence *(sanity)*, comprehension, intellect, intelligence *(intellect)*, reason *(sound judgment)*. SEE MAIN ENTRY
mental constitution disposition *(inclination)*, frame *(mood)*
mental cultivation edification
mental decay insanity
mental deficiency insanity
mental derangement insanity
mental disease insanity, paranoia
mental dissociation lunacy
mental equilibrium competence *(sanity)*, sanity
mental faculty intellect, intelligence *(intellect)*, judgment *(discernment)*
mental giant mastermind
mental grasp comprehension, information *(knowledge)*
mental health competence *(sanity)*, sanity
mental hospital asylum *(hospital)*
mental illness lunacy
mental image concept, impression, notion, perception, phantom, recollection, remembrance *(recollection)*, sense *(feeling)*
mental imbalance lunacy
mental impression concept, perception
mental incapacity insanity
mental infirmities insanity
mental instability insanity
mental institution asylum *(hospital)*
mental outlook position *(point of view)*
mental picture recollection
mental poise common sense
mental representation concept
mental reservation ambivalence
mental sickness insanity, lunacy
mental toil labor *(exertion)*
mental unsoundness insanity
mental view impression, perspective
mentality caliber *(mental capacity)*, comprehension, intellect, intelligence *(intellect)*, sagacity, sense *(intelligence)*, temperament
mentally aberrant lunatic
mentally appreciate discern *(detect with the senses)*
mentally capable competent
mentally deficient non compos mentis
mentally diseased non compos mentis SEE MAIN ENTRY
mentally ill lunatic, non compos mentis
mentally sick non compos mentis
mentally sound normal *(sane)*, sane
mentally unbalanced lunatic
mentally unsound non compos mentis
mentation reflection *(thought)*
mentio mention *(reference)*
mention adduce, advise, allude, attribution, citation *(attribution)*, cite *(state)*, comment *(noun)*, comment *(verb)*, communicate, convey *(communicate)*, designate, disclose, disclosure *(act of disclosing)*, enumerate, expression *(comment)*, impart, indication, inform *(notify)*, innuendo, intimation, itemize, notice *(announcement)*, notice *(observe)*, notification, notify, observation, observe *(remark)*, refer *(direct attention)*, reference *(allusion)*, reference *(citation)*, referral, relate *(tell)*, remark *(noun)*, remark *(verb)*, report *(disclose)*, reveal, signify *(inform)*, specify, tip *(clue)*. SEE MAIN ENTRY
mention in detail itemize
mention one by one enumerate
mention specifically enumerate
mentioned aforesaid
mentioned previously aforesaid
mentioning reference *(citation)*
mentiri lie *(falsify)*
mentis acies perception
mentis compos sane
mentor mastermind
mentors faculty *(teaching staff)*
Mephistophelian diabolic
mephitic deadly, harmful, insalubrious, malignant, pernicious, pestilent
mercantile commercial, industrial, retail. SEE MAIN ENTRY
mercantile business commerce, industry *(business)*, trade *(commerce)*
mercantile relations commerce, trade *(commerce)*
mercantilism commerce
mercari buy
mercator dealer, merchant
mercatura commerce
mercaturam trade
mercatus market *(business)*, trade *(commerce)*
mercenarius mercenary
mercenary employee, illiberal, parsimonious, penurious, venal. SEE MAIN ENTRY
merces fee *(charge)*, pay, recompense, rent, wage
merces mutare barter
merces vetitae contraband
merchandise barter, cargo, commodities, deal, freight, handle *(trade)*, item, output, paraphernalia *(personal belongings)*, product, sell, stock in trade, trade. SEE MAIN ENTRY
merchandise list inventory
merchandise sent consignment
merchandise specification invoice *(itemized list)*
merchandiser dealer, merchant
merchandising business *(commerce)*, commerce, commercial, mercantile, trade *(commerce)*
merchant dealer, supplier, vendor. SEE MAIN ENTRY
merchantable marketable
merchantry business *(commerce)*, commerce, deal, exchange, trade *(commerce)*
merciful benevolent, charitable *(lenient)*, humane, lenient, placable, propitious, sensitive *(easily affected)*
mercifulness clemency, humanity *(humaneness)*, lenience, pity
merciless brutal, cruel, diabolic, harmful, harsh, inexorable, malevolent, malicious, obdurate, relentless, remorseless, ruthless, unrelenting, vicious SEE MAIN ENTRY
mercilessness atrocity, brutality, cruelty
mercurial capricious, inconsistent, irresolute, moving *(in motion)*, undependable, unpredictable, untrustworthy, variable, volatile. SEE MAIN ENTRY
mercurialness inconsistency
mercy benevolence *(disposition to do good)*, clemency, condonation, consideration *(sympathetic regard)*, humanity *(humaneness)*, lenience, pity, understanding *(tolerance)*
mere marginal, minor, naked *(lacking embellishment)*, only *(no more than)*, simple. SEE MAIN ENTRY

merely only, purely *(simply),* solely *(purely)*
merere earn
meretricious dishonest, disreputable, fraudulent, pretentious *(ostentatious),* tawdry. SEE MAIN ENTRY
meretriciousness bad faith
merge amalgamate, annex *(add),* attach *(join),* bond *(hold together),* cement, coincide *(concur),* combine *(join together),* commingle, conjoin, connect *(join together),* consolidate *(unite),* converge, desegregate, federalize *(associate),* federate, include, incorporate *(include),* join *(bring together),* organize *(unionize),* pool, unite SEE MAIN ENTRY
merge in desegregate
merged compound, concordant, concurrent *(united),* conjoint, federal, joint, miscellaneous
merger accession *(annexation),* affiliation *(amalgamation),* cartel, coalescence, coalition, combination, concert, consolidation, consortium *(business cartel),* federation, integration *(amalgamation),* integration *(assimilation),* meeting *(encounter),* syndicate, trust *(combination of businesses)*
merging centralization, coalescence, coalition, concerted, concordant
meridian pinnacle
merit caliber *(quality),* consequence *(significance),* credit *(recognition),* earn, importance, probity, quality *(excellence),* quality *(grade),* rate, rectitude, right *(righteousness),* significance, value, weight *(importance),* worth SEE MAIN ENTRY
merit as compensation earn
merited condign, due *(owed),* entitled, equitable, fair *(just),* just, justifiable, rightful, suitable
meriting blame peccant *(culpable)*
meriting censure culpable
meriting condemnation culpable
meritless unworthy
meritoria lodging
meritorious cogent, conscientious, exemplary, high-minded, incorruptible, justifiable, laudable, major, moral, reputable, sterling, unimpeachable
meritoriousness merit, validity
meritum merit
meritus condign, equitable, just
merriment enjoyment *(pleasure)*
merry jocular
merrymaking jocular
merus genuine, unadulterated
merx commodities, merchandise
mesh intertwine
mesh together engage *(involve)*
mesh with comport *(agree with)*
meshing interlocking
mesial central *(situated near center),* intermediate
mesne intermediate. SEE MAIN ENTRY
mess confuse *(create disorder),* imbroglio, pollute, predicament, quagmire, quantity, shambles, snarl
mess up confuse *(create disorder),* disrupt, spoil *(impair)*
message communication *(statement),* disclosure *(something disclosed),* intelligence *(news),* issuance, note *(brief comment),* notice *(announcement),* notification, proclamation, report *(detailed account).* SEE MAIN ENTRY
messenger forerunner, harbinger, informer *(a person who provides information),* liaison, plenipotentiary, proxy, representative *(proxy),* spokesman
messuage homestead
messy disordered
metabolize convert *(change use)*
metage measurement
metamorphic protean
metamorphose alter, change, convert *(change use),* modify *(alter),* transform
metamorphoses SEE MAIN ENTRY
metamorphosis conversion *(change)*
metaphor example
metaphorical comparative
metaphysical incomprehensible
metari measure
metastasis transition
mete allocate, allot, apportion, assess *(appraise),* bestow, calculate, disburse *(distribute),* dispense, distribute, divide *(distribute),* dole, measure, parcel, partition, periphery, split. SEE MAIN ENTRY
mete out administer *(tender),* allot, apportion, arbitrate *(adjudge),* assign *(allot),* contribute *(supply),* disperse *(disseminate),* dispose *(apportion),* divide *(distribute),* dole, inflict, partition, present *(make a gift),* prorate, render *(administer)*
meteoric brief, ephemeral, transient
meteoric rise SEE MAIN ENTRY
meteorical ephemeral
meter measure
meterable appreciable
meterage measurement
metes confines, outline *(boundary)*
method act *(undertaking),* arrangement *(ordering),* arrangement *(plan),* array *(order),* avenue *(means of attainment),* campaign, conduct, conduit *(channel),* contrivance, course, device *(contrivance),* direction *(course),* disposition *(final arrangement),* expedient, facility *(instrumentality),* form *(arrangement),* instrumentality, key *(solution),* manner *(behavior),* means *(opportunity),* mode, modus operandi, policy *(plan of action),* practice *(custom),* practice *(procedure),* procedure, process *(course),* regularity, rule *(guide),* scheme, science *(technique),* strategy, style, system, technicality, usage. SEE MAIN ENTRY
method of action manner *(behavior)*
method of attack avenue *(means of attainment)*
method of business dealings
method of communication forum *(medium)*
method of expression forum *(medium)*
method of living modus vivendi
method of treatment cure
methodical precise, procedural, punctilious, regular *(orderly),* systematic. SEE MAIN ENTRY
methodicalness array *(order),* regularity
methodization classification
methodize adjust *(regulate),* classify, codify, coordinate, disentangle, fix *(arrange),* orchestrate, organize *(arrange),* pigeonhole, regulate *(adjust),* sort, tabulate
methodology array *(order),* modus operandi, order *(arrangement),* procedure, process *(course)*
meticulosity diligence *(perseverance),* interest *(concern)*
meticulous accurate, careful, circumspect, close *(rigorous),* conscientious, detailed, discriminating *(judicious),* exact, faithful *(diligent),* literal, painstaking, particular *(exacting),* precise, punctilious, punctual, strict, subtle *(refined),* thorough. SEE MAIN ENTRY
meticulously faithfully
meticulousness caution *(vigilance),* diligence *(care),* particularity, rigor
metier calling, career, industry *(business),* pursuit *(occupation),* trade *(occupation),* work *(employment)*
meting out apportionment
metiri gauge
metropolis city
metropolitan civic, civil *(public)*
metropolitan area city
mettle character *(personal quality),* frame *(mood),* prowess *(bravery),* spirit
mettlesome undaunted
metuere fear
metus fear
metus timor misgiving
mew imprison
miasmal deleterious, destructive, harmful, insalubrious, malignant, peccant *(unhealthy)*
miasmatic destructive, insalubrious, malignant
miasmatical insalubrious, malignant
miasmic deadly, destructive, insalubrious
microscopic impalpable
mid average *(midmost),* intermediate
middle average *(midmost),* center *(central position),* central *(situated near center),* interior, intermediate, mediocre, mesne. SEE MAIN ENTRY
middle class average *(midmost)*
middle distance center *(central position)*
middle grade average *(midmost)*
middle ground compromise
middle man representative *(proxy)*
middle point center *(central position)*
middle position center *(central position)*
middle state mediocrity
middleman agent, broker, conduit *(intermediary),* dealer, factor *(commission merchant),* go-between, interagent, intermediary, medium, merchant, procurator
middlemost average *(midmost),* central *(situated near center)*
middling average *(midmost),* fair *(satisfactory),* imperfect, marginal, mediocre, nondescript, ordinary, passable, usual
midmost central *(situated near center),* intermediate
midmost point center *(central position)*
midpoint center *(central position),* norm
midst center *(central position)*
midway en route
mien appearance *(look),* aspect, behavior, complexion, conduct, demeanor, deportment, manner *(behavior),* presence *(poise),* semblance, state *(condition)*
miff aggravate *(annoy)*
miffed resentful
might degree *(magnitude),* dint, force *(strength),* influence, main force, potential, prowess *(bravery),* puissance, quality *(excellence),* severity, sinew, strength. SEE MAIN ENTRY
mightiness dint, dominance, eminence, force *(strength),* influence, potential, predominance, puissance, strength
mightless powerless
mighty efficient, grandiose, important *(significant),* in full force, inexpugnable, influential, irresistible, omnipotent, potent, powerful, predominant, prevailing *(having superior force),* prodigious *(enormous),* spartan, strong, vehement

migrate leave *(depart)*, move *(alter position)*, part *(leave)*. SEE MAIN ENTRY
migration immigration
migratory moving *(in motion)*, transient, unsettled
mild civil *(polite)*, innocuous, lenient, patient, peaceable, permissive, placable, placid SEE MAIN ENTRY
mild-tempered patient
milden mollify, relax
mildewed stale
mildly fairly *(moderately)*
mildness amenity, humanity *(humaneness)*, lenience, moderation
mileage space
milestone cornerstone, crossroad *(turning point)*, event, landmark *(significant change)*, step. SEE MAIN ENTRY
milieu atmosphere, case *(set of circumstances)*, environment, section *(vicinity)*
militancy belligerency
militant aggressor, contentious, litigious, offensive *(taking the initiative)*, pugnacious, radical *(favoring drastic change)*, spartan
militant aggressor SEE MAIN ENTRY
militaristic offensive *(taking the initiative)*, pugnacious
military evolutions strategy
military science strategy
military tribunal SEE MAIN ENTRY
militate influence, operate. SEE MAIN ENTRY
militate against counter, counteract, countervail, oppugn
milk exploit *(take advantage of)*
millstone incumbrance *(burden)*
mime impersonate, mock *(imitate)*, parody
mimesis part *(role)*
mimic impersonate, jape, mock *(imitate)*, pose *(impersonate)*, pretend
mimicking caricature
mimicry caricature, parody, ridicule, travesty
minacious ominous, pending *(imminent)*, portentous *(ominous)*, prophetic
minacious force menace
minacity menace
minae threat
minatorial imminent, portentous *(ominous)*, prophetic
minatory aleatory *(perilous)*, dangerous, imminent, ominous, portentous *(ominous)*, prophetic, sinister, unpropitious
mince the truth prevaricate
mind animus, attend *(heed)*, beware, care *(be cautious)*, care *(regard)*, comprehension, conatus, concern *(care)*, conscience, conviction *(persuasion)*, frame *(mood)*, hear *(give attention to)*, heed, intellect, intelligence *(intellect)*, intent, memory *(retention)*, note *(notice)*, obey, observe *(watch)*, preserve, propensity, reason *(sound judgment)*, regard *(pay attention)*, submit *(yield)*, will *(desire)*. SEE MAIN ENTRY
mind set position *(point of view)*
minded prone
mindful careful, circumspect, cognizant, conscious *(aware)*, discreet, faithful *(diligent)*, familiar *(informed)*, judicious, knowing, meticulous, particular *(exacting)*, perceptive, politic, prudent, sensitive *(discerning)* SEE MAIN ENTRY
mindfulness caution *(vigilance)*, comprehension, diligence *(care)*, discretion *(quality of being discreet)*, interest *(concern)*, knowledge *(awareness)*, notice *(heed)*, observation, perception, realization, recollection, regard *(attention)*, sense *(feeling)*, sensibility
mindless blind *(not discerning)*, heedless, irrational, lax, negligent, non compos mentis, oblivious, opaque, perfunctory, reckless, unaware
mindlessness disinterest *(lack of interest)*, disregard *(unconcern)*
mine bomb, contrive, extract, fund
mingle combine *(join together)*, confuse *(create disorder)*, desegregate, join *(associate oneself with)*, unite
mingle confusedly confound
mingled complex, compound, conglomerate, promiscuous
minglement incorporation *(blend)*, melange
mingling concrescence, integration *(amalgamation)*, integration *(assimilation)*
miniature model, tenuous
minify diminish, lessen
minim minimum, scintilla
minimal minor, remote *(small)*. SEE MAIN ENTRY
minimalize discount *(minimize)*
minime suspicax unsuspecting
minimization curtailment, deduction *(diminution)*, understatement
minimize allay, commute, decrease, depreciate, dilute, diminish, disparage, lessen, misprize, palliate *(abate)*, reduce, remit *(relax)*, underestimate. SEE MAIN ENTRY
minimum minimal, minor, modicum, nominal, paucity. SEE MAIN ENTRY
minimum wage SEE MAIN ENTRY
minimus inappreciable
minister administer *(conduct)*, caretaker *(one fulfilling the function of office)*, contribute *(assist)*, deputy, incumbent, officiate, operate, pander, proctor, supply
minister to accommodate, aid, assist, attend *(take care of)*, bear *(yield)*, bestow, care *(regard)*, concern *(care)*, cure, foster, preserve, relieve *(give aid)*, remedy, serve *(assist)*, support *(assist)*
ministerial administrative, executive. SEE MAIN ENTRY
ministering angel samaritan
ministerium service *(assistance)*
ministers government *(political administration)*
ministrant ancillary *(auxiliary)*, benefactor, samaritan, subservient
ministrare supply
ministration administration, aid *(help)*, aid *(subsistence)*, attendance, behalf, bureaucracy, direction *(guidance)*, help, relief *(aid)*, service *(assistance)*
ministry aid *(help)*, aid *(subsistence)*, bureau, control *(supervision)*, department, relief *(aid)*
minor adolescent, child, collateral *(immaterial)*, dependent *(adjective)*, dependent *(noun)*, frivolous, immaterial, inappreciable, incidental, inconsequential, inconsiderable, infant, inferior *(lower in position)*, juvenile *(adjective)*, juvenile *(noun)*, minimal, negligible, nonessential, null *(insignificant)*, petty, secondary, slight, subaltern, subordinate, unessential. SEE MAIN ENTRY
minor amount modicum
minor officer of the law marshal
minor part detail
minor point technicality
minor under guardianship dependent
minor under protectorship dependent
minoris aestimare underestimate
minoris facere underestimate
minority adolescence, nonage, paucity. SEE MAIN ENTRY
minors children
mintage money
minted monetary
minuere curtail, diminish, extenuate
minui suffer *(sustain loss)*
minus save
minute accurate, capsule, conscientious, detailed, entry *(record)*, exact, impalpable, inconsiderable, meticulous, minimal, minor, negligible, nominal, notation, note *(brief comment)*, outline *(synopsis)*, paltry, paraphrase, petty, record, remote *(small)*, report *(detailed account)*, scarce, slight, summary, synopsis, tenuous, trivial. SEE MAIN ENTRY
minute account specification
minute application diligence *(care)*
minute attention diligence *(care)*, interest *(concern)*, scrutiny
minute circumstance particularity
minute examination cross-examination
minute investigation indagation
minute part detail
minute quantity iota
minute study diligence *(care)*
minute thought diligence *(care)*
minutely careful meticulous
minutely correct punctilious, punctual
minuteness diligence *(care)*, interest *(concern)*, particularity
minutes register, transcript
minutia particular
minutiae circumstances, technicality
minutus paltry, petty
miracle phenomenon *(unusual occurrence)*. SEE MAIN ENTRY
miraculous incomprehensible, ineffable, portentous *(eliciting amazement)*, prodigious *(amazing)*, remarkable, special, unprecedented
mirage deception, figment, phantom
miratio surprise
mire pollute
mirror copy, impersonate, mock *(imitate)*, reproduce
mirth-loving jocular
mirthful jocular
mirthless solemn
mirus eccentric
misaddress misdirect
misadminister misgovern, mismanage
misadministration maladministration, misconduct
misadventure accident *(misfortune)*, adversity, casualty, catastrophe, debacle, disaster, miscarriage, misfortune, quirk *(accident)*, tragedy
misadvise misdirect, misguide, misinform, mislead
misadvised ill-advised, ill-judged, inadvisable. SEE MAIN ENTRY
misalliance disaccord, incongruity, misjoinder
misanthropic cynical
misapplication abuse *(corrupt practice)*, catachresis, conversion *(misappropriation)*, distortion, exploitation, maladministration, misappropriation, misdoing, misrepresentation, misusage, misuse, waste. SEE MAIN ENTRY
misapplied inapplicable, inappropriate
misapplied name misnomer
misapply abuse *(misuse)*, bilk, convert *(misappropriate)*, embezzle, exploit *(take*

advantage of), misemploy, mismanage, pervert, purloin, slant
misapply funds defalcate
misapprehend err, misconceive, misconstrue, misinterpret, misjudge, misread, mistake, misunderstand
misapprehension catachresis, fallacy, misestimation, misjudgment
misappropriate abuse *(misuse),* bilk, divert, embezzle, exploit *(take advantage of),* hold up *(rob),* impropriate, jostle *(pickpocket),* misemploy, mismanage, peculate, pilfer, plagiarize, poach, purloin, rob. SEE MAIN ENTRY
misappropriate funds embezzle
misappropriate intrusted funds embezzle
misappropriate money defalcate
misappropriation abuse *(corrupt practice),* embezzlement, larceny, misapplication, misusage, misuse, plagiarism, theft. SEE MAIN ENTRY
misappropriation of funds conversion *(misappropriation)*
misarrange disorganize
misarrangement disturbance
misbecoming inappropriate
misbegetting bar sinister
misbegot illegitimate *(born out of wedlock)*
misbegotten illegitimate *(born out of wedlock)*
misbehave disobey, lapse *(fall into error)*
misbehaved disorderly
misbehaving delinquent *(guilty of a misdeed),* disobedient, disorderly
misbehavior bad repute, culpability, delinquency *(misconduct),* disregard *(omission),* fault *(responsibility),* guilt, impropriety, malfeasance, miscarriage, mischief, misconduct, misdeed, misdoing, transgression, violation
misbelief error, fallacy
misbelieve doubt *(distrust),* misdoubt
misbeliever heretic
misbelieving doubtful
misbrand mislabel
miscalculate err, misapprehend, misconceive, misinterpret, misjudge, mistake, misunderstand. SEE MAIN ENTRY
miscalculated fallacious, ill-judged, incorrect, inexact, inflated *(overestimated)*
miscalculation confusion *(ambiguity),* error, fallacy, fault *(mistake),* miscue, misestimation, misjudgment
miscalling misnomer
miscarriage accident *(misfortune),* disaster, failure *(lack of success).* SEE MAIN ENTRY
miscarriage of justice error, inequity, injustice, misjudgment
miscarry fail *(lose)*
miscellaneous composite, conglomerate, diverse, heterogeneous, manifold, multifarious, multiple, omnibus, promiscuous. SEE MAIN ENTRY
miscellaneous collection melange
miscellany assemblage, compilation, conglomeration, diversity, melange
miscere combine *(join together),* disorganize, unite
mischance accident *(misfortune),* adversity, calamity, casualty, catastrophe, debacle, fatality, miscarriage, misfortune, quirk *(accident)*
mischaracterize mislabel
mischief disservice, harm, misdoing. SEE MAIN ENTRY
mischief-maker delinquent, malefactor
mischievous harmful, malevolent, malicious, noxious, peccant *(culpable),* pernicious, sinister, vicious, wrongful
miscitation catachresis
miscite bear false witness, distort, falsify, misrepresent
misclassify mislabel
miscolor camouflage, cloak, distort, falsify, misinform, misrepresent, slant
miscomprehend misapprehend
miscomputation error, misestimation, misjudgment
miscompute err, miscalculate, misjudge
misconceive misapprehend, miscalculate, misconstrue, misinterpret, misjudge, mistake, misunderstand. SEE MAIN ENTRY
misconception catachresis, confusion *(ambiguity),* error, fallacy, misapplication, misestimation, misjudgment. SEE MAIN ENTRY
misconduct blame *(culpability),* crime, culpability, disregard *(omission),* fault *(responsibility),* guilt, indiscretion, maladministration, malpractice, miscarriage, mischief, misdeed, misdoing, misemploy, misfeasance, misguide, mishandle *(mismanage),* mismanage, misprision, misrule, offense, transgression, vice. SEE MAIN ENTRY
misconduct oneself offend *(violate the law)*
misconducted misadvised
misconjecture error, miscalculate, misconceive, misestimation, misinterpret
misconstructed fallacious
misconstruction catachresis, distortion, fallacy, falsification, misapplication, misjudgment, misrepresentation
misconstrue distort, err, misapprehend, miscalculate, misconceive, misinterpret, misjudge, misread, mistake, misunderstand, slant. SEE MAIN ENTRY
misconstrued incorrect
miscounseled ill-advised
miscount error, miscalculate
miscreancy wrong
miscreant bad *(offensive),* convict, delinquent, hoodlum, immoral, iniquitous, malefactor, nefarious, outlaw, profane, racketeer, sinister, wrongdoer
miscue SEE MAIN ENTRY
misdealing bribery, crime, disingenuous, disreputable, machiavellian, racket
misdeed crime, delinquency *(misconduct),* disservice, fault *(responsibility),* guilt, illegality, lapse *(expiration),* malfeasance, misconduct, misdemeanor, misdoing, misfeasance, misprision, offense, onus *(blame),* tort, transgression, vice, wrong. SEE MAIN ENTRY
misdeed punishable by imprisonment felony
misdeem misapprehend, miscalculate, misconceive, misinterpret, misjudge, misread, misunderstand
misdemeanant convict, criminal, culpable, delinquent, lawbreaker, malefactor, wrongdoer
misdemeanor crime, delict, guilt, misconduct, misdeed, misdoing, offense. SEE MAIN ENTRY
misdenominate mislabel
misdescribe distort, mislabel, mislead, misrepresent
misdesignate mislabel
misdirect convert *(misappropriate),* corrupt, deceive, delude, disorient, distort, divert, dupe, ensnare, exploit *(take advantage of),* illude, misemploy, misgovern, misguide, mishandle *(mismanage),* misinform, mislabel, mislead, mismanage, palter, slant. SEE MAIN ENTRY
misdirected errant, inappropriate, misadvised
misdirection abuse *(corrupt practice),* digression, distortion, maladministration, misrule
misdo misemploy, mismanage
misdoer delinquent, wrongdoer
misdoing crime, criminality, culpability, delinquency *(misconduct),* disservice, guilt, infringement, malfeasance, mischief, misconduct, misdeed, misdemeanor, misfeasance, offense, tort, transgression, wrong. SEE MAIN ENTRY
misdoubt apprehension *(fear),* cloud *(suspicion),* doubt *(suspicion),* doubt *(distrust),* mistrust, suspect *(distrust),* suspicion *(mistrust).* SEE MAIN ENTRY
miseducate distort, misdirect, misguide, misinform, mislead
misemploy abuse *(misuse),* convert *(misappropriate),* exploit *(take advantage of),* mishandle *(maltreat),* mismanage, mistreat, persecute. SEE MAIN ENTRY
misemploy funds defalcate
misemployment abuse *(corrupt practice),* conversion *(misappropriation),* misapplication, misappropriation, misusage, misuse, waste
miserabilis deplorable, moving *(evoking emotion)*
miserable deplorable, disconsolate, lamentable, lugubrious, paltry, pessimistic, poor *(inferior in quality).* SEE MAIN ENTRY
misereri sympathize
miseria adversity
misericordia humanity *(humaneness),* pity
misericors humane
miserly illiberal, parsimonious, penurious
misery calamity, disaster, distress *(anguish),* pain, pessimism, prostration. SEE MAIN ENTRY
misesteem misjudge
misestimate distort, miscalculate, misconceive, misjudge, overestimate
misestimation misjudgment. SEE MAIN ENTRY
misexplain distort, misrepresent
misexplanation catachresis, distortion, misapplication
misexplication catachresis, misapplication
misexposition catachresis
misexpress distort
misfeasance bad faith, crime, delict, fault *(responsibility),* guilt, infringement, maladministration, misconduct, misdeed, misdemeanor, misdoing, misprision, offense, tort, transgression. SEE MAIN ENTRY
misfeasor convict, delinquent, lawbreaker
misfigured fallacious, incorrect, inexact
misfire miscarriage
misfit misjoinder
misfortunate unfavorable
misfortune adversity, calamity, casualty, catastrophe, debacle, detriment, disaster, failure *(lack of success),* fatality, hardship, harm, infliction, loss, plight, predicament, quagmire, tragedy, trouble. SEE MAIN ENTRY
misgive doubt *(distrust),* misdoubt, mistrust, suspect *(distrust)*

misgiving apprehension *(fear),* cloud *(suspicion),* disturbance, doubt *(indecision),* doubt *(suspicion),* expectation, fear, fright, incertitude, premonition, qualm, reluctance, scruple, stress *(strain),* suspicion *(mistrust).* SEE MAIN ENTRY
misgovern exploit *(take advantage of),* mismanage, mistreat. SEE MAIN ENTRY
misgovernment anarchy, lynch law, maladministration, malfeasance, misconduct, misrule
misguidance error, maladministration, misconduct, misrepresentation, misrule
misguide deceive, delude, dupe, ensnare, equivocate, fabricate *(make up),* illude, lie *(falsify),* misdirect, misgovern, misinform, mislabel, mislead, mismanage, misrepresent, misstate, palter, prevaricate. SEE MAIN ENTRY
misguided astray, ill-advised, inadvisable, injudicious, misadvised
mishandle abuse *(misuse),* exploit *(take advantage of),* ill use, maltreat, misemploy, misguide, mismanage, mistreat, persecute. SEE MAIN ENTRY
mishandling abuse *(corrupt practice),* abuse *(physical misuse),* maladministration, misapplication, misrule, misuse
mishap accident *(misfortune),* adversity, casualty, catastrophe, debacle, misfortune, quirk *(accident),* situation, tragedy. SEE MAIN ENTRY
misidentify mislabel, misread, mistake
misinform betray *(lead astray),* bilk, cloak, deceive, delude, distort, equivocate, fabricate *(make up),* hoodwink, illude, lie *(falsify),* misdirect, misguide, mislabel, mislead, misstate, palter, prevaricate. SEE MAIN ENTRY
misinformation distortion, false pretense, misstatement
misinformed misadvised
misinstruct distort, misdirect, misguide, misinform, mislead
misinstructed misadvised
misinstruction distortion, propaganda
misinterpret distort, err, misapprehend, misconceive, misconstrue, misjudge, misread, mistake, misunderstand, slant. SEE MAIN ENTRY
misinterpretation catachresis, distortion, error, fallacy, misapplication, misestimation, misjudgment. SEE MAIN ENTRY
misinterpreted inexact
misjoinder SEE MAIN ENTRY
misjoined incongruous
misjudge err, misapprehend, miscalculate, misconceive, misconstrue, misinterpret, misprize, mistake, misunderstand, overestimate, underestimate. SEE MAIN ENTRY
misjudged incorrect, inopportune, untimely
misjudging credulous
misjudgment catachresis, error, fallacy, fault *(mistake),* indiscretion, misapplication, miscue, misestimation, overstatement. SEE MAIN ENTRY
mislabel SEE MAIN ENTRY
mislaid lost *(taken away)*
mislay dislocate, disorient, lose *(be deprived of)*
mislead betray *(lead astray),* brutalize, circumvent, cloak, confound, confuse *(bewilder),* corrupt, deceive, defraud, delude, disorient, distort, divert, dupe, ensnare, equivocate, evade *(deceive),* fabricate *(make up),* fake, feign, hoodwink, illude, inveigle, lie *(falsify),* misdirect, misguide, misinform, mislabel, misrepresent, misstate, obscure, overreach, palter, pervert, pettifog, pretend, prevaricate. SEE MAIN ENTRY
misleader decoy
misleading assumed *(feigned),* deceptive, delusive, dishonest, disingenuous, equivocal, evasive, fallacious, false *(inaccurate),* fictitious, fraudulent, illusory, incorrect, lying, meretricious, ostensible, propaganda, sophistic, specious, untrue
misleading enlargement exaggeration
misleading notion fallacy
misled astray, misadvised
misled by deception blind *(not discerning)*
mislike disaffect
mismanage convert *(misappropriate),* exploit *(take advantage of),* fail *(neglect),* misemploy, misgovern, misguide, mistreat, muddle. SEE MAIN ENTRY
mismanagement abuse *(corrupt practice),* incompetence, maladministration, malfeasance, misapplication, misconduct, misdoing, misrule, misusage, misuse
mismark mislabel
mismatch conflict, incongruity, misjoinder
mismatched different, disproportionate, dissimilar, inapplicable, inapt, incommensurate, incongruous, inept *(inappropriate),* unrelated, unsuitable
mismated different, incongruous, opposite
misname mislabel
misnaming misnomer
misnomer SEE MAIN ENTRY
misperceive misunderstand
misplace dislocate, disorganize, disorient, lose *(be deprived of)*
misplaced anomalous, inapplicable, inappropriate, inapt, inept *(inappropriate),* lost *(taken away)*
misprint error
misprision contempt *(disdain),* crime, delict, delinquency *(failure of duty),* dereliction, guilt, misconduct, misdoing, neglect, nonfeasance, offense. SEE MAIN ENTRY
misprize contemn, depreciate, derogate, discount *(disbelieve),* disdain, disfavor, disparage, humiliate, minimize, underestimate. SEE MAIN ENTRY
mispronunciation misusage
misquotation catachresis, distortion, falsification, misrepresentation
misquote distort, falsify, misrepresent, slant
misread distort, misconstrue, misinterpret, misjudge, mistake, misunderstand. SEE MAIN ENTRY
misreading catachresis
misreckon distort, err, misapprehend, miscalculate, misconceive, misinterpret, misjudge, misunderstand
misreckoning error, misestimation
misrender palter, slant
misrendering catachresis, distortion
misreport bear false witness, distort, falsify, feign, misrepresent, misrepresentation, misstate, palter
misreported inaccurate, inexact
misrepresent cloak, deceive, delude, disguise, distort, equivocate, evade *(deceive),* fabricate *(make up),* fake, falsify, feign, invent *(falsify),* lie *(falsify),* misguide, misinform, misinterpret, mislabel, mislead, misrepresent, misstate, overestimate, palter, perjure, pervert, pretend, prevaricate, slant. SEE MAIN ENTRY
misrepresentation abuse *(corrupt practice),* artifice, bad faith, catachresis, color *(deceptive appearance),* deceit, deception, distortion, evasion, false pretense, falsehood, falsification, forgery, fraud, hoax, lie, misstatement, overstatement, perjury, pretense *(pretext),* pretext, sham, sophistry, story *(falsehood),* subreption, understatement. SEE MAIN ENTRY
misrepresentative evasive, fallacious, false *(not genuine),* fictitious, lying, mendacious
misrepresented assumed *(feigned),* mendacious, spurious
misrule anarchy, lynch law, maladministration, misemploy, misgovern, mismanage, mistreat, oppression. SEE MAIN ENTRY
miss fail *(neglect),* ignore, lack, lose *(be deprived of),* miscue, need, omit, overlook *(disregard),* pretermit, require *(need).* SEE MAIN ENTRY
miss an opportunity fail *(neglect)*
miss the mark fail *(lose)* SEE MAIN ENTRY
missend mismanage
misserved aggrieved *(victimized)*
misshape contort, deface, distort
misshapen blemished, repulsive
missile bomb
missing deficient, delinquent *(overdue),* devoid, insufficient, lost *(taken away),* truant, vacuous
missio release
mission agency *(legal relationship),* assignment *(task),* business *(affair),* business *(occupation),* calling, charge *(responsibility),* charge *(empower),* commitment *(responsibility),* delegation *(envoy),* deputation *(delegation),* design *(intent),* embassy, end *(intent),* function, goal, job, objective, occupation *(vocation),* purpose, role. SEE MAIN ENTRY
mission of the ambassador embassy
missive dispatch *(message),* note *(brief comment)*
missives correspondence *(communication by letters)*
misspend dissipate *(expend foolishly),* misemploy
misstate delude, equivocate, fabricate *(make up),* falsify, feign, invent *(falsify),* lie *(falsify),* misguide, misinform, mislabel, mislead, misrepresent, palter, prevaricate, slant. SEE MAIN ENTRY
misstated inaccurate, inexact, mendacious
misstatement abuse *(corrupt practice),* color *(deceptive appearance),* error, false pretense, falsehood, falsification, lie, miscue, misestimation, misrepresentation, overstatement, perjury, pretext, story *(falsehood).* SEE MAIN ENTRY
misstatement of fact misrepresentation. SEE MAIN ENTRY
misstep delinquency *(misconduct),* fault *(mistake),* indiscretion, lapse *(expiration),* lapse *(fall into error),* miscue. SEE MAIN ENTRY
missum facere discharge *(dismiss)*
mist obfuscate
mistakable uncertain *(ambiguous)*
mistake catachresis, defect, err, error, failure *(lack of success),* fallacy, indiscretion, lapse *(expiration),* misapplication, misapprehend, miscalculate, miscarriage, misconstrue, miscue, misdeed, misestimation, misinterpret, misjudge, misjudgment, misread, misstatement, misunderstand, oversight *(carelessness),* wrong. SEE MAIN ENTRY

mistake of the court injustice
mistaken errant, erroneous, fallacious, false *(inaccurate)*, faulty, illogical, improper, inaccurate, incorrect, misadvised, unsound *(fallacious)*. SEE MAIN ENTRY
mistaken belief error
mistaken idea fallacy
mistaken judgment error
misteach distort, misdirect, misguide, misinform, mislead, misrepresent
misterm misnomer
misthink misjudge
misticket mislabel
mistimed inauspicious, inopportune, premature, untimely
mistiness indistinctness
mistitle mislabel
mistranslate distort, misinterpret, misread
mistranslated inexact
mistranslation catachresis, distortion, error, misapplication
mistreat abuse *(misuse)*, abuse *(victimize)*, exploit *(take advantage of)*, ill use, maltreat, misemploy, persecute. SEE MAIN ENTRY
mistreatment abuse *(physical misuse)*, disservice, misuse, molestation, oppression, violation, wrong
mistrust apprehension *(fear)*, cloud *(suspicion)*, disbelieve, discount *(disbelieve)*, discredit, doubt *(suspicion)*, doubt *(distrust)*, incredulity, misdoubt, misgiving, qualm, rejection, suspect *(distrust)*. SEE MAIN ENTRY
mistrustful cynical, doubtful, incredulous, leery, resentful, suspicious *(distrustful)*
mistrustfulness cloud *(suspicion)*, doubt *(suspicion)*, incredulity, misgiving
mistrusting doubtful
misty inconspicuous, indistinct, opaque, unclear
misunderstand err, misapprehend, misconceive, misconstrue, misinterpret, misjudge, misread, mistake
misunderstanding argument *(contention)*, catachresis, conflict, difference, error, fault *(mistake)*, incompatibility *(difference)*, misapplication, miscue, misestimation, misjudgment, rift *(disagreement)*. SEE MAIN ENTRY
misunderstood vague
misusage abuse *(corrupt practice)*, abuse *(physical misuse)*, catachresis, distortion, misapplication, misappropriation, mischief, misuse, waste. SEE MAIN ENTRY
misuse abuse *(corrupt practice)*, conversion *(misappropriation)*, convert *(misappropriate)*, dissipate *(expend foolishly)*, embezzle, endanger, exploit *(take advantage of)*, exploitation, harass, harm, harrow, ill use, manipulate *(control unfairly)*, misapplication, misappropriation, misemploy, mishandle *(maltreat)*, mishandle *(mismanage)*, mismanage, mistreat, misusage, molest *(annoy)*, persecute, perversion, pervert, purloin, taint *(corrupt)*, violation, waste. SEE MAIN ENTRY
misuse entrusted monies defalcate
misuse of funds misapplication
misuse of power oppression
misuse of words distortion, error, misapplication
misused aggrieved *(harmed)*
misventure disaster
mite modicum
mitigare allay, assuage, extenuate, mitigate, mollify
mitigate abate *(lessen)*, adjust *(resolve)*, allay, alleviate, ameliorate, assuage, commute, curb, decrease, dilute, diminish, ease, extenuate, justify, lessen, lull, meliorate, moderate *(temper)*, modify *(moderate)*, mollify, obtund, palliate *(abate)*, relax, relieve *(free from burden)*, remedy, remit *(relax)*, soothe, subside. SEE MAIN ENTRY
mitigating narcotic, palliative *(abating)*. SEE MAIN ENTRY
mitigating circumstance justification
mitigating circumstances extenuating circumstances
mitigating factor SEE MAIN ENTRY
mitigatio mitigation
mitigation abatement *(reduction)*, decrease, diminution, excuse, extenuating circumstances, justification, moderation, mollification, relief *(release)*, remission, solace. SEE MAIN ENTRY
mitigative narcotic, palliative *(abating)*
mitiorem facere mitigate
mitis lenient
mittere cast *(throw)*, discharge *(shoot)*, dispatch *(send off)*, remit *(send payment)*, send
mittimus citation *(charge)*, commitment *(confinement)*. SEE MAIN ENTRY
mix agitate *(shake up)*, amalgamate, combine *(join together)*, commingle, conjoin, consolidate *(strengthen)*, consolidate *(unite)*, denature, desegregate, diffuse, incorporate *(include)*, integration *(amalgamation)*, intersperse, join *(bring together)*, merge, pool, solution *(substance)*, unite. SEE MAIN ENTRY
mix together commingle
mix up agitate *(shake up)*, confuse *(bewilder)*, confuse *(create disorder)*, discompose, disrupt, muddle, obfuscate, perplex
mix-up embroilment, entanglement *(confusion)*
mixed composite, compound, conglomerate, conjoint, dissimilar, diverse, heterogeneous, inextricable, joint, miscellaneous, multifarious, multiple, nonsectarian, promiscuous. SEE MAIN ENTRY
mixed up labyrinthine
mixing concrescence
mixture coalescence, coalition, consolidation, diversity, incorporation *(blend)*, melange, merger, solution *(substance)*
mixup pandemonium
mnemonic reminder
mnemonic device reminder
moan deplore, plaint
mob assemblage, mass *(body of persons)*
mob law anarchy
mob rule anarchy, lynch law
mob swayer demagogue
mobile moving *(in motion)*, protean
mobilis movable, volatile
mobilization campaign
mobilize call *(summon)*, consolidate *(unite)*, convene, dispatch *(send off)*, employ *(make use of)*, impel
mobilized ready *(prepared)*
mobocracy lynch law
mobster hoodlum, racketeer
mock copy, deceptive, delusive, disdain, disgrace, disparage, false *(not genuine)*, flout, harass, humiliate, illude, imitation, jape, jeer, meretricious, misrepresent, pillory, pose *(impersonate)*, quasi, sham, simulate, spurious, synthetic, untrue. SEE MAIN ENTRY
mockery caricature, dishonor *(shame)*, disparagement, disrespect, falsification, irony, parody, pretense *(ostentation)*, ridicule, travesty
mocking caustic, cynical, disdainful
mode avenue *(means of attainment)*, conduit *(channel)*, course, form *(arrangement)*, habit, instrumentality, manner *(behavior)*, means *(opportunity)*, method, modus operandi, parlance, practice *(custom)*, practice *(procedure)*, procedure, style, tenor, usage, way *(channel)*. SEE MAIN ENTRY
mode of action behavior, conduct
mode of behavior conduct
mode of communication forum *(medium)*
mode of expression context, phraseology
mode of living modus vivendi
mode of management course, policy *(plan of action)*, practice *(procedure)*, system
mode of operation avenue *(means of attainment)*, modus operandi, procedure, process *(course)*, strategy. SEE MAIN ENTRY
mode of procedure course, expedient, maneuver *(tactic)*, modus operandi, practice *(custom)*
mode of proceeding manner *(behavior)*
mode of reasoning dialectic
mode of speech phraseology
mode of use procedure
model absolute *(ideal)*, build *(construct)*, case *(example)*, code, copy, criterion, design *(construction plan)*, epitome, example, exemplar, exemplary, forge *(produce)*, form *(arrangement)*, illustration, instance, laudable, make, norm, paradigm, paragon, paramount, pattern, precedent, principle *(axiom)*, professional *(stellar)*, prototype, representative *(example)*, rule *(guide)*, sample, specimen, standard, style, symbol, typical. SEE MAIN ENTRY
model after mock *(imitate)*
model instance precedent
model of virtue paragon
model oneself after pose *(impersonate)*
moderari control *(regulate)*, modify *(moderate)*
moderate adjust *(regulate)*, allay, alleviate, alter, arbitrate *(conciliate)*, assuage, average *(standard)*, controlled *(restrained)*, curb, de minimus, ease, extenuate, fair *(satisfactory)*, imperfect, intercede, intermediate, judge, judicious, lenient, lessen, marginal, mediate, mediocre, minimal, mitigate, mollify, negligible, nominal, nonpartisan, obtund, officiate, palliate *(abate)*, passable, peaceable, regulate *(adjust)*, relax, relieve *(free from burden)*, remit *(relax)*, restrain, soothe, subdue, subside, usual. SEE MAIN ENTRY
moderate in severity mitigate
moderated qualified *(conditioned)*, tempered
moderately good fair *(satisfactory)*
moderately large major
moderateness continence, moderation, neutrality, temperance
moderatio control *(supervision)*, restraint, temperance
moderation composure, continence, control *(restriction)*, lenience, mitigation, regulation *(management)*, remission, restraint, temperance. SEE MAIN ENTRY
moderatism moderation
moderator arbiter, arbitrator, chairman, go-between, intermediary, judge, magistrate

moderator procurator
moderator referee, umpire
modern contemporary, novel, present *(current)*, progressive *(advocating change)*, sophisticated, unprecedented, unusual. SEE MAIN ENTRY
modernist pioneer
modernization development *(progression)*, innovation, renewal
modernize meliorate, modify *(alter)*, reconstruct, renew *(refurbish)*, renovate
modest de minimus, diffident, inconsiderable, inconspicuous, insubstantial, marginal, mediocre, minimal, minor, negligible, nominal, paltry, slight, unaffected *(sincere)*, unobtrusive, unpretentious. SEE MAIN ENTRY
modestly fairly *(moderately)*
modesty decorum, propriety *(correctness)*
modicum minimum, paucity, scintilla. SEE MAIN ENTRY
modicus reasonable *(fair)*, unpretentious
modifiable ambulatory, open-ended, pliable, protean, provisional, variable
modification abatement *(reduction)*, amendment *(correction)*, correction *(change)*, curtailment, innovation, qualification *(condition)*, transition, treatment. SEE MAIN ENTRY
modification of the law amendment *(legislation)*
modifications vicissitudes
modificatory restrictive
modified qualified *(conditioned)*, tempered
modified by conditions conditional, dependent
modify abate *(lessen)*, adapt, alter, amend, change, convert *(change use)*, influence, moderate *(temper)*, qualify *(condition)*, reform, relax, restrict, revise, transform, treat *(process)*, vary. SEE MAIN ENTRY
modify by excisions delete, edit
modify sentence commute
modifying mitigating, palliative *(abating)*, restrictive
modifying cause catalyst
modulate adapt, alleviate, alter, change, lessen, limit, obtund, palliate *(abate)*, regulate *(adjust)*, relax
modulation inflection, remission
modulatory palliative *(abating)*
module entity
modus kind, method, mode, moderation, restriction, style
modus operandi course
modus operandi procedure. SEE MAIN ENTRY
modus vivendi SEE MAIN ENTRY
moiety segment. SEE MAIN ENTRY
moil commotion
mold character *(personal quality)*, delineate, disposition *(inclination)*, fabricate *(construct)*, facsimile, forge *(produce)*, form, frame *(construct)*, influence, make, manufacture, militate, model, norm, nurture, organize *(unionize)*, pattern, prototype, resemblance. SEE MAIN ENTRY
moldable facile, flexible, malleable, pliable, pliant, sequacious
molded together inseparable
molder decay
moldering decadent
molding creation, edge *(border)*, facsimile, manufacture
moldy stale
moles bulk
molest abuse *(victimize)*, brutalize, debauch, distress, disturb, endanger, harrow, hector, irritate, misemploy, mishandle *(maltreat)*, mistreat, pique, plague, press *(goad)*. SEE MAIN ENTRY
molestation abuse *(physical misuse)*, disturbance, mischief, nuisance. SEE MAIN ENTRY
moleste ferre resent
molestia dissatisfaction
molestus irksome, oppressive
mollification reconciliation. SEE MAIN ENTRY
mollify allay, assuage, disarm *(set at ease)*, mitigate, moderate *(temper)*, modify *(moderate)*, pacify, placate, propitiate, reconcile, remedy, soothe, subdue. SEE MAIN ENTRY
mollifying palliative *(abating)*
mollire mollify
molliri relent
mollis malleable, pliant, resilient, sensitive *(easily affected)*, susceptible *(responsive)*
Molotov cocktail bomb
moment date, degree *(magnitude)*, emphasis, import, importance, interest *(concern)*, occasion, phase *(period)*, point *(period of time)*, significance, weight *(importance)*. SEE MAIN ENTRY
moment of change landmark *(significant change)*
momentarily pro tempore
momentariness insignificance
momentary brief, ephemeral, immediate *(imminent)*, pending *(imminent)*, temporary, transient, transitory, volatile
momentous cardinal *(outstanding)*, consequential *(substantial)*, considerable, critical *(crucial)*, crucial, decisive, important *(significant)*, key, major, material *(important)*, notable, noteworthy, remarkable, serious *(grave)*, stellar, strategic. SEE MAIN ENTRY
momentousness importance, magnitude, materiality *(consequence)*, significance
momentum headway, impetus. SEE MAIN ENTRY
momentum importance, stress *(strain)*
momumental notable
monad individual, unit *(item)*
monarchy realm
monas individual
monens hortative
monere admonish *(warn)*, caution
moneta currency
monetary commercial, financial, fiscal, mercantile, pecuniary. SEE MAIN ENTRY
monetary benefit interest *(profit)*
monetary clause ad damnum clause
monetary exchange commerce
monetary gain interest *(profit)*
monetary help maintenance *(support of spouse)*
monetary remuneration compensation, indemnification
monetary reservoir bank
monetary return pay
monetary theory finance
monetary unit cash
monetary value expense *(cost)*
money assets, capital, cash, currency, finance, payment *(remittance)*, possession *(property)*, principal *(capital sum)*, remuneration, substance *(material possessions)*. SEE MAIN ENTRY
money back refund
money box bank
money chest coffer
money coming in income, proceeds
money conscious mercenary, provident *(frugal)*
money dealings finance
money due debt, setoff
money earned earnings
money expended cost *(expenses)*, expenditure, expense *(cost)*, overhead
money going out disbursement *(funds paid out)*
money hungry mercenary
money illegally acquired graft
money in actual use currency
money in bank deposit
money invested security *(stock)*
money matters finance
money order check *(instrument)*, draft, note *(written promise to pay)*
money owed debt
money paid collection *(payment)*
money paid for passage fare
money saving economic
money sent remittance
money's worth tariff *(bill)*
money-conscious economical
money-making finance, gainful, profitable
money-saving economical
moneyed opulent, prosperous, solvent
moneyless bankrupt, destitute, insolvent, poor *(underprivileged)*
moneylessness poverty
moneymaking lucrative
moneys cash
moneys borrowed loan
moneys expended disbursement *(funds paid out)*
moneys paid out disbursement *(funds paid out)*
monger broker, dealer, merchant, vendor
monitio premonition
monition admonition, caution *(warning)*, caveat, citation *(charge)*, deterrence, deterrent, dispatch *(message)*, guidance, indication, intelligence *(news)*, notice *(warning)*, notification, symptom, warning. SEE MAIN ENTRY
monitor audit, bystander, chairman, check *(inspect)*, examine *(study)*, overhear, patrol, proctor, procurator, superintendent, symptom. SEE MAIN ENTRY
monitorial hortative, prophetic
monitory informatory, ominous, portentous *(ominous)*, presageful, prophetic
monitum premonition
monitus warning
monocratic dictatorial
monohemerous temporary
monolithical solid *(compact)*
monologue peroration
monomachy contest *(dispute)*
monomania obsession
monomaniac bigot
monopolistic organization trust *(combination of businesses)*
monopolium monopoly
monopolize immerse *(engross)*, occupy *(engage)*, possess. SEE MAIN ENTRY
monopolize the thoughts occupy *(engage)*
monopoly consortium *(business cartel)*, exclusion, franchise *(license)*, trust *(combination of businesses)*. SEE MAIN ENTRY
monosyllabic inarticulate
monotone prosaic
monotonous insistent, jejune *(dull)*, lifeless *(dull)*, pedestrian, ponderous, prolix, prosaic, repeated, repetitious, stale, usual

monster prodigious *(enormous)*
monstrosity atrocity
monstrous arrant *(onerous)*, bad *(offensive)*, delinquent *(guilty of a misdeed)*, diabolic, flagrant, gross *(flagrant)*, heinous, inexcusable, inordinate, malignant, nefarious, odious, offensive *(offending)*, outrageous, prodigious *(enormous)*, reprehensible, repulsive, unconscionable. SEE MAIN ENTRY
monstrousness bestiality, disrepute
monument landmark *(conspicuous object)*, remembrance *(commemoration)*. SEE MAIN ENTRY
monumental noteworthy, prodigious *(enormous)*, remarkable. SEE MAIN ENTRY
monumentum monument
mood atmosphere, climate, disposition *(inclination)*, emotion, spirit, state *(condition)*, tenor
moodish fractious
moody despondent, disconsolate, fractious, froward, inconsistent, petulant, resentful, restive
moonshiner bootlegger
moored firm, stable
moot debate, dubious, equivocal, pose *(propound)*, posit, problematic, propound, undecided. SEE MAIN ENTRY
moot point problem, thesis
mope brood
mora check *(bar)*, delay
moral blameless, clean, conscientious, ethical, high-minded, honest, incorruptible, just, law-abiding, meritorious, proper, reputable, scrupulous, signification, upright. SEE MAIN ENTRY
moral behavior ethics
moral certainty certitude
moral compulsion coercion
moral conduct ethics
moral consciousness conscience, responsibility *(conscience)*
moral degeneracy bad repute
moral excellence principle *(virtue)*, probity
moral faculty conscience, responsibility *(conscience)*
moral insensibility brutality
moral judgment ethics
moral necessity duty *(obligation)*
moral obligation allegiance, conscience, duty *(obligation)*, ethics, responsibility *(conscience)*
moral philosophy ethics
moral practice ethics
moral principles conscience, ethics
moral qualities character *(personal quality)*
moral rectitude ethics, honor *(good reputation)*, principle *(virtue)*. SEE MAIN ENTRY
moral responsibility obligation *(duty)*
moral science casuistry
moral sense conscience, responsibility *(conscience)*
moral soundness integrity
moral strength ethics, integrity
moral tone ethics
moral turpitude bad repute
moral weakness foible
morale confidence *(faith)*
moralis ethical
moralism maxim
morality ethics, integrity, principle *(virtue)*, probity, propriety *(correctness)*, rectitude, responsibility *(conscience)*, right *(righteousness)*. SEE MAIN ENTRY
morally fairly *(impartially)*
morally abandoned reprobate
morally evil profligate *(corrupt)*
morally impure lewd
morally unrestrained lewd
morals conduct, ethics, probity, right *(righteousness)*
morari pause
moratorium adjournment, cancellation, cessation *(interlude)*, deferment, delay, discontinuance *(interruption of a legal action)*, extension *(postponement)*, hiatus, pause, pendency, reprieve. SEE MAIN ENTRY
moratory late *(tardy)*
morbid malignant, ominous, peccant *(unhealthy)*, pessimistic, pestilent
morbidly meditate brood
morbiferous deleterious, malignant, pernicious, pestilent
morbific deleterious, harmful, insalubrious, malignant, peccant *(unhealthy)*, pernicious, pestilent
morbifical insalubrious, malignant, pestilent
morbus disease
mordacious caustic, harsh, incisive, malignant, scathing, virulent. SEE MAIN ENTRY
mordant astringent, bitter *(penetrating)*, harsh, incisive, mordacious, severe, trenchant
mordax caustic, cynical, incisive, scathing
mordent caustic
more additional, ancillary *(auxiliary)*
more advantageous preferable
more desirable preferable
more elevated superior *(higher)*
more in demand preferable
more or less inexact, on or about
more pleasing preferable
more popular preferable
more select preferable
more than due overdue
more than enough copious, excess, superfluous
more than half majority *(greater part)*
more than one multiple, several *(plural)*
more than one can tell innumerable
more than sufficient superfluous
more time extension *(postponement)*
morem gerere comply
moreover also
mores behavior, character *(personal quality)*
mores decorum
mori die
moribund decadent, in extremis
moronic fatuous, non compos mentis, obtuse, opaque
morose disconsolate, lugubrious, pessimistic
morosis incapacity
morosus fractious
morsel iota, minimum
mortal character *(an individual)*, conscious *(awake)*, deadly, ephemeral, lethal, live *(conscious)*, pernicious, person, pestilent. SEE MAIN ENTRY
mortal body person
mortal remains corpse
mortalis person
mortalitas mortality
mortality death, demise *(death)*, fatality. SEE MAIN ENTRY
mortalness mortality
mortals humanity *(mankind)*
mortar cement
mortem obire die
mortgage cloud *(incumbrance)*, encumber *(financially obligate)*, encumbrance, hypothecation, pawn. SEE MAIN ENTRY
mortgage holder obligee
mortgaged fully secured
mortgagee creditor, obligee
mortgagor debtor, obligor
mortgatee backer
mortifer deadly, lethal
mortiferous deadly, fatal, insalubrious, lethal
mortification disgrace, embarrassment, ignominy
mortify badger, demean *(make lower)*, discompose, disgrace, embarrass, humiliate, offend *(insult)*, plague. SEE MAIN ENTRY
mortuus dead, defunct
mos habit, practice *(procedure)*, usage
mosaic composite, compound, miscellaneous
most majority *(greater part)*, maximum *(pinnacle)*, utmost. SEE MAIN ENTRY
most carefully selected group elite
most complete definitive
most considerable principal
most desirable best
most distant extreme *(last)*, ultimate
most eminent superlative
most excellent best
most frequently as a rule, generally
most important cardinal *(outstanding)*, master, principal
most important character protagonist
most important point emphasis
most influential leading *(ranking first)*
most often as a rule, generally
most powerful principal, sovereign *(absolute)*
most precise definitive
most recent last *(preceding)*
most remote extreme *(last)*, ultimate
mostly as a rule, purely *(simply)*, quasi
mot catchword
mote minimum
mother parents
mother country home *(place of origin)*
motherhood maternity
motherland home *(place of origin)*
motherliness maternity
motif content *(meaning)*, subject *(topic)*. SEE MAIN ENTRY
motile moving *(in motion)*
motion application, call *(appeal)*, campaign, circulation, course, overture, petition, prayer, procedure, proposal *(suggestion)*, recommendation, request, suggestion, transition. SEE MAIN ENTRY
motion docket calendar *(list of cases)*
motion in limine SEE MAIN ENTRY
motionless firm, idle, inactive, indolent, otiose, placid, rigid, stable, stagnant, static, torpid
motionlessness inaction, inertia
motivate cause, coax, evoke, further, impel, induce, influence, inspire, lobby, originate, persuade, prevail *(persuade)*, prevail upon, prompt, provoke, spirit, stimulate, urge. SEE MAIN ENTRY
motivated by a desire for money mercenary
motivated by greed mercenary
motivating provocative
motivating force catalyst, stimulus
motivating idea end *(intent)*, purpose
motivation catalyst, cause *(reason)*, determinant, end *(intent)*, impulse, incentive, instigation, origination, persuasion, provocation, rationale, reason *(basis)*
motivator abettor
motive animus, basis, cause *(reason)*, design *(intent)*, desire, determinant, end

(intent), ground, impetus, impulse, incentive, intent, moving *(in motion)*, origination, point *(purpose)*, provocation, purpose, rationale, reason *(basis)*, source, stimulus, target. SEE MAIN ENTRY
motiveless arbitrary and capricious
motley composite, compound, diverse, heterogeneous, miscellaneous, multifarious
motor road causeway
motorway causeway
motto expression *(comment)*, phrase
motus commotion, disturbance, insurrection, mutiny, rebellion, revolt, sedition
moulder degenerate
mouldering dilapidated
mount accrue *(increase)*, increase, originate, progress
mount guard protect
mounted accrued
mourn deplore, repent
mourn for regret
mourn with sympathize
mournful despondent, disconsolate, lamentable, lugubrious, querulous, solemn
mourning disconsolate
mouth entrance, enunciate, express, phrase, recite, utter
mouthpiece medium, protagonist, spokesman. SEE MAIN ENTRY
mouthy flatulent, fustian, inflated *(bombastic)*
movable ambulatory, amenable, disposable, open *(persuasible)*, pliant, possession *(property)*, protean, receptive, suasible, susceptible *(responsive)*. SEE MAIN ENTRY
movable article of property chattel
movable property effects
movables chattel, commodities, merchandise, paraphernalia *(personal belongings)*, possessions, property *(possessions)*
movant petitioner
move act *(undertaking)*, carry *(transport)*, constrain *(compel)*, dislocate, displace *(remove)*, further, impress *(affect deeply)*, incite, influence, inspire, interest, maneuver *(tactic)*, maneuver, motivate, operate, operation, persuade, pose *(propound)*, prevail *(persuade)*, prevail upon, proffer, prompt, propose, propound, provoke, reach, reason *(persuade)*, recommend, remove *(transfer)*, spirit, step, stimulate, transport, undertaking *(enterprise)*, urge, vacate *(leave)*, venture. SEE MAIN ENTRY
move across cross *(intersect)*
move ahead continue *(persevere)*, endure *(last)*, keep *(continue)*, proceed *(go forward)*, progress, resume
move aimlessly loiter
move at an accelerated rate of speed race
move away part *(leave)*, quit *(evacuate)*
move back ebb, retreat
move backward regress
move by persuasion prevail upon
move fast hasten
move forward gain, impel, proceed *(go forward)*
move furtively lurk
move in waves fluctuate, oscillate
move into occupy *(take possession)*
move near approach
move off abandon *(physically leave)*
move on dispatch *(send off)*, leave *(depart)*, progress
move onward progress
move out evacuate, move *(alter position)*, part *(leave)*, vacate *(leave)*
move quickly hasten
move secretly prowl
move speedily hasten
move strongly impress *(affect deeply)*
move to locate
move to action constrain *(compel)*, motivate, stimulate
move to and fro oscillate, vacillate
move to anger provoke
move toward approach, border *(approach)*, gravitate
move under cover prowl
move up expedite, prefer, promote *(advance)*, raise *(advance)*
move up and down beat *(pulsate)*
moveant applicant *(petitioner)*
moved inclined
movement activity, band, campaign, circulation, course, denomination, dispatch *(promptness)*, operation, outflow, progress, transition, transmittal. SEE MAIN ENTRY
movement forward progress
movement of population immigration
movement toward adulthood growth *(evolution)*
movement toward maturity growth *(evolution)*
mover advocate *(counselor)*, catalyst, special interest
movere impress *(affect deeply)*, influence
moving convincing, eloquent, impulsive *(impelling)*, incisive, itinerant, persuasive, potent, prevailing *(having superior force)*, profound *(intense)*, progressive *(going forward)*, sensitive *(easily affected)*. SEE MAIN ENTRY
moving cause motive
moving force impetus
moving power motive
moving spirit catalyst, motive
movingly expressive eloquent
mow down obliterate
much innumerable. SEE MAIN ENTRY
much the same approximate, comparable *(capable of comparison)*, pendent
much touted renowned
much used trite
muchness quantity
muck pollute
muckrake disapprove *(condemn)*, expose. SEE MAIN ENTRY
muckraking disparagement
mucky sordid
muddle blind *(obscure)*, complex *(entanglement)*, confound, confuse *(bewilder)*, confuse *(create disorder)*, confusion *(turmoil)*, discompose, disorder *(lack of order)*, disorganize, disorient, embroilment, imbroglio, obfuscate, perplex, plight, quagmire, turmoil. SEE MAIN ENTRY
muddled complex, labyrinthine
muddleheaded opaque
muddy opaque, pollute, unclear
muffle cloak, disguise, repress, shroud, stifle, subdue, suppress
muffled covert, indistinct
muffler damper *(stopper)*
mug assail
mulcere soothe
mulct bilk, deceive, defraud, deprive, dupe, exact, fine *(noun)*, fine *(verb)*, forfeiture *(thing forfeited)*, peculate, penalize, punishment, seize *(confiscate)*, steal, trover. SEE MAIN ENTRY
mulctuary penal, punitive
mulish inflexible, intractable, obdurate, pertinacious, recalcitrant, restive, uncontrollable
mull muse
mull over brood, consider, deliberate, ponder, reflect *(ponder)*, review, study, weigh. SEE MAIN ENTRY
multa fine, penalty
multare fine, sentence
multifarious composite, compound, diverse, manifold, miscellaneous, multifold, multiple. SEE MAIN ENTRY
multifariousness difference, diversification, diversity
multifold manifold, multiple. SEE MAIN ENTRY
multiform compound, dissimilar, diverse, heterogeneous, manifold, miscellaneous, multifarious, multifold, protean
multiformity diversification, diversity
multigenerous multifarious, multifold
multilateral trade commerce
multiloquent voluble
multipartite bicameral
multiphase protean
multiple composite, compound, manifold, multifold, repeated. SEE MAIN ENTRY
multiplex complex, complex *(entanglement)*, composite, compound, manifold
multiplex miscellaneous, multifarious, multifold, multiple
multiplicare proliferate
multiplicate manifold, multifold
multiplication accession *(enlargement)*, growth *(increase)*
multiplicity diversity, quantity. SEE MAIN ENTRY
multiplied accrued
multiply accrue *(increase)*, accumulate *(enlarge)*, bear *(yield)*, compound, enlarge, expand, heighten *(augment)*, increase, proliferate, propagate *(increase)*, pullulate, reproduce. SEE MAIN ENTRY
multiplying cumulative *(increasing)*, cumulative *(intensifying)*
multipotent influential, powerful
multisyllabic sesquipedalian
multitude assemblage, assembly, body *(collection)*, collection *(assembly)*, conglomeration, congregation, mass *(body of persons)*, plurality, populace, quantity. SEE MAIN ENTRY
multitudinary profuse
multitudinous innumerable, manifold, multifold, multiple, multiplicity, myriad, populous, profuse, rife
multitudinousness quantity
multitudo mass *(body of persons)*, plurality
mum laconic, speechless, taciturn, unresponsive
mummery parody
mundane civil *(public)*, material *(physical)*, physical, profane, prosaic. SEE MAIN ENTRY
mundivagant moving *(in motion)*
mundus clean
munerari present *(make a gift)*
municipal civic, civil *(public)*, local, public *(affecting people)*
municipal code ordinance
municipal regulation bylaw, ordinance
municipality city, community
municipalization condemnation *(seizure)*
municipalize condemn *(seize)*
munificence benevolence *(disposition to do good)*, charity, donation, goodwill, largess *(generosity)*, philanthropy
munificent benevolent, charitable *(benevolent)*, liberal *(generous)*, nonprofit, philanthropic, profuse. SEE MAIN ENTRY

munificus liberal *(generous)*
muniment ammunition, certificate, charter *(license),* form *(document)*
muniments deed
munimentum safeguard
munition ammunition, gun
munitions bomb, weapons
munus calling, department, duty *(obligation),* function, gift *(present),* office, post
munus obire discharge *(perform)*
murder assassination, destroy *(efface),* dispatch *(act of putting to death),* dispatch *(put to death),* extinguish, homicide, killing, manslaughter, slay. SEE MAIN ENTRY
murder by stealth assassination
murder victim corpse
murderer criminal, lawbreaker SEE MAIN ENTRY
murderous deadly, diabolic, fatal, lethal, malignant, pernicious, pestilent, ruthless, sinister
murderous assault killing
mure detain *(hold in custody)*
murkiness indistinctness
murky obscure *(faint),* privy, unclear
murmur speak
muscle sinew, strength
muscular powerful
muse brood, concentrate *(pay attention),* consider, digest *(comprehend),* observe *(remark),* ponder, reflect *(ponder),* speculate *(conjecture),* study. SEE MAIN ENTRY
museful cogitative, pensive
mushroom proliferate
musing contemplation, hindsight, introspection, pensive, preoccupation, reflection *(thought)*
must requirement, requisite
must-carry rules SEE MAIN ENTRY
muster call *(summon),* collect *(gather),* collection *(assembly),* convene, garner, levy, marshal, meet, raise *(collect),* recruit, rendezvous *(noun),* rendezvous *(verb),* roll
muster up call *(summon)*
mustering company *(assemblage)*
musty stale
mutabilis mutable
mutabilitas inconsistency
mutability irregularity
mutable aleatory *(uncertain),* ambulatory, convertible, faithless, inconsistent, irresolute, noncommittal, pliable, protean, unpredictable, unsettled. SEE MAIN ENTRY
mutare alter, innovation, modify *(alter),* vary
mutate convert *(change use),* transform, vary
mute inarticulate, moderate *(temper),* repress, speechless, stifle, subdue, taciturn, unresponsive. SEE MAIN ENTRY
mutilare mutilate
mutilate damage, deface, destroy *(efface),* disable, harm, maim, spoil *(impair).* SEE MAIN ENTRY
mutilated broken *(fractured),* defective, imperfect, marred
mutilation defacement, defect, detriment, harm
mutineer insurgent, malcontent
mutineering disloyalty, insurrection
mutinous contumacious, disobedient, disorderly, insubordinate, irresponsible, lawless, radical *(favoring drastic change),* recalcitrant, renitent, restive, unruly
mutinousness disloyalty, outbreak
mutiny defect, defiance, defy, desertion, disloyalty, disobey, infidelity, insurrection, outbreak, rebel, rebellion, resistance, revolt, secede, sedition, treason. SEE MAIN ENTRY
mutter speak
mutual cognate, collective, common *(shared),* concordant, correlative, joint, reciprocal, related. SEE MAIN ENTRY
mutual accord conciliation
mutual agreement arrangement *(understanding),* bargain, composition *(agreement in bankruptcy),* conciliation, consensus, contract, indenture, pact, policy *(contract),* quid pro quo. SEE MAIN ENTRY
mutual appreciation rapport
mutual assent agreement *(concurrence),* arrangement *(understanding)*
mutual assistance coaction, concert
mutual attraction affection
mutual aversion feud
mutual company partnership
mutual concern coalition
mutual concession adjustment, composition *(agreement in bankruptcy),* compromise, conciliation
mutual consideration comity, quid pro quo
mutual dependence mutuality
mutual exchange interview
mutual exclusiveness antithesis, difference
mutual forgiveness reconciliation
mutual friendliness rapprochement
mutual intercourse contact *(association)*
mutual ownership pool
mutual pledge agreement *(contract),* bargain, compact, contract, pact, understanding *(agreement)*
mutual profit boom *(prosperity)*
mutual promise agreement *(concurrence),* arrangement *(understanding),* compact, contract, mutual understanding, pact
mutual relation mutuality
mutual relationship privity
mutual respect comity
mutual sympathy consensus
mutual transfer assignment *(transfer of ownership),* delivery
mutual understanding accommodation *(adjustment),* accord, adjustment, agreement *(concurrence),* bargain, cartel, compatibility, conciliation, consensus, covenant, quid pro quo. SEE MAIN ENTRY
mutual undertaking arrangement *(understanding),* bargain, contract, indenture, league, policy *(contract)*
mutuality coaction, rapport, rapprochement, reciprocity, relation *(connection),* relationship *(connection).* SEE MAIN ENTRY
mutuality of interest privity
mutually agreeable consensual
mutually agreed concerted
mutually assent agree *(contract)*
mutually opposed opposite
mutually related correlative
mutually understood consensual
mutuari borrow
mutus mute, speechless
mutuum loan
mutuus mutual *(reciprocal),* reciprocal
muzzle constraint *(restriction),* curb, disadvantage, disarm *(divest of arms),* discipline *(control),* hamper, inhibit, prevent, repress, restrict, stifle, strangle, withhold
myriad innumerable, manifold, multiple, profuse. SEE MAIN ENTRY
myriads quantity
mysterious covert, elusive, enigmatic, esoteric, evasive, furtive, hidden, inapprehensible, incomprehensible, indefinable, indefinite, indistinct, ineffable, inexplicable, inscrutable, obscure *(abstruse),* oracular, peculiar *(curious),* private *(confidential),* privy, problematic, recondite, secret, surreptitious, uncanny, uncertain *(ambiguous),* undisclosed, vague. SEE MAIN ENTRY
mysteriousness indistinctness
mystery enigma, problem, question *(issue),* secret. SEE MAIN ENTRY
mystic covert, esoteric, hidden, inapprehensible, incomprehensible, inexplicable, mysterious, recondite
mystical covert, esoteric, hidden, inapprehensible, incomprehensible, inexplicable, mysterious, oracular, recondite, sacrosanct. SEE MAIN ENTRY
mysticism mystery
mystification confusion *(ambiguity)*
mystified incognizant, lost *(disoriented)*
mystify confound, confuse *(bewilder),* delude, disorient, elude, equivocate, hoodwink, obfuscate, perplex
mystifying enigmatic, labyrinthine, mysterious, peculiar *(curious),* uncanny, uncertain *(ambiguous)*
myth fiction, figment, story *(falsehood).* SEE MAIN ENTRY
mythic fictitious, illusory
mythical fictitious. SEE MAIN ENTRY
mythological fictitious, illusory

N

nafarius heinous
nag annoy, bicker, browbeat, hector, importune, irritate, obsess, plague, request
nagging critical (faultfinding), petulant, querulous
naive credulous, inexperienced, ingenuous, puerile, unaccustomed, unaffected (sincere), unsuspecting. SEE MAIN ENTRY
naiveness credulity
naivete credulity, nescience
naked manifest, perceivable, perceptible. SEE MAIN ENTRY
name appoint, assign *(designate),* bear *(adduce),* call *(title),* call *(title),* character *(reputation),* cite *(state),* classify, cognomen, define, delegate, denominate, denomination, denounce *(inform against),* designate, designation *(symbol),* distinction (reputation), elect (choose), identify, induct, instate, invest *(vest),* label, mention, nominate, notoriety, phrase, pigeonhole, prestige, reputation, select, specify, stipulate, term *(expression),* title *(designation).* SEE MAIN ENTRY
name expressly enumerate
name for office nominate
name inaccurately mistake
name incorrectly mislabel
name one by one enumerate
name to fill an appointment delegate
named aforesaid, before mentioned, said, select. SEE MAIN ENTRY
named representative nominee *(candidate),* officer
nameless anonymous, ineffable
namely a savoir
namesake call *(title)*
naming appointment *(act of designating),* call *(title),* nomination, selection *(choice)*
nancisci obtain
narcissism pride
narcissistic orgulous
narcotic cannabis. see main entry

narcotic preparation drug
narcotic substance drug
narcotical narcotic
narcotize drug
narrare narrative
narrate communicate, convey *(communicate)*, detail *(particularize)*, inform *(notify)*, recite, recount, relate (tell)
narratio account *(report)*, narration, recital, story (narrative)
narration account *(report)*, recital, report (detailed account), representation *(statement)*, story *(narrative)*. SEE MAIN ENTRY
narrative description, descriptive, journal, narration, recital, representation *(statement)*, scenario, statement. SEE MAIN ENTRY
narrator informant
narrow attenuate, constrict *(compress)*, decrease, illiberal, limit, limited, minimal, moderate *(temper)*, one-sided, parochial, partial *(part)*, precise, provincial, qualify *(condition)*, reduce, restrict, restrictive, specialize, specific, tenuous, uncompromising. SEE MAIN ENTRY
narrow means indigence, poverty, privation
narrow reading SEE MAIN ENTRY
narrow search indagation, inquiry *(systematic investigation)*
narrow-minded dogmatic, illiberal, narrow, one-sided, parochial, partial *(biased)*, provincial, unbending
narrow-minded person pedant
narrow-mindedness intolerance, prejudice *(preconception)*
narrowing centralization, decrease
narrowly tailored SEE MAIN ENTRY
narrowness intolerance
nascence nascency
nascency birth *(beginning)*, origin *(source)*, origination. SEE MAIN ENTRY
nascent inchoate, incipient, initial, original *(initial)*, primary. SEE MAIN ENTRY
nastiness mischief
nasty bad *(offensive)*, bitter *(penetrating)*, harmful, heinous, loathsome, malignant, objectionable, obnoxious, odious, offensive *(offending)*, perverse, repulsive, severe, unsavory, vicious
nasty blow disaster
natal native *(inborn)*, original *(initial)*
nation nationality, polity, populace, population, public, state *(political unit)*. SEE MAIN ENTRY
national domestic *(indigenous)*, federal, public *(affecting people)*. SEE MAIN ENTRY
national culture civilization
national group nationality
national status nationality
nationality blood, polity. SEE MAIN ENTRY
nationalization condemnation *(seizure)*
nationalize condemn *(seize)*, naturalize *(make a citizen)*. SEE MAIN ENTRY
nationwide public *(affecting people)*
native born *(innate)*, citizen, domestic *(indigenous)*, domiciliary, hereditary, inhabitant, inherent, innate, intrinsic *(belonging)*, local, natural, organic, original *(initial)*, prime *(original)*, regional, resident. SEE MAIN ENTRY
native character disposition *(inclination)*
native environment home *(domicile)*
native ground home *(place of origin)*
native grown domestic *(indigenous)*
native hearth home *(place of origin)*
native land home *(place of origin)*, nationality
native reason common sense
native rights SEE MAIN ENTRY
native soil home *(place of origin)*
native tendency instinct
natives population
nativity birth *(emergence of young)*, genesis, nascency, nationality, origin *(source)*, origination
nativus natural
natura character *(personal quality)*, disposition *(inclination)*, essence
natura et ingenium gift *(flair)*
natural bodily, born *(innate)*, common *(customary)*, conventional, familiar *(customary)*, genuine, habitual, informal, ingenuous, inherent, innate, legitimate *(lawfully conceived)*, naive, native *(inborn)*, normal *(regular)*, organic, physical, prevailing *(current)*, real, realistic, regular *(conventional)*, simple, spontaneous, unaffected *(sincere)*, undistorted, unobtrusive, unpretentious, usual, veridical. SEE MAIN ENTRY
natural ability gift *(flair)*, specialty *(special aptitude)*
natural course practice *(custom)*
natural courtesy decorum
natural disposition tendency
natural fitness disposition *(inclination)*
natural impulse conatus
natural liking affinity *(regard)*
natural meaning connotation
natural quality gift *(flair)*
natural right equity *(justice)*
natural sagacity common sense
natural science ecology
natural sense instinct, proclivity
natural state matter of course
natural tendency conatus, disposition *(inclination)*, instinct, predisposition
natural turn of mind character *(personal quality)*
naturalistic realistic
naturalize adopt, inure *(accustom)*. SEE MAIN ENTRY
naturally consequently, generally
naturalness informality
nature animus, center *(essence)*, character *(personal quality)*, characteristic, color *(complexion)*, complexion, composition *(makeup)*, consequence *(significance)*, content *(meaning)*, content *(structure)*, disposition *(inclination)*, essence, frame *(mood)*, kind, personality, posture *(attitude)*, predisposition, quality *(attribute)*, quality *(grade)*, spirit, temperament, tendency, tenor, trait. SEE MAIN ENTRY
nature study ecology
naught nullity
naughtiness mischief
naughty improper, iniquitous, peccant *(culpable)*, perverse, reprehensible, reprobate
naulum fare
nauseate repel *(disgust)*
nauseating loathsome, obnoxious, offensive *(offending)*, repugnant *(exciting aversion)*, repulsive, unsavory
nauseous loathsome, repulsive, unsavory
navigable open *(accessible)*, passable
navigate direct *(show)*, oversee
navus active
ne plus ultra absolute *(ideal)*
ne plus ultra maximum *(pinnacle)*
ne'er-do-well derelict
near border *(approach)*, cognate, congruous, contiguous, forthcoming, future, immediate *(not distant)*, imminent, inevitable, instant, local, pending *(imminent)*, present *(current)*, proximate, quasi. SEE MAIN ENTRY
near at hand close *(near)*, future, immediate *(imminent)*, imminent, instant, present *(attendant)*
near by immediate *(not distant)*
near death in extremis
near in time present *(current)*
near one's end in extremis
near relation next of kin
nearby close *(near)*, local, present *(attendant)*. SEE MAIN ENTRY
nearest proximate. SEE MAIN ENTRY
nearest blood relation next of kin
nearest relative by blood next of kin
nearing forthcoming, immediate *(imminent)*, imminent
nearing completion determinable *(liable to be terminated)*
nearly almost
nearly accurate approximate, inexact
nearly allied consanguineous
nearly correct approximate, inexact
nearly equal approximate *(adjective)*, approximate *(verb)*
nearly perfect approximate *(adjective)*
nearly related consanguineous
nearly resembling approximate *(adjective)*
nearly rival approximate *(verb)*
nearness comparison, connection *(abutment)*, presence *(attendance)*, propinquity *(proximity)*, relation *(connection)*, relationship *(connection)*
nearness of blood propinquity *(kinship)*
nearness of relation propinquity *(kinship)*
neat meticulous, unadulterated
nebulose nebulous
nebulosity indistinctness, opacity
nebulosus nebulous
nebulous debatable, elusive, enigmatic, equivocal, inconspicuous, indistinct, inexpressive, obscure *(faint)*, opaque, recondite, uncertain *(ambiguous)*, vague. SEE MAIN ENTRY
nebulousness incomprehensible
necessaries maintenance *(support of spouse)*
necessarii kindred
necessarily a priori, consequently
necessarily connected appurtenant
necessarius indispensable, inevitable, integral, requisite, unavoidable *(inevitable)*, urgent
necessary binding, cardinal *(basic)*, central *(essential)*, compelling, compulsory, desideratum, essential *(required)*, exigent, fundamental, imperative, important *(urgent)*, indispensable, integral, mandatory, material *(important)*, need *(requirement)*, obligatory, peremptory *(imperative)*, primary, requisite, unavoidable *(inevitable)*, urgent. SEE MAIN ENTRY
necessary attribute necessity, need *(requirement)*
necessary component necessity, need *(requirement)*
necessary condition prerequisite
necessary item prerequisite
necessary party SEE MAIN ENTRY
necessary to life vital
necessitas compulsion *(coercion)*, necessary, necessity
necessitate call *(demand)*, coerce, compel, constrain *(compel)*, enforce, entail, exact, force *(coerce)*, impose *(enforce)*, press *(constrain)*, require *(compel)*, require *(need)*. SEE MAIN ENTRY

necessitated bound, indispensable, man-datory, necessary *(required)*, obligatory, requisite
necessitation duress, enforcement, force *(compulsion)*, requirement, requisition
necessities necessary, sustenance
necessities of life maintenance *(support of spouse)*
necessitous destitute, exigent, impecunious, important *(urgent)*, mandatory, necessary *(required)*, poor *(underprivileged)*, urgent
necessitousness emergency, indigence, necessary, need *(deprivation)*, poverty
necessitude force *(compulsion)*, necessary, need *(deprivation)*, privation
necessitudo affinity *(family ties)*
necessity burden, coercion, compulsion *(coercion)*, desideratum, enforcement, exigency, force *(compulsion)*, market *(demand)*, necessary, need *(deprivation)*, need *(requirement)*, obligation *(duty)*, poverty, prerequisite, pressure, priority, privation, requirement, requisition, sine qua non. SEE MAIN ENTRY
necrosis demise *(death)*
nectarean savory
nectareous palatable, sapid, savory. SEE MAIN ENTRY
need absence *(omission)*, compulsion *(obsession)*, contribution *(indemnification)*, dearth, deficiency, desideratum, emergency, entail, exigency, foible, force *(compulsion)*, indigence, insufficiency, lack, market *(demand)*, necessary, necessity, paucity, poverty, prerequisite, pressure, privation, requirement, requisition, stress *(strain)*. SEE MAIN ENTRY
need for action emergency
needed essential *(required)*, exigent, fundamental, important *(urgent)*, indispensable, integral, necessary *(required)*, requisite, vital
needed item prerequisite
needful destitute, essential *(required)*, exigent, imperative, integral, poor *(underprivileged)*, requisite
needfulness emergency, priority
neediness indigence, poverty, privation
needing perfunctory
needing outside support dependent
needle annoy, harrow, harry *(harass)*, irritate, pique, plague, stimulus
needless excess, excessive, expendable, extraneous, gratuitous *(unwarranted)*, injudicious, inordinate, nonessential, redundant, superfluous, undue *(excessive)*, unessential, unnecessary, unwarranted. SEE MAIN ENTRY
needlessness redundancy
needy destitute, impecunious, penurious, poor *(underprivileged)*
needy circumstances indigence, poverty
nefandus heinous
nefarious bad *(offensive)*, blameful, blameworthy, contemptible, contemptuous, delinquent *(guilty of a misdeed)*, diabolic, dishonest, disreputable, felonious, flagrant, heinous, immoral, inexpiable, iniquitous, irregular *(improper)*, malignant, objectionable, obnoxious, outrageous, peccant *(culpable)*, profligate *(corrupt)*, reprehensible, reprobate, scandalous, sinister. SEE MAIN ENTRY
nefarious act tortious act
nefariousness atrocity, delinquency *(misconduct)*, disrepute
nefarius felon, nefarious
nefas atrocity
nefastus inauspicious
negans negative
negare deny *(contradict)*, deny *(refuse to grant)*
negate abolish, abrogate *(annul)*, adeem, annul, cancel, challenge, contradict, contravene, controvert, counter, counteract, countercharge, countervail, demonstrate *(protest)*, deny *(contradict)*, disaccord, disaffirm, disallow, disapprove *(reject)*, disavow, disobey, disown *(deny the validity)*, disprove, dissent *(withhold assent)*, fight *(counteract)*, gainsay, impugn, neutralize, nullify, oppose, prohibit, protest, rebut, recant, refute, repeal, repudiate, rescind, revoke, vacate *(void)*, vitiate. SEE MAIN ENTRY
negated null *(invalid)*, null and void
negating contradictory
negatio denial, negation
negation absence *(omission)*, ademption, annulment, answer *(judicial response)*, answer *(reply)*, antipode, cancellation, confutation, contradiction, contravention, counterargument, declination, defeasance, denial, disagreement, disapprobation, disapproval, discharge *(annulment)*, disclaimer, prohibition, refusal, rejection, renunciation, repudiation, rescision, retraction, revocation. SEE MAIN ENTRY
negation of allegations demurrer
negative challenge, contradict, contrary, disadvantageous, disapprove *(reject)*, disavow, disown *(deny the validity)*, dispute *(contest)*, dissent *(withhold assent)*, negate, opposite, perverse, prohibit, rebut, recusant, refuse, veto, vitiate. SEE MAIN ENTRY
negative advertising SEE MAIN ENTRY
negative answer denial, refusal
negative compulsion coercion
negative evidence answer *(judicial response)*, contradiction
negative result miscarriage
negativistic perverse
negatory antipathetic *(oppositional)*, contradictory, contrary, negative
neglect blame *(culpability)*, break *(violate)*, default, delinquency *(failure of duty)*, dereliction, desuetude, disinterest *(lack of interest)*, disobey, disregard *(omission)*, disregard *(unconcern)*, disregard, disrepair, disuse, eschew, exclude, ignore, inconsideration, indifference, laches, laxity, leave *(allow to remain)*, maladministration, mismanage, misprision, nonpayment, nonperformance, nonuse, omission, omit, overlook *(disregard)*, override, oversight *(carelessness)*, pretermit, procrastinate, rebuff, reject, rejection, repudiate, shirk, shun, spurn. SEE MAIN ENTRY
neglect of duty delict, nonfeasance
neglect of obligation delinquency *(failure of duty)*
neglect one's duty default
neglect to obey disoblige
neglect to perform omission
neglected derelict *(abandoned)*, outmoded
neglectful blameful, careless, derelict *(negligent)*, disobedient, heedless, improvident, imprudent, inadvertent, lax, negligent, oblivious, otiose, perfunctory, reckless, remiss, thoughtless, truant. SEE MAIN ENTRY
neglectful of obligation delinquent *(overdue)*
neglectfulness dereliction, disinterest *(lack of interest)*, disregard *(omission)*, disregard *(unconcern)*, laches, laxity, negligence, sloth
neglecting derelict *(negligent)*
neglection breach
neglector of duty delinquent
neglegens careless, heedless, lax, negligent, reckless, regardless, remiss, thoughtless
neglegentia laxity, neglect, negligence
neglegere disregard, ignore, neglect
negligence delinquency *(failure of duty)*, dereliction, disinterest *(lack of interest)*, disregard *(unconcern)*, fault *(responsibility)*, incompetence, inconsideration, indifference, inertia, laches, lapse *(expiration)*, laxity, maladministration, misconduct, misprision, neglect, nonfeasance, nonperformance, omission, oversight *(carelessness)*. SEE MAIN ENTRY
negligence per se SEE MAIN ENTRY
negligent blameful, blameworthy, careless, delinquent *(guilty of a misdeed)*, disobedient, heedless, improvident, inadvertent, indolent, injudicious, lax, oblivious, perfunctory, reckless, remiss, slipshod, thoughtless. SEE MAIN ENTRY
negligent act tort
negligent act of injury delict
negligent offense delict
negligent wrongdoing delict
negligibility inconsequence
negligible collateral *(immaterial)*, de minimus, expendable, inapposite, inappreciable, inconsiderable, insufficient, minor, nominal, nonessential, null *(insignificant)*, paltry, petty, slight, trivial, unessential. SEE MAIN ENTRY
negotia commerce
negotiable assignable, conditional, heritable. SEE MAIN ENTRY
negotiable instrument coupon, debenture, draft, letter of credit, note *(written promise to pay)*, security *(stock)*. SEE MAIN ENTRY
negotiable paper check *(instrument)*, draft, note *(written promise to pay)*, security *(stock)*
negotiables portfolio, securities, stock *(shares)*
negotiant adjuster, advocate *(counselor)*, agent, arbiter, arbitrator, broker, intermediary, liaison, medium
negotiate arbitrate *(conciliate)*, assign *(transfer ownership)*, close *(agree)*, compromise *(settle by mutual agreement)*, confer *(consult)*, deal, debate, deliberate, dicker, discuss, haggle, intercede, judge, lobby, mediate, reconcile, settle, trade, transact, treat *(process)*. SEE MAIN ENTRY
negotiated agreed *(harmonized)*, contractual, res judicata
negotiated agreement contract
negotiation adjustment, collective bargaining, commerce, compromise, conciliation, conference, counteroffer, deal, intercession, mediation, meeting *(conference)*, parley, settlement, trade *(commerce)*, transaction, treaty. SEE MAIN ENTRY
negotiation process mediation
negotiations conference
negotiator adjuster, advocate *(counselor)*, agent, arbiter, arbitrator, broker, conduit *(intermediary)*. SEE MAIN ENTRY
negotiator dealer

negotiator go-between, interagent, intermediary, judge, liaison, medium, spokesman
negotium employment, occupation *(vocation)*, pursuit *(occupation)*, transaction
neighbor adjoin, border *(approach)*, juxtapose
neighborhood civic, community, district, local, locality, location, region, regional, section *(vicinity)*, site, venue, vicinity. SEE MAIN ENTRY
neighboring adjacent, close *(near)*, contiguous, immediate *(not distant)*, proximate
neighborliness comity, concordance, consideration *(sympathetic regard)*, rapprochement
neighborly benevolent
neither more nor less coequal
nemesis punishment, reprisal, retribution, revenge, vengeance
neologism jargon *(technical language)*
neology jargon *(technical language)*
neophyte amateur, novice, probationer *(one being tested)*. SEE MAIN ENTRY
neophytism preparation
neoteric novel
neoterical novel
neoterism innovation
nepenthe drug
nepotism SEE MAIN ENTRY
nequam bad *(offensive)*
nequitia knavery
nerve audacity, confidence *(faith)*, prowess *(bravery)*, reassure, temerity
nerveless powerless
nervous suspicious *(distrustful)*, unsettled
nervousness hesitation, misgiving, panic, qualm, stress *(strain)*, trepidation
nervus sinew
nervy insolent
nescience ignorance. SEE MAIN ENTRY
nescient blind *(not discerning)*, incognizant, opaque, unaware
nescius unaware
nest habitation *(dwelling place)*
nest egg fund, store *(depository)*
net capture, earn, ensnare, gain, realize *(obtain as a profit)*, trap. SEE MAIN ENTRY
net profit dividend, proceeds
net quantity amount *(quantity)*, amount *(result)*
net return income
nettle aggravate *(annoy)*, badger, discompose, disturb, hector, incense, irritate, offend *(insult)*, pique, plague, provoke. SEE MAIN ENTRY
network complex *(development)*, conjunction, league. SEE MAIN ENTRY
neutral dispassionate, equitable, evenhanded, impartial, independent, intermediate, liberal *(broad minded)*, noncommittal, nonmilitant, nonpartisan, objective, openminded, peaceable, unbiased, unprejudiced. SEE MAIN ENTRY
neutralism neutrality
neutrality candor *(impartiality)*, disinterest *(lack of prejudice)*, objectivity, peace. SEE MAIN ENTRY
neutralization of forces balance *(equality)*
neutralize compensate *(counterbalance)*, counteract, countervail, cross *(disagree with)*, disable, disarm *(divest of arms)*, disqualify, dissolve *(terminate)*, frustrate, negate, nullify, outbalance, prevent, remedy, vitiate. SEE MAIN ENTRY
neutralized ineffective, ineffectual
neutralizer offset
neutralizing preventive
neutrius partis neutral
never sine die
never again sine die
never cease keep *(continue)*, persist
never changing immutable
never ending continuous
never idle diligent, industrious
never late punctual
never the same atypical
never tiring diligent
never to be forgotten critical *(crucial)*
never varying immutable
never-ceasing chronic, permanent, perpetual
never-dying perpetual
never-ending continual *(perpetual)*, durable, incessant, permanent, protracted
never-endingness perpetuity
never-fading perpetual
never-failing infallible, perpetual
never-stopping chronic, permanent, perpetual
never-tiring painstaking, pertinacious
never-wearying pertinacious
nevertheless notwithstanding, regardless
new contemporary, current, de novo, inexperienced, novel, recent, sophisticated, unaccustomed, unacquainted, unprecedented, unsettled, unusual. SEE MAIN ENTRY
new arrival novice
new beginning continuation *(resumption)*
new departure creation
new device innovation
new edition revision *(corrected version)*
new energy resurgence
new hearing rehearing
new idea innovation
new method innovation
new offer counteroffer
new outbreak recrudescence
new phase innovation
new start continuation *(resumption)*, renewal
new version revival
newborn child
newcomer neophyte, novice, probationer *(one being tested)*, stranger, successor
newest last *(preceding)*
newfangled unprecedented, unusual
newly anew, de novo
newly arrived recent
newly come novel
news communication *(statement)*, disclosure *(something disclosed)*, dispatch *(message)*, information *(facts)*, notice *(announcement)*, notification, publicity, report *(detailed account)*, story *(narrative)*. SEE MAIN ENTRY
news article story *(narrative)*
news blackout censorship
news business press
news gatherers press
news item story *(narrative)*
news story report *(detailed account)*
newsmen press
newspaper organ
newspaper report story *(narrative)*
newspaper world press
newspaperman press
newspapers press
newsworthy notable, noteworthy. SEE MAIN ENTRY
newswriters press
newsy informative, informatory
next a savoir, ensuing, future, immediate *(imminent)*, imminent, inevitable, proximate, subsequent, thereafter. SEE MAIN ENTRY
next generation offspring
next in line successor
next of kin affiliation *(bloodline)*, blood, kindred. SEE MAIN ENTRY
next to adjacent, contiguous, immediate *(not distant)*
nexus attachment *(act of affixing)*, connection *(fastening)*, contact *(touching)*, liaison, privity, relation *(connection)*, sequence. SEE MAIN ENTRY
nice palatable. SEE MAIN ENTRY
nice appreciation decorum.
niceness amenity
nicety decorum, discretion *(quality of being discreet)*, nuance, specification
nickname cognomen, sobriquet
niggard penurious
niggardly economical, illiberal, nonsubstantial *(not sufficient)*, paltry, parsimonious, penurious, slight
niggling inconsequential
nigh approximate, close *(near)*, forthcoming, future, immediate *(imminent)*, present *(attendant)*, present *(current)*, proximate
night stick cudgel
nihil nonentity
nihil ad rem pertinet irrelevant
nihilism anarchy, lynch law
nihilist insurgent, malcontent
nihilistic disorderly, incendiary
nihility nullity
nil blank *(emptiness)*
nim steal
nimble alert *(agile)*, deft, rapid
nimble-fingered deft
nimble-witted perspicacious
nimbleness dispatch *(promptness)*
nimiety plethora, redundancy, surfeit, surplus
nimious inordinate
nimium excess
nimius excessive, gross *(total)*, undue *(excessive)*
nip foil, thwart
nip in the bud deter
nisus conatus
nisus endeavor
nitid lucid
no decision deadlock
no longer conventional outmoded
no longer customary outdated, outmoded
no longer fashionable outdated
no longer in perfect condition marred
no longer in style outdated
no longer in use obsolete
no longer law null *(invalid)*, null and void
no longer living dead, deceased, defunct
no longer prevailing outdated, outmoded
no longer prevalent outdated
no longer stylish outdated
no longer young old
no matter when whenever
no matter who whoever
no more defunct
no one nonentity
no relation alien *(unrelated)*, apart
no reputation disrepute
no repute dishonor *(shame)*, disrepute

no standing dishonor *(shame)*
nobilis notorious
nobility character *(reputation)*, distinction *(reputation)*, elite, eminence, prestige
noble heroic, high-minded, illustrious, laudable, law-abiding, magnanimous, meritorious, moral, prominent, proud *(self-respecting)*, reputable, scrupulous, sterling, superior *(excellent)*. SEE MAIN ENTRY
noble-minded magnanimous
nobleness integrity, principle *(virtue)*, right *(righteousness)*
nobody nonentity
nocens harmful, prejudicial
nocent harmful, lethal, noxious, pernicious, pestilent
nocere harm
nocuous bad *(offensive)*, deleterious, harmful, inadvisable, lethal, malignant, peccant *(unhealthy)*, pestilent, sinister
nod recognition
nod assent to coincide *(concur)*
nod of approbation approval
noesis insight, perception
noise outcry, pandemonium. SEE MAIN ENTRY
noise abroad circulate, divulge, proclaim, propagate *(spread)*
noiseless mute, speechless
noiselessness silence
noisiness brawl
noisome deleterious, detrimental, fatal, harmful, harsh, heinous, insalubrious, malignant, noxious, objectionable, obnoxious, peccant *(unhealthy)*, pernicious, pestilent, repugnant *(exciting aversion)*, repulsive, sinister. SEE MAIN ENTRY
noisy blatant *(obtrusive)*, loquacious
noisy quarrel altercation, fracas
noisy strife commotion
nol-pros quit *(discontinue)*
nolition reluctance
nollo contendere SEE MAIN ENTRY
nollo presequi SEE MAIN ENTRY
nom de plume sobriquet
nomad migrant
nomadic moving *(in motion)*
nomen entry *(record)*, prestige
nomen alienum alias
nomen deferre indict
nomenclature call *(title)*, classification, denomination
nominal immaterial, inconsiderable, negligible, null *(insignificant)*, trivial. SEE MAIN ENTRY
nominalness insignificance
nominare call *(title)*, designate, nominate
nominate charge *(empower)*, delegate, designate, induct, instate, invest *(vest)*, propose, select. SEE MAIN ENTRY
nominatio nomination
nomination appointment *(act of designating)*, assignment *(designation)*, deputation *(selection of delegates)*, selection *(choice)*. SEE MAIN ENTRY
nomination contest primary
nominative competition primary
nominative contest primary
nominative election primary
nominator licensor
nomine nominal
nominee candidate, contender, licensee. SEE MAIN ENTRY
nomography jurisprudence
nomology jurisprudence
nomothetic decretal, due *(regular)*, lawful
nomothetical de jure
non aptus incongruous
non compos mentis SEE MAIN ENTRY
non credere disbelieve
non idoneus inapposite, inappropriate, unsatisfactory
non legitimus felonious, illegitimate *(illegal)*, unlawful
non necessarius needless, unnecessary
non obsequi disobedient
non occurrence noncompliance *(nonobservance)*
non rectus indirect
non salable unmarketable
non sequitur anacoluthon. SEE MAIN ENTRY
non specific unspecified
non valere inapplicable
non verisimilis improbability
non voluntarius involuntary
non-esse blank *(emptiness)*
non-executionary judgment declaratory judgment
non-uniform atypical
nonabolishable noncancellable
nonabstract actual
nonacceptance declination, denial, disapproval, disdain, dishonor *(nonpayment)*, exclusion, impugnation, negation, refusal, rejection. SEE MAIN ENTRY
nonactual baseless
nonadherence breach, contempt *(disobedience to the court)*, dishonor *(nonpayment)*
nonadhering broken *(unfulfilled)*, nonconforming
nonadmission bar *(obstruction)*, disqualification *(rejection)*, exclusion, ostracism, prohibition
nonadmission of employees lockout
nonage adolescence, minority *(infancy)*. SEE MAIN ENTRY
nonaggresive nonmilitant
nonaggressive lax
nonagreement disaccord, discord, discrepancy, disparity, dispute, dissension, dissent *(difference of opinion)*, dissent *(nonconcurrence)*, exception *(objection)*, impugnation, incompatibility *(difference)*, negation, nonconformity, variance *(disagreement)*
nonaligned neutral, nonpartisan
nonannullable noncancellable
nonapparent covert
nonappearance absence *(nonattendance)*, concealment, leave *(absence)*. SEE MAIN ENTRY
nonapproval disapprobation, disapproval, disparagement, dissatisfaction, exception *(objection)*, reversal
nonassent dissension, dissent *(nonconcurrence)*
nonattendance leave *(absence)*, nonappearance
nonattendant truant
nonavailability desuetude
nonbeing absence *(omission)*, nonentity, nullity
nonbelligerence neutrality
nonbelligerent neutral
noncancellable SEE MAIN ENTRY
nonchalance disinterest *(lack of interest)*, indifference
nonchalant careless, casual, dispassionate, informal. SEE MAIN ENTRY
nonchallengeable noncontestable
noncitizen alien
noncohesive disconnected
noncombatance neutrality
noncombatant neutral, nonmilitant
noncombative nonmilitant, peaceable
noncomformity contest *(dispute)*
noncommittal guarded, neutral. SEE MAIN ENTRY
noncomplete clause SEE MAIN ENTRY
noncompletion breach, deficiency, delinquency *(failure of duty)*, dishonor *(nonpayment)*, failure *(falling short)*, frustration, laxity, miscarriage, neglect, nonperformance
noncompletion of a task delinquency *(failure of duty)*
noncompliance contempt *(disobedience to the court)*, declination, defiance, dishonor *(nonpayment)*, disregard *(omission)*, dissent *(difference of opinion)*, dissidence, impugnation, informality, infraction, insurrection, negation, neglect, nonperformance, offense, refusal, resistance, revolt, sedition, transgression. SEE MAIN ENTRY
noncompliance with law crime
noncompliant disobedient, dissident, insubordinate, nonconforming, perverse
noncompulsory disjunctive *(alternative)*, extraneous, needless, unnecessary
nonconcurrence dissension, dissidence, nonconformity
nonconformance resistance
nonconformant nonconsenting
nonconforming dissident, eccentric, individual, licentious. SEE MAIN ENTRY
nonconformism deviation
nonconformist deviant, dissident, eccentric, heretic, lawless, malcontent, novel, original *(creative)*, recusant
nonconformity breach, deviation, difference, disaccord, discrepancy, disparity, dissent *(nonconcurrence)*, dissidence, exception *(exclusion)*, incompatibility *(inconsistency)*, incongruity, inconsistency, inequality, informality, irregularity, noncompliance *(nonobservance)*, quirk *(idiosyncrasy)*, schism. SEE MAIN ENTRY
nonconformity to fact falsehood
nonconsent declination, denial, disagreement, disapproval, dissent *(nonconcurrence)*, dissent *(withhold assent)*, impugnation, negation, refusal
nonconsenting SEE MAIN ENTRY
nonconsideration exclusion
nonconstitutional illicit
noncontent nonconsenting
noncontestable SEE MAIN ENTRY
noncontinuance cloture
noncontinuous discrete, disjunctive *(tending to disjoin)*
noncontroversial incontestable, incontrovertible, unimpeachable
noncontrovertible noncontestable
noncooperating contentious, disinclined, hostile
noncooperation contempt *(disobedience to the court)*, defiance, dereliction, disaccord, division *(act of dividing)*, impugnation, nonperformance
noncooperative recalcitrant
noncooperator malcontent
noncorroboration negation
noncriminal civil *(public)*
nondebatable noncontestable
nondescript indefinite, usual. SEE MAIN ENTRY
nondisputable noncontestable
nondivisible indivisible, inseparable
nondomicile nonresidence

nondurable ephemeral, temporary
none the less notwithstanding
noneccliastical civil *(public)*
nonelastic immutable, inflexible
nonemployment disuse, nonuse
nonentity blank *(emptiness)*, nullity. SEE MAIN ENTRY
nonerasable noncancellable
nonessential circumstantial, collateral *(immaterial)*, excessive, expendable, extraneous, extrinsic, immaterial, inconsequential, inconsiderable, minor, needless, petty, slight, supplementary, tangential, trivial, unessential. SEE MAIN ENTRY
nonessentiality immateriality
nonesuch exemplar, paragon, phenomenon *(unusual occurrence)*
nonetheless regardless
nonexclusive competitive *(open)*, generic
nonexistence absence *(omission)*, blank *(emptiness)*, nonentity, nullity
nonexistent fictitious, insubstantial. SEE MAIN ENTRY
nonexpectation bombshell, improbability
nonexpert unprofessional
nonfatal nontoxic
nonfeasance crime, delict, dereliction, dishonor *(nonpayment)*, laches, laxity, misconduct, neglect, nonperformance, omission. SEE MAIN ENTRY
nonfertile barren
nonfinal interlocutory
nonfulfillment default, defeat, deficiency, delinquency *(failure of duty)*, delinquency *(shortage)*, dishonor *(nonpayment)*, failure *(falling short)*, frustration, laxity, miscarriage, mistrial, neglect, nonfeasance, nonperformance
nonfulfillment of one's hopes dissatisfaction
nonfulfilment abortion *(fiasco)*, breach
nonfunctional expendable, otiose
nonfunctioning otiose
nongregarious unapproachable
nonhabitancy nonresidence
nonhabitation nonresidence
nonhampering laissez faire
nonidentical different, dissimilar
nonimitation deviation, difference
nonimitative original *(initial)*
nonimmunity danger
noninclusion bar *(obstruction)*, dispensation *(exception)*, disqualification *(rejection)*, exception *(exclusion)*, exclusion, omission, ostracism, prohibition, rejection, removal
noninfringement laissez faire
noninhabitance nonresidence
noninhabitancy nonresidence
nonintentional occurrence quirk *(accident)*
noninterference freedom, home rule, laissez faire, latitude, liberty, neutrality
noninterfering neutral
nonintermeddling laissez faire
noninterruption laissez faire
nonintervention home rule, laissez faire, latitude, neutrality
noninterventionist neutral
nonintrusion laissez faire
noninvolvement disinterest *(lack of interest)*, disinterest *(lack of prejudice)*, objectivity
nonirritating innocuous, nontoxic
nonjuring recusant
nonlegal felonious, illicit, impermissible, lawless
nonlethal nontoxic
nonliability condonation, dispensation *(exception)*, immunity, impunity
nonliable clear *(free from criminal charges)*
nonliteral translation paraphrase
nonmalignant harmless, innocuous, nontoxic
nonmaterial impalpable
nonmilitant SEE MAIN ENTRY
nonmilitary civil *(public)*
nonobjective subjective
nonobligatory disjunctive *(alternative)*
nonobservance breach, contempt *(disobedience to the court)*, default, delinquency *(failure of duty)*, dereliction, desuetude, deviation, dishonor *(nonpayment)*, disregard *(omission)*, disregard *(unconcern)*, dissent *(nonconcurrence)*, failure *(falling short)*, indifference, informality, infraction, infringement, neglect, offense, oversight *(carelessness)*, repudiation, transgression, violation
nonobservance of law crime
nonobservance of rules infraction
nonobservant broken *(unfulfilled)*, disorderly, dissident, heedless, lawless, nonconforming, recusant
nonobviousness SEE MAIN ENTRY
nonoccupance nonresidence
nonoccupancy nonresidence
nonoccupation nonresidence
nonofficial private *(not public)*
nonpacific contentious
nonpareil exemplar, outstanding *(prominent)*, paragon, phenomenon *(unusual occurrence)*, primary, prime *(most valuable)*, singular, superior *(excellent)*, superlative, unique, unusual
nonparticipance neutrality
nonparticipant neutral
nonparticipating neutral, otiose
nonparticipation abstention, neutrality
nonpartisan impartial, independent, liberal *(broad minded)*, neutral, objective, unbiased, unprejudiced. SEE MAIN ENTRY
nonpartisanship candor *(impartiality)*, disinterest *(lack of prejudice)*, neutrality, objectivity
nonpayer delinquent
nonpaying penurious
nonpayment debt, delinquency *(shortage)*. SEE MAIN ENTRY
nonpayment at maturity dishonor *(nonpayment)*
nonperformance breach, default, deficiency, delinquency *(failure of duty)*, dereliction, failure *(falling short)*, frustration, laches, laxity, miscarriage, neglect, nonfeasance. SEE MAIN ENTRY
nonperishable indelible, indestructible
nonpermanent interlocutory, provisional
nonpermanent agreement modus vivendi
nonpermanent arrangement modus vivendi
nonpertinent extraneous, gratuitous *(unwarranted)*
nonphased. SEE MAIN ENTRY
nonphysical immaterial, incorporeal, intangible
nonplus confound, confuse *(bewilder)*, confusion *(ambiguity)*, discompose, disorient, disturb, embarrass, obfuscate, perplex, perturb, quagmire, quandary
nonpoisonous harmless, nontoxic
nonporous solid *(compact)*
nonpractice nonperformance
nonpresence absence *(nonattendance)*, nonappearance, nonresidence
nonproblematical noncontestable
nonproducing barren
nonproductive barren
nonprofessional layman, volunteer
nonprofit SEE MAIN ENTRY
nonprohibitive permissive
nonprosecution compurgation, impunity
nonpublic private *(not public)*, privy
nonquestionable noncontestable
nonrational arbitrary
nonrecognition disdain, insentience
nonrecurrent desultory
nonrefutable noncontestable
nonrescindable noncancellable
nonresidence SEE MAIN ENTRY
nonresident foreign
nonresistance acquiescence, capitulation, compliance, deference, discipline *(obedience)*, resignation *(passive acceptance)*
nonresistant passive, resigned, susceptible *(unresistent)*
nonresisting obeisant, passive, patient, pliable, pliant
nonresponsibility dispensation *(exception)*
nonresumption impasse
nonretention alienation *(transfer of title)*, assignment *(transfer of ownership)*, cession, desuetude, devolution
nonretractable noncancellable
nonreversible indefeasible, irreversible, irrevocable, noncancellable, permanent
nonsacred mundane
nonscientific illogical
nonsectarian SEE MAIN ENTRY
nonsense jargon *(unintelligible language)*, platitude
nonsensical fatuous, incredible, inexpressive, irrational, ludicrous, lunatic, puerile, unreasonable
nonsensical language jargon *(unintelligible language)*
nonsensical talk jargon *(unintelligible language)*, prattle
nonsensicality non sequitur
nonsensicalness jargon *(unintelligible language)*, non sequitur
nonspecialist layman
nonspecific broad, generic, indefinite, indeterminate
nonspiritual material *(physical)*, mundane, physical
nonstandard anomalous
nonstop consecutive, continual *(connected)*, incessant
nonsubjective objective
nonsubjectivity objectivity
nonsubsistence blank *(emptiness)*
nonsubstantial intangible. SEE MAIN ENTRY
nonsuccess miscarriage, mistrial
nonsuit dismissal *(termination of a proceeding)*. SEE MAIN ENTRY
nonsystematic haphazard
nontampering laissez faire
nontenancy nonresidence
nontoxic harmless, innocuous. SEE MAIN ENTRY
nontransferable inalienable
nontranslucent opaque
nonuniform anomalous, desultory, deviant, disjointed, disordered, disparate,

dissimilar, distinct *(distinguished from others)*, divergent, heterogeneous, individual, intermittent, miscellaneous, multifarious, nonconforming, protean, sporadic, unique
nonuniformity deviation, difference, discrepancy, disparity, distinction *(difference)*, diversity, exception *(exclusion)*, incompatibility *(inconsistency)*, inequality, nonconformity
nonuse abatement *(extinguishment)*, abolition, cancellation, desuetude, discontinuance *(act of discontinuing)*, disuse. SEE MAIN ENTRY
nonutilization nonuse
nonvenomous harmless, nontoxic
nonviolence moderation
nonviolent harmless, nonmilitant
nonvirulent harmless, nontoxic
nonworker parasite
norm code, criterion, cross section, example, law, paradigm, pattern, rule *(guide)*, standard. SEE MAIN ENTRY
norma canon, rule *(guide)*, standard
normal accustomed *(customary)*, average *(standard)*, common *(customary)*, conventional, customary, exemplary, familiar *(customary)*, habitual, mediocre, natural, ordinary, prevailing *(current)*, prevalent, regular *(conventional)*, routine, sane, typical, usual. SEE MAIN ENTRY
normalcy competence *(sanity)*, sanity
normality competence *(sanity)*, sanity
normalize adjust *(regulate)*, naturalize *(acclimate)*, regulate *(adjust)*
normally as a rule, generally, invariably
normalness competence *(sanity)*
normative average *(standard)*, exemplary
noscere recognize *(acknowledge)*
noscitare recognize *(perceive)*
noscitur a sociis SEE MAIN ENTRY
not abide conflict, disapprove *(reject)*
not abiding dissenting
not able unable
not able to be conveyed inalienable
not absolute conditional, qualified *(conditioned)*
not abundant scarce
not accept abrogate *(rescind)*, conflict, disagree, disallow, disapprove *(reject)*, disavow, disbelieve, disclaim, disdain, disoblige, disown *(deny the validity)*, dissent *(withhold assent)*
not accepting dissenting
not accidental express
not according to law illegal, illegitimate *(illegal)*, illicit
not accountable immune, privileged
not admissible SEE MAIN ENTRY
not admit disapprove *(reject)*, disavow, disclaim, disown *(deny the validity)*, doubt *(distrust)*
not admitted inadmissible
not agree differ *(vary)*, dispute *(contest)*, dispute *(debate)*, dissent *(differ in opinion)*
not agreeing dissenting
not alien native *(domestic)*
not allow estop, forbid
not allowed illegal, illicit, inadmissible
not allowed by law unlawful
not answerable clear *(unencumbered)*, exempt, immune
not apocryphal authentic
not applicable irrelevant
not approve disapprove *(reject)*, disavow, dissent *(withhold assent)*
not approved illegal, illicit
not argued over uncontested
not ascertained indeterminate
not ashamed unabashed
not authenticated unsupported
not authorized by law illegal
not averruncated chronic
not axiomatic controversial, disputable
not badly fairly *(moderately)*
not baneful nontoxic
not believe disbelieve, doubt *(distrust)*
not belonging disordered
not biased impartial
not binding invalid, void *(invalid)*
not blamable inculpable
not bother with disregard
not budge hold out *(resist)*
not by chance express
not capable of annulment irreversible
not capable of being introduced as evidence inadmissible
not care for disfavor, neglect, pretermit
not certain conditional, uncertain *(ambiguous)*
not challenged uncontested
not charged gratuitous *(given without recompense)*
not charged for free *(at no charge)*, gratuitous *(given without recompense)*
not choosy indiscriminate
not clear ambiguous, nebulous, uncertain *(ambiguous)*
not clear to the mind intangible
not close remote *(secluded)*
not cohesive disjunctive *(tending to disjoin)*
not commercial residential
not committed to writing parol
not comparable alien *(unrelated)*, disparate, dissimilar
not compare with differ *(vary)*
not complete partial *(part)*
not completed partial *(part)*
not completely formed inchoate
not compliant contumacious
not comply disallow, disobey
not comply with disoblige
not compromise hold out *(resist)*
not compulsory disjunctive *(alternative)*
not concealed manifest
not confirm demur, disallow, disavow, disown *(deny the validity)*
not conform conflict, deviate, differ *(vary)*
not conforming dissenting
not conforming to the usual anomalous
not connected with immaterial
not consenting dissident
not consider disapprove *(reject)*, disdain, disregard, dissent *(withhold assent)*
not considered ineligible
not contradictory consistent
not cooperate disobey
not countenance disapprove *(reject)*, enjoin
not countenanced SEE MAIN ENTRY
not covered by law illegal, illicit
not current outdated
not dangerous nontoxic
not deadly nontoxic
not declared openly implicit
not decreased undiminished
not defend dissent *(withhold assent)*
not definite intangible
not deleterious nontoxic
not designated indeterminate
not discharged delinquent *(overdue)*
not disconcerted unabashed
not dispose of hold *(possess)*
not disposed reluctant
not disputed uncontested
not do justice to derogate
not domestic alien *(foreign)*
not easily governed intractable
not easily worn out durable
not eligible ineligible
not elusive tangible
not employed unemployed
not endowed with life defunct
not enough deficient, inadequate, insufficiency, insufficient
not enslaved free *(enjoying civil liberty)*
not entirely quasi
not equal to incapable
not equate differ *(vary)*
not equitable unfair. SEE MAIN ENTRY
not established unsupported
not evident underlying
not excessive reasonable *(fair)*
not existing defunct
not expressed implicit
not expressed by writing parol
not extinct extant
not extraordinary nondescript
not extreme reasonable *(fair)*
not false authentic, true *(authentic)*
not faulty true *(authentic)*
not fictitious actual, authentic, documentary, true *(authentic)*
not final inconclusive, interlocutory
not find tenable disbelieve
not fit unworthy
not fitting gratuitous *(unwarranted)*, unacceptable
not fixed aleatory *(uncertain)*, ambulatory, indeterminate
not fixed in extent indeterminate
not fluctuating fixed *(settled)*
not following disproportionate, gratuitous *(unwarranted)*
not for publication confidential
not foreign domestic *(indigenous)*, native *(domestic)*
not forfeitable indefeasible
not forget remember
not fully executed inchoate
not genuine synthetic
not give up hold out *(resist)*
not guilty acquitted, blameless, clean, clear *(free from criminal charges)*, inculpable, irreprehensible. SEE MAIN ENTRY
not have any part of conflict, disapprove *(reject)*
not hear disregard
not hear of dismiss *(put out of consideration)*
not heed disobey, disregard
not hold with dissent *(withhold assent)*
not honest dishonest, fraudulent
not honorable blameworthy. SEE MAIN ENTRY
not ideal faulty
not identical distinct *(distinguished from others)*
not imaginary actual
not immediate remote *(not proximate)*
not important immaterial
not imported domestic *(indigenous)*
not impossible allowable
not improbable credible
not improper allowable
not in action defunct
not in bondage free *(enjoying civil liberty)*

not in force defunct, void *(invalid)*
not in keeping disproportionate
not in use vacant
not in vogue outdated, outmoded
not inclined reluctant
not include censor, disregard
not included inadmissible
not including save
not indigenous alien *(foreign)*
not indiginous foreign
not integrated disjunctive *(tending to disjoin)*
not intended unpremeditated
not lasting ephemeral
not legitimate want of jurisdiction
not lessened undiminished
not liable blameless, exempt, immune
not like disfavor
not limited by conditions unconditional
not listen disobey, disregard
not long past recent
not lost extant
not lying candid
not made certain indeterminate
not maintain disavow, disown *(deny the validity)*, disown *(refuse to acknowledge)*
not manifest impalpable, ulterior
not mature undue *(not owing)*
not merely supposed actual
not met delinquent *(overdue)*
not mind disobey
not modern old, outdated
not modified unqualified *(unlimited)*
not narrow-minded liberal *(broad minded)*
not native alien *(foreign)*, foreign
not natural artificial, synthetic
not naturalized alien *(foreign)*
not near remote *(secluded)*
not nearby remote *(secluded)*
not necessitated gratuitous *(unwarranted)*
not nervous secure *(confident)*
not obey disobey, disoblige
not objectionable allowable
not obscure manifest, naked *(perceptible)*
not observant of the law lawless
not observe dishonor *(refuse to pay)*, overstep
not occupied vacant
not odd nondescript
not of high standards unprofessional
not of material nature incorporeal
not on point irrelevant
not on time overdue
not open private *(not public)*
not openly expressed tacit
not owing solvent
not paid on time delinquent *(overdue)*
not part with hold *(possess)*
not partial competitive *(open)*, general, impartial
not particular generic, open-ended
not particularly designated indeterminate
not pass disavow
not pay default, dishonor *(refuse to pay)*
not perfect fallible
not perfectly accurate approximate
not permanent transitory
not permit enjoin
not permitted illegal, illegitimate *(illegal)*, illicit. SEE MAIN ENTRY
not permitting passage impervious
not permitting penetration impervious
not pernicious nontoxic
not pertaining to immaterial, irrelevant
not pertinent gratuitous *(unwarranted)*, immaterial, improper, irrelevant
not plain ambiguous, uncertain *(ambiguous)*
not plainly apparent implicit
not plentiful scarce
not pliable intractable
not positive indefinite
not possessing life dead
not precise indeterminate
not private public *(open)*
not privileged competitive *(open)*
not proceed with cancel, forbear
not protracted brief
not public residential, secret
not readily discerned impalpable
not readily salable unmarketable
not receivable as evidence inadmissible
not receivable in evidence inadmissible
not reciprocal unilateral
not reputable disreputable
not required elective *(voluntary)*
not resist comply
not respect contemn, decry, disdain, disfavor
not respectable blameworthy, disreputable
not responsible clean, clear *(unencumbered)*, exempt, immune, not guilty
not restorable chronic
not restricted exempt
not retain displace *(remove)*, waive
not reveal conceal
not right errant, improper
not satisfying deficient
not scared secure *(confident)*
not select general
not selective indiscriminate
not sensitive to insusceptible *(resistant)*
not settled indeterminate
not sharp indefinite
not significant irrelevant
not similar dissimilar
not singular nondescript
not speak well of censure, decry
not special generic, nondescript
not specific open-ended
not spiritual corporal
not spurious authentic
not straightforward mendacious
not subject immune, privileged
not subject to exempt
not subject to a payment gratuitous *(given without recompense)*
not subject to regulation free *(enjoying civil liberty)*
not submit hold out *(resist)*, oppose
not subordinate substantive
not substantiated unsupported. SEE MAIN ENTRY
not succeed fail *(lose)*
not sufficient insufficient
not suitable improper
not support counter, disapprove *(reject)*
not sure conditional, uncertain *(questionable)*
not tainted blameless
not take kindly to disapprove *(condemn)*
not tampered with authentic
not the same different, disparate, distinct *(distinguished from others)*
not think about disregard
not think of disregard
not thought much of disreputable
not to be abrogated indefeasible
not to be admitted inadmissible
not to be allowed inadmissible
not to be annulled indefeasible
not to be avoided obligatory
not to be believed disputable
not to be changed immutable
not to be communicated confidential
not to be delayed exigent
not to be disclosed confidential
not to be disputed demonstrable, inappealable
not to be evaded obligatory
not to be made void indefeasible
not to be moved immutable
not to be overlooked considerable, exigent
not to be quoted confidential, unofficial
not to be recommended blameworthy
not to be spoken of confidential
not to the point irrelevant
not to the purpose irrelevant
not too difficult practicable
not toxiferous nontoxic
not trouble oneself disregard
not true dishonest, fraudulent, illusory
not unique nondescript
not up to expectation inadequate
not up to normal deficient
not up to par deficient, unsatisfactory
not use neglect, waive
not vague tangible, unambiguous
not valid illegal, null *(invalid)*, null and void. SEE MAIN ENTRY
not varying fixed *(settled)*
not vital incidental, inconsequential, irrelevant, minor
not wanted inadmissible
not weaken hold out *(resist)*
not well off impecunious
not well-founded baseless
not whole semi
not wholly in part
not working unemployed
not worth considering inconsiderable
not worth mentioning minor
not worthy of notice inconsiderable
not written nuncupative, parol
not yet carried into operation executory
not yet due undue *(not owing)*
not yet payable undue *(not owing)*
not yield hold out *(resist)*, oppose
nota brand, stamp, stigma, symptom, trait
notabilis notable
notability character *(reputation)*, clout, distinction *(reputation)*, eminence, emphasis, feature *(characteristic)*, importance, materiality *(consequence)*, notoriety, prestige, reputation, significance, status
notable appreciable, cardinal *(outstanding)*, considerable, conspicuous, critical *(crucial)*, extraordinary, famous, illustrious, important *(significant)*, influential, major, manifest, momentous, noteworthy, obvious, outstanding *(prominent)*, palpable, paramount, perceivable, perceptible, portentous *(eliciting amazement)*, prominent, remarkable, renowned, reputable, salient, special, unusual. SEE MAIN ENTRY
notable disaster catastrophe
notable feature consequence *(significance)*
notableness materiality *(consequence)*
notably particularly
notam homini inurere brand *(mark)*

notare brand *(mark)*, characterize, designate
notarize SEE MAIN ENTRY
notary notary public. SEE MAIN ENTRY
notatio notice *(heed)*, notice *(observe)*, observation
notation comment, marginalia, memorandum, reminder, symbol. SEE MAIN ENTRY
note attend *(heed)*, book, capsule, check *(instrument)*, comment *(noun)*, comment *(verb)*, coupon, denote, designate, discern *(detect with the senses)*, dispatch *(message)*, distinction *(reputation)*, draft, eminence, emphasis, enter *(record)*, entry *(record)*, hear *(give attention to)*, heed, importance, indicant, indication, indicator, interest *(concern)*, invoice *(bill)*, itemize, marginalia, memorandum, mention *(reference)*, mention, muse, notation, notice *(announcement)*, notice *(observe)*, observation, observe *(watch)*, outline *(synopsis)*, perceive, perception, pierce *(discern)*, prestige, record *(noun)*, record *(verb)*, regard *(esteem)*, regard *(pay attention)*, remark *(noun)*, remark *(verb)*, remind, reminder, report *(detailed account)*, reputation, respect, set down, significance, study, summary, symbol, transmittal, witness *(have direct knowledge of)*. SEE MAIN ENTRY
note differences discriminate *(distinguish)*, distinguish
note down register
note of explanation comment
note the distinctions discern *(discriminate)*, secern
note the similarities and differences compare
note the time of date
notebook file
noted famous, illustrious, notable, notorious, outstanding *(prominent)*, popular, renowned. SEE MAIN ENTRY
notedness notoriety
notes caption, currency, register
noteworthiness distinction *(reputation)*, eminence, importance, prestige
noteworthy certain *(specific)*, considerable, distinctive, extraordinary, famous, important *(significant)*, influential, major, momentous, notable, outstanding *(prominent)*, particular *(specific)*, peculiar *(distinctive)*, portentous *(eliciting amazement)*, prodigious *(amazing)*, rare, remarkable, renowned, special, stellar, uncanny, uncommon, unusual. SEE MAIN ENTRY
nothing blank *(emptiness)*, nonentity, nullity. SEE MAIN ENTRY
nothing but mere
nothingness blank *(emptiness)*, nonentity, nullity
nothus bastard, illegitimate *(born out of wedlock)*
notice admonition, advice, appreciate *(comprehend)*, attend *(heed)*, caution *(warning)*, caveat, character *(reputation)*, citation *(charge)*, comment, consider, declaration, detect, discern *(detect with the senses)*, disclosure *(something disclosed)*, dispatch *(message)*, dun, find *(discover)*, hear *(perceive by ear)*, heed, information *(facts)*, intelligence *(news)*, issuance, monition *(warning)*, notification, observation, observe *(watch)*, perceive, perception, pierce *(discern)*, pronouncement, publication *(disclosure)*, publicity, recognition, recognize *(perceive)*, regard *(attention)*, regard *(pay attention)*, report *(detailed account)*, symptom, ultimatum, witness *(have direct knowledge of)*. SEE MAIN ENTRY
notice critically review
notice of an action lis pendens
notice of an appearance SEE MAIN ENTRY
notice of appearance SEE MAIN ENTRY
notice of claim demand
notice of danger warning
notice of pending suit lis pendens
notice of right lis pendens
notice on file lis pendens
notice to appear citation *(charge)*, monition *(legal summons)*
noticeable apparent *(perceptible)*, appreciable, blatant *(conspicuous)*, conspicuous, determinable *(ascertainable)*, distinct *(clear)*, distinctive, evident, flagrant, manifest, naked *(perceptible)*, noteworthy, obvious, open *(in sight)*, ostensible, overt, palpable, patent, perceivable, perceptible, prominent, salient, scrutable
noticeably fairly *(clearly)*
notification admonition, advice, caveat, citation *(charge)*, communication *(statement)*, declaration, directive, disclosure *(act of disclosing)*, disclosure *(something disclosed)*, dispatch *(message)*, information *(facts)*, issuance, monition *(legal summons)*, monition *(warning)*, notice *(announcement)*, proclamation, profession *(declaration)*, pronouncement, publication *(disclosure)*, publicity, report *(detailed account)*, subpoena. SEE MAIN ENTRY
notification of legal action service *(delivery of legal process)*
notification to appear summons, venire
notificatory declaratory
notified acquainted, informed *(having information)*
notifier informant, informer *(a person who provides information)*
notify admonish *(advise)*, advise, alert, annunciate, apprise, communicate, contact *(communicate)*, convey *(communicate)*, correspond *(communicate)*, disabuse, disclose, disseminate, enlighten, enunciate, forewarn, herald, inform *(notify)*, issue *(publish)*, mention, notice *(give formal warning)*, portend, predict, promulgate, propagate *(spread)*, relate *(tell)*, report *(disclose)*, reveal, signify *(inform)*. SEE MAIN ENTRY
notify of danger caution
notify publicly issue *(publish)*
notify to appear subpoena, summon
notifying informatory
noting down registration
notio idea, notion
notion apprehension *(perception)*, assumption *(supposition)*, concept, idea, impression, opinion *(belief)*, perception, sense *(feeling)*, suspicion *(uncertainty)*. SEE MAIN ENTRY
notional allusive, delusive, fictitious, illusory, inconsistent, insubstantial, nonexistent, quixotic
notoriety bad repute, character *(reputation)*, common knowledge, disgrace, dishonor *(shame)*, ill repute, infamy, opprobrium, prestige, publicity, reputation, scandal, stigma. SEE MAIN ENTRY
notorious apparent *(perceptible)*, blatant *(conspicuous)*, conspicuous, disreputable, famous, flagrant, outrageous, overt, prominent, proverbial, public *(known)*, renowned, scandalous, unmistakable. SEE MAIN ENTRY
notorious criminal outlaw
notoriousness character *(reputation)*, stigma
notus acquainted, familiar *(customary)*, notorious
notwithstanding regardless. SEE MAIN ENTRY
nought nonentity
nourish abet, bear *(support)*, cultivate, foster, maintain *(sustain)*, nurture, preserve, promote *(organize)*, support *(assist)*, sustain *(prolong)*
nourishing conservation, salubrious, salutary
nourishment preservation, sustenance
nouveau riche philistine
novare innovation
novation SEE MAIN ENTRY
novel different, noteworthy, original *(creative)*, portentous *(eliciting amazement)*, recent, unaccustomed, uncommon, unique, unprecedented, unusual. SEE MAIN ENTRY
novelty innovation
novice amateur, apprentice, neophyte, probationer *(one being tested)*, protégé. SEE MAIN ENTRY
novitiate apprentice, preparation, probationer *(one being tested)*
novus eccentric, extraordinary, novel, unprecedented
now instantly
now and forever SEE MAIN ENTRY
now and then sporadic
now to be accounted for a savoir
now to be announced a savoir
now to be described a savoir
now to be enunciated a savoir
now to be itemized a savoir
now to be listed a savoir
now to be mentioned a savoir
now to be narrated a savoir
now to be presented a savoir
now to be read a savoir
now to be recited a savoir
now to be recounted a savoir
now to be reported a savoir
now to be set forth a savoir
now to be stated a savoir
now to follow a savoir
nowhere to be found lost *(taken away)*
noxia guilt
noxious bad *(inferior)*, contemptible, deadly, deleterious, detrimental, fatal, harmful, harsh, inimical, insalubrious, lethal, malignant, objectionable, obnoxious, offensive *(offending)*, peccant *(unhealthy)*, pernicious, pestilent, repulsive, sinister, tainted *(contaminated)*, toxic, unfavorable, virulent. SEE MAIN ENTRY
noxiousness harm
noxius deleterious, harmful, obnoxious, pernicious, prejudicial
nuance difference, differential, technicality. SEE MAIN ENTRY
nubilous indistinct
nucleation centralization
nucleus center *(essence)*, consequence *(significance)*, cornerstone, gravamen, main point, mainstay. SEE MAIN ENTRY
nudge jostle *(bump into)*
nugatorius invalid, nugatory
nugatory collateral *(immaterial)*, expendable, futile, inactive, inadequate, inconsequential, inconsiderable, ineffective, ineffectual, invalid, minor, negligible, null *(insignificant)*, null *(invalid)*, null and void, otiose, paltry, petty, powerless, slight, trivial, unavailing, unproductive, void *(invalid)*. SEE MAIN ENTRY

nugatory check bad check
nugatory trial mistrial
nugax frivolous
nuisance aggravation *(annoyance)*, disadvantage, mischief, molestation. SEE MAIN ENTRY
nuisance value SEE MAIN ENTRY
null inactive, ineffective, ineffectual, invalid, lifeless *(dead)*, nugatory, vacuous, void *(invalid)*. SEE MAIN ENTRY
null and void nugatory, otiose, powerless, void *(invalid)*. SEE MAIN ENTRY
nullifiable defeasible, voidable
nullification abatement *(extinguishment)*, abolition, ademption, annulment, cancellation, countermand, defeasance, destruction, discharge *(annulment)*, discharge *(release from obligation)*, disclaimer, discontinuance *(act of discontinuing)*, dissolution *(termination)*, mistrial, negation, repudiation, rescision, retraction, reversal, revocation. SEE MAIN ENTRY
nullified null *(invalid)*, null and void
nullifier offset
nullify abate *(extinguish)*, abolish, abrogate *(annul)*, abrogate *(rescind)*, adeem, alleviate, annul, balk, cancel, contravene, counteract, destroy *(void)*, disable, disavow, discharge *(release from obligation)*, disinherit, disown *(deny the validity)*, disprove, dissolve *(terminate)*, eliminate *(eradicate)*, expunge, extinguish, extirpate, frustrate, invalidate, kill *(defeat)*, negate, neutralize, obliterate, override, overrule, overthrow, quash, recall *(call back)*, recant, renege, repeal, repudiate, rescind, revoke, supersede, vacate *(void)*, vitiate, withdraw. SEE MAIN ENTRY
nullify a marriage divorce
nullify one's gains overreach
nullifying avoidance *(cancellation)*, cancellation
nullity blank *(emptiness)*, invalidity, mistrial, nonentity. SEE MAIN ENTRY
nullius filius bastard
nullius momenti immaterial
nullo modo fieri potest impossible
numb drug, insusceptible *(uncaring)*, obtund, torpid
number amount *(quantity)*, calculate, contain *(comprise)*, enumerate, itemize, quantity, quota. SEE MAIN ENTRY
number of people population
numbering census, poll *(canvass)*
numberless frequent, infinite, innumerable, myriad, profuse
numerare pay
numerate enumerate
numeration amount *(quantity)*, census, computation, poll *(canvass)*
numerous copious, frequent, manifold, multifarious, multifold, multiple, myriad, populous, profuse, rife. SEE MAIN ENTRY
numerousness multiplicity
numerus quantity
numismatical monetary, pecuniary
nummarius venal
nummary financial, pecuniary
nummi principal *(capital sum)*
nummulary monetary
nummus money
nunc pro tunc SEE MAIN ENTRY
nuncupative parol, verbal. SEE MAIN ENTRY
nundinae market *(business)*
nundination trade *(commerce)*
nuntiare inform *(notify)*
nuntius innuendo, intelligence *(news)*, intimation
nuptiae marriage *(wedlock)*
nuptial conjugal. SEE MAIN ENTRY
nuptial agreements SEE MAIN ENTRY
nuptial bond cohabitation *(married state)*, coverture, marriage *(wedlock)*, matrimony
nuptial state matrimony
nuptial tie cohabitation *(married state)*, marriage *(wedlock)*, matrimony
nuptialis nuptial
nurse cure, foster, maintain *(sustain)*, nurture, promote *(organize)*, protect
nursing conservation
nursing home asylum *(hospital)*
nursling infant
nurture abet, aid, assist, care *(regard)*, conjure, cultivate, discipline *(train)*, educate, foster, keep *(shelter)*, maintain *(sustain)*, mature, preservation, promote *(organize)*. SEE MAIN ENTRY
nurture a belief opine
nutriment sustenance
nutrire foster, nurture
nutrition sustenance
nutritious salubrious, salutary
nutritive salubrious, salutary

O

oafish obtuse, opaque, provincial
oafishness opacity
oath adjuration, affirmation, asseveration, assurance, attestation, avouchment, confirmation, covenant, obligation *(duty)*, pledge *(binding promise)*, profession *(declaration)*, promise, undertaking *(pledge)*, vow. SEE MAIN ENTRY
oath-giving affirmation
oath-taking affirmation
obaeratus indebted
obducere envelop
obduracy resolution *(decision)*, tenacity
obdurate callous, cold-blooded, disobedient, implacable, incorrigible, inexorable, inflexible, insusceptible *(uncaring)*, intractable, pertinacious, recusant, relentless, remorseless, reprobate, resolute, restive, rigid, ruthless, severe, strict, unaffected *(uninfluenced)*, unalterable, unbending, uncompromising, uncontrollable, unrelenting, unyielding, willful. SEE MAIN ENTRY
obdurescere insensible
obedience adherence *(devotion)*, adhesion *(loyalty)*, allegiance, capitulation, compliance, deference, duty *(obligation)*, fealty, homage, loyalty, resignation *(passive acceptance)*, servitude
obedient amenable, controlled *(restrained)*, faithful *(loyal)*, law-abiding, lawful, licit, loyal, obeisant, obsequious, passive, pliable, pliant, sequacious, servile, subservient, tractable, true *(loyal)*, yielding. SEE MAIN ENTRY
obediently faithfully, respectfully
obeisance conformity *(obedience)*, homage, honor *(outward respect)*, prostration, respect
obeisant obedient, passive, pliant, sequacious, servile, subservient. SEE MAIN ENTRY
obey abide, accede *(concede)*, adhere *(maintain loyalty)*, bear *(tolerate)*, comply, conform, fulfill, hear *(give attention to)*, heed, observe *(obey)*, pander, submit *(yield)*, surrender *(yield)*, yield *(submit)*. SEE MAIN ENTRY
obey orders conform
obey regulations conform
obey rules conform
obeyed powerful
obfuscate blind *(obscure)*, camouflage, confound, confuse *(bewilder)*, disorganize, disorient, muddle, obnubilate, obscure. SEE MAIN ENTRY
obfuscated lost *(disoriented)*, nebulous, opaque
obfuscation concealment, evasion, obscuration, opacity, pretext
object article *(commodity)*, cause *(reason)*, collide *(clash)*, complain *(criticize)*, condemn *(ban)*, conflict, confront *(oppose)*, connotation, content *(meaning)*, contest, counter, demonstrate *(protest)*, demur, deprecate, design *(intent)*, destination, determinant, differ *(disagree)*, discord, disaffirm, disagree, disallow, disapprove *(reject)*, disown *(deny the validity)*, dissent *(withhold assent)*, doubt *(distrust)*, end *(intent)*, entity, expostulate, fight *(counteract)*, goal, idea, intent, intention, item, motive, negate, oppose, oppugn, point *(purpose)*, predetermination, project, purpose, pursuit *(goal)*, reason *(basis)*, recipient, reject, remonstrate, reprehend, signification, target. SEE MAIN ENTRY
object frivolously cavil
object lesson admonition. SEE MAIN ENTRY
object of responsibility charge *(custody)*
object of study specialty *(special aptitude)*
object of the action gist *(ground for a suit)*
object produced as evidence exhibit
object submitted in proof of facts exhibit
object to challenge, complain *(criticize)*, criticize *(find fault with)*, disapprove *(condemn)*, discriminate *(treat differently)*, disfavor, dispute *(contest)*, except *(object)*, refuse. SEE MAIN ENTRY
objectify substantiate
objecting critical *(faultfinding)*, disobedient, dissenting, dissident, nonconsenting, remonstrative
objection admonition, complaint, condemnation *(blame)*, criticism, demurrer, denial, disadvantage, disagreement, disapprobation, disapproval, disparagement, dissent *(difference of opinion)*, dissent *(nonconcurrence)*, drawback, grievance, ground, misgiving, negation, nonconformity, opposition, outcry, reaction *(opposition)*, rejection, reluctance, remonstrance, reprimand, reproach, scruple, stricture. SEE MAIN ENTRY
objection to a pleading demurrer
objectionable bad *(inferior)*, bad *(offensive)*, blameful, blameworthy, contemptuous, disreputable, heinous, immoral, impermissible, improper, inadmissible, inadvisable, inappropriate, inapt, ineligible, inept *(inappropriate)*, inexcusable, iniquitous, injudicious, invidious, loathsome, obnoxious, odious, offensive *(offending)*, peccable, reprehensible, repugnant *(exciting aversion)*, repulsive, unacceptable, undesirable, undue *(excessive)*, unendurable, unfit, unjustifiable, unsatisfactory, unsavory, unsuitable, unwarranted. SEE MAIN ENTRY

objective actual, candid, cause *(reason)*, desideratum, design *(intent)*, destination, dispassionate, end *(intent)*, equitable, evenhanded, factual, fair *(just)*, focus, goal, impartial, intent, intention, just, liberal *(broad minded)*, mission, motive, neutral, nonpartisan, open-minded, point *(purpose)*, predetermination, project, purpose, pursuit *(goal)*, rational, substantive, target, unbiased, unprejudiced. SEE MAIN ENTRY
objective certainty certification *(certainness)*, certitude
objective certitude certainty
objective necessity compulsion *(coercion)*
objectivity candor *(impartiality)*, disinterest *(lack of prejudice)*, fairness, justice. SEE MAIN ENTRY
objector appellant, disputant, malcontent
objects commodities
objuration disparagement, imprecation
objurgate admonish *(warn)*, blame, castigate, censure, contemn, criticize *(find fault with)*, defame, deprecate, disapprove *(condemn)*, expostulate, lash *(attack verbally)*, rebuke, remonstrate, reprehend, reprimand, reproach. SEE MAIN ENTRY
objurgation aspersion, bad repute, blame *(culpability)*, charge *(accusation)*, condemnation *(blame)*, contempt *(disdain)*, contumely, denunciation, diatribe, disapprobation, obloquy, remonstrance, reprimand, reproach, revilement, stricture. SEE MAIN ENTRY
objurgatory blameful, contemptible, critical *(faultfinding)*, derogatory, remonstrative, scandalous
oblation benefit *(conferment)*, grant
obliga agreement *(contract)*
obligare bind *(obligate)*, pledge *(promise the performance of)*
obligate compel, constrain *(compel)*, detail *(assign)*, encumber *(financially obligate)*, entail, exact, force *(coerce)*, guarantee, necessitate, press *(constrain)*, require *(compel)*. SEE MAIN ENTRY
obligate oneself contract, promise *(vow)*, undertake
obligated accountable *(responsible)*, bound, contractual, indebted, indentured, liable
obligation agreement *(contract)*, allegiance, arrears, assurance, bond, burden, charge *(cost)*, charge *(lien)*, charge *(responsibility)*, cloud *(incumbrance)*, commitment *(responsibility)*, compact, compulsion *(coercion)*, condition *(contingent provision)*, contract, coverage *(insurance)*, debit, debt, delinquency *(shortage)*, duress, enforcement, excise, expense *(cost)*, incumbrance *(lien)*, job, liability, lien, mortgage, need *(requirement)*, pledge *(binding promise)*, policy *(contract)*, pressure, promise, provision *(clause)*, rate, recognizance, requirement, responsibility *(accountability)*, restriction, security *(stock)*, specialty *(contract)*, trust *(custody)*, undertaking *(commitment)*, undertaking *(pledge)*, weight *(burden)*. SEE MAIN ENTRY
obligation accrued due
obligation incurred cost *(expenses)*
obligation of investigation SEE MAIN ENTRY
obligation repudiated delict
obligatorily will shall
obligatoriness responsibility *(accountability)*
obligatory binding, choate lien, compelling, compulsory, conclusive *(determinative)*, contractual, essential *(required)*, imperative, indispensable, involuntary, mandatory, necessary *(required)*, peremptory *(imperative)*, positive *(prescribed)*, prescriptive, requisite, strict, unavoidable *(inevitable)*. SEE MAIN ENTRY
obligatus indebted
oblige accommodate, aid, assist, bear *(support)*, bestow, bind *(obligate)*, call *(demand)*, coerce, compel, constrain *(compel)*, delegate, detail *(assign)*, dictate, enjoin, exact, excise *(levy a tax)*, force *(coerce)*, help, impose *(enforce)*, impose *(subject)*, let *(permit)*, necessitate, order, pander, patronize *(condescend toward)*, press *(constrain)*, require *(compel)*, suffer *(permit)*, supply, tolerate. SEE MAIN ENTRY
obliged accountable *(responsible)*, bound, indebted, indentured, liable
obliged in law liable
obligee SEE MAIN ENTRY
obligement enforcement, obligation *(duty)*
obliging accommodation *(adjustment)*, beneficial, benevolent, binding, charitable *(lenient)*, civil *(polite)*, favorable *(expressing approval)*, malleable, obedient, obeisant, philanthropic, pliable, propitious, sequacious, yielding
obligingness amenability, benevolence *(disposition to do good)*, clemency, comity, consideration *(sympathetic regard)*, indulgence
obligor debtor. SEE MAIN ENTRY
oblinere smear
obliquation indirection *(indirect action)*
oblique circuitous, deceptive, deviant, indirect, labyrinthine, sinuous. SEE MAIN ENTRY
oblique allusion innuendo
oblique hint insinuation
obliqueness indirection *(deceitfulness)*, indirection *(indirect action)*
obliquitous deceptive, sinister
obliquity bad faith, bad repute, corruption, crime, deception, delinquency *(misconduct)*, improbity, indirection *(deceitfulness)*, indirection *(indirect action)*, vice, wrong
obliquus indirect, oblique *(slanted)*
obliterate abate *(extinguish)*, abolish, adeem, annul, cancel, deface, delete, destroy *(efface)*, dissolve *(terminate)*, eliminate *(eradicate)*, eradicate, expunge, extinguish, extirpate, negate, nullify, overthrow, overturn, quash, remove *(eliminate)*, repeal, rescind. SEE MAIN ENTRY
obliterated lost *(taken away)*, null *(invalid)*, null and void
obliteration abatement *(extinguishment)*, abolition, annulment, catastrophe, censorship, defacement, destruction, dissolution *(termination)*, obscuration, removal
obliteration of grievances pardon
oblitterare expunge
oblivion disregard *(unconcern)*, nullity
obliviosus oblivious
oblivious careless, heedless, inadvertent, incognizant, lax, negligent, unaware. SEE MAIN ENTRY
obliviousness disinterest *(lack of interest)*, disregard *(unconcern)*, negligence
obloquial calumnious
obloquious calumnious
obloquy aspersion, attaint, bad repute, blame *(culpability)*, contempt *(disdain)*, contumely, criticism, defamation, degradation, denunciation, diatribe, disgrace, dishonor *(shame)*, disparagement, disrepute, ignominy, infamy, malediction, notoriety, odium, opprobrium, ostracism, phillipic, profanity, reproach, revilement, scandal, shame, slander, stricture. SEE MAIN ENTRY
obnoxious bad *(offensive)*, blameworthy, contemptuous, disreputable, heinous, invidious, loathsome, nefarious, objectionable, odious, offensive *(offending)*, reprehensible, repugnant *(exciting aversion)*, repulsive, undesirable, unendurable, unsavory. SEE MAIN ENTRY
obnoxiousness bad repute, disrepute, indecency
obnoxium reddere subject
obnoxius dependent, liable
obnubliate SEE MAIN ENTRY
oboediens obedient
oboedire obey
obreptitious collusive, sly, stealthy, surreptitious
obruere overwhelm
obrussa criterion
obscene depraved, lascivious, lewd, licentious, objectionable, prurient, repulsive, salacious, scurrilous, suggestive *(risqué)*. SEE MAIN ENTRY
obscene art pornography
obscene literature pornography
obscenitas obscenity
obscenity debauchery, pornography, turpitude. SEE MAIN ENTRY
obscenus obscene
obscuration indistinctness, opacity. SEE MAIN ENTRY
obscure allusive, ambiguous, blind *(concealed)*, camouflage, clandestine, cloak, complex, conceal, confound, cover *(conceal)*, de minimus, debatable, difficult, disguise, disorganize, disorient, elusive, enigmatic, ensconce, enshroud, envelop, equivocal, esoteric, hidden, hide, impalpable, inapprehensible, incomprehensible, inconspicuous, indefinable, indefinite, indeterminate, inexplicable, inscrutable, minor, mysterious, nebulous, obfuscate, obliterate, obnubilate, opaque, oracular, plant *(covertly place)*, privy, recondite, secret, shroud, stealthy, ulterior, uncertain *(ambiguous)*, unclear, underlying, unspecified, vague. SEE MAIN ENTRY
obscure information secret
obscure meaning ambiguity
obscure question enigma
obscure statement enigma
obscured hidden, lost *(taken away)*
obscurity ambiguity, complication, concealment, indistinctness, mystery, nonappearance, obscuration, opacity, privacy
obscurus inconspicuous, indistinct, inscrutable, lurid
obsecrare appeal, plead *(implore)*, request
obsecrate importune, solicit
obsecratio entreaty
obsecration call *(appeal)*, claim *(legal demand)*, dun, entreaty, imprecation, request
obsequens subservient, yielding
obsequi defer *(put off)*, defer *(yield in judgment)*, obey
obsequious law-abiding, passive, sequacious, servile, subservient, yielding. SEE MAIN ENTRY
obsequiousness allegiance, discipline *(obedience)*

obsequium compliance
obserere lock
observable appreciable, blatant *(conspicuous),* clear *(apparent),* conspicuous, determinable *(ascertainable),* discernible, manifest, naked *(perceptible),* obvious, open *(in sight),* ostensible, palpable, patent, perceivable, perceptible, scrutable, visible *(noticeable)*
observably particularly
observably different distinct *(distinguished from others)*
observance acquiescence, adherence *(devotion),* allegiance, ceremony, compliance, conformity *(obedience),* contemplation, custom, discharge *(performance),* discipline *(obedience),* habit, manner *(behavior),* notice *(heed),* practice *(procedure),* prescription *(custom),* remembrance *(commemoration),* scrutiny. SEE MAIN ENTRY
observance of form formality
observance of obligation allegiance
observant alert *(vigilant),* circumspect, conscientious, conscious *(aware),* law-abiding, obedient, perspicacious, punctilious, receptive, sensible, sensitive *(discerning),* vigilant
observant of decorum punctilious
observant of form formal
observantia homage, respect
observantly faithfully
observare heed, keep *(fulfill),* observe *(obey),* observe *(watch),* regard *(pay attention)*
observatio observation
observation apprehension *(perception),* comment, comprehension, concept, conclusion *(determination),* dictum, diligence *(care),* discovery, estimate *(idea),* examination *(study),* generalization, indagation, inference, inspection, judgment *(discernment),* notice *(heed),* outlook, perception, pronouncement, regard *(attention),* remark, research, scrutiny, sense *(intelligence),* statement, surveillance, test. SEE MAIN ENTRY
observation post standpoint
observe abide, bear *(tolerate),* check *(inspect),* comment, comply, conform, consider, detect, discern *(detect with the senses),* discover, examine *(study),* express, find *(discover),* fulfill, heed, keep *(fulfill),* mention, monitor, note *(notice),* notice *(observe),* obey, patrol, perceive, perform *(adhere to),* peruse, phrase, pierce *(discern),* police, probe, regard *(pay attention),* relate *(tell),* remark, scrutinize, spy, study, survey *(examine),* witness *(have direct knowledge of).* SEE MAIN ENTRY
observe discipline conform
observer bystander, eyewitness, spy, witness
observing circumspect
obses hostage
obsess harass, occupy *(engage).* SEE MAIN ENTRY
obsessed fanatical, lunatic, pensive
obsessed with addicted
obsessing compelling
obsessio blockade *(barrier)*
obsession dipsomania, phobia, preoccupation, requirement. SEE MAIN ENTRY
obsessional compelling
obsessive compelling, fanatical
obsidio blockade *(barrier)*
obsistere withstand
obsolescence desuetude, disuse
obsolescent obsolete, outdated, outmoded
obsolete defunct, inactive, old, outdated, outmoded. SEE MAIN ENTRY
obsoleteness desuetude
obsoletus dilapidated, obsolete, stale
obstacle bar *(obstruction),* barrier, blockade *(barrier),* check *(bar),* complication, damper *(stopper),* deterrence, deterrent, detriment, disadvantage, drawback, encumbrance, fetter, handicap, hindrance, impasse, impediment, interruption, nuisance, obstruction, pitfall, predicament, problem, prohibition, restraint, stay. SEE MAIN ENTRY
obstare prevent, withstand
obstinacy contempt *(disobedience to the court),* contest *(dispute),* reluctance, resistance, resolution *(decision),* tenacity
obstinate contentious, contumacious, difficult, disobedient, froward, immutable, impervious, implacable, incorrigible, inexorable, inflexible, insusceptible *(uncaring),* intractable, obdurate, persistent, pertinacious, perverse, proud *(conceited),* purposeful, recalcitrant, recusant, relentless, resolute, restive, rigid, steadfast, unbending, uncompromising, uncontrollable, unruly, unyielding, willful
obstinatus inflexible, pertinacious, willful
obstreperous blatant *(obtrusive),* disobedient, disorderly, intractable, perverse, recalcitrant, uncontrollable, unruly
obstruct abrogate *(annul),* arrest *(stop),* balk, ban, bar *(hinder),* block, check *(restrain),* clog, condemn *(ban),* constrain *(restrain),* constrict *(inhibit),* contain *(restrain),* control *(restrain),* counter, curb, debar, defer *(put off),* delay, detain *(restrain),* deter, disadvantage, discontinue *(break continuity),* disrupt, estop, fight *(counteract),* foil, forbid, forestall, frustrate, halt, hamper, hinder, hold up *(delay),* impede, inconvenience, inhibit, interdict, interfere, interpose, interrupt, keep *(restrain),* lock, obturate, occlude, oppose, oppugn, preclude, prevent, prohibit, repulse, resist *(oppose),* restrain, restrict, shut, stall, stave, stay *(halt),* stem *(check),* stifle, stop, suppress, thwart, toll *(stop),* trammel, withstand. SEE MAIN ENTRY
obstruct action encumber *(hinder)*
obstruct by opposition discourage
obstruct one's vision blind *(deprive of sight)*
obstruct the course of descent escheat
obstruct the view of cloak, enshroud
obstruct work strike *(refuse to work)*
obstructed arrested *(checked),* blind *(impassable),* broken *(interrupted),* impervious
obstructer deterrent
obstructio obstruction
obstruction barrier, blockade *(barrier),* check *(bar),* cloud *(incumbrance),* complication, constraint *(restriction),* damper *(stopper),* deadlock, deterrence, deterrent, disadvantage, encumbrance, estoppel, fetter, filibuster, frustration, halt, handicap, hindrance, impasse, impediment, impugnation, interruption, obstacle, onus *(burden),* predicament, prohibition, resistance, restraint, stay, trouble. SEE MAIN ENTRY
obstruction of justice misprision
obstruction to congressional action filibuster
obstructionism constraint *(restriction),* contempt *(disobedience to the court)*
obstructionist assailant, disputant, malcontent. SEE MAIN ENTRY
obstructive deterrent, preventive, prohibitive *(restrictive)*
obstruent obstruction
obstupefacere confound
obsuration concealment
obtain accept *(take),* acquire *(receive),* attain, buy, derive *(receive),* educe, engage *(hire),* evoke, extract, gain, glean, induce, inherit, occupy *(take possession),* perform *(adhere to),* possess, preempt, procure, purchase, raise *(collect),* reach, realize *(obtain as a profit),* reap, receive *(acquire),* recover, recruit, redeem *(repurchase),* succeed *(attain).* SEE MAIN ENTRY
obtain a mortgage borrow
obtain a return profit, realize *(obtain as a profit)*
obtain a victory beat *(defeat),* earn
obtain again repossess
obtain by any means acquire *(secure)*
obtain by compulsion enforce, extort
obtain by course of law recover
obtain by force enforce, impose *(enforce)*
obtain by reasoning derive *(deduce)*
obtain by search find *(discover)*
obtain exclusive possession monopolize
obtain in an unlawful manner extort
obtain insurance insure
obtain knowledge of overhear
obtain money by false pretenses cheat
obtain money on false pretenses defraud, peculate
obtain money under false pretenses defalcate
obtain payment collect *(recover money)*
obtain the use of borrow
obtain under false pretenses peculate
obtain unlawfully extort
obtainable available, open *(accessible),* possible, potential, practicable, vulnerable
obtainer consumer
obtaining by force extortion
obtaining by threat extortion
obtaining national defense secrets espionage
obtaining of classified information espionage
obtainment adverse possession, collection *(accumulation),* distraint, receipt *(act of receiving),* recovery *(repossession),* takeover
obtainment of property acquisition
obtegere cover *(pretext)*
obtemperans obedient
obtemperare conform
obtest importune, petition, pray, request, solicit
obtestatio appeal, entreaty
obtestation call *(appeal),* dun
obtrectare decry, defame, depreciate
obtrectatio disparagement
obtrectation bad repute
obtrude accroach, encroach, impinge, impose *(intrude),* interpose, intervene, intrude, invade, overstep. SEE MAIN ENTRY
obtrude on compel
obtrusion deterrent, encroachment, intrusion
obtrusive brazen, bumptious, contemptuous, flagrant, intrusive, prominent. SEE MAIN ENTRY
obtrusiveness pretense *(ostentation)*
obtund assuage, impair, palliate *(abate),* soothe, subdue. SEE MAIN ENTRY
obturate balk, deter, occlude. SEE MAIN ENTRY

obturation blockade *(limitation)*, obstruction
obtuse blind *(not discerning)*, fatuous, impervious, inexpressive, opaque, unaffected *(uninfluenced)*. SEE MAIN ENTRY
obtuseness ignorance, opacity
obtusus obtuse
obumbrate obfuscate
obverse adverse *(opposite)*, antipode, contra, contradictory, contraposition, contrary, counterpart *(complement)*
obviate balk, bar *(hinder)*, deter, estop, forestall, overrule, overthrow, prevent, remove *(eliminate)*, stay *(halt)*, supersede. SEE MAIN ENTRY
obviation SEE MAIN ENTRY
obvious absolute *(conclusive)*, apparent *(perceptible)*, arrant *(definite)*, blatant *(conspicuous)*, coherent *(clear)*, comprehensible, conspicuous, distinct *(clear)*, elementary, evident, explicit, flagrant, gross *(flagrant)*, lucid, manifest, naked *(perceptible)*, open *(in sight)*, ostensible, outright, overt, palpable, patent, pellucid, perceivable, perceptible, prominent, public *(known)*, salient, scrutable, stark, tangible, unambiguous, undeniable, unmistakable. SEE MAIN ENTRY
obvious interpretation connotation, content *(meaning)*
obvious meaning connotation, content *(meaning)*
obvious sense connotation, content *(meaning)*
obviously fairly *(clearly)*
occasio occasion, opportunity
occasion access *(opening)*, avail *(bring about)*, cause, chance *(fortuity)*, create, day in court, engender, entail, event, evoke, experience *(encounter)*, generate, happening, incident, inspire, occurrence, opportunity, particular, point *(period of time)*, prompt, provoke, qualification *(fitness)*. SEE MAIN ENTRY
occasional casual, infrequent, intermittent, periodic, sporadic, uncommon, unusual
occasioner author *(originator)*
occasions circumstances
occidere kill *(murder)*, perish, slay
occisio murder
occlude balk, bar *(exclude)*, bar *(hinder)*, block, clog, constrict *(inhibit)*, debar, hinder, lock, obstruct, seal *(close)*, shut, stop. SEE MAIN ENTRY
occlusion blockade *(limitation)*, damper *(stopper)*, deterrent, obstruction
occulere conceal
occult blind *(obscure)*, cloak, covert, elusive, esoteric, hidden, incomprehensible, inexplicable, inscrutable, mysterious, obfuscate, obnubilate, obscure, recondite, secret, uncertain *(ambiguous)*, undisclosed
occultare disguise
occultari abscond
occultate camouflage
occultation obscuration
occultism mystery
occultness mystery
occultus hidden, inscrutable, latent, mysterious, secret, stealthy
occupancy enjoyment *(use)*, habitation *(act of inhabiting)*, inhabitation *(act of dwelling in)*, occupation *(possession)*, ownership, possession *(ownership)*, seisin, tenancy, tenure. SEE MAIN ENTRY
occupant citizen, denizen, domiciliary, habitant, inhabitant, inmate, lessee, lodger, resident, tenant. SEE MAIN ENTRY
occupant of an office incumbent
occupare assume *(seize)*, encroach, invest *(fund)*, occupy *(engage)*, occupy *(take possession)*
occupatio occupation *(possession)*, pursuit *(occupation)*, taking
occupation appointment *(position)*, calling, capacity *(job)*, career, employment, enjoyment *(use)*, enterprise *(undertaking)*, function, habitation *(act of inhabiting)*, industry *(activity)*, inhabitation *(act of dwelling in)*, job, labor *(work)*, livelihood, occupancy, office, position *(business status)*, post, practice *(professional business)*, profession *(vocation)*, project, province, seisin, specialty *(special aptitude)*, tenancy, tenure, undertaking *(enterprise)*, work *(employment)*. SEE MAIN ENTRY
occupational technical
occupatum employ *(engage services)*
occupiable habitable
occupied full, pensive, populous, residential
occupier citizen, denizen, domiciliary, habitant, inhabitant, inmate, lessee, lodger, occupant, resident, tenant
occupy consist, dwell *(reside)*, engage *(involve)*, hold *(possess)*, immerse *(engross)*, inhabit, interest, monopolize, own, possess, preempt, reside. SEE MAIN ENTRY
occupy oneself with address *(direct attention to)*, commit *(perpetrate)*, devote, notice *(observe)*, ply
occupy the attention interest
occupy the chair manage, officiate, preside
occupy the mind with concentrate *(pay attention)*
occupy the thoughts with concentrate *(pay attention)*, focus, ponder
occupying situated
occupying the same domicile cohabitation *(living together)*
occur accrue *(arise)*, appear *(materialize)*, ensue, supervene. SEE MAIN ENTRY
occur again recur
occur at the same time concur *(coexist)*
occur concurrently concur *(coexist)*
occurrence appearance *(emergence)*, case *(example)*, case *(set of circumstances)*, contingency, development *(outgrowth)*, event, experience *(encounter)*, happening, incident, occasion, particular, predicament, situation. SEE MAIN ENTRY
occurrences circumstances
occurring current
occurring after death posthumous
occurring again periodic
occurring at the same time concurrent *(at the same time)*
occurring by chance fortuitous
occurring in an instant instantaneous
occurring simultaneously coincidental
occurring together coincidental
ochlocracy lynch law
oculis captus blind *(not discerning)*
odd dissimilar, eccentric, inappropriate, irregular *(not usual)*, ludicrous, noteworthy, novel, original *(creative)*, particular *(specific)*, peculiar *(curious)*, singular, unaccustomed, uncanny, uncommon, unique, unusual. SEE MAIN ENTRY
oddity exception *(exclusion)*, irregularity, quirk *(idiosyncrasy)*, speciality, specialty *(distinctive mark)*, trait. SEE MAIN ENTRY
oddment discard
oddments balance *(amount in excess)*
oddness irregularity
odds advantage, contraposition, discord, disagreement, edge *(advantage)*, embroilment, feud, probability, variance *(disagreement)*
odiosus irksome, odious, repulsive
odiosus molestus offensive *(offending)*
odious antipathetic *(distasteful)*, bad *(offensive)*, base *(bad)*, blameworthy, contemptible, disgraceful, disreputable, gross *(flagrant)*, heinous, invidious, libelous, loathsome, nefarious, notorious, objectionable, obnoxious, offensive *(offending)*, outrageous, reprehensible, repugnant *(exciting aversion)*, repulsive, scandalous, sordid. SEE MAIN ENTRY
odiousness bad repute, disrepute, odium
odium alienation *(estrangement)*, attaint, bad repute, contempt *(disdain)*, criticism, degradation, discredit, disgrace, disrepute, hatred, ignominy, ill will, infamy, malice, notoriety, obloquy, opprobrium. SEE MAIN ENTRY
odium rancor
odium scandal, shame
odorari trace *(follow)*
of construe *(translate)*
of a different kind dissimilar
of a previous fashion outdated, outmoded
of a previous style outdated, outmoded
of all sorts dissimilar
of an equal size commensurable
of any description whatever
of any kind or sort whatever
of bad character disreputable
of consequence cogent
of course consequently. SEE MAIN ENTRY
of decisive importance critical *(crucial)*
of doubtful certainty disputable
of doubtful meaning equivocal
of equal dignity coequal
of equal duration commensurate
of equal extent commensurate
of equal force equivalent
of equal length or volume commensurable
of equal power coequal
of equal rank commensurate
of equal value equivalent
of equal weight equivalent
of every description miscellaneous
of everyday occurrence typical
of external origin alien *(unrelated)*
of foreign origin alien *(foreign)*
of frequent occurrence typical
of general utility beneficial, practical
of good omen auspicious
of great age outdated
of great consequence critical *(crucial)*, decisive, important *(significant)*
of great extent copious, far reaching
of great import SEE MAIN ENTRY
of great magnitude important *(significant)*
of great scope complete *(all-embracing)*, far reaching, omnibus
of great weight important *(significant)*
of greater influence superior *(higher)*
of hidden meaning enigmatic
of high standing important *(significant)*
of high station important *(significant)*
of higher rank superior *(higher)*
of highest excellence prime *(most valuable)*
of humble birth ignoble

of ill fame disreputable, notorious
of ill repute notorious
of illicit union illegitimate *(born out of wedlock)*
of importance considerable, critical *(crucial)*, important *(significant)*, indispensable
of inestimable value invaluable
of law jural
of lawful parentage legitimate *(lawfully conceived)*
of less importance inferior *(lower in position)*
of like rank coequal
of little account immaterial, inappreciable, negligible
of little consequence negligible, nonessential, paltry, trivial
of little importance inapposite, inappreciable, negligible, nonessential
of little moment collateral *(immaterial)*
of little value paltry
of little weight frivolous
of long duration chronic, durable
of long standing conventional, customary, durable
of loose morals brazen
of low character ignoble
of low extraction caitiff, ignoble
of low origin caitiff
of low station ignoble
of lower rank subaltern
of many kinds dissimilar
of mean extraction caitiff
of mean origin caitiff
of minor importance de minimus, inconsequential
of mixed character miscellaneous
of moment crucial
of necessity compelling, consequently
of no account de minimus, expendable, frivolous, inconsequential, minor, nonessential, null *(insignificant)*, paltry, unessential
of no avail unavailing
of no binding force null *(invalid)*, null and void
of no concern nonessential
of no consequence immaterial, inconsequential, inconsiderable, insubstantial, nonessential, unessential
of no effect null *(insignificant)*, null *(invalid)*, null and void
of no essential consequence immaterial
of no importance immaterial, nonessential
of no legal weight null and void
of no moment immaterial, inconsiderable, negligible, null *(insignificant)*
of no repute blameworthy
of no significance immaterial, negligible, nonessential
of no validity null *(invalid)*, null and void
of no value null *(insignificant)*
of no weight null *(invalid)*
of note considerable, crucial
of old outdated
of one accord concurrent *(united)*, consensual, consenting
of one mind consensual
of promise auspicious
of recent occurrence recent
of regular recurrence continual *(connected)*
of repute credible
of right de jure
of second rank minor
of service beneficial, disposable, effective *(efficient)*
of short duration provisional
of small account petty, slight
of small importance nonessential, slight
of small moment petty
of small value paltry
of sound judgment normal *(sane)*
of supreme importance crucial
of that kind cognate
of that sort cognate
of the best quality prime *(most valuable)*
of the blood consanguineous
of the moment current
of the old order outdated
of the old school outdated, outmoded
of the origin reputed authentic
of the present current
of the quality of a felon felonious
of the same degree equal
of the same family consanguineous, interrelated
of the same kind consanguineous
of the same mind collective, concordant, consensual
of the same rank coequal, equal
of the same stock akin *(related by blood)*
of this date current
of todays date current
of uncertain issue doubtful
of uncertain significance equivocal
of unknown authorship anonymous
of unsound mind deranged, lunatic, non compos mentis
of use disposable, effective *(efficient)*
of value beneficial
of various kinds miscellaneous
of vital importance critical *(crucial)*, essential *(required)*
of which wherein
off stale
off guard heedless, negligent, unaware, unsuspecting
off the charts SEE MAIN ENTRY
off the mark improper
off the point immaterial
off the record confidential, unofficial
off the subject impertinent *(irrelevant)*, irrelevant
off the topic immaterial, irrelevant
off-center astray
off-color improper, suggestive *(risqué)*
off-the-record private *(confidential)*
offbeat unusual
offed SEE MAIN ENTRY
offence crime
offend affront, aggravate *(annoy)*, annoy, antagonize, bait *(harass)*, disoblige, distress, estrange, harry *(harass)*, hector, humiliate, irritate, mistreat, persecute, pique, plague, provoke, repel *(disgust)*, trespass. SEE MAIN ENTRY
offend against the law violate
offended aggrieved *(victimized)*, resentful
offender convict, criminal, delinquent, felon, lawbreaker, malefactor, outlaw, pariah, racketeer, recidivist, wrongdoer. SEE MAIN ENTRY
offender against society outlaw
offender against the law malefactor
offender under suspension of sentence probationer *(released offender)*
offendere disoblige, offend *(insult)*
offending delinquent *(guilty of a misdeed)*, felonious, offensive *(offending)*, repugnant *(exciting aversion)*. SEE MAIN ENTRY
offensa disfavor, dissatisfaction
offense assault, crime, delict, delinquency *(misconduct)*, disrespect, exception *(objection)*, felony, foray, guilt, indiscretion, infraction, injury, injustice, misconduct, misdeed, misdemeanor, misdoing, misfeasance, misprision, onset *(assault)*, provocation, resentment, transgression, umbrage, violation, wrong. SEE MAIN ENTRY
offense against the law crime, guilt, misdemeanor, misfeasance
offense against the state crime
offense punishable by imprisonment felony
offense specific right SEE MAIN ENTRY
offenseless blameless
offensio dissatisfaction, offense
offensive antipathetic *(distasteful)*, bad *(offensive)*, blatant *(obtrusive)*, calumnious, contemptible, contemptuous, foray, gross *(flagrant)*, heinous, impertinent *(insolent)*, inelegant, insolent, invidious, lewd, litigious, loathsome, lurid, noxious, objectionable, obnoxious, obscene, odious, onset *(assault)*, outrageous, peccant *(culpable)*, presumptuous, profligate *(corrupt)*, pugnacious, reprehensible, repugnant *(exciting aversion)*, repulsive, salacious, scandalous, scurrilous, unacceptable, unbecoming, unendurable, unsatisfactory, unsavory, unseemly, vicious. SEE MAIN ENTRY
offensive action battery
offensive office environment SEE MAIN ENTRY
offensive to decency obscene
offensive to modesty obscene
offensively assertive blatant *(obtrusive)*
offensively obtrusive blatant *(obtrusive)*
offensiveness guilt, obscenity
offer adduce, administer *(tender)*, bear *(yield)*, bid, hold out *(deliberate on an offer)*, introduce, invitation, overture, pose *(propound)*, present *(introduce)*, present *(make a gift)*, proffer, proposal *(suggestion)*, propose, proposition, propound, remit *(submit for consideration)*, tender. SEE MAIN ENTRY
offer a discount rebate
offer a job to delegate
offer a post delegate
offer a word of caution forewarn, notice *(give formal warning)*
offer advice exhort
offer an explanation explain
offer an explanation of interpret
offer an inducement coax, suborn
offer an opinion advise
offer an opinion to counsel
offer as an exhibit introduce
offer assurances to assure *(give confidence to)*
offer collateral ensure, pawn, pledge *(deposit)*
offer compensation indemnify
offer counsel admonish *(advise)*, advise, charge *(instruct on the law)*
offer evidence present *(introduce)*
offer for consideration move *(judicially request)*
offer for inspection exhibit
offer for sale handle *(trade)*, sell, vend
offer in defense justify
offer in exchange displace *(replace)*
offer performance offer *(tender)*
offer reparation indemnify
offer resistance confront *(oppose)*, hold out *(resist)*, oppose, parry, resist *(oppose)*, withstand

offer sacrifice propitiate
offer satisfaction indemnify
offer to give dedicate
offer to the public issue *(publish),* post
offered unsolicited, voluntary
offered price bid
offerer client
offering benefit *(conferment),* bribe, contribution *(donation),* dedication, donation, gratuity *(present),* introduction, largess *(gift),* tip *(gratuity)*
offering a problem difficult
offering as an exhibit introduction
offering evidence probative
offerre offer *(propose)*
offertory benefit *(conferment)*
offhand cursory, impulsive *(rash),* informal, nonchalant, perfunctory, slipshod, unpremeditated
offhandedness informality
office agency *(commission),* appointment *(position),* bureau, business *(occupation),* calling, career, chamber *(compartment),* chapter *(branch),* duty *(obligation),* employment, firm, function, mission, occupation *(vocation),* organ, position *(business status),* post, profession *(vocation),* province, pursuit *(occupation),* sphere, title *(position),* trade *(occupation),* work *(employment).* SEE MAIN ENTRY
office bearer official
office force personnel
office holder clerk, functionary
office hunter candidate
office seeker candidate, politician
office worker clerk
office-seeker contender
officebearer incumbent
officeholder caretaker *(one fulfilling the function of office),* incumbent, officer, official, politician
officeholders authorities
officer caretaker *(one fulfilling the function of office),* functionary, incumbent, key man, magistrate, marshal, official, peace officer, proctor SEE MAIN ENTRY
officer in charge caretaker *(one fulfilling the function of office)*
officer of court counsel, counselor
officer of state caretaker *(one fulfilling the function of office),* legislator, politician
officer of the court administrator, attorney, esquire. SEE MAIN ENTRY
officer of the law marshal, peace officer
officer who carries out orders of the court marshal
officers management *(directorate),* police
officers of instruction faculty *(teaching staff)*
officers of the law police
official actual, certain *(fixed),* choate lien, civic, clerk, ex officio, factual, formal, functionary, genuine, incumbent, indubious, legitimate *(rightful),* magistrate, notary public, officer, politician, valid. SEE MAIN ENTRY
official announcement charter *(declaration of rights)*
official bulletin declaration
official call monition *(legal summons),* process *(summons),* summons
official correspondence dispatch *(message)*
official count census
official court order summons
official criminal charge information *(charge)*
official document charter *(license)*
official enumeration of inhabitants census
official enumeration of the population census
official headquarters of an ambassador embassy
official inquiry investigation
official misconduct crime, criminality, delict, guilt, misfeasance, offense SEE MAIN ENTRY
official mission embassy
official notice citation *(charge),* monition *(legal summons),* process *(summons),* summons
official order mittimus, summons
official procedure bureaucracy
official publication document, proclamation
official receiver assessor
official reception ceremony
official reckoning census
official recognition mention *(tribute)*
official record instrument *(document)*
official registration census
official reply answer *(judicial response)*
official representative legislator, plenipotentiary
official writing certificate, instrument *(document)*
officialdom bureaucracy
officially utter pronounce *(pass judgment)*
officially withdraw repeal
officials authorities, hierarchy *(persons in authority),* management *(directorate)*
officiary official
officiate administer *(conduct),* exercise *(discharge a function),* govern, handle *(manage),* manage, moderate *(preside over),* operate, oversee, preside, rule *(govern).* SEE MAIN ENTRY
officiate at conduct
officiating executive, ministerial
officiation bureaucracy, direction *(guidance)*
officio fungi officiate
officious dictatorial, obtrusive
officium courtesy, duty *(obligation),* function, obligation *(duty),* office, subjection
offprint copy
offset adeem, compensate *(counterbalance),* contra, counteract, countervail, cover *(provide for),* equipoise, negate, neutralize, nullify, outbalance, overreach, reaction *(opposition),* setoff. SEE MAIN ENTRY
offset bad debts redeem *(satisfy debts)*
offsetting contribution *(indemnification)*
offsetting claim setoff
offshoot affiliate, consequence *(conclusion),* corollary, descendant, development *(outgrowth),* organ, outgrowth. SEE MAIN ENTRY
offshoots offspring
offspring affinity *(family ties),* blood, child, children, descendant, family *(household),* issue *(progeny),* offshoot, outcome, outgrowth, posterity, product, progeny, succession. SEE MAIN ENTRY
oft repeated proverbial, trite
oft-repeated customary, frequent, ordinary, periodic, typical
often chronic. SEE MAIN ENTRY
often done frequent
often met with common *(customary)*
oftentime periodic
old antique, elderly, obsolete, outdated, outmoded, prior, stale, traditional, trite. SEE MAIN ENTRY
old age longevity
old campaigner veteran
old fashioned antique
old soldier veteran
old-fashioned defunct, obsolete, outdated, outmoded
old-time outdated
old-world outdated, outmoded
olden old, outdated
older antique
oldest prime *(original)*
oldness longevity
oligopoly monopoly
olio melange
omega close *(conclusion),* end *(termination)*
omen anticipate *(prognosticate),* caution *(warning),* forerunner, harbinger, herald, indicant, indication, portend, precursor, predict, premonition, presage, threat, token, warning
ominate forewarn, portend, predict, presage, prognosticate
ominous aleatory *(perilous),* bleak *(not favorable),* dangerous, dire, imminent, inauspicious, insalubrious, oracular, pending *(imminent),* portentous *(ominous),* presageful, prophetic, suggestive *(evocative),* unfavorable, unpropitious. SEE MAIN ENTRY
omission breach, default, deficiency, deficit, delinquency *(failure of duty),* dereliction, desuetude, dishonor *(nonpayment),* dispensation *(exception),* exception *(exclusion),* exclusion, failure *(falling short),* fault *(mistake),* flaw, infraction, laches, miscue, neglect, negligence, nonfeasance, nonperformance, offense, ostracism, rejection, removal, renunciation. SEE MAIN ENTRY
omission of a court injustice
omission of duty delinquency *(failure of duty)*
omission of obligation delinquency *(failure of duty)*
omission prohibited by law crime
omissive remiss
omit abrogate *(rescind),* bar *(exclude),* censor, delete, eliminate *(exclude),* except *(exclude),* exclude, fail *(neglect),* forgo, forswear, ignore, neglect, obliterate, overlook *(disregard),* pretermit, prohibit, relegate, remove *(eliminate),* set aside *(annul).* SEE MAIN ENTRY
omit using conserve
omit what is due default
omitted null *(invalid),* null and void
omittere abandon *(withdraw),* disregard, omit
omitting perfunctory, save
omnibus SEE MAIN ENTRY
omniform protean
omnino in toto
omnipotence force *(strength),* influence, predominance, supremacy
omnipotens omnipotent
omnipotent compelling, in full force, indomitable, influential, irresistible, powerful, predominant, strong. SEE MAIN ENTRY
omnipresent ubiquitous
omnis total
omniscient expert, learned. SEE MAIN ENTRY
omnivorous gluttonous
omnivorousness greed

on a footing with coequal
on a level with coequal
on a par coequal, commensurate, equal
on a par with coequal, equivalent
on a proper scale commensurate
on a suitable scale commensurate
on account of ad hoc, in furtherance
on account of this a priori, consequently
on all counts in toto
on approval elective *(selective)*
on bad terms inimical
on behalf of in furtherance, in lieu of. SEE MAIN ENTRY
on call available, disposable, ready *(prepared)*
on condition that provided
on duty operative
on edge restive
on even terms commensurate, equal, pro rata
on familiar terms intimate
on fire perfervid
on guard alert *(vigilant)*, circumspect, noncommittal, provident *(showing foresight)*, safe, vigilant
on hand present *(attendant)*
on intimate terms familiar *(informed)*
on no occasion sine die
on oath promissory
on one side only ex parte
on one's deathbed in extremis
on one's guard careful
on one's word promissory
on one's word of honor promissory
on or about SEE MAIN ENTRY
on paper holographic, in writing
on par comparable *(equivalent)*
on point SEE MAIN ENTRY
on presentation prima facie *(self-evident)*
on purpose purposely. SEE MAIN ENTRY
on record documentary
on schedule punctual
on that account a priori, consequently
on that ground a priori
on the agenda at issue, forthcoming
on the alert careful
on the anniversary per annum
on the application of one party ex parte
on the basis of a year per annum
on the brink of almost
on the confines of contiguous
on the contrary contra
on the decline regressive
on the docket forthcoming. SEE MAIN ENTRY
on the edge peripheral
on the edge of contiguous
on the face of the matter prima facie *(self-evident)*
on the first view prima facie *(self-evident)*
on the fringe of society derelict *(abandoned)*
on the grounds SEE MAIN ENTRY
on the horizon forthcoming, pending *(imminent)*, prospective
on the increase cumulative *(increasing)*
on the journey en route
on the level SEE MAIN ENTRY
on the market available
on the other hand contra. SEE MAIN ENTRY
on the record SEE MAIN ENTRY
on the road en route
on the same footing coequal
on the same level equal
on the same matter pari materia
on the spot present *(attendant)*, present *(current)*
on the verge of almost
on the wane decadent, dilapidated
on the way en route, imminent
on the whole as a rule, generally. SEE MAIN ENTRY
on this account consequently
on time prompt, punctual
once late *(defunct)*, whenever
once more anew, de novo
oncoming forthcoming, imminent, onset *(commencement)*, pending *(imminent)*
one exclusive *(singular)*, individual, indivisible, sole, unit *(item)*, whole *(unified)*
one after another consecutive
one after the other consecutive
one and all en banc, in solido
one and the same same
one at a time respectively
one authorized to deliver a verdict juror
one by one respectively
one called to the bar advocate *(counselor)*, counselor, jurist
one engaged in a manual enterprise artisan
one engaged in buying and selling dealer
one excluded from some privilege alien
one held in captivity captive
one held in confinement captive
one held in subjegation captive
one holding land of another tenant
one implicated in the commission of a crime offender
one instigating an action complainant
one not legally competent minor
one occupying another's land tenant
one occupying real property tenant
one of constituent *(part)*
one of an adjudgment body juror
one of several parts installment
one of several payments installment
one of successive parts installment
one of the clientele customer
one of the contents component
one of the purchasing public customer
one seeking cure patient
one seeking relief patient
one sided ex parte, inequitable. SEE MAIN ENTRY
one skilled in an industrial art artisan
one suspected of a crime suspect
one sworn to deliver a verdict juror
one thing in return for another quid pro quo
one to whom a fee is conveyed feoffee
one to whom seisin passes feoffee
one to whom something is entrusted trustee
one to whom title is passed feoffee
one trained in a mechanic trade artisan
one undergoing therapy patient
one undergoing treatment patient
one using real property tenant
one who affirms declarant
one who applies for relief petitioner
one who asserts declarant
one who asserts a demand claimant
one who attests deponent
one who bears witness bystander, deponent
one who breaks the law offender
one who brings an action plaintiff
one who claims a right claimant
one who commits a crime offender
one who commits larceny embezzler
one who dispenses justice judge
one who enfeoffs another feoffor
one who exacts assessor
one who files an application for relief petitioner
one who flees fugitive
one who formulates laws legislator
one who gives a corporeal hereditament feoffor
one who gives assistance good samaritan
one who gives evidence deponent
one who gives or makes laws legislator
one who gives testimony witness
one who handles property for another fiduciary
one who has attained legal majority adult
one who has land landholder
one who has no specialized training layman
one who has not come of age infant
one who has not reached his majority infant
one who helps another good samaritan
one who helps to pass laws legislator
one who imposes a charge assessor
one who inherits heir, legatee
one who is enfeoffed feoffee
one who is unfriendly foe
one who levies assessor
one who makes an affidavit deponent
one who obtains evidence first hand eyewitness
one who opposes foe, opponent
one who personally observes an occurrence eyewitness
one who proclaims declarant
one who receives beneficiary
one who remains holdover
one who renders aid good samaritan
one who requests relief petitioner
one who sells for factorage factor *(commission merchant)*
one who stays on holdover
one who supplies criminal information to the police informer *(one providing criminal information)*
one who testifies to what he has seen eyewitness
one who testifies under oath affirmant, deponent
one who transacts business for another fiduciary
one who transfers property by deed feoffor
one who transfers real property to another feoffor
one's due birthright
one's duty charge *(responsibility)*
one's own land demesne
one's people blood
one-sided ex parte, illiberal, interested, parochial, partial *(biased)*, unequal *(unjust)*, unfair, unilateral
one-sided conception distortion
one-sided view distortion
one-sidedness favoritism, inequity, intolerance, partiality, predetermination, prejudice *(preconception)*
one-time late *(defunct)*, previous
one-track mind compulsion *(obsession)*
oneness agreement *(concurrence)*, concordance, conformity *(agreement)*, entity,

facsimile, identity *(individuality)*, identity *(similarity)*, peace, personality, union *(unity)*
onerare encumber *(financially obligate)*, load
onerous bad *(offensive)*, operose, oppressive, ponderous. SEE MAIN ENTRY
onesidedness foregone conclusion
ongoing chronic, live *(existing)*, open-ended, progressive *(going forward)*, protracted. SEE MAIN ENTRY
onlooker bystander, eyewitness, witness
only exclusive *(singular)*, mere, sole, solely *(singly)*. SEE MAIN ENTRY
onrush onset *(assault)*
onset assault, birth *(beginning)*, genesis, inception, nascency, origin *(source)*, origination, outset, start, threshold *(commencement)*. SEE MAIN ENTRY
onset with force assault
onslaught assault, battery, incursion, onset *(assault)*, outbreak, violence
onus allegiance, burden, commitment *(responsibility)*, duty *(tax)*, handicap, imposition *(excessive burden)*, incumbrance *(burden)*, liability, penalty, requirement, weight *(burden)*. SEE MAIN ENTRY
onus cargo, encumbrance, freight
onus imponere load
onus probandi cloud *(suspicion)*
onward vanward
onward motion progress
ooze exude, outflow
opacity density, indistinctness, obscuration. SEE MAIN ENTRY
opaque impervious, inapprehensible, indefinable, indefinite, obtuse. SEE MAIN ENTRY
opaqueness density, obscuration, opacity
open aleatory *(uncertain)*, apparent *(perceptible)*, available, bare, bona fide, break *(separate)*, candid, commence, conspicuous, denude, direct *(forthright)*, equivocal, establish *(launch)*, evident, explicit, flagrant, generate, honest, impartial, indeterminate, ingenuous, initiate, launch *(initiate)*, liberal *(broad minded)*, liberal *(not literal)*, manifest *(adjective)*, manifest *(verb)*, naive, naked *(perceptible)*, obvious, open-minded, originate, outstanding *(unresolved)*, overt, passable, patent, penetrable, perceivable, perceptible, preface, pullulate, receptive, reveal, scrutable, simple, split, spread, straightforward, suasible, subject *(exposed)*, susceptible *(unresistent)*, unaffected *(sincere)*, unbiased, undecided, unmistakable, unprejudiced, unrestricted, unsettled, vacant, vulnerable. SEE MAIN ENTRY
open a passage admit *(give access)*
open a path admit *(give access)*
open a road admit *(give access)*
open a route admit *(give access)*
open a trade deal
open act overt act
open again reopen
open an account with deal
open an entryway admit *(give access)*
open an inlet admit *(give access)*
open breach feud
open contest competition
open court bench
open declaration avowal, oath
open discussion meeting *(conference)*, panel *(discussion group)*
open enemy foe
open fire discharge *(shoot)*
open fire upon attack
open forum panel *(discussion group)*
open market market place, trade *(commerce)*
open mart market *(business)*
open out compound
open position access *(opening)*
open quarrel feud
open statement of affirmation avouchment
open the mind disabuse
open the way for facilitate
open to disposable
open to all general
open to attack helpless *(defenseless)*
open to choice disjunctive *(alternative)*, elective *(selective)*
open to criticism blameful, blameworthy, reprehensible
open to debate debatable, disputable, litigious, polemic
open to discussion controversial, debatable, disputable, forensic, moot, pending *(unresolved)*, polemic, uncertain *(questionable)*
open to dispute debatable
open to doubt controversial, debatable, disputable, doubtful, implausible, incredible, ludicrous, problematic, suspicious *(questionable)*, unbelievable
open to error undependable
open to objection irregular *(improper)*
open to proof theoretical
open to question controversial, debatable, disputable, doubtful, dubitative, equivocal, indefinite, indeterminate, litigious, moot, pending *(unresolved)*, polemic, suspicious *(questionable)*, uncertain *(questionable)*. SEE MAIN ENTRY
open to suggestion receptive
open to suggestions amenable
open to suspicion debatable, disputable, doubtful, implausible, incredible, unbelievable
open to the public competitive *(open)*
open to the vision evident
open to various interpretations ambiguous, uncertain *(ambiguous)*
open to view apparent *(perceptible)*, evident, expose, perceivable, perceptible, present *(introduce)*
open up bare, exhibit, liberate, manifest, unveil
open-ended SEE MAIN ENTRY
open-handed philanthropic
open-handedness philanthropy
open-minded dispassionate, impartial, liberal *(broad minded)*, objective, open *(persuasible)*, progressive *(advocating change)*, receptive, suasible, unbiased. SEE MAIN ENTRY
open-mindedness disinterest *(lack of prejudice)*, objectivity
open-mouthed speechless
opened penetrable
openhanded benevolent, charitable *(benevolent)*, donative, liberal *(generous)*
openhandedness largess *(generosity)*
openhearted liberal *(generous)*
opening access *(right of way)*, admission *(entry)*, admittance *(means of approach)*, chance *(fortuity)*, egress, entrance, first appearance, hiatus, inception, initial, loophole, margin *(spare amount)*, occasion, onset *(commencement)*, opportunity, original *(initial)*, origination, outlet, outset, portal, preamble, preface, preliminary, prelude, preparatory, rift *(gap)*, start. SEE MAIN ENTRY
opening argument opening statement
opening of negotiations overture
opening statement SEE MAIN ENTRY
openly fairly *(clearly)*
openminded unprejudiced
openmindedness fairness
openness candor *(straightforwardness)*, honesty, latitude
opera effort, service *(assistance)*
operable functional, practicable
operant active, functional
operate administer *(conduct)*, commit *(perpetrate)*, conduct, control *(regulate)*, employ *(make use of)*, exercise *(use)*, exert, exploit *(make use of)*, function, handle *(manage)*, manage, manipulate *(utilize skillfully)*, militate, ply, transact, wield. SEE MAIN ENTRY
operate jointly concur *(agree)*
operating active, in full force
operating company corporation
operating expenses overhead
operation act *(undertaking)*, activity, calling, campaign, commission *(act)*, conduct, course, deal, enterprise *(undertaking)*, instrumentality, management *(judicious use)*, maneuver *(tactic)*, manner *(behavior)*, method, modus operandi, performance *(execution)*, performance *(workmanship)*, practice *(procedure)*, process *(course)*, scheme, system, transaction, undertaking *(enterprise)*, usage. SEE MAIN ENTRY
operational effective *(operative)*, functional, operative, practical
operational before retroactive
operative constructive *(creative)*, functional, ministerial, potent, practical, prevailing *(having superior force)*, procedural, valuable, viable. SEE MAIN ENTRY
operative with respect to the past nunc pro tunc
operator actor, artisan, dealer
operire close *(terminate)*, cover *(pretext)*
operose difficult, diligent, industrious, oppressive, painstaking. SEE MAIN ENTRY
operosus painstaking
opes strength
opiate cannabis, drug, narcotic *(adjective)*, narcotic *(noun)*
opifex artisan
opinabilis hypothetical
opinari guess, opine
opine advise, comment, construe *(comprehend)*, counsel, deem, determine, gauge, guess, presume, presuppose, surmise, suspect *(think)*. SEE MAIN ENTRY
opinio belief *(state of mind)*, character *(reputation)*, conviction *(persuasion)*, expectation, faith, impression, presumption, reputation, supposition
opinio praeiudicata prejudice *(preconception)*
opinion adjudication, advice, apprehension *(perception)*, assumption *(supposition)*, award, belief *(state of mind)*, concept, conclusion *(determination)*, conjecture, conviction *(persuasion)*, decree, deduction *(conclusion)*, determination, dictum, estimate *(idea)*, estimation *(calculation)*, finding, guidance, holding *(ruling of a court)*, idea, impression, judgment *(discernment)*, judgment *(formal court decree)*, notion, observation, position *(point of view)*, posture *(attitude)*, presumption, prognosis, pronouncement, recommendation, regard *(esteem)*, sense *(feeling)*, stand *(position)*, standpoint, supposition, theory. SEE MAIN ENTRY

opinion of the court finding, ruling
opinion of the jury verdict
opinionated dogmatic, illiberal, inexorable, inflexible, narrow, obdurate, parochial, prejudicial, pretentious *(pompous)*, uncontrollable, unyielding
opinionated person bigot, pedant
opinionative dogmatic, inexorable, inflexible, obdurate, parochial
opinionativeness discrimination *(bigotry)*
opinionist bigot
opitulari assist
oppidan civil *(public)*, denizen, resident
oppignerare pawn
oppignerare pledge *(promise the performance of)*
oppilate obstruct, occlude
oppilation damper *(stopper)*
opponent adversary, contender, contestant, contradictory, disputant, foe, litigant, plaintiff, rival. SEE MAIN ENTRY
opponent in a lawsuit litigant
opportune appropriate, auspicious, convenient, favorable *(advantageous)*, felicitous, fit, fitting, proper, propitious, seasonable, suitable. SEE MAIN ENTRY
opportune moment opportunity
opportune time opportunity
opportuneness expedience, feasibility, timeliness
opportunism bribery
opportunist machiavellian
opportunistic mercenary
opportunities choice *(alternatives offered)*
opportunity access *(opening)*, behalf, call *(option)*, day in court, latitude, occasion, option *(choice)*, possibility, privilege. SEE MAIN ENTRY
opportunity to obtain goods on time credit *(delayed payment)*
opportunus eligible, opportune, seasonable
oppose answer *(reply)*, antagonize, argue, block, challenge, collide *(clash)*, compensate *(counterbalance)*, compete, complain *(criticize)*, condemn *(ban)*, conflict, contend *(dispute)*, contest, contradict, contrast, contravene, controvert, counter, counteract, countervail, cross *(disagree with)*, defy, demonstrate *(protest)*, demur, deprecate, differ *(disagree)*, disaccord, disaffirm, disagree, disallow, disapprove *(reject)*, discourage, disobey, disown *(deny the validity)*, dissent *(differ in opinion)*, dissent *(withhold assent)*, engage *(involve)*, except *(object)*, expostulate, fight *(battle)*, fight *(counteract)*, forbid, frustrate, gainsay, grapple, hamper, impugn, negate, object, oppugn, parry, polarize, preclude, prevent, prohibit, proscribe *(prohibit)*, protest, rebel, rebut, refuse, refute, reject, remonstrate, renounce, repel *(drive back)*, repulse, restrain, stem *(check)*, thwart, trammel, withstand. SEE MAIN ENTRY
oppose as false impugn
oppose by argument dispute *(contest)*
oppose by contrary proof countercharge
opposed adverse *(hostile)*, antipathetic *(oppositional)*, averse, contradictory, contrary, different, discordant, disinclined, disobedient, hostile, inimical, negative, opposite, reluctant, renitent, repugnant *(incompatible)*, unfavorable
opposed to contra *(adverb)*, contra *(preposition)*. SEE MAIN ENTRY
opposer adversary, contender, contestant, disputant, foe, opponent
opposing antipathetic *(oppositional)*, competitive *(antagonistic)*, contradictory, contrary, contravention, discordant, disobedient, dissenting, dissident, hostile, inimical, litigious, negative, opposite, preventive, recalcitrant, renitent, repugnant *(incompatible)*. SEE MAIN ENTRY
opposing causes conflict
opposing counsel SEE MAIN ENTRY
opposing litigant opponent
opposing party adversary, complainant, contestant, foe, opponent, party *(litigant)*. SEE MAIN ENTRY
opposing suit counterclaim
opposite antipathetic *(oppositional)*, antipode, antithesis, contra *(adverb)*, contra *(noun)*, contradictory, contraposition, contrary *(adjective)*, contrary *(noun)*, discordant, hostile, inverse, negative, offset, opponent, pertinent. SEE MAIN ENTRY
opposite camp foe
opposite evidence answer *(judicial response)*
opposite extreme antipode, contradiction
opposite in character contrary
opposite in nature contrary
opposite number peer
opposite pole antipode, antithesis
opposite side antipode, contraposition, foe, opponent
opposite to contra
oppositely contra
oppositeness antipode, contradiction, contradistinction, difference, dissent *(difference of opinion)*
opposites contradiction
opposition antipode, antithesis, argument *(contention)*, belligerency, check *(bar)*, collision *(dispute)*, competition, condemnation *(blame)*, conflict, confrontation *(altercation)*, contender, contest *(competition)*, contest *(dispute)*, contestant, contradiction, contradistinction, contraposition, contrary, contravention, controversy *(argument)*, counterargument, criticism, defiance, deterrence, deterrent, difference, disaccord, disagreement, disapprobation, disapproval, discord, dispute, dissatisfaction, dissent *(difference of opinion)*, dissent *(nonconcurrence)*, dissidence, division *(act of dividing)*, exception *(objection)*, feud, ill will, impediment, impugnation, incompatibility *(difference)*, mutiny, negation, objection, offset, opponent, outcry, protest, rebellion, rebuff, rejection, remonstrance, restraint, revolt, rival, strife, struggle, variance *(disagreement)*. SEE MAIN ENTRY
opposition to allegations demurrer
oppositional contradictory, contrary, discordant, hostile
oppositionist adversary, contender, contestant, disputant
oppositive antipathetic *(oppositional)*, contradictory
opposure confrontation *(altercation)*, contempt *(disdain)*
oppress abuse *(victimize)*, badger, bait *(harass)*, brutalize, coerce, constrain *(restrain)*, contemn, discommode, dominate, exploit *(take advantage of)*, harass, harry *(harass)*, ill use, maltreat, mistreat, overload, persecute, plague, pressure, prey, subdue, subject, tax *(overwork)*. SEE MAIN ENTRY
oppressed aggrieved *(victimized)*
oppression adversity, burden, coercion, compulsion *(coercion)*, cruelty, encumbrance, extortion, force *(compulsion)*, grievance, ground, incumbrance *(burden)*, infliction, injustice, molestation, pressure, servitude, thrall, weight *(burden)*. SEE MAIN ENTRY
oppressive bad *(offensive)*, brutal, cruel, detrimental, dictatorial, disastrous, forcible, harsh, malignant, onerous, ponderous, severe, tyrannous. SEE MAIN ENTRY
oppressive act ground
oppressive exaction blackmail, coercion, extortion
oppressive taskmaster dictator
oppressor dictator, hoodlum
opprimere overwhelm, repress, stifle
opprobrious bad *(offensive)*, blameful, blameworthy, calumnious, contemptible, contemptuous, disgraceful, disreputable, heinous, insolent, loathsome, notorious, objectionable, obnoxious, offensive *(offending)*, outrageous, reprehensible, scandalous, scurrilous
opprobrium aspersion
opprobrium attaint, bad repute, blame *(culpability)*, contempt *(disdain)*, contumely, criticism, degradation, denunciation, disapprobation, discredit, disdain, disgrace, dishonor *(shame)*, disrepute, ignominy, infamy, notoriety, obloquy, odium, reproach, revilement, scandal, shame, slander, vilification. SEE MAIN ENTRY
oppugn answer *(reply)*, assail, assault, attack, collide *(clash)*, confront *(oppose)*, contest, contradict, counteract, disaffirm, disagree, disprove, gainsay, hold out *(resist)*, oppose, refute, repulse, resist *(oppose)*. SEE MAIN ENTRY
oppugnance resistance
oppugnancy belligerency, conflict, contest *(dispute)*, contravention, disagreement, impugnation, mutiny, opposition
oppugnant adversary, antipathetic *(oppositional)*, competitive *(antagonistic)*, contrary, discordant, hostile, malevolent, opposite, recalcitrant, recusant
oppugnare assail, attack, impugn
oppugnatio assault
oppugnation belligerency, defiance, opposition, resistance
opt decide, espouse
opt for choose, elect *(choose)*. SEE MAIN ENTRY
optative solicitous
optimal best
optimas prime *(most valuable)*
optimates elite
optimism confidence *(faith)*, faith, longanimity
optimistic sanguine
optimum ceiling, utmost
optimus best, superlative
option choice *(alternatives offered)*, conatus, discretion *(power of choice)*, election *(choice)*, franchise *(right to vote)*, latitude, preference *(choice)*, suffrage, volition, vote. SEE MAIN ENTRY
optional discretionary, disjunctive *(alternative)*, elective *(voluntary)*, extraneous, needless, nonessential, spontaneous, unnecessary, voluntary
optionally SEE MAIN ENTRY
optionality discretion *(power of choice)*
opulence boom *(prosperity)*, prosperity
opulency boom *(prosperity)*

opulent copious. SEE MAIN ENTRY
opulentus opulent
opus enterprise *(undertaking)*, performance *(workmanship)*, product, work *(effort)*
ora edge *(border)*
oracular indefinite, mysterious, omniscient, portentous *(ominous)*, profound *(esoteric)*, prophetic. SEE MAIN ENTRY
oral language, nuncupative, parol, verbal. SEE MAIN ENTRY
oral communication conversation, discourse, parlance, parley, speech. SEE MAIN ENTRY
oral contention argument *(contention)*, fight *(argument)*
oral declaration nuncupative
oral evidence affirmance *(legal affirmation)*, deposition. SEE MAIN ENTRY
oral examination interview
oral expression speech
oral statement under oath deposition
oral testimony nuncupative
orare plead *(implore)*, pray, sue
orate address *(talk to)*, declaim, discourse, recite
oratio language, speech
oration bombast, declamation, diatribe, discourse, peroration, recital, speech.
orationem attribuere personify
orationem facere discourse
orationem habere discourse
oratorical flatulent, inflated *(bombastic)*, nuncupative, orotund
oratorical display declamation, peroration
oratory declamation, parlance, phraseology, rhetoric *(skilled speech)*, speech
orb sphere, zone
orbis circuit
orbit ambit, area *(province)*, bailiwick, capacity *(sphere)*, circuit, province, purview, realm, scope, sphere
orbus orphan
orchestrate compose. SEE MAIN ENTRY
ordain award, bestow, command, constitute *(establish)*, decide, dictate, direct *(order)*, impose *(enforce)*, induct, invest *(vest)*, necessitate, nominate, order, pass *(approve)*, pass *(determine)*, predetermine, prescribe, require *(compel)*
ordain by law enact, pass *(approve)*
ordained entitled, inevitable, mandatory, necessary *(inescapable)*, positive *(prescribed)*, rightful
ordained by custom prescriptive
ordained by legislation legislative
ordaining legislative
ordainment designation *(naming)*, nomination, ordinance, selection *(choice)*
ordeal aggravation *(annoyance)*, burden, infliction, nuisance, pain, trouble. SEE MAIN ENTRY
order adjudge, adjudicate, adjudication, agenda, appointment *(act of designating)*, arbitrate *(adjudge)*, arrange *(methodize)*, authority *(documentation)*, award *(noun)*, award *(verb)*, book, buy, call *(demand)*, canon, caveat, chain *(series)*, charge *(command)*, choice *(decision)*, class, classification, coerce, command, compel, constrain *(compel)*, control *(regulate)*, course, decree *(noun)*, decree *(verb)*, delegate, demand *(noun)*, demand *(verb)*, denomination, detail *(assign)*, determination, dictate *(noun)*, dictate *(verb)*, directive, disposition *(determination)*, disposition *(final arrangement)*, draft, edict, enact, enjoin, exact, fiat, finding, force *(coerce)*, form *(arrangement)*, formation, govern, hierarchy *(arrangement in a series)*, holding *(ruling of a court)*, impose *(enforce)*, injunction, insist, instruct *(direct)*, instruction *(direction)*, judgment *(formal court decree)*, law, legislate, lineup, manage, mandamus, mandate, manner *(kind)*, method, mittimus, modus operandi, monition *(legal summons)*, opinion *(judicial decision)*, orchestrate, ordinance, organization *(structure)*, organize *(arrange)*, peace, pigeonhole, precept, prescribe, prescription *(directive)*, press *(constrain)*, procedure, program, purchase, register, regularity, regulate *(adjust)*, regulate *(manage)*, regulation *(rule)*, request *(noun)*, request *(verb)*, require *(compel)*, requirement, requisition, rule *(guide)*, rule *(legal dictate)*, rule *(govern)*, ruling, scheme, sentence, sequence, society, sodality, sort, statute, subpoena *(noun)*, subpoena *(verb)*, succession, summon, system, uniformity, warrant *(judicial writ)*, writ. SEE MAIN ENTRY
order authorizing a search search warrant
order back recommit, remand
order by law legalize
order for payment draft
order not to do forbid
order of business calendar *(record of yearly periods)*
order of cases calendar *(list of cases)*
order of penalty sentence
order of succession hierarchy *(arrangement in a series)*
order of the court adjudication, award, decree, holding *(ruling of a court)*, ruling, sentence. SEE MAIN ENTRY
order of the day agenda, docket, practice *(custom)*, practice *(procedure)*
order on a bank check *(instrument)*
order to appear subpoena *(noun)*, subpoena *(verb)*, summon, summons
order to appear in court subpoena *(noun)*
order with authority command
ordered decretal, systematic
ordering allotment, array *(order)*, classification, disposition *(final arrangement)*, distribution *(arrangement)*
orderless casual, disjointed, disordered, disorderly, haphazard, indiscriminate, random, slipshod
orderliness decorum, diligence *(care)*, method, peace, regularity, system
orderly meticulous, normal *(regular)*, peaceable, right *(suitable)*, systematic, uniform
orderly arrangement classification, method
orderly arrangement of papers file
orderly combination system
orderly disposition method
ordinance act *(enactment)*, brevet, bylaw, canon, code, codification, dictate, direction *(order)*, directive, edict, enactment, law, precept, prescription *(directive)*, regulation *(rule)*, rubric *(authoritative rule)*, rule *(legal dictate)*, statute, writ. SEE MAIN ENTRY
ordinances legislation *(enactments)*
ordinare arrange *(methodize)*, fix *(arrange)*, organize *(arrange)*
ordinarily as a rule, generally, invariably
ordinariness mediocrity
ordinarius regular *(conventional)*
ordinary accustomed *(customary)*, average *(standard)*, common *(customary)*, conventional, customary, daily, familiar *(customary)*, general, habitual, household *(familiar)*, imperfect, informal, jejune *(dull)*, mediocre, mundane, nondescript, normal *(regular)*, orthodox, passable, pedestrian, poor *(inferior in quality)*, prevalent, prosaic, regular *(conventional)*, trite, typical, usual. SEE MAIN ENTRY
ordinary course practice *(custom)*
ordinary judgment common sense
ordinary manner custom
ordinary run norm
ordinary run of things matter of course
ordinary sense common sense
ordinary state matter of course
ordinary wear and tear SEE MAIN ENTRY
ordinate nominate
ordinatio disposition *(final arrangement)*
ordination appointment *(act of designating)*, brevet, citation *(charge)*, classification, dedication, delegation *(assignment)*, designation *(naming)*, dictate, installation, nomination, ordinance, selection *(choice)*
ordo class, degree *(station)*, order *(arrangement)*, regularity, sequence
organ chapter *(branch)*, publication *(printed matter)*. SEE MAIN ENTRY
organic bodily, born *(innate)*, fundamental, native *(inborn)*, natural, physical. SEE MAIN ENTRY
organic law constitution
organic remains corpse
organism entity, individual
organization array *(order)*, association *(connection)*, building *(business of assembling)*, bureaucracy, business *(commercial enterprise)*, campaign, cartel, centralization, chamber *(body)*, citation *(attribution)*, classification, committee, company *(enterprise)*, complex *(development)*, composition *(makeup)*, concern *(business establishment)*, content *(structure)*, corporation, denomination, disposition *(final arrangement)*, distribution *(arrangement)*, facility *(institution)*, firm, form *(arrangement)*, formation, institute, league, method, order *(arrangement)*, practice *(procedure)*, regulation *(management)*, scheme, society, sodality, structure *(composition)*, syndicate, system, union *(labor organization)*. SEE MAIN ENTRY
organization of a commercial concern incorporation *(formation of a business entity)*
organization of a company incorporation *(formation of a business entity)*
organization to aid the needy foundation *(organization)*
organize arrange *(methodize)*, classify, codify, compose, constitute *(establish)*, contrive, coordinate, create, disentangle, establish *(launch)*, fabricate *(construct)*, federalize *(associate)*, federate, file *(arrange)*, fix *(arrange)*, form, frame *(construct)*, frame *(formulate)*, make, marshal, orchestrate, pigeonhole, plan, plot, program, provide *(arrange for)*, regulate *(adjust)*, scheme, sort, tabulate. SEE MAIN ENTRY
organize a corporation incorporate *(form a corporation)*
organized systematic, tactical
organized body federation
organized body for charity foundation *(organization)*
organized group committee, party *(political organization)*, society

organized illegal activity racket
organized knowledge science *(study)*
organized labor union *(labor organization)*
organized labor union SEE MAIN ENTRY
organized observation experiment
organized refusal to work strike
organized society facility *(institution)*
organizer architect, author *(originator)*, chief, developer, promoter
organizer of business enterprises promoter
organizer of commercial enterprises promoter
organizing conception impression
orgiastic gluttonous
orgulous proud *(conceited)*. SEE MAIN ENTRY
orgy debauchery
orient apprise, inform *(notify)*
orientation guidance, perspective, standpoint
origin affiliation *(bloodline)*, ancestry, basis, birth *(beginning)*, bloodline, cause *(reason)*, derivation, descent *(lineage)*, determinant, embryo, family *(common ancestry)*, foundation *(basis)*, genesis, ground, inception, lineage, nascency, nationality, onset *(commencement)*, outset, parentage, paternity, progenitor, reason *(basis)*, source, start. SEE MAIN ENTRY
original authentic, causative, fertile, genuine, incipient, initial, native *(domestic)*, native *(inborn)*, natural, nonconforming, noteworthy, novel, old, organic, paradigm, particular *(individual)*, pattern, peculiar *(distinctive)*, preliminary, primary, primordial, productive, prototype, resourceful, rudimentary, sample, source, true *(authentic)*, underlying, undistorted, unique, unprecedented, unusual. SEE MAIN ENTRY
original meaning connotation
original sum principal *(capital sum)*
original work creation
originality identity *(individuality)*, legitimacy, nonconformity, personality. SEE MAIN ENTRY
originally ab initio
originate accrue *(arise)*, build *(construct)*, cause, commence, compose, conceive *(invent)*, conjure, constitute *(establish)*, create, embark, engender, establish *(launch)*, forge *(produce)*, frame *(construct)*, frame *(formulate)*, generate, induce, initiate, inspire, invent *(produce for the first time)*, launch *(initiate)*, legislate, maintain *(commence)*, make, manufacture, produce *(manufacture)*, propagate *(increase)*, provoke, result, stem *(originate)*, unveil. SEE MAIN ENTRY
originate from evolve
originate in emanate
originating causal
origination ancestry, birth *(beginning)*, building *(business of assembling)*, creation, derivation, embryo, formation, genesis, inception, invention, manufacture, nascency, onset *(commencement)*, outset, source, start. SEE MAIN ENTRY
originative causal, causative, constructive *(creative)*, fertile, original *(creative)*, prime *(original)*, productive, rudimentary
originator architect, developer, predecessor. SEE MAIN ENTRY
origo ancestry, lineage, origin *(ancestry)*, origin *(source)*, primogenitor, source
ornament embellish, motif
ornamental aesthetic
ornamentation bombast, motif
ornamented elaborate, pretentious *(ostentatious)*
ornare provide *(supply)*
ornate elaborate, grandiose, meretricious, pretentious *(ostentatious)*
ornatus pretentious *(ostentatious)*
ornery malicious
orotund flatulent, fustian, grandiose, histrionic, turgid. SEE MAIN ENTRY
orotundity bombast, declamation, fustian, histrionics, peroration
orphan SEE MAIN ENTRY
orphaned solitary
orphaned child orphan
orphaned infant orphan
orphic recondite
orthodox conventional, dogmatic, parochial, popular, proper, rigid, strict, traditional, typical, uncompromising, uniform, usual. SEE MAIN ENTRY
orthodoxus orthodox
orthodoxy doctrine, dogma
ortus birth *(beginning)*
os impudens indiscretion
oscillate alternate *(fluctuate)*, beat *(pulsate)*, hesitate, vacillate. SEE MAIN ENTRY
oscillating irresolute, variable
oscillation hesitation, indecision, trepidation
oscitancy inertia, languor
oscitant lifeless *(dull)*, otiose, phlegmatic
osculate contact *(touch)*, juxtapose
osmose penetrate, permeate
osmosis SEE MAIN ENTRY
ossified solid *(compact)*. SEE MAIN ENTRY
ostendere evince, prove, reflect *(mirror)*
ostensibility probability
ostensible apparent *(presumptive)*, circumstantial, colorable *(plausible)*, evident, manifest, naked *(perceptible)*, overt, patent, plausible, probable, purported, putative, specious. SEE MAIN ENTRY
ostensible motive pretext
ostensible purpose pretense *(pretext)*, pretext
ostensible reason excuse, pretense *(pretext)*, pretext
ostensibly prima facie *(self-evident)*
ostent presence *(poise)*
ostentare flaunt
ostentatio pretense *(ostentation)*
ostentation bombast, histrionics, jactation, rodomontade
ostentatious elaborate, grandiose, histrionic, inflated *(bombastic)*, tawdry. SEE MAIN ENTRY
ostentatiousness pretense *(ostentation)*
ostentum phenomenon *(unusual occurrence)*
ostium entrance
ostracism banishment, boycott, exclusion, expulsion, ignominy, prohibition, rejection, segregation *(isolation by races)*. SEE MAIN ENTRY
ostracization banishment
ostracize bar *(exclude)*, condemn *(ban)*, defame, denounce *(condemn)*, eliminate *(exclude)*, exclude, expel, ignore, isolate, proscribe *(denounce)*, reject, relegate, renounce, seclude, spurn, transport
other additional, alter ego, ancillary *(auxiliary)*
other choice alternative *(substitute)*
other extreme antipode, antithesis, contradiction, contrary
other half alter ego
other person alter ego
other self alter ego
other side foe, opponent
other than different
other wordly immaterial
otherness contraposition, nonconformity
otherwise contra. SEE MAIN ENTRY
otherwise called alias
otherwise known as alias
otherwise known by alias
otherwise named alias
otherwordly demote
otherworldliness immateriality
otiose futile, inactive, indolent, nugatory, passive, redundant, stagnant, torpid, unproductive. SEE MAIN ENTRY
otiosity sloth
otiosus idle, unemployed
otium ease, inaction, peace
oust deport *(banish)*, depose *(remove)*, disinherit, dislocate, dislodge, dismiss *(discharge)*, disown *(refuse to acknowledge)*, displace *(remove)*, dispossess, divest, eject *(evict)*, eject *(expel)*, eliminate *(exclude)*, evict, exclude, expel, reject, relegate, remove *(dismiss from office)*, supersede, supplant. SEE MAIN ENTRY
oust from office depose *(remove)*
ouster deportation, discharge *(dismissal)*, dismissal *(discharge)*, disqualification *(rejection)*, disseisin, eviction, expulsion, layoff, rejection. SEE MAIN ENTRY
ouster by paramount title eviction
ousting banishment, defeasance, discharge *(dismissal)*, removal
out of devoid
out of accord discordant
out of bounds excessive, extreme *(exaggerated)*, illicit, impermissible, inordinate, undue *(excessive)*. SEE MAIN ENTRY
out of cash poor *(underprivileged)*
out of character inappropriate, inapt, incongruous, inept *(inappropriate)*, undesirable, unseemly, unsuitable
out of circulation rare
out of control uncontrollable, uncurbed, unruly
out of danger safe
out of debt solvent
out of employment unemployed
out of fashion defunct, outmoded
out of favor blameful, repugnant *(exciting aversion)*
out of focus indistinct, nebulous, unclear
out of funds bankrupt, insolvent
out of hand uncurbed
out of humor petulant
out of joint disproportionate
out of keeping anomalous, disproportionate, inapplicable, inappropriate, inapt, incommensurate, incongruous, inept *(inappropriate)*, unbecoming, undesirable, unfit, unsuitable, untimely
out of limits inordinate
out of line nonconforming
out of money bankrupt, destitute, impecunious, insolvent, poor *(underprivileged)*
out of one's bearings astray
out of one's mind lunatic, non compos mentis
out of one's reckoning astray
out of one's senses lunatic, non compos mentis
out of one's wits non compos mentis
out of order anomalous, defective, deviant, disjointed, disordered, disorderly, faulty, imperfect, irregular *(not usual)*, irrelevant. SEE MAIN ENTRY

out of place disordered, disproportionate, immaterial, impertinent *(irrelevant)*, improper, inapplicable, inappropriate, inapt, incongruous, inept *(inappropriate)*, irregular *(improper)*, irregular *(not usual)*, irrelevant, peculiar *(curious)*, unbecoming, unfit, unseemly, unsuitable, untimely
out of pocket SEE MAIN ENTRY
out of pocket expenses SEE MAIN ENTRY
out of proportion disparate, disproportionate, extreme *(exaggerated)*, inapt, incommensurate, inept *(inappropriate)*
out of reach difficult, inaccessible, infeasible, insuperable, insurmountable, unapproachable, unattainable
out of sight covert, hidden, inconspicuous, lost *(taken away)*
out of sorts petulant
out of step deviant, nonconforming, unorthodox
out of the common run eccentric, prodigious *(amazing)*
out of the ordinary anomalous, different, distinct *(distinguished from others)*, eccentric, extraordinary, irregular *(not usual)*, noteworthy, original *(creative)*, peculiar *(curious)*, peculiar *(distinctive)*, portentous *(eliciting amazement)*, prodigious *(amazing)*, rare, singular, specific, unaccustomed, unusual. SEE MAIN ENTRY
out of the question impossible, impracticable, ineligible, infeasible, insuperable, insurmountable, unattainable. SEE MAIN ENTRY
out of the regular order extraordinary
out of the way circuitous, indirect, irrelevant, peculiar *(curious)*, remote *(secluded)*, scarce, uncommon
out of touch inaccessible
out of use obsolete, outmoded
out of view blind *(concealed)*, hidden
out of work unemployed
out-and-out outright
out-of-date obsolete, outdated, outmoded
out-of-fashion outdated
out-of-sorts restive
out-of-the-way immaterial, private *(secluded)*, unapproachable
out-of-use outdated
outbalance countervail, outweigh. SEE MAIN ENTRY
outbreak bluster *(commotion)*, brawl, embroilment, fracas, furor, inception, insurrection, mutiny, onset *(commencement)*, outburst, outset, rebellion, revolt, revolution, riot, start, strife, threshold *(commencement)*. SEE MAIN ENTRY
outburst bluster *(commotion)*, furor, outbreak, outflow, riot, spate, strife, violence. SEE MAIN ENTRY
outcast derelict *(abandoned)*, derelict, ineligible, notorious, pariah, undesirable
outclass beat *(defeat)*, surpass
outcome amount *(result)*, answer *(solution)*, cessation *(termination)*, choice *(decision)*, conclusion *(outcome)*, consequence *(conclusion)*, corollary, denouement, development *(outgrowth)*, effect, end *(termination)*, finding, holding *(ruling of a court)*, issuance, output, product, result. SEE MAIN ENTRY
outcry disparagement, exception *(objection)*, expletive, noise, pandemonium, panic, plaint, protest. SEE MAIN ENTRY
outdated obsolete, outmoded. SEE MAIN ENTRY
outdistance transcend
outdo beat *(defeat)*, outbalance, outweigh, overcome *(surmount)*, surmount, surpass, transcend
outer peripheral
outer boundary periphery
outer district frontier
outer edge edge *(border)*, extremity *(furthest point)*, frontier, limit
outer edges confines
outer limit ambit
outer line limit
outer part frontier, periphery
outer point limit
outermost extreme *(last)*, last *(final)*, peripheral
outface defy, oppugn, parry
outfit assemblage, band, clothe, furnish, supply
outfitter materialman
outflank beat *(defeat)*
outflow issuance. SEE MAIN ENTRY
outgo cost *(expenses)*, disbursement *(act of disbursing)*, disbursement *(funds paid out)*, expenditure, expense *(cost)*, issuance, outlay
outgrowth amount *(result)*, boom *(prosperity)*, conclusion *(outcome)*, consequence *(conclusion)*, corollary, denouement, effect, offshoot, outcome, result. SEE MAIN ENTRY
outgush outflow
outland peripheral
outlander alien
outlandish eccentric, ludicrous, peculiar *(curious)*, prodigious *(amazing)*, unaccustomed, unusual
outlandishness quirk *(idiosyncrasy)*
outlast endure *(last)*, persevere, persist, remain *(continue)*, subsist
outlaw ban, bar *(exclude)*, condemn *(ban)*, convict, criminal, debar, deport *(banish)*, disfranchise, eliminate *(exclude)*, exclude, expatriate, expel, felon, foe, forbid, hoodlum, isolate, lawless, malefactor, pariah, proscribe *(denounce)*, proscribe *(prohibit)*, recidivist, relegate, seclude, thief, wrongdoer. SEE MAIN ENTRY
outlawed felonious, illegal, illegitimate *(illegal)*, illicit, impermissible, unlawful
outlawing expulsion
outlawry banishment, criminality, lynch law, prohibition
outlay bear the expense, charge *(cost)*, cost *(expenses)*, disburse *(pay out)*, disbursement *(act of disbursing)*, disbursement *(funds paid out)*, expenditure, expense *(cost)*, invest *(fund)*, investment, maintenance *(upkeep)*, overhead, payment *(act of paying)*, price, spend. SEE MAIN ENTRY
outlet catharsis, egress, issuance, loophole, market *(demand)*, store *(business)*. SEE MAIN ENTRY
outline ambit, arrangement *(plan)*, blueprint, border, border *(bound)*, boundary, brief, capsule, characterize, circumscribe *(define)*, circumscribe *(surround by boundary)*, compendium, complexion, condense, configuration *(confines)*, configuration *(form)*, construe *(translate)*, delineate, delineation, demarcate, depict, describe, description, design *(construction plan)*, digest, digest *(summarize)*, dimension, direction *(course)*, edge *(border)*, form *(arrangement)*, hedge, inform *(notify)*, mete, mode, pandect *(treatise)*, pattern, periphery, plan, plot, portray, practice *(procedure)*, program *(noun)*, program *(verb)*, project, prospectus, render *(depict)*, report *(disclose)*, represent *(portray)*, scenario, schedule, scheme, suggestion, summary, synopsis. SEE MAIN ENTRY
outline on the law brief
outlined compact *(pithy)*
outlined before hand intentional
outlined beforehand deliberate, express, premeditated
outlines confines, frontier
outlive endure *(last)*, last, remain *(continue)*, subsist
outlook conviction *(persuasion)*, opinion *(belief)*, perspective, platform, position *(point of view)*, posture *(attitude)*, side, stand *(position)*, standpoint. SEE MAIN ENTRY
outlying peripheral, provincial
outlying area frontier
outlying borders frontier
outlying districts frontier
outmaneuver beat *(defeat)*, circumvent, dupe, elude, ensnare, illude, pettifog, surmount, surpass, thwart
outmatch surpass
outmode succeed *(follow)*
outmoded obsolete, outdated. SEE MAIN ENTRY
outmost peripheral
outnumber surpass
outplay beat *(defeat)*, surpass
outpoint beat *(defeat)*, outbalance
outpost border, frontier, periphery
outpour issuance, outburst, outflow. SEE MAIN ENTRY
outpouring boom *(prosperity)*
output product, profit, result. SEE MAIN ENTRY
outrage abuse *(physical misuse)*, bait *(harass)*, cruelty, defilement, delinquency *(misconduct)*, dishonor *(shame)*, disregard *(lack of respect)*, disservice, disturb, flout, ground, harass, harrow, mischief, misdoing, offend *(insult)*, offense, persecute, perturb, vice, wrong. SEE MAIN ENTRY
outraged resentful
outrageous arrant *(onerous)*, deplorable, diabolic, disgraceful, disorderly, drastic, egregious, excessive, exorbitant, extreme *(exaggerated)*, flagrant, gross *(flagrant)*, heinous, inept *(inappropriate)*, inexcusable, inordinate, insolent, irrational, nefarious, notorious, offensive *(offending)*, presumptuous, scandalous, unconscionable, undue *(excessive)*, unwarranted. SEE MAIN ENTRY
outrageous act misdeed
outrageousness exaggeration
outrange beat *(defeat)*
outrank outweigh, predominate *(outnumber)*, surpass, transcend
outre egregious
outreach circumvent
outright candid, stark, total, unequivocal, unqualified *(unlimited)*, wholly. SEE MAIN ENTRY
outrival beat *(defeat)*, outbalance, outweigh, overcome *(surmount)*, predominate *(outnumber)*, surmount, surpass, transcend
outrivalry competition
outrun surpass. SEE MAIN ENTRY
outset genesis, inception, nascency, onset *(commencement)*, origination, prelude, start. SEE MAIN ENTRY
outshine overcome *(surmount)*, surpass, transcend
outside alien *(foreign)*, alien *(unrelated)*, border, contour *(outline)*, exempt, extremity *(furthest point)*, extrinsic, foreign, peripheral, periphery. SEE MAIN ENTRY

outside surface periphery
outside the law felonious, illegal, illegitimate *(illegal)*, illicit, impermissible
outside the question immaterial
outsider alien, pariah, stranger
outskirt margin *(outside limit)*, penumbra
outskirts border, edge *(border)*, frontier, periphery, vicinity
outsmart dupe, overreach
outsourcing SEE MAIN ENTRY
outspoken brazen, candid, clear *(apparent)*, direct *(forthright)*, explicit, express, honest, ingenuous, parol, straightforward, unaffected *(sincere)*. SEE MAIN ENTRY
outspokenness candor *(straightforwardness)*
outspread broad, deploy, expand, spread
outstanding best, blatant *(conspicuous)*, critical *(crucial)*, delinquent *(overdue)*, due *(owed)*, extraordinary, famous, flagrant, important *(significant)*, infrequent, leading *(ranking first)*, major, master, momentous, notable, noteworthy, open *(in sight)*, overdue, particular *(specific)*, past due, payable, portentous *(eliciting amazement)*, preferential, principal, prominent, receivable, remarkable, renowned, residuary, salient, special, stellar, uncommon, unpaid, unsettled, unusual. SEE MAIN ENTRY
outstanding debt arrears, bad debt, cloud *(incumbrance)*, delinquency *(shortage)*, due, nonpayment, obligation *(liability)*
outstanding feature emphasis, gist *(ground for a suit)*, highlight, main point
outstanding item feature *(special attraction)*
outstanding property feature *(characteristic)*
outstanding quality importance
outstream outflow
outstretch expand
outstretched broad
outstrip outbalance, overcome *(surmount)*, predominate *(outnumber)*, surpass, transcend
outvie outbalance, surpass, transcend
outward ostensible, specious, superficial
outward act overt act
outward appearance color *(deceptive appearance)*, complexion, feature *(appearance)*
outward flow outflow
outward form configuration *(form)*, formality, semblance
outward look appearance *(look)*
outward perception impression
outward show appearance *(look)*, presence *(poise)*, pretense *(ostentation)*
outward sweep outflow
outwardly seem assume *(simulate)*
outweigh convince, nullify, outbalance, override, predominate *(outnumber)*, surpass, transcend. SEE MAIN ENTRY
outweighing preponderance
outwit betray *(lead astray)*, circumvent, defeat, dupe, elude, ensnare, evade *(deceive)*, frustrate, hoodwink, illude, overreach
outwitting fraud
outworn obsolete, outdated, outmoded
ovation respect
over complete *(ended)*, de novo
over again anew, de novo. SEE MAIN ENTRY
over against contra
over all throughout *(all over)*
over and above a fortiori, also
over pass traverse
over-all complete *(all-embracing)*
over-coloring distortion
over-harsh brutal
overabound overload
overabounding profuse
overabundance overage, plethora, surfeit, surplus. SEE MAIN ENTRY
overabundant excess, needless, rampant. SEE MAIN ENTRY
overact overreach
overacted histrionic
overacting histrionics
overage surplus. SEE MAIN ENTRY
overall comprehensive, omnibus. SEE MAIN ENTRY
overall theme motif
overanxiety apprehension *(fear)*
overanxious diffident
overapprehensive diffident
overassess overestimate
overassessment exaggeration, surcharge
overawe browbeat, deter, intimidate
overbalance outbalance, outweigh
overbear beat *(defeat)*, browbeat, repress, subdue, subjugate
overbearing brutal, dictatorial, disdainful, dogmatic, inflated *(vain)*, insolent, onerous, oppressive, orgulous, peremptory *(absolute)*, presumptuous, proud *(conceited)*, severe, supercilious, tyrannous. SEE MAIN ENTRY
overbid beat *(defeat)*
overblown inflated *(bombastic)*
overboard extreme *(exaggerated)*
overboldness audacity
overburden disadvantage, exploit *(take advantage of)*, harass, impact, mishandle *(maltreat)*, mistreat, overload, persecute, surcharge
overcalculate overestimate
overcareful meticulous
overcast obnubilate, obscure
overcaution hesitation
overcautious careful
overcharge exploitation, overdraw, premium *(excess value)*, surcharge, usury
overcharged disproportionate, inordinate
overcloud blind *(obscure)*, obnubilate, obscure
overcoloring caricature
overcome attach *(seize)*, beat *(defeat)*, carry away, defeat, disconsolate, drunk, hijack, impose *(subject)*, outbalance, override, overturn, overwhelm, prevail *(triumph)*, repress, subdue, subject, subjugate, suppress, surmount. SEE MAIN ENTRY
overcome another's resistence prevail upon
overcome by argument convince, impugn
overcome by liquor drunk
overcoming prevailing *(having superior force)*
overcommit overextend
overconfidence temerity
overconfident precipitate, presumptuous, reckless
overconscientious particular *(exacting)*
overcount overestimate
overcritical critical *(faultfinding)*, nonconsenting, particular *(exacting)*, querulous
overcriticalness disparagement
overcrowd impact
overdaring audacity
overdevelop overextend
overdo distort, overestimate, over-indulge, overload, overreach
overdone extreme *(exaggerated)*, outrageous
overdose overload, surfeit
overdraft deficit
overdramatize distort
overdramatized pretentious *(pompous)*
overdraw dissipate *(expend foolishly)*. SEE MAIN ENTRY
overdrawing caricature
overdrawn inflated *(overestimated)*, past due
overdrive harass, ill use
overdue back *(in arrears)*, dilatory, late *(tardy)*, outstanding *(unpaid)*, past due. SEE MAIN ENTRY
overdue bill arrears
overdue payment arrears, due
overeat overindulge
overemotional fanatical, sensitive *(easily affected)*
overemphasis exaggeration, histrionics, hyperbole
overenlargement hyperbole
overenthusiasm exaggeration
overenthusiastic fanatical
overestimate magnify. SEE MAIN ENTRY
overestimation caricature, overstatement
overexercise tax *(overwork)*
overexert overload, tax *(overwork)*
overexertion stress *(strain)*
overexpand overextend
overextend overdraw, overreach. SEE MAIN ENTRY
overfamiliar presumptuous
overfastidious particular *(exacting)*
overfatigue tax *(overwork)*
overfeed overload
overfill overload
overflood inundate
overflow balance *(amount in excess)*, cataclysm, inundate, outflow, overage, plethora, surfeit, surplus
overflowing cataclysm, copious, demonstrative *(expressive of emotion)*, excess, excessive, full, inordinate, profuse, replete, superfluous
overfullness surfeit
overgenerous profuse
overgorge overindulge
overgratify overindulge
overgrow overlap
overhang overlap, project *(extend beyond)*
overhanging imminent, pending *(imminent)*
overhasty careless, imprudent, premature, reckless
overhaul check *(inspect)*, fix *(repair)*, modify *(alter)*, remedy, renew *(refurbish)*, repair *(noun)*, repair *(verb)*, reparation *(keeping in repair)*, revise, scrutinize
overhauled renascent
overhauling reorganization, revision *(process of correcting)*
overhead cost *(expenses)*, expense *(cost)*, maintenance *(upkeep)*. SEE MAIN ENTRY
overhear eavesdrop. SEE MAIN ENTRY
overheat burn
overindulge carouse
overindulgence greed. SEE MAIN ENTRY
overjoyed ecstatic

overjudge overestimate
overlap contact *(touch)*, encroachment. SEE MAIN ENTRY
overlaud overestimate
overlay overcome *(overwhelm)*, overlap
overlie overlap
overload disadvantage, impact, overcome *(overwhelm)*, plethora, surcharge, surfeit, tax *(overwork)*. SEE MAIN ENTRY
overlook administer *(conduct)*, check *(inspect)*, condone, contemn, control *(regulate)*, disregard, exclude, excuse, forgive, ignore, misprize, monitor, neglect, palliate *(excuse)*, pardon, patrol, peruse, police, preside, pretermit, remit *(release from penalty)*, review, superintend, survey *(examine)*. SEE MAIN ENTRY
overlook an offense condone
overlooker chief, custodian *(protector)*, principal *(director)*
overlooking condonation, disregard *(unconcern)*, oblivious, oversight *(control)*
overly unduly. SEE MAIN ENTRY
overly bold presumptuous
overly confident presumptuous
overly decorated pretentious *(ostentatious)*
overly hasty precipitate
overly liberal profligate *(extravagant)*
overly passionate perfervid
overly trustful credulous
overmaster beat *(defeat)*, defeat, overthrow, repress, subject
overmastering abduction
overmatch beat *(defeat)*, outbalance, overcome *(surmount)*
overmeasure balance *(amount in excess)*, overage, overestimate, surplus
overmeticulous particular *(exacting)*
overmuch disproportionate, excess, excessive, exorbitant, inordinate, needless, redundant, superfluous, undue *(excessive)*, unnecessary, unwarranted
overpass overstep, surmount, transcend
overplentiful needless
overplus balance *(amount in excess)*, expendable, overage, plethora, redundancy, remainder *(remaining part)*, surplus
overpoise outweigh
overpower beat *(defeat)*, carry away, check *(restrain)*, defeat, force *(coerce)*, hijack, obsess, outweigh, overcome *(overwhelm)*, overcome *(surmount)*, override, overthrow, overturn, overwhelm, repress, subdue, subjugate, supplant, suppress, surmount, upset. SEE MAIN ENTRY
overpowered with emotion ecstatic
overpowering compelling, formidable, in full force, indomitable, invincible, irresistible, moving *(evoking emotion)*, onerous, oppressive, powerful, predominant, severe, strong
overpowering fright panic
overpraise doxology, exaggeration, overestimate
overpraised inflated *(overestimated)*
overpriced inflated *(overestimated)*
overprize magnify, overestimate
overprized inflated *(overestimated)*
overproud inflated *(vain)*, orgulous
overrate magnify, overestimate
overrated inflated *(overestimated)*
overreach betray *(lead astray)*, impose *(intrude)*. SEE MAIN ENTRY
override abolish, abrogate *(rescind)*, beat *(defeat)*, browbeat, cancel, foil, frustrate, insist, invalidate, negate, nullify, overlap, overrule, preclude, predominate *(command)*, prevent, repeal, repudiate, rescind, revoke, supersede, thwart. SEE MAIN ENTRY
overriding compelling, primary, reversal
overrule abolish, abrogate *(rescind)*, annul, cancel, disaffirm, disown *(deny the validity)*, dominate, invalidate, negate, nullify, override, predominate *(command)*, prevent, quash, reject, repeal, repudiate, rescind, subjugate, supersede, vacate *(void)*, withdraw. SEE MAIN ENTRY
overruled null *(invalid)*, null and void
overruling cancellation, cardinal *(basic)*, compelling, considerable, critical *(crucial)*, predominant, prevailing *(having superior force)*, primary, rejection, rescision, reversal
overrun balance *(amount in excess)*, despoil, harass, impinge, incursion, invade, overlap, overstep, overthrow, overwhelm, permeate, spread, surplus, trespass
overrunning cataclysm, intrusion
oversee administer *(conduct)*, censor, check *(inspect)*, conduct, control *(regulate)*, direct *(supervise)*, discipline *(control)*, govern, maintain *(sustain)*, manage, moderate *(preside over)*, monitor, officiate, operate, overlook *(superintend)*, police, predominate *(command)*, preside, regulate *(manage)*, rule *(govern)*, superintend, survey *(examine)*. SEE MAIN ENTRY
overseer administrator, caretaker *(one caring for property)*, caretaker *(one fulfilling the function of office)*, chairman, chief, custodian *(protector)*, director, employer, guardian, official, principal *(director)*, procurator, superintendent, warden
oversensitive hot-blooded
overset overthrow, overturn, prostration, subversion, subvert
overshadow minimize, obfuscate, obnubilate, obscure, outweigh, overcome *(surmount)*, predominate *(command)*, shroud, surpass, transcend. SEE MAIN ENTRY
overshadowing critical *(crucial)*, dominant, important *(significant)*, obscuration
overshoot overreach
overshy diffident
oversight administration, auspices, control *(supervision)*, delinquency *(failure of duty)*, direction *(guidance)*, disregard *(unconcern)*, error, failure *(falling short)*, fault *(mistake)*, inconsideration, laxity, management *(supervision)*, miscue, neglect, negligence, nonpayment, omission, protection, supervision, surveillance. SEE MAIN ENTRY
overspend dissipate *(expend foolishly)*, overdraw
overspread diffuse, dissipate *(spread out)*, inundate, overlap, penetrate, permeate, pervade, radiate, spread
overstate distort, magnify, misrepresent, overestimate, slant
overstated extreme *(exaggerated)*, inflated *(overestimated)*
overstatement bombast, distortion, exaggeration, hyperbole, misrepresentation. SEE MAIN ENTRY
overstep accroach, encroach, impinge, impose *(intrude)*, infringe, transcend, trespass. SEE MAIN ENTRY
overstep boundaries impinge
overstepping encroachment, incursion, infraction, invasion, malfeasance
overstrain dissipate *(expend foolishly)*, harass, overdraw, overload, tax *(overwork)*
overstress magnify
overstressed inflated *(overestimated)*
overstretch overdraw
overstuff overload
oversufficient needless
oversupply balance *(amount in excess)*, overage, plethora, redundancy, surfeit, surplus
oversweet nectarious
overt apparent *(perceptible)*, blatant *(conspicuous)*, candid, clear *(apparent)*, comprehensible, conspicuous, evident, lucid, manifest, naked *(perceptible)*, obvious, open *(in sight)*, ostensible, palpable, patent, pellucid, perceivable, perceptible, public *(known)*, salient, scrutable, unmistakable. SEE MAIN ENTRY
overt act SEE MAIN ENTRY
overtake beat *(defeat)*, invade, reach
overtask exploit *(take advantage of)*, mistreat, overload
overtax exploit *(take advantage of)*, harass, misemploy, mistreat, overcome *(overwhelm)*, overload, persecute
overtaxing onerous
overthrow beat *(defeat)*, commotion, debacle, defeat *(noun)*, defeat *(verb)*, destroy *(efface)*, dislodge, dissolution *(termination)*, eliminate *(eradicate)*, insurrection, invalidate, kill *(defeat)*, miscarriage, negate, overcome *(surmount)*, overturn, overwhelm, plunder, prostration, quash, rebel, rebellion, refute, repulse, rescision, revolt, revolution, sedition, subject, subjugate, subversion, subvert, supplant, suppress, surmount, upset. SEE MAIN ENTRY
overthrow of authority outbreak, revolution
overthrowing reversal
overtire exhaust *(deplete)*, tax *(overwork)*
overtone implication *(inference)*, innuendo, intimation, suggestion
overtop outbalance, outweigh, predominate *(outnumber)*, transcend
overtrump beat *(defeat)*
overtrustfulness credulity
overture bid, invitation, preface, prelude, proposal *(suggestion)*, proposition, threshold *(commencement)*. SEE MAIN ENTRY
overturn abolish, debacle, destroy *(efface)*, disaffirm, disorient, disrupt, disturb, extirpate, kill *(defeat)*, nullify, override, overrule, overthrow, prostration, quash, rebellion, revolt, subversion, subvert, surmount, upset, vitiate. SEE MAIN ENTRY
overturn of authority revolution
overturn of government revolution
overturning havoc
overuse exploit *(take advantage of)*, overload, tax *(overwork)*
overused trite
overvaluation exaggeration
overvalue magnify, overestimate
overvalued inflated *(overestimated)*
overview inquiry *(systematic investigation)*. SEE MAIN ENTRY
overweening disdainful, inflated *(vain)*, orgulous, presumptuous, proud *(conceited)*, supercilious
overweigh convince, outbalance, outweigh, overload
overweight ponderous
overwelm quash
overwhelm beat *(defeat)*, controvert, defeat, devastate, force *(coerce)*, hijack, immerse *(engross)*, inundate, overload, overthrow, overturn, subdue, subjugate, suppress, upset. SEE MAIN ENTRY

overwhelming compelling, formidable, indomitable, ineffable, invincible, irresistible, lurid, moving *(evoking emotion),* omnipotent, oppressive, powerful, prodigious *(amazing),* remarkable, resounding, strong. SEE MAIN ENTRY
overwhelming part bulk
overwork exploit *(take advantage of),* harass, misemploy, mistreat, overload, persecute
overwrought demonstrative *(expressive of emotion),* frenetic
overzealous extreme *(exaggerated),* fanatical
owe overdraw. SEE MAIN ENTRY
owe money overdraw
owed delinquent *(overdue),* receivable
owing accountable *(responsible),* delinquent *(overdue),* due *(owed),* indebted, outstanding *(unpaid),* payable, receivable, unpaid, unsettled
owing nothing solvent
own hold *(possess),* occupy *(take possession),* particular *(individual),* personal *(individual),* possess, profess *(avow),* recognize *(acknowledge),* remain *(occupy).* SEE MAIN ENTRY
own exclusively monopolize
own up betray *(disclose),* confess
owned jointly common *(shared)*
owner employer, holder, lessor, principal *(director),* proprietor, shareholder, tenant. SEE MAIN ENTRY
owner of an estate in land landholder, landlord, landowner
owner of land landowner
owner of lands landlord
owner of real estate landowner
owner of real property landowner
owner of tenements landlord
owner of the fee landholder, landowner
owner of the fee simple absolute landholder
owner's mark brand
owner's sign brand
ownership adverse possession, claim *(right),* dominion *(absolute ownership),* enjoyment *(use),* occupancy, occupation *(possession),* property *(possessions),* right *(entitlement),* seisin, stake *(interest),* substance *(material possessions),* tenancy, title *(right).* SEE MAIN ENTRY

P

pace patrol, perambulate, rate, step
pace off measure
pacem conciliare mediate
pacesetter pioneer
pachydermatous impervious, insusceptible *(uncaring).* SEE MAIN ENTRY
pacifiable placable
pacific harmonious, neutral, patient, peaceable, placid
pacificate mollify, pacify, placate, propitiate, soothe
pacification conciliation, expiation, mollification, peace, reconciliation
pacificatory nonmilitant, peaceable
pacifier go-between
pacifistic neutral, nonmilitant, peaceable
pacify allay, alleviate, assuage, disarm *(set at ease),* ease, lull, moderate *(temper),* mollify, palliate *(abate),* placate, propitiate, reconcile, redress, soothe. SEE MAIN ENTRY
pacifying palliative *(abating)*
pacisci agree *(contract),* close *(agree),* covenant
pack assemblage, band, cargo, impact, load, overload, quantity
pack away hoard
pack close impact
pack in impact
pack tightly constrict *(compress)*
pack together impact
package bargaining collective bargaining
packages cargo, freight
packed compact *(dense),* full, pithy, populous, replete, solid *(compact)*
packed together solid *(compact)*
packed with meaning sententious
packet assemblage
packman dealer
packwoman dealer
pact accordance *(compact),* adjustment, agree *(contract),* agreement *(contract),* arrangement *(understanding),* assurance, bargain, cartel, compact, condition *(contingent provision),* contract, covenant, deal, guaranty, indenture, league, mutual understanding, obligation *(duty),* peace, policy *(contract),* promise, protocol *(agreement),* settlement, specialty *(contract),* stipulation, treaty, understanding *(agreement).* SEE MAIN ENTRY
pact before marriage antenuptial agreement
pactio bargain, compact, covenant, pact, treaty
paction assurance, contract, pact, promise
pactum compact, confederacy *(compact),* contract, covenant, indenture, league, pact, settlement, stipulation
pad inflate
padded profuse, prolix
padlock handcuff, lock
paean doxology
paedeutic disciplinary *(educational)*
paenitendus regrettable
paenitens repentant
paenitet contrite
page call *(summon)*
paid mercenary
pain aggravate *(annoy),* annoy, distress *(anguish),* distress, irritate, nuisance, offend *(insult),* perturb, pique, plague. SEE MAIN ENTRY
pain and suffering SEE MAIN ENTRY
pain reliever narcotic
pain-killing narcotic
pained aggrieved *(harmed),* disconsolate, resentful
painful cruel, insufferable, lamentable, loathsome, oppressive, pernicious, repugnant *(exciting aversion),* severe. SEE MAIN ENTRY
painkiller drug, narcotic
painless innocuous
pains burden, effort, endeavor, labor *(exertion),* struggle
painstaking careful, circumspect, conscientious, difficult, diligence *(care),* diligent, elaborate, faithful *(diligent),* industrious, meticulous, operose, particular *(exacting),* pertinacious, precise, sedulous, thorough. SEE MAIN ENTRY
paint delineate, describe, portray
paint a picture delineate
pair connect *(join together),* join *(bring together)*
pair with combine *(act in concert),* commingle
paired attached *(annexed),* concurrent *(united),* conjoint, conjugal, correlative
palatable popular, sapid, savory. SEE MAIN ENTRY
palatial elaborate
palaver confer *(consult),* conference, council *(assembly),* speak, speech. SEE MAIN ENTRY
pale ambit, border, capacity *(sphere),* circuit, district, locality, nebulous, obscure *(faint),* outline *(boundary),* periphery, sphere. SEE MAIN ENTRY
paleness indistinctness
palimony SEE MAIN ENTRY
palingenesis reconversion, revival
palinode retraction
pall veil
palladian omniscient
palladium bulwark, protection, safeguard, security *(safety)*
palliate abate *(lessen),* allay, alleviate, ameliorate, assuage, commute, condone, cure, drug, extenuate, forgive, justify, lessen, lull, meliorate, mitigate, moderate *(temper),* mollify, obtund, redress, relieve *(give aid),* remedy, remit *(relax),* soothe. SEE MAIN ENTRY
palliation abatement *(reduction),* extenuating circumstances, justification, mitigation, moderation, mollification, relief *(release),* solace
palliative cure, drug, medicinal, mitigating, narcotic *(adjective),* narcotic *(noun),* panacea, remedial, remedy *(that which corrects),* salutary. SEE MAIN ENTRY
palliative circumstances extenuating circumstances
palm off foist
palm off fraudulently foist
palming prestidigitation
palmy prosperous
palmy days prosperity
palpability density, materiality *(physical existence)*
palpable actual, apparent *(perceptible),* appreciable, arrant *(definite),* bodily, coherent *(clear),* comprehensible, concrete, corporal, corporeal, distinct *(clear),* evident, lucid, manifest, material *(physical),* obvious, overt, pellucid, perceivable, perceptible, physical, ponderable, sensible, substantive, tangible, unmistakable. SEE MAIN ENTRY
palpable episode fact
palpably fairly *(clearly)*
palpably false unbelievable
palpitate beat *(pulsate)*
palsied powerless
palter equivocate, evade *(deceive),* fabricate *(make up),* feign, haggle, lie *(falsify),* misrepresent, perjure, pettifog, prevaricate. SEE MAIN ENTRY
palter with the truth distort
paltriness immateriality, inconsequence, insignificance
paltry de minimus, deficient, frivolous, inappreciable, inconsequential, inconsiderable, inferior *(lower in quality),* insubstantial, insufficient, minimal, minor, negligible, nonsubstantial *(not sufficient),* nugatory, null *(insignificant),* petty, poor *(inferior in quality),* scarce, slight, tenuous. SEE MAIN ENTRY
paltry few minority *(outnumbered group)*
pamper pander
pamper excessively overindulge
pampering indulgence, lenience, lenient
panacea cure. SEE MAIN ENTRY
panache pretense *(ostentation)*

pandect abstract, capsule, compendium, constitution, digest, hornbook, outline *(synopsis)*, summary. SEE MAIN ENTRY
pandemic general, omnibus, predominant, prevailing *(current)*, prevalent, rife. SEE MAIN ENTRY
pandemonium bluster *(commotion)*, brawl, commotion, confusion *(turmoil)*, disorder *(lack of order)*, embroilment, furor, noise, outcry, panic, riot, shambles, turmoil. SEE MAIN ENTRY
pander SEE MAIN ENTRY
panegyric mention *(tribute)*
panegyrical favorable *(expressing approval)*
panel array *(jury)*, band, chamber *(body)*, jury, meeting *(conference)*. SEE MAIN ENTRY
panel of judges bench, chamber *(body)*, forum *(court)*, tribunal
pang *pain*
pangs of conscience remorse
panhandler parasite
panic fear, fright, frighten, pandemonium, phobia, trepidation. SEE MAIN ENTRY
panoplied armed, safe
panoply ammunition, protection. SEE MAIN ENTRY
panorama scene
panoramic comprehensive
pansophic learned, omniscient
pansophical omniscient
pantomine mock *(imitate)*
panurgic practiced
paper blank *(form)*, certificate, document, instrument *(document)*, pandect *(treatise)*
paper credit letter of credit
paper money check *(instrument)*, currency, debenture
papers credentials, data, dossier
paphian lascivious, salacious
par peer, similar
par worth. SEE MAIN ENTRY
paraclete advocate *(counselor)*
parade demonstrate *(protest)*, display, flaunt, histrionics, lineup, pretense *(ostentation)*, produce *(offer to view)*. SEE MAIN ENTRY
parade conspicuously flaunt
paradigm case *(example)*, example, exemplar, instance, model, pattern, prototype, sample, specimen, standard. SEE MAIN ENTRY
paradigma paradigm
paradigmatic exemplary
paradisiacal placid
paradox enigma. SEE MAIN ENTRY
paradoxical debatable, disputable, impossible, inconsistent, inexplicable, ironic, problematic. SEE MAIN ENTRY
paragon exemplar, expert, model, pattern, prototype, representative *(example)*, standard. SEE MAIN ENTRY
paragraph chapter *(division)*, clause, subheading, title *(division)*
parallel agreed *(harmonized)*, akin *(germane)*, analogous, coequal, coextensive, cognate, collateral *(accompanying)*, commensurable, comparable *(capable of comparison)*, compare, comparison, concerted, concomitant, concurrent *(at the same time)*, congruous, connection *(relation)*, consensual, consonant, constructive *(inferential)*, correlate, correlative, correspond *(be equivalent)*, equivalent, mutual *(reciprocal)*, peer, reciprocal, relate *(establish a connection)*, reproduce, resemblance, same, similar, tantamount. SEE MAIN ENTRY
parallel relation analogy
paralleling commensurate
parallelism analogy, identity *(similarity)*, parity, propinquity *(similarity)*
parallelize compare
paralogical sophistic
paralogism fallacy, non sequitur
paralogistic fallacious, illogical
paralogize distort
paralysis deadlock, inaction, inertia
paralysis of authority lynch law
paralytic disabled *(made incapable)*, powerless
paralyze debar, disable, disarm *(divest of arms)*, fetter, impair, impede, inhibit, prevent, stall
paralyzed disabled *(made incapable)*, helpless *(powerless)*, powerless
paralyzing chilling effect, disabling
parameter guideline
paramount absolute *(ideal)*, best, cardinal *(outstanding)*, central *(essential)*, critical *(crucial)*, dominant, important *(significant)*, influential, leading *(ranking first)*, major, master, material *(important)*, necessary *(required)*, noteworthy, outstanding *(prominent)*, peremptory *(imperative)*, predominant, preferential, prevailing *(having superior force)*, primary, prime *(most valuable)*, principal, professional *(stellar)*, salient, sovereign *(absolute)*, stellar, superior *(higher)*, superlative, vital. SEE MAIN ENTRY
paramount law constitution
paramountcy hegemony, importance, influence, predominance, preponderance, prestige, primacy, significance, stress *(accent)*, supremacy
paramountly a fortiori
paranoia insanity. SEE MAIN ENTRY
parapet bulwark
paraph sign
paraphernalia effects, goods. SEE MAIN ENTRY
paraphrase construe *(translate)*, elucidate, explain, plagiarize, quote, recapitulate, repeat *(state again)*, restatement. SEE MAIN ENTRY
paraphrased repeated
paraphrasis paraphrase
parasite SEE MAIN ENTRY
parasitize prey
paratus ready *(prepared)*
parcel installment, lot, moiety, part *(separate)*, property *(land)*, ration, real estate, reapportion, subdivide. SEE MAIN ENTRY
parcel of land plot *(land)*, section *(vicinity)*
parcel out allocate, allot, apportion, disburse *(distribute)*, dispense, disperse *(disseminate)*, dispose *(apportion)*, distribute, divide *(distribute)*, dole, marshal, mete, partition, prorate, sort, split. SEE MAIN ENTRY
parcel out again redistribute
parcel out to delegate
parceling out disbursement *(act of disbursing)*, distribution *(apportionment)*
parcelling division *(act of dividing)*
parcels paraphernalia *(personal belongings)*
parcener heir
parcere forbear
parch burn
parcus close *(rigorous)*, frugal, parsimonious
pardon absolution, absolve, acquit, acquittal, amnesty, clear, clemency, compurgation, condonation, condone, discharge *(release from obligation)*, discharge *(liberate)*, dispensation *(exception)*, emancipation, exculpate, excuse, exonerate, exoneration, extenuate, forgive, free, grace, grace period, impunity, indulgence, liberate, liberation, longanimity, overlook *(excuse)*, palliate *(excuse)*, purge *(wipe out by atonement)*, quit *(free of)*, release, remission, remit *(release from penalty)*, respite *(reprieve)*, vindicate. SEE MAIN ENTRY
pardonable allowable, defensible, justifiable. SEE MAIN ENTRY
pardoned clear *(free from criminal charges)*, free *(relieved from a burden)*
pardoning clemency, lenient, palliative *(excusing)*
pardonment release
pare curtail, decrease, denude, diminish, discount *(minimize)*, excise *(cut away)*, lessen, minimize, rebate, retrench
pare down curtail
paregoric narcotic
parens parents, progenitor
parent ancestor, author *(originator)*, derivation, precursor, primogenitor, progenitor, source. SEE MAIN ENTRY
parentage adoption *(affiliation)*, affiliation *(bloodline)*, affinity *(family ties)*, ancestry, birth *(lineage)*, blood, bloodline, citation *(attribution)*, derivation, descent *(lineage)*, family *(common ancestry)*, filiation, lineage, origin *(ancestry)*, origination, paternity, race, source. SEE MAIN ENTRY
parental paternal
parenthesis insertion
parenthesize interpose
parenthetic incidental, nonessential
parenthetical nonessential. SEE MAIN ENTRY
parenthetically among
parenthood maternity, origin *(ancestry)*
parentless child orphan
parents ancestry. SEE MAIN ENTRY
parents and children household
parere bear *(yield)*, comply, generate, heed, obey
pari materia SEE MAIN ENTRY
pariah derelict. SEE MAIN ENTRY
paring economy *(frugality)*
parity analogy, balance *(equality)*, correspondence *(similarity)*, equipoise, identity *(similarity)*, resemblance. SEE MAIN ENTRY
park locate, lodge *(house)*, stay *(rest)*
parkway causeway
parlance conference, language, phraseology, rhetoric *(skilled speech)*, speech. SEE MAIN ENTRY
parlay bet, build *(augment)*, compound. SEE MAIN ENTRY
parley communicate, confer *(consult)*, conference, confrontation *(act of setting face to face)*, consult *(ask advice of)*, conversation, converse, council *(assembly)*, deliberate, discourse, discuss, mediate, mediation, meet, meeting *(conference)*, negotiate, negotiation, session, speak, treat *(process)*. SEE MAIN ENTRY
parliament chamber *(body)*, council *(assembly)*, legislature
parliamentarian legislator
parlor chamber *(compartment)*
parlous aleatory *(perilous)*
parlous state peril
parochial illiberal, narrow, provincial, regional. SEE MAIN ENTRY
parochialis parochial
parody caricature, distort, jape, mock *(imitate)*, pose *(impersonate)*, travesty. SEE MAIN ENTRY

parol noncupative. SEE MAIN ENTRY
parole discharge *(liberate)*, free, liberate, liberation, probation, undertaking *(pledge)*, verbal. SEE MAIN ENTRY
parole evidence rule SEE MAIN ENTRY
paroled free *(relieved from a burden)*, unbound
parolee convict, probationer *(released offender)*
paroxysm outbreak, outburst
parrot copy, impersonate, mock *(imitate)*, recite, repeat *(state again)*
parry avert, bicker, block, defense, dispute *(debate)*, divert, elude, equivocate, prevaricate, prevent, rebut, refute, repel *(drive back)*, reply, resist *(oppose)*, respond, retort. SEE MAIN ENTRY
parrying avoidance *(evasion)*
pars clause, constituent *(part)*, department, faction, ingredient, installment, item, proportion, segment, share *(interest)*, side, subdivision
pars interior chamber *(compartment)*
pars minima minimum
parsimonia economy *(frugality)*
parsimonious economical, frugal, illiberal, penurious, provident *(frugal)*. SEE MAIN ENTRY
part alienate *(estrange)*, alight, aspect, assignment *(task)*, bifurcate, break *(separate)*, chapter *(division)*, circuit, component, constituent *(part)*, courtroom, depart, department, detach, detail, dichotomize, disband, discontinue *(break continuity)*, disengage, disjoint, disperse *(scatter)*, dissociate, dissolve *(separate)*, divide *(separate)*, divorce, element, equity *(share of ownership)*, estrange, excerpt, factor *(ingredient)*, feature *(characteristic)*, ingredient, interest *(ownership)*, isolate, item, leave *(depart)*, lot, luxate, member *(constituent part)*, moiety, organ, phase *(aspect)*, proportion, province, quit *(evacuate)*, ration, region, remove *(eliminate)*, retire *(retreat)*, role, section *(division)*, section *(vicinity)*, segment, separate, sever, share *(interest)*, split, subdivision, title *(division)*, unit *(item)*. SEE MAIN ENTRY
part and parcel constituent *(part)*
part company avoid *(evade)*, disband, estrange, move *(alter position)*, separate, split
part exemplifying a mass cross section
part exemplifying a number cross section
part of the bargain counteroffer
part payment deposit, installment
part payment of a debt installment
part ways separate
part with abandon *(relinquish)*, alienate *(transfer title)*, attorn, bestow, cede, disown *(refuse to acknowledge)*, forfeit, forgo, forswear, jettison, lose *(be deprived of)*, parcel, relinquish, renounce, spend, surrender *(give back)*. SEE MAIN ENTRY
part with life die
partage split
partake contribute *(assist)*, engage *(involve)*, involve *(participate)*, participate. SEE MAIN ENTRY
partake in cooperate
partake in a symposium discuss
partake of contribute *(assist)*
partaken privy
partaker accessory, accomplice, participant, partner, party *(participant)*
parted discrete, disjunctive *(tending to disjoin)*, separate
partes office, part *(role)*, role
partes hominis agere impersonate
partial deficient, ex parte, illiberal, imperfect, inchoate, inequitable, interested, one-sided, parochial, partisan, preferential, prone, semi, unequal *(unjust)*, unjust. SEE MAIN ENTRY
partial change modification
partial excuse extenuating circumstances
partial payment installment
partial similarity analogy
partial to inclined, willing *(desirous)*
partial truth evasion
partialism favoritism
partiality affection, affinity *(regard)*, bias, favoritism, foregone conclusion, inclination, inequality, inequity, injustice, intolerance, nepotism, penchant, preconception, predetermination, predilection, predisposition, preference *(choice)*, prejudice *(preconception)*, proclivity, propensity, tendency. SEE MAIN ENTRY
partially in part, piecemeal
partible divisible, divisive, separable, severable
particeps participant, partner
particeps criminis abettor, accessory, accomplice, cohort, colleague, copartner *(coconspirator)*
participant accessory, accomplice, actor, contestant, contributor *(contributor)*, partisan, partner, privy. SEE MAIN ENTRY
participate assist, connive, contribute *(assist)*, cooperate, engage *(involve)*, espouse, federalize *(associate)*, federate, join *(associate oneself with)*, partake. SEE MAIN ENTRY
participate in commit *(perpetrate)*, compete
participate in an unlawful scheme conspire
participate surreptitiously connive
participate with combine *(act in concert)*
participating common *(shared)*, concurrent *(united)*
participation affiliation *(connectedness)*, assistance, association *(connection)*, collusion, connivance, contact *(association)*, coverage *(scope)*, integration *(assimilation)*, interest *(ownership)*, league, partnership. SEE MAIN ENTRY
participation in fraud collusion
participator accessory, accomplice, colleague, confederate, consociate, contributor *(contributor)*, member *(individual in a group)*, participant, partner, party *(participant)*
participatory common *(shared)*, mutual *(collective)*
particle constituent *(part)*, element, iota, minimum, modicum, part *(portion)*, scintilla. SEE MAIN ENTRY
particular accurate, certain *(specific)*, circumspect, concrete, conscientious, detail, detailed, distinct *(clear)*, distinct *(distinguished from others)*, distinctive, exact, express, faithful *(diligent)*, feature *(characteristic)*, individual, item, meticulous, painstaking, peculiar *(distinctive)*, personal *(individual)*, point *(item)*, precise, proper, punctilious, singular, special, specific, specification, strict, technicality, term *(provision)*, unusual. SEE MAIN ENTRY
particular aptitude penchant
particular characteristic specialty *(distinctive mark)*
particular charge complaint, count
particular course of action procedure
particular item specialty *(distinctive mark)*
particular manner of proceeding course
particular matter specialty *(distinctive mark)*
particular object article *(commodity)*
particular object of pursuit specialty *(special aptitude)*
particular one individual
particular part component
particular point specialty *(distinctive mark)*
particular point of time date
particularity characteristic, color *(complexion)*, detail, differential, diligence *(care)*, habit, identity *(individuality)*, particular, personality, property *(distinctive attribute)*, quality *(attribute)*, quality *(grade)*, quirk *(idiosyncrasy)*, speciality, specialty *(distinctive mark)*, technicality, trait. SEE MAIN ENTRY
particularization designation *(naming)*, specification
particularize delineate, depict, describe, designate, detail *(particularize)*, differentiate, distinguish, itemize, portray, recount, relate *(tell)*, specify
particularized descriptive, detailed
particularly a fortiori. SEE MAIN ENTRY
particularness discretion *(quality of being discreet)*, particularity
particulars circumstances, description, story *(narrative)*
partim partial *(part)*, partial *(relating to a part)*
parting divergent, division *(act of dividing)*, egress, estrangement, leave *(absence)*, rift *(disagreement)*, rift *(gap)*, separation
parting with cession
partiri parcel, part *(separate)*
partisan addict, advocate *(espouser)*, backer, ex parte, inequitable, interested, one-sided, parochial, partial *(biased)*, party *(participant)*, political, politician, preferential, prejudicial, proponent. SEE MAIN ENTRY
partisan competition primary
partisan conflict faction
partisan contest primary
partisan election primary
partisan outlook posture *(attitude)*
partisanism bias, inequity, nepotism, politics
partisanship bias, constituency, faction, favor *(partiality)*, favoritism, indorsement, inequity, injustice, nepotism, partiality, predilection, prejudice *(preconception)*. SEE MAIN ENTRY
partitio division *(act of dividing)*
partition allot, allotment, apportion, apportionment, assign *(allot)*, assignment *(allotment)*, barrier, bifurcate, chapter *(division)*, classify, decentralization, demarcate, dichotomize, disassociation, dispensation *(act of dispensing)*, disperse *(disseminate)*, disperse *(scatter)*, distribution *(apportionment)*, divide *(separate)*, division *(act of dividing)*, parcel, part *(separate)*, schism, segregation *(separation)*, sever, split *(noun)*, split *(verb)*, subdivide, subdivision. SEE MAIN ENTRY
partitioned bipartite, disconnected, disjunctive *(tending to disjoin)*
partitioned space chamber *(compartment)*
partitionment apportionment

partly in part
partner accessory, accomplice, assistant, associate, coactor, coadjutant, coconspirator, cohort, colleague, confederate, connect *(join together)*, consociate, consort, conspirer, contributor *(contributor)*, copartner *(business associate)*, member *(individual in a group)*, participant, partisan, party *(participant)*. SEE MAIN ENTRY
partner in crime accessory, accomplice, coactor, coconspirator, conspirer, copartner *(coconspirator)*
partner in wrongdoing accomplice, coconspirator
partnered conjoint, conjugal, corporate *(associate)*
partnership affiliation *(connectedness)*, association *(connection)*, coaction, coalition, community, company *(enterprise)*, consortium *(business cartel)*, consortium *(marriage companionship)*, contribution *(participation)*, cooperative, firm, integration *(assimilation)*, league, matrimony, merger, pool, sodality, syndicate. SEE MAIN ENTRY
parts contents
parturient fertile
parturition birth *(emergence of young)*
partus embryo
party actor, amicus curiae, appellant, applicant *(petitioner)*, assemblage, character *(an individual)*, complainant, constituency, contender, contributor *(contributor)*, denomination, individual, litigant, participant, person, petitioner, privy, side. SEE MAIN ENTRY
party against whom a complaint is lodged defendant
party against whom charges are pending defendant
party answering a summons or bill respondent
party competition primary
party contest primary
party election primary
party in power management *(directorate)*
party leadership politics
party line platform, policy *(plan of action)*
party machine party *(political organization)*
party making an affidavit deponent
party member partisan, politician
party planks platform
party politics politics
party system politics
party to a suit accuser, appellant, claimant, complainant, contender, contestant, litigant, suitor
party to an instrument comaker
party to the suit plaintiff
party who is sued defendant
party who sues plaintiff
party-liner partisan
parum candidus disingenuous
parum clarus indistinct
parum distinctus inarticulate
parum insignis inconspicuous
parum procedere miscarriage
parvi facere disregard
parvo emere rate
parvus limited
pasquinade parody, ridicule
pass alienate *(transfer title)*, circulate, confirm, constitute *(establish)*, convey *(transfer)*, decide, enact, experience *(encounter)*, expire, exude, forgo, franchise *(license)*, give *(grant)*, grant *(transfer formally)*, incident, key *(passport)*, legislate, outbalance, penetrate, perambulate, perish, permit, plight, posture *(situation)*, predicament, pretermit, promote *(advance)*, surmount, surpass, transcend, transfer, transmit, traverse. SEE MAIN ENTRY
pass an opinion determine, find *(determine)*
pass and repass beat *(pulsate)*
pass away decease, die, expire, perish. SEE MAIN ENTRY
pass back regress
pass by disdain, disregard, ignore, neglect, omit, reject
pass by devise descend
pass by inheritance descend
pass by operation of law descend
pass by succession descend
pass by will demise
pass censure on condemn *(blame)*, convict, denounce *(condemn)*
pass censure upon disapprove *(condemn)*
pass current circulate
pass down attorn, confer *(give)*, contribute *(supply)*, convey *(transfer)*, demise, endow, render *(deliver)*
pass down from generation to generation descend
pass for assume *(simulate)*, displace *(replace)*, impersonate, pose *(impersonate)*, profess *(pretend)*
pass from one to another circulate
pass from point to point traverse
pass in the mind occur *(come to mind)*
pass into enter *(go in)*
pass judgment adjudge, adjudicate, arbitrate *(adjudge)*, award, conclude *(decide)*, decide, decree, determine, find *(determine)*, hold *(decide)*, rule *(decide)*. SEE MAIN ENTRY
pass judgment upon sentence
pass laws legislate
pass off fake, pretend
pass off another's ideas as one's own plagiarize
pass off another's writings as one's own plagiarize
pass off as genuine foist
pass off for disguise, misrepresent
pass on abalienate, annunciate, comment, convey *(communicate)*, decease, deliver, descend, die, perish, proceed *(go forward)*, transfer, transmit
pass on again recover
pass on information annunciate, notice *(give formal warning)*
pass on to bequeath
pass orders instruct *(direct)*
pass out disburse *(distribute)*, disperse *(disseminate)*, divide *(distribute)*, parcel
pass out of sight disappear
pass over alienate *(transfer title)*, condone, discount *(disbelieve)*, disdain, dismiss *(put out of consideration)*, exclude, excuse, grant *(transfer formally)*, ignore, neglect, omit, overlook *(disregard)*, override, pretermit, reject, remit *(release from penalty)*
pass over to bequeath
pass round circulate
pass sentence adjudicate, award, decide, determine, rule *(decide)*
pass sentence on condemn *(punish)*, convict
pass sentence upon judge, pronounce *(pass judgment)*
pass through endure *(suffer)*, perambulate, permeate, pervade, traverse
pass time in idleness loiter
pass title convey *(transfer)*
pass to devolve
pass to another lapse *(cease)*
pass under review censor, judge, notice *(observe)*, peruse
pass unfavorable judgment upon disapprove *(condemn)*
pass up disapprove *(reject)*, disavow, refuse. SEE MAIN ENTRY
pass upon award, rule *(decide)*
pass without notice ignore
passable admissible, allowable, average *(standard)*, fair *(satisfactory)*, imperfect, marginal, mediocre, pardonable, penetrable, unobjectionable. SEE MAIN ENTRY
passableness mediocrity
passably fairly *(moderately)*
passage access *(right of way)*, admission *(entry)*, admittance *(means of approach)*, avenue *(route)*, chapter *(division)*, circulation, clause, conversion *(change)*, entrance, entry *(entrance)*, excerpt, fare, ingress, osmosis, progress, reconversion, transition, transmittal
passage at arms affray
passage money fare
passage out egress, outlet
passage taken from a book excerpt
passages approaches
passageway access *(right of way)*, admission *(entry)*, admittance *(means of approach)*, avenue *(route)*, entrance, portal
passbook ledger
passe outdated, outmoded
passed allowed
passed away dead, deceased, defunct, lifeless *(dead)*
passed down hereditary
passed on deceased, late *(defunct)*, lifeless *(dead)*
passer-by bystander
passing brief, circulation, cursory, ephemeral, extremity *(death)*, itinerant, moving *(in motion)*, promotion *(advancement)*, provisional, temporary, transient, transition, volatile
passing away death, demise *(death)*, in extremis, transitory
passing into law legalization
passing judgment conviction *(finding of guilt)*
passing of seisin feoffment
passing over omission
passing word mention *(reference)*
passion affection, ardor, emotion, furor, obsession, penchant, propensity, spirit. SEE MAIN ENTRY
passionate demonstrative *(expressive of emotion)*, eager, ecstatic, fanatical, fervent, hot-blooded, impulsive *(rash)*, intense, serious *(devoted)*, vehement, zealous
passionateness ardor
passionless cold-blooded, controlled *(restrained)*, dispassionate, languid, lifeless *(dull)*, nonchalant, perfunctory, phlegmatic, stoical
passive dormant, indolent, insensible, languid, lifeless *(dull)*, obedient, otiose, patient, phlegmatic, pliant, resigned, sequacious, servile, stagnant, static, stoical, torpid, unobtrusive, yielding. SEE MAIN ENTRY
passive agreement acquiescence
passive consent acquiescence
passiveness capitulation, inaction, inertia, resignation *(passive acceptance)*

passivity capitulation, inaction, inertia, languor, resignation *(passive acceptance)*, sloth
passport credentials, permit
password catchword
past back *(in arrears)*, defunct, former, last *(preceding)*, obsolete, old, outdated, outmoded, previous, prior. SEE MAIN ENTRY
past bearing insufferable, unendurable
past comprehension inapprehensible, inscrutable
past cure incorrigible, irredeemable, irremediable
past dispute categorical, certain *(positive)*, cogent, inappealable, incontestable, incontrovertible, indubious, irrefutable, positive *(incontestable)*, uncontroverted, undeniable, undisputed
past due delinquent *(overdue)*, late *(tardy)*, outstanding *(unpaid)*, overdue. SEE MAIN ENTRY
past enduring insufferable, unendurable
past help irremediable
past hope incorrigible, irrecoverable, irredeemable
past mending irredeemable, irremediable
past recall irredeemable, irretrievable
past the time for payment overdue
paste combine *(join together)*
pastiche melange
pastoral placid
pat suitable, usual
patch fix *(repair)*, flaw, parcel, plot *(land)*, repair, restore *(renew)*
patch up fix *(repair)*, renew *(refurbish)*, restore *(renew)*
patch up a quarrel placate
patching repair
patchwork melange
patefacere detect, manifest, reveal
patefactio common knowledge, disclosure *(act of disclosing)*
patens open *(unclosed)*
patent apparent *(perceptible)*, appreciable, blatant *(conspicuous)*, charter *(license)*, clear *(apparent)*, comprehensible, conspicuous, evident, explicit, lucid, manifest, naked *(perceptible)*, obvious, open *(in sight)*, ostensible, overt, palpable, pellucid, perceivable, perceptible, permit, unmistakable. SEE MAIN ENTRY
patently bad arrant *(onerous)*
patently offensive obscene
patere open *(accessible)*
paternal consanguineous. SEE MAIN ENTRY
paternal parentage paternity
paternity descent *(lineage)*, filiation, parentage. SEE MAIN ENTRY
paternus hereditary, paternal
path access *(right of way)*, admission *(entry)*, admittance *(means of approach)*, avenue *(route)*, conduit *(channel)*, outlet, way *(channel)*. SEE MAIN ENTRY
pathetic deplorable, disconsolate, lamentable, paltry
pathfinder pioneer, precursor
pathless impervious
pathogenic contagious, insalubrious
pathway way *(channel)*
pati bear *(tolerate)*, let *(permit)*, suffer *(permit)*
patience composure, diligence *(perseverance)*, indulgence, lenience, longanimity, moderation, resignation *(passive acceptance)*, sufferance, temperament, temperance, tolerance, understanding *(tolerance)*. SEE MAIN ENTRY
patiens patient, phlegmatic
patient charitable *(lenient)*, lenient, peaceable, persistent, pertinacious, placid, resigned, sedulous, steadfast, stoical. SEE MAIN ENTRY
patient endurance longanimity, sufferance
patientia sufferance
patois phraseology
patriarch ancestor, parents, precursor, predecessor, primogenitor
patriarchal consanguineous, paternal
patriarchs ancestry
patriciate society
patrilinear consanguineous
patrimonial paternal, testamentary
patrimonium birthright, heritage
patrimony bequest, birthright, estate *(hereditament)*, hereditament, heritage
patriotic faithful *(loyal)*, loyal
patrius paternal
patrocinium patronage *(power to appoint jobs)*
patrol perambulate, police, protect, traverse. SEE MAIN ENTRY
patrolman peace officer, warden
patron abettor, advocate *(counselor)*, advocate *(espouser)*, backer, benefactor, client, consumer, contributor *(giver)*, customer, donor, employer, good samaritan, guardian, member *(individual in a group)*, partisan, promoter, proponent, samaritan, sponsor. SEE MAIN ENTRY
patron of professional servies client
patronage advantage, advocacy, aid *(help)*, aid *(subsistence)*, auspices, charge *(custody)*, charity, control *(supervision)*, favor *(sanction)*, goodwill, guidance, help, nepotism, protection, safekeeping, support *(assistance)*, trade *(commerce)*. SEE MAIN ENTRY
patroness donor
patronize deign, finance, foster, help, nurture, prefer, preserve, promote *(organize)*, protect, sponsor, subscribe *(promise)*, subsidize, support *(assist)*. SEE MAIN ENTRY
patronizer client, patron *(regular customer)*
patronizing inflated *(vain)*, orgulous, proud *(conceited)*, supercilious
patronus advocate *(counselor)*, patron *(influential supporter)*, spokesman
patronymic call *(title)*
pattern array *(order)*, compose, configuration *(form)*, constant, content *(structure)*, contrive, create, criterion, delineation, example, exemplar, form *(arrangement)*, habit, make, manner *(behavior)*, model, modus operandi, motif, norm, order *(arrangement)*, paradigm, practice *(custom)*, prototype, rule *(guide)*, specimen, stamp, standard, structure *(composition)*, style, system. SEE MAIN ENTRY
pattern after copy, mock *(imitate)*
pattern bargaining collective bargaining
pattern of words phraseology
patterned boiler plate, periodic, regular *(orderly)*
patterning creation
patternless disordered
patulous open *(unclosed)*
patulus open *(unclosed)*
pauciloquent brief, laconic, mute, succinct, taciturn
paucitas paucity
paucity dearth, deficiency, deficit, delinquency *(shortage)*, insignificance, insufficiency, need *(deprivation)*, poverty. SEE MAIN ENTRY
paululum modicum
paulum modicum
pauperism bankruptcy, indigence, poverty, privation
pauperize deplete, deprive
pauperized bankrupt, impecunious, poor *(underprivileged)*
paupertas poverty
pause cease, cessation *(interlude)*, defer *(put off)*, delay, discontinuance *(act of discontinuing)*, doubt *(hesitate)*, extension *(postponement)*, halt *(noun)*, halt *(verb)*, hesitate, hiatus, interruption, interval, lapse *(break)*, leave *(absence)*, lull, misdoubt, moratorium, pendency, procrastinate, qualm, recess *(noun)*, recess *(verb)*, remain *(stay)*, remission, reprieve, respite *(interval of rest)*, rest *(cease from action)*, stay *(rest)*, stop. SEE MAIN ENTRY
pausing dilatory, hesitant
pave the way expedite, facilitate, precede, provide *(arrange for)*
paved road causeway
paved way causeway
pavor consternation, fear, fright, panic
pawn captive, deposit, security *(pledge)*. SEE MAIN ENTRY
pax peace
pay advance *(allowance)*, commission *(fee)*, compensation, contribute *(supply)*, cover *(provide for)*, defray, disburse *(pay out)*, disbursement *(funds paid out)*, earnings, expend *(disburse)*, fund, income, indemnify, inure *(benefit)*, liquidate *(determine liability)*, offer *(tender)*, payment *(remittance)*, post, profit, recoup *(reimburse)*, remit *(send payment)*, remunerate, remuneration, requital, revenue, reward, satisfy *(discharge)*, spend, subsidize, tender, wage. SEE MAIN ENTRY
pay a debt quit *(repay)*
pay a price for buy
pay allegiance adhere *(maintain loyalty)*
pay an indemnity bear the expense, defray, quit *(repay)*
pay and settle liquidate *(determine liability)*
pay attention devote, hear *(give attention to)*, heed, notice *(observe)*, observe *(watch)*
pay attention to care *(be cautious)*, care *(regard)*, concern *(care)*, consider, note *(notice)*, observe *(obey)*, oversee
pay back bear *(yield)*, contribute *(indemnify)*, indemnify, quit *(repay)*, rebate, reciprocate, recoup *(reimburse)*, recriminate, refund, reimburse, repay, replace, retaliate, return *(refund)*
pay cash for buy
pay compensation bear the expense, defray, indemnify
pay damages bear the expense, compensate *(remunerate)*, contribute *(indemnify)*. SEE MAIN ENTRY
pay debts liquidate *(determine liability)*
pay deference honor
pay dividends disperse *(disseminate)*
pay for bear the expense, buy, compensate *(remunerate)*, defray, finance, fund, purchase, sponsor, subsidize
pay heed devote, observe *(watch)*
pay heed to note *(notice)*
pay homage honor
pay homage to regard *(hold in esteem)*, yield *(submit)*

pay honor dedicate
pay in advance prepay
pay in full bear the expense, compensate *(remunerate)*, discharge *(pay a debt)*, quit *(repay)*, satisfy *(discharge)*
pay in kind repay
pay little attention to minimize
pay little heed to minimize
pay load freight
pay no attention discount *(disbelieve)*, disregard, neglect
pay no attention to disobey, ignore, pretermit
pay no heed discount *(disbelieve)*
pay no heed to ignore, neglect
pay no mind discount *(disbelieve)*
pay no regard to dismiss *(put out of consideration)*, disregard, neglect, pretermit
pay off disburse *(pay out)*, discharge *(pay a debt)*, quit *(repay)*, satisfy *(discharge)*. SEE MAIN ENTRY
pay old debts quit *(repay)*
pay on demand bear the expense
pay one's way defray
pay out disperse *(disseminate)*, divide *(distribute)*, dole, expend *(disburse)*, mete
pay reparations defray, indemnify
pay respect to defer *(yield in judgment)*
pay respects honor
pay the bill bear the expense
pay the costs bear the expense, defray
pay the equivalent compensate *(remunerate)*
pay the penalty repent
pay the value compensate *(remunerate)*
pay towards subsidize
pay tribute belaud, bestow, honor, regard *(hold in esteem)*
pay up discharge *(pay a debt)*, satisfy *(discharge)*
pay wages bear the expense, compensate *(remunerate)*
pay-off commission *(fee)*
pay-out payoff *(payment in full)*
payable delinquent *(overdue)*, outstanding *(unpaid)*, receivable, unpaid. SEE MAIN ENTRY
payee beneficiary, heir, holder, recipient, transferee. SEE MAIN ENTRY
paying beneficial, compensatory, gainful, lucrative, productive, profitable
paying back contribution *(indemnification)*, expiation, reimbursement, restitution
paying for collection *(payment)*
paying guest tenant
paying off discharge *(payment)*
payload cargo
payment amortization, binder, charge *(cost)*, collection *(payment)*, commission *(fee)*, compensation, consideration *(recompense)*, contribution *(indemnification)*, correction *(punishment)*, cost *(expenses)*, deposit, disbursement *(funds paid out)*, downpayment, earnings, expenditure, expense *(cost)*, expiation, fee *(charge)*, handsel, honorarium, income, indemnification, indemnity, out of pocket, outlay, pay, payroll, pension, perquisite, price, prize, profit, rate, receipt *(voucher)*, recompense, reimbursement, relief *(legal redress)*, remittance, remuneration, rent, reparation *(indemnification)*, requital, restitution, retainer, retribution, revenue, reward, satisfaction *(discharge of debt)*, settlement, tip *(gratuity)*, toll *(effect)*, toll *(tax)*, trover, wage. SEE MAIN ENTRY
payment beforehand advance *(allowance)*
payment for delay demurrage
payment for expenses refund
payment for misconduct fine
payment for services payroll
payment for the right of carriage fare
payment in lieu composition *(agreement in bankruptcy)*
payment of damages compensation
payments overhead
payments past due arrears
payoff effect
payor transferor
payroll SEE MAIN ENTRY
peace composure, concordance, lull, reconciliation. SEE MAIN ENTRY
peace of mind composure
peace offering reparation *(indemnification)*
peace officer marshal. SEE MAIN ENTRY
peace officers police
peace-loving nonmilitant, peaceable
peaceable neutral, nonmilitant, patient, placid. SEE MAIN ENTRY
peaceful dispassionate, harmonious, neutral, nonmilitant, peaceable, placid
peaceful of mind complacent
peacefulness composure
peacelike peaceable
peacemaker go-between, intermediary, referee, umpire
peacemaking compromise, conciliation, intercession, reconciliation
peak ceiling, culmination, maximum *(amplitude)*, pinnacle
pealing resounding
peasant ignoble
pecability offense
peccability bad repute, blame *(culpability)*, culpability, delinquency *(misconduct)*, frailty, impeachability
peccable blameful, blameworthy, imperfect, profane, reprehensible, sinister. SEE MAIN ENTRY
peccadillo guilt, impropriety, malfeasance, misconduct, misdeed, misdemeanor, misdoing, misfeasance
peccancy culpability, delinquency *(misconduct)*, guilt, malfeasance, misdeed
peccans offender, peccant *(culpable)*
peccant bad *(offensive)*, blameful, blameworthy, culpable, delinquent *(guilty of a misdeed)*, disgraceful, errant, guilty, iniquitous, malignant, nefarious, objectionable, offensive *(offending)*, profane, profligate *(corrupt)*, reprehensible, reprobate, sinister. SEE MAIN ENTRY
peccare lapse *(fall into error)*, offend *(violate the law)*
peccatum error, fault *(responsibility)*, lapse *(expiration)*, misconduct, misdeed, offense, transgression
peculate bilk, cheat, convert *(misappropriate)*, defalcate, defraud, impropriate, loot, mulct *(defraud)*, poach, purloin, rob, steal. SEE MAIN ENTRY
peculation bad faith, bad repute, conversion *(misappropriation)*, embezzlement, larceny, misappropriation, misusage, theft. SEE MAIN ENTRY
peculator embezzler, hoodlum, thief
peculiarity SEE MAIN ENTRY
peculiar anomalous, certain *(particular)*, certain *(specific)*, different, distinct *(distinguished from others)*, distinctive, eccentric, express, extraordinary, irregular *(not usual)*, ludicrous, nonconforming, noteworthy, novel, particular *(individual)*, particular *(specific)*, personal *(individual)*, prodigious *(amazing)*, remarkable, several *(separate)*, singular, specific, suspicious *(questionable)*, unaccustomed, uncanny, uncommon, unique, unusual. SEE MAIN ENTRY
peculiar expression phrase
peculiar feature aspect
peculiar idiom characteristic, specialty *(distinctive mark)*
peculiar temperament specialty *(distinctive mark)*
peculiaris specific
peculiarities color *(complexion)*, personality
peculiarity character *(personal quality)*, characteristic, differential, distinction *(difference)*, feature *(characteristic)*, habit, identity *(individuality)*, irregularity, nonconformity, property *(distinctive attribute)*, quality *(attribute)*, quirk *(idiosyncrasy)*, speciality, specialty *(distinctive mark)*, technicality, trait
peculiarity of phrasing phraseology
peculiarly particularly
pecunia fund, income, money, remittance
pecunia praesens cash
pecuniae aversor embezzler
pecuniae residuae arrears
pecuniam mutuam dare capitalize *(provide capital)*
pecuniam redigere realize *(obtain as a profit)*
pecuniaria finance
pecuniarius pecuniary
pecuniary commercial, financial, fiscal, monetary. SEE MAIN ENTRY
pecuniary aid alimony, consideration *(recompense)*, pension
pecuniary assistance alimony
pecuniary burden charge *(cost)*, charge *(lien)*
pecuniary due debit
pecuniary management finance
pecuniary penalty amercement, fine, forfeiture *(thing forfeited)*
pecuniary punishment fine
pecuniary resource bank
pecuniary resources assets, capital, cash, possessions, property *(possessions)*
pecunious opulent, prosperous, solvent
pedagogic didactic, disciplinary *(educational)*. SEE MAIN ENTRY
pedagogical disciplinary *(educational)*
pedagogue SEE MAIN ENTRY
pedagogy education, guidance, instruction *(teaching)*
pedant SEE MAIN ENTRY
pedantic dogmatic, inflated *(bombastic)*, learned, sesquipedalian. SEE MAIN ENTRY
pedantical learned
pedantry diligence *(care)*
peddle barter, handle *(trade)*, sell, vend
peddler dealer, merchant, vendor
pedem referre retreat
pederasty sodomy
pedestal cornerstone
pedestrian inferior *(lower in quality)*, mundane, nondescript, ordinary, prevalent, prosaic, stale, usual. SEE MAIN ENTRY
pedestrianize perambulate
pedigree ancestry, blood, bloodline, descent *(lineage)*, origin *(ancestry)*, parentage
pedogogic informative
peel denude
peep spy
peer contributor *(contributor)*, copartner *(business associate)*, delve, spy. SEE MAIN ENTRY

peer at examine *(study)*, observe *(watch)*
peer into frisk, investigate, peruse, scrutinize
peerage society
peerless absolute *(ideal)*, best, inestimable, invaluable, laudable, noteworthy, outstanding *(prominent)*, paramount, premium, priceless, prime *(most valuable)*, rare, singular, sterling, superior *(excellent)*, superlative, unapproachable, unique, unusual
peeve bait *(harass)*, irritate
peevish fractious, froward, perverse, petulant, querulous, resentful, restive, sensitive *(easily affected)*
pejoration decline
pejorative calumnious, derogatory, libelous. SEE MAIN ENTRY
pelf spoils
pellicere lure
pellucid clear *(apparent)*, cognizable, coherent *(clear)*, comprehensible, distinct *(clear)*, lucid. SEE MAIN ENTRY
pellucidus lucid, pellucid
pelt beat *(strike)*, lash *(strike)*
pen close *(enclosed area)*, detain *(hold in custody)*, enclose, lock, note *(record)*, restrict
pen in confine, encompass *(surround)*
pen up repress
penal disciplinary *(punitory)*, punitive. SEE MAIN ENTRY
penal colony penitentiary, prison
penal institution jail, penitentiary, prison, reformatory
penal restraint bondage
penal retribution correction *(punishment)*, cost *(penalty)*, discipline *(punishment)*, forfeiture *(thing forfeited)*, penalty, punishment, sanction *(punishment)*
penal servitude bondage, correction *(punishment)*
penal settlement penitentiary
penalization condemnation *(punishment)*, conviction *(finding of guilt)*, correction *(punishment)*, cost *(penalty)*, forfeiture *(thing forfeited)*, punishment
penalize condemn *(punish)*, convict, demote, discipline *(punish)*, fine, mulct *(fine)*, punish. SEE MAIN ENTRY
penalizing punitive
penalty amercement, condemnation *(punishment)*, conviction *(finding of guilt)*, correction *(punishment)*, damages, disadvantage, discipline *(punishment)*, expense *(sacrifice)*, fine, forfeiture *(thing forfeited)*, imposition *(tax)*, infliction, punishment, reparation *(indemnification)*, reprisal, retribution, sanction *(punishment)*, sentence, surcharge, trover. SEE MAIN ENTRY
penalty for delay demurrage
penalty imposed on an offender punishment
penalty phase SEE MAIN ENTRY
penance cost *(penalty)*, discipline *(punishment)*, penalty, punishment
penance doer penitent
penates household *(domestic)*
penchant affection, animus, bias, characteristic, conatus, disposition *(inclination)*, favor *(partiality)*, favoritism, inclination, partiality, predilection, predisposition, proclivity, propensity, tendency. SEE MAIN ENTRY
pencraft handwriting
pendant addition, appendix *(accession)*, appurtenance, complement, correlate, counterpart *(complement)*
pendency cessation *(interlude)*. SEE MAIN ENTRY
pendent dependent. SEE MAIN ENTRY
pendere pay
pending ad interim, conditional, forthcoming, future, outstanding *(unresolved)*, undecided, unsettled, until. SEE MAIN ENTRY
pendulate alternate *(fluctuate)*, beat *(pulsate)*, fluctuate, oscillate
penes quos est reipublica government *(political administration)*
penetrabilis penetrable
penetrability danger
penetrable cognizable, coherent *(clear)*, comprehensible, passable, scrutable, vulnerable. SEE MAIN ENTRY
penetralia privacy
penetrare penetrate
penetrate break *(fracture)*, delve, encroach, impress *(affect deeply)*, interpose, invade, lancinate, permeate, pervade, pierce *(lance)*, solve, spread. SEE MAIN ENTRY
penetrating acute, incisive, interrogative, mordacious, perspicacious, potent, profound *(esoteric)*, profound *(intense)*, sensitive *(discerning)*, trenchant
penetration comprehension, encroachment, entrance, incursion, inflow, infusion, insertion, insight, judgment *(discernment)*, osmosis, perception, sagacity
penetrative trenchant
penitence remorse
penitent contrite, remorseful, repentant. SEE MAIN ENTRY
penitential contrite, penitent, remorseful, repentant
penitentiary cell, jail, prison, reformatory. SEE MAIN ENTRY
penitus defixus inveterate
penitus insitus inveterate
penmanship handwriting, script
penned holographic
penniless bankrupt, destitute, impecunious, insolvent, penurious, poor *(underprivileged)*
pennilessness indigence, poverty
penny-conscious frugal
penny-pinching parsimonious
penological disciplinary *(punitory)*
penology discipline *(punishment)*
penscript script
pensio installment
pension annuity, capitalize *(provide capital)*. SEE MAIN ENTRY
pensioner dependent, protégé
pensive cogitative, grave *(solemn)*, serious *(grave)*, solemn. SEE MAIN ENTRY
pensiveness contemplation, introspection, preoccupation
penumbra SEE MAIN ENTRY
penuria dearth, insufficiency
penurious illiberal, impecunious, parsimonious, poor *(underprivileged)*, provident *(frugal)*. SEE MAIN ENTRY
penury bankruptcy, dearth, deficiency, indigence, need *(deprivation)*, poverty, privation
people community, family *(common ancestry)*, humanity *(mankind)*, nationality, populace, population, race. SEE MAIN ENTRY
people delegated delegation *(envoy)*
peopled populous
peoples of the earth humanity *(mankind)*
pepper intersperse
per thereby
per annum SEE MAIN ENTRY
per capita SEE MAIN ENTRY
per contra contra
per day per diem
per diem SEE MAIN ENTRY
per head per capita
per miscere confound
per vim factus forcible
peragrare perambulate, prowl
perambulate SEE MAIN ENTRY
perceivable apparent *(perceptible)*, appreciable, blatant *(conspicuous)*, clear *(apparent)*, coherent *(clear)*, comprehensible, conspicuous, determinable *(ascertainable)*, discernible, distinct *(clear)*, evident, manifest, naked *(perceptible)*, obvious, open *(in sight)*, ostensible, palpable, patent, perceptible, tangible, visible *(noticeable)*. SEE MAIN ENTRY
perceivable dissimilarity distinction *(difference)*, identity *(individuality)*
perceive appreciate *(comprehend)*, comprehend *(understand)*, conceive *(comprehend)*, conjure, construe *(comprehend)*, deem, detect, discern *(detect with the senses)*, discover, find *(discover)*, identify, judge, note *(notice)*, notice *(observe)*, observe *(watch)*, pierce *(discern)*, read, realize *(understand)*, regard *(pay attention)*, spy, understand. SEE MAIN ENTRY
perceive as true presume
perceive clearly differentiate, distinguish
perceive differences secern
perceive something audible hear *(perceive by ear)*
perceive the worth of appreciate *(value)*
perceived cognizable, foreseeable
perceived from accompanying words noscitur a sociis
perceived happening fact
perceiving reasonable *(rational)*
percellere disconcert
percent proportion, share *(interest)*
percentage commission *(fee)*, moiety, part *(portion)*, per capita, proportion, quota, ration, share *(interest)*. SEE MAIN ENTRY
percentage compensation commission *(fee)*
percentage of ownership interest *(ownership)*
percept concept, idea
perceptible appreciable, ascertainable, bodily, clear *(apparent)*, cognizable, coherent *(clear)*, comprehensible, concrete, conspicuous, determinable *(ascertainable)*, discernible, distinct *(clear)*, evident, manifest, obvious, open *(in sight)*, ostensible, overt, palpable, patent, perceivable, ponderable, scrutable, tangible, visible *(in full view)*. SEE MAIN ENTRY
perceptibly fairly *(clearly)*
perception cognition, comprehension, concept, detection, discovery, discretion *(quality of being discreet)*, discrimination *(good judgment)*, estimate *(idea)*, idea, impression, insight, judgment *(discernment)*, knowledge *(awareness)*, precognition, reaction *(response)*, realization, reason *(sound judgment)*, recognition, sagacity, scienter, sense *(feeling)*, sense *(intelligence)*, sensibility, understanding *(comprehension)*, vision *(dream)*. SEE MAIN ENTRY
perception of difference diagnosis
perceptive acute, cognizant, conscious *(aware)*, discreet, discriminating *(judicious)*, judicious, juridical, knowing, lucid, omniscient, perspicacious, politic, profound

(*esoteric*), receptive, responsive, sapient, sensible, sensitive (*discerning*), sensitive (*easily affected*), subtle (*refined*), vicarious (*delegated*). SEE MAIN ENTRY
perceptiveness judgment (*discernment*), knowledge (*awareness*)
perceptivity sensibility
perch rest (*be supported by*), seat
percipere hear (*perceive by ear*), perceive
percipience cognition, insight, judgment (*discernment*), knowledge (*awareness*), perception, sagacity
percipiency insight, reason (*sound judgment*)
percipient circumspect, cognizant, conscious (*aware*), judicious, juridical, knowing, omniscient, perceptive, perspicacious, reasonable (*rational*), sensitive (*discerning*). SEE MAIN ENTRY
percolate permeate
percontatio inquiry (*request for information*), interrogation
percussion collision (*accident*)
percutere beat (*strike*)
perdere destroy (*efface*), lose (*be deprived of*), spoil (*impair*)
perdition adversity, destruction, miscarriage, subversion
perditus immoral, incorrigible, profligate (*corrupt*), reprobate
perdu hidden, recondite
perducere conduct
perdurable chronic, constant, durable, infinite, infrangible, permanent, perpetual, persistent, stable
perdure endure (*last*), last, persist, remain (*continue*), subsist
perduring live (*existing*), permanent
peregrinate perambulate, prowl
peregrine foreign
peregrinus alien, foreign
peremptory compelling, compulsory, de-cisive, dictatorial, dogmatic, inappealable, insistent, mandatory, severe, supercilious, tyrannous, unequivocal. SEE MAIN ENTRY
peremptory challenge SEE MAIN ENTRY
peremptory claim demand
peremptory demand dun
peremptory refusal rebuff
perennial chronic, consecutive, constant, continual (*connected*), continuous, immutable, incessant, indestructible, permanent, unremitting
perenniality perpetuity
perennis permanent, perpetual
pererration vagrancy
perfect absolute (*ideal*), accurate, amend, attain, best, blameless, cap, complete, consummate, definitive, develop, elaborate, enhance, faithful (*true to fact*), felicitous, finish, fulfill, infallible, intact, mature, meritorious, peremptory (*absolute*), pure, rectify, renew (*refurbish*), renovate, right (*suitable*), ripe, thorough, unblemished, unimpeachable. SEE MAIN ENTRY
perfect a routine practice (*train by repetition*)
perfect substitute alter ego
perfected choate lien, elaborate
perfected condition maturity
perfectible corrigible
perfection amendment (*correction*), maturity, progress. SEE MAIN ENTRY
perfectionism casuistry, particularity
perfectly purely (*positively*)
perfectly sure positive (*confident*)
perferre enact, endure (*suffer*)
perfervid eager, fervent, intense, vehement, zealous. SEE MAIN ENTRY
perfervor ardor
perficere consummate, dispatch (*dispose of*), perfect, perform (*execute*)
perfidia infidelity, treason
perfidiosus faithless, perfidious
perfidious bad (*offensive*), collusive, contemptible, dishonest, disingenuous, disobedient, evasive, faithless, false (*disloyal*), felonious, fraudulent, insidious, irresponsible, lying, machiavellian, malevolent, mendacious, outrageous, recreant, tortuous (*corrupt*), undependable, unreliable, unscrupulous, untrue, untrustworthy. SEE MAIN ENTRY
perfidiousness bad faith, bad repute, corruption, dishonesty, disloyalty, indirection (*deceitfulness*), infidelity
perfidus faithless, false (*disloyal*), perfidious
perfidy artifice, bad faith, bad repute, breach, bribery, collusion, corruption, deceit, dishonesty, disloyalty, duplicity, false pretense, fraud, indirection (*deceitfulness*), infidelity, treason, turpitude. SEE MAIN ENTRY
perforable penetrable
perforare pierce (*lance*)
perforate enter (*penetrate*), lancinate, penetrate, pervade, pierce (*lance*)
perforated penetrable
perforation split
perform abide, commit (*perpetrate*), comply, comport (*behave*), demonstrate (*establish*), dispatch (*dispose of*), effectuate, execute (*accomplish*), exercise (*discharge a function*), fulfill, function, implement, inflict, keep (*fulfill*), make, obey, observe (*obey*), officiate, operate, perpetrate, pretend, pursue (*carry on*), realize (*make real*), recite, render (*administer*), transact. SEE MAIN ENTRY
perform a circuit detour, deviate
perform a function avail (*be of use*)
perform by turns alternate (*take turns*), reciprocate
perform on militate
perform reciprocally alternate (*take turns*)
perform repeatedly practice (*train by repetition*)
perform responsively alternate (*take turns*), reciprocate
perform sentry duty patrol
perform the duties of practice (*engage in*)
perform the functions of practice (*engage in*)
performability feasibility
performable facile, possible, potential, practicable, viable
performance act (*undertaking*), conduct, course, finality, fruition, function, histrionics, infliction, operation, part (*role*), proceeding, process (*course*), realization, role, transaction. SEE MAIN ENTRY
performance of executive duties administration
performance owed obligation (*duty*)
performed complete (*ended*)
performer actor
performing active, operative
perfringere breach
perfugium refuge
perfunctoriness disinterest (*lack of interest*), laxity
perfunctory careless, casual, cursory, inadequate, informal, lax, superficial. SEE MAIN ENTRY
pergere continue (*persevere*)
periculum danger, experiment, hazard, risk, venture
peril danger, endanger, hazard, jeopardize, jeopardy, menace, pitfall, risk, threat, venture. SEE MAIN ENTRY
perilous dangerous, disastrous, insalubrious, insecure, noxious, ominous, peccant (*unhealthy*), portentous (*ominous*), precarious
perilousness danger, jeopardy
perimeter ambit, border, boundary, configuration (*confines*), confines, contour (*outline*), enclosure, frontier, guideline, limit, margin (*outside limit*), mete, outline (*boundary*), periphery, purview, range, zone. SEE MAIN ENTRY
perimeters realm
perimetric peripheral
perimetrical peripheral
perimetros periphery
period age, annum, cycle, date, duration, expiration, life (*period of existence*), moratorium, tenure, term (*duration*), time. SEE MAIN ENTRY
period of allowance grace period
period of being under legal age minority (*infancy*)
period of being under statutory age minority (*infancy*)
period of decrease decline
period of detention quarantine
period of existence lifetime
period of indulgence grace period
period of isolation quarantine
period of legal immaturity nonage
period of legal minority nonage
period of life lifetime
period of obligatory delay moratorium
period of rest lull
period of survival life (*period of existence*), lifetime
period of testing probation
period of time date, duration, phase (*period*)
period of tolerance grace period
period of trial probation
periodic disjunctive (*tending to disjoin*), habitual, infrequent, intermittent, regular (*orderly*), repeated, sporadic. SEE MAIN ENTRY
periodic payment installment, premium (*insurance payment*)
periodic returns from property or labor income
periodical habitual, journal, organ, publication (*printed matter*), regular (*orderly*), serial, sporadic
periodicity frequency, regularity
peripatetic itinerant (*adjective*), itinerant (*noun*), moving (*in motion*), pedestrian
peripheral collateral (*immaterial*), expendable, extraneous, extrinsic, minor, nonessential, null (*insignificant*). SEE MAIN ENTRY
peripheral group minority (*outnumbered group*)
periphery ambit, border, boundary, contour (*outline*), edge (*border*), frontier, margin (*outside limit*), mete, outline (*boundary*), zone. SEE MAIN ENTRY
periphrasis digression, indirection (*indirect action*)
periphrastic indirect, redundant, turgid
periphrastical indirect
perire perish
perish decease, die, expire, succumb. SEE MAIN ENTRY

perishable ephemeral, nonsubstantial *(not sturdy)*, temporary, transient
perished deceased, defunct, late *(defunct)*, lifeless *(dead)*, lost *(taken away)*
peritia experience *(background)*, skill
peritus acquainted, familiar *(informed)*, proficient
periurare perjure
periurium perjury
periurium facere perjure
perjure palter, prevaricate. SEE MAIN ENTRY
perjure oneself bear false witness, fabricate *(make up)*, frame *(charge falsely)*, lie *(falsify)*, misrepresent
perjured dishonest, fraudulent, lying, mendacious, perfidious
perjured testimony frame up
perjury deceit, dishonesty, falsification, fiction, hypocrisy, misstatement, subreption. SEE MAIN ENTRY
perlegere peruse
perlustrare perambulate
permanence constant, continuity, indestructibility, perpetuity, survival
permanent chronic, constant, continual *(perpetual)*, conventional, durable, fixed *(securely placed)*, fixed *(settled)*, immutable, indefeasible, indelible, indestructible, infinite, ingrained, irreversible, irrevocable, last *(final)*, noncancellable, perpetual, stable, standing, static, unalterable. SEE MAIN ENTRY
permanent attachment to real property fixture
permanent exclusion expulsion, ouster
permanent legal address home *(domicile)*
permanent resident inhabitant
permanent structure monument
permanere endure *(last)*, last, pursue *(carry on)*
permeable penetrable
permeare diffuse
permeate diffuse, imbue, penetrate, pervade, spread. SEE MAIN ENTRY
permeation infusion, osmosis
permeative ubiquitous
permetiri measure
permiscere confuse *(bewilder)*, muddle
permissibility admissibility, legitimacy
permissible admissible, allowable, allowed, lawful, legal, licit, potential. SEE MAIN ENTRY
permissible evidence admissible evidence
permissibleness legality
permissio leave *(permission)*
permission acquiescence, admittance *(acceptance)*, assent, capacity *(authority)*, charter *(sanction)*, concession *(authorization)*, consent, discretion *(power of choice)*, dispensation *(exception)*, favor *(sanction)*, franchise *(license)*, indorsement, indulgence, liberty, license, permit, privilege, sanction *(permission)*, sufferance, title *(right)*, warrant *(authorization)*. SEE MAIN ENTRY
permission to defer payment credit *(delayed payment)*
permission to rent lease
permissioned allowed
permissive SEE MAIN ENTRY
permit abide, accede *(concede)*, allow *(authorize)*, allow *(endure)*, approval, assent, authorize, bear *(tolerate)*, bestow, capacity *(authority)*, certify *(approve)*, charge *(empower)*, charter *(license)*, charter *(sanction)*, concede, concession *(authorization)*, condone, confirm, consent *(noun)*, consent *(verb)*, copyright, dispensation *(exception)*, empower, enable, enfranchise, exemption, franchise *(license)*, freedom, grant *(concede)*, invest *(vest)*, key *(passport)*, leave *(allow to remain)*, license, palliate *(excuse)*, patent, qualify *(meet standards)*, receive *(permit to enter)*, recognize *(acknowledge)*, sanction *(permission)*, sanction, tolerate, vouchsafe, warrant *(authorization)*, yield *(submit)*. SEE MAIN ENTRY
permit by law legalize
permit to borrow lend, loan
permit to vote enfranchise
permittance acquiescence, leave *(permission)*
permitted admissible, allowed, due *(regular)*, entitled, justifiable, lawful, licit, open *(accessible)*, pardonable, permissible, potential, privileged, public *(open)*, rightful, unrestricted
permitted by law legal
permittere concede, countenance, devolve, grant *(concede)*, grant *(transfer formally)*, suffer *(permit)*
permitting charitable *(lenient)*, consenting
permutable aleatory *(uncertain)*, ambulatory, convertible, protean
permutatio exchange, interchange
permutation exchange, mutuality
permute alternate *(take turns)*, change, convert *(change use)*
perniciosus deadly, detrimental, disastrous, fatal, pernicious
pernicious bad *(offensive)*, deadly, deleterious, destructive, detrimental, disadvantageous, disastrous, fatal, harmful, heinous, immoral, inadvisable, incendiary, inimical, iniquitous, insalubrious, lethal, malevolent, malicious, malignant, nefarious, noxious, objectionable, obnoxious, oppressive, pestilent, prejudicial, sinister, toxic, vicious, virulent. SEE MAIN ENTRY
perniciousness fatality, harm
perorate converse, declaim, discourse
peroratio peroration
peroration close *(conclusion)*. SEE MAIN ENTRY
perperam misunderstand
perperam accipere misconceive
perpetrate execute *(accomplish)*, operate, perform *(execute)*. SEE MAIN ENTRY
perpetration act *(undertaking)*, commission *(act)*, course, discharge *(performance)*, infliction, performance *(execution)*
perpetual chronic, constant, continuous, durable, habitual, immutable, incessant, indestructible, infinite, periodic, permanent, stable, standing, unlimited, unremitting. SEE MAIN ENTRY
perpetually invariably
perpetualness perpetuity
perpetuate continue *(prolong)*, establish *(entrench)*, keep *(continue)*, maintain *(carry on)*, persevere, preserve, prolong, remain *(continue)*, sustain *(prolong)*, uphold. SEE MAIN ENTRY
perpetuated lasting, permanent, perpetual, standing
perpetuating honorary
perpetuation continuance, continuation *(prolongation)*, longevity, perpetuity, preservation, remembrance *(commemoration)*
perpetuitas continuance, continuation *(prolongation)*, continuity, perpetuity
perpetuity continuity, indestructibility. SEE MAIN ENTRY
perpetuo comitari inseparable
perpetuus continual *(perpetual)*, incessant, indestructible
perplex agitate *(perturb)*, badger, bait *(harass)*, confound, confuse *(bewilder)*, discommode, discompose, disconcert, disorganize, disturb, obfuscate, perturb. SEE MAIN ENTRY
perplexed lost *(disoriented)*
perplexing complex, debatable, difficult, disputable, dubious, enigmatic, equivocal, indefinable, labyrinthine, mysterious, peculiar *(curious)*, problematic, recondite, uncertain *(ambiguous)*, vague
perplexing state of affairs imbroglio
perplexity cloud *(suspicion)*, complication, confusion *(ambiguity)*, dilemma, doubt *(indecision)*, enigma, ignorance, impasse, incertitude, paradox, predicament, quagmire, quandary
perplexus indistinct, labyrinthine
perquisite bounty, gratuity *(present)*, pay, prerogative, privilege, reward, tip *(gratuity)*. SEE MAIN ENTRY
perquisites bonus, paraphernalia *(personal belongings)*, revenue
perquisition examination *(study)*, indagation, probe, quest
perscribere record, register
perscrutari investigate, scrutinize
perscrutatio scrutiny
perscrutation indagation, probe
persecute abuse *(violate)*, badger, bait *(harass)*, brutalize, endanger, exploit *(take advantage of)*, harrow, harry *(harass)*, hector, ill use, irritate, maltreat, mishandle *(maltreat)*, mistreat, pique, plague, press *(goad)*, provoke. SEE MAIN ENTRY
persecuted aggrieved *(victimized)*
persecuting brutal, callous, illiberal, malignant
persecution abuse *(physical misuse)*, cruelty, infliction, injustice, intolerance, molestation, oppression
persecutor bigot
persecutor bar SEE MAIN ENTRY
persequi prosecute *(carry forward)*
perseverance continuance, continuation *(prolongation)*, industry *(activity)*, longanimity, purpose, resolution *(decision)*, tenacity, tolerance
perseverant diligent, insistent, lasting, patient, persistent, relentless, sedulous, steadfast, strong, undaunted, unrelenting, unremitting, unyielding, zealous
perseverare continue *(persevere)*, keep *(continue)*
persevere adhere *(persist)*, bear *(tolerate)*, continue *(persevere)*, endeavor, endure *(last)*, hold out *(resist)*, insist, keep *(continue)*, last, maintain *(carry on)*, persist, prolong, pursue *(carry on)*, recur, remain *(continue)*, resist *(withstand)*, stay *(continue)*. SEE MAIN ENTRY
persevere at ply
persevere in prosecute *(carry forward)*
perseverence prowess *(bravery)*. SEE MAIN ENTRY
persevering chronic, diligent, durable, faithful *(diligent)*, indelible, indestructible, indomitable, industrious, inexorable, inflexible, insistent, live *(existing)*, painstaking, patient, permanent, persistent, pertinacious, purposeful, relentless, resolute, sedulous, steadfast, strong, undaunted, unrelenting, unremitting, unyielding
persist continue *(persevere)*, endure *(last)*, exist, hold out *(resist)*, insist, keep

(continue), last, maintain (carry on), persevere, prosecute (carry forward), pursue (carry on), recur, remain (continue), repeat (do again), resist (withstand), stay (continue), subsist. SEE MAIN ENTRY
persist in adhere (persist), bear (tolerate)
persistence continuance, continuation (prolongation), diligence (perseverance), industry (activity), longevity, purpose, resolution (decision), tenacity, tolerance, uniformity
persistency diligence (perseverance), tenacity
persistent chronic, continual (connected), diligent, durable, faithful (diligent), frequent, immutable, incessant, indelible, industrious, inexorable, infinite, insistent, lasting, patient, permanent, perpetual, pertinacious, purposeful, relentless, repeated, resolute, sedulous, stable, steadfast, strong, undaunted, unrelenting, unremitting, unyielding, zealous. SEE MAIN ENTRY
persistent exertion diligence (perseverance)
persistere continue (persevere), persevere, persist, pursue (carry on)
persisting chronic, durable, indelible, indestructible, inexorable, insistent, irrevocable, lasting, live (existing), patient, permanent, pertinacious, undaunted
persisting in error perverse
persisting in fault perverse
persnickety particular (exacting)
person actor, character (an individual), individual. SEE MAIN ENTRY
person accused of crime suspect
person affording evidence witness
person appointed to administer affairs trustee
person coming from a foreign country alien
person employing advice client
person entrusted with property of another fiduciary
person from foreign parts alien
person full of character individual
person in authority chairman, chief, incumbent, official, principal (director)
person in charge caretaker (one fulfilling the function of office), chief, executor, principal (director)
person in possession holder, lessee
person in responsibility executor
person making a feoffment feoffor
person named to carry out the provisions of a will executor
person of age adult
person of experience veteran
person of importance key man
person of intellect mastermind
person of interest SEE MAIN ENTRY
person of repute key man, paragon
person of voting age adult
person represented client
person represented by counsel client
person responsible official
person under 18 years of age minor
person under 18 years old infant
person under arrest captive, prisoner
person under guardianship dependent
person under legal age juvenile, minor
person under the age of majority infant
person who conveys a fee feoffor
person who flees justice fugitive
person who is not of full age infant, minor
person who makes a claim claimant
person who makes allegations declarant
person who writes author (writer)
person with a grievance claimant
personage body (person), character (an individual), individual, person
personal intimate, particular (individual), private (confidential), privy, several (separate), subjective, unofficial. SEE MAIN ENTRY
personal allowance alimony
personal bearing behavior, conduct, deportment, manner (behavior)
personal bias prejudice (preconception)
personal characteristic identity (individuality), specialty (distinctive mark)
personal chattels which are not in possession intangible
personal effect chattel
personal effects assets, movable, paraphernalia (personal belongings), property (possessions)
personal equation characteristic
personal estate goods, paraphernalia (personal belongings)
personal gain earnings
personal hatred malice
personal identity personality
personal judgment assumption (supposition), conviction (persuasion), estimate (idea)
personal mark personality
personal matter confidence (relation of trust), secret
personal presence appearance (look)
personal property effects, movable, paraphernalia (personal belongings), personalty, possessions
personal property capable of being inherited hereditament
personal reasons motive
personal representative administrator, executor
personal resources assets, personalty, property (possessions)
personal right not reduced to possession intangible
personal security pledge (security)
personal style manner (behavior)
personal traits character (personal quality)
personal wrong tort
personality character (an individual), character (personal quality), disposition (inclination), identity (individuality), individual, presence (poise), property (distinctive attribute), temperament. SEE MAIN ENTRY
personalize call (title)
personalized private (not public), subjective
personally in person
personally solicit lobby
personalty chattel, effects, estate (property), movable, paraphernalia (personal belongings), possessions
personate assume (simulate), copy, feign, impersonate, mock (imitate), pose (impersonate)
personation caricature, copy
personhood laws SEE MAIN ENTRY
personification embodiment
personify characterize, depict, embody, impersonate. SEE MAIN ENTRY
personifying exemplary
personnel copartner (business associate)
personnel employee, staff. SEE MAIN ENTRY
persons humanity (mankind), populace, population, public
persons in office authorities
persons in power hierarchy (persons in authority)
persons of commanding influence authorities
persons summoned to attend the court as jurymen panel (jurors)
personship identity (individuality)
perspective aspect, opinion (belief), outlook, standpoint, vision (dream). SEE MAIN ENTRY
perspicacious acute, circumspect, cognizant, discriminating (judicious), judicious, juridical, lucid, perceptive, sapient, sensitive (discerning)
perspicaciousness comprehension, experience (background), perception, sagacity
perspicacitas sagacity
perspicacity caliber (mental capacity), discretion (quality of being discreet), discrimination (good judgment), insight, judgment (discernment), perception, sagacity, sense (intelligence). SEE MAIN ENTRY
perspicax acute, perspicacious
perspicuity discrimination (good judgment)
perspicuous appreciable, clear (apparent), cognizable, coherent (clear), comprehensible, evident, explicit, lucid, manifest, obvious, open (in sight), ostensible, overt, palpable, patent, perceivable, perceptible, unambiguous, unmistakable. SEE MAIN ENTRY
perspicuousness judgment (discernment)
perspicuus comprehensible, distinct (clear), lucid, manifest, obvious
perstare persevere, persist
perstringere refer (direct attention)
persuable reasonable (rational)
persuadable amenable, open (persuasible), open-minded, pliable, receptive, suasible, susceptible (responsive)
persuade agitate (activate), assure (give confidence to), bait (lure), coax, convince, counsel, exhort, incite, induce, influence, inspire, inveigle, lobby, motivate, prejudice (influence), pressure, prevail upon, prompt, reason (persuade), recommend, urge. SEE MAIN ENTRY
persuade against caution, deter, discourage
persuade by argument convince
persuade not to work picket
persuade oneself presuppose
persuade to believe error delude
persuaded affirmative, certain (positive), definite, positive (confident)
persuadere convince, prevail (persuade), prevail upon
persuaders lobby
persuading hortative, moving (evoking emotion)
persuasibility amenability, credulity
persuasible amenable, credulous, open-minded, pliable, suasible
persuasio belief (state of mind), faith
persuasion belief (something believed), concept, conclusion (determination), credence, denomination, dogma, force (compulsion), guidance, idea, incentive, inducement, instigation, motive, opinion (belief), patronage (power to appoint jobs), pressure, propaganda, seduction, standpoint, surety (certainty). SEE MAIN ENTRY
persuasive believable, cogent, colorable (plausible), convincing, determinative, eloquent, hortative, prevailing (having supe-

rior force), provocative, sound, specious, strong. SEE MAIN ENTRY
persuasive facts evidence
persuasiveness inducement
persuasory persuasive
pert brazen, impertinent *(insolent),* insolent, presumptuous
pertain appertain, correspond *(be equivalent),* refer *(direct attention),* relate *(establish a connection).* SEE MAIN ENTRY
pertain to affiliate, concern *(involve),* connect *(relate)*
pertaining correlative, pertinent, relative *(relevant)*
pertaining to comparative, germane, incident, relevant
pertaining to business commercial
pertaining to financial matters fiscal
pertaining to government finances fiscal
pertaining to home household *(domestic)*
pertaining to law jural
pertaining to litigation actionable
pertaining to merchants commercial
pertaining to monetary receipts and expenditures fiscal
pertaining to one's household domestic *(household)*
pertaining to ownership proprietary
pertaining to property proprietary
pertaining to the courts forensic
pertaining to the family domestic *(household),* household *(domestic)*
pertaining to the home domestic *(household)*
pertaining to the law forensic
pertaining to the public revenues fiscal
pertaining to the public treasury fiscal
pertaining to the whole community common *(shared)*
pertaining to trade commercial
pertinacia tenacity
pertinacious diligent, faithful *(diligent),* inexorable, inflexible, insistent, intractable, obdurate, patient, persistent, purposeful, relentless, resolute, sedulous, steadfast, unrelenting, unremitting, unyielding. SEE MAIN ENTRY
pertinaciousness tenacity
pertinacity diligence *(perseverance),* tenacity. SEE MAIN ENTRY
pertinax contumacious, froward, inflexible, pertinacious, willful
pertinence connection *(relation),* interest *(concern),* propriety *(appropriateness),* qualification *(fitness),* relation *(connection),* relationship *(connection),* relevance
pertinent akin *(germane),* applicable, apposite, appropriate, felicitous, fit, germane, interrelated, intrinsic *(belonging),* material *(important),* noteworthy, related, relative *(relevant),* relevant, suitable, tangential. SEE MAIN ENTRY
pertinent to comparative
pertinere concern *(involve),* relate *(establish a connection)*
pertinere ad apply *(pertain)*
pertness disrespect
perturb badger, bait *(harass),* discommode, discompose, disconcert, disorganize, disorient, disrupt, distress, disturb, embarrass, harrow, molest *(annoy),* obfuscate, perplex, pique, provoke, upset. SEE MAIN ENTRY
perturbance panic
perturbare confuse *(bewilder),* disconcert, disorganize, disturb
perturbate agitate *(perturb),* perturb
perturbatio confusion *(turmoil)*
perturbation apprehension *(fear),* commotion, confusion *(ambiguity),* consternation, distress *(anguish),* disturbance, embarrassment, instigation, misgiving, panic, quandary, trepidation, turmoil
perturbed frenetic, unsettled
perturbing enigmatic
perturbo perturb
perusal analysis, discovery, examination *(study),* indagation, inquiry *(systematic investigation),* inspection, scrutiny. SEE MAIN ENTRY
peruse check *(inspect),* examine *(study),* observe *(watch),* probe, read, regard *(pay attention),* scrutinize, study, survey *(examine).* SEE MAIN ENTRY
peruse carefully concentrate *(pay attention)*
pervade diffuse, enter *(penetrate),* imbue, obsess, penetrate, permeate, spread. SEE MAIN ENTRY
pervadere penetrate
pervading ubiquitous
pervagari perambulate
pervasive broad, ubiquitous
perverse arbitrary, contentious, contumacious, difficult, disobedient, fractious, froward, intractable, opposite, petulant, restive, sinister, unruly, unyielding, vicious. SEE MAIN ENTRY
perverseness contempt *(disobedience to the court)*
perversion abuse *(corrupt practice),* debauchment, distortion, lie, misapplication, misstatement, misusage, misuse, sodomy, travesty, vice. SEE MAIN ENTRY
perversion of integrity corruption
perversion of the truth evasion
perversion of truth false pretense, falsehood, indirection *(deceitfulness),* perjury, story *(falsehood)*
perversity bad repute
perversus incorrect, perverse
pervert abuse *(misuse),* adulterate, bear false witness, brutalize, camouflage, contort, corrupt, damage, debase, debauch, degenerate, denature, deteriorate, distort, falsify, harm, infect, invent *(falsify),* lie *(falsify),* misconceive, misconstrue, misemploy, misguide, mislead, mismanage, misread, misrepresent, misstate, mistreat, misunderstand, palter, pollute, prevaricate, slant, subvert, taint *(corrupt),* vitiate. SEE MAIN ENTRY
perverted depraved, dissolute, immoral, mendacious, perverse, tainted *(corrupted)*
pervicacious intractable, obdurate, pertinacious, recalcitrant, restive, unreasonable, unyielding
pervicax pertinacious
pervious amenable, disposable, open *(persuasible),* passable, penetrable, pliable, suasible
pervius penetrable
pervulgatus prevalent, trite
pessimism damper *(depressant).* SEE MAIN ENTRY
pessimistic cynical, despondent, disconsolate, ominous. SEE MAIN ENTRY
pest nuisance
pester annoy, badger, discompose, harass, harry *(harass),* hector, importune, irritate, molest *(annoy),* perturb, pique, plague, press *(goad)*
pestering vexatious
pestiferous contagious, dangerous, deadly, harmful, insalubrious, lethal, malignant, noxious, pernicious
pestilence nuisance
pestilens insalubrious, pestilent
pestilent insalubrious, lethal, noxious, peccant *(unhealthy),* toxic. SEE MAIN ENTRY
pestilential deleterious, detrimental, harmful, insalubrious, lethal, malignant, pernicious, pestilent
pet animal, popular
petard bomb
peter out perish, subside
petere petition, solicit
petit petty
petitio application, plea
petition appeal, application, apply *(request),* bill *(formal declaration),* call *(appeal),* call *(appeal to),* canvass, claim *(demand),* complaint, cross-examine, entreaty, importune, invitation, motion, move *(judicially request),* plead *(implore),* pray, prayer, press *(beseech),* request *(noun),* request *(verb),* requisition, solicit, sue, suit. SEE MAIN ENTRY
petition for intercede, request
petition for release habeas corpus
petitionary solicitous
petitioner accuser, actor, appellant, applicant *(petitioner),* candidate, claimant, complainant, contender, litigant, malcontent, party *(litigant),* plaintiff, special interest, suitor, undersigned. SEE MAIN ENTRY
petitioner for legal redress complainant
petitioners lobby
petitor contestant, plaintiff
petrification congealment
petrified ossified
petrify browbeat, frighten, intimidate
pettifog cheat, circumvent. SEE MAIN ENTRY
pettifogger SEE MAIN ENTRY
pettifoggery artifice, bad faith, bribery, false pretense, knavery. SEE MAIN ENTRY
pettifogging bunko, hoax, immoral
pettiness immateriality
pettish fractious, petulant, querulous
petty de minimus, frivolous, illiberal, inappreciable, inconsequential, inconsiderable, insubstantial, minor, nominal, nugatory, null *(insignificant),* paltry, parsimonious, penurious, provincial, puerile, slight, tenuous, trivial. SEE MAIN ENTRY
petty detail technicality
petty dishonesty pettifoggery
petulans petulant
petulant argumentative, brazen, fractious, froward, perverse, querulous. SEE MAIN ENTRY
phalanx band, mass *(body of persons)*
phantasm phantom
phantasmal delusive, illusory
phantom SEE MAIN ENTRY
pharisaism hypocrisy
phase aspect, duration, transition. SEE MAIN ENTRY
phenomenal extraordinary, infrequent, noteworthy, portentous *(eliciting amazement),* prodigious *(amazing),* unusual. SEE MAIN ENTRY
phenomenon experience *(encounter),* happening, occurrence, vision *(dream).* SEE MAIN ENTRY
philanthropic benevolent, charitable *(benevolent),* donative, humane, liberal

(generous), magnanimous, meritorious, nonprofit. SEE MAIN ENTRY
philanthropic gift charity
philanthropic institution foundation *(organization)*
philanthropist benefactor, contributor *(giver)*, donor, good samaritan, patron *(influential supporter)*, samaritan. SEE MAIN ENTRY
philanthropize bestow, dedicate
philanthropy benefit *(conferment)*, benevolence *(act of kindness)*, benevolence *(disposition to do good)*, charity, dedication, donation, favor *(act of kindness)*, goodwill, help, largess *(generosity)*. SEE MAIN ENTRY
philippic denunciation
philippic outcry, revilement, stricture. SEE MAIN ENTRY
philistine ordinary. SEE MAIN ENTRY
philoprogenitive fertile, prolific
philosophaster pedant
philosophia moralis ethics
philosophic patient, stoical
philosophical cogitative, logical, profound *(esoteric)*, theoretical
philosophize reason *(conclude)*, speculate *(conjecture)*
philosophy doctrine, posture *(attitude)*, principle *(axiom)*, theory. SEE MAIN ENTRY
philosophy of law jurisprudence
phlegm disinterest *(lack of interest)*, languor, sloth
phlegmatic dispassionate, indolent, languid, lifeless *(dull)*, obtuse, otiose, passive, stagnant, torpid. SEE MAIN ENTRY
phlegmatical languid, phlegmatic, stagnant
phobia apprehension *(fear)*, fear, fright, panic, paranoia. SEE MAIN ENTRY
phoenix revival
phonate enunciate
phonation intonation, speech
phonic nuncupative, oral
phoniness falsification
phony bogus, fictitious, fraudulent, imitation, specious
photographic descriptive
photostat duplicate
phrase chapter *(division)*, clause, denominate, express, observe *(remark)*, relate *(tell)*, speak, term *(expression)*. SEE MAIN ENTRY
phraseology language, parlance, rhetoric *(skilled speech)*, speech. SEE MAIN ENTRY
phrasing language, phraseology, rhetoric *(skilled speech)*
phrenetic fanatical
phrenetical fanatical
phylactery reminder
phylum race
physic drug *(noun)*, drug *(verb)*
physical bodily, concrete, corporal, corporeal, mundane, tangible. SEE MAIN ENTRY
physical appearance demeanor
physical being body *(person)*, materiality *(physical existence)*
physical condition health
physical derangement disease
physical element component
physical force compulsion *(coercion)*
physical hurt injury
physical limit capacity *(maximum)*
physical nature materiality *(physical existence)*
physical power force *(strength)*
physically strong powerful
physicalness materiality *(physical existence)*
physiognomy appearance *(look)*, feature *(appearance)*
physique body *(person)*, configuration *(form)*
placular penitent
piaculum expiation
picayune inconsequential, insubstantial, minor, negligible, petty, trivial
pick alternative *(option)*, appoint, choice *(alternatives offered)*, choose, cull, decide, decision *(election)*, discretion *(power of choice)*, elect *(choose)*, election *(choice)*, extract, option *(choice)*, prefer, reap, screen *(select)*, select, volition, vote
pick a quarrel bicker
pick one's pockets jostle *(pickpocket)*
pick out appoint, choose, cull, eviscerate, except *(exclude)*, extract, prefer
pick up elevate, gain, glean, heighten *(elevate)*, obtain, overhear, procure, purchase, reap, receive *(acquire)*. SEE MAIN ENTRY
picked preferable, select
picked out preferred *(favored)*
pickeer hold up *(rob)*
picket demonstrate *(protest)*. SEE MAIN ENTRY
pickings spoils
pickle imbroglio
pickpocket hoodlum
pickpocketing larceny
picky particular *(exacting)*
pictorial descriptive, suggestive *(evocative)*
picture characterize, conceive *(comprehend)*, concept, contour *(outline)*, delineate, depict, describe, design *(construction plan)*, detail *(particularize)*, draw *(depict)*, exemplify, portray, recount, render *(depict)*, represent *(portray)*, symbol, vision *(dream)*. SEE MAIN ENTRY
picturize delineate
piddling inconsiderable, paltry, petty, puerile
piece commingle, component, constituent *(part)*, detail, element, gun, item, lot, member *(constituent part)*, minimum, moiety, parcel, part *(portion)*, ration, repair, segment, story *(narrative)*, unit *(item)*. SEE MAIN ENTRY
piece of apparatus appliance
piece of architecture building *(structure)*, edifice
piece of ground lot
piece of information item, particular
piece of land parcel, plot *(land)*, premises *(buildings)*
piece of landed property estate *(property)*
piece of legislation measure
piece of news item
piece together combine *(join together)*, consolidate *(unite)*, devise *(invent)*, fabricate *(construct)*, frame *(construct)*, join *(bring together)*, make, merge, solve
pieced together conjoint
piecemeal SEE MAIN ENTRY
pierce break *(fracture)*, enter *(penetrate)*, impress *(affect deeply)*, inject, lancinate, penetrate, pervade. SEE MAIN ENTRY
piercing acute, bitter *(penetrating)*, caustic, harsh, incisive, interrogative, mordacious, perspicacious, profound *(intense)*, trenchant
piercing of the corporate veil SEE MAIN ENTRY
pietas affection
pig-headed obdurate
pigeonhearted recreant
pigeonhole classify, defer *(put off)*, file *(arrange)*, hold up *(delay)*, partition, postpone, procrastinate, set aside *(reserve)*. SEE MAIN ENTRY
piger stagnant
piggish insatiable
pigheaded pertinacious
pignerare pawn
pignoration security *(pledge)*
pignus bail, mortgage, pledge *(security)*, security *(stock)*
pignus judiciale charge *(lien)*, cloud *(incumbrance)*
pignus legale cloud *(incumbrance)*
piker bettor
pile agglomeration, assemblage, collect *(gather)*, collection *(accumulation)*, cumulation, hoard, load, selection *(collection)*
pile up accumulate *(amass)*, compound, hoard, keep *(shelter)*, set aside *(reserve)*, store
pileup collision *(accident)*
pilfer despoil, embezzle, hold up *(rob)*, jostle *(pickpocket)*, loot, peculate, poach, purloin, rob, steal. SEE MAIN ENTRY
pilferage larceny, misappropriation, theft
pilferer burglar, criminal, embezzler, thief
pilfering burglary, embezzlement, housebreaking, plagiarism, spoliation, theft
piling up cumulative *(increasing)*
pillage despoil, devastate, harry *(plunder)*, havoc, hold up *(rob)*, loot, pilfer, pirate *(take by violence)*, plunder *(noun)*, plunder *(verb)*, prey, prize, rape, rob, seize *(confiscate)*, spoils, spoliation, steal. SEE MAIN ENTRY
pillager burglar, criminal, thief, vandal
pillaging burglary, foray, predatory, rapacious, spoliation
pillar mainstay
pillory brand *(stigmatize)*, defame, denigrate, denounce *(condemn)*, disgrace, dishonor *(deprive of honor)*, smear. SEE MAIN ENTRY
pilot administer *(conduct)*, conduct, control *(regulate)*, govern, manage, manipulate *(utilize skillfully)*, moderate *(preside over)*, officiate, operate, overlook *(superintend)*, oversee, prescribe, preside, superintend
pilotage direction *(guidance)*, management *(supervision)*
pilpulistic argumentative
pin fix *(make firm)*
pin down restrict
pinch constrict *(compress)*, dearth, plight, predicament, privation, quagmire, retrench, stress *(strain)*
pinch hitter substitute
pinchbeck spurious
pinched impecunious, narrow
pine languish
pine away languish
pinion contain *(restrain)*, handcuff *(noun)*, handcuff *(verb)*, restrict, trammel
pinnacle ceiling, culmination. SEE MAIN ENTRY
pinpoint designate, discover, locate. SEE MAIN ENTRY
pioneer commence, forerunner, initiate, originate, precede, precursor. SEE MAIN ENTRY
pious tartuffish, zealous
piquancy instigation
piquant hot-blooded, incisive, moving *(evoking emotion)*, palatable, provocative, sapid, savory

pique affront, aggravate *(annoy)*, annoy, badger, bait *(harass)*, discommode, discompose, dissatisfaction, disturb, harrow, harry *(harass)*, incense, interest, irritate, malice, molest *(annoy)*, offend *(insult)*, perturb, plague, provoke, resentment, stimulate, umbrage. SEE MAIN ENTRY
piqued bitter *(reproachful)*, petulant, resentful
piracy pillage, robbery, spoliation
pirate abduct, copy, criminal, hijack, hold up *(rob)*, impropriate, loot, pillage, plagiarize, plunder, poach, prey, seize *(confiscate)*, spoil *(pillage)*, steal, thief. SEE MAIN ENTRY
piratic larcenous
piratical larcenous, rapacious
piste brand
pistol gun
pit against alienate *(estrange)*, counter, counteract
pit against one another polarize
pitch elevate, inflection, intonation, launch *(project)*, precipitate *(throw down violently)*
pitch into attack
piteous deplorable, lamentable, lugubrious. SEE MAIN ENTRY
pitfall hazard, trap, trouble. SEE MAIN ENTRY
pith center *(essence)*, contents, corpus, essence, gist *(substance)*, import, main point, significance, signification, subject *(topic)*, substance *(essential nature)*
pith of a matter gist *(ground for a suit)*
pithless languid, powerless
pithy brief, concise, eloquent, laconic, sententious, succinct. SEE MAIN ENTRY
pithy saying catchword, maxim
pitiable deplorable, lamentable
pitiful deplorable, lamentable, paltry, poor *(inferior in quality)*
pitiless brutal, callous, cold-blooded, cruel, diabolic, harmful, harsh, implacable, inexorable, malevolent, relentless, remorseless, ruthless, severe, unaffected *(uninfluenced)*, unrelenting, unresponsive
pitilessness brutality, malice
pittance paucity, ration
pitted blemished, marred
pitted-against SEE MAIN ENTRY
pitting of strength competition
pitting of strengths contest *(competition)*
pitting of wits competition
pity lenience, relent, sympathize. SEE MAIN ENTRY
pitying lenient
pivot cornerstone, crossroad *(turning point)*
pivotal cardinal *(basic)*, causative, central *(essential)*, critical *(crucial)*, crucial, decisive, indispensable, material *(important)*. SEE MAIN ENTRY
pivotal argument base *(foundation)*
pivotal point gravamen, main point. SEE MAIN ENTRY
placabilis peaceable, placable
placability amenability, benevolence *(disposition to do good)*, lenience, longanimity
placable lenient, nonmilitant. SEE MAIN ENTRY
placableness lenience
placare pacify, placate, propitiate, soothe
placate disarm *(set at ease)*, lull, mollify, pacify, propitiate, reconcile, soothe. SEE MAIN ENTRY
placation conciliation, mollification
placative nonmilitant
placatus dispassionate
place allocate, area *(province)*, base *(place)*, building *(structure)*, case *(set of circumstances)*, character *(reputation)*, circuit, class, deploy, dispose *(apportion)*, employ *(engage services)*, fix *(arrange)*, habitation *(dwelling place)*, identify, inhabitation *(place of dwelling)*, instate, levy, locality, locate, location, lodge *(house)*, lodge *(reside)*, marshal, organize *(arrange)*, pigeonhole, pinpoint, plant *(place firmly)*, position *(situation)*, post, premises *(buildings)*, prestige, recall *(remember)*, recognize *(perceive)*, recollect, region, remember, residence, role, scene, seat, set down, site *(noun)*, site *(verb)*, situs, source, stand *(witness' place in court)*, status, territory. SEE MAIN ENTRY
place a cloud on encumber *(financially obligate)*
place a false construction on misinterpret
place a value on calculate, estimate, evaluate
place a wrong construction on misinterpret
place against contrast
place an erroneous construction on misinterpret
place an instrument in a place of deposit file *(place among official records)*
place at one's disposal extend *(offer)*, present *(make a gift)*
place at ones disposal hold out *(deliberate on an offer)*
place authority vest
place before introduce, preface
place between interpose
place by itself isolate
place close together juxtapose
place control vest
place for safe keeping depository
place in a category classify, partition, pigeonhole
place in a dubious position compromise *(endanger)*
place in a former state reinstate
place in a receptacle deposit *(place)*
place in an office delegate
place in authority nominate
place in charge of delegate
place in command nominate
place in confinement arrest *(apprehend)*, commit *(institutionalize)*, imprison, jail
place in custody again rearrest
place in danger jeopardize
place in durance confine, contain *(restrain)*, detain *(hold in custody)*
place in juxtaposition border *(approach)*, compare, contrast
place in office elect *(select by a vote)*, hire, induct, instate, nominate
place in official custody of the clerk file *(place among official records)*
place in order apportion, arrange *(methodize)*, classify, file *(arrange)*, fix *(arrange)*, marshal, organize *(arrange)*, sort
place in the condition of natural born subjects naturalize *(make a citizen)*
place in the foreground adduce
place in the possession of deliver
place in the protection of entrust
place in the record enter *(record)*
place into enter *(insert)*, inject, interject
place limitations border *(bound)*, clog
place near border *(approach)*, juxtapose
place next to juxtapose
place of abode habitation *(dwelling place)*, home *(domicile)*, household, inhabitation *(place of dwelling)*
place of assignation rendezvous
place of birth home *(place of origin)*
place of business address, market *(business)*, market place, office
place of business traffic market place
place of buying and selling market *(business)*, market place
place of commerce market *(business)*, market place
place of concealment cache *(hiding place)*
place of confinement jail, penitentiary
place of deposit cache *(storage place)*, depository, treasury
place of detention penitentiary
place of dwelling abode, home *(domicile)*
place of education institute
place of employment office
place of entry entrance
place of existence home *(domicile)*
place of exit egress
place of habitation building *(structure)*, house
place of immunity asylum *(hiding place)*
place of imprisonment penitentiary
place of jurisdiction venue
place of meeting rendezvous
place of occupancy domicile
place of one's domestic affections home *(domicile)*
place of protection refuge
place of refuge asylum *(hiding place)*, home *(domicile)*, shelter *(protection)*
place of residence apartment, domicile, dwelling, habitation *(dwelling place)*, home *(domicile)*, inhabitation *(place of dwelling)*, lodging, residence
place of rest home *(domicile)*, lodging
place of safety cache *(storage place)*, haven, refuge
place of settlement homestead
place of trade market *(business)*, market place
place of traffic market *(business)*
place on record cast *(register)*, file *(place among official records)*
place out of bounds exclude
place outside the protection of the law outlaw
place parallel border *(approach)*
place permanently fix *(make firm)*
place reliance in trust
place reliance on confide *(trust)*
place side by side adjoin, juxtapose
place the blame for lodge *(bring a complaint)*
place the blame on impute, incriminate
place the responsibility for impute
place to live in home *(domicile)*
place trust in delegate, rely
place under a liquid immerse *(plunge into)*
place under arrest apprehend *(arrest)*
place under federal administration federalize *(place under federal control)*
place under federal rule federalize *(place under federal control)*
place under government control nationalize

place under interdiction enjoin
place under protective custody confine
place under the ban enjoin
place upon a list empanel
place where justice is administered court, judicatory
place where one lives home *(domicile)*
placed situated
placed in advance preferred *(given priority)*
placement arrogation, assignation, classification, disposition *(final arrangement)*, distribution *(apportionment)*, distribution *(arrangement)*, installation, location, order *(arrangement)*, organization *(structure)*, rating, situs
placement against contraposition
placement opposite contraposition
placere interest
placet brevet
placid complacent, patient, peaceable, stoical. SEE MAIN ENTRY
placidity composure, longanimity
placidness composure
placidus dispassionate, peaceable, placid
placing array *(order)*, introduction
placing in confinement commitment *(confinement)*
placing in office appointment *(act of designating)*, assignment *(designation)*, designation *(naming)*
placitum decision *(judgment)*
placitum decree, dogma
plagiarism counterfeit. SEE MAIN ENTRY
plagiarize copy, fake, pirate *(reproduce without authorization)*, steal. SEE MAIN ENTRY
plagiary counterfeit
plague annoy, badger, bait *(harass)*, discommode, discompose, disease, disturb, dun, embarrass, harass, harm, harrow, harry *(harass)*, hector, ill use, importune, infliction, irritate, mistreat, molest *(annoy)*, nuisance, obsess, persecute, perturb, pique, press *(goad)*, prey, provoke, trouble. SEE MAIN ENTRY
plagued by conscience penitent
plagueful pestilent
plaguesome invidious
plain apparent *(perceptible)*, arrant *(definite)*, blatant *(conspicuous)*, clear *(apparent)*, coherent *(clear)*, comprehensible, conspicuous, direct *(forthright)*, elementary, evident, exact, explicit, express, flagrant, genuine, household *(familiar)*, ingenuous, jejune *(dull)*, lucid, manifest, mere, mundane, naive, naked *(lacking embellishment)*, naked *(perceptible)*, nondescript, obvious, only *(no more than)*, open *(in sight)*, ostensible, overt, palpable, patent, pedestrian, pellucid, perceivable, perceptible, prosaic, salient, scrutable, simple, stark, tangible, unaffected *(sincere)*, unambiguous, unequivocal, unmistakable, unpretentious, usual, visible *(in full view)*
plain English plain language
plain interpretation explanation
plain language SEE MAIN ENTRY
plain meaning connotation, content *(meaning)*
plain sense common sense
plain speaking plain language
plain speech plain language
plain to be seen patent, perceivable
plain words plain language
plain-speaking bona fide, honest
plain-spoken straightforward
plainly fairly *(clearly)*, only, purely *(simply)*, solely *(purely)*
plainness honesty, informality
plainspeaking honesty
plainspoken unaffected *(sincere)*
plaint charge *(accusation)*, complaint, denunciation, outcry. SEE MAIN ENTRY
plaintful querulous
plaintiff actor, claimant, complainant, litigant, party *(litigant)*, suitor. SEE MAIN ENTRY
plaintiff's allegations pleading
plaintiff's initiatory pleading complaint
plaintive disconsolate, lugubrious, querulous
plait intertwine. SEE MAIN ENTRY
plan agenda, blueprint, building *(business of assembling)*, calculate, campaign, conceive *(invent)*, conspiracy, conspire, contemplation, content *(structure)*, contour *(outline)*, contrivance, contrive, course, delineation, design *(construction plan)*, design *(intent)*, device *(contrivance)*, devise *(invent)*, direction *(course)*, enterprise *(undertaking)*, expedient, forethought, form *(arrangement)*, frame *(construct)*, frame *(formulate)*, frame *(prearrange)*, goal, idea, intend, intent, intention, maneuver, method, model, motif, motive, order *(arrangement)*, organization *(structure)*, originate, pattern, platform, ploy, policy *(plan of action)*, prearrange, predetermine, preparation, procedure, process *(course)*, program *(noun)*, program *(verb)*, project, proposal *(report)*, proposal *(suggestion)*, propose, proposition, prospect *(outlook)*, prospectus, provide *(arrange for)*, purpose, purview, resolution *(formal statement)*, resolve *(decide)*, schedule, scheme *(noun)*, scheme *(verb)*, set down, stratagem, strategy, structure *(composition)*, subterfuge, system, target, undertaking *(attempt)*, undertaking *(enterprise)*, way *(channel)*. SEE MAIN ENTRY
plan a crime conspire
plan an unlawful act conspire
plan mischief plot
plan of action platform, polity, practice *(procedure)*, procedure, strategy
plan of attack design *(intent)*, maneuver *(tactic)*, strategy
plan of campaign policy *(plan of action)*
plan of offensive campaign
plan on anticipate *(expect)*, expect *(anticipate)*
plan out devise *(invent)*
plan secretly conspire, plot
plan strategy maneuver
plan to commit a crime conspire
plane degree *(station)*
plane in toto
plane surface area *(surface)*
planless haphazard
planned aforethought, deliberate, express, foreseeable, forthcoming, future, intentional, knowing, premeditated, prospective, purposeful, strategic, tactical, willful
planned beforehand aforethought, premeditated
planned campaign maneuver *(tactic)*, strategy
planned course of action forethought
planned disbursement budget
planned for future
planned in advance deliberate, express, premeditated
planned place of arrival destination
planner accessory, accomplice, architect, catalyst, coactor, conspirer, contractor, developer, promoter
planning agenda
planning ahead forethought
planning board commission *(agency)*
plans calendar *(record of yearly periods)*
plant deposit *(place)*, embed, engender, establish *(entrench)*, fix *(make firm)*, frame up, inculcate, initiate, inseminate, insertion, instate, repose *(place)*. SEE MAIN ENTRY
plant the evidence frame *(prearrange)*
planted situated
plastic flexible, pliable, pliant, sequacious, tractable
plasticity amenability
plat intertwine, plot *(land)*
platform policy *(plan of action)*, polity, prospectus, stand *(witness' place in court)*, strategy. SEE MAIN ENTRY
platitude SEE MAIN ENTRY
platitudinous ordinary, pedestrian, prosaic, trite
plaudit mention *(tribute)*
plausibility common sense, credibility, likelihood, possibility, probability. SEE MAIN ENTRY
plausible apparent *(presumptive)*, believable, convincing, defensible, justifiable, ostensible, persuasive, possible, presumptive, probable, rational, reasonable *(rational)*, specious, tenable, viable. SEE MAIN ENTRY
plausible excuse alibi
play bet, latitude, parlay *(bet)*, performance *(workmanship)*, pretend
play a direct part affect
play a leading part predominate *(command)*
play a long shot bet
play a part involve *(participate)*, mock *(imitate)*, pose *(impersonate)*
play a part in participate
play a trick dupe
play a trick on delude
play act pretend
play against counter, counteract
play at cross purposes conflict, counteract
play down disparage
play false betray *(lead astray)*, cheat, illude, pretend
play favorites prefer
play for bet
play for money gamble
play for stakes gamble
play for time procrastinate
play havoc with disorganize, prejudice *(injure)*
play one false ensnare
play out discontinue *(abandon)*
play safe hedge
play the market invest *(fund)*, speculate *(chance)*
play the part assume *(simulate)*
play tricks upon jape
play truant flee
play up magnify
play upon dupe
play upon words distort
play-act simulate
playact palter
playbook script
player bettor
player for stakes bettor
playful jocular
playfulness mischief

plaza market place
plea advocacy, allegation, answer *(judicial response),* argument *(pleading),* call *(appeal),* claim *(legal demand),* contention *(argument),* counterargument, entreaty, invitation, nollo contendere, petition, pleading, prayer, pretense *(pretext),* request, response. SEE MAIN ENTRY
plea in being elsewhere alibi
plea in rebuttal answer *(judicial response),* confutation, counterargument, rejoinder
plead address *(petition),* adduce, allege, answer *(reply),* answer *(respond legally),* bear *(adduce),* depose *(testify),* exhort, importune, intercede, petition, pray, press *(beseech),* pressure, reason *(persuade),* respond, solicit, sue. SEE MAIN ENTRY
plead a cause against a third party implead
plead for advocate, bear *(support),* call *(appeal to),* defend, justify, request, side
plead guilty repent. SEE MAIN ENTRY
plead in favor of advocate
plead innocent SEE MAIN ENTRY
plead one's case advocate, assert
plead one's cause advocate, assert, defend, justify
plead with call *(appeal to)*
pleader advocate *(counselor),* apologist, attorney, claimant, counsel, intermediary, jurist, petitioner, proponent, suitor
pleading argument *(pleading),* persuasion, plea, precatory. SEE MAIN ENTRY
pleading in a civil action complaint
pleadings matter *(case),* plea
pleasant attractive, desirable *(pleasing),* harmonious, jocular, palatable, sapid, savory. SEE MAIN ENTRY
pleasantness amenity
please obey, pacify, pander, placate, propitiate, satisfy *(fulfill).* SEE MAIN ENTRY
pleased complacent, inclined, proud *(self-respecting)*
pleased with oneself inflated *(vain)*
pleasing attractive, harmonious, palatable, popular, sapid, savory
pleasingness amenity
pleasurable desirable *(pleasing),* palatable, sapid
pleasure benefit *(betterment),* satisfaction *(fulfilment),* treat, will *(desire).* SEE MAIN ENTRY
pleasureful desirable *(pleasing)*
plebeian ordinary, uncouth
plebian ignoble
plebicola demagogue
plebis dux demagogue
plebiscite election *(selection by vote),* poll *(casting of votes),* referendum. SEE MAIN ENTRY
plebiscitum enactment
plebs populace
pledge adjuration, agree *(contract),* agreement *(contract),* allegiance, assurance, assure *(insure),* avouch *(guarantee),* bail, bear *(adduce),* bind *(obligate),* binder, bond *(secure a debt),* charge *(lien),* cloud *(incumbrance),* commitment *(responsibility),* compact, contract *(noun),* contract *(verb),* covenant, coverage *(insurance),* deal, debenture, deposit, due, duty *(obligation),* guarantee, guaranty, hostage, hypothecation, insurance, lien, loan, mortgage, oath, pact, pawn, profess *(avow),* profession *(declaration),* promise, promise *(vow),* responsibility *(accountability),* specialty *(contract),* stipulate, subscribe *(promise),* undertake, undertaking *(bond),* undertaking *(commitment),* underwrite, vouch, vow, warrant *(guaranty),* warranty. SEE MAIN ENTRY
pledge for the payment of a debt mortgage
pledge of security mortgage
pledge one's credit promise *(vow)*
pledge one's honor promise *(vow)*
pledge one's word avouch *(guarantee),* promise *(vow),* undertake
pledge oneself promise *(vow)*
pledged agreed *(promised),* bound, contractual, fully secured, loyal
pledged word contract, specialty *(contract),* undertaking *(pledge)*
pledgee creditor
pledges ties
pledgor debtor, obligor
plenary complete *(all-embracing),* detailed, full, gross *(total),* radical *(extreme),* thorough, unmitigated, unqualified *(unlimited).* SEE MAIN ENTRY
plenipotent omnipotent, powerful
plenipotentiaries deputation *(delegation)*
plenipotentiary deputy, omnipotent, spokesman, substitute. SEE MAIN ENTRY
plenitude capacity *(maximum),* sufficiency
plenitudinous replete
plenteous ample, copious, multiple, replete, rife
plentiful considerable, copious, liberal *(generous),* ordinary, profuse, replete, rife, substantial, usual
plentifulness boom *(prosperity),* plethora, quorum
plentitude boom *(prosperity),* maximum *(amplitude).* SEE MAIN ENTRY
plenty overage, plethora, prosperity, quantity, quorum, store *(depository),* sufficiency, surfeit
plenum body *(collection),* chamber *(body),* corpus, meeting *(conference),* quorum, session
plenus full
pleonasm redundancy, tautology
pleonastic extraneous, needless, prolix, redundant, repetitious, turgid
pleonastical prolix, repetitious
plethora sufficiency. SEE MAIN ENTRY
plethoric excessive, full, replete, turgid
plexiform sinuous
pliability amenability, credulity
pliable amenable, facile, flexible, malleable, passive, pliant, resilient, sequacious, suasible, tractable, yielding. SEE MAIN ENTRY
pliancy amenability, compliance, credulity, discipline *(obedience)*
pliant amenable, facile, flexible, malleable, obedient, obeisant, passive, patient, pliable, resilient, sequacious, suasible, susceptible *(responsive),* tractable, yielding. SEE MAIN ENTRY
plight case *(set of circumstances),* condition *(state),* emergency, imbroglio, position *(situation),* posture *(situation),* predicament, problem, promise *(vow),* quagmire, quandary, situation, state *(condition).* SEE MAIN ENTRY
plight one's honor promise *(vow)*
plight one's word promise *(vow)*
plod bear *(tolerate),* labor, persevere, persist
plodding operose, painstaking, patient, pedestrian, pertinacious, stable, steadfast
plot cabal, campaign, confederacy *(conspiracy),* connivance, connive, conspiracy, conspire, contrivance, contrive, delineate, delineation, forethought, location, lot, machination, maneuver *(trick),* maneuver, parcel, plan *(noun),* plan *(verb),* prearrange, program, property *(land),* real estate, ruse, scenario, scheme *(noun),* scheme *(verb),* section *(vicinity),* stratagem. SEE MAIN ENTRY
plot an action in advance conspire
plot craftily conspire
plot of ground parcel, section *(vicinity)*
plot of land parcel, section *(vicinity)*
plot together conspire
plotted deliberate, premeditated, tactical
plotter coactor, conspirator, conspirer
plotting artful, collusion, collusive, insidious, machiavellian, malevolent, perfidious, sly
ploy artifice, machination, plot *(secret plan),* stratagem. SEE MAIN ENTRY
pluck cull, eviscerate, prowess *(bravery)*
pluck out excise *(cut away),* extirpate
plucking out avulsion, evulsion
pluckless languid, phlegmatic
plucky indomitable, spartan
plug clog, damper *(stopper),* obstruction, occlude, shut, stem *(check),* stop
plug away labor, persevere, persist
plug up block, clog
plum prize
plumb probe
plunder despoil, devastate, hijack, hold up *(rob),* loot, pillage *(noun),* pillage *(verb),* pirate *(take by violence),* prey, prize, rape, rob, spoil *(pillage),* spoils, spoliation, steal. SEE MAIN ENTRY
plunder by stealth poach
plunderage burglary, pillage, rape, spoils, spoliation
plunderer burglar, criminal, vandal
plundering burglary, foray, havoc, housebreaking, larcenous, predatory, rapacious, robbery, spoliation
plunderous larcenous
plunge decline, depress, risk, speculate *(chance),* venture
plunge ahead race
plunge in pierce *(lance)*
plunge into embark, occupy *(engage)*
plunge into a liquid immerse *(plunge into)*
plunger bettor
plural multiple
plurality majority *(greater part),* mass *(body of persons),* multiplicity, preponderance. SEE MAIN ENTRY
plures esse predominate *(outnumber)*
plus advantage, also, balance *(amount in excess),* further
ply cajole, employ *(make use of),* importune, labor, manipulate *(utilize skillfully),* occupy *(engage),* propensity, wield. SEE MAIN ENTRY
ply one's task attempt
ply one's trade labor
plying bribery
poach hold up *(rob),* impose *(intrude),* pilfer, purloin, steal. SEE MAIN ENTRY
poached trade contraband
poached traffic contraband
pock-marked blemished
pocket obtain, receive *(acquire),* steal
pococurante careless, casual, cold-blooded, inactive, insusceptible *(uncaring),* lax, lifeless *(dull),* nonchalant

pococurantism disinterest *(lack of interest)*
poena expiation, penalty, punishment, retribution
poenalis penal
poetic original *(creative)*
poignant bitter *(penetrating)*, moving *(evoking emotion)*. SEE MAIN ENTRY
point case *(set of circumstances)*, consequence *(significance)*, content *(meaning)*, contention *(argument)*, degree *(station)*, detail, direct *(show)*, edge *(border)*, end *(termination)*, feature *(characteristic)*, gist *(ground for a suit)*, import, intent, issue *(matter in dispute)*, item, location, matter *(subject)*, motive, object, objective, occasion, particular, period, phase *(aspect)*, phase *(period)*, pinnacle, posture *(situation)*, property *(distinctive attribute)*, purpose, refer *(direct attention)*, remark, signification, situs, standpoint, subject *(topic)*, target, technicality, term *(provision)*, tip *(clue)*. SEE MAIN ENTRY
point at denounce *(inform against)*, strive
point at issue matter *(subject)*, subject *(topic)*
point in common analogy
point in dispute problem, question *(issue)*
point in question issue *(matter in dispute)*, matter *(subject)*
point of connotation
point of cessation destination
point of comparison criterion, example, norm, precedent
point of concentration focus
point of convergence center *(central position)*, focus
point of difference characteristic, distinction *(difference)*, specialty *(distinctive mark)*
point of disembarkation destination
point of etiquette decorum
point of no return crossroad *(turning point)*
point of observation outlook, perspective
point of resemblance analogy
point of time date, phase *(period)*
point of view concept, conviction *(persuasion)*, idea, opinion *(belief)*, outlook, perception, perspective, platform, posture *(attitude)*, side, stand *(position)*, standpoint. SEE MAIN ENTRY
point out apprise, bear *(adduce)*, charge *(instruct on the law)*, comment, convey *(communicate)*, demonstrate *(establish)*, denote, designate, direct *(show)*, disabuse, discriminate *(distinguish)*, enumerate, exhibit, explain, impart, indicate, inform *(notify)*, instruct *(teach)*, itemize, manifest, mention, quote, reason *(persuade)*, remind, select, signify *(denote)*, specify
point out an essential difference distinguish
point to allude, ascribe, attribute, bear *(adduce)*, cite *(state)*, connote, evince, exemplify, implicate, imply, indicate, mention, predict, presage
point to be settled problem
point up dwell *(linger over)*
point-blank direct *(forthright)*
pointed acute, compact *(pithy)*, conspicuous, direct *(forthright)*, eloquent, explicit, incisive, laconic, mordacious, persuasive, pithy, sententious, trenchant
pointedly fairly *(clearly)*, knowingly, purposely
pointer indicant, indication, indicator, suggestion, tip *(clue)*
pointing out designation *(naming)*, reference *(citation)*
pointless immaterial, inapposite, insipid, null *(insignificant)*, pedestrian, unavailing, unreasonable. SEE MAIN ENTRY
pointlessness immateriality
points of comparison analogy
poise composure, confidence *(faith)*, decorum, demeanor, deportment. SEE MAIN ENTRY
poison contaminate, degenerate, infect, pervert, pollute, taint *(contaminate)*, virulent, vitiate. SEE MAIN ENTRY
poisoned deadly, peccant *(unhealthy)*, tainted *(contaminated)*
poisoning contaminate, detriment
poisonous deadly, deleterious, fatal, harmful, incendiary, insalubrious, lethal, malevolent, malignant, noxious, obnoxious, peccant *(unhealthy)*, pernicious, pestilent, ruthless, toxic, virulent
poke delve, jostle *(bump into)*, loiter
poke fun at jape, mock *(deride)*
poke into frisk, probe
poker-faced inexpressive, inscrutable
polarity antipode, antithesis, conflict, penchant, reaction *(opposition)*
polarize SEE MAIN ENTRY
polarized hostile
pole cudgel, end *(termination)*, extremity *(furthest point)*
polemic argumentative, contention *(argument)*, disputable, dispute, litigious. SEE MAIN ENTRY
polemical argumentative, contentious, controversial, dissenting, forensic, litigious, polemic. SEE MAIN ENTRY
polemicist disputant
polemics argument *(contention)*, contest *(dispute)*, controversy *(argument)*, disaccord, disagreement, fight *(argument)*, strife
polemist contender
poles apart distinct *(distinguished from others)*
police censor, moderate *(preside over)*, patrol, peace officer, regulate *(manage)*, rule *(govern)*. SEE MAIN ENTRY
police constable peace officer
police force police
police officer peace officer
police officers police
police tipper informer *(one providing criminal information)*
policeman peace officer
policewoman peace officer
policy course, direction *(course)*, platform, polity, practice *(procedure)*, principle *(axiom)*, procedure, process *(course)*, program, rule *(guide)*, scheme, strategy, system. SEE MAIN ENTRY
policy-fixing meeting caucus
polis city
polish amend, complete, cultivate, decorum, discretion *(quality of being discreet)*, edit, embellish, enhance, meliorate, revise
polished civil *(polite)*, literate
polished manners courtesy, decorum
polite diplomatic, discreet, formal, obeisant
polite act courtesy
polite regard respect
politely respectfully
politeness comity, consideration *(sympathetic regard)*, courtesy, decorum, deference, propriety *(correctness)*, protocol *(etiquette)*, respect
politic diplomatic, discreet, favorable *(advantageous)*, judicial, judicious, juridical, provident *(showing foresight)*, prudent, sensible, solid *(sound)*, strategic, subtle *(refined)*, tactical. SEE MAIN ENTRY
political civic, civil *(public)*. SEE MAIN ENTRY
political affairs politics
political agitator malcontent
political aspirant candidate
political body congress
political community government *(political administration)*
political competition primary
political confluence caucus
political contention primary
political contestant candidate
political corruption graft
political disorder anarchy
political division state *(political unit)*
political election primary
political independence freedom, home rule, liberty
political influence politics
political involvement politics
political leaders government *(political administration)*
political machine party *(political organization)*
political maneuvers politics
political methods politics
political partisanship politics
political prisoner hostage
political process politics
political question SEE MAIN ENTRY
political regime government *(political administration)*
political representative nominee *(candidate)*
political rivalry primary
political spin SEE MAIN ENTRY
political strategy politics
political subdivision venue
political system regime
political theater SEE MAIN ENTRY
political upheaval insurrection, revolt, revolution
politically independent autonomous *(self governing)*, sovereign *(independent)*
politician demagogue, lawmaker, legislator. SEE MAIN ENTRY
politicians government *(political administration)*
politico lawmaker, politician
politicos government *(political administration)*
politics SEE MAIN ENTRY
polity body *(collection)*, community, constituency, government *(political administration)*, nationality, policy *(plan of action)*, public, society, state *(political unit)*. SEE MAIN ENTRY
poll canvass, cast *(register)*, census, election *(selection by vote)*, inquiry *(request for information)*, plebiscite, primary, referendum, vote *(noun)*, vote *(verb)*. SEE MAIN ENTRY
pollage tax
polliceri promise *(vow)*
pollinate inseminate
pollinize inseminate
polluere stain
pollute abuse *(violate)*, adulterate, contaminate, corrupt, damage, debase,

degenerate, denature, deteriorate, disgrace, harm, impair, infect, misemploy, mistreat, pervert, smear, stain, sully, taint *(contaminate)*, tarnish, vitiate. SEE MAIN ENTRY
polluted dissolute, harmful, profane, salacious, tainted *(contaminated)*
pollution contaminate, detriment, misusage, perversion. SEE MAIN ENTRY
pollution control ecology
poltergeist phantom
poltroon recreant
poltroonish caitiff
polygamous SEE MAIN ENTRY
polymorphic protean
polymorphous protean
polysyllabic profundity bombast
pommel impinge
pomp pretense *(ostentation)*, solemnity
pomposity bombast, fustian, pretense *(ostentation)*, pride, rhetoric *(insincere language)*
pompous dictatorial, flatulent, formal, fustian, grandiose, inflated *(bombastic)*, inflated *(vain)*, orgulous, orotund, presumptuous, proud *(conceited)*, supercilious, turgid. SEE MAIN ENTRY
pompous prolixity bombast
pompous speech rhetoric *(insincere language)*
pompousness pretense *(ostentation)*, rhetoric *(insincere language)*
ponder brood, concentrate *(pay attention)*, consider, debate, deliberate, doubt *(hesitate)*, muse, reason *(conclude)*, speculate *(conjecture)*, study, weigh. SEE MAIN ENTRY
ponder over deliberate
ponder reasons for and against deliberate
ponderable appreciable. SEE MAIN ENTRY
ponderare ponder
pondered deliberate, intentional
pondering cogitative, consideration *(contemplation)*, contemplation, deliberation, reflection *(thought)*
ponderosus ponderous
ponderous jejune *(dull)*, major, oppressive, pedestrian. SEE MAIN ENTRY
ponderousness weight *(burden)*
pondus importance, influence, pressure, stress *(strain)*, validity
ponere invest *(fund)*, propose
poniard pierce *(lance)*
ponzi scheme SEE MAIN ENTRY
pool combination, combine *(act in concert)*, concert, consolidation, consortium *(business cartel)*, contribution *(participation)*, cooperate, federalize *(associate)*, federation, fund, join *(associate oneself with)*, join *(bring together)*, league, partnership, syndicate, trust *(combination of businesses)*, unite. SEE MAIN ENTRY
pool one's interests federate
pooled common *(shared)*, conjoint
poor base *(inferior)*, deficient, deplorable, destitute, devoid, impecunious, imperfect, inadept, inadequate, inferior *(lower in quality)*, insubstantial, insufficient, lamentable, marginal, mediocre, negligible, paltry, perfunctory, slipshod, unfavorable, unsatisfactory. SEE MAIN ENTRY
poor administration maladministration
poor chance improbability
poor circumstances indigence, poverty
poor judgment error, indiscretion, misestimation, misjudgment
poor opinion disparagement
poor prospect improbability
poor quality work noncompliance *(improper completion)*
poor reputation ignominy
poor usage misapplication
poor visiblity indistinctness
poorly adapted disproportionate, unsuitable
poorly advised misadvised
poorly defined inconspicuous, unclear, vague
poorly done perfunctory
poorly off impecunious
poorly qualified inexperienced
poorly seen inconspicuous, unclear
poorly timed untimely
poorness dearth, indigence, mediocrity, poverty
populace community, nationality, population, public. SEE MAIN ENTRY
populacy population
popular common *(customary)*, common *(shared)*, competitive *(open)*, current, customary, familiar *(customary)*, famous, general, household *(familiar)*, illustrious, meritorious, ordinary, prescriptive, prevailing *(current)*, prevalent, proverbial, public *(known)*, regular *(conventional)*, renowned, rife, routine, sapid, select, typical, usual. SEE MAIN ENTRY
popular agitator demagogue
popular choice referendum
popular decision poll *(casting of votes)*, referendum, suffrage
popular favor character *(reputation)*, distinction *(reputation)*, reputation
popular regard affection
popular report hearsay
popular repute notoriety
popular ringleader catalyst
popular vote referendum
popularity character *(reputation)*, notoriety
popularize elucidate, explain
popularly believed consensual
populate dwell *(reside)*
populated populous
population community, populace, public, society. SEE MAIN ENTRY
populous compact *(dense)*, copious, manifold, rife. SEE MAIN ENTRY
populus public
pore over consider, notice *(observe)*, peruse, read, reflect *(ponder)*, study
pornographic lascivious, lewd, obscene, prurient, salacious, suggestive *(risqué)*
pornography obscenity. SEE MAIN ENTRY
porous penetrable
port complexion, conduct, deportment, destination, haven, manner *(behavior)*
portage carriage
portage fee fare
portal admittance *(means of approach)*, entrance, margin *(outside limit)*, outlet. SEE MAIN ENTRY
portare bear *(support)*
portend anticipate *(prognosticate)*, forewarn, indicate, predict, presage, prognosticate, promise *(raise expectations)*, threaten. SEE MAIN ENTRY
portendance caveat
portendere portend, presage
portending evil ominous, portentous *(ominous)*, sinister
portending happiness auspicious
portendment caveat
portent caution *(warning)*, forerunner, harbinger, indicant, indication, phenomenon *(unusual occurrence)*, precursor, premonition, significance, threat, token, warning. SEE MAIN ENTRY
portention caveat
portentous dire, imminent, important *(significant)*, ominous, oracular, presageful, prophetic, unusual. SEE MAIN ENTRY
porter caretaker *(one caring for property)*
porterage carriage
portfolio dossier. SEE MAIN ENTRY
portio installment, share *(interest)*
portion allotment, article *(distinct section of a writing)*, assignment *(allotment)*, chapter *(division)*, commission *(fee)*, component, detail, dole, element, equity *(share of ownership)*, excerpt, factor *(ingredient)*, heritage, installment, interest *(ownership)*, lot, member *(constituent part)*, moiety, parcel, part *(separate)*, partition, phase *(aspect)*, proportion, prorate, quantity, quota, ration, region, segment, share *(interest)*, subdivide, title *(division)*. SEE MAIN ENTRY
portion off allocate
portion out allocate, allot, apportion, assign *(allot)*, dispense, disperse *(disseminate)*, distribute, divide *(distribute)*, measure, parcel, partition, reapportion
portion out again reassign
portion out equitably apportion
portioning division *(act of dividing)*
portorium tax, toll *(tax)*
portraiture representation *(statement)*
portray characterize, copy, delineate, denote, depict, describe, detail *(particularize)*, draw *(depict)*, exemplify, impersonate, mock *(imitate)*, pose *(impersonate)*, pretend, recite, recount, relate *(tell)*, render *(depict)*, reproduce, signify *(denote)*. SEE MAIN ENTRY
portray by example exemplify
portray falsely fake
portray in words delineate, describe
portrayal caricature, delineation, description, narration, part *(role)*, representation *(statement)*, story *(narrative)*, symbol
portus haven
poscere require *(compel)*
pose disguise, offer *(propose)*, palter, perplex, posit, position *(point of view)*, posture *(attitude)*, pretense *(ostentation)*, propose, propound, role. SEE MAIN ENTRY
pose as assume *(simulate)*, fake, impersonate, purport
posed specious
poser enigma
posit comment, infer, pose *(propound)*, postulate, presume, presuppose, propound, surmise, suspect *(think)*. SEE MAIN ENTRY
posited assumed *(inferred)*, situated
position advantage, aspect, calling, capacity *(job)*, career, case *(set of circumstances)*, character *(reputation)*, claim *(assertion)*, class, condition *(state)*, conviction *(persuasion)*, degree *(station)*, employment, file *(arrange)*, job, livelihood, locality, locate, location, marshal, occupation *(vocation)*, office, opinion *(belief)*, opinion *(judicial decision)*, outlook, perspective, platform, plight, post, posture *(attitude)*, posture *(situation)*, predicament, prestige, principle *(axiom)*, profession *(vocation)*, proposition, pursuit *(occupation)*, reputation, role, seat, side, site *(noun)*, site *(verb)*, situation, situs, stand *(position)*, stand *(witness' place in court)*, standpoint, state *(condition)*, status, supposition, thesis, trade

(occupation), venue, work *(employment)*. SEE MAIN ENTRY
position in society character *(reputation)*, reputation
position of influence authority *(power)*, patronage *(power to appoint jobs)*
position of power authority *(power)*
position paper pandect *(treatise)*
position together juxtapose
positioned situated
positions premises *(hypotheses)*
positive absolute *(conclusive)*, actual, affirmative, authentic, axiomatic, categorical, certain *(fixed)*, clear *(certain)*, conclusive *(determinative)*, convincing, decisive, definite, demonstrable, distinct *(clear)*, dogmatic, explicit, express, incontrovertible, indubious, inexorable, irrefutable, obdurate, peremptory *(absolute)*, pure, resounding, secure *(confident)*, stark, strict, substantive, tangible, undisputed, unequivocal, unmistakable, unrefutable, well-grounded. SEE MAIN ENTRY
positive action course
positive assertion allegation, avouchment
positive declaration affirmance *(legal affirmation)*, allegation, assertion, asseveration, averment
positive fact certification *(certainness)*
positive statement affirmance *(legal affirmation)*, affirmation, allegation, assertion, asseveration, averment, avouchment, avowal, declaration
positively de facto, fairly *(clearly)*, ipso facto
positively declared alleged
positively direct enjoin
positiveness belief *(state of mind)*, certainty, certification *(certainness)*, certitude, confidence *(faith)*, conviction *(persuasion)*, surety *(certainty)*, weight *(credibility)*
positivistic dogmatic
positus situated
posse possibility
possess appropriate, comprehend *(include)*, impropriate, keep *(shelter)*, obsess, obtain, occupy *(take possession)*, own, remain *(occupy)*, retain *(keep in possession)*. SEE MAIN ENTRY
possess authority handle *(manage)*, rule *(govern)*
possess oneself of assume *(seize)*, distrain
possessed diabolic, fanatical, frenetic, lunatic
possessed of immunity exempt, immune
possessed of knowledge cognizant
possessing double meaning equivocal
possessing merit meritorious
possessing unlimited power omnipotent
possessio domain *(land owned)*, estate *(property)*, holding *(property owned)*, occupancy, possession *(ownership)*, possession *(property)*, possessions, retention, tenure
possession acquisition, chattel, compulsion *(obsession)*, dominion *(absolute ownership)*, enjoyment *(use)*, habitation *(act of inhabiting)*, holding *(property owned)*, interest *(ownership)*, item, occupancy, receipt *(act of receiving)*, seisin, tenancy, title *(right)*. SEE MAIN ENTRY
possession and control trust *(custody)*
possession of full rights emancipation
possessione depellere dispossess
possessions assets, commodities, effects, estate *(property)*, goods, merchandise, movable, paraphernalia *(personal belongings)*, personalty, property *(possessions)*. SEE MAIN ENTRY
possessive jealous, mercenary
possessiveness greed
possessor bearer
possessor holder
possessor lessee, lodger, occupant, proprietor, tenant
possessor of descent heir
possessorship dominion *(absolute ownership)*, ownership, seisin, tenancy
possibility access *(opening)*, contingency, feasibility, likelihood, opportunity, potential, probability, proposal *(suggestion)*, prospect *(outlook)*, prospect *(prospective patron)*, risk, suggestion. SEE MAIN ENTRY
possibility of injury risk
possibility of loss risk
possible conditional, contingent, convincing, debatable, future, plausible, potential, practicable, presumptive, probable, prospective, viable. SEE MAIN ENTRY
possible client prospect *(prospective patron)*
possible customer prospect *(prospective patron)*
possible patron prospect *(prospective patron)*
possibleness chance *(possibility)*, likelihood, potential
possidere hold *(possess)*, own, tenure
post annunciate, appointment *(position)*, bond *(secure a debt)*, book, calling, career, convey *(communicate)*, dispatch *(send off)*, employment, enter *(record)*, induct, inform *(notify)*, inscribe, issue *(publish)*, itemize, location, notify, office, organ, pawn, pledge *(deposit)*, position *(business status)*, pursuit *(occupation)*, record, register, role, seat, send, set down, situation, stand *(witness' place in court)*, standpoint, title *(position)*, trade *(occupation)*, work *(employment)*. SEE MAIN ENTRY
post mortem posthumous
post on redirect
post road causeway
postal communication dispatch *(message)*
postdate succeed *(follow)*
posted acquainted, cognizant, informed *(having information)*, knowing, situated
posterior back *(in reverse)*, ensuing
posterior subsequent
posteritas posterity
posterity descendant, heir, offspring, progeny, succession. SEE MAIN ENTRY
postern portal
posterus future
postfix attachment *(thing affixed)*
posthaste rapid
posthumous SEE MAIN ENTRY
postnote memorandum
postpone adjourn, continue *(adjourn)*, defer *(put off)*, delay, discontinue *(break continuity)*, hold up *(delay)*, impede, procrastinate, recess, stall, suspend. SEE MAIN ENTRY
postponed arrested *(checked)*, late *(tardy)*
postponed payment bill *(invoice)*
postponement adjournment, cessation *(interlude)*, continuance, deferment, delay, discontinuance *(act of discontinuing)*, moratorium, pendency, reprieve
postponement of penalty reprieve
postscript addendum, allonge, codicil, insertion, rider
postulant claimant
postulare arraign
postulate assumption *(supposition)*, avow, claim *(legal demand)*, comment *(noun)*, comment *(verb)*, concept, condition *(contingent provision)*, conjecture, deduction *(conclusion)*, generalization, guess, hypothesis, infer, inference, maxim, opine, pose *(propound)*, posit, presume, presumption, presuppose, principle *(axiom)*, propose, proposition, propound, require *(compel)*, supposition, suspicion *(uncertainty)*, theory, thesis. SEE MAIN ENTRY
postulate of reason principle *(axiom)*
postulated assumed *(inferred)*, presumptive, requisite, theoretical
postulates premises *(hypotheses)*
postulatio claim *(legal demand)*, pretense *(pretext)*, request, requisition
postulation condition *(contingent provision)*, conjecture, conviction *(persuasion)*, deduction *(conclusion)*, generalization, hypothesis, inference, prolepsis, request, suspicion *(uncertainty)*, thesis
postulational presumptive
postulatory theoretical
postulatum inference
posture appearance *(look)*, aspect, case *(set of circumstances)*, color *(complexion)*, complexion, condition *(state)*, conduct, conviction *(persuasion)*, demeanor, deportment, disguise, manner *(behavior)*, opinion *(belief)*, outlook, position *(point of view)*, position *(situation)*, predicament, presence *(poise)*, profess *(pretend)*, role, situation, state *(condition)*, status. SEE MAIN ENTRY
pot cannabis, stake *(award)*
potable palatable
potare carouse
potation alcohol, dipsomania, inebriation
potence dint, force *(strength)*, main force, puissance, sinew
potency caliber *(quality)*, clout, competence *(ability)*, dint, efficiency, faculty *(ability)*, force *(strength)*, influence, leverage, main force, potential, power, prestige, puissance, quality *(excellence)*, sinew, strength, validity, weight *(importance)*. SEE MAIN ENTRY
potens influential, predominant
potent assertive, capable, cogent, compelling, considerable, convincing, efficient, in full force, indomitable, inexpugnable, influential, irresistible, omnipotent, operative, persuasive, powerful, predominant, prevailing *(having superior force)*, productive, sound, sovereign *(absolute)*, strong, valid, virtual. SEE MAIN ENTRY
potentia influence, predominance
potential chance *(possibility)*, constructive *(inferential)*, likelihood, possibility, possible, prospective, viable, virtual. SEE MAIN ENTRY
potentialis potential *(adjective)*, potential *(noun)*
potentiality ability, capacity *(aptitude)*, chance *(possibility)*, feasibility, likelihood, possibility, quality *(excellence)*
potentially liable at risk
potentiate empower
potestas ability, dominion *(supreme authority)*, license, opportunity, permission, possibility, power, warrant *(authorization)*
potestatem facere authorize, empower
potestates authorities

pother furor, hector, perplex, perturb, pique, plague, turmoil
potior preferable
potiorem outweigh
potpourri melange
poultice drug
pounce upon attack, oppugn, seize *(confiscate)*
pound beat *(pulsate)*, beat *(strike)*, cell, enclosure, lash *(strike)*, strike *(assault)*
pour forth emit, issue *(send forth)*, outpour, speak
pour in imbue, penetrate
pour out emit, issue *(send forth)*, outpour
pour out of emanate
pour over inundate
pourboire bonus, bounty
pourparler caucus
poverty dearth, deficiency, indigence, paucity, privation. SEE MAIN ENTRY
poverty-stricken bankrupt, destitute, impecunious, penurious, poor *(underprivileged)*
power advantage, capacity *(aptitude)*, capacity *(authority)*, catalyst, clout, control *(supervision)*, credit *(recognition)*, dint, dominance, dominion *(supreme authority)*, droit, faculty *(ability)*, force *(strength)*, government *(administration)*, hegemony, influence, jurisdiction, license, main force, management *(directorate)*, occupation *(possession)*, option *(contractual provision)*, patronage *(power to appoint jobs)*, potential, predominance, prerogative, pressure, prestige, primacy, puissance, quality *(excellence)*, range, realm, regime, right *(entitlement)*, sinew, strength, supremacy, title *(right)*, validity, warrant *(authorization)*, weight *(importance)*. SEE MAIN ENTRY
power of choice latitude, liberty, volition
power of choosing discretion *(power of choice)*, will *(desire)*
power of determination will *(desire)*
power of directing pressure
power of disposal dominion *(absolute ownership)*
power of entrance ingress
power of impelling clout, pressure
power over trust *(custody)*
power to choose latitude, liberty, option *(choice)*
power to grasp ideas comprehension
power to reason intellect, intelligence *(intellect)*
power to understand comprehension, understanding *(comprehension)*
power-crazed dictatorial
power-hungry dictatorial
power-mad dictatorial
powerful assertive, cogent, consequential *(substantial)*, considerable, convincing, decisive, drastic, efficient, eloquent, forcible, important *(significant)*, incisive, indomitable, inexpugnable, influential, intense, intensive, irresistible, omnipotent, persuasive, potent, predominant, prevailing *(having superior force)*, prominent, sound, sovereign *(absolute)*, strong, trenchant, valid, vehement, virtual. SEE MAIN ENTRY
powerfully expressive eloquent
powerfulness dint, force *(strength)*, influence, main force, potential, sinew
powerless harmless, inactive, inadequate, ineffective, ineffectual, inept *(incompetent)*, insipid, insubstantial, languid, nonsubstantial *(not sturdy)*, null *(insignificant)*, null *(invalid)*, otiose, unable, untenable. SEE MAIN ENTRY
powerless group minority *(outnumbered group)*
powerlessness disability *(physical inability)*, fault *(weakness)*, impotence, impuissance, inability, inefficacy, insentience
powerpacked powerful
powers hierarchy *(persons in authority)*
powers that be authorities, authority *(power)*, bureaucracy
practicability feasibility, potential
practicable appropriate, beneficial, effective *(efficient)*, functional, justifiable, potential, practical, probable, suitable, viable. SEE MAIN ENTRY
practicableness feasibility
practical beneficial, constructive *(creative)*, effective *(efficient)*, efficient, functional, ministerial, politic, practicable, pragmatic, purposeful, realistic, viable, virtual. SEE MAIN ENTRY
practical attitude pragmatism
practical demonstration illustration
practical discernment common sense
practical joke hoax
practical knowledge common sense, experience *(background)*
practical management administration
practical wisdom experience *(background)*
practicality common sense, expedience, feasibility, pragmatism, utility *(usefulness)*, utilization
practicalness pragmatism
practice business *(occupation)*, calling, conduct, course, custom, dealings, deportment, discipline *(training)*, employ *(make use of)*, employment, exercise *(discharge a function)*, exercise *(use)*, expedient, experience *(background)*, habit, manner *(behavior)*, method, mode, operate, operation, perform *(adhere to)*, ply, position *(business status)*, prescription *(custom)*, procedure, profession *(vocation)*, protocol *(etiquette)*, pursue *(carry on)*, pursuit *(occupation)*, qualify *(meet standards)*, resort, rule *(guide)*, system, trade *(occupation)*, usage, use. SEE MAIN ENTRY
practice chicanery cheat, circumvent, deceive, defraud, delude, dupe, illude, profess *(pretend)*
practice deception deceive, mislead
practice economy retrench
practice exclusively specialize
practice extravagance dissipate *(expend foolishly)*
practice fraud cheat, mulct *(defraud)*
practice fraud upon defraud, delude
practice gaming gamble
practice of spying on others espionage
practice upon one's credulity delude
practiced cognizant, competent, convincing, deft, expert, facile, familiar *(informed)*, literate, proficient, qualified *(competent)*, resourceful, veteran. SEE MAIN ENTRY
practiced hand expert, specialist, veteran
practiced individual professional
practicing lawyer jurist
practicing plural marriage polygamous
practitioner addict, attorney, esquire, expert, professional, specialist. SEE MAIN ENTRY
practitioner of the law jurist
praebere furnish, provide *(supply)*
praeceps precipitate
praeceptum maxim, precept, regulation *(rule)*, rule *(legal dictate)*
praecidere abridge *(shorten)*
praecipere forestall, instruct *(direct)*
praecipitare precipitate *(hasten)*, precipitate *(throw down violently)*
praecipue particularly
praecipuus cardinal *(basic)*, cardinal *(outstanding)*, salient, special
praecurrentia precursory
praecursor precursor
praeda plunder
praedabundus predatory
praedari plunder, prey
praedatorius predatory
praedial proprietary
praedicare declare, proclaim, publish
praedicatio declaration, publication *(disclosure)*
praedicere predict
praedium liberum freehold
praeesse superintend
praefari preface
praefatio preface
praefectus official, superintendent
praefinire predetermine
praegravare encumber *(financially obligate)*
praeiudicare preconceive, prejudge
praeiudicata opinio preconception
praematurus premature
praemeditatio premeditation
praemium prize, recompense, remuneration
praemium proponere reward
praemonere forewarn
praenomen call *(title)*
praenuntius forerunner, harbinger, precursor
praeoccupatio preoccupation
praeoptare prefer
praepollens predominant
praepollere predominate *(command)*
praeponere prefer
praepositio preference *(priority)*
praesagire presage
praesagium misgiving
praesciens foreseeable
praescribere instruct *(direct)*, prescribe
praescriptum instruction *(direction)*, precept, rule *(legal dictate)*
praesens immediate *(at once)*, imminent, instantaneous, present *(attendant)*, present *(current)*
praesentia presence *(attendance)*
praesertim particularly
praeses guardian
praesidere preside
praesidium patronage *(power to appoint jobs)*, protection
praestantia eminence
praestantior superior *(excellent)*
praestare ascendant, evince, indorse
praestituere predetermine
praeterire ignore, overlook *(superintend)*
praetermissio omission
praetermittere omit
praetervehi pass *(advance)*
praetextum pretext
praetextus color *(deceptive appearance)*
praetor judge
praetorium headquarters
praevaricatio collusion
praevenire forestall
praevertere anticipate *(prognosticate)*

pragmatic constructive *(inferential),* effective *(efficient),* functional, realistic. SEE MAIN ENTRY
pragmatic sanction charter *(sanction)*
pragmatism expedience. SEE MAIN ENTRY
pragmatize justify
praise advocacy, belaud, doxology, estimation *(esteem),* honor *(outward respect),* honor, laudation, mention *(tribute),* recommend, recommendation, regard *(hold in esteem),* remembrance *(commemoration),* respect. SEE MAIN ENTRY
praised popular
praiseworthy exemplary, laudable, meritorious, moral, professional *(stellar)*
praiseworthy quality merit
praising favorable *(expressing approval)*
prankishness mischief
prate bombast, prattle
prattle jargon *(unintelligible language),* prattle, speech. SEE MAIN ENTRY
prattling loquacious
prava rerum administratio maladministration
pravitas distortion
pravus immoral, sinister
praxis course, manner *(behavior)*
pray apply *(request),* importune, request. SEE MAIN ENTRY
pray for petition
prayer call *(appeal),* entreaty, petition, request. SEE MAIN ENTRY
pre-trial inquiries interrogatories
preach address *(talk to),* declaim, educate, inculcate, recite
preaching instruction *(teaching),* propaganda
preamble overture, preface *(noun),* preface *(verb),* prelude, threshold *(commencement).* SEE MAIN ENTRY
preannounce anticipate *(prognosticate),* predict, prognosticate
preannouncement prognosis
preapprehend preconceive
preapprehension bias, inequity, preconception, predetermination, predisposition
prearrange devise *(invent),* frame *(prearrange),* maneuver, plan, plot, predetermine. SEE MAIN ENTRY
prearrange fraudulently frame *(charge falsely),* frame *(prearrange)*
prearranged aforethought, deliberate, express, intentional, premeditated, stated
prearrangement premeditation
precari pray
precarious aleatory *(perilous),* debatable, insecure, noxious, uncertain *(questionable),* unreliable, unsound *(not strong),* untrustworthy, volatile, vulnerable. SEE MAIN ENTRY
precariousness danger, doubt *(indecision),* hazard, jeopardy, peril, predicament, risk
precatio prayer
precatory SEE MAIN ENTRY
precaution caution, discretion *(quality of being discreet),* panoply, preparation, prudence, safeguard. SEE MAIN ENTRY
precautional solid *(sound)*
precautionary circumspect, noncommittal, preparatory, preventive, provident *(showing foresight),* prudent, solid *(sound)*
precautious careful, circumspect, discreet, noncommittal, provident *(showing foresight),* prudent, solid *(sound),* vigilant
precede antecede, preface. SEE MAIN ENTRY
precedence advantage, importance, magnitude, preference *(priority),* prestige, priority, reputation, significance, supremacy. SEE MAIN ENTRY
precedent aforesaid, antecedent, authority *(documentation),* before mentioned, code, criterion, finding, forerunner, holding *(ruling of a court),* judgment *(formal court decree),* last *(preceding),* law, mode, model, pattern, precursor, precursory, preparatory, prescription *(custom),* previous, prior, prototype, standard, stare decisis. SEE MAIN ENTRY
precedential exemplary
preceding aforesaid, antecedent, before mentioned, former, old, precursory, preferred *(given priority),* preliminary, preparatory, previous, prior, said. SEE MAIN ENTRY
preceding instance precedent
precept act *(enactment),* authority *(documentation),* belief *(something believed),* brevet, canon, charge *(command),* citation *(charge),* code, codification, constitution, dictate, direction *(order),* directive, doctrine, dogma, edict, guidance, holding *(ruling of a court),* injunction, instruction *(direction),* law, mandate, maxim, order *(judicial directive),* precedent, prescription *(directive),* principle *(axiom),* recommendation, regulation *(rule),* rubric *(authoritative rule),* rule *(legal dictate),* technicality, writ. SEE MAIN ENTRY
preceptive decretal, disciplinary *(educational),* informative, prescriptive
preceptor pedagogue
preceptoral disciplinary *(educational)*
precepts code, platform
precepts on securities blue sky law
preces entreaty, imprecation, request
precinct bailiwick, circuit, close *(enclosed area),* department, district, province, region, territory
precincts confines, vicinity
preciosity bombast
precious inestimable, invaluable, premium, priceless, rare, sterling, valuable. SEE MAIN ENTRY
preciousness bombast
precipitance dispatch *(promptness),* haste, inconsideration
precipitancy dispatch *(promptness),* haste, inconsideration
precipitant careless, impulsive *(rash),* precipitate
precipitate careless, cause, evoke, expedite, hasten, heedless, impel, imprudent, impulsive *(rash),* induce, injudicious, inspire, launch *(project),* originate, premature, reckless, thoughtless, unexpected. SEE MAIN ENTRY
precipitation congealment, dispatch *(promptness),* haste
precipitous impulsive *(rash),* precipitate
precipitousness dispatch *(promptness),* haste
précis abridgment *(condensation)*
precis abstract, capsule, compendium, condense
precise absolute *(conclusive),* accurate, actual, appropriate, brief, certain *(particular),* certain *(specific),* circumspect, close *(rigorous),* coherent *(clear),* conscientious, detailed, distinct *(clear),* draconian, exact, explicit, express, factual, faithful *(true to fact),* laconic, literal, meticulous, narrow, painstaking, particular *(exacting),* positive *(incontestable),* prompt, proper, punctilious, punctual, rigid, sententious, specific, strict, stringent, subtle *(refined),* systematic, true *(authentic),* unambiguous, verbatim. SEE MAIN ENTRY
precise amount face amount
precise moment point *(period of time)*
precisely faithfully
precisely bounded definite
precisely formulated specific
preciseness particularity, rigor
precisian precise
precision particularity, regularity, rigor, truth, veracity
precision tool appliance
preclude bar *(exclude),* bar *(hinder),* block, censor, clog, condemn *(ban),* constrain *(restrain),* debar, disable, disqualify, eliminate *(exclude),* enjoin, estop, exclude, fight *(counteract),* forbid, forestall, halt, hamper, impede, interdict, interfere, obstruct, occlude, preempt, prevent, prohibit, reject, restrict, stay *(halt),* stop, supersede, thwart, withstand. SEE MAIN ENTRY
precluded barred
precluding unless
preclusion bar *(obstruction),* blockade *(limitation),* check *(bar),* constraint *(restriction),* damper *(stopper),* deterrence, deterrent, disqualification *(rejection),* embargo, estoppel, exception *(exclusion),* exclusion, hindrance, impasse, obstacle, obstruction, ostracism, preemption, prohibition. SEE MAIN ENTRY
preclusion by act estoppel
preclusion by conduct estoppel
preclusion of work lockout
preclusive exclusive *(limited),* preventive, prohibitive *(restrictive),* restrictive
precognition SEE MAIN ENTRY
precognitive prophetic
precognize anticipate *(prognosticate),* preconceive
preconceive anticipate *(expect),* forejudge, opine, predetermine, prejudge, preordain, presume, presuppose. SEE MAIN ENTRY
preconceived aforethought, prejudicial
preconceived idea bias, foregone conclusion, inequity, preconception, prejudice *(preconception)*
preconceived liking preference *(choice)*
preconceived notion inequity, prejudice *(preconception)*
preconception bias, expectation, inequity, intolerance, opinion *(belief),* partiality, predetermination, predisposition, prejudice *(preconception).* SEE MAIN ENTRY
preconceptual prejudicial
preconcert orchestrate, plan, plot, prearrange, program
preconclude forejudge, preconceive, predetermine, prejudge, preordain, presuppose
preconclusion foregone conclusion, preconception, predetermination, predisposition
precondemn prejudge
precondition necessity, need *(requirement),* prerequisite, requirement, sine qua non. SEE MAIN ENTRY
preconsider predetermine, prejudge, preordain
preconsideration forethought, predisposition, premeditation
preconsidered aforethought, deliberate, intentional, premeditated
precontrive plan, prearrange

precontrived premeditated
precurse portend
precursive aforesaid, antecedent, before mentioned, ominous, oracular, precursory, preliminary, previous, prophetic
precursor ancestor, ascendant, caution *(warning)*, forerunner, harbinger, indicator, parents, pioneer, precedent, predecessor, primogenitor, progenitor. SEE MAIN ENTRY
precursory aforesaid, antecedent, before mentioned, elementary, incipient, last *(preceding)*, ominous, oracular, original *(initial)*, preliminary, preparatory, previous, prior. SEE MAIN ENTRY
predaceous larcenous
predacious predatory, rapacious
predate antecede, antedate
predative predatory
predatory larcenous, rapacious. SEE MAIN ENTRY
predatory incursion foray
predecessor ancestor, ascendant, forerunner, parents, pioneer, precedent, precursor, primogenitor, progenitor. SEE MAIN ENTRY
predecessors ancestry
predecide forejudge, preconceive, predetermine, prejudge, preordain, presuppose
predecision foregone conclusion, predetermination, predisposition
predecisive prejudicial
predeliberate preordain
predeliberated aforethought, deliberate, premeditated
predeliberation forethought, goal, plan, predetermination, premeditation
predesign contrive, frame *(prearrange)*, plan, prearrange, scheme
predesigned deliberate, intentional, premeditated
predesigned conclusion foregone conclusion
predestinate prearrange, predetermine
predestination predetermination
predestine prearrange, predetermine, preordain
predestined forthcoming, future, inevitable
predeterminated premeditated
predetermination animus, bias, design *(intent)*, foregone conclusion, forethought, goal, intent, preconception, predisposition, prejudice *(preconception)*, premeditation. SEE MAIN ENTRY
predetermine anticipate *(prognosticate)*, devise *(invent)*, forejudge, frame *(prearrange)*, necessitate, orchestrate, plan, prearrange, preconceive, prejudge, prejudice *(influence)*, preordain, presuppose, program, scheme
predetermined aforethought, deliberate, express, fixed *(settled)*, intentional, premeditated, stated
predetermined conclusion foregone conclusion
predetermined course of events predetermination
predevised premeditated
predicament case *(set of circumstances)*, complication, condition *(state)*, confusion *(ambiguity)*, deadlock, dilemma, emergency, entanglement *(involvement)*, imbroglio, impasse, occurrence, peril, pitfall, plight, position *(situation)*, posture *(situation)*, problem, quagmire, quandary, situation, state *(condition)*. SEE MAIN ENTRY
predicate ascribe, assume *(suppose)*, attribute, avow, cite *(state)*, claim *(maintain)*, contend *(maintain)*, declare, express, pose *(propound)*, posit, postulate, propound, surmise. SEE MAIN ENTRY
predication affirmance *(authentication)*, affirmation, assertion, claim *(assertion)*, pronouncement
predict anticipate *(prognosticate)*, calculate, caution, expect *(consider probable)*, forewarn, portend, preconceive, presage, prognosticate, promise *(raise expectations)*. SEE MAIN ENTRY
predictable foreseeable, regular *(conventional)*
predicted foreseeable, forseen, forthcoming, future, imminent
predicting omniscient, oracular
prediction premonition, prognosis, prospect *(outlook)*
prediction of danger monition *(warning)*
prediction of misfortune misgiving
predictive oracular, prophetic, provident *(showing foresight)*
predictory prophetic
predilection affinity *(regard)*, animus, bias, character *(personal quality)*, characteristic, choice *(decision)*, compulsion *(obsession)*, conatus, conviction *(persuasion)*, desire, disposition *(inclination)*, favor *(partiality)*, foregone conclusion, inclination, inequity, partiality, penchant, position *(point of view)*, predisposition, preference *(choice)*, prejudice *(preconception)*, presumption, proclivity, propensity, standpoint, vote. SEE MAIN ENTRY
predispose anticipate *(expect)*, bait *(lure)*, convince, preconceive, predetermine, prejudice *(influence)*, prevail upon, slant
predispose to conduce
predisposed inclined, parochial, partial *(biased)*, partisan, prone, ready *(willing)*, susceptible *(unresistent)*
predisposition affection, animus, bias, conatus, conviction *(persuasion)*, disposition *(inclination)*, foregone conclusion, habit, inclination, instinct, partiality, penchant, personality, position *(point of view)*, predilection, prejudice *(preconception)*, presumption, proclivity, propensity, tendency. SEE MAIN ENTRY
predispositional prejudicial
predominance advantage, dominance, force *(strength)*, hegemony, influence, majority *(greater part)*, occupation *(possession)*, patronage *(power to appoint jobs)*, power, precedence, preponderance, prestige, puissance, supremacy. SEE MAIN ENTRY
predominancy clout, dominance, influence, occupation *(possession)*, predominance, primacy, supremacy
predominant cardinal *(outstanding)*, causative, compelling, considerable, customary, dominant, forcible, influential, leading *(ranking first)*, omnipotent, potent, prevailing *(current)*, prevailing *(having superior force)*, prevalent, primary, prime *(most valuable)*, principal, rife, salient, sovereign *(absolute)*, stellar. SEE MAIN ENTRY
predominant part bulk, generality *(bulk)*, majority *(greater part)*
predominantly the same in strict conformity
predominate beat *(defeat)*, dominate, outbalance, outweigh, prevail *(be in force)*, prevail *(triumph)*, rule *(govern)*, surpass, transcend. SEE MAIN ENTRY
predominating dominant, master, prevailing *(having superior force)*
predominating influence hegemony
predomination predominance, preponderance, prestige, primacy, supremacy
predominent prominent, remarkable
preeminence advantage, character *(reputation)*, eminence, precedence, preference *(priority)*, preponderance, prestige, primacy, priority, reputation, significance, supremacy
preeminent absolute *(ideal)*, best, cardinal *(outstanding)*, compelling, conspicuous, dominant, famous, important *(significant)*, influential, leading *(ranking first)*, master, meritorious, notable, noteworthy, outstanding *(prominent)*, paramount, primary, prime *(most valuable)*, principal, professional *(stellar)*, prominent, renowned. SEE MAIN ENTRY
preeminently particularly
preeminently bad arrant *(onerous)*
preempt attach *(seize)*, distrain, preclude, sequester *(seize property)*. SEE MAIN ENTRY
preemption taking. SEE MAIN ENTRY
preengagement reservation *(engagement)*
preestablish contrive, prearrange, predetermine, preordain, program
preestimate preconception, prejudge, presuppose
preexamine canvass
preexist precede
preexistent aforesaid, antecedent, before mentioned, former, preexisting, previous, prior
preexisting old, preliminary. SEE MAIN ENTRY
prefabrication building *(business of assembling)*
preface caption, forerunner, overture, preamble, prelude. SEE MAIN ENTRY
prefatorial previous
prefatory antecedent, before mentioned, elementary, inchoate, incipient, initial, last *(preceding)*, precursory, preliminary, preparatory, previous, prior
prefatory note preamble, preface
prefer choose, discriminate *(treat differently)*, favor, proffer, promote *(advance)*, relish, screen *(select)*, select. SEE MAIN ENTRY
prefer a claim impeach, litigate, prosecute *(charge)*, sue
prefer a petition call *(appeal to)*, pray
prefer a request call *(appeal to)*, plead *(implore)*, pray
prefer a request to petition
prefer an appeal call *(appeal to)*
prefer charges accuse, arraign, book, complain *(charge)*, impeach, incriminate, indict, involve *(implicate)*, lodge *(bring a complaint)*, present *(prefer charges)*, prosecute *(charge)*
preferability choice *(decision)*
preferable preferred *(favored)*, select, superior *(excellent)*. SEE MAIN ENTRY
preference advantage, bias, choice *(decision)*, conatus, discrimination *(bigotry)*, disposition *(inclination)*, election *(choice)*, favor *(partiality)*, favoritism, inclination, inequity, option *(choice)*, partiality, patronage *(power to appoint jobs)*, penchant, poll *(casting of votes)*, position *(point of view)*, precedence, predilection, predisposition, prejudice *(preconception)*, prerogative, primary, priority, propensity, referendum,

selection *(choice)*, volition, vote, will *(desire)*. SEE MAIN ENTRY
preferential adoptive, preferred *(favored)*. SEE MAIN ENTRY
preferential treatment favor *(partiality)*, inequity, nepotism, partiality
preferment behalf, preference *(priority)*, progress, promotion *(advancement)*
preferment of charges complaint
preferred popular, preferable, preferential, select, superior *(excellent)*. SEE MAIN ENTRY
preferred provider organization SEE MAIN ENTRY
preferred standing preference *(priority)*. SEE MAIN ENTRY
preferring of charges accusation
preferror of charges complainant
prefigurate portend, presage, presuppose
prefiguration caution *(warning)*, caveat, prognosis
prefigurative prophetic
prefigure forewarn, portend, presage, presuppose
prefigurement forerunner, prognosis
pregnability danger
pregnable disabled *(made incapable)*, helpless *(defenseless)*, indefensible, open *(accessible)*, penetrable, powerless, untenable, vulnerable
pregnant eloquent, productive, replete, strategic
prehension adhesion *(affixing)*, arrest, condemnation *(seizure)*, disseisin, understanding *(comprehension)*
preindicate portend, predict, presage
preindication symptom
preindicative prophetic
preinstruct initiate
prejudge forejudge, opine, preconceive, predetermine, prejudice *(influence)*, preordain, presume, presuppose. SEE MAIN ENTRY
prejudged conclusion foregone conclusion
prejudgment bias, foregone conclusion, inequity, intolerance, partiality, preconception, predetermination, predilection, prejudice *(preconception)*
prejudicate forejudge, prejudge
prejudication bias, preconception
prejudice bias, damage, detriment, disadvantage *(noun)*, disadvantage *(verb)*, discrimination *(bigotry)*, drawback, exclusion, favor *(partiality)*, favoritism, foregone conclusion, hatred, inclination, inequality, inequity, influence, injury, injustice, intolerance, ostracism, partiality, penchant, preconception, predetermination, predilection, predisposition, preference *(choice)*, proclivity, segregation *(isolation by races)*, slant, tendency. SEE MAIN ENTRY
prejudiced disadvantaged, ex parte, exclusive *(limited)*, illiberal, inequitable, interested, one-sided, parochial, partial *(biased)*, subjective, unequal *(unjust)*, unfair, unjust
prejudiced view foregone conclusion, preconception
prejudicial adverse *(negative)*, detrimental, disadvantageous, unfavorable. SEE MAIN ENTRY
prejudicial delay laches
prelect declaim, discourse, inculcate, recite
prelection discourse, harangue, peroration
preliminaries preparation
preliminary antecedent, before mentioned, inchoate, last *(preceding)*, original *(initial)*, overture, precursory, preparatory, previous, prior. SEE MAIN ENTRY
preliminary comment preface
preliminary condition need *(requirement)*, prerequisite
preliminary drawing design *(construction plan)*
preliminary negotiation overture
preliminary part prelude
preliminary statement preface
preliminary step preparation
prelude overture, preamble, preface *(noun)*, preface *(verb)*, threshold *(commencement)*. SEE MAIN ENTRY
preludial last *(preceding)*, precursory, preliminary, preparatory, prior
preluding aforesaid
preludious last *(preceding)*, precursory
prelusion preamble, preface, prelude
prelusive antecedent, last *(preceding)*, original *(initial)*, precursory, preliminary, preparatory, previous, prior
prelusory aforesaid, antecedent, last *(preceding)*, original *(initial)*, precursory, preliminary, preparatory, previous
premature undue *(not owing)*. SEE MAIN ENTRY
premeditate intend, plan, plot, ponder, prearrange, predetermine, scheme
premeditated aforethought, deliberate, express, intentional, willful. SEE MAIN ENTRY
premeditation conference, consideration *(contemplation)*, deliberation, forethought, goal, predetermination. SEE MAIN ENTRY
premeditative circumspect
premier initial
premise assume *(suppose)*, assumption *(supposition)*, basis, foundation *(basis)*, generalization, ground, inference, postulate *(noun)*, postulate *(verb)*, presumption, proposition, supposition, thesis. SEE MAIN ENTRY
premised apparent *(presumptive)*
premises apartment, area *(province)*, building *(structure)*, part *(place)*, property *(land)*, structure *(edifice)*. SEE MAIN ENTRY
premium bonus, bounty, gratuity *(present)*, payment *(remittance)*, perquisite, price, prize, profit, reward. SEE MAIN ENTRY
premium bond coupon
premium certificate coupon
premium for the use of money interest *(profit)*
premonish admonish *(warn)*, anticipate *(prognosticate)*, expostulate, forewarn, portend, predict, prognosticate
premonishment notice *(warning)*, premonition
premonition caveat, misgiving, prognosis. SEE MAIN ENTRY
premonitive portentous *(ominous)*
premonitor indication, symptom
premonitory ominous, portentous *(ominous)*, prophetic
premonitory sign harbinger, indication, symptom
premonstrate portend, predict, presage, prognosticate
premunition precaution, preparation
prenomen call *(title)*
prenotice prognosis
prenotification notice *(warning)*, premonition, tip *(clue)*
prenotify caution
prenotion bias, foregone conclusion, inequity, precognition, preconception, predetermination
prentice neophyte
preoccupation compulsion *(obsession)*, contemplation, interest *(concern)*, obsession. SEE MAIN ENTRY
preoccupied oblivious
preoccupy immerse *(engross)*, obsess, occupy *(engage)*, preempt
preordain predetermine. SEE MAIN ENTRY
preordained inevitable
preorder prearrange
preordination foregone conclusion
preparation building *(business of assembling)*, composition *(makeup)*, creation, direction *(guidance)*, discipline *(training)*, edification, education, experience *(background)*, instruction *(teaching)*, manufacture, performance *(workmanship)*, plan, precursor, prelude, provision *(act of supplying)*, qualification *(fitness)*. SEE MAIN ENTRY
preparation of laws legislation *(lawmaking)*
preparative preliminary, preparatory
preparatory precursory, preliminary, previous, prior. SEE MAIN ENTRY
prepare arrange *(plan)*, charge *(instruct on the law)*, compile, conceive *(invent)*, contrive, devise *(invent)*, discipline *(train)*, educate, establish *(launch)*, fix *(arrange)*, forewarn, frame *(construct)*, induct, initiate, instill, instruct *(teach)*, make, nurture, originate, plan, plot, practice *(train by repetition)*, prearrange, produce *(manufacture)*, provide *(arrange for)*, qualify *(meet standards)*, scheme
prepare a complaint address *(petition)*
prepare a formal request address *(petition)*
prepare a petition address *(petition)*
prepare an estimate evaluate
prepare for anticipate *(expect)*, expect *(anticipate)*, forestall
prepare for crops cultivate
prepare for publication edit
prepare for the worst caution
prepare something specious fake
prepare the ground precede
prepared aforethought, alert *(vigilant)*, circumspect, competent, defensible, discreet, expert, familiar *(informed)*, fit, inclined, informed *(educated)*, practiced, provident *(showing foresight)*, prudent, resourceful, ripe, tactical
prepared announcement statement
prepared for sale commercial
prepared speech peroration
prepared text statement
preparedness diligence *(care)*, maturity, prudence, qualification *(fitness)*
preparer precursor
preparing prospective
prepay SEE MAIN ENTRY
prepense aforethought, deliberate
prepollence dominance, hegemony, influence, power, predominance, preponderance
prepollency dominance, influence, power, predominance, preponderance
prepollent influential, paramount, sovereign *(absolute)*
preponderance dominance, generality *(bulk)*, majority *(greater part)*, plurality. SEE MAIN ENTRY
preponderancy generality *(bulk)*, plurality, preponderance

preponderant cardinal *(basic)*, cardinal *(outstanding)*, compelling, dominant, influential, predominant, prevailing *(having superior force)*, prevalent, prime *(most valuable)*
preponderate beat *(defeat)*, dominate, outbalance, outweigh, predominate *(outnumber)*, prevail *(be in force)*, prevail *(triumph)*
preponderating prevailing *(having superior force)*
preponderation generality *(bulk)*, majority *(greater part)*, preponderance
prepositional preparatory
prepositive before mentioned
prepossess forejudge, preconceive, slant
prepossess unfavorably prejudice *(influence)*
prepossessed interested, one-sided, parochial, partial *(biased)*, prejudicial, unequal *(unjust)*, unjust
prepossessing attractive, palatable, sapid
prepossession compulsion *(obsession)*, foregone conclusion, inequity, partiality, preconception, predetermination, predilection, predisposition, prejudice *(preconception)*, preoccupation
preposterous excessive, exorbitant, impossible, incredible, inept *(inappropriate)*, inordinate, irrational, ludicrous, outrageous, prohibitive *(costly)*, unconscionable, unreasonable, unseemly. SEE MAIN ENTRY
prepotency dint, dominance, influence, predominance
prepotent dominant, forcible, influential, master, omnipotent, paramount, potent, sovereign *(absolute)*
prequisiteness need *(requirement)*
prerequirement condition *(contingent provision)*, necessary, necessity, need *(requirement)*
prerequisite attornment, compulsory, condition *(contingent provision)*, important *(urgent)*, integral, mandatory, necessary *(required)*, necessary, necessity, obligatory, qualified *(conditioned)*, requirement, requisite, sine qua non. SEE MAIN ENTRY
preresolution predetermination, premeditation
preresolve prearrange, predetermine, preordain
preresolved aforethought, premeditated
prerogative authority *(right)*, birthright, capacity *(authority)*, droit, enjoyment *(use)*, franchise *(license)*, franchise *(right to vote)*, freedom, impunity, liberty, license, option *(contractual provision)*, prescription *(claim of title)*, privilege, right *(entitlement)*, suffrage, title *(right)*. SEE MAIN ENTRY
presage anticipate *(prognosticate)*, caution *(warning)*, forerunner, forewarn, harbinger, herald, indicant, indicate, indication, misgiving, portend, precognition, precursor, predict, premonition, prognosis, prognosticate, promise *(raise expectations)*, threat, threaten, warning. SEE MAIN ENTRY
presaged forseen
presageful inauspicious, ominous, portentous *(ominous)*, prophetic, sinister. SEE MAIN ENTRY
presagement prognosis
presaging ominous, oracular, portentous *(ominous)*, prophetic
presaging good fortune auspicious
prescience precognition
prescient omniscient, prophetic, vigilant
prescribe administer *(conduct)*, admonish *(advise)*, advise, advocate, allocate, assign *(designate)*, authorize, call *(demand)*, caution, command, constitute *(establish)*, counsel, decree, define, detail *(assign)*, dictate, direct *(order)*, drug, enact, govern, impose *(enforce)*, instruct *(direct)*, order, pass *(approve)*, recommend, require *(compel)*, rule *(govern)*, urge. SEE MAIN ENTRY
prescribe a task instruct *(direct)*
prescribe by law constitute *(establish)*
prescribe laws legislate
prescribe punishment condemn *(punish)*, convict, determine, pronounce *(pass judgment)*, sentence
prescribe the law charge *(instruct on the law)*
prescribed arrested *(checked)*, boiler plate, certain *(specific)*, fixed *(settled)*, juridical, legal, licit, limited, mandatory, necessary *(required)*, prescriptive, qualified *(conditioned)*, stated, traditional
prescribed by law lawful, legal
prescribed code of conduct decorum
prescribed form constant, criterion, custom, formality, law, matter of course, policy *(plan of action)*, practice *(procedure)*
prescribed method of action proceeding
prescribed mode of action proceeding
prescribed procedure ceremony
prescribed punishment conviction *(finding of guilt)*, fine, penalty, sentence
prescribed system course
prescribed usage practice *(procedure)*
prescriber arbiter
prescript act *(enactment)*, bylaw, canon, citation *(charge)*, code, dictate, direction *(order)*, directive, fiat, injunction, mandate, measure, order *(judicial directive)*, ordinance, precept, prescription *(directive)*, regulation *(rule)*, requirement
prescription assignment *(designation)*, brevet, bylaw, canon, citation *(charge)*, cloud *(incumbrance)*, code, codification, condition *(contingent provision)*, constitution, dictate, direction *(order)*, directive, drug, fiat, guidance, law, mandate, measure, order *(judicial directive)*, practice *(custom)*, recommendation, regulation *(rule)*, requirement, rubric *(authoritative rule)*, rule *(legal dictate)*, title *(right)*, usage. SEE MAIN ENTRY
prescriptive compulsory, decretal, formal, legislative, orthodox, rightful, traditional, unalienable. SEE MAIN ENTRY
prescriptive right droit
prescriptivism SEE MAIN ENTRY
prescripts legislation *(enactments)*
preselect reserve
presence attendance, behavior, complexion, conduct, demeanor, deportment, manner *(behavior)*, phenomenon *(manifestation)*, posture *(attitude)*, specter, vision *(dream)*. SEE MAIN ENTRY
presence in court appearance *(coming into court)*
presence of mind common sense, composure, discretion *(quality of being discreet)*, prudence
present actual, adduce, allege, bear *(adduce)*, benefit *(conferment)*, bestow, confer *(give)*, contribute *(supply)*, contribution *(donation)*, convey *(transfer)*, current, de facto, dedicate, disclose, display, dole, donation, endow, endowment, endue, exhibit, expose, exposit, express, extant, extend *(offer)*, fund, furnish, gift *(present)*, give *(grant)*, grant, grant *(transfer formally)*, hold out *(deliberate on an offer)*, impart, initiate, instruct *(teach)*, introduce, largess *(gift)*, leave *(give)*, manifest, mete, offer *(tender)*, pass *(determine)*, pay, perquisite, phrase, plead *(allege in a legal action)*, portray, pose *(propound)*, post, produce *(offer to view)*, proffer, pronounce *(speak)*, propose, propound, provide *(supply)*, recite, remark, remit *(submit for consideration)*, render *(deliver)*, replenish, serve *(deliver a legal instrument)*, submit *(give)*, supply, tender, unveil. SEE MAIN ENTRY
present a case show cause
present an answer appear *(attend court proceedings)*
present an opportunity extend *(offer)*
present an ultimatum call *(demand)*, charge *(assess)*
present argument show cause
present as proof cite *(state)*
present as worthy recommend
present cause show cause
present day contemporary, current
present facts communicate
present falsely pretend
present for acceptance offer *(tender)*
present for acceptance or rejection extend *(offer)*
present for consideration exhibit
present for payment tender
present formally introduce
present information inform *(notify)*
present itself arise *(appear)*, occur *(come to mind)*
present itself to the mind occur *(come to mind)*
present money fund
present money for safekeeping deposit *(submit to a bank)*
present one's claim call *(demand)*, charge *(assess)*, demand
present oneself appear *(attend court proceedings)*, comport *(behave)*, demean *(deport oneself)*, report *(present oneself)*
present reason show cause
present reasons against argue
present reasons for argue
present reasons for and against debate
present the appearance appear *(seem to be)*, demean *(deport oneself)*
present the meaning of expound
present to the court for acceptance introduce
present to the view appear *(materialize)*
present to view denude, disinter, exhibit
present varied opinions debate, discuss
present with bias prejudice *(influence)*
present-day present *(current)*
present-time present *(current)*
presentability admissibility
presentable admissible, passable
presentably fairly *(moderately)*
presentation account *(report)*, application, benefit *(conferment)*, bid, cession, claim *(assertion)*, clarification, concession *(authorization)*, contribution *(donation)*, declaration, dedication, disclosure *(something disclosed)*, dispensation *(act of dispensing)*, donation, endowment, exhibit, experience *(encounter)*, expression *(manifestation)*, gift *(present)*, gratuity *(present)*, inheritance, installation, introduction,

largess *(gift)*, notice *(announcement)*, overture, presence *(poise)*, profession *(declaration)*, program, proposal *(suggestion)*, proposition, publicity, representation *(statement)*, resolution *(formal statement)*, reward, role, style
presentation of arguments and evidence hearing
presentation of basics opening statement
presentation of data opening statement
presentation of essentials opening statement
presentation of evidence corroboration
presentation of testimony hearing
presentation of the documentation opening statement
presentation of the evidence opening statement
presentation of the facts opening statement
presentation to the public publication *(disclosure)*
presentation to view disclosure *(act of disclosing)*
presented alleged
presenter contributor *(giver)*, donor, grantor
presentient ominous, portentous *(ominous)*, prophetic
presentiment apprehension *(fear)*, expectation, fear, foregone conclusion, inequity, misgiving, precognition, preconception, premonition
presenting donative
presenting favorable conditions propitious
presenting few difficulties convenient
presenting information informatory
presently in due course, instantly
presentment charge *(accusation)*, claim *(legal demand)*, dedication, dispensation *(act of dispensing)*, endowment, expression *(manifestation)*, indictment, largess *(gift)*. SEE MAIN ENTRY
preservation bulwark, conservation, continuation *(prolongation)*, custody *(supervision)*, defense, ecology, maintenance *(support of spouse)*, panoply, protection, safekeeping, security *(safety)*, shelter *(protection)*, support *(assistance)*, ward. SEE MAIN ENTRY
preservation from harm custody *(supervision)*
preservation from injury custody *(supervision)*
preservation of the same conditions status quo
preservative preventive, prophylactic, protective
preserve adhere *(maintain loyalty)*, conserve, continue *(prolong)*, ensconce, fund, harbor, hoard, hold *(possess)*, keep *(shelter)*, maintain *(sustain)*, perpetuate, prolong, protect, protection, record, rescue, reserve, retain *(keep in possession)*, save *(conserve)*, sustain *(prolong)*, uphold. SEE MAIN ENTRY
preserve a memory remember
preserve permanently as a public record file *(place among official records)*
preserve public order police
preserve public tranquility police
preserved intact, lasting, permanent, safe
preserver guardian
preserving conservation
presettle prepay
preshow forewarn, portend, presage
preside direct *(supervise)*, manage, officiate, overlook *(superintend)*. SEE MAIN ENTRY
preside over administer *(conduct)*, conduct, control *(regulate)*, direct *(supervise)*, dominate, govern, handle *(manage)*, hear *(give a legal hearing)*, manage, operate, regulate *(manage)*, render *(administer)*, rule *(govern)*
presidency management *(directorate)*
president chief, key man
presider chairman
presiding executive
presiding officer chairman, director
presidium board, management *(directorate)*
presignify caution, portend, predict, presage, prognosticate
press attach *(seize)*, bait *(lure)*, call *(appeal to)*, call *(demand)*, claim *(demand)*, coax, coerce, compel, constrain *(compel)*, constrict *(compress)*, demand, desire, duress, enforce, exact, exhort, exigency, force *(coerce)*, hasten, impact, impede, importune, impose *(enforce)*, incite, inculcate, insist, jostle *(bump into)*, lobby, motivate, plead *(implore)*, pray, pressure *(noun)*, pressure *(verb)*, prompt, solicit, spirit, urge, weigh. SEE MAIN ENTRY
press a claim dun, sue
press advice on charge *(instruct on the law)*
press agentry publicity
press back repress
press by entreaty importune
press down depress
press earnestly insist
press in embed, inject
press in court litigate
press into service resort
press notice publicity, story *(narrative)*
press on impel, proceed *(go forward)*, progress
press onward continue *(persevere)*, endure *(last)*, keep *(continue)*, progress
press out distill
press together constrict *(compress)*, impact
pressed by duty bound
pressed into smaller compass compact *(dense)*
pressed together cohesive *(compact)*, compact *(dense)*, solid *(compact)*
pressing compelling, compulsory, critical *(crucial)*, crucial, essential *(required)*, exigent, grave *(important)*, imperative, important *(urgent)*, indispensable, insistent, major, mandatory, obligatory, onerous, operose, peremptory *(imperative)*, relentless, requisite, serious *(grave)*, urgent, vital. SEE MAIN ENTRY
pressing concern requirement
pressing necessity emergency, exigency
pressing need emergency, prerequisite
pressing requirement market *(demand)*
pressure aggravation *(annoyance)*, bribery, cajole, coerce, coercion, compel, compulsion *(coercion)*, constrain *(compel)*, constraint *(restriction)*, dint, duress, encumbrance, enforcement, exigency, force *(compulsion)*, force *(strength)*, hasten, impetus, impulse, inducement, influence, instigation, leverage, lobby, main force, persuasion, power, predicament, provocation, requirement, stress *(strain)*, weight *(burden)*. SEE MAIN ENTRY
pressure group faction, lobby, special interest
prestige advantage, character *(reputation)*, clout, credit *(recognition)*, distinction *(reputation)*, eminence, importance, influence, power, precedence, primacy, reputation, respect, status. SEE MAIN ENTRY
prestigious outstanding *(prominent)*
prestigitation SEE MAIN ENTRY
presumable apparent *(presumptive)*, believable, circumstantial, colorable *(plausible)*, constructive *(inferential)*, ostensible, plausible, presumptive, probable
presumably prima facie *(self-evident)*, reputedly
presume assume *(suppose)*, deem, expect *(consider probable)*, forejudge, guess, infer, intend, opine, postulate, preconceive, predetermine, prejudge, presuppose, prognosticate, read, surmise, suspect *(think)*, trust. SEE MAIN ENTRY
presume on accroach
presumed assumed *(inferred)*, constructive *(inferential)*, deductible *(provable)*, forseen, presumptive, putative, theoretical
presumed wrongdoer suspect
presuming obtrusive, presumptuous
presumption assumption *(supposition)*, concept, condition *(contingent provision)*, conjecture, disrespect, expectation, generalization, inequity, opinion *(belief)*, position *(point of view)*, preconception, predetermination, probability, prognosis, prospect *(outlook)*, rationale, speculation *(conjecture)*, supposition. SEE MAIN ENTRY
presumption of innocense SEE MAIN ENTRY
presumptive circumstantial, colorable *(plausible)*, deductible *(provable)*, probable, putative, speculative, theoretical. SEE MAIN ENTRY
presumptuous brazen, impertinent *(insolent)*, insolent, obtrusive, orgulous, orotund, proud *(conceited)*, supercilious. SEE MAIN ENTRY
presumptuousness contumely, disrespect, temerity
presupposal foregone conclusion, inference, preconception, predetermination
presuppose assume *(suppose)*, forejudge, guess, opine, postulate, preconceive, predetermine, prejudge, presume, surmise, suspect *(think)*. SEE MAIN ENTRY
presupposed assumed *(inferred)*, presumptive
presupposition assumption *(supposition)*, condition *(contingent provision)*, conjecture, conviction *(persuasion)*, foregone conclusion, generalization, idea, inference, opinion *(belief)*, preconception, predetermination, presumption, prolepsis, theory
presurmise conjecture, expectation, foregone conclusion, forejudge, preconceive, preconception, predetermination, predetermine, prejudge, premonition, presume, presuppose
pretend claim *(demand)*, cloak, copy, evade *(deceive)*, fabricate *(make up)*, fake, false *(not genuine)*, feign, invent *(falsify)*, lie *(falsify)*, misrepresent, mock *(imitate)*, palter, prevaricate, purport, simulate, specious, spurious. SEE MAIN ENTRY
pretend not to see ignore
pretend to be assume *(simulate)*, impersonate, pose *(impersonate)*

pretended artificial, assumed *(feigned)*, deceptive, delusive, evasive, fictitious, hypothetical, illusory, imitation, mendacious, ostensible, purported, specious, synthetic, tartuffish
pretender fake, pedant
pretense appearance *(look)*, artifice, bad faith, color *(deceptive appearance)*, counterfeit, cover *(pretext)*, deceit, disguise, excuse, false pretense, falsehood, falsification, fraud, histrionics, hoax, hypocrisy, imposture, indirection *(deceitfulness)*, misstatement, pretext, rodomontade, role, sham, story *(falsehood)*, subterfuge. SEE MAIN ENTRY
pretense of virtue hypocrisy
pretension artifice, disguise, droit, hypocrisy, jactation, pretense *(ostentation)*, pretext, rhetoric *(insincere language)*, rodomontade
pretentious flatulent, fustian, grandiose, histrionic, inflated *(bombastic)*, inflated *(vain)*, orotund, tawdry. SEE MAIN ENTRY
pretentious speech fustian
pretentious talk rodomontade
pretentiousness bombast, pretense *(ostentation)*, rhetoric *(insincere language)*
preterition disregard *(omission)*
pretermission default, disregard *(omission)*, failure *(falling short)*, omission
pretermit defer *(put off)*, disregard, neglect. SEE MAIN ENTRY
preternatural mysterious, peculiar *(curious)*, uncanny
pretexed purported
pretext artifice, bad faith, color *(deceptive appearance)*, deception, disguise, evasion, excuse, false pretense, falsehood, ruse, stratagem, subterfuge. SEE MAIN ENTRY
pretexted assumed *(feigned)*
pretiosissimus invaluable, priceless
pretiosus valuable
pretium bribe, charge *(cost)*, price, ransom, worth
pretrial examination proceedings discovery
pretty attractive
pretty good passable
pretty well fairly *(moderately)*
prevail carry *(succeed)*, coax, continue *(persevere)*, convert *(persuade)*, dominate, endure *(last)*, last, outbalance, outweigh, pass *(satisfy requirements)*, persevere, persist, predominate *(command)*, remain *(continue)*, subsist, succeed *(attain)*, surpass, transcend. SEE MAIN ENTRY
prevail against resist *(withstand)*, withstand
prevail on govern. SEE MAIN ENTRY
prevail over beat *(defeat)*, defeat, kill *(defeat)*, operate, overcome *(surmount)*, override, prejudice *(influence)*, prescribe, surmount
prevail upon affect, bait *(lure)*, browbeat, coax, constrain *(compel)*, convince, exhort, incite, induce, influence, inspire, motivate, persuade, reason *(persuade)*, urge
prevail with arbitrate *(conciliate)*
prevailing accustomed *(customary)*, cardinal *(outstanding)*, coercion, common *(customary)*, convincing, current, customary, dominant, familiar *(customary)*, force *(compulsion)*, forcible, general, influential, leading *(ranking first)*, master, ordinary, orthodox, popular, potent, powerful, predominant, prevalent, prime *(most valuable)*, principal, regular *(conventional)*, rife, successful, typical, usual. SEE MAIN ENTRY
prevailing attitudes climate
prevailing conditions climate
prevailing form protocol *(etiquette)*
prevailing idea motif
prevailing standards climate
prevailing style mode
prevailing taste custom, mode
prevalence boom *(prosperity)*, custom, frequency, mode, preponderance, usage
prevalent common *(customary)*, conventional, current, customary, dominant, extensive, familiar *(customary)*, frequent, general, habitual, household *(familiar)*, influential, master, material *(important)*, ordinary, popular, predominant, present *(current)*, prevailing *(current)*, proverbial, rampant, regular *(conventional)*, rife, routine, typical, usual. SEE MAIN ENTRY
prevaricate bear false witness, cheat, circumvent, deceive, equivocate, evade *(deceive)*, fabricate *(make up)*, feign, invent *(falsify)*, lie *(falsify)*, mislead, misrepresent, misstate, palter, pettifog, pretend. SEE MAIN ENTRY
prevaricating deceptive, disingenuous, disreputable, equivocal, mendacious, oblique *(evasive)*, untrue
prevarication ambivalence, deceit, deception, dishonesty, evasion, false pretense, falsehood, falsification, fiction, fraud, indirection *(deceitfulness)*, lie, perjury, story *(falsehood)*, subreption, subterfuge
prévenance comity
prevene antecede
prevenience expectation
prevenient aforesaid, antecedent, before mentioned, precursory, preliminary, previous, prior, said
prevent arrest *(stop)*, avert, balk, ban, bar *(exclude)*, bar *(hinder)*, block, censor, clog, condemn *(ban)*, constrain *(restrain)*, counter, counteract, countervail, debar, delay, detain *(restrain)*, disqualify, disrupt, eliminate *(exclude)*, enjoin, estop, exclude, fight *(counteract)*, foil, forbid, forestall, frustrate, halt, hamper, impede, inhibit, interdict, interfere, interpose, keep *(restrain)*, obstruct, obturate, occlude, oppose, parry, preclude, prohibit, proscribe *(prohibit)*, repel *(drive back)*, resist *(oppose)*, restrain, restrict, stave, stay *(halt)*, stem *(check)*, stifle, stop, suppress, thwart, withstand. SEE MAIN ENTRY
prevent crime police
prevent from being discovered enshroud
prevent from being seen enshroud
prevent offenses against the state police
prevent passage clog, shut
prevent publication censor
prevent temporarily hinder
preventative offset, preventive, prophylactic, restrictive
prevented arrested *(checked)*
preventing prohibitive *(restrictive)*
prevention bar *(obstruction)*, barrier, constraint *(restriction)*, control *(restriction)*, damper *(stopper)*, deterrence, deterrent, disadvantage, fetter, frustration, halt, impediment, obstruction, obviation, prohibition, restraint, stay, veto. SEE MAIN ENTRY
prevention of accomplishment frustration
prevention of congressional action filibuster
prevention of waste economy *(frugality)*
preventive barrier, prohibitive *(restrictive)*, prophylactic, protective, restrictive, salutary. SEE MAIN ENTRY
preventive custody constraint *(imprisonment)*, detention
preventive detention constraint *(imprisonment)*
preventive measure panoply, safeguard
preventive measures precaution
preview precursor
previous aforesaid, antecedent, before mentioned, former, last *(preceding)*, late *(defunct)*, precursory, preexisting, preliminary, prior, said. SEE MAIN ENTRY
previous consideration forethought
previous deliberation premeditation
previous design forethought
previous reflection forethought, premeditation
previous to heretofore, theretofore
previously heretofore
previously called alias
previously in mind aforethought
previously mentioned previous, said
previously named said. SEE MAIN ENTRY
previously referred to said
previously specified aforesaid
prevision premonition
prewarn admonish *(warn)*, caution, forewarn, presage
prewarning caveat, premonition
prey pillage, prize, victim. SEE MAIN ENTRY
prey on plague, plunder
prey on the mind obsess
prey upon bait *(harass)*, endanger, harass, loot
preyed upon aggrieved *(harmed)*
preying rapacious
price bid, charge *(cost)*, collection *(payment)*, evaluate, expenditure, expense *(cost)*, fare, fee *(charge)*, gratuity *(bribe)*, par *(face amount)*, rate *(noun)*, rate *(verb)*, recompense, value, worth. SEE MAIN ENTRY
price charged face value *(price)*
price increase inflation *(decrease in value of currency)*
price list tariff *(bill)*
price of a ticket fare
price of corruption gratuity *(bribe)*
price of passage fare
price of redemption ransom
price of retaking ransom
price of retrieval ransom
priceless inestimable, invaluable, prime *(most valuable)*, rare. SEE MAIN ENTRY
pricing charge *(assess)*
prick enter *(penetrate)*, lancinate, penetrate, pierce *(lance)*, provocation
pricking bitter *(penetrating)*
pride SEE MAIN ENTRY
prideful inflated *(vain)*, orgulous, pretentious *(pompous)*, proud *(conceited)*, supercilious
prig steal
prim formal, pretentious *(pompous)*
prima facie content *(meaning)*. SEE MAIN ENTRY
primacy advantage, dominance, dominion *(supreme authority)*, emphasis, force *(strength)*, importance, magnitude, power, precedence, prestige, priority, regime, significance, stress *(accent)*, supremacy. SEE MAIN ENTRY
primal cardinal *(basic)*, central *(essential)*, incipient, initial, original *(initial)*, prime *(original)*, primordial, principal, rudimentary, underlying

primarily a fortiori, ab initio, particularly
primarius leading *(ranking first)*
primary cardinal *(basic)*, causative, central *(essential)*, critical *(crucial)*, dominant, elementary, essential *(inherent)*, essential *(required)*, fundamental, important *(significant)*, inchoate, incipient, indispensable, initial, integral, leading *(ranking first)*, master, material *(important)*, organic, original *(initial)*, paramount, preliminary, prime *(original)*, primordial, principal, rudimentary, salient, simple, stellar, substantive, ultimate, underlying, vital. SEE MAIN ENTRY
primary care SEE MAIN ENTRY
primary constituent necessity
primary element center *(essence)*, consequence *(significance)*, content *(meaning)*
primary meaning connotation, content *(meaning)*, gist *(substance)*
primary rights SEE MAIN ENTRY
primate chief
prime bonus
prime cardinal *(basic)*, cardinal *(outstanding)*, dominant, edify, educate, important *(significant)*, initiate, instruct *(teach)*, leading *(ranking first)*, major, master, meritorious, necessary *(required)*, notable, original *(initial)*, paramount, premium, primary, primordial, principal, professional *(stellar)*, ripe, salient, select, sterling, superlative. SEE MAIN ENTRY
prime constituent center *(essence)*, main point, sine qua non
prime ingredient center *(essence)*, main point, sine qua non
prime ingredients character *(personal quality)*
prime motive derivation
prime mover aggressor, architect, author *(originator)*, determinant, promoter, protagonist, reason *(basis)*
primed acquainted, fit, informed *(having information)*, ready *(prepared)*, ripe
primer hornbook
primeval incipient, original *(initial)*, prime *(original)*, primordial
primigenial original *(initial)*, primordial
primitive brutal, elementary, incipient, obsolete, organic, original *(initial)*, outdated, outmoded, prime *(original)*, primordial, rudimentary. SEE MAIN ENTRY
primogenitor ancestor, derivation, progenitor. SEE MAIN ENTRY
primogenitors parentage
primogeniture birthright
primordial original *(initial)*, prime *(original)*, rudimentary. SEE MAIN ENTRY
primus cardinal *(basic)*, cardinal *(outstanding)*, elementary, fundamental, initial, primary, prime *(original)*, principal
princeliness philanthropy
princely charitable *(benevolent)*, liberal *(generous)*, magnanimous, meritorious, outstanding *(prominent)*, philanthropic
princeps chief, leading *(ranking first)*, principal
principal accomplice, assets, cardinal *(basic)*, cash, central *(essential)*, chairman, chief, corpus, critical *(crucial)*, director, dominant, fundamental, important *(significant)*, leading *(ranking first)*, major, material *(important)*, necessary *(required)*, noteworthy, outstanding *(prominent)*, paramount, predominant, primary, prime *(most valuable)*, professional *(stellar)*, prominent, protagonist, salient, stellar, substantive, superlative, vital. SEE MAIN ENTRY
principal backer mainstay
principal character protagonist
principal item feature *(special attraction)*
principal maintainer mainstay
principal part body *(main part)*, bulk, center *(essence)*, cornerstone, generality *(bulk)*, gist *(ground for a suit)*, gravamen, majority *(greater part)*, principal *(capital sum)*
principal person chief
principal point gist *(ground for a suit)*, main point
principal support mainstay
principal supporter mainstay
principal sustainer mainstay
principal thoroughfare avenue *(route)*
principalis fundamental, primary, principal
principally ab initio, as a rule, generally, particularly
principatus predominance, supremacy
principia premises *(hypotheses)*
principium maxim
principium origin *(source)*
principle article *(precept)*, basis, belief *(something believed)*, color *(complexion)*, conscience, consequence *(significance)*, conviction *(persuasion)*, cornerstone, corpus, criterion, doctrine, dogma, generality *(vague statement)*, ground, honor *(good reputation)*, integrity, law, maxim, precept, prescription *(directive)*, probity, reason *(basis)*, rectitude, right *(righteousness)*, rule *(legal dictate)*, substance *(essential nature)*, thesis, veracity. SEE MAIN ENTRY
principle of law stare decisis
principle part component
principled bona fide, conscientious, equitable, ethical, high-minded, honest, juridical, just, law-abiding, meritorious, moral, reputable, scrupulous, strict
principles code, ethics, honesty, pandect *(code of laws)*, platform, policy *(plan of action)*, polity
principles of government constitution
principles of morality ethics
print brand *(mark)*, circulate, copy *(noun)*, copy *(verb)*, impression, issue *(publish)*, post, publish, stamp
printed holographic
printing publication *(printed matter)*, script
prints fingerprints
prior aforesaid, antecedent, back *(in arrears)*, before mentioned, former
prior last *(preceding)*
prior precursory, preexisting, preferred *(given priority)*, preliminary, preparatory, previous, said. SEE MAIN ENTRY
prior condition prerequisite
prior determination premeditation
prior instance authority *(documentation)*, precedent
prior measure precaution, preparation
prior planning forethought
prior right prerogative, priority
prior thought forethought
prior to heretofore, theretofore
priority importance, magnitude, materiality *(consequence)*, precedence, preferential, prerogative, privilege, significance. SEE MAIN ENTRY
prison bondage, captivity, cell, constraint *(imprisonment)*, detention, jail, penitentiary, reformatory. SEE MAIN ENTRY
prison house cell, prison
prisonbreaker fugitive
prisoner captive, convict, hostage, inmate. SEE MAIN ENTRY
prisoner at the bar convict
prisoner behind bars convict
prisoner of state convict
prisonhouse jail, penitentiary
pristine initial, original *(initial)*, primordial
pristinus former
privacy concealment, confidence *(relation of trust)*, obscuration. SEE MAIN ENTRY
private blind *(concealed)*, confidence *(relation of trust)*, confidential, covert, esoteric, furtive, interior, internal, intimate, obscure *(remote)*, personal *(individual)*, privy, remote *(secluded)*, residential, secret, several *(separate)*, solitary, surreptitious. SEE MAIN ENTRY
private affair confidence *(relation of trust)*, secret
private communication secret
private enterprise business *(commercial enterprise)*, commerce
private language jargon *(technical language)*
private matter secret
private property possessions
private right of action SEE MAIN ENTRY
private understanding contract
private war feud
private wrong tort
privateering larcenous
privately alone *(solitary)*, in person
privateness privacy
privation abridgment *(disentitlement)*, bankruptcy, cost *(penalty)*, curtailment, dearth, deficiency, denial, detriment, expense *(sacrifice)*, foreclosure, indigence, injury, loss, need *(deprivation)*, paucity, poverty. SEE MAIN ENTRY
privation of seisin disseisin
privatus personal *(private)*, private *(not public)*
privilege advantage, allow *(authorize)*, authorize, birthright, capacity *(authority)*, charter *(sanction)*, claim *(right)*, concession *(authorization)*, dispensation *(exception)*, droit, easement, empower, enable, exclusion, exemption, franchise *(license)*, franchise *(right to vote)*, free, freedom, grant *(concede)*, immunity, impunity, invest *(vest)*, let *(permit)*, liberty, license, option *(contractual provision)*, palliate *(excuse)*, patent, permit, prerogative, prize, right *(entitlement)*, sanction. SEE MAIN ENTRY
privilege to publish copyright
privilege to reproduce copyright
privileged entitled, exempt, free *(not restricted)*, immune, preferential, rightful, unalienable. SEE MAIN ENTRY
privileged class elite, society
privileged communication confidence *(relation of trust)*, secret
privileged information secret
privity chain *(nexus)*, nexus. SEE MAIN ENTRY
privy mysterious, personal *(private)*, private *(confidential)*, secret, stealthy. SEE MAIN ENTRY
privy council bench
privy to familiar *(informed)*
prizable valuable
prize bounty, consideration *(recompense)*, honor, hush money, paragon, prefer, preferential, premium *(excess value)*, prime *(most valuable)*, profit, raise *(advance)*, recognition, recommend, regard

(hold in esteem), reward, select, spoils, stake *(award)*. SEE MAIN ENTRY
pro forma SEE MAIN ENTRY
pro hoc vici SEE MAIN ENTRY
pro life SEE MAIN ENTRY
pro rata per capita. SEE MAIN ENTRY
pro re valere equivalent
pro tem pro tempore
pro tempore SEE MAIN ENTRY
pro-choice SEE MAIN ENTRY
probabilis plausible
probabilitas likelihood
probability chance *(possibility)*, expectation, likelihood, possibility, presumption, prospect *(outlook)*, supposition. SEE MAIN ENTRY
probable apparent *(presumptive)*, believable, circumstantial, constructive *(inferential)*, deductible *(provable)*, foreseeable, future, possible, presumptive, reasonable *(rational)*. SEE MAIN ENTRY
probable cause SEE MAIN ENTRY
probare approve, establish *(show)*, evince, prove, recommend, verify *(confirm)*, vindicate
probate SEE MAIN ENTRY
probatio probation. SEE MAIN ENTRY
probation examination *(test)*, preparation. SEE MAIN ENTRY
probationary tentative
probationer apprentice, novice. SEE MAIN ENTRY
probative tentative
probative matter evidence
probatory probative
probe analysis, analyze, audit, canvass, check *(inspect)*, consider, cross-examination, cross-examine, cross-questioning, delve, examine *(interrogate)*, examine *(study)*, frisk, hearing, hunt, indagation, inquire, inquiry *(request for information)*, inquiry *(systematic investigation)*, interrogation, investigate, investigation, penetrate, peruse, pursuit *(chase)*, pursuit *(effort to secure)*, question *(inquiry)*, research, scrutinize, scrutiny, search, study, trace *(follow)*, traverse, trial *(experiment)*. SEE MAIN ENTRY
probe into research
probe to the bottom delve
prober detective
probing interrogative, judgment *(discernment)*
probitas honesty, integrity, probity, rectitude
probity candor *(impartiality)*, conscience, credibility, ethics, fairness, good faith, honesty, honor *(good reputation)*, integrity, justice, principle *(virtue)*, rectitude, right *(righteousness)*, trustworthiness, truth, veracity. SEE MAIN ENTRY
problem disadvantage, enigma, foible, grievance, hindrance, impasse, issue *(matter in dispute)*, matter *(subject)*, misfortune, nuisance, pitfall, plight, quagmire, question *(issue)*, thesis, trouble. SEE MAIN ENTRY
problematic debatable, difficult, disputable, doubtful, inauspicious, uncertain *(questionable)*. SEE MAIN ENTRY
problematical controversial, debatable, inauspicious, moot, problematic, uncertain *(questionable)*, undecided, vague
probrosus disgraceful, scandalous, scurrilous
probrum discredit, infamy, reproach
probus honest, moral, upright
procacious bumptious, impertinent *(insolent)*, insolent. SEE MAIN ENTRY
procacity temerity
procedural SEE MAIN ENTRY
procedural due process SEE MAIN ENTRY
procedural law adjective law
procedure agenda, avenue *(means of attainment)*, campaign, conduct, constant, course, direction *(course)*, expedient, form *(arrangement)*, maneuver *(tactic)*, manner *(behavior)*, matter of course, method, mode, modus operandi, operation, policy *(plan of action)*, polity, practice *(custom)*, proceeding, process *(course)*, rule *(guide)*, scheme, step, strategy, system. SEE MAIN ENTRY
proceed accrue *(arise)*, arise *(occur)*, continue *(resume)*, develop, emanate, ensue, occur *(happen)*, pass *(advance)*, progress, pursue *(carry on)*, redound, remain *(continue)*, reopen, result, resume, stem *(originate)*. SEE MAIN ENTRY
proceed against civilly prosecute *(charge)*
proceed against criminally prosecute *(charge)*
proceed by stratagem circumvent, devise *(invent)*, maneuver
proceed from arise *(originate)*, result
proceed to assume *(undertake)*
proceed with conduct, discharge *(perform)*, maintain *(carry on)*, prosecute *(carry forward)*, transact
proceeding business *(affair)*, continuation *(resumption)*, day in court, event, expedient, experience *(encounter)*, happening, incident, lawsuit, manner *(behavior)*, occurrence, operation, procedure, progressive *(going forward)*, step, suit, transaction, trial *(legal proceeding)*. SEE MAIN ENTRY
proceeding from antecedent to consequent a priori
proceeding without cessation continual *(connected)*
proceeding without interruption continual *(connected)*
proceedings affairs, case *(lawsuit)*, cause *(lawsuit)*, dealings, matter *(case)*, record, register, strategy
proceeds commission *(fee)*, earnings, income, output, product, profit, rent, revenue. SEE MAIN ENTRY
process avenue *(means of attainment)*, conduit *(channel)*, course, expedient, instrumentality, manufacture, method, mode, modus operandi, operation, practice *(procedure)*, procedure, proceeding, search warrant, step, subpoena, system, transaction, treatment, warrant *(judicial writ)*. SEE MAIN ENTRY
process in law controversy *(lawsuit)*
process of extinguishment of rights foreclosure
process of governing bureaucracy
process of proving proof
processing treatment
procession chain *(series)*, order *(arrangement)*, sequence, serial, succession
proclaim affirm *(claim)*, annunciate, appoint, argue, avouch *(avow)*, avow, bear *(adduce)*, certify *(attest)*, circulate, command, communicate, convey *(communicate)*, declaim, declare, decree, disclose, divulge, enunciate, express, herald, inform *(notify)*, issue *(publish)*, manifest, notify, observe *(remark)*, plead *(allege in a legal action)*, posit, post, prescribe, profess *(avow)*, promulgate, pronounce *(speak)*, propagate *(spread)*, publish, report *(disclose)*, signify *(inform)*, speak, utter. SEE MAIN ENTRY
proclaimed alleged, public *(known)*
proclaimer harbinger, informant, informer *(a person who provides information)*
proclaimor declarant
proclamation adjudication, avouchment, canon, charge *(command)*, charter *(declaration of rights)*, communication *(statement)*, declaration, decree, dictate, directive, disclosure *(act of disclosing)*, disclosure *(something disclosed)*, divulgation, issuance, notice *(announcement)*, notification, order *(judicial directive)*, ordinance, publication *(disclosure)*, publicity, report *(detailed account)*. SEE MAIN ENTRY
proclamatory declaratory
proclivis inclined, prone
proclivitas predisposition, proclivity, propensity, tendency
proclivity affinity *(regard)*, bias, character *(personal quality)*, characteristic, conatus, conviction *(persuasion)*, desire, disposition *(inclination)*, favor *(partiality)*, favoritism, frame *(mood)*, habit, inclination, instinct, liability, partiality, penchant, position *(point of view)*, predisposition, preference *(choice)*, propensity, standpoint, tendency. SEE MAIN ENTRY
procrastinare procrastinate
procrastinate defer *(put off)*, hesitate, hold up *(delay)*, neglect, protract *(prolong)*, stall. SEE MAIN ENTRY
procrastinating dilatory
procrastination cessation *(interlude)*, deferment, delay, laches, neglect, pause. SEE MAIN ENTRY
procrastinative dilatory, indolent, remiss
procrastinatory dilatory
procreant fertile
procreare propagate *(increase)*
procreate bear *(yield)*, create, produce *(manufacture)*, propagate *(increase)*, pullulate, reproduce
procreation creation
procreative causative, fertile, prolific
procreator ancestor, ascendant, parents, predecessor, primogenitor, progenitor
procreators ancestry
proctor advocate *(counselor)*, deputy, director, factor *(commission merchant)*, plenipotentiary, procurator, superintendent. SEE MAIN ENTRY
proctorage supervision
proctorship control *(supervision)*
procurable disposable, open *(accessible)*
procuracy agency *(legal relationship)*, delegation *(envoy)*
procurare administer *(conduct)*, administer *(tender)*, oversee, superintend
procuratio administration, government *(administration)*, supervision
procuration acquisition, agency *(legal relationship)*, delegation *(assignment)*, deputation *(selection of delegates)*, recovery *(repossession)*
procurator agent, attorney, barrister, deputy, director jurist, proctor. SEE MAIN ENTRY
procurator factor *(commission merchant)*, proxy
procuratory vicarious *(delegated)*
procure acquire *(secure)*, attain, buy, coax, contrive, derive *(receive)*, educe, engage *(hire)*, evoke, gain, glean, hire, lobby, obtain, occupy *(take possession)*, pander,

purchase, raise *(collect)*, realize *(obtain as a profit)*, reap, receive *(acquire)*, recover. SEE MAIN ENTRY
procure another to commit perjury suborn
procure by effort earn
procure indirectly suborn
procure title to buy, purchase
procurement acquisition, adverse possession, provision *(act of supplying)*, recovery *(repossession)*, takeover
procurer consumer, go-between
prod coax, coerce, constrain *(compel)*, impel, jostle *(bump into)*, press *(goad)*, pressure, prompt, remind, reminder, spirit, stimulate, stimulus, urge
prodding provocation
prodere betray *(disclose)*, deliver, give *(grant)*
prodesse avail *(be of use)*, contribute *(assist)*
prodigal dissolute, improvident, inordinate, liberal *(generous)*, needless, portentous *(eliciting amazement)*, profligate *(extravagant)*, profuse, superfluous, unrestrained *(not repressed)*. SEE MAIN ENTRY
prodigality delinquency *(misconduct)*, inconsideration, largess *(generosity)*, misapplication, neglect, waste
prodigalize dissipate *(expend foolishly)*
prodigious far reaching, noteworthy, portentous *(eliciting amazement)*, special, unusual. SEE MAIN ENTRY
prodigium phenomenon *(unusual occurrence)*
prodigy mastermind
prodition bad repute, bribery
prodromal before mentioned
prodrome precursor
produce adduce, avail *(bring about)*, bear *(adduce)*, bear *(yield)*, build *(construct)*, cargo, cause, commodities, compose, conjure, constitute *(compose)*, create, develop, discharge *(perform)*, effectuate, engender, evoke, exhibit, fabricate *(construct)*, form, formulate, frame *(construct)*, frame *(formulate)*, furnish, generate, germinate, goods, induce, inspire, invent *(produce for the first time)*, make, manufacture, merchandise, occasion, offer *(tender)*, originate, output, perpetrate, proceeds, product, profit, propagate *(increase)*, provide *(supply)*, pullulate, realize *(make real)*, realize *(obtain as a profit)*. SEE MAIN ENTRY
produce a change affect
produce a good effect profit
produce a good result profit
produce an effect affect
produce an example illustrate
produce an instance exemplify, quote
produce conviction convince
produce counterfeit money forge *(counterfeit)*
produce equilibrium compensate *(counterbalance)*
produce evidence verify *(confirm)*
produce injury inflict
produce rapidly proliferate
produce the evidence bear *(adduce)*
produced alleged
produced materials commodities
producer author *(originator)*, derivation, determinant, maker
producere adduce, promote *(advance)*
producing creation
producing a powerful effect forcible
producing abundantly copious
producing boredom lifeless *(dull)*
producing ennui lifeless *(dull)*
product amount *(result)*, conclusion *(outcome)*, consequence *(conclusion)*, development *(outgrowth)*, effect, invention, item, outcome, output, proceeds, result
product of imagination fiction, idea
product of the imagination figment
production boom *(increase)*, boom *(prosperity)*, building *(business of assembling)*, business *(commerce)*, composition *(makeup)*, creation, discharge *(performance)*, disclosure *(act of disclosing)*, formation, fruition, industry *(business)*, manifestation, manufacture, operation, origination, outcome, output, performance *(execution)*, performance *(workmanship)*, realization. SEE MAIN ENTRY
production and distribution commerce
productive beneficial, causal, causative, constructive *(creative)*, copious, effective *(efficient)*, efficient, fertile, gainful, lucrative, operative, original *(creative)*, potent, profitable, prolific, purposeful. SEE MAIN ENTRY
productiveness creation, efficiency, utility *(usefulness)*
productivity boom *(prosperity)*, creation, utility *(usefulness)*
products commodities, goods, stock in trade. SEE MAIN ENTRY
proelium committere fight *(battle)*
proem overture, preamble, preface, prelude
proemial elementary, incipient, original *(initial)*, preliminary, preparatory, prior
profanation blasphemy, profanity
profane abuse *(violate)*, contaminate, debase, diabolic, mundane, obscene, pollute. SEE MAIN ENTRY
profane interjection expletive
profane language profanity
profane oath blasphemy
profaneness blasphemy, profanity
profanity imprecation. SEE MAIN ENTRY
profanus profane
profectio start
proferre adduce, postpone, publish, quote
profess affirm *(claim)*, allege, annunciate, assert, assume *(simulate)*, assure *(insure)*, avouch *(avow)*, avow, bear *(adduce)*, claim *(maintain)*, concede, contend *(maintain)*, declare, depose *(testify)*, enunciate, palter, posit, pretend, purport, testify. SEE MAIN ENTRY
professed alleged, ostensible, purported, putative, specious
professed belief doctrine, dogma, principle *(axiom)*
professed purpose pretense *(pretext)*, pretext
professio profession *(declaration)*
profession admission *(disclosure)*, affirmation, appointment *(position)*, assertion, asseveration, averment, avowal, business *(occupation)*, calling, career, conviction *(persuasion)*, cover *(pretext)*, declaration, disclosure *(act of disclosing)*, disclosure *(something disclosed)*, employment, expression *(comment)*, industry *(business)*, job, labor *(work)*, livelihood, mission, occupation *(vocation)*, office, position *(business status)*, post, pretext, pronouncement, pursuit *(occupation)*, testimony, trade *(occupation)*, work *(employment)*. SEE MAIN ENTRY
profession of faith principle *(axiom)*
professional ethical, expert *(adjective)*, expert *(noun)*, learned, practitioner, specialist, technical. SEE MAIN ENTRY
professional advice holding *(ruling of a court)*
professional decision holding *(ruling of a court)*
professional error of judgment malpractice
professional ethics conscience
professional fee retainer
professional force staff
professional language jargon *(technical language)*
professional laxness malpractice
professional misconduct malpractice
professional neglect malpractice
professional negligence malpractice
professional staff staff
professional standards ethics
professional vocabulary jargon *(technical language)*
professionalism specialty *(special aptitude)*. SEE MAIN ENTRY
professor pedagogue, specialist
professorate faculty *(teaching staff)*
professorial learned
professors faculty *(teaching staff)*
proffer adduce, bestow, bid, contribute *(supply)*, extend *(offer)*, give *(grant)*, hold out *(deliberate on an offer)*, introduce, invitation, offer *(propose)*, offer *(tender)*, overture, pose *(propound)*, present *(make a gift)*, proposal *(suggestion)*, propose, propound, remit *(submit for consideration)*, tender. SEE MAIN ENTRY
proffer payment offer *(tender)*
proffered unsolicited
proficere profit, progress
proficiency ability, caliber *(mental capacity)*, capacity *(aptitude)*, competence *(ability)*, efficiency, experience *(background)*, facility *(easiness)*, faculty *(ability)*, force *(strength)*, gift *(flair)*, knowledge *(learning)*, performance *(workmanship)*, potential, prowess *(ability)*, science *(technique)*, skill, specialty *(special aptitude)*. SEE MAIN ENTRY
proficient artful, capable, cognizant, competent, deft, effective *(efficient)*, efficient, expert, familiar *(informed)*, informed *(educated)*, learned, literate, practiced, professional *(trained)*, qualified *(competent)*, resourceful, sciential, specialist, veteran. SEE MAIN ENTRY
proficient person expert, specialist
proficient practitioner professional
proficisci leave *(depart)*
proficuous beneficial
profile brief, characterize, configuration *(form)*, contour *(outline)*, contour *(shape)*, cross section, delineate, delineation, description, outline *(boundary)*
profit advantage, avail *(bring about)*, bear *(yield)*, behalf, benefit *(betterment)*, boom *(prosperity)*, capitalize *(seize the chance)*, collect *(recover money)*, commission *(fee)*, dividend, earn, earnings, edification, gain, inure *(benefit)*, output, pay, perquisite, proceeds, prosperity, realization, realize *(obtain as a profit)*, reap, revenue, succeed *(attain)*, utility *(usefulness)*, worth. SEE MAIN ENTRY
profit and loss account budget
profit and loss statement ledger
profit by employ *(make use of)*, exploit *(make use of)*

profit by cheating prey
profit by swindling prey
profit from conversion of assets income
profit from money loaned interest *(profit)*
profit from sale income
profit making boom *(prosperity)*
profitability utility *(usefulness)*
profitable beneficial, constructive *(creative)*, copious, effective *(efficient)*, favorable *(advantageous)*, fertile, functional, gainful, lucrative, practical, productive, salutary, successful, valuable. SEE MAIN ENTRY
profitableness expedience, feasibility, worth
profiteering exploitation, graft, mercenary
profiteri avow, declare, offer *(propose)*
profiting prosperous
profitless barren, disadvantageous, futile, ineffective, ineffectual, unavailing, unproductive
profits earnings, income
profits from employment earnings
profits of commerce income
profligacy bad repute, debauchery, delinquency *(misconduct)*, vice
profligate delinquent *(guilty of a misdeed)*, depraved, disreputable, dissolute, immoral, improvident, iniquitous, lawless, lecherous, lewd, licentious, nefarious, obscene, prodigal, profuse, promiscuous, reprobate, salacious, scandalous, tainted *(corrupted)*, unscrupulous, vicious, wrongdoer. SEE MAIN ENTRY
profligatus profligate *(extravagant)*, reprobate
profluence boom *(prosperity)*
profluency boom *(prosperity)*
profluent progressive *(going forward)*
profound convincing, esoteric, intense, learned, obscure *(abstruse)*, recondite, sapient. SEE MAIN ENTRY
profound application diligence *(care)*
profound attention diligence *(care)*
profound study diligence *(care)*
profound thought diligence *(care)*, preoccupation
profugus fugitive
profundity sagacity
profuse copious, excess, excessive, inordinate, liberal *(generous)*, loquacious, manifold, multiple, prolific, replete, rife, superfluous, undue *(excessive)*, voluble. SEE MAIN ENTRY
profuseness boom *(prosperity)*, plethora, sufficiency, surfeit, tautology
profusion boom *(prosperity)*, overage, plethora, quantity, spate, store *(depository)*, sufficiency, surfeit, waste
profusive copious
profusus profuse
progenerate propagate *(increase)*, reproduce
progenerative fertile
progenies issue *(progeny)*, offspring, progeny
progenitive prolific
progenitor ancestor, ascendant, derivation, forerunner, parents, predecessor. SEE MAIN ENTRY
progenitors lineage, parentage
progenitorship paternity
progeniture bloodline
progeny child, children, descendant, family *(household)*, offspring, posterity, succession. SEE MAIN ENTRY
prognose predict
prognosis caution *(warning)*. SEE MAIN ENTRY
prognostic caution *(warning)*, harbinger, indicant, indication, indicator, menace, oracular, precursor, prophetic, provident *(showing foresight)*, symptom, warning
prognosticate expect *(consider probable)*, forewarn, herald, portend, predict, presage, promise *(raise expectations)*. SEE MAIN ENTRY
prognostication prognosis
prognosticative precursory, prophetic
program arrange *(methodize)*, arrange *(plan)*, calendar *(record of yearly periods)*, campaign, course, direction *(course)*, docket, enterprise *(undertaking)*, method, plan, platform, policy *(plan of action)*, polity, practice *(procedure)*, procedure, prospectus, register, schedule, set down, strategy, system, undertaking *(enterprise)*. SEE MAIN ENTRY
program of action arrangement *(plan)*, device *(contrivance)*, method, proposition, scheme
program of business agenda
program of operation agenda
progredi progress
progress accession *(enlargement)*, accrue *(arise)*, advance *(progression)*, advancement *(improvement)*, augmentation, boom *(increase)*, boom *(prosperity)*, civilization, continue *(persevere)*, develop, development *(progression)*, edification, endure *(last)*, enlarge, evolve, expand, germinate, growth *(evolution)*, headway, increase, inflow, keep *(continue)*, move *(alter position)*, pass *(advance)*, persist, proceed *(go forward)*, promotion *(advancement)*, pursue *(strive to gain)*, reform, remain *(continue)*, renew *(begin again)*, resume, succeed *(attain)*, transition. SEE MAIN ENTRY
progress to maturity development *(progression)*
progressing live *(existing)*
progression accession *(enlargement)*, advance *(progression)*, advancement *(improvement)*, array *(order)*, boom *(increase)*, boom *(prosperity)*, chain *(series)*, civilization, continuity, cycle, gamut, headway, hierarchy *(arrangement in a series)*, order *(arrangement)*, progress, promotion *(advancement)*, reform, sequence, serial, step, succession, way *(manner)*
progressive continuous, corrigible, direct *(uninterrupted)*, liberal *(broad minded)*, radical *(favoring drastic change)*, sophisticated. SEE MAIN ENTRY
progressive course process *(course)*
progressive growth development *(progression)*
progressiveness boom *(prosperity)*
progressivism reform
progressus advance *(progression)*, development *(progression)*, progress
prohibere avert, debar, exclude, hinder, preclude, prevent, stop
prohibit abolish, abrogate *(annul)*, abrogate *(rescind)*, ban, bar *(exclude)*, bar *(hinder)*, block, censor, clog, condemn *(ban)*, constrain *(restrain)*, contain *(restrain)*, control *(restrain)*, counter, curb, debar, deny *(refuse to grant)*, disfranchise, disqualify, dissent *(withhold assent)*, eliminate *(exclude)*, enjoin, estop, exclude, fetter, forbid, forestall, halt, inhibit, interdict, interfere, keep *(restrain)*, lock, negate, obstruct, occlude, oppose, preclude, prevent, refuse, reject, repel *(drive back)*, repress, restrain, restrict, revoke, stay *(halt)*, stop, suppress, withhold. SEE MAIN ENTRY
prohibit by legal injunction enjoin
prohibited barred, illegal, illegitimate *(illegal)*, illicit, impermissible, improper, inadmissible, irregular *(improper)*, unauthorized, unlawful
prohibited articles contraband
prohibited by law illegal, illegitimate *(illegal)*
prohibited import contraband
prohibiting penal
prohibition bar *(obstruction)*, barrier, censorship, check *(bar)*, coercion, constraint *(imprisonment)*, constraint *(restriction)*, control *(restriction)*, countermand, denial, deterrence, embargo, estoppel, exclusion, fetter, halt, injunction, limitation, obstacle, obstruction, ostracism, proscription, refusal, rejection, restraint, restriction, temperance, veto. SEE MAIN ENTRY
prohibitionary restrictive
prohibitive exclusive *(limited)*, inordinate, preventive, restrictive. SEE MAIN ENTRY
prohibitory prohibitive *(restrictive)*, restrictive
project arrange *(plan)*, campaign, cast *(throw)*, contrive, device *(contrivance)*, emanate, endeavor, enterprise *(undertaking)*, impel, overlap, plan, prearrange, precipitate *(throw down violently)*, predetermine, program *(noun)*, program *(verb)*, proposition, propound, pursuit *(occupation)*, scheme *(noun)*, scheme *(verb)*, send, undertaking *(business)*, undertaking *(enterprise)*, venture. SEE MAIN ENTRY
projected forthcoming, prospective, speculative
projected campaign project
projected goal design *(intent)*
projected law bill *(proposed act)*
projected scheme project
projecting prominent
projection design *(construction plan)*, plan
projector architect
prolatio extension *(expansion)*
prolegomenon preamble, preface
prolepsis SEE MAIN ENTRY
proles offspring
proletarian ignoble
proletariat populace
proliferate bear *(yield)*, increase, propagate *(increase)*, pullulate, reproduce. SEE MAIN ENTRY
proliferation augmentation, boom *(increase)*, boom *(prosperity)*
proliferative productive, prolific
proliferous productive, prolific
prolific beneficial, copious, fertile, productive, profuse, rampant. SEE MAIN ENTRY
prolix flatulent, loquacious, profuse, prosaic, protracted, turgid. SEE MAIN ENTRY
prolixity SEE MAIN ENTRY
prolocutor procurator, spokesman
prologue preamble, prelude, threshold *(commencement)*
prolong compound, conserve, defer *(put off)*, delay, dwell *(linger over)*, expand, hold up *(delay)*, increase, keep *(continue)*, last, maintain *(carry on)*, perpetuate, persevere, preserve, procrastinate, remain *(continue)*, stay *(continue)*. SEE MAIN ENTRY
prolongate dwell *(linger over)*
prolongation adjournment, advance *(increase)*, boom *(increase)*, continuance,

deferment, delay, extension *(postponement)*, longevity, survival
prolonged chronic, continuous, prolix, protracted
prolonged outburst of denunciation diatribe
prolusion preface
promenade perambulate
prominence character *(reputation)*, clout, consequence *(significance)*, distinction *(reputation)*, eminence, emphasis, honor *(outward respect)*, importance, materiality *(consequence)*, notoriety, prestige, reputation, significance, status, stress *(accent)*, weight *(importance)*. SEE MAIN ENTRY
prominens prominent
prominent appreciable, blatant *(conspicuous)*, clear *(apparent)*, conspicuous, critical *(crucial)*, famous, flagrant, illustrious, important *(significant)*, influential, leading *(ranking first)*, manifest, momentous, naked *(perceptible)*, notable, noteworthy, notorious, obtrusive, obvious, open *(in sight)*, palpable, paramount, particular *(specific)*, patent, perceivable, perceptible, primary, prime *(most valuable)*, principal, remarkable, renowned, reputable, salient, stellar, unusual. SEE MAIN ENTRY
prominent aspect main point
prominent detail highlight
prominent object landmark *(conspicuous object)*
prominent part highlight
prominent point main point
prominently fairly *(clearly)*, particularly
promiscuous haphazard, immoral, indiscriminate, lascivious, licentious, random. SEE MAIN ENTRY
promiscuus indiscriminate, miscellaneous, promiscuous
promise agree *(contract)*, allegiance, assurance, assure *(insure)*, bestow, bind *(obligate)*, bond, bond *(secure a debt)*, commitment *(responsibility)*, compact, condition *(contingent provision)*, contract *(noun)*, contract *(verb)*, cosign, covenant, coverage *(insurance)*, depose *(testify)*, duty *(obligation)*, ensure, expectation, guarantee, insurance, oath, obligation *(duty)*, pact, pledge *(binding promise)*, possibility, potential, predict, presage, probability, proffer, prognosis, prognosticate, prospect *(outlook)*, recognizance, responsibility *(accountability)*, security *(pledge)*, stipulate, stipulation, swear, testament, undertake, undertaking *(pledge)*, underwrite, vouch, vow, warrant *(guaranty)*, warranty. SEE MAIN ENTRY
promise ill impend
promise solemnly pledge *(promise the performance of)*
promise to contribute subscribe *(promise)*
promise to pay coverage *(insurance)*
promise to pay another's debt guaranty
promise to set aside reservation *(engagement)*
promise under seal specialty *(contract)*
promised contractual, forseen, forthcoming, indentured, prospective
promising auspicious, favorable *(advantageous)*, possible, probable, promissory, propitious, viable
promising to underwrite promissory
promisor surety *(guarantor)*
promissory SEE MAIN ENTRY
promissory note bond, draft, security *(pledge)*
promissory oath pledge *(binding promise)*
promissory obligation bill *(formal declaration)*
promissum pledge *(binding promise)*, promise, vow
promittere hold out *(deliberate on an offer)*, proffer
promote advocate, aid, ameliorate, assist, avail *(be of use)*, bear *(support)*, capitalize *(provide capital)*, conduce, continue *(persevere)*, cultivate, develop, elevate, enhance, expedite, facilitate, favor, foment, foster, further, hasten, heighten *(augment)*, help, honor, inure *(benefit)*, lobby, motivate, notify, nurture, originate, prefer, preserve, prompt, propagate *(spread)*, provoke, raise *(advance)*, recommend, sanction, serve *(assist)*, side, sponsor, subsidize, support *(assist)*, sustain *(prolong)*, urge. SEE MAIN ENTRY
promote a cause defend
promote public health and safety police
promote racial harmony desegregate
promote racial mixing desegregate
promoter abettor, advocate *(espouser)*, backer, benefactor, coactor, conspirer, developer, disciple, partisan, patron *(influential supporter)*, sponsor. SEE MAIN ENTRY
promoting beneficial
promoting health salutary
promotion advance *(progression)*, advancement *(improvement)*, advocacy, aid *(help)*, behalf, benefit *(betterment)*, development *(progression)*, elevation, headway, progress, propaganda, publicity, relief *(aid)*, support *(assistance)*. SEE MAIN ENTRY
promotor coactor
promovere promote *(advance)*
prompt abet, acute, advocate, agitate *(activate)*, cause, coax, convince, counsel, enjoin, evoke, exhort, expeditious, hint, immediate *(at once)*, impel, incite, indication, induce, influence, initiate, inspire, instantaneous, instruct *(direct)*, motivate, originate, persuade, prevail *(persuade)*, provoke, punctual, ready *(prepared)*, recommend, remind, reminder, spirit, stimulate, summary, urge. SEE MAIN ENTRY
prompte readily
prompted inclined
prompter abettor, advocate *(counselor)*, catalyst, special interest
prompting advice, cause *(reason)*, guidance, impulsive *(impelling)*, incentive, inducement, instigation, invitation, moving *(evoking emotion)*, persuasion, provocation, suggestion
promptitude dispatch *(promptness)*
promptly as soon as feasible, forthwith, instantly, readily
promptuary bank, cache *(storage place)*, repository
prompture suggestion
promptus expeditious, prompt, ready *(prepared)*
promulgare promulgate
promulgate annunciate, bear *(adduce)*, circulate, convey *(communicate)*, decree, diffuse, disclose, disseminate, divulge, enunciate, herald, inform *(notify)*, issue *(publish)*, notify, posit, proclaim, propagate *(spread)*, report *(disclose)*, reveal, signify *(inform)*, spread. SEE MAIN ENTRY
promulgate a decree instruct *(direct)*
promulgate an order command, instruct *(direct)*
promulgated alleged, public *(known)*
promulgatio notice *(announcement)*, notice *(give formal warning)*, notification
promulgation charter *(declaration of rights)*, declaration, divulgation, issuance, notification, proclamation, pronouncement, publication *(disclosure)*, publicity
promulgatory declaratory
prone inclined, partial *(biased)*, ready *(willing)*, subject *(exposed)*. SEE MAIN ENTRY
prone to addicted
prone to believe credulous
prone to display of feeling demonstrative *(expressive of emotion)*
prone to emotional display demonstrative *(expressive of emotion)*
prone to error fallible
prone to inaccuracy fallible
proneness affection, bias, character *(personal quality)*, characteristic, conatus, disposition *(inclination)*, favor *(partiality)*, favoritism, frame *(mood)*, inclination, instinct, liability, penchant, position *(point of view)*, predilection, predisposition, preference *(choice)*, proclivity, propensity, tendency
proneness to error frailty
pronounce adjudicate, affirm *(claim)*, affirm *(declare solemnly)*, allege, annunciate, argue, assert, avouch *(avow)*, avow, award, certify *(attest)*, communicate, convey *(communicate)*, decide, declare, decree, determine, enunciate, express, issue *(publish)*, judge, pass *(determine)*, phrase, posit, profess *(avow)*, recite, rule *(decide)*, speak, try *(conduct a trial)*, utter. SEE MAIN ENTRY
pronounce a judgment conclude *(decide)*, determine. SEE MAIN ENTRY
pronounce as an official act find *(determine)*
pronounce distinctly enunciate
pronounce formally adjudge, arbitrate *(adjudge)*
pronounce free from guilt exonerate
pronounce guilty determine, sentence
pronounce in a distinct manner enunciate
pronounce innocent of wrong excuse
pronounce judgment arbitrate *(adjudge)*, award, condemn *(punish)*, convict, deem, opine, pass *(determine)*, rule *(decide)*, sentence
pronounce legal authorize, certify *(approve)*, legalize, notarize
pronounce not guilty acquit, clear, vindicate
pronounce on award
pronounce sentence condemn *(punish)*, convict
pronounced alleged, clear *(apparent)*, conspicuous, distinct *(clear)*, evident, flagrant, lucid, manifest, nuncupative, obvious, open *(in sight)*, palpable, prominent, salient, unmistakable, verbal
pronouncement adjudication, affirmance *(authentication)*, affirmance *(legal affirmation)*, affirmation, allegation, assertion, asseveration, averment, avouchment, avowal, award, charter *(declaration of rights)*, choice *(decision)*, conclusion *(determination)*, confession, declaration, decree, determination, dictum, disposition *(determination)*, edict, fiat, finding, holding *(ruling of a court)*, issuance, judgment *(formal

court decree), law, notice *(announcement),* notification, observation, opinion *(judicial decision),* order *(judicial directive),* proclamation, profession *(declaration),* publication *(disclosure),* remark, resolution *(formal statement),* ruling, sentence, speech, statement, surety *(certainty).* SEE MAIN ENTRY
pronouncement by a court award, holding *(ruling of a court)*
pronouncement of a jury verdict
pronunciamento canon, issuance, pronouncement
pronunciamiento decree
pronunciation speech, stress *(accent)*
pronuntiare enunciate, issue *(publish),* proclaim, pronounce *(pass judgment)*
pronuntiatio declamation, publication *(disclosure)*
pronus prone, propensity
prooemium preface, prelude
proof certification *(attested copy),* certification *(certainness),* confirmation, corroboration, counterargument, data, design *(construction plan),* document, documentation, evidence, ground, safe, strength, testimony, token. SEE MAIN ENTRY
proof by a witness deposition, testimony
proof legally presented at trial evidence
proof of absence alibi
proof of authority credentials
proof of delivery receipt *(proof of receiving)*
proof of facts evidence
proof of guilt conviction *(finding of guilt)*
proof of identity identification
proof of payment receipt *(proof of receiving)*
proof of the validity of a will probate
proof of the will probate
prop bear *(support),* bolster, elevate, help, mainstay, reinforcement, rest *(be supported by),* uphold
propaedeutic didactic, informative
propaedeutical informative
propaedeutics education
propaganda persuasion. SEE MAIN ENTRY
propagandist advocate *(espouser)*
propagandistic persuasive
propagandize convert *(persuade),* convince, inculcate, instill, misinform, persuade, prevail *(persuade),* promote *(organize)*
propagare extend *(enlarge)*
propagate bear *(yield),* circulate, diffuse, disperse *(disseminate),* disseminate, notify, originate, proclaim, produce *(manufacture),* proliferate, promulgate, reproduce, spread. SEE MAIN ENTRY
propagated public *(known)*
propagatio extension *(expansion)*
propagation maternity, publication *(disclosure),* publicity, report *(detailed account),* transmittal
propagator advocate *(espouser)*
propel cast *(throw),* constrain *(compel),* dispatch *(send off),* impel, launch *(project),* move *(alter position),* precipitate *(throw down violently),* project *(impel forward),* provoke, send, spirit, stimulate, urge. SEE MAIN ENTRY
propel oneself proceed *(go forward)*
propellant impetus
propellants ammunition
propense prone, ready *(willing)*
propenseness predisposition, propensity
propensio penchant
propensio animi bias
propension character *(personal quality),* penchant, predisposition, propensity
propensity affinity *(regard),* animus, aptitude, bias, character *(personal quality),* characteristic, conatus, conviction *(persuasion),* desire, disposition *(inclination),* favor *(partiality),* frame *(mood),* habit, inclination, instinct, partiality, penchant, position *(point of view),* predilection, predisposition, preference *(choice),* proclivity, standpoint, tendency. SEE MAIN ENTRY
propensus inclined, propensity
proper accurate, admissible, allowable, applicable, appropriate, due *(regular),* eligible, equitable, evenhanded, fit, fitting, formal, honest, juridical, just, justifiable, lawful, legal, licit, meritorious, moral, official, orthodox, permissible, precise, reasonable *(fair),* reasonable *(rational),* relevant, right *(suitable),* rightful, seasonable, several *(separate),* suitable, tenable, unprejudiced. SEE MAIN ENTRY
proper behavior protocol *(etiquette)*
proper for judicial examination justiciable
proper for judicial review justiciable
proper formality propriety *(correctness)*
proper name call *(title)*
proper occasion opportunity
proper thing to do decorum
proper time opportunity, timeliness
proper title heading
proper to be examined in courts of justice justiciable
proper to public debate forensic
properantia haste
properare hasten
properatio dispatch *(promptness),* haste
properly as a matter of right, fairly *(impartially)*
properly qualified competent
properly timed punctual, seasonable
properness decorum, propriety *(appropriateness),* propriety *(correctness)*
propertied opulent
properties commodities
property assets, capital, characteristic, chattel, demesne, differential, domain *(land owned),* dominion *(absolute ownership),* effects, fee *(estate),* freehold, goods, holding *(property owned),* interest *(ownership),* land, merchandise, money, paraphernalia *(personal belongings),* parcel, personalty, plot *(land),* possessions, premises *(buildings),* principal *(capital sum),* quality *(attribute),* quality *(grade),* real estate, realty, remainder *(estate in property),* resource, securities, share *(stock),* specialty *(distinctive mark),* stock *(shares),* substance *(material possessions),* territory, trait. SEE MAIN ENTRY
property holder landholder, landowner, lessee
property illegally acquired graft
property leased leasehold
property obtained by descent inheritance
property obtained by devise inheritance
property owner landholder, landowner, lessor, shareholder
property permanently affixed to the realty immovable
property right lien
property saved salvage
property which may descend to an heir hereditament
prophesied foreseeable, forseen
prophesy anticipate *(prognosticate),* expect *(consider probable),* forewarn, portend, predict, presage, prognosis, prognosticate, promise *(raise expectations)*
prophetic oracular, portentous *(ominous).* SEE MAIN ENTRY
prophetical portentous *(ominous),* prophetic
prophylactic preventive, protective, remedial, salutary. SEE MAIN ENTRY
prophylaxis deterrence
propiatory penitent
propietory owner landlord
propinquitas affinity *(family ties),* relationship *(family tie)*
propinquity blood, connection *(relation),* corollary, kinship, relation *(connection),* vicinity. SEE MAIN ENTRY
propinquus approximate, close *(near),* related, relation *(kinship),* relative
propitiable nonmilitant
propitiare propitiate
propitiate arbitrate *(conciliate),* disarm *(set at ease),* mollify, pacify, placate, reconcile, redeem *(satisfy debts),* redress, soothe. SEE MAIN ENTRY
propitiated agreed *(harmonized)*
propitiating compensatory
propitiation collection *(payment),* conciliation, expiation, mollification, reconciliation
propitiator go-between, intermediary, referee
propitiatory nonmilitant
propitious auspicious, beneficial, favorable *(advantageous),* fitting, opportune, seasonable, viable. SEE MAIN ENTRY
propitiousness expedience, opportunity
propitius propitious
propone hold out *(deliberate on an offer)*
proponent advocate *(espouser),* apologist. SEE MAIN ENTRY
proponere exhibit, issue *(publish)*
proporting distribution *(apportionment)*
proportion allotment, caliber *(measurement),* coordinate, differential, quota, ration, regularity, share *(interest).* SEE MAIN ENTRY
proportionable cognate, proportionate
proportional commensurable, commensurate, congruous, harmonious, proportionate, relative *(comparative)*
proportionate adequate, commensurable, commensurate, congruous, correlative, dispense, harmonious, pro rata, relative *(comparative),* suitable. SEE MAIN ENTRY
proportionately per capita, pro rata
proportioned coextensive, elegant
proportionment apportionment
proportions area *(surface),* degree *(magnitude),* dimension, magnitude
proposal advice, agenda, application, bid, bill *(proposed act),* campaign, conspiracy, invitation, measure, motion, motive, nomination, overture, plan, platform, policy *(plan of action),* prescription *(directive),* program, project, proposition, recommendation, request, resolution *(formal statement),* strategy, suggestion. SEE MAIN ENTRY
propose advise, advocate, argue, counsel, extend *(offer),* hold out *(deliberate on an offer),* initiate, intend, move *(judicially request),* nominate, plan, pose *(propound),* posit, present *(introduce),* proffer, propound, raise *(advance),* recommend, remit *(submit for consideration),* resolve *(decide),* submit *(give),* tender. SEE MAIN ENTRY

propose a motion move *(judicially request)*
propose a question inquire
propose an action formally move *(judicially request)*
propose as a candidate nominate
propose legal instructions charge *(instruct on the law)*
proposed apparent *(presumptive)*, tentative
proposed act measure
proposed action agenda, design *(intent)*, plan, platform, policy *(plan of action)*, strategy
proposed enactment bill *(proposed act)*
proposed law bill *(proposed act)*
proposed measure motion
proposed regulation bill *(proposed act)*
proposed rule bill *(proposed act)*
proposed sequence of action design *(intent)*
proposed statute bill *(proposed act)*
proposer of a law lawmaker
proposer of legislation lawmaker
propositio proposition
proposition advice, affirmance *(legal affirmation)*, agenda, application, basis, bid, business *(affair)*, campaign, claim *(assertion)*, clause, contention *(argument)*, invitation, issue *(matter in dispute)*, matter *(subject)*, measure, motion, overture, plan, platform, policy *(plan of action)*, principle *(axiom)*, project, proposal *(suggestion)*, question *(issue)*, rationale, recommendation, resolution *(formal statement)*, strategy, suggestion, theory, thesis, ultimatum. SEE MAIN ENTRY
propositional apparent *(presumptive)*
propositum intention, matter *(subject)*, object, project, purpose, strategy
propound adduce, admonish *(advise)*, advocate, allege, annunciate, argue, assert, avouch *(avow)*, avow, bear *(adduce)*, claim *(maintain)*, defend, hold *(decide)*, issue *(publish)*, offer *(propose)*, posit, postulate, proffer, propose, submit *(give)*, utter. SEE MAIN ENTRY
propounded alleged
proprietary ownership, proprietor. SEE MAIN ENTRY
proprietary rights occupation *(possession)*
proprietas character *(personal quality)*, characteristic, feature *(characteristic)*, property *(distinctive attribute)*, trait
proprieties protocol *(etiquette)*
proprietor employer, landholder, landlord, landowner, principal *(director)*, tenant
proprietorship adverse possession, dominion *(absolute ownership)*, enjoyment *(use)*, interest *(ownership)*, occupancy, occupation *(possession)*, ownership, possession *(ownership)*, tenancy, title *(right)*
propriety admissibility, aptitude, behalf, behavior, conduct, decorum, deportment, expedience, formality, integrity, justice, qualification *(fitness)*, rectitude, right *(righteousness)*
proprius distinctive, essential *(required)*, individual, inherent, innate, particular *(specific)*, specific, typical
propugnaculum bulwark, safeguard
propulsare parry, repulse, stave
propulsion impetus
propulsive compelling, impulsive *(impelling)*
propulsive force impetus
prorate allocate, allot, apportion, charge *(assess)*, disburse *(distribute)*, distribute, divide *(distribute)*, parcel, partition. SEE MAIN ENTRY
prorogare prolong
prorogate postpone
prorogation adjournment, cloture, deferment, delay, dissolution *(termination)*
prorogue adjourn, continue *(adjourn)*, defer *(put off)*, postpone, procrastinate, recess
prorsus in toto
proruption outbreak, outburst
prosaic average *(standard)*, jejune *(dull)*, languid, lifeless *(dull)*, mediocre, mundane, nondescript, ordinary, pedestrian, ponderous, stale, trite, typical, usual. SEE MAIN ENTRY
prosaical mediocre, ordinary, prosaic
proscribe ban, bar *(hinder)*, block, border *(bound)*, censor, condemn *(ban)*, constrain *(restrain)*, debar, eliminate *(exclude)*, enjoin, exclude, forbid, forswear, inhibit, interdict, limit, order, outlaw, prohibit, reject, relegate, renounce, repudiate, restrain, restrict, sentence. SEE MAIN ENTRY
proscribed barred, illegal, illegitimate *(illegal)*, illicit, impermissible, unauthorized
proscribed form procedure
proscribed person pariah
proscribere outlaw, proscribe *(prohibit)*
proscriptio proscription
proscription bar *(obstruction)*, boycott, check *(bar)*, constraint *(restriction)*, deterrence, deterrent, direction *(order)*, injunction, limitation, mandate, obstacle, obstruction, ostracism, prohibition, refusal, rejection, renunciation, restraint, veto. SEE MAIN ENTRY
proscriptive prohibitive *(restrictive)*, restrictive
proscriptus outlaw
proscrit discard
prosecute accuse, arraign, complain *(charge)*, incriminate, lodge *(bring a complaint)*, pursue *(carry on)*. SEE MAIN ENTRY
prosecute an inquiry delve
prosecute one's case plead *(argue a case)*
prosecute to a conclusion close *(terminate)*, conclude *(complete)*, consummate, follow-up
prosecuting attorney district attorney, prosecutor. SEE MAIN ENTRY
prosecution action *(proceeding)*, arraignment, complainant, complaint, cross-examination, proceeding, prosecutor, pursuit *(chase)*. SEE MAIN ENTRY
prosecution history estoppel SEE MAIN ENTRY
prosecutor accuser, complainant, district attorney, jurist. SEE MAIN ENTRY
prosecutorial complaint information *(charge)*
proselyte partisan, persuade
proselytism persuasion
proselytize convert *(persuade)*, persuade
prosequi pursue *(chase)*
prospect chance *(possibility)*, contemplation, customer, expectation, likelihood, motive, opportunity, possibility, potential, probability. SEE MAIN ENTRY
prospection expectation
prospective apparent *(presumptive)*, forthcoming, future, immediate *(imminent)*, imminent, pending *(imminent)*, proximate. SEE MAIN ENTRY
prospective buyer patron *(regular customer)*
prospective client prospect *(prospective patron)*
prospective customer prospect *(prospective patron)*
prospector speculator
prospectus issuance, plan, program, proposition. SEE MAIN ENTRY
prosper auspicious
prosper earn, gain, prevail *(triumph)*, progress, succeed *(attain)*
prospering successful
prosperitas prosperity
prosperity welfare. SEE MAIN ENTRY
prosperous beneficial, opulent, successful. SEE MAIN ENTRY
prosperous issue boom *(prosperity)*
prosperous outcome boom *(prosperity)*
prosperousness boom *(prosperity)*, prosperity, welfare
prosperus favorable *(advantageous)*, prosperous
prospicience expectation
prostitute betray *(lead astray)*, corrupt, deteriorate, misemploy, mistreat, pervert, pollute
prostitution misusage, perversion
prostrate disable, helpless *(powerless)*, overcome *(overwhelm)*, overthrow, servile, subservient
prostration impuissance. SEE MAIN ENTRY
prosy jejune *(dull)*, mundane, pedestrian, prolix, prosaic, stale, usual
protagonist abettor, backer. SEE MAIN ENTRY
protean aleatory *(uncertain)*, mutable, pliable, variable. SEE MAIN ENTRY
protect care *(be cautious)*, care *(regard)*, conceal, conserve, cover *(guard)*, defend, ensconce, enshroud, ensure, envelop, foster, harbor, hedge, keep *(shelter)*, maintain *(sustain)*, patrol, police, preserve, save *(rescue)*, screen *(guard)*, shroud, side, sponsor, support *(assist)*, sustain *(prolong)*, uphold. SEE MAIN ENTRY
protect against loss insure
protect from injury preserve
protected exempt, guarded, immune, impervious, inexpugnable, insusceptible *(resistant)*, safe, secure *(free from danger)*
protecting conservation, preventive
protection adoption *(affiliation)*, advantage, auspices, behalf, blackmail, bulwark, charge *(custody)*, conservation, coverage *(insurance)*, custody *(supervision)*, defense, direction *(guidance)*, ecology, gratuity *(bribe)*, haven, immunity, impunity, inviolability, lodging, panoply, patronage *(support)*, precaution, preservation, refuge, reinforcement, safeguard, safekeeping, security *(safety)*, shield, support *(assistance)*, surveillance, trust *(custody)*, veil, ward. SEE MAIN ENTRY
protection against loss indemnity, insurance
protection money bribe
protective paternal, preventive, prophylactic, salutary. SEE MAIN ENTRY
protective covering panoply
protective custody constraint *(imprisonment)*, detention, preservation, safekeeping
protective device barrier
protective fire barrage
protective order SEE MAIN ENTRY
protective outfit panoply
protector advocate *(counselor)*, apologist, backer, benefactor, guardian, peace officer, proponent, samaritan, shield, sponsor, warden

protectorship adoption *(affiliation),* auspices, control *(supervision),* management *(supervision),* patronage *(support)*
protectory cache *(hiding place)*
protegé disciple. SEE MAIN ENTRY
proteiform pliable, protean
protervitas audacity
protest admonition, avow, challenge, complain *(criticize),* complaint, conflict, confront *(oppose),* contention *(opposition),* counter, counteract, cross *(disagree with),* demur, denial, deprecate, differ *(disagree),* disaccord *(noun),* disaccord *(verb),* disaffirm, disagree, disallow, disapprobation, disapprove *(reject),* disavow, disown *(deny the validity),* disparagement, dissension, dissent *(withhold assent),* drawback, except *(object),* exception *(objection),* expostulate, fight *(counteract),* gainsay, impugnation, negate, negation, nonconformity, object, objection, oppose, opposition, oppugn, outcry, picket, prohibit, reaction *(opposition),* refuse, reject, remonstrance, remonstrate, renounce, reprehend, repudiate, resist *(oppose),* resistance. SEE MAIN ENTRY
protest against counter, counteract, decry, denounce *(condemn),* inveigh, reproach
protest against a ruling exception *(objection)*
protest frivolously cavil
protestant dissident, heretic, recusant, reluctant
protestation avowal, complaint, contention *(opposition),* criticism, denial, disapprobation, disapproval, dissension, drawback, exception *(objection),* impugnation, negation, nonconformity, opposition, outcry, remonstrance
protested bill bad debt
protester malcontent
protesting dissenting, dissident, nonconsenting, remonstrative
prothonotary clerk
protocol bill *(proposed act),* decorum, mode, practice *(procedure),* rule *(guide),* treaty. SEE MAIN ENTRY
protogenic primordial
protomorphic rudimentary
protoplast prototype
prototypal primordial
prototype constant, exemplar, model, paradigm, pattern, rule *(guide),* sample, standard. SEE MAIN ENTRY
protract compound, continue *(prolong),* delay, enlarge, extend *(enlarge),* hold up *(delay),* increase, last, procrastinate, prolong, sustain *(prolong).* SEE MAIN ENTRY
protracted chronic, profuse, prolix. SEE MAIN ENTRY
protraction adjournment, advance *(increase),* boom *(increase),* continuance, continuation *(prolongation),* continuity, filibuster, longevity
protrude overlap, project *(extend beyond)*
protrudent salient
protruding obtrusive, prominent, salient
protrusive obtrusive, prominent, salient
protuberant obtrusive, prominent, salient
protuberate project *(extend beyond)*
proud disdainful, inflated *(vain),* supercilious. SEE MAIN ENTRY
proud contempt disdain
provable convincing. SEE MAIN ENTRY
prove ascertain, bear *(adduce),* cite *(state),* confirm, convince, corroborate, demonstrate *(establish),* disabuse, document, establish *(show),* evince, manifest, reason *(persuade),* substantiate, support *(corroborate),* sustain *(confirm),* testify, validate, verify *(confirm).* SEE MAIN ENTRY
prove acceptable satisfy *(fulfill)*
prove blameless exonerate
prove false disprove, rebut, refute
prove guiltless exculpate
prove inadequate fail *(lose)*
prove innocent absolve, acquit, clear
prove not guilty absolve, exculpate, exonerate
prove one's point convince
prove the contrary contradict, disprove, negate
prove the truth of justify
prove the validity of a will probate
prove to be a participant in involve *(implicate)*
prove to be wrong disprove
prove to the contrary disprove
prove treacherous defect
prove unreliable fail *(neglect)*
prove unsatisfactory fail *(lose)*
prove useless fail *(lose)*
prove warranted justify
proved dependable, reliable, unrefutable, valid
proved innocent acquitted
proved strength proof
provehere promote *(advance),* raise *(advance)*
proven dependable, irrefutable, official, sound, undeniable, unrefutable
proven name goodwill
provenance birth *(lineage),* derivation, genesis, origination, source
provender replenish
provenience derivation, origination, source
proverb maxim, phrase
proverbial trite. SEE MAIN ENTRY
proverbial saying maxim
provide accommodate, avail *(bring about),* bear *(yield),* bequeath, bestow, clothe, dispense, enable, endow, endue, fund, furnish, give *(grant),* hoard, impart, lend, make, pander, present *(make a gift),* procure, produce *(manufacture),* recruit, render *(administer),* replenish, sell, stipulate, supply, transmit, yield *(produce a return).* SEE MAIN ENTRY
provide against forestall
provide an answer respond
provide an opportunity extend *(offer)*
provide capital finance, invest *(fund)*
provide capital again refinance
provide capital for capitalize *(provide capital),* subsidize
provide financing subsidize
provide for bear *(support),* capitalize *(provide capital),* expect *(anticipate),* fund, maintain *(sustain),* nurture, plan, preserve, sponsor, subsidize, support *(assist)*
provide funds finance
provide funds for capitalize *(provide capital),* subsidize
provide funds for again refinance
provide justification palliate *(excuse),* support *(justify)*
provide means enable
provide money finance, fund, invest *(fund)*
provide money for capitalize *(provide capital),* subsidize
provide refuge harbor
provide safety harbor
provide sanctuary harbor, preserve
provide subvention finance
provide the answer countercharge, resolve *(solve)*
provide the means implement
provide the wherewithal fund
provide with administer *(tender),* lend, render *(administer)*
provide with a motive motivate
provide with an alibi excuse
provide with documents document
provide with information instruct *(teach)*
provide with nomenclature call *(title),* identify, label
provide with proof document
provided SEE MAIN ENTRY
provided with arms armed
provided without charge free *(at no charge),* gratuitous *(given without recompense)*
providence discretion *(quality of being discreet),* economy *(frugality),* precaution, preparation, provision *(act of supplying),* prudence
provident acute, careful, economical, frugal, judicious, juridical, politic, preparatory, preventive, prudent, vigilant. SEE MAIN ENTRY
providentia forethought
providential auspicious, favorable *(advantageous),* fitting, fortuitous, opportune, propitious, prosperous
provider materialman, supplier
providere provide *(arrange for)*
providing donative
providing evidence probative
providing proof probative
providing sanctuary conservation
providus circumspect, vigilant
province ambit, bailiwick, capacity *(sphere),* circuit, coverage *(scope),* department, district, division *(administrative unit),* domain *(sphere of influence),* jurisdiction, locality, part *(role),* pursuit *(occupation),* purview, realm, region, role, section *(vicinity),* sphere, territory. SEE MAIN ENTRY
provincia department, province, sphere
provincial local, naive, narrow, parochial, regional. SEE MAIN ENTRY
provincialism prejudice *(preconception)*
proving cogent, convincing
provise stipulation
provision accommodation *(adjustment),* aid, alimony, article *(distinct section of a writing),* attornment, bear *(yield),* bestow, budget, clause, condition *(contingent provision),* contribution *(donation),* dispensation *(act of dispensing),* donation, endowment, forethought, fund, furnish, inheritance, limitation, precaution, preparation, principle *(axiom),* qualification *(condition),* ration, replenish, reservation *(condition),* reserve, resource, safeguard, stock *(store),* supply, title *(division),* ultimatum. SEE MAIN ENTRY
provision for damages ad damnum clause
provision of the law statute
provisional conditional, contingent, dubious, empirical, interim, interlocutory, qualified *(conditioned),* restrictive, speculative, subject *(conditional),* surrogate, temporary, tentative, transient, transitory, uncertain *(questionable),* vicarious *(substitutional).* SEE MAIN ENTRY
provisional hypothesis proposition

provisional measure stopgap
provisional remedy SEE MAIN ENTRY
provisional settlement modus vivendi
provisionally pro tempore, provided
provisionary conditional, qualified *(conditioned)*
provisioner supplier
provisioning equipment
provisions ammunition, cargo, maintenance *(support of spouse)*, merchandise, stock in trade, store *(depository)*, sustenance
provisions of a law legislation *(enactments)*
proviso arrangement *(understanding)*, article *(distinct section of a writing)*, attornment, clause, condition *(contingent provision)*, need *(requirement)*, option *(contractual provision)*, prerequisite, provision *(clause)*, qualification *(condition)*, requirement, reservation *(condition)*, salvo, specification, term *(provision)*, ultimatum. SEE MAIN ENTRY
provisory conditional, dependent, interim, interlocutory, provisional, qualified *(conditioned)*, restrictive, tentative, transient
provocare defy
provocateur catalyst
provocatio appeal, defiance
provocation aggravation *(annoyance)*, catalyst, incentive, inducement, influence, instigation, motive, reason *(basis)*, stimulus. SEE MAIN ENTRY
provocative catalyst, impertinent *(insolent)*, incentive, inducement, invitation, moving *(evoking emotion)*, offensive *(taking the initiative)*, persuasive, presumptuous, provocation, salacious, sapid, suggestive *(evocative)*, suggestive *(risqué)*, vexatious. SEE MAIN ENTRY
provocator aggressor, demagogue
provoke aggravate *(annoy)*, agitate *(activate)*, annoy, antagonize, badger, bait *(harass)*, bait *(lure)*, cause, coax, contrive, discommode, discompose, evoke, exacerbate, foment, generate, harass, harrow, harry *(harass)*, hector, incense, incite, inspire, irritate, lobby, mistreat, molest *(annoy)*, occasion, offend *(insult)*, originate, persecute, perturb, pique, plague, press *(goad)*, prompt, spirit, stimulate, urge. SEE MAIN ENTRY
provoke desire lure, motivate
provoke hatred alienate *(estrange)*, incense
provoke hatred against disaffect
provoke ire incense
provoked aggrieved *(harmed)*, bitter *(reproachful)*
provoker demagogue
provoking moving *(evoking emotion)*, offensive *(taking the initiative)*, persuasive, provocative, sapid, vexatious
provost plenipotentiary
prowess ability, efficiency, skill. SEE MAIN ENTRY
prowl lurk, perambulate, pursue *(chase)*. SEE MAIN ENTRY
prowl after hunt
prowler burglar
prowling burglary, stealthy
proxies deputation *(delegation)*
proximal adjacent, approximate, close *(near)*, contiguous, proximate
proximate approximate, border *(approach)*, close *(near)*, contiguous, immediate *(not distant)*, present *(attendant)*. SEE MAIN ENTRY
promixate cause SEE MAIN ENTRY
proximate to situated
proximity presence *(attendance)*, propinquity *(similarity)*, vicinity
proximity of blood degree *(kinship)*
proximus proximate, related
proxy agency *(legal relationship)*, agent, attorney in fact, conduit *(intermediary)*, deputy, plenipotentiary, proctor, procurator, replacement, substitute, surrogate. SEE MAIN ENTRY
proxyship delegation *(assignment)*
prudence caution *(vigilance)*, common sense, continence, deliberation, diligence *(care)*, discretion *(quality of being discreet)*, discrimination *(good judgment)*, economy *(frugality)*, expedience, precaution, preparation, sagacity, sense *(intelligence)*, temperance. SEE MAIN ENTRY
prudens circumspect, deliberate, discreet, judicious, knowing, politic, prudent, reasonable *(rational)*, sensible, tactical
prudent acute, careful, circumspect, deliberate, diplomatic, discreet, economical, frugal, guarded, judicial, judicious, juridical, noncommittal, politic, provident *(frugal)*, provident *(showing foresight)*, responsive, safe, sensible, solid *(sound)*, vigilant. SEE MAIN ENTRY
prudent conduct management *(judicious use)*
prudentia caution *(vigilance)*, discretion *(quality of being discreet)*, discrimination *(good judgment)*, prudence, sagacity, sense *(intelligence)*
prudential judicial, judicious, juridical, politic, provident *(showing foresight)*, prudent, solid *(sound)*
prudently contrived politic
prune decrease, diminish, minimize, retrench
prurience pornography
prurient dissolute, immoral, lascivious, lecherous, lewd, salacious. SEE MAIN ENTRY
pry delve, force *(break)*, hunt, research, spy
pry into examine *(study)*, frisk, inquire, peruse, probe, scrutinize, search
prying encroachment, interest *(concern)*, interrogative, obtrusive
pseudo false *(not genuine)*, imitation, quasi, spurious, surrogate, synthetic
pseudonym sobriquet
pseudonymous quasi
psyche spirit
psychiatric hospital asylum *(hospital)*
psychiatric ward asylum *(hospital)*
psychological habits character *(personal quality)*
psychologically abnormal non compos mentis
psychopathic non compos mentis
psychotic non compos mentis
puberty adolescence
pubes adult
pubescence adolescence
pubescent juvenile, minor
public blatant *(conspicuous)*, civic, common *(shared)*, competitive *(open)*, conspicuous, famous, manifest, national, open *(accessible)*, overt, patent, political, populace, population. SEE MAIN ENTRY
public address peroration
public announcement canon, charter *(declaration of rights)*, declaration, issuance, proclamation, publication *(disclosure)*
public attorney district attorney, jurist
public avowal proclamation
public building edifice
public business utility *(public service)*
public company utility *(public service)*
public corporation utility *(public service)*
public declaration avouchment
public disclosure common knowledge
public disgrace dishonor *(shame)*
public distribution publicity
public disturbance commotion
public domain SEE MAIN ENTRY
public economy finance
public enemy convict, criminal, foe, outlaw
public entwinement SEE MAIN ENTRY
public esteem character *(reputation)*, distinction *(reputation)*
public favor goodwill, prestige
public forum SEE MAIN ENTRY
public industry utility *(public service)*
public inquest hearing
public knowledge common knowledge
public manners conduct
public notice common knowledge, declaration, notoriety, proclamation, publicity
public office holder official
public opinion poll *(canvass)*
public opponent foe
public option SEE MAIN ENTRY
public pleader district attorney
public proceeding hearing
public prosecutor complainant, district attorney, prosecutor
public recognition mention *(tribute)*
public relations publicity
public reproach bad repute, infamy
public revenue finance
public sale auction
public sale of property auction
public servant caretaker *(one fulfilling the function of office)*, legislator, politician
public servants government *(political administration)*
public service nonprofit, politics. SEE MAIN ENTRY
public speaking declamation, rhetoric *(skilled speech)*
public spirit philanthropy
public statement charter *(declaration of rights)*
public support goodwill
public treasury bank
public uprising revolution
public wrong crime
public-spirited philanthropic
publicare condemn *(seize)*, confiscate
publication charter *(declaration of rights)*, declaration, disclosure *(act of disclosing)*, disclosure *(something disclosed)*, issuance, pandect *(treatise)*, proclamation, pronouncement, publicity. SEE MAIN ENTRY
publicist attorney, barrister, promoter
publicists press
publicity issuance, notice *(announcement)*, notification, notoriety, promotion *(encouragement)*, story *(narrative)*. SEE MAIN ENTRY
publicize annunciate, bare, communicate, correspond *(communicate)*, denude, disseminate, divulge, herald, issue *(publish)*, notify, proclaim, promulgate, propagate *(spread)*, publish, spread, utter. SEE MAIN ENTRY
publicized notorious
publicizer harbinger
publicly accuse condemn *(blame)*, denounce *(condemn)*, denounce *(inform against)*

publicly indecent lewd
publicly known common *(customary)*
publicly owned national
publicly recognized standing character *(reputation)*
publicness common knowledge
publicus common *(shared)*, official, political, public *(known)*
publish annunciate, apprise, bear *(adduce)*, circulate, convey *(communicate)*, disclose, disseminate, divulge, enunciate, expose, herald, inform *(notify)*, manifest, notice *(give formal warning)*, notify, post, proclaim, promulgate, propagate *(spread)*, report *(disclose)*, reveal, signify *(inform)*, speak, spread, utter. SEE MAIN ENTRY
publish a falsehood libel
publish abroad disseminate
published patent, public *(known)*
publishers press
puckishness mischief
pudency embarrassment
pueri child, children
puerile inept *(incompetent)*, jejune *(lacking maturity)*. SEE MAIN ENTRY
puerile person juvenile
puerilis juvenile *(adjective)*, juvenile *(noun)*, puerile
puerility adolescence, minority *(infancy)*. SEE MAIN ENTRY
puff up inflate
puffed inflated *(enlarged)*
puffed up inflated *(enlarged)*, proud *(conceited)*, supercilious, turgid
puffery overstatement, rodomontade
puffy inflated *(enlarged)*
pugilatio fight *(battle)*
pugilist contender
pugna affray, fight *(argument)*, fray
pugnacious argumentative, contentious, hostile, litigious, perverse, petulant, polemic, querulous, spartan. SEE MAIN ENTRY
pugnaciousness belligerency
pugnacity belligerency
pugnare contend *(dispute)*
pugnax contentious
puisne inferior *(lower in position)*
puissance clout, dint, influence, main force, potential, power, predominance, quality *(excellence)*, strength, validity. SEE MAIN ENTRY
puissant cogent, compelling, considerable, efficient, in full force, indomitable, inexpugnable, influential, irresistible, om-nipotent, potent, powerful, predominant
puissant prevailing *(having superior force)*
puissant strong
puling querulous
pull draw *(attraction)*, draw *(extract)*, educe, evulsion, extract, predominance, pressure, stress *(strain)*
pull aside divert
pull back retreat, withdraw
pull different ways bicker
pull down derogate, subvert
pull in discipline *(control)*, inhibit
pull into shape frame *(formulate)*
pull out abandon *(withdraw)*, disinter, educe, eviscerate, extirpate, extract, leave *(depart)*, quit *(evacuate)*, relinquish, renege, secede
pull strings influence, lobby, manipulate *(control unfairly)*
pull strings for prefer
pull the strings predominate *(command)*
pull together cooperate, unite
pull up disinter
pull up by the roots extirpate, obliterate
pull wires manipulate *(control unfairly)*
pullalare pullulate
pulling out evulsion
pullulate germinate, increase, propagate *(increase)*. SEE MAIN ENTRY
pulsare beat *(strike)*
pulse beat *(pulsate)*
pulseless lifeless *(dead)*
pulverize break *(fracture)*, destroy *(efface)*
pulverized broken *(fractured)*
pummel beat *(strike)*, fight *(battle)*, lash *(strike)*
pump up inflate
punch beat *(strike)*
punctilio decorum, formality, particular, protocol *(etiquette)*
punctilious accurate, close *(rigorous)*, conscientious, detailed, diligent, draconian, exact, meticulous, painstaking, particular *(exacting)*, precise, rigid, strict. SEE MAIN ENTRY
punctiliously faithfully
punctiliousness decorum, particularity
punctual exact, expeditious, instant, precise, prompt. SEE MAIN ENTRY
punctuality dispatch *(promptness)*, regularity
punctualness dispatch *(promptness)*
punctuate discontinue *(break continuity)*, interrupt, reaffirm
punctuated disjunctive *(tending to disjoin)*
punctum vote
punctum temporis instant
puncture break *(fracture)*, debunk, enter *(penetrate)*, lancinate, penetrate, pierce *(lance)*
pundit mastermind. SEE MAIN ENTRY
pungent bitter *(acrid tasting)*, caustic, incisive, mordacious, trenchant
punic faith bad faith
punire condemn *(punish)*
punish beat *(strike)*, convict, fine, inflict, mulct *(fine)*, penalize, repay, reprehend. SEE MAIN ENTRY
punish by pecuniary penalty fine
punish with death execute *(sentence to death)*
punishable culpable, delinquent *(guilty of a misdeed)*, illegal, impermissible
punishable act tortious act
punishable by law illicit
punishable offense misdemeanor
punishing cruel, disciplinary *(punitory)*, harsh, penal, punitive
punishing experience condemnation *(punishment)*
punishment condemnation *(punishment)*, conviction *(finding of guilt)*, cost *(penalty)*, expiation, forfeiture *(act of forfeiting)*, forfeiture *(thing forfeited)*, infliction, penalty, reprisal, retribution, revenge, sentence, vengeance. SEE MAIN ENTRY
punishment fixed by law penalty
punishment prescribed by law penalty
punishment without trial lynch law
punition condemnation *(punishment)*, conviction *(finding of guilt)*, correction *(punishment)*, punishment, reprisal
punitive disciplinary *(punitory)*, penal, severe, vindictive. SEE MAIN ENTRY
punitive action reprisal, retribution, revenge
punitive damages SEE MAIN ENTRY
punitory penal, punitive, vindictive
punt bet
punter bettor
puny negligible, null *(insignificant)*, paltry, petty
pupil disciple, neophyte, novice, protégé
purblind opaque
purchasable mercenary, venal
purchase acquire *(secure)*, buy, deal, leverage, procure, takeover, trade *(commerce)*, trade, transaction. SEE MAIN ENTRY
purchase from patronize *(trade with)*
purchase money price
purchase on time credit *(delayed payment)*
purchase on trust credit *(delayed payment)*
purchase price cost *(price)*
purchase without a guaranty caveat emptor
purchase without a warranty caveat emptor
purchased at one's risk caveat emptor
purchaser client, consumer, customer, patron *(regular customer)*. SEE MAIN ENTRY
purchaser of goods consumer
purchaser of goods from another customer
purchaser of stolen goods fence
purchaser of stolen property fence
pure absolute *(ideal)*, authentic, blameless, clean, clear *(apparent)*, genuine, honest, inculpable, inviolate, moral, natural, original *(initial)*, pellucid, simple, stark, sterling, theoretical, true *(authentic)*, unadulterated, unblemished, upright. SEE MAIN ENTRY
pure in heart clean
pure-hearted clean
purebred genuine
purely only, solely *(purely)*. SEE MAIN ENTRY
purgare absolve, acquit, justify, vindicate
purgatio justification
purgation absolution, acquittal, catharsis, clemency, confession
purgatorial penitent
purge absolve, catharsis, clear, decontaminate, deplete, deportation, discharge *(liberate)*, dismiss *(discharge)*, displace *(remove)*, eliminate *(eradicate)*, eradicate, exclusion, exonerate, expel, expulsion, expurgate, extirpate, free, oust, pardon, removal, remove *(eliminate)*. SEE MAIN ENTRY
purge oneself confess
purged clear *(free from criminal charges)*
purified sacrosanct
purify decontaminate, expurgate, fix *(repair)*, meliorate. SEE MAIN ENTRY
purify by removing the foreign and nonessential distill
purifying medicinal, remedial
puritanic severe, uncompromising
puritanical draconian, rigid, severe, strict, stringent, tartuffish, uncompromising
purity honor *(good reputation)*, integrity, rectitude
purlieu bailiwick, periphery, vicinity
purlieus border, locality, location, part *(place)*, region, section *(vicinity)*
purloin abduct, bilk, carry away, cheat, defalcate, deprive, despoil, embezzle, hold up *(rob)*, impropriate, jostle *(pickpocket)*, loot, peculate, pilfer, pirate *(reproduce without authorization)*, plunder, poach, rob, steal. SEE MAIN ENTRY
purloiner embezzler, hoodlum, thief

purloining embezzlement, theft
purloinment burglary, theft
purport amount *(result)*, bespeak, connotation, consequence *(significance)*, content *(meaning)*, context, cornerstone, design *(intent)*, gist *(substance)*, import, intent, main point, materiality *(consequence)*, meaning, point *(purpose)*, pretend, signification, signify *(denote)*, spirit, substance *(essential nature)*, tenor, value. SEE MAIN ENTRY
purported ostensible, putative, specious. SEE MAIN ENTRY
purpose animus, basis, cause *(reason)*, contemplation, content *(meaning)*, cornerstone, design *(intent)*, destination, end *(intent)*, forethought, function, goal, ground, idea, impetus, intend, intent, intention, mission, motive, object, objective, plan, predetermination, project, pursuit *(goal)*, purview, reason *(basis)*, resolution *(decision)*, resolve *(decide)*, signification, undertaking *(attempt)*, use, volition, will *(desire)*. SEE MAIN ENTRY
purpose in view design *(intent)*
purposed aforethought, deliberate, intentional, tactical, willful
purposeful decisive, deliberate, earnest, express, industrious, intense, intentional, knowing, persistent, pertinacious, resolute, serious *(devoted)*, tactical, voluntary, willful. SEE MAIN ENTRY
purposefully knowingly, purposely
purposefulness diligence *(perseverance)*
purposeless arbitrary and capricious, casual, expendable, nugatory, random, unavailing, unintentional, unwitting, vacuous
purposely SEE MAIN ENTRY
purposive aforethought, express, purposeful
purse reward, stake *(award)*, treasury
purser comptroller
pursuance course, endeavor, industry *(activity)*
pursuant to SEE MAIN ENTRY
pursue adhere *(persist)*, approach, assume *(undertake)*, attempt, bait *(harass)*, chase, continue *(persevere)*, delve, desire, endeavor, exercise *(discharge a function)*, follow-up, hunt, inquire, keep *(continue)*, maintain *(carry on)*, persevere, ply, practice *(engage in)*, prosecute *(carry forward)*, race, remain *(continue)*, research, resume, search, specialize, strive, study, trace *(follow)*, undertake. SEE MAIN ENTRY
pursue a claim sue
pursue a course perform *(execute)*
pursue an inquiry audit, canvass, investigate, probe, research
pursue in court litigate
pursue relentlessly persist
pursuer addict
pursuit activity, assignment *(task)*, business *(occupation)*, calling, career, course, design *(intent)*, employment, endeavor, enterprise *(undertaking)*, function, industry *(activity)*, industry *(business)*, inquiry *(systematic investigation)*, labor *(work)*, livelihood, market *(demand)*, mission, objective, occupation *(vocation)*, operation, position *(business status)*, post, practice *(professional business)*, probe, profession *(vocation)*, project, quest, research, specialty *(special aptitude)*, struggle, trade *(occupation)*, undertaking *(business)*, undertaking *(enterprise)*, work *(employment)*. SEE MAIN ENTRY
pursuit by a law enforcement agency prosecution *(criminal trial)*
pursuits affairs
purulent toxic
purus clean, pure, unblemished, unconditional
purvey bear *(yield)*, fund, furnish, pander, provide *(supply)*, replenish, supply
purveyance provision *(act of supplying)*
purveyor supplier
purview area *(province)*, coverage *(scope)*, jurisdiction, scope. SEE MAIN ENTRY
push cajole, coerce, constrain *(compel)*, dispatch *(send off)*, exhort, foray, force *(coerce)*, impact, impel, impetus, importune, impulse, incite, jostle *(bump into)*, launch *(project)*, main force, pressure *(noun)*, pressure *(verb)*, project *(impel forward)*, promote *(organize)*, prompt, provoke, spirit, stimulus, struggle, urge. SEE MAIN ENTRY
push ahead expedite, proceed *(go forward)*
push aside divert, doubt *(hesitate)*, hold up *(delay)*, ignore, misprize, postpone, procrastinate, relegate
push away dispel, eject *(expel)*, parry, stave
push back repel *(drive back)*, repulse
push forward expedite, facilitate
push into browbeat
push on hasten, move *(alter position)*, proceed *(go forward)*, progress
push out dislodge, eject *(expel)*
push through dispatch *(send off)*, expedite
push together impact
push too far incense, tax *(overwork)*
push toward pursue *(strive to gain)*
push up promote *(advance)*
pushing impulsive *(impelling)*
pushy eager, obtrusive
pusillanimity fear
pusillanimous caitiff, recreant. SEE MAIN ENTRY
pusillus paltry
put deposit *(place)*, dispose *(incline)*, impute, introduce, locate, lodge *(house)*, phrase, plant *(place firmly)*, raise *(advance)*, repose *(place)*, situated, submit *(give)*. SEE MAIN ENTRY
put a barrier around enclose, include
put a damper on discourage
put a false appearance on misrepresent
put a false appearance upon disguise
put a false construction on distort, misconceive, misread, misrepresent, misunderstand
put a false construction upon perjure, profess *(pretend)*
put a false sense on distort, misconstrue, mistake
put a mark on brand *(mark)*
put a mark upon label
put a meaning on comment, construe *(translate)*
put a restraint upon check *(restrain)*
put a stop to cease, check *(restrain)*, clog, close *(terminate)*, condemn *(ban)*, constrain *(restrain)*, desist, deter, eliminate *(eradicate)*, enjoin, estop, finish, hold up *(delay)*, interrupt, quit *(discontinue)*, strangle, toll *(stop)*
put a wrong construction on misread, misunderstand
put aboard load
put about circulate
put across explain
put ahead conduce
put along side border *(approach)*
put alongside compare, juxtapose
put an approximate price on estimate
put an embargo on bar *(hinder)*, condemn *(ban)*
put an end to abate *(extinguish)*, annul, cancel, cease, check *(restrain)*, condemn *(ban)*, destroy *(void)*, discontinue *(abandon)*, dispatch *(put to death)*, eliminate *(eradicate)*, enjoin, estop, expunge, extinguish, extirpate, finish, halt, interrupt, quash, quit *(discontinue)*, stay *(halt)*, stop, subvert, terminate
put an erroneous construction on distort, misunderstand
put an indication on brand *(mark)*
put an interpretation construe *(translate)*
put an obligation upon commit *(entrust)*
put aside abandon *(relinquish)*, defer *(put off)*, eliminate *(exclude)*, except *(exclude)*, exclude, forfeit, hoard, hold up *(delay)*, isolate, keep *(shelter)*, postpone, pretermit, reserve, select, set aside *(reserve)*, waive
put asunder disconnected, divorce
put at a disadvantage embarrass, penalize
put at ease assure *(give confidence to)*
put at hazard compromise *(endanger)*, pawn
put at interest deposit *(submit to a bank)*
put at stake pawn
put away keep *(shelter)*, preserve, retain *(keep in possession)*, set aside *(reserve)*
put back reconstitute, reinstate, renew *(begin again)*, replace, restore *(return)*
put back into service reinstate
put before instruct *(teach)*
put behind bars imprison, jail, lock
put beside juxtapose
put between interject, intersperse
put beyond the protection of the law outlaw
put by store
put close together juxtapose
put confidence in rely, trust
put down cast *(register)*, defeat, demean *(make lower)*, derogate, dispatch *(put to death)*, enter *(record)*, humiliate, kill *(defeat)*, quash, repress, stifle, subdue, subjugate
put faith in confide *(trust)*, rely
put first preface
put forth argue, communicate, emit, exert, extend *(offer)*, issue *(publish)*, move *(judicially request)*, offer *(propose)*, pass *(determine)*, plead *(allege in a legal action)*, posit, postulate, present *(introduce)*, profess *(avow)*, propound, publish, pullulate, submit *(give)*. SEE MAIN ENTRY
put forth an effort attempt, strive
put forth effort try *(attempt)*
put forth for acceptance offer *(propose)*
put forth for consideration offer *(propose)*
put forward alleged, circulate, claim *(maintain)*, conduce, declare, extend *(offer)*, flaunt, hold out *(deliberate on an offer)*, introduce, issue *(publish)*, move *(judicially request)*, offer *(propose)*, plead *(allege in a legal action)*, pose *(propound)*, posit, postulate, prefer, profess *(avow)*, proffer, propose, propound, submit *(give)*, tender

put forward for consideration extend *(offer)*, introduce, offer *(propose)*
put forward in opposition object
put goods in load
put in enter *(insert)*, interpose, introduce
put in a bad light defame, denounce *(condemn)*, pillory
put in a cell constrain *(imprison)*, imprison
put in a claim for call *(demand)*, desire
put in a conspicuous place expose
put in accord arbitrate *(conciliate)*
put in action apply *(put in practice)*, employ *(make use of)*, enforce, execute *(accomplish)*, exercise *(use)*, exert, manipulate *(utilize skillfully)*
put in an affidavit avouch *(avow)*, plead *(allege in a legal action)*
put in an appearance appear *(attend court proceedings)*, emerge, issue *(send forth)*, report *(present oneself)*. SEE MAIN ENTRY
put in array classify, file *(arrange)*, organize *(arrange)*
put in bodily fear menace
put in care of charge *(empower)*, confide *(trust)*
put in charge entrust
put in check balk, counter
put in commission assign *(designate)*, delegate, invest *(vest)*
put in concealment blind *(obscure)*, camouflage, plant *(covertly place)*
put in condition fix *(repair)*
put in custody commit *(institutionalize)*
put in danger expose
put in durance arrest *(apprehend)*
put in duress arrest *(apprehend)*, seize *(apprehend)*
put in execution commence
put in fear browbeat, intimidate, menace
put in for request
put in force administer *(conduct)*, authorize, constitute *(establish)*, effectuate, enact, enforce, execute *(accomplish)*, implement, impose *(enforce)*, legislate, pass *(approve)*, perform *(adhere to)*, perform *(execute)*
put in good condition fix *(repair)*
put in hazard endanger
put in in a bad light denigrate
put in irons fetter, handcuff, imprison, trammel
put in jeopardy compromise *(endanger)*, endanger
put in motion agitate *(shake up)*, dispatch *(send off)*, establish *(launch)*, exercise *(discharge a function)*, impel, launch *(initiate)*, move *(alter position)*
put in one's hands delegate
put in operation apply *(put in practice)*, capitalize *(seize the chance)*, employ *(make use of)*, enforce
put in opposition confront *(oppose)*, oppose, polarize
put in order classify, emend, file *(arrange)*, fix *(arrange)*, fix *(repair)*, marshal, orchestrate, organize *(arrange)*, pigeonhole, regulate *(adjust)*, repair, restore *(renew)*, settle, sort
put in other words construe *(translate)*, elucidate, explain
put in pawn pledge *(deposit)*
put in peril expose
put in place locate
put in pledge pawn
put in possession bequeath, devolve, grant *(transfer formally)*, instate, seize *(confiscate)*, vest

put in practice exercise *(use)*, exploit *(make use of)*, implement, perform *(adhere to)*, ply
put in production manufacture
put in proper order fix *(arrange)*
put in readiness arrange *(methodize)*
put in repair fix *(repair)*, restore *(renew)*
put in restraint apprehend *(arrest)*
put in safekeeping delegate
put in shape fix *(repair)*
put in slyly foist
put in stealthily foist
put in the hands of commit *(entrust)*, endow
put in the place of change, displace *(replace)*, supersede
put in uniform clothe
put in view expose
put in words communicate, enunciate, express
put in writing enter *(record)*, inscribe, note *(record)*, record
put into inject
put into a cage imprison
put into a receptacle enclose
put into a systematic form orchestrate
put into a temper incense
put into action exercise *(discharge a function)*, expedite, exploit *(make use of)*, perpetrate
put into bodily form embody
put into circulation circulate, diffuse, dispel, issue *(publish)*, publish
put into condition remedy
put into disorder confound
put into effect enact, enforce, exercise *(discharge a function)*, implement, operate, pass *(approve)*, perpetrate, ply, render *(administer)*
put into execution enforce
put into force inflict
put into isolation confine
put into language phrase
put into motion cast *(throw)*. SEE MAIN ENTRY
put into operation exploit *(make use of)*, manipulate *(utilize skillfully)*
put into practice exercise *(discharge a function)*, operate, transact
put into shape formulate, frame *(formulate)*, organize *(arrange)*, remedy, renew *(refurbish)*, repair
put into the hands of deliver
put into words observe *(remark)*, phrase, relate *(tell)*, speak
put money down bet
put off adjourn, delay, deter, hold up *(delay)*, pause, postpone, pretermit, procrastinate, stall, stave, suspend
put off a decision doubt *(hesitate)*
put off the scent misdirect
put off the track divert, obfuscate
put off to a future time hold up *(delay)*
put on betray *(lead astray)*, levy, pretend, prevaricate, specious
put on a false front pretend
put on a firm basis establish *(entrench)*
put on a pedestal elevate, honor
put on an act fake
put on board load
put on deceitfully assume *(simulate)*
put on display produce *(offer to view)*
put on guard caution, forewarn, portend
put on one's guard alert, notice *(give formal warning)*
put on paper note *(record)*, record
put on payroll hire

put on record cast *(register)*, enter *(record)*, file *(place among official records)*, note *(record)*, record, set down
put on sale sell
put on speed hasten
put on the retired list discharge *(dismiss)*
put on the scale weigh
put on the stage produce *(offer to view)*
put on trial hear *(give a legal hearing)*, impeach, sue
put one's case plead *(argue a case)*
put one's mind to concentrate *(pay attention)*
put one's trust in swear
put one's veto to condemn *(ban)*
put one's veto upon bar *(hinder)*
put oneself out endeavor
put out depose *(remove)*, disadvantage, disappointed, discompose, dislodge, disoblige, displace *(remove)*, eject *(evict)*, exclude, expel, extinguish, issue *(publish)*, oust, perturb, provoke, publish, remove *(dismiss from office)*
put out at interest invest *(fund)*
put out of action disable
put out of combat disarm *(divest of arms)*
put out of commission impair
put out of countenance bait *(harass)*, humiliate, pique
put out of house by legal process evict
put out of humor irritate, provoke
put out of joint luxate
put out of matrimony divorce
put out of mind dismiss *(put out of consideration)*
put out of order disorganize, upset
put out of place luxate
put out of possession depose *(remove)*, eject *(evict)*
put out of sight blind *(obscure)*, cloak, cover *(conceal)*, hide, plant *(covertly place)*
put out of the way dispatch *(put to death)*
put out of wedlock divorce
put over continue *(adjourn)*
put over to a future date continue *(adjourn)*
put pressure on bait *(harass)*, browbeat, coerce, constrain *(compel)*, enforce, insist, lobby, press *(constrain)*, press *(goad)*
put questions to examine *(interrogate)*
put right disabuse, edit, emend, help, redress, repair, restore *(renew)*
put side by side juxtapose
put something across bilk
put something over bilk, dupe, illude
put something over on betray *(lead astray)*
put straight disabuse
put the blame on charge *(accuse)*, convict, impeach
put through attain, pass *(approve)*, prosecute *(carry forward)*
put through a deal dicker
put through paces discipline *(train)*
put to call *(appeal to)*, pose *(propound)*
put to a wrong use convert *(misappropriate)*
put to advantage capitalize *(seize the chance)*
put to death destroy *(efface)*, dispatch *(put to death)*, execute *(sentence to death)*, extinguish, kill *(murder)*, slay
put to death according to law execute *(sentence to death)*

put to flight repel *(drive back)*, repulse
put to inconvenience discommode
put to press publish
put to rest lull
put to rights rectify
put to rout beat *(defeat)*
put to service capitalize *(seize the chance)*, employ *(make use of)*, exploit *(make use of)*
put to shame brand *(stigmatize)*, denigrate, humiliate, pillory, reproach, sully
put to sleep drug, lull
put to the proof prove
put to the test probe, prove
put to the vote choose
put to use apply *(put in practice)*, employ *(make use of)*, exercise *(use)*, exploit *(make use of)*, profit, resort
put to work employ *(engage services)*, engage *(hire)*, exercise *(use)*, exploit *(make use of)*, hire, retain *(employ)*
put to wrong use exploit *(take advantage of)*
put together affix, annex *(add)*, attach *(join)*, cement, collect *(gather)*, commingle, connect *(join together)*, consolidate *(strengthen)*, consolidate *(unite)*, constitute *(compose)*, create, devise *(invent)*, fabricate *(construct)*, forge *(produce)*, form, formulate, frame *(construct)*, incorporate *(include)*, join *(bring together)*, make, manufacture
put under an injunction condemn *(ban)*, enjoin, forbid
put under an interdiction condemn *(ban)*, enjoin
put under arrest apprehend *(arrest)*, confine, constrain *(imprison)*, detain *(hold in custody)*, immure
put under contract engage *(hire)*
put under duress kidnap
put under embargo enjoin
put under lock and key imprison
put under obligation compel, constrain *(compel)*, force *(coerce)*, press *(constrain)*
put under prohibition condemn *(ban)*
put under restraint arrest *(apprehend)*, check *(restrain)*, coerce, confine, constrain *(imprison)*, constrain *(restrain)*, control *(restrain)*, detain *(hold in custody)*, fetter, hold up *(delay)*, imprison, jail, restrict
put under suspicion compromise *(endanger)*
put under the ban enjoin
put under water immerse *(plunge into)*
put up build *(construct)*, invest *(fund)*, nominate, pledge *(deposit)*, proffer
put up a front fake
put up a petition move *(judicially request)*
put up a request call *(appeal to)*, plead *(implore)*
put up a sign post
put up a struggle parry
put up for sale handle *(trade)*, sell, vend
put up petitions pray
put up the money finance, lend, sponsor
put up with authorize, bear *(tolerate)*, endure *(suffer)*, forbear, submit *(yield)*, suffer *(permit)*, tolerate
put upon record inscribe
putare impression
putative plausible, presumptive. SEE MAIN ENTRY
putrefaction deterioration, spoilage
putrefied tainted *(contaminated)*
putrefy decay, degenerate, infect, spoil *(impair)*, taint *(contaminate)*
putrescence spoilage
putrid loathsome, offensive *(offending)*, tainted *(contaminated)*
putridity deterioration
putting in custody commitment *(confinement)*
putting in order disposition *(determination)*
putting off deferment, delay
putting out expulsion
putting together accession *(annexation)*
puzzle complication, confound, confuse *(bewilder)*, confusion *(ambiguity)*, dilemma, disconcert, disturb, enigma, hoodwink, involution, muddle, mystery, obfuscate, paradox, perplex, pose *(propound)*, problem, question *(issue)*, secret. SEE MAIN ENTRY
puzzle out solve
puzzle over doubt *(hesitate)*, ponder, reflect *(ponder)*, speculate *(conjecture)*
puzzled lost *(disoriented)*
puzzlement ambiguity, cloud *(suspicion)*, confusion *(ambiguity)*, dilemma, quandary
puzzling debatable, difficult, elusive, enigmatic, equivocal, esoteric, hidden, inapprehensible, incomprehensible, indefinable, inexplicable, inexpressive, inscrutable, labyrinthine, mysterious, opaque, peculiar *(curious)*, problematic, recondite, uncertain *(ambiguous)*
puzzling alternative dilemma
puzzling problem enigma
pylon portal
pyramid build *(augment)*, parlay *(exploit successfully)*
pyramid scheme SEE MAIN ENTRY
pyromania arson
pyrotic caustic
pythonic ominous, portentous *(ominous)*, prophetic

Q

quack fake
quackery abortion *(fiasco)*, fraud, hypocrisy
quadrate comport *(agree with)*
quadrate with cohere *(adhere)*
quaerere investigate, speculate *(conjecture)*
quaesitor judge
quaestio inquest, inquiry *(systematic investigation)*, interrogation, question *(inquiry)*, subject *(topic)*, trial *(legal proceeding)*
quaestuosus gainful, lucrative
quaestus earnings, income, profit
quaff carouse
quagmire impasse, pitfall, plight, qu-andary. SEE MAIN ENTRY
quaint eccentric, nonconforming, novel, outdated, outmoded
quake beat *(pulsate)*, cataclysm
quaking trepidation
qualification caliber *(mental capacity)*, capacity *(aptitude)*, capacity *(authority)*, clause, condition *(contingent provision)*, control *(restriction)*, correction *(change)*, degree *(academic title)*, discipline *(training)*, discretion *(quality of being discreet)*, doubt *(indecision)*, drawback, education, experience *(background)*, extenuating circumstances, faculty *(ability)*, gift *(flair)*, limitation, modification, necessary, necessity, performance *(workmanship)*, potential, preparation, propensity, provision *(clause)*, reservation *(condition)*, restriction, salvo, sine qua non, specialty *(special aptitude)*, term *(provision)*. SEE MAIN ENTRY
qualifications competence *(ability)*
qualified admissible, capable, competent, conditional, deft, dependent, desirable *(qualified)*, eligible, entitled, expert, familiar *(informed)*, fit, literate, practiced, professional *(trained)*, proficient, sciential, suitable, veteran. SEE MAIN ENTRY
qualified endorsement without recourse
qualified immunity SEE MAIN ENTRY
qualified person expert, mastermind, specialist
qualified practitioner professional
qualify allay, allow *(authorize)*, alter, delegate, discipline *(train)*, empower, enable, enfranchise, extenuate, instill, instruct *(teach)*, lessen, moderate *(temper)*, modify *(alter)*, modify *(moderate)*, palliate *(abate)*, pass *(satisfy requirements)*, restrict, satisfy *(fulfill)*, specialize, validate. SEE MAIN ENTRY
qualifying mitigating, palliative *(excusing)*, preparatory, restrictive
qualifying factors circumstances
qualifying reasons extenuating circumstances
qualities character *(personal quality)*, temperament
quality characteristic, color *(complexion)*, complexion, condition *(state)*, differential, feature *(characteristic)*, gift *(flair)*, intonation, merit, meritorious, premium, property *(distinctive attribute)*, select, speciality, specialty *(distinctive mark)*, status, sterling, trait, value, weight *(importance)*, worth. SEE MAIN ENTRY
quality of being certain certainty
quality of being equal and fair equity *(justice)*
quality of being singular identity *(individuality)*
quality of execution performance *(workmanship)*
quality of work performance *(workmanship)*
quality-minded particular *(exacting)*
qualm apprehension *(fear)*, doubt *(indecision)*, doubt *(suspicion)*, fear, hesitation, misgiving, scruple, suspicion *(mistrust)*. SEE MAIN ENTRY
qualmish diffident, disinclined, hesitant
qualmishness doubt *(indecision)*, doubt *(suspicion)*
qualms reluctance
quandary complication, confusion *(ambiguity)*, deadlock, dilemma, disturbance, doubt *(indecision)*, imbroglio, impasse, incertitude, indecision, plight, predicament, problem, quagmire. SEE MAIN ENTRY
quantification appraisal, measurement, rating
quantified definite
quantify calculate, measure, pinpoint, rate. SEE MAIN ENTRY
quantitas quantity
quantity bulk, conglomeration, corpus, extent, measurement, part *(portion)*, quota, ration, selection *(collection)*, unit *(item)*. SEE MAIN ENTRY
quantity produced output
quantum bulk, proportion, quantity, quota
quantum meruit SEE MAIN ENTRY
quantum of proof SEE MAIN ENTRY
quarantine captivity, confine, constraint *(imprisonment)*, contain *(enclose)*, detain

(hold in custody), detention, durance, exclude, immure, insulate, isolate, ostracism, seclude, sequester *(seclude)*. SEE MAIN ENTRY
quarantine station captivity
quarrel altercation, argument *(contention)*, bicker, brawl, challenge, collide *(clash)*, commotion, conflict *(noun)*, conflict *(verb)*, confrontation *(altercation)*, contend *(dispute)*, contention *(opposition)*, contest *(dispute)*, contradict, contravention, controversy *(argument)*, disaccord *(noun)*, disaccord *(verb)*, disagree, disagreement, dissension, dissent *(differ in opinion)*, dissidence, embroilment, feud, fight *(argument)*, fracas, fray, incompatibility *(difference)*, object, outbreak, split, strife, struggle, variance *(disagreement)*. SEE MAIN ENTRY
quarrel noisily brawl
quarrel over contest, dispute *(contest)*
quarreling abusive, argument *(contention)*, conflict, contention *(opposition)*, discord, dissenting, dissident
quarrelsome argumentative, contentious, disorderly, dissenting, fractious, litigious, negative, petulant, polemic, pugnacious, querulous
quarrelsomeness contention *(opposition)*
quarry extract, victim
quarter circuit, deposit *(place)*, disjoint, district, dwell *(reside)*, harbor, indulgence, lenience, locality, locate, location, lodge *(house)*, lodge *(reside)*, part *(place)*, pity, region, territory
quartered situated
quarters building *(structure)*, domicile, dwelling, habitation *(dwelling place)*, home *(domicile)*, house, inhabitation *(place of dwelling)*, lodging, premises *(buildings)*, residence
quash abate *(extinguish)*, abolish, abrogate *(annul)*, cancel, censor, condemn *(ban)*, contain *(restrain)*, discharge *(release from obligation)*, disinherit, dissolve *(terminate)*, eliminate *(eradicate)*, enjoin, expunge, extinguish, extirpate, invalidate, kill *(defeat)*, negate, nullify, obliterate, overcome *(surmount)*, overthrow, overwhelm, prohibit, refute, repeal, rescind, revoke, subjugate, suppress, upset, vacate *(void)*, vitiate, withdraw. SEE MAIN ENTRY
quash the conviction clear
quashed invalid, lifeless *(dead)*, null *(invalid)*, null and void
quashing avoidance *(cancellation)*, deterrence, dismissal *(termination of a proceeding)*, rescision
quasi imitation. SEE MAIN ENTRY
quasi pendent
quasi spurious, synthetic
quaver beat *(pulsate)*
queer eccentric, irregular *(not usual)*, ludicrous, noteworthy, peculiar *(curious)*, prodigious *(amazing)*, singular, unaccustomed
queerness quirk *(idiosyncrasy)*
quell abate *(extinguish)*, allay, alleviate, arrest *(stop)*, assuage, beat *(defeat)*, cancel, cease, condemn *(ban)*, contain *(restrain)*, decrease, defeat, destroy *(efface)*, deter, diminish, eliminate *(eradicate)*, enjoin, expunge, extinguish, extirpate, halt, impede, kill *(defeat)*, lull, moderate *(temper)*, mollify, obliterate, obtund, overcome (surmount), override, overthrow, overturn, overwhelm, pacify, palliate *(abate)*, prevail *(triumph)*, prohibit, quash, remit *(relax)*, repress, restrain, soothe, stay *(halt)*, stem *(check)*, stifle, stop, strangle, subdue, subject, subjugate, suppress. SEE MAIN ENTRY
quell suspicion disarm *(set at ease)*
quelling palliative *(abating)*
quench allay, assuage, cancel, deter, discourage, extinguish, inhibit, quash, repress, satisfy *(fulfill)*, soothe, stifle, suppress
quenchless hot-blooded, indomitable, insatiable
querela grievance, plaint
queribundus querulous
querimonia complaint, grievance, plaint
querimonious querulous
querulous fractious, froward, litigious, particular *(exacting)*, petulant, reluctant, resentful. SEE MAIN ENTRY
querulousness dissatisfaction
querulus querulous
query challenge, check *(inspect)*, cross-examination, cross-examine, cross-questioning, dispute *(contest)*, doubt *(distrust)*, examine *(interrogate)*, impugn, inquire, inquiry *(request for information)*, interrogation, pose *(propound)*, question *(inquiry)*. SEE MAIN ENTRY
quest agency *(legal relationship)*, attempt, campaign, cross-examination, delve, discovery, endeavor, hunt, indagation, inquest, probe, pursue *(chase)*, pursuit *(chase)*, pursuit *(effort to secure)*, research *(noun)*, research *(verb)*, undertaking *(attempt)*, undertaking *(enterprise)*, venture. SEE MAIN ENTRY
question analyze, canvass, challenge, check *(inspect)*, consult *(ask advice of)*, contest, cross-examine, disbelieve, discount *(disbelieve)*, doubt *(indecision)*, doubt *(distrust)*, enigma, examine *(interrogate)*, hesitate, impugn, incertitude, incredulity, inquire, inquiry *(request for information)*, inquiry *(systematic investigation)*, investigate, issue *(matter in dispute)*, matter *(subject)*, misdoubt, mistrust, pose *(propound)*, probe, problem, qualm, scruple, scrutinize, suspect *(distrust)*, suspicion *(uncertainty)*, thesis. SEE MAIN ENTRY
question and answer interview
question at issue conflict, controversy *(argument)*, issue *(matter in dispute)*
question in one's mind doubt *(suspicion)*
question the truth of dispute *(contest)*
question under oath examine *(interrogate)*. SEE MAIN ENTRY
questionability cloud *(suspicion)*, ill repute, improbability
questionable blameworthy, contestable, controversial, debatable, disputable, doubtful, dubious, dubitative, equivocal, implausible, indefinite, lewd, ludicrous, moot, outrageous, problematic, speculative, tentative, unbelievable, undecided, unethical, unscrupulous, unsound *(fallacious)*, unsustainable, untenable, untrustworthy, vague. SEE MAIN ENTRY
questionableness ill repute
questionary form *(document)*, poll *(canvass)*
questioned moot
questioning conversation, cross-examination, cross-questioning, cynical, dissenting, doubtful, inconvincible, incredulous, indagation, inquest, inquisitive, interest *(concern)*, interrogation, interrogative, interrogatories, investigation, leery, research, skeptical, test
questioning integrity impeachment
questioning under oath examination *(test)*
questioning witness's veracity impeachment
questionless axiomatic, certain *(positive)*, clear *(certain)*, decisive, definite, incontrovertible, irrefutable, undisputed, unimpeachable
questionlessness certainty
questionnaire blank *(form)*, form *(document)*, poll *(canvass)*. SEE MAIN ENTRY
questions interrogatories
queue assemblage, lineup. SEE MAIN ENTRY
qui conventui praeest chairman
qui facit actor
qui oppugnat assailant
qui sibi placet complacent
qui vulnerari potest vulnerable
quibble equivocate, haggle, prevaricate, tergiversate. SEE MAIN ENTRY
quibbling excuse salvo
quick alert *(agile)*, artful, born *(alive)*, brief, cursory, deft, expeditious, facile, immediate *(at once)*, impulsive *(rash)*, instantaneous, live *(conscious)*, perfunctory, perspicacious, precipitate, proficient, prompt, rapid, ready *(prepared)*, summary, volatile. SEE MAIN ENTRY
quick discharge dispatch *(promptness)*
quick judgment discretion *(quality of being discreet)*
quick of apprehension perceptive, sapient, sensitive *(discerning)*
quick riddance dispatch *(promptness)*
quick sense perception
quick-tempered hot-blooded, sensitive *(easily affected)*
quick-witted acute, perspicacious, sapient
quicken expedite, facilitate, precipitate *(hasten)*, promise *(raise expectations)*
quickening acceleration, cumulative *(intensifying)*, revival
quickly forthwith, instantly, readily
quickly executed summary
quickly performed summary
quickness dispatch *(promptness)*, efficiency, facility *(easiness)*, haste, judgment *(discernment)*, sagacity, skill
quickness of perception intelligence *(intellect)*
quid center *(essence)*
quid pro quo collection *(payment)*. SEE MAIN ENTRY
quidam certain *(specific)*
quiddity center *(essence)*, character *(personal quality)*, content *(meaning)*, essence, gist *(substance)*, main point
quies ease, inaction
quiescence cessation *(interlude)*, composure, inaction, inertia, languor, lull, peace, silence. SEE MAIN ENTRY
quiescency abeyance, lull, silence
quiescent dormant, lifeless *(dull)*, mute, passive, patient, peaceable, placid, stagnant, static
quiet allay, alleviate, diffident, diminish, dormant, ease, inconspicuous, laconic, lifeless *(dull)*, lull (noun), lull *(verb)*, moderate *(temper)*, moderation, mollify, mute, obtund, pacify, palliate *(abate)*, patient, peace, peaceable, placate, placid, private *(secluded)*, remit *(relax)*, repress, silence, solemn, soothe, speechless, static, strangle, subdue, subside, taciturn, unobtrusive, unpretentious. SEE MAIN ENTRY

quiet down lull
quieten lull
quieting palliative *(abating)*
quietly persevering patient
quietness peace, silence
quietude composure, privacy, silence. SEE MAIN ENTRY
quietus denouement
quietus extremity *(death)*
quietus inactive, placid
quietus release, remission
quintessence center *(essence)*, character *(personal quality)*, characteristic, consequence *(significance)*, content *(meaning)*, cornerstone, corpus, essence, gist *(substance)*, main point, spirit. SEE MAIN ENTRY
quintessential best
quirk compulsion *(obsession)*, speciality, specialty *(distinctive mark)*. SEE MAIN ENTRY
quit abandon *(physically leave)*, abandon *(relinquish)*, abandon *(withdraw)*, cease, comport *(behave)*, defect, demean *(deport oneself)*, demit, discontinue *(abandon)*, evacuate, forfeit, forgo, forswear, halt, leave *(depart)*, part *(leave)*, pay, recoup *(reimburse)*, relinquish, remise, renege, renounce, resign, retire *(conclude a career)*, retreat, secede, shirk, stop, vacate *(leave)*, withdraw, yield *(submit)*. SEE MAIN ENTRY
quit of free *(relieved from a burden)*
quit work strike *(refuse to work)*
quitclaim cede, remise. SEE MAIN ENTRY
quite the contrary contra
quittance acquittal, amnesty, collection *(payment)*, compensation, contribution *(indemnification)*, expiation, honorarium, payment *(act of paying)*, payment *(remittance)*, quitclaim, receipt *(proof of receiving)*, recompense, remission, remittance, remuneration, reparation *(indemnification)*, reprieve, requital, restitution, revenge, reward, satisfaction *(discharge of debt)*, trover, wage
quitting abdication, desertion, resignation *(relinquishment)*
quiver beat *(pulsate)*
quivering trepidation
quixotic SEE MAIN ENTRY
quixotical quixotic
quiz check *(inspect)*, cross-examine, examination *(test)*, examine *(interrogate)*, inquire, test. SEE MAIN ENTRY
quizzical inquisitive, interrogative, ironic, skeptical, suspicious *(distrustful)*
quo nihil efficitur inconclusive
quod abalienari non potest inalienable
quod comprehendi incomprehensible
quod contra dicitur objection
quod contra leges fit illegal, illicit
quod defendi non potest indefensible
quod eodem tempore est contemporaneous
quod est admirabile contraque opinionem omnium paradox
quod everti non potest indestructible
quod ex lege legal, licit
quod fiere non potest impracticable
quod fieri non potest impossible
quod indecorum est impropriety
quod nihil ad rem est impertinent *(irrelevant)*
quod nihil excusationis habet inexcusable
quod refutari non potest inappealable, incontrovertible
quod restat remainder *(remaining part)*
quod satis est sufficiency
quod tangi non potest impalpable
quondam former, prior
quorum minimum. SEE MAIN ENTRY
quota quorum, ration. SEE MAIN ENTRY
quotation attribution, bid, charge *(cost)*, citation *(attribution)*, cost *(price)*, estimate *(approximate cost)*, excerpt, price, rate, reference *(citation)*, value, worth. SEE MAIN ENTRY
quote cite *(state)*, excerpt, extract, recite, refer *(direct attention)*, repeat *(state again)*. SEE MAIN ENTRY
quoted passage excerpt, reference *(citation)*
quoted price bid, cost *(price)*, face value *(price)*, tariff *(bill)*
quotidian daily
quotidianus customary, ordinary
quotidie daily
quoting reference *(citation)*
quotum proportion, share *(interest)*

R

rabble-rouser demagogue, malcontent
rabid deranged, extreme *(exaggerated)*, fanatical, outrageous, vehement, zealous
rabidity furor, passion
race competition, contest *(competition)*, descent *(lineage)*, hasten, origin *(ancestry)*, strife. SEE MAIN ENTRY
race hatred discrimination *(bigotry)*
race prejudice discrimination *(bigotry)*
race-conscious admissions process SEE MAIN ENTRY
racial balance integration *(assimilation)*
racial harmonization integration *(assimilation)*
racial harmony integration *(assimilation)*
racial prejudice segregation *(isolation by races)*
racialism discrimination *(bigotry)*, segregation *(isolation by races)*
racism discrimination *(bigotry)*, intolerance, segregation *(isolation by races)*
rack plague
rack the brains ponder
racket bluster *(commotion)*, brawl, bunko, commotion, disorder *(lack of order)*, noise, outcry, pandemonium. SEE MAIN ENTRY
racketeer malefactor, outlaw. SEE MAIN ENTRY
rackety disorderly
racking insufferable
racy lurid, suggestive *(risqué)*
radiant ecstatic, illustrious
radiare radiate
radiate cast *(throw)*, circulate, deploy, diffuse, dispel, disseminate, dissipate *(spread out)*, dissolve *(disperse)*, emanate, emit, pervade, spread, transmit. SEE MAIN ENTRY
radiating divergent
radical demagogue, drastic, extreme *(exaggerated)*, fanatical, insurgent, malcontent, outrageous, total, unusual, vital. SEE MAIN ENTRY
radically new measure innovation
radicated permanent
radius boundary
raffish blatant *(obtrusive)*, caitiff, ignoble
raffle bet, lottery
rag mock *(deride)*
rage furor, mode, outbreak, outburst, passion, style, violence
rage against inveigh
raging disorderly, lunatic, outrageous, severe
raid attack, bait *(harass)*, depredation, despoil, devastate, encroach, encroachment, foray, harry *(plunder)*, impinge, incursion, invade, invasion, loot, onset *(assault)*, outbreak, pillage *(noun)*, pillage *(verb)*, plunder *(noun)*, plunder *(verb)*, prey, spoil *(pillage)*, spoliation. SEE MAIN ENTRY
raider burglar, vandal
raiding burglary, housebreaking, predatory
rail demonstrate *(protest)*, inveigh
rail at flout, reprimand, reproach
railing aspersion, diatribe
raillery ridicule
rainmaker SEE MAIN ENTRY
raise accrue *(increase)*, adopt, ameliorate, boom *(increase)*, build *(augment)*, build *(construct)*, collect *(recover money)*, compound, develop, discipline *(train)*, elevate, enhance, enlarge, excise *(levy a tax)*, expand, foster, frame *(construct)*, heighten *(augment)*, heighten *(elevate)*, honor, increase, increment, levy, magnify, meliorate, originate, parlay *(exploit successfully)*, prefer, produce *(manufacture)*, promote *(advance)*, promotion *(advancement)*, recruit, uphold. SEE MAIN ENTRY
raise a demand necessitate
raise a hue and cry against censure, decry, impugn
raise a question challenge, doubt *(distrust)*
raise a question as to impugn
raise a suspicion doubt *(distrust)*
raise above the proper value inflate
raise aloft elevate, heighten *(elevate)*
raise anger incense
raise apprehension dissuade, frighten
raise apprehensions browbeat, menace
raise contributions collect *(recover money)*
raise expectations assure *(give confidence to)*
raise frivolous objection to cavil
raise funds collect *(recover money)*
raise hopes promise *(raise expectations)*
raise objections challenge, counter, demur, differ *(disagree)*, disaffirm, disagree, dissent *(withhold assent)*, protest, remonstrate
raise objections frivolously cavil
raise one's voice against challenge, decry, dissent *(withhold assent)*, impugn, inveigh
raise questions impugn
raise specious objection to cavil
raise spirits invoke
raise taxes toll *(exact payment)*
raise to a higher position elevate
raise to distinction honor
raise troops recruit
raise up one's voice pray
raised prominent
raised path causeway
raised road causeway
raised voice outcry
raison d'être basis SEE MAIN ENTRY
rake off decrease
rake through frisk
rakeoff gratuity *(bribe)*
rakish dissolute, lecherous, licentious
rally assemblage, call *(summon)*, caucus, coax, collection *(assembly)*, combine *(act in concert)*, congregate, convene, help, incite, join *(bring together)*, meet, provoke, reassure, stimulate
rally around side

rally round cooperate
rally to bear *(support)*, maintain *(sustain)*
ram constrict *(compress)*, impact
ram in inject
ramble detour, digress, perambulate, prowl
rambler itinerant
rambling circuitous, desultory, discursive *(digressive)*, indirect, labyrinthine, loquacious, profuse, prolix, sinuous, voluble. SEE MAIN ENTRY
rambling talk jargon *(unintelligible language)*
ramification organ
ramified divergent
ramify bifurcate, radiate, spread
rammed compact *(dense)*
rampage bluster *(commotion)*, brawl *(noun)*, brawl *(verb)*, commotion, confusion *(turmoil)*, outburst, pandemonium, passion, violence
rampageous uncontrollable
rampancy passion
rampant disorderly, hot-blooded, predominant, prevailing *(current)*, prevalent, rife, uncontrollable, unrestrained *(not repressed)*, unruly, vehement. SEE MAIN ENTRY
rampart barrier, buffer zone, bulwark, mainstay, security *(safety)*, shield
ramshackle dilapidated
rancid loathsome, stale, tainted *(contaminated)*
rancor alienation *(estrangement)*, cruelty, feud, ill will, malice, odium, spite, umbrage, vengeance. SEE MAIN ENTRY
rancorous bitter *(reproachful)*, caustic, harsh, hostile, invidious, malevolent, malignant, mordacious, negative, relentless, ruthless, scathing, spiteful, vindictive, virulent
random astray, desultory, discursive *(digressive)*, disordered, disorderly, fortuitous, haphazard, indiscriminate, unpredictable. SEE MAIN ENTRY
random luck act of god, happenstance
random sample cross section
randomness incoherence
range area *(province)*, capacity *(aptitude)*, chain *(series)*, circuit, classify, coverage *(scope)*, degree *(magnitude)*, direction *(course)*, extent, file *(arrange)*, fix *(arrange)*, gamut, hierarchy *(arrangement in a series)*, jurisdiction, latitude, magnitude, perambulate, prowl, purview, region, scene, scope, sort, space, sphere. SEE MAIN ENTRY
range of choice latitude
range of meaning connotation, context
range of view coverage *(scope)*, perspective
range of vision perspective
range together juxtapose
ranger migrant
ranging discursive *(digressive)*
rank calculate, class, classify, codify, condition *(state)*, credit *(recognition)*, criticize *(evaluate)*, degree *(station)*, depraved, estimate, evaluate, excessive, fertile, file *(arrange)*, fix *(arrange)*, gauge, loathsome, marshal, materiality *(consequence)*, measure, obnoxious, odious, organize *(arrange)*, pigeonhole, precedence, prestige, productive, quality *(excellence)*, rate, rating, repulsive, reputation, sort, status, tabulate, title *(position)*, unmitigated. SEE MAIN ENTRY
rank first surpass
ranking classification, degree *(station)*, master, outstanding *(prominent)*, rating
rankle affront, aggravate *(annoy)*, annoy, bait *(harass)*, harass, irritate
rankling malice, resentment
ransack despoil, devastate, foray, harry *(plunder)*, loot, pillage *(noun)*, pillage *(verb)*, pirate *(take by violence)*, plunder, prey, spoil *(pillage)*, spoliation
ransom blackmail, extricate, free, pay, redeem *(repurchase)*, rescue. SEE MAIN ENTRY
ransom factor SEE MAIN ENTRY
ransomed free *(relieved from a burden)*
rant bombast, declaim, fustian, outpour, reprimand, rodomontade
rant at reproach
ranter bigot, demagogue
ranting bluster *(speech)*, fustian, incoherence, lunatic
rap beat *(strike)*
rapacious confiscatory, insatiable, larcenous, mercenary, predatory. SEE MAIN ENTRY
rapaciousness desire, extortion
rapacity bad repute, extortion, larceny, pillage
rapax rapacious
rape molest *(subject to indecent advances)*. SEE MAIN ENTRY
rapere rape, seize *(apprehend)*
rapid cursory, expeditious, impulsive *(rash)*, instantaneous, precipitate, summary. SEE MAIN ENTRY
rapidity dispatch *(promptness)*, haste
rapidly instantly
rapidus rapid
rapina pillage, plunder, robbery
rapine depredation, larceny, pillage, plunder, rape, spoliation
rapport accordance *(understanding)*, compatibility, concert, concordance, connection *(relation)*, contact *(association)*, peace, rapprochement, relationship *(connection)*, understanding *(agreement)*. SEE MAIN ENTRY
rapprochement arbitration, comparison
rapprochement reconciliation. SEE MAIN ENTRY
rapscallion degenerate, malefactor
rapt ecstatic, pensive
rapt attention diligence *(care)*, obsession, preoccupation
raptorial predatory
rapture passion
rapturous ecstatic
raptus abduction
rare extraordinary, individual, inestimable, infrequent, meritorious, nonconforming, notable, noteworthy, novel, obscure *(remote)*, original *(creative)*, peculiar *(curious)*, portentous *(eliciting amazement)*, priceless, remarkable, scarce, select, singular, special, sporadic, unaccustomed, uncanny, uncommon, unique, unprecedented, unusual, valuable. SEE MAIN ENTRY
rare occurrence improbability, phenomenon *(unusual occurrence)*
rarefy cultivate, decontaminate
rareness dearth, paucity
rari aditus inaccessible, unapproachable
rarity exception *(exclusion)*, improbability, irregularity, phenomenon *(unusual occurrence)*, specialty *(distinctive mark)*
rarus infrequent, rare, scarce, sporadic, uncommon
rascal malefactor
rascality artifice, deception, ill repute, improbity, knavery, mischief, misdoing
rascally artful, lawless, machiavellian, profligate *(corrupt)*, reprobate, sinister, unconscionable
rash blind *(not discerning)*, careless, heedless, hot-blooded, ill-advised, ill-judged, impolitic, improvident, imprudent, irresponsible, negligent, precipitate, premature, presumptuous, spontaneous, thoughtless, unpolitic, unpremeditated
rashness audacity, haste, inconsideration, indiscretion, inexpedience, neglect, temerity
rasp erode, irritate
rasure annulment, cancellation
ratable ad valorem
rate amount *(sum)*, assess *(appraise)*, assessment *(levy)*, calculate, caliber *(quality)*, charge *(cost)*, charge *(assess)*, classify, criticize *(evaluate)*, differential, duty *(tax)*, earnings, estimate *(approximate cost)*, estimate, evaluate, expense *(cost)*, frequency, gauge, inveigh, measure, organize *(arrange)*, par *(face amount)*, pigeonhole, price, rebuke, reprehend, worth. SEE MAIN ENTRY
rate below the true value underestimate
rate incorrectly misjudge
rate of pay wage
rate too low underestimate
rather than in lieu of
rather well fairly *(moderately)*
ratification acceptance, acknowledgment *(acceptance)*, adoption *(acceptance)*, affirmance *(authentication)*, affirmation, approval, assent, certification *(attested copy)*, charter *(sanction)*, confirmation, consent, corroboration, indorsement, jurat, legalization, proof, sanction *(permission)*, stamp, subscription, support *(corroboration)*. SEE MAIN ENTRY
ratified allowed, choate lien, nunc pro tunc
ratified agreement contract
ratifier surety *(guarantor)*, undersigned
ratify accept *(assent)*, accredit, acknowledge *(respond)*, affirm *(uphold)*, agree *(comply)*, approve, assent, attest, bear *(adduce)*, bestow, certify *(approve)*, certify *(attest)*, concur *(agree)*, confirm, consent, corroborate, cosign, countenance, countersign, embrace *(accept)*, endorse, fix *(make firm)*, indorse, pass *(approve)*, recommend, sanction, seal *(solemnize)*, sign, subscribe *(sign)*, substantiate, support *(corroborate)*, sustain *(confirm)*, validate. SEE MAIN ENTRY
rating assessment *(estimation)*, class, disapprobation, estimate *(approximate cost)*, estimation *(calculation)*, measurement, reprimand, reproach, status. SEE MAIN ENTRY
ratio differential, proportion, quota, share *(interest)*. SEE MAIN ENTRY
ratio account *(evaluation)*, expedient, ground, method, mode, motive, phase *(aspect)*, process *(course)*, reason *(basis)*, reference *(allusion)*, reflection *(thought)*, scheme *(noun)*, scheme *(verb)*, style, theoretical, theory
ratio decidendi authority *(documentation)*
ratio iudiciorum judicatory
ratiocinari reason *(conclude)*
ratiocinate debate, deduce, deliberate, ponder, reason *(conclude)*
ratiocinatio ratiocination
ratiocination contemplation, deduction *(conclusion)*, deliberation, dialectic, judgment *(discernment)*. SEE MAIN ENTRY
ratiocinative deductible *(provable)*, discursive *(analytical)*, logical, pensive, rational, reasonable *(rational)*, sensible

ratiocinatory discursive *(analytical),* logical, pensive
ration allocate, allot, allotment, budget, disburse *(distribute),* dispense, distribute, divide *(distribute),* dole, mete, moiety, parcel, provision *(something provided),* quota, reapportion, share *(interest).* SEE MAIN ENTRY
rational colorable *(plausible),* conscious *(aware),* convincing, deductive, discriminating *(judicious),* discursive *(analytical),* judicial, judicious, juridical, justifiable, logical, lucid, normal *(sane),* plausible, possible, pragmatic, reasonable *(rational),* sane, sapient, sensible, solid *(sound),* tenable. SEE MAIN ENTRY
rational faculty common sense, intellect, intelligence *(intellect),* judgment *(discernment),* sense *(intelligence)*
rationale argument *(pleading),* basis, cause *(reason),* construction, explanation, ground, motive, reason *(basis).* SEE MAIN ENTRY
rationalism dialectic
rationalistic discursive *(analytical)*
rationality coherence, common sense, competence *(sanity),* comprehension, discrimination *(good judgment),* intellect, intelligence *(intellect),* judgment *(discernment),* pragmatism, ratiocination, reason *(sound judgment),* sagacity, sanity, sense *(intelligence)*
rationalization deduction *(conclusion),* dialectic, excuse, justification, ratiocination
rationalize comment, deduce, deduct *(conclude by reasoning),* ponder, reason *(conclude).* SEE MAIN ENTRY
rationalizing dialectic
rationcinate construe *(comprehend),* deduct *(conclude by reasoning)*
ratione praeditus rational
rationem inire embark
rationem rei responsibility *(accountability)*
rationes dispungere audit
rationi consentaneus reasonable *(fair)*
rationing control *(restriction),* distribution *(apportionment),* division *(act of dividing)*
rationis expers irrational
rationis particeps reasonable *(rational)*
rattle confuse *(bewilder),* discompose, perplex
rattle the saber brandish
ratum facere sanction
ravage beat *(defeat),* catastrophe, consumption, damage, debacle, despoil, destroy *(efface),* devastate, disaster, extirpate, harm, harry *(plunder),* havoc, loot, obliterate, overthrow, pillage, plunder, prejudice *(injure),* prey, prostration, rape, spoil *(pillage),* wear and tear. SEE MAIN ENTRY
ravagement defilement
ravager aggressor, assailant, vandal
ravaging depredation, disastrous, larcenous, predatory
rave against lash *(attack verbally)*
ravel ascertain, disorganize, elucidate, snarl
raveled disordered, inextricable, labyrinthine, problematic
raven despoil, prey
ravening predatory, rapacious
ravenous eager, gluttonous, predatory, rapacious
ravenousness greed
ravin plunder, spoils
raving bluster *(speech),* bombast, frenetic, incoherence, insanity, lunatic, non compos mentis, zealous
ravish abduct, carry away, mishandle *(maltreat),* molest *(subject to indecent advances),* prey
ravishing attractive, provocative
ravishment abduction, rape
raw imperfect, incompetent, inept *(incompetent),* inexperienced, mordacious, premature, puerile, unaccustomed, unversed
raw materials commodities
rawness ignorance, nescience
raze abolish, destroy *(efface),* devastate, eliminate *(eradicate),* expunge, extinguish, extirpate, obliterate, plunder
razzia foray, pillage, plunder
re carere dispense
re liber free *(relieved from a burden)*
re multari forfeit
re uti avail *(bring about)*
re vacuus devoid
re-charged double jeopardy
re-litigated double jeopardy
re-prosecuted double jeopardy
re-tried double jeopardy
reach abut, accede *(succeed),* attain, capacity *(aptitude),* capacity *(maximum),* capacity *(sphere),* contact *(communicate),* contact *(touch),* coverage *(scope),* degree *(magnitude),* extent, gamut, impress *(affect deeply),* jurisdiction, magnitude, obtain, pass *(satisfy requirements),* purview, range, scope, succeed *(attain).* SEE MAIN ENTRY
reach a compromise settle
reach a conclusion infer
reach a decision decide
reach a new high surpass
reach a peak culminate
reach a verdict decide
reach an official decision rule *(decide)*
reach beyond overreach
reach manhood develop
reach of mind caliber *(mental capacity),* comprehension, intellect, intelligence *(intellect)*
reach one's goal attain
reach over overlap, overreach
reach the end of exhaust *(deplete)*
reach the goal consummate
reach the highest point culminate
reach the zenith culminate
reach to adjoin
reach too far overreach
reachable available, disposable, open *(accessible),* passable, public *(open),* vulnerable
reacknowledge reconfirm
reacquire collect *(recover money),* reclaim, recoup *(regain),* recover, repossess
react perceive, reply, respond, return *(respond).* SEE MAIN ENTRY
reacting responsive
reaction answer *(reply),* consequence *(conclusion),* effect, emotion, estimate *(idea),* impression, opinion *(belief),* repercussion, reply, reprisal, response. SEE MAIN ENTRY
reactionary hostile, illiberal, malcontent, renitent
reactionist malcontent
reactivate reconstitute
reactivation recrudescence
reactive responsive, sensitive *(easily affected),* susceptible *(responsive)*
read peruse, predict, study. SEE MAIN ENTRY
read as one pari materia
read back repeat *(state again)*
read in tandem pari materia
read incorrectly misread
read the future predict
read together pari materia
read up on research
read with respect of another pari materia
readable cognizable
readapt attune
readdress redirect
readily SEE MAIN ENTRY
readily impressed susceptible *(responsive)*
readily influenced pliant
readily mastered facile
readily perceived palpable
readily seen palpable
readily wrought tractable
readiness amenability, diligence *(care),* dispatch *(promptness),* facility *(easiness),* faculty *(ability),* gift *(flair),* inclination, maturity, opportunity, plan, predisposition, preparation, proclivity, propensity, qualification *(fitness)*
readiness to believe credulity
readiness to give largess *(generosity)*
reading declamation, rendition *(explication)*
reading matter publication *(printed matter)*
readjust adapt, attune, modify *(alter),* redress, rehabilitate, remedy, renovate, repair
readjust downward depreciate
readjustment accommodation *(adjustment),* correction *(change),* reconversion, rehabilitation, renewal, reorganization, reparation *(keeping in repair)*
readminister redistribute
readmit renew *(begin again)*
ready artful, available, competent, discipline *(train),* eager, expeditious, facile, fit, inclined, instant, present *(current),* proficient, prompt, prone, provide *(arrange for),* provident *(showing foresight),* punctual, ripe, willing *(desirous),* zealous. SEE MAIN ENTRY
ready ability facility *(easiness)*
ready cash capital
ready for use disposable, effective *(operative)*
ready money cash, currency
ready-tongued voluble
readying discipline *(training),* preparation
reaffirm avouch *(avow),* certify *(attest),* plead *(allege in a legal action),* reconfirm, reiterate, repeat *(state again).* SEE MAIN ENTRY
reaffirmation recital, restatement SEE MAIN ENTRY
reaffirmed nunc pro tunc
real absolute *(conclusive),* actual, apparent *(perceptible),* authentic, bona fide, certain *(positive),* concrete, convincing, corporeal, de facto, definite, documentary, factual, faithful *(true to fact),* genuine, legitimate *(rightful),* material *(physical),* natural, objective, peremptory *(absolute),* physical, ponderable, pure, realistic, reliable, rightful, sterling, substantial, substantive, tangible, true *(authentic),* veridical. SEE MAIN ENTRY
real content gist *(substance)*
real episode fact
real estate demesne, domain *(land owned),* estate *(property),* fee *(estate),* holding *(property owned),* immovable, land, parcel, premises *(buildings),* property *(land),* realty. SEE MAIN ENTRY

real estate trespass encroachment
real experience fact
real interpretation connotation
real meaning connotation
real property demesne, domain *(land owned)*, fee *(estate)*, freehold, holding *(property owned)*, immovable, property *(land)*, real estate, realty. SEE MAIN ENTRY
real property capable of being inherited hereditament
real property holder landholder, landowner
real property owner landholder, landowner
real property subject to a lease leasehold
real security bond, charge *(lien)*, cloud *(incumbrance)*, hostage, lien, mortgage, pledge *(security)*
real sense connotation
real size area *(surface)*
realignment transition
realism pragmatism, truth
realistic accurate, actual, candid, descriptive, factual, faithful *(true to fact)*, natural, pragmatic, reasonable *(rational)*, sane, true *(authentic)*. SEE MAIN ENTRY
realistic attitude pragmatism
realisticness pragmatism
reality fact, fait accompli, gist *(substance)*, honesty, materiality *(physical existence)*, substance *(essential nature)*, truth, validity. SEE MAIN ENTRY
realizable cognizable, coherent *(clear)*, comprehensible, disposable, passable, possible, potential, practicable
realization acquisition, appreciation *(increased value)*, cessation *(termination)*, cognition, commission *(act)*, comprehension, conclusion *(determination)*, creation, denouement, development *(outgrowth)*, discharge *(performance)*, embodiment, end *(termination)*, fait accompli, fruition, insight, knowledge *(awareness)*, occurrence, outcome, perception, performance *(execution)*, phenomenon *(manifestation)*, profit, recognition, satisfaction *(fulfilment)*, sense *(feeling)*, understanding *(comprehension)*. SEE MAIN ENTRY
realization in advance advancement *(loan)*
realize accomplish, acquire *(secure)*, appreciate *(comprehend)*, apprehend *(perceive)*, attain, avail *(bring about)*, collect *(recover money)*, commit *(perpetrate)*, complete, comprehend *(understand)*, conceive *(comprehend)*, conjure, construe *(comprehend)*, consummate, detect, discern *(detect with the senses)*, discharge *(perform)*, discover, dispatch *(dispose of)*, earn, effectuate, execute *(accomplish)*, find *(discover)*, fulfill, gain, implement, invent *(produce for the first time)*, note *(notice)*, notice *(observe)*, obtain, pass *(satisfy requirements)*, perceive, pierce *(discern)*, procure, produce *(manufacture)*, profit, reap, receive *(acquire)*, recognize *(acknowledge)*, recover, solve, substantiate, succeed *(attain)*. SEE MAIN ENTRY
realize in cash liquidate *(convert into cash)*
realize the worth of appreciate *(value)*
realized cognizable, complete *(ended)*, fully executed *(consummated)*
realized from accompanying words noscitur a sociis
reallocate reapportion, reassign
reallocation reclassification, removal
reallot reapportion, reassign, redistribute
reallotment reclassification
really purely *(positively)*
realm ambit, area *(province)*, bailiwick, capacity *(sphere)*, circuit, coverage *(scope)*, demesne, department, district, domain *(sphere of influence)*, jurisdiction, part *(role)*, province, region, scope, sphere, territory. SEE MAIN ENTRY
realness honesty, legitimacy, reality, validity
realtor broker
realty demesne, domain *(land owned)*, estate *(property)*, fee *(estate)*, freehold, holding *(property owned)*, property *(land)*, real estate. SEE MAIN ENTRY
reanalysis reclassification
reanalyze reexamine
reanimate recall *(call back)*, recreate, renew *(refurbish)*, renovate, restore *(renew)*, resurrect
reanimated renascent
reanimation recrudescence, renewal, repair, resurgence, revival
reap acquire *(receive)*, attain, earn, gain, procure, profit, realize *(obtain as a profit)*, receive *(acquire)*, succeed *(attain)*. SEE MAIN ENTRY
reap profits gain
reap rewards gain
reap the benefit of capitalize *(seize the chance)*, gain
reap the fruits profit
reappear recur, return *(go back)*
reappearance recrudescence, resurgence, revival
reappearing periodic, renascent
reappoint reapportion, reassign, reinstate
reapportion redistribute. SEE MAIN ENTRY
reapportionment reclassification
reappraise reassess
reappreciate reassess
reapprise reassess
reappropriate reassign
reapprove reconfirm
rear discipline *(train)*, educate, foster, last *(final)*, nurture
rearmost back *(in reverse)*, final
rearrange alter, convert *(change use)*, disturb, edit, modify *(alter)*, reapportion, reconstruct, redistribute, reform, restore *(renew)*. SEE MAIN ENTRY
rearrangement exchange, interchange, reclassification, renewal, reorganization
rearrest SEE MAIN ENTRY
rearward back *(in reverse)*
reason analyze, answer *(solution)*, basis, common sense, competence *(sanity)*, comprehension, construe *(comprehend)*, contention *(argument)*, debate, deduce, deduct *(conclude by reasoning)*, deliberate, derive *(deduce)*, discrimination *(good judgment)*, end *(intent)*, excuse, gist *(ground for a suit)*, ground, impetus, incentive, infer, intellect, intelligence *(intellect)*, justice, justification, motive, point *(item)*, point *(purpose)*, ponder, postulate, rationale, rationalize, read, reflect *(ponder)*, sagacity, sanity, sense *(intelligence)*, solution *(answer)*, stimulus, treat *(process)*, understanding *(comprehension)*. SEE MAIN ENTRY
reason about discuss, treat *(process)*
reason against oppugn
reason earnestly against expostulate
reason for action motive
reason for disapproval objection
reason for legal pursuit cause of action
reason for relief cause of action
reason for which suit is commenced gist *(ground for a suit)*
reason out deliberate, solve
reason the point deliberate
reason to believe clue
reason to complain grievance
reason upon argue
reason with counsel, discuss
reasonability admissibility, competence *(sanity)*
reasonable adequate, amenable, colorable *(plausible)*, considerable, convincing, discriminating *(judicious)*, equitable, fair *(satisfactory)*, impartial, judicial, judicious, just, justifiable, logical, normal *(sane)*, objective, open-minded, ostensible, peaceable, placable, plausible, possible, practicable, pragmatic, probable, rational, receptive, right *(correct)*, right *(suitable)*, rightful, sane, sensible, solid *(sound)*, suitable, tenable, unprejudiced, upright, viable. SEE MAIN ENTRY
reasonable chance likelihood, opportunity, probability, prospect *(outlook)*
reasonable claim cause of action
reasonable excuse justification
reasonable ground likelihood
reasonable presumption likelihood
reasonable prospect likelihood
reasonable supposition presumption
reasonableness common sense, equity *(justice)*, expedience, fairness, feasibility, justice, moderation, pragmatism, probability, propriety *(appropriateness)*, sanity
reasonably anticipated foreseeable
reasonably good fair *(satisfactory)*
reasonably sufficient adequate
reasoned deductive, deliberate, intentional, judicial, logical, premeditated
reasoned judgment adjudication, conclusion *(determination)*, deduction *(conclusion)*, determination
reasoning contemplation, dialectic, discursive *(analytical)*, judgment *(discernment)*, justification, pensive, ratiocination, rational, rationale, reflection *(thought)*, speculation *(conjecture)*. SEE MAIN ENTRY
reasoning faculties judgment *(discernment)*
reasoning faculty intellect, intelligence *(intellect)*
reasoning power intellect, intelligence *(intellect)*, judgment *(discernment)*, sagacity
reasonless deranged, irrational, lunatic, misadvised
reassemble recall *(call back)*
reassembling repair
reassembly collection *(assembly)*
reassert avouch *(avow)*, plead *(allege in a legal action)*, reaffirm, reiterate, repeat *(state again)*
reassertation recital
reassertion restatement
reassess SEE MAIN ENTRY
reassessment rehearing
reassign reapportion, recover, redistribute, relocate, remand. SEE MAIN ENTRY
reassignment reclassification
reassort reapportion, redistribute
reassorting reclassification
reassortment reclassification
reassume recoup *(regain)*
reassurance assurance, certainty, certification *(attested copy)*, coverage

(insurance), solace, surety *(certainty)*, trust *(confidence)*
reassure assure *(give confidence to)*, certify *(attest)*, corroborate, insure. SEE MAIN ENTRY
reassure oneself ascertain
reassured positive *(confident)*, sanguine, secure *(confident)*
reassurement certification *(attested copy)*
reassuring favorable *(expressing approval)*, propitious
reauthenticate reconfirm
reave hold up *(rob)*, pillage, plunder
reawaken renew *(refurbish)*
reawakening revival
rebate discount *(reduce)*, refund *(noun)*, refund *(verb)*, reimburse, reimbursement, repay, restitution. SEE MAIN ENTRY
rebegin continue *(resume)*
rebel defect, defy, demagogue, disobey, fight *(battle)*, insurgent, malcontent, pariah, resist *(oppose)*, secede, strike *(refuse to work)*. SEE MAIN ENTRY
rebellio insurrection
rebellion anarchy, commotion, defiance, disloyalty, disturbance, infidelity, insurrection, mutiny, outbreak, outburst, resistance, revolt, revolution, riot, sedition, subversion, treason. SEE MAIN ENTRY
rebellion against the government treason
rebellious contumacious, disobedient, disorderly, dissident, fractious, froward, impertinent *(insolent)*, insubordinate, intractable, irresponsible, lawless, pugnacious, radical *(favoring drastic change)*, recalcitrant, recusant, restive, unruly
rebelliousness defiance
rebellis insurgent
rebirth reconversion, renewal, resurgence, revival
reborn renascent
rebound reaction *(opposition)*, reflect *(mirror)*, repercussion, return *(go back)*
rebounding resounding
rebuff abrogate *(annul)*, censure, check *(bar)*, confront *(oppose)*, contemn, contempt *(disdain)*, controvert, counter, counteract, decline *(reject)*, disallow, disapprove *(condemn)*, disapprove *(reject)*, disdain *(noun)*, disdain *(verb)*, disfavor, disoblige, disown *(refuse to acknowledge)*, disrespect, dissent *(withhold assent)*, eliminate *(exclude)*, exclude, fight *(counteract)*, impeach, parry, reaction *(opposition)*, rebut, refusal, refuse, reject, rejection, renounce, renunciation, repel *(drive back)*, repulse, resist *(oppose)*, resistance, reversal, shun, spurn. SEE MAIN ENTRY
rebuffing negative
rebuild copy, fix *(repair)*, reclaim, reconstitute, reconstruct, recreate, rehabilitate, renew *(refurbish)*, renovate, repair, reproduce, restore *(renew)*, resurrect
rebuilding rehabilitation, reorganization, reparation *(keeping in repair)*
rebukable reprehensible
rebuke admonish *(warn)*, admonition, aspersion, bad repute, blame *(culpability)*, blame, castigate, censure, complain *(criticize)*, condemn *(blame)*, condemnation *(blame)*, criticize *(find fault with)*, denounce *(condemn)*, denunciation, diatribe, disapprobation, disapprove *(condemn)*, disparagement, exception *(objection)*, impeachment, lash *(attack verbally)*, objection, objurgation, odium, outcry, penalize, rebuff *(noun)*, rebuff *(verb)*, remonstrance, remonstrate, reprehend, reprimand *(noun)*, reprimand *(verb)*, reproach *(noun)*, reproach *(verb)*, reversal, stricture. SEE MAIN ENTRY
rebuking critical *(faultfinding)*, remonstrative
rebut answer *(reply)*, answer *(respond legally)*, contradict, contravene, controvert, countercharge, countervail, disaccord, disaffirm, disallow, disown *(deny the validity)*, disprove, dispute *(debate)*, gainsay, impugn, negate, oppose, refute, reply, respond, retaliate, retort, return *(respond)*. SEE MAIN ENTRY
rebut the charge countercharge
rebuttal answer *(judicial response)*, answer *(reply)*, argument *(pleading)*, confutation, contradiction, contravention, counterargument, defense, denial, disagreement, plea, pleading, reply, response. SEE MAIN ENTRY
rebuttable presumption SEE MAIN ENTRY
rebutter confutation, counterargument
rebutting contradictory, contrary, negative
rebutting evidence answer *(judicial response)*, contradiction
recalcitrance contempt *(disobedience to the court)*, contest *(dispute)*, defiance, resistance, revolt, tenacity
recalcitrancy defiance
recalcitrant adverse *(hostile)*, contentious, contumacious, deviant, disinclined, disobedient, disorderly, dissident, fractious, incorrigible, indomitable, insubordinate, insusceptible *(uncaring)*, intractable, lawless, nonconsenting, obdurate, recusant, reluctant, renitent, restive, uncontrollable, unreasonable, unruly, unyielding, vicious. SEE MAIN ENTRY
recalcitrantly unwillingly
recalcitrate confront *(oppose)*, disobey, oppose, oppugn, rebel, resist *(oppose)*
recalcitration defiance, opposition, reaction *(opposition)*
recalculate reassess
recall abjuration, abrogate *(rescind)*, ademption, annul, cancel, cancellation, countermand, defeasance, depose *(remove)*, disavow, discharge *(annulment)*, discharge *(release from obligation)*, disinherit, hindsight, nullify, recant, reclaim, recognition, recognize *(perceive)*, recollect, recollection, redeem *(repurchase)*, remember, remembrance *(recollection)*, renege, repeal, repossess, rescind, rescision, retain *(keep in possession)*, retraction, retrospect, revocation, revoke, withdraw. SEE MAIN ENTRY
recall to life cure, resurrect
recalling cancellation, memory *(retention)*
recalling to mind honorary
recant abrogate *(rescind)*, cancel, disaffirm, disavow, disclaim, disinherit, disown *(deny the validity)*, negate, nullify, renounce, repent, repudiate, rescind, revoke, tergiversate, vacate *(void)*, withdraw. SEE MAIN ENTRY
recantare recant
recantation abjuration, abolition, bad faith, cancellation, countermand, denial, disclaimer, negation, rejection, renunciation, repudiation, rescision, retraction, reversal, revocation
recap scenario, summary
recapitulate compile, copy, digest *(summarize)*, itemize, quote, recite, recount, reiterate, repeat *(state again)*, review. SEE MAIN ENTRY
recapitulated compact *(pithy)*
recapitulation account *(report)*, capsule, compendium, digest, hornbook, narration, outline *(synopsis)*, paraphrase, recital, report *(detailed account)*, restatement, retrospect, review *(official reexamination)*, scenario, statement, story *(narrative)*, summary, synopsis
recapitulatory repetitious
recapture rearrest, recoup *(regain)*, recover, recovery *(repossession)*, redeem *(repurchase)*, repossess, rescue, salvage
recast alter, change, convert *(change use)*, modify *(alter)*, reconstruct, recreate, reform *(noun)*, reform *(verb)*, revise, tempered, transform
recasting reorganization
recede decrease, depart, diminish, ebb, erode, escheat, regress, retire *(retreat)*, retreat, revert, subside, withdraw
recede from view disappear
recedence capitulation
recedere ebb, retire *(retreat)*
receding regressive
receipt acceptance, binder, quitclaim, realization. SEE MAIN ENTRY
receipt for payment binder
receipt in full payment *(act of paying)*
receipted payment collection *(payment)*, satisfaction *(discharge of debt)*
receipts capital, earnings, income, proceeds, profit, revenue
receivable delinquent *(overdue)*, passable. SEE MAIN ENTRY
receival acquisition
receive accept *(take)*, congregate, draw *(extract)*, embrace *(encircle)*, endure *(suffer)*, gain, hold *(possess)*, inherit, instate, obtain, partake, possess, procure, realize *(obtain as a profit)*, reap, tolerate. SEE MAIN ENTRY
receive a false idea misconstrue
receive a false impression err, misapprehend, miscalculate, misconceive, misconstrue, misinterpret, misread, mistake
receive a legacy inherit
receive a wrong idea misinterpret
receive a wrong impression misconceive, misread, mistake, misunderstand
receive an endowment inherit
receive an incorrect impression misinterpret, misread
receive an instrument officially file *(place among official records)*
receive as right inherit
receive by bequest inherit
receive by devise inherit
receive by law of descent inherit
receive by succession inherit
receive compensation earn
receive information overhear
receive information aurally hear *(perceive by ear)*
receive knowledge of overhear
receive money collect *(recover money)*
receive notice beware
receive payment collect *(recover money)*
receive property as an heir inherit
receive with approval accept *(take)*
received common *(customary)*, popular
received maxim principle *(axiom)*
receiver assignee, bearer, beneficiary, catchall, disciple, fence, feoffee, heir, holder, recipient. SEE MAIN ENTRY
receiver of stolen goods fence
receiver of stolen property fence
receiving acquisition, assumption *(adoption)*, receptive

recent current, novel, present *(current)*. SEE MAIN ENTRY
receptacle catchall, coffer, depository, enclosure, receiver, repository, treasury
receptaculum depository, refuge, repository, shelter *(protection)*
reception acquisition, adoption *(acceptance)*, assumption *(adoption)*, ceremony, entrance, receipt *(act of receiving)*. SEE MAIN ENTRY
reception room chamber *(compartment)*
receptive available, inclined, liberal *(broad minded)*, open *(persuasible)*, open-minded, passive, penetrable, perceptive, pliable, pliant, responsive, suasible, susceptible *(responsive)*, willing *(not averse)*. SEE MAIN ENTRY
receptiveness acceptance, amenability
receptor receiver
recertify reconfirm
recess abeyance, adjourn, adjournment, cloture, continue *(adjourn)*, defer *(put off)*, discontinuance *(act of discontinuing)*, discontinue *(break continuity)*, extension *(postponement)*, furlough, halt, hiatus, holiday, interruption, interval, lapse *(break)*, leave *(absence)*, lull, moratorium, pause, pendency, remission, respite *(interval of rest)*, rest *(cease from action)*. SEE MAIN ENTRY
recession capitulation, decline, erosion, outflow. SEE MAIN ENTRY
recessive regressive
rechannel recover
recharge reassess, replenish
recharging renewal
recheck reconfirm, reexamine, review
recidere relapse *(noun)*, relapse *(verb)*
recidivate relapse, return *(go back)*. SEE MAIN ENTRY
recidivation recrudescence, relapse
recidivism relapse, reversion *(act of returning)*. SEE MAIN ENTRY
recidivist convict, criminal, delinquent, felon, malefactor, outlaw. SEE MAIN ENTRY
recidivistic regressive
recidivous incorrigible, regressive, reprobate
recipe system
recipere admit *(give access)*, enfranchise
recipience acquisition, assumption *(adoption)*, receipt *(act of receiving)*
recipient assignee, bearer, beneficiary, devisee, donee, grantee, heir, holder, legatee, payee, receiver, receptive, subject *(object)*, transferee, trustee. SEE MAIN ENTRY
recipient of a fee feoffee
recipient of stolen goods fence
recipient of stolen property fence
reciprocal coequal, cognate, common *(shared)*, complement, correlate, correlative, counterpart *(complement)*, equivalent, related, same. SEE MAIN ENTRY
reciprocal action reaction *(response)*, repercussion
reciprocal agreement mutual understanding
reciprocal commitment mutual understanding
reciprocal concession composition *(agreement in bankruptcy)*
reciprocal exchange interchange
reciprocal feeling consortium *(marriage companionship)*
reciprocal trade commerce
reciprocality mutuality, quid pro quo, reciprocity
reciprocalize correspond *(be equivalent)*
reciprocally attached conjoint
reciprocalness mutuality, reciprocity
reciprocate beat *(pulsate)*, repay, retaliate, return *(respond)*. SEE MAIN ENTRY
reciprocating mutual *(reciprocal)*
reciprocation exchange, interchange, mutuality, quid pro quo, reciprocity, reply, reprisal, retribution, revenge
reciprocative convertible, mutual *(reciprocal)*, reciprocal, responsive
reciprocator correlate
reciprocity comity, exchange, mutuality, quid pro quo, rapprochement, relationship *(connection)*. SEE MAIN ENTRY
reciprocity of obligation agreement *(concurrence)*
recision abolition, retraction
recission revocation
recital account *(report)*, declamation, delineation, disclosure *(act of disclosing)*, disclosure *(something disclosed)*, discourse, instruction *(teaching)*, mention *(reference)*, narration, report *(detailed account)*, restatement, specification, speech, statement, story *(narrative)*. SEE MAIN ENTRY
recitation declamation, declaration, delineation, disclosure *(act of disclosing)*, discourse, instruction *(teaching)*, mention *(reference)*, narration, parlance, peroration, proclamation, recital, reference *(citation)*, remark, report *(detailed account)*, rhetoric *(skilled speech)*, speech, statement, story *(narrative)*
recite allege, assert, cite *(state)*, converse, convey *(communicate)*, declaim, delineate, depict, detail *(particularize)*, discourse, discuss, inform *(notify)*, mention, phrase, pronounce *(speak)*, quote, recapitulate, recount, relate *(tell)*, remark, repeat *(state again)*, report *(disclose)*, speak, utter. SEE MAIN ENTRY
recite a spell invoke
recite an incantation invoke
recited aforesaid, repeated, verbal
reckless careless, heedless, hot-blooded, ill-advised, ill-judged, impolitic, improvident, imprudent, impulsive *(rash)*, injudicious, misadvised, negligent, precipitate, prodigal, profligate *(extravagant)*, profuse, remiss, thoughtless, unpolitic, wanton. SEE MAIN ENTRY
reckless expenditure misapplication
reckless homocide manslaughter
recklessness audacity, inconsideration, indiscretion, neglect, negligence, temerity
reckon assess *(appraise)*, calculate, consider, criticize *(evaluate)*, determine, estimate, evaluate, guess, infer, judge, measure, opine, presuppose, rate, speculate *(conjecture)*, suspect *(think)*
reckon among contain *(comprise)*
reckon from some point in time date
reckon on expect *(anticipate)*
reckon up sum
reckon with pay
reckoner accountant, comptroller
reckoning accounting, amount *(sum)*, appraisal, assessment *(estimation)*, bill *(invoice)*, census, computation, consideration *(contemplation)*, consideration *(recompense)*, contribution *(indemnification)*, cost *(price)*, determination, dun, estimate *(approximate cost)*, estimate *(idea)*, estimation *(calculation)*, expiation, invoice *(bill)*, measurement, pay, payment *(act of paying)*, recovery *(award)*
reclaim claim *(demand)*, collect *(recover money)*, cure, fix *(repair)*, meliorate, purge *(wipe out by atonement)*, reconstruct, recoup *(regain)*, recover, redeem *(repurchase)*, reform, rehabilitate, renew *(refurbish)*, repossess, rescue. SEE MAIN ENTRY
reclaimable corrigible
reclaimed renascent, repentant
reclaimed materials salvage
reclamare remonstrate
reclamatio remonstrance
reclamation compensation, progress, recovery *(award)*, recovery *(repossession)*, redemption, reform, rehabilitation, renewal, replacement, replevin, restitution, revival, salvage. SEE MAIN ENTRY
reclass reassess, redistribute
reclassification SEE MAIN ENTRY
reclassify reapportion, redistribute
recline repose *(rest)*, rest *(be supported by)*
reclusive solitary
recognition acknowledgment *(acceptance)*, adoption *(acceptance)*, appreciation *(perception)*, apprehension *(perception)*, approval, assent, certification *(certification of proficiency)*, character *(reputation)*, charter *(sanction)*, cognition, comprehension, concession *(compromise)*, franchise *(license)*, identification, knowledge *(awareness)*, notice *(heed)*, notoriety, perception, realization, reason *(sound judgment)*, recollection, remembrance *(recollection)*, respect, reward, scienter, sense *(intelligence)*, understanding *(comprehension)*. SEE MAIN ENTRY
recognizable apparent *(perceptible)*, appreciable, arrant *(definite)*, ascertainable, cognizable, coherent *(clear)*, comprehensible, conspicuous, discernible, distinct *(clear)*, explicit, manifest, naked *(perceptible)*, obvious, open *(in sight)*, palpable, pellucid, perceivable, perceptible, ponderable, prominent, solvable, unambiguous, unmistakable, visible *(noticeable)*
recognizably fairly *(clearly)*
recognizance binder, concession *(compromise)*, guaranty, identification, remembrance *(recollection)*, specialty *(contract)*. SEE MAIN ENTRY
recognize acknowledge *(verify)*, admit *(concede)*, appreciate *(comprehend)*, apprehend *(perceive)*, assent, authorize, bear *(tolerate)*, bestow, comprehend *(understand)*, concede, confirm, countenance, detect, diagnose, discern *(detect with the senses)*, find *(discover)*, grant *(concede)*, hear *(perceive by ear)*, heed, identify, notice *(observe)*, perceive, pierce *(discern)*, realize *(understand)*, recall *(remember)*, recollect, remember, spy, witness *(have direct knowledge of)*. SEE MAIN ENTRY
recognize as different distinguish
recognize as distinct discern *(discriminate)*
recognize as separate differentiate, discriminate *(distinguish)*
recognize authority of acknowledge *(verify)*
recognize the worth of appreciate *(value)*
recognized allowed, common *(customary)*, customary, familiar *(customary)*, famous, household *(familiar)*, influential, master, ordinary, orthodox, outstanding *(prominent)*, predominant, prescriptive, proverbial, public *(known)*, putative, renowned, right *(suitable)*, salient
recognized because of continued possession prescriptive

recognized by law jural, legitimate *(rightful)*
recognized by the law legal
recognized condition necessity
recognized from accompanying words noscitur a sociis
recognized maxim principle *(axiom)*
recognized principles polity
recognized through use prescriptive
recoil rebuff, refuse, repercussion, retreat, revert
recoil from eschew, shun
recoil from with pride disdain
recoiling reluctance, resilient
recolere resume
recollect identify, recall *(remember)*, recognize *(perceive)*, remember, retain *(keep in possession)*. SEE MAIN ENTRY
recollection hindsight, identification, memory *(retention)*, recognition, retrospect. SEE MAIN ENTRY
recollective suggestive *(evocative)*
recommence continue *(resume)*, proceed *(continue)*, renew *(begin again)*, reopen, resume
recommencement continuation *(resumption)*, renewal
recommend admonish *(advise)*, advise, advocate, authorize, bestow, coax, counsel, countenance, exhort, incite, indorse, instruct *(direct)*, offer *(propose)*, prefer, prompt, propose, propound, refer *(send for action)*, urge. SEE MAIN ENTRY
recommend against expostulate
recommend points of law charge *(instruct on the law)*
recommend to pardon condone
recommendable desirable *(qualified)*
recommendation advice, advocacy, auspices, determination, dictum, direction *(guidance)*, guidance, holding *(ruling of a court)*, judgment *(formal court decree)*, patronage *(support)*, proposal *(suggestion)*, proposition, suggestion, tip *(clue)*. SEE MAIN ENTRY
recommendations credentials
recommendatory advisory, favorable *(expressing approval)*
recommended preferential
recommender arbiter
recommission reassign
recommit confine, rearrest, remand. SEE MAIN ENTRY
recommit to custody commit *(institutionalize)*
recommitment rendition *(restoration)*
recompensation in value compensation
recompense alimony, bear the expense, brokerage, collect *(recover money)*, collection *(payment)*, commission *(fee)*, compensate *(remunerate)*, compensation, contribute *(indemnify)*, contribution *(indemnification)*, cover *(provide for)*, damages, disburse *(pay out)*, disbursement *(funds paid out)*, discharge *(payment)*, discharge *(pay a debt)*, earnings, expiation, fee *(charge)*, honorarium, indemnification, indemnify, indemnity, pay *(noun)*, pay *(verb)*, payment *(act of paying)*, payment *(remittance)*, payroll, perquisite, price, prize, quit *(repay)*, reciprocate, recoup *(reimburse)*, recovery *(award)*, refund *(noun)*, refund *(verb)*, reimburse, reimbursement, relief *(legal redress)*, remedy *(legal means of redress)*, remit *(send payment)*, remittance, remunerate, remuneration, reparation *(indemnification)*, repay, requital, restitution, restore *(return)*, retainer, revenue, reward, satisfaction *(discharge of debt)*, satisfy *(discharge)*, trover, wage. SEE MAIN ENTRY
recompense for past loss indemnify
recompenser insurer
recompensive compensatory
recompose reconstruct
reconcilable apposite, concordant, congruous, consonant, correlative, placable, suitable
reconcile adapt, agree *(comply)*, arbitrate *(conciliate)*, comport *(agree with)*, compromise *(settle by mutual agreement)*, conform, correspond *(be equivalent)*, disarm *(set at ease)*, mediate, mollify, pacify, placate, propitiate, rationalize, settle, unite. SEE MAIN ENTRY
reconcile oneself to submit *(yield)*
reconciled agreed *(harmonized)*, consensual, patient, resigned
reconcilement accordance *(compact)*, accordance *(understanding)*, adjustment, conciliation, condonation, consensus, intercession, rapprochement, reconciliation
reconciler adjuster, arbiter, arbitrator, go-between, intermediary, referee, umpire
reconciliatio accommodation *(adjustment)*
reconciliation accordance *(compact)*, accordance *(understanding)*, adjustment, arrangement *(understanding)*, compatibility, concession *(compromise)*, conciliation, expiation, intercession, mediation, mollification, pact, peace, rapprochement, settlement. SEE MAIN ENTRY
reconcinnare renew *(refurbish)*
recondite complex, difficult, equivocal, esoteric, hidden, inapprehensible, incomprehensible, inexplicable, learned, mysterious, nebulous, oblique *(evasive)*, obscure *(abstruse)*, opaque, private *(confidential)*, privy, profound *(esoteric)*, secret. SEE MAIN ENTRY
recondite knowledge secret
reconditeness ambiguity
recondition change, fix *(repair)*, reconstitute, reconstruct, rehabilitate, renew *(refurbish)*, renovate, repair, restore *(renew)*, resurrect, transform
reconditioned renascent
reconditioning repair, reparation *(keeping in repair)*
reconditus recondite
reconfine rearrest
reconfirm SEE MAIN ENTRY
reconfirmed nunc pro tunc
reconnaissance examination *(study)*, inspection, observation, research
reconnoiter check *(inspect)*, examine *(study)*, investigate, observe *(watch)*, oversee, patrol, perambulate, spy, study, survey *(examine)*
reconnoiterer spy
reconnoitering discovery
reconsider appeal, reexamine, review, revise. SEE MAIN ENTRY
reconsideration appeal, hindsight, retrospect, review *(official reexamination)*
reconstitute convert *(change use)*, reconstruct, reform, rehabilitate, reinforce, reinstate, renew *(refurbish)*, renovate, reproduce, restore *(renew)*. SEE MAIN ENTRY
reconstituted renascent
reconstitution reclassification, reform, rehabilitation, renewal, reorganization, replacement
reconstruct alter, change, convert *(change use)*, copy, emend, fix *(repair)*, modify *(alter)*, reconstitute, recreate, reform, rehabilitate, renew *(refurbish)*, renovate, repair, repeat *(do again)*, reproduce, restore *(renew)*, revise, transform. SEE MAIN ENTRY
reconstructed renascent, tempered
reconstruction conversion *(change)*, correction *(change)*, reform, rehabilitation, remembrance *(recollection)*, renewal, reorganization, repair, reparation *(keeping in repair)*, replacement
reconvene recall *(call back)*
reconversion SEE MAIN ENTRY
reconvert reconstitute, rehabilitate, renew *(refurbish)*, renovate, transform
record account *(report)*, bill *(invoice)*, book, calendar *(list of cases)*, calendar *(record of yearly periods)*, cast *(register)*, ceiling, date, deed, docket, document, documentation, dossier, enroll, evidence, file, form *(document)*, impanel, index *(relate)*, inscribe, inscription, instrument *(document)*, inventory, journal, ledger, marginalia, memorandum, notation, note *(brief comment)*, register *(noun)*, register *(verb)*, render *(depict)*, report *(detailed account)*, roll, set down, story *(narrative)*, transcript. SEE MAIN ENTRY
record book ledger
record keeper clerk
record keeping registration
record of credits and debits ledger
record of money transactions ledger
record of proceedings docket
record of the court file
record of yearly periods calendar *(record of yearly periods)*
record the vote poll
record-breaking best. SEE MAIN ENTRY
recordari recall *(remember)*, recollect, remember
recordatio recollection
recordation SEE MAIN ENTRY
recorded documentary, in writing
recorded expression of a formal judgment award, holding *(ruling of a court)*
recorded information dossier, file
recorded item entry *(record)*
recorded material document, documentation, dossier
recorder accountant, amanuensis, clerk, notary public
recording record, registration, transcript
recording secretary amanuensis
records credentials, proof
recount census, converse, convey *(communicate)*, delineate, depict, detail *(particularize)*, disabuse, inform *(notify)*, itemize, mention, notify, quote, recapitulate, recite, relate *(tell)*, repeat *(state again)*, report *(disclose)*. SEE MAIN ENTRY
recountal narration, recital, restatement, story *(narrative)*
recounted narrative
recounting narration, recital, report *(detailed account)*, restatement
recoup collect *(recover money)*, outbalance, recover, redeem *(repurchase)*, repossess, restore *(return)*. SEE MAIN ENTRY
recoupable deductible *(capable of being deducted from taxes)*
recouping recovery *(repossession)*
recoupment compensation, expiation, indemnity, recompense, recovery *(award)*, refund, reimbursement, replevin,

restitution, salvage, satisfaction *(discharge of debt)*, setoff, trover
recourse alternative *(option)*, tool. SEE MAIN ENTRY
recourse to some higher power appeal
recourse to the principles of natural justice equity *(justice)*
recover collect *(recover money)*, cure, hold *(possess)*, obtain, occupy *(take possession)*, reap, reclaim, recoup *(regain)*, redeem *(repurchase)*, renew *(refurbish)*, repossess, rescue. SEE MAIN ENTRY
recover knowledge recognize *(perceive)*
recover knowledge of recall *(remember)*, remember
recover property evict
recoverable corrigible
recovery adverse possession, boom *(prosperity)*, compensation, cure, damages, expiation, improvement, out of pocket, progress, recompense, redemption, reform, repair, replacement, replevin, restitution, resurgence, revival, salvage, trover. SEE MAIN ENTRY
recovery of property replevin
recovery of property from another's possession eviction
recreance sedition
recreancy bad faith, desertion, disloyalty, infidelity, lapse *(expiration)*, recidivism, sedition
recreant caitiff, convict, criminal, degenerate, delinquent, disgraceful, disreputable, faithless, false *(disloyal)*, felon, iniquitous, lawless, peccable, reprehensible, reprobate, untrue. SEE MAIN ENTRY
recreare reassure
recreate copy, portray, reconstruct, renew *(refurbish)*, renovate, repeat *(do again)*, reproduce, restore *(renew)*. SEE MAIN ENTRY
recreated renascent
recreation enjoyment *(pleasure)*, reform, rehabilitation, revival
recreation time leave *(absence)*
recremental excess
recrementitial excess
recrementitious excess
recriminate answer *(respond legally)*, blame, censure, charge *(accuse)*, countercharge, denounce *(condemn)*, dispute *(contest)*, impeach, reprehend, reprimand, return *(respond)*. SEE MAIN ENTRY
recrimination answer *(judicial response)*, charge *(accusation)*, condemnation *(blame)*, contention *(opposition)*, denunciation, incrimination
recriminative critical *(faultfinding)*
recrudesce recur, relapse
recrudescence relapse, renewal. SEE MAIN ENTRY
recrudescency recrudescence, relapse, renewal
recruit disciple, employ *(engage services)*, enroll, hire, induct, novice, prospect *(prospective patron)*, retain *(employ)*, supply, volunteer. SEE MAIN ENTRY
rectifiable corrigible
rectification accommodation *(adjustment)*, adjustment, collection *(payment)*, compensation, correction *(change)*, reform, relief *(legal redress)*, remedial statute, remedy *(legal means of redress)*, reorganization, repair, reparation *(keeping in repair)*, revision *(process of correcting)*
rectify adjust *(resolve)*, ameliorate, amend, attune, cure, disabuse, edit, emend, fix *(repair)*, meliorate, modify *(alter)*, purge *(purify)*, redress, reform, regulate *(adjust)*, rehabilitate, remedy, renew *(refurbish)*, repair, restore *(renew)*, revise, settle. SEE MAIN ENTRY
rectilineal direct *(straight)*
rectitude conscience, credibility, ethics, fairness, good faith, honor *(good reputation)*, integrity, justice, merit, principle *(virtue)*, probity, propriety *(correctness)*, right *(righteousness)*, trustworthiness, veracity. SEE MAIN ENTRY
rectus direct *(forthright)*, proper, right *(righteousness)*
recumbency abeyance, prostration
recumbent inactive, passive
recuperare recover
recuperate cure, progress
recuperation cure, rehabilitation, resurgence, revival
recuperative medicinal, remedial, salubrious
recuperatory medicinal
recur occur *(happen)*, repeat *(do again)*. SEE MAIN ENTRY
recurrence continuation *(resumption)*, cycle, frequency, habit, recrudescence, redundancy, regularity, relapse, renewal, resurgence, revival. SEE MAIN ENTRY
recurrent chronic, consecutive, habitual, incessant, insistent, intermittent, iterative, periodic, repeated, repetitious, routine, sporadic, typical, usual
recurring chronic, habitual, intermittent, iterative, periodic, regular *(orderly)*, repeated, repetitious, routine, sporadic. SEE MAIN ENTRY
recurring period cycle
recurring theme motif
recusancy contempt *(disobedience to the court)*, contest *(dispute)*, defiance, disagreement, dissidence, nonconformity, resistance, schism, sedition, violation
recusant contumacious, disobedient, dissenting, dissident, insubordinate, lawless, malcontent, nonconsenting, radical *(favoring drastic change)*, recalcitrant, restive. SEE MAIN ENTRY
recusare decline *(reject)*, protest
recusatio protest, refusal
recuse SEE MAIN ENTRY
red neck bigot
red tape bureaucracy. SEE MAIN ENTRY
redact edit, formulate, revise. SEE MAIN ENTRY
redaction correction *(change)*
redargue disaccord
redarguere disprove, rebut, refute
redargution confutation
reddere refund, reimburse, render *(deliver)*, repay, restore *(return)*, return *(refund)*
reddition restitution
rede advice
redeem buy, collect *(recover money)*, cure, defray, discharge *(pay a debt)*, disenthrall, extricate, free, fulfill, indemnify, liberate, liquidate *(convert into cash)*, outbalance, pardon, purchase, purge *(wipe out by atonement)*, reclaim, recoup *(regain)*, recover, reform, refund, rehabilitate, renovate, repossess, rescue, restore *(return)*, save *(conserve)*. SEE MAIN ENTRY
redeemable corrigible, payable, receivable
redeemable part coupon
redeemer benefactor, customer, good samaritan
redeliberate reconsider
redelivery replevin
redemption discharge *(payment)*, freedom, indemnification, indemnity, liberation, progress, ransom, recovery *(repossession)*, rehabilitation, replevin, restitution, salvage. SEE MAIN ENTRY
redemption slip coupon
redemptive compensatory
redesign renew *(refurbish)*
redetain rearrest
redimire intertwine
redintegrare renew *(begin again)*
redintegrate fix *(repair)*, rehabilitate, renew *(refurbish)*, renovate, restore *(renew)*
redintegrated renascent
redintegration reconversion, rehabilitation, repair, revival
redire return *(go back)*
redirect divert. SEE MAIN ENTRY
redisperse reapportion
redistribute reapportion, reassign, subdivide. SEE MAIN ENTRY
redistributing reclassification
redistribution reclassification
redistrict reapportion
reditus proceeds, rent, revenue
redivide reapportion, reassign, redistribute, subdivide
redivivus renascent
redo emend, reconstitute, reconstruct, recreate, reform, renew *(refurbish)*, repeat *(do again)*, reproduce, restore *(renew)*, transform
redolent suggestive *(evocative)*
redone repeated
redouble accrue *(increase)*, accumulate *(enlarge)*, expand, intensify, reinforce, reiterate
redoubled repeated
redoubling augmentation, renewal
redoubtable formidable, indomitable, inexpugnable
redound result. SEE MAIN ENTRY
redraft edit, redact
redress adjust *(resolve)*, collection *(payment)*, compensate *(remunerate)*, contribution *(indemnification)*, cure *(noun)*, cure *(verb)*, disbursement *(funds paid out)*, equity *(justice)*, fix *(repair)*, habeas corpus, help, recompense, recourse, recovery *(award)*, rectify, reform, reimburse, reimbursement, remedy, renew *(refurbish)*, repair, reparation *(indemnification)*, repent, requital, restitution, restore *(return)*, satisfaction *(discharge of debt)*, trover. SEE MAIN ENTRY
redressible wrong cause of action
reduce abate *(lessen)*, abridge *(shorten)*, abstract *(summarize)*, allay, alleviate, assuage, attenuate, beat *(defeat)*, commute, condense, constrict *(compress)*, curtail, debilitate, decrease, demean *(make lower)*, demote, deplete, depose *(remove)*, depress, derogate, digest *(summarize)*, diminish, discount *(minimize)*, divest, erode, expend *(consume)*, extenuate, impair, lessen, minimize, mitigate, moderate *(temper)*, modify *(moderate)*, mollify, palliate *(abate)*, rebate, relax, remit *(relax)*, restrict, retrench, subdue, subjugate. SEE MAIN ENTRY
reduce a punishment commute
reduce expenses retrench
reduce forces disarm *(divest of arms)*
reduce in asperity commute
reduce in intensity attenuate
reduce in quality debase

reduce in severity allay
reduce in strength attenuate, disarm *(divest of arms)*, extenuate
reduce tension ease
reduce the armament disarm *(divest of arms)*
reduce the edge obtund
reduce the mark-up discount *(reduce)*
reduce the purchasing value of depreciate
reduce the strength of depreciate, dilute
reduce the violence obtund
reduce to a code codify
reduce to a digest codify
reduce to a formula formulate
reduce to ashes deflagrate
reduce to chaos mismanage
reduce to extreme purity and strength distill
reduce to inferior rank demote
reduce to method regulate *(adjust)*
reduce to nothing annul, destroy *(efface)*, extinguish
reduce to nought annul
reduce to order arrange *(methodize)*, classify, codify, file *(arrange)*, orchestrate, organize *(arrange)*, pigeonhole, sort
reduce to subjection repress
reduce to the ranks demote, humiliate
reduce volume constrict *(compress)*
reduced brief, inferior *(lower in position)*, insolvent, minimal, nominal, poor *(underprivileged)*. SEE MAIN ENTRY
reduced circumstances poverty, privation
reduced in means destitute
reduced to a writing in writing
reduced to beggary poor *(underprivileged)*
reducing mitigating
reducing to order classification
reductio ad absurdum counterargument
reduction abatement *(reduction)*, abridgment *(condensation)*, abstract, capsule, curtailment, decrease, deduction *(diminution)*, deterioration, diminution, discount, erosion, mitigation, moderation, mollification, rebate, refund, relief *(release)*, remission
reduction in rank degradation
reduction to order method
redundance overage, redundancy, sufficiency, surfeit, surplus
redundancy overage, prolixity, surplus, tautology. SEE MAIN ENTRY
redundant excess, excessive, expendable, extraneous, inordinate, iterative, needless, nonessential, profuse, prolix, repetitious, superfluous, turgid, unnecessary. SEE MAIN ENTRY
redundantia redundancy
redundare redound
redundent repeated
reduplicate copy, plagiarize, repeat *(do again)*, reproduce
reduplicated repeated
reduplicative repeated, repetitious
reecho copy
reechoed repetitious
reeducation rehabilitation
reeking offensive *(offending)*
reel off recite
reembark renew *(begin again)*, reopen
reenact repeat *(do again)*
reenactment duplicate
reendorse reconfirm
reendorsed nunc pro tunc
reenforce reconfirm, relieve *(give aid)*
reengage reassign
reenter renew *(begin again)*, return *(go back)*
reestablish continue *(resume)*, copy, reclaim, reconfirm, reconstitute, reconstruct, recreate, reform, rehabilitate, reinforce, reinstate, relocate, renovate, reopen, restore *(return)*, return *(go back)*
reestablished nunc pro tunc, renascent
reestablishment continuation *(resumption)*, reclassification, reconversion, rehabilitation, renewal, reorganization, resurgence, revival
reestimate reassess
reevaluate reassess, reconsider
reexamination appeal, cross-examination, cross-questioning, hindsight, rehearing, retrospect
reexamine appeal, audit, check *(inspect)*, cross-examine, reconsider, review, revise. SEE MAIN ENTRY
reface meliorate
refashion amend, convert *(change use)*, copy, fix *(repair)*, reconstruct, recreate, reform, rehabilitate, renew *(refurbish)*, renovate, reproduce, restore *(renew)*
refashioned renascent
refellere controvert, disprove, refute
refer appertain, apply *(pertain)*, assign *(transfer ownership)*, confer *(consult)*, delegate, hint, pertain, quote, relegate, remit *(submit for consideration)*, submit *(give)*. SEE MAIN ENTRY
refer back recommit
refer to allude, appeal, ascribe, bear *(adduce)*, cite *(state)*, concern *(involve)*, connote, consult *(seek information from)*, denote, mention, specify
refer to for information consult *(seek information from)*
refer to legal authorities cite *(state)*
referable to comparative
referee adjudicate, arbiter, arbitrate *(conciliate)*, arbitrator, decide, determine, go-between, hear *(give a legal hearing)*, intercede, intermediary, judge *(noun)*, judge *(verb)*, mediate, negotiate, umpire. SEE MAIN ENTRY
reference attribution, citation *(attribution)*, connection *(relation)*, connotation, derivation, documentation, excerpt, guidance, indication, innuendo, insinuation, intimation, recommendation, referral, relation *(connection)*, relevance, reminder. SEE MAIN ENTRY
reference book directory
reference form form *(document)*
reference work directory
references credentials
referendary arbitrator
referendum election *(selection by vote)*, plebiscite, poll *(casting of votes)*. SEE MAIN ENTRY
referent mention *(reference)*
referential comparative, leading *(guiding)*, suggestive *(evocative)*
referment reference *(allusion)*, reference *(citation)*, referral
referral reference *(citation)*. SEE MAIN ENTRY
referre enter *(record)*, move *(judicially request)*, recapitulate, recount, refer *(send for action)*, render *(deliver)*, report *(disclose)*, restore *(return)*, submit *(give)*
referrence delegation *(assignment)*
referrential pertinent
referring comparative, delegation *(assignment)*, germane, pertinent, relative *(relevant)*
referring to relevant
reficere fix *(repair)*, reconstruct, renew *(refurbish)*, renovate, repair
refill replenish, supply
refilled replete
refinance SEE MAIN ENTRY
refine amend, clarify, compound, cultivate, decontaminate, develop, edit, elaborate, emend, enhance, expurgate, meliorate, modify *(alter)*, perfect, purge *(purify)*, reform. SEE MAIN ENTRY
refined aesthetic, choate lien, civil *(polite)*, discreet, elegant, meritorious, punctilious
refined discrimination discretion *(quality of being discreet)*
refined manners decorum
refined taste decorum
refinement amendment *(correction)*, amenity, civilization, clarification, courtesy, decorum, development *(progression)*, discretion *(quality of being discreet)*, presence *(poise)*, propriety *(correctness)*, reform. SEE MAIN ENTRY
refining revision *(process of correcting)*
refinish renew *(refurbish)*
refit fix *(repair)*, rehabilitate, renew *(refurbish)*, renovate, repair, restore *(renew)*
refitting renewal, repair
reflect brood, characterize, deliberate, muse, pause, radiate, rationalize, reason *(conclude)*. SEE MAIN ENTRY
reflect again reconsider
reflect discredit upon discommend, disgrace, dishonor *(deprive of honor)*
reflect dishonor upon discredit, disgrace
reflect honor on dedicate
reflect honor upon bestow
reflect over deliberate
reflect poorly upon denigrate, disparage
reflect shame upon disgrace
reflect upon brand *(stigmatize)*, consider, deliberate, denounce *(condemn)*, ponder, study, weigh
reflecting circumspect, discreet, judicious, juridical
reflection apprehension *(perception)*, bad repute, comment, concept, consideration *(contemplation)*, contemplation, criticism, deliberation, dialectic, discredit, hindsight, idea, impression, innuendo, introspection, memory *(retention)*, observation, opinion *(belief)*, penumbra, remark, repercussion, resemblance. SEE MAIN ENTRY
reflective aforethought, circumspect, cogitative, deliberate, pensive, profound *(esoteric)*, rational, solemn SEE MAIN ENTRY
reflex controlled *(restrained)*, repercussion
reflex action instinct
refluence outflow
refluent regressive
reflux decrease, outflow
refocillate recreate
reform ameliorate, amend, change, convert *(change use)*, convert *(persuade)*, correction *(change)*, development *(progression)*, emend, fix *(repair)*, meliorate, modify *(alter)*, progress, reconstitute, reconstruct, recreate, rectify, redeem *(satisfy debts)*, repair *(noun)*, repair *(verb)*, repent, reproduce, restore *(renew)*, revision *(process of correcting)*, transform. SEE MAIN ENTRY
reform school reformatory
reformable corrigible

reformation amendment *(correction)*, correction *(change)*, development *(progression)*, reform, rehabilitation, renewal, reorganization, repair
reformational corrigible, disciplinary *(punitory)*, progressive *(advocating change)*
reformative disciplinary *(punitory)*, medi-cinal, progressive *(advocating change)*, remedial, repentant
reformatory corrigible, disciplinary *(punitory)*, jail, penitentiary, prison, progressive *(advocating change)*, repentant. SEE MAIN ENTRY
reformed penitent, renascent, repentant
reformed character penitent
reformer insurgent, malcontent
reformers lobby
refractoriness contempt *(disobedience to the court)*
refractory contumacious, difficult, disobedient, disorderly, fractious, froward, hostile, incorrigible, indomitable, inflexible, insubordinate, intractable, lawless, obdurate, perverse, recalcitrant, restive, uncontrollable, unruly, unyielding, vicious
refrain cease, desist, eschew, forbear, shun, stop, withhold. SEE MAIN ENTRY
refrain from avoid *(evade)*, forgo, forswear, waive
refrain from action forbear
refrain from noticing ignore
refrain from punishing condone
refrain from using conserve
refrain from working strike *(refuse to work)*
refraining avoidance *(evasion)*
refraining from involvement laissez faire
refraining from utterance mute
refrainment abstention
refresh meliorate, reassure, reconstruct, recreate, renew *(refurbish)*, renovate, repair, replenish, restore *(renew)*
refresh one's memory recall *(remember)*
refresh the memory remind
refreshed renascent
refreshing palatable, sapid, unusual
refreshment enjoyment *(pleasure)*, renewal, revival, solace, treat
refuel replenish
refuge asylum *(hiding place)*, asylum *(protection)*, bulwark, cache *(hiding place)*, haven, home *(domicile)*, inhabitation *(place of dwelling)*, lodging, protection, shelter *(protection)*, shelter *(tax benefit)*, shield. SEE MAIN ENTRY
refugee alien
refugee prisoner fugitive
refugium refuge
refulgent lucid
refund bear the expense, compensate *(remunerate)*, consideration *(recompense)*, defray, discharge *(payment)*, discharge *(pay a debt)*, indemnify, indemnity, quit *(repay)*, rebate *(noun)*, rebate *(verb)*, reciprocate, recoup *(reimburse)*, reimburse, reimbursement, repay, replace, replacement, restitution, restore *(return)*. SEE MAIN ENTRY
refunding compensatory
refundment refund
refurbish fix *(repair)*, meliorate, reconstruct, rehabilitate, reinforce, renew *(refurbish)*, renovate, repair
refurbishment reparation *(keeping in repair)*
refusal bar *(obstruction)*, declination, disapproval, disclaimer, exclusion, negation, noncompliance *(nonobservance)*, ostracism, prohibition, rebuff, rejection, renunciation, repudiation, resistance. SEE MAIN ENTRY
refusal of agreement dissension
refusal of approval veto
refusal of bail bondage
refusal of consent declination
refusal to accept dishonor *(nonpayment)*
refusal to answer demurrer
refusal to be provoked longanimity
refusal to become involved laissez faire
refusal to believe cloud *(suspicion)*, doubt *(suspicion)*
refusal to comply mutiny
refusal to do business boycott
refusal to furnish work lockout
refusal to obey disregard *(omission)*, infraction
refusal to obey orders contempt *(disobedience to the court)*
refusal to pay default, dishonor *(nonpayment)*, nonpayment
refusal to sanction veto
refuse abrogate *(annul)*, ban, bar *(exclude)*, censor, condemn *(ban)*, constrain *(restrain)*, debar, decline *(reject)*, disaffirm, disallow, disapprove *(reject)*, disavow, dismiss *(put out of consideration)*, disobey, disoblige, dissent *(withhold assent)*, forbid, forgo, forswear, hold out *(resist)*, prohibit, proscribe *(prohibit)*, protest, rebuff, refrain, reject, renounce, shirk, spurn, waive, withhold. SEE MAIN ENTRY
refuse approval forbid
refuse assent disaccord, disagree, dissent *(withhold assent)*
refuse assent to disapprove *(reject)*
refuse bail imprison
refuse consent disapprove *(reject)*, forbid, hold out *(resist)*
refuse credence disavow, disbelieve, disown *(deny the validity)*, impugn
refuse payment dishonor *(refuse to pay)*
refuse permission ban, censor, interdict, prohibit, proscribe *(prohibit)*
refuse to accept contest, contradict, decline *(reject)*, disaccord, disavow, disown *(deny the validity)*, except *(object)*, reject, repudiate, spurn
refuse to acknowledge deny *(contradict)*, disaccord, disallow, disavow, ignore, repudiate
refuse to admit contest, deny *(contradict)*, disaccord, disavow, disbelieve, disown *(deny the validity)*, dissent *(withhold assent)*, exclude, gainsay, ignore
refuse to agree disagree
refuse to allow deny *(contradict)*, deny *(refuse to grant)*, disallow, forbid, inhibit
refuse to associate with isolate
refuse to authorize forbid
refuse to believe disbelieve, doubt *(distrust)*
refuse to bestow deny *(refuse to grant)*
refuse to confirm disapprove *(reject)*
refuse to conform cross *(disagree with)*, rebel
refuse to consent disaccord
refuse to consider exclude, reject
refuse to corroborate disallow, disavow, disown *(deny the validity)*
refuse to credit disbelieve
refuse to disclose withhold
refuse to give deny *(refuse to grant)*
refuse to give permission forbid
refuse to give up endure *(last)*, persevere, persist
refuse to grant constrain *(restrain)*, disallow
refuse to hear disregard, ignore
refuse to honor dishonor *(refuse to pay)*
refuse to honor a commitment renege
refuse to honor a promise renege
refuse to include exclude
refuse to know disregard
refuse to notice ignore
refuse to obey disobey
refuse to oblige disoblige
refuse to permit deny *(refuse to grant)*, forbid
refuse to ratify disapprove *(reject)*
refuse to receive disapprove *(reject)*
refuse to recognize disown *(refuse to acknowledge)*, neglect
refuse to regard disregard
refuse to sanction disapprove *(reject)*
refuse to see exclude
refuse to submit resist *(withstand)*, withstand
refuse to supply deny *(refuse to grant)*
refuse to support rebel, secede
refuse to sustain overrule
refuse to tolerate persecute
refuse to trust doubt *(distrust)*
refuse to waste conserve
refuse to yield endure *(last)*, persevere, resist *(oppose)*
refused inadmissible
refusing disinclined, dissident, nonconsenting, reluctant
refusing to admit dissenting
refusing to agree dissenting, irreconcilable
refusing to harmonize irreconcilable
refusing to obey contumacious
refusing to relent persistent
refutability cloud *(suspicion)*
refutable contestable, controversial, debatable, defeasible, disputable, dubious, dubitative, litigable, untenable
refutal answer *(reply)*, contradiction
refutare controvert
refutation answer *(judicial response)*, argument *(pleading)*, confutation, contradiction, counterargument, defeat, demurrer, denial, negation, opposition, plea, repudiation
refutative contradictory, contrary
refutatory contradictory, contrary
refute answer *(reply)*, avoid *(cancel)*, conflict, contradict, contravene, controvert, countercharge, countervail, cross *(disagree with)*, debate, defeat, disaccord, disaffirm, disagree, disallow, disown *(deny the validity)*, disprove, dispute *(contest)*, dispute *(debate)*, gainsay, impugn, invalidate, negate, oppose, oppugn, overthrow, parry, rebut, reply. SEE MAIN ENTRY
refute by argument countercharge
refuting contradictory, contrary, dissenting, negative
regain collect *(recover money)*, reclaim, recover, redeem *(repurchase)*, repossess
regaining recovery *(repossession)*
regainment recovery *(repossession)*
regard affection, appertain, apply *(pertain)*, aspect, caution *(vigilance)*, character *(reputation)*, complexion, concern *(interest)*, concern *(care)*, concern *(involve)*, consider, consideration *(sympathetic regard)*, credit *(recognition)*, deem, defer *(yield in judgment)*, deference, diligence *(care)*, discern

(detect with the senses), estimation (esteem), hear (give attention to), heed, homage, honor (good reputation), honor (outward respect), honor, interest (concern), keep (fulfill), mention (tribute), note (notice), notice (heed), notice (observe), observation, observe (watch), opine, outlook, perceive, perception, prestige, presuppose, prudence, recognition, reputation, respect, surmise, worth. SEE MAIN ENTRY
regard as apprehend (perceive)
regard as axiomatic postulate, presume
regard as wrong disapprove (condemn)
regard carefully check (inspect), concentrate (pay attention), examine (study), focus, scrutinize
regard indulgently excuse
regard likely expect (consider probable)
regard studiously peruse
regard unfavorably disfavor
regard upon deliberate
regard with blame disapprove (condemn)
regard with favor favor
regard with kindness favor
regard with proud contempt disdain
regard with sorrow deplore
regard with suspicion doubt (distrust), mistrust
regardful careful, circumspect, cognizant, conscientious, conscious (aware), discreet, judicious, meticulous, obedient, painstaking, particular (exacting), politic, preventive, prudent, vigilant
regardfully respectfully
regardfulness discretion (quality of being discreet), interest (concern), notice (heed)
regarding pertinent, wherein
regardless careless, cursory, derelict (negligent), inadvertent, insusceptible (uncaring), lax, negligent, perfunctory, thoughtless. SEE MAIN ENTRY
regardless of irrespective
regardlessness disregard (lack of respect), disregard (omission), disregard (unconcern), inconsideration, negligence
regauge reassess
regency dominion (supreme authority), hegemony, hierarchy (persons in authority), predominance, regime
regeneracy revival
regenerate change, convert (change use), cure, fix (repair), meliorate, penitent, reclaim, reconstitute, reconstruct, recreate, reform, renew (begin again), renew (refurbish), renovate, repeat (do again), restore (renew), resurrect, transform
regenerated renascent
regenerateness reconversion
regeneration development (progression), reconversion, reform, rehabilitation, rene-wal, resurgence, revival
regenesis reconversion, resurgence, revival
regent plenipotentiary, sovereign (absolute), substitute
regere direct (supervise), govern, manage
regignere reproduce
regime hierarchy (persons in authority), management (directorate), system, tenure. SEE MAIN ENTRY
regimen control (supervision)
regimen regime, regulation (rule), system
regiment control (regulate), manage, marshal, orchestrate, organize (arrange), oversee. SEE MAIN ENTRY
regimentation distribution (arrangement), form (arrangement), regulation (management)
regio direction (course), district, region, section (vicinity), territory
region area (province), bailiwick, capacity (sphere), circuit, coverage (scope), district, division (administrative unit), domain (sphere of influence), locality, location, parcel, province, realm, scope, seat, section (vicinity), sphere, territory, vicinity, zone. SEE MAIN ENTRY
regional local, native (domestic), parochial, provincial. SEE MAIN ENTRY
register account (evaluation), book, calendar (list of cases), calendar (record of yearly periods), date, digest (comprehend), docket, document, empanel, enroll, enter (record), file, file (place among official records), form (document), impanel, inscribe, inventory, itemize, join (associate oneself with), journal, ledger, marginalia, notary public, notation, poll (canvass), poll, program, record (noun), record (verb), roll, set down, subscribe (promise), survey (poll), tabulate. SEE MAIN ENTRY
register of cases calendar (list of cases)
register one's vote cast (register)
registered person member (individual in a group)
registerer notary public
registering census
registrar accountant, clerk, comptroller, notary public
registration census, entry (record), poll (canvass), reservation (engagement), subscription. SEE MAIN ENTRY
registration book register
registry docket, file, form (document), ledger, registration, roll
règlement act (enactment)
reglement bylaw
regnancy government (administration)
regnant dominant, master, paramount, powerful, predominant
régnant prevailing (having superior force)
regnant rife, sovereign (absolute)
regnare rule (govern)
regradation reclassification
regrade retreat
regrater broker
regress decline, deteriorate, escheat, recidivate, relapse (noun), relapse (verb), reversion (act of returning), revert. SEE MAIN ENTRY
regression decline, lapse (expiration), recidivism, recrudescence, relapse, reversion (act of returning)
regressive decadent. SEE MAIN ENTRY
regret deplore, dissatisfaction, refuse, remorse, repent. SEE MAIN ENTRY
regret profoundly deplore
regretful contrite, penitent, remorseful, repentant
regretfulness remorse
regrets refusal
regrettable deplorable, lamentable. SEE MAIN ENTRY
regretted regrettable
regretting contrite, repentant
regroup redistribute
regrouping reclassification
regula canon, law, maxim, principle (axiom), rule (guide), standard
regular accustomed (customary), chronic, consistent, constant, continual (connected), conventional, customary, daily, familiar (customary), general, habitual, household (familiar), mundane, natural, ordinary, periodic, prevailing (current), prevalent, punctual, repeated, routine, systematic, traditional, typical, uniform, usual. SEE MAIN ENTRY
regular arrangement method
regular employment pursuit (occupation)
regular performance norm
regular procedure matter of course
regular proceeding process (course)
regular recurrence regularity
regular return cycle, regularity
regularity arrangement (ordering), array (order), constant, form (arrangement), frequency, method, organization (structure), system, uniformity. SEE MAIN ENTRY
regularity of action method
regularity of recurrence cycle, frequency
regularize adapt, codify, coordinate, modify (alter), naturalize (acclimate), regulate (adjust)
regularly as a rule, generally, invariably
regularness regularity
regulate administer (conduct), arbitrate (conciliate), arrange (methodize), attune, check (inspect), conduct, coordinate, determine, direct (supervise), discipline (control), file (arrange), fix (arrange), govern, handle (manage), manage, manipulate (utilize skillfully), marshal, mitigate, moderate (preside over), modify (moderate), officiate, operate, orchestrate, organize (arrange), oversee, palliate (abate), police, preclude, prescribe, preside, prohibit, qualify (condition), rule (govern), superintend. SEE MAIN ENTRY
regulated periodic, regular (orderly), safe, systematic
regulated by conditional, dependent
regulating adjustment, leading (guiding)
regulation act (enactment), administration, boiler plate, bureaucracy, bylaw, canon, check (bar), codification, condition (contingent provision), constitution, control (supervision), criterion, custody (supervision), dictate, direction (guidance), direction (order), discipline (training), disposition (final arrangement), edict, enactment, familiar (customary), fiat, government (administration), instruction (direction), law, management (supervision), mandate, measure, moderation, ordinance, ordinary, precept, prescription (directive), principle (axiom), quota, requirement, restriction, rubric (authoritative rule), rule (legal dictate), statute, supervision, supremacy, writ. SEE MAIN ENTRY
regulation by a system classification
regulation by law code, edict
regulation by statute code, edict, legalization
regulation of finances economy (economic system)
regulations code, legislation (enactments), mode, protocol (etiquette). SEE MAIN ENTRY
regulative administrative
regulatory civic, disciplinary (punitory)
rehabilitate cure, fix (repair), meliorate, reconstruct, recreate, rectify, reform, reinstate, renew (refurbish), renovate, repair, restore (renew). SEE MAIN ENTRY
rehabilitated renascent
rehabilitation correction (change), improvement, progress, reconversion,

remedy *(legal means of redress)*, rendition *(restoration)*, renewal, reorganization, repair, reparation *(keeping in repair)*. SEE MAIN ENTRY
rehash copy, repeat *(state again)*, restatement
rehear appeal, reconsider
rehearing appeal. SEE MAIN ENTRY
rehearsal discipline *(training)*, preparation
rehearse practice *(train by repetition)*, recite, review
rehearsed repeated
rehire reinstate
rei adiacere abut
rei adversari militate
rei deditus addicted
rei obstare militate
reicere rebuff, reject, repudiate
reidentification remembrance *(recollection)*
reidentify recognize *(perceive)*, remember
reiectio rejection, renunciation
reify substantiate
reign dominion *(supreme authority)*, govern, government *(administration)*, hegemony, influence, jurisdiction, power, predominance, predominate *(command)*, preside, prevail *(triumph)*, regime, rule *(govern)*, term *(duration)*. SEE MAIN ENTRY
reign of terror lynch law, oppression
reign over dominate, handle *(manage)*
reigning influential, master, paramount, powerful, predominant, rife, sovereign *(absolute)*
reimburse bear the expense, compensate *(remunerate)*, contribute *(indemnify)*, defray, disburse *(pay out)*, indemnify, pay, quit *(repay)*, rebate, reciprocate, refund, remunerate, repay, replace, restore *(return)*, return *(refund)*, satisfy *(discharge)*. SEE MAIN ENTRY
reimbursement collection *(payment)*, commission *(fee)*, compensation, consideration *(recompense)*, contribution *(indemnification)*, damages, disbursement *(funds paid out)*, discharge *(payment)*, honorarium, indemnification, indemnity, pay, payment *(act of paying)*, payment *(remittance)*, rebate, receipt *(voucher)*, recompense, refund, remittance, remuneration, reparation *(indemnification)*, restitution, satisfaction *(discharge of debt)*. SEE MAIN ENTRY
reimbursing compensatory
reimprison rearrest
rein constraint *(restriction)*, damper *(stopper)*, disadvantage, fetter, hamper, oversee, subdue
rein in constrict *(inhibit)*, detain *(restrain)*, discipline *(control)*, inhibit, repress, stem *(check)*, withhold. SEE MAIN ENTRY
reinaugurate reinstate
reincarcerate remand
reincarnate resurrect
reincarnation revival
reindoctrination rehabilitation
reinfection recrudescence
reinforce accumulate *(enlarge)*, aid, assist, bear *(support)*, bear *(yield)*, compound, corroborate, develop, enhance, heighten *(augment)*, help, preserve, side, supplement, support *(assist)*, support *(corroborate)*, sustain *(confirm)*, sustain *(prolong)*. SEE MAIN ENTRY
reinforced strong
reinforcement aid *(help)*, assistance, augmentation, boom *(increase)*, help, mainstay, relief *(aid)*. SEE MAIN ENTRY
reinless lawless, uncurbed
reinquire reexamine
reinquiry rehearing, review *(official reexamination)*
reins bondage
reins of government bureaucracy
reinstall reassign, reinstate, renew *(begin again)*, replace, restore *(return)*
reinstate continue *(resume)*, proceed *(continue)*, reclaim, remit *(release from penalty)*, renew *(begin again)*, replace, restore *(return)*, surrender *(give back)*. SEE MAIN ENTRY
reinstatement continuation *(resumption)*, rehabilitation, renewal, replacement, restitution
reinstitute continue *(resume)*, renew *(begin again)*, reopen, repeat *(do again)*
reinstitution continuation *(resumption)*
reinstitutionalize remand
reinsurance coverage *(insurance)*
reinsure certify *(attest)*
reintegrate reconstitute, rehabilitate, renew *(refurbish)*
reintroduce renew *(begin again)*
reinvest refinance, reinstate
reinvest with restore *(return)*
reinvestigate reexamine
reinvigorate fix *(repair)*, meliorate, recruit, rehabilitate, reinforce, remedy, renew *(refurbish)*, renovate, restore *(renew)*
reinvigoration rehabilitation, renewal
reipublicae forma organization *(association)*, polity
reissue circulate, copy, redistribute, renewal
reiterant iterative, repetitious
reiterate copy, dwell *(linger over)*, quote, reaffirm, recapitulate, recite, recount, repeat *(state again)*, review. SEE MAIN ENTRY
reiterated repeated
reiteration narration, platitude, recital, redundancy, restatement. SEE MAIN ENTRY
reiterative frequent, incessant, insistent, repetitious
reive hold up *(rob)*
rejail rearrest
reject abrogate *(annul)*, bar *(exclude)*, censor, challenge, condemn *(ban)*, contemn, decry, defect, demonstrate *(protest)*, demur, deny *(refuse to grant)*, deprecate, differ *(disagree)*, disaccord, disaffirm, disallow, disavow, disbelieve, discard, disclaim, discriminate *(treat differently)*, disdain, disfavor, dismiss *(put out of consideration)*, disobey, disoblige, disown *(deny the validity)*, disqualify, dissent *(withhold assent)*, eliminate *(exclude)*, eschew, exclude, expel, fight *(counteract)*, forgo, forswear, gainsay, ignore, oppose, outlaw, overrule, prohibit, proscribe *(denounce)*, rebuff, refuse, relegate, relinquish, remove *(eliminate)*, renounce, repudiate, repulse, resign, select, set aside *(annul)*, spurn, waive. SEE MAIN ENTRY
reject as erroneous deny *(contradict)*
reject as inadmissable disapprove *(reject)*
reject as untrue disbelieve
reject by subsequent action overrule
reject by subsequent decision overrule
rejected derelict *(abandoned)*, disreputable, inadmissible, ineligible, obsolete, outdated, outmoded, poor *(inferior in quality)*, undesirable, unsatisfactory
rejecting disqualification *(rejection)*, negative
rejection abandonment *(repudiation)*, abjuration, bar *(obstruction)*, boycott, breach, check *(bar)*, criticism, declination, denial, disapprobation, disapproval, disclaimer, disdain, dishonor *(nonpayment)*, dismissal *(termination of a proceeding)*, disparagement, disqualification *(rejection)*, exception *(objection)*, exclusion, expulsion, impugnation, intolerance, layoff, negation, nonconformity, objection, ostracism, prohibition, proscription, rebuff, refusal, removal, renunciation, repudiation, reversal, veto. SEE MAIN ENTRY
rejective reluctant
rejoice in relish
rejoicing enjoyment *(pleasure)*
rejoin acknowledge *(respond)*, answer *(reply)*, answer *(respond legally)*, countercharge, meet, rebut, reply, respond, retort, return *(respond)*. SEE MAIN ENTRY
rejoinder answer *(judicial response)*, answer *(reply)*, confutation, contradiction, counterargument, counterclaim, reaction *(response)*, reply, response. SEE MAIN ENTRY
rejoining responsive
rejudge reassess, reconsider
rejuvenate cure, fix *(repair)*, recreate, renew *(refurbish)*, renovate, repair, restore *(renew)*, resurrect. SEE MAIN ENTRY
rejuvenated renascent
rejuvenation renewal, reparation *(keeping in repair)*, resurgence, revival
rejuvenescence revival
rekindle renew *(refurbish)*, resurrect
relabi relapse
relapse crossroad *(turning point)*, decline, escheat, lapse *(expiration)*, recidivate, recidivism, recrudescence, regress, renewal, repeat *(do again)*, return *(go back)*, reversion *(act of returning)*. SEE MAIN ENTRY
relapsing regressive
relate admit *(concede)*, allege, allude, appertain, apply *(pertain)*, assert, communicate, compare, connect *(relate)*, contact *(communicate)*, converse, convey *(communicate)*, correspond *(be equivalent)*, correspond *(communicate)*, delineate, depict, depose *(testify)*, detail *(particularize)*, disabuse, divulge, impart, inform *(notify)*, involve *(implicate)*, involve *(participate)*, notify, pertain, phrase, recapitulate, recite, recount, refer *(direct attention)*, remark, repeat *(state again)*. SEE MAIN ENTRY
relate ideas converse
relate to affiliate, concern *(involve)*
related affiliated, akin *(germane)*, allied, analogous, associated, coadunate, cognate, collateral *(accompanying)*, comparable *(capable of comparison)*, consanguineous, consonant, correlative, germane, interrelated, pertinent, relative *(relevant)*, relevant, similar, tangential. SEE MAIN ENTRY
related by affinity next of kin
related to incident
relatedness association *(connection)*, chain *(nexus)*, connection *(relation)*, degree *(kinship)*
relater informer *(a person who provides information)*
relating akin *(germane)*, germane, pertinent, reference *(citation)*, relative *(relevant)*
relating to apposite, cognate, comparative, correlative, incident

relating to a penalty penal
relating to a will testate
relating to accounts fiscal
relating to method procedural
relating to money matters fiscal
relating to moral action ethical
relating to one side only ex parte
relating to the family domestic *(household)*
relating to the home domestic *(household)*
relating to the management of revenue fiscal
relating to the mechanics of a lawsuit procedural
relating to traffic industrial
relatio report *(detailed account)*
relation affiliation *(bloodline)*, affiliation *(connectedness)*, affinity *(family ties)*, analogy, association *(connection)*, attribution, chain *(nexus)*, collation, contact *(association)*, correlate, delineation, disclosure *(act of disclosing)*, kinship, mention *(reference)*, narration, nexus, privity, proportion, recital, relationship *(connection)*, relationship *(family tie)*, relative, relevance, report *(detailed account)*, representation *(statement)*, story *(narrative)*. SEE MAIN ENTRY
relation by birth kindred
relation by blood affinity *(family ties)*, kindred, next of kin
relation by consanguinity kindred
relational comparative, pertinent, relative *(relevant)*
relations blood, dealings, kindred, next of kin
relationship affiliation *(bloodline)*, affiliation *(connectedness)*, affinity *(family ties)*, association *(connection)*, chain *(nexus)*, connection *(relation)*, contact *(association)*, filiation, kinship, nexus, privity, propinquity *(kinship)*, proportion, rapport, relation *(connection)*, relation *(kinship)*, relevance. SEE MAIN ENTRY
relationship between persons degree *(kinship)*
relative apposite, cognate, commensurable, commensurate, comparative, consanguineous, correlative, germane, proportionate, related, relation *(kinship)*, relevant. SEE MAIN ENTRY
relative estimate comparison, proportion
relative estimation comparison
relative position aspect, degree *(station)*, relation *(connection)*
relative quantity differential
relative to incident
relative to the manner of proceeding procedural
relativeness analogy
relatives kindred, next of kin
relativity analogy, chain *(nexus)*, proportion
relator complainant, informant
relax ease, impair, lull, mollify, recess, relent, relieve *(free from burden)*, repose *(rest)*, rest *(cease from action)*, soothe, subside. SEE MAIN ENTRY
relax severity commute
relaxation enjoyment *(pleasure)*, informality, leave *(absence)*, mitigation, mollification, pause, remission, respite *(interval of rest)*
relaxation of control freedom
relaxation of law dispensation *(exception)*. SEE MAIN ENTRY
relaxed informal
relay deliver, disseminate, pass *(advance)*, send. SEE MAIN ENTRY
relay ideas converse
release absolution, acquit, acquittal, amnesty, assign *(transfer ownership)*, authorize, bestow, catharsis, cede, cession, clear, clemency, composition *(agreement in bankruptcy)*, condone, deed, disband, discharge *(liberation)*, discharge *(dismiss)*, discharge *(liberate)*, disencumber, disengage, disentangle, disenthrall, dismiss *(discharge)*, dispel, disposition *(transfer of property)*, dissociate, emancipation, enable, enfranchise, excuse, exemption, exoneration, extricate, exude, free, freedom, immunity, issuance, issue *(publish)*, layoff, let *(permit)*, liberate, liberation, notice *(announcement)*, notification, palliate *(excuse)*, pardon *(noun)*, pardon *(verb)*, parole *(noun)*, parole *(verb)*, privilege, probation, proclaim, publication *(disclosure)*, publicity, quit *(free of)*, receipt *(proof of receiving)*, redeem *(repurchase)*, redemption, relieve *(free from burden)*, relinquish, remise, remission, remit *(release from penalty)*, report *(detailed account)*, rescue, respite *(reprieve)*, settlement, terminate, vindicate, waiver. SEE MAIN ENTRY
release conditionally parole
release from an obligation exonerate
release from attachment disengage
release from bondage disenthrall
release from charge immunity
release from custody discharge *(liberation)*, emancipation, liberate
release from debt satisfaction *(discharge of debt)*
release from duty immunity
release from employment dismissal *(discharge)*
release from imprisonment parole
release from imputation absolve
release from liability exemption, exonerate
release from matrimonial status divorce
release from matrimony divorce
release from obligation dispensation *(exception)*, excuse, exemption, palliate *(excuse)*
release from penalty pardon
release from pressure ease
release from prison parole SEE MAIN ENTRY
release from punishment absolution, pardon *(noun)*, pardon *(verb)*
release from restraint disenthrall, extricate, free
release from wedlock divorce
released clear *(free from criminal charges)*, exempt, free *(relieved from a burden)*, immune, public *(known)*, unbound
released convict probationer *(released offender)*
released criminal probationer *(released offender)*
released felon probationer *(released offender)*
released lawbreaker probationer *(released offender)*
released malefactor probationer *(released offender)*
released prisoner probationer *(released offender)*
released transgressor probationer *(released offender)*
released wrongdoer probationer *(released offender)*
releasing from custody liberation
releasor licensor
relegate assign *(transfer ownership)*, bar *(exclude)*, delegate, detail *(assign)*, dislodge, remand, remit *(submit for consideration)*, seclude, set aside *(annul)*. SEE MAIN ENTRY
relegate to commit *(entrust)*
relegatio banishment
relegation assignment *(transfer of ownership)*, proscription, rejection, removal
relent comply, condone, relax, submit *(yield)*, succumb, surrender *(yield)*, yield *(submit)*. SEE MAIN ENTRY
relentless callous, close *(rigorous)*, cold-blooded, cruel, dictatorial, diligent, draconian, faithful *(diligent)*, immutable, implacable, inexorable, inflexible, ironclad, malicious, obdurate, patient, persistent, pertinacious, recalcitrant, remorseless, resolute, rigid, ruthless, sedulous, serious *(devoted)*, severe, stable, steadfast, unalterable, unbending, uncompromising, unrelenting, unyielding. SEE MAIN ENTRY
relentlessness cruelty, diligence *(perseverance)*, rigor, severity
relet sublet
relevance connection *(relation)*, consequence *(significance)*, importance, interest *(concern)*, materiality *(consequence)*, propriety *(appropriateness)*, qualification *(fitness)*, relation *(connection)*, relationship *(connection)*, significance. SEE MAIN ENTRY
relevancy relationship *(connection)*. SEE MAIN ENTRY
relevant akin *(germane)*, applicable, apposite, appropriate, congruous, correlative, felicitous, fit, fitting, germane, important *(significant)*, interrelated, material *(important)*, pertinent, proper, related, suitable, valuable. SEE MAIN ENTRY
relevant conduct SEE MAIN ENTRY
relevant fact evidence
relevant instance illustration
relevant material evidence
relevant to all general
relevy reassess
reliability adhesion *(loyalty)*, candor *(straightforwardness)*, certainty, certification *(certainness)*, constant, credibility, honor *(good reputation)*, loyalty, trustworthiness. SEE MAIN ENTRY
reliable accurate, authentic, believable, bona fide, candid, certain *(fixed)*, certain *(positive)*, cogent, conscientious, constant, convincing, credible, definite, dependable, diligent, factual, faithful *(loyal)*, fiduciary, honest, incorruptible, indestructible, infallible, loyal, meritorious, official, positive *(incontestable)*, reputable, safe, scrupulous, secure *(sound)*, solid *(sound)*, stable, staunch, steadfast, strong, tenable, true *(authentic)*, true *(loyal)*. SEE MAIN ENTRY
reliableness certification *(certainness)*
reliably faithfully
reliance confidence *(faith)*, credence, credit *(delayed payment)*, faith, mainstay, prospect *(outlook)*, security *(safety)*, trust *(confidence)*, weight *(credibility)*. SEE MAIN ENTRY
reliance on principle *(axiom)*, surety *(certainty)*
reliant dependent
relic holdover, reminder, token
relief abatement *(reduction)*, aid *(help)*, aid

(subsistence), benefit *(betterment)*, benevolence *(act of kindness)*, charity, contour *(outline)*, contour *(shape)*, cure, help, immunity, mitigation, mollification, panacea, reinforcement, remedial statute, remedy *(legal means of redress)*, remedy *(that which corrects)*, remission, reparation *(indemnification)*, replacement, service *(assistance)*, solace, substitute, support *(assistance)*. SEE MAIN ENTRY
relief from exoneration
relieve abate *(lessen)*, aid, allay, alleviate, assist, assuage, commute, cure, demote, diminish, discharge *(dismiss)*, discharge *(liberate)*, discharge *(release from obligation)*, disencumber, disentangle, divest, ease, excuse, exonerate, extricate, free, help, meliorate, mitigate, mollify, pacify, palliate *(abate)*, redress, release, remedy. SEE MAIN ENTRY
relieve from accusation exonerate
relieve of dispossess
relieve of blame exonerate
relieve of burden vindicate
relieve of complication disentangle
relieve of liability exonerate
relieve of obligation disengage
relieve of responsibility discharge *(release from obligation)*
relieve of something detrimental cure
relieve pressure soothe
relieved free *(relieved from a burden)*, prominent
relieved from liability exempt
reliever backer
relieving curative, mitigating, palliative *(abating)*
religiosus conscientious, scrupulous
religious sacrosanct, solemn
religious order denomination, society
religiously faithfully
relinguish bestow
relinquere leave *(give)*, relinquish
relinquish annul, attorn, cease, cede, confer *(give)*, contribute *(supply)*, convey *(transfer)*, demit, disavow, discontinue *(abandon)*, disown *(refuse to acknowledge)*, forfeit, forgo, forswear, lapse *(cease)*, leave *(allow to remain)*, quit *(discontinue)*, release, remise, remit *(relax)*, renounce, resign, retire *(conclude a career)*, secede, set aside *(annul)*, surrender *(give back)*, vacate *(leave)*, vacate *(void)*, waive, withdraw, yield *(submit)*. SEE MAIN ENTRY
relinquish life die, perish
relinquished derelict *(abandoned)*
relinquishing claim to cession
relinquishment abandonment *(desertion)*, abandonment *(discontinuance)*, abdication, cancellation, capitulation, cession, concession *(compromise)*, denial, dereliction, desuetude, disclaimer, disposition *(transfer of property)*, expense *(sacrifice)*, pardon, release, remission, renunciation, waiver SEE MAIN ENTRY
relinquishment by gift disposition *(transfer of property)*
reliquum remainder *(remaining part)*
reliquus balance *(amount in excess)*
relish enjoyment *(pleasure)*, penchant, propensity. SEE MAIN ENTRY
relishable palatable, preferable, sapid
relive recall *(remember)*, recollect, remember
reload replenish
relocate remove *(transfer)*. SEE MAIN ENTRY
reluct contend *(dispute)*, demonstrate *(protest)*, fight *(battle)*, oppugn, parry
reluctance disincentive, doubt *(indecision)*, hesitation, misgiving, resistance, scruple. SEE MAIN ENTRY
reluctance to believe cloud *(suspicion)*, doubt *(suspicion)*, incredulity
reluctant averse, disinclined, disobedient, hesitant, renitent, restive. SEE MAIN ENTRY
reluctant to punish placable
reluctantly unwillingly
reluctate oppugn, parry, resist *(oppose)*
relume burn
rely SEE MAIN ENTRY
rely on confide *(trust)*, rely, trust
rely on fortune bet
rely upon confide *(trust)*
relying on based on
relying upon subject *(conditional)*
rem administrare administer *(conduct)*
rem amittere forfeit
rem attingere abut
rem bene succeed *(attain)*
rem concedere waive
rem dissimulare connive, disguise
rem faciliorem reddere facilitate
rem hereditate accipere inherit
rem hominem flagitare importune
rem homini adsignare assign *(allot)*
rem integram relinquere abeyance
rem invenire detect
rem longius prosequi dwell *(linger over)*
rem praestare vouch
rem pro re pacisci barter
rem re mutare barter
rem relinquere abandon *(withdraw)*
rem sibi adrogare assume *(seize)*
rem simulare appearance *(look)*
rem tempore tribuere date
rem tempori adsignare date
rem testari attest
remade renascent
remail redirect
remain cease, dwell *(reside)*, endure *(last)*, exist, halt, inhabit, keep *(continue)*, last, lodge *(reside)*, persevere, persist, reside, resist *(withstand)*, stay *(continue)*, stay *(rest)*, subsist. SEE MAIN ENTRY
remain alive endure *(last)*, exist, subsist
remain firm determine, hold out *(resist)*
remain hidden elude
remain unchanged persist
remain unconverted disbelieve
remain undiscovered elude
remain valid endure *(last)*
remainder balance *(amount in excess)*, complement, discard, dower, holdover, overage, residual, surplus. SEE MAIN ENTRY
remainder over reversion *(remainder of an estate)*
remaining durable, habitation *(act of inhabiting)*, lasting, live *(existing)*, net, permanent, persistent, residuary, superfluous
remaining course alternative *(option)*
remaining courses choice *(alternatives offered)*
remaining options choice *(alternatives offered)*
remaining period unexpired term
remaining portion balance *(amount in excess)*, holdover, remainder *(remaining part)*
remaining time unexpired term
remains balance *(amount in excess)*, corpse, remainder *(remaining part)*, residual, salvage
remake change, convert *(change use)*, copy, fix *(repair)*, reconstitute, reconstruct, recreate, reform, rehabilitate, renew *(refurbish)*, renovate, repeat *(do again)*, reproduce, restore *(renew)*, transform
remaking reform, rehabilitation, reorganization
remand bondage, confine, constraint *(imprisonment)*, detain *(hold in custody)*, recommit, relegate, remit *(submit for consideration)*. SEE MAIN ENTRY
remand to custody commit *(institutionalize)*
remanded arrested *(apprehended)*
remanded into custody arrested *(apprehended)*
remanding to custody commitment *(confinement)*
remanent superfluous
remanere remain *(stay)*
remark acknowledge *(respond)*, comment *(noun)*, comment *(verb)*, convey *(communicate)*, dictum, disclosure *(something disclosed)*, express, expression *(comment)*, mention *(reference)*, muse, observation, phrase, pronouncement, speak, statement. SEE MAIN ENTRY
remark on mention
remark upon comment
remarkable considerable, conspicuous, egregious, extraordinary, famous, illustrious, important *(significant)*, major, material *(important)*, meritorious, momentous, nonconforming, notable, noteworthy, outstanding *(prominent)*, paramount, peculiar *(curious)*, perceivable, portentous *(eliciting amazement)*, prime *(most valuable)*, prodigious *(amazing)*, prominent, renowned, salient, singular, special, unaccustomed, uncanny, uncommon, unusual. SEE MAIN ENTRY
remarkably particularly
remarriage digamy
remeasure reapportion, reassess
remediable corrigible
remediable by an action at law actionable
remedial curative, medicinal, progressive *(advocating change)*, salubrious, salutary. SEE MAIN ENTRY
remedial justice equity *(justice)*
remedial measure remedial statute, remedy *(legal means of redress)*, remedy *(that which corrects)*
remedial statute SEE MAIN ENTRY
remediless inoperable *(incurable)*, irredeemable, irremediable, irreparable, irreversible, irrevocable
remedium relief *(release)*, remedy *(that which corrects)*, remedy
remedy adjust *(resolve)*, alleviate, amend, amendment *(correction)*, assuage, correction *(change)*, cure *(noun)*, cure *(verb)*, disabuse, drug, emend, fix *(repair)*, habeas corpus, help *(noun)*, help *(verb)*, panacea, recourse, rectify, redress, reform, regulate *(adjust)*, relief *(legal redress)*, relieve *(give aid)*, remedial statute, repair *(noun)*, repair *(verb)*, reparation *(indemnification)*, reparation *(keeping in repair)*, restore *(renew)*. SEE MAIN ENTRY
remember occur *(come to mind)*, recognize *(perceive)*, recollect, retain *(keep in possession)*, review. SEE MAIN ENTRY
remember with sorrow repent
rememberable notable
remembrance contribution *(donation)*, hindsight, impression, memory *(commemoration)*, monument, recognition, recollection, reminder, retrospect, reward, token. SEE MAIN ENTRY

rememoration retrospect

remind advise, notify, prompt. SEE MAIN ENTRY

remind oneself remember

reminder admonition, monument, note *(brief comment)*, notice *(announcement)*, suggestion. SEE MAIN ENTRY

remindful suggestive *(evocative)*

reminisce recall *(remember)*, recollect, remember

reminiscence recollection, remembrance *(recollection)*, retrospect

reminiscent suggestive *(evocative)*

reminiscential suggestive *(evocative)*

reminisci recollect, remember

remise alienate *(transfer title)*, cede, pass *(advance)*. SEE MAIN ENTRY

remiss careless, delinquent *(guilty of a misdeed)*, delinquent *(overdue)*, derelict *(negligent)*, dilatory, disobedient, improvident, lax, negligent, oblivious, overdue, perfunctory, slipshod, thoughtless, truant. SEE MAIN ENTRY

remissio abatement *(extinguishment)*, abatement *(reduction)*, remission

remission absolution, acquittal, cessation *(interlude)*, collection *(payment)*, diminution, discontinuance *(act of discontinuing)*, exoneration, halt, lull, pause, relief *(release)*. SEE MAIN ENTRY

remission of guilt pardon

remissness culpability, dereliction, disregard *(omission)*, laches, laxity, neglect, negligence, omission, oversight *(carelessness)*

remissus languid, lax, negligent

remit absolve, acquit, alleviate, bear *(yield)*, bear the expense, bequeath, bestow, compensate *(remunerate)*, condone, contribute *(indemnify)*, contribute *(supply)*, defray, delay, deliver, diminish, discontinue *(break continuity)*, dispatch *(send off)*, excuse, free, give *(grant)*, lessen, lull, offer *(tender)*, present *(make a gift)*, recommit, reimburse, reinstate, relax, release, relent, remand, remise, remunerate, restore *(return)*, satisfy *(discharge)*, subside, suspend, transmit. SEE MAIN ENTRY

remit a penalty exonerate

remit the penalty palliate *(excuse)*

remit to custody commit *(institutionalize)*

remittal recovery *(award)*

remittance amortization, benefit *(conferment)*, collection *(payment)*, consideration *(recompense)*, delivery, disbursement *(funds paid out)*, discharge *(payment)*, expenditure, expense *(cost)*, installment, pay, payment *(act of paying)*, payment *(remittance)*, pension, transmittal. SEE MAIN ENTRY

remittance for delay demurrage

remitted clear *(free from criminal charges)*

remittent intermittent, periodic, sporadic

remitter restitution

remittere abate *(lessen)*, remand, remit *(relax)*

remitting compensatory

remitting to custody commitment *(confinement)*

remnant balance *(amount in excess)*, discard, end *(termination)*, overage

remodel convert *(change use)*, emend, modify *(alter)*, reconstitute, reconstruct, recreate, reform, renew *(refurbish)*, renovate, restore *(renew)*, transform

remodeling development *(progression)*, rehabilitation, reorganization, repair

remold convert *(change use)*, modify *(alter)*, reconstitute, reconstruct, revise, transform

remolded tempered

remonstrance admonition, blame *(culpability)*, complaint, criticism, diatribe, disapprobation, disapproval, discredit, dispute, dissension, exception *(objection)*, objection, opposition, protest, reply, reprimand. SEE MAIN ENTRY

remonstrant remonstrative

remonstrate admonish *(warn)*, argue, blame, castigate, caution, censure, challenge, complain *(criticize)*, demonstrate *(protest)*, denounce *(condemn)*, deter, disaccord, disagree, disapprove *(condemn)*, discourage, dissuade, expostulate, fault, oppose, oppugn, protest, reason *(persuade)*, reprimand. SEE MAIN ENTRY

remonstrate against decry

remonstrate with rebuke

remonstration disapprobation, disapproval, dispute, opposition, protest

remonstrative hortative. SEE MAIN ENTRY

remora handicap, obstacle, obstruction. SEE MAIN ENTRY

remorseful contrite, penitent, repentant. SEE MAIN ENTRY

remorseful person penitent

remorsefulness remorse

remorseless brutal, callous, cold-blooded, cruel, incorrigible, obdurate, relentless, ruthless, sinister, unaffected *(uninfluenced)*, unrelenting. SEE MAIN ENTRY

remorselessness cruelty

remote foreign, immaterial, impertinent *(irrelevant)*, inaccessible, inapposite, inappropriate, inconsequential, irrelevant, private *(secluded)*, remote *(secluded)*, solitary, unapproachable. SEE MAIN ENTRY

remote cause SEE MAIN ENTRY

remote district frontier

remotion removal

remotus remote *(not proximate)*

removable deductible *(capable of being deducted from taxes)*, defeasible, moving *(in motion)*

removal absence *(nonattendance)*, avoidance *(cancellation)*, banishment, deduction *(diminution)*, defeasance, deportation, discharge *(dismissal)*, distress *(seizure)*, eviction, evulsion, exception *(exclusion)*, exclusion, expropriation *(divestiture)*, expulsion, flight, foreclosure, homicide, layoff, leave *(absence)*, loss, obviation, ouster, rejection, replacement. SEE MAIN ENTRY

removal from a job dismissal *(discharge)*

removal from a position dismissal *(discharge)*

removal from employment discharge *(dismissal)*

removal from office dismissal *(discharge)*

removal of a cause out of court dismissal *(termination of a proceeding)*

removal of discrimination integration *(assimilation)*

removal of errors correction *(change)*, revision *(process of correcting)*

remove abscond, abstract *(separate)*, adeem, bowdlerize, cancel, carry away, debar, deduct *(reduce)*, delete, deport *(banish)*, detach, discharge *(dismiss)*, discharge *(release from obligation)*, disencumber, disinter, dislocate, dislodge, dismiss *(discharge)*, dispel, dispossess, dissociate, divest, eject *(evict)*, eject *(expel)*, eliminate *(eradicate)*, eliminate *(exclude)*, eradicate, evacuate, evict, except *(exclude)*, excise *(cut away)*, exclude, expel, expunge, extirpate, extract, hold up *(rob)*, impound, move *(alter position)*, obliterate, oust, overthrow, part *(leave)*, reject, relegate, rescind, retire *(retreat)*, retrench, revoke, seclude, sequester *(seclude)*, succeed *(follow)*, superannuate, supersede, supplant, suspend, transfer, transport, vacate *(leave)*, withdraw. SEE MAIN ENTRY

remove a disability enable

remove a hindrance disencumber

remove a restraint disencumber

remove all sign of expunge

remove all trace of expunge

remove an essential part eviscerate

remove an impediment disencumber

remove bodily carry away

remove doubt ascertain, reassure

remove errors edit, emend

remove falsehood disabuse

remove faults amend

remove fear reassure

remove from abandon *(physically leave)*

remove from legal office disbar

remove from life dispatch *(put to death)*

remove from office demote, discharge *(dismiss)*, dismiss *(discharge)*, oust

remove from premises eject *(evict)*

remove from private ownership nationalize

remove from the practice of law disbar

remove from the roll of attorneys disbar

remove misunderstanding resolve *(solve)*

remove one's anxieties lull

remove one's fears lull

remove oneself flee, quit *(evacuate)*, retreat, secede

remove pollutants decontaminate

remove suspicion disarm *(set at ease)*

remove the errors fix *(repair)*

remove the obstacles permit

remove the traces obliterate

remove unhealthy agents decontaminate

remove utterly eradicate

removed alone *(solitary)*, apart, discrete, distinct *(distinguished from others)*, inaccessible, insular, insusceptible *(uncaring)*, irrelative, obscure *(remote)*, private *(secluded)*, remote *(not proximate)*, remote *(secluded)*, separate, solitary, unapproachable

removed from bondage free *(enjoying civil liberty)*, sovereign *(independent)*

removere remove *(transfer)*, seclude

rempublicam gubernare administer *(conduct)*

remunerari compensate *(remunerate)*, remunerate

remunerate bear the expense, contribute *(indemnify)*, defray, disburse *(pay out)*, indemnify, pay, quit *(repay)*, recoup *(reimburse)*, reimburse, remit *(send payment)*, repay, satisfy *(discharge)*. SEE MAIN ENTRY

remunerate for injury compensate *(remunerate)*

remuneratio recompense, remuneration

remuneration advance *(allowance)*, alimony, annuity, boom *(prosperity)*, brokerage, collection *(payment)*, commission *(fee)*, compensation, consideration *(recompense)*, contribution *(indemnification)*, disbursement *(funds paid out)*, earnings, fee *(charge)*, honorarium, income, indemnification, indemnity,

out of pocket, pay, payment *(remittance)*, payroll, pension, perquisite, profit, recompense, recovery *(award)*, reimbursement, remittance, rent, requital, restitution, retainer, revenue, reward, satisfaction *(discharge of debt)*, wage. SEE MAIN ENTRY
remuneration for injury compensation
remuneration for injury suffered damages
remunerative beneficial, compensatory, gainful, lucrative, productive, profitable, valuable. SEE MAIN ENTRY
remunerator insurer
renaissance reconversion, renewal, resurgence, revival
renascence renewal, resurgence, revival
renascent SEE MAIN ENTRY
rencounter conflict, confrontation *(act of setting face to face)*, confrontation *(altercation)*, fight *(battle)*, struggle
rend break *(fracture)*, destroy *(efface)*, dichotomize, disjoint, disperse *(scatter)*, force *(break)*, lancinate, luxate, separate, sever, split. SEE MAIN ENTRY
rend asunder disrupt, sever
render administer *(tender)*, allocate, avail *(bring about)*, bear *(yield)*, bear the expense, bequeath, bestow, cede, construe *(translate)*, contribute *(supply)*, define, discharge *(perform)*, dispense, offer *(tender)*, pay, present *(make a gift)*, proffer, rebate, recite, recount, remit *(send payment)*, satisfy *(discharge)*, supply, tender, transact, yield *(produce a return)*. SEE MAIN ENTRY
render a decision pass *(determine)*
render a document imperfect mutilate
render a judgment pass *(determine)*. SEE MAIN ENTRY
render a service accommodate, function
render a service to promote *(organize)*
render a task easier facilitate
render accordant adapt, attune, comport *(agree with)*, conform, regulate *(adjust)*
render an account convey *(communicate)*, depict
render an account of speak
render an attorney's license null and void disbar
render assistance enable, facilitate, help, relieve *(give aid)*, subsidize
render averse deter, disaffect, discourage, dissuade
render better emend, meliorate, nurture, repair
render broad expand
render central focus
render certain ascertain, assure *(give confidence to)*, assure *(insure)*
render chaotic degenerate
render clear explicate
render compatible arbitrate *(conciliate)*
render competent empower, enable
render complete conclude *(complete)*, consummate
render concordant arbitrate *(conciliate)*, reconcile
render deathless perpetuate
render defective vitiate
render definite ascertain
render different convert *(change use)*, transform
render difficult encumber *(hinder)*, hinder
render dim blind *(obscure)*
render evil brutalize, pervert
render eyeless blind *(deprive of sight)*
render feeble impair
render few deduct *(reduce)*, diminish
render filthy pollute
render flustered embarrass
render free clear, discharge *(liberate)*, disenthrall, quit *(free of)*
render harmless decontaminate, disarm *(divest of arms)*
render help aid, contribute *(assist)*, serve *(assist)*
render helpless disable
render honor to dedicate
render humble humiliate
render ill at ease embarrass
render illegible deface, expunge, obliterate
render impassable stop
render imperceptible obliterate
render imperfect mutilate
render impossible forbid. SEE MAIN ENTRY
render impotent disable, disqualify
render impure taint *(contaminate)*
render in a better form modify *(alter)*
render incompetent disable
render ineffective destroy *(void)*
render inefficacious vitiate
render inert dissolve *(terminate)*, neutralize
render inimical antagonize
render innocuous disarm *(divest of arms)*
render inoperative neutralize, vacate *(void)*
render insufficient deplete
render intelligible clarify, comment, construe *(translate)*, solve
render invalid cancel, frustrate, nullify, repeal, rescind
render invisible blind *(obscure)*, cloak, conceal, enshroud, hide, plant *(covertly place)*, shroud
render judgment adjudicate
render larger expand
render less decrease, discount *(minimize)*, minimize
render less difficult commute, ease, facilitate
render less excusable aggravate *(exacerbate)*
render less painful soothe
render less tolerable aggravate *(exacerbate)*
render lip service palter
render manifest exemplify
render more compact condense
render necessary call *(demand)*, necessitate
render neutral neutralize
render no longer opposed arbitrate *(conciliate)*
render null extirpate, perish
render null and void abolish, adeem, annul, disown *(deny the validity)*, frustrate, negate. SEE MAIN ENTRY
render payment disburse *(pay out)*, expend *(disburse)*
render powerless disable, disarm *(divest of arms)*, handcuff, stall
render precise characterize, define
render putrid decay
render safe assure *(insure)*, hedge, police
render sanitary decontaminate
render service pander
render sightless blind *(deprive of sight)*
render smaller diminish
render solid consolidate *(strengthen)*, fix *(make firm)*
render spurious adulterate, fake
render sterile decontaminate
render strong nurture
render suspect impugn
render threadlike attenuate
render uncertain blind *(obscure)*, confuse *(bewilder)*, disorganize, disorient, perplex
render unclean infect, smear
render unfit disable, disqualify
render up abandon *(relinquish)*, restore *(return)*, surrender *(give back)*
render useful capitalize *(seize the chance)*, inure *(benefit)*
render useless cancel, eliminate *(eradicate)*
render vain foil
render visionless blind *(deprive of sight)*
render void adeem, annul, cancel, discharge *(release from obligation)*
render weak debilitate, dilute, disarm *(divest of arms)*
render worse aggravate *(exacerbate)*, exacerbate
renderable accountable *(explainable)*
rendered stable fixed *(securely placed)*
rendering delivery, design *(construction plan)*, explanation, paraphrase, rendition *(explication)*
rendering explicit clarification
rendering incisive clarification
rendering legal advice representation *(acting for others)*
rendering legal assistance representation *(acting for others)*
rendering unequivocal clarification
rendering unmistakable clarification
rendering void avoidance *(cancellation)*
rendezvous appointment *(meeting)*, meeting *(encounter)*, session. SEE MAIN ENTRY
rending separation
rendition delineation, explanation, narration, paraphrase, performance *(execution)*, recital. SEE MAIN ENTRY
renegade fugitive, insurgent, malcontent, pariah, recreant
renege abandon *(withdraw)*, annul, cancel, default, defect, deny *(refuse to grant)*, nullify, refuse, renounce, rescind, revoke, tergiversate, withdraw. SEE MAIN ENTRY
renew amend, continue *(resume)*, cure, fix *(repair)*, meliorate, proceed *(continue)*, recollect, reconstitute, reconstruct, recreate, recur, reform, rehabilitate, relapse, remedy, renovate, reopen, repair, repeat *(do again)*, replenish, reproduce, resume, resurrect. SEE MAIN ENTRY
renew memories remind
renewable corrigible
renewable energy SEE MAIN ENTRY
renewal continuation *(resumption)*, recrudescence, reform, rehabilitation, repair, reparation *(keeping in repair)*, replacement, resurgence, revival. SEE MAIN ENTRY
renewed renascent, repeated
renitant contumacious
renitence reaction *(opposition)*, reluctance, resistance
renitency conflict, reaction *(opposition)*, reluctance
renitent adverse *(hostile)*, disinclined, disobedient, hostile, insusceptible *(uncaring)*, recalcitrant, reluctant, restive, rigid, unbending, unyielding. SEE MAIN ENTRY
renounce abandon *(relinquish)*, abrogate *(annul)*, cede, decline *(reject)*, defect, demit, deny *(refuse to grant)*, disaffirm, disapprove *(reject)*, disavow, disclaim,

discontinue *(abandon)*, disdain, disinherit, disown *(refuse to acknowledge)*, eliminate *(exclude)*, exclude, forbear, forfeit, forgo, forswear, leave *(allow to remain)*, negate, overrule, quit *(discontinue)*, rebel, rebuff, recant, refrain, refuse, reject, relinquish, repel *(drive back)*, repudiate, rescind, resign, revoke, set aside *(annul)*, spurn, surrender *(give back)*, tergiversate, waive, yield *(submit)*. SEE MAIN ENTRY

renounce citizenship expatriate

renounce claim to cede, forgo

renounce rights of citizenship expatriate

renouncement abandonment *(repudiation)*, abjuration, ademption, denial, desertion, disclaimer, rebuff, refusal, renunciation, repudiation, resignation *(relinquishment)*, reversal, revocation

renovare continue *(resume)*, recreate, renew *(refurbish)*

renovate convert *(change use)*, fix *(repair)*, meliorate, reconstitute, reconstruct, recreate, rectify, reform, rehabilitate, renew *(refurbish)*, restore *(renew)*, transform. SEE MAIN ENTRY

renovated renascent

renovatio renewal

renovation correction *(change)*, development *(progression)*, reform, rehabilitation, renewal, repair, reparation *(keeping in repair)*, replacement

renovize renovate

renown character *(reputation)*, distinction *(reputation)*, eminence, notoriety, prestige, reputation

renowned conspicuous, famous, household *(familiar)*, illustrious, influential, notable, noteworthy, notorious, outstanding *(prominent)*, prodigious *(amazing)*, prominent, public *(known)*, reputable. SEE MAIN ENTRY

rent charge *(cost)*, lease, let *(lease)*, rift *(gap)*, schism, split, sublease, sublet. SEE MAIN ENTRY

rent out lease, let *(lease)*, sublease, sublet

rent payer lessee, lodger, tenant

rental rent

rentee lessee

renter lessee, lodger, occupant, tenant

renting tenancy

renueve decline *(reject)*

renumeration proceeds

renunciate disallow

renunciation abandonment *(repudiation)*, abdication, abjuration, ademption, cancellation, confutation, continence, declination, denial, desertion, disclaimer, disdain, expense *(sacrifice)*, rebuff, refusal, rejection, repudiation, rescision, resignation *(relinquishment)*, retraction, reversal, waiver. SEE MAIN ENTRY

renunciatory ambulatory

renuntiare report *(disclose)*, revoke

renuntiatio report *(detailed account)*

reobtain recoup *(regain)*, recover

reoccupation salvage

reoccupy reclaim

reoccur recur

reoccurrence relapse

reopen appeal, continue *(resume)*, renew *(begin again)*. SEE MAIN ENTRY

reopening appeal, continuation *(resumption)*, renewal

reordering reclassification

reorganization development *(progression)*, progress, reclassification, reconversion, rehabilitation, repair, replacement. SEE MAIN ENTRY

reorganize alter, change, convert *(change use)*, emend, meliorate, reconstitute, reconstruct, recreate, reform, reinforce, renew *(begin again)*, renovate, restore *(renew)*, resurrect, transform, vary

repair correction *(change)*, cure, emend, maintenance *(upkeep)*, meliorate, rectify, redress, reform *(noun)*, reform *(verb)*, rehabilitate, rehabilitation, remedy, renew *(refurbish)*, renewal, renovate, reparation *(keeping in repair)*, restore *(renew)*. SEE MAIN ENTRY

repairable corrigible

repaired renascent

repairing correction *(change)*

reparable corrigible

reparare fix *(repair)*, recover, repair

reparation collection *(payment)*, compensation, consideration *(recompense)*, contribution *(indemnification)*, damages, discharge *(payment)*, indemnification, justice, payment *(remittance)*, recompense, recovery *(award)*, redemption, rehabilitation, reimbursement, relief *(legal redress)*, remedy *(legal means of redress)*, remittance, rendition *(restoration)*, repair, replacement, requital, restitution, retribution, satisfaction *(discharge of debt)*, satisfaction *(fulfilment)*, trover. SEE MAIN ENTRY

reparation for loss out of pocket

reparative compensatory, curative, remedial, salubrious, salutary

reparative measure remedy *(legal means of redress)*

reparatory remedial, salutary

repartee answer *(reply)*

repartition dispensation *(act of dispensing)*, distribution *(apportionment)*, reapportion, redistribute

repast treat

repay bear the expense, compensate *(remunerate)*, defray, disburse *(pay out)*, discharge *(pay a debt)*, indemnify, rebate, reciprocate, recoup *(reimburse)*, refund, reimburse, remit *(send payment)*, remunerate, replace, restore *(return)*, retaliate, return *(refund)*, satisfy *(discharge)*. SEE MAIN ENTRY

repay for a loss compensate *(remunerate)*

repay in kind retaliate

repaying compensatory

repayment collection *(payment)*, commission *(fee)*, compensation, consideration *(recompense)*, contribution *(indemnification)*, disbursement *(funds paid out)*, discharge *(payment)*, expiation, indemnification, indemnity, out of pocket, pay, rebate, recompense, recovery *(award)*, refund, reimbursement, reparation *(indemnification)*, reprisal, requital, restitution, retribution, revenge, satisfaction *(discharge of debt)*, vengeance

repayment for injury sustained damages

repayment for loss damages

repeal abate *(extinguish)*, abatement *(extinguishment)*, abolish, abolition, abrogate *(rescind)*, adeem, ademption, annul, cancel, cancellation, countermand, defeasance, discharge *(annulment)*, discharge *(release from obligation)*, discharge *(release from obligation)*, discontinue *(abandon)*, dissolution *(termination)*, invalidate, negate, negation, nullify, overrule, quash, renege, repudiate, repudiation, rescind, rescision, retraction, reversal, revocation, revoke, supersede, vacate *(void)*, withdraw. SEE MAIN ENTRY

repealed lifeless *(dead)*, null *(invalid)*, null and void

repeat circulate, copy, insist, mock *(imitate)*, propagate *(spread)*, quote, reaffirm, recapitulate, recite, recount, recur, reflect *(mirror)*, reiterate, relate *(tell)*, renew *(begin again)*, reopen, reproduce, speak. SEE MAIN ENTRY

repeat by rote recite

repeat from memory recite

repeat offender recidivist

repeated consecutive, continuous, frequent, habitual, incessant, insistent, iterative, ordinary, periodic, persistent, repetitious, routine, usual. SEE MAIN ENTRY

repeated relapse into crime recidivism

repeatedly invariably

repeatedly recognized common *(customary)*

repeater gun

repeating chronic, repetitious

repel alienate *(estrange)*, antagonize, arrest *(stop)*, confront *(oppose)*, counter, decline *(reject)*, deter, disapprove *(reject)*, disavow, discourage, disfavor, disoblige, exclude, forswear, hold out *(resist)*, oppose, outlaw, parry, rebuff, refuse, refute, reject, renounce, repulse, resist *(oppose)*, spurn, stave, stem *(check)*, withstand. SEE MAIN ENTRY

repelled averse

repellence repudiation

repellent antipathetic *(distasteful)*, contemptible, contemptuous, insusceptible *(resistant)*, loathsome, obnoxious, odious, offensive *(offending)*, repugnant *(exciting aversion)*, repulsive, sordid, undesirable

repellere parry, rebuff, rebut, repel *(drive back)*, repulse, stave

repelling loathsome, offensive *(offending)*, repugnant *(exciting aversion)*, repulsive, unsavory

repent reform, regret. SEE MAIN ENTRY

repentance remorse

repentant contrite, penitent, remorseful. SEE MAIN ENTRY

repentant person penitent

repenting remorseful. SEE MAIN ENTRY

repercuss repel *(drive back)*, repulse

repercussion conclusion *(outcome)*, effect, outgrowth, reaction *(response)*. SEE MAIN ENTRY

repercussive resounding

reperire detect, invent *(produce for the first time)*

reperta invention

repertory cache *(storage place)*, depository, treasury

repetere renew *(begin again)*, resume

repetition copy, duplicate, frequency, habit, narration, redundancy, relapse, renewal, restatement, tautology. SEE MAIN ENTRY

repetitional insistent, repeated, repetitious

repetitionary insistent, repeated, repetitious

repetitious chronic, incessant, iterative, repeated. SEE MAIN ENTRY

repetitive chronic, consecutive, frequent, iterative, prolix, redundant, repeated, repetitious

repetitiveness cycle, frequency

rephrase construe *(translate),* elucidate, explain, quote, recapitulate, reiterate, repeat *(state again)*
rephrasing restatement
repine complain *(criticize),* deplore, languish, regret
repiner malcontent
repititious redundant
replace accede *(succeed),* change, convert *(change use),* cover *(provide for),* discharge *(dismiss),* disinherit, rebate, reconstitute, recoup *(regain),* recoup *(reimburse),* redistribute, refund, reimburse, reinstate, relocate, remand, remove *(dismiss from office),* renew *(refurbish),* renovate, repay, replenish, represent *(substitute),* restore *(return),* succeed *(follow),* superannuate, supersede, supplant. SEE MAIN ENTRY
replace with displace *(replace)*
replaceable corrigible, expendable
replacement alternative *(substitute),* correction *(change),* cover *(substitute),* defeasance, discharge *(dismissal),* exchange, novation, preemption, refund, reimbursement, reparation *(keeping in repair),* restitution, stopgap, subrogation, substitute, succedaneum, successor. SEE MAIN ENTRY
replacing acting, subrogation
replay restatement
replenish bear *(yield),* bestow, provide *(supply),* recruit, reinforce, renew *(refurbish),* supply. SEE MAIN ENTRY
replenished replete
replenishment reinforcement, renewal
replere replenish
replete copious, detailed, full, intact, profuse, rife. SEE MAIN ENTRY
repleteness plethora
repletion overage, plethora, sufficiency, surfeit
repletus full
replevied attached *(seized)*
replevin reclaim, recoup *(regain),* recovery *(repossession),* redeem *(repurchase),* redemption. SEE MAIN ENTRY
replevy attach *(seize),* distrain, reclaim, recoup *(regain),* recover, recovery *(repossession),* redeem *(repurchase),* repossess, sequester *(seize property)*
replica copy, counterpart *(parallel),* duplicate, facsimile, fake, model, resemblance, semblance
replicate copy, repeat *(do again),* reproduce, retort. SEE MAIN ENTRY
replication acknowledgment *(acceptance),* answer *(judicial response),* answer *(reply),* counterargument, reply, response
replier respondent
reply acknowledge *(respond),* acknowledgment *(acceptance),* answer *(respond legally),* confutation, correspond *(communicate),* counterargument, countercharge, plea, pleading, reaction *(response),* rebut, rejoinder, respond, response, retort, return *(respond).* SEE MAIN ENTRY
reply to a charge answer *(judicial response)*
replying responsive
reponder reconsider
reponere repay, replace, reserve
report annunciate, apprise, betray *(disclose),* bill *(invoice),* book, canvass, comment, communication *(statement),* conclusion *(determination),* convey *(communicate),* delineate, delineation, depict, detail *(particularize),* disabuse, disclose, disclosure *(something disclosed),* dispatch *(message),* disseminate, divulge, document, enlighten, enter *(record),* entry *(record),* file, finding, form *(document),* hearsay, herald, holding *(ruling of a court),* inform *(notify),* intelligence *(news),* issuance, judgment *(formal court decree),* memorandum, mention *(reference),* mention, narration, notice *(announcement),* notification, notify, observation, opinion *(judicial decision),* outline *(synopsis),* portray, post, proclaim, promulgate, pronouncement, propagate *(spread),* publication *(disclosure),* publicity, publish, quote, recital, recite, record, recount, relate *(tell),* rendition *(explication),* repeat *(state again),* repercussion, report *(disclose),* representation *(statement),* reputation, review *(critical evaluation),* scenario, signify *(inform),* speak, statement, story *(narrative),* summary, tip *(clue).* SEE MAIN ENTRY
report against accuse, denounce *(inform against),* inform *(betray)*
report inaccurately misinform
report intended to delude canard
reported alleged, documentary, narrative, public *(known),* putative, stated
reportedly reputedly
reporter bystander, deponent, informant, informer *(a person who provides information),* spy, witness
reporters press
reporting informatory
repose abeyance, composure, desist, leave *(absence),* lull, pause, peace, prostration, recess, remain *(stay),* rest *(cease from action),* stay *(rest).* SEE MAIN ENTRY
reposeful complacent, placid
reposing inactive
reposit deposit *(place),* hoard, repose *(place),* store
reposition relocate
repository arsenal, bank, cache *(storage place),* catchall, depository, hoard, recipient, treasury. SEE MAIN ENTRY
repossess reclaim, recoup *(regain),* recover, redeem *(repurchase).* SEE MAIN ENTRY
repossession redemption, replevin, salvage
reprehend admonish *(warn),* blame, castigate, cavil, censure, charge *(accuse),* complain *(charge),* complain *(criticize),* condemn *(blame),* criticize *(find fault with),* decry, defame, denounce *(condemn),* disapprove *(condemn),* discredit, fault, lash *(attack verbally),* protest, rebuke, remonstrate, reprimand, reproach. SEE MAIN ENTRY
reprehendendus reprehensible
reprehendere blame, censure, criticize *(find fault with),* rebuke, reprehend, reprimand
reprehensibility culpability, guilt
reprehensible bad *(offensive),* blameful, blameworthy, contemptible, delinquent *(guilty of a misdeed),* disreputable, gross *(flagrant),* guilty, heinous, inexcusable, inexpiable, iniquitous, loathsome, nefarious, obnoxious, odious, offensive *(offending),* outrageous, peccable, peccant *(culpable),* scandalous, sinister, unjustifiable, unseemly, vicious. SEE MAIN ENTRY
reprehensio blame *(culpability),* reprimand, stricture
reprehension bad repute, blame *(culpability),* condemnation *(blame),* conviction *(finding of guilt),* criticism, denunciation, diatribe, disapprobation, disapproval, discredit, disparagement, impugnation, objurgation, onus *(blame),* reprimand, reproach, revilement, stricture
reprehensive critical *(faultfinding)*
represent advise, bare, bear *(adduce),* characterize, comport *(behave),* connote, construe *(comprehend),* convey *(communicate),* copy, delineate, denote, depict, draw *(depict),* exemplify, illustrate, impersonate, lobby, manifest, portray, purport, render *(depict),* replace, signify *(denote),* simulate, specify. SEE MAIN ENTRY
represent as assume *(simulate)*
represent as resembling compare
represent by diagram delineate
represent by outlines delineate
represent by words describe
represent falsely cheat, falsify, lie *(falsify),* misrepresent, palter
represent fictitiously feign, profess *(pretend)*
represent fraudulently misrepresent
represent in words portray, relate *(tell)*
represent incorrectly mislabel, misrepresent
represent oneself demean *(deport oneself)*
represent oneself to be impersonate
represent pictorially delineate
represent to oneself conjure
representation agency *(legal relationship),* assertion, brief, color *(deceptive appearance),* concept, copy, cross section, definition, delineation, deputation *(delegation),* design *(construction plan),* designation *(symbol),* disclosure *(act of disclosing),* disguise, duplicate, election *(selection by vote),* embodiment, example, illustration, indicant, manifestation, model, narration, paraphrase, part *(role),* performance *(workmanship),* profession *(declaration),* proxy, recital, rendition *(explication),* resemblance, role, sample, semblance, substitute, suggestion, symbol. SEE MAIN ENTRY
representation by words delineation
representation in language expression *(comment)*
representational descriptive, detailed, realistic, representative, vicarious *(substitutional)*
representative acting, advocate *(counselor),* agent, broad, broker, case *(example),* conduit *(intermediary),* congruous, demonstrative *(illustrative),* deputy, descriptive, employee, epitome, example, exemplary, factor *(commission merchant),* functionary, general, indicant, instance, intermediary, lawmaker, legislator, liaison, nominee *(delegate),* normal *(regular),* ordinary, plenipotentiary, politician, proctor, procurator, proxy, realistic, replacement, sample, several *(separate),* specimen, spokesman, substitute, surrogate, typical, usual. SEE MAIN ENTRY
representative in Congress lawmaker
representative of the decedent executor
representative sampling cross section
representative section cross section
representative selection case *(example),* cross section, example, excerpt, instance, sample, specimen
representatives chamber *(body),* commission *(agency),* committee, delegation *(envoy),* deputation *(delegation),* government *(political administration)*
representing acting, congruous, in lieu of
repress allay, ban, bar *(hinder),* bind *(restrain),* capture, clog, condemn *(ban),* confine, constrain *(restrain),* constrict *(inhibit),*

contain *(restrain)*, counteract, curb, deter, disadvantage, dominate, enjoin, extinguish, hamper, hold up *(delay)*, inhibit, interdict, kill *(defeat)*, limit, moderate *(temper)*, overturn, prevent, prohibit, quash, restrain, restrict, stifle, stop, strangle, subdue, subject, suppress, trammel, withhold. SEE MAIN ENTRY
repressed arrested *(checked)*
repressing limiting
repressing emotion stoical
repression censorship, coercion, constraint *(restriction)*, control *(restriction)*, deterrence, deterrent, disadvantage, discipline *(obedience)*, duress, fetter, force *(compulsion)*, oppression, prohibition, restraint
repressive dictatorial, prohibitive *(restrictive)*, restrictive
repressive governor dictator
reprieve abeyance, absolution, absolve, acquit, acquittal, amnesty, clear, clemency, compurgation, condonation, condone, discharge *(liberation)*, discharge *(release from obligation)*, emancipation, excuse, exoneration, forgive, grace, grace period, immunity, impunity, palliate *(excuse)*, pardon *(noun)*, pardon *(verb)*, parole, postpone, release, relief *(release)*, remission, remit *(release from penalty)*, stay, stay *(halt)*, vindicate. SEE MAIN ENTRY
reprieved blameless, clear *(free from criminal charges)*, free *(relieved from a burden)*
reprimand admonish *(warn)*, admonition, bad repute, blame, castigate, censure, complain *(criticize)*, condemn *(punish)*, condemnation *(blame)*, criticism, criticize *(find fault with)*, denounce *(condemn)*, denunciation, diatribe, disapprobation, disapprove *(condemn)*, discipline *(punishment)*, disparagement, fault, impeach, impeachment, lash *(attack verbally)*, objurgation, outcry, penalize, punish, punishment, rebuff, rebuke, remonstrance, reprehend, reproach *(noun)*, reproach *(verb)*. SEE MAIN ENTRY
reprimanded blameful, blameworthy
reprimanding remonstrative
reprimere restrain, stifle, suppress
reprint copy *(noun)*, copy *(verb)*, transcript
reprisal conviction *(finding of guilt)*, counterattack, exchange, penalty, reaction *(opposition)*, requital, retribution, revenge, vengeance. SEE MAIN ENTRY
reproach admonition, aspersion, attaint, bad repute, blame *(culpability)*, blame, castigate, censure, charge *(accusation)*, complain *(charge)*, complain *(criticize)*, condemn *(blame)*, condemnation *(blame)*, contemn, contempt *(disdain)*, contempt *(disobedience to the court)*, contumely, criticism, criticize *(find fault with)*, denigrate, denounce *(condemn)*, denunciation, diatribe, disapprobation, disapproval, disapprove *(condemn)*, discredit, disgrace, dishonor *(shame)*, dishonor *(deprive of honor)*, disparagement, guilt, ignominy, impeach, impeachment, incrimination, indictment, infamy, lash *(attack verbally)*, notoriety, objurgation, obloquy, odium, onus *(stigma)*, opprobrium, outcry, rebuff, rebuke, remonstrance, remonstrate, reprehend, reprimand *(noun)*, reprimand *(verb)*, revilement, scandal, shame, slander, stigma, stricture. SEE MAIN ENTRY
reproach oneself regret
reproachability bad character
reproachable blameful, blameworthy, delinquent *(guilty of a misdeed)*, guilty, reprehensible
reproachableness culpability
reproached accused *(attacked)*, disreputable
reproachful blameful, contemptible, contemptuous, critical *(faultfinding)*, ignoble, remonstrative
reproachful accusation incrimination
reproaching contemptuous
reprobacy bad faith, delinquency *(misconduct)*
reprobate bad *(offensive)*, blame, blameful, blameworthy, censure, complain *(charge)*, condemn *(ban)*, convict, criminal, criticize *(find fault with)*, delinquent *(guilty of a misdeed)*, delinquent, denounce *(condemn)*, disapprove *(condemn)*, disgraceful, dissolute, felon, immoral, incorrigible, inexcusable, iniquitous, judge, lecherous, lewd, malefactor, nefarious, peccable, peccant *(culpable)*, perverse, rebuff, recidivist, recreant, reject, reprehend, reprehensible, reprimand, reproach, sentence, spurn, tainted *(corrupted)*, vandal, vicious, wrongdoer. SEE MAIN ENTRY
reprobation abandonment *(repudiation)*, admonition, bad repute, blame *(culpability)*, condemnation *(blame)*, contempt *(disdain)*, conviction *(finding of guilt)*, correction *(punishment)*, denunciation, discredit, disdain, disparagement, impugnation, ostracism, outcry, phillipic, rejection, remonstrance, renunciation, reprimand, reproach, revilement, stricture
reprobative blameful, blameworthy, contemptible, critical *(faultfinding)*, remonstrative
reprobatory remonstrative
reprobe reexamine
reproduce bear *(yield)*, copy, mock *(imitate)*, portray, proliferate, propagate *(increase)*, pullulate, quote, recreate, reflect *(mirror)*, rehabilitate, reiterate, render *(depict)*, renew *(refurbish)*, repeat *(do again)*, trace *(delineate)*. SEE MAIN ENTRY
reproduce fraudulently forge *(counterfeit)*
reproduce in kind proliferate
reproduce rapidly proliferate
reproduced renascent, repeated
reproducing plagiarism
reproduction boom *(increase)*, copy, counterpart *(parallel)*, duplicate, facsimile, fake, maternity, plagiarism, renewal, replacement, resemblance, revival, sham, transcript
reproof admonition, aspersion, bad repute, blame *(culpability)*, charge *(accusation)*, condemnation *(blame)*, contempt *(disdain)*, conviction *(finding of guilt)*, criticism, denunciation, diatribe, disapprobation, discipline *(punishment)*, disparagement, impeachment, objurgation, ostracism, rebuff, remonstrance, reprimand, reproach, revilement, stricture. SEE MAIN ENTRY
reprovable blameful, blameworthy, guilty, reprehensible
reproval contempt *(disdain)*, correction *(punishment)*, disapprobation, objurgation, remonstrance, reprimand
reprove admonish *(warn)*, advise, blame, browbeat, castigate, censure, comment, complain *(criticize)*, condemn *(blame)*, condemn *(punish)*, criticize *(find fault with)*, denigrate, deter, disapprove *(condemn)*, discipline *(punish)*, discourage, fault, impeach, lash *(attack verbally)*, penalize, rebuff, rebuke, remonstrate, reprehend, reprimand, reproach
reproved accused *(attacked)*
reproving critical *(faultfinding)*, remonstrative
reptilian heinous
republic polity
republish copy
repudiare disclaim, disown *(deny the validity)*, disown *(refuse to acknowledge)*, reject, repudiate
repudiate abandon *(relinquish)*, abolish, abrogate *(annul)*, abrogate *(rescind)*, adeem, annul, answer *(reply)*, cancel, challenge, condemn *(blame)*, contemn, contradict, controvert, cross *(disagree with)*, decline *(reject)*, default, defect, demur, deny *(contradict)*, deprecate, differ *(disagree)*, disaccord, disaffirm, disagree, disallow, disapprove *(condemn)*, disapprove *(reject)*, disavow, disclaim, disdain, dishonor *(refuse to pay)*, disinherit, disobey, disoblige, disown *(deny the validity)*, disown *(refuse to acknowledge)*, dissent *(withhold assent)*, except *(object)*, exclude, forfeit, forswear, gainsay, ignore, invalidate, leave *(allow to remain)*, negate, nullify, oust, overrule, picket, prohibit, proscribe *(prohibit)*, protest, rebuff, rebut, recall *(call back)*, recant, refuse, refute, reject, renounce, repel *(drive back)*, repulse, rescind, resign, revoke, secede, set aside *(annul)*, spurn, waive. SEE MAIN ENTRY
repudiated broken *(unfulfilled)*, derelict *(abandoned)*
repudiating dissenting, negative
repudiatio denial, rejection, renunciation, repudiation
repudiation abandonment *(desertion)*, abjuration, abolition, ademption, breach, cancellation, condemnation *(blame)*, confutation, contempt *(disobedience to the court)*, countermand, declination, default, denial, desertion, disapprobation, disapproval, discharge *(annulment)*, disclaimer, discredit, disdain, disqualification *(rejection)*, dissent *(nonconcurrence)*, exclusion, impugnation, infringement, negation, nonpayment, ouster, prohibition, protest, rebuff, refusal, rejection, renunciation, rescision, retraction, reversal, revocation. SEE MAIN ENTRY
repudiation of a marriage divorce
repudiation of employment lockout
repudiation of one's duty delinquency *(failure of duty)*
repudiation of payment dishonor *(nonpayment)*
repudiation of the allegations demurrer
repudiative ambulatory
repudiatory ambulatory
repudium divorce
repugn disaccord, disagree, expostulate, oppose
repugnance antipode, contempt *(disdain)*, disapprobation, incompatibility *(difference)*, malice, odium, phobia, reluctance, resistance. SEE MAIN ENTRY
repugnancy disapprobation
repugnans contradictory, repugnant *(exciting aversion)*
repugnant adverse *(hostile)*, antipathetic *(distasteful)*, averse, bad *(offensive)*, contemptible, contemptuous, contradictory, heinous, inimical, loathsome, malevolent, negative, objectionable, obnoxious, odious,

offensive *(offending)*, repulsive, unacceptable, unfavorable, unsavory. SEE MAIN ENTRY
repugnantia contradiction, incongruity
repugnare conflict, object
repugning dissenting
repulsa defeat, rebuff
repulse beat *(defeat)*, block, contemn, disallow, disavow, disdain *(noun)*, disdain *(verb)*, disfavor, disown *(refuse to acknowledge)*, dissent *(withhold assent)*, eliminate *(exclude)*, exclude, fight *(counteract)*, kill *(defeat)*, oppose, parry, rebuff *(noun)*, rebuff *(verb)*, refusal, reject, rejection, renounce, repel *(disgust)*, repel *(drive back)*, resist *(oppose)*, spurn, stem *(check)*, withstand. SEE MAIN ENTRY
repulsion contempt *(disobedience to the court)*, disdain, malice, renunciation, resistance
repulsive antipathetic *(distasteful)*, bad *(offensive)*, contemptible, contemptuous, contumacious, loathsome, lurid, objectionable, obnoxious, odious, offensive *(offending)*, repugnant *(exciting aversion)*, undesirable. SEE MAIN ENTRY
repulsiveness odium
repurchase redemption
reputability distinction *(reputation)*, honesty, honor *(good reputation)*, integrity, probity, rectitude, regard *(esteem)*
reputable conscientious, credible, dependable, high-minded, honest, incorruptible, influential, law-abiding, meritorious, moral, outstanding *(prominent)*, reliable, renowned, scrupulous, unimpeachable. SEE MAIN ENTRY
reputableness character *(reputation)*, credit *(recognition)*
reputare reconsider, weigh
reputation credit *(recognition)*, notoriety, prestige, regard *(esteem)*. SEE MAIN ENTRY
repute character *(reputation)*, credit *(recognition)*, distinction *(reputation)*, eminence, honesty, honor *(good reputation)*, importance, notoriety, prestige, regard *(esteem)*, reputation, respect
reputed putative SEE MAIN ENTRY
reputedly SEE MAIN ENTRY
request application, call *(appeal)*, call *(appeal to)*, canvass, charge *(command)*, claim *(demand)*, demand, desire, dun *(noun)*, dun *(verb)*, entreaty, importune, invitation, lobby, mandate, market *(demand)*, motion, move *(judicially request)*, petition *(noun)*, petition *(verb)*, plead *(implore)*, prayer, press *(beseech)*, pressure, require *(need)*, requirement, requisition, solicit, subpoena, urge. SEE MAIN ENTRY
request another decision appeal
request for another decision appeal
request for payment bill *(invoice)*
request for relief petition, prayer
request for retrial appeal
request for review appeal
request for the aid of the court prayer
request reexamination appeal
request reopening of a case appeal
request the presence of call *(summon)*
request to appear summons
request to perform demand
requested important *(urgent)*, popular
requesting insistent
requestion reexamine
require appoint, bind *(obligate)*, call *(demand)*, claim *(demand)*, coerce, command, compel, constrain *(compel)*, decree, demand, dictate, dun, enforce, enjoin, entail, exact, force *(coerce)*, impose *(enforce)*, impose *(subject)*, insist, instruct *(direct)*, lack, levy, necessitate, need, order, prescribe, press *(constrain)*, request, tax *(levy)*, tax *(overwork)*. SEE MAIN ENTRY
require a tax excise *(levy a tax)*
require authoritatively dictate, exact
require compliance impose *(enforce)*, subpoena, summon
require of others call *(demand)*
require to attend subpoena, summon
required binding, bound, compulsory, exigent, forcible, fundamental, imperative, important *(urgent)*, indispensable, integral, mandatory, obligatory, positive *(prescribed)*, requisite, urgent, vital
required assumption presumption
required by custom prescriptive
required by law legal
required item necessity, need *(requirement)*
required legal assumption presumption
required manner practice *(procedure)*
required to attend venire
requirement appointment *(act of designating)*, article *(precept)*, burden, call *(appeal)*, call *(option)*, canon, charge *(command)*, claim *(legal demand)*, compulsion *(coercion)*, condition *(contingent provision)*, demand, desideratum, dictate, directive, duress, enforcement, exigency, instruction *(direction)*, mandate, market *(demand)*, necessary, necessity, ordinance, precept, prerequisite, provision *(clause)*, qualification *(condition)*, request, requisition, sine qua non, ultimatum, writ. SEE MAIN ENTRY
requirement of polite society decorum
requirement to appear process *(summons)*
requirement to attend subpoena
requirere require *(need)*
requiring perfunctory
requiring immediate attention exigent, imperative
requiring immediate care exigent
requiring no effort convenient
requiring prompt action exigent
requisite attornment, binding, burden, central *(essential)*, compulsory, condition *(contingent provision)*, demand, desideratum, essential *(required)*, fundamental, imperative, important *(urgent)*, indispensable, integral, mandatory, necessary *(required)*, necessary, necessity, need *(requirement)*, obligatory, positive *(prescribed)*, prerequisite, primary, qualification *(condition)*, requirement, requisition, reservation *(condition)*, substantive, ultimatum, vital. SEE MAIN ENTRY
requisiteness need *(requirement)*, priority
requisition application, arrogation, call *(appeal)*, call *(option)*, call *(demand)*, canon, charge *(command)*, claim *(demand)*, desideratum, dun, exact, excise *(levy a tax)*, importune, mandate, market *(demand)*, monition *(legal summons)*, move *(judicially request)*, petition *(noun)*, petition *(verb)*, pray, prayer, request *(noun)*, request *(verb)*, require *(compel)*, requirement. SEE MAIN ENTRY
requisition to the court application
requisitioned necessary *(required)*
requisitory confiscatory, requisite
requital collection *(payment)*, compensation, consideration *(recompense)*, contribution *(indemnification)*, exchange, expiation, honorarium, indemnification, interchange, recompense, remuneration, reprisal, restitution, retribution, revenge, reward, satisfaction *(discharge of debt)*, trover. SEE MAIN ENTRY
requite defray, disburse *(pay out)*, indemnify, reciprocate, recoup *(reimburse)*, recriminate, refund, reimburse, remit *(send payment)*, remunerate, repay, retaliate, retort, satisfy *(discharge)*
requited reciprocal
requitement contribution *(indemnification)*, indemnification, indemnity, recompense, requital, restitution, retribution, reward, satisfaction *(discharge of debt)*, trover. SEE MAIN ENTRY
rerank reassess
res article *(commodity)*, article *(distinct section of a writing)*, commodities
res corpus
res effects, fact, issue *(matter in dispute)*, item, matter *(subject)*, occurrence, point *(item)*, possession *(property)*, possessions, substance *(essential nature)*
res adversae adversity
res arcana secret
res atrox atrocity
res commodata loan
res cuius actio est actionable
res ficta fiction
res ipsa loquitor SEE MAIN ENTRY
res judicata adjudication. SEE MAIN ENTRY
res mira phenomenon *(unusual occurrence)*
res occulta mystery, secret
res repetundae extortion
res secundae prosperity
res simillima counterpart *(parallel)*
res summa main point
res venales merchandise
resanction reconfirm
rescind abate *(extinguish)*, abolish, adeem, annul, cancel, disavow, discharge *(release from obligation)*, disclaim, disinherit, disown *(deny the validity)*, invalidate, negate, nullify, overrule, quash, recall *(call back)*, recant, renege, repeal, revoke, vacate *(void)*, vitiate, withdraw. SEE MAIN ENTRY
rescind an attorney's license to practice disbar
rescinded null *(invalid)*, null and void
rescindere abrogate *(rescind)*, invalidate, quash, repeal, rescind, revoke
rescinding cancellation
rescindment abatement *(extinguishment)*, abolition, ademption, annulment, cancellation, countermand, defeasance, rescision, retraction, revocation
rescission abandonment *(repudiation)*, abolition, ademption, avoidance *(cancellation)*, cancellation, countermand, defeasance, discharge *(annulment)*, discharge *(release from obligation)*, dissolution *(termination)*, negation, repudiation, reversal. SEE MAIN ENTRY
rescribere answer *(reply)*
rescript canon, citation *(charge)*, correction *(change)*, dictate, direction *(order)*, directive, fiat, issuance, law, monition *(legal summons)*, order *(judicial directive)*, proclamation, requirement, revision *(corrected version)*, transcript
rescrutinize reexamine
rescuable corrigible

rescue aid *(help)*, aid, clear, disencumber, disenthrall, extricate, free, help, liberate, liberation, palliate *(excuse)*, preserve, quit *(free of)*, ransom, recovery *(repossession)*, redeem *(repurchase)*, redemption, relief *(aid)*, salvage. SEE MAIN ENTRY
rescue from imprisonment disenthrall
rescue from oppression disenthrall
rescue from slavery disenthrall
rescued free *(relieved from a burden)*
rescuer benefactor, good samaritan
research analysis, analyze, audit, canvass, delve, examination *(study)*, examine *(study)*, experiment, indagation, inquire, inquiry *(systematic investigation)*, investigation, peruse, probe, quest, scrutinize, scrutiny, study, test. SEE MAIN ENTRY
reseat reinstate
resell recover
resemblance analogy, comparison, correspondence *(similarity)*, identity *(similarity)*, parity, propinquity *(similarity)*, relation *(connection)*, same, semblance. SEE MAIN ENTRY
resemble appear *(seem to be)*, approximate, correspond *(be equivalent)*, demean *(deport oneself)*. SEE MAIN ENTRY
resembling akin *(germane)*, analogous, comparable *(capable of comparison)*, congruous, correlative, identical, similar
resembling truth specious. SEE MAIN ENTRY
resent contemn
resentful bitter *(reproachful)*, malevolent, malicious, malignant, restive, spiteful, vindictive. SEE MAIN ENTRY
resentfulness resentment
resentive resentful
resentment dissension, ground, ill will, malice, odium, rancor, spite, umbrage. SEE MAIN ENTRY
reservation adjournment, condition *(contingent provision)*, doubt *(indecision)*, limitation, misgiving, modification, objection, provision *(clause)*, qualification *(condition)*, registration, restriction, retention, salvo, selection *(choice)*. SEE MAIN ENTRY
reservations reluctance
reservatory repository, treasury
reserve adjourn, bank, cash, composure, cumulation, doubt *(indecision)*, engage *(hire)*, fund *(noun)*, fund *(verb)*, garner, hoard, hold up *(delay)*, keep *(shelter)*, margin *(spare amount)*, misgiving, predetermine, provision *(something provided)*, register, resource, restraint, retain *(employ)*, retain *(keep in possession)*, save *(hold back)*, stock *(store)*, stopgap, store *(depository)*, store, strangle, treasury, withhold. SEE MAIN ENTRY
reserve fund resource, treasury
reserved diffident, discreet, formal, guarded, inarticulate, laconic, mute, noncommittal, private *(not public)*, privy, taciturn, unapproachable, unobtrusive, unresponsive
reserved amount margin *(spare amount)*
reserves assets, capital, hoard. SEE MAIN ENTRY
reservoir arsenal, cache *(storage place)*, depository, fund, repository, stock *(store)*, store *(depository)*, sufficiency. SEE MAIN ENTRY
reset adjust *(regulate)*
resettle relocate
reshape camouflage, convert *(change use)*, distort, modify *(alter)*, reform, repair
reshaped tempered
reship redirect
reside dwell *(reside)*, lodge *(reside)*, remain *(occupy)*. SEE MAIN ENTRY
reside in inhabit, occupy *(take possession)*
reside together cohabit
residence abode, address, apartment, building *(structure)*, domicile, dwelling, habitation *(act of inhabiting)*, habitation *(dwelling place)*, headquarters, home *(domicile)*, homestead, house, household, inhabitation *(place of dwelling)*, lodging, occupancy, occupation *(possession)*, seat. SEE MAIN ENTRY
residencer citizen
residences premises *(buildings)*
residency abode, domicile, inhabitation *(place of dwelling)*, residence, tenancy
resident citizen, constituent *(member)*, denizen, domiciliary, habitant, inhabitant, inmate, lessee, lodger, occupant, tenant. SEE MAIN ENTRY
residential habitable, household *(domestic)*. SEE MAIN ENTRY
residential building development *(building)*
residentiary denizen, habitant, household *(domestic)*, inhabitant, lodger, occupant, resident
residents populace, population
resider citizen, habitant, lodger, occupant, resident
residere subside
residing habitation *(act of inhabiting)*
residing together cohabitation *(living together)*
residual balance *(amount in excess)*, net, residuary, superfluous. SEE MAIN ENTRY
residual estate remainder *(estate in property)*
residual portion balance *(amount in excess)*
residual time unexpired term
residuals remainder *(remaining part)*
residuary alluvion, net, residual, superfluous. SEE MAIN ENTRY
residue balance *(amount in excess)*, overage, remainder *(remaining part)*, residual, reversion *(remainder of an estate)*, surplus
residuum balance *(amount in excess)*
residuum remainder *(remaining part)*
residuum residual
residuum surplus
resign abandon *(relinquish)*, cede, defect, demit, depart, discontinue *(abandon)*, forgo, leave *(depart)*, quit *(discontinue)*, reconcile, relent, relinquish, remise, renounce, retire *(conclude a career)*, secede, submit *(yield)*, succumb, surrender *(give back)*, withdraw, yield *(submit)*. SEE MAIN ENTRY
resign oneself bear *(tolerate)*
resign oneself to comply, endure *(suffer)*
resignation abdication, acceptance, capitulation, cession, desertion, longanimity, renunciation, sufferance, tolerance. SEE MAIN ENTRY
resigned complacent, passive, patient, stoical. SEE MAIN ENTRY
resignedness acquiescence, capitulation
resilient corrigible. SEE MAIN ENTRY
resist challenge, collide *(clash)*, conflict, confront *(oppose)*, contest, counter, counteract, countervail, cross *(disagree with)*, decline *(reject)*, defy, demonstrate *(protest)*, disaccord, disaffirm, disallow, disapprove *(reject)*, disobey, dissent *(withhold assent)*, fight *(battle)*, fight *(counteract)*, hamper, hold up *(delay)*, object, oppose, oppugn, parry, rebel, rebuff, refuse, repel *(drive back)*, repulse, stem *(check)*, withstand. SEE MAIN ENTRY
resist change persevere
resist lawful authority rebel
resist openly defy
resistance conflict, contempt *(disobedience to the court)*, contention *(opposition)*, contest *(dispute)*, contravention, defiance, deterrence, disadvantage, disapproval, fight *(battle)*, impediment, impugnation, mutiny, negation, opposition, protest, reaction *(opposition)*, rebellion, rebuff, refusal, reluctance, revolt, struggle. SEE MAIN ENTRY
resistance against attack defense
resistance movement rebellion
resistance to authority contempt *(disobedience to the court)*, sedition
resistance to change inertia
resistance to government insurrection, revolution
resistant antipathetic *(oppositional)*, contumacious, disobedient, dissident, durable, inexorable, infrangible, nonconsenting, recalcitrant, recusant, renitent, rigid, unbending
resistence collision *(dispute)*
resister adversary, disputant, malcontent
resistere counteract, hold out *(resist)*, withstand
resisting chronic, cohesive *(sticking)*, disorderly, dissenting, indomitable, opposite, renitent, spartan, unyielding
resisting authority contumacious
resisting control contumacious, restive
resistive adverse *(hostile)*, disobedient, insubordinate, intractable, negative, opposite, perverse, preventive, recalcitrant, unruly
resistless forcible, indomitable, inexpugnable, invincible, irresistible, passive, resigned, susceptible *(unresistent)*, unavoidable *(inevitable)*
resite relocate
resolute decisive, definite, diligent, earnest, faithful *(loyal)*, fanatical, heroic, indomitable, inexorable, inflexible, loyal, obdurate, patient, peremptory *(absolute)*, persistent, pertinacious, purposeful, relentless, sedulous, serious *(devoted)*, spartan, staunch, steadfast, strong, true *(loyal)*, unalterable, unbending, uncompromising, undaunted, unyielding. SEE MAIN ENTRY
resolutely faithfully
resoluteness prowess *(bravery)*, resolution *(decision)*, spirit, tenacity, will *(desire)*
resolution act *(enactment)*, adhesion *(loyalty)*, adjudication, animus, answer *(solution)*, arbitration, award, bill *(proposed act)*, choice *(decision)*, conclusion *(determination)*, consequence *(conclusion)*, decision *(judgment)*, declaration, decree, denouement, determination, diligence *(perseverance)*, disposition *(determination)*, finding, forethought, goal, holding *(ruling of a court)*, intent, intention, judgment *(formal court decree)*, key *(solution)*, opinion *(judicial decision)*, outcome, project, proposition, purpose, result, ruling, solution *(answer)*, spirit, suggestion, tenacity, volition, will *(desire)*. SEE MAIN ENTRY
resolution by a jury verdict
resolution of the court finding
resolvable determinable *(ascertainable)*, solvable

resolve animus, arbitrate *(adjudge)*, arrange *(methodize)*, ascertain, choice *(decision)*, choose, conclude *(decide)*, conclusion *(determination)*, contemplation, decide, design *(intent)*, determination, determine, discharge *(perform)*, endeavor, find *(determine)*, fix *(settle)*, forethought, goal, hold *(decide)*, intend, intent, intention, judge, plan *(noun)*, plan *(verb)*, predetermination, purpose, reason *(conclude)*, resolution *(decision)*, rule *(decide)*, settle, solve. SEE MAIN ENTRY
resolve a discord attune
resolve beforehand prearrange, predetermine, prejudge, preordain
resolve into change
resolved decisive, deliberate, indomitable, inexorable, inflexible, intense, intentional, patient, peremptory *(absolute)*, persistent, pertinacious, purposeful, res judicata, resolute, sedulous, serious *(devoted)*, spartan, steadfast, uncompromising, unrelenting, unyielding. SEE MAIN ENTRY
resonance intonation
resonant full, orotund
resort device *(contrivance)*, expedient, refuge, resource, stopgap. SEE MAIN ENTRY
resort to employ *(make use of)*, exploit *(make use of)*
resort to arms belligerency, fight *(battle)*
resort to superior authority appeal
resounding powerful. SEE MAIN ENTRY
resource chattel, expedient, help, holding *(property owned)*, instrumentality, means *(funds)*, possession *(property)*, recourse, reserve, tool. SEE MAIN ENTRY
resourceful artful, competent, deft, original *(creative)*, practiced, productive. SEE MAIN ENTRY
resourcefulness common sense, discretion *(quality of being discreet)*, efficiency
resourceless helpless *(defenseless)*
resources advantage, assets, capital, cash, effects, estate *(property)*, finance, fund, goods, livelihood, means *(funds)*, money, paraphernalia *(personal belongings)*, personalty, possessions, principal *(capital sum)*, property *(possessions)*, provision *(something provided)*, reserve, stock in trade, substance *(material possessions)*. SEE MAIN ENTRY
respect abide, character *(reputation)*, comity, complexion, comply, concede, concern *(care)*, concern *(involve)*, consideration *(sympathetic regard)*, courtesy, credit *(recognition)*, decorum, defer *(yield in judgment)*, deference, estimation *(esteem)*, fealty, heed, homage, honor, keep *(fulfill)*, mention *(tribute)*, obey, observe *(obey)*, particular, perform *(adhere to)*, prestige, regard *(esteem)*, regard *(hold in esteem)*, reputation, worth. SEE MAIN ENTRY
respectability character *(reputation)*, decorum, distinction *(reputation)*, honesty, honor *(good reputation)*, propriety *(correctness)*, reputation
respectable considerable, ethical, fair *(satisfactory)*, high-minded, honest, incorruptible, influential, law-abiding, moral, proper, reliable, reputable, upright
respected influential, outstanding *(prominent)*, popular, prominent, reputable
respectful civil *(polite)*, obedient, obeisant, servile
respectful deportment decorum
respectfulness comity, deference
respectfully SEE MAIN ENTRY
respecting relative *(relevant)*, wherein
respective certain *(specific)*, particular *(individual)*, specific
respectively per capita, pro rata. SEE MAIN ENTRY
respectlessness ingratitude
respectus regard *(esteem)*, retrospect
respicere consider, regard *(hold in esteem)*
respite abeyance, adjournment, cessation *(interlude)*, clemency, continue *(adjourn)*, defer *(put off)*, deferment, extension *(postponement)*, furlough, halt, hiatus, immunity, interruption, interval, leave *(absence)*, lull, moratorium, pause, pendency, recess, relief *(aid)*, relief *(release)*, remission, remit *(release from penalty)*, reprieve, stay, stay *(halt)*. SEE MAIN ENTRY
respite from impending punishment reprieve
resplendent illustrious
respond answer *(reply)*, correspond *(communicate)*, countercharge, obey, rebut, reciprocate, remark, reply, retort. SEE MAIN ENTRY
respond conclusively countercharge
respondeat superior SEE MAIN ENTRY
responded to reciprocal
respondence answer *(reply)*, response
respondent contender, defendant, litigant, open *(persuasible)*, party *(litigant)*, responsive. SEE MAIN ENTRY
responder respondent
respondere answer *(reply)*, reply, retort, return *(respond)*
responsal response
response acknowledgment *(acceptance)*, answer *(reply)*, consequence *(conclusion)*, counterargument, effect, emotion, impression, plea, rejoinder, repercussion, reply, sensibility. SEE MAIN ENTRY
response to an action appearance *(coming into court)*
responsibility agency *(legal relationship)*, allegiance, assignment *(task)*, burden, business *(affair)*, competence *(ability)*, duty *(obligation)*, function, integrity, job, labor *(work)*, liability, obligation *(duty)*, onus *(blame)*, onus *(burden)*, part *(role)*, position *(business status)*, rectitude, requirement, trust *(custody)*, weight *(burden)*. SEE MAIN ENTRY
responsible actionable, amenable, blameful, blameworthy, bound, causative, competent, culpable, dependable, diligent, liable, lucid, moral, normal *(sane)*, reliable, sane, solid *(sound)*, true *(loyal)*
responsible for at fault
responsibleness charge *(responsibility)*
responsibly faithfully
responsio reply
responsive favorable *(expressing approval)*, flexible, open *(persuasible)*, openminded, perceptive, pliable, pliant, receptive, resilient, sensitive *(discerning)*, suasible, willing *(not averse)*. SEE MAIN ENTRY
responsive allegations pleading
responsive offer counteroffer
responsive to change flexible, resilient
responsiveness amenability, sensibility
responsum reply
respublica community, realm
rest abeyance, cessation *(interlude)*, complement, composure, deposit *(place)*, desist, extension *(postponement)*, furlough, halt *(noun)*, halt *(verb)*, hiatus, holiday, inaction, inertia, interval, leave *(absence)*, lodge *(reside)*, lull, moratorium, pause *(noun)*, pause *(verb)*, recess *(noun)*, recess *(verb)*, relief *(release)*, remain *(stay)*, remainder *(remaining part)*, remission, repose *(rest)*, respite *(interval of rest)*, stop. SEE MAIN ENTRY
rest assured opine
rest in peace die
rest period pause
restate construe *(translate)*, copy, elucidate, explain, quote, reaffirm, recapitulate, reiterate, repeat *(state again)*. SEE MAIN ENTRY
restate briefly review
restated repeated
restatement narration, paraphrase, recital, redundancy, summary. SEE MAIN ENTRY
restation relocate
rested on based on
restful placid
restiff restive
resting dormant, inactive, static
resting place destination, haven, home *(domicile)*
restinguere extinguish
restituere fix *(repair)*, reconstruct, redress, rehabilitate, reinstate
restitute bear the expense, recoup *(reimburse)*, replace, restore *(renew)*. SEE MAIN ENTRY
restitution collection *(payment)*, consideration *(recompense)*, contribution *(indemnification)*, damages, disbursement *(funds paid out)*, discharge *(payment)*, expiation, indemnification, indemnity, out of pocket, payment *(act of paying)*, payment *(remittance)*, recompense, recovery *(award)*, refund, rehabilitation, reimbursement, relief *(legal redress)*, remedy *(legal means of redress)*, remuneration, rendition *(restoration)*, reparation *(indemnification)*, replacement, requital, satisfaction *(discharge of debt)*, trover. SEE MAIN ENTRY
restitutive compensatory, medicinal, remedial
restitutory compensatory
restive adverse *(hostile)*, contumacious, disinclined, disobedient, disorderly, fractious, froward, insubordinate, intractable, lawless, recalcitrant, recusant, uncontrollable, unruly, willful. SEE MAIN ENTRY
restiveness contempt *(disobedience to the court)*, disturbance
restless frenetic, moving *(in motion)*, restive, unsettled
restlessness commotion, diligence *(perseverance)*, disturbance, outburst, trepidation
restock replenish
restorable corrigible
restoral reparation *(keeping in repair)*
restoration acquittal, collection *(payment)*, compensation, continuation *(resumption)*, contribution *(indemnification)*, correction *(change)*, damages, indemnification, indemnity, out of pocket, progress, reconversion, recovery *(repossession)*, redemption, rehabilitation, reimbursement, relief *(legal redress)*, renewal, reorganization, repair, reparation *(indemnification)*, reparation *(keeping in repair)*, replacement, restitution, resurgence, revival
restoration of harmony arrangement *(understanding)*, reconciliation
restoration to health cure
restorative curative, cure, medicinal, palliative *(abating)*, panacea, remedial,

remedy *(that which corrects),* salubrious, salutary
restorative agent panacea
restore bear *(yield),* bestow, continue *(resume),* contribute *(indemnify),* cure, emend, fix *(repair),* indemnify, meliorate, quit *(repay),* rebate, reconstitute, reconstruct, recoup *(reimburse),* recreate, rectify, redress, reform, refund, rehabilitate, reimburse, reinstate, remand, remedy, renew *(refurbish),* renovate, repair, repay, resurrect, return *(refund),* surrender *(give back).* SEE MAIN ENTRY
restore courage to reassure
restore equilibrium adjust *(regulate),* regulate *(adjust)*
restore harmony arbitrate *(conciliate),* attune, disarm *(set at ease),* mediate, pacify, placate, reconcile, settle
restore one's faith assure *(give confidence to)*
restore permission authorize
restore to a state of peace pacify
restore to a state of tranquillity pacify
restore to assurance reassure
restore to confidence reassure
restore to equilibrium compensate *(counterbalance)*
restore to friendship reconcile
restore to liberty enfranchise
restore to office reinstate
restore to power reinstate
restored renascent
restrain allay, apprehend *(arrest),* arrest *(apprehend),* arrest *(stop),* balk, ban, bar *(hinder),* block, border *(bound),* cancel, capture, censor, check *(restrain),* clog, commit *(institutionalize),* condemn *(ban),* confine, constrain *(imprison),* constrain *(restrain),* constrict *(inhibit),* continue *(adjourn),* curb, debar, deter, diminish, discipline *(control),* discourage, disqualify, enclose, enjoin, estop, fetter, foil, forbear, forbid, govern, halt, hamper, hinder, hold up *(delay),* immure, impede, imprison, inhibit, interdict, jail, limit, lock, mitigate, moderate *(temper),* mollify, obstruct, occlude, police, preclude, prevent, prohibit, proscribe *(prohibit),* repress, restrict, rule *(govern),* stay *(halt),* stem *(check),* stifle, stop, strangle, subdue, subjugate, suppress, thwart, toll *(stop),* trammel, withhold. SEE MAIN ENTRY
restrain by injunction enjoin
restrain motion fetter
restrain movement fetter
restrained arrested *(apprehended),* arrested *(checked),* bound, controlled *(restrained),* frugal, limited, passive, patient, peaceable, reasonable *(fair),* taciturn, unobtrusive
restraining compulsory, limiting, preventive, prohibitive *(restrictive),* restrictive
restraining device barrier
restraining order injunction
restraint apprehension *(act of arresting),* arrest, bar *(obstruction),* barrier, bondage, captivity, censorship, check *(bar),* cloud *(incumbrance),* coercion, commitment *(confinement),* composure, compulsion *(coercion),* constraint *(restriction),* continence, control *(restriction),* custody *(incarceration),* damper *(stopper),* detention, deterrence, deterrent, disadvantage, discipline *(obedience),* disincentive, durance, embargo, estoppel, fetter, force *(compulsion),* handicap, hindrance, impediment, incarceration, incumbrance *(lien),* injunction, limitation, moderation, obstacle, obstruction, prohibition, propriety *(correctness),* quota, restriction, retention, servitude, stay, temperance, veto. SEE MAIN ENTRY
restraint of movement quarantine
restraints confines
restrengthen compound
restrict abridge *(divest),* bar *(exclude),* block, border *(bound),* capture, censor, check *(restrain),* clog, compel, condemn *(ban),* confine, constrain *(imprison),* constrain *(restrain),* constrict *(inhibit),* contain *(restrain),* control *(restrain),* debar, detain *(restrain),* deter, disadvantage, discipline *(control),* disfranchise, disqualify, enclose, enjoin, estop, exclude, fetter, forbid, halt, hamper, hinder, impede, inhibit, interdict, jail, keep *(restrain),* limit, lock, modify *(moderate),* occlude, preclude, prevent, prohibit, proscribe *(prohibit),* qualify *(condition),* repress, restrain, specialize, toll *(stop),* trammel, withhold. SEE MAIN ENTRY
restrict access condemn *(ban),* confine, constrain *(restrain),* picket, police
restrict in area constrict *(compress)*
restricted arrested *(checked),* certain *(specific),* conditional, confidential, dependent, exclusive *(limited),* limited, local, narrow, partial *(biased),* personal *(private),* private *(not public),* privy, qualified *(conditioned),* regional, specific, without recourse. SEE MAIN ENTRY
restricted goods contraband
restricted to a small area parochial
restricted to a small scope parochial
restricting limiting
restriction abridgment *(disentitlement),* arrest, barrier, blockade *(limitation),* bondage, censorship, check *(bar),* commitment *(confinement),* compulsion *(coercion),* condition *(contingent provision),* constraint *(imprisonment),* custody *(incarceration),* damper *(stopper),* decrease, detention, deterrence, deterrent, disadvantage, duress, economy *(frugality),* embargo, enclosure, encumbrance, estoppel, fetter, force *(compulsion),* guideline, hindrance, impediment, incarceration, injunction, limitation, moderation, modification, obstacle, obstruction, prohibition, provision *(clause),* qualification *(condition),* quota, reservation *(condition),* restraint, salvo, veto. SEE MAIN ENTRY
restriction on movement bondage, detention, durance
restriction on personal liberty incarceration
restrictive arbitrary and capricious, binding, compulsory, exclusive *(limited),* limiting, preventive, proprietary. SEE MAIN ENTRY
restrictive practice constraint *(restriction),* control *(restriction)*
restrictus parsimonious
restringe restrict
restructuring reorganization
restudy reexamine
restyle change, convert *(change use),* transform
restyling revision *(process of correcting)*
resubstantiate reconfirm
result adjudication, answer *(solution),* award, conclusion *(determination),* conclusion *(outcome),* consequence *(conclusion),* denouement, destination, determination, development *(outgrowth),* effect, emanate, end *(termination),* ensue, evolve, finding, follow-up, holding *(ruling of a court),* issuance, judgment *(formal court decree),* occur *(happen),* outcome, outgrowth, output, proceeds, product, redound, stem *(originate),* supervene, toll *(effect).* SEE MAIN ENTRY
result ascertained conclusion *(determination),* determination
result from accrue *(arise)*
result in produce *(manufacture)*
result of judicial inquest conclusion *(determination)*
resultance conclusion *(outcome),* outgrowth
resultant amount *(result),* ancillary *(subsidiary),* consequential *(deducible),* constructive *(creative),* deductive, derivative, development *(outgrowth),* effect, end *(termination),* ensuing, outcome, outgrowth, residuary, result
resultant action conclusion *(outcome),* consequence *(conclusion),* effect
resulting ancillary *(subsidiary),* derivative, ensuing
resulting from contingent, dependent
resultless futile, otiose
resume brief. SEE MAIN ENTRY
resumé capsule, dossier
resume proceed *(continue),* recur, renew *(begin again),* reopen, repeat *(do again),* return *(go back)*
resumption recrudescence, renewal, resurgence, revival. SEE MAIN ENTRY
resupply replenish
resurge renew *(refurbish)*
resurgence recrudescence, resurgence, revival. SEE MAIN ENTRY
resurgent corrigible, renascent
resurrect disinter, renew *(refurbish),* renovate, repair. SEE MAIN ENTRY
resurrected renascent
resurrection rehabilitation, renewal, repair, resurgence, revival
resuscitate cure, recall *(call back),* remedy, renew *(refurbish),* restore *(renew),* resurrect. SEE MAIN ENTRY
resuscitated renascent
resuscitation rehabilitation, renewal, resurgence, revival
retabulating reclassification
retail recount, vend. SEE MAIN ENTRY
retail store market *(business)*
retailer dealer, merchant, vendor
retain continue *(prolong),* detain *(hold in custody),* employ *(engage services),* enclose, engage *(hire),* fund, hire, hoard, hold *(possess),* keep *(shelter),* occupy *(take possession),* own, perpetuate, possess, prolong, recall *(remember),* remain *(occupy),* remember, reserve, save *(hold back),* store, understand. SEE MAIN ENTRY
retain exclusive control monopolize
retain exclusive possession monopolize
retain in custody impound
retain the impression of recognize *(perceive)*
retain the services of employ *(engage services)*
retainer compensation, consociate, deposit, downpayment, honorarium. SEE MAIN ENTRY
retainer of counsel client
retaining reservation *(engagement)*
retaining fee compensation, retainer
retainment employment, reservation *(engagement),* retention
retake attach *(seize),* reclaim, recoup *(regain),* recover, rescue

retaking replevin
retaliate answer *(reply)*, penalize, punish, rebut, reciprocate, recriminate, repay, resist *(oppose)*, return *(respond)*. SEE MAIN ENTRY
retaliation counterattack, exchange, interchange, reaction *(opposition)*, reprisal, requital, retribution, revenge, vengeance. SEE MAIN ENTRY
retaliative malevolent, reciprocal, ruthless, vindictive
retaliatory disciplinary *(punitory)*, malevolent, penal, punitive, reciprocal, vindictive
retaliatory punishment revenge
retard bar *(hinder)*, block, check *(restrain)*, clog, condemn *(ban)*, constrict *(inhibit)*, control *(restrain)*, curb, debar, defer *(put off)*, delay, diminish, disadvantage, discontinue *(break continuity)*, encumber *(hinder)*, enjoin, foil, hamper, hinder, hold up *(delay)*, impede, inhibit, interfere, interrupt, keep *(restrain)*, obstruct, occlude, preclude, prevent, procrastinate, protract *(prolong)*, stall, stem *(check)*, thwart, trammel, withstand. SEE MAIN ENTRY
retard decay keep *(shelter)*
retard flow shut
retardant preventive
retardare hinder, impede
retardation check *(bar)*, damper *(stopper)*, delay, deterrent, disadvantage, encumbrance, filibuster, hindrance, impediment, restraint
retarded arrested *(checked)*, disadvantaged, late *(tardy)*
retardment check *(bar)*, disadvantage, filibuster, hindrance, impediment
retax reassess
retell copy, quote, reaffirm, recapitulate, recite, recount, reiterate, relate *(tell)*, repeat *(state again)*, review
retelling narration, recital, redundancy, restatement
retentio detention, retention
retention apprehension *(act of arresting)*, arrest, enjoyment *(use)*, occupancy, occupation *(possession)*, remembrance *(recollection)*, reservation *(engagement)*. SEE MAIN ENTRY
retentive memory retrospect
rethink reconsider
reticent discreet, guarded, inarticulate, laconic, mute, noncommittal, taciturn, unobtrusive, unresponsive
reticular sinuous
reticulate intertwine
retinere detain *(restrain)*, hold up *(delay)*, keep *(fulfill)*, keep *(restrain)*, restrain, withhold
retire abandon *(withdraw)*, demit, depart, discharge *(dismiss)*, discontinue *(abandon)*, dislodge, ebb, flee, leave *(depart)*, part *(leave)*, quit *(discontinue)*, quit *(evacuate)*, recess, rest *(cease from action)*, retreat, secede, seclude, sequester *(seclude)*, superannuate, supplant, withdraw. SEE MAIN ENTRY
retire from office demit
retire from sight seclude
retired former, obsolete, outmoded
retirement abandonment *(desertion)*, cessation *(termination)*, end *(termination)*, expiration, layoff, leave *(absence)*, obscuration, privacy, removal, resignation *(relinquishment)*
retirement benefits pension
retirement income annuity, pension
retirement of a debt discharge *(payment)*
retiring diffident, inconspicuous, unobtrusive, unpretentious
retold repeated
retort answer *(reply)*, answer *(reply)*, confutation, counterargument, counterattack, countercharge, plea, rebut, recriminate, refute, rejoinder, reply *(noun)*, reply *(verb)*, respond, response, return *(respond)*. SEE MAIN ENTRY
retort a charge recriminate
retortion counterattack
retouch emend, enhance, fix *(repair)*, renew *(refurbish)*, repair, restore *(renew)*
retouching repair
retrace copy, recall *(remember)*, reexamine, repeat *(do again)*, review. SEE MAIN ENTRY
retrace one's steps return *(go back)*
retract abandon *(withdraw)*, abolish, abrogate *(annul)*, abrogate *(rescind)*, adeem, annul, cancel, disaffirm, disavow, discharge *(release from obligation)*, disclaim, disinherit, disown *(deny the validity)*, invalidate, negate, nullify, overrule, recant, renege, repeal, repudiate, rescind, revoke, secede, vacate *(void)*, withdraw. SEE MAIN ENTRY
retractare recant, revise
retractation defeasance, discharge *(annulment)*, negation, repudiation, retraction, revocation. SEE MAIN ENTRY
retracting cancellation
retraction abjuration, abolition, ademption, annulment, breach, cancellation, correction *(change)*, countermand, defeasance, denial, negation, renunciation, repudiation, rescision, reversal, revocation. SEE MAIN ENTRY
retractory willful
retranslate construe *(translate)*
retransmit recover
retread repair
retreat abandon *(physically leave)*, abandon *(withdraw)*, asylum *(hiding place)*, avoid *(evade)*, avoidance *(evasion)*, chamber *(compartment)*, decline, disappear, ebb, evacuate, flee, flight, give *(yield)*, haven, leave *(absence)*, leave *(depart)*, part *(leave)*, privacy, quit *(evacuate)*, refuge, removal, renege, resign, return *(go back)*, revert, seclude, shelter *(protection)*, vacate *(leave)*, withdraw. SEE MAIN ENTRY
retrench curtail, decrease, diminish. SEE MAIN ENTRY
retrenchment curtailment, decrease
retrial appeal, rehearing
retribution condemnation *(punishment)*, conviction *(finding of guilt)*, correction *(punishment)*, discipline *(punishment)*, justice, punishment, relief *(legal redress)*, reprisal, revenge, vengeance. SEE MAIN ENTRY
retributive compensatory, disciplinary *(punitory)*, penal, punitive, reciprocal, vindictive
retributive action sanction *(punishment)*
retributive justice condemnation *(punishment)*, conviction *(finding of guilt)*, correction *(punishment)*, discipline *(punishment)*, penalty, punishment, reprisal, retribution
retributive punishment revenge, vengeance
retrievable corrigible
retrieval compensation, out of pocket, recovery *(repossession)*, redemption, replevin, restitution, salvage, trover
retrieve collect *(recover money)*, reap, reclaim, recoup *(regain)*, recover, redeem *(repurchase)*, remedy, repossess, rescue. SEE MAIN ENTRY
retrievement trover
retroaction decline, reaction *(opposition)*, repercussion, reversion *(act of returning)*
retroactive ex post facto. SEE MAIN ENTRY
retroactive application SEE MAIN ENTRY
retroactive effect nunc pro tunc
retrocede escheat, regress, relapse, retire *(retreat)*, retreat. SEE MAIN ENTRY
retrocedent regressive
retrocession decline, relapse, reversion *(act of returning)*
retrogradation decline, degradation, deterioration, lapse *(expiration)*, recidivism, relapse, reversion *(act of returning)*
retrograde decadent, decay, depreciate, deteriorate, recidivate, regress, regressive, relapse, return *(go back)*, revert
retrogress decay, degenerate, deteriorate, regress, relapse, revert
retrogression decline, degradation, deterioration, lapse *(expiration)*, recidivism, reconversion, relapse, reversion *(act of returning)*
retrogressive back *(in reverse)*, bad *(offensive)*, decadent, regressive
retrospect hindsight, recall *(remember)*, recapitulate, recollect, remembrance *(recollection)*. SEE MAIN ENTRY
retrospection hindsight, recollection, remembrance *(recollection)*
retrospective back *(in reverse)*
retrospective effect nunc pro tunc
retrospectively heretofore
retroversion reconversion, relapse, reversion *(act of returning)*
retrovert escheat, relapse, revert
retrude repel *(drive back)*, repulse
retry appeal, reconsider. SEE MAIN ENTRY
return annuity, answer *(reply)*, answer *(reply)*, bear *(yield)*, benefit *(betterment)*, commission *(fee)*, compensate *(remunerate)*, compensation, consideration *(recompense)*, continuation *(resumption)*, contribute *(indemnify)*, contribution *(indemnification)*, discharge *(payment)*, dividend, escheat, indemnification, indemnity, output, pay, payment *(act of paying)*, perquisite, poll *(canvass)*, proceed *(continue)*, profit, quit *(repay)*, reaction *(response)*, rebate, reciprocate, reciprocity, recommit, recompense, reconversion, recoup *(reimburse)*, recovery *(repossession)*, recrudescence, recur, redemption, refund *(noun)*, refund *(verb)*, regress, rehabilitation, reinstate, relapse *(noun)*, relapse *(verb)*, remand, remuneration, rendition *(restoration)*, renewal, rent, reparation *(indemnification)*, repay, repeat *(do again)*, reply *(noun)*, reply *(verb)*, reprisal, requital, response, restitution, retaliate, retort, retribution, revenue, reversion *(act of returning)*, revert, revival, reward, salvage, satisfaction *(discharge of debt)*, surrender *(give back)*, trover, yield *(produce a return)*. SEE MAIN ENTRY
return an accusation recriminate
return an answer respond
return in money income
return money paid out indemnify
return on capital income
return the charge recriminate
return to continue *(resume)*, renew *(begin again)*, reopen, resume

return to prison remand
return to the original state fix *(repair)*
returned reciprocal
returned check bad check
returning chronic, incessant, periodic
returning at intervals chronic, periodic
returns earnings, proceeds
retusus obtuse
réunion assemblage
reunion collection *(assembly)*, conciliation, congregation, meeting *(conference)*, rapprochement, reconciliation
reunite call *(summon)*, collect *(gather)*, conjoin, convene, meet, pacify, reconcile
reus criminal
reutter recapitulate, reiterate
reuttered repeated
revalidate reconfirm
revalidated nunc pro tunc
revalue reassess
revamp amend, convert *(change use)*, edit, emend, fix *(repair)*, modify *(alter)*, reconstruct, recreate, redact, rehabilitate, renew *(refurbish)*, renovate, repair, revise, transform. SEE MAIN ENTRY
revamping renewal, reparation *(keeping in repair)*
revampment amendment *(correction)*, correction *(change)*
reveal adduce, admit *(concede)*, apprise, bare, betray *(disclose)*, circulate, communicate, confess, construe *(translate)*, convey *(communicate)*, declare, denude, depict, detect, disabuse, disclose, disinter, display, divulge, enlighten, evidence, exhibit, explain, explicate, expose, expound, find *(discover)*, impart, inform *(betray)*, inform *(notify)*, interpret, issue *(publish)*, locate, manifest, mention, notice *(give formal warning)*, notify, produce *(offer to view)*, profess *(avow)*, promulgate, publish, relate *(tell)*, report *(disclose)*, resolve *(solve)*, signify *(denote)*, signify *(inform)*, speak, unveil, utter. SEE MAIN ENTRY
reveal itself arise *(appear)*, occur *(come to mind)*
reveal oneself report *(present oneself)*
reveal something private confide *(divulge)*
reveal the answer resolve *(solve)*
reveal to public notice exhibit
revealed comprehensible, evident, manifest, naked *(perceptible)*, obvious, open *(in sight)*, overt, palpable, patent, pellucid, perceivable, perceptible, public *(known)*
revealing demonstrative *(illustrative)*, descriptive, disclosure *(act of disclosing)*, informative, informatory
revealment admission *(disclosure)*, confession, disclosure *(act of disclosing)*, disclosure *(something disclosed)*, discovery, expression *(manifestation)*, publication *(disclosure)*, publicity
revel carouse
revel in relish
revelation admission *(disclosure)*, answer *(solution)*, communication *(statement)*, declaration, disclosure *(something disclosed)*, discovery, exhibit, expression *(manifestation)*, information *(knowledge)*, manifestation, notice *(announcement)*, notification, publication *(disclosure)*, publicity, report *(detailed account)*, testimony, vision *(dream)*
revelatory informatory
revelry treat
revenant phantom, specter
revenge counterattack, penalize, rancor, repay, reprisal, retaliate, retribution, vengeance. SEE MAIN ENTRY
revengeful malevolent, malignant, resentful, ruthless, spiteful, vindictive
revengefulness belligerency, rancor, reprisal, revenge, spite, vengeance
revenue boom *(prosperity)*, capital, duty *(tax)*, earnings, finance, income, money, pay, perquisite, proceeds, profit, rent, resource, substance *(material possessions)*, wage. SEE MAIN ENTRY
reverberant resounding
reverberating resounding
reverberation reaction *(response)*, repercussion
reverberatory resounding
revere honor, regard *(hold in esteem)*. SEE MAIN ENTRY
revered outstanding *(prominent)*, reputable, sacrosanct
reverence courtesy, estimation *(esteem)*, fealty, homage, honor *(outward respect)*, honor, interest *(concern)*, regard *(esteem)*, regard *(hold in esteem)*, respect
reverenced reputable
reverend sacrosanct
reverent obeisant
reverenter respectfully
reverential obedient, obeisant, sequacious, solemn
reverently respectfully
reverie contemplation, figment, introspection, preoccupation, reflection *(thought)*
reversal annulment, cancellation, countermand, defeasance, discharge *(annulment)*, negation, nollo prosequi, reconversion, recrudescence, relapse, repudiation, rescision, retraction, reversion *(act of returning)*, revocation. SEE MAIN ENTRY
reverse abrogate *(annul)*, abrogate *(rescind)*, adverse *(opposite)*, annul, antipathetic *(oppositional)*, antipode, antithesis, cancel, contra, contradict, contradictory, contraposition, contrary, counteract, counterpart *(complement)*, debacle, disaffirm, discharge *(release from obligation)*, disown *(deny the validity)*, escheat, hostile, invalidate, inverse, misfortune, negate, negative, nullify, opposite, override, overrule, overthrow, overturn, plight, quash, recant, recrudescence, regress, regressive, relapse *(noun)*, relapse *(verb)*, renege, repeal, repudiate, rescind, retreat, reversion *(act of returning)*, revert, revoke, tragedy, trouble, upset, vacate *(void)*, vitiate, withdraw. SEE MAIN ENTRY
reverse direction return *(go back)*
reversed back *(in reverse)*, inverse, null *(invalid)*, null and void, opposite, regressive
reverseless indefeasible, indelible, irreversible, irrevocable, permanent
reversible ambulatory, capricious, convertible
reversing cancellation
reversion continuation *(resumption)*, decline, defeasance, devolution, heritage, lapse *(expiration)*, nollo prosequi, recidivism, reconversion, recovery *(repossession)*, recrudescence, relapse, remainder *(remaining part)*, restitution, resurgence, reversal. SEE MAIN ENTRY
reversion rights SEE MAIN ENTRY
reversion to the government escheatment
reversion to the state escheatment
reversional ambulatory, regressive
reversionary regressive
reversionary estate remainder *(estate in property)*
revert disorganize, escheat, recur, regress, relapse, repeat *(do again)*, return *(go back)*, revoke. SEE MAIN ENTRY
revert to the state escheat
reverti lapse *(cease)*, return *(go back)*
reverting reversion *(act of returning)*
revest reinstate, restore *(return)*
review account *(report)*, analysis, analyze, appeal *(noun)*, appeal *(verb)*, audit, canvass, capsule, censor, check *(inspect)*, comment, compendium, consideration *(contemplation)*, contemplation, criticism, criticize *(evaluate)*, cross-questioning, deliberate, digest, diligence *(care)*, discretion *(power of choice)*, discuss, evaluate, examination *(study)*, examine *(study)*, frisk, habeas corpus, hindsight, hornbook, indagation, inquest, inspection, investigate, judge, judgment *(discernment)*, monitor, muse, narration, notice *(observe)*, observe *(watch)*, overlook *(superintend)*, peruse, ponder, probe *(noun)*, probe *(verb)*, recall *(remember)*, recapitulate, recital, recollect, reconsider, reexamine, reiterate, remember, repeat *(state again)*, report *(detailed account)*, restatement, retrospect, revise, revision *(process of correcting)*, scenario, scrutinize, scrutiny, study, summary, survey *(examine)*, survey *(poll)*, synopsis, test, trial *(experiment)*. SEE MAIN ENTRY
review of things past hindsight
reviewer juror
reviewers of fact jury
revile attack, blame, condemn *(blame)*, contemn, decry, defame, denigrate, denounce *(condemn)*, derogate, disapprove *(condemn)*, discommend, flout, inveigh, lash *(attack verbally)*, libel, malign, rebuke, reprimand, reproach. SEE MAIN ENTRY
revilement bad repute, contempt *(disdain)*, contumely, criticism, denunciation, diatribe, disapprobation, discredit, disdain, disparagement, libel, malediction, obloquy, outcry, phillipic, rejection, reprimand, reproach, slander, vilification. SEE MAIN ENTRY
revilement of religion blasphemy
reviling abusive, aspersion, contemptuous, diatribe
revindication recovery *(repossession)*
revisable corrigible
revisal amendment *(correction)*, correction *(change)*, revision *(process of correcting)*
revise adapt, amend, change, convert *(change use)*, edit, emend, modify *(alter)*, qualify *(condition)*, rectify, reform, remedy, renew *(refurbish)*, review, transform, treat *(process)*. SEE MAIN ENTRY
revise one's thoughts reconsider
revised current, tempered
revised edition correction *(change)*, revision *(corrected version)*
revising reorganization
revision amendment *(correction)*, correction *(change)*, development *(progression)*, innovation, reform, renewal, reorganization. SEE MAIN ENTRY
revisional ambulatory, corrigible
revisionist malcontent
revisit return *(go back)*
revisory ambulatory
revitalize renew *(refurbish)*, resurrect. SEE MAIN ENTRY

revival recrudescence, rehabilitation, renewal, repair, resurgence. SEE MAIN ENTRY
revival in the mind remembrance *(recollection)*
revive change, copy, cure, develop, fix *(repair)*, meliorate, recall *(call back)*, recall *(remember)*, recollect, recreate, rehabilitate, reinstate, remedy, renew *(begin again)*, renew *(refurbish)*, renovate, reopen, repair, restore *(renew)*, resurrect. SEE MAIN ENTRY
revived de novo, renascent
revivement rehabilitation
revivification recrudescence, rehabilitation, renewal, resurgence, revival
revivified renascent
revivify cure, fix *(repair)*, recall *(call back)*, rehabilitate, remedy, renovate, restore *(renew)*, resurrect
revivifying remedial
reviviscence recrudescence, revival
reviviscency recrudescence
reviviscent salubrious
revocable ambulatory, defeasible, voidable. SEE MAIN ENTRY
revocare recall *(call back)*
revocatio revocation
revocation abatement *(extinguishment)*, abjuration, abolition, ademption, annulment, cancellation, countermand, defeasance, denial, discharge *(annulment)*, discharge *(release from obligation)*, disclaimer, dissolution *(termination)*, mistrial, negation, repudiation, rescision, retraction, reversal. SEE MAIN ENTRY
revocation of orders countermand
revocatory ambulatory
revoke abate *(extinguish)*, abolish, abrogate *(rescind)*, adeem, annul, bear false witness, cancel, debar, disavow, discharge *(release from obligation)*, discontinue *(abandon)*, disinherit, disown *(deny the validity)*, dissolve *(terminate)*, invalidate, kill *(defeat)*, negate, nullify, override, overrule, prohibit, proscribe *(prohibit)*, recall *(call back)*, recant, refuse, renege, repeal, repudiate, rescind, vacate *(void)*, withdraw. SEE MAIN ENTRY
revoke one's license to practice law disbar
revoked null *(invalid)*, null and void
revokement abjuration, abolition, ademption, annulment, cancellation, countermand, defeasance, dissolution *(termination)*, negation, rescision, reversal, revocation
revoking cancellation, revocation
revolt conflict, contest *(dispute)*, defect, defiance, disagree, disloyalty, disobey, disturbance, fight *(battle)*, infidelity, insurrection, mutiny, outbreak, outburst, overthrow, protest, rebel, rebellion, reject, rejection, repel *(disgust)*, resistance, revolution, riot, secede, sedition, strike *(refuse to work)*, subversion, treason. SEE MAIN ENTRY
revolted averse
revolter insurgent, malcontent
revolting bad *(offensive)*, heinous, loathsome, lurid, objectionable, obnoxious, odious, offensive *(offending)*, repugnant *(exciting aversion)*, repulsive, unsavory
revolution anarchy, cycle, defiance, disturbance, innovation, insurrection, mutiny, outbreak, outburst, rebellion, resistance, revolt, sedition, subversion, treason. SEE MAIN ENTRY
revolutionary demagogue, disorderly, incendiary, insubordinate, insurgent, lawless, malcontent, radical *(favoring drastic change)*, restive
revolutionist insurgent, malcontent
revolutionize change, disobey, overthrow, rebel, reform, transform
revolve muse
revolve in the mind ponder, reflect *(ponder)*, study
revolver gun
revulsion contempt *(disdain)*, disapprobation, hatred, odium. SEE MAIN ENTRY
reward benefit *(conferment)*, bonus, bounty, commission *(fee)*, compensate *(remunerate)*, compensation, consideration *(recompense)*, disburse *(pay out)*, earnings, fee *(charge)*, grant, gratuity *(present)*, pay *(noun)*, pay *(verb)*, perquisite, prize, profit, recognition, recompense, remunerate, remuneration, repay, requital, retribution, revenue, tip *(gratuity)*. SEE MAIN ENTRY
reward for a loss compensate *(remunerate)*
reward for an injury compensate *(remunerate)*
reward for injury compensation
reward for loss compensation
reward for service bounty, compensation, honorarium, perquisite, wage
reward of labor earnings
reward of office earnings
rewarder donor, grantor
rewardful compensatory, lucrative
rewarding compensatory, gainful, lucrative, profitable, valuable
reweigh reconsider
reword construe *(translate)*, quote, recapitulate, recount, reiterate, repeat *(state again)*, review
reworded repeated
rewording paraphrase, rendition *(explication)*, restatement
rework amend, edit, emend, modify *(alter)*, reconsider, reconstruct, redact, reform, renew *(refurbish)*, revise
rewrite amend, copy, correction *(change)*, edit, emend, modify *(alter)*, redact, revise, revision *(corrected version)*. SEE MAIN ENTRY
rewriting revision *(process of correcting)*
rezone reapportion, reassign
rhapsodical ecstatic
rhetoric bombast, declamation, fustian, language, parlance, phraseology, speech. SEE MAIN ENTRY
rhetorica rhetoric *(skilled speech)*
rhetorical flatulent, inflated *(bombastic)*, orotund, turgid, voluble
rhetorical discourse peroration
rhetorical phrase expletive
rhetorical presentation discourse
rhetorical word expletive
rhetoricalness bombast
rhetorize declaim
rhythm regularity
rhythmic intermittent, periodic, regular *(orderly)*
rhythmical periodic
rialto market *(business)*
ribald blameworthy, blatant *(obtrusive)*, disreputable, inelegant, lascivious, lewd, obscene, offensive *(offending)*, prurient, salacious, scurrilous, suggestive *(risqué)*
ribaldry obscenity
rich copious, elaborate, eloquent, fertile, full, nectarious, opulent, productive, profuse, prolific, prosperous, resounding, savory, strong, successful. SEE MAIN ENTRY
riches assets, cash, hoard, money, prosperity, substance *(material possessions)*
richly endowed opulent
richness boom *(prosperity)*, plethora, prosperity
rickety imperfect
ricochet repercussion
rid dislodge, eject *(evict)*, extirpate, free *(relieved from a burden)*, relieve *(free from burden)*, relinquish. SEE MAIN ENTRY
rid of deception disabuse
rid of defects emend
rid oneself of forgo, jettison, renounce
riddance catharsis, deportation, estrangement, exclusion, layoff, privation, rejection, removal
riddle enigma, mystery, penetrate, problem
riddled penetrable
rider addendum, allonge, amendment *(legislation)*, appendix *(supplement)*. SEE MAIN ENTRY
ridicile discommend
ridicula imitatio parody
ridicule contemn, contempt *(disdain)*, decry, derogate, disdain, disgrace, dishonor *(shame)*, disparage, disparagement, disrespect, flout, humiliate, illude, impeach, jape, jeer, libel, malign, minimize, misprize, mock *(deride)*, offend *(insult)*, parody, pillory, smear, travesty. SEE MAIN ENTRY
ridicule irresponsibly cavil
ridiculing cynical, disdainful
ridiculous fatuous, incredible, inept *(inappropriate)*, irrational, ludicrous, unreasonable, untenable
ridiculousness incongruity
ridiculum ridicule
ridiculus jocular
rife general, ordinary, populous, predominant, prevailing *(current)*, prevalent, profuse, rampant, replete, usual. SEE MAIN ENTRY
rifle despoil, gun, loot, pirate *(take by violence)*, plunder, poach, steal
rifler burglar
rift alienation *(estrangement)*, disaccord, disassociation, dissension, estrangement, flaw, hiatus, schism, split, strife. SEE MAIN ENTRY
rig furnish, manipulate *(control unfairly)*
right accurate, actual, allowable, applicable, appropriate, birthright, capacity *(authority)*, cause of action, certain *(positive)*, condign, cure, dominion *(absolute ownership)*, droit, due, eligible, emend, equitable, equity *(share of ownership)*, ethical, exact, factual, fairness, fit, fix *(repair)*, franchise *(license)*, honest, intangible, interest *(ownership)*, juridical, just, justice, liberty, license, licit, option *(contractual provision)*, patent, possession *(ownership)*, prerogative, prescription *(claim of title)*, privilege, proper, propriety *(appropriateness)*, qualification *(fitness)*, real, reasonable *(rational)*, rectify, rectitude, redress, remedy, repair, rightful, share *(interest)*, sound, stake *(interest)*, suitable, title *(right)*, true *(authentic)*, truth, undistorted. SEE MAIN ENTRY
right answer solution *(answer)*
right arm mainstay
right away instantly
right dealing equity *(justice)*
right hand mainstay
right note decorum
right now instantly
right of action cause of action

right of choice discretion *(power of choice)*, franchise *(right to vote)*, latitude, liberty, option *(choice)*, patronage *(power to appoint jobs)*
right of entry access *(right of way)*, ingress
right of future enjoyment reversion *(remainder of an estate)*
right of future possession reversion *(remainder of an estate)*
right of literary property copyright
right of ownership interest *(ownership)*
right of passage easement
right of possession dominion *(absolute ownership)*, fee *(estate)*, ownership
right of put and call call *(option)*
right of recovery cause of action. SEE MAIN ENTRY
right of representation franchise *(right to vote)*
right of retention possession *(ownership)*
right of succession reversion *(remainder of an estate)*
right of use easement
right of way easement
right thing to do decorum
right time opportunity
right to adjudicate authority *(right)*
right to buy or sell option *(contractual provision)*
right to command authority *(right)*
right to control SEE MAIN ENTRY
right to counsel SEE MAIN ENTRY
right to decide freedom
right to determine authority *(right)*
right to die SEE MAIN ENTRY
right to dispose of property charge *(lien)*
right to enforce charge on property mechanics lien
right to enforce charge upon property lien
right to enter ingress
right to life SEE MAIN ENTRY
right to personal things intangible
right to precedence priority
right to preference priority
right to privacy SEE MAIN ENTRY
right to profits accruing patent
right to property dominion *(absolute ownership)*
right to recovery intangible
right to relief cause of action
right to remain silent SEE MAIN ENTRY
right to retain occupation *(possession)*
right to settle issues authority *(right)*
right to vote suffrage
right, title and interest in land estate *(property)*
right-hand man assistant
right-minded clean, high-minded, law-abiding, meritorious, moral. SEE MAIN ENTRY
right-of-way priority
righteous clean, conscientious, equitable, ethical, high-minded, just, law-abiding, meritorious, moral, proper, pure, reputable, right *(correct)*, upright. SEE MAIN ENTRY
righteously fairly *(impartially)*
righteousness equity *(justice)*, ethics, honor *(good reputation)*, integrity, justice, merit, principle *(virtue)*, probity, rectitude
rightful actual, allowed, appropriate, blameless, bona fide, due *(regular)*, felicitous, genuine, juridical, just, legal, legitimate *(rightful)*, licit, right *(correct)*, sound, suitable, true *(authentic)*, unalienable. SEE MAIN ENTRY
rightful possession dominion *(absolute ownership)*, interest *(ownership)*
rightful power authority *(right)*, prerogative
rightful strength force *(legal efficacy)*
rightfully as a matter of right, duly, fairly *(impartially)*
rightfulness equity *(justice)*, fairness, justice, legality, legitimacy, principle *(virtue)*
righting correction *(change)*
rightly fairly *(impartially)*
rightness expedience, fairness, honesty, propriety *(appropriateness)*, qualification *(fitness)*
rights and privileges birthright
rigid close *(rigorous)*, draconian, exact, factual, firm, fixed *(securely placed)*, formal, inflexible, ironclad, irreconcilable, literal, meticulous, narrow, orthodox, particular *(exacting)*, pertinacious, precise, provincial, punctilious, relentless, renitent, severe, solid *(compact)*, static, strict, stringent, unalterable, unbending, uncompromising, unmitigated, unrelenting, unyielding. SEE MAIN ENTRY
rigid control censorship
rigid routine bureaucracy
rigidity formality, rigor
rigidly faithfully, invariably
rigidness formality, particularity, rigor
rigidus inflexible, rigid, stark, strict, unbending
rigor severity. SEE MAIN ENTRY
rigorist bigot
rigorous accurate, callous, draconian, harsh, inflexible, intense, ironclad, meticulous, onerous, oppressive, particular *(exacting)*, precise, punctilious, rigid, severe, strict, stringent, unrelenting. SEE MAIN ENTRY
rigorous proof certification *(certainness)*
rigorous search indagation, probe
rigorousness rigor, severity
rile badger, bait *(harass)*, disaffect, discompose, harry *(harass)*, incense, irritate, offend *(insult)*, pique
rim border, boundary, edge *(border)*, frontier, limit, margin *(outside limit)*, mete, outline *(boundary)*, periphery
rima rift *(gap)*, split
rimari ferret, probe *(noun)*, probe *(verb)*
ring cabal, enclose, encompass *(surround)*, hedge, league, syndicate
ringing resounding
ringleader demagogue, pioneer
riot anarchy, belligerency, bluster *(commotion)*, brawl *(noun)*, brawl *(verb)*, disorder *(lack of order)*, embroilment, fracas, imbroglio, insurrection, outbreak, pandemonium, rebel, rebellion, sedition. SEE MAIN ENTRY
rioter insurgent, malcontent
riotous disobedient, disorderly, drunk, lawless, licentious, uncontrollable, unruly
rip lancinate, rend, split *(noun)*, split *(verb)*
rip out eviscerate
riparian fluvial, littoral
riparian right SEE MAIN ENTRY
ripe ready *(prepared)*. SEE MAIN ENTRY
ripe to submit for judicial review justiciable
ripen develop, mature, progress
ripeness opportunity
ripening growth *(evolution)*
riposte answer *(reply)* counterattack, countercharge, reply, response, retort, return *(respond)*. SEE MAIN ENTRY
ripping out avulsion, evulsion
rise advancement *(improvement)*, appearance *(emergence)*, appreciate *(increase)*, appreciation *(increased value)*, augmentation, boom *(increase)*, build *(augment)*, commence, disobey, elevation, emerge, genesis, growth *(increase)*, inception, increase, increment, inflate, inflation *(increase)*, nascency, onset *(commencement)*, origination, outset, progress *(noun)*, progress *(verb)*, promotion *(advancement)*, pullulate, rebel, result, start, stem *(originate)*. SEE MAIN ENTRY
rise above outbalance, outweigh, overcome *(surmount)*, predominate *(outnumber)*, surmount, surpass, transcend
rise against confront *(oppose)*
rise and fall fluctuate
rise from accrue *(arise)*
rise in arms rebel
rise in hostility before accost
rise in value appreciate *(increase)*, appreciation *(increased value)*
risible ludicrous
rising insurrection, outbreak, outburst, progressive *(going forward)*, prominent, prosperous, rebellion, revolt, sedition
rising generation children
rising insubordination commotion
rising prices boom *(prosperity)*
risk bet, compromise *(endanger)*, danger, endanger, endeavor, expose, gamble, hazard, invest *(fund)*, jeopardize, jeopardy, parlay *(bet)*, pawn, peril, pitfall, speculate *(chance)*, threat, venture. SEE MAIN ENTRY
risk exposure to harm endanger
risk one's money invest *(fund)*
risk/reward analysis SEE MAIN ENTRY
risk taker speculator
risk-taker bettor
risk-taking hot-blooded, impulsive *(rash)*
riskful aleatory *(perilous)*, precarious
risks pitfall
risky aleatory *(perilous)*, dangerous, impulsive *(rash)*, insalubrious, insecure, noxious, precarious, speculative, toxic, vulnerable
risky undertaking venture
risqué brazen
risque improper, lewd, lurid, obscene, salacious, scurrilous
rite ceremony, custom, form *(arrangement)*, formality
ritual behavior, ceremony, custom, form *(arrangement)*, formal, formality, process *(course)*, propriety *(correctness)*, remembrance *(commemoration)*, routine, solemn, way *(manner)*
ritual behavior SEE MAIN ENTRY
ritualism behavior
ritualistic formal
ritualistically pro forma
ritualize formalize
ritually pro forma
ritus ceremony, formality
rival adversary, antagonize, compete, competitive *(antagonistic)*, conflict, confront *(oppose)*, contend *(dispute)*, contender, contestant, counteract, disputant, foe, jealous, outbalance, peer, resist *(oppose)*, surpass, transcend. SEE MAIN ENTRY
rivaling comparative, competitive *(antagonistic)*
rivalry belligerency, competition, conflict, contention *(opposition)*, contest *(competition)*, impugnation, strife. SEE MAIN ENTRY

rivalship contest *(competition)*
rive break *(separate)*, dichotomize, disjoint, disperse *(scatter)*, force *(break)*, lancinate, luxate, rend, separate, sever, split
riven broken *(fractured)*
riverine fluvial
rivery fluvial
rivet the attention occupy *(engage)*
rivet the mind occupy *(engage)*
rivet the thoughts occupy *(engage)*
riveted immutable, stable, steadfast
rixa affray, altercation, brawl
rixari brawl, dispute *(contest)*
road access *(right of way)*, admission *(entry)*, admittance *(means of approach)*, avenue *(route)*, causeway, course, way *(channel)*. SEE MAIN ENTRY
roadway admission *(entry)*, avenue *(route)*, causeway, way *(channel)*
roam perambulate, prowl
roamer itinerant, pedestrian
roaming discursive *(digressive)*, moving *(in motion)*, shifting, transient, vagrancy
roar barrage, pandemonium
rob defalcate, deprive, despoil, harry *(plunder)*, hold up *(rob)*, impropriate, loot, peculate, pilfer, pillage, pirate *(take by violence)*, plunder, prey, purloin, spoil *(pillage)*, steal. SEE MAIN ENTRY
rob of freedom subjugate
robber burglar, criminal, outlaw, thief, vandal
robbery burglary, housebreaking, plunder, spoliation, theft. SEE MAIN ENTRY
robbing burglary
robe clothe
roborant medicinal, remedial, salubrious, salutary
robur strength
robust durable, strong
robustness health, puissance, sinew, strength
robustus strong
rock lull, oscillate, vacillate
rocklike durable
rodomontade bombast, exaggeration, fustian, jactation. SEE MAIN ENTRY
rogare petition, pray, request, sue
rogatio bill *(proposed act)*, motion, proposition, question *(inquiry)*, request
rogue convict, delinquent, hoodlum, malefactor
roguery deception, improbity, knavery, mischief, misdoing
roguish false *(disloyal)*, immoral, jocular, machiavellian, reprobate, unscrupulous
roguishness knavery, mischief
roil agitate *(activate)*, annoy, badger, discompose, disturb, hector, pique, plague, provoke
roisterer hoodlum
role agency *(legal relationship)*, assignment *(task)*, capacity *(job)*, conduct, duty *(obligation)*, function, job, office, position *(business status)*, profession *(vocation)*. SEE MAIN ENTRY
roll docket, file, record, register, schedule. SEE MAIN ENTRY
roll back decrease, diminish
roll into one collect *(gather)*, consolidate *(unite)*
roll on proceed *(go forward)*
roll out spread
roll-over clause SEE MAIN ENTRY
rollicking jocular
rolling fluvial
rolling in riches opulent
romance figment
romantic quixotic
rompish jocular
roof ceiling, shelter *(protection)*
rookie novice
room capacity *(maximum)*, chamber *(compartment)*, coverage *(scope)*, dwell *(reside)*, freedom, inhabit, latitude, margin *(spare amount)*, part *(place)*, scope, space. SEE MAIN ENTRY
room for improvement foible
room in which a court of law is held courtroom
room in which a lawcourt is held courtroom
room to spare margin *(spare amount)*
room together cohabit
room used for the application of the laws courtroom
room used for the public administration of justice courtroom
room where justice is administered courtroom
roomer inmate, lessee, lodger, occupant
rooming together cohabitation *(living together)*
rooms lodging
roomy capacious
roorback canard
root basis, bloodline, cause *(reason)*, derivation, determinant, embed, establish *(entrench)*, fix *(make firm)*, foundation *(basis)*, genesis, gist *(substance)*, gravamen, ground, hunt, origin *(source)*, origination, plant *(place firmly)*, reason *(basis)*, source. SEE MAIN ENTRY
root of dissension contention *(argument)*
root out destroy *(efface)*, disinter, extirpate, ferret, solve
root up disinter
rooted firm, fixed *(settled)*, habitual, immutable, indelible, ingrained, inveterate, organic, permanent, prescriptive, situated, stable, steadfast, traditional
rooted belief conviction *(persuasion)*
rootless baseless, solitary
rope handcuff
rope off demarcate, isolate, seclude
roseate auspicious, propitious
roster record, register, roll
rot decay, degenerate, spoil *(impair)*, spoilage, taint *(contaminate)*
rotate oscillate, vary
rotation cycle, order *(arrangement)*, sequence
rotten heinous, marred, odious, profligate *(corrupt)*, repulsive, stale, tainted *(contaminated)*, tainted *(corrupted)*
rotting decadent, dissolution *(disintegration)*
rough astringent, blatant *(obtrusive)*, brutal, disorderly, harsh, hoodlum, imperfect, impertinent *(insolent)*, inelegant, inexact, mishandle *(maltreat)*, mordacious, provincial, severe, stringent, uncouth. SEE MAIN ENTRY
rough calculation estimate *(approximate cost)*, estimation *(calculation)*
rough cast design *(construction plan)*
rough copy design *(construction plan)*
rough draft delineation
rough guess estimate *(approximate cost)*, estimation *(calculation)*
rough outline configuration *(form)*
rough representation design *(construction plan)*
rough sketch contour *(outline)*
roughness irregularity
round chain *(series)*, cycle, stabilize
round body sphere
round table panel *(discussion group)*, session
round up convene, cull
round-about astray
roundabout circuitous, devious, discursive *(digressive)*, indirect, labyrinthine, oblique *(evasive)*, sinuous, tortuous *(bending)*
roundabout action indirection *(indirect action)*
roundabout course detour
roundabout way digression
roundaboutness indirection *(indirect action)*
roundly wholly
rouse agitate *(activate)*, bait *(harass)*, coax, disturb, evoke, exhort, foment, hasten, impel, impress *(affect deeply)*, incite, interest, motivate, persuade, perturb, pique, prompt, provoke, spirit, stimulate, urge. SEE MAIN ENTRY
rouser demagogue
rousing moving *(evoking emotion)*, persuasive
rout beat *(defeat)*, debacle, defeat, dispel, miscarriage, overcome *(surmount)*, prostration, repel *(drive back)*, repulse, subjugate, surmount
rout out expel, purge *(purify)*
route access *(right of way)*, admission *(entry)*, admittance *(means of approach)*, conduit *(channel)*, course, direction *(course)*, send, way *(channel)*. SEE MAIN ENTRY
routes approaches
routine accustomed *(customary)*, behavior, conventional, custom, customary, daily, familiar *(customary)*, habit, habitual, manner *(behavior)*, matter of course, method, mode, modus operandi, mundane, normal *(regular)*, operation, perfunctory, practice *(custom)*, practice *(procedure)*, procedure, process *(course)*, regular *(conventional)*, rule *(guide)*, system, systematic, trite, usage, usual. SEE MAIN ENTRY
routine event matter of course
routine happening matter of course
routine procedure custom
routinely invariably
rove digress, perambulate, prowl
rover itinerant, migrant, pedestrian
roving circuitous, discursive *(digressive)*, moving *(in motion)*, shifting, transient, vagrancy
row affray, altercation, bluster *(commotion)*, brawl *(noun)*, brawl *(verb)*, chain *(series)*, commotion, confrontation *(altercation)*, disaccord, embroilment, fight *(argument)*, fracas, fray, imbroglio, pandemonium, riot, strife, trouble, turmoil
rowdiness brawl, fracas
rowdy blatant *(obtrusive)*, disorderly, pugnacious, uncontrollable, unruly
royal outstanding *(prominent)*, sovereign *(absolute)*
rub contact *(touch)*
rub away diminish, erode
rub off deface, obliterate
rub out censor, deface, delete, destroy *(efface)*, expunge, extirpate, obliterate
rub the wrong way irritate
rubber check bad check
rubbery resilient
rubbing away erosion

rubric article *(precept),* bylaw, caption, code, constitution, dictate, direction *(order),* law, measure, precept, prescription *(directive),* principle *(axiom),* statute, title *(designation).* SEE MAIN ENTRY
rubricate embellish
ruckus noise
ruction brawl, commotion, fracas, fray, noise, pandemonium
rude blatant *(obtrusive),* brazen, caitiff, caustic, contemptuous, disdainful, disorderly, impertinent *(insolent),* inelegant, insolent, obtrusive, offensive *(offending),* perverse, presumptuous, provincial, uncouth, unseemly. SEE MAIN ENTRY
rude behavior disrespect
rude reproach disparagement
rudeness contempt *(disobedience to the court),* contumely, disparagement, disregard *(lack of respect),* disrespect, ingratitude, rebuff, temerity
rudiment cornerstone, element, embryo, foundation *(basis),* necessity
rudimental elementary, inchoate, incipient, original *(initial),* rudimentary, ultimate
rudimentary cardinal *(basic),* elementary, fundamental, inchoate, incipient, initial, minimal, organic, original *(initial),* prime *(original),* primordial, simple, ultimate, underlying. SEE MAIN ENTRY
rudimentary state embryo
rudis inexperienced, novice, uncouth, unversed
rue deplore, regret, remorse, repent
rueful contrite, despondent, lamentable, penitent, remorseful, repentant
ruffian aggressor, delinquent, hoodlum, malefactor
ruffianism brutality, misdoing
ruffianly disorderly
ruffle aggravate *(annoy),* agitate *(shake up),* annoy, badger, discompose, disconcert, disorient, disrupt, disturb, harry *(harass),* incense, irritate, molest *(annoy),* perturb, pique, plague
rugged brutal, powerful, severe, solid *(sound),* strong
ruggedness health
ruin bankruptcy, betray *(lead astray),* catastrophe, consumption, damage *(noun),* damage *(verb),* debacle, debauch, decay, decline, defeat, despoil, destroy *(efface),* destruction, deterioration, detriment, devastate, disable, disaster, dissolution *(termination),* extinguish, failure *(lack of success),* fatality, foil, harm *(noun),* harm *(verb),* havoc, impair, loss, miscarriage, mischief, misemploy, misfortune, obliterate, overturn, pervert, pillage, plunder, prejudice *(injure),* prostration, spoil *(impair),* stain, subversion, subvert, thwart, upset. SEE MAIN ENTRY
ruin one's eyesight blind *(deprive of sight)*
ruin one's prospects disappoint
ruinable destructible
ruinate despoil, destroy *(efface),* pillage, spoil *(impair)*
ruination adversity, bankruptcy, catastrophe, consumption, damage, debacle, defeat, defilement, destruction, deterioration, detriment, disaster, disrepair, dissolution *(termination),* havoc, prostration, subversion, waste, wear and tear
ruined bad *(inferior),* bad *(offensive),* bankrupt, depraved, dilapidated, imperfect, insolvent, irredeemable, irremediable, irreparable, marred, poor *(underprivileged)*
ruiner vandal
ruining disastrous, fatal
ruinous adverse *(negative),* bad *(offensive),* deadly, deleterious, diabolic, dire, disastrous, fatal, harmful, insalubrious, malevolent, malignant, noxious, pernicious, regrettable
ruinous price toll *(effect)*
ruinousness adversity, disaster
rule act *(enactment),* adjudge, adjudicate, arbitrate *(adjudge),* array *(order),* award, belief *(something believed),* brevet, bureaucracy, bylaw, canon, codification, coerce, command, conclude *(decide),* condition *(contingent provision),* constant, control *(regulate),* criterion, decide, decree, determine, dictate *(noun),* dictate *(verb),* direct *(order),* direct *(supervise),* direction *(order),* doctrine, dogma, dominate, dominion *(supreme authority),* edict, enactment, enjoin, fiat, find *(determine),* govern, government *(administration),* habit, handle *(manage),* hegemony, hold *(decide),* influence, instruction *(direction),* law, legislate, manage, mandamus, mandate, manipulate *(control unfairly),* matter of course, maxim, measure *(noun),* measure *(verb),* method, mode, norm, occupation *(possession),* operate, opinion *(judicial decision),* order *(judicial directive),* order, ordinance, oversee, pass *(determine),* pattern, police, power, practice *(procedure),* precedent, precept, predominance, predominate *(command),* prescription *(directive),* preside, prevail *(triumph),* primacy, principle *(axiom),* procedure, pronounce *(pass judgment),* regime, regulate *(manage),* rubric *(authoritative rule),* ruling, stare decisis, statute, subject, superintend, supremacy, technicality, try *(conduct a trial),* wield. SEE MAIN ENTRY
rule against overrule
rule dishonestly misgovern
rule for future determinations precedent
rule for future guidance precedent
rule of action platform, policy *(plan of action),* principle *(axiom)*
rule of conduct canon, law
rule of law SEE MAIN ENTRY
rule of might oppression
rule of proceeding formality
rule of reason SEE MAIN ENTRY
rule on judge
rule out delete, deter, dismiss *(put out of consideration),* disqualify, eliminate *(exclude),* exclude, negate, obliterate, overrule, prevent
rule over dominate, predominate *(command),* subjugate
rule upon adjudicate
rule-abiding obedient
ruled positive *(prescribed)*
ruler arbitrator
rulers authorities, hierarchy *(persons in authority)*
rulership government *(administration)*
rules code, mode, protocol *(etiquette)*
rules and regulations codification, criterion
rules of business practice *(procedure)*
rules of conduct decorum
rules of war strategy
ruling act *(enactment),* adjudication, authority *(documentation),* award, canon, central *(essential),* code, conclusion *(determination),* condition *(contingent provision),* conviction *(finding of guilt),* decree, determination, dictate, dominant, edict, enactment, finding, influential, judgment *(formal court decree),* mandate, master, measure, omnipotent, opinion *(judicial decision),* order *(judicial directive),* potent, powerful, predominant, prescription *(directive),* prevailing *(having superior force),* primary, principal, pronouncement, requirement, rubric *(authoritative rule),* sentence, sovereign *(absolute),* verdict. SEE MAIN ENTRY
ruling of the court award, decree
ruling passion obsession
ruling power government *(political administration)*
ruling whim obsession
rulings codification, legislation *(enactments)*
ruminant cogitative, pensive
ruminate brood, concentrate *(pay attention),* consider, deliberate, muse, ponder, reflect *(ponder),* speculate *(conjecture),* study, weigh
rumination consideration *(contemplation),* contemplation, deliberation, dialectic, hindsight, reflection *(thought),* speculation *(conjecture).* SEE MAIN ENTRY
ruminative cogitative, pensive
rummage delve
rumor canard, circulate
rumor hearsay
rumor spread
rumor about circulate
rumored reputedly
rumpere infringe, violate
rumpus bluster *(commotion),* fray, furor, imbroglio, pandemonium, riot, turmoil
run abscond, chain *(series),* conduct, exude, flee, function, hierarchy *(arrangement in a series),* manage, manipulate *(utilize skillfully),* market *(demand),* moderate *(preside over),* officiate, operate, race, rule *(govern).* SEE MAIN ENTRY
run a race race
run across find *(discover)*
run afoul of collide *(clash)*
run after chase, hunt, pursue *(chase)*
run against collide *(clash),* conflict, counteract, fight *(counteract),* jostle *(bump into),* oppugn
run at attack
run at cross purposes conflict
run at cross-purposes collide *(clash)*
run away abandon *(physically leave),* abscond, defect, escape, evacuate, flee, leave *(depart),* quit *(evacuate),* retreat
run away with jostle *(pickpocket),* kidnap
run checks on check *(inspect),* poll, probe
run counter check *(restrain),* confront *(oppose),* counteract
run counter to antagonize, collide *(clash),* conflict, confront *(oppose),* contradict, contravene, counteract, countervail, cross *(disagree with),* disaccord, disaffirm, except *(object),* fight *(counteract),* oppugn
run down brutalize, decrease, defame, degenerate, denigrate, deplete, depreciate, derogate, diminish, disapprove *(condemn),* disparage, lessen, minimize, misprize, mistreat, old, pillory, pursue *(chase),* reprehend, reprimand, sully, underestimate
run foul of collide *(clash)*
run from shirk
run in opposition to conflict, counter, counteract

run in pursuit chase
run into impinge, pervade
run into debt overdraw
run into each other collide *(crash against)*
run its course cease
run low diminish
run of luck prosperity
run of the mill mediocre, prevalent, regular *(conventional)*, trite
run off flee, publish
run off with carry away, hold up *(rob)*, jostle *(pickpocket)*, kidnap, poach
run on keep *(continue)*, persevere
run out close *(terminate)*, expire, lapse *(cease)*, terminate
run over inundate, invade, overlap, overstep, recapitulate, repeat *(state again)*, review
run parallel to correspond *(be equivalent)*
run riot brawl
run swiftly race
run tests on check *(inspect)*
run the chance incur
run the risk bet
run through exhaust *(deplete)*, penetrate, permeate, pervade, pierce *(lance)*, spend
run together collide *(crash against)*, commingle
runabout itinerant
runagate fugitive
runaway elusive, fugitive
rundle step
rung degree *(station)*, step
runic mysterious
runner bootlegger, candidate
running consecutive, continuous, fluvial, management *(judicious use)*
running account ledger
running away flight
running counter to dissenting, opposition
running expense cost *(expenses)*
running expenses maintenance *(upkeep)*
running out expiration
runoff outflow
runthrough hornbook
rupture alienation *(estrangement)*, break *(fracture)*, controversy *(argument)*, disassociation, disrupt, embroilment, estrangement, feud, force *(break)*, rend, rift *(gap)*, schism, separate, separation, sever, split, variance *(disagreement)*
ruptured broken *(fractured)*
ruse artifice, bunko, canard, deception, device *(contrivance)*, evasion, expedient, fake, false pretense, fraud, hoax, imposture, machination, maneuver *(trick)*, plot *(secret plan)*, ploy, pretense *(pretext)*, pretext, stratagem, subterfuge. SEE MAIN ENTRY
rush dispatch *(promptness)*, dispatch *(send off)*, expedite, haste, hasten, outbreak, outburst, precipitate *(hasten)*, race, spate. SEE MAIN ENTRY
rush off dispatch *(send off)*
rush through hasten
rush to a conclusion presuppose
rush to conclusion prejudge
rush upon assail, attack, inundate
rushed perfunctory, precipitate
rushing rapid
rushing in incursion
rustic inelegant, ingenuous, simple, uncouth
rusticate retreat
rusty old
ruth lenience, pity
ruthful placable
ruthless brutal, cold-blooded, cruel, diabolic, draconian, harsh, malevolent, malicious, malignant, relentless, remorseless, severe, uncompromising, unrelenting, unscrupulous. SEE MAIN ENTRY
ruthlessness atrocity, brutality, cruelty, oppression, rancor, severity, violence
ruttish lecherous, lewd, licentious, salacious
rutty lewd

S

sabotage damage, disable, disloyalty, pillage, spoil *(impair)*, subversion. SEE MAIN ENTRY
saboteurs conspirers. SEE MAIN ENTRY
saccharine nectarious
sack depredation, despoil, devastate, foray, harry *(plunder)*, havoc, hold up *(rob)*, loot, pillage *(noun)*, pillage *(verb)*, pirate *(take by violence)*, plunder *(noun)*, plunder *(verb)*, spoliation
sacrament of marriage matrimony
sacramental sacrosanct, solemn
sacred ineffable, infrangible, inviolate, sacrosanct, solemn. SEE MAIN ENTRY
sacrifice abandon *(relinquish)*, cost *(penalty)*, extirpate, forbear, forfeit, forswear, lose *(be deprived of)*, loss, relinquish, renunciation, suffer *(sustain loss)*, waive, yield *(submit)*. SEE MAIN ENTRY
sacrifice pride condescend *(deign)*
sacrificed lost *(taken away)*
sacrilege blasphemy
sacrilegious profane
sacrilegiousness blasphemy
sacrosanct infrangible. SEE MAIN ENTRY
sad deplorable, despondent, disconsolate, grave *(solemn)*, lamentable, lugubrious, pessimistic, regrettable, remorseful. SEE MAIN ENTRY
sadden depress, discourage, distress
saddening lamentable
saddle disadvantage, encumber *(hinder)*, load, overcome *(overwhelm)*, overload
saddle with tax *(overwork)*
sadistic brutal, cruel, diabolic, ruthless
sadness damper *(depressant)*, distress *(anguish)*
saepire enclose
safe bank, cache *(storage place)*, coffer, depository, guarded, immune, impervious, indubious, inexpugnable, innocuous, intact, nontoxic, reliable, repository, salutary, secure *(free from danger)*, solid *(sound)*, treasury. SEE MAIN ENTRY
safe conduct protection, security *(safety)*
safe deposit box coffer
safe haven SEE MAIN ENTRY
safe place cache *(hiding place)*, cache *(storage place)*, refuge
safe retreat cache *(hiding place)*
safe workplace SEE MAIN ENTRY
safe-deposit box depository
safe-deposite vault bank
safebreaker burglar
safecracker burglar
safeguard asylum *(protection)*, auspices, barrier, bear *(support)*, bulwark, concern *(care)*, conserve, cover *(protection)*, cover *(guard)*, coverage *(insurance)*, custody *(supervision)*, defend, discretion *(quality of being discreet)*, ensconce, ensure, foster, guarantee, guaranty, guardian, harbor, hedge, keep *(shelter)*, maintain *(sustain)*, panoply, patrol, police, precaution, preparation, preserve, protect, protection, rescue, save *(rescue)*, screen *(guard)*, security *(safety)*, shield, ward. SEE MAIN ENTRY
safeguarded guarded, safe
safeguarding conservation, preservation, preventive, prophylactic, protective
safehold asylum *(hiding place)*
safekeeper guardian
safekeeping charge *(custody)*, conservation, custody *(incarceration)*, custody *(supervision)*, preservation, protection, ward. SEE MAIN ENTRY
safeness security *(safety)*
safety asylum *(protection)*, inviolability, preservation, protection, refuge, shelter *(protection)*, trust *(custody)*. SEE MAIN ENTRY
safety from prosecution immunity
safety valve SEE MAIN ENTRY
safety valve provisions SEE MAIN ENTRY
sag give *(yield)*, languish
saga account *(report)*, report *(detailed account)*, story *(narrative)*. SEE MAIN ENTRY
sagacious cognizant, discriminating *(judicious)*, judicial, judicious, juridical, learned, lucid, omniscient, perspicacious, politic, profound *(esoteric)*, prudent, rational, reasonable *(rational)*, resourceful, sapient, sensible, solid *(sound)*, subtle *(refined)*. SEE MAIN ENTRY
sagaciousness insight, perception, sagacity, sense *(intelligence)*
sagacitas perception, sagacity
sagacity caliber *(mental capacity)*, common sense, comprehension, discretion *(quality of being discreet)*, discrimination *(good judgment)*, insight, intelligence *(intellect)*, judgment *(discernment)*, perception, reason *(sound judgment)*, sense *(intelligence)*. SEE MAIN ENTRY
sagax acute, judicious, perceptive, perspicacious
sage cognizant, expert, judicial, judicious, juridical, learned, lucid, mastermind, oracular, pedagogue, perspicacious, profound *(esoteric)*, prudent, rational, sapient, sensible, solid *(sound)*. SEE MAIN ENTRY
sage maxim principle *(axiom)*
sage reflection maxim
sageness comprehension
sagesse discretion *(quality of being discreet)*
said aforesaid, before mentioned, oral, stated. SEE MAIN ENTRY
said again repeated
said aloud oral
said in a preceding part aforesaid
sainted sacrosanct
saintly laudable
sake advantage, reason *(basis)*
salable disposable, marketable, negotiable, valuable
salable commodities merchandise
salable commodity item, product
salacious depraved, dissolute, immoral, lascivious, lecherous, lewd, lurid, obscene, prurient, scurrilous, suggestive *(risqué)*. SEE MAIN ENTRY
salaciousness obscenity, pornography
salacity debauchery, obscenity, pornography
salaried worker employee
salary commission *(fee)*, compensate *(remunerate)*, compensation, earnings,

honorarium, income, pay, payment *(remittance)*, payroll, recompense, revenue, wage
sale conveyance, disposition *(transfer of property)*, trade *(commerce)*, transaction. SEE MAIN ENTRY
sale by bid auction
sale by outcry auction
sale proceeds income
sale to the highest bidder auction
sales trade *(commerce)*
salesman dealer, vendor
salesmanship persuasion
salesperson dealer, merchant
saleswoman dealer
salience emphasis, importance, interest *(concern)*, materiality *(consequence)*, significance
saliency emphasis
salient arrant *(definite)*, clear *(apparent)*, distinctive, evident, important *(significant)*, manifest, material *(important)*, notable, noteworthy, open *(in sight)*, outstanding *(prominent)*, palpable, paramount, perceivable, perceptible, prominent, remarkable. SEE MAIN ENTRY
salient characteristic aspect
salient feature main point
salient point content *(meaning)*, cornerstone, feature *(characteristic)*, gist *(ground for a suit)*, gravamen, highlight, landmark *(significant change)*, main point, significance. SEE MAIN ENTRY
salient quality feature *(characteristic)*
salire frisk
salle chamber *(compartment)*
sally outburst
salubrious beneficial, medicinal, remedial, safe, salutary. SEE MAIN ENTRY
salubriousness health
salubrity health
salus health, maintenance *(upkeep)*, security *(safety)*
salutaris beneficial, remedial, salutary
salutary beneficial, contributory, favorable *(advantageous)*, medicinal, profitable, prophylactic, remedial, salubrious. SEE MAIN ENTRY
salutation remembrance *(commemoration)*
salute honor, recognize *(acknowledge)*, salvo
salutiferous beneficial, medicinal, remedial, salubrious, salutary. SEE MAIN ENTRY
salvage recover, recovery *(repossession)*, rehabilitate, renew *(refurbish)*, renewal, renovate, repair, reparation *(keeping in repair)*, replevin, rescue, save *(conserve)*. SEE MAIN ENTRY
salvageable corrigible
salvaged renascent
salvation discharge *(liberation)*, emancipation, mainstay, preservation, protection, redemption, rehabilitation, release, relief *(aid)*, safekeeping, salvage, security *(safety)*
salve assuage, cure *(noun)*, cure *(verb)*, pacify, placate, relieve *(give aid)*, soothe
salvo barrage, discharge *(shot)*, reservation *(condition)*. SEE MAIN ENTRY
salvus intact
samaritan SEE MAIN ENTRY
Samaritanism benevolence *(disposition to do good)*
same analogous, cognate, equal, equivalent, similar, uniform. SEE MAIN ENTRY
same conditions status quo
same line of descent family *(common ancestry)*
same-sex marriage SEE MAIN ENTRY
same strain family *(common ancestry)*
sameness constant, correspondence *(similarity)*, facsimile, identity *(similarity)*, par *(equality)*, parity, regularity, resemblance, semblance
sample case *(example)*, check *(inspect)*, cross section, example, exemplary, illustration, instance, model, paradigm, partake, pattern, poll, prototype, representative, representative *(example)*, specimen. SEE MAIN ENTRY
samples selection *(collection)*
sanare cure
sanatio cure
sanative medicinal, remedial, salutary
sanatory medicinal, remedial, salubrious, salutary
sancire confirm, sanction
sanctification elevation
sanctified inviolate, sacrosanct, solemn
sanctify authorize, elevate, purge *(purify)*. SEE MAIN ENTRY
sanctify by custom inure *(accustom)*
sanctimonious tartuffish
sanctimoniousness blasphemy, hypocrisy. SEE MAIN ENTRY
sanctimony hypocrisy
sanctio enactment, ratification
sanction abide, accept *(assent)*, acceptance, accredit, acquiescence, adoption *(acceptance)*, advantage, advocacy, advocate, allow *(authorize)*, appoint, approval, approve, assent *(noun)*, assent *(verb)*, authority *(documentation)*, authorize, bear *(support)*, bear *(tolerate)*, bestow, bind *(obligate)*, brevet, capacity *(authority)*, certify *(approve)*, concede, concession *(authorization)*, concur *(agree)*, confirm, confirmation, consent *(noun)*, consent *(verb)*, constitute *(establish)*, copyright, corroborate, countenance, countersign, decree, delegate, discretion *(power of choice)*, dispensation *(exception)*, droit, embrace *(accept)*, empower, enable, endorse, enfranchise, favor, fiat, force *(compulsion)*, franchise *(license)*, grant *(concede)*, indorse, indorsement, indulgence, invest *(vest)*, leave *(permission)*, legality, legalization, legalize, legislate, legitimate, let *(permit)*, liberty, license, option *(contractual provision)*, pass *(approve)*, permission, permit *(noun)*, permit *(verb)*, prefer, prerogative, privilege, promote *(organize)*, qualify *(meet standards)*, ratification, reassure, recommend, recommendation, right *(entitlement)*, seal *(solemnize)*, sign, subscription, sufferance, sustain *(confirm)*, title *(right)*, tolerate, uphold, validate, vest, warrant *(authorization)*. SEE MAIN ENTRY
sanction a claim authorize
sanction by law legalize
sanctionability admissibility
sanctionable admissible, allowable, licit
sanctionableness admissibility, legality
sanctioned admissible, allowable, allowed, due *(regular)*, entitled, juridical, justifiable, lawful, legal, legitimate *(rightful)*, licit, official, permissible, privileged, rightful, statutory, traditional, valid
sanctioned by custom legitimate *(rightful)*
sanctioned by law de jure, jural, lawful, legitimate *(rightful)*, permissible
sanctioned by legal authority legitimate *(rightful)*
sanctioned by the law allowed
sanctioned effectiveness force *(legal efficacy)*
sanctioned potency force *(legal efficacy)*
sanctions codification
sanctitas inviolability
sanctity good faith, honesty
sanctuary asylum *(hiding place)*, asylum *(protection)*, bulwark, haven, preservation, protection, refuge, security *(safety)*, shelter *(protection)*, shield. SEE MAIN ENTRY
sanctum sanctorum asylum *(hiding place)*
sanctus conscientious, incorruptible, inculpable, irreprehensible, moral, unimpeachable
sane lucid, rational, sensible. SEE MAIN ENTRY
sanemindedness competence *(sanity)*
saneness competence *(sanity)*, sanity
sang-froid dispassionate
sanguinary deadly, ruthless
sanguine SEE MAIN ENTRY
sanguine expectation faith
sanguineness belief *(state of mind)*, confidence *(faith)*, faith
sanguineous sanguine
sanguis blood
sanitary remedial, salutary
sanitary cordon quarantine
sanitas health
sanitize decontaminate
sanitorium asylum *(hospital)*
sanity reason *(sound judgment)*. SEE MAIN ENTRY
sans pareil best
sansculottic insubordinate
sanus sane
sap eviscerate, exhaust *(deplete)*, impair
sap the strength of debilitate
sapid palatable, savory. SEE MAIN ENTRY
sapience caliber *(mental capacity)*, common sense, judgment *(discernment)*, sagacity, sense *(intelligence)*. SEE MAIN ENTRY
sapiency sagacity
sapiens judicious, sapient
sapient acute, discriminating *(judicious)*, judicial, judicious, juridical, learned, literate, omniscient, oracular, perspicacious, prudent, reasonable *(rational)*, sensible, solid *(sound)*. SEE MAIN ENTRY
sapiential sensible
sapless languid, powerless
saporous sapid
sarcasm diatribe, irony, ridicule
sarcastic bitter *(reproachful)*, cynical, incisive, insolent, ironic, offensive *(offending)*, trenchant. SEE MAIN ENTRY
sarcastical cynical, incisive, ironic
sardonic bitter *(reproachful)*, cynical, disdainful, ironic
satanic cruel
satanic diabolic
satanic heinous, malevolent, malignant, sinister
sate assuage, satisfy *(fulfill)*
sated full
satellite offshoot, partisan
satiate assuage, pacify, satisfy *(fulfill)*. SEE MAIN ENTRY
satiate to excess overindulge
satiated full, replete
satiation plethora, surfeit
satietas surfeit
satiety plethora, sufficiency, surfeit
satire caricature, distortion, irony, parody, ridicule

satiric incisive, ironic
satirical incisive, ironic
satirize jape, mock *(deride)*, mock *(imitate)*
satisdatio warranty
satisfactio reparation *(indemnification)*
satisfaction amortization, benefit *(betterment)*, compensation, conciliation, consideration *(recompense)*, contribution *(indemnification)*, discharge *(payment)*, enjoyment *(pleasure)*, expiation, fruition, indemnification, offset, out of pocket, payment *(act of paying)*, pride, proof, recompense, recovery *(award)*, refund, relief *(legal redress)*, remuneration, reparation *(indemnification)*, requital, restitution, retribution, revenge, settlement, surfeit, trover. SEE MAIN ENTRY
satisfaction for damage compensation
satisfaction for injury compensation
satisfaction in full payoff *(payment in full)*
satisfactorily fairly *(moderately)*
satisfactoriness mediocrity, sufficiency
satisfactory adequate, ample, competent, eligible, mediocre, palatable, prima facie *(legally sufficient)*, right *(suitable)*, suitable, unobjectionable. SEE MAIN ENTRY
satisfactory evidence proof
satisfactory notice adequate notice
satisfiable placable
satisfied certain *(positive)*, complacent, definite, full, indubious, peaceable, positive *(confident)*, proud *(self-respecting)*, replete, successful
satisfy assuage, assure *(give confidence to)*, compensate *(remunerate)*, comply, contribute *(indemnify)*, convince, disarm *(set at ease)*, discharge *(pay a debt)*, fulfill, keep *(fulfill)*, liquidate *(determine liability)*, obey, observe *(obey)*, pacify, pander, pay, perform *(adhere to)*, placate, propitiate, reassure, recoup *(reimburse)*, redeem *(satisfy debts)*, redress, refund, reimburse, remedy, remit *(send payment)*, remunerate, repay, restore *(return)*, return *(refund)*, supply, vouchsafe. SEE MAIN ENTRY
satisfy a claim defray
satisfy by evidence convince, persuade
satisfy by proof convince, persuade
satisfy desires pander
satisfy in advance prepay
satisfy in full discharge *(pay a debt)*
satisfy oneself ascertain
satisfy requirements pass *(satisfy requirements)*
satisfy to excess overindulge
satisfying adequate, compensatory, sapid
saturate imbue, inject, inundate, overload, penetrate, permeate, pervade, replenish
saturated drunk, full, replete
saturation maximum *(amplitude)*, osmosis, plethora, sufficiency, surfeit. SEE MAIN ENTRY
saturnine disconsolate, grave *(solemn)*, lugubrious
satyric dissolute, lascivious, prurient, salacious
satyrical lascivious, salacious
sauciness disrespect
saucy brazen, impertinent *(insolent)*, insolent, obtrusive, offensive *(offending)*, presumptuous
saunter perambulate
savage assail, brutal, cold-blooded, cruel, disorderly, harsh, hot-blooded, malevolent, malicious, malignant, mistreat, ruthless, severe, vicious. SEE MAIN ENTRY
savageness brutality, cruelty
savagery atrocity, bestiality, brutality, cruelty, severity, violence
savant expert, mastermind, specialist
save conserve, deposit *(submit to a bank)*, extricate, free, fund, garner, glean, hold *(possess)*, keep *(shelter)*, maintain *(sustain)*, perpetuate, preserve, protect, release, remedy, renew *(refurbish)*, rescue, reserve, retain *(keep in possession)*, store, sustain *(prolong)*, unless. SEE MAIN ENTRY
save from disencumber
save from loss conserve
save harmless indemnify
save up fund, hoard, set aside *(reserve)*
saved free *(relieved from a burden)*
saved from bondage free *(enjoying civil liberty)*
saving conservation, economical, economy *(frugality)*, hoard, penurious, preservation, provident *(frugal)*, prudent, reservation *(engagement)*
saving clause loophole, reservation *(condition)*, salvo
savings capital, fund, reserve, store *(depository)*
savings clause SEE MAIN ENTRY
savior samaritan
savoir faire common sense, discretion *(quality of being discreet)*
savor partake, relish
savorless insipid, stale
savory palatable, sapid. SEE MAIN ENTRY
saw maxim, phrase
say allege, claim *(maintain)*, comment, communicate, contend *(maintain)*, converse, declare, enunciate, express, observe *(remark)*, phrase, posit, pronounce *(speak)*, purport, referendum, relate *(tell)*, remark, speak, speech, suffrage. SEE MAIN ENTRY
say again recapitulate, reiterate, repeat *(state again)*
say by heart recite
say in advance preface
say in defense support *(justify)*
say in reply answer *(reply)*, countercharge, retort, return *(respond)*
say less than the truth perjure
say no challenge
say no to ban
say over repeat *(state again)*
say repeatedly reiterate
say-so SEE MAIN ENTRY
say under oath depose *(testify)*, witness *(attest to)*
say yes concur *(agree)*
saying catchword, expression *(comment)*, maxim, phrase, remark
scab pariah
scabrous lurid, obscene, salacious, scurrilous. SEE MAIN ENTRY
scaena scene
scaenicus histrionic, histrionics
scald burn
scalding caustic
scale caliber *(measurement)*, chain *(series)*, differential, index *(gauge)*, magnitude, surmount. SEE MAIN ENTRY
scale down decrease, diminish, discount *(minimize)*, minimize
scale of prices tariff *(bill)*
scaled proportionate
scamp degenerate, derelict, malefactor
scamper race
scampish disorderly, profligate *(corrupt)*
scampishness knavery
scan analyze, canvass, check *(inspect)*, frisk, investigate, monitor, observe *(watch)*, patrol, peruse, probe, read, regard *(pay attention)*, research, scrutinize, search, study, survey *(examine)*
scandal defamation, discredit, disgrace, dishonor *(shame)*, ignominy, infamy, notoriety, odium, opprobrium, shame, slander. SEE MAIN ENTRY
scandalize contemn, defame, discredit, disgrace, libel, pillory, repel *(disgust)*
scandalizing flagrant
scandalous arrant *(onerous)*, bad *(offensive)*, blameworthy, calumnious, contemptuous, delinquent *(guilty of a misdeed)*, disgraceful, disorderly, flagrant, ignoble, inexpiable, iniquitous, lewd, libelous, licentious, nefarious, notorious, outrageous, peccant *(culpable)*, regrettable, vicious. SEE MAIN ENTRY
scandalum magnatum stigma
scant deficient, inadequate, inappreciable, insubstantial, insufficient, marginal, minimal, minor, negligible, nonsubstantial *(not sufficient)*, paltry, petty, poor *(inferior in quality)*, remote *(small)*, scarce, slight, tenuous. SEE MAIN ENTRY
scant of devoid
scant respect disparagement
scantiness austerity, dearth, deficit, delinquency *(shortage)*, insignificance, insufficiency, need *(deprivation)*, paucity, poverty
scantity poverty
scantling minimum
scantness dearth, insufficiency, paucity, poverty
scanty de minimus, deficient, imperfect, inappreciable, insufficient, marginal, minimal, negligible, nominal, nonsubstantial *(not sufficient)*, paltry, partial *(relating to a part)*, petty, trivial
scapegrace degenerate
scar deface, defacement, onus *(stigma)*, stigma
scarce barren, deficient, infrequent, insufficient, minimal, nonsubstantial *(not sufficient)*, paltry, rare, uncommon, unusual. SEE MAIN ENTRY
scarcely almost
scarceness dearth, insignificance, paucity, poverty
scarcity dearth, deficiency, deficit, delinquency *(shortage)*, indigence, insufficiency, need *(deprivation)*, paucity, poverty
scare browbeat, discourage, fear, fright, frighten, intimidate, menace, start, trepidation. SEE MAIN ENTRY
scared caitiff
scarify lash *(attack verbally)*
scarifying critical *(faultfinding)*
scarlet lewd, licentious, salacious
scarred marred
scathe damage, disable, harm *(noun)*, harm *(verb)*, lash *(attack verbally)*, persecute
scathed marred
scatheful adverse *(negative)*, malevolent, malignant, noxious, scathing, sinister
scatheless inviolate, safe
scathing bitter *(penetrating)*, critical *(faultfinding)*, harsh, incisive, mordacious, trenchant. SEE MAIN ENTRY
scatter break *(fracture)*, deploy, diffuse, disband, disburse *(distribute)*, dislocate, disorganize, dispel, dispense, dissipate *(spread out)*, dissociate, dissolve *(disperse)*,

distribute, intersperse, radiate, repel *(drive back),* spread
scatter abroad disperse *(disseminate),* disperse *(scatter)*
scatter thinly dissipate *(spread out)*
scatter to the winds dissipate *(spread out)*
scatter widely dissipate *(spread out)*
scatterbrained fatuous, thoughtless
scattered disconnected, sporadic
scattering circulation, decentralization, havoc
scavenge prowl
sceleratus criminal, felon, guilty
scelestus felon
scenario SEE MAIN ENTRY
scene locality, location, region, territory, vicinity. SEE MAIN ENTRY
scene of destruction shambles
scene of disorder shambles
scent clue, trace *(follow)*
scepter supremacy
schedule agenda, arrange *(plan),* book, calendar *(list of cases),* calendar *(record of yearly periods),* docket, empanel, impanel, invoice *(itemized list),* plan *(noun),* plan *(verb),* policy *(contract),* program *(noun),* program *(verb),* register *(noun),* register *(verb),* roll, scheme, set down. SEE MAIN ENTRY
schedule of affairs agenda
schedule of articles inventory
schedule of duties tariff *(duties)*
schedule of events calendar *(record of yearly periods)*
schedule of items and their respective prices invoice *(itemized list)*
scheduled forthcoming, future, prospective
scheduling codification, economy *(frugality)*
schema arrangement *(plan)*
schematic arrangement array *(order)*
schematism arrangement *(ordering)*
schematize arrange *(methodize),* coordinate, devise *(invent)*
scheme agenda, arrangement *(plan),* artifice, avenue *(means of attainment),* blueprint, cabal, campaign, circumvent, codification, connivance, connive, conspiracy, conspire, contrivance, contrive, course, design *(intent),* device *(contrivance),* devise *(invent),* direction *(course),* endeavor, enterprise *(undertaking),* expedient, forethought, form *(arrangement),* frame *(formulate),* goal, hoax, intend, intent, machination, maneuver *(tactic),* maneuver *(trick),* maneuver, mode, organization *(structure),* plan *(noun),* plan *(verb),* platform, plot *(secret plan),* plot, ploy, policy *(plan of action),* practice *(procedure),* procedure, process *(course),* program, project, proposal *(suggestion),* proposition, prospectus, racket, ruse, stratagem, strategy, suggestion, system. SEE MAIN ENTRY
scheme of arrangement configuration *(form),* method
schemeful collusive
schemer architect, coactor, conspirator, conspirer
schemery collusion, confederacy *(conspiracy),* strategy
scheming artful, collusion, collusive, deceptive, devious, diplomatic, dishonest, disingenuous, evasive, fraudulent, insidious, machiavellian, perfidious, recreant, sinister, sly, unconscionable, untrue
schism alienation *(estrangement),* contention *(opposition),* difference, disaccord, disassociation, discord, dissension, dissent *(difference of opinion),* dissidence, division *(act of dividing),* estrangement, fight *(argument).* SEE MAIN ENTRY
schisma schism
schismatic contentious, divisive, heretic, hostile, polemic, recusant
schismatize conflict
scholar disciple, expert, pedagogue, specialist
scholarly didactic, diligent, disciplinary *(educational),* learned, literate, profound *(esoteric)*
scholarship education, knowledge *(learning)*
scholastic didactic, disciplinary *(educational),* informative, literate
scholium clarification, comment, note *(brief comment)*
school discipline *(train),* edify, educate, instill, institute, instruct *(teach),* organization *(association),* practice *(train by repetition),* style
school oneself study
schooled familiar *(informed),* informed *(educated),* knowing, learned, literate, sciential
schooling discipline *(training),* edification, education, experience *(background),* guidance, instruction *(teaching)*
schoolman pedagogue
schoolmaster pedagogue
schoolteacher pedagogue
science SEE MAIN ENTRY
science of law jurisprudence
science of legal relations jurisprudence
science of monetary relations finance
science of oratory rhetoric *(skilled speech)*
science of teaching education
science of wealth finance
sciens expert, familiar *(informed),* knowing, proficient
scienter SEE MAIN ENTRY
scientia knowledge *(learning),* science *(study),* skill
sciential SEE MAIN ENTRY
scientific objective, precise, real, sound, technical, valid
scientific determination diagnosis
scindere split
scintilla iota, minimum. SEE MAIN ENTRY
sciolist pedant
sciolistic superficial
scion child, descendant, heir, offshoot, offspring, posterity, successor
scions progeny
scissile destructible, divisible, severable
scission decentralization, division *(act of dividing),* severance, split
scissura split
scissure rift *(gap),* split
scitum resolution *(decision)*
scoff derogate, disdain *(noun),* disdain *(verb),* disparage, flout, humiliate, jape, jeer, mock *(deride)*
scoff at contemn, discommend, reject
scoffing cynical, disregard *(lack of respect),* disrespect, impertinent *(insolent),* skeptical
scofflaw delinquent. SEE MAIN ENTRY
scold castigate, denounce *(condemn),* disapprove *(condemn),* fault, inveigh, rebuke, remonstrate, reprehend, reprimand, reproach. SEE MAIN ENTRY
scolding critical *(faultfinding),* criticism, diatribe, disparagement, objurgation, obloquy, outcry, rebuff, reprimand, reproach
sconce fine, penalty
scope area *(province),* capacity *(aptitude),* capacity *(maximum),* capacity *(sphere),* connotation, content *(meaning),* contents, context, degree *(magnitude),* extent, gamut, intent, latitude, magnitude, opportunity, province, purview, range, region, scene, space, sphere. SEE MAIN ENTRY
scope of review SEE MAIN ENTRY
scope of vision perspective
scorch burn, deflagrate
scorched earth policy SEE MAIN ENTRY
scorching bitter *(penetrating)*
score bill *(invoice),* calculate, carry *(succeed),* census, computation, inveigh, poll, sum *(tally)*
score a success attain, succeed *(attain)*
scorify burn
scorn affront, contemn, contempt *(disdain),* decry, disapprove *(reject),* disavow, disdain *(noun),* disdain *(verb),* dishonor *(shame),* disoblige, disown *(refuse to acknowledge),* disparage, disparagement, disregard *(lack of respect),* disrespect, exclude, flout, forswear, humiliate, ignore, illude, infamy, minimize, misprize, mock *(deride),* odium, pillory, rebuff, rejection, renounce, repulse, ridicule, shame, spurn, vilification. SEE MAIN ENTRY
scorn of the consequences audacity
scorned derelict *(abandoned),* undesirable
scornful bitter *(reproachful),* contemptuous, cynical, disdainful, inflated *(vain),* orgulous, pejorative, supercilious
scornful imitation ridicule
scornful insolence contumely
scornful treatment contumely
scornfulness contumely, disdain
scorning disdain
scorse trade
scot tax
scotch stem *(check)*
scoundrel convict, hoodlum, malefactor, wrongdoer
scoundrelism corruption, knavery
scoundrelly sinister
scour decontaminate, frisk, perambulate, purge *(purify),* search
scourge catastrophe, disaster, discipline *(punishment),* discipline *(punish),* disease, harm *(noun),* harm *(verb),* lash *(strike),* nuisance, persecute, plague, punish
scourging correction *(punishment)*
scout forerunner, observe *(watch),* patrol, pioneer, precede, precursor, reject, search, spurn, spy
scramble bluster *(commotion),* brawl, commingle, competition, confound, disorganize, disorient, dispatch *(promptness),* fracas, fray, muddle, race. SEE MAIN ENTRY
scrambled composite, miscellaneous, promiscuous
scrap bicker, brawl, reject, salvage
scrape entanglement *(involvement),* erode, imbroglio, misdeed, misdoing, plight, predicament, quagmire
scrape together glean
scraping obsequious
scrapped derelict *(abandoned)*
scrappy sporadic
scratch deface, defacement
scratch out censor, deface, delete, destroy *(efface),* expunge, obliterate

scratched marred
scrawl script
scream outcry
screaming blatant *(obtrusive)*, flagrant
screed declamation, philippic
screen blind *(obscure)*, buffer zone, camouflage, cloak, conceal, cover *(pretext)*, cover *(conceal)*, disguise *(noun)*, disguise *(verb)*, ensconce, enshroud, envelop, harbor, hedge, hide, lodge *(house)*, maintain *(sustain)*, obfuscate, obliterate, obnubilate, obscure, panoply, plant *(covertly place)*, preserve, protect, safeguard, shelter *(protection)*, shield, shroud, sort, suppress, veil. SEE MAIN ENTRY
screen from observation blind *(obscure)*, camouflage
screen from sight blind *(obscure)*, camouflage
screen off insulate
screen out reject, seclude
screened allusive, blind *(concealed)*, clandestine, covert, hidden, immune, impalpable, indiscernible, latent, mysterious, safe
screened from danger safe
screening protective
scriba clerk, notary public
scribbled holographic
scribe amanuensis, clerk, inscribe, notary public, note *(record)*
scribere legislate
scrimmage affray, brawl *(noun)*, brawl *(verb)*, fight *(battle)*, fray, struggle
scrimping austerity, parsimonious
scrinium portfolio
script handwriting, scenario. SEE MAIN ENTRY
scription handwriting, script
scriptor author *(writer)*
scriptorial holographic
scriptory in writing
scriptural holographic
scrivener amanuensis, clerk, notary public
scrofulous lurid, salacious
scrounger parasite
scrub decontaminate, poor *(inferior in quality)*
scrubby ignoble, poor *(inferior in quality)*
scrumptious palatable, sapid
scruple demur, doubt *(hesitate)*, hesitate, hesitation, misdoubt, qualm, refuse. SEE MAIN ENTRY
scruples conscience, integrity, reluctance, responsibility *(conscience)*
scrupulosity honesty, particularity
scrupulous accurate, bona fide, candid, careful, clean, close *(rigorous)*, conscientious, credible, equitable, evenhanded, exact, factual, fair *(just)*, high-minded, honest, impartial, incorruptible, just, law-abiding, literal, meticulous, moral, orthodox, painstaking, particular *(exacting)*, precise, punctilious, punctual, reliable, reputable, right *(correct)*, straightforward, strict, undistorted, upright, vigilant. SEE MAIN ENTRY
scrupulously fairly *(impartially)*, faithfully
scrupulousness adhesion *(loyalty)*, fairness, honesty, honor *(good reputation)*, integrity, particularity, principle *(virtue)*, probity, rectitude, responsibility *(conscience)*, rigor
scrupulus embarrassment
scrutable cognizable, coherent *(clear)*, solvable. SEE MAIN ENTRY
scrutari probe *(noun)*, probe *(verb)*
scrutation indagation, scrutiny
scrutinization analysis, investigation
scrutinize analyze, audit, canvass, check *(inspect)*, concentrate *(pay attention)*, consider, criticize *(evaluate)*, discern *(detect with the senses)*, examine *(study)*, frisk, inquire, investigate, monitor, notice *(observe)*, observe *(watch)*, overlook *(superintend)*, oversee, peruse, probe, regard *(pay attention)*, research, review, search, spy, study, survey *(examine)*. SEE MAIN ENTRY
scrutinizing circumspect, inquisitive, interrogative
scrutiny analysis, contemplation, cross-examination, cross-questioning, diligence *(care)*, discovery, examination *(study)*, indagation, inquiry *(request for information)*, inquiry *(systematic investigation)*, inspection, interrogation, investigation, notice *(heed)*, observation, perception, probe, question *(inquiry)*, regard *(attention)*, research, review *(official reexamination)*, surveillance, test, trial *(experiment)*. SEE MAIN ENTRY
scud race
scuffle affray, altercation, belligerency, brawl *(noun)*, brawl *(verb)*, commotion, confrontation *(altercation)*, fight *(battle)*, fight *(battle)*, fracas, fray, struggle
sculpture contour *(shape)*
scurrile calumnious, libelous, salacious, scurrilous
scurrilis scurrilous
scurrility aspersion, bad repute, contempt *(disdain)*, contumely, diatribe, disapprobation, expletive, slander
scurrillity obscenity
scurrilous blatant *(obtrusive)*, calumnious, ignoble, lewd, libelous, malignant, salacious, scandalous. SEE MAIN ENTRY
scurry dispatch *(promptness)*
scurvy iniquitous, objectionable, odious, poor *(inferior in quality)*
scuttlebutt report *(rumor)*
scutum shield
se abstinere refrain
se applicare recourse
se conferre recourse
se coniungere join *(associate oneself with)*
se continere refrain
se defendere answer *(reply)*
se interponere intrude, mediate
se opponere confront *(oppose)*
se recipere retreat
se rei dedere address *(talk to)*
se submittere condescend *(deign)*
seaboard littoral
seacoast littoral
seal bar *(hinder)*, brand, brand *(mark)*, complete, conclude *(complete)*, conclude *(decide)*, confirm, confirmation, determine, fix *(settle)*, lock, notarize, occlude, sanction *(permission)*, shut, sign, stamp, subscribe *(sign)*, symbol, validate. SEE MAIN ENTRY
seal of secrecy censorship
seal the doom of determine
seal up contain *(enclose)*, immure, repress
sealed blind *(impassable)*, impervious, necessary *(inescapable)*, undisclosed
sealed record SEE MAIN ENTRY
sealing off blockade *(enclosure)*
sear burn, deflagrate
search audit, canvass, chase, cross-examination, delve, endeavor, examination *(study)*, experiment, ferret, indagation, inquest, inquire, inquiry *(request for information)*, inquiry *(systematic investigation)*, interrogation, investigation, market *(demand)*, peruse, probe, pursue *(chase)*, pursuit *(chase)*, pursuit *(effort to secure)*, quest, question *(inquiry)*, research *(noun)*, research *(verb)*, scrutinize, scrutiny, survey *(examine)*, test, trace *(follow)*, undertaking *(attempt)*, undertaking *(enterprise)*. SEE MAIN ENTRY
search for delve, hunt
search for an answer consult *(seek information from)*
search for information inquiry *(request for information)*
search into check *(inspect)*, inquire, investigate, probe, scrutinize, study
search into facts cross-examination, inquest
search laboriously delve
search made for useful military information espionage
search one's pockets frisk
search out hunt, locate, spy
search through delve, frisk
search warrant SEE MAIN ENTRY
searching inquisitive, interrogative, quest, vigilant
searching examination probe
searching inquiry analysis, cross-examination, hearing, investigation
searching investigation indagation
seared callous, impervious
searing insufferable, scathing
seashore littoral
seaside littoral
season duration, inure *(accustom)*, lifetime, mature, moderate *(temper)*, period, phase *(period)*, term *(duration)*. SEE MAIN ENTRY
seasonable apposite, favorable *(advantageous)*, fit, fitting, opportune, prompt, proper, propitious, punctual, relevant, suitable
seasonableness timeliness
seasonal intermittent, periodic, regular *(orderly)*. SEE MAIN ENTRY
seasoned elderly, expert, practiced, ripe, sapid, veteran
seasoning experience *(background)*
seat address, embed, headquarters, instate, locality, standpoint, venue. SEE MAIN ENTRY
seat of judgment bench
seat of justice bar *(court)*, bench
seated situated
secede defect, leave *(depart)*, quit *(discontinue)*, renege, withdraw. SEE MAIN ENTRY
secede from abandon *(physically leave)*, relinquish
secern SEE MAIN ENTRY
secernere distinguish, isolate
secession desertion, lapse *(expiration)*, resignation *(relinquishment)*, revolt, schism
seclude blind *(obscure)*, camouflage, cloak, conceal, condemn *(ban)*, confine, cover *(conceal)*, ensconce, enshroud, harbor, hide, immure, insulate, isolate, protect, shroud. SEE MAIN ENTRY
seclude oneself lurk, retire *(retreat)*, retreat
secluded clandestine, covert, evasive, hidden, obscure *(remote)*, secret, separate, solitary, unapproachable

secludere seclude
seclusion concealment, exclusion, obscuration, privacy, quarantine
seclusive private *(secluded)*, remote *(secluded)*
second abet, abettor, advocate, aid, approve, assist, assistant, backer, bear *(support)*, concur *(agree)*, confirm, countersign, deputy, endorse, help, indorse, justify, point *(period of time)*, proctor, promote *(organize)*, recommend, replacement, side, support *(assist)*, uphold. SEE MAIN ENTRY
second best poor *(inferior in quality)*
second examination review *(official reexamination)*
second legal marriage digamy
second marriage digamy
second nature habit
second rank circumstantial
second self alter ego
second thoughts hesitation, hindsight
second time de novo
second to none best, cardinal *(outstanding)*, paramount, premium, primary, superior *(excellent)*, superlative
second view hindsight
second-rate inferior *(lower in quality)*, mediocre, poor *(inferior in quality)*
second-story thief burglar
secondary ancillary *(subsidiary)*, circumstantial, collateral *(immaterial)*, contributory, deputy, derivative, extrinsic, incidental, inferior *(lower in position)*, minor, null *(insignificant)*, pendent, peripheral, plenipotentiary, replacement, slight, subaltern, subordinate, subservient, subsidiary, succedaneum, supplementary, unessential. SEE MAIN ENTRY
secondary evidence hearsay
secondary group minority *(outnumbered group)*
secondary implied meaning connotation
secondary rights SEE MAIN ENTRY
seconded SEE MAIN ENTRY
seconder advocate *(counselor)*, advocate *(espouser)*, assistant, backer, benefactor, colleague, partisan, proponent
secondhand evidence hearsay
seconding accommodation *(backing)*, advocacy, help
secrecy concealment, confidence *(relation of trust)*, evasion, mystery, obscuration, privacy. SEE MAIN ENTRY
secret anonymous, clandestine, confidence *(relation of trust)*, confidential, covert, enigma, enigmatic, esoteric, furtive, hidden, inscrutable, interior, intimate, mysterious, mystery, personal *(private)*, private *(confidential)*, privy, recondite, seal *(close)*, sequester *(seclude)*, sly, stealthy, surreptitious, ulterior, uncanny, undisclosed. SEE MAIN ENTRY
secret agent spy
secret approval connivance
secret association collusion
secret communication confidence *(relation of trust)*
secret fraudulent understanding collusion
secret group cabal
secret observation espionage
secret place cache *(hiding place)*
secret plot cabal
secret storehouse cache *(storage place)*
secret understanding collusion
secret understanding for fraud collusion
secret watching espionage
secretary amanuensis, clerk
secrete blind *(obscure)*, camouflage, cloak, conceal, cover *(conceal)*, emit, ensconce, enshroud, exude, harbor, hide, plant *(covertly place)*
secrete oneself lurk
secreted blind *(concealed)*, hidden
secretion concealment
secretive clandestine, evasive, furtive, laconic, mysterious, noncommittal, oblique *(evasive)*, sly, stealthy, surreptitious, taciturn, unresponsive
secretiveness concealment, evasion, mystery, privacy
secretness evasion
secretus mysterious, secret, separate
sect class, denomination, side, society, split
sectarian heretic, one-sided, parochial, partisan *(adjective)*, partisan *(noun)*, specific
sectarianism intolerance, schism
sectarism schism
sectarist pariah
sectary advocate *(espouser)*, backer, pariah, partisan
section article *(distinct section of a writing)*, chamber *(compartment)*, chapter *(branch)*, chapter *(division)*, circuit, clause, component, constituent *(part)*, cross *(intersect)*, decentralization, denomination, department, detail, dichotomize, disjoint, district, divide *(separate)*, division *(act of dividing)*, element, heading, ingredient, installment, locality, location, member *(constituent part)*, moiety, organ, parcel, part *(place)*, part *(portion)*, part *(separate)*, partition, phase *(aspect)*, pigeonhole, province, region, segment, separate, share *(interest)*, split, subdivision, subheading, territory, title *(division)*. SEE MAIN ENTRY
section head caption
sectional broken *(fractured)*, local, partial *(part)*, partial *(relating to a part)*, provincial, regional
sectionalism intolerance
sectionalize dichotomize, divide *(separate)*, parcel, partition, separate
sector chapter *(division)*, component, constituent *(part)*, department, ingredient, locality, parcel, region, segment, subdivision. SEE MAIN ENTRY
secular civil *(public)*, material *(physical)*, mundane, profane
secundarius secondary
secundum leges fit legal
secundus fair *(satisfactory)*, prosperous
securable available, disposable, open *(accessible)*
secure accept *(take)*, adhere *(fasten)*, affix, arrest *(apprehend)*, attach *(join)*, attach *(seize)*, attain, bar *(hinder)*, bind *(restrain)*, bond *(hold together)*, bond *(secure a debt)*, buy, cement, certain *(positive)*, collect *(recover money)*, combine *(join together)*, conserve, convincing, cosign, cover *(guard)*, definite, derive *(receive)*, detain *(hold in custody)*, earn, educe, employ *(engage services)*, engage *(hire)*, ensconce, ensure, evoke, fetter, firm, fix *(make firm)*, fixed *(securely placed)*, gain, guarantee, handcuff, harbor, hijack, hold *(possess)*, inexpugnable, infallible, infrangible, inviolate, keep *(shelter)*, lock, maintain *(sustain)*, obtain, permanent, police, positive *(confident)*, possess, preserve, procure, protect, purchase, reap, receive *(acquire)*, recover, reliable, repossess, restrict, retain *(employ)*, retain *(keep in possession)*, safe, seal *(close)*, shut, solid *(sound)*, sponsor, stabilize, stable, steadfast, strong, succeed *(attain)*, underwrite, vouch. SEE MAIN ENTRY
secure against damage indemnify
secure against loss assure *(insure)*, indemnify, insure
secure by force constrain *(compel)*
secure exclusive control monopolize
secure exclusive possession monopolize
secure for a consideration buy, purchase
secure from capture inexpugnable, invincible
secure payment collect *(recover money)*
secure retreat asylum *(hiding place)*
secure the services of hire
secure with chains fetter
secured firm, guarded
secured by law inalienable
secured debenture security *(stock)*
securely fixed firm
securement distraint
secureness certainty, security *(safety)*
securing accession *(annexation)*
securities portfolio. SEE MAIN ENTRY
securities law blue sky law
securities oversight blue sky law
securities rules blue sky law
securities statutes blue sky law
security accommodation *(backing)*, assurance, asylum *(protection)*, bail, binder, bond, bulwark, certainty, charge *(lien)*, check *(instrument)*, cloud *(incumbrance)*, confidence *(faith)*, deposit, guaranty, handsel, hostage, hypothecation, indemnity, inviolability, letter of credit, lien, mainstay, mortgage, pledge *(security)*, precaution, preservation, protection, recognizance, refuge, reliance, safeguard, safekeeping, share *(stock)*, shelter *(protection)*, shelter *(tax benefit)*, shield, specialty *(contract)*, stock *(shares)*, undertaking *(bond)*, undertaking *(pledge)*, ward, warrant *(guaranty)*. SEE MAIN ENTRY
security against damage indemnity
security against loss coverage *(insurance)*, indemnity, insurance
security against violence inviolability
security for a debt mortgage
security officer peace officer
security on property charge *(lien)*, cloud *(incumbrance)*, lien, mechanics lien
securus safe
secus procedere miscarriage
sedare allay, assuage, lull
sedate peaceable, phlegmatic, solemn
sedateness composure, decorum, moderation
sedative drug, narcotic *(adjective)*, narcotic *(noun)*, palliative *(abating)*
sedentary inactive, torpid
sedes dwelling, foundation *(basis)*, inhabitation *(place of dwelling)*, residence, seat
sediment alluvion
seditio insurrection, mutiny, rebellion, revolt, sedition
sedition anarchy, bad faith, bad repute, defiance, disloyalty, infidelity, insurrection, mutiny, rebellion, resistance, revolt, subversion, treason. SEE MAIN ENTRY
seditionary insurgent, malcontent
seditionem rebel

seditionist malcontent
seditiosus insubordinate
seditious lawless, nonconsenting, restive. SEE MAIN ENTRY
seditiousness bad faith, disloyalty, infidelity, sedition
seduce bait *(lure)*, betray *(lead astray)*, brutalize, corrupt, entice, inveigle, lure, mislead, persuade, prevail *(persuade)*, suborn
seducement bribery, seduction
seduction debauchery, debauchment, rape. SEE MAIN ENTRY
seductive attractive, provocative, suggestive *(risqué)*
sedulity diligence *(perseverance)*, industry *(activity)*
sedulous active, diligent, faithful *(diligent)*, industrious, painstaking, patient, persistent, pertinacious, purposeful, relentless, resolute, stable, steadfast, unrelenting, unremitting, unyielding, zealous. SEE MAIN ENTRY
sedulousness diligence *(perseverance)*, industry *(activity)*
sedulus industrious, painstaking, sedulous
see apprehend *(perceive)*, comprehend *(understand)*, conceive *(comprehend)*, detect, discern *(detect with the senses)*, discover, note *(notice)*, notice *(observe)*, observe *(watch)*, perceive, pierce *(discern)*, realize *(understand)*, recognize *(perceive)*, regard *(pay attention)*, spy, witness *(have direct knowledge of)*. SEE MAIN ENTRY
see about check *(inspect)*
see as distinct discern *(discriminate)*
see at a glance discern *(detect with the senses)*
see in retrospect recall *(remember)*
see the difference diagnose, discern *(discriminate)*, discriminate *(distinguish)*
see through construe *(comprehend)*, dispatch *(dispose of)*, execute *(accomplish)*, follow-up, implement
see to attend *(take care of)*, handle *(manage)*, maintain *(sustain)*, manage, superintend
seeable appreciable, discernible, manifest, open *(in sight)*, ostensible, palpable, perceivable, perceptible, scrutable, visible *(in full view)*
seed children, embryo, inseminate, posterity, progeny
seedy poor *(inferior in quality)*
seek apply *(request)*, chase, delve, endeavor, ferret, frisk, hunt, petition, probe, pursue *(chase)*, pursue *(strive to gain)*, request, research, search, strive, trace *(follow)*, try *(attempt)*
seek a clue delve
seek accord close *(agree)*
seek advice confer *(consult)*, counsel, refer *(send for action)*
seek as due claim *(demand)*
seek by request sue
seek counsel consult *(ask advice of)*
seek facts from consult *(seek information from)*
seek guidance consult *(ask advice of)*
seek information inquire
seek information regarding investigate, probe
seek legal redress litigate
seek redress address *(petition)*
seek reexamination appeal
seek reference of a case from one court to another appeal
seek review of a case appeal
seek the opinion of consult *(ask advice of)*
seek to attempt
seek to attain pursue *(strive to gain)*
seek to persuade counsel
seeker candidate, special interest, suitor
seeking inquisitive, quest
seeking to avoid evasive
seeking to elude evasive
seeking to evade evasive
seem comport *(behave)*, demean *(deport oneself)*, pretend
seem like appear *(seem to be)*
seem to be demean *(deport oneself)*
seeming apparent *(presumptive)*, colorable *(plausible)*, constructive *(inferential)*, deceptive, ostensible, plausible, presumptive, probable, specious
seeming contradiction paradox
seemingly prima facie *(self-evident)*, reputedly
seemingly but not actually quasi
seemingly fair colorable *(plausible)*
seemingly sound colorable *(plausible)*
seemingly valid colorable *(plausible)*
seemingly worthy of acceptance plausible
seemliness conduct, decorum, expedience, propriety *(appropriateness)*
seemly appropriate, felicitous, fit, fitting, proper, right *(suitable)*, rightful, seasonable, suitable
seep exude, outflow, permeate
seep in penetrate, pervade
seepage osmosis
seer bystander, eyewitness
seesaw beat *(pulsate)*, oscillate, vacillate
seethe burn
segment chapter *(division)*, component, constituent *(part)*, cross *(intersect)*, dichotomize, disjoint, divide *(separate)*, element, factor *(ingredient)*, installment, member *(constituent part)*, moiety, parcel *(noun)*, parcel *(verb)*, part *(portion)*, partition, section *(division)*, separate, sever, share *(interest)*, split, subdivision, subheading. SEE MAIN ENTRY
segmental partial *(relating to a part)*
segmentation disassociation, division *(act of dividing)*, split. SEE MAIN ENTRY
segmentum segment
segnitia sloth
segregare seclude
segregate classify, demarcate, differentiate, dissociate, divide *(separate)*, estrange, exclude, insulate, isolate, relegate, remove *(eliminate)*, screen *(select)*, seclude, select, separate, sequester *(seclude)*, sever, sort, split. SEE MAIN ENTRY
segregated remote *(secluded)*, separate
segregation discrimination *(differentiation)*, division *(act of dividing)*, estrangement, exception *(exclusion)*, exclusion, expulsion, intolerance, ostracism, quarantine, removal, selection *(choice)*, severance, split. SEE MAIN ENTRY
seigniory domain *(land owned)*
seignorage dominion *(absolute ownership)*
seisin dominion *(absolute ownership)*, enjoyment *(use)*, holding *(property owned)*, inheritance, interest *(ownership)*, land, ownership, paraphernalia *(personal belongings)*, possession *(ownership)*. SEE MAIN ENTRY
seiunctio segregation *(separation)*
seiungere detach, isolate
seize abridge *(divest)*, adopt, annex *(arrogate)*, apprehend *(arrest)*, arrest *(apprehend)*, capture, carry away, confiscate, construe *(comprehend)*, deprive, despoil, distrain, divest, embrace *(accept)*, garnish, grapple, harry *(plunder)*, hijack, impound, impress *(procure by force)*, impropriate, kidnap, levy, loot, obsess, obtain, occupy *(take possession)*, pilfer, pirate *(take by violence)*, plunder, possess, preempt, prey, procure, purloin, receive *(acquire)*, repossess, rob, takeover, usurp. SEE MAIN ENTRY
seize again rearrest
seize and appropriate confiscate, garnish
seize as forfeited to the public treasury confiscate
seize by authority confiscate
seize by legal warrant arrest *(apprehend)*
seize for public use nationalize
seize for the government nationalize
seize from private control federalize *(place under federal control)*
seize from state control federalize *(place under federal control)*
seize legally book
seize power federalize *(place under federal control)*, usurp
seize summarily attach *(seize)*
seize the advantage beat *(defeat)*
seize wrongfully infringe
seized arrested *(apprehended)*
seized articles contraband
seized goods contraband
seizing attachment *(seizure)*, confiscatory, distress *(seizure)*
seizure adverse possession, apprehension *(act of arresting)*, appropriation *(taking)*, arrest, arrogation, disseisin, forfeiture *(act of forfeiting)*, garnishment, infringement, levy, occupation *(possession)*, onset *(assault)*, plunder, sequestration, taking
seizure and appropriation distraint
seizure and transference extradition
seizure of a privilege forfeiture *(act of forfeiting)*
seizure of private property for public use expropriation *(right of eminent domain)*
seizure of property by the government expropriation *(right of eminent domain)*
seizure of property in the public interest expropriation *(right of eminent domain)*
seizure to procure satisfaction of a debt distraint
sejunction division *(act of dividing)*
seldom happening infrequent
seldom met with scarce, uncommon
seldom occurring infrequent
seldom seen infrequent, rare
select adopt, appoint, best, cast *(register)*, certain *(specific)*, choose, compile, cull, decide, delegate, designate, digest *(summarize)*, edit, elect *(choose)*, exclusive *(limited)*, extract, inestimable, meritorious, nominate, particular *(specific)*, personal *(individual)*, prefer, preferential, premium, prime *(most valuable)*, private *(not public)*, rare, recruit, restrictive, specialize, specific, specify, valuable. SEE MAIN ENTRY
select and arrange compile
select as one's own adopt
select body elite

select boundaries locate
select few elite
select for office elect *(select by a vote)*
select jurors empanel
select passage excerpt
selected particular *(specific)*, preferable, preferential, preferred *(favored)*, select
selectee licensee, nominee *(delegate)*
selection adoption *(acceptance)*, alternative *(option)*, appointment *(act of designating)*, assignment *(designation)*, assumption *(adoption)*, choice *(alternatives offered)*, choice *(decision)*, compilation, decision *(election)*, designation *(naming)*, discretion *(power of choice)*, election *(choice)*, excerpt, manner *(kind)*, nomination, nominee *(candidate)*, option *(choice)*, patronage *(power to appoint jobs)*, poll *(casting of votes)*, preference *(choice)*, primary, referendum, volition, vote. SEE MAIN ENTRY
selection for office by vote election *(selection by vote)*
selection of words phraseology
selective adoptive, discretionary, discriminating *(distinguishing)*, discriminating *(judicious)*, disjunctive *(alternative)*, exclusive *(limited)*, particular *(exacting)*, preferential, restrictive
selectiveness particularity
selector licensor
self identity *(individuality)*
self consistent consonant
self-abasing obeisant, repentant
self-abnegation capitulation
self-absorption introspection
self-accusation confession, remorse
self-accusatory remorseful, repentant
self-accusing contrite, penitent
self-acting spontaneous
self-admiration pride
self-admiring pretentious *(pompous)*
self-applauding inflated *(vain)*, orgulous, pretentious *(pompous)*, proud *(conceited)*
self-applause pride
self-approval pride
self-assertive obtrusive
self-assurance composure, surety *(certainty)*
self-assured assertive, positive *(confident)*
self-centered inflated *(vain)*
self-centred orgulous
self-command composure, continence, discipline *(obedience)*
self-communing pensive, reflection *(thought)*
self-communion introspection
self-condemnation confession, remorse
self-condemnatory contrite, remorseful, repentant
self-condemned penitent
self-confident positive *(confident)*
self-conquest discipline *(obedience)*
self-conscious diffident, histrionic
self-consciousness embarrassment
self-consequence consequence *(significance)*
self-consistent consistent
self-contained autonomous *(independent)*
self-containment home rule
self-content complacent
self-contradiction paradox
self-contradictory illogical, impossible
self-control continence, longanimity, moderation, restraint, sufferance, temperance, will *(desire)*
self-controlled controlled *(restrained)*, dispassionate, nonchalant, patient, stoical
self-convicted contrite, penitent, repentant
self-conviction remorse, surety *(certainty)*
self-counsel introspection, reflection *(thought)*
self-criticism remorse
self-denial austerity, continence, discipline *(obedience)*, restraint, temperance
self-denouncing repentant
self-denunciatory contrite
self-derived power home rule
self-determination discretion *(power of choice)*, freedom, home rule, liberty, suffrage
self-determined autonomous *(self governing)*, nonpartisan, sovereign *(independent)*, spontaneous
self-determined being character *(an individual)*
self-directing autonomous *(self governing)*, free *(enjoying civil liberty)*, nonpartisan, sovereign *(independent)*
self-direction discipline *(obedience)*, home rule, liberty
self-discipline continence, will *(desire)*
self-disciplined stoical
self-doubt doubt *(indecision)*
self-effacing diffident, unobtrusive
self-esteem pride
self-esteeming pretentious *(pompous)*
self-evident apparent *(perceptible)*, axiomatic, certain *(positive)*, clear *(apparent)*, coherent *(clear)*, comprehensible, conspicuous, convincing, discernible, distinct *(clear)*, ostensible, palpable
self-evident proposition principle *(axiom)*
self-evident truth principle *(axiom)*
self-exaltation pride
self-examination introspection
self-existent peremptory *(absolute)*
self-explanatory comprehensible
self-flattering orgulous
self-glorification jactation, pride
self-glorifying inflated *(vain)*, orgulous, pretentious *(pompous)*
self-governed sovereign *(independent)*
self-governing free *(enjoying civil liberty)*, independent, nonpartisan
self-government freedom, home rule, liberty, suffrage
self-importance consequence *(significance)*, pride
self-important consequential *(substantial)*, inflated *(vain)*, orgulous, pretentious *(pompous)*, proud *(conceited)*
self-imposed task campaign
self-inspection introspection
self-knowledge introspection
self-lauding inflated *(vain)*, orgulous
self-legislation home rule
self-magnifying orgulous
self-mastery discipline *(obedience)*
self-possession composure, sufferance
self-praising orgulous
self-regulation discipline *(obedience)*
self-reliance home rule
self-reliant autonomous *(independent)*, independent, spartan
self-reproach remorse
self-reproachful contrite, penitent, repentant
self-reproaching remorseful
self-reproof remorse
self-reproving repentant
self-respect integrity
self-restraint austerity, composure, continence, discipline *(obedience)*, sufferance, temperance
self-rule freedom
self-ruling autonomous *(self governing)*, free *(enjoying civil liberty)*, sovereign *(independent)*
self-sacrifice philanthropy
self-satisfaction pride
self-satisfied complacent, inflated *(vain)*, orgulous, pretentious *(pompous)*, proud *(conceited)*
self-scrutiny introspection
self-seeking venal
self-study introspection
self-subsistence home rule
self-subsistent independent
self-sufficiency home rule
self-sufficient autonomous *(independent)*, insular
self-support home rule
self-supporting autonomous *(independent)*, independent
self-willed pertinacious, perverse, voluntary
selfhood identity *(individuality)*, personality
selfish illiberal, insatiable, mercenary, parsimonious, penurious, thoughtless. SEE MAIN ENTRY
selfishness greed
selfless dispassionate, liberal *(generous)*, philanthropic
selflessness largess *(generosity)*, philanthropy
selfness identity *(individuality)*, personality. SEE MAIN ENTRY
selfsameness resemblance. SEE MAIN ENTRY
sell deal, handle *(trade)*, liquidate *(convert into cash)*, persuade, trade, vend. SEE MAIN ENTRY
sell assets liquidate *(convert into cash)*
sell at the market handle *(trade)*
sell below par discount *(reduce)*
sell into slavery subjugate
sell out betray *(disclose)*, betray *(lead astray)*
seller creditor, dealer, merchant, supplier, vendor
selling alienation *(transfer of title)*
selling price price
selvedge border
semantics meaning
semaphore indicator
semasiology meaning
semblance analogy, complexion, correspondence *(similarity)*, disguise, face value *(first blush)*, facsimile, identity *(similarity)*, parity, presence *(poise)*, pretense *(pretext)*, pretext, propinquity *(similarity)*, reflection *(image)*, resemblance. SEE MAIN ENTRY
semi SEE MAIN ENTRY
seminal original *(initial)*
seminar conference, meeting *(conference)*, panel *(discussion group)*, parley
semiprocessed inchoate
sempiternal constant, continual *(perpetual)*, durable, infinite, permanent, perpetual
sempiternus indelible, perpetual
senate legislature
senator lawmaker, legislator
senatus consultum decree

send consign, delegate, deliver, dispatch *(send off)*, dispel, displace *(remove)*, project *(impel forward)*, radiate, refer *(send for action)*, remand, remit *(submit for consideration)*, remove *(transfer)*, transfer, transmit, transport. SEE MAIN ENTRY
send a final demand charge *(assess)*
send a message correspond *(communicate)*, transmit
send abroad diffuse
send an order instruct *(direct)*
send an order for call *(demand)*
send as deputy delegate
send away deport *(banish)*, dislodge, dismiss *(discharge)*, dispatch *(send off)*, displace *(remove)*, evacuate, expatriate, rebuff, relegate, repulse
send back disavow, recommit, reflect *(mirror)*, remand, restore *(return)*
send flying dispel, launch *(project)*, precipitate *(throw down violently)*
send for call *(summon)*, request, subpoena, summon
send forth cast *(throw)*, circulate, diffuse, discharge *(shoot)*, dispatch *(send off)*, emit, launch *(project)*, outpour, precipitate *(throw down violently)*, radiate, remove *(transfer)*, send
send forward redirect
send headlong impel, launch *(project)*, precipitate *(throw down violently)*
send home dispel
send money remit *(send payment)*
send off cast *(throw)*, dismiss *(discharge)*, launch *(project)*, project *(impel forward)*
send on redirect, transmit
send on a commission delegate
send on a mission delegate
send on an errand delegate
send out delegate, emit, issue *(publish)*, outpour, send
send payment remit *(send payment)*
send regrets refuse
send through the mail dispatch *(send off)*
send to an asylum commit *(institutionalize)*
send to jail arrest *(apprehend)*, commit *(institutionalize)*, confine, imprison
send to prison apprehend *(arrest)*, commit *(institutionalize)*, constrain *(imprison)*, immure, imprison, jail
send to the bottom immerse *(plunge into)*
send word communicate, inform *(notify)*
sending consignment, delivery, transmittal
sending away deportation
sending to another state for trial extradition
sending to jail commitment *(confinement)*
senescence deterioration
senescent elderly
senility caducity
senior adult, chief, principal *(director)*, superior *(higher)* SEE MAIN ENTRY
senior court appellate court
senior statesman veteran
seniority age, authority *(power)*, longevity, precedence, predominance, preference *(priority)*, primacy, priority. SEE MAIN ENTRY
sensation emotion, impression, reaction *(response)*, sense *(feeling)*, sensibility. SEE MAIN ENTRY
sensational blatant *(conspicuous)*, lurid, moving *(evoking emotion)*
sensationalism exaggeration
sense apprehend *(perceive)*, apprehension *(perception)*, competence *(sanity)*, comprehension, connotation, construction, content *(meaning)*, contents, context, detect, expedience, gist *(substance)*, import, impression, intellect, intelligence *(intellect)*, main point, meaning, perceive, perception, prudence, reaction *(response)*, reason *(sound judgment)*, sagacity, sanity, signification, spirit, substance *(essential nature)*, tenor, understanding *(comprehension)*. SEE MAIN ENTRY
sense of danger apprehension *(fear)*
sense of disgrace ignominy
sense of duty adhesion *(loyalty)*, allegiance, charge *(responsibility)*, commitment *(responsibility)*, conscience, responsibility *(conscience)*
sense of language parlance
sense of moral right conscience
sense of obligation responsibility *(conscience)*
sense of proportion perspective
sense of responsibility adhesion *(loyalty)*, honor *(good reputation)*
sense of right and wrong conscience, ethics, responsibility *(conscience)*. SEE MAIN ENTRY
sense of shame disgrace, ignominy
sense perception impression
senseless fatuous, frivolous, ill-advised, impolitic, inexpressive, insensible, irrational, ludicrous, lunatic, misadvised, non compos mentis, obtuse, opaque, puerile, unpolitic, unreasonable, unsound *(fallacious)*, vacuous. SEE MAIN ENTRY
senseless prate platitude
senseless talk jargon *(unintelligible language)*
senselessness inexpedience, insentience
senses competence *(sanity)*
sensibility cognition, perception, pragmatism, realization, reason *(sound judgment)*. SEE MAIN ENTRY
sensible colorable *(plausible)*, conscious *(aware)*, discreet, familiar *(informed)*, functional, judicial, judicious, justifiable, lucid, normal *(sane)*, perceptive, perspicacious, physical, plausible, politic, pragmatic, prudent, rational, reasonable *(rational)*, responsive, sane, sapient, solid *(sound)*, viable. SEE MAIN ENTRY
sensible to cognizant
sensibleness common sense, expedience, pragmatism, reason *(sound judgment)*, sanity
sensilis sensitive *(discerning)*
sensitive charitable *(lenient)*, circumspect, discreet, hot-blooded, moving *(evoking emotion)*, open *(persuasible)*, perceptive, receptive, responsive, susceptible *(responsive)*, susceptible *(unresistent)*. SEE MAIN ENTRY
sensitiveness discretion *(quality of being discreet)*, emotion, sensibility
sensitivity discretion *(quality of being discreet)*, insight, sensibility, understanding *(tolerance)*
sensory experience perception
sensory perception impression
sensu carere insensible, insusceptible *(uncaring)*
sensual dissolute, mundane, obscene, physical, salacious
sensuous lascivious, physical
sensus content *(meaning)*, sense *(feeling)*
sent to prison arrested *(apprehended)*
sentence adjudge, adjudication, clause, condemn *(punish)*, condemnation *(punishment)*, convict, conviction *(finding of guilt)*, decide, decree, determination, discipline *(punish)*, finding, holding *(ruling of a court)*, judge, judgment *(formal court decree)*, opinion *(judicial decision)*, penalize, penalty, punish, ruling, verdict. SEE MAIN ENTRY
sentenced blameworthy
sentencing commitment *(confinement)*, conviction *(finding of guilt)*
sententia content *(meaning)*, conviction *(persuasion)*, expression *(comment)*, holding *(ruling of a court)*, meaning, motion, opinion *(judicial decision)*, resolution *(decision)*, standpoint, tenor, verdict, vote
sententiam dicere comment
sententiosus sententious
sententious axiomatic, brief, compact *(pithy)*, incisive, laconic, pithy, proverbial, succinct. SEE MAIN ENTRY
sententious saying maxim
sententious utterance maxim
sentient conscious *(aware)*, perceptive, responsive, sensitive *(discerning)*
sentiment affection, conviction *(persuasion)*, emotion, idea, notion, opinion *(belief)*, position *(point of view)*, posture *(attitude)*, reaction *(response)*, spirit. SEE MAIN ENTRY
sentimental sensitive *(easily affected)*
sentimental attachment affection
sentimentality affection
sentinel guardian, protect
sentire perceive
sentry caretaker *(one caring for property)*, guardian, warden
separabilis severable
separable divisible, divisive, moving *(in motion)*, severable. SEE MAIN ENTRY
separable part of a certificate coupon
separare apart, detach, divide *(separate)*, part *(separate)*, separate, sever
separate alienate *(estrange)*, alone *(solitary)*, apart, bifurcate, bipartite, classify, cross *(intersect)*, cull, demarcate, detach, dichotomize, different, disaffect, disband, disconnected, discontinue *(abandon)*, discontinue *(break continuity)*, discrete, discriminate *(distinguish)*, disengage, disentangle, disjoint, disjunctive *(tending to disjoin)*, disorganize, disparate, disperse *(scatter)*, dissociate, distill, distinct *(distinguished from others)*, distinguish, divide *(separate)*, estrange, except *(exclude)*, excise *(cut away)*, exclusive *(singular)*, extract, extrinsic, foreign, impertinent *(irrelevant)*, individual, insular, insulate, interrupt, irrelative, isolate, liberate, luxate, particular *(individual)*, particular *(specific)*, private *(secluded)*, purge *(purify)*, relegate, remove *(eliminate)*, screen *(select)*, secede, seclude, sequester *(seclude)*, sequester *(seize property)*, sever, singular, sole, solitary, sort, split, sporadic, subdivide, substantive, unrelated, withdraw. SEE MAIN ENTRY
separate as different differentiate
separate existence entity
separate from quit *(evacuate)*
separate in two dichotomize
separate into categories organize *(arrange)*
separate maintenance alimony, estrangement

separate oneself retire *(retreat)*
separate oneself from part *(leave)*
separate paragraph item
separate part chamber *(compartment)*, chapter *(division)*, section *(division)*
separate ticket coupon
separated apart, bicameral, bipartite, broken *(fractured)*, disconnected, discrete, inaccessible, individual, irrelative, peculiar *(distinctive)*, remote *(secluded)*, separate, solitary, unapproachable
separately respectively
separateness difference, nonconformity, privacy
separating divergent
separatio separation
separation alienation *(estrangement)*, decentralization, dichotomy, disassociation, discrimination *(differentiation)*, dissolution *(disintegration)*, diversification, division *(act of dividing)*, estrangement, evulsion, exception *(exclusion)*, exclusion, expulsion, hiatus, liberation, ostracism, privacy, quarantine, removal, rift *(gap)*, schism, section *(division)*, selection *(choice)*, severance, split, subdivision. SEE MAIN ENTRY
separation by races segregation *(isolation by races)*
separation money alimony
separatism nonconformity
separatist heretic
separative discriminating *(distinguishing)*, distinctive
separatus distinct *(distinguished from others)*, particular *(specific)*, separate
seperate select
sept family *(common ancestry)*
septic deleterious, peccant *(unhealthy)*
sequacious passive, pliable, pliant, resilient. SEE MAIN ENTRY
sequel codicil, development *(outgrowth)*, effect, follow-up, outgrowth
sequela codicil
sequence array *(order)*, chain *(series)*, continuity, cycle, method, order *(arrangement)*, outcome, succession. SEE MAIN ENTRY
sequence of events calendar *(record of yearly periods)*
sequent consecutive, corollary, derivative, future, outcome, proximate, subsequent, successive
sequential ancillary *(subsidiary)*, consecutive, consequential *(deducible)*, continuous, ensuing, narrative, subsequent, successive
sequester attach *(seize)*, collect *(recover money)*, confiscate, deprive, distrain, exclude, garnish, impound, impress *(procure by force)*, insulate, isolate, remove *(eliminate)*, seclude, seize *(confiscate)*, withdraw. SEE MAIN ENTRY
sequestered attached *(seized)*, privy, remote *(secluded)*
sequestrate attach *(seize)*, condemn *(seize)*, confiscate, deprive, distrain, garnish, impound, impress *(procure by force)*, remove *(eliminate)*, seize *(confiscate)*, sequester *(seize property)*, withdraw
sequestrating confiscatory
sequestration attachment *(seizure)*, disseisin, distraint, distress *(seizure)*, expropriation *(divestiture)*, privation, removal, taking. SEE MAIN ENTRY
sequi pursue *(chase)*, pursue *(strive to gain)*
serendipitous beneficial
serendipity happenstance
serene complacent, patient, peaceable, phlegmatic, placid
serenity composure, peace
serere propagate *(spread)*
serial cognate, consecutive, intermittent, journal, periodic, progressive *(going forward)*. SEE MAIN ENTRY
serialization distribution *(arrangement)*, sequence
serialized consecutive
seriate classify, consecutive
seriatim consecutive
seriation hierarchy *(arrangement in a series)*
series assemblage
series chain *(series)*
series hierarchy *(arrangement in a series)*
series sequence
series serial, succession
series of events proceeding, program
series of measures process *(course)*
serious chronic, critical *(crucial)*, dangerous, dire, earnest, exigent, grave *(important)*, grave *(solemn)*, important *(significant)*, insistent, major, momentous, pensive, pernicious, persistent, pertinacious, purposeful, resolute, solemn, steadfast, urgent. SEE MAIN ENTRY
serious accident casualty
serious calamity catastrophe
serious infraction of the law crime
serious thought consideration *(contemplation)*
seriously purely *(positively)*
seriously dangerous deadly
seriousness consequence *(significance)*, contemplation, degree *(magnitude)*, diligence *(care)*, import, importance, magnitude, severity, significance, solemnity, weight *(importance)*
serius grave *(important)*, serious *(grave)*
sermo discourse, language
sermon declamation, diatribe, instruction *(teaching)*, objurgation, peroration, reprimand, speech
sermonize address *(talk to)*, declaim, discourse, inculcate, speak
serpentiform circuitous
serpentile circuitous
serpentine artful, circuitous, devious, indirect, insidious, labyrinthine, sinuous, subtle *(insidious)*, tortuous *(bending)*
serpentoid circuitous
serried compact *(dense)*, solid *(compact)*
servant employee
servantry personnel
servants personnel, staff
servare conserve, preserve
serve abet, accommodate, aid, assist, attend *(take care of)*, avail *(be of use)*, bestow, care *(regard)*, contribute *(assist)*, dispense, divide *(distribute)*, fulfill, function, help, inure *(benefit)*, obey, officiate, order, pander, perform *(execute)*, promote *(organize)*, provide *(arrange for)*, supply. SEE MAIN ENTRY
serve as exercise *(discharge a function)*
serve as a substitute succeed *(follow)*
serve in the capacity of perform *(execute)*
serve notice caution, communicate, contact *(communicate)*, notify
serve the people rule *(govern)*
serve the purpose satisfy *(fulfill)*
serve with a writ call *(summon)*
service adhesion *(loyalty)*, agency *(legal relationship)*, aid *(help)*, aid, avail *(be of use)*, benevolence *(act of kindness)*, bureaucracy, employment, fix *(repair)*, help, homage, maintain *(sustain)*, maintenance *(upkeep)*, office, post, profit, promotion *(encouragement)*, purpose, repair, reparation *(keeping in repair)*, servitude, usage, use, utility *(usefulness)*, worth. SEE MAIN ENTRY
service road causeway
serviceability means *(opportunity)*, use, utility *(usefulness)*, utilization
serviceable constructive *(creative)*, convenient, disposable, effective *(efficient)*, functional, instrumental, ministerial, operative, passable, practical, pragmatic, profitable, subservient, valuable
serviceableness worth
services agency *(legal relationship)*
serviceway easement
servicing provision *(act of supplying)*
servile dependent, ignoble, obedient, obsequious, passive, pliable, pliant, sequacious, subaltern, subservient
servilis servile
servility amenability, discipline *(obedience)*, fealty, homage
serving adequate, part *(portion)*, provision *(act of supplying)*, ration
serving as a deterrent exemplary
serving as a model exemplary
serving as a pattern exemplary
serving as a sample exemplary
serving as a warning exemplary
serving as an adjunct ancillary *(auxiliary)*
serving as an aid ancillary *(auxiliary)*
serving as an instance exemplary
serving to commemorate honorary
serving to declare declaratory
serving to distinguish distinctive
servire serve *(assist)*
servitium servitude
servitude adhesion *(loyalty)*, bondage, homage, restraint, subjection, thrall. SEE MAIN ENTRY
servitus servitude, subjection, thrall
sescenti myriad
sesquipedalian turgid. SEE MAIN ENTRY
sesquipedalian words bombast
sesquipedalianism fustian
sesquipedalism bombast
sesquipedality bombast
session caucus, chamber *(body)*, congregation, meeting *(conference)*, phase *(period)*, term *(duration)*. SEE MAIN ENTRY
session of the court forum *(court)*
sessions bar *(court)*
set adjust *(resolve)*, assemblage, assess *(appraise)*, assign *(designate)*, cement, chain *(series)*, chronic, class, confederacy *(compact)*, crystallize, customary, deposit *(place)*, designate, embed, firm, fix *(make firm)*, fix *(settle)*, fixed *(securely placed)*, formal, habitual, inexorable, ingrained, instate, inveterate, levy, locate, permanent, pertinacious, plant *(place firmly)*, positive *(prescribed)*, prescribe, prescriptive, prevalent, ready *(prepared)*, repose *(place)*, resolute, rigid, routine, situated, society, stabilize, unyielding, usual
set a figure evaluate
set a name to subscribe *(sign)*
set a price on estimate, evaluate
set a question at rest find *(determine)*
set a snare for entrap
set a task bind *(obligate)*, direct *(order)*
set a trap for ambush, dupe, ensnare, entrap, hunt

set a value on calculate, estimate, evaluate, gauge, measure, rate
set about assume *(undertake)*, endeavor, occupy *(engage)*, undertake
set above others prefer
set abroach dispel
set adrift derelict *(abandoned)*
set afloat originate
set afoot initiate
set against alienate *(estrange)*, antagonize, counter, counteract, disaffect, discourage, estrange, oppose
set an earlier date antedate
set apart allocate, characterize, choose, dedicate, demarcate, designate, devote, different, disconnected, discriminate *(distinguish)*, distinct *(distinguished from others)*, distinguish, estrange, except *(exclude)*, exclude, exempt, hoard, hold *(possess)*, insulate, isolate, label, preferred *(favored)*, relegate, remove *(eliminate)*, reserve, sacrosanct, seclude, select, separate *(adjective)*, separate *(verb)*, sequester *(seize property)*, set aside *(reserve)*, sever. SEE MAIN ENTRY
set apart as different differentiate
set apart for special use dedicate
set aright fix *(repair)*
set as a goal intend, pursue *(strive to gain)*
set aside abandon *(relinquish)*, abolish, abrogate *(rescind)*, allocate, annul, cancel, dedicate, defer *(put off)*, designate, devote, disapprove *(reject)*, disavow, discharge *(release from obligation)*, disclaim, dismiss *(put out of consideration)*, disown *(deny the validity)*, dispel, eliminate *(exclude)*, exclude, hoard, hold *(possess)*, hold up *(delay)*, isolate, leave *(allow to remain)*, negate, null *(invalid)*, null and void, override, overrule, postpone, rebuff, reject, repeal, repudiate, rescind, reserve, seclude, sequester *(seize property)*, succeed *(follow)*, supersede, vacate *(void)*, waive. SEE MAIN ENTRY
set astir foment, inspire, promise *(raise expectations)*
set asunder disconnected, dispel, dissolve *(separate)*
set at ease assure *(give confidence to)*, satisfy *(fulfill)*
set at large clear, disencumber, disenthrall, extricate, free, liberate, release
set at liberty acquit, clear, discharge *(liberate)*, disengage, disenthrall, enfranchise, extricate, free, liberate, pardon, parole, quit *(free of)*, release
set at naught counteract, disavow, lessen, minimize, misprize, underestimate
set at nought decry, disown *(deny the validity)*, spurn
set at odds alienate *(estrange)*, antagonize, disaffect
set at rest complete *(ended)*, conclude *(complete)*, dispatch *(dispose of)*, settle, through
set at variance alienate *(estrange)*, estrange
set back check *(restrain)*, constrict *(inhibit)*, delay, hinder
set before pose *(propound)*
set bounds limit
set bounds to demarcate
set by hoard
set conflagration arson
set down alight, avow, browbeat, enter *(record)*, express, formulate, itemize, note *(record)*, record, render *(deliver)*. SEE MAIN ENTRY
set down to attribute
set eyes on discern *(detect with the senses)*
set firmly embed, plant *(place firmly)*
set foot in enter *(go in)*
set for a later time continue *(adjourn)*
set form formality, matter of course, procedure
set format procedure
set forth allege, alleged, argue, assert, cite *(state)*, commence, communicate, contend *(maintain)*, declare, delineate, demonstrate *(establish)*, depict, detail *(particularize)*, exhibit, exposit, expound, express, interject, issue *(publish)*, manifest, pass *(determine)*, plead *(allege in a legal action)*, portray, posit, present *(introduce)*, proclaim, profess *(avow)*, proffer, promulgate, propose, propound, quit *(evacuate)*, reason *(persuade)*, recite, recount, relate *(tell)*, render *(depict)*, report *(disclose)*, signify *(inform)*, stated, trace *(delineate)*. SEE MAIN ENTRY
set forth evidence bare
set forth in a will testamentary
set forth in words express
set forth the character of characterize
set forth the meaning interpret
set free absolve, acquit, clear, condone, discharge *(liberate)*, disencumber, disengage, disentangle, disenthrall, dismiss *(discharge)*, dissociate, enfranchise, exculpate, exonerate, extricate, free *(relieved from a burden)*, free, liberate, palliate *(excuse)*, pardon, parole, quit *(free of)*, release, relieve *(free from burden)*, rescue, unbound, vindicate
set going create, dispatch *(send off)*, establish *(launch)*, impel, initiate, launch *(initiate)*, originate
set going again renew *(begin again)*
set guidelines organize *(arrange)*
set in remain *(stay)*
set in array organize *(arrange)*
set in motion expedite, exploit *(make use of)*, generate, impel, implement, incite, launch *(initiate)*, launch *(project)*, maintain *(commence)*, manipulate *(utilize skillfully)*, motivate, originate, preface, undertake
set in operation commence, establish *(launch)*, maintain *(commence)*
set in opposition contrast
set in order apportion, arrange *(methodize)*, classify, coordinate, distribute, file *(arrange)*, fix *(arrange)*, marshal, orchestrate, organize *(arrange)*
set in place locate, settle
set limitations constrict *(inhibit)*
set limits constrict *(inhibit)*
set little store by underestimate
set loose release, rescue
set moving impel
set no store by disbelieve, flout
set no value on decry
set of facts case *(set of circumstances)*
set of maneuvers strategy
set of questions examination *(test)*
set of rules codification, law, protocol *(etiquette)*
set of standards protocol *(etiquette)*
set of tactics program
set of terms article *(precept)*, counteroffer, settlement
set off abandon *(physically leave)*, compensate *(counterbalance)*, countervail, demarcate, differentiate, discriminate *(distinguish)*, offset, outbalance, part *(leave)*. SEE MAIN ENTRY
set off against contrast
set off by opposition contrast
set one back deter, hold up *(delay)*, impede
set one's hand and seal notarize
set one's hand and seal to certify *(attest)*
set one's name to sign
set oneself against conflict, confront *(oppose)*, disapprove *(condemn)*
set out allocate, depart, embark, leave *(depart)*, manifest, part *(leave)*, produce *(offer to view)*, quit *(evacuate)*
set out to attempt
set phrase expression *(comment)*
set purpose animus, design *(intent)*, goal, intention, objective, project
set right attune, debunk, disabuse, emend, fix *(repair)*, inform *(notify)*, rectify, redress, regulate *(adjust)*, reveal
set side by side compare, juxtapose
set store by honor
set straight disabuse, emend, inform *(notify)*, informed *(having information)*, redeem *(satisfy debts)*, reform, remedy
set terms contract
set the date date
set to brawl, fight *(battle)*
set to music orchestrate
set to rights file *(arrange)*, rectify
set to work employ *(engage services)*, engage *(hire)*, exert, exploit *(make use of)*, hire, manipulate *(utilize skillfully)*, occupy *(engage)*
set too high an estimate overestimate
set up build *(construct)*, capitalize *(provide capital)*, constitute *(establish)*, create, devise *(invent)*, establish *(launch)*, fabricate *(construct)*, frame *(construct)*, frame *(formulate)*, initiate, make, marshal, organize *(unionize)*, originate, plan, plant *(place firmly)*, structure *(composition)*
set up an inquiry analyze, canvass, delve
set up housekeeping lodge *(reside)*
set up in business capitalize *(provide capital)*, finance
set upon accost, assail, assault, earnest, oppugn, persistent
set upon with force assault, attack
set upon with violence assail, assault
set-off counterclaim, drawback
set-to affray, controversy *(argument)*, fracas
setback adversity, casualty, damper *(depressant)*, debacle, decline, defeat, delay, disadvantage, disaster, hindrance, impediment, misfortune, plight, relapse, toll *(effect)*, trouble. SEE MAIN ENTRY
setdown disgrace
setoff indemnity
setting atmosphere, case *(set of circumstances)*, posture *(situation)*, scene, site, vicinity
setting a price appraisal
setting apart appropriation *(allotment)*, dedication, discrimination *(differentiation)*, segregation *(separation)*
setting aside avoidance *(cancellation)*, repudiation
setting aside for a particular purpose dedication
setting aside of specific property levy
setting forth narration, representation *(statement)*
setting forth in words expression *(comment)*

setting free discharge *(liberation)*, emancipation, parole, release
setting the value appraisal
settle accommodate, adjudge, adjudicate, adjust *(resolve)*, administer *(conduct)*, agree *(comply)*, agree *(contract)*, arbitrate *(adjudge)*, arbitrate *(conciliate)*, arrange *(methodize)*, award, choose, close *(agree)*, compromise *(settle by mutual agreement)*, concede, conclude *(complete)*, conclude *(decide)*, decide, deposit *(place)*, determine, discharge *(pay a debt)*, dwell *(reside)*, embed, hold *(decide)*, intercede, judge, liquidate *(determine liability)*, locate, lodge *(reside)*, lull, mediate, negotiate, pacify, pay, plant *(place firmly)*, reconcile, recoup *(reimburse)*, refund, reimburse, remit *(send payment)*, remunerate, repose *(place)*, repose *(rest)*, reside, rest *(cease from action)*, return *(refund)*, rule *(decide)*, satisfy *(discharge)*, settle, stabilize, stipulate, subside, sustain *(confirm)*. SEE MAIN ENTRY
settle a debt quit *(repay)*
settle a dispute mediate
settle accounts discharge *(pay a debt)*, satisfy *(discharge)*
settle accounts with collect *(recover money)*, compensate *(remunerate)*
settle accounts with the debtors and creditors liquidate *(determine liability)*
settle amicably accommodate
settle an account quit *(repay)*
settle by authoritative decision arbitrate *(adjudge)*
settle by conciliation mediate
settle by covenant agree *(contract)*
settle by decree rule *(decide)*
settle differences arbitrate *(conciliate)*, compromise *(settle by mutual agreement)*, mediate, pacify
settle disputes negotiate
settle firmly consolidate *(strengthen)*
settle in occupy *(take possession)*
settle in advance prepay
settle in one's mind conclude *(decide)*, determine
settle on elect *(choose)*
settle on by deliberate will resolve *(decide)*
settle order on notice settle
settle terms stipulate
settle upon conclude *(decide)*, descend, determine, fund, leave *(give)*, resolve *(decide)*
settled absolute *(conclusive)*, agreed *(harmonized)*, categorical, certain *(fixed)*, certain *(positive)*, certain *(specific)*, chronic, complete *(ended)*, contractual, definite, durable, firm, immutable, incontrovertible, indefeasible, ingrained, irrevocable, necessary *(inescapable)*, prescriptive, resolute, serious *(devoted)*, situated, stable, standing, stated, steadfast, through, unalterable, unavoidable *(not voidable)*, unyielding
settled belief conviction *(persuasion)*
settled decision adjudication, holding *(ruling of a court)*
settled determination intention
settled disposition practice *(custom)*
settled judgment conviction *(persuasion)*
settled law code
settled method formality. SEE MAIN ENTRY
settled principle law, principle *(axiom)*
settled procedure method, system
settled purpose animus, design *(intent)*, objective
settled upon preferred *(favored)*
settled without appeal clear *(certain)*
settlement accommodation *(adjustment)*, accord, accordance *(compact)*, adjustment, agreement *(concurrence)*, agreement *(contract)*, alimony, alluvion, arbitration, arrangement *(understanding)*, bargain, choice *(decision)*, compensation, composition *(agreement in bankruptcy)*, compromise, concession *(compromise)*, conciliation, consequence *(conclusion)*, consideration *(recompense)*, contract, denouement, descent *(declination)*, determination, discharge *(payment)*, disposition *(determination)*, disposition *(final arrangement)*, dower, expiation, habitation *(act of inhabiting)*, habitation *(dwelling place)*, honorarium, nollo contendere, outcome, pact, pay, payment *(act of paying)*, payoff *(payment in full)*, recompense, reconciliation, refund, remuneration, reparation *(indemnification)*, restitution, satisfaction *(discharge of debt)*, treaty. SEE MAIN ENTRY
settlement by authoritative decision holding *(ruling of a court)*, opinion *(judicial decision)*
settlement by mutual agreement composition *(agreement in bankruptcy)*
settlement of an estate administration
settlement of differences conciliation
settlement of difficulties mediation
settlement of dispute mediation
settlement on account composition *(agreement in bankruptcy)*, discharge *(payment)*
settler domiciliary, habitant, inhabitant, migrant, pioneer, referee, resident
settling conclusion *(determination)*
settlings alluvion
setup content *(structure)*, device *(contrivance)*, method, order *(arrangement)*
sever break *(separate)*, detach, dichotomize, disband, discontinue *(abandon)*, discontinue *(break continuity)*, disengage, disjoint, dissociate, dissolve *(separate)*, divide *(separate)*, divorce, estrange, excise *(cut away)*, interrupt, isolate, luxate, part *(separate)*, partition, rend, separate, split, subdivide. SEE MAIN ENTRY
sever one's connections secede
sever the unity of possession partition
severable divisible, divisive, separable. SEE MAIN ENTRY
several diverse, manifold, multiple. SEE MAIN ENTRY
severally respectively
severance decentralization, dichotomy, dismissal *(discharge)*, division *(act of dividing)*, estrangement, exception *(exclusion)*, interruption, schism, separation, split. SEE MAIN ENTRY
severance of relations estrangement
severe astringent, bitter *(penetrating)*, brutal, callous, caustic, close *(rigorous)*, critical *(faultfinding)*, crucial, cruel, dictatorial, draconian, drastic, harsh, incisive, inexorable, insufferable, intense, mordacious, onerous, oppressive, pejorative, precise, relentless, rigid, scathing, serious *(grave)*, spartan, strict, trenchant, tyrannous, uncompromising, unmitigated, unrelenting. SEE MAIN ENTRY
severe censure denunciation
severe discipline austerity
severe weather SEE MAIN ENTRY
severed bipartite, broken *(fractured)*, disconnected, disjunctive *(tending to disjoin)*, separate
severence disassociation
severitas austerity, rigor, severity, solemnity
severity austerity, cruelty, oppression, violence. SEE MAIN ENTRY
severus rigid, serious *(grave)*, severe, solemn, strict
sex-ridden lascivious
sexton caretaker *(one caring for property)*
sexual abuse SEE MAIN ENTRY
sexual assault rape SEE MAIN ENTRY
sexual deviation sodomy
sexual unfaithfulness of a married person adultery
sexually abuse molest *(subject to indecent advances)*
sexually assault molest *(subject to indecent advances)*
sexual harassment SEE MAIN ENTRY
sexually impure lewd
sexually indecent lewd
sexually indulgent lecherous
sexy obscene, salacious, suggestive *(risqué)*
shabby decadent, dilapidated, inferior *(lower in quality)*, penurious, poor *(inferior in quality)*, slipshod
shabby work noncompliance *(improper completion)*
shackle arrest *(apprehend)*, constrain *(imprison)*, contain *(restrain)*, detain *(restrain)*, disadvantage, encumber *(hinder)*, estop, fetter *(noun)*, fetter *(verb)*, hamper, handcuff *(noun)*, handcuff *(verb)*, hinder, hindrance, impede, impediment, lock, obstruction, repress, restrain, restraint, restrict, trammel
shade blind *(obscure)*, camouflage, cloak, conceal, ensconce, enshroud, hide, minimum, nuance, obfuscate, obnubilate, obscuration, obscure, penumbra, phantom, plant *(covertly place)*, protect, screen *(guard)*, veil
shade into consolidate *(unite)*
shade of difference differential, nuance
shade of meaning nuance
shaded impalpable
shadiness ill repute, improbity, knavery
shading obscuration
shadow alter ego, blind *(obscure)*, cloak, conceal, damper *(depressant)*, ensconce, hide, indistinctness, nuance, obnubilate, penumbra, specter, spy, trace *(follow)*
shadowed nebulous
shadowiness indistinctness
shadowing obscuration
shadowy blind *(concealed)*, dubious, elusive, equivocal, impalpable, inconspicuous, intangible, mysterious, nebulous, obscure *(faint)*, opaque, unclear, vague
shady furtive, machiavellian, unethical
shady reputation disrepute, opprobrium, turpitude
shake beat *(pulsate)*, brandish, discompose, disturb, intersperse, jostle *(bump into)*, perturb
shake off dispel
shake one's faith deter
shake up agitate *(perturb)*, churn, discompose, disturb, perturb
shakedown blackmail
shaking trepidation
shaky diffident, insecure, precarious
shall SEE MAIN ENTRY
shallow barren, cursory, fatuous, frivolous, puerile, superficial, trivial, volatile
shallowness immateriality, insignificance

sham artifice, bogus, cloak, colorable *(specious)*, cover *(pretext)*, deceit, deception, deceptive, delusive, disguise, duplicity, evasion, fabricate *(make up)*, fake, false *(not genuine)*, false pretense, feign, fictitious, forgery, fraud, fraudulent, hoax, imitation, imposture, invent *(falsify)*, mendacious, meretricious, misrepresent, pretend, pretense *(ostentation)*, pretense *(pretext)*, pretext, prevaricate, profess *(pretend)*, recreant, role, ruse, spurious, subterfuge. SEE MAIN ENTRY
shambles havoc. SEE MAIN ENTRY
shame attaint, bad repute, defame, degradation, demean *(make lower)*, denigrate, derogate, discredit, disgrace *(noun)*, disgrace *(verb)*, disparage, disrepute, embarrass, embarrassment, expose, humiliate, ignominy, ill repute, infamy, notoriety, obloquy, odium, onus *(stigma)*, opprobrium, ostracism, reproach, scandal, stigma, sully, tarnish. SEE MAIN ENTRY
shame into browbeat
shamefacedness disgrace
shameful arrant *(onerous)*, contemptible, depraved, diffident, disgraceful, disreputable, gross *(flagrant)*, heinous, ignoble, inexcusable, inexpiable, iniquitous, nefarious, notorious, obscene, paltry, peccant *(culpable)*, profligate *(corrupt)*, reprehensible, salacious, scandalous, unseemly
shameful notoriety disgrace
shamefulness bad repute, defilement, dishonor *(shame)*, disrepute
shameless arrant *(onerous)*, brazen, contemptible, depraved, dishonest, disreputable, dissolute, flagrant, immoral, impertinent *(insolent)*, insolent, lascivious, lewd, machiavellian, notorious, obscene, outrageous, presumptuous, profane, profligate *(corrupt)*, prurient, remorseless, reprobate, salacious, scurrilous, suggestive *(risqué)*, tainted *(corrupted)*, unabashed, vicious
shamelessness temerity
shanghai abduct, carry away, kidnap
shanghaling abduction
shape body *(main part)*, build *(construct)*, color *(complexion)*, complexion, compose, condition *(state)*, configuration *(form)*, create, criterion, delineate, delineation, devise *(invent)*, dimension, fabricate *(construct)*, feature *(appearance)*, forge *(produce)*, form *(arrangement)*, form, formalize, formulate, frame *(construct)*, frame *(formulate)*, influence, make, militate, mode, motif, organization *(structure)*, pattern, phenomenon *(manifestation)*, posture *(situation)*, specter, state *(condition)*, structure *(composition)*, style, vision *(dream)*. SEE MAIN ENTRY
shape a course arrange *(plan)*, plan
shape out a course contrive
shape up crystallize, develop
shapeless disordered, indefinite, indeterminate
shapelessness confusion *(turmoil)*
shaping building *(business of assembling)*, creation, determinative
share allocate, allot, apportion, assign *(allot)*, claim *(right)*, contribute *(supply)*, convey *(communicate)*, disburse *(distribute)*, dispensation *(act of dispensing)*, dispense, distribute, divide *(distribute)*, dividend, dole, engage *(involve)*, holding *(property owned)*, interest *(ownership)*, involve *(participate)*, member *(constituent part)*, moiety, part *(portion)*, partake, participate, partition, pool, proportion, quota, ration, reciprocate, segment, split, stake *(interest)*, subdivide. SEE MAIN ENTRY
share an address cohabit
share and share alike per capita
share bed and board cohabit
share buyer customer
share grief sympathize
share in cooperate, partake, participate
share of profits commission *(fee)*
share out mete
share secrets confide *(divulge)*
share sorrow sympathize
share-out coupon
shared concurrent *(united)*, joint, mutual *(collective)*
shared among several common *(shared)*
shared by two or more common *(shared)*
shareholder contributor *(contributor)*, member *(individual in a group)*, participant. SEE MAIN ENTRY
shareholding contribution *(participation)*
sharer contributor *(contributor)*, copartner *(business associate)*, member *(individual in a group)*, participant, partner, party *(participant)*
shares securities
sharing cognate, contribution *(participation)*, distribution *(apportionment)*, division *(act of dividing)*
sharp acute, artful, bitter *(acrid tasting)*, caustic, cheat, close *(rigorous)*, cognizant, deft, distinct *(clear)*, harsh, incisive, intensive, machiavellian, mordacious, mulct *(defraud)*, perceptive, perspicacious, politic, profound *(intense)*, resourceful, responsive, sapient, scathing, severe, sly, subtle *(refined)*, trenchant, vigilant
sharp censure reprimand
sharp criticism reproach
sharp practice artifice, knavery, maneuver *(trick)*, misdoing, pettifoggery, ruse
sharp sight perception
sharp words reprimand
sharp-edged acute
sharp-sighted perspicacious
sharp-tempered fractious
sharp-witted acute, artful, perspica-cious
sharpen enhance, intensify
sharpening cumulative *(intensifying)*
sharper bettor
sharply defined precise
sharpness discretion *(quality of being discreet)*, insight, perception, propensity, rigor, sagacity, sensibility, severity
sharpness of mind judgment *(discernment)*
shatter break *(fracture)*, discompose, disintegrate, extinguish, extirpate, force *(break)*, overcome *(overwhelm)*, overthrow, rend
shattered broken *(fractured)*, disabled *(made incapable)*
shave decrease, minimize
shave off diminish
she who has expired decedent
sheaf assemblage
sheath cover *(protection)*
sheathe cover *(guard)*, ensconce, enshroud, envelop, protect, shroud
shed cast *(throw)*, denude, eliminate *(exclude)*, emit, outpour, radiate
shed light on clarify SEE MAIN ENTRY
shed light upon comment, elucidate, enlighten, explain, explicate, exposit, resolve *(solve)*, solve
shed tears over deplore
sheepish diffident
sheer absolute *(complete)*, mere, naked *(lacking embellishment)*, outright, pure, stark, thorough, unmitigated
sheer force main force
sheer power main force
sheer terror panic
sheet of flame conflagration
shell bomb, frame *(structure)*
shelling barrage
shelter asylum *(hiding place)*, asylum *(protection)*, building *(structure)*, bulwark, cache *(hiding place)*, cloak, cover *(protection)*, cover *(guard)*, dwelling, ensconce, enshroud, harbor, haven, hedge, hide, house, immure, keep *(shelter)*, lodging, maintain *(sustain)*, panoply, preserve, protect, protection, receive *(permit to enter)*, refuge, safekeeping, screen *(guard)*, security *(safety)*, shield, shroud, veil. SEE MAIN ENTRY
shelter for the afflicted asylum *(hospital)*
sheltered blind *(concealed)*, covert, guarded, immune, safe, secure *(free from danger)*
sheltering conservation, protective
shelterless helpless *(defenseless)*
shelve continue *(adjourn)*, defer *(put off)*, delay, hold up *(delay)*, postpone, pretermit, procrastinate, protract *(stall)*, reserve, retire *(retreat)*, set aside *(reserve)*, superannuate, suspend
shepherd protect
sheriff peace officer
shibboleth catchword
shield blind *(obscure)*, bulwark, conceal, conserve, cover *(protection)*, cover *(guard)*, defend, disguise *(noun)*, disguise *(verb)*, ensconce, enshroud, envelop, harbor, hedge, lodge *(house)*, maintain *(sustain)*, obfuscate, panoply, preserve, protect, protection, safeguard, save *(rescue)*, screen *(guard)*, shelter *(protection)*, veil. SEE MAIN ENTRY
shield from danger preserve
shield from injury preserve
shielded exempt, guarded, immune, impervious, safe
shielding conservation, preservation, preventive, protective
shift conversion *(change)*, convert *(change use)*, convey *(transfer)*, conveyance, digress, diversification, divert, equivocate, exchange, expedient, fluctuate, hoax, innovation, maneuver, oscillate, palter, period, phase *(period)*, pretext, prevaricate, reconversion, removal, remove *(transfer)*, replacement, ruse, stratagem, subterfuge, tergiversate, transfer, transform, transition, vacillate, vary
shift from its place displace *(remove)*
shift in topic digression
shift the blame recriminate
shifting discursive *(digressive)*, faithless, moving *(in motion)*, sporadic, temporary, variable. SEE MAIN ENTRY
shiftless idle, improvident, indolent, irresponsible, remiss, truant
shiftlessness sloth, vagrancy
shifty dishonest, disingenuous, evasive, fraudulent, furtive, machiavellian, perfidious, sly, subtle *(insidious)*, undependable, unreliable, unscrupulous, untrue, untrustworthy

shillelagh cudgel
shindy riot
shining illustrious
shining example exemplar
ship consign, deliver, dispatch *(send off)*, send, transmit, transport. SEE MAIN ENTRY
shipload cargo
shipment cargo, carriage, consignment, delivery, freight
shipments outflow
shipper carrier, dealer
shipping cargo, carriage, consignment
shirk default, disobey, fail *(neglect)*, neglect, refuse, shun. SEE MAIN ENTRY
shirk one's duty default
shirking disinclined, truant
shiver beat *(pulsate)*, break *(fracture)*, rend, split
shivered broken *(fractured)*
shoal plurality, superficial
shock bombshell, collision *(accident)*, frighten, intimidate, overwhelm, perturb, repel *(disgust)*, repercussion, stimulus, surprise, upset. SEE MAIN ENTRY
shock with sudden fear frighten
shock-proof callous
shocking arrant *(onerous)*, deplorable, disgraceful, flagrant, gross *(flagrant)*, heinous, immoral, loathsome, lurid, notorious, odious, offensive *(offending)*, outrageous, portentous *(eliciting amazement)*, reprehensible, repulsive, scandalous, unexpected
shoddiness disrepute
shoddy inferior *(lower in quality)*, poor *(inferior in quality)*, tawdry
shoot emit, inject, launch *(project)*, precipitate *(throw down violently)*, send
shoot at attack
shoot forth pullulate
shoot forward project *(impel forward)*
shoot upward expand
shooting SEE MAIN ENTRY
shop business *(commercial enterprise)*, market *(business)*, store *(business)*, trade
shop at patronize *(trade with)*
shop goods merchandise
shop with patronize *(trade with)*
shopkeeper dealer, merchant
shoplift steal
shopman dealer, merchant
shopper consumer, customer, patron *(regular customer)*
shopperson dealer
shopping center market *(business)*, market place
shopwoman dealer
shopworn stale, trite
shore margin *(outside limit)*
shore up bolster, maintain *(carry on)*
short brief, caustic, compact *(pithy)*, concise, cursory, deficient, delinquent *(overdue)*, devoid, ephemeral, impecunious, imperfect, inadequate, incommensurate, insufficient, laconic, minimal, perfunctory, petulant, poor *(underprivileged)*, scarce, succinct, transient. SEE MAIN ENTRY
short fall insufficiency
short letter note *(brief comment)*
short measure delinquency *(shortage)*, insufficiency
short of devoid, save
short of cash impecunious
short of funds impecunious, indebted
short of money destitute, impecunious, poor *(underprivileged)*
short supply dearth, deficiency, delinquency *(shortage)*, insufficiency
short version summary
short-lived ephemeral, temporary, transient, volatile
short-tempered fractious, hot-blooded, petulant
short-term acting, brief
shortage absence *(omission)*, dearth, deficiency, deficit, delinquency *(shortage)*, insufficiency, need *(deprivation)*, paucity, poverty. SEE MAIN ENTRY
shortcoming breach, decrement, defect, deficiency, deficit, disadvantage, disqualification *(factor that disqualifies)*, failure *(falling short)*, fault *(weakness)*, flaw, foible, frailty, handicap, inability, insufficiency, lapse *(expiration)*, onus *(blame)*, vice. SEE MAIN ENTRY
shorten abstract *(summarize)*, commute, condense, constrict *(compress)*, curtail, decrease, digest *(summarize)*, diminish, discount *(minimize)*, lessen, minimize, reduce, retrench. SEE MAIN ENTRY
shortened compact *(pithy)*, concise, minimal
shortening curtailment, decrease, decrement, deduction *(diminution)*
shortening of time acceleration
shortly in due course, instantly
shortness deficit, delinquency *(shortage)*, disrespect
shortness of supply need *(deprivation)*
shortsighted ill-advised, ill-judged, imprudent, misadvised. SEE MAIN ENTRY
shotgun gun
shoulder assume *(undertake)*, bear *(support)*, bolster, maintain *(sustain)*, underwrite
shout outcry
shove impact, impel, impetus, jostle *(bump into)*
shove aside avert
show adduce, appearance *(look)*, argue, bare, bear *(adduce)*, betray *(disclose)*, brandish, cite *(state)*, clarify, color *(deceptive appearance)*, demean *(deport oneself)*, demonstrate *(establish)*, denote, denude, depict, designate, detail *(particularize)*, discipline *(train)*, disinter, display, document, edify, educate, emerge, evince, exhibit, explain, expose, express, expression *(manifestation)*, flaunt, histrionics, hypocrisy, illustrate, indicate, instruct *(teach)*, manifest, manifestation, performance *(workmanship)*, phenomenon *(manifestation)*, portray, present *(introduce)*, pretense *(ostentation)*, pretense *(pretext)*, pretext, produce *(offer to view)*, prove, purport, render *(depict)*, represent *(portray)*, semblance, signify *(denote)*, specify, testify, unveil. SEE MAIN ENTRY
show a difference differentiate
show a relationship connect *(relate)*
show affinity connect *(relate)*
show an aversion discriminate *(treat differently)*
show an image reflect *(mirror)*
show as cognate connect *(relate)*
show as kindred connect *(relate)*
show bias discriminate *(treat differently)*
show by example demonstrate *(establish)*, exemplify, illustrate
show cause SEE MAIN ENTRY
show clearly prove
show clemency relax, remit *(release from penalty)*
show concern for deplore
show consideration for favor
show contempt for flout
show contrast differ *(vary)*
show correspondence compare
show courtesy defer *(yield in judgment)*
show determination adhere *(persist)*
show devotion adhere *(maintain loyalty)*
show disagreement demonstrate *(protest)*
show disapproval blame, demonstrate *(protest)*
show disrespect humiliate
show evidence cite *(state)*
show favor bestow, vouchsafe
show favor to favor
show forbearance bear *(tolerate)*
show grounds for show cause
show hostility collide *(clash)*, menace
show ill will antagonize, ill use, mistreat
show improvement develop
show in receive *(permit to enter)*
show indecision alternate *(fluctuate)*, vacillate
show indignation resent
show indirectly imply
show itself arise *(appear)*, occur *(come to mind)*
show manner comport *(behave)*
show mercy condone, palliate *(excuse)*, relent, remit *(release from penalty)*, sympathize
show mien comport *(behave)*
show no mercy persecute
show no pity persecute
show no respect minimize
show off expose, flaunt
show oneself report *(present oneself)*
show opinion publicly demonstrate *(protest)*
show opposition demonstrate *(protest)*
show phases change
show pity relax
show preference discriminate *(treat differently)*, prefer
show prejudice discriminate *(treat differently)*
show promise portend
show proof cite *(state)*
show regard for observe *(obey)*
show regret for repent
show relation connect *(relate)*
show reluctance challenge
show resemblance connect *(relate)*
show respect defer *(yield in judgment)*, honor
show signs evince
show signs of promise *(raise expectations)*
show similarity connect *(relate)*
show tenderness sympathize
show the fallacy of disprove
show the meaning of construe *(comprehend)*
show to be an abettor involve *(implicate)*
show to be analagous compare
show to be false disprove
show to be just justify
show to be similar compare
show unfair bias favor
show up emerge
show variety deviate, differ *(vary)*, fluctuate, vary
showable manifest
shower barrage, sufficiency
shower upon bestow, load
showiness pretense *(ostentation)*
showing apparent *(perceptible)*, clear *(apparent)*, demonstrative *(illustrative)*,

disclosure *(act of disclosing)*, evident, exhibit, explanation, expression *(manifestation)*, illustration, lineup, manifestation, perceivable, perceptible, proof, salient, visible *(in full view)*. SEE MAIN ENTRY
showing homage obeisant
showing lack of judgment injudicious
showing of criminal defendants lineup
showing of criminals for inspection and identification lineup
showing of possible suspects lineup
showing of suspected criminals lineup
showing poor judgment ill-judged, injudicious
showmanship histrionics
shown clear *(apparent)*, ostensible, perceptible
showpiece sample
showy elaborate, flagrant, grandiose, histrionic, inflated *(vain)*, meretricious, orotund, pretentious *(ostentatious)*, prominent, tawdry
shred iota
shrewd artful, judicious, machiavellian, perceptive, perspicacious, politic, practiced, prudent, resourceful, sapient, sensible, sly, subtle *(insidious)*
shrewd diagnosis discretion *(quality of being discreet)*
shrewdness discretion *(quality of being discreet)*, discrimination *(good judgment)*, forethought, insight, perception, prudence, sagacity, sense *(intelligence)*
shrewish fractious, petulant, querulous
shrine monument, reminder
shrink abridge *(shorten)*, commute, condense, constrict *(compress)*, decrease, deduct *(reduce)*, depreciate, depress, diminish, disoblige, ebb, erode, lessen, minimize, reduce, retreat, shirk, subside. SEE MAIN ENTRY
shrink from eschew, mistrust, shun
shrinkage curtailment, decline, decrease, decrement, deduction *(diminution)*, diminution, erosion
shrinking decrease, diffident, disinclined, hesitant, reluctant, unobtrusive
shrive clear, excuse, forgive, palliate *(excuse)*, purge *(wipe out by atonement)*, redeem *(satisfy debts)*
shrivel decay, degenerate
shriver penitent
shroud blind *(obscure)*, camouflage, cloak, conceal, cover *(conceal)*, disguise, ensconce, enshroud, envelop, harbor, hide, obfuscate, obliterate, obnubilate, obscure, plant *(covertly place)*, protect, screen *(guard)*, suppress, veil. SEE MAIN ENTRY
shrouded blind *(concealed)*, clandestine, covert, esoteric, furtive, hidden, impalpable, inconspicuous, secret, stealthy
shrouded in mystery esoteric, inexplicable, problematic
shrug off ignore
shrunk compact *(pithy)*
shuck denude
shuffle beat *(pulsate)*, bilk, equivocate, evade *(deceive)*, exchange, palter, prevaricate
shun avoid *(evade)*, default, disapprove *(reject)*, disavow, discriminate *(treat differently)*, disdain, elude, eschew, forgo, forswear, leave *(allow to remain)*, neglect, refrain, refuse, reject, repulse, shirk, spurn, stave. SEE MAIN ENTRY
shunned derelict *(abandoned)*, undesirable
shunning avoidance *(evasion)*, boycott, disapprobation, disapproval, elusive, reluctant
shunt avert, divert, set aside *(annul)*
shut blind *(impassable)*, impervious, obturate, occlude. SEE MAIN ENTRY
shut away remote *(secluded)*
shut down close *(terminate)*, conclude *(complete)*, discontinue *(abandon)*, shut
shut in bind *(restrain)*, border *(bound)*, circumscribe *(surround by boundary)*, confine, contain *(enclose)*, detain *(hold in custody)*, enclose, encompass *(surround)*, fetter, jail, keep *(restrain)*, occlude. SEE MAIN ENTRY
shut off ban, bar *(hinder)*, block, clog, occlude
shut out ban, bar *(exclude)*, barred, condemn *(ban)*, debar, discharge *(dismiss)*, eliminate *(exclude)*, exclude, lock, prohibit, relegate, restrict, seclude, select
shut up block, immure, jail, keep *(restrain)*, lock
shut-in patient
shut-off blind *(impassable)*
shutdown blockade *(limitation)*, close *(conclusion)*, halt, strike
shutter protect
shutting out renunciation
shy deficient, diffident, guarded, hesitant, insufficient, precipitate *(throw down violently)*
shy at refuse
shy away from avoid *(evade)*, shun
shy from mistrust
shy of leery
shyness reluctance
sib interrelated, relative
sibi adsumere usurp
sibylic prophetic
sibylline oracular, portentous *(ominous)*, prophetic
sick individual patient
sick person patient
sicken degenerate, disable, languish, repel *(disgust)*
sickening heinous, loathsome, objectionable, odious, offensive *(offending)*, repulsive, unsavory
sickling patient
sickly languid, powerless, unsound *(not strong)*
sickness disability *(physical inability)*, disease, disorder *(abnormal condition)*, pain, prostration
side border, choose, edge *(border)*, faction, phase *(aspect)*. SEE MAIN ENTRY
side against counter, counteract, disapprove *(reject)*, fight *(counteract)*, oppugn
side by side along, contiguous
side issue development *(outgrowth)*
side road causeway
side with concur *(agree)*, conform, cooperate, espouse, involve *(participate)*, join *(associate oneself with)*, maintain *(sustain)*, unite
side-partner consociate
sidelong indirect
sidereal stellar
sideslip digression
sidestep avoidance *(evasion)*, detour, digress, digression, parry
sidetrack digress, divert
siege assault, barrage, belligerency, invasion, onset *(assault)*, outbreak. SEE MAIN ENTRY
sieve screen *(select)*, sort
sift analyze, censor, cull, discriminate *(distinguish)*, screen *(select)*, scrutinize, select, sort, study
sifting analysis
sigh plaint
sigh for deplore
sight appearance *(look)*, detect, discern *(detect with the senses)*, notice *(observe)*, perception, phenomenon *(manifestation)*, phenomenon *(unusual occurrence)*, recognize *(perceive)*, scene, spy, witness *(have direct knowledge of)*. SEE MAIN ENTRY
sight draft check *(instrument)*
sighted perceivable, perceptible
sighting detection, discovery
sightly attractive
sigil brand, stamp
sigmoid circuitous
sign authorize, brand, brand *(mark)*, call *(title)*, clue, designation *(symbol)*, device *(distinguishing mark)*, earmark, expression *(manifestation)*, forerunner, harbinger, index *(catalog)*, indicant, indication, indicator, indorse, label, manifestation, notarize, phenomenon *(manifestation)*, precursor, premonition, seal *(solemnize)*, symbol, symptom, threat, title *(designation)*, token, witness *(attest to)*. SEE MAIN ENTRY
sign a name to subscribe *(sign)*
sign and seal notarize
sign away alienate *(transfer title)*, cede, devolve, forgo, relinquish
sign in empanel, register
sign legally notarize
sign on join *(associate oneself with)*
sign one's name on indorse
sign over alienate *(transfer title)*, assign *(transfer ownership)*, grant *(transfer formally)*, lend. SEE MAIN ENTRY
sign up employ *(engage services)*, enroll, recruit, register
signal admonition, clue, contact *(communicate)*, denote, direct *(order)*, forewarn, illustrious, important *(significant)*, indicant, indicate, indication, manifestation, material *(important)*, momentous, notable, noteworthy, notify, particular *(specific)*, peculiar *(curious)*, remarkable, symbol, symptom. SEE MAIN ENTRY
signal by which one is summoned process *(summons)*
signalize indicate
signally particularly
signatory surety *(guarantor)*, undersigned
signature call *(title)*, indicant, subscription
signboard indicant
signed contractual
signed and delivered instrument deed
signed and sealed contractual
signed notice receipt *(proof of receiving)*
signer affiant, surety *(guarantor)*, undersigned
signet brand, trademark
significance clout, connotation, construction, content *(meaning)*, degree *(magnitude)*, distinction *(reputation)*, import, importance, interest *(concern)*, magnitude, main point, materiality *(consequence)*, meaning, notoriety, point *(purpose)*, prestige, purpose, relevance, signification, spirit, stress *(accent)*, substance *(essential nature)*, tenor, validity, value, weight *(importance)*. SEE MAIN ENTRY
significant central *(essential)*, consequential *(substantial)*, considerable,

constructive *(creative)*, critical *(crucial)*, crucial, decisive, determinative, indispensable, key, major, material *(important)*, momentous, necessary *(required)*, notable, noteworthy, outstanding *(prominent)*, paramount, prominent, remarkable, salient, special, strategic, substantial, unusual, valuable
significant detail necessity
significant event landmark *(significant change)*
significant feature highlight
significant occurrence landmark *(significant change)*
significant part content *(meaning)*
significare allude, denote, express, hint, imply, indicate, portend, purport
significatio content *(meaning)*, hint, import, indication, innuendo, insinuation, intimation, meaning, significance, signification
signification assignment *(designation)*, connotation, consequence *(significance)*, content *(meaning)*, corpus, designation *(naming)*, implication *(inference)*, import, manifestation, meaning, significance, substance *(essential nature)*, symbol, tenor, title *(designation)*. SEE MAIN ENTRY
signified implied
signify allude, bear *(adduce)*, bespeak, communicate, connote, construe *(translate)*, convey *(communicate)*, denominate, denote, depict, designate, evidence, exemplify, hint, indicate, inform *(notify)*, manifest, notify, portend, predict, presage, prognosticate, promise *(raise expectations)*, purport, refer *(direct attention)*, represent *(portray)*. SEE MAIN ENTRY
signify assent acknowledge *(respond)*, concur *(agree)*
signing up registration
signit stamp
signory domain *(sphere of influence)*
signpost indication, landmark *(conspicuous object)*
signs indicia
signum stamp, symbol
silence allay, concealment, lull *(noun)*, lull *(verb)*, peace, placate, repress, stifle, stop, strangle, subdue, suppress. SEE MAIN ENTRY
silent inarticulate, mute, noncommittal, speechless, stealthy, tacit, taciturn
silentium silence
silhouette configuration *(form)*, contour *(outline)*, contour *(shape)*, delineate, delineation
sill threshold *(entrance)*
silly fatuous, frivolous, inept *(inappropriate)*, ludicrous, puerile, superficial, vacuous
silly talk jargon *(unintelligible language)*
similar akin *(germane)*, analogous, approximate, cognate, commensurable, commensurate, comparable *(capable of comparison)*, congruous, consonant, correlative, equal, equivalent, identical, pendent, same, tantamount, uniform. SEE MAIN ENTRY
similar appearance analogy
similar form analogy
similar item cover *(substitute)*
similar relation analogy
similar to comparative
similarity analogy, conformity *(agreement)*, identity *(similarity)*, par *(equality)*, parity, relation *(connection)*, resemblance, same, semblance. SEE MAIN ENTRY
similarly also
similative congruous
simile example
similis analogous, similar
similitude analogy, correlate, correspondence *(similarity)*, identity *(similarity)*, propinquity *(similarity)*, relation *(connection)*, resemblance, semblance
similitudinous comparative
similitudo analogy, resemblance
simiitude parity
simoniacal mercenary
simple coherent *(clear)*, comprehensible, credulous, elementary, facile, fatuous, genuine, household *(familiar)*, ingenuous, innocuous, lucid, mere, mundane, naive, naked *(lacking embellishment)*, narrow, nominal, obtuse, only *(no more than)*, opaque, ordinary, pellucid, puerile, pure, rudimentary, stark, unadulterated, unaffected *(sincere)*, unobtrusive, unpretentious, unsuspecting. SEE MAIN ENTRY
simple job sinecure
simple meaning connotation
simple-minded non compos mentis, obtuse, opaque, simple
simpleness credulity, ignorance
simplex candid, categorical, honest, ingenuous, naive, open *(persuasible)*, simple, straightforward, unaffected *(sincere)*, unconditional, unpretentious
simplicity credulity, honesty, ignorance, informality, opacity
simplification clarification, definition, explanation, illustration, paraphrase
simplified elementary, simple
simplify clarify, elucidate, enlighten, explain, explicate, exposit, expound, facilitate, interpret. SEE MAIN ENTRY
simplistic statement generality *(vague statement)*
simply only, solely *(purely)*
simul simultaneous
simulacrum color *(deceptive appearance)*
simulacrum deception
simulacrum disguise
simulacrum distortion
simulacrum embodiment
simulacrum imitation, semblance, sham
simulare feign, pretend
simulate copy, disguise, fake, feign, forge *(counterfeit)*, misrepresent, mock *(imitate)*, pose *(impersonate)*, pretend, profess *(pretend)*, reflect *(mirror)*. SEE MAIN ENTRY
simulated artificial, false *(not genuine)*, imitation, specious, spurious, surrogate
simulatio disguise, pretext
simulation color *(deceptive appearance)*, copy, counterfeit, decoy, disguise, fake, false pretense, plagiarism, pretense *(pretext)*, pretext, sham
simulatione pretense *(pretext)*
simulative artificial
simulatus false pretense, ostensible
simultaneity synchronism
simultaneous coincidental, collateral *(accompanying)*, concerted, concomitant, contemporaneous, instant, instantaneous. SEE MAIN ENTRY
simultaneous discharge of shots salvo
simultaneousness synchronism
simultas feud
sin guilt, misdeed, transgression, trespass, vice, wrong. SEE MAIN ENTRY
sin-laden diabolic
since thereafter
sincere candid, direct *(forthright)*, earnest, faithful *(loyal)*, fervent, genuine, honest, ingenuous, pure, reliable, scrupulous, serious *(devoted)*, simple, straightforward, true *(loyal)*, veridical. SEE MAIN ENTRY
sincerely faithfully
sinceritas honesty
sincerity candor *(straightforwardness)*, honesty, integrity, probity, truth, veracity
sincerus genuine, honest, real, simple, unadulterated
sine certamine uncontested
sine corpore immaterial
sine die SEE MAIN ENTRY
sine nomine anonymous
sine qua non center *(essence)*, cornerstone. SEE MAIN ENTRY
sinecure SEE MAIN ENTRY
sinere let *(permit)*, suffer *(permit)*
sinew prowess *(bravery)*. SEE MAIN ENTRY
sinewless languid, powerless
sinewy powerful
sinful arrant *(onerous)*, bad *(offensive)*, delinquent *(guilty of a misdeed)*, depraved, diabolic, disgraceful, immoral, iniquitous, malignant, nefarious, outrageous, peccant *(culpable)*, profane, profligate *(corrupt)*, reprehensible, reprobate, salacious, sinister
sinfulness guilt, vice
sing out proclaim
sing the praises of belaud
singe burn, deflagrate
single exclusive *(singular)*, express, individual, particular *(individual)*, particular *(specific)*, simple, singular, sole, solitary, sporadic, unilateral, unique, whole *(unified)*. SEE MAIN ENTRY
single case particular
single item entity
single out cull, differentiate, except *(exclude)*, extract, label, prefer, screen *(select)*, select
single piece entity
single-minded intense, pertinacious, purposeful, steadfast
single-mindedness adhesion *(loyalty)*, diligence *(care)*, loyalty, obsession
singled out preferred *(favored)*
singlehearted faithful *(loyal)*
singleness identity *(individuality)*, particularity, purpose, uniformity
singleness of heart loyalty
singleness of purpose diligence *(perseverance)*
singleton item
singly only, respectively, retail
singula detail
singular certain *(particular)*, certain *(specific)*, different, distinct *(distinguished from others)*, distinctive, eccentric, extraordinary, individual, infrequent, irregular *(not usual)*, nonconforming, notable, noteworthy, novel, only *(sole)*, original *(creative)*, particular *(individual)*, particular *(specific)*, peculiar *(curious)*, peculiar *(distinctive)*, personal *(private)*, portentous *(eliciting amazement)*, prodigious *(amazing)*, rare, remarkable, renowned, several *(separate)*, sole, special, unaccustomed, uncanny, uncommon, unilateral, unique, unprecedented, unusual. SEE MAIN ENTRY
singularis individual, rare, remarkable, singular, unique
singularity differential, feature *(characteristic)*, identity *(individuality)*, irregularity, nonconformity, particularity, personality, property *(distinctive attribute)*, quality *(attribute)*, quirk *(idiosyncrasy)*, speciality, specialty *(distinctive mark)*, technicality, trait

singularly particularly
sinister arrant *(onerous)*, bad *(offensive)*, blameworthy, diabolic, dire, heinous, malevolent, malignant, nefarious, odious, ominous, pernicious, portentous *(ominous)*, unfavorable, unpropitious. SEE MAIN ENTRY
sinistrous disastrous
sink decay, decrease, degenerate, depreciate, depress, ebb, immerse *(plunge into)*, invest *(fund)*, languish, subside
sink away perish
sink back relapse
sink in penetrate
sink into enter *(penetrate)*
sink to a lower condition degenerate
sinkage decline
sinking decadent, decline, decrease, depression, descent *(declination)*, relapse
sinless blameless, incorruptible, inculpable, innocent, irreprehensible, not guilty, pure, unblemished, unimpeachable
sinlessness innocence
sinner convict, offender, wrongdoer
sinning diabolic, iniquitous
sinuate circuitous, sinuous, tortuous *(bending)*
sinuated tortuous *(bending)*
sinuation involution
sinuosity complication, involution
sinuosus sinuous
sinuous circuitous, complex, devious, indirect, labyrinthine, oblique *(evasive)*, tortuous *(bending)*. SEE MAIN ENTRY
sire ascendant, author *(originator)*, generate, originate, progenitor, propagate *(increase)*, reproduce
sired in wedlock legitimate *(lawfully conceived)*
sisyphean operose
sit in conclave deliberate
sit in council deliberate
sit in judgment adjudge, adjudicate, arbitrate *(adjudge)*, decide, determine, find *(determine)*, hear *(give a legal hearing)*, judge, try *(conduct a trial)*
site building *(structure)*, circuit, habitation *(dwelling place)*, locality, location, part *(place)*, pinpoint, scene, seat, situs, venue. SEE MAIN ENTRY
sitting session
sitting room chamber *(compartment)*
situate allocate, deposit *(place)*, establish *(entrench)*, locate, lodge *(house)*, pinpoint, plant *(place firmly)*, site
situated SEE MAIN ENTRY
situated at the farthest limit extreme *(last)*
situation aspect, capacity *(job)*, career, case *(set of circumstances)*, condition *(state)*, degree *(station)*, employment, environment, experience *(encounter)*, livelihood, locality, occasion, occupation *(vocation)*, occurrence, office, perspective, plight, position *(business status)*, post, predicament, pursuit *(occupation)*, region, site, situs, standpoint, state *(condition)*, status, title *(position)*, trade *(occupation)*. SEE MAIN ENTRY
situations circumstances
situs circuit, site. SEE MAIN ENTRY
situs locality, situated, situation
sizable appreciable, considerable, major, prodigious *(enormous)*, substantial
sizableness mass *(weight)*
size arrange *(methodize)*, bulk, calculate, caliber *(measurement)*, classify, dimension, extent, magnitude, mass *(weight)*, maximum *(amplitude)*, measure, measurement, sort, space. SEE MAIN ENTRY
size up gauge
sizzle burn
skeleton capsule, configuration *(form)*, contour *(outline)*, design *(construction plan)*, foundation *(basis)*, frame *(structure)*, outline *(synopsis)*, summary
skeleton plan delineation
skeptic heretic
skeptical cynical, dubious, inconvincible, incredulous, leery, suspicious *(distrustful)*. SEE MAIN ENTRY
skepticalness doubt *(suspicion)*, incredulity, misgiving
skepticism cloud *(suspicion)*, doubt *(suspicion)*, incredulity, misgiving, qualm, reluctance, suspicion *(mistrust)*
sketch abridge *(shorten)*, abridgment *(condensation)*, blueprint, brief, capsule, contour *(outline)*, contrive, delineate, delineation, depict, description, design *(construction plan)*, draw *(depict)*, frame *(construct)*, frame *(formulate)*, indicate, narration, outline *(synopsis)*, portray, program, prospectus, render *(depict)*, scenario, story *(narrative)*, trace *(delineate)*
sketch in outline delineate
sketch out arrange *(plan)*, delineate, devise *(invent)*
sketchy deficient, inchoate, partial *(relating to a part)*, perfunctory, unclear
skewer penetrate, pierce *(lance)*
skill ability, capacity *(aptitude)*, competence *(ability)*, discretion *(quality of being discreet)*, efficiency, experience *(background)*, facility *(easiness)*, faculty *(ability)*, gift *(flair)*, knowledge *(learning)*, performance *(workmanship)*, potential, propensity, prowess *(ability)*, qualification *(fitness)*, science *(technique)*, specialty *(special aptitude)*. SEE MAIN ENTRY
skilled competent, deft, efficient, expert, facile, familiar *(informed)*, learned, literate, practiced, professional *(trained)*, proficient, qualified *(competent)*, veteran
skilled hand expert, specialist
skilled in commerce commercial
skilled laborer artisan
skilled occupation career
skilled person specialist
skilled practitioner expert, professional, specialist
skilled technician professional
skilled worker artisan, specialist
skillful artful, capable, competent, deft, effective *(efficient)*, efficient, expert, facile, familiar *(informed)*, practiced, professional *(trained)*, proficient, qualified *(competent)*, resourceful, sciential, subtle *(refined)*, tactical
skillful in handling others diplomatic
skillful management strategy
skillful treatment management *(judicious use)*
skillfulness competence *(ability)*, efficiency, experience *(background)*, faculty *(ability)*, gift *(flair)*, performance *(workmanship)*, prowess *(ability)*, science *(technique)*, specialty *(special aptitude)*
skim border *(approach)*, read, review
skimpy deficient, marginal, petty, scarce
skin denude
skin-deep superficial
skip ignore, neglect, omit, pretermit
skirmish affray, collision *(dispute)*, commotion, confront *(oppose)*, confrontation *(altercation)*, contend *(dispute)*, contest *(dispute)*, disaccord, fight *(battle)*, fight *(battle)*, fray
skirt border, border *(approach)*, detour, digress, embrace *(encircle)*, margin *(outside limit)*, outline *(boundary)*
skirting circuitous
skirts confines, edge *(border)*, periphery
skittish restive
skulduggery bunko, knavery
skulk lurk, prowl
skulking recreant, sly, stealthy
skyrocket increase
skyscraper edifice
slab part *(portion)*
slack careless, derelict *(negligent)*, indolent, languid, lax, negligent, otiose, remiss, truant
slack off subside
slacken alleviate, commute, decrease, delay, ease, hold up *(delay)*, impede, lessen, moderate *(temper)*, pause, relax, subdue, subside
slackening mollification
slackness informality, laxity, neglect, negligence, sloth
slake allay, assuage, satisfy *(fulfill)*, soothe
slam beat *(strike)*
slam into collide *(crash against)*
slander aspersion, defamation, defame, denigrate, disparage, libel, malign, smear, tarnish, vilification. SEE MAIN ENTRY
slanderous calumnious, derogatory
slant aspect, character *(personal quality)*, complexion, favoritism, inclination, intolerance, misrepresent, outlook, perspective, position *(point of view)*, prejudice *(preconception)*, prejudice *(influence)*, side, stand *(position)*, tendency. SEE MAIN ENTRY
slanted inclined, one-sided, prejudicial
slanting oblique *(slanted)*
slap beat *(strike)*, lash *(strike)*, strike *(assault)*
slapp suit SEE MAIN ENTRY
slapdash cursory, superficial
slash commute, decrease, deduct *(reduce)*, lancinate, minimize, rebate, rend, split
slash prices discount *(reduce)*
slashing incisive, mordacious
slate docket, lash *(attack verbally)*, program, punish, rebuke, reprehend, reproach, set down
slatternly sordid
slaughter aberemurder, dispatch *(put to death)*, eliminate *(eradicate)*, extinguish, homicide, kill *(murder)*, killing, slay
slaughtering killing, lethal
slaughterous deadly, fatal
slave captive
slavery bondage, captivity, restraint, servitude, subjection, thrall
slavish loyal, obsequious, pliable, pliant, sequacious, servile, subservient
slavishness bondage
slay destroy *(efface)*, dispatch *(put to death)*, execute *(sentence to death)*, extinguish, kill *(murder)*. SEE MAIN ENTRY
slaying aberemurder, assassination, homicide, killing
sleave involution
sleazy poor *(inferior in quality)*, tawdry
sleep repose *(rest)*
sleep at lodge *(reside)*
sleeping dormant
sleepless industrious
sleepy torpid

sleight false pretense, imposture, maneuver *(trick)*
sleight of hand prestidigitation
sleightful delusive, evasive
slender insubstantial, insufficient, minimal, slight, subtle *(refined)*, tenuous
slender means poverty
sleuth research, spy
slice part *(portion)*, ration, rend, segment, share *(interest)*, split
slick deft, machiavellian
slide ebb
slide back relapse
slight affront, aspersion, bad repute, brief, contemn, de minimus, deficient, delinquency *(failure of duty)*, depreciate, discommend, discount *(disbelieve)*, disdain, disoblige, disparage, disregard *(lack of respect)*, disrespect, flout, frivolous, humiliate, ignore, impalpable, inappreciable, inconsequential, inconsiderable, insubstantial, insufficient, lessen, minimal, minimize, minor, misprize, neglect *(noun)*, neglect *(verb)*, negligible, nominal, nonsubstantial *(not sturdy)*, nugatory, offend *(insult)*, omit, paltry, pardonable, petty, pretermit, rebuff *(noun)*, rebuff *(verb)*, reject, rejection, remote *(small)*, spurn, superficial, tenuous, trivial, underestimate. SEE MAIN ENTRY
slight change modification
slight indication hint
slight mention hint
slight trace suggestion
slighting calumnious, contemptuous, derogatory, pejorative
slighting language disparagement
slim insubstantial, insufficient, minimal, remote *(small)*, slight, trivial
sling project *(impel forward)*
slink lurk, prowl
slink away shirk
slip coupon, delinquency *(failure of duty)*, deviate, ebb, err, error, failure *(falling short)*, fault *(mistake)*, indiscretion, label, lapse *(expiration)*, lapse *(fall into error)*, miscalculate, miscue, misdeed, misdoing, misstatement, omission, oversight *(carelessness)*, receipt *(proof of receiving)*, transgression
slip and fall case SEE MAIN ENTRY
slip away elude, escape, leave *(depart)*, move *(alter position)*, retreat
slip away from abandon *(physically leave)*
slip back ebb, escheat, recidivate, relapse
slip from virtue lapse *(fall into error)*
slip into penetrate
slip off move *(alter position)*
slip out elude, evade *(elude)*
slip up miscalculate, mistake
slippery deceptive, elusive, evasive, insecure, machiavellian, perfidious, precarious, sly, undependable, untrustworthy
slipshod careless, cursory, inaccurate, lax, negligent. SEE MAIN ENTRY
slipshodness disorder *(lack of order)*
slit lancinate, sever, split *(noun)*, split *(verb)*
sliver minimum
slivered broken *(fractured)*
slogan catchword, phrase
sloping oblique *(slanted)*
sloppiness laxity
sloppy careless, repulsive, slipshod
slot split
sloth inaction, inertia, languor, laxity, neglect. SEE MAIN ENTRY
slothful idle, inactive, indolent, lax, lifeless *(dull)*, negligent, otiose, remiss, truant
slough denude, jettison
slovenliness laxity, neglect
slovenly disorderly, lax, negligent, slipshod, sordid
slow check *(restrain)*, constrict *(inhibit)*, delay, deliberate, hesitant, languid, late *(tardy)*, obtuse, otiose, phlegmatic, torpid. SEE MAIN ENTRY
slow down alleviate, check *(restrain)*, delay, diminish, encumber *(hinder)*, hinder, impede, moderate *(temper)*, obstruct, prolong
slow in understanding opaque
slow motion languor
slow pace languor
slow to believe inconvincible, incredulous
slow to take offense peaceable
slow up delay, hold up *(delay)*
slow-moving deliberate, ponderous
slow-paced deliberate
slow-wittedness opacity
slowed down arrested *(checked)*
slowing down decrease
slowness delay, hesitation, languor, opacity
slug beat *(strike)*
sluggish despondent, inactive, indolent, languid, lax, lifeless *(dull)*, otiose, phlegmatic, ponderous, stagnant, torpid
sluggishness inaction, inertia, languor, sloth
slumber repose *(rest)*
slumbering dormant
slumberous narcotic
slump decline, decrease *(noun)*, decrease *(verb)*, depress, depression, languish
slur aspersion, brand *(stigmatize)*, contemn, defamation, defame, denounce *(condemn)*, denunciation, depreciate, discommend, discredit, disgrace *(noun)*, disgrace *(verb)*, dishonor *(shame)*, dishonor *(deprive of honor)*, disparage, ignominy, libel *(noun)*, libel *(verb)*, malign, notoriety, obloquy, onus *(stigma)*, opprobrium, reproach, scandal, slander, smear, spurn, stigma, sully, tarnish. SEE MAIN ENTRY
slur over ignore, minimize
slush fund hush money
sly artful, covert, deceptive, devious, disingenuous, furtive, insidious, machiavellian, mendacious, secret, stealthy, subtle *(insidious)*, unscrupulous. SEE MAIN ENTRY
slyness artifice, evasion, indirection *(deceitfulness)*, knavery
smack beat *(strike)*
small brief, deficient, impalpable, inappreciable, inconsiderable, minimal, minor, negligible, nominal, null *(insignificant)*, paltry, petty, remote *(small)*, slight, tenuous, trivial. SEE MAIN ENTRY
small amount iota, minimum, modicum, scintilla
small cavity cell
small chance improbability
small group minority *(outnumbered group)*
small hope improbability
small number minority *(outnumbered group)*, paucity
small parcel of land lot
small part member *(constituent part)*, segment
small percentage minority *(outnumbered group)*
small proportion minority *(outnumbered group)*
small quantity iota, minimum, minority *(outnumbered group)*, modicum, paucity, scintilla
small room cell
small-minded parochial, parsimonious, provincial
smaller minor
smaller group minority *(outnumbered group)*
smaller part minority *(outnumbered group)*
smallest minimal
smallness inconsequence, insignificance
smallness of number dearth
smart omniscient, rapid, resourceful. SEE MAIN ENTRY
smarten embellish
smarting bitter *(penetrating)*, painful
smartness perception, sagacity, sense *(intelligence)*
smash break *(fracture)*, debacle, defeat, extirpate, force *(break)*, obliterate, spoil *(impair)*, strike *(assault)*, strike *(collide)*, subdue
smash into collide *(crash against)*
smash up collide *(clash)*
smear attaint, brand *(stigmatize)*, contemn, deface, defacement, defamation, defame, denigrate, denounce *(condemn)*, denunciation, disgrace, dishonor *(shame)*, dishonor *(deprive of honor)*, disparage, libel *(noun)*, libel *(verb)*, malign, pillory, slander, spread, stain, stigma, sully, tarnish, vilification. SEE MAIN ENTRY
smearing calumnious, defilement, pejorative
smelt burn
smirch attaint, brand, brand *(stigmatize)*, defamation, defame, denigrate, derogate, disgrace *(noun)*, disgrace *(verb)*, dishonor *(deprive of honor)*, ignominy, infect, malign, onus *(stigma)*, opprobrium, pillory, pollute, shame, smear, stain, stigma, sully, tarnish
smirched tainted *(contaminated)*
smite beat *(strike)*, harm, impress *(affect deeply)*, kill *(murder)*, lash *(strike)*, plague, punish, strike *(assault)*
smoke out expose
smoke screen disguise, subterfuge
smokiness indistinctness
smoky indistinct
smolder burn
smoldering dormant
smooth allay, alleviate, deft, facile, facilitate, help, machiavellian, moderate *(temper)*, mollify, pacify, placate, placid, practiced, soothe. SEE MAIN ENTRY
smooth over disarm *(set at ease)*
smoothe expedite
smoothly diplomatic, readily
smoothness facility *(easiness)*, uniformity
smother assuage, extinguish, hamper, inhibit, prohibit, repress, stifle, strangle, subdue, suppress, withhold
smudge brand *(stigmatize)*, deface, defacement, onus *(stigma)*, stain, sully, tarnish
smug complacent, pretentious *(pompous)*
smuggle hide
smuggled commerce contraband
smuggled goods contraband
smuggled trade contraband

smuggled traffic contraband
smuggler bootlegger, criminal
smugness pride
smut obscenity, pornography
smutch onus *(stigma)*
smuttiness obscenity
smutty profane, prurient, salacious, suggestive *(risqué)*
snag block, complex *(entanglement)*, damper *(stopper)*, entanglement *(confusion)*, impediment, obstacle, obstruct, obstruction, snarl, trouble
snakelike circuitous, tortuous *(bending)*
snaky circuitous, malevolent, sinuous
snap impulsive *(rash)*, rend, split, spontaneous, unpremeditated
snap back retort
snappish fractious, perverse, petulant
snappy expeditious, petulant
snare ambush, artifice, bait *(lure)*, deceive, deception, ensnare, entrap, hunt, inveigle, mislead, pitfall, ruse, trap *(noun)*, trap *(verb)*
snaring bribery
snarl altercation, complex *(entanglement)*, confuse *(create disorder)*, entanglement *(confusion)*, involution, perplex, perturb. SEE MAIN ENTRY
snarled complex, inextricable, labyrinthine, problematic
snarling perverse, petulant
snatch hijack, kidnap, poach, purloin, steal, trap
snatching appropriation *(taking)*, distress *(seizure)*
sneak cloak, deceive, lurk, prowl
sneak and peek warrant SEE MAIN ENTRY
sneak off escape
sneak thief burglar, criminal
sneakiness deceit, fraud
sneaking clandestine, devious, furtive, machiavellian, perfidious, recreant, sly, stealthy
sneaky covert, deceptive, evasive, fraudulent, furtive, lying, machiavellian, perfidious, sly, stealthy, surreptitious
sneer disdain, disparage, disrespect, flout, humiliate, jeer, mock *(deride)*, ridicule, spurn
sneer at denigrate, derogate, discommend, disdain, minimize, misprize
sneering cynical, disdainful
snicker mock *(deride)*
snigger mock *(deride)*
sniggering ridicule
snobbery pride
snobbish disdainful, exclusive *(limited)*, pretentious *(pompous)*
snobby disdainful, exclusive *(limited)*
snoop spy *(noun)*, spy *(verb)*
snooper spy *(noun)*
snooty disdainful
snowy clean
snub affront, curb, disdain, disregard *(lack of respect)*, disregard, disrespect, humiliate, ignore, offend *(insult)*, ostracism, rebuff *(noun)*, rebuff *(verb)*, reject, rejection, repulse, shun, spurn
snuff out obliterate, stifle, strangle
so-called ostensible, purported, specious
so-so mediocre
soak imbue, immerse *(plunge into)*, overload, permeate, pervade
soak through penetrate
soaked full
sober deliberate, disconsolate, discriminating *(judicious)*, earnest, grave *(solemn)*, lucid, major, moderate *(temper)*, objective, peaceable, pensive, phlegmatic, prudent, rational, sane, sensible, serious *(grave)*, solemn
sober-minded sane
sober-mindedness common sense
sobered penitent
soberness solemnity, temperance
sobriety common sense, continence, deliberation, moderation, reason *(sound judgment)*, sagacity, solemnity, temperance
sobriquet call *(title)*, cognomen. SEE MAIN ENTRY
sociable amicable, harmonious
social civil *(public)*, public *(affecting people)*
social adjustment civilization
social behavior conduct
social climber philistine
social code decorum
social conduct decorum
social elevation civilization
social graces conduct, decorum
social group public, sodality
social procedures decorum
social rank class
social responsibility obligation *(duty)*
social security SEE MAIN ENTRY
social status class
social usage custom, decorum
socialize nationalize
societal civil *(public)*, national, public *(affecting people)*
societas association *(connection)*, combination, company *(assemblage)*, confederacy *(compact)*, league, partnership, syndicate
societas clandestina cabal
society chamber *(body)*, civilization, coalition, community, confederacy *(compact)*, institute, league, nationality, populace, population, public, sodality. SEE MAIN ENTRY
socius associate, consort, partner
socius criminis accessory, accomplice, cohort, colleague, copartner *(coconspirator)*
sodalis associate
sodalitas facility *(institution)*, foundation *(organization)*, institute
sodality body *(collection)*, cartel, coalition, corporation, league, organization *(association)*, partnership, society, union *(labor organization)*. SEE MAIN ENTRY
sodomy SEE MAIN ENTRY
soft charitable *(lenient)*, flexible, lenient, malleable, pliant, yielding. SEE MAIN ENTRY
soft job sinecure
soften allay, alleviate, assuage, commute, ease, extenuate, give *(yield)*, mitigate, moderate *(temper)*, modify *(moderate)*, mollify, obtund, palliate *(abate)*, propitiate, relax, relent, remit *(relax)*, soothe, subdue
softened malleable
softening mitigating, mitigation, mollification, palliative *(abating)*
softening circumstances extenuating circumstances
softhearted benevolent, charitable *(lenient)*, lenient, placable, sensitive *(easily affected)*
softheartedness benevolence *(disposition to do good)*, lenience
softness lenience, mollification
soil brand *(stigmatize)*, debase, deface, denigrate, depreciate, disgrace, infect, onus *(stigma)*, pervert, pillory, pollute, smear, stain, sully, taint *(contaminate)*, tarnish
soiled blemished, tainted *(contaminated)*
soiling defacement
sojourn dwell *(reside)*, habitation *(act of inhabiting)*, inhabit, inhabitation *(act of dwelling in)*, lodge *(reside)*, reside, stop
sojourner denizen, habitant, inhabitant, lodger, occupant, resident
sojournment habitation *(act of inhabiting)*, presence *(attendance)*
solace alleviate, assuage, assure *(give confidence to)*, benefit *(betterment)*, reassure, sympathize. SEE MAIN ENTRY
solatium compensation, consideration *(recompense)*, expiation, pay, payment *(remittance)*, recompense, reward, satisfaction *(discharge of debt)*
solatium solace
solatium trover
solder cement, connect *(join together)*
soldier-like spartan
soldierly heroic, spartan
soldiership strategy
sole exclusive *(singular)*, individual, singular, solitary, unique. SEE MAIN ENTRY
sole control of a commodity monopoly
solecism catachresis, irregularity, misuse
solecistic anomalous, faulty, incorrect
solecistical faulty, incorrect
solely only. SEE MAIN ENTRY
solemn critical *(crucial)*, earnest, important *(significant)*, major, sacrosanct, serious *(grave)*. SEE MAIN ENTRY
solemn affirmation affidavit, affirmation, averment, oath
solemn agreement testament
solemn appropriation dedication
solemn assertion assurance, vow
solemn averment affirmance *(legal affirmation)*, affirmation, asseveration, attestation, avouchment, confirmation, declaration, surety *(certainty)*
solemn avowal adjuration, affirmance *(legal affirmation)*, affirmation, asseveration, attestation, avouchment, confirmation, declaration, oath, surety *(certainty)*
solemn declaration affirmation, asseveration, attestation, avouchment, certification *(attested copy)*, commitment *(responsibility)*, confirmation, deposition, jurat, oath, pledge *(binding promise)*, surety *(certainty)*, vow
solemn entreaty call *(appeal)*, prayer
solemn feeling solemnity
solemn invocation oath
solemn mockery blasphemy
solemn observance ceremony
solemn promise assurance, testament, vow
solemn request petition
solemn word pledge *(binding promise)*
solemn writing instrument *(document)*
solemnity ceremony, formality, importance. SEE MAIN ENTRY
solemnization ceremony, remembrance *(commemoration)*
solemnize formalize, keep *(fulfill)*
solemnly affirm avouch *(avow)*, certify *(attest)*
solemnly promise assure *(insure)*
solemnly request petition
solicit apply *(request)*, bait *(lure)*, call *(appeal to)*, desire, importune, inquire, lobby, petition, plead *(implore)*, pray, pressure, pursue *(strive to gain)*, request, urge. SEE MAIN ENTRY

solicitation SEE MAIN ENTRY
solicit earnestly importune
solicit insistently bait *(harass)*, importune
solicit votes lobby
solicitant applicant *(petitioner)*, claimant, petitioner
solicitation call *(appeal)*, dun, entreaty, instigation, invitation, persuasion, request, seduction
solicitor advocate *(counselor)*, agent, attorney, barrister, claimant, counsel, counselor, esquire, jurist, lawyer, petitioner, practitioner, procurator, representative *(proxy)*, special interest, suitor. SEE MAIN ENTRY
solicitorial forensic, juridical
solicitors bar *(body of lawyers)*
solicitous benevolent, interested, protective, zealous. SEE MAIN ENTRY
solicitousness benevolence *(disposition to do good)*, consideration *(sympathetic regard)*
solicitude benevolence *(disposition to do good)*, concern *(interest)*, consideration *(sympathetic regard)*, interest *(concern)*, precaution
solid authentic, axiomatic, bodily, cogent, cohesive *(compact)*, compact *(dense)*, compound, concrete, corporeal, dependable, firm, fixed *(securely placed)*, indomitable, inflexible, infrangible, intact, material *(physical)*, meritorious, ossified, secure *(sound)*, sound, stable, staunch, strong, substantive, tangible, unyielding, valid, well-grounded, whole *(undamaged)*. SEE MAIN ENTRY
solid substance corpus
solid vote consensus
solidarity coaction, conciliation, confederacy *(compact)*, corpus, integration *(assimilation)*, merger
solidification adhesion *(affixing)*, agglomeration, coalescence, congealment, consolidation
solidified compact *(dense)*, concrete, ossified, solid *(compact)*
solidify amalgamate, cement, cohere *(adhere)*, consolidate *(strengthen)*, consolidate *(unite)*, crystallize, establish *(entrench)*, fix *(make firm)*, unite. SEE MAIN ENTRY
solidity certainty, common sense, congealment, density, materiality *(physical existence)*, strength
solidness congealment
solidus concrete, durable, firm, solid *(sound)*
soliloquize recite
soliloquy peroration
solitariness privacy
solitary derelict *(abandoned)*, exclusive *(singular)*, individual, insular, nonconforming, only *(sole)*, private *(secluded)*, remote *(secluded)*, separate, sole. SEE MAIN ENTRY
solitary abode cell
solitude privacy
solitudo privacy
solitus accustomed *(customary)*, typical
sollemnis periodic
sollers resourceful
sollertia skill
sollicitare harass, molest *(annoy)*, perplex, pique
sollicitudo concern *(interest)*, misgiving, trouble
sollicitus solicitous
solo alone *(solitary)*, apart, solitary
soluble solvable
solus apart, sole, solitary
solutio solution *(answer)*
solution conclusion *(determination)*, denouement, determination, disposition *(determination)*, explanation, finding, opinion *(judicial decision)*, outcome, panacea, remedy *(legal means of redress)*. SEE MAIN ENTRY
solution to difficulties panacea
solutus exempt, free *(not restricted)*, independent
solvable determinable *(ascertainable)*. SEE MAIN ENTRY
solve adjust *(resolve)*, ascertain, construe *(comprehend)*, elucidate, explain, expound, find *(discover)*, interpret, remedy, settle. SEE MAIN ENTRY
solvent solid *(sound)*, solution *(substance)*. SEE MAIN ENTRY
solvere annul, defray, disburse *(pay out)*, disengage, free
somatic bodily, corporal, physical, tangible
somatical bodily
somber bleak *(not favorable)*, bleak *(severely simple)*, despondent, disconsolate, grave *(solemn)*, lifeless *(dull)*, lugubrious, ominous, portentous *(ominous)*, solemn. SEE MAIN ENTRY
sombrous bleak *(not favorable)*, bleak *(severely simple)*
some several *(plural)*
somebody character *(an individual)*, person
someone character *(an individual)*, person
something added appurtenance, augmentation
something constructively affixed to real property fixture
something equivalent quid pro quo
something for something quid pro quo
something immovable from realty fixture
something like cognate, pendent
something of value consideration *(recompense)*
something over and above bonus
something owed due
something owing mortgage
something physically annexed to realty fixture
something produced by capital income
something to be imitated example
somewhat fairly *(moderately)*, in part
somewhere about on or about
somnifacient narcotic
somniferous narcotic
somnific narcotic
somnolence languor
somnolency languor
somnolent torpid
sonitus noise
sonorous orotund, resounding, sesquipedalian
sons progeny
soon in due course, instantly
soon to be prospective
soon to happen prospective
sooner than due premature
sooner than intended premature
soothe allay, alleviate, assuage, cure, lessen, lull, moderate *(temper)*, mollify, pacify, placate, propitiate, relieve *(give aid)*, remedy, remit *(relax)*, sympathize. SEE MAIN ENTRY
soother narcotic
soothing medicinal, mitigation, mollification, narcotic, palliative *(abating)*, placid, remedial
soothsay predict, presage, prognosticate
sop bribe, gratuity *(bribe)*
sophism fallacy, non sequitur
sophistic deceptive, ill-founded, illogical, illusory, incorrect, specious. SEE MAIN ENTRY
sophistical deceptive, fallacious, ill-founded, illogical, illusory, incorrect, sophistic, specious, subtle *(insidious)*, unsound *(fallacious)*
sophistical excuse evasion
sophisticate denature, evade *(deceive)*, expert, mislead, pervert, prevaricate, veteran
sophisticated elegant, practiced, subtle *(refined)*, veteran. SEE MAIN ENTRY
sophistication civilization, experience *(background)*, perversion
sophistry casuistry, fallacy, non sequitur, subterfuge. SEE MAIN ENTRY
sophomoric inexperienced
soporiferous narcotic
soporific drug, narcotic *(adjective)*, narcotic *(noun)*, pedestrian
sorcery prestidigitation
sordid penurious, poor *(inferior in quality)*. SEE MAIN ENTRY
sordidus illiberal, sordid
sore bitter *(penetrating)*, pain, painful, resentful
soreness pain, resentment, umbrage
sorosis sodality
sorriness remorse
sorrow distress *(anguish)*, pain, plaint, remorse, tragedy. SEE MAIN ENTRY
sorrow for regret
sorrow over deplore
sorrowful bitter *(reproachful)*, contrite, deplorable, despondent, disconsolate, grave *(solemn)*, lamentable, lugubrious, penitent, pessimistic, remorseful, repentant
sorrowfulness pessimism
sorry contrite, deplorable, ignoble, lamentable, nonsubstantial *(not sturdy)*, paltry, penitent, poor *(inferior in quality)*, remorseful, repentant
sorry plight predicament
sors capital, lottery, principal *(capital sum)*
sort class, classify, codify, distribute, file *(arrange)*, fix *(arrange)*, form *(arrangement)*, kind, manner *(kind)*, organize *(arrange)*, pigeonhole, screen *(select)*, tabulate. SEE MAIN ENTRY
sort out cull, diagnose, differentiate, discriminate *(distinguish)*, fix *(arrange)*, part *(separate)*, select
sort systematically fix *(arrange)*
sortable applicable, fit
sortie affray, incursion
sortitio lottery
sottish drunk
sought after popular
soul center *(essence)*, consequence *(significance)*, essence, person, personality, spirit, substance *(essential nature)*
soul-searching contrite
soul-stirring profound *(intense)*
soulless cold-blooded
sound authentic, cogent, communicate, credible, defensible, discriminating *(judicious)*, durable, fiduciary, firm, fixed

(securely placed), honest, indomitable, intact, intonation, inviolate, judicious, juridical, justifiable, legitimate *(rightful),* licit, logical, lucid, meritorious, noise, normal *(sane),* persuasive, phrase, plausible, positive *(incontestable),* pragmatic, pronounce *(speak),* rational, reasonable *(rational),* reliable, safe, sane, scrupulous, secure *(sound),* sensible, stable, staunch, strong, thorough, true *(authentic),* unblemished, undeniable, utter, valid, viable, well-grounded. SEE MAIN ENTRY
sound bite SEE MAIN ENTRY
sound forth proclaim
sound judgment discretion *(quality of being discreet),* expedience
sound mind competence *(sanity)*
sound moral principle integrity
sound out inquire
sound perception common sense
sound reasoning discretion *(quality of being discreet),* discrimination *(good judgment).* SEE MAIN ENTRY
sound sense common sense
sound stewardship economy *(frugality)*
sound the alarm alert, caution
sound thinking pragmatism
sound understanding common sense, sanity
sounded oral
sounding resounding
soundless mute, speechless
soundlessness lull, silence
soundmindedness competence *(sanity),* sanity
soundness certainty, competence *(sanity),* health, honesty, legitimacy, quality *(excellence),* sanity, strength, validity, welfare
soundness of body health
soundness of mind competence *(sanity)*
sour aggravate *(annoy),* bitter *(acrid tasting),* dyseptic, petulant, severe, spoil *(impair),* stale
sour-tempered bitter *(reproachful),* dyseptic, petulant
source authority *(power),* basis, cause *(reason),* citation *(attribution),* connotation
source derivation
source determinant, documentation, embryo, genesis, inception, informant, informer *(a person who provides information),* onset *(commencement),* origination, parentage, progenitor, prototype, reason *(basis),* reference *(citation),* resource, spy, start. SEE MAIN ENTRY
source material derivation, reference *(citation)*
source of danger peril
source of income livelihood
source of perplexity problem
source of risk hazard, peril
soured bitter *(acrid tasting),* stale
sourish bitter *(acrid tasting)*
souse immerse *(plunge into),* permeate
souvenir remembrance *(commemoration),* reminder, token
sovereign autonomous *(self governing),* dominant, free *(enjoying civil liberty),* government *(political administration),* independent, master, national, nonpartisan, omnipotent, paramount, powerful, predominant, superlative. SEE MAIN ENTRY
sovereign immunity SEE MAIN ENTRY
sovereign state nationality
sovereign unit state *(political unit)*
sovereignty bureaucracy, capacity *(authority),* dominance, dominion *(supreme authority),* hierarchy *(persons in authority),* home rule, influence, jurisdiction, polity, predominance, primacy, regime, supremacy
sow diffuse, dissipate *(spread out),* distribute, inseminate, plant *(place firmly),* spread
sow dissension alienate *(estrange),* disaffect
sow the seeds of cause
space arrange *(methodize),* atmosphere, coverage *(scope),* distribute, extent, latitude, margin *(spare amount),* pause, range, region, scope. SEE MAIN ENTRY
space of time duration, phase *(period)*
space-saving compact *(dense)*
spacious broad, capacious, open *(unclosed)*
spaciousness capacity *(maximum),* extent, space
span comprehend *(include),* connect *(relate),* duration, encompass *(include),* extent, gamut, include, life *(period of existence),* lifetime, magnitude, measure, measurement, period, phase *(period),* purview, range, scope, space, term *(duration)*
span of years lifetime
spangle embellish
spar bicker, compete, contend *(dispute),* fight *(battle)*
spare ancillary *(auxiliary),* balance *(amount in excess),* bear *(tolerate),* bestow, condone, conserve, dole, excess, excessive, expendable, fund, insufficient, keep *(shelter),* needless, nonessential, overage, palliate *(excuse),* preserve, release, relent, relinquish, remit *(release from penalty),* residuary, superfluous, supplementary, surplus, sustain *(prolong),* unnecessary
spare no effort endeavor, persevere
spare no pains endeavor
spared clear *(free from criminal charges),* free *(relieved from a burden),* immune
spargere disseminate, spread
sparing conservation, deficient, devoid, economical, economy *(frugality),* frugal, illiberal, lenient, parsimonious, penurious, placable, provident *(frugal),* prudent, release, scarce
sparing no pains painstaking
sparing of words brief, inarticulate, laconic, sententious, taciturn
sparing use temperance
spark iota, scintilla
sparkle spirit
sparring belligerency
sparse barren, deficient, infrequent, insufficient, petty, scarce, sporadic. SEE MAIN ENTRY
sparseness delinquency *(shortage),* insignificance, insufficiency, paucity, poverty
sparsity dearth, deficiency, delinquency *(shortage),* paucity
spartan draconian
spartan frugal, stoical. SEE MAIN ENTRY
spasm outbreak, outburst
spasmodic broken *(interrupted),* desultory, disjointed, disjunctive *(tending to disjoin),* intermittent, periodic, sporadic, unpredictable, variable
spat bicker, brawl, contend *(dispute)*
spate plethora. SEE MAIN ENTRY
spatium magnitude, space
spatium interiectum interval
spatium temporis term *(duration)*
spatter defame, diffuse, pillory, pollute, stain, sully
spawn create, engender, offspring, proliferate, propagate *(increase),* reproduce
spe depellere disappoint
speak avow, communicate, convey *(communicate),* declaim, discourse, enunciate, express, phrase, recite, relate *(tell),* remark, utter. SEE MAIN ENTRY
speak about report *(disclose)*
speak against cross *(disagree with),* disapprove *(reject),* gainsay, protest
speak clearly enunciate
speak derisively jeer
speak disparagingly of decry
speak evil defame
speak evil of derogate, malign, smear
speak falsely bear false witness, feign, misrepresent, perjure, prevaricate
speak for plead *(argue a case),* promote *(organize),* represent *(substitute),* uphold
speak formally pronounce *(speak)*
speak highly of recommend
speak ill defame
speak ill of censure, complain *(criticize),* decry, defame, denigrate, denounce *(condemn),* derogate, discommend, dishonor *(deprive of honor),* disparage, malign, pillory, reproach, sully
speak in favor of advocate, justify
speak logically reason *(persuade)*
speak of bespeak, circulate, connote, discuss, mention
speak of slightingly defame
speak on discuss
speak on oath attest
speak one's mind communicate
speak out disclose, manifest
speak publicly declaim
speak rhetorically declaim
speak slightingly jeer, lessen
speak slightingly of decry, derogate, discommend, misprize
speak the truth disclose
speak to address *(talk to)*
speak up for plead *(argue a case)*
speak well of recommend
speak with converse
speaker amicus curiae, chairman, plenipotentiary, spokesman. SEE MAIN ENTRY
speaking conversation
speaking by delegated authority acting
speaking for another representation *(acting for others)*
spear penetrate, pierce *(lance)*
special ad hoc, certain *(particular),* certain *(specific),* considerable, distinct *(distinguished from others),* distinctive, exclusive *(singular),* extraordinary, individual, momentous, nonconforming, notable, noteworthy, outstanding *(prominent),* particular *(individual),* particular *(specific),* peculiar *(distinctive),* preferential, preferred *(favored),* rare, remarkable, singular, specific, technical, uncommon, unique, unusual. SEE MAIN ENTRY
special ability gift *(flair)*
special attention emphasis
special attraction feature *(special attraction)*
special case exception *(exclusion)*
special characteristic specialty *(distinctive mark)*
special concern emphasis
special dispensation variance *(exemption)*

special endowment gift *(flair)*
special favor distinction *(reputation)*
special interest SEE MAIN ENTRY
special interest group lobby
special interests lobby
special intonation emphasis
special item specialty *(distinctive mark)*
special line of work specialty *(special aptitude)*
special marking distinction *(difference)*
special matter specialty *(distinctive mark)*
special occurrence phenomenon *(unusual occurrence)*
special point detail, particular, particularity, specialty *(distinctive mark)*, specification, technicality
special points circumstances
special price discount
special privilege dispensation *(exception)*, exemption, immunity, license
special privileges patronage *(support)*
special project specialty *(special aptitude)*
special right prerogative
special significance emphasis
special skill specialty *(special aptitude)*
special study specialty *(special aptitude)*
specialist expert, mastermind, practitioner, professional. SEE MAIN ENTRY
speciality characteristic, identity *(individuality)*, technicality. SEE MAIN ENTRY
specialization calling, pursuit *(occupation)*, specialty *(special aptitude)*. SEE MAIN ENTRY
specialize practice *(engage in)*, restrict, select, study. SEE MAIN ENTRY
specialize in occupy *(engage)*, practice *(engage in)*
specialized professional *(trained)*, technical
specialized administrative unit bureau
specialized language jargon *(technical language)*
specialized terminology jargon *(technical language)*
specialized unit bureau
specialized vocabulary jargon *(technical language)*
specializer expert, specialist
specially particularly
specially prepared express
specially provided for privileged
specially selected premium, prime *(most valuable)*
specially trained person expert
specialness speciality
specialties commodities
specialty bailiwick, business *(occupation)*, caliber *(mental capacity)*, calling, capacity *(sphere)*, career, characteristic, department, employment, feature *(special attraction)*, identity *(individuality)*, merchandise, occupation *(vocation)*, penchant, position *(business status)*, practice *(professional business)*, profession *(vocation)*, province, pursuit *(occupation)*, trade *(occupation)*, trait, work *(employment)*. SEE MAIN ENTRY
specie cash, currency, money
species apparent *(perceptible)*, appearance *(look)*, color *(complexion)*
species denomination, kind, manner *(kind)*
species pretext, semblance
species of proof evidence
specific actual, certain *(particular)*, concrete, descriptive, detailed, exact, explicit, express, particular *(individual)*, particular, personal *(individual)*, point *(item)*, precise, regional, said, special, technical, technicality. SEE MAIN ENTRY
specific aptness penchant
specific confinement limitation
specific curtailment limitation
specific moment point *(period of time)*
specific quality characteristic, identity *(individuality)*, particularity, penchant, property *(distinctive attribute)*, specialty *(distinctive mark)*
specifically particularly
specification assignment *(designation)*, caption, clarification, classification, clause, condition *(contingent provision)*, delineation, description, designation *(naming)*, detail, diagnosis, item, limitation, particular, prerequisite, provision *(clause)*, qualification *(condition)*, report *(detailed account)*, requirement, reservation *(condition)*, selection *(choice)*, stipulation, technicality, term *(provision)*, ultimatum. SEE MAIN ENTRY
specification of details bill *(formal declaration)*
specifications pattern
specificity identity *(individuality)*
specificness specialty *(distinctive mark)*
specifics data, information *(facts)*
specified aforesaid, certain *(particular)*, certain *(specific)*, conditional, express, stated
specified income payable for life annuity, pension
specified period of time date
specify allocate, allot, amplify, annunciate, assign *(designate)*, call *(title)*, characterize, cite *(state)*, classify, communicate, convey *(communicate)*, define, delineate, denominate, depict, describe, designate, detail *(particularize)*, diagnose, disabuse, distinguish, enumerate, explain, identify, index *(relate)*, interject, itemize, label, mention, nominate, pinpoint, portray, postulate, qualify *(condition)*, quote, report *(disclose)*, select, signify *(inform)*, stipulate. SEE MAIN ENTRY
specify in greater detail amplify
specify limits border *(bound)*
specify the particulars of delineate
specify the peculiarities of characterize
specimen case *(example)*, entity, example, illustration, instance, model, representative *(example)*. SEE MAIN ENTRY
specimen paragon, pattern, sample
speciosus specious
specious deceptive, delusive, ostensible, purported, sophistic, untenable. SEE MAIN ENTRY
specious argument non sequitur
specious reasoning non sequitur, sophistry
speciously attractive meretricious
speckled marred
spectacle phenomenon *(manifestation)*, phenomenon *(unusual occurrence)*, scene, vision *(dream)*. SEE MAIN ENTRY
spectacular conspicuous
spectare aspect, observe *(watch)*, survey *(examine)*, witness *(have direct knowl-edge of)*
spectator bystander, eyewitness
spectator et testis eyewitness
specter phantom, reflection *(image)*, spirit, vision *(dream)*. SEE MAIN ENTRY
spectral immaterial, insubstantial
speculari spy
speculate bet, gamble, guess, invest *(fund)*, muse, opine, parlay *(bet)*, ponder, postulate, presume, presuppose, prognosticate, reflect *(ponder)*, surmise, suspect *(think)*. SEE MAIN ENTRY
speculate with endanger
speculation conjecture, consideration *(contemplation)*, contemplation, estimate *(idea)*, estimation *(calculation)*, hypothesis, inference, investment, opinion *(belief)*, postulate, presumption, prospect *(outlook)*, rationale, reflection *(thought)*, risk, sense *(feeling)*, supposition, suspicion *(uncertainty)*, theory, thesis, venture. SEE MAIN ENTRY
speculatist bettor
speculative cogitative, controversial, debatable, deliberate, disputable, doubtful, dubious, hypothetical, indeterminate, inquisitive, insecure, moot, pensive, presumptive, putative, tentative, theoretical, undecided, unpredictable, unsettled, unsound *(fallacious)*. SEE MAIN ENTRY
speculator bettor. SEE MAIN ENTRY
speculator spy
speculatory presumptive, speculative, theoretical
speech declamation, discourse, language, parlance, peroration, phraseology, remark. SEE MAIN ENTRY
speech-making rhetoric *(skilled speech)*
speechification declamation
speechless mute, taciturn. SEE MAIN ENTRY
speechlessness silence
speechmaker spokesman
speed dispatch *(promptness)*, dispatch *(send off)*, expedite, haste, help, precipitate *(hasten)*, promote *(organize)*, race
speed along dispatch *(send off)*, hasten
speed on its way dispatch *(send off)*
speed track causeway
speed up expedite, facilitate, precipitate *(hasten)*
speeded adjudication accelerated judgment
speedily instantly
speediness dispatch *(promptness)*
speedup acceleration
speedway causeway
speedy brief, cursory, expeditious, immediate *(at once)*, instant, instantaneous, perfunctory, precipitate, prompt, rapid, ready *(prepared)*, summary
speedy completion dispatch *(promptness)*
speedy disposition dispatch *(promptness)*
speedy transaction dispatch *(promptness)*
speedy trial SEE MAIN ENTRY
spell duration, hiatus, interval, period, phase *(period)*, prognosticate, recess, respite *(interval of rest)*, term *(duration)*
spell danger caution
spell out clarify, comment, define, describe, elucidate, enlighten, explain, explicate, exposit, expound
spellbind coax
spellbinding eloquent
spend bestow, consume, defray, deplete, disburse *(pay out)*, dissipate *(expend foolishly)*, exert, exhaust *(deplete)*, expend *(consume)*, expend *(disburse)*, pay. SEE MAIN ENTRY
spend lavishly dissipate *(expend foolishly)*

spend more than one has overdraw
spend one's time in occupy *(engage)*
spend wastefully dissipate *(expend foolishly)*
spendable disposable
spending outlay, payment *(act of paying)*
spendings disbursement *(funds paid out)*, expenditure, overhead
spendthrift improvident, prodigal, profligate *(extravagant)*, profuse
spent irredeemable, irretrievable, powerless
sperare expect *(anticipate)*
spernere disdain
spes chance *(possibility)*, expectation
sphaera sphere
sphere ambit, area *(province)*, bailiwick, circuit, coverage *(scope)*, department, district, jurisdiction, position *(business status)*, province, pursuit *(occupation)*, purview, range, realm, region, scene, scope, zone. SEE MAIN ENTRY
sphere of activity calling
sphere of occupation appointment *(position)*
spheroid sphere
sphinx-like mysterious
sphinxian mysterious
spice spirit
spicy obscene, salacious, suggestive *(risqué)*
spike penetrate, pierce *(lance)*
spill outflow, outpour
spill over inundate
spin SEE MAIN ENTRY
spin out prolong
spineless irresolute, obsequious, powerless
spiral sinuous
spiral inflation boom *(prosperity)*
spiriferous circuitous
spirit ardor, complexion, connotation, content *(meaning)*, disposition *(inclination)*, emotion, frame *(mood)*, gist *(substance)*, gravamen, life *(vitality)*, motivate, phantom, prowess *(bravery)*, specter, tenor. SEE MAIN ENTRY
spirit away abduct, carry away, hold up *(rob)*, kidnap, purloin
spirit of the law equity *(justice)*
spirited alert *(agile)*, eager, expeditious, fervent, trenchant, unrestrained *(not repressed)*, volatile. SEE MAIN ENTRY
spiritedness life *(vitality)*
spiriting away abduction
spiritless caitiff, disconsolate, grave *(solemn)*, inactive, inexpressive, insensible, insipid, lifeless *(dull)*, nonchalant, otiose, pedestrian, phlegmatic, prosaic, recreant, torpid
spiritlessness disinterest *(lack of interest)*
spirits alcohol
spiritual incorporeal, intangible, sacrosanct, solemn
spiritual upbuilding edification
spirituality immateriality
spiritualness immateriality
spit pierce *(lance)*
spite antagonize, cruelty, disoblige, harass, harrow, ill will, malice, mistreat, plague, rancor, resentment. SEE MAIN ENTRY
spiteful bilious, bitter *(reproachful)*, contemptuous, cruel, dyseptic, harmful, hostile, invidious, malevolent, malicious, malignant, mordacious, outrageous, pejorative, perverse, petulant, resentful, scathing, sinister, vicious, vindictive, virulent. SEE MAIN ENTRY
spitefulness ill will, malice, rancor, spite
splash pretense *(ostentation)*, sully
splay deploy, radiate, spread
spleen resentment, umbrage
spleenful bilious, fractious, malevolent, malignant, perverse, petulant
spleeny fractious, perverse
splendid elegant, illustrious, meritorious, premium, prime *(most valuable)*, proud *(self-respecting)*, sterling. SEE MAIN ENTRY
splendidus illustrious
splendor prestige
splendorous illustrious
splenetic bitter *(reproachful)*, fractious, froward, perverse, petulant, querulous, resentful, restive
splenetical petulant
splice combine *(join together)*, connection *(fastening)*, intertwine, join *(bring together)*
spliced conjoint
splinter break *(fracture)*, rend, separate, sever, split
splinter party faction
splintered broken *(fractured)*
split alienation *(estrangement)*, apportion, bifurcate, break *(separate)*, controversy *(argument)*, cross *(intersect)*, detach, dichotomize, dichotomy, disaccord *(noun)*, disaccord *(verb)*, disagree, disassociation, discord, discrepancy, disjoint, divide *(separate)*, division *(act of dividing)*, divisive, estrangement, feud, force *(break)*, isolate, mete, part *(separate)*, partial *(part)*, rend, rift *(disagreement)*, rift *(gap)*, schism, separate *(adjective)*, separate *(verb)*, separation, sever, sort, subdivide, variance *(disagreement)*. SEE MAIN ENTRY
split again reapportion
split hairs bicker, pettifog
split off break *(separate)*
split up disintegrate, disperse *(scatter)*, disrupt, dissolve *(separate)*, dissolve *(terminate)*, divorce, parcel, partition, prorate, separate
splitting division *(act of dividing)*
splotch defacement, stain
splurge pretense *(ostentation)*, spend
spoil adulterate, corrupt, damage, decay, deface, depreciate, deteriorate, disable, eviscerate, foil, frustrate, harm, hold up *(rob)*, infect, loot, misemploy, mismanage, pervert, pillage, pirate *(take by violence)*, pollute, prejudice *(injure)*, prey, prize, stain, sully, taint *(contaminate)*, thwart, vitiate. SEE MAIN ENTRY
spoil excessively overindulge
spoil the look of deface
spoilage decrement, dissolution *(disintegration)*. SEE MAIN ENTRY
spoilate pirate *(take by violence)*
spoiled decadent, marred, stale, tainted *(contaminated)*
spoiler burglar, vandal
spoiling burglary, damage, decadent
spoils plunder, stake *(award)*. SEE MAIN ENTRY
spoken nuncupative, oral, verbal
spoken expression language
spoken in confidence confidential
spoken language speech
spoken out loud oral
spoken word language, parlance, speech
spokesman advocate *(counselor)*, advocate *(espouser)*, go-between, informer *(a person who provides information)*, interagent, liaison, plenipotentiary, procurator, proponent, representative *(proxy)*. SEE MAIN ENTRY
spokesperson liaison, medium, plenipotentiary
spokeswoman advocate *(counselor)*, advocate *(espouser)*
spolia spoils
spoliare spoil *(pillage)*
spoliate despoil, harry *(plunder)*, loot, pillage, plunder, prey, spoil *(pillage)*
spoliatio robbery
spoliation depredation, deterioration, dissolution *(disintegration)*, havoc, pillage, plunder, rape. SEE MAIN ENTRY
spoliatory predatory
sponge parasite
spongy resilient
sponsio guarantee, recognizance
sponsor avouch *(guarantee)*, backer, bestow, capitalize *(provide capital)*, creditor, espouse, finance, guarantee, guardian, invest *(fund)*, nurture, partisan, patron *(influential supporter)*, promote *(organize)*, promoter, proponent, protect, surety *(guarantor)*, underwrite. SEE MAIN ENTRY
sponsor again refinance
sponsorship accommodation *(backing)*, advocacy, aid *(help)*, appropriation *(donation)*, auspices, behalf, favor *(sanction)*, goodwill, guidance, indorsement, patronage *(support)*, promotion *(encourage-ment)*
spontaneity impulse
spontaneous elective *(voluntary)*, fortuitous, impulsive *(rash)*, informal, ingenuous, prompt, unaffected *(sincere)*, unintentional, unpremeditated. SEE MAIN ENTRY
spontaneous inclination impulse
spontaneus spontaneous
sporadic broken *(interrupted)*, infrequent, intermittent, periodic. SEE MAIN ENTRY
sporadical sporadic
sport bet, contest *(competition)*, flaunt, ridicule
sport with dupe
sporting fair *(just)*
sporting event contest *(competition)*
sportive jocular
sportsmanlike fair *(just)*
spot deface, defacement, detect, discern *(detect with the senses)*, locality, location, notice *(observe)*, onus *(stigma)*, part *(place)*, position *(situation)*, quagmire, region, seat, stain, standpoint, stigma, sully, tarnish, witness *(have direct knowledge of)*
spotless absolute *(ideal)*, clean, inviolate, irreprehensible, moral, pure, unblemished, unimpeachable
spotlight publicity
spotted blemished, marred
spotting detection
spotty sporadic
spousal marriage *(wedlock)*, matrimony
spousal support SEE MAIN ENTRY
spouse consort. SEE MAIN ENTRY
spout exude, outflow, outlet, outpour, recite
sprawl expand, spread
spray barrage, discharge *(shot)*
spread accumulate *(enlarge)*, augmentation, boom *(increase)*, cast *(throw)*, circulate, circulation, coverage *(scope)*, deploy, diffuse, disburse *(distribute)*, dispel, disperse *(disseminate)*, dissipate *(spread out)*, dissolve *(disperse)*, distribute, division *(act of*

dividing), enlarge, expand, growth *(increase),* herald, increase, inflate, inflated *(enlarged),* inflation *(increase),* issue *(publish),* magnify, pervade, post, proliferate, promulgate, publish, radiate, scope, utter. SEE MAIN ENTRY
spread a report circulate, disseminate
spread about diffuse
spread abroad circulate, diffuse, disperse *(disseminate),* divulge, post, proclaim, promulgate, propagate *(spread),* public *(known)*
spread an evil report malign
spread around diffuse
spread far and wide diffuse, disseminate
spread out compound, disperse *(disseminate),* expand, far-reaching, open *(unclosed),* prolix
spread out in area extend *(enlarge)*
spread out in battle formation deploy
spread over dissipate *(spread out),* expand, overlap
spread through permeate, pervade
spread too far overextend
spread too thin overextend
spread widely diffuse, disperse *(scatter)*
spread-out extensive
spreading boom *(increase),* broad, circulation, contagious, extension *(expansion),* extensive, rampant
spreading abroad divulgation
spree carouse
sprightliness life *(vitality)*
sprightly alert *(agile),* jocular, resilient, volatile
spring accrue *(arise),* derivation, ensue, fund, origination, proceed *(go forward),* reason *(basis),* redound, result, source, stem *(originate)*
spring forth arise *(originate)*
spring from emanate, evolve
spring up arise *(originate),* issue *(send forth),* pullulate, supervene
spring upon attack
springhead derivation, source
springy resilient
sprinkle dissipate *(spread out),* distribute, intersperse, spread
sprinkling minimum
sprint race
sprite phantom, specter
sprout germinate, outgrowth, proliferate, pullulate, stem *(originate)*
sprout from redound
sprouting boom *(increase),* growth *(evolution)*
spruce up embellish
spry alert *(agile)*
spun out prolix
spunk resolution *(decision)*
spunkless languid, phlegmatic
spur abet, agitate *(activate),* bait *(harass),* catalyst, cause *(reason),* exhort, hasten, impel, impetus, incentive, motivate, precipitate *(hasten),* prevail upon, provocation, provoke, spirit, stimulate, stimulus, urge
spur of necessity compulsion *(coercion),* force *(compulsion)*
spur on incite, prompt
spurious artificial, assumed *(feigned),* bogus, deceptive, delusive, dishonest, disingenuous, disreputable, erroneous, false *(not genuine),* fictitious, fraudulent, imitation, lying, mendacious, meretricious, specious, synthetic, unfounded, untrue. SEE MAIN ENTRY
spurious issue bastard
spuriousness bad faith, false pretense
spurn bar *(exclude),* condescend *(patronize),* contemn, decline *(reject),* decry, demonstrate *(protest),* disallow, disapprove *(reject),* disavow, disclaim, discommend, discount *(disbelieve),* disdain, disoblige, disown *(refuse to acknowledge),* disregard, disrespect, dissent *(withhold assent),* eliminate *(exclude),* exclude, fight *(counteract),* flout, forswear, humiliate, mock *(deride),* rebuff *(noun),* rebuff *(verb),* refuse, reject, renounce, repel *(drive back),* repudiate, repulse, set aside *(annul),* shun. SEE MAIN ENTRY
spurning denial, disdain, negative, rejection, renunciation
spurt acceleration, dispatch *(promptness),* emit, outburst, outflow, outpour, race
spy conspirator, discern *(detect with the senses),* informant, observe *(watch),* recognize *(perceive).* SEE MAIN ENTRY
spy against subvert
spy upon spy
spying espionage
squabble affray, altercation, bicker, brawl *(noun),* brawl *(verb),* confrontation *(altercation),* contend *(dispute),* contest *(dispute),* controversy *(argument),* disaccord *(noun),* disaccord *(verb),* embroilment, fight *(argument),* fight *(battle),* fracas, strife
squad assemblage, band
squalid destitute, repulsive, sordid
squall fracas
squander consume, lose *(be deprived of),* misemploy, mishandle *(mismanage),* overdraw
squandered irredeemable, lost *(taken away)*
squandering consumption, improvident, misapplication, prodigal, profligate *(extravagant),* profuse, waste
square close *(enclosed area),* compensate *(counterbalance),* fair *(just),* market place, parcel, pay, refund, regulate *(adjust),* rightful, upright
square accounts discharge *(pay a debt),* pay, repay
square measure dimension
square with comport *(agree with)*
squash depress, extinguish, kill *(defeat),* obliterate, repress, stifle
squat inhabit, lodge *(reside),* reside, rest *(be supported by),* usurp
squatter habitant
squeal divulge
squealer informer *(one providing criminal information)*
squeamish disinclined, reluctant
squeamishness reluctance
squeeze constrain *(compel),* constrict *(compress),* exact, impact
squeeze out distill
squeeze together consolidate *(strengthen)*
squeezed together compact *(dense)*
squelch abolish, counteract, defeat, extinguish, quash, refute, stifle, strangle
squib parody, ridicule
squirt emit
stab enter *(penetrate),* lancinate, penetrate, pierce *(lance)*
stabbing bitter *(penetrating)*
stabile stable
stabilire establish *(entrench),* instate
stabilis constant *(adjective),* constant *(noun),* durable, firm, immovable, immutable, permanent, solid *(sound),* stable, steadfast
stabilitate establish *(entrench)*
stability certainty, composure, constant, equipoise, indestructibility, prowess *(bravery),* responsibility *(conscience),* security *(safety),* uniformity. SEE MAIN ENTRY
stabilization balance *(equality)*
stabilize adjust *(regulate),* compensate *(counterbalance),* establish *(entrench),* fix *(make firm),* settle. SEE MAIN ENTRY
stable certain *(fixed),* constant, demonstrable, dependable, durable, firm, fixed *(securely placed),* indelible, indomitable, infallible, irrevocable, permanent, perpetual, rational, regular *(orderly),* reliable, secure *(free from danger),* secure *(sound),* solid *(sound),* static, staunch, steadfast, strong, unalterable, unyielding. SEE MAIN ENTRY
stable equilibrium balance *(equality)*
stable state status quo
stabulare stall
stack assemblage, bulk, hoard, load, store *(depository)*
staff committee, cudgel, employ *(engage services),* hire, mainstay, personnel, unit *(department).* SEE MAIN ENTRY
staff members staff
staff person employee
staff with engage *(hire)*
stage degree *(station),* direct *(supervise),* duration, period, phase *(period),* point *(period of time),* portray, scene, term *(duration)*
stage of advancement degree *(station)*
stage of life age
stage setting scene
stagecraft histrionics
stagger overcome *(overwhelm),* vacillate
staggering incredible, ineffable, portentous *(eliciting amazement),* unbelievable
staggering belief ludicrous
stagnans stagnant
stagnant inactive, indolent, languid, lifeless *(dull),* static, torpid. SEE MAIN ENTRY
stagnate languish
stagnating barren, otiose, stagnant
stagnation desuetude, inaction, inertia, languor
stagy histrionic
staid earnest, phlegmatic, solemn
stain attaint, brand, brand *(stigmatize),* damage, debase, deface, defacement, demean *(make lower),* denigrate, depreciate, derogate, discredit *(noun),* discredit *(verb),* disgrace *(noun),* disgrace *(verb),* dishonor *(shame),* dishonor *(deprive of honor),* disparage, disrepute, flaw, humiliate, ignominy, infamy, infect, onus *(stigma),* opprobrium, pervert, pillory, pollute, scandal, shame, smear, stigma, sully, tarnish. SEE MAIN ENTRY
stain one's reputation malign
stain the character of defame
stained blemished, marred, tainted *(contaminated)*
stainless absolute *(ideal),* blameless, clean, honest, infallible, inviolate, irreprehensible, meritorious, pure, unblemished, unimpeachable
stainlessness honesty
stake bet, binder, bond *(secure a debt),* claim *(right),* compromise *(endanger),* deposit, dominion *(absolute ownership),* downpayment, endanger, equity *(share of ownership),* gamble, guarantee, guaranty,

holding *(property owned)*, interest *(ownership)*, jeopardize, lien, loan, parlay *(bet)*, pawn, pledge *(security)*, pledge *(deposit)*, right *(entitlement)*, risk, speculate *(chance)*, title *(right)*. SEE MAIN ENTRY
stake money handsel, pledge *(security)*
stake one's credit promise *(vow)*
stake out border *(bound)*, demarcate
stale dilapidated, languid, lifeless *(dull)*, mundane, obsolete, old, ordinary, outdated, outmoded, pedestrian, prosaic, repetitious, trite, usual. SEE MAIN ENTRY
stale comment platitude
stalemate abeyance, check *(restrain)*, deadlock, draw *(tie)*, halt, impasse, impede, stall. SEE MAIN ENTRY
staleness disuse
stalk approach, hunt, perambulate, pursuit *(chase)*
stall arrest *(stop)*, balk, block, chamber *(compartment)*, clog, constrict *(inhibit)*, continue *(adjourn)*, debar, defer *(put off)*, delay *(noun)*, delay *(verb)*, detain *(restrain)*, disadvantage, extension *(postponement)*, hold up *(delay)*, impasse, inconvenience, obstruct, pause, postpone, procrastinate, remit *(relax)*, stand *(witness' place in court)*, stem *(check)*, stop, store *(business)*, suspend. SEE MAIN ENTRY
stall for time delay
stalling filibuster
stalwart cohort, colleague, heroic, indomitable, pertinacious, powerful, purposeful, sedulous, spartan, stable, staunch, strong, undaunted
stalwartness strength
stamina force *(strength)*, health, longanimity, prowess *(bravery)*, puissance, sinew, strength, tenacity, tolerance
stamp brand, brand *(mark)*, embed, indicant, indicator, label *(noun)*, label *(verb)*, seal *(solemnize)*, speciality, specialty *(distinctive mark)*, tenor, validate. SEE MAIN ENTRY
stamp incorrectly mislabel
stamp of approval confirmation, indorsement, ratification, sanction *(permission)*
stamp out eliminate *(eradicate)*, eradicate, extirpate, obliterate
stamped monetary
stamped with approval permissible, popular
stampede panic
stance manner *(behavior)*, opinion *(belief)*. SEE MAIN ENTRY
stanch cease, firm, incorruptible, indomitable, infallible, occlude, pertinacious, reliable, resolute, solid *(sound)*, stable, stem *(check)*, stop, true *(loyal)*, unyielding
stanchly faithfully
stanchness adhesion *(loyalty)*, fidelity, loyalty
stand bear *(tolerate)*, desist, endure *(last)*, endure *(suffer)*, halt, lie *(be sustainable)*, opine, opinion *(belief)*, outlook, remain *(stay)*, resist *(withstand)*, resistance, stay *(rest)*, thesis, tolerate. SEE MAIN ENTRY
stand against counter, counteract, disapprove *(reject)*, fight *(counteract)*, oppugn
stand aghast fear
stand aloof eschew
stand apart deviate
stand around loiter
stand aside abandon *(withdraw)*, demit, quit *(discontinue)*, resign, retire *(conclude a career)*
stand behind espouse, preserve, sanction, side, sponsor, subsidize
stand between intercede, part *(separate)*
stand by adhere *(maintain loyalty)*, adjoin, assist, contribute *(assist)*, countenance, help, indorse, keep *(fulfill)*, maintain *(sustain)*, recommend, side, subsidize, uphold
stand clear eschew
stand down demit
stand facing confront *(encounter)*
stand fast endure *(last)*, hold out *(resist)*, persevere, remain *(continue)*, remain *(stay)*, resist *(withstand)*, subsist, withstand
stand firm adhere *(persist)*, bear *(adduce)*, claim *(maintain)*, confront *(oppose)*, hold out *(resist)*, insist, last, maintain *(sustain)*, persevere, remain *(continue)*, resist *(withstand)*, withstand
stand firm against oppose
stand for connote, denote, exemplify, indicate, replace, represent *(portray)*, signify *(denote)*
stand guard patrol, police
stand in replacement
stand in awe fear
stand in for displace *(replace)*
stand in need of require *(need)*
stand in relation concern *(involve)*
stand in relation to pertain
stand in stead of supersede
stand in the place of represent *(substitute)*
stand in the way balk, bar *(hinder)*, block, check *(restrain)*, delay, estop, hinder, hold up *(delay)*, impede, inconvenience, interpose, obstruct
stand in the way of clog
stand off deadlock
stand one's ground maintain *(sustain)*
stand opposite confront *(encounter)*
stand out project *(extend beyond)*
stand out in opposition contrast
stand over discipline *(control)*, moderate *(preside over)*
stand sentinel patrol, police
stand still halt, pause, rest *(cease from action)*
stand the cost bear the expense, defray
stand the cost of disburse *(pay out)*
stand the hazard bet
stand the strain bear *(tolerate)*
stand the test pass *(satisfy requirements)*
stand together conform, cooperate
stand up against challenge, defy
stand up for defend, espouse, justify, plead *(argue a case)*, support *(justify)*, uphold
stand up to disown *(deny the validity)*, fight *(battle)*, fight *(counteract)*, oppugn, resist *(withstand)*, withstand
stand-in alter ego, cover *(substitute)*, substitute, surrogate
standard broad, bylaw, canon, code, constant, conventional, cornerstone, criterion, customary, decorum, designation *(symbol)*, epitome, example, exemplar, familiar *(customary)*, general, habitual, household *(familiar)*, law, mediocre, model, mundane, norm, normal *(regular)*, ordinary, paradigm, paragon, pattern, popular, precedent, prevalent, principle *(axiom)*, pro forma, prototype, rate, regular *(conventional)*, repeated, representative, routine, rule *(guide)*, stare decisis, typical, uniform, usual. SEE MAIN ENTRY
standard for comparison exemplar, paragon
standard for imitation exemplar
standard letter form *(document)*
standard of care SEE MAIN ENTRY
standard of comparison criterion, example, sample
standard of criticism criterion, pattern
standard of judgment criterion, pattern
standard of perfection exemplar
standard of review SEE MAIN ENTRY
standard of value money
standard practice constant
standard procedure avenue *(means of attainment)*, constant, modus operandi. SEE MAIN ENTRY
standardization uniformity
standardization of laws codification
standardize adapt, adjust *(regulate)*, conform, orchestrate, organize *(arrange)*, regulate *(adjust)*. SEE MAIN ENTRY
standardized boiler plate, industrial, normal *(regular)*, systematic, typical
standardness mediocrity
standards conscience, ethics
standards of conduct ethics
standards of professional behavior ethics
standby colleague
standing caliber *(quality)*, case *(set of circumstances)*, character *(reputation)*, class, credit *(recognition)*, degree *(station)*, eminence, extant, honor *(good reputation)*, lasting, posture *(situation)*, prestige, quality *(excellence)*, quality *(grade)*, reputation, situation, stagnant, state *(condition)*, static, status. SEE MAIN ENTRY
standing apart distinct *(distinguished from others)*
standing by ready *(prepared)*
standing committee commission *(agency)*
standing in the place of acting
standing order decree, law, rule *(guide)*, rule *(legal dictate)*
standing out conspicuous, evident, manifest, noteworthy, obvious, patent, salient
standing out clearly evident
standoff draw *(tie)*
standoffish unapproachable
standpoint conviction *(persuasion)*, outlook, perspective, position *(point of view)*, posture *(attitude)*, side, stand *(position)*. SEE MAIN ENTRY
standstill cessation *(interlude)*, check *(bar)*, cloture, deadlock, desuetude, halt, hiatus, impasse, interruption, lull, moratorium, pause, remission
staple item, stock in trade
staples commodities, goods, merchandise, provision *(something provided)*
star feature *(special attraction)*, master. SEE MAIN ENTRY
starched formal, punctilious, rigid
starchy rigid
stare abide, continue *(prolong)*
stare scrutinize
stare decisis SEE MAIN ENTRY
staring stark
stark naked *(lacking embellishment)*, palpable, severe, unmitigated. SEE MAIN ENTRY
starlike stellar
starring outstanding *(prominent)*
starry stellar
start arise *(originate)*, cause, commence, conceive *(invent)*, create, embark, embryo, establish *(launch)*, generate, genesis, impel, impetus, inception, incite, initiate,

launch *(initiate)*, maintain *(commence)*, nascency, onset *(commencement)*, originate, origination, outset, overt act, postulate, preface, prelude, stem *(originate)*, threshold *(commencement)*, undertake, unveil. SEE MAIN ENTRY
start a corporation incorporate *(form a corporation)*
start a fight attack
start a lawsuit litigate
start a war attack
start afresh resume
start again relapse, renew *(begin again)*, resume
start an action complain *(charge)*, litigate
start forward again resume
start fresh relapse
start out arise *(originate)*, depart, embark
start over reopen
start up induct
starting elementary, incipient, initial, nascency, original *(initial)*, preliminary, preparatory, prime *(original)*, rudimentary
starting before retroactive
starting point base *(foundation)*, derivation, embryo, inception, onset *(commencement)*, origin *(source)*, origination, outset, postulate
startle disconcert, disturb, frighten, menace, upset
startler bombshell
startling lurid, peculiar *(curious)*, portentous *(eliciting amazement)*, prodigious *(amazing)*, unanticipated, uncommon, unexpected, unforeseeable, unusual
starvation poverty, privation
starved deficient, poor *(underprivileged)*
stash deposit *(place)*
state acknowledge *(declare)*, adduce, affirm *(claim)*, allege, annunciate, aspect, assert, avouch *(avow)*, avow, caliber *(quality)*, case *(set of circumstances)*, claim *(maintain)*, comment, contend *(maintain)*, converse, convey *(communicate)*, declare, disabuse, enunciate, exposit, express, inform *(notify)*, interject, issue *(publish)*, mention, notify, observe *(remark)*, phase *(period)*, phrase, plead *(allege in a legal action)*, plight, polity, pose *(propound)*, posit, position *(situation)*, posture *(situation)*, predicament, proclaim, profess *(avow)*, pronounce *(speak)*, public *(affecting people)*, publish, purport, quagmire, recite, recount, relate *(tell)*, remark, remind, report *(disclose)*, signify *(inform)*, situation, speak, status, stipulate, swear, testify, utter, verify *(swear)*. SEE MAIN ENTRY
state a fact testify
state a grievance complain *(charge)*
state a truth testify
state affairs politics
state again reiterate
state an untruth misrepresent
state as fact bear *(adduce)*
state as true allege, assert, avouch *(avow)*, avow
state authoritatively command
state by items itemize
state by way of objection object
state directly express
state emphatically certify *(attest)*, contend *(maintain)*, plead *(allege in a legal action)*, speak
state falsely misrepresent
state fully expound
state highway causeway
state hospital asylum *(hospital)*
state in detail expound, specify
state in nonexplicit terms imply
state incorrectly misstate
state institution asylum *(hospital)*
state management bureaucracy, government *(administration)*
state managers government *(political administration)*
state misleadingly misstate
state occasion ceremony
state of a married woman coverture
state of affairs case *(set of circumstances)*, circumstances, plight, posture *(situation)*
state of anxiety fear
state of being condition *(state)*
state of being different difference
state of being equal parity
state of being public common knowledge
state of being unused desuetude
state of disorder disturbance
state of doubt quandary
state of equilibrium balance *(equality)*
state of excitability ardor
state of excitement affection
state of feeling frame *(mood)*
state of health health
state of inaction deadlock, impasse
state of indebtedness arrears, cloud *(incumbrance)*, mortgage
state of indecision deadlock
state of inertia deadlock
state of matrimony cohabitation *(married state)*, coverture
state of mind frame *(mood)*
state of neutralization deadlock
state of no progress impasse
state of not being satisfied dissatisfaction
state of order array *(order)*, system
state of refinement civilization
state of siege belligerency
state of suspense doubt *(indecision)*
state of terror panic
state of violence shambles
state of war belligerency
state on oath bear *(adduce)*
state one's case plead *(argue a case)*, speak
state one's terms dicker
state opposition demonstrate *(protest)*, object
state positively affirm *(claim)*
state precisely specify
state servant caretaker *(one fulfilling the function of office)*
state something in detail elaborate
state systematically formulate
state the meaning of define
state the meaning precisely define
state under oath swear
state with conviction affirm *(claim)*, argue, avouch *(avow)*, avow, certify *(attest)*, express, speak
state's attorney district attorney, prosecution *(government agency)*, prosecutor
statecraft government *(administration)*
stated alleged, assumed *(inferred)*, certain *(positive)*, certain *(specific)*, convincing, definite, nuncupative, verbal. SEE MAIN ENTRY
stated as a premise theoretical
stated authoritatively positive *(prescribed)*
stated in a writing in writing
stated in writing in writing
stated maintenance pension
stated term condition *(contingent provision)*
stated terms contract
statehood nationality
stateliness solemnity
stately elegant, proud *(self-respecting)*, solemn
statement account *(evaluation)*, acknowledgment *(avowal)*, admission *(disclosure)*, affidavit, affirmation, allegation, amount *(sum)*, assertion, attestation, avowal, bill *(invoice)*, budget, caption, census, certification *(attested copy)*, claim *(assertion)*, comment, confession, declaration, dictum, disclosure *(something disclosed)*, dispatch *(message)*, dun, expression *(comment)*, invoice *(bill)*, issuance, ledger, mention *(reference)*, note *(brief comment)*, notice *(announcement)*, notification, observation, postulate, proclamation, profession *(declaration)*, pronouncement, prospectus, publication *(disclosure)*, recital, remark, rendition *(explication)*, report *(detailed account)*, resolution *(formal statement)*, speech, suggestion, testimony, title *(division)*. SEE MAIN ENTRY
statement alleged in defense plea
statement alleged in justification plea
statement by way of illustration dictum
statement of a cause of action count
statement of account budget, invoice *(bill)*
statement of belief principle *(axiom)*
statement of claim demand
statement of debits and credits account *(evaluation)*
statement of defense argument *(pleading)*, justification, plea, pleading
statement of facts averment, avouchment, bill *(formal declaration)*, declaration, testimony. SEE MAIN ENTRY
statement of general truth maxim
statement of indebtedness bill *(invoice)*
statement of meaning definition
statement of obligations invoice *(bill)*
statement of particulars specification
statement of pecuniary transactions account *(evaluation)*
statement of position principle *(axiom)*
statement of the case brief
statement of the costs estimate *(approximate cost)*
statement of the plaintiff's cause complaint
statement offered in proof argument *(pleading)*
statement on oath affirmance *(legal affirmation)*, affirmation, averment, avowal, deposition, pledge *(binding promise)*
statement particularizing debts due invoice *(bill)*
statement recorded in a book entry *(record)*
statement tending to prove a point argument *(pleading)*
statement under oath affidavit, deposition
statement which answers the charges plea
statement which confirms information on an affidavit jurat
statements on behalf of the defense plea
statements that describe delineation

statemongers government *(political administration)*
stateroom chamber *(compartment)*
statesman politician
statesmanship discretion *(quality of being discreet)*, government *(administration)*, politics
statesmen government *(political administration)*
static certain *(fixed)*, dormant, immutable, inactive, permanent, rigid, stagnant, torpid. SEE MAIN ENTRY
static condition status quo
statical static
statim instantly
station appointment *(position)*, base *(place)*, building *(structure)*, caliber *(quality)*, character *(reputation)*, class, condition *(state)*, department, locality, locate, location, lodge *(house)*, lodge *(reside)*, office, plant *(place firmly)*, plight, position *(business status)*, position *(situation)*, post, posture *(situation)*, prestige, reputation, seat, situation, stand *(witness' place in court)*, standpoint, state *(condition)*, status, title *(position)*, venue
stationary firm, permanent, stable, stagnant, standing, static, steadfast. SEE MAIN ENTRY
stationed situated
statistic computation, poll *(canvass)*
statistical inquiry census, investigation
statistician accountant, actuary
statistics census, information *(facts)*
statuere constitute *(establish)*, determine, establish *(launch)*, fix *(settle)*, instate, resolve *(decide)*
stature capacity *(authority)*, elevation, magnitude. SEE MAIN ENTRY
status caliber *(quality)*, case *(set of circumstances)*, character *(reputation)*, class, credit *(recognition)*, degree *(station)*, honor *(good reputation)*, precedence, prestige, quality *(excellence)*, rating, reputation, situation, title *(position)*. SEE MAIN ENTRY
status condition *(state)*, phase *(aspect)*, position *(situation)*, posture *(situation)*, state *(condition)*
status quo SEE MAIN ENTRY
statutable law-abiding, lawful, legitimate *(rightful)*, licit
statute act *(enactment)*, authority *(documentation)*, canon, code, codification, constitution, edict, enactment, law, measure, ordinance, precept, prescription *(directive)*, regulation *(rule)*, rubric *(authoritative rule)*, rule *(legal dictate)*. SEE MAIN ENTRY
statute book code, codification, pandect *(code of laws)*
statute law code, codification
statute of frauds SEE MAIN ENTRY
statutes legislation *(enactments)*
statutory due *(regular)*, forensic, law-abiding, lawful, legal, legislative, legitimate *(rightful)*, licit, rightful, valid. SEE MAIN ENTRY
statutory cogency force *(legal efficacy)*
statutory law enactment
staunch constrict *(inhibit)*, dependable, faithful *(loyal)*, loyal, purposeful, steadfast, strong. SEE MAIN ENTRY
staunch belief conviction *(persuasion)*, faith
staunch loyalty faith
staunchness constant
stave in break *(fracture)*
stave off avert, contain *(restrain)*, defer *(put off)*, deter, dissuade, forestall, hold up *(delay)*, parry, postpone, prevent, procrastinate, repel *(drive back)*, thwart, withstand
stay abeyance, adjournment, arrest *(stop)*, balk, ban, bar *(hinder)*, barrier, block, cease, cessation *(interlude)*, clog, cloture, cohere *(adhere)*, constrict *(inhibit)*, continuance, continue *(adjourn)*, curb, defer *(put off)*, delay *(noun)*, delay *(verb)*, desist, detain *(restrain)*, dwell *(reside)*, encumbrance, endure *(last)*, estop, exist, extension *(postponement)*, forestall, halt *(noun)*, halt *(verb)*, impede, inhabit, inhabitation *(act of dwelling in)*, keep *(continue)*, keep *(restrain)*, last, lodge *(reside)*, lull, mainstay, obstruct, occupy *(take possession)*, pause *(noun)*, pause *(verb)*, persevere, persist, postpone, preclude, prevent, prohibit, prohibition, remain *(continue)*, remission, repress, reprieve, reside, resist *(withstand)*, respite *(interval of rest)*, rest *(cease from action)*, restraint, stem *(check)*, stop, subsist, suspend, toll *(stop)*, uphold, withstand. SEE MAIN ENTRY
stay alive exist, subsist
stay away shirk
stay away from shun
stay incognito prowl
stay of execution reprieve, respite *(reprieve)*. SEE MAIN ENTRY
stay on continue *(persevere)*, last
stay order injunction
stay together cohabit, consolidate *(unite)*
stayed arrested *(checked)*
staying durable, infallible, lasting, live *(existing)*, permanent, persistent
staying power diligence *(perseverance)*, resolution *(decision)*, sinew
stead behalf, help *(noun)*, help *(verb)*, site
steadfast chronic, constant, continual *(connected)*, dependable, diligent, durable, faithful *(loyal)*, firm, fixed *(securely placed)*, immutable, indelible, industrious, inexorable, inflexible, loyal, patient, permanent, persistent, pertinacious, purposeful, relentless, reliable, resolute, sedulous, serious *(devoted)*, solid *(sound)*, stable, staunch, strong, true *(loyal)*, uncompromising, unrelenting, unyielding. SEE MAIN ENTRY
steadfast belief faith
steadfastly faithfully
steadfastness adherence *(devotion)*, adhesion *(loyalty)*, allegiance, constant, diligence *(perseverance)*, faith, fealty, fidelity, industry *(activity)*, loyalty, resolution *(decision)*, tenacity. SEE MAIN ENTRY
steadily faithfully, in good faith, invariably
steadiness constant, diligence *(perseverance)*, indestructibility, longanimity, moderation, regularity, resolution *(decision)*
steady bear *(support)*, consecutive, constant, continual *(connected)*, continuous, controlled *(restrained)*, dependable, direct *(uninterrupted)*, dispassionate, establish *(entrench)*, firm, fixed *(securely placed)*, immutable, incessant, industrious, inexorable, infallible, loyal, patient, permanent, persistent, pertinacious, punctual, purposeful, regular *(orderly)*, reliable, resolute, serious *(devoted)*, solid *(sound)*, stabilize, stable, staunch, steadfast, strong, true *(loyal)*, undaunted, uniform, unyielding, well-grounded
steady advance progress
steady application diligence *(perseverance)*
steady demand market *(demand)*
steal acquire *(secure)*, carry away, convert *(misappropriate)*, defalcate, deprive, despoil, impropriate, jostle *(pickpocket)*, loot, lurk, mulct *(defraud)*, peculate, pilfer, pillage, pirate *(reproduce without authorization)*, pirate *(take by violence)*, plagiarize, plunder, poach, prowl, purloin, rob, spoil *(pillage)*, usurp. SEE MAIN ENTRY
steal away abscond, elude, escape, kidnap
stealer burglar, hoodlum, thief
stealing acquisition, burglary, embezzlement, housebreaking, misappropriation, plagiarism, robbery, theft
stealth evasion
stealthful stealthy
stealthiness concealment, evasion
stealthy artful, clandestine, covert, evasive, furtive, insidious, machiavellian, mysterious, privy, sly, subtle *(insidious)*, surreptitious. SEE MAIN ENTRY
steamship company carrier
steeled impervious
steeled against callous
steely rigid, unaffected *(uninfluenced)*
steep immerse *(plunge into)*, oblique *(slanted)*, permeate, pervade
steeped in poison deadly
steeped in vice vicious
steepness elevation
steer administer *(conduct)*, direct *(show)*, direct *(supervise)*, govern, manage, manipulate *(utilize skillfully)*, militate, moderate *(preside over)*, officiate, operate, overlook *(superintend)*, oversee, prescribe, preside, regulate *(manage)*, superintend
steer clear shirk. SEE MAIN ENTRY
steer clear of shun
steer for pursue *(strive to gain)*
steerage direction *(guidance)*, management *(judicious use)*, regulation *(management)*, supervision
steered direct *(straight)*
steering guidance, leading *(guiding)*, management *(supervision)*
steering committee management *(directorate)*
steeve load
stellar leading *(ranking first)*, master, principal. SEE MAIN ENTRY
stem block, bloodline, cease, check *(restrain)*, confront *(oppose)*, constrict *(inhibit)*, derivation, enjoin, halt, obstruct, parentage, race, repulse, resist *(oppose)*, source, stay *(halt)*, stop, withstand. SEE MAIN ENTRY
stenographic copy transcript
stentorian powerful
step act *(undertaking)*, degree *(station)*, expedient, operation, perambulate, phase *(period)*, procedure, proceeding, venture. SEE MAIN ENTRY
step aside deviate
step-by-step SEE MAIN ENTRY
step down alight, diminish, quit *(discontinue)*, resign
step in enter *(go in)*, intercede, intervene
step up expand, increase, intensify
step up to approach
stepping up a pace acceleration
steps campaign
steps in the prosecution of an action proceeding
stereotyped boiler plate, familiar *(customary)*, mundane, ordinary, routine, trite, typical, usual

stereotyped saying platitude
sterile barren, ineffective, ineffectual, otiose, unproductive
sterilis unproductive
sterilize decontaminate
sterilized pure
sterling genuine, high-minded, honest, laudable, meritorious, priceless, professional *(stellar)*. SEE MAIN ENTRY
stern astringent, bitter *(penetrating)*, harsh, particular *(exacting)*, relentless, rigid, serious *(grave)*, severe, solemn, strict, stringent, unapproachable, unbending, unrelenting, unyielding. SEE MAIN ENTRY
sternly just inexorable
sternness cruelty, rigor, severity
stew imbroglio
steward caretaker *(one caring for property)*, proctor, procurator, substitute, superintendent, supplier
stewards management *(directorate)*
stewardship control *(supervision)*, custody *(supervision)*, generalship, government *(administration)*, management *(supervision)*, supervision, surveillance
stick bond *(hold together)*, cement, cohere *(adhere)*, cudgel, lancinate, pierce *(lance)*
stick at refuse
stick close cohere *(adhere)*
stick in enter *(insert)*, plant *(place firmly)*
stick on to cohere *(adhere)*
stick out project *(extend beyond)*
stick to adhere *(fasten)*, adhere *(persist)*, keep *(continue)*, maintain *(carry on)*, maintain *(sustain)*, persevere, persist, pursue *(carry on)*
stick together adhere *(fasten)*, cohere *(adhere)*, combine *(join together)*, consolidate *(unite)*
stick up hold up *(rob)*
stick up for side
sticker brand, label
stickiness adhesion *(affixing)*
sticking coherent *(joined)*, cohesive *(sticking)*
sticking out manifest
sticking together adherence *(adhesion)*, coherence, coherent *(joined)*
stickle haggle, refuse, remonstrate
stickler bigot
stickling restive
stickup man burglar
stiff close *(rigorous)*, draconian, formal, immutable, indomitable, inflexible, ossified, ponderous, potent, precise, punctilious, renitent, restrictive, rigid, severe, solid *(compact)*, strict, stringent, strong, unbending, unyielding
stiffen fix *(make firm)*
stiffened ossified
stiffness formality
stifle arrest *(stop)*, cloak, clog, constrict *(inhibit)*, debar, diminish, extinguish, forestall, impair, inhibit, keep *(restrain)*, repress, restrain, restrict, stop, suppress, thwart, withhold. SEE MAIN ENTRY
stifle competition monopolize
stifled clandestine
stifling censorship, deadly, disadvantage, oppressive
stigma attaint, bad repute, brand, discredit, disgrace, dishonor *(shame)*, disparagement, ignominy, infamy, notoriety, obloquy, opprobrium, reproach, scandal, shame. SEE MAIN ENTRY
stigmatism brand
stigmatization denunciation, notoriety
stigmatize charge *(accuse)*, defame, denigrate, denounce *(condemn)*, discredit, disgrace, dishonor *(deprive of honor)*, disparage, humiliate, incriminate, involve *(implicate)*, lessen, pillory, smear, stain, sully, tarnish
stigmatizing calumnious
still allay, alleviate, assuage, dead, dormant, idle, lull, moderate *(temper)*, mollify, mute, notwithstanding, pacify, palliate *(abate)*, peaceable, placate, placid, regardless, repress, soothe, stagnant, stall, standing, static, stifle, strangle, suppress. SEE MAIN ENTRY
still existing extant
still in debate pending *(unresolved)*
still to be found extant
stillare distill
stilling palliative *(abating)*
stillness abeyance, inaction, insentience, lull, pause, peace, silence
stilted formal, histrionic, inflated *(bombastic)*, orotund, pretentious *(pompous)*, turgid
stiltedness formality
stimulant catalyst, cause *(reason)*, drug, impulse, incentive, inducement, motive, provocation, stimulus
stimulare spirit
stimulate abet, agitate *(activate)*, bait *(lure)*, cause, coax, develop, elicit, evoke, exhort, expedite, foment, foster, impel, incite, induce, influence, inspire, motivate, originate, promise *(raise expectations)*, prompt, provoke, renew *(begin again)*, spirit, urge. SEE MAIN ENTRY
stimulated inclined
stimulater inducement
stimulating causative, constructive *(creative)*, impulsive *(impelling)*, moving *(evoking emotion)*, provocative, remedial, salubrious
stimulation aggravation *(exacerbation)*, cause *(reason)*, development *(progression)*, inducement, instigation, motive, origination, provocation, reason *(basis)*, stimulus
stimulative inducement, moving *(evoking emotion)*, provocative, stimulus
stimulator catalyst, stimulus
stimulus cause *(reason)*, impetus, incentive, inducement, motive, origination, provocation. SEE MAIN ENTRY
stimulus instigation
stimulus program SEE MAIN ENTRY
sting affront, aggravate *(annoy)*, irritate, pique, provoke, stimulus
stinginess austerity
stinging bitter *(penetrating)*, caustic, harsh, incisive, mordacious, offensive *(offending)*, scathing, severe, trenchant
stinging words diatribe
stingy illiberal, nonsubstantial *(not sufficient)*, parsimonious, penurious, provident *(frugal)*
stint assignment *(task)*, austerity, insufficiency, period. SEE MAIN ENTRY
stinted devoid, limited, slight
stinting frugal, illiberal, limiting, parsimonious
stintless liberal *(generous)*
stipend alimony, annuity, commission *(fee)*, consideration *(recompense)*, endowment, honorarium, loan, pay, payment *(remittance)*, payroll, pension, perquisite, subsidy, wage
stipendium campaign, pay
stipulari stipulate
stipulate agree *(contract)*, bear *(adduce)*, designate, determine, mention, posit, promise *(vow)*, select, signify *(inform)*, specify. SEE MAIN ENTRY
stipulated agreed *(promised)*, contractual, stated
stipulatio stipulation
stipulation adjustment, agreement *(contract)*, assignment *(designation)*, attornment, bargain, clause, compact, condition *(contingent provision)*, consent, contract, covenant, designation *(naming)*, indenture, option *(contractual provision)*, pact, prerequisite, promise, protocol *(agreement)*, provision *(clause)*, qualification *(condition)*, reservation *(condition)*, security *(pledge)*, selection *(choice)*, specialty *(contract)*, specification, term *(provision)*, ultimatum, undertaking *(pledge)*. SEE MAIN ENTRY
stipulation to compensate for loss insurance
stipulative conditional
stipulatory qualified *(conditioned)*
stir agitate *(shake up)*, commingle, commotion, discompose, emotion, foment, furor, impress *(affect deeply)*, incite, industry *(activity)*, interest, noise, outburst, pandemonium, perturb, prompt, provoke, turmoil
stir to anger irritate
stir up agitate *(activate)*, churn, disrupt, disturb, engender, foment, incite, motivate, perturb, pique, press *(goad)*, promote *(organize)*, provoke, spirit, stimulate
stirps ancestry, family *(common ancestry)*
stirps issue *(progeny)*, lineage, offspring, parentage
stirps race
stirring momentous, moving *(evoking emotion)*, noteworthy, portentous *(eliciting amazement)*, provocative, sapid, solemn
stock average *(standard)*, blood, bloodline, boiler plate, cargo, commodities, cumulation, derivation, descent *(lineage)*, familiar *(customary)*, family *(common ancestry)*, fund *(noun)*, fund *(verb)*, furnish, garner, goods, hoard, household *(familiar)*, kindred, merchandise, nationality, nondescript, ordinary, origin *(ancestry)*, parentage, possessions, posterity, prevailing *(current)*, prevalent, progeny, prosaic, provide *(supply)*, provision *(something provided)*, race, regular *(conventional)*, repeated, replenish, reserve, resource, routine, stock in trade, store *(depository)*, store, supply, trite, typical, usual. SEE MAIN ENTRY
stock agreement call *(option)*
stock book inventory
stock company corporation
stock in trade commodities, goods, merchandise, possessions, product, resource. SEE MAIN ENTRY
stock list inventory
stock market exchange
stock pile reserve
stock saying catchword
stock sheet inventory
stock up hoard
stockade bulwark, jail
stocked replete
stockholder member *(individual in a group)*, shareholder. SEE MAIN ENTRY

stockholder of record shareholder
stockholding share *(stock)*
stockowner shareholder
stockpile accumulate *(amass)*, collection *(accumulation)*, cumulation, fund, garner, hoard *(noun)*, hoard *(verb)*, provision *(something provided)*, store *(depository)*, store
stockroom cache *(storage place)*
stocks portfolio, securities
stocks and bonds portfolio
stodgy lifeless *(dull)*, pedestrian
stoic patient, resigned, spartan, unaffected *(uninfluenced)*
stoical controlled *(restrained)*, dispassionate, patient, phlegmatic, resigned, spartan, unaffected *(uninfluenced)*. SEE MAIN ENTRY
stoicism continence, discipline *(obedience)*, longanimity, resignation *(passive acceptance)*, sufferance, tolerance
stolen article contraband
stolen articles plunder
stolen goods contraband, plunder, spoils
stolid dispassionate, jejune *(dull)*, opaque, phlegmatic, ponderous
stolidity opacity
stolidness opacity
stomach endure *(suffer)*, tolerate
stomachus resentment
stony insensible, obdurate, ossified, phlegmatic, rigid, severe, unaffected *(uninfluenced)*
stony-hearted brutal, malignant, relentless, ruthless, severe
stool pigeon informant
stoop comply, condescend *(deign)*, decline *(fall)*, deign, succumb, vouchsafe
stop adjourn, balk, ban, bar *(hinder)*, barrier, block, blockade *(barrier)*, cease, cessation *(interlude)*, check *(bar)*, check *(restrain)*, clog, close *(terminate)*, cloture, conclude *(complete)*, condemn *(ban)*, constrict *(inhibit)*, contain *(restrain)*, debar, delay, desist, destination, desuetude, detain *(restrain)*, deter, deterrence, discontinuance *(act of discontinuing)*, discontinue *(abandon)*, disqualify, disrupt, dissolve *(terminate)*, dwell *(reside)*, embargo, encumbrance, end *(termination)*, enjoin, estop, expiration, expire, finality, finish, forbear, forbid, forestall, forgo, halt *(noun)*, halt *(verb)*, hesitate, hiatus, hold up *(delay)*, impasse, impede, impediment, inhibit, interdict, interfere, interrupt, interruption, keep *(restrain)*, kill *(defeat)*, lapse *(cease)*, leave *(allow to remain)*, lock, lodge *(reside)*, lull, moratorium, obstacle, obstruct, obstruction, occlude, palliate *(abate)*, parry, preclude, prevent, prohibit, prohibition, quash, quit *(discontinue)*, recess *(noun)*, recess *(verb)*, refrain, remission, remit *(relax)*, reprieve, resist *(oppose)*, respite *(interval of rest)*, rest *(cease from action)*, restrain, restraint, restrict, shut, stall, stay, stay *(halt)*, stay *(rest)*, stem *(check)*, stifle, strangle, suppress, suspend, terminate, thwart, withstand. SEE MAIN ENTRY
stop & frisk SEE MAIN ENTRY
stop an advance halt
stop and consider pause
stop at nothing persevere
stop in progress by hindrances impede
stop look and listen beware
stop payment default, dishonor *(refuse to pay)*
stop short balk, clog, halt
stop the progress of estop
stop the way estop
stop to consider doubt *(hesitate)*
stop up block, clog, obstruct, obturate, occlude, shut
stop work cease, rest *(cease from action)*, strike *(refuse to work)*
stopgap expedient, substitute, temporary. SEE MAIN ENTRY
stopover halt
stoppage abeyance, bar *(obstruction)*, blockade *(limitation)*, cessation *(termination)*, check *(bar)*, close *(conclusion)*, cloture, damper *(stopper)*, deadlock, defeasance, deferment, desuetude, discontinuance *(act of discontinuing)*, embargo, encumbrance, end *(termination)*, expiration, extremity *(death)*, filibuster, finality, halt, hiatus, impediment, interruption, layoff, lull, miscarriage, moratorium, obstacle, obviation, pause, prohibition, recess, remission, restraint, stay, strike
stoppage of use desuetude
stoppage of work lockout
stopped arrested *(checked)*, broken *(interrupted)*
stopped-up blind *(impassable)*
stopper bar *(obstruction)*, check *(bar)*, damper *(stopper)*, obstacle, obstruction, obturate, shut, stop
stopping-place destination
stopple damper *(stopper)*, stop
storage arsenal, cache *(storage place)*, coffer, conservation, cumulation, depository, preservation
store business *(commercial enterprise)*, collection *(accumulation)*, conceal, cumulation, deposit *(place)*, depository, fund *(noun)*, fund *(verb)*, garner, hoard *(noun)*, hoard *(verb)*, keep *(shelter)*, load, market *(business)*, merchandise, provision *(something provided)*, quantity, replenish, repose *(place)*, reserve *(noun)*, reserve *(verb)*, resource, stock in trade, sufficiency, treasury. SEE MAIN ENTRY
store away reserve
store in the archives file *(place among official records)*
store of knowledge education
store of provisions cache *(storage place)*
store secretly hoard
store up accumulate *(amass)*, conserve, hoard, reserve, set aside *(reserve)*
storehouse bank, cache *(storage place)*, depository, repository, reserve, store *(depository)*, treasury
storehouse for safekeeping cache *(storage place)*
storekeeper dealer, merchant
storeroom cache *(storage place)*, repository
storm assail, attack, barrage, bluster *(commotion)*, cataclysm, demonstrate *(protest)*, furor, incursion, onset *(assault)*, pandemonium, passion, strike *(assault)*, turmoil. SEE MAIN ENTRY
storm against inveigh
stormer aggressor
storming barrage
stormless placid
stormy disorderly, severe, unruly
story falsehood, figment, item, myth, recital, scenario, statement. SEE MAIN ENTRY
storylike narrative
storytelling narration
stout firm, heroic, indomitable, ponderous, powerful, spartan, strong
stout heart prowess *(bravery)*
stout-hearted spartan
stouthearted heroic, undaunted
stoutness puissance, strength
stow deposit *(place)*, garner, hoard, load
stow away harbor, hide, hoard, store
straddle pause, tergiversate
strages havoc
straggle spread
straight clean, direct *(uninterrupted)*, ethical, naked *(lacking embellishment)*, right *(direct)*, straightforward, unadulterated, unbending, undistorted. SEE MAIN ENTRY
straight course rectitude, right *(righteousness)*
straight-out SEE MAIN ENTRY
straight-thinking pragmatic
straightaway direct *(straight)*, forthwith, right *(direct)*
straighten fix *(repair)*, organize *(arrange)*, rectify
straighten out arrange *(methodize)*, disabuse, disentangle, fix *(arrange)*, fix *(settle)*, negotiate, regulate *(adjust)*, settle
straightforward absolute *(conclusive)*, bona fide, candid, clear *(apparent)*, cognizable, coherent *(clear)*, compact *(pithy)*, credible, direct *(forthright)*, explicit, honest, ingenuous, irreprehensible, law-abiding, lucid, outright, pellucid, right *(direct)*, simple, unaffected *(sincere)*, unequivocal, upright. SEE MAIN ENTRY
straightforwardness probity, rectitude
straightness rectitude
straightway instantly
strain aggravation *(annoyance)*, ancestry, blood, bloodline, burden, descent *(lineage)*, distill, distort, effort, encumber *(hinder)*, endeavor *(noun)*, endeavor *(verb)*, exert, exhaust *(deplete)*, family *(common ancestry)*, feud, force *(break)*, harass, ill will, labor *(exertion)*, labor, mistreat, overextend, overload, overstep, pressure, purge *(purify)*, race, screen *(select)*, strive, struggle, tax *(overwork)*, try *(attempt)*, work *(effort)*
strain of invective diatribe
strain out distill
strain the meaning distort
strain the sense distort
strain the truth distort, perjure
strained relations contest *(dispute)*, disaccord, discord
strained sense catachresis, distortion
straining operose
strait emergency, entanglement *(involvement)*, plight, quagmire
strait-laced provincial, severe, stringent
straitened poor *(underprivileged)*
straitened circumstances poverty
straitened means privation
straitlaced restrictive, rigid, strict, unbending
straits poverty, predicament
strange eccentric, extraneous, extrinsic, foreign, incongruous, ineffable, inexplicable, irregular *(not usual)*, irrelative, ludicrous, mysterious, noteworthy, novel, obscure *(remote)*, peculiar *(curious)*, prodigious *(amazing)*, rare, remarkable, suspicious *(questionable)*, unaccustomed, unacquainted, uncanny, uncommon, uncouth, unrelated, unusual. SEE MAIN ENTRY
strange behavior quirk *(idiosyncrasy)*

strange occurrence quirk *(idiosyncrasy)*
strange person stranger
strangeness irregularity, nonconformity, quirk *(idiosyncrasy)*
stranger alien. SEE MAIN ENTRY
strangle extinguish, inhibit, repress, stifle, suppress. SEE MAIN ENTRY
strangulare strangle
strangulate constrict *(inhibit)*, stifle
strangulation blockade *(limitation)*, constraint *(restriction)*
strap fetter, handcuff
strapped impecunious, poor *(underprivileged)*
strapping powerful, strong
stratagem act *(undertaking)*, artifice, campaign, contrivance, deception, design *(intent)*, device *(contrivance)*, expedient, false pretense, hoax, instrumentality, machination, maneuver *(tactic)*, maneuver *(trick)*, operation, plot *(secret plan)*, ploy, policy *(plan of action)*, practice *(procedure)*, pretext, ruse, scheme, trap. SEE MAIN ENTRY
strategem plan, subterfuge
strategic cardinal *(basic)*, critical *(crucial)*, diplomatic, necessary *(required)*, subtle *(refined)*, tactical. SEE MAIN ENTRY
strategic item necessity, need *(requirement)*
strategical necessary *(required)*, strategic, tactical
strategics contrivance
strategist catalyst, coactor, conspirator, conspirer, expert, mastermind. SEE MAIN ENTRY
strategists management *(directorate)*
strategy campaign, design *(intent)*, direction *(course)*, discretion *(quality of being discreet)*, expedient, forethought, machination, maneuver *(tactic)*, plan, practice *(procedure)*, procedure, process *(course)*, program, proposition, ruse, scheme, stratagem, system. SEE MAIN ENTRY
stratification order *(arrangement)*
stratum class
straw man SEE MAIN ENTRY
stray detour, deviant, deviate, digress, lapse *(fall into error)*, miscalculate, prowl, random, sporadic
strayed lost *(disoriented)*
straying astray, deviation, discursive *(digressive)*, divergent, indirection *(indirect action)*, shifting, truant
streak frame *(mood)*
stream issue *(send forth)*, outflow, outpour
stream of abuse diatribe
stream of correspondence dispatch *(message)*
stream out emanate
streaming copious, fluvial
streamline simplify *(make easier)*
streamy fluvial
street avenue *(route)*, causeway
street number address
street vendor dealer
strenghten sustain *(confirm)*
strength amount *(quantity)*, degree *(magnitude)*, dint, emphasis, faculty *(ability)*, health, main force, mainstay, potential, predominance, protection, prowess *(bravery)*, puissance, sinew, tenacity, tolerance, validity. SEE MAIN ENTRY
strength of character discipline *(obedience)*
strength of will diligence *(perseverance)*, discipline *(obedience)*
strengthen aid, bear *(support)*, compound, concentrate *(consolidate)*, corroborate, develop, document, edify, empower, enable, endue, enforce, enhance, establish *(entrench)*, heighten *(augment)*, help, intensify, justify, magnify, nurture, reassure, recruit, reinforce, side, supplement, support *(corroborate)*, sustain *(prolong)*. SEE MAIN ENTRY
strengthened insusceptible *(resistant)*, protective
strengthener reinforcement
strengthening boom *(increase)*, consolidation, corroboration, cumulative *(increasing)*, cumulative *(intensifying)*, development *(progression)*, enforcement, help, remedial, support *(corroboration)*
strengthful strong
strengthless helpless *(powerless)*, languid, nonsubstantial *(not sturdy)*, null *(invalid)*, null and void, powerless
strengthlessness impotence, impuissance
strenuous difficult, intense, intensive, onerous, operose, oppressive, painstaking SEE MAIN ENTRY
strenuous effort endeavor, pursuit *(effort to secure)*
strenuousness effort, industry *(activity)*
strenuus spartan
strepitus noise
stress aggravation *(annoyance)*, argue, assert, certify *(attest)*, compulsion *(coercion)*, contend *(maintain)*, duress, dwell *(linger over)*, emphasis, enunciate, force *(compulsion)*, inflection, insist, plead *(allege in a legal action)*, pressure *(noun)*, pressure *(verb)*, pronounce *(speak)*, reaffirm, remind, work *(effort)*. SEE MAIN ENTRY
stressed alleged
stretch capacity *(maximum)*, capacity *(sphere)*, develop, distort, distortion, duration, embellish, enlarge, exaggeration, expand, extend *(enlarge)*, extent, falsify, gamut, increase, inflate, magnify, magnitude, overextend, overstep, period, phase *(period)*, prolong, purview, range, scope, slant, space, spread, stress *(strain)*, sustain *(prolong)*. SEE MAIN ENTRY
stretch a point magnify
stretch out deploy, expand, extend *(enlarge)*, spread
stretch the meaning distort
stretch the truth fabricate *(make up)*, perjure, prevaricate
stretch too far overextend
stretchable flexible, malleable, pliable
stretched inflated *(enlarged)*
stretching continuation *(prolongation)*, extension *(expansion)*
strew diffuse, dispel, disperse *(disseminate)*, disseminate, dissipate *(spread out)*, spread
stricken disconsolate
strict astringent, close *(rigorous)*, conscientious, draconian, drastic, exact, explicit, factual, faithful *(true to fact)*, inflexible, intense, ironclad, literal, meticulous, narrow, orthodox, painstaking, particular *(exacting)*, precise, punctilious, punctual, rigid, severe, stringent, tyrannous, unbending, uncompromising. SEE MAIN ENTRY
strict construction SEE MAIN ENTRY
strict control force *(compulsion)*
strict disciplinarian dictator
strict examination indagation, probe
strict honesty integrity
strict inquiry analysis, examination *(study)*, hearing, indagation, investigation
strict interpretation explanation
strict isolation quarantine
strict meaning SEE MAIN ENTRY
strict order array *(order)*
strict procedure bureaucracy
strict scrutiny SEE MAIN ENTRY
strict search indagation
striction deterrence, hindrance
strictly faithfully
strictly defined definite
strictly honest clean
strictly to the letter verbatim
strictness austerity, particularity, rigor, severity
stricture admonition, aspersion, bad repute, condemnation *(blame)*, correction *(punishment)*, denunciation, discredit, obloquy, obstruction, ostracism, outcry, reprimand, revilement, slander. SEE MAIN ENTRY
stride perambulate, step
strident discordant, harsh
stridulous harsh
strife altercation, argument *(contention)*, belligerency, competition, contention *(opposition)*, contest *(dispute)*, controversy *(argument)*, disaccord, disagreement, discord, dispute, dissension, dissidence, embroilment, feud, fight *(argument)*, fray, labor *(exertion)*, outbreak, outburst, resistance, revolt, variance *(disagreement)*, work *(effort)*. SEE MAIN ENTRY
strike assault *(noun)*, assault *(verb)*, attack, beat *(pulsate)*, boycott, collide *(crash against)*, contact *(touch)*, defiance, fight *(battle)*, find *(discover)*, impact, impinge, impress *(affect deeply)*, inflict, mistreat, onset *(assault)*, reach, rebel, rebellion, resist *(oppose)*, resistance, revolt. SEE MAIN ENTRY
strike a balance adjust *(regulate)*, compensate *(counterbalance)*, compromise *(settle by mutual agreement)*, discharge *(pay a debt)*. SEE MAIN ENTRY
strike a bargain barter, close *(agree)*, dicker, settle
strike a light burn
strike against collide *(crash against)*, jostle *(bump into)*
strike at accost, collide *(crash against)*, contend *(dispute)*, oppugn
strike back conflict, confront *(oppose)*, counter, recriminate, resist *(oppose)*, retaliate
strike forcibly against each other collide *(crash against)*
strike hard impress *(affect deeply)*
strike home impress *(affect deeply)*
strike in with involve *(participate)*
strike off decrease, deduct *(reduce)*, delete, discount *(reduce)*, rebate
strike off the roll discharge *(dismiss)*
strike off the roll of lawyers disbar
strike one as being appear *(seem to be)*
strike out annul, deface, delete, edit, eliminate *(eradicate)*, eradicate, expunge, expurgate, obliterate, redact
strike sightless blind *(deprive of sight)*
strike the first blow attack
strike together jostle *(bump into)*
strike visionless blind *(deprive of sight)*
strike with overwhelming fear frighten, menace
striking arrant *(definite)*, clear *(apparent)*, conspicuous, distinct *(clear)*, eloquent,

flagrant, insistent, manifest, notable, obvious, open *(in sight)*, palpable, particular *(specific)*, portentous *(eliciting amazement)*, powerful, prodigious *(amazing)*, prominent, remarkable, salient, special, unusual
striking part highlight
striking qualities character *(personal quality)*
striking together collision *(accident)*
strikingly particularly
string assemblage, handcuff, sequence
string out dispel, protract *(stall)*
stringency austerity, rigor, severity
stringent astringent, close *(rigorous)*, compulsory, draconian, harsh, inflexible, ironclad, particular *(exacting)*, relentless, rigid, severe, strict, uncompromising. SEE MAIN ENTRY
strip abridge *(divest)*, deduct *(reduce)*, demote, denude, deprive, despoil, disarm *(divest of arms)*, divest, erode, expose, harry *(plunder)*, loot, minimize, pillage, plunder, prey, remove *(eliminate)*, unveil
strip of disguise expose
strip of right disqualify
stripling juvenile
strive attempt, compete, contend *(dispute)*, endeavor, exert, labor, oppose, try *(attempt)*, undertake. SEE MAIN ENTRY
strive against conflict, dispute *(contest)*, oppose, oppugn, repel *(drive back)*, resist *(oppose)*
strive for pursue *(strive to gain)*
striver contender
striving competitive *(antagonistic)*, struggle
striving for effect flagrant, histrionic
striving for superiority competition
stroke calamity, expedient, maneuver *(tactic)*, operation
stroll perambulate, prowl
strong assertive, categorical, cogent, cohesive *(compact)*, compelling, convincing, disorderly, drastic, durable, firm, forcible, in full force, indomitable, inexpugnable, influential, infrangible, insusceptible *(resistant)*, intense, intensive, irresistible, omnipotent, orotund, persuasive, potent, powerful, predominant, prevailing *(having superior force)*, profound *(intense)*, reliable, resilient, resounding, secure *(sound)*, solid *(sound)*, sound, spartan, stable, staunch, steadfast, substantial, tenable, unyielding, valid, vehement, well-grounded. SEE MAIN ENTRY
strong arm tactics coercion
strong aversion odium
strong connection adhesion *(loyalty)*
strong contrast antithesis
strong demand market *(demand)*
strong discomfort pain
strong dissension dissension
strong feeling passion
strong language expletive
strong point specialty *(special aptitude)*
strong probability presumption
strong request dun
strong-minded inexorable, obdurate, purposeful, unbending
strong-willed earnest, hot-blooded, inexorable, inflexible, obdurate, persistent, pertinacious, purposeful, resolute, steadfast
strongbox coffer, treasury
stronghold bulwark, mainstay, protection, refuge, shelter *(protection)*
strongly attached close *(intimate)*, intimate
strongroom bank
structural fundamental, organic
structural composition configuration *(form)*
structural design configuration *(form)*
structure body *(main part)*, complex *(development)*, composition *(makeup)*, configuration *(form)*, construction, contour *(outline)*, contour *(shape)*, corpus, delineation, edifice, fabricate *(construct)*, form, formation, motif, order *(arrangement)*, temperament. SEE MAIN ENTRY
structures premises *(buildings)*
structuring building *(business of assembling)*
struggle affray, campaign, commotion, compete, conflict, confront *(oppose)*, confrontation *(altercation)*, contend *(dispute)*, contention *(opposition)*, contest *(competition)*, contest, effort, embroilment, endeavor *(noun)*, endeavor *(verb)*, engage *(involve)*, fight *(battle)*, grapple, labor, onus *(burden)*, opposition, persevere, pursuit *(effort to secure)*, resistance, strife, strive, work *(effort)*. SEE MAIN ENTRY
struggle against dispute *(contest)*, fight *(battle)*
struggle for pursue *(strive to gain)*
struggle for superiority competition
struggler candidate
strut flaunt, perambulate
strutting inflated *(vain)*
stub coupon, receipt *(proof of receiving)*
stubborn callous, chronic, contentious, difficult, disobedient, fractious, froward, impervious, incorrigible, indomitable, inexorable, inflexible, insusceptible *(uncaring)*, intractable, obdurate, persistent, pertinacious, perverse, pugnacious, purposeful, recalcitrant, relentless, resolute, restive, rigid, severe, unbending, uncontrollable, unrelenting, unruly, unyielding
stubborn person bigot
stubbornly disobedient contumacious
stubbornly rebellious contumacious
stubbornness defiance, diligence *(perseverance)*, tenacity
stuck inextricable
student disciple, neophyte, novice, protégé
studere adhere *(maintain loyalty)*, favor, study
studied aforethought, deliberate, elaborate, intentional, literate, nonchalant, premeditated, purposeful, tactical, willful
studies education
studiosus partial *(biased)*, zealous
studious diligent, industrious, learned, literate, pensive. SEE MAIN ENTRY
studiously purposely
studiousness diligence *(care)*, interest *(concern)*
studium ardor, inclination, interest *(concern)*, predilection, predisposition, pursuit *(chase)*, regard *(esteem)*
study analysis, analyze, audit, brood, canvass, check *(inspect)*, consider, consideration *(contemplation)*, contemplation, deliberate, deliberation, diligence *(care)*, hornbook, indagation, inquire, inquiry *(systematic investigation)*, inspection, knowledge *(learning)*, monitor, observation, overlook *(superintend)*, pandect *(treatise)*, peruse, ponder, preoccupation, probe, read, reason *(conclude)*, reflect *(ponder)*, reflection *(thought)*, research *(noun)*, research *(verb)*, review *(official reexamination)*, review, scrutinize, scrutiny, subject *(topic)*, survey *(examine)*, test, treatment, trial *(experiment)*, weigh. SEE MAIN ENTRY
study book hornbook
study deeply concentrate *(pay attention)*
study in detail investigate, probe
study in silence muse
study of ecosystems ecology
study of environs ecology
study of surroundings ecology
study quietly muse
study systematically examine *(study)*
stuff load
stuffed compact *(dense)*, full, replete
stuffy orotund, pedestrian
stultification constraint *(restriction)*
stultify balk, check *(restrain)*, clog, deter, disable, foil, frustrate, thwart
stultus irrational
stumble miscalculate, miscue, mistake
stumble on find *(discover)*, locate
stumbling incompetent
stumbling block bar *(obstruction)*, barrier, blockade *(barrier)*, complication, deadlock, deterrence, disadvantage, handicap, obstacle
stump confuse *(bewilder)*
stumper enigma, problem
stun drug, impress *(affect deeply)*, overcome *(overwhelm)*, overwhelm
stunned speechless
stunt lessen
stupefacient drug, narcotic
stupefaction bombshell
stupefactive narcotic
stupefied insensible, lifeless *(dull)*, phlegmatic, speechless, torpid
stupefy confuse *(bewilder)*, drug, lull, muddle, obfuscate
stupendous grandiose, portentous *(eliciting amazement)*, prodigious *(enormous)*, remarkable, special
stuperous torpid
stupid fatuous, impolitic, incompetent, inexpressive, irrational, obtuse, opaque, thoughtless, torpid, unpolitic, vacuous
stupidity opacity
stupidness opacity
stupor inertia, insentience, prostration, sloth
stuprare dishonor *(deprive of honor)*
stuprate debauch
stupration rape
stuprum debauchery, seduction
sturdiness health, prowess *(bravery)*, strength
sturdy durable, firm, indestructible, inexpugnable, solid *(sound)*, stable, strong
style call *(title)*, character *(personal quality)*, cognomen, color *(complexion)*, complexion, conduct, custom, denominate, form *(arrangement)*, habit, identify, manner *(behavior)*, manner *(kind)*, means *(opportunity)*, mode, modus operandi, motif, nominate, parlance, personality, phrase, phraseology, practice *(custom)*, presence *(poise)*, property *(distinctive attribute)*, structure *(composition)*, temperament, usage. SEE MAIN ENTRY
style of arrangement content *(structure)*, organization *(structure)*
style of penmanship handwriting
styleless outdated, outmoded
stylish current, elegant, popular
stymie balk, clog, constrict *(inhibit)*, debar, delay, disadvantage, estop, forestall, frustrate, hamper, imbroglio,

inconvenience, keep *(restrain)*, obstruct, parry, stay *(halt)*, stifle, stop, thwart. SEE MAIN ENTRY
sua sponte free *(enjoying civil liberty)* SEE MAIN ENTRY
sua voluntate free *(enjoying civil liberty)*
suable actionable
suadere advocate
suasible amenable, open *(persuasible)*, pliable. SEE MAIN ENTRY
suasion instigation, persuasion
suasive cogent, convincing, hortative, persuasive. SEE MAIN ENTRY
suasor advocate *(counselor)*, spokesman
suavis palatable
suavity courtesy
sub hasta vendere auction
subaltern ancillary *(subsidiary)*, assistant, ignoble, inferior *(lower in position)*, minor, secondary, slight, subordinate, subservient. SEE MAIN ENTRY
subalternate subaltern
subauscultare overhear
subcategory subdivision
subcenturio subaltern
subclass subdivision
subcommittee caucus
subconscious perception impression
subdere foist
subditus false *(not genuine)*
subdivide apportion, break *(separate)*, codify, dichotomize, disjoint, file *(arrange)*, parcel, part *(separate)*, partition, pigeonhole, sever, sort, split. SEE MAIN ENTRY
subdivided bipartite
subdivisible divisible
subdivision affiliate, chapter *(branch)*, chapter *(division)*, class, component, constituent *(part)*, decentralization, denomination, department, detail, dichotomy, lot, member *(constituent part)*, offshoot, organ, part *(portion)*, province, section *(division)*, segment, split, subheading. SEE MAIN ENTRY
subdivisional local, regional
subdivisive divisive
subdolous deceptive, machiavellian, surreptitious
subdolus sly
subdual control *(restriction)*, subjection
subduce withdraw
subducere steal
subduct decrease, deduct *(reduce)*, discount *(reduce)*, except *(exclude)*, excise *(cut away)*, retrench, withdraw
subduction curtailment, decrease, deduction *(diminution)*
subdue allay, alleviate, arrest *(stop)*, beat *(defeat)*, browbeat, capture, confine, constrain *(restrain)*, contain *(restrain)*, control *(restrain)*, defeat, diminish, disarm *(set at ease)*, dominate, extinguish, foil, halt, impose *(subject)*, lessen, lull, moderate *(temper)*, modify *(moderate)*, mollify, overcome *(surmount)*, override, overthrow, overturn, overwhelm, pacify, palliate *(abate)*, prevail *(triumph)*, quash, repress, restrain, stifle, strangle, subject, subjugate, suppress, surmount. SEE MAIN ENTRY
subdued dispassionate, passive, placid, solemn, unobtrusive
subduing bondage, mitigating, palliative *(abating)*
subgrade poor *(inferior in quality)*
subgroup chapter *(division)*, class, classification, part *(portion)*, section *(division)*, subdivision, subheading
subhead caption
subheading caption, subdivision. SEE MAIN ENTRY
subicere forge *(counterfeit)*, hint, subject
subiectio forgery
subiectus subject *(conditional)*
subigere compel
subit occur *(come to mind)*
subitaneous unexpected, unforeseeable
subitus instantaneous
subiungere subdue
subject article *(commodity)*, article *(distinct section of a writing)*, captive, compel, constrain *(compel)*, content *(meaning)*, contents, dependent, dominate, inferior *(lower in position)*, object, passive, question *(issue)*, require *(compel)*, servile, subdue, subjugate, subordinate, subservient, thesis. SEE MAIN ENTRY
subject for inquiry issue *(matter in dispute)*, matter *(subject)*
subject matter content *(meaning)*, contents, context, matter *(subject)*, tenor. SEE MAIN ENTRY
subject of controversy discrepancy
subject of dispute cause *(lawsuit)*, conflict, controversy *(argument)*, discrepancy, problem
subject of inquiry question *(inquiry)*
subject of thought contents
subject to conditional, contingent, dependent, incident, liable, provided
subject to a charge encumber *(financially obligate)*
subject to a handicap penalize
subject to a liability encumber *(financially obligate)*
subject to a pecuniary penalty fine
subject to action of court of justice justiciable
subject to analysis examine *(study)*
subject to another jurisdiction foreign
subject to argument debatable, disputable
subject to authority impose *(subject)*
subject to be concluded determinable *(liable to be terminated)*
subject to being abrogated defeasible
subject to being annulled defeasible
subject to being cancelled defeasible
subject to being divested defeasible
subject to being invalidated defeasible
subject to being repealed defeasible
subject to being retracted defeasible
subject to being revoked defeasible, voidable
subject to being taken away defeasible
subject to being withdrawn defeasible
subject to cancellation determinable *(liable to be terminated)*, voidable
subject to chance conditional, insecure
subject to change ambulatory, conditional, indefinite, insecure, mutable, provisional
subject to contention debatable, forensic
subject to contravention debatable
subject to control impose *(subject)*
subject to controversy debatable, disputable, forensic, moot, polemic
subject to dependence impose *(subject)*
subject to discontinuance determinable *(liable to be terminated)*
subject to examination analyze, audit, canvass, cross-examine, monitor
subject to influence impose *(subject)*
subject to loss endanger
subject to measurement determinable *(ascertainable)*
subject to penalty condemn *(punish)*, penalize, punish
subject to preference disjunctive *(alternative)*
subject to pressure enforce
subject to punishment discipline *(punish)*, penalize
subject to questioning examine *(interrogate)*
subject to revisal corrigible
subject to scrutiny check *(inspect)*, examine *(study)*, frisk, inquire, monitor, peruse, probe
subject to strain distress
subject to termination determinable *(liable to be terminated)*
subject to terms conditional, contingent, provisional, qualified *(conditioned)*, without recourse
subject to verification inconclusive
subjected subordinate
subjection acquiescence, allegiance, bondage, captivity, duress, force *(compulsion)*, homage, oppression, prostration, servitude, thrall. SEE MAIN ENTRY
subjection to responsibility *(accountability)*
subjection to death mortality
subjection to fate fatality
subjection to force compulsion *(coercion)*
subjective partial *(biased)*, personal *(private)*. SEE MAIN ENTRY
subjective belief credence
subjectivity intolerance, prejudice *(preconception)*
subjoin affix, annex *(add)*, append, attach *(join)*, compound, connect *(join together)*, join *(bring together)*
subjoined attached *(annexed)*
subjoiner adjoiner
subjoining accession *(annexation)*
subjugate abduct, beat *(defeat)*, coerce, confine, constrain *(restrain)*, defeat, discipline *(control)*, dominate, impose *(subject)*, jail, manage, overcome *(surmount)*, overthrow, overwhelm, repress, restrain, subdue, subject, surmount. SEE MAIN ENTRY
subjugated to inferior *(lower in position)*
subjugation abduction, bondage, captivity, duress, force *(compulsion)*, oppression, servitude, subjection, thrall
subjunction accession *(annexation)*, addition, attachment *(act of affixing)*, rider
sublation removal
sublease rent, sublet. SEE MAIN ENTRY
sublet lease, rent, sublease. SEE MAIN ENTRY
sublevatio relief *(release)*
sublimate elevate, purge *(purify)*
sublime illustrious, meritorious, outstanding *(prominent)*
sublunar mundane
sublunary mundane
submerge censor, immerse *(engross)*, immerse *(plunge into)*, overcome *(overwhelm)*, overwhelm
submerged latent
submerse immerse *(plunge into)*
submission acquiescence, adhesion *(loyalty)*, allegiance, amenability, application, argument *(pleading)*, assent, bid, capitulation, compliance, concession *(compromise)*, conciliation, conformity *(obedience)*, deference, discipline

(obedience), homage, longanimity, proposal (suggestion), proposition, prostration, rendition (restoration), resignation (passive acceptance), servitude, subjection, sufferance, thrall, tolerance
submission to a court's jurisdiction appearance (coming into court)
submissive malleable, obedient, obeisant, obsequious, passive, patient, pliable, pliant, powerless, resigned, sequacious, servile, subordinate, subservient, tractable, yielding
submissive to correction corrigible
submissively faithfully, respectfully
submissiveness acquiescence, adhesion (loyalty), amenability, capitulation, conformity (obedience), deference, discipline (obedience), homage, loyalty, resignation (passive acceptance)
submit abide, accede (concede), admonish (advise), advise, argue, bear (adduce), bestow, cede, concede, conform, counsel, defer (yield in judgment), extend (offer), forbear, give (grant), hear (give attention to), hold out (deliberate on an offer), index (docket), introduce, move (judicially request), obey, offer (propose), offer (tender), pose (propound), posit, proffer, propose, propound, refer (send for action), render (deliver), serve (assist), succumb, surrender (yield), tender. SEE MAIN ENTRY
submit a formal request move (judicially request)
submit for determination defer (yield in judgment)
submit in evidence exhibit
submit in judgment to defer (yield in judgment)
submit oneself to appear (attend court proceedings)
submit the case rest (end a legal case)
submit to allow (endure), bear (tolerate), comply, concede, endure (suffer), tolerate
submit without complaint forbear
submittal acquiescence, capitulation, cession, deference
suborder class
subordinate ancillary (subsidiary), assistant, coadjutant, dependent, derivative, employee, extrinsic, impose (subject), incidental, inferior (lower in position), minor, obsequious, passive, pliant, secondary, sequacious, servile, slight, subaltern, subject (conditional), subject, subservient, subsidiary, supplementary, tangential. SEE MAIN ENTRY
subordinate group minority (outnumbered group)
subordinate part adjunct, member (constituent part)
subordinate position subordinate
subordination allegiance, array (order), bondage, conformity (obedience), servitude, subjection
subordination to rules discipline (obedience)
suborn bait (lure), coax, convince, corrupt, inveigle, persuade, taint (corrupt). SEE MAIN ENTRY
subornare suborn
subornation gratuity (bribe)
subornative persuasive
subpoena call (summon), charge (command), citation (charge), direction (order), monition (legal summons), process (summons), serve (deliver a legal instrument), summon, venire, warrant (judicial writ). SEE MAIN ENTRY
subpoema duces tecum SEE MAIN ENTRY
subrent lease, rent, sublease, sublet
subreption deceit, fraud, misstatement. SEE MAIN ENTRY
subreptitious collusive
subrogate change, replace, succeed (follow), supersede, supplant
subrogation replacement. SEE MAIN ENTRY
subscribe attest, bear (adduce), close (agree), corroborate, enroll, hear (give attention to), join (associate oneself with), notarize, register, sign, subsidize. SEE MAIN ENTRY
subscribe to abide, accede (concede), advocate, agree (comply), assent, assure (insure), authorize, coincide (concur), concur (agree), contribute (assist), countenance, defer (yield in judgment), embrace (accept), espouse, indorse, maintain (sustain), profess (avow), promote (organize), sanction, sponsor
subscriber affiant, contributor (giver), donor, notary public, proponent, surety (guarantor), undersigned
subscribere sign
subscript addendum, codicil, rider
subscription advance (allowance), advocacy, affirmance (judicial sanction), aid (help), confirmation, consent, favor (sanction), grant, sanction (permission), vow. SEE MAIN ENTRY
subsection department, subheading
subsequent consecutive, derivative, ensuing, future, prospective, proximate, secondary, successive. SEE MAIN ENTRY
subsequent meditation hindsight
subsequent reflection hindsight
subsequently thereafter
subsequently set down a savoir
subserve aid, assist, avail (be of use), foster, inure (benefit), pander, promote (organize), subsidize
subservience adhesion (loyalty), bondage, homage, servitude
subserviency subjection
subservient dependent, inferior (lower in position), obedient, obeisant, obsequious, passive, pliant, subordinate, subsidiary. SEE MAIN ENTRY
subside decrease, diminish, ebb, lessen. SEE MAIN ENTRY
subsidence decline, decrease, descent (declination), lull, remission
subsidiarius subsidiary
subsidiary affiliate, appurtenance, appurtenant, chapter (branch), circumstantial, contingent, derivative, extraneous, extrinsic, incident, incidental, inferior (lower in position), minor, offshoot, organ, pendent, secondary, slight, subaltern, subordinate, subservient, supplementary. SEE MAIN ENTRY
subsidiary group minority (outnumbered group)
subsidiary law code
subsidium help, relief (aid), support (assistance)
subsidization alimony, pension
subsidize assist, capitalize (provide capital), contribute (supply), endow, finance, fund, maintain (sustain), pay, supplement, support (assist). SEE MAIN ENTRY
subsidize again refinance
subsidizer backer
subsidy aid (help), aid (subsistence), alimony, annuity, assistance, benefit (conferment), commission (fee), consideration (recompense), contribution (donation), donation, endowment, grant, loan, maintenance (support of spouse), payment (act of paying), pension, perquisite. SEE MAIN ENTRY
subsist continue (persevere), endure (last), exist, last, remain (continue), stay (continue). SEE MAIN ENTRY
subsist of contain (comprise)
subsistence aid (help), livelihood, maintenance (support of spouse), subsidy, support (assistance), sustenance
subsistence level austerity, poverty
subsistent extant, inherent
subsistere halt
subspecies class
substance amount (quantity), article (commodity), body (main part), bulk, capsule, center (essence), connotation, consequence (significance), construction, content (meaning), contents, contour (shape), cornerstone, corpus, element, essence, gist (ground for a suit), gravamen, import, importance, main point, materiality (physical existence), meaning, money, object, point (purpose), property (possessions), reality, significance, signification, spirit, structure (composition), sum (tally), value. SEE MAIN ENTRY
substance of a charge complaint
substandard deficient, perfunctory, poor (inferior in quality)
substantiable deductible (provable)
substantial actual, appreciable, capacious, cardinal (basic), cogent, cohesive (compact), concrete, considerable, convincing, corporal, corporeal, critical (crucial), durable, far reaching, firm, grave (important), important (significant), major, material (important), material (physical), meritorious, momentous, opulent, organic, outstanding (prominent), physical, pithy, prodigious (enormous), secure (sound), solid (sound), sound, stable, staunch, substantive, tangible, valid. SEE MAIN ENTRY
substantial cause gravamen
substantial cause shown SEE MAIN ENTRY
substantial form contour (shape)
substantial meaning connotation, content (meaning), gist (substance)
substantial number bulk
substantial part bulk
substantial part of a complaint gist (ground for a suit)
substantial quantity bulk
substantial rise of prices inflation (decrease in value of currency)
substantiality certainty, character (personal quality), cornerstone, corpus, embodiment, importance, materiality (consequence), materiality (physical existence), reality, significance, strength
substantialize embody, substantiate
substantially as a rule
substantially true candid
substantialness materiality (physical existence), reality, strength
substantiate affirm (uphold), attest, bear (adduce), cite (state), corroborate, demonstrate (establish), document, establish (show), maintain (sustain), probate, prove, quote, realize (make real), seal (solemnize), support (corroborate), sustain (confirm), uphold, validate, verify (confirm), witness (attest to). SEE MAIN ENTRY
substantiated incident fact
substantiation affirmance (authentication), affirmation, attestation, certification (attested copy), confirmation, corroboration, documentation, evidence, jurat,

proof, ratification, realization, reference *(citation)*, reference *(recommendation)*, support *(corroboration)*. SEE MAIN ENTRY
substantiative demonstrative *(illustrative)*. SEE MAIN ENTRY
substantive actual, appreciable, cardinal *(basic)*, concrete, corporeal, de facto, necessary *(required)*, organic, physical, ponderable, solid *(sound)*, substantial, tangible, virtual
substantive due process SEE MAIN ENTRY
substantive issue SEE MAIN ENTRY
substituere replace
substantive issue SEE MAIN ENTRY
substitutable equivalent, expendable
substitute agent, alienate *(transfer title)*, alternate *(take turns)*, change, commute, conduit *(intermediary)*, convert *(change use)*, cover *(provide for)*, delegate, deputy, devolve, disjunctive *(alternative)*, displace *(replace)*, exchange, false *(not genuine)*, imitation, liaison, offset, plenipotentiary, procurator, provisional, proxy, quid pro quo, replace, replacement, representative *(proxy)*, secondary, stopgap, succedaneum, supersede, supplant, surrogate, transform. SEE MAIN ENTRY
substitute for succeed *(follow)*
substitutes choice *(alternatives offered)*
substituting for acting
substitution contribution *(indemnification)*, cover *(substitute)*, devolution, exchange, novation, preemption, proxy, recompense, replacement, representation *(acting for others)*, representative *(proxy)*, stopgap, subrogation, substitute, succedaneum
substitution of counsel SEE MAIN ENTRY
substitutional disjunctive *(alternative)*, surrogate
substitutive convertible, disjunctive *(alternative)*
substructure foundation *(basis)*
subsume classify, comprise, encompass *(include)*, include, pigeonhole. SEE MAIN ENTRY
subterfuge artifice, bad faith, color *(deceptive appearance)*, concealment, contrivance, cover *(pretext)*, deception, evasion, excuse, expedient, false pretense, hoax, imposture, machination, maneuver *(trick)*, pretense *(pretext)*, pretext, ruse, scheme, stratagem. SEE MAIN ENTRY
subterranean clandestine
subtile imponderable, subtle *(refined)*
subtilis acute, exact
subtilize clarify, differentiate
subtitle caption
subtle artful, discreet, furtive, impalpable, inconspicuous, insidious, obscure *(faint)*, politic, recondite, sly, surreptitious. SEE MAIN ENTRY
subtle communication reference *(allusion)*
subtle difference differential, nuance
subtle maneuver device *(contrivance)*
subtlety discretion *(quality of being discreet)*, evasion, nuance, subterfuge, technicality
subtract abridge *(shorten)*, curtail, decrease, deduct *(reduce)*, dilute, diminish, discount *(reduce)*, eradicate, except *(exclude)*, excise *(cut away)*, lessen, minimize, rebate, remove *(eliminate)*, retrench, withdraw. SEE MAIN ENTRY
subtract from derogate
subtraction curtailment, decrease, decrement, deduction *(diminution)*, discount, exception *(exclusion)*, removal. SEE MAIN ENTRY
suburbs vicinity
subvenire assist, help
subvention alimony, annuity, benefit *(conferment)*, contribution *(donation)*, dispensation *(act of dispensing)*, donation, grant, help, pension, subsidy
subventionize subsidize
subversion bad faith, counterargument, disloyalty, mutiny, rebellion, revolt, sedition, treason. SEE MAIN ENTRY
subversionary harmful
subversive activities subversion
subversive activity bad faith, disloyalty, espionage
subversives SEE MAIN ENTRY
subvert corrupt, destroy *(efface)*, disturb, harm, overthrow, overturn, pervert, supplant, upset. SEE MAIN ENTRY
subverter insurgent
subvertere abolish, overturn, subvert, upset
succedaneum alternative *(substitute)*, stopgap. SEE MAIN ENTRY
succedere succeed *(follow)*, supersede
succeed accomplish, attain, avail *(bring about)*, carry *(succeed)*, complete, discharge *(perform)*, dispatch *(dispose of)*, displace *(replace)*, effectuate, ensue, execute *(accomplish)*, gain, implement, pass *(satisfy requirements)*, prevail *(triumph)*, reach, replace, supersede, supervene, supplant. SEE MAIN ENTRY
succeed in reaching attain, earn
succeed to inherit
succeeding consecutive, ensuing, future, proximate, subsequent, successive
succeeding generation descendant
succeeding generations posterity, progeny
success advantage, benefit *(betterment)*, fruition, progress, prosperity, satisfaction *(fulfilment)*, welfare. SEE MAIN ENTRY
successful auspicious, effective *(efficient)*, felicitous, lucrative, operative, prevailing *(having superior force)*, profitable, prosperous. SEE MAIN ENTRY
successful remedial treatment cure
successfulness prosperity
succession birth *(lineage)*, bloodline, chain *(series)*, continuity, cycle, devolution, frequency, hierarchy *(arrangement in a series)*, sequence, subrogation. SEE MAIN ENTRY
succession of acts course
succession of property inheritance
succession of property rights devolution
successions vicissitudes
successive consecutive, direct *(uninterrupted)*, disjunctive *(tending to disjoin)*, ensuing, periodic, progressive *(going forward)*, regular *(orderly)*, repeated. SEE MAIN ENTRY
successive phases vicissitudes
successive portion installment, serial
successive relationship privity
successively gaining in force cumulative *(increasing)*
successively waxing in force cumulative *(increasing)*
successiveness continuity
successless disappointed, unavailing
successlessness miscarriage
successor descendant, devisee, heir, offspring, replacement, transferee. SEE MAIN ENTRY
successors posterity
successorship succession
succinct brief, compact *(pithy)*, concise, laconic, pithy, proverbial, sententious. SEE MAIN ENTRY
succor abet, accommodation *(backing)*, aid *(help)*, aid, alleviate, assist, assistance, avail *(be of use)*, bear *(support)*, benefit *(betterment)*, benevolence *(act of kindness)*, bolster, contribute *(assist)*, contribution *(donation)*, favor, foster, help *(noun)*, help *(verb)*, nurture, relief *(aid)*, relieve *(give aid)*, remedy, serve *(assist)*, service *(assistance)*, soothe, support *(assistance)*
succorer benefactor, good samaritan, samaritan, sponsor
succulent palatable, sapid
succumb accede *(concede)*, cede, comply, concede, decease, expire, fail *(lose)*, hear *(give attention to)*, languish, lose *(undergo defeat)*, obey, perish, quit *(discontinue)*, relent, submit *(yield)*, surrender *(yield)*, yield *(submit)*. SEE MAIN ENTRY
succumb to death die
succumbere succumb
succurrere help
suceed in winning beat *(defeat)*
such being the case consequently
sudden brief, immediate *(at once)*, impulsive *(rash)*, precipitate, spontaneous, summary, unanticipated, unexpected, unforeseeable, unforeseen. SEE MAIN ENTRY
sudden attack assault, bombshell, foray
sudden burst bombshell
sudden contact collision *(accident)*
sudden death fatality
sudden desire impulse
sudden excursion outburst
sudden fear consternation, panic
sudden force impulse
sudden happening accident *(chance occurrence)*
sudden misfortune disaster
sudden peril emergency
sudden terror fright
suddenness dispatch *(promptness)*
sue appeal, call *(appeal to)*, claim *(demand)*, complain *(charge)*, importune, litigate, prosecute *(charge)*. SEE MAIN ENTRY
sue a third party implead
sue for request
suffer abide, allow *(endure)*, bear *(tolerate)*, consent, forbear, languish, let *(permit)*, permit, recognize *(acknowledge)*, sanction, tolerate, vouchsafe. SEE MAIN ENTRY
suffer a deprivation lose *(be deprived of)*
suffer a relapse relapse
suffer by comparison lose *(undergo defeat)*
suffer death die
suffer defeat lose *(undergo defeat)*, quit *(discontinue)*, yield *(submit)*
suffer loss decrease, lose *(be deprived of)*
suffer pain endure *(suffer)*
suffer privation lack
suffer to occur allow *(endure)*, authorize
sufferable allowable, permissible
sufferance acquiescence, charter *(sanction)*, consent, dispensation *(exception)*, franchise *(license)*, indulgence, leave *(permission)*, longanimity, resignation *(passive acceptance)*, sanction *(permission)*, tolerance, understanding *(tolerance)*. SEE MAIN ENTRY
suffered allowable
sufferer victim

suffering adversity, discipline *(punishment)*, distress *(anguish)*, hardship, misfortune, pain, prostration, sanction *(punishment)*, sufferance, toll *(effect)*, trouble. SEE MAIN ENTRY
suffering privation poor *(underprivileged)*
suffice avail *(bring about)*, bear *(tolerate)*, fulfill, satisfy *(fulfill)*
suffice to defray cover *(provide for)*
sufficience quorum
sufficiency admissibility, competence *(ability)*, minimum, quorum, satisfaction *(fulfilment)*, store *(depository)*. SEE MAIN ENTRY
sufficient adequate, ample, commensurate, competent, fair *(satisfactory)*, operative, suitable. SEE MAIN ENTRY
sufficient amount minimum
sufficient evidence proof
sufficient for the purpose adequate
sufficient foundation SEE MAIN ENTRY
sufficient in law legal
sufficient notice adequate notice
sufficient number quorum
sufficient on its face prima facie *(legally sufficient)*
sufficient on the pleadings prima facie *(legally sufficient)*
sufficient proof SEE MAIN ENTRY
sufficient quantity quorum
sufficient to make out a case prima facie *(legally sufficient)*
sufficiently strong prima facie *(legally sufficient)*
sufficientness sufficiency
sufficing adequate, commensurate
suffisant complacent
suffix codicil
sufflate inflate
sufflation inflation *(increase)*
suffocate extinguish, impede, repress, stifle
suffocating deadly, oppressive
suffragari favor, support *(assist)*
suffrage discretion *(power of choice)*, franchise *(right to vote)*. SEE MAIN ENTRY
suffragia election *(choice)*
suffragium suffrage, vote
suffragium ferre vote
suffuscus dun
suffuse penetrate, permeate, pervade, spread
sugary nectarious
suggest admonish *(advise)*, advise, advocate, allude, bespeak, charge *(instruct on the law)*, coax, connote, convey *(communicate)*, counsel, denote, evidence, hint, hold out *(deliberate on an offer)*, implicate, imply, indicate, instruct *(direct)*, mention, nominate, offer *(propose)*, pose *(propound)*, postulate, present *(introduce)*, proffer, promise *(raise expectations)*, prompt, propose, propound, purport, raise *(advance)*, recommend, refer *(direct attention)*, remark, remind, signify *(denote)*, submit *(give)*. SEE MAIN ENTRY
suggest a proposed claim counsel
suggest a proposed contention counsel
suggest conclusions of law charge *(instruct on the law)*
suggest itself occur *(come to mind)*
suggested constructive *(inferential)*, implicit, implied, tacit
suggested meaning implication *(inference)*
suggested plan suggestion
suggester catalyst, special interest
suggestibility credulity
suggestible open *(persuasible)*, pliant
suggesting advisory, demonstrative *(illustrative)*, precatory
suggestio falsi color *(deceptive appearance)*
suggestion advice, advocacy, connotation, expedient, guidance, hint, hypothesis, implication *(inference)*, indicant, indication, innuendo, insinuation, intimation, mention *(reference)*, notion, nuance, plan, possibility, postulate, proposal *(suggestion)*, proposition, recommendation, reference *(allusion)*, reminder, request, suspicion *(uncertainty)*, tip *(clue)*. SEE MAIN ENTRY
suggestive allusive, apparent *(presumptive)*, circumstantial, demonstrative *(illustrative)*, implicit, leading *(guiding)*, lewd, portentous *(ominous)*, precatory, provocative, prurient, salacious. SEE MAIN ENTRY
sui generus SEE MAIN ENTRY
sui iuris sovereign *(independent)*
suit accommodate, action *(proceeding)*, agree *(comply)*, calculate, call *(appeal)*, case *(lawsuit)*, cause *(lawsuit)*, chain *(series)*, claim *(legal demand)*, clothe, comport *(agree with)*, concur *(agree)*, conform, entreaty, matter *(case)*, proceeding, prosecution *(criminal trial)*, satisfy *(fulfill)*, trial *(legal proceeding)*. SEE MAIN ENTRY
suit at law action *(proceeding)*, case *(lawsuit)*, cause *(lawsuit)*, lawsuit, matter *(case)*, proceeding, trial *(legal proceeding)*
suit in equity lawsuit
suit in law action *(proceeding)*, controversy *(lawsuit)*, suit
suit one's purpose avail *(be of use)*
suit to extinguish the equity of redemption foreclosure
suitability admissibility, aptitude, competence *(ability)*, decorum, expedience, propriety *(appropriateness)*, qualification *(fitness)*, relevance, timeliness, use, utility *(usefulness)*. SEE MAIN ENTRY
suitable adequate, admissible, allowable, allowed, applicable, apposite, appropriate, available, commensurate, competent, condign, consonant, constructive *(creative)*, convenient, correlative, desirable *(qualified)*, disposable, eligible, entitled, fair *(just)*, fair *(satisfactory)*, favorable *(advantageous)*, felicitous, fit, fitting, habitable, harmonious, just, justifiable, opportune, pertinent, practical, prima facie *(legally sufficient)*, proper, qualified *(competent)*, reasonable *(fair)*, relative *(relevant)*, relevant, right *(suitable)*, rightful, sciential, seasonable, valuable, viable. SEE MAIN ENTRY
suitable circumstance chance *(fortuity)*, opportunity
suitable for living in habitable
suitable for use functional
suitable notice adequate notice
suitable occasion opportunity
suitable time occasion, opportunity, timeliness
suitableness decorum, expedience, propriety *(appropriateness)*, qualification *(fitness)*, relevance
suite chain *(series)*
suited agreed *(harmonized)*, apposite, appropriate, capable, convenient, correlative, fit, fitting, opportune, proper, sciential, suitable
suited to youth juvenile
suitedness qualification *(fitness)*
suiting congruous, felicitous, harmonious
suitor appellant, claimant, complainant, contender, contestant, litigant, party *(litigant)*, plaintiff, special interest. SEE MAIN ENTRY
sulk brood
sulky resentful, restive
sullen despondent, resentful, restive
sullied blemished, marred, tainted *(contaminated)*
sully brand *(stigmatize)*, contaminate, debauch, deface, defame, denigrate, depreciate, derogate, disapprove *(condemn)*, disgrace, disparage, humiliate, infect, pillory, pollute, smear, stain, taint *(contaminate)*, tarnish, vitiate. SEE MAIN ENTRY
sullying defilement
sum aggregate, amount *(quantity)*, amount *(result)*, computation, consideration *(recompense)*, content *(meaning)*, corpus, entirety, expenditure, expense *(cost)*, face amount, face value *(price)*, import, principal *(capital sum)*, quantity, substance *(essential nature)*, totality. SEE MAIN ENTRY
sum and substance capsule, center *(essence)*, content *(meaning)*, context, corpus, gist *(ground for a suit)*, gist *(substance)*, gravamen, materiality *(consequence)*, scenario
sum asked for cost *(price)*
sum charged expense *(cost)*
sum derived from a sale proceeds
sum entrusted loan
sum of money fund
sum of money borrowed loan
sum of money lent loan
sum owed debt
sum owing debit
sum paid for carrying a passenger fare
sum shown face amount
sum stated face amount
sum total aggregate, amount *(result)*, corpus, in solido, principal *(capital sum)*, quantity, sum *(total)*, whole
sum up condense, criticize *(evaluate)*, digest *(summarize)*, recapitulate, repeat *(state again)*, review
sumere presume
sumless innumerable, myriad
summa amount *(quantity)*
summarily dispossess eject *(evict)*
summariness dispatch *(promptness)*
summarium epitome, summary, synopsis
summarization narration. SEE MAIN ENTRY
summarize abridge *(shorten)*, condense, extract, lessen, recapitulate, recount, repeat *(state again)*, review. SEE MAIN ENTRY
summarized brief, compact *(pithy)*, concise, laconic, sententious
summary abridgment *(condensation)*, abstract, account *(report)*, brief *(adjective)*, brief *(noun)*, capsule, compact *(pithy)*, compendium, concise, cursory, decisive, digest, direct *(forthright)*, narration, pandect *(treatise)*, paraphrase, pithy, prompt, proposal *(report)*, prospectus, recital, report *(detailed account)*, restatement, scenario, statement, succinct, sum *(tally)*, synopsis. SEE MAIN ENTRY
summary of facts story *(narrative)*
summary on the law brief
summary punishment by mob lynch law

summate sum
summation account *(report),* amount *(sum),* computation, corpus, denouement, outline *(synopsis),* synopsis. SEE MAIN ENTRY
summed up compact *(pithy)*
summing up recital
summisse respectfully
summit caucus, ceiling, culmination, meeting *(conference),* panel *(discussion group),* paragon, parley, pinnacle
summit conference parley
summit talk parley
summital cardinal *(basic)*
summitry negotiation
summon convene, evoke, invoke, prosecute *(charge),* request, require *(compel),* serve *(deliver a legal instrument),* subpoena. SEE MAIN ENTRY
summon back recall *(call back)*
summon by incantation invoke
summon forth call *(summon),* educe, elicit, evoke
summon to court subpoena
summon up evoke, recall *(remember),* recollect, remember
summons charge *(accusation),* charge *(command),* direction *(order),* invitation, monition *(legal summons),* subpoena, venire, warrant *(judicial writ).* SEE MAIN ENTRY
summons to appear and answer monition *(legal summons)*
summus ascendant, extreme *(last),* paramount, unqualified *(unlimited)*
sumptio assumption *(supposition),* postulate
sumptious profuse
sumptuary financial, pecuniary
sumptuous elaborate
sumptus outlay, waste
sumptus minuere retrench
sunder bifurcate, break *(separate),* disband, discontinue *(abandon),* discontinue *(break continuity),* disengage, disjoint, disrupt, dissociate, dissolve *(separate),* divide *(separate),* divorce, estrange, interrupt, isolate, lancinate, luxate, part *(separate),* rend, separate, sever, split, subdivide
sunderance disassociation, division *(act of dividing),* interruption, severance, split
sundered disconnected, discrete, separate
sundering estrangement, separation
sundry composite, diverse, manifold, miscellaneous, multiple, several *(plural)*
sung famous
sunset law SEE MAIN ENTRY
sunshine laws SEE MAIN ENTRY
suo arbitrio discretion *(power of choice)*
super superlative
super pac SEE MAIN ENTRY
superable possible
superabundance boom *(prosperity),* plethora, redundancy, sufficiency, surfeit, surplus
superabundant copious, excess, excessive, expendable, inordinate, multiple, needless, redundant, superfluous, unwarranted
superadd compound, supplement
superadded additional
superannuate SEE MAIN ENTRY
superannuated antique, old, outdated, outmoded, powerless
superare beat *(defeat),* defeat, outweigh, predominate *(command),* prevail *(triumph)*
superb meritorious, portentous *(eliciting amazement),* preferential, premium, prime *(most valuable),* professional *(stellar),* sterling. SEE MAIN ENTRY
superbia intolerance
superbire rampant
superbus supercilious
supercharge overload
supercherie bunko
supercilious cynical, disdainful, insolent, orgulous, presumptuous, proud *(conceited).* SEE MAIN ENTRY
superciliousness disdain, disrespect, pride
superego conscience
supereminence eminence, primacy
supereminent cardinal *(outstanding),* master, outstanding *(prominent),* paramount, primary, prime *(most valuable),* principal
supererogate surpass
supererogative excess, superfluous, unnecessary
supererogatory excess, excessive, expendable, inordinate, needless, nonessential, superfluous, unnecessary
superexcellent superior *(excellent),* superlative
superficial artificial, careless, casual, cursory, frivolous, inconsequential, insubstantial, minor, nominal, nugatory, null *(insignificant),* perfunctory, pretentious *(ostentatious),* remote *(small),* trivial. SEE MAIN ENTRY
superficially pro forma
superficies area *(surface)*
superfine best, premium, subtle *(refined),* superlative
superfluity balance *(amount in excess),* boom *(prosperity),* exaggeration, plethora, redundancy, remainder *(remaining part),* surfeit, surplus
superfluous disproportionate, excess, excessive, expendable, extraneous, gratuitous *(unwarranted),* inordinate, needless, nonessential, profuse, redundant, undue *(excessive),* unessential, unnecessary, unwarranted. SEE MAIN ENTRY
superfluousness balance *(amount in excess),* exaggeration, plethora, tautology
superfund SEE MAIN ENTRY
superhighway causeway
superimpose overlap
superinduce affect, cause
superintend administer *(conduct),* check *(inspect),* conduct, control *(regulate),* direct *(supervise),* discipline *(control),* govern, handle *(manage),* manage, officiate, operate, oversee, patrol, police, prescribe, preside, regulate *(manage),* rule *(govern).* SEE MAIN ENTRY
superintendence administration, agency *(legal relationship),* auspices, charge *(custody),* control *(supervision),* custody *(supervision),* direction *(guidance),* government *(administration),* jurisdiction, management *(supervision),* occupation *(possession),* oversight *(control),* regulation *(management),* safekeeping, supervision, supremacy, surveillance
superintendency generalship
superintendent caretaker *(one caring for property),* caretaker *(one fulfilling the function of office),* director, employer, guardian, official, principal *(director),* procurator, warden. SEE MAIN ENTRY
superintendents management *(directorate)*
superintending administrative
superior absolute *(ideal)*
superior ascendant
superior best, chief, disdainful, dominant, employer, important *(significant),* inflated *(vain),* irresistible, meritorious, notable, outstanding *(prominent),* paramount, predominant, preferable, preferential, premium, prime *(most valuable),* principal *(director).* SEE MAIN ENTRY
superior prior
superior professional *(stellar),* select, special, sterling, superlative, unapproachable, valuable
superior group elite
superior individual paragon
superior situation advantage
superiority advantage, dint, distinction *(reputation),* edge *(advantage),* eminence, hegemony, importance, influence, merit, precedence, predominance, preponderance, prestige, pride, primacy, priority, quality *(excellence),* status, strength, stress *(accent),* supremacy, value
superiority in number plurality
superlatio exaggeration
superlative absolute *(ideal),* best, bombast, cardinal *(outstanding),* exaggeration, meritorious, outstanding *(prominent),* paramount, portentous *(eliciting amazement),* premium, prime *(most valuable),* rare, sterling, superior *(excellent),* unapproachable, utmost. SEE MAIN ENTRY
supernatural mysterious, peculiar *(curious),* uncanny
supernatural being spirit
supernormal best, extraordinary, mysterious, prodigious *(amazing),* unusual
supernumerary ancillary *(auxiliary),* copious, excess, excessive, expendable, needless, redundant, superfluous, unwarranted
superplus balance *(amount in excess),* surplus
supersaturate overload
supersaturated inordinate
supersaturation overage, plethora, surfeit, surplus
superscription caption, heading, inscription, label, rubric *(title),* title *(designation)*
supersede abolish, abrogate *(rescind),* accede *(succeed),* annul, disinherit, dislodge, displace *(replace),* leave *(allow to remain),* override, overrule, replace, succeed *(follow),* supplant, upset. SEE MAIN ENTRY
superseded null *(invalid),* null and void, outdated, outmoded
supersedence preemption
superseder alternative *(substitute)*
supersedere forbear
superseding cause SEE MAIN ENTRY
supersedure replacement, subrogation
supersession cancellation, defeasance, preemption, replacement, subrogation
superstruct build *(construct)*
superstructure building *(structure)*
supervacaneous superfluous
supervacaneus redundant, superfluous, unnecessary
supervacuus superfluous, unnecessary
supervene ensue, succeed *(follow).* SEE MAIN ENTRY
supervenient additional, extraneous, incidental, needless, nonessential, supplementary
supervenire intervene, supervene
supervention preemption

supervise administer *(conduct)*, care *(regard)*, check *(inspect)*, conduct, control *(regulate)*, discipline *(control)*, govern, handle *(manage)*, manage, moderate *(preside over)*, officiate, operate, overlook *(superintend)*, oversee, police, predominate *(command)*, preside, regulate *(manage)*, rule *(govern)*, superintend. SEE MAIN ENTRY
supervise communications censor
supervising administrative, leading *(guiding)*
supervising director chief
supervision administration, agency *(legal relationship)*, auspices, charge *(custody)*, direction *(guidance)*, generalship, guidance, jurisdiction, observation, oversight *(carelessness)*, oversight *(control)*, protection, regime, regulation *(management)*, safekeeping, supremacy, surveillance. SEE MAIN ENTRY
supervisor administrator, caretaker *(one caring for property)*, chairman, director, employer, guardian, official, principal *(director)*, procurator, superintendent, warden. SEE MAIN ENTRY
supervisor of accounts comptroller
supervisor of an estate administrator
supervisors management *(directorate)*
supervisorship generalship
supervisory administrative, leading *(guiding)*, predominant
supervisory official warden
supine inactive, indolent, insensible, languid, lifeless *(dull)*, otiose, passive, phlegmatic, ponderous, stagnant, torpid
supineness disinterest *(lack of interest)*, inertia, languor, sloth
suppeditare defray, furnish, provide *(supply)*, supply
suppeditate supply
supplant abolish, accede *(succeed)*, dislodge, displace *(replace)*, replace, succeed *(follow)*, supersede. SEE MAIN ENTRY
supplantation replacement, subrogation
supplanter alternative *(substitute)*, replacement, substitute
supplanting exchange, preemption, subrogation
supple flexible, malleable, obedient, passive, pliable, pliant, servile, yielding
supplement accrue *(increase)*, addendum, addition, additive, adjunct, affix, aid, allonge, amendment *(correction)*, amendment *(legislation)*, annex *(add)*, append, appurtenance, attach *(join)*, attachment *(thing affixed)*, augmentation, boom *(increase)*, codicil, complement, compound, corollary, correlate, enlarge, expand, extend *(enlarge)*, increase, increment, insertion, offshoot, reinforce, reinforcement, replenish, rider. SEE MAIN ENTRY
supplement to a will codicil
supplemental additional, ancillary *(auxiliary)*, collateral *(accompanying)*, expendable, extrinsic, incidental, nonessential, pendent, subsidiary, superfluous, supplementary, unnecessary. SEE MAIN ENTRY
supplementary additional, ancillary *(auxiliary)*, collateral *(accompanying)*, expendable, extraneous, incidental, nonessential, subsidiary, unnecessary. SEE MAIN ENTRY
supplementary device attachment *(thing affixed)*
supplementation accession *(annexation)*, accession *(enlargement)*, addendum, continuation *(resumption)*, development *(progression)*, extension *(expansion)*, insertion
supplementum reinforcement
supplere replenish
suppletive supplementary
suppletory supplementary
supplex petitioner
suppliant special interest, suitor
supplicant petitioner, suitor
supplicate call *(appeal to)*, desire, importune, plead *(implore)*, pray, press *(beseech)*, request, solicit, sue
supplication call *(appeal)*, entreaty, intercession, prayer, request
supplicatory solicitous
supplicium execute *(sentence to death)*
supplied with arms armed
supplier contributor *(giver)*, materialman. SEE MAIN ENTRY
supplies equipment, goods, merchandise, paraphernalia *(apparatus)*, store *(depository)*, sustenance
supply bear *(yield)*, bestow, clothe, contribute *(supply)*, cumulation, dole, endow, endue, fund *(noun)*, fund *(verb)*, furnish, give *(grant)*, hoard, lend, maintain *(sustain)*, pander, present *(make a gift)*, provision *(something provided)*, quantity, recruit, replenish, reserve, resource, stock *(store)*, stock in trade, store *(depository)*, sufficiency, yield *(produce a return)*. SEE MAIN ENTRY
supply accommodations for lodge *(house)*
supply aid abet, assist, bear *(support)*, capitalize *(provide capital)*, inure *(benefit)*, lend, nurture, serve *(assist)*, subsidize
supply an equivalent replace
supply base headquarters
supply deficiencies replenish
supply funds loan
supply money finance
supply on hand stock in trade
supply or furnish with reference index *(relate)*
supply support bear *(support)*, capitalize *(provide capital)*, subsidize
supply the necessities of support *(assist)*
supply the wants of accommodate
supply with a subsidy capitalize *(provide capital)*
supply with an epithet call *(title)*
supply with means enable, endow
supplying commercial, donative
supplying another's place representation *(acting for others)*
supponere foist, forge *(counterfeit)*
support abet, abettor, accommodate, accommodation *(backing)*, adhere *(maintain loyalty)*, adhesion *(loyalty)*, advantage, advocacy, advocate *(espouser)*, advocate, affirm *(uphold)*, aid *(help)*, aid *(subsistence)*, aid, alimony, allegiance, allow *(authorize)*, approval, approve, assist, assistance, attest, auspices, base *(foundation)*, basis, bear *(tolerate)*, behalf, benevolence *(act of kindness)*, bolster, bulwark, capitalize *(provide capital)*, care *(regard)*, certification *(attested copy)*, charity, charter *(sanction)*, choose, concur *(agree)*, confederate, confirm, confirmation, conform, consent *(noun)*, consent *(verb)*, conservation, contribute *(assist)*, cornerstone, corroborate, corroboration, cosign, countenance, countersign, coverage *(insurance)*, defend, defense, demonstrate *(establish)*, document, documentation, ecology, embrace *(accept)*, enable, encourage, endorse, enforcement, espouse, expedite, favor *(sanction)*, favor, fealty, finance, foster, foundation *(basis)*, frame *(structure)*, goodwill, grant *(concede)*, ground, guarantee, guaranty, help *(noun)*, help *(verb)*, indorse, indorsement, invest *(fund)*, involve *(participate)*, justify, keep *(continue)*, keep *(shelter)*, let *(permit)*, livelihood, loyalty, mainstay, maintain *(sustain)*, nurture, palliate *(excuse)*, partisan, pass *(approve)*, patronage *(support)*, patronize *(trade with)*, pay *(noun)*, pay *(verb)*, pension, preservation, preserve, promote *(organize)*, protect, protection, prove, quote, reassure, recommend, recommendation, reinforce, reinforcement, reliance, relief *(aid)*, resource, safekeeping, sanction *(permission)*, sanction, seal *(solemnize)*, security *(safety)*, service *(assistance)*, shelter *(protection)*, side, sponsor, subscribe *(promise)*, subsidize, substantiate, sustain *(confirm)*, sustenance, underwrite, uphold, verify *(confirm)*, vouch. SEE MAIN ENTRY
support again refinance
support an analogy correspond *(be equivalent)*
support by authority authorize
support the expense of disburse *(pay out)*, expend *(disburse)*
supportability corroboration
supportable convincing, deductible *(provable)*, defensible, provable, tenable
supportable by law valid
supported by authority allowed
supporter abettor, accomplice, advocate *(espouser)*, apologist, assistant, backer, benefactor, coactor, coadjutant, coconspirator, cohort, confederate, contributor *(giver)*, copartner *(coconspirator)*, disciple, partisan, patron *(influential supporter)*, patron *(regular customer)*, promoter, proponent, surety *(guarantor)*, undersigned. SEE MAIN ENTRY
supporting ancillary *(auxiliary)*, instigation, propitious, underlying
supporting evidence corroboration, documentation. SEE MAIN ENTRY
supporting structure foundation *(basis)*
supportive benevolent, demonstrative *(illustrative)*
supposable apparent *(presumptive)*, colorable *(plausible)*, constructive *(inferential)*, ostensible, possible, theoretical
supposal assumption *(supposition)*, condition *(contingent provision)*, conjecture, deduction *(conclusion)*, estimate *(idea)*, estimation *(calculation)*, generalization, hypothesis, inference, postulate, supposition
suppose anticipate *(expect)*, deduce, deduct *(conclude by reasoning)*, deem, estimate, expect *(consider probable)*, gauge, generalize, guess, infer, opine, presume, presuppose, reason *(conclude)*, speculate *(conjecture)*, surmise, suspect *(think)*. SEE MAIN ENTRY
supposed apparent *(presumptive)*, assumed *(inferred)*, hypothetical, ostensible, plausible, presumptive, probable, putative
supposedly reputedly
supposition concept, condition *(contingent provision)*, conjecture, conviction *(persuasion)*, deduction *(conclusion)*, estimate *(idea)*, estimation *(calculation)*, generalization, ground, hypothesis, idea, inference, notion, opinion *(belief)*, perception,

postulate, presumption, prognosis, proposition, speculation *(conjecture)*, suspicion *(uncertainty)*, theory, thesis. SEE MAIN ENTRY
suppositional apparent *(presumptive)*, assumed *(inferred)*, disputable, doubtful, dubious, hypothetical, ill-founded, illusory, indefinite, moot, plausible, presumptive, speculative, theoretical, unfounded, unsupported
suppositionary apparent *(presumptive)*
suppositious debatable
suppositious check bad check
supposititious presumptive, unfounded, unsupported
suppositive apparent *(presumptive)*, hypothetical, presumptive, theoretical
suppress abate *(lessen)*, abolish, allay, arrest *(stop)*, ban, beat *(defeat)*, camouflage, censor, check *(restrain)*, cloak, clog, coerce, conceal, condemn *(ban)*, confine, constrain *(restrain)*, constrict *(inhibit)*, contain *(restrain)*, control *(restrain)*, counter, countervail, curb, debar, defeat, detain *(restrain)*, disadvantage, eliminate *(eradicate)*, enjoin, ensconce, expurgate, extinguish, fetter, forestall, hamper, hide, hold up *(delay)*, inhibit, keep *(restrain)*, limit, moderate *(temper)*, negate, obliterate, obscure, obstruct, overthrow, overturn, overwhelm, palliate *(abate)*, prevail *(triumph)*, prohibit, quash, repress, restrain, restrict, revoke, shroud, stay *(halt)*, stem *(check)*, stifle, stop, strangle, subdue, subject, subjugate, trammel, withhold. SEE MAIN ENTRY
suppress competition monopolize
suppressed arrested *(checked)*, clandestine, hidden, inadmissible, inconspicuous, undisclosed
suppressing limiting
suppressio veri color *(deceptive appearance)*
suppression abatement *(reduction)*, bar *(obstruction)*, censorship, concealment, constraint *(restriction)*, control *(restriction)*, countermand, defeasance, deterrence, deterrent, disadvantage, dissolution *(termination)*, fetter, obstacle, oppression, prohibition, quota, removal, restraint, servitude
suppression of sound silence
suppression of the truth concealment
suppression of truth bad faith, false pretense, misstatement, story *(falsehood)*
suppressive dictatorial, prohibitive *(restrictive)*, restrictive
supprimere suppress, withhold
supputation census
supremacy advantage, authority *(power)*, capacity *(authority)*, dominance, dominion *(supreme authority)*, eminence, force *(strength)*, hegemony, importance, influence, possession *(ownership)*, power, precedence, predominance, primacy, priority, regime, significance. SEE MAIN ENTRY
supreme absolute *(ideal)*, best, cardinal *(outstanding)*, central *(essential)*, crucial, definitive, dictatorial, dominant, final, important *(significant)*, influential, leading *(ranking first)*, major, master, meritorious, omnipotent, outstanding *(prominent)*, paramount, predominant, prevailing *(having superior force)*, primary, prime *(most valuable)*, principal, sovereign *(absolute)*, superior *(excellent)*, superlative, ultimate, unapproachable, utmost. SEE MAIN ENTRY
supreme authority predominance, supremacy
supreme contempt disdain
supreme law constitution
supremely particularly
supremeness power, primacy, supremacy
suppression of evidence SEE MAIN ENTRY
surcease cease, cessation *(termination)*, close *(terminate)*, conclude *(complete)*, desist, expire, quit *(discontinue)*
surcharge overload. SEE MAIN ENTRY
sure affirmative, axiomatic, believable, certain *(fixed)*, certain *(positive)*, clear *(certain)*, constant, dependable, dogmatic, explicit, incontrovertible, indubious, inevitable, infallible, irrefutable, necessary *(inescapable)*, pertinacious, positive *(confident)*, positive *(incontestable)*, real, reliable, safe, secure *(confident)*, stable, staunch, true *(loyal)*, unambiguous, unavoidable *(inevitable)*, unequivocal, unmistakable, unrefutable. SEE MAIN ENTRY
sure assumption certitude
sure presumption certainty, certitude
sure to happen inevitable
surely admittedly, fairly *(clearly)*
sureness certainty, certification *(certainness)*, certitude, confidence *(faith)*, conviction *(persuasion)*, credence, faith, reliance, surety *(certainty)*, trust *(confidence)*
surety accommodation *(backing)*, assurance, bail, bond, certainty, certitude, confidence *(faith)*, coverage *(insurance)*, credence, deposit, downpayment, faith, guaranty, insurer, recognizance, safeguard, security *(pledge)*, sponsor, warrant *(guaranty)*. SEE MAIN ENTRY
surface bare, cursory, dimension, emerge, issue *(send forth)*, ostensible, side, superficial
surfeit balance *(amount in excess)*, overage, overload, plethora, satisfy *(fulfill)*, sufficiency, surplus, tautology. SEE MAIN ENTRY
surfeited full, replete
surge growth *(increase)*, increase, increment, inflate, inflation *(increase)*, inundate, issue *(send forth)*. SEE MAIN ENTRY
surging fluvial
surly fractious, froward, harsh, impertinent *(insolent)*, perverse, petulant, resentful
surmisable colorable *(plausible)*, ostensible, presumptive, probable
surmisal estimate *(idea)*, estimation *(calculation)*
surmise anticipate *(expect)*, apprehend *(perceive)*, assumption *(supposition)*, concept, conclusion *(determination)*, conjecture, deduce, deduct *(conclude by reasoning)*, deduction *(conclusion)*, deem, estimate *(idea)*, estimation *(calculation)*, expect *(consider probable)*, gauge, generalize, guess, hypothesis, idea, infer, inference, opine, opinion *(belief)*, perception, postulate *(noun)*, postulate *(verb)*, preconceive, presume, presumption, presuppose, prognosticate, rationale, speculate *(conjecture)*, speculation *(conjecture)*, supposition, suspect *(think)*, suspicion *(uncertainty)*, theory. SEE MAIN ENTRY
surmised approximate, inexact
surmount beat *(defeat)*, defeat, kill *(defeat)*, negotiate, overthrow, overwhelm, prevail *(triumph)*, transcend. SEE MAIN ENTRY
surmount obstacles succeed *(attain)*
surmountable possible
surname call *(title)*
surpass beat *(defeat)*, outbalance, outweigh, override, predominate *(outnumber)*, prevail *(triumph)*, surmount, transcend. SEE MAIN ENTRY
surpassing best, infringement, preferable, superlative
surplus balance *(amount in excess)*, bonus, boom *(prosperity)*, excess, excessive, expendable, needless, net, overage, plethora, profuse, redundancy, redundant, remainder *(estate in property)*, remainder *(remaining part)*, residual, residuary, superfluous, surfeit, unnecessary. SEE MAIN ENTRY
surplus time unexpired term
surplusage balance *(amount in excess)*, bonus, overage, plethora, surfeit, surplus
surprisal bombshell. SEE MAIN ENTRY
surprise bombshell, fortuitous, overwhelm, unforeseeable, unforeseen. SEE MAIN ENTRY
surprise package bombshell
surprised unaware
surprising coincidental, fortuitous, noteworthy, peculiar *(curious)*, portentous *(eliciting amazement)*, prodigious *(amazing)*, remarkable, unaccustomed, unanticipated, uncommon, unexpected, unusual
surrebut rebut, reply, retort, return *(respond)*
surrebuttal answer *(judicial response)*, counterargument, reply
surrebutter answer *(judicial response)*, counterargument, response
surrejoin answer *(respond legally)*, rebut, reply, retort, return *(respond)*
surrejoinder answer *(judicial response)*, confutation, counterargument, response
surrender abandon *(relinquish)*, abandonment *(discontinuance)*, abdication, accede *(concede)*, alienate *(transfer title)*, alienation *(transfer of title)*, bear *(yield)*, cancellation, capitulation, cede, cession, concession *(compromise)*, deliver, delivery, desuetude, discontinue *(abandon)*, disposition *(transfer of property)*, expense *(sacrifice)*, forfeit, forgo, give *(grant)*, give *(yield)*, introduce, leave *(allow to remain)*, obey, perish, prostration, quit *(discontinue)*, relinquish, remise, render *(deliver)*, rendition *(restoration)*, renounce, resign, resignation *(passive acceptance)*, resignation *(relinquishment)*, submit *(yield)*, succumb, vacate *(leave)*, waive, waiver, withdraw, yield *(submit)*. SEE MAIN ENTRY
surrender of an individual extradition
surrender of control abdication
surrender to another assign *(transfer ownership)*
surrendered resigned
surrendered to addicted
surrendering obeisant
surreptitious clandestine, collusive, covert, dishonest, disingenuous, evasive, fraudulent, furtive, hidden, insidious, mysterious, privy, secret, sly, stealthy, unobtrusive. SEE MAIN ENTRY
surreptitiousness bad faith, deceit, dishonesty, false pretense, fraud, improbity
surripere pilfer, purloin, steal
surrogate attorney in fact, conduit *(intermediary)*, deputy, judge, plenipotentiary, proctor, proxy, replace, replacement, substitute. SEE MAIN ENTRY
surrogation replacement, subrogation
surround border *(bound)*, circumscribe *(surround by boundary)*, contain *(enclose)*, delimit, detain *(hold in custody)*, embrace *(encircle)*, enclose, enshroud, envelop, hedge, include. SEE MAIN ENTRY

surrounded by difficulties difficult
surrounding blockade *(enclosure)*, local
surrounding area periphery
surrounding facts circumstances
surrounding influence climate
surrounding space periphery
surroundings atmosphere, circumstances, climate, context, environment, locality, scene, section *(vicinity)*, vicinity
surveillance bondage, contemplation, direction *(guidance)*, espionage, inspection, management *(supervision)*, notice *(heed)*, observation, precaution, scrutiny, supervision. SEE MAIN ENTRY
survey analysis, analyze, appraisal, assessment *(estimation)*, canvass, check *(inspect)*, compendium, delineate, digest *(summarize)*, estimate, examination *(study)*, examine *(study)*, gauge, inquire, inquiry *(request for information)*, inquiry *(systematic investigation)*, inspection, investigate, measure, measurement, monitor, observation, observe *(watch)*, overlook *(superintend)*, pandect *(treatise)*, peruse, poll *(canvass)*, poll, question *(inquiry)*, regard *(pay attention)*, research, retrospect, review *(official reexamination)*, review, scrutinize, scrutiny, study, test. SEE MAIN ENTRY
survey carefully traverse
survey of time past hindsight
surveyable appreciable, determinable *(ascertainable)*
surveying discovery
surviorship longevity
survival life *(period of existence)*, longevity. SEE MAIN ENTRY
survival studies ecology
survivance longevity
survive endure *(last)*, exist, keep *(continue)*, last, persevere, persist, remain *(continue)*, subsist. SEE MAIN ENTRY
surviving durable, extant, lasting, live *(existing)*, net, outstanding *(unpaid)*, permanent, perpetual
survivor heir
susceptibility bias, character *(personal quality)*, credulity, danger, peril, predisposition, probability, sensibility, tendency. SEE MAIN ENTRY
susceptible liable, open *(accessible)*, open *(persuasible)*, penetrable, pliant, receptive, responsive, sensitive *(easily affected)*, subject *(exposed)*, vulnerable, willing *(not averse)*. SEE MAIN ENTRY
susceptible of apportionment divisible
susceptible of division divisible
susceptible of proof provable
susceptibleness peril
susceptive pliant, sensitive *(easily affected)*, susceptible *(responsive)*
susceptivity credulity, peril
suscipere assume *(undertake)*, incur, undertake
suspect assume *(suppose)*, controversial, debatable, deem, disbelieve, discount *(disbelieve)*, disputable, doubt *(distrust)*, dubitative, expect *(consider probable)*, guess, incredible, infer, leery, ludicrous, misdoubt, mistrust, opine, presume, presumptive, presuppose, surmise, suspicious *(questionable)*, unbelievable, uncertain *(questionable)*. SEE MAIN ENTRY
suspected criminal suspect
suspecting cynical, inconvincible, incredulous, leery, skeptical, suspicious *(distrustful)*
suspectum reddere incriminate
suspend adjourn, arrest *(stop)*, balk, bar *(exclude)*, cancel, cease, close *(terminate)*, continue *(adjourn)*, debar, defer *(put off)*, desist, discharge *(dismiss)*, discontinue *(abandon)*, discontinue *(break continuity)*, dismiss *(discharge)*, disrupt, forestall, halt, hold up *(delay)*, impede, inhibit, interrupt, leave *(allow to remain)*, negate, nullify, obstruct, palliate *(abate)*, pause, postpone, pretermit, procrastinate, prohibit, quit *(discontinue)*, recess, remit *(relax)*, remove *(dismiss from office)*, revoke, stop, toll *(stop)*. SEE MAIN ENTRY
suspend charges pardon
suspend from the practice of law disbar
suspend from the profession of law disbar
suspend operation close *(terminate)*
suspend work strike *(refuse to work)*
suspended arrested *(checked)*, broken *(interrupted)*, disjunctive *(tending to disjoin)*, dormant, inactive, null *(invalid)*, null and void, static
suspended animation inaction
suspended judgment doubt *(indecision)*
suspense doubt *(indecision)*, expectation, pendency, remission. SEE MAIN ENTRY
suspenseful conditional, pending *(unresolved)*
suspension abandonment *(discontinuance)*, abeyance, adjournment, cancellation, cessation *(interlude)*, check *(bar)*, cloture, deferment, delay, desuetude, discontinuance *(act of discontinuing)*, disuse, expulsion, extension *(postponement)*, halt, hiatus, inaction, interruption, lull, moratorium, nonuse, ostracism, pause, pendency, remission, rescision, respite *(interval of rest)*, solution *(substance)*, stay. SEE MAIN ENTRY
suspension of activity extension *(postponement)*
suspension of business failure *(bankruptcy)*
suspension of consciousness insentience
suspension of disbelief credence
suspension of employment layoff
suspension of execution reprieve
suspension of hostilities peace
suspension of punishment reprieve
suspension of work furlough, leave *(absence)*, strike
suspicari surmise, suspect *(think)*
suspicio doubt *(suspicion)*, notion, suspicion *(mistrust)*
suspicion apprehension *(fear)*, conjecture, idea, incredulity, inference, opinion *(belief)*, qualm, speculation *(conjecture)*, suggestion, supposition. SEE MAIN ENTRY
suspicionem habere suspect *(think)*
suspiciosus suspicious *(distrustful)*
suspicious cynical, debatable, disputable, disreputable, guarded, implausible, inconvincible, incredible, incredulous, jealous, leery, resentful, skeptical, unbelievable, uncertain *(questionable)*, vigilant. SEE MAIN ENTRY
suspiciousness bad faith, bad repute, doubt *(suspicion)*, incredulity, suspicion *(mistrust)*
sustain adhere *(persist)*, affirm *(uphold)*, aid, allow *(authorize)*, allow *(endure)*, approve, authorize, bear *(adduce)*, bear *(support)*, bear *(tolerate)*, bolster, care *(regard)*, certify *(attest)*, concur *(agree)*, confirm, conserve, continue *(persevere)*, continue *(prolong)*, corroborate, countenance, defend, demonstrate *(establish)*, document, endure *(last)*, endure *(suffer)*, finance, foster, fund, harbor, help, indorse, justify, keep *(continue)*, keep *(shelter)*, last, nurture, pass *(approve)*, perpetuate, persevere, persist, preserve, prolong, promote *(organize)*, protect, provide *(supply)*, reaffirm, reassure, remain *(continue)*, retain *(keep in possession)*, side, sponsor, subsidize, supply, support *(assist)*, support *(corroborate)*, uphold, vouch, witness *(attest to)*. SEE MAIN ENTRY
sustain by authority authorize
sustain damage suffer *(sustain loss)*
sustainable convincing, deductible *(provable)*, provable
sustainable in law valid
sustained chronic, constant, continual *(connected)*, continuous, durable, habitual, incessant, lasting, live *(existing)*, permanent, persistent, safe
sustained action continuance
sustained by dependent
sustained trial endeavor, pursuit *(effort to secure)*
sustainer abettor, backer, benefactor, mainstay, partisan
sustaining conservation, continuation *(prolongation)*, corroboration, salutary
sustainment aid *(help)*, aid *(subsistence)*, ecology, livelihood, tolerance
sustenance aid *(help)*, aid *(subsistence)*, alimony, behalf, continuation *(prolongation)*, contribution *(donation)*, ecology, help, livelihood, mainstay, maintenance *(support of spouse)*, relief *(aid)*, support *(assistance)*. SEE MAIN ENTRY
sustentare sustain *(prolong)*, uphold
sustentation alimony, conservation, sustenance
sustentative salubrious, salutary
sustinere bear *(tolerate)*, endure *(suffer)*, preserve, sustain *(prolong)*, uphold
swaddle envelop
swag contraband, spoils
swagger flaunt, jactation, pride, rodomontade
swaggering bluster *(speech)*, inflated *(vain)*, insolent
swallow consume, endure *(suffer)*, tolerate
swallow up obliterate, overcome *(overwhelm)*
swamp immerse *(plunge into)*, inundate, overcome *(overwhelm)*
swank jactation
swap barter, exchange, interchange, replace, replacement, trade *(commerce)*
swarm assemblage, mass *(body of persons)*, meet
swarming populous, profuse, rife
swashbuckling rodomontade
swatch sample
swathe enshroud, envelop
sway advantage, authority *(power)*, bailiwick, beat *(pulsate)*, coax, convert *(persuade)*, convince, dint, dispose *(incline)*, dominance, dominate, dominion *(supreme authority)*, force *(strength)*, government *(administration)*, hegemony, induce, influence *(noun)*, influence *(verb)*, inspire, inveigle, lobby, manage, motivate, oscillate, patronage *(power to appoint jobs)*, persuade, power, predominance, predominate

(*command*), prejudice (*influence*), preside, pressure, prestige, prevail (*persuade*), prevail upon, primacy, supremacy, vacillate, wield. SEE MAIN ENTRY
swayable open (*persuasible*), pliable, pliant, suasible, susceptible (*responsive*)
swayed one-sided, partial (*biased*), partisan
swaying convincing, persuasive
swear acknowledge (*declare*), assure (*insure*), attest, avouch (*avow*), avow, bear (*adduce*), certify (*attest*), depose (*testify*), evidence, plead (*allege in a legal action*), promise (*vow*), testify, witness (*attest to*). SEE MAIN ENTRY
swear an affidavit certify (*attest*)
swear an oath avouch (*avow*), promise (*vow*)
swear by trust
swear falsely bear false witness, cloak, frame (*charge falsely*), lie (*falsify*), perjure
swear in delegate
swear off forgo, refrain, renounce
swear the truth avouch (*avow*)
swear to vouch
swear under oath depose (*testify*)
swearer affiant, bystander, deponent, juror, witness
swearing adjuration, affirmation, attestation, averment, avouchment, blasphemy, certification (*attested copy*), confirmation, expletive, imprecation, oath, profanity
swearing-in SEE MAIN ENTRY
swearing off denial, renunciation
sweep coverage (*scope*), extent, gamut, range, scope, space
sweep aside rescind
sweep away eliminate (*eradicate*), eradicate, obliterate
sweep out purge (*purify*)
sweep through patrol, perambulate
sweeping broad, complete (*all-embracing*), comprehensive, extensive, far reaching, general, generic, inclusive, omnibus, outright, prevailing (*current*), prevalent, radical (*extreme*), thorough, unqualified (*unlimited*)
sweeping change revolution
sweepstake lottery
sweet attractive, nectarious, sapid, savory
sweet-tempered benevolent
swell accrue (*increase*), accumulate (*enlarge*), boom (*increase*), build (*augment*), develop, enlarge, expand, extend (*enlarge*), growth (*increase*), increase, inflate, inflation (*increase*), magnify, proliferate, spread
swell the ranks recruit
swelled inflated (*enlarged*), turgid
swelling accession (*enlargement*), boom (*increase*), cumulative (*increasing*), growth (*increase*), inflation (*increase*), orotund, plethora
swelling utterance bombast
swerve depart, detour, deviate, deviation, digress, digression, divert, indirection (*indirect action*), oscillate
swerving deviation
swift brief, expeditious, impulsive (*rash*), instantaneous, precipitate, prompt, rapid, ready (*prepared*), summary
swift execution dispatch (*promptness*)
swift rate dispatch (*promptness*)
swiftly instantly
swiftness haste
swindle bait (*lure*), betray (*lead astray*), bilk, bunko, cheat, circumvent, deceive, deception, defalcate, defraud, delude, dupe, embezzle, embezzlement, fake, false pretense, hoax, hoodwink, illude, imposture, larceny, misappropriation, mislead, mulct (*defraud*), peculate, purloin. SEE MAIN ENTRY
swindled aggrieved (*harmed*)
swindler criminal, delinquent, embezzler, outlaw, thief
swindling fraud, imposture, larceny, theft
swing beat (*pulsate*), beat (*strike*), brandish, fluctuate, oscillate, vacillate, wield
switch alternate (*take turns*), barter, change, conversion (*change*), convert (*change use*), displace (*replace*), lash (*strike*), reciprocate, remove (*transfer*), replace, replacement, subrogation, transform. SEE MAIN ENTRY
switch around change
switched off disconnected
swollen full, fustian, inflated (*enlarged*), orotund, pretentious (*pompous*), proud (*conceited*), supercilious, turgid
swollen diction bombast
swollen language fustian
swoon prostration
sworn agreed (*promised*). SEE MAIN ENTRY
sworn declarant SEE MAIN ENTRY
sworn enemy foe
sworn evidence affidavit, affirmance (*legal affirmation*), affirmation, attestation, certification (*attested copy*), deposition
sworn pledge oath
sworn promise oath
sworn statement adjuration, affidavit, affirmation, asseveration, oath
sycophant parasite. SEE MAIN ENTRY
sycophantic obsequious, sequacious, servile, subservient
syllabus capsule, compendium, outline (*synopsis*), pandect (*treatise*), plan, program, prospectus, summary
syllogism corollary
symbiosis coalescence
symbol device (*distinguishing mark*), earmark, indicant, indication, indicator, manifestation, representative (*example*), substitute, suggestion, token, trademark. SEE MAIN ENTRY
symbolic nominal, representative, suggestive (*evocative*). SEE MAIN ENTRY
symbolical representative
symbolization connotation
symbolize connote, denote, depict, exemplify, personify, replace, represent (*portray*), signify (*denote*)
symbolized tacit
symbols indicia
symbolum symbol
symmetric equal
symmetrical coequal, coextensive, equal, regular (*orderly*)
symmetrical scales balance (*equality*)
symmetry analogy, arrangement (*ordering*), balance (*equality*), constant, correspondence (*similarity*), equipoise, parity, proportion, regularity, uniformity
sympathetic charitable (*lenient*), concerted, concordant, consensual, lenient, open (*persuasible*), patient, propitious, receptive, sensitive (*easily affected*), susceptible (*responsive*), vicarious (*delegated*). SEE MAIN ENTRY
sympathetic perception discretion (*quality of being discreet*)
sympathize relent, sponsor. SEE MAIN ENTRY
sympathize with concur (*agree*)
sympathizer advocate (*espouser*), backer, disciple, partisan, proponent, samaritan, sponsor
sympathizing benevolent, charitable (*lenient*), vicarious (*delegated*)
sympathy affinity (*regard*), concordance, condonation, goodwill, humanity (*humaneness*), lenience, pity, sensibility, solace, tolerance, understanding (*tolerance*). SEE MAIN ENTRY
symphonize orchestrate
symphysis concrescence
symposiac parley
symposiarch chairman
symposium assemblage, conference, meeting (*conference*), panel (*discussion group*), parley
symptom indicant, indication, indicator, manifestation, symbol, warning. SEE MAIN ENTRY
symptomatology diagnosis
synchronal commensurate, concurrent (*at the same time*), consonant, contemporaneous, simultaneous
synchronic simultaneous
synchronical simultaneous
synchronism SEE MAIN ENTRY
synchronistic concurrent (*at the same time*), contemporaneous, simultaneous
synchronistical concurrent (*at the same time*), simultaneous
synchronization consensus
synchronize coincide (*concur*), conform, coordinate
synchronized congruous, consonant
synchronous concurrent (*at the same time*), congruous, contemporaneous, simultaneous
syncophantic vexatious
syncretize combine (*act in concert*), embody, federalize (*associate*), unite
syndic functionary, procurator
syndicate amalgamate, association (*alliance*), business (*commercial enterprise*), cartel, coalition, combine (*act in concert*), committee, confederacy (*compact*), consortium (*business cartel*), corporation, enterprise (*economic organization*), federation, institute, merger, organization (*association*), partnership, pool, trust (*combination of businesses*). SEE MAIN ENTRY
synergetic associated, joint. SEE MAIN ENTRY
synergic concerted, concomitant, concurrent (*united*), consensual
synergism collusion, synergy
synergy collusion, concert. SEE MAIN ENTRY
syngrapha bill (*invoice*), bond, instrument (*document*)
synod council (*assembly*), meeting (*conference*), session
synonym call (*title*), definition, same
synonymity identity (*similarity*), propinquity (*similarity*)
synonymous coequal, coextensive, cognate, congruous, equivalent, identical, same, similar, tantamount. SEE MAIN ENTRY
synopsis abridgment (*condensation*), abstract, brief, capsule, compendium, digest, pandect (*treatise*), paraphrase, prospectus, restatement, scenario, summary. SEE MAIN ENTRY
synopsize abridge (*shorten*), abstract (*summarize*), condense
synoptic broad, compact (*pithy*), comprehensive, concise, succinct

syntaxis classification
synthesis building *(business of assembling)*, centralization, coalescence, composition *(makeup)*, embodiment, formation, manufacture
synthesize consist, consolidate *(unite)*, embody, make
synthetic assumed *(feigned)*, false *(not genuine)*, imitation, spurious. SEE MAIN ENTRY
system arrangement *(plan)*, array *(order)*, avenue *(means of attainment)*, bureaucracy, codification, complex *(development)*, course, device *(contrivance)*, doctrine, form *(arrangement)*, hierarchy *(arrangement in a series)*, institute, means *(opportunity)*, method, mode, modus operandi, order *(arrangement)*, practice *(procedure)*, procedure, process *(course)*, program, rule *(guide)*, scheme, strategy, usage. SEE MAIN ENTRY
system of belief doctrine
system of distributing wealth economy *(economic system)*
system of drill discipline *(training)*
system of exchanges commerce
system of government polity
system of knowledge education, science *(study)*
system of law code
system of laws codification, jurisprudence
system of morals ethics
system of reckoning time calendar *(record of yearly periods)*
system of regulations codification
system of rules code, protocol *(etiquette)*
systematic arrangement of cases calendar *(list of cases)*
systematic arrangement of laws codification
systematic search indagation, investigation
systematic secret observation of the words and conduct of others espionage
systematic training discipline *(training)*, education
systematical systematic
systematically invariably
systematization arrangement *(ordering)*, array *(order)*, centralization, classification, distribution *(arrangement)*, form *(arrangement)*, formation, order *(arrangement)*, organization (structure), regulation *(management)*
systematization of laws codification
systematize adjust *(regulate)*, arrange (methodize), classify, codify, conform, contrive, coordinate, distribute, file (arrange), fix *(arrange)*, frame *(construct)*, marshal, orchestrate, organize *(arrange)*, pigeonhole, police, regulate *(adjust)*, sort, tabulate
systematized tactical
systemic physical
systemize codify
systemless haphazard, indiscriminate

T

T.N.T. bomb
tab invoice *(bill)*
tabernacle domicile, dwelling, habitation *(dwelling place)*
tabescere languish
tabid dilapidated
table calendar *(record of yearly periods)*, continue *(adjourn)*, defer *(put off)*, delay, doubt *(hesitate)*, hold up *(delay)*, postpone, procrastinate, suspend
table of cases calendar *(list of cases)*
table of charges tariff *(bill)*
tables census
tabling deferment
taboo ban, exclude, forbid, illicit, inhibit, prohibition, proscribe *(prohibit)*, restraint, restrict, veto
tabula document, instrument *(document)*, inventory, roll, schedule
tabula rasa blank *(emptiness)*
tabulae register
tabular register of the year calendar *(record of yearly periods)*
tabulas referre register
tabulate book, cast *(register)*, codify, enter *(record)*, enumerate, fix *(arrange)*, itemize, pigeonhole, poll, record, register, sort, survey *(poll)*. SEE MAIN ENTRY
tabulation census, codification, poll *(canvass)*, registration
tacere speechless
tacit allusive, constructive *(inferential)*, covert, implicit, implied, indirect, undisclosed. SEE MAIN ENTRY
tacit assent acquiescence
tacit inference implication *(inference)*
tacitly assumed constructive *(inferential)*
taciturn inarticulate, laconic, mute, noncommittal, unresponsive. SEE MAIN ENTRY
taciturnitas silence
taciturnus taciturn
tacitus implicit, tacit
tack avenue *(means of attainment)*
tack together combine *(join together)*
tackle attack, endeavor, grapple, occupy *(engage)*, ply, strive, try *(attempt)*, undertake
tact consideration *(sympathetic regard)*, courtesy, decorum, discretion *(quality of being discreet)*, prudence
tactful diplomatic, judicious, politic, subtle *(refined)*
tactfulness discretion *(quality of being discreet)*
tactic expedient, machination, method, plan, plot *(secret plan)*, stratagem. SEE MAIN ENTRY
tactical strategic. SEE MAIN ENTRY
tactician mastermind
tactics artifice, campaign, contrivance, direction *(course)*, manner *(behavior)*, modus operandi, practice *(procedure)*, procedure, process *(course)*, scheme, strategy. SEE MAIN ENTRY
tactile bodily, material *(physical)*, palpable, tangible
taction contact *(touching)*
tactless thoughtless, unpolitic
tactlessness disrespect, impropriety, indiscretion
tactual tangible
taeter loathsome
tag brand, brand *(mark)*, call *(title)*, catchword, classify, label *(noun)*, label *(verb)*, nominate, pigeonhole, rate, title *(designation)*
tag incorrectly mislabel
tail end *(termination)*
tail end extremity *(furthest point)*
tailor conform, transform
tailor-made fit
taint adulterate, attaint, bad repute, brand, brand *(stigmatize)*, contaminate *(noun)*, contaminate *(verb)*, contemn, corrupt, damage, debase, defame, degenerate, depreciate, derogate, deteriorate, disadvantage, discredit *(noun)*, discredit *(verb)*, disease, disgrace *(noun)*, disgrace *(verb)*, dishonor *(shame)*, dishonor *(deprive of honor)*, disparage, disrepute, humiliate, ignominy, impair, infamy, infect, misemploy, notoriety, onus *(stigma)*, opprobrium, pervert, pillory, pollute, prejudice *(injure)*, reproach, scandal, shame, smear, stain, stigma, sully, tarnish. SEE MAIN ENTRY
tainted blameworthy, blemished, imperfect, marred, odious, peccable, peccant *(unhealthy)*, sinister, unsound *(not strong)*. SEE MAIN ENTRY
taintless absolute *(ideal)*, blameless, clean, pure, unblemished
take acquire *(secure)*, adopt, apprehend *(arrest)*, appropriate, attach *(seize)*, carry *(transport)*, derive *(receive)*, despoil, endure *(suffer)*, excise *(levy a tax)*, gain, hijack, impound, impress *(procure by force)*, inherit, loot, obtain, partake, pilfer, plunder, preempt, procure, profit, purloin, reap, receive *(acquire)*, seize *(apprehend)*, seize *(confiscate)*, sequester *(seize property)*, spoils, transport, trust, usurp. SEE MAIN ENTRY
take a beating lose *(undergo defeat)*
take a break rest *(cease from action)*
take a breather pause
take a census poll
take a chance bet, gamble, parlay *(bet)*, speculate *(chance)*, try *(attempt)*
take a circuitous route detour
take a constitutional perambulate
take a crack at endeavor
take a decisive step choose, conclude *(decide)*, determine
take a different course deviate
take a dim view of disapprove *(condemn)*
take a fancy to prefer
take a lease rent
take a life slay
take a part in participate
take a part of participate
take a recess recess
take a rest recess
take a roll call poll
take a roundabout course detour
take a share of partake
take a stand posit, resolve *(decide)*
take a stand against counter, disagree, oppose, rebut
take a temporary route detour
take a turn reciprocate
take a vow promise *(vow)*
take a walk perambulate
take account of note *(notice)*, ponder
take action complain *(charge)*, endeavor, execute *(accomplish)*, implement, militate, perform *(execute)*, strive
take advantage deceive
take advantage of bait *(lure)*, bilk, capitalize *(seize the chance)*, defraud, delude, dupe, employ *(make use of)*, ensnare, exploit *(make use of)*, illude, manipulate *(control unfairly)*, mislead
take after copy, mock *(imitate)*
take alarm fear
take amiss misapprehend, resent
take an account of calculate
take an active part in contribute *(assist)*, partake, participate

take an advance borrow
take an airing perambulate
take an alternate highway detour
take an alternate route detour
take an indirect way detour
take an interest in participate
take an oath promise *(vow)*
take another's place displace *(replace)*
take apart break *(separate)*, disjoint, dissolve *(separate)*
take as an axiom postulate
take as an heir inherit
take as one's own assume *(seize)*, impropriate
take authority hold *(possess)*
take away abduct, abridge *(divest)*, abridge *(shorten)*, adeem, carry away, decrease, deduct *(reduce)*, depreciate, deprive, dilute, diminish, dislodge, displace *(remove)*, distrain, divest, excise *(cut away)*, hijack, hold up *(rob)*, jostle *(pickpocket)*, kidnap, lessen, plunder, remove *(eliminate)*, withdraw
take away an essential part eviscerate
take away from confiscate, disinherit
take back adeem, bear false witness, disavow, disclaim, recall *(call back)*, recant, recoup *(regain)*, repossess, rescind, withdraw
take back again collect *(recover money)*
take birth arise *(originate)*
take by assault capture, carry away, hijack
take by authority apprehend *(arrest)*, arrest *(apprehend)*
take by craft ensnare
take by descent inherit
take by force abduct, capture, despoil, hijack, kidnap, levy, pirate *(take by violence)*, rob
take by fraud defalcate, defraud, dupe, embezzle, purloin
take by illegal methods poach
take by inheritance inherit
take by stealth carry away
take by strategem ensnare
take by succession inherit
take by theft hold up *(rob)*
take by unfair methods poach
take captive apprehend *(arrest)*, arrest *(apprehend)*, capture, carry away, constrain *(imprison)*, detain *(hold in custody)*, hijack, immure
take care beware, heed
take care of assume *(undertake)*, concern *(care)*, conduct, control *(regulate)*, cover *(guard)*, foster, keep *(shelter)*, maintain *(sustain)*, operate, preserve, preside, protect, serve *(assist)*, support *(assist)*
take charge assume *(undertake)*, command, govern, preside, takeover, usurp
take charge of arrest *(apprehend)*, conduct, maintain *(sustain)*, manage, moderate *(preside over)*, operate
take cognizance notice *(observe)*
take cognizance of hear *(perceive by ear)*, heed, note *(notice)*, observe *(watch)*, regard *(pay attention)*, witness *(have direct knowledge of)*
take command direct *(supervise)*, federalize *(place under federal control)*, govern, hold *(possess)*, takeover
take control federalize *(place under federal control)*
take control of accept *(take)*
take counsel confer *(consult)*, consult *(ask advice of)*
take counsel with oneself deliberate
take disciplinary action condemn *(punish)*
take dishonestly hold up *(rob)*, purloin
take down demean *(make lower)*, demote, enter *(record)*, note *(record)*, record
take effect occur *(happen)*
take employment occupy *(engage)*
take evasive action counter, elude, parry
take evidence investigate
take exception complain *(criticize)*, conflict, cross *(disagree with)*, demur, differ *(disagree)*, differ *(vary)*, disaccord, disagree, disapprove *(reject)*, dispute *(contest)*, dissent *(differ in opinion)*, except *(object)*, expostulate, object, oppugn, protest, remonstrate, reprehend
take exception to challenge, complain *(criticize)*, confront *(oppose)*, contest, denounce *(condemn)*, disapprove *(condemn)*, disapprove *(reject)*, disclaim, gainsay, oppose, reject, renounce, resent
take exception to the allegations demurrer
take feloniously embezzle, hold up *(rob)*, purloin
take flight abscond, disappear, escape, evacuate, flee, move *(alter position)*, quit *(evacuate)*, retreat
take for deem
take for granted assume *(suppose)*, guess, postulate, presume, presuppose, suspect *(think)*, trust
take for oneself impropriate
take for public use condemn *(seize)*
take forcibly carry away
take form crystallize, develop, evolve
take fright fear
take from adeem, diminish, discount *(reduce)*, occupy *(take possession)*
take heed beware
take hold of accept *(take)*, grapple, sequester *(seize property)*
take illegally convert *(misappropriate)*, pirate *(reproduce without authorization)*, poach
take in acquire *(receive)*, betray *(lead astray)*, bilk, comprehend *(include)*, comprehend *(understand)*, defraud, delude, dupe, embrace *(encircle)*, encompass *(include)*, entrap, illude, include, incorporate *(include)*, instate, mislead, realize *(understand)*, reap, receive *(acquire)*, receive *(permit to enter)*, recruit, seize *(apprehend)*
take in exchange displace *(replace)*
take in hand undertake
take into account calculate, consider, discuss, heed, notice *(observe)*, provide *(arrange for)*
take into consideration appreciate *(comprehend)*, concern *(care)*, deliberate, muse, notice *(observe)*
take into custody apprehend *(arrest)*, arrest *(apprehend)*, book, capture, confine, constrain *(imprison)*, detain *(hold in custody)*, distrain, enclose, immure, impound, jail, restrain, seize *(apprehend)*
take into employ employ *(engage services)*
take into legal custody impound
take into one's employ engage *(hire)*
take into preventive custody arrest *(apprehend)*
take into protective custody arrest *(apprehend)*
take into service employ *(engage services)*, engage *(hire)*, hire
take issue collide *(clash)*, differ *(disagree)*, differ *(vary)*, disagree
take issue with antagonize, contradict, counter, counteract, demurrer, disown *(deny the validity)*, dispute *(contest)*, dissent *(differ in opinion)*, gainsay, impugn, oppose. SEE MAIN ENTRY
take it to be deem
take its course occur *(happen)*
take leave abandon *(physically leave)*, dissociate, leave *(depart)*, part *(leave)*, quit *(evacuate)*, retire *(conclude a career)*, retire *(retreat)*
take leave of quit *(evacuate)*
take liberties infringe
take life dispatch *(put to death)*
take lodgings lodge *(reside)*
take measures frame *(formulate)*, perpetrate, plan, plot, provide *(arrange for)*
take minutes record
take no account of disregard, flout, override
take no denial compel, constrain *(compel)*, insist, persevere, persist, press *(constrain)*
take no interest disregard
take no note ignore, neglect
take no note of disregard
take no notice dismiss *(put out of consideration)*, ignore, neglect, overlook *(disregard)*
take no notice of disregard
take no part in refrain
take no stock in disbelieve
take note heed, observe *(watch)*, spy
take note of concern *(care)*, peruse
take notice appreciate *(comprehend)*, heed, note *(notice)*, observe *(watch)*, perceive, regard *(pay attention)*
take notice of attend *(heed)*
take off decrease, deduct *(reduce)*, diminish, discount *(reduce)*, rebate
take off on mock *(imitate)*
take offense resent
take offensive action attack
take on adopt, attempt, contend *(dispute)*, embark, endeavor, engage *(involve)*, fight *(battle)*, grapple, hire, occupy *(engage)*
take on cargo load
take on character crystallize
take on credit borrow
take on loan borrow
take on oneself assume *(undertake)*
take on the aspect appear *(seem to be)*
take on the manner appear *(seem to be)*, demean *(deport oneself)*
take one to court prosecute *(charge)*
take one's choice choose
take one's departure abandon *(physically leave)*, part *(leave)*
take one's leave abandon *(physically leave)*
take one's life away dispatch *(put to death)*
take one's meaning construe *(comprehend)*
take one's oath affirm *(declare solemnly)*, attest, avow, bear *(adduce)*, certify *(attest)*, testify, witness *(attest to)*
take one's stand against antagonize, counteract
take oneself away quit *(evacuate)*
take order crystallize
take orders obey
take origin arise *(originate)*
take out delete, distill, except *(exclude)*, excise *(cut away)*, exclude, expunge, extract, remove *(eliminate)*, select

take out of context abstract *(separate)*
take out of the place of interment disinter
take over accroach, annex *(arrogate)*, appropriate, attach *(seize)*, condemn *(seize)*, confiscate, distrain, hold *(possess)*, impound, impropriate, manage, obtain, occupy *(take possession)*, preempt, preside, prevail *(triumph)*, succeed *(follow)*, supplant. SEE MAIN ENTRY
take over another's duties displace *(replace)*
take pains endeavor, strive
take part combine *(act in concert)*, compete, engage *(involve)*, involve *(participate)*, join *(associate oneself with)*, occupy *(engage)*, participate
take part in conspire, cooperate, espouse, partake
take part in a demonstration picket
take part with assist, conspire, cooperate
take patiently allow *(endure)*, bear *(tolerate)*, endure *(suffer)*, tolerate
take place arise *(occur)*, occur *(happen)*, supervene
take pleasure in relish
take poorly resent
take possession acquire *(secure)*, annex *(arrogate)*, collect *(recover money)*, condemn *(seize)*, evict, obtain, possess, receive *(acquire)*, takeover, usurp
take possession for public use eminent domain
take possession of accept *(take)*, adopt, attach *(seize)*, capture, confiscate, distrain, hold up *(rob)*, impound, impress *(procure by force)*, impropriate, preempt, procure, repossess, seize *(confiscate)*. SEE MAIN ENTRY
take precautions beware, care *(be cautious)*, caution, forestall
take precedence beat *(defeat)*, override, surpass, transcend. SEE MAIN ENTRY
take precedence over outweigh
take prisoner apprehend *(arrest)*, arrest *(apprehend)*, capture, carry away, confine, detain *(hold in custody)*, hijack, restrain, seize *(apprehend)*
take prisoner again rearrest
take responsibility underwrite
take responsibility for sponsor
take retribution retaliate
take revenge retaliate
take rooms lodge *(reside)*
take shape crystallize, develop, evolve
take sides bicker, involve *(participate)*
take something from derogate
take steps devise *(invent)*, frame *(formulate)*, maneuver, perform *(execute)*, plot, proceed *(go forward)*, provide *(arrange for)*, strive
take stock calculate, check *(inspect)*, observe *(watch)*, survey *(poll)*
take stock of criticize *(evaluate)*, examine *(study)*, muse, notice *(observe)*, pe-ruse
take summarily annex *(arrogate)*, attach *(seize)*, confiscate
take surreptitiously abduct
take the chair officiate
take the chances of bet
take the dimensions calculate
take the edge off obtund
take the first step embark, launch *(initiate)*, originate
take the initiative attack, commence, initiate, originate
take the lead command, initiate, launch *(initiate)*, originate, precede, predominate *(command)*
take the necessary measure SEE MAIN ENTRY
take the offensive attack, fight *(battle)*, oppugn
take the opportunity capitalize *(seize the chance)*
take the part of assume *(simulate)*, impersonate, pose *(impersonate)*, represent *(substitute)*, side, support *(assist)*
take the place of accede *(succeed)*, displace *(replace)*, succeed *(follow)*, supersede, supplant
take the semblance of assume *(simulate)*
take the stand testify
take the yield reap
take time stall
take time out pause, recess, rest *(cease from action)*
take to prefer
take to account impeach
take to court litigate, sue
take to mean understand
take to one's heels flee
take to oneself embrace *(accept)*, impropriate
take to pieces break *(separate)*, disable
take to safety rescue
take to task castigate, condemn *(blame)*, denounce *(condemn)*, disapprove *(condemn)*, discipline *(punish)*, fault, lash *(attack verbally)*, punish, rebuke, reprehend, reproach
take training practice *(train by repetition)*
take trouble strive
take umbrage alienate *(estrange)*, resent
take under consideration deliberate, ponder
take unlawful possession rob
take unlawfully steal
take up adopt, assume *(undertake)*, discharge *(pay a debt)*, embark, embrace *(accept)*, endeavor, espouse, immerse *(engross)*, levy, occupy *(engage)*, ply, specialize, undertake
take up abode locate, reside
take up again continue *(resume)*, proceed *(continue)*, resume
take up an inquiry canvass, probe
take up an option choose
take up arms fight *(battle)*, rebel
take up in conference discuss
take up membership join *(associate oneself with)*
take up one's abode dwell *(reside)*
take up quarters lodge *(reside)*
take up residence dwell *(reside)*, inhabit, reside
take up residence in lodge *(reside)*, occupy *(take possession)*
take upon oneself endeavor, pledge *(promise the performance of)*, promise *(vow)*, undertake
take vengeance retaliate
take vengeance on punish
take warning beware
take wing disappear
take without proof assume *(suppose)*, presume
take wrongfully hold up *(rob)*, purloin
take wrongly misapprehend
take-off travesty
take-over disseisin, sequestration
take-over of property eviction
taken lost *(taken away)*, preferred *(favored)*
taken advantage of aggrieved *(victimized)*
taken by force by the authorities arrested *(apprehended)*
taken for granted apparent *(presumptive)*, assumed *(inferred)*, ordinary, tacit
taken into custody arrested *(apprehended)*
taken prisoner arrested *(apprehended)*
takeover condemnation *(seizure)*
taker bearer, customer, extortionist, grantee, payee, volunteer
taking acquisition, apprehension *(act of arresting)*, arrogation, confiscatory, disseisin, distress *(seizure)*, plagiarism. SEE MAIN ENTRY
taking away abduction, removal
taking back retraction
taking by undue exercise of power blackmail, extortion
taking counsel deliberation
taking different courses divergent
taking effect before retroactive
taking exception dissenting
taking for public use expropriation *(right of eminent domain)*
taking hold apprehension *(act of arresting)*
taking information interrogation
taking issue with dissenting
taking of human life murder
taking of life aberemurder
taking of private land by the government expropriation *(right of eminent domain)*
taking of property for public use condemnation *(seizure)*
taking on assumption *(adoption)*
taking possession appropriation *(taking)*, condemnation *(seizure)*, disseisin
taking the law in one's own hands lynch law
taking the place of another vicarious *(delegated)*
taking without compensation disseisin
takings earnings, spoils
takings clause SEE MAIN ENTRY
tale falsehood, myth, narration, story *(narrative)*
tale telling narration
talebearer informant
talent aptitude, caliber *(mental capacity)*, capacity *(aptitude)*, competence *(ability)*, faculty *(ability)*, gift *(flair)*, penchant, performance *(workmanship)*, potential, proclivity, propensity, sense *(intelligence)*, skill, specialty *(special aptitude)*. SEE MAIN ENTRY
talented artful, deft, practiced, proficient, resourceful, veteran
talesmen jury
talion punishment, reprisal
talionic disciplinary *(punitory)*, punitive
talk communicate, conversation, converse, declaim, declamation, discourse *(noun)*, discourse *(verb)*, interview, language, parlance, parley, peroration, phrase, recite, recount, report *(detailed account)*, report *(rumor)*, scandal, speak, speech, utter. SEE MAIN ENTRY
talk about discuss, mention, remark
talk down to condescend *(patronize)*, patronize *(condescend toward)*

talk insincerely palter
talk into convert *(persuade)*, exhort, induce, influence, motivate, prevail upon
talk it over discuss
talk nonsense prattle
talk of circulate, discuss
talk out discuss
talk out of dissuade, expostulate
talk over confer *(consult)*, consult *(ask advice of)*, discourse, discuss, reason *(persuade)*
talk together discourse, discuss
talkative demonstrative *(expressive of emotion)*, flatulent, loquacious, voluble
talked about renowned
talked of famous, illustrious, notable
talked-about household *(familiar)*
talked-of household *(familiar)*
talking loquacious
talking big bluster *(speech)*
talks conference
tall story myth
tall talk rodomontade
tallage assessment *(levy)*, duty *(tax)*
tallness elevation
tally account *(evaluation)*, amount *(sum)*, bill *(invoice)*, calculate, census, comport *(agree with)*, computation, poll *(canvass)*, poll, record. SEE MAIN ENTRY
tally sheet inventory
tame alleviate, dominate, harmless, insipid, jejune *(dull)*, lifeless *(dull)*, malleable, moderate *(temper)*, obedient, passive, peaceable, pedestrian, phlegmatic, placid, prosaic, resigned, soothe, subdue, subject, subjugate
tameable corrigible
tamper disturb. SEE MAIN ENTRY
tamper with adulterate, contaminate, damage, denature, falsify, pervert, suborn, vitiate
tangency connection *(abutment)*, contact *(touching)*
tangent close *(near)*, proximate, tangential
tangential proximate. SEE MAIN ENTRY
tangere adjoin, affect
tangibility embodiment, materiality *(physical existence)*
tangible actual, apparent *(perceptible)*, appreciable, bodily, certain *(positive)*, concrete, corporal, corporeal, de facto, manifest, material *(physical)*, palpable, perceivable, perceptible, physical, substantive. SEE MAIN ENTRY
tangible assets estate *(property)*, merchandise, principal *(capital sum)*, property *(possessions)*
tangible form embodiment
tangible object entity
tangible proof fact
tangibles estate *(property)*, property *(possessions)*
tangibly fairly *(clearly)*
tangle complex *(entanglement)*, disorganize, engage *(involve)*, implicate, intertwine, involution, perplex, snarl
tangled complex, compound, disordered, disorderly, inextricable, intricate, labyrinthine, problematic, recondite, sinuous
tangly inextricable
tangy palatable
tankage capacity *(maximum)*
tantalization bribery, incentive, seduction
tantalize bait *(lure)*, interest, lure
tantalized eager
tantalizing provocative, sapid
tantamount coequal, comparable *(equivalent)*, equal, equivalent, identical. SEE MAIN ENTRY
tantamount to constructive *(inferential)*, virtual
tap impinge
tap the lines eavesdrop
taper attenuate, converge, decrease, diminish, lessen
taper off subside
tapering narrow
tar brand *(stigmatize)*
tardare delay, hold up *(delay)*
tardiness delay
tardus phlegmatic
tardy back *(in arrears)*, dilatory, overdue, remiss
targe panoply
target design *(intent)*, destination, end *(intent)*, goal, intention, object, objective, purpose, pursuit *(goal)*, victim. SEE MAIN ENTRY
tariff duty *(tax)*, excise, fare, imposition *(tax)*, levy, tax. SEE MAIN ENTRY
tarnish attaint, brand *(stigmatize)*, contaminate, debase, deface, defacement, defame, demean *(make lower)*, denigrate, depreciate, derogate, discredit *(noun)*, discredit *(verb)*, disgrace *(noun)*, disgrace *(verb)*, dishonor *(shame)*, dishonor *(deprive of honor)*, disparage, humiliate, ignominy, infamy, infect, onus *(stigma)*, opprobrium, pillory, pollute, reproach, scandal, shame, smear, stain, stigma, sully, taint *(corrupt)*. SEE MAIN ENTRY
tarnished blemished, disgraceful, marred
tarnished honor attaint, disgrace, dishonor *(shame)*, ignominy, scandal, shame
tarriance delay
tarry delay, dwell *(reside)*, lodge *(reside)*, loiter, pause, procrastinate, prolong, reside, stop
tarrying deferment
tart astringent, bitter *(acrid tasting)*, caustic
Tartuffish SEE MAIN ENTRY
task act *(undertaking)*, agency *(legal relationship)*, burden, business *(affair)*, calling, campaign, capacity *(job)*, charge *(responsibility)*, duty *(obligation)*, duty *(tax)*, employment, endeavor, enterprise *(undertaking)*, exact, function, job, labor *(work)*, mission, operation, part *(role)*, post, project, pursuit *(occupation)*, role, specialty *(special aptitude)*, tax *(overwork)*, trade *(occupation)*, undertaking *(business)*, undertaking *(enterprise)*, venture, work *(employment)*. SEE MAIN ENTRY
task undertaken undertaking *(attempt)*
taskmaster employer, principal *(director)*, superintendent
taste discretion *(quality of being discreet)*, mode, partake, partiality, predilection, predisposition, propensity, propriety *(correctness)*, sensibility, style. SEE MAIN ENTRY
tasteful aesthetic, attractive, elegant, felicitous, fit, palatable, proper
tastefulness decorum
tasteless disreputable, inelegant, insipid, jejune *(dull)*, pedestrian, stale, tawdry
tastelessness indecency
tasty nectarious, palatable, sapid, savory
tattle betray *(disclose)*, divulge, inform *(notify)*, report *(rumor)*
taught informed *(educated)*, knowing
taunt badger, bait *(harass)*, denigrate, discompose, disparage, jape, jeer, mock *(deride)*, offend *(insult)*, pique, plague, press *(goad)*, provocation, provoke, ridicule. SEE MAIN ENTRY
taunting critical *(faultfinding)*, instigation
taut firm, rigid
tautness stress *(strain)*
tautologic redundant
tautological iterative, redundant
tautology redundancy. SEE MAIN ENTRY
tawdry blatant *(obtrusive)*, meretricious, poor *(inferior in quality)*, pretentious *(ostentatious)*. SEE MAIN ENTRY
tax assessment *(levy)*, charge *(cost)*, charge *(assess)*, encumber *(hinder)*, exact, excise, excise *(levy a tax)*, exhaust *(deplete)*, fine, force *(coerce)*, impose *(enforce)*, levy *(noun)*, levy *(verb)*, rebuke, reproach, require *(compel)*, tariff *(duties)*, toll *(exact payment)*. SEE MAIN ENTRY
tax collector assessor
tax gatherer assessor
tax haven shelter *(tax benefit)*
tax man assessor
tax on demand duty *(tax)*
tax one's energies strive
tax receiver assessor
tax sanctuary shelter *(tax benefit)*
tax taker assessor
taxation ad valorem, duty *(tax)*, excise, levy, tax
taxer assessor
taxing onerous, oppressive
taxis classification
teach communicate, convey *(communicate)*, disabuse, edify, educate, elucidate, enlighten, explain, impart, inculcate, inform *(notify)*, initiate, instill, nurture. SEE MAIN ENTRY
teach a lesson to punish
teach by example demonstrate *(establish)*
teach by examples illustrate
teach wickedness brutalize, pervert
teachable corrigible, malleable, pliable, sequacious, tractable
teacher pedagogue
teachers faculty *(teaching staff)*
teaching didactic, direction *(guidance)*, discipline *(field of study)*, doctrine, edification, education, experience *(background)*, guidance, informatory, maxim, precept, preparation, propaganda
teaching body faculty *(teaching staff)*
teaching personnel faculty *(teaching staff)*
teachings doctrine
team band
team of employees personnel
team up federalize *(associate)*, involve *(participate)*
team up with combine *(act in concert)*, join *(associate oneself with)*
teammate coadjutant, contributor *(contributor)*, member *(individual in a group)*, partner
teamwork coaction, concert, contribution *(participation)*, cooperative
teamworker contributor *(contributor)*, partner
tear divide *(separate)*, lancinate, mutilate, race, rend, separate, sever, split
tear apart disjoint, mutilate
tear assunder part *(separate)*

tear asunder force *(break)*, rend
tear away deprive
tear down obliterate, refute
tear into attack
tear loose extricate
tear off denude
tear oneself away part *(leave)*
tear out eliminate *(eradicate)*, eviscerate, excise *(cut away)*, extirpate
tear to pieces extirpate
tear up disorganize
tearable divisible
tearful disconsolate, lugubrious, querulous
tearing division *(act of dividing)*, separation
tearing away avulsion
tearing down destruction
tearing off avulsion
tearless callous
tease badger, bait *(harass)*, bait *(lure)*, cajole, discompose, harrow, harry *(harass)*, hector, irritate, jape, mock *(deride)*, molest *(annoy)*, offend *(insult)*, perplex, pique, plague, press *(goad)*, provoke. SEE MAIN ENTRY
teaser enigma
technic instrumentality. SEE MAIN ENTRY
technical industrial. SEE MAIN ENTRY
technical term technicality
technicality detail. SEE MAIN ENTRY
technician artisan, expert, specialist
technique avenue *(means of attainment)*, discretion *(quality of being discreet)*, expedient, facility *(instrumentality)*, instrumentality, method, mode, modus operandi, performance *(workmanship)*, specialty *(special aptitude)*, strategy, style, system, treatment
technological industrial
technology SEE MAIN ENTRY
tectum ceiling, habitation *(dwelling place)*, inhabitation *(place of dwelling)*
tectus inscrutable
tedious jejune *(dull)*, lifeless *(dull)*, mundane, onerous, pedestrian, ponderous, prolix, prosaic, repetitious, trite, usual. SEE MAIN ENTRY
teem propagate *(increase)*, pullulate
teeming copious, full, manifold, populous, productive, profuse, prolific, replete, rife
teemless barren
teen juvenile
teenager adolescent, juvenile, minor
teeter beat *(pulsate)*
teetotalism temperance
tegere cloak, shroud
telecommunications SEE MAIN ENTRY
telegram dispatch *(message)*
telegraphic laconic, sententious
telescope abridge *(shorten)*, abstract *(summarize)*, constrict *(compress)*
telescoped compact *(pithy)*
telic purposeful
tell annunciate, apprise, betray *(disclose)*, communicate, constrain *(compel)*, convey *(communicate)*, declare, depict, detail *(particularize)*, direct *(order)*, disclose, divulge, enunciate, express, herald, impart, inform *(notify)*, instruct *(direct)*, mention, notify, observe *(remark)*, order, phrase, posit, proclaim, profess *(avow)*, pronounce *(speak)*, propagate *(spread)*, publish, recite, recount, remark, remind, report *(disclose)*, reveal, signify *(inform)*, speak, utter. SEE MAIN ENTRY
tell a falsehood fabricate *(make up)*, falsify, lie *(falsify)*, misguide, mislead, misrepresent, misstate, perjure, prevaricate
tell a lie bear false witness, fabricate *(make up)*, misguide, misstate, perjure, prevaricate
tell a secret confide *(divulge)*
tell again recapitulate, repeat *(state again)*
tell all confess
tell an untruth lie *(falsify)*, misguide, mislead, misstate, prevaricate
tell apart differentiate, discriminate *(distinguish)*
tell details detail *(particularize)*
tell falsehoods about frame *(charge falsely)*
tell fortunes predict, prognosticate
tell from differentiate
tell fully detail *(particularize)*
tell how explain
tell in detail recount
tell lies misrepresent
tell lies about frame *(charge falsely)*
tell of bespeak, connote, evidence, signify *(denote)*
tell on betray *(disclose)*
tell over repeat *(state again)*
tell particulars detail *(particularize)*
tell secrets inform *(betray)*
tell the future predict
tell the meaning define
tell the meaning of denote
tell the truth bare, disabuse
tell vividly delineate, depict, portray
tell with assurance of secrecy confide *(divulge)*
teller bystander, deponent, harbinger, informer *(a person who provides information)*
telling caveat, cogent, conversation, demonstrative *(illustrative)*, determinative, disclosure *(act of disclosing)*, eloquent, incisive, informatory, noteworthy, persuasive, potent, powerful, recital, strategic, trenchant
tellurian mundane
telluric mundane
temblor cataclysm
temerarious careless, hot-blooded, impolitic, improvident, imprudent, impulsive *(rash)*, injudicious, lax, negligent, remiss, unpolitic. SEE MAIN ENTRY
temerarius heedless, ill-advised, imprudent, injudicious, precipitate
temeritas temerity
temerity audacity. SEE MAIN ENTRY
temerous negligent, reckless
temper abate *(lessen)*, adapt, adjust *(regulate)*, allay, alleviate, alter, animus, assuage, character *(personal quality)*, commute, complexion, curb, disposition *(inclination)*, extenuate, frame *(mood)*, lessen, mitigate, modify *(moderate)*, mollify, palliate *(abate)*, passion, posture *(attitude)*, qualify *(condition)*, regulate *(adjust)*, relax, soothe, spirit, subdue
temperament character *(personal quality)*, color *(complexion)*, conatus, condition *(state)*, disposition *(inclination)*, frame *(mood)*, personality, posture *(attitude)*, predisposition, property *(distinctive attribute)*, spirit, tendency, trait. SEE MAIN ENTRY
temperamental fractious, sensitive *(easily affected)*
temperance austerity, clemency, constraint *(restriction)*, continence, longanimity, moderation, prudence, restraint. SEE MAIN ENTRY
temperantia continence, control *(supervision)*, moderation, temperance
temperare control *(restrain)*, forbear, modify *(moderate)*
temperate charitable *(lenient)*, controlled *(restrained)*, dispassionate, judicious, normal *(sane)*, peaceable, reasonable *(fair)*. SEE MAIN ENTRY
temperateness continence, moderation, temperance
temperatio organization *(structure)*
tempered reasonable *(fair)*. SEE MAIN ENTRY
tempering abatement *(reduction)*, mitigating, palliative *(abating)*
tempermental demonstrative *(expressive of emotion)*
tempest bluster *(commotion)*, commotion, furor, outburst, turmoil
tempestivus ripe, seasonable
tempestuous disorderly, outrageous, severe, vehement. SEE MAIN ENTRY
template pattern
tempo rate
temporal civil *(public)*, corporeal, ephemeral, material *(physical)*, mundane, physical, profane, temporary, transient, transitory
temporarily pro tempore
temporarily established provisional
temporary acting, brief, ephemeral, interim, interlocutory, provisional, tentative, transient, transitory, vicarious *(substitutional)*. SEE MAIN ENTRY
temporary accommodation loan
temporary agreement modus vivendi
temporary arrangement modus vivendi, stopgap
temporary closing lockout
temporary deprivation layoff
temporary discharge layoff
temporary escape reprieve
temporary existence mortality
temporary expedient replacement, stopgap, substitute
temporary halt moratorium
temporary inaction cessation *(interlude)*
temporary possession occupancy, tenancy
temporary quiet lull
temporary refuge asylum *(hiding place)*
temporary relief moratorium, reprieve
temporary route detour
temporary settlement modus vivendi
temporary stillness lull
temporary stop extension *(postponement)*, hiatus, pendency
temporary stoppage respite *(interval of rest)*
temporary substitute stopgap
temporary suspension extension *(postponement)*, layoff
temporary suspension of the execution of a sentence reprieve
temporis intervallum interim
temporis spatium duration
temporize delay, stall, suspend
tempt bait *(lure)*, cajole, coax, entice, entrap, interest, inveigle, lure, motivate, prompt. SEE MAIN ENTRY
temptare attempt, try *(attempt)*
temptation bribery, cause *(reason)*, hush money, incentive, provocation, seduction
tempted eager
temptestuousness bluster *(commotion)*

tempting attractive, bribery, palatable, persuasive, provocative, sapid, savory
tempus date, emergency, occasion
temulentus drunk
tenability credibility
tenable believable, colorable *(plausible)*, convincing, defensible, inexpugnable, persuasive, reasonable *(rational)*. SEE MAIN ENTRY
tenableness credibility
tenacious chronic, cohesive *(sticking)*, diligent, dogmatic, durable, indestructible, indivisible, industrious, inexorable, infallible, inflexible, inseparable, insistent, intractable, obdurate, patient, permanent, persistent, purposeful, relentless, resolute, sedulous, serious *(devoted)*, stable, steadfast, strong, unrelenting, unremitting, unyielding, willful. SEE MAIN ENTRY
tenaciousness adherence *(adhesion)*, adherence *(devotion)*, adhesion *(loyalty)*, diligence *(perseverance)*, strength, tenacity
tenacitas tenacity
tenacity adherence *(adhesion)*, adherence *(devotion)*, adhesion *(loyalty)*, diligence *(perseverance)*, industry *(activity)*, longanimity, purpose, resolution *(decision)*, retention, rigor, strength. SEE MAIN ENTRY
tenancy duration, enjoyment *(use)*, habitation *(act of inhabiting)*, inhabitation *(act of dwelling in)*, ownership, possession *(ownership)*, seisin, term *(duration)*, time. SEE MAIN ENTRY
tenant denizen, dwell *(reside)*, habitant, inhabit, inhabitant, lessee, lodge *(reside)*, lodger, occupant, reside, resident. SEE MAIN ENTRY
tenant-landlord agreement lease
tenantable habitable
tenanted populous
tenantless devoid
tenantry inhabitation *(act of dwelling in)*
tenative interim
tenax close *(rigorous)*, parsimonious, penurious
tend care *(regard)*, concern *(care)*, contribute *(assist)*, dispose *(incline)*, foster, gravitate, keep *(shelter)*, pander, prefer, preserve, serve *(assist)*
tend to conduce
tend to show evidence
tend toward discriminate *(treat differently)*, gravitate
tendency animus, aptitude, bias, character *(personal quality)*, characteristic, color *(complexion)*, conatus, direction *(course)*, disposition *(inclination)*, habit, inclination, instinct, mode, penchant, position *(point of view)*, predilection, predisposition, probability, proclivity, propensity, quality *(grade)*, standpoint, temperament, tenor. SEE MAIN ENTRY
tendency to change the mind indecision
tendency to waver indecision
tender benevolent, bestow, bid, cede, confer *(give)*, contribute *(indemnify)*, contribute *(supply)*, dispense, extend *(offer)*, introduce, invitation, overture, pay, pose *(propound)*, present *(make a gift)*, proffer, proposal *(suggestion)*, propose, proposition, propound, remit *(send payment)*, remit *(submit for consideration)*, satisfy *(discharge)*, submit *(give)*. SEE MAIN ENTRY
tender age nonage
tender feeling affection
tender in advance prepay
tender offer SEE MAIN ENTRY
tender one's resignation abandon *(withdraw)*, demit, resign, retire *(conclude a career)*
tender passion affection
tender payment disburse *(pay out)*
tender performance offer *(tender)*
tenderfoot neophyte
tenderhearted sensitive *(easily affected)*
tenderness affection, affinity *(regard)*, benevolence *(disposition to do good)*, consideration *(sympathetic regard)*
tending inclined, prone
tending to attract attention conspic-uous
tending to cause death deadly, malignant, pernicious, pestilent
tending to elude elusive
tending to escape elusive
tending to evade evasive
tending to excite lustful desires obscene
tending to impair prejudicial
tending to obstruct prejudicial
tending to slip away elusive
tenement estate *(property)*
tenere detain *(restrain)*, hold *(possess)*, interest, occupy *(engage)*, own, possess, restrain, retain *(keep in possession)*
tenet article *(precept)*, belief *(something believed)*, concept, conviction *(persuasion)*, doctrine, dogma, idea, law, precept, principle *(axiom)*, rule *(legal dictate)*, thesis
tenets platform
tenor complexion, condition *(state)*, connotation, content *(meaning)*, context, degree *(magnitude)*, gist *(substance)*, import, main point, meaning, mode, signification, spirit, substance *(essential nature)*, temperament. SEE MAIN ENTRY
tense rigid
tenseness stress *(strain)*
tension conflict, disaccord, feud, ill will, pressure, stress *(strain)*. SEE MAIN ENTRY
tensity stress *(strain)*
tentative conditional, hesitant, interlocutory, problematic, provisional, speculative, uncertain *(questionable)*, undecided, unsettled, vicarious *(substitutional)*. SEE MAIN ENTRY
tentative approach proposition
tentative explanation hypothesis
tentative law hypothesis
tentative statement proposition, suggestion
tentativeness hesitation
tenuis inconsiderable, negligible, petty, poor *(inferior in quality)*, slight
tenuitas poverty
tenuous illusory, insubstantial, marginal, nonsubstantial *(not sturdy)*, null *(insignificant)*, slight. SEE MAIN ENTRY
tenure domain *(land owned)*, duration, enjoyment *(use)*, occupancy, occupation *(possession)*, ownership, period, phase *(period)*, seisin, tenancy, term *(duration)*, time, title *(right)*. SEE MAIN ENTRY
tenure by lease leasehold
tepidity disinterest *(lack of interest)*
tergiversari equivocate, prevaricate
tergiversate abandon *(relinquish)*, defect, equivocate, leave *(depart)*, palter, prevaricate, quit *(discontinue)*, rebel, recant, secede. SEE MAIN ENTRY
tergiversating false *(disloyal)*, regressive, undependable, unreliable, untrustworthy
tergiversatio evasion
tergiversation breach, evasion, reversal, revolt, sedition
tergiversator pariah
term call *(title)*, call *(title)*, clause, condition *(contingent provision)*, define, denominate, denomination, duration, expiration, finality, identify, label, life *(period of existence)*, lifetime, option *(contractual provision)*, period, phase *(period)*, phrase, provision *(clause)*, purview, qualification *(condition)*, session, technicality, tenure, time, title *(division)*. SEE MAIN ENTRY
term of activity life *(period of existence)*
term of effectiveness life *(period of existence)*
term of imprisonment captivity
term of life age
term of reference article *(distinct section of a writing)*
terminable defeasible, determinable *(liable to be terminated)*. SEE MAIN ENTRY
terminal border, conclusive *(settled)*, destination, end *(termination)*, extreme *(last)*, final, finality, last *(final)*, mete, ultimate
terminal point destination, end *(termination)*, extremity *(furthest point)*, objective
terminally ill in extremis
terminare finish, limit
terminate abate *(extinguish)*, abolish, abrogate *(rescind)*, adjourn, annul, cancel, cap, cease, complete, conclude *(complete)*, consummate, culminate, decide, desist, destroy *(void)*, discontinue *(abandon)*, eliminate *(eradicate)*, expire, extinguish, finish, halt, lapse *(cease)*, liquidate *(convert into cash)*, obstruct, overthrow, palliate *(abate)*, quash, quit *(discontinue)*, rest *(cease from action)*, result, shut, slay, stop. SEE MAIN ENTRY
terminate a trial rest *(end a legal case)*
terminate business affairs liquidate *(convert into cash)*
terminate work strike *(refuse to work)*
terminated complete *(ended)*, dead, defunct, through
terminated trial mistrial
terminating final, last *(final)*
termination abatement *(extinguishment)*, adjournment, barrier, border, cancellation, close *(conclusion)*, conclusion *(outcome)*, denouement, destination, desuetude, discharge *(performance)*, discontinuance *(act of discontinuing)*, discontinuance *(interruption of a legal action)*, effect, end *(termination)*, expiration, extremity *(death)*, extremity *(furthest point)*, finality, frontier, halt, lapse *(expiration)*, layoff, moratorium, rescision, resignation *(relinquishment)*, result. SEE MAIN ENTRY
termination of a pregnancy abortion *(feticide)*
termination of an action dismissal *(termination of a proceeding)*, nonsuit
termination of cohabitation estrangement
termination of employment layoff
termination of life death, homicide
termination of marital cohabitation separation
termination of membership expulsion
terminational complete *(ended)*, definitive, final, last *(final)*
terminative complete *(ended)*, conclusive *(settled)*, definitive, extreme *(last)*, final, last *(final)*, ultimate

terminology denomination, language, parlance, phraseology
terminus boundary
terminus cessation *(termination)*
terminus close *(conclusion)*, denouement
terminus destination, end *(termination)*, extremity *(furthest point)*, finality
terminus limit
terminus mete, periphery
termless indeterminate, infinite, open-ended, unlimited
termly intermittent
termor lodger
terms adjustment, arrangement *(understanding)*, case *(set of circumstances)*, compromise, posture *(situation)*, premises *(hypotheses)*, settlement. SEE MAIN ENTRY
terms for agreement contract
terms imposed circumstances
terms proposed counteroffer, proposition
terra district
terra firma cornerstone
terrae filius nonentity
terrain land, locality, parcel, region, territory, zone
terrene mundane
terrestrial mundane
terrible deplorable, dire, formidable, gross *(flagrant)*, heinous, lamentable, loathsome, nefarious, pestilent, regrettable, sinister. SEE MAIN ENTRY
terrible accident disaster
terrifc meritorious. SEE MAIN ENTRY
terrific prodigious *(enormous)*
terrify endanger, frighten, intimidate, menace
terrifying formidable
territorial local, regional
territorial division district
territorial range of authority jurisdiction
territorial shape dimension
territory area *(province)*, bailiwick, capacity *(sphere)*, circuit, district, domain *(sphere of influence)*, dominion *(absolute ownership)*, estate *(property)*, freehold, jurisdiction, locality, location, parcel, possessions, property *(land)*, province, purview, realm, region, scope, section *(vicinity)*, site, space, venue, vicinity, zone. SEE MAIN ENTRY
territory for defense buffer zone
terror fear. SEE MAIN ENTRY
terror fright
terror panic, phobia, trepidation. SEE MAIN ENTRY
terrorism anarchy, lynch law. SEE MAIN ENTRY
terrorist assailant, criminal. SEE MAIN ENTRY
terrorist activity SEE MAIN ENTRY
terrorist cell SEE MAIN ENTRY
terrorize bait *(harass)*, coerce, endanger, frighten, harass, intimidate, threaten
terse cohesive *(compact)*, compact *(pithy)*, laconic, pithy, sententious, succinct
test attempt, canon, check *(inspect)*, criterion, endeavor, experiment, indagation, question *(inquiry)*, research, survey *(poll)*, trial *(experiment)*, try *(attempt)*, venture. SEE MAIN ENTRY
test case criterion
test of endurance contest *(competition)*
testable deductible *(provable)*, incontrovertible, irrefutable
testament certificate, codicil, will *(testamentary instrument)*. SEE MAIN ENTRY
testamentary heritable. SEE MAIN ENTRY
testamentary declaration testament
testamentary decree testament
testamentary disposition bequest, conveyance, demise *(conveyance)*
testamentary gift bequest, legacy
testamentum testament, will *(testamentary instrument)*
testari depose *(testify)*, testify, witness *(attest to)*
testate SEE MAIN ENTRY
testator contributor *(giver)*, decedent, grantor
tested conclusive *(determinative)*, definite, dependable, genuine, indubious, meritorious, safe
testee subject *(object)*
testem facere attest
testificari attest, depose *(testify)*, testify, witness *(attest to)*
testificatio attestation
testification affirmation, attestation, averment, avouchment, certification *(attested copy)*, corroboration, deposition, reference *(recommendation)*
testification under oath affidavit
testified to alleged
testifier affiant, affirmant, bystander, deponent, eyewitness, witness
testify acknowledge *(verify)*, affirm *(declare solemnly)*, avouch *(avow)*, avow, bear *(adduce)*, bespeak, certify *(attest)*, inform *(notify)*, manifest, posit, promise *(vow)*, verify *(swear)*, vouch. SEE MAIN ENTRY
testify against inform *(betray)*
testify to attest, corroborate, establish *(show)*, report *(disclose)*, witness *(attest to)*
testilying SEE MAIN ENTRY
testimonial affirmation, deposition, monument, recommendation, remembrance *(commemoration)*, reminder, respect
testimonial averment admission *(disclosure)*
testimonials credentials
testimonium affirmation
testimonium attestation, deposition, evidence *(noun)*, evidence *(verb)*, proof, testimony
testimonium dicere witness *(attest to)*
testimonium per tabulas datum affidavit
testimony adjuration, admission *(disclosure)*, affirmance *(legal affirmation)*, affirmation, attestation, avowal, certification *(attested copy)*, corroboration, deposition, disclosure *(something disclosed)*, proof, reference *(recommendation)*, statement. SEE MAIN ENTRY
testing trial *(experiment)*
testing program experiment, research
testis witness
testy fractious, perverse, petulant, querulous, spiteful
tether fix *(make firm)*, handcuff, restrict, trammel
tethered fixed *(securely placed)*
text content *(meaning)*, contents, context, hornbook, meaning, phraseology, scenario, script, subject *(topic)*
textbook hornbook
textual literal
textualism SEE MAIN ENTRY
thalamus chamber *(compartment)*
thankful indebted
thankless undesirable, unrequited
thanklessness ingratitude
thanks recognition
that being so consequently
that being the case consequently
that is a savoir
that is to say a savoir
that may be determined determinable *(ascertainable)*
that which a person owes to another obligation *(duty)*
that which attaches attachment *(act of affixing)*
that which furnishes proof evidence
that which is comprehended coverage *(scope)*
that which is decided holding *(ruling of a court)*
that which is due from a person obligation *(duty)*
that which is owed debit
that which is owing due, obligation *(liability)*, responsibility *(accountability)*
that which is proper decorum
that which tends to prove evidence
thaumaturgy mystery
the accused defendant
the act of tracing delineation
the bench forum *(court)*
the case basic facts
the court judge
the deceased dead
the defense litigant
the defunct dead
the departed dead
the entirety *in solido*
the facts in the matter basic facts
the facts of the case basic facts
the following a savoir
the government prosecution *(government agency)*
the late dead
the late lamented dead
the legal fraternity bar *(body of lawyers)*
the most possible utmost
the other side contra
the outvoted minority *(outnumbered group)*
the people district attorney, prosecution *(government agency)*
the prosecuting attorney prosecution *(government agency)*
the prosecution contender, district attorney
the state district attorney, prosecution *(government agency)*
the succeeding a savoir
the unforeseen bombshell
the whole sum *(total)*
the whole story basic facts
theater scene
theatralis pretentious *(pompous)*
theatrecraft histrionics
theatric histrionic
theatrical grandiose, histrionic, meretricious, orotund
theatricalism histrionics
theatricality histrionics, pretense *(ostentation)*
theatricalness histrionics
theft burglary, conversion *(misappropriation)*, embezzlement, housebreaking, larceny, misappropriation, plunder, robbery, spoliation. SEE MAIN ENTRY
theft of money entrusted to one's care embezzlement

theft of money entrusted to one's management embezzlement
theistic sacrosanct
theme content *(meaning)*, motif, question *(issue)*, subject *(topic)*, thesis
theme of inquiry question *(inquiry)*
themes contents
then late *(defunct)*. SEE MAIN ENTRY
then again also
theologic sacrosanct
theological sacrosanct
theorem inference, postulate, prescription *(directive)*, principle *(axiom)*, supposition
theorems premises *(hypotheses)*
theoretical debatable, disputable, indefinite, intangible, moot, nonexistent, presumptive, speculative. SEE MAIN ENTRY
theorization generalization, speculation *(conjecture)*
theorize assume *(suppose)*, derive *(deduce)*, generalize, guess, opine, ponder, postulate, presume, presuppose, prognosticate, rationalize, reason *(conclude)*, reflect *(ponder)*, speculate *(conjecture)*, surmise, suspect *(think)*
theory assumption *(supposition)*, concept, conjecture, conviction *(persuasion)*, deduction *(conclusion)*, generalization, hypothesis, idea, inference, opinion *(belief)*, perception, proposition, rationale, speculation *(conjecture)*, supposition, thesis. SEE MAIN ENTRY
theory of business finance
theory of fiscal relations finance
therapeutic curative, cure, medicinal, palliative *(abating)*, remedial, salubrious, salutary
therapeutical medicinal, salubrious
therapy treatment
there SEE MAIN ENTRY
thereafter ex post facto. SEE MAIN ENTRY
thereby SEE MAIN ENTRY
therefore consequently
therein herein, wherein
theretofore SEE MAIN ENTRY
thersitical scandalous
thesaurus treasury
theses premises *(hypotheses)*
thesis conjecture, contents, deduction *(conclusion)*, hypothesis, inference, opinion *(belief)*, postulate, proposition, subject *(topic)*, supposition, theory. SEE MAIN ENTRY
thews sinew
thick cohesive *(compact)*, compact *(dense)*, impervious, obtuse, opaque, ossified, populous, rife, solid *(compact)*
thick-headed opaque
thick-skinned callous, impervious
thick-witted opaque
thick-wittedness opacity
thicken crystallize
thickened ossified
thickening congealment
thicket assemblage
thickheaded obtuse
thickheadedness opacity
thickly settled populous
thickness caliber *(measurement)*, congealment, density, opacity
thief burglar, convict, criminal, embezzler, hoodlum, lawbreaker, outlaw. SEE MAIN ENTRY
thieve carry away, defalcate, despoil, embezzle, hold up *(rob)*, impropriate, loot, pilfer, pillage, pirate *(take by violence)*, plunder, purloin, steal
thievery burglary, conversion *(misappropriation)*, embezzlement, housebreaking, larceny, misappropriation, plagiarism, racket, robbery, spoliation, theft
thieving larcenous
thievish furtive, larcenous, stealthy
thievishness dishonesty
thin deficient, dilute, diminish, excise *(cut away)*, extenuate, insubstantial, insufficient, jejune *(dull)*, lessen, minimal, minimize, narrow, nonsubstantial *(not sufficient)*, reduce, slight, tenuous
thin out deploy, dilute, diminish, lessen
thin with liquid dilute
thing article *(commodity)*
things effects
things as they are status quo
things for sale goods
think deduce, deduct *(conclude by reasoning)*, deem, expect *(consider probable)*, guess, muse, opine, presume, presuppose, rationalize, reason *(conclude)*, reflect *(ponder)*, speculate *(conjecture)*, surmise. SEE MAIN ENTRY
think about consider, devote, digest *(comprehend)*, muse, regard *(pay attention)*, study
think ahead plan, scheme
think anxiously brood
think back remember
think back to recall *(remember)*
think better prefer
think better of reconsider, repent
think carefully deliberate
think credible assume *(suppose)*
think deeply ponder
think differently differ *(disagree)*, differ *(vary)*, disagree
think highly of recommend, regard *(hold in esteem)*
think ill of disapprove *(condemn)*
think intensely concentrate *(pay attention)*
think it over doubt *(hesitate)*
think likely assume *(suppose)*, deduce, deduct *(conclude by reasoning)*, expect *(consider probable)*, guess, presume
think little of disparage, disregard, minimize
think logically rationalize
think no more of dismiss *(put out of consideration)*
think nothing of disdain, disregard, minimize
think of conjure, initiate, invent *(produce for the first time)*, recollect
think on ponder
think one deserves claim *(demand)*
think out calculate, scheme, solve
think over brood, deliberate, muse, pause, reconsider
think probable assume *(suppose)*
think reprehensible disapprove *(condemn)*
think through reason *(conclude)*
think too little of underestimate
think twice beware, hesitate, pause
think unworthy of notice disdain
think up conjure, create, frame *(formulate)*, invent *(produce for the first time)*, make, originate
think well of regard *(hold in esteem)*
think wrong disapprove *(condemn)*
thinkable colorable *(plausible)*, plausible, possible, potential, viable
thinker mastermind
thinking assumption *(supposition)*, circumspect, cogitative, conviction *(persuasion)*, dialectic, opinion *(belief)*, ratiocination, rational, reason *(sound judgment)*, reflection *(thought)*, sapient, sensible. SEE MAIN ENTRY
thinking out deliberation
thinly scattered scarce
thinness immateriality, paucity
thinning out erosion
thirst desire, need *(deprivation)*
thirst for need
thorny impracticable, precarious
thorough accurate, circumspect, complete *(all-embracing)*, comprehensive, conscientious, definitive, detailed, diligent, faithful *(diligent)*, industrious, ingrained, intensive, judicious, meticulous, outright, painstaking, particular *(exacting)*, plenary, precise, punctilious, radical *(extreme)*, scrupulous, systematic, total, unmitigated. SEE MAIN ENTRY
thoroughfare causeway
thoroughgoing circumspect, complete *(all-embracing)*, comprehensive, diligent, intensive, meticulous, particular *(exacting)*, radical *(extreme)*, systematic, thorough, total, trenchant
thoroughgoingness diligence *(care)*
thoroughly in toto, purely *(positively)*
thoroughness caution *(vigilance)*, diligence *(care)*
those holding power authorities
those in command authorities
those in control authorities
those of influence authorities
those who rule authorities
though regardless
thought apprehension *(perception)*, concept, consideration *(sympathetic regard)*, contemplation, deliberation, idea, notice *(heed)*, notion, opinion *(belief)*, perspective, point *(item)*, proposal *(suggestion)*, ratiocination, reason *(sound judgment)*, remark, suggestion, theory. SEE MAIN ENTRY
thought beforehand forethought
thought out intentional, premeditated
thought-out deliberate
thought-provoking sapid, suggestive *(evocative)*
thoughtful benevolent, careful, circumspect, cogitative, deliberate, discreet, discriminating *(judicious)*, earnest, intentional, judicial, judicious, pensive, politic, profound *(esoteric)*, provident *(showing foresight)*, prudent, rational, sensible
thoughtful regard consideration *(sympathetic regard)*
thoughtfulness benevolence *(disposition to do good)*, consideration *(sympathetic regard)*, contemplation, courtesy, deliberation, discretion *(quality of being discreet)*, discrimination *(good judgment)*, forethought, interest *(concern)*, introspection, largess *(generosity)*
thoughtless blind *(not discerning)*, careless, casual, cursory, derelict *(negligent)*, fatuous, heedless, hot-blooded, ill-judged, impolitic, improvident, imprudent, impulsive *(rash)*, inadvertent, injudicious, irrational, irresponsible, lax, misadvised, negligent, oblivious, perfunctory, perverse, precipitate, reckless, remiss, slipshod, unpremeditated, unwitting, vacuous. SEE MAIN ENTRY
thoughtlessness disinterest *(lack of interest)*, disregard *(lack of respect)*, inconsideration, indiscretion, ingratitude, laxity, neglect, oversight *(carelessness)*, temerity

thoughts of the past hindsight, retrospect
thrall captive, durance, servitude, subjection. SEE MAIN ENTRY
thralldom bondage, custody *(incarceration)*, durance, servitude, thrall
thrash beat *(strike)*, lash *(strike)*
thrashing battery
thrasonical orgulous
thread nexus
threadbare trite
threadbare phrase platitude
threat apprehension *(fear)*, coercion, danger, dun, duress, hazard, jeopardy, menace, peril, pitfall, ultimatum, warning. SEE MAIN ENTRY
threaten bait *(harass)*, brandish, challenge, coerce, compel, endanger, exact, forewarn, frighten, hector, impend, intimidate, jeopardize, menace, portend, presage, promise *(raise expectations)*. SEE MAIN ENTRY
threatening abusive, chilling effect, dangerous, formidable, imminent, insalubrious, noxious, ominous, pending *(imminent)*, pestilent, portentous *(ominous)*, precarious, pugnacious, sinister, unpropitious
threatening harm imminent
threatful ominous
thresh beat *(strike)*
threshold cornerstone, entrance, margin *(outside limit)*, onset *(commencement)*, outline *(boundary)*, outset, start. SEE MAIN ENTRY
thrift austerity, economy *(frugality)*, moderation, prudence
thriftiness austerity, economy *(frugality)*, moderation
thriftless improvident, prodigal, profligate *(extravagant)*, profuse
thrifty economic, economical, frugal, parsimonious, provident *(frugal)*, prudent
thrifty use management *(judicious use)*
thrill enjoyment *(pleasure)*, passion. SEE MAIN ENTRY
thrilled ecstatic, proud *(self-respecting)*
thrilling moving *(evoking emotion)*, provocative
thrive gain, germinate, increase, prevail *(triumph)*, proliferate, succeed *(attain)*
thriving cumulative *(increasing)*, prosperous, successful
thriving condition prosperity
thriving conditions boom *(prosperity)*
thriving economy boom *(prosperity)*
throb beat *(pulsate)*
throbbing painful
throe outbreak, outburst
throng assemblage, collection *(assembly)*, congregate, mass *(body of persons)*, meet
thronged populous
throttle occlude, shut, stifle
throttle down curb
through arrant *(definite)*, complete *(ended)*, hereby, thereby. SEE MAIN ENTRY
through and through outright
through road causeway
through the medium of hereby, thereby
throughout ad interim, wholly. SEE MAIN ENTRY
throughway way *(channel)*
throw emit, impel, launch *(project)*, project *(impel forward)*, send
throw a veil over camouflage, conceal
throw aside forgo, reject
throw away abandon *(relinquish)*, dislodge, dispel, jettison, relinquish
throw back reflect *(mirror)*, repulse
throw dishonor upon brand *(stigmatize)*, disgrace
throw doubt upon impugn
throw down overthrow, precipitate *(throw down violently)*, subvert
throw headlong precipitate *(throw down violently)*
throw into confusion agitate *(perturb)*, confound, confuse *(bewilder)*, confuse *(create disorder)*, discompose, disconcert, dislocate, disorganize, disorient, misdirect, muddle, obfuscate, perturb
throw into disorder confuse *(create disorder)*, disorganize, disorient
throw into prison arrest *(apprehend)*, immure
throw light upon define, elucidate, explain, explicate, exposit, interpret, resolve *(solve)*, solve
throw off abandon *(relinquish)*, dispel, emit, repel *(drive back)*
throw off heat radiate
throw off the scent obfuscate
throw oneself upon attack
throw open admit *(give access)*, manifest
throw open to inquiry canvass
throw out discharge *(dismiss)*, dislodge, displace *(remove)*, eject *(evict)*, eject *(expel)*, eliminate *(exclude)*, emit, exclude, expel, oust, pose *(propound)*, propound, radiate, reject, relegate
throw out of gear luxate
throw out of joint dislocate
throw out of order agitate *(shake up)*, dislocate, disorganize, disorient, muddle
throw over overthrow
throw overboard jettison
throwback reversion *(act of returning)*
throwing out disqualification *(rejection)*, expulsion
thrown away lost *(taken away)*
thrown overboard derelict *(abandoned)*
thrust emphasis, foray, gravamen, impetus, impinge, impulse, launch *(project)*, onset *(assault)*, operation, project *(impel forward)*. SEE MAIN ENTRY
thrust at accost, assail, assault, oppugn
thrust back repel *(drive back)*
thrust in impact, inject, interject, interpose, intrude, plant *(place firmly)*
thrust oneself intrude
thrust oneself in impose *(intrude)*
thrust out deport *(banish)*, dislodge, eject *(evict)*, eject *(expel)*, eliminate *(exclude)*, evict, exclude, expel, oust
thrust under immerse *(plunge into)*
thrust upon surreptitiously foist
thrustful compelling, decisive
thrusting out deportation
thruway causeway
thug assailant
thumb peruse
thumb through read
thumbnail sketch brief
thump beat *(pulsate)*
thumping prodigious *(enormous)*
thunder barrage, outbreak, outburst
thunder against inveigh, reprimand
thunder forth proclaim
thunderbolt bombshell
thunderclap bombshell
thunderous resounding
thunderstruck speechless
thus a fortiori, consequently. SEE MAIN ENTRY
thusly a priori, consequently
thwart annoy, arrest *(stop)*, avert, balk, bar *(hinder)*, beat *(defeat)*, block, check *(restrain)*, circumvent, condemn *(ban)*, constrict *(inhibit)*, contain *(restrain)*, contravene, counter, countervail, defeat, deter, disadvantage, discontinue *(break continuity)*, discourage, disrupt, encumber *(hinder)*, enjoin, estop, fight *(counteract)*, foil, forestall, frustrate, halt, hamper, hold up *(delay)*, impede, inconvenience, interdict, interfere, interrupt, keep *(restrain)*, kill *(defeat)*, obstruct, occlude, oppugn, overreach, override, parry, preclude, prevent, prohibit, repulse, resist *(oppose)*, stay *(halt)*, stem *(check)*, stop, toll *(stop)*, trammel, withstand. SEE MAIN ENTRY
thwarted disappointed
thwarted expectation frustration
thwarter deterrence, deterrent
thwarting defeat, disadvantageous, frustration, preventive
ticket brand, coupon, fare, key *(passport)*, label *(noun)*, label *(verb)*, pigeonhole, trademark
ticket incorrectly mislabel
ticket of leave permit
ticklish insecure, precarious
tidal wave cataclysm
tide outflow
tide over continue *(adjourn)*
tide turning SEE MAIN ENTRY
tidewater littoral
tidings intelligence *(news)*, report *(detailed account)*, story *(narrative)*
tidy compact *(pithy)*, meticulous
tie adherence *(adhesion)*, adherence *(devotion)*, adhesion *(loyalty)*, attachment *(act of affixing)*, chain *(nexus)*, charge *(lien)*, combine *(join together)*, connect *(join together)*, connection *(fastening)*, connection *(relation)*, contact *(association)*, deadlock, fetter *(noun)*, fetter *(verb)*, handcuff, kinship, liaison, marriage *(intimate relationship)*, nexus, prevent, privity, propinquity *(kinship)*, relate *(establish a connection)*, relation *(connection)*, relationship *(connection)*, restrain, trammel
tie down fetter
tie in with correspond *(be equivalent)*, involve *(implicate)*, pertain
tie one's hands handcuff
tie the hands of handcuff
tie together intertwine
tie up constrict *(inhibit)*, encumber *(hinder)*, handcuff, restrict, trammel
tie-in relation *(connection)*, relevance
tied bound, cohesive *(sticking)*, compound, equal, inextricable, interrelated, related
tied down indentured
tied in with relevant
tied together conjoint
tier degree *(station)*
ties SEE MAIN ENTRY
ties of blood affiliation *(bloodline)*, degree *(kinship)*, filiation
ties of family blood
ties of race affiliation *(bloodline)*
tiff bicker, brawl
tight cohesive *(compact)*, compact *(dense)*, fixed *(securely placed)*, illiberal, impervious, parsimonious, solid *(compact)*
tight situation predicament, problem, quagmire

tight spot imbroglio, predicament
tight-lipped mute
tighten adhere *(fasten)*, constrict *(compress)*
tightfisted illiberal
tightly knit compact *(dense)*
tightness stress *(strain)*
til until
till ad interim, bank, coffer, cultivate, treasury
tilt bicker, compete
tilted oblique *(slanted)*
timbre intonation
time annum, chance *(fortuity)*, date *(noun)*, date *(verb)*, duration, life *(period of existence)*, lifetime, occasion, opportunity, period, phase *(period)*, point *(period of time)*, term *(duration)*, timeliness. SEE MAIN ENTRY
time ahead prospect *(outlook)*
time during which anything occurs date
time from birth to death life *(period of existence)*
time interval period
time of life age
time of war belligerency
time off furlough, holiday
time out halt, pause, recess
time payment loan
time saving economic
time stretch period
time without end perpetuity
time worn antique
time-honored conventional, familiar *(customary)*, illustrious, inveterate, prescriptive, traditional
time-saving economical
timed punctual
timeful seasonable
timeless durable, incessant, infinite
timelessness perpetuity
timeliness dispatch *(promptness)*, expedience. SEE MAIN ENTRY
timely apposite, appropriate, favorable *(advantageous)*, felicitous, fitting, opportune, prompt, propitious, punctual, seasonable, suitable
timely care precaution
timere fear
timeserving undependable
timetable calendar *(list of cases)*, calendar *(record of yearly periods)*, schedule
timeworn dilapidated, obsolete, old, stale
timid diffident, hesitant, irresolute, recreant
timidity fear
timor fear
timorous diffident, recreant
timorousness fear
tincture minimum, penetrate
tinge minimum, stain
tingere imbue
tingling ecstatic
tinker repair
tinsel meretricious, tawdry
tint stain
tiny impalpable, minimal, remote *(small)*, tenuous
tip bonus, bounty, edge *(border)*, end *(termination)*, extremity *(furthest point)*, gratuity *(present)*, herald, inform *(notify)*, intelligence *(news)*, perquisite, pinnacle, recommendation, reward, suggestion. SEE MAIN ENTRY
tip off notify
tip over upset
tipped informed *(having information)*, oblique *(slanted)*
tipper informant, informer *(a person who provides information)*
tipping oblique *(slanted)*
tipple carouse
tipster bystander, informant, informer *(one providing criminal information)*, informer *(a person who provides information)*
tiptop superlative
tirade bombast, declamation, denunciation, diatribe, disparagement, harangue, obloquy, philippic, revilement, stricture
tire exhaust *(deplete)*, succumb
tire out tax *(overwork)*
tired languid, lifeless *(dull)*
tiredness languor, prostration
tireless diligent, faithful *(diligent)*, industrious, persistent, undaunted
tirelessness diligence *(perseverance)*
tiresome irksome, jejune *(dull)*, lifeless *(dull)*, operose, painful, pedestrian, prolix, prosaic, vexatious
tiring irksome, operose, oppressive
tiro probationer *(one being tested)*
titallative sapid
titanic prodigious *(enormous)*, strong
tithe tax, toll *(tax)*
titillate bait *(lure)*, interest
titillating attractive, provocative, salacious, sapid, suggestive *(risqué)*
title caption, claim *(right)*, degree *(academic title)*, denominate, denomination, designation *(symbol)*, dominion *(absolute ownership)*, fee *(estate)*, heading, interest *(ownership)*, label, nominate, ownership, possession *(ownership)*, prerogative, privilege, prize, right *(entitlement)*, seisin, stake *(interest)*, subheading, term *(expression)*. SEE MAIN ENTRY
title deed debenture
title impairment incumbrance *(lien)*
title incorrectly mislabel
title of honor degree *(academic title)*
titleholder landholder, landowner
tittle iota, minimum, scintilla
titular nominal
titulary nominal
titulus inscription
to until
to a certain extent in part, quasi
to a degree fairly *(moderately)*, in part
to a limited extent fairly *(moderately)*, in part
to all appearances prima facie *(self-evident)*
to all intents and purposes as a rule
to be future, prospective
to be believed convincing
to be decided disputable
to be depended on credible, official
to be expected foreseeable, probable
to be had available, disposable
to be paid delinquent *(overdue)*, due *(owed)*
to be relied upon credible
to be similiar correspond *(be equivalent)*
to be supposed apparent *(presumptive)*
to be trusted official
to blame delinquent *(guilty of a misdeed)*, guilty
to bring to completion consummate
to bring together desegregate
to come forthcoming, future, immediate *(imminent)*, inevitable, prospective
to each according to his share per capita, pro rata
to infinity ad infinitum
to no end unavailing
to no purpose unavailing
to one's advantage beneficial
to one's liking attractive
to some extent fairly *(moderately)*
to that end a priori, consequently
to the contrary contra
to the end throughout *(all over)*
to the letter faithfully, literal, verbatim
to the point applicable, apposite, brief, cogent, cohesive *(compact)*, compact *(pithy)*, concise, explicit, felicitous, germane, laconic, pertinent, relevant, sententious, succinct
to the purpose apposite, effective *(efficient)*, felicitous, fit, pertinent, practical, relevant
to the same degree equal
to the time when until
to this day through *(until now)*
to wit a savoir
toady pander, truckle
toadying obsequious, sequacious, subservient
toast honor
toddler infant
together along, conjoint, en masse, intact. SEE MAIN ENTRY
together with also
togetherness integration *(assimilation)*
toil effort, endeavor *(noun)*, endeavor *(verb)*, industry *(activity)*, labor *(work)*, labor, persevere, strive, work *(effort)*
toil unceasingly persist
toiler employee
toilsome onerous, operose, oppressive
token binder, bounty, brand, clue, coupon, denote, designation *(symbol)*, device *(distinguishing mark)*, expression *(manifestation)*, guaranty, indicant, indication, indicator, money, nominal, null *(insignificant)*, perquisite, precursor, prize, remembrance *(commemoration)*, security *(pledge)*, specialty *(distinctive mark)*, symbol, symptom. SEE MAIN ENTRY
token payment binder, installment, pledge *(security)*
tokens indicia
told acquainted, informed *(having information)*, narrative, oral, parol, stated
told in confidence confidential
tolerability admissibility, mediocrity
tolerable admissible, allowable, allowed, considerable, fair *(satisfactory)*, imperfect, marginal, mediocre, passable, permissible, reasonable *(fair)*, unobjectionable
tolerableness mediocrity
tolerably fairly *(moderately)*
tolerance acceptance, benevolence *(disposition to do good)*, charter *(sanction)*, clemency, composure, consent, disinterest *(lack of prejudice)*, dispensation *(exception)*, franchise *(license)*, goodwill, indulgence, leave *(permission)*, lenience, longanimity, permission, privilege, resignation *(passive acceptance)*, sanction *(permission)*, sufferance, temperance. SEE MAIN ENTRY
tolerans patient
tolerant benevolent, charitable *(lenient)*, dispassionate, lenient, liberal *(broad minded)*, nonmilitant, open-minded, patient, peaceable, permissive, receptive, resigned, stoical, unbiased, unprejudiced
tolerantia tolerance

tolerantly fairly *(impartially)*
tolerare bear *(tolerate)*, endure *(suffer)*, tolerate
tolerate abide, accept *(assent)*, allow *(endure)*, authorize, concede, condescend *(deign)*, condone, consent, endure *(suffer)*, forbear, let *(permit)*, palliate *(excuse)*, permit, receive *(permit to enter)*, recognize *(acknowledge)*, resist *(withstand)*, sanction, submit *(yield)*, suffer *(permit)*, vouchsafe. SEE MAIN ENTRY
tolerated allowable, allowed
tolerating permissive
toleratio sufferance
toleration acceptance, approval, charter *(sanction)*, clemency, consent, disinterest *(lack of prejudice)*, dispensation *(exception)*, indulgence, lenience, longanimity, resignation *(passive acceptance)*, sanction *(permission)*, sufferance, temperance, tolerance, understanding *(tolerance)*
toll assessment *(levy)*, charge *(cost)*, duty *(tax)*, exact, excise, fare, fee *(charge)*, imposition *(tax)*, levy, price, tax. SEE MAIN ENTRY
tollere abolish, cancel
tome publication *(printed matter)*
tonality intonation
tone character *(personal quality)*, color *(complexion)*, complexion, inflection, intonation, manner *(behavior)*, means *(opportunity)*, parlance, phraseology, property *(distinctive attribute)*, stress *(accent)*, style, tenor
tone deaf SEE MAIN ENTRY
tone down allay, commute, diminish, moderate *(temper)*, modify *(moderate)*, mollify, subdue
tone of voice intonation
tongue language, speech
tongue lash reproach
tongue-lashing denunciation, diatribe, malediction, obloquy, phillipic
tongue-tied inarticulate, mute, speechless
tonguey loquacious
tonic cure, medicinal, panacea, remedial, salubrious, salutary
tonnage cargo
too also
too difficult insurmountable
too early premature
too familiar trite
too few insufficiency
too hard difficult, impracticable, insurmountable
too little deficient, insufficient, nonsubstantial *(not sufficient)*
too many overage
too much disproportionate, overage
too small nonsubstantial *(not sufficient)*
too soon premature
too zealous perfervid
tool appliance, device *(mechanism)*, embellish, expedient, facility *(instrumentality)*, instrumentality, medium, resource. SEE MAIN ENTRY
tools paraphernalia *(apparatus)*
toothsome palatable
top cardinal *(outstanding)*, ceiling, culminate, culmination, leading *(ranking first)*, major, outbalance, outweigh, paramount, pinnacle, prime *(most valuable)*, surmount, surpass, transcend
top-match SEE MAIN ENTRY
top people elite
top person key man
top-flight master, renowned
top-level best, major
top-level meeting caucus
top-notch best, premium, select
top-rank notable
top-secret confidential
topic caption, context, heading, matter *(subject)*, question *(issue)*, thesis
topic for discussion matter *(subject)*
topic under consideration issue *(matter in dispute)*
topical current, present *(current)*
topical outline hornbook
topics affairs, contents
toploftiness pride
toplofty insolent, supercilious
topmost best, leading *(ranking first)*, primary
topmost point culmination
topping superior *(excellent)*
topple obliterate, overthrow, overturn, subvert, upset
torment annoy, badger, bait *(harass)*, discompose, distress *(anguish)*, distress, endanger, harass, harrow, harry *(harass)*, hector, ill use, inflict, infliction, irritate, mistreat, molest *(annoy)*, obsess, oppression, pain, persecute, pique, plague, press *(goad)*, prey, provoke, trouble. SEE MAIN ENTRY
tormenting caustic, painful
tormentum gun
torpedo bomb
torpescence sloth
torpescent lifeless *(dull)*, otiose, torpid
torpid dormant, inactive, indolent, insipid, jejune *(dull)*, languid, lifeless *(dull)*, otiose, phlegmatic, powerless, stagnant, static. SEE MAIN ENTRY
torpidity inaction, languor, sloth
torpidness languor
torpor inaction, inertia, languor, sloth
torporifc narcotic
torporific insensible, obtuse, stagnant, torpid
torquere harrow, harry *(harass)*
torrefy deflagrate
torrent outbreak, outburst, spate
torrid hot-blooded
torsion involution
torsional tortuous *(bending)*
tort delict, delinquency *(misconduct)*, misconduct. SEE MAIN ENTRY
tortile circuitous, sinuous, tortuous *(bending)*
tortility involution
tortious illicit
tortious act SEE MAIN ENTRY
tortiously illegally
tortuose indirect. SEE MAIN ENTRY
tortuosity involution
tortuous caustic, circuitous, complex, cruel, devious, labyrinthine, machiavellian, sinuous. SEE MAIN ENTRY
tortuousness involution
torture badger, cruelty, endanger, ill use, inflict, infliction, irritate, mistreat, pique, plague, prey, punish
torturous insufferable, painful
torturous interference SEE MAIN ENTRY
toss beat *(pulsate)*, cast *(throw)*, launch *(project)*, precipitate *(throw down violently)*, send
toss aside forswear
toss out jettison
toss overboard jettison
toss up bet
tot infant
total absolute *(complete)*, aggregate *(noun)*, aggregate *(verb)*, amount *(quantity)*, categorical, collective, complete *(all-embracing)*, comprehensive, comprise, computation, corpus, detailed, entirety, face amount, face value *(price)*, full, in solido, inclusive, maximum *(amplitude)*, outright, peremptory *(absolute)*, plenary, poll, pure, radical *(extreme)*, stark, sum, survey *(poll)*, thorough, unqualified *(unlimited)*, whole *(undamaged)*, whole *(unified)*. SEE MAIN ENTRY
total loss miscarriage
totalitarian dictator, dictatorial
totalitarianism oppression
totality aggregate, complex *(development)*, corpus, entirety, finality, in solido, principal *(capital sum)*, quantity, sum *(total)*, whole. SEE MAIN ENTRY
totalize calculate
totally in toto, purely *(positively)*, wholly
totalness entirety, totality
tote carry *(transport)*, transport
totem designation *(symbol)*
totter vacillate
tottering insecure, precarious
totus entirety, total
touch abut, adjoin, appertain, apply *(pertain)*, connect *(join together)*, correspond *(be equivalent)*, disarm *(set at ease)*, impinge, impress *(affect deeply)*, interest, minimum, nuance, overlap, reach, suggestion
touch off launch *(initiate)*
touch on connote, indicate, refer *(direct attention)*
touch up embellish, emend, enhance, fix *(repair)*, meliorate, modify *(alter)*, repair, revise
touch upon allude, comment, mention, pertain
touchable palpable, tangible
touched lunatic
touching adjacent, close *(near)*, contiguous, moving *(evoking emotion)*, persuasive, profound *(intense)*, proximate, tangential, wherein
touchstone standard
touchy fractious, perverse, petulant, querulous, resentful, sensitive *(easily affected)*
tough durable, indestructible, indomitable, insusceptible *(resistant)*, insusceptible *(uncaring)*, ossified, pertinacious, rigid, severe, strong, unyielding. SEE MAIN ENTRY
toughen inure *(accustom)*
toughened callous, incorrigible, insusceptible *(uncaring)*, ossified
toughness main force, strength, tenacity
tour perambulate, period, phase *(period)*
touring moving *(in motion)*
tournament contest *(competition)*
tourner la loi circumvent
tourney contest *(competition)*, fight *(battle)*, oppose
tournure contour *(outline)*
tousle agitate *(shake up)*, discompose
tout bystander, inform *(notify)*
tout au contraire contradictory
tout le contraire contrary
towardly seasonable
tower edifice
tower above overcome *(surmount)*, transcend
tower of strength mainstay
tower over surpass
towering prodigious *(enormous)*, salient

town civic, community
townsman denizen, habitant, resident
toxic deadly, deleterious, detrimental, fatal, harmful, insalubrious, lethal, malignant, noxious, peccant *(unhealthy)*, pernicious, pestilent, virulent. SEE MAIN ENTRY
toxic tort SEE MAIN ENTRY
toxicant deadly, pernicious, pestilent
toxiferous lethal, malignant, pernicious, pestilent
trace copy, deduce, deduct *(conclude by reasoning)*, delineate, derive *(deduce)*, detect, ferret, find *(discover)*, follow-up, hint, hunt, impression, indication, iota, locate, minimum, pursue *(chase)*, research, scintilla, search, solve, suggestion, suspicion *(uncertainty)*. SEE MAIN ENTRY
trace out delineate
trace the outline of delineate
trace to ascribe
traceable deductible *(provable)*
tracing copy, delineation, outline *(boundary)*, pattern
tracing back derivation
track chase, delve, detect, follow-up, investigate, pursue *(chase)*, research, search, trace *(follow)*
track down ferret, hunt, locate, search, trace *(follow)*
track mentally investigate
tract district, land, lot, pandect *(treatise)*, parcel, plot *(land)*, property *(land)*, province, section *(vicinity)*, territory, thesis
tract of land premises *(buildings)*
tractabilis palpable, tangible, tractable
tractability amenability, compliance, credulity
tractable amenable, corrigible, facile, flexible, malleable, obedient, open *(persuasible)*, passive, patient, pliable, pliant, receptive, resigned, resilient, sequacious, servile, suasible, subservient, willing *(not averse)*, yielding. SEE MAIN ENTRY
tractableness compliance
tractare manage, manipulate *(utilize skillfully)*, wield
tractate pandect *(treatise)*
tractatio management *(supervision)*
tractile pliable, pliant, tractable
traction stress *(strain)*
tractus region
tradable marketable
trade barter, business *(commerce)*, business *(occupation)*, buy, calling, career, commerce, commercial, deal *(noun)*, deal *(verb)*, dealings, devolve, dicker, employment, exchange, handle *(trade)*, industry *(business)*, interchange, job, labor *(work)*, livelihood, mercantile, occupation *(vocation)*, office, position *(business status)*, practice *(professional business)*, profession *(vocation)*, pursuit *(occupation)*, reciprocate, sale, vend, work *(employment)*. SEE MAIN ENTRY
trade association union *(labor organization)*
trade by exchange barter
trade fair market *(business)*
trade in handle *(trade)*, sell
trade name brand
trade off barter
trade secret SEE MAIN ENTRY
trade sign trademark
trade with deal
trademark brand, denomination, designation *(symbol)*, device *(distinguishing mark)*, indicant, symbol. SEE MAIN ENTRY
trader broker, dealer, merchant, speculator, supplier, vendor
tradere deliver, surrender *(yield)*
tradesman artisan, dealer, vendor
tradesperson dealer, merchant
tradeswoman dealer
trading business *(commerce)*, commerce, commercial
trading house market *(business)*
trading place market place
trading post market *(business)*
tradition custom, habit, myth, prescription *(custom)*, propriety *(correctness)*, solemnity, usage
tradition-bound conventional
traditional accustomed *(customary)*, common *(customary)*, conventional, customary, familiar *(customary)*, formal, habitual, hereditary, ordinary, orthodox, prescriptive, proverbial, regular *(conventional)*, standing, typical, usual. SEE MAIN ENTRY
traditionalism custom
traditionalist philistine
traditionality custom
traditionally invariably
traditionary traditional
traditive prescriptive, traditional
traduce defame, denigrate, denounce *(condemn)*, deprecate, depreciate, derogate, discommend, disoblige, disparage, lessen, libel, malign, pillory, reproach, smear, sully
traducement aspersion, bad repute, defamation, denunciation, dishonor *(shame)*, obloquy, revilement, slander, vilification
traducere transfer
traducing libelous
traffic business *(commerce)*, commerce, deal, dealings, exchange, trade *(commerce)*, trade
traffic by exchange barter
traffic in deal, handle *(trade)*, sell
traffic of commodities commerce
traffic with communicate, patronize *(trade with)*
trafficker dealer
tragedy adversity, calamity, casualty, catastrophe, debacle, disaster, fatality, misfortune. SEE MAIN ENTRY
tragic deplorable, dire, disastrous, fatal, lamentable
tragical deplorable, dire, disastrous
tragoedia tragedy
trahere derive *(receive)*, prolong
traiectio exaggeration
trail chase, delve, follow-up, hunt, pursue *(chase)*, search, spy, stem *(originate)*, trace *(follow)*
trail blazer pioneer
trailing subsequent
train chain *(series)*, cultivate, edify, educate, empower, foster, inculcate, initiate, instill, instruct *(teach)*, nurture, specialize, succession
train by instruction discipline *(train)*
train in study
train of thought idea
trained competent, expert, familiar *(informed)*, informed *(educated)*, literate, practiced, professional *(trained)*, proficient, qualified *(competent)*, resourceful, sciential, technical, veteran
trained person expert, practitioner, professional, specialist
trained personnel expert
trainee neophyte, novice, protégé
trainer pedagogue
training competence *(ability)*, direction *(guidance)*, disciplinary *(educational)*, edification, education, experience *(background)*, guidance, instruction *(teaching)*, preparation
trainload cargo
trait character *(personal quality)*, characteristic, differential, feature *(characteristic)*, habit, particularity, property *(distinctive attribute)*, quality *(attribute)*, specialty *(distinctive mark)*, symptom. SEE MAIN ENTRY
traitor conspirer, insurgent, malcontent
traitoriousness disloyalty
traitorous disobedient, faithless, false *(disloyal)*, perfidious, recreant, untrue
traitorousness bad faith, infidelity
traits personality
traject deliver, project *(impel forward)*
trammel bar *(hinder)*, block, check *(bar)*, confine, constrain *(imprison)*, constraint *(restriction)*, contain *(restrain)*, control *(restrain)*, curb, debar, detain *(hold in custody)*, detain *(restrain)*, disadvantage, enclose, enclosure, encumber *(hinder)*, fetter *(noun)*, fetter *(verb)*, hamper, handcuff *(noun)*, handcuff *(verb)*, hinder, impede, impediment, obstacle, obstruct, obstruction, occlude, repress, restrain, restrict. SEE MAIN ENTRY
tramontane stranger
tramp perambulate, prowl, step, traverse
tramper derelict
trample spurn, subjugate
trample on damage, mistreat, violate
trample upon beat *(defeat)*, break *(violate)*
trance insentience, preoccupation
trangression infringement
tranmission conveyance
tranquil complacent, dispassionate, patient, peaceable, placid
tranquil mind composure
tranquility longanimity, peace, solace
tranquilization mollification, remission
tranquilize allay, alleviate, assuage, disarm *(set at ease)*, lull, moderate *(temper)*, mollify, pacify, placate, propitiate, remit *(relax)*, soothe, subdue
tranquilizer narcotic
tranquilizing narcotic, palliative *(abating)*
tranquillitas composure, ease
tranquillity composure, lull
tranquillus dispassionate, placid
transact commit *(perpetrate)*, conduct, dicker, discharge *(perform)*, execute *(accomplish)*, manage, negotiate, perform *(adhere to)*, perpetrate, trade. SEE MAIN ENTRY
transact business handle *(trade)*
transact business with patronize *(trade with)*
transact with patronize *(trade with)*
transaction act *(undertaking)*, agreement *(contract)*, business *(commerce)*, commission *(act)*, deal, event, exchange, interchange, occurrence, operation, proceeding, process *(course)*, sale, trade *(commerce)*, treatment, undertaking *(business)*. SEE MAIN ENTRY
transactions affairs, dealings
transcedent sacrosanct
transcend beat *(defeat)*, outbalance, outweigh, overcome *(surmount)*, overstep, prevail *(triumph)*, surmount, surpass. SEE MAIN ENTRY

transcendant prime *(most valuable)*
transcendence infringement, supremacy
transcendency supremacy
transcendent best, notable, outstanding *(prominent)*, paramount, primary, superior *(excellent)*, superlative
transcendental mysterious, obscure *(abstruse)*, paramount, recondite
transcendere surmount
transcending infringement
transcribe copy, enter *(record)*
transcript copy, record. SEE MAIN ENTRY
transcript of minutes of commitment mittimus
transcript of testimony deposition
transcription record, transcript
transcursion transgression
transect dichotomize
transfer abalienate, assignment *(transfer of ownership)*, attorn, bear *(yield)*, cargo, carriage, cede, cession, confer *(give)*, consign, consignment, convert *(change use)*, conveyance, copy, deed, defect, delegate, delivery, demise *(conveyance)*, deport *(banish)*, devise *(give)*, devolution, devolve, dispatch *(send off)*, dispensation *(act of dispensing)*, displace *(remove)*, displace *(replace)*, disposition *(transfer of property)*, exchange, give *(grant)*, grant *(transfer formally)*, impart, move *(alter position)*, reassign, refer *(send for action)*, relegate, remand, removal, replacement, sale, send, subrogation, supplant, transmit, transmittal, transport. SEE MAIN ENTRY
transfer again recover
transfer among the living inter vivos
transfer back recover
transfer by deed abalienate, deliver
transfer by will abalienate, demise
transfer by writing grant *(transfer formally)*
transfer control to the government nationalize
transfer for a consideration sell
transfer for sale consign
transfer of property conveyance, devolution, feoffment
transfer of property as security for a debt mortgage
transfer of security mortgage
transfer of title conveyance
transfer ownership alienate *(transfer title)*, bequeath, demise, devolve, grant *(transfer formally)*, pass *(advance)*
transfer ownership to the government nationalize
transfer property deliver
transfer right deliver
transfer title convey *(transfer)*, pass *(advance)*
transfer to devolve
transfer to an earlier date antedate
transfer to another assign *(transfer ownership)*
transfer to another authority extradition
transferable assignable, contagious, heritable, negotiable
transferee assignee, bearer, consumer, devisee, feoffee, heir, legatee, licensee, payee, recipient. SEE MAIN ENTRY
transference alienation *(transfer of title)*, assignment *(transfer of ownership)*, carriage, consignment, conveyance, deed, delivery, demise *(conveyance)*, devolution, disposition *(transfer of property)*, extradition, removal, subrogation, takeover, transition, transmittal
transferor carrier, feoffor, licensor. SEE MAIN ENTRY
transferral delivery
transferre transfer
transferred bailment
transferred by a legacy testamentary
transferred by bequest testamentary
transferred by devise testamentary
transferring consignment
transfigere pierce *(lance)*
transfiguration development *(progression)*
transfigure affect, change, convert *(change use)*, denature, distort, meliorate, modify *(alter)*, transform, vary
transfix pierce *(lance)*
transform adapt, alter, change, convert *(change use)*, denature, distort, meliorate, modify *(alter)*, renew *(begin again)*, vary. SEE MAIN ENTRY
transformable convertible, protean
transformation conversion *(change)*, development *(progression)*, reconversion, reorganization, transition
transformations vicissitudes
transformed tempered
transfuse deliver, inject, permeate, pervade
transfuse the sense construe *(translate)*
transgredi pass *(advance)*
transgress accroach, break *(violate)*, contravene, disobey, encroach, impose *(intrude)*, infringe, lapse *(fall into error)*, offend *(violate the law)*, overstep, trespass, violate
transgress established bounds impinge
transgressed broken *(unfulfilled)*
transgressing blameworthy, culpable, delinquent *(guilty of a misdeed)*, diabolic, felonious, guilty, peccant *(culpable)*
transgression bad repute, breach, contravention, criminality, culpability, delinquency *(misconduct)*, disregard *(omission)*, encroachment, fault *(responsibility)*, felony, guilt, illegality, infraction, injustice, invasion, malfeasance, mischief, misconduct, misdeed, misdemeanor, misdoing, misfeasance, misprision, offense, onus *(blame)*, tort, vice, violation, wrong. SEE MAIN ENTRY
transgressive disobedient, lawless, unlawful
transgressor convict, criminal, degenerate, delinquent, felon, lawbreaker, malefactor, offender, outlaw, recidivist, vandal, wrongdoer. SEE MAIN ENTRY
transhipment removal
transient acting, brief, ephemeral, interim, interlocutory, lodger, moving *(in motion)*, mutable, profane, provisional, shifting, temporary, transitory, unsettled, volatile. SEE MAIN ENTRY
transient arrangement modus vivendi
transientness insignificance, mortality
transigere transact
transire omit, pass *(advance)*
transit circulation, reconversion, transition
transitio transition
transition circulation, conversion *(change)*, reconversion. SEE MAIN ENTRY
transitional intermediate, mesne, moving *(in motion)*, progressive *(going forward)*, provisional, temporary
transitive temporary
transitorily pro tempore
transitoriness mortality
transitory brief, ephemeral, interlocutory, profane, provisional, shifting, temporary, transient, volatile. SEE MAIN ENTRY
translatable accountable *(explainable)*, determinable *(ascertainable)*
translate define, deliver, elucidate, explain, explicate, interpret, render *(depict)*, transform
translate incorrectly misread
translate into action exercise *(discharge a function)*
translate orally interpret
translaticius conventional, ordinary
translation construction, definition, explanation, paraphrase, rendition *(explication)*, restatement
translocate deliver, move *(alter position)*
translocation carriage, extradition, removal, transmittal
transmigration circulation, immigration, transition
transmigratory moving *(in motion)*
transmissible assignable, contagious, hereditary, heritable, negotiable
transmission alienation *(transfer of title)*, assignment *(transfer of ownership)*, circulation, consignment, contact *(association)*, conveyance, delivery, demise *(conveyance)*, devolution, osmosis, publication *(disclosure)*, transmittal
transmission of knowledge declaration, notification
transmission of title feoffment
transmissive contagious
transmit annunciate, assign *(transfer ownership)*, bestow, cede, circulate, communicate, confer *(give)*, consign, contribute *(supply)*, convey *(communicate)*, convey *(transfer)*, correspond *(communicate)*, delegate, deliver, demise, descend, devise *(give)*, devolve, dispatch *(send off)*, disseminate, give *(grant)*, grant *(transfer formally)*, impart, issue *(send forth)*, leave *(give)*, notify, pass *(advance)*, propagate *(spread)*, radiate, redirect, remit *(submit for consideration)*, remove *(transfer)*, send, transfer, transport. SEE MAIN ENTRY
transmit by will devise *(give)*
transmit disease infect
transmit payment remit *(send payment)*
transmittable assignable
transmittal assignment *(transfer of ownership)*, conveyance, delivery, demise *(conveyance)*, remittance. SEE MAIN ENTRY
transmittance delivery, transmittal
transmittere transfer, transmit, transport
transmittible negotiable
transmogrify alter, change, convert *(change use)*, transform
transmutable convertible
transmutation conversion *(change)*, transition
transmute alter, change, convert *(change use)*, denature, modify *(alter)*, transform, vary
transparent clear *(apparent)*, direct *(forthright)*, evident, explicit, ingenuous, lucid, manifest, obvious, open *(in sight)*, pellucid, perceivable, unambiguous. SEE MAIN ENTRY
transpierce enter *(penetrate)*, lancinate, penetrate, pierce *(lance)*
transpiration experience *(encounter)*, happening

transpire arise *(occur)*, ensue, occur *(happen)*, pass *(advance)*
transplacement removal
transplant consign, deliver, transport
transplantation insertion, removal, transmittal
transplendent illustrious
transport carry *(transport)*, consign, convey *(transfer)*, deliver, deport *(banish)*, expatriate, move *(alter position)*, passion, relegate, transfer, transmit. SEE MAIN ENTRY
transport back recover
transport company carrier
transportable property movable
transportables movable
transportare transport
transportation carriage, removal, transmittal
transportation charge fare
transportation fee fare
transportation of commodities commerce
transportation of goods commerce
transported ecstatic
transposable convertible
transposal delivery, exchange
transpose convert *(change use)*, convey *(transfer)*, displace *(replace)*, move *(alter position)*
transposed inverse
transposition delivery, exchange, replacement
transshape convert *(change use)*, transform
transshipment carriage
transubstantiate change, convert *(change use)*, modify *(alter)*, transform
transudation outflow
trap ambush, artifice, bait *(lure)*, deceive, deception, decoy, dupe, ensnare, entrap, frame up, hunt, imposture, inveigle, lock, maneuver *(trick)*, mislead, obstruct, occlude, pitfall, stratagem. SEE MAIN ENTRY
trapping chattel
trappings paraphernalia *(personal belongings)*
trashy inferior *(lower in quality)*, poor *(inferior in quality)*, trivial
traumatize damage
travail disaster, effort, endeavor, hardship, labor, strive
travel perambulate. SEE MAIN ENTRY
travel over traverse
travelable passable
traveled passable
traveler afoot pedestrian
traveling moving *(in motion)*, progressive *(going forward)*
traveller itinerant
travelling itinerant
traversable passable
traversal contravention, counterargument, demurrer, disapproval, impugnation, intersection, negation, opposition, prohibition
traverse answer *(reply)*, balk, circumvent, collide *(clash)*, contest, contradict, contravene, counteract, countervail, cross *(disagree with)*, cross *(intersect)*, demonstrate *(protest)*, demur, deny *(contradict)*, disaccord, disaffirm, disagree, disavow, disobey, disown *(deny the validity)*, disprove, dispute *(contest)*, fight *(counteract)*, gainsay, hinder, negate, oppugn, patrol, perambulate, prohibit, protest, refuse, refute, reject, repel *(drive back)*, thwart. SEE MAIN ENTRY
traverse the outline of delineate
traversing negative
travesty caricature, distortion, jape, mock *(imitate)*, parody, ridicule. SEE MAIN ENTRY
treacherous aleatory *(perilous)*, bad *(offensive)*, collusive, cruel, dangerous, detrimental, dishonest, faithless, false *(disloyal)*, fraudulent, harmful, insecure, insidious, insubordinate, irresponsible, lying, machiavellian, malevolent, malicious, malignant, nefarious, perfidious, pernicious, precarious, recreant, ruthless, sinister, sly, tortuous *(corrupt)*, undependable, unreliable, unscrupulous, untrue, untrustworthy, vicious, virulent
treacherous killing assassination
treacherousness bad faith, dishonesty, false pretense, improbity
treachery bad faith, collusion, deceit, disloyalty, false pretense, fraud, infidelity, knavery, machination, pettifoggery, sedition, treason
tread perambulate, step
tread on mistreat, spurn
treading warily diffident
treason disloyalty, infidelity, mutiny, rebellion, sedition. SEE MAIN ENTRY
treasonable faithless, false *(disloyal)*, perfidious, recreant, untrue
treasonable activities disloyalty
treasonable alliance confederacy *(conspiracy)*, conspiracy
treasonous disobedient, faithless, false *(disloyal)*, insubordinate, perfidious
treasure cash, conserve, foster, fund, garner, hoard, keep *(shelter)*, money, possession *(property)*, possessions, preserve, protect, regard *(hold in esteem)*, store *(depository)*, store, substance *(material possessions)*, sufficiency
treasure house treasury
treasure up hoard
treasured valuable
treasurehouse repository
treasurer comptroller
treasury arsenal, coffer, repository, selection *(collection)*, store *(depository)*. SEE MAIN ENTRY
treasury note check *(instrument)*
treat adjust *(resolve)*, comment, cure, drug, enjoyment *(pleasure)*, manage, relieve *(give aid)*, remedy. SEE MAIN ENTRY
treat abusively mishandle *(maltreat)*
treat as a special case except *(exclude)*, exclude
treat as human personify
treat badly mistreat
treat cruelly ill use
treat differently favor
treat ill mishandle *(maltreat)*
treat improperly mishandle *(maltreat)*, violate
treat in a condescending way patronize *(condescend toward)*
treat poorly persecute
treat rudely ignore
treat thoroughly exhaust *(try all possibilities)*
treat unfairly ill use
treat unkindly ill use
treat with contempt disdain, flout, mock *(deride)*
treat with derision mock *(deride)*
treat with discourtesy offend *(insult)*
treat with disdain flout, spurn
treat with disfavor disgrace
treat with disrespect humiliate, mock *(deride)*
treat with indignity disoblige, humiliate, offend *(insult)*
treat with indulgence bear *(tolerate)*, forbear
treat with insolence hector, jeer
treat with partiality favor, prefer
treat with reserve mistrust
treat with scorn mock *(deride)*
treat without due respect disregard
treat without reverence violate
treated tempered
treatise hornbook
treatise on the law hornbook
treatment analysis, design *(construction plan)*, expedient, management *(judicious use)*, pandect *(treatise)*, practice *(procedure)*, process *(course)*, relief *(aid)*, usage. SEE MAIN ENTRY
treaty bargain, compact, league, mutual understanding, pact, peace, promise, protocol *(agreement)*, stipulation. SEE MAIN ENTRY
treaty-making negotiation
trek perambulate, traverse
trekker migrant
tremble beat *(pulsate)*
trembling trepidation
tremendous far reaching, major, portentous *(eliciting amazement)*, prodigious *(enormous)*
tremor cataclysm, trepidation
tremulous diffident
tremulousness trepidation
trench on intrude, overstep
trench upon impinge
trenchant active, acute, bitter *(penetrating)*, brief, caustic, cogent, compelling, concise, eloquent, incisive, mordacious, pithy, potent, powerful, scathing, succinct. SEE MAIN ENTRY
trend bias, conatus, direction *(course)*, gravitate, mode, style, tendency, tenor
trend downward decline *(fall)*
trending inclined
trepan bait *(lure)*, deception, ensnare
trepidatio trepidation
trepidation apprehension *(fear)*, cloud *(suspicion)*, consternation, disturbance, fear, fright, misgiving, panic, phobia, stress *(strain)*, suspicion *(mistrust)*. SEE MAIN ENTRY
trepidity trepidation
trespass accroach, breach, break *(violate)*, delinquency *(misconduct)*, disobey, disregard *(omission)*, encroach, encroachment, impinge, impose *(intrude)*, infraction, infringe, infringement, intrude, intrusion, invade, invasion, lapse *(fall into error)*, misdeed, misdoing, obtrude, offend *(violate the law)*, overstep, transgression, violate, violation, wrong. SEE MAIN ENTRY
trespasser malefactor
trespassing disobedient, housebreaking, infringement, intrusive, peccant *(culpable)*
triable illicit, justiciable. SEE MAIN ENTRY
triable act tortious act
trial action *(proceeding)*, cause *(lawsuit)*, conatus, contest *(competition)*, cross-examination, day in court, discipline *(punishment)*, distress *(anguish)*, effort, endeavor, experiment, grievance, hearing, indagation, infliction, inquiry *(systematic investigation)*, inspection, lawsuit, matter *(case)*, misfortune, nuisance, plight, predicament, preliminary, proceeding, prosecution *(criminal trial)*, quagmire, stress *(strain)*,

suit, tentative, test, trouble, undertaking *(attempt)*, undertaking *(enterprise)*, venture. SEE MAIN ENTRY
trial at the bar hearing
trial balloon SEE MAIN ENTRY
trial by jury hearing
trial in court hearing
trial list calendar *(list of cases)*
trial of a case action *(proceeding)*
trial of superiority competition
trial of the issues action *(proceeding)*
tribe affinity *(family ties)*, assemblage, band, blood, family *(common ancestry)*, house, origin *(ancestry)*, parentage, progeny, society
tribuere attribute, render *(deliver)*
tribulation burden, distress *(anguish)*, misfortune, quagmire, trouble
tribunal bar *(court)*, bench, board, chamber *(body)*, council *(assembly)*, court, forum *(court)*, judicatory, judicature, judiciary, jury. SEE MAIN ENTRY
tributary contributory, inferior *(lower in position)*
tribute bounty, contribution *(donation)*, duty *(tax)*, gift *(present)*, honor *(outward respect)*, payment *(remittance)*, recognition, recommendation, remembrance *(commemoration)*, respect, reward, tax
trick artifice, bait *(lure)*, betray *(lead astray)*, bilk, bunko, canard, circumvent, deceive, deception, decoy, defraud, delude, device *(contrivance)*, dupe, ensnare, evade *(deceive)*, evasion, expedient, fake, false pretense, foist, hoax, hoodwink, illude, imposture, inveigle, knavery, machination, maneuver, mislead, misrepresent, mulct *(defraud)*, overreach, pettifog, plot *(secret plan)*, ploy, pretense *(pretext)*, pretext, racket, ruse, sham, stratagem, subterfuge. SEE MAIN ENTRY
trickery artifice, collusion, deceit, deception, duplicity, falsification, frame up, fraud, hoax, hypocrisy, imposture, knavery, pettifoggery, prestidigitation, pretense *(pretext)*, pretext, ruse, sham
trickiness deception, dishonesty, fraud, improbity, knavery, pettifoggery
trickish fraudulent, machiavellian
trickle distill, exude, paucity
tricksy jocular
tricky deceptive, delusive, devious, disingenuous, evasive, fraudulent, illusory, insidious, intricate, lying, machiavellian, perfidious, sly, sophistic, strategic, subtle *(insidious)*, surreptitious, unconscionable
tried conclusive *(determinative)*, convincing, dependable, expert, indubious, loyal, reliable, staunch, steadfast, true *(loyal)*, veteran
tried for the same crime double jeopardy
trier array *(jury)*
trier of fact juror
trier of the facts array *(jury)*
triers of fact jury, panel *(jurors)*
trifle palter, paucity, pettifog, scintilla, technicality
trifle amount modicum
trifle with mock *(deride)*
trifling collateral *(immaterial)*, de minimus, expendable, frivolous, inappreciable, inconsequential, inconsiderable, insubstantial, marginal, minor, negligible, nominal, nonessential, nugatory, null *(insignificant)*, paltry, petty, slight, superficial, tenuous, trivial, unessential
trigger launch *(initiate)*, originate
trim abridge *(shorten)*, color *(complexion)*, commute, compact *(pithy)*, curtail, decrease, deduct *(reduce)*, edit, embellish, lessen
trimming curtailment, reprimand
trip misguide, overreach
trip and fall case SEE MAIN ENTRY
trip up entrap
triste disconsolate
tristis grave *(important)*, solemn
tristitia depression, solemnity
trite inexpressive, lifeless *(dull)*, mediocre, mundane, nondescript, ordinary, pedestrian, prosaic, stale. SEE MAIN ENTRY
trite expression phrase, platitude
trite phrase platitude
trite remark platitude
trite saying platitude
tritus customary, trite
triumph carry *(succeed)*, kill *(defeat)*, pass *(satisfy requirements)*, reach, succeed *(attain)*, supremacy
triumph over beat *(defeat)*, defeat, overcome *(surmount)*, overwhelm, subdue, subject, subjugate, surmount, surpass
triumphal prevailing *(having superior force)*
triumphant prevailing *(having superior force)*, successful
trivia detail
trivial collateral *(immaterial)*, de minimus, frivolous, immaterial, inapposite, inconsequential, inconsiderable, insubstantial, mediocre, minor, negligible, nominal, nonessential, nugatory, null *(insignificant)*, paltry, peripheral, petty, remote *(small)*, slight, superficial, tenuous, unessential, usual. SEE MAIN ENTRY
triviality immateriality, inconsequence, insignificance, mediocrity, platitude, technicality
troop assemblage, band
trope call *(title)*
trophy prize
troth adherence *(devotion)*, adhesion *(loyalty)*, faith, loyalty, profession *(declaration)*, reliance, undertaking *(pledge)*
trothless faithless, false *(disloyal)*, perfidious
trouble aggravate *(annoy)*, agitate *(perturb)*, annoy, badger, bait *(harass)*, burden, disaster, discommode, discompose, disorient, distress *(anguish)*, distress, disturb, embarrass, emergency, encumber *(hinder)*, fracas, grievance, harass, hector, inconvenience, mischief, misfortune, molest *(annoy)*, nuisance, obsess, pandemonium, perplex, persecute, perturb, pique, plague, plight, predicament, press *(goad)*, problem, quagmire, strife, turmoil. SEE MAIN ENTRY
trouble maker delinquent
trouble oneself endeavor, strive
trouble-maker demagogue
troubled disconsolate, pessimistic, unsettled
troublemaker malcontent
troublesome difficult, froward, invidious, irksome, operose, oppressive, painful, perverse, problematic, uncontrollable, undesirable, unruly, vexatious
troubling painful
troublous bad *(offensive)*, harmful
trounce beat *(strike)*, browbeat, defeat, lash *(strike)*, punish, reprehend, reprimand
troupe assemblage, band, body *(collection)*, organization *(association)*
trover recovery *(repossession)*. SEE MAIN ENTRY
trow presuppose, surmise
truancy absence *(nonattendance)*, dereliction, nonappearance, nonperformance
truant disobedient. SEE MAIN ENTRY
truce cessation *(interlude)*, conciliation, halt, interruption, interval, lull, pause, peace, treaty
trucidare kill *(defeat)*
truck trade *(commerce)*
truckage carriage
truckle SEE MAIN ENTRY
truckle to pander
truckling servile, subservient
truckload cargo
truculence atrocity, brutality
truculency brutality
truculent brutal, cold-blooded, harsh, hostile, malevolent, malicious, malignant, offensive *(offending)*, perverse, relentless, ruthless, sinister
trudge perambulate
true absolute *(conclusive)*, accurate, actual, authentic, candid, convincing, credible, de facto, definite, dependable, direct *(straight)*, documentary, factual, faithful *(loyal)*, faithful *(true to fact)*, genuine, honest, incontrovertible, literal, loyal, positive *(incontestable)*, proper, pure, real, reliable, rightful, serious *(devoted)*, solid *(sound)*, sound, staunch, steadfast, sterling, unadulterated, undistorted, unrefutable, unyielding, valid, veridical. SEE MAIN ENTRY
true believer disciple
true bill accusation
true charge accusation
true dimensions area *(surface)*
true incident fact
true meaning connotation, gist *(substance)*
true to fact exact, literal
true to form normal *(regular)*
true to life descriptive, natural
true to nature undistorted
true to scale candid
true to the facts actual, candid, certain *(positive)*, honest
true to the letter actual, verbatim
true to type typical
truehearted honest, loyal, moral, true *(loyal)*
trueness adhesion *(loyalty)*, allegiance, fidelity, loyalty, validity
truism platitude, postulate, principle *(axiom)*
truly admittedly, de facto, faithfully, in good faith, ipso facto
trump outbalance
trump up fabricate *(make up)*, frame *(prearrange)*, invent *(falsify)*, misrepresent, palter, perjure
trump up a charge frame *(charge falsely)*
trumped up colorable *(specious)*, ill-founded, lying, unfounded, untrue
trumped up story myth
trumped-up fictitious
trumped-up charge frame up
trumped-up story frame up
trumpery deception, falsification
trumpet circulate, herald, inform *(notify)*, proclaim, propagate *(spread)*, publish
truncare mutilate
truncate commute, condense, deduct *(reduce)*, excise *(cut away)*, mutilate, remove *(eliminate)*

truncheon beat *(strike)*, cudgel, lash *(strike)*
trunk road causeway
truss bear *(support)*
trust agency *(legal relationship)*, cartel, charge *(custody)*, commit *(entrust)*, commitment *(responsibility)*, confederacy *(compact)*, confidence *(faith)*, consortium *(business cartel)*, credence, credulity, entrust, expectation, faith, league, loan, mission, office, pool, prospect *(outlook)*, protégé, reliance, rely, security *(safety)*. SEE MAIN ENTRY
trust to chance bet, parlay *(bet)*
trust to keep secret confide *(divulge)*
trust with delegate
trustable dependable, incorruptible
trusted authentic, convincing, credible, dependable, fiduciary, intimate, undisputed
trustee administrator, comptroller, executor, fiduciary, guardian, nominee *(delegate)*, receiver, representative *(proxy)*, substitute, transferee. SEE MAIN ENTRY
trustees commission *(agency)*, committee
trusteeship charge *(custody)*, custody *(supervision)*, ward
truster disciple
trustful sanguine, unsuspecting
trustfulness credulity
trustiness adhesion *(loyalty)*, fidelity, honor *(good reputation)*, probity
trusting convincing, credulous, naive, positive *(confident)*, sanguine, unsuspecting
trustingly faithfully
trustless irresponsible
trustworthily faithfully
trustworthiness adhesion *(loyalty)*, certification *(certainness)*, credibility, fidelity, honesty, honor *(good reputation)*, integrity, loyalty, principle *(virtue)*, probity, rectitude, responsibility *(conscience)*, trust *(confidence)*, veracity, weight *(credibility)*. SEE MAIN ENTRY
trustworthy accurate, authentic, believable, bona fide, candid, cogent, conscientious, convincing, credible, demonstrable, dependable, diligent, factual, faithful *(loyal)*, fiduciary, harmless, high-minded, honest, incorruptible, infallible, ingenuous, law-abiding, loyal, moral, official, positive *(incontestable)*, real, reliable, reputable, safe, scrupulous, secure *(sound)*, solid *(sound)*, staunch, steadfast, tenable, thorough, true *(authentic)*, true *(loyal)*, upright
trusty believable, conscientious, dependable, incorruptible, infallible, law-abiding, loyal, reliable, secure *(sound)*, solid *(sound)*, staunch, true *(loyal)*
truth fact, honesty, maxim, principle *(virtue)*, probity, reality, right *(righteousness)*, validity, veracity. SEE MAIN ENTRY
truth telling credible
truth-speaking straightforward
truth-telling veridical
truthful accurate, actual, candid, credible, direct *(forthright)*, honest, ingenuous, literal, precise, real, realistic, reliable, right *(correct)*, scrupulous, sound, straightforward, true *(authentic)*, unaffected *(sincere)*, undistorted, upright, valid, veridical. SEE MAIN ENTRY
truthfully faithfully
truthfulness credibility, honesty, integrity, probity, veracity
truthless dishonest, disingenuous, evasive, fallacious, false *(inaccurate)*, fraudulent, lying, mendacious, untrue
truthlessness bad faith, dishonesty, improbity
try adjudicate, adopt, attempt, check *(inspect)*, endeavor *(noun)*, endeavor *(verb)*, exert, harrow, harry *(harass)*, hear *(give a legal hearing)*, judge, pursuit *(effort to secure)*, resort, strive, test, undertake. SEE MAIN ENTRY
try a case hear *(give a legal hearing)*, judge
try conclusions reason *(conclude)*
try for pursue *(strive to gain)*, strive
try hard attempt
try one's best attempt, pursue *(strive to gain)*, strive
try one's fortune bet
try one's luck bet, gamble, speculate *(chance)*
try one's patience badger, bait *(harass)*, provoke
try the cause adjudicate, hear *(give a legal hearing)*
try the patience discompose, pique, plague
try to find hunt
try to obtain pursue *(strive to gain)*
try to overtake chase
trying onerous, operose, oppressive, painful, severe, vexatious
trying situation predicament
tryout experiment, test
tryst appointment *(meeting)*, rendezvous
tueri preserve
tuitio preservation
tuition direction *(guidance)*, edification, education, experience *(background)*, guidance
tuitionary disciplinary *(educational)*
tumble agitate *(shake up)*, disorganize, subvert, upset
tumid flatulent, fustian, grandiose, inflated *(bombastic)*, inflated *(enlarged)*, orotund, pretentious *(pompous)*, turgid
tumidity bombast
tumidness bombast
tumidus inflated *(bombastic)*, inflated *(enlarged)*, pretentious *(pompous)*
tumult affray, anarchy, belligerency, bluster *(commotion)*, brawl, commotion, confusion *(turmoil)*, disorder *(lack of order)*, disturbance, embroilment, entanglement *(confusion)*, fracas, fray, furor, imbroglio, noise, outcry, pandemonium, revolution, riot, turmoil
tumultuary disordered, disorderly
tumultuous disordered, disorderly. SEE MAIN ENTRY
tumultuous assault affray
tumultuousness bluster *(commotion)*, disorder *(lack of order)*
tumultus affray, commotion, disturbance, revolt, riot
tune adjust *(regulate)*
tune down diminish
tunnel penetrate
turba band, commotion, riot, turmoil
turbare muddle
turbatio disturbance
turbid inextricable, opaque, unclear
turbulence bluster *(commotion)*, commotion, confusion *(turmoil)*, disorder *(lack of order)*, disturbance, embroilment, furor, irregularity, pandemonium, revolution, severity, turmoil
turbulency turmoil
turbulent disordered, disorderly, hot-blooded, unruly, vehement
turbulentus insubordinate
turgent turgid
turgescence bombast, inflation *(increase)*, plethora, rodomontade
turgescent orotund, pretentious *(pompous)*, proud *(conceited)*
turgid flatulent, fustian, grandiose, inflated *(bombastic)*, inflated *(enlarged)*, orotund, pretentious *(pompous)*, proud *(conceited)*. SEE MAIN ENTRY
turgid language fustian
turgidity bombast, inflation *(increase)*
turgidness inflation *(increase)*
turgidus inflated *(enlarged)*
turmoil affray, anarchy, bluster *(commotion)*, brawl, commotion, conflict, disorder *(lack of order)*, disturbance, embroilment, emotion, fracas, fray, furor, havoc, imbroglio, misrule, outcry, pandemonium, panic, riot, shambles. SEE MAIN ENTRY
turn alter, avert, contort, contour *(shape)*, convert *(change use)*, crossroad *(turning point)*, deviate, digress, gift *(flair)*, occurrence, opportunity, oscillate, posture *(situation)*, predisposition, prejudice *(influence)*, proclivity, quirk *(accident)*, slant, spoil *(impair)*, tendency, transform, transition. SEE MAIN ENTRY
turn a deaf ear to ignore
turn adrift dispel, evict
turn against antagonize, confront *(oppose)*, rebel
turn aside avert, deter, detour, deviate, discourage, divert, eschew, estop, expostulate, impede, parry, prevent, shun, stave, thwart
turn attention devote
turn attention to note *(notice)*
turn away abandon *(relinquish)*, alienate *(estrange)*, avert, decline *(reject)*, depose *(remove)*, disaffect, disapprove *(reject)*, disclaim, disfavor, dismiss *(discharge)*, exclude, parry, prevent, rebuff, repulse
turn away from disavow, eschew, shun
turn awry distort
turn back disavow, escheat, parry, regress, revert
turn down decline *(reject)*, disapprove *(reject)*, disoblige, refuse, spurn
turn from change, disapprove *(reject)*, disavow, discourage, disfavor, refuse, renounce
turn from a purpose dissuade
turn from sin redeem *(satisfy debts)*
turn in retire *(retreat)*
turn informer betray *(disclose)*, denounce *(inform against)*
turn into change, evolve, vary
turn into cash realize *(obtain as a profit)*
turn into money liquidate *(convert into cash)*, realize *(obtain as a profit)*
turn loose discharge *(dismiss)*, discharge *(liberate)*, disenthrall, free, liberate, parole
turn of expression phrase, phraseology
turn of mind disposition *(inclination)*, position *(point of view)*, spirit
turn of the tide crossroad *(turning point)*
turn off alienate *(estrange)*, shut
turn on recriminate
turn one's back on abandon *(physically leave)*, ignore, quit *(evacuate)*, relinquish
turn one's back upon disdain

turn one's gaze upon peruse
turn out deport *(banish)*, depose *(remove)*, discharge *(dismiss)*, disinherit, dislodge, dismiss *(discharge)*, displace *(remove)*, dispossess, eject *(evict)*, eliminate *(exclude)*, evict, exclude, expel, expose, fabricate *(construct)*, formulate, make, manufacture, oust, produce *(manufacture)*, remove *(dismiss from office)*, result, supplant
turn out by industrial process manufacture
turn out of doors evict
turn out of house and home evict
turn out of one's way deviate
turn out of possession eject *(evict)*
turn over alienate *(transfer title)*, attorn, cede, consign, deal, deliver, devolve, give *(grant)*, lend, muse, reflect *(ponder)*, serve *(deliver a legal instrument)*, subvert
turn over for safekeeping entrust
turn over in one's mind consider
turn over in the mind ponder, reason *(conclude)*, speculate *(conjecture)*
turn over to commit *(entrust)*, delegate, relegate
turn renegade tergiversate
turn selfishly to one's own account exploit *(take advantage of)*
turn state's evidence confess
turn tail retreat
turn the attention to observe *(watch)*, occupy *(engage)*
turn the eyes on observe *(watch)*
turn the leaves of peruse
turn the mind to occupy *(engage)*
turn the tables on recriminate
turn to call *(appeal to)*, consult *(ask advice of)*
turn to account employ *(make use of)*, exercise *(use)*, expend *(consume)*, exploit *(make use of)*, gain, inure *(benefit)*, profit
turn to for help resort
turn to for support resort
turn to good account capitalize *(seize the chance)*
turn to one's advantage capitalize *(seize the chance)*
turn to scorn disdain
turn to the side avert
turn to use employ *(make use of)*
turn up discover, disinter, emerge
turn upside down overthrow, upset
turnabout reversal, reversion *(act of returning)*
turnaround reversion *(act of returning)*
turned about inverse
turned around back *(in reverse)*
turned to bone ossified
turning circuitous, critical *(crucial)*, indirect, sinuous, strategic, tortuous *(bending)*
turning aside obviation
turning over to a foreign state extradition
turning to account exploitation
turnkey warden
turnout result
turnpike causeway
turns on SEE MAIN ENTRY
turpis disgraceful, obscene, scandalous, vicious
turpitude bad faith, bad repute, corruption, defilement, delinquency *(misconduct)*, discredit, dishonor *(shame)*, disrepute, guilt, knavery, misconduct, misdoing, perversion, shame, vice, wrong. SEE MAIN ENTRY
turpitudinous bad *(offensive)*
turpitudo disgrace, dishonor *(shame)*, ignominy, obscenity
tussle affray, belligerency, commotion, fight *(battle)*, fight *(battle)*, fracas, grapple, struggle
tutari protect
tutela charge *(custody)*, protection
tutelage aid *(help)*, auspices, charge *(custody)*, direction *(guidance)*, edification, education, guidance, instruction *(teaching)*, patronage *(support)*, protection, safekeeping, ward
tutelar guardian
tutelary protective
tutor edify, educate, enlighten, instill, instruct *(teach)*, nurture, pedagogue
tutored familiar *(informed)*
tutorial didactic, disciplinary *(educational)*
tutoring direction *(guidance)*, education, guidance, instruction *(teaching)*
tutors faculty *(teaching staff)*
tutus safe
twaddle prattle
tweaking SEE MAIN ENTRY
twelve months annum
twice-bereaved child orphan
twice-told repeated
twin alter ego, correlate, counterpart *(parallel)*, duplicate, identical, same, similar
twine contort
twine together intertwine
twinge of conscience qualm
twining circuitous
twist camouflage, complex *(entanglement)*, contort, disorganize, distort, distortion, falsify, intertwine, involution, mutilate, palter, prejudice *(influence)*, quirk *(accident)*, quirk *(idiosyncrasy)*, slant, snarl, tendency
twist and turn contort
twist the meaning distort, misinterpret, misstate, misunderstand
twist the meaning of camouflage, misread, misrepresent
twist the sense distort
twist the truth pretend, prevaricate
twist the words distort, misconstrue
twistable malleable
twisted disordered, inextricable, labyrinthine, peccable, sinuous, tortuous *(bending)*, unreasonable
twisting circuitous, indirect, labyrinthine, sinuous, tortuous *(bending)*
twit jape, jeer, mock *(deride)*
two-faced faithless, false *(disloyal)*, machiavellian, recreant, tartuffish, undependable, unreliable, unscrupulous, untrue, untrustworthy
two-facedness duplicity
two-part trial SEE MAIN ENTRY
two-sided bilateral, mutual *(reciprocal)*, reciprocal
two-way mutual *(reciprocal)*
type case *(example)*, characteristic, class, classification, classify, color *(complexion)*, criterion, denomination, designation *(symbol)*, form *(arrangement)*, instance, kind, manner *(kind)*, personality, pigeonhole, resemblance, style
typical average *(standard)*, boiler plate, broad, common *(customary)*, conventional, customary, demonstrative *(illustrative)*, familiar *(customary)*, general, habitual, mediocre, mundane, natural, nondescript, normal *(regular)*, ordinary, orthodox, prevailing *(current)*, prevalent, regular *(conventional)*, representative, usual. SEE MAIN ENTRY
typical component epitome
typical example representative *(example)*, sample
typical instance example, representative *(example)*
typical part epitome
typical performance norm
typicus typical
typification epitome
typify depict, exemplify, personify, represent *(portray)*, signify *(denote)*
typifying exemplary, representative
tyrannical brutal, cruel, dictatorial, oppressive, relentless, severe, strict, stringent, tyrannous
tyrannical leader dictator
tyrannize bait *(harass)*, harass, mishandle *(maltreat)*, mistreat, tax *(overwork)*
tyrannized aggrieved *(harmed)*
tyrannous brutal, dictatorial. SEE MAIN ENTRY
tyranny cruelty, injustice, oppression, severity, thrall
tyrant dictator
tyro neophyte, novice
tyrranize brutalize, dominate

U

uber productive
ubiquitary present *(current)*, ubiquitous
ubiquitous broad, present *(current)*. SEE MAIN ENTRY
ugly loathsome, odious, repulsive, scandalous
ugsome SEE MAIN ENTRY
ukase citation *(charge)*, declaration, decree, directive, fiat, order *(judicial directive)*, requirement
ulciscendi cupidus vindictive
ulcisci punish, retaliate
ullage deficiency
ulterior additional, undisclosed. SEE MAIN ENTRY
ultimate categorical, ceiling, conclusive *(determinative)*, conclusive *(settled)*, definitive, extreme *(last)*, final, forthcoming, future, last *(final)*, prospective. SEE MAIN ENTRY
ultimate cause derivation, determinant, gist *(ground for a suit)*
ultimate end design *(intent)*
ultimate motive determinant
ultimate point extremity *(furthest point)*
ultimate purpose intention, object
ultimate result issuance
ultimately hereafter *(eventually)*, in due course
ultimatum canon, charge *(command)*, claim *(legal demand)*, condition *(contingent provision)*, demand, dictate, dun, mandate, notice *(warning)*, requirement, warning. SEE MAIN ENTRY
ultimus extreme *(last)*, final, ultimate
ultio revenge, vengeance
ultra vires SEE MAIN ENTRY
ultracritical critical *(faultfinding)*
ultraist radical *(favoring drastic change)*
ultramodern sophisticated
ultrareligious fanatical
ululant blatant *(obtrusive)*
umbrage alienation *(estrangement)*, dissatisfaction, malice, offense, resentment. SEE MAIN ENTRY
umbrageous mysterious, resentful

umpirage collective bargaining
umpire decide, go-between, intercede, judge *(noun)*, judge *(verb)*, mediate, negotiate, referee, rule *(decide)*. SEE MAIN ENTRY
unabashed brazen, impertinent *(insolent)*, insolent, presumptuous. SEE MAIN ENTRY
unabated undiminished, unremitting
unabetted alone *(unsupported)*, solitary, unsupported
unable disabled *(deprived of legal right)*, helpless *(powerless)*, inadept, inadequate, incapable, incompetent, inept *(incompetent)*, otiose, powerless, unfit, unqualified *(not competent)*. SEE MAIN ENTRY
unable to be annulled irrevocable, unavoidable *(not voidable)*
unable to be bought inalienable, incorruptible
unable to be corrected irremediable
unable to be discredited unimpeachable
unable to be disposed of inalienable
unable to be evaded compulsory
unable to be expressed ineffable
unable to be fixed irremediable
unable to be investigated inscrutable
unable to be overcome invincible
unable to be pacified irreconcilable
unable to be quelled invincible
unable to be remedied irremediable
unable to be spoken ineffable
unable to be subjugated invincible
unable to exist without dependent
unable to find the way lost *(disoriented)*
unable to make both ends meet bankrupt
unable to make ends meet impecunious, poor *(underprivileged)*
unable to pay indebted, insolvent
unable to pay matured debts bankrupt
unable to resist eager
unable to satisfy creditors bankrupt
unable to speak mute, speechless
unable to utter articulate sound mute
unable to yield barren
unabridged full, gross *(total)*, intact, thorough
unabridgedly in toto
unacceptable blameful, ineligible, inferior *(lower in quality)*, invidious, nonsubstantial *(not sufficient)*, objectionable, repugnant *(exciting aversion)*, undesirable, unendurable, unsatisfactory, unsuitable. SEE MAIN ENTRY
unacceptableness bad repute
unacceptance disapproval
unaccepted outdated, outmoded, unorthodox
unaccessible inaccessible
unaccidental voluntary
unaccommodating disinclined, froward, invidious, perverse, restive, thoughtless
unaccompanied alone *(unsupported)*, separate, singular, sole, solitary
unaccomplished amateur, executory, inadept
unaccountable arbitrary, clear *(unencumbered)*, immune, inapprehensible, incomprehensible, indefinable, inexplicable, inscrutable, lawless, mysterious, nonconforming, peculiar *(curious)*, prodigious *(amazing)*, uncanny, uncurbed, unforeseeable, unpredictable. SEE MAIN ENTRY
unaccredited unauthorized
unaccustomed extraordinary, inexperienced, nonconforming, peculiar *(curious)*, prodigious *(amazing)*, special, unacquainted, uncommon, unusual. SEE MAIN ENTRY
unachievability impossibility
unachievable difficult, impossible, impracticable, inaccessible, infeasible, insuperable, insurmountable, unattainable
unacknowledged anonymous, unrequited, unspecified
unacquaintance ignorance
unacquainted blind *(not discerning)*, incognizant, inexperienced, insensible, unaccustomed, unaware, unversed. SEE MAIN ENTRY
unacquirability unavailability
unacquirable inaccessible, unattainable
unacquired devoid
unactivated lifeless *(dull)*
unactivity neglect
unactual delusive, illusory, nominal
unadaptable nonconforming, otiose, rigid
unadapted improper, incompetent, ineligible, inexperienced, unfit, unqualified *(not competent)*
unadjustable irreconcilable, nonconforming
unadjusted outstanding *(unresolved)*, unsettled
unadministered executory
unadorned clear *(apparent)*, naked *(lacking embellishment)*, nondescript, simple
unadroit amateur, inadept, inept *(incompetent)*
unadult juvenile
unadulterate decontaminate
unadulterated authentic, genuine, honest, naked *(lacking embellishment)*, natural, pure, simple, sterling, true *(authentic)*. SEE MAIN ENTRY
unadulteration honesty
unadvantageous deleterious
unadventurous careful, safe
unadvertised ulterior
unadvisable adverse *(negative)*, disadvantageous, inappropriate, injudicious
unadvised hot-blooded, imprudent, impulsive *(rash)*, incognizant, unaware
unaffected bona fide, direct *(forthright)*, dispassionate, exempt, genuine, honest, impartial, impervious, inexpressive, ingenuous, insensible, insusceptible *(uncaring)*, irreconcilable, naive, neutral, nonchalant, simple, straightforward, true *(authentic)*, unpretentious. SEE MAIN ENTRY
unaffected by immune
unaffected by injury intact, inviolate
unaffectedness candor *(straightforwardness)*, honesty, informality
unaffiliated alien *(unrelated)*, apart, disconnected, extraneous, foreign, independent, irrelative, separate, unrelated
unaffirmative negative
unaffirmed debatable, disputable, unauthorized
unafraid secure *(confident)*, spartan, unabashed, undaunted
unaggressive harmless, nonmilitant
unaging immutable
unagitated peaceable, phlegmatic, placid
unagreeing discordant
unagressive languid
unaided alone *(unsupported)*, helpless *(defenseless)*, solitary, unilateral, unsupported
unaimed haphazard, indiscriminate, random
unaired undisclosed
unalarmed undaunted
unalert negligent
unalertness neglect, negligence
unalienable SEE MAIN ENTRY
unalike atypical, dissimilar, heterogeneous
unallayed persistent, undiminished
unalleviated chronic
unallied alien *(unrelated)*, apart, disconnected, extraneous, foreign, impertinent *(irrelevant)*, inapposite, independent, individual, irrelative, irrelevant, separate, unrelated
unallocated unclaimed
unallowable impermissible, improper, inexcusable, inexpiable, unjustifiable
unallowed felonious, illegitimate *(illegal)*, illicit, *ultra vires*, unlawful
unalloyed genuine, simple, sterling, unadulterated
unalluring undesirable, unsavory
unalterability indestructibility
unalterable firm, immutable, indefeasible, indelible, inevitable, inexorable, inflexible, ironclad, irreconcilable, irreversible, irrevocable, necessary *(inescapable)*, obdurate, peremptory *(absolute)*, permanent, resolute, rigid, stable, steadfast, unalienable. SEE MAIN ENTRY
unalterableness resistance
unalterably invariably
unaltered certain *(positive)*, durable, intact, inviolate, unaffected *(uninfluenced)*, uniform
unambiguity certification *(certainness)*, certitude
unambiguous accurate, axiomatic, categorical, certain *(fixed)*, certain *(positive)*, clear *(apparent)*, coherent *(clear)*, comprehensible, conclusive *(determinative)*, demonstrable, direct *(forthright)*, distinct *(clear)*, explicit, express, incontestable, incontrovertible, lucid, pellucid, precise, unequivocal, unmistakable. SEE MAIN ENTRY
unambiguously fairly *(clearly)*
unambitious diffident, lax
unamenable impervious, inflexible
unamiable bitter *(reproachful)*
unamicable malevolent
unample deficient
unamusing pedestrian
unanimated inexpressive, insipid, languid, lifeless *(dead)*
unanimity accordance *(understanding)*, agreement *(concurrence)*, compatibility, concert, conciliation, consensus, peace, rapprochement, understanding *(agreement)*
unanimous concordant, consensual, harmonious
unanimously in toto
unannexed disconnected, discrete, disjunctive *(tending to disjoin)*, individual
unannounced undisclosed, unexpected
unanswerable certain *(fixed)*, cogent, immune, incontrovertible, irrefutable, positive *(incontestable)*, sound, uncurbed, undeniable, undisputed, unequivocal, unrefutable
unanswered unrequited
unanswering unresponsive
unanticipated impulsive *(rash)*, premature, unexpected, unforeseeable, unforeseen. SEE MAIN ENTRY
unanticipated event accident *(chance occurrence)*

unanxious peaceable, phlegmatic, secure *(confident)*
unapologizing incorrigible
unapparent blind *(concealed)*, hidden, impalpable, inconspicuous, indiscernible, intangible, latent, obscure *(abstruse)*, obscure *(faint)*, potential, undisclosed
unappealable certain *(fixed)*, final
unappealing objectionable, unacceptable, undesirable
unappeasability contention *(opposition)*
unappeasable implacable, insatiable, irreconcilable, relentless, remorseless, uncontrollable, unrelenting
unappetizing bitter *(acrid tasting)*, repugnant *(exciting aversion)*, unsavory
unapplied theoretical, unclaimed
unappreciable paltry
unappreciativeness ingratitude
unapprehensive careless, lax, phlegmatic, spartan, unabashed, undaunted
unapprised blind *(not discerning)*, unaware
unapprized incognizant, unacquainted, unwitting
unapproachability unavailability
unapproachable difficult, disdainful, inaccessible, remote *(secluded)*, unattainable. SEE MAIN ENTRY
unapproached best, paramount
unappropriated unclaimed
unapprovable undesirable
unapproved unauthorized, unorthodox
unapproving hostile, nonconsenting
unapt disproportionate, impertinent *(irrelevant)*, inadept, inadequate, inapplicable, inapposite, inappropriate, inapt, incompetent, inept *(inappropriate)*, inept *(incompetent)*, irrelevant, powerless, unbecoming, unsatisfactory, unseemly, unsuitable
unaptness disqualification *(factor that disqualifies)*, impropriety
unarm disarm *(divest of arms)*
unarmed helpless *(defenseless)*, powerless
unarmored helpless *(defenseless)*
unaroused dormant, insensible, insusceptible *(uncaring)*, lifeless *(dull)*, nonchalant
unarranged casual, complex, disordered, haphazard, random
unartificial natural
unascertained debatable, disputable, dubious, inconclusive, indefinite, outstanding *(unresolved)*, pending *(unresolved)*, provisional, unconfirmed, undecided
unashamed brazen, dissolute, unabashed
unasked unsolicited
unasked for unclaimed
unaspiring lax
unassailability incontestability, inviolability, security *(safety)*
unassailable categorical, certain *(positive)*, clear *(certain)*, defensible, definitive, immune, inappealable, incontestable, inexpugnable, infallible, insuperable, insurmountable, invincible, irreprehensible, safe, secure *(free from danger)*, tenable, unimpeachable. SEE MAIN ENTRY
unassembled disordered
unassenting dissident, involuntary
unassertive obsequious, passive, pliant, resigned, sequacious, servile, subservient
unassimilated discrete, individual
unassisted alone *(unsupported)*, solitary, unsupported
unassociated alien *(unrelated)*, apart, disconnected, discrete, disjunctive *(tending to disjoin)*, extraneous, foreign, independent, individual, irrelative, remote *(secluded)*, separate, unrelated
unassumed honest
unassuming diffident, direct *(forthright)*, honest, inconspicuous, ordinary, unaffected *(sincere)*, unobtrusive, unpretentious
unassumingly respectfully
unassumingness informality
unassured conditional, dubious, hesitant, insecure, noncommittal, precarious, provisional
unassured purchase caveat emptor
unatonable inexcusable, inexpiable
unattach disengage, remove *(eliminate)*
unattached apart, disconnected, discrete, free *(not restricted)*, independent, individual, irrelative, moving *(in motion)*, separate, sovereign *(independent)*, unrelated, unsettled
unattackability security *(safety)*
unattackable defensible, immune, inexpugnable, insuperable, insurmountable, safe, secure *(free from danger)*, tenable
unattainability impossibility, unavailability
unattainable impossibility, impossible, inaccessible, infeasible, insuperable, insurmountable, unapproachable. SEE MAIN ENTRY
unattended alone *(unsupported)*, separate, sole, solitary. SEE MAIN ENTRY
unattended to perfunctory
unattested unconfirmed, uncorroborated, unfounded, unsupported
unattractive unacceptable, undesirable, unsavory
unauthentic artificial, assumed *(feigned)*, bogus, dishonest, dubious, fraudulent, illusory, imitation, invalid, spurious, unsound *(fallacious)*, unsustainable
unauthenticated dubious, unconfirmed, uncorroborated, unfounded, unsupported, untrustworthy
unauthenticity bad faith
unauthorative uncorroborated
unauthoritative dubious, ineffective, ineffectual, unofficial
unauthorization illegality
unauthorized disorderly, felonious, illegal, illegitimate *(illegal)*, illicit, impermissible, improper, irregular *(improper)*, null *(invalid)*, null and void, ultra vires, unlawful, unofficial, unwarranted, wrongful. SEE MAIN ENTRY
unauthorized assumption of property conversion *(misappropriation)*
unauthorized borrowing plagiarism
unauthorized copy counterfeit
unauthorized reproduction fake
unavailability absence *(omission)*, impossibility. SEE MAIN ENTRY
unavailable difficult, inaccessible, scarce, unattainable
unavailing disadvantageous, expendable, futile, ineffective, ineffectual, needless, nugatory, null *(insignificant)*, otiose, powerless, unproductive. SEE MAIN ENTRY
unavoidable certain *(fixed)*, certain *(positive)*, compelling, compulsory, exigent, forthcoming, imperative, important *(urgent)*, indispensable, inevitable, irrevocable, mandatory, necessary *(inescapable)*, obligatory, peremptory *(imperative)*, undeniable. SEE MAIN ENTRY
unavowed ulterior
unawaited unexpected
unawaited event bombshell
unawakened dormant
unaware heedless, incognizant, insensible, lax, oblivious, reckless, unacquainted, unsuspecting, unwitting. SEE MAIN ENTRY
unawareness ignorance, insentience, nescience
unawares unknowingly
unawed unabashed
unbacked unsound *(not strong)*, unsupported
unbalance discompose, disorganize, disorient, disturb, inequality, obsess
unbalanced deranged, disproportionate, inequitable, insecure, *non compos mentis*, partial *(biased)*, unequal *(unequivalent)*, unsettled
unbalanced mind insanity
unbar disencumber, disengage, disenthrall
unbarred open *(accessible)*, public *(open)*
unbased baseless, ill-founded, insubstantial
unbearable deplorable, insufferable, intolerable, loathsome, objectionable, obnoxious, odious, offensive *(offending)*, onerous, oppressive, painful, repulsive, unendurable. SEE MAIN ENTRY
unbeatable indomitable, inexpugnable, infallible, insuperable, insurmountable, invincible, irresistible, premium. SEE MAIN ENTRY
unbeaten prosperous, successful
unbecoming improper, inapposite, inappropriate, inapt, incongruous, inept *(inappropriate)*, objectionable, undesirable, undue *(excessive)*, unfit, unseemly, unsuitable. SEE MAIN ENTRY
unbefitting disproportionate, improper, inapposite, inappropriate, inapt, inept *(inappropriate)*, unbecoming, undesirable, undue *(excessive)*, unfit, unprofessional, unsatisfactory, unseemly
unbefriended helpless *(defenseless)*
unbeguile disabuse
unbeholdable indiscernible, intangible
unbelief cloud *(suspicion)*, doubt *(suspicion)*, suspicion *(mistrust)*
unbelievable debatable, disputable, doubtful, implausible, impossible, incredible, ludicrous, remarkable, suspicious *(questionable)*, uncanny. SEE MAIN ENTRY
unbeliever heretic
unbelieving cynical, inconvincible, incredulous, leery, skeptical
unbellicose nonmilitant, peaceable
unbelligerent nonmilitant, peaceable
unbend condescend *(deign)*, relent
unbending callous, draconian, firm, formal, immutable, implacable, inexorable, inflexible, insusceptible *(uncaring)*, intractable, ironclad, irreconcilable, obdurate, orthodox, parochial, pertinacious, precise, relentless, resolute, rigid, severe, strict, unalterable, uncompromising, unrelenting, unyielding. SEE MAIN ENTRY
unbenevolent cruel, scathing, sinister
unbent direct *(straight)*
unbeseeming unbecoming, unsuitable
unbetraying loyal, true *(loyal)*
unbias candor *(impartiality)*
unbiased broad, discriminating *(judicious)*, dispassionate, equal, equitable, evenhanded, factual, fair *(just)*, honest, impartial, judicial, juridical, just, liberal *(broad minded)*, neutral, nonpartisan, objective, open-minded, receptive, undistorted, unprejudiced. SEE MAIN ENTRY

unbiased impulse common sense
unbiasedly fairly *(impartially)*
unbiasedness disinterest *(lack of prejudice)*, fairness
unbidden lawless, spontaneous, unsolicited, voluntary, willing *(uncompelled)*
unbigoted equitable, impartial, judicial, just, liberal *(broad-minded)*, neutral, nonpartisan, objective, open-minded, unbiased, unprejudiced
unbind break *(separate)*, disband, disencumber, disengage, disenthrall, dissociate, divide *(separate)*, extricate, free, liberate, remove *(eliminate)*, rescue, separate, sever, split
unbinding liberation
unblamable blameless, clean, inculpable, innocent, irreprehensible, pardonable, unimpeachable
unblameworthy blameless, inculpable, irreprehensible, unimpeachable, unobjectionable
unblemished absolute *(ideal)*, blameless, clean, incorruptible, intact, inviolate, irreprehensible, not guilty, pure, unimpeachable. SEE MAIN ENTRY
unblenched undaunted
unblenching heroic, spartan
unblended simple
unblest profane
unblindfold disabuse
unblocked open *(accessible)*
unblurred clear *(apparent)*, cognizable, coherent *(clear)*, conspicuous
unblushing brazen, callous, lascivious, nonchalant, salacious, unabashed
unboastful diffident
unbodied incorporeal
unbolt disengage, parole
unborn nonexistent
unborrowed native *(domestic)*, original *(creative)*
unbosom divulge
unbought free *(at no charge)*, gratis, gratuitous *(given without recompense)*, impartial, just, loyal
unbound clear *(unencumbered)*, exempt, free *(not restricted)*, independent, sovereign *(independent)*, uncurbed, unqualified *(unlimited)*, unrestricted. SEE MAIN ENTRY
unbounded absolute *(complete)*, competitive *(open)*, excessive, indefinite, indeterminate, infinite, open-ended, unconditional, unlimited, unmitigated, unrestrained *(not in custody)*, unrestricted
unbowdlerized salacious
unbreakable indivisible, inexpugnable, infrangible, ironclad
unbreathed undisclosed
unbribable honest, incorruptible, just, law-abiding
unbribed clean, evenhanded, impartial, just, loyal
unbridgeable insuperable
unbridled clear *(unencumbered)*, disorderly, dissolute, free *(not restricted)*, hot-blooded, incendiary, independent, inordinate, intemperate, lecherous, open-ended, prodigal, profuse, uncurbed, unrestrained *(not in custody)*, unrestrained *(not repressed)*, unrestricted, unruly
unbridled authority SEE MAIN ENTRY
unbroadened provincial
unbroken consecutive, continual *(connected)*, continuous, direct *(straight)*, direct *(uninterrupted)*, gross *(total)*, incessant, intact, inviolate, safe, unremitting
unbroken line chain *(series)*
unbroken order array *(order)*
unbruised intact
unbuckle disengage
unburden alleviate, disencumber, ease, free, mitigate, release, relieve *(free from burden)*
unburdened clear *(free from criminal charges)*, clear *(unencumbered)*, free *(relieved from a burden)*
unbury disinter
unbusied inactive
unbusinesslike inexperienced, unprofessional
uncage parole
uncalculated fortuitous, imprudent, unintentional, unpremeditated
uncalculating careless, impulsive *(rash)*, injudicious, negligent, precipitate
uncalled for disproportionate, excessive, extraneous, gratuitous *(unwarranted)*, inapplicable, inappropriate, nonessential
uncalled-for exorbitant, expendable, inordinate, needless, otiose, redundant, superfluous, unclaimed, undue *(excessive)*, unessential, unnecessary, unsolicited, unwarranted
uncamouflaged obvious, patent
uncandid devious, disingenuous, lying, mendacious, sly, untrue
uncanny mysterious. SEE MAIN ENTRY
uncanonical unorthodox
uncaptivating insipid, lifeless *(dull)*, pedestrian
uncarcerated person SEE MAIN ENTRY
uncared for derelict *(abandoned)*
uncareful slipshod
uncaring callous, cold-blooded, heedless, lax, nonchalant, obdurate, oblivious, obtuse, perfunctory, phlegmatic, slipshod, unaffected *(uninfluenced)*
uncase denude, unveil
uncatholic parochial
uncaught free *(not restricted)*, unbound
uncaused baseless
unceasing chronic, continual *(connected)*, continual *(perpetual)*, continuous, durable, incessant, industrious, infinite, live *(existing)*, open-ended, patient, permanent, perpetual, persistent, standing, undiminished, unremitting
uncensored intact, lurid
uncensurable blameless, clear *(free from criminal charges)*, irreprehensible, laudable, meritorious, unimpeachable, unobjectionable
unceremonial informal
unceremonious informal, presumptuous
unceremoniousness informality
uncertain ambiguous, approximate, capricious, casual, conditional, controversial, debatable, difficult, disputable, dubious, elusive, equivocal, fallible, hesitant, inconclusive, inconvincible, indefinite, indeterminate, insecure, intangible, irresolute, leery, moot, mutable, nebulous, noncommittal, pending *(unresolved)*, precarious, problematic, reluctant, shifting, skeptical, speculative, sporadic, subject *(conditional)*, suspicious *(questionable)*, unclear, unconfirmed, undecided, undependable, unforeseeable, unpredictable, unsettled, untrustworthy, vague. SEE MAIN ENTRY
uncertain event condition *(contingent provision)*, contingency
uncertain state doubt *(indecision)*
uncertainness doubt *(indecision)*, hesitation, incertitude, quandary
uncertainty ambivalence, chance *(possibility)*, confusion *(ambiguity)*, contingency, dilemma, doubt *(indecision)*, hazard, hesitation, improbability, incertitude, incredulity, indecision, jeopardy, misgiving, peril, possibility, qualm, quandary, reluctance, risk, scruple, speculation *(risk)*, venture. SEE MAIN ENTRY
uncertainty of meaning ambiguity
uncertified controversial, dubious, unauthorized, unconfirmed, unsupported
unchain break *(separate)*, disencumber, disengage, disenthrall, dissociate, free, liberate, parole, rescue
unchained free *(not restricted)*, unbound, uncurbed
unchaining liberation, release
unchallengeable axiomatic, clear *(certain)*, conclusive *(determinative)*, equitable, evenhanded, incontrovertible, indefeasible, inexpugnable, irrebuttable, irrefutable, irreprehensible, just, positive *(incontestable)*, sound, tenable, unalienable, uncontested, undisputed, unimpeachable
unchallenged accurate, consensual, permissible, uncontested, uncontroverted, undisputed, unequivocal
unchangeability indestructibility
unchangeable categorical, certain *(positive)*, conclusive *(determinative)*, consonant, durable, fixed *(settled)*, immutable, inappealable, indefeasible, indelible, inevitable, inflexible, infrangible, ironclad, irreconcilable, irredeemable, irreversible, irrevocable, loyal, noncancellable, obdurate, orthodox, patient, permanent, stable, unalterable, unavoidable *(not voidable)*, unbending, uncompromising, unyielding
unchangeableness constant
unchangeably invariably
unchanged consonant, infallible, literal, regular *(conventional)*, unaffected *(uninfluenced)*
unchanging certain *(fixed)*, consistent, consonant, constant, continual *(connected)*, definite, dependable, equal, fixed *(settled)*, immutable, inexorable, infallible, ironclad, loyal, permanent, persistent, resolute, stable, standing, steadfast, uniform, unremitting
uncharacteristic improper, novel
uncharged free *(at no charge)*
uncharitable exclusive *(limited)*, illiberal, mordacious, parsimonious, scathing
uncharitableness rancor
uncharming pedestrian
unchartered illegal, impermissible, ultra vires, unauthorized, unsettled
unchary impulsive *(rash)*
unchaste dissolute, immoral, lascivious, lecherous, lewd, licentious, obscene, peccable, promiscuous, prurient, salacious
unchastised clear *(free from criminal charges)*
unchastity obscenity, vice
unchecked exempt, free *(not restricted)*, independent, intemperate, live *(existing)*, permanent, persistent, rampant, unbound, unconditional, unconfirmed, uncurbed, unlimited, unqualified *(unlimited)*, unrestrained *(not in custody)*, unrestrained *(not repressed)*, unrestricted. SEE MAIN ENTRY
uncheerful grave *(solemn)*, pessimistic
uncheerfulness pessimism

uncheery grave *(solemn)*, pessimistic
unchivalrous ignoble, illiberal
unchosen ineligible
uncircumscribed far reaching, omnipotent
uncircumspect careless, derelict *(negligent)*, hot-blooded, imprudent, impulsive *(rash)*, lax, negligent, reckless, remiss
uncircumspection indiscretion
uncivil blatant *(obtrusive)*, contemptuous, disdainful, disorderly, impertinent *(insolent)*, offensive *(offending)*, perverse, uncouth
uncivilized brutal, caitiff, disorderly, vicious
unclaimed anonymous, derelict *(abandoned)*. SEE MAIN ENTRY
unclarified equivocal, opaque
unclarity opacity
unclasp disengage
unclassifiable individual, nonconforming, nondescript, unusual
unclassified complex, disjointed, disordered, miscellaneous, peculiar *(curious)*
unclean insalubrious, lewd, prurient, repulsive, salacious, tainted *(contaminated)*
unclean hands SEE MAIN ENTRY
uncleanliness defilement
uncleanness defilement
unclear difficult, elusive, equivocal, impalpable, inarticulate, incomprehensible, inconspicuous, indefinable, indefinite, indeterminate, indistinct, inexact, inscrutable, nebulous, oblique *(evasive)*, obscure *(faint)*, opaque, pending *(unresolved)*, uncertain *(ambiguous)*, unspecified, vague. SEE MAIN ENTRY
unclearness confusion *(ambiguity)*, incoherence, indistinctness, obscuration, opacity
unclever inadept, inept *(incompetent)*, unversed
unclinch break *(separate)*
uncloak bare, denude, expose, find *(discover)*, reveal, unveil
unclog disencumber
unclogged open *(unclosed)*
unclosed competitive *(open)*, penetrable
unclothe bare, denude
unclouded clear *(apparent)*, comprehensible, conspicuous, distinct *(clear)*, manifest, open *(in sight)*, perceivable, pure
uncoerced autonomous *(independent)*, free *(not restricted)*, voluntary
uncohesive desultory, disconnected, disjointed
uncoil spread
uncollaborated unsupported
uncollected outstanding *(unpaid)*, payable, unpaid, unsettled
uncollectible debt bad debt
uncolored accurate, factual, fair *(just)*, genuine, honest, impartial, just, objective, open-minded, true *(authentic)*, unbiased, unprejudiced
uncombined simple, unadulterated
uncomely unbecoming
uncomfortable egregious, lamentable, oppressive, painful
uncomfortableness dissatisfaction
uncomforting callous, harsh
uncommanded unauthorized
uncommendable blameful, blameworthy, disorderly, inappropriate, objectionable, peccable, reprehensible, scandalous, sinister, unethical
uncommissioned unauthorized
uncommitted impartial, independent, neutral, noncommittal, nonpartisan
uncommon anomalous, distinct *(distinguished from others)*, distinctive, eccentric, extraordinary, individual, infrequent, momentous, nonconforming, noteworthy, novel, original *(creative)*, particular *(specific)*, peculiar *(distinctive)*, prodigious *(amazing)*, rare, remarkable, scarce, singular, special, specific, unaccustomed, uncanny, unique, unorthodox, unusual. SEE MAIN ENTRY
uncommonly particularly
uncommonness paucity
uncommunicated undisclosed
uncommunicative laconic, mute, noncommittal, phlegmatic, surreptitious, taciturn, unresponsive
uncommunicativeness loophole
uncompassionate callous, cruel, draconian, inexorable, obdurate, relentless, remorseless, ruthless, unaffected *(uninfluenced)*, unrelenting, unresponsive
uncompassionateness cruelty
uncompelled autonomous *(independent)*, impartial, nonpartisan, spontaneous, voluntary
uncompensated due *(owed)*, unpaid, unrequited
uncomplaining patient, resigned
uncomplaisant perverse, reluctant, restive
uncompleted deficient, executory, imperfect, inchoate, incipient, insufficient, partial *(part)*, partial *(relating to a part)*, rudimentary
uncomplex elementary
uncompliant broken *(unfulfilled)*, disobedient, lawless, perverse, recalcitrant, recusant, restive, unruly
uncomplicate simplify *(make easier)*
uncomplicated elementary, naked *(lacking embellishment)*, simple
uncomplimentary critical *(faultfinding)*, derogatory, pejorative
uncomplimentary remark disparagement
uncomplying contumacious, disobedient, insubordinate, lawless, nonconsenting, recalcitrant, reluctant, restive, unruly
uncompounded simple, unadulterated
uncomprehended hidden
uncomprehending blind *(not discerning)*, obtuse, opaque
uncomprehension nescience
uncompromising close *(rigorous)*, dictatorial, draconian, formal, immutable, implacable, inexorable, inflexible, ironclad, irreconcilable, obdurate, orthodox, particular *(exacting)*, patient, pertinacious, precise, punctilious, purposeful, radical *(favoring drastic change)*, relentless, resolute, rigid, scathing, sedulous, serious *(devoted)*, severe, stable, steadfast, strict, stringent, thorough, tyrannous, unbending, unrelenting, unyielding, willful. SEE MAIN ENTRY
uncompromisingness rigor
unconceal bare, expose, find *(discover)*, manifest, unveil
unconcealed comprehensible, evident, manifest, naked *(perceptible)*, obvious, open *(in sight)*, overt, palpable, patent, pellucid, perceivable, perceptible, salient, scrutable, unmistakable
unconcern dereliction, disinterest *(lack of interest)*, indifference, laxity, neglect, negligence, sloth
unconcerned careless, casual, cold-blooded, controlled *(restrained)*, derelict *(negligent)*, heedless, insusceptible *(uncaring)*, lax, negligent, neutral, nonchalant, obdurate, perfunctory, phlegmatic, reckless, remiss, secure *(confident)*, thoughtless, torpid, truant, unabashed, unaffected *(uninfluenced)*, undaunted, unresponsive. SEE MAIN ENTRY
unconcise prolix
unconcluded outstanding *(unresolved)*, pending *(unresolved)*
unconcrete intangible
unconcreteness impalpability
uncondemned blameless, clear *(free from criminal charges)*
unconditional absolute *(complete)*, categorical, complete *(all-embracing)*, comprehensive, outright, peremptory *(absolute)*, strict, unlimited, unmitigated, unqualified *(unlimited)*, unrestricted. SEE MAIN ENTRY
unconditional authority SEE MAIN ENTRY
unconditional inheritance fee *(estate)*
unconditionally purely *(positively)*
unconditioned absolute *(conclusive)*, categorical, peremptory *(absolute)*
uncondoling callous
unconfident dubious, hesitant, insecure
unconfined broad, competitive *(open)*, exempt, free *(not restricted)*, open-ended, plenary, unbound, unconditional, uncurbed, unlimited, unrestrained *(not in custody)*, unrestricted. SEE MAIN ENTRY
unconfirmable unsustainable
unconfirmed debatable, disputable, dubious, ill-founded, inconclusive, provisional, speculative, uncertain *(questionable)*, uncorroborated, unsupported. SEE MAIN ENTRY
unconfirmed account hearsay
unconfirmed report hearsay, report *(rumor)*
unconformable disparate, disproportionate, dissident, dissimilar, inapplicable, inapposite, inappropriate, incommensurate, irreconcilable, irregular *(not usual)*, lawless, nonconforming, original *(creative)*, peculiar *(curious)*, peculiar *(distinctive)*, recusant, repugnant *(incompatible)*, rigid, unique, unorthodox, unrelated. SEE MAIN ENTRY
unconforming eccentric, peculiar *(distinctive)*, recusant
unconformity breach, controversy *(argument)*, deviation, difference, disaccord, disagreement, discrepancy, disparity, dissent *(difference of opinion)*, dissidence, distinction *(difference)*, diversity, exception *(exclusion)*, incompatibility *(inconsistency)*, incongruity, inconsistency, inequality, irregularity, nonconformity, quirk *(idiosyncrasy)*, variance *(disagreement)*
unconfused coherent *(clear)*, comprehensible, distinct *(distinguished from others)*, unambiguous
unconfusedly fairly *(clearly)*
unconfusing explicit, unmistakable
unconfutability certainty
unconfutable clear *(certain)*, convincing, incontrovertible, irrefutable, positive *(incontestable)*, solid *(sound)*, sound, unimpeachable, unrefutable
unconfuted certain *(positive)*, cogent, definite
uncongenial inapposite, inapt, incongruous, inept *(inappropriate)*, offensive *(offending)*, unsuitable

unconnected alien *(unrelated),* apart, collateral *(immaterial),* desultory, disconnected, discrete, disjunctive *(tending to disjoin),* foreign, gratuitous *(unwarranted),* impertinent *(irrelevant),* inapposite, inconsequential, independent, individual, irrelative, irrelevant, obscure *(remote),* remote *(secluded),* separate, solitary, unrelated. SEE MAIN ENTRY
unconquerable formidable, indomitable, inexpugnable, infallible, insuperable, insurmountable, invincible, irresistible, powerful, spartan
unconquered independent, sovereign *(independent)*
unconscienced recreant, unconscionable
unconscientious inaccurate
unconscientiousness bad faith, neglect
unconscionable excessive, exorbitant, immoral, inordinate, outrageous, perfidious, prohibitive *(costly),* reprobate, unethical, unwarranted, usurious. SEE MAIN ENTRY
unconscionable delay laches
unconscionable rate of interest usury
unconscionability SEE MAIN ENTRY
unconscious blind *(not discerning),* incognizant, insensible, involuntary, oblivious, torpid, unaware, unintentional, unsuspecting, unwitting
unconsciously unknowingly
unconsciousness disregard *(unconcern),* ignorance, insentience
unconsecrated profane
unconsenting disinclined, disobedient, dissenting, dissident, nonconsenting, recusant, reluctant, restive
unconsentingly unwillingly
unconsidered haphazard, ill-advised, ill-judged, impulsive *(rash),* injudicious, irrational, misadvised, unpremeditated
unconsolable disconsolate
unconsoling callous, harsh
unconsonant hostile, inapplicable, inapposite, inappropriate, inapt, inept *(inappropriate)*
unconspicuous unobtrusive
unconstitutional illegal, illicit, impermissible, unauthorized, unlawful
unconstitutionality prohibition
unconstrained absolute *(complete),* autonomous *(independent),* candid, clear *(unencumbered),* direct *(forthright),* ingenuous, lawless, open-ended, simple, spontaneous, unbound, uncurbed, unqualified *(unlimited),* unrestrained *(not in custody),* unrestrained *(not repressed),* unrestricted, voluntary, willful
unconstraint freedom, honesty, informality, latitude, liberty
uncontained unrestricted
uncontaminated pure, unadulterated
uncontemplated unanticipated, unexpected
uncontemporary outdated
uncontentious nonmilitant, peaceable
uncontestable arrant *(definite),* irrefutable, manifest, palpable, unmistakable
uncontested axiomatic, categorical, clear *(certain),* conclusive *(determinative),* consensual, definite, definitive, indubious, uncontroverted. SEE MAIN ENTRY
uncontradictable incontestable, incontrovertible
uncontradicted consensual, uncontested, uncontroverted
uncontrite incorrigible
uncontrived spontaneous, straightforward
uncontrollable hot-blooded, incorrigible, inexorable, intractable, necessary *(inescapable),* obdurate, recalcitrant, restive, unavoidable *(inevitable),* unruly, unyielding. SEE MAIN ENTRY
uncontrolled autonomous *(independent),* capricious, disorderly, drunk, exempt, impulsive *(rash),* independent, intemperate, irresponsible, lawless, licentious, open-ended, rampant, sensitive *(easily affected),* sovereign *(independent),* spontaneous, unbound, uncurbed, unlimited, unqualified *(unlimited),* unrestrained *(not repressed),* unrestricted
uncontroversial clear *(certain),* consensual, inappealable, irrefutable, uncontested, undisputed, unrefutable
uncontroverted consensual, uncontested. SEE MAIN ENTRY
unconventional anomalous, deviant, divergent, eccentric, individual, informal, irregular *(not usual),* licentious, nonconforming, novel, original *(creative),* peculiar *(curious),* prodigious *(amazing),* unaccustomed, uncommon, unorthodox, unusual
unconventionality exception *(exclusion),* informality, nonconformity, quirk *(idiosyncrasy)*
unconversable unresponsive
unconversant blind *(not discerning),* inexperienced, unaccustomed, unacquainted, unversed
unconverted negative
unconveyed undisclosed
unconvinced incredulous, leery, negative, undecided
unconvincing doubtful, implausible, incredible, ludicrous, problematic, suspicious *(questionable),* unbelievable
uncooperated reluctant
uncooperative adverse *(hostile),* contentious, disinclined, disobedient, froward, hostile, perverse, recalcitrant, unresponsive
uncoordinated disordered, incongruous, random, slipshod
uncopied honest, original *(creative)*
uncorked open *(unclosed)*
uncorrectable chronic
uncorrectness misestimation
uncorroborated baseless, inconclusive, unconfirmed, unsupported. SEE MAIN ENTRY
uncorrupt blameless, conscientious, credible, decontaminate, ethical, evenhanded, high-minded, impartial, incorruptible, inculpable, just, moral, pure, reputable, straightforward, upright
uncorrupted blameless, clean, dispassionate, ethical, evenhanded, fair *(just),* high-minded, impartial, inviolate, just, law-abiding, literal, moral, pure, unadulterated
uncorruptibility rectitude
uncorruptible credible
uncountable innumerable, myriad
uncounted innumerable, multiple, myriad
uncounterfeited authentic, bona fide, genuine, honest, unaffected *(sincere),* veridical
uncouple break *(separate),* detach, disband, disjoint, dissociate, dissolve *(separate),* divide *(separate),* divorce, separate, sever
uncoupled disconnected
uncoupling division *(act of dividing),* separation
uncourageous caitiff, recreant
uncourteous uncouth
uncourtliness disrespect
uncourtly disorderly, inelegant, presumptuous, provincial, uncouth
uncouth blatant *(obtrusive),* ignoble, impertinent *(insolent),* inelegant, provincial. SEE MAIN ENTRY
uncovenanted purchase caveat emptor
uncover bare, betray *(disclose),* convey *(communicate),* denude, detect, disabuse, disclose, discover, disinter, divest, divulge, evidence, exhibit, expose, find *(discover),* inform *(betray),* locate, manifest, present *(introduce),* produce *(offer to view),* reveal, unveil
uncovered apparent *(perceptible),* clear *(apparent),* conspicuous, distinct *(clear),* helpless *(defenseless),* open *(in sight),* open *(unclosed),* overt, palpable
uncovering disclosure *(act of disclosing),* discovery, expression *(manifestation),* manifestation
uncovery disclosure *(act of disclosing)*
uncreated nonexistent
uncreative trite
uncredulousness cloud *(suspicion),* doubt *(suspicion)*
uncringing unabashed
uncritical casual, favorable *(expressing approval),* indiscriminate, promiscuous, unnecessary
uncritical acceptance credulity
uncrown overthrow
uncrowning abdication
unctious subservient
unculpable blameless, clean, pardonable
uncultivated idle, ignoble, inelegant, natural, uncouth
uncultured blatant *(obtrusive),* imperfect, inelegant, uncouth
uncurbed clear *(unencumbered),* disorderly, dissolute, free *(not restricted),* independent, inordinate, intemperate, intractable, irresponsible, lawless, licentious, prodigal, profuse, unrestrained *(not in custody),* unrestrained *(not repressed),* unruly. SEE MAIN ENTRY
uncurrent outdated, outmoded
uncurtain bare, denude, manifest, reveal, unveil
uncurtained palpable
uncustomarily particularly
uncustomary anomalous, extraordinary, informal, infrequent, nonconforming, noteworthy, novel, original *(creative),* peculiar *(curious),* portentous *(eliciting amazement),* prodigious *(amazing),* rare, singular, special, unaccustomed, uncommon, unprecedented, unusual
uncut gross *(total),* intact, undiminished
undamaged intact, safe, undiminished
undaring judicious, noncommittal, safe
undaunted diligent, heroic, indomitable, patient, persistent, pertinacious, relentless, resolute, spartan, steadfast, unabashed. SEE MAIN ENTRY
undauntedness audacity, diligence *(perseverance)*
undebased unadulterated
undebatable undisputed
undecayed intact
undeceitful direct *(forthright)*

undeceitfulness honesty
undeceive debunk, disabuse, inform *(notify),* reveal
undeceived conscious *(aware),* informed *(having information)*
undeceiving direct *(forthright)*
undeceptive direct *(forthright),* unaffected *(sincere)*
undeceptiveness honesty, probity
undecided aleatory *(uncertain),* conditional, controversial, debatable, disputable, equivocal, hesitant, impartial, indefinite, indeterminate, irresolute, moot, mutable, noncommittal, outstanding *(unresolved),* pending *(unresolved),* pliant, problematic, provisional, tentative, uncertain *(questionable),* unsettled. SEE MAIN ENTRY
undecidedness ambivalence, doubt *(indecision),* qualm
undecipherability incoherence
undecipherable complex, inapprehensible, indistinct, inexplicable, inexpressive
undeciphered hidden, mysterious
undeclared implied, tacit, undisclosed
undecorated naked *(lacking embellishment),* simple
undeducted from gross *(total)*
undefaced intact
undefeatable indefeasible, insuperable, insurmountable
undefeated prosperous, successful
undefended helpless *(defenseless),* open *(accessible),* susceptible *(unresistent),* untenable
undefiled blameless, inviolate, pure, unadulterated, unblemished
undefinable inapprehensible, ineffable. SEE MAIN ENTRY
undefined equivocal, inconspicuous, indefinite, indeterminate, indistinct, nebulous, open-ended, unclear, unspecified, vague
undeflected direct *(straight)*
undefrayed delinquent *(overdue)*
undeft inadept, inept *(incompetent)*
undeftness disqualification *(factor that disqualifies),* inability, incompetence
undelectable unsavory
undeleted gross *(total)*
undeliberate unintentional
undemanded unclaimed
undemanding facile, lax, lenient
undemanding chore sinecure
undemanding job sinecure
undemanding task sinecure
undemocratic dictatorial
undemolished intact
undemonstrable debatable, disputable, problematic, unsustainable, untenable
undemonstrated debatable, disputable, dubious, inconclusive, speculative, unconfirmed, uncorroborated, unsupported
undemonstrative controlled *(restrained),* dispassionate, passive, phlegmatic, placid, stoical
undeniability certainty, certitude, incontestability
undeniable axiomatic, believable, categorical, certain *(fixed),* certain *(positive),* clear *(certain),* cogent, conclusive *(determinative),* convincing, credible, definite, definitive, evident, factual, incontestable, incontrovertible, indefeasible, indubious, irrefutable, lucid, necessary *(inescapable),* noncontestable, obvious, official, positive *(incontestable),* real, reliable, uncontested, undisputed, unequivocal, unimpeachable, unmistakable, unrefutable. SEE MAIN ENTRY
undeniable fact fait accompli
undeniably admittedly, fairly *(clearly)*
undenied accurate
undenominational nonsectarian
undependability dishonesty, improbity
undependable dishonest, disobedient, faithless, fallible, false *(disloyal),* insecure, irresponsible, machiavellian, perfidious, precarious, recreant, unpredictable, unreliable, untrustworthy. SEE MAIN ENTRY
under inferior *(lower in position),* subaltern
under a sense of impending death in extremis
under a vow bound
under advisement at issue
under arms armed
under arrest arrested *(apprehended),* in custody. SEE MAIN ENTRY
under average poor *(inferior in quality)*
under ban illicit, impermissible
under compulsion bound
under consideration at issue, pending *(unresolved)*
under control bailment, systematic
under cover safe
under discussion debatable, disputable, moot
under examination at issue, debatable
under fiduciary control in trust
under inquiry controversial
under legal obligation actionable, liable
under lock and key in custody
under necessity bound
under oath promissory. SEE MAIN ENTRY
under obligation accountable *(responsible),* actionable, bound, indebted, indentured, liable
under one's hand holographic
under par minimal
under shelter immune
under surveillance guarded
under the circumstances consequently
under the control of conditional
under the influence of addicted
under the influence of liquor drunk
under the mark minimal
under the surface internal, latent
underage juvenile
underage person minor
underbid haggle
underbred ignoble
undercover cache *(hiding place),* clandestine, collusive, confidential, covert, furtive, hidden, mysterious, private *(confidential),* sly, stealthy, surreptitious, unobtrusive
undercover agent spy
undercover man bystander, spy
undercover work espionage
underestimate depreciate, derogate, discount *(minimize),* lessen, minimize, misprize. SEE MAIN ENTRY
underestimating pejorative
underestimation disregard *(lack of respect),* understatement
undergo allow *(endure),* bear *(tolerate),* endure *(suffer),* tolerate
undergo eclipse disappear
undergo evolution evolve
undergo the cost of disburse *(pay out)*
undergo the expense of disburse *(pay out)*
undergrade poor *(inferior in quality)*
underground clandestine, covert, furtive, hidden, surreptitious, unobtrusive
underground activity sedition
underhand clandestine, covert, furtive, machiavellian, mysterious, oblique *(evasive),* sly, stealthy, subtle *(insidious),* surreptitious, unscrupulous
underhand dealing bad faith, collusion, dishonesty, evasion, knavery, pettifoggery
underhand participation connivance
underhand practice pettifoggery
underhanded clandestine, collusive, deceptive, dishonest, disingenuous, false *(disloyal),* fraudulent, hidden, insidious, machiavellian, oblique *(evasive),* sly, unethical. SEE MAIN ENTRY
underhanded act maneuver *(trick)*
underhanded complicity connivance
underhanded practice deceit
underhandedness deceit, dishonesty, false pretense, fraud, illegality, improbity, indirection *(deceitfulness)*
underived original *(creative),* primordial
underlease rent
underlet rent, sublease, sublet
underlie inspire
underline insist, reaffirm
underling assistant, coadjutant
underlining emphasis
underlying cardinal *(basic),* central *(essential),* fundamental, latent, organic, original *(initial),* primary, rudimentary, substantive, virtual. SEE MAIN ENTRY
underlying principle basis, cause *(reason),* foundation *(basis)*
undermine check *(restrain),* corrupt, countervail, debilitate, disable, disarm *(divest of arms),* discommode, disqualify, foil, frustrate, hamper, hold up *(delay),* impair, invalidate, overreach, plot, pollute, rebel, smear, subvert, supplant, thwart. SEE MAIN ENTRY
undermine one's belief deter, impugn
undermining detrimental
undermost cardinal *(basic),* underlying
underpin bolster
underpinning foundation *(basis)*
underplot collusion, connivance, conspiracy, machination
underpraise depreciate, minimize
underprice discount *(reduce),* minimize, underestimate
underprize depreciate, misprize, underestimate
underrate depreciate, derogate, discommend, disparage, lessen, minimize, misprize, underestimate
underreckon depreciate, derogate, minimize, misprize, underestimate
underripe premature
underscoring emphasis
undersell discount *(reduce)*
undersign corroborate, cosign, indorse, notarize, seal *(solemnize),* sign, subscribe *(sign),* witness *(attest to)*
undersigned SEE MAIN ENTRY
undersized minimal
understand agree *(comply),* appreciate *(comprehend),* apprehend *(perceive),* conceive *(comprehend),* construe *(comprehend),* deduce, deduct *(conclude by reasoning),* digest *(comprehend),* discover, find *(discover),* infer, interpret, perceive, pierce *(discern),* presume, presuppose, read, recognize *(perceive),* resolve *(solve),* solve, surmise, suspect *(think),* sympathize. SEE MAIN ENTRY
understand by construe *(comprehend)*
understand fully comprehend *(understand)*

understand improperly misconstrue
understand incorrectly miscalculate, misinterpret, misread
understand the meaning of construe *(comprehend)*
understand wrongly misunderstand
understandability coherence
understandable ascertainable, cognizable, coherent *(clear)*, comprehensible, elementary, explicit, lucid, obvious, pardonable, pellucid, perceptible, ponderable, reasonable *(rational)*, scrutable, simple, unambiguous. SEE MAIN ENTRY
understandable language plain language
understandably fairly *(clearly)*
understanding accord, accordance *(understanding)*, adjustment, affection, agreement *(concurrence)*, agreement *(contract)*, apprehension *(perception)*, attornment, bargain, belief *(state of mind)*, benevolence *(disposition to do good)*, benevolent, caliber *(mental capacity)*, charitable *(lenient)*, cognition, cognizant, common sense, compact, comprehension, concept, conciliation, concordance, conscious *(aware)*, consideration *(sympathetic regard)*, consortium *(marriage companionship)*, construction, contract, conviction *(persuasion)*, covenant, deal, discrimination *(good judgment)*, estimate *(idea)*, experience *(background)*, humanity *(humaneness)*, inference, information *(knowledge)*, insight, intellect, intelligence *(intellect)*, judgment *(discernment)*, juridical, knowing, knowledge *(awareness)*, league, lenience, longanimity, notion, omniscient, option *(contractual provision)*, pact, patient, perception, perceptive, perspicacious, placable, policy *(contract)*, promise, protocol *(agreement)*, quid pro quo, rapport, rapprochement, rational, realization, reason *(sound judgment)*, receptive, reconciliation, sagacity, sane, sanity, scienter, sense *(feeling)*, sense *(intelligence)*, sensible, sensitive *(discerning)*, settlement, specialty *(contract)*, stipulation, term *(provision)*, tolerance, treaty, vicarious *(delegated)*. SEE MAIN ENTRY
understanding before marriage antenuptial agreement
understandings dealings
understate discount *(minimize)*, distort, minimize, misrepresent
understatement SEE MAIN ENTRY
understood assumed *(inferred)*, clear *(apparent)*, cognizable, coherent *(clear)*, consensual, constructive *(inferential)*, contractual, familiar *(customary)*, implicit, implied, indirect, lucid, prescriptive, tacit
understood by a select few esoteric
understood by the initiated esoteric
understood from accompanying words noscitur a sociis
understudy replace, replacement, substitute
understudy for displace *(replace)*
undertake agree *(contract)*, attempt, close *(agree)*, commence, contract, embark, endeavor, engage *(involve)*, generate, incur, initiate, launch *(initiate)*, maintain *(commence)*, occupy *(engage)*, originate, participate, pledge *(promise the performance of)*, ply, practice *(engage in)*, promise *(vow)*, strive, try *(attempt)*, underwrite. SEE MAIN ENTRY
undertake by contract contract
undertake responsibility answer *(be responsible)*
undertaking activity, agreement *(contract)*, appointment *(position)*, assumption *(adoption)*, bail, burden, business *(affair)*, business *(occupation)*, calling, campaign, charge *(responsibility)*, commitment *(responsibility)*, contract, covenant, coverage *(insurance)*, endeavor, enterprise *(undertaking)*, expedient, indenture, industry *(business)*, job, labor *(work)*, livelihood, maneuver *(tactic)*, mission, occupation *(vocation)*, operation, part *(role)*, plan, pledge *(binding promise)*, post, practice *(professional business)*, proceeding, profession *(vocation)*, project, prosecution *(criminal trial)*, pursuit *(effort to secure)*, pursuit *(occupation)*, role, specialty *(contract)*, transaction, vow, work *(effort)*. SEE MAIN ENTRY
undertakings dealings
undervaluation disregard *(lack of respect)*, understatement
undervalue depreciate, derogate, discommend, discount *(minimize)*, discount *(reduce)*, disparage, humiliate, lessen, minimize, misprize, underestimate
underworker assistant
underworld activity racket
underworld character criminal, outlaw, racketeer
underworld gangster racketeer
underwrite assure *(insure)*, authorize, avouch *(guarantee)*, bond *(secure a debt)*, close *(agree)*, cosign, ensure, guarantee, indorse, promise *(vow)*, sign, sponsor, subscribe *(sign)*, subsidize, vouch. SEE MAIN ENTRY
underwrite again refinance
underwrite against loss insure
underwriter insurer, surety *(guarantor)*
underwriting coverage *(insurance)*
undeserved disproportionate, undue *(excessive)*, unjust
undeserving disproportionate, unworthy
undeserving of censure irreprehensible
undesignated anonymous, unspecified
undesigned fortuitous, inadvertent, random, unexpected, unforeseen, unintentional, unpremeditated, unwitting
undesigned occurrence accident *(chance occurrence)*, quirk *(accident)*
undesigning direct *(forthright)*, ingenuous, simple, straightforward, unaffected *(sincere)*
undesirability bad character, detriment, disqualification *(factor that disqualifies)*, inexpedience
undesirable antipathetic *(distasteful)*, bad *(inferior)*, bad *(offensive)*, delinquent, deplorable, gratuitous *(unwarranted)*, ill-advised, improper, imprudent, inadvisable, inappropriate, inapt, ineligible, inept *(inappropriate)*, inferior *(lower in quality)*, injudicious, inopportune, loathsome, needless, objectionable, repugnant *(exciting aversion)*, sordid, unacceptable, unendurable, unfit, unsatisfactory, unsavory, unsuitable. SEE MAIN ENTRY
undesirableness inexpedience
undesired unacceptable, unsolicited
undesirous averse
undespairing sanguine
undestroyable indelible, indestructible, infallible, noncancellable, permanent, perpetual
undestroyed chronic, extant, intact, inviolate, lasting, live *(existing)*
undestructive nontoxic
undetached interested, one-sided, partisan
undetachment bias, inequity, nepotism, predetermination
undetected blind *(concealed)*, hidden, latent, potential, undisclosed
undetermination ambivalence
undetermined casual, conditional, debatable, disputable, dubious, equivocal, indefinite, irresolute, moot, outstanding *(unresolved)*, pending *(unresolved)*, problematic, provisional, speculative, uncertain *(questionable)*, undecided, unsettled, vague
undeterminedness doubt *(indecision)*
undeveloped deficient, dormant, imperfect, inadequate, inexperienced, juvenile, latent, partial *(relating to a part)*, premature, rudimentary
undeveloped stage embryo
undeviating accurate, boiler plate, certain *(positive)*, comparable *(equivalent)*, consistent, consonant, constant, direct *(straight)*, equal, exact, factual, immutable, industrious, intense, literal, loyal, patient, persistent, pertinacious, purposeful, regular *(conventional)*, relentless, resolute, right *(direct)*, rigid, sedulous, sequacious, stable, steadfast, straightforward, unalterable, undistorted, uniform, unrelenting, unyielding
undeviatingly faithfully, invariably
undevout profane
undexterous inadept
undextrous amateur
undifferentiating indiscriminate
undignified blatant *(obtrusive)*, disreputable, inappropriate, inelegant, unbecoming, unprofessional, unseemly
undiligent negligent
undiluted honest, unadulterated
undiminished complete *(all-embracing)*, gross *(total)*, intact, outright, plenary, whole *(undamaged)*. SEE MAIN ENTRY
undiminished quantity entirety
undiplomatic impolitic, unpolitic
undirected astray, casual, discursive *(digressive)*, fortuitous, haphazard, indiscriminate, random
undiscernable impalpable
undiscernible inconspicuous, indefinite, intangible, nebulous
undiscerning blind *(not discerning)*, cursory, heedless, ill-judged, inadvertent, injudicious, insensible, oblivious, obtuse, perfunctory, promiscuous, unaware
undischarged unpaid
undisciplined capricious, disobedient, disordered, disorderly, inexperienced, intractable, irresponsible, lawless, licentious, uncurbed, unrestrained *(not repressed)*, unversed
undisclosable private *(confidential)*
undisclosed clandestine, covert, esoteric, furtive, hidden, mysterious, personal *(private)*, potential, privy, secret, stealthy, surreptitious, ulterior. SEE MAIN ENTRY
undiscordant consonant
undiscouraged patient, persistent, undaunted
undiscoverability mystery
undiscoverable inapprehensible, indiscernible, inexplicable, inscrutable
undiscovered latent, potential
undiscriminating promiscuous
undisguise bare
undisguised accurate, apparent *(perceptible)*, authentic, bona fide, candid, clear

(apparent), coherent *(clear)*, conspicuous, distinct *(clear)*, evident, explicit, factual, genuine, honest, ingenuous, lucid, manifest, naked *(lacking embellishment)*, obvious, open *(in sight)*, overt, palpable, patent, pellucid, realistic, true *(authentic)*, undistorted, unmistakable
undisguising direct *(forthright)*, honest
undismayed unabashed, undaunted
undispassionate one-sided, partisan
undispassionateness bias, inequity
undisputable indefeasible, sound
undisputed accurate, axiomatic, categorical, certain *(fixed)*, certain *(positive)*, clear *(certain)*, consensual, convincing, definite, definitive, factual, general, resounding, true *(authentic)*, uncontested, uncontroverted, unequivocal, unimpeachable. SEE MAIN ENTRY
undissembling bona fide, candid, honest, straightforward
undissimulating honest
undissolvable inseparable
undissolved solid *(compact)*
undistinctive usual
undistinguished marginal, mediocre, mundane, nondescript, obscure *(faint)*, ordinary, unpretentious, usual
undistorted accurate, authentic, bona fide, candid, direct *(straight)*, distinct *(clear)*, factual, genuine, honest, literal, realistic, sound, straightforward, true *(authentic)*, unadulterated. SEE MAIN ENTRY
undistracted pertinacious, steadfast
undisturbed dispassionate, inviolate, patient, peaceable, phlegmatic, placid, sane, secure *(confident)*, stoical
undiversified uniform
undividable indivisible, inseparable
undivided complete *(all-embracing)*, concurrent *(united)*, gross *(total)*, intact, outright, total, undiminished
undivided attention diligence *(care)*, diligence *(perseverance)*, interest *(concern)*, obsession
undividedly in toto
undividedness entirety, integration *(assimilation)*, whole
undivisible whole *(unified)*
undivulgable private *(confidential)*
undivulged esoteric, hidden, secret, ulterior, undisclosed
undo abolish, abrogate *(annul)*, beat *(defeat)*, betray *(lead astray)*, counteract, denude, disengage, disorganize, disown *(deny the validity)*, dissociate, dissolve *(separate)*, dissolve *(terminate)*, frustrate, invalidate, liberate, overreach, overrule, part *(separate)*, subvert, upset, vitiate. SEE MAIN ENTRY
undoable impracticable, inoperable *(impracticable)*
undogmatic open-minded
undoing annulment, defeasance, defeat, destruction, detriment, disaster, dissolution *(disintegration)*, prostration, reversal
undone irredeemable, irreparable
undoubtable cogent, irrefutable, noncontestable, palpable, real
undoubted absolute *(conclusive)*, axiomatic, certain *(positive)*, clear *(certain)*, cogent, conclusive *(determinative)*, decisive, definitive, uncontested, uncontroverted, undisputed, unimpeachable, unmistakable
undoubtedly admittedly, fairly *(clearly)*
undoubtful certain *(positive)*, indubious
undoubting affirmative, certain *(positive)*, credulous, definite, pertinacious, positive *(confident)*, sanguine, unsuspecting
undramatic insipid, jejune *(dull)*
undrape bare, denude, expose, manifest, unveil
undress denude, expose, unveil
undrilled inexperienced, unversed
undue disproportionate, drastic, excess, excessive, exorbitant, extreme *(exaggerated)*, gratuitous *(unwarranted)*, improper, inadmissible, inapposite, inappropriate, inapt, inept *(inappropriate)*, inordinate, outrageous, prohibitive *(costly)*, redundant, unauthorized, unfit, unreasonable, unseemly, unwarranted, usurious, wrongful. SEE MAIN ENTRY
undue amount overage, plethora
undue delay laches. SEE MAIN ENTRY
undue expansion of currency inflation *(decrease in value of currency)*
undue influence coercion, pressure. SEE MAIN ENTRY
undueness breach, exaggeration, inequity
undulate beat *(pulsate)*, circuitous, oscillate, vacillate
undulated circuitous
undulating circuitous
undulative circuitous
undulatory circuitous, tortuous *(bending)*
unduly arbitrary and capricious. SEE MAIN ENTRY
unduteousness breach, nonperformance
undutiful broken *(unfulfilled)*, disobedient, irresponsible, untrue
undutifulness breach, contempt *(disobedience to the court)*, infidelity, nonperformance
undying chronic, constant, durable, immutable, incessant, indestructible, infallible, infinite, permanent, persistent. SEE MAIN ENTRY
unearned increment gratuity *(present)*
unearth ascertain, betray *(disclose)*, delve, detect, disclose, discover, disinter, educe, expose, ferret, find *(discover)*, locate, manifest, probe, research, reveal, solve, trace *(follow)*
unearthing detection, discovery
unearthly intangible, nonsubstantial *(not sturdy)*, uncanny
unease pain, scruple
uneasiness apprehension *(fear)*, concern *(interest)*, distress *(anguish)*, embarrassment, fear, misgiving, qualm, scruple, trepidation
uneasiness of mind dissatisfaction
uneasy restive, unsettled
uneconomical improvident, prodigal, prolix
unedited intact
uneducated unversed
uneffective unqualified *(not competent)*
unelaborate unpretentious
unelapsed period unexpired term
unelevated insipid
unembarrassed brazen, unabashed
unembellished naked *(lacking embellishment)*, simple
unembodied incorporeal
unembroidered honest, literal, undistorted
unemotional clinical, cold-blooded, controlled *(restrained)*, dispassionate, inexpressive, insusceptible *(uncaring)*, phlegmatic, unresponsive. SEE MAIN ENTRY
unemotional consideration common sense
unemphatic insipid
unemployable impracticable
unemployed idle, inactive, otiose, truant, vacant. SEE MAIN ENTRY
unemployment disuse, inaction
unemployment insurance SEE MAIN ENTRY
unempowered inadequate, incapable, ineffectual, powerless, unauthorized
unenclosed open *(accessible)*
unencumbered exempt, free *(relieved from a burden)*, immune, independent, unbound, unrestrained *(not in custody)*. SEE MAIN ENTRY
unendangered safe
unended live *(existing)*
unending chronic, continual *(perpetual)*, continuous, direct *(uninterrupted)*, durable, far reaching, immutable, incessant, infinite, myriad, open-ended, permanent, perpetual, protracted, rife, unlimited
unendorsed unauthorized, unofficial
unendorsed purchase caveat emptor
unendowed disabled *(deprived of legal right)*, disabled *(made incapable)*, inadept, powerless
unendowment incompetence
unendurable insufferable, intolerable, loathsome, objectionable, obnoxious, odious, offensive *(offending)*, oppressive, painful. SEE MAIN ENTRY
unenduring ephemeral, temporary, transient, transitory
unenforceable void *(invalid)*
unengaged unemployed
unenlightened blind *(not discerning)*, ill-judged, incognizant, insensible, opaque, unacquainted, unaware
unenlightenment ignorance, nescience
unenlivened jejune *(dull)*, lifeless *(dull)*, nondescript, pedestrian
unenslaved free *(enjoying civil liberty)*, independent, sovereign *(independent)*
unentangled free *(not restricted)*
unenterprising careful, indolent, lax, lifeless *(dull)*
unentertaining insipid, jejune *(dull)*, lifeless *(dull)*, pedestrian, prosaic
unenthralled free *(enjoying civil liberty)*, independent
unenthusiastic disinclined, lifeless *(dull)*, nonchalant, perfunctory
unentitled impermissible, ineligible, unauthorized, unwarranted
unequal broken *(interrupted)*, disparate, disproportionate, heterogeneous, incommensurate, incompetent, insufficient, partial *(biased)*, peculiar *(distinctive)*, unconscionable, unfair, unjust. SEE MAIN ENTRY
unequal to deficient, inadept, inadequate
unequaled absolute *(ideal)*, best, cardinal *(outstanding)*, leading *(ranking first)*, noteworthy, paramount, premium, priceless, prime *(most valuable)*, professional *(stellar)*, rare, select, singular, superior *(excellent)*, superlative, unapproachable, unique, unprecedented, unusual
unequalled extraordinary, inestimable, invaluable
unequalness difference
unequipped incapable, incompetent, ineligible, powerless, unfit, unqualified *(not competent)*

unequivocal absolute *(conclusive)*, axiomatic, categorical, certain *(positive)*, clear *(apparent)*, clear *(certain)*, cogent, cognizable, coherent *(clear)*, conclusive *(determinative)*, constant, credible, decisive, definite, demonstrable, distinct *(clear)*, dogmatic, evident, explicit, express, incontestable, incontrovertible, indubious, irrefutable, lucid, official, outright, palpable, peremptory *(absolute)*, positive *(incontestable)*, precise, reliable, unambiguous, unmistakable, unrefutable, vehement. SEE MAIN ENTRY
unequivocally fairly *(clearly)*, purely *(positively)*
unequivocalness belief *(state of mind)*, certainty, certitude, incontestability, surety *(certainty)*
uneradicated lasting
unerasable chronic, indelible, permanent, perpetual
unerased lasting
unerring absolute *(conclusive)*, accurate, actual, certain *(fixed)*, certain *(positive)*, clean, clear *(certain)*, definite, effective *(efficient)*, exact, factual, incorruptible, inculpable, infallible, irreprehensible, literal, moral, positive *(incontestable)*, precise, reliable, secure *(sound)*, solid *(sound)*, strict, unblemished. SEE MAIN ENTRY
unerringly faithfully
unerroneous actual, factual, real
unescorted solitary
unessayed unsettled
unessential collateral *(immaterial)*, expendable, extraneous, extrinsic, gratuitous *(unwarranted)*, immaterial, inapposite, inconsequential, inconsiderable, irrelevant, minor, needless, negligible, nonessential, null *(insignificant)*, petty, remote *(small)*, secondary, slight, superfluous, supplementary, unnecessary. SEE MAIN ENTRY
unestablished inconclusive, unconfirmed, unfounded
unethical dishonest, disingenuous, disreputable, fraudulent, immoral, machiavellian, profligate *(corrupt)*, unconscionable, unprofessional, unscrupulous. SEE MAIN ENTRY
unethical use exploitation
unevasible necessary *(inescapable)*
unevasive clear *(apparent)*, cognizable
uneven broken *(interrupted)*, disordered, disorderly, disparate, disproportionate, inequitable, one-sided, partial *(biased)*, sporadic, unequal *(unequivalent)*, unfair, unpredictable, variable
unevenness diversity, flaw, incoherence, inequality, irregularity
uneventful mundane, unavailing
unevident impalpable, inconspicuous, ulterior, unclear
unexact indefinite
unexacted unclaimed
unexacting casual, flexible
unexaggerated authentic, bona fide, exact, factual, honest, literal, naked *(lacking embellishment)*, sound, true *(authentic)*, undistorted
unexalted mundane
unexamined perfunctory
unexampled extraordinary, original *(creative)*, peculiar *(curious)*, portentous *(eliciting amazement)*, prodigious *(amazing)*, rare, renowned, singular, special, uncommon, unique, unprecedented
unexcelled absolute *(ideal)*, cardinal *(outstanding)*, leading *(ranking first)*, paramount, professional *(stellar)*, select, superior *(excellent)*, superlative, unapproachable
unexceptionability admissibility
unexceptionable admissible, clean, irreprehensible, mediocre, unimpeachable, unobjectionable
unexceptional average *(standard)*, fair *(satisfactory)*, familiar *(customary)*, nondescript, normal *(regular)*, ordinary, regular *(conventional)*, typical, usual
unexceptionality mediocrity
unexcercised unversed
unexcessiveness temperance
unexcitable controlled *(restrained)*, peaceable, phlegmatic
unexcited dispassionate, nonchalant, peaceable, phlegmatic, placid, unaffected *(uninfluenced)*
unexciting insipid, jejune *(dull)*, mediocre, nondescript, ordinary, trite
unexclusive comprehensive
unexcused delay laches
unexecuted executory, inchoate
unexempt from actionable, subject *(exposed)*
unexercised inactive
unexisting devoid, nonexistent
unexpectant unsuspecting
unexpected coincidental, fortuitous, impulsive *(rash)*, nonconforming, original *(creative)*, peculiar *(curious)*, precipitate, unanticipated, unforeseeable, unforeseen, unintentional, unprecedented, unpredictable, unusual, unwitting. SEE MAIN ENTRY
unexpected event bombshell, surprise
unexpected happening emergency
unexpected misfortune accident *(chance occurrence)*
unexpected occurrence accident *(chance occurrence)*, happenstance, surprise
unexpectedness chance *(possibility)*
unexpended net
unexpired term SEE MAIN ENTRY
unexplainable inapprehensible, inexplicable, mysterious, undefinable
unexplained dubious, equivocal, hidden, mysterious, undisclosed
unexplained delay laches
unexplicit impalpable, unclear
unexplored unsettled
unexplored ground mystery
unexposed blind *(concealed)*, hidden, immune, latent, potential, safe, undisclosed
unexpressed implicit, indirect, potential, tacit, ulterior, undisclosed
unexpressive mute
unexpurgated gross *(total)*, intact, lurid, salacious
unextravagant reasonable *(fair)*
unextreme reasonable *(fair)*
unfabricated authentic, factual, genuine, honest, true *(authentic)*
unfacile inadept, inept *(incompetent)*
unfactual inaccurate, incorrect, lying
unfactualness error
unfaded intact, undiminished
unfading chronic, durable, indelible, indestructible, infallible, live *(existing)*, permanent, perpetual
unfailing certain *(fixed)*, certain *(positive)*, credible, definite, dependable, durable, faithful *(loyal)*, inevitable, infallible, lasting, live *(existing)*, loyal, permanent, perpetual, persistent, reliable, secure *(sound)*, solid *(sound)*, stable, staunch, steadfast, true *(loyal)*, unremitting
unfair inequitable, iniquitous, one-sided, partial *(biased)*, sinister, unconscionable, unequal *(unjust)*, unethical, unjust, unreasonable, unscrupulous, unwarranted, wrongful. SEE MAIN ENTRY
unfair action injustice
unfair choice dilemma
unfair judgment misjudgment
unfair prejudice SEE MAIN ENTRY
unfairly call to account frame *(charge falsely)*
unfairness bad faith, discrimination *(bigotry)*, grievance, inequality, inequity, injustice, misjudgment, nepotism, prejudice *(injury)*, wrong
unfaith bad faith
unfaithful broken *(unfulfilled)*, derelict *(negligent)*, dishonest, disobedient, faithless, false *(disloyal)*, fraudulent, perfidious, recreant, untrue, untrustworthy
unfaithfulness adultery, bad faith, breach, dereliction, disloyalty, infidelity
unfaithworthiness bad faith
unfaithworthy irresponsible, precarious
unfaked authentic, bona fide, genuine, honest, undistorted, veridical
unfallacious actual, real, true *(authentic)*
unfallen blameless, irreprehensible
unfalse actual, credible, true *(loyal)*
unfaltering continuous, definite, diligent, direct *(uninterrupted)*, industrious, inexorable, infallible, patient, persistent, pertinacious, purposeful, relentless, resolute, sedulous, serious *(devoted)*, stable, staunch, steadfast, undaunted
unfamiliar extraordinary, foreign, incognizant, inexperienced, inexplicable, noteworthy, novel, peculiar *(curious)*, prodigious *(amazing)*, rare, recondite, special, unaccustomed, unacquainted, uncanny, uncommon, unprecedented, unusual, unversed
unfamiliar with unaware
unfamiliarity ignorance, insentience
unfamiliarly particularly
unfashionable deviant, eccentric, nonconforming, obsolete, original *(creative)*, outdated, outmoded, unorthodox
unfasten detach, disencumber, disengage, disentangle, disjoint, free, liberate, remove *(eliminate)*, sever
unfastened discrete, free *(not restricted)*, insecure, moving *(in motion)*, open *(unclosed)*, unbound
unfathomability mystery
unfathomable complex, inapprehensible, inarticulate, incomprehensible, indefinable, indeterminate, inexpressive, innumerable, inscrutable, myriad, mysterious, opaque, profound *(intense)*, unlimited
unfathomableness mystery, opacity
unfavorable adverse *(negative)*, averse, bleak *(not favorable)*, deleterious, derogatory, disadvantageous, disastrous, harmful, inadvisable, inapposite, inauspicious, inimical, inopportune, lamentable, noxious, prejudicial, regrettable, sinister, unpropitious, unsatisfactory, unsuitable, untimely. SEE MAIN ENTRY
unfavorable circumstance disadvantage
unfavorable remark stricture
unfavorable to health insalubrious, peccant *(unhealthy)*
unfavorable verdict conviction *(finding of guilt)*
unfavorableness disadvantage

unfavorably known notorious
unfearing unabashed, undaunted
unfeasable insuperable
unfeasibility impossibility
unfeasible impossible, impracticable, inoperable *(impracticable)*, insurmountable, unattainable
unfeeling brutal, callous, cold-blooded, cruel, dispassionate, harsh, insensible, insusceptible *(uncaring)*, lifeless *(dead)*, lifeless *(dull)*, malevolent, malicious, nonchalant, obdurate, obtuse, perfunctory, phlegmatic, relentless, ruthless, severe, torpid, unaffected *(uninfluenced)*, unresponsive
unfeelingness brutality, ingratitude, insentience
unfeigned authentic, bona fide, genuine, honest, naive, real, straightforward, true *(authentic)*
unfeigning direct *(forthright)*, genuine, honest, unaffected *(sincere)*
unfenced open *(accessible)*
unfertile barren, lifeless *(dull)*, otiose
unfetter break *(separate)*, disencumber, disengage, disentangle, disenthrall, extricate, free, liberate, parole, release, rescue
unfettered clear *(unencumbered)*, free *(not restricted)*, independent, lawless, unbound, unrestrained *(not in custody)*, unrestrained *(not repressed)*, unrestricted
unfettering freedom, liberation, release
unficticious veridical
unfictitious authentic, genuine, honest, true *(authentic)*, undistorted
unfigurative literal
unfilled available, insatiable, vacant, vacuous, void *(empty)*
unfilled place access *(opening)*
unfinalized inchoate, partial *(relating to a part)*
unfinished defective, deficient, executory, imperfect, inchoate, insufficient, interim, outstanding *(unresolved)*, partial *(part)*, partial *(relating to a part)*, rudimentary, semi
unfirm insubstantial
unfit amateur, bad *(inferior)*, bad *(offensive)*, detrimental, disabled *(deprived of legal right)*, disabled *(made incapable)*, disqualify, faulty, ill-advised, improper, inadept, inadequate, inadmissible, inapplicable, inapposite, inappropriate, inapt, incapable, incompetent, incongruous, ineligible, inept *(inappropriate)*, injudicious, inopportune, insufficient, powerless, unable, unbecoming, undesirable, undue *(excessive)*, unqualified *(not competent)*, unsatisfactory, unseemly, unsuitable, unworthy. SEE MAIN ENTRY
unfitness disability *(legal disqualification)*, disability *(physical inability)*, disqualification *(factor that disqualifies)*, illegality, impotence, impropriety, inability, incapacity, incompetence, incongruity, inexpedience
unfitted disabled *(made incapable)*, inadept, inadequate, inadmissible, inapplicable, inappropriate, incompetent, ineligible, insufficient, unbecoming
unfittedness disqualification *(factor that disqualifies)*
unfitting disproportionate, improper, inadvisable, inapplicable, inapposite, inappropriate, inapt, incongruous, ineligible, inept *(inappropriate)*, unfit, unprofessional, unseemly, unsuitable
unfittingness impropriety, incongruity, inexpedience
unfix disengage, free
unfixable irremediable
unfixed casual, debatable, disputable, free *(not restricted)*, indeterminate, irresolute, pending *(unresolved)*, unbound, undecided, unsettled, unspecified
unflagging faithful *(diligent)*, industrious, infallible, patient, permanent, persistent, pertinacious, purposeful, sedulous, stable, steadfast. SEE MAIN ENTRY
unflappable nonchalant
unflattering calumnious, derogatory, harsh, pejorative
unfledged inexperienced, jejune *(lacking maturity)*, juvenile
unfleshly incorporeal, intangible
unflimsy strong
unflinching heroic, indomitable, patient, pertinacious, purposeful, relentless, resolute, spartan, stable, steadfast, unabashed, undaunted
unflowing stagnant
unfluctuating equal
unflustered phlegmatic
unfold bare, betray *(disclose)*, clarify, construe *(translate)*, crystallize, denude, deploy, develop, disabuse, disclose, educe, elucidate, evolve, expand, explain, explicate, expose, exposit, expound, find *(discover)*, interpret, manifest, produce *(offer to view)*, recount, reveal, simplify *(clarify)*, solve, spread, unveil
unfold the meaning of explicate
unfold the sense of explicate
unfolding denouement, detection, development *(progression)*, disclosure *(act of disclosing)*, explanation, growth *(evolution)*, happening, manifestation
unfoldment disclosure *(act of disclosing)*
unfool disabuse
unforbidden admissible, allowable, allowed, permissible, unrestricted
unforced ingenuous, nonpartisan, spontaneous, voluntary, willing *(uncompelled)*
unforeseeable unpredictable. SEE MAIN ENTRY
unforeseen fortuitous, haphazard, unanticipated, unexpected, unintentional. SEE MAIN ENTRY
unforeseen accident casualty
unforeseen adversity misfortune
unforeseen circumstance complication
unforeseen circumstances SEE MAIN ENTRY
unforeseen condition emergency
unforeseen contingency surprise
unforeseen event quirk *(accident)*, surprise
unforeseen occurrence accident *(chance occurrence)*, contingency, emergency, happenstance, quirk *(accident)*, surprise
unforewarned unaware
unforfeitable inalienable
unforgettable indelible, notable, noteworthy, outstanding *(prominent)*, remarkable, special
unforgivable inexcusable, inexpiable, peccant *(culpable)*, unjustifiable
unforgiving callous, implacable, irreconcilable, obdurate, relentless, remorseless, resentful, ruthless, unrelenting, vindictive
unforgoable obligatory
unforgotten indelible
unformed premature
unforthcoming noncommittal
unfortified disabled *(made incapable)*, helpless *(defenseless)*, indefensible, open *(accessible)*, powerless, untenable
unfortunate adverse *(negative)*, deplorable, derelict *(abandoned)*, dire, harmful, inopportune, lamentable, ominous, regrettable, unfavorable, unpropitious, unsuitable. SEE MAIN ENTRY
unfortunate accident casualty
unfortunate consequence cost *(penalty)*
unfortunate event accident *(misfortune)*, disaster
unfortunate occurence casualty
unfortunate occurrence misfortune
unfortunate person victim
unfounded baseless, delusive, erroneous, fallacious, false *(inaccurate)*, fictitious, gratuitous *(unwarranted)*, ill-founded, illogical, inaccurate, insubstantial, sophistic, specious, unsupported, untrue, unwarranted. SEE MAIN ENTRY
unfounded conclusion non sequitur
unfounded story canard
unfrequent infrequent
unfrequented private *(secluded)*, remote *(secluded)*
unfriended derelict *(abandoned)*
unfriendliness alienation *(estrangement)*, estrangement, ill will, incompatibility *(difference)*, ostracism, rancor
unfriendly adverse *(hostile)*, antipathetic *(oppositional)*, contentious, inimical, malevolent, perverse, pugnacious, recusant, unfavorable, vicious, virulent
unfriendly feeling ill will
unfrightened secure *(confident)*, undaunted
unfrock denude
unfrugal improvident, prodigal
unfruitful barren, disadvantageous, futile, ineffective, ineffectual, nugatory, otiose, unproductive
unfruitfulness inefficacy
unfulfilled deficient, executory
unfulfillment nonperformance
unfulfillment of an assignment delinquency *(failure of duty)*
unfulfillment of duty delinquency *(failure of duty)*
unfunctional impracticable
unfurl bare, deploy, spread
unfurled open *(unclosed)*
unfurnished deficient, void *(empty)*
unfussy inaccurate
ungainly incompetent, inelegant, inept *(incompetent)*, uncouth
ungallant perverse
ungallantness disrespect
ungarbled honest, literal
ungarrulous laconic, taciturn
ungathered outstanding *(unpaid)*
ungenerous illiberal, parsimonious, penurious
ungenteel blatant *(obtrusive)*, disorderly, ignoble, inelegant, presumptuous, unbecoming, unseemly
ungentle brutal, caustic, disorderly, harsh, hot-blooded, scathing, severe
ungentlemanlike disorderly
ungentlemanliness disrespect
ungentlemanly blatant *(obtrusive)*, disorderly, illiberal, uncouth
ungenuine artificial, assumed *(feigned)*, bogus, dishonest, disingenuous, fraudulent, imitation, mendacious, spurious

ungenuineness bad faith
ungermane alien *(unrelated)*, inapplicable, inapposite, inappropriate, inconsequential, nonessential, peripheral, unrelated
ungerminating barren
ungettable unattainable
ungifted amateur, inadept
ungiving insusceptible *(uncaring)*
unglue disengage
ungodly mundane, profane
ungovernable contumacious, disobedient, froward, hot-blooded, incorrigible, indomitable, insubordinate, intractable, lawless, obdurate, perverse, recalcitrant, restive, uncontrollable, unruly, unyielding
ungoverned disorderly, lawless, licentious, uncurbed, unrestrained *(not repressed)*
ungraceful inelegant, provincial
ungracious abusive, blatant *(obtrusive)*, harsh, impertinent *(insolent)*, invidious, offensive *(offending)*, perverse, severe
ungraciousness disrespect
ungratefulness ingratitude
ungratifying nonsubstantial *(not sufficient)*, unsatisfactory
ungrounded baseless, erroneous, fallacious, false *(inaccurate)*, ill-founded, illogical, incorrect, insubstantial, nonsubstantial *(not sturdy)*, sophistic, unfounded, unsound *(fallacious)*
ungrudging benevolent, dispassionate, liberal *(generous)*, magnanimous, philanthropic
ungrudgingness philanthropy
unguaranteed purchase caveat emptor
unguarded careless, helpless *(defenseless)*, improvident, imprudent, indefensible, lax, open *(accessible)*, perfunctory, unaware, unsuspecting, untenable, vulnerable. SEE MAIN ENTRY
unguardedness danger
unguided astray, haphazard, ill-judged, random
unguilty blameless, clean
unhabitual unusual
unhabituated inexperienced, unaccustomed
unhallow pollute
unhallowed mundane, profane
unhamper disencumber, disengage, disentangle, extricate
unhampered clear *(unencumbered)*, free *(not restricted)*, unrestrained *(not in custody)*, unrestrained *(not repressed)*
unhandsome unbecoming, unseemly
unhandy impracticable, incompetent, inept *(incompetent)*
unhappiness damper *(depressant)*, dissatisfaction, distress *(anguish)*, pessimism
unhappiness with one's lot dissatisfaction
unhappy bitter *(reproachful)*, deplorable, despondent, disconsolate, lamentable, lugubrious, pessimistic, regrettable
unharmable secure *(free from danger)*
unharmed intact, inviolate, safe
unharmonious hostile, inapplicable, inapposite, inappropriate
unharmoniousness conflict, discord
unharness disencumber, extricate, parole
unharnessing release
unhasty deliberate
unhazarded safe
unhazardous harmless, nontoxic, reliable
unhealable chronic
unhealthful deleterious, insalubrious, pernicious, pestilent
unhealthiness disease
unhealthy deadly, deleterious, detrimental, disadvantageous, harmful, inadvisable, insalubrious, lethal, noxious, pernicious, pestilent, unsound *(not strong)*
unhealthy air air pollution
unhealthy situation peril
unheard diffident, ineffable
unheard of extraordinary, implausible, ludicrous, noteworthy, novel, original *(creative)*, peculiar *(curious)*, portentous *(eliciting amazement)*, prodigious *(amazing)*, uncanny, uncommon, unprecedented, unusual. SEE MAIN ENTRY
unhearing heedless, insensible
unheeded perfunctory
unheedful derelict *(negligent)*, heedless, inadvertent, negligent, perfunctory
unheedfulness disregard *(lack of respect)*, disregard *(unconcern)*, neglect
unheeding derelict *(negligent)*, heedless, inadvertent, lax, negligent, oblivious, perfunctory, reckless, remiss, unaware
unhelpful detrimental, disadvantageous, inadvisable, perverse
unheralded undisclosed, unexpected, unforeseen
unheroic peccable
unhesitating categorical, certain *(positive)*, clear *(certain)*, decisive, definite, immediate *(at once)*, positive *(confident)*, prompt, purposeful, secure *(confident)*, stable, steadfast
unheterodox orthodox
unhidden comprehensible, conspicuous, distinct *(clear)*, evident, manifest, obvious, open *(in sight)*, overt, palpable, patent, pellucid, perceivable, perceptible, scrutable
unhindered clear *(unencumbered)*, free *(not restricted)*, independent, unbound, uncurbed, unrestrained *(not in custody)*, unrestrained *(not repressed)*
unhinge confuse *(bewilder)*, discompose, disjoint, impair, luxate, obsess
unhinged lunatic
unhistorical fictitious
unhitch disengage
unholiness blasphemy
unholy mundane, profane
unhook disengage
unhopeful despondent
unhostile amicable, nonmilitant, propitious
unhouse displace *(remove)*
unhurried deliberate
unhurriedness deliberation
unhurt intact, inviolate, safe, whole *(undamaged)*
unhygienic insalubrious, peccant *(unhealthy)*
unicus singular, sole, unique
unidealism pragmatism
unidealistic mercenary, pragmatic, realistic
unidentical different, dissimilar, diverse
unidentifiable nondescript
unidentified anonymous
unification accession *(annexation)*, affiliation *(amalgamation)*, centralization, coalescence, coalition, combination, confederacy *(compact)*, consolidation, federation, incorporation *(blend)*, incorporation *(formation of a business entity)*, integration *(amalgamation)*, joinder, league, meeting *(encounter)*, merger, pool, relationship *(connection)*, sodality, union *(unity)*
unified coadunate, collective, concurrent *(united)*, conjoint, consonant, intact, joint, mutual *(collective)*
unifier connection *(fastening)*
uniform boiler plate, clothe, coequal, comparable *(equivalent)*, concordant, consistent, consonant, equal, identical, proportionate, regular *(orderly)*, repeated, routine, same, similar, systematic. SEE MAIN ENTRY
uniformity adjustment, agreement *(concurrence)*, arrangement *(ordering)*, array *(order)*, conciliation, conformity *(agreement)*, consensus, constant, correspondence *(similarity)*, identity *(similarity)*, method, parity, regularity, resemblance, semblance, union *(unity)*. SEE MAIN ENTRY
uniformly invariably
unify amalgamate, cohere *(adhere)*, collect *(gather)*, combine *(join together)*, conjoin, consolidate *(strengthen)*, conspire, crystallize, desegregate, federalize *(associate)*, federate, include, join *(bring together)*, merge, organize *(unionize)*, pool, unite
unilateral ex parte *(adjective)*, ex parte *(adverb)*. SEE MAIN ENTRY
unimaginable implausible, impossible, incomprehensible, incredible, ineffable, infeasible, peculiar *(curious)*, prodigious *(amazing)*, unbelievable
unimaginative lifeless *(dull)*, mundane, obtuse, ordinary, parochial, pedestrian, prosaic, sequacious, stale, trite, usual
unimagined actual, factual, real, sound, true *(authentic)*
unimitated distinct *(distinguished from others)*, distinctive, genuine, individual, noteworthy, original *(creative)*, peculiar *(distinctive)*, uncommon, unique
unimitative eccentric, special
unimpaired complete *(all-embracing)*, intact, inviolate, safe, undiminished, whole *(undamaged)*
unimparted undisclosed
unimpassioned dispassionate, insipid, insusceptible *(uncaring)*, jejune *(dull)*, languid, lifeless *(dull)*, nonchalant, open-minded, phlegmatic, placid, prosaic, stoical
unimpeachability certainty, certification *(certainness)*, certitude, incontestability
unimpeachable absolute *(conclusive)*, accurate, actual, axiomatic, believable, blameless, certain *(positive)*, clean, clear *(certain)*, conclusive *(determinative)*, definite, definitive, demonstrable, ethical, factual, genuine, inappealable, incontestable, incontrovertible, incorruptible, infallible, irrebuttable, irrefutable, irreprehensible, just, laudable, law-abiding, loyal, meritorious, not guilty, official, positive *(incontestable)*, provable, real, reputable, secure *(sound)*, solid *(sound)*, sound, true *(authentic)*, unalienable, undeniable, unobjectionable, unrefutable, upright. SEE MAIN ENTRY
unimpeached inculpable
unimpeded exempt, free *(not restricted)*, free *(relieved from a burden)*, passable, uncurbed, unrestrained *(not in custody)*
unimperiled secure *(free from danger)*
unimportance immateriality, inconsequence, insignificance, mediocrity
unimportant collateral *(immaterial)*, expendable, frivolous, futile, immaterial, inapposite, inappreciable, inconsequential, inconsiderable, inferior *(lower in position)*,

insubstantial, irrelevant, mediocre, minimal, minor, negligible, nominal, nonessential, nugatory, null *(insignificant)*, paltry, peripheral, petty, remote *(small)*, secondary, slight, tenuous, trivial, unessential, unnecessary
unimposing diffident, unobtrusive
unimpressed callous, nonchalant, unaffected *(uninfluenced)*
unimpressible callous, cold-blooded, dispassionate, inexorable, insusceptible *(uncaring)*, stoical, unresponsive, unyielding
unimpressionable callous, clinical, dispassionate, unresponsive
unimpressive poor *(inferior in quality)*, usual
unimprison free
unimprovable irremediable
uninclined disinclined, reluctant
unincreased undiminished
unindebted compensatory, solvent
unindoctrinated unversed
uninduced nonpartisan
uninfluenceable impervious, unresponsive, unyielding
uninfluenced dispassionate, fair *(just)*, impartial, impervious, independent, judicial, just, liberal *(broad minded)*, loyal, neutral, nonpartisan, objective, open-minded, unbiased, unprejudiced
uninfluential ineffective, ineffectual, minor, null *(insignificant)*, powerless
uninfluential group minority *(outnumbered group)*
uninformed blind *(not discerning)*, incognizant, inexperienced, unacquainted, unaware, unversed, unwitting
uninformedness nescience
uninhabited devoid, solitary, unsettled, vacant, void *(empty)*
uninhibited candid, intemperate, uncurbed
uninhibitedness freedom, latitude, liberty
uniniquitous blameless
uninitiated incompetent, inexperienced, unaccustomed, unversed
uninjured intact, inviolate, safe, unblemished
uninjurious harmless, innocuous, nontoxic, salutary
uninspired insipid, jejune *(dull)*, languid, lifeless *(dull)*, mundane, perfunctory, unaffected *(uninfluenced)*
uninspiring insipid, jejune *(dull)*, lifeless *(dull)*, mediocre, pedestrian, prosaic
uninstructed incognizant
unintellectualism illiteracy
unintellectuality ignorance
unintelligence ignorance, nescience
unintelligent fatuous, irrational, obtuse, opaque, vacuous
unintelligibility ambiguity, incoherence, opacity
unintelligible ambiguous, disconnected, equivocal, inapprehensible, inarticulate, incomprehensible, indefinite, indistinct, inexplicable, inexpressive, inscrutable, mysterious, nebulous, obscure *(abstruse)*, opaque, recondite, uncertain *(ambiguous)*, unclear
unintelligible talk jargon *(unintelligible language)*
unintelligibleness obscuration
unintended fortuitous, haphazard, inadvertent, involuntary, unexpected, unforeseeable, unforeseen, unintentional, unpremeditated, unwitting
unintentional fortuitous, haphazard, inadvertent, involuntary, spontaneous, unexpected, unpremeditated, unwitting. SEE MAIN ENTRY
unintentional happening contingency
unintentional homicide manslaughter
unintentional mistake oversight *(carelessness)*
unintentional murder manslaughter
unintentional omission oversight *(carelessness)*
unintentionality quirk *(accident)*
unintentionally unknowingly
uninterested cold-blooded, derelict *(negligent)*, insusceptible *(uncaring)*, languid, lax, nonchalant, perfunctory, unresponsive
uninteresting insipid, lifeless *(dull)*, mediocre, mundane, nondescript, pedestrian, prosaic, stale, usual
unintermitted continual *(connected)*
unintermitted continuance perpetuity
unintermittedness continuity
unintermittent continuous, incessant, unremitting
unintermitting chronic, continuous, durable, incessant, relentless
uninterrupted chronic, consecutive, constant, continual *(connected)*, continuous, durable, incessant, permanent, perpetual, progressive *(going forward)*, unremitting
uninterrupted connection continuity
uninterrupted existence perpetuity
uninterrupted in course consecutive
uninterruptedness continuity, perpetuity
uninterruption continuity
uninured unaccustomed
uninvented genuine, honest
uninventive lifeless *(dull)*, pedestrian
uninvited unsolicited
uninvited attendance intrusion
uninvited entry intrusion
uninviting antipathetic *(distasteful)*, bleak *(severely simple)*, objectionable, repulsive, unacceptable, undesirable, unsavory
uninvolved clean, cognizable, dispassionate, irreprehensible, neutral, noncommittal, not guilty, perfunctory, simple
union accession *(annexation)*, adhesion *(affixing)*, adhesion *(loyalty)*, affiliation *(amalgamation)*, assemblage, association *(alliance)*, cabal, cartel, centralization, chain *(nexus)*, chamber *(body)*, coaction, coalescence, coalition, cohabitation *(married state)*, coherence, collusion, combination, compatibility, composition *(makeup)*, conciliation, confederacy *(compact)*, conformity *(agreement)*, conjunction, connection *(abutment)*, connection *(fastening)*, consensus, consolidation, consortium *(business cartel)*, contact *(association)*, contact *(touching)*, contribution *(participation)*, cooperative, corporation, coverture, federation, incorporation *(blend)*, incorporation *(formation of a business entity)*, institute, integration *(amalgamation)*, intersection, joinder, league, marriage *(intimate relationship)*, matrimony, meeting *(encounter)*, melange, merger, nexus, pact, pool, reconciliation, relationship *(connection)*, session, society, sodality, syndicate. SEE MAIN ENTRY
union of action coaction
union of factions coalition
unionize consolidate *(unite)*, federalize *(associate)*, federate
unions ties
unique certain *(particular)*, different, distinct *(distinguished from others)*, distinctive, eccentric, exclusive *(singular)*, extraordinary, individual, inestimable, irregular *(not usual)*, nonconforming, noteworthy, novel, only *(sole)*, original *(creative)*, particular *(individual)*, particular *(specific)*, peculiar *(distinctive)*, portentous *(eliciting amazement)*, prodigious *(amazing)*, rare, remarkable, renowned, scarce, several *(separate)*, singular, sole, special, specific, unaccustomed, unapproachable, uncommon, unprecedented, unusual. SEE MAIN ENTRY
unique feature distinction *(difference)*
uniquely particularly
uniqueness characteristic, difference, distinction *(difference)*, identity *(individuality)*, irregularity, nonconformity, particularity, personality, specialty *(distinctive mark)*
unirritable dispassionate
unison accordance *(compact)*, agreement *(concurrence)*, concert, consensus, consent, rapprochement, synchronism, union *(unity)*
unisonant consonant
unisonous consonant
unit band, component, entity, factor *(ingredient)*, ingredient, item, member *(constituent part)*, organ. SEE MAIN ENTRY
unit of being entity
unit of composition component, ingredient
unite accumulate *(amass)*, adhere *(fasten)*, affiliate, affix, aggregate, agree *(comply)*, amalgamate, annex *(add)*, attach *(join)*, bond *(hold together)*, border *(approach)*, call *(summon)*, cement, cohere *(adhere)*, coincide *(concur)*, collect *(gather)*, combine *(act in concert)*, combine *(join together)*, commingle, compile, concentrate *(consolidate)*, congregate, conjoin, connect *(join together)*, conspire, contact *(touch)*, convene, converge, correspond *(be equivalent)*, desegregate, federalize *(associate)*, federate, include, incorporate *(include)*, involve *(participate)*, join *(associate oneself with)*, join *(bring together)*, lock, meet, merge, organize *(unionize)*, pool, reconcile, relate *(establish a connection)*. SEE MAIN ENTRY
unite by compact federate
unite efforts concur *(agree)*
unite efforts with participate
unite for a common purpose organize *(unionize)*
unite in a federation federate
unite in a league federalize *(associate)*, federate
unite ones efforts cooperate
unite with concur *(agree)*, cooperate, participate, side
united affiliated, associated, attached *(annexed)*, coadunate, coherent *(joined)*, cohesive *(sticking)*, collective, composite, compound, concerted, concordant, concurrent *(united)*, conglomerate, conjoint, conjugal, consensual, federal, harmonious, indivisible, infrangible, inseparable, interrelated, joint, mutual *(collective)*, nuptial, solid *(compact)*. SEE MAIN ENTRY
united action coaction, conjunction, synergy

united body faction
united front merger
uniting accession *(annexation)*, concerted, concordant, concrescence
unity accordance *(compact)*, adhesion *(affixing)*, affiliation *(amalgamation)*, agreement *(concurrence)*, cartel, centralization, coalition, coherence, compatibility, complex *(development)*, concert, conciliation, concordance, consent, identity *(similarity)*, peace, propinquity *(similarity)*, rapprochement, relationship *(connection)*, totality, uniformity. SEE MAIN ENTRY
unius diei ephemeral
universal boiler plate, collective, common *(shared)*, competitive *(open)*, comprehensive, familiar *(customary)*, general, generic, nonsectarian, prevailing *(current)*, prevalent, proverbial, rife, total, ubiquitous, uniform, unlimited, usual, whole *(unified)*. SEE MAIN ENTRY
universal cure panacea
universal forgiveness of past offenses amnesty
universal principle doctrine
universal remedy panacea
universality generality *(bulk)*, whole
universalize generalize
universally always *(without exception)*
universally known common *(customary)*
universally recognized familiar *(customary)*, famous, household *(familiar)*
universe generalize
university institute
universus total
univocal definite, unambiguous
unjaundiced impartial, neutral, objective, open-minded, reasonable *(rational)*, receptive, unbiased, undistorted, unprejudiced
unjealous dispassionate
unjoined apart, disconnected, discrete, disjunctive *(tending to disjoin)*, individual
unjoint disjoint, displace *(remove)*, luxate
unjoyful pessimistic
unjust delinquent *(guilty of a misdeed)*, inequitable, iniquitous, one-sided, partial *(biased)*, peccant *(culpable)*, prejudicial, severe, unconscionable, unfair, unjustifiable, unreasonable, unscrupulous, unwarranted, wrongful. SEE MAIN ENTRY
unjust acquisition graft
unjust action injustice
unjust burden imposition *(excessive burden)*
unjust decision inequity
unjust deed ground
unjust enrichment SEE MAIN ENTRY
unjust opinion misjudgment
unjust performance malfeasance
unjust requirement imposition *(excessive burden)*
unjustifiable baseless, blameful, blameworthy, disproportionate, immoral, indefensible, inexcusable, inexpiable, iniquitous, peccant *(culpable)*, reprehensible, sinister, unequal *(unjust)*, unjust, unreasonable, untenable, unwarranted, wanton. SEE MAIN ENTRY
unjustified arbitrary, gratuitous *(unwarranted)*, illegal, partial *(biased)*, unauthorized, undue *(excessive)*, unjustifiable, unwarranted
unjustly call to account frame *(charge falsely)*
unjustly involve frame *(charge falsely)*
unjustly severe tyrannous
unjustness ground, inequity, nepotism
unkempt disordered, inelegant
unkind caustic, cold-blooded, cruel, harsh, invidious, malevolent, mordacious, pernicious, ruthless, scathing, severe
unkindly harsh
unkindness cruelty, disservice, ill will, inconsideration, severity
unknot break *(separate)*, disengage, disentangle, extricate
unknowable inapprehensible, incomprehensible, inexplicable, inscrutable
unknowing blind *(not discerning)*, incognizant, insensible, unacquainted, unaware, unintentional, unversed, unwitting
unknowingly SEE MAIN ENTRY
unknowingness ignorance, nescience
unknowledgeable unversed
unknown anonymous, blind *(concealed)*, clandestine, covert, defunct, disputable, hidden, inexplicable, mysterious, obscure *(remote)*, secret, surreptitious, ulterior, undisclosed, unprecedented. SEE MAIN ENTRY
unknown information secret
unknown person stranger
unlace disengage
unladylike blatant *(obtrusive)*, disorderly, unbecoming
unlatch disengage
unlatched open *(unclosed)*
unlavish economical, provident *(frugal)*
unlawful broken *(unfulfilled)*, delinquent *(guilty of a misdeed)*, felonious, illegal, illegitimate *(illegal)*, illicit, immoral, impermissible, unauthorized, unscrupulous, unwarranted, wrongful. SEE MAIN ENTRY
unlawful acquisition larceny
unlawful act burglary, miscarriage, offense, tortious act
unlawful action malfeasance
unlawful appropriation conversion *(misappropriation)*
unlawful bait bribe
unlawful begetting bar sinister
unlawful breaking and entering burglary
unlawful carnal connection adultery
unlawful carnal knowledge adultery
unlawful carnality adultery
unlawful combination conspiracy
unlawful compensation bribe
unlawful compulsion coercion
unlawful contrivance conspiracy
unlawful conversion larceny
unlawful departure desertion
unlawful detention detainer
unlawful encouragement bribery
unlawful entry intrusion
unlawful force violence
unlawful gain graft
unlawful gift bribe
unlawful gratuity bribe
unlawful hitting battery
unlawful homicide aberemurder, assassination
unlawful invasion encroachment
unlawful killing murder
unlawful obstruction nuisance
unlawful obtainer extortionist
unlawful plan conspiracy
unlawful practice guilt
unlawful restriction detainer
unlawful retention detainer
unlawful scheme conspiracy
unlawful sexual intercourse sodomy
unlawful striking battery
unlawful taking extortion, larceny
unlawful touching battery
unlawful use of another's property conversion *(misappropriation)*
unlawful use of power misfeasance
unlawfully illegally
unlawfully begotten illegitimate *(born out of wedlock)*
unlawfully deprive purloin
unlawfully seize kidnap
unlawfulness burglary, criminality, illegality, injustice, prohibition
unlearned jejune *(lacking maturity)*, unversed
unlearnedness ignorance, illiteracy, nescience
unleash free
unlegalized illicit
unlegislated illicit
unless SEE MAIN ENTRY
unlessened undiminished
unlettered unversed
unliable immune
unliberal parochial
unlicensed felonious, illegitimate *(illegal)*, impermissible, inexperienced, ultra vires, unauthorized, unlawful
unlikable objectionable, undesirable
unlike different, disparate, dissimilar, distinct *(distinguished from others)*, distinctive, diverse, heterogeneous, peculiar *(distinctive)*, unequal *(unequivalent)*, unrelated. SEE MAIN ENTRY
unlike others distinct *(distinguished from others)*
unlikelihood improbability
unlikeliness improbability
unlikely disputable, doubtful, dubious, implausible, impossible, incredible, infeasible, unbelievable, unfit
unlikely to cause harm innocuous
unlikely to cause injury innocuous
unlikeness contraposition, deviation, difference, discrepancy, disparity, distinction *(difference)*, distortion, diversity, identity *(individuality)*, incompatibility *(inconsistency)*, incongruity, inconsistency, inequality, nonconformity, specialty *(distinctive mark)*
unlimited absolute *(complete)*, copious, dictatorial, far reaching, indefinite, indeterminate, infinite, innumerable, inordinate, intemperate, myriad, omnibus, open-ended, peremptory *(absolute)*, perpetual, plenary, unbound, unrestrained *(not in custody)*, unrestrained *(not repressed)*, unrestricted. SEE MAIN ENTRY
unlimited in power omnipotent
unlimited inheritance fee *(estate)*
unlimited sovereignty home rule
unlink detach
unlinked disconnected
unliquidated delinquent *(overdue)*, outstanding *(unpaid)*
unliquidated claim liability, obligation *(liability)*
unlively grave *(solemn)*, jejune *(dull)*, lifeless *(dull)*, pedestrian, ponderous
unload alleviate, deplete, diminish, disencumber, dislodge, ease, relieve *(free from burden)*, remove *(eliminate)*, vend
unlock disencumber, disengage, disenthrall, dissociate, find *(discover)*, solve
unlocked open *(accessible)*, open *(unclosed)*
unlooked for fortuitous, unanticipated, unexpected, unforeseeable

unloose break *(separate),* diffuse, disencumber, disengage, disentangle, dissociate, extricate, liberate, part *(separate),* rescue, separate
unloosen disjoint, extricate
unloquacious laconic, mute, taciturn
unlovable odious
unloyal broken *(unfulfilled),* faithless
unloyalty bad faith
unlucid blind *(not discerning)*
unlucky dire, harmful, inauspicious, ominous, regrettable, unfavorable
unlucky accident misfortune
unlucky happening misfortune
unlucky person victim
unmaintainable unsustainable, untenable
unmake annul, destroy *(void),* disorganize, extirpate, obliterate
unmaking cancellation, destruction
unmalleable immutable, inflexible, intractable, ironclad, obdurate, rigid, uncontrollable
unmanacle disenthrall, free
unmanageable contumacious, disobedient, disordered, disorderly, fractious, froward, impossible, impracticable, incorrigible, indomitable, inexorable, inflexible, intractable, obdurate, perverse, ponderous, recalcitrant, restive, uncontrollable, unruly, unyielding, wanton. SEE MAIN ENTRY
unmanifested latent, potential
unmanly ignoble, recreant, unseemly
unmanned devoid
unmannered disorderly, offensive *(offending)*
unmannerliness disrespect
unmannerly brazen, disdainful, disorderly, impertinent *(insolent),* inelegant, insolent, obtrusive, offensive *(offending),* perverse, uncouth
unmannerly conduct disrespect
unmarked intact, usual
unmarketable SEE MAIN ENTRY
unmarketable check bad check
unmarred intact, pure, unblemished, unimpeachable
unmarry divorce, separate
unmask admit *(concede),* bare, betray *(disclose),* clarify, detect, disabuse, disclose, divulge, expose, find *(discover),* inform *(betray),* manifest, produce *(offer to view),* report *(disclose),* reveal, unveil
unmasked naked *(lacking embellishment),* obvious, palpable, patent, scrutable
unmasking admission *(disclosure),* disclosure *(act of disclosing),* manifestation
unmasterable insuperable, insurmountable
unmatched different, disparate, dissimilar, diverse, heterogeneous, inestimable, leading *(ranking first),* only *(unrepeated),* original *(creative),* paramount, premium, prime *(most valuable),* solitary, superlative, unequal *(unequivalent),* unique, unprecedented, unrelated, unusual
unmatured premature
unmeaningful null *(insignificant)*
unmeant fortuitous, inadvertent, unintentional, unpremeditated, unwitting
unmeasured copious, indeterminate, infinite, innumerable, intemperate, open-ended
unmeditated involuntary
unmeet improper, inappropriate, inapt, inept *(inappropriate),* unbecoming, undesirable, unseemly
unmelting callous
unmemorable usual
unmentionable confidential, ineffable
unmentioned tacit, ulterior, undisclosed
unmerciful brutal, callous, cold-blooded, cruel, harsh, inexorable, malignant, obdurate, relentless, remorseless, ruthless, severe, unrelenting
unmeretricious elegant
unmerited undue *(excessive),* unjust
unmetaphorical literal
unmethodical capricious, casual, desultory, disordered, disorderly, haphazard, indiscriminate, informal, unpredictable
unmeticulous casual, inexact, slipshod
unmilitant harmless, nonmilitant, peaceable
unmindful blind *(not discerning),* careless, casual, cold-blooded, cursory, derelict *(negligent),* disobedient, dispassionate, heedless, impulsive *(rash),* inadvertent, incognizant, insensible, lax, negligent, nonchalant, oblivious, perfunctory, reckless, remiss, thoughtless, unaware, unwitting
unmindfully unknowingly
unmindfulness disinterest *(lack of interest),* disregard *(lack of respect),* disregard *(unconcern),* neglect, negligence
unmingled pure, simple, sterling, unadulterated
unmistakability certainty
unmistakable absolute *(conclusive),* arrant *(definite),* axiomatic, certain *(fixed),* certain *(positive),* clear *(apparent),* clear *(certain),* cognizable, coherent *(clear),* comprehensible, conclusive *(determinative),* conspicuous, definite, demonstrable, evident, explicit, factual, incontrovertible, irrefutable, lucid, manifest, naked *(perceptible),* obvious, open *(in sight),* palpable, particular *(specific),* perceivable, perceptible, positive *(incontestable),* salient, unambiguous, unequivocal. SEE MAIN ENTRY
unmistakableness surety *(certainty)*
unmistakably fairly *(clearly)*
unmistakably bad arrant *(onerous)*
unmistaken accurate, actual, proper, real, true *(authentic)*
unmitigable hot-blooded, relentless
unmitigated absolute *(conclusive),* categorical, chronic, comprehensive, disorderly, drastic, gross *(flagrant),* harsh, intensive, outright, pure, rigid, severe, stark, thorough, unqualified *(unlimited).* SEE MAIN ENTRY
unmitigating chronic
unmixed absolute *(conclusive),* pure, simple, strong, unadulterated
unmodern obsolete
unmodest brazen
unmodifiable irrevocable, permanent, unalterable
unmodified unqualified *(unlimited)*
unmolested safe
unmoneyed bankrupt, destitute, impecunious, poor *(underprivileged)*
unmoral immoral
unmotivated fortuitous
unmovable firm, impervious, inexorable, inflexible, permanent, pertinacious
unmoved callous, cold-blooded, impervious, inexpressive, insensible, insusceptible *(uncaring),* irreconcilable, nonchalant, peaceable, placid, steadfast, stoical, unaffected *(uninfluenced),* unresponsive
unmoved by entreaties inexorable
unmoved by pity relentless
unmoving firm, inactive, rigid, stagnant, static
unmuddied clean
unmurmuring patient
unmuzzled uncurbed
unnamable ineffable
unnamed anonymous, unspecified
unnatural anomalous, artificial, cruel, diabolic, histrionic, illegitimate *(born out of wedlock),* irregular *(not usual),* peculiar *(curious),* synthetic, unaccustomed, uncanny, unusual
unnatural carnal intercourse sodomy
unnatural habit perversion
unnatural sexual intercourse sodomy
unnaturalized alien *(foreign)*
unnaturalness bestiality, false pretense, irregularity, pretense *(ostentation)*
unnavigable impervious
unneat slipshod
unnecessary circumstantial, excess, excessive, expendable, extraneous, gratuitous *(unwarranted),* inconsequential, inordinate, minor, needless, nonessential, null *(insignificant),* otiose, redundant, superfluous, undue *(excessive),* unessential, unwarranted. SEE MAIN ENTRY
unnecessary addition expletive
unnecessary inclusion expletive
unnecessary loss waste
unnecessary prolongation laches
unneeded excess, excessive, expendable, extraneous, gratuitous *(unwarranted),* needless, nonessential, otiose, undue *(excessive),* unessential, unnecessary
unnerve disable, discommode, discourage, disturb, frighten, intimidate, menace, perturb, upset
unnerved disconsolate, powerless, unsettled
unnerving formidable
unnervous dispassionate
unnotable petty
unnoteworthiness immateriality, inconsequence, insignificance, mediocrity
unnoteworthy average *(standard),* inapposite, mediocre, minor, negligible, nonessential
unnoticeable impalpable, inconspicuous, indiscernible, minor
unnoticed inconspicuous, latent
unnoticing heedless, inadvertent, oblivious
unnourishing deficient
unnumberable myriad
unnumbered infinite, innumerable, multiple, myriad, profuse
unobjectionability admissibility
unobjectionable admissible, allowable, blameless, clean, fair *(satisfactory),* innocuous, irreprehensible, mediocre, nontoxic, palatable, pardonable, unimpeachable. SEE MAIN ENTRY
unobliging thoughtless
unobnoxious innocuous
unobscure comprehensible, palpable
unobscured palpable
unobservable impalpable
unobservance breach, contempt *(disobedience to the court),* neglect, negligence
unobservant blind *(not discerning),* broken *(unfulfilled),* careless, derelict *(negligent),* heedless, inadvertent, lax, oblivious, perfunctory, reckless, thoughtless, unaware, unorthodox
unobserved blind *(concealed),* defunct, hidden, inconspicuous
unobserving blind *(not discerning),* lax
unobstructed clear *(unencumbered),* free *(not restricted),* open *(accessible),* open

(in sight), passable, patent, unbound, uncurbed, unrestrained *(not in custody)*, unrestricted
unobstrusive diffident
unobtainability impossibility, unavailability
unobtainable impossible, inaccessible, infeasible, insuperable, scarce, unapproachable, unattainable
unobtainableness impossibility
unobtrusive covert, furtive, inconspicuous, unpretentious. SEE MAIN ENTRY
unobvious impalpable, inconspicuous, ulterior, unclear
unoccupied devoid, idle, open *(accessible)*, otiose, solitary, unemployed, unsettled, vacant, vacuous, void *(empty)*
unoffended dispassionate
unoffending blameless, clean, innocent, innocuous, irreprehensible
unofficered devoid
unofficial informal, interim, private *(not public)*, uncorroborated. SEE MAIN ENTRY
unopened impervious
unoperative ineffective, ineffectual
unopinionated impartial, liberal *(broad minded)*
unopinioned impartial
unopposed consensual
unopposing passive
unordered casual, indeterminate
unordinary extraordinary, momentous, nonconforming, novel, original *(creative)*, unaccustomed
unorganized casual, complex, disordered, haphazard, indiscriminate, random, slipshod
unoriginal familiar *(customary)*, lifeless *(dull)*, ordinary, pedestrian, prosaic, trite, usual
unornamented naked *(lacking embellishment)*
unorthodox deviant, eccentric, informal, nonconforming, novel, original *(creative)*, peculiar *(curious)*, skeptical, uncommon, unusual. SEE MAIN ENTRY
unorthodoxness nonconformity
unorthodoxy blasphemy, deviation, informality, irregularity, nonconformity, quirk *(idiosyncrasy)*
unostentatious diffident, inconspicuous, unobtrusive, unpretentious
unovercomable insuperable
unowed undue *(not owing)*
unowned derelict *(abandoned)*
unpacifiable implacable
unpacific contentious, offensive *(taking the initiative)*, pugnacious
unpaid delinquent *(overdue)*, due *(owed)*, free *(at no charge)*, gratuitous *(given without recompense)*, overdue, payable, receivable, unsettled. SEE MAIN ENTRY
unpaid amount delinquency *(shortage)*
unpaid bill arrears
unpaid debt arrears, obligation *(liability)*
unpaid dues nonpayment
unpaid for gratis, gratuitous *(given without recompense)*
unpaid worker volunteer
unpainstaking inaccurate
unpaired dissimilar, solitary
unpalatable bitter *(acrid tasting)*, loathsome, objectionable, odious, offensive *(offending)*, repugnant *(exciting aversion)*, repulsive, undesirable, unendurable, unsavory. SEE MAIN ENTRY
unparalled renowned
unparalleled best, cardinal *(outstanding)*, extraordinary, inestimable, invaluable, leading *(ranking first)*, major, nonconforming, noteworthy, only *(unrepeated)*, original *(creative)*, outstanding *(prominent)*, paramount, portentous *(eliciting amazement)*, premium, prime *(most valuable)*, rare, remarkable, singular, special, superior *(excellent)*, superlative, unapproachable, uncommon, unique, unprecedented, unusual. SEE MAIN ENTRY
unpardonable blameful, felonious, inexcusable, inexpiable, peccant *(culpable)*, reprehensible, unjustifiable
unpardoning callous
unparticular casual, indiscriminate
unpassable impervious
unpassionate dispassionate
unpatent impalpable
unpatriotic faithless
unpatterned disordered
unpayable irredeemable
unpeaceful contentious, litigious, offensive *(taking the initiative)*, pugnacious
unpeacefulness belligerency
unpent free *(not restricted)*
unpeopled devoid
unperceivability nonappearance
unperceivable impalpable, inconspicuous, indiscernible, intangible
unperceived blind *(concealed)*, hidden, ulterior
unperceiving blind *(not discerning)*, heedless
unperceptive inadvertent, insensible
unperfected partial *(relating to a part)*
unperfidious bona fide, candid, loyal, true *(loyal)*
unperfidiousness responsibility *(conscience)*
unperforated impervious
unperformability impossibility
unperformable impracticable, insurmountable, unattainable
unperformed executory, partial *(part)*
unperilous reliable
unperjured accurate, bona fide, candid, honest, straightforward, true *(authentic)*, veridical
unpermitted unauthorized
unpersevering otiose, truant
unpersuadable inexorable
unpersuaded disinclined
unperturbed cold-blooded, dispassionate, patient, phlegmatic
unperverted undistorted
unphysical intangible
unpierceable impervious
unpin disengage
unpitying callous, cruel, harsh, obdurate, relentless, remorseless, ruthless, unrelenting
unplagiarized authentic
unplain equivocal, impalpable, inarticulate, indefinable, indistinct, obscure *(faint)*, opaque, unclear
unplainness indistinctness, opacity
unplanned coincidental, fortuitous, haphazard, spontaneous, unforeseeable, unpremeditated
unplanned happening quirk *(accident)*
unplausible suspicious *(questionable)*
unpleasant bitter *(acrid tasting)*, deplorable, invidious, loathsome, objectionable, obnoxious, odious, offensive *(offending)*, outrageous, painful, repugnant *(exciting aversion)*, repulsive, unacceptable, undesirable, unendurable, unsatisfactory, unsavory
unpleasant sound noise
unpleasing deplorable, objectionable, obnoxious, offensive *(offending)*, unacceptable, undesirable, unsavory
unplentiful scarce
unpliable immutable, inflexible, unyielding
unpliant inflexible, ironclad, rigid, strong, unalterable, unbending
unplug detach
unpoetic prosaic
unpoetical mundane, pedestrian, prosaic
unpointed jejune *(dull)*
unpolished blatant *(obtrusive)*, caitiff, imperfect, impertinent *(insolent)*, inelegant, provincial, uncouth
unpolite perverse
unpoliteness disrespect
unpolitic SEE MAIN ENTRY
unpollute decontaminate
unpolluted inviolate, pure
unpopular odious, repugnant *(exciting aversion)*, unacceptable, undesirable
unpopularity ill repute, ill will, odium
unpopulated bleak *(exposed and barren)*
unpositive conditional
unpossessed derelict *(abandoned)*, unclaimed, vacant
unpossessed of devoid
unpowerful incapable
unpracticability impossibility
unpracticed inexperienced, outdated, outmoded, unaccustomed, unversed
unpraiseworthy blameful, blameworthy, unbecoming, unseemly
unprecedented extraordinary, nonconforming, noteworthy, novel, portentous *(eliciting amazement)*, prodigious *(amazing)*, renowned, singular, special, uncommon, unforeseeable, unique, unusual. SEE MAIN ENTRY
unprecise approximate, casual, faulty, liberal *(not literal)*
unpreciseness misestimation, misjudgment
unpredictability chance *(possibility)*, happenstance
unpredictable conditional, debatable, fallible, haphazard, undependable, unforeseeable, unreliable. SEE MAIN ENTRY
unpredicted fortuitous, unexpected, unforeseeable, unforeseen
unprejudice disinterest *(lack of prejudice)*
unprejudiced dispassionate, equal, equitable, evenhanded, factual, fair *(just)*, impartial, judicial, juridical, just, liberal *(broad minded)*, neutral, nonpartisan, objective, reasonable *(rational)*, receptive, unbiased, undistorted. SEE MAIN ENTRY
unprejudicedness candor *(impartiality)*
unpremeditated fortuitous, haphazard, impulsive *(rash)*, inadvertent, involuntary, random, spontaneous, unexpected, unintentional, unwitting. SEE MAIN ENTRY
unpremeditated murder manslaughter
unpremeditation inconsideration, quirk *(accident)*
unprepared impulsive *(rash)*, lax, premature, spontaneous, unaware, unfit, unpremeditated, unqualified *(not competent)*, unversed, vulnerable
unprepared for precipitate, unexpected, unforeseeable
unpreparedness disqualification *(factor that disqualifies)*, laxity

unpreparing improvident
unprepossessed dispassionate, impartial, neutral, open-minded, unprejudiced
unprepossessing repulsive
unpresentable blatant *(obtrusive)*, unseemly
unpretended bona fide, genuine, honest, true *(authentic)*
unpretending direct *(forthright)*, genuine, honest, unaffected *(sincere)*, veridical
unpretentious bona fide, diffident, direct *(forthright)*, genuine, honest, inconspicuous, simple, unaffected *(sincere)*. SEE MAIN ENTRY
unpretentiousness candor *(straightforwardness)*
unprevalent unusual
unpreventable certain *(fixed)*, compulsory, inevitable, necessary *(inescapable)*, unavoidable *(inevitable)*
unprevented free *(not restricted)*, unbound, uncurbed, unrestrained *(not in custody)*
unprincipaled dissolute
unprincipled baseless, delinquent *(guilty of a misdeed)*, depraved, diabolic, dishonest, disingenuous, disreputable, false *(disloyal)*, heinous, illicit, immoral, inexcusable, iniquitous, lawless, machiavellian, peccable, peccant *(culpable)*, perfidious, profligate *(corrupt)*, reprehensible, reprobate, sinister, unconscionable, unethical, unfair, unjust, unscrupulous, vicious
unprincipled politician demagogue
unprintable profane, salacious
unprocessed inchoate
unproclaimed undisclosed
unprocreant barren
unprocurable inaccessible, unattainable
unproductive barren, futile, ineffective, ineffectual, inept *(incompetent)*, nugatory, otiose, unavailing. SEE MAIN ENTRY
unproductive trial mistrial
unproductivity miscarriage
unprofaned inviolate
unprofessional unethical
SEE MAIN ENTRY
unprofessional conduct incompetence, malpractice, misconduct
unprofessional treatment malpractice
unproficiency disqualification *(factor that disqualifies)*, inability, incapacity, incompetence, maladministration
unproficient inadept, inept *(incompetent)*, unversed
unprofitability detriment, inexpedience
unprofitable barren, detrimental, disadvantageous, expendable, futile, idle, inadvisable, ineffective, ineffectual, injudicious, needless, nugatory, otiose, unavailing, unproductive
unprogressive decadent, static
unprogressiveness inaction
unprohibited admissible, allowable, allowed, lawful, licit, permissible, public *(open)*
unprolific barren, otiose, unproductive
unprolonged brief
unpromising inauspicious, ominous, pessimistic, sinister, unfavorable, unfit, unpropitious, untimely
unprompted impulsive *(rash)*, spontaneous, voluntary
unprompted will conatus
unpronounceable ineffable
unpronounced impalpable, implicit, inconspicuous, tacit, undisclosed
unpropitiating implacable
unpropitious adverse *(hostile)*, antipathetic *(oppositional)*, detrimental, dire, disadvantageous, harmful, inauspicious, inimical, inopportune, ominous, pernicious, portentous *(ominous)*, regrettable, sinister, unfavorable, untimely. SEE MAIN ENTRY
unprosperous impecunious, poor *(underprivileged)*
unprosperousness poverty
unprotected dangerous, helpless *(defenseless)*, indefensible, insecure, open *(in sight)*, precarious, susceptible *(unresistent)*, untenable, vulnerable
unprovable unsustainable
unproved inconclusive, theoretical, unconfirmed, unsupported
unproved theory hypothesis
unproven debatable, disputable, inconclusive, speculative, theoretical, unconfirmed, uncorroborated, unfounded, unsupported
unprovided deficient, devoid
unprovided for poor *(underprivileged)*
unproviding improvident
unprovocativeness disincentive
unprovoked gratuitous *(unwarranted)*, wanton
unpublicized undisclosed
unpublished secret, undisclosed
unpugnacious nonmilitant, peaceable
unpunctilious casual
unpunctual back *(in arrears)*, dilatory, late *(tardy)*, untimely
unpunctuality irregularity
unpunishable immune
unpunished clear *(free from criminal charges)*
unpurposed unwitting
unpurposeful unintentional, unpremeditated
unpushing diffident
unqualification certainty, disability *(legal disqualification)*
unqualified absolute *(complete)*, affirmative, categorical, certain *(positive)*, clear *(certain)*, complete *(all-embracing)*, comprehensive, decisive, definite, demonstrable, disabled *(deprived of legal right)*, disabled *(made incapable)*, free *(not restricted)*, inadept, inadmissible, inapplicable, inapt, incapable, incompetent, ineligible, inept *(inappropriate)*, inept *(incompetent)*, inexperienced, insufficient, omnibus, outright, peremptory *(absolute)*, plenary, positive *(incontestable)*, powerless, stark, thorough, total, unable, unconditional, unequivocal, unfit, unmitigated, unrestricted, unversed, unworthy. SEE MAIN ENTRY
unqualifiedness disability *(legal disqualification)*, disqualification *(factor that disqualifies)*, incompetence
unquashable noncancellable
unquelled disorderly, hot-blooded
unquenchable indomitable, insatiable, powerful
unquenched hot-blooded
unquestionability certainty, certification *(certainness)*, incontestability
unquestionable absolute *(conclusive)*, accurate, authentic, axiomatic, believable, categorical, certain *(fixed)*, certain *(positive)*, clear *(certain)*, cogent, conclusive *(determinative)*, de facto, decisive, definitive, demonstrable, evident, factual, genuine, incontestable, incontrovertible, indefeasible, inevitable, infallible, irrebuttable, irrefutable, lucid, manifest, noncontestable, obvious, palpable, pellucid, peremptory *(absolute)*, positive *(incontestable)*, probable, real, reliable, solid *(sound)*, tenable, true *(authentic)*, uncontested, undeniable, unequivocal, unimpeachable, unmistakable, unrefutable. SEE MAIN ENTRY
unquestionableness certainty, certification *(certainness)*, certitude, surety *(certainty)*
unquestionably admittedly, fairly *(clearly)*
unquestioned axiomatic, certain *(fixed)*, certain *(positive)*, clear *(certain)*, consensual, decisive, definite, infallible, proverbial, uncontested, uncontroverted, undisputed
unquestioning categorical, credulous, positive *(confident)*, unsuspecting
unquestioning acceptance faith
unquestioning belief credulity
unquiet restive
unratified unauthorized, unconfirmed, uncorroborated
unravel ascertain, clarify, construe *(translate)*, detect, discover, disengage, disentangle, elucidate, explain, extricate, find *(discover)*, interpret, resolve *(solve)*, separate, simplify *(make easier)*, solve, spread
unraveled elementary
unraveling denouement
unraveling of plot denouement
unravelment development *(progression)*, evulsion
unreachable impervious, inaccessible, unapproachable, unattainable
unreacting unresponsive
unread unversed
unreadable inapprehensible, pedestrian, unclear
unready back *(in arrears)*, late *(tardy)*, premature, unqualified *(not competent)*
unreal artificial, assumed *(feigned)*, bogus, delusive, dishonest, erroneous, false *(not genuine)*, fictitious, fraudulent, hypothetical, illusory, impalpable, inaccurate, insubstantial, nonexistent, spurious, unsound *(fallacious)*, untrue
unrealistic infeasible, quixotic, subjective
unreality figment, myth, phantom
unrealizable impracticable, inaccessible, insurmountable
unrealized possible, potential
unrealizing incognizant, insensible, unaware
unreasonable arbitrary, baseless, contumacious, disproportionate, drastic, excessive, exorbitant, extreme *(exaggerated)*, fanatical, ill-advised, ill-judged, impolitic, impossible, impracticable, improper, inexcusable, inexpiable, infeasible, inordinate, irrational, ludicrous, misadvised, oppressive, outrageous, partial *(biased)*, perverse, prohibitive *(costly)*, sophistic, unconscionable, undue *(excessive)*, unfair, unjust, unjustifiable, unsound *(fallacious)*, untenable, unwarranted, usurious. SEE MAIN ENTRY
unreasonable amplification exaggeration
unreasonable bias prejudice *(preconception)*
unreasonable delay laches
unreasonable fear paranoia
unreasonable fright paranoia

unreasonably resolute fanatical
unreasoned arbitrary, injudicious, irrational, unsound *(fallacious)*
unreasoned alarm phobia
unreasoned fear phobia
unreasoning fatuous, ill-judged, irrational, opaque, thoughtless, vacuous
unreasoning fear panic
unreceivable inadmissible
unreceptive impervious
unrecognizable impalpable, inapprehensible, incomprehensible, indiscernible, indistinct, inexplicable, unclear
unrecognizing oblivious
unrecompensed gratis, gratuitous *(given without recompense)*, outstanding *(unpaid)*, unpaid, unrequited
unreconciled adverse *(hostile)*, contradictory, disinclined, irreconcilable, polemic
unrecoverable irretrievable
unredeemable profligate *(corrupt)*
unredeemed diabolic
unreduced complete *(all-embracing)*, gross *(total)*, intact, undiminished, whole *(undamaged)*
unrefined blatant *(obtrusive)*, disreputable, impertinent *(insolent)*, improper, inelegant, provincial, uncouth, unseemly
unreflecting blind *(not discerning)*, irrational, misadvised, thoughtless
unreflective thoughtless
unreformable incorrigible
unrefreshed languid
unrefutability incontestability
unrefutable clear *(certain)*, convincing, inappealable, positive *(incontestable)*, solid *(sound)*, unimpeachable. SEE MAIN ENTRY
unrefuted accurate, actual, certain *(positive)*, definite, factual
unregarded indiscernible, perfunctory
unregenerate lascivious, lecherous, profligate *(corrupt)*, remorseless, reprobate
unregretful incorrigible
unregretting incorrigible
unregular intermittent
unregulated disorderly
unrehearsed fortuitous, spontaneous, unpremeditated
unreined free *(not restricted)*, independent, intemperate, lawless, licentious, uncurbed, unrestrained *(not repressed)*
unrelated alien *(unrelated)*, different, disconnected, dissimilar, extraneous, foreign, gratuitous *(unwarranted)*, heterogeneous, immaterial, impertinent *(irrelevant)*, inapposite, inconsequential, individual, irrelative, irrelevant. SEE MAIN ENTRY
unrelatedness difference, inconsequence
unrelaxed rigid
unrelaxing industrious, patient, persistent, pertinacious
unrelenting brutal, callous, cold-blooded, constant, cruel, dictatorial, diligent, faithful *(diligent)*, immutable, implacable, inexorable, inflexible, ironclad, obdurate, patient, pertinacious, recalcitrant, relentless, remorseless, resolute, rigid, ruthless, sedulous, severe, unbending, uncompromising, undaunted, vindictive. SEE MAIN ENTRY
unreliability dishonesty, improbity, knavery
unreliable capricious, dangerous, debatable, dishonest, disobedient, disputable, dubious, faithless, fallible, false *(disloyal)*, false *(inaccurate)*, fraudulent, insecure, irresponsible, mutable, perfidious, precarious, recreant, uncertain *(questionable)*, undependable, unpredictable, unsound *(not strong)*, untrustworthy, variable. SEE MAIN ENTRY
unrelievable chronic
unreligious profane
unreluctant willing *(not averse)*
unremarkable mediocre, nondescript, usual
unremarkableness mediocrity
unremedied chronic
unremittent chronic
unremitting chronic, close *(rigorous)*, consecutive, continual *(connected)*, continuous, diligent, faithful *(diligent)*, incessant, industrious, patient, persistent, pertinacious, relentless, sedulous, stable, strong, uncompromising. SEE MAIN ENTRY
unremorseful remorseless
unremorsefulness cruelty
unremoved lasting, present *(attendant)*, present *(current)*
unremunerated unpaid, unrequited
unremunerative unproductive
unrenowned obscure *(remote)*
unrepaid unrequited
unrepair deterioration
unrepealable irrevocable, permanent, perpetual
unrepealed lasting
unrepeated desultory, unique
unrepentant incorrigible, profligate *(corrupt)*, recusant, remorseless
unrepining resigned
unreplenished devoid, inadequate
unreplying unresponsive
unrepresentative anomalous, atypical
unrepressed disorderly, hot-blooded, uncurbed, unrestrained *(not repressed)*
unreproachable blameless
unreproached blameless, inculpable
unreproved blameless, inculpable
unrequested unsolicited
unrequired expendable, needless, nonessential, redundant, unnecessary
unrequisitioned unclaimed
unrequited outstanding *(unpaid)*, unpaid. SEE MAIN ENTRY
unresembling dissimilar
unresentful placable
unreserve honesty
unreserved absolute *(complete)*, bona fide, brazen, candid, complete *(all-embracing)*, comprehensive, direct *(forthright)*, ingenuous, public *(open)*, unaffected *(sincere)*, unqualified *(unlimited)*, unrestrained *(not repressed)*
unreservedly in toto
unresigned recusant
unresistant passive, yielding
unresisting obedient, obeisant, passive, patient, peaceable, resigned, servile, stoical, yielding
unresistingness capitulation
unresolved debatable, disputable, doubtful, dubious, equivocal, hesitant, indefinite, indeterminate, irresolute, noncommittal, undecided, unsettled
unrespectability bad character, bad repute, ignominy, notoriety
unrespectable disreputable, ignoble, notorious
unrespected blameworthy
unresponding unresponsive
unresponsive cold-blooded, dispassionate, impervious, insensible, insusceptible *(uncaring)*, lifeless *(dull)*, noncommittal, obdurate, perfunctory, phlegmatic, unaffected *(uninfluenced)*. SEE MAIN ENTRY
unrest confusion *(turmoil)*, disorder *(lack of order)*, disturbance, embroilment, strife, trepidation, turmoil
unrestful restive
unrestorable irreversible, irrevocable
unrestored languid
unrestrainable uncontrollable
unrestrained absolute *(complete)*, capricious, clear *(unencumbered)*, competitive *(open)*, demonstrative *(expressive of emotion)*, direct *(forthright)*, dissolute, exempt, free *(not restricted)*, gluttonous, immune, informal, ingenuous, inordinate, intemperate, irresponsible, lecherous, licentious, privileged, prodigal, profligate *(extravagant)*, rampant, unbound, uncurbed, unlimited, unqualified *(unlimited)*, unrestricted, unruly, unscrupulous, voluntary. SEE MAIN ENTRY
unrestraint debauchery, freedom, honesty, latitude
unrestricted absolute *(complete)*, autonomous *(independent)*, competitive *(open)*, complete *(all-embracing)*, comprehensive, copious, dictatorial, exempt, general, immune, omnibus, open *(accessible)*, open-ended, peremptory *(absolute)*, plenary, public *(open)*, sovereign *(independent)*, unbound, unconditional, unlimited, unqualified *(unlimited)*. SEE MAIN ENTRY
unrestricted inheritance fee *(estate)*
unretarded undiminished
unreturnable irreversible
unreturned unrequited
unrevealable private *(confidential)*
unrevealed blind *(concealed)*, clandestine, confidential, furtive, hidden, impalpable, inscrutable, latent, mysterious, personal *(private)*, privy, secret, stealthy, ulterior, undisclosed
unrevengeful placable
unreversed live *(existing)*
unrevised inexact
unrevived lifeless *(dead)*
unrevoked live *(existing)*
unrewarded barren, due *(owed)*, unpaid, unrequited
unrewarding barren, needless, unproductive
unriddle ascertain, elucidate, explicate, expound, solve
unrighteous blameworthy, culpable, diabolic, immoral, iniquitous, lawless, nefarious, peccable, peccant *(culpable)*, reprehensible, reprobate, sinister, vicious
unrighteousness guilt, injustice, misdoing, offense, wrong
unrigorous liberal *(not literal)*
unrigorousness informality, laxity
unripe inexperienced, premature
unripeness minority *(infancy)*
unrivaled absolute *(ideal)*, best, paramount, premium, prime *(most valuable)*, professional *(stellar)*, superlative, unique, unprecedented, unusual
unrivaled effort main force
unrivalled leading *(ranking first)*, superior *(excellent)*
unrobe denude, unveil
unroll spread
unromantic pragmatic, realistic
unroot disinter, eradicate
unrooted unsettled
unrooting evulsion

unroutine unusual
unruffled callous, controlled *(restrained)*, dispassionate, nonchalant, patient, peaceable, phlegmatic, placid, stoical
unruliness anarchy, commotion, contempt *(disobedience to the court)*, defiance, disturbance, irregularity, lynch law, misrule, outbreak, outburst, pandemonium, riot
unruly disobedient, disordered, disorderly, fractious, froward, indomitable, insubordinate, intemperate, intractable, licentious, perverse, restive, uncontrollable, uncurbed, vicious. SEE MAIN ENTRY
unsacred mundane, profane
unsacredness blasphemy
unsafe aleatory *(perilous)*, dangerous, deadly, destructible, harmful, insalubrious, insecure, noxious, precarious, speculative, susceptible *(unresistent)*, toxic, unsound *(not strong)*, untrustworthy, vulnerable
unsafe object hazard
unsafety jeopardy, peril
unsagacious unpolitic
unsaid implicit, tacit, undisclosed
unsaintly profane
unsalable barren, unmarketable
unsalaried unpaid
unsame dissimilar
unsanctified mundane, profane
unsanctioned illegal, illegitimate *(illegal)*, illicit, impermissible, null *(invalid)*, null and void, ultra vires, unauthorized, unlawful, unwarranted
unsanitary insalubrious
unsated insatiable
unsatisfaction dissatisfaction
unsatisfactoriness mediocrity
unsatisfactory antipathetic *(distasteful)*, deficient, deleterious, deplorable, detrimental, faulty, imperfect, inadequate, inadvisable, inferior *(lower in quality)*, nonsubstantial *(not sufficient)*, objectionable, paltry, poor *(inferior in quality)*, unacceptable, undesirable, unfavorable, unsuitable. SEE MAIN ENTRY
unsatisfied delinquent *(overdue)*, disappointed, insatiable, outstanding *(unpaid)*, payable. SEE MAIN ENTRY
unsatisfied hopes frustration
unsatisfying nonsubstantial *(not sufficient)*, unsatisfactory, unsuitable
unsavory bitter *(acrid tasting)*, disreputable, insipid, loathsome, objectionable, offensive *(offending)*, repugnant *(exciting aversion)*, repulsive, unendurable. SEE MAIN ENTRY
unsay disclaim, recall *(call back)*, recant
unsaying retraction
unscarred intact
unscathed intact, inviolate, safe
unscholarliness ignorance, illiteracy
unscholarly unprofessional
unschooled inexperienced, naive, unversed
unscientific illogical, inexact
unscintillating insipid, pedestrian
unscramble ascertain, clarify, elucidate, explain, find *(discover)*, interpret, resolve *(solve)*, solve
unscratched intact
unscreen bare, denude, disclose, find *(discover)*, manifest, produce *(offer to view)*
unscreened obvious, palpable
unscrew disengage
unscrupulous arrant *(onerous)*, delinquent *(guilty of a misdeed)*, depraved, diabolic, dishonest, disingenuous, disreputable, faithless, false *(disloyal)*, fraudulent, immoral, insidious, lawless, machiavellian, peccant *(culpable)*, perfidious, recreant, sly, tortuous *(corrupt)*, unconscionable, unethical. SEE MAIN ENTRY
unscrupulous agitator demagogue
unscrupulous haranguer demagogue
unscrupulousness bad faith, bad repute, corruption, dishonesty, fraud, improbity
unseal bare, disclose, reveal, unveil
unsealed open *(accessible)*, open *(unclosed)*
unsearchable inscrutable
unsearchableness opacity
unseasonable improper, inapposite, inappropriate, inapt, inept *(inappropriate)*, inopportune, premature, undue *(not owing)*, unsuitable, untimely
unseasoned inexperienced, juvenile, unaccustomed
unseat demote, depose *(remove)*, discharge *(dismiss)*, dislocate, dislodge, dismiss *(discharge)*, displace *(remove)*, disturb, divest, oust, overthrow, supplant
unseating discharge *(dismissal)*, removal
unsecluded open *(in sight)*
unseconded alone *(unsupported)*, solitary, unsupported
unsecurable inaccessible, unattainable
unseeable inconspicuous, indiscernible, intangible
unseeableness nonappearance
unseeing blind *(not discerning)*, blind *(sightless)*, heedless, inadvertent, incognizant, insensible
unseemingliness indecency
unseemliness impropriety
unseemly blatant *(obtrusive)*, brazen, delinquent *(guilty of a misdeed)*, disgraceful, disorderly, disproportionate, ill-advised, illicit, improper, inappropriate, inapt, inelegant, inept *(inappropriate)*, notorious, objectionable, slipshod, unbecoming, uncouth, undesirable, undue *(excessive)*, unfit, unprofessional, unsatisfactory, unsuitable, wrongful. SEE MAIN ENTRY
unseen blind *(concealed)*, clandestine, covert, furtive, hidden, inconspicuous, latent, potential, secret, stealthy, surreptitious, ulterior, underlying, undisclosed, unobtrusive
unselected miscellaneous
unselective promiscuous
unselfconscious ingenuous
unselfish benevolent, charitable *(benevolent)*, humane, liberal *(generous)*, magnanimous, meritorious, philanthropic
unselfish person good samaritan
unselfishness benevolence *(disposition to do good)*, charity, consideration *(sympathetic regard)*, disinterest *(lack of prejudice)*, humanity *(humaneness)*, largess *(generosity)*, philanthropy
unsensible ill-judged, impolitic, inadvisable, irrational, misadvised, unreasonable
unsensibleness inexpedience
unsentimental dispassionate, pragmatic
unsentimentality pragmatism
unseparated composite
unsepulcher disinter
unserious frivolous
unserviceable impracticable, ineffective, ineffectual, nugatory, otiose, unavailing
unserviceable check bad check
unsettle agitate *(perturb)*, confuse *(bewilder)*, confuse *(create disorder)*, discompose, dislocate, disorganize, disorient, disrupt, disturb, inconvenience, muddle, obfuscate, perplex, perturb, upset
unsettled aleatory *(uncertain)*, conditional, debatable, delinquent *(overdue)*, deranged, disorderly, disputable, due *(owed)*, frenetic, hesitant, inconclusive, indefinite, indeterminate, insecure, irresolute, lunatic, moot, moving *(in motion)*, mutable, *non compos mentis*, noncommittal, outstanding *(unpaid)*, outstanding *(unresolved)*, payable, pending *(unresolved)*, precarious, problematic, protean, provisional, restive, speculative, tentative, uncertain *(questionable)*, unconfirmed, undecided, unpaid, unsound *(not strong)*, unspecified, vague, variable. SEE MAIN ENTRY
unsettled in one's mind *non compos mentis*
unsettled in opinion doubtful
unsettled opinion doubt *(indecision)*, indecision
unsettlement confusion *(turmoil)*, disturbance, doubt *(indecision)*
unsevered complete *(all-embracing)*, intact, undiminished
unshacking liberation
unshackle disencumber, disengage, disenthrall, extricate, free, liberate, parole, rescue
unshackled free *(not restricted)*, independent, uncurbed, unrestrained *(not in custody)*, unrestricted
unshackling emancipation
unshaded candid, patent
unshakable certain *(positive)*, dogmatic, incontrovertible, indubious, pertinacious, safe
unshakable opinion conviction *(persuasion)*
unshakable trust faith
unshakeable infrangible, ironclad, stable, staunch
unshaken constant, definite, dispassionate, inexorable, patient, pertinacious, positive *(confident)*, resolute, secure *(confident)*, stable, steadfast, unabashed, undaunted
unshaken belief credence
unshape deface, mutilate
unshared personal *(private)*, solitary
unshatterable infrangible
unshattered intact
unsheathe bare, denude, evidence, expose, withdraw
unsheltered bleak *(exposed and barren)*, dangerous, helpless *(defenseless)*, insecure, open *(in sight)*, precarious
unshield bare
unshielded helpless *(defenseless)*, insecure, open *(accessible)*, open *(in sight)*, precarious, vulnerable
unshifting chronic, fixed *(settled)*, permanent, unremitting
unshocked nonchalant
unshorn gross *(total)*
unshortened gross *(total)*
unshown unconfirmed
unshrewd unpolitic
unshrinking heroic, indomitable, pertinacious, purposeful, relentless, spartan, unabashed, undaunted
unshroud bare, denude, disclose, find *(discover)*, manifest, reveal

unshrouded palpable
unshut open *(unclosed)*
unsightliness defacement
unsightly poor *(inferior in quality)*, repulsive, unseemly
unsigned anonymous
unsimilar dissimilar
unsimulated authentic, bona fide, genuine, honest, real, unaffected *(sincere)*
unskilled amateur, incompetent, inexperienced, unaccustomed, unversed
unskilled person novice
unskilled practitioner layman
unskillful inadept, incapable, incompetent, inept *(incompetent)*
unskillfulness abortion *(fiasco)*, disqualification *(factor that disqualifies)*, inability, incapacity, inefficacy
unslackening chronic
unslanted objective, unbiased, unprejudiced
unslantedness disinterest *(lack of prejudice)*
unsleeping industrious, vigilant
unslumbering vigilant
unsmoothness irregularity
unsnap disengage
unsober drunk
unsociable disdainful, taciturn, unapproachable, unresponsive
unsociableness ostracism
unsoftened unmitigated
unsoftening unrelenting
unsoiled blameless, clean, unblemished
unsolicited SEE MAIN ENTRY
unsolicitous cold-blooded, heedless, remiss
unsolicitousness disinterest *(lack of interest)*
unsolid insubstantial, intangible, nonsubstantial *(not sturdy)*
unsolidity impalpability
unsolvable insurmountable
unsolved doubtful, equivocal, pending *(unresolved)*
unsophisticated credulous, elementary, honest, inexperienced, ingenuous, naive, provincial, simple, unadulterated, unaffected *(sincere)*, usual
unsophistication credulity
unsorted disjointed, haphazard, miscellaneous
unsought unclaimed, undesirable, unsolicited
unsound bad *(inferior)*, baseless, defective, deficient, dubious, erroneous, fallacious, false *(inaccurate)*, faulty, ill-judged, illogical, imperfect, impolitic, improper, inaccurate, inadvisable, inconsequential, incorrect, injudicious, insecure, insubstantial, insufficient, irrational, misadvised, *non compos mentis*, nonsubstantial *(not sturdy)*, peccable, precarious, sophistic, unreasonable, unreliable, untenable, untrustworthy. SEE MAIN ENTRY
unsound argument fallacy
unsound check bad check
unsound mind insanity
unsoundness disability *(physical inability)*, disease, frailty, inexpedience, invalidity
unsoundness of mind insanity, lunacy
unsparing benevolent, charitable *(benevolent)*, close *(rigorous)*, copious, liberal *(generous)*, philanthropic, profuse, relentless, ruthless, severe, trenchant, unqualified *(unlimited)*, unrelenting
unsparingness philanthropy
unsparkling insipid, lifeless *(dull)*, pedestrian
unspeakable ineffable, offensive *(offending)*, profane, remarkable
unspecific indiscriminate
unspecified anonymous, broad, collective, generic, indefinite, indeterminate, inexact, nonsectarian, vague. SEE MAIN ENTRY
unspecious authentic, bona fide, honest
unspeciousness honesty
unspent net, residuary
unspiced insipid
unspied latent, surreptitious
unspirited inactive, insipid, jejune *(dull)*, languid, lifeless *(dull)*, nonchalant
unspiritual civil *(public)*, corporeal, lecherous, material *(physical)*, mundane, physical
unspoiled intact
unspoken implicit, implied, tacit
unsporting unfair
unspotted blameless, clean, infallible, inviolate, pure, unblemished
unspurious authentic, bona fide, factual, genuine, honest, real, true *(authentic)*
unspuriousness honesty
unstable aleatory *(uncertain)*, capricious, dangerous, ephemeral, faithless, fallible, inconsistent, indefinite, insecure, irresponsible, mutable, *non compos mentis*, nonsubstantial *(not sturdy)*, peccable, precarious, temporary, transient, transitory, undependable, unpredictable, unreliable, unsettled, unsound *(not strong)*, untrustworthy, variable, volatile
unstaffed devoid
unstaid moving *(in motion)*, unsettled
unstained clean, inviolate, pure
unstated tacit
unstationary moving *(in motion)*
unsteadfast faithless, false *(disloyal)*, insecure, irresolute, mutable, noncommittal, precarious, undependable, unpredictable, untrustworthy, variable
unsteadfastness bad faith, disloyalty
unsteadiness doubt *(indecision)*, inconsistency, indecision, irregularity
unsteady broken *(interrupted)*, dangerous, disorderly, inconsistent, infrequent, insecure, irresolute, irresponsible, mutable, noncommittal, powerless, precarious, sporadic, undependable, unpredictable, unreliable, unsettled, unsound *(not strong)*, variable, volatile
unstereotyped informal
unstick detach, disengage
unstinted absolute *(complete)*, full, profuse, unqualified *(unlimited)*
unstinting benevolent, charitable *(benevolent)*, copious, liberal *(generous)*, philanthropic, profuse
unstirred callous, dispassionate, inactive, insusceptible *(uncaring)*, nonchalant, obdurate, unaffected *(uninfluenced)*
unstirring placid, stagnant
unstoppable infallible
unstopped chronic, continual *(connected)*, continual *(perpetual)*, continuous, direct *(uninterrupted)*, free *(not restricted)*, live *(existing)*, rampant
unstoppered open *(unclosed)*
unstopping chronic, persistent
unstraightforward devious, disingenuous, oblique *(evasive)*
unstraightforward action indirection *(indirect action)*
unstraightforwardness dishonesty, improbity, indirection *(deceitfulness)*
unstrain ease
unstrained harmonious
unstrained meaning connotation
unstrap disengage
unstrengthened dangerous, helpless *(defenseless)*, insipid, languid, powerless
unstrict flexible, inaccurate, informal, lax, lenient, liberal *(not literal)*
unstrictness latitude
unstruck unaffected *(uninfluenced)*
unstrung powerless
unstudied casual, ingenuous, perfunctory, simple, spontaneous, unpremeditated, unversed
unsturdy nonsubstantial *(not sturdy)*
unstylish outdated, outmoded
unsubduable indomitable, inexpugnable, insurmountable, invincible
unsubdued undaunted
unsubject immune
unsubjected free *(enjoying civil liberty)*, independent, sovereign *(independent)*
unsubmissive contumacious, disobedient, disorderly, incorrigible, indomitable, intractable, lawless, nonconforming, nonconsenting, recalcitrant, recusant, renitent, restive, uncontrollable, unruly
unsubmissiveness contempt *(disobedience to the court)*
unsubsiding chronic
unsubstantial baseless, delusive, erroneous, futile, ill-founded, illusory, immaterial, impalpable, imponderable, incorporeal, insubstantial, intangible, negligible, nominal, nonsubstantial *(not sturdy)*, null *(insignificant)*, otiose, precarious, slight, tenuous, unfounded, unsound *(fallacious)*, unsound *(not strong)*, untrue
unsubstantiality blank *(emptiness)*, immateriality, nonentity
unsubstantialness impalpability, nonentity
unsubstantiated baseless, implausible, inconclusive, theoretical, unconfirmed, uncorroborated, unsupported
unsuccessful disappointed, futile, inadept, ineffective, ineffectual, otiose, regrettable, unavailing, unproductive
unsuccessful attempt failure *(lack of success)*
unsuccessful trial mistrial
unsuccessfulness frustration
unsuccessive broken *(interrupted)*, desultory, disjointed, disjunctive *(tending to disjoin)*, intermittent, sporadic
unsufferable painful
unsufficing deficient, inadequate, insufficient, nonsubstantial *(not sufficient)*
unsuitability disability *(legal disqualification)*, disqualification *(factor that disqualifies)*, impropriety, incongruity, inexpedience, misdoing
unsuitable bad *(inferior)*, bad *(offensive)*, detrimental, disproportionate, gratuitous *(unwarranted)*, ill-advised, imperfect, improper, inadmissible, inadvisable, inapplicable, inapposite, inappropriate, inapt, incapable, incompetent, incongruous, inconsistent, ineligible, inept *(inappropriate)*, injudicious, inopportune, irrelevant, objectionable, unacceptable, unauthorized, unbecoming, undesirable, undue *(excessive)*, unfit, unprofessional, unsatisfactory, unseemly, wrongful. SEE MAIN ENTRY
unsuitable action impropriety

unsuitable for practical use impracticable
unsuitableness disability *(legal disqualification),* impropriety, incompatibility *(inconsistency),* inconsistency
unsuitably timed untimely
unsuited gratuitous *(unwarranted),* improper, inapplicable, inapposite, inappropriate, incapable, ineligible, inept *(inappropriate),* inopportune, insufficient, unbecoming, unfavorable, unfit, unqualified *(not competent),* unsuitable
unsuitedness disability *(legal disqualification)*
unsullied blameless, clean, irreprehensible, pure, unblemished
unsunderable indivisible, inseparable
unsupplied deficient, devoid, void *(empty)*
unsupportable baseless, ill-founded, illusory, insubstantial, unfounded
unsupported baseless, helpless *(defenseless),* ill-founded, inconclusive, powerless, solitary, unauthorized, unconfirmed, uncorroborated, unfounded. SEE MAIN ENTRY
unsupported by evidence inconclusive
unsupposed actual
unsuppressed chronic, intemperate, lawless, uncurbed, unmitigated, unrestrained *(not in custody),* unrestrained *(not repressed)*
unsure aleatory *(uncertain),* conditional, controversial, debatable, disputable, doubtful, dubious, equivocal, fallible, hesitant, inconclusive, indefinite, insecure, leery, noncommittal, precarious, skeptical, uncertain *(questionable),* undecided, undependable, unpredictable, vague. SEE MAIN ENTRY
unsure of oneself diffident
unsureness doubt *(indecision),* hazard, hesitation, incertitude, indecision, peril, suspicion *(uncertainty)*
unsurmountable insurmountable
unsurpassable inestimable, prime *(most valuable)*
unsurpassed absolute *(ideal),* cardinal *(outstanding),* dominant, infallible, leading *(ranking first),* paramount, premium, primary, prime *(most valuable),* professional *(stellar),* superior *(excellent),* superlative, unapproachable. SEE MAIN ENTRY
unsurprising usual
unsusceptibility resistance
unsusceptible callous, cold-blooded, dispassionate, immune, obdurate, phlegmatic
unsusceptible of change certain *(positive)*
unsuspected blind *(concealed),* covert, latent, surreptitious
unsuspected event surprise
unsuspecting credulous, definite, incognizant, insensible, naive, secure *(confident),* unaware, unsuspecting, unwitting. SEE MAIN ENTRY
unsuspectingly unknowingly
unsuspectingness credulity
unsuspicious credulous, definite, ingenuous, naive, unsuspecting
unsuspiciousness credulity
unsustainable baseless, debatable, disputable, doubtful, dubitative, erroneous, ill-founded, illogical, insubstantial, untenable. SEE MAIN ENTRY
unsustained baseless, debatable, disputable, unsupported
unswayable impervious, inflexible
unswayed dispassionate, fair *(just),* impartial, judicial, just, liberal *(broad minded),* loyal, neutral, nonpartisan, objective, open-minded, receptive, unaffected *(uninfluenced),* unbiased, unprejudiced
unsweet bitter *(acrid tasting)*
unswerring purposeful
unswerving constant, direct *(straight),* industrious, loyal, patient, persistent, pertinacious, relentless, resolute, right *(correct),* right *(direct),* sedulous, serious *(devoted),* stable, steadfast, straightforward, true *(loyal),* undistorted, uniform, unremitting
unswerving fidelity adhesion *(loyalty)*
unswervingly faithfully
unsymmetric irregular *(not usual)*
unsymmetrical disproportionate, irregular *(not usual)*
unsympathetic callous, cold-blooded, cruel, harsh, insusceptible *(uncaring),* obdurate, relentless, ruthless, unaffected *(uninfluenced),* unrelenting, unresponsive
unsympathizing callous, cruel
unsynthetic authentic, genuine, honest, natural, real, sterling, unaffected *(sincere),* veridical
unsystematic capricious, casual, desultory, discursive *(digressive),* disjointed, disordered, disorderly, haphazard, indiscriminate, sporadic, unpredictable
untactful impolitic, unpolitic
untaint decontaminate
untainted absolute *(ideal),* blameless, infallible, pure, unblemished, unimpeachable
untaken available, unclaimed
untalented amateur, inadept
untalkative laconic, mute, taciturn
untalked of undisclosed
untamed brutal, lawless, unmitigated, vicious
untangle ascertain, elucidate, explain, explicate, rectify, resolve *(solve),* solve
untarnishable incorruptible
untarnished absolute *(ideal),* clean, pure, unblemished
untasteful inelegant, unbecoming, unseemly
untastefulness indecency
untaught spontaneous, unversed
untaught state ignorance
untaxed free *(at no charge)*
untempered intemperate, unmitigated
untenable baseless, disabled *(deprived of legal right),* doubtful, helpless *(defenseless),* ill-founded, illogical, implausible, inadequate, indefensible, insubstantial, invalid, ludicrous, nonsubstantial *(not sturdy),* sophistic, unbelievable, unfounded, unreasonable, unsound *(fallacious),* unsupported, unsustainable, vulnerable. SEE MAIN ENTRY
untenableness invalidity
untenanted devoid, vacant, void *(empty)*
untender harsh
unterrified undaunted
untested inconclusive, novel
untested opinion theory
unthankfulness ingratitude
unthinkability impossibility
unthinkable implausible, impossible, incomprehensible, incredible, infeasible, ludicrous, prodigious *(amazing),* unbelievable
unthinking careless, fatuous, heedless, ill-judged, impolitic, impulsive *(rash),* inadvertent, involuntary, irrational, lax, misadvised, negligent, opaque, perfunctory, reckless, remiss, spontaneous, superficial, thoughtless, unintentional, unpremeditated, unwitting, vacuous
unthinkingness disregard *(unconcern)*
unthorough cursory, lax, negligent, partial *(relating to a part),* perfunctory
unthought of perfunctory, unanticipated, unexpected, unforeseeable, unforeseen
unthoughtful ill-judged, irrational, lax, misadvised, thoughtless
unthoughtfulness inexpedience, temerity
unthreatened immune, safe, secure *(free from danger)*
unthreatening harmless
unthriftiness waste
unthrifty improvident, prodigal, profligate *(extravagant),* profuse
untidiness laxity
untidy disordered, disorderly, lax, slipshod
untie break *(separate),* disencumber, disengage, disentangle, disenthrall, extricate, free, liberate, remove *(eliminate),* separate, sever, split
untied free *(not restricted),* unbound
until ad interim. SEE MAIN ENTRY
until the conclusion of throughout *(during)*
untimeliness impropriety, inexpedience
untimely improper, inapposite, inappropriate, inapt, inauspicious, inept *(inappropriate),* inopportune, overdue, premature, regrettable, undue *(not owing),* unexpected, unfavorable, unsuitable. SEE MAIN ENTRY
untimid undaunted
untiring diligent, faithful *(diligent),* incessant, industrious, painstaking, patient, persistent, pertinacious, resolute, sedulous, stable, steadfast, unremitting
untitled ignoble
untold esoteric, hidden, indefinite, innumerable, multiple, myriad, mysterious, personal *(private),* secret, tacit, undisclosed, unlimited
untolerating parochial
untomb disinter
untorn intact
untouchable dispassionate, immune, impalpable, inalienable, intangible
untouched cold-blooded, immune, impartial, insensible, insusceptible *(uncaring),* intact, inviolate, natural, nonchalant, obdurate, pure, unadulterated, unaffected *(uninfluenced)*
untoward adverse *(hostile),* deplorable, detrimental, disproportionate, inadvisable, inapposite, inappropriate, inapt, inauspicious, inept *(inappropriate),* lawless, perverse, regrettable, uncontrollable, unfavorable, unpropitious, unruly, unsatisfactory, unsuitable
untraceable irretrievable
untractable fractious, immutable
untraditional divergent, unprecedented, unusual
untrained disorderly, incompetent, inexperienced, unaccustomed
untrained individual novice
untrained person layman
untrammel disencumber, rescue
untrammeled clear *(unencumbered),* free *(not restricted),* unbound, unrestrained *(not in custody),* unrestricted

untransferable unalienable
untranslatable indefinable, ineffable, undefinable
untransparent equivocal, opaque
untraveled provincial
untreacherous candid, incorruptible, loyal, true *(loyal)*
untreacherousness responsibility *(conscience)*
untried inconclusive, inexperienced, moot, novel, unaccustomed, unconfirmed, unsettled
untrodden unsettled
untroubled cold-blooded, harmonious, peaceable, phlegmatic, placid, positive *(confident)*. SEE MAIN ENTRY
untrue bogus, broken *(unfulfilled)*, colorable *(specious)*, deceptive, delusive, dishonest, erroneous, faithless, fallacious, false *(disloyal)*, false *(inaccurate)*, fictitious, fraudulent, inaccurate, incorrect, invalid, lying, mendacious, perfidious, recreant, spurious, unfounded, unreliable, unsound *(fallacious)*, unsustainable, untrustworthy. SEE MAIN ENTRY
untrue declaration falsehood
untrue statement misrepresentation, story *(falsehood)*
untrue story myth
untrueness bad faith
untrustful cynical, suspicious *(distrustful)*
untrustiness bad faith
untrusting incredulous, skeptical, suspicious *(distrustful)*
untrustworthiness bad faith, dishonesty, improbity, indirection *(deceitfulness)*, knavery
untrustworthy dangerous, dishonest, disingenuous, disreputable, faithless, fallible, false *(disloyal)*, fraudulent, inaccurate, insecure, irresponsible, machiavellian, perfidious, precarious, recreant, sinister, suspicious *(distrustful)*, uncertain *(questionable)*, undependable, unreliable, unsound *(not strong)*, unsustainable, untrue. SEE MAIN ENTRY
untrusty irresponsible
untruth canard, deceit, deception, defamation, dishonesty, false pretense, falsehood, fiction, figment, lie, misrepresentation, misstatement, myth, perjury, pretense *(pretext)*, pretext, story *(falsehood)*, subreption, subterfuge
untruthful dishonest, disingenuous, disreputable, evasive, fraudulent, lying, machiavellian, mendacious, perfidious, untrue
untruthful report canard, fiction
untruthfulness bad faith, deceit, deception, dishonesty, false pretense, falsification, fraud, improbity, indirection *(deceitfulness)*, misrepresentation, misstatement
unturned direct *(straight)*, straightforward
untutored inexperienced
untutored intelligence instinct
untwist disentangle, simplify *(clarify)*
untying division *(act of dividing)*, liberation, release
untypical anomalous, dissimilar, infrequent, unusual
ununiformity inequality, irregularity
unus sole
unusable expendable, impracticable, inapplicable, otiose, unfit
unused defunct, expendable, idle, inexperienced, novel, unemployed, vacant
unusual anomalous, different, distinct *(distinguished from others)*, eccentric, extraordinary, foreign, individual, infrequent, irregular *(not usual)*, lurid, momentous, nonconforming, noteworthy, novel, original *(creative)*, particular *(individual)*, particular *(specific)*, patent, peculiar *(distinctive)*, portentous *(eliciting amazement)*, rare, remarkable, scarce, singular, special, specific, unaccustomed, uncommon, unexpected, unforeseeable, unique, unorthodox, unprecedented. SEE MAIN ENTRY
unusual circumstance phenomenon *(unusual occurrence)*
unusual happening phenomenon *(unusual occurrence)*
unusual incident phenomenon *(unusual occurrence)*
unusual occurrence surprise
unusual task onus *(burden)*
unusually particularly
unusualness irregularity, quirk *(idiosyncrasy)*
unutilized vacant
unutterable ineffable
unutterable contempt disdain
unvalidated unconfirmed, uncorroborated, unsupported
unvanquishable insurmountable, invincible
unvanquished independent, prevailing *(having superior force)*, sovereign *(independent)*, successful
unvaried boiler plate, equal, literal, ordinary, pedestrian, prosaic, stale, uniform, usual
unvarnished accurate, genuine, honest, literal, naked *(lacking embellishment)*, simple, true *(authentic)*, unadulterated
unvarnished truth honesty
unvarying certain *(positive)*, chronic, comparable *(equivalent)*, constant, continual *(perpetual)*, equal, fixed *(settled)*, invariably, normal *(regular)*, permanent, persistent, regular *(orderly)*, steadfast, uniform, unremitting
unveil admit *(concede)*, bare, clarify, denude, detect, disabuse, disclose, disinter, divulge, educe, exhibit, expose, find *(discover)*, manifest, present *(introduce)*, produce *(offer to view)*, reveal. SEE MAIN ENTRY
unveiled comprehensible, naked *(lacking embellishment)*, palpable, scrutable
unveiling admission *(disclosure)*, denouement, disclosure *(act of disclosing)*, manifestation
unvenal incorruptible
unvendible unmarketable
unventilated impervious
unventured unsettled
unveracious dishonest, evasive, false *(inaccurate)*, fraudulent, incorrect, lying, mendacious, untrue
unveraciousness bad faith
unveracity bad faith, deception, false pretense, misrepresentation
unveridical mendacious
unverifiable controversial, debatable, disputable, dubious, hypothetical, unsustainable
unverified inconclusive, unconfirmed, uncorroborated, unsupported
unverified comments hearsay
unverified news hearsay, report *(rumor)*
unverified supposition conjecture
unverity bad faith
unversed blind *(not discerning)*, inexperienced, unaccustomed, unacquainted, unaware. SEE MAIN ENTRY
unvexed complacent, patient
unviable impracticable, insurmountable
unvindictive placable
unviolated clean, inviolate
unvirtuous bad *(offensive)*, blameworthy, delinquent *(guilty of a misdeed)*, diabolic, dishonest, dissolute, fraudulent, immoral, lewd, peccable, peccant *(culpable)*, profane, promiscuous, prurient, salacious
unvirtuousness delinquency *(misconduct)*
unvisited solitary
unvivid insipid, lifeless *(dull)*, pedestrian
unvocal inarticulate, mute, speechless, taciturn
unvocalizing mute
unvoiced implicit, tacit, undisclosed
unvoidable noncancellable
unwakened dormant
unwanted derelict *(abandoned)*, ineligible, needless, otiose, unacceptable, undesirable, unsolicited
unwariness disregard *(unconcern)*, inconsideration, indiscretion, neglect, negligence
unwarlike nonmilitant
unwarned unaware, unsuspecting
unwarped direct *(straight)*, nonpartisan, objective, open-minded, unbiased, undistorted, unprejudiced
unwarrantable disproportionate, felonious, illegal, illicit, improper, indefensible, inexcusable, lawless, untenable, unwarranted
unwarrantable intrusion nuisance
unwarranted baseless, disproportionate, exorbitant, extreme *(exaggerated)*, ill-founded, illegal, illicit, inconsequential, inexcusable, irregular *(improper)*, irrelevant, lawless, nonessential, outrageous, profuse, prohibitive *(costly)*, sophistic, ultra vires, unauthorized, unconscionable, undue *(excessive)*, unfounded, unjust, unlawful, unreasonable, unsound *(fallacious)*. SEE MAIN ENTRY
unwarranted conclusion anacoluthon, non sequitur
unwarranted purchase caveat emptor
unwary careless, heedless, hot-blooded, impolitic, improvident, imprudent, injudicious, lax, misadvised, negligent, reckless, unaware, unpolitic
unwasteful economical, frugal
unwastefulness austerity
unwatchful derelict *(negligent)*, heedless, lax, negligent, perfunctory, reckless, remiss, thoughtless
unwatchfulness disregard *(unconcern)*, laxity, neglect, negligence
unwavering certain *(positive)*, constant, definite, diligent, faithful *(diligent)*, faithful *(loyal)*, fixed *(settled)*, indomitable, industrious, inexorable, infallible, intense, loyal, patient, permanent, persistent, pertinacious, positive *(confident)*, purposeful, resolute, stable, staunch, steadfast, straightforward, true *(loyal)*, unalterable, unrelenting, unyielding
unweakened powerful, undiminished
unwearied patient, unremitting
unwearying diligent, incessant, patient, persistent, pertinacious, sedulous
unweighable imponderable

unweighed casual, perfunctory
unwelcome invidious, unacceptable, undesirable, unsatisfactory, unsolicited
unwelcome suggestion intrusion
unwell unsound *(not strong)*
unwholesome detrimental, harmful, immoral, insalubrious, noxious, obnoxious, obscene, peccant *(unhealthy)*, pernicious, sinister
unwholesome condition disease
unwieldy impracticable, onerous, ponderous
unwilled involuntary
unwilling adverse *(hostile)*, averse, disinclined, disobedient, dissident, evasive, intractable, involuntary, nonconsenting, recalcitrant, recusant, reluctant, remiss, renitent, restive. SEE MAIN ENTRY
unwilling to accept inconvincible, incredulous
unwilling to care insusceptible *(uncaring)*
unwilling to give parsimonious
unwilling to pay penurious
unwillingness contempt *(disobedience to the court)*, declination, disincentive, hesitation, refusal, reluctance, resistance, scruple
unwillingness to believe incredulity
unwillingly SEE MAIN ENTRY
unwind spread
unwise detrimental, disadvantageous, fatuous, ill-advised, ill-judged, impolitic, imprudent, inadvisable, inapt, inept *(inappropriate)*, injudicious, irrational, misadvised, puerile, reckless, unfit, unpolitic, unreasonable. SEE MAIN ENTRY
unwiseness indiscretion, inexpedience
unwished undesirable, unsolicited
unwitnessed unconfirmed
unwitting incognizant, insensible, unintentional. SEE MAIN ENTRY
unwittingly unknowingly
unwitty pedestrian
unwonted different, nonconforming, original *(creative)*, unforeseeable, unusual
unworkability impossibility
unworkable impossible, impracticable, infeasible, inoperable *(impracticable)*, insurmountable, otiose. SEE MAIN ENTRY
unworldliness ignorance
unworldly incorporeal, inexperienced, naive
unworn intact, undiminished
unworried nonchalant, phlegmatic
unworthiness frailty
unworthy blameful, blameworthy, contemptible, delinquent *(guilty of a misdeed)*, disgraceful, disreputable, ignoble, odious, peccant *(culpable)*, poor *(inferior in quality)*, reprehensible, scandalous, undesirable, unethical, unfit, unsatisfactory. SEE MAIN ENTRY
unworthy of belief suspicious *(questionable)*
unworthy of confidence untrustworthy
unworthy of consideration inappreciable, inconsiderable
unworthy of notice inappreciable, inconsiderable
unworthy of regard negligible, petty
unworthy of respect notorious
unworthy of serious consideration de minimus, paltry, puerile
unworthy of serious notice frivolous
unworthy of trust untrustworthy
unwrap bare, denude, expose, unveil
unwritten nuncupative, oral, parol, prescriptive, verbal
unwritten law custom, equity *(justice)*
unyielding barren, callous, chronic, disobedient, dogmatic, durable, fanatical, firm, formidable, froward, immutable, impervious, implacable, impossible, indelible, indestructible, indomitable, industrious, inexorable, inexpugnable, infallible, inflexible, insusceptible *(resistant)*, insusceptible *(uncaring)*, intractable, invincible, ironclad, irreconcilable, obdurate, oppressive, parsimonious, particular *(exacting)*, patient, permanent, persistent, pertinacious, perverse, recalcitrant, relentless, resolute, restive, rigid, sedulous, serious *(devoted)*, severe, solid *(compact)*, stable, staunch, steadfast, strict, stringent, strong, unaffected *(uninfluenced)*, unalterable, unbending, uncompromising, unmitigated, unproductive, unrelenting, unruly, willful. SEE MAIN ENTRY
unyieldingness resistance, rigor, tenacity
unyoke disencumber, dissociate, divorce, separate
unzealous disinclined
up for discussion arguable, debatable
up in arms inimical, resentful
up in the air debatable
up to effective *(efficient)*, proficient, sciential, until
up to date contemporary, current, progressive *(advocating change)*, sophisticated
up to par palatable
up to standard fairly *(moderately)*
up to the mark coequal
up to the minute contemporary, current, sophisticated
up to the time of until
up to this time heretofore
up-to-date novel, present *(current)*, prevailing *(current)*, recent
up-to-the-minute novel, present *(current)*
upbear bear *(support)*
upbraid blame, castigate, cavil, censure, complain *(criticize)*, condemn *(blame)*, criticize *(find fault with)*, denounce *(condemn)*, disapprove *(condemn)*, fault, harass, impeach, lash *(attack verbally)*, rebuke, remonstrate, reprehend, reprimand, reproach. SEE MAIN ENTRY
upbraiding critical *(faultfinding)*, criticism, denunciation, diatribe, objurgation, outcry, reprimand, reproach, revilement
upbringing education, instruction *(teaching)*
upbuild build *(construct)*, edify
upcoming forthcoming, future, immediate *(imminent)*, imminent, instant, pending *(imminent)*, prospective, proximate
updated version revision *(corrected version)*
upend overthrow, overturn, upset
upgrade ameliorate, amend, elevate, enhance, inure *(benefit)*, meliorate, promote *(advance)*
upgrading boom *(prosperity)*
upgrowth boom *(increase)*, boom *(prosperity)*, development *(progression)*
upheaval bluster *(commotion)*, cataclysm, commotion, confusion *(turmoil)*, disaster, furor, havoc, mutiny, outburst, rebellion, revolution, shambles, strife, subversion, turmoil. SEE MAIN ENTRY
uphill operose
uphold adhere *(maintain loyalty)*, advocate, aid, approve, bear *(support)*, bolster, certify *(approve)*, concur *(agree)*, confirm, continue *(prolong)*, corroborate, defend, demonstrate *(establish)*, document, espouse, establish *(show)*, indorse, justify, maintain *(sustain)*, pass *(approve)*, preserve, promote *(organize)*, prove, reassure, recommend, sanction, side, sponsor, subsidize, substantiate, support *(assist)*, sustain *(confirm)*, sustain *(prolong)*, underwrite, vouch, witness *(attest to)*. SEE MAIN ENTRY
uphold in evidence corroborate, establish *(show)*, support *(corroborate)*, sustain *(confirm)*
upholder abettor, advocate *(counselor)*, advocate *(espouser)*, apologist, backer, benefactor, mainstay, partisan, patron *(influential supporter)*, proponent
upholding conservation, corroboration
upkeep alimony, conservation, maintenance *(support of spouse)*, overhead, preservation, promotion *(encouragement)*, safekeeping, support *(assistance)*, sustenance. SEE MAIN ENTRY
uplift edify, elevate, elevation, enhance, heighten *(elevate)*, meliorate, promotion *(advancement)*, raise *(advance)*, reassure, reform
uplifting edification
upmost prominent
upper circles elite
upper class society
upper classes elite
upper extremity maximum *(pinnacle)*, pinnacle
upper hand advantage, edge *(advantage)*, predominance
upper limit capacity *(maximum)*
upperhand supremacy
uppermost best, cardinal *(basic)*, cardinal *(outstanding)*, primary
uppish proud *(conceited)*, supercilious
uppity proud *(conceited)*, supercilious
upraise elevate, enhance, heighten *(elevate)*, raise *(advance)*, uphold
upright blameless, clean, conscientious, credible, dependable, equitable, ethical, evenhanded, fair *(just)*, high-minded, incorruptible, innocent, irreprehensible, just, law-abiding, licit, meritorious, moral, pure, reliable, reputable, right *(correct)*, scrupulous, sterling, straightforward, unaffected *(sincere)*, unimpeachable. SEE MAIN ENTRY
upright distance elevation
upright moral character integrity
uprighteousness justice
uprightly faithfully
uprightness candor *(straightforwardness)*, conscience, credibility, equity *(justice)*, ethics, fairness, good faith, honesty, honor *(good reputation)*, integrity, merit, principle *(virtue)*, probity, rectitude, responsibility *(conscience)*, right *(righteousness)*, trustworthiness
uprightness of character integrity
uprisen disorderly
uprising anarchy, commotion, defiance, disturbance, insurrection, mutiny, outbreak, rebellion, resistance, revolt, revolution, riot, sedition, subversion. SEE MAIN ENTRY
uproar bluster *(commotion)*, brawl, commotion, confusion *(turmoil)*, disorder *(lack of order)*, disturbance, embroilment, fracas, fray, furor, imbroglio, noise, outbreak, outburst, outcry, pandemonium, riot, shambles, turmoil. SEE MAIN ENTRY

uproarious disorderly
uproariousness noise, pandemonium
uproot destroy *(efface)*, dislodge, eliminate *(eradicate)*, eradicate, evict, exclude, extirpate, overthrow, overturn, reject, remove *(eliminate)*, supplant
uprooting evulsion, rejection
ups and downs vicissitudes
upset agitate *(perturb)*, annoy, beat *(defeat)*, counterargument, debacle, defeat, disaster, discommode, discompose, disconcert, discourage, dislocate, disorganize, disorient, disrupt, distress, disturb, embarrass, foil, harrow, hold up *(delay)*, kill *(defeat)*, muddle, obfuscate, override, overrule, overthrow, overturn, perplex, perturb, pique, prostration, rebellion, subversion, subvert, supplant, surmount, unsettled. SEE MAIN ENTRY
upsetting oppressive, unsatisfactory
upshot amount *(result)*, conclusion *(outcome)*, consequence *(conclusion)*, denouement, development *(outgrowth)*, effect, end *(termination)*, holding *(ruling of a court)*, issuance, outcome, result
upstanding high-minded, law-abiding, moral, right *(correct)*, upright
upstandingness honesty, integrity, rectitude
upsurge advance *(progression)*, boom *(increase)*, boom *(prosperity)*, inflate, inflation *(increase)*
upswing headway
uptrend development *(progression)*
upturn in prices inflation *(decrease in value of currency)*
upward curve boom *(prosperity)*
upward trend boom *(prosperity)*
uranic stellar
urban civic, civil *(public)*
urban district city
urban place city
urbana record
urbane civil *(polite)*, sophisticated
urbanitas courtesy
urbanity courtesy
urbanization city, development *(building)*
urbs city
urge abet, admonish *(advise)*, advocate, argue, assert, bait *(harass)*, bait *(lure)*, cajole, call *(appeal to)*, caution, charge *(instruct on the law)*, coax, compel, constrain *(compel)*, counsel, demand, desire *(noun)*, desire *(verb)*, exact, exhort, foment, force *(coerce)*, hold out *(deliberate on an offer)*, impel, impetus, importune, incite, inculcate, influence, insist, inspire, inveigle, lobby, motivate, persuade, petition, plead *(implore)*, pray, press *(beseech)*, pressure, prevail *(persuade)*, prevail upon, promote *(organize)*, prompt, provocation, reason *(persuade)*, recommend, request, solicit, stimulus. SEE MAIN ENTRY
urge against expostulate, forewarn, remonstrate
urge as a reason allege
urge forward compel, constrain *(compel)*, expedite, impel, precipitate *(hasten)*, press *(constrain)*
urge in court litigate
urge not to dissuade
urge on agitate *(activate)*, expedite, hasten, spirit
urge persistently pray
urge reasons for assert, defend, justify, plead *(argue a case)*
urge repeatedly pray
urge to take heed forewarn
urge upon offer *(propose)*, tender
urgency compulsion *(coercion)*, dispatch *(promptness)*, emergency, exigency, force *(compulsion)*, haste, importance, necessity, need *(requirement)*, pressure, priority, requirement, stress *(accent)*, stress *(strain)*. SEE MAIN ENTRY
urgent compulsory, critical *(crucial)*, crucial, essential *(required)*, exigent, grave *(important)*, imperative, indispensable, insistent, mandatory, necessary *(required)*, obligatory, peremptory *(imperative)*, provocative, requisite, vehement, vital. SEE MAIN ENTRY
urgent need exigency
urgent request prayer
urgent requirement necessity, need *(requirement)*
urger demagogue
urgere impel, press *(beseech)*, urge
urging impulsive *(impelling)*, inducement, influence, instigation, invitation
urging by force compulsion *(coercion)*
urging by moral constraint compulsion *(coercion)*
urging by physical constraint compulsion *(coercion)*
usability utility *(usefulness)*, utilization
usable applicable, available, beneficial, constructive *(creative)*, disposable, effective *(operative)*, eligible, functional, malleable, passable, ripe, viable. SEE MAIN ENTRY
usage consumption, custom, function, management *(judicious use)*, manner *(behavior)*, means *(opportunity)*, mode, phraseology, practice *(custom)*, prescription *(custom)*, procedure, use. SEE MAIN ENTRY
use apply *(put in practice)*, consumption, employ *(make use of)*, exert, exhaust *(deplete)*, expend *(consume)*, exploit *(make use of)*, exploitation, function, handle *(manage)*, help, impropriate, manipulate *(control unfairly)*, manipulate *(utilize skillfully)*, means *(opportunity)*, ownership, parlay *(exploit successfully)*, patronize *(trade with)*, ply, practice *(custom)*, prescription *(custom)*, profit, purpose, resort, spend, treat *(process)*, usage, utility *(usefulness)*, value, wield, worth. SEE MAIN ENTRY
use and title patent
use another's services employ *(engage services)*
use arguments plead *(argue a case)*
use as an agent employ *(engage services)*
use badly exploit *(take advantage of)*, ill use
use carefully conserve
use dispiteously mishandle *(maltreat)*, mistreat, persecute
use evasions tergiversate
use false evidence frame *(prearrange)*
use for one's own needs bilk
use force upon coerce
use frugally conserve
use hard mistreat, tax *(overwork)*
use improperly abuse *(misuse)*, exploit *(take advantage of)*
use in support of propositions of law cite *(state)*
use of words parlance, phraseology
use one's authority police
use one's best endeavors attempt
use one's discretion choose
use one's imagination compose
use one's influence lobby
use one's option choose
use premises rent
use selfishly exploit *(take advantage of)*
use sparingly conserve
use subterfuge tergiversate
use threats threaten
use thriftily conserve
use trickery palter
use up consume, deplete, diminish, dissipate *(expend foolishly)*, exhaust *(deplete)*, expend *(consume)*, spend
use up available remedies exhaust *(try all possibilities)*
use violence force *(coerce)*
use wrongfully infringe
use wrongly abuse *(misuse)*, exploit *(take advantage of)*, ill use, misemploy, mishandle *(maltreat)*, mishandle *(mismanage)*, mistreat
useable operative, purposeful
used dilapidated, old, trite
used as a deterrent exemplary
used as a model exemplary
used as a specimen exemplary
used by all common *(shared)*
used to familiar *(informed)*
used up irredeemable
used with another thing appurtenant
useful applicable, beneficial, constructive *(creative)*, contributory, convenient, disposable, effective *(efficient)*, favorable *(advantageous)*, functional, gainful, instrumental, lucrative, ministerial, operative, potent, practical, pragmatic, productive, profitable, purposeful, salutary, subservient, valuable, viable. SEE MAIN ENTRY
useful office service *(assistance)*
usefulness consequence *(significance)*, expedience, feasibility, importance, service *(assistance)*, use, utilization, value
useless disabled *(made incapable)*, expendable, futile, impracticable, inadequate, incapable, incompetent, ineffective, ineffectual, inept *(incompetent)*, invalid, needless, nugatory, null *(insignificant)*, null *(invalid)*, null and void, otiose, paltry, powerless, redundant, superfluous, trivial, unable, unavailing, unfit, unproductive, unsatisfactory, void *(invalid)*. SEE MAIN ENTRY
useless check bad check
useless consumption waste
useless expenditure misapplication
useless trial mistrial
user customer
usher conduct, harbinger, precursor
usher in herald, induct, initiate, introduce, originate, precede, preface, receive *(permit to enter)*
using through *(by means of)*
using evasion evasive
using the help of through *(by means of)*
using up consumption
usitatus current, customary, habitual
usuage enjoyment *(use)*
usual accustomed *(customary)*, average *(standard)*, common *(customary)*, conventional, customary, daily, familiar *(customary)*, frequent, general, habitual, household *(familiar)*, jejune *(dull)*, lifeless *(dull)*, mediocre, mundane, nondescript, normal *(regular)*, ordinary, orthodox, pedestrian, prescriptive, prevailing *(current)*, pro forma, prosaic, regular *(conventional)*, rife, routine, typical. SEE MAIN ENTRY
usual custom matter of course, practice *(custom)*

usual manner custom
usual method practice *(custom)*
usual occurrence matter of course
usual practice matter of course
usual procedure habit, matter of course
usual thing matter of course
usual way practice *(procedure)*
usually as a rule, generally, invariably
usually understood common *(customary)*
usualness frequency
usufruct benefit *(betterment)*
usufructuary beneficiary. SEE MAIN ENTRY
usufructuary right SEE MAIN ENTRY
usura interest *(profit)*
usurious mercenary. SEE MAIN ENTRY
usurp abridge *(divest)*, accroach, adopt, annex *(arrogate)*, assume *(seize)*, attach *(seize)*, condemn *(seize)*, depose *(remove)*, deprive, dislodge, impropriate, infringe, invade, levy, overstep, preempt, seize *(confiscate)*, steal, supplant, takeover, trespass. SEE MAIN ENTRY
usurp for public use eminent domain
usurpation arrogation, assumption *(seizure)*, distress *(seizure)*, infringement
usurpatory confiscatory
usurped attached *(seized)*
usury exploitation. SEE MAIN ENTRY
usus misuse, practice *(procedure)*, routine, use
usus perversus abuse *(corrupt practice)*, misapplication
utensil appliance, device *(mechanism)*, expedient, instrument *(tool)*, tool
utensils paraphernalia *(apparatus)*
utile functional
utilis beneficial, profitable, salutary
utilitarian beneficial, disposable, effective *(efficient)*, functional, practical, pragmatic, purposeful, subservient, valuable
utilitarianism casuistry
utilitas expedience, use
utility advantage, appliance, behalf, benefit *(betterment)*, expedience, feasibility, function, help, instrument *(tool)*, profit, propriety *(appropriateness)*, use, value, worth. SEE MAIN ENTRY
utilizable applicable, disposable, functional, practical
utilization benefit *(betterment)*, consumption, enjoyment *(use)*, exploitation, management *(judicious use)*, usage, use. SEE MAIN ENTRY
utilization for profit exploitation
utilize adopt, apply *(put in practice)*, capitalize *(seize the chance)*, consume, employ *(make use of)*, exercise *(use)*, exert, exploit *(make use of)*, manipulate *(utilize skillfully)*, ply, profit, resort, wield. SEE MAIN ENTRY
utilize for profit bilk, capitalize *(seize the chance)*
utmost cardinal *(basic)*, cardinal *(outstanding)*, ceiling, extreme *(last)*, maximum *(amplitude)*, primary, prime *(most valuable)*, superlative. SEE MAIN ENTRY
utmost care diligence *(care)*
utmost extent ceiling, pinnacle
utmost height ceiling, culmination, pinnacle
utmost point extremity *(furthest point)*
utopian quixotic
utter absolute *(complete)*, arrant *(definite)*, comment, communicate, complete *(all-embracing)*, confess, converse, declare, disclose, disseminate, enunciate, express, gross *(flagrant)*, mention, observe *(remark)*, outright, phrase, proclaim, profess *(avow)*, pronounce *(speak)*, publish, pure, recite, relate *(tell)*, remark, reveal, speak, stark, thorough, total, unconditional, unequivocal, unmitigated, unqualified *(unlimited)*. SEE MAIN ENTRY
utter a falsehood bear false witness, misrepresent, palter, perjure
utter again repeat *(state again)*
utter an oath swear
utter contempt disdain
utter disapproval denunciation
utter force main force
utter formally pronounce *(pass judgment)*, pronounce *(speak)*
utter forth pronounce *(speak)*, speak
utter invective inveigh
utter judicial sentence pronounce *(pass judgment)*
utter judicial sentence against convict, determine
utter reliability certification *(certainness)*
utter with conviction certify *(attest)*, claim *(maintain)*, contend *(maintain)*, issue *(publish)*, posit, speak
utter words speak
utterance comment, communication *(statement)*, confession, disclosure *(something disclosed)*, observation, parlance, phrase, pronouncement, publicity, remark, speech, statement. SEE MAIN ENTRY
uttered nuncupative, oral, parol, stated, verbal
uttered with conviction alleged
uttering disclosure *(act of disclosing)*
utterly in toto, purely *(positively)*, wholly
utterly disperse dispel
utterly illogical irrational
utterly overlook ignore
utterly senseless *non compos mentis*
uttermost ceiling, extreme *(last)*

V

vacancy access *(opening)*, blank *(emptiness)*
vacant available, barren, devoid, idle, inexpressive, thoughtless, vacuous, void *(empty)*. SEE MAIN ENTRY
vacate abolish, abrogate *(rescind)*, adeem, avoid *(cancel)*, cancel, cease, depart, disappear, discontinue *(abandon)*, dismiss *(discharge)*, disown *(deny the validity)*, evacuate, leave *(depart)*, move *(alter position)*, negate, nullify, quash, quit *(evacuate)*, recant, relinquish, renege, repeal, rescind, resign, retire *(conclude a career)*, retire *(retreat)*, retreat, revoke, secede, withdraw. SEE MAIN ENTRY
vacate office abandon *(withdraw)*, demit
vacate one's seat demit
vacated null *(invalid)*, null and void, open *(accessible)*
vacating abandonment *(desertion)*, abdication, avoidance *(cancellation)*
vacatio exemption, immunity
vacation abdication, abolition, ademption, avoidance *(cancellation)*, cancellation, countermand, defeasance, furlough, holiday, leave *(absence)*, pause, recess *(noun)*, recess *(verb)*, resignation *(relinquishment)*. SEE MAIN ENTRY
vacatur ademption, cancellation, revocation. SEE MAIN ENTRY
vaccinate inject
vacillant irresolute
vacillare vacillate
vacillate alternate *(fluctuate)*, beat *(pulsate)*, doubt *(hesitate)*, hesitate, oscillate, pause, tergiversate, vary. SEE MAIN ENTRY
vacillating capricious, dubious, faithless, hesitant, inconsistent, irresolute, irresponsible, moving *(in motion)*, mutable, noncommittal, shifting, undecided, undependable, unreliable, unsettled, volatile
vacillation ambivalence, doubt *(indecision)*, hesitation, incertitude, inconsistency, indecision
vacillatory irresolute, undecided
vacuefacere vacate *(leave)*
vacuitas exemption
vacuity nullity, opacity
vacuous barren, devoid, fatuous, inexpressive, jejune *(dull)*, opaque, thoughtless, vacant, void *(empty)*. SEE MAIN ENTRY
vacuousness blank *(emptiness)*
vacuum blank *(emptiness)*, need *(deprivation)*
vacuus blank *(emptiness)*, free *(relieved from a burden)*, idle, unemployed, vacant, void *(empty)*
vadimonium guarantee
vadimonium deserere default
vadium promise, security *(pledge)*
vadium mortuum charge *(lien)*, cloud *(incumbrance)*
vadium vivum charge *(lien)*
vafer sly
vagabond moving *(in motion)*
vagabondage vagrancy
vagabondism vagrancy
vagari err, prowl
vagarious capricious
vagary notion, quirk *(idiosyncrasy)*
vagrancy SEE MAIN ENTRY
vagrant derelict, indirect, moving *(in motion)*, variable
vague allusive, ambiguous, broad, debatable, disputable, dubious, equivocal, evasive, impalpable, imponderable, inapprehensible, inarticulate, incomprehensible, inconspicuous, indefinite, indeterminate, indistinct, inexact, inexpressive, inscrutable, insubstantial, intangible, nebulous, noncommittal, oblique *(evasive)*, obscure *(faint)*, opaque, open-ended, problematic, uncertain *(ambiguous)*, unclear, undecided, undefinable, unspecified. SEE MAIN ENTRY
vague impression hint
vague suggestion hint
vagueness ambiguity, confusion *(ambiguity)*, doubt *(indecision)*, ignorance, incertitude, indistinctness, obscuration, opacity
vagus discursive *(digressive)*
vail largess *(gift)*
vain baseless, futile, ineffective, ineffectual, invalid, nugatory, orgulous, otiose, presumptuous, pretentious *(pompous)*, proud *(conceited)*, unavailing
vain attempt abortion *(fiasco)*, failure *(lack of success)*, miscarriage. SEE MAIN ENTRY
vain effort abortion *(fiasco)*, miscarriage
vain pretensions pride
vainglorious grandiose, inflated *(bombastic)*, orgulous, orotund, pretentious *(pompous)*, proud *(conceited)*, supercilious
vainglorious boasting rodomontade
vainglory bombast, jactation, pride, rodomontade

valens strong
valere avail *(be of use)*
valetudo health
valiancy prowess *(bravery)*
valiant heroic, indomitable, spartan, undaunted. SEE MAIN ENTRY
valid accurate, actual, adequate, allowed, authentic, certain *(positive)*, cogent, convincing, de facto, deductible *(provable)*, demonstrable, documentary, effective *(efficient)*, effective *(operative)*, factual, genuine, honest, lawful, legal, legitimate *(rightful)*, licit, official, operative, persuasive, potent, real, reasonable *(rational)*, right *(correct)*, right *(suitable)*, rightful, solid *(sound)*, substantial, suitable, true *(authentic)*, unrefutable, viable. SEE MAIN ENTRY
valid notice adequate notice
valid potentiality force *(legal efficacy)*
validate accredit, affirm *(uphold)*, approve, attest, authorize, bear *(adduce)*, certify *(approve)*, certify *(attest)*, confirm, constitute *(establish)*, corroborate, cosign, demonstrate *(establish)*, document, endorse, establish *(show)*, formalize, indorse, legalize, legitimate, notarize, pass *(approve)*, prove, quote, sanction, seal *(solemnize)*, sign, substantiate, support *(corroborate)*, sustain *(confirm)*, verify *(confirm)*, witness *(attest to)*. SEE MAIN ENTRY
validate a will probate
validated allowed, choate lien
validation acknowledgment *(avowal)*, affirmance *(authentication)*, affirmation, approval, avowal, certification *(attested copy)*, confirmation, consent, corroboration, documentation, evidence, legalization, ratification, sanction *(permission)*, stamp, subscription, support *(corroboration)*. SEE MAIN ENTRY
validation of a testament probate
validification attestation, corroboration, reference *(recommendation)*
validity honesty, legality, legitimacy, quality *(excellence)*, strength, weight *(credibility)*. SEE MAIN ENTRY
validity proceedings probate
validly admittedly
validus compelling
valor prowess *(bravery)*
valorization ad valorem, rating
valorize calculate, gauge
valorous heroic, spartan, undaunted. SEE MAIN ENTRY
valorousness prowess *(bravery)*
valuable beneficial, chattel, considerable, constructive *(creative)*, crucial, functional, gainful, important *(significant)*, inestimable, instrumental, invaluable, lucrative, material *(important)*, meritorious, possession *(property)*, practical, priceless, productive, profitable, purposeful, sterling, subservient. SEE MAIN ENTRY
valuables assets, estate *(property)*, property *(possessions)*
valuate assess *(appraise)*, calculate, gauge
valuation account *(evaluation)*, appraisal, appreciation *(perception)*, assessment *(estimation)*, census, charge *(cost)*, computation, conclusion *(determination)*, cost *(price)*, estimate *(approximate cost)*, estimation *(calculation)*, expense *(cost)*, idea, measurement, par *(face amount)*, price, rate, rating, regard *(esteem)*, value, worth. SEE MAIN ENTRY
value amount *(sum)*, assess *(appraise)*, calculate, caliber *(quality)*, charge *(cost)*, charge *(assess)*, cost *(price)*, criticize *(evaluate)*, degree *(magnitude)*, emphasis, estimate *(approximate cost)*, estimate, evaluate, expense *(cost)*, gauge, honor, importance, judge, magnitude, materiality *(consequence)*, measure, merit, par *(face amount)*, prefer, price, quality *(excellence)*, rate *(noun)*, rate *(verb)*, recommend, regard *(esteem)*, regard *(hold in esteem)*, significance, signification, utility *(usefulness)*, weight *(importance)*, worth. SEE MAIN ENTRY
value added tax ad valorem
value in exchange par *(face amount)*
value incorrectly misconceive
value received income, proceeds, profit
valued at ad valorem
valueless barren, expendable, futile, needless, negligible, nugatory, null *(insignificant)*, null *(invalid)*, null and void, otiose, paltry, poor *(inferior in quality)*, unavailing, unfit
valueless check bad check
values ethics
vamp modify *(alter)*, repair
vandal SEE MAIN ENTRY
vandalism defacement, pillage
vandalize damage
vandimonium deserere default
vanguard forerunner, pioneer, precursor
vanish depart, disappear, dissipate *(spread out)*, evacuate, expire, leave *(depart)*, perish, quit *(evacuate)*
vanished defunct, irretrievable, lost *(taken away)*
vanishing elusive, ephemeral, transient
vanishment nonappearance
vanitas nullity
vanity jactation, pride
vanload cargo
vanquish beat *(defeat)*, defeat, demean *(make lower)*, foil, humiliate, kill *(defeat)*, overcome *(surmount)*, overturn, overwhelm, repress, restrain, subdue, subject, subjugate, succeed *(attain)*, suppress, surmount, upset. SEE MAIN ENTRY
vanquishment defeat, prostration
vantage edge *(advantage)*, leverage
vantage point perspective, stand *(position)*, standpoint
vanus delusive, fallacious, futile, illusory, unavailing, unfounded, void *(invalid)*
vanward SEE MAIN ENTRY
vapid insipid, jejune *(dull)*, languid, lifeless *(dull)*, prosaic, stale
vapid expression platitude
vapidity opacity
vapor phantom
vaporable volatile
vaporing inflated *(vain)*, rodomontade
vaporizable volatile
vaporize disappear
vaporize and condense distill
vaporous immaterial, volatile
variability deviation, diversity, irregularity
variable aleatory *(uncertain)*, ambulatory, atypical, broken *(interrupted)*, capricious, faithless, inconsistent, mutable, open-ended, periodic, pliable, protean, sporadic, undependable, unpredictable, untrustworthy. SEE MAIN ENTRY
variableness irregularity
variance alienation *(estrangement)*, argument *(contention)*, conflict, contest *(dispute)*, contradiction, contravention, controversy *(argument)*, deviation, difference, digression, disaccord, disagreement, discord, discrepancy, disparity, dispute, dissent *(difference of opinion)*, dissent *(nonconcurrence)*, dissidence, distinction *(difference)*, estrangement, feud, fight *(argument)*, incompatibility *(difference)*, incompatibility *(inconsistency)*, incongruity, inconsistency, inequality, nonconformity, nuance, rift *(disagreement)*, split, strife. SEE MAIN ENTRY
variant deviant, different, differential, discordant, distinction *(difference)*, divergent, diverse, heterogeneous, peculiar *(distinctive)*, variable
variare vary
variation deviation, difference, digression, discrepancy, disparity, distinction *(difference)*, diversification, diversity, inequality, innovation, irregularity, modification, nonconformity. SEE MAIN ENTRY
variations vicissitudes
varied complex, composite, compound, conglomerate, different, disparate, dissimilar, diverse, heterogeneous, miscellaneous, multifarious, multifold, multiple. SEE MAIN ENTRY
variegate alter, change, vary
variegated composite, compound, dissimilar, diverse, heterogeneous, manifold, miscellaneous, multifarious, multifold, promiscuous
variegation difference, diversity
varietal different
varietas difference
variety class, color *(complexion)*, denomination, difference, diversity, kind, manner *(kind)*, nonconformity, selection *(collection)*
variety store market *(business)*
variform dissimilar, heterogeneous, miscellaneous, multifold
various different, dissimilar, diverse, heterogeneous, manifold, miscellaneous, multifarious, multiple
variously called alias
variously known as alias
variousness diversity
varius discursive *(digressive)*, manifold, miscellaneous, multifarious, unsettled
varnish embellish, invent *(falsify)*, mislead, slant
varnished mendacious
vary alter, alternate *(fluctuate)*, change, collide *(clash)*, conflict, convert *(change use)*, detour, deviate, differ *(vary)*, disaccord, disagree, fluctuate, modify *(alter)*, oscillate, replace, transform. SEE MAIN ENTRY
vary from depart
varying desultory, different, dissenting, divergent, diverse, heterogeneous, protean, shifting. SEE MAIN ENTRY
vassal dependent
vassalage thrall
vast capacious, extensive, far reaching, general, inclusive, prodigious *(enormous)*, unlimited
vastatio havoc
vastness degree *(magnitude)*, gamut, magnitude, measurement, space
vasty capacious
vatic ominous, oracular, prophetic
vaticinal foreseeable, ominous, oracular, prophetic
vaticinari predict
vaticinate anticipate *(prognosticate)*, forewarn, portend, predict, presage, prognosticate
vaticination prognosis

vault bank, coffer, depository, surmount, treasury
vaunt jactation
vauntful inflated *(vain)*
vaunting orgulous
vecordia insanity
vectigal duty *(tax)*, income, revenue, tax, toll *(tax)*
vectura fare
veer detour, deviate, digress, divert, slant, vary
vegatating lifeless *(dull)*
vegetate germinate, languish, pullulate
vegetating insensible
vegetation inaction, inertia, languor
vegetative inactive, lifeless *(dull)*
vehemence force *(compulsion)*, outburst, passion, violence
vehemens compelling
vehement categorical, demonstrative *(expressive of emotion)*, eager, fervent, forcible, hot-blooded, incisive, insistent, intense, intensive, powerful. SEE MAIN ENTRY
vehement condemnation denunciation
vehement desire passion
vehement speech harangue
vehicle expedient, forum *(medium)*, go-between, instrument *(tool)*, instrumentality, interagent, intermediary, medium, tool. SEE MAIN ENTRY
vehicle for escape loophole
vehiculum carriage
veil blind *(obscure)*, camouflage, cloak, conceal, cover *(conceal)*, disguise, ensconce, enshroud, envelop, hide, obfuscate, obnubilate, obscure, plant *(covertly place)*, protect, screen *(guard)*, shroud, suppress. SEE MAIN ENTRY
veil the brightness blind *(obscure)*
veiled allusive, clandestine, covert, enigmatic, equivocal, esoteric, furtive, hidden, impalpable, inconspicuous, indiscernible, latent, mysterious, oblique *(evasive)*, obscure *(faint)*, personal *(private)*, secret, stealthy, surreptitious
veiled information secret
veiled observation insinuation
veiled remark insinuation
vein phraseology, tenor
velare cover *(pretext)*, cover *(conceal)*, shroud
velitation confrontation *(altercation)*, contention *(opposition)*
velleity will *(desire)*
vellicare cavil
velocity haste, rate
velox rapid
venal bad *(offensive)*, blameful, blameworthy, lawless, machiavellian, mercenary, penurious, unjust. SEE MAIN ENTRY
venalis marketable, mercenary, venal
venality bad faith, bad repute, bribery, corruption, disloyalty
venari hunt
vend barter, handle *(trade)*, sell. SEE MAIN ENTRY
vendee consumer, customer, patron *(regular customer)*
vendere sell
vendetta feud, rancor, reprisal, revenge, vengeance
vendible item, marketable, negotiable
vendibles commodities, goods, merchandise, stock in trade
venditation jactation
vendition sale
vendor dealer, merchant. SEE MAIN ENTRY
vendor of stolen goods fence
vendor of stolen property fence
vendue auction
veneer cover *(protection)*, disguise
venemous malicious, scathing, spiteful
venerable antique, outstanding *(prominent)*, popular, sacrosanct, solemn. SEE MAIN ENTRY
venerate defer *(yield in judgment)*, honor, regard *(hold in esteem)*
venerated reputable, sacrosanct
venerating obedient
veneration estimation *(esteem)*, fealty, homage, honor *(outward respect)*, interest *(concern)*, regard *(esteem)*, respect
vengeance punishment, rancor, reprisal, retribution, revenge, spite. SEE MAIN ENTRY
vengeful resentful, ruthless, vindictive. SEE MAIN ENTRY
vengefulness rancor, reprisal, resentment, retribution, revenge, vengeance
venia amnesty, indulgence, pardon, remission
venial allowable
venire SEE MAIN ENTRY
venom malice, odium, rancor, resentment, severity, spite
venomous bitter *(penetrating)*, bitter *(reproachful)*, caustic, dangerous, deadly, deleterious, fatal, harmful, insalubrious, lethal, malevolent, malignant, peccant *(unhealthy)*, pejorative, pernicious, perverse, pestilent, resentful, ruthless, sinister, toxic, vicious, virulent
venomousness rancor
vent bare, convey *(communicate)*, denude, disabuse, disclose, expose, express, exude, outlet, outpour, promulgate, propagate *(spread)*, relate *(tell)*, reveal, signify *(inform)*, spread, utter
ventilate bare, circulate, consult *(ask advice of)*, proclaim, propagate *(spread)*, publish, relate *(tell)*
ventilate a question reason *(persuade)*
ventilated public *(known)*
ventilation catharsis, publicity, report *(detailed account)*
venture activity, attempt, bet, business *(commercial enterprise)*, compromise *(endanger)*, embark, endeavor *(noun)*, endeavor *(verb)*, enterprise *(undertaking)*, experience *(encounter)*, experiment, invest *(fund)*, investment, livelihood, mission, occupation *(vocation)*, occurrence, offer *(propose)*, operation, parlay *(bet)*, presume, project, pursuit *(effort to secure)*, pursuit *(occupation)*, risk, speculate *(chance)*, speculate *(conjecture)*, speculation *(risk)*, strive, try *(attempt)*, undertake, undertaking *(business)*, undertaking *(enterprise)*. SEE MAIN ENTRY
venture a conjecture postulate
venture a supposition postulate
venture capital capitalize *(provide capital)*
venture on commence
venture upon assume *(undertake)*
venturer bettor, speculator
ventures business *(commerce)*
venturesome aleatory *(perilous)*, hot-blooded, imprudent, impulsive *(rash)*, insecure, resourceful
venturesomeness temerity
venturous aleatory *(perilous)*, imprudent, impulsive *(rash)*, insecure
venue locality. SEE MAIN ENTRY
venustus felicitous
veracious accurate, actual, bona fide, candid, certain *(positive)*, clean, credible, demonstrable, dependable, direct *(forthright)*, documentary, factual, honest, incontrovertible, ingenuous, literal, real, realistic, reliable, right *(correct)*, sound, straightforward, strict, true *(authentic)*, undistorted, unrefutable, upright, veridical. SEE MAIN ENTRY
veraciously faithfully
veraciousness honesty, probity, veracity
veracity credibility, honesty, probity, reality, rectitude, truth, validity. SEE MAIN ENTRY
verbal loquacious, nuncupative, oral, parol. SEE MAIN ENTRY
verbal abuse malediction, obloquy, philippic, revilement
verbal assault barrage, malediction
verbal attack malediction, vilification
verbal communication discourse
verbal conflict argument *(contention)*
verbal contention contest *(dispute)*, dispute
verbal contest fight *(argument)*
verbal controversy dispute
verbal engagement contest *(dispute)*, dispute
verbal evidence affirmance *(legal affirmation)*
verbal exposition discourse
verbal expression speech
verbal intercourse conversation, discourse, interview, language, parlance, parley, speech
verbal onslaught diatribe
verbal portraiture delineation
verbalism expression *(comment)*, term *(expression)*
verbalize communicate, enunciate, express, phrase, pronounce *(speak)*, relate *(tell)*, remark
verbatim accurate, exact, faithfully, literal. SEE MAIN ENTRY
verberare beat *(strike)*, lash *(strike)*
verbiage bombast, fustian, language, prattle, prolixity, tautology
verbose flatulent, inflated *(bombastic)*, loquacious, profuse, prolific, prolix, redundant, voluble
verbosity fustian, prolixity, tautology
verbosus loquacious, prolix
verbum expression *(comment)*, term *(expression)*, verbal
verdant inexperienced
verdict adjudication, answer *(solution)*, award, conclusion *(determination)*, consequence *(conclusion)*, conviction *(finding of guilt)*, decision *(judgment)*, decree, determination, finding, holding *(ruling of a court)*, result, ruling, sentence. SEE MAIN ENTRY
verdict after judicial inquiry finding
verdict of not guilty acquittal, compurgation
verecunde respectfully
verecundia homage
verecundus diffident
vereri fear
verge border, border *(approach)*, boundary, dispose *(incline)*, edge *(border)*, extremity *(furthest point)*, limit, margin *(outside limit)*, outline *(boundary)*, periphery, side
verge on abut, approach, connect *(join together)*
verge upon border *(approach)*, contact *(touch)*
verging contiguous, immediate *(not distant)*, proximate

verging on adjacent
veri similis probable
veri similitudo likelihood, probability
veridical bona fide, candid, cogent, direct *(forthright)*, factual, genuine, honest, reliable, straightforward, true *(authentic)*. SEE MAIN ENTRY
veridicality honesty, integrity, veracity
verifiability corroboration
verifiable accurate, ascertainable, authentic, certain *(positive)*, deductible *(provable)*, determinable *(ascertainable)*, indubious, provable, tangible, true *(authentic)*, veridical
verifiable excuse alibi
verifiable happening fact
verificate SEE MAIN ENTRY
verification acknowledgment *(acceptance)*, affirmance *(authentication)*, affirmation, approval, attestation, avowal, certainty, certification *(attested copy)*, confirmation, consent, corroboration, document, documentation, evidence, experiment, jurat, proof, reference *(recommendation)*, support *(corroboration)*. SEE MAIN ENTRY
verificative demonstrative *(illustrative)*, probative
verificative excuse alibi
verificatory provable
verified official
verify affirm *(uphold)*, ascertain, assure *(insure)*, attest, avouch *(guarantee)*, bear *(adduce)*, certify *(attest)*, check *(inspect)*, confirm, corroborate, demonstrate *(establish)*, depose *(testify)*, document, ensure, establish *(show)*, evidence, find *(discover)*, identify, prove, quote, recognize *(perceive)*, reveal, seal *(solemnize)*, substantiate, support *(corroborate)*, sustain *(confirm)*, testify, validate, witness *(attest to)*. SEE MAIN ENTRY
verify a testament probate
verify again reconfirm
verifying convincing, demonstrative *(illustrative)*
verifying statement jurat
verisimilar believable, circumstantial, credible, probable
verisimilis colorable *(plausible)*, plausible
verisimilitude credibility, probability
verisimilous probable
veritable absolute *(conclusive)*, actual, authentic, candid, de facto, definite, documentary, genuine, honest, real, sound, true *(authentic)*, unrefutable, valid
veritably admittedly
veritas reality, truth, veracity
verity honesty, reality, truth, validity, veracity
vermicular tortuous *(bending)*
vermiculate tortuous *(bending)*
vermiculated tortuous *(bending)*
vernacular language, native *(domestic)*, ordinary, prevailing *(current)*, prevalent, regional, usual
vernal juvenile
vernile servile
versant learned
versari employ *(engage services)*
versari in re concern *(involve)*
versatile artful, mutable, pliable, protean, resourceful. SEE MAIN ENTRY
versatility ability, amenability
verse maker author *(writer)*
versed cognizant, competent, expert, familiar *(informed)*, informed *(educated)*, learned, qualified *(competent)*
version construction, paraphrase
versus contra
versus contra
versutus artful
vertex ceiling, crossroad *(intersection)*
verus actual, authentic, candid, essential *(required)*, real, right *(righteousness)*, sterling, true *(authentic)*
verve ardor, emotion, life *(vitality)*, passion, spirit
very stark. SEE MAIN ENTRY
very fine impalpable, premium
very thorough complete *(all-embracing)*
vesanus frenetic
vesicate burn
vest admit *(give access)*, bestow, dedicate, empower. SEE MAIN ENTRY
vest in bequeath, commit *(entrust)*, delegate, repose *(place)*. SEE MAIN ENTRY
vest with a title authorize
vested immutable, prescriptive
vested interest birthright, claim *(right)*, equity *(share of ownership)*, prescription *(claim of title)*, right *(entitlement)*, title *(right)*
vested interest in land fee *(estate)*, freehold
vested right birthright, charter *(sanction)*, droit, due, prerogative, prescription *(claim of title)*
vestibule entrance
vestigium indication
vestire clothe
vestis mutata disguise
vetare condemn *(ban)*, disallow, forbid
veteran expert *(adjective)*, expert *(noun)*, practiced, specialist. SEE MAIN ENTRY
vetitus felonious, illegal, illicit, unlawful
veto ban, countermand, debar, decline *(reject)*, disapproval, disapprove *(reject)*, disavow, exclude, forbid, forestall, inhibit, interdict, negate, nonconformity, prevent, prohibit, prohibition, protest, refusal, refuse, reject, rejection, renunciation, repudiation, restraint, restrict, stem *(check)*. SEE MAIN ENTRY
vetoed impermissible
vetus old, stale
vetustus old
vex affront, aggravate *(annoy)*, annoy, badger, bait *(harass)*, discommode, discompose, distress, disturb, embarrass, harass, harrow, harry *(harass)*, hector, incense, inconvenience, irritate, mistreat, molest *(annoy)*, obsess, offend *(insult)*, perplex, perturb, pique, plague, press *(goad)*, provoke, repel *(disgust)*. SEE MAIN ENTRY
vexare harass, harrow, harry *(harass)*, molest *(annoy)*, persecute, pique, plague
vexatio molestation, oppression
vexation burden, damage, dissatisfaction, distress *(anguish)*, grievance, molestation, nuisance, provocation
vexatious invidious, operose, oppressive, perverse, provocative. SEE MAIN ENTRY
vexatious litigation SEE MAIN ENTRY
vexed aggrieved *(harmed)*, bitter *(reproachful)*
vexed question dilemma, problem
vexing provocative, unsatisfactory
via direction *(course)*, facility *(instrumentality)*, method, mode
via through *(from beginning to end)*
viability feasibility, possibility
viable live *(conscious)*, permissible, possible, virtual. SEE MAIN ENTRY
viableness possibility
viatical agreement SEE MAIN ENTRY
viatical settlement SEE MAIN ENTRY
vibrant strong. SEE MAIN ENTRY
vibrare brandish
vibrate beat *(pulsate)*, vacillate
vicar deputy, proctor, spokesman
vicarial surrogate
vicarious derivative, secondary, surrogate. SEE MAIN ENTRY
vicarius deputy, proxy, representative *(proxy)*, surrogate
vice bad repute, flaw, foible, guilt, mens rea, mischief, misdoing, sodomy, wrong. SEE MAIN ENTRY
vice versa contra, contrary
vice-ridden profane, profligate *(corrupt)*
vicegerent deputy
viceregent procurator
viceroy plenipotentiary
vicinage area *(province)*, locality, location, propinquity *(proximity)*, region, section *(vicinity)*
vicinal adjacent, close *(near)*, present *(attendant)*, proximate
vicinitas section *(vicinity)*
vicinity area *(province)*, locality, location, region, site. SEE MAIN ENTRY
vicinus adjacent
vicious bad *(offensive)*, brutal, cruel, dangerous, delinquent *(guilty of a misdeed)*, diabolic, harmful, heinous, hostile, inexcusable, inexpiable, iniquitous, malevolent, malicious, malignant, noxious, peccant *(culpable)*, pernicious, profligate *(corrupt)*, reprehensible, reprobate, ruthless, severe, spiteful, tainted *(corrupted)*, unjustifiable, unscrupulous. SEE MAIN ENTRY
viciousness bestiality, cruelty, delinquency *(misconduct)*, guilt, malice, spite
vicissitudes circumstances. SEE MAIN ENTRY
vicissitudinous unpredictable
vicissitudo reciprocity
vicitimize ill use
victim cadaver, captive, corpse, patient, subject *(object)*. SEE MAIN ENTRY
victima victim
victimization abuse *(physical misuse)*, atrocity, bunko, cruelty, oppression
victimize bait *(harass)*, betray *(lead astray)*, bilk, deceive, defeat, dupe, endanger, ensnare, exploit *(take advantage of)*, extort, harass, illude, inveigle, mishandle *(maltreat)*, mistreat, palter, persecute, prey, slay. SEE MAIN ENTRY
victorious prevailing *(having superior force)*, successful
victory supremacy
victual nurture, supply
victualer supplier
victuals sustenance
victus livelihood, maintenance *(support of spouse)*, sustenance
videlicet a savoir
videor apparent *(perceptible)*
videre witness *(have direct knowledge of)*. SEE MAIN ENTRY
videri appear *(seem to be)*
vie strive
vie for endeavor
vie with compete, contend *(dispute)*, contest, fight *(battle)*, grapple
view advice, apprehend *(perceive)*, apprehension *(perception)*, aspect, assumption *(supposition)*, complexion, concept, conclusion *(determination)*, conviction *(persuasion)*, coverage *(scope)*, credence, design

(intent), detect, discern *(detect with the senses),* estimate *(idea),* idea, intent, notice *(observe),* notion, observation, observe *(watch),* opine, opinion *(belief),* perception, perspective, pierce *(discern),* platform, position *(point of view),* posture *(attitude),* purview, reaction *(response),* recognize *(perceive),* regard *(pay attention),* scene, scrutinize, side, spy, stand *(position),* standpoint, study, surmise, survey *(examine),* suspect *(think),* theory, witness *(have direct knowledge of).* SEE MAIN ENTRY
view as deem
view from all sides ponder
view retrospectively review
view with a scornful eye disdain, flout
view with deliberation ponder
view with disfavor censure, deprecate, disapprove *(condemn),* discommend, disfavor, expostulate
view with dissatisfaction resent
view with favor countenance
view with regret deplore
viewable apparent *(perceptible),* discernible, perceivable, perceptible, visible *(in full view)*
viewer bystander, eyewitness
viewership bystander
viewless inconspicuous
viewpoint aspect, conviction *(persuasion),* idea, opinion *(belief),* outlook, perception, perspective, position *(point of view),* posture *(attitude),* side, stand *(position),* standpoint. SEE MAIN ENTRY
vigil notice *(heed),* precaution, surveillance
vigilance diligence *(care),* notice *(heed),* precaution, prudence, regard *(attention),* surveillance, ward
vigilans vigilant
vigilant careful, circumspect, conscious *(aware),* discreet, guarded, leery, meticulous, protective, provident *(showing foresight).* SEE MAIN ENTRY
vigilence diligence *(perseverance)*
vignette brief
vigor ardor, diligence *(perseverance),* dint, effort, force *(strength),* health, industry *(activity),* life *(vitality),* main force, prowess *(bravery),* puissance, sinew, spirit, strength
vigorless powerless
vigorous active, compelling, forcible, indomitable, intense, intensive, irresistible, potent, powerful, resolute, resounding, strong, trenchant. SEE MAIN ENTRY
vigorous enunciation emphasis
vigorously effective drastic
vigorousness ardor, effort, force *(strength),* sinew
vile arrant *(onerous),* bad *(offensive),* blameful, caitiff, contemptible, contemptuous, deplorable, depraved, disgraceful, heinous, ignoble, iniquitous, loathsome, machiavellian, malignant, nefarious, objectionable, obnoxious, obscene, odious, offensive *(offending),* paltry, peccant *(culpable),* profligate *(corrupt),* reprobate, repulsive, scurrilous, vicious. SEE MAIN ENTRY
vileness delinquency *(misconduct),* dishonor *(shame),* disrepute, obscenity, shame, turpitude, vice
vilification aspersion, bad repute, condemnation *(blame),* contumely, denunciation, diatribe, dishonor *(shame),* disparagement, disrespect, impeachment, imprecation, libel, malediction, obloquy, opprobrium, outcry, phillipic, profanity, reproach, revilement, scandal, slander. SEE MAIN ENTRY
vilify brand *(stigmatize),* condemn *(blame),* contemn, decry, defame, denigrate, denounce *(condemn),* derogate, discommend, dishonor *(deprive of honor),* disparage, humiliate, inveigh, lash *(attack verbally),* lessen, libel, malign, pillory, reprimand, reproach, smear, sully, tarnish
vilifying calumnious, libelous, pejorative
vilipend blame, brand *(stigmatize),* censure, contemn, decry, defame, denigrate, denounce *(condemn),* deprecate, derogate, disapprove *(condemn),* discommend, disoblige, disparage, lash *(attack verbally),* lessen, malign, reprimand, reproach, smear, sully
vilipendency bad repute, disapprobation, disparagement, disrespect
vilis paltry
villa estate *(property)*
villager habitant, resident
villain convict, criminal, hoodlum, malefactor, wrongdoer
villainous bad *(offensive),* contemptible, delinquent *(guilty of a misdeed),* felonious, heinous, inexpiable, iniquitous, malevolent, malignant, nefarious, notorious, obnoxious, outrageous, peccant *(culpable),* recreant, reprehensible, sinister, unscrupulous, vicious. SEE MAIN ENTRY
villainousness corruption, delinquency *(misconduct),* knavery
villainy atrocity, corruption, delinquency *(misconduct),* knavery, mischief, misdeed, misdoing, wrong
vim industry *(activity),* life *(vitality),* spirit
vincere beat *(defeat),* defeat, establish *(show),* outweigh, overrule, predominate *(command),* prevail *(triumph)*
vincibility danger
vincible disabled *(made incapable),* helpless *(defenseless),* inadequate, indefensible, penetrable, powerless, untenable, vulnerable
vincibleness danger
vincula fetter, incarceration
vincula ties
vinculo matrimonii cohabitation *(married state)*
vinculum chain *(series),* fetter
vinculum nexus
vindicable defensible, justifiable, pardonable, tenable, unobjectionable
vindicate absolve, acquit, bear *(adduce),* bear *(support),* clear, condone, exculpate, excuse, exonerate, extenuate, forgive, free, justify, liberate, maintain *(sustain),* palliate *(excuse),* pardon, rationalize, remit *(release from penalty),* substantiate, support *(corroborate),* support *(justify),* sustain *(confirm),* uphold. SEE MAIN ENTRY
vindicate a right claim *(demand)*
vindicate a title claim *(demand)*
vindicate from unjust reproach exculpate
vindicated acquitted, blameless, clear *(free from criminal charges)*
vindicating palliative *(excusing)*
vindicatio assertion
vindication absolution, acquittal, advocacy, compurgation, condonation, corroboration, exoneration, indemnity, justification, liberation, pardon, reason *(basis),* support *(corroboration)*
vindicative palliative *(excusing)*
vindicator proponent
vindicatory defensible, palliative *(excusing),* vindictive
vindicta revenge, vengeance
vindictive implacable, malevolent, malicious, malignant, punitive, relentless, resentful, ruthless, severe, spiteful. SEE MAIN ENTRY
vindictive oath imprecation
vindictiveness rancor, reprisal, resentment, retribution, revenge, spite, vengeance
vinegarish bitter *(acrid tasting)*
vintage age, old
violare infringe, offend *(violate the law),* violate
violate betray *(lead astray),* contravene, damage, debauch, disobey, encroach, endanger, impinge, impose *(intrude),* infringe, invade, misemploy, mishandle *(maltreat),* mistreat, molest *(subject to indecent advances),* overstep, pollute, taint *(corrupt),* trespass. SEE MAIN ENTRY
violate a confidence betray *(disclose),* inform *(betray)*
violate a contract infringe
violate a law infringe
violate a privilege infringe
violate a regulation infringe
violate one's oath defect
violate rules mismanage
violate the confidence of inform *(betray)*
violate the truth falsify
violated broken *(unfulfilled)*
violating disobedient
violatio infraction, infringement
violation abuse *(corrupt practice),* abuse *(physical misuse),* breach, contravention, debauchment, defilement, delict, delinquency *(misconduct),* disregard *(omission),* encroachment, guilt, incursion, infraction, infringement, invasion, irregularity, misdeed, misdoing, misprision, misusage, misuse, offense, perversion, rape, rebellion, sedition, transgression, wrong. SEE MAIN ENTRY
violation of a contract infringement
violation of a duty delict
violation of a law infringement
violation of a legal duty tort
violation of a privilege infringement
violation of a regulation infringement
violation of allegiance bad faith, disloyalty, treason
violation of an oath perjury
violation of another's rights assault
violation of duty bad faith, default
violation of law breach, crime, felony, guilt, infraction, misdemeanor, misfeasance, offense
violation of oath infidelity
violation of orders contempt *(disobedience to the court),* infraction, offense
violation of professional code malpractice
violation of professional duty malpractice
violation of right injustice, wrong
violation of the law illegality
violation of the marriage vows adultery
violation of trust dishonesty, disloyalty
violative broken *(unfulfilled),* disobedient, lawless
violator aggressor, assailant, offender
violator of laws malefactor

violator of the law outlaw
violence affray, belligerency, brutality, commotion, cruelty, embroilment, havoc, infliction, infringement, injury, outburst, passion, severity, strife. SEE MAIN ENTRY
violent brutal, demonstrative *(expressive of emotion)*, disorderly, drastic, extreme *(exaggerated)*, forcible, hot-blooded, malignant, pernicious, pestilent, precipitate, severe, strong, uncontrollable, vehement, virulent. SEE MAIN ENTRY
violent anger passion
violent animosity malice
violent behavior outbreak
violent change revolution
violent contact collision *(accident)*
violent death fatality, homicide, killing, murder
violent disagreement dissension
violent separation avulsion
violent upheaval cataclysm
violentia violence
viperine dangerous
viperous dangerous, malevolent, spiteful
vires ability, strength
virgin unadulterated
virile potent, spartan, strong
virility strength
virtual constructive *(inferential)*. SEE MAIN ENTRY
virtue caliber *(quality)*, ethics, honesty, honor *(good reputation)*, integrity, merit, probity, rectitude, right *(righteousness)*, veracity
virtueless bad *(offensive)*, base *(bad)*, delinquent *(guilty of a misdeed)*, diabolic, inexpiable, peccable, profane, salacious
virtuosity performance *(workmanship)*, prowess *(ability)*, specialty *(special aptitude)*
virtuoso expert, specialist
virtuous blameless, clean, conscientious, ethical, evenhanded, high-minded, incorruptible, inculpable, innocent, innocuous, irreprehensible, just, laudable, law-abiding, meritorious, moral, proper, pure, reputable, right *(correct)*, right *(suitable)*, sterling, upright
virtuous conduct ethics
virtuously faithfully
virtuousness ethics, integrity, principle *(virtue)*
virtus merit, prowess *(bravery)*, worth
virulence fatality, force *(strength)*, harm, rancor, severity, spite
virulency fatality, spite
virulent antipathetic *(distasteful)*, bitter *(penetrating)*, caustic, chronic, dangerous, deleterious, fatal, harsh, insalubrious, lethal, malevolent, malicious, malignant, mordacious, noxious, peccant *(unhealthy)*, pernicious, pestilent, ruthless, scathing, sinister, spiteful, toxic, vicious. SEE MAIN ENTRY
virulently inimical malignant
virus disease
vis compulsion *(coercion)*, efficiency, essence, faculty *(ability)*, force *(strength)*, impetus, import, importance, influence, life *(vitality)*, meaning, power, pressure, significance, signification, stock *(store)*
vis-à-vis antipode, contra, contrary, hostile
visa permission, permit
visage aspect, complexion, feature *(appearance)*, presence *(poise)*, semblance
viscidity adhesion *(affixing)*
viscosity adhesion *(affixing)*
viscous coherent *(joined)*
visé confirmation
visible apparent *(perceptible)*, appreciable, bodily, clear *(apparent)*, coherent *(clear)*, conspicuous, discernible, distinct *(clear)*, evident, extant, flagrant, manifest, naked *(perceptible)*, obvious, open *(in sight)*, ostensible, overt, palpable, patent, perceivable, perceptible, prominent, remarkable, salient, tangible, unmistakable. SEE MAIN ENTRY
visible effect impression
visible form embodiment
visible sign symbol
visible token indicant
visibly fairly *(clearly)*
vision phantom, phenomenon *(manifestation)*, sagacity, standpoint. SEE MAIN ENTRY
visionary delusive, illusory, impossible, infeasible, insubstantial, nonexistent, quixotic, theoretical
visioned original *(creative)*
visionless blind *(sightless)*
visit appointment *(meeting)*, attend *(be present at)*, inhabit
visit punishment discipline *(punish)*, penalize
visitation adversity, misfortune, presence *(attendance)*
visor enshroud, veil
vista aspect, scene, vision *(sight)*
visual discernible, perceivable, perceptible
visual examination inspection
visual impact face value *(first blush)*
visualization concept, perception
visualize compose, conceive *(comprehend)*, conjure, discern *(detect with the senses)*, invent *(produce for the first time)*
visualized distinct *(clear)*
visualizing original *(creative)*
vita life *(period of existence)*
vita decedere die
vital born *(alive)*, cardinal *(basic)*, central *(essential)*, compulsory, critical *(crucial)*, crucial, exigent, fundamental, important *(urgent)*, indispensable, integral, live *(conscious)*, major, mandatory, material *(important)*, necessary *(required)*, obligatory, primary, requisite, strategic, substantive, urgent, viable. SEE MAIN ENTRY
vital center seat
vital concern main point, sine qua non
vital element center *(essence)*
vital essence spirit
vital part center *(essence)*, consequence *(significance)*, ingredient, necessity, need *(requirement)*, prerequisite, requirement, substance *(essential nature)*
vital principle gist *(substance)*
vital statistics census
vitalic vital
vitalis vital
vitality ardor, force *(strength)*, health, prowess *(bravery)*, puissance, spirit, strength
vitalization birth *(beginning)*
vitalize generate, stimulate
vitalized born *(alive)*
vitalness need *(requirement)*, priority
vitals necessary, necessity
vitare avoid *(evade)*, eschew, shun
vitiare adulterate, corrupt, debase, debauch, falsification, falsify, vitiate
vitiate abolish, adulterate, annul, contaminate, corrupt, damage, debase, debauch, degenerate, denature, deteriorate, disable, dissolve *(terminate)*, infect, invalidate, neutralize, nullify, pervert, pollute, revoke, spoil *(impair)*, subvert, sully, taint *(corrupt)*. SEE MAIN ENTRY
vitiated depraved, profligate *(corrupt)*, reprobate, stale, tainted *(corrupted)*
vitiation annulment, contaminate, damage, debauchment, fault *(weakness)*, invalidity, perversion, rescision
vitiis inficere infect
vitiosus faulty, vicious
vitium fallacy, flaw, foible, guilt
vitriol disapprobation
vitriolic bitter *(reproachful)*, malevolent, malignant, mordacious, scathing
vituperare blame, censure, condemn *(blame)*, decry, rebuke, reprimand
vituperate castigate, condemn *(blame)*, contemn, defame, denigrate, denounce *(condemn)*, impeach, inveigh, lash *(attack verbally)*, malign, pillory, rebuke, reprimand, reproach
vituperatio blame *(culpability)*, obloquy, reprimand
vituperation aspersion, condemnation *(blame)*, contumely, denunciation, diatribe, disparagement, imprecation, malediction, obloquy, outcry, philippic, profanity, revilement, stricture, vilification
vituperative calumnious, contemptuous, harsh, libelous, pejorative
vivacity ardor, life *(vitality)*, spirit
vivid acute, clear *(apparent)*, coherent *(clear)*, descriptive, detailed, distinct *(clear)*, eloquent, intense, profound *(intense)*, strong, suggestive *(evocative)*. SEE MAIN ENTRY
vividly fairly *(clearly)*
vividness strength
vivification birth *(emergence of young)*, revival
vivified conscious *(awake)*
vivify generate, heighten *(augment)*, stimulate
vixenish petulant, querulous
vizard veil
vocable term *(expression)*
vocabulary language, parlance, phraseology
vocabulum term *(expression)*
vocal nuncupative, oral, parol
vocal embodiment of thought expression *(comment)*
vocalism intonation
vocalization parlance, speech
vocalize communicate, enunciate, observe *(remark)*, phrase, pronounce *(speak)*, remark
vocalized oral
vocare call *(title)*
vocation appointment *(position)*, business *(occupation)*, calling, career, employment, job, labor *(work)*, livelihood, mission, position *(business status)*, post, practice *(professional business)*, profession *(vocation)*, pursuit *(occupation)*, specialty *(special aptitude)*, trade *(occupation)*, work *(employment)*
vocational technical
voces outcry
vociferance noise
vociferate interject
vociferatio outcry
vociferation noise, outcry, pandemonium
vociferous blatant *(obtrusive)*, loquacious
vogue custom, market *(demand)*, mode, style, usage

vogue word catchword
voice circulate, communicate, disclose, divulge, enunciate, express, intonation, mention, observe *(remark)*, phrase, poll *(casting of votes)*, pronounce *(speak)*, propose, propound, recite, referendum, remark, report *(disclose)*, reveal, signify *(inform)*, spokesman, suffrage, utter. SEE MAIN ENTRY
voice change inflection
voice disapproval reprehend
voiced nuncupative, oral, parol, stated, verbal
voiceless mute, speechless
voicing expression *(comment)*
void abate *(extinguish)*, abolish, abrogate *(annul)*, abrogate *(rescind)*, absence *(omission)*, adeem, annul, avoid *(cancel)*, barren, blank *(emptiness)*, cancel, defunct, deplete, discontinue *(abandon)*, disown *(deny the validity)*, eliminate *(eradicate)*, eradicate, inactive, ineffective, ineffectual, inexpressive, invalid, lifeless *(dead)*, nugatory, null *(invalid)*, null and void, nullify, nullity, overrule, recall *(call back)*, recant, repeal, rescind, revoke, supersede, vacant, vacuous. SEE MAIN ENTRY
void check bad check
void of deficient, devoid
void of contents barren
void of feeling insensible
void of reason irrational
void of suspicion certain *(positive)*, credible, naive
void of taste insipid
void of truth dishonest, fraudulent, mendacious
void the license of an attorney disbar
void trial mistrial
voidable defeasible. SEE MAIN ENTRY
voidance abatement *(extinguishment)*, abolition, ademption, annulment, avoidance *(cancellation)*, cancellation, countermand, defeasance, discharge *(annulment)*, discharge *(release from obligation)*, dissolution *(termination)*, exclusion, repudiation, rescision, retraction, reversal
voiding cancellation, reversal
voidness invalidity
voir dire SEE MAIN ENTRY
volaticus volatile
volatile brief, ephemeral, inconsistent, irresolute, mutable, temporary, transient, transitory, variable. SEE MAIN ENTRY
volatility inconsistency
volcanic vehement
volcano outburst
volens voluntary
volitient deliberate, spontaneous, voluntary
volition animus, conatus, discretion *(power of choice)*, election *(choice)*, forethought, intent, purpose, will *(desire)*. SEE MAIN ENTRY
volitional deliberate, discretionary, spontaneous, voluntary, willful, willing *(desirous)*
volitionally purposely
volitionary voluntary
volitive deliberate, discretionary, permissive, spontaneous, willful
volley barrage, discharge *(shot)*, salvo
voluble loquacious. SEE MAIN ENTRY
volume bulk, capacity *(maximum)*, coverage *(scope)*, degree *(magnitude)*, magnitude, publication *(printed matter)*, quantity
voluminous capacious, copious
voluntarily purposely, readily
voluntariness conatus, purpose
voluntarius spontaneous, voluntary
voluntary consenting, deliberate, gratis, gratuitous *(given without recompense)*, spontaneous, unsolicited, willful, willing *(not averse)*. SEE MAIN ENTRY
voluntary acknowledgment admission *(disclosure)*
voluntary activity conatus
voluntary association affiliation *(amalgamation)*, merger
voluntary attestment under oath affidavit
voluntary conveyance largess *(gift)*
voluntary decision alternative *(option)*
voluntary exile privacy
voluntary oversight connivance
voluntary relinquishment waiver
voluntary work campaign
voluntary worker volunteer
voluntas inclination, volition, will *(desire)*
volunteer hold out *(deliberate on an offer)*, pose *(propound)*, proffer, tender, unpaid. SEE MAIN ENTRY
volunteered unsolicited
volute sinuous
voracious eager, gluttonous, predatory, rapacious
voraciousness greed
voracity greed
votary addict, advocate *(counselor)*, advocate *(espouser)*, colleague, disciple, partisan, proponent
vote cast *(register)*, decide, franchise *(right to vote)*, plebiscite, poll *(casting of votes)*, primary, referendum, suffrage. SEE MAIN ENTRY
vote against disapprove *(reject)*, protest, reject
vote down disapprove *(reject)*, fight *(counteract)*
vote favorably pass *(approve)*
vote for confirm, side
vote in legislate, pass *(approve)*
vote into office elect *(select by a vote)*, nominate
vote of confidence adhesion *(loyalty)*
vote to accept adopt
vote-casting election *(selection by vote)*
voted consensual
voter constituent *(member)*
voter ID law SEE MAIN ENTRY
voters constituency
voting age majority *(adulthood)*
voting district constituency
voting list constituency
voting power franchise *(right to vote)*
votum prayer
vouch affirm *(declare solemnly)*, avouch *(avow)*, avouchment, avow, certify *(attest)*, contend *(maintain)*, depose *(testify)*, posit, promise *(vow)*, seal *(solemnize)*, swear, vow. SEE MAIN ENTRY
vouch for accredit, affirm *(uphold)*, assure *(insure)*, attest, authorize, avouch *(guarantee)*, bear *(adduce)*, certify *(attest)*, confirm, corroborate, cosign, depose *(testify)*, guarantee, indorse, recommend, side, sponsor, support *(corroborate)*, underwrite, verify *(swear)*, witness *(attest to)*
vouch for as genuine certify *(attest)*
vouched alleged
vouched for promissory
voucher affiant, affirmant, assurance, bond, certificate, corroboration, coupon, deponent, draft, guaranty, note *(written promise to pay)*, permit, receipt *(proof of receiving)*, reference *(recommendation)*, security *(pledge)*, surety *(guarantor)*, warrant *(authorization)*, warranty
vouchers credentials
vouching adjuration, advocacy, averment, deposition, reference *(recommendation)*
vouchsafe accede *(concede)*, allow *(authorize)*, authorize, bestow, cede, condescend *(deign)*, deign, give *(grant)*, grant *(concede)*, let *(permit)*, patronize *(condescend toward)*, present *(make a gift)*, sanction. SEE MAIN ENTRY
vouchsafed allowed
vouchsafement concession *(authorization)*, consent, disposition *(transfer of property)*, indulgence, leave *(permission)*, license, privilege, sanction *(permission)*
vouchsafer contributor *(giver)*, donor
vow adjuration, asseveration, assurance, assure *(insure)*, avouch *(avow)*, avouchment, avow, bear *(adduce)*, claim *(maintain)*, commitment *(responsibility)*, oath, pledge *(binding promise)*, pledge *(promise the performance of)*, profession *(declaration)*, promise, promise *(vow)*, surety *(certainty)*, swear, undertake, undertaking *(pledge)*, verify *(swear)*. SEE MAIN ENTRY
vox call *(appeal)*, expression *(comment)*, verbal
voyager itinerant
voyaging moving *(in motion)*
vulgar blatant *(obtrusive)*, caitiff, depraved, ignoble, impertinent *(insolent)*, inelegant, lewd, licentious, lurid, meretricious, obnoxious, obscene, odious, poor *(inferior in quality)*, profane, scurrilous, tawdry, unbecoming, uncouth, unseemly. SEE MAIN ENTRY
vulgare propagate *(spread)*
vulgarian blatant *(obtrusive)*
vulgarity indecency, obscenity, pornography, profanity
vulgarize corrupt, debase
vulgus mass *(body of persons)*
vulnerability danger, frailty, jeopardy, liability, peril, risk
vulnerable destructible, helpless *(defenseless)*, inadequate, indefensible, insecure, liable, open *(accessible)*, penetrable, precarious, subject *(exposed)*, susceptible *(unresistent)*, untenable. SEE MAIN ENTRY
vulnerable point fault *(weakness)*, peril
vulnerableness frailty
vulnerary medicinal
vulpine artful, insidious, machiavellian, sly, subtle *(insidious)*, surreptitious
vulturine predatory, rapacious
vulturish predatory
vulturous predatory, rapacious
vying competitive *(antagonistic)*
vying for ascendance competition
vying with comparative, contravention

W

wag brandish
wage commission *(fee)*, exercise *(discharge a function)*, fee *(charge)*, income, payment *(remittance)*, perquisite, ply, recompense. SEE MAIN ENTRY
wage earner employee
wage war engage *(involve)*, fight *(battle)*
wager bet, gamble, lottery, parlay *(bet)*, pawn, risk, speculate *(chance)*, speculation *(risk)*, stake *(award)*, venture

wagerer bettor, speculator
wages compensation, earnings, income, pay, payroll, revenue
waggery mischief
waggish jocular
waggishness mischief
waggle brandish
waif orphan
wail outcry, plaint
wailful querulous
wait cessation *(interlude)*, defer *(put off)*, deferment, delay, discontinue *(break continuity)*, forbear, halt *(noun)*, halt *(verb)*, hesitate, last, moratorium, pause, procrastinate, remain *(stay)*, respite *(interval of rest)*, stay, stay *(rest)*. SEE MAIN ENTRY
wait for anticipate *(expect)*, expect *(anticipate)*, forestall
wait on pander, serve *(assist)*
wait upon attend *(take care of)*
waiting expectation, ready *(prepared)*
waiting period moratorium
waive abrogate *(rescind)*, discontinue *(abandon)*, discontinue *(break continuity)*, forbear, forfeit, forgo, forswear, leave *(allow to remain)*, refrain, reject, relinquish, remit *(release from penalty)*, renounce, surrender *(give back)*, yield *(submit)*. SEE MAIN ENTRY
waive privilege condescend *(deign)*
waive punishment condone
waived exempt
waiver cancellation, cession, quitclaim, rejection, release, renunciation. SEE MAIN ENTRY
wake incite, inspire
wake up foment
wakeful vigilant
wakefulness diligence *(care)*
waken foment
walk patrol, perambulate
walk a beat patrol
walk away move *(alter position)*, quit *(evacuate)*
walk in enter *(go in)*
walk of life business *(occupation)*, calling, position *(business status)*, profession *(vocation)*
walk off move *(alter position)*
walk off with hold up *(rob)*, jostle *(pickpocket)*, poach
walk out quit *(evacuate)*, secede, strike *(refuse to work)*
walk through perambulate
walker pedestrian
walkout strike
wall barrier. SEE MAIN ENTRY
wall in enclose, encompass *(surround)*, envelop, restrain, restrict
wall of flame conflagration
wall up block, immure
walled in area enclosure
wallow carouse
wan disconsolate, languid
wander digress, perambulate
wander about prowl
wander aimlessly loiter
wander from the subject deviate
wanderer derelict, itinerant, migrant
wandering circuitous, discursive *(digressive)*, incoherence, indirect, itinerant, labyrinthine, lost *(disoriented)*, lunatic, moving *(in motion)*, prolix, shifting, truant, unsettled, vagrancy
wane decline, decline *(fall)*, decrease *(noun)*, decrease *(verb)*, degenerate, deteriorate, diminish, ebb, end *(termination)*, lessen, outflow, relapse, subside
waning attrition, decrease, old
want absence *(omission)*, conatus, dearth, deficiency, desideratum, desire *(noun)*, desire *(verb)*, exigency, failure *(falling short)*, foible, indigence, insufficiency, lack, market *(demand)*, need *(deprivation)*, need, paucity, poverty, privation, request, require *(need)*, requirement, requisition, will *(desire)*. SEE MAIN ENTRY
want of ability disqualification *(factor that disqualifies)*, inability
want of activity inertia
want of adaptation incompatibility *(difference)*
want of agreement incompatibility *(difference)*, incompatibility *(inconsistency)*
want of attention disinterest *(lack of interest)*
want of authority want of jurisdiction
want of capacity inability. SEE MAIN ENTRY
want of caution audacity, impropriety, temerity
want of certainty cloud *(suspicion)*
want of circumspection impropriety
want of comprehension insanity
want of confidence cloud *(suspicion)*, doubt *(indecision)*, doubt *(suspicion)*, fear, qualm
want of consideration ingratitude
want of duty laches, maladministration
want of esteem disrepute, disrespect
want of faith cloud *(suspicion)*, doubt *(indecision)*, doubt *(suspicion)*, incredulity
want of fidelity story *(falsehood)*
want of forbearance discrimination *(bigotry)*, intolerance
want of formality informality
want of harmony conflict, impugnation, inconsistency, opposition
want of integrity dishonesty
want of interest disinterest *(lack of interest)*
want of jurisdiction SEE MAIN ENTRY
want of knowledge ignorance. SEE MAIN ENTRY
want of legal capacity disability *(legal disqualification)*
want of legal qualification disability *(legal disqualification)*
want of loyalty disloyalty
want of method irregularity, pandemonium
want of moral strength frailty
want of notice disregard *(unconcern)*
want of originality platitude
want of power inability
want of principle abuse *(corrupt practice)*, bad repute, corruption, perversion
want of reason insanity
want of respect disparagement
want of sensibility insentience
want of skill disqualification *(factor that disqualifies)*, inability
want of success abortion *(fiasco)*
want of thought disregard *(lack of respect)*, disregard *(unconcern)*, negligence
want of toleration intolerance
want of transparency opacity
want of trust doubt *(suspicion)*
wantage dearth, need *(deprivation)*
wanted important *(urgent)*, indispensable, popular, requisite
wanting defective, deficient, delinquent *(overdue)*, destitute, devoid, faulty, imperfect, inadept, inadequate, insufficient, marginal, nonsubstantial *(not sufficient)*, paltry, partial *(part)*, partial *(relating to a part)*, perfunctory, poor *(inferior in quality)*, scarce, solicitous, unsatisfactory, vacuous, void *(empty)*
wanting discretion imprudent
wanting in candor disingenuous
wanting in probity dishonest, fraudulent
wanting in proportion disproportionate
wanton flagrant, hot-blooded, imprudent, lascivious, lecherous, lewd, licentious, malicious, needless, obscene, outrageous, prodigal, profuse, promiscuous, prurient, reckless, salacious, suggestive *(risqué)*, unrestrained *(not repressed)*, unruly, unscrupulous. SEE MAIN ENTRY
wanton destruction waste
wanton disregard malice
wantonly wicked conduct atrocity
wantonness delinquency *(misconduct)*, vice
war contend *(dispute)*, contest *(dispute)*, fight *(battle)*, strife
war hammer cudgel
war of words argument *(contention)*, contest *(dispute)*, fight *(argument)*
war with engage *(involve)*
ward bailiwick, charge *(custody)*, control *(supervision)*, dependent, district, division *(administrative unit)*, juvenile, minor, orphan, preservation, protect, protégé, region. SEE MAIN ENTRY
ward off avert, contain *(restrain)*, counter, debar, deter, estop, forestall, parry, prevent, repel *(drive back)*, repulse, shun, stall, stave, stop, thwart
warden caretaker *(one caring for property)*, guardian, superintendent. SEE MAIN ENTRY
wardenship auspices, control *(supervision)*
warder guardian, warden
warding off defense, preventive
wardship adoption *(affiliation)*, auspices, charge *(custody)*, control *(supervision)*, custody *(supervision)*, management *(supervision)*, preservation, protection, safekeeping
ware cargo, item
warehouse cache *(storage place)*, depository, repository, store
wares cargo, commodities, merchandise, stock in trade
warfare belligerency, campaign, fight *(battle)*, outbreak, strife
wariness caution *(vigilance)*, deliberation, diligence *(care)*, discretion *(quality of being discreet)*, doubt *(suspicion)*, notice *(heed)*, precaution
warlike disorderly, inimical, litigious, malevolent, offensive *(taking the initiative)*, pugnacious, spartan
warlikeness belligerency
warm benevolent, charitable *(lenient)*, moving *(evoking emotion)*
warmhearted benevolent, humane
warmheartedness benevolence *(disposition to do good)*
warmth affection
warmth of feeling ardor
warn advise, alert, apprise, caution, counsel, deter, discourage, exhort, forewarn, herald, inform *(notify)*, notice *(give formal warning)*, notify, portend, predict, presage, remind, remonstrate, reprimand. SEE MAIN ENTRY
warn against admonish *(warn)*
warn beforehand forewarn

warn in advance forewarn
warned informed *(having information)*
warner informer *(a person who provides information)*
warning admonition, advice, caveat, deterrent, forerunner, harbinger, hortative, indication, indicator, intelligence *(news)*, notification, precaution, precursor, premonition, remonstrance, remonstrative, reprimand, symptom, threat, tip *(clue)*, ultimatum. SEE MAIN ENTRY
warning notice dun
warning sign caveat, symptom
warp corrupt, deface, distort, mutilate, pervert, predisposition, prejudice *(influence)*, propensity, slant, tendency
warped defective, depraved, dissolute, faulty, imperfect, one-sided, peccable, tainted *(corrupted)*, unjust, unsound *(not strong)*
warped idea misestimation
warped impression misestimation
warped judgment distortion, misestimation
warrant affirm *(uphold)*, allow *(authorize)*, assure *(insure)*, authorize, avouch *(guarantee)*, award, basis, bear *(adduce)*, bind *(obligate)*, bond, bond *(secure a debt)*, brevet, canon, capacity *(authority)*, certificate, certify *(attest)*, charge *(empower)*, citation *(charge)*, claim *(maintain)*, commitment *(responsibility)*, concession *(authorization)*, confirmation, consent *(noun)*, consent *(verb)*, contend *(maintain)*, corroborate, coverage *(insurance)*, delegate, delegation *(assignment)*, direction *(order)*, dispensation *(exception)*, draft, droit, empower, ensure, flat, grant *(concede)*, guarantee, guaranty, indorsement, injunction, justify, leave *(permission)*, let *(permit)*, license, monition *(legal summons)*, order, permit *(noun)*, permit *(verb)*, pledge *(promise the performance of)*, power, precept, prerogative, privilege, promise *(vow)*, proof, reassure, requirement, right *(entitlement)*, sponsor, subscribe *(promise)*, surety *(certainty)*, undertaking *(pledge)*, uphold, validate, verify *(swear)*, vouch, vow, witness *(attest to)*. SEE MAIN ENTRY
warrant of commitment mittimus
warrantability admissibility
warrantable admissible, allowable, colorable *(plausible)*, defensible, justifiable, licit, permissible, reasonable *(rational)*, tenable
warrantableness admissibility, legality
warranted admissible, agreed *(promised)*, allowed, condign, entitled, fully secured, juridical, justifiable, legal, licit, rightful, valid
warranted by law lawful
warranting advocacy
warrantless search SEE MAIN ENTRY
warrantor backer, surety *(guarantor)*
warranty assurance, bond, certainty, consent, contract, covenant, coverage *(insurance)*, guaranty, pact, pledge *(binding promise)*, promise, recognizance, security *(pledge)*, specialty *(contract)*, warrant *(guaranty)*. SEE MAIN ENTRY
warranty against loss insurance
wartime belligerency
wary alert *(vigilant)*, circumspect, deliberate, diffident, guarded, inconvincible, leery, noncommittal, provident *(showing foresight)*, prudent, skeptical, suspicious *(distrustful)*, vigilant
wash permeate
wash away purge *(purify)*
waspish fractious, perverse, petulant, querulous, resentful
wastage consumption, decrement, spoilage, waste, wear and tear
waste barren, bleak *(exposed and barren)*, consume, consumption, decrement, degenerate, deplete, destroy *(efface)*, deteriorate, diminish, discard, dissipate *(expend foolishly)*, erode, erosion, exhaust *(deplete)*, expend *(consume)*, havoc, impair, lose *(be deprived of)*, loss, misapplication, misemploy, mishandle *(mismanage)*, mistreat, pillage, prey, prostration, spoil *(pillage)*, spoilage. SEE MAIN ENTRY
waste away decay, diminish, ebb, languish, lessen
waste time procrastinate
wasted futile, irredeemable, lost *(taken away)*, otiose, stale, unavailing, unsound *(not strong)*
wasteful barren, careless, improvident, inordinate, intemperate, needless, prodigal, profligate *(extravagant)*, profuse, superfluous, unavailing, unproductive
wasteful expenditure misapplication
wastefulness consumption, misapplication, waste
wasting decadent, deleterious, fatal, waste
wasting away decadent
wastrel degenerate, derelict
watch charge *(custody)*, check *(inspect)*, concern *(care)*, custody *(supervision)*, harbor, heed, monitor, note *(notice)*, notice *(heed)*, notice *(observe)*, observation, oversee, patrol, peruse, police, precaution, preserve, regard *(attention)*, regard *(pay attention)*, safekeeping, scrutinize, spy, superintend, surveillance, survey *(examine)*, ward, witness *(have direct knowledge of)*. SEE MAIN ENTRY
watch closely examine *(study)*
watch diligently police
watch for expect *(anticipate)*
watch out beware
watch out for care *(be cautious)*
watch over attend *(take care of)*, care *(be cautious)*, care *(regard)*, cover *(guard)*, ensconce, foster, keep *(shelter)*, maintain *(sustain)*, overlook *(superintend)*, oversee, preserve, protect
watch secretely spy
watched over guarded
watcher bystander, eyewitness, spy
watchful alert *(vigilant)*, careful, circumspect, conscious *(aware)*, diligent, discreet, guarded, leery, meticulous, noncommittal, precise, preventive, protective, provident *(showing foresight)*, suspicious *(distrustful)*, vigilant
watchful care oversight *(control)*
watchfulness caution *(vigilance)*, deliberation, diligence *(care)*, discretion *(quality of being discreet)*, notice *(heed)*, observation, oversight *(control)*, precaution, prudence, regard *(attention)*, surveillance, ward
watchman caretaker *(one caring for property)*, guardian, warden
watchword catchword, indicant, phrase
water dilute
water down denature, lessen
waterfront littoral
waterlog permeate
watermark brand
waterproof impervious
watershed crossroad *(turning point)*
waterside littoral
watertight impervious
wave beat *(pulsate)*, brandish, display, flaunt, fluctuate
wave brazenly flaunt
wave conspicuously flaunt
wave ostentatiously flaunt
waver alternate *(fluctuate)*, beat *(pulsate)*, doubt *(hesitate)*, fluctuate, hesitate, misdoubt, oscillate, pause, vacillate, vary
wavering capricious, doubt *(indecision)*, dubious, faithless, hesitant, hesitation, intermittent, irresolute, irresponsible, moving *(in motion)*, mutable, noncommittal, shifting, sporadic, undecided, undependable, unpredictable, unreliable, unsettled, untrustworthy, variable, volatile. SEE MAIN ENTRY
wax expand, inflate, proliferate, pullulate
waxen flexible
waxing inflation *(increase)*
way access *(right of way)*, admission *(entry)*, admittance *(means of approach)*, avenue *(means of attainment)*, avenue *(route)*, conduct, conduit *(channel)*, demeanor, deportment, direction *(course)*, expedient, facility *(instrumentality)*, form *(arrangement)*, habit, instrumentality, key *(solution)*, manner *(behavior)*, method, mode, modus operandi, ploy, practice *(custom)*, practice *(procedure)*, presence *(poise)*, procedure, process *(course)*, state *(condition)*, style, system, temperament, treatment. SEE MAIN ENTRY
way in access *(right of way)*, entrance, ingress
way of acting behavior, conduct
way of approach access *(right of way)*
way of doing things design *(intent)*, practice *(procedure)*
way of escape loophole
way of life behavior, modus vivendi
way of living modus vivendi
way of operation procedure
way of thinking conviction *(persuasion)*, outlook, perspective, position *(point of view)*, posture *(attitude)*, principle *(axiom)*
way out egress, loophole, outlet
way over land easement
way through access *(right of way)*
way to ingress
wayfaring itinerant, moving *(in motion)*, vagrancy
waylay accost, ambush, assail, attack, carry away, ensnare, jostle *(pickpocket)*, kidnap
waymark landmark *(conspicuous object)*
ways approaches, conduct, deportment, means *(opportunity)*, policy *(plan of action)*, presence *(poise)*
ways and means avenue *(means of attainment)*, modus operandi, process *(course)*
wayward disobedient, disorderly, dissolute, eccentric, froward, insubordinate, intractable, lawless, opposite, peccable, perverse, restive, unruly, unyielding, variable
waywardness delinquency *(misconduct)*
weak defective, deficient, dependent, fallible, harmless, helpless *(powerless)*, imperfect, inactive, inadequate, incapable, inconclusive, indistinct, ineffective, ineffectual, insipid, insubstantial, insufficient, invalid, jejune *(dull)*, languid, lifeless *(dull)*, marginal, nonsubstantial *(not sturdy)*, obscure *(faint)*, poor *(inferior in*

quality), powerless, unsatisfactory, unsound *(not strong)*, untenable, vulnerable. SEE MAIN ENTRY
weak group minority *(outnumbered group)*
weak point disadvantage, fault *(weakness)*, flaw, foible, frailty, vice
weak side foible, frailty
weak spot flaw
weak-eyed blind *(sightless)*
weak-minded caitiff
weaken adulterate, alleviate, attenuate, countervail, damage, debase, debilitate, denature, deplete, depreciate, depress, derogate, deteriorate, dilute, diminish, disable, disadvantage, disarm *(divest of arms)*, encumber *(hinder)*, erode, eviscerate, exhaust *(deplete)*, extenuate, impair, languish, lapse *(fall into error)*, lessen, moderate *(temper)*, mollify, obtund, prejudice *(injure)*, relapse, relax, remit *(relax)*, tax *(overwork)*, vitiate. SEE MAIN ENTRY
weaken in force attenuate
weaken the resolution of discourage
weakened decadent, disadvantaged, old
weakening damage, decrease, disabling, mitigation, operose, relapse
weakly nonsubstantial *(not sturdy)*
weakness caducity, defect, deficiency, detriment, disability *(physical inability)*, disadvantage, disease, flaw, foible, frailty, impotence, impuissance, incapacity, inefficacy, languor, penchant, predisposition, propensity, prostration, vice
weakness of character foible
weal boom *(prosperity)*, prosperity, welfare
wealth assets, boom *(prosperity)*, economy *(economic system)*, effects, finance, income, means *(funds)*, money, personalty, possessions, principal *(capital sum)*, prosperity, resource, store *(depository)*, substance *(material possessions)*, sufficiency. SEE MAIN ENTRY
wealthy prosperous, successful. SEE MAIN ENTRY
wean alienate *(estrange)*, withdraw
wean away disaffect
weapon bomb, cudgel, gun
weaponless powerless
weapons ammunition. SEE MAIN ENTRY
wear consumption, degenerate, depreciate, endure *(last)*, erode, erosion, flaunt, keep *(continue)*, usage
wear and tear decrement, defacement. SEE MAIN ENTRY
wear away consume, decay, degenerate, diminish, erode, expire, languish, lessen, spend
wear down diminish, erode, harass, prevail *(persuade)*, tax *(overwork)*
wear down by friction erode
wear out consume, deplete, diminish, exhaust *(deplete)*, impair, misemploy, mistreat, spend, tax *(overwork)*
wear the aspect appear *(seem to be)*
wearful irksome
weariness inertia, languor, prostration
wearing chronic, irksome, operose, oppressive
wearing away attrition, erosion
wearing down by friction erosion
wearisome irksome, jejune *(dull)*, lifeless *(dull)*, mundane, onerous, operose, oppressive, ordinary, painful, pedestrian, ponderous, prolix, prosaic, trite, vexatious
weary exhaust *(deplete)*, lugubrious, otiose, tax *(overwork)*
weary load onus *(burden)*
wearying irksome, lifeless *(dull)*, operose, ponderous
weather atmosphere, bear *(tolerate)*, endure *(last)*, endure *(suffer)*, erode, maintain *(sustain)*, resist *(withstand)*, withstand
weatherbeaten dilapidated
weathered old
weave incorporate *(include)*
weave a plot scheme
web intertwine, involution
wed connect *(join together)*, join *(bring together)*, unite
wedded composite, concurrent *(united)*, conjoint, conjugal, nuptial
wedded state cohabitation *(married state)*, coverture, marriage *(wedlock)*, matrimony
wedded status cohabitation *(married state)*
wedded to addicted
wedding marriage *(wedlock)*
wedding a second time digamy
wedge impact
wedged inextricable
wedlock cohabitation *(married state)*, matrimony
weed cannabis, delete, edit, eliminate *(exclude)*, excise *(cut away)*, exclude, expurgate, screen *(select)*
weed out diminish, eliminate *(eradicate)*, eradicate, expel, extirpate, lessen, reject, select
ween opine, surmise
weep exude
weep over deplore, regret, repent
weeping disconsolate, outcry, repentant
weigh assess *(appraise)*, brood, compare, consider, criticize *(evaluate)*, debate, deliberate, determine, diagnose, digest *(comprehend)*, estimate, gauge, judge, measure, muse, pause, ponder, rate, reason *(conclude)*, reflect *(ponder)*, review, speculate *(conjecture)*, study, survey *(examine)*. SEE MAIN ENTRY
weigh against countervail
weigh down disadvantage, encumber *(hinder)*, load, overcome *(overwhelm)*, overload, overwhelm, tax *(overwork)*
weigh in the mind deliberate
weigh more than outweigh
weigh on harass
weigh on the mind obsess
weigh out mete
weighable appreciable, ponderable
weighed deliberate, tactical
weighing contemplation, deliberation, discrimination *(differentiation)*, estimation *(calculation)*, judgment *(discernment)*, reflection *(thought)*
weight burden, clout, corpus, degree *(magnitude)*, dint, dominance, eminence, emphasis, import, importance, incumbrance *(burden)*, influence, interest *(concern)*, load, magnitude, materiality *(consequence)*, onus *(burden)*, power, predominance, pressure, prestige, primacy, significance, stress *(accent)*. SEE MAIN ENTRY
weight of numbers majority *(greater part)*, plurality
weight of the evidence SEE MAIN ENTRY
weighted inequitable, unfair
weightiness import, importance, interest *(concern)*, magnitude, materiality *(consequence)*, significance
weightless intangible
weighty cogent, compelling, consequential *(substantial)*, critical *(crucial)*, determinative, dominant, grave *(important)*, important *(significant)*, key, major, material *(important)*, momentous, onerous, oppressive, persuasive, ponderous, potent, powerful, predominant, prevailing *(having superior force)*, prominent, serious *(grave)*, solid *(sound)*, sound, urgent
weird mysterious, peculiar *(curious)*, prodigious *(amazing)*, uncanny
welcome desirable *(pleasing)*, embrace *(accept)*, palatable, sapid
welcoming receptive
weld cement, join *(bring together)*, lock, merge
welded conjoint, inseparable
welfare advantage, behalf, benefit *(betterment)*, boom *(prosperity)*. SEE MAIN ENTRY
well fund, source
well based well-grounded
well being prosperity
well defined visible *(in full view)*
well done professional *(stellar)*
well enough fairly *(moderately)*
well established fixed *(settled)*
well founded well-grounded
well off prosperous. SEE MAIN ENTRY
well provided for opulent
well thought of popular, reputable
well thought out strategic
well to do prosperous
well-acquainted familiar *(informed)*
well-adapted apposite, politic
well-advised cognizant, discreet, discriminating *(judicious)*, juridical, politic, prudent, reasonable *(rational)*, sensible
well-armed armed
well-balanced proportionate
well-based authentic, true *(authentic)*
well-behaved civil *(polite)*, malleable, obedient
well-being benefit *(betterment)*, boom *(prosperity)*, health, welfare. SEE MAIN ENTRY
well-bred civil *(polite)*, proper
well-brought up civil *(polite)*
well-built solid *(sound)*, stable, strong
well-chosen felicitous
well-chosen moment crossroad *(turning point)*
well-conducted moral
well-considered aforethought, circumspect, deliberate, judicious, premeditated
well-constructed solid *(sound)*
well-defined absolute *(conclusive)*, accurate, certain *(specific)*, clear *(apparent)*, coherent *(clear)*, conspicuous, definite, distinct *(clear)*, manifest, obvious, perceivable, perceptible, precise, tangible, unambiguous, unmistakable
well-deserved condign
well-developed explicit, ripe
well-devised politic, premeditated
well-disciplined spartan
well-disposed inclined, peaceable, prone, propitious
well-doer benefactor
well-done meritorious, right *(suitable)*
well-drawn descriptive, distinct *(clear)*
well-earned condign
well-educated cognizant, familiar *(informed)*, informed *(educated)*, learned, literate
well-established ingrained, solid *(sound)*
well-expressed felicitous
well-fitted competent, fit
well-fixed opulent

well-founded actual, authentic, axiomatic, believable, cogent, convincing, de facto, legitimate *(rightful)*, presumptive, provable, reasonable *(rational)*, solid *(sound)*, sound, tenable, true *(authentic)*. SEE MAIN ENTRY
well-founded opinion conviction *(persuasion)*
well-grounded actual, authentic, believable, cogent, cognizant, convincing, credible, de facto, informed *(educated)*, justifiable, legitimate *(rightful)*, presumptive, provable, rational, solid *(sound)*, sound, stable, tenable, true *(authentic)*, valid. SEE MAIN ENTRY
well-grounded hope likelihood, prospect *(outlook)*
well-grounded possibility likelihood
well-informed cognizant, knowing, learned, literate, omniscient, politic
well-intentioned benevolent, meritorious, propitious
well-judged politic
well-knit cohesive *(compact)*
well-known blatant *(conspicuous)*, common *(customary)*, customary, familiar *(customary)*, famous, household *(familiar)*, illustrious, important *(significant)*, influential, master, mundane, prevailing *(current)*, prevalent, prominent, proverbial, public *(known)*, renowned, reputable, salient, trite, usual. SEE MAIN ENTRY
well-liked popular
well-made solid *(sound)*, strong
well-mannered civil *(polite)*
well-marked clear *(apparent)*, coherent *(clear)*, conspicuous, definite, distinct *(clear)*, manifest, perceivable, perceptible, prominent
well-matched concurrent *(united)*, uniform
well-meaning benevolent, propitious
well-meant benevolent
well-off opulent, successful
well-ordered systematic
well-organized systematic
well-paying gainful, lucrative, profitable
well-performed right *(suitable)*
well-planned artful, tactical
well-pleased proud *(self-respecting)*
well-populated populous
well-posted knowing
well-principled honest, law-abiding
well-provided copious, full, replete
well-qualified expert, fit, practiced, professional *(trained)*, proficient
well-read cognizant, informed *(educated)*, learned, literate
well-received popular
well-recognized household *(familiar)*, influential
well-regarded influential
well-regulated regular *(orderly)*, right *(suitable)*, systematic
well-rounded informed *(educated)*, learned
well-satisfied proud *(self-respecting)*
well-seen clear *(apparent)*, conspicuous, manifest, prominent
well-situated opulent, prosperous, successful
well-spoken civil *(polite)*
well-stocked copious, full, replete
well-suited appropriate, fit, qualified *(competent)*, sciential
well-supplied full, rife
well-taught learned, literate
well-thought-out tactical
well-timed felicitous, fit, opportune, punctual, seasonable
well-timed initiative crossroad *(turning point)*
well-to-do opulent, successful
well-trained learned
well-trodden familiar *(customary)*, mundane, ordinary, routine, usual
well-versed cognizant, familiar *(informed)*, informed *(educated)*, knowing, proficient
well-wisher proponent, samaritan
well-worn ordinary
well-written cognizable
wellhead source
wellspring origin *(source)*, origination, source
welter commotion, imbroglio, shambles, turmoil
wergild reparation *(indemnification)*
whack lash *(strike)*
wharton rule SEE MAIN ENTRY
whatever SEE MAIN ENTRY
whatsoever whatever.. SEE MAIN ENTRY
wheedle inveigle
whelm overcome *(overwhelm)*
when ad interim, whenever
whenever SEE MAIN ENTRY
whereabouts locality, scene. SEE MAIN ENTRY
whereby hereby, thereby. SEE MAIN ENTRY
wherefore consequently, reason *(basis)*
wherein herein. SEE MAIN ENTRY
whereon wherein
whereupon wherein
wherewithal assets, expedient, instrumentality, means *(funds)*, means *(opportunity)*, money, resource, substance *(material possessions)*, sufficiency
whet stimulate, stimulus
whet one's interest interest
whichever whatever
while ad interim, duration, period. SEE MAIN ENTRY
whilom former
whim notion
whimpering querulous
whimsical arbitrary and capricious, capricious, original *(creative)*
whine plaint
whiner malcontent
whining querulous
whiny petulant, querulous
whip beat *(strike)*, churn, punish
whirl commotion
whisper imply, report *(rumor)*, suggestion, tip *(clue)*
whistle-blower SEE MAIN ENTRY
whit iota, minimum, scintilla
white clean
whittle abridge *(shorten)*, diminish
whiz race
whoever SEE MAIN ENTRY
whole absolute *(complete)*, aggregate, amount *(quantity)*, collective, corpus, detailed, entirety, full, gross *(total)*, intact, inviolate, plenary, principal *(capital sum)*, pure, radical *(extreme)*, safe, total, totality, undiminished. SEE MAIN ENTRY
whole attention diligence *(care)*, obsession
whole mind diligence *(care)*
whole range gamut
wholeness body *(collection)*, corpus, entirety, finality, sum *(total)*, whole
wholesale destruction conflagration
wholesale trader dealer
wholesaler dealer
wholesome clean, remedial, salubrious, salutary, unaffected *(sincere)*
wholesomeness health
wholly in toto, solely *(singly)*. SEE MAIN ENTRY
wholly inadequate SEE MAIN ENTRY
whomever whoever
whomsoever whoever
whopping prodigious *(enormous)*
whorled circuitous
whosoever whoever
wicked arrant *(onerous)*, bad *(offensive)*, base *(bad)*, contemptible, delinquent *(guilty of a misdeed)*, depraved, diabolic, felonious, harmful, heinous, ignoble, illicit, immoral, impermissible, incorrigible, inexpiable, iniquitous, irregular *(improper)*, malevolent, malicious, malignant, nefarious, outrageous, peccant *(culpable)*, pernicious, perverse, profane, profligate *(corrupt)*, reprehensible, reprobate, scandalous, sinister, tainted *(corrupted)*, unjust, unjustifiable, unscrupulous, vicious. SEE MAIN ENTRY
wicked action misdeed
wicked deed misdeed, misdemeanor, misdoing
wickedness atrocity, corruption, delinquency *(misconduct)*, dishonor *(shame)*, disrepute, mischief, misdoing, perversion, turpitude, vice, wrong
wide broad, capacious, comprehensive, copious, extensive, far reaching, generic, inclusive, liberal *(not literal)*, open *(unclosed)*
wide awake vigilant
wide currency coverage *(scope)*
wide of the mark improper
wide open penetrable
wide-awake careful
wide-embracing complete *(all-embracing)*
wide-open open-ended, patent
wide-reaching comprehensive, extensive, omnibus
wide sweeping SEE MAIN ENTRY
widely accepted prevailing *(current)*, prevalent
widely extended extensive
widely known common *(customary)*, household *(familiar)*, illustrious, prevalent, proverbial, public *(known)*, trite
widely read informed *(educated)*, learned, literate
widely recognized predominant
widely used conventional
widen accrue *(increase)*, compound, deploy, develop, enlarge, expand, extend *(enlarge)*, increase, magnify, project *(extend beyond)*, spread, supplement
widening augmentation, cumulative *(increasing)*, extension *(expansion)*
widespread broad, collective, common *(customary)*, comprehensive, current, extensive, familiar *(customary)*, far reaching, general, household *(familiar)*, omnibus, ordinary, predominant, prevailing *(current)*, prevalent, rampant, rife. SEE MAIN ENTRY
widow's estate dower
widow's portion dower
width caliber *(measurement)*, extent, gamut
wield brandish, employ *(make use of)*, exercise *(use)*, exert, exploit *(make use of)*, handle *(manage)*, manipulate *(utilize skillfully)*, militate, ply. SEE MAIN ENTRY
wield authority govern, handle *(manage)*, manage, preside

wield influence prevail upon
wield restraint over hold *(possess)*
wielding power forcible
wieldy flexible
wife consort, spouse
wifedom coverture
wild disobedient, disorderly, ill-judged, licentious, ludicrous, lunatic, outrageous, precipitate, promiscuous, rampant, reckless, uncontrollable, unrestrained *(not repressed)*, unruly, vehement
wild being animal
wild confusion riot
wild uproar pandemonium
wild-fire conflagration
wildness furor, irregularity, pandemonium, violence
wile artifice, bunko, contrivance, deception, device *(contrivance)*, false pretense, hoax, imposture, machination, maneuver *(trick)*, ploy, pretext, ruse, stratagem
wiles knavery
wiliness artifice, dishonesty, fraud
will animus, choose, conatus, contribute *(supply)*, decision *(election)*, demise, descend, design *(intent)*, desire, determine, discretion *(power of choice)*, elect *(choose)*, forethought, give *(grant)*, latitude, leave *(give)*, predetermination, purpose, resolution *(decision)*, resolve *(decide)*, tenacity, testament, volition. SEE MAIN ENTRY
will addendum codicil
will and bequeath descend, devise *(give)*
will power discipline *(obedience)*, resolution *(decision)*
will supplement codicil
will to bequeath, devise *(give)*
will validation proceeding probate
will verification proceeding probate
willed deliberate
willful arbitrary and capricious, deliberate, disobedient, express, froward, hot-blooded, inexorable, inflexible, intentional, intractable, obdurate, pertinacious, premeditated, purposeful, recalcitrant, restive, spontaneous, unbending, uncontrollable, unruly, unyielding, voluntary. SEE MAIN ENTRY
willful abandonment desertion
willful burning of property arson
willful disregard contempt *(disobedience to the court)*
willful distortion of the truth perjury
willful falsehood perjury
willful telling of a falsehood perjury
willful telling of a lie perjury
willfully purposely
willfully contrary froward
willfully disregard ignore
willfully disrespectful contumacious
willfulness forethought
willing available, consenting, eager, favorable *(expressing approval)*, inclined, malleable, obedient, obeisant, pliable, pliant, prone, receptive, resigned, solicitous, tractable, zealous. SEE MAIN ENTRY
willing consent assent
willing help aid *(help)*, charity
willing to forgive lenient, placable
willing to yield to influence of others flexible
willingly purposely, readily
willingness acquiescence, adhesion *(loyalty)*, amenability, assent, conformity *(obedience)*, consent, deference, goodwill, predisposition, sanction *(permission)*, volition. SEE MAIN ENTRY
willingness to comply compliance
willingness to forgive clemency, condonation
willingness to please consideration *(sympathetic regard)*
willingness to purchase market *(demand)*
willowy flexible
willpower strength
wilt languish, perish
wilted dilapidated, stale
wily artful, collusive, deceptive, delusive, devious, disingenuous, fraudulent, insidious, machiavellian, politic, sly, subtle *(insidious)*, surreptitious
wily device contrivance, machination
win acquire *(receive)*, carry *(succeed)*, earn, gain, inveigle, obtain, prevail *(triumph)*, reap, receive *(acquire)*, succeed *(attain)*
win an argument convert *(persuade)*
win back recoup *(regain)*, recover
win over convert *(persuade)*, convince, disarm *(set at ease)*, persuade, placate, prejudice *(influence)*, prevail *(persuade)*, prevail upon, propitiate, reason *(persuade)*, reconcile
win the battle beat *(defeat)*
wind contort
wind up close *(terminate)*, complete, expire, finish, terminate
windfall profit
winding circuitous, indirect, labyrinthine, sinuous, tortuous *(bending)*
window-dressing pretense *(ostentation)*
windup close *(conclusion)*, defeasance, denouement
windy loquacious, orotund
wing affiliate, organ, protection
winged rapid
winning popular, prevailing *(having superior force)*, prize, sapid, successful
winning over persuasion
winnings earnings, profit, spoils, stake *(award)*
winnow cull, distinguish, screen *(select)*, select, separate
winsome sapid
wipe away deface, expunge
wipe off expunge
wipe out delete, destroy *(efface)*, dissolve *(terminate)*, eliminate *(eradicate)*, expunge, extinguish, extirpate, obliterate, rescind, revoke, stop
wipe out illiteracy educate
wiretap eavesdrop
wiry resilient, strong
wisdom caliber *(mental capacity)*, cognition, common sense, comprehension, discretion *(quality of being discreet)*, experience *(background)*, information *(knowledge)*, insight, intelligence *(intellect)*, knowledge *(learning)*, reason *(sound judgment)*, sagacity, sense *(intelligence)*, understanding *(comprehension)*. SEE MAIN ENTRY
wise cognizant, conduct, discreet, discriminating *(judicious)*, expert, favorable *(advantageous)*, fit, judicial, judicious, learned, manner *(behavior)*, omniscient, oracular, perceptive, perspicacious, politic, profound *(esoteric)*, prudent, rational, reasonable *(rational)*, sapient, sensible, solid *(sound)*
wise man mastermind
wise saying maxim
wiseness sense *(intelligence)*
wish conatus, desire, end *(intent)*, market *(demand)*, predisposition, purpose, request, volition, will *(desire)*
wish for desire, lack
wishful eager
wistful pensive
with along
with a high degree of certainty high probability
with a valid will testate
with alacrity expeditious
with all reasonable speed forthwith
with all respect respectfully
with allegiance faithfully
with an executed will testate
with an iron hand dictatorial
with assurance fairly *(clearly)*
with authority as a matter of right
with cause for cause
with certainty fairly *(clearly)*
with compliance respectfully
with confidence fairly *(clearly)*
with constancy faithfully
with deference respectfully
with dispatch expeditious
with due deference respectfully
with due respect respectfully
with fealty faithfully
with fidelity faithfully
with force of law obligatory
with forethought aforethought, deliberate, express, premeditated, purposely
with free will purposely
with full effect in full force
with full force in full force
with funds solvent
with good credit solvent
with good faith faithfully
with intent purposely
with justice fairly *(impartially)*
with justification for cause
with knowledge knowingly
with license liberal *(not literal)*
with meager funds poor *(underprivileged)*
with means opulent
with no exception complete *(all-embracing)*, total
with no mistake exact
with nothing missing intact
with premeditation purposely
with reasonable dispatch forthwith, immediate *(at once)*
with reference to apposite, comparative, pertinent
with regard to comparative
with relation to comparative
with scanty funds poor *(underprivileged)*
with secret design clandestine
with simplicity ingenuous
with speed expeditious, instantly
with the aid of thereby
with the end in sight determinable *(liable to be terminated)*
with the greater force a fortiori
with the highest respect respectfully
with the stipulation provided
with the understanding provided
with this proviso provided
with validity de facto
withdraw abolish, abscond, adeem, annul, cancel, cease, debar, deduct *(reduce)*, demit, depart, diminish, disavow, discontinue *(abandon)*, disengage, disinherit, disinter, dissociate, ebb, evacuate, excise *(cut away)*, extract, flee, forfeit, hold up *(rob)*, invalidate, leave *(depart)*, part *(leave)*, quash, quit *(discontinue)*, quit *(evacuate)*, recall *(call back)*, recant, recess, refrain, refuse, relinquish, remove *(eliminate)*, renege, repeal, repudiate, rescind,

resign, retire *(retreat)*, retreat, revoke, secede, seclude, sequester *(seclude)*, superannuate, vacate *(leave)*. SEE MAIN ENTRY
withdraw clandestinely abscond
withdraw from eschew, forgo, forswear, stop
withdraw from association disband
withdraw from observation conceal
withdraw from one's native land expatriate
withdraw one's objections concede
withdraw one's support defect
withdraw the affections of alienate *(estrange)*, disaffect
withdrawal abandonment *(desertion)*, abandonment *(discontinuance)*, abdication, absence *(nonattendance)*, ademption, alienation *(estrangement)*, cancellation, cloture, countermand, deduction *(diminution)*, defeasance, discontinuance *(act of discontinuing)*, discontinuance *(interruption of a legal action)*, egress, estrangement, evulsion, exception *(exclusion)*, outflow, privacy, recess, removal, renunciation, repudiation, rescision, resignation *(relinquishment)*, retraction, revocation, schism, severance
withdrawal of a sentence reprieve
withdrawal of the charge compurgation, exoneration
withdrawing cancellation
withdrawment ademption
withdrawn inarticulate, null *(invalid)*, null and void, taciturn, unapproachable. SEE MAIN ENTRY
wither decay, decline *(fall)*, degenerate, diminish, languish, perish
withered ineffective, ineffectual, stale
withering bitter *(penetrating)*, consumption, decadent, dilapidated, harsh, regressive, scathing, supercilious
withheld arrested *(checked)*
withhold arrest *(stop)*, condemn *(ban)*, constrain *(restrain)*, constrict *(inhibit)*, debar, defer *(put off)*, deny *(refuse to grant)*, disinherit, forbear, hamper, hide, hoard, hold up *(delay)*, inhibit, keep *(restrain)*, refrain, repress, reserve, restrain, retain *(keep in possession)*, stifle, strangle. SEE MAIN ENTRY
withhold action forbear
withhold approval disaccord, disallow
withhold approval from disapprove *(reject)*
withhold assent demur, differ *(disagree)*, differ *(vary)*, disaccord, disbelieve, expostulate, hold out *(resist)*
withhold consent disoblige, forbid, hold out *(resist)*, refuse
withhold judgment doubt *(hesitate)*, misdoubt
withhold one's assent disapprove *(reject)*
withhold payment default, dishonor *(refuse to pay)*
withhold permission ban, censor, disapprove *(reject)*, forbid
withhold reliance doubt *(distrust)*
withholding reservation *(engagement)*
withholding approval dissenting
withholding assent dissenting
withholding of patronage boycott
within herein, wherein
within appropriate time provided timeliness
within boundary lines internal
within bounds fairly *(moderately)*
within reach available, disposable, facile, open *(accessible)*, passable, possible, practicable, present *(attendant)*
within reason fairly *(moderately)*
within sight of almost
within the bounds of possiblity practicable
within the law allowed, de jure, jural, juridical, law-abiding, lawful, legal, legitimate *(rightful)*, licit, permissible, rightful, statutory
within the range of possibility possible
within the realm of possibility plausible, possible
withold conceal
withold information conceal
without devoid, peripheral, save, unless
without a bend direct *(straight)*
without a name anonymous
without a penny poor *(underprivileged)*
without a preference impartial
without a shade of doubt categorical
without a shred of evidence SEE MAIN ENTRY
without a sign of life dead
without a stain clean
without a wait instantly
without adequate ability incompetent
without adequate determining principle arbitrary
without aid helpless *(defenseless)*
without airs unpretentious
without animation languid
without any lapse of time instantly
without appeal categorical, final, irrevocable, mandatory, obligatory
without assent unwillingly
without authority illegal, illicit, null *(invalid)*, null and void, powerless, unofficial
without base baseless
without basis baseless, gratuitous *(unwarranted)*, ill-founded, illogical, insubstantial, unfounded, unsupported
without bearings lost *(disoriented)*
without belief incredulous, leery
without bias fairly *(impartially)*
without blame blameless
without blemish infallible
without body incorporeal
without bound indeterminate, profuse
without cause baseless
without caution reckless
without ceasing incessant
without ceremony informal, unofficial
without cessation continuous
without charge gratis, gratuitous *(given without recompense)*
without choice compulsory, mandatory, obligatory
without circumlocution direct *(straight)*
without companions solitary
without company solitary
without comparison best, prime *(most valuable)*
without compensation gratuitous *(given without recompense)*
without compulsion voluntary
without concern perfunctory
without conditions unconditional
without confusion simple
without connection foreign, impertinent *(irrelevant)*, irrelative
without consent involuntary, unwillingly
without consequence null *(insignificant)*
without consideration arbitrary, gratis, gratuitous *(given without recompense)*, heedless, oblivious, thoughtless
without constraint voluntary
without content devoid
without contents void *(empty)*
without context alien *(unrelated)*
without cost free *(at no charge)*
without current stagnant
without date sine die
without deductions gross *(total)*
without defect unblemished
without defense blameful, blameworthy, inexcusable, inexpiable
without delay as soon as feasible, immediate *(at once)*, instant, instantaneous, instantly, prompt
without depth immaterial
without dexterity inadept
without difference equivalent, same
without distinction comparable *(equivalent)*, fairly *(impartially)*, identical
without divergence direct *(straight)*
without doubt decisive, definitive, demonstrable, indubious, undisputed
without effect ineffective, ineffectual
without employment unemployed
without end ad infinitum, durable, indeterminate, infinite, permanent, perpetual, profuse
without enthusiasm perfunctory
without equal inestimable
without error exact
without exaggeration literal
without exception invariably
without excuse blameful, inexcusable, inexpiable, peccant *(culpable)*, unjustifiable
without exit blind *(impassable)*
without experience inexperienced
without faith inconvincible, incredulous, leery
without fault blameless
without favor fairly *(impartially)*
without favoritism impartial
without force helpless *(powerless)*, insipid, languid, nonsubstantial *(not sturdy)*, powerless
without foresight improvident
without form intangible
without formality informal
without foundation gratuitous *(unwarranted)*, ill-founded, illogical, insubstantial, nonsubstantial *(not sturdy)*, unfounded, unsupported
without funds impecunious
without guile ingenuous
without harm innocent
without heart cold-blooded
without hesitation instantly
without honor perfidious, recreant
without hope irredeemable
without insight blind *(not discerning)*
without integrity immoral, unscrupulous
without interruption continuous, incessant
without issue barren
without judgment irrational
without judicial authority want of jurisdiction. SEE MAIN ENTRY
without knowledge inexperienced
without law lawless
without legal authority illegally
without legal effect null *(invalid)*, null and void
without legal efficacy invalid
without legal force null *(invalid)*, null and void, void *(invalid)*
without legal sanction illegally
without life dead, defunct, lifeless *(dead)*

without limit indeterminate, infinite, profuse
without limitation peremptory *(absolute)*
without limits open-ended
without loss intact, undiminished, whole *(undamaged)*
without meaning null *(insignificant)*
without measure indeterminate, infinite
without method disordered
without modesty proud *(conceited)*
without monetary inducement gratis
without monetary reward gratis
without money impecunious
without motion stagnant
without nerves dispassionate
without notice instantly, unaware
without novelty stale
without number infinite, myriad, unlimited
without offense innocent
without omission in toto, total
without omissions complete *(all-embracing)*
without order haphazard
without originality sequacious
without parallel paramount, superlative
without particularizing generally
without pecuniary gain gratis
without perceptible time lapse instantaneous
without physical substance intangible
without pity ruthless
without plausibility insubstantial
without potency null *(invalid)*, null and void
without power of appeal inappealable
without power of choice involuntary
without power to harm innocuous
without precision inexact
without prejudice fairly *(impartially)*
without price inestimable, invaluable, priceless
without probity dishonest, fraudulent
without prudence impulsive *(rash)*, reckless
without qualification absolute *(complete)*
without question decisive, definitive, indubious, undisputed
without rational basis capricious
without reality baseless, insubstantial, unfounded
without reason arbitrary, baseless, irrational, ludicrous
without recompense gratis
without recourse SEE MAIN ENTRY
without reference irrespective
without reference to irrelevant
without regard insusceptible *(uncaring)*
without regard to regardless. SEE MAIN ENTRY
without regrets relentless
without relation alien *(unrelated)*, heterogeneous, irrelative
without reliance in suspect *(distrust)*
without reproach blameless, clean
without repute notorious
without reservations unconditional
without reserve categorical, demonstrative *(expressive of emotion)*
without resources destitute, devoid
without respect or regard to irrespective
without respect to regardless
without restraint inordinate. SEE MAIN ENTRY
without results unproductive
without reward gratis
without rhyme or reason irrational
without risk harmless, immune, nontoxic, safe
without scruples unscrupulous
without shame unabashed
without significance null *(insignificant)*
without sound basis ill-founded
without specified limits open-ended
without spirit languid
without stain unblemished
without stint profuse
without stopping incessant
without strings unrestricted
without substance ill-founded, immaterial, incorporeal, null *(insignificant)*, unfounded
without substantial cause arbitrary
without succor helpless *(defenseless)*
without suspicion unsuspecting
without taste inelegant, insipid
without tendency to harm innocuous
without the appearance of life dead
without the name of the author anonymous
without thought impulsive *(rash)*
without truth dishonest, disingenuous, fraudulent
without value null *(invalid)*, null and void
without vanity diffident
without vitality powerless
without warmth cold-blooded, dispassionate
without warranty as is
without weight immaterial, ineffective, ineffectual
without will involuntary
withstand allow *(endure)*, collide *(clash)*, counteract, defy, endure *(last)*, endure *(suffer)*, hold out *(resist)*, last, parry, repel *(drive back)*, repulse. SEE MAIN ENTRY
withstanding resistance
witless fatuous, irrational, obtuse, opaque
witlessly unknowingly
witness attest, avow, bystander, bystander, corroboration, declarant, deponent, depose *(testify)*, discern *(detect with the senses)*, indicator, informant, notarize, note *(notice)*, notice *(observe)*, perceive, pierce *(discern)*, regard *(pay attention)*, subscribe *(sign)*, verify *(swear)*, vouch. SEE MAIN ENTRY
witness against informer *(one providing criminal information)*
witness as to character bystander
witness box stand *(witness' place in court)*
witness stand stand *(witness' place in court)*
witness to bear *(adduce)*
witness to a crime bystander
witness who gives testimony deponent
witnessing attestation, observation, reference *(recommendation)*
wittingly knowingly, purposely
witty jocular
wizardry prowess *(ability)*
wobbly insubstantial, nonsubstantial *(not sturdy)*
woe disaster, distress *(anguish)*, pain, plaint, tragedy
woebegone disconsolate, lugubrious
woeful blameworthy, dire, disconsolate, lamentable, lugubrious, regrettable
wolfish predatory, rapacious
womanhood majority *(adulthood)*
wonder phenomenon *(unusual occurrence)*, reflect *(ponder)*, surprise
wonder about ponder, speculate *(conjecture)*
wonderful meritorious, noteworthy, portentous *(eliciting amazement)*, prodigious *(amazing)*, remarkable, special
wondering incredulous
wonderment phenomenon *(unusual occurrence)*, surprise
wonderwork phenomenon *(unusual occurrence)*
wondrous noteworthy, portentous *(eliciting amazement)*, prodigious *(amazing)*, remarkable
wont custom, manner *(behavior)*, usage
wonted boiler plate, conventional, customary, familiar *(customary)*, habitual, inveterate, ordinary, orthodox, prescriptive, prevailing *(current)*, regular *(conventional)*, usual
wontedness custom
woo persuade, prevail *(persuade)*
wooden rigid
word canon, disclosure *(something disclosed)*, intelligence *(news)*, phrase, pledge *(binding promise)*, profession *(declaration)*, promise, remark, term *(expression)*, undertaking *(pledge)*, vow. SEE MAIN ENTRY
word for word faithfully, literal, verbatim *(adjective)*, verbatim *(adverb)*
word group phrase
word of command instruction *(direction)*
word of explanation comment, note *(brief comment)*
word of honor pledge *(binding promise)*, profession *(declaration)*, vow
word picture delineation
wordage language, parlance
wordiness fustian, prolixity
wording language, phraseology, rhetoric *(skilled speech)*
wordless mute, speechless, tacit
wordlessness silence
words speech
wordy flatulent, loquacious, profuse, prolific, prolix, redundant, turgid, voluble
work activity, appointment *(position)*, assignment *(task)*, burden, business *(occupation)*, calling, career, cultivate, duty *(obligation)*, effectuate, employ *(make use of)*, employment, endeavor, exert, exploit *(make use of)*, function *(noun)*, function *(verb)*, industry *(activity)*, industry *(business)*, job, labor, livelihood, manage, manipulate *(utilize skillfully)*, militate, mission, occupation *(vocation)*, office, operate, perform *(execute)*, performance *(execution)*, performance *(workmanship)*, perpetrate, ply, position *(business status)*, post, profession *(vocation)*, publication *(printed matter)*, pursuit *(occupation)*, role, strive, struggle, wield. SEE MAIN ENTRY
work a change adapt, affect
work a cure remedy
work against antagonize, collide *(clash)*, counter, counteract, countervail, fight *(counteract)*, hinder, interfere
work as a team cooperate, federalize *(associate)*
work at endeavor, occupy *(engage)*, practice *(engage in)*, practice *(train by repetition)*
work at cross purposes counter
work done fait accompli
work evil mistreat
work for foster, help, pursue *(strive to gain)*, serve *(assist)*

work for a judge clerk
work for hire SEE MAIN ENTRY
work force personnel
work hard labor, strive
work in interject, intersperse
work in the service of pander
work in unison combine *(act in concert)*
work into a passion incense, provoke
work jointly concur *(agree)*
work on lobby, treat *(process)*
work out calculate, compose, devise *(invent)*, dispatch *(dispose of)*, fix *(settle)*, implement, maneuver, negotiate, perpetrate, plan, plot, program, scheme, settle, solve
work out differences mediate
work out in detail develop
work over emend, modify *(alter)*, redact, revise
work party personnel
work place office
work side by side with cooperate
work stoppage lockout, strike
work to excess overload
work together combine *(act in concert)*, consolidate *(unite)*, cooperate, federalize *(associate)*, involve *(participate)*, participate
work toward conduce
work unceasingly adhere *(persist)*, persevere, persist
work unflaggingly persevere, persist
work up churn, compose, foment, frame *(formulate)*, perturb, pique, provoke, scheme, stimulate
work upon affect, constrain *(compel)*, influence, motivate
workability feasibility, potential
workable demonstrable, determinable *(ascertainable)*, fit, functional, operative, possible, potential, practicable, practical, solvable, viable
workableness feasibility
workaday household *(familiar)*, ordinary, prevailing *(current)*, regular *(conventional)*, usual
workday mundane
worked up frenetic
worker apprentice, artisan, employee
worker of iniquity criminal, delinquent
workers personnel, staff
workfellow contributor *(contributor)*, partner
working active, effective *(operative)*, functional, operative
working ability performance *(workmanship)*
working arrangement modus vivendi
working assets capital, cash
working capital finance, money, principal *(capital sum)*
working in concert association *(connection)*
working people personnel
working plan device *(contrivance)*, method
working proposition device *(contrivance)*
working together coaction, connivance
workingman artisan
workingwoman artisan
workless idle, unemployed
workman artisan, employee
workwoman artisan
world-wide nonsectarian, ubiquitous. SEE MAIN ENTRY
world-wise veteran
worldliness experience *(background)*
worldly civil *(public)*, material *(physical)*, mundane, physical, profane
worldly belongings possessions
worldly substance effects
worldly wisdom common sense
worldly-minded mundane
worldwide prevailing *(current)*, prevalent, rife
worn dilapidated, old, trite, unsound *(not strong)*
worn out decadent, dilapidated, old, stale, trite
worrisome problematic
worry agitate *(perturb)*, apprehension *(fear)*, badger, bait *(harass)*, concern *(interest)*, discommode, discompose, distress *(anguish)*, distress, disturb, embarrass, fear, harry *(harass)*, hector, interest *(concern)*, mistreat, molest *(annoy)*, nuisance, pain, perplex, perturb, pique, plague, press *(goad)*, qualm. SEE MAIN ENTRY
worsen aggravate *(exacerbate)*, decay, degenerate, depreciate, deteriorate, exacerbate, harm, impair
worsening aggravation *(exacerbation)*
worship honor *(outward respect)*, regard *(hold in esteem)*, respect
worshiped sacrosanct
worshipful solemn
worst dire, subdue, subject, upset
worth advantage, amount *(sum)*, benefit *(betterment)*, caliber *(quality)*, charge *(cost)*, connotation, credit *(recognition)*, emphasis, estimate *(approximate cost)*, expense *(cost)*, face value *(price)*, magnitude, materiality *(consequence)*, merit, par *(face amount)*, prestige, price, quality *(excellence)*, quality *(grade)*, rate, respect, significance, signification, value. SEE MAIN ENTRY
worth a great deal opulent
worth considering material *(important)*
worth imitating meritorious
worthiness expedience, honesty, integrity, merit, qualification *(fitness)*, rectitude, right *(righteousness)*, value, worth
worthless barren, contemptible, delinquent *(guilty of a misdeed)*, expendable, frivolous, futile, ignoble, immaterial, inconsequential, inconsiderable, ineffective, ineffectual, insubstantial, needless, nugatory, null *(insignificant)*, null *(invalid)*, null and void, otiose, paltry, petty, poor *(inferior in quality)*, reprobate, trivial, unable, unavailing, unproductive, unsound *(fallacious)*, unworthy
worthless argument fallacy
worthless check bad check
worthless person degenerate
worthless trial mistrial
worthlessness immateriality
worthwhile beneficial, gainful, laudable, lucrative, meritorious, productive, profitable, purposeful
worthy capable, condign, constructive *(creative)*, desirable *(qualified)*, entitled, exemplary, fit, high-minded, justifiable, laudable, meritorious, moral, premium, qualified *(competent)*, reputable, scrupulous, sterling, suitable, unimpeachable, upright, valuable
worthy of attention extraordinary
worthy of belief authentic, credible, fiduciary
worthy of blame culpable, sinister
worthy of choice preferable, qualified *(competent)*
worthy of confidence credible, loyal, official
worthy of consideration considerable, major
worthy of contempt disgraceful
worthy of credence convincing, credible, fiduciary, plausible
worthy of estimation laudable
worthy of fame meritorious
worthy of imitation exemplary
worthy of note remarkable
worthy of notice influential, notable, noteworthy, paramount, salient
worthy of praise meritorious
worthy of regard extraordinary
worthy of remark major, notable, noteworthy, paramount, salient
worthy of trust reliable
would-be specious
wound damage, disable, harm, inflict, infliction, maim, mistreat, mutilate, offend *(insult)*, prejudice *(injure)*, provoke
wound the feelings affront
woundable vulnerable
wounded aggrieved *(harmed)*, marred
wounded pride resentment
wounding harmful, offensive *(offending)*
woven compound
wrack prostration
wraith phantom
wrangle altercation, argument *(contention)*, belligerency, bicker, brawl *(noun)*, brawl *(verb)*, challenge, collide *(clash)*, conflict *(noun)*, conflict *(verb)*, confront *(oppose)*, confrontation *(altercation)*, contend *(dispute)*, contest *(dispute)*, contravention, controversy *(argument)*, debate, dicker, disaccord, disagree, dispute, dispute *(debate)*, dissidence, fight *(argument)*, fracas, haggle, oppugn, strife
wrangler disputant, malcontent
wrangling altercation, argument *(contention)*, contention *(opposition)*, contentious, discord, dissension, dissenting, hostile
wrap clothe, cover *(guard)*, encompass *(surround)*, ensconce, enshroud, envelop, hide, obnubilate, obscure, plant *(covertly place)*, shroud
wrap around envelop
wrapper enclosure
wrath ill will, malice, passion, resentment, umbrage
wreak inflict
wreathe intertwine
wreathed tortuous *(bending)*
wreck damage *(noun)*, damage *(verb)*, debacle, despoil, destroy *(efface)*, devastate, disable, mutilate, obliterate, pillage, prejudice *(injure)*, prostration, spoil *(impair)*
wrecker vandal
wrecking activities defacement
wrench contort, deprive, distort, exact, force *(break)*, luxate, sever
wrench away from confiscate
wrench the meaning distort
wrench the sense distort
wrenching extortion
wrest contort, deprive, exact, extort, levy, seize *(confiscate)*, sequester *(seize property)*, slant, succeed *(attain)*, usurp
wrest away from confiscate
wrest from abridge *(divest)*, acquire *(secure)*, coerce

wrest property from evict
wrester extortionist
wresting avulsion, extortion
wresting money by force extortion
wrestle compete, grapple
wrestle with confront *(oppose)*, fight *(battle)*
wretched deplorable, derelict *(abandoned)*, disconsolate, heinous, lamentable, lugubrious, obnoxious, paltry, peccant *(culpable)*, pessimistic, poor *(inferior in quality)*
wretchedness disrepute, distress *(anguish)*, pessimism, prostration
wring distill, exact, extort, press *(constrain)*
wring away from confiscate
wringing extortion
wrinkle artifice, contort
writ brevet, canon, certificate, charge *(command)*, citation *(charge)*, direction *(order)*, directive, document, habeas corpus, monition *(legal summons)*, precept, process *(summons)*, search warrant, subpoena, summons. SEE MAIN ENTRY
writ for deliverance from illegal confinement habeas corpus
writ of summons citation *(charge)*
writ to gain freedom habeas corpus
write communicate, compile, compose, correspond *(communicate)*, frame *(construct)*, inscribe, note *(record)*, record, subscribe *(sign)*
write a prescription prescribe
write about treat *(process)*
write down book, enter *(record)*, note *(record)*, record
write in enter *(record)*
write notes for edit
write off obliterate. SEE MAIN ENTRY
write up report *(disclose)*
write-off bad debt
write-up publicity
writer amanuensis
writhe beat *(pulsate)*, contort
writing charter *(declaration of rights)*, communication *(statement)*, entry *(record)*, handwriting, instrument *(document)*, memory *(commemoration)*, proposal *(report)*, publication *(printed matter)*, script, testament
writing delivered as the evidence of an agreement instrument *(document)*
writing that discredits libel
writing which gives formal expression to a legal act instrument *(document)*
writings correspondence *(communication by letters)*
written documentary, holographic
written accusation indictment, information *(charge)*, libel
written agreement covenant, lease
written announcement resolution *(formal statement)*
written application for relief petition
written assurance vow
written authorization proxy
written certificate bill *(formal declaration)*
written characters script
written complaint bill *(formal declaration)*
written constitution code
written contract certificate
written copy transcript
written declaration under oath deposition
written declaration upon oath affidavit
written discourse publication *(printed matter)*
written document form *(document)*
written evidence affirmance *(legal affirmation)*, certificate, certification *(attested copy)*
written expression language
written formal expression instrument *(document)*
written instrument coupon
written instrument of contingency escrow
written law act *(enactment)*, code, codification, constitution, statute
written material document, record
written matter inscription, script
written notification to appear in court summons
written off derelict *(abandoned)*
written order holding *(ruling of a court)*, instruction *(direction)*, mandate
written permission charter *(license)*, license
written pledge covenant
written precept of imprisonment mittimus
written record entry *(record)*, register
written requests for information interrogatories
written requirement specification
written statement averment
written statement of defense pleading
written statement under oath affidavit
written statements of accusation pleading
written terms contract
written word language
wrong abuse *(violate)*, affront, arrant *(onerous)*, at fault, blame *(culpability)*, blameworthy, crime, culpable, damage *(noun)*, damage *(verb)*, delict, delinquency *(misconduct)*, disservice, errant, erroneous, fallacious, false *(inaccurate)*, faulty, felonious, grievance, ground, guilt, harm, harrow, heinous, illicit, immoral, impermissible, improper, inaccurate, inadmissible, inadvisable, inapplicable, inapposite, incorrect, infraction, infringement, iniquitous, injury, injustice, inopportune, irregular *(improper)*, mendacious, mens rea, mischief, misconduct, misdeed, misdemeanor, misdoing, misfeasance, mishandle *(maltreat)*, mistreat, nefarious, objectionable, offense, peccant *(culpable)*, persecute, perverse, prejudice *(injury)*, prejudice *(injure)*, reprehensible, sinister, sophistic, tort, transgression, unethical, unfit, unjust, unjustifiable, unseemly, unsound *(fallacious)*, unsustainable, untenable, untrue, vice, vicious, violation, wrongful. SEE MAIN ENTRY
wrong application misapplication
wrong arising from affirmative action misfeasance
wrong course detour, error
wrong designation misnomer
wrong doing infringement
wrong estimation misjudgment
wrong implementation noncompliance *(improper completion)*
wrong impression error, misestimation
wrong interpretation catachresis, distortion, misapplication
wrong name misnomer
wrong reasoning non sequitur
wrong statement misstatement
wrong usage catachresis, misapplication
wrong use abuse *(corrupt practice)*, misapplication, misusage, misuse
wrong verdict injustice
wrong-doer delinquent
wrongdoer convict, criminal, felon, hoodlum, lawbreaker, malefactor, offender, recidivist. SEE MAIN ENTRY
wrongdoer released from prison probationer *(released offender)*
wrongdoing criminality, culpability, delinquency *(misconduct)*, felony, guilt, injustice, knavery, mens rea, mischief, misconduct, misdeed, misfeasance, offense, tort, transgression, turpitude, vice
wronged aggrieved *(victimized)*
wrongful arrant *(onerous)*, blameful, blameworthy, felonious, illegal, illegitimate *(illegal)*, illicit, impermissible, improper, irregular *(improper)*, lawless, outrageous, peccant *(culpable)*, unauthorized, unjust, unlawful, unscrupulous, unwarranted. SEE MAIN ENTRY
wrongful act tort, tortious act. SEE MAIN ENTRY
wrongful action malfeasance
wrongful action of a public official misprision
wrongful appropriation embezzlement
wrongful assumption conversion *(misappropriation)*
wrongful conduct malfeasance. SEE MAIN ENTRY
wrongful conversion of property misappropriation
wrongful displacement asportation
wrongful dispossession disseisin
wrongful entry encroachment
wrongful exaction extortion
wrongful exercise of dominion conversion *(misappropriation)*
wrongful impoundment detainer
wrongful ingress encroachment
wrongful keeping detainer
wrongful performance of a normally legal act misfeasance
wrongful removal asportation
wrongful taking larceny, theft
wrongful transfer asportation
wrongful use misapplication, misappropriation. SEE MAIN ENTRY
wrongfully illegally
wrongfulness infringement, misdoing, misfeasance, offense
wrongheaded perverse
wrongly advised misadvised
wrongly timed inappropriate
wrongness error
wrongous unlawful
wrought up frenetic
wrought with labor elaborate

Y

yard close *(enclosed area)*, curtilage
yardage space
yardstick criterion. SEE MAIN ENTRY
yarn myth
yawning open *(unclosed)*, penetrable
year annum
yearly per annum
yearly payment annuity, premium *(insurance payment)*
yearn for lack, need
yearning desire, eager, predisposition, solicitous, will *(desire)*

years age, longevity
years of existence lifetime
yeilding resignation *(passive acceptance)*
yell outcry
yellow recreant
yen desire
yet notwithstanding. SEE MAIN ENTRY
yet to be forthcoming
yield abandon *(relinquish)*, abide, accede *(concede)*, accommodate, accrue *(arise)*, acknowledge *(verify)*, allow *(endure)*, bestow, cede, concede, concur *(agree)*, condescend *(deign)*, condone, confer *(give)*, confess, conform, consent, defer *(yield in judgment)*, engender, forfeit, forgo, forswear, fund, furnish, germinate, grant *(concede)*, hear *(give attention to)*, let *(permit)*, lose *(undergo defeat)*, obey, outcome, outgrowth, output, proceeds, produce *(manufacture)*, product, profit, quit *(discontinue)*, redound, relax, release, relent, relinquish, resign, result, revenue, succumb, supply, vouchsafe, waive. SEE MAIN ENTRY
yield assent accede *(concede)*, agree *(comply)*, certify *(approve)*, coincide *(concur)*, conform, grant *(concede)*, permit
yield gain inure *(benefit)*
yield in opinion to defer *(yield in judgment)*
yield passage to admit *(give access)*
yield profit inure *(benefit)*
yield results make
yield returns gain, profit
yield to comply, observe *(obey)*, recognize *(acknowledge)*
yield to the wishes of others truckle
yielding amenable, capitulation, cession, charitable *(lenient)*, compliance, concession *(compromise)*, conformity *(obedience)*, consenting, constructive *(creative)*, disposition *(transfer of property)*, facile, fertile, flexible, lenient, malleable, obedient, obeisant, obsequious, operative, passive, patient, permissive, pliable, pliant, powerless, productive, prolific, release, renunciation, resignation *(relinquishment)*, resigned, resilient, sequacious, subjection, susceptible *(unresistent)*, tractable, willing *(not averse)*. SEE MAIN ENTRY
yielding abundantly copious
yieldingness amenability, compliance
yoke bondage, curb, fetter, incorporate *(include)*, join *(bring together)*, lock, subjection, thrall
young child, inexperienced, juvenile, progeny
young boy child
young descendant child
young girl child
young people children
young person adolescent, infant, juvenile, minor
younger generation children, offspring
youngling adolescent, child, juvenile, minor
youngster adolescent, child, infant, juvenile, minor
youngsters children
your honor judge. SEE MAIN ENTRY
youth adolescence, adolescent, child, children, infant, juvenile, minor, minority *(infancy)*, nonage
youthful inexperienced, juvenile
youthfulness minority *(infancy)*

Z

zeal adhesion *(loyalty)*, ardor, compulsion *(obsession)*, diligence *(perseverance)*, emotion, industry *(activity)*, life *(vitality)*, loyalty, passion, predisposition, purpose, spirit
zealot addict, bigot, partisan
zealotist partisan
zealotry resolution *(decision)*
zealous eager, earnest, faithful *(loyal)*, fanatical, fervent, hot-blooded, industrious, intense, intensive, painstaking, pertinacious, purposeful, ready *(willing)*, resolute, sedulous, serious *(devoted)*, steadfast, thorough, true *(loyal)*, unyielding, vehement, willing *(desirous)*. SEE MAIN ENTRY
zealous advocates lobby
zealous attachment affection
zealousness diligence *(perseverance)*, industry *(activity)*
zenith ceiling, culmination, pinnacle
zero blank *(emptiness)*
zest enjoyment *(pleasure)*, life *(vitality)*
zestful eager, fervent, ready *(willing)*
zestfulness life *(vitality)*
zigzag circuitous, indirect, indirection *(indirect action)*, sinuous, tortuous *(bending)*
zonal regional
zone area *(province)*, circuit, coverage *(scope)*, demarcate, department, district, division *(administrative unit)*, enclosure, insulate, locality, location, purview, region, scope, territory, vicinity. SEE MAIN ENTRY
zoning SEE MAIN ENTRY
zoning laws SEE MAIN ENTRY

CPSIA information can be obtained
at www.ICGtesting.com
Printed in the USA
LVHW080538170519
618172LV00001B/1/P